# VOX

## Modern

# SPANISH

### and

# ENGLISH

## Dictionary

# VOX

# Modern

# SPANISH
## and
# ENGLISH
## Dictionary

**English-Spanish/Spanish-English**

Dictionary Compiled by
the Editors of Biblograf, S.A.

North American Edition Prepared by
the Editors of NTC Publishing Group

*NTC Publishing Group*

In Spanish, the best, by definition

**Library of Congress Cataloging-in-Publication Data**
is available from the United States Library of Congress.

Published by NTC Publishing Group
A division of NTC/Contemporary Publishing Group, Inc.
4255 West Touhy Avenue, Lincolnwood (Chicago), Illinois 60646-1975 U.S.A.
Printed in the United States of America
Library of Congress Catalog Number: 86-61160
International Standard Book Number: 0-8442-7990-0 (cloth)
0-8442-7988-9 (vinyl)
28  27  26  25  24  23  22  21  20  19  18  17  16  15  14  13  12  11

# CONTENTS

# CONTENTS

# PREFACE

For educators, students, business people, tourists, and the general public, a dictionary provides answers to all kinds of questions about language. The *VOX Modern Spanish and English Dictionary* has been designed as a reference tool that offers a bridge of understanding between the two languages, as well as between the two cultures. Far more than a mere lexicon, this dictionary presents broad lexical, grammatical, and cultural information in a concise and practical form that will assure its extensive, daily use.

All of the sections of the *VOX Modern* dictionary help the reader derive the most benefit from one single reference source without having to consult countless grammar books, almanacs, or other reference works. The entries contain many examples of current word usage so that the reader may select the precise word or expression. There are other labor-saving features, as well. Irregular verbs are generally conjugated as part of the main verb entry, rather than being marked with an asterisk and requiring the reader to look elsewhere for the models of irregular verbs. Also among the entries is terminology from business, science, the arts, and culture.

Preceding the English-Spanish section and the Spanish-English section is a summary of grammar that gives the reader a quick reference that clarifies the most frequently confused rules. To this end also, a pronunciation guide is offered for each language.

The dictionary also contains a section of more than 3,500 idioms and expressions in English and Spanish and appendices with tables of weights and measures, monetary units, and temperatures; six detailed maps; and common abbreviations in the two languages. There is a section with examples of appropriate phrases in each language to aid in translating or writing business correspondence and, to assure that the reader chooses the exact word, there is a bilingual list of false cognates.

Without a doubt, the North American edition of the *VOX Modern Spanish and English Dictionary* offers a practical and up-to-date tool that is easy to use and completely reliable.

# PRÓLOGO

Para educadores, alumnos, comerciantes, turistas y la pública en general, un diccionario provee las respuestas a todas clases de preguntas linguísticas. El *VOX Modern Spanish and English Dictionary* ha sido concebido como un instrumento de trabajo y de consulta que ofrece un puente de entendimiento tanto entre las dos lenguas como entre las dos culturas. Mucho más que un simple léxico, este diccionario ofrece amplios datos léxicos, gramaticales y culturales en una forma concisa y práctica que asegurará su uso extensivo diario.

Todas las secciones del diccionario *VOX Modern* ayudan al lector a sacar mayor provecho de una sola obra sin tener que buscar en una infinidad de libros gramaticales, almanaques u otras obras de consulta. Los artículos contienen muchos ejemplos del uso actual de las palabras para que el lector escoja la palabra o expresión exacta. Hay también otras economías de trabajo. Las irregularidades de los verbos figuran como parte del mismo artículo en vez de indicarse con asterisco para que el lector tenga que buscar en otra parte los modelos de verbos irregulares. Además, entre los artículos se encuentra la terminología del comercio, la ciencia, las artes y la cultura.

Antes de la sección inglés-español y la español-inglés, se encuentra un resumen gramatical que da al lector un medio rápido de consulta sobre los casos de dificultad más frecuentes. A este fin también se ofrece una lista que provee ejemplos de la pronunciación de cada idioma.

El diccionario contiene también una sección de más de 3.500 modismos y expresiones en inglés y español. Y en los apéndices, ofrece al lector tablas de pesas y medidas, unidades monetarias, temperaturas, seis mapas detallados y abreviaturas comunes en los dos idiomas. Hay una sección de ejemplos de correspondencia comercial con frases apropiadas en cada idioma, y para asegurar que el lector escoja la palabra exacta, hay una lista bilingüe de cognados falsos.

Sin duda, la edición norteamericana del *VOX Modern Spanish and English Dictionary* tiene la seguridad de ofrecer un instrumento práctico y al día, de fácil manejo y digno de toda confianza.

# INGLÉS-ESPAÑOL
# ENGLISH-SPANISH

# OBSERVACIONES

Al consultar este Diccionario, el lector ha de tener en cuenta que:

- Dentro de cada artículo, la palabra o el grupo de palabras correspondiente a cada una de las acepciones del vocablo inglés constituyen una entidad separada y numerada.

- Los ejemplos, frases y modos no se dan, como es corriente en esta clase de Diccionarios, al final del artículo, sino que van agregados a la acepción a que corresponden, con lo cual ilustran mejor el sentido de ésta.

- En general, los ejemplos, frases y modos, se dan, dentro de cada acepción, en el siguiente orden: grupos de nombre y adjetivo o compuestos formados por palabras separadas; oraciones con verbo expreso, y modos adverbiales, conjuntivos, etc.

- Las frases y modos no atribuibles a ninguna acepción determinada tienen lugar independiente y numerado dentro del artículo.

- Los compuestos formados por palabras separadas se encuentran en el artículo correspondiente a su primer elemento. Los compuestos cuyos elementos van unidos por un guión o formando una sola palabra se hallarán como artículos independientes.

- Los sinónimos y aclaraciones encerradas entre corchetes sirven para determinar el sentido en que han de tomarse las palabras que se dan como traducción.

- A este fin se usan también abreviaturas de materia, uso, etc., cuya interpretación se da en la lista correspondiente. (V. Abreviaturas usadas en este diccionario.)

Para completar las indicaciones de naturaleza gramatical que se dan en los artículos del Diccionario, se incluye una sección gramatical referente a temas concretos. No se trata de dar con ella, ni siquiera en resumen, toda la doctrina gramatical del inglés, sino de ofrecer al lector (especialmente de habla española) un medio rápido de consulta sobre los casos de dificultad más frecuentes.

- Un asterisco en el cuerpo de un artículo indica que la palabra española que precede sólo tiene uso en América.

El lector encontrará en este Diccionario secciones de referencia que facilitarán su aprendizaje y uso del idioma. Por ejemplo, en el centro del Diccionario se encuentra una lista de más de tres mil idiomas y expresiones: Español-Inglés e Inglés-Español.

Además se incluyen en los apéndices:

- False Cognates and ''Part-Time'' Cognates
- Monetary Units / Unidades monetarias
- Weights and Measures / Pesas y medidas
- Numbers / Numerales
- Temperature / La temperatura
- Abreviaturas más usadas en inglés
- Abbreviations Most Commonly Used in Spanish
- Business Correspondence in Spanish / La carta comercial en español
- Maps/Mapas

# ABREVIATURAS USADAS EN ESTE DICCIONARIO

| | |
|---|---|
| *abrev.* | abreviatura |
| *adj.*, adj. | adjetivo |
| *adv.*, adv. | adverbio |
| AER. | aerostación |
| AGR. | agricultura |
| AJED. | ajedrez |
| ÁLG. | álgebra |
| ANAT. | anatomía |
| ant. | antiguamente; anticuado |
| ARIT. | aritmética |
| ARM. | armaduras; armas |
| ARQ. | arquitectura |
| ARQUEOL. | arqueología |
| *art.* | artículo |
| ARTILL. | artillería |
| ASTR. | astronomía; astrología |
| AUTO. | automóvil; automovilismo |
| *aux.* | verbo auxiliar |
| AVIA. | aviación |
| BACT. | bacteriología |
| B. ART. | bellas artes |
| BIB. | Biblia |
| BIOL. | biología |
| BIOQUÍM. | bioquímica |
| BOT. | botánica |
| CARN. | carnicería |
| CARP. | carpintería |
| CERÁM. | cerámica |
| CINEM. | cinematografía |
| CIR. | cirugía |
| COC. | cocina |
| COM. | comercio |
| *compar.* | comparativo |
| Cond. | Condicional |
| *conj.* | conjunción |
| CONJUG. | Conjugación |
| CONSTR. | construcción |
| *contr.* | contracción |
| CORR. | Correos |
| COST. | costura |
| CRISTAL. | cristalografía |
| CRON. | cronología |
| *def.* | definido; defectivo |
| DEP. | deportes |
| DER. | derecho; forense |
| desp. | despectivo |
| desus. | desusado |
| *dial.* | dialectal |
| DIB. | dibujo |
| *dim.* | diminutivo |
| ECLES. | eclesiástico; iglesia |
| ECON. | economía |
| E. U. | Estados Unidos |
| ELECT. | electricidad |
| ENTOM. | entomología |
| EQUIT. | equitación |
| ESC. | escultura |
| ESGR. | esgrima |
| esp. | especialmente |
| *f.* | femenino; nombre femenino |
| fam. | familiar |
| FERROC. | ferrocarriles |
| fig. | figurado |
| FIL. | filosofía |
| FÍS. | física |
| FISIOL. | fisiología |
| FORT. | fortificación |
| FOT. | fotografía |
| gal. | galicismo |
| GEOGR. | geografía |
| GEOL. | geología |
| GEOM. | geometría |
| ger., GER. | gerundio |
| gralte. | generalmente |
| GRAM. | gramática |
| HIST. | historia |
| ICT. | ictiología |
| *impers.* | verbo impersonal |
| IMPR. | imprenta |
| IND. | industria |
| *indef.* | indefinido |
| INDIC., indic. | indicativo |
| INF., inf. | infinitivo |
| ING. | ingeniería |
| Ingl. | Inglaterra |
| *interj.* | interjección |
| *interr.*, *interrog.* | interrogativo |
| *intr.* | verbo intransitivo |
| irón. | irónico |
| *irreg.* | irregular |
| JOY. | joyería |
| lat. | latín |

| | | | |
|---|---|---|---|
| LIT. | literatura | S. | sur |
| LITURG. | liturgia | s. | nombre substantivo |
| loc. | locución | simplte. | simplemente |
| LÓG. | lógica | SUBJ. | Subjuntivo |
| | | superl. | superlativo |
| m. | masculino; nombre | | |
| | masculino | TEAT. | teatro |
| MAR. | marina; marítimo | TÉCN. | técnica |
| MAT. | matemáticas | TELEF. | telefonía |
| may. | mayúscula | TELEGR. | telegrafía |
| MEC. | mecánica | TELEV. | televisión |
| MED. | medicina | TEOL. | teología |
| METAL. | metalurgia | TOP. | topografía |
| METEOR. | meteorología | tr., tr. | verbo transitivo |
| MÉTR. | métrica | TRIG. | trigonometría |
| MIL. | militar; milicia | | |
| MIN. | minería | us. | usado |
| min. | minúscula | | |
| MINER. | mineralogía | V. | Véase |
| MIT. | mitología | vulg. | vulgarismo |
| MÚS. | música | VET. | veterinaria |
| n. pr. | nombre propio | ZOOL. | zoología |
| num. | numeral | | |
| ORNIT. | ornitología | | |
| PART. PAS. | Participio pasivo | | |
| pers. | persona(s); personal | | |
| pl. | plural | | |
| poc. us. | poco usado | | |
| poét. | poético | | |
| POL. | política | | |
| pop. | popular | | |
| por ext. | por extensión | | |
| pos. | posesivo | | |
| p. p., p. p. | participio pasivo | | |
| pref. | prefijo | | |
| prep. | preposición | | |
| Pres., pres. | presente | | |
| Pret., pret. | pretérito | | |
| pron. | pronombre | | |
| pron. rel. | pronombre relativo | | |
| QUÍM. | química | | |
| RADIO. | radiotelefonía; radiotelegrafía | | |
| ref. | verbo reflexivo | | |
| REL. | religión | | |

# PRONUNCIACIÓN FIGURADA DE LA LENGUA INGLESA

Normas para su interpretación*

| Signos | Sonidos |
| --- | --- |
| a | Sonido parecido al de la a de mano. |
| *a* | Sonido más obscuro y cerrado que la a de seda. |
| æ | Sonido intermedio entre el de la a de mano y el de la e de seda. |
| ai | Sonido del diptongo ai de aire. |
| au | Sonido del diptongo au de lauro. |
| e | Sonido parecido al de la e de seda. |
| ei | Sonido del diptongo ei de veis. |
| ø | En sílaba tónica, sonido parecido al de la œ francesa de *coeur*. En sílaba átona, sonido más obscuro, como el de la e francesa de *le*. |
| i | Sonido intermedio entre la i de ánimo y la e de dicen. |
| ɪ | Sonido parecido al de la i de pila, pero más cerrado y más largo. |
| iu | Sonido del diptongo iu de triunfo. |
| o | Sonido parecido al de la o de volar. |
| *o* | Sonido parecido al de la o española de soy, pero más largo y cerrado. |
| ou | Sonido parecido al del diptongo ou de bou. |
| u | Sonido parecido al de la u de mulo. |
| b | Sonido parecido al de la b de barón, pero algo más explosivo. |
| ch | Sonido de la ch de mucho. |
| d | Sonido de la d de dar. |
| đ | Sonido parecido al de la d de seda. |
| f | Sonido parecido al de la f de fe. |
| g | Sonido de la g de garra. |
| j | Sonido aspirado, parecido a la j de juerga, pero más breve y suave. |
| dȳ | Sonido parecido al de la g y la j de las palabras francesas *général* y *jambe*. |
| ȳ | Sonido parecido al anterior, pero más suave. |
| k | Sonido de la c de casa. |
| l | Sonido parecido al de la l de lana. |
| m | Sonido de la m de mano. |
| n | Sonido de la n de nadie. |
| ng | Sonido parecido al de la n de tan, pero seguido de un leve sonido velar. |

* Hemos querido dar la mayor sencillez posible a la pronunciación figurada que ofrecemos entre paréntesis al principio de cada artículo porque estimamos que su objeto sólo puede ser orientar a los lectores que ya posean un conocimiento general de la pronunciación inglesa. Ésta debe aprenderse de viva voz. Su exposición requeriría prolijas explicaciones o el empleo del alfabeto fonético, cuya interpretación no se halla al alcance de los profanos.

| Signos | Sonidos |
|--------|---------|
| ñ | Sonido de la ñ de **cañón**. |
| p | Sonido de la p de **pan**. |
| r | Sonido semivocal que se articula con la punta de la lengua hacia atrás y sin hacerla vibrar. |
| ʳ | Sonido parecido al anterior, pero mucho más débil, que en algunos casos llega a perderse. Cuando va precedido de una vocal tónica, ésta queda alargada. Después de una vocal átona, muchos no lo pronuncian. |
| s | Sonido parecido al de la s de **sal**. |
| s̄ | Sonido de la s francesa de *rose* y la catalana de *casa*. |
| sh | Sonido parecido al de la ch francesa de *machine* y al de la x catalana de *xàfec*. |
| t | Sonido parecido al de la t de **tan**, pero pronunciado con la punta de la lengua más próxima a los alvéolos. |
| v | Sonido labiodental de la v de **valle**. |
| w | Sonido parecido al de la u de **hueso**. |
| y | Sonido de la y de **yugo**. |
| z | Sonido parecido al de la z de **zorro**, pero más suave. |
| (·) | El punto volado (·) indica que sobre la vocal o diptongo que lo precede recae el acento tónico de la palabra. |

# RESUMEN DE GRAMÁTICA INGLESA

## ARTÍCULO / ARTICLES

El inglés tiene dos clases de artículo: el definido y el indefinido.

* Artículo definido: **the**. Es invariable y corresponde a *el, la, los, las* y (en ciertos casos) *lo*.

* Artículo indefinido: **a** o **an**. Se usa para el singular en todos los géneros.
  —La forma **a** se usa: a) delante de consonantes (incluyendo entre ellas la **h** aspirada, la **w** y la **y**); b) delante de **u, eu** y **ew**, cuando suenan como en **use, European** y **ewe**, y delante de **o**, cuando suena como en **one**.
  —El plural español *unos* y *unas* se traduce al inglés por el adjetivo **some**: he had some papers in his hand, tenía unos papeles en la mano.

NOTA: El uso que hace el español del artículo determinado en expresiones como: me lavo *las* manos, ponte *el* sombrero, él se ha roto *el* brazo, no existe en inglés. Estas expresiones se traducen por: I wash my hands, put on your hat, he has broken his arm.

## GÉNERO / GENDER

Por regla general, en inglés, son

* **Masculinos**. Los nombres que significan varón o animal macho: **man** (hombre); **knight** (caballero); **bull** (toro).

* **Femeninos**. Los que significan mujer o animal hembra: **woman** (mujer); **spinster** (solterona); **lady** (dama); **cow** (vaca).

* **Comunes**. Como en español, los de persona de una sola terminación para los dos géneros: **friend** (amigo, -ga); **neighbor** (vecino, -na); **companion** (compañero, -ra).

* **Neutros**. Los nombres de cosa concretos o abstractos; los de animales cuando no se especifica su sexo; los que significan niño [niño o niña indiferentemente] o niño de pecho como **child** o **baby**.

*Excepciones:*
* Los nombres de países, barcos y máquinas son generalmente del género femenino: **Poland** has lost her independence, Polonia ha perdido su independencia; she was a fine **ship**, era un hermoso barco.

### Indicación del género
Hay cierto número de nombres que tienen palabras distintas para cada género: **man** (hombre); **woman** (mujer); **father** (padre); **mother** (madre); **widow** (viuda); **widower** (viudo); **bull** (toro); **cow** (vaca); **rooster** (gallo); **hen** (gallina), etc.

En los demás casos, el género se infiere del contexto (**she is an orphan**, ella es huérfana), o se distingue:

* Por medio de las terminaciones femeninas **-ess, -ix** o **-ine**: actor, **actress** (actor, actriz); duke, **duchess** (duque, duquesa); testator, **testatrix** (testador, testadora); hero, **heroine** (héroe, heroína).

* Por medio de **male, female, woman**, etc., en función de adjetivo o de los pronombres **he-**, **she-** como prefijos: **female fish** (pez hembra); **woman lawyer** (abogada, licenciada); **he-goat** (macho cabrío); **she-ass** (asna, jumenta).

* Por medio de palabras compuestas en que uno de los elementos expresa el género: **man-servant** (criado); **maidservant** (criada); **bull-elephant** (elefante), **doe-hare** (liebre hembra), **cock-sparrow** (gorrión).

## PLURAL (Sustantivos) / THE PLURAL OF NOUNS
### Regla general

En inglés la desinencia del plural es una s que se añade a la forma propia del singular: bale, **bales**; chair, **chairs**.

*Observ.:* Los nombres terminados en **se, ce, ge** y **ze** ganan una sílaba en el plural al tomar la s, ya que la **e** muda se pronuncia como [i]: **fence** [fens], valla; pl. **fences** ['fensiz], vallas.

**Excepciones y casos particulares**

- Toman **es** en el plural:

  —Los nombres terminados en **o** precedida de consonante: virago, **viragoes**; potato, **potatoes**.

    Sin embargo, los nombres de formación moderna o de origen extranjero hacen el plural en s: auto, **autos**; contralto, **contraltos**; dynamo, **dynamos**; memento, **mementos**; piano, **pianos**.

  —Los nombres terminados en **s, sh, ch** (con sonido de *ch*), **x** y **z**: brass, **brasses**; bush, **bushes**; wrench, **wrenches**; box, **boxes**; chintz, **chintzes**.

  *Observ.:* Los terminados en **ex** hacen el plural en **exes** o **ices**; los terminados en **ix** lo hacen en **ixes** o **ices**: vortex, **vortexes** o **vortices**; appendix, **appendixes** o **appendices**.

- Los nombres terminados en **f** o **fe** hacen el plural en **ves**: half, **halves**; knife, **knives**; wolf, **wolves**.

  —Se exceptúan: **dwarf, gulf, safe, still-life, strife** y los terminados en **ff, ief** y **oof**, que hacen el plural en s: dwarf, **dwarfs**; cliff, **cliffs**; belief, **beliefs**; roof, **roofs**. Sin embargo, *thief* hace **thieves**.

  —Algunos tienen plural doble en **fs** y en **ves**, como: beef, **beefs** y **beeves**; hoof, **hoofs** y **hooves**; scarf, **scarfs** y **scarves**; wharf, **wharfs** y **wharves**.

- Los nombres terminados en **quy** o en **y** precedida de consonante hacen el plural cambiando la **y** en **ies**: colloquy, **colloquies**; cry, **cries**; oddity, **oddities**.

  —Sin embargo, los nombres propios terminados en y, con muy raras excepciones, hacen el plural en s: Henry, **Henrys**.

- Algunos nombres son invariables: **sheep** (carnero, carneros); **swine** (cerdo, cerdos). Otros tienen formas propias para el singular y para el plural: child, **children**; die, **dice**; foot, **feet**; man, **men**; mouse, **mice**; woman, **women**; tooth, **teeth**.

## GENITIVO / THE GENITIVE CASE

En ciertos casos, el inglés expresa el genitivo añadiendo una s apostrofada (**'s**) al nombre del poseedor y poniendo sin artículo el nombre de lo poseído (**John's father**, el padre de Juan). Es lo que se llama *caso genitivo* o *genitivo sajón*.

**Se omite la s** (nunca el apóstrofe):

- Después de un nombre en plural terminado en s: the **birds'** nests, los nidos de los pájaros.

- Después de un nombre en singular cuya última sílaba empiece con s: **Moses'** law, la ley de Moisés.

- Después de un nombre propio latino, griego o extranjero terminado en s, es o x: **Cassius'** dagger, el puñal de Casio; **Achilles'** heel, el talón de Aquiles. Nótese, sin embargo: **Venus's** beauty, la hermosura de Venus.

- Después de un nombre terminado en s o ce, cuando va seguido de **sake**: for **goodness'** sake!, ¡por Dios!; for **conscience'** sake, por conciencia.

**Casos especiales**

- Puede usarse con elipsis del nombre de la cosa poseída cuando éste significa *iglesia, hospital, casa, tienda*: **St. Paul's**, la catedral de San Pablo; at my **aunt's**, en casa de mi tía; I am going to the **grocer's**, voy a la tienda de comestibles. También se usa con elipsis en casos como: this car is my **father's**, este coche es de mi padre; Is this your hat? No, it is **Mr. Brown's**; Este sombrero es el suyo? No, es el del señor Brown.

- Si hay más de dos nombres propios de poseedor, el signo del genitivo se pone detrás del último: **Mary and Robert's** brother, el hermano de María y Roberto.

# ADJETIVO / ADJECTIVES

El adjetivo inglés es invariable. Una misma forma sirve para todos los géneros en singular y en plural: an old man, un hombre viejo; an old house, una casa vieja; these trees are old, estos árboles son viejos.

## Lugar del adjetivo

Por regla general, el adjetivo (cuando no tiene función de predicado) precede al sustantivo que califica o determina: a clever man, un hombre inteligente; a long journey, un largo viaje.

El adjetivo va pospuesto:

- Cuando lleva un complemento: a man worthy of esteem, un hombre digno de aprecio.
- Cuando completa el sentido del verbo: he found the plot absurd, halló absurdo el argumento.
- Cuando equivale a una oración subordinada: the garden proper is not very large, el jardín propiamente dicho no es muy grande.
- Cuando significa de alto, de ancho, de edad, etc.: the tree is twenty feet high, el árbol tiene veinte pies de alto.
- Cuando califica un pronombre terminado en -thing o -body: there is nothing strange about that, eso no tiene nada de extraño.
- En algunas denominaciones de cargo, empleo, etc. y en ciertas expresiones procedentes del francés: accountant general, jefe de contabilidad; court martial, consejo de guerra.
- Los adjetivos worth, ill, left (que queda), missing y los compuestos con el prefijo a- suelen usarse sólo como predicados. Si alguno de ellos se aplica directamente al sustantivo, debe ir detrás de éste: a life worth preserving, una vida que merece ser conservada; he has only three dollars left, sólo le quedan tres dólares.
- La palabra alone va siempre detrás del nombre o el pronombre: leave him alone, déjalo solo.

## El sustantivo usado como adjetivo

En inglés puede usarse un sustantivo para calificar a otro sustantivo. En este caso el primero va inmediatamente antes del segundo: coal ship, barco carbonero; pocket knife, navaja.

## El comparativo y el superlativo

Al comparativo español *tan...como,* corresponde el inglés as...as para la afirmación, y so...as para la negación: my house is as beautiful as yours, mi casa es tan hermosa como la de usted; my house is not so beautiful as yours, mi casa no es tan hermosa como la de usted.

Al comparativo *más* (o *menos*)*...que,* corresponde el inglés more (o less)...than: my house is more (o less) beautiful than yours, mi casa es más (o menos) hermosa que la de usted.

El inglés no lleva desinencia propia para el superlativo absoluto. Este superlativo se forma anteponiendo al adjetivo los adverbios very, most, etc.: very high, altísimo; most excellent, excelentísimo.

Al superlativo relativo *el más* (o *el menos*)*... de,* corresponde el inglés the most (o the least)... in [delante de un nombre de lugar] u of [delante de los demás nombres]: the most populous quarter in town, el barrio más populoso de la ciudad; the least brave man of the regiment, el hombre menos valiente del regimiento.

Sin embargo, el comparativo correspondiente a *más...* y el superlativo correspondiente a *el más...* suelen formarse, cuando se trata de adjetivos monosílabos y de algunos bisílabos, añadiendo -er y -est respectivamente a la forma del positivo. Así, de short (corto) se hace shorter (más corto) y shortest (el más corto).

Al agregar -er y -est a la forma del positivo, la terminación de éste queda modificada en los casos siguientes:

- Adjetivos terminados en -e. Pierden la -e: nice, nicer, nicest; large, larger, largest.
- Adjetivos terminados en -y precedida de consonante. Cambian la -y en -i: burly, burlier, burliest.
- Adjetivos monosílabos terminados en consonante precedida de vocal breve. Doblan la consonante: big, bigger, biggest; fat, fatter, fattest.

**Observaciones:**

No se pueden usar las formas en **-er** y **-est** con adjetivos compuestos con el prefijo **a-**, ni con los terminados en **-al**, **-ed**, **-ful**, **-ic**, **-ile**, **-ive**, **-ose** y **-ous**: **alive, mortal, aged, rustic, fragile, massive, verbose, famous.**

## NUMERALES / NUMERALS

### Algunas particularidades

**Cardinales**

- Los números compuestos de decenas y unidades (a partir de *veinte*) se expresan poniendo las unidades a continuación de las decenas, separadas por un guión: **twenty-one** (21); **forty-six** (46).

- Los números de cien, ciento, mil, un millón, etc., se expresan así: **a** o **one hundred; a** o **one thousand; a** o **one million.** Generalmente se usa **a** para los números redondos y **one** con los demás: **a hundred men,** cien hombres; **one hundred sixty** dollars, ciento sesenta dólares.

 A doscientos, trescientos, dos mil, tres mil, etc., corresponden **two hundred, three hundred, two thousand, three thousand,** etc.

**Ordinales**

- Los ordinales (excepto los tres primeros: **first, second, third**) se forman añadiendo **th** a la forma del cardinal: **four** (cuatro), **fourth** (cuarto); **seven** (siete), **seventh** (séptimo).

 Al recibir la desinencia del ordinal, el cardinal queda modificado en los casos siguientes:
 —**five** y **twelve** cambian la **v** en **f: fifth, twelfth.**
 —**eight** pierde la **t: eighth.**
 —**nine** pierde la **e: ninth.**
 —**twenty, thirty,** etc., cambian la **y** en **ie: twentieth, thirtieth,** etc.
 En los números compuestos, sólo toma la forma de ordinal el último elemento: **thirty-first, twenty-second, forty-third, fifty-eighth.**

- Cuando el ordinal se aplica al nombre de un soberano se escribe con mayúscula y se le antepone el artículo: Henry **the Fourth,** Enrique cuarto; Pius **the Twelfth,** Pío doce.

## PRONOMBRE PERSONAL / PERSONAL PRONOUNS

### Formas del pronombre personal

| *Personas* | *Oficio* | *Singular* | | *Plural* | |
|---|---|---|---|---|---|
| 1.ª | sujeto<br>complemento<br>reflexivo | I<br>me<br>myself | masc.<br>y fem. | we<br>us<br>ourselves | masc.<br>y fem. |
| 2.ª | sujeto<br>complemento<br>reflexivo | thou, you<br>thee, you<br>thyself, yourself | masc.<br>y fem. | ye, you<br>you<br>yourselves | masc.<br>y fem. |
| 3.ª | sujeto<br><br><br>complemento<br><br><br>reflexivo | he<br>she<br>it<br>him<br>her<br>it<br>himself<br>herself<br>itself | (masc.)<br>(fem.)<br>(neut.)<br>(masc.)<br>(fem.)<br>(neut.)<br>(masc.)<br>(fem.)<br>(neut.) | they<br><br><br>them<br><br><br><br>themselves | todos<br>los<br>géneros |

**Observaciones**

• El pronombre complemento indirecto lleva la preposición to: she promised it **to me**, ella me la prometió.

Sin embargo, con ciertos verbos, se puede omitir el **to** a condición de poner el complemento indirecto delante del directo: my father gave **me** this book, mi padre me dio este libro.

Con **to tell** y **to answer**, se usa siempre esta última forma: he told **me** what had happened, me contó lo que había ocurrido.

• Después de los verbos seguidos de una partícula, el pronombre personal complemento directo se coloca entre el verbo y la partícula. Así a *he took off his coat* (se quitó el abrigo), corresponderá *he took it off*, se lo quitó.

• **All**, con un pronombre personal, se coloca después de éste; **all of**, delante: they **all**, **all of** them, todos, todos ellos o ellas.

• Después de las preposiciones **about, around, behind, with** y de las que indican movimiento, el inglés emplea el pronombre personal no reflexivo en vez del reflexivo: she brought her workbasket **with her**, ella trajo consigo su neceser de costura; he looked **behind him**, miró detrás de sí.

• El pronombre personal usado como antecedente de un relativo forma las expresiones **he who** o **that, she who** o **that**, etc., equivalentes a las españolas *el que, aquel que, la que,* etc.

Sin embargo, en el lenguaje moderno no se dice they **who** o **that**, sino those **who** o **that**, los que, aquellos que.

• **They** puede ser sujeto de una oración impersonal, como: they say that, dicen que, se dice que.

• Las formas reflexivas del pronombre personal se usan también para reforzar el pronombre sujeto: I saw it **myself**, yo mismo lo vi.

## POSESIVO (Adjetivo y pronombre) / POSSESSIVE ADJECTIVES AND PRONOUNS

Los adjetivos y pronombres posesivos ingleses son invariables por lo que se refiere a la cosa poseída. Sólo concuerdan con el nombre del posesor.

### Adjetivos

*Singular*

| | | |
|---|---|---|
| 1.ª persona: | **my** | mi, mis |
| 2.ª persona: | **thy, your** | tu, tus* |
| 3.ª persona: | **his** | su, sus [de él] |
| | **her** | su, sus [de ella] |
| | **its** | su, sus [de ello; de un animal o cosa en género neutro] |

*Plural*

| | | |
|---|---|---|
| 1.ª persona: | **our** | nuestro, nuestra, nuestros, nuestras |
| 2.ª persona: | **your** | tu, tus; vuestro, vuestra; vuestros, vuestras; su, sus [de usted o ustedes] |
| 3.ª persona: | **their** | su, sus [de ellos, de ellas, tanto para el masc. y el fem. como para el neutro] |

**Observaciones:**

• Cuando el adjetivo posesivo se refiere a dos o más nombres de género diferente se pone en masculino: all the pupils, **boys** and **girls**, were there, **each** carrying **his** little present, todos los alumnos, niños y niñas, estaban allí llevando cada uno su pequeño regalo.

• Cuando no hay idea de posesión, suele sustituirse el adjetivo posesivo por el genitivo con **of**: the remembrance **of it**, su recuerdo; the directions for the use **of them**, las instrucciones para su uso.

# Pronombres

*Singular*

| | | |
|---|---|---|
| 1.ª persona: | **mine** | el mío, la mía, los míos, las mías |
| 2.ª persona: | **thine, yours** | el tuyo, la tuya, los tuyos, las tuyas* |
| 3.ª persona: | **his** | el suyo, la suya, los suyos, las suyas [de él] |
| | **hers** | el suyo, la suya, los suyos, las suyas [de ella] |
| | **its own** | el suyo, la suya, los suyos, las suyas [de un animal o cosa en género neutro] |

*Plural*

| | | |
|---|---|---|
| 1.ª persona: | **ours** | el nuestro, la nuestra, los nuestros, las nuestras |
| 2.ª persona: | **yours** | el tuyo, la tuya, los tuyos, las tuyas; el vuestro, la vuestra, los vuestros, las vuestras; el suyo, la suya, los suyos, las suyas [de usted o de ustedes] |
| 3.ª persona: | **theirs** | el suyo, la suya, los suyos, las suyas [de ellos, de ellas, tanto para el masc. y el fem. como para el neutro] |

**Observaciones:**

- Cuando el pronombre posesivo va después del verbo **to be** puede traducirse también por el posesivo español sin artículo: this hat is **mine**, este sombrero es mío (o es el mío).
- El pronombre posesivo precedido de of equivale al adjetivo español *mío, tuyo,* etc., o *a uno de mis, de tus,* etc.: a friend **of mine**, un amigo mío, uno de mis amigos.

---

*El adjetivo posesivo thy y el pronombre **thine** sólo se usan en poesía, en la Biblia y en las oraciones. En el lenguaje corriente se usa your y yours para la segunda persona del singular, lo mismo que para la del plural.

## CONJUGACIÓN DE VERBOS / CONJUGATION OF VERBS

La conjugación regular de un verbo inglés comprende un número de formas muy reducido. En todos los tiempos personales se usa la misma forma para todas las personas del singular y del plural, con excepción de la tercera persona del singular del presente de indicativo y de la segunda del singular del presente y el pretérito de indicativo.

*Observación:* La segunda persona del singular (que se forma añadiendo st a la forma propia del tiempo) sólo se emplea en poesía, en la oración y en la Biblia. En el lenguaje corriente se emplea la forma del plural, lo mismo para éste que para el singular. Así, **you** dance equivale, según los casos, a *tú bailas, usted baila, vosotros bailáis* o *ustedes bailan.*

### Presente de indicativo

Tiene la forma del infinitivo sin to para la primera persona del singular y todas las del plural: I, we, you, they dance.

### La tercera persona del singular

Se forma añadiendo es o s a la forma del infinitivo.

Toma **es:**

- En los verbos cuyo infinitivo termina en **ch, sh, ss, x** o **z:** reaches, brushes, passes, boxes, buzzes.
- En los verbos **to do** y **to go:** does, goes.

Toma **s:**

- En los verbos cuyo infinitivo termina en una e muda, una vocal o un diptongo: dances, lives, baas, sees, draws, knows.
- En aquellos cuyo infinitivo termina en una consonante que *no* es **ch, sh, ss, x** o **z:** sobs, packs, rings, kills, hears, bleats.

**Observaciones:**

- Los verbos terminados en y precedida de consonante cambian la y en ie: cry, cries; fly, flies. Los terminados en y precedida de vocal no cambian la y: buy, buys; play, plays.

- Los verbos terminados en **ce, se** o **ge** y los terminados en **ch, sh, ss, x** o **z,** ganan fonéticamente una sílaba al tomar la desinencia de la tercera persona del singular: dance, dances; buzz, buzzes; brush, brushes.

## Pretérito de indicativo

La forma del pretérito de indicativo distingue, una de otra, dos clases de verbos:

**Verbos débiles**

Forman el pretérito y el participio pasivo añadiendo **ed, d** o **t** a la forma del infinitivo: walk, **walked;** live, lived. Algunos acortan (no cambian) la vocal de la raíz y añaden **t:** keep, **kept; sweep, swept.**

**Observaciones:**

- Los verbos débiles terminados en y precedida de consonante cambian la y en ie al tomar la desinencia del pretérito y del participio pasivo: cry, cried; spy, spied. Los terminados en y precedida de vocal no cambian la y: cloy, cloyed; play, played. Por excepción, **to lay** y **to pay** hacen el pretérito y el participio pasivo en **aid:** laid y paid.

- Los verbos que terminan en una consonante dental ganan fonéticamente una sílaba al tomar la desinencia del pretérito y el participio pasivo: blind, blinded; wait, waited.

- Los verbos monosílabos y los polisílabos acentuados en la última sílaba, cuando terminan en una vocal breve seguida de una sola consonante, doblan ésta en el pretérito, el participio pasivo y el gerundio: fit, **fitted, fitting;** bar, **barred, barring;** compel, **compelled, compelling.**
  Cuando la consonante final es **l** precedida de una sola vocal, pueden doblar la **l** aunque no estén acentuados en la última sílaba: travel, traveled o travelled.

**Verbos fuertes**

Forman el pretérito y el participio pasivo cambiando la vocal de la raíz y añadiendo o no **e, en, n** o **ne.** Generalmente tienen el pretérito diferente del participio pasivo: break, **broke, broken;** bear (llevar), **born, borne.**

*Advertencia:* Los pretéritos, participios pasivos y gerundios de los verbos fuertes, así como los de otros que ofrezcan particularidades de forma u ortografía, se encontrarán en el cuerpo de este Diccionario al final del artículo correspondiente a cada verbo.

## Futuro de indicativo

Se forma anteponiendo **shall** o **will** al infinitivo sin **to** (véase lo referente al uso de **shall** y **will** en los respectivos artículos de este Diccionario): I **shall** come, yo vendré; we **will** come, nosotros vendremos; you **will** come, tú vendrás, usted vendrá, vosotros vendréis, ustedes vendrán; he **will** come, él vendrá; they **will** come, ellos vendrán.

## Potencial

Se forma anteponiendo **should** y **would** al infinitivo sin **to** (véase lo referente al uso de **should** y **would** en los respectivos artículos de este Diccionario): I **should** come, yo vendría; we **would** come, nosotras vendríamos; you **would** come, tú vendrías, usted vendría, vosotros vendríais, ustedes vendrían; he **would** come, él vendría; they **would** come, ellos vendrían.

## Imperativo

El imperativo inglés sólo tiene una forma propia que es la del infinitivo sin **to** y sólo se usa para las segundas personas: come, ven, venga usted, venid, vengan ustedes.

Para las personas 1.ª y 3.ª hay que recurrir a una oración formada con el verbo **to let:** let us **see,** veamos.

## Tiempos compuestos

Se forman, como en español, con el verbo auxiliar **to have** (haber) y el participio pasivo.
*Ejemplos:*
I **have played**, yo he jugado; he **has played**, él ha jugado (pretérito perfecto).
I **had played**, yo había jugado o hube jugado (pretérito pluscuamperfecto o pretérito anterior).
I **shall have played**, yo habré jugado; he **will have played**, él habrá jugado (futuro perfecto).
I **should have played**, yo habría jugado; he **would have played**, él habría jugado (potencial compuesto o perfecto).

## Conjugación continua

Además de esta forma de conjugación, el inglés tiene otra llamada *continua* que se forma con el auxiliar **to be** y el gerundio del verbo: **I am coming, I was coming**. Esta forma se usa para indicar una acción en curso de realización, o sea no terminada.

En el presente, corresponde a un presente español del verbo en cuestión o de una oración del verbo *estar:* **I am writing** a letter, escribo una carta o estoy escribiendo una carta.

En el pretérito simple corresponde a un imperfecto español: **he was writing** a letter, él escribía una carta o estaba escribiendo una carta.

*Observación:* La forma continua no puede usarse para expresar una acción instantánea o definitiva, como tampoco una acción habitual o permanente. Así no se dirá: **I am forgiving** him, **the sun is setting** every day, **he is being** her father, sino: **I forgive** him, **the sun sets** every day, **he is** her father.

## INFINITIVO / THE INFINITIVE

Por regla general, el infinitivo va precedido de la partícula **to**, que en muchos casos equivale a las preposiciones *a* o *para.*

**Infinitivo sin to**
El infinitivo se usa sin **to:**

- Después de los auxiliares defectivos **shall, will, can, may** y **must:** I **shall write** to him, le escribiré; you **cannot speak** French, usted no sabe hablar francés; we **must be** quiet, hemos de callar.
  —Nótese que después de **ought** se usa el infinitivo con **to:** you **ought to know** it, usted debería saberlo.
- Después de **to dare** y **to need** usados como auxiliares: he **dared not speak** to him, él no se atrevió a hablarle; they **need not fear**, no tienen por qué temer.
- Después de los verbos que expresan sensación o percepción, como **to hear, to see, to feel, to behold, to observe, to watch**, etc.: I **hear** him **speak** in the hall, le oigo hablar en el vestíbulo; I **felt** the child **tremble** in my arms, sentí al niño temblar en mis brazos.
- Después de los verbos **to let** (dejar, permitir), **to bid** (ordenar, mandar) y **to make** (hacer que se ejecute una acción): **let** me **read** this letter, déjeme leer esta carta; he **bade** her **open** the door, le mandó abrir la puerta.
  —Sin embargo, en la voz pasiva, estos verbos van seguidos del infinitivo con **to:** I **was let to read** the letter, se me dejó leer la carta.
- Después de **and, or, than** y **but** en oraciones como: they decided to **stop** there **and wait** for him, decidieron detenerse allí y esperarle; he was told to be quiet **or go**, se le dijo que se callara o que se fuera; she did nothing other **than laugh**, ella no hizo más que reír.
- En ciertas oraciones interrogativas o exclamatorias: a father **not love** his son!, ¡un padre no querer a su hijo!
- Después de las locuciones **had better, had rather, would rather**, etc.: you **had better wait**, vale más que espere.

**Infinitivo traducido por el subjuntivo o el indicativo**
El infinitivo inglés se traduce algunas veces por un subjuntivo y, aun, por un indicativo español.
*Ejemplos:* he asked me **to pay** the bill, me pidió que pagase la cuenta; the captain ordered the soldiers **to bring** the prisoner, el capitán ordenó a los soldados que trajesen el prisionero; I want him **to do** this, quiero que él haga esto; they expect him **to go** soon, esperan que se irá pronto.

## GERUNDIO / THE GERUND

El gerundio inglés, o sea la forma verbal terminada en **-ing**, puede hacer varios oficios y generalmente se traduce, según los casos:

**Como gerundio**
Por el gerundio español: he was **waiting** for me, él me estaba esperando.

**Como participio—adjetivo**
* Por un participio activo: **cutting** tool, instrumento cortante; in a **surprising** manner, de un modo sorprendente.

* Por un participio pasivo: an **amusing** book, un libro entretenido; **lying** on a sofa, echado en un sofá.

* Por un adjetivo, o por una expresión equivalente a éste: a **calculating** person, una persona calculadora, interesada; **hunting** season, temporada de caza; **sewing** machine, máquina de coser.
  *Observación:* Por su naturaleza verbal puede tener un complemento directo. En este caso se traduce por *que* y un verbo en tiempo personal: a package **containing** six pairs of gloves, un paquete *que* contiene seis pares de guantes.

**Como infinitivo o nombre verbal**
* Por un infinitivo nominal: before **speaking**, antes de hablar; an organization for **helping** the poor, una organización para socorrer a los pobres.

* Por *que* y un verbo en tiempo personal (generalmente en subjuntivo): this door needs **painting**, esta puerta necesita que la pinten.

* Por un sustantivo: he was engaged in the **reading** of that book, estaba ocupado en la lectura de aquel libro.

*Observaciones:*
—**On**, delante de la forma verbal en **-ing**, se traduce generalmente por *al* seguido de un infinitivo: **on** arriving, *al* llegar.
—Cuando un nombre va delante de la forma en **-ing**, debe ponerse en genitivo si es de los que lo admiten: my father was annoyed at Peter's **coming** so late, mi padre estaba enojado de que Pedro viniese tan tarde (o porque Pedro venía tan tarde).
—Si en lugar del nombre hay un pronombre, éste debe tomar la forma del posesivo: would you mind **my opening** the window?, ¿le molestaría que yo abriese la ventana?

## NEGACIÓN / EXPRESSING NEGATION

**Construcción de la oración negativa**
* Cuando el verbo es **to be** o **to have**; **to dare** o **to need** (como auxiliares), o alguno de los defectivos **shall, will, can, may, must** o **ought**, la negación se expresa poniendo **not** inmediatamente después del verbo: they **are not** here, no están aquí; he **dared not** come, no se atrevía a venir; John **will not** win the prize, Juan no ganará el premio; if I **may not** go, si no puedo ir.
  *Observ.:* El presente **can not** se escribe en una sola palabra: **cannot.**

* Cuando el verbo es otro cualquiera en tiempo simple, la negación se expresa por medio del auxiliar **to do** seguido de **not**; el verbo toma la forma invariable del infinitivo sin **to**: I **do not** see it, no lo veo; he **does not** play, él no juega; her father **did not** come, su padre no vino.
  En los tiempos compuestos no se usa **do, does, did** y se pone **not** inmediatamente después del auxiliar: he **has not seen** it, él no lo ha visto.
  *Observ.:* Con **dare** la negación puede expresarse también así, pero el verbo regido lleva **to**: they **did not dare to come**, no se atrevieron a venir.

* En las oraciones interrogativas, **not** se pone después del sujeto si éste es un pronombre y antes de él si es un nombre: do **you not** see it?, ¿no lo ve usted?; **did not** (o **didn't**) **your brother** win the prize?, ¿no ganó el premio su hermano?

- En el infinitivo y en el gerundio se antepone **not** al verbo: **not** to understand, no entender; **not** understanding, no entendiendo.

- En el imperativo se antepone **do not** al verbo: **do not** (o **don't**) laugh, no rías (ría usted, rían ustedes, riáis); **do not** (o **don't**) let them come, que no vengan.

- En el lenguaje corriente **not** se contrae frecuentemente con **do** o con otros verbos: **don't** (do not); **didn't** (did not); **aren't** (are not); **can't** (cannot); **isn't** (is not); **won't** (will not); etc.

- Cuando el carácter negativo de la oración está determinado por palabras como **never**, **no**, **nobody**, **nothing**, **nowhere**, **by no means**, no se usa **not** ni el auxiliar **to do**: it is **never** too late, nunca es tarde; I have **no** time, no tengo tiempo.

## INTERROGACIÓN / INTERROGATIVES

### Construcción de la oración interrogativa

- Cuando el verbo es **to be** o **to have**; **to dare** o **to need** (como auxiliares) o algún defectivo como **shall**, **will**, **can**, **may**, **must** o **ought**, el sujeto va inmediatamente después del verbo: are they here?, ¿están aquí?; have you any money?, ¿tiene usted dinero?; dare you go there?, ¿se atreve usted a ir allí?; need he do it?, ¿necesita hacerlo?; can this boy write?, ¿sabe escribir este niño?

- Cuando el verbo es otro cualquiera en tiempo simple, la oración se construye con el auxiliar **to do**, que va delante del sujeto; el verbo toma la forma invariable del infinitivo sin **to**: do you see this tree?, ¿ve usted este árbol?; did your brother win the race?, ¿ganó la carrera su hermano?
  —En los tiempos compuestos no se usa **do, does, did** y el sujeto va inmediatamente después del auxiliar: have you seen the house?, ¿ha visto usted la casa?

- Cuando la oración empieza con un pronombre interrogativo sujeto del verbo o con un adjetivo interrogativo que acompaña al sujeto, no se usa **do, did** y no hay inversión del sujeto: who wins the prize?, ¿quién gana el premio?; what happened to him?, ¿qué le pasó?; which pillars support the arch?, ¿qué pilares sostienen el arco?

- Después de un adverbio interrogativo la oración se construye como se ha indicado: how long will they remain here?, ¿cuánto tiempo permanecerán aquí?

## CONJUGACIÓN DE TO HAVE (TENER), HAD (TENÍA, TUVE), HAD (TENIDO)

### INDICATIVO

|  | Afirmación | Negación | Interrogación (Negación) |
|---|---|---|---|
| **Presente** | *yo tengo*<br>I have<br>he, she, it has<br>we, you, they have | *yo no tengo*<br>I have not<br>he, she, it has not<br>we, you, they have not | *¿(no) tengo yo?*<br>have I (not)?<br>has he, she, it (not)?<br>have we, you, they (not)? |
| **Pretérito (Past)** | *yo tenía, tuve*<br>I had<br>you had, etc. | *yo no tenía, tuve*<br>I had not<br>you had not, etc. | *¿(no) tenía, tuve yo?*<br>had I (not)?<br>had you (not)?, etc. |
| **Futuro simple** | *yo tendré*<br>I, we shall have<br>you, he, they will have | *yo no tendré*<br>I, we shall not have<br>you, he, they will not have | *¿(no) tendré yo?*<br>shall I, we (not) have?<br>will you, he, they (not) have? |

|  | Afirmación | Negación | Interrogación (Negación) |
|---|---|---|---|
| **Condicional simple** | *yo tendría*<br>I, we should have<br>you, he, they would have | *yo no tendría*<br>I, we should not have<br>you, he, they would not have | *¿(no) tendría yo?*<br>should I, we (not) have?<br>would you, he, they (not) have? |
| **Pretérito perfecto** | *yo he tenido*<br>I, we, you, they have had<br>he has had | *yo no he tenido*<br>I, we, you, they have not had<br>he has not had | *¿(no) he tenido yo?*<br>have I, we, you, they (not) had?<br>has he (not) had? |
| **Pretérito plusc.** | *yo había tenido*<br>I, you...had had | *yo no había tenido*<br>I, you...had not had | *¿(no) había tenido yo?*<br>had I, you...(not) had? |
| **Futuro perfecto** | *yo habré tenido*<br>I, we shall have had<br>you, he, they will have had | *yo no habré tenido*<br>I, we shall not have had<br>you, he, they will not have had | *¿(no) habré yo tenido?*<br>shall I, we (not) have had?<br>will he, you, they (not) have had? |
| **Condicional compuesto** | *yo habría tenido*<br>I, we should have had<br>you, he, they would have had | *yo no habría tenido*<br>I, we should not have had<br>you, he, they would not have had | *¿(no) habría yo tenido?*<br>should I, we (not) have had?<br>would you, he, they (not) have had? |

IMPERATIVO

| Afirmación | Negación |
|---|---|
| *tenga yo* | *no tenga yo* |
| let me have | don't let me have |
| have | don't have, etc. |
| let him (her, it) have | |
| let us have | |
| have | |
| let them have | |

| | |
|---|---|
| PARTICIPIO PRES. } | having |
| GERUNDIO } | *teniendo* |
| PARTICIPIO PAS. | had |
| | *tenido* |
| INFINITIVO SIMPLE | (not) to have |
| | *(no) tener* |
| INFINITIVO COMP. | to have had |
| | *haber tenido* |

## CONJUGACIÓN DE **TO BE** (SER, ESTAR), WAS (ERA, FUI), BEEN (SIDO)

INDICATIVO

| | | Afirmación | Negación | Interrogación (Negación) |
|---|---|---|---|---|
| Presente | | *yo soy*<br>I am<br>he, she, it is<br>we, you, they are | *yo no soy*<br>I am not<br>he, she, it is not<br>we, you, they are not | *¿ (no) soy yo?*<br>am I (not)?<br>is he, she, it (not)?<br>are we, you, they (not)? |
| Pretérito (Past) | | *yo era, fui*<br>I, he was<br>we, you, they were | *yo no era, fui*<br>I, he was not<br>we, you, they were not | *¿ (no) era, fui yo?*<br>was I, he (not)?<br>were we, you, they (not)? |
| Futuro simple | | *yo seré*<br>I, we shall be<br>he, you, they will be | *yo no seré*<br>I, we shall not be<br>he, you, they will not be | *¿ (no) seré yo?*<br>shall I, we (not) be?<br>will you, he, they (not) be? |
| Condicional simple | | *yo sería*<br>I, we should be<br>he, you, they would be | *yo no sería*<br>I, we should not be<br>he, you, they would not be | *¿ (no) sería yo?*<br>should I, we (not) be?<br>would you, he, they (not) be? |
| Pretérito perfecto | | *yo he sido*<br>I, we, you, they have been<br>he has been | *yo no he sido*<br>I, we, you, they have not been<br>he has not been | *¿ (no) he sido yo?*<br>have I, we, you, they (not) been?<br>has he (not) been? |
| Pretérito plusc. | | *yo había sido*<br>I, you...had been | *yo no había sido*<br>I, you...had not been | *¿ (no) había sido yo?*<br>had I, you...(not) been? |
| Futuro perfecto | | *yo habré sido*<br>I, we shall have been<br>you, he, they will have been | *yo no habré sido*<br>I, we shall not have been<br>you, he, they will not have been | *¿ (no) habré yo sido?*<br>shall I, we (not) have been?<br>will you, he, they (not) have been? |
| Condicional compuesto | | *yo habría sido*<br>I, we should have been<br>you, he, they would have been | *yo no habría sido*<br>I, we should not have been<br>you, he, they would not have been | *¿ (no) habría yo sido?*<br>should I, we (not) have been?<br>would you, he, they (not) have been? |

IMPERATIVO

| Afirmación | Negación |
|---|---|
| *sea yo*<br>let me be<br>be<br>let him (her, it) be<br>let us be<br>be<br>let them be | *no sea yo*<br>don't let me be<br>don't be, etc. |

| PARTICIPIO PRES.<br>GERUNDIO } | being<br>*siendo* |
|---|---|
| PARTICIPIO PAS. | been<br>*sido* |
| INFINITIVO SIMPLE | (not) to be<br>*(no) ser* |
| INFINITIVO COMP. | to have been<br>*haber sido* |

# CONJUGACIÓN DE UN VERBO REGULAR

**to look** (mirar), **looked** (miraba, miré), **looked** (mirado)

INDICATIVO

|  | Afirmación | Negación | Interrogación (Negación) |
|---|---|---|---|
| **Presente** | *yo miro*<br>I look<br>you look<br>he, she, it looks<br>we, you, they look | *yo no miro*<br>I do not look<br>you do not look<br>he, she, it does not look<br>we, you, they do not look | *¿(no) miro yo?*<br>do I (not) look?<br>do you (not) look?<br>does he, she, it (not) look?<br>do we, you, they (not) look? |
| **Pretérito (Past)** | *yo miré, miraba*<br>I looked<br>you looked<br>he looked, etc. | *yo no miré, miraba*<br>I did not look<br>you did not look<br>he did not look, etc. | *¿(no) miré, miraba yo?*<br>did I (not) look?<br>did you (not) look?<br>did he (not) look?, etc. |
| **Futuro simple** | *yo miraré*<br>I, we shall look<br>you, he, they will look | *yo no miraré*<br>I, we shall not look<br>you, he, they will not look | *¿(no) miraré yo?*<br>shall I, we (not) look?<br>will you, he, they (not) look? |
| **Condicional simple** | *yo miraría*<br>I, we should look<br>you, he, they would look | *yo no miraría*<br>I, we should not look<br>you, he, they would not look | *¿(no) miraría yo?*<br>should I, we (not) look?<br>would you, he, they (not) look? |
| **Pretérito perfecto** | *yo he mirado*<br>I, we, you, they have looked<br>he has looked | *yo no he mirado*<br>I, we, you, they have not looked<br>he has not looked | *¿(no) he mirado yo?*<br>have I, we, you, they (not) looked?<br>has he (not) looked? |
| **Pretérito plusc.** | *yo había mirado*<br>I, you...had looked | *yo no había mirado*<br>I, you...had not looked | *¿(no) había mirado yo?*<br>had I, you...(not) looked? |
| **Futuro perfecto** | *yo habré mirado*<br>I, we shall have looked<br>you, he, they will have looked | *yo no habré mirado*<br>I, we shall not have looked<br>you, he, they will not have looked | *¿(no) habré yo mirado?*<br>shall I, we (not) have looked?<br>will you, he, they (not) have looked? |
| **Condicional compuesto** | *yo habría mirado*<br>I, we should have looked<br>you, he, they would have looked | *yo no habría mirado*<br>I, we should not have looked<br>you, he, they would not have looked | *¿(no) habría yo mirado?*<br>should I, we (not) have looked?<br>would you, he, they (not) have looked? |

IMPERATIVO

| Afirmación | Negación |
|---|---|
| *mire yo* | *no mire yo* |
| let me look | don't let me look |
| look | don't look, etc. |
| let him (her, it) look | |
| let us look | |
| look | |
| let them look | |

| | |
|---|---|
| PARTICIPIO PRES. <br> GERUNDIO | looking <br> *mirando* |
| PARTICIPIO PAS. | looked <br> *mirado* |
| INFINITIVO SIMPLE | (not) to look <br> *(no) mirar* |
| INFINITIVO COMP. | to have looked <br> *haber mirado* |

## CONJUGACIÓN DE UN VERBO IRREGULAR

**to go** (ir), **went** (iba, fui), **gone** (ido)

INDICATIVO

| | Afirmación | Negación | Interrogación (Negación) |
|---|---|---|---|
| **Presente** | *yo voy* <br> I go <br> you go <br> he, she, it goes <br> we, you, they go | *yo no voy* <br> I do not go <br> you do not go <br> he, she, it does not go <br> we, you, they do not go | *¿ (no) voy yo?* <br> do I (not) go? <br> do you (not) go? <br> does he, she, it (not) go? <br> do we, you, they (not) go? |
| **Pretérito (Past)** | *yo iba, fui* <br> I went <br> you went <br> he went, etc. | *yo no iba, fui* <br> I did not go <br> you did not go <br> he did not go, etc. | *¿ (no) fui, iba yo?* <br> did I (not) go? <br> did you (not) go? <br> did he (not) go?, etc. |
| **Futuro simple** | *yo iré* <br> I, we shall go <br> you, he, they will go | *yo no iré* <br> I, we shall not go <br> you, he, they will not go | *¿ (no) iré yo?* <br> shall I, we (not) go? <br> will you, he, they (not) go? |
| **Condicional simple** | *yo iría* <br> I, we should go <br> you, he, they would go | *yo no iría* <br> I, we should not go <br> you, he, they would not go | *¿ (no) iría yo?* <br> should I, we (not) go? <br> would you, he, they (not) go? |

|  | Afirmación | Negación | Interrogación (Negación) |
|---|---|---|---|
| **Pretérito perfecto** | *yo he ido*<br>I, we, you, they have gone<br>he has gone | *yo no he ido*<br>I, we, you, they have not gone<br>he has not gone | *¿(no) he ido yo?*<br>have I, we, you, they (not) gone?<br>has he (not) gone? |
| **Pretérito plusc.** | *yo había ido*<br>I, you...had gone | *yo no había ido*<br>I, you...had not gone | *¿(no) había ido yo?*<br>had I, you...(not) gone? |
| **Futuro perfecto** | *yo habré ido*<br>I, we shall have gone<br>you, he, they will have gone | *yo no habré ido*<br>I, we shall not have gone<br>you, he, they will not have gone | *¿(no) habré yo ido?*<br>shall I, we (not) have gone?<br>will you, he, they (not) have gone? |
| **Condicional compuesto** | *yo habría ido*<br>I, we should have gone<br>you, he, they would have gone | *yo no habría ido*<br>I, we should not have gone<br>you, he, they would not have gone | *¿(no) habría yo ido?*<br>should I, we (not) have gone?<br>would you, he, they (not) have gone? |

IMPERATIVO

| Afirmación | Negación |
|---|---|
| *vaya yo*<br>let me go<br>go<br>let him (her, it) go<br>let us go<br>go<br>let them go | *no vaya yo*<br>don't let me go<br>don't go, etc. |

| | |
|---|---|
| PARTICIPIO PRES.<br>GERUNDIO } | going<br>*yendo* |
| PARTICIPIO PAS. | gone<br>*ido* |
| INFINITIVO SIMPLE | (not) to go<br>*(no) ir* |
| INFINITIVO COMP. | to have gone<br>*haber ido* |

# SUBJUNTIVO / THE SUBJUNCTIVE MOOD

El inglés no tiene formas propias para el subjuntivo, excepto en el verbo to be, cuyo presente de subjuntivo es **be** y cuyo pretérito de subjuntivo es **were** para todas las personas del singular y del plural: whoever he **be**, quienquiera que sea; if I **were** in his place, si yo estuviese en su lugar.

En todo otro caso, el inglés expresa el subjuntivo mediante: a) el infinitivo; b) una forma de indicativo; c) una forma compuesta con los auxiliares **may** o **might** y **should**.

**Por regla general:**

- Cuando la acción expresada por el subjuntivo es pensada como cierta, se usa el infinitivo o el indicativo: tell him **to go away**, dígale que se vaya; as you **please**, como usted quiera o guste; wait till he **comes**, aguarde hasta que él venga.

- Cuando la acción es pensada como incierta, dudosa o simplemente deseada, se usa una forma compuesta con may, might o should.

  **May, might** se usan:
  —Para expresar la idea del verbo *poder*: however strong he **might be**, por fuerte que fuese.
  —Para expresar un deseo, una orden: **may** he live long, que viva muchos años.
  —En oraciones finales después de **that, in order that, so that** (para que, a fin de que): he went away **that** they **might** not **find** him in the house, se fue para que no le encontrasen en la casa.

  Se usa **should:**
  —Después de **that** (conjunción *que*): he seemed to expect **that** I **should assent** to this, parecía esperar que yo asintiese a esto; **that** I **should be** so unfortunate!, ¡que sea yo tan desgraciado!
  —Después de conjunciones condicionales o concesivas, como **if, though, even though,** etc.: **if** he **should come**, si él viniese; **though** he **should come**, aunque él viniese.
  —Después de lest: I shall keep your book **lest** you **should lose** it, guardaré tu libro para que no lo pierdas.

**Observaciones:**

- **If** puede omitirse en ciertos casos a condición de poner el sujeto detrás de **should, had** o **were**: should **he** know it, si él lo supiese; had **I** known it, si yo lo hubiese sabido; were **I** in his place, si yo estuviese en su lugar.

- Después de **for fear that** se usa **should** en el presente y **should** o **might** en el pretérito: he is running away **for fear that** his father **should punish** him, huye por miedo de que su padre le castigue; he ran away for fear that his father **should** (o **might**) **punish** him, huyó por miedo de que su padre lo castigase.

# ADVERBIO / ADVERBS

El inglés tiene muchos adverbios derivados de adjetivo, análogos a los españoles terminados en *-mente*. Se forman añadiendo -ly al adjetivo. Así de bad, se forma **badly**; de bright, **brightly**, etc.

Esta forma de derivación tiene las siguientes alteraciones:

- Los adjetivos terminados en **-le** pierden esta terminación: possible, **possibly**; tolerable, **tolerably**.
- Los terminados en **-ue** pierden la e: due, **duly**; true, **truly**.
- Los terminados en **-ll** sólo añaden la y: dull, **dully**; full, **fully**.
- Los terminados en **-y** cambian esta letra en i: guilty, **guiltily**; showy, **showily**.

## Lugar del adverbio

Cuando modifica una palabra que no es el verbo:

- Por regla general, va delante de la palabra que modifica: **seriously** ill, gravemente enfermo; **very** well, muy bien; **long** before, mucho antes.
  —Se exceptúan **enough**, que siempre va detrás de la palabra que modifica: good **enough** for me, suficientemente bueno para mí; y **ago**, que siempre va detrás de las palabras que expresan el período de tiempo: two years **ago**, hace dos años.

Cuando modifica al verbo:

- Si el verbo es transitivo, el adverbio no puede separar el verbo del complemento directo: va delante del verbo o después del complemento. En los tiempos compuestos, puede ir también después del verbo auxiliar: he **easily** defeated his opponent, he defeated his opponent **easily**, ha derrotado fácilmente a su adversario.

  —Sin embargo, cuando el complemento directo consta de muchas palabras o está complementado por una oración, el adverbio puede ir entre el verbo y el complemento directo: he rewarded **liberally** all those who had served his father, recompensó liberalmente a todos los que habían servido a su padre.

- Si el verbo es intransitivo, el adverbio va después del verbo, tanto en los tiempos simples como en los compuestos: she has sung **wonderfully**, ha cantado maravillosamente.

  —Sin embargo, algunos adverbios, como **suddenly, promptly**, etc., pueden ir después del auxiliar de los tiempos compuestos: the wind has **suddenly** risen, el viento ha soplado de pronto.

- Si el verbo es **to be**, el adverbio suele ir después del verbo o después del auxiliar de los tiempos compuestos: he is **always** silent, siempre está callado.

- Como en español, el adverbio va al principio de la oración cuando modifica la oración entera o cuando se quiere dar mayor fuerza a la expresión: **meanwhile**, I was writing the letter, entretanto yo escribía la carta.

Casos particulares

No yendo con el verbo **to be**, los adverbios **also, even, first, once** y **quite**, los de tiempo indefinido y los seminegativos como **almost, nearly, hardly, only** y **scarcely**, van siempre entre el sujeto y el verbo o después del auxiliar de los tiempos compuestos: he **never** spoke about it, él nunca ha hablado de ello.

En cambio, los adverbios de tiempo **early, late, today, tonight** y los polisílabos como **yesterday, presently**, etc.; los de lugar; los de cantidad, y los de modo **very well, badly** y **worse**, van al final de la oración: they arrived **late**, ellos llegaron tarde.

### El comparativo y el superlativo

El comparativo y el superlativo de los adverbios se forman como los del adjetivo. Algunos tienen formas propias que se encontrarán en los artículos correspondientes de este Diccionario.

## PREPOSICIÓN / PREPOSITIONS

### Traslado de la preposición

La preposición mediante la cual el verbo rige a un complemento se puede trasladar al final de la oración:

- En las oraciones interrogativas: whom are you speaking **to**? (o sea: **to** whom are you speaking?), ¿a quién habla usted?

- En las subordinadas que empiezan por un pronombre relativo: I did not know the man whom I was speaking **with** (o the man **with** whom I was speaking), yo no conocía al hombre con quien estaba hablando.

Esta construcción es obligatoria cuando el pronombre relativo es **that**, ya sea expreso o elíptico: he has the book (**that**) you are looking for, él tiene el libro que usted busca.

### Omisión de la preposición

En algunas frases adverbiales o prepositivas y en ciertas expresiones, se omiten las preposiciones:

at: (at) every moment, en todo momento; (at) full speed, a toda velocidad; (at) that hour, entonces; (at) the next moment, un momento después; he looked (at) me in the face, me miró a la cara.

of: on board (of) the ship, a bordo del buque; (of) what use is this to me?, ¿de qué me sirve esto?

with: (with) tooth and nail, con dientes y uñas, encarnizadamente, desesperadamente.

## COMPLEMENTOS DIRECTO E INDIRECTO / DIRECT AND INDIRECT OBJECTS

En inglés, el complemento directo se construye siempre sin preposición. El complemento indirecto suele llevar preposición.

En la construcción regular, el complemento directo va inmediatamente después del verbo y el complemento indirecto, después del directo: John has explained his conduct, Juan ha explicado su conducta; John has explained his conduct to Peter, Juan ha explicado su conducta a Pedro.

### Cambios de lugar del complemento

Con ciertos verbos, como to allow, to answer, to bring, to do, to get, to give, to lend, to owe, to send, to show, to take, to teach, to tell, to write, etc., el complemento indirecto puede ir delante del directo. En este caso no lleva preposición: he gave his son a book, dio un libro a su hijo.

Pero cuando estos dos complementos son pronombres, el acusativo precede siempre al dativo: John gave it to him, Juan se lo dio.

### El complemento directo va delante del verbo:

- Para dar mayor realce al complemento: he had two fine horses: **the black one** he gave to his son, **the white one** to his daughter, tenía dos hermosos caballos: el negro lo dio a su hijo; el blanco, a su hija.

- Cuando el complemento es un pronombre relativo o interrogativo: the man **that** (o **whom**) we saw, el hombre que vimos; **what** do you see?, ¿qué ve usted?

- Cuando va precedido de un adjetivo interrogativo: **which road** must I take?, ¿qué camino he de tomar?

- En las oraciones exclamativas precedidas de **what**: **what nonsense** you talk!, ¡qué tonterías dice usted!; **what a beautiful book** he has written!, ¡qué hermoso libro ha escrito!

### Omisión del complemento directo

El complemento directo se omite frecuentemente cuando es un pronombre relativo: the man **(that** o **whom)** we were looking for, el hombre que buscábamos.

## MAYÚSCULAS / CAPITAL LETTERS

### Se escriben con mayúscula:

- Las mismas palabras que llevan mayúscula en español.
- Las derivadas de nombres propios: **Aristotelian, Aristotelianism, Christian, Christianity, Victorian.**
- Los nombres de pueblos, razas, naciones, tribus y lenguas con sus compuestos y derivados: **Angles, Anglo-Norman, Anglican, Chinaman, Chinese, French, Hispanic, Hispanophile, Inca, Incan.**
- Los de credos o confesiones, de religiones o sectas y de las órdenes religiosas, con sus derivados: **Apostles' Creed, Augsburg Confession, Catholic, Catholicism, Protestant, Protestantism.**
- Los de instituciones, congresos, exposiciones, cuerpos legisladores, organizaciones, partidos políticos, etc.: **Congress of Vienna, Columbian Exposition, House of Representatives, Spanish Army.**
- Los de tratados, batallas, acontecimientos históricos, períodos, épocas, eras: **Treaty of Westphalia, Battle of Verdun, Revolutionary War, Middle Ages, Jurassic, Christian Era, Before Christ.**
- Los de los días de la semana, de los meses del año y de las fiestas: **Monday, June, Good Friday, Mother's Day.**
- Los de calle, plaza, etc.: **Madison Avenue, Trafalgar Square, Central Park.**
- Los de las estaciones del año y los de ciertas ideas abstractas cuando se quieren personificar: **Spring, Winter, Autumn.**
- Los de los tipos, clases, órdenes, familias, etc., de plantas y animales: **Monocotyledones, Platanaceae, Mammalia, Ursidae.**
- Las palabras que constituyen el saludo de las cartas, comunicaciones, etc.: **Dear Father.**
- Las palabras State, Territory, Dominion, Province, Department, etc., cuando forman parte del nombre de una división determinada: **the State of Texas, the Dominion of Canada.**
- La palabra Church cuando se aplica a una iglesia determinada: **Roman Catholic Church, St. Peter's Church.**
- I (pronombre, *yo*) y O (interjeccion).

**A, a** (ei) *s*. A, a [vocal]. *2* MÚS. la.
**a** *art. indef.* un, una. V. ARTÍCULO (cuadro gramatical). *2* un tal, cierto: ~ *Mr. Brown*, un tal (o cierto) señor Brown. *3* el, la, al, a la, por, cada [con valor distributivo]: *two dollars* ~ *yard*, dos dólares la (o cada) yarda. *4 what* ~...!, ¡qué...! *5 such* ~..., tal..., tan...
**Aaron** (e·ørøn) *n. pr.* Aarón.
**abaca** (abaka·) *s*. abacá.
**aback** (abæk·k) *adv.* atrás, hacia atrás. *2* MAR. en facha. *3* fig. *to take* ~, sorprender, desconcertar.
**abacus** (æ·bakøs) *s*. ábaco.
**abaft** (abæ·ft) *adv.* MAR. a popa, hacia popa.
**abandon** (abæ·ndøn) *s*. abandono, naturalidad, desenvoltura. *2* desenfreno.
**abandon (to)** *tr.* abandonar. *2 ref.* abandonarse, entregarse.
**abandoned** (-d) *adj* abandonado. *2* vicioso, depravado.
**abandonment** (-mønt) *s*. abandono, dejación; entrega de sí mismo. *2* abandono, desamparo. *3* desenfreno.
**abase (to)** (abei·s) *tr.* humillar. *2* rebajar, envilecer.
**abasement** (-mønt) *s*. humillación. *2* degradación, envilecimiento.
**abash (to)** (abæ·sh) *tr.* correr, avergonzar, confundir, desconcertar.
**abashment** (-mønt) *s*. vergüenza, confusión.
**abate (to)** (abei·t) *tr.* rebajar, reducir, disminuir, moderar. *2* deducir, quitar. *3* DER. suprimir, anular. *4 intr.* menguar, disminuir, amainar, calmarse, ceder, remitir.
**abatement** (-mønt) *s*. disminución. *2* mitigación, moderación. *3* rebaja, deducción. *4* DER. supresión, anulación.
**abatis** (æ·batis) *s*. FORT. tala.
**abattoir** (æbætua·ʳ) *s*. matadero.
**abbacy** (æ·basi) *s*. abadía, abadiado, abiadato.
**abbatial** (æbei·shal) *adj.* abacial, abadengo.
**abbess** (æ·bis) *f*. abadesa.
**abbey** (æ·bi) *s*. abadía, monasterio.
**abbot** (æ·bøt) *m*. abad.
**abbotship** (-ship) *s*. ABBACY.
**abbreviate (to)** (abri·vieit) *tr.* abreviar.
**abbreviation** (-ei·shøn) *s*. abreviación. *2* abreviatura.
**abbreviature** (-viachuʳ) *s*. compendio, resumen.

**abdicate (to)** (æ·bdikeit) *intr.* abdicar.
**abdication** (-kei·shøn) *s*. abdicación.
**abdomen** (æ·bdømen) *s*. abdomen.
**abdominal** (æbda·minal) *adj.* abdominal.
**abdominous** (-nøs) *adj.* panzudo.
**abducent** (æbdiu·sønt) *adj.* FISIOL. abductor.
**abduct (to)** (æbdø·kt) *tr.* raptar, secuestrar. *2* FISIOL. producir la abducción de.
**abduction** (æbdø·kshøn) *s*. rapto, robo, secuestro. *2* FISIOL. abducción.
**abductor** (æbdø·ktøʳ) *s*. raptor, secuestrador. *2* ANAT. abductor.
**abeam** (abı·m) *adv.* MAR. por el través.
**abed** (abe·d) *adv.* en cama, acostado.
**abelmosk** (ei·bølmask) *s*. BOT. abelmosco.
**aberrance, -cy** (æbe·rans, -si) *s*. error, extravío. *2* H. NAT. anormalidad.
**aberrant** (æbe·rant) *s*. aberrante, extraviado.
**aberration** (æbørei·shøn) *s*. aberración.
**abet (to)** (abe·t) *tr.* alentar, consentir, ayudar [delito o delincuente]. ¶ Pret. y p. p.: *abetted;* ger.: *-tting.*
**abetment** (abe·tmønt) *s*. ayuda, complicidad.
**abetter, abettor** (abe·tør) *s*. fautor, instigador, cómplice.
**abhor (to)** (æbjo·ʳ) *tr.* aborrecer, detestar, repugnar.
**abhorrence** (æbjo·røns) *s*. aborrecimiento, detestación.
**abhorrent** (-rønt) *adj.* aborrecible, detestable. *2* opuesto, incompatible. *3* que aborrece.
**abidance** (abai·dans) *s*. estancia, permanencia. *2* observancia [de leyes, reglas, etc.].
**abide (to)** (abai·d) *intr.* morar, habitar. *2* quedarse, permanecer. *3* mantenerse, continuar [en un estado o condición]. *4 to* ~ *by*, apoyar, estar con o por; mantener [lo dicho, una opinión, etc.]; cumplir, observar; conformarse con, atenerse a. *5 tr.* esperar, aguardar. *6* sufrir, tolerar, aguantar. ¶ Pret. y p. p.: *abode* o *abided.*
**abiding** (abai·ding) *adj.* permanente, durable. *2* observante. *3* ~ *place*, domicilio, morada.
**Abietineae** (æbieti·nii) *s. pl.* BOT. abietáceas.
**abigail** (æ·bigeil) *s*. fig. doncella, camarera.
**ability** (abi·liti) *s*. habilidad, capacidad, talento, aptitud, ingenio. *2* poder, facultad; posibilidades.
**abintestate** (æbinte·steit) *adj.* abintestato.

**abject** (æ·bdỹekt) *adj.* abyecto.
**abjection** (æbdỹe·kshøn), **abjectness** (-tnis) *s.* abyección.
**abjuration** (æbdỹurei·shøn) *s.* abjuración.
**abjure (to)** (æbdyū·ʳ) *tr.* abjurar.
**ablation** (æblei·shøn) *s.* ablación.
**ablative** (æ·blativ) *adj.-s.* ablativo.
**ablaze** (ablei·š) *adv.* y *adj.* ardiendo, en llamas. 2 *adj.* resplandeciente. 3 fig. encendido.
**able** (ei·bøl) *adj.* que puede: *to be* ~, poder. 2 hábil, diestro, capaz, compete`nte. 3 DER. capaz.
**able-bodied** *adj.* sano, robusto, válido.
**abloom** (ablu·m) *adj.* y *adv.* en flor; floreciente.
**ablush** (ablø·sh) *adj.* y *adv.* ruborizado.
**ablution** (æblu·shøn) *s.* ablución.
**ably** (ei·bli) *adv.* hábilmente, inteligentemente.
**abnegate (to)** (æ·bnigeit) *tr.* renunciar, negarse [algo] a sí mismo. 2 abjurar.
**abnegation** (-gei·shøn) *s.* renuncia, abnegación.
**abnormal** (æbno·ʳmal) *adj.* anormal.
**abnormality** (-mæ·liti) *s.* anormalidad.
**abnormity** (-miti) *s.* anomalía; monstruosidad.
**aboard** (abo·ʳd) *adv.* a bordo. 2 en un tren, etc.: *all* ~!, ¡viajeros al tren! 3 MAR. junto a: *to keep the land* ~, costear.
**abode** (abou·d) *pret.* y *p. p.* de TO ABIDE. 2 *s.* morada, domicilio. 3 estancia [en un lugar].
**abolish (to)** (aba·lish) *tr.* abolir, suprimir.
**abolishment** (-mønt), **abolition** (æboli·shøn) *s.* abolición, supresión.
**abolitionist** (-ist) *s.* abolicionista.
**A-bomb** (ei·bam) *s.* bomba atómica.
**abominable** (aba·minabøl) *adj.* abominable.
**abominate (to)** (aba·mineit) *tr.* abominar, abominar de.
**abomination** (-nei·shøn) *s.* abominación.
**aboriginal** (æbori·dỹinal) *adj.-s.* aborigen.
**aborigines** (-dỹinis) *s. pl.* aborígenes.
**abort (to)** (abo·t) *intr.* abortar.
**abortion** (abo·ʳshøn) *s.* aborto. 2 fracaso.
**abortive** (abo·ʳtiv) *adj.-s.* abortivo. 2 *adj.* abortado, malograḍo.
**abound (to)** (aba·nd) *intr.* abundar.
**about** (abau·t) *prep.* cerca de, junto a, alrededor, en torno de. 2 por, en [un espacio, lugar, etc.]: *to play* ~ *the garden*, jugar en el jardín. 3 encima, consigo, en [una pers. o cosa]: *have you much money* ~ *you?*, ¿lleva usted mucho dinero [encima]? 4 tocante a, con respecto a, sobre, acerca de, de, en: *to speak* ~, hablar de; *to think* ~, pensar en. 5 poco más o menos, sobre, cosa de, unos, unas. 6 hacia, a eso de: ~ *zero*, sobre cero; ~ *las times*, estar al día. 7 ocupado en, cuidando de. 8 *to be* ~ *to* [con un inf.], estar a punto de, estar para, ir a.
9 *adv.* alrededor, en torno, por todas partes, aquí y allí, circularmente, en contorno: *all* ~, por todas partes. 10 casi, aproximadamente. 11 en sentido o posición opuesta: *to face* ~, volverse, dar media vuelta.
**about-face** *s.* media vuelta.
**above** (abø·v) *prep.* sobre, encima de, por encima de; superior a, fuera de: ~ *my strength*, superior a mis fuerzas; ~ *my reach*, fuera de mi alcance; ~ *mean actions*, incapaz de acciones mezquinas. 2 arriba de, más de o más que. 3 ~ *all*, sobre todo, principalmente.
4 *adv.* arriba, en lo alto. 5 antes, anteriormente, más arriba [en un escrito].
6 *adj.* antedicho, arriba expresado; anterior, precedente. 7 *s.* lo antedicho, lo dicho o mencionado más arriba.

**aboveboard** (-bo·ʳd) *adv.* abiertamente, francamente. 2 *adj.* franco, sincero.
**abracadabra** (æbrakadæ·bra) *s.* abracadabra.
**abrade (to)** (æbrei·d) *tr.* desgastar.
**Abraham** (ei·brajæm) *n. pr.* Abrahán.
**abrasion** (æbrei·ỹøn) *s.* abrasión.
**abrasive** (æbrei·šiv) *adj.-s.* abrasivo.
**abreast** (abre·st) *adv.* de frente [uno al lado de otro]: *four* ~, a cuatro de frente. 2 *to keep* ~ *of the times*, estar al día. 3·MAR. por el través.
**abridge (to)** (abri·dỹy) *tr.* abreviar, acortar. 2 resumir, compendiar. 3 privar, despojar.
**abridg(e)ment** (-mønt) *s.* abreviación, acortamiento. 2 compendio. 3 privación, merma.
**abroad** (abro·d) *adv.* fuera de casa; en el extranjero, al extranjero. 2 sobre un gran espacio, hasta lejos. 3 suelto, en libertad; en circulación por todas partes: *to set* ~, divulgar, propalar; *there is a rumor* ~, corre la voz. 4 *to be all* ~, estar equivocado.
**abrogate (to)** (æ·brogeit) *tr.* abrogar.
**abrupt** (abrø·pt) *adj.* abrupto, escarpado. 2 brusco. 3 precipitado, súbito. 4 inconexo [estilo].
**abruption** (-shøn) *s.* rotura, desgajamiento.
**abruptness** (-nis) *s.* escabrosidad [de un terreno]. 2 brusquedad. 3 precipitación.
**abscess** (æ·bses) *s.* MED. absceso.
**abscissa** (æbsi·sa) *s.* GEOM. abscisa.
**abscission** (-shøn) *s.* CIR. abscisión.
**abscond (to)** (æbsca·nd) *intr.* esconderse. 2 huir, substraerse a la justicia.
**absence** (æ·bsøns) *s.* ausencia: *leave of* ~, permiso [a un militar o funcionario]. 2 falta de asistencia. 3 falta, carencia. 4 ~ *of mind*, distracción, abstracción.
**absent** (æ·bsønt) *adj.* ausente. 2 distraído.
**absent oneself (to)** (æbse·nt) *ref.* ausentarse.
**absentee** (æbsøntı·) *s.* ausente. 2 absentista.
**absenteeism** (-išm) *s.* absentismo. 2 costumbre de faltar al trabajo.
**absent-minded** *adj.* distraído, abstraído.
**absinth, absinthe** (æ·bsinz) *s.* ajenjo.
**absolute** (æ·bsoliut) *adj.* absoluto. 2 categórico. 3 autoritario, perentorio. 4 *s.* lo absoluto.
**absolutely** (-li) *adv.* absolutamente. 2 categóricamente, terminantemente.
**absolution** (æ·bsoliu·shøn) *s.* absolución.
**absolutism** (æ·bsoliutišm) *s.* absolutismo.
**absolutist** (-ist) *adj.-s.* absolutista.
**absolve (to)** (æbsa·lv) *tr.* absolver. 2 perdonar, remitir.
**absorb (to)** (æbsoʳb) *tr.* absorber. 2 *ref.* abstraerse, enfrascarse.
**absorbed** (-d) *adj.* absorbido. 2 embebido, absorto.
**absorbent** (-ønt) *adj.-s.* absorbente: ~ *cotton*, algodón hidrófilo.
**absorber** (-øʳ) *s.* absorbente. 2 MEC. amortiguador.
**absorbing** (-ing) *adj.* absorbente [que interesa o preocupa].
**absorption** (æbso·ʳoshøn) *s.* absorción. 2 embebecimiento, enfrascamiento.
**abstain (to)** (æbstei·n) *intr.* abstenerse.
**abstainer** (-øʳ) *s.* abstemio.
**abstemious** (æbstı·miøs) *adj.* abstemio. 2 sobrio, templado. 3 de abstinencia [día].
**abstention** (æbste·nshøn) *s.* abstención.
**abstergent** (æbstøʳdỹønt) *adj.-s.* abstergente.
**abstersion** (-shøn) *s.* abtersión.
**abstinence, abstinency** (æ·bstinøns, -i) *s.* abstinencia. 2 sobriedad, templanza.
**abstinent** (æ·bstinønt) *adj.* abstinente.

**abstract** (æ·bstrǽkt) *adj.* abstracto: *in the* ~, en abstracto. *2 s.* extracto, resumen, compendio.

**abstract (to)** (æbstrǽ·kt) *tr.* abstraer. *2* sustraer, robar. *3* distraer [apartar la atención de uno]. *4* resumir, compendiar.

**abstracted** (æbstrǽ·ktid) *adj.* abstraído. *2* distraído.

**abstraction** (æbstrǽ·kshøn) *s.* abstracción. *2* distracción, ensimismamiento. *3* sustracción, hurto. *4* retiro, recogimiento.

**abstractive** (æbstrǽ·ktiv) *adj.* abstractivo.

**abstruse** (æbstru·s) *adj.* abstruso.

**absurd** (æbsø·ᵈd) *adj.* absurdo.

**absurdity** (-iti) *s.* absurdidad, absurdo.

**abulia** (æbiu·lia) *s.* abulia.

**abundance** (abø·ndans) *s.* abundancia.

**abundant** (abø·ndant) *adj.* abundante: ~ *in* o *with*, abundante en, lleno de.

**abuse** (abiu·š) *s.* abuso. *2* corruptela. *3* maltrato, insultos, denuestos.

**abuse (to)** *tr.* abusar de. *2* maltratar, denostar, denigrar, hablar mal de.

**abusive** (abiu·siv) *adj.* abusivo. *2* injurioso, insultante.

**abut (to)** (abø·t) *intr. to* ~ *on, upon* o *against*, terminar en; lindar, confinar con; empalmar con; estribar en. ¶ Pret. y p. p.: *abutted;* ger.: *-tting.*

**abutment** (-mønt) *s.* punto donde estriba algo; estribo, contrafuerte. *2* contigüidad [de terrenos]; linde. *3* CARP. empalme.

**abysm** (abi·šm) *s.* ABYSS.

**abysmal** (-al) *adj.* ABYSSAL.

**abyss** (abi·s) *s.* abismo.

**abyssal** (abi·sal) *adj.* abismal, abisal. *2* insondable.

**Abyssinia** (æbisi·nia) *n. pr.* Abisinia.

**Abyssinian** (-n) *adj.-s.* abisinio.

**acacia** (akei·sha) *s.* BOT. acacia.

**academic** (ækade·mik) *adj.-s.* académico. *2 s.* universitario.

**academical** (-al) *adj.* académico. *2* teórico.

**academicals** (-s) *s. pl.* traje o distintivos usados en ciertas universidades.

**academician** (ækade·mishan) *s.* académico.

**academy** (akæ·dømi) *s.* academia. *2* colegio, escuela. *3* (con may.) Academia [de Platón].

**acalephan** (ækøle·fan) *adj.-s.* acalefo.

**acanthaceous** (ækænze·shøs) *adj.* acantáceo.

**acanthopterygian** (ækænzaptøri·ŷian) *adj.-s.* ICT. acantopterigio.

**acanthus** (ækæ·nzøs) *s.* BOT., ARQ. acanto.

**acarid** (æ·kørid) *s.* acárido.

**acarus** (æ·karøs), *pl.* **-ri** (-ri o -rai) *s.* ácaro.

**acaulescent** (ækole·sønt) *adj.* BOT. acaule.

**accede (to)** (æksi·d) *intr.* acceder, asentir. *2* ascender, subir [a un cargo o dignidad].

**accelerate (to)** (ækse·løreit) *tr* acelerar, apresurar. *2 intr.* acelerarse, apresurarse.

**acceleration** (-ei·shøn) *s.* aceleración.

**accelerative** (-tiv) *adj.* acelerador, -triz.

**accelerator** (-tør) *s.* acelerador.

**accent** (æ·ksent) *s.* acento. *2* dejo, tonillo.

**accent (to)** (ækse·nt) *tr.* acentuar.

**accentuate (to)** (ækse·nchueit) *tr.* acentuar. *2* intensificar.

**accentuation** (-ei·shøn) *s.* acentuación.

**accept (to)** (ækse·pt) *tr.* aceptar. *2* admitir [como cierto], creer. *3* entender, interpretar.

**acceptable** (-abøl) *adj.* aceptable, admisible. *2* acepto, grato, bien recibido.

**acceptance** (-ans) *s.* aceptación, admisión. *2* aceptación, buena acogida. *3* COM. aceptación.

**acceptation** (ei·shøn) *s.* acepción, sentido.

**acceptor** (-tøʳ) *s.* aceptador, aceptante.

**acces** (æ·kses) *s.* acceso [en todos sus sentidos]. *2* aumento, añadidura.

**accessible** (ækse·sibøl) *adj.* accesible. *2* asequible.

**accession** (-shøn) *s.* asentimiento. *2* entrada [en un grupo, etc.]. *3* advenimiento, subida [a un cargo o dignidad]. *4* aumento, agregación. *5* MED., DER. accesión.

**accessit** (-sit) *s.* accésit.

**accessory** (-sori) *adj.* accesorio, adicional. *2* que contribuye o tiene complicidad. *3 s.* accesorio. *4* cómplice, encubridor, inductor: ~ *after the fact*, encubridor; ~ *before the fact*, cómplice, inductor.

**accidence** (æ·ksidøns) *s.* GRAM. los accidentes.

**accident** (æ·ksidønt) *s.* accidente. *2* casualidad. *3* percance.

**accidental** (ækside·ntal) *adj.* accidental. *2* casual, imprevisto. *3 m.* accidente [lo no esencial]. *4* MÚS. accidental, accidente.

**acclaim** (æklei·m) *s.* aclamación [grito].

**acclaim (to)** *tr.-intr.* aclamar. *2* proclamar.

**acclamation** (ækl;amei·shøn) *s.* aclamación.

**acclimate (to)** (æklai·mit) *tr.-intr.* ACCLIMATIZE.

**acclimation** (æklimei·shøn), **acclimatization** (æklaimatišei·shøn) *s.* aclimatación.

**acclimatize (to)** (æklai·mataiš) *tr.* aclimatar. *2 intr.* aclimatarse.

**acclivity** (ækli·viti) *s.* cuesta, pendiente.

**accolade** (ækolei·d) *s.* acolada, espaldarazo. *2* MÚS. corchete, barra.

**accommodate (to)** (aka·modeit) *tr.* acomodar, ajustar, amoldar. *2* arreglar, reconciliar. *3* acomodar, proveer [del]; servir, hacer un favor [a]. *4* hospedar, alojar. *5 intr.* conformarse, avenirse. *6* tener cabida [para].

**accommodating** (-ing) *adj.* servicial, complaciente, amable.

**accommodation** (-ei·shøn) *s.* acomodación, adaptación. *2* acomodamiento, arreglo, conciliación. *3* complacencia, carácter servicial. *4* servicio, favor: ~ *bill*, o *simplte. accommodation*, letra de favor. *5* cabida, sitio; alojamiento [en un hotel]. *6* FISIOL. acomodación. *7 pl.* facilidades, comodidades.

**accompaniment** (akø·mpanimønt) *s.* acompañamiento.

**accompanist** (-nist) *s.* MÚS. acompañante.

**accompany (to)** (akø·mpani) *tr.* acompañar. ¶ Pret. y p. p.: *accompanied.*

**accomplice** (aka·mplis) *s.* cómplice.

**accomplish (to)** (aka·mplish) *tr.* hacer, ejecutar, acabar, llevar a cabo, cumplir. *2* lograr. *3* dotar, adornar [física o moralmente].

**accomplished** (-t) *adj.* cumplido, perfecto, consumado. *2* culto, instruido; distinguido.

**accomplishment** (-mønt) *s.* realización, ejecución, cumplimiento. *2* logro. *3 pl.* talentos, habilidades.

**accord** (aka·ᵈd) *s.* acuerdo, concierto, armonía: *with one* ~, unánimemente, de consuno. *2* acuerdo, convenio. *3* MÚS. concordancia, acorde. *4 of one's own* ~, espontáneamente.

**accord (to)** *tr.* concordar, poner de acuerdo. *2* conciliar. *3* otorgar, conceder. *4 intr.* convenir, estar de acuerdo; concordar.

**accordance** (-ans) *s.* acuerdo, conformidad: *in* ~ *with*, de acuerdo con.

**accordant** (-ant) *adj.* acorde. *2* conforme, consonante, correspondiente.

**according** (-ing) *adj.* acorde, conforme, armónico. 2 ACCORDINGLY: ~ *to*, según, conforme a; ~ *to him*, según él.

**accordingly** (-li) *adv.* de conformidad, de acuerdo [con]. 2 en consecuencia, por lo tanto.

**accordion** (akaˑ*r*diøn) *s.* acordeón.

**accordionist** (-ist) *s.* acordeonista.

**accost (to)** (akaˑst) *tr.* abordar, hablar, dirigirse [a uno].

**account** (akauˑnt) *s.* cuenta [cálculo, cómputo; estado de cantidades o partidas]: ~ *current*, cuenta corriente; *to settle accounts*, ajustar cuentas; *on* ~, a cuenta. 2 cuenta [que se da o pide]: *to call to* ~, pedir cuentas. 3 causa, razón, motivo: *on* ~ *of*, a causa de, en atención a; *on no* ~, de ningún modo. 4 explicación. 5 relación, informe, relato, descripción. 6 cuenta, interés: *for* ~ *of*, por cuenta de; *to turn to* ~, sacar provecho de, hacer útil. 7 importancia: *of no* ~, sin importancia, despreciable. 8 *to take into* ~, tener en cuenta.

**account (to)** *tr.* tener por, estimar, considerar, juzgar. 2 *intr. to* ~ *for*, responder de; dar cuenta de; explicar, justificar.

**accountability** (-abiˑliti) *s.* responsabilidad.

**accountable** (-abøl) *adj.* responsable. 2 explicable.

**accountant** (-ant) *s.* contador, perito mercantil, tenedor de libros.

**accounting** (-ing) *s.* contabilidad. 2 estado de cuentas. 3 explicación, justificación.

**accouter, accoutre (to)** (akuˑtø*r*) *tr.* vestir, ataviar, equipar.

**accouterment, accoutrement** (akuˑtø*r*mønt) *s.* vestido, atavíos. 2 equipo [del soldado].

**accredit (to)** (ækreˑdit) *tr.* acreditar. | No tiene el sentido de abonar en cuenta. 2 creer, dar crédito. 3 atribuir, imputar.

**accredited** (-id) *adj.* acreditado. 2 creído, aceptado.

**accrescent** (ækreˑsønt) *adj.* BOT. acrescente.

**accretion** (ækriˑshøn) *s.* acrecimiento. 2 MINER. acreción. 3 DER. accesión.

**accrual** (ækruˑøl) *s.* incremento, acumulación.

**accrue (to)** (ækruˑ) *intr.* aumentar, crecer, acumularse. 2 provenir, resultar.

**accumulate (to)** (akiuˑmiuleit) *tr.* acumular; atesorar. 2 *intr.* aumentar, acumularse.

**accumulation** (-leiˑshøn) *s.* acumulación, amontonamiento. 2 *pl.* ahorros.

**accumulative** (-iv) *adj.* acumulativo. 2 acumulado.

**accumulator** (-ø*r*) *s.* acumulador, amontonador. 2 ELECT. acumulador.

**accuracy** (æˑkiurøsi) *s.* exactitud, corrección, precisión. 2 cuidado, esmero.

**accurate** (æˑkiurit) *adj.* exacto, correcto, fiel. 2 preciso, de precisión. 3 cuidadoso, esmerado.

**acurateness** (-nis) *s.* ACCURACY.

**accursed, accurst** (akøˑ*r*st) *adj.* maldito, maldecido. 2 execrable. 3 afligido, perseguido [por una enfermedad, la desgracia]. 4 infausto.

**accusal** (akiuˑšal) *s.* ACCUSATION.

**accusation** (akiušeiˑshøn) *s.* acusación. 2 denuncia. 3 imputación, cargo.

**accusative** (akiuˑšativ) *adj.-s.* GRAM. 1 acusativo.

**accusatory** (-tori) *adj.* acusatorio.

**accuse (to)** (akiuˑš) *tr.* acusar, denunciar. 2 culpar, tachar, tildar [de].

**accused** (-d) *s.* acusado.

**accuser** (-ø*r*) *s.* acusador.

**accustom (to)** (akøˑstøm) *tr.* acostumbrar.

**accustomed** (-d) *adj.* acostumbrado, avezado; que acostumbra. 2 acostumbrado, usual.

**ace** (eis) *s.* as. 2 punto, tanto. 3 *within an* ~ *of*, a punto de, a dos dedos de.

**acephalous** (eiseˑfaløs) *adj.* acéfalo.

**acerb** (asøˑ*r*b) *adj.* acerbo.

**acerbate (to)** (æˑsø*r*beit) *tr.* agriar. 2 exasperar.

**acerbity** (æsøˑ*r*biti) *s.* acerbidad, aspereza, rigor.

**acescent** (æseˑsønt) *adj.* acescente.

**acetabulum** (æsitæˑbiuløm) *s.* acetábulo.

**acetate** (æˑsiteit) *s.* acetato.

**acetic** (æsiˑtic) *adj.* acético.

**acetone** (æˑsitoun) *s.* QUÍM. acetona.

**acetose** (æsiˑtous), **acetous** (-tøs) *adj.* acetoso.

**acetylene** (æseˑtilin) *s.* acetileno.

**Achaea** (akiˑa) *n. pr.* Acaya.

**Achaean** (akiˑan) *adj.-s.* aqueo.

**ache** (eich) *s.* nombre de la letra *h*.

**ache** (eik) *s.* dolor [continuo]; achaque, mal.

**ache (to)** *intr.* doler [dar dolor]: *my head aches*, me duele la cabeza. 2 sentir pena, sufrir. 3 *to* ~ *to*, desear, anhelar.

**achene** (akiˑn) *s.* BOT. aquenio.

**achieve (to)** *tr.* acabar, llevar a cabo, realizar. 2 lograr, conseguir. 3 *intr.* triunfar.

**achievement** (-mønt) *s.* realización, ejecución. 2 logro. 3 proeza, hazaña.

**Achilles** (akiˑlïš) *n. pr.* Aquiles.

**aching** (eiˑng) *adj.* dolorido, doliente. 2 deseoso, anheloso. 3 *s.* dolencia. 4 dolor, pena. 5 anhelo.

**achromatism** (ækrouˑmatišm) *s.* acromatismo.

**acicular** (æsiˑkiular) *adj.* acicular.

**acid** (æˑsid) *adj.-s.* ácido. 2 *s.* acre, mordaz.

**acidity** (æsiˑditi), **acidness** (æˑsidnis) *s.* acidez. 2 acritud.

**acidulate (to)** (æsiˑdiuleit) *tr.* acidular.

**acidulous** (-løs) *adj.* acídulo.

**acierate (to)** (æˑsiøreit) *tr.* acerar.

**acknowledge (to)** (æknaˑlidý) *tr.* reconocer, confesar. 2 agradecer. 3 *to* ~ *receipt*, acusar recibo. 4 der. autenticar.

**acknowledgement** (-mønt) *s.* reconocimiento, confesión. 2 expresión de gratitud. 3 acuse de recibo. 4 der. autenticación.

**acme** (æˑmi) *s.* pináculo, punto culminante, apogeo. 2 MED. acmé.

**acne** (æˑkni) *s.* MED. acné, barros.

**acolyte** (æˑkolait) *s.* acólito.

**acolythate** (ækaˑlizeit) *s.* acolitado.

**aconite** (æˑkonait) *s.* acónito.

**acorn** (eiˑko*r*n) *s.* bellota.

**acotyledonous** (eikatiliˑdønøs) *adj.* acotiledóneo.

**acoustic** (akuˑstic) *adj.* acústico.

**acoustics** (-s) *s.* acústica.

**acquaint (to)** (akueiˑnt) *tr.* enterar, informar, familiarizar, hacer saber o conocer: *to be acquainted with*, saber, estar enterado de; conocer, tener trato con.

**acquaintance** (-ans) *s.* conocimiento [de una cosa]. 2 trato, relación. 3 conocido [pers.].

**acquaintanceship** (-ship) *s.* conocimiento, trato, relaciones.

**acquiesce** (akuieˑs) *intr.* asentir, consentir, conformarse, allanarse.

**acquiescence** (-øns) *s.* aquiescencia, conformidad.

**acquiescent** (-ønt) *adj.* anuente, conforme.

**acquire (to)** (akuaiˑ*r*) *tr.* adquirir. 2 contraer [hábitos, etc.].

**acquirement** (-mønt) *s.* adquisición. 2 *pl.* saber, conocimientos.

**acquisition** (ækuiˑšishøn) *s.* adquisición.

**acquisitive** (ækui·šitiv) *adj.* adquisitivo. 2 codicioso, ahorrativo.

**acquit (to)** (*akui*·t) *tr.* descargar [de una deuda, etc.]. *2* absolver [declarar inocente]. *3* pagar, satisfacer. *4 ref.* desempeñar [un cometido], cumplir, portarse: *to ~ oneself well*, portarse bien; quedar bien, lucirse. ¶ Pret. y p. p.: *acquitted;* ger.: *-tting.*

**acquittal** (-al) *s.* descargo [de deuda]. *2* recibo, quitanza, finiquito.

**acre** (ei·kɵ<sup>r</sup>) *s.* acre [40.47 a.].

**acreage** (ei·kɵridẙ) *s.* extensión en acres.

**acrid** (æ·krid) *adj.* acre.

**acridity** (ækri·diti) *s.* acritud, acrimonia.

**acrimonious** (ækrimou·niɵs) *adj.* acre. *2* áspero, mordaz, sarcástico.

**acrimoniousness** (-nis), **acrimony** (æ·krimouni) *s.* acritud, acrimonia. *2* aspereza, mordacidad.

**acritude** (æ·kritiud) *s.* acritud.

**acrobat** (æ·krobæt) *s.* acróbata.

**acrobatic** (æ·krobæ·tic) *adj.* acrobático.

**acrobatics** (-s), **acrobatism** (æ·krobatišm) *s.* acrobacia, acrobatismo.

**acromion** (ækrou·miɵn) *s.* ANAT. acromio(n.

**acropolis** (ækra·polis) *s.* acrópolis.

**across** (akro·s) *prep.* a través, por, sobre, de una parte a otra de: *~ country*, a campo traviesa. *2* al otro lado de: *~ the way*, enfrente, en la acera de enfrente. *3* atravesado, cruzando. *4 to come* o *to run ~*, tropezar, topar con. *5 adv.* de través, al través, al otro lado, cruzado, en cruz. *6* ELECT. en paralelo.

**acrostic** (akro·stic) *adj.-s.* acróstico.

**acroterium** (ækrotɪ·triɵm) *s.* ARQ. acrotera.

**acrylic** (akri·lik) *adj.* QUÍM. acrílico.

**act** (ækt) *s.* acto, hecho, acción: *~ of God*, fuerza mayor, caso fortuito; *in the (very) ~*, in fraganti. *2* TEAT. acto. *3* ley, decreto. *4 pl.* actos [de los apóstoles].

**act (to)** *intr.* obrar, actuar, conducirse, portarse: *to ~ as*, hacer de; *to ~ for*, representar [a uno]. *2* funcionar [un órgano]. *3* obrar, influir. *4* TEAT. representar. *5* fingir. *6 tr.* interpretar, desempeñar [un papel]; fingirse. *7* fingir, simular. *8* interinar.

**acting** (æ·kting) *adj.* que obra. *2* interino, suplente. *3* que finge. *4 s.* acción, efecto. *5* TEAT. desempeño. *6* fingimiento.

**actinia** (ækti·nia) *s.* actinia.

**actinic** (ækti·nic) *adj.* actínico.

**actinism** (æ·ktinišm) *s.* actinismo.

**actinium** (ækti·niɵm) *s.* QUÍM. actinio.

**action** (æ·kshɵn) *s.* acción: *to take ~*, tomar medidas; DER. proceder [contra]. | No tiene el sentido de acción de una compañía anónima. *2* mecanismo [de un piano, órgano, etc.]. *3* cierre [de fusil].

**actionable** (-abɵl) *adj.* DER. perseguible.

**activate (to)** (æ·ktiveit) *tr.* QUÍM., BIOL. activar.

**active** (æ·ktiv) *adj.* activo. *2* vivo, ligero. *3* vigoroso, enérgico. *4* en actividad. *5* vigente.

**actively** (-li) *adv.* activamente. *2* acuciosamente.

**activity** (ækti·viti) *s.* actividad, agilidad, vivacidad, vigor. *2 pl.* actividades.

**actor** (æ·ktɵ<sup>r</sup>) *s.* actor [en un suceso]. *2* TEAT., DER. actor.

**actress** (æ·ktris) *s.* actriz.

**actual** (æ·kchual) *adj.* real, efectivo, de hecho; propiamente dicho. *2* actual.

**actuality** (ækchuæ·liti) *s.* realidad.

**actually** (æ·kchuali) *adv.* realmente, efectivamente, de hecho.

**actuary** (æ·kchueri) *s.* escribano. *2* actuario de seguros.

**actuate (to)** (æ·kchueit) *tr.* actuar, poner en acción; mover, impulsar.

**acuity** (akiu·iti) *s.* acuidad, agudeza.

**acumen** (akiu·min) *s.* cacumen, perspicacia.

**acuminate** (-eit) *adj.* BOT. acuminado.

**acute** (akiu·t) *adj.* agudo.

**acute-angled** *adj.* GEOM. acutángulo.

**acuteness** (akiu·tnis) *s.* agudeza [intensidad; sutileza; perspicacia].

**ad** (æd) *s. fam.* anuncio [en los periódicos].

**adage** (æ·didẙ) *s.* adagio, refrán.

**adagio** (ada·dẙou) *s.* MÚS. adagio.

**Adam** (æ·dam) *n. pr.* Adán: *Adam's apple*, fam. nuez [de la garganta].

**adamant** (æ·damænt) *s.* adamante. *2 adj.* adamantino. *3* inexorable.

**adamantine** (ædamæ·ntin) *adj.* adamantino.

**adapt (to)** (adæ·pt) *tr.* adaptar.

**adaptable** (adæ·ptabɵl) *adj.* adaptable. *2* aplicable.

**adaptation** (ædæptei·shɵn) *s.* adaptación.

**adapter** (adæ·ptɵ<sup>r</sup>) *s.* adaptador. *2* QUÍM. alargadera.

**add (to)** (æd) *tr.* añadir, agregar. *2 tr.-intr.* sumar: *to ~ up*, sumar, totalizar. *3 to ~ to*, aumentar, acrecentar.

**addendum** (æde·ndɵm), *pl.* **-da** (-dæ) *s.* adición, aditamento. *2 pl.* addenda.

**adder** (æ·dɵ<sup>r</sup>) *s.* ZOOL. víbora. *2* culebra.

**addict** (æ·dikt) *s.* persona aficionada al uso de [un narcótico, etc.].

**addict (to)** (adi·kt) *tr.* dedicar, aplicar, consagrar. *2 ref.* dedicarse, entregarse, darse (a).

**addicted** (-id) *adj.* aficionado, dado, entregado (a). *2* apasionado (por), partidario [de].

**addiction** (adi·kshɵn) *s.* afición, apego.

**addition** (ædi·shɵn) *s.* adición, añadidura; aditamento: *in ~ to*, además de. *3* ARIT. adición, suma.

**additional** (-al) *adj.* adicional. *2 s.* aditamento.

**addle** (æ·dɵl) *adj.* huero, podrido, vacío, vano.

**addle (to)** *tr.* enhuerar. *2* hacer estéril. *3* embrollar, confundir.

**addle-brained, addle-pated** *adj.* mentecato.

**address** (æ·dres o adre·s) *s.* discurso, plática, alocución. *2* dedicatoria. *3* acción o manera de hablar a otro; palabra: *form of ~*, tratamiento. *4* dirección, sobrescrito. *5* destreza, habilidad. *6* garbo, donaire. *7 pl.* corte, galanteo.

**address (to)** *tr.* dirigir [la palabra, un ruego, etc.]. *2* dirigir la palabra, arengar, hacer una petición a [uno o unos]. *3* dirigir, enviar. *4* COM. consignar. *5* cortejar, galantear. *6 ref.* dirigirse [a una pers.]; dedicarse, aplicarse.

**addressee** (adre·si) *s.* destinatario.

**adduce (to)** (ædiu·s) *tr.* aducir.

**adduction** (ædɵ·kshɵn) *s.* aducción.

**adductor** (ædɵ·ktɵ<sup>r</sup>) *s.* ANAT. músculo aductor.

**Adele** (æde·l) *n. pr.* Adela.

**adenoid** (æ·dɵnoid) *adj.* adenoideo. *2 s. pl.* vegetaciones adenoideas.

**adept** (ade·pt) *adj. y s.* adepto, iniciado. *2* experto, perito.

**adequacy** (æ·dikuɵsi) *s.* calidad de adecuado. *2* suficiencia.

**adequate** (æ·dikuit) *adj.* adecuado, proporcionado, suficiente.

**adhere (to)** (ædjɪ·ʳ) *intr.* adherir, adherirse. *2* tener apego.
**adherence** (-øns) *s.* adhesión, apego.
**adherent** (-ønt) *adj.* adherente. *2* adhesivo. *3 s.* adherido, adicto, partidario, seguidor.
**adherer** (-øʳ) *s.* ADHERENT.
**adhesion** (ædjɪ·ɏøn) *s.* adherencia. *2* adhesión.
**adhesive** (ædjɪ·siv) *adj.-s.* adhesivo.
**adieu** (adiu·) *interj.* ¡adiós! *2 s.* adiós, despedida: *to bid ~*, despedirse.
**adipose** (æ·dipous) *adj.* adiposo.
**adit** (æ·dit) *s.* MIN. socavón. *2* entrada, acceso.
**adjacent** (ædɏei·sønt) *adj.* adyacente.
**adjectival** (ædjɛktai·val) *adj.* adjetival, adjetivo.
**adjective** (æ·djɛktiv) *adj.-s.* adjetivo.
**adjoin (to)** (adɏoi·n) *tr.* unir, anexar. *2* asociar. *3* lindar con. *4 intr.* lindar, colindar, estar contiguo.
**adjoining** (-ing) *adj.* contiguo, inmediato.
**adjourn (to)** (adɏø·ʳn) *tr.* aplazar, trasladar, suspender. *2 intr.* levantar la sesión. *3* levantarse, suspenderse [la sesión]; terminar sus sesiones [una asamblea]. *4* trasladarse.
**adjournment** (-mønt) *s.* aplazamiento, suspensión, clausura. *2* DER. espera.
**adjudge (to)** (adɏø·dɏ) *tr.* adjudicar. *2* juzgar [un asunto]; decidir, sentenciar. *3 intr.* fallar, dictar sentencia.
**adjudgement** (-mønt) *s.* adjudicación. *2* decisión, fallo.
**adjudicate (to)** (adɏu·dikeit) *tr.* declarar judicialmente. *2* juzgar [un asunto]. *3 intr.* juzgar, actuar como juez.
**adjudication** (adɏudikei·shøn) *s.* juicio, fallo.
**adjunct** (æ·dɏønkt) *adj.* adjunto, accesorio. *2 s.* aditamento, cosa accesoria. *3* adjunto, ayudante. *4* GRAM. modificativo.
**adjunction** (ædɏø·nkshøn) *s.* adjunción, agregación.
**adjuration** (ædɏurei·shøn) *s.* conjuro, ruego encarecido, orden solemne.
**adjure (to)** (adɏu·ʳ) *tr.* conjurar, rogar encarecidamente, ordenar solemnemente.
**adjust (to)** (adɏø·st) *tr.* ajustar, arreglar [diferencias, cuentas, etc.]. *2* ajustar, acomodar, adaptar. *3* reglar, graduar, enfocar, ajustar [un instrumento]. *4 intr.* ajustarse, acomodarse.
**adjuster** (-øʳ) *s.* ajustador. *2* mediador. *3* comisario de averías. *4* MEC. mecanismo regulador.
**adjustment** (-mønt) *s.* arreglo, composición. *2* liquidación (de cuentas). *3* acomodación, adaptación. *4* regulación, corrección (de un instrumento).
**adjutancy** (æ·dɏutansi) *s.* ayudantía.
**adjutant** (æ·dɏutant) *s.* ayudante. *2* ORN. marabú de la India.
**adjuvant** (ædɏu·vant) *adj.* adyuvante.
**adminicle** (ædmi·nikøl) *s.* adminículo, ayuda.
**administer (to)** (ædmi·nistøʳ) *tr.-intr.* administrar. *2 tr.* dar, propinar. *3* dirigir [los negocios públicos]; ejercer [un cargo]; aplicar [las leyes]. *4 to ~ an oath*, tomar juramento. *5* intr. *to ~ to*, contribuir a.
**administration** (ædministrei·shøn) *s.* administración [acción]. *2* dirección, gobierno. *3* gobierno, ministerio; tiempo que dura el mando de un gobierno, un ministro, etc.
**administrative** (ædmi·nistreitiv) *adj.* administrativo. *2* gubernativo.
**administrator** (-treitøʳ) *s.* administrador; gobernante, director. *2* DER. curador.

**admirable** (æ·dmirabøl) *adj.* admirable.
**admiral** (æ·dmiral) *s.* almirante. *2* capitana [nave].
**admiralty** (æ·dmiralti) *s.* almirantazgo. *2* ministerio de marina. *3 Court of ~*, tribunal marítimo; ~ *law*, derecho marítimo, código marítimo.
**Admiralty Islands** *s. pl.* GEOGR. Islas Almirantes.
**admiration** (ædmirei·shøn) *s.* admiración.
**admire (to)** (ædmai·ʳ) *tr.* admirar. *2 intr.* admirarse.
**admirer** (-øʳ) *s.* admirador. *2* apasionado, gran aficionado.
**admiring** (-ing) *adj.* admirativo. *2* admirado [que admira]. *3* enamorado.
**admissible** (ædmi·sibøl) *adj.* admisible, concesible. *2* lícito, permitido.
**admission** (ædmi·shøn) *s.* admisión, entrada, acceso. *2* precio de la entrada. *3* ingreso, entrada [en una escuela, etc.]. *4* reconocimiento [de la certeza de una cosa], concesión.
**admit (to)** (ædmi·t) *tr.* admitir, dar entrada a. *2* reconocer, confesar, conceder. *3 intr. to ~ of*, admitir, permitir, sufrir. ¶ Pret. y p. p.: *admitted;* ger.: *admitting.*
**admittance** (-ans) *s.* admisión, entrada: *no ~*, se prohíbe la entrada.
**admittedly** (-itly) *adv.* reconocidamente.
**admix** (to) (ædmi·ks) *tr.* mezclar.
**admixtion** (-shøn), **admixture** (-chu·ʳ) *s.* mixtura, mezcla. *2* ingrediente.
**admonish (to)** (ædma·nish) *tr.* advertir, prevenir. *2* amonestar, exhortar.
**admonishment** (-mønt), **admonition** (-i·shøn) *s.* advertencia, admonición. *2* amonestación, exhortación.
**admonitive** (ædma·nitiv), **admonitory** (-tori) *adj.* exhortatorio.
**adnate** (æ·dneit) *s.* adnato.
**ado** (adu·) *s.* ruido, alboroto, ajetreo; trabajo, dificultad.
**adobe** (adou·bi) *s.* (E.U.) adobe.
**adolescence, -cy** (ædole·søns, -i) *s.* adolescencia.
**Adolph** (æ·dalf) *n. pr.* Adolfo.
**adonic** (ada·nik) *adj. y s.* adónico.
**Adonis** (ada·nis) *n. pr. y s.* Adonis.
**adopt (to)** (ada·pt) *tr.* adoptar. *2* aprobar [una proposición].
**adoption** (ada·pshøn) *s.* adopción. *2* aprobación [de una proposición].
**adoptive** (ada·ptiv) *adj.* adoptivo.
**adorable** (ado·rabøl) *adj.* adorable.
**adoration** (ædorei·shøn) *s.* adoración. *2* culto, veneración.
**adore (to)** (ado·ʳ) *tr.* adorar.
**adorer** (ado·røʳ) *s.* adorador.
**adorn (to)** (ado·ʳn) *tr.* adornar, ornar.
**adornment** (-mønt) *s.* adorno, ornamento.
**adrenalin** (ædre·nalin) *s.* adrenalina.
**Adrian** (ei·drian) *n. pr.* Adrián. *2* Adriano.
**Adriatic** (eidriæ·tic) *adj. y s.* Adriático.
**adrift** (adri·ft) *adv. y adj.* MAR. a la deriva, al garete. *2* fig. sin rumbo; divagando.
**adroit** (adroi·t) *adj.* diestro, hábil.
**adroitness** (-nis) *s.* destreza, habilidad.
**adulate (to)** (æ·diuleit) *tr.* adular.
**adulation** (-ei·shøn) *s.* adulación.
**adulator** (æ·diuleitøʳ) *s.* adulador.
**adulatress** (-tris) *s.* aduladora.
**adult** (adø·lt) *adj. y s.* adulto.

**adulterate** (adø·ltøreit) *adj.* adúltero, adulterino. 2 falso, contrahecho.
**adulterate (to)** *tr.* adulterar, sofisticar.
**adulteration** (-ei·shøn) *s.* adulteración.
**adulterer** (-ø^r) *s.* adúltero.
**adulteress** (-is) *s.* adúltera.
**adulterine** (-in) *adj.* adulterino.
**adulterize (to)** (-aiš) *intr.* adulterar [cometer adulterio].
**adulterous** (-øs) *adj.* adúltero.
**adultery** (-i) *s.* adulterio.
**adultness** (adø·ltnis) *s.* edad adulta.
**adumbrate (to)** (ædø·mbreit) *tr.* bosquejar. 2 anunciar, presagiar. 3 sombrear.
**adumbration** (-brei·shøn) *s.* bosquejo. 2 anuncio, presagio. 3 sombra.
**adust** (adø·st) *adj.* adusto, abrasado, tostado.
**advance** (ædvæ·ns) *s.* avance. 2 adelanto. 3 progreso, mejora, ascenso. 3 anticipo. 4 alza, aumento [de precio o valor]. 5 *in* ~, al frente, adelante; de antemano, por adelantado. 6 *pl.* primeros pasos para entablar un asunto, una conversación, etc.; insinuaciones, proposiciones. 7 *adj.* ~ *guard*, MIL. avanzada; ~ *payment*, adelanto, anticipo.
**advance (to)** *tr.* adelantar, avanzar. 2 ascender, promover [a uno]. 3 acrecentar, mejorar, fomentar. 4 apresurar. 5 adelantar, anticipar [dinero]. 6 proponer, insinuar, alegar, enunciar. 7 subir [el precio]. 8 *intr.* adelantarse, avanzar. 9 adelantar, progresar; medrar. 10 subir [de precio].
**advanced** (ædvæ·nst) *adj.* avanzado. 2 superior [no elemental]: ~ *algebra*, álgebra superior. 3 ~ *in years*, entrado en años.
**advancement** (ædvæ·nsmønt) *s.* adelantamiento, fomento. 2 ascenso, promoción, elevación. 3 adelanto, progreso. 4 anticipo [de dinero].
**advantage** (ædvæ·ntidƫy) *s.* ventaja [superioridad, condición favorable]; conveniencia, comodidad: *to have the* ~ *of one*, llevar ventaja a uno; *to show to* ~, lucir, hacer brillar; *to take of*, aprovecharse de.
**advantage (to)** *tr.* adelantar, promover, favorecer, beneficiar.
**advantageous** (ædvantei·dȳøs) *adj.* ventajoso, conveniente, provechoso, útil.
**advent** (æ·dvent) *s.* advenimiento. 2 adviento.
**adventitious** (ædventi·shøs) *adj.* adventicio.
**adventive** (ædven·tiv) *adj.* BOT. advenedizo.
**adventure** (ædven·chø^r) *s.* aventura. 2 especulación comercial.
**adventure (to)** *tr.* aventurar, arriesgar. 2 *ref.* arriesgarse; atreverse, osar.
**adventurer** (-ø^r) *s.* aventurero.
**adventuresome** (-søm) *adj.* ADVENTUROUS.
**adventuress** (-is) *s.* aventurera.
**adventurous** (-øs) *adj.* aventurero, emprendedor, arrojado. 2 aventurado, arriesgado.
**adverb** (æ·dvø^rb) *s.* adverbio.
**adverbial** (ædvø·^rbial) *adj.* adverbial.
**adversary** (æ·dvø^rseri) *s.* adversario. 2 *the Adversary*, el enemigo, Satanás.
**adversative** (ædvø·^rsativ) *adj.* adversativo.
**adverse** (æ·dvø^rs) *adj.* adverso.
**adversity** (ædvø·^rsiti) *s.* adversidad.
**advert (to)** (ædvø·^rt) *intr. to* ~ *to*, referirse, aludir a: hacer notar.
**advertence, -cy** (-øns, -i) *s.* advertencia, atención, cuidado.
**advertent** (-ønt) *adj.* atento, cuidadoso.

**advertise** o **-tize (to)** (ædvø·^rtaiš) *tr.* avisar, informar. 2 *tr.-intr.* COM. anunciar.
**advertisement** (ædvø·^rtišmønt) *s.* aviso. 2 COM. anuncio.
**advertiser** o **-tizer** (ædvø^rtai·šø^r) *s.* avisador. 2 anunciador, anunciante.
**advertising** (-ing) *s.* publicidad, propaganda.
**advice** (ædvai·s) *s.* consejo, dictamen, parecer. 2 COM. aviso, noticia.
**advice-boat** *s.* MAR. aviso [embarcación].
**advisable** (-šabøl) *adj.* aconsejable, prudente.
**advise (to)** (ædvai·š) *tr.* aconsejar. 2 avisar, advertir. 3 *intr.* aconsejarse, consultar.
**advised** (-d) *adj.* avisado, aconsejado. 2 deliberado, premeditado.
**advisedly** (-li) *adv.* deliberadamente.
**advisement** (ædvai·šmønt) *s.* consideración, estudio.
**adviser** (-ø^r) *s.* aconsejador, consejero, asesor.
**advisory** (-ori) *adj.* asesor, consultivo.
**advocacy** (æ·dvocasi) *s.* abogacía, defensa. 2 intercesión.
**advocate** (æ·dvokeit) *s.* abogado, defensor, intercesor. 2 partidario.
**advocate (to)** *tr.* abogar por, en favor de; defender, propugnar.
**adz, adze** (adš) *s.* azuela.
**ædile** (i·dail) *s.* edil.
**Aegean** (idȳi·an) *adj.* Egeo: ~ *Sea*, Mar Egeo.
**ægis** (i·dȳis) *s.* égida, escudo.
**Aeneas** (ini·as) *n. pr.* Eneas.
**Aeolian** (iou·lian) *adj.* eolio, eólico. 2 [con min.] *æolian harp*, arpa eólica.
**Aeolus** (iou·løs) *n. pr.* MIT. Eolo.
**aeon** (i·øn) *s.* eón. 2 evo.
**aerate (to)** (ei·øreit) *tr.* someter a la aeración.
**aeration** (eiørei·shøn) *s.* aeración.
**aerial** (ei·rial) *adj.* aéreo. 2 atmosférico. 3 etéreo. 4 *s.* RADIO. antena.
**aerie** (e·ri) *s.* EYRIE.
**aeriform** (ei·rørifo^rm) *adj.* aeriforme.
**aerobe** (ei·øroub) *s.* aerobio.
**aerodrome** (ei·ørodroum) *s.* aeródromo.
**aerodynamic** (eiørodainæ·mik) *adj.* aerodinámico.
**aerodynamics** (-s) *s.* aerodinámica.
**aerolite** (ei·ørolait) *s.* aerolito.
**aeromancy** (ei·øromænsi) *s.* aeromancia.
**aerometer** (eiøra·mitø^r) *s.* aerómetro.
**aeronaut** (ei·øronot) *s.* aeronauta.
**aeronautic** (eiørono·tik) *adj.* aeronáutico.
**aeronautics** (-s) *s.* aeronáutica.
**aeroplane** (ei·øroplein) *s.* aeroplano.
**aeroscope** (ei·øroskoup) *s.* aeroscopio.
**aerostat** (ei·ørostæt) *s.* aerostato.
**aerostatic** (-stæ·tik) *adj.* aerostático.
**aerostatics** (-s) *s.* aerostática.
**aerostation** (ei·ørostei·shøn) *s.* aerostación.
**aeroview** (ei·øroviu) *s.* fotografía aérea.
**Aesculapius** (eskiulei·piøs) *n. pr.* Esculapio.
**Aesop** (i·sap) *n. pr.* Esopo.
**aesthete** (e·szit) *s.* esteta.
**aesthetic** (esze·tik) *adj.* estético.
**aesthetics** (-s) *s.* estética.
**aesthetician** (-tishan) *s.* estético.
**aestival** (e·stival) *adj.* estival.
**aether** (i·zø^r) *s.* éter.
**aetherial** (iziri·al) *adj.* etéreo.
**Aetna** (e·tna) *n. pr.* Etna.
**afar** (afa·^r) *adv.* lejos, a lo lejos: ~ *off*, muy distante; a lo lejos.
**affability** (æfabi·liti) *s.* afabilidad.

**affable** (æ·fabøl) *adj.* afable.
**affair** (æfe·ʳ) *s.* asunto, negocio, cuestión, lance; amorío, aventura. *2* MIL. acción, encuentro. *3* objeto, cosa.
**affect (to)** (afe·kt) *tr.* tener afición a, gustar de. *2* frecuentar. *3* tomar [cierta forma, disposición, etc.]. *4* afectar, fingir. *5* afectar, alterar, influir en. *6* afectar, conmover.
**affectation** (æfektei·shøn) *s.* afectación.
**affected** (afe·ktid) *adj.* afectado. *2* dado a la afectación. *3* inclinado, afecto.
**affecting** (afe·kting) *adj.* conmovedor, patético. *2* concerniente a.
**affection** (afe·kshøn) *s.* afecto, cariño. *2* inclinación, propensión. *3* afección, impresión. *4* afecto [del alma]. *5* MED. afección. *6* cualidad, propiedad.
**affectionate** (-it) *adj.* afectuoso, cariñoso, tierno.
**affective** (afe·ktiv) *adj.* afectivo. *2* emotivo.
**afferent** (æ·førønt) *adj.* aferente.
**affiance** (afai·ans) *s.* confianza. *2* palabra de casamiento, esponsales.
**affiance (to)** *tr.-ref.* prometer en matrimonio.
**affidavit** (æfidei·vit) *s.* declaración jurada; afidávit.
**affiliate** (afi·lieit) *adj.-s.* afiliado.
**affiliate (to)** *tr.* afiliar, asociar. *2* adoptar, prohijar. *3* establecer o atribuir la paternidad de; referir a un origen. *4* intr. to ~ with, afiliarse a.
**affiliation** (-ei·shøn) *s.* afiliación. *2* prohijamiento. *3* atribución de la paternidad u origen.
**affined** (afai·nd) *adj.* afín.
**affinity** (afi·niti) *s.* afinidad.
**affirm (to)** (afø·ʳm) *tr.* afirmar, aseverar. *2* DER. confirmar, ratificar [un fallo, etc.].
**affirmation** (æføʳmei·shøn) *s.* afirmación, aserción. *2* DER. confirmación, ratificación.
**affirmative** (aføʳmativ) *adj.* afirmativo. *2 s.* afirmativa.
**affix** (æ·fiks) *s.* añadidura. *2* afijo.
**affix (to)** *tr.* pegar, añadir. *2* poner [una firma, un sello, etc.]. *3* atribuir, aplicar. *4* afijar.
**afflatus** (æflei·tøs) *s.* aflato, inspiración.
**afflict (to)** (afli·kt) *tr.* afligir. *2* aquejar: *to be afflicted with*, padecer de.
**afflicting** (-ing) *adj.* aflictivo, penoso.
**affliction** (afli·kshøn) *a.* aflicción. *2* desgracia, calamidad. *3* achaque, mal.
**affluence** (æfluøns) *s.* afluencia, aflujo. *2* afluencia, abundancia. *3* riqueza, opulencia.
**affluent** (æ·fluønt) *adj.* abundante. *2* rico, opulento. *3 s.* GEOGR. afluente.
**afflux** (æ·fløks) *s.* aflujo.
**afford (to)** (afo·ʳd) *tr.* producir, dar, deparar, proporcionar, ofrecer. *2* soportar, permitirse [un gasto, el lujo de, etc.]; poder, tener medios o recursos para. | Gralte. con *can, could, might*, etc.
**afforest (to)** (afa·rist) *tr.* convertir en bosque.
**affranchise** (afræ·nchaiš) *tr.* ENFRANCHISE.
**affray** (afrei·) *s.* riña, pendencia.
**affreight (to)** (afrei·t) *tr.* fletar.
**affreightment** (-mønt) *s.* fletamiento.
**affright** (afrai·t) *s.* terror, espanto.
**affright (to)** *tr.* asustar, aterrar.
**affront** (afrø·nt) *s.* afrenta, insulto, desaire.
**affront (to)** *tr.* afrentar. *2* afrontar, arrostrar.
**affusion** (afiu·ŷøn) *s.* afusión.
**Afghan** (æ·fgan) *adj.-s.* afgano.
**afield** (afi·ld) *adv.* al campo, en el campo; fuera, lejos.

**afire** (afai·ʳ) *adv.* ardiendo.
**aflame** (aflei·m) *adj.-adv.* en llamas; inflamado.
**afloat** (aflou·t) *adj.-adv.* flotante, a flote. *2* en circulación. *3* sin rumbo. *4* inundado.
**afoot** (afu·t) *adv.* a pie. *2* en marcha; en preparación.
**afore** (afo·øʳ) *adv.* delante. *2* MAR. a proa.
**aforegoing** (-gouing) *adj.* anterior, precedente.
**aforementioned** (-menshønd), **aforesaid** (-sed) *adj.* mencionado, antedicho, susodicho.
**aforethought** (-zot) *adj.* premeditado. *2 s.* premeditación.
**aforetime** (-taim) *adj.* antiguamente.
**afoul** (afau·l) *adj.* y *adv.* MAR. en colisión; enredado.
**afraid** (afrei·d) *adj.* asustado, temeroso, que teme: *to be ~*, tener miedo.
**afresh** (afre·sh) *adv.* de nuevo, otra vez.
**Africa** (æ·frika) *n. pr.* GEOGR. África.
**African** (-n) *adj.-s.* africano.
**aft** (æft) *adv.* MAR. a popa, en popa.
**after** (æ·ftøʳ) *prep.* después de, detrás de, tras, en seguimiento de, en busca de, por: *the day ~ tomorrow*, pasado mañana; *to inquire ~ a friend*, preguntar por un amigo; ~ *all*, después de todo. *2* en imitación de, en conformidad con, según, a la [manera de]. *3 adv.* después, luego: *soon ~*, poco después. *4 adj.* posterior, ulterior, siguiente, subsiguiente. *5* MAR. de popa. *6 conj.* después que, o de que.
**afterdamp** (-dæmp) *s.* MIN. gases de explosión.
**afterdeck** (-dek) *s.* MAR. cubierta de popa.
**after-dinner** (-dinøʳ) *adj.* de sobremesa.
**afterglow** (-glou) *s.* resplandor crepuscular.
**after-hours** (-au·ʳs) *s. pl.* horas extraordinarias.
**aftermath** (-mæz) *s.* segunda siega, renadío. *2* consecuencias, resultados.
**aftermost** (-moust) *adj.* posterior, último.
**afternoon** (-nu·n) *s.* la tarde.
**afterpiece** (-pis) *s.* sainete, entremés.
**aftertaste** (-teist) *s.* resabio, dejo, gustillo.
**afterthought** (-zot) *s.* idea que se ocurre a uno después de un acto, etc.
**afterward** (-wøʳd), **afterwards** (-wøʳdš) *adv.* después, pues, luego.
**again** (agei·n) *adv.* de nuevo, otra vez, segunda vez, aún: *come ~*, vuelva usted; *again and ~*, muchas veces; *as much ~*, otro tanto más; *now and ~*, de vez en cuando; *never ~*, nunca más. *2* por otra parte, además, asimismo.
**against** (age·nst) *prep.* contra; ~ *time*, contra el reloj. *2* enfrente de. *3* junto a, cerca de. *4* en contraste con, comparado con.
**agalloch** (agæ·lok) *s.* agáloco.
**agami** (æ·gami) *s.* ORN. agamí.
**agape** (æ·gapi) *s.* HIST. ágape.
**agape** (agei·p) *adj.* y *adv.* boquiabierto.
**agaric** (æ·garik) *s.* agárico.
**agate** (æ·git) *s.* MINER. ágata.
**Agatha** (æ·gaza) *n. pr.* Águeda.
**agave** (ægei·vi) *s.* agave, pita.
**age** (ei·dŷ) *s.* edad: *full ~*, mayoría de edad; *of ~*, mayor de edad; *under ~*, menor de edad. *2* vejez, senectud. *3* siglo, centuria. *4* generación [de hombres]. *5 pl.* mucho tiempo, una eternidad.
**age (to)** *intr.-tr.* envejecer. *2 tr.* añejar.
**aged** (ei·dŷid) *adj.* viejo, anciano; envejecido. *2* de [tantos años de] edad: ~ *twelve*, de doce años.
**ageing** (ei·dŷing) *s.* AGING.
**ageless** (ei·dŷilis) *adj.* eternamente joven.
**agency** (ei·dŷønsi) *s.* acción, operación, obra: *free ~*, libre albedrío. *2* mediación, intervención;

medio, influencia. *3* COM. agencia, factoría, representación.

**agenda** (adȳ·nda) *s.* agenda. *2* orden del día.

**agent** (ei·dȳønt) *adj.* agente. *2 s.* agente [lo que produce un efecto]. *3* agente, factor, representante.

**agglomerate** (ægla·møreit) *adj.-s.* aglomerado.

**agglomerate (to)** *tr.* aglomerar. *2 intr.* aglomerarse.

**agglomeration** (-ei·shøn) *s.* aglomeración.

**agglutinant** (aglu·tinant) *adj.-s.* aglutinante.

**agglutinate** (-nit) *adj.* aglutinado.

**agglutinate (to)** (-neit) *tr.* aglutinar.

**agglutination** (-nei·shøn) *s.* aglutinación.

**agglutinative** (-neitiv) *adj.* aglutinante.

**aggrandize (to)** (æ·grændaiš) *tr.* agrandar. *2* engrandecer, elevar.

**aggrandizement** (agrændi·šmønt) *s.* agrandamiento. *2* engrandecimiento.

**aggravate (to)** (æ·graveit) *tr.* agravar. *2* irritar, exasperar.

**aggravating** (-ing) *adj.* agravante. *2* irritante, exasperante.

**aggravation** (-i·shøn) *s.* agravamiento. *2* agravante. *3* irritación, exasperación.

**aggregate** (æ·grigeit) *adj.* agregado, reunido, conjunto, total. *2 s.* agregado, conjunto, totalidad: *in the* ~, en conjunto, en total.

**aggregate (to)** *tr.* agregar, juntar. *2* sumar, ascender a [un total].

**aggregately** (-li) *adv.* colectivamente, en junto.

**aggregation** (-ei·shøn) *s.* agregación. *2* agregado, colección, conjunto, total.

**aggression** (agre·shøn) *s.* agresión.

**aggressive** (-siv) *adj.* agresivo.

**aggressor** (-søʳ) *s.* agresor.

**aggrieve** (agrı·v) *tr.* afligir, apenar. *2* vejar, oprimir.

**aghast** (agæ·st) *adj.* espantado, horrorizado. *2* estupefacto.

**agile** (æ·dȳil) *adj.* ágil, vivo, pronto.

**agility** (adȳi·liti) *s.* agilidad, expedición, prontitud.

**aging** (ei·dȳing) *s.* envejecimiento. *2* añejamiento.

**agio** (æ·dȳiou) *s.* agio.

**agiotage** (-tidȳ) *s.* agiotaje.

**agitate (to)** (æ·dȳiteit) *tr.* agitar. *2* conmover. *3* debatir, discutir. *4* maquinar, discurrir. *5 intr.* agitar la opinión pública.

**agitation** (-ei·shøn) *s.* agitación. *2* examen, discusión.

**agitator** (-tøʳ) *s.* agitador.

**agleam** (aglı·m) *adj. y adv.* brillante, centelleante.

**aglet** (æ·glit) *s.* herrete. *2 pl.* MIL. cordones.

**aglow** (aglou·) *adj. y adv.* encendido, ardiente.

**agnail** (æ·gneil) *s.* panadizo, uñero.

**agnate** (æ·gneit) *adj.-s.* agnado.

**agnation** (ægnei·shøn) *s.* agnación.

**Agnes** (æ·gnis) *n. pr.* Inés.

**agnostic** (ægna·stik) *adj.-s.* agnóstico.

**agnosticism** (-tisišm) *s.* agnosticismo.

**Agnus Dei** (æ·gnøs dei·i) *s.* agnusdéi.

**ago** (agou·) *adv.* atrás, hace, ha: *two years* ~, dos años atrás, hace dos años.

**agog** (aga·g) *adv.* ansiosamente, con viva curiosidad. *2 adj.* anhelante, excitado, curioso.

**agoing** (agou·ing) *adv.* en acción, en movimiento.

**agonist** (æ·gonist) *s.* agonista, luchador.

**agonistic** (ægoni·stic) *adj.* agonístico.

**agonize (to)** (æ·gonaiš) *intr.* agonizar, sufrir angustiosamente, retorcerse de dolor. *2* hacer grandes esfuerzos. *3 tr.* atormentar.

**agony** (æ·goni), *pl.* **-nies** (-niš) *s.* agonía. *2* angustia, aflicción extrema. *3* paroxismo.

**agora** (æ·gøra), *pl.* **-ræ** (-ri) *s.* ágora.

**agouti** (agu·ti) *s.* ZOOL. agutí.

**agraffe** (agræ·f) *s.* broche.

**agrarian** (agrei·rian) *adj.-s.* agrario.

**agree (to)** (agrı·) *intr.* asentir, consentir. *2* concordar, cuadrar, conformarse. *3* avenirse, estar o ponerse de acuerdo, convenir. *4* venir bien, sentar bien. *5* GRAM. concordar.

**agreeable** (agrı·abøl) *adj.* agradable. *2* conforme, conveniente. *3 fam.* que quiere, que consiente, que acepta.

**agreeably** (-bli) *adv.* agradablemente. *2* de acuerdo [con], conformemente [a].

**agreement** (agrı·mønt) *s.* acuerdo, convenio, pacto, avenencia. *2* armonía, unión. *3* acuerdo, conformidad, concordancia.

**agricultural** (ægrico·lchøral) *adj.* agrícola.

**agriculturalist** (-ist) *s.* AGRICULTURIST.

**agriculture** (æ·grikølchøʳ) *s.* agricultura.

**agriculturist** (ægriko·lchørist) *s.* agricultor.

**agrimony** (æ·grimoni) *s.* BOT. agrimonia.

**agronomic(al** (ægrona·mik(al) *adj.* agronómico.

**agronomics** (-s), **agronomy** (agra·nømi) *s.* agronomía.

**aground** (agrau·nd) *adv.* MAR. encallado, varado: *to run* ~, encallar, varar.

**ague** (ei·giu) *s.* fiebre intermitente. *2* escalofrío.

**ah!** (a) *interj.* ¡ah!, ¡ay!

**ahead** (aje·d) *adv.* delante, al frente, a la cabeza; más allá de, adelante: *to be* ~, ir delante; llevar la delantera; *to go* ~, avanzar; ~ *of time*, adelantado, antes de tiempo. *2* MAR. por la proa, avante.

**ahem!** (aje·m) *interj.* ¡eh!, ¡ejem!

**ahoy** (ajoi·) *inter.* MAR. ¡ah!: *ship* ~*!*, ¡ah del barco!

**aid** (eid) *s.* ayuda, auxilio, socorro: *first* ~, primeros auxilios. *2* ayudante, auxiliar.

**aid (to)** *tr.* ayudar, auxiliar, socorrer. *2* apoyar, coadyuvar.

**aide-de-camp** (ei·døkæ·mp) *s.* MIL. edecán.

**aigret, aigrette** (ei·gret) *s.* ORN. garzota. *2* gargota, penacho, airón.

**ail (to)** (eil) *tr.* afligir, molestar, aquejar. *2 intr.* sufrir, estar indispuesto.

**ailanthus** (eila·nzos) *s.* BOT. ailanto.

**aileron** (ei·løran) *s.* AVIA. alerón.

**ailing** (ei·ling) *adj.-s.* enfermo, achacoso.

**ailment** (ei·lmønt) *s.* dolencia, padecimiento, achaque.

**aim** (eim) *s.* puntería, encaro, acción de asestar, de dirigir [un arma, un golpe, etc.]. *2* blanco [al que se tira]; *to miss one's* ~, errar el tiro. *3* mira, designio, fin.

**aim (to)** *intr.* apuntar [con un arma]; dirigir un golpe, la intención, el propósito [a]; poner la mira [en]; tratar [de]. *2 tr.* apuntar, asestar, encarar, dirigir [un arma, un golpe, etc.].

**aimless** (ei·mlis) *adj.* sin objeto, sin designio.

**ain't** (eint) *contr. vulg.* de *am not, is not, are not, have not* y *has not.*

**air** (e·øʳ) *s.* aire [fluido, atmósfera, viento]: *open* ~, aire libre; *in the* ~, en el aire, en el ambiente; indeciso, incierto; *on the* ~, RADIO. transmitiendo. *2* céfiro, aura. *3* ambiente. *4* aire, semblante, actitud, continente, aspecto. *5* afectación, tono: *to put on airs*, darse tono. *6* manifestación, divulgación: *to give it* ~; decirlo, manifestarlo; *to take* ~, ser conocido, divulgarse. *7* MÚS. aire, tonada. *8 adj.* de aire, neumático; aé-

reo, aeronáutico; de aviación: ~ *base*, base aérea; ~ *castle*, castillo en el aire; ~ *force*, fuerzas aéreas; ~ *gun*, escopeta de aire comprimido; ~ *hostess*, AVIA. azafata; ~ *mail*, correo aéreo; ~ *pump*, máquina neumática, bomba de aire; ~ *raid*, ataque aéreo.
**air (to)** *tr.* airear, orear. *2* ventilar. *3* secar [al aire o al calor]. *4* exhibir, ostentar. *5* emitir, divulgar. *6 intr.* tomar el aire.
**airbrush** (-brøsh) *s.* PINT. pistola.
**air-conditioned** *adj.* con aire acondicionado.
**aircraft** (-kraft) *s.* aeronave o avión: ~ *carrier*, portaaviones.
**airdrome** (-droum) *s.* aeródromo.
**airfoil** (-foil) *s.* AVIA. superficie de sustentación.
**airified** (-ifaid) *adj.* hecho a la ligera, sin fundamento. *2* presumido, entonado.
**airiness** (-inis) *s.* viveza, vivacidad. *2* ligereza, superficialidad.
**airing** (-ing) *s.* paseo, excursión [para tomar el aire]. *2* oreo.
**airlift** (-lift) *s.* puente aéreo.
**airline** (-lain) *s.* línea aérea.
**airman** (-mæn) *s.* aviador.
**airplane** (-plein) *s.* aeroplano.
**airport** (-pořt) *s.* aeropuerto.
**airship** (-ship) *s.* aeronave.
**airsick** (-sik) *adj.* mareado en el aire.
**airsickness** (-nis) *s.* mareo en avión.
**airstrip** (-strip) *s.* AVIA. pista.
**airtight** (-tait) *adj.* hermético, herméticamente cerrado.
**airway** (-wei) *s.* línea aérea, vía aérea. *2* MIN. pozo o galería de ventilación.
**airy** (-i) *adj.* airoso, oreado. *2* etéreo, sutil, vaporoso. *3* ágil, ligero. *4* alegre, vivo. *5* delicado, gracioso. *6* vano, sin fundamento. *7* ligero, superficial.
**aisle** (ail) *s.* pasillo [en un teatro, etc.]. *2* ARQ. nave lateral. *3* calle de árboles.
**Aix-la-Chapelle** (e·la-chapel) *n. pr.* Aquisgrán.
**ajar** (adÿa·ř) *adj.* entreabierto, entornado. *2* en pugna, en desacuerdo.
**akimbo** (aki·mbou) *adj.* en jarras.
**akin** (aki·n) *adj.* pariente. *2* semejante.
**alabaster** (æ·labæstø̌ř) *s.* alabastro.
**alabastrine** (ælabæ·strin) *adj.* alabastrino.
**alacrity** (alæ·criti) *s.* alacridad, presteza.
**Aladdin** (alæ·din) *n. pr.* Aladino.
**Alans** (a·lanš) *s.* HIST. alanos.
**alar** (ei·lař) *adj.* alado. *2* BOT. axilar.
**alarm** (ala·řm) *s.* alarma. *2* mecanismo despertador; timbre de alarma: ~ *clock*, despertador.
**alarm (to)** *tr.* alarmar. *2* alertar.
**alarming** (-ing) *adj.* alarmante.
**alarmist** (-ist) *s.* alarmista.
**alarum clock** (alæ·røm) *s.* ant. (Ingl.) despertador.
**alas** (alæ·s) *interj.* ¡ay!, ¡guay!
**alate(d** (ei·leit(id) *adj.* alado.
**alatern** (alatø̌·řn) *s.* BOT. aladierna.
**alb** (ælb) *s.* LITURG. alba.
**albacore** (æ·lbacouř) *s.* ICT. albacora.
**Albanian** (ælbei·nian) *adj.-s.* albanés.
**albatros** (æ·lbatrøs) *s.* albatros.
**albeit** (olbi·it) *conj.* aunque, bien que.
**Albert** (æ·lbǫřt) *n. pr.* Alberto.
**albinism** (æ·lbinišm) *s.* albinismo.
**albino** (ælbai·nou), *pl.* **-nos** *s.* albino.
**Albion** (æ·lbiøn) *n. pr.* Albión.
**albugo** (ælbiu·gou) *s.* MED. albugo.
**album** (æ·lbøm) *s.* álbum.

**albumen** (ælbiu·møn) *s.* albumen. *2* albúmina.
**albumin** (ælbiu·min) *s.* albúmina.
**albuminoid** (-oid) *adj.* albuminoideo. *2 s.* albuminoide.
**albuminous** (-øs) *adj.* albuminoso.
**albuminuria** (-iu·ria) *s.* albuminuria.
**alburnum** (ælbø̌·řnøm) *s.* BOT. alburno.
**alchemist** (æ·lkemist) *s.* alquimista.
**alchemy** (æ·lkemi) *s.* alquimia.
**alcohol** (æ·lcojol) *s.* QUÍM. alcohol.
**alcoholic** (ælcojo·lic) *adj.* alcohólico. *2 s. pl.* líquidos espirituosos.
**alcoholism** (æ·lcojolišm) *s.* alcoholismo.
**alcoholize (to)** (-aiš) *tr.* alcoholizar.
**alcoholometer** (-a·mitǫř) *s.* alcoholímetro.
**Alcoran** (ælcora·n) *s.* alcorán.
**alcove** (æ·lcouv) *s.* hueco o nicho [en una habitación]; alcoba. *2* cenador, glorieta.
**aldehyde** (æ·ldijaid) *s.* aldehído.
**alder** (o·ldø̌ř) *s.* aliso. *2* ~ *buckthorn*, arraclán.
**alderman** (-mæn) *s.* teniente de alcalde.
**Aldine** (o·ldin) *adj.* aldino.
**ale** (eil) *s.* cerveza inglesa muy fuerte.
**aleatory** (ei·liatori) *adj.* aleatorio.
**alee** (alı·) *adv.* MAR. a sotavento.
**alehouse** (ei·ljaus) *s.* cervecería, taberna.
**alembic** (ale·mbik) *s.* alambique.
**Aleppo** (æle·pou) *n. pr.* Alepo: *Aleppo pine*, pincarrasco.
**alert** (alø̌ř t) *adj.* alerta, vigilante. *2* vivo, dispuesto. *3 s.* MIL. alarma: *on the* ~, alerta, sobre aviso.
**alert (to)** *tr.* alertar.
**alertness** (-nis) *s.* vigilancia. *2* viveza, presteza.
**alette** (æle·t) *s.* ARQ. aleta.
**alewife** (ei·luaif) *s.* cervecera, tabernera.
**Alexander** (æligšæ·ndøř) *n. pr.* Alejandro.
**Alexandrie** (-ndria) *n. pr.* GEOGR. Alejandría.
**Alexandrine** (-drin) *s.* verso alejandrino.
**alfalfa** (ælfæ·lfa) *s.* (E.U.) alfalfa.
**alfaqui** (a·lfaki) *s.* alfaquí.
**alga** (æ·lga), *pl.* **algae** (æ·ldÿi) *s.* alga.
**algebra** (æ·ldÿebra) *s.* álgebra.
**algebraic(al** (ældÿebrei·ik(al) *adj.* algebraico, algébrico.
**algebraist** (æ·ldÿebreist) *s.* MAT. algebrista.
**Algeria** (æ·ldÿi·ria) *n. pr.* GEOGR. Argelia.
**Algerian** (-n), **Algerine** (ældÿeri·n) *adj.-s.* argelino.
**algid** (æ·ldÿid) *adj.* álgido.
**algidity** (ældÿi·diti) *s.* algidez.
**Algiers** (æ·ldÿi·řs) *n. pr.* GEOGR. Argel.
**algorism** (æ·lgorišm) *s.* algoritmia.
**algous** (æ·lgøs) *adj.* algoso.
**alias** (ei·lias) *adv.-s.* alias.
**alibi** (æ·libai) *s.* coartada.
**Alice** (æ·lis) *n. pr.* Alicia.
**alidade** (æ·lideid) *s.* alidada.
**alien** (ei·liøn) *adj.* ajeno, extraño. *2 adj.-s.* forastero, extranjero.
**alien (to)** *tr.* ALIENATE.
**alienable** (æbøl) *adj.* alienable, enajenable.
**alienate (to)** (-eit) *tr.* alienar, enajenar.
**alienation** (-ei·shøn) *s.* alienación, enajenación. *2* alejamiento, desvío, enajena.
**alienism** (-išm) *s.* extranjería. *2* frenopatía.
**alienist** (-ist) *s.* alienista.
**aliferous** (æ·li·førøs) *adj.* alífero, alígero.
**alight** (alai·t) *adj. y adv.* encendido, iluminado; ardiendo.
**alight (to)** *intr.* bajar, apearse. *2* caer, ir a caer, posarse. *3* dar, topar [con].
**align (to)** (alai·n) *tr.* alinear. *2 intr.* alinearse.

**alignment** (-mønt) *s.* alineación.
**alike** (*alai·*k) *adj.* igual, semejante. *2 adv.* igualmente, del mismo modo.
**aliment** (æ·limønt) *s.* alimento.
**alimental** (ælime·ntal) *adj.* nutritivo.
**alimentary** (-tari) *adj.* alimentario. *2* alimenticio. *3* ~ *canal*, tubo digestivo.
**alimentation** (-ei·shøn) *s.* alimentación.
**alimony** (æ·limoni) *s.* DER. alimentos.
**aline (to)** *tr.-intr.* TO ALIGN.
**alinement** *s.* ALIGNMENT.
**aliped** (æ·liped) *adj.* alípedo.
**aliquant** (æ·likuant) *adj.* alicuanta.
**aliquot** (æ·likuat) *adj.* alícuota.
**alive** (*alai·*v) *adj.* vivo, viviente. *2* vivo, en actividad, no extinguido. *3* vivo, activo: *to look* ~, menearse, darse prisa. *4* ~ *with,* lleno de [cosas que abundan u hormiguean]. *5* ~ *to,* sensible a, despierto para.
**alkalescent** (ælkæle·sønt) *adj.* alcalescente.
**alkali** (ælkali) *s.* álcali.
**alkalimetry** (-li·metri) *s.* alcalimetría.
**alkaline** (-lain) *adj.* alcalino.
**alkaline-earth** *adj.* QUÍM. alcalino-térreo.
**alkalinity** (-li·niti) *s.* alcalinidad.
**alkaloid** (-loid) *s.* alcaloide.
**alkaloidal** (loidal) *adj.* alcaloideo.
**alkanet** (æ·lkanet) *s.* BOT. orcaneta, onoquiles. *2* ancusa.
**all** (ol) *adj.* todo, toda, todos, todas: ~ *of us,* todos nosotros. *2 pron.* todo, conjunto, totalidad: *after* ~, después de todo, al fin y al cabo; *at* ~, en absoluto, del todo; siquiera; *not at* ~, de ninguna manera; no hay de qué; *for* ~, a pesar de; *for* ~ *I know,* que yo sepa, quizás, posiblemente. *3* todos, todo el mundo: ~ *and singular,* ~ *and sundry,* todos y cada uno. *4 adv.* del todo, completamente, muy: ~ *but,* casi; por poco; ~ *in,* agotado, rendido de fatiga; ~ *of sudden,* de pronto, de repente; ~ *out,* fam. agotado, rendido; equivocado, confundido; con energía; ~ *right,* sano y salvo, bien de salud; bueno, buena persona, competente, satisfactorio; bien; ~ *right!,* ¡bueno!, ¡está bien!, ¡conformes!; ~ *round,* por todas partes; ~ *the better,* tanto mejor; ~ *the same,* sin embargo, a pesar de todo; ~ *there,* listo, despierto; cuerdo.
**Allah** (æ·la) *n. pr.* Alá.
**allantois** (ælæ·ntois) *s.* BIOL. alantoides.
**allay (to)** (alei·) *tr.* aliviar, mitigar, calmar. *2* aquietar, apaciguar.
**allayment** (-mønt) *s.* alivio.
**allegation** (æligei·shøn) *s.* alegación. *2* DER. alegato.
**allege (to)** (æle·dẏ) *tr.* alegar, afirmar, sostener.
**alleged** (-d) *adj.* alegado, supuesto.
**allegiance** (æli·dẏans) *s.* obediencia, fidelidad [a un soberano, etc.]. *2* homenaje, pleito homenaje.
**allegoric(al** (æligo·rik(al) *adj.* alegórico.
**allegorize (to)** (æ·ligoraiš) *tr.-intr.* alegorizar.
**allegory** (æ·ligori) *s.* alegoría.
**allegretto** (æløgre·tou) *s.* MÚS. alegreto.
**allegro** (æle·grou) *s.* MÚS. alegro.
**alleluia** (ælilu·ẏa) *s.* e *interj.* aleluya.
**allergic** (alo·ʳdẏik) *adj.* alérgico.
**allergy** (æ·løʳdẏi) *s.* alergia.
**alleviate (to)** (ali·vieit) *tr.* aliviar, mitigar.
**alleviation** (-ei·shøn) *s.* alivio, mitigación.
**alley** (æ·li) *s.* calleja, callejón. *2* calle de árboles; camino entre setos. *3* bolera.

**All Fools' Day** *s.* primero de abril, especie de día de los Inocentes.
**all fours (on)** *adv.* a cuatro patas, a gatas.
**Allhallows** (oljæ·louš) *s.* día de Todos los Santos.
**alliance** (ala·ians) *s.* alianza.
**allied** (alai·d) *adj.* aliado. *2* afin. *3* emparentado.
**allies** (alai·š) *s. pl.* [de ALLY] aliados.
**alligator** (æligei·tøʳ) *s.* ZOOL. caimán. *2* BOT. ~ *pear,* aguacate.
**alliteration** (alitørei·shøn) *s.* aliteración.
**alliterative** (-rei·tiv) *adj.* aliterado.
**allocate (to)** (æ·lokeit) *tr.* señalar, asignar. *2* colocar, situar.
**allocation** (-kei·shøn) *s.* asignación, distribución.
**allocution** (ælokiu·shøn) *s.* alocución.
**allodium** (ælou·diøm) *s.* alodio.
**allopathist** (ala·pazist) *s.* alópata.
**allopathy** (ala·pazi) *s.* alopatía.·
**allot (to)** (ala·t) *tr.* repartir, distribuir, asignar, adjudicar. ¶ Pret. y p. p.: *allotted;* ger.: *-tting.*
**allotment** (-mønt) *s.* reparto, asignación. *2* parte, porción, lote.
**allotropism** (æla·tropišm), **allotropy** (-tropi) *s.* alotropía.
**allow (to)** (alau·) *tr.* conceder, dar, asignar. *2* dejar, permitir, consentir. *3* conceder, reconocer [como cierto]. *4* COM. descontar, rebajar. *5 intr. to* ~ *of,* permitir, admitir. *6 to* ~ *for,* tener en cuenta; dejar [espacio, etc.] para.
**allowable** (-abøl) *adj.* aceptable, permisible, lícito.
**allowance** (-ans) *s.* concesión, asignación [acción]. *2* permiso, autorización. *3* asignación, pensión, subsidio: *family* ~, subsidio familiar. *4* ración. *5* COM. descuento, bonificación, tara. *6* TÉCN. tolerancia. *7 to make* ~ *for,* tener en cuenta; ser indulgente con.
**alloy** (æloi·) *s.* liga, aleación. *2* fig. mezcla, impureza.
**alloy (to)** (æloi·) *tr.* ligar, alear [metales]. *2* fig. adulterar, desvirtuar.
**alloyage** (-idẏ) *s.* aleación [operación].
**all-powerful** *adj.* omnipotente, todopoderoso.
**all-round** *adj.* apto o que sirve para muchas cosas. *2* general, comprensivo.
**All Saints' day** *s.* día de Todos los Santos.
**All Souls' day** *s.* día de Difuntos.
**allspice** (o·lspais) *s.* pimienta inglesa.
**allude (to)** (aliu·d) *intr.* aludir, referirse.
**allure (to)** (aliu·øʳ) *tr.* atraer, tentar, seducir; inducir [con cebo o halago].
**allurement** (-mønt) *s.* tentación, seducción. *2* atractivo, encanto. *3* incentivo, cebo.
**alluring** (-ing) *adj.* seductor, tentador, halagüeño.
**allusion** (aliu·ẏøn) *s.* alusión.
**allusive** (aliu·siv) *adj.* alusivo.
**alluvial** (aliu·vial) *adj.* aluvial.
**alluvion** (-viøn) *s.* aluvión.
**alluvium** (-viøm) *s.* GEOL. aluvión.
**all-wave** *adj.* RADIO. de toda onda.
**ally** (alai·), *pl.* **allies** (-š) *s.* aliado.
**ally (to)** *tr.* aliar. *2* unir, relacionar. *3 intr.* aliarse. ¶ Pret. y p. p.: *allied.*
**almagest** (æ·lmadẏest) *s.* almagesto.
**almanac** (o·lmanæk) *s.* almanaque.
**alme(h** (æ·lmi) *s.* almea.
**almighty** (olmai·ti) *adj.* omnipotente, todopoderoso: *the Almighty,* el Todopoderoso [Dios]. *2* fam. grande, terrible.
**almond** (a·mønd) *s.* almendra: ~ *brittle,* crocante. *2* amígdala.
**almoner** (æ·lmønøʳ) *s.* limosnero.

**almonry** (æ·lmønri) *s.* lugar donde se distribuyen limosnas.
**almost** (*o*·lmoust) *adv.* casi; por poco.
**alms** (amŝ) *s.* limosna, caridad: ~ *box*, cepillo para las limosnas.
**almshouse** (a·mŝjaus) *s.* hospicio, casa de caridad.
**almucantar** (ælmiukæ·nta<sup>r</sup>) *s.* almicantarat.
**aloe** (æ·lou) *s.* BOT. áloe [planta].
**aloes** (æ·lous) *s.* áloe, acíbar [jugo]. 2 BOT. ~ *wood*, agáloco, palo áloe.
**aloft** (*alo*·ft) *adv.* arriba, en alto.
**alone** (*alou*·n) *adj.* solo. 2 solitario. 3 único, exclusivo. 4 *adv.* sólo, exclusivamente.
**along** (*alo*·ng) *adv.* a lo largo, por lo largo. 2 con uno o unos: *come* ~, ven o venid conmigo o con nosotros; ~ *with*, con, junto con. 3 adelante. 4 pop. ~ *of*, por o a causa de. 5 *all* ~, todo el tiempo, desde el principio. 6 *prep.* a lo largo de.
**alongshore** (-sho·<sup>r</sup>) *adv.* a lo largo de la costa, de la orilla.
**alongside** (-said) *adv.* y *prep.* a lo largo de, al costado de; lado a lado: ~ *of*, junto a.
**aloof** (alu·f) *adv.* a distancia. 2 *adj.* apartado, distante, frío, reservado: *to keep* o *stand* ~, mantenerse apartado, no mezclarse, retraerse.
**aloofness** (-nis) *s.* alejamiento, retraimiento, reserva, frialdad.
**alopecia** (ælopi·sia) *s.* alopecia.
**aloud** (alau·d) *adv.* alto, en voz alta.
**alpaca** (ælpæ·ka) *s.* alpaca.
**alpenstock** (æ·lpinstak) *s.* bastón de alpinista.
**alpha** (æ·lfa) *s.* alfa.
**alphabet** (æ·lfabet) *s.* alfabeto.
**alphabetic**(**al** (ælfabe·tik(*a*l) *adj.* alfabético.
**Alphonso** (ælfa·nsou) *n. pr.* Alfonso.
**alpine** (æ·lpain) *adj.* alpino, alpestre.
**alpinism** (æ·lpiniŝm) *s.* alpinismo.
**alpinist** (-nist) *s.* alpinista.
**alpist** (æ·lpist) *s.* alpiste.
**Alps** (ælps) *n. pr.* Alpes.
**already** (olre·di) *adv.* ya.
**Alsace** (æ·lsæs) *n. pr.* Alsacia.
**Alsatian** (ælsei·shan) *adj.-s.* alsaciano.
**also** (*o*·lsou) *adv.* también, asimismo, además.
**Altaic** (æltei·k) *adj.* altaico.
**altar** (*o*·lta<sup>r</sup>) *s.* altar: ~ *boy*, monaguillo; ~ *cloth*, sabanilla, mantel de altar.
**altar-piece** *s.* retablo.
**alter** (**to**) (*o*·ltø<sup>r</sup>) *tr.* alterar, cambiar, modificar. 2 *intr.* alterarse, modificarse.
**alterable** (-abøl) *adj.* alterable.
**alteration** (-ei·shøn) *s.* alteración, cambio, modificación.
**altercate** (**to**) (æ·lto<sup>r</sup>keit) *intr.* altercar.
**altercation** (-ei·shøn) *s.* altercado, disputa.
**alternant** (oltø·<sup>r</sup>nant) *adj.* ALTERNATING. 2 *s.* MAT. alternante.
**alternate** (*o*·ltø<sup>r</sup>nit) *adj.* alternado, alternativo, alterno. 2 alternante. 3 *s.* suplente.
**alternate** (**to**) (*o*·ltø<sup>r</sup>neit) *tr.* alternar. 2 *intr.* alternar, turnar.
**alternating** (-ing) *adj.* ELECT., MAT. alterna [corriente, función].
**alternation** (-ei·shøn) *s.* alternación, alternancia, turno.
**alternative** (oltø·<sup>r</sup>nativ) *adj.* alternativo. 2 GRAM., LÓG. disyuntivo. 3 *s.* alternativa [opción].
**alternator** (*o*·ltø<sup>r</sup>neitø<sup>r</sup>) *s.* ELECT. alternador.
**althea** (ælzi·a) *s.* altea. 2 rosa de Siria.
**although** (olðou·) *conj.* aunque, aun cuando, si bien, bien que, a pesar de que.

**altimetry** (ælti·mitri) *s.* altimetría.
**altisonant** (-son*a*nt), **altisonous** (-sonøs) *adj.* altisonante, retumbante.
**altitude** (æ·ltitiud) *s.* altitud, altura, elevación. 2 ASTR., GEOM. altura.
**alto** (æ·ltou) *adj.-s.* MÚS. contralto. 2 *s.* viola.
**altogether** (oltuge·ðø<sup>r</sup>) *adv.* enteramente, del todo. 2 en conjunto. 3 *s.* conjunto, totalidad.
**alto-relievo** (æltoril·vou) *s.* alto relieve.
**altruism** (æ·ltruiŝm) *s.* altruismo.
**altruist** (-ist) *s.* altruista.
**altruistic** (-i·stic) *adj.* altruista.
**alum** (æ·løm) *s.* alumbre.
**alumina** (æliu·mina) *s.* QUÍM. alúmina.
**aluminite** (-ait) *s.* MINER. aluminita.
**aluminium** (æliumi·niøm) *s.* ALUMINUM.
**aluminum** (-øm) *s.* QUÍM. aluminio.
**alumna** (alæ·mna) *s.* alumna o ex alumna.
**alumnus** (-nøs) *s.* alumno o ex alumno.
**alunite** (æliu·nait) *s.* alunita.
**alveolar** (ælvi·ola<sup>r</sup>) *adj.* alveolar.
**alveolus** (-oløs) *s.* alvéolo. 2 celdilla.
**alvine** (æ·lvin o -vain) *adj.* alvino.
**always** (*o*·lweiŝ) *adv.* siempre.
**am** (æm) *1.ª pers. del pres. de ind.* de TO BE.
**amadou** (æ·madu) *s.* yesca.
**amain** (amei·n) *adv.* vehementemente, vigorosamente. 2 a toda prisa.
**amalgam** (amæ·lgam) *s.* amalgama.
**amalgamate** (**to**) (-eit) *tr.* amalgamar. 2 reunir, fusionar [sociedades, etc.].
**amanita** (æmanai·ta) *s.* BOT. amanita.
**amanuensis** (æmæniue·nsis) *s.* amanuense.
**amaranth** (æ·marænz) *s.* BOT. amaranto.
**amaranthine** (æmaræ·nzin) *adj.* de amaranto. 2 purpúreo. 3 inmarcesible, imperecedero.
**Amaryllidaceae** (æmarilidei·sii) *s. pl.* amarilidáceas.
**amass** (**to**) (amæ·s) *tr.* juntar, amontonar, acumular.
**amateur** (æmatø·<sup>r</sup>) *adj.-s.* aficionado.
**amateurish** (-ish) *adj.* propio de un aficionado, defectuoso, chapucero.
**amative** (æ·mativ) *adj.* amativo.
**amatorial** (æma·to·rial), **amatory** (æ·matori) *adj.* amatorio.
**amaurosis** (æmorou·sis) *s.* MED. amaurosis.
**amaze** (**to**) (amei·ŝ) *tr.* asombrar, pasmar.
**amazed** (-d) *adj.* asombrado, pasmado, atónito.
**amazing** (-ing) *adj.* asombroso, pasmoso.
**Amazon** (æ·mazan) *s.* MIT. Amazona. 2 [con min.] marimacho. 3 *n. pr.* Amazonas [río].
**ambages** (æ·mbidŷis) *s. pl.* ambages.
**ambagious** (æmbei·dŷøs) *adj.* ambagioso.
**ambassador** (æmbæ·sadø<sup>r</sup>) *m.* embajador.
**ambassadorship** (-ship) *s.* embajada [cargo].
**ambassadress** (-dris) *s.* embajadora.
**amber** (æ·mbø<sup>r</sup>) *s.* ámbar, succino. 2 BOT. corazoncillo. 3 *adj.* ambarino, de ámbar.
**amber** (**to**) *tr.* ambarar. 2 dar color de ámbar.
**ambergris** (æ·mbø<sup>r</sup>gris) *s.* ámbar gris.
**ambidexter** (æmbide·kstø<sup>r</sup>) *adj.-s.* ambidextro. 2 fig. doble, falso, de dos caras.
**ambidexterity** (-te·riti) *s.* calidad de ambidextro. 2 fig. doblez, falsedad.
**ambidextrous** (æmbide·kstrøs) *adj.* AMBIDEXTER.
**ambient** (æ·mbient) *adj.* ambiente.
**ambiuity** (æmbigiui·ti) *s.* ambigüedad.
**ambiguous** (æmbi·giuøs) *adj.* ambiguo.
**ambit** (æ·mbit) *s.* ámbito, recinto.
**ambition** (æmbi·shøn) *s.* ambición.

**ambition (to)** *tr.* ambicionar.
**ambitious** (-søs) *adj.* ambicioso. 2 deseoso, ávido.
**amble** (æ·mbøl) *s.* portante, paso de ambladura.
**amble (to)** *intr.* amblar.
**ambler** (æ·mbløʳ) *s.* caballo amblador.
**ambo** (æ·mbou) *s.* ambón.
**Ambrose** (æ·mbrous) *n. pr.* Ambrosio.
**ambrosia** (æmbrou·šia) *s.* ambrosía.
**ambrosial** (-l) *adj.* delicioso, celestial.
**ambry** (æ·mbri) *s.* armario, alacena; despensa.
**ambulacrum** (æmbiulei·krøm) *s.* ZOOL. ambulacro.
**ambulance** (æ·mbiulans) *s.* ambulancia [hospital; vehículo].
**ambulant** (-ant) *adj.* ambulante.
**ambulation** (-ei·shøn) *s.* ambulación, paseo.
**ambulatory** (-tori) *adj.* ambulante, ambulatorio. 2 *s.* ARQ. galería.
**ambuscade** (æ·mbøskeid) *s.* AMBUSH.
**ambuscade (to)** *tr.-intr.* TO AMBUSH.
**ambush** (æ·mbush) *s.* emboscada, acecho.
**ambush (to)** *tr.* emboscar. 2 poner una emboscada a. 3 *intr.* estar emboscado, al acecho.
**ameer** (amɪ·ʳ) *s.* AMIR.
**ameliorate (to)** (amɪ·lioreit) *tr.* mejorar. 2 *intr.* mejorar, mejorarse.
**amelioration** (-ei·shøn) *s.* mejora, mejoramiento.
**amen** (ame·n) *interj.* amén.
**amenability** (aminabi·liti) *s.* responsabilidad. 2 docilidad.
**amenable** (ami·nabøl) *adj.* responsable. 2 sujeto [a]. 3 dócil.
**amend (to)** (ame·nd) *tr.* enmendar, corregir, mejorar. 2 *intr.* enmendarse. 3 restablecerse.
**amendment** (-mønt) *s.* enmienda, enmendadura; remedio, mejora. 2 enmienda [a un proyecto de ley]. 3 AGR. enmienda.
**amends** (ame·nds) *s.* satisfacción, reparación, compensación: *to make ~ for*, dar cumplida satisfacción por, reparar, resarcir.
**amenity** (ame·niti) *s.* amenidad. 2 afabilidad.
**amenorrhea** (amenørɪ·a) *s.* amenorrea.
**ament** (æ·ment) *s.* BOT. amento.
**amerce (to)** (amø·ʳs) *tr.* multar; castigar.
**amercement** (-mønt) *s.* multa.
**America** (ame·rika) *n. pr.* GEOGR. América.
**American** (-n) *adj.-s.* americano. 2 norteamericano. 3 BOT. ~ *aloe*, pita, magüey.
**Americanism** (-nišm) *s.* americanismo.
**Americanist** (-nist) *s.* americanista.
**Americanize (to)** (-naiš) *tr.* americanizar.
**amethyst** (æ·mizist) *s.* amatista.
**amiability** (eimiabi·liti) *s.* amabilidad.
**amiable** (ei·miabøl) *adj.* amable, afable, bondadoso.
**amianthus** (æmiæ·nzøs) *s.* amianto.
**amicability** (æmikabi·liti) *s.* calidad de amistoso.
**amicable** (æ·mikabøl) *adj.* amigable, amistoso.
**amice** (æ·mis) *s.* amito.
**amid** (ami·d) *prep.* en medio de, entre, rodeado por.
**amide** (æ·mid o æ·mid) *s.* QUÍM. amida.
**amidships** (ami·dships) *adv.* MAR. en medio del buque.
**amidst** (ami·dst) *prep.* AMID.
**amine** (æmɪ·n) *s.* QUÍM. amina.
**amir** (ami·ʳ) *s.* emir.
**amiss** (ami·s) *adv.* erradamente, mal; de más, fuera de lugar o del caso: *to take ~*, llevar a mal; *it is not ~*, no está de más, es conveniente. 2 *adj.*

errado, malo, impropio, inoportuno, desarreglado.
**amity** (æ·miti) *s.* amistad, buena inteligencia.
**ammeter** (æ·mitøʳ) *s.* amperímetro.
**ammonia** (æmou·nia) *s.* amoníaco [gas]: ~ *water*, agua amoniacal.
**ammoniac** (æmou·niæk) *s.* amoniaco [goma].
**ammoniac(al** (æmonai·k(al) *adj.* amoniacal.
**ammonite** (æ·monait) *s.* amonita [fósil]. 2 (con may.) BIB. amonita.
**ammonium** (æmou·niøm) *s.* amonio.
**ammunition** (æmiuni·shøn) *s.* MIL. munición, municiones.
**ammunition (to)** *tr.* municionar.
**amnesia** (æmnɪ·šia) *s.* MED. amnesia.
**amnesty** (æ·mnesti) *s.* amnistía.
**amnesty (to)** *tr.* amnistiar. ¶ Pret. y p. p.: *amnestied.*
**amnicola** (æmni·kola) *adj.* amnícola.
**amnion** (æ·mniøn) *s.* BIOL. amnios.
**amock** (oma·k) *adv.* AMUCK.
**amœba** (æmɪ·ba) *s.* ZOOL. amiba.
**amomum** (æmou·møn) *s.* amomo.
**among(st** (ama·ng(st) *prep.* entre, en medio de, en el número de.
**amoral** (eima·ral) *adj.* amoral.
**amorality** (eimoræ·liti) *s.* amoralidad.
**amorous** (æ·mørøs) *adj.* amoroso, tierno. 2 enamoradizo. 3 enamorado.
**amorphous** (amo·ʳføs) *adj.* amorfo, informe.
**amortization** (amoʳtišei·shøn) *s.* amortización.
**amortize (to)** (amo·ʳtaiš) *tr.* amortizar.
**amount** (amau·nt) *s.* cantidad, suma. 2 importe. 3 cuantía, valor.
**amount (to)** *intr.* ~ *to*, montar, sumar, importar, ascender a; equivaler a.
**amour** (amu·ʳ) *s.* amores, amorío.
**amourette** (æmure·t) *s.* amorío.
**ampere** (æ·mpiʳ) *s.* amperio.
**amperemeter** (-mitøʳ) *s.* AMMETER.
**ampersand** (æ·mpøʳsænd) *s.* el signo & [y].
**Amphibia** (æmfi·bia) *s. pl.* ZOOL. anfibios.
**amphibian** (-n) *s.* ZOOL. anfibio.
**amphibious** (-biøs) *adj.* anfibio.
**amphibole** (æ·mfiboul) *s.* MINER. anfibol.
**amphibological** (æmfibola·dýkal) *adj.* anfibológico.
**amphibology** (æmfiba·lodýi) *s.* anfibología.
**amphibrach** (æ·mfibræk) *s.* anfíbraco.
**amphictyon** (æmfi·ktiøn) *s.* anfiction.
**amphimacer** (æmfi·masøʳ) *s.* anfímacro.
**amphisbena** (æmfisbɪ·na) *s.* ZOOL. anfisbena.
**amphiscii** (æmfi·shiai) *s. pl.* anfiscios.
**amphitheater, -tre** (æ·mfiziatøʳ) *s.* anfiteatro.
**Amphitryon** (æmfi·triøn) *n. pr.* y *s.* Anfitrión.
**amphora** (æ·mfora) *s.* ánfora.
**ample** (æ·mpøl) *adj.* amplio. 2 extenso, capaz, holgado. 3 suficiente, cumplido, abundante.
**ampliation** (æmpliei·shøn) *s.* ampliación. 2 DER. aplazamiento de fallo.
**amplification** (-fikei·shøn) *s.* amplificación. 2 ampliación. 3 ÓPT. aumento.
**amplifier** (æ·mplifaiøʳ) *s.* amplificador, ampliador. 2 ELECT. amplificador. 3 RADIO. altavoz.
**amplify (to)** (æ·mplifai) *tr.* amplificar, ampliar. 2 extender, aumentar, exagerar. 3 *intr.* extenderse en los detalles, explayarse. ¶ Pret. y p. p.: *amplified.*
**amplitude** (-tiud) *s.* amplitud.
**amply** (æ·mpli) *adv.* ampliamente, latamente, abundantemente.

ampoule (æmpu·l) s. ampolla, inyectable.
amputate (to) (æ-mpiuteit) tr. amputar.
amputation (-tei·shøn) s. amputación.
amuck (amø·k) adv. furiosamente: to run ~, atacar ciegamente, a todo el mundo.
amulet (æ·miulit) s. amuleto.
amuse (to) (amiu·š) tr. entretener, divertir, hacer gracia a. 2 ref. distraerse, divertirse.
amusement (-mønt) s. entretenimiento, solaz, diversión, pasatiempo.
amusing (-ing) adj. entretenido, divertido, gracioso, humorístico.
amygdala (ami·gdala) s. ANAT. amígdala.
Amygdalaceae (-lei·sii) s. pl. BOT. amigdaláceas.
amyl (æ·mil) s. QUÍ. amilo. 2 adj. amílico.
amylic (æ·milic) adj. amílico.
an (æn) art. indef. un, una. V. ARTÍCULO (cuadro gramatical).
ana (ei·na) s. colección de dichos o anécdotas.
Anabaptism (ænabæ·ptišm) s. anabaptismo.
Anabaptist (-tist) s. anabaptista.
anachronic(al (ænakra·nik(al) adj. anacrónico.
anachronism (ænæ·kronišm) s. anacronismo.
anaconda (ænaka·nda) s. ZOOL. anaconda.
Anacreon (anæ·krian) n. pr. Anacreonte.
Anacreontic (anækria·ntik) adj. anacreóntico. 2 s. anacreóntica.
anaemia (æni·mia) s. MED. anemia.
anaemic (-ic) adj. anémico.
anaerobe (ænei·øroub) s. BIOL. anaerobio.
anaesthesia (æneszi·šia) s. anestesia.
anaesthetic (-ze·tik) adj.-s. anestésico.
anaesthetist (æne·szitist) s. anestesiador.
anaesthetize (to) (-taiš) tr. anestesiar.
anaglyph (æ·naglif) s. anáglifo.
anagoge (ænagou·dÿi) s. anagoge.
anagram (æ·nagræm) s. anagrama.
anal (ei·nal) adj. ANAT. anal.
analecta (ænale·kta), analects (æ·nalekts) s. pl. analectas.
analgesia (ænældÿi·sia) s. analgesia.
analgesic (-šic) adj.-s. analgésico.
analogical (ænala·dÿical) adj. de analogía; fundado en ella.
analogize (to) (anæ·lodÿaiš) tr.-intr. explicar o razonar por analogía.
analogous (anæ·logøs) adj. análogo, semejante, correspondiente.
analogue (æ·nalag) s. cosa análoga.
analogy (anæ·lodÿi) s. analogía, correlación, correspondencia.
analysis (anæ·lisis) s. análisis.
analyst (æ·nalist) s. analizador, analista.
analytic(al (ænali·tik(al) adj. analítico.
analytics (-s) s. analítica. 2 geometría analítica.
analyze (to) (æ·nalaiš) tr. analizar.
anana(s) (ana·nas) s. anana, ananás.
anapaest, anapest (æ·napest) s. anapesto.
anaphrodisia (ænæfrodi·šia) s. anafrodisia.
anaphylaxis (ænafilæ·ksis) s. MED. anafilaxis.
anarchic(al (æna·ʳkik(al) adj. anárquico.
anarchism (æ·naʳkišm) s. anarquismo.
anarchist (-kist) adj.-s. anarquista.
anarchistic (-kistik) adj. anarquista.
anarchy (æ·naʳki) s. anarquía.
anastigmatic (ænæstigmæ·tik) adj. ÓPT. anastigmático.
anastomose (to) (anæ·stomouš) intr. anastomizarse.
anastomosis (anestomou·sis) s. anastomosis.
anastrophe (anæ·strofi) s. anástrofe.

anathema (ænæ·zima) s. anatema. 2 cosa maldita.
anathematize (to) (-taiš) tr. anatematizar.
Anatolia (ænatou·lia) n. pr. GEOGR. Anatolia.
Anatolian (-n) adj.-s. anatolio.
anatomic(al (ænata·mik(al) adj. anatómico.
anatomist (anæ·tomist) s. anatomista, disector.
anatomize (to) (-maiš) tr. anatomizar, disecar.
anatomy (-mi) s. anatomía. 2 disección, análisis. 3 fig. esqueleto, persona flaca.
ancestor (æ·nsestøʳ) s. progenitor, antepasado.
ancestral (ænse·stral) adj. de los antepasados, hereditario, solariego.
ancestry (æ·nsestri) s. linaje, prosapia, abolengo.
anchor (æ·ngkøʳ) s. ancla, áncora. 2 RELOJ. áncora. 3 tirante, riostra; lo que sirve para sujetar, retener o amarrar.
anchor (to) (æ·ngkøʳ) tr. sujetar con el ancla. 2 sujetar, asegurar, fijar, empotrar. 3 intr. anclar, echar el ancla.
anchorage (æ·ngkøridÿ) s. anclaje. 2 ancladero. 3 sitio donde puede asegurarse una cosa.
anchoress (-is) s. mujer anacoreta.
anchoret (-ret), anchorite (-rait) s. anacoreta.
anchorless (-lis) adj. sin ancla; inseguro; errante.
anchovy (æ·nchouvi) s. ICT. anchoa, boquerón.
ancient (ei·nshønt) adj. antiguo. 2 anciano. 3 pl. los antiguos, la antigüedad.
anciently (-li) adv. antiguamente.
ancillary (æ·nsileri) adj. auxiliar, subordinado.
and (ænd) conj. y, e; ~ so forth, ~ so on, etcétera; y así sucesivamente. 2 con: bread ~ butter, pan con mantequilla. 3 a, de: to go ~ see, ir a ver; to try ~ teach, tratar de enseñar.
Andalusia (ændalu·ÿa) n. pr. GEOGR. Andalucía.
Andalusian (-n) adj.-s. andaluz.
andante (ænde·nti) adv.-s. MÚS. andante.
andantino (-i·nou) adv.-s. MÚS. andantino.
Andean (ændi·an) adj. andino.
Andes (æ·ndiš) n. pr. GEOGR. Andes.
andirons (ændaiøʳns) s. pl. morillos.
Andrew (æ·ndru) n. pr. Andrés.
androecium (ændri·shiøm) s. BOT. andróceo.
androgynous (ændra·dÿnøs) adj. andrógino.
anecdotal (æ·nikdoutal) adj. anecdótico.
anecdote (æ·nikdout) s. anécdota.
anecdotic(al (ænikda·tik(al) adj. ANECDOTAL.
anemia, s, anemic adj. ANAEMIA, ANAEMIC. .
anemograph (æne·mogræf) s. anemógrafo.
anemometer (ænima·mitøʳ) s. anemómetro.
anemone (ane·moni) s. BOT. anemone, anemona: sea ~, ZOOL. anemone de mar.
anemoscope (æne·moskoup) s. anemoscopio.
aneroid (æ·nøroid) adj. aneroide.
anesthesia, anesthetic, etc. ANAESTHESIA, ANAESTHETIC, etc.
aneurism (æ·niurišm) s. aneurisma.
anew (aniu·) adv. nuevamente, de nuevo, otra vez: to read ~, volver a leer.
anfractuosity (ænfrækchua·siti) s. anfractuosidad; sinuosidad.
anfractuous (ænfræ·kchuøs) adj. anfractuoso; sinuoso.
angel (ei·ndÿøl) s. ángel. 2 pop. caballo blanco, pagano. 3 ICT. ~ fish, peje ángel.
angelic (ændÿe·lik) adj. angélico, angelical.
angelica (ændÿe·lika) s. BOT. angélica.
angelical (-l) adj. ANGELIC.
Angelus (æ·ndÿeløs) adj. Ángelus.
anger (æ·ngøʳ) s. cólera, ira, enojo.
anger (to) tr. encolerizar, enfurecer, enojar.

angina (ændÿai·na) s. angina: ~ *pectoris*, angina de pecho.
angiology (ændÿia·lodÿi) s. angiología.
angiospermous (ændÿiøspø·ʳmøs) *adj*. BOT. angiospermo.
angle (æ·ngøl) s. ángulo: *to be at an ~ of*, formar un ángulo de. *2* rincón, esquina, codo, recodo. *3* punto de vista, aspecto. *4* anzuelo.
angle (to) *tr*. pescar con caña en [un río, etc.]. *2 intr*. pescar con caña; fig. *to ~ for*, tratar de conseguir o conquistar.
Angles (æ·ngøls) *s. pl*. anglos.
angled (æ·ngøld) *adj*. anguloso, esquinado.
angler (æ·ngløʳ) s. pescador de caña. *2* pejesapo, rape.
anglesite (æ·ngløsait) s. anglesita.
Anglican (æ·nglikan) *adj.-s*. anglicano.
Anglicanism (-išm) s. anglicanismo.
Anglicism (æ·nglisišm) s. anglicismo.
Anglicize (to) (-aiš) *tr*. inglesar.
angling (æ·ngling) s. pesca con caña.
Anglo-Indian (æ·nglo) *adj.-s*. angloindio.
Anglophile (-fail) *adj.-s*. anglófilo.
Anglophobe (-foub) *adj.-s*. anglófobo.
Anglo-Saxon *adj.-s*. anglosajón.
angrily (æ·ngrili) *adj*. coléricamente, airadamente.
angry (æ·ngri) *adj*. colérico, airado, enojado. *2* furioso, embravecido. *3* MED. irritado.
anguish (æ·ngüish) s. angustia, congoja, ansia, aflicción, dolor, tormento.
anguish (to) *tr*. angustiar, acongojar, atormentar.
angular (æ·ngiular) *adj*. angular. *2* anguloso. *3* seco, huesudo, tieso.
angularity (-læ·riti) s. angulosidad.
anhelation (ænjilei·shøn) s. anhélito.
anhydride (ænjai·drid) s. anhídrido.
anhydrous (-drøs) *adj*. anhidro.
anil (æ·nil) s. BOT. añil, índigo.
anile (æ·nail) *adj*. de vieja que chochea.
anilin(e (æ·nilin) s. QUÍM. anilina.
animadversion (ænimæ·dvøʳshøn) s. crítica, censura, reproche.
animadvert (to) (-vøʳt) *intr*. censurar, criticar. | Con *on* o *upon*.
animal (æ·nimal) s. animal. *2* bestia, bruto. *3 adj*. animal. *4 ~ spirits*, vivacidad, animación.
animalcule (ænimæ·lkiul) s. animálculo.
animality (-liti) s. animalidad.
animalize (to) (æ·nimalaiš) *tr*. animalizar.
animate (æ·nimit) *adj*. animado [viviente; que tiene animación].
animate (to) *tr*. animar.
animated (-id) *adj*. animado: ~ *cartoon*, dibujo animado. *2* vivo, vigoroso.
animation (animei·shøn) s. animación; vida, calor, movimiento.
animism (æ·nimišm) s. animismo.
animosity (ænima·siti) s. animosidad.
animus (æ·nimøs) s. ánimo, intención. *2* animosidad.
anion (æ·naløn) s. QUÍM., FÍS. anión.
anise (æ·nis) s. anís [planta y semilla].
aniseed (æ·nisiid) s. anís [semilla].
anisette (ænise·t) s. anisete.
anisopetalous (ænaisope·taløs) *adj*. anisopétalo.
ankle (æ·ngkøl) s. tobillo.
anklet (æ·ngklit) s. ajorca [para el tobillo].
ankylose (to) (æ·nkilous) *tr*. anquilosar. *2 intr*. anquilosarse.
ankylosis (-lou·sis) s. anquilosis.

Ann, Anne (æ·n), Anna (æ·na) *n. pr*. Ana.
annalist (æ·nalist) s. analista, cronista.
annals (æ·nals) *s. pl*. anales.
Annamese (ænamı·š), *pl*. **-ese** *adj.-s*. anamita.
annato (ænæ·tou) s. BOT. achiote, bija.
anneal (to) (anı·l) *tr*. templar, recocer. *2* fig. fortalecer.
annelid (æ·nelid) *adj.-s*. anélido.
annex (ane·ks) s. anexo, aditamento, apéndice. *2* dependencia, edificio anexo.
annex (to) *tr*. anexar, anexionar. *2* unir, añadir. *3* poner [una firma].
annexation (-ei·shøn) s. anexión.
annexed (ane·kst) *adj*. anexo, anejo, adjunto.
annihilate (to) (anai·ileit) *tr*. aniquilar.
annihilation (-ei·shøn) 's. aniquilación, aniquilamiento.
anniversary (ænivø·ʳsari) *adj*. aniversario, anual. *2* s. aniversario.
annotate (to) (æ·noteit) *tr*. anotar, apostillar.
annotation (ænotei·shøn) s. anotación [acción]. *2* anotación, acotación, nota.
annotator (-tøʳ) s. anotador.
announce (to) (anau·ns) *tr*. anunciar, hacer saber, proclamar, declarar.
announcement (-mønt) s. anuncio, notificación, declaración.
announcer (-øʳ) s. anunciador, nuncio. *2* locutor [de radio].
annoy (to) (anoi) *tr*. molestar, incomodar, fastidiar.
annoyance (-ans) s. molestia, incomodidad, fastidio, aburrimiento. *2* lata, pejiguera.
annoyer (-øʳ) s. molestador, persona enfadosa.
annoying (-ing) *adj*. molesto, fastidioso, enfadoso, engorroso.
annual (æ·nyual) *adj*. anual. *2* s. LITURG. aniversario. *3* anuario.
annuary (æ·nyueri) s. anuario.
annuity (æniu·iti) s. anualidad, pensión; renta vitalicia.
annul (to) (anø·l) *tr*. anular, invalidar. *2* abolir. *3* borrar, destruir.
annular (æ·nyular) *adj*. anular.
annulate(d (anyulei·tid) *adj*. anillado.
annulet (æ·nyulit) s. anillito. *2* ARQ., ZOOL. anillo.
annulment (anø·lmønt) s. anulación.
annunciate (to) (ænø·nshieit) *tr*. TO ANNOUNCE.
annunciation (-ei·shøn) s. anuncio, anunciación.
annunciator (-ei·tøʳ) s. anunciador. *2* MEC. indicador. *3* ELECT. indicador de llamadas.
anode (æ·nod) s. ELECT. ánodo.
anodyne (æ·nodain) *adj.-s*. anodino.
anoint (to) (anoi·nt) *tr*. untar. *2* ungir, consagrar. *3* administrar la Extremaunción.
anointing (-ing), anointment (-mønt) s. unción, óleo. *2* untadura.
anomalism (ana·mališm) s. anomalía.
anomalistic (anamali·stik) *adj*. anomalístico.
anomalous (ana·maløs) *adj*. anómalo.
anomalousness (-nis), anomaly (-li) s. anomalía.
anon (ana·n) *adv*. pronto, luego, en seguida.
anonym (æ·nonim) s. anónimo [pers.]. *2* pseudónimo.
anonymous (ana·nimøs) *adj*. anónimo.
anorexia (ænore·ksia) s. MED. anorexia.
anosmia (æna·šmia) s. anosmia.
another (anø·ðøʳ) *adj.-pron*. otro, otra.
anserine (æ·nsørain) *adj*. ansarino. *2* fig. tonto, necio.

**answer** (æ·nsø<sup>r</sup>) *s.* respuesta, contestación. *2* explicación, solución [de un problema, enigma, etc.].
**answer (to)** *tr.-intr.* respónder, contestar, reponer: *to ~ back,* replicar, ser respondón. *2* responder, corresponder [guardar, conformidad o correspondencia]. *3 tr.* responder, refutar. *4* responder [a esperanzas, deseos, necesidades, etc.]; convenir [a un designio]. *5* obedecer [a una acción, una fuerza]. *6 intr.* servir, llenar el objeto. *7 to ~ for,* responder por o de; ser o hacerse responsable de.
**answerable** (-abøl) *adj.* responsable. *2* correspondiente; conforme. *3* discutible, refutable.
**ant** (ænt) *s.* ENT. hormiga: *~ bear,* oso hormiguero; *~ lion,* hormiga león.
**anta** (æ·nta) *s.* ARQ. anta.
**Antaeus** (ænti·øs) *n. pr.* Anteo.
**antagonism** (æntæ·gonišm) *s.* antagonismo.
**antagonist** (-ist) *s.* antagonista.
**antagonistic** (-i·stik) *s.* antagónico.
**antagonize (to)** (-aiš) *tr.* oponerse a, contrarrestar. *2* provocar el antagonismo, la enemistad de.
**antaphrodisiac** (æntæfrodi·šilaek) *adj.-s.* antiafrodisíaco.
**antarctic** (ænta·<sup>r</sup>tik) *adj.* antártico. *2 s.* tierras antárticas.
**antarthritic** (-zri·tik) *adj.* antiartrítico.
**antecede (to)** (æntisɪ·d) *intr.* anteceder, preceder.
**antecedence, -cy** (-ens, -i) *s.* predecesión.
**antecedent** (-ønt) *adj.-s.* antecedente, precedente, anterior. *2 s.* antecedente. *3 pl.* antepasados.
**antecedently** (-li) *adv.* anteriormente.
**antecessor** (æntise·sø<sup>r</sup>) *s.* antecesor, predecesor.
**antechamber** (æ·nticheimbø<sup>r</sup>) *s.* antecámara, antesala.
**antechoir** (-kuaiø<sup>r</sup>) *s.* antecoro.
**antedate** (æ·ntideit) *s.* antedata.
**antedate (to)** *tr.* antedatar. *2* adelantar; retrotraer.
**antediluvian** (-diliu·vian) *adj.* antediluviano.
**antelope** (æ·nteloup) *s.* antílope.
**antemeridian** (æntimøri·dian) *adj.* antemeridiano.
**antenatal** (æntinei·tal) *adj.* prenatal.
**antenna** (ænte·na), *pl.* -**nae** (-ni) ZOOL. antena. *2 (pl.* -**nas)** RADIO. antena.
**antenuptial** (antinø·pshal) *adj.* antenupcial.
**antependium** (-pe·ndiøm) *s.* antipendio.
**antepenultimate** (-pinø·lt(imit) *adj.* y *s.* antepenúltima [sílaba].
**anterior** (ænti·riø<sup>r</sup>) *adj.* anterior.
**anteriority** (æntiria·riti) *s.* anterioridad.
**anteroom** (æ·ntirum) *s.* antesala, vestíbulo.
**anthem** (æ·nzøm) *s.* antífona. *2* himno.
**anther** (æ·nzø<sup>r</sup>) *s.* antera.
**antheridium** (ænzøri·diøm) *s.* anteridio.
**anthill** (æ·ntjil) *s.* hormiguero [montículo].
**anthological** (ænzola·dy̆kal) *adj.* antológico.
**anthology** (ænza·lody̆i) *s.* antología.
**Anthony** (æ·ntoni) *n. pr.* Antonio.
**anthozoan** (ænzošou·an) *adj.* y *s.* ZOOL. antozoario, antozoo.
**anthracene** (æ·nzrasɪn) *s.* QUÍM. antraceno.
**anthracite** (æ·nzrasait) *s.* antracita.
**anthrax** (æ·nzræks) *s.* MED. ántrax. *2* MED. carbunco.
**anthropoid** (æ·nzropoid) *adj.-s.* antropoideo.
**anthropologic(al** (-pola·dy̆ik(al) *adj.* antropológico.
**anthropologist** (-pa·lody̆ist) *s.* antropólogo.
**anthropology** (-pa·lody̆i) *s.* antropología.

**anthropometric(al** (-pome·trik(al) *adj.* antropométrico.
**anthropometry** (-pa·metri) *s.* antropometría.
**anthropomorphism** (-pomo·<sup>r</sup>fism) *s.* antropomorfismo.
**anthropomorphous** (-pomo·<sup>r</sup>føs) *adj.* antropomorfo.
**anthropophagi** (-pa·fady̆ai) *s. pl.* antropófagos.
**anthropophagite** (-fady̆ait) *s.* antropófago.
**anthropophagous** (-fagøs) *adj.* antropófago.
**anthropophagy** (-fay̆i) *s.* antropofagia.
**anti-** (ænti) *pref.* anti-.
**antiaircraft** (æntie·ø<sup>r</sup>kraft) *adj.* antiaéreo.
**antialcoholic** (-ælkojo·lik) *adj.* antialcohólico.
**antiar** (æ·tia<sup>r</sup>) *s.* antiar [árbol y veneno].
**antibiotic** (-baia·tik) *adj.-s.* antibiótico.
**antibody** (-ba·di) *s.* anticuerpo.
**antic** (æ·ntik) *adj.* grotesco, estrafalario. *2 s.* zapateta, cabriola. *3* bufón, payaso. *4 pl.* bufonadas, travesuras.
**anticatarrhal** (æntikata·ral) *adj.* anticatarral.
**Antichrist** (æ·ntikraist) *s.* antecristo.
**anticipate (to)** (ænti·sipeit) *tr.* anticipar, adelantar [una acción, un suceso]. *2* anticiparse, adelantarse a. *3* prevenir, impedir. *4* prever, esperar. *5* prometerse [un placer, etc.]; gozar o experimentar de antemano. *6* gastar por adelantado.
**anticipation** (-pei·shøn) *s.* anticipación [acción, efecto]. *2* intuición o impresión de lo que va a suceder. *3* expectación, esperanza, goce anticipado.
**anticlerical** (-kle·rikal) *adj.* anticlerical.
**anticolonialism** (-kolou·niališm) *s.* anticolonialismo.
**anticonstitutional** (-konstitiu·shønal) *adj.* anticonstitucional.
**anticyclone** (-sai·kloun) *s.* anticiclón.
**antidiptheritic** (-difzøri·tik) *adj.* antidiftérico.
**antidote** (æ·ntidout) *s.* antídoto.
**antiferment** (-fø<sup>r</sup>mønt) *s.* antifermento.
**antifreeze** (-fri·š) *adj.* anticongelante.
**antifriction** (-frikshøn) *s.* MEC. antifricción.
**antigen** (æ·ntidy̆øn) *s.* antígeno.
**antihydrophobic** (-jaidrofou·bik) *adj.* antirrábico.
**anti-knock** (-nak) *adj.* antidetonante [gasolina].
**Antillean** (ænti·lian) *adj.-s.* antillano.
**Antilles** (ænti·liš) *n. pr.* GEOGR. Antillas.
**antilogarithm** (-logariðm) *s.* MAT. antilogaritmo.
**antilogy** (-lody̆i) *s.* antilogía.
**antimilitarism** (-mi·litarišm) *s.* antimilitarista.
**antimonial** (-mou·nial) *adj.* antimonial.
**antimony** (æ·ntimouni) *s.* QUÍM. antimonio.
**antinomy** (ænti·nomi) *s.* antinomia.
**antioch** (æ·ntiak) *s.* GEOGR. Antioquía.
**Antiochus** (æntai·okøs) *n. pr.* Antíoco.
**antipathetic(al** (æntipaze·tik(al) *adj.* antipático. *2* antagónico, opuesto.
**antipathy** (ænti·pazi) *s.* antipatía, aversión.
**antiphon** (æ·ntiføn) *s.* antífona.
**antiphrasis** (ænti·frasis) *s.* antífrasis.
**antipodal** (-podal) *adj.* antípoda.
**antipode** (æn·tipoud) *s.* lo contrario u opuesto.
**antipodean** (æntipodi·an) *adj.* ANTIPODAL.
**antipodes** (ænti·podiš) *s. pl.* GEOGR. antípodas.
**antipope** (-poup) *s.* antipapa.
**antipyretic** (antipaire·tik) *adj.-s.* antipirético.
**antipyrin(e** (-pai·rin) *s.* antipirina.
**antiquarian** (-kue·rian) *s.* anticuario.
**antiquary** (æ·ntikueri) *s.* anticuario.
**antiquate (to)** (æ·ntikueit) *tr.* anticuar.
**antiquated** (-id) *adj.* anticuado.

**antique** (æntɪ·k) *adj.* antiguo. *2 s.* antigüedad, antigualla.
**antiqueness** (-nis) *s.* antigüedad [calidad].
**antiquity** (-kuiti) *s.* antigüedad. *2* ancianidad, vejez. *3 pl.* antigüedades.
**antiscians** (ænti·shanš), **antiscii** (-shiai) *s. pl.* antiscios.
**anti-Semite** (-se·mait) *s.* antisemita.
**anti-Semitic** (-semi·tik) *adj.* antisemita, antisemítico.
**antisepsis** (-se·psis) *s.* antisepsia.
**antiseptic** (-se·ptik) *adj.-s.* antiséptico.
**antiskid** (æ·ntiskid) *adj.* antideslizante.
**antisocial** (æntisou·shal) *adj.* antisocial.
**antispasmodic** (-spæšma·dik) *adj.-s.* antiespasmódico.
**antistrophe** (anti·strof) *s.* antistrofa.
**antitank** (æntitæ·nk) *adj.* antitanque.
**antitetanic** (-titænik) *adj.* antitetánico.
**antithesis** (ænti·zesis) *s.* antítesis.
**antithetical** (æntize·tikal) *adj.* antitético.
**antitoxin** (-ta·ksin) *s.* antitoxina.
**antitragus** (anti·tragøs) *s.* antitrago.
**antitrust** (æntitrø·st) *adj.* opuesto a los trusts.
**antituberculous** (-tiubø·ʳkiuløs) *adj.* antituberculoso.
**antler** (æntlø ʳ) *s.* asta, cuerna [de venado].
**antlered** (æ·ntlø ʳ) *adj.* provisto de cuerdas o adornado con ellas.
**antoecians** (anti·shans), **antoeci** (æ-sai) *m. pl.* GEOGR. antecos.
**Antoinette** (æntuane·t) *n. pr.* Antonieta.
**antonomasia** (æntonomei·ŷia) *s.* antonomasia.
**Antony** (æ·ntoni) *n. pr.* Antonio.
**antonym** (æ·ntonim) *s.* antónimo.
**Antwerp** (æ·ntwø ʳp) *n. pr.* GEOGR. Amberes.
**anuran** (æniu·ram) *adj.-s.* anuro.
**anus** (ei·nøs) *s.* ANAT. ano.
**anvil** (æ·nvil) *s.* yunque, bigornia. *2* ANAT. yunque.
**anxiety** (ængšai·øti) *s.* ansiedad, inquietud, desasosiego. *2* ansia, anhelo, afán.
**anxious** (æ·nkshøs) *adj.* ansioso, inquieto, desasosegado. *2* ansioso, anheloso, afanoso. *3* angustioso, penoso.
**any** (-e·ni) *adj.* cualquier, todo, todos los, algún, alguno; [en frases negativas] ninguno, ninguno: ~ *place,* cualquier parte, en cualquier parte; *I have not* ~ *book,* no tengo ningún libro; *at* ~ *rate,* de todos modos; sea como sea. *2* tiene sentido partitivo y en este caso suele no traducirse: *have you* ~ *money?,* ¿tiene usted dinero? *3* todo [la mayor cantidad, etc., posible]: *at* ~ *cost,* a toda costa.
   *4 pron.* alguno, alguna, algunos, alguien; [en frases negativas] ninguno, ninguna, nadie: *if* ~, si lo hay.
   *5 adv.* en alguna extensión, en algún grado, algo. | A veces no se traduce: ~ *more,* más, más tiempo; *not...* ~ *longer,* ya no.
**anybody** (e·nibadi) *pron.* alguien, alguno: [en frases negativas] ninguno, nadie. *2* cualquiera, todos, todo el mundo.
**anyhow** (e·nijau) *adv.* de cualquier modo. *2* de todos modos, sin embargo. *3* en todo caso, como quiera que sea; sea lo que fuere.
**anyone** (e·niuøn) *pron.* ANYBODY.
**anything** (e·nizing) *pron.* algo, alguna cosa, cualquier cosa, todo cuanto; [con negación] nada. *2 as* ~, *like* ~, por demás.
**anyway** (e·niuei) *adv.* de todos modos, en cualquier caso. *2* sin embargo. *3* de cualquier modo, sin orden.
**anywhere** (e·nijue ʳ) *adv.* doquiera, en todas partes; en cualquier parte, adondequiera; *not* ~, en ninguna parte, a ninguna parte.
**anywise** (e·niwaiš) *adv.* de cualquier modo.
**aorist** (ei·ørist) *s.* aoristo.
**aorta** (eio·ʳta) *s.* ANAT. aorta.
**apace** (apei·s) *adv.* aprisa, rápidamente.
**Apache** (apæ·chi) *adj.-s.* apache.
**apanage** (æ·panidŷ) *s.* APPANAGE.
**apart** (apa·ʳt) *adv.* aparte; a un lado. *2* separadamente, de por sí. *3* en piezas: *to take* ~, desarmar, desmontar.
**apartment** (-mønt) *s.* aposento. *2* cuarto piso, apartamento.
**apathetic** (æpaze·tik) *adj.* apático, indiferente.
**apathy** (æ·pazi) *s.* apatía, indiferencia.
**ape** (eip) *s.* ZOOL. mono, mico, simio. *2* fig. mona, imitador.
**ape (to)** *tr.* imitar, remedar.
**Apennines** (æ·pønainš) *n. pr.* GEOGR. Apeninos.
**aperiodic** (eipiria·dik) *adj.* aperiódico.
**apéritif** (æperiti·f) *s.* aperitivo.
**aperture** (æ·pø ʳchø ʳ) *s.* abertura [oficio, portillo, etc.].
**apery** (ei·pøri) *s.* remedo, monada.
**apetalous** (eipe·taløs) *adj.* apétalo.
**apex** (ei·peks) *s.* ápice, cúspide, vértice, cumbre.
**aphaeresis** (æfe·røsis) *s.* aféresis.
**aphasia** (æfei·ŷia) *s.* afasia.
**aphelion** (æfi·liøn) *s.* ASTR. afelio.
**apheresis** (æfe·røsis) *s.* APHAERESIS.
**aphid** (ei·fid), **aphis** (-fiš) *s.* ENT. áfido.
**aphonia** (eifou·nia) *s.* afonía.
**aphonic** (eifa·nik) *adj.* afónico.
**aphonous** (æ·fonøs) *adj.* áfono.
**aphorism** (æ·førišm) *s.* aforismo.
**aphrodisia** (æfrødi·ŷia) *s.* afrodisia.
**aphrodisiac** (-i·ŷiak) *adj.-s.* afrodisíaco.
**aphta** (æ·fza) *s.* MED. afta.
**aphtous** (æ·fzøs) *adj.* aftoso.
**apiary** (ei·pieri) *s.* colmenar.
**apical** (æ·pikal) *adj.* apical.
**apiculture** (eipikøl·chø ʳ) *s.* apicultura.
**apiculturist** (-ist) *s.* apicultor.
**apiece** (apı·s) *adv.* cada uno, a cada uno, por barba, por cabeza.
**apish** (ei·pish) *adj.* simiesco. *2* que imita servilmente. *3* necio.
**aplomb** (aplo·m) *s.* aplomo, seguridad. *2* aplomo, verticalidad.
**apnea, apnoea** (æpni·a) *s.* apnea.
**Apocalypse** (apa·kalips) *s.* Apocalipsis.
**apocopate (to)** (apa·kopeit) *tr.* apocopar.
**apocope** (apa·kopi) *s.* apócope.
**Apocrypha** (apa·krifa) *s. pl.* libros apócrifos.
**apocryphal** (-l) *adj.* apócrifo.
**apocynaceous** (aposinei·shøs) *adj.* apocináceo.
**apod** (æ·pad) *s.* ápodo.
**apodal** (æ·padal) *adj.* ápodo.
**apodosis** (æpa·dosis) *s.* apódosis.
**apogee** (æ·podŷi) *s.* apogeo.
**Apolline** (æ·palin) *adj.* APOLLONIAN.
**Apolo** (æpa·lou) *n. pr.* Apolo.
**Apollonian** (æpalou·nian) *adj.* apolíneo.
**apologetic(al** (apalodŷe·tik(al) *adj.* apologético. *2* de excusa.
**apologetically** (-i) *adv.* apologéticamente. *2* en tono de excusa.
**apologetics** (-tiks) *s.* apologética.

**apologist** (apa·lodỹist) *s.* apologista.
**apologize (to)** (-aiš) *intr.* excusarse, disculparse, presentar excusas.
**apologue** (æ·polag) *s.* apólogo.
**apology** (apa·lodỹi) *s.* apología. *2* excusa, disculpa. *3* cosa que suple la falta de otra.
**apophthegm** (æ·pozem) *s.* APOTHEGM.
**apophyge** (æpa·fidỹi) *s.* apófige.
**apophysis** (-sis), *pl.* **-sis** (siš) *se* apófisis.
**apoplectic** (æpople·ktik) *adj.-s.* apoplético.
**apoplexy** (æpopleksi) *s.* MED. apoplejía.
**apostasy** (apa·stasi) *s.* apostasía.
**apostate** (-teit) *s.* apóstata, renegado. *2 adj.* falso, pérfido.
**apostatize (to)** (-tataiš) *intr.* apostatar.
**aposteme** (æ·pastem) *s.* apostema.
**apostle** (apa·søl) *s.* apóstol.
**apostleship** (-ship), **apostolate** (-leit) *s.* apostolado.
**apostolic(al** (æpøsta·lik(al) *adj.* apostólico.
**apostrophe** (apa·strofi) *s.* apóstrofe. *2* apóstrofo.
**apostrophize (to)** (apa·strofaiš) *tr.* apostrofar. *2* señalar con un apóstrofo.
**apothecary** (apa·zikeri) *s.* boticario, farmacéutico.
**apothegm** (æ·pozem) *s.* apotegma.
**apothem** (æ·pozem) *s.* GEOM. apotema.
**apotheosis** (æpaziou·sis) *s.* apoteosis.
**apotheosize (to)** (æpa·ziosaiš) *tr.* deificar.
**appa(l (to)** (æpo·l) *tr.* espantar, aterrar. *2* desmayar, desanimar. ¶ Pret. y p. p.: *appalled;* ger.: *-lling.*
**appalling** (-ing) *adj.* espantoso, aterrador.
**appanage** (æ·panidỹi) *s.* infantazgo. *2* patrimonio, atributo [cosa o cualidad inherente].
**apparatus** (æparei·tøs) *s.* aparato, dispositivo.
**apparel** (apæ·rel) *s.* ropa, vestido. *2* MAR. aparejo [de un buque].
**apparel (to)** *tr.* vestir, trajear. *2* adornar.
**apparent** (ape·rønt) *adj.* claro, manifiesto, evidente. *2* aparente. *3* sensible [horizonte].
**apparently** (-li) *adv.* claramente, evidentemente. *2* al parecer, por lo visto.
**apparition** (æpari·shøn) *s.* aparición.
**apparitor** (apæ·ritøʳ) *s.* alguacil; bedel.
**appeal** (apɪ·l) *s.* apelación. *2* llamamiento; petición, súplica, clamor. *3* recurso [a un medio; a una autoridad o testimonio]. *4* atracción, atractivo, interés.
**appeal (to)** *intr.* DER. apelar. *2* apelar, recurrir [a una pers. o cosa]; suplicar; hacer llamamiento a. *3* remitirse [a uno], poner por testigo. *4* mover, atraer, interesar.
**appealing** (apɪ·ling) *adj.* suplicante. *2* atrayente. *3* que despierta interés o simpatía.
**appear (to)** (apɪ·ʳ) *intr.* aparecer, aparecerse, parecer, salir, mostrarse, asomar, brotar, surgir. *2* salir [un periódico]. *3* comparecer, presentarse. *4* parecer, semejar.
**appearance** (apɪ·rans) *s.* aparición, aparecimiento; llegada, entrada. *2* DER. comparecencia. *3* apariencia. *4* aspecto, traza, porte. *5* viso, vislumbre. *6 pl.* apariencias.
**appease (to)** (apɪ·š) *tr.* aplacar, calmar. *2* sosegar, aquietar, apaciguar. *3* desenojar.
**appeasement** (-mønt) *s.* alivio, aplacamiento. *2* aquietamiento. *3* apaciguamiento, desenojo.
**appeaser** (-øʳ) *s.* aplacador, apaciguador.
**appellant** (ape·lant) *adj.-s.* apelante.
**appellation** (æpelei·shøn) *s.* denominación, nombre, título.

**appelative** (ape·lativ) *adj.* GRAM. apelativo, común. *2 s.* apelativo, nombre.
**appellee** (æpelɪ·) *s.* DER. apelado.
**append (to)** (ape·ndi) *tr.* atar, colgar, añadir [una cosa a otra].
**appendage** (-idỹ) *s.* dependencia, accesorio, aditamento, apéndice.
**appendant** (-ant) *adj.* anexo, accesorio; colgante. *2 s.* cosa o pers. adjunta o dependiente.
**appendicitis** (-disai·tis) *s.* MED. apendicitis.
**appendix** (-diks) *s.* apéndice.
**apperception** (æpøˑʳse·pshøn) *s.* apercepción.
**appertain (to)** (æpøʳtei·n) *intr.* pertenecer, tocar, atañer. *2* ser relativo [a].
**appetence, -cy** (æ·pitøns, -si) *s.* apetencia, deseo. *2* FÍS., QUÍM. afinidad.
**appetite** (æ·pitait) *s.* apetito.
**appetitive** (-iv) *adj.* apetitivo.
**appetizer** (æ·pitaišøʳ) *s.* aperitivo.
**appetizing** (-ing) *adj.* apetitoso. *2* tentador, incitante.
**Appian Way** (æ·pian) *s.* Vía Apia.
**applaud (to)** (aplo·d) *tr.-intr.* aplaudir. *2 tr.* alabar, encomiar.
**applause** (aplo·š) *s.* aplauso.
**applausive** (aplo·siv) *adj.* laudatorio.
**apple** (æ·pøl) *s.* BOT. manzana, poma: ~ *mint,* mastranzo; ~ *tree,* manzano. *2* ~ *of the eye,* pupila, niña del ojo; fig. niña de los ojos.
**applejack** (-dỹæk) *s.* aguardiente de manzanas.
**apple-pie order** *s.* orden perfecto.
**appliance** (aplai·ans) *s.* instrumento, utensilio, aparato, medio, artificio. *2* aplicación, empleo.
**applicable** (æ·plikabøl) *adj.* aplicable.
**applicant** (æ·plikant) *s.* solicitante, peticionario. *2* pretendiente, aspirante.
**application** (æplikei·shøn) *s.* aplicación. *2* emplasto, untura. *3* petición, solicitud.
**applied** (æplai·d) *pret.* y *p. p.* de TO APPLY.
**appliqué** (æplike·) *s.* aplicación [adorno sobrepuesto].
**apply (to)** (aplai·) *tr.* aplicar. *2 intr.* aplicarse, referirse, ser apropiado [a]. *3* ~ *to ~ for,* pedir, solicitar; *to ~ to,* recurrir a, pedir a. *4 ref.* aplicarse, consagrarse, dedicarse [a]. ¶ Pret. y p. p.: *applied.*
**appogiatura** (apadỹatu·ra) *s.* MÚS. apoyatura.
**appoint (to)** (apoi·nt) *tr.* fijar, señalar, determinar, establecer, prescribir. *2* ordenar, decretar. *3* asignar, destinar. *4* nombrar, designar, comisionar. *5* proveer, amueblar.
**appointee** (apointɪ·) *s.* persona nombrada o electa.
**appointment** (apoi·ntmønt) *s.* señalamiento, fijación. *2* decreto, mandato. *3* cita, hora dada. *4* nombramiento, designación. *5* empleo, puesto. *6 pl.* equipo; mobiliario.
**apportion (to)** (apo·ʳshøn) *tr.* prorratear, distribuir.
**apportionment** (-mønt) *s.* prorrateo, prorrata. *2* repartimiento.
**appose (to)** (æpou·š) *tr.* poner, aplicar. *2* yuxtaponer.
**apposite** (æ·pošit) *adj.* apropiado, conveniente, oportuno, a propósito.
**apposition** (æpoši·shøn) *s.* aposición. *2* adición, yuxtaposición.
**appraisal** (aprei·šal) *s.* apreciación, estimación, valoración, tasación.
**appraise (to)** (aprei·š) *tr.* apreciar, estimar, valorar, tasar.
**appraisement** (-mønt) *s.* APPRAISAL.

**appraiser** (-ø$^r$) *s.* estimador, tasador.
**appreciable** (apri·shiabøl) *adj.* apreciable, estimable, sensible, perceptible.
**appreciate (to)** (-sieit) *tr.* apreciar, estimar, valuar, tasar. *2* estimar, agradecer. *3* aumentar el valor de. *4 intr.* aumentar de valor.
**appreciation** (-ei·shøn) *s.* apreciación, aprecio. *2* agradecimiento. *3* aumento de valor.
**apprehend (to)** (æprije·nd) *tr.* aprehender, prender. *2* FIL. aprehender. *3* comprender, percibir. *4* temer, recelar.
**apprehension** (-shøn) *s.* aprehensión, prisión, captura. *2* FIL. aprehensión. *3* comprensión. *4* temor, recelo.
**apprehensive** (-siv) *adj.* aprehensivo. *2* inteligente, perspicaz. *3* consciente [de algo]. *4* temeroso, receloso [de]; que teme [por].
**apprentice** (apre·ntis) *s.* aprendiz.
**apprentice (to)** *tr.* poner de aprendiz.
**apprise, apprize (to)** (aprai·ś) *tr.* informar, avisar, enterar. *2* ant. TO APPRAISE.
**approach** (aprou·ch) *s.* proximidad, aproximación. *2* acceso, entrada. *3* tentativas, primeros pasos [para una amistad, un negocio, etc.]; acción de abordar [a una pers., un estudio, etc.], de enfocar [un problema, etc.]. *4 pl.* cercanías. *5* FORT. aproches.
**approach (to)** *intr.* acercarse, aproximarse; avecinarse. *2 tr.* acercar, aproximar. *3* acercarse a. *4* dirigirse [a uno], hablarle de un asunto, hacerle proposiciones. *5* abordar, enfocar [un asunto]; tocar [un tema].
**approachable** (-abøl) *adj.* accesible, abordable.
**approbate (to)** (æ·probeit) *tr.* (E. U.) aprobar, sancionar.
**approbation** (-ei·shøn) *s.* aprobación.
**appropriate** (aprou·prieit) *adj.* apropiado. *2* propio, peculiar.
**appropriate (to)** *tr.* destinar [a un uso]; asignar, votar [una cantidad]. *2* apropiarse.
**appropriation** (-ei·shøn) *s.* apropiación. *2* (E. U.) crédito, asignación [votados].
**approval** (apru·val) *s.* aprobación. *2* COM.on ~, a prueba.
**approve (to)** (apru·v) *tr.* aprobar, sancionar; confirmar, ratificar. *2* probar, demostrar; acreditar [de]. *3 intr.* to ~ of, aprobar, hallar de su gusto.
**approvingly** (-ingli) *adv.* con aprobación.
**approximate** (apra·ksimit) *adj.* próximo, cercano. *2* aproximado.
**approximate (to)** (-meit) *tr.* aproximar. *2* aproximarse a. *3 intr.* aproximarse, acercarse.
**approximately** (-li) *adv.* aproximadamente.
**approximation** (-ei·shøn) *s.* aproximación.
**approximative** (-ativ) *adj.* aproximado, aproximativo.
**appulse** (æ·pøls) *s.* ASTR. apulso.
**appurtenance** (apø·$^r$tønans) *s.* pertenencia, dependencia, accesorio.
**apricot** (ei·prikat) *s.* BOT. albaricoque: ~ *tree*, albaricoquero.
**April** (ei·pril) *s.* abril.
**April Fool's Day** *s.* ALL FOOL'S DAY.
**apriorism** (eipraiou·rišm) *s.* apriorismo.
**apron** (ei·prøn) *s.* delantal, mandil: *tied to the* ~ *strings of*, dominado por [la madre, la mujer, etc.]. *2* batiente [de un dique]. *3* MEC. plancha de protección. *4* MAR. albitana.
**apropos** (æpropou') *adj.* pertinente, oportuno. *2 adv.* a propósito.
**apse** (æps) *s.* ARQ. ábside.

**apsis** (æ·psis) *s.* ASTR. ápside.
**apt** (æpt) *adj.* apto. *2* listo, hábil, pronto. *3* adecuado. *4* propenso, expuesto, capaz.
**apterous** (æ·ptørøs) *adj.* ZOOL. áptero.
**aptitude** (æ·ptitiud), **aptness** (æ·ptnis) *s.* aptitud. *2* propensión, disposición, facilidad.
**aquafortis** (æ·kuafo$^r$tis) *s.* B. ART. aguafuerte.
**aquafortist** (-fo·$^r$tist) *s.* aguafuertista.
**aquamarine** (-mari·n) *s.* MINER. aguamarina.
**aquarelle** (ækuare·l) *s.* acuarela.
**aquarellist** (-ist) *s.* acuarelista.
**aquarium** (akue·riøm) *s.* acuario.
**Aquarius** (-riøs) *n. pr.* ASTR. acuario.
**aquatic(al** (akue·tikal) *adj.* acuático.
**aquatint** (æ·kuatint) *s.* acuatinta.
**aqueduct** (æ·kuidøkt) *s.* acueducto.
**aqueous** (ei·kuiøs) *adj.* ácueo, acuoso.
**aquiline** (æ·kuilin) *adj.* aquilino, aguileño.
**aquose** (ei·kuous) *adj.* ACQUEOUS.
**Arab** (æ·rab) *adj.-s.* árabe. *2 s.* caballo árabe. *3 street* ~, pillete, golfillo.
**arabesque** (ærabe·sk) *adj.-s.* arabesco.
**Arabian** (arei·bian) *adj.* arábico, arábigo. *2 the Arabian Nights*, Las mil y una noches. *3 s.* árabe.
**Arabic** (æ·rabik) *adj.* arábigo. *2 s.* árabe, arábico [idioma].
**Arabist** (-bist) *s.* arabista.
**arable** (æ·rabøl) *adj.* labrantío, cultivable.
**arachnida(n** (aræ·knid(an) *adj.-s.* arácnido.
**arachnoid** (-noid) *adj.* aracnoideo. *2 adj.-s.* arácnido. *3* ANAT. aracnoides.
**Aragonese** (ærægoni·ś) *adj.-s.* aragonés.
**Aramaic** (æramei·ik) *adj.* arameo.
**Araucanian** (ærokei·nian) *adj.-s.* araucano.
**araucaria** (æroke·ria) *s.* BOT. araucaria.
**arbalest, arbalist** (a·$^r$balist) *s.* ballesta [arma]. *2* arbalestrilla.
**arbiter** (a·$^r$bitø$^r$) *s.* árbitro, arbitrador.
**arbitrage** (a·$^r$bitrȳ) *s.* arbitraje.
**arbitral** (-tral) *adj.* arbitral.
**arbitrament** (a$^r$·bi·tramønt) *s.* arbitramento. *2* arbitrio, albedrío.
**arbitrary** (a·$^r$bitreri) *adj.* arbitrario. *2* discrecional. *3* despótico, autocrático.
**arbitrate (to)** (-treit) *tr.-intr.* arbitrar, juzgar, decidir.
**arbitration** (a$^r$bitrei·shøn) *s.* arbitraje, arbitramento.
**arbitrator** (a·$^r$bitreitø$^r$) *m.* árbitro. *2* arbitrador, amigable componedor.
**arbor** (a·$^r$bø$^r$) *s.* MEC. árbol. *2* ARBOUR.
**arboreal** (a$^r$bo·rial) *adj.* arbóreo.
**arborescent** (a$^r$bore·sønt) *adj.* arborescente.
**arboretum** (a$^r$bori·tøm) *s.* jardín botánico de árboles.
**arboriculture** (æ·$^r$børikølchø$^r$) *s.* arboricultura.
**arboriculturist** (-ist) *s.* arboricultor.
**arborist** (a·$^r$børist) *s.* arborista.
**arbor-vitæ** (a·$^r$bø$^r$ vai·ti) *s.* BOT., ANAT. árbol de la vida.
**arbour** (a·$^r$bø$^r$) *s.* cenador, glorieta, emparrado.
**arbutus** (a·$^r$biu·tøs) *s.* BOT. madroño [planta].
**arc** (a$^r$k) *s.* GEOM., ASTR., ELECT. arco.
**arc (to)** *tr.* ELECT. formar arco.
**arcade** (a·$^r$keid) *s.* ARQ. arcada. *2* soportal, galería.
**Arcadia** (a·$^r$keid·ia) *n. pr.* Arcadia.
**Arcadian** (a$^r$·kei·dian) *adj.-s.* arcadio, árcade. *2 adj.* arcádico.
**Arcady** (a·$^r$keidi) *n. pr.* ARCADIA.
**arcane** (a$^r$·kei·n) *adj.* arcano.
**arcanum** (a$^r$·kei·nøm), *pl.* **-na** (-na) *s.* arcano.

**arch** (aᵣch) s. ARQ. arco; bóveda. 2 ANAT. cayado [de la aorta]. 3 adj. travieso, picaresco. 4 astuto, socarrón. 5 principal, insigne.
**arch (to)** tr. arquear, encarcar. 2 abovedar. 3 intr. arquearse. 4 formar bóveda.
**archaelogic(al** (aᵣkiola·dŷik(al) adj. arqueológico.
**archaelogist** (aᵣkia·lodŷist) s. arqueólogo.
**archaeology** (aᵣkia·lodŷi) s. arqueología.
**archaic** (aᵣkei·k) adj. arcaico.
**archaism** (aᵣkeišm) s. arcaísmo.
**archaize (to)** (a·ᵣkeiaiš) intr. arcaizar.
**archangel** (a·kei·ndŷøl) s. arcángel.
**archangelic** (aᵣkændŷe·lik) f. arcangélico.
**archbishop** (a·ᵣchbishøp) s. arzobispo.
**archbishopric** (aᵣchdbi·shøprik) s. arzobispado.
**archdeacon** (aᵣchdɪ·køn) s. arcediano.
**archdeaconry** (-ri) s. arcedianato.
**archdiocese** (-dai·søs) s. archidiócesis.
**archducal** (-diu·kal) adj. archiducal.
**archduchess** (-dø·chis) s. archiduquesa.
**archduchy** (-dø·chi) s. archiducado.
**archduke** (-diu·k) s. archiduque.
**arched** (aᵣcht) adj. arqueado, abovedado.
**archegonium** (aᵣkigou·niøm) s. BOT. arquegonio.
**archeologic(al,** etc. ARCHAEOLOGIC(AL, etc.
**archer** (a·ᵣchøᵣ) s. arquero, flechero.
**archeress** (-is) s. arquera.
**archery** (-i) s. tropa de arqueros. 2 tiro de arco.
**archetype** (a·ᵣkitaip) s. arquetipo.
**archiepiscopal** (aᵣkiipi·skopal) adj. arzobispal.
**archil** (a·ᵣkil) s. BOT. urchilla.
**archimandrite** (-mæ·ndrait) s. archimandrita.
**Archimedean** (aᵣkimɪ·diαn) adj. de Arquímedes: ~ screw, rosca de Arquímedes.
**Archimedes** (-diš) n. pr. Arquímedes.
**archipelago** (aᵣkipe·lagou) s. archipiélago.
**architect** (a·ᵣkitekt) s. arquitecto.
**architectonic** (aᵣkitekta·nik), **architectural** (aᵣkite·kchøral) adj. arquitectónico.
**architecture** (a·ᵣkitekchøᵣ) s. arquitectura.
**architrave** (a·ᵣkitreiv) s. ARQ. arquitrabe.
**archives** (a·ᵣkaivš) s. pl. archivo.
**archivist** (a·ᵣkivist) s. archivero.
**archivolt** (a·ᵣkivoult) s. archivolta.
**archly** (a·ᵣchli) adv. con travesura, con picardía.
**archon** (a·ᵣkan) s. arconte.
**archpriest** (a·ᵣchprɪst) s. gran sacerdote. 2 arcipreste.
**archway** (a·ᵣchuei) s. entrada en forma de arco; pasaje abovedado.
**arctic** (a·ᵣktik) adj. ártico: Arctic Circle, círculo polar ártico; ~ fox, zorro azul. 2 s. región ártica.
**arcuate** (a·ᵣkiueit) adj. arqueado.
**arcuation** (-ei·shøn) s. arcuación. 2 ARQ. sistema de arcos.
**ardency** (a·ᵣdønsi) s. ardor.
**ardent** (a·ᵣdønt) adj. ardiente: ~ spirits, licores espirituosos. 2 encendido, brillante.
**ardo(u)r** (a·ᵣdøᵣ) s. ardor. 2 celo, entusiasmo, ardimiento.
**arduous** (a·ᵣdiuøs) adj. arduo, difícil. 2 riguroso. 3 enérgico. 4 escarpado, escabroso.
**are** (aᵣ) pl. del pres. de indic. de TO BE.
**are** (e·øᵣ) s. área (medida).
**area** (e·ria) s. área (superficie, espacio). 2 patio bajo que da acceso a la parte delantera de los sótanos.
**areca** (ari·ka) s. BOT. areca. 2 nuez de areca.
**arena** (arɪ·na) s. arena, arenas, liza, redondel, ruedo.

**arenaceous** (ærinei·shøs), **arenose** (æ·rinous) adj. arenáceo, arenoso, arenisco.
**areola** (ærɪ·ola) s. ANAT., MED. aréola.
**areometer** (æria·mitøᵣ) s. areómetro.
**Areopagus** (æria·pagøs) s. areópago.
**argent** (æ·ᵣdŷønt) s. BLAS. argén.
**argentiferous** (aᵣdŷønti·førøs) adj. argentífero.
**Argentina** (aᵣdŷøntɪ·na) n. pr. Argentina.
**argentine** (a·ᵣdŷøntin) adj. argentino. 2 s. metal blanco.
**Argentine, Argentinean** (aᵣdŷønti·nian) adj.-s. argentino [de la Argentina].
**argil** (a·ᵣdŷil) s. arcilla, alfar.
**argilous** (aᵣdŷi·løs) adj. arcilloso.
**argon** (a·ᵣgan) s. QUÍM. argón.
**Argonaut** (a·ᵣgønot) s. argonauta.
**argue (to)** (a·ᵣgiu) intr. argüir, argumentar. 2 tr.-intr. discutir. 3 tr. argüir (probar, indicar). 4 to ~ into, persuadir a; to ~ out of, disuadir de.
**arguer** (a·ᵣgiuøᵣ) s. arguyente. 2 discutidor.
**argument** (a·ᵣgiumønt) s. argumento. 2 debate, discusión, disputa.
**argumentation** (-mentei·shøn) s. argumentación. 2 debate, discusión.
**argumentative** (-me·ntativ) adj. argumentativo, dialéctico. 2 argumentador, discutidor.
**Argus** (a·ᵣgøs) n. pr. MIT. Argos.
**argute** (a·ᵣgiu·t) adj. astuto, sagaz. 2 estridente.
**aria** (a·ria) s. MÚS. aria.
**Arian** (e·rian) adj.-s. arriano.
**Arianism** (-išm) s. arrianismo.
**arid** (æ·rid) adj. árido.
**aridity** (ari·diti) s. aridez.
**Aries** (e·riiš) n. pr. ASTR. Aries.
**aright** (arai·t) adv. bien, correctamente.
**aril** (æ·ril) s. BOT. arilo.
**arise (to)** (arai·š) intr. subir, elevarse. 2 levantarse. 3 aparecer, surgir. 4 presentarse, suscitarse. 5 originarse. ¶ Pret.: arose; p. p.: arisen.
**Aristarch** (ærista·ᵣk) n. pr. y s. Aristarco.
**aristocracy** (ærista·krasi) s. aristocracia.
**aristocrat** (æri·stokræt) s. aristócrata.
**aristocratic(al** (-æ·tik(al) adj. aristocrático.
**Aristophanes** (-ta·fanis) n. pr. Aristófanes.
**Aristotelian** (-totɪ·lian), **Aristotelic** (-toti·lik) adj. aristotélico.
**Aristotle** (-ta·tøl) n. pr. Aristóteles.
**arithmetic** (ari·zmetik) s. aritmética.
**arithmetical** (arizme·tikal) adj. aritmético.
**arithmetician** (arizmeti·shan) s. aritmético.
**Arius** (arai·øs) n. pr. Arrio.
**ark** (aᵣk) s. arca [caja]. 2 arca (de Noé). 3 ~ of the covenant, Arca de la Alianza. 4 (E.U.) chalana.
**arm** (aᵣm) s. ANAT. brazo: ~ band, brazal; ~ in ~, de bracero, cogidos del brazo. 2 fig. brazo [poder, fuerza, autoridad]. 3 brazo [de animal, de palanca, de mar, de ancla, de sillón, etc.]. 4 rama [de árbol]. 5 arma: under arms, sobre las armas; to arms!, ¡a las armas!
**arm (to)** tr. armar [con armas]; fortalecer. 2 proveer [de armadura, un imán, de lentes, un telescopio, etc.]. 3 intr.-ref. armarse.
**armada** (aᵣma·da) s. armada, escuadra: the Armada, la Armada Invencible.
**armadillo** (aᵣmædi·lou) s. armadillo.
**armament** (a·ᵣmamønt) s. armamento.
**armature** (a·ᵣmachøᵣ) s. armadura [defensiva]. 2 H. NAT. órganos de defensa. 3 ELECT., MAGNET. armadura. 4 ELECT. inducido.
**armchair** (a·ᵣmcheᵣ) s. sillón, butaca.
**Armenian** (aᵣmɪ·nian) adj.-s. armenio.

**armet** (aˑ<sup>r</sup>met) *s.* almete.
**armful** (aˑ<sup>r</sup>mful) *s.* brazado.
**armillary** (aˑ<sup>r</sup>mileri) *adj.* armilar.
**armings** (aˑ<sup>r</sup>mmings) *s.* MAR. empavesada.
**armistice** (aˑ<sup>r</sup>mistis) *s.* armisticio.
**armless** (aˑ<sup>r</sup>mlis) *adj.* inerme. *2* manco.
**armlet** (aˑ<sup>r</sup>mlit) *s.* pequeño brazo de mar. *2* brazal.
**armor, armored, armory,** etc. ARMOUR, ARMOURED, ARMOURY, etc.
**armorial** (aˑ<sup>r</sup>moˑrial) *adj.* heráldico: ~ *berings,* escudo de armas. *2 s.* libro de heráldica.
**armour** (aˑ<sup>r</sup>møʳ) *s.* armadura [defensiva]. *2* coraza, blindaje.
**armoured** (-d) *adj.* armado [cubierto con armadura]. *2* acorazado, blindado. *3* ~ *concrete,* hormigón armado.
**armourer** (-øʳ) *s.* armero [pers.].
**armoury** (aˑrmøri) *s.* heráldica. *2* armería, arsenal. *3* (E.Ú.) fábrica de armas.
**armpit** (aˑ<sup>r</sup>mpit) *s.* sobaco, axila.
**army** (aˑ<sup>r</sup>mi) *s.* ejército: ~ *chaplain,* capellán castrense; ~ *corps,* cuerpo de ejército.
**arnica** (aˑ<sup>r</sup>nika) *s.* BOT., FARM. árnica.
**aroma** (arouˑma) *s.* aroma, fragancia.
**aromatic(al** (æromæˑtik(al) *adj.* aromático.
**aromatics** (-s) *s. pl.* aromas, especias.
**aromatize** (to) (arouˑmataiš) *tr.* aromatizar.
**arose** (arouˑš) *pret.* de *arise.*
**around** (arauˑnd) *adv.* alrededor, en derredor, en torno, a la redonda, en circuito. *2* por todas partes. *3* en la dirección opuesta. *4 prep.* alrededor de. *5* por, de un lado a otro de. *6* al volver, a la vuelta de: ~ *the corner,* a la vuelta de la esquina.
**arousal** (arauˑsal) *s.* despertamiento.
**arouse** (to) (arauˑš) *tr.* despertar. *2* mover, excitar.
**arpeggio** (aʳpeˑỹiou) *s.* arpegio.
**arquebus** (aˑ<sup>r</sup>kiubøs) *s.* HARQUEBUS.
**arraign** (to) (areiˑn) *tr.* acusar, hacer cargos a. *2* DER. procesar.
**arraignment** (-mønt) *s.* acusación. *2* DER. procesamiento.
**arrange** (to) (areiˑndỹ) *tr.* arreglar, poner en orden, disponer, clasificar, ordenar. *2* disponer, preparar. *3* fijar, acordar [un plan, etc.]. *4* MÚS. arreglar, adaptar. *5 intr.* convenirse; tomar disposiciones [para].
**arrangement** (-mønt) *s.* arreglo, ordenamiento. *2* orden, disposición. *3* arreglo, convenio. *4* MÚS. arreglo.
**arrant** (æˑrant) *adj.* acabado, consumado, insigne, de siete suelas.
**arras** (æˑras) *s.* tapiz de Arrás.
**array** (areiˑ) *s.* orden, formación. *2* pompa, aparato. *3* atavío, gala.
**array** (to) *tr.* formar, poner en orden [las tropas]. *2* adornar, ataviar.
**arrearage** (ariˑøridỹ) *s.* atraso. *2 pl.* ARREARS.
**arrears** (ariˑøʳs) *s. pl.* atrasos, caídos.
**arrest** (areˑst) *s.* arresto, detención, prisión. *2* paro, detención. *3* MEC. tope.
**arrest** (to) *tr.* arrestar, detener, prender. *2* atraer, fijar [la atención, la mirada]. *3* parar, detener, contener.
**arresting** (-ing) *adj.* notable, sorprendente.
**arris** (æˑris) *s.* ARQ. arista.
**arrival** (araiˑval) *s.* llegada, arribo. *2* llegado [pers.].
**arrive** (to) (araiˑv) *intr.* llegar. *2* tener éxito, triunfar.
**arrogance, -cy** (æˑrogans, -si) *s.* arrogancia, soberbia, altanería.

**arrogant** (æˑrogant) *adj.* arrogant, altanero.
**arrogate** (to) (æˑrogeit) *tr.* atribuir indebidamente. *2 to* ~ *oneself,* arrogarse.
**arrow** (æˑrou) *s.* flecha, saeta.
**arrowhead** (-jed) *s.* punta de flecha. BOT. sagitaria.
**arrowroot** (-rut) *s.* BOT. arrurruz.
**arrowy** (æˑroui) *adj.* aflechado. *2* fig. veloz, cortante, penetrante.
**arsenal** (aˑ<sup>r</sup>sinal) *s.* MIL. arsenal.
**arsenic** (aˑ<sup>r</sup>sinik) *s.* QUÍM. arsénico.
**arsenic(al** (aˑ<sup>r</sup>seˑnik(al) *adj.* arsenical.
**arson** (aˑ<sup>r</sup>søn) *s.* incendio provocado.
**art** (aˑ<sup>r</sup>t) ant. *2.ª pers. del sing. del pres. de ind. de* TO BE.
**art** *s.* arte: *arts and crafts,* artes y oficios.
**arterial** (aˑ<sup>r</sup>tiˑrial) *adj.* arterial.
**arterialize** (-aiš) *tr.* arterializar.
**arteriole** (-riol) *s.* ANAT. arteriola.
**arteriosclerosis** (-osclirouˑsis) *s.* MED. arteriosclerosis.
**artery** (aˑ<sup>r</sup>tøri) *s.* ANAT. arteria.
**Artesian** (aˑ<sup>r</sup>tiˑsian) *adj.* artesiano.
**artful** (aˑ<sup>r</sup>tful) *adj.* artero, ladino, astuto, artificioso. *2* diestro, ingenioso.
**artfully** (-i) *adv.* arteramente, ladinamente. *2* diestramente, con arte.
**arthritis** (aˑ<sup>r</sup>zraiˑtis) *s.* artritis.
**arthritism** (aˑ<sup>r</sup>zritišm) *s.* artritismo.
**arthropod** (aˑ<sup>r</sup>zropad) *s.* ZOOL. artrópodo.
**Arthur** (aˑ<sup>r</sup>zøʳ) *n. pr.* Arturo.
**artichoke** (aˑ<sup>r</sup>tichouk) *s.* BOT. alcachofa.
**article** (aˑ<sup>r</sup>tikøl) *s.* artículo. *2* cláusula, estipulación: *articles of marriage,* capítulos matrimoniales; *articles of war,* código militar. *3* punto, detalle, particular. *4* objeto, cosa. *5* ZOOL. artejo, segmento articulado.
**article** (to) *tr.* formular en artículos. *2* escriturar, contratar. *3* poner [a uno] de aprendiz bajo contrato. *4* acusar, hacer cargos.
**articular** (aˑ<sup>r</sup>tiˑkiulaʳ) *adj.* articular.
**articulate** (aˑ<sup>r</sup>tiˑkiulit) *adj.* articulado. *2* claro, distinto. *3 s.* ZOOL. articulado.
**articulate** (to) (aˑ<sup>r</sup>tiˑkiuleit) *tr.* articular. *2* enunciar. *3 intr.* articularse.
**articulation** (aˑ<sup>r</sup>tikiuleiˑshøn) *s.* articulación.
**artifice** (aˑ<sup>r</sup>tifis) *s.* artificio. *2* ardid, treta.
**artificer** (aˑ<sup>r</sup>tiˑfisøʳ) *s.* artífice. *2* inventor, autor. *3* MIL. artificiero.
**artificial** (aˑ<sup>r</sup>tifiˑshal) *adj.* artificial. *2* afectado, fingido. *3* DER. jurídica [persona].
**artificiality** (-fishiæˑliti), **artificialness** (-fiˑshalnis) *s.* calidad de artificial. *2* afectación, falta de naturalidad.
**artillerist** (aˑ<sup>r</sup>tiˑlørist) *s.* artillero.
**artillery** (aˑ<sup>r</sup>tiˑløri) *s.* artillería.
**artilleryman** (-mæn) *s.* artillero.
**artiodactyl** (aˑ<sup>r</sup>tiodæˑktil) *adj.-s.* artiodáctilo.
**artisan** (aˑ<sup>r</sup>tizan) *s.* artesano.
**artist** (aˑ<sup>r</sup>tist) *s.* artista.
**artistic** (aˑ<sup>r</sup>tiˑstik) *adj.* artístico.
**artistically** (-ali) *adv.* artísticamente.
**artistry** (aˑ<sup>r</sup>tiˑstri) *s.* talento artístico, arte.
**artless** (aˑ<sup>r</sup>tlis) *adj.* natural, sencillo, ingenuo. *2* torpe, sin arte.
**arum** (eˑrøm) *s.* BOT. aro, yaro.
**aruspex** (arøˑspeks), **aruspice** (aræˑspis) *s.* arúspice.
**Aryan** (eˑrian) *adj.* ario.
**as** (æs) *s.* as [peso; moneda].
**as** (æs) *adv.* como, tal como, cual [de la manera que]: ~ *you please,* como usted guste. *2* como

[igual que; en calidad de; según, conforme]: ~ *a friend*, como, o en calidad de, amigo; ~ *if*, ~ *though*, como si; ~ *it were*, como si dijéramos; ~ *usual*, como de costumbre. *3* así como. *4* tan, como [comparativos]: ~ *slippery* ~ *an eel*, (tan) escurridizo como una anguila. *5 conj.* mientras, cuando, según, a medida que. *6* como, ya que, puesto que. *7* a pesar de: *young* ~ *he is*, a pesar de ser joven. *8* que: *the same* ~, el mismo que. *9* Otros usos: ~ *far* ~, hasta, hasta donde; ~ *good* ~, como si fuera, prácticamente; ~ *for*, ~ *to*, en cuanto a, respecto a; ~ *long* ~, mientras, con tal que; ~ *much*, otro tanto, eso, eso mismo, lo mismo; ~ *per*, según; ~ *well*, también, además; ~ *yet*, aún, todavía, hasta ahora.

**asafetida, asafoetida** (æsafe·tida) *s.* BOT. asafétida.

**asarabacca** (æsɑrabæ·ka) *s.* BOT. ásaro.

**asbestos** (æsbe·støs) *s.* asbesto.

**ascarid** (æ·skɑrid) *s.* ascáride.

**ascend** (ase·nd) *intr.* ascender, subir, elevarse. *2 tr.* subir [una cuesta, etc.]; subir a.

**ascendance, -cy** (-ans, -ansi) *s.* ascendiente [dominio moral, influencia].

**ascendant** (-ant) *adj.* ascendente. *2* superior, predominante. *3 s.* ascendiente [padre, abuelo]. *4* supremacía, poder, influencia.

**ascendence, -cy** (-øns, -ønsi) *s.* ASCENDANCE, -CY.

**ascendent** (-ønt) *adj.-s.* ASCENDANT.

**ascending** (-ing) *adj.* ascendente.

**ascension** (ase·nshøn) *s.* ascensión. *2* (con may.) Ascensión [de N. S.].

**ascensional** (-al) *adj.* ascensional.

**ascent** (ase·nt) *s.* ascensión, subida, elevación. *2* ascenso, promoción. *3* cuesta, pendiente.

**ascertain (to)** (æsøʳtei·n) *tr.* averiguar, hallar, determinar, cerciorarse de.

**ascertainment** (-mønt) *s.* averiguación.

**ascetic** (ase·tik) *adj.* ascético. *2 s.* asceta.

**asceticism** (-tisišm) *s.* ascetismo.

**ascians** (æ·shianš) *s. pl.* ascios.

**ascidian** (asi·dian) *s.* ZOOL. ascidia.

**ascomycete** (æskomaisı·t) *s.* BOT. ascomiceto.

**ascon** (æ·skøn) *s.* BOT. ascón.

**ascus** (æ·skøs) *s.* BOT. asca.

**ascribe (to)** (askrai·b) *tr.* atribuir, imputar.

**ascription** (askri·pshøn) *s.* atribución, imputación.

**asepsis** (ase·psis) *s.* asepsia.

**aseptic** (ase·ptik) *adj.* aséptico.

**asexual** (eise·kshual) *adj.* asexual.

**ash** (æsh), *pl.* **ashes** *s.* ceniza: ~ *tray*, cenicero [de fumador]. *2* BOT. fresno. *3 pl.* ceniza, cenizas. *4* restos mortales.

**Ash Wednesday** *s.* miércoles de ceniza.

**ashamed** (ashei·md) *adj.* avergonzado: *to be* ~, avergonzarse.

**ashen** (æ·shøn) *adj.* fresnal. *2* ceniciento.

**ashlar** (æ·shlaʳ) *s.* sillar, piedra de talla.

**ashore** (asho·ʳ) *adv.* MAR. en tierra, a tierra: *to go* ~, desembarcar; *to run* ~, encallar.

**ashpan** (æ·shpæn) *s.* cenicero [de estufa, hogar, etc.].

**ashy** (æ·shi) *adj.* ceniciento: ~ *pale*, pálido, lívido.

**Asia** (ei·sha) *n. pr.* GEOGR. Asia.

**Asian** (-n), **Asiatic** (eishiæ·tik) *adj.-s.* asiático.

**aside** (asai·d) *adv.* al lado, a un lado, aparte: ~ *from this*, esto aparte, fuera de esto. *2 s.* TEAT. aparte.

**asinine** (æ·sinain) *adj.* asinino, asnal.

**ask (to)** (æsk) *tr.* preguntar [una cosa]; preguntar [a uno]. *2* pedir, solicitar, rogar que. *3* requerir, exigir [hacer necesario]. *4* invitar, convidar. | A veces con *out*. *5 fam.* amonestar [publicar las amonestaciones de]. *6 intr. to* ~ *after, for* o *about*, preguntar por. *7 to* ~ *for*, pedir [una cosa].

**askance** (askæ·ns), **askant** (-nt) *adv.* al sesgo, de soslayo, de reojo, de refilón. *2* con desdén, con recelo.

**askew** (askiu·) *adv.* al sesgo, oblicuamente. *2 adj.* sesgado, oblicuo.

**asking** (æ·sking) *s.* acción de pedir; ruego, petición. *2 fam.* publicación de amonestaciones.

**aslant** (aslæ·nt) *adv.* oblicuamente, en posición inclinada. *2 adj.* inclinado. *3 prep.* al través de.

**asleep** (aslı·p) *adj.-adv.* dormido, durmiendo. *2* adormecido, entumecido.

**aslope** (aslou·p) *adv.-adj.* en declive.

**asp** (æsp) *s.* ZOOL. áspid. *2* BOT. tiemblo.

**asparagus** (æspæ·ragøs) *s.* BOT. espárrago. *2* COC. espárragos.

**aspect** (æ·spekt) *s.* aspecto. *2* aire, semblante.

**aspen** (æ·spøn) *s.* tiemblo, álamo temblón. *2 adj.* tembloroso.

**aspergillum** (-ỹi·løm) *s.* hisopo, asperges.

**asperity** (æspe·riti) *s.* aspereza.

**asperse (to)** (æspø·ʳs) *tr.* difamar, calumniar. *2* asperjar.

**aspersion** (-shøn) *s.* difamación, calumnia. *2* aspersión.

**asphalt** (æ·sfalt) *s.* asfalto.

**asphalt (to)** *tr.* asfaltar.

**asphaltic** (æsfo·ltik) *adj.* asfáltico.

**asphodel** (æ·sfødel) *s.* BOT. asfódelo, gamón.

**asphyxia** (æsfi·ksia) *s.* asfixia.

**asphyxiate (to)** (-sieit) *tr.* asfixiar.

**asphyxiation** (-sie·shøn) *s.* asfixia.

**aspic** (æ·spik) *s.* ZOOL. áspid. *2* espliego. *3* gelatina con carne picada, jugo de tomate, etc.

**aspirant** (aspai·rant) *s.* aspirante, pretendiente.

**aspirate** (æ·spirit) *adj.-s.* aspirado [sonido].

**aspirate (to)** (æ·spireit) *tr.* GRAM., FONÉT. aspirar. *2* aspirar, sorber.

**aspiration** (-ei·shøn) *s.* aspiración. *2* anhelo.

**aspirator** (æspirei·toʳ) *s.* aspirador.

**aspire (to)** (aspai·ʳ) *intr.* aspirar a, ambicionar. | Gralte. con *to* o *after*. *2* elevarse [como una llama, etc.].

**aspirin** (æ·spirin) *s.* aspirina.

**aspiring** (aspai·ring) *adj.* ambicioso, con aspiraciones.

**asquint** (askui·nt) *adv.* de través, de soslayo.

**ass** (æs) *s.* ZOOL. asno, burro, jumento. *2 fig.* asno, majadero.

**assagai** (æ·sagai) *s.* azagaya.

**assail (to)** (asei·l) *tr.* asaltar, atacar, acometer. *2* asediar, acosar.

**assailant** (-ant) *adj.-s.* atacante, agresor. *2* atracador.

**assassin** (asæ·sin) *s.* asesino.

**assassinate (to)** (-eit) *tr.* asesinar.

**assassination** (-ei·shøn) *s.* asesinato.

**assault** (asolt) *s.* MIL., ESGR. asalto. *2* ataque, acometida. *3* agresión; atraco. *4* DER. ~ *and battery*, injurias y golpes.

**assault (to)** *tr.* asaltar. *2* atacar, acometer. *3* saltear, atracar.

**assay** (asei) *s.* ensaye; contraste. *2* QUÍM. ensayo. *3* ESSAY[1].

**assay (to)** *tr.* ensayar, aquilatar, contrastar [metales]. *2* QUÍM. ensayar. *3* analizar, experimentar. *4* tentar, intentar.

**assayer** (asei·ø^r) *s.* ensayador [dé metales]; contraste.

**assemblage** (ase'mblidỹ) *s.* reunión [acción]. *2* reunión, agregado, conjunto, multitud, concurso. *3* MEC., CARP. montaje.

**assemble (to)** (-bøl) *tr.* congregar, reunir, juntar, agrupar. *2* MEC., CARP. montar, armar. *3 intr.* reunirse.

**assembly** (-bli) *s.* asamblea, junta. *2* reunión, fiesta [de sociedad]. *3* concurrencia, concurso. *4* MEC., CARP. montaje, armazón. *5* MEC. grupo, juego, unidad.

**assent** (ase·nt) *s.* asenso, asentimiento, aquiescencia, beneplácito.

**assent (to)** *intr.* asentir, consentir.

**assentient** (ase·nshiønt) *adj.-s.* que asiente.

**assert (to)** (asø·^rt) *tr.* aseverar, afirmar. *2* mantener, defender, hacer valer. *3 to* ~ *oneself*, imponerse, hacer valer sus derechos; hacerse sentir.

**assertion** (-shøn) *s.* aserción, aserto. *2* mantenimiento, reivindicación.

**assertive** (asø·^rtiv) *adj.* asertivo; dogmático.

**assess (to)** (ase·s) *tr.* ámillarar; evaluar [para la aplicación de impuestos]. *2* fijar [una indemnización, impuesto, etc.]. *3* imponer una contribución a.

**assessment** (-mønt) *s.* amillaramiento, avalúo. *2* imposición, repartimiento [de contribuciones]. *3* tasa de tributación. *4* dividendo pasivo.

**assessor** (-ø^r) *s.* DER. asesor. *2* tasador de la propiedad para efectos fiscales.

**asset** (æ·set) *s.* COM. partida del activo. *2* fig. recurso, medio, etc., con que se cuenta. *3 pl.* COM. activo. *4* haber, capital, fondos, créditos.

**asseverate (to)** (ase·vøreit) *tr.* aseverar.

**asseveration** (-rei·shøn) *s.* aseveración.

**assiduity** (æsidiu·iti) *s.* asiduidad.

**assiduous** (æsi·diuøs) *adj.* asiduo. *2* constante, laborioso.

**assign (to)** (asai·n) *tr.* asignar. *2* destinar, designar. *3* adscribir, atribuir. *4* DER. ceder, transferir, consignar.

**assignation** (æsignei·shøn) *s.* asignación; designación, destinación, atribución. *2* DER. cesión. *3* cita [para encontrarse]. | Tómase gralte. en mala parte.

**assignment** (asai·nmønt) *s.* ASSIGNATION 1 y 2. *2* DER. escritura de cesión.

**assimilable** (asi·milabøl) *adj.* asimilable. *2* semejante.

**assimilate (to)** (asi·mileit) *tr.* asimilar. *2 intr.* FISIOL. asimilarse.

**assimilation** (-le·shøn) *s.* asimilación.

**Assisi** (asi·ši) *n. pr.* GEOGR. Asís.

**assist (to)** (asi·st) *tr.* asistir, ayudar, socorrer. *2 intr.* asistir, estar presente.

**assistance** (-ans) *s.* asistencia, ayuda, socorro. *2* asistencia (presencia). *3* concurrencia [pers. presentes].

**assistant** (-ant) *s.* ayudante, auxiliar, adjunto; acólito. *2 adj.* auxiliar, segundo, sub-: ~ *manager*, subdirector.

**assize** (asai·š) *s.* tasa, tipo. *2 pl.* sesiones de un tribunal.

**associate** (asou·shieit) *adj.* asociado; adjunto. *2 s.* asociado, socio, consocio. *3* compinche; cómplice.

**associate (to)** *tr.* asociar. *2 intr.* asociarse. *3* juntarse, acompañarse.

**association** (-ei·shøn) *s.* asociación. *2* ~ *football*, fútbol, balompié.

**assonance** (æ·sønans) *s.* asonancia.

**assonant** (-ant) *adj.-s.* asonante.

**assonate (to)** (-eit) *intr.* asonar, asonantar.

**assort (to)** (asø·^rt) *tr.* ordenar, clasificar, agrupar con. *2* surtir [de cosas varias]. *3 intr.* cuadrar, convenir. *4* juntarse, asociarse.

**assorted** (-id) *adj.* surtido, variado. *2* apareado.

**assortment** (-mønt) *s.* ordenación, clasificación. *2* surtido, variedad.

**assuage (to)** (asuei·dỹ) *tr.* suavizar, mitigar, aliviar, calmar. *2* apaciguar, ablandar.

**assuagement** (-mønt) *s.* mitigación, alivio.

**assuasive** (asuei·siv) *adj.* mitigativo, calmante.

**assume (to)** (asiu·m) *tr.* aşumir. *2* arrogarse, usurpar. *3* tomar, adoptar [una forma, actitud, etc.]. *4* simular. *5* suponer, dar por sentado. *6 intr.* ser arrogante o presuntuoso.

**assumed** (-d) *adj.* supuesto, dado por sentado. *2* supuesto, falso, fingido.

**assuming** (-ing) *adj.* arrogante, altivo; presuntuoso.

**assumption** (asø·mpshøn) *s.* asunción. *2* arrogación. *3* adopción [de una actitud, etc.]. *4* suposición, supuesto. *5* (con may.) Asunción [de la Virgen].

**assumptive** (-tiv) *adj.* supositivo; supuesto. *2* arrogante, presuntuoso.

**assurance** (ashu·rans) *s.* seguridad [que se tiene o que se da], certidumbre, convicción. *2* seguridad, confianza en sí mismo. *3* aplomo, descaro. *4* COM. seguro; aseguramiento.

**assure (to)** (ashu·^r) *tr.* asegurar, afirmar, certificar. *2* infundir confianza. *3* asegurar [hacer cierto o seguro]. *4* COM. asegurar.

**assured** (-d) *adj.* seguro, cierto. *2* confiado, atrevido, audaz. *3* COM. asegurado.

**assurer** (ashu·rø^r) *s.* asegurador.

**Assyria** (asi·ria) *n. pr.* HIST. Asiria.

**Assyrian** (asi·rian) *adj.-s.* Asirio.

**astatic** (eistæ·tik) *adj.* astático.

**asterisk** (æ·størisk) *s.* asterisco.

**astern** (astø·^rn) *adv.* MAR. a popa, por la popa.

**asteroid** (æ·støroid) *s.* ASTR. asteroide.

**asthenia** (æszi·nia) *s.* MED. astenia.

**asthenic** (æsze·nik) *adj.-s.* asténico.

**asthma** (æ·šma) *s.* asma.

**asthmatic** (æšmæ·tik) *adj.-s.* asmático.

**astigmatic** (æstigmæ·tik) *adj.* ÓPT. astigmático.

**astigmatism** (æsti·gmatišm) *s.* astigmatismo.

**astir** (astø·^r) *adv.* en movimiento, en actividad. *2* levantado (de la cama).

**astonish (to)** (asta·nish) *tr.* asombrar, pasmar, sorprender.

**astonished** (-t) *adj.* atónito, asombrado, pasmado.

**astonishing** (-ing) *adj.* asombroso, pasmo, sorpresa.

**astonishment** (-mønt) *s.* asombro, pasmo, sorpresa.

**astound (to)** (astau·nd) *tr.* pasmar, sorprender. *2* aturdir, aterrar.

**astounding** (-ing) *adj.* asombroso, pasmoso.

**astraddle** (astra·døl) *adv.* a horcajadas.

**astragal** (æ·stragal) *s.* ARQ., ARTILL. astrágalo.

**astragalus** (æstræ·galøs) *s.* ANAT., BOT. astrágalo.

**astrak(h)an** (æ·strakan) *s.* astracán [piel].

**astral** (æ·stral) *adj.* astral.

**astrand** (astræ·nd) *adv.* MAR. encallado, varado.

**astray** (astrei·) *adv.-adj.* descaminado, extraviado, errado: *to go* ~, descarriarse, extraviarse.

**astriction** (æstri·kshøn) *s.* astricción.

**astride** (astrai·d) *adv.* a horcajadas. *2 prep.* a caballo de; a horcajadas en.
**astringe (to)** (astri·ndŷ) *tr.* astreñir, astringir, constreñir.
**astringency** (-ønsi) *s.* astringencia. *2* severidad, austeridad.
**astringent** (-ønt) *adj.-s.* astringente. *2 adj.* severo, austero.
**astrochemistry** (æstroke·mistri) *s.* astroquímica.
**astrolabe** (æ'stroleib) *s.* astrolabio.
**astrologer** (æstra·lodŷøʳ) *s.* astrólogo.
**astrologic(al** (æstrola·dŷik(al) *adj.* astrológico.
**astrology** (æstra·lodŷi) *s.* astrología.
**astronaut** (æ·stronot) *s.* astronauta.
**astronautics** (æ·strono·tiks) *s.* astronáutica.
**astronomer** (æstra·nomøʳ) *s.* astrónomo.
**astromic(al** (æstrona·mik(al) *adj.* astronómico.
**astronomy** (æstra·nomi) *s.* astronomía.
**astrophysics** (æstrofi·šiks) *s.* astrofísica.
**astrut** (astrø·t) *adj.* hinchado [de orgullo]; que anda con orgullo.
**Asturian** (æstiu·rian) *adj.-s.* asturiano.
**astute** (æstiu·t) *adj.* astuto, sagaz.
**asunder** (asø·ndøʳ) *adj.* separado. *2 adv.* en dos, en pedazos: *to cut ~*, partir en dos, en pedazos.
**asylum** (asai·løm) *s.* asilo, refugio. *2* acogida, sagrado. *3* casa de beneficencia; manicomio.
**asymmetric(al** (eisime·trik(al) *adj.* asimétrico.
**asymmetry** (eisi·mitri) *s.* asimetría.
**asymptote** (æ·simtout) *s.* asíntota.
**asystole** (eisi·stoli) *s.* MED. asistolia.
**at** (æt) *prep.* en, a, de, con, cerca de, delante de con significaciones varias. | A veces no se traduce: *look ~ him*, miradle. *2* Con ciertos nombres, equivale a un gerundio: *~ work*, trabajando.
**atavism** (æ·tavišm) *s.* atavismo.
**atavistic** (ætavi·stik) *adj.* atávico.
**ate** (eit) *pret.* de TO EAT.
**atelier** (æ·tøliei) *s.* taller, estudio.
**atheism** (ei·ziišm) *s.* ateísmo.
**atheist** (ei·ziist) *s.* ateo.
**atheistic(al** (eizii·stik(al) *adj.* ateo, ateísta.
**atheneum** (æzini·øm) *s.* ateneo.
**Athenian** (æzi·nian) *adj.-s.* ateniense.
**Athens** (æ·zins) *n. pr.* Atenas.
**athirst** (azø·ʳst) *adj.* sediento.
**athlete** (æ·zlit) *s.* atleta.
**athletic** (æzle·tik) *adj.* atlético.
**athletics** (-s) *s.* atletismo.
**at-home** *s.* horas en que se reciben visitas.
**athwart** (azwo·ʳt) *adv.-prep.* al través o por el través [de]; atravesado [en]. *2* contrariamente [a], contra.
**atilt** (ati·lt) *adv.* en posición inclinada. *2* lanza en ristre.
**atlantes** (ætlæ·ntiš) *s. pl.* ARQ. atlantes.
**Atlantic** (-tik) *adj.* atlántico. *2 n. pr.* GEOGR. Atlántico.
**Atlantis** (-tis) *n. pr.* Atlántida.
**atlas** (æ·tlas) *s.* atlas. *2* ARQ. atlante. *3* (con may.) MIT. Atlante; GEOGR. Atlas.
**atmosphere** (ætmøsfi·ʳ) *s.* atmósfera.
**atmospheric(al** (-fe·rik(al) *adj.* atmosférico.
**atmospherics** (-fe·riks) *s. pl.* RADIO. parásitos atmosféricos.
**atoll** (æta·l) *s.* atolón.
**atom** (æ·tøm) *s.* átomo.
**atomic(al** (æta·mik(al) *adj.* atómico.
**atomize (to)** (æ·tømaiš) *tr.* atomizar, pulverizar.
**atomizer** (-øʳ) *s.* pulverizador.

**atone (to)** (atou·n) *intr.-tr.* reparar, dar satisfacción, compensar, expiar. | Gralte. con *for*.
**atonement** (-mønt) *s.* reparación, compensación, expiación.
**atonic** (æta·nik) *adj.* GRAM. átono. *2* MED. atónico.
**atony** (æ·tøni) *s.* atonía.
**atop** (ata·p) *prep.-adv.* encima.
**atrabiliary** (æ·trabilieri), **atrabilious** (ætrabiliøs) *adj.* atrabiliario, melancólico.
**atrium** (ei·triøm) *s.* atrio.
**atrocious** (atrou·shøs) *s.* atroz. *2* abominable.
**atrocity** (atra·siti) *s.* atrocidad.
**atrophy** (æ·trofi) *s.* atrofia.
**atrophy (to)** *tr.* producir atrofia. *2 intr.* atrofiarse.
**attach (to)** (atæ·ch) *tr.* atar, ligar, vincular; pegar, adherir, unir, sujetar, enganchar, prender. *2* granjearse el afecto de. *3* agregar, adscribir. *4* dar, atribuir [valor, importancia, etc.]. *5* DER. embargar, secuestrar. *6 intr.* acompañar, ser inherente. *7 ref.* unirse, adherirse. *8* cobrar afecto.
**attaché** (atachei·) *s.* agregado [diplomático].
**attachment** (atæ·chmønt) *s.* adadura, unión, enlace, conexión, fijación. *2* accesorio. *3* apego, afecto, adhesión. *4* DER. embargo, incautación, secuestro.
**attack** (ætæ·k) *s.* ataque, embestida, agresión. *2* MED. ataque.
**attack (to)** *tr.* atacar [acometer, embestir: combatir], agredir. *2* MÚS., QUÍM., MED. atacar.
**attain (to)** (atei·n) *tr.* lograr, obtener. *2 tr. e intr.* alcanzar llegar [a una edad, un punto, etc.].
**attainable** (atei·nabøl) *adj.* asequible, obtenible, realizable.
**attainder** (atei·ndøʳ) *s.* DER. proscripción, muerte civil.
**attainment** (-mønt) *s.* logro, consecución, adquisición. *2 pl.* dotes, prendas, saber.
**attaint (to)** (atei·nt) *tr.* DER. proscribir. *2* manchar, deshonrar. *3* viciar, corromper.
**attar** (æ·taʳ) *s.* esencia [esp. de rosas].
**attemper (to)** (ate·mpøʳ) *tr.* temperar, moderar. *2* atemperar, acomodar.
**attempt** (ate·mpt)*s.* intento, prueba, esfuerzo, tentativa. *2* atentado [contra la vida].
**attempt (to)** *tr.* intentar, procurar, probar a. *2* atacar, atentar contra.
**attend (to)** (ate·nd) *tr.* atender a, cuidar de. *2* asistir [a un enfermo]. *3* acompañar, servir, escoltar. *4* asistir, concurrir a. *5* acompañar, seguir [como efecto o consecuencia], ser inherente a. *6* esperar [a que suceda algo]. *7 intr. to ~ to*, atender a, hacer caso de, ocuparse de. *8 to ~ on* o *upon*, servir a.
**attendance** (-ans) *s.* asistencia, servicio. *2* cuidado, vigilancia. *3* asistencia, presencia. *4* concurrencia, concurso. *5* séquito, acompañamiento. *6* espera.
**atendant** (-ant) *adj.* acompañante. *2 s.* servidor. *3* acompañante, seguidor. *4* asistente, concurrente. *5 pl.* séquito, acompañamiento.
**attention** (ate·nshøn) *s.* atención. *2* MIL. *to stand to ~*, cuadrarse; *attention!*, ¡firmes! *3 pl.* atenciones, obsequios.
**attentive** (ate·ntiv) *adj.* atento [que pone atención]. *2* atento, obsequioso.
**attenuate** (ate·niueit) *adj.* atenuado, disminuido, diluido. *2* delgado.
**attenuate (to)** *tr.* atenuar, disminuir, diluir, debilitar. *2* adelgazar.
**attenuation** (ateniuei·shøn) *s.* atenuación, dismi-

nución, debilitación, extenuación. *2* dilución. *3* adelgazamiento.

**attest (to)** (ate·st) *tr.-intr.* atestar, testificar, atestiguar, certificar. *2 tr.* autenticar.

**attestation** (ætestei·shøn) *s.* atestación, testimonio, prueba. *2* autenticación. *3* certificación.

**Attic** (æ·tik) *adj.* ático: ~ *salt*, sal ática.

**attic** *s.* ARQ. ático, buhardilla.

**atticism** (æ·tisišm) *s.* aticismo.

**Attila** (æ·tila) *n. pr.* Atila.

**attire** (atai·ʳ) *s.* traje, vestido, atavío.

**attire (to)** *tr.* vestir, ataviar. *2* engalanar.

**attitude** (æ·titiud) *s.* actitud. *2* AVIA. posición.

**attitudinize** (ætitiu·dinaiš) *intr.* obrar con afectación.

**attorney** (atø·ʳni) *s.* apoderado, poderhabiente, procurador, agente: ~ *at law*, procurador judicial; abogado; *private* ~, apoderado, representante; *by* ~, por poder. *2* ~ *general*, fiscal de la Corona o de la República. *3* (E.U.) *district* ~ fiscal de distrito.

**attract (to)** (atræ·ct) *tr.* atraer. *2* llamar [la atención].

**attraction** (atræ·kshøn) *s.* atracción. *2* atractivo.

**attractive** (atræ·ktiv) *adj.* atractivo, atrayente. *2* agradable, simpático.

**attractiveness** (-nis) *s.* fuerza atractiva. *2* atractivo, simpatía.

**attribute** (æ·tribiut) *s.* atributo.

**attribute (to)** *tr.* atribuir.

**attribution** (ætribiu·shøn) *s.* atribución.

**attributive** (ætri·biutiv) *adj.* atributivo. *2 adj.-s.* GRAM. calificativo.

**attrite** (atrai·t) *adj.* atrito.

**attrition** (ætri·shøn) *s.* atrición. *2* roce, fricción, desgaste.

**attune (to)** (atiu·n) *tr.* armonizar, acordar. *2* MÚS. afinar.

**aubade** (ou·bæd) *s.* MÚS. alborada.

**auburn** (o·bøʳn) *adj.* castaño rojizo.

**auction** (o·kshøn) *s.* subasta, almoneda, remate. *2* ~ *bridge*, bridge subastado.

**auction (to)** *tr.* subastar, almonedar.

**auctionneer** (okshønı·ʳ) *s.* subastador.

**auctionneer (to)** *tr.* TO AUCTION.

**audacious** (odei·shøs) *adj.* audaz, osado. *2* atrevido, descarado.

**audaciousness** (-nis), **audacity** (odæ·siti) *s.* audacia, osadía. *2* atrevimiento, descaro.

**audibility** (odibi·liti) *s.* calidad de audible.

**audible** (o·dibøl) *adj.* audible.

**audience** (o·diøns) *s.* acción de escuchar. *2* auditorio, público. *3* audiencia (entrevista).

**audio-frequency** (o·diou) *s.* RAD. audiofrecuencia.

**audit** (o·dit) *s.* intervención, revisión, ajuste [de cuentas].

**audit (to)** *tr.* intervenir, revisar [cuentas].

**audition** (odi·shøn) *s.* audición.

**auditive** (o·ditiv) *adj.* auditivo.

**auditor** (o·ditøʳ) *s.* interventor, revisor de cuentas. *2* ordenador de pagos. *3* oyente. *4* auditor.

**auditorium** (odito·riøm) *s.* sala de conferencias, de conciertos, etc.; paraninfo.

**auditory** (o·ditori) *s.* auditorio, concurrencia. *2* AUDITORIUM. *3 adj.* auditorio.

**auger** (o·gøʳ) *s.* barrena, taladro, berbiquí.

**aught** (ot) *pron.* ant. algo, alguna cosa. *2* (con negación) nada.

**augment (to)** (ogme·nt) *tr.* aumentar. *2* abultar, engrosar. *3 intr.* aumentar, crecer.

**augmentation** (-ei·shøn) *s.* aumento, acrecentamiento, añadidura.

**augmentative** (-ativ) *adj.-s.* aumentativo.

**augur** (o·gøʳ) *s.* augur. *2* agorero, adivino.

**augur (to)** *tr.-intr.* augurar, pronosticar, presagiar.

**augury** (o·giuri) *s.* augurio, pronóstico. *2* auguración.

**August** (o·gøst) *s.* agosto.

**august** (ogø·st) *adj.* augusto.

**Augustine** (o·gøstin) *n. pr.* Agustín.

**Augustinian** (ogøsti·nian) *adj.-s.* agustino, agustiniano.

**augustness** (ogø·stnis) *s.* majestad, grandeza.

**Augustus** (ogø·støs) *n. pr.* Augusto.

**auk** (ok) *s.* ORN. alca.

**aulic** (o·lic) *adj.* áulico.

**aunt** (ænt o ant) *s.* tía.

**auntie, aunty** (æ·nti) *s.* tiíta.

**aura** (o·ra) *s.* aura, céfiro. *2* efluvio, emanación. *3* MED., ORN. aura.

**aural** (o·ral) *adj.* del oído.

**aureola** (orı·ola), **aureole** (o·rioul) *s.* aureola.

**aureole (to)** *tr.* aureolar.

**aureomycin** (oriomai·sin) *s.* FARM. aureomicina.

**aureous** (o·riøs) *adj.* áureo.

**auricle** (o·rikøl) *s.* aurícula.

**auricula** (ori·kiula) *s.* ZOOL. apéndice en forma de oreja. *2* BOT. oreja de oso.

**auricular** (ori·kiulaʳ) *adj.* auricular.

**auriferous** (ori·førøs) *adj.* aurífero.

**auriga** (orai·ga) *s.* auriga.

**aurist** (o·rist) *s.* otólogo.

**aurochs** (o·raks) *s.* ZOOL. uro.

**aurora** (oro·ra) *s.* aurora: ~ *australis*, aurora austral; ~ *borealis*, aurora boreal.

**auscultate (to)** (o·skølteit) *tr.* MED. auscultar.

**auscultation** (oskøltei·shøn) *s.* auscultación.

**auspicate (to)** (o·spikeit) *tr.* augurar. *2* dar buen principio a.

**auspice** (o·spis) *s.* auspicio.

**auspicious** (ospi·shøs) *adj.* próspero, feliz, favorable, propicio.

**austere** (ostı·ʳ) *adj.* austero. *2* sencillo, sin adornos. *3* grave, serio.

**austereness** (-nis), **austerity** (oste·riti) *s.* austeridad. *2* gravedad, seriedad.

**Austin** (o·stin) *n. pr.* Agustín.

**austral** (ostral) *adj.* austral.

**Australia** (ostrei·lia) *n. pr.* GEOGR. Australia.

**Australian** (-n) *adj.-s.* australiano.

**Austria** (o·stria) *n. pr.* GEOGR. Austria.

**Austrian** (-n) *adj.-s.* austríaco.

**autarchy** o **-ky** (o·taʳki) *s.* autarquía.

**authentic(al** (oze·ntik(al) *adj.* auténtico. *2* fiel, fidedigno.

**authenticate (to)** (-tikeit) *tr.* autenticar, autorizar, legalizar.

**authenticity** (-ti·siti) *s.* autenticidad.

**author** (o·zøʳ) *s.* autor; escritor.

**authoress** (-nis) *s.* autora; escritora.

**authoritarian** (ozarite·rian) *adj.-s.* autoritario.

**authoritative** (oza·riteitiv) *adj.* autorizado, que tiene autoridad. *2* autoritario. *3* imperativo, terminante.

**authority** (oza·riti) *s.* autoridad: *on the best* ~, de buena tinta. *2* autorización, licencia. *3 pl.* autoridades. *4* consejeros, junta directiva.

**authorization** (ozørišei·shøn) *s.* autorización.

**authorize (to)** (o·zøraiš) *tr.* autorizar, facultar, dar autoridad o poder. *2* justificar. *3* autorizar, sancionar.

**authorship** (oˑzøᵣship) s. calidad o profesión de autor o escritor. 2 paternidad literaria.
**auto** (oˑtou) s. fam. auto, automóvil.
**autobiography** (otobaiaˑgrafi) s. autobiografía.
**autobus** (oˑtobøs) s. autobús.
**autocar** (-kaᵣ) s. autocar. 2 automóvil.
**autochthon** (otaˑkzøn) s. autóctono.
**autochthonous** (-øs) adj. autóctono.
**autoclave** (oˑtokleiv) s. autoclave.
**autocracy** (otaˑkrɑsi) s. autocracia.
**autocraft** (oˑtokræt) s. autócrata.
**auto-da-fe** (otodɑfeiˑ) s. auto de fe.
**autodrome** (oˑtodroum) s. autódromo.
**autogenous** (otaˑdȳinøs) adj. autógeno.
**autogiro** o **-gyro** (otodȳaiˑrou) s. autogiro.
**autograph** (otogræf) adj.-s. autógrafo. 2 s. copia autográfica.
**autography** (otaˑgrafi) s. autografía.
**autoist** (oˑtoist) s. fam. automovilista.
**automat** (oˑtomæt) s. (E.U.) bar o restaurante de servicio automático.
**automatic** (otomæˑtic) adj. automático.
**automation** (-eiˑshøn) s. automación.
**automatization** (otomætišeiˑshøn) s. automatización.
**automaton** (otaˑmatan) s. autómata.
**automobile** (otomouˑbil) s. automóvil.
**automobilism** (-išm) s. automovilismo.
**automobilist** (-ist) adj.-s. automovilista.
**automotive** (-tiv) adj. automotor, triz.
**autonomic** (otonaˑmik) adj. autonómico.
**autonomous** (otaˑnomøs) adj. autónomo.
**autonomy** (-mi) s. autonomía.
**autopsy** (oˑtapsi) s. autopsia.
**autosuggestion** (otosødtyeˑschøn) s. autosugestión.
**autumn** (otaˑm) s. otoño.
**autumnal** (-nal) adj. otoñal.
**auxiliary** (ogšiˑliari) adj. auxiliar.
**avail** (aveiˑl) s. provecho, utilidad, eficacia.
**avail (to)** intr. servir, ser útil, llenar el objeto. 2 tr. aprovechar, servir, valer [a uno]. 3 ref. to ~ oneself of, aprovechar, valerse de.
**availability** (aveilabiˑliti) s. disponibilidad. 2 utilidad, eficacia. 3 validez.
**available** (aveiˑlabøl) adj. aprovechable, disponible. 2 obtenible.
**avalanche** (æˑvalænch) s. salud.
**avarice** (æˑvaris) s. avaricia, codicia.
**avaricious** (ævariˑshøs) adj. avaro, avariento.
**avariciousness** (-nis) s. AVARICE.
**avatar** (ævataˑᵣ) s. avatar.
**avaunt** (avoˑnt) interj. ant. ¡fuera!, ¡atrás!
**Ave Maria** (aˑvi marˑtˑa) s. avemaría.
**avenge (to)** (aveˑndȳ) tr. vengar.
**avenger** (-øᵣ) s. vengador.
**avengress** (-øris) f. vengadora.
**avenue** (æˑviniu) s. avenida, paseo, alameda. 2 vía, entrada, pasadizo.
**aver (to)** (avoˑᵣ) tr. afirmar, asegurar, declarar. ¶ Pret. y p. p.: averred; ger.; -rring.
**average** (æˑvøridȳ) s. promedio, término medio: on an ~, por término medio. 2 prorrata. 3 lo corriente, lo común. 4 MAR. avería. 5 adj. medio, de promedio. 6 ordinario, corriente.
**average (to)** intr. hacer un promedio de. 2 tr. determinar el promedio de. 3 prorratear.
**averment** (avøˑᵣmønt) s. aseveración.
**Avernus** (avøˑᵣnøs) s. Averno.
**averse** (avøˑᵣs) adj. contrario, opuesto, renuente.

**aversion** (avoˑᵣshøn) s. aversión. 2 repugnancia. 3 cosa aborrecida.
**avert (to)** (avˑᵣt) tr. apartar, desviar. 2 impedir, evitar, conjurar.
**aviary** (eiˑvieri) s. pajarera.
**aviate (to)** (-eit) intr. ant. volar [en avión].
**aviation** (-eiˑshøn) s. ant. aviación.
**aviator** (eiˑvieitøᵣ) s. ant. aviador.
**aviculture** (eiˑvikølchøᵣ) s. avicultura.
**avid** (æˑvid) adj. ávido.
**avidity** (aviˑditi) s. avidez, codicia.
**avocado** (ævokaˑdou) s. BOT. aguacate.
**avocation** (ævokeiˑshøn) s. distracción, pasatiempo, afición. 2 ocupación, negocio.
**avocet** (æˑvoset) s. ORN. avoceta.
**avoid (to)** (avoiˑd) tr. evitar, eludir, rehuir. 2 anular, invalidar.
**avoidance** (-ans) s. evitación. 2 DER. anulación.
**avoirdupois** (ævøᵣøpoiˑš) s. sistema de pesos cuya unidad es la libra de 16 onzas.
**avouch (to)** (avauˑch) tr. afirmar; decir. 2 probar, garantizar. 3 reconocer, confesar.
**avow (to)** (avauˑ) tr. confesar, reconocer.
**avowal** (-al) s. confesión, reconocimiento.
**avowed** (avauˑd) adj. confesado, declarado, manifiesto.
**avuncular** (avøˑnkiulaᵣ) adj. de tío.
**await (to)** (aueiˑt) tr.-intr. aguardar, esperar.
**awake** (aueiˑk) adj. despierto. 2 atento, vigilante. 3 ~ to, consciente de.
**awake (to)** tr. despertar. 2 intr. despertar, despertarse. ¶ Pret.: awoke; p. p.: awaked, awaken o awoke.
**awaken** (-øn) tr. e intr. TO AWAKE.
**awakening** (-øning) s. despertamiento, despertar.
**award** (auoˑᵣd) s. sentencia, decisión; laudo. 2 concesión, adjudicación. 3 premio, galardón.
**award (to)** tr. DER. adjudicar. 2 dar, conceder, otorgar, conferir. 3 tributar [elogios].
**aware** (aueˑᵣ) adj. sabedor, enterado, consciente de: to be ~ of, saber, darse cuenta de.
**awareness** (-nis) s. conocimiento, conciencia [de un hecho].
**awash** (auaˑsh) adj.-adv. MAR. a flor de agua.
**away** (aueiˑ) adv. lejos, a distancia, fuera, afuera, alejándose: to be ~, estar fuera, ausente; to go ~, irse, ausentarse. | Indica libertad o continuidad en la acción: talk ~, hable usted; diga usted lo que quiera; he was firing ~, iba disparando. 2 interj. ¡fuera de ahí!
**awe** (o) s. temor. 2 temor reverencial. 3 asombro, sobrecogimiento.
**awe (to)** tr. atemorizar, sobrecoger.
**awesome** (oˑsøm) adj. impotente.
**awestricken** (ostrikøn), **awestruck** (oˑstrøk) adj. atemorizado, sobrecogido.
**awful** (oˑful) adj. atroz, horrible. 2 tremendo, espantoso, imponente. 3 fam. enorme, muy malo, muy feo.
**awfully** (-i) adv. atrozmente, terriblemente. 2 fam. muy, mucho, enormemente.
**awhile** (ajuaiˑl) adv. un rato, algún tiempo.
**awkward** (oˑkuaᵣd) adj. torpe, encogido, desmañado, desgarbado. 2 embarazoso, delicado, difícil. 3 de mal manejar.
**awkwardness** (-nis) s. torpeza, desmaña. 2 encogimiento, cortedad.
**awl** (ol) s. lezna, punzón. 2 MEC. lengüeta.
**awn** (on) s. BOT. arista, raspa.
**awning** (oˑning) s. toldo, tendal, entalamadura. 2 marquesina. 3 MAR. toldo, toldilla.

**awoke** (auou·k) *pret.* y *p. p.* de TO AWAKE.
**awry** (arai·) *adv.* de través. *2* erradamente, descaminadamente. *3 adj.* torcido, ladeado. *4* errado, descaminado.
**ax, axe** (aks) *s.* hacha, destral, segur.
**ax, axe (to)** *tr.* hachear.
**axial** (æ·ksial) *adj.* axil, axial.
**axil** (æ·ksil) *s.* BOT. axila.
**axilla** (æksi·la) *s.* BOT., ZOOL. axila.
**axillar** (a·ksila$^r$), **axillary** (-leri) *s.* axilar.
**axiom** (æ·ksiøm) *s.* axioma.
**axiomatic** (æksiømæ·tik) *adj.* axiomático.
**axis** (æ·ksis) *s.* eje. *2* ANAT. axis.
**axle** (æ·ksøl) *s.* eje [de rueda]; árbol [de máquina]. *2* bolo [de escalera].

**axletree** (-trı) *s.* eje [de carruaje].
**axoloti** (æ·ksolatøl) *s.* ZOOL. ajolote.
**axon(e** (æ·ksøn) ANAT. cilindroeje.
**ay** (ai) *adv.* sí.
**aye** (ei) *adv.* siempre.
**aye-aye** (ai·ai) *s.* ZOOL. ayeaye.
**azalea** (aše·lia) *s.* BOT. azalea.
**azarole** (æ·šaroul) *s.* BOT. acerola.
**azedarach** (aše·daræk) *s.* BOT. acederaque.
**azimuth** (æ·šimøz) *s.* ASTR. acimut.
**azoic** (ašou·ik) *adj.* azoico.
**azote** (æ·šout) *s.* QUÍM. ázoe.
**Aztec** (æ·štek) *adj.-s.* azteca.
**azure** (æ·ÿø$^r$) *adj.-s.* azul celeste. *2 s.* azur.
**azurite** (æ·ÿorait) *s.* MINER. azurita.
**azymous** (æ·šimøs) *adj.* ázimo.

# B

**B, b** (bi) *s.* B, b, segunda letra del alfabeto inglés. *2* MÚS. si.

**baa** (ba) *s.* be [balido].

**baa (to)** *intr.* balar.

**Babbit metal** (bæ·bit) *s.* metal antifricción.

**babble** (bæ·bøl) *s.* charla, cháchara. *2* balbuceo. *3* murmullo [de una corriente].

**babble (to)** *intr.* charlar. *2* balbucear. *3* murmurar [una corriente]. *4 tr.* decir [lo que debería callarse].

**babbler** (bæ·blø^r) *s.* charlatán, hablador.

**babbling** (bæ·bling) *s.* charla, garrulería.

**babe** (beib) *s.* BABY.

**Babel, babel** (bei·bøl) *s.* babel, confusión, algarabía.

**babiroussa** (bæbiru·sa) *s.* ZOOL. babirusa.

**baboon** (bæbu·n) *s.* ZOOL. babuino, mandril.

**babouche** (bæbu·sh) *s.* babucha.

**baby** (bei·bi) *s.* criatura, rorro, bebé, nene, niño. *2* benjamín. *3 adj.* de niño; infantil; pequeño. *4 ~ sitter,* niñera por horas, canguro.

**baby (to)** *tr.* tratar como niño, mimar. ¶ Pret. y p. p.: *babied.*

**babyish** (-ish) *adj.* pueril, infantil.

**Babylon** (bæ·bilan) *n. pr.* HIST. Babilonia.

**Babylonian** (bæbila·nian) *adj.-s.* babilonio. *2 adj.* babilónico, de Babilonia.

**baccalaureate** (bækalo·rit) *s.* bachillerato.

**baccarat** (bækara) *s.* bacará [juego].

**bacchanal** (bæ·kanal), **bacchanalian** (bækanelian) *adj.* bacanal. *2* ebrio. *3 s.* discípulo de Baco; borracho, calavera.

**Bacchanalia** (-ne·lia) *s. pl.* bacanales. *2* [ús. en sing.] bacanal, orgía.

**Bacchanals** (bæ·kanelš) *s. pl.* bacanales.

**bacchante** (bæka·nti) *s.* bacante.

**Bacchic** (bæ·kik) *adj.* báquico.

**Bacchus** (bæ·køs) *n. pr.* MIT. Baco.

**bachelor** (bæ·chølø^r) *m.* soltero, célibe; *old ~,* solterón. *2* bachiller.

**bachelorhood** (-jud) *s.* soltería [del hombre].

**bachelor's button** *s.* nombre del azulejo, la centaurea y otras plantas.

**bacillus** (bæsi·løs) *s.* bacilo.

**back** (bæk) *s.* espalda [del hombre]; lomo, cerro [de un animal]; espinazo; *to turn one's ~ on* o *upon,* abandonar, desertar; volver la espalda a; *behind one's ~,* a espaldas de uno; *on one's ~,* a cuestas; de espaldas, boca arriba. *2* espalda, dorso, envés, revés [de una cosa]; trasera, fondo, parte de atrás. *3* espaldar [de coraza]. *4* respaldo [de silla, etc.]. *5* lomo [de libro]. *6* canto, lomo, recazo [de cuchillo]. *7* parte convexa [de una cosa arqueada]. *8* FÚTBOL defensa. *9* TEAT. foro.

*10 adj.* posterior, dorsal, trasero, que está atrás; interior, apartado; *~ door,* puerta trasera o excusada. *11* atrasado [renta, número de un periódico]. *12* que vuelve, que va hacia atrás, dirigido hacia atrás. *13 adv.* atrás, hacia atrás, en situación apartada: *to go ~,* retroceder. *14* de vuelta, de regreso, en reciprocidad, en pago: *to come ~,* volver, regresar; *to give ~,* devolver. *15* en ocultación o retención: *to keep ~,* callar; retener.

*16 interj.* ¡atrás!

**back (to)** *tr.* apoyar, sostener, respaldar, secundar. *2* apostar por o a. *3* empujar o tirar hacia atrás, hacer recular. *4* formar, estar en o resguardar la espalda, el dorso, el envés o el lomo de. *5* respaldar [un escrito]. *6* MAR. engalgar. *7* montar [un caballo]. *8 pop.* llevar a cuestas. *9 to ~ up,* sostener, apoyar. *10 to ~ water,* MAR. ciar. *11 intr.* recular, retroceder. *12 to ~ down, to ~ out,* volverse atrás.

**backbite (to)** (bæ·kbait) *intr.-tr.* murmurar [de]; criticar, calumniar [a uno]. ¶ Pret.: *backbit;* p. p.: *backbit* o *-bitten;* ger.: *backbitting.*

**backbiter** (-ø^r) *s.* murmurador, calumniador.

**backbone** (bæ·kboun) *s.* espinazo, columna vertebral. *2 fig.* firmeza, nervio, resistencia.

**backdoor** (bæ·kdoø^r) *adj.* clandestino, secreto.

**backdown** (-daun) *s. fam.* retractación, palinodia.

**backer** (bæ·kø^r) *s.* apoyador, respaldador, financiador, partidario. *2* el que apuesta.

**backfire** (bæ·kfai^r) *s.* AUTO. petardeo.

**backfire (to)** *intr.* AUTO. petardear.

**backgammon** (-gæmøn) *s.* chaquete.

**background** (-graund) *s.* fondo, último término, lontananza. *2* fondo [de un dibujo, etc.].

**backhand(ed)** (bækjæ·nd(id)) *adj.* de revés, dado con la mano vuelta. *2* inclinada a la izquierda [escritura]. *3* insincero, irónico. *4* desmañado.

**backing** (bæ·king) *s.* apoyo, sostén. *2* garantía. *3* lo que sostiene o refuerza por detrás, forro. *4* azogado [de un espejo]. *5* retroceso.

**backpiece** (-pɪs) s. espaldar [de armadura].
**backset** (-set) s. contratiempo, contrariedad. 2 remanso, contracorriente.
**backshop** (-shap) s. trastienda; rebotica.
**backside** (-said) s. espalda, parte de atrás. 2 trasero, tafanario.
**backslide** (-slaid) *intr.* deslizarse hacia atrás. 2 recaer, reincidir, volver a un estado de culpa o atraso.
**backspacer** (-peisøʳ) s. tecla de retroceso.
**backstairs** (bakste·ʳs) *adj.* de intriga, secreto, clandestino.
**backstitch** (bæ·kstitch) s. pespunte.
**backstitch (to)** *tr.* pespunt(e)ar.
**backward** (-woʳd) *adj.* dirigido hacia atrás, retrógrado, retrospectivo. 2 que retrocede. 3 dicho o hecho al revés. 4 atrasado; tardío. 5 lento, tardo. 6 lerdo, torpe. 7 corto, tímido. 8 renuente.
**backward(s** (-woʳd(s) *adv.* hacia atrás, atrás. 2 al revés. 3 de espaldas. 4 a reculones.
**backwardation** (-ei·shøn) s. doble [en Bolsa].
**backwater** (-uøtøʳ) s. remanso.
**backwoods** (-wuds) s. *pl.* (E.U.) región de bosques alejada de los centros de población.
**bacon** (bei·køn) s. tocino [esp. el entreverado].
**bacteria** (bækti·ria) *pl.* de BACTERIUM.
**bacteriology** (-a·lodyi) s. bacteriología.
**bacterium** (bækti·riøm) s. bacteria.
**bad** (bæd) *adj.* malo, mal: ~ *form*, mala educación. 2 malo, enfermo. 3 podrido [huevo]. 4 incobrable [deuda]. 5 falsa [moneda]. 6 *adv.* mal: ~ *looking*, feo, de mal aspecto. 7 s. mal, lo malo: *to go to the* ~, perderse, arruinarse; *from* ~ *to worse*, de mal en peor.
**bade** *pret.* de TO BID.
**badge** (bæ·dyi) s. insignia, distintivo, placa, condecoración. 2 divisa, símbolo.
**badger** (-øʳ) s. ZOOL. tejón.
**badger (to)** *tr.* molestar, atormentar.
**badinage** (bæ·dinidy) s. broma, burla, chanza.
**badly** (bæ·dli) *adv.* mal, malamente: ~ *off*, en mal estado o situación; maltrecho. 2 muy mucho. 3 gravemente.
**badminton** (bæ·dmintøn) s. volante [juego].
**badness** (bæ·dnis) s. maldad [calidad de malo]; mala calidad.
**baffle** (bæ·føl) s. confusión, desconcierto [de uno]. 2 MEC. pantalla; deflector.
**baffle (to)** *tr.* confundir, desconcertar, chasquear. 2 burlar, frustrar. 3 desviar, detener.
**bag** (bæg) s. saco, bolsa, talega. 2 cartera, valija; maletín, saco de mano; bolso, monedero. 3 zurrón, morral. 4 ANAT. bolsa, saco. 5 bolsa [en la piel o en la ropa].
**bag (to)** *tr.* embolsar, ensacar, meter en el zurrón. 2 cazar, pescar, atrapar, coger. 3 *intr.* abolsarse, hacer bolsa. 4 hincharse, abotagarse. ¶ Pret. y p. p.: *bagged;* ger.: *bagging.*
**bagasse** (bagæ·s) s. bagazo.
**bagatelle** (bægate·l) s. bagatela.
**baggage** (bæ·gidy) s. (E.U. y Can.) equipaje [de viaje]. 2 MIL. bagaje. 3 pelandusca. 4 fam. picaruela.
**baggy** (bæ·gi) *adj.* holgado, flojo, que hace bolsas.
**bagnio** (bæ·nou) s. baño [prisión de esclavos]. 2 lupanar.
**bagpipe** (bæ·gpaip) s. MÚS. gaita, cornamusa.
**bagpiper** (-ø·) s. gaitero.
**bah** (ba) *interj.* ¡bah!
**bail** (beil) s. DER. fianza. 2 DER. fiador. 3 asa [de

cubo o caldero]. 4 arco [que sostiene un toldo]. 5 achicador. 6 aro, cerco, zuncho.
**bail (to)** *tr.* DER. dar fianza por [uno]. 2 poner en libertad bajo fianza. 3 achicar [sacar agua]. 4 zunchar, asegurar con aros. 5 *intr.* AVIA. *to* ~ *out*, tirarse con paracaídas.
**bailey** (bei·li) s. muralla o patio de un castillo o fortaleza.
**bailiff** (bei·lif) s. baile [ant. magistrado]. 2 administrador, mayordomo. 3 alguacil, corchete.
**bailiwick** (bei·liuik) s. bailía. 2 mayordomía. 3 alguacilazgo.
**bairn** (beʳn) s. [Esc.] niño, niña.
**bait** (beit) s. cebo, carnada. 2 fig. cebo, señuelo, anzuelo: *to take the* ~, tragar el anzuelo. 3 pienso.
**bait (to)** *tr.* cebar [poner cebo; atraer con cebo]. 2 dar un pienso a. 3 atormentar, acosar, hostigar.
**baize** (beiš) s. bayeta.
**bake** (beik) s. cocción al horno. 2 cosa cocida al horno.
**bake (to)** *tr.* cocer, asar, etc., al horno. 2 secar, endurecer [por la acción del calor]; calcinar. 3 *intr.* hornear. 4 cocerse [en el horno]. 5 secarse, endurecerse [al sol, etc.].
**bakelite** (bei·kølait) s. baquelita.
**baker** (bei·køʳ) s. hornero, panadero: *baker's dozen,* docena de fraile.
**bakery** (-i) s. horno, panadería, tahona.
**baking** (bei·king) s. cochura, cocción [al horno]; ~ *powder*, levadura química. 2 hornada.
**balance** (bæ·lans) s. balanza [instrumento]. 2 ASTR. Libra. 3 contrapeso. 4 equilibrio. 5 comparación, estimación. 6 COM. balance. 7 COM. saldo, alcance. 8 volante [de reloj]. 9 MEC. ~ *wheel*, volante. *10* ~ *of trade*, balanza comercial.
**balance (to)** *tr.* pesar [en la balanza]. 2 estimar, comparar. 3 equilibrar; nivelar. 4 balancear, contrapesar. 5 COM. saldar, finiquitar. 6 *intr.* estar en equilibrio. 7 equilibrarse, compensarse. 8 balancear[se; vacilar.
**balancer** (-øʳ) s. pesador. 2 equilibrista. 3 ELECT. estabilizador. 4 ENT. balancín [de díptero].
**balas** (bæ·las) s. balaje [rubí].
**balcony** (bæ·lkøni) s. balcón; galería exterior. 2 TEAT. galería, anfiteatro.
**bald** (bold) *adj.* calvo. 2 desnudo, pelado. 3 escueto. 4 pobre [estilo].
**baldachin** (bæ·ldakin) s. baldaquín.
**balderdash** (bo·ldøʳdæsh) s. vaciedades, tonterías, monserga.
**bald-faced** *adj.* cariblanco, careto.
**baldly** (-li) *adv.* desnudamente, escuetamente. 2 pobremente.
**baldness** (-nis) s. calvicie. 2 desnudez [falta de pelo, plumas, adornos, etc.].
**baldric** (bol·arik) s. tahalí.
**bale** (beil) s. bala, fardo. 2 poét. mal, dolor.
**bale (to)** *tr.* embalar, enfardar, empacar. 2 MAR. achicar.
**Balearic** (bæliæ·rik) *adj.* balear, baleárico.
**balefire** (bei·lfaiʳ) s. almenara, hoguera.
**baleful** (bei·lful) *adj.* funesto, pernicioso.
**balk** (bok) s. AGR. caballón. 2 yerro, desliz. 3 fracaso, contrariedad. 4 impedimento. 5 viga. 6 BILLAR. cabaña; casa; cuadro.
**balk (to)** *tr.* evitar. 2 burlar, desbaratar, contrariar. 3 malograr, perder. 4 *intr.* plantarse, resistirse. 5 repropiarse.
**Balkan** (bo·lkan) *adj.* balcánico.
**ball** (bol) s. bola, globo, esfera. 2 pelota. 3 bala

[proyectil redondo]. *4* ovillo; burujo. *5* yema [del pulgar o del dedo]. *6* AGR. cepellón. *7* baile [fiesta].
**ball (to)** *tr.* ovillar. *2* apelotonar, convertir en bola. *3* intr. *to ~ up*, apelotonarse.
**ballad** (bæ·lad) *s.* balada. *2* canción, copla.
**ballast** (bæ·last) *s.* lastre. *2* grava, balasto.
**ballast (to)** *tr.* lastrar. *2* balastar; afirmar.
**ballet** (bæ·lei) *s.* baile de espectáculo.
**ballista** (bali·sta) *s.* balista.
**ballistic** (bali·stik) *adj.* balístico.
**ballistics** (-s) *s.* balística.
**balloon** (balu·n) *s.* globo [aerostático; juguete]. *2* QUÍM. balón.
**balloon (to)** *intr.* ir en globo. *2* hincharse.
**ballot** (bæ·lot) *s.* balota; papeleta de voto, candidatura. *2* votación, sufragio.
**ballot (to)** *intr.* y *tr.* votar. *2* insacular.
**ball-point pen** *s.* bolígrafo.
**ballroom** (bo·lrum) *s.* salón de baile.
**balm** (bam) *s.* bálsamo. *2* aroma, perfume. *3* BOT. melisa, cidronela, toronjil.
**balmy** (ba·mi) *adj.* balsámico, calmante, reparador. *2* suave [clima, tiempo]. *3* fam. chiflado, idiota.
**balsam** (bo·lsam) *s.* bálsamo. *2* BOT. balsamina [de jardín]. *3 ~ apple*, balsamina [cucurbitácea].
**balsamic** (bolsæ·mik) *adj.* balsámico.
**Balthasar** (balza·sa^r) *n. pr.* Baltasar.
**Baltic** (bo·ltik) *adj.* báltico.
**baluster** (bæ·løstø^r) *s.* balaustre.
**balustrade** (bæløstrei·d) *s.* balaustrada.
**bamboo** (bambu·) *s.* BOT. bambú.
**bamboozle** (-sløl) *s.* engaño, embeleco.
**bamboozle (to)** *tr.* engañar, embaucar, burlar.
**bamboozler** (-šlø^r) *s.* engañador, embaucador.
**ban** (bæn) *s.* proclama, edicto. *2* proscripción. *3* excomunión, entredicho. *4 pl.* BANNS.
**ban (to)** *tr.* proscribir, desterrar. *2* excomulgar, anatematizar. *3* prohibir.
**banal** (bæ·nal) *adj.* trivial, común, trillado.
**banality** (-iti) *s.* trivialidad, vulgaridad.
**banana** (banæ·na) *s.* BOT. plátano, banana.
**band** (bænd) *s.* faja, venda, fleje, cinta, tira [para atar]; vencejo, vilorta; sortija de cigarro. *2* abrazadera, zuncho. *3* faja, cenefa, cinta, lista, zona. *4* ARQ. filete, listón. *5* RADIO. banda [de ondas]. *6* MEC. correa. *7* MÚS. banda, música. *8* banda, cuadrilla, partida.
**band (to)** *tr.* atar, fajar, vendar, precintar. *2* acuadrillar, juntar. *3* intr. *to ~ together*, acuadrillarse, juntarse.
**bandage** (bæ·ndidỹ) *s.* venda, vendaje.
**bandanna** (bændæ·na) *s.* pañuelo de hierbas.
**bandbox** (bæ·ndbaks) *s.* sombrerera [caja].
**banderol(e** (bæ·ndøroul) *s.* banderola.
**bandit** (bæn·dit) *s.* bandido, bandolero.
**banditry** (bæ·nditri) *s.* bandidaje, bandolerismo.
**bandog** (bæ·ndog) *s.* mastín, perro de presa.
**bandoleer, bandolier** (bændolɪ·^r) *s.* bandolera.
**bandore** (bæ·ndø^r) *s.* bandurria.
**band-saw** *s.* sierra sin fin.
**bandy** (bæ·ndi) *adj.* arqueado, torcido hacia afuera.
**bandy (to)** ) *tr.* lanzar, tirar de un lado a otro. *2* cambiar [palabras, golpes, etc.]. *3* intr. discutir, contender.
**bandy-legged** *adj.* estevado.
**bane** (bein) *s.* muerte, ruina, daño, perdición. *2* veneno.

**baneful** (bei·nful) *adj.* letal, funesto, pernicioso, venenoso.
**banewort** (-uø^rt) *s.* planta venenosa.
**bang** (bæng) *s.* golpe, porrazo [que resuena], portazo, detonación. *2* flequillo [de cabello]. *3 adv.* con estrépito, con golpe. *4* de repente, impetuosamente.
**bang (to)** *tr.* golpear [haciendo ruido]: *to ~ the door*, dar un portazo. *2* aporrear, apalear, maltratar. *3* sobrepujar. *4* cortar el cabello en flequillo. *5* intr. hacer estrépito.
**banian** (bæ·nian) *s.* baniano.
**banish (to)** (bæ·nish) *tr.* desterrar, proscribir. *2* expulsar. *3* ahuyentar, desechar.
**banishment** (-mønt) *s.* destierro, proscripción, expulsión.
**banister** (bæ·nistø^r) *s.* balaustre. *2 pl.* balaustrada, barandilla.
**banjo** (bæ·ndýou) *s.* banjo.
**bank** (bænk) *s.* ribazo, talud. *2* lomo [de tierra]. *3* margen, orilla [de río o lago]. *4* peralte [de carretera]. *5* banco [de arena]. *6* masa [de nubes]. *7* hilera, batería [de remos, teclas, lámparas, etc.]. *8* banda [del billar]. *9* COM. banco: *~ note, ~ bill*, billete de banco; *~ vault*, cámara acorazada. *10* hucha, alcancía. *11* banca [en el juego].
**bank (to)** *tr.* amontonar [formando dique o talud]; aporcar, cubrir. | Gralte. con *up*. *2* proteger, represar [con dique o reparo]. *3* juntar en serie o batería. *4* depositar en un banco. *5* intr. hacer negocios de banca. *6* tener dinero en un banco. *7 to ~ up*, elevarse formando lomo o talud; AVIA. inclinarse al virar. *8 to ~ on*, contar con.
**banker** (-ø^r) *s.* banquero.
**banking** (bæ·nking) *s.* banca [negocio]. *2 adj.* bancario de banca: *~ house*, casa de banca.
**bankrupt** (bæ·nkrøpt) *adj.-s.* insolvente, quebrado, falldo, arruinado.
**bankrupt (to)** *tr.* hacer quebrar; arruinar.
**bankruptcy** (-si) *s.* quiebra, bancarrota.
**banner** (bæ·nø^r) *s.* bandera, estandarte, pendón.
**banneret** (-et) *s.* caballero con bandera.
**banns** (bæns) *s.* amonestaciones.
**banquet** (bæ·nkuit) *s.* banquete, festín.
**banquet (to)** *tr.-intr.* banquetear.
**bantam** (bæ·ntam) *s.* ORN. gallina enana.
**bantam-weight** *s.* BOX. peso gallo.
**banter** (bæ·ntø^r) *s.* burla, chanza, vaya.
**banter (to)** *tr.* embromar, dar vaya. *2* intr. bromear, chancearse.
**bantling** (bæ·ntling) *s.* pequeñuelo, pequeñuela.
**banyan** (bæ·nian) *s.* BANIAN.
**baobab** (bei·oubæb) *s.* baobab.
**baptism** (bæ·ptism) *s.* bautismo. *2* bautizo.
**baptismal** (bæpti·šmal) *s.* bautismal; *~ name*, nombre de pila.
**Baptist** (bæ·ptist) *s.* bautista. *2* baptista.
**baptistery** (bæ·ptistøri) *s.* baptisterio.
**baptize (to)** (bæ·ptaiš) *tr.* bautizar.
**baptizer** (-ø^r) *s.* bautista, bautizante.
**bar** (ba^r) *s.* barra, barrote, varilla. *2* barra [de plata, oro, etc.]. *3* GEOGR. barra, alfaque. *4* tranca [de puerta]. *5* raya, faja, lista. *6* barrera, valla, reja. *7* barra [de un tribunal o asamblea]. *8* DER. estrados. *9* abogacía, foro; colegio de abogados. *10* mostrador [de taberna o restaurante]; sala donde está; bar. *11* MÚS. barra, compás. *12* FÍS. bar. *13 prep.* excepto, salvo.
**bar (to)** *tr.* atrancar [una puerta]. *2* barrear. *3* listar, rayar. *4* MÚS. dividir en compases. *5* obs-

truir; obstar, impedir, prohibir. ¶ Pret. y p. p.:
*barred;* ger.: *barring.*
**Barabbas** (baræ·bas) *n. pr.* Barrabás.
**barb** (ba$^r$b) *s.* púa, lengüeta [de flecha, anzuelo,
etc.]. *2* barbilla [de pez]. *3* caballo árabe. *4 pl.*
barbas [de pluma].
**barb (to)** *tr.* armar con púas o lengüetas.
**barbarian** (barbe·rian) *adj.-s.* bárbaro [de los pueblos bárbaros; no civilizado].
**barbaric** (ba$^r$bæ·rik) *s.* bárbaro, barbárico.
**barbarism** (ba·$^r$barišm) *s.* barbarismo. *2* barbarie.
**barbarity** (ba·bæ·riti) *s.* barbarie, crueldad.
**barbarize (to)** (ba·$^r$baraiš) *tr.-intr.* barbarizar. *2*
volver o volverse bárbaro.
**barbarous** (ba·$^r$barøs) *adj.* bárbaro.
**Barbary** (ba·$^r$bikiu) *n. pr.* GEOGR. Berbería.
**barbecue** (ba·$^r$bikiu) *s.* barbacoa [parrilla; carne].
**barbecue (to)** *tr.* asar un animal entero; churrasquear.
**barbed** (ba·$^r$bd) *adj.* armado con púas o lengüetas:
~ *wire,* alambre con púas, espino artificial.
**barbel** (ba·$^r$bøl) *s.* barbilla [de pez]. *2* barbo.
**bar-bell** *s.* GIMN. barra con pesas.
**barber** (ba·$^r$bø$^r$) *s.* barbero: *barber's shop,* barbería.
**barberry** (ba·$^r$børi) *s.* bérbero, agracejo.
**barbet** (ba·$^r$bet) *s.* perro de aguas.
**barbican** (ba·$^r$bikan) *s.* FORT. barbacana.
**barcarol** (ba·$^r$karoul) *s.* barcarola.
**bard** (ba$^r$d) *s.* bardo; vate. *2* barda [del caballo]. *3*
COC. albardilla.
**bard (to)** *tr.* COC. albardillar, embozorrar.
**bare** (be$^r$) *adj.* desnudo; descubierto: *to lay* ~, desnudar, descubrir. *2* pelado, raso. *3* raído. *4* desprovisto de. *5* mero, puro, solo. *6* liso, sencillo.
**bare (to)** *tr.* desnudar, despojar, descubrir.
**barebone** (-boun) *s.* esqueleto [persona flaca].
**barefaced** (-feist) *adj.* descarado, desfachatado, insolente, atrevido.
**barefoot** (-fut), **barefooted** (-id) *adj.* descalzo.
**bareheaded** (-jedid) *adj.* descubierto, destocado.
**barelegged** (-legid) *adj.* en pernetas.
**barely** (-li) *adv.* desnudamente. *2* apenas, escasamente. *3* insuficientemente.
**barenecked** (-nekt) *adj.* descotado.
**bareness** (-nis) *s.* desnudez. *2* desabrigo. *3* miseria,
escasez.
**bargain** (ba·$^r$gin) *s.* trato, convenio, ajuste, negocio: *into the* ~, de más, por añadidura. *2* ganga,
buen negocio: *at a* ~, muy barato.
**bargain (to)** *intr.* negociar, ajustar un trato; regatear: *I did not* ~ *for it,* fig. no esperaba yo esto.
*2 tr.* vender, negociar, trocar.
**bargaining** (-ing) *s.* trato, regateo.
**barge** (ba$^r$dž) *s.* barcaza, gabarra. *2* chalupa. *3*
HOUSEBOAT.
**barge (to)** *intr.* moverse, meterse, entrometerse.
**bargeman** (-mæn) *s.* barquero, gabarrero.
**barilla** (bari·la) *s.* barrilla, sosa.
**baritone** (bæritoun) *s.* QUÍM. bario.
**barium** (be·riøm) *s.* QUÍM. bario.
**bark** (ba$^r$k) *s.* corteza [de árbol]; casca. *2* ladrido.
*3* fam. tos. *4* MAR. bricbarca, barca.
**bark (to)** *tr.* curtir [con casca]. *2* descortezar. *3*
rozar, desollar. *4* cubrir con corteza. *5 intr.* ladrar.
**barker** (-ø$^r$) *s.* descortezador. *2* animal ladrador. *3*
voceador.
**barkentine** (ba·$^r$køntin) *s.* barca goleta.
**barking** (-ing) *s.* ladrido. *2 adj.* ladrador.
**barley** (ba·$^r$li) *s.* BOT. cebada; alcacer.

**barm** (ba$^r$m) *s.* levadura [esp. de cerveza].
**barmaid** (ba·$^r$meid) *s.* camarera, moza de taberna.
**barman** (ba·$^r$mæn) *s.* mozo de taberna, barman.
**barmy** (ba·$^r$mi) *adj.* espumoso. *2* fig. chiflado.
**barn** (ba$^r$n) *s.* granero, pajar; cobertizo.
**barnacle** (ba·$^r$nakøl) *s.* acial. *2* ORN. barnacla. *3* bellota de mar, percebe. *4 pl.* gafas.
**barn-owl** *s.* ORN. lechuza.
**barnyard** (-ya$^r$d) *s.* corral [de granja]: ~ *fowl,* ave
de corral.
**barometer** (barə·mitø$^r$) *s.* barómetro.
**baron** (bæ·røn) *s.* barón. *2* magnate.
**baronage** (-idỹ) *s.* baronía [dignidad].
**baroness** (-is) *s.* baronesa.
**baronet** (-et) *s.* baronet.
**baronetage** (-idỹ), **baronetcy** (-si) *s.* título o dignidad de baronet.
**baronial** (barou·nial) *adj.* del barón o la baronía.
**barony** (bæ·røni) *s.* baronía.
**baroque** (barou·k) *adj.* barroco.
**barouche** (baru·sh) *s.* birlocho.
**barque** (ba$^r$k) *s.* especie de bricbarca.
**barrack (to)** (bæ·rak) *tr.* acuartelar, poner en cuar-
teles. *2* DEP. abuchear. *3 intr.* alojarse en cuar-
teles.
**barracks** (bæ·raks) *s. pl.* cuartel [edificio].
**barracuda** (baraku·da) *s.* ICT. picuda.
**barrage** (bara·dỹ) *s.* barrera. *2* presa [en un río,
etc.].
**barratry** (bæ·ratri) *s.* MAR. baratería.
**barrel** (bæ·røl) *s.* barril, tonel. *2* cañón, cilindro. *3*
cañón [de un arma; de la pluma de ave]. *4*
cuerpo [de bomba]. *5* MEC. cilindro, tambor. *6*
cubo [de reloj]. *7* tronco [de un cuadrúpedo].
**barrel (to)** *tr.* embarrilar, entonelar. ¶ Pret. y p. p.:
*barreled* o *-lled;* ger.: *barreling* o *-lling.*
**barren** (bæ·røn) *adj.* estéril, infecundo, infructuoso. *2* árido, yermo. *3* falto, desprovisto de. *4*
*s.* yermo, erial.
**barricade** (bærikei·d) *s.* barricada.
**barricade (to)** *tr.* fortificar u obstruir con barricada.
**barrier** (bæ·riø$^r$) *s.* barrera, valla, empalizada. *2*
barrera, obstáculo.
**barring** (ba·ring) *prep.* excepto, salvo, quitando.
**barrister** (bæ·ristø$^r$) *s.* abogado.
**barroom** (ba·$^r$rum) *s.* cantina, bar.
**barrow** (bæ·rou) *s.* angarillas, parihuela. *2* carrito
de mano, carretilla. *3* túmulo [montículo]. *4*
cerdo castrado.
**bartender** (ba·$^r$tendø$^r$) *s.* BARMAN.
**barter** (ba·$^r$tø$^r$) *s.* trueque, cambio, cambalache.
**barter (to)** *tr.-intr.* trocar, cambiar, permutar,
cambalachear.
**Bartholomew** (barza·lømiu) *n. pr.* Bartolomé.
**baryta** (bærai·ta) *s.* QUÍM. barita.
**barytone** (bæ·ritoun) *s.* BARITONE.
**basal** (bei·sal) *s.* basal. *2* básico.
**basalt** (bæsolt) *s.* basalto.
**basaltic** (-ik) *adj.* basáltico.
**basan** (bæ·san) *s.* badana.
**bascule** (bæ·skiul) *s.* báscula [aparato para levantar un puente].
**base** (beis) *adj.* inferior, de baja calidad, de poco
valer. *2* bajo, de baja ley [metal, moneda]. *3*
bajo, ruin, vil. *4* MÚS. bajo, grave. *5* base, que
sirve de base. *6 s.* base. *7* basa, basamento, pie,
zócalo.
**base (to)** *tr.* basar, fundar, fundamentar. *2 intr.* basarse, estar basado.
**baseball** (-bol) *s.* béisbol.

**baseboard** (-boᵳd) *s.* zócalo [en una pared]. *2* rodapié. *3* tablero que sirve de base.
**baseless** (-lis) *adj.* sin base; infundado.
**basement** (-mønt) *s.* basamento. *2* sótano, cuarto bajo.
**bash (to)** (bæsh) *tr.* quebrar o aplastar a golpes.
**bashful** (-ful) *adj.* vergonzoso, tímido, encogido, modesto, ruboroso.
**basic** (bei·sik) *adj.* básico.
**basidium** (basi·diøm) *s.* BOT. basidio.
**Basil** (bei·sil) *n. pr.* Basilio.
**basil** (bæ·sil) *s.* BOT. albahaca. *2* badana.
**basilar** (-aᵳ) *adj.* basilar.
**basilic(a** (bæ·silik(a) *s.* basílica.
**basilisk** (bæ·silisk) *s.* basilisco.
**basin** (bei·sin) *s.* jofaina, palangana, bacía, cubeta, lebrillo. *2* taza, pilón [de fuente]. *3* dársena. *4* GEOGR. cuenca, valle, hoya. *5* estanque.
**basinet** (bæ·sinet) *s.* bacinete.
**basis** (bei·sis) *s.* base, fundamento. *2* ARQ., ZOOL., BOT. base.
**bask (to)** (bæks) *intr.* calentarse, estarse expuesto [al sol, a un calor agradable]. *2 tr.* calentar, asolear.
**basket** (bæ·skit) *s.* cesto, cesta, canasta, cuévano. *2* barquilla [de globo].
**basketball** (-bol) *s.* baloncesto.
**basket-handle** *adj.* ARQ. carpanel [arco].
**basket-work** *s.* cestería; obra de cestería o que la imita.
**basketry** (bæ·skøtri) *s.* cestería.
**Balse** (bal) *n. pr.* GEOGR. Basilea.
**Basque** (bask) *adj.-s.* vasco. *2 s.* vascuence.
**bas-relief** (ba-rilıf) *s.* bajo relieve.
**bass** (bæs) *s.* ICT. róbalo, lobina. *2* ICT. perca. *3* BOT. liber. *4* fibra de ciertas plantas.
**bass** (beis) *adj.* MÚS. bajo, grave: ~ *viol,* violón. *2 s.* MÚS. bajo.
**basset** (bæ·sit) *s.* perro de patas muy cortas.
**bassinet** (-sinet) *s.* cuna de mimbres. *2* BASINET.
**basso** (bæ·sou) *s.* MÚS. bajo.
**bassoon** (bæsu·n) *s.* MÚS. bajón, piporro; fagot.
**basswood** (bæ·swud) *s.* BOT. tilo americano.
**bast** (bæst) *s.* liber, fibra.
**bastard** (bæ·staᵳd) *adj.-s.* bastardo. *2 adj.* degenerado. *3* IMPR. ~ *title,* anteportada.
**bastardize (to)** (-aiš) *tr.* declarar bastardo. *2 intr.* bastardear, degenerar.
**bastardy** (-i) *s.* bastardía.
**baste (to)** (beist) *tr.* hilvanar, embastar. *2* fam. apalear. *3* COC. lardear, lardar.
**bastinado** (bæstinei·dou) *s.* bastonazo. *2* paliza.
**bastinado (to)** *tr.* apalear.
**bastings** (bæ·stings) *s. pl.* hilvanes.
**bastion** (bæ·schøn) *s.* bastión, baluarte.
**bat** (bæt) *s.* ZOOL. murciélago. *2* palo, bate, raqueta [para ciertos juegos]. *3* pedazo de ladrillo, tejoleta.
**bat (to)** *tr.* golpear con el bate. *2* mover: *to* ~ *the eyelashes,* parpadear.
**batch** (bæch) *s.* hornada, cochura. *2* cantidad de cosas que se producen, se emplean, se necesitan, etc., de una vez. *3* fam. soltero.
**bate (to)** (beit) *tr.* rebajar, disminuir. *2* cortar, contener: *with bated breath,* con aliento entrecortado. *3 intr.* disminuir.
**bath** (bæz) *s.* baño. *2* bañera [recipiente]. *3 pl.* baños [edificio; balneario].
**bathe (to)** (beið) *tr.* bañar. *2 intr.* bañarse.
**bather** (-øᵳ) *s.* bañista [que se baña].

**bathhouse** (bæ·zjaus) *s.* casa de baños. *2* caseta de baño.
**bathrobe** (-roub) *s.* albornoz, bata.
**bathroom** (-rum) *s.* cuarto de baño.
**bathtub** (-tøb) *s.* bañera, baño.
**bathymetry** (bæzi·metri) *s.* batimetría.
**bating** (bei·ting) *prep.* excepto, exceptuando.
**batiste** (bætı·st) *s.* batista.
**batman** (bæ·tmæn) *s.* MIL. asistente, ordenanza.
**baton** (bæ·tøøn) *s.* bastón [de mando]. *2* MÚS. batuta.
**baton (to)** *tr.* bastonear.
**batrachian** (batrei·kian) *adj.-s.* batracio.
**batsman** (bæ·tsmæn) *s.* jugador de pelota con bate.
**battalion** (batæ·liøn) *s.* batallón.
**batten** (bæ·tøn) *s.* tabla [para entarimar]; lata, listón. *3* batán [del telar].
**batten (to)** *tr.* reforzar o asegurar con listones. *2* cebar, engordar. *3 intr.* engordar, medrar.
**batter** (bæ·tøᵳ) *s.* COC. pasta, batido. *2* pasta de yeso. *3* talud, releje [de un muro].
**batter (to)** *tr.* batir, golpear. *2* MIL. batir, cañonear. *3* romper, abollar, estropear: *to* ~ *down,* demoler. *4* ataludar [un muro]. *5 intr.* tener talud [un muro].
**battered** (-d) *adj.* hecho una pasta. *2* derruido, estropeado, abollado.
**battering** (-in) *adj.* MIL. de batir: ~ *ram,* ariete.
**battery** (-i) *s.* batería. *2* DER. agresión.
**battle** (bæ·tøl) *s.* batalla, combate, lucha: ~ *front,* frente de combate.
**battle (to)** *intr.* batallar, luchar.
**battled** (bæ·tøld) *adj.* almenado.
**battledore** (-døᵳ) *s.* raqueta [para jugar al volante]. *2* pala [de lavandera].
**battlefield** (-fild) *s.* campo de batalla.
**battlement** (-mønt) *s.* almenaje, muro almenado.
**battleship** (-ship) *s.* acorazado.
**bauble** (bo·bøl) *s.* chuchería, fruslería; perifollo. *2* cetro de bufón.
**baulk (to)** (bok) *intr.* TO BALK.
**Bavaria** (bave·ria) *n. pr.* GEOGR. Baviera.
**Bavarian** (-n) *adj.-s.* bávaro.
**bawd** (bod) *s.* alcahuete, ta.
**bawd (to)** ) *intr.* alcahuetear.
**bawdiness** (bo·di[nis) *adj.* obscenidad.
**bawdy** (bo·di) *adj.* obsceno, verde.
**bawl (to)** (bol) *intr.-tr.* gritar, vociferar; berrear.
**bawler** (bo·løᵳ) *s.* voceador, vocinglero, gritador, gritón.
**bay** (bei) *adj.-s.* bayo [caballo]. *2 s.* bahía, ensenada, abra. *3* entrada de un llano en una cordillera. *4* ARQ. intercolumnio, vano, entrepaño. *5* ojo [de puente]. *6* ventana salediza: ~ *window,* mirador, cierro de cristales. *7* compartimiento [de cuadra; de granero o henil]. *8* ladrido [esp. del perro que persigue]. *9* acorralamiento: *at* ~, acorralado, acosado; haciendo frente a los que le acosan. *10* laurel.
**bay (to)** *intr.* ladrar. *2 tr.* ladrar a. *3* acorralar.
**bayadere** (baiadi·øᵳ) *s.* bayadera.
**bayberry** (bei·beri) *s.* BOT. arrayán brabántico; su fruto. *2* fruto del laurel.
**bayonet** (bei·ønit) *s.* bayoneta.
**bayonet (to)** *tr.* herir con bayoneta. *2* cargar a la bayoneta.
**baza(a)r** (bæza·ᵳ) *s.* bazar. *2* feria o tómbola benéfica.
**bazooka** (bašu·ka) *s.* cañón lanzacohetes.
**be (to)** (bı) *intr.* ser: *so* ~ *it,* así sea. *2* existir, vivir.

*3* celebrarse, efectuarse. *4* tener [una edad]: *he is fifty* o *fifty years old*, tiene cincuenta años. *5* estar, hallarse, encontrarse; verse: *he is ill*, está enfermo; *I am obliged to do it*, me veo obligado a hacerlo. *6* llevar [tiempo] en un sitio. *7* Precedido de *there* se traduce por haber [impers.]: *there is something*, hay algo. *8* En ciertos casos, la oración se traduce por una del verbo tener: *to ~ hungry*, tener hambre, tener apetito; *to ~ right*, tener razón. *9* Otros sentidos: *to ~ at [a thing]*, estar ocupado en, estar haciendo [una cosa]; *it is not for me to say*, no soy yo quien ha de decir; *it is to ~ regretted*, es de lamentar. *10 impers.* hacer, haber: *it is cold*, hace frío; *it is foggy*, hay niebla; *it is now a year*, hace un año. *11 aux.* Forma la voz pasiva: *she is loved*, ella es amada. *12* Forma los tiempos compuestos de ciertos verbos intransitivos: *he is gone*, se ha ido. *13* Con un gerundio denota acción que se está realizando o que se va a realizar: *I am coming*, vengo; *he was going to speak*, él iba a hablar. *14* Con un infinitivo equivale a haber de, tener que: *I am to go out*, he de salir; *what are we to do?*, ¿qué hemos de hacer? ¶ CONJUG. INDIC. Pres.: *am, art, is; are*. | Pret.: *was, was, was; were*. | SUBJ. Pres. *be*. | Pret.: *were*. PART. PAS.: . | GER.: *being*.

**beach** (bi·ch) *s.* playa. *2* guijo.

**beach (to)** *intr.-tr.* MAR. encallar, varar [en la playa].

**beachy** (-i) *adj.* playado. *2* cubierto de guijo.

**beacon** (bi·kən) *s.* almenara. *2* atalaya [torre, eminencia]. *3* faro, farola, fanal. *4* baliza, señal. *5* radiofaro.

**beacon (to)** *tr.* iluminar, guiar. *2* guarnecer de faros, señales, etc. *3 intr.* brillar [como un faro].

**bead** (bid) *s.* cuenta [de rosario]. *2* cuenta, abalorio, agallón. *3* glóbulo, grano, gota, burbuja. *4* ARQ., QUÍM. perla. *5* pallón. *6* punto [de un arma de fuego]. *7* moldura convexa; junquillo, astrágalo. *8* reborde redondeado. *9 pl.* sarta de cuentas; rosario.

**bead (to)** *tr.* adornar con cuentas o abalorios. *2 intr.* burbujear, ser espumoso.

**beading** (-ing) *s.* cuentas, abalorios. *2* BEAD. *3* espuma [en un licor].

**beadle** (bi·dəl) *s.* alguacil, macero. *2* pertiguero. *3* bedel.

**beady** (bi·di) *adj.* parecido a un abalorio: *~ eyes*, ojos pequeños, redondos y brillantes. *2* espumoso [licor].

**beagle** (bi·gəl) *s.* sabueso.

**beak** (bik) *s.* pico [de ave, de vasija, de un objeto]. *2* pitorro. *3 fig.* nariz. *4* promontorio. *5* mechero [de gas]. *6* MAR., BOT. espolón. *7* MÚS. boquilla. *8 pop.* juez, magistrado.

**beaker** (-ø·r) *s.* copa o vaso de boca ancha. *2* QUÍM. vaso de precipitados.

**beaky** (-i) *adj.* picudo, narigudo.

**beam** (bim) *s.* viga, madero. *2* astil [de balanza o romana]. *3* enjulio; plegador [de telar]. *4* MEC. balancín. *5* lanza [de coche]. *6* bao. *7* manga [de un buque]: *on the ~*, por el través. *8* rayo, haz de rayos [de luz, calor, etc.].

**beam (to)** *tr.* emitir [luz, calor, etc.]. *2 intr.* destellar, brillar. *2* sonreír.

**beaming** (-ing) *adj.* brillante, resplandeciente. *2* radiante, sonriente.

**beamy** (-i) *adj.* BEAMING. *2* macizo como una viga.

**bean** (bin) *s.* BOT. haba; alubia, habichuela, judía.

*2* grano, semilla [de café o cacao]. *3 fam.* cabeza, chola.

**bear** (be·r) *s.* oso, osa. *2 fig.* bajista [en Bolsa]. *3* ASTR. *Great Bear*, Osa Mayor; *Little Bear*, Osa Menor.

**bear (to)** *tr.* llevar [una carga; una inscripción, una señal, una fecha; un nombre; espada, arma; una insignia, etc.]. *2* dar, producir, rendir. *3* dar [hijos]; dar a luz. *4* sostener, soportar. *5* sufrir, padecer; tolerar, aguantar, resistir. *6* tener [un aspecto, una cualidad; responsabilidad, parte, etc.]. *7* tener, profesar [amor, etc.]; guardar [rencor]. *8* tener, guardar [relación, analogía, etc.]. *9* hacer bajar [los valores]. *10* Otros sentidos: *to ~ a hand*, ayudar; *to ~ company*, hacer compañía; *to ~ in mind*, tener presente; *to ~ oneself*, portarse, conducirse; *to ~ witness*, dar testimonio.

*11 intr.* tener aguante, resistir. *12* ser paciente. *13* inclinarse, dirigirse o estar situado hacia. *14 to ~ on* o *upon*, referirse, aplicarse a; versar sobre; apuntar a [hablando de un arma]; pesar, tener efecto sobre. *15 to ~ up*, tener valor, mantenerse firme. ¶ Pret.: *bore*; p. p.: *borne*.

**beard** (bi·rd) *s.* barba [pelo]. *2* barbilla [de pez]. *3* lengüeta [de flecha]. *4* raspas [de la espiga].

**beard (to)** *tr.* mesar, arrancar las barbas. *2* desafiar, retar.

**bearded** (-id) *adj.* barbado, barbudo. *2* aristado. *3* barbato [cometa].

**beardless** (-lis) *adj.* imberbe, carilampiño. *2* desraspado, mocho [trigo].

**bearer** (be·rø·r) *s.* portador. *2* dador [de una carta]. *3* camillero. *4* andero. *5* ARQ., MEC. soporte, caballete, asiento. *6* árbol fructífero.

**bearing** (be·ring) *s.* porte, conducción. *2* presión, acción sobre. *3* producción [de frutos, flores, etc.]. *4* conducta, porte, aire, continente. *5* paciencia, aguante. *6* ARQ., MEC. apoyo, sostén. *7* MEC. cojinete. *8* MAR. orientación, situación, marcación, demora. *9* relación, conexión. *10* intención, fuerza; sentido [de lo que se dice]. *11 pl.* armas, blasones. *12 adj.* de apoyo, de contacto. *13* productivo, que lleva: *fruit ~*, fructífero.

**bearish** (-ish) *adj.* rudo, brusco, osuno.

**bear's-ear** *s.* BOT. oreja de oso.

**bearskin** (be·ø·r·skin) *s.* piel de oso. *2* birretina.

**beast** (bist) *s.* bestia, animal. *2* hombre brutal.

**beastly** (-li) *s.* bestial, brutal; horrible.

**beat** (bit) *s.* golpe; latido, pulsación; son repetido. *2* toque [en el tambor]. *3* tictac [del reloj]. *4* MÚS. tiempo [del compás]. *5* ronda, recorrido [de un guardia, un vigilante, etc.].

**beat (to)** *tr.* pegar, apalizar. *2* golpear, aporrear, azotar. *3* moler, sacudir [golpeando], machacar. *4* tocar [el tambor o en el tambor]. *5* batir [metales; huevos]. *6* hollar [un camino]. *7* batir, vencer, derrotar. *8* ganar, aventajar, sobrepujar. *9* marcar con golpes o movimientos: *to ~ time*, llevar el compás. *10* MONT. batir [el monte, etc.]. *11 to ~ a retreat*, emprender la retirada. *12 intr.* batir, golpear [en]; llamar [a la puerta]; ludir. *13* latir, palpitar, vibrar. *14* MAR. voltejear. *15 to ~ about the bush*, fig. andar con rodeos. ¶ Pret.: *beat*; p. p.: *beaten*.

**beaten** (-n) *adj.* batido. *2* trillado [camino]. *3* vencido; cansado, agotado.

**beater** (-ø·r) *s.* batidor, golpeador, apaleador. *2* vencedor. *3* MONT. batidor.

**beatific(al** (biati·fik(al) *f.* beatífico.

**beatification** (biætifikei·shøn) *s.* beatificación.
**beatify (to)** (biæ·tifai) *tr.* beatificar.
**beating** (bɪ·ting) *s.* paliza. *2* golpeo. *3* latido, pulsación. *4* ojeo. *5* MAR. voltejeo.
**beatitude** (biæ·titiud) *s.* beatitud. *2 the Beatitudes*, las bienaventuranzas.
**beau** (bou), *pl.* **beaux** o **beaus** *s.* elegante, lechuguino. *2* galán, cortejo.
**beauteous** (biu·tiøs) *adj.* BEAUTIFUL.
**beautiful** (biu·tiful) *adj.* hermoso, bello. *2* lindo, precioso.
**beautify (to)** (biu·tifai) *tr.* hermosear, embellecer, adornar, acicalar. *2 intr.* hermosearse, embellecerse. ¶ Pret. y p. p.: *beautified.*
**beauty** (biu·ti) *s.* belleza, hermosura, perfección: ~ *spot*, lunar, postizo. *2* belleza, beldad [mujer].
**beaver** (bɪ·vøʳ) *s.* castor [animal, piel, pelo, fieltro, tela]. *2* sombrero de copa. *3* ARM. babera. *4* ARM. visera.
**becalm (to)** (bika·m) *tr.* calmar, sosegar, serenar. *2* detener [a un buque] la falta de viento.
**became** (bikei·m) *pret.* de TO BECOME.
**because** (biko·š) *conj.* porque. *2 ~ of*, a causa de, por causa de.
**beccafico** (bekafɪ·kou) *s.* ORN. papafigo.
**bechance (to)** (bichæ·ns) *tr.* e *intr.* ocurrir, suceder, acontecer.
**beck** (bek) *s.* seña [con la cabeza o la mano]; *at one's ~ and call*, a la disposición de uno. *2* riachuelo.
**beck (to)** *tr.-intr.* TO BECKON.
**beckon** (be·køn) *s.* BECK.
**beckon (to)** *tr.* llamar, indicar algo [a uno] por señas. *2 intr.* hacer señas.
**becloud (to)** (biklau·d) *tr.* obscurecer, anublar.
**become (to)** (bikø·m) *tr.* convenir, cuadrar, sentar, caer o ir bien; ser propio o decoroso. *2 intr.* volverse, hacerse, convertirse en, llegar a ser; ponerse: *to ~ angry*, ponerse furioso, enojarse; *to ~ old*, hacerse viejo, envejecer. *3 to ~ of*, ser de, parar en, hacerse: *what has become of Peter?*, ¿qué ha sido, o se ha hecho de Pedro? ¶ Pret.: *became*; p. p.: *become.*
**becoming** (-ing) *adj.* que sienta, va o está bien. *2* adecuado, conveniente, propio, decoroso. *3* apuesto.
**bed** (bed) *s.* cama, lecho, yacija: *to go to ~*, acostarse. *2* GEOGR. lecho, álveo, cauce, madre. *3* solera [de acequia]. *4* macizo, cuadro, tabla [de jardín o huerto]. *5* asiento, base, cimiento. *6* MAR. basada. *7* ALBAÑ. lecho. *8* lecho, capa, estrato, yacimiento.
**bed (to)** *tr.* acostar. *2* dar cama. *3* asentar, dar asiento o base. *4* plantar, sembrar [en cuadros o tablas]. *5* disponer en capas. *6 intr.* acostarse; yacer. ¶ Pret. y p. p.: *bedded*; ger.: *bedding.*
**bedabble (to)** (bidæ·bøl) *tr.* mojar, rociar.
**bedaub (to)** (bido·b) *tr.* embadurnar. *2* TO BEDIZEN.
**bedazzle (to)** (bidæ·šøl) *tr.* deslumbrar.
**bedbug** (be·dbug) *s.* ENT.. chinche.
**bedchamber** (-cheimbøʳ) *s.* alcoba, dormitorio.
**bedclothes** (-clouðš) *s. pl.* ropas de cama.
**bedcover** (-køvøʳ) *s.* cubrecama.
**bedding** (-ing) *s.* colchones y ropa de cama. *2* cama [para el ganado]. *3* ALBAÑ., MEC. asiento. *4* empotramiento. *5* estratificación.
**bedeck (to)** (bide·k) *tr.*adornar, engalanar, ataviar.
**bedevil** (bide·vøl) *tr.* endemoniar. *2* hechizar. *3* enredar. *4* enloquecer.
**bedew (to)** (bidiu·) *tr.* rociar, regar.
**bedim (to)** (bidi·m) *tr.* oscurecer, ofuscar.

**bedizen** (bidai·šøn) *tr.* emperejilar.
**bedlam** (be·dlam) *s.* casa de orates, manicomio. *2* belén, confusión, desbarajuste.
**bedlamite** (-ait) *s.* loco, orate.
**Bedouin** (be·duin) *adj.-s.* beduino. *2* nómada.
**bedpan** (be·dpæn) *s.* chata, silleta. *2* calentador de cama.
**bedplate** (-pleit) *s.* MEC. bancada, platina.
**bedraggle** (bidræ·gøl) *tr.* ensuciar arrastrando por el suelo, el lodo, etc.
**bedrid(en** (be·drid(øn) *adj.* postrado en cama.
**bedrock** (-rak) *s.* lecho de roca, roca firme. *2* fig. fondo, base, fundamento.
**bedroom** (-rum) *s.* alcoba, dormitorio.
**bedside** (-said) *s.* lado de la cama, cabecera.
**bedsore** (-soʳ) *s.* encentadura, úlcera de decúbito.
**bedspread** (-spred) *s.* cobertor, cubrecama.
**bedspring** (-spring) *s.* colchón de muelles, somier.
**bedstead** (-sted) *s.* armadura de la cama.
**bestraw** (-stro) *s.* BOT. cuajaleche.
**bedtime** (be·dtaim) *s.* hora de acostarse.
**bee** (bɪ) *s.* ENT. abeja: ~ *eater*, ORN. abejaruco. *2* reunión, tertulia.
**beech** (bɪch) *s.* BOT. haya.
**beechen** (-øn) *adj.* de haya.
**beechnut** (-nøt) *s.* fabuco, hayuco.
**beef** (bɪf) *s.* carne de vaca, buey o toro. *2* res vacuna de matadero. *3* fam. músculo, fuerza muscular.
**beefeater** (-itøʳ) *s.* alabardero.
**beefsteak** (-stek) *s.* biftec, bisté.
**beehive** (bɪ·jaiv) *s.* colmena.
**beekeeper** (bɪkɪ·pøʳ) *s.* colmenero.
**bee-line** *s.* línea recta, derechura: *to make a ~ for*, ir en línea recta hacia.
**Beelzebub** (bie·lššibøb) *n. pr.* Belcebú.
**been** (lbin) *p. p.* de TO BE.
**beer** (bɪ·ʳ) *s.* cerveza.
**beerhouse** (-) *s.* cervecería.
**beeswax** (bɪ·šuæks) *s.* cera de abejas.
**beet** (bɪt) *s.* remolacha.
**beetle** (bɪ·tøl) *s.* ENT. escarabajo. *2* ENT. cucaracha. *3* pisón, aplanadera. *4* mazo; mano, majadero. *5* TEJ. batán. *6 adj.* saliente.
**beetle (to)** *tr.* apisonar; majar. *2* batanar. *3 intr.* salir, sobresalir.
**beetrave** (bɪ·treiv), **beetrot** (-rut) *s.* BEET.
**beeves** (bivš) *s. pl.* reses vacunas.
**befall (to)** (bifo·l) *intr.-tr.* ocurrir, acontecer, sobrevenir. ¶ Pret.: *befell*; p. p.: *befallen.*
**befit (to)** (bifi·t) *intr.* convenir, cuadrar, sentar bien; ser propio o digno de. ¶ Pret. y p. p.: *befitted*; ger.: *befitting.*
**befitting** (-ing) *adj.* conveniente, adecuado, digno de. *2* propio, decoroso.
**befog (to)** (bifo·g) *tr.* envolver en niebla. *2* fig. confundir, obscurecer. ¶ Pret. y p. p.: *befogged*; ger.: *befogging.*
**befool (to)** (bifu·l) *tr.* engañar. *2* entontecer.
**before** (bifo·ʳ) *adv.* antes, anteriormente, primero. *2* delante, al frente, enfrente. *3 prep.* antes de o que. *4* delante de, enfrente de; ante, en presencia de.
**beforehand** (-jænd) *adv.* de antemano, con antelación: *to be ~ with*, anticiparse a. *2 adj.* hecho de antemano.
**befoul (to)** (bifau·l) *tr.* ensuciar, emporcar.
**befriend (to)** (bifre·nd) *tr.* tratar como amigo; favorecer, amparar, proteger.
**befuddle (to)** (bifu·døl) *tr.* turbar los sentidos.
**beg (to)** (beg) *tr.* pedir, mendigar, solicitar; rogar.

*2* Ús. por cortesía: *I ~ to inform you that,* he de comunicarle que. *3 to ~ the question,* cometer petición de principio. *4 intr.* pedir limosna. ¶ Pret. y p. p.: *begged;* ger.: *begging.*

**began** (bigæ·n) *pret.* de TO BEGIN.

**beget (to)** (bige·t) *tr.* engendrar [procrear, originar]. ¶ Pret.: *begot;* p. p.: *begotten* o *-got.*

**begettal** (-al) *s.* engendramiento.

**beggar** (be·gaʳ) *s.* mendigo, pordiosero. *2* pobre, miserable. *3* pícaro, bribón.

**beggar (to)** *tr.* empobrecer, arruinar. *2* agotar, apurar.

**beggarly** (-li) *adj.* pobre, miserable; mezquino. *2 adv.* pobremente.

**begging** (be·ging) *adj.* mendicante. *2 s.* acción de pedir; mendicación, pordioseo.

**begin (to)** (bigi·n) *tr.* e *intr.* empezar, comenzar, principiar. *2 tr.* iniciar. *3 intr.* nacer [tomar principio]. ¶ Pret.: *began;* p. p.: *begun;* ger.: *beginning.*

**beginner** (-øʳ) *s.* principiante, novicio, novato. *2* iniciador, originador.

**beginning** (-ing) *s.* principio, comienzo, iniciación; albores. *2* principio, causa, origen.

**begird (to)** (bigøˑʳd) *tr.* ceñir, rodear.

**begone!** (bigo·n) *interj.* ¡fuera!, ¡vete!

**begonia** (bigouˑnia) *s.* begonia.

**begot** (biga·t) *pret.* y *p. p.* de TO BEGET.

**begotten** (-øn) *p. p.* de TO BEGET.

**begrime (to)** (bigrai·m) *tr.* tiznar, ensuciar.

**begrudge (to)** (bigrøˑdÿ) *tr.* TO GRUDGE.

**beguile (to)** (bigai·l) *tr.* engañar, seducir: *to ~ of,* estafar, defraudar. *2* entretener [el ocio], pasar [el tiempo].

**beguiler** (-øʳ) *s.* engañador.

**begun** (bigø·n) *p. p.* de TO BEGIN.

**behalf** (bijæ·f) *s.* nombre, cuenta, interés, defensa: *in ~ of,* en interés de, en defensa de; *on ~ of,* en nombre de; por cuenta de.

**behave (to)** (bijei·v) *intr.-ref.* obrar, proceder, conducirse, portarse. *2* portarse bien.

**behavio(u)r** (-iøʳ) *s.* proceder, conducta, comportamiento. *2* BIOL., MEC. comportamiento.

**behead (to)** (bije·d) *tr.* decapitar, descabezar.

**beheading** (-ing) *s.* decapitación.

**beheld** (bije·ld) *pret.* y *p. p.* de TO BEHOLD.

**behind** (bijai·nd) *adv.* detrás. *2* a la zaga, en zaga. *3* atrás, hacia atrás. *4 prep.* detrás de; después de: *~ time,* tarde, con retraso.

**behindhand** (-jænd) *adv.* con retraso, con atraso. *2* en déficit. *3 adj.* atrasado, retrasado.

**behold (to)** (bijou·ld) *tr.* ver, mirar, contemplar, observar. ¶ Pret. y p. p.: *beheld.*

**beholden** (-øn) *s.* obligado [por gratitud]; deudor [de beneficios].

**beholder** (-øʳ) *s.* espectador, observador.

**behoof** (bijuˑf) *s.* provecho, utilidad, interés.

**behoove** (bijuˑv), **behove (to)** (bijou·v) *intr.* tocar, atañer, corresponder, incumbir. *2* importar, ser necesario.

**being** (brˑing) *ger.* de TO BE: siendo, estando; que es o está. *2 s.* ser, existencia. *3* estado, condición. *4* ser, ente, criatura, esencia, substancia.

**bejewel (to)** (biÿu·l) *tr.* enjoyar.

**belabo(u)r** (to) (bilei·bøʳ) *tr.* pegar, apalear, maltratar. *2* trabajar [una materia].

**belated** (-tid) *adj.* retardado, tardío. *2* sorprendido por la noche.

**belaying pin** (bile·ing) *s.* MAR. cabilla.

**belch** (belch) *s.* eructo.

**belch (to)** *intr.* eructar. *2 tr.* vomitar [llamas, injurias, etc.].

**beldam** (bel·dam) *s.* vieja, bruja, arpía.

**beleaguer (to)** (bilrˑgøʳ) *tr.* sitiar, cercar, rodear.

**beleaguerer** (-øʳ) *s.* sitiador.

**belfry** (be·lfri) *s.* campanario, torre.

**Belgian** (be·ldÿian) *adj.-s.* belga.

**Belgium** (be·ldÿiøm) *n. pr.* GEOGR. Bélgica.

**Belgrade** (belgrei·d) *n. pr.* Belgrado.

**belie (to)** (bilai·) *tr.* desmentir, contradecir. *2* disfrazar, falsear. *3* calumniar. *4* defraudar [una esperanza].

**belief** (bilrˑf) *s.* creencia. *2* credo, religión, opinión, convicción. *3* REL. fe. *4* fe, confianza.

**believe (to)** (bilrˑv) *tr.-intr.* creer. *2* pensar, opinar [bien, mal, etc., de].

**believer** (-øʳ) *s.* creyente, fiel.

**believing** (-ing) *adj.* creyente.

**belittle (to)** (bili·tøl) *tr.* empequeñecer. *2* rebajar, hablar con desprecio de.

**bell** (bel) *s.* campana; campanilla; timbre: *~ boy,* botones; *~ glass, ~ jar,* campana de vidrio; *~ ringer,* campanero, esquila, cascabel. *3* tañido de campanas, campanada: *passing ~,* doble [por los difuntos]. *4* BOT. carola acampanada. *5* pabellón [de trompeta, etc.]. *6* MÚS. *~ tree,* chinesco.

**bell (to)** *tr.* poner campanilla, etc.: *to ~ the cat,* poner el cascabel al gato. *2* acampanar. *3 intr.* crecer en forma de campana. *4* bramar [el ciervo].

**belladonna** (belada·na) *s.* belladona.

**belle** (bel) *f.* bella, beldad.

**bellflower** (be·lflauøʳ) *s.* BOT. campánula, farolillo.

**bellicose** (be·likous) *adj.* belicoso.

**bellied** (be·lid) *adj.* ventrudo, panzudo.

**belligerence, -cy** (bili·dÿørøns, -i) *s.* beligerancia. *2 adj.* belicoso, guerrero.

**belligerent** (bili·dÿørønt) *adj.-s.* beligerante. *2 adj.* belicoso, guerrero.

**bellman** (be·lmæn) *s.* campanillero, pregonero.

**bellmouthed** (-mauzt) *adj.* abocardado.

**bellow** (be·lou) *s.* bramido, mugido, berrido, rugido.

**bellow (to)** *intr.* bramar, mugir, berrear, rugir. *2* vociferar.

**bellows** (be·lous) *s. sing.* y *pl.* fuelle.

**belly** (be·li) *s.* vientre, panza, barriga. *2* estómago.

**belly (to)** *tr.* hinchar, combar, abultar. *2 intr.* pandear. *3* hincharse [las velas].

**bellyful** (-ful) *s.* panzada, hartazgo.

**belong (to)** (bilo·ng) *intr.* pertenecer. *2* tocar, corresponder, incumbir; ser propio [de]. *3* ser [de un lugar].

**belongings** (-ings) *s. pl.* pertenencias. *2* efectos, bártulos.

**beloved** (bilø·v(i)d) *adj.* querido, amado, dilecto. *2 s.* persona amada.

**below** (bilou·) *adv.* abajo, debajo. *2* en el infierno. *3* más abajo [en un escrito]. *4 prep.* bajo, debajo de, por debajo de: *~ zero,* bajo cero. *5* indigno de.

**belt** (belt) *s.* cinturón, cinto, faja, ceñidor; *to hit below the ~,* dar un golpe bajo. *2* [lo que rodea]. *3* ARQ. cinta, faja. *4* ASTR., GEOGR. zona. *5* correa de transmisión. *6 ~ conveyor,* correa o banda transportadora.

**belt (to)** *tr.* ceñir, rodear, fajar. *2* poner correa [a una máquina]. *3 fam.* dar correazos.

**belting** (-ing) *s.* cinturones, correas.

**belvedere** (belvidrˑʳ) *s.* belvedere. *2* cenador.

**bemire** (bimai·ʳ) *tr.* arrastrar por el fango, enlodar, manchar.

**bemoan (to)** (bimou·n) *tr.* llorar, lamentar, deplorar.

**bemuse (to)** (bimiu·š) *tr.* aturdir, atontar.

**bench** (bench) *s.* banco, escaño; banqueta [asiento]. *2* consejo, tribunal. *3* asiento de los jueces. *4* judicatura. *5* MAR., MIN. bancada. *6* banco [de artesano]. *7* ~ *show*, exposición canina.

**bench (to)** *tr.* proveer de bancos. *2* sentar en un banco. *3* poner en un tribunal. *4* exhibir [perros]. *5 intr.* ocupar un banco.

**bend** (bend) *s.* inclinación. *2* curvatura, curva, recodo, meandro. *3* codo, ángulo. *4* MAR. nudo, gaza. *5* BLAS. barra.

**bend (to)** *tr.* encorvar, enarcar, combar, doblar, torcer, acodillar: *to* ~ *the knee*, doblar la rodilla. *2* poner en tensión; armar [el arco]. *3* inclinar. *4* dirigir, volver, encaminar: *to* ~ *one's efforts*, dirigir sus esfuerzos. *5* doblegar, someter. *6* MAR. atar, entalingar, envergar. *7 intr.* encorvarse, combarse, doblegarse, torcerse. *8* desviarse, torcer. *9* inclinarse. *10* dirigirse, tender. *11* aplicarse. ¶ Pret. y p. p.: *bent*.

**bending** (be·nding) *s.* acción de torcer, doblar, etc.; flexión; cimbreo. *2* recodo, revuelta.

**beneath** (binɪ·z) *adv.* abajo, debajo. *2 prep.* bajo, debajo de. *3* por debajo [en rango, dignidad, etc.]. *4* indigno de.

**benedicte** (benidi·siti) *s.* benedícite.

**Benedict** (be·nidikt) *n. pr.* Benito, Benedicto.

**Benedictine** (benidi·ktin) *adj.-s.* benedictino.

**benediction** (-di·kshøn) *s.* bendición.

**benefaction** (-æ·kshøn) *s.* beneficio, merced, gracia, donación.

**benefactor** (-fæ·ktøʳ) *s.* bienhechor. *2* donador, fundador.

**benefactress** (-fæ·ktris) *s.* bienhechora. *2* donadora, fundadora.

**benefice** (be·nifis) *s.* beneficio [feudal o eclesiástico].

**beneficence** (bine·fisøns) *s.* beneficencia, bondad, caridad.

**beneficent** (-ønt) *adj.* benéfico, bondadoso, caritativo.

**beneficial** (benifi·shal) *adj.* beneficioso, provechoso.

**beneficiary** (benifi·shari) *adj.* beneficial. *2 s.* ECLES. beneficiado. *3* beneficiario.

**benefit** (be·nifit) *s.* beneficio, favor. *2* beneficio, bien, utilidad, provecho; disfrute. *3* TEAT. beneficio.

**benefit (to)** *tr.* beneficiar, aprovechar [a uno]. *2 intr.* beneficiarse.

**benevolence** (bine·valøns) *s.* benevolencia, caridad, humanidad. *2* gracia, merced.

**benevolent** (-ønt) *adj.* benévolo, bondadoso, caritativo.

**Bengal** (bengol) *n. pr.* GEÓGR. Bengala.

**Bengalese** (bengali·š), **Bengali** (bengo·li) *adj.-s.* bengalí.

**benighted** (binai·tid) *adj.* sorprendido por la noche. *2* rodeado de tinieblas. *3* ignorante.

**benign** (binai·n) *adj.* benigno, afable. *2* propicio. *3* benigno [clima, enfermedad].

**benignancy** (bini·gnansi) *s.* benignidad, afabilidad.

**benignant** (-nant) *adj.* benigno, afable, bondadoso. *2* favorable, beneficioso.

**benignity** (bini·gniti) *s.* benignidad. *2* favor, merced.

**Benjamin** (be·ndẏømin) *n. pr.* Benjamín. *2 s.* [con min.] benjuí.

**bent** (bent) *pret.* y *p. p.* de TO BEND. *2 adj.* torcido, encorvado, doblado. *3* ~ *on* o *upon*, empeñado en, resuelto a. *4 s.* encorvamiento, curvatura. *5* inclinación, propensión, tendencia, afición. *6* declive. *7* capacidad de resistencia. *8* BOT. nombre de varias plantas.

**benthos** (be·nzøs) *s.* BIOL. bentos.

**benumb (to)** (binø·m) *tr.* entumecer, aterir. *2* entorpecer, embotar.

**benzene** (be·nšin o benši·n) *s.* benceno.

**benzine** (be·nšin) *s.* bencina [del petróleo].

**benzoin** (be·nšoin) *s.* benzoina. *2* benjuí.

**bequeath (to)** (bikui·ð o -kui·z) *tr.* legar, dejar.

**bequether** (-øʳ) *s.* testador, el que lega.

**bequest** (bikue·st) *s.* legado, manda.

**berate (to)** (birei·t) *tr.* reñir, reprender.

**Berber** (bø·ʳbeʳ) *adj.-s.* bereber.

**bereave (to)** (birɪ·v) *tr.* privar, desposeer de. *2* desolar, desconsolar; dejar [la muerte] sin un ser querido. ¶ Pret. y p. p.: *bereaved* o *bereft*.

**bereavement** (-mønt) *s.* privación, despojo. *2* soledad, desamparo, duelo; pérdida de un ser querido.

**bereft** (bire·ft) *pret.* y *p. p.* de TO BEREAVE.

**beret** (be·rei) *s.* boina.

**berg** (bø·ʳg) *s.* ICEBERG.

**bergamot** (bø·ʳgamat) *s.* BOT. bergamoto. *2* bergamota. *3* sándalo de jardín.

**Berlin** (bø·ʳli·n) *n. pr.* GEOGR. Berlín. *2 s.* [con min.] berlina [coche, auto].

**Bern** (bø·ʳn o be·ʳn) *n. pr.* GEOGR. Berna.

**Bernard** (bø·ʳnaʳd) *n. pr.* Bernardo.

**berry** (be·ri) *s.* baya. *2* nombre de otros frutos como la mora, la fresa, etc.

**berth** (bø·ʳz) *s.* MAR. espacio para maniobrar: *to give a wide* ~ *to*, evitar, apartarse de. *2* anclaje, amarradero. *3* dársena. *4* camarote, litera. *5* fam. empleo, destino.

**berth (to)** *tr.* MAR. amarrar. *2* dar litera o empleo.

**Bertha** (bø·ʳza) *n. pr.* Berta.

**beryl** (be·ri·l) *s.* MINER. berilo.

**beseech (to)** (bisi·ch) *tr.* pedir, implorar; suplicar, rogar. ¶ Pret. y p. p.: *besought* o *beseeched*.

**beseecher** (-øʳ) *s.* rogador, suplicante.

**beseem (to)** (bisi·m) *tr.-intr.* cuadrar, estar bien. *2* ser propio o decoroso.

**beset (to)** (bise·t) *tr.* asediar, estrechar, acosar. *2* cercar, rodear. *3* adornar, tachonar. ¶ Pret. y p. p.: *beset*; ger.: *besetting*.

**besetting** (-ing) *adj.* constante, dominante: ~ *sin*, flaco, vicio dominante.

**beside** (bisai·d) *adv.* cerca, al lado. *2* además. *3 prep.* al lado de, cerca de, junto a. *4* en comparación de. *5* fuera de: ~ *oneself*, fuera de sí; ~ *the point*, que no viene al caso.

**besides** (-š) *adv.* además, por otra parte, asimismo. *2 prep.* además de. *3* excepto, fuera de.

**besiege (to)** (bisi·ÿ) *tr.* sitiar. *2* asediar, acosar.

**besieger** (-øʳ) *s.* sitiador; asediador.

**besmear (to)** (bismɪ·ʳ) *tr.* embadurnar, untar.

**besmirch (to)** (bismø·ʳch) *tr.* manchar, ensuciar. *2* mancillar.

**besom** (bɪ·šøm) *s.* escoba. *2* retama.

**besot (to)** (bisa·t) *tr.* entontecer, embrutecer. *2* enamorar tontamente. ¶ Pret. y p. p.: *besotted*; ger.: *besotting*.

**besought** (biso·t) *pret.* y *p. p.* de TO BESEECH.

**bespangle (to)** (bispæ·ngøl) *tr.* adornar con lentejuelas o cosas brillantes.

**bespatter** (bispæ·tø<sup>r</sup>) *tr.* salpicar, manchar.
**bespeak (to)** (bispɪ·k) *tr.* apalabrar, encargar, hacer reservar. *2* indicar, denotar, pronosticar. *3* poét. hablar [a uno]. ¶ Pret.: *bespoke;* p. p.: *bespoken* o *-spoke.*
**bespread (to)** (bispre·d) *tr.* cubrir [esparciendo]. *2* esparcir, tender. ¶ Pret. y p. p.: *bespread.*
**besprinkle (to)** (bispri·ngkøl) *tr.* rociar, salpicar, espolvorear, sembrar.
**best** (best) *adj. superl.* de GOOD; mejor, óptimo, superior: ~ *girl,* novia, amiga preferida; ~ *man,* padrino de boda; ~ *seller,* éxito de librería, libro de mayor venta; *it is* ~, es mejor. *2* mayor [en extensión]: *the* ~ *part of,* la mayor parte de. *3 adv.* super. de WELL: mejor; mucho; más: *the* ~ *known,* el más conocido.
*4 s.* lo mejor, lo más: *to do one's* ~, esmerarse; *to get the* ~ *of,* llevar la ventaja a; vencer; *to make the* ~ *of,* sacar el mejor partido de; *at* ~, *at the* ~, en el mejor de los casos; a lo más; *for the* ~, con la mejor intención; conducente al bien, a lo mejor.
*5 pron. the* ~, el mejor, el que más.
**bestead** (biste·d) *adj.* situado. *2* rodeado de peligros, etc.
**bestead (to)** *tr.* servir, aprovechar, ayudar.
**bestial** (be·stial) *adj.* bestial, brutal, abrutado.
**bestiality** (bestiæ·liti) *s.* bestialidad.
**bestialize (to)** (be·stialaiš) *tr.* embrutecer.
**bestiary** (be·stieri) *s.* bestiario.
**bestir (to)** (bistø·<sup>r</sup>) *tr.* mover, animar, incitar: *to* ~ *oneself,* menearse, afanarse.
**bestow (to)** (bistou·) *tr.* dar, conceder, otorgar, dispensar, conferir. *2* gastar, emplear.
**bestowal** (-al) *s.* concesión, dádiva, don. *2* empleo, dedicación [de tiempo, etc.].
**bestower** (-ø<sup>r</sup>) *s.* donador, dispensador.
**bestrew (to)** (bistru·) *tr.* cubrir, sembrar [de]. *2* cubrir, estar esparcido sobre. ¶ Pret.: *bestrewed;* p. p.: *bestrewn* o *-trewed.*
**bestride (to)** (bistrai·d) *tr.* montar [a horcajadas]. *2* estar [sobre algo] a horcajadas. *3* cruzar [de un tranco]. ¶ Pret.: *bestrode;* p. p.: *bestridden* o *bestrid.*
**bet** (bet) *s.* apuesta.
**bet (to)** *tr.-intr.* apostar [dinero, etc.]; *to* ~ *on,* apostar a o por. ¶ Pret. y p. p.: *bet* o *betted;* ger.: *betting.*
**beta** (bei·ta) *s.* beta [letra griega].
**betake (to)** (bitei·k) *ref.* recurrir, acudir. *2* ir, trasladarse. *3* aplicarse, darse. ¶ Pret.: *betook;* p. p.: *betaken.*
**betel** (bɪtøl) *s.* BOT. betel.
**bethink** (bizi·nk) *tr.-ref.* hacer memoria de, acordarse de, caer en la cuenta de, pensar, considerar. ¶ Pret. y p. p.: *bethought.*
**Bethlehem** (be·zlijem) *n. pr.* GEOGR. Belén.
**bethought** (bizo·t) *pret.* y *p. p.* de TO BETHINK.
**betide (to)** (bitai·d) *tr.-intr.* ocurrir, acaecer, suceder. *2 tr.* presagiar, indicar.
**betime(s** (bitai·m(s) *adv.* con tiempo, a tiempo. *2* pronto, temprano.
**betoken (to)** (bitou·køn) *tr.* presagiar, anunciar. *2* indicar, denotar, dar muestras de.
**betony** (be·tøni) *s.* BOT. betónica.
**betook** (bitu·k) *pret.* de TO BETAKE.
**betray (to)** (bitrei·) *tr.* traicionar, vender, entregar, hacer traición. *2* inducir, llevar [a error, a un peligro, etc.]. *3* revelar, descubrir; mostrar, dejar ver.

**betrayal** (-al) *s.* traición. *2* revelación [de un secreto, un sentimiento, etc.].
**betroth (to)** (bitro·z) *tr.-intr.* desposar, prometer: *to be* o *become betrothed,* desposarse, prometerse.
**betrothal** (-al) *s.* desposorio; noviazgo.
**betrothed** (-t) *adj.-s.* prometido, novio, futuro.
**better** (be·tø<sup>r</sup>) *adj.* compar. de GOOD: mejor; ~ *half,* fig. costilla, cara, mitad; *to get* ~, mejorarse. *2* mayor, más: *the* ~ *part,* la mayor parte.
*3 adv.* comp. de WELL; mejor: ~ *off,* en mejor posición; mejor librado.
*4 s.* lo mejor; ventaja, superioridad: *to change for the* ~, mejorar, mejorarse; *to get the* ~ *of,* aventajar, llevar ventaja, vencer; *all the* ~, *so much the* ~, mejor, tanto mejor. *5* apostante. *6 pl.* superiores, mayores, los que son más [que uno].
**better (to)** *tr.* mejorar, adelantar, favorecer. *2* aventajar, sobrepujar. *3 intr.* mejorar, mejorarse.
**betterment** (-mønt) *s.* mejora, mejoramiento, adelanto.
**bettor** (-ø<sup>r</sup>) *s.* apostante.
**Betty** (-i) *n. pr. dim.* de ELIZABETH.
**between** (bitu·n) *adv.* entremedias, en medio. *2 prep.* entre [una pers. o cosa y otra u otras]: ~ *whiles,* a intervalos.
**betwixt** (bitui·kst) *adv.-prep.* BETWEEN.
**bevel** (be·vøl) *s.* ángulo oblicuo, bisel, chaflán. *2* baivel, falsa regla. *3 adj.* oblicuo, biselado, achaflanado. *4* MEC. cónico.
**bevel (to)** *tr.* biselar, chaflanar. *2* ARQ. falsear. ¶ Pret. y p. p.: *beveled* o *-lled;* ger.: *beveling* o *-lling.*
**beverage** (be·vøridẏ) *s.* bebida, brebaje.
**bevy** (be·vi) *s.* bandada. *2* grupo [de mujeres].
**bewail (to)** (biuei·l) *tr.* llorar, lamentar, deplorar. *2 intr.* lamentarse, plañir.
**beware (to)** (biue·<sup>r</sup>) *tr.* guardarse, recelarse de, tener cuidado con: *beware!,* ¡cuidado [con]!. ¶ Sólo se usa en INFIN. e IMPER.
**bewilder (to)** (biui·ldø<sup>r</sup>) *tr.* desconcertar, desorientar, aturdir, atolondrar, turbar.
**bewilderment** (-mønt) *s.* desconcierto, desorientación, aturdimiento, confusión, perplejidad.
**bewitch (to)** (biui·ch) *tr.* embrujar, hechizar, encantar, fascinar.
**bewitcher** (-ø<sup>r</sup>) *s.* hechicero, encantador.
**bewitchment** (-mønt) *s.* hechizo, embrujamiento. *2* encanto, fascinación.
**bey** (bei) *s.* bey.
**beyond** (biya·nd) *adv.* más allá, al otro lado, allende, a lo lejos. *2 prep.* detrás de, al lado de, más allá de, allende. *3* fuera de, excepto, salvo. *4* fuera de o excediendo los límites o posibilidades de: ~ *doubt,* fuera de duda; ~ *measure,* sobremanera; ~ *oneself,* fuera de sí. *5 s.* el otro mundo, el más allá.
**bezant** (be·šant) *s.* besante.
**bezel** (be·šøl) *s.* bisel. *2* JOY. faceta. *3* JOY. engaste. *4* sello [de una sortija].
**bezel (to)** *tr.* biselar, achaflanar.
**bezique** (beši·k) *s.* juego de naipes.
**bias** (bai·as) *s.* sesgo, oblicuidad. *2* tendencia, predisposición; parcialidad, prejuicio. *3* RADIO. tensión de rejilla. *4 adj.* sesgado.
**bias (to)** *tr.* torcer, inclinar, influir, predisponer. ¶ Pret. y p. p.: *biased* o *-ssed;* ger.: *biasing* o *-ssing.*
**bib** (bib) *s.* barbero, pechero. *2* pechera [de delantal].

**bib (to)** *tr.-intr.* beber, empinar el codo. ¶ Pret. y p. p.: *bibbed;* ger.: *-bbing.*
**bibasic** (baibei·sik) *adj.* bibásico.
**bibber** (bi·bøʳ) *s.* bebedor.
**Bible** (bai·bøl) *s.* Biblia.
**biblical** (bi·blikal) *adj.* bíblico.
**bibliography** (biblia·grafi) *s.* bibliografía.
**bibliophile** (bi·bliofail o -fil) *s.* bibliófilo.
**bibulous** (bi·biuløs) *adj.* esponjoso, absorbente. *2* bebedor, borrachín.
**bicameral** (baikæ·møral) *adj.* bicameral.
**bicarbonate** (baika·ʳbønit) *s.* bicarbonato.
**bice** (bais) *s.* azul o verde pálidos.
**bicephalous** (baisep·faløs) *adj.* bicéfalo.
**biceps** (bai·seps) *adj.-s.* ANAT. bíceps.
**bicker** (bi·køʳ) *s.* disputa, quisquilla.
**bicker (to)** *intr.* disputar, altercar. *2* murmurar [un arroyo, etc.]. *3* temblar, destellar, chisporrotear [una luz, etc.].
**bickering** (-ing) *s.* disputa, altercado.
**biconcave** (baika·nkeiv) *adj.* bicóncavo.
**biconvex** (baika·nveks) *adj.* biconvexo.
**bicuspid** (baikø·spid) *adj.* bicúspide.
**bicycle** (bai·sikøl) *s.* bicicleta.
**bicycle (to)** *intr.* ir en bicicleta.
**bicyclist** (-siklist) *s.* biciclista.
**bid** (bid) *s.* licitación, oferta, puja. *2* declaración [en el bridge].
**bid (to)** *tr.* anunciar, expresar, ofrecer: *to ~ good bye,* decir adiós; *to defiance,* desafiar, retar. *2* ofrecer [un precio], pujar, licitar. *3* ordenar, mandar, pedir. *4* invitar. *5* declarar [en el bridge]. *6 intr.* hacer una oferta, licitar. *7 to ~ fair to,* prometer, dar indicios de. ¶ Pret.: *bade;* p. p.: *bidden;* ger.: *bidding.* | En las acepciones 2 y 5, pret. y p. p.: *bid.*
**bidder** (-øʳ) *s.* licitador, postor. *2* declarante [en el bridge].
**bidding** (-ing) *s.* licitación, postura. *2* mandato, ruego; invitación.
**bide (to)** (baid) *tr.-intr.* ABIDE: *to ~ one's time,* esperar la ocasión, la oportunidad. ¶ Pret.: *bode, bade* o *bided;* p. p.: *bided.*
**bident** (bai·dent) *s.* bidente.
**bidet** (bide·t) *s.* bidé. *2* caballito, jaca.
**biding** (bai·ding) *s.* espera. *2* residencia, permanencia.
**biennial** (baie·nial) *adj.* bienal.
**biennium** (-niøm) *s.* bienio.
**bier** (bɪ·ʳ) *s.* andas, féretro.
**biffid** (bai·fid) *adj.* bífido.
**bifocal** (baifou·kal) *adj.* bifocal.
**bifurcate** (bai·føʳkeit) *adj.* bifurcado.
**bifurcate (to)** *tr.* dividir en dos puntas o ramales. *2 intr.* bifurcarse.
**bifurcation** (-kei·shøn) *s.* bifurcación.
**big** (big) *adj.* grande, importante: *~ game,* caza mayor; *~ bug,* fig. fam. personaje. *2* corpulento, voluminoso, hinchado. *3* imponente. *4* fuerte [voz]. *5* jactancioso, pomposo, amenazador. *6* preñada, lleno. *7 adv.* mucho. *8* pomposamente, jactanciosamente: *to talk ~,* echar bravatas.
**bigamist** (bi·gamist) *s.* bígamo.
**bigamous** (-møs) *adj.* bígamo.
**bigamy** (-mi) *s.* bigamia.
**bigger** (bi·gøʳ) *adj. compar.* de BIG.
**biggest** (bi·gist) *adj. superl.* de BIG.
**biggish** (bi·gish) *adj.* grandote.
**big-headed** *adj.* cabezón. *2* engreído.
**big-hearted** *adj.* magnánimo, valeroso.

**bight** (bait) *s.* MAR. seno de un cabo, gaza. *2* meandro, recodo. *3* ensenada, cala.
**bigmouthed** (bi·gmauzt) *adj.* bocudo. *2* hablador. *3* gritón.
**bigot** (bi·gøt) *s.* fanático, intolerante.
**bigoted** (-id) *adj.* fanático, intolerante.
**bigotry** (-ri) *s.* fanatismo, intolerancia.
**bigwig** (bi·gwig) *s.* fam. personaje.
**bilabial** (bailæ·bial) *adj.* FONÉT. bilabial.
**bilander** (bi·landøʳ) *s.* balandra.
**bilateral** (bailæ·tøral) *adj.* bilateral.
**bilberry** (bi·lberi) *s.* BOT. arándano.
**bile** (bail) *s.* bilis, hiel. *2* fig. cólera, mal humor.
**bilge** (bildÿ) *s.* barriga [de tonel]. *2* MAR. pantoque, sentina.
**bilge (to)** *intr.* MAR. sufrir una vía de agua, hacer agua. *2* hacer barriga, abultar.
**biliary** (bi·liari) *adj.* biliar.
**bilingual** (baili·ngual) *adj.* bilingüe.
**bilious** (bi·liøs) *adj.* bilioso.
**bilk** (bilk) *s.* estafa, trampa. *2* estafador, tramposo.
**bilk (to)** *s.* estafar, defraudar.
**Bill** (bil) *n. pr.* dim. de WILLIAM.
**bill** *s.* pico [de ave]. *2* mandíbulas [de tortuga]. *3* MAR. punta de la uña [del ancla]; extremo [de verga]. *4* pica, alabarda. *5* hocino, podón. *6* cuenta, nota, factura, relación, estado, lista: *~ of fare,* minuta, lista de platos; *~ of lading,* conocimiento de embarque. *7* billete, cédula, documento, letra, pagaré: *~ of exchange,* letra de cambio. *8* patente, certificado. *9* cartel, programa [de teatro], prospecto, hoja. *10* DER. escrito. *11* proyecto de ley; ley.
**bill (to)** *tr.* cargar en cuenta. *2* facturar. *3* anunciar por carteles; poner carteles en. *4 intr.* juntar los picos [las palomas]: *to ~ and coo,* fig. besarse, arrullarse.
**billboard** (bi·lboʳd) *s.* cartelera.
**billet** (bi·lit) *s.* billete, esquela. *2* MIL. boleta. *3* MIL. alojamiento. *4* puesto, colocación, destino. *5* trozo de leña. *6* barra [de oro o hierro].
**billet (to)** *tr.* MIL. alojar. *2* aposentar, colocar.
**billhead** (bi·ljed) *s.* impreso para facturas. *2* encabezamiento de factura.
**billhook** (-juk) *s.* podón.
**billiard** (bi·liaʳd) *adj.* de billar. *2 s.* (E.U.) carambola.
**billiards** (-s) *s.* billar.
**billingsgate** (bi·lingsgeit) *s.* lenguaje soez.
**billion** (bi·liøn) *s.* (Ingl.) billón. *2* (E.U.) mil millones.
**billow** (bi·lou) *s.* oleada, golpe de mar. *2* ola, ondulación.
**billow (to)** *intr.* undular. *2* levantarse como una ola.
**billowy** (-i) *adj.* ondeante, agitado. *2* ondulado. *3* hinchado como una ola.
**Billy** (bi·li) *n. pr.* dim. de WILLIAM. *2 s.* [con mín.] cachiporra. *3 ~ goat,* macho cabrío.
**bimane** (bai·mein) *s.* bímano.
**bimanous** (bi·manøs) *adj.* bímano.
**bimetallism** (baime·tališm) *s.* bimetalismo.
**bimonthly** (baimø·nzli) *adj.* bimestral. *2* quincenal. *3 s.* publicación bimestral o quincenal. *4 adv.* bimestralmente. *5* quincenalmente.
**bin** (bin) *s.* caja, arca, arcón, depósito, recipiente.
**binary** (bai·neri) *adj.* binario.
**bind** (baind) *s.* lazo, ligadura. *2* MÚS. ligado.
**bind (to)** *tr.* ligar, liar, envolver, ceñir, atar, amarrar, sujetar, unir. *2* vendar. *3* ribetear, guar-

necer. *4* trabar, dar consistencia. *5* encuadernar. *6* FISIOL. estreñir, restriñir. *7* obligar, compeler, comprometer. *8* escriturar, contratar [a
uno]. *9 intr.* trabarse, endurecerse, pegarse. *10*
obligar. ¶ Pret. y p. p.: *bound.*
**binder** (-ø<sup>r</sup>) *s.* atador. agavilladora [máquina]. *3*
ribeteador. *4* encuadernador. *5* carpeta, cu-
bierta [para papeles]. *6* aglutinante, cemento. *7*
riostra.
**bindery** (-øri) *s.* encuadernación [taller].
**binding** (-ing) *s.* atadura, ligamiento. *2* venda,
tira, faja, ligadura. *3* COST. ribeteado; ribete,
guarnición. *4* encuadernación: *full* ~, pasta entera; *half* ~, media pasta. *5* trabadura; lo que
traba o espesa. *6 adj.* que ata, une, traba, etc. *7*
obligatorio, valedero. *8* MED. estíptico.
**bindweed** (-uid) *s.* BOT. enredadera; correhuela.
**binnacle** (bi·nakøl) *s.* bitácora.
**binocle** (bi·nøkøl) *s.* binóculo, gemelos.
**binocular** (baina·kiula<sup>r</sup>) *adj.* binocular. *2 s. pl.* ÓPT.
gemelos.
**binomial** (bainou·mial) *s.* binomio.
**biochemistry** (baioke·mistri) *s.* bioquímica.
**biogeny** (-ȳ·ni) *s.* biogenia.
**biographer** (baia·grafø<sup>r</sup>) *s.* biógrafo.
**biography** (-grafi) *s.* biografía.
**biologic(al** (baiola·dȳk(al) *adj.* biológico.
**biologist** (baia·lodȳist) *s.* biólogo.
**biology** (-lodȳi) *s.* biología.
**biophysics** (baiofi·siks) *s.* biofísica.
**bipartite** (baipa·<sup>r</sup>tait) *adj.* bipartido.
**biped** (bai·ped) *adj.-s.* bípedo.
**bipedal** (-al) *adj.* bipede; bípedo.
**biplane** (bai·plein) *adj.-s.* biplano.
**bipolar** (baipou·la<sup>r</sup>) *adj.* bipolar.
**birch** (bø<sup>r</sup>c) *s.* BOT. abedul. *2* vara de abedul.
**birch (to)** *tr.* azotar, castigar.
**birchen** (-øn) *adj.* de abedul.
**bird** (bø<sup>r</sup>d) *s.* ave, pájaro: ~ *of paradise,* ave del
Paraíso; ~ *of passage,* ave de paso; ~ *of prey,* ave
de rapiña; *birds of a feather,* gente de una misma
calaña.
**bird (to)** *intr.* pajarear, cazar pájaros.
**birdcall** (-kol) *s.* reclamo; añagaza.
**birdcatcher** (-kæchø<sup>r</sup>) *m.* pajarero, parancero.
**birding** (-ing) *s.* caza de pájaros.
**birdlime** (-laim) *s.* liga, ajonje.
**bird's-eye view** *s.* lo que se ve a vista de pájaro;
ojeada general.
**bird's-nest (to)** *intr.* coger nidos.
**birefringent** (bairifri·nȳønt) *adj.* birrefringente.
**bireme** (bai·rim) *s.* birreme.
**biretta** (bire·ta) *s.* bonete [de eclesiástico].
**birth** (bø<sup>r</sup>z) *s.* nacimiento: ~ *rate,* natalidad; *by* ~,
de nacimiento. *2* cuna, origen. *3* linaje, alcur-
nia. *4* parto.
**birthday** (-dei) *s.* natalicio, cumpleaños.
**birthmark** (-ma<sup>r</sup>k) *s.* antojo, lunar.
**birthplace** (-pleis) *s.* lugar de nacimiento; pueblo
natal.
**birthright** (-rait) *s.* derecho de nacimiento. *2* primogenitura.
**bis** (bis) *adv.* MÚS. bis.
**Biscay** (bi·skei) *n. pr.* Vizcaya.
**biscuit** (bi·skit) *s.* galleta, bizcocho. *2* CERÁM. bizcocho.
**bisect (to)**(baise·kt) *tr.* bisecar.
**bisector** (-ø<sup>r</sup>) *s.* bisectriz.
**bishop** (bi·shøp) *s.* ECLES. obispo. *2* AJED. alfil.
**bishopric** (-rik) *s.* obispado. *2* diócesis. *3* episcopado [dignidad].

**bisk** (bisk) *s.* sopa sustanciosa.
**bismuth** (bi·śmøz) *s.* QUÍM. bismuto.
**bison** (bai·søn) *s.* ZOOL. bisonte.
**bissextile** (bise·kstil) *adj.* bisiesto.
**bister, bistre** (bi·stø<sup>r</sup>) *s.* bistre.
**bistort** (bi·sto<sup>r</sup>t) *s.* BOT. bistorta.
**bistoury** (bi·sturi) *s.* bisturí.
**bisulcate** (baisø·lkeit) *adj.* bisulco.
**bit** (bit) *s.* pedazo, trozo, pedacito; migaja, pizca,
un poco, un momento: *not a* ~, ni pizca. *2* bocado [de comida]. *3* bocado [del freno]. *4* paletón [de llave]. *5* broca, taladro. *6* boca, corte [de
herramienta].
**bit (to)** *tr.* enfrenar [el caballo]. *2* refrenar. ¶ Pret.
y p. p.: *bitted;* ger.: *bitting.*
**bitch** (bich) *s.* ZOOL. perra; loba; zorra. *2* fam. ramera.
**bite** (bait) *s.* mordedura. *2* mordisco. *3* bocado,
tentempié. *4* picadura [de insecto, etc.]. *5* resquemo [en el paladar]. *6* sensación cortante [del
aire, del frío].
**bite (to)** *tr.-intr.* morder, mordiscar, dentellar. *2*
picar [un insecto, etc.]. *3* resquemar, escocer [la
pimienta, etc.]. *4* cortar [el frío, el aire]. *5* morder, atacar [un ácido, etc.]. *6* MEC. morder, agarrar. *7 tr.* tascar [el freno]. *8* engañar, pegarla. *9*
*intr.* picar, morder el anzuelo. ¶ Pret.: *bit;* p. p.:
*bit* o *bitten.*
**biter** (-ø<sup>r</sup>) *s.* mordedor. *2* engañador.
**biting** (-ing) *adj.* punzante, penetrante. *2* mordaz,
sarcástico. *3* picante [al gusto]. *4* mordedor.
**bitt** (bit) *s.* bita.
**bitten** (-øn) *p. p.* de TO BITE.
**bitter** (bi·tø<sup>r</sup>) *adj.* amargo. *2* áspero, agrio, duro,
cruel, agudo, intenso. *3* mordaz, sarcástico. *4*
enconado, encarnizado. *5 s.* amargor, amargura. *6 pl.* amargo [licor].
**bittern** (-n) *s.* ORN. avetoro.
**bitterness** (-nis) *s.* amargor, amargura. *2* acritud.
*3* dureza, crueldad. *4* rencor. *5 s.* encono.
**bittersweet** (-suit) *adj.* agridulce. *2 s.* lo agridulce.
*3* BOT. dulcamara.
**bitterwort** (-wo<sup>r</sup>t) *s.* BOT. genciana.
**bitumen** (bitiu·møn) *s.* MINER. betún.
**bituminous** (-minøs) *adj.* bituminoso.
**bivalent** (baivei·lønt) *adj.* bivalente.
**bivalve** (bai·vælv) *adj.* bivalvo.
**bivouac** (bi·vuæk) *s.* vivac, vivaque.
**bivouac (to)** *intr.* vivaquear.
**biweekly** (baiu·kli) *adj.* bisemanal.
**bizarre** (biša·<sup>r</sup>) *adj.* raro, original, extravagante.
**blab** (blæb) *s.* hablador. *2* chismoso. *3* charla, habladuría, chisme.
**blab (to)** *tr.* revelar, divulgar. *2 intr.* chismear. ¶
Pret. y p. p.: *blabbed;* ger.: *blagging.*
**blabber** (-ø<sup>r</sup>) *s.* hablador, chismoso; soplón.
**black** (blæk) *adj.* negro: ~ *art,* nigromancia; ~
*beetle,* cucaracha; ~ *currant* BOT. casis, grosella
negra; ~ *friar,* dominico; ~ *lead,* grafito, lápiz
plomo; ~ *monk,* benedictino; *Black Sea,* Mar
Negro; ~ *sheep,* fig. garbanzo negro; *in* ~ *and
white,* por escrito. *2* moreno, atezado. *3* puro
[café]. *4* hosco, ceñudo, terrible, amenazador. *5*
~ *and blue,* lívido, amoratado. *6 adv.* amenazadoramente. *7 s.* negro. *8* luto. *9* moreno, mulato.
*10 pl.* luto. *11* colgaduras de luto.
**black (to)** *tr.* ennegrecer. *2* embetunar, lustrar, dar
bola. *3 intr.* ennegrecerse, negrear. *4 to* ~ *out,*
apagar las luces [como precaución]; desmayarse, perder el sentido.
**blackamoor** (-amu<sup>r</sup>) *s.* negro [esp. africano].

**black-and-blue** adj. acardenalado.
**blackball** (-bol) s. bola negra. 2 betún, bola.
**blackball (to)** tr. dar bola negra. 2 embetunar.
**blackberry** (-beri) s. BOT. zarza. 2 zarzamora.
**blackbird** (-bøʳd) s. ORN. mirlo.
**blackboard** (-boʳd) s. pizarra, encerado.
**blackdam** (-dæmp) s. MIN. mofeta.
**blacken** (-øn) tr. dar o teñir de negro; embetunar. 2 ennegrecer, oscurecer. 3 denigrar, infamar. 4 intr. ennegrecerse, oscurecerse.
**blackface** (-feis) s. IMPR. letra negrilla.
**blackguard** (blæ·gaʳd) s. pillo, bribón, sinvergüenza.
**blackhead** (blæ·kjed) s. espinilla, comedón. 2 ORN. pato marino.
**blacking** (-ing) s. ennegrecimiento. 2 betún, bola, lustre.
**blackish** (-ish) adj. negruzco, oscuro.
**black jack** s. bandera negra [de pirata]. 2 rompecabezas, porra.
**blackleg** (-leg) s. estafador, tramposo. 2 obrero no sindicado; esquirol.
**blackmail** (-meil) s. chantaje.
**blackmail (to)** tr. hacer un chantaje a.
**blackmailer** (-øʳ) s. chantajista.
**blackness** (-nis) s. negrura, oscuridad.
**black-out** s. apagón. 2 desmayo; vértigo de los aviadores.
**blacksmith** (-miz) s. herrero, forjador.
**blackthorn** (-zoʳn) s. BOT. endrino.
**bladder** (blæ·døʳ) s. ANAT., ZOOL. vejiga. 2 vejiga, ampolla. 3 BOT. ~ senna, espantalobos.
**blade** (bleid) s. hoja [de arma, de herramienta]. 2 fig. espada [arma; esgrimidor]. 3 persona lista, decidida, calavera; valentón. 4 pala [de remo]; paleta [de hélice, etc.]. 5 ANAT. parte ancha y plana de un órgano. 6 lámina [de ballena]. 7 limbo [de hoja]. 8 hoja, brizna [de hierba o cereal]. 9 ELECT. cuchilla [de interruptor].
**bladebone** (-boun) s. omóplato, paletilla.
**bladesmith** (-miz) s. espadero, cuchillero.
**blain** (blein) s. ampolla, pústula.
**blamable** (blei·mabøl) adj. reprensible, censurable, culpable.
**blame** (bleim) s. reprobación, censura, reproche, tacha. 2 culpa, responsabilidad.
**blame (to)** tr. reprobar, censurar, reprochar, culpar: to be to ~, tener la culpa, merecer reproche.
**blameful** (-ful) adj. de reproche, de censura. 2 culpable, reprochable.
**blameless** (-lis) adj. irreprochable, intachable, sin culpa.
**blamer** (-øʳ) s. censurador, reprochador.
**blameworthy** (-uøʳdi) adj. reprensible, censurable, culpable.
**blanch (to)** (blænch o blanch) tr. blanquear, blanquecer. 2 hacer palidecer. 3 COC. escaldar; pelar. 4 intr. palidecer; ponerse blanco.
**Blanche** (blænch) n. pr. Blanca.
**blancher** (-øʳ) s. blanqueador. 2 blanquecedor.
**blanc-mange** (blama·nỹ) s. manjar blanco.
**bland** (blænd) adj. blando, suave, dulce, melifluo.
**blandish (to)** (blæ·ndish) tr. halagar, lisonjear, acariciar, engatusar.
**blandishment** (-mønt) s. halago, lisonja, caricia, zalamería.
**blank** (blænk) adj. pálido, descolorido. 2 en blanco: ~ check, cheque en blanco; fig. carta blanca. 3 vacío, desierto; desnudo; sin interés; sin afectos, sin esperanzas, infructuoso. 4 sin bala [cartucho]. 5 desconcertado, confuso. 6

vago, inexpresivo [mirada, etc.]. 7 blanco, suelto [verso]. 8 s. blanco, espacio, hueco. 9 ARQ. vano. 10 hoja, formulario. 11 diana [de un blanco]. 12 cospel.
**blanket** (blæ·nkit) s. manta [de cama o de abrigo], frazada. 2 capa, manto [de nieve, etc.]. 3 adj. general, comprensivo.
**blanket (to)** tr. cubrir, tapar. 2 mantear.
**blankly** (blæ·nkli) adv. inexpresivamente, desconcertadamente. 2 directamente, a quema ropa. 3 completamente.
**blare** (bleʳ) s. sonido [de la trompeta]; rugido, fragor.
**blare (to)** intr. sonar [la trompeta o como la trompeta]. 2 tr. gritar.
**blarney** (bla·ʳni) s. lisonja, zalamería.
**blaspheme (to)** (blæsfɪ·m) intr. blasfemar. 2 tr. blasfemar contra.
**blasphemer** (-øʳ) s. blasfemo.
**blasphemous** (-møs) adj. blasfemo.
**blasphemy** (blæ·sfimi) s. blasfemia.
**blast** (blæst) s. ráfaga, bocanada, golpe [de viento]. 2 soplo [de un fuelle]; corriente, chorro [de aire, vapor, etc.]. 3 añublo, agostamiento. 4 hálito pernicioso. 5 sonido fuerte [de trompeta, bocina, silbato, etc.]. 6 explosión, voladura. 7 carga [de un barreno].
**blast (to)** tr. añublar, agostar, marchitar, destruir, arruinar. 2 maldecir, infamar. 4 volar [con explosivos].
**blasting** (blæ·esting) s. marchitamiento, agostamiento, añublo. 2 destrucción. 3 voladura.
**blastuta** (blæ·schula) s. BIOL. blástula.
**blatant** (blei·tant) adj. vocinglero, ruidoso. 2 vulgar, llamativo.
**blather** (blæ·døʳ) s. charlatán. 2 charla.
**blather (to)** intr.-tr. charlar, decir tonterías.
**blatherer** (-øʳ) s. charlatán, hablador.
**blaze** (bleiʃ) s. llama, llamarada. 2 hoguera, incendio. 3 luz brillante, ardor [del sol, etc.]. 4 brillo, resplandor, esplendor. 5 explosión, arrebato, estallido. 6 mancha blanca [en la cara de un animal].
**blaze (to)** intr. arder, llamear. 2 brillar, resplandecer. 3 to ~ away, disparar o ir disparando [con un arma de fuego]. 4 tr. encender, inflamar. 5 publicar, proclamar.
**blazer** (-øʳ) s. chaqueta de deporte de colores vivos.
**blazing** (-ing) adj. llameante, resplandeciente. 2 patente, evidente.
**blazon** (blei·søn) s. blasón. 2 ostentación, divulgación, publicación.
**blazon (to)** tr. BLAS. blasonar. 2 mostrar, publicar, proclamar. 3 adornar.
**blazoner** (blei·šnøʳ) s. blasonista.
**blazonry** (blei·šønri) s. blasón. 2 esplendor, decoración brillante.
**bleach (to)** (blɪch) tr. blanquear [tejidos]; emblanquecer, descolorar. 2 poner pálido. 3 intr. ponerse blanco, descolorirse. 4 palidecer.
**bleacher** (-øʳ) s. blanqueador.
**bleachery** (-i) s. taller de blanqueo.
**bleaching** (-ing) s. blanqueo.
**bleak** (blɪk) adj. desierto, yermo, desolado, frío, helado, triste.
**blear** (blɪʳ) adj. empañado, legañoso [ojo]. 2 confuso, borroso.
**blear (to)** tr. empañar, hacer legañoso. 2 nublar [la vista]. 3 ofuscar.
**bleared** (-d) adj. BLEAR.

**blear-eyed** *adj.* legañoso.
**bleat** (blɪt) *s.* balido.
**bleat (to)** *intr.* balar.
**bleating** (-ing) *s.* balido. *2 adj.* balador.
**bleb** (bleb) *s.* ampolla, vejiga. *2* burbuja.
**bled** (bled) *pret.* y *p. p.* de TO BLEED.
**bleed (to)** (blɪd) *intr.* sangrar; verter su sangre. *2* exudar savia. *3* manar [como de una herida]. *4 tr.* sangrar [a un enfermo, un árbol, etc.]. *5* sacar dinero [a uno]. ¶ Pret. y p. p.: *bled.*
**bleeder** (blɪ·døʳ) *s.* sangrador.
**bleeding** (-ing) *adj.* sangrante.
**blemish** (ble·mish) *s.* tacha, defecto, imperfección. *2* mancha, desdoro, borrón.
**blemish (to)** *tr.* manchar, afear, empañar.
**blemishless** (-lis) *adj.* inmaculado, intachable.
**blench (to)** (blench) *intr.* cejar, retroceder, acobardarse. *2 tr.-intr.* TO BLANCH.
**blend** (blend) *s.* mezcla, combinación. *2* PINT. gradación.
**blend (to)** *tr.* mezclar, combinar, fundir. *2* PINT. matizar, armonizar. *3 intr.* mezclarse, combinarse. *4* pasar insensiblemente de un matiz, etc., a otro. ¶ Pret. y p. p.: *blended* o *blent.*
**blende** (blend) *s.* blenda.
**blent** (blent) *pret.* y p. p. de TO BLEND.
**bless (to)** (bles) *tr.* bendecir. *2* agraciar, favorecer, dotar. *3* guardar, proteger; ~ *me!*, ¡válgame Dios! *4* santiguar, persignar. ¶ Pret. y p. p.: *blessed* o *blest.*
**blessed** (ble·sid) *adj.* bendito; santo, bienaventurado, feliz, dichoso. *2* Santísimo. *3* beato, beatificado.
**blessedness** (-nis) *s.* santidad, beatitud, bienaventuranza, felicidad.
**blessing** (ble·sing) *s.* bendición. *2* don, beneficio, gracia. *3* culto, adoración.
**blest** (blest) *p. p.* de TO BLESS.
**blet** (blet) *s.* podredumbre incipiente de la fruta.
**blet (to)** *intr.* pasarse [la fruta].
**blew** (blu) *pret.* de TO BLOW.
**blight** (blait) *s.* lo que daña las plantas; añublo, tizón, roya, pulgón, etc.
**blight (to)** *tr.* añublar, secar, agostar, marchitar. *2* frustrar, malograr.
**blind** (blaind) *adj.* ciego. *2* de ciego, para ciegos, hecho a ciegas. *3* oculto, secreto. *4* oscuro, tenebroso. *5* ~ *alley*, callejón sin salida. *6 s.* pantalla, mampara, persiana, transparente, cortinilla. *7* pantalla [pers.]; engaño, disfraz, fachada, pretexto, subterfugio. *8* anteojera [del caballo]. *9* CAZA. tollo. *10* FORT. blinda.
**blind (to)** *tr.* cegar [quitar la vista]. *2* deslumbrar, ofuscar, obcecar. *3* vendar [los ojos].
**blindage** (-idy̆) *s.* MIL. blindaje, blinda.
**blinders** (-øʳs) *s. pl.* anteojeras [de caballo].
**blindfold** (-fould) *adj.* vendado [de ojos]. *2* ciego, ofuscado. *3* hecho a ciegas. *4 s.* ardid, engaño.
**blindfold (to)** *tr.* vendar los ojos. *2* poner una venda en los ojos, ofuscar; despistar.
**blindman's-buff** (-mans bøf) *s.* gallina ciega [juego].
**blindness** (-nis) *s.* ceguedad, ceguera. *2* ofuscación, obcecación.
**blink** (blindk) *s.* pestañeo, guiño, guiñada. *2* destello, reflejo, ardentía.
**blink (to)** *intr.* parpadear, pestañear. *2* oscilar [una luz]. *3 intr.-tr.* mirar con los ojos entornados; fig. hacer la vista gorda.
**blinkard** (blɪ·nkaʳd) *s.* cegarrita.

**blinker** (-øʳ) *s.* pop. ojo. *2* luz intermitente. *3 pl.* BLINDERS.
**bliss** (bliss) *s.* bienaventuranza, gloria, felicidad. *2* arrobamiento, embeleso.
**blissful** (bli·sful) *adj.* bienaventurado, dichoso.
**blissfulness** (-nis) *s.* suprema felicidad.
**blister** (bli·støʳ) *s.* vejiga, ampolla. *2* vejigatorio. *3* burbuja [en el vidrio].
**blister (to)** *intr.* ampollarse. *2 tr.* ampollar, levantar ampollas en.
**blite** (blait) *s.* BOT. bledo.
**blithe** (blaiz), **blitheful** (-ful), **blithesome** (-søm) *adj.* alegre, gozoso, jocundo, jovial.
**blizzard** (bli·šaʳd) *s.* ventisca, tempestad. *2* descarga [de tiros].
**bloat (to)** (blout) *tr.* hinchar. *2* curar arenques. *3 intr.* hincharse; abotagarse; engreírse.
**bloated** (blou·tid) *adj.* hinchado, abotagado. *2* engreído.
**bloater** (-øʳ) *s.* arenque ahumado.
**blobber** (bla·bøʳ) *adj.* blubber.
**block** (blak) *s.* bloque. *2* trozo grande, toza, tarugo, adoquín. *3* tajo [de madera]. *4* fam. cabeza, chola. *5* fig. zoquete [pers.]. *6* motón, polea de aparejo. *7* MEC. dado, cubo. *8* zapata [de freno]. *9* cepo [de yunque]. *10* horma [de sombrero]. *11* CARP. calzo, alza, coda. *12* manzana, *cuadra [de casas]. *13* paquete [de acciones]; lote, partida. *14* bloc [de papel]. *15* obstáculo. *16* MEC. tope. *17* DEP. parada. *18* FERROC. tramo. *19* cuadrito [de sellos de correo]. *20* MED. bloqueo.
**block (to)** *tr.* obstruir, cerrar, bloquear, atascar. *2* ALBAÑ. tapiar, condenar. *3* parar [la pelota]. *4* encerrar [un peón]. *5* calzar [una rueda].
**blockade** (blakei·d) *s.* MIL. bloqueo, asedio. *2* obstrucción.
**blockade (to)** *tr.* MIL. bloquear. *2* obstruir.
**blockhead** (bla·kjed) *s.* tonto, bolonio, zopenco.
**block-house** *s.* MIL. blocao.
**blockish** (bla·kish) *adj.* tonto, estúpido.
**blond, blonde** (bland) *adj.* y *s.* rubio, blondo.
**blood** (blød) *s.* sangre: ~ *pressure*, presión arterial; *to make one's* ~ *run cold*, helar la sangre; *in cold* ~, a sangre fría. *2* asesinato, efusión de sangre. *3* ira, cólera. *4* temperamento, vida. *5* alcurnia, prosapia. *6* hombre animoso. *7* petimetre, calavera. *8* raza, animal de pura raza.
**blood-curdling** *adj.* horripilante, que hiela la sangre.
**bloodguilty** (-gilti) *adj.* culpable de homicidio o asesinato.
**bloodhound** (-jaund) *s.* sabueso.
**bloodless** (-lis) *adj.* pálido, exangüe. *2* incruento. *3* flojo, sin espíritu. *4* frío, insensible.
**bloodletter** (-letøʳ) *s.* sangrador.
**bloodletting** (-leting) *s.* sangría, flebotomía.
**bloodshed** (-shed) *s.* derramamiento o efusión de sangre; matanza.
**bloodshot** (-shat) *adj.* inyectado en sangre [ojo].
**bloodstone** (-stoun) *s.* MINER. hematíes. *2* MINER. heliotropo.
**bloodsucker** (-søkøʳ) *s.* ZOOL. y fig. sanguijuela.
**bloodthirsty** (-zøʳsti) *adj.* sanguinario.
**bloody** (-i) *adj.* sangriento, cruento. *2* ensangrentado, sanguinolento. *3* encarnizado, sanguinario. *4* vulg. maldito.
**bloody (to)** *tr.* ensangrentar. ¶ Pret. y p. p.: *bloodied.*
**bloom** (blum) *s.* BOT. flor, flores [colectivamente]. *2* floración, florecimiento: *in* ~, florido, en flor.

*3* frescura, lozanía. *4* color rosado [de las mejillas]. *5* flor, polvillo [de ciertas frutas y hojas]. *6* tocho, lingote.
**bloom (to)** *intr.* florecer, estar en flor. *2* lozanear, aparecer con toda su frescura, belleza o esplendor. *3 tr.* hacer florecer. *4* dar frescura o lozanía.
**bloomers** (blu·mø<sup>r</sup>s) *s. pl.* ant. pantalones femeninos de deporte.
**blooming** (-ing) *adj.* florido, en flor. *2* floreciente. *3* fresco, lozano. *4* vulg. maldito.
**bloomy** (-i) *adj.* florido. *2* lozano.
**blossom** (bla·søm) *s.* flor [que da fruto]; flores [de un árbol frutal]. *2* flor [de la vida, de la juventud]; lozanía, perfección.
**blossom (to)** *intr.* florecer, florar. *2* abrirse [las flores]. *3* florecer, prosperar.
**blot** (blat) *s.* borrón, mancha.
**blot (to)** *tr.* emborronar, manchar. *2* mancillar, empañar; afear. *3* secar [lo escrito]. *4* oscurecer, eclipsar. *5 to* ~ *out*, tachar, borrar. *6 intr.* correrse [la tinta], pasarse [el papel]. ¶ Pret. y p. p.: *blotted;* ger.: *-tting.*
**blotch** (bla·ch) *s.* mancha, borrón. *2* pústula, roncha.
**blotch (to)** *tr.* emborronar. *2* cubrir de pústulas.
**blotter** (bla·tø<sup>r</sup>) *s.* papel secante, teleta. *2* borrador, libro de apuntes.
**blotting paper** (bla·ting) *s.* papel secante.
**blotting pad** *s.* secafirmas.
**blouse** (blaus) *s.* blusa.
**blow** (blou) *s.* golpe, porrazo: ~ *with a hammer*, martillazo; *to come to blows*, venir a las manos, pegarse. *2* golpe, revés, desgracia, desastre. *3* soplido; trompetazo; ~ *of a horn*, bocinazo. *4* resoplido. *5* acción de sonarse las narices. *6* soplo [de aire]. *7* bot. florescenncia. *8* pop. fanfarrón.
**blow (to)** *tr.* soplar. *2* tocar [la trompeta, el silbato, etc.]: *to* ~ *one's own trumpet*, alabarse. *3* divulgar. *4* impeler, abrir, etc.[una cosa el aire]. *5* hinchar, inflar. *6* cansar, fatigar. *7* volar, hacer estallar. *8* bot. echar [flores]. *9 to* ~ *off steam*, dejar salir el vapor; fig. desahogarse. *10 to* ~ *one's nose*, sonarse las narices. *11 to* ~ *out*, apagar; elect. fundir; volar: *to* ~ *one's brains out*, levantarse la tapa de los sesos. *12* impers. hacer viento. *13 intr.* soplar. *14* resoplar, jadear. *15* sonar [la trompeta, etc.]. *16* hincharse, inflarse. *17* abrirse [las flores]. *18 to* ~ *hot an cold*, estar entre sí y no, vacilar. *19 to* ~ *out*, estallar; apagarse; elect. fundirse. ¶ Pret.: *blew;* p. p.: *blown.*
**blower** (-ø<sup>r</sup>) *s.* soplador. *2* mec. ventilador. *3* soplador. *4* pop. fanfarrón.
**blowfly** (-flai) *s.* ent. moscarda.
**blowgun** (-gøn) *s.* cerbatana, bodoquera.
**blown** (-n) *p. p.* de to blow. *2* jadeante, rendido.
**blowoff** (-of) *s.* escape, salida [de vapor, etc.].
**blowout** (-aut) *s.* reventón, ruptura [por presión interior]. *2* quema [de un fusible]. *3* pop. banquete.
**blowpipe** (-paip) *s.* soplete. *2* cerbatana.
**blowtorch** (-to<sup>r</sup>ch) *s.* lámpara de soldar.
**blowy** (-i) *adj.* ventoso. *2* ligero.
**blowzy** (blau·si) *adj.* coloradote. *2* desaliñado.
**blubber** (blø·bø<sup>r</sup>) *s.* lloro, llanto. *2* ortiga de mar. *3* grasa de ballena. *4 adj.* abultado, hinchado.
**blubber (to)** *intr.* llorar, sollozar. *2 tr.* decir llorando.
**blubber-lipped** *adj.* bezudo, jetudo.
**bludgeon** (blø·dyøn) *s.* porra, cachiporra.

**bludgeon (to)** *tr.* apalear. *2* amedrentar, intimidar.
**blue** (blu) *adj.* azul: ~ *devils*, hipocondría; alucinaciones del delirium tremens; ~ *streak*, relámpago, rayo; fig. cosa rápida. *2* lívido, amoratado. *3* rígido, puritano. *4* triste. *5 s.* azul [color]. *6 the* ~, el cielo, el mar. *7 pl. the blues*, tristeza, murria, melancolía. *8* baile de origen negro.
**blue (to)** *tr.* azular. *2* dar azulete. *3* pavonear.
**Bluebeard** (-bi<sup>r</sup>d) *s.* Barba azul.
**blueberry** (-beri) *s.* arándano.
**bluebotte** (-batøl) *s.* ent. moscón. *2* bot. aciano, azulejo.
**blueing** (-ing) *s.* bluing.
**blueprint** (-print) *s.* cianotipia. *2* cianotipo.
**bluestocking** (-staking) *s.* mujer literata. *2* marisabidilla.
**bluet** (blu·it) *s.* bot. aciano, azulejo.
**bluff** (bløf) *adj.* mar. ancha, abultada [amura, proa]. *2* escarpado, enhiesto. *3* rudo, francote. *4 s.* escarpa, risco, farallón. *5* farol, envite falso. *6* falso alarde de fuerzas, recursos, etc.; baladronada.
**bluff (to)** *intr.* hacer un farol [en el juego]. *2 intr.-tr.* tratar de intimidar o disuadir con un falso alarde de fuerzas, recursos, etc.
**bluffness** (-nis) *s.* rudeza, franqueza, brusquedad.
**bluing** (blu·ing) *s.* pavonado. *2* azulete.
**bluish** (bu·ish) *adj.* azulado, azulino.
**blunder** (blø·ndø<sup>r</sup>) *s.* disparate, equivocación, yerro, pifia, plancha.
**blunder (to)** *intr.* equivocarse, hacer disparates, pifias, planchas. *2* moverse torpemente, tropezar. *3 tr.* estropear [un negocio]. *4* decir con torpeza o indiscreción.
**blunderbuss** (-bøs) *s.* trabuco.
**blunderer** (-ø<sup>r</sup>) *s.* torpe, chapucero.
**blunderhead** (-jed) *s.* torpe, estúpido.
**blunt** (blønt) *adj.* embotado, despuntado, romo. *2* embotado, insensible; torpe, obtuso. *3* franco, brusco, descortés.
**blunt (to)** *tr.* embotar. *2* despuntar, poner romo. *3* adormecer, mitigar. *4 intr.* embotarse.
**bluntly** (-li) *adv.* claramente, bruscamente.
**bluntness** (-nis) *s.* embotamiento. *2* brusquedad, aspereza.
**blur** (blø<sup>r</sup>) *s.* borrón, mancha. *2* cosa borrosa.
**blur (to)** *tr.* manchar, empañar. *2* hacer borroso o confuso. *3* nublar, oscurecer [la vista, el entendimiento]. *4 intr.* oscurecerse, ponerse borroso. ¶ Pret. y p. p.: *blurred;* ger.: *blurring.*
**blurt (to)** (blø<sup>r</sup>t) *s.* decir o soltar bruscamente o indiscretamente.
**blush** (bløsh) *s.* rubor, sonrojo. *2* color encendido.
**blush (to)** *intr.* ruborizarse, sonrojarse. *2* tomar un color encendido.
**blushful** (-ful) *s.* ruboroso, modesto. *2* encendido, róseo.
**blushing** (-ing) *adj.* ruborizado; encendido. *2 s.* rubor, sonrojo.
**blushless** (-lis) *adj.* desvergonzado.
**bluster** (blø·stø<sup>r</sup>) *s.* borrasca ruidosa. *2* ruido, tumulto; violencia, furor. *3* sonido fuerte. *4* fanfarria, gritos, amenazas.
**bluster (to)** *intr.* soplar recio [el viento]; ser ventoso [el tiempo]. *2* tempestear, fanfarrear, bravear. *3 tr.* intimidar con gritos y amenazas.
**blusterer** (-ø<sup>r</sup>) *s.* fanfarrón, perdonavidas.
**blustering** (-ing), **blustery** (-i) *adj.* violento [viento]. *2* ventoso. *3* tempestuoso, ruidoso, tumultuoso. *4* fanfarrón, jactancioso.

**boa** (bou·a) *s.* boa.
**boar** (boʳ) *s.* verraco. *2* jabalí.
**board** (boʳd) *s.* tabla, tablero [de madera]. *2* anaquel. *3* tablilla [de anuncios]. *4* ELECT. cuadro. *5* mesa puesta, comida, pensión, pupilaje. *6* mesa [para una junta o consejo]; junta, consejo: *Board of Admiralty*, Consejo superior de Marina; ~ *of directors*, consejo de administración; junta directiva; *Board of Education*, Consejo de Instrucción Pública. *7* cartón. *8* MAR. bordo: *free on* ~, franco a bordo. *9* canto, borde, orilla. *10* MAR. borda. *11* MAR. bordada. *12 pl.* tablazón. *13* TEAT. escenario, tablas.
**board (to)** *tr.* entarimar, enmaderar. *2* tomar o poner a pupilaje. *3* abordar. *4* subir a un tren, a un buque. *5 intr.* estar de pupilo.
**boarder** (-øʳ) *s.* abordador. *2* huésped, pupilo, pensionista.
**boarding** (-ing) *s.* tablazón. *2* entablado. *3* tabique de tablas. *4* MAR. abordaje. *5* pensión, hospedaje: ~ *house*, casa de huéspedes; ~ *school*, internado.
**boast** (boust) *s.* jactancia, ostentación, vanagloria, alarde, baladronada.
**boast (to)** *intr.* jactarse, alardear, blasonar, vanagloriarse. *2 tr.* ponderar, decantar. *3* ostentar, tener.
**boastful** (-ful) *adj.* jactancioso.
**boastless** (-lis) *adj.* sencillo, sin ostentación.
**boat** (bout) *s.* bote, barca, lancha; barco, buque, nave, embarcación: ~ *hook*, bichero. *2* LITURG. naveta. *3* salsera.
**boat (to)** *tr.* poner o llevar en un bote, barco, etc. *2 intr.* ir en bote, lancha, etc.
**boathouse** (-jaus) *s.* cobertizo para botes.
**boating** (-ing) *s.* paseo en lancha o bote. *2* transporte en barca. *3* manejo de un bote.
**boatman** (-mæn) *s.* botero, barquero.
**boatswain** (bou·søn o bou·tswen) *s.* MAR. contramaestre.
**Bob** (bab) *n. pr. dim.* de ROBERT.
**bob** *s.* lenteja [de péndulo]. *2* pilón [de romana]. *3* plomo [de plomada]. *4* corcho [en la pesca con anzuelo]. *5* cierto cebo para pescar. *6* cola cortada [de un caballo]. *7* pelo [esp. de mujer o de niño] cortado a la altura del cogote. *8* meneo, sacudida, movimiento de lo que sube y baja; saludo, reverencia. *9* adorno colgante. *10* peluquín. *11* fam. chelín.
**bob (to)** *tr.* cortar [la cola]. *2* cortar [el pelo] a la altura del cogote. *3* menear, sacudir, hacer subir y bajar. *4 intr.* menearse [con sacudidas]. ¶ Pret. y p. p.: *bobbed;* ger.: *bobbing.*
**bobbin** (ba·bin) *s.* bolillo, majaderillo. *2* carrete, bobina; canilla, broca.
**bobby** (ba·bi) *s.* fam. [Ingl.] policía [agente].
**bobsled** (ba·bsled), **bobsleigh** (-slei) *s.* trineo pequeño.
**bobtail** (-teil) *adj.* rabón. *2 s.* rabo mocho. *3* animal rabón.
**bobtail (to)** *tr.* cortar la cola a.
**bobwig** (-uig) *s.* peluquín.
**boce** (bous) *s.* ICT. boga.
**bode** (boud) *pret.* y *p. p.* de TO BIDE.
**bode (to)** *tr.-intr.* anunciar, presagiar: *to* ~ *ill* o *well*, ser un mal o buen presagio. *2* pronosticar, prever.
**bodice** (ba·dis) *s.* jubón, corpiño, cuerpo [de vestido].
**bodiless** (ba·dilis) *adj.* sin cuerpo. *2* incorpóreo.

**bodily** (-li) *adj.* corporal. *2 adv.* en persona. *3* todos juntos, en peso.
**bodkin** (ba·dkin) *s.* COST. punzón. *2* pasacintas. *3* espadilla [para el pelo]. *4* ant. puñal.
**body** (ba·di) *s.* FÍS., QUÍM., GEOM., METAF. cuerpo. *2* cuerpo [de una pers., un animal, un vestido, un escrito, etc.]. *3* persona, individuo. *4* nave [de iglesia]. *5* caja, carrocería [de un coche, etc.]. *6* MÚ. caja, tubo [de instrumento]. *7* cuerpo [grueso, consistencia, etc.]. *8* masa, extensión: ~ *of water*, extensión de agua. *9* grupo, conjunto, cuerpo, gremio, clase: *in a* ~, en masa. *body (to)* *tr.* dar forma a. *2* materializar, representar. ¶ Pret. y p. p.: *bodied.*
**bodyguard** (-gaʳd) *s.* guardia personal. *2* séquito.
**Boer** (bouʳ) *adj.-s.* bóer.
**bog** (bag) *s.* pantano, marjal, cenagal, tremedal. *2* turbera.
**bog (to)** *tr.-intr.* hundir o hundirse en un pantano; atollar, atollarse. ¶ Pret. y p. p.: *bogged;* ger.: *bogging.*
**bogey** (bou·gi) *s.* duende, coco.
**boggle** (-gøl) *s.* espantada [del caballo]. *2* vacilación, indecisión. *3* chapucería, disparate.
**boggle (to)** *intr.* retroceder asustado. *2* vacilar, titubear. *3* hacer disparates.
**boggy** (ba·gi) *adj.* pantanoso, turboso.
**bogie** (bou·gi) *s.* carretilla; vagoneta de carga. *2* FERROC. bogui. *3* BOGEY.
**bogle** (bou·gøl) *s.* duende, coco. *2* aversión.
**bogus** (bou·gøs) *adj.* (E.U) falso, ficticio.
**bogy** (-gil) *s.* BOGEY.
**Bohemian** (bouji·mian) *adj.-s.* bohemio.
**boil** (boil) *s.* hervor, ebullición. *2* divieso.
**boil (to)** *intr.* hervir, bullir: *to* ~ *over*, salirse [un líquido al hervir]; fig. estar excitado, fuera de sí. *2* cocerse [en un líquido]. *3 tr.* hacer hervir, cocer, herventar: *to* ~ *down*, reducir por cocción; condensar, abreviar.
**boiler** (-øʳ) *s.* marmita, olla, caldero. *2* caldera. *3* cocedor.
**boilermaker** (-meikøʳ) *s.* calderero.
**boiling** (-ing) *s.* hervor, ebullición; cocción: ~ *point*, punto de ebullición.
**boisterous** (boi·størøs) *adj.* estrepitoso, ruidoso, bullicioso, tumultuoso. *3* violento, tempestuoso.
**boisterousness** (-nis) *s.* turbulencia, tumulto, ruido, vocinglería.
**bold** (bould) *adj.* intrépido, valiente. *2* atrevido, audaz. *3* descarado. *4* escarpado, acantilado. *5* claro, preciso, bien delineado.
**bold-faced** (-feist) *adj.* descarado. *2* IMPR. negra [letra].
**boldness** (-nis) *s.* intrepidez. *2* audacia. *3* atrevimiento, descaro.
**bole** (boul) *s.* tronco [de árbol]. *2* bol [arménico].
**bolero** (bole·rou) *s.* bolero.
**bolide** (bou·laid) *s.* bólido.
**boll** (boul) *s.* cápsula [del lino, del algodón].
**bollard** (ba·laʳd) *s.* MAR. bolardo.
**Bolshevik** (ba·lshevik) *s.* bolchevique.
**Bolshevism** (-višm) *s.* bolchevismo.
**Bolshevist** (-vist) *adj.-s.* bolchevista.
**bolster** (bou·lstøʳ) *s.* cabezal, travesaño [de cama]. *2* cojín, almohadón, almohadilla. *3* ARQ. zapata. *4* refuerzo, sostén, soporte.
**bolster (to)** *tr.* apoyar con almohadón. *2* apoyar, sostener. *3* apuntalar.
**bolstering** (-ing) *s.* apoyadero, apoyo.
**bolsterwork** (-uøʳk) *s.* ARQ. almohadillado.

**bolt** (boult) *s.* saeta, virote. *2* rayo, centella: ~ *from the blue*, suceso inopinado. *3* suceso o acción repentinos; salto rápido, fuga. *4* perno, tornillo, clavija. *5* cerrojo, pasador, pestillo, falleba. *6* cerrojo [del fusil]. *7* tamiz [para harina]. *8* rollo [de paño o papel pintado]. *9 adv.* de repente, como una flecha; rígidamente: ~ *upright*, derecho, tieso.
**bolt (to)** *tr.* echar el cerrojo a, acerrojar. *2* empernar. *3* arrojar, expeler. *4* engullir sin masticar. *5* cerner, tamizar. *6 intr.* salir, entrar, etc., de repente; echar a correr, huir. *7* desbocarse [el caballo].
**bolter** (-øʳ) *s.* cedazo, tamiz.
**bolthead** (-jed) *s.* matraz.
**boltrope** (-roup) *s.* relinga [de vela].
**bolus** (bou·løs) *s.* FARM. bolo. *2* bolo alimenticio.
**bomb** (bam) *s.* bomba [proyectil]; artefacto explosivo: ~ *shelter*, refugio antiaéreo.
**bomb (to)** *tr.-intr.* bombardear.
**bombard** (bamba·ʳd) *s.* bombarda.
**bombard (to)** *tr.* bombardear.
**bombardier** (bambaʳdɪ·ʳ) *s.* bombardero.
**bombardment** (-a·ʳdmønt) *s.* bombardeo.
**bombardon** (ba·mbaʳdøn) *s.* MÚS. bombardón.
**bombast** (ba·mbæst) *s.* ampulosidad.
**bombastic** (-bæ·stik) *adj.* ampuloso, campanudo, altisonante.
**bomber** (ba·møʳ) *s.* bombardero. *2* avión de bombardeo.
**bombshell** (-shel) *s.* bomba, granada.
**bonbon** (ba·nban) *s.* bombón.
**bond** (band) *s.* atadura, amarra, traba. *2* lazo, vínculo, nexo. *3* trabazón. *4* pacto, compromiso. *5* ARQ. aparejo. *6* QUÍM. enlace. *7* fiador [pers.]. *8* depósito [de mercancías] hasta el pago de derechos. *9* COM. bono, obligación. *10 pl.* cadenas, cautiverio. *11 adj.* sujeto, esclavizado.
**bond (to)** *tr.* unir, ligar, vincular. *2* hipotecar. *3* poner como garantía; dar fianza. *4* depositar [mercancías] hasta el pago de derechos.
**bondage** (-idẙ) *s.* esclavitud, servidumbre, sujeción.
**bondholder** (-jouldøʳ) *s.* tenedor de bonos, obligacionista.
**bondman** (-mæn) *s.* esclavo, siervo.
**bondsman** (-smæn) *s.* fiador, garante. *2* BONDMAN.
**bondstone** (-stoun) *s.* perpiaño.
**bone** (boun) *s.* hueso: ~ *of contention*, materia de desavenencia; *to have a* ~ *to pick with someone*, tener algo que discutir con uno; *to make no bones*, no tener empacho [en]. *2* cuesco [de fruta]. *3* espina [de pescado]. *4* ballena [de corsé, etc.]. *5* ficha [de dominó]. *6 pl.* esqueleto, armazón. *7* dados. *8* especie de castañuelas.
**bone (to)** *tr.* deshuesar. *2* quitar la espina [a un pescado]. *3* emballenar.
**bonebreaker** (-breikøʳ) *s.* ORN. quebrantahuesos.
**boneless** (-lis) *adj.* sin huesos; mollar.
**bonesetter** (-setøʳ) *s.* algebrista, ensalmador.
**bonfire** (ba·nfaiʳ) *s.* hoguera, fogata.
**bonhomie** (ba·nomi) *s.* afabilidad.
**Boniface** (ba·nifeis) *n. pr.* Bonifacio. *2 s.* hostelero, mesonero.
**bonito** (boni·tous) *s.* ICT. bonito.
**bonnet** (ba·nit) *s.* capota, sombrero [de mujer]. *2* gorro. *3* boina escocesa. *4* tocado de plumas [de los pieles rojas]. *5* MEC. sombrerete, casquete. *6* AUTO. capó, cubierta. *7* FORT., ZOOL. bonete. *8* MAR. boneta.
**bonnet (to)** *tr.-ref.* cubrir [la cabeza].

**bonny** (ba·ni) *adj.* hermoso, lindo; bueno.
**bonus** (bou·nøs) *s.* prima, gratificación, plus. *2* dividendo extraordinario.
**bony** (bou·ni) *adj.* óseo; oseoso. *2* huesudo.
**bonze** (banš) *s.* bonzo.
**boo** (bu) *s.* grita. *2 interj.* ¡fuera!, ¡bu!
**boo (to)** *tr.-intr.* abuchear, silbar.
**booby** (bu·bi) *s.* bobo. *2* torpe, desmañado.
**book** (buk) *s.* libro: *the Book*, la Biblia; *to bring to* ~, llamar a capítulo. *2* libreta, cuaderno. *3* libreto.
**book (to)** *tr.* anotar, inscribir [en un libro o registro]. *2* tomar, sacar, hacerse reservar [pasaje, localidades, etc.]. *3* contratar [a un artista].
**bookbinder** (-baindøʳ) *m.* encuadernador.
**bookbinding** (-bainding) *s.* encuadernación.
**bookcase** (-keis) *s.* armario o estante para libros, librería.
**bookie** (bu·ki) *s.* BOOKMAKER 2.
**booking** (-ing) *s.* registro, asiento. *2* reserva, venta, compra [de pasajes, localidades, etc.]: ~ *office*, despacho de pasajes o localidades.
**bookish** (-ish) *adj.* estudioso. *2* libresco.
**bookkeeper** (-kɪpøʳ) *s.* tenedor de libros.
**bookkeeping** (-kɪping) *s.* teneduría de libros.
**booklet** (-lit) *s.* librito, folleto, opúsculo.
**bookmaker** (-meikøʳ) *s.* el que hace los libros. *2* corredor de apuestas [en las carreras].
**bookmark** (-maʳk) *s.* registro [señal en un libro].
**bookseller** (-se·løʳ) *s.* librero.
**bookshop** (-shap) *s.* librería [tienda].
**bookstall** (-tol) *s.* puesto o quiosco de librería.
**bookstore** (-stoʳ) *s.* BOOKSHOP.
**bookworm** (-uøʳm) *s.* polilla de los libros. *2 fig.* ratón de biblioteca.
**boom** (bum) *s.* estampido, retumbo. *2 fig.* auge, popularidad o prosperidad rápida y creciente; crecimiento rápido [de una ciudad, etc.]; alza rápida [de un artículo]. *3* MAR. botalón, botavara. *4* cadena [de puerto o río]. *5* aguilón [de grúa].
**boom (to)** *intr.* retumbar, tronar. *2* estar en auge, en prosperidad rápida y creciente; estar en alza sostenida [un artículo]. *3 tr.* fomentar, hacer prosperar rápidamente. *4* lanzar, anunciar con gran propaganda.
**boomerang** (bu·møræng) *s.* bomerang.
**boon** (bun) *s.* don, dádiva; merced. *2* bendición, dicha. *3 adj.* alegre, jovial.
**boor** (buʳ) *s.* patán. *2* grosero, mal educado.
**boorish** (-ish) *adj.* rústico, rudo, grosero.
**boost** (bust) *s.* (E.U.) empujón, ayuda. *2* alza [de los precios, el voltaje, etc.].
**boost (to)** *tr.* (E.U) empujar, ayudar. *2* hacer subir [los precios, el voltaje, etc.].
**boot** (but) *s.* bota, botina: ~ *hook*, tirabotas; ~ *tree*, horma para el calzado; *to give one the* ~, fig. despedir a uno. *2* borceguí [de tormento]. *3* provecho, ganancia: *to* ~, además, por añadidura.
**boot (to)** *tr.* calzar las botas. *2* dar un puntapié. *3* *to* ~ *it*, ir a pie. *4 intr.* calzarse las botas. *4* servir, aprovechar.
**bootblack** (-blæk) *m.* limpiabotas.
**booth** (buz) *s.* casilla, quiosco; puesto. *2* cabina [telefónica, etc.].
**bootjack** (bu·tjaek) *s.* sacabotas.
**bootlace** (-leis) *s.* cordón para los zapatos.
**bootleg (to)** *tr.-intr.* (E.U) contrabandear [en bebidas alcohólicas]. ¶ Pret. y p. p.: *bootlegged*; ger.: *-gging*.

**bootlegger** (-ǿ<sup>r</sup>) *s.* (E.U) contrabandista de bebidas alcohólicas.
**boots** (buts) *s.* limpiabotas de hotel.
**booty** (bu·ti) *s.* botín, presa. *2* ganancia, premio. *3* saqueo.
**booze** (buš) *s.* fam. bebida; borrachera.
**booze (to)** *intr.* empinar el codo.
**borage** (bo·eidý) *s.* borraja.
**borate** (bo·reit) *s.* borato.
**borax** (bo·ræks) *s.* bórax.
**border** (bo·ʳdǿ<sup>r</sup>) *s.* borde, orilla, margen. *2* frontera, límite, confín; (E.U) fronteras de la civilización. *3* orla, ribete. *4* repulgo, dobladillo. *5* arriate [de jardín]. *6 pl.* TEAT. bambalinas.
**border (to)** *tr.* orlar. *2* orillar, ribetear. *3* estar en el borde de. *4* intr. *to* ~ *on* o *upon,* confinar o lindar con; rayar en.
**borderland** (-laænd) *s.* zona fronteriza.
**bordeline** (-lain) *s.* frontera, límite.
**bore** (bo<sup>r</sup>) *pret.* de TO BEAR.
**bore** *s.* taladro, barreno [agujero]. *2* ánima, alma [hueco interior]. *3* calibre [de un tubo]; luz [de un pozo]. *4* lata [cosa fastidiosa]. *5* latoso, pelmazo, posma.
**bore (to)** *tr.* horadar, taladrar, perforar. *2* abrir [un agujero, un pozo, etc.]. *3* aburrir, fastidiar, dar la lata a.
**boreal** (borial) *adj.* boreal.
**Boreas** (-rias) *s.* MIT., METEOR. bóreas.
**boredom** (bo·ʳdøm) *s.* fastidio, aburrimiento, tedio.
**borer** (bo·rø<sup>r</sup>) *s.* perforador. *2* barrena, taladro, broca. *3* MIN. sonda. *4* latoso, pelmazo.
**boric** (bo·rik) *adj.* bórico.
**born** (bo<sup>r</sup>n) *p. p.* de TO BEAR; nacido. *2* de nacimiento, nato.
**borne** *p. p.* de TO BEAR.
**boron** (bo·ran) *s.* boro.
**borough** (bø·rou) *s.* villa; burgo. *2* distrito municipal.
**borrow (to)** (ba·rou) *tr.* tomar o pedir prestado. *2* apropiarse [una idea, etc.].
**borrowed** (ba·roud) *adj.* prestado.
**boscage** (ba·skidý) *s.* boscaje.
**bosh** (bash) *s.* palabrería, tonterías.
**bosky** (ba·ski) *adj.* nemoroso, arbolado.
**bosom** (bu·šøm) *s.* pecho, seno [parte exterior del pecho]. *2* pecho, corazón [sede de los afectos, etc.]. *3* COST. pechera. *4* seno [parte interna, cavidad]. *5 adj.* querido, íntimo: ~ *friend,* amigo íntimo.
**bosom (to)** *tr.* guardar en el pecho. *2* ocultar.
**Bosporus** (ba·spørøs) *n. pr.* GEOGR. Bósforo.
**boss** (bos) *s.* protuberancia; bollo, bollón; giba. *2* cazoleta [de broquel]. *3* ARQ. clave en relieve. *4* fam. amo, patrón, jefe; (E.U) cacique.
**boss (to)** *tr.* repujar, trabajar de relieve. *2 tr.-intr.* mandar, dominar.
**bossage** (bo·sidý) *s.* ARQ. almohadillado.
**bossism** (-iøm) *s.* caciquismo.
**bossy** (-i) *adj.* mandón, autoritario.
**bot** (bat) *s.* ENT. rezno.
**botanic(al** (botæ·nik(al) *adj.* botánico.
**botanist** (ba·tanist) *s.* botánico.
**bonatize** (-aiš) *intr.* herborizar.
**botany** (-i) *s.* botánica.
**botch** (bach) *s.* remiendo, chapucería, chafallo.
**botch (to)** *tr.* remendar chapuceramente, chafallar.
**botchy** (-i) *adj.* remendado. *2* chapucero.
**botfly** (ba·tflai) *s.* ENT. moscardón.

**both** (bouz) *adj.* y *pron.* ambos, entrambos, el uno y el otro, los dos: ~ *of them,* los dos; ~ *his friends,* sus dos amigos. *2 conj.* al mismo tiempo, a la vez; tanto ...como: ~ *good and cheap,* bueno y barato a la vez; ~ *A and B,* tanto A como B.
**bother** (ba·ðø<sup>r</sup>) *s.* preocupación. *2* fastidio, molestia; persona o cosa molesta. *3* inconveniente.
**bother (to)** *tr.* preocupar, fastidiar, molestar. *2 intr.* preocuparse, molestarse: *to* ~ *about,* preocuparse de; *to* ~ *to,* molestarse en.
**botheration** (-ei·shøn) *s.* fastidio, molestia. *2 interj.* ¡demonio!
**bothersome** (-søm) *adj.* molesto, fastidioso.
**bottle** (ba·tøl) *s.* botella, frasco, pomo. *2* zaque, bota. *3* haz [de heno].
**bottle (to)** *tr.* embotellar: *to* ~ *up,* embotellar [naves]; contener [la ira, etc.].
**bottleflower** (-flauø<sup>r</sup>) *s.* aciano.
**bottleneck** (-nek) *s.* gollete [de botella]. *2* estrechura, camino estrecho. *3* obstáculo.
**bottling** (ba·tling) *s.* embotellado.
**bottom** (ba·tøm) *s.* fondo [de una cosa, del mar, de un río]: *at* ~, en el fondo, en realidad. *2* base, fundamento. *3* asiento [de silla o vasija]. *4* pie [parte inferior]; lo último, lo más bajo. *5* fondo [de buque]; casco, nave. *6* fam. trasero. *7 pl.* heces, poso. *8* hondonada. *9 adj.* fundamental. *10* del fondo, del pie, más bajo, último.
**bottom (to)** *tr.* poner fondo o asiento a. *2* fundar, basar. *3* profundizar. *4 intr.* basarse.
**bottomless** (-lis) *adj.* sin fondo; insondable.
**boudoir** (budua·<sup>r</sup>) *s.* gabinete [de señora].
**bouffe** (buf) *adj.* MÚS. bufo.
**bough** (bau) *s.* rama [de árbol].
**bought** (bot) *pret.* y *p. p.* de TO BUY.
**bougie** (bu·dýi) *s.* CIR. sonda, candelilla.
**bouillon** (bu·lian) *s.* COC. caldo.
**boulder** (bou·ldø<sup>r</sup>) *s.* pedrejón, canto rodado.
**boulevard** (bu·lva<sup>r</sup>) *s.* bulevar.
**boulter** (bou·ltø<sup>r</sup>) *s.* palangre.
**bounce** (bauns) *s.* golpazo. *2* salto, brinco, bote, rebote. *3* bravata, fanfarronada. *4* mentira. *5* fam. (E.U) despido.
**bounce (to)** *tr.* hacer botar. *2* fam. (E.U) echar, despedir [a uno]. *3 intr.* lanzarse, saltar. *4* botar, rebotar. *5* fanfarronear.
**bouncer** (-ǿ<sup>r</sup>) *s.* guapo, fanfarrón. *2* embustero. *3* embuste. *4* cosa grande.
**bouncing** (-ing) *adj.* fuerte, robusto. *2* exagerado.
**bound** (baund) *pret.* y *p. p.* de TO BIND. *2 adj.* obligado. *3* encuadernado. *4* estreñido. *5* destinado a, que ha de o tiene que: ~ *to fail,* destinado a fracasar. *6* ~ *for,* con destino a, rumbo a.
**bound** *s.* límite, término, confín. *2* salto, brinco, bote.
**bound (to)** *tr.* limitar, circunscribir, encerrar. *2 intr.* saltar, brincar, botar. *3 to* ~ *on* o *with,* limitar, confinar con.
**boundary** (-ari) *s.* límite, linde, confín, término frontera: ~ *stone,* hito, mojón.
**bounden** (-øn) *adj.* obligado. *2* obligatorio, forzoso.
**boundless** (-lis) *adj.* ilimitado, infinito, vasto.
**bounteous** (bau·ntiøs), **bountiful** (bau·ntiful) *adj.* dadivoso, liberal, generoso. *2* amplio, abundante, copioso.
**bounty** (-i) *s.* liberalidad, generosidad, munificencia. *2* don, merced. *3* prima, subvención.
**bouquet** (bukei·) *s.* ramillete. *2* aroma [del vino].
**bourdon** (bu·ʳdøn) *s.* bordón [bastón; registro del órgano].

**bourgeois** (bu<sup>r</sup>ẙua·) *adj.*-*s.* burgués.
**bourgeoisie** (-si·) *s.* burguesía.
**bourgeon** (bø·<sup>r</sup>ẙøn) *s.* BOT. yema, brote.
**bourgeon** (to) *intr.* brotar, retoñar.
**bourn(e** (bou<sup>r</sup>n) *s.* riachuelo. 2 linde. 3 meta.
**bourse** (bu<sup>r</sup>s) *s.* bolsa, lonja.
**bout** (baut) *s.* rato [de hacer o de dedicarse a algo]; mano [de un juego]; asalto [de esgrima]; combate, encuentro. 2 probatura. 3 ataque [de una enfermedad].
**bovine** (bou·vain) *adj.* bovino, vacuno.
**bow** (bau) *s.* inclinación, reverencia, saludo. 2 MAR. proa; amura.
**bow** (bou) *s.* arco [arma]. 2 arco, curva. 3 MÚS. arco. 4 ojo [de la llave, de las tijeras]. 5 lazo, lazada: ~ *tie*, corbata de lazo. 6 arzón delantero. 7 ~ *compass*, bigotera.
**bow** (to) (bau) *intr.* arquear, doblar. 2 MÚS. tocar con arco. 3 *intr.* arquearse, doblarse.
**bowel** (bau·uøl) *s.* intestino. 2 *pl.* intestinos, vientre. 3 fig. entrañas [lo más oculto].
**bowel** (to) *tr.* destripar, sacar las tripas.
**bower** (bau·ø<sup>r</sup>) *s.* glorieta, cenador, emparrado, enramada. 2 casita rústica. 3 gabinete, retrete. 4 MAR. ancla de leva.
**bower** (bou·ø<sup>r</sup>) *s.* músico de arco.
**bowery** (bau·øri) *adj.* frondoso, emparrado, sombreado.
**bowie-knife** (bou·i) *s.* cuchillo de monte.
**bowl** (boul) *s.* cuenco, escudilla, bol; copa. 2 palangana, jofaina. 3 hueco, concavidad. 4 taza [de fuente]. 5 platillo [de balanza]. 6 palita [de cuchara]. 7 cazoleta [de pipa]. 8 bola, bocha. 9 *pl.* juego de bochas.
**bowl** (to) *tr.* hacer rodar. 2 tirar [la bola]; tumbar con una bola. 3 *intr.* jugar a bochas o a los bolos.
**bowlegged** (bou·legd) *adj.* estevado.
**bowler** (bou·lø<sup>r</sup>) *s.* jugador de bochas o de bolos. 2 [Ingl.] sombrero hongo.
**bowline** (bou·lin) *s.* MAR. bolina.
**bowling** (-ing) *s.* juego de bochas o de bolos.
**bowman** (-mæn) *s.* arquero. 2 (bau mæn) MAR. remero de proa.
**bowsprit** (-sprit) *s.* bauprés.
**bowstring** (-tring) *s.* cuerda de arco.
**bow-window** *s.* ARQ. mirador de planta curva.
**bowwow** (bau·uau) *s.* guau, ladrido.
**bowwow** (to) *intr.* ladrar. 2 gruñir, regañar.
**box** (baks) *s.* caja, cajita, estuche. 2 cajón, cofre, arca, baúl. 3 hucha. 4 MEC. buje, cubo, caja, manguito, cojinete. 5 apartado [de correos]. 6 pescante [de carruaje]. 7 casilla, garita. 8 compartimiento, departamento. 9 TEAT. palco. 10 bofetón, puñetazo. 11 BOT. boj. 12 ~ *calf*, cuero de becerro curtido al cromo. 13 TEAT. ~ *office*, taquilla.
**box** (to) *tr.* meter en caja, embalar. 2 apuñear, abofetear. 3 *intr.* boxear.
**boxer** (-sø<sup>r</sup>) *s.* boxeador. 2 embalador.
**boxing** (-ing) *s.* boxeo. 2 embalaje.
**boxthorn** (-zø<sup>r</sup>n) *s.* arto, cambronera.
**boxwood** (-wud) *s.* boj.
**boy** (boi) *s.* niño, muchacho: ~ *scout*, muchacho explorador. 2 muchacho, chico [hombre joven; término cariñoso o familiar]. 3 mozo, criado.
**boyar** (bo·ẙa<sup>r</sup>) *s.* boyardo.
**boycott** (-cat) *s.* boicot; boicoteo.
**boycott** (to) *tr.* boicotear.
**boyhood** (-jud) *s.* muchachez. 2 los muchachos.
**boyish** (-ish) *adj.* de muchacho. 2 amuchachado.
**bra** (bra) *s.* BRASSIÈRE.

**braccate** (bræ·keit) *adj.* ORN. calzado.
**brace** (breis) *s.* abrazadera, grapa, refuerzo, sostén. 2 MEC. riostra, tirante, viento, puntal. 3 berbiquí. 4 MAR. braza. 5 par [de pistolas, etc.]. 6 IMPR. corchete. 7 CIR. braguero. 8 *pl.* tirantes [del pantalón].
**brace** (to) *tr.* atar, trabar, arriostrar, apuntar, ensamblar, asegurar. 2 atesar, atirantar. 3 MAR. bracear. 4 IMPR. abrazar con corchete. 5 cercar, ceñir. 6 vigorizar. 7 dar ánimo. 8 *intr.* animarse, cobrar ánimo.
**bracelet** (brei·slit) *s.* brazalete, ajorca, pulsera.
**bracer** (bre·sø<sup>r</sup>) *s.* ARN. brazal. 2 abrazadera, laña. 3 cinto, venda. 4 MED. tónico.
**brachial** (bræ·kial) *adj.* ANAT. braquial.
**brachycephalic** (brakisøfæ·lik) *adj.* braquicéfalo.
**bracing** (brei·sing) *adj.* tónico, vigorizante.
**bracken** (bræ·køn) *s.* helecho. 2 helechal.
**bracket** (bræ·kit) *s.* cartela, ménsula, repisa, palomilla. 2 brazo de lámpara fijo en una pared o columna. 3 anaquel, rinconera. 4 IMPR. corchete. 5 IMPR. paréntesis rectangular. 6 clase, categoría.
**brackish** (bræ·kish) *adj.* salobre.
**bract** (bræ·kt) *s.* BOT. bráctea.
**bractlet** (-lit) *s.* BOT. bractéola.
**brad** (bræd) *s.* clavito, estaquilla, saetín.
**brag** (bræg) *s.* jactancia, fanfarronada, alarde. 2 fanfarrón, farolero. 3 juego de naipes.
**brag** (to) *intr.* jactarse, alardear, fanfarronear. ¶ Pret. y p. p.: *bragged;* ger.: *bragging.*
**braggadocio** (brægadou·shiou) *s.* fanfarrón. 2 fanfarria.
**braggart** (bræ·ga<sup>r</sup>t) *adj.*-*s.* jactancioso, baladrón.
**bragger** (bræ·gø<sup>r</sup>) *s.* jaque, fanfarrón.
**Brahman** (bra·mæn) *s.* brahman, brahmin.
**Brahmanism** (-išm) *s.* brahmanismo.
**Brahmin** (bra·min) *s.* brahmín, brahmán.
**braid** (breid) *s.* trenza. 2 trencilla, galón, cordoncillo, alamar.
**braid** (to) *tr.* trenzar. 2 atar [el cabello]. 3 galonear, trencillar, guarnecer.
**brail** (breil) *s.* MAR. candaliza.
**brail** (to) *tr.* MAR. cargar [las velas].
**brain** (brein) *s.* ANAT. cerebro, seso: ~ *fever*, fiebre cerebral. 2 esp. *pl.* cabeza, inteligencia, seso.
**brain** (to) *tr.* romper la cabeza.
**brainless** (-lis) *adj.* sin seso, mentecato.
**brainsick** (-sik) *adj.* loco. 2 de loco.
**brainy** (-i) *adj.* inteligente, talentudo.
**braise** (to) (brei·š) *tr.* rehogar [la carne].
**braize** *s.* ICT. pagro.
**brake** (brei·k) *s.* freno [de máquina o vehículo]. 2 guimbalete. 3 agramadera. 4 amasadora mecánica [de panadero]. 5 AGR. grada, rastra. 6 break [coche]. 7 BOT. helecho. 8 matorral, mato, jaral.
**brake** (to) *tr.* frenar. 2 amasar [pan]. 3 agramar. 4 AGR. gradar.
**brakeman** (-mæn) *s.* guardafrenos.
**bramble** (bræ·mbøl) *s.* zarza. 2 *pl.* zarzal.
**brambly** (bræ·mbli) *adj.* zarzoso.
**brambling** (-ing) *s.* ORN. pinzón real.
**bran** (bræn) *s.* salvado, afrecho.
**branch** (branch) *s.* rama [de árbol, de familia, etc.]. 2 ramo [de una ciencia, arte, etc.]. 3 ramal [vía férrea, camino, conducción, etc.]. 4 sección, departamento. 5 COM. sucursal. 6 brazo [de río, de candelero, etc.]. 7 candil [de cuerna]. 8 pierna [de compás]. 9 *adj.* filial, sucursal.
**branch** (to) *intr.* echar ramas. 2 ramificarse, bifurcarse; partir de un punto [una rama, un ramal].

| Gralte. con *off* o *out*. *3 to* ~ *out*, extender sus actividades. *4 tr.* dividir en ramas, bifurcar.

**branchia** (bræ·nkia) *s.* ZOOL. branquia.

**branchial** (-l) *adj.* branquial.

**branchy** (bra·nchi) *adj.* ramoso.

**brand** (brænd) *s.* tizón, tea. *2 poét.* antorcha. *3 poét.* espada. *4* hierro [para marcar; marca]. *5* baldón, estigma. *6* marca de fábrica; clase.

**brand (to)** *tr.* marcar [con hierro o marca de fábrica]. *2* grabar [en la mente]. *3* estigmatizar.

**brandish** (-ish) *s.* ESGR. floreo, molinete.

**brandish (to)** *tr.* blandir, blandear.

**brand-new** *adj.* completamente nuevo, nuevecito, flamante.

**brandy** (-i) *s.* aguardiente, coñac.

**bran-new** *adj.* BRAND-NEW.

**brant** (brænt) *s.* ganso silvestre.

**brash** (brash) *s.* escombros, broza. *3* MED. acedia.

**brasier** (brei·ȳøʳ) *s.* BRAZIER.

**brass** (bræs) *s.* latón, azófar, metal; bronce. *2* MÚS. metal [instrumentos]: ~ *band*, charanga. *3* descaro, desfachatez.

**brass (to)** *tr.* revestir de latón, de metal.

**brassart** (bræ·saʳt) *s.* brazal.

**brassière** (brašɪ·ʳ) *s.* sostén [prenda femenina].

**brassy** (bræ·si) *adj.* de latón. *2* bronco, metálico. *3* descarado, desvergonzado.

**brat** (bræt) *s.* desp. niño, mocoso.

**bravado** (brava·dou) *s.* baladronada; cosa que uno hace para demostrar su valentía.

**brave** (brei·v) *adj.* bravo, valiente. *2 poét.* airoso, elegante. *3* honrado. *4 s.* valiente.

**brave (to)** *tr.* arrostrar, desafiar, retar.

**bravery** (-øri) *s.* bravura, intrepidez. *2* esplendor, ornato; galas.

**bravo** (bra·vous) *s.* asesino a sueldo. *2 interj.* ¡bravo!

**brawl** (brol) *s.* reyerta, alboroto, tumulto. *2* ruido, fragor [de un torrente, etc.].

**brawl (to)** *intr.* reñir, alborotar, vociferar. *2* hacer ruido o fragor [un torrente, etc.].

**brawler** (-øʳ) *s.* camorrista, alborotador.

**brawn** (bron) *s.* músculo, carne dura. *2* carne de cerdo adobada.

**brawny** (-i) *adj.* musculoso, fornido.

**bray** (brei) *s.* rebuzno. *2* sonido bronco.

**bray (to)** *intr.* rebuznar. *2* hacer un sonido bronco. *3 tr.* moler, triturar.

**braze (to)** (breiš) *tr.* soldar con latón. *2* broncear.

**brazen** (brei·šn) *adj.* de latón. *2* broncíneo; bronceado. *3* descarado, desvergonzado.

**brazen (to)** *tr.* dar atrevimiento o descaro. *2 to* ~ *it out*, sostener o llevar a cabo con decisión o descaro.

**brazen-faced** *adj.* descarado, desvergonzado.

**brazier** (brei·ȳøʳ) *s.* latonero. *2* brasero [para calentarse].

**Brazil** (braši·l) *n. pr.* GEOGR. Brasil. *2 s.* (con min.) palo brasil.

**braziletto** (brašile·tou) *s.* brasilete.

**Brazilian** (braši·lian) *adj.* y *s.* brasileño.

**breach** (brɪch) *s.* brecha, portillo, abertura. *2* rotura, fractura. *3* hernia. *4* ruptura, desavenencia. *5* infracción, quebrantamiento, violación: ~ *of the peace*, alteración del orden público; ~ *of promise*, incumplimiento de la palabra de matrimonio.

**breach (to)** *tr.* abrir brecha o boquete en.

**bread** (bred) *s.* pan [de harina, etc.]; sustento diario]: ~ *crumb*, miga de pan; pan rallado; *to*

*know on which side one's* ~ *is buttered*, saber uno donde le aprieta el zapato.

**bread (to)** *tr.* COC. empanar.

**breadth** (bredz) *s.* anchura, ancho. *2* envergadura. *3* extensión, latitud, holgura. *4* amplitud [de juicio, de ideas].

**breadthwise** (-uaiš) *adv.* a lo ancho.

**break** (breik) *s.* break [coche]. *2* rotura, ruptura, rompimiento. *3* comienzo: ~ *of the day*, amanecer. *4* abertura, grieta. *5* interrupción, pausa, hueco, claro. *6* clara [en el tiempo]. *7* fuga, evasión. *8* ELECT. corte [en un circuito]. *9* GEOL. falla. *10* BILLAR tacada. *11* MÚS. gallo. *12* fig. (E.U) plancha. *13* (E.U) suerte, oportunidad.

**break (to)** *tr.* romper, quebrar, fracturar, hender, partir, quebrantar. *2* deshacer, descomponer. *3* agramar. *4* romper [filas]. *5* forzar [una puerta]. *6* abrir [un camino, etc.]. *7* templar, amortiguar. *8* parar [un golpe]. *9* penetrar, atravesar. *10* interrumpir, hacer cesar. *11* quebrantar, infringir. *12* hacer fracasar. *13* someter, dominar; domar. *14* causar la quiebra de, arruinar. *15* MIL. degradar. *16* abrumar. *17* comunicar, divulgar; dar [una noticia]. *18* PINT. templar [los colores]. *19 to* ~ *cover*, salir del escondite. *20* ~ *down*, demoler; anonadar; descomponer, analizar. *21 to* ~ *ground*, romper la tierra; comenzar una empresa. *22 to* ~ *in*, forzar la entrada; domar [un caballo]. *23 to* ~ *someone of a bad habit*, quitar un vicio a uno. *24 to* ~ *the record*, batir la marca. *25 to* ~ *up*, desmenuzar; romper; forzar; disolver [una reunión]; levantar [la casa, el campo]. *26 to* ~ *wind*, ventosear.

*27 intr.* romperse, abrirse, partirse. *28* quebrantarse [la salud]. *29* salir [un grito]; estallar [la tormenta]. *30* prorrumpir. *31* irrumpir. *32* abrirse, reventarse. *33* disolverse, disiparse. *34* romper [con uno]. *35* fallar, cascarse [la voz]. *36* estropearse. *37* debilitarse, perder la salud. *38* aparecer, salir, nacer, brotar, apuntar, comenzar. *39* divulgarse. *40 to* ~ *away*, soltarse; escapar. *41 to* ~ *down*, parar por avería; irse abajo; abatirse; perder la salud; prorrumpir en llanto. *42 to* ~ *forth*, brotar; estallar; prorrumpir. *43 to* ~ *out*, estallar, desatarse, empezar. *44 to* ~ *up*, disolverse, disgregarse; levantar [una sesión].

¶ Pret.: *broke*; p. p.: *broken*.

**breakage** (-i·dy̆) *s.* rotura. *2* indemnización por cosas rotas [en el transporte, etc.].

**breakdown** (-daun) *s.* caída, vuelco, derrumbamiento. *2* fracaso. *3* paro, interrupción, avería. *4* MED. colapso; agotamiento.

**breaker** (-øʳ) *s.* rompedor. *2* quebrantador. *3* roturador. *4* ELECT. disyuntor. *5* ola que rompe, cachón.

**breakfast** (-fast) *s.* desayuno, almuerzo.

**breakfast (to)** *intr.* desayunarse, almorzar.

**breakneck** (-nek) *s.* despeñadero, precipicio. *2 adj.* precipitado, rápido.

**breakup** (-øp) *s.* disolución, disgregación. *2* separación, dispersión.

**breakwater** (-uotøʳ) *s.* rompeolas.

**bream** (brim) *s.* ICT. brema; sargo.

**breast** (brest) *s.* pecho, seno [del cuerpo humano]. *2* pecho, seno, mama, teta [de mujer]; tetilla [de hombre]. *3* pecho [de animal]; pechuga [de ave]. *4* pechera [de una prenda]. *5* parte frontal [de una cosa]. *6* fig. pecho, corazón [interior del hombre].

**breast (to)** *tr.* arrostrar, luchar con.

**breastbone** (-boun) *s.* ANAT. esternón. *2* ORN. quilla.
**breastpin** (-pin) *s.* alfiler de pecho, broche.
**breastplate** (-pleit) *s.* peto [de armadura]. *2* petral. *3* pectoral, racional [de los judíos].
**breastwork** (-wøᵗk) *s.* FORT. parapeto. *2* MAR. propao.
**breath** (brez) *s.* hálito, aliento, respiración, resuello: *out of* ~, sin aliento, sofocado; *under one's* ~, en voz baja. *2* fig. vida. *3* hálito, soplo [de aire]. *4* soplo, instante. *5* respiro, descanso. *6* susurro.
**breathable** (brı-ðabøl) *adj.* respirable.
**breathe (to)** (brıð) *intr.* alentar, respirar, resollar. *2* respirar, descansar. *3* soplar [un aire suave]. *4* *tr.* respirar [el aire]. *5* exhalar: *to* ~ *one's last,* dar el último suspiro. *6* dar un descanso. *7* susurrar, decir, revelar. *8* infundir.
**breather** (-øᵗ) *s.* respirador. *2* viviente. *3* inspirador. *4* respiro, descanso.
**breathing** (-ing) *s.* respiración. *2* hálito. *3* inspiración, sugestión. *4* descanso, pausa. *5* momento.
**breathless** (-lis) *adj.* muerto. *2* jadeante, sin aliento. *3* intenso, expectante.
**bred** (bred) *pret.* y *p. p.* de TO BREED.
**breech** (brıch) *s.* trasero, posaderas. *2* recámara, culata [un arma].
**breech (to)** *tr.* poner calzones. *2* azotar, zurrar.
**breeches** (brı-chiš) *s. pl.* calzones, bragas, pantalón corto; fam. pantalones: *to wear the* ~, llevar los pantalones [la mujer].
**breeching** (-ching) *s.* retranca, cejadero.
**breed** (brıd) *s.* casta, raza, progenie. *2* clase, especie.
**breed (to)** *tr.* engendrar. *2* criar [animales]; dar, producir [flores, frutos, etc.]. *3* criar, educar. *4* *intr.* criarse. *5* producirse, originarse. ¶ Pret. y p. p.: *bred.*
**breeder** (-øᵗ) *s.* criador; productor. *2* animal reproductor.
**breeding** (-ing) *s.* cría, crianza; producción. *2* crianza, educación. *3* urbanidad, modales.
**breeze** (brıš) *s.* brisa, airecillo. *2* fam. excitación, enojo. *3* fam. rumor, murmuración.
**breezy** (-i) *adj.* oreado. *2* airoso, vivo, animado. *3* vivaracho, desenvuelto.
**brethren** (bre-ðrin) *s. pl.* hermanos, cofrades.
**Breton** (bre-tøn) *adj.-s.* bretón.
**breve** (briv) *s.* MÚS. breve.
**brevet** (brøve-t) *s.* título, despacho. *2* MIL. graduación honoraria; grado.
**brevet (to)** *tr.* MIL. graduar.
**breviary** (brı-vieri) *s.* breviario.
**brevity** (bre-viti) *s.* brevedad; concisión.
**brew** (bru) *s.* bebida preparada, mezcla, infusión.
**brew (to)** *tr.* hacer [cerveza]. *2* preparar [el té, un ponche, etc.]. *3* urdir, tramar. *4* *intr.* hacer cerveza. *5* prepararse, amenazar [una tempestad, etc.].
**brewage** (-dȳ) *s.* BREW.
**brewer** (-øᵗ) *s.* cervecro [que hace cerveza].
**brewry** (-øri), **brewhouse** (-jaus) *s.* cervecería, fábrica de cerveza.
**briar** (brai-øᵗ) *s.* BRIER.
**bribe** (braib) *s.* soborno, cohecho [dinero, etc.]. *2* cebo, incentivo.
**bribe (to)** *tr.* sobornar, cohechar.
**bribery** (-øri) *s.* soborno, cohecho [acción].
**bric-a-brac** (brı-kabræk) *s.* artículos de arte, antigüedades.
**brick** (brik) *s.* ladrillo; ladrillos. *2* fam. persona excelente, simpática.

**brick (to)** *tr.* enladrillar.
**brickbat** (-bæt) *s.* pedazo de ladrillo.
**bricklayer** (-leiøᵗ) *s.* albañil.
**brickmaker** (-meikøᵗ) *s.* ladrillero.
**brickyard** (-iaᵗd) *s.* ladrillar.
**bridal** (brai-dal) *adj.* nupcial. *2* de la novia. *3* *s.* boda.
**bride** (braid) *s.* novia, desposada.
**bridegroom** (-grum) *s.* novio, desposado.
**bridesmaid** (-šmeid) *s.* dama de honor [en una boda].
**bridesman** (-šmæn) *s.* padrino de boda.
**bridge** (bridȳ) *s.* puente [para pasar un río, etc.]. *2* caballete [de la nariz]. *3* MÚS., ODON., QUÍM. puente. *4* MAR. puente de mando. *5* BILL. violín. *6* bridge [juego]. *7* ELECT. conexión en paralelo.
**bridge (to)** *tr.* pontear. *2* salvar, cubrir [un espacio].
**bridgehead** (-jed) *s.* MIL. cabeza de puente.
**bridle** (brai-døl) *s.* EQUIT. brida: ~ *path,* camino de herradura. *2* freno, sujeción. *3* ANAT. frenillo. *4* MAR. poa.
**bridle (to)** *tr.* embridar. *2* refrenar, dominar. *3* erguir la cabeza, engallarse.
**bridoon** (brindu·n) *s.* bridón, filete.
**brief** (brıf) *adj.* breve, corto, conciso, lacónico, seco. *2* fugaz, pasajero. *3 s.* breve [apostólico]. *4* resumen, compendio. *5* DER. informe, escrito: ~ *bag,* cartera [para documentos].
**briefless** (-lis) *adj.* sin pleitos [abogado].
**brier** (brai·øᵗ) *s.* BOT. escaramujo. *2* BOT. zarza. *3* BOT. brezo. *4* pipa de brezo.
**briery** (-i) *adj.* zarzoso.
**brig** (brig) *s.* MAR. bergantín; bricbarca.
**brigade** (brigei·d) *s.* brigada.
**brigade (to)** *tr.* reunir en brigada.
**brigadier** (brigadı·øᵗ) *s.* brigadier.
**brigand** (bri·gand) *s.* bandido, bandolero.
**brigandage** (-idȳ) *s.* bandolerismo.
**brigantine** (bri·gantin) *s.* bergantín, goleta.
**bright** (brait) *adj.* brillante. *2* lustroso. *3* luminoso, resplandeciente. *4* límpido. *5* vibrante [sonido]. *6* vivo [color]. *7* claro, ilustre. *8* alegre. *9* inteligente, perspicaz. *10* vivo, animado.
**brighten (to)** (-øn) *tr.* abrillantar. *2* avivar, animar, alegrar. *3* enaltecer. *4* *intr.* cobrar brillo. *5* avivarse, alegrarse. *6* aclararse.
**brightness** (-nis) *s.* brillo, brillantez. *2* claridad, luz. *3* alegría, viveza. *4* agudeza de ingenio.
**brill** (bril) *s.* ICT. rodaballo.
**brilliance, -cy** (bri·lians, -si) *s.* brillantez, brillo, resplandor. *2* esplendor, lustre.
**brilliant** (bri·liant) *adj.* brillante. *2 s.* brillante [piedra].
**brilliantine** (-in) *s.* brillantina.
**brim** (brim) *s.* borde, orilla. *2* borde [de una vasija]. *3* ala [de sombrero].
**brim (to)** *tr.* llenar hasta el borde. *2* *intr.* rebosar. *3* asomar [las lágrimas]. ¶ Pret. y p. p.: *brimmed;* ger.: *brimming.*
**brimful** (-ful) *adj.* lleno hasta el borde.
**brimless** (-lis) *adj.* sin borde o ala.
**brimmer** (-øᵗ) *s.* copa o vaso lleno.
**brimstone** (-stoun) *s.* azufre.
**brindled** (bri·ndøld) *adj.* leonado, rayado [animal].
**brine** (brain) *s.* salmuera; agua salada. *2* fig. mar. *3* poét. lágrimas.
**brine (to)** *tr.* poner en salmuera.
**bring (to)** (bring) *tr.* traer, llevar [en varios sentidos]. *2* acarrear, producir, causar. *3* poner [en

un estado, condición, etc.]. *4* inducir [persuadir].' *5* DER. intentar [una acción]. *6* aportar, aducir. *7* rentar. *8 to ~ about*, efectuar, realizar; traer, ocasionar. *9 to ~ down*, bajar, hacer caer, derribar; abatir, humillar; reducir. *10 to ~ forth*, dar [fruto]; dar a luz; poner de manifiesto, aducir. *11 to ~ forward*, presentar; aducir; COM. llevar a otra cuenta. *12 to ~ in*, entrar, introducir; producir, rentar; presentar [un proyecto, etc.]; dar [un fallo]. *13 to ~ out*, sacar; publicar; presentar. *14 to ~ round*, ganar, persuadir; devolver la salud. *15 to ~ to*, hacer volver en sí. *16 to ~ to bear*, aplicar; apuntar, asestar. *17 to ~ up*, subir; criar, educar; traer, presentar, llevar [ante]; parar, detener; *to ~ up by hand*, criar con biberón; *to ~ up the rear*, cerrar la marcha. ¶ Pret. y p. p.: *brought*.

**bringing-up** *s.* crianza, educación [de un niño].

**brink** (brink) *s.* borde, orilla, extremidad; *on the ~ of*, al borde, a punto de.

**briny** (bri·ni) *adj.* salobre, salado.

**briquette** (brike·t) *s.* aglomerado.

**brisk** (brisk) *adj.* vivo, activo, animado. *2* ágil, ligero, rápido. *3* fresco [viento]. *4* espumoso [licor].

**brisk up (to)** *tr.* avivar, activar, apresurar. *2 intr.* animarse; apresurarse.

**brisket** (bri·skit) *s.* pecho [de una res].

**briskness** (bris·knis) *s.* viveza, actividad, vivacidad.

**bristle** (bri·søl) *s.* cerda, porcipelo.

**bristle (to)** *tr.* erizar. *2 intr.* erizarse, erizar [el pelo, etc.]; encresparse. *3 to ~ with*, estar erizado de.

**bristly** (bri·sli) *adj.* cerdoso, hirsuto.

**Bristol board** (bri·støl) *s.* cartulina.

**Britain [Great]** (bri·tøn) *n. pr.* GEOGR. Gran Bretaña.

**Britannia** (britæ·nia) *n. pr.* Britania, la Gran Bretaña, el Imperio Británico.

**British** (bri·tish) *adj.* británico, inglés. *2 s.* britano, inglés.

**Briton** (bri·tøn) *s.* brítano.

**Brittany** (bri·tani) *n. pr.* GEOGR. Bretaña.

**brittle** (bri·tøl) *adj.* quebradizo, friable. *2* vidrioso, irritable.

**broach** (brouch) *s.* espetón, asador. *2* lezna, punzón. *3* CARP. broca, mecha. *4* aguja, chapitel. *5* broche, prendedor.

**broach (to)** *tr.* espetar, ensartar. *2* espitar. *3* empezar, decentar. *4* hacer público; mencionar por primera vez.

**broad** (brod) *adj.* ancho. *2* anchuroso. *3* amplio, extenso, lato. *4* claro, obvio. *5* tolerante, comprensivo. *6* esencial, general. *7* vulgar, grosero, libre, atrevido. *8* cerrado, dialectal. *9 in ~ day*, en pleno día.

**broadcast** (-kæst) *s.* esparcimiento; siembra al voleo. *2* emisión de radio.

**broadcast (to)** *tr.* esparcir, difundir. *2* sembrar al voleo. *3* radiar, emitir por radio. ¶ Pret. y p. p.: *broadcast*, y también, refiriéndose a la radio; *broadcasted*.

**broadcasting** (-ing) *s.* radiodifusión: *~ station*, emisora de radio.

**boadcloth** (-kloz) *s.* paño fino.

**broaden (to)** (-øn) *tr.* ensanchar. *2 intr.* ensancharse.

**broad-minded** *adj.* liberal, tolerante, despreocupado.

**broadside** (-said) *s.* MAR. costado [de un buque], andana. *2* MAR. andanada. *3* IMPR. hoja suelta,

grande. *3* CINEM. lámpara o batería que ilumina fuertemente.

**broadsword** (so·d) *s.* espadón, montante.

**broadwise** (-wuaiš) *adv.* a lo ancho, por lo ancho.

**brocade** (brokei·d) *s.* brocado.

**brocaded** (-id) *adj.* brochado; recamado.

**broccoli** (bra·koli) *s.* BOT. brécol, bróculi.

**brochure** (broshu·ø^r) *s.* folleto.

**brock** (bra·k) *s.* ZOOL. tejón.

**brocket** (-it) *s.* gamo de dos años.

**brogue** (brou·g) *s.* abarca. *2* acento irlandés.

**broil** (broil) *s.* asado a la parrilla. *2* calor intenso. *3* riña, alboroto, tumulto.

**broil (to)** *tr.* asar a la parrilla. *2* achicharrar. *3 intr.* asarse; achicharrarse.

**broiler** (-ø^r) *s.* COC. parrilla. *2* pollo asadero. *3* camorrista.

**broiling** (-ing) *adj.* ardiente, achicharrador.

**brocke** (brouk) *pret.* de TO BREAK. *2 adj.* pop. arruinado.

**broken** (brou·køn) *p. p.* de TO BREAK. *2 adj.* roto, cascado. *3* roturado. *4* quebrada [línea]. *5* accidentado [suelo]. *6* suelto, disgregado. *7* interrumpido, entrecortado. *8* fragmentario. *9* quebrantado, debilitado. *10* arruinado.

**broken-down** *adj.* abatido. *2* deshecho, descompuesto. *3* quebrantado. *4* arruinado.

**brokenly** (-li) *adv.* interrumpidamente, a ratos. *2* entrecortadamente.

**broker** (brou·kø^r) *s.* COM. corredor, agente. *2* bolsista. *3* (Ingl.) chamarilero; tasador y vendedor de objetos embargados.

**brokerage** (-dy) *s.* corretaje, correduría.

**bromatology** (broumɑta·lodȳi) *s.* bromatología.

**bromide** (brou·mid) *s.* QUÍM. bromuro.

**bromine** (brou·min) *s.* QUÍM. bromo.

**bronchi** (bra·nkai) *s. pl.* bronquios.

**bronchial** (-kial) *adj.* bronquial.

**bronchitis** (-kaitiš) *s.* bronquitis.

**bronchopneumonia** (brankoniumou·nia) *s.* bronconeumonía.

**bronchus** (bra·nkøs) *s.* bronquio.

**bronco** (bra·nkou) *s.* caballo pequeño y medio salvaje de Norteamérica.

**bronze** (branš) *s.* bronce.

**bronze (to)** *tr.* broncear. *2 intr.* broncearse.

**brooch** (brouch) *s.* broche; alfiler de pecho.

**brood** (brud) *s.* cría, pollada, nidada, lechigada. *2* progenie. *3* casta.

**brood (to)** *tr.* empollar, incubar. *2* cobijar. *3* tramar, fraguar. *4 intr.* encobar. *5* meditar, cavilar. | Gralte. con *on* u *over*.

**brooder** (-ø^r) *s.* clueca. *2* incubadora. *3* rumión, caviloso.

**broody** (-i) *adj.* clueca. *2* caviloso, melancólico.

**brook** (bruk) *s.* arroyo, riachuelo.

**brook (to)** *tr.* sufrir, aguantar, tolerar.

**brooklet** (-lit) *s.* arroyuelo.

**broom** (brum) *s.* escoba. *2* BOT. escoba; retama de escobas.

**broomstick** (-stik) *s.* palo de escoba.

**broth** (broz) *s.* COC. caldo.

**brothel** (bra·ðøl) *s.* burdel.

**brother** (brøðø^r) *s.* hermano. *2* cofrade, colega.

**brotherhood** (-jud) *s.* hermandad, hermanazgo. *2* hermandad, cofradía.

**brother-in-law** *s.* cuñado, hermano político.

**brotherly** (-li) *adj.* fraterno; fraternal. *2 adv.* fraternalmente.

**brougham** (bru·am) *s.* berlina [coche].

**brought** (brot) *pret.* y *p. p.* de TO BRING.

**brow** (brau) *s.* ANAT. ceja. *2* frente, entrecejo. *3* semblante. *4* cresta, cima, cumbre.

**browbeat (to)** (-bɪt) *tr.* intimidar, aturrullar [con miradas o palabras]. ¶ Pret. *browbeat;* p. p.: *browbeaten.*

**brown** (braun) *adj.* pardo, moreno, castaño, bazo: ~ *paper,* papel de estraza o de embalar; ~ *race,* raza cobriza; *in a* ~ *study,* absorto en sus pensamientos. *2 s.* pardo, moreno, castaño [color].

**brown (to)** *tr.* poner moreno; broncear. *2* COC. tostar, dorar. *3 intr.* tostarse.

**browning** (-ing) *s.* pistola automática.

**brownstone** (-stoun) *s.* arenisca de color obscuro.

**browse** (brauš) *s.* pimpollos, hojas tiernas [que roza el ganado]. *2* roza, ramoneo.

**browse (to)** *tr.* rozar, ramonear; pacer.

**bruise** (bruš) *s.* magulladura, cardenal, contusión. *2* maca [en la fruta]. *3* abolladura.

**bruise (to)** *tr.* magullar, contundir. *2* machucar, abollar. *3* majar, machacar.

**bruiser** (-ø<sup>r</sup>) *s.* boxeador. *2* majador.

**bruit (to)** (brut) *tr.* esparcir, publicar, divulgar. *2* dar fama.

**brume** (bru·m) *s.* bruma, neblina.

**brumous** (-øs) *adj.* brumoso.

**brunette** (brune·t) *adj.-s.* morena, trigueña.

**brunt** (brønt) *s.* choque, embate; lo más recio [de una lucha, etc.].

**brush** (brøsh) *s.* cepillo, bruza; escobilla. *2* brocha, pincel. *3* hopo [rabo peludo]. *4* cepilladura. *5* roce. *6* ramojo, broza. *7* matorral, maleza. *8* escaramuza.

**brush (to)** *tr.* cepillar, frotar, restregar; pasar la brocha, el pincel. *2* rozar, rasar, empujar [al pasar]: *to* ~ *aside,* apartar; desechar.

**brushmaker** (-meikø<sup>r</sup>) *s.* brucero.

**brushwood** (-wud) *s.* ramojo, broza. *2* matorral, zarzal.

**brushy** (brø·shi) *adj.* matoso. *2* hirsuto.

**brusque** (brøsk) *adj.* brusco, rudo.

**brusque (to)** *tr.* tratar con rudeza.

**brusqueness** (-nis) *s.* brusquedad.

**Brussels** (brø·sølš) *n. pr.* GEOGR. Bruselas. *2 s.* ~ *sprouts,* coles de Bruselas.

**brutal** (bru·tal) *adj.* brutal, bestial, cruel.

**brutality** (brutæ·liti) *s.* brutalidad, crueldad.

**brutalize** (bru·talaiš) *tr.* volver brutal. *2* tratar brutalmente. *3 intr.* bestializarse.

**brute** (brut) *s.* bruto [animal; pers. brutal]. *2 adj.* brutal, bruto.

**brutify (to)** (bru·tifai) *tr.* embrutecer. *2 intr.* embrutecerse. ¶ Pret. y p. p.: *brutified.*

**brutish** (bru·tish) *adj.* abrutado, brutal, bestial. *2* estúpido. *3* sensual, grosero.

**bryology** (braia·lodẏi) *s.* briología.

**bryony** (brai·øni) *s.* brionia, nueza.

**bubal** (biu·bal) *s.* búbalo.

**bubble** (bø·bøl) *s.* burbuja, ampolla, pompa. *2* borbolleo. *3* quimera, ilusión. *4* ~ *gum,* chicle hinchable.

**bubble (to)** *intr.* burbujear, borbollar, hervir. *2* murmurar [un río, etc.]. *3 to* ~ *over,* rebosar.

**bubbly** (bø·bli) *adj.* burbujeante, espumoso.

**bubo** (biu·bou) *s.* MED. bubón.

**bubonic** (biuba·nik) *adj.* bubónico.

**buccal** (bø·kal) *adj.* bucal.

**buccaneer** (bøkanɪ·<sup>r</sup>) *s.* bucanero.

**bucentaur** (biuse·nto<sup>r</sup>) *s.* bucentauro.

**buck** (bøk) *s.* ZOOL. macho cabrío: gamo; macho de otros animales. *2* petimetre. *3* lejía, colada. *4* salto de carnero. *5* fam. dólar.

**buck (to)** *tr.* colar [ropa]. *2* tirar [al jinete] el caballo. *3* romper [mineral]. *4* embestir; oponerse, resistir. *5 intr.* dar un salto de carnero. *6 tr.-intr.* animar, animarse.

**bucket** (bo·kit) *s.* cubo, herrada, balde. *2* cangilón [de noria]; paleta [de rueda hidráulica]; cuchara [de excavadora, etc.].

**buckle** (bø·kol) *s.* hebilla. *2* alabeo.

**buckle (to)** *tr.* abrochar, enhebillar. *2* alabear. *3 intr.* alabearse. *4 to* ~ *for,* prepararse para; *to* ~ *to,* aplicarse a.

**buckler** (bø·klø<sup>r</sup>) *s.* broquel, rodela, escudo.

**buckram** (-kram) *s.* zangala. *2* tiesura.

**buckshot** (-shat) *s.* posta [perdigón].

**buckskin** (-skin) *s.* ante [piel].

**buckthorn** (-zo<sup>r</sup>n) *s.* BOT. espino cerval. *2* BOT. aladierna.

**buckwheat** (-juit) *s.* BOT. alforfón.

**bucolic** (biuka·lik) *adj.* bucólico. *2 s.* bucólica [poema].

**bud** (bød) *s.* yema, botón, brote, pimpollo, capullo: *in the* ~, fig. en su principio.

**bud (to)** *intr.* brotar, pimpollecer, florecer. *2* empezar a desarrollarse. *3 tr.* injertar de escudete. ¶ Pret. y p. p.: *budded;* ger.: *budding.*

**Buddha** (bu·da) *n. pr.* Buda.

**Buddhism** (bu·dišm) *s.* budismo.

**budding** (bø·ding) *adj.* en capullo, en ciernes.

**budge** (bødẏ) *s.* piel de cordero [en peletería]. *2 adj.* grave, solemne, pomposo.

**budge (to)** *tr.* mover. *2 intr.* moverse, menearse.

**budget** (bø·dẏit) *s.* presupuesto. *2* saco [de noticias, etc.].

**budget (to)** *tr.-intr.* presuponer, presupuestar.

**buff** (bøf) *adj.* de ante, anteado. *2 s.* ante [piel].

**buff (to)** *tr.* pulir con ante. *2* parar [un golpe]; amortiguar [un choque].

**buffalo** (bø·falou) *s.* ZOOL. búfalo; su piel.

**buffer** (bø·fø<sup>r</sup>) *s.* MEC. amortiguador [de choques]. *2* FERROC. tope.

**buffet** (bø·fit) *s.* bofetada, puñada. *2* embate. *3* aparador [mueble]. *4* ambigú. *5* bar [de estación, etc.]. *6* caja [de órgano].

**buffet (to)** (bø·fit) *tr.* abofetear, pegar. *2* batir, combatir, aporrear. *3 intr.* luchar [con].

**buffing block** *s.* FERROC. tope.

**buffoon** (bøfu·n) *s.* bufón, payaso. *2 adj.* bufón.

**buffoonery** (-øri) *s.* bufonada.

**buffy** (bø·fi) *adj.* anteado.

**bug** (bøg) *s.* insecto, bicho. *2* [Ingl.] chinche.

**bugaboo** (-abu), **bugbear** (-be<sup>r</sup>) *s.* coco, bu, espantajo.

**buggy** (-i) *adj.* lleno de bichos. *2* pop. chiflado. *3 s.* especie de calesa.

**bugle** (biu·gøl) *s.* MIL. clarín, corneta. *2* MÚS. bugle. *3* BOT. consuelda menor. *4* cañutillo [abalorio]. *5* MÚS. ~ *horn,* cuerno de caza.

**bugler** (biu·glø<sup>r</sup>) *s.* clarín, corneta, etc. [pers.].

**bugloss** (biu·glas) *s.* BOT. buglosa.

**buhl** (bul), **buhlwork** (-uø<sup>r</sup>k) *s.* taracea, marquetería. *2* ~ *saw,* segueta.

**build** (bild) *s.* estructura. *2* forma, figura, talle.

**build (to)** *tr.* construir, edificar, labrar, erigir. *2* fabricar, crear. *3* fundar, cimentar. *4 intr. to* ~ *on,* o *upon,* contar con. ¶ Pret. y p. p.: *built.*

**builder** (-ø<sup>r</sup>) *s.* constructor, edificador. *2* maestro de obras.

**building** (-ing) *s.* construcción, edificación. *2* edificio, casa, fábrica, obra.

**built** (bilt) *pret.* y *p. p.* de TO BUILD.

**bulb** (bølb) *s.* BOT., ZOOL. bulbo. *2* ELECT. bombilla.

3 bola o depósito [de termómetro o barómetro].
4 pera de goma.
**bulbous** (-øs) *adj.* bulboso.
**Bulgarian** (bølgue·ri*a*n) *adj.-s.* búlgaro.
**bulge** (bø·ldŷ) *s.* protuberancia, pandeo, panza. 2
BILDE.
**bulge (to)** *intr.* hacer bulto; pandearse.
**bulgy** (-i) *adj.* abultado, prominente, pandeado.
**bulk** (bølk) *s.* bulto, volumen, tamaño, corpulencia. 2 mole, balumba. 3 la mayor parte, el grueso. 4 cabida [de un buque]. 5 COM. *in* ~, a granel, suelto.
**bulk (to)** *intr.* abultar, hacer bulto. 2 tener importancia.
**bulkhead** (-jed) *s.* mamparo.
**bulky** (-i) *adj.* abultado, voluminoso, macizo, pesado.
**bull** (bul) *s.* ZOOL. toro; ~ *ring*, plaza de toros. 2 ASTR. Tauro. 3 macho de algunos animales. 4 COM. alcista. 5 bula [pontificia]. 6 despropósito.
**bull (to)** *tr.* COM. *to* ~ *the market*, hacer subir la Bolsa.
**bulla** (bu·la) *s.* bula [sello].
**bulbaiting** (bu·lbeiting) *s.* lucha de perros y toros.
**bulldog** (-dog) *s.* perro dogo. 2 revólver de gran calibre.
**bulldozer** (bu·ldousø*r*) *s.* valentón. 2 excavadora, buldozer.
**bullet** (bu·lit) *s.* bala [de fusil o pistola]. 2 plomo [de la caña de pescar].
**bulletin** (bu·løtin) *s.* boletín. 2 comunicado.
**bullfight** (bu·lfait) *s.* corrida de toros.
**bullfighter** (-ø*r*) *s.* torero.
**bullfighting** (-ing) *s.* tauromaquia, toreo, toros.
**bullfinch** (bul·finch) *s.* ORN. pinzón real.
**bullhead** (-jed) *s.* ORN. chorlito. 2 fam. tonto, cabezota. 3 nombre de varios peces.
**bullion** (bu·li*ø*n) *s.* oro o plata en barras. 2 pasamanería de oro o plata. 3 COM. metálico.
**bullish** (bu·lish) *adj.* disparatado. 2 en alza, alcista.
**bullock** (bu·løk) *s.* buey.
**bull-roarer** *s.* bramadera [juguete].
**bull's-eye** *s.* ARQ., MAR. ojo de buey. 2 diana [de un blanco]. 3 linterna sorda.
**bully** (bu·li) *s.* matón, valentón; el que maltrata a los débiles. 2 *adj.* fam. (E. U.) magnífico, excelente.
**bully (to)** *tr.* intimidar con gritos o amenazas; maltratar [a los débiles]. 2 *intr.* fanfarronear. ¶ Pret. y p. p.: *bullied.*
**bulrush** (bu·lrøsh) *s.* BOT. anea; junco.
**bulwark** (-ua*r*k) *s.* baluarte. 2 rompeolas. 3 MAR. amurada.
**bulwark (to)** *tr.* abaluartar.
**bum** (bøm) *s.* (E. U.) juerga; jira. 2 (E. U.) vago, gorrón. 3 vulg. trasero.
**bumbailif** (bømbei·lif) *s.* alguacil.
**bumblebee** (bø·mbølbı) *s.* ENT. abejarrón, abejorro.
**bump** (bømp) *s.* choque, encontrón, coscorrón, porrazo, batacazo. 2 chichón. 3 protuberancia. 4 sacudida [del avión].
**bump (to)** *tr.-intr.* golpear; chocar [con], dar [contra].
**bumper** (-ø*r*) *s.* lo que golpea. 2 parachoques. 3 FERROC. tope. 4 copa o vaso lleno.
**bumpkin** (-kin) *adj.* presuntuoso.
**bumpy** (bø·mpi) *adj.* abollado. 2 lleno de baches. 3 AVIA. agitado [aire].

**bun** (bøn) *s.* bollo [panecillo]. 2 moño, castaña. 3 rato [de conejo o liebre].
**bunch** (bønch) *s.* manojo, haz, mazo, ristra. 2 racimo. 3 macolla. 4 grupo, hato. 5 giba.
**bunch (to)** *tr.* juntar, amanojar, arracimar. 2 *intr.* juntarse, arracimarse.
**buncombe** (bø·ncøm) *s.* faramalla.
**bundle** (bø·ndøl) *s.* atado, manojo, mazo, haz. 2 bulto, envoltorio, paquete, lío, fajo.
**bundle (to)** *tr.* liar, atar, empaquetar, envolver: *to* ~ *up*, arropar. 2 tr.-intr. *to* ~ *off* o *out*, enviar, despedir precipitadamente; salir precipitadamente.
**bung** (bøng) *s.* tapón de tonel.
**bung (to)** *tr.* tapar [un tonel]. 2 tapar, obstruir.
**bungalow** (-alou) *s.* casita de una sola planta con veranda.
**bungle** (-øl) *s.* chapucería; torpeza.
**bungle (to)** *tr.* chafallar, estropear; hacer torpemente. 2 *intr.* obrar con torpeza.
**bungler** (-lø*r*) *s.* chapucero.
**bunion** (bø·niøn) *s.* juanete [del pie].
**bunk** (bønk) *s.* tarima, litera [para dormir].
**bunk (to)** *tr.* dormir en litera. 2 acostarse.
**bunker** (bø·nkø*r*) *s.* arcón. 2 MAR. carbonera. 3 GOLF hoyo de arena.
**bunny** (bø·ni) *s.* fam. conejito, ardilla.
**bunt** (bønt) *s.* MAR. bolsa [de red]; seno [de vela]. 2 empellón; topetazo. 3 (Ingl.) cola de conejo o liebre. 4 añubio, tizón.
**bunt (to)** *tr.* empellar; topetar.
**bunting** (-ing) *s.* lanilla [para banderas]. 2 empavesado. 3 nombre del hortelano y otros pájaros.
**buntline** (-lain) *s.* briol.
**buoy** (boi) *s.* boya, baliza.
**buoy (to)** *tr.* mantener a flote. 2 sostener, animar. 3 aboyar.
**buoyancy** (-ansi) *s.* propiedad de flotar. 2 fuerza ascensional. 3 elasticidad [del ánimo]; alegría, animación. 4 tendencia [de los precios, valores, etc.] a subir de nuevo.
**buoyant** (-ant) *adj.-s.* que flota o sostiene a flote. 2 elástico, ligero, alegre, animado, vivaz.
**bur** (bø*r*) *s.* erizo [de castaña]. 2 carda [de cardencha]. 3 BOT. bardana, cadillo. 4 TEJ. mota, nudillo. 5 arandela [de lanza].
**bur (to)** ) *tr.* TEJ. desmotar. ¶ Pret. y p. p.: *burred; ger.: -rring.*
**burbot** (bø·*r*bøt) *s.* ICT. lota.
**burden** (bø·*r*døn) *s.* carga [que se transporta]. 2 fig. carga, peso, gravamen. 3 MAR. porte, tonelaje. 4 poét. estribillo. 5 tema, idea principal.
**burden (to)** *tr.* cargar, agobiar, gravar.
**burdensome** (-søm) *adj.* gravoso, pesado, agobiador.
**burdock** (bø·*r*dak) *s.* BOT. bardana; cadillo.
**bureau** (biu·rou) *s.* escritorio [mesa]. 2 despacho, oficina; negociado, departamento.
**bureaucracy** (biura·krasi) *s.* burocracia.
**bureaucrat** (-kræt) *s.* burócrata.
**burette** (biure·t) *s.* bureta.
**burg** (bø*r*g) *s.* BOROUGH.
**burgeon** (bø·*r*ŷøn) *s.* BOURGEON.
**bourgeon (to)** *intr.* TO BOURGEON.
**burgess** (bø·*r*dŷis) *s.* burgués, ciudadano libre.
**burgh** (bø*r*g) *s.* municipio escocés.
**burglar** (bø·*r*gla*r*) *s.* ladrón [que roba con escalo].
**burglary** (-i) *s.* robo con escalo.
**burgle (to)** (bø·*r*gøl) *intr.* robar con escalo.
**burgomaster** (bø·*r*gomæstø*r*) *s.* burgomaestre.
**burgonet** (bø·*r*gonet) *s.* borgoñota.

**Burgundy** (bø·ᵣgøndi) *n. pr.* Borgoña.
**burial** (bø·rial) *s.* entierro, sepelio.
**burin** (biu·rin) *s.* buril, cincel.
**burl** (bøᵣl) *s.* TEJ. mota, nudillo. 2 CARP. nudo.
**burl (to)** *tr.* desmotar, despinzar.
**burlap** (bø·ᵣlæp) *s.* harpillera.
**burlesque** (bø·ˢlesk) *adj.* burlesco.
**burlesque (to)** *tr.* parodiar, ridiculizar.
**burly** (bø·ᵣli) *adj.* corpulento, fornido. 2 nudoso.
**Burma** (bø·ᵣmæ) *n. pr.* GEOGR. Birmania.
**Burmese** (-ɪ·š) *adj.-s.* birmano.
**burn** (bøᵣn) *s.* quemadura. 2 quema. 3 cocción [de
ladrillos]. 4 (Esc.) riachuelo.
**burn (to)** *tr.* quemar, abrasar, incendiar, inflamar:
*to ~ up*, quemar, consumir del todo: *to ~ the
midnight oil*, quemarse las cejas. 2 quemar,
abrasar [la lengua, el paladar, etc.]. 3 AGR. ahor-
nagar. 4 cocer [ladrillos, etc.]. 5 calcinar. 6 hacer [quemando]. 7 cauterizar. 8 tostar, atezar. 9
*intr.* arder, quemarse, abrasarse. 10 encenderse,
inflamarse. 11 *to ~ out*, pasarse [el fuego], quemarse [un fusible, motor, etc.]; fundirse [una
bombilla]. ¶ Pret. y p. p.: *burned* o *burnt*.
**burner** (-øᵣ) *s.* quemador. 2 mechero, piquera. 3
punta de soplete.
**burnet** (-it) *s.* BOT. sanguisorba.
**burning** (-ing) *adj.* ardiente, encendido, abrasador. 2 ustorio. 3 vehemente. 4 urente.
**burnish** (bø·ᵣnish) *s.* bruñido, pulimento.
**burnish (to)** *tr.* bruñir, pulir. 2 FOT. satinar.
**burnisher** (-øᵣ) *s.* bruñidor, pulidor. 2 FOT. satina-
dor.
**burnous** (bø·ᵣnøs) *s.* albornoz.
**burnt** (bøᵣnt) *prep.* y *p. p.* de TO BURN.
**burr** (bøᵣ) *s.* BUR. 2 piedra amoladera. 3 METEOR.
halo. 4 DENT. buril. 5 METAL. rebaba. 6 zumbido,
chirrido [de insecto]. 8 pronunciación gutural
de la *r*.
**burr (to)** *tr.-intr.* pronunciar la *r* con sonido gutural.
**burrow** (bø·rou) *s.* madriguera, conejera. 2 galería, excavación.
**burrow (to)** *intr.-tr.* minar [como los conejos]. 2
*intr.* amadrigarse. 3 buscar, investigar.
**burrstone** (bø·ᵣstoun) *s.* piedra de molino.
**bursar** (bø·ᵣsaᵣ) *s.* tesorero. 2 becario.
**bursary** (-i) *s.* tesorería. 2 beca.
**burse** (bøᵣs) *s.* bolsa. 2 bolsa de corporales.
**burst** (bøᵣst) *s.* explosión, estallido, reventón. 2 esfuerzo supremo. 3 ráfaga [de tiros].
**burst (to)** *intr.* reventar, estallar, volar, hacer explosión; romperse, abrirse. 2 aparecer, entrar,
salir, etc., súbitamente o con violencia. 3 prorrumpir. 4 rebosar. 5 *tr.* reventar, romper, hacer
estallar. ¶ Pret. y p. p.: *burst*.
**bury (to)** (be·ri) *tr.* enterrar. 2 sepultar. 3 soterrar;
esconder, ocultar. ¶ Pret. y p. p.: *buried*.
**burying** (-ing) *s.* entierro.
**bus** (bøs) *s.* fam. ómnibus, autobús.
**busby** (bø·sbai) *s.* birretina.
**bush** (bush) *s.* arbusto, mata. 2 matorral, maleza.
3 ramo [de taberna]. 4 hopo [de zorra]. 5 BUS-
HING.
**bush (to)** *tr.* sostener o cubrir con matas. 2 MEC.
guarnecer de buje, forro, etc. 3 *intr.* crecer espeso.
**bushel** (bu·shøl) *s.* medida para áridos.
**bushhammer** (-jæmøᵣ) *s.* escoda.
**bushing** (-ing) *s.* MEC. buje, boquilla, casquillo, forro [de metal].
**Bushman** (-mæn) *s.* bosquimano.

**bushy** (-i) *adj.* matoso. 2 espeso, peludo.
**busily** (bi·šili) *adv.* activamente. 2 atareadamente.
**business** (bi·šnis) *s.* oficio, ocupación, quehacer,
trabajo, asunto: *to mean ~*, obrar o hablar en
serio; *mind your own ~*, no se meta en lo que no
le importa. 2 negocio, comercio, tráfico. 3 negocio, casa, establecimiento, empresa.
**businesslike** (-laik) *adj.* metódico, ordenado. 2
práctico, expeditivo. 3 formal, directo.
**busk** (bøsk) *s.* ballena o hierro [de corsé].
**buskin** (bø·skin) *s.* borceguí. 2 coturno.
**busman** (bø·smæn) *s.* conductor de autobús.
**buss** (bøs) *s.* beso, beso sonoro.
**bust** (bøst) *s.* busto. 2 pop. fracaso. 3 pop. borrachera.
**bust (to)** *tr.* pop. reventar, romper. 2 *tr.-intr.* (E.U.)
arruinar, arruinarse.
**bustard** (bø·staᵣd) *s.* ORN. avutarda; sisón.
**bustle** (bø·søl) *s.* movimiento, agitación, bullicio;
diligencia oficiosa. 2 polisón.
**bustle (to)** *tr.-intr.* bullir, menearse, no parar.
**bustler** (bø·stløᵣ) *s.* bullebulle.
**busy** (bi·ši) *adj.* ocupado, atareado. 2 activo, diligente. 3 bullicioso, entrometido.
**busy (to)** *tr.* ocupar, emplear; atarear. 2 *ref.* ocuparse, atarearse. ¶ Pret. y p. p.: *busied*.
**busybody** (-badi) *s.* entremetido, fisgón, chismoso.
**but** (bøt) *prep.-conj.* excepto, fuera de, menos,
sino: *last ~ one*, el penúltimo; *no one ~ you*,
nadie sino usted. 2 *conj.* pero, empero, mas. 3
que no, sin que, que. 4 *I cannot ~*, no puedo
menos de, no puedo dejar de. 5 *adv.* sólo, no más
que. 6 *all ~*, casi, por poco. 7 *~ for*, a no ser por.
8 *s.* pero [objeción, dificultad].
**butane** (biu·tein) *s.* butano.
**butcher** (bu·choᵣ) *s.* carnicero. 2 matarife. 3 hombre sanguinario.
**butcher (to)** *tr.-intr.* matar, sacrificar [reses]. 2 fig.
matar cruelmente, asesinar.
**butcherly** (-li) *adj.* de carnicero. 2 sanguinario, salvaje.
**butchery** (-i) *s.* matadero. 2 oficio de carnicero. 3
matanza, carnicería.
**butler** (bø·tløᵣ) *s.* mayordomo; despensero.
**butlery** (-i) *s.* despensa.
**butt** (but) *s.* extremo o cabo grueso; culata, mocho, mango. 2 cepa; tocón [de árbol]. 3 colilla
[de cigarro]. 4 terrero, blanco [de tiro]. 5 pipa,
tonel. 6 ESGR. estocada. 7 topetada. 8 límite, término.
**butt (to)** *tr.-intr.* topetar, acornear; topar. 2 *tr.* apoyar [en]. 3 MEC. juntar a tope. 4 *intr. to ~ in* o
*into*, entrometerse; *to ~ out*, salir, sobresalir.
**butte** (but) *s.* mota, colina aislada.
**butter** (bø·tøᵣ) *s.* manteca [de leche o vegetal]. 2
pasta, mermelada.
**butter (to)** *tr.* untar con manteca o mantequilla. 2
fam. adular.
**buttercup** (-køp) *s.* BOT. botón de oro.
**butterfly** (-flai) *s.* ENT. mariposa.
**butterine** (-in) *s.* margarina.
**buttery** (bø·tøri) *s.* despensa. 2 *adj.* mantecoso. 3
fam. adulador, zalamero.
**buttock** (bo·tøk) *s.* nalga. 2 *pl.* trasero, posaderas.
**button** (bø·tøn) *s.* botón [de vestido, de florete]. 2
botón, tirador, pulsador. 3 BOT. botón, capullo.
4 ARTILL. cascabel. 5 *pl.* botones [criadito].
**button (to)** *tr.* abotonar. 2 ESGR. dar un botonazo a.
3 *intr.* abotonarse.
**buttonhole** (-jout) *s.* ojal, presilla.

**buttonhole (to)** *tr.* ojalar. *2* asir por la solapa [para obligar a escuchar].
**buttonhook** (-juk) *s.* abotonador.
**buttress** (bø·tris) *s.* ARQ. contrafuerte, estribo, machón, arbotante. *2* fig. apoyo, sostén.
**buttress (to)** *tr.* estribar, sostener.
**butyric** (biuti·ric) *adj.* butírico.
**buxom** (bø·ksøm) *adj.* lozana, garrida.
**buy (to)** (bai) *tr.* comprar, mercar: *to* ~ *off*, librarse de [con dinero]; comprar [a uno]; *to* ~ *out*, comprar la parte de un socio o el negocio de un competidor. *2* comprar, sobornar. *3 intr.* comprar, hacer compras. ¶ Pret. y p. p.: *bought*.
**buyer** (-ør) *s.* comprador.
**buzz** (bøš) *s.* zumbido, susurro, murmullo.
**buzz (to)** *intr.* zumbar, susurrar, murmurar. *2* circular [un rumor]. *3* moverse, andar.
**buzzard** (bø·šaʳd) *s.* ORN. alfaneque; dardabasi.
**buzzer** (bø·šøʳ) *s.* zumbador.
**by** (bai) *prep.* junto a, cerca de, al lado de, cabe. *2* por [indicando lugar del movimiento o de la acción; agente, causa; modo, medio]. *3* de [hecho de; nacido de]. *4* a, con, de, en, por, etc. [expresando relaciones varias]: ~ *day*, de día; ~ *degrees*, por grados; ~ *dint of*, a fuerza de; ~ *far*, con mucho; ~ *the dozen*, por docenas; ~ *train*, en tren, por tren; ~ *oneself*, solo, sin ayuda; ~ *itself*, de por sí; *one* ~ *one*, de uno en uno. *5* ~

*and* ~, pronto, luego. *6* ~ *the bye*, ~ *the way*, de paso, entre paréntesis, a propósito.
*7 adj.* lateral, apartado; secundario.
*8 adv.* cerca, al lado, por el lado. *9* aparte; *to put* ~, guardar, ahorrar.
**by-blow** (-blou) *s.* golpe indirecto; accidente imprevisto.
**bye** *s.* cosa secundaria. *2 adj.* BY *7*.
**by-election** *s.* elección parcial.
**bygone** (bai·gon) *adj.* pasado. *2 s.* lo pasado; *let bygones be bygones*, olvidemos lo pasado.
**by-lane** *s.* sendero o camino apartado.
**by-law** (-lo) *s.* reglamento, ordenanzas, estatutos.
**by-name** (-neim) *s.* sobrenombre, apodo.
**bypass** (-pæs) *s.* camino o canal de derivación; desvío. *2* MEC. y ELECT. derivación.
**bypath** (-pæz) *s.* vereda, atajo.
**byplay** (-plei) *s.* TEAT. escena muda; juego escénico.
**by-product** *adj.* subproducto, derivado.
**bystander** (-stændøʳ) *s.* espectador, el que está presente. *2 pl.* circunstantes.
**by-street** *s.* callejuela, travesía.
**byway** (-uei) *s.* camino desviado.
**byword** (-uøʳ) *s.* objeto de burla u oprobio. *2* apodo. *3* dicho, refrán.
**Byzantine** (bizæ·ntin) *adj.-s.* bizantino.
**Byzantium** (baišæ·nshiøn) *n. pr.* Bizancio.

# C

**C, c** (sı) *s.* C, c, tercera letra del alfabeto inglés. *2* MÚS. do.

**cab** (kæb) *s.* cabriolé. *2* coche de punto; taxi. *3* cabina [de maquinista de tren o de conductor de camión].

**cabal** (kabæ·l) *s.* cábala, intriga. *2* camarilla.

**cabal (to)** *intr.* intrigar, maquinar. ¶ Pret. y p. p.: *caballed;* ger.: *-lling.*

**cabala** (kæ·bala) *s.* cábala [de los judíos].

**cabalistic(al** (kæbali·stik(al) *adj.* cabalístico.

**caballer** (kabæ·løʳ) *s.* maquinador.

**cabaret** (kæbarei·) *s.* cabaret, café o restaurante con atracciones. *2* taberna.

**cabbage** (kæ·bidỹ) *s.* BOT. col, berza, repollo. *2* COC. coles.

**cabbage (to)** *intr.* repollar.

**cabby** (kæ·bi) *s.* CABMAN.

**cabin** (kæ·bin) *s.* cabaña, choza. *2* MAR. cámara, camarote: ~ *boy,* grumete; camarero. *3* cabina [de avión].

**cabin (to)** *intr.* vivir en cabaña o choza. *2 tr.* encerrar en cabaña o parte estrecha.

**cabinet** (kæ·binit) *s.* gabinete [ministerio; colección; aposento]. *2* bargueño, armario, vitrina, escaparate. *3* mueble [de un aparato de radio]. *4* IMPR. chibalete. *5 adj.* ministerial. *6* de gabinete. *7* privado, confidencial.

**cabinetmaker** (-meikøʳ) *s.* ebanista.

**cabinetmaking** (-meiking), **cabinetwork** (-uøʳk) *s.* ebanistería.

**cable** (kei·bøl) *s.* cable, maroma. *2* TELEGR. cable; cablegrama: ~ *address,* dirección cablegráfica. *3* *cable's length,* cable [medida].

**cable (to)** *tr.* cablegrafiar.

**cablegram** (-græm) *s.* cablegrama.

**cabman** (kæ·bmæn) *s.* cochero de punto; taxista.

**caboodle** (kabu·døl) *s.* (E.U.) *the whole* ~, todo el hato.

**caboose** (kabu·s) *s.* MAR. fogón, cocina. *2* FERROC. (E.U.) furgón de cola.

**cabotage** (kæ·bøtidỹ) *s.* MAR. cabotaje.

**cabriolet** (kæbriolei·) *s.* cabriolé.

**cacao** (kaka·ou) *s.* cacao [árbol, semilla].

**cachalot** (kæ·shalat) *s.* ZOOL. cachalote.

**cache** (kæsh) *s.* escondite, escondrijo.

**cache (to)** *tr.* esconder.

**cachet** (kæshei·) *s.* FARM. sello.

**cachexia** (kæke·ksia) *s.* caquexia.

**cachinnation** (kækinei·shøn) *s.* risotada.

**cacique** (kası·k) *s.* cacique [indio].

**cackle** (kæ·køl) *s.* cacareo, cloqueo. *2* risa parecida a un cloqueo. *3* cháchara.

**cackle (to)** *intr.* cacarear, cloquear. *2* reirse. *3* charchear.

**cackler** (kæ·kløʳ) *s.* cacareador. *2* chismoso; parlanchín.

**cackling** (-ing) *s.* CACKLE. *2* graznido.

**cacodyl** (kæ·kodil) *s.* QUÍM. cacodilo.

**cacodylate** (-eit) *s.* QUÍM. cacodilato.

**cacomistle** (kæ·kømisøl) *s.* ZOOL. cacomiztle, basáride.

**cacophony** (kæka·føni) *s.* cacofonía.

**cactaceous** (kæktei·shøs) *adj.* BOT. cactáceo.

**cactus** (kæ·ktøs) *s.* cacto.

**cad** (kæd) *s.* canalla, grosero, malcriado.

**cadastre, -ter** (kadæ·støʳ) *s.* catastro.

**cadaver** (kadæ·vøʳ) *s.* cadáver.

**cadaveric** (kadave·rik), **cadaverous** (kadæ·vørøs) *adj.* cadavérico.

**caddie** (kæ·di) *s.* hombre o muchacho que lleva las mazas de los jugadores de golf.

**caddis** (-dis) *s.* jerguilla.

**caddish** (-dish) *adj.* grosero, mal criado.

**caddy** (-di) *s.* lata o cajita para el té. *2* CADDIE.

**cade** (keid) *adj.* manso, favorito [animal]. *2 s.* BOT. enebro.

**cadence** (kei·døns) *s.* cadencia. *2* ritmo. *3* modulación.

**cadenced** (-t) *adj.* cadencioso, rítmico.

**cadent** (kei·dønt) *adj.* caliente. *2* cadencioso.

**cadenza** (kade·nša) *s.* MÚS. cadencia.

**cadet** (kade·t) *s.* hijo o hermano menor. *2* cadete.

**cadge (to)** (kædỹ) *tr.-intr.* mendigar, gorronear.

**cadi** (ka·di o kei·di) *s.* cadí.

**cadmium** (kæ·dmiøm) *s.* QUÍM. cadmio.

**cadre** (ka·døʳ) *s.* armazón. *2* cuadro [de oficiales].

**caduceus** (kadiu·siøs) *s.* caduceo.

**caducity** (kadiu·siti) *s.* caducidad. *2* caduquez.

**caducous** (kadiu·køs) *adj.* caduco.

**caecal** (sı·kal) *adj.* cecal.

**caecum** (sı·køm) *s.* intestino ciego.

**Caesar** (sı·šøʳ) *n. pr.* César.

**Caesarean** (-še·rian) *adj.* cesáreo.

**Caesarism** (sı·šørišm) *s.* cesarismo.

**caesium** (sı·šiøm) *s.* QUÍM. cesio.

**caesura** (siỹu·ra) *s.* cesura.

cafe (kæfei·) s. café [establecimiento].
cafeteria (kæføti·ria) s. restaurante o café de autoservicio.
caffein(e (kæ·fiin) s. QUÍM. cafeína.
caftan (kæ·ftan) s. caftán.
cage (keiγ̂) s. jaula. 2 camarín [de ascensor].
cage (to) tr. enjaular.
cageling (-ling) s. ave enjaulada.
Caiaphas (kai·afas) n. pr. Caifás.
caique (kar·k) s. caique.
cagey (kei·dγ̂i) adj. ladino, zorro.
cairn (keʳn) s. montón de piedras que sirve de señal.
caisson (kei·søn) s. cajón de municiones. 2 ARTILL. armón, furgón. 3 ING. cajón hidráulico. 4 MAR. camello. 5 ARQ. artesón.
caitiff (kei·tif) adj. ruin, cobarde. 2 s. miserable, canalla.
cajole (to) (kadγ̂ou·l) tr. engatusar, enlabiar, persuadir con halagos.
cajoler (-øʳ) s. engatusador, zalamero.
cajolery (-i) s. engatusamiento. 2 halago, zalamerías.
cake (keik) s. galleta, bizcocho, torta, pastel, bollo. 2 pastilla, pan [de jabón, cera, etc.].
cake (to) intr. hacerse una pasta, una masa dura, una costra.
cakewalk (-wøk) s. cake-walk.
calaba (kæ·laba) s. calambuco.
calabash (kæ·labæsh) s. BOT. calabaza vinatera, güira. 2 vasija hecha de calabaza.
Calabrian (kælei·brian) adj.-s. calabrés.
calamary (kæ·lameri) s. ZOOL. calamar.
calamine (kæ·lamain) s. calamina.
calamint (kæ·lamint) s. BOT. calaminta.
calamitous (kalæ·mitøs) adj. calamitoso.
calamity (-miti) s. calamidad. 2 desgracia, infortunio.
calamus (kæ·lamøs) s. BOT. ácoro.
calander (kalæ·ndøʳ) s. ORN. calandria.
calash (kalæ·sh) s. calesa, carretela. 2 capota [de coche, de señora].
calcaneum (kalkei·niøm) s. ANAT. calcáneo.
calcareous (kælke·riøs) adj. calcáreo.
calceate (kæ·lsieit), calced (kælst) adj. calzado [religioso].
calceolaria (kælsiøle·ria) s. calceolaria.
calcic (kæ·lsik) adj. cálcico.
calcify (to) (kæ·lsifai) tr. calcificar. 2 intr. calcificarse. ¶ Pret. y p. p.: calcified.
calcination (-shøn) s. calcinación.
calcine (to) (kæ·lsin) tr. calcinar. 2 intr. calcinarse.
calcium (kæ·lsiøm) s. calcio.
calculable (kæ·lkiulabøl) adj. calculable.
calculate (to) (-leit) tr. calcular. 2 [esp. en p. p.] adaptar a un fin. 3 intr. hacer cálculos. 4 contar [con]; confiar [en o que].
calculating (-ing) adj. calculador.
calculation (-ei·shøn) s. calculación, cálculo.
calculator (-tøʳ) s. calculador, calculista. 2 máquina calculadora.
calculose (kæ·lkiulous) adj. calculoso.
calculus (-løs) s. MAT., MED. cálculo.
caldron (ko·ldrøn) s. caldera, caldero, paila.
calendar (kæ·lindaʳ) s. calendario, almanaque. 2 lista de asuntos. 3 santoral.
calendar (to) tr. poner en el calendario. 2 poner en lista [para ser juzgado, discutido, etc.].
calender (kæ·lindøʳ) s. calandria [máquina]. 2 derviche mendicante.
calender (to) tr. calandrar.

calends (kæ·lindš) s. pl. calendas.
calf (kaf), calves (kavš) s. ZOOL. becerro, ternero, becerra, ternera. 2 fam. bobo. 3 pantorrilla.
calfskin (ka·fskin) s. becerro [piel].
caliber (kæ·libøʳ) s. CALIBRE.
calibrate (to) (-breit) tr. calibrar, graduar.
calibration (-brei·shøn) s. calibración, graduación.
calibre (kæ·libøʳ) s. calibre. 2 capacidad, aptitud.
calicie (kæ·likøl) s. calículo.
calico (kæ·licou) s. calicó, indiana.
calif, califate, CALIPH, CALIPHATE.
Californian (kalifo·ʳnian) adj.-s. californiano, califórnico, calofornio.
caliga (kæ·liga) s. cáliga.
caliginous (kæli·dγ̂inøs) adj. caliginoso.
caliper (kæ·lipøʳ) o pl. calipers s. compás de calibres o de espesores. 2 pie de rey.
caliph (kei·lif) s. califa.
caliphate (kæ·lifeit) s. califato.
calisthenics (kælisze·niks) s. calistenia.
calix s. CALYX.
calk (kok) s. ramplón [de herradura]. 2 hierro [para zapatos].
calk (to) tr. proveer de ramplones. 2 herrar [zapatos]. 3 calcar [un dibujo]. 4 TO CAULK.
call (kol) s. llamada, llamamiento. 2 citación, convocación. 3 toque, grito, etc., de señal o llamada. 4 CAZA reclamo, chilla. 5 llamada o conversación telefónica. 6 grito [de ave o animal]. 7 demanda, exigencia. 8 obligación, derecho, motivo. 9 visita [que se hace]; escala [de un buque]. 10 declaración [en el bridge]. 11 adj. de llamada, que llama: ~ boy, botones; TEAT. avisador.
call (to) tr. llamar [dar voces a, hacer venir, atraer, etc.]. 2 convocar. 3 anunciar, proclamar, pregonar. 4 invocar, apelar a. 5 llamar [al que duerme]. 6 pasar lista. 7 llamar, apellidar, denominar, tratar de. 8 to ~ attention to, llamar la atención sobre. 9 to ~ down, hacer bajar; fam. censurar, reprender. 10 to ~ forth, hacer salir; poner de manifiesto o en acción. 11 to ~ names, insultar de palabra. 12 to ~ off, llamar a otra parte; aplazar, suspender. 13 to ~ out, llamar [desde afuera]; desafiar; evocar. 14 to ~ to account, pedir cuentas; reprender. 15 to ~ to order, llamar al orden; abrir la sesión. 16 to ~ up, hacer subir; hacer surgir; evocar, recordar; poner a debate; llamar por teléfono.
17 intr. gritar, dar voces. 18 hacer una visita; detenerse [en]; MAR. hacer escala [en]. 19 to ~ for, pedir, exigir, requerir, necesitar.
calla (kæ·la) s. cala, lirio de agua.
caller (ko·løʳ) s. llamador [pers.]. 2 visita, visitante.
calligrapher (kæli·graføʳ) s. calígrafo.
calligraphy (kæli·grafi) s. caligrafía.
calling (ko·ling) s. profesión, oficio, ministerio. 2 visita, visiteo. 3 llamamiento.
Calliope (kælai·api) s. MIT. Calíope.
calliper (kæ·lipøʳ) s. CALIPER.
callisthenics (kælisze·niks) s. calistenia.
callosity (kæla·siti) s. callosidad, callo.
callcus (kæ·løs) adj. calloso. 2 fig. duro, insensible.
callousness (-nis) s. CALLOSITY. 2 fig. dureza, insensibilidad.
callow (kæ·lou) adj. implume. 2 joven, inexperto.
callus (kæ·løs) s. callo, dureza.
calm (kam) s. calma, sosiego. 2 serenidad, sangre

fría. 3 MAR. calma. 4 *adj.* en calma, sosegado; tranquilo, sereno.
**calm (to)** *tr.* calmar, sosegar, tranquilizar, apaciguar. 2 *intr.* calmar[se, sosegarse, abonanzar. | Gralte. con *down.*
**calmative** (-ativ) *adj.-s.* calmante.
**calmness** (-nis) *s.* CALM.
**calmy** (-i) *adj.* poét. tranquilo, apacible.
**calomel** (kæ·lomel) *s.* calomelanos.
**caloric** (kalo·rik) *adj.-s.* calórico.
**calorie** (kæ·lori) *s.* caloría.
**calorific** (kæløri·fik) *adj.* calorífico.
**calory** (kæ·løri) *s.* caloría.
**calotte** (kæla·t) *s.* casquete, gorro. 2 solideo.
**caltrop** (kæ·ltrøp) *s.* BOT., MIL. abrojo.
**calumet** (kæ·liumet) *s.* pipa de los indios de Norteamérica.
**calumniate (to)** (kalø·mnieit) *tr.* calumniar.
**calumniatio** (-ei·shon) *s.* calumnia.
**calumniator** (kalø·mnietø·ʳ) *s.* calumniador.
**calumnious** (-mniøs) *adj.* calumnioso.
**calumny** (kæ·lømni) *s.* calumnia.
**Calvary** (kæ·lvari) *n. pr.* Calvario.
**calve (to)** (kæv) *intr.* parir [la vaca].
**Calvinism** (kæ·lvinišm) *s.* calvinismo.
**Calvinist** (-ist) *s.* calvinista.
**calvities** (kælvi·shiis) *s.* calvicie.
**calycle** (kæ·likøl) *s.* calículo.
**calyx** (kei·liks) *s.* BOT. cáliz. 2 ANAT. pelvis [del riñón].
**cam** (kæm) *s.* MEC. cama, leva, levador.
**camail** (kamei·l) *s.* almófar.
**camaraderie** (kamara·døri) *s.* camaradería.
**camber** (kæ·mbø·ʳ) *s.* comba, curvatura, bombeo.
**camber (to)** *tr.* combar, arquear. 2 *intr.* combarse, arquearse.
**cambist** (kæ·mbist) *s.* cambista.
**cambium** (kæ·mbiom) *s.* BOT. cambium.
**cambric** (kei·mbrik) *s.* cambray, batista.
**came** (keim) *pret.* de TO COME.
**camel** (kæ·møl) *s.* ZOOL., MAR. camello.
**camellia** (kamı·lia) *s.* camelia.
**cameo** (kæ·miou) *s.* camafeo.
**camera** (kæ·møra) *s.* despacho particular del juez. 2 cámara apostólica. 3 ANAT. cámara. 4 máquina fotográfica. 5 ~ *lucida,* cámara clara o lúcida; ~ *obscura,* cámara oscura.
**cameraman** (-mæn) *s.* operador de tomavistas, operador cinematográfico.
**Cameroons** (kæ·mørunš) *n. pr.* GEOGR. Camerún.
**Camillus** (kami·løs) *n. pr.* Camilo.
**camion** (kæ·miøn) *s.* camión, carro bajo y fuerte.
**camisado** (kæmisei·dou) *s.* MIL. encamisada.
**camisole** (kæ·misoul) *s.* camiseta, cubrecorsé.
**camlet** (kæ·mlit) *s.* camelote [tela].
**camomile** (kæ·momail) *s.* BOT. camomila, manzanilla.
**camouflage** (kæ·møflaỹ) *s.* camuflaje.
**camouflage (to)** *tr.* camuflar.
**camp** (kæmp) *s.* campamento. 2 ranchería. 3 MIL. campo. 4 servicio o vida militar. 5 *adj.* ~ *bed,* lecho de campaña; ~ *chair,* silla de tijera.
**camp (to)** *tr.-intr.* acampar.
**campaign** (kæmpei·n) *s.* campaña [militar, política, etc.].
**campaign (to)** *intr.* salir a campaña. 2 hacer campaña o propaganda.
**campaigner** (-ø·ʳ) *s.* veterano. 2 propagandista.
**campanile** (kæmpanı·li) *s.* campanil, campanario.
**campanula** (-pæ·niula) *s.* BOT. campánula.
**campanulaceous** (-ei·shøs) *adj.* campanuláceo.

**campeachy-wood** (kæmpı·chi) *s.* palo campeche.
**camper** (kæ·mpøʳ) *s.* acampador.
**campfire** (-faiʳ) *s.* fuego u hoguera de campamento.
**camphor** (kæ·mføʳ) *s.* alcanfor: ~ *tree,* alcanforero.
**camphor, camphorate (to)** (-eit) *tr.* alcanforar.
**camping** (kæ·mping) *s.* campamento.
**campus** (kæ·mpøs) *s.* (E.U) patio, jardín, recinto [de una universidad].
**camshaft** (kæ·mshæft) *s.* MEC. árbol de levas.
**can** (kæn) *s.* vaso, jarro, bote, lata [de metal]: ~ *opener,* abrelatas.
**can** *aux.* poder o saber [hacer una cosa]. ¶ Pret. y cond.: *could.* | Sólo se usa con las formas *can* y *could* en el presente y pretérito del indicativo o subjuntivo y en el condicional.
**can (to)** *tr.* enlatar, conservar en latas. ¶ Pret. y p. p.: *canned;* ger.: *-nning.*
**Canaanite** (kei·nanait) *adj.-s.* cananeo.
**Canadian** (kanei·dian) *adj.-s.* canadiense.
**canal** (kanæ·l) *s.* canal; acequia. 2 ANAT. canal, conducto, tubo. 3 ARQ. canal, estría.
**canalization** (kanælišei·shøn) *s.* canalización.
**canalize (to)** (kanæ·laiš) *tr.* canalizar.
**canapé** (kanapei) *s.* canapé [de caviar, etc.].
**canary** (kane·ri) *s.* ORN. canario. 2 color de canario. 3 vino de Canarias.
**Canary Islands** *n. pr.* Islas Canarias.
**canasta** (kænæ·sta) *s.* canasta [juego].
**cancel** (kæ·nsøl) *s.* cancelación. 2 IMPR. supresión. 3 MÚS. becuadro.
**cancel (to)** *tr.* cancelar. 2 rescindir. 3 neutralizar. 4 borrar, tachar. 5 inutilizar [un sello]. 6 MÚS. poner becuadro. 7 IMPR. suprimir. 8 MAT. eliminar. ¶ Pret. y p. p.: *canceled* o *-lled;* ger.: *canceling* o *-lling.*
**cancellate** (-lit) *adj.* BIOL. reticular.
**cancer** (kæ·nsør) *s.* MED. cáncer. 2 [con may.] ASTR. Cáncer.
**cancerate (to)** (-eit) *intr.* cancerarse.
**cancerous** (-øs) *adj.* canceroso.
**cancroid** (kæ·nkroid) *adj.* cancroideo. 2 *s.* cancroide.
**candelabrum** (kændølei·brøm) *s.* candelabro.
**candent** (kæ·ndønt), **candescent** (kænde·sønt) *adj.* candente.
**candid** (kæ·ndid) *adj.* franco, sincero. 2 imparcial. 3 cándido, ingenuo.
**candidate** (-dit) *s.* candidato. 2 aspirante, pretendiente. 3 graduando.
**candidature** (-dachøøʳ), **candidacy** (-si) *s.* candidatura [aspiración, propuesta].
**candidness** (kæ·ndidnis) *s.* sinceridad, franqueza. 2 candor, ingenuidad.
**candied** (kæ·ndid) *pret.* y *p. p.* de TO CANDY. 2 confitado, escarchado, garapiñado.
**candle** (kæ·ndøl) *s.* vela, bujía; candela. 2 FÍS. bujía.
**candleholder** (-jouldøʳ) *s.* candelero.
**candlelight** (-lait) *s.* luz de vela; luz artificial.
**Candlemas** (-mas) *s.* Candelaria [fiesta].
**candlestick** (-stik) *s.* candelero; palmatoria.
**candlewick** (-uik) *s.* pábilo.
**cando(u)r** (kæ·ndøʳ) *s.* candor, sinceridad, franqueza. 2 imparcialidad.
**candy** (kæ·ndi) *s.* azúcar cande. 2 dulce, bombón, confite, caramelo.
**candy (to)** *tr.* confitar, escarchar, garapiñar. 2 endulzar. 3 *intr.* cubrirse de azúcar cristalizado. ¶ Pret. y p. p.: *candied.*
**cane** (kein) *s.* BOT. caña, rota, junco [de Indias];

bejuco; caña de azúcar. 2 bastón; ~ *stand*, bastonera.
**cane (to)** *tr.* bastonear. 2 poner asiento de rejilla a.
**canephorus** (kæne·forøs) *s.* canéfora.
**Canicula** (kani·kiula) *n. pr.* ASTR. Canícula, Sirio.
**canicular** (-ʳ) *adj.* canicular.
**canid** (kæ·nid) *s.* ZOOL. cánido.
**canine** (kæ·nain) *adj.-s.* canino.
**canister** (kæ·nistøʳ) *s.* bote, lata [para té, tabaco, etc.].
**canker** (kæ·nkøʳ) *s.* úlcera maligna. 2 BOT. cancro. 3 fig. cáncer [lo que corroe].
**canker (to)** *tr.* ulcerar, gangrenar. 2 cancerar, corromper. 3 *intr.* cancerarse, corromperse. 4 agriarse [el carácter, etc.].
**cankerous** (-øs) *adj.* maligno, gangrenoso, corrosivo.
**canna** (kæ·na) *s.* BOT. cañacoro.
**cannaceous** (canei·shøs) *adj.* canáceo.
**canned** (kænd) *adj.* en conserva, en lata.
**cannery** (kæ·nøri) *s.* fábrica de conservas.
**cannibal** (kæ·nibal) *adj.-s.* caníbal.
**cannibalism** (-išm) *s.* canibalismo.
**cannikin** (kæ·nikin) *s.* vaso de metal. 2 cubo, balde.
**cannon** (kæ·non) *s.* ARTILL. cañón; cañones, artillería: ~ *fodder*, carne de cañón. 2 MEC. manguito. 3 caña [de cuadrúpedo]. 4 BILLAR carambola.
**cannonade** (-ei·d) *s.* cañoneo.
**cannonade (to)** *tr.* cañonear.
**cannoneer** (-iøʳ) *s.* artillero.
**cannot** (kæ·nat) forma compuesta de *can* y *not*.
**cannula** (kæ·niula) *s.* cánula.
**canny** (kæ·ni) *adj.* sagaz, prudente, cuerdo. 2 cómodo. 3 agradable. 4 apuesto.
**canoe** (kanu·) *s.* canoa; piragua.
**canon** (kæ·nøn) *s.* canónigo. 2 canon, regla. 3 ECLES., LITURG., MÚS. canon. 4 IMPR. canon. 5 ~ *law*, derecho canónico.
**canoness** (-is) *s.* canonesa.
**canonic** (kana·nik) *adj.* canónico.
**canonical** (-al) *adj.* canónico. 2 canonical. 3 aceptado, establecido.
**canonicals** (-als) *s. pl.* vestiduras sacerdotales.
**canonicate** (-eit) *s.* canonicado, canonjía.
**canonist** (kæ·nønist) *s.* canonista.
**canonization** (-iøei·shøn) *s.* canonización.
**canonize (to)** (-aiš) *tr.* canonizar.
**canonry** (-ri) *s.* CANONICATE.
**canopy** (kæ·nøpi) *s.* dosel, baldaquino, palio, pabellón. 2 doselete. 3 bóveda [del cielo].
**canopy (to)** *tr.* endoselar. ¶ Pret. y p. p.: *canopied*.
**canorous** (kanou·røs) *adj.* canoro.
**can't** (kænt) contr. de *can* y *not*.
**cant** (kænt) *s.* canto, esquina. 2 inclinación, sesgo. 3 bisel. 4 tumbo, vaivén. 5 jerga, jerigonza. 6 lenguaje gazmoño, hipocresía. 7 *adj.* inclinado, sesgado. 8 de una jerga. 9 gazmoño, hipócrita.
**cant (to)** *tr.* inclinar, ladear; volcar. 2 arrojar, lanzar. 3 *intr.* inclinarse, volcarse. 4 hablar en jerga o con gazmoñería.
**cantankerous** (kæntæ·nkørøs) *adj.* avinagrado, intratable,quisquilloso.
**cantata** (kænta·ta) *s.* cantata.
**canteen** (kænti·n) *s.* cantimplora [frasco]. 2 cantina, taberna.
**canter** (kæ·ntøʳ) *s.* medio galope.
**canter (to)** *intr.* ir a medio galope.
**Canterbury** (kæntøʳbe·ri) *n. pr.* GEOGR. Cantórbery. 2 BOT. ~ *bell*, farolillo.
**cantharides** (kænzæ·ridiš) *s.* cantáridas.

**canticle** (kæ·ntikøl) *s.* cántico.
**cantilever** (kæantile·vøʳ) *s.* ARQ. modillón, cónsola. 2 ~ *bridge*, puente de contrapeso.
**cantle** (kæ·ntøl) *s.* pedazo, porción. 2 borrén o arzón trasero.
**canton** (kæ·ntøn) *s.* cantón, distrito. 2 BLAS. cantón.
**canton (to)** *tr.* acantonar, acuartelar.
**cantonal** (-al) *adj.* cantonal.
**cantonment** (-mønt) *s.* acantonamiento; cuartel, campamento.
**cantor** (kæ·ntøʳ) *s.* chantre.
**canvas** (kæ·nvas) *s.* lona. 2 cañamazo. 3 vela, velamen. 4 PINT. lienzo.
**canvass** *s.* recorrido en busca de votos, pedidos, etc. 2 examen, discusión.
**canvass (to)** *tr.-intr.* recorrer una población o distrito en busca de votos, pedidos, etc. 2 *tr.* examinar, discutir.
**canvasser** (-øʳ) *s.* el que solicita votos, pedidos, etc.; agente electoral; corredor.
**canyon** (kæ·niøn) *s.* GEOGR. (E.U.) cañón, hondonada.
**canzonet** (kænšøne·t) *s.* cancioncilla.
**caoutchouc** (kau·chuk) *s.* caucho.
**cap** (kæp) *s.* gorra; gorro; cofia; birrete; bonete; capelo: *to set one's* ~ *at*, querer conquistar para novio. 2 cima, cumbre. 3 MEC. casquete, casquillo, sombrerete. 4 tapa [de ciertas cosas]. 5 cápsula [de botella o para fulminante]. 6 caballete [de chimenea]. 7 chapa [de brújula]. 8 GEOM. casquete. 9 sombrero [de seta].
**cap (to)** *tr.* cubrir [la cabeza]. 2 poner tapa, casquillo, cápsula, etc., a. 3 cubrir, coronar, acabar. 4 sobrepujar. 5 *tr.-intr.* saludar descubriéndose. ¶ Pret. y p. p.: *capped*; ger.: *capping*.
**capability** (keipabi·liti) *s.* capacidad, aptitud.
**capable** (kei·pabøl) *s.* capaz [de hacer algo]. 2 susceptible [de]. 3 capaz, apto, competente.
**capacious** (kapei·shøs) *adj.* capaz, espacioso.
**capaciousness** (-nis) *s.* espaciosidad, anchura.
**capacitate (to)** (kapæ·siteit) *tr.* capacitar.
**capacity** (-iti) *s.* capacidad. 2 facultad, poder, posibilidad. 3 calidad, condición: *in the* ~ *of*, en calidad de. 4 DER. competencia.
**cap-a-pie** (kæpapı·) *adv.* de pies a cabeza; de punta en blanco.
**caparison** (kapæ·rišøn) *s.* caparazón, gualdrapa.
**caparison (to)** *tr.* engualdrapar, enjaezar. 2 vestir ricamente.
**cape** (keip) *s.* capotillo, capa corta. 2 esclavina, manteleta. 3 cabo, promontorio. 4 *n. pr. Cape Town*, Ciudad del Cabo.
**capelin** (kæ·pølin) *s.* ICT. capelán.
**capeline** *s.* ARM., CIR. capellina.
**caper** (kei·pøʳ) *s.* cabriola, zapateta; travesura. 2 BOT. alcaparro; alcaparra.
**caper (to)** *intr.* cabriolar, triscar, retozar.
**capercailye** (kæpøʳkei·li) *s.* urogallo.
**Capetown** (kei·ptaum) *n. pr.* GEOGR. Ciudad del Cabo.
**capillarity** (kæpilæ·riti) *s.* capilaridad.
**capillary** (kæ·pileri) *adj.* capilar. 2 *s.* vaso capilar.
**capital** (kæ·pital) *adj.* capital. 2 primordial, vital, importante. 3 excelente. 4 *adj.-s.* mayúscula, versal [letra]. 5 *s.* COM. capital, principal. 6 capital [en oposición a trabajo]. 7 capital [población]. 8 ARQ. capitel.
**capitalism** (-išm) *s.* capitalismo.
**capitalist** (-ist) *adj.-s.* capitalista.

**capitalize (to)** (-aiš) *tr.* capitalizar. *2* escribir con mayúscula.
**capitation** (kapitei·shøn) *s.* capitación.
**Capitol** (kæ·pitøl) *s.* Capitolio.
**capitular** (kapi·chølɑ<sup>r</sup>) *adj.-s.* capitular.
**capitulary** (-leri) *adj.-s.* capitular. *2 s.* capitulario.
**capitulate (to)** (-leit) *intr.* capitular.
**capitulation** (-lei·shøn) *s.* capitulación [pacto; rendición].
**capon** (kei·pøn) *s.* capón [pollo, etc.].
**capotasto** (kapota·stou) *s.* MÚS. cejuela.
**capote** (kapou·t) *s.* capote [prenda]. *2* capota.
**Cappadocian** (kapadou·shan) *adj.-s.* capadocio.
**capped** (kæpt) *pret.* y *p. p.* de TO CAP.
**caprice** (kaprɪ·s) *s.* capricho, antojo.
**capricious** (-shøs) *adj.* caprichoso, antojadizo.
**Capricorn** (kæ·prico·<sup>r</sup>n) *s.* ASTR. Capricornio.
**caprifig** (kæ·prifig) *s.* BOT. cabrahigo.
**caprine** (kæ·prain) *adj.* caprino.
**capriole** (kæ·prioul) *s.* cabriola. *2* corveta.
**capriole (to)** *intr.* cabriolar, corvetear.
**capsize (to)** (kæ·psaiš) *tr.-intr.* volcar, dar vuelta. *2* MAR. volver o volverse quilla arriba; zozobrar.
**capstan** (-stan) *s.* cabrestante.
**capstone** (-toun) *s.* ARQ. coronamiento.
**capsular** (-siulɑ<sup>r</sup>) *adj.* capsular.
**capsule** (-siul) *s.* cápsula.
**captain** (-tin) *s.* capitán.
**captain (to)** *tr.* capitanear.
**captaincy** (-si), **captainship** (-ship) *s.* capitanía.
**caption** (-shøn) *s.* captura, prisión. *2* título, encabezamiento. *3* texto [de un grabado, etc.]. *4* CINEM. subtítulo.
**captious** (-shøs) *adj.* capcioso. *2* reparón, quisquilloso.
**captivate (to)** (-tiveit) *tr.* cautivar.
**captivating** (-ing) *adj.* cautivador, encantador, seductor.
**captive** (kæ·tiv) *adj.-s.* cautivo. *2 adj.* de cautiverio.
**captivity** (-ti·viti) *s.* cautividad, cautiverio.
**captor** (kæ·ptø<sup>r</sup>) *s.* aprehensor; apresador.
**capture** (-chø<sup>r</sup>) *s.* captura. *2* apresamiento. *3* presa, botín, prisionero. *4* MIL. toma.
**capture (to)** *tr.* capturar, prender. *2* apresar. *3* MIL. tomar.
**capuchin** (kæ·piuchin) *s.* capilla, capucho; capuchón [de dama]. *2* mono capuchino. *3* paloma de toca. *4* [con may.] capuchino [fraile].
**capucine** (kæ·piusin) *s.* BOT. capuchina. *2* color anaranjado.
**capybara** (kæpiba·ra) *s.* ZOOL. capiguara, carpincho.
**car** (ka<sup>r</sup>) *s.* carruaje, carro, carreta. *2* coche, automóvil. *3* tranvía. *4* FERROC. (E.U.) vagón. *5* caja [de ascensor]. *6* barquilla [de globo].
**carabao** (karaba·ou) *s.* ZOOL. carabao.
**carabineer** (kæ·rabinɪ<sup>r</sup>) *s.* carabinero [soldado].
**caracal** (ka·rakal) *s.* ZOOL. caracal.
**caracole** (kæ·rakoul) *s.* EQUIT. caracol, caracoleo.
**caracole (to)** *intr.* caracolear.
**carafe** (kæ·raf) *s.* garrafa.
**carambole** (kæ·ramboul) *s.* carambola por tablas.
**caramel** (kæ·ramøl) *s.* caramelo. *2* azúcar quemado.
**caramelize (to)** *tr.* caramelizar.
**carapace** (kæ·rapeis) *s.* ZOOL. carapacho, caparazón.
**carat** (kæ·rat) *s.* quilate.
**caravan** (kæ·ravæn) *s.* caravana. *2* (Ingl.) coche habitación.

**caravansary** (kæravæ·nsari), **caravanserai** (-rai) *s.* caravanera, caravanseray.
**caravel** (kæ·ravel) *s.* MAR. carabela.
**caraway** (-uei) *s.* BOT. alcaravea.
**carbide** (ka·<sup>r</sup>baid) *s.* carburo.
**carbon** (ka·<sup>r</sup>bøn) *s.* QUÍM. carbono. *2* ELECT., FOT. carbón. *3* ~ *paper,* papel carbón.
**carbonaceous** (-ei·shøs) *adj.* carbonoso.
**Carbonarism** (ka·<sup>r</sup>bønarišm) *s.* carbonarismo.
**carbonate** (-eit) *s.* carbonato.
**carbonate (to)** *tr.* carbonatar.
**carbonic** (ka<sup>r</sup>ba·nik) *adj.* carbónico.
**carboniferous** (ka<sup>r</sup>bøni·førøs) *adj.* carbonífero.
**carbonization** (ka<sup>r</sup>bønišei·shøn) *s.* carbonización.
**carbonize (to)** (ka·<sup>r</sup>bønaiš) *tr.* carbonizar.
**carborundum** (ka<sup>r</sup>børø·ndøm) *s.* carborundo.
**carboy** (ka·<sup>r</sup>boi) *s.* bombona, garrafón.
**carbuncle** (ka<sup>r</sup>bø·nkøl) *s.* carbunclo, carbúnculo. *2* MED. carbunco.
**carburet** (ka·<sup>r</sup>biuret) *s.* carburo.
**carburet (to)** *tr.* carburar ¶ Pret. y p. p.: *carbureted,* o *-tted;* ger.: *carbureting* o *-tting.*
**carburetant** (-ant) *adj.-s.* carburante.
**carburet(t)or** (-ø<sup>r</sup>) *s.* carburador.
**carcanet** (ka·<sup>r</sup>kanet) *s.* gargantilla, collar.
**carcase, carcass** (ka·<sup>r</sup>kas) *s.* CARN. res muerta. *2* cadáver, carroña. *3* cuerpo, corpachón. *4* armazón, esqueleto. *5* carcasa. *6* MAR. casco.
**carcinoma** (ka<sup>r</sup>sinou·ma) *s.* carcinoma.
**card** (ka<sup>r</sup>d) *s.* carta, naipe: ~ *sharper,* tramposo, fullero. *2* fam. tipo, sujeto. *3* tarjeta; participación, invitación; felicitación; cédula, ficha. *4* minuta; lista de vinos. *5* carnet, programa. *6* carda, cardencha *7* almohaza.
**cardamon** (ka·<sup>r</sup>damøn) *s.* BOT. cardamomo.
**cardan** (ka·<sup>r</sup>dan) *adj.* MEC. cardán.
**cardboard** (ka·<sup>r</sup>bo<sup>r</sup>d) *s.* cartón, cartulina.
**cardcase** (ks·<sup>r</sup>keis) *s.* tarjetero.
**carder** (ka·<sup>r</sup>dø<sup>r</sup>) *s.* cardador [pers.]. *2* máquina de cardar.
**cardia** (ka·<sup>r</sup>dia) *s.* ANAT. cardias.
**cardiac** (ka·<sup>r</sup>diæk) *adj.-s.* cardíaco.
**cardigan** (ka·<sup>r</sup>digan) *s.* chaqueta de punto.
**cardinal** (ka·<sup>r</sup>dinal) *adj.* cardinal. *2* cardenalicio: ~ *hat,* capelo. *3 s.* ECLES. cardenal. *4* ORN. ~ *bird,* cardenal.
**cardinalate** (-eit) *s.* cardenalato.
**cardiogram** (ka·<sup>r</sup>diogræm) *s.* cardiograma.
**cardiography** (ka<sup>r</sup>dia·grafi) *s.* cardiografía.
**cardiology** (-lodẙi) *s.* cardiología.
**cardiologist** (-ist) *s.* cardiólogo.
**cardoon** (ka<sup>r</sup>du·n) *s.* BOT. cardo comestible.
**cardsharp** (ka·<sup>r</sup>dsha<sup>r</sup>p) *s.* fullero.
**care** (ke<sup>r</sup>) *s.* preocupación, inquietud. *2* cuidado, solicitud, esmero, atención, cautela: *take* ~*!,* ¡cuidado! *3* cuidado, cargo, custodia.
**care (to)** *intr.* [gralte. con *about* o *for*] preocuparse, inquietarse, cuidar de; importarle a uno; apreciar, querer, hacer caso, gustarle a uno; *he cares for me,* él me quiere; *I don't* ~, me tiene sin cuidado. *2* desear, tener ganas de.
**careen** (karı·n) *s.* MAR. carena, carenadura.
**careen (to)** *tr.* MAR. dar a la banda; carenar. *2* inclinar, volcar. *3 intr.* MAR. escorar; dar bandazos.
**careenage** (-idẙ) *s.* carenadura. *2* carenero.
**career** (kare·<sup>r</sup>) *s.* carrera [paso rápido; curso; progreso que hace uno; profesión].
**career (to)** *intr.* galopar, correr.
**careful** (ke·<sup>r</sup>ful) *adj.* cuidadoso, preocupado,

atento, solícito. *2* detenido, esmerado. *3* cauteloso, providente.

**carefully** (-i) *adv.* cuidadosamente, etc.

**careless** (-lis) *adj.* descuidado, negligente. *2* que no tiene en cuenta, que no considera. *3* desatento. *4* indiferente. *5* despreocupado. *6* irreflexivo, atolondrado. *7* libre de cuidados. *8* hecho o dicho sin atención o advertencia.

**caress** (kare·s) *s.* caricia, halago, mimo.

**caress (to)** *tr.* acariciar, halagar, mimar.

**caretaker** (ke·ʳteikøʳ) *s.* cuidador, custodio, guardián, vigilante; el que cuida de una casa y vive en ella.

**careworn** (-uøʳn) *adj.* agobiado por los cuidados, devorado por la inquietud. *2* trasojado.

**cargo** (ka·ʳgou) *s.* MAR. carga, cargamento. *2* barco de carga.

**Carib** (kæ·rib), **Caribbean** (kæribɪ·an) *adj.-s.* caribe.

**caribou** (kæribu·) *s.* ZOOL. caribú.

**caricature** (kæ·rikachøʳ) *s.* caricatura.

**caricature (to)** *tr.* caricaturizar.

**caricaturist** (-ist) *s.* caricaturista.

**caries** (kei·riš) *s.* caries.

**carillon** (kæ·rilan) *s.* carillon. *2* toque de carillón.

**carillon (to)** *intr.* tocar el carillón. ¶ Pret. y p. p.: *carillonned;* ger.: *-nning.*

**carious** (kei·riøs) *adj.* cariado.

**carking** (ka·ʳking) *adj.* molesto, inquietante.

**carline thistle** (ka·ʳlin) *s.* BOT. ajonjera, carlina.

**Carlism** (ka·ʳlišm) *s.* carlismo.

**Carlist** (-list) *s.* carlista.

**carload** (-loud) *s.* carretada. *2* carga de un vagón.

**Carlovingian** (kaʳløvi·ndÿian) *adj.* Carlovingio.

**carman** (ka·ʳmæn) *s.* carretero. *2* conductor [de tranvía].

**Carmelite** (ka·qmølait) *adj.-s.* carmelita.

**carmine** (ka·ʳmin) *s.* carmín. *2 adj.* carmíneo.

**carnage** (ka·ʳnidÿ) *s.* carnicería, matanza.

**carnal** (-nal) *adj.* carnal [de la carne, sensual, terrenal].

**carnality** (kaʳnæ·liti) *s.* carnalidad.

**carnation** (-nei·shøn) *adj.-s.* encarnado [color de carne]. *2 s.* clavel, clavel doble.

**carnelian** (-nɪ·lian) *s.* CORNELIAN.

**carnival** (-nival) *s.* carnaval. *2* orgía.

**Carnivora** (kaʳni·vøra) *s. pl.* carnívoros.

**carnivorous** (-vørøs) *adj.* carnívoro.

**carnose** (ka·ʳnous) *adj.* carnoso.

**carnosity** (kaʳna·siti) *s.* carnosidad.

**carob** (kæ·røb) *s.* BOT. algarrobo; ~ *bean,* algarroba.

**carol** (kæ·røl) *s.* canto alegre, villancico.

**carol (to)** *intr.* cantar villancicos; cantar alegremente. ¶ Pret. y p. p.: *caroled* o *-lled;* ger.: *caroling* o *-lling.*

**Caroline** (kæ·rølain) *n. pr.* Carolina. *2 ~ Islands,* Islas Carolinas.

**Carolingian** (kærøli·ndÿian) *adj.-s.* carolingio.

**carom** (kæ·røm) *s.* BILLAR. carambola.

**carom (to)** *intr.* hacer carambola.

**carotid** (kara·tid) *adj.-s.* carótida.

**carousal** (karau·sal) *s.* orgía, juerga.

**carouse (to)** *intr.* hacer una juerga, emborracharse.

**carp** (kaʳp) *s.* ICT. carpa.

**carp (to)** *intr.* criticar, censurar.

**carpal** (ka·ʳpal) *adj.-s.* ANAT. carpiano.

**Carpathian** (kaʳpei·zian) *adj.* Cárpato.

**carpel** (ka·ʳpøl) *s.* carpelo.

**carpenter** (ka·ʳpøntøʳ) *s.* carpintero.

**carpentry** (-tri) *s.* carpintería [arte, oficio]. *2* maderamen.

**carper** (ka·ʳpøʳ) *s.* criticón, reparón.

**carpet** (ka·ʳpøt) *s.* alfombra, tapiz. *2* tapete.

**carpet (to)** *tr.* alfombrar, entapizar.

**carpetbag** (-bæg) *s.* maleta, saco de noche.

**carping** (ka·ʳping) *adj.* criticón, reparón.

**carpus** (ka·ʳpøs) *s.* ANAT. carpo.

**carrack** (kæ·rak) *s.* carraca [galeón].

**carriage** (kæ·ridÿ) *s.* carruaje, coche; ~ *and four,* coche de cuatro caballos. *2* FERROC. (Ing.) vagón, coche. *3* ARTILL. cureña. *4* MEC. carro [de una máquina]. *5* porte, transporte, acarreo. *6* aire, porte, continente [de una pers.].

**Carrie** (kæ·ri) *n. pr. dim.* de CAROLINE.

**carrier** (kæ·riøʳ) *s.* portador. *2* porteador, empresa de transportes. *3* mandadero; ordinario, cosario. *4* recipiente, etc., donde se lleva algo. *5* RADIO. onda portadora. *6* ~ *pigeon,* paloma mensajera.

**carrion** (kæ·riøn) *s.* carroña. *2 adj.* carroño, inmundo.

**carronade** (kæ·røneid) *s.* carronada.

**carrot** (kæ·røt) *s.* zanahoria.

**carroty** (-i) *adj.* bermejo [pelo]. *2* pelirrojo.

**carry** (kæ·ri) *s.* transporte en hombros. *2* alcance [de un arma].

**carry (to)** *tr.* llevar, traer, acarrear, conducir, portear, transportar. *2* llevar [encima, consigo, en sí]. *3* entrañar, incluir. *4* sostener, soportar. *5* dirigir, impulsar. *6* entusiasmar, convencer. *7* arrebatar, tomar, conquistar, lograr, ganar. *8* dar, producir [frutos]. *9* hacer aprobar [una moción, etc.]. *10* ARIT. llevar. *11 to ~ away,* quitar, llevarse; arrebatar, entusiasmar. *12 to ~ forward, to ~ over,* COM. llevar a otra página, columna, etc. *13 to ~ off,* llevarse; ganar; hacer pasar; arrostrar. *14 to ~ on,* continuar; practicar, ejercer. *15 to ~ oneself,* portarse, conducirse. *16 to ~ one's point,* salirse con la suya. *17 to ~ out,* llevar a cabo. *18 to ~ the day,* quedar victorioso. *19 to ~ through,* llevar a término; tramitar. *20 to ~ weight,* pesar, influir. *21 intr.* portear. *22* alcanzar, llegar [la voz, un tiro, etc.]. ¶ Pret. y p. p.: *carried.*

**carry-over** *s.* sobrante, reserva. *2* COM. suma anterior.

**cart** (kaʳt) *s.* carro, carromato, carreta. *2* especie de tílburí. *3* carro de mano. *4 ~ wheel,* rueda de carro; GIMN. vuelta que se da de lado sobre manos y pies.

**cart (to)** *tr.* acarrear, acarrear.

**cartage** (-idÿ) *s.* carretaje, acarreo, transporte.

**carte** (kaʳt) *s.* ESGR. cuarta. *2* carta, lista [de platos]. *3 ~ blanche,* carta blanca.

**cartel** (kæ·rtel o ka·ʳtøl) *s.* cartel [de desafío]. *2* ECON., POL. cartel.

**carter** (ka·ʳtøʳ) *s.* carretero; acarreador.

**Cartesian** (kaʳtɪ·šan) *adj.-s.* cartesiano.

**Carthage** (ka·ʳzidÿ) *n. pr.* Cartago.

**Carthaginian** (kaʳzadÿi·nian) *adj.-s.* cartaginés.

**Carthusian** (kaʳziu·ÿan) *adj.-s.* cartujo.

**cartilage** (ka·ʳtilidÿ) *s.* cartílago.

**cartilaginous** (-ædÿinøs) *adj.* cartilaginoso.

**cartload** (-ka·ʳtloud) *s.* carretada.

**cartman** (-mæn) *s.* carretero, carrero.

**cartographer** (kaʳta·graføʳ) *s.* cartógrafo.

**cartography** (-fi) *s.* cartografía.

**cartomancy** (ka·ʳtømænsi) *s.* cartomancia.

**carton** (ka·ʳtøn) *s.* caja de cartón. *2* diana [de un blanco].

cartoon (ka<sup>r</sup>tu·n) *s*. PINT. cartón. *2* caricatura. *3* película de dibujos animados.

cartoonist (-ist) *s*. caricaturista.

cartouche (ka-<sup>r</sup>tush) *s*. ARQ. cartela. *2* orla [de mapa, etc.]. *3* MIL. cartucho [de papel].

cartridge (-tridȳ) *s*. cartucho [de arma]; ~ *belt*, canana.

cartway (-tuei) *s*. camino carretero.

cartwright (-rait) *s*. carretero [que hace carros].

caruncle (kæ·rønkøl) *s*. caruncula.

carve (to) (ka<sup>r</sup>v) *tr*. tallar, esculpir, cincelar, grabar. *2* cortar, trinchar [carne].

carvel (ka<sup>r</sup>·vøl) *s*. carabela.

carven (-vøn) *adj*. grabado, esculpido.

carver (-vø<sup>r</sup>) *s*. tallista, escultor. *2* trinchante [pers.]. *3* cuchillo de trinchar.

carving (-ing) *s*. entalladura, talla, escultura. *2* arte cisoria.

caryatid (kæriæ·tid) *s*. cariátide.

caryophyllaceous (kæriofilei·shøs) *adj*. cariofiláceo.

caryopsis (karia·psis) *s*. BOT. cariópside.

cascade (kæ·skeid) *s*. cascada.

cascade (to) *intr*. caer en forma de cascada.

cascarilla (kæskarɪ·la) *s*. BOT., FARM. cascarilla.

case (keis) *s*. caso [suceso, ejemplo, coyuntura, etc.]: *in any* ~, en todo caso; *in* ~, en caso de que. *2* GRAM., MED., DER. caso. *3* estado, situación. *4* argumentos o pruebas [en pro o en contra de algo]; lo que uno sostiene. *5* DER. acción, pleito, causa. *6* caja, estuche, vaina, funda, cubierta, carpeta, neceser. *7* MEC. camisa, forro. *8* cápsula [de cartucho]. *9* marco, arco, bastidor [de puerta, ventana, etc.]. *10* IMPR. caja.

case (to) *tr*. embalar, encajonar, enfundar, cubrir, borrar.

casein (kei·siin) *s*. caseína.

casemate (kei·smeit) *s*. FORT. casamata.

casement (-mønt) *s*. ventana de bisagras [hoja]. *2* capa, cubierta.

caseous (kei·siøs) *adj*. caseoso.

cash (kæsh) *s*. numerario, efectivo, dinero contante: ~ *register*, caja registradora; ~ *down*, a toca teja; ~ *on delivery*, contra reembolso. *2* COM. caja. *3* pago al contado. *4* *adj.-adv*. al contado.

cash (to) *tr*. cobrar, hacer efectivo [un cheque, etc.].

cashbook *s*. libro de caja.

cashbox *s*. caja [para el dinero].

cashew (kashu·) *s*. BOT. anacardo.

cashier (kæshi·ø<sup>r</sup>) *s*. cajero, contador.

cashier (to) *tr*. destituir. *2* MIL. degradar.

cashmere (kæ·shmiø<sup>r</sup>) *s*. cachemir, casimir.

Casimir (kæ·simi<sup>r</sup>) *n. pr*. Casimiro.

casing (kei·sing) *s*. cubierta, envoltura, camisa, forro, revestimiento. *2* cubierta [de neumático]. *3* COST. jareta.

casino (kasi·nou) *s*. casino.

cask (kæsk) *s*. casco, tonel, cuba, barrica, barril.

cask (to) *tr*. entonelar, embarrilar.

casket (ka·skit) *s*. arqueta, cofrecito.

Caspian Sea (kæ·spian) *n. pr*. Mar Caspio.

casque (kæsk) *s*. casco, yelmo, almete.

cassation (kæsei·shøn) *s*. casación.

cassava (kæsa·va) *s*. mandioca.

casserole (kæ·søroul) *s*. cacerola.

cassia (kæ·sha) *s*. casia.

cassimere (kæ·simɪ<sup>r</sup>) *s*. casimir.

cassino (kasi·nou) *s*. cierto juego de naipes.

cassis (kasi·s) *s*. BOT. casis.

cassock (kæ·søk) *s*. sotana. *2* casacón.

cassowary (kæ·søueri) *s*. casuario.

cast (kæst) *s*. echada, lanzamiento, tirada. *2* tiro, alcance [de una piedra, etc.]. *3* fundición, vaciado; pieza fundida o vaciada. *4* molde [que se saca]; mascarilla; impronta. *5* IMPR. plancha. *6* aspecto; disposición, tendencia. *7* matiz, tono. *8* TEAT. reparto; cuadro de actores. *9* *to have a* ~ *in one eye*, ser bizco de un ojo. *10* p. p. de TO CAST. *11* *adj*. lanzado, vaciado, fundido, etc.: ~ *iron*, hierro colado, fundición.

cast (to) *tr*. echar, lanzar, tirar, arrojar. *2* verter, derramar. *3* despedir, desechar. *4* perder [una herradura, las hojas, etc.]; soltar, mudar [la pluma, la piel]. *5* arrojar [luz]; proyectar [sombra]. *6* derribar, tumbar. *7* tornar, disponer, arreglar. *8* fundir, vaciar, moldear. *9* volver, poner [los ojos, el pensamiento, etc.]. *10* hacer [cuentas]. *11* TEAT. repartir [los papeles]. *12* dar, depositar [un voto]. *13* *to* ~ *anchor*, echar anclas. *14* *to* ~ *aside*, desechar. *15* *to* ~ *lots*, echar suertes. *16* *intr*. echar el anzuelo. *17* sumar, hacer cálculos. *18* alabearse, deformarse. *19* *to* ~ *about*, buscar, discurrir, hacer planes.
¶ Pret. y p. p.: *cast*.

Castalides (-æ·lids) *s. pl*. MIT. Castálidas.

castanets (kæ·stanets) *s. pl*. castañuelas.

castaway (ka·stauei) *s*. desechado, abandonado. *2* MAR. perdido. *3* *s*. náufrago. *4* fig. réprobo, proscrito.

caste (kast) *s*. casta, clase [social].

castellan (ka·stølan) *s*. castellano, alcaide [de un castillo].

castellated (-eitid) *adj*. encastillado, fortificado.

caster (ka·stø<sup>r</sup>) *s*. echador. *2* el que hace sumas, cálculos o pronósticos. *3* vaciador, fundidor. *4* vinagrera. *5* ruedecilla [de muebles]. *6* *pl*. vinagreras.

castigate (to) (kæ·stigeit) *tr*. castigar, corregir.

castigation (-ei·shøn) *s*. castigo; corrección.

Castile (kæsti·l) *n. pr*. Castilla.

Castilian (-ian) *adj.-s*. castellano [de Castilla].

casting (kæ·sting) *s*. echada. *2* fundición, vaciado. *3* alabeo. *4* distribución, arreglo, plan, modelo. *5* *adj*. ~ *vote*, voto decisivo, de calidad.

cast-iron *adj*. de hierro colado. *2* fuerte, duro.

castle (kæ·søl) *s*. castillo, alcázar: ~ *in Spain*, ~ *in the air*, fig. castillo en el aire. *2* AJED. torre.

castle (to) *intr*. AJED. enrocar.

cast off *adj*. abandonado, desechado. *2* de desecho.

castor (ka·stø<sup>r</sup>) *s*. castóreo. *2* sombrero de castor. *3* CASTER *4* y *5*. *4* ~ *oil*, aceite de ricino.

castoreum (kastou·riøm) *s*. castóreo.

castrate (to) (kæ·streit) *tr*. castrar, capar.

castration (-ei·shon) *s*. castración, capadura.

castrator (-tø<sup>r</sup>) *s*. castrador.

casual (kæ·śiual) *adj*. casual, fortuito. *2* ocasional. *3* transeúnte, volandero. *4* hecho o dicho como al descuido.

casually (-i) *adv*. por accidente; ocasionalmente. *2* como al descuido, sin darle importancia.

casualty (-uti) *s*. accidente, desgracia, siniestro. *2* MIL. baja, pérdida. *3* víctima [de un accidente].

casuist (kæ·śiuist) *s*. casuista.

casuistic(al (kæśiui·stik(al) *adj*. casuístico.

casuistry (-tri) *s*. casuística.

cat (kæt) *s*. ZOOL. gato, gata: *cat's cradle*, cunas [juego de niños]; *cat's paw*, intrumento, persona de quien se sirve otra. *2* ZOOL. felino. *3* MAR. aparejo de gata. *4* tala, toña [palito].

cataclysm (kæ·taclišm) *s*. cataclismo.

catacomb (-koum) *s*. catacumba.

**catafalque** (-fælk) *s.* catafalco.
**Catalan** (-lən) *adj.-s.* catalán.
**catalectic** (kætale·ktik) *adj.* cataléctico.
**catalepsy** (-le·psi) *s.* catalepsia.
**cataleptic** (-le·ptik) *adj.* cataléptico.
**catalogue** (kæ·talag) *s.* catálogo.
**catalogue (to)** *tr.* catalogar.
**Catalonia** (kætalou·nia) *n. pr.* Cataluña.
**catalpa** (katæ·lpa) *s.* BOT. catalpa.
**catalysis** (katæ·lisis) *s.* catálisis.
**catalyst** (kæ·talist), **catalyzer** (-laišøᵣ) *s.* catalizador.
**catamaran** (kætamaræ·n) *s.* MAR. especie de balsa. *2* mujer pendenciera.
**catamount** (kæ·tamaunt), **catamountain** (-ing) *s.* ZOOL. gato montés; lince; leopardo.
**cataplasm** (kæ·taplæšm) *s.* POULTICE.
**catapult** (kæ·tapølt) *s.* catapulta. *2* tirador [para lanzar piedrecitas, etc.].
**catapult (to)** *tr.* catapultar.
**cataract** (kæ·tarækt) *s.* GEOGR., MED. catarata.
**catarrh** (kata·ᵣ) *s.* catarro.
**catarrhal** (-ral) *adj.* catarral.
**catastrophe** (katæ·strofi) *s.* catástrofe. *2* GEOL. cataclismo.
**catbird** (kæ·tbøᵣd) *s.* pájaro americano.
**catboat** (kæ·tbout) *s.* MAR. laúd.
**catcall** (kæ·tkol) *s.* silbido, silba, abucheo.
**catcall (to)** *tr.* silbar, abuchear.
**catch** (kæch) *s.* cogedura, asimiento, captura. *2* botín, pesca, redada. *3* pregunta insidiosa, trampa. *4* lo que detiene o sujeta: gancho, trinquete, tope, cerradero, pestillo, pasador, etc. *5* interrupción brusca. *6* trocito, rato. *7* atractivo, buen partido. *8 adj.* atractivo, insidioso, que sujeta, etc.: ~ *question*, pregunta insidiosa; ~ *bolt*, picaporte.
**catch (to)** *tr.* coger, asir, agarrar, retener, sujetar. *2* coger, pescar, cazar, atrapar. *3* coger, pillar [una enfermedad]; contagiarse de. *4* coger, sorprender. *5* comprender, penetrar. *6* engranar, endentar. *7* recoger [en un recipiente]. *8* atraer [la atención, la mirada]. *9* fam. atizar [un golpe]. *10 to* ~ *fire*, encenderse, inflamarse. *11 to* ~ *hold of*, agarrarse a; apoderarse de. *12 to* ~ *one's breath*, contener bruscamente el aliento. *13 intr.* enredarse, engancharse, trabarse. *14* prender el fuego, etc. *15* contagiarse, ser pegadizo. *16 to* ~ *at*, tratar de coger. *17 to* ~ *up*, ponerse al día.
¶ Pret. y p. p.: *caught.*
**catcher** (kæ·tchøᵣ) *s.* el o lo que coge, sujeta, etc. *2* DEP. cátcher.
**catching** (-ing) *adj.* contagioso, pegadizo. *2* atractivo.
**catchpenny** (kæ·chpeni) *s.* baratija, sacadineros. *2 adj.* de pacotilla.
**catchpole, catchpoll** (-poul) *s.* alguacil.
**catchup** (-øp) *s.* salsa hecha con jugo de setas, tomates, etc.
**catchword** (-wøᵣd) *s.* IMPR. reclamo. *2* TEAT. pie. *3* lema [de un partido, etc.].
**catchy** (kæ·chi) *adj.* CATCHING. *2* intermitente.
**catechesis** (kætøki·sis) *s.* catequesis, catequismo.
**catechetic(al** (katøke·tik(al) *adj.* catequístico.
**catechism** (kæ·tøkišm) *s.* catecismo.
**catechist** (-ist) *s.* catequista.
**catechize (to)** (-kaiš) *tr.* catequizar. *2* interrogar.
**catechu** (kæ·tøchu) *s.* catecú, cato.
**catechumen** (kætikiu·møn) *s.* catecúmeno.
**categoric(al** (kætiga·rik(al) *adj.* categórico.

**category** (kæ·tigøri) *s.* categoría.
**catenary** (kæ·tineri) *adj.-s.* catenaria.
**catenate (to)** (kæ·tineit) *tr.* encadenar, concadenar.
**catenation** (-ei·shøn) *s.* encadenamiento, concadenación.
**cater (to)** (kei·tøᵣ) *intr.* abastecer, proveer.
**caterer** (-tørøᵣ) *s.* abastecedor, proveedor.
**caterpillar** (kæ·tøᵣpilaᵣ) *s.* ENT. oruga.
**caterwaul** (-uol) *s.* maullido.
**caterwaul (to)** *intr.* maullar.
**catfish** (cæ·tfish) *s.* ICT. siluro; barbo.
**catgut** (-gøt) *s.* catgut. *2* cuerda de tripa.
**cathartic** (kaza·ᵣtik) *adj.-s.* catártico, purgante.
**cathead** (kæ·tjed) *s.* serviola.
**cathedra** (kæzɪ·dra) *s.* cátedra [asiento del maestro; dignidad pontificia o episcopal].
**cathedral** (kæzɪ·dral) *s.* catedral. *2 adj.* catedral, catedralicio. *3* episcopal.
**Catherine** (kæ·zørin) *n. pr.* Catalina: ~ *wheel*, rueda de fuegos artificiales; ARQ. rosa, rosetón.
**catheter** (kæ·zøtør) *s.* catéter.
**cathode** (kæ·zoud) *s.* cátodo.
**cathodic** (-ik) *adj.* catódico.
**catholic** (kæ·zølik) *adj.* católico, universal. *2* [con may.] *adj.-s.* REL. católico.
**catholicism** (kaza·lisišm) *s.* catolicismo.
**catholicity** (kæzøli·siti) *s.* catolicidad.
**cation** (kæ·taiøn) *s.* QUÍ., FÍS. catión.
**catkin** (kæ·tkin) *s.* BOT. amento, candelilla.
**catlike** (-laik) *adj.* gatuno, gatesgo.
**catmint** (-mint) *s.* BOT. hierba gatera.
**Cato** (kei·tou) *n. pr.* Catón.
**Catonian** (keitou·nian) *adj.* catoniano.
**cat-o'-nine-tails** *s.* azote con nueve ramales.
**catoptrics** (kata·ptriks) *s.* catóptrica.
**cat's-eye** *s.* MINER. ojo de gato.
**catsup** (kæ·tsøp) *s.* CATCHUP.
**cattail** (-teil) *s.* BOT. espadaña; anea.
**cattish** (-tish) *adj.* gatuno, gatesgo.
**cattle** (kæ·tøl) *s.* ganado, reses; ganado vacuno; cabeza de ganado: ~ *bell*, esquila. *2* desp. gentuza.
**cattleman** (-mæn) *s.* ganadero.
**Caucasian** (kokei·shan) *adj.-s.* caucásico.
**Caucasus** (ko·kasøs) *n. pr.* GEOGR. Cáucaso.
**caucus** (ko·køs) *s.* junta política.
**caudal** (ko·dal) *adj.* ZOOL. caudal.
**caudate** (ko·deit) *adj.* caudado, caudato.
**caudle** (ko·døl) *s.* bebida confortante.
**caul** (kol) *s.* redaño. *2* membrana que envuelve al feto.
**cauldron** (ko·ldrøn) *s.* caldero, caldera.
**cauliflower** (ko·liflauøᵣ) *s.* BOT. coliflor.
**caulk (to)** (kok) *tr.* MAR. calafatear. *2* tapar las rendijas de.
**caulker** (ko·køᵣ) *s.* calafate.
**causal** (ko·šal) *adj.* causal.
**causality** (kosæ·liti) *s.* causalidad.
**causate (to)** (ko·šeit) *tr.* causar, originar.
**causative** (ko·šativ) *adj.* causativo.
**cause** (koš) *s.* causa [de un efecto; motivo, autor]. *2* causa [en que se toma interés o partido]: *common* ~, causa común. *3* DER. causa, pleito.
**cause (to)** *tr.* causar. *2* hacer [con un inf.]; hacer que, inducir a, impeler a.
**causeless** (-lis) *adj.* inmotivado, infundado.
**causer** (ko·šøᵣ) *s.* causante, causador.
**causeway** (ko·šwei), **causey** (-i) *s.* paso firme que cruza un pantano, etc.; calzada, arrecife.
**causidical** (koši·dikal) *adj.* causídico.
**caustic** (ko·stik) *adj.-s.* cáustico.

**causticity** (kosti·siti) *s.* causticidad.
**cauter** (ko·tø$^r$) *s.* cauterio [instrumento].
**cauterize (to)** (ko·tøraiš) *tr.* cauterizar.
**cautery** (ko·tøri) *s.* cauterio.
**caution** (ko·shøn) *s.* caución, cautela, precaución. 2 aviso, amonestación, advertencia.
**caution (to)** *tr.* cautelar, advertir, avisar; amonestar.
**cautious** (ko·shøs) *adj.* cauto, precavido, prudente, circunspecto.
**cautiousness** (-nis) *s.* cautela, precaución, prudencia.
**cavalcade** (kæ·valkeid) *s.* cabalgata.
**cavalier** (kæ·valiø$^r$) *s.* caballero [noble]. 2 jinete. 3 caballero, galán [de una dama]. 4 *adj.* alegre, desenvuelto. 5 altivo, brusco.
**cavaliery** (-li) *adv.* caballerescamente. 2 altivamente, bruscamente.
**cavalry** (kæ·valri) *s.* MIL. caballería.
**cave** (kiev) *s.* cueva, caverna; antro: ~ *dweller*, cavernícola.
**cave (to)** *tr.* excavar, hundir. 2 *intr.* to ~ *in*, hundirse [el suelo, etc.]; fam. ceder, rendirse.
**cavern** (kæ·vø$^r$n) *s.* caverna, antro.
**cavernous** (-øs) *adj.* cavernoso.
**cavesson** (kæ·vøsøn) *s.* cabezón de serreta.
**caviar** (kæ·via$^r$) *s.* cavial, caviar.
**cavicorn** (kæ·vikø$^r$n) *adj.-s.* ZOOL. cavicornio.
**cavil** (kæ·vil) *s.* quisquilla, objeción frívola, sutileza, argucia.
**cavil (to)** *intr.* buscar quisquillas; poner tachas o reparos nimios. ¶ Pret. y p. p.: *caviled* o *-lled;* ger.: *caviling* o *-lling.*
**caviller** (-ø$^r$) *s.* reparón.
**cavity** (kæ·viti) *s.* cavidad.
**cavy** (kei·vi) *s.* nombre que se da al cobayo, al carpincho, al agutí, etc.
**caw** (ko) *s.* graznido.
**caw (to)** *intr.* graznar.
**cay** (kei) *s.* cayo, isleta.
**Cayenne** (kaie·n) *n. pr.* Cayena.
**cayenne pepper** *s.* pimentón.
**cayman** (kei·man) *s.* ZOOL. caimán.
**cease** (sis) *s.* cesación: *without* ~, sin cesar.
**cease (to)** *intr.* cesar [no continuar]. 2 *tr.* poner fin a, parar, acabar, dejar de.
**ceaseless** (sı·slis) *adj.* incesante, continuo.
**Cecil** (si·sil o se·sil) *n. pr.* Cecilio.
**Cecilia** (sisi·lia) *n. pr.* Cecilia.
**cecity** (se·siti) *s.* ceguera.
**cecum** *s.* CAECUM. .
**cedar** (sı·da$^r$) *s.* BOT. cedro.
**cedarn** (sı·da$^r$n) *adj.* poét. cedrino.
**cede (to)** (sıd) *tr.* ceder, traspasar.
**cedilla** (sidi·la) *s.* cedilla.
**cedrine** (si·drin) *adj.* cedrino.
**ceil (to)** (sıl) *tr.* poner cielo raso.
**ceiling** (sı·ling) *s.* techo, cielo raso. 2 AVIA. techo, altura máxima.
**celadon** (se·ladøn) *s.* verdeceledón.
**celandine** (se·landain) *s.* BOT. celidonia.
**celebrant** (se·løbrant) *s.* celebrante.
**celebrate** (se·løbreit) *tr.* celebrar, solemnizar. 2 celebrar, alabar. 3 *intr.* celebrar [decir misa]. 4 divertirse.
**celebrated** (se·løbreitid) *adj.* célebre, famoso.
**celebration** (-ei·shøn) *s.* celebración. 2 fiesta.
**celebrity** (søle·briti) *s.* celebridad.
**celerity** (-riti) *s.* celeridad.
**celery** (se·løri) *s.* BOT. apio.
**celestial** (søle·schal) *adj.* celestial, celeste, célico:

*Celestial Empire*, Imperio Celeste, China. 2 *s.* chino. 3 morador del cielo.
**celiac** (sı·liæk) *adj.* COELIAC.
**celibacy** (se·libasi) *s.* celibato, soltería.
**celibate** (se·libeit) *adj.-s.* célibe.
**cell** (sel) *s.* celda. 2 célula. 3 celdilla, hueco, nicho, cavidad, alvéolo. 4 ELECT. par, elemento [de pila]; pila simple.
**cellar** (se·la$^r$) *s.* sótano, cueva. 2 bodega [para vinos].
**cellaret** (selare·t) *s.* frasquera; licorera.
**cellist** (che·list) *s.* violoncelista.
**cello** (che·lou) *s.* violoncelo.
**cellophane** (se·lofein) *s.* celofana.
**cellular** (se·liula$^r$) *adj.* celular, celuloso.
**cellule** (-liul) *s.* celdilla, celulilla.
**celluloid** (-oid) *s.* celuloide.
**cellulose** (-ous) *adj.* celuloso. 2 *s.* celulosa.
**Celt** (selt) *s.* celta.
**Celtiberian** (-ibi·rian) *adj.* celtibérico. 2 *adj.-s.* celtíbero.
**Celtic** (se·ltik) *adj.* céltico.
**cement** (søme·nt) *s.* cemento; mortero, argamasa; masilla. 2 ANAT., GEOL., METAL. cemento. 3 lazo de unión, vínculo.
**cement (to)** *tr.* unir o cubrir con cemento, etc. 2 afianzar, consolidar. 3 METAL. cementar. 4 *intr.* unirse, consolidarse.
**cementation** (-ei·shøn) *s.* unión, consolidación. 2 METAL. cementación.
**cemetery** (se·møteri) *s.* cementerio.
**cenacle** (se·nakøl) *s.* cenáculo.
**cenobite** (se·nobait) *s.* cenobita.
**cenobium** (senou·biøm), **cenoby** (se·nobi) *s.* cenobio.
**cenotaph** (se·notæf) *s.* cenotafio.
**cense (to)** (sens) *tr.* incensar, turificar.
**censer** (-ø$^r$) *s.* incensario.
**censor** (se·nsø$^r$) *s.* censor.
**censor (to)** *tr.* censurar [libros, etc.].
**censorial** (senso·rial) *adj.* censorio.
**censorious** (-riøs) *adj.* censurador, severo, rígido. 2 crítico, de censura.
**censorship** (se·nsø$^r$ship) *s.* censura [oficio].
**censual** (se·nshual) *adj.* censual.
**censure** (se·nshø$^r$) *s.* censura, crítica, reprobación. 2 censura [pena].
**censure (to)** *tr.* censurar, criticar, reprobar.
**census** (se·nsøs) *s.* censo, padrón. 2 DER. censo.
**cent** (sent) *s.* centavo [moneda]. 2 ciento, en frases como: *per* ~, por ciento.
**centaur** (se·ntø$^r$) *s.* MIT. centauro.
**centaury** (-i) *s.* BOT. centaura, centaurea.
**centenarian** (sentine·rian) *adj.-s.* centenario [pers.].
**centenary** (se·ntineri) *adj.* centenario, secular. 2 *s.* centenario [cien años, conmemoración].
**centennial** (sente·nial) *adj.* centenario, secular. 2 *s.* centenario [conmemoración].
**center, to center,** etc. = CENTRE, TO CENTRE, etc.
**centesimal** (sente·simal) *adj.* centesimal.
**centiare** (se·ntieø$^r$) *s.* centiárea.
**centigrade** (-greid) *adj.* centígrado.
**centigram[me** (-græm) *s.* centigramo.
**centilitre** o **-liter** (-litø$^r$) *s.* centilitro.
**centime** (santı·m) *s.* céntimo.
**centimetre,** o **-meter** (-ntimitø$^r$) *s.* centímetro.
**centipede** (se·ntipıd) *s.* ZOOL. ciempiés.
**cento** (se·ntou) *s.* centón.
**central** (se·ntral) *adj.* central; céntrico. 2 *s.* central [telefónica]. 3 telefonista.
**centralism** (-išm) *s.* centralismo.

**centralize (to)** (-aiš) *tr.* centralizar.
**centre** (se·ntøʳ) *s.* centro. *2* fuente [de energía]. *3* ARQ. cimbra.
**centre (to)** *tr.* centrar. *2* concentrar [en]. *3* ÓPT. ajustar, enfocar. *4* ARQ. cimbrar. *5 intr.* estar centrado [en]: *to ~ round*, girar en torno de.
**centreboard** (-boʳd) *s.* orza de quilla.
**centrepiece** (-pɪs) *s.* centro de mesa. *2* rosetón [de techo].
**centric(al** (se·ntrik(al) *adj.* céntrico, central.
**centrifugal** (sentri·fiugal), **centrifuge** (se·ntrifiudў) *adj.* centrífugo. *2 s.* centrifugadora.
**centrifuge (to)** *tr.* centrifugar.
**centripetal** (sentri·petal) *adj.* centrípeto.
**centrosome** (se·ntrosoum) *s.* BIOL. centrosoma.
**centrosphere** (se·ntrosfɪʳ) *s.* GEOL., BIOL. centroesfera.
**centumvir** (sentø·mviʳ) *s.* centunviro.
**centuple** (se·ntiupøl) *adj.* céntuplo.
**centuple (to)** *tr.* centuplicar.
**centuplicate** (sentiu·plikeit) *adj.* centuplicado.
**centuplicate (to)** *tr.* centuplicar.
**centurion** (sentiu·riøn) *s.* centurión.
**century** (se·nchøri) *s.* centuria. *2* siglo.
**cephalic** (sefæ·lik) *adj.* cefálico.
**cephalopod** (se·falopad) *adj.-s.* ZOOL. cefalópodo.
**cephalothorax** (-zou·ræks) *s.* ZOOL. cefalotórax.
**Cepheus** (si·fiøs) *n. pr.* MIT., ASTR. Cefeo.
**ceramic** (siræ·mik) *adj.* cerámico.
**ceramics** (-s) *s.* cerámica.
**ceramist** (se·ræmist) *s.* ceramista.
**cerastes** (seræ·stiš) *s.* ZOOL. cerasta.
**cerate** (sɪ·reit) *s.* cerato.
**cerated** (-id) *adj.* encerado.
**Cerberus** (sø·ʳbørøs) *n. pr.-s.* Cancerbero.
**cere** (sɪʳ) *s.* ORN. cera.
**cereal** (sɪ·rial) *adj.-s.* cereal.
**cerebellum** (seribe·løm) *s.* ANAT. cerebelo.
**cerebral** (se·røbral) *adj.* cerebral.
**cerebrum** (se·ribrøm) *s.* ANAT. cerebro. *2* encéfalo.
**cerecloth** (si·øʳcloz) *s.* encerado, hule.
**ceremonial** (serimou·nial) *adj.-s.* ceremonial.
**ceremonious** (serimou·niøs) *adj.* ceremonioso. *2* ceremonial.
**ceremony** (se·rimøni) *s.* ceremonia. *2* cumplido, formalidad, etiqueta.
**cereous** (sɪ·riøs) *adj.* céreo.
**Ceres** (si·rɪš) *n. pr.* Ceres.
**cerium** (sɪ·riøm) *s.* QUÍM. cerio.
**certain** (sø·ʳtøn) *adj.* fijo, determinado. *2* cierto, seguro, indudable, infalible, inevitable, positivo. *3* cierto, seguro, convencido [de algo]. *4 a ~*, cierto [en sentido indeterminado]; un tal. *5 s. for ~*, de fijo, con toda seguridad.
**certainly** (-li) *adv.* ciertamente, indudablemente, por cierto. *2* seguramente, sin falta.
**certainty** (-ti) *s.* certeza, certidumbre, seguridad. *2* cosa cierta, segura.
**certifiable** (sø·ʳtifaiabøl) *adj.* certificable. *2* loco.
**certificate** (sø·ʳti·fikit) *s.* certificado, partida. *2* acta [notarial]. *3* título [para ejercer ciertas profesiones]. *4* COM. *~ of stock*, título, acción.
**certificate (to)** (-eit) *tr.* certificar. *2* proveer de título o certificado.
**certifier** (sø·ʳtifaiøʳ) *s.* certificador.
**certify (to)** (sø·ʳtifai) *tr.* certificar, afirmar, asegurar. *2* MED. declarar loco. ¶ P. p.: *certified*.
**certitude** (sø·ʳtitiud) *s.* certeza, certidumbre.
**cerulean** (søru·lian), **-leous** (-liøs) *adj.* cerúleo.
**cerumen** (søru·møn) *s.* cerumen.
**ceruse** (sɪ·rus) *s.* cerusa, albayalde.

**cervical** (sø·ʳvikal) *adj.* cervical.
**Cervidae** (sø·ʳvidi) *s. pl.* ZOOL. cérvidos.
**cervine** (sø·ʳvin) *adj.* cervino.
**cervix** (sø·ʳviks) *s.* cerviz.
**cesium** (sɪ·šiøm) *s.* QUÍM. cesio.
**cespitose** (si·spitous) *adj.* cespitoso.
**cessation** (sesei·shøn) *s.*cesación, paro, suspensión.
**cession** (se·shøn) *s.* cesión.
**cessionary** (se·shøneri) *adj.-s.* cesionario.
**cesspool** (se·spul) *s.* pozo negro, sumidero.
**cesura** *s.* CAESURA.
**cetacean** (sitei·shan) *adj.* y *s.* ZOOL. cetáceo.
**cetaceous** (-shøs) *adj.* cetáceo.
**Ceylon** (si·lan) *n. pr.* Ceilán.
**Ceylonese** (silani·š) *adj.-s.* cingalés.
**chafe** (cheif) *s.* roce; rozadura, excoriación, sahorno. *2* irritación, impaciencia.
**chafe (to)** *tr.* calentar frotando. *2* rozar, excoriar. *3* enojar, irritar. *4 intr.* rozar [con]. *5* rozarse, sahornarse. *6* rabiar, impacientarse.
**chafer** (-øʳ) *s.* calentador [vasija]. *2* lo que roza. *3* COCKCHAFER.
**chafery** (-i) *s.* fragua, forja.
**chaff** (chaf) *s.* ahechaduras, barcia, granzas, paja menuda; broza. *2* broma, vaya.
**chaff (to)** *tr.* embromar, dar vaya.
**chaffer** (chæ·føʳ) *s.* regateo.
**chaffer (to)** *tr.* regatear. *2 to ~ away*, gastar, pasar [el tiempo, etc.].
**chafferer** (-øʳ) *s.* regatón [que regatea].
**chaffinch** (chæ·finch) *s.* ORN. pinzón.
**chafing-dish** (chei·fing) *s.* escalfador [braserillo].
**chagrin** (shagri·n) *s.* mortificación, desazón, disgusto.
**chagrin (to)** *tr.* mortificar, disgustar.
**chain** (chein) *s.* cadena [serie de eslabones, de cosas o de sucesos]; *~ gang*, cadena de presidiarios; *~ stitch*, punto de cadencia. *2* cadena de agrimensor. *3* cadenilla. *4* WARP 1. *5 pl.* cadenas, esclavitud.
**chain (to)** *tr.* encadenar. *2* esclavizar. *3* enlazar, unir.
**chainwork** (-uøʳk) *s.* labor de cadeneta.
**chair** (cheʳ) *s.* silla, sillón, sitial. *2* asiento de juez; cátedra; presidencia: *to take the ~*, presidir. *3* silla de manos. *4* FERROC. cojinete.
**chairman** *s.* presidente. *2* silletero.
**chairwoman** *s.* presidenta.
**chaise** (cheiš) *s.* coche, silla, volante, calesín. *2* silla de posta.
**chalcedony** (kælse·døni) *s.* calcedonia.
**chalcography** (kæ·lkagrafi) *s.* calcografía.
**Chaldaic** (kældei·k) *adj.* caldaico.
**Chaldea** (kældɪ·a) *n. pr.* HIST. Caldea.
**Chaldean** (-n) *adj.-s.* caldeo.
**chalet** (sha·lei) *s.* chalet.
**chalice** (chæ·lis) *s.* cáliz.
**chalk** (chok) *s.* cresta; marga. *2* tiza, yeso; clarión.
**chalk (to)** *tr.* enyesar, mezclar con yeso. *2* margar. *3* dibujar o marcar con tiza. *4* entizar.
**chalky** (cho·ki) *adj.* yesoso. *2* blanquecino, pálido. *3* FOT. duro.
**challenge** (chæ·lindў) *s.* desafío, reto. *2* DEP. disputa [de un título]. *3* discusión, impugnación. *4* DER. recusación. *5* MIL. quién vive.
**challenge (to)** *tr.* desafiar, retar. *2* reclamar, merecer [atención, respeto, etc.]. *3* disputar, discutir, impugnar, poner en duda. *4* DER. recusar. *5* MIL. dar el quién vive.

**challenger** (-ø$^r$) *s.* desafiador, retador. *2* DEP. aspirante a un título.

**chamade** (shæma·d) *s.* MIL. llamada.

**chamber** (chei·mbø$^r$) *s.* cámara, aposento: ~ *pot*, vaso de noche. *2* cámara [legislativa, de comercio, etc.]; sala [de tribunal]. *3* cámara, compartimiento, cavidad. *4* ARTILL. recámara.

**chamberlain** (-lin) *s.* chambelán, camarlengo.

**chambermaid** (-meid) *s.* camarera, sirvienta.

**chameleon** (kamɪ·liøn) *s.* camaleón.

**chamfer** (chæ·mfø$^r$) *s.* chaflán, bisel. *2* canal, estria.

**chamfer (to)** *tr.* achaflanar, biselar. *2* acanalar.

**chamois** (shæ·mua) *s.* ZOOL. gamuza. *2* gamuza [piel].

**chamomile** (kæ·mømail) *s.* BOT. manzanilla, camomila.

**champ (to)** (chæmp) *tr.* mordiscar, mascar; tascar: *to ~ the bit*, tascar el freno.

**champagne** (shæ·mpein) *s.* champán, champaña.

**champaign** *s.* campiña. *2 adj.* abierto, llano, raso.

**champion** (chæ·mpiøn) *s.* campeón, paladín, defensor. *2* DEP. campeón.

**champion (to)** *tr.* defender, abogar por.

**championess** (-is) *f.* campeona; defensora.

**championship** (-ship) *s.* campeonato.

**chance** (chans) *s.* ventura, suerte. *2* azar, albur, accidente, casualidad: *by ~*, por casualidad, por ventura. *3* oportunidad, coyuntura. *4* riesgo, peligro. *5* probabilidad, posibilidad. *6 adj.* casual, fortuito, accidental.

**chance (to)** *intr.* acaecer, suceder, encontrarse [por acaso], acertar a.

**chancel** (chæ·nsøl) *s.* presbiterio [de iglesia].

**chancellery** (-øri) *s.* cancillería.

**chancellor** (-ø$^r$) *s.* canciller. *2* magistrado presidente. *3 Chancellor of the Exchequer*, (Ingl.) Ministro de Hacienda.

**chancery** (chæ·nsøri) *s.* nombre de ciertos tribunales.

**chancre** (shæ·nkø$^r$) *s.* chancro.

**chancy** (chæ·nsi) *adj.* arriesgado.

**chandelier** (shændøli·ø$^r$) *s.* lámpara, araña.

**chandler** (shæ·ndlø$^r$) *s.* cerero, velero. *2* tendero. *3* abastecedor de buques.

**change** (chei·ndȝ) *s.* cambio, alteración, variación, mudanza, transformación, mutación. *2* cambio, trueque, sustitución. *3* muda [de ropa]. *4* cambio [de un billete]; vuelta [de un pago]. *5* suelto, moneda suelta. *6* novedad, variedad: *for a ~*, para variar, para cambiar de aire. *7* lonja, Bolsa.

**change (to)** *tr.* cambiar, alterar, variar, mudar, transformar, convertir, trocar. *2* cambiar de, mudar de: *to ~ colour*, demudarse, ruborizarse. *3* mudar las ropas de. *4 intr.* cambiar, variar, transformarse. *5* corregirse.

**changeable** (-øbøl) *adj.* cambiable. *2* mudable, variable, voluble, inconstante. *3* cambiante, tornasolado.

**changeful** (-ful) *adj.* cambiante. *2* mudable, variable, inconstante.

**changeless** (-lis) *adj.* inmutable, constante.

**changeling** (-ling) *s.* niño cambiado por otro. *2* idiota.

**changer** (-ø$^r$) *s.* cambiador, cambista.

**channel** (chæ·nøl) *s.* cauce, lecho, álveo. *2* canal [porción de mar], canalizo: *English Channel*, Canal de la Mancha. *3* zanja, reguera. *4* conducto, vía. *5* ranura, canal, estría.

**channel (to)** *tr.* acanalar, estriar. *2* encauzar, con-

ducir. ¶ Pret. y p. p.: *channeled* o *-lled;* ger.: *channeling* o *-lling*.

**chant** (chant) *s.* canción, canto. *2* canto llano, salmodia. *3* sonsonete.

**chant (to)** *tr.* cantar, entonar; salmodiar. *2* celebrar cantando.

**chanter** (-ø$^r$) *s.* cantor. *2* chantre.

**chantey** (-i) *s.* MAR. saloma.

**chanticleer** (chæntikli·ø$^r$) *s.* gallo [ave].

**chantress** (cha·ntris) *s.* cantora.

**chantry** (cha·ntri) *s.* ECLES. capilla.

**chaos** (kei·øs) *s.* caos.

**chaotic** (keia·tik) *adj.* caótico.

**chap** (chæp) *s.* fam. muchacho. *2* fam. sujeto. *3* grieta, raja. *4* carrillo, quijada. *5 pl.* (E.U.) chaparreras.

**chap (to)** *tr.* resquebrajar, agrietar. *2 intr.* resquebrajarse, agrietarse. ¶ Pret. y p. p.: *chapped;* ger.: *-pping*.

**chape** (cheip) *s.* boquilla o contera [de vaina]. *2* patilla [de hebilla].

**chapel** (chæ·pøl) *s.* capilla [para el culto]. *2* capilla [de música]. *3* personal [de una imprenta].

**chaperon** (shæ·pøroun) *s.* caperuza. *2* persona mayor que acompaña y protege a una joven; carabina.

**chaperon (to)** *tr.* acompañar y proteger a una joven, servirle de carabina.

**chapfallen** (chæ·pfoløn) *adj.* alicaído, cariacontecido.

**chaplain** (chæ·plin) *s.* capellán.

**chaplaincy** (-si), **chaplainship** (-ship) *s.* capellanía.

**chaplet** (chæ·plit) *s.* guirnalda. *2* sarta, rosario. *3* collar, gargantilla. *4* ARQ. moldura de cuentas.

**chapman** (-mæn) *s.* buhonero.

**chappy** (chæ·pi) *adj.* rajado, agrietado.

**chapter** (chæ·ptø$^r$) *s.* capítulo [de un libro]. *2* ECLES. capítulo, cabildo. *3* LITURG. capítula.

**char** (cha$^r$) *s.* trabajo a jornal o por horas. *2* especie de trucha.

**char (to)** *tr.* carbonizar; socarrar. *2 intr.* trabajar a jornal o por horas. ¶ Pret. y p. p.: *charred;* ger.: *charring*.

**charabanc** (charabæ·ng) *s.* charabán.

**character** (kæ·raktø$^r$) *s.* carácter [en todos sus sentidos]. *2* calidad, condición. *3* letra [de una pers.]..*4* fama, reputación. *5* referencias, certificado de conducta. *6* descripción. *7* HIST., LIT. personaje. *8* TEAT. papel. *9* sujeto, tipo.

**character (to)** *tr.* grabar, inscribir.

**characteristic** (-i·stik) *s.* característica.

**characteristic(al** (-i·stik(al) *adj.* característico, distintivo.

**characterization** (-išei·shøn) *s.* caracterización. *2* representación, descripción.

**characterize (to)** (-aiš) *tr.* caracterizar. *2* representar, describir.

**characterless** (-lis) *adj.* sin carácter.

**charade** (shara·d) *s.* charada.

**charbon** (sha·$^r$ban) *s.* MED. carbunco.

**charcoal** (cha·$^r$koul) *s.* carbón de leña; carbón animal. *2* DIB. carboncillo.

**chard** (cha·$^r$d) *s.* BOT. acelga. *2* penca de alcachofa.

**chare** *s.*, **to chare** *intr.* CHAR 1; TO CHAR 2.

**charge** (cha·$^r$dȝ) *s.* carga [de un arma, un horno, etc.]. *2* peso [moral]. *3* cargo, obligación, custodia, cuidado. *4* encargo, cometido. *5* persona o cosa de que uno está encargado. *6* orden, mandato. *7* carga, gravamen. *8* precio, costa. *9* com. cargo [en cuenta]. *10* cargo, acusación. *11* MIL. carga, ataque. *12* BLAS. blasón.

**charge (to)** *tr.* cargar [un arma, un horno, etc.; saturar, llenar]. *2* confiar, encargar, cometer. *3* mandar, exhortar. *4* cargar, gravar, imponer. *5* cobrar, pedir, llevar [un precio]. *6* COM. adeudar, cargar. *7* poner como blasón [en el escudo]. *8 to* ~ *with*, acusar, tachar de. *9 tr.-intr.* cargar, embestir. *10* cobrar [caro, barato, etc.].

**charger** (cha·ʳdy̌øʳ) *s.* corcel; caballo de guerra. *2* cargador. *3* ant. fuente [plato].

**charily** (che·rili) *adv.* con cuidado. *2* parcamente.

**chariot** (chæ·riøt) *s.* carro [de guerra]. *2* carroza ligera.

**charioteer** (chariøti·øʳ) *s.* auriga.

**charism** (kæ·rišm) *s.* carisma.

**charitable** (chæ·ritabøl) *adj.* caritativo.

**charity** (chæ·riti) *s.* caridad [virtud]. *2* caridad, limosna. *3* beneficencia; institución benéfica.

**charivari** (shariva·ri) *s.* cencerrada.

**charlatan** (sha·ʳlɑtan) *s.* charlatán, curandero.

**charlatanism** (-išm) *s.* charlatanismo.

**Charles** (chaʳlš) *n. pr.* Carlos.

**Charle's Waim** (cha·rlšiš uein) *s.* Osa Mayor.

**Charlotte** (cha·ʳløt) *n. pr.* Carlota.

**charm** (chaʳm) *s.* encantamiento. *2* amuleto. *3* encanto, embeleso, hechizo, atractivo, gracia. *4* dije.

**charm (to)** *tr.* encantar, hechizar. *2* embelesar, cautivar, prendar.

**charmer** (-øʳ) *s.* encantador, hechicero.

**charming** (-ing) *s.* encantador, hechicero, embelesador.

**charnel** (cha·ʳnøl) *adj.* sepulcral: ~ *house*, osario, carnero.

**Charon** (kei·røn) *n. pr.* MIT. Carón.

**chart** (cha·ʳt) *s.* carta de marear. *2* mapa, plano. *2* cuadro, gráfica.

**chart (to)** *tr.* trazar [un mapa, rumbo, etc.].

**charter** (cha·ʳtøʳ) *s.* carta constitucional o de privilegio. *2* patente, título; escritura. *3* COM. *charter* o ~ *party*, fletamento.

**charter (to)** *tr.* estatuir. *2* conceder privilegio o patente. *3* fletar [un buque]; alquilar [un vehículo].

**chartographer, chartography** = CARTOGRAPHER, CARTOGRAPHY.

**Chartreuse** (chaʳtrø·š) *s.* Cartuja. *2* (con min.) chartreuse [licor].

**charwoman** (cha·ʳwumæn) *s.* asistencia, mujer empleada en los trabajos domésticos.

**chary** (che·ri) *adj.* cuidadoso [de]. *2* circunspecto; receloso [de]. *3* económico, frugal, parco.

**chase** (cheis) *s.* caza, persecución. *2* montería. *3* partida de cazadores. *4* res, etc., que se persigue. *5* muesca, ranura, encaje. *6* ARTILL. caña. *7* IMPR. rama.

**chase (to)** *tr.* cazar, dar caza a, perseguir. *2* ahuyentar. *3* cincelar. *4* JOY. engastar, montar.

**chaser** (-øʳ) *s.* cazador, perseguidor. *2* cincelador. *3* engastador. *4* avión de caza.

**chasm** (kæšm) *s.* quiebra, grieta, abismo, sima. *2* hueco, laguna, vacío.

**chasseur** (shasø·ʳ) *s.* MIL. cazador. *2* botones [criado].

**chassis** (shæsi·) *s.* chasis.

**chaste** (cheist) *adj.* casto. *2* puro, castizo, neto. *3* BOT. ~ *tree*, agnocasto, sauzgatillo.

**chasten (to)** (chei·søn) *tr.* castigar, corregir. *2* depurar [el estilo, etc.]. *3* moderar, templar.

**chasteness** (chei·stnis) *s.* CHASTITY.

**chastise (to)** (chæ·staiš) *tr.* castigar, corregir.

**chastisement** (chæ·stišmønt) *s.* castigo, corrección.

**chastity** (chæ·stiti) *s.* castidad. *2* LIT., B. ART. pureza, corrección, simplicidad.

**chasuble** (chæ·siubøl) *s.* casulla.

**chat** (chæt) *s.* charla, plática, conversación. *2* ORN. nombre de algunos pájaros.

**chat (to)** *intr.* charlar, platicar.

**chatelaine** (sha·tølein) *s.* castellana. *2* cadena con dijes.

**chattels** (chæ·tølš) *s.* enseres, bienes muebles.

**chatter** (chæ·tøʳ) *s.* charla, parloteo. *2* chirrido [de aves]. *3* castañeteo [de dientes]. *4* MEC. vibración, traqueteo.

**chatter (to)** *intr.* charlar, parlotear. *2* chirriar [las aves]. *3* castañetear [los dientes]. *4* MEC. vibrar, traquetear.

**chatterbox** (-baks) *s.* parlanchín, tarabilla.

**chatty** (chæ·ti) *adj.* hablador, parlero. *2* de conversación.

**chauffeur** (shoufø·ʳ) *s.* chófer.

**chauvinism** (shou·vinišm) *s.* patriorería.

**cheap** (chip) *adj.-adv.* barato. *2* adj. ordinario, de pacotilla, de mal gusto; despreciable.

**cheapen (to)** (-øn) *tr.* abaratar. *2* depreciar. *3* intr. abaratarse.

**cheat** (chit) *s.* timo, estafa, fraude, trampa. *2* timador, tramposo, fullero.

**cheat (to)** *intr.* engañar, estafar, defraudar, timar. *2* burlar, frustrar. *3* intr. hacer trampas.

**cheater** (chi·tøʳ) *s.* timador, estafador, tramposo, fullero.

**cheatery** (-i), **cheating** (chi·ting) *s.* timo, estafa, trampa, fullería.

**check** (chek) *s.* detención, interrupción. *2* rechazo. *3* restricción, represión, refrenamiento, freno. *4* obstáculo, impedimento. *5* MEC. tope. *6* contratiempo. *7* comprobación, verificación, repaso. *8* señal, visto bueno. *9* talón, contraseña [de equipajes, de guardarropa, etc.]. *10* COM. cheque, talón. *11* cuenta [de restaurante]. *12* cuadro, jaquel, escaque; dibujo o tela a cuadros. *13* AJED. jaque. *14* resquebrajadura.

**check (to)** *tr.* parar, detener, contener, reprimir, poner coto a, moderar. *2* comprobar, verificar, repasar. | A veces con *up*. *3* marcar [con una señal]. *4* facturar [equipajes]. *5* hacer cuadros en. *6* AJED. dar jaque. *7* intr. detenerse. *8* corresponder punto por punto. *9* resquebrajarse.

**checkbook** (-buk) *s.* talonario de cheques.

**checker** (-øʳ) *s.* refrenador. *2* comprobador, revisor. *3* dibujo a cuadros. *4* (E.U.) peón [del juego de damas]. *5 pl.* (E.U.) damas [juego].

**checker (to)** *tr.* formar escaques o cuadros en. *2* abigarrar, dar variedad.

**checkered** (-d) *adj.* ajedrezado, a cuadros. *2* fig. variado, accidentado.

**checking account** (-ing) *s.* cuenta corriente [en un banco].

**checkmate** (-meit) *s.* jaque mate.

**checkmate (to)** *tr.* AJED. dar mate. *2* desbaratar, frustrar. *3* derrotar.

**checkroom** (che·krum) *s.* (E.U.) vestuario, guardarropa [de restaurante, etc.]; depósito de equipajes.

**checkup** (-øp) *s.* comprobación. *2* MED. reconocimiento general.

**cheek** (chik) *s.* mejilla; carrillo. *2* fig. descaro, tupé. *3* lado [de un objeto]. *4* larguero, montante, jamba. *5* MEC. quijada.

**cheekbone** (-boun) *s.* pómulo.

**cheeky** (-i) *s.* descarado.
**cheep** (chɪp) *s.* pío, chirrido [de ave].
**cheep (to)** *intr.* piar, chirriar.
**cheer** (chɪˑʳ) *s.* alegría, ánimo; estado de ánimo: *be of good* ~, alegraos, tened ánimo. *2* viandas, comida. *3* viva, vítor.
**cheer (to)** *tr.* alegrar, animar, alentar, consolar. *2* vitorear, aclamar, aplaudir.
**cheerful** (-ful) *adj.* alegre, animado, jovial, placentero.
**cheerio** (chɪˑriou) *interj.* ¡hola!, ¡adiós! [como saludo jovial].
**cheerlees** (chɪˑʳlis) *adj.* triste, sombrío.
**cheery** (chɪˑri) *adj.* CHEERFULL.
**cheese** (chɪˑs) *s.* queso: ~ *cake*, quesadilla, ~ *rennet*, BOT. cuajaleche.
**cheesy** (chɪˑsi) *adj.* cáseo, caseoso.
**chef** (shef) *s.* cocinero.
**chelicera** (kiliˑsøra) *s.* quelícero.
**chelonian** (kilouˑnian) *s.* ZOOL. quelonio.
**chemical** (keˑmikal) *adj.* químico. *2 s.* substancia química.
**chemise** (shømɪˑš) *s.* camisa [de mujer]. *2* FORT. camisa.
**chemisette** (shømišeˑt) *s.* camiseta [de mujer].
**chemist** (keˑmist) *s.* químico. *2* farmacéutico.
**chemistry** (-si) *s.* química.
**chenille** (shønɪˑl) *s.* felpilla.
**cheque** (chek) *s.* CHECK 10.
**chequer** *s.* CHECKER 3, 4 y 5.
**cherish (to)** (cheˑrish) *tr.* acariciar. *2* apreciar, querer. *3* cuidar, criar, cultivar, fomentar. *4* alimentar, abrigar [un sentimiento].
**cherry** (cheˑri) *s.* BOT. cereza; cerezo. *2* ~ *laurel*, lauroceraso.
**cherub** (cheˑrøb) *s.* querube, querubín.
**cherubic(al** (chøruˑbik(al) *adj.* angélico.
**chervil** (chøˑʳvil) *s.* BOT. perifollo.
**chess** (ches) *s.* ajedrez.
**chessboard** (-boˑʳd) *s.* tablero de ajedrez.
**chessman** (-mæn) *s.* trebejo, pieza de ajedrez.
**chest** (chest) *s.* cofre, arca, caja, baúl: ~ *of drawers*, cómoda. *2* MEC. caja, receptáculo. *3* pecho, tórax.
**chested** (-id) *adj.* de pecho: *broad-chested*, de pecho ancho.
**chestnut** (-nøt) *s.* BOT. castaña. *2* castaño [árbol; madera; color]. *3* caballo castaño. *4* fam. cuento o chiste gastados.
**cheval-de-frise** (chøˑvældøfriš) *s.* MIL. caballo de Frisa.
**cheval-glass** (chøˑval) *s.* espejo de vestir.
**chevalier** (shevaliˑøʳ) *s.* caballero [de una orden].
**cheviot** (cheˑviøt) *s.* TEJ. cheviot.
**chevron** (sheˑvrøn) *s.* cheurón. *3* MIL. galón en figura de cheurón.
**chew** (chu) *s.* mascadura. *2* mascada.
**chew (to)** *tr.* mascar, masticar. *2* *tr.-intr.* rumiar, meditar.
**chewing gum** (-ing) *s.* goma de mascar.
**chiaroscuro** (kiaroskiuˑrou) *s.* claroscuro.
**chibouk** (chibuˑk) *s.* chibuquí.
**chicane** (shiˑkein) *s.* triquiñuela, argucia.
**chicane (to)** *intr.* trapacear, andar con triquiñuelas. *2* *tr.* embrollar, enredar.
**chicanery** (shikeiˑnøri) *s.* triquiñuela, argucia, enredo legal.
**chick** (chick), **chicken** (chiˑkøn) *s.* pollo, polluelo [de ave de corral]. *2* fig. jovencito, niño.
**chicken-hearted** *adj.* tímido; cobarde.
**chicken-pox** *s.* viruelas locas.

**chickpea** (chiˑkpɪ) *s.* BOT. garbanzo.
**chickweed** (chiˑkwɪd) *s.* BOT. álsine.
**chicle** (chiˑkøl) *s.* chicle.
**chicory** (chiˑkøri) *s.* BOT. achicoria.
**chide (to)** (chaid) *tr.* reñir, reprender; reprobar. *2* gruñir, refunfuñar. ¶ Pret.: *child* o *chided;* p. p.: *chidden* o *chided.*
**chiding** (-ing) *s.* reprensión, reprimenda.
**chief** (chɪˑf) *adj.* principal, mayor, supremo; primero, en jefe. *2 s.* jefe, cabeza, caudillo: *in* ~, en jefe. *3* BLAS. jefe.
**chiefless** (-lis) *adj.* sin jefe.
**chiefly** (-li) *adv.* principalmente, mayormente, sobre todo.
**chieftain** (-tin) *s.* jefe, capitán, caudillo.
**chiffon** (shiˑfan) *s.* gasa, soplillo [tela].
**chiffonier** (shiføniˑʳ) *s.* cómoda alta con espejo.
**chignon** (shiˑñan) *s.* moño, castaña.
**chigoe** (chiˑgou) *s.* ENT. nigua.
**chiblain** (chiˑlblein) *s.* sabañón.
**child** (chaiˑld), *pl.* **children** (chiˑldrøn) *s.* niño, niña; criatura: *with* ~, encinta. *2* hijo, hija.
**childbirth** (-bøˑʳz) *s.* parto, alumbramiento.
**childhood** (-jud) *s.* infancia, niñez.
**childish** (-ish) *adj.* infantil, pueril. *2* aniñado.
**childishness** (-nis) *s.* puerilidad.
**childless** (-lis) *adj.* sin hijos.
**childlike** (-laik) *adj.* infantil, pueril, de niño. *2* aniñado.
**children** (chiˑldrøn) *s. pl.* de CHILD.
**Chilean** (chiˑlian) *adj.-s.* chileno.
**chili** (chiˑli) *s.* pimiento, chile, *ají.
**chill** (chɪˑl) *s.* frío [sensación]. *2* escalofrío, estremecimiento. *3* frialdad. *4* enfriamiento [del entusiasmo, etc.], desaliento. *5* resfriado. *6 adj.* frío, desapacible; glacial.
**chill (to)** *tr.* enfriar, helar; resfriar. *2* desalentar. *3* *intr.* enfriarse, calofriarse.
**chilly** (chiˑli) *adj.* que siente frío, calofriado. *2* friolento. *3* frío, glacial.
**chimaera** *s.* CHIMERA.
**chime** (chaim) *s.* juego de campanas. *2* campaneo, repique. *3* ritmo, armonía. *4* concordancia, conformidad.
**chime (to)** *tr.* tocar, tañer [campanas]. *2* dar [la hora]. *3* *intr.* sonar [las campanas]. *4* sonar con armonía. *5* armonizar, concordar.
**chimera** (kaimiˑra) *s.* MIT. quimera. *2* quimera, ilusión.
**chimerical** (kaimeˑrikal) *adj.* quimérico.
**chimney** (chiˑmni) *s.* chimenea: ~ *sweeper*, deshollinador. *2* hogar, chimenea francesa: ~ *piece*, delantero de chimenea. *3* tubo de lámpara.
**chimpanzee** (chimpænšiˑ) *s.* chimpancé.
**chin** (chin) *s.* barba, barbilla, mentón: ~ *strap*, carrillera, barboquejo.
**China** (chaiˑna) *n. pr.* China.
**china** *s.* china, porcelana, loza.
**Chinaman** (-mæn) *s.* chino.
**chinaware** (-ueˑʳ) *s.* porcelana, loza.
**chinchilla** (chinchiˑla) *s.* ZOOL. chinchilla.
**chine** (chain) *s.* espinazo, lomo. *2* solomo.
**chine (to)** *tr.* deslomar.
**Chinese** (chainɪˑš) *adj.* chino, chinesco, sínico. *2 s.* chino [pers.; idioma].
**chink** (chink) *s.* grieta, raja; rendija, resquicio. *2* tintineo. *3* pop. dinero.
**chink (to)** *tr.* agrietar, hender, rajar. *2* *intr.-tr.* tintinar, hacer tintinar.
**chinky** (chiˑnki) *adj.* hendido, rajado. *2* resquebradizo.

**chintz** (chintš) *s.* zaraza, indiana.
**chip** (chip) *s.* astilla, lasca, desportilladura, viruta, brizna, pedacito. *2* ficha [en el juego]. *3 pl.* patatas a la inglesa.
**chip (to)** *tr.* cortar, picar. *2* astillar, descantillar, desportillar. *3 intr.* romperse, desportillarrse, desconcharse. *4* chillar, piar [ciertos pájaros]. ¶ Pret. y p. p.: *chipped;* ger.: *-pping.*
**chipmunk** (-mønk) *s.* zool. ardilla listada.
**chirk** (chøᵏk) *s.* fam. (E.U.) animado, de buen humor.
**chirograph** (kai·rogræf) *s.* quirógrafo.
**chiromancer** (kai·romænsøᵣ) *s.* quiromántico.
**chiromancy** (kai·romænsøᵣ) *s.* quiromántico.
**chiromancy** (-mænsi) *s.* quiromancia.
**chiropodist** (kaira·podist) *s.* quirópodo.
**chiropteran** (kaira·ptøran) *s.* quiróptero.
**chirp** (chøᵣp) *s.* chirrido, pío, gorjeo. *2* canto o voz alegre.
**chirp (to)** *intr.* chirriar, piar, gorjear. *2* cantar o hablar alegremente.
**chirping** (-ing), **chirpy** (-pi) *adj.* parlero. *2* alegre, animado.
**chirrup** (chi·røp) *s.* chirrido, gorjeo; voz que lo imita.
**chirrup (to)** *intr.* chirriar, gorjear; silbar.
**chisel** (chi·šøl) *s.* cincel. *2* escoplo, formón. *3* cortafrío.
**chisel (to)** *tr.* cincelar. *2* escoplear. ¶ Pret. y p. p.: *chiseled* o *-lled;* ger.: *chiseling* o *-lling.*
**chit** (chit) *s.* desp. chiquillo, chiquilla. *2* bot. brote, grillo.
**chit (to)** *tr.* quitar los brotes.
**chitchat** (chi·tchæt) *s.* charla, palique.
**chitin** (kai·tin) *s.* quitina.
**chitterlings** (chi·tøᵣlingš) *s. pl.* mondongo de cerdo frito o asado.
**chivalric** (shi·valrik) *adj.* caballeresco.
**chivalrous** (shi·valrøs) *adj.* caballeroso.
**chivalry** (shi·valri) *s.* caballería [institución; empresa o dignidad de caballero]. *2* caballerosidad.
**chive** (chaiv) *s.* bot. cebollino.
**chlamys** (klei·mis) *s.* clámide.
**chloral** (klo·ral) *s.* quím. cloral.
**chlorate** (-reit) *s.* quím. clorato.
**chloride** (-raid) *s.* quím. cloruro.
**chlorine** (-rin) *s.* quím. cloro.
**chloroform (to)** *tr.* cloroformizar.
**chlorophyll** (klorou·sis) *s.* clorofila.
**chlorosis** (klorou·sis) *s.* clororis.
**chlorotic** (klora·tik) *adj.* clorótico.
**choana** (kouæ·na) *s.* anat. coana.
**chock** (chok) *s.* calzo, cuña. *2* mar. taco. *3 adv.* completamente.
**chock (to)** *tr.* calzar, acuñar, afianzar. *2* tapar [un hueco]; llenar, atestar.
**chock-full** *adj.* colmado, repleto, atestado.
**chocolate** (cho·kølit) *s.* chocolate: ~ *cup,* jícara; ~ *pot,* chocolatera.
**choice** (cho·is) *s.* escogimiento, selección, elección, preferencia. *2* opción, alternativa. *3* cosa escogida. *4* la flor, lo más escogido. *5 adj.* escogido, selecto, exquisito.
**choiceness** (-nis) *s.* excelencia, exquisitez. *2* discernimiento, delicadeza.
**choir** (kuai·øᵣ) *s.* coro.
**choke** (chouk) *s.* ahogo, estrangulación. *2* mec. obturador. *3* elect. ~ *coil,* bobina de reacción.
**choke (to)** *tr.* ahogar, sofocar. *2* estrangular. *3* aga-

rrotar. *4* reprimir. *5* obstruir, atorar. *6 intr.* ahogarse, atragantarse. *7* atorarse.
**chokedamp** (-dæ·mp) *s.* anhídrido carbónico de las minas de carbón.
**choker** (-øᵣ) *s.* ahogador. *2* tapaboca. *3* corbatín. *4* mec. obturador [del carburador]. *5* elect. bobina de reacción.
**choler** (ka·løᵣ) *s.* cólera, enojo. *2* bilis.
**cholera** (-a) *s.* med. cólera.
**choleric** (-ik) *s.* colérico, iracundo. *2* med. colérico.
**cholesterin** (køle·størin) *s.* colesterina.
**chondriome** (ka·ndrioum) *s.* condrioma.
**choose (to)** (chuš) *tr.* escoger, elegir. *2* preferir, optar por; decidir, querer [hacer algo]. *3 intr.* escoger, querer. ¶ Pret.: *chose;* p. p.: *chosen.*
**chooser** (-øᵣ) *s.* escogedor.
**choosey, choosy** (chu·ši) *adj.* (E.U.) delicado, melindroso.
**chop** (chap) *s.* corte, tajo. *2* tajada; chuleta. *3* grieta, raja. *4* mec. quijada. *5* cambio, trueque. *6 pl.* fauces; boca, entrada. *7* cosa desmenuzada.
**chop (to)** *tr.* cortar, tajar; picar [carne, etc.]: *to* ~ *off,* cortar [separar]. *2* hender, rajar. *3* desbastar. *4* trocar. *5 intr.* dar golpes de hacha, cuchillo, etc. *6* saltar [el viento]; variar, cambiar. ¶ Pret. y p. p.: *chopped;* ger.: *chopping.*
**chophouse** (-jaus) *s.* figón.
**chopper** (-øᵣ) *s.* hacha, hacheta. *2* cuchilla de carnicero.
**chopping** (-ing) *s.* tajadura, picadura; ~ *block,* tajo, tajadero; ~ *knife,* tajadera [cuchilla]. *2 adj.* choppy.
**choppy** (-i) *adj.* picado [mar]. *2* variable [viento]. *3* mudable. *4* cortado, incoherente. *5* agrietado.
**chopsticks** (-stiks) *s.* palillos chinos [para comer].
**choral** (ko·ral) *adj.-s.* mús. coral.
**chord** (ko·ᵣd) *s.* mús., geom. cuerda. *2* fig. cuerda sensible. *3* mús. acorde. *4* anat. cuerda, cordón.
**chore** (choᵣ) *s.* (E.U.) quehacer, faena.
**chorea** (kori·a) *s.* med. corea.
**choree** (kori·) *s.* coreo.
**choreography** (koria·grafi) *s.* coreografía.
**choriamb** (ko· riæmb) *s.* coriambo.
**chorion** (ko·riøn) *s.* anat. corión.
**chorist** (ko·rist), **chorister** (-øᵣ) *s.* corista.
**chorography** (kora·grafi) *s.* corografía.
**choroid** (ko·roid) *adj.-s.* anat. coroides.
**chorus** (ko·røs) *s.* mús. coro: *in* ~, a coro. *2* teat. coro, conjunto. *3* estribillo [de canción].
**chorus (to)** *tr.-intr.* cantar o hablar a coro. *2 tr.* hacer coro a.
**chose** (chouš) *pret.* de to choose.
**chosen** (-øn) *p. p.* de to choose.
**chough** (chøf) *s.* orn. chova.
**chouse** (chaus) *s.* fam. engaño, estafa.
**chouse (to)** *tr.* fam. engañar, estafar.
**chow** (chau) *s.* perro chino.
**chow-chow** *s.* mezcla de encurtidos o de frutas en conserva.
**chrematistic** (kremati·stik) *adj.* crematístico.
**chrism** (kri·šm) *s.* liturg. crisma.
**chrismatory** (-atori) *s.* crismera.
**Christ** (kraist) *n. pr.* Cristo.
**christen** (to) (kri·søn) *tr.* bautizar, cristianar.
**Christendom** (-d) *s.* cristiandad.
**christening** (-ing) *s.* bautizo, bautismo. *2 adj.* bautismal.
**Christian** (kri·schan) *adj.-s.* cristiano: ~ *name,* nombre de pila.
**Christianism** (-išm) *s.* cristianismo.

Christianity (krischiæ·niti) s. cristianidad. 2 cristianismo.
Christianize (kri·schanaiš) tr. cristianizar.
Christine (kristı·n) n. pr. Cristina.
Christmas (kri·smas) s. Navidad; pascuas de Navidad: ~ carol, villancico; ~ Eve, nochebuena.
Christopher (kri·støfø^r) n. pr. Cristóbal.
chromatic (kroumæ·tik) adjt. cromático.
chromatics (-tiks) s. cromática.
chrome (kroum), chromium (-iøm) s. QUÍM. cromo.
chromium plate (to) tr. cromar.
chromo (krou·mo), chromolitograph (-li·zogræf) s. cromo, cromolitografía.
chromosome (krou·mosoum) s. BIOL. cromosoma.
chronic (kra·nik) adj. crónico, inveterado.
chronicle (kra·nikøl) s. crónica.
chronicle (to) tr. narrar en una crónica. 2 intr. escribir crónicas.
chronicler (kra·niclø^r) s. cronista.
chronograph (kra·nogræf) s. cronógrafo.
chronologic(al (kranola·dÿik(al) adj. cronológico.
chronology (krona·lodÿi) s. cronología.
chronometer (-mitø^r) s. cronómetro.
chronometry (-metri) s. cronometría.
chrysalid (kri·salid), chrysalis (-lis) s. crisálida.
chrysanthemum (krisæ·nzimøm) s. BOT. crisantemo.
chrysoberyl (kri·souberil) s. MINER. crisoberilo.
chub (chøb) s. ICT. coto.
chubby (chø·bi) adj. regordete, gordinflón.
chuck (chøk) s. mamola, golpecito debajo de la barba. 2 cloqueo. 3 echada. 4 MEC. calzo, cuña; nuez o mandril de torno; portaherraminta.
chuck (to) intr. cloquear. 2 tr. hacer la mamola, dar un golpecito debajo de la barba. 3 echar, tirar, arrojar.
chuckle (cho·køl) s. risita, risa ahogada. 2 cloqueo.
chuckle (to) intr. reír entre dientes, con risa ahogada. 2 cloquear.
chuckle head s. tonto, zoquete.
chufa (chu·fa) s. BOT. chufa.
chum (chøm) s. fam. camarada. 2 condiscípulo.
chum (to) intr. fam. ser camarada. ¶ Pret. y p. p.: chummed; ger.: chumming.
chummy (-i) adj. íntimo [amigo]. 2 sociable.
chump (chømp) s. zoquete, tarugo. 2 lomo [de carnero]. 3 fam. chola. 4 fam. tonto.
chunk (chønk) s. pedazo corto y grueso. 2 persona o caballo rechonchos.
chunky (-i) adj. rechoncho.
church (chø^rch) s. iglesia: Church of England, Iglesia Anglicana; Roman Catholic Church, Iglesia Católica.
church (to) tr. llevar a la iglesia [para bautizar, etc.].
churchman (-mæn) s. eclesiástico, clérigo. 2 miembro de una iglesia.
churchwarden (-wo^r·døn) s. obrero, fabriquero.
churchyard (-ia^rd) s. cementerio.
churl (chø·^rl) s. patán, palurdo. 2 grosero. 3 tacaño.
churlish (-ish) adj. rústico, rudo, grosero, intratable. 2 ruin, avaro.
churn (chø^rn) s. mantequera [para hacer manteca].
churn (to) tr. batir [en una mantequera], mazar. 2 agitar, revolver.
chute (shut) s. cascada, rabión. 2 conducto o canal por donde se hace bajar algo.
chyle (kail) s. FISIOL. quilo.
chylification (kailifikei·shøn) s. quilificación.

chyme (kaim) s. FISIOL. quimo.
chymification (kaimifikei·shøn) s. quimificación.
cibol (si·bøl) s. BOT. cebolleta. 2 BOT. chalote.
ciborium (sibou·riøm) s. ciborio. 2 copón.
cicada (sikei·da) s. ENT. cigarra, chicharra.
cicatrice (si·katris) s. cicatriz.
cicatricle (sikatri·køl), cicatricula (-kula) s. galladura.
cicatrix s. CICATRICE.
cicatrization (-šei·shøn) s. cicatrización.
cicatrize (to) (si·katraiš) tr. cicatrizar. 2 intr. cicatrizarse.
cicely (si·søli) s. BOT. perifollo oloroso.
Cicero (si·sørou) n. pr. Cicerón.
cicerone (chichørou·ni) s. cicerone.
cicuta (sikiu·ta) s. cicuta.
cider (sai·dø^r) s. sidra.
cigar (siga·^r) s. cigarro puro, tabaco: ~ case, cigarrera, petaca; ~ holder, boquilla.
cigarette (sigøre·t) s. cigarrillo, pitillo: ~ case, pitillera; ~ paper, papel de fumar.
ciliary (si·lieri) adj. ciliar.
ciliate (si·lieit) adj. H. NAT. ciliado.
cilice (si·lis) s. cilicio.
Cimbrian (si·mbrian) adj.-s. cimbro.
cinch (sinch) s. (E.U.) cincha. 2 fam. (E.U.) ganga; cosa fácil o segura.
cinch (to) tr. (E.U.) cinchar. 2 apretar, ceñir.
cinchona (sinkou·na) s. BOT. quino: ~ bark, quina.
cincture (si·nkchø^r) s. cinto, cincho, cingudo. 2 cerca, cercado.
cincture (to) tr. ceñir, cercar, rodear.
cinder (si·ndø^r) s. brasa; carbonilla. 2 pol. cenizas, pavesas, rescoldo.
Cinderella (sindøre·la) s. Cenicienta.
cinema (si·nima) s. (esp. Ingl.) cine, cinema.
cinematograph (sinimæ·togræf) s. cinematógrafo.
cinematography (-mata·grafi) s. cinematografía.
cineraria (sinøre·ria) s. BOT. cineraria.
cinerary (si·nøreri) adj. cinerario.
cinereous (sini·riøs) adj. cinéreo, ceniciento.
Cingalese (singæli·š) adj.-s. cingalés.
cingulum (si·ngiuløm) s. cíngulo.
cinnabar (si·naba^r) s. cinabrio.
cinnamon (si·namøn) s. canela: ~ tree, canelo.
cinquefoil (si·ngkfoil) s. BOT. cincoenrama. 2 ventana de cinco lóbulos.
cipher (sai·fø^r) s. cero: a mere ~, un cero a la izquierda. 2 cifra [número; escritura secreta; monograma].
cipher (to) tr. cifrar [escribir en cifra]. 2 expresar con cifras; calcular.
Circassian (sø^r·kæ·shan) adj.-s. circasiano.
circensian (sø^r·se·nshan) adj. circense.
circio (sø·^rkøl) s. círculo, circunferencia. 2 anillo, redondel, corro, ruedo. 3 ASTR. órbita. 4 círculo, ámbito, esfera, grupo. 5 TEAT. gradería. 6 círculo vicioso. 7 ciclo, serie.
circle (to) tr. circuir, rodear, circundar. 2 intr. girar; dar vueltas.
circlet (sø·^rklit) s. circulito, anillo. 2 brazalete, diadema.
circuit (sø·^rkit) s. circuito: ~ breaker, ELECT. cortacircuitos. 2 ámbito, radio. 3 rodeo; vuelta, recorrido. 4 ASTR. revolución.
circuitous (sø^r·kiui·tøs) adj. tortuoso, indirecto.
circular (sø·^rkula^r) adj. circular, redondo. 2 s. circular [carta].
circulate (to) (sø·^rkiuleit) intr. circular. 2 poner en circulación; propalar, esparcir.

**circulating** (-ing) *adj.* circulante. *2* MAT. periódica [fracción].

**circulation** (-ei·shøn) *s.* circulación.

**circulatory** (sø·ʳkiulátori) *adj.* circulatorio.

**circumambient** (sø·ʳkømæ·mbiønt) *adj.* circumambiente.

**circumcise (to)** (sø·ʳkømsaiš) *tr.* circuncidar.

**circumcised** (-d) *adj.* circunciso.

**circumcision** (-si·ȳøn) *s.* circuncisión.

**circumference** (sø·ʳkø·mførøns) *s.* circunferencia.

**circumflex** (sø·ʳkømfleks) *adj.* circunflejo. *2* que lleva acento circunflejo. *3* ANAT. encorvado. *4 s.* acento circunflejo.

**circumfuse (to)** (-fiuš) *tr.* verter o difundir alrededor.

**circumjacent** (-dȳei·søn) *adj.* circunvecino.

**circumlocution** (sø·ʳkømloukiu·shøn) *s.* circunlocución, circunloquio.

**circumnavigate (to)** (næ·vigeit) *tr.* circumnavegar.

**circumpolar** (-pou·laʳ) *adj.* circumpolar.

**circumscribe** (-skrai·b) *tr.* circunscribir.

**circumscription** (-skrip·shøn) *s.* circunscripción.

**circumspect** (sø·ʳkømspekt) *adj.* circunspecto, prudente.

**circumspection** (sø·ʳkømspe·kshøn) *s.* circunspección, prudencia.

**circumstance** (sø·ʳkømstæns) *s.* circunstancia. *2* detalle, pormenor. *3* ceremonia, formalidad. *4 pl.* medios, posición económica.

**circumstantial** (sø·ʳkømstæ·nshal) *adj.* circunstancial. *2* circunstanciado. *3* DER. ~ *evidence*, prueba iniciaria, indicios vehementes.

**circumstantially** (-li) *adv.* circunstancialmente. *2* detalladamente.

**circumstantitate (to)** (-shieit) *tr.* detallar, referir circunstanciadamente.

**circumvallate (to)** (-væ·leit) *tr.* circunvalar.

**circumvent (to)** (-vent) *tr.* engañar, embaucar; entrampar. *2* rodear, evitar.

**circumvolution** (-vølu·shøn) *s.* circunvolución. *2* rodeo, circunloquio.

**circus** (sø·ʳkøs) *s.* circo [romano]. *2* circo, circo ecuestre. *3* plaza redonda, glorieta. *4* GEOL. circo.

**cirque** (sø·ʳk) *s.* CIRCO 1, 2 y 4. *2* círculo, anillo.

**cirrhosis** (sirou·sis) *s.* cirrosis.

**cirrhotic** (sirou·tik) *adj.* cirrótico.

**cirriped** (si·riped) *adj.-s.* ZOOL. cirrípedo; cirrópodo.

**cirrus** (si·røs) *s.* BOT., ZOOL., METEOR. cirro.

**cisalpine** (sisæ·lpain) *adj.* cisalpino.

**cissoid** (si·soid) *s.* GEOM. cisoide.

**cist** (sist) *s.* ARQUEOL. arquilla.

**cistaceous** (sistei·shøs) *adj.* BOT. cistáceo.

**Cistercian** (sistø·ʳshan) *adj.-s.* cisterciense.

**cistern** (si·støʳn) *s.* cisterna.

**cistus** (si·støs) *s.* BOT. jara.

**citadel** (saitei·tadøl) *s.* ciudadela.

**citation** (saitei·shøn) *s.* cita, citación, mención. *2* DER., MIL. citación.

**cite (to)** (sait) *tr.* citar, llamar. *2* citar, aducir, mencionar.

**cithara** (si·zara) *s.* MÚS. cítara.

**cithern** (si·zøʳn) *s.* MÚS. especie de laúd.

**citizen** (si·tišøn) *s.* ciudadano. *2* habitante, vecino.

**citizenship** (-ship) *s.* ciudadanía.

**citrate** (si·treit) *s.* QUÍM. citrato.

**citric** (-trik) *adj.* QUÍM. cítrico.

**citrine** (-trin) *adj.* citrino.

**citron** (-trøn) *s.* cidra: ~ *tree*, cidro. *2* acitrón.

**citrus fruits** *s. pl.* agrios.

**city** (si·ti) *s.* ciudad. *2 the City*, barrio comercial y bancario de Londres. *3 adj.* municipal, de la ciudad, urbano.

**civet** (si·vit) *s.* civeto, algalia: ~ *cat*, civeta.

**civic** (si·vik) *adj.* cívico. *2* ciudadano.

**civil** (si·vil) *adj.* civil: ~ *servant*, funcionario público. *2* cortés, urbano.

**civilian** (sivi·lian) *adj.* de paisano. *2 s.* paisano [no militar]. *3* jurisperito.

**civility** (-liti) *s.* civilidad, cortesía, urbanidad. *2* amabilidad, atención [acto].

**civilization** (-šei·shøn) *s.* civilización.

**civilize (to)** (si·vilaiš) *tr.* civilizar.

**civilized** (-d) *adj.* civilizado.

**civilly** (si·vili) *adv.* civilmente, cortésmente.

**civism** (si·višm) *s.* civismo, patriotismo.

**clack** (klæk) *s.* charla, parloteo. *2* cítola. *3* golpe seco, golpeteo. *4* ~ *valve*, chapaleta.

**clack (to)** *intr.* charlar. *2* golpetear, tabletear.

**clad** (klæd) *adj.* vestido, cubierto. *2* investido.

**claim** (kleim) *s.* demanda, reclamación, reivindicación. *2* derecho, título, pretensión. *3* MIN. pertenencia.

**claim (to)** *tr.* reclamar, exigir, pedir, tener derecho. *2* reivindicar. *3* denunciar [una mina]. *4* afirmar, declarar.

**claimant** (-ant) *s.* reclamante, demandante. *2* persona que reivindica un título, derecho, etc.; pretendiente [a un trono]. *3* MIN. denunciante.

**clairvoyance** (kleʳvo·ians) *s.* clarividencia.

**clairvoyant** (-iant) *s.* clarividente. *2* vidente.

**clam** (klæm) *s.* almeja, telina.

**clam (to)** *intr.* pescar almejas. *2* ser pegajoso. ¶ Pret. y p. p.: *clammed;* ger.: *clamming.*

**clamant** (-ant) *adj.* clamoroso; apremiante.

**clamber (to)** (klæ·mbøʳ) *intr.* trepar, encaramarse, gatear.

**clamminess** (klæ·minis) *s.* viscosidad.

**clammy** (klæ·mi) *adj.* viscoso, pegajoso; frío y húmedo.

**clamor, to clamor** = CLAMOUR, TO CLAMOUR.

**clamorous** (klæ·mørøs) *adj.* clamoroso, ruidoso, tumultuoso.

**clamour** (klæ·møʳ) *s.* clamor, clamoreo, griterío, estruendo.

**clamour (to)** *intr.-tr.* clamar, clamorear, gritar.

**clamp** (klæmp) *s.* CARP. cárcel. *2* MEC. pieza o instrumento para apretar o sujetar; tornillo de banco o de sujeción, mordaza, abrazadera, etc. *3* ELECT. borne. *4* pisada fuerte.

**clamp (to)** *tr.* sujetar, unir [con tornillo, abrazadera, etc.]. *2 intr.* pisar recio.

**clan** (klæn) *s.* clan.

**clandestine** (klænde·stin) *adj.* clandestino.

**clang** (klæng) *s.* sonido metálico, resonante.

**clang (to)** *intr.* sonar, resonar. *2 tr.* golpear haciendo resonar.

**clango(u)r** (klæ·ngøʳ) *s.* clangor, estruendo.

**clank** (klænk) *s.* sonido metálico de golpe o choque.

**clank (to)** *intr.* sonar, resonar al chocar. *2 tr.* hacer sonar [cadenas, etc.].

**clannish** (klæ·nish) *adj.* de clan; cerrado, exclusivo.

**clap** (klæp) *s.* ruido o golpe seco: ~ *of thunder*, trueno. *2* palmada. *3* aplauso.

**clap (to)** *tr.* batir, golpear: *to* ~ *the hands*, palmotear, -aplaudir. *2* dar una palmada. *3* cerrar dando golpe. *4* aplicar, poner. *5 intr.* sonar con golpe seco. *6* guachapear. ¶ Pret. y p. p.: *clapped* o *clapt;* ger.: *clapping.*

**clapboard** (-boᵣd) *s.* tabla de chilla.
**clapper** (-øᵣ) *s.* palmoteador. *2* TEAT. alabardero. *3* cítola. *4* tableta, tejoleta. *5* badajo. *6* fig. la lengua. *7* carraca [instrumento]. *8* chapaleta.
**claptrap** (-træp) *s.* faramalla. *2 adj.* de faramalla, insincero; de relumbrón.
**Clare** (kleᵣ) *n. pr.* Clara.
**clarence** (klæ·røns) *s.* clarens [coche].
**claret** (klæ·ret) *s.* clarete [vino].
**clarification** (klærifikei·shøn) *s.* clarificación.
**clarify (to)** (klæ·rifai) *tr.* clarificar, purificar. *2* aclarar, esclarecer. *3 intr.* clarificarse, aclararse.
**clarinet** (klærine·t) *s.* clarinete [instrumento].
**clarinettist** (-ist) *s.* clarinete [músico].
**clarion** (klæ·riøn) *s.* clarín.
**clarionet** (klæriøne·t) *s.* CLARINETE.
**clarity** (klæ·riti) *s.* claridad.
**clary** (kle·ri) *s.* BOT. amaro, esclarea.
**clash** (klæsh) *s.* ruido, estruendo [de choque, caída, etc.]. *2* choque, encuentro. *3* oposición, conflicto.
**clash (to)** *intr.* sonar [al chocar]. *2* chocar, entrechocarse. *3* estar en oposición, en conflicto. *4 tr.* hacer chocar, golpear.
**clasp** (klæsp) *s.* broche, cierre, manecilla, pieza que une, cierra o sujeta: ~ *knife*, navaja. *2* abrazo, apretón.
**clasp (to)** *tr.* abrochar, cerrar, sujetar [con broche, cierre, etc.]. *2* asir, agarrar. *3* abrazar, estrechar.
**class** (klas) *s.* clase [grupo, categoría, etc.]. *2* clase [en la eneñanza]. *3 fam.* distinción, elegancia. *4* MIL. promoción, reemplazo.
**class (to)** *tr.* clasificar.
**classic** (klæ·sik) *adj.-s.* clásico.
**classical** (-al) *adj.* clásico.
**clascicism** (klæ·sisišm) *s.* clasicismo.
**classicist** (-sist) *s.* clasicista.
**classification** (klæsifikei·shøn) *s.* clasificación.
**classify (to)** (klæ·sifai) *tr.* clasificar. ¶ Pret. y p. p.: *classified.*
**classmate** (kla·smeit) *s.* condiscípulo.
**classroom** (-rum) *s.* clase, aula.
**classy** (kla·si) *adj. fam.* elegante, de categoría.
**clastic** (klæ·stik) *adj.* clástico.
**clatter** (klæ·tøᵣ) *s.* martilleo, guachapeo; ruido repetido como el de pasos o golpes. *2* alboroto, gresca. *3* charla.
**clatter (to)** *intr.* hacer un ruido repetido como el de pasos o golpes; resonar, guachapear. *2* charlar. *3 tr.* hacer sonar.
**Claude** (klod), **Claudius** (klo·diøs) *n. pr.* Claudio.
**clause** (klo·š) *s.* GRAM. oración breve, subordinada. *2* cláusula, estipulación.
**claustral** (klo·stral) *adj.* claustral.
**claustrophobia** (klostrofou·bia) *s.* claustrofobia.
**clavate(d** (klei·veit(id) *adj.* BOT., ZOOL. en forma de clava.
**clavichord** (klæ·vikøᵣd) *s.* clavicordio.
**clavicle** (klæ·vikøl) *s.* clavícula.
**claw** (klo) *s.* ZOOL. garfa, garra, presa. *2* uña [de insecto; de pétalo]; pinza [de crustáceo]. *3* MEC. uña, garfio; orejas: ~ *hammer,* martillo de orejas; *fam.* frac.
**claw (to)** *tr.-intr.* arañar, arpar, rasgar, desgarrar. *2 tr.* agarrar.
**clay** (klei) *s.* arcilla, tierra, barro, greda: ~ *pit,* barrera; gredal. *2* tiza.
**clay (to)** *tr.* embarrar; arcillar; engredar.
**clayey** (klei·i), **clayish** (-ish) *adj.* arcilloso.

**claymore** (klei·moᵣ) *s.* espada escocesa.
**clean** (klın) *adj.* limpio: *to make* ~, limpiar. *2* puro, honesto. *3* libre, despejado. *4* neto, distinto. *5* completo. *6* bien formado, bien proporcionado. *7 adv.* limpiamente. *8* completamente, enteramente.
**clean (to)** *tr.* limpiar. *2* asear; desempolvar; quitar las manchas de; desengrasar. *3* lavar [la vajilla]. *4* mondar. *5* descombrar. *6* depurar, purificar.
**clean-cut** *adj.* bien cortado; claro, preciso, definido.
**clenaer** (-øᵣ) *s.* limpiador. *2* detergente. *3* quitamanchas.
**cleaning** (ing) *s.* limpia, limpieza. *2* monda. *3 pl.* limpiaduras, mondaduras.
**cleanlily** (-lili) *adv.* CLEANLY.
**cleanlines** (-linis) *s.* limpieza, aseo, pulidez.
**cleanly** (-li) *adj.* limpio, curioso, aseado. *2 adv.* limpiamente.
**cleanness** (-nis) *s.* limpieza [calidad, estado]. *2* pureza, inocencia. *3* elegancia [de estilo].
**cleanse (to)** (klenš) *tr.* limpiar, lavar. *2* purificar, depurar, purgar. *3* absterger.
**cleanser** (-øᵣ) *s.* limpiador, lavador, purificador. *2* purgante.
**clean-shaven** *adj.* bien afeitado.
**clear** (kli·øᵣ) *adj.* claro. | No tiene los sentidos de ralo, poco espeso y poco subido [color]. *2* limpio, puro. *3* sereno, despejado. *4* brillante [metal]. *5* terso, fresco [cutis, etc.]. *6* liso, raso, abierto. *7* libre [de culpa, de estorbos, de deudas, etc.], desembarazado, despejado, desenredado, expedito. *8* líquido, neto. *9* apartado, alejado: *to keep* ~ *of,* no acercarse a. *10* preciso, definido. *11* seguro [de una cosa]. *12 s.* claro, espacio. *13* PINT. luz, claros. *14 adv.* claramente. *15* enteramente, absolutamente.
**clear (to)** *tr.* aclarar [clarificar; dispar; hacer inteligible]. *2* aclarar [el semblante, la voz]. *3* limpiar [de impurezas, etc.]; librar [de estorbos], despejar, desocupar: *to* ~ *the table,* levantar la mesa. *4* justificar, absolver. *5* desenredar, desembrollar. *6* saltar, salvar [un espacio]. *7* pagar, liquidar. *8* cancelar [una hipoteca]. *9* desempeñar; librar de cargas u obligaciones. *10* despachar [un buque] en la aduana. *11* sacar [un beneficio]. *12* AGR. desmontar, rozar. *13* mondar [un árbol]. *14 to* ~ *up,* desembarazar, limpiar, dilucidar.
*15 intr.* aclararse, serenarse. *16* desembarazarse, desenredarse. *17* COM. liquidar cuentas. *18 to* ~ *up,* serenarse, desencapotarse; arreglarse [una situación].
**clearage** (-idÿ) *s.* despejo; descombro, desmonte.
**clearance** (-ans) *s.* despejo [acción]. *2* MEC. huelgo, juego, espacio libre o muerto. *3* despacho [de aduana]. *4* compensación [de cheques, etc.]. *5* COM. ~ *sale,* liquidación de existencias.
**clear-cut** *adj.* bien perfilado, bien definido.
**clear-headed** *adj.* inteligente.
**clearing** (-ing) *s.* aclaramiento, despejo. *2* justificación, exculpación. *3* AGR. desmonte. *4* claro, raso; terreno desarbolado. *5* COM. liquidación, compensación: ~ *house,* cámara de compensación.
**clearly** (-li) *adv.* claramente.
**clearness** (-nis) *s.* claridad.
**clear-sighted** *adj.* clarividente, perspicaz.
**cleat** (klıt) *s.* listón, soporte. *2* tojino. *3* MAR. cornamusa. *4* ELECT. aislador.

**cleavage** (klɪ·vidȳ) *s.* hendidura, división. *2* MINER. crucero.

**1) cleave (to)** (klɪv) *tr.-intr.* pegarse, adherirse. *2* apegarse. ¶ Pret. y p. p.: *cleaved.*

**2) cleave (to)** *tr.* hender, rajar, cortar, dividir. *2 intr.* henderse, partirse. *3* abrirse. ¶ Pret.: *cleft, cleaved* o *clove*; p. p.: *cleft, cleaved* o *cloven.*

**cleavers** (-ø^rŝ) *s.* BOT. amor de hortelano.

**clef** (klef) *s.* MÚS. clave, llave.

**cleft** (kleft) *adj.* hendido, partido. *2 s.* hendidura, raja, grieta, rendija.

**clematis** (kle·matis) *s.* BOT. clemátide.

**clemency** (kle·mønsi) *s.* clemencia. *2* benignidad [del tiempo].

**clement** (kle·mønt) *adj.* clemente. *2* suave [tiempo].

**clench** (klench) *s.* agarro, presión.

**clench (to)** *tr.* fijar, asegurar. *2* remachar, roblar. *3* apretar [los puños, los dientes]. *4* agarrar, empuñar.

**clencher** (-ø^r) *s.* CLINCHER.

**clepsydra** (kle·psidra) *s.* clepsidra.

**cleptomania** (kleptomei·nia) *s.* cleptomanía.

**clerestory** (cli·^rstori) *s.* claraboya lateral [de una iglesia, estación, etc.].

**clergy** (klø·^rdȳi) *s.* clero; clerecía.

**clergyman** (-mæn) *s.* clérigo, eclesiástico, sacerdote, pastor.

**cleric** (kle·rik) *s.* clérigo.

**clerical** (-al) *adj.* clerical; eclesiástico. *2* de oficinista.

**clerk** (klø^rk) *s.* empleado, dependiente, pasante, escribiente, secretario, actuario. *2* sacristán. *3* clérigo. *4* ant. docto, erudito.

**clever** (kle·vø^r) *adj.* diestro, hábil, mañoso. *2* listo, avisado, capaz, inteligente. *3* (E.U) complaciente.

**cleverness** (-nis) *s.* destreza, habilidad, maña. *2* talento.

**clew** (klu) *s.* ovillo. *2* MAR. puño de escota; su anillo. *3* pista, indicio.

**clew (to)** *tr.* MAR. cargar los puños de [una vela].

**click** (klik) *s.* golpecito seco; su sonido. *2* seguro, fiador, trinquete.

**click (to)** *intr.-tr.* sonar o hacer sonar con uno o más golpecitos secos. *2 intr.* hacer tictac.

**client** (klai·ønt) *s.* cliente.

**clientele** (kklaiønte·l) *s.* clientela.

**cliff** (klif) *s.* risco, precipicio, escarpa, farallón, acantilado.

**cliffy** (-i), **clifty** (-ti) *adj.* escarpado, acantilado; riscoso.

**climacteric** (klaimækte·rik) *adj.* climatérico. *2 s.* período climatérico.

**climate** (klai·mit) *s.* clima.

**climatic(al** (klaimæ·tik[al) *adj.* climático.

**climatology** (klaimata·lodȳi) *s.* climatología.

**climax** (klai·mæks) *s.* RET. climax. *2* punto culminante o crítico; cenit, colmo.

**climb** (klaim) *s.* trepa, subida, ascenso.

**climb (to)** *intr.* trepar, subir, escalar. *2 intr.* trepar, subir, elevarse, encaramarse: *to ~ down*, bajar; desistir.

**climber** (-ø^r) *s.* trepador, escalador. *2* BOT. enredadera. *3* ORN. trepadora.

**clime** (klaim) *s.* clima, región.

**clinch** (klinch) *s.* remache, robladura. *2* argumento irrebatible. *3* agarro; lucha cuerpo a cuerpo.

**clinch (to)** *tr.* TO CLENCH. *2* MAR. entalingar. *3* cerrar

[un trato]. *4 intr.* agarrarse, abrazarse estrechamente.

**clincher** (-ø^r) *s.* remachador. *2* roblón, laña. *3* argumento decisivo.

**cling (to)** (kling) *intr.* asirse, aferrarse, adherirse, pegarse. *2* persistir. ¶ Pret. y p. p.: *clung.*

**clinging** (-ing) *adj.* adhesivo. *2* adherido, colgante.

**clingy** (-i) *adj.* adhesivo, tenaz.

**clinic** (kli·nik) *adj.* clínico. *2 s.* clínica [enseñanza]. *3* clínica, dispensario [de hospital].

**clinical** (-al) *adj.* clínico.

**clinician** (klini·shan) *s.* clínico.

**clink** (klink) *s.* tintín.

**clink (to)** *tr.* hacer tintinear. *2 intr.* tintinear.

**clinker** (-ø^r) *s.* ladrillo muy duro. *2* pedazo de escoria. *3 ~ work*, obra de tingladillo.

**Clio** (klai·ou) *n. pr.* MIT. Clío.

**clip** (klip) *s.* grapa, pinza, sujetapapeles, clip. *2* cargador [de pistola, etc.]. *3* tijeretazo, corte. *4* recorte. *5* cercenadura. *6* esquileo. *7* fam. golpe.

**clip (to)** *tr.* abrazar, sujetar. *2* cortar, recortar, cercenar, acortar. *3* esquilar, trasquilar. *4* fam. arrear [un golpe]. *5 intr.* correr, moverse con rapidez. ¶ Pret. y p. p.: *clipped*; ger.: *clipping.*

**clipper** (-ø^r) *s.* recortador, cercenador, esquilador. *2* cizalla. *3* MAR., AVIA. clíper.

**clipping** (-ing) *s.* recorte, cercenadura. *2* recorte, retal; recorte de prensa. *3 adj.* que recorta, etc. *4* fam. rápido. *5* fam. estupendo.

**clique** (klɪk) *s.* pandilla, camarilla.

**cloaca** (klouei·ka) *s.* cloaca.

**cloak** (klouk) *s.* capa, manto. *2* fig. capa, excusa, pretexto.

**cloak (to)** *tr.* encapar, cubrir. *2* encubrir, embozar, disimular.

**cloakroom** (-rum) *s.* guardarropa [en un teatro, etc.].

**clock** (klak) *s.* reloj [de mesa o pared]: *what o'clock is it?*, ¿qué hora es? *2* cuadrado [de las medias].

**clock (to)** *tr.* cronometrar.

**clockmaker** (-meikø^r) *s.* relojero.

**clockwise** (-waiŝ) *adv.-adj.* en el sentido de las saetas del reloj.

**clockwork** (-wø^rk) *s.* mecanismo de relojería. *2 adj.* regular, automático.

**clod** (klad) *s.* terrón, gleba. *2* tierra, suelo, césped. *3* gaznápiro, zoquete.

**clod (to)** *intr.* aterronarse. *2 tr.* tirar terrones. ¶ Pret. y p. p.: *clodded*; ger.: *-dding.*

**clodhopper** (-japø^r) *s.* patán. *3* destripaterrones.

**clog** (klag) *s.* traba, embarazo, obstáculo, estorbo. *2* zueco, chanclo, chapín.

**clog (to)** *tr.* cargar, embarazar, estorbar, entorpecer. *2* obstruir. *3 intr.* apiñarse, aterronarse. *4* obstruirse. ¶ Pret. y p. p.: *clogged*; ger.: *clogging.*

**cloggy** (kla·gi) *adj.* aterronado. *2* pegajoso. *3* embarazoso, entorpecedor.

**cloister** (kloi·stø^r) *s.* ARQ., REL. claustro.

**cloister (to)** *tr.* enclaustrar. *2* proveer de claustro.

**cloisterer** (-ø^r) *m.* monje, religioso.

**cloistral** (kloi·stral) *adj.* claustral.

**1) close** (klouŝ) *s.* fin, conclusión. *2* cierre, clausura. *3* lucha cuerpo a cuerpo. *4* MÚS. cadencia.

**2) close** (klous) *adj.* cerrado. *2* cercado, encerrado, acotado. *3* apretado, ajustado. *4* secreto. *5* reservado [pers.]. *6* mal ventilado. *7* cubierto, pesado, sofocante [tiempo]. *8* agarrado, mezquino. *9* espeso, tupido, compacto. *10* próximo, contiguo, inmediato. *11* reñido, muy igualado. *12* COM. retraído [dinero]. *13* exacto, fiel. *14* estrecho, riguroso, cuidadoso, detenido, concienzudo. *15* estrecho, íntimo [amistad, etc.]. *16* breve, conciso. *17* limitado, restringido. *18* ~ *quarters,* contacto inmediato. *19* ~ *season,* veda. *20 adv.* cerca. *21* de cerca, estrechamente, apretadamente. *22* a raíz. *23* ~ *by,* muy cerca. *24 s.* cercado, recinto.

**close (to)** (klouš) *tr.* cerrar. *2* tapar, obstruir. *3* apretar, tupir. *4* cercar, rodear. *5* concluir, ultimar. *6* clausurar. *7 to* ~ *in,* encerrar. *8 intr.* cerrarse. *9* acercarse. *10* luchar, agarrarse: *to* ~ *with,* cerrar contra. *11* terminar, acabarse. *12* ponerse de acuerdo. *13 to* ~ *in,* acercarse rodeando; cerrar [la noche].

**closed** (-d) *adj.* cerrado, concluido, etc. *2* ~ *season,* veda.

**closefisted** (klou·sfistid) *adj.* tacaño.

**closely** (klou·sli) *adv.* estrechamente, etc.

**closeness** (klou·snis) *s.* encierro, estrechez. *2* densidad, apretamiento. *3* proximidad. *4* intimidad. *5* unión, dependencia. *6* mala ventilación. *7* reserva, cautela. *8* tacañería. *9* fidelidad, exactitud.

**closet** (kla·šit) *s.* gabinete, camarín. *2* retrete, excusado. *3* armario, alacena.

**closet (to)** *tr.* encerrar en un aposento [para una entrevista reservada].

**close-up** *s.* fotografía tomada de cerca.

**closure** (klou·ȳøʳ) *s.* cierre. *2* fin, conclusión. *3* POL. guillotina parlamentaria.

**clot** (klat) *s.* grumo, coágulo, cuajarón.

**clot (to)** *intr.* agrumarse, coagularse, cuajarse. ¶ Pret. y p. p.: *clotted;* ger.: *clotting.*

**cloth** (kloz) *s.* paño, tela. *2* trapo, paño [para limpiar]. *3* mantel. *4* vestido clerical; clero. *5* MAR. lona.

**clothbound** (-baund) *adj.* encuadernado en tela.

**clothe (to)** (klou·ð) *tr.* vestir. *2* revestir, investir. ¶ Pret. y p. p.: *clothed* o *clad.*

**clothes** (klouš o klou·ðš) *s. pl.* vestido, vestuario, ropa: ~ *hanger,* ~ *tree,* colgador, percha.

**clothesline** (-lain) *s.* cuerda para tender la ropa.

**clothesman** (clou·šmæn) *s.* prendero, ropavejero.

**clothier** (klou·ðiøʳ) *s.* pañero, ropero.

**clothing** (-ðing) *s.* ropa, vestidos. *2* MAR. velas. *3* revestimiento.

**Clotilda** (klouti·lda) *n. pr.* Clotilde.

**clotted** (kla·tid), **clotty** (-ti) *adj.* grumoso, coagulado.

**cloud** (klaud) *s.* nube; nublado: *under a* ~, bajo sospecha; en desgracia.

**cloud (to)** *tr.* nublar, anublar. *2* oscurecer, empeñar, manchar. *3 intr.* anublarse.

**cloudburst** (klau·dbøʳst) *s.* aguacero, chaparrón.

**cloudily** (-ili) *adv.* nebulosamente.

**cloudless** (-lis) *adj.* sereno, sin nubes.

**cloudy** (-i) *adj.* nuboso; nublado. *2* nebuloso. *3* vaporoso. *4* oscuro, sombrío. *5* turbo. *6* nubarrado.

**clough** (kløf) *s.* quebrada, cañada.

**clout** (klaut) *s.* cíbica, cibicón. *2* rodilla, trapo. *3* pañal, metedor. *4* remiendo. *5* fam. bofetada. *6* ~ *nail,* clavo de zapato.

**clout (to)** *tr.* cubrir, vendar. *2* remendar toscamente. *3* fam. abofetear.

**clove** (klouv) *s.* clavo [de especia]. *2* diente [de ajo]. *3 pret.* de TO CLEAVE.

**cloven** (klou·vøn) *p. p.* de TO CLEAVE. *2 adj.* partido, hendido: ~ *foot,* ~ *hoof,* pata hendida.

**clover** (klou·vøʳ) *s.* trébol: *in* ~, regaladamente, en la abundancia.

**Clovis** (klou·vis) *n. pr.* Clodoveo.

**clown** (klaun) *s.* payaso, clown. *2* rústico, patán.

**clownish** (-ish) *adj.* de payaso. *2* rústico, zafio; grosero.

**cloy (to)** (kloi) *tr.* hartar, hastiar, empalagar.

**cloying** (-ing), **cloysome** (-søm) *adj.* hastioso, empalagoso.

**club** (kløb) *s.* clava, porra, garrote. *2* maza [de gimnasia]. *3* DEP. bate; palo [de golf]. *4* basto, trébol [de la baraja]. *5* club, círculo, sociedad. *6* ~ *moss,* licopodio.

**club (to)** *tr.* apalear. *2* unir, juntar. *3 intr.* apiñarse. *4* unirse [para un fin], pagar cada uno su escote. ¶ Pret. y p. p.: *clubbed;* ger.: *clubbing.*

**clubbed** (-d) *adj.* en forma de clava.

**clubfooted** (-futid) *adj.* zopo del pie.

**clubman** (-mæn) *s.* socio de un club.

**cluck** (kløk) *s.* cloqueo.

**cluck (to)** ) *intr.* cloquear.

**clue** (klu) *s.* indicio, pista, guía, clave.

**clump** (klømp) *s.* grupo [de árboles]. *2* masa, terrón, zoquete. *3* suela gruesa. *4* pisada fuerte.

**clump (to)** *tr.* agrupar. *2 intr.* agruparse. *2* andar pesadamente.

**clumsiness** (klø·mšinis) *s.* torpeza, desmaña. *2* tosquedad, pesadez.

**clumsy** (klø·mši) *adj.* torpe, desmañado, chapucero. *2* tosco, pesado.

**clung** (kløng) *pret.* y *p. p.* de TO CLING.

**cluster** (klø·støʳ) *s.* racimo, macolla, piña, ramo. *2* grupo, hato, agregado. *3* enjambre.

**cluster (to)** *intr.* arracimarse, agruparse. *2 tr.* apiñar, agrupar.

**clustery** (-i) *adj.* arracimado, apiñado, agrupado.

**clutch** (kløch) *s.* uña, garra. *2* agarro, presa, dominio, poder. *3* MEC. embrague: *to push in the* ~, embragar. *4* nidada.

**clutch (to)** *tr.* asir, agarrar, empuñar, apretar. *2 intr. to* ~ *at,* tratar de coger, asir con avidez.

**clutter** (kløtøʳ) *s.* desorden, confusión. *2* barahúnda.

**clutter (to)** *tr.* desordenar. *2 intr.* alborotar; atropellarse.

**clyster** (kli·støʳ) *s.* clíster, enema.

**coach** (kouch) *s.* coche, carroza, diligencia. *2* vagón de pasajeros. *3* profesor particular. *4* DEP. preparador.

**coach (to)** *tr.* llevar en coche. *2* preparar [para exámenes, etc.]; dar lecciones a, adiestrar. *3 intr.* ir en coche. *4 to* ~ *with,* tomar lecciones de [un profesor].

**coaching** (-ing) *s.* lecciones particulares. *2* preparación, adiestramiento.

**coachmaker** (-meikøʳ) *s.* carrocero.

**coachman** (-mæn) *s.* cochero.

**coaction** (koæ·kshøn) *s.* coacción.

**coadjutor** (kouæ·dȳøtøʳ) *s.* coadjutor, ayudante.

**coadunate (to)** (-diuneit) *tr.* coadunar.

**coagulant** (-giulant) *adj.-s.* coagulante.

**cogulate (to)** (-leit) *tr.* coagular, cuajar. *2 intr.* coagularse, cuajarse.

**coagulation** (-ei·shøn) *s.* coagulación.

**coagulum** (kouæ·giuløm) *s.* coágulo.

**coal** (koul) *s.* carbón [materia]: ~ *basin,* cuenca hullera; ~ *oil,* petróleo, aceite mineral; ~ *tar,* alquitrán de hulla. *2* ascua, brasa: *to haul,* o *drag, over the coals,* reñir, poner como un trapo. *3* ORN. ~ *titmouse,* azabache.

**coal (to)** *tr.* carbonear; carbonizar. *2* proveer de carbón. *3 intr.* proveerse de carbón.

**coalbox** (-baks), **coalbin** (-bin) *s.* carbonera.

**coalesce (to)** (koua̸le·s) *intr.* unirse, incorporarse, fundirse.

**coalescence** (-øns) *s.* unión, fusión.

**coalition** (-li·shøn) *s.* unión, fusión. *2* coalición.

**coalmouse** (kou·lmaus) *s.* ORN. azabache.

**coalpit** (kou·lpit) *s.* mina de carbón.

**coaly** (-i) *adj.* carbonoso.

**coalyard** (-ya<sup>r</sup>d) *s.* carbonería, almacén de carbón.

**coaming** (kou·ming) *s.* MAR. brazola.

**coarse** (ko·<sup>r</sup>s) *adj.* tosco, grosero, ordinario, basto. *2* vulgar, chabacano, soez. *3* áspero, grueso.

**coarsen (to)** (-øn) *tr.-intr.* volver o volverse tosco, burdo, grueso o grosero.

**coarsenes** (-nis) *s.* tosquedad, basteza. *2* ordinariez, vulgaridad, grosería.

**coast** (koust) *s.* costa; litoral. *2* (E.U. y Can.) pendiente, deslizadero.

**coast (to)** *intr.* navegar cerca de la costa, perlongar. *2* (E.U. y Can.) deslizarse cuesta abajo [en trineo, bicicleta, etc.]. *3 tr.* MAR. COSTEAR.

**coastal** (kou·stal) *adj.* costanero.

**coaster** (-tø<sup>r</sup>) *s.* práctico de costa. *2* buque de cabotaje. *3* (E.U. y Can.) deslizadero, tobogán.

**coasting** (-ing) *s.* cabotaje.

**coastline** (-lain) *s.* litoral, línea de la costa.

**coat** (kout) *s.* chaqueta, *saco; casaca; abrigo: *to turn one's* ~, volver casaca. *2* capa, mano [de pintura, etc.]. *3* MEC. cubierta, revestimiento. *4* ANAT. tegumento, túnica. *5* ZOOL. capa, pelaje, plumaje. *6* cota [de malla]. *7 ~ of arms*, escudo de armas.

**coat (to)** *tr.* cubrir, revestir. *2* dar una capa o mano a; azogar.

**coati** (koa·ti) *s.* coatí.

**coating** (kou·ting) *s.* capa, mano, revestimiento.

**coax (to)** (kouks) *tr.* halagar, engatusar. *2* obtener con halagos.

**coaxer** (-ø<sup>r</sup>) *s.* engatusador.

**coaxial** (kouæ·ksial) *adj.* coaxial.

**cob** (kab) *s.* pedazo redondo. *2* carozo, zuro [de maíz]. *3* jaca. *4* cisne macho. *5* variedad de gaviota. *6* ZOOL. araña. *7* duro [español].

**cobalt** (kou·bolt) *s.* cobalto.

**cobble** (ka·bøl) *s.* guijarro.

**cobble (to)** *tr.* empedrar con guijarros [calles]. *2* *tr.-intr.* componer [zapatos]; chapucear.

**cobbler** (ka·blø<sup>r</sup>) *s.* zapatero remendón. *2* chapucero.

**cobblestone** (ka·bølstoun) *s.* guijarro.

**cobnut** (ka·bnøt) *s.* avellana grande.

**cobra** (kou·bra) *s.* ZOOL. cobra.

**cobweb** (ka·bweb) *s.* telaraña.

**cobwebbed** (-d) *adj.* telarañoso.

**coca** (kou·ka) *s.* BOT. coca, *hayo.

**cocain[e** (koukei·n) *s.* cocaína.

**cocculus** (ka·kiuløs) *s.* BOT. coca de Levante.

**coccus** (ka·køs) *s.* coco [bacteria].

**coccyx** (ka·ksiks) *s.* ANAT. cóccix.

**cochineal** (ka·chinɪ) *s.* cochinilla, grana: ~ *insect*, cochinilla [insecto].

**cock** (kak) *s.* gallo [ave]. *2* macho de un ave. *3* fig. gallo, amo; campeón. *4* veleta. *5* llave, espita; grifo. *6* gatillo, can [de escopeta]. *7* estilo, gnomon. *8* montón [de heno]. *9* inclinación hacia arriba; ladeo.

**cock (to)** *intr.* gallear, darse tono. *2 tr.* amartillar [un arma de fuego]. *3* levantar, dar una inclinación airosa o provocativa a. *4* amontonar heno, etc.

**cockade** (kakei·d) *s.* escarapela, cucarda.

**cock-a-doodle-do** (ka·kadudøldu) *s.* quiquiriquí.

**cockatoo** (kakatu) *s.* ORN. cacatúa.

**cockatrice** (ka·katris) *s.* basilisco.

**cockboat** (ka·kbout) *s.* bote, barquilla.

**cockchafer** (ka·kcheifø<sup>r</sup>) *s.* abejorro [coleóptero].

**cocked hat** (kakt) *s.* sombrero de tres picos.

**cocker** (ka·kø<sup>r</sup>) *s.* sabueso pequeño.

**cocker (to)** *tr.* acariciar, mimar.

**cockerel** (ka·kørel) *s.* pollo, gallito.

**cock-fight(ing** *s.* riña de gallos.

**cock-horse** *s.* caballito mecedor.

**cockle** (ka·køl) *s.* berberecho. *2* barquichuelo. *3* cúpula de horno. *4* BOT. cizaña; ballico.

**cockle (to)** *tr.* arrugar. *2 intr.* arrugarse.

**cocklebur** (-bø<sup>r</sup>) *s.* bardana, cadillo.

**cockleshell** (-shel) *s.* concha de berberecho. *2* fig. cascarón de nuez [barco].

**cockloft** (ka·kloft) *s.* desván.

**cockney** (ka·kni) *s.* londinense de la clase popular.

**cockpit** (ka·kpit) *s.* gallera [reñidero de gallos]. *2* TEAT. cazuela. *3* AVIA. cabina del piloto.

**cockroach** (-rouch) *s.* ENT. cucaracha.

**cockscomb** (-scoum) *s.* cresta de gallo. *2* COXCOMB.

**cockspur** (-pu<sup>r</sup>) *s.* espolón de gallo.

**cocksure** (-shu<sup>r</sup>) *adj.* segurísimo. *2* muy seguro de sí mismo.

**cocktail** (-teil) *s.* combinado, cóctel; ~ *shaker*, coctelera.

**coco(a** (kou·kou) *s.* BOT. coco; cocotero.

**cocoa** *s.* cacao [árbol, polvo y bebida].

**cocoanut, coconut** (-nøt) *s.* coco [fruto].

**cocoon** (køku·n) *s.* ENT. capullo.

**cocoonery** (-nøri) *s.* criadero de gusanos de seda.

**coction** (ka·kshøn) *s.* cocción.

**cod** (kad) *s.* bacalao, abadejo. *2* copo [de red]. *3* escroto.

**cod (to)** *tr.* fam. engañar.

**coda** (kou·dæ) *s.* MÚS. coda.

**coddle (to)** *tr.* consentir, mimar.

**code** (koud) *s.* código. *2* cifra, clave.

**codein** (koudi·in) *s.* codeína.

**codex** (kou·deks) *s.* códice.

**codfish** (ka·dfish) *s.* bacalao, abadejo.

**codger** (ka·dy̆ø<sup>r</sup>) *s.* fam. tipo; chiflado.

**codicil** (ka·disil) *s.* codicilo.

**codification** (kadifikei·shøn) *s.* codificación.

**codify (to)** (ka·difai) *tr.* codificar. ¶ Pret. y p. p.: *codified.*

**codling** (ka·dling) *s.* bacalao pequeño. *2* variedad de manzana.

**coeducation** (kouedy̆ukei·shøn) *s.* coeducación.

**coefficient** (-efi·shønt) *adj.-s.* coeficiente.

**cœlenterate** (sile·ntøreit) *adj.-s.* celentéreo.

**cœliac** (sɪ·liæk) *adj.* celíaco.

**cœlom** (sɪ·lom) *s.* ZOOL. celoma.

**coerce (to)** (kouø·<sup>r</sup>s) *tr.* coercer. *2* forzar, obligar.

**coercion** (-shøn) *s.* coerción. *2* coacción, compulsión.

**coercive** (-siv) *adj.* coercitivo. *2* coactivo.

**coetaneous** (kouitei·niøs) *adj.* coetáneo.

**coeval** (kou·val) *adj.-s.* coevo.

**coexist (to)** (koui·gšist) *intr.* coexistir.

**coexistence** (-ši·støns) *s.* coexistencia.

**cofee** (ko·fi) *s.* café [grano; bebida; planta]: ~ *tree*, cafeto.

**coffeehouse** (-jaus) *s.* café [establecimiento].

**coffeepot** (-pat) *s.* cafetera [utensilio].

**coffeeroom** (-rum) *s.* café, bar [de hotel].

**coffer** (ko·fø<sup>r</sup>) *s.* cofre, arca. *2* ARQ. artesón.

**cofferdam** (-dæm) *s.* ataguía, caja dique.

**coffin** (ko·fin) *s.* ataúd, féretro, caja. *2* casco [de caballería]: ~ *bone,* VET. bolillo.
**cog** (cag) *s.* diente [de engranaje]. *2* CARP. espiga, lengüeta. *3* botequín. *4* engaño.
**cog (to)** *tr.* dentar [una rueda]. *2* CARP. ensamblar. *3* hacer trampas con [los dados]. *4* engañar. ¶ Pret. y p. p.: *cogged;* ger.: *-gging.*
**cogency** (kou·dȳønsi) *s.* fuerza [lógica o moral].
**cogent** (-ønt) *adj.* poderoso, convincente.
**cogged** (kæ·gd) *adj.* MEC. dentado. *2* cargado [dado].
**cogitate (to)** (ka·dȳiteit) *intr.* meditar, reflexionar.
**cogitation** (-tei·shøn) *s.* cogitación.
**cognac** (kou·ñæk) *s.* coñac.
**cognate** (ka·gneit) *adj.-s.* cognado. *2 adj.* afín; análogo.
**cognation** (-nei·shøn) *s.* cognación.
**cognition** (kagni·shøn) *s.* cognición.
**cognitive** (ka·gnitiv) *adj.* cognoscitivo.
**cognizable** (-šabøl) *adj.* cognoscible. *2* DER. de la competencia de.
**cognizance** (-šans) *s.* conocimiento, noticia. *2* divisa, distintivo. *3* DER. competencia.
**cognizant** (-šant) *adj.* sabedor, enterado.
**cognize (to)** (ka·gnaiš) *tr.* conocer, reconocer.
**cognomen** (kagnou·møn) *s.* cognomento.
**cognoscible** (kagna·sibøl) *adj.* cognoscible, conocible.
**cognoscitive** (-tiv) *adj.* cognoscitivo.
**cogwheel** (ka·gjuıl) *s.* rueda dentada.
**cohabit (to)** (koujæ·bit) *intr.* cohabitar.
**coheir** (koue·øʳ) *s.* coheredero.
**coheiress** (-ris) *s.* coheredera.
**cohere (to)** (kouji·øʳ) *intr.* adherirse, pegarse, unirse. *2* adaptarse.
**coherence** (-øns), **coherency** (-ønsi) *s.* coherencia.
**coherent** (-ønt) *adj.* coherente.
**coherer** (-øʳ) *s.* cohesor.
**cohesion** (koujı·ȳøn) *s.* cohesión.
**cohesive** (-siv) *adj.* cohesivo.
**cohort** (kou·joʳt) *s.* cohorte.
**coif** (koif) *s.* cofia, gorra, papalina. *2* birrete.
**coif (to)** *tr.* cubrir la cabeza.
**coiffure** (kua·fiuʳ) *s.* tocado, peinado.
**coign** (coin) *s.* esquina, ángulo.
**coil** (koil) *s.* rollo [de cuerda, etc.]; rosca, espiral, vuelta, aduja. *2* ELECT. carrete, bobina. *3* serpentín [de alambique]. *4* rizo [de cabello].
**coil (to)** *tr.* arrollar, enrollar, adujar. *2 intr.* enrollarse, enroscarse.
**coin** (koin) *s.* moneda. *2* dinero. *3* cuña.
**coin (to)** *tr.* acuñar, batir; amonedar. *2* forjar, inventar.
**coinage** (koi·nidȳ) *s.* acuñación. *2* sistema monetario. *3* forja, invención.
**coincide** (kouinsai·d) *intr.* coincidir.
**coincidence** (koui·nsidøns) *s.* coincidencia.
**coincident** (-ønt) *adj.* coincidente.
**coiner** (koi·nøʳ) *s.* acuñador. *2* monedero falso. *3* forjador, inventor.
**coinsurance** (-shu·rans) *s.* coaseguro.
**coir** (koiʳ) *s.* bonote, fibra de coco.
**coition** (koui·shøn) *s.* coito, cópula.
**coke** (kouk) *s.* cok, coque.
**cola** (kou·la) *s.* FARM. cola.
**colander** (kø·landøʳ) *s.* colador, pasador [utensilio].
**colchicum** (ka·lkikøm) *s.* BOT. cólquico.
**cold** (kould) *adj.* frío: ~ *chisel,* cortafrío; ~ *cream,* colcrén; ~ *meat,* fiambre; *to be* ~, estar frío; tener frío; *it is* ~, hace frío; *in* ~ *blood,* a sangre

fría. *2* desalentador; desalentado. *3* débil, perdido [rastro, pista]. *4* desnudo [sin adornos o comentarios]: *the* ~ *fact,* los hechos desnudos. *5 s.* frío. *6* catarro, resfriado: *to take* ~, resfriarse.
**cold-blooded** *adj.* de sangre fría. *2* friolento. *3* atroz, despiadado, cruel.
**coldly** (-li) *adv.* fríamente.
**coldness** (-nis) *s.* frialdad.
**cold-storage** *adj.* frigorífico.
**cole** (koul) *s.* col. *2* colza.
**Coleoptera** (koulia·ptøra) *s. pl.* ENT. coleópteros.
**colewort** (kou·lwøʳt) *s.* COLE.
**colic** (ka·lik) *adj.-s.* cólico.
**Coliseum** (kalisı·øm) *s.* coliseo.
**colitis** (kolai·tis) *s.* MED. colitis.
**collaborate (to)** (kølæ·børeit) *intr.* colaborar.
**collaboration** (-rei·shøn) *s.* colaboración.
**collaborator** (-rei·tøʳ) *s.* colaborador.
**collapse** (kølæps) *s.* derrumbamiento, hundimiento, desplome. *2* fracaso, ruina. *3* MED. colapso.
**collapse (to)** *intr.* derrumbarse, hundirse, desplomarse. *2* fracasar. *3* sufrir colapso. *4* plegarse, doblarse.
**collapsible** (-ibøl) *adj.* plegable, desmontable.
**collar** (ka·laʳ) *s.* cuello [de una prenda]. *2* cuello postizo, valona, golilla, etc. *3* collar. *4* MEC. collar, manguito, aro. *5* collera. *6* ARQ. collarino.
**collar (to)** *tr.* poner collar o collera. *2* coger por el cuello de la chaqueta; prender.
**collarbone** (-boun) *s.* clavícula.
**collaret[te** (kalare·t) *s.* cuello de encaje o piel.
**collate** (kølei·t) *tr.* colacionar, cotejar. *2* ECLES. colacionar, colar. *3* DER. colacionar.
**collateral** (kølæ·tøral) *adj.* colateral. *2* paralelo. *3* accesorio, indirecto, subordinado. *4* COM. subsidiario. *5 m.* COM. garantía subsidiaria.
**collation** (kølei·shøn) *s.* colación, cotejo. *2* colación, refacción. *3* DER., ECLES. colación.
**colleague** (ka·lıg) *s.* colega.
**colleague (to)** (køl·g) *intr.* coligarse.
**collect** (ka·lekt) *s.* LITURG. colecta.
**collect (to)** (køle·kt) *tr.* congregar. *2* juntar, recoger, coleccionar. *3* colegir, inferir. *4* recaudar, cobrar: ~ *on delivery,* contra reembolso. *5 to* ~ *oneself,* serenarse, reponerse. *6 intr.* congregarse, acumularse.
**collectable** (-abøl) *adj.* cobrable.
**collected** (-id) *adj.* reunido, juntado. *2* sereno, sosegado, dueño de sí mismo.
**collectedness** (-nis) *s.* calma, serenidad.
**collectible** (-ibøl) *adj.* cobrable, cobradero.
**collection** (køle·kshøn) *s.* reunión [acción]. *2* recogida. *3* cobro, recaudación. *4* colecta, cuestación. *5* colección. *6* recopilación.
**collective** (køle·ktiv) *adj.* colectivo. *2* formado por unión o agregación.
**collectivism** (-išm) *s.* colectivismo.
**collectivity** (-ti·viti) *s.* colectividad.
**collectivize (to)** (køle·ktivaiš) *tr.* colectivizar.
**collector** (køle·ktø·) *s.* colector, coleccionista. *2* compilador. *3* recaudador, cobrador. *4* ELECT. colector.
**college** (ka·lidȳ) *s.* colegio [corporación]. *2* colegio [donde se cursan estudios superiores].
**collegial** (køl·dȳial) *adj.* colegial.
**collegian** (-dȳian) *s.* individuo o estudiante de un colegio.
**collegiate** (-dȳieit) *adj.* colegiado. *2* colegial [iglesia].
**collet** (kæ·lit) *s.* MEC. collar. *2* JOY. engaste.

**collide (to)** (kølai·d) *tr.* chocar, topar. *2* estar en conflicto, oponerse.

**collie** (ka·li) *s.* (Esc.) perro de pastor.

**collier** (ka·liø^r) *s.* minero [de carbón]. *2* barco carbonero. *3* tratante en carbón.

**colliery** (-i) *s.* mina o comercio de carbón.

**colligate (to)** (ka·ligeit) *tr.* enlazar, relacionar.

**collimation** (kølimei·shøn) *s.* colimación.

**collimator** (-tø^r) *s.* colimador.

**collision** (køli·ȳøn) *s.* colisión, choque. *2* oposición, conflicto.

**collocate (to)** (ka·lokeit) *tr.* colocar, disponer.

**collocation** (-ei·shøn) *s.* colocación, disposición.

**colloid** (ka·loid) *adj.-s.* FÍS., QUÍM. coloide.

**colloidal** (køloi·dal) *adj.* coloidal.

**collop** (ka·løp) *s.* tajada; pedacito.

**colloquial** (kølou·kuial) *adj.* familiar [lenguaje, acepción, etc.].

**colloquialism** (-ism) *s.* estilo o expresión familiar.

**colloquy** (ka·lokui) *s.* coloquio, conversación.

**collude (to)** (kølu·d) *intr.* coludir.

**collusion** (kølu·ȳøn) *s.* colusión, confabulación.

**collusive** (-siv) *adj.* colusorio.

**collyrium** (kali·riøm) *s.* colirio.

**colocynth** (ka·losinz) *s.* BOT. coloquíntida.

**Cologne** (kølou·n) *n. pr.* GEOGR. Colonia. *2 s.* agua de colonia.

**Colombian** (kølø·mbian) *adj.-s.* colombiano.

**colon** (kou·løn) *s.* ANAT. colon. *2* ORT. dos puntos.

**colonel** (kø^rnøl) *s.* MIL. coronel.

**colonelcy** (-si), **colonelship** (-ship) *s.* coronelía.

**colonial** (kolou·nial) *adj.* colonial: ~ *period*, [Am.] coloniaje.

**colonialism** (-išm) *s.* colonialismo.

**colonist** (ka·lonist) *s.* colono [de una colonia].

**colonize** (ka·lonaiš) *tr.* colonizar. *2 intr.* establecerse en una colonia.

**colonizer** (-ø^r) *s.* colonizador.

**colonnade** (kaløneï·d) *s.* columnata.

**colony** (ka·loni) *s.* colonia.

**colophon** (ka·løføn) *s.* colofón.

**colophony** (kølo·føni) *s.* colofonía.

**color, coloration,** etc. COLOUR, COLOURATON, etc.

**colorific** (køløri·fik) *adj.* colorativo.

**colorimeter** (-mitø^r) *s.* colorímetro.

**colorimetry** (-metri) *s.* colorimetría.

**colossal** (køla·sal), **colossean** (kaløsï·an) *adj.* colosal.

**Colosseum** (kaløsï·øm) *s.* COLISEUM.

**colossus** (kola·søs) *s.* coloso.

**colostrum** (kola·strøm) *s.* calostro.

**colour** (kø·lø^r) *s.* color: *off* ~, pálido, indispuesto; (E.U.) verde, escabroso; *to lose* ~, palidecer. *2* colorido. *3* tinte, matiz. *4* apariencia, visos; excusa, pretexto: *under* ~ *of*, so color de, bajo pretexto de. *5* palo [en los naipes]. *6* [esp. en *pl.*] bandera, pabellón, enseña.

**colour (to)** *tr.* colorar, colorear, pintar, teñir, iluminar. *2* colorear, paliar, disfrazar. *3 intr.* colorearse. *4* enrojecer.

**colourable** (-abøl) *adj.* especioso.

**colouration** (-ei·shøn) *s.* coloración, colorido.

**colour-blind** *adj.-s.* daltoniano [pers.].

**coloured** (-d) *adj.* coloreado, pintado, teñido. *2* de color [negro, mulato, etc.]. *3* especioso, adornado, exagerado.

**colourful** (-ful) *adj.* lleno de colorido. *2* vívido, pintoresco, variado.

**colouring** (-ing) *s.* color, colorido. *2* colorante. *3* apariencia especiosa.

**colourist** (-ist) *s.* colorista.

**colourless** (-lis) *adj.* incoloro; descolorido.

**colporteur** (ka·lpo^rtø^r) *s.* distribuidor de libros o folletos religiosos.

**colt** (koult) *s.* ZOOL. potro. *2* joven sin juicio. *3* azote con nudo. *4* (con may.) revólver Colt.

**colter** (-ø^r) *s.* cuchilla [del arado].

**coltish** (-ish) *adj.* juguetón, retozón.

**coltsfoot** (-sfut) *s.* BOT. tusílago.

**columbary** (ka·lømbari) *s.* columbario. *2* palomar.

**Columbian** (kølø·mbian) *adj.* colombino.

**columbine** (ka·lømbain) *adj.* columbino. *2 s.* BOT. aguileña. *3* [con may.] *n. pr.* Colombina.

**Columbus** (kølø·mbøs) *n. pr.* Colón.

**column** (ka·løm) *s.* columna. *2* sección [de un periódico].

**columned** (-d) *adj.* con columnas.

**columniation** (-niei·shøn) *s.* columnata.

**colure** (koliu·^r) *s.* ASTR., GEOGR. coluro.

**colza** (kou·lša) *s.* BOT. colza.

**coma** (kou·ma) *s.* MED. coma. *2* ASTR. cabellera. *3* BOT. vilano.

**comatose** (kou·matous) *adj.* comatoso.

**comb** (koum) *s.* peine [para el pelo]. *2* peineta. *3* peine, carda, rastrillo. *4* almohaza. *5* cresta [de ave, de animal, de ola]. *6* API. panal.

**comb (to)** *tr.* peinar, carmenar. *2* cardar, rastrillar. *3* registrar [en busca de algo]. *4 intr.* romper, encresparse [las olas].

**combat** (ka·mbæt) *s.* combate, lucha.

**combat (to)** *tr.-intr.* combatir.

**combatant** (ka·mbatant) *adj.* luchador, combativo. *2 s.* combatiente.

**combative** (kømbø·tiv) *adj.* combativo, belicoso.

**comber** (kou·mø^r) *s.* peinador, cardador. *2* peinadora [máquina]. *3* ola con cresta.

**combination** (kambinei·shøn) *s.* combinación; mezcla. *2* unión, liga. *3* combinación [prenda femenina].

**combine** (ka·mbain) *s.* monipodio, confabulación. *2* AGR. cosechadora.

**combine (to)** (kømbai·n) *tr.* combinar. *2 intr.* combinarse. *3* confabularse; maquinar, conspirar.

**combing** (kou·ming) *s.* peinadura; rastrillaje. *2 pl.* peinaduras.

**combustibility** (kømbøstibi·liti) *s.* combustibilidad.

**combustible** (-bø·stibøl) *adj.-s.* combustible.

**combustion** (-shøn) *s.* combustión. *2* agitación, tumulto.

**comby** (kou·mi) *adj.* apanalado.

**come (to)** (køm) *intr.* venir, llegar, acercarse. *2* venir, provenir. *3* avanzar, aparecer, salir. *4* pasar, suceder. *5* entrar [en acción, en contacto, etc.]. *6* ascender [a un total], ser lo mismo [que]. *7 to* ~ *about*, ocurrir; MAR. virar. *8 to* ~ *across*, topar con. *9 to* ~ *apart* o *asunder*, dividirse, desunirse. *10 to* ~ *back*, volver, retroceder. *11 to* ~ *by*, pasar; obtener. *12 to* ~ *down*, bajar, descender; caer; *to* ~ *down with*, pagar [dinero]. *13 to* ~ *forth*, salir, aparecer. *14 to* ~ *forward*, avanzar, presentarse. *15 to* ~ *in*, entrar. *16 to* ~ *near*, acercarse. *17 to* ~ *of age*, llegar a la mayoría de edad. *18 to* ~ *off*, efectuarse; salir [bien, mal, etc.]; despegarse, desprenderse. *19 to* ~ *on*, avanzar; proseguir; entrar; medrar; ~ *on!*, ¡venga!, ¡vamos! *20 to* ~ *out*, salir; debutar; ponerse de largo; *to* ~ *out with*, decir, revelar. *21 to* ~ *round*, llegar, volver; reponerse; ceder, asentir. *22 to* ~ *to*, volver en sí; consentir, ceder; MAR. anclar; orzar. *23 to* ~ *to terms*, ceder, aceptar condiciones. *24 to* ~ *together*, juntarse. *25 to*

~ *true*, realizarse. 26 *to* ~ *up*, subir; aparecer; acercarse [a], estar a la altura [de]. 27 *to* ~ *upon*, caer sobre; dar con. ¶ Pret.: *came*; p. p.: *come*.

**comedian** (kømɪ·dian) *s.* cómico, comediante. 2 comediógrafo.

**comedienne** (kømidie·n) *s.* cómica, comedianta.

**comedist** (ka·mødist) *s.* comediógrafo.

**comedown** (kø·mdaun) *s.* caída, revés de fortuna.

**comedy** (ka·mødi) *s.* comedia.

**comeliness** (kø·mlinis) *s.* gentileza, apostura. 2 propiedad, decoro.

**comely** (kø·mli) *adj.* gentil, apuesto, bien parecido. 2 decente.

**come-off** *s.* fam. excusa, escapatoria.

**comer** (kø·møʳ) *s.* viniente, llegado.

**comestible** (køme·stibøl) *adj.-s.* comestible.

**comet** (ka·mit) *s.* ASTR. cometa.

**comfit** (kø·mfit) *s.* confitura seca.

**comfort** (kø·mføʳt) *s.* consuelo, alivio, confortación. 2 solaz. 3 comodidad, bienestar, regalo.

**comfort (to)** *tr.* confortar, fortificar. 2 aliviar, consolar. 3 alentar, animar, alegrar.

**comfortable** (-abøl) *adj.* confortable. 2 cómodo. 3 desahogada [posición]; regular, suficiente. 4 consolador. 5 *s.* (E.U) colcha, edredón.

**comforter** (-øʳ) *s.* confortador, consolador: *the Comforter*, el Espíritu Santo. 2 bufanda. 3 (E.U) COMFORTABLE 5.

**comfortless** (-lis) *adj.* triste, desolado. 2 desconsolado. 3 incómodo.

**comfrey** (kø·mfri) *s.* BOT. CONSUELDA.

**comic** (ka·mik) *adj.* cómico, bufo, burlesco; gracioso. 2 *s. pl.* historieta cómica ilustrada.

**comical** (-al) *adj.* cómico.

**comicalness** (-nis) *s.* comicidad, gracia.

**coming** (kø·ming) *adj.* próximo, venidero. 2 *s.* venida, llegada. 3 ~ *out*, salida; puesta de largo.

**comitia** (komi·shia) *s. pl.* comicios.

**comity** (ka·miti) *s.* urbanidad, cortesía.

**comma** (ka·ma) *s.* GRAM., MÚS. coma. 2 *inverted commas*, comillas.

**command** (kømæ·nd) *s.* orden, mandato. 2 mando, dirección; poder, dominio; disposición. 3 dominio, conocimiento [de una lengua, etc.]. 4 vista, perspectiva. 5 MIL. comandancia.

**command (to)** *tr.* mandar, ordenar. 2 mandar, comandar, dirigir. 3 dominar. 4 disponer de. 5 imponer, merecer [respeto, etc.]. 6 *intr.* mandar, imperar.

**commandant** (kamandæ·nt) *s.* comandante [el que manda].

**commander** (kømæ·ndøʳ) *s.* comandante, jefe, caudillo. 2 comendador.

**commandery** (-ri) *s.* comandancia. 2 encomienda.

**commanding** (-ing) *adj.* que manda. 2 imperativo, autoritario; imponente. 3 dominante.

**commandment** (-mønt) *s.* mando, comando. 2 mandato, orden: *the Ten Commandments*, los mandamientos de la ley de Dios.

**commando** (kømæ·ndou) *s.* MIL. comando [grupo de soldados].

**commeasurable** (køme·ÿurabøl) *s.* conmensurable.

**commemorable** (-morabøl) *adj.* memorable.

**commemorate (to)** (-møreit) *tr.* conmemorar.

**commemoration** (-ei·shøn) *s.* conmemoración.

**commence (to)** (køme·ns) *tr.* comenzar, empezar, iniciar, entablar. 2 *intr.* comenzar, principiar.

**commencement** (-mønt) *s.* comienzo, principio.

**commend (to)** (køme·nd) *tr.* encomendar. 2 recomendar, alabar.

**commendable** (-abøl) *adj.* recomendable, loable.

**commendation** (-ei·shøn) *s.* encomio, alabanza.

**commendatory** (køme·ndatori) *adj.* comendatorio, laudatorio.

**commender** (køme·ndøʳ) *s.* alabador.

**commensal** (køme·nsal) *adj.-s.* comensal.

**commensurable** (køme·nshurabøl) *adj.* conmensurable. 2 proporcionado.

**commensurate** (-reit) *adj.* proporcionado, correspondiente.

**commensurate (to)** *tr.* conmensurar; proporcionar.

**comment** (ka·ment) *s.* comento, comentario.

**comment (to)** *intr.* comentar. | Gralte. con *in* o *upon*.

**commentary** (ka·mønteri) *s.* comentario, glosa.

**commentator** (-ei·tøʳ), **commenter** (-øʳ) *s.* comentador, comentarista.

**commerce** (ka·møʳs) *s.* comercio, tráfico. 2 comercio [trato, comunicación].

**commercial** (kømø·ʳshal) *adj.* comercial, mercantil.

**commination** (køminei·shøn) *s.* conminación, amenaza.

**commingle (to)** (kømi·ngøl) *tr.* mezclar. 2 *intr.* mezclarse, unirse, barajarse.

**comminute (to)** (ka·miniut) *tr.* quebrantar, triturar.

**comminution** (-iu·shøn) *s.* trituración. 2 CIR. fractura conminuta.

**commiserate (to)** (kømi·søreit) *tr.* compadecer.

**commiseration** (-ei·shøn) *s.* conmiseración.

**commissariat** (kamise·riat) *s.* administración militar. 2 comisariado.

**commissary** (ka·miseri) *s.* comisario, delegado. 2 intendente militar. 3 economato [almacén].

**commission** (kømi·shøn) *s.* comisión, perpetración. 2 comisión, misión, encargo, cometido. 3 COM. comisión. 4 comisión, junta. 5 MIL. despacho, nombramiento. 6 *to put into* ~, poner [un buque] en servicio.

**commission (to)** *tr.* comisionar, encargar, facultar, delegar, nombrar.

**commissioned** (-d) *adj.* comisionado. 2 MIL. ~ *officer*, oficial [desde alférez para arriba]; *non* ~ *officer*, sargento, cabo, clase.

**comissioner** (-øʳ) *s.* comisionado. 2 apoderado, factor. 3 comisario.

**commissure** (ka·mishuʳ) *s.* comisura.

**commit (to)** (kømi·t) *tr.* cometer, perpetrar. 2 cometer, encargar. 3 confiar, depositar, entregar. 4 encarcelar. 5 comprometer: *to* ~ *oneself*, comprometerse, soltar prendas. ¶ Pret. y p. p.: *committed*; ger.: *committing*.

**commitment** (-mønt), **committal** (-al) *s.* comisión, perpetración. 2 acción de confiar, de entregar; auto de prisión; encarcelamiento. 3 compromiso, promesa.

**committee** (kømi·ti) *s.* comisión, comité, junta, delegación.

**commix** (kømi·ks) *tr.* mezclar. 2 *intr.* mezclarse.

**commixtion** (kømi·kshøn), **commixture** (-chøʳ) *s.* conmixtion, mezcla.

**commode** (kømou·d) *s.* cómoda. 2 lavabo cubierto. 3 sillico.

**commodious** (kømou·diøs) *adj.* cómodo, conveniente. 2 espacioso, holgado.

**commodiousness** (-nis) *s.* comodidad, espaciosidad, holgura.

**commodity** (køma·diti) *s.* artículo [de consumo], género, producto. *2* comodidad, conveniencia.

**commodore** (ka·mødø<sup>r</sup>) *s.* MAR. comodoro.

**common** (ka·møn) *adj.* común [de varios, de la mayoría]: ~ *crier*, pregonero; ~ *sense*, sentido común. *2* común, vulgar, corriente, ordinario. *3* raso [soldado]. *4* adocenado, trivial. *5* regular, usual. *6* GRAM., MAT. común. *7* *s.* lo común. *8 pl.* pueblo, estado llano. *9* tierras comunales. *10 the Commons, the House of Commons*, la Cámara de los Comunes.

**commonable** (-abøl) *adj.* comunal.

**commonalty** (-alti) *s.* común, comunidad.

**commoner** (-ø<sup>r</sup>) *s.* plebeyo. *2* miembro de la Cámara de los Comunes.

**commonplace** (-pleis) *adj.* común, vulgar, trivial. *2 s.* lugar común, trivialidad. *3* apunte, nota.

**commonweal** (-uıl) *s.* bien público.

**commonwealth** (-uelz) *s.* nación, república, cosa pública. *2* comunidad de naciones.

**commotion** (kømou·shøn) *s.* conmoción, agitación. *2* levantamiento, alboroto, tumulto; revuelo.

**commove (to)** (kømu·v) *tr.* conmover, alterar, agitar.

**communal** (ka·miunal) *adj.* comunal.

**commune** (ka·miun) *s.* comunicación, comunión, trato.

**commune (to)** *intr.* conversar, estar en comunión o trato íntimo. *2* (E.U) comulgar.

**communicable** (kømiu·nikabøl) *adj.* comunicable, transmisible. *2* comunicativo.

**communicant** (kant) *adj.-s.* comunicante. *2 s.* comulgante.

**communicate (to)** (-keit) *tr.* comunicar, participar. *2* comunicar, transmitir. *3* *tr.-intr.* comulgar [dar o recibir la comunión]. *4 intr.* comunicarse. *5* consultar, conferenciar.

**communication** (-ei·shøn) *s.* comunicación [acción de comunicar o comunicarse], trato, correspondencia. *2* transmisión [de calor, movimiento, etc.]. *3* noticia, mensaje. *4* acceso, paso. *5 pl.* comunicaciones.

**communicative** (kømiu·nikeitiv) *adj.* comunicativo, expansivo.

**communicatory** (-katori) *adj.* comunicatorio.

**communion** (kømiu·niøn) *s.* comunión. *2 Holy Communion*, la Sagrada Comunión.

**communism** (ka·miunišm) *s.* comunismo.

**communist** (-ist) *adj.* comunista.

**communistic** (-i·stik) *adj.* comunista.

**community** (kømiu·niti) *s.* comunidad [calidad de común]. *2* comunidad, común, público, sociedad. *3* comunidad [religiosa, etc.]. *4* vecindario, municipio, barrio.

**commutable** (-tabøl) *adj.* conmutable.

**commutate** (ka·miuteit) *tr.* ELECT. CONMUTAR.

**commutation** (-ei·shøn) *s.* conmutación, cambio, trueque. *2* FERROC. (E.U) ~ *ticket*, abono.

**commutator** (-ø<sup>r</sup>) *s.* ELECT. conmutador. *2* ELECT. colector.

**commute** (kømiu·t) *tr.* conmutar, cambiar, substituir. *2* cambiar una forma de pago por otra; igualar, tomar abono para. *3* ELECT. conmutar. *4 intr.* FERROC. (E.U) abonarse.

**compact** (ka·mpakt) *s.* pacto, convenio, trato. *2* polvera de bolsillo.

**compact** (kømpæ·ct) *adj.* compacto, denso, apretado, comprimido. *2* breve, conciso. *3* ~ *of*, compuesto de.

**compact (to)** *tr.* apretar, comprimir, condensar, hacer compacto. *2* hacer o componer [de].

**compactness** (-nis) *s.* compacidad, densidad, tamaño reducido. *2* firmeza, solidez.

**companion** (kømpæ·niøn) *s.* compañero, ra; camarada. *2* acompañante. *3* caballero [de ciertas órdenes]. *4* MAR. carroza, chupeta: ~ *way*, escalera de cámara.

**companionable** (-abøl) *adj.* sociable, afable.

**companionship** (-ship) *s.* compañerismo, camaradería. *2* unión, compañía.

**company** (ka·mpani) *s.* compañía [efecto de acompañar; personas que acompañan]. *2* compañía, gremio, sociedad. *3* grupo, banda. *4* COM., TEAT. compañía. *5* MAR. tripulación. *6* banda [de música]. *7* visitas, invitados; vida de sociedad.

**comparable** (ka·mparabøl) *adj.* comparable.

**comparative** (kømpæ·rativ) *adj.* comparativo. *2* relativo [no absoluto]. *3* comparado [filológia, etc.].

**comparatively** (-li) *adv.* comparativamente. *2* relativamente.

**compare** (kømpe·ø<sup>r</sup>) *s.* comparación: *beyond* ~, sin comparación.

**compare (to)** *tr.* comparar. *2* cotejar, confrontar. *3* parangonar, equiparar. *4 intr.* poderse comparar.

**comparison** (kømpæ·rišøn) *s.* comparación [acción y efecto]. *2* RET. comparación, símil.

**compartment** (kømpa·<sup>r</sup>tmønt) *s.* compartimiento, departamento, división; cajoncito, gaveta. *2* BLAS. cuartel.

**compass** (kø·mpas) *s.* área, ámbito, recinto, circunferencia. *2* alcance, esfera, círculo [de acción, etc.]. *3* límites, moderación. *4* (a veces en *pl.*) compás [instrumento]. *5* brújula: ~ *card*, rosa náutica. *6* MÚS. extensión [de la voz o de un instrumento].

**compass (to)** *tr.* idear, planear. *2* conseguir. *3* comprender, entender. *4* circuir, cercar. *5* rodear, contornear.

**compassable** (-abøl) *adj.* asequible.

**compassion** (kømpæ·shøn) *s.* compasión.

**compassionable** (-abøl) *adj.* compasible, lastimoso.

**compassionate** (-it) *adj.* compasivo.

**compassionate (to)** (-eit) *tr.* compadecer.

**compatibility** (kømpætibi·liti) *s.* compatibilidad.

**compatible** (-pæ·tibøl) *adj.* compatible.

**compatriot** (kømpei·triøt) *adj.-s.* compatriota. *2* compatricio, paisano.

**compeer** (kømpi·ø<sup>r</sup>) *s.* igual, par. *2* compañero.

**compel (to)** (kømpe·l) *tr.* compeler, constreñir, obligar, forzar. *2* imponer [respeto, silencio, etc.]. ¶ Pret. y p. p.: *compelled;* ger.: *-lling.*

**compellent** (-ønt) *adj.* compulsivo.

**compend** (ka·mpend) *s.* compendio.

**compendious** (kømpe·ndiøs) *adj.* compendioso, breve, sucinto, sumario.

**compendium** (-diøm) *s.* compendio, resumen, epítome, sumario.

**compensate (to)** (ka·mpenseit) *tr.* compensar, contrapesar. *2* resarcir, indemnizar. *3* recompensar. *4 intr. to* ~ *for*, compensar.

**compensation** (-ei·shøn) *s.* compensación.

**compensator** (ka·mpenseitø<sup>r</sup>) *s.* compensador.

**compete (to)** (kømpı·t) *intr.* competir, contender, rivalizar.

**competence** (ka·mpitøns), **competency** (-si) *s.* competencia, aptitud. *2* medios de vida, buen

pasar. *3* cantidad suficiente. *4* DER. competencia.
**competent** (-ønt) *adj.* competente, capaz. *2* suficiente, adecuado, idóneo. *3* DER. competente.
**competition** (kømpiti·shøn) *s.* competición, competencia, rivalidad. *2* certamen, concurso, oposición. *3* COM. competencia.
**competitive** (kømpe·titiv) *adj.* de competición, de competencia.
**competitor** (-tø\[r\]) *s.* competidor, rival, contrincante. *2* opositor.
**compilation** (kampilei·shøn) *s.* compilación, recopilación.
**compile (to)** (kømpai·l) *tr.* compilar, recopilar.
**compiler** (-ø\[r\]) *s.* compilador, recopilador.
**complacence** (kømplei·søns), **complacency** (-si) *s.* complacencia, contento. *2* satisfacción de sí mismo.
**complacent** (-ønt) *adj.* satisfecho de sí mismo. *2* complaciente.
**complain (to)** (kømplei·n) *intr.* quejarse, lamentarse. *2* querellarse, demandar.
**complainant** (-ant) *s.* querellante, demandante.
**complainer** (-ø\[r\]) *s.* el que se queja.
**complaint** (-t) *s.* queja, lamento. *2* queja, agravio. *3* DER. demanda; reclamación. *4* mal, enfermedad.
**complaisance** (kømplei·šans) *s.* condescendencia, amabilidad, cortesía.
**complaisant** (-ant) *adj.* complaciente, amable, atento, cortés.
**complement** (ka·mplimønt) *s.* complemento. *2* cantidad o número total [asignados]. *3* MAR. dotación.
**complement (to)** *tr.* complementar, completar.
**complemental** (-me·ntal) *adj.* completivo.
**complementary** (-tari) *adj.* complementario.
**complete** (kømpli·t) *adj.* completo. *2* concluido. *3* acabado, consumado. *4* pleno, absoluto.
**complete (to)** *tr.* completar. *2* acabar, concluir, consumar. *3* efectuar.
**completion** (kømpli·shøn) *f.* complemento, perfección, acabamiento. *2* realización.
**completive** (-tiv) *adj.* completivo.
**complex** (ka·mpleks) *adj.* complejo, complexo. *2* complicado, intrincado. *3* s. complejo.
**complexion** (kømple·kshøn) *s.* cutis, tez, color. *2* temperamento, carácter. *3* aspecto, cariz.
**complexional** (-al) *adj.* temperamental.
**complexioned** (-d) *adj.* de tal o cual tez, cutis o temperamento.
**complexity** (kømple·ksiti), **complexness** (-nis) *s.* complejidad.
**compliance** (kømplai·ans) *s.* condescendencia, docilidad, sumisión, obediencia. *2* anuencia, consentimiento: *3 in* ~ *with,* conforme a.
**compliant** (-ant) *adj.* complaciente, condescendiente. *2* dócil, obediente, sumiso.
**complicacy** (ka·mplikasi) *s.* complicación; complejidad.
**complicate** (-keit) *adj.* complicado.
**complicated** (-id) *adj.* complicado, intrincado.
**complication** (-ei·shøn) *s.* complicación.
**complicity** (kømpli·siti) *s.* complicidad. *2* complejidad, complicación.
**compliment** (ka·mplimønt) *s.* cumplimiento, cumplido, lisonja, galantería, requiebro. *2* atención, fineza; regalo, obsequio. *3 pl.* saludos, respetos.
**compliment (to)** *tr.* cumplimentar, felicitar, obsequiar. *2* lisonjear, alabar, requebrar.

**complimentary** (-me·ntari) *adj.* obsequioso, galante, lisonjero. *2* de alabanza, de felicitación. *3* de regalo; gratuito.
**complin\[e** (ka·mplin) *s.* LITURG. completas.
**complot** (ka·mplat) *s.* complot, conspiración.
**complot (to)** (kampla·t) *tr.* tramar. *2 intr.* conspirar. ¶ Pret. y p. p.: *complotted;* ger.: *complotting.*
**comply (to)** (kømplai·) *intr.* (gralte. con *with*) condescender, acceder. *2* complacer, obedecer, cumplir, llenar, conformarse. ¶ Pret. y p. p.: *complied.*
**component** (kømpou·nent) *adj.-s.* componente.
**comport (to)** (kømpo·\[r\]t) *intr.* concordar, convenir. *2 ref.* comportarse, conducirse.
**comportment** (-mønt) *s.* comportamiento.
**compose (to)** (kømpou·š) *tr.* componer [formar, integrar]. *2* IMPR., LIT., MÚS., PINT. componer. *3* redactar, escribir. *4* concertar, arreglar, ordenar, disponer. *5* calmar, serenar.
**composed** (-d) *adj.* compuesto [de]. *2* sosegado, tranquilo, sereno.
**composedness** (kømpou·šidnis) *s.* compostura, sosiego, serenidad, mesura.
**composer** (kømpou·sø\[r\]) *s.* autor, escritor. *2* compositor. *3* cajista. *4* apaciguador.
**composite** (kømpa·šit) *adj.* compuesto [no simple]. *2* mixto. *3* ARQ., BOT. compuesto. *4 s.* compuesto; mixtura. *5* BOT. flor compuesta.
**composition** (kampoši·shøn) *s.* composición. *2* tema, redacción [escolar]. *3* arreglo, transacción. *4* compuesto; mixtura.
**compositor** (kømpa·šitø\[r\]) *s.* IMPR. cajista.
**compost** (ka·mpoust) *s.* AGR. abono, estiércol.
**compost (to)** *tr.* abonar, estercolar.
**composure** (kømpou·ỹø\[r\]) *s.* calma, serenidad, sangre fría.
**compote** (ka·mpout) *s.* compota.
**compound** (ka·mpaund) *adj.* compuesto [formado por unión o combinación]. *2* ARIT. complejo. *3* COM. compuesto [interés]. *4* MEC. compound. *5 s.* compuesto; mezcla. *6* recinto, empalizada.
**compound (to)** (kampau·nd) *tr.* componer, confeccionar; combinar, mezclar. *2* arreglar, transigir. *3 intr.* pactar, avenirse, transigir.
**compounder** (-ø\[r\]) *s.* mezclador, preparador. *2* el que pacta o transige.
**comprehend (to)** (kamprije·nd) *tr.* comprender, entender. *2* comprender, contener, incluir.
**comprehensible** (-sibøl) *adj.* comprensible.
**comprehension** (-shøn) *s.* comprensión.
**comprehensive** (-siv) *adj.* comprensivo. *2* amplio, extenso.
**comprehensiveness** (-nis) *s.* comprensión, inteligencia. *2* amplitud, extensión.
**compress** (ka·mpres) *s.* compresa.
**compress (to)** (kømpre·s) *tr.* comprimir. *2* apretar, condensar, reducir.
**compressibility** (-ibi·liti) *s.* comprensibilidad.
**compression** (kømpre·shøn) *s.* comprensión. *2* reducción, condensación.
**compressor** (-sø\[r\]) *s.* compresor.
**comprise (to)** (kømprai·š) *tr.* comprender, incluir, abrazar, constar de.
**compromise** (ka·mprømaiš) *s.* transacción, arreglo, componenda. *2* término medio. *3* DER. compromiso.
**compromise (to)** *tr.* componer, arreglar [por vía de transacción]. *2* comprometer [poner en peligro, etc.]. *3 intr.* transigir, hacer concesiones.
**comptroller** (køntrou·lø\[r\]) *s.* interventor.

**compulsion** (kømpø·lshøn) *s.* compulsión, constreñimiento, coacción.

**compulsory** (-sori) *adj.* compulsivo. *2* obligatorio.

**compunction** (kømpø·nkshøn) *s.* compunción, remordimiento, escrúpulo.

**compunctious** (-søs) *adj.* compungido, contrito.

**compurgation** (kampøᵣgei·shøn) *s.* compurgación.

**computation** (kampiutei·shøn) *s.* computación, cómputo, cuenta, cálculo.

**compute (to)** (kømpiu·t) *tr.* computar, calcular, estimar.

**computer** (-øᵣ) *s.* calculador. *2* máquina calculadora.

**comrade** (ka·mræd) *s.* compañero, camarada.

**con** (kan) *adv.-s.* contra. V. PRO.

**con (to)** *tr.* estudiar, aprender. *2* gobernar [un buque]. ¶ Pret. y p. p.: *conned;* ger.: *conning.*

**concatenate** (kankæ·tineit) *adj.* concadenado.

**concatenate (to)** *tr.* concadenar.

**concatenation** (-ei·shøn) *s.* concatenación.

**concave** (ka·nkeiv) *adj.* cóncavo. *2 s.* concavidad, bóveda.

**concaveness** (-nis), **concavity** (-kæ·viti) *s.* concavidad.

**conceal (to)** (kønsi·l) *tr.* ocultar, esconder, disimular, tapar, encubrir.

**concealment** (-mønt) *s.* ocultación, encubrimiento, disimulación. *2* escondite, escondrijo.

**concede (to)** (kønsi·d) *tr.* conceder, reconocer. *2* conceder, otorgar. *3 intr.* hacer concesiones.

**conceit** (kønsi·t) *s.* vanidad, presunción, orgullo, engreimiento. *2* concepto, opinión. *3* concepto, expresión ingeniosa o afectada. *4* capricho, fantasía.

**conceited** (-id) *adj.* engreído, presumido, pagado de sí mismo.

**conceivable** (kønsi·vabøl) *adj.* concebible, imaginable.

**conceive (to)** (kønsi·v) *tr.* concebir [en todas sus acepciones]. *2* comprender. *3* creer, suponer. *4* expresar, formular. *5 intr.* concebir [la hembra].

**concenter (to)** TO CONCENTRE.

**concentrate** (ka·nsøntreit) *adj.* concentrado.

**concentrate (to)** *tr.* concentrar, reconcentrar. *2* enfocar. *3 intr.* concentrarse, reconcentrarse.

**concentration** (-ei·shøn) *s.* concentración. *2* reconcentración.

**concentre (to)** (kønse·ntøᵣ) *tr.* concentrar, reunir en un centro común. *2 intr.* concentrarse; tener un centro común.

**concentric(al** (-trik(al) *adj.* concéntrico.

**concentus** (kønse·tøs) *s.* concento.

**concept** (kæ·nsept) *s.* concepto, noción, idea.

**conception** (kønse·pshøn) *s.* concepción. *2* concepto, idea; noción, comprensión.

**conceptual** (-chual) *adj.* conceptual.

**concern** (kønsøᵣn) *s.* interés, afecto. *2* preocupación, inquietud, ansiedad. *3* interés, parte. *4* concernencia, incumbencia. *5* lo que importa; importancia. *6* asunto. *7* negocio, empresa, establecimiento.

**concern (to)** *tr.* concernir, atañer. *2* importar, interesar, afectar. *3* preocupar, inquietar. *4 ref.* interesarse, preocuparse.

**concerned** (-t) *adj.* interesado, comprometido. *2* preocupado, inquieto.

**concerning** (-ing) *prep.* tocante a, acerca de.

**concernment** (-mønt) *s.* concernencia. *2* interés, importancia. *3* interés, parte. *4* asunto. *5* preocupación, inquietud.

**concert** (ka·nsøᵣt) *s.* concierto, acuerdo: *in* ~, de concierto. *2* MUS. concierto.

**concert (to)** (kønsø·ᵣt) *tr.* concertar, convenir. *2* planear, disponer. *3 intr.* concertarse.

**concertina** (kansøᵣtɪ·na) *s.* concertina.

**concertmaster** (ka·nsøᵣtmæstøᵣ) *s.* MÚS. concertino.

**concerto** (kønche·ᵣtou) *s.* MÚS. concierto [composición].

**concession** (kønse·shøn) *s.* concesión.

**concessionary** (-eri) *s.* concesionario. *2 adj.* otorgado por concesión.

**concessive** (kønse·siv) *adj.* concesivo.

**conch** (kank o kanch) *s.* caracol marino; caracola. *2* ARQ. concha.

**conchiferous** (kanki·førøs) *adj.* conchífero.

**conchoid** (ka·nkoid) *s.* concoide.

**conchoidal** (kankoi·dal) *adj.* concoide, concoideo.

**conchology** (kanka·lodÿi) *s.* conquiliología.

**conciliar** (kønsi·liaᵣ) *adj.* conciliar.

**conciliate (to)** (kønsi·lieit) *tr.* conciliar [ganar, atraerse], propiciar, apaciguar. *2* conciliar [doctrinas, etc.].

**conciliation** (-ei·shøn) *s.* conciliación.

**conciliatory** (kønsi·liatori) *adj.* conciliatorio.

**concise** (kønsai·s) *adj.* conciso, breve.

**conciseness** (-nis) *s.* concisión.

**concision** (kønsi·ÿøn) *s.* concisión. *2* corte, cortadura.

**conclave** (ka·nkleiv) *s.* cónclave.

**conclude (to)** (kønklu·d) *tr.* concluir, dar fin a. *2* concluir, hacer [un tratado, etc.]. *3* concluir, inferis. *4* decidir, determinar. *5 intr.* concluir, finalizar. *6* formar un juicio definitivo.

**conclusion** (kønclu·ÿøn) *s.* conclusión [en todas sus acepciones]. *2* decisión final, resultado. *3* final, despedida [de una carta].

**conclusive** (-siv) *adj.* conclusivo. *2* concluyente.

**concoct (to)** (kønka·kt) *tr.* mezclar, preparar, confeccionar. *2* urdir, tramar, forjar, inventar.

**concoction** (-shøn) *s.* mezcla, preparado. *2* trama, maquinación, invención.

**concomitance, -cy** (kønka·mitans, -si) *s.* concomitancia.

**concomitant** (-nt) *adj.-s.* concomitante.

**concord** (ka·koᵣd) *s.* concordia, armonía. *2* acuerdo, convenio. *3* GRAM., MÚS. concordia.

**concordance** (kanko·ᵣdans) *s.* concordancia, armonía, conformidad. *2* concordancias [índice].

**concordant** (-ant) *adj.* concordante, concorde, conforme.

**concordat** (kanko·ᵣdat) *s.* concordato.

**concourse** (ka·nkoᵣs) *s.* concurso, concurrencia [de cosas]. *2* concurso, concurrencia, gentío.

**concrescence** (kønkre·søns) *s.* concrescencia.

**concrete** (ka·nkrit) *adj.* concreto [no abstracto; concrecionado]. *2* de hormigón. *3 s.* lo concreto. *4* hormigón.

**concrete (to)** (kønkrɪ·t) *tr.* concrecionar, solidificar. *2* cubrir con hormigón. *3 intr.* concrecionarse, cuajarse.

**concretion** (kønkrɪ·shøn) *s.* concreción. *2* solidificación, coagulación.

**concubinage** (kankiu·binidÿ) *s.* concubinato.

**concubine** (ka·nkiubain) *f.* concubina.

**concupiscence** (kankiu·pisøns) *s.* concupiscencia.

**concupiscent** (-sønt) *adj.* concupiscente.

**concur (to)** (kønkø·ᵣ) *intr.* concurrir, coincidir. *2* cooperar. *3* concurrir, convenir, hallarse de acuerdo. ¶ Pret. y p. p.: *concurred;* ger.: *concurring.*

**concurrence** (-røns), **concurrency** (-si) *s.* concurrencia, coincidencia, conjunción. *2* acuerdo, consenso. *3* cooperación, ayuda. *4* competencia, rivalidad.

**concurrent** (-rønt) *adj.* concurrente, coincidente, coexistente. *2 s.* contribuidor. *3* rival, competidor.

**concuss** (kønkø·s) *tr.* sacudir, agitar. *2* coaccionar.

**concussion** (kønkø·shøn) *s.* concusión, sacudida, golpe. *2* MED. conmoción.

**condemn** (to) (kønde·m) *tr.* condenar. *2* desahuciar [a un enfermo]. *3* confiscar, expropiar.

**condemnation** (kandemnei·shøn) *s.* condenación.

**condemnatory** (kande·mnatori) *adj.* condenatorio.

**condensate** (kønde·nseit) *s.* producto de una condensación.

**condensation** (-ei·shøn) *s.* condensación.

**condense** (to) (kønde·ns) *tr.* condensar. *2* reducir, abreviar. *3 intr.* condensarse. *4* expresarse con concisión.

**condenser** (-ø$^r$) *s.* condensador.

**condensing** (-ing) *adj.* condensador.

**condescend** (to) (kandise·nd) *intr.* dignarse, acomodarse a un inferior; tomar un aire de protección o de superioridad.

**condescendence** (-øns), **condescension** (-se·nshøn) *s.* dignación, actitud afable de protección o superioridad.

**condign** (køndai·n) *adj.* condigno.

**condiment** (ka·ndimønt) *s.* condimento.

**condisciple** (køndi·sipøl) *s.* condiscípulo.

**condition** (køndi·shøn) *s.* condición, requisito. *2* condición, estado, circunstancia [de las cosas]. *3* condición [social]; estado [de las personas]. *4* estado físico [de los cuerpos].

**condition** (to) *tr.* condicionar. *2* estipular, convenir. *3* acondicionar [el aire, etc.].

**conditional** (-al) *adj.* condicional. *2 adj.-s.* GRAM. potencial [modo].

**conditioned** (-d) *adj.* condicionado. *2* acondicionado.

**condole** (to) (køndou·l) *intr.* condolerse, dar el pésame. | Gralte. con *with*.

**condolement** (-mønt), **condolence** (-øus) *s.* condolencia, lástima, pésame.

**condominium** (kandomi·niøm) *s.* condominio.

**condonation** (køndounei·shøn) *s.* perdón, olvido [de agravio o culpa].

**condone** (to) (køndou·n) *tr.* perdonar, olvidar [un agravio o culpa].

**condor** (ka·ndø$^r$) *s.* cóndor [ave; moneda].

**conduce** (to) (køndiu·s) *tr.* conducir, tender, contribuir.

**conducive** (-iv) *adj.* conducente.

**conduct** (ka·ndøkt) *s.* conducta, comportamiento. *2* conducta, gobierno, manejo. *3* MIL. escolta.

**conduct** (to) (køndø·kt) *tr.* conducir, guiar, llevar, escoltar, acompañar. *2* conducir, dirigir, mandar. *3* FÍS. conducir [el calor, etc.]. *4* MÚS. dirigir.

**conductibility** (-ibi·liti) *s.* conductibilidad.

**conduction** (køndø·kshøn) *s.* conducción [de un líquido, del calor, de la electricidad]; traída.

**conductive** (-tiv) *adj.* conductivo. *2* FÍS. conductor.

**conductivity** (-iti) *adj.* conductividad; conductibilidad.

**conductor** (-tø$^r$) *s.* conductor, guía. *2* MÚS. director. *3* cobrador [de tranvía]; (E.U) revisor [de tren]. *4* FÍS. conductor.

**conductress** (-tris) *s.* conductora, directora.

**conduit** (ka·ndit) *s.* conducto. *2* caño, encañado, tubería, canalización.

**condyle** (ka·ndil) *s.* ANAT. cóndilo.

**cone** (koun) *s.* GEOM., BOT. cono. *2* cucurucho. *3* pilón [de azúcar].

**coney** (kou·ni) *s.* conejo, gazapo.

**confabulate** (to) (kønfæ·biuleit) *intr.* confabular, platicar, departir.

**confabulation** (-ei·shøn) *s.* confabulación, plática.

**confection** (kønfe·kshøn) *s.* confección, preparación. *2* confitura, dulce. *3* confección [ropa hecha].

**confection** (to) *tr.* preparar, confitar.

**confectionary** (-ari) *adj.* confitado, de confitería.

**confectioner** (-ø$^r$) *s.* confitero, repostero.

**confectionery** (-eri) *s.* confitería, repostería. *2* dulces, confituras.

**confederacy** (kønfe·dørasi) *s.* confederación, coalición, liga. *2* asociación [para un acto delictivo], complicidad.

**confederate** (-eit) *adj.-s.* confederado, aliado. *2* socio, compinche, cómplice.

**confederate** (to) *tr.* confederar, unir. *2 intr.* confederarse, unirse.

**confederation** (ei·shøn) *s.* confederación.

**confer** (to) (kønfø·$^r$) *tr.* conferir, dar, otorgar. *2* dar, comunicar [una cualidad, etc., a una cosa]. *3* conferir, comparar. *4 intr.* conferir, conferenciar. ¶ Pret. y p. p.: *conferred*; ger.: *conferring*.

**conference** (ka·nførøns) *s.* conferencia, junta, entrevista.

**conferment** (kønfø·$^r$mønt) *s.* acción de conferir o dar.

**conferrer** (kønfø·rø$^r$) *s.* el que confiere o da.

**confess** (to) (kønfe·s) *tr.* confesar [pecados, etc.]. confesar, reconocer. *3* confesar [oír en confesión]. *4 intr.* confesarse.

**confessed** (-t) *adj.* confesado, declarado, reconocido.

**confession** (kønfe·shøn) *s.* confesión. *2* religión, credo. *3* profesión [de fe].

**confessional** (-al), **confessionary** (-eri) *adj.* confesional. *2 s.* confesonario.

**confessor** (kønfe·sø$^r$) *s.* confesor. *2* confesante.

**confetti** (kønfe·ti) *s.* confeti.

**confidant** *m.*, **confidante** (kanfidæ·nt) *f.* confidente [de una persona].

**confide** (to) (kønfai·d) *intr.* confiar [poner la fe o confianza en]. *2 tr.* confiar [un secreto, un objeto, etc.].

**confidence** (ka·nfidøns) *s.* confianza, fe, seguridad. *2* confianza, presunción, atrevimiento. *3* confidencia.

**confident** (-ønt) *adj.* seguro, que tiene fe o confianza. *2* confiado, presuntuoso, atrevido. *3* confidente [pers.].

**confidential** (kanfide·nshal) *adj.* confidencial, reservado. *2* de confianza.

**confiding** (kønfai·ding) *adj.* confiado, crédulo.

**configurate** (to) (kønfi·giureit) *tr.* configurar.

**configuration** (-ei·shøn) *s.* configuración.

**configure** (-giu$^r$) *tr.* configurar.

**confine** (ka·nfain) *s.* confín, límite, término.

**confine** (to) *intr.* confinar, lindar. *2 tr.* limitar, restringir. *3* encerrar; recluir: *to be confined*, estar de parto; *to be confined to bed*, guardar cama.

**confineless** (-lis) *adj.* ilimitado.

**confinement** (-mønt) *s.* encierro, reclusión, cautiverio. *2* alumbramiento; sobreparto. *3* restricción, limitación.

**confirm** (to) (kønfø·$^r$m) *tr.* confirmar, corroborar, revalidar, ratificar. *2* confirmar, fortalecer. *3* ECLES. confirmar.

**confirmation** (-ei·shøn) *s.* confirmación, corroboración. *2* ECLES. confirmación.

**confirmed** (kønfø·ᵣmd) *adj.* confirmado. *2* inveterado.

**confiscate (to)** (ka·nfiskeit) *tr.* confiscar; decomisar.

**confiscation** (ei·shøn) *s.* confiscación; decomiso.

**confiteor** (ka·nfitiøʳ) *s.* confiteor.

**confiture** (ka·nfichøʳ) *s.* confitura, dulce.

**conflagration** (kanfkagrei·shøn) *s.* conflagración, incendio.

**conflict** (ka·nflikt) *s.* conflicto, lucha, choque, pugna, antagonismo.

**conflict (to)** *intr.* chocar, estar en conflicto, en pugna.

**confluence** (ka·nfluøns) *s.* confluencia. *2* concurso [de gentes].

**confluent** (-ønt) *adj.* confluente. *2 s.* confluencia, confluente. *3* río confluente.

**conflux** (ka·nfløks) *s.* CONFLUENCE.

**conform (to)** (kønfo·ᵣm) *tr.* conformar, acomodar, ajustar. *2 intr.* conformarse, acomodarse, cumplir, obedecer.

**conformable** (-abøl) *adj.* conforme, acorde, consonante, proporcionado. *2* sumiso, obediente.

**conformation** (-ei·shøn) *s.* conformación, forma, estructura. *2* adaptación.

**conformist** (kønfo·ᵣmist) *s.* conformista.

**conformity** (-iti) *s.* conformidad, concordancia, consonancia. *2* obediencia.

**confound (to)** (kønfau·nd) *tr.* confundir [mezclar, desordenar, embrollar]. *2* CONFUSE *2. 3* confundir, equivocar. *4* desbaratar, frustrar. *5* interj. ~ *it!*, ¡maldito sea!

**confounded** (-id) *adj.* confuso. *2* vulg. maldito, condenado, dichoso.

**confraternity** (kanfratø·ᵣniti) *s.* confraternidad. *2* cofradía, hermandad, sociedad.

**confront (to)** (kønfrø·nt) *tr.* confrontar, enfrentar, carear. *2* confrontar, cotejar. *3* arrostrar, hacer frente a.

**confrontation** (-ei·shøn), **confrontment** (kønfrø·ntmønt) *s.* confrontación, careo.

**Confucianism** (kønfiu·shanis̄m) *s.* confucianismo.

**Confucius** (-shøs) *n. pr.* Confucio.

**confuse (to)** (kønfiu·s̄) *tr.* confundir [mezclar, embrollar], oscurecer. *2* confundir, turbar, avergonzar; desconcertar, desorientar. *3* confundir, equivocar.

**confused** (-d) *adj.* confuso. *2* perplejo, desconcertado.

**confusion** (kønfiu·ȳøn) *s.* confusión.

**confutation** (kanfiutei·shøn) *s.* confutación.

**confute (to)** (kønfiu·t) *tr.* confutar. *2* confundir [en la disputa].

**congé** (ka·nȳei) *s.* despedida; despido.

**congeal (to)** (kønȳi·l) *tr.* congelar, helar. *2* cuajar, coagular. *3 intr.* congelarse, helarse, cuajarse.

**congealment** (-mønt) *s.* congelación.

**congee** (ka·nȳi) *s.* CONGÉ.

**congelation** (-ei·shøn) *s.* congelación. *2* solidificación.

**congener** (ka·ndȳinøʳ) *s.* congénere.

**congeneric** (kandȳøne·rik) *adj.* congénere.

**congenial** (kønȳi·nial) *adj.* congenial. *2* afín, análogo, concordante. *3* que conviene al gusto o a la naturaleza de uno; simpático.

**congeniality** (-iti), **congenialness** (-nis) *s.* conformidad, afinidad; simpatía. *2* calidad de lo que conviene al gusto o a la naturaleza de uno.

**congenital** (kønȳe·nital) *adj.* congénito.

**conger** (ca·ngøʳ), **conger eel** *s.* ICT. congrio.

**congeries** (køndȳi·riis̄) *s.* congerie.

**congest (to)** (køndȳe·st) *tr.* congestionar. *2 intr.* congestionarse.

**congested** (-id) *adj.* congestionado. *2* BOT. apiñado.

**congestion** (køndȳe·schøn) *s.* congestión.

**conglobate** (kønglou·beit) *adj.* conglobado.

**conglobate (to)** *tr.* conglobar.

**conglomerate** (køngla·mørit) *adj.-s.* conglomerado. *2 adj.* apiñado, denso.

**conglomerate (to)** (-reit) *tr.* conglomerar. *2 intr.* conglomerarse.

**conglutinate** (kønglu·tineit) *adj.* conglutinado.

**conglutinate (to)** *tr.* conglutinar. *2 intr.* conglutinarse.

**Congo** (ka·ngou) *n. pr.* GEOGR. Congo. *2 adj.-s.* congoleño.

**congo(l)ese** (kangou[l]i·s̄) *adj.-s.* congoleño.

**congratulate** (køngræ·chuleit) *tr.* congratular, felicitar, dar el parabién.

**congratulation** (-ei·shøn) *s.* congratulación, felicitación, enhorabuena.

**congratulatory** (køngræ·chulatori) *adj.* congratulatorio.

**congregate (to)** (ka·ngrigeit) *tr.* congregar, juntar, reunir. *2 intr.* congregarse, juntarse.

**congregation** (-ei·shøn) *s.* congregación. *2* reunión, agregado. *3* concurso, auditorio. *4* grey; feligresía.

**congregational** (-al) *adj.* de congregación; colectivo. *2* perteneciente a una grey o feligresía.

**congress** (ka·ngris) *s.* congreso, asamblea, reunión. *2* (con may.) Congreso [cámara legislativa]. *4* (E.U) conjunto de las dos Cámaras legislativas.

**congressman** (-mæn), **congresswoman** (-wumæn) *f.* congresista. *2* diputado. *3* (E.U) miembro del Congreso.

**congruence, congruency** (ka·ngruøns, -i) *s.* congruencia, consonancia, conformidad. *2* MAT., TEOL. congruencia.

**congruent** (ka·ngruønt) *adj.* congruente, congruo, consonante, conforme. *2* MAT. congruente.

**congruity** (køngru·iti) *s.* CONGRUENCE.

**congruous** (ka·ngruøs) *adj.* CONGRUENT.

**conic** (ka·nik) *adj.* cónico, coniforme. *2 s.* GEOM. sección cónica.

**conical** (-al) *adj.* cónico.

**conicalness** (-nis) *s.* conicidad.

**conifer** (kou·niføʳ) *s.* BOT. conífera.

**coniferous** (-røs) *adj.* conífero.

**coniform** (kou·nifoʳm) *adj.* coniforme.

**conirostral** (kounira·stral) *adj.* ORN. conirrostro.

**conjectural** (køndȳe·kchøral) *adj.* conjetural.

**conjecture** (-kchøʳ) *s.* conjetura, presunción.

**conjecture (to)** *tr.* conjeturar, presumir.

**conjoin (to)** (køndȳoi·n) *tr.* unir, juntar, asociar. *2 intr.* unirse, juntarse, asociarse.

**conjoint** (-t) *adj.* unido. *2* aunado. *3 s.* asociado, aliado.

**conjointly** (-li) *adv.* conjuntamente, mancomunadamente.

**conjugal** (ka·ndȳugal) *adj.* conyugal.

**conjugate** (ka·ndȳugeit) *adj.* conjugado. *2* GRAM. de la misma derivación. *3 s.* BOT. conjugada [alga].

**conjugate (to)** *tr.* unir, enlazar. *2* BIOL., GRAM. conjugar. *3 intr.* BIOL. conjugarse.

**conjugation** (-ei·shøn) *s.* unión, conjunción. *2* BIOL., GRAM. conjugación.

**conjunct** (køndȳø·nkt) *adj.* unido, conjunto, asociado.

**conjunction** (køndÿø·nshøn) *s.* conjunción, unión. *2* ASTR., GRAM. conjunción.
**conjunctiva** (køndÿønktai·va) *s.* ANAT. conjuntiva.
**conjunctive** (køndÿø·nktiv) *adj.* conjuntivo. *2* conjunto.
**conjunctivitis** (-tivai·tis) *s.* MED. conjuntivitis.
**conjunctly** (køndÿø·nktli) *adv.* conjuntamente.
**conjuncture** (-chø$^r$) *s.* coyuntura, circunstancias. *2* ASTR. conjunción.
**conjuration** (kandÿurei·shøn) *s.* conjuro [ruego]. *2* conjuro, sortilegio. *3* prestidigitación.
**conjure** (køndÿu·ø$^r$) *tr.* conjurar, rogar, implorar. *2* evocar [a un espíritu, etc.]; conjurar, exorcizar. *3* producir, enviar, hacer aparecer o desaparecer, etc., por [o como por] arte mágica. *4 to* ~ *up*, evocar; traer a la memoria o a la imaginación. *6 intr.* practicar las artes mágicas. *7* hacer juegos de manos.
**conjurement** (køndÿu·ø$^r$mønt) *s.* conjuro, exorcismo. *2* adjuración.
**conjurer, conjuror** (ka·ndÿørø$^r$) *s.* hechicero, mago. *2* prestidigitador, ilusionista.
**connate** (kanei·t) *adj.* innato. *2* afín. *3* connato.
**connatural** (kanæ·chøral) *adj.* connatural. *2* de igual naturaleza.
**connect (to)** (køne·kt) *tr.* unir, enlazar, coordinar. *2* conectar. *3* relacionar, asociar. *4* poner en comunicación. *5 intr.* unirse, enlazarse, tener conexión. *6* FERROC. enlazar, empalmar.
**connected** (-id) *adj.* unido, enlazado, conexo. *2* relacionado. *3* emparentado. *4* coherente, que tiene ilación.
**connectedly** (-li) *adv.* con coherencia.
**connecting** (-ing) *adj.* de unión o conexión; ~ *link*, eslabón; ~ *rod*, MEC. biela.
**connection** (køne·kshøn) *s.* conexión, unión, enlace. *2* coherencia, ilación. *3* relación, analogía, respecto. *4* relación [de amistad, comercial, etc.], parentesco. *5* pariente, deudo. *6* clientela. *7* secta. *8* medio de comunicación. *9* FERROC. empalme.
**connective** (-tiv) *adj.* conectivo, conjuntivo. *2 s.* GRAM. palabra que enlaza.
**connexion** *s.* CONNECTION.
**connivance** (kønai·vans) *s.* connivencia, consentimiento.
**connive (to)** (køvai·v) *intr.* disimular o tolerar culpablemente. *2* BOT. ser conniviente.
**connivent** (-ønt) *adj.* BOT. ser conniviente.
**conniver** (-ø$^r$) *s.* consentidor, cómplice.
**connoisseur** (kanisø·$^r$) *s.* perito, conocedor.
**connotation** (kanotei·shøn) *s.* connotación.
**connote (to)** (kønou·t) *tr.* connotar. *2* suponer [traer consigo].
**connubial** (køniu·bial) *adj.* connubial.
**conoid** (kou·noid) *s.* conoide.
**conoidal** (konoi·dal) *adj.* conoide, conoidal.
**conquer** (ka·nkø$^r$) *tr.* conquistar. *2* vencer, dominar. *3* vencer, superar. *4 intr.* triunfar.
**conquerable** (-øbøl) *adj.* conquistable. *2* domable. *3* vencible, superable.
**conqueror** (-ø$^r$) *s.* conquistador. *2* vencedor, sojuzgador.
**conquest** (ka·nkuest) *s.* conquista.
**Conrad** (ka·nræd) *n. pr.* Conrado.
**consaguineous** (kansængüi·niøs) *adj.* consanguíneo.
**consanguinity** (-niti) *s.* consanguinidad.
**conscience** (ka·nshøns) *s.* conciencia [esp. en sentido moral]: *in (all)* ~, en conciencia; en verdad.

**conscienceless** (-lis) *adj.* sin conciencia, desalmado.
**conscientious** (kanshie·nshøs) *adj.* concienzudo, escrupuloso, detenido. *2* de conciencia.
**conscientiousness** (-nis) *s.* conciencia, rectitud, escrupulosidad.
**conscious** (ka·nshøs) *adj.* consciente. *2* que se da cuenta, que se percata.
**consciousness** (-nis) *s.* FIL., PSIC. conciencia. *2* conciencia [de una cosa]. *3* conocimiento, sentimiento, sentido, estado consciente.
**conscript** (ka·nskript) *adj.* conscripto. *2* reclutado. *3 s.* recluta, quinto.
**conscript (to)** (kønskri·pt) *tr.* MIL. alistar, reclutar.
**conscription** (-kri·pshøn) *s.* alistamiento, reclutamiento [forzoso].
**consecrate** (ka·nsikreit) *adj.* consagrado.
**consecrate (to)** *tr.* consagrar. *2 intr.* LITURG. consagrar.
**consecration** (-ei·shøn) *s.* consagración. *2* dedicación.
**consecrator** (-ø$^r$) *s.* consagrante.
**consecution** (kansikiu·shøn) *s.* ilación. *2* sucesión, serie.
**consecutive** (kønse·kiutiv) *adj.* consecutivo. *2* sucesivo.
**consensual** (kønse·nshual) *adj.* consensual.
**consensus** (-søs) *s.* consenso, acuerdo general.
**consent** (kønse·nt) *s.* consentimiento, asentimiento, aquiescencia, aprobación, permiso: *all with one* ~, unánimemente.
**consent (to)** *intr.* consentir, acceder, estar de acuerdo.
**consentaneous** (kønsentei·niøs) *adj.* unánime. *2* conforme [a], consonante [con].
**consentient** (kønse·nshiønt) *adj.* anuente. *2* acorde, unánime.
**consequence** (ka·nsikuøns) *s.* consecuencia, resultado: *in* ~ *of*, de resultas de, a consecuencia de. *2* consecuencia, deducción. *3* importancia, entidad.
**consequent** (-kuønt) *adj.* consecuente, consiguiente. *2* lógico. *3 s.* consecuencia, resultado. *4* LÓG., MAT. consecuente.
**consequential** (-kue·nshal) *adj.* consiguiente. *2* importante [pers.]. *3* pomposo, engreído.
**consequently** (kønse·kuøntli) *adv.* por consiguiente, por ende, en consecuencia.
**conservancy** (kønsø·$^r$vansi) *s.* conservación, cuidado.
**conservant** (-vant) *adj.* conservador, preservador.
**conservation** (-ei·shøn) *s.* conservación.
**conservatism** (kønsø·$^r$vatišm) *s.* conservadurismo.
**conservative** (-tiv) *adj.* conservativo, conservador. *2 adj.-s.* POL. conservador.
**conservatoire** (kansø$^r$vatua·$^r$) *s.* conservatorio.
**conservator** (ka·nsø$^r$veitø$^r$) *s.* conservador, protector.
**conservatory** (kønsø·$^r$vatori) *adj.-s.* conservatorio. *2 s.* invernáculo, invernadero.
**conservatrix** (ka·nsø$^r$veitriks) *s.* conservadora, protectora.
**conserve** (kønsø·$^r$v) *s.* conserva, confitura.
**conserve (to)** *tr.* conservar, mantener. *2* confitar.
**conserver** (-ø$^r$) *s.* conservador. *2* confitero.
**consider (to)** (lønsi·dø$^r$) *tr.* considerar, pensar, tener en cuenta. *2* examinar, estudiar. *3* considerar, juzgar, tener por. *4* considerar [tratar con respeto o bondad].
**considerable** (-øbøl) *adj.* considerable. *2* notable, importante [pers.].

**considerate** (-it) *adj.* considerado [para con los demás]. *2* reflexivo, circunspecto, mirado.
**considerateness** (-itnis) *s.* consideración [para con los demás]. *2* prudencia, circunspección, moderación.
**consideration** (-ei·shøn) *s.* consideración [acción de considerar]; examen, estudio. *2* motivo, razón. *3* consideración, respeto, benevolencia. *4* importancia. *5* retribución, precio.
**considering** (kønsi·døring) *prep.* considerando [que], en atención a.
**consideringly** (-li) *adv.* con reflexión, seriamente.
**consign (to)** (kønsai·n) *tr.* COM. consignar. *2* consignar, confiar, depositar, entregar, relegar.
**consignation** (-ei·shøn) *s.* COM. consignación. *2* consignación, entrega.
**consignee** (konsaini·) *s.* consignatario.
**consigner** *s.* CONSIGNOR.
**consignment** (konsai·nmønt) *s.* COM. consignación; remesa, envío; partida.
**consignor** (kønsai·nø^r) *s.* consignador.
**consist (to)** (kønsi·st) *intr.* consistir. *2* componerse, constar [de]. *3* concordar, ser compatible [con].
**consistence, -cy** (-øns) *s.* consistencia. *2* congruencia, consonancia, compatibilidad. *3* consecuencia [en la conducta].
**consistent** (-ønt) *adj.* consistente, sólido, estable. *2* congruente, consonante, compatible. *3* consecuente [en la conducta].
**consistory** (kønsi·stori) *s.* consistorio.
**consolable** (kønsou·labøl) *adj.* consolable.
**consolation** (kansolei·shøn) *s.* consolación, consuelo, alivio.
**consolatory** (kønsou·latori) *adj.* consolatorio.
**console** (ka·nsoul) *s.* cónsola. *2* ARQ. cartela; repisa.
**console (to)** (kønsou·l) *tr.* consolar, confortar.
**consolidate** (kønsa·lideit) *tr.* consolidar, solidar. *2* unir, fusionar. *3* intr. consolidarse, solidarse. *4* unirse, fusionarse.
**consolidation** (-eishøn) *s.* consolidación. *2* COM. fusión, unión [de entidades].
**consols** (ka·nsouls) *s. pl.* (Ingl.) títulos de la deuda consolidada.
**consommé** (kansømei·) *s.* consumado, caldo.
**consonance, -cy** (ka·nsønans, -si) *s.* consonancia, conformidad. *2* MÚS. consonancia.
**consonant** (-ant) *adj.* consonante, cónsono, conforme. *2 adj.-s.* GRAM. consonante.
**consonous** (-nøs) *adj.* cónsono, armonioso.
**consort** (ka·nso^rt) *s.* consorte, cónyuge. *2* compañero. *3* MAR. buque que acompaña a otro.
**consort (to)** (kønso·^rt) *intr.* juntarse, acompañarse. *2* concordar, armonizar. *3 tr.* casar, asociar.
**consortium** (-shiøm) *s.* consorcio.
**conspectus** (kønspe·ktøs) *s.* ojeada general, sumario, compendio.
**conspicuity** (kønspikiu·iti) *s.* visibilidad, claridad. *2* nombradía.
**conspicuous** (kønspi·kiuøs) *adj.* conspicuo, eminente. *2* notable. *3* visible, manifiesto.
**conspiracy** (-pi·rasi) *s.* conspiración, complot.
**conspirator** (-ratø^r) *s.* conspirador.
**conspire (to)** (kønspai·^r) *intr.* conspirar, conjurarse. *2 tr.* planear, tramar.
**conspirer** (-rø^r) *s.* conspirador.
**constable** (ka·nstabøl) *s.* condestable. *2* alguacil. *3* policía [uniformado].
**constableship** (-ship) *s.* condestablía.
**constabulary** (kønstæ·biuleri) *s.* policía uniformada.

**Constance** (ka·nstans) *n. pr.* Constancia. *2 n. pr.* Constancio.
**constancy** (-i) *s.* constancia [firmeza, perseverancia]. *2* fidelidad. *3* persistencia.
**constant** (ka·nstant) *adj.* constante [firme, perseverante; durable]. *2* leal. *3* continuo, prsistente. *4 s.* MAT. constante.
**Constantine** (-tin o -tain) *n. pr.* Constantino.
**Constantinople** (kanstæntinou·pøl) *n. pr.* GEOGR. Constantinopla.
**constellation** (kanstelei·shøn) *s.* constelación.
**consternate (to)** (ka·nstø^rneit) *tr.* consternar.
**consternation** (-ei·shøn) *s.* consternación; terror, espanto.
**constipate (to)** (ka·nstipeit) *tr.* estreñir.
**constipation** (-ei·shøn) *s.* MED. estreñimiento.
**constituency** (kønsti·chuønsi) *s.* distrito electoral; electores de un distrito. *2* grupo de comitentes.
**constituent** (-ønt) *adj.* constitutivo, componente. *2* POL. constituyente. *3* elector, electoral. *4 s.* componente. *5* comitente, poderdante, mandante. *6* electo^r [de un diputado].
**constitute (to)** (ka·nstitiut) *tr.* constituir. *2* nombrar, hacer. *3* establecer, instituir. *4 ref.* constituirse en o por.
**connectedly** (-li) *adv.* con coherencia.
**constitution** (kanstitiu·shøn) *s.* constitución. *2* complexión; temperamento.
**constitutional** (-al) *adj.* constitucional. *2 s. fam.* paseíto.
**constitutionality** (-æ·liti) *s.* constitucionalidad.
**constitutive** (ka·nstitiutiv) *adj.-s.* constitutivo. *2 adj.* legislativo.
**constrain** (kønstrei·n) *adj.-s.* constitutivo. *2 adj.* legislativo.
**constrain (to)** (kønstrei·n) *tr.* constreñir, obligar. *2* estrechar, apretar. *3* restringir, reprimir, contener.
**constrained** (-d) *adj.* constreñido. *2* forzado, violento; encogido, embarazado: ~ *smile*, sonrisa forzada.
**constraint** (-t) *s.* constreñimiento, coacción, fuerza, apremio. *2* represión, contención. *3* embarazo, violencia.
**constrict (to)** (kønstri·kt) *tr.* constreñir, apretar, estrechar. *2* atar, ligar.
**constriction** (-kshøn) *s.* constricción, encogimiento.
**constrictor** (-tø^r) *s.* constrictor. *2* ZOOL. boa.
**constringe (to)** (kønstri·ndỹ) *tr.* constreñir, apretar, contraer.
**construct (to)** (kønstrø·kt) *tr.* construir, fabricar, hacer. *2* idear, componer. *3* GRAM. construir.
**constructer** (-ø^r) *s.* constructor.
**construction** (-kshøn) *s.* construcción [acción de construir]. *2* construcción, edificio, artefacto. *3* interpretación, sentido que se atribuye. *4* GRAM. construcción.
**constructive** (-tiv) *adj.* constructivo. *2* implícito, inferido, sobrentendido.
**constructor** (-tø^r) *s.* constructor.
**construe (to)** (kønstru·) *tr.* GRAM. construir. *2* traducir. *3* interpretar, explicar.
**consubstantial** (kønsøbstæ·nshal) *adj.* consubstancial.
**consubstantiation** (-shiei·shøn) *s.* consubstanciación.
**consuetude** (ka·nsuitiud) *s.* uso, costumbre.
**consuetudinary** (-tiu·dineri) *adj.* consuetudinario, de costumbre.
**consul** (ka·nsøl) *s.* cónsul.

consular (ka·nsiula$^r$) *adj.* consular.
consulate (-lit) *s.* consulado.
consulship (ka·nsølship) *s.* consulado [dignidad o cargo].
consult (to) (kønsø·lt) *tr.-intr.* consultar. 2 *tr.* tener en cuenta. 3 *intr.* deliberar, conferenciar.
consultation (kansøltei·shøn) *s.* consultación, consulta. 2 junta, deliberación.
consultative (kansø·ltativ) *adj.* consultivo.
consulter (-tø$^r$) *s.* consultor, consultante.
consulting (-ting) *adj.* consultante. 2 consultor, llamado a consulta. 3 de consulta: ~ *office,* consultorio.
consume (to) (kønsiu·m) *tr.* consumir. 2 gastar, disipar. 3 *consumed with,* absorbido por, muerto de. 4 *intr.* consumirse, deshacerrse.
consumedly (-idli) *adv.* extremadamente.
consumer (-ø$^r$) *s.* consumidor.
consummate (kansø·mit) *adj.* consumado. 2 completo, extremado.
consummate (to) (ka·nsømeit) *tr.* consumar.
consummation (kansømei·shøn) *s.* consumación. 2 complemento, perfección.
consumption (-shøn) *s.* consunción, consumimiento, consumición. 2 gasto, consumo. 3 MED. consunción; tisis.
consumptive (-tiv) *adj.* consuntivo. 2 *adj.-s.* MED. tísico.
contact (ka·ntækt) *s.* contacto: ~ *breaker,* ELECT. interruptor. 3 *pl.* contactos, relaciones.
contact (to) *tr.* ponerse o estar en contacto con.
contagion (køntei·dÿøn) *s.* contagio.
contagious (-dÿøs) *adj.* contagioso, pegadizo.
contain (to) (kønte·in) *tr.* contener, encerrar, incluir; tener cabida para. 2 MAT. ser múltiplo de. 3 contener, reprimir.
container (-ø$^r$) *s.* continente, recipiente, caja, vasija, envase.
contaminate (to) (køntæ·mineit) *tr.* contaminar. 2 impurificar, adulterar.
contamination (-nei·shøn) *s.* contaminación. 2 impurificación.
contemn (to) (kønte·m) *tr.* despreciar, menospreciar.
contemner (-nø$^r$) *tr.* despreciador.
contemplate (to) (ka·ntempleit) *tr.* contemplar [con los ojos o la mente]. 2 proponerse, proyectar; tener intención de. 3 *intr.* meditar, reflexionar.
contemplation (-ei·shøn) *s.* contemplación [con los ojos o la mente]. 2 espera, consideración [de algo] como probable. 3 intención, propósito [de].
contemplative (kønte·mplativ) *adj.* contemplativo.
contemporaneous (-rei·niøs) *adj.* contemporáneo.
contemporary (kønte·mpøreri) *adj.-s.* contemporáneo, coetáneo. 2 *s.* colega [dicho de periódicos].
contempt (kønte·mpt) *s.* desprecio, menosprecio, desdén. 2 DER. ~ *of court,* desacato a un juez o tribunal.
contemptible (-ibøl) *adj.* despreciable. 2 desdeñable.
contemptuous (kønte·mpchuøs) *adj.* despreciativo, despectivo, desdeñoso.
contemptuousness (-nis) *s.* desprecio, desdén.
contend (to) (kønte·nd) *intr.* contender. 2 competir, oponerse. 3 luchar, esforzarse, bregar. 4 *tr.* sostener, afirmar.
contendent (-ønt) *adj.* contendiente.

contender (-ø$^r$) *s.* contendedor, contendiente. 2 competidor. 3 sostenedor, mantenedor.
content (ka·ntent) *s.* contenido, capacidad, cabida, extensión, volumen. 2 *pl.* contenido [de un recipiente o de un libro]: *table of contents,* tabla de materias, índice general.
content (kønte·nt) *adj.* contento, satisfecho. 2 *s.* contento, contentamiento, satisfacción.
content (to) (tr. contentar, satisfacer.
contented (-id) *adj.* contento, satisfecho; tranquilo, resignado.
contention (kønte·nshøn) *s.* contención, contienda, disputa. 2 afirmación, lo que uno sostiene. 3 tema u objeto de disputa.
contentious (-shøs) *adj.* contencioso, disputador. 2 contencioso, litigioso.
contentment (kønte·ntmønt) *s.* contentamiento, contento.
conterminal (kantø·$^r$minal), conterminous (-nøs) *adj.* contérmino, limítrofe.
contest (ka·ntest) *s.* contienda, lucha, lid. 2 disputa, litigio. 3 torneo, competición, concurso, certamen.
contest (to) (kønte·st) *tr.* disputar, luchar por. 2 negar, discutir, controvertir, impugnar. 3 *intr.* contender, competir, litigar.
contestable (-abøl) *adj.* contestable, discutible.
contestant (-ant) *s.* contendiente. 2 impugnador, oponente.
contestation (kantestei·shøn) *s.* altercación, contestación.
context (ka·ntekst) *s.* contexto.
contexture (kønte·kschø$^r$) *s.* contextura. 2 tejido, enlazamiento.
contiguity (kantigiu·iti) *s.* contigüidad, inmediación. 2 continuidad.
contiguous (kønti·giuøs) *adj.* contiguo, inmediato, próximo.
continence, continency (ka·ntinøns, -i) *s.* continencia, templanza, castidad.
continent (ka·ntinønt) *adj.* continente, templado, casto. 2 *s.* GEOGR. continente.
continental (kantine·ntal) *adj.* continente, templado, casto. 2 *s.* GEOGR. continente.
continental (kantine·ntal) *adj.* continental. 2 *s.* habitante de la Europa continental.
contingence (kønti·ndÿøns) *s.* contacto, tangencia.
contingency (-i) *s.* contingencia. 2 eventualidad.
contingent (-ønt) *adj.* contingente, eventual, accidental. 2 *s.* contingente, contingencia. 3 contingente, cuota.
continual (kønti·niual) *adj.* continuo, incesante.
continuance (-ans) *s.* continuación, persistencia. 2 duración. 3 DER. aplazamiento.
continuate (-eit) *adj.* continuo, ininterrumpido.
continuation (-ei·shøn) *s.* continuación. 2 prolongación, extensión.
continuative (-eitiv) *adj.* continuativo.
continue (to) (kønti·niu) *tr.* continuar. 2 prolongar. 3 persistir en. 4 mantener, perpetuar. 5 prorrogar, aplazar. 6 *intr.* continuar, seguir, proseguir, durar.
continued (-d) *adj.* continuado, continuo, prolongado, seguido. 2 MAT. continua [fracción].
continuity (kantiniu·iti) *s.* continuidad. 2 continuo. 3 CINEM. guión.
continuous (kønti·niuøs) *adj.* continuo.
continuum (-niuøm) *s.* continuo, todo.
contort (to) (kønto·$^r$t) *tr.* torcer, retorcer.
contortion (-to·$^r$shøn) *s.* contorsión.
contortionist (-ist) *s.* contorsionista.

**contour** (ka·ntu<sup>r</sup>) *s.* contorno, perfil. *2* perímetro. *3* TOP. curva de nivel.

**contour (to)** *tr.* contornear, perfilar.

**contraband** (ka·ntrabænd) *s.* contrabando. *2 adj.* de contrabando, ilegal.

**contrabandist** (-ist) *s.* contrabandista.

**contrabass** (ka·ntrabeis) *s.* MÚS. contrabajo.

**contraceptive** (-se·ptiv) *adj.* anticoncepcional.

**contract** (ka·ntrækt) *s.* contrato. *2* contrata. *3* DER. escritura. *4* esponsales. *5* GRAM. forma contraída.

**contract (to)** (køntræ·kt) *tr.* contraer, reducir, encoger, estrechar, fruncir, arrugar. *2* GRAM. contraer, acortar [una palabra]. *3* contratar, pactar. *4* contraer [matrimonio, una enfermedad, etc.]. *5 intr.* contraerse, reducirse, encogerse. *6* contratar.

**contracted** (-id) *adj.* contraído, fruncido. *2* abreviado. *3* estrecho, mezquino. *4* escaso. *5* contratado, pactado.

**contractile** (køntræ·ktil) *adj.* contráctil.

**contractility** (-ti·liti) *s.* contractilidad.

**contracting** (køntræ·kting) *adj.* contractivo. *2* contratante. *3* contrayente.

**contraction** (-shøn) *s.* contracción. *2* reducción, encogimiento. *3* estrechez [de miras]. *4* reducción [de créditos, etc.].

**contractor** (-tø<sup>r</sup>) *s.* contratante. *2* contratista.

**contractual** (-chual) *adj.* contractual.

**contradict (to)** (kantradi·kt) *tr.* contradecir. *2* desmentir, negar.

**contradicter** (-ø<sup>r</sup>) *s.* contradictor.

**contradiction** (-di·kshøn) *s.* contradicción. *2* lo que envuelve contradicción en sí.

**contradictory** (-di·ktori) *adj.* contradictorio. *2* contrario, opuesto. *3 s.* LÓG. contradictoria.

**contradistinction** (-disti·nkshøn) *s.* distinción por oposición o contraste: *in ~ to*, por oposición a.

**contraindicate (to)** (-i·ndikeit) *tr.* MED. contraindicar.

**contraindication** (-kei·shøn) *s.* MED. contraindicación.

**contralto** (køntræ·ltou) *s.* MÚS. contralto.

**contraposition** (kantrapouši·shøn) *s.* contraposición.

**contraption** (køntræ·pshøn) *s.* desp. artefacto, artilugio.

**contrariety** (kantrarai·iti) *s.* contrariedad, oposición. *2* cosa contraria u opuesta.

**contrariness** (ka·ntrerinis) *s.* contrariedad, oposición. *2* terquedad.

**contrariwise** (-uaiš) *adv.* al contrario, inversamente, al revés. *2* tercamente.

**contrary** (ka·ntreri) *adj.* contrario. *2* adverso. *3* dado a la oposición, díscolo, terco. *4* adv. *~ to*, contrariamente a; contra, en contra de; al contrario de. *5 s.* cada una de dos cosas contrarias. *6* lo contrario: *on the ~*, al contrario; *to the ~*, en contrario, en contra.

**contrast** (ka·ntræst) *s.* contraste; contraposición.

**contrast (to)** (køntræ·st) *tr.* hacer contrastar. *2 intr.* contrastar.

**contravene (to)** (kantravi·n) *tr.* contravenir. *2* contradecir, discutir.

**contravener** (-ø<sup>r</sup>) *s.* contraventor, infractor.

**contravention** (-ve·nshøn) *s.* contravención, infracción.

**contribute (to)** (køntri·biut) *tr.* contribuir con, aportar, donar. *2* colaborar con [un artículo] en un periódico. *3 intr.* contribuir [a].

**contribution** (kantribiu·shøn) *s.* contribución [ac-

ción de contribuir]. *2* contribución, aportación, cuota, donativo. *3* colaboración [en un periódico]. *4* contribución [de guerra].

**contributor** (køntri·biutø<sup>r</sup>) *s.* contribuidor. *2* colaborador [de un periódico].

**contrite** (ka·ntrait) *adj.* contrito.

**contrition** (køntri·shøn) *s.* contrición.

**contrivance** (køntrai·vans) *s.* inventiva. *2* traza, artificio, invención, medio, arbitrio. *3* utensilio, aparato, artefacto, mecanismo. *4* plan, idea.

**contrive (to)** (køntrai·v) *tr.* idear, inventar, discurrir. *2* maquinar, tramar. *3* procurar, lograr. *4 intr.* hacer planes, darse maña.

**contriver** (-ø<sup>r</sup>) *s.* autor, inventor, causante. *2* maquinador. *3* arbitrista.

**control** (køntrou·l) *s.* mando, poder, dominio, autoridad. *2* sujeción, freno. *3* gobierno, dirección. *4* inspección, intervención, fiscalización. *5* verificación, comprobación. *6* MEC. mando, control, regulación; *~ board*, cuadro de control; *~ lever*, palanca de mando.

**control (to)** *tr.* dominar, sujetar, reprimir. *2* gobernar, dirigir, controlar. *3* inspeccionar, revisar, fiscalizar, intervenir, regular. ¶ Pret. y p. p.: *controlled;* ger.: *-lling.*

**controller** (-ø<sup>r</sup>) *s.* director, interventor, inspector, superintendente. *2* MEC., ELECT. regulador; aparato de manejo. *3* MAR. estopor.

**controversial** (kantrovø·<sup>r</sup>shal) *adj.* de controversia, polémico.

**controversialist** (-ist) *s.* controversista.

**controversy** (ka·ntrovø<sup>r</sup>si) *s.* controversia, polémica disputa.

**controvert (to)** (kantrovø·<sup>r</sup>t) *tr.-intr.* controvertir. *2 tr.* negar, contradecir.

**contumacious** (kantiumei·shøs) *adj.* contumaz, rebelde.

**contumacy** (ka·ntiumasi) *s.* contumacia, rebeldía. *2* desobediencia, desacato [a la autoridad].

**contumelious** (kantiumi·liøs) *adj.* contumelioso, injurioso.

**contumely** (ka·ntiumili) *s.* contumelia.

**contuse (to)** (køntiu·š) *tr.* contundir, magullar.

**contusion** (køntiu·ŷøn) *s.* contusión.

**contusive** (-šiv) *adj.* contundente.

**conundrum** (kønø·ndrøm) *s.* acertijo, rompecabezas.

**convalesce (to)** (kanvale·s) *intr.* convalecer.

**convalescence** (-øns) *s.* convalecencia.

**convalescent** (-ønt) *adj.* convaleciente.

**convection** (kønve·kshøn) *s.* conducción, transmisión. *2* FÍS. convección.

**convene (to)** (kønvi·n) *tr.* reunir, convocar. *2* citar, emplazar. *3 intr.* reunirse.

**convenience, -cy** (-iøns, -si) *s.* conveniencia, utilidad, comodidad, oportunidad: *at your ~*, cuando buenamente pueda. *2* retrete. *3 pl.* comodidades.

**convenient** (-iønt) *adj.* conveniente, oportuno. *2* a propósito. *3* cómodo. *4* próximo, a mano.

**convent** (ka·nvønt) *s.* convento.

**conventicle** (kønven·tikøl) *s.* conventículo.

**convention** (kønve·nshøn) *s.* convocación. *2* asamblea, convención. *3* convención, convenio. *4* costumbre o regla comúnmente aceptada, convencionalismo.

**conventional** (-al) *adj.* convencional. *2* convenido, pactado. *3* corriente, tradicional, clásico. *4 s.* convencional.

**conventionalism** (-išm) *s.* convencionalismo.

**conventionality** (kønvenshønæ·liti) *s.* calidad de

convencional. *2* regla o práctica establecida por el uso.
**conventual** (kønve·nchuɑl) *adj.* conventual.
**converge (to)** (kønvø<sup>r</sup>·dȳ) *intr.* converger. *2 tr.* hacer converger.
**convergence, -cy** (-øns, -i) *s.* convergencia.
**convergent** (-ønt) *adj.* convergente.
**conversable** (kønvø·<sup>r</sup>sabøl) *adj.* conversable. *2* propio para la conversación.
**conversance, -cy** (ka·nvø<sup>r</sup>sɑns, -i) *s.* familiaridad, conocimiento.
**conversant** (-ɑnt) *adj.* ~ *with*, que tiene trato con; versado, entendido en.
**conversation** (kɑnvø<sup>r</sup>sei·shøn) *s.* conversación. *2* familiaridad, conocimiento.
**conversationalist** (-ɑlist) *s.* conversador.
**converse** (ka·nvø<sup>r</sup>s) *adj.* inverso, opuesto. *2 s.* lo inverso, lo opuesto. *3* conversación; trato.
**converse (to)** (kønvø·<sup>r</sup>s) *intr.* conversar. *2* tener trato.
**conversely** (-li) *adv.* a la inversa, recíprocamente.
**conversion** (kønvø·<sup>r</sup>shøn) *s.* conversión [en todos sus sentidos]. *2* inversión, transposición.
**conversive** (kønvø·<sup>r</sup>siv) *adj.* conversivo.
**convert** (ka·nvø<sup>r</sup>t) *s.* convertido, converso.
**convert (to)** (kønvø·<sup>r</sup>s) *intr.* conversar. *2* tener trato.
**conversely** (-li) *adv.* a la inversa, recíprocamente.
**conversion** (kønvø·<sup>r</sup>shøn) *s.* conversión [en todos sus sentidos]. *2* inversión, transposición.
**conversive** (kønvø·<sup>r</sup>siv) *adj.* conversivo.
**convert** (ka·nvø<sup>r</sup>t) *s.* convertido, converso.
**convert (to)** (kønvø·<sup>r</sup>t) *tr.* convertir [en todos sus sentidos]. *2* invertir, transponer. *3 intr.* convertirse.
**converter** (-ø<sup>r</sup>) *s.* convertidor.
**convertible** (-ibøl) *adj.* convertible. *2* AUTO. descapotable.
**convex** (ka·nveks) *adj.* convexo. *2 s.* convexidad.
**convexity** (kønve·ksiti) *s.* convexidad.
**convey (to)** (kønvei·) *tr.* llevar, transportar. *2* conducir, transmitir, comunicar, enviar. *3* dar [idea, información, etc.]. *4* ceder, transferir [bienes].
**conveyance** (-ɑns) *s.* transporte, conducción. *2* comunicación, transmisión. *3* medio de transporte, vehículo. *4* DER. cesión, traspaso. *5* DER. escritura de traspaso.
**conveyer, -yor** (-ø<sup>r</sup>) *s.* portador, llevador. *2* DER. cedente. *3 adj.-s.* MEC. transportador.
**convict** (kønvi·kt) *s.* reo convicto; condenado. *2* penado, presidiario.
**convict (to)** *tr.* DER. declarar culpable; probar la culpabilidad de. *2* convencer [de error].
**conviction** (kønvi·kshøn) *s.* DER. prueba o declaración de culpabilidad. *3* convicción, convencimiento.
**convince (to)** (kønvi·ns) *tr.* convencer.
**convincing** (-ing) *adj.* convincente.
**convivial** (kønvi·viɑl) *adj.* convival. *2* sociable, jovial.
**conviviality** (-æ·liti) *s.* jovialidad, buen humor.
**convocation** (kɑnvokei·shøn) *s.* convocación, llamamiento. *2* asamblea.
**convoke (to)** (kønvou·k) *s.* convocar, reunir.
**convolute** (ka·nvoliut) *adj.* convoluto, enroscado.
**convolution** (-liu·shøn) *s.* convolución, circunvolución.
**convolve (to)** (kønva·lv) *tr.* enrollar, retorcer. *2 intr.* enroscarse, retorcerse.

**convolvulaceous** (-viulei·shøs) *adj.* BOT. convolvuláceo.
**convolvulus** (-viuløs) *s.* BOT. convólvulo.
**convoy** (ka·nvoi) *s.* convoy.
**convoy (to)** (kønvoi·) *tr.* convoyar.
**convulse (to)** (kønvø·ls) *tr.* convulsionar; crispar. *2 intr.* sufrir convulsión; crisparse: *to be convulsed with laughter*, desternillarse de risa.
**convulsion** (kønvø·lshøn) *s.* convulsión. *2 pl.* ataque de risa.
**convulsive** (kønvø·lsiv) *adj.* convulsivo.
**coo** (ku) *s.* arrullo.
**coo (to)** *intr.* arrullar; arrullarse.
**cooing** (-ing) *adj.* arrullador. *2* enamorado. *3 s.* arrullo.
**cook** (kuk) *s.* cocinero, cocinera.
**cook (to)** *tr.-intr.* cocer, guisar, cocinar. *2 tr.* echar a perder, hacer fracasar. *3 to* ~ *up*, urdir; amañar, falsear.
**cooker** (ku·kø<sup>r</sup>) *s.* cocedor. *2* hornilla, fogón.
**cookery** (-i) *s.* cocina [arte; lugar].
**cookie** (ku·ki) *s.* bizcochito, galletita.
**cooking** (-ng) *s.* cocina [arte]. *2* acción de guisar, cocción. *3 adj.* de cocina; para cocer.
**cookshop** (-shap) *s.* casa de comidas.
**cooky** (-i) *s.* fam. cocinera. *2* COOKIE.
**cool** (kul) *adj.* fresco [algo frío]. *2* frío, tibio, indiferente. *3* frío [hecho con frialdad]. *4* sereno, osado. *5 s.* fresco, frescor, frescura.
**cool (to)** *tr.* refrescar, enfriar, entibiar: *to* ~ *one's heels*, estar esperando. *2* orear. *3* templar, calmar. *4 intr.* refrescarse, enfriarse, entibiarse. *5* calmarse.
**cooler** (-ø<sup>r</sup>) *s.* enfriador. *2* enfriadera. *3* refrigerador.
**coolie** (ku·li) *s.* peón chino o indio.
**cooling** (ku·ling) *adj.* refrescante. *2* refrigerador. *3* atemperador.
**coolish** (-lish) *adj.* fresquito.
**coolness** (ku·lnis) *s.* fresco, frescura, frescor. *2* frialdad. *3* serenidad.
**coomb, coombe** (kum) *s.* vallecito estrecho.
**coop** (kup) *s.* caponera, gallinero. *2* fam. cárcel. *3* cuba, barril.
**coop (to)** *tr.* encerrar, enjaular.
**cooper** (ku·pø<sup>r</sup>) *s.* cubero, tonelero.
**cooper (to)** *tr.-intr.* hacer toneles.
**cooperage** (-idȳ) *s.* tonelería.
**co-operate (to)** (koua·pøreit) *intr.* cooperar, coadyuvar.
**co-operation** (-rei·shøn) *s.* cooperación.
**co-operative** (-rativ) *adj.* cooperativo. *2 s.* cooperativa [sociedad].
**co-ordinate** (kouo·<sup>r</sup>dinit) *adj.* coordinado; del mismo orden, clase, etc. *2* MAT. coordenado, de las coordenadas. *3 s.* MAT. coordenada.
**co-ordinate (to)** (-neit) *tr.* coordinar. *2 intr.* coordinarse.
**coot** (kut) *s.* ORN. foja.
**cop** (kap) *s.* fam. policía, polizonte. *2* TEJ. enrollamiento cónico.
**copaiba** (koupei·bɑ) *s.* copaiba.
**copal** (kou·pɑl) *s.* copal.
**copartner** (koupa·<sup>r</sup>tnø<sup>r</sup>) *s.* socio. *2* copartícipe.
**cope** (koup) *s.* capa pluvial. *2* COPING. *3* lo que cubre; bóveda, cúpula.
**cope (to)** *tr.* cubrir. *2 intr. to* ~ *with*, contender, rivalizar con; habérselas o poder con; hacer frente a.
**copeck** (kou·pek) *s.* copeck.

**Copenhaguen** (kapønje·gøn) *n. pr.* GEOGR. Copenhague.

**copestone** (kou·pstoun) *s.* ALBAÑ. piedra de albardilla. *2* fig. fin, coronamiento.

**copier** (ka·piøʳ) *s.* copiador, imitador. *2* copista.

**coping** (kou·ping) *s.* ALBAÑ. albardilla.

**copious** (kou·piøs) *adj.* copioso, abundante. *2* profuso, exuberante, rico.

**copper** (ka·pøʳ) *s.* QUÍM. cobre. *2* moneda de cobre. *3* caldera. *4* pop. policía, polizonte. *5* grabado en cobre. *6 adj.* de cobre, cobrizo.

**copper (to)** *tr.* forrar de cobre, encobrar.

**copperas** (-as) *s.* caparrosa verde, aceche.

**copperish** (-ish) *adj.* cobrizo, cobreño.

**copperplate** (-pleit) *s.* lámina de cobre; grabado en cobre.

**coppersmith** (-smiz) *s.* calderero.

**coppery** (-i) *adj.* cobrizo, cobreño.

**coppice** (ka·pis), **coppice woods** *s.* bosquecillo, soto. *2* tallar. *3* maleza.

**copra** (ka·pra) *s.* copra.

**copse** (kaps) *s.* COPPICE. *2* matorral.

**Copt** (kapt) *s.* copto.

**Coptic** (ka·ptic) *adj.* cóptico, copto.

**copula** (ka·piula) *s.* GRAM., LÓG. cópula. *2* ANAT. ligamento.

**copulate (to)** (ka·piuleit) *tr.* unir. *2 intr.* copularse.

**copulation** (-lei·shøn) *s.* unión. *2* cópula, ayuntamiento.

**copulative** (-lativ) *adj.* copulativo.

**copy** (ka·pi) *s.* copia, reproducción, imitación. *2* ejemplar [de un libro]; número [de un periódico]. *3* muestra, modelo [para copiar]. *4* IMPR. original, manuscrito. *5 rough* ~, borrador.

**copy (to)** *tr.* copiar. *2* imitar, remedar.

**copybook** (-buk) *s.* cuaderno de escritura. *2 adj.* común, trillado.

**copying** (-ing) *adj.* de copiar. *2 s.* copia, imitación [acción].

**copyist** (-ist) *s.* COPIER.

**copyright** (-rait) *s.* [derechos de] propiedad literaria: ~ *by,* es propiedad de.

**copyright (to)** *tr.* registrar la propiedad literaria de.

**coquet (to)** (kake·t) *intr.* coquetear. ¶ Pret. y p. p.: *coquetted;* ger.: *coquetting.*

**coquetry** (kou·ketri) *s.* coquetería. *2* coqueteo.

**coquette** (koke·t) *s.* coqueta [mujer].

**coquettish** (-ish) *adj.* coqueta. *2* de coqueta, de coquetería.

**coracoid** (ka·rakid) *adj.-s.* ANAT. coracoides.

**coral** (ka·ral) *s.* coral. *2* chupador; sonajero. *3 adj.* de coral, coralino.

**coralline** (-in) *adj.* coralino. *2 s.* BOT., ZOOL. coralina.

**corbel** (ko·ʳbøl) *s.* ARQ. ménsula, repisa, modillón; voladizo. *2* ARQ. zapata.

**corbel (to)** *tr.* ARQ. sostener con ménsulas, etc.; disponer un voladizo. *2 intr.* ARQ. sobresalir, volar.

**corbie** (ko·ʳbi) *s.* BLAS. cuervo.

**cord** (ko·ʳd) *s.* cordón, cordel, bramante. *2* cuerda, dogal. *3* TEJ. . cordoncillo. *4* TEJ. pana. *5* ELECT. flexible. *6* ANAT. cuerda, cordón, tendón. *7 pl.* pantalones de pana.

**cord (to)** *tr.* encordelar. *2* guarnecer con cordón.

**cordage** (-idÿ) *s.* cordaje, cordería.

**cordate** (-eit) *adj.* BOT. acorazonado.

**corded** (-id) *adj.* encordelado. *2* de cuerda. *3* TEJ. que forma cordoncillo.

**cordial** (ko·ʳdÿal o -dial) *adj.* cordial. *2 s.* cordial, licor espirituoso.

**cordiality** (-æ·liti) *s.* cordialidad.

**cordially** (ko·ʳdÿali) *adv.* cordialmente.

**cordite** (ko·ʳdait) *s.* cordita.

**cordon** (-døn) *s.* cordón [para adorno], cíngulo. *2* cordón [de tropa, etc.]. *3* ARQ. cordón.

**Cordova** (ko·ʳdova) *n. pr.* GEOGR. Córdoba.

**Cordovan** (-n) *adj.-s.* cordobés. *2 s.* (con min.) cordobán.

**corduroy** (ko·ʳdiuroi) *s.* TEJ. pana. *2 pl.* pantalones o vestido de pana.

**cordwain** (ko·ʳduein) *s.* cordobán.

**core** (ko·ʳ) *s.* corazón, centro, alma, núcleo, parte interior. *2* substancia, esencia, médula, fondo. *3* corazón [de una fruta, de la madera].

**core (to)** *tr.* quitar el corazón o centro a.

**Corean** (ka·rian) *adj.-s.* coreano.

**coregency** (kouri·dÿønsi) *s.* corregencia.

**coregent** (-dÿønt) *s.* corregente.

**corespondent** (kourispa·ndønt) *s.* cómplice del demandado en una demanda de divorcio por adulterio.

**coriaceous** (koriei·shos) *adj.* coriáceo, correoso.

**coriander** (koriæ·ndøʳ) *s.* BOT. cilantro.

**Corinth** (kori·nz) *n. pr.* GEOGR. Corinto.

**Corinthian** (-ian) *adj.-s.* corintio.

**cork** (ko·ʳk) *s.* corcho. *2* tapón de corcho. *3* BOT. suber. *4* BOT. ~ *oak,* ~ *tree,* alcornoque.

**cork (to)** *tr.* tapar [con corcho], encorchar. *2* tiznar con corcho quemado.

**corking** (-ing) *adj.* fam. estupendo, de primera.

**corkscrew** (-scru) *s.* sacacorchos: ~ *curl,* tirabuzón.

**corky** (-i) *adj.* de corcho; corchoso.

**cormophytic** (ko·ʳmøfitik) *adj.* BOT. cormofita.

**cormorant** (ko·ʳmørant) *s.* ORN. cormorán, cuervo marino. *2* fig. glotón; avaro.

**corn** (ko·ʳn) *s.* grano, trigo, cereal. *2* (E.U.) maíz. *3* mies [no segada]. *4* callo, ojo de gallo: ~ *doctor,* callista. *5* ORN. ~ *crake,* rey de codornices.

**corn (to)** *tr.* salar, curar, acecinar. *2* granular.

**corncob** (-kab) *s.* (E.U.) carozo, zuro [del maíz].

**cornea** (ko·ʳnia) *s.* ANAT. córnea.

**cornel** (ko·ʳnel) *s.* BOT. cornejo.

**cornelian** (ko·ʳnɪ·lian) *s.* MINER. cornalina.

**corneous** (ko·ʳniøs) *adj.* córneo.

**corner** (ko·ʳnøʳ) *s.* ángulo, esquina, esconce, recodo. *2* pico [del sombrero, etc.]. *3* rabillo [del ojo]. *4* cantonera. *5* rincón: ~ *bracket,* ~ *shelf,* rinconera. *6* aprieto, apuro. *7* COM. acaparamiento, monopolio. *8* FÚTBOL córner, saque de esquina.

**corner (to)** *tr.* arrinconar, acorralar, poner en un aprieto. *2* COM. acaparar, monopolizar.

**cornered** (-d) *adj.* que tiene ángulos o picos. *2* acorralado, en un aprieto. *3* acaparado.

**cornerstone** (-stoun) *s.* piedra angular. *2* primera piedra.

**cornet** (ko·ʳne·t) *s.* corneta de llaves, cornetín. *2* cucurucho. *3* toca de las hermanas de la caridad. *4* ant. alférez, portaestandarte. *5* MAR. corneta.

**cornet(t)ist** (-ist) *s.* cornetín [músico].

**cornfield** (ko·ʳnfɪld) *s.* sembrado.

**cornflower** (-flauøʳ) *s.* BOT. aciano, azulejo.

**cornice** (ko·ʳnis) *s.* ARQ. cornisa.

**cornucopia** (ko·ʳniukou·pia) *s.* cornucopia, cuerno de la abundancia.

**cornute(d** (ko·ʳniu·ti(d) *adj.* cornudo.

**Cornwall** (ko·ʳnuol) *n. pr.* GEOGR. Cornualles.

**corny** (ko·ʳni) *adj.* de los callos; con callos [en los pies]. *3* abundante en grano.

**corolla** (kora·la) *s.* BOT. corola.

corollary (ka·røleri) s. corolario.
corona (kørou·na), pl. -nas o -nae (-ni) s. ANAT., ASTR., METEOR. corona. 2 corona [tonsura; rosario].
coronal (-l) adj. coronal. 2 s. ANAT. coronal. 3 corona, guirnalda.
coronary (ka·roneri) adj. coronario.
coronation (karonei·shøn) s. coronación.
coroner (ka·ronøʳ) s. funcionario encargado de investigar, en una especie de juicio, si una muerte ha sido debida a causas naturales o no.
coronet (-ronet) s. corona [de noble]. 2 diadema [adorno]. 3 VET. corona [del casco].
corporal (ko·ʳpøral) adj. corporal. 2 s. LITURG. corporal. 3 MIL. cabo.
corporality (-æ·liti) s. corporalidad.
corporate (ko·ʳporit) adj. conjunto, colectivo, social. 2 constituido legalmente en corporación, sociedad o compañía.
corporation (-ræ·shøn) s. corporación, gremio. 2 COM. sociedad, compañía. 3 ayuntamiento, cabildo.
corporative (ko·ʳporeitiv) adj. corporativo.
corporeal (koʳpou·rial) adj. corpóreo. 2 material, tangible.
corporeity (koʳpoʳ·iti) s. corporeidad.
corposant (ko·ʳpošænt) s. MAR. fuego de Santelmo.
corps (kouʳ) s. cuerpo [agregado de personas].
corpse (køʳps) s. cadáver.
corpulence, -cy (kø·ʳpiuløns, -i) s. corpulencia.
corpulent (-ønt) adj. corpulento.
corpus (ko·ʳpøs) s. cuerpo [de escritos, etc.]. 2 ECLES. Corpus Christi, Corpus, Corpus Cristi.
corpuscle (ko·ʳpøsøl) s. corpúsculo. 2 FISIOL. glóbulo.
corral (køræ·l) s. (E.U.) corral, cercado.
corral (to) tr. (E.U.) acorralar [el ganado].
correct (kore·kt) adj. correcto. 2 exacto, justo.
correct (to) tr. corregir.
correction (køre·kshøn) s. corrección, enmienda. 2 corrección, castigo.
correctional (-al) adj. correccional, penal. 2 s. reformatorio.
correctitude (køre·ktitiud) s. corrección [en la conducta].
corrective (-tive) adj.-s. correctivo.
correctness (-nis) s. corrección [calidad de correcto]; exactitud.
corrector (-øʳ) s. corrector, enmendador.
correlate (to) (ka·røleit) tr. poner en correlación. 2 intr. tener correlación.
correlation (karølei·shøn) s. correlación.
correlative (køre·lativ) adj.-s. correlativo [que tiene correlación].
correspond (to) (karispa·nd) intr. corresponder, corresponderse, responder [tener proporción o analogía, convenir]. 2 corresponderse [escribirse].
correspondence (-øns) s. correspondencia [proporción, analogía, conveniencia]. 2 correspondencia [por escrito].
correspondency (-i) s. CORRESPONDENCE 1.
correspondent (-ønt) adj. correspondiente [análogo, conforme, conveniente]. 2 s. correspondiente; corresponsal.
corresponding (-ing) adj. CORRESPONDENT 1. 2 correspondiente [que corresponde por escrito].
corridor (ka·ridøʳ) s. corredor, pasillo.
corrigible (ka·ridȳibøl) adj. corregible.
corroborant (køra·børant) adj.-s. corroborante.
corroborate (to) (-eit) tr. corroborar, confirmar.

corroboration (-ei·shøn) s. corroboración.
corroborative (køra·børativ) adj. corroborativo. 2 adj.-s. corroborante, tónico.
corrode (to) (kørou·d) tr. corroer; roer. 2 intr. corroerse.
corrodent (-ønt) adj.-s. CORROSIVE.
corrosion (kørou·ȳøn) s. corrosión.
corrosive (-siv) adj.-s. corrosivo.
corrugate (to) (ka·rugeit) tr. arrugar, contraer. 2 plegar, ondular.
corrugate(d (-id) adj. arrugado; ondulado.
corrupt (køra·pt) adj. corrupto. 2 corrompido. 3 adulterado [texto].
corrupt (to) tr. corromper. 2 adulterar, falsear. 3 intr. corromperse.
corrupter (-øʳ) s. corruptor, corrompedor.
corruptible (-ibøl) adj. corruptible.
corruption (køra·pshøn) s. corrupción.
corruptless (køra·ptlis) adj. incorruptible.
corruptress (-ris) s. corruptora.
corsage (ko·ʳsidȳ) s. cuerpo [de vestido], corpiño.
corsair (-eʳ) s. corsario. 2 buque corsario.
corselet (ko·ʳslit) s. coselete. 2 especie de corsé ligero.
corset (-sit) s. corés: ~ cover, cubrecorsé.
corset (to) tr. encorsetar.
Corsica (-sika) n. pr. GEOGR. Córcega.
Corsican (-n) adj.-s. corso [de Córcega].
corslet (ko·ʳslit) s. CORSELET 1.
cortege (-teȳ) s. comitiva, cortejo, séquito.
cortical (-tikal) adj. cortical.
cortisone (-šon) s. cortisona.
corundum (korø·ndøm) s. MINER. corindón.
coruscate (to) (ko·røskeit) intr. coruscar, brillar.
corvette (koʳve·t) s. MAR. corbeta.
corvine (ko·ʳvain) adj. ZOOL. córvido.
corybant (ko·ribant) s. coribante.
corymb (ko·rim) s. BOT. corimbo.
coryphaeus (korifɪ·øs) s. corifeo.
coryphée (ko·rifei·) s. primera bailarina.
coryza (kørai·ša) s. MED. coriza.
cosecant (kousɪ·kant) s. TRIG. cosecante.
cosher (-shøʳ) tr. mimar, regalar.
cosily (-šili) adv. cómodamente, confortablemente.
cosine (kou·sain) s. TRIG. coseno.
cosmetic (kašme·tik) adj.-s. cosmético.
cosmic(al (ka·šmik(al) adj. cósmico. 2 vasto, grandioso. 3 ordenado, armónico.
cosmogony (kašma·goni) s. cosmogonía.
cosmographer (-graføʳ) s. cosmógrafo.
cosmography (-grafi) s. cosmografía.
cosmology (-lodȳi) s. cosmología.
cosmonaut (ka·šmønot) s. cosmonauta.
cosmopolitan (-møpa·litan) adj.-s. cosmopolita.
cosmopolitanism, cosmopolitism (-išm) s. cosmopolitismo.
cosmopolite (-ma·pølait) adj.-s. COSMOPOLITAN.
cosmos (ka·smøs) s. cosmos.
Cossack (ka·sæk) adj.-s. cosaco.
cosset (ka·sit) s. cordero favorito.
cosset (to) tr. acariciar, mimar.
cost (kost) s. coste, costo, costa, precio, expensas: at all costs, at any ~, a toda costa. 2 DER. costas.
cost (to) intr. costar, valer.
costal (ka·stal) adj. ANAT. costal.
costard (ka·staʳd) s. variedad de manzana. 2 fam. chola.
coster (monger (kastøʳ(møngøʳ) s. vendedor ambulante de frutas, pescado, etc.
costive (ka·stiv) adj. estreñido. 2 fig. agarrado.

**costiveness** (-nis) *s.* estreñimiento.

**costliness** (kóstlinis) *s.* suntuosidad.

**costly** (kó·stli) *adj.* costoso, caro. *2* suntuoso.

**costmary** (ka·stmeri) *s.* BOT. atanasia.

**costume** (ka·stium) *s.* traje, vestido. *2* traje de época, disfraz: ~ *ball*, baile de trajes. *3 pl.* TEAT. vestuario.

**costume (to)** *tr.* vestir; disfrazar.

**costumer** (-ǿr), **-mier** (ɪ·ǿr) *s.* sastre de teatro.

**cosy** (kou·ši) *adj.* cómodo, agradable. *2* contento, satisfecho. *3* (Ingl.) hablador, sociable.

**cot** (kat) *s.* choza. *2* catre, coy, camita. *3* sitio para animales domésticos.

**cotangent** (koutæ·ndỹønt) *s.* TRIG. cotangente.

**cote** (kout) *s.* corral, aprisco. *2* COT *3*.

**coterie** (kou·tøri) *s.* tertulia, corrillo.

**cothurnus** (kozø·ʳnøs) *s.* coturno.

**cotill(i)on** (koti·liøn) *s.* cotillón.

**cotise** (ka·tis) *s.* BLAS. cotiza.

**cottage** (ka·tidỹ) *s.* cabaña, casita. *2* hotelito; casita de campo. *3* ~ *cheese*, requesón.

**cottager** (-ǿr) *s.* el que vive en un COTTAGE. *2* campesino, labrador.

**cotter** (ka·tǿr) *s.* MEC. chaveta, pasador.

**cotton** *s.* algodón: ~ *powder*, algodón pólvora; ~ *wool*, algodón en rama. *2* BOT. algodonero. *3* BOT. pelusa. *4* BOT. ~ *thistle*, cardo borriquero. *5* BOT. ~ *trez*, chopo; ceiba. *6 pl.* géneros de algodón.

**cotton (to)** *tr.* algodonar. *2* mimar. *3 intr.* avenirse, hacer buenas migas. *4* tomar cariño.

**cottonwood** (-wud) *s.* BOT. chopo americano.

**cottony** (-i) *adj.* algodonoso.

**cotyledon** (katiɾ·døn) *s.* BOT. cotiledón.

**couch** (kauch) *s.* cama, lecho, yacija. *2* canapé, meridiana. *3* capa, tonga. *4* madriguera. *5* BOT. ~ *grass*, grama del Norte.

**couch (to)** *tr.* acostar, tender. *2* poner en capas. *3* incrustar, bordar. *4* expresar [con palabras]. *5* bajar, agachar. *6* calar, enristrar [una pica, lanza, etc.]. *7* MED. batir [las cataratas]. *8 intr.* acostarse, tenderse. *9* agacharse. *10* esconderse, estar al acecho.

**couchant** (-ənt) *adj.* BLAS. acostado.

**cougar** (ku·gaʳ) *s.* ZOOL. puma, jaguar.

**cough** (kof) *s.* tos. *2* carraspeo.

**cough (to)** *intr.* toser. *2* carraspear. *3* expectorar.

**coughing** (-ing) *s.* tos, tosidura.

**could** (cud) *pret.* del *aux.* CAN.

**coulisse** (kulɪ·s) *s.* corredera [ranura]. *2* TEAT. bastidor; entre bastidores.

**coulomb** (kula·m) *s.* ELECT. culombio.

**coulter** (kou·ltǿr) *s.* COLTER.

**council** (kau·nsil) *s.* concilio. *2* consejo, junta. *3* ayuntamiento, concejo.

**councilman** (-mæn) *s.* concejal.

**council(l)or** (-ǿr) *s.* consejero [de un consejo]. *2* concejal.

**counsel** (kau·nsøl) *s.* consejo, parecer; deliberación, consulta. *2* designio, pensamiento: *to keep one's own* ~, callar lo que uno piensa o se propone. *3* asesor; abogado; abogados que asesoran o defienden a uno.

**counsel (to)** *tr.* aconsejar; asesorar.

**counsel(l)or** (-ǿr) *s.* consejero. *2* consiliario. *3* abogado.

**count** (kaunt) *s.* cuenta, cuento, cálculo, cómputo. *2* contaje. *3* suma, total. *4* conde [no inglés].

**count (to)** *tr.* contar, numerar, computar. *2* considerar, tener por. *3 intr.* contar [formar cuentas]. *4* ser tenido en cuenta, valer. *5 to* ~ *on*, contar con, confiar en.

**countenance** (kau·ntǿnans) *s.* cara, rostro, semblante, expresión del rostro; serenidad: *to change (one's)* ~, demudarse; *to keep one's* ~, no alterarse, no inmutarse, no reírse; *to put out of* ~, turbar, desconcertar. *2* favor, apoyo, aprobación: *to give* ~ *to*, TO COUNTENANCE.

**countenance (to)** *tr.* favorecer, apoyar, aprobar, alentar.

**counter** (kau·ntǿr) *s.* ficha, tanto. *2* contador, computador. *3* contador, mostrador [mesa]. *4* MAR. bovedilla. *5* ZAP. contrafuerte. *6* ESGR. contra. *7* 'lo opuesto. *8 adv.* contrariamente, contra.

**counter (to)** *tr.* oponerse a. *2 intr.* devolver un golpe; responder [a una pregunta, etc.] con otra.

**counteract** (-æ·ct) *tr.* contrarrestar, neutralizar.

**counterattack** (-ɑtæ·k) *s.* contraataque.

**counterattack (to)** *tr.-intr.* contraatacar.

**counterbalance** (-bæ·lans) *s.* contrabalanza, contrapeso; compensación.

**counterbalance (to)** *tr.* contrabalancear, contrapesar; compensar.

**countercheck** (-che·k) *s.* oposición, rechazo. *2* segunda comprobación.

**countercheck (to)** *tr.* resistir, contrarrestar. *2* comprobar por segunda vez.

**countercurrent** (-cǿrønt) *s.* contracorriente.

**counterdie** (-dai) *s.* contramatriz, punzón.

**counterdike** (-daik) *s.* contradique.

**counterespionage** (-e·spiønidỹ) *s.* contraespionaje.

**counterfeit** (-fit) *adj.* falso, contrahecho. *2* fingido. *3 s.* falsificación, imitación; moneda falsa.

**counterfeit (to)** *tr.* falsificar, contrahacer. *2* fingir, simular.

**counterfeiter** (-ǿr) *s.* falsario, falsificador. *2* simulador.

**counterfoil** (-foil) *s.* matriz [de un cheque, etc.].

**counterfort** (-foʳt) *s.* ARQ. contrafuerte.

**counterfugue** (-fiu·g) *s.* MÚS. contrafuga.

**counterindication** (-indiei·shøn) *s.* MED. contraindicación.

**counterlight** (-lait) *s.* contraluz.

**countermand** (-mænd) *s.* contraorden.

**countermand (to)** *tr.* contramandar.

**countermarch** (-maʳch) *s.* contramarcha.

**countermarch (to)** *intr.* contramarchar.

**countermark** (-maʳk) *s.* contramarca.

**countermark (to)** *tr.* contramarcar.

**countermine** (-main) *s.* contramina.

**countermine (to)** *tr.* contraminar.

**counteroffensive** (-ofe·nsiv) *s.* contraofensiva.

**counteroffer** (-ofǿr) *s.* contraoferta.

**counterpane** (-pein) *s.* colcha, cobertor.

**counterpart** (-paʳt) *s.* duplicado, trasunto, imagen. *2* parte que corresponde a otra. *3* MÚS. contrapaso.

**counterpoint** (-point) *s.* MÚS. contrapunto.

**counterpoise** (-poiš) *s.* contrapeso. *2* equilibrio.

**counterpoise (to)** *tr.* contrapesar, equilibrar.

**counterpunch** (-pønch) *s.* contrapunzón.

**Counter Reformation** *s.* Contrarreforma.

**counterrevolution** (-røvoliu·shøn) *s.* contrarrevolución.

**counterscarp** (-skaʳp) *s.* FORT. contraescarpa.

**countersign** (-sain) *s.* refrendata. *2* MIL. contraseña.

**countersign (to)** *tr.* refrendar, visar.

**countersink** (-si·nk) *s.* MEC. avellanador. *2* MEC. avellanado.

**countersink (to)** *tr.* MEC. avellanar. ¶ Pret. y p.p.: *countersunk.*

**countersunk** (-sønk) *adj.* MEC. avellanado. *2* MEC. de cabeza embutida.
**countervail (to)** (-veil) *tr.* contrapesar, equivaler. *2* contrarrestar.
**counterweigh (to)** (-uel) *tr.* contrapesar.
**counterweight** (-ueit) *s.* contrapeso, pesa.
**counterwork (to)** (-uøᶠk) *tr.* contrarrestar.
**countess** (kau·ntis) *s.* condesa.
**countinghouse** (kau·ntinjaus) *s.* COM. despacho, escritorio, oficina.
**countless** (kau·ntlis) *adj.* incontable, innumerable, sin cuento.
**countrified** (kø·ntrifaid) *adj.* rural, campesino.
**country** (kø·ntri) *s.* país, nación, región, comarca. *2* tierra, patria. *3* campo, campiña. *4* *adj.* del campo, rural, campestre, campesino.
**country-dance** *s.* contradanza.
**countryfolk** (-fouk) *s.* gente del campo. *2* lugareños. *3* paisanos, compatricios.
**countryman** (-mæn) *s.* compatriota, paisano. *2* campesino, aldeano.
**countryseat** (-sıt) *s.* residencia señorial en el campo.
**countryside** (-said) *s.* campo, campiña. *2* distrito rural.
**county** (kau·nti) *s.* condado. *2* distrito, provincia.
**coup** (cu) *s.* golpe maestro.
**coupé** (kupei·) *s.* cupé.
**couple** (kø·pøl) *s.* par, pareja. *2* lo que une dos cosas; trailla.
**couple (to)** *tr.* aparear, emparejar. *2* unir, acoplar, conectar, enganchar. *3* *intr.* aparearse.
**couplet** (kø·plit) *s.* pareado. *2* copla, cuplé.
**coupon** (ku·pan) *s.* cupón.
**courage** (kø·ridỹ) *s.* coraje, valor, ánimo, denuedo.
**courageous** (kørei·dỹøs) *adj.* valeroso, valiente, animoso, denodado.
**courier** (ku·riøᶠ) *s.* correo, mensajero, expreso.
**course** (koᶠs) *s.* curso, marcha. *2* camino, trayecto, recorrido. *3* rumbo, derrotero. *4* MAR. rumbo. *5* MAR. punto del compás. *6* serie, curso [de los sucesos]; curso, transcurso [del tiempo]. *7* salida, circulación, expansión. *8* línea [de conducta]. *9* carrera [en la vida]. *10* curso [de estudios], asignatura. *11* DEP. pista, campo. *12* plato, servicio [de una comida]. *13* capa, tongada. *14* ALBAÑ. hilada. *15* MIN. galería. *16* MAR. papahigo. *17* *pl.* regla, menstruo. *18* *adv.* *of* ~, naturalmente, desde luego, por supuesto.
**course (to)** *tr.* correr por. *2* hacer correr. *3* dar caza, perseguir. *4* *intr.* correr. *5* corretear.
**courser** (-øᶠ) *s.* cazador. *2* perro corredor. *3* corcel.
**court** (koᶠt) *s.* patio; atrio. *2* callejón sin salida; plazuela cerrada. *3* pista [de tenis, etc.]. *4* corte [de un soberano]. *5* corte [que se hace a una pers.]. *6* estrados, sala de justicias. *7* tribunal. *8* consejo superior. *9* ~ *card*, figura [de la baraja]. *10* ~ *plaster*, tafetán inglés.
**court (to)** *tr.* cortejar. *2* galantear. *3* solicitar, buscar.
**courteous** (kø·ᶠtiøs) *adj.* cortés, atento.
**courteously** (-li) *adv.* cortésmente.
**courtesan** (kou·ᶠtiśan) *s.* cortesana.
**courtesy** (kø·ᶠtisi) *s.* cortesía, urbanidad. *2* amabilidad, fineza, atención. *3* favor, gracia.
**courtier** (kø·ᶠtiøᶠ) *s.* cortesano, palaciego.
**courtlike** (-laik) *adj.* cortesano, elegante.
**courtly** (-li) *adj.* cortesano. *2* elegante, refinado. *3* obsequioso, adulador. *4* *adv.* cortésmente.
**court-martial** *s.* consejo de guerra.
**courtship** (-ship) *s.* cortejo, galanteo. *2* noviazgo.

**courtyard** (-iaᶠd) *s.* patio.
**couscous** (kusku·s) *s.* alcuzcuz.
**cousin** (kø·śøn) *s.* primo, prima: ~ *german*, primo hermano, prima hermana.
**cove** (kouv) *s.* abra, ancón, cala, ensenada. *2* ARQ. miembro cóncavo. *3* *fam.* tipo, individuo.
**cove (to)** *tr.* ARQ. abovedar.
**covenant** (kø·vønant) *s.* convenio, pacto; contrato. *2* BIB. alianza, testamento.
**covenant (to)** *tr.* pactar, estipular. *2* *intr.* pactar, convenirse.
**covenanter** (-øᶠ) *s.* pactante, contratante. *2* presbiteriano escocés.
**cover** (kø·vøᶠ) *s.* tapa, tapadera, cobertera. *2* cubierta, envoltura, funda, forro. *3* sobre, sobrecarta. *4* ENCUAD. tapa, cubierta. *5* portada [de una revista]. *6* tapete, cobertor. *7* abrigo, refugio, cubierto, techado, albergue. *8* *fig.* pantalla, velo. *9* capa, pretexto. *10* cubierto [servicio de mesa]. *11* huidero [de la caza], maleza. *12* COM. provisión de fondos. *13* *under* ~ *of*, a favor de [la oscuridad, etc.]; so pretexto de.
**cover (to)** *tr.* cubrir, tapar. *2* recubrir, revestir, forrar. *3* abrigar, arropar. *4* proteger, resguardar. *5* MIL. cubrir [la retirada]. *6* empollar [huevos]. *7* tapar, ocultar, disimular, encubrir. *8* comprender, abarcar, incluir. *9* recorrer [una distancia]. *10* COM. cubrir [gastos, riesgos, etc.]. *11* ARTILL., FORT. dominar [un espacio]. *12* apuntar [a uno] con un arma. *13* cubrir, fecundar. *14* *intr.* cubrirse. *15* COM. hacer provisión de fondos.
**coverage** (-idỹ) *s.* cantidad o espacio cubiertos. *2* riesgos que cubre una póliza de seguro. *3* cobertura [del papel moneda].
**covering** (-ing) *s.* acción de cubrir. *2* cubierta, techado. *3* cubierta, envoltura, ropa, abrigo. *4* tegumento.
**coverlet** (-lit), **coverlid** (-lid) *tr.* tapete. *2* colcha, cobertor.
**coversed sine** (kou·vøᶠst sain) *s.* MAT. coseno verso.
**covert** (kø·vøᶠt) *adv.* cubierto, abrigado. *2* escondido, secreto. *3* encubierto, disimulado. *4* *s.* abrigo, refugio. *5* ORN. cobija [pluma].
**coverture** (-chøᶠ) *s.* abrigo, defensa.
**covet (to)** (kø·vit) *tr.* codiciar, desear, ambicionar.
**covetous** (-øs) *adj.* codicioso.
**covetousness** (-nis) *s.* codicia, avidez.
**covey** (kø·vi) *s.* nidada, pollada. *2* bandada.
**cow** (kau) *s.* ZOOL. vaca. *2* ZOOL. hembra del alce, la foca, etc.
**cow (to)** *tr.* acobardar, amilanar.
**coward** (kau·aᶠd) *adj.-s.* cobarde.
**cowardice** (-is) *s.* cobardía.
**cowardly** (-li) *adj.* cobarde, pusilánime. *2* *adv.* cobardemente.
**cowbell** (-bel) *s.* cencerro.
**cowboy** (-boi) *s.* (E.U.) vaquero, jinete vaquero.
**cower (to)** (-øᶠ) *intr.* agacharse [por miedo o frío].
**cowhide** (-jaid) *s.* cuero [de vaca o toro]. *2* zurriago de cuero, rebenque.
**cowhide (to)** *tr.* azotar, zurriagar.
**cowl** (kaul) *s.* cogulla. *2* capucha, capucho. *3* sombrerete [de chimenea]. *4* AUTO. bóveda del tablero. *5* AVIA. cubierta del motor.
**cowled** (-d) *adj.* encapuchado.
**cowlick** (kau·lik) *s.* remolino [de cabellos].
**cowling** (-ling) *s.* COWL 5.
**cowpox** (-paks) *s.* vacuna [de vaca].
**cowslip** (-slip) *s.* BOT. primavera. *2* BOT. (E.U.) hierba centella.
**coxa** (ka·ksa) *s.* ANAT. cadera. *2* ENT. coxa.

**coxal** (-l) *adj.* coxal.
**coxcomb** (ka·kskoum) *s.* petimetre, presumido, fatuo. *2* gorro de bufón. *3* BOT. moco de pavo.
**coxcombry** (-ri) *s.* fatuidad, presunción.
**coxswain** (ka·ksuein) *s.*MAR. nostramo. *2* patrón de un bote de regatas.
**coy** (koi), **coyish** (-ish) *adj.* recatada, tímida, esquiva; que se hace la tímida o esquiva.
**coyness** (-nis) *s.* modestia, timidez; afectación de modestia o timidez.
**coyote** (kaiou·ti) *s.* ZOOL. coyote.
**coz** (kaš) *s.* fam. primo, prima.
**cozen** (ka·søn) *tr.* engañar, estafar.
**cozenage** (-idȳ) *s.* engaño, estafa.
**cozy** (kou·ši) *adj.* COSY.
**crab** (kræb) *s.* ZOOL. cámbaro, cangrejo de mar. *2* ENT. *crab* o ~ *louse*, ladilla. *3* cascarrabias. *4* MEC. molinete; carro de grúa. *5* *adj.* agrio, avinagrado. *6* BOT. ~ *apple*, manzana silvestre.
**crab (to)** *tr.* censurar, agriamente. ¶ Pret. y p. p.: *crabbed;* ger.: *-bbing.*
**crabbed** (-id) *adj.* gruñón, avinagrado. *2* obscuro, enrevesado. *3* irregular, apretada [letra].
**crabby** (-i) *adj.* CRABBED 1 y 2.
**crack** (kræk) *s.* crujido, chasquido, restallido; estampido: *the* ~ *of doom*, el juicio final. *2* fam. golpe seco. *3* fam. instante. *4* rotura, hendidura, grieta, raja, rendija. *5* bronquedad [de la voz cuando se muda]. *6* tornillo flojo, chifladura. *7* *adj.* fam. de primera.
**crack (to)** *intr.* crujir, restallar. *2* reventar, estallar, rajarse, resquebrajarse, agrietarse, cuartearse: *to* ~ *up*, fracasar; arruinarse; estrellarse. *3* cascarse, enronquecerse [la voz]. *4* fam. volverse loco. *5* *tr.* romper, rajar, hender, resquebrajar. *6* trastornar, enloquecer. *7* hacer restallar. *8* QUÍM. someter a destilación fraccionada. *9* fam. *to* ~ *a bottle*, beber una botella. *10* fam. *to* ~ *jokes*, hacer chistes, bromear. *11* *to* ~ *up*, elogiar, bombear; estrellar.
**crackbrain** (-brein) *s.* chiflado, medio loco.
**cracker** (-øʳ) *s.* petardo, triquitraque. *2* especie de galleta. *3* *pl.* cascanueces.
**crackle** (-øl) *s.* crujido, chasquido, crepitación. *2* B. ART. superficie finamente agrietada.
**crackle (to)** *intr.* crujir, chasquear, crepitar.
**crackling** (-ing) *s.* CRACKLE 1. *2* corteza de tocino asada. *3* chicharrón.
**cracknel** (-nøl) *s.* galletita crujiente. *2* chicharrón.
**crackpot** (-pat) *s.* pop. chiflado.
**cracksman** (-mæn) *s.* pop. BURGLAR.
**crack-up** (øp) *m.* hundimiento [físico o mental]. *2* AVIA. aterrizaje violento.
**cracky** (-i) *adj.* rajado. *2* que se raja fácilmente.
**Cracow** (krei·kou) *s.* GEOGR. Cracovia.
**cradle** (-døl) *s.* cuna [para niños; niñez,origen]. *2* armazón, soporte, etc., en forma de cuna. *3* TELÉF. horquilla. *4* MAR. cuna, basada. *5* andamio colgante. *6* MIN. artesa oscilante.
**cradle (to)** *tr.* acunar, mecer. *2* poner o tener en una cuna. *3* *intr.* estar en la cuna.
**craft** (kraft) *s.* arte, destreza. *2* oficio, profesión; gremio. *3* artificio, astucia, artería. *4* treta, maña. *5* embarcación; embarcaciones.
**craftiness** (-inis) *s.* astucia, artería.
**craftsman** (-smæn) *s.* artesano. *2* artífice.
**craftsmanship** (-ship) *s.* arte, habilidad [en un oficio]. *2* artesanía.
**crafty** (kra·fti) *adj.* astuto, artero, artificioso.
**crag** (kræg) *s.* risco, despeñadero.

**cragged** (-id), **craggy** (-i) *adj.* escarpado, riscoso, áspero, fragoso.
**crake** (kreik) *s.* ORN. rey de codornices. *2* ORN. rascón.
**cram** (kræm) *s.* apretura; atiborramiento. *2* atracón. *3* preparación [para exámenes]. *4* CRAMMER.
**cram (to)** *tr.* henchir, atestar, atiborrar. *2* atracar [de comida]. *3* meter apretando o llenando, embutir. *4* fam. preparar [para exámenes]. *5* *intr.* atracarse [de comida]. *6* fam. estudiar, empollar [para aprender en poco tiempo]. ¶ Pret. y p. p.: *crammed;* ger.: *cramming.*
**crambo** (-bou) *s.* juego de hallar consonantes.
**crammer** (-øʳ) *s.* preparador [para exámenes]. *2* pop. mentira.
**cramp** (kræmp) *s.* calambre, rampa. *2* laña, grapa. *3* MEC. CLAMP 1 y 2. *4* fig. aprieto, estrechez. *5* fig. sujeción, traba.
**cramp (to)** *tr.* dar calambres; entumecer. *2* fig. restringir, trabar. *3* apretar, sujetar; engrapar.
**cramp-iron** *s.* laña, grapa.
**crampon** (kræmpøn) *s.* BOT. raicilla aérea. *2* gancho para trepar. *3* pieza con puntas para andar sobre el hielo. *4* *pl.* tenazas de garfios [para elevar piedras, etc.].
**cranberry** (kræ·nberi) *s.* BOT. arándano agrio.
**crane** (krein) *s.* ORN. grulla. *2* MEC. grúa, árgana. *3* MAR. abanico. *4* brazo o pescante giratorio. *5* sifón, cantimplora.
**crane (to)** *tr.* levantar con grúa. *2* estirar [el cuello]. *3* *intr.* estirar el cuello [para ver mejor].
**crane-fly** *s.* ENT. típula.
**crane's-bill** *s.* BOT. variedad de geranio.
**cranial** (krei·nial) *adj.* craneal.
**cranium** (-niøm) *s.* ANAT. cráneo.
**crank** (kræŋk) *s.* MEC. cigüeña, manubrio, manivela; codo, palomilla. *2* fantasía, capricho, humorada. *3* maniático, chiflado. *4* *adj.* CRANKY.
**crank (to)** *tr.* doblar, acodar. *2* mover, etc., con manivela.
**crankcase** (-keis) *s.* MEC. cárter de cigüeñal.
**crankle** (kræ·nkøl) *s.* recodo, repliegue, vuelta.
**crankle (to)** *intr.* serpentear, zigzaguear.
**crankshaft** (-shæft) *s.* MEC. cigüeñal.
**cranky** (-i) *adj.* chiflado, estrafalario. *2* irritable. *3* caprichoso, raro. *4* inseguro, desvencijado. *5* torcido, sinuoso.
**crannied** (kræ·ni) *adj.* grietoso.
**cranny** (kræ·ni) *s.* grieta, hendedura, rendija. *2* rincón, hueco.
**crape** (kreip) *s.* crespón.
**craps** (kræps) *s.* juego de dados.
**crapulence** (kræ·piuløns) *s.* crápula, intemperancia.
**crash** (kræsh) *s.* estallido, estampido, estrépito [de cosas que chocan o se rompen]. *2* caída, choque, acción de estrellarse. *3* COM. quiebra, bancarrota.
**crash (to)** *tr.* romper, estrellar. *2* poner, mover, hacer chocar, etc., con estrépito. *3* *intr.* estallar, romperse, chocar, estrellarse. *4* COM. quebrar, hacer bancarrota.
**crass** (kræs) *adj.* espeso, basto, grosero. *2* craso, estúpido.
**crassitude** (kræ·sitiud), **crassness** (-nis) *s.* grosería, tosquedad; estupidez.
**crassulaceous** (kræsiulei·shøs) *adj.* BOT. crasuláceo.
**Crassus** (krøsøs) *n. pr.* Craso.
**crate** (kreit) *s.* canasta, banasta. *2* cesta o embalaje de listones.

**crater** (krei·tø<sup>r</sup>) *s.* cráter. *2* crátera. *3* (con may.) ASTR. Copa, Cráter.

**craunch (to)** (kronch) *tr.* TO CRUNCH.

**cravat** (krəvæ·t) *s.* corbata, pañuelo para el cuello.

**crave (to)** (kreiv) *tr.* pedir, implorar. *2* ansiar, anhelar. *3 intr. to* ~ *after* o *for*, pedir, implorar; ansiar, anhelar.

**craven** (-vøn) *adj.-s.* cobarde. *2 to cry* ~, rendirse.

**craving** (-ving) *s.* deseo, anhelo, ansia, sed.

**craw** (cro) *s.* buche.

**crawfish** (cro·fish) *s.* ZOOL. langosta [de mar].

**crawl** (kro·l) *s.* reptación, arrastramiento; marcha lenta. *2* crol [modo de nadar]. *3* criadero de tortugas.

**crawl (to)** *intr.* reptar, arrastrarse; gatear. *2* fig. arrastrarse servilmente. *3* andar o moverse lentamente. *4* nadar haciendo el crol. *5* sentir hormigueo. *6 to* ~ *with*, estar lleno de [cosas que bullen u hormiguean].

**crawler** (-ø<sup>r</sup>) *s.* reptil. *2* planta rastrera. *3* MEC. tractor de oruga.

**crayfish** (krei·fish) *s.* CRAWFISH.

**crayon** (-øn) *s.* DIB. barrita de lápiz, pastel, etc. *2* dibujo al lápiz, pastel, etc. *3* ELECT. carbón.

**crayon (to)** *tr.* dibujar al lápiz, pastel, etc. *2* fig. esbozar, planear.

**craze** (kreiš) *s.* manía, antojo, chifladura, moda. *2* locura, demencia. *3* resquebrajadura [de un barniz o esmalte].

**craze (to)** *tr.* trastornar [el juicio]; enloquecer. *2* resquebrajar finamente el barniz de. *3 intr.* volverse loco. *4* resquebrajarse finamente [un barniz].

**crazed** (-d) *s.* loco. *2* lleno de pequeñas resquebrajaduras.

**crazy** (-i) *adj.* agrietado, roto, cascado, desvencijado, ruinoso. *3* loco, insensato. *4* extravagante. *5* fig. loco [por].

**creak (to)** (krik) *intr.* crujir, rechinar, chirriar.

**creaking** (-ing) *s.* crujido, rechinamiento, chirrido. *2 adj.* CREAKY.

**creaky** (-i) *adj.* crujiente, rechinante, chirriante.

**cream** (krim) *s.* crema, nata [de la leche]. *2* fig, flor, flor y nata. *3* crema [cosmético]. *4* COC. crema [sopa]. *5* ~ *of tartar*, crémor tártaro.

**cream (to)** *intr.* criar nata. *2 tr.* desnatar. *3* preparar con nata.

**creamery** (-øri) *s.* lechería, mantequería.

**creamy** (-i) *s.* cremoso. *2* fig. meloso.

**crease** (kris) *s.* pliegue, doblez, arruga. *2* raya [del pantalón].

**crease (to)** *tr.* plegar, doblar, arrugar. *2* ENC. filetear. *3 intr.* arrugarse.

**creasy** (-i) *adj.* arrugado, lleno de arrugas.

**create (to)** (kriei·t) *tr.* crear, criar [producir Dios de la nada]. *2* crear [en los demás sentidos]. *3* producir, causar. *4* hacer [conde, marqués, etc.].

**creation** (-shøn) *s.* creación [acción; cosa creada]. *2* la creación, el universo. *3* acción de hacer conde, marqués, etc.

**creative** (-tiv) *adj.* creador.

**creativeness** (-nis) *s.* facultad creadora, inventiva.

**creator** (kriei·tø<sup>r</sup>) *s.* creador. *2 The Creator*, el Creador, Dios.

**creatress** (-tris) *s.* creadora.

**creature** (kri·chø<sup>r</sup>) *s.* criatura [cosa creada]. *2* hechura, instrumento [de otro]. *3* ser viviente. *4* individuo, persona [a veces desp.].

**crèche** (kresh) *s.* nacimiento, belén. *2* casa cuna.

**credence** (kri·døns) *s.* creencia, crédito, fe. *2* credencia.

**credential** (kride·nshal) *adj.* credencial. *2 s. pl.* credenciales.

**credibility** (kredibi·liti) *s.* credibilidad.

**credible** (kre·dibøl) *adj.* creíble, creedero.

**credit** (-dit) *s.* crédito, asenso, fe. *2* autoridad [para ser creído]. *3* crédito, buena reputación. *4* influencia, valimiento. *5* honor, honra, lo que honra o enaltece. *6* COM. crédito: *on* ~, a crédito, al fiado. *7* COM. haber. *8* fig. *to give someone* ~ *for*, atribuir a uno [una cualidad, etc.].

**credit (to)** *tr.* dar crédito a, creer. *2* COM. acreditar, abonar. *3 to* ~ *someone with*, atribuir a uno [una cualidad, etc.].

**creditable** (-abøl) *adj.* loable, honroso, meritorio.

**creditor** (-ø<sup>r</sup>) *s.* acreedor. *2* COM. haber, partida del haber.

**Credo** (kri·dou) *s.* LITÚRG., MÚS. credo.

**credulity** (krediu·liti) *s.* credulidad.

**creed** (krid) *s.* credo [símbolo; conjunto de doctrinas]. *2* creencia, religión.

**creek** (krik) *s.* abra o cala estrecha. *2* (E.U.) ría; riachuelo. *3* rincón, recodo.

**creel** (kril) *s.* cesta de pescador. *2* TEJ. fileta.

**creep** (krip) *s.* arrastramiento, deslizamiento. *2 pl. the creeps*, hormigueo, escalofrío, horror.

**creep (to)** *intr.* arrastrarse, serpear, gatear; correr [los insectos]; extenderse, trepar [las plantas rastreras o trepadoras]. *2* deslizarse, insinuarse; penetrar, invadir, acercarse, entrar, salir, etc., lenta, insensible o furtivamente. | Gralte. con *in, out, on* o *upon*. *3* fig. arrastrarse servilmente. *4* sentir hormigueo, escalofrío. *5* MAR. rastrear. ¶ Pret. y p. p.: *crept*.

**creeper** (-ø<sup>r</sup>) *s.* lo que se arrastra, insecto, reptil. *2* BOT. enredadera. *3* ORN. nombre de varios pájaros. *4* garabato, arpeo.

**creepy** (-i) *adj.* lento. *2* que produce hormigueo o escalofrío; que lo siente.

**creese** (kris) *s.* cris [arma].

**cremate (to)** (kri·meit) *tr.* incinerar.

**cremation** (krimei·shøn) *s.* cremación, incineración.

**crematory** (kri·matori) *s.* horno crematorio.

**crenate(d** (kri·neit(id) *adj.* BOT. festeoneado.

**crenel(l)ate(d** (kre·nøleit(id) *adj.* almenado. *2* BOT. festeoneado.

**creole** (kri·oul) *adj.-s.* criollo.

**creosote** (kri·osout) *s.* QUÍM. creosota.

**crepe, crêpe** (kreip) *s.* TEJ. crespón.

**crepitate (to)** (kre·piteit) *intr.* crepitar. *2* chirriar, chisporrotear [al fuego].

**crepitation** (-ei·shøn) *s.* crepitación. *2* chisporroteo.

**crept** (krept) *pret.* y *p. p.* de TO CREEP.

**crepuscular** (krepø·skiula<sup>r</sup>) *adj.* crepuscular.

**crepuscle** (-kiul) *s.* crepúsculo.

**crescendo** (kreše·ndou) *adv.-s.* MÚS. crescendo.

**crescent** (kre·sønt) *adj.* creciente. *2 s.* media luna. *3* cosa en figura de media luna. *4* creciente [de la luna]; luna creciente.

**cress** (kres) *s.* BOT. lepidio, mastuerzo.

**cresset** (kre·sit) *s.* fogaril, tedero. *2* fig. tea, antorcha.

**crest** (krest) *s.* cresta. *2* penacho, copete. *3* crestón. *4* cimera. *5* BLAS. timbre. *6* cima, cumbre. *7* fig. coraje; orgullo.

**crest (to)** *tr.* coronar, cubrir. *2* alcanzar la cresta de. *2* BLAS. timbrar. *4 intr.* erguirse. *5* encresparse [las olas].

**crested lark** (-id) *s.* ORN. cochevís, cogujada.
**crestfallen** (fɔløn) *adj.* cabizbajo, abatido, alicaído.
**cretaceous** (kritei·shøs) *adj.* cretáceo.
**Cretan** (krɪ·tan) *adj.-s.* cretense.
**cretin** (krɪ·tin) *s.* cretino.
**cretinism** (-išm) *s.* cretinismo.
**cretonne** (kre·tan) *s.* TEJ. cretona.
**crevasse** (krøva·s) *s.* GEOL. grieta.
**crevice** (kre·vis) *s.* raja, hendedura, rendija.
**crew** (kru) *s.* MAR., AVIA. tripulación, equipaje. *2* equipo, cuadrilla; banda. *3* Pret. de TO CROW.
**crewel** (kru·øl) *s.* lana para bordar.
**crib** (krib) *s.* pesebre. *2* nacimiento, belen. *3* camita [de niño]. *4* casucha, chiribitil. *5* arcón, granero, depósito. *6* emparrillado; refuerzo. *7* HIDR. cajón. *8* hurto; plagio. *9* fam. chuleta [para el que se examina].
**crib (to)** *tr.* encerrar. *2* hurtar, plagiar. ¶ Pret. y p. p.: *cribbed;* ger.: *cribbing.*
**cribbage** (kri·bidỹ) *s.* juego de naipes.
**cribble** (kri·bøl) *s.* criba, harnero.
**cribble (to)** *tr.* cribar, cerner. *2* GRAB. puntear.
**crick** (krik) *s.* tortícolis, calambre.
**cricket** (kri·kit) *s.* ENT. grillo. *2* cricquet [juego]. *3* escabel, taburete.
**cricketer** (-øʳ) *s.* jugador de cricquet.
**cricoid** (krai·koid) *adj.-s.* ANAT. cricoides.
**cried** (kraid) *pret.* y *p. p.* de TO CRY.
**crier** (krai·øʳ) *s.* pregonero. *2* voceador.
**crime** (kraim) *s.* delito. *2* crimen.
**criminal** (kri·minal) *adj.* delictivo, delictuoso; criminal. *2* DER. penal. *3* *s.* delincuente; criminal.
**criminalist** (-ist) *s.* criminalista.
**criminate (to)** (kri·mineit) *tr.* acriminar, acusar. *2* censurar, reprobar.
**criminous** (-nøs) *adj.* delictuoso, criminoso.
**crimp** (krimp) *adj.* rizado. *2* quebradizo, friable. *3* *s.* rizado. *4* rizador.
**crimp (to)** *tr.* rizar, encrespar. *2* plegar, ondular. *3* amoldar, dar forma.
**crimpy** (-i) *adj.* rizado. *2* arrugado.
**crimson** (kri·mšøn) *adj.-s.* carmesí, rojo.
**crimson (to)** *tr.* teñir de carmesí. *2* *intr.* enrojecerse. *3* sonrojarse.
**cringe** (krindỹ) *s.* obsequiosidad servil, adulación, bajeza.
**cringe (to)** *intr.* encogerse [ante un peligro, dolor, etc.]. *2* arrastrarse [servilmente], adular.
**cringing** (-ing) *adj.* bajo, vil, rastrero.
**crinite** (krai·nait) *adj.* crinito.
**crinkle** (kri·nkøl) *s.* arruga, rizo, sinuosidad, ondulación.
**crinkle (to)** *tr.* rizar, arrugar. *2* *intr.* ondularse, rizarse, arrugarse.
**crinoid** (krai·noid) *adj.-s.* ZOOL. crinoideo.
**crinoline** (kri·nølin) *s.* tela de crin. *2* miriñaque.
**cripple** (kri·pøl) *s.* cojo, manco, lisiado, tullido, inválido. *2* MAR. desmantelado, desarbolado.
**cripple (to)** *tr.* encojar, mancar, lisiar, estropear: *2* MAR. desmantelar, desarbolar. *3* *intr.* lisiarse. *4* cojear.
**crippled** (-d) *adj.* lisiado, tullido.
**crisis** (krai·sis) *s.* crisis.
**crisp** (krisp) *adj.* crespo, rizado. *2* tieso, crujiente. *3* quebradizo, seco, bien tostado. *4* gráfico, expresivo. *5* vivo, chispeante. *6* decidido, resuelto. *7* vigorizante, tónico [aire, frío].
**crisp (to)** *tr.* encrespar, rizar. *2* hacer quebradizo, tostar bien. *3* hacer crujir. *4* *intr.* encresparse, rizarse.

**crispation** (krispei·shøn) *s.* encrespadura. *2* crispatura.
**crisping iron** *s.* encrespador.
**crispy** (kri·spi) *adj.* crespo, rizado. *2* crujiente, quebradizo. *3* CRISP. 7.
**criss-cross** (kri·skros) *adj.* cruzado, entrecruzado. *2* *adv.* CROSSWISE.
**criterion** (kraiti·riøn) *s.* criterio.
**critic** (kri·tik) *s.* crítico. *2* censurador. *3* crítica.
**critical** (kri·tikal) *adj.* crítico. *2* exacto, escrupuloso. *3* de censura.
**criticism** (-tisišm) *s.* crítica [juicio crítico]. *2* crítica, censura.
**criticize (to)** (-tisaiš) *tr.-intr.* criticar.
**critique** (kritɪ·k) *s.* crítica [arte; juicio crítico].
**croak** (krouk) *s.* graznido [de cuervo]. *2* croar [de rana].
**croak (to)** *intr.* graznar, crascitar. *2* croar. *3* gruñir, refunfuñar. *4* fam. morir.
**Croatia** (kroei·sha) *n. pr.* GEOGR. Croacia.
**Croatian** (-shan) *adj.-s.* croata.
**croceous** (krou·shøs) *adj.* crocino.
**crochet** (kroshei·) *s.* ganchillo [labor].
**crochet (to)** *tr.* hacer [algo] con ganchillo. *2* *intr.* hacer ganchillo.
**crock** (krak) *s.* vasija de barro o loza, cacharro.
**crockery** (-øri) *s.* cacharros, loza, vidriado.
**crocodile** (kra·kodail) *s.* ZOOL. cocodrilo.
**Croesus** (krɪ·søs) *n. pr.* y fig. Creso.
**croft** (kroft) *s.* (Ingl.) pejugal; cercado.
**cromlech** (kra·mlek) *s.* ARQUEOL. crónlech.
**crone** (kroun) *s.* vieja arrugada.
**Cronus** (krou·nøs) *n. pr.* MIT. Cronos.
**crony** (krou·ni) *s.* camarada, compinche.
**crook** (kruk) *s.* curva, curvatura, cosa encorvada. *2* gancho, garfio. *3* cayado. *4* MÚS. tudel. *5* artificio, trampa. *6* fam. estafador, fullero, bribón.
**crook (to)** *tr.* torcer, encorvar. *2* *intr.* torcerse, encorvarse.
**crookback** (-bæk), **crookbacked** (bækt) *adj.-s.* jorobado, corcovado.
**crooked** (-id) *adj.* corvo, encorvado, ganchudo, torcido, deformado. *2* tórcido, avieso, falto de honradez, falso, fraudulento.
**crooklegged** (-legid) *adj.* patituerto.
**croon (to)** (krun) *tr.-intr.* canturrear. *2* cantar ciertas canciones exagerando el sentimiento.
**crop** (krap) *s.* cosecha. *2* cultivo, producción. *3* cabello o barba que crece. *4* acción de cortar corto o al rape; cabello corto o cortado al rape. *5* corte en la oreja [de un animal]. *6* buche [de ave]. *7* mango de látigo, látigo corto. *8* pl. campos, mieses, trigos.
**crop (to)** *tr.* segar, cosechar, coger. *2* cultivar, sembrar [una tierra]. *3* despuntar, cercenar, desmochar; trasquilar, desorejar. *4* *intr.* dar cosechas. *5* pacer. *6 to ~ out* o *forth*, aparecer, salir. *7* MIN. *to ~ out* o *up*, aflorar.
**crop-eared** *adj.* desorejado.
**cropper** (-øʳ) *s.* cosechador. *2* aparcero. *3* recortador. *4* ORN. paloma buchona.
**croquet** (kroukei·) *s.* croquet [juego].
**croquette** (krouke·t) *s.* COC. croqueta.
**crosier** (krou·šøʳ) *s.* báculo pastoral.
**cross** (kros) *s.* cruz [instrumento de suplicio; la de Nuestro Señor; imagen de ella; pena, trabajo; insignia de una orden]. *2* signo de la cruz. *3* cruz [señal o cosa en forma de cruz]. *4* cruce [de líneas, caminos, etc.]. *5* ELECT. cruce. *6* cruzamiento, mezcla [de razas, características, etc.]. *7* oposición, disputa. *8* *adj.* en cruz, atravesado,

transversal: ~ *street*, travesía, calle transversal; ~ *vault*, ARQ. bóveda por arista. *9* contrario, adverso. *10* recíproco: ~ *reference*, referencia, remisión [en un libro]. *11* COM. cruzado [cheque]. *12* malhumorado, enojado, regañón: *to be* ~, enfurruñarse. *13* ~ *grain*, repelo [de la madera].

**cross (to)** *tr.* signar, santiguar, persignar. *2* tachar, tildar, rayar. | Gralte. con *off* o *out*. *3* marcar con cruces. *4* cruzar, atravesar; fig. *to* ~ *one's mind*, ocurrírsele a uno. *5* cruzar [un cheque]. *6* cruzar, poner en cruz: *to* ~ *swords*, cruzar las espadas, reñir. *7* cruzarse con. *8* cruzar [razas o castas]. *9* estorbar [los planes, étc., de uno]. *10* *intr.* estar al través. *11* cruzarse. *12* cortarse, intersecarse. *13 to* ~ *over*, pasar al otro lado.

**crossbar** (-ba<sup>r</sup>) *s.* tranca [de puerta]. *2* travesaño.

**cross-bearer** *s.* cruciferario.

**crossbill** (-bill) *s.* ORN. piquituerto.

**crossbow** (-bou) *s.* ballesta [arma].

**crossbowman** (mæn) *s.* ballestero.

**crossbred** (-bred) *adj.-s.* cruzado, híbrido, mestizo.

**crossbreed** (-brɪd) *s.* casta cruzada. *2* planta o animal cruzado, híbrido, mestizo.

**crosbreed (to)** *tr.* cruzar [animales o plantas].

**cross-country** *adj.* que se hace a campo traviesa. *2 s.* carrera a campo traviesa.

**crosscut** (-køt) *s.* corte transversal. *2* atajo. *3* entrecruzamiento. *4 adj.* cortado al través; para cortar al través.

**crossed** (-t) *adj.* cruzado. *2* de través, transversal.

**cross-examination** *s.* DER. repregunta.

**cross-examine (to)** *tr.* DER. repreguntar.

**cross-eyed** *adj.* bizco.

**cross-fire** *s.* MIL. fuego cruzado. *2* tiroteo [de preguntas, etc.].

**cross-grained** *adj.* de grano o fibra diagonal o irregular. *2* difícil, terco, irritable.

**crossing** (-ing) *s.* acción de signar o persignar; santiguada. *2* cruce [acción]. *3* cruce, intersección, encrucijada: *level* ~, FERROC. paso a nivel. *4* paso, vado [de un río]. *5* MAR. travesía. *6* cruzamiento [de castas]. *7* estorbo, oposición [a los planes, etc., de uno].

**cross-legged** *adj.-adv.* con las piernas cruzadas.

**crosslet** (-lit) *s.* crucecita.

**crossly** (-li) *adv.* con enojo o mal humor.

**crossness** (-nis) *s.* enojo, enfado, mal humor.

**crosspiece** (-pis) *s.* travesaño.

**cross-purpose** *s.* hecho contrario; designio opuesto: *at cross-purposes*, interpretándose mal; contradiciéndose o haciéndose la contra sin querer. *2 pl.* juego de los despropósitos.

**cross-question** *s.* DER. pregunta. *2* interrogatorio detenido.

**cross-question (to)** *tr.* DER. repreguntar. *2* estrechar a preguntas.

**crossroad** (-roud) *s.* travesía [camino]; atajo. *2* cruce, encrucijada. *3 pl.* punto crítico, momento crucial.

**cross-section paper** *s.* papel cuadriculado.

**cross-staff** (-tæf) *s.* escuadra de agrimensor. *2* MAR. ballestilla.

**cross-stitch** *s.* COST. punto cruzado o de cruz.

**crosstie** (-tai) *s.* FERROC. traviesa.

**crosstree** (-trɪ) *s.* MAR. cruceta.

**crosswalk** (-uok) *s.* cruce señalado [en una calle].

**crossway** (-uei) *s.* CROSSROAD.

**crossways** (-ueis), **crosswise** (uaiš) *adv.* de través. *2* en cruz. *3* al revés, mal, en contra.

**crossword** (-uø<sup>r</sup>d), **crossword puzzle** *s.* crucigrama.

**crotalum** (kra·taløm) *s.* MÚS. crótalo.

**crotch** (krach) *s.* horquilla, horca [para sostener algo]. *2* horcadura, cruz, bifurcación. *3* horcajadura.

**crotchet** (kra·chit) *s.* ganchito. *2* MÚS. negra. *3* capricho, rareza, excentricidad.

**crotchety** (-i) *adj.* caprichoso, raro, excéntrico.

**crouch (to)** (krauch) *intr.* agacharse, agazaparse, acuclillarse. *2* arrastrarse [servilmente].

**croup** (krup) *s.* anca, grupa. *2* MED. crup, garrotillo.

**croupier** (kru·piø<sup>r</sup>) *s.* crupié.

**crow** (krou) *s.* ORN. cuervo; grajo; corneja; chova: *to eat* ~, fam. cantar la palinodia; *as the* ~ *flies*, fig. en linea recta. *2* canto [del gallo]. *3* palanca, alzaprima.

**crow (to)** *intr.* cantar [el gallo]. *2* jactarse, bravear, gallear; cantar victoria. *3* gorjear [el niño]. ¶ Pret.: *crowed* o *crew*.

**crowbar** (krou·ba<sup>r</sup>) *s.* palanca, alzaprima, pie de cabra.

**crowd** (kraud) *s.* multitud, muchedumbre, tropel [de pers. o cosas], gentío, apretura. *2* turba, masa, populacho, vulgo. *3* fam. grupo, pandilla.

**crowd (to)** *tr.* apretar, apiñar, amontonar. *2* atestar, llenar. *3* *intr.* agolparse, apiñarse, amontonarse.

**crowded** (-id) *adj.* atestado, abarrotado, de bote en bote.

**crowfoot** (-fut), *pl.* **foots** *s.* BOT. ranúnculo, botón de oro. *2* (*pl.* **-feet**) MIL. abrojo. *3* MAR. araña.

**crown** (kraun) *s.* corona [para la cabeza; dignidad real, reino; premio, galardón]: ~ *prince*, príncipe, heredero; ~ *princess*, princesa heredera; esposa del príncipe heredero. *2* ANAT. coronilla; cabeza. *3* cima, cumbre, parte superior. *4* complemento, colmo. *5* copa [de árbol, de sombrero]. *6* ARQ. coronamiento. *7* corona [de diente]. *8* corona [moneda; esp. la inglesa de 5 chelines]. ¶ Pret. ~ *grafting*, injerto de coronilla. *10* ~ *saw*, sierra circular.

**crown (to)** *tr.* coronar [en todos sus sentidos]: *to* ~ *it all*, para colmo, por remate.

**crowning** (-ing) *s.* coronamiento, remate.

**crownlet** (-lit) *s.* coronita.

**crow's-foot** *s.* pata de gallo [arrugas]. *2* CROWFOOT.

**crozier** *s.* CROSIER.

**crucial** (kru·shal) *adj.* crucial.

**cruciate** (-shieit) *adj.* cruciforme.

**crucible** (-sibøl) *s.* crisol.

**crucifer** (-sifø<sup>r</sup>) *s.* cruciferario. *2* BOT. crucífero.

**cruciferous** (krusi·førøs) *adj.* BOT. crucífero.

**crucifix** (kru·sifiks) *s.* crucifijo.

**crucifixion** (-krusifi·kshøn) *s.* crucifixión.

**cruciform** (kru·sifo<sup>r</sup>m) *adj.* cruciforme.

**crucify (to)** (-sifai) *tr.* crucificar. *2* mortificar; atormentar. ¶ Pret. y p p.: *crucified*.

**crude** (krud) *adj.* crudo [sin cocer, sin preparar]; imperfecto, mal acabado, no sazonado; bruto [sin refinar]. *2* crudo, desnudo [sin atenuantes]. *3* tosco, basto, rudo. *4* brusco, descortés.

**crudity** (-iti) *s.* crudeza. *2* imperfección, tosquedad.

**cruel** (kru·øl) *adj.* cruel. *2* despiadado, atroz.

**cruelty** (-ti) *s.* crueldad, inhumanidad, atrocidad.

**cruet** (kru·it) *s.* ampolla, vinagrera. *2* vinajera. *3* *cruet* o ~ *stand*, vinagreras.

**cruise** (kru·š) *s.* MAR., AVIA. crucero [acción de cruzar; viaje].

**cruise (to)** *tr.* MAR., AVIA. cruzar, navegar, viajar. *2* circular [un taxi] en busca de pasaje.

**cruiser** (-ø$^r$) *s.* buque o pers. que realiza un crucero. *2* MAR. crucero [buque].
**cruller** (krø·lø$^r$) *s.* (E.U.) buñuelo.
**crumb** (krøm) *s.* miga [del pan]. *2* pedacito, mendrugo, migaja.
**crumb (to)** *tr.* migar, desmenuzar, desmigajar. *2* empanar [con pan rallado].
**crumble (to)** (krø·mbøl) *tr.* desmenuzar, deshacer. *2 intr.* desmenuzarse, deshacerse, desmoronarse, derrumbarse.
**crumbly** (-bli) *adj.* desmenuzable, friable.
**crumby** (-bi) *adj.* blando, lleno de migas.
**crumpet** (-pit) *s.* especie de bollo.
**crumple (to)** (-pøl) *tr.* arrugar, chafar, ajar, apabullar. *2 intr.* arrugarse, encogerse, aplastarse.
**crunch (to)** (krønch) *tr.* mascar haciendo crujir; ronzar, tascar. *2* hacer crujir [bajo los pies, etc.]. *3 intr.* crujir [al ser mascado, pisado, etc.].
**crupper** (krø·pø$^r$) *s.* baticola, grupera. *2* grupa.
**crural** (kru·ral) *adj.* ANAT. crural.
**crusade** (krusei·d) *s.* cruzada.
**crusade (to)** *intr.* tomar parte en una cruzada.
**crusader** (-ø$^r$) *s.* cruzado [pers.].
**crush** (krøsh) *s.* compresión, presión, aplastamiento, machacamiento, estrujamiento. *2* apretura, apiñamiento, aglomeración.
**crush (to)** *tr.* aplastar, machacar, quebrantar, moler, triturar. *2* machucar, estrujar, exprimir. *3* aplastar, sojuzgar, oprimir, abrumar. *4* destruir, aniquilar.
**crusher** (-ø$^r$) *s.* el o lo que aplasta, machaca, oprime, etc. *2* fam. argumento o respuesta contundente, decisiva.
**crust** (krøst) *s.* corteza [de pan, queso, etc.]. *2* mendrugo. *3* corteza [terrestre]. *4* costra. *5* MED. postilla. *6* pasta [de un pastel]. *7* ZOOL. carapacho.
**crust (to)** *tr.* encostrar, incrustar. *2 intr.* encostrarse.
**crustacean** (krøstei·shian) *adj.-s.* ZOOL. crustáceo.
**crustaceous** (-shøs) *adj.* crustáceo.
**crustation** (-shøn) *s.* costra, incrustación.
**crusty** (krø·sti) *adj.* costroso. *2* rudo, áspero, brusco.
**crutch** (krøch) *s.* muleta [de cojo]. *2* horquilla, puntal. *3* horcajadura.
**crux** (krøks) *s.* cosa difícil, enigma. *2* el quid, lo esencial.
**cry** (krai) *s.* grito. *2* alarido. *3* lamento, lloro, llanto: *to have a good ~*, desahogarse llorando. *4* gritería, clamor: *much ~ and little wool*, es más el ruido que las nueces. *5* pregón. *6* voz pública. *7* jauría, muta, ladridos de la jauría. *8 a far ~*, una gran distancia o diferencia.
**cry (to)** *intr.-tr.* gritar. *2* vocear, pregonar. *3 intr.* aullar. *4* llorar, lamentarse. *5 tr.* exclamar. *6* pedir: *to ~ quarter*, pedir cuartel. *7* proclamar, pregonar. *8 to ~ down*, rebajar, desacreditar. *9 to ~ for*, pedir llorando o a gritos; llorar de: *to ~ for help*, pedir socorro; *to ~ for joy*, llorar de alegría. *10 to ~ off*, deshacer [un trato, etc.]. *11 to ~ one's eyes out*, llorar amargamente. *12 to ~ out*, gritar, vociferar. *13 to ~ up*, ensalzar, alabar. ¶ Pret. y p. p.: *cried*.
**crying** (-ing) *s.* grito, griterío; lloro, llanto. *2 adj.* que grita o llora. *3* patente, notorio. *4* enorme, atroz, odioso.
**crypt** (kript) *s.* cripta.
**cryptic(al** (-tik(al) *adj.* secreto, oculto, enigmático.
**cryptogam** (-togæm) *s.* BOT. criptógama.
**cryptogamous** (kripta·gamøs) *adj.* criptógamo.
**cryptogram** (kri·ptogræm) *s.* criptograma.

**cryptography** (kripta·grafi) *s.* criptografía.
**crystal** (kri·stal) *s.* cristal. *2* RADIO. galena. *3 adj.* de cristal, cristalino.
**crystalline** (-in) *adj.* cristalino. *2 s.* ANAT. cristalino [del ojo].
**crystallization** (-išei·shøn) *s.* cristalización.
**crystallize (to)** (-aiš) *tr.* cristalizar. *2 intr.* cristalizar(se.
**crystallography** (-a·grafi) *s.* cristalografía.
**cub** (køb) *s.* cachorro. *2* ballenato. *3* fig. mocoso, joven mal educado.
**cubage** (kiu·bidȳ) *s.* cubicación.
**Cuban** (-ban) *adj.-s.* cubano.
**cube** (kiub) *s.* GEOM., MAT. cubo. *2 adj.* MAT. *~ root*, raíz cúbica.
**cube (to)** *tr.* cubicar.
**cubeb** (kiu·beb) *s.* BOT. cubeba.
**cubic(al** (-bik(al) *adj.* cúbico.
**cubicle** (-bikøl) *s.* cubículo.
**cubism** (-bišm) *s.* cubismo.
**cubist** (-bist) *s.* cubista.
**cubit** (-bit) *s.* codo [medida]. *2* ANAT. cúbito.
**cubital** (-al) *adj.* cubital. *2* codal.
**cuboid** (-boid) *adj.-s.* ANAT. cuboides. *2 s.* GEOM. paralelepípedo rectángulo.
**cuckold** (kø·køld) *s.* cornudo [marido].
**cuckold (to)** *tr.* encornudar.
**cuckoo** (ku·ku) *s.* ORN. cuclillo, cuco. *2* cucú [canto]. *3 ~ clock*, reloj de cuco.
**cuckoopint** (-pint) *s.* BOT. aro, alcatraz.
**cucumber** (kiu·kømbø$^r$) *s.* BOT. cohombro; pepino.
**cucurbit** (kukø·$^r$bit) *s.* cucúrbita. *2* BOT. calabaza.
**cucurbitaceous** (-ei·shøs) *adj.* BOT. cucurbitáceo.
**cud** (kød) *s.* lo que rumia un rumiante: *to chew the ~*, fig. rumiar, meditar.
**cuddle (to)** (kø·døl) *tr.* abrazar, tener en brazos [para acariciar, dar calor, etc.]. *2 intr.* estar abrazado o arrimado a.
**cuddy** (-di) *s.* MAR. camareta. *2* pequeño aposento. *3* alacena.
**cudgel** (kø·dȳøl) *s.* garrote corto, porra.
**cudgel (to)** *tr.* apalear, aporrear: *to ~ one's brains*, devanarse los sesos. ¶ Pret. y p. p.: *cudgeled* o *-lled*; ger.: *cudgeling* o *-lling*.
**cue** (kiu) *s.* señal, indicación [para hacer algo]; indirecta, sugestión. *2* TEAT. pie. *3* BILL. taco. *4* coleta. *5* cola [de personas].
**cuff** (køf) *s.* puño [de camisa o vestido]: *~ links*, gemelos [de puño]. *2* doblez, vuelta [de pantalón]. *3* bofetada, sopapo, puñetazo. *4 pl.* HANDCUFFS.
**cuff (to)** *tr.* abofetear, apuñear, pegar. *2 intr.* dar puñetazos, boxear.
**cuirass** (kuira·s) *s.* coraza.
**cuirassier** (kuirasi·ø$^r$) *s.* coracero.
**cuisine** (kuiši·n) *s.* cocina [arte].
**culinary** (kiu·lineri) *adj.* culinario.
**cull (to)** (køl) *tr.* escoger, elegir, entresacar. *2* coger [frutos, flores, etc.].
**cullender** (kø·løndø$^r$) *s.* COLANDER.
**cullion** (-liøn) *s.* belitre, bribón.
**culm** (kølm) *s.* BOT. caña [tallo]. *2* cisco [carbón].
**culminant** (kø·lminant) *adj.* culminante. *2* dominante, predominante.
**culminate (to)** (-neit) *tr.* culminar.
**culmination** (-nei·shøn) *s.* culminación.
**culpability** (kølpabi·liti) *s.* culpabilidad.
**culpable** (kø·lpabøl) *adj.* culpable.
**culprit** (-prit) *s.* culpable, reo, delincuente.
**cult** (kølt) *s.* culto. *2* secta religiosa.
**cultism** (-išm) *s.* LIT. culteranismo.

cultist (-ist) s. culterano.
cultivable (kø·ltivabøl) adj. cultivable.
cultivate (to) (-veit) tr. cultivar. 2 civilizar.
cultivated (-id) adj. cultivado. 2 culto, ilustrado, instruido.
cultivation (-ei·shøn) s. cultivo. 2 cultura, refinamiento.
cultivator (kø·ltiveitø') s. cultivador. 2 agricultor. 3 AGR. escarificador.
cultual (kø·lchual) adj. cultual.
culture (-chø') adj. cultura. 2 cultivo. 3 producción, cría.
culture (to) tr. cultivar. 2 educar, refinar.
cultured (-chø'd) adj. culto, ilustrado.
culverin (kø·lvørin) s. ARTILL. culebrina.
culvert (kø·lvø't) s. alcantarilla [en un camino]; atarjea.
cumber (to) (kø·mbø') tr. embarazar, estorbar, cargar, molestar, causar engorro.
cumbersome (-søm) adj. embarazoso, engorroso, pesado, incómodo, difícil de mover o manejar.
cumbrance (-brans) s. ENCUMBRANCE.
cumbrous (-brøs) adj. CUMBERSOME.
cum(m)in (kø·min) s. BOT. comino [planta].
cuminseed (-sid) s. BOT. comino [semilla].
cumulate (kiu·miuleit) tr. cumular, acumular, amontonar. 2 intr. acumularse, amontonarse.
cumulation (-ei·shøn) s. acumulación, amontonamiento.
cumulative (-miulativ) adj. cumulativo.
cumulus (-miuløs), pl. -li (-li) s. cúmulo, montón. 2 METEOR. cúmulo.
cuneal (-nial), cuneate(d (-nieit(id) cuneiform (-niifø'm) adj. cuneiforme.
cunning (kø·ning) adj. hábil, diestro, ingenioso. 2 sagaz, astuto, taimado. 3 (E.U.) gracioso, mono. 4 s. habilidad, destreza, ingenio. 5 astucia, maña, artería. 6 ardid, artificio.
cup (køp) s. taza, jícara; copa o hueco en forma de copa: ~ and ball, boliche [juguete]. 2 copa, trago: in one's cups, bebido, achispado. 3 copa [trofeo]. 4 cáliz [vaso]. 5 BOT. cúpula; cáliz; corola. 6 ANAT. glena. 7 ELECT. campana [aislador]. 8 cubeta [de barómetro]. 9 ASTR. (con may.) Copa.
cup (to) tr. poner ventosas a. 2 ahuecar en formə de copa. ¶ Pret. y p. p.: cupped; ger.: -pping.
cupbearer (køpbe·rø') s. copero, escanciador.
cupboard (kø·pbo'd) s. aparador, armario, alacena.
cupel (kiu·pøl) s. METAL. copela.
cupel (to) tr. copelar.
cupful (kø·pful) s. copa, taza [contenido].
Cupid (kiu·pid) n. pr. MIT. Cupido. 2 s. (con min.) amorcillo.
cupidity (-pi·diti) s. codicia, avidez, avaricia.
cupola (-pøla) s. ARQ., MAR. cúpula. 2 METAL. cubilote.
cupreous (-priøs) adj. cobrizo, cobreño.
cupric (-pric) adj. QUÍM. cúprico.
cupule (-piul) s. BOT. cúpula.
cupuliferous (kiupiuli·førøs) adj. BOT. cupulífero.
cur (kø') s. desp. perro, gozque. 2 canalla, hombre vil.
curable (kiu·rabøl) adj. curable.
curaçao (kiurasou·) s. curasao.
curacy (kiu·rasi) s. coadjutoría.
curare (kura·ri) s. BOT., QUÍM. curare.
curassow (kiu·rasou) s. ORN. guaco.
curate (kiu·reit) s. coadjutor, teniente cura.
curative (-rativ) adj. curativo.

curator (kiurei·tø') s. DER. curador. 2 conservador, guardián, administrador.
curatrix (-triks) f. de CURATOR.
curb (kø'b) s. barbada [del freno]. 2 fig. sujeción, restricción, freno. 3 bordillo, encintado. 4 brocal [de pozo].
curb (to) tr. refrenar, contener, reprimir, sujetar.
curbstone (-stoun) s. piedra de encintado. 2 CURB 3 y 4.
curcuma (kø·'kiuma) s. cúrcuma.
curd (kø'd) s. cuajada. 2 requesón.
curd (to) tr. cuajar, coagular. 2 intr. cuajarse, coagularse.
curdle (to) (kø·'døl) tr. cuajar, coagular, espesar; helar [la sangre]. 2 intr. cuajarse, coagularse, engrumecerse; helarse.
cure (kiu·ø') s. cura, curación, remedio. 2 cura [de almas]. 3 feligresía, parroquia. 4 acción de curar pescado, madera, etc.
cure (to) tr. curar, remediar. 2 curar [pescado, madera, etc.]; vulcanizar [caucho]. 3 intr. curarse.
curfew (kø·'fiu) s. queda, toque de queda.
curia (kiu·ria) s. curia [de los ant. romanos]. 2 curia [papal].
curie (-ri) s. FÍS. curie.
curio (-riou) s. curiosidad, antigüedad, objeto curioso.
curiosity (kiuria·siti) s. curiosidad [deseo de saber o averiguar]. 2 lo curioso [de una cosa]. 3 curiosidad, objeto raro o curioso.
curious (kui·riøs) adj. curioso [deseoso de saber o averiguar]. 2 curioso, raro, singular. 3 minucioso. 4 primoroso.
curiousness (-nis) s. CURIOSITY 1 y 2. 2 delicadeza, primor.
curl (kø'l) s. rizo, bucle, sortija, tirabuzón. 2 espiral [de humo, etc.]. 3 curva, sinuosidad. 4 encorvadura, enroscamiento, abarquillamiento.
curl (to) tr. rizar, ensortijar, encrespar. 2 torcer, encorvar, enroscar, abarquillar: to ~ one's lip, hacer un gesto de desprecio con los labios. 3 intr. rizarse, ensortijarse. 4 encorvarse, enroscarse, abarquillarse.
curlew (kø·'liu) s. ORN. zarapito.
curling (-ling) s. rizado, ensortijamiento, encorvadura. 2 juego en que se hacen correr unas piedras sobre el hielo. 3 adj. de rizar: ~ irons, ~ tongs, rizador, encrespador, tenacillas.
curly (-li) adj. rizado, rizoso, ensortijado, crespo, ondulado.
curmudgeon (kø'ma·dỹøn) s. avaro, tacaño.
currant (kø·rant) s. uva o pasa de Corinto. 2 grosella. 3 BOT. grosellero.
currency (kø·rønsi) s. curso, circulación. 2 valor corriente. 3 moneda corriente, dinero. 4 dinero en circulación.
current (kø·rønt) adj. corriente, que corre: ~ account, COM. cuenta corriente. 2 corriente [generalmente aceptado]; común, general; en boga, reinante; en circulación. 3 presente, actual. 4 corrida [letra]. 5 s. corriente. 6 curso, marcha, progresión.
curricle (kø·rikøl) s. carrocín.
curriculum (køri·kiuløm) s. plan de estudios.
currier (kø·riø') s. curtidor, zurrador.
curriery (-riri) s. tenería.
curry (kø·ri) s. condimento de origen indio. 2 plato sazonado con él.
curry (to) tr. zurrar, adobar [pieles]. 2 almohazar. 3 COC. sazonar con CURRY. 4 fig. to ~ favour, adular. ¶ Pret. y p. p.: curried.

**curry-comb** *s.* almohaza, rascadera.
**curse** (køᵣs) *s.* maldición, imprecación, anatema.
2 juramento, voto, reniego. 3 azote, calamidad.
**curse (to)** *tr.* maldecir. 2 afligir, azotar [con males, calamidades, etc.]. 3 *intr.* jurar, renegar, echar votos.
**cursed** (køᵣsid) *adj.* maldito, abominable, execrable.
**cursive** (-siv) *adj.-s.* cursiva [letra].
**cursor** (køᵣsøᵣ) *s.* MEC. cursor.
**cursory** (-i) *adj.* superficial, sumario, rápido, hecho sin detención, por encima o de pasada.
**curt** (køᵣt) *adj.* corto, breve, conciso. 2 brusco, seco.
**curtail (to)** (køᵣtei·l) *tr.* acortar, cercenar, mutilar. 2 abreviar, reducir, restringir, escatimar.
**curtailment** (-mønt) *s.* acortamiento, abreviación, reducción.
**curtain** (køᵣtin) *s.* cortina [paño colgante; cosa que oculta]: *to draw the ~,* correr la cortina, correr un velo. 2 TEAT. telón [de boca]: *behind the ~,* entre bastidores, en secreto. 3 FORT. cortina.
**curtain (to)** *tr.* encortinar. 2 velar, ocultar.
**curtation** (koᵣtei·shøn) *s.* ASTR. curtación.
**curtesy, curtsy** (køᵣtsi) *s.* cortesía, reverencia [saludo femenino].
**curtesy, curtsy (to)** *intr.* hacer una cortesía o reverencia [la mujer]. ¶ Pret. y p. p.: *curtsied.*
**curule** (kiu·rul) *adj.* curul.
**curvate(d** (køᵣveit(id) *adj.* corvo, encorvado.
**curvation** (-ei·shøn) *s.* encorvadura.
**curvature** (køᵣvachøᵣ) *s.* curvatura.
**curve** (køᵣv) *adj.* curvo, encorvado. 2 *s.* curva.
**curve (to)** *tr.* encorvar, torcer, combar. 2 *intr.* encorvarse, torcerse; describir una curva.
**curvet** (køᵣvet o køᵣve·t) *s.* corveta, corcovo. 2 retozo, brinco.
**curvet (to)** *intr.* corvetear, corcovear. 2 retozar, brincar. ¶ Pret. y p. p.: *-ted* o *-tted; ger.: -ting* o *-tting.*
**curvilinear** (køᵣvili·niaᵣ) *adj.* curvilíneo.
**curvity** (køᵣviti) *s.* curvidad.
**cushion** (ku·shøn) . cojín, almohadón, almohadilla. 2 BILL. banda. 3 MEC. amortiguador. 4 ARQ. almohadón. 5 VET. ranilla [del casco].
**cushion (to)** *tr.* proveer de cojines. 2 sentar o poner sobre cojín. 3 suavizar, apagar [la voz]. 4 MEC. amortiguar, acojinar. 5 ahogar [quejas, etc.].
**cusp** (køsp) *s.* cúspide. 2 cuerno [de la luna].
**cuspidor** (-øᵣ) *s.* escupidera.
**cuss** (køs) *s.* (E.U.) reniego, terno. 2 desp. bicho, individuo.
**cussedness** (kø·sidnis) *s.* (E.U.) terquedad; mal genio.
**custard** (køstaᵣd) *s.* flan; natillas.
**custard-apple** *s.* BOT. guanábana.
**custodian** (køstou·dian) *s.* custodio, guardián.
**custody** (kø·stødi) *s.* custodia, guarda. 2 prisión, detención; encarcelamiento: *to take into ~,* detener, prender. 3 custodia [de la orden franciscana].
**custom** (kø·støm) *s.* costumbre, hábito, uso, usanza. 2 DER. costumbre. 3 parroquia, clientela; hecho de ser parroquiano o cliente. 4 *pl.* derechos de aduana: *customs officer,* aduanero, vista de aduanas. 5 *adv.-adj.* a medida, por encargo; que hace algo a medida o por encargo.
**customable** (-abøl) *adj.* sujeto al pago de derechos de aduana.
**customary** (-eri) *adj.* acostumbrado, de costumbre, habitual, usual. 2 DER. consuetudinario.

**customer** (-øᵣ) *s.* parroquiano, cliente. 2 fam. tipo, individuo.
**custom-free** *adj.* libre de derechos de aduana.
**customhouse** (-jaus) *s.* aduana: *~ broker,* agente de aduanas.
**custom-made** *adj.* hecho a medida.
**cut** (køt) *s.* corte, cortadura, incisión. 2 tajo, cuchillada. 3 lámina, grabado [esp. en madera]. 4 labra, tallado [de la piedra, etc.]. 5 corte, reducción. 6 corte [en los naipes]. 7 trozo [de carne], tajada. 8 zanja, foso, cortadura. 9 camino directo: *short ~,* atajo. 10 corte, estilo [de un vestido]. 11 hechura, forma, figura. 12 golpe dado con el canto de algo, golpe cortante. 13 palabra o acto que hiere; desaire, ofensa. 14 acto de negar el saludo a uno. 15 falta [a clase]. 16 pret. y p. p. de TO CUT: cortado, tallado, interrumpido, etc.
**cut (to)** *tr.* cortar, hender, partir, dividir, separar: *to ~ the throat,* degollar. 2 cortar [un vestido, etc.]. 3 segar. 4 abrir, excavar. 5 cortar, interrumpir, interceptar. 6 cortar [el suministro de agua, gas, etc.]. 7 reducir, acortar. 8 recortar. 9 trinchar. 10 labrar, esculpir, tallar, cincelar, grabar. 11 cortar, cruzar [una línea o superficie a otra]. 12 atravesar, abrirse paso en; surcar [el agua]; hender [el aire]. 13 cortar, alzar [los naipes]. 15 castrar [un animal]. 16 dar un golpe vivo [con un látigo, etc.]. 17 herir [lastimar los sentimientos de]. 18 faltar a [una clase]; dejar [una costumbre, etc.]; desentenderse de. 19 dejar de tratarse con, negar el saludo a. 20 diluir, aguar, adulterar [un licor]. 21 templar [un color]. 22 golpear de cierto modo la pelota. 23 parar [un motor]. 24 *to ~ a caper,* hacer una cabriola. 25 *to ~ a figure,* hacer papel [en sociedad, etc.]. 26 *to ~ down,* derribar [cortando]; rebajar, reducir. 27 *to ~ ice,* tener peso o influencia. 28 *to ~ in,* mezclar, introducir en; ELECT. conectar, intercalar. 29 *to ~ off,* cortar, separar; llevarse, quitar la vida prematuramente; poner fin a; cortar [la comunicación, la retirada, el encendido, etc.]. 30 *to ~ out,* cortar [quitar o hacer cortando], dividir; quitar, separar, suprimir; desconectar; preparar, trazar; hacer formar. 31 *to ~ short,* interrumpir bruscamente.
32 *intr.* cortar: *to ~ both ways,* ser arma de dos filos. 33 salir [un diente, los dientes]. 34 pasar [con rapidez o por el camino más corto], atajar. 35 *to ~ in,* intervenir, meter baza.
¶ CONJUG. pret. y p. p.: *cut;* ger.: *cutting.*
**cutaneous** (kiutei·niøs) *adj.* cutáneo.
**cutaway coat** (kø·tauel) *s.* chaqué.
**cute** (kiut) *adj.* listo, astuto. 2 (E.U.) lindo, mono.
**cuticle** (kiu·tikøl) *s.* cutícula.
**cutlass** (kø·tlas) *s.* machete; sable de abordaje, sable corto.
**cutler** (-løᵣ) *s.* cuchillero.
**cutlery** (-løri) *s.* cuchillería.
**cutlet** (-lit) *s.* COC. chuleta.
**cutoff** (-of) *s.* atajo. 2 MEC. cortavapor.
**cutout** (-aut) *s.* recortado, figura recortada. 2 ELECT. cortacircuito.
**cutpurse** (-pøᵣs) *s.* cortabolsas, ratero.
**cutter** (-øᵣ) *s.* cortador. 2 tallador, grabador. 3 MEC. cuchilla, fresa. 4 MAR. cúter. 5 MAR. escampavía. 6 pequeño trineo.
**cutthroat** (-zrout) *s.* asesino.
**cutting** (-ing) *adj.* cortante. 2 frío, penetrante. 3 hiriente, incisivo, mordaz. 4 *s.* corte, cortadura,

incisión. *5* recorte, retazo. *6* alce [de los naipes].
*7* talla [de la piedra, etc.]. *8* AGR. esqueje, estaca.
**cuttlebone** (kø·tølboun) *s.* jibión.
**cuttlefish** (-fish) *s.* ZOOL. jibia, sepia. *2* por ext. calamar, pulpo, etc.
**cutwater** (kø·tuotø^r) *s.* tajamar.
**cuvette** (kiuve·t) *s.* FOT. cubeta.
**cyanic** (saiæ·nic) *adj.* QUÍM. ciánico. *2* BOT. azulado.
**cyanide** (sai·anaid) *s.* QUÍM. cianuro.
**Cybele** (si·bøli) *n. pr.* MIT. Cibeles.
**cybernetics** (saibø^rne·tics) *s.* cibernética.
**Cyclades** (si·kladiš) *n. pr.* GEOGR. Cícladas.
**cyclamen** (si·klamin) *s.* BOT. ciclamino, pamporcino.
**cycle** (sai·cøl) *s.* ciclo. *2* ELECT. período. *3* biciclo, triciclo.
**cycle (to)** *intr.* ir en bicicleta.
**cyclic(al** (-klic(al) *adj.* cíclico.
**cycling** (-kling) *s.* ciclismo. *2* acción de ir en bicicleta.
**cyclism** (-klišm) *s.* ciclismo.
**cyclist** (-ist) *s.* ciclista.
**cycloid** (-kloid) *s.* GEOM. cicloide.
**cyclone** (-kloun) *s.* METEOR. ciclón.
**cyclopa(e)dia** (saiklopɪ·dia) *s.* ENCYCLOPAEDIA.
**Cyclopean** (saiklopɪ·an), **Cyclopic** (-kla·pic) *adj.* ciclópeo, ciclópico, gigantesco.
**Cyclops** (sai·klaps) *s.* MIT. cíclope.
**cyclorama** (saiklora·ma) *s.* ciclorama.
**cyclostyle** (-tail) *s.* ciclostilo.
**cyclotron** (sai·klotran) *s.* FÍS. ciclotrón.
**cygnet** (si·gnit) *s.* pollo del cisne.

**cylinder** (si·lindø^r) *s.* GEOM., MEC. cilindro. *2* cuerpo cilíndrico, rodillo.
**cylindric(al** (sili·ndrik(al) *adj.* cilíndrico.
**cyma** (sai·ma), **cymatium** (simei·shiøm) *s.* ARQ. cimacio, gola.
**cymbal** (si·mbal) *s.* MÚS. címbalo, platillos.
**cyme** (saim) *s.* BOT. cima.
**cymose** (-ous) *adj.* BOT. cimoso.
**cynegetic** (sinidỹe·tik) *adj.* cinegético.
**cynic** (si·nik) *adj.-s.* FIL. cínico.
**cynical** (-al) *adj.* FIL. cínico. *2* pesimista.
**cynicism** (-sišm) *s.* FIL. cinismo. *2* pesimismo.
**Cynosure** (sai·nøỹu^r) *s.* ASTR. Cinosura. *2* (con min.) blanco de las miradas.
**cyperaceous** (saipørei·shøs) *adj.* BOT. ciperáceo.
**cypher** (sai·fø^r) *s.* CIPHER.
**cypress** (-pres) *s.* BOT. ciprés.
**Cyprian** (si·prian) *n. pr.* Cipriano. *2* *adj.-s.* chipriota.
**Cyprus** (sai·prøs) *n. pr.* GEOGR. Chipre.
**Cyril** (si·ril) *n. pr.* Cirilo.
**Cyrus** (sai·røs) *n. pr.* Ciro.
**cyst** (sist) *s.* quiste.
**cystic** (si·stic) *adj.* ANAT. cístico.
**cystis** (si·stis) *s.* CYST.
**cystitis** (sistai·tis) *s.* MED. cistitis.
**Cytherea** (sizirɪ·a) *n. pr.* MIT. Citerea.
**cytisus** (si·tisøs) *s.* BOT. citiso, codeso.
**cytoplasm** (sai·toplæšm) *s.* BIOL. citoplasma.
**czar** (ša^r) *s.* zar
**czarevitch** (ša·revich) *s.* zarevitz.
**czarevna** (šare·vna) *s.* zarina.
**Czecho-Slovakia** (che·kou·slova·kia) *n. pr.* GEOGR. Checoslovaquia.

# D

**D, d** (dɪ) s. D, d, cuarta letra del alfabeto inglés. *2* MÚS. re.

**dab** (dæb) s. golpecito, toque ligero, picotazo leve. *2* pincelada, untadura. *3* ICT. platija. *4* fig. hacha [pers. diestra en algo].

**dab (to)** tr. dar golpecitos a, picar, picotear. *2* chapotear [con una esponja, un paño mojado, etc.]. *3* dar brochazos o pinceladas ligeras; aplicar [algo] con ellos. ¶ Pret. y p. p.: *dabbed;* ger.: *dabbing.*

**dabble (to)** (dæ·bøl) tr. rociar, salpicar, mojar, humedecer. *2* dar golpecitos a. *3* intr. chapotear [en el agua]. *4* hacer algo o meterse en algo en pequeña escala, como aficionado.

**dabbler** (dæ·blør) s. diletante, aficionado.

**dabchick** (-chik) s. ORN. somorgujo.

**dabster** (dæ·bstør) s. DAB 4.

**dace** (deis) s. ICT. albur, dardo, breca.

**dachsund** (da·ksjunt) s. perro de patas muy cortas.

**Dacia** (dei·sha) n. pr. GEOGR. Dacia.

**Dacian** (dei·shan) adj.-s. dacio.

**dactyl** (dæ·ctil) s. MET. dáctilo.

**dactylology** (dæctila·lodŷi) s. dactilología.

**dactylography** (-grafi) s. estudio de las huellas digitales. *2* dactilología.

**dactyloscopy** (-skopi) s. dactiloscopia.

**dad** (dæd), **daddie, daddy** (-i) s. fam. papá, papaíto, taita.

**daddy-longlegs** s. ENT. típula. *2* ZOOL. segador [arácnido].

**dado** (dei·dou) s. ARQ. dado, neto. *2* rodapié, friso, alizar.

**Daedalus** (dɪ·deløs) n. pr. MIT. Dédalo.

**daffodil** (dæ·fodil) s. BOT. narciso, trompón.

**daft** (dæft) adj. tonto, chiflado, loco.

**dagger** (dæ·gør) s. daga, puñal: *to be at daggers drawn,* fig. estar a matar. *2* IMPR. obelisco.

**dago** (dei·gou) s. (E.U. y Can.) desp. italiano, español o portugués.

**daguerrotype** (dage·røtaip) s. daguerrotipo.

**dahlia** (da·lia) s. BOT. dalia.

**daily** (dei·li) adj. diario, cotidiano. *2* diurno. *3* s. periódico diario. *4* adv. diariamente, cotidianamente, cada día.

**daintily** (dei·ntili) adv. delicadamente, exquisitamente.

**dainty** (dei·nti) adj. delicado, primoroso, exquisito, elegante, refinado. *2* sabroso, delicioso. *3* delicado, exigente. *4* s. bocado exquisito, golosina.

**dairy** (de·ri) s. lechería. *2* quesería. *3* vaquería: ~ *farm,* granja lechera.

**dairymaid** (-meid) s. lechera [pers.].

**dairyman** (-mæn) s. lechero.

**dais** (dei·is) s. tarima, estrado. *2* (gal.) dosel.

**daisy** (dei·si) s. BOT. margarita, maya, vellorita.

**dale** (deil) s. cañada, hondonada, valle.

**dalliance** (dæ·lians) s. jugueteo, devaneo.

**dally (to)** (dæ·li) intr. jugar, juguetear, coquetear. *2* perder el tiempo. *3* tardar, entretenerse. *4* tr. *to* ~ *away,* pasar, perder [el tiempo].

**Dalmatia** (dælmei·shia) n. pr. GEOGR. Dalmacia.

**Dalmatian** (-n) adj.-s. dálmata.

**dalmatic** (dælme·tik) s. dalmática.

**daltonism** (da·ltønišm) s. MED. daltonismo.

**dam** (dæm) s. dique, presa. *2* embalse, pantano. *3* madre [en ganadería].

**dam (to)** tr. represar, embalsar. *2* cerrar, obstruir. ¶ Pret. y p. p.: *dammed;* ger.: *-mming.*

**damage** (dæ·midŷ) tr. daño, perjuicio, detrimento. *2* COM. avería, siniestro. *3* pl. daños y perjuicios. *4* indemnización.

**damage (to)** tr. dañar, perjudicar, deteriorar. *2* intr. deteriorarse, averiarse.

**damaging** (-ing) adj. perjudicial, nocivo.

**Damascene** (dæ·masin) adj. y s. damasceno. *2* (con min.) adj. damasquino.

**damascene (to)** (dæmasɪ·n) tr. damasquinar.

**Damascus** (dæmæ·skøs) n. pr. GEOGR. Damasco.

**damask** (dæ·mask) s. damasco [tejido]. *2* damasquinado, ataujía. *3* adj. damasceno. *4* adamascado. *5* damasquino.

**damask (to)** tr. damasquinar. *2* adamascar.

**damaskeen (to)** (dæmaskɪ·n) tr. TO DAMASCENE.

**dame** (deim) s. dama, señora. *2* fam. mujer.

**damn** (dæm) s. maldición. *2* fig. *I don't care a* ~, me importa un bledo.

**damn (to)** tr. TEOL. condenar. *2* condenar, reprobar. *3* maldecir. *4* intr. echar ternos.

**damnable** (-nabøl) adj. condenable, detestable, abominable.

**damnation** (-ei·shøn) s. condenación, perdición.

**damned** (dæ·mnd) adj. condenado, réprobo. *2* fig. condenado, maldito, detestable. *3* adv. sumamente.

**damnify (to)** (-nifai) tr. damnificar.

**damp** (dæmp) *adj.* húmedo, mojado. *2 s.* humedad. *3* fig. desaliento. *4* MIN. grisú, mofeta.
**damp (to)** *tr.* humedecer, mojar. *2* ahogar, apagar, amortiguar. *3* enfriar [los ánimos]; desalentar. *4 intr.* humedecerse. *5* desalentarse.
**dampen (to)** (-øn) *tr.* (esp. E.U.) TO DAMP.
**damper** (dæ·mpøʳ) *s.* apagador, amortiguador. *2* regulador de tiro [de chimenea]. *3* MÚS. apagador [del piano]; sordina. *4* desalentador.
**dampness** (-nis) *s.* humedad.
**damsel** (dæ·mšøl) *s.* damisela.
**damson** (dæ·mšøn) *s.* ciruela damascena.
**Dan** (dæn) *n. pr.* BIB. Dan. *2* dim. de Daniel.
**dance** (dæns) *s.* danza, baile.
**dance (to)** *intr.* danzar, bailar: *to ~ attendance on,* servir obsequiosamente a. *2* bailar [un baile]. *3* hacer bailar.
**dancer** (-øʳ) *s.* bailador, ra. *2* bailarín, danzarín, na. *3* pl. parejas de baile.
**dancing** (-ing) *s.* danza, baile [acción]. *2 adj.* de baile, que baila: *~ girl,* bailarina.
**dandelion** (dæ·ndilaiøn) *s.* BOT. amargón, diente de león.
**dander** (dæ·ndøʳ) *s.* fam. ira, enojo.
**dandify (to)** (dæ·ndifai) *s.* acicalar, componer.
**dandle (to)** (dæ·ndøl) *tr.* hacer saltar [a un niño] sobre las rodillas. *2* mimar, acariciar.
**dandler** (-løʳ) *s.* niñero.
**dandruff** (dæ·ndrøf) *s.* caspa.
**dandy** (dæ·ndi) *adj. y s.* dandi, elegante, gomoso. *2 adj.* fam. estupendo.
**dandyism** (-išm) *s.* dandismo.
**Dane** (dein) *s.* danés, dinamarqués. *2* perro danés.
**danewort** (-uøʳt) *s.* BOT. cimicaria, yezgo.
**danger** (dei·ndjøʳ) *s.* peligro, riesgo, escollo.
**dangerous** (-øs) *adj.* peligroso. *2* de cuidado, grave.
**dangerously** (-li) *adv.* peligrosamente, gravemente.
**dangle (to)** (dæ·ngøl) *tr.* hacer balancear [en el aire]. *2 intr.* colgar, pender, bambolearse. *3 to ~ after,* rondar, andar detrás de.
**Danish** (dei·nish) *adj. y s.* danés, dinamarqués.
**dank** (dønk) *adj.* liento, húmedo.
**danseuse** (dansø·š) *s.* bailarina.
**Dantesque** (dænte·sk) *adj.* dantesco.
**Danube** (dæ·niub) *n. pr.* GEOGR. Danubio.
**Danubian** (dæniu·bian) *adj.* danubiano.
**Daphne** (dæ·fni) *n. pr.* MIT. Dafne. *2 s.* (con min.). BOT. adelfilla.
**dapper** (dæ·pøʳ) *adj.* vivaracho. *2* atildado, pulcro, elegante.
**dapple** (dæ·pøl) *adj.* DAPPLED.
**dapple (to)** *tr.* manchar, salpicar de manchas.
**dappled** (-d) *adj.* manchado, moteado. *2* rodado [caballo].
**dare** (deʳ) *s.* fam. reto, desafío.
**dare (to)** *tr.* atreverse a, osar. *2* arrostrar, desafiar. *3* desafiar, retar [a hacer algo]. ¶ Pret.: *dared* o *durst;* p. p.: *dred.*
**daredevil** (-de·vøl) *adj. y s.* atrevido, temerario.
**daring** (dæ·ring) *adj.* atrevido, osado. *2* emprendedor. *3 s.* atrevimiento, osadía.
**Darius** (dara·iøs) *n. pr.* Darío.
**dark** (daʳk) *adj.* oscuro: *~ room,* cuarto oscuro; *it grows ~,* oscurece, anochece. *2* moreno negruzco. *3* negro, sombrío, triste, infausto. *4* amenazador, siniestro. *5* negro, perverso, atroz. *6* callado, reservado. *7* secreto, enigmático. *8* ignorante. *9 ~ lantern,* linterna sorda. *10 s.* oscuridad; sombra, noche, tinieblas. *11* ignorancia: *in the ~,* a oscuras, en la ignorancia de una cosa.

**darken (to)** (-øn) *tr.* oscurecer, ensombrecer. *2* anublar. *3* entristecer. *4* cegar, ofuscar. *5* embrollar, confundir. *6* denigrar, manchar. *7 intr.* obscurecerse, ensombrecerse.
**darkle (to)** (-øl) *intr.* acechar en la oscuridad.*2* oscurecerse.
**darkling** (-ling) *adj.* oscuro. *2 adv.* a oscuras.
**darkly** (-li) *adv.* oscuramente. *2* misteriosamente. *3* secretamente. *4* sombríamente.
**darkness** (-nis) *s.* oscuridad. *2* tinieblas, lobreguez. *3* tristeza. *4* ignorancia, maldad. *5* reserva, secreto.
**darksome** (-søm) *s.* poét. oscuro, sombrío.
**darky** (-i) *s.* fam. negro, mulato.
**darling** (da·ʳling) *adj.* amado, querido. *2 s.* ser querido: *my ~,* vidita, amor mío.
**darn** (daʳn) *s.* zurcido.
**darn (to)** *tr.* zurcir.
**darnel** (da·ʳnøl) *s.* BOT. cizaña, joyo.
**darning** (da·ʳning) *s.* zurcidura, zurcido.
**dart** (daʳt) *s.* dardo, flecha, venablo. *2* rehilete, flechilla. *3* aguijón [de insecto]. *4* ARQ. dardo. *5* movimiento rápido.
**dart (to)** *tr.* lanzar, tirar, arrojar, despedir. *2 intr.* lanzarse, precipitarse.
**Darwinism** (da·ʳuinišm) *s.* darvinismo.
**Darwinist** (-ist) *s.* darvinista.
**dash** (dæsh) *s.* arremetida. *2* golpe, choque, embate: *at a ~,* de un golpe. *3* chapaleteo. *4* movimiento súbito. *5* DEP. carrera corta y rápida. *6* trazo, plumada, raya, guión largo. *7* TELEGR. raya. *8* un poco, unas gotas, un chorrito. *9* ostentación: *to cut a ~,* hacer gran papel. *10* empuje, energía, brío. *11* DASHBOARD.
**dash (to)** *tr.* golpear, romper, estrellar. *2* arrojar, lanzar. *3* rociar, salpicar. *4* echar, mezclar. *5* frustrar, destruir. *6* desanimar. *7 to ~ off,* escribir o hacer aprisa. *8 to ~ out,* rayar, tachar. *9 intr.* moverse, arrojarse con ímpetu: *to ~ out,* salir corriendo. *10* chocar, estrellarse, batir. *11* fachendear.
**dashboard** (-boʳd) *s.* guardafangos. *2* AUTO. salpicadero.
**dashing** (dæ·shing) *adj.* enérgico, brioso, arrollador. *2* ostentoso, vistoso.
**dastard** (dæ·staʳd) *adj. y s.* cobarde, vil.
**dastardize (to)** (-aiš) *tr.* acobardar.
**dastardly** (-li) *adj.* cobarde, vil.
**data** (dei·ta) *s.* datos, detalles.
**datary** (dei·tari) *s.* dataria. *2* datario.
**date** (deit) *s.* fecha, data. *2* cita [para verse]. *3* época, período. *4* ahora, el presente: *down to ~,* hasta ahora; *out of ~,* anticuado, desusado, pasado de moda; *up to ~,* hasta ahora; al día; a la última. *5* BOT. dátil: *~ palm,* datilera, palmera. *6* ZOOL. *~ shell,* dátil [molusco].
**date (to)** *tr.* datar, fechar. *2* contar [por años, etc.]. *3* pop. dar cita [a uno]. *4 intr.* anticuarse. *5 to ~ from,* llevar fecha de; datar de.
**dated** (-id) *adj.* datado, fechado. *2* anticuado.
**dateless** (-lis) *adj.* sin fecha. *2* inmemorial.
**dater** (-øʳ) *s.* fechador.
**dative** (-tiv) *adj. y s.* GRAM. dativo.
**datum** (-øm) *s.* dato.
**daub** (dob) *s.* unto, embadurnadura. *2* PINT. pintarrajo.
**daub (to)** *tr.* untar, embadurnar. *2* pintarrajear.
**dauber** (-øʳ) *s.* embadurnador. *2* pintamonas. *3* cepillo, etc., para embadurnar.
**daubing** (-ing) *s.* embadurnamiento. *2* afeite.
**dauby** (-i) *adj.* untuoso, pegajoso. *2* pintarrajeado.

**daughter** (do·tø<sup>r</sup>) *s.* hija.
**daughter-in-law** *s.* nuera, hija política.
**daughterly** (-li) *adj.* filial, de hija.
**daunt (to)** (dont) *tr.* acobardar, intimidar, asustar, arredrar, desanimar.
**dauntless** (-lis) *adj.* impávido, intrépido.
**dauphin** (do·fin) *s.* delfín [de Francia].
**dauphiness** (-is) *s.* delfina.
**davit** (dæ·vit) *s.* MAR. pescante; serviola.
**Davy** (dei·vi) *n. pr.* dim. de DAVID.
**daw** (do) *s.* ORN. corneja.
**dawdle (to)** (do·døl) *intr.* haronear, perder el tiempo.
**dawdler** (do·dlø<sup>r</sup>) *s.* ocioso, paseante.
**dawn** (don) *s.* alba, aurora, amanecer, madrugada. 2 fig. comienzo, albor, albores.
**dawn (to)** *intr.* amanecer, alborear, clarear, romper el día. 2 apuntar asomar. 3 *to ~ on* o *upon*, empezar a ser visto o comprendido por.
**dawning** (-ing) *s.* alba, amanecer. 2 fig. *first dawnings*, albores.
**day** (dei) *s.* día: *~ of doom, Day of Judgment*, día del juicio; *~ off*, día de asueto, día libre; *day's run*, MAR. singladura; *all ~ long*, todo el día; *by ~*, de día; *by the ~*, por día; *~ by ~* o *~ in, ~ out*, día tras día; *from ~ to ~*, de día en día; *some fine ~*, un buen día, el mejor día; *the ~ after tomorrow*, pasado mañana; *the ~ before yesterday*, anteayer; *up to this ~*, hasta hoy. 2 jornada, jornal [horas de trabajo]. 3 luz del día. 4 *pl.* días, tiempo, época: *in the days of old*, antaño. 5 *adj.* de día, diurno; a jornal, de jornal: *~ school*, escuela diurna, sin internado; *~ labour*, trabajo a jornal; *~ labourer*, jornalero.
**daybook** (-buk) *s.* COM. libro diario.
**daybreak** (-breik) *s.* alba, amanecer.
**daydream** (-drim) *s.* ensueño, ilusión, quimera, castillo en el aire.
**dayfly** (-flai) *s.* ENT. cachipolla, efímera.
**daylight** (-lait) *s.* luz del día, luz natural.
**daylong** (-long) *adj.* de todo el día. 2 *adv.* todo el día.
**dayspring** (-spring) *s.* alba, albor.
**daystar** (-sta<sup>r</sup>) *s.* lucero del alba.
**daytime** (-taim) *s.* día [de sol a sol]: *in the ~*, de día.
**daywork** (-uø<sup>r</sup>k) *s.* jornada, jornal.
**daze** (deiš) *s.* deslumbramiento, aturdimiento: *to be in a ~*, estar aturdido.
**daze (to)** *tr.* deslumbrar, ofuscar, aturdir.
**dazzle** (dæ·søl) *s.* deslumbramiento. 2 brillo.
**dazzle (to)** *tr.* deslumbrar, ofuscar. 2 *intr.* deslumbrarse. 3 brillar.
**dazzling** (-šling) *adj.* deslumbrador.
**deacon** (di·køn) *s.* diácono.
**deaconess** (-is) *s.* diaconisa.
**deaconry** (-ri), **deaconship** (-ship) *s.* diaconato, diaconado; diaconía.
**dead** (ded) *adj.* muerto [en todas sus acepciones]: *Dead Sea*, GEOGR. Mar Muerto. 2 difunto, finado. 3 inerte, inanimado. 4 insensible, sordo, indiferente. 5 estéril, inútil. 6 frío, sin fervor, sin energía, gastado. 7 apagado [volcán, brasa, etc.]. 8 sordo [sonido]. 9 mate. 10 uniforme, monótono. 11 despoblado. 12 seguro, cierto, certero: *~ shot*, tirador certero. 13 absoluto, completo, profundo: *~ calm*, calma profunda; MAR. calma chicha. 14 imitada, condenada [puerta, ventana]. 15 mortal, terrible. 16 ELECT. inactivo, sin corriente. 17 insípido, desbravado, que ya no fermenta. 18 Otros sentidos: *~ end*, callejón sin

salida; RADIO. punto muerto; *~ heat*, DEP. empate [en una carrera]; *~ reckoning*, MAR. estima; *~ stop*, parada en seco; paro completo.
 *19 adv.* absolutamente, completamente, del todo. *20 de pronto. 21 directamente. 22 exactamente.
 *23 s.* lo más callado, muerto, etc., de: *the ~ of night*, el silencio de la noche; *the ~ of winter*, lo más crudo del invierno. *24* usado como plural: *the ~*, los muertos.
**deaden (to)** (de-døn) *tr.* amortiguar. 2 retardar, frenar. 3 apagar [el sonido, el brillo]. 4 hacer insípido, desbravado. 5 *intr.* amortiguarse, apagarse.
**deadhead** (de·djed) *s.* el que tiene pase [en el teatro, etc.]. 2 MAR. bolardo.
**dead-letter office** *s.* CORR. departamento de cartas devueltas o no reclamadas.
**deadliness** (-linis) *s.* calidad de mortífero.
**deadlock** (-lak) *s.* detención, paro, situación sin salida, punto muerto.
**deadly** (-li) *adj.* mortal, mortífero, letal. 2 mortal [odio, enemigo, palidez, etc.]. 3 intenso, sumo. 4 capital [pecado]. 5 *adv.* mortalmente, sumamente.
**dead-nettle** *s.* BOT. ortiga muerta.
**dead-stick landing** *s.* AVIA. aterrizaje con el motor parado.
**dead-struck** *adj.* aterrado, anonadado.
**deaf** (def) *adj.* sordo [pers. o animal]: *~ and dumb*, sordomudo; *to turn a ~ ear*, hacerse el sordo. 2 sordo, apagado [sonido].
**deafen (to)** (-øn) *tr.* asordar, ensordecer. 2 apagar [un sonido].
**deafening** (-ing) *adj.* ensordecedor.
**deaf-mute** *adj.-s.* sordomudo.
**deafness** (de·fnis) *s.* sordera.
**deal** (dil) *s.* porción, cantidad: *a good ~ [of]*, bastante; *a great ~ [of]*, mucho. 2 trato, negociación. 3 trato [que se da o recibe]. 4 distribución, reparto. 5 mano [de un juego de naipes]. 6 tabla [de pino o abeto]. 7 política económica.
**deal (to)** *tr.* distribuir, repartir, dispensar. *~ Gralte. con out.* 2 arrear [un golpe, etc.]. 3 dar [naipes]. 4 *intr. to ~ in*, tratar, comerciar, negociar. 5 *to ~ by* o *with*, portarse [con uno], tratarlo. 6 *to ~ with*, tratar con; tratar de o sobre; ocuparse en o de; intervenir en; habérselas con. ¶ Pret. y p. p.: *dealt*.
**dealer** (di·lø<sup>r</sup>) *s.* comerciante, negociante, tratante. 2 distribuidor. 3 *plain ~*, hombre sincero; *double ~*, hombre falso.
**dealing** (-ling) *s.* proceder, comportamiento: *fair ~*, buena fe; *double ~*, doblez, mala fe. 2 *pl.* trato, relaciones. 3 tratos, negocios.
**dealt** (delt) pret. y p. p. de TO DEAL.
**dean** (din) *s.* deán. 2 decano.
**deanery** (-øri), **deanship** (-ship) *s.* deanato, deanazgo. 2 decanato.
**dear** (di·ø<sup>r</sup>) *adj.* querido, caro, amado, estimado, preciado. 2 caro, costoso. 3 *Dear Sir, Dears Messrs.*, muy señor mío, muy señores míos [en las cartas]. 4 *s.* persona querida. 5 persona amable, excelente. 6 interj. *~ me!*, ¡Dios mío! 9 *adv.* caro.
**dearly** (-li) *adv.* amorosamente, tiernamente. 2 caro, caramente.
**dearth** (dø<sup>r</sup>z) *s.* carestía, hambre. 2 escasez, falta.
**deary** (di·øri) *s.* vidita, amor mío.
**death** (dez) *s.* muerte: *the Death*, la muerte, la descarnada: *to ~, to the ~*, a muerte, hasta la

muerte; sumamente; ~ *to...!*, ¡muera...! *2* defunción, fallecimiento, óbito. *3 adj.* de muerte, de difuntos, de defunción: ~ *bell,* ~ *knell,* ~ *toll,* toque de difuntos; ~ *certificate,* partida de defunción; ~ *duties,* derechos sucesorios; ~ *mask,* mascarilla [de un difunto]; ~ *penalty,* pena de muerte; ~ *rate,* mortalidad; ~ *rattle,* estertor de la muerte.

**deathbed** (-bed) *s.* lecho de muerte.

**deathblow** (-blou) *s.* golpe mortal.

**deathful** (-ful) *adj.* mortal, letal, mortífero.

**deathless** (-lis) *adj.* inmortal; imperecedero.

**deathlike** (-laik) *adj.* DEATHLY 1.

**deathly** (-li) *adj.* mortal, de muerte, letárgico, cadavérico. *2 adv.* mortalmente; sumamente.

**deathtrap** (-træp) *s.* lugar peligroso, trampa.

**deathwatch** (-uøtch) *s.* velatorio. *2* guardia de un reo de muerte.

**debacle** (dibæ·køl) *s.* deshielo [en un río]; avenida que lo sigue. *2* desastre, ruina.

**debar (to)** (diba·ᵣ) *tr.* excluir [de]. *2* privar, prohibir. ¶ Pret. y p. p.: *debarred;* ger.: *-rring.*

**debark (to)** (diba·ᵣk) *tr.-intr.* desembarcar. *2 tr.* descortezar [un árbol].

**debarkation** (-ei·shøn) *s.* desembarco, desembarque.

**debase (to)** (dibei·s) *tr.* rebajar, degradar, envilecer, deshonrar. *2* adulterar, viciar.

**debasement** (-mønt) *s.* degradación, envilecimiento. *2* adulteración.

**debatable** (dibei·tabøl) *adj.* discutible.

**debate** (dibei·t) *s.* debate, discusión.

**debate (to)** *tr.-intr.* debatir, discutir. *2 intr.* deliberar, reflexionar.

**debauch** (di·boch) *s.* exceso, orgía, libertinaje.

**debauch (to)** *tr.* seducir, corromper. *2 intr.* entregarse al libertinaje.

**debauchee** (di·boshı) *s.* libertino.

**debaucher** (dibo·shøʳ) *s.* seductor, corruptor.

**debauchery** (-i) *s.* libertinaje, intemperancia. *2* corrupción. *3 pl.* orgías.

**debenture** (dibe·nchøʳ) *s.* COM. obligación, bono. *2* abonaré de la aduana.

**debilitate (to)** (dibi·liteit) *tr.* debilitar, enervar.

**debility** (dibi·liti) *s.* debilidad.

**debit** (de·bit) *s.* COM. debe. *2* COM. débito, adeudo, cargo. *3* COM. ~ *balance,* saldo deudor.

**debit (to)** *tr.* COM. adeudar, cargar [en cuenta].

**debonair** (debone·øʳ) *adj.* afable, jovial.

**Deborah** (de·bora) *n. pr. f.* Débora.

**debouch (to)** (dibu·sh) *intr.* desembocar, salir.

**debouchment** (-mønt) *s.* desembocadura.

**debris** (debrı·) *s.* ruinas, escombros, restos. *2* GEOL. deyecciones.

**debt** (det) *s.* deuda, débito: *National* ~, deuda pública; *to run into* ~, endeudarse.

**debtor** (de·tøʳ) *s.* deudor.

**debut** (debiu·) *s.* TEAT. estreno, debut. *2* entrada en sociedad [de una joven].

**debutant** (-tan) *adj.-s.* debutante.

**debutante** (-tant) *adj.-s.* debutante. *2* díc. de la joven que hace su entrada en sociedad.

**decade** (de·keid) *s.* década, decenio.

**decadence, -cy** (de·kadøns, -si) *s.* decadencia, ocaso.

**decadent** (-ønt) *adj.-s.* decadente. *2* decadentista.

**decagon** (de·kagøn) *s.* GEOM. decágono.

**decagram, decagramme** (de·kagæm) *s.* decagramo.

**decahedron** (dekaji·drøn) *s.* GEOM. decaedro.

**decalcomania** (dikakoumei·nia) *s.* calcomanía.

**decalitre, decaliter** (de·kalitøʳ) *s.* decalitro.

**decalogue** (-log) *s.* decálogo.

**decametre, decameter** (-mitøʳ) *s.* decámetro.

**decamp (to)** (dikæ·mp) *intr.* decampar. *2* largarse, huir.

**decanal** (de·kanal) *adj.* del deán o del decano.

**decant (to)** (dikæ·nt) *tr.* decantar. *2* trasegar.

**decantation** (-ei·shøn) *s.* decantación. *2* trasiego.

**decanter** (dikæ·ntøʳ) *s.* ampolla, garrafa.

**decapitate (to)** (dikæ·piteit) *tr.* decapitar.

**decapitation** (-ei·shøn) *s.* decapitación.

**decapod** (de·kapad) *adj.-s.* ZOOL. decápodo.

**decasyllable** (dekasi·labøl) *s.* decasílabo.

**decay** (dikei·) *s.* decaimiento, decadencia. *2* ruina, desmedro. *3* putrefacción, podredumbre. *4* MED. caries.

**decay (to)** *intr.* decaer, descaecer, declinar, venir a menos. *2* arruinarse, deteriorarse. *3* pudrirse. *4* pasarse, marchitarse. *5* MED. cariarse. *6 tr.* arruinar, echar a perder.

**decease** (disı·t) *s.* defunción, fallecimiento.

**decease (to)** *intr.* morir, fallecer.

**deceased** (-t) *adj.-s.* difunto, finado.

**deceit** (disı·t) *s.* engaño, dolo, falacia. *2* artificio, superchería.

**deceitful** (-ful) *adj.* engañoso, doloso, falaz. *2* falso, engañador.

**deceivable** (disı·vabøl) *adj.* engañadizo.

**deceive (to)** (disı·v) *tr.* engañar. *2* defraudar, burlar.

**deceiver** (-øʳ) *s.* engañador.

**December** (dise·mbøʳ) *s.* diciembre.

**decemvir** (dise·mvøʳ) *s.* decenviro.

**decency** (dı·sønsi) *s.* decencia. *2* decoro. *3 pl.* conveniencias sociales.

**decennial** (dise·nial) *adj.* decenal.

**decennium** (-niøm) *m.* decenio.

**decent** (dı·sønt) *adj.* decente. *2* razonable, regular.

**decenter (to)** (dise·ntøʳ) *tr.* TO DECENTRE.

**decentralize (to)** (dise·ntralaiš) *tr.* descentralizar.

**decentre (to)** (dise·ntøʳ) *tr.* descentrar.

**deception** (disep·shøn) *s.* decepción, engaño.

**deceptive** (-tiv) *adj.* engañoso, falaz.

**dechristianize (to)** (dikri·stianaiš) *tr.* descristianizar.

**decide (to)** (disai·d) *tr.-intr.* decidir: *to* ~ *to,* decidir o decidirse a [hacer algo].

**decided** (-id) *adj.* decidido. *2* definido, indudable, categórico.

**deciduous** (-ŷuøs) *adj.* H. NAT. caedizo, caduco.

**decigram(me** (de·sigræm) *s.* decigramo.

**decilitre, deciliter** (-litøʳ) *s.* decilitro.

**decimal** (-mal) *adj.* decimal.

**decimate (to)** (-meit) *tr.* diezmar.

**decimation** (-ei·shøn) *s.* acción de diezmar. *2* estrago, mortandad.

**decimetre, decimeter** (-mitøʳ) *s.* decímetro.

**decipher (to)** (disai·føʳ) *tr.* descifrar.

**decision** (disi·ŷøn) *s.* decisión, resolución, acuerdo. *2* decisión, firmeza.

**decisive** (disai·siv) *adj.* decisivo. *2* conclusivo. *3* decidido, firme.

**deck** (dek) *s.* MAR. cubierta, puente: *between decks,* entrepuente. *2* MEC. sección o parte plana. *3* piso [de un autobús, etc.]. *4* techo [de vagón]. *5* baraja. *6* baceta, monte [en los naipes].

**deck (to)** *tr.* vestir, ataviar, adornar. *2* cubrir, revestir.

**deckle** o **deckle edge** (de·køl) *s.* barba [del papel].

**declaim (to)** (diklei·m) *intr.-tr.* declamar. *2 intr.* perorar.

**declaimer** (-ør) *s*. declamador, perorador.
**declamation** (-ei·shøn) *s*. declamación. *2* perorata.
**declamatory** (diklæ·matori) *adj*. declamatorio.
**declaration** (diklarei·shøn) *s*. declaración. *2* aserto. *3* manifiesto.
**declarative, -tory** (diklæ·rativ, -tori) *adj*. declaratorio. *2* afirmativo, enunciativo.
**declare (to)** (dikle·ør) *tr.-ref*. declarar. *2 tr.* manifestar, afirmar. *3* intr. *to ~ for* o *against*, declararse partidario o enemigo de.
**declaredly** (-idly) *adv*. declaradamente.
**declension** (dikle·nshøn) *s*. GRAM., MAGNET. declinación. *2* declive. *3* decadencia, caída.
**declination** (deklinei·shøn) *s*. ASTR., MAGNET. declinación. *2* desviación, apartamiento. *3* declive. *4* negativa, acción de rehusar.
**decline** (dikla·in) *s*. declinación, decadencia, ocaso, fin. *2* decaimiento, consunción. *3* mengua, baja. *4* declive.
**decline (to)** *tr*. inclinar, bajar. *2* desviar. *3* rehusar, negarse a; renunciar. *4* GRAM. declinar. *5 intr.* inclinarse, bajar. *6* desviarse. *7* declinar, decaer, venir a menos. *8* menguar, ir de baja.
**declivity** (-viti) *s*. declividad, declive.
**declutch (to)** (diclø·ch) *tr*. MEC. desembragar.
**decoction** (dika·kshøn) *s*. decocción, cocimiento.
**decode (to)** (dikou·d) *tr*. descifrar [lo escrito en cifra].
**decollate (to)** (dika·leit) *tr*. degollar, decapitar.
**decollation** (-lei·shøn) *s*. degollación.
**decolleté** (deikaltei·) *adj*. escotado [vestido].
**decolorant** (dika·lørant) *adj.-s*. decolorante.
**decolo(u)rate** (dika·løreit), **decolo(u)rize (to)** (-raiš) *tr*. decolorar, descolorar, descolorir.
**decompose (to)** (dikømpøu·š) *tr*. descomponer [separar los elementos de; pudrir]. *2 intr.* descomponerse.
**decomposition** (dikampoši·shøn) *s*. descomposición.
**decompression** (dikømpre·shøn) *s*. descompresión.
**decontaminate (to)** (dikøntæ·mineit) *tr*. desinfectar.
**decorate (to)** (de·køreit) *tr*. decorar, adornar, embellecer. *2* condecorar.
**decoration** (-rei·shøn) *s*. decoración, ornamentación; ornamento, adorno. *2* condecoración.
**decorative** (de·kørativ) *adj*. decorativo, ornamental.
**decorator** (-reitør) *s*. decorador, adornista.
**decorous** (de·kørøs) *adj*. decoroso, correcto.
**decorticate (to)** (diko·ʳtikeit) *tr*. descortezar, mondar, pelar.
**decorum** (diko·røm) *s*. decoro.
**decoy** (dikoi·) *s*. señuelo, reclamo, cimbel. *2* añagaza. *3* entruchón, gancho [pers.].
**decoy (to)** *tr*. reclamar, atraer con señuelo. *2* atraer a un peligro, emboscada, etc.
**decrease** (dikrı·s) *s*. decrecimiento, disminución. *2* menguante [de la luna].
**decrease (to)** *intr*. decrecer, disminuir, menguar. *2 tr*. disminuir, reducir.
**decreasing** (-ing) *adj*. decreciente.
**decree** (dikrı·) *s*. decreto, orden, edicto, mandato.
**decree (to)** *tr*. decretar, ordenar, mandar.
**decrement** (de·krimønt) *s*. decremento.
**decrepit** (dikre·pit) *adj*. decrépito, caduco.
**decrepitude** (-tiud) *s*. decrepitud, caduquez.
**decrescent** (dikre·sønt) *adj*. decreciente.
**decretal** (dikrı·tal) *adj.-s*. decretal. *2 s. pl.* decretales.

**decrial** (dikrai·al) *s*. descrédito, rebaja, censura.
**decrier** (-ør) *s*. censurador, denigrador.
**decry (to)** (dikrai·) *tr*. desacreditar, rebajar, censurar. *2* desvalorizar.
**decubitus** (dikiu·bitøs) *s*. decúbito.
**decumbent** (dikø·mbønt) *adj*. decumbente.
**decuple** (de·kiupøl) *adj.-s*. décuplo.
**decuple (to)** *tr*. decuplicar.
**decurion** (dikiu·riøn) *s*. decurión.
**decurrent** (dikø·rønt) *adj*. BOT. decurrente.
**decussate** (dikø·seit) *adj*. decusado.
**dedicate (to)** (de·dikeit) *tr*. dedicar [un libro, etc.].
**dedication** (-ei·shøn) *s*. dedicación. *2* dedicatoria. *3* advocación [de una iglesia].
**deduce (to)** (didiu·s) *tr*. deducir, inferir. *2* hacer derivar.
**deducible** (-ibøl) *adj*. deducible, inferible.
**deduct (to)** (didø·kt) *tr*. deducir, rebajar, descontar, restar.
**deduction** (didø·kshøn) *s*. deducción, rebaja, descuento. *2* deducción, inferencia.
**deductive** (-tiv) *adj*. deductivo.
**deed** (dıd) *s*. hecho; acción, obra, acto; realidad: *in ~*, de hecho, en verdad. *2* hazaña, proeza. *3* DER. escritura, instrumento.
**deed (to)** *tr*. DER. transferir por escritura o instrumento.
**deem (to)** (dım) *tr.-intr*. juzgar, creer, pensar, estimar, considerar.
**deep** (dıp) *adj*. hondo, profundo. *2* espeso [nieve, etc.]. *3* alta [hierba]. *4* hundido, sumergido [en]; cubierto [de]. *5* impenetrable, abstruso. *6* penetrante, sagaz. *7* astuto. *8* grave, grande. *9* absorto, embebido, enfrascado, muy metido [en]. *10* agudo, intenso, extremo, cordial. *11* grave [sonido]. *12* oscuro [color]. *13* riguroso [luto]. *14* de profundidad, de espesor; hundido hasta [cierta profundidad].
*15 adv*. hondamente, profundamente, muy, mucho. *16* muy adentro: *~ into the night*, muy entrada la noche.
*17 s*. profundidad. *18* piélago, abismo, sima. *19* misterio.
**-deep**, elemento final de compuestos como: *ankle-deep*, *knee-deep*, metido hasta los tobillos, las rodillas.
**deep-chested** *adj*. ancho de pecho.
**deepen (to)** (-øn) *tr*. ahondar, intensificar. *2* oscurecer. *3* hacer más grave [un sonido]. *4 intr.* ahondarse, intensificarse, oscurecerse, hacerse más grave.
**deep-felt** *adj*. hondamente sentido.
**deep-laid** *adj*. dispuesto con astucia.
**deepness** (-nis) *s*. profundidad, intensidad. *2* penetración, sagacidad.
**deep-rooted** *adj*. profundamente arraigado.
**deer** (di·ør) *s*. ZOOL. ciervo, venado: *red ~*, ciervo común; *fallow ~*, gramo.
**deerskin** (-skin) *s*. piel de venado.
**deface (to)** (difei·s) *tr*. borrar, desfigurar, mutilar, estropear, afear.
**defacement** (-mønt) *s*. desfiguración, mutilación, estropeo, afeamiento.
**de facto** (di·fæ·ctou) loc. de hecho.
**defalcate (to)** (difælkeit) *intr*. desfalcar, cometer desfalcos.
**defalcation** (-ei·shøn) *s*. desfalco.
**defamation** (defamei·shøn) *s*. difamación, infamación.
**defamatory** (difæ·matori) *adj*. difamatorio, infamatorio.

**defame (to)** (difei·m) *tr.* difamar, infamar.
**defamer** (-ø<sup>r</sup>) *s.* difamador, infamador.
**default** (difo·lt) *s.* falta, defecto, carencia. 2 descuido, negligencia; incumplimiento; falta de pago. *3* no comparecencia; DER. rebeldía.
**default (to)** *tr.-intr.* dejar de cumplir, faltar [a un deber, obligación, etc.]; no pagar. *2 intr.* DEP. no comparecer, estar en rebeldía. *3 tr.* DER. declarar en rebeldía.
**defaulter** (-ø<sup>r</sup>) *s.* el que falta o no cumple. *2* desfalcador. *3* DER. rebelde.
**defeat** (difi·t) *s.* derrota, vencimiento. *2* frustración.
**defeat (to)** *tr.* derrotar, vencer. *2* desbaratar, frustrar. *3* DER. anular.
**defeatist** (-ist) *adj.-s.* derrotista.
**defecate (to)** (de·fikeit) *tr.-intr.* defecar.
**defecation** (-ei·shøn) *s.* defecación.
**defect** (dife·kt) *s.* defecto.
**defection** (dife·kshøn) *s.* defección.
**defective** (dife·ktiv) *adj.* defectivo, defectuoso. *2* GRAM. defectivo. *3* corto, deficiente. *4 s.* PSIC. deficiente [pers.].
**defence** (dife·ns) *s.* defensa. *2 pl.* FORT. defensas.
**defenceless** (-lis) *adj.* indefenso, inerme.
**defend (to)** (dife·nd) *tr.-ref.* defender.
**defendant** (-ant) *adj.* que defiende. *2 s.* DER. demandado; acusado, procesado.
**defender** (-ø<sup>r</sup>) *s.* defensor. *2* campeón, abogado.
**defense, defenseless,** etc. = DEFENCE, DEFENCELESS, etc.
**defensible** (dife·nsibøl) *adj.* defendible.
**defensive** (-siv) *adj.* defensivo. *2 s.* defensiva: *on the ~,* a la defensiva.
**defer (to)** (difø·<sup>r</sup>) *tr.* diferir, aplazar, retardar. *2* remitir [al juicio, etc. de]. *3* esperar. *4 to ~ to,* deferir a, ceder a. ¶ Pret. y p. p.: *deferred;* ger.: *-rring.*
**deference** (de·førøns) *s.* deferencia.
**deferent** (-ønt) *adj.* deferente, respetuoso. *2* ASTR., ANAT. deferente.
**deferential** (deføre·nshal) *adj.* DEFERENT 1.
**deferment** (difø·<sup>r</sup>mønt) *s.* dilación, aplazamiento.
**deferred** (difø·rd) *pret.* y *p. p.* de TO DEFER.
**defiance** (difai·ans) *s.* desafío, reto, provocación: *to bid ~ to, to set at ~,* desafiar; *in ~ of,* a despecho de.
**defiant** (-ant) *adj.* desafiador, provocativo.
**deficiency** (difi·shønsi) *s.* deficiencia. *2* falta, insuficiencia. *3* COM. déficit. *4* MED. carencia.
**deficient** (-shønt) *adj.* deficiente. *2* falto, insuficiente. *3* faltante.
**deficit** (de·fisit) *s.* déficit. *2 adj.* deficitario.
**defier** (difai·ø<sup>r</sup>) *s.* desafiador, retador.
**defilade (to)** (defilei·d) *tr.* MIL. desenfilar.
**defile** (di·fail) *s.* desfiladero.
**defile (to)** (difai·l) *tr.* manchar, ensuciar. *2* mancillar, deshonrar, profanar. *3 intr.* MIL. desfilar.
**defilement** (-mønt) *s.* ensuciamiento. *2* mancilla, deshonra, profanación.
**define (to)** (difai·n) *tr.* definir.*2* delimitar, circunscribir. *3* distinguir, caracterizar.
**definite** (de·finit) *adj.* definido; *~ article,* artículo definido o determinado. *2* claro, preciso, terminante.
**definition** (defini·shøn) *s.* definición. *2* precisión, claridad [de una imagen, etc.].
**definitive** (difi·nitiv) *adj.* definitivo. *2* definido. *3* que distingue o define.
**definitor** (definai·tø<sup>r</sup>) *s.* ECLES. definidor.

**deflagrate (to)** (de·flagreit) *intr.* deflagrar. *2 tr.* hacer deflagrar.
**deflate (to)** (diflei·t) *tr.* desinflar, deshinchar. *2* ECON. reducir la inflación. *3 intr.* deshincharse.
**deflation** (-ei·shøn) *s.* desinflamiento. *2* ECON. deflación.
**deflect (to)** (difle·kt) *tr.* desviar, apartar. *2 intr.* desviarse, apartarse.
**deflection** (difle·kshøn) *s.* desvío, desviación. *2* MEC. deflexión.
**defloration** (deflorei·shøn) *s.* desfloración. *2* desflorecimiento. *3* selección.
**deflower (to)** (diflau·ø<sup>r</sup>) *tr.* desflorar [ajar, deslustrar; violar]. *3* despojar de flores.
**defoliate (to)** (difou·lieit) *tr.* deshojar. *2 intr.* deshojarse.
**deforce (to)** (difo·<sup>r</sup>s) *tr.* DER. detentar.
**deforest (to)** (difa·rist) *tr.* despoblar de árboles.
**deform (to)** (difo·<sup>r</sup>m) *tr.* deformar. *2* desfigurar, afear. *3* degradar, envilecer.
**deformed** (-d) *adj.* deformado. *3* deforme, feo, monstruoso.
**deformity** (-iti) *s.* deformidad, fealdad.
**defrauder** (-ø<sup>r</sup>) *s.* defraudador.
**defraud (to)** (difro·d) *tr.* defraudar, estafar.
**defray (to)** (difrei·) *tr.* costear, sufragar, pagar.
**defrayal** (-al) *s.* pago, acción de costear o sufragar.
**defreeze (to)** (difrı·š) *tr.* descongelar.
**deft** (deft) *s.* ágil, diestro, hábil, mañoso.
**defunct** (difø·nkt) *adj.-s.* difunto.
**defy (to)** (difai·) *tr.* desafiar. *2* retar, provocar. *3* arrostrar. *4* despreciar, contravenir.
**degeneracy** (didÿe·nørasi) *s.* degeneración. *2* degradación, perversión.
**degenerate** (-nørit) *adj.-s.* degenerado.
**degenerate (to)** (-nøreit) *intr.* degenerar.
**degeneration** (-ei·shøn) *s.* degeneración.
**deglutition** (digluti·shøn) *s.* deglución.
**degradation** (degradei·shøn) *s.* degradación. *2* degeneración, disminución, deterioro.
**degrade (to)** (digrei·d) *tr.* degradar. *2* minorar, rebajar, reducir. *3 intr.* degradarse.
**degrading** (-ing) *adj.* degradante.
**degrease (to)** (digrı·s) *tr.* desgrasar.
**degree** (digrı·) *s.* grado [en todas sus acepciones, menos en la de voluntad, gusto y en la de grado militar]: *by degrees,* gradualmente; *to a ~,* algo, en cierto modo, hasta cierto punto; sumamente. *2* rango, categoría.
**degustation** (digøstei·shøn) *f.* degustación.
**dehiscence** (diji·søns) *s.* BOT. dehiscencia.
**dehiscent** (-sønt) *adj.* BOT. dehiscente.
**dehorn (to)** (dıjø·<sup>r</sup>n) *tr.* descornar.
**dehumanize (to)** (dıjiu·manaiš·) *tr.* deshumanizar.
**dehydrate (to)** (dıjai·dreit) *tr.* deshidratar.
**deice (to)** (dıai·s) *tr.* AVIA. descongelar.
**deicide** (dı·isaid) *s.* deicida. *2* deicidio.
**deific(al** (dii·fik(al) *adj.* deífico.
**deify (to)** (dı·ifai) *tr.* deificar, divinizar.
**deign (to)** (dein) *intr.* dignarse. *2 tr.* dignarse dar.
**deigning** (-ing) *s.* dignación.
**Deipara** (dıi·para) *adj.* deípara.
**deism** (dı·išm) *s.* deísmo.
**deist** (dı·ist) *s.* deísta.
**deity** (dı·iti) *s.* deidad. *2 the Deity,* Dios.
**deject (to)** (didÿe·kt) *tr.* abatir, desanimar.
**dejected** (-id) *adj.* abatido, desanimado.
**dejection** (didÿe·kshøn) *s.* abatimiento, desánimo. *2* FISIOL. deyección.
**delate (to)** (dilei·t) *tr.* delatar, denunciar.
**delation** (-ei·shøn) *s.* delación.

**delay** (dilei) *s.* dilación, demora, tardanza, retraso.

**delay (to)** *tr.* dilatar, diferir, aplazar, retardar, demorar. *2 intr.* tardar, retrasarse, entretenerse.

**delectable** (dile·ktabøl) *adj.* deleitable, deleitoso.

**delectation** (ei·shøn) *s.* deleite, delectación.

**delegacy** (de·løgasi) *s.* DELEGATION.

**delegate** (de·løgeit) *adj.-s.* delegado, comisionado. *2 s.* lugarteniente, comisario.

**delegate (to)** (tr. delegar, comisionar, diputar.

**delegation** (-ei·shøn) *s.* delegación, diputación, comisión.

**delete (to)** (dilɪ·t) *tr.* borrar, tachar, suprimir.

**deleterious** (deløti·riøs) *adj.* deletéreo. *2* nocivo, pernicioso.

**deletion** (dilɪ·shøn) *s.* tachadura, supresión.

**deliberate** (dili·børit) *adj.* deliberado, premeditado, hecho de intento. *2* cauto, circunspecto. *3* lento, pausado.

**deliberate (to)** (-børeit) *tr.* reflexionar, pensar, considerar, premeditar. *2 intr.* deliberar, consultar. *3* vacilar, dudar.

**deliberately** (-ly) *adv.* deliberadamente. *2* a sabiendas. *3* pausadamente.

**deliberation** (-ei·shøn) *s.* deliberación, premeditación, reflexión. *2* deliberación [acción de deliberar].

**deliberative** (dili·børativ) *adj.* deliberativo. *2* deliberante.

**delicacy** (de·likasi) *s.* delicadeza, delicadez. *2* finura, sensibilidad [de un instrumento, etc.]. *3* exigencia, miramiento. *4* refinamiento, exquisitez, primor. *5* cosa delicada, lujo, golosina.

**delicate** (de·likit) *adj.* delicado. *2* mirado, considerado. *3* exquisito, primoroso. *4* de gusto exigente.

**delicateness** (-nis) *adj.* delicadeza, delicadez.

**delicatessen** (delikate·søn) *s. pl.* fiambre, queso, conservas, etc.; tienda en que se venden.

**delicious** (dili·shøs) *adj.* delicioso. *2* sabroso.

**delight** (dilai·t) *s.* deleite, delicia, placer, gozo, encanto.

**delight (to)** *tr.* deleitar, encantar, dar gusto, recrear. *2 intr.* deleitarse, gozarse, complacerse.

**delightful** (-ful) *adj.* deleitable, deleitoso, delicioso, ameno, exquisito, encantador.

**delightsome** (-søm) *adj.* deleitoso, placentero.

**Delilah** (dilai·la) *n. pr.* Dalila.

**delimit(ate (to)** (dili·mit(eit) *tr.* delimitar.

**delineament** (-niamønt) *s.* DELINEATION.

**delineate (to)** (-nieit) *tr.* delinear, trazar, bosquejar. *2* pintar, describir.

**delineation** (-ei·shøn) *s.* delineación, traza, bosquejo. *2* pintura, descripción.

**delineator** (-nieitøʳ) *s.* delineador, dibujante.

**delinquency** (dili·nkuønsi) *s.* delincuencia. *2* culpa, falta.

**delinquent** (-kuønt) *adj.-s.* delincuente, culpable. *2* moroso [deudor].

**delisquesce (to)** (delikue·s) *intr.* liquidarse lentamente.

**deliquescence** (-øns) *s.* delicuescencia.

**deliquescent** (-ønt) *adj.* delicuescente.

**delirious** (dili·riøs) *adj.* delirante, desvariado.

**delirium** (-riøm) *s.* delirio, desvarío. *2* MED. ~ *tremens,* delirium tremens.

**deliver (to)** (dili·vøʳ) *tr.* libertar. *2* librar, salvar. *3* entregar, dar; rendir, resignar. ~ *Gralte.* con *over* o *up.* *4* despachar [un pedido]; repartir [géneros, correspondencia]. *5* descargar [un golpe]; lanzar, tirar. *6* recitar; pronunciar [dis-

cursos]; emitir [conceptos]. *7 to be delivered of a child,* dar a luz un hijo.

**deliverance** (-ans) *s.* liberación, rescate, salvación. *2* DER. traspaso. *3* dictamen, declaración.

**deliverer** (-øʳ) *s.* libertador, salvador. *2* entregador. *3* repartidor [de paquetes, etc.].

**delivery** (-i) *s.* liberación, rescate. *2* entrega, dación. *3* remesa, reparto [de géneros o correspondencia]. *4* lo entregado. *5* pronunciación [de un discurso, etc.], elocuencia, dicción; manera de expresarse o de cantar. *6* DEP. acción o manera de tirar o lanzar. *7* parto, alumbramiento.

**dell** (del) *s.* hondonada, cañada, vallecito.

**delouse (to)** (dilou·s) *tr.* despiojar.

**Delphian** (de·lfian), **Delphic** (-fik) *adj.* délfico.

**delta** (de·lta) *s.* delta.

**deltoid** (-oid) *adj.-s.* deltoides.

**delude (to)** (diliu·d) *tr.* engañar, deludir.

**deluding** (-ing) *adj.* engañoso, delusorio.

**deluge** (de·liudÿ) *s.* diluvio. *2* inundación.

**deluge (to)** *tr.* inundar.

**delusion** (dilui·ÿøn) *s.* engaño, decepción, error, ilusión.

**delusive** (-siv), **delusory** (-sori) *adj.* engañoso, delusivo, mentiroso, ilusorio.

**delve (to)** (delv) *tr.-intr.* cavar, ahondar, inquirir, escudriñar.

**demagnetize (to)** (dɪmæ·gnetiaĭ) *tr.* desimantar.

**demagogic** (demaga·dÿik) *adj.* demagógico.

**demagogue** (de·magag) *s.* demagogo.

**demagogy** (-gadÿi) *s.* demagogia.

**demand** (dimæ·nd) *s.* demanda, petición, requerimiento; *on* ~, COM. a la presentación. *2* COM., ECON., DER. demanda. *3* pregunta.

**demand (to)** *tr.* demandar, pedir, requerir, exigir, reclamar. *2* preguntar.

**demandant** (-ant) *s.* DER. demandante.

**demanding** (-ing) *adj.* exigente.

**demarcate (to)** (dima·ʳkeit) *tr.* demarcar, deslindar.

**demarcation** (-kei·shøn) *s.* demarcación, deslinde.

**demarche** (dema·ʳsh) *s.* paso, gestión.

**demean (to)** (dimɪ·n) *tr.* rebajar, degradar. *2 ref.* portarse, conducirse. *3* rebajarse, degradarse.

**demeano(u)r** (-øʳ) *s.* conducta, comportamiento. *2* aire, porte.

**dement (to)** (dime·nt) *tr.* dementar, enloquecer.

**demented** (-id) *adj.* demente, insano.

**dementia** (dime·nshia) *s.* demencia, locura.

**demerit** (dime·rit) *s.* demérito, desmerecimiento.

**demesne** (dimei·n o -mɪn) *s.* heredad. *2* región, territorio. *3 fig.* dominio, campo.

**demi-** (de·mi-) *pref.* semi-.

**demigod** (-gad) *s.* semidiós.

**demijohn** (-dÿan) *s.* damajuana, castaña.

**demilitarize (to)** (dɪmi·litaraĭ) *tr.* desmilitarizar.

**demineralization** (dɪminøralĭsei·shøn) *s.* MED. desmineralización.

**demise** (dimai·ĭ) *s.* fallecimiento. *2* transmisión de la corona. *2* DER. transmisión de dominio.

**demise (to)** *tr.* DER. transmitir, transferir.

**demi-semi-quaver** *s.* MÚS. fusa.

**demission** (dimi·shøn) *s.* dimisión, abdicación.

**demit (to)** (dimi·t) *tr.* dimitir, renunciar.

**demiurge** (de·miøʳdÿ) *s.* demiurgo.

**demobilize (to)** (dɪmou·bilaĭ) *tr.* MIL. desmovilizar.

**democracy** (dima·krasi) *s.* democracia.

**democrat** (de·møkræt) *s.* demócrata.

**democratic (al** (-ik(al) *adj.* democrático.

**democratize (to)** (dima·krataĭ) *tr.* democratizar.

**demographic** (dimɡræ·fik) *adj.* demográfico.
**demography** (dima·grafi) *s.* demografía.
**demoiselle** (demuaše·l) *s.* ORN. zaida.
**demolish (to)** (dima·lish) *tr.* demoler. *2* arrasar, derruir, destruir.
**demolishment** (-mønt), **demolition** (-shøn) *s.* demolición. *2* destrucción.
**demon** (-dımøn) *m.* demonio.
**demonetize (to)** (dima·netaiš) *tr.* desmonetizar.
**demoniac** (dimou·niæk) *adj.* demoníaco. *2 adj.-s.* endemoniado, energúmeno.
**demoniacal** (dimønai·akal) *adj.* DEMONIAC 1.
**demonology** (dimøna·lodÿi) *s.* demonología.
**demonstrable** (dima·nstrabøl) *adj.* demostrable.
**demonstrate (to)** (de·mønstrei·t) *tr.* demostrar, hacer ver, probar.
**demonstration** (-ei·shøn) *s.* demostración. *2* COM. exposición, presentación [de un artículo]. *3* manifestación pública.
**demonstrative** (dima·nstrativ) *adj.* demostrativo.
**demonstrator** (de·mønstreitøʳ) *s.* demostrador. *2* POL. manifestante.
**demoralize (to)** (dima·ralaiš) *tr.* desmoralizar.
**Demosthenes** (dima·szønis) *n. pr.* Demóstenes.
**demotic** (dima·tik) *adj.* demótico.
**demount (to)** (dımau·nt) *tr.* desmontar, desarmar.
**demulcent** (dimø·lsønt) *adj.* demulcente.
**demur** (dimø·ʳ) *s.* irresolución, vacilación. *2* objeción, escrúpulo, reparo.
**demur (to)** *intr.* objetar, poner dificultades. *2* vacilar, fluctuar. ¶ Pret. y p. p.: *demurred;* ger.: *-rring.*
**demure** (dimiu·ʳ) *adj.* grave, serio, formal. *2* recatado. *3* gazmoño.
**demurrage** (dimø·ridÿ) *s.* COM. estadía.
**demurrer** (dimø·røʳ) *s.* el que objeta o pone reparos. *2* DER. excepción.
**den** (den) *s.* cubil, guarida. *2* cueva, antro. *3* cochitril. *4* fig. rincón, cuarto de estudio o retiro.
**denarius** (dine·riøs) *s.* denario.
**denationalize (to)** (dınæ·shønalaiš) *tr.* desnacionalizar.
**denaturalize (to)** (-churlaiš) *tr.* desnaturalizar.
**denature (to)** (dınei·chøʳ) *tr.* QUÍM. desnaturalizar.
**dendrite** (de·ndrait) *s.* dendrita.
**dendrology** (dendra·lodÿi) *s.*dendrología.
**denegation** (denigei·shøn) *s.* negación, negativa.
**dengue** (de·ngei) *s.* MED. dengue.
**deniable** (dinai·abøl) *adj.* negable.
**denial** (dinai·al) *s.* negación, negativa, contradicción. *2* denegación, negativa.
**denier** (dinai·øʳ) *s.* negador, contradictor.
**denier** (deni·øʳ) *s.* dinero [moneda, medida].
**denigrate (to)** (de·nigreit) *tr.* denigrar. *2* ennegrecer.
**denigration** (-ei·shøn) *s.* denigración.
**Denis, Denys** (de·nis) *n. pr. m.* Dionisio.
**denizen** (de·nišøn) *s.* ciudadano, vecino, habitante. *2* (Ingl.) extranjero naturalizado.
**Denmark** (de·nmaʳk) *n. pr.* GEOGR. Dinamarca.
**denominate (to)** (dina·mineit) *tr.* denominar, llamar.
**denomination** (-ei·shøn) *s.* denominación. *2* clase, categoría. *3* secta, comunión.
**denominative** (-eitiv) *adj.* denominativo.
**denominator** (-eitøʳ) *s.* MAT. denominador.
**denote (to)** (dinou·t) *tr.* denotar. *2* indicar, señalar.
**denouement** (deinu·man) *s.* desenlace.
**denounce (to)** (dinau·ns) *tr.* denunciar. *2* anunciar, presagiar.
**denouncement** (-mønt) *s.* denunciación, denuncia.

**dense** (dens) *adj.* denso, espeso, apretado, tupido. *2* crasa [ignorancia]; profunda [estupidez]. *3* estúpido.
**denseness** (-nis) *s.* densidad, espesor. *2* estupidez.
**densimeter** (densi·mitøʳ) *s.* densímetro.
**density** (de·nsiti) *s.* densidad. *2* espesor [de un bosque, etc.].
**dent** (dent) *s.* mella, escotadura, hoyo, abolladura. *2* MEC. diente.
**dent (to)** *tr.* mellar, abollar.
**dental** (de·ntal) *adj.* dental, dentario: ~ *surgeon,* dentista. *2 s.* dental [consonante].
**dentate (d** (de·nteit(id) *adj.* BOT., ZOOL. dentado.
**denticle** (de·ntikøl) *s.* dentículo.
**denticulate (d** (denti·kiuleit(id) *adj.* denticulado.
**dentifrice** (de·ntifris) *adj.-s.* dentífrico.
**dentil** (-til) *s.* ARQ. dentículo, dentellón.
**dentilabial** (dentilei·bial) *adj.* FONÉT. labiodental.
**dentin(e** (de·ntin) *s.* ANAT. dentina.
**dentirostral** (dentira·stral) *adj.* ORN. dentirrostro.
**dentist** (de·ntist) *s.* dentista.
**dentistry** (-ri) *s.* cirugía dental, odontología.
**dentition** (denti·shøn) *s.* dentición. *2* dentadura.
**denture** (de·nchøʳ) *s.* dentadura [esp. la postiza].
**denudation** (diniudei·shøn) *s.* denudación.
**denude (to)** (diniu·d) *tr.* denudar, desnudar, despojar.
**denunciate (to)** (dinø·nshieit) *tr.* TO DENOUNCE.
**denunciation** (-ei·shøn) *s.* denuncia, acusación, estigmatización pública. *2* denuncia [de un tratado].
**denutrition** (dınutri·shøn) *s.* desnutrición.
**deny (to)** (dinai·) *tr.* negar: *to ~ oneself,* negarse a sí mismo; negarse a recibir [a uno].
**deodar** (dı·odaʳ) *s.* BOT. cedro, deodara.
**deodorant** (diou·dørant) *adj.-s.* desodorante.
**deodorize (to)** (-raiš) *tr.* desodorar.
**deodorizer** (-øʳ) *s.* desodorante.
**deontology** (dianta·lodÿi) *s.* deontología.
**deoxidize (to)** (dıa·csidaiš) *tr.* QUÍM. desoxidar.
**depart (to)** (dipa·ʳt) *intr.* partir, salir, irse, retirarse. *2* morir: *the departed,* los difuntos. *3* apartarse, desviarse, salirse de; desistir: *to ~ from life,* morir.
**department** (-mønt) *s.* departamento, ministerio, ramo, sección, negociado, despacho.
**departmental** (-tal) *adj.* de un ramo o departamento.
**departure** (dipa·ʳchuʳ) *s.* partida, marcha, salida. *2* muerte, fallecimiento. *3* apartamiento, desviación, abandono [de una regla, proceder, plan, etc.].
**depauperate (to)** (dıpo·pørei·t) *tr.* depauperar.
**depauperize (to)** (dıpo·pøraiš) *tr.* librar de pobres. *2* sacar de la pobreza.
**depend (to)** (dipe·nd) *intr.* pender, colgar. *2* depender. *3* estar pendiente, sin decidir. *4 to ~ on, o upon,* depender de, estribar en; confiar en, contar con, estar seguro de.
**dependable** (-abøl) *adj.* seguro, fidedigno, confiable.
**dependant** (-ant) *s.* DEPENDENT 4.
**dependence** (-døns) *s.* dependencia [subordinación; estado de lo condicionado, anexo o que se sigue a una cosa]. *2* dependencia [de otros para cubrir las propias necesidades]. *3* confianza, fe, seguridad. *4* apoyo, sostén; aquello con que se cuenta.
**dependency** (-si) *s.* DEPENDENCE 2. *2* dependencia [lo que depende]. *3* posesión, protectorado.
**dependent** (dipe·ndønt) *adj.* dependiente. *2* subor-

dinado, anexo. *3* pendiente, colgante. *4 s.* persona mantenida por otra, carga de familia.

**depict** (dipi·kt), **depicture (to)** (dipi·kchø<sup>r</sup>) *tr.* pintar, representar, retratar, describir.

**depilate (to)** (de·pileit) *tr.* depilar.

**depilation** (-ei·shøn) *s.* depilación.

**depilatory** (dipi·lǝtori) *adj.-s.* depilatorio.

**deplete (to)** (diplı·t) *tr.* vaciar, agotar, esquilmar.

**depletion** (diplı·shøn) *s.* vaciamiento, agotamiento.

**deplorable** (diplo·rbøl) *adj.* deplorable, lamentable, lastimoso.

**deplore (to)** (diplo·<sup>r</sup>) *tr.* deplorar, lamentar, llorar.

**deploy (to)** (diploi·) *tr.* MIL. desplegar. *2 intr.* MIL. desplegarse.

**deployment** (-mønt) *s.* MIL. despliegue.

**deplume (to)** (dıplu·m) *tr.* desplumar.

**depolarize** (dıpou·laraiš) *tr.* FÍS. despolarizar.

**depone (to)** (dipou·n) *tr.-intr.* DEPOSE 2.

**deponent** (-ønt) *adj.* GRAM. deponente. *2 s.* DER. deponente. *3* verbo deponente.

**depopulate (to)** (dıpa·piuleit) *tr.* despoblar, deshabitar. *2 intr.* despoblarse [de habitantes].

**depopulation** (-ei·shøn) *s.* despoblación.

**deport (to)** (dipo·rt) *tr.* deportar, desterrar. *2 to ~ oneself,* portarse, conducirse.

**deportation** (-ei·shøn) *s.* deportación.

**deportment** (dipo·<sup>r</sup>tmønt) *s.* conducta, proceder, comportamiento, porte, maneras.

**deposal** (dipou·šal) *s.* DEPOSITION 1.

**depose (to)** (dipou·š) *tr.* deponer, destronar, destituir. *2 tr.-intr.* deponer, declarar.

**deposit** (dipa·šit) *s.* depósito [cosa depositada; poso, sedimento]: *on ~,* en depósito. *2* arras, señal. *3* GEOL. yacimiento.

**deposit (to))** *tr.* depositar. *2* sedimentar. *3 intr.* depositarse, sedimentarse.

**depositary** (-eri) *s.* depositario. *2* depósito, almacén.

**deposition** (depøši·shøn) *s.* deposición, destitución. *2* B. ART. descendimiento. *3* DER. deposición, declaración. *4* depósito [acción].

**depositor** (dipa·šitø<sup>r</sup>) *s.* depositante; cuentacorrentista, imponente.

**depository** (-tori) *s.* depositaria; depósito [donde se deposita]. *2* depositario.

**depot** (dı·pou) *s.* depósito, almacén. *2* MIL., FISIOL. depósito. *3* FERROC. (E.U.) estación.

**depravation** (depravei·shøn) *s.* depravación.

**deprave (to)** (diprei·v) *tr.* depravaȓ. *2* corromper, viciar.

**depravity** (dipræ·viti) *s.* depravación. *2* acción depravada.

**deprecate (to)** (de·prikeit) *tr.* deprecar. *2* desaprobar, censurar.

**deprecation** (-ei·shøn) *s.* deprecación. *2* desaprobación.

**depreciate** (diprı·shieit) *tr.* depreciar. *2* despreciar, desestimar, rebajar. *3 intr.* depreciarse.

**depreciation** (-ei·shøn) *s.* depreciación. *2* desprecio, desestimación.

**depredate (to)** (de·prideit) *tr.* depredar.

**depredation** (-ei·shøn) *s.* depredación. *2 pl.* estragos.

**depress (to)** (dipre·s) *tr.* deprimir. *2* abatir, desanimar. *3* bajar, inclinar. *4* disminuir la actividad, bajar el tono, el precio, de. *5* MAT. reducir el grado de.

**depression** (dipre·shøn) *s.* depresión. *2* abatimiento, desánimo. *3* crisis [económica].

**depressive** (-siv) *adj.* depresivo. *2* deprimente.

**deprivación** (deprivei·shøn) *s.* privación, desposesión. *2* falta, carencia, pérdida.

**deprive (to)** (diprai·v) *tr.* privar, despojar, desposeer. *2* destituir.

**depth** (depz) *s.* profundidad, hondura. *2* grueso, espesor. *3* fondo [lo más profundo o alejado], lo hondo. *4* abismo. *5* mitad, corazón: *in the ~ of night,* en mitad de la noche. *6* gravedad [del sonido], intensidad [del color]. *7* sagacidad. *8* MAR. puntal. *9 out of one's ~,* perdiendo pie [en el agua]; metido en algo superior a los alcances de uno.

**depurate (to)** (de·piureit) *tr.* depurar, purificar.

**depurative** (-iv) *adj.-s.* MED. depurativo.

**deputation** (depiutei·shøn) *s.* diputación, delegación, comisión.

**depute (to)** (dipiu·t) *tr.* diputar, delegar. *2* nombrar [a uno] agente, comisario o lugarteniente.

**deputy** (de·piuti) *s.* diputado. *2* delegado, agente, comisario, lugarteniente. *3 adj.* segundo, teniente, vice.

**derail (to)** (direi·l) *tr.* hacer descarrilar. *2 intr.* descarrilar.

**derailment** (-mønt) *s.* descarrilamiento.

**derange (to)** (direi·ndӯ) *tr.* desarreglar, descomponer, trastornar. *2* trastornar el juicio a. *3* interrumpir, estorbar.

**derrangement** (-mønt) *s.* desarreglo, desconcierto. *2* perturbación mental.

**deratization** (dıræ·tišei·shøn) *s.* desratización.

**Derby** (dø·<sup>r</sup>bi) *n. pr.* GEOGR. Derby. *2* carrera anual de caballos que se celebra en Epsom (Inglaterra).

**derby** *s.* (E.U.) sombrero hongo.

**derelict** (de·rølikt) *adj.* derrelicto, abandonado. *2* negligente. *3 s.* MAR. derrelicto. *4* persona o cosa abandonada.

**dereliction** (derøli·kshøn) *s.* abandono, dejación. *2* desamparo. *3* negligencia culpable.

**deride (to)** (dirai·d) *tr.* burlarse, mofarse de, ridiculizar.

**derision** (diri·ӯøn) *s.* mofa, escarnio, irrisión.

**derisive** (dirai·siv) *adj.* de burla, de mofa.

**derisory** (-sori) *adj.* DERISIVE. *2* irrisorio, ridículo.

**derivation** (derivei·shøn) *s.* derivación [deducción, descendencia]. *2* GRAM., MAT., MED. derivación. *3* origen, procedencia, origen.

**derivative** (diri·vativ) *adj.-s.* derivativo. *2* derivado. *3 s.* MAT. derivada.

**derive (to)** (dirai·v) *tr.* derivar, sacar, deducir. *2* GRAM., ELECT. derivar. *3 intr.* derivar, derivarse, provenir.

**derived** (-d) *adj.* derivado. *2* ELECT. en derivación.

**derm** (dø<sup>r</sup>m), **derma** (dø·<sup>r</sup>ma) *s.* dermis.

**dermal** (dø·<sup>r</sup>mal) *adj.* DERMIC.

**dermatology** (dø·<sup>r</sup>mata·lødӯi) *s.* dermatología.

**dermic** (dø·<sup>r</sup>mik) *adj.* dérmico, cutáneo.

**dermis** (dø·<sup>r</sup>mis) *s.* DERM.

**derogate (to)** (de·røgeit) *intr. to ~ from,* restar, mermar, ser en mengua de; obrar de manera que desdice del [rango, posición, etc. de uno].

**derogation** (-eishøn) *s.* derogación, mengua, menoscabo. *2* acción de desdecir de.

**derogative** (dira·gativ), **derogatory** (-tori) *adj.* que rebaja o menoscaba, que es en mengua o desprecio de. *2* despectivo.

**derrick** (de·rik) *s.* grúa, cabria. *2* torre de perforación o extracción [de petróleo, etc.].

**dervish** (dø·<sup>r</sup>vish) *s.* derviche.

**descant (to)** (de·skænt) *intr.* comentar, disertar [sobre].

**descend (to)** (dise·nd) *intr.* descender; bajar: *to ~ from*, descender de, derivarse de; *to ~ to*, descender a, rebajarse a. *2* caer [la lluvia, etc.]. *3 to ~ on* o *upon*, caer sobre, invadir, hacer un desembarco en. *4 tr.* bajar [recorrer bajando].

**descendant** (-ant) *adj.-s.* descendiente. *2 adj.* descendente.

**descendent** (-ønt) *adj.* descendente. *2* descendiente.

**descending** (-ing) *adj.* descendente.

**descent** (-dise·nt) *s.* descenso, bajada, baja; caida. *2* nacimiento, origen, linaje, abolengo. *3* descendencia. *4* grado descendente; generación. *5* pendiente, bajada; escalera. *6* MIL. incursión, desembarco.

**describe (to)** (diskrai·b) *tr.* describir.

**description** (diskri·pshøn) *s.* descripción. *2* clase, género, especie, calidad, linaje.

**descriptive** (-tiv) *adj.* descriptivo.

**descry (to)** (diskrai·) *tr.* descubrir, avistar, divisar, distinguir, columbrar. ¶ Pret. y p. p.: *descried*.

**desecrate (to)** (de·sicreit) *tr.* profanar.

**desensitize (to)** (dise·nsitaiš) *tr.* desensibilizar.

**1) desert** (dišø·ʳt) *s.* mérito, valía. *2 pl.* merecimiento, merecido, premio o castigo merecido.

**2) desert** (de·šøʳt) *adj.* desierto. *2 s.* desierto, yermo.

**desert (to)** (dišø·ʳt) *tr.* abandonar, dejar, desemparar. *2 tr.-intr.* desertar.

**deserter** (-øʳ) *m.* desertor, tránsfuga.

**desertion** (dišø·ʳshøn) *s.* abandono, desamparo. *2* deserción.

**deserve (to)** (dišø·ʳv) *tr.-intr.* merecer.

**deservedly** (-idli) *adv.* merecidamente.

**deserving** (dišø·ʳving) *adj.* merecedor, digno de, acreedor a, meritorio. *2 s.* merecimiento.

**desiccate (to)** (de·sikeit) *tr.* desecar, secar. *2* pasar [higos, etc.]. *3 intr.* desecarse.

**desiccative** (-keitiv), **desiccatory** (katori) *adj.-s.* desecativo.

**desideratum** (disidørei·tøm) *s.* desideratum.

**design** (dišai·n) *s.* plan, proyecto. *2* intención, mira, propósito, designio: *by ~*, de intento; *to have designs on*, proponerse algo contra. *3* dibujo, diseño, plano, modelo. *4* invención artística.

**design (to)** *tr.* designar, destinar. *2* idear, proyectar, tramar, maquinar. *3* proponerse. *4* trazar, diseñar. *5 intr.* hacer diseños, planes, proyectos.

**designate (to)** (de·šigneit) *tr.* indicar, señalar. *2* denotar. *3* designar [denominar; destinar].

**designation** (-ei·shøn) *s.* acción de señalar o indicar. *2* denominación, nombre, título. *3* designación.

**designedly** (dišai·nidli) *adv.* adrede, de intento.

**designer** (dišai·nøʳ) *s.* diseñador, dibujante. *2* inventor, planeador. *3* maquinador, intrigante.

**designing** (-ning) *adj.* artero, insidioso, intrigante.

**desinence** (de·sinøns) *s.* GRAM. desinencia.

**desirable** (disai·rabøl) *adj.* deseable, apetecible.

**desire** (disai·øʳ) *s.* deseo. *2* anhelo, ansia.

**desire (to)** *tr.* desear, anhelar, ansiar. *2* rogar, pedir.

**desirous** (-røs) *adj.* deseoso, anheloso, ganoso.

**desist (to)** (diši·st) *intr.* desistir. *2 tr.* cesar de.

**desistance** (-ans) *s.* desistimiento, cesación.

**desk** (desk) *s.* pupitre, escritorio, bufete, buró. *2* (E.U.) púlpito.

**desman** (de·sman) *s.* ZOOL. desmán.

**desolate** (de·sølit) *adj.* desolado, desierto, solitario; triste. *2* solo, desconsolado.

**desolate (to)** (de·soleit) *tr.* desolar, asolar, devastar. *2* afligir, desconsolar.

**desolation** (-ei·shøn) *s.* desolación. *2* soledad.

**despair** (dispe·øʳ) *s.* desesperación; desesperanza.

**despair (to)** *intr.* desesperar; desesperanzarse.

**despairing** (-ing) *adj.* desesperado, sin esperanza.

**despatch (to)** = DISPATCH (TO).

**desperado** (despørei·dou) *s.* facineroso; malhechor peligroso.

**desperate** (de·spørit) *adj.* desesperado. *2* arriesgado, temerario. *3* grave, terrible, violento. *4* heroico [remedio].

**desperation** (-ei·shøn) *s.* desesperación.

**despicable** (de·spikabøl) *adj.* despreciable, bajo, vil.

**despisable** (dispai·šbøl) *adj.* despreciable.

**despise (to)** (dispai·š) *tr.* despreciar, menospreciar.

**despite (to)** (dispai·t) *s.* malquerencia, inquina. *2* despecho. *3 prep. despite* (o *~ of, in ~ of*) a despecho de, a pesar de, pese a.

**despiteful** (-ful) *adj.* lleno de odio, malévolo, maligno, rencoroso.

**despoil (to)** (dispoi·l) *tr.* despojar, privar [de]. *2* saquear, robar.

**despollation** (dispouliei·shøn) *s.* despojo; saqueo.

**despond (to)** (dispa·nd) *intr.* desalentarse, descorazonarse.

**despondence, -cy** (-øns, -si) *s.* desaliento, desánimo, abatimiento.

**despondent** (-ønt), **desponding** (-ing) *adj.* desalentado, desanimado, abatido.

**despot** (de·spat) *s.* déspota, tirano.

**despotic(al** (despa·tik(al) *adj.* despótico.

**despotism** (de·spøtišm) *s.* despotismo.

**desquamate (to)** (de·skuameit) *intr.* MED. descamarse.

**desquamation** (-ei·shøn) *s.* MED. descamación.

**dessert** (dišø·ʳt) *s.* postres.

**destination** (destinei·shøn) *s.* destinación, destino.

**destine (to)** (de·stin) *tr.* destinar.

**destiny** (-i) *s.* destino, sino, suerte; hado.

**destitute** (de·stitiud) *adj.* destituido, falto, desprovisto. *2* desvalido, menesteroso.

**destitute (to)** *tr.* destituir, privar.

**destitution** (destitiu·shøn) *s.* destitución, privación, falta. *2* miseria, indigencia.

**destroy (to)** (distroi·) *tr.* destruir. *2* demoler. *3* romper, destrozar. *4* aniquilar, exterminar, matar: *to ~ oneself*, suicidarse. *5* minar, consumir.

**destroyer** (-øʳ) *s.* destructor, destruidor. *2* MAR. destructor.

**destruction** (distrø·kshøn) *s.* destrucción; ruina; muerte. *2* perdición.

**destructive** (-tiv) *adj.* destructivo.

**desuetude** (de·suitiud) *s.* desuso.

**desultory** (de·søltori) *adj.* intermitente, discontinuo, deshilvanado, inconexo; que salta de un tema a otro.

**detach (to)** (ditæ·ch) *tr.* desatar, desligar. *2* despegar, desunir, separar. *3* MIL. destacar.

**detachable** (-abøl) *adj.* separable, desmontable, de quita y pon.

**detached** (ditæ·cht) *adj.* aislado, suelto, separado. *2* desinteresado. *3* imparcial.

**detachment** (-mønt) *s.* separación, desprendimiento. *2* despego, alejamiento, indiferencia; desapasionamiento. *3* MIL. destacamento.

**detail** (ditei·l) *s.* detalle, pormenor: *in ~*, en detalle. *2* MIL. pequeño destacamento.

**detail (to)** *tr.* detallar, especificar, enumerar. *2* MIL. destacar.

**detain (to)** (ditei·n) *tr.* detener, parar; entretener, retardar. *2* retener, detentar. *3* contener, represar. *4* tener preso [a uno].

**detect** (dite·kt) *tr.* descubrir, averiguar, hallar, percibir. *2* RADIO. detectar.

**detecter** (-ø^r) *s.* DETECTOR.

**detection** (-shøn) *s.* descubrimiento, averiguación. *2* RADIO. detección.

**detective** (-tiv) *adj.* que descubre. *2* policíaco: ~ *story*, novela policíaca. *3 s.* detective.

**detector** (-tø^r) *s.* descubridor. *2* MEC. indicador. *3* RADIO. detector.

**detent** (dite·nt) *s.* MEC. trinquete, fiador, seguro.

**detention** (dite·nshøn) *s.* detención [acción]. *2* detención, prisión, encierro. *3* DER. retención, detentación.

**deter (to)** (ditø·^r) *tr.* detener, disuadir, impedir. ¶ Pret. y p. p.: *deterred;* ger.: *-rring.*

**deterge (to)** (ditø·^rdÿ) *tr.* deterger.

**detergent** (-ønt) *adj.-s.* detergente, detersivo.

**deteriorate** (diti·rioreit) *tr.* deteriorar. *2* empeorar. *3 intr.* deteriorarse, decaer, empeorar.

**deterioration** (-ei·shøn) *s.* deterioración; empeoramiento.

**determent** (ditø·^rmønt) *s.* disuasión. *2* estorbo, impedimento.

**determinant** (ditø·^rminant) *adj.-s.* determinante.

**determinate** (-nit) *adj.* determinado. *2* definitivo.

**determination** (-ei·shøn) *s.* determinación [acción y efecto de determinar]. *2* decisión, fallo. *3* determinación, voluntad decidida. *4* H. NAT. clasificación.

**determine** (to)** (ditø·^rmin) *tr.* determinar. *2 intr.* determinarse, decidirse. | Gralte. con *on.*

**determined** (-d) *adj.* determinado, decidido, resuelto.

**determinism** (ditø·^rmišm) *s.* FIL. determinismo.

**deterrent** (ditø·rønt) *adj.* disuasivo. *2 s.* lo que disuade; freno, impedimento.

**detersion** (ditø·^rshøn) *s.* detersión.

**detersive** (-iv) *adj.-s.* detersivo.

**detest (to)** (dite·st) *tr.* detestar, aborrecer.

**detestable** (-abøl) *adj.* detestable, aborrecible.

**detestation** (-ei·shøn) *s.* detestación.

**dethrone (to)** (dizrou·n) *tr.* destronar.

**dethronement** (-mønt) *s.* destronamiento.

**detonate (to)** (de·toneit) *intr.* detonar, estallar. *2 tr.* hacer estallar.

**detonation** (-ei·shøn) *s.* detonación.

**detonator** (de·toneitø^r) *s.* detonador.

**detour** (ditu·^r) *s.* desvío; vuelta, rodeo. *2* manera indirecta.

**detract (to)** (ditra·kt) *tr.* detraer, quitar, restar. *2* detraer, detractar. *3 intr. to ~ from,* menoscabar, rebajar, hacer desmerecer.

**detraction** (-kshøn) *s.* detracción, calumnia, maledicencia.

**detractor** (-ktø^r) *s.* detractor, calumniador.

**detriment** (de·trimønt) *s.* detrimento, perjuicio.

**detrimental** (-me·ntal) *adj.* perjudicial, nocivo.

**detrition** (ditri·shøn) *s.* desgaste.

**detritus** (ditrai·tøs) *s.* detrito.

**detune (to)** (ditiu·n) *tr.* RADIO. desintonizar.

**deuce** (dius) *s.* dos [en naipes o dados]. *2* demonios, diantre: *what the ~ ...?,* ¿qué demonios...?

**deuced** (diu·sid) *adj.* endemoniado, del demonio [malo, extremado].

**Deuteronomy** (diutøra·nømi) *s.* Deuteronomio.

**devaluate (to)** (divæ·liueit) *tr.* desvalorizar.

**devaluation** (-ei·shøn) *s.* devalorización, devaluación.

**devastate** (de·vasteit) *tr.* devastar, asolar.

**devastation** (-ei·shøn) *s.* devastación, asolamiento.

**develop (to)** (dive·løp) *tr.* desenvolver, desarrollar. *2* fomentar, mejorar. *3* explotar [una mina, etc.]; urbanizar, edificar [un terreno], ensanchar [una población]. *4* desplegar, mostrar. *5* echar [pelo, hojas, etc.]. *6* FOT. revelar. *8 intr.* desarrollarse, evolucionar.

**developer** (-ø^r) *s.* FOT. revelador.

**development** (-mønt) *s.* desarrollo, desenvolvimiento. *2* crecimiento, progreso. *3* evolución. *4* fomento, explotación, urbanización. *5* caserío nuevo, ensanche. *6* acontecimiento, hecho nuevo. *7* AJED., MAT. desarrollo. *8* FOT. revelado.

**deviate (to)** (dı·vieit) *intr.* desviarse, apartarse, divergir.

**deviation** (-ei·shøn) *s.* desviación. *3* extravío, error.

**device** (divai·s) *s.* artificio, invención; traza, proyecto. *2* aparato, dispositivo, mecanismo. *3* ardid, recurso, expediente. *4* dibujo [de tela, bordado, etc.]. *5* vidisa, empresa, lema, mote. *6 pl.* voluntad, antojo.

**deviceful** (-ful) *adj.* inventivo, ingenioso.

**devil** (de·vøl) *s.* demonio, diablo: *poor ~,* pobre diablo, desgraciado; *between the ~, and the deep sea,* entre la espada y la pared; *the ~!,* ¡demonio!, ¡diantre! *2* aprendiz de impresor. *3* escritor a sueldo. *4* nombre de varias máquinas.

**devil (to)** *tr.* hacer diabólico. *2* COC. condimentar con mucho picante. ¶ Pret. y p. p.: *deviled* o *-lled;* ger.: *deviling* o *-lling.*

**devilish** (-ish) *adj.* diabólico. *2* endemoniado, endiablado; extremado.

**devilkin** (-kin) *s.* diablejo, diablillo.

**devilment** (-mønt) *s.* diablura, diablería.

**devilry** (-ri) *s.* diablura, diablería. *2* acción diabólica; maldad, crueldad.

**devil's-darning-needle** *s.* ENT. libélula, caballito del diablo. *2* BOT. aguja de pastor o de Venus.

**deviltry** (-tri) *s.* devilry.

**devious** (dı·viøs) *adj.* desviado, apartado, extraviado. *2* tortuoso. *3* indirecto. *4* errante.

**devisal** (divai·šal) *s.* invención.

**devise** (divai·š) *s.* DER. legado.

**devise (to)** *tr.* inventar, idear, discurrir. *2* DER. legar. *3 intr.* formar planes.

**devisee** (diviši·^r) *s.* DER. legatario.

**devitalize (to)** (divai·talaiš) *tr.* privar de vitalidad.

**devold** (divoi·d) *adj.* falto, desprovisto, exento.

**devoir** (de·vua^r) *s.* deber. *2 pl.* homenaje, respetos.

**devolution** (devoliu·shøn) *s.* entrega, traspaso. *2* transmisión por sucesión. *3* BIOL. degeneración.

**devolve (to)** (diva·lv) *tr.* transmitir, traspasar. *2 intr.* pasar [por sucesión]; recaer, tocar, incumbir, corresponder.

**Devonian** (devou·nian) *adj.-s.* GEOL. devoniano, devónico.

**devote (to)** (divou·t) *tr.* consagrar, dedicar, aplicar. *2* destinar, condenar.

**devoted** (-id) *adj.* consagrado, dedicado, aplicado. *2* destinado, condenado. *3* devoto, ferviente, celoso. *4* adicto, fiel, apegado.

**devotee** (devoı·^r) *s.* devoto, beato. *2* fanático, partidario ardiente.

**devotion** (divou·shøn) *s.* devoción. *2* fervor, celo. *3* afecto, lealtad. *4 pl.* devociones.

**devotional** (-al) *adj.* devoto, de devoción.

**devour (to)** (divau·^r) *tr.* devorar.

**devouring** (-ing) *adj.* devorador.

**devout** (divau·t) *adj.* devoto, piadoso. 2 fervoroso, sincero, cordial.

**dew** (diu) *s.* rocío; sereno, relente.

**dew (to)** *tr.* rociar, refrescar. 2 *intr.* rociar, formarse el rocío.

**dewberry** (-beri) *s.* BOT. zarzamora.

**dewclaw** (-klo) *s.* ZOOL. dedo rudimentario [del perro].

**dewdrop** (-drap) *s.* gota de rocío.

**dewlap** (-læp) *s.* papada.

**dewy** (-i) *adj.* cubierto de rocío; parecido al rocío.

**dexter** (de·kstø$^r$) *adj.* derecho, diestro. 2 de buen augurio.

**dexterity** (-iti) *s.* destreza, habilidad.

**dexterous** (-tørøs) *adj.* diestro, hábil.

**dextral** (-tral) *adj.* derecho, diestro.

**dextrin(e** (-trin) *s.* QUÍM. dextrina.

**dextrose** (-trous) *s.* QUÍM. dextrosa.

**dey** (dei) *s.* dey.

**diabetes** (daiabɪ·tis) *s.* MED. diabetis.

**diabetic** (-be·tik) *adj.-s.* diabético.

**diablerie, -ry** (dia·bløri) *s.* brujería, magia negra. 2 diablura.

**diabolic (al** (daiaba·lik(al) *adj.* diabólico.

**diabolo** (diæ·bølou) *s.* diábolo [juguete].

**diaconal** (daiæ·konal) *adj.* diaconal.

**diaconate** (-koneit) *s.* diaconato.

**diacoustics** (daiaku·stiks) *s.* diacústica.

**diacritic** (-kri·tik) *adj.-s.* diacrítico.

**diacritical** (-al) *adj.* DIACRITIC.

**diadelphous** (-de·lføs) *adj.* BOT. diadelfo.

**diadem** (dai·adem) *s.* diadema.

**diaeresis** (daie·risis) *s.* diéresis.

**diagnose (to)** (daiægnou·s) *tr.* diagnosticar.

**diagnosis** (-is) *s.* diagnosis. 2 diagnóstico.

**diagnosticate (to)** (-eit) *tr.* diagnosticar.

**diagonal** (daiæ·gonal) *adj.-s.* diagonal.

**diagram** (dai·agræm) *s.* diagrama, esquema.

**diagram (to)** *tr.* hacer el diagrama de; esquematizar.

**dial** (dai·al) *s.* reloj de sol, cuadrante. 2 esfera [de reloj]. 3 disco [de teléfono]. 4 RADIO. dial.

**dial (to)** *tr.* TELEF. marcar. 2 RADIO. sintonizar. ¶ Pret. y p. p.: *dialed* o *-lled*; ger.: *-ling* o *-lling*.

**dialect** (dai·alekt) *s.* dialecto. 2 *adj.* dialectal.

**dialectic (al** (daiale·ktik(al) *adj.* dialéctico.

**dialectician** (-ti·shan) *s.* dialéctico.

**dialectics** (daiale·ktiks) *s.* dialéctica.

**dial(l)ing** (-ling) *s.* gnomónica.

**dialogic (al** (daialo·dȳik(al) *adj.* dialogal, dialogístico.

**dialogism** (daiæ·lodȳišm) *s.* dialogismo, diálogo.

**dialogist** (-dȳist) *s.* dialoguista.

**dialogistic (al** (daialodȳi·stik(al) *adj.* dialogístico.

**dialogize (to)** (daiæ·lodȳaiš) *intr.* TO DIALOGUE.

**dialogue** (dai·alag) *s.* diálogo.

**dialogue (to)** *intr.* dialogar.

**dialysis** (daiæ·lisis) *s.* QUÍM. diálisis.

**dialyze (to)** (dai·alaiš) *tr.* QUÍM. dializar.

**dialyzer** (-ø$^r$) *s.* dializador.

**diamantiferous** (daiamænti·førøs) *adj.* diamantífero.

**diamantine** (daiamæ·ntin) *adj.* diamantino.

**diametral** (-metral), **diametrical** (daiame·trical) *adj.* diametral.

**diameter** (daiæ·metø$^r$) *s.* diámetro.

**diamond** (dai·amønd) *s.* diamante; ~ *cutter*, diamantista. 2 GEOM. rombo. 3 rombo [palo de la baraja].

**diandrous** (dai·ændrøs) *adj.* BOT. diandro.

**diapason** (daiapei·šøn) *s.* MÚS. diapasón.

**diaper** (dai·apø$^r$) *s.* lienzo adamascado. 2 culero, pañal. 3 labor o adorno de motivos que se repiten indefinidamente.

**diaper (to)** *tr.* adamascar. 2 labrar o adornar con motivos que se repiten indefinidamente.

**diaphaneity** (daiafanɪ·iti) *s.* diafanidad.

**diaphanous** (daiæ·fanøs) *adj.* diáfano.

**diaphragm** (dai·afræm) *s.* diafragma.

**diaphysis** (daiæ·fisis) *s.* ANAT. diáfisis.

**diapositive** (daiapa·šitiv) *s.* FOT. diapositiva.

**diarrhea, diarrhoea** (daiarɪ·a) *s.* MED. diarrea.

**diarthrosis** (-a$^r$zrou·sis) *s.* ANAT. diartrosis.

**diary** (dai·ari) *s.* diario, dietario.

**Diaspora** (daiæ·spøra) *s.* Diáspora.

**diastase** (dai·ateis) *s.* QUÍM. diastasa.

**diastole** (daiæ·støli) *s.* FISIOL. diástole.

**diathermia** (daiazø·$^r$mia), **diathermy** (-mi) *s.* MED. diatermia.

**diatom** (dai·atam) *s.* BOT. diatomea.

**diatonic** (-ata·nik) *adj.* MÚS. diatónico.

**diatribe** (-atraib) *s.* diatriba.

**dibble** (di·bøl) *s.* plantador [instrumento].

**dibble (to)** *tr.* plantar con plantador. 2 hacer hoyos [en la tierra].

**dibs** (dibs) *s. pl.* taba [juego]. 2 fam. dinero.

**dibstone** (-toun) *s.* piedrecita, taba, etc., para jugar.

**dice** (dais) *s. pl.* dados: ~ *box*, cubilete. 2 cubitos.

**dice (to)** *intr.* jugar a los dados. 2 *tr.* cortar en cubitos.

**dicer** (-ø$^r$) *s.* jugador de dados.

**dichotomy** (daika·tømi) *s.* dicotomía.

**dichorism** (dai·kroišm) *s.* FÍS. dicroísmo.

**Dick** (dik) *n. pr.* Ricardito.

**dickens** (di·kønš) *s.* fam. demonio, diantre.

**dicker** (di·kø$^r$) *s.* (E.U.) trato, cambalache.

**dicker (to)** *intr.* (E.U.) tratar, regatear.

**dick(e)y** (di·ki) *s.* camisolín. 2 delantal, babero. 3 pajarito. 4 AUT. asiento del conductor; trasera [de coche].

**dicotyledon** (daikatilɪ·døn) *s.* BOT. dicotiledónea.

**dicotyledonous** (-dønøs) *adj.* BOT. dicotiledóneo.

**dictaphone** (di·ktafoun) *s.* dictáfono.

**dictate** (di·kteit) *s.* dictado [inspiración, mandato].

**dictate (to)** *tr.* dictar. 2 *intr.* mandar.

**dictation** (-ei·shøn) *s.* dictado [acción de dictar; lo dictado]. 2 mandato, imposición.

**dictator** (-ei·tø$^r$) *s.* dictador.

**dictatorial** (diktato·rial) *adj.* dictatorial.

**dictatorship** (diktei·tø$^r$ship), **dictature** (-shø$^r$) *s.* dictadura.

**diction** (di·kshøn) *s.* dicción, estilo, lenguaje.

**dictionary** (di·kshøneri) *s.* diccionario, léxico.

**dictum** (di·ctøm), *pl.* **-ta** *s.* sentencia, aforismo.

**did** (did) *pret.* de TO DO.

**didactic(al** (daidæ·ktik(al) *adj.* didáctico.

**didactics** (-tiks) *s.* didáctica.

**diddle (to)** (di·døl) *tr.* estafar. 2 perder [el tiempo]. 3 zarandearse.

**didn't** (di·dønt) contrac. de *did* y *not*.

**1) die** (dai), *pl.* **dice** (dais) *s.* dado [para jugar]. 2 cubito.

**2) die**, *pl.* **dies** *s.* ARQ. dado, neto. 3 MEC. troquel, cuño. 4 MEC. cojinete de la terraja.

**1) die (to)** *intr.* morir, fallecer, acabar, fenecer, extinguirse. 2 agostarse, marchitarse. 3 *to* ~ *of laughing*, desternillarse de risa. 4 *to be dying for* o *to*, morirse por, desear ardientemente. ¶ Pret. y p. p.: *died*; ger.: *dying*.

**2) die (to)** *tr.* cortar o estampar con troquel. ¶ Pret. y p. p.: *died;* ger.: *dieing.*
**die-hard** *adj.-s.* POL. intransigente.
**dielectric** (daiile·ktrik) *adj.-s.* dieléctrico.
**dieresis** (daie·risis) *s.* DIAERESIS.
**diesinker** (dai·sinkø^r) *s.* grabador en hueco.
**diesis** (-esis) *s.* MÚS. diesi.
**diestock** (-stak) *s.* MEC. terraja.
**diet** (dai·et) *s.* MED. dieta, régimen alimenticio. *2* dieta [asamblea].
**dietetics** (daiete·tiks) *s.* dietética.
**differ (to)** (di·fø^r) *intr.* diferir, diferenciarse, distinguirse; discrepar, disentir. *2* reñir, tener una diferencia.
**difference** (-øns) *s.* diferencia. *2* disparidad, desigualdad. *3* distinción [que se hace entre pers. o cosas]. *4* cambio, alteración: *it makes no ~,* es igual, lo mismo da. *5* divergencia, discrepancia.
**difference (to)** *tr.* diferenciar, distinguir.
**different** (-ønt) *adj.* diferente, distinto. *2* diferente de lo usual; poco corriente.
**differential** (diføre·nshal) *adj.* diferencial. *2 s.* MAT., MEC. diferencial.
**differentiate (to)** (-shieit) *tr.* diferenciar, distinguir. *2 intr.* diferenciarse.
**differentiation** (-ei·shøn) *s.* diferenciación.
**difficult** (di·fikølt) *adj.* difícil. *2* dificultoso, trabajoso. *3* apurado, penoso.
**difficulty** (-i) *s.* dificultad. *2* obstáculo, objeción, reparo, inconveniente. *3* apuro, aprieto.
**diffidence** (di·fidøns) *s.* falta de confianza en sí mismo; cortedad, timidez, apocamiento.
**diffident** (-dønt) *adj.* que desconfía de sí mismo; tímido, apocado.
**diffluent** (di·fluønt) *adj.* difluente.
**diffract (to)** (difræ·kt) *tr.* FÍS. difractar. *2 intr.* difractarse.
**diffraction** (difræ·kshøn) *s.* difracción.
**diffuse** (difiu·s) *adj.* difuso.
**diffuse (to)** (difiu·š) *tr.* difundir. *2* esparcir, diseminar. *3 intr.* difundirse.
**diffused** (-d) *adj.* difundido. *2* difuso, disperso.
**diffuser** (difiu·šø^r) *s.* difusor.
**diffusion** (-ȳøn) *s.* difusión.
**dig** (dig) *s.* hurgonazo, metido, codazo o golpe parecido. *2* fam. pulla, sarcasmo.
**dig (to)** *tr.* cavar, excavar, ahondar, ahoyar. *2* escarbar. *3* extraer, buscar, hacer, abrir, etc., cavando o escarbando: *to ~ out o up,* extraer, desenterrar. *4* clavar, hundir [las uñas, un cuchillo, etc.]. *5* dar un metido a, hurgar, aguijonear, picar. *6 intr.* cavar. *7* clavarse, entrar, penetrar. *8* fam. trabajar de firme. ¶ Pret. y p. p.: *dug* o *digged;* ger.: *digging.*
**digest** (dai·dȳest) *s.* compendio, recopilación. *2* DER. digesto.
**digest (to)** (daidȳe·st) *tr.* digerir. *2* resumir, recopilar. *3 intr.* digerirse.
**digester** (-ø^r) *s.* digestor. *2* MED. digestivo. *3* compendiador, recopilador.
**digestion** (daiȳe·stshøn) *s.* digestión.
**digestive** (-stiv) *adj.* digestivo.
**digger** (di·gø^r) *s.* cavador. *2* azada. *3* máquina cavadora.
**digging** (-ing) *s.* cava, excavación. *2 pl.* lo que se saca cavando. *3* mina [esp. de oro o diamantes]. *4* fam. domicilio, alojamiento.
**digit** (di·dȳit) *s.* ZOOL. dedo. *2* dedo [medida]. *3* número dígito. *4* ASTR. dígito.
**digital** (-al) *adj.* digital.
**digitalin** (didȳite·lin) *s.* FARM. digitalina.

**digitalis** (-tei·lis) *s.* BOT. digital.
**digitate(d** (di·dȳiteit(id) *adj.* digitado.
**digitigrade** (di·dȳitigreid) *adj.* ZOOL. digitígrado.
**dignified** (di·gnifaid) *adj.* dignificado; enaltecido. *2* digno, serio, grave; noble, majestuoso.
**dignify (to)** (-fai) *tr.* dignificar, enaltecer. ¶ Pret. y p. p.: *dignified.*
**dignitary** (-teri) *s.* dignatario.
**dignity** (di·gniti) *s.* dignidad. *2* honor. *3* rango, elevación.
**digraph** (dai·græf) *s.* dígrafo.
**digress (to)** (digre·s) *intr.* desviarse del tema, divagar.
**digression** (-ei·shøn) *s.* digresión.
**dihedral** (daiji·dral) *adj.* GEOM. diedro.
**dike** (daik) *s.* dique, malecón, represa. *2* zanja, acequia.
**dike (to)** *tr.* proteger con dique. *2* avenar [un terreno].
**dilacerate (to)** (dilæ·søreit) *tr.* romper, desgarrar; dilacerar.
**dilapidate (to)** (-pideit) *tr.* arruinar, estropear, echar a perder. *2* dilapidar.
**dilapidated** (-id) *adj.* ruinoso, estropeado, viejo, en mal estado.
**dilatability** (daileitabi·liti) *s.* dilatabilidad.
**dilatation** (dilatei·shøn) *s.* dilatación.
**dilate (to)** (dai·leit) *tr.* dilatar. *2 intr.* dilatarse. *3 to ~ in o upon,* extenderse, explayarse, sobre.
**dilation** (dailei·shøn) *s.* DILATATION.
**dilative** (-tiv) *adj.* dilativo.
**dilatory** (di·latori) *adj.* dilatorio. *2* tardo, lento, moroso.
**dilemma** (dile·ma) *s.* dilema. *2* disyuntiva.
**dilettante** (diløtæ·nti), *pl.* **-tes** o **-ti** (-ti) *s.* diletante, aficionado.
**diligence** (di·lidȳøns) *s.* diligencia, cuidado, aplicación, asiduidad. *2* diligencia [coche].
**diligent** (-ønt) *adj.* diligente, aplicado, activo, solícito, cuidadoso.
**dill** (dil) *s.* BOT. eneldo.
**dilly-dally (to)** (di·lidæli) *intr.* holgazanear, perder el tiempo.
**diluent** (di·liuønt) *adj.-s.* diluente.
**dilute (to)** *tr.* diluir, desleír. *2* aguar. *3 intr.* diluirse; desleírse.
**dilution** (diliu·shøn) *s.* dilución, desleimiento.
**diluvial** (-vial) *adj.* diluvial.
**diluvian** (-vian) *adj.* diluviano.
**dim** (dim) *adj.* oscuro, opaco. *2* anublado, caliginoso. *3* empañado, deslustrado. *4* vago, confuso. *5* apagado, débil. *6* cegato. *7* obtuso, torpe.
**dim (to)** *tr.* oscurecer, ofuscar, anublar. *2* empañar, deslustrar. *3* hacer confuso, indistinto. *4* amortiguar [una luz]. *5 intr.* oscurecerse.
**dime** (daim) *s.* diezmo. *2* (E.U.) diez centavos.
**dimension** (dime·nshøn) *s.* dimensión.
**diminish (to)** (dimi·nish) *tr.* disminuir. *2* empequeñecer. *3* abatir, humillar. *4 intr.* disminuir, menguar.
**diminution** (diminiu·shøn) *s.* disminución.
**diminutive** (dimi·niutiv) *adj.-s.* diminutivo. *2 adj.* pequeño, minúsculo.
**dimissory** (di·misori) *adj.* dimisorio.
**dimity** (di·miti) *s.* cotonada.
**dimmer** (di·mø^r) *s.* amortiguador [de luz]. *2* AUT. luz de cruce.
**dimness** (di·mnis) *s.* semioscuridad, penumbra. *2* oscuridad, anublamiento.
**dimorphism** (daimo·^rfišm) *s.* dimorfismo.
**dimorphous** (-føs) *adj.* dimorfo.

**dimple** (di·mpøl) *s.* hoyuelo.
**dimple (to)** *tr.-intr.* formar o formarse hoyuelos [en].
**dimpled** (-d), **dimply** (-pli) *adj.* que tiene hoyuelos.
**din** (din) *s.* fragor, estrépito, estruendo, batahola.
**din (to)** *tr.* golpear con ruido; ensordecer, aturdir. *2* clamorear; repetir con pesadez. *3 intr.* resonar, hacer estrépito.
**dine (to)** (dain) *intr.* comer [hacer la comida principal]. *2 tr.* tener convidado a comer.
**diner** (-ø<sup>r</sup>) *s.* comensal [en una comida]. *2* FERROC. vagón restaurante.
**ding-a-ling** (di·ngalin) *s.* tintín.
**ding-dong** (di·ndan) *s.* din don [sonido]. *2 adj.* disputado, con ventaja alterna [carrera, etc.].
**dingey, dinghy** (di·ngɪ) *s.* MAR. bote.
**dinginess** (di·ndȳinis) *s.* suciedad, empañamiento.
**dingle** (di·ngøl) *s.* cañada, vallecito umbroso.
**dingo** (di·ngou) *s.* ZOOL. dingo [perro salvaje].
**dingy** (di·ndȳi) *adj.* oscuro, negruzco, sucio, deslucido; sórdido. *2 s.* DINGEY.
**dining car** (dai·nig) *s.* FERROC. vagón restaurante.
**dining-room** *s.* comedor [pieza].
**dinner** (di·nø<sup>r</sup>) *s.* comida [principal], banquete: ~ *coat*, ~ *jacket*, smoking.
**dinosaur** (dai·noso<sup>r</sup>) *s.* PALEONT. dinosaurio.
**dinothere** (dai·nozi<sup>r</sup>) *s.* PALEONT. dinoterio.
**dint** (dint) *s.* golpe, abolladura. *2 adv. by .* of, a puro, a fuerza de.
**dint (to)** *tr.* abollar.
**diocesan** (daia·sisan) *adj.-s.* diocesano.
**diocese** (dai·øsis) *s.* diócesis.
**Diocletian** (daiokli·shan) *n. pr.* Diocleciano.
**dioecions** (dai·shøs) *adj.* BOT. dioico.
**Dionysius** (daioni·shiøs) *n. pr.* Dionisio.
**Dioniysos** o **-sus** (-shøs) *n. pr.* MIT. Dioniso.
**diopter** (daia·ptø<sup>r</sup>) *s.* dioptra. *2* dioptría.
**dioptric** (-trik) *adj.* dióptrico. *2 s.* DIOPTER 2.
**dioptrics** (-triks) *s.* dióptrica.
**diorama** (daiora·ma) *s.* diorama.
**diorite** (dai·orait) *s.* MINER. diorita.
**dioxide** (daia·ksaid) *s.* QUÍM. bióxido.
**dip** (dip) *s.* zambullida, inmersión, baño corto. *2* declive, pendiente, depresión, inclinación, grado de inclinación. *3* baño [en que se sumerge una cosa]. *4* GEOL. buzamiento.
**dip (to)** *tr.* zambullir, sumergir, bañar, mojar. *2* sacar [con cuchara, etc.]; achicar. *3* bajar, inclinar [banderas, etc.]. *4 intr.* zambullirse, sumergirse; bajar, inclinarse. *5* meter la mano, un cucharón, etc. [en un sitio para sacar algo]. *6* hacer pendiente [un terreno]. *7* GEOL. buzar. *8* descender rápidamente. *9* desaparecer [bajo una superficie o nivel]. *10* investigar, penetrar. *11* meterse [en algo]. ¶ Pret. y P. P.: *dipped;* ger. *dipping.*
**diphtheria** (difzi·ria) *s.* MED. difteria.
**diphtherial** (-al), **diphtheritic** (-i·tik) *adj.* diftérico.
**diphthong** (di·fzong) *s.* diptongo.
**diphtong, diphtongize (to)** (-gaiš) *tr.* diptongar.
**diplodocus** (diploda·køs) *s.* PALEONT. diplodoco.
**diploma** (diplou·ma) *s.* diploma.
**diplomacy** (-si) *s.* diplomacia.
**diplomat** (di·plomæt) *s.* diplomático.
**diplomate** (di·plomit) *adj.* diplomado, titulado.
**diplomatic(al** (diplomæ·tik(al) *adj.* diplomático.
**diplomatics** (-tiks) *s.* diplomacia. *2* diplomática.
**diplomatist** (diplou·matist) *s.* diplomático.
**dipper** (di·pø<sup>r</sup>) *s.* cazo, cacillo, cucharón. *2* MEC. cuchara [de excavadora]. *3* ASTR. The Dipper, el Carro.

**dipsomania** (dipsoumei·nia) *s.* dipsomanía.
**dipsomaniac** (-niæk) *s.* dipsómano.
**dipter** (di·ptø<sup>r</sup>) *s.* ENT. díptero.
**dipteral** (-al) *adj.* ARQ., ENT. díptero.
**dipteran** (-an) *adj.-s.* ENT. díptero.
**dipteros** (-rous) *adj.* ARQ. díptero.
**dipterous** (-røs) *adj.* ENT. díptero.
**diptych** (di·ptik) *s.* díptica. *2* díptico.
**dire** (dai·ø<sup>r</sup>) *adj.* horrible, horrendo. *2* extremo, sumo.
**direct** (dire·kt) *adj.* directo. *2* recta [línea de descendencia]. *3* inmediato. *4* claro, categórico. *5* franco, sincero. *6* ELECT. continua [corriente]. *7* GRAM. ~ *object*, complemento directo. *8 adv.* directamente [esp. en compuestos].
**direct (to)** *tr.* dirigir. *2* encaminar, encauzar. *3* mandar, encargar; decir [a uno lo que ha de hacer], dar instrucciones a. *4* dedicar [una obra a uno]. *5 intr.* dirigir, servir de guía.
**directer** (-ø<sup>r</sup>) *s.* DIRECTOR.
**direction** (dire·kshøn) *s.* dirección. *2* consejo de administración, junta directiva. *3* sobrescrito. *4 pl.* mandato, orden, encargo; instrucciones.
**directional** (-al) *adj.* de dirección.
**directive** (dire·ktiv) *adj.* director, directivo. *2* dirigible, gobernable. *3 s.-pl.* directrices.
**directly** (dire·ktli) *adv.* directamente. *2* inmediatamente, en seguida. *3* exactamente, completamente. *4* francamente. *5* sinceramente. *6 conj.* fam. en cuanto, tan pronto como.
**directness** (-nis) *s.* derechura. *2* franqueza, lealtad, rectitud.
**director** (-ø<sup>r</sup>) *s.* director. *2* caudillo, guía. *3* gerente; consejero [de una compañía], individuo de una junta directiva. *4 adj.* MAT. director, directriz.
**directorate** (-ørit) *s.* dirección [cargo]. *2* consejo de administración, junta directiva, directorio.
**directory** (-ori) *adj.* directorio. *2 s.* libro de reglas o instrucciones. *3* guía [libro con direcciones]: *telephone* ~, guía telefónica.
**directress** (dire·ktris) *s.* directora.
**directrix** (-iks) *s.* GEOM. directriz.
**direful** (dai·ø<sup>r</sup>ful) *adj.* horrendo, terrible, espantoso.
**dirge** (dø<sup>r</sup>dȳ) *s.* endecha, treno, canto fúnebre.
**dirigible** (di·ridȳibøl) *adj.-s.* dirigible.
**diriment** (di·rimønt) *s.* dirimente.
**dirk** (dø<sup>r</sup>k) *s.* daga escocesa. *2* puñal.
**dirt** (dø<sup>r</sup>t) *s.* tierra, barro, lodo. *2* suciedad, mugre, porquería, inmundicia, basura. *3* bajeza, vileza.
**dirt-cheap** *adj. y adv.* muy barato, baratísimo.
**dirty** (-i) *adj.* enlodado, manchado, mugriento, sucio. *2* concho, indecente. *3* bajo, vil, despreciable. *4* malo [tiempo, mar, etc.]. *5* ~ *trick*, perrada, cochinada.
**dirty (to)** *tr.* ensuciar, manchar, enlodar.
**disability** (disabi·liti) *s.* impotencia, incapacidad, inhabilidad. *2* inutilidad [para el trabajo].
**disable (to)** (disei·bøl) *tr.* inutilizar, imposibilitar, incapacitar, inhabilitar. *2* lisiar. *3* MAR. desaparejar, desmantelar.
**disablement** (-mønt) *s.* incapacitación, inhabilitación. *2* invalidez [física]. *3* MAR. desmantelamiento.
**disabuse (to)** (disabiu·š) *tr.* desengañar, sacar del error o del engaño.
**disaccord** (disa·ko<sup>r</sup>d) *s.* desacuerdo, disensión.
**disaccord (to)** *intr.* discordar, disentir.
**disaccustom (to)** (-kø·støm) *tr.* desacostumbrar.
**disadjust (to)** (-dȳø·st) *tr.* desajustar, desarreglar.

disadvantage (-dvæ·ntidẙ) *s.* desventaja. *2* inconveniente. *3* detrimento.

disadvantage (to) *tr.* perjudicar, dañar.

disadvantageous (-dvæntei·dẙøs) *adj.* desventajoso, perjudicial, inconveniente.

disaffect (to) (disafe·kt) *tr.* indisponer, enemistar.

disaffected (-id) *adj.* desafecto.

disaffection (-fe·kshøn) *s.* desafección, desafecto.

disagregate (disa·grigeit) *tr.* disgregar.

disagree (to) (disagrı·) *intr.* desconvenir, disonar. *2* discordar, discrepar, diferir. *3* disentir. *4* desavenirse, estar en pugna. *5 to ~ with,* no estar de acuerdo con; no probar, sentar mal.

disagreeable (-abøl) *adj.* desagradable, ingrato. *2* desabrido, descortés.

disagreement (-grı·mønt) *s.* discordancia, discrepancia, desacuerdo, disconformidad. *2* disentimiento. *3* disensión, desavenencia.

disallow (to) (-lau·) *tr.-intr.* desaprobar. *2 tr.* denegar, rechazar.

disappear (to) (-pi·ø') *intr.* desaparecer.

disappearance (-ans) *s.* desaparición.

disappoint (to) (-poi·nt) *tr.* privar [de lo que uno espera]; defraudar, burlar, frustrar; chasquear, decepcionar, desilusionar; ·contrariar. *2* dejar plantado.

disappointment (-mønt) *s.* desilusión, desengaño, decepción. *2* frustración, chasco, contrariedad.

disapprobation (-probei·shøn), disapproval (-pru·val) *s.* desaprobación, censura.

disapprove (to) (-pru·v) *tr.* desaprobar. *2* no aprobar, rechazar [un proyecto, etc.]. *3 intr. to ~ of,* no aprobar, no hallar de su gusto.

disarm (to) (disa·'m) *tr.* desarmar [quitar las armas; aplacar, apaciguar]. *2 intr.* desarmarse. *3* MIL. efectuar el desarme.

disarmament (-amønt) *s.* desarme.

disarrange (disarei·ndẙ) *tr.* desarreglar, desordenar, descomponer.

disarray (-rei·) *s.* desorden, confusión. *2* desatavío, desaliño, trapillo.

disarray (to) *tr.* desarreglar, desordenar. *2* derrotar. *3* desaliñar, desnudar.

disarticulate (to) (disa'ti·kiuleit) *tr.* desarticular.

disassemble (to) (disase·mbøl) *tr.* desmontar, desarmar [un artefacto].

disassimilation (dišasimilei·shøn) *s.* desasimilación.

disassociate (to) (-sou·shieit) *tr.* disociar.

disaster (diša·stø') *s.* desastre.

disastrous (-trøs) *adj.* desastroso.

disavow (to) (disavau·) *tr.* repudiar, desconocer, negar. *2* desautorizar, desaprobar.

disavowal (-al), disavowment (-mønt) *s.* repudiación, desconocimiento. *2* desautorización, desaprobación.

disband (to) (disbæ·nd) *tr.* disolver [una banda, etc.]; despedir, licenciar [huestes]. *2 intr.* dispersarse, desbandarse.

disbar (to) (disba·') *tr.* expulsar del foro.

disbark (to) (-k) *tr.* descortezar.

disbelief (disbilı·f) *s.* incredulidad.

disbelieve (to) (-v) *tr.-intr.* descreer; no creer; no dar fe.

disburden (to) (-bø·'døn) *tr.* descargar, aligerar. *2* descargarse de.

disburse (to) (-bø·'s) *tr.* desembolsar. *2* gastar.

disbursement (-mønt) *s.* desembolso. *2* gasto.

disc (disk) *s.* disco.

discalced (-kæ·lst) *adj.* descalzo [religioso].

discard (-ka·'d) *s.* descarte. *2* cosa desechada, desecho.

discard (to) *tr.-intr.* NAIPES. descartarse [de]. *2 intr.* descartar, desechar; abandonar, dejar de usar. *3* despedir, destituir.

discern (to) (disø·'n) *tr.* discernir, distinguir. *2* ver, distinguir, descubrir, percibir.

discernible (-ibøl) *adj.* discernible. *2* perceptible, visible.

discerning (-ing) *adj.* discernidor. *2* inteligente, sagaz, perspicaz.

discernment (-mønt) *s.* discernimiento. *2* buen criterio, gusto, juicio recto.

discharge (discha·'dẙ) *s.* descarga [de un buque, de un arma, etc.]. *2* tiro, disparo. *3* ARQ., ELECT. descarga. *4* salida, derrame [de un líquido]; desagüe. *5* líquido que sale, gasto. *6* supuración. *7* pus, humor [despedidos]. *8* descargo. *9* exoneración, absolución. *10* pago [de una deuda]. *11* cumplimiento, desempeño. *12* recibo, quitanza. *13* liberación [de un preso]. *14* despido, destitución. *15* MIL. licenciamiento, licencia.

discharge (to) *tr.* descargar. *2* dejar [sus pasajeros un tren, etc.]. *3* disparar [un arma, un proyectil]. *4* verter [sus aguas]. *5* despedir, arrojar, echar [fuera de sí]. *6* desembarazar [de]. *7* exonerar, absolver. *8* poner en libertad [un preso]. *9* saldar, pagar. *10* cumplir [un deber], desempeñar [un cometido]. *11* relevar, [de servicio]; despedir, destituir. *12* MIL. licenciar. *13 intr.* descargarse. *14* dispararse [un arma]. *15* salir, desaguar.

disciple (disai·pøl) *s.* discípulo, seguidor, secuaz.

disciplinant (di·siplinant) *s.* disciplinante.

disciplinarian (disipline·rian) *s.* ordenancista, rigorista.

disciplinary (di·siplineri) *adj.* disciplinario.

discipline (di·siplin) *s.* disciplina. *2* enseñanza, doctrina. *3* educación, ejercicio. *4* castigo.

discipline (to) *tr.* disciplinar. *2* enseñar, educar. *3* castigar, corregir.

disclaim (to) (disklei·m) *tr.* negar, desconocer, repudiar. *2* DER. renunciar.

disclose (to) (-klou·s) *tr.* descubrir, destapar. *2* revelar, exponer, divulgar, publicar.

disclosure (-klou·ẙø') *s.* descubrimiento, revelación, declaración.

discobolus (diska·boløs) *s.* discóbolo.

discolo(u)r (to) (-kø·lø') *tr.* descolorir, desteñir; alterar el color, manchar. *2 intr.* descolorirse, desteñirse.

discolo(u)ration (-ei·shøn) *s.* descolorimiento. *2* mancha [donde se ha alterado el color].

discomfit (to) (diskø·mfit) *tr.* derrotar. *2* burlar, frustrar, desconcertar.

discomfiture (-mfichø') *s.* derrota. *2* frustración, desconcierto. *3* decepción.

discomfort (-mfø't) *s.* incomodidad, molestia. *2* malestar.

discomfort (to) *tr.* incomodar, molestar. *2* afligir.

discommend (to) (-køme·nd) *tr.* censurar.

discompose (to) (-kømpou·š) *tr.* turbar, desconcertar, agitar. *2* desarreglar.

discomposure (-pou·ẙø') *s.* turbación, desconcierto, agitación. *2* desorden, desarreglo.

disconcert (to) (-kønsø·'t) *tr.* desconcertar, desbaratar. *2* desconcertar, confundir, turbar.

disconnect (-køne·kt) *tr.* desunir, separar, disociar. *2* MEC., ELECT. desacoplar, desconectar, desenchufar.

**disconnected** (-id) *adj.* desconectado. *2* inconexo, incoherente.

**disconnection, disconnexion** (-ne·kshøn) *s.* desunión, separación. *2* inconexión, incoherencia.

**disconsolate** (-ka·nsolit) *adj.* desconsolado.

**disconsolateness** (-nis) *s.* desconsuelo.

**discontent** (-kønte·nt) *s.* descontento, disgusto. *2 adj.* descontento, disgustado.

**discontent (to)** *tr.* descontentar, disgustar.

**discontented** (-id) *adj.* descontento, disgustado. *2* descontentadizo.

**discontentment** (-mønt) *s.* descontento, mal humor.

**discontinuance** (diskønti·niuans), **discontinuation** (-ei·shøn) *s.* discontinuación, interrupción, intermisión, suspensión, cesación.

**discontinue (to)** (-niu) *tr.* discontinuar, interrumpir, suspender, hacer cesar. *2* dejar [una suscripción o abono]. *3 intr.* no continuar, interrumpirse, cesar.

**discontinuity** (diskantinu·ti) *s.* discontinuidad.

**discontinuous** (-niuøs) *adj.* discontinuo.

**discord** (di·skord) *s.* discordia. *2* MÚS. discordancia, disonancia.

**discord (to)** *intr.* desconvenir, discordar.

**discordance, -cy** (-ko·ᵣdans, -si) *s.* discordancia. *2* disonancia.

**discordant** (-dant) *adj.* discordante, discorde.

**discount** (-kau·nt) *s.* descuento; rebaja, bonificación.

**discount (to)** *tr.* descontar, rebajar, reducir. *2* COM. descontar. *3* desestimar, no tener en cuenta.

**discountenance** (-ønans) *s.* desaprobación, desagrado.

**discountenance (to)** *tr.* desconcertar, turbar, avergonzar. *2* no alentar o apoyar; desaprobar.

**discourage (to)** (-kø·ridỹ) *tr.* descorazonar, desalentar. *2* reprimir o impedir desaprobando, disuadir.

**discourse** (-ko·ᵣs) *s.* discurso; disertación. *2* plática, conversación.

**discourse (to)** *intr.* disertar, discurrir, hablar, conversar.

**discourteous** (-kø·ᵣtiøs) *adj.* descortés.

**discourtesy** (-kø·ᵣtiši) *s.* descortesía.

**discover (to)** (-kø·vøᵣ) *tr.* descubrir, hallar. *2* descubrir, revelar, manifestar.

**discoverer** (-øᵣ) *s.* descubridor.

**discovery** (-i) *s.* descubrimiento, hallazgo.

**discredit** (-kre·dit) *s.* descrédito; deshonra. *2* desconfianza, duda.

**discredit (to)** *tr.* desacreditar; deshonrar. *2* no creer, dudar de, desconfiar de.

**discreditable** (-abøl) *adj.* deshonroso.

**discreet** (-krɪ·t) *adj.* discreto [que procede con discreción]; juicioso, cuerdo, prudente.

**discreetness** (-nis) *s.* discreción, sensatez, cordura, prudencia.

**discrepance, -cy** (kre·pans, -si) *s.* discrepancia.

**discrepant** (-pant) *adj.* discrepante.

**discrete** (-krɪ·t) *adj.* discontinuo, separado. *2* MAT. discreto. *3* FIL. abstracto.

**discretion** (-kei·shøn) *s.* discreción [sensatez, reserva]; juicio, discernimiento. *2* discreción, arbitrio: *at the ~ of*, a la discreción de.

**discretional** (-al), **discretionary** (-eri) *adj.* discrecional.

**discretive** (di·skritiv) *adj.* disyuntivo. *2* que distingue.

**discriminant** (diskri·minant) *s.* MAT. discriminante.

**discriminate** (-minit) *adj.* distinto, diferenciado.

**discriminate (to)** (-eit) *tr.* discernir, distinguir, diferenciar; discriminar. *2 intr.* hacer diferencias, distinciones [en favor o en contra].

**discriminating** (-ing) *adj.* que distingue finamente, agudo. *2* distintivo. *3* que hace diferencias, parcial.

**discrimination** (-ei·shøn) *s.* discernimiento. *2* diferencia, distinción, discriminación. *3* trato diferente.

**discriminative** (diskri·mineitiv), **discriminatory** (-atori) *adj.* discernidor. *2* distintivo. *3* que hace diferencias.

**discrown (to)** (-krau·n) *tr.* deponer, destronar.

**discursive** (-kø·ᵣsiv) *adj.* digresivo, descosido; extenso, lato. *2* razonado, no intuitivo.

**discus** (di·skøs) *s.* DEP. disco.

**discuss (to)** (diskø·s) *tr.-intr.* discutir. *2* ventilar, dilucidar; hablar de.

**discussion** (-shøn) *s.* discusión [debate, examen].

**disdain** (-dei·n) *s.* desdén, menosprecio.

**disdain (to)** (tr. desdeñar, menospreciar. *2* desdeñarse de.

**disdainful** (-ful) *adj.* desdeñoso. *2* altanero.

**disease** (-dišɪ·š) *s.* enfermedad, mal, afección, dolencia.

**disease (to)** *tr.* enfermar, hacer daño.

**diseased** (-d) *adj.* enfermo; morboso.

**disembark (to)** (-emba·ᵣk) *tr.-intr.* desembarcar.

**disembarkation** (-ei·shøn), **disembarkment** (-mønt) *s.* desembarque. *2* desembarco.

**disembarrass (to)** (-embæ·ras) *tr.* desembarazar. *2* despejar. *3* zafar.

**disembody (to)** (-emba·di) *tr.* desencarnar. *2* licenciar [huestes]. ¶ Pret. y p. p.: *disembodied.*

**disembogue (-bou·g)** *intr.* desembocar. *2 tr.* vaciar [sus aguas]. *3 tr.-intr.* arrojar [lavas, etc.].

**disembowel (-bau·øl)** *tr.* desentrañar, destripar.

**disembroil (to)** (-broi·l) *tr.* desembrollar.

**disenchant (to)** (-encha·nt) *tr.* desencantar.

**disencumber (-kø·mbøᵣ)** *tr.* desembarazar, descargar [de lo que embaraza]; descombrar.

**disengage (-gei·dỹ)** *tr.* desasir, soltar, desenredar, desembarazar, librar. *2* librar, eximir, desligar [de una obligación, etc.]. *3 intr.* zafarse, desasirse, soltarse, librarse. *4* MIL. despegarse.

**disengaged (-d)** *adj.* desembarazado, libre. *2* suelto, desasido, despegado. *3* vacante. *4* desocupado, sin empleo.

**disentangle (to)** (-tæ·ngøl) *tr.* desenredar, desenmarañar, desembrollar; zafar.

**disentomb** (-tu·m) *tr.* desenterrar, exhumar.

**disestablish (to)** (disestæ·blish) *tr.* separar [la Iglesia] del Estado.

**disesteem** (-estɪ·m) *s.* desestima.

**disesteem (to)** *tr.* desestimar, no estimar.

**disfavour** (-fei·vøᵣ) *s.* disfavor. *2* desagrado, malquerencia. *3* desgracia [pérdida del favor].

**disfavour (to)** *tr.* desfavorecer, desairar.

**disfigure (to)** (-fi·giuᵣ) *tr.* desfigurar, afear.

**disfigurement** (-mønt) *s.* desfiguración, afeamiento. *2* mancha, borrón, cosa que afea.

**disgarnish (to)** (-ga·ᵣnish) *tr.* desguarnecer.

**disgorge (to)** (-go·ᵣdỹ) *tr.* arrojar, vomitar, desembuchar. *2* devolver [lo robado].

**disgrace** (-grei·s) *s.* desgracia [pérdida del favor]. *2* deshonor, deshonra, vergüenza, oprobio. *3* baldón, mancha.

**disgrace (to)** *tr.* hacer perder el favor. *2* deshonrar, causar oprobio. *3* afear.

**disgraceful** (-ful) *adj.* deshonroso, vergonzoso, ignominioso.

**disgracious** (-grei·shøs) *adj.* falto de gracia.

**disgregation** (-grøgei·shøn) *s.* disgregación.

**disgruntle** (-grø·ntøl) *tr.* enfadar, disgustar.

**disguise** (-gaiš) *s.* disfraz. *2* embozo, rebozo, fingimiento.

**disguise (to)** *tr.* disfrazar. *2* enmascarar, ocultar, encubrir, disimular.

**disgust** (-gøst) *s.* aversión, hastío, repugnancia, asco.

**disgust (to)** *tr.* hastiar, repugnar, asquear.

**disgusting** (-ing) *adj.* repugnante, asqueroso.

**dish** (dish) *s.* plato, fuente: ~ *rack*, escurreplatos. *2* plato [manjar]. *3* concavidad. *4 pl.* vajilla.

**dish (to)** *tr.* servir, poner en platos. *2* aderezar, disponer. *3* burlar, frustrar. *4 intr.* hacerse cóncavo.

**dishabille** (disabi·l) *s.* trapillo, vestido casero.

**dishabituate** (-jabi·chueit) *tr.* deshabituar.

**disharmony** (-ja·ʳmoni) *s.* falta de armonía, discordancia.

**dishcloth** (di·shkloz) *s.* albero.

**dishearten (to)** (disja·ʳtøn) *tr.* descorazonar.

**dished** (di·sht) *adj.* cóncavo.

**dishevel (to)** (dishe·vøl) *tr.* desgreñar, despeinar; desarreglar. ¶ Pret. y p. p.: *disheveled* o *-lled;* ger.: *-ling* o *-lling.*

**dishful** (dish·ful) *s.* plato, fuente [contenido].

**dishonest** (disa·nist) *adj.* falto de honradez, ímprobo, falso. *2* poco honrado, ilícito, deshonroso.

**dishonesty** (-i) *s.* improbidad, falta de honradez.

**dishono(u)r** (disa·nøʳ) *s.* deshonor, deshonra. *2* afrenta. *3* COM. falta de pago o de aceptación de un efecto.

**dishono(u)r (to)** *tr.* deshonorar. *2* deshonrar, infamar. *3* afrentar. *4* COM. no pagar o no aceptar [un efecto].

**dishono(u)rable** (-abøl) *adj.* deshonroso. *3* poco honrado.

**dishpan** (di·shpæn) *s.* lebrillo de fregar platos.

**dishwasher** (-uoshøʳ) *s.* lavaplatos.

**disillusion** (disilu·ÿøn) *s.* desilusión, desengaño.

**disillusion, disillusionize (to)** (-aiš) *tr.* desilusionar.

**disinclination** (-inklinei·shøn) *s.* desafición, aversión.

**disincline** (-inklai·n) *tr.* desinclinar.

**disinfect (to)** (-infe·kt) *tr.* desinfectar.

**disinfectant** (-ant) *s.* desinfectante.

**disinfection** (-fe·kshøn) *s.* desinfección.

**disingenuous** (-indÿe·niuøs) *adj.* falso, insincero.

**disinherit** (-je·rit) *tr.* desheredar.

**disinheritance** (-ans) *s.* desheredamiento.

**disintegrate (to)** (-tigrei·t) *tr.* desintegrar, disgregar, deshacer, desmoronar. *2 intr.* desintegrarse, deshacerse, desmoronarse.

**disintegration** (-ei·shøn) *s.* desintegración, disgregación.

**disinter (to)** (disi·ntøʳ) *tr.* desenterrar, exhumar. ¶ Pret. y p. p.: *-rred;* ger.: *-rring.*

**disinterest** (-tørest) *s.* perjuicio. *2* desinterés. *2* indiferencia.

**disinterest (to)** *tr.* despojar de interés o de motivos interesados. *2 ref.* desinteresarse.

**desinterested** (-id) *adj.* desinteresado. *2* que no tiene beneficio en una cosa. *3* imparcial.

**disjoin (to)** (disÿoi·n) *tr.* desjuntar, desunir, separar. *2 intr.* desunirse, separarse.

**disjoint** (-t) *tr.* desarticular, descoyuntar, dislocar, desquiciar, devencijar. *2* desunir, separar. *3 intr.* desarticularse, dislocarse.

**disjointed** (-id) *adj.* desarticulado, descoyuntado. *2* inconexo, incoherente.

**disjunction** (-jø·nkshøn) *s.* disyunción. *2* separación.

**disjunctive** (-tiv) *adj.-s.* disyuntivo. *2 s.* disyuntiva.

**disk** (disk) *s.* disco [pieza circular]. *2* ASTR., BOT., ZOOL. disco.

**dislike** (dislai·k) *s.* aversión, antipatía, aborrecimiento.

**dislike (to)** *tr.* tener aversión o antipatía a, detestar; no encontrar de su gusto.

**dislocate (to)** (di·slokeit) *tr.* dislocar, descoyuntar. *2* desarreglar.

**dislocation** (-ei·shøn) *s.* dislocación.

**dislodge (to)** (disla·dÿ) *tr.* desalojar, echar fuera.

**disloyal** (-lo·ial) *adj.* desleal.

**disloyalty** (-ti) *s.* deslealtad.

**dismal** (di·smal) *adj.* triste, lúgubre, tétrico. *2* funesto, desgraciado. *3 pl. the dismals,* tristeza, melancolía.

**dismantle (to)** (dismæ·ntøl) *tr.* desmantelar. *2* desguarnecer, desamoblar. *3* MEC. desmontar.

**dismast (to)** (-mæ·st) *tr.* MAR. desarbolar.

**dismay** (-mei·) *s.* desmayo, desaliento. *2* consternación, espanto.

**dismay (to)** *tr.* desanimar, espantar, aterrar.

**dismember** (-me·mbøʳ) *tr.* desmembrar.

**dismemberment** (-mønt) *s.* desmembración.

**dismiss (to)** (-mi·s) *tr.* despedir [hacer salir; dar permiso para irse]; disolver [una junta, etc.]. *2* despedir, destituir, separar, licenciar. *3* desechar, alejar del pensamiento; deshacerse [de un asunto].

**dismissal** (-al), **dismission** (-shøn) *s.* despido [invitación a retirarse]. *2* despido, destitución. *3* acción de desechar.

**dismount (to)** (-mau·nt) *tr.* desmontar [apear]. *2* desmontar [la artillería, una joya, etc.]. *3 intr.* desmontar, apearse.

**disobedience** (-obi·diøns) *s.* desobediencia.

**disobedient** (-diønt) *adj.* desobediente, insumiso, rebelde.

**disobey (to)** (-obei·) *tr.-intr.* desobedecer.

**disoblige** (-oblai·dÿ) *tr.* desobligar. *2* no complacer, ser desatento con. *3* molestar, ofender.

**disobliging** (-ing) *adj.* poco complaciente, desatento. *2* molesto, ofensivo.

**disorder** (-o·ʳdøʳ) *s.* desorden. *2* trastorno, desarreglo; enfermedad. *3* enajenación mental.

**disorder (to)** *tr.* desordenar. *2* desarreglar, perturbar, trastornar.

**disorderly** (-li) *adj.* desordenado, desarreglado. *2* alborotador, escandaloso: ~ *conduct,* faltas contra la moral o el orden público. *3 adv.* desordenadamente.

**disorganization** (-oʳganišei·shøn) *s.* desorganización.

**disorganize (to)** (-o·ʳganaiš) *tr.* desorganizar.

**disorientate (to)** (-o·rienteit) *tr.* desorientar.

**disorientation** (-ei·shøn) *s.* desorientación.

**disown (to)** (-ou·n) *tr.* repudiar; desconocer, negar; renegar de.

**disparage (to)** (-pæ·ridÿ) *tr.* desacreditar, despreciar, rebajar. *2* desdorar, hacer desmerecer.

**disparagement** (-mønt) *s.* detracción, menosprecio. *2* desdoro, descrédito.

**disparate** (di·sparit) *adj.* dispar, disparejo, discorde. *2 s.* una de dos cosas dispares.

**disparity** (-i) *s.* disparidad.
**dispart (to)** (-pa·ᶜt) *tr.* despartir, dividir. *2 intr.* dividirse.
**dispassionate** (-pæ·shønit) *adj.* desapasionado, sereno, frío, imparcial.
**dispatch** (-pæ·ch) *s.* despacho [acción]. *2* expedición, prontitud. *3* despacho, parte, comunicación. *4* MAR. ~ *boat,* aviso.
**dispatch (to)** *tr.* despachar [enviar, expedir; matar; comer]. *2* despachar, concluir, apresurar.
**dispel (to)** (-pe·l) *tr.* dispersar, disipar. *2 intr.* dispersarse, disiparse. ¶ Pret. y p. p.: *-lled;* ger.: *-lling.*
**dispendious** (-pe·ndiøs) *adj.* dispendioso.
**dispensary** (-sari) *s.* dispensario farmacéutico.
**dispensation** (-ei·shøn) *s.* dispensación, distribución, administración. *2* gobierno. *3* providencia divina. *4* dispensa, exención. *5* ley, religión.
**dispensatory** (dispe·nsatori) *s.* farmacopea.
**dispense (to)** (-pe·ns) *tr.* dispensar, distribuir, conceder. *2* administrar [justicia]. *3* despachar [medicamentos]. *4* dispensar, eximir, excusar. ❦ *intr. to ~ with,* prescindir de.
**dispeople (to)** (-pi·pøl) *tr.* despoblar.
**dispersal** (-pø·ᶜsal) *s.* dispersión.
**disperse** (-pø·ᶜs) *adj.* disperso.
**disperse (to)** *tr.* dispersar. *2* disipar, desvanecer. *3* esparcir. *4 intr.* dispersarse, esparcirse; disiparse.
**dispersed** (-t) *adj.* dispersado, disperso.
**dispersion** (-pø·ᶜshøn) *s.* dispersión. *2* disipación, desvanecimiento. *3* esparcimiento, difusión.
**dispirit (to)** (-pi·rit) *tr.* desalentar, desanimar.
**dispiritedness** (-idnis) *s.* desaliento, desánimo.
**displace (to)** (-plei·s) *tr.* cambiar de sitio, remover, desalojar, quitar el sitio a. *2* MAR. desplazar. *3* destituir, separar.
**displacement** (-mønt) *s.* remoción, traslado. desalojamiento. *2* destitución, separación. *3* MAR. desplazamiento. *4* GEOL. falla, quiebra.
**displant** (-plænt) *tr.* desplantar.
**display** (-plei·) *s.* despliegue, exhibición, manifestación. *2* ostentación, alarde. *3* pompa, fausto.
**display (to)** *tr.* desplegar, abrir, extender. *2* exponer, poner de manifiesto. *3* exhibir, lucir, ostentar. *4* MAR. enarbolar.
**displease (to)** (-plɪ·š) *tr.* desplacer, desagradar, descontentar. *2* disgustar, enojar, ofender.
**displeasure** (-ple·ȳøᶜ) *s.* desplacer, desagrado, descontento, enojo. *2* desgracia, disfavor. *3* disgusto, sinsabor.
**displume (to)** (-plu·m) *tr.* desplumar.
**disport** (-po·ᶜt) *s.* juego, diversión.
**disport (to)** *tr.* divertir. *2 intr.* juguetear, divertirse.
**disposal** (-pou·šal) *s.* disposición, colocación, arreglo [acción]. *2* DISPOSITION 4. *3* acción de deshacerse [de]; donación, venta, enajenación.
**dispose (to)** (-pouₛ·š) *tr.* disponer, arreglar, ordenar. *2* disponer, establecer, determinar. *3* disponer, inclinar el ánimo de. *4 intr. to ~ of,* disponer de; deshacerse de; despachar, consumir; dar, vender, enajenar.
**disposition** (-poši·shøn) *s.* disposición, arreglo, ordenación. *2* condición, genio, humor. *3* tendencia, inclinación, propensión. *4* disposición [acción o facultad de disponer]. *5 pl.* disposiciones [que se toman].
**dispositioned** (-t) *adj.* de tal o cual condición, genio, humor, etc.

**dispossess (to)** (-pøse·s) *tr.* desposeer. *2* DER. desahuciar, lanzar.
**dispossession** (-se·shøn) *s.* desposeimiento. *2* DER. desahucio, lanzamiento.
**dispraise** (disprei·š) *s.* desalabanza, censura.
**dispraise (to)** *tr.* desalabar, censurar.
**disproof** (-pru·f) *s.* refutación.
**disproportion** (-propo·ᶜshøn) *s.* desproporción.
**disproportion (to)** *tr.* desproporcionar.
**disproportionate** (-it) *adj.* desproporcionado.
**disproval** (-pru·val) *s.* refutación, confutación.
**disprove** (-pru·v) *tr.* refutar, confutar.
**disputable** (-piu·tabøl) *adj.* disputable, discutible.
**disputant** (-tant) *adj.-s.* disputador.
**disputation** (-ei·shøn) *s.* disputa, debate.
**disputatious** (-ei·shøs) *adj.* disputador, reparón.
**dispute** (-piu·t) *s.* disputa, discusión. *2* controversia. *3* litigio, pleito.
**dispute (to)** *tr.-intr.* disputar, discutir. *2* controvertir. *3 intr.* impugnar, poner en duda.
**disputeless** (-lis) *adj.* indiscutible.
**disqualification** (-kualifikei·shøn) *s.* inhabilitación, incapacidad, impedimento. *2* DEP. descalificación.
**disqualify (to)** (-kua·lifai) *tr.* inhabilitar, incapacitar. *2* DEP. descalificar.
**disquiet** (-kuai·øt) *s.* inquietud, desasosiego.
**disquiet (to)** (-t) *tr.* inquietar, intranquilizar, desasosegar, atormentar.
**disquietness** (-nis), **disquietude** (-iud) *s.* DISQUIET.
**disquisition** (-kuiši·shøn) *s.* disquisición.
**disregard** (-riga·ᶜd) *s.* desatención, descuido, olvido, desprecio. *2* desconsideración, desaire.
**disregard (to)** *tr.* desatender, descuidar, olvidar, despreciar, no hacer caso [de]. *2* desconsiderar, desairar.
**disregardful** (-ful) *adj.* desatento, descuidado, que no hace caso.
**disrelish** (-re·lish) *s.* repugnancia, aversión.
**disreputable** (-re·piutabøl) *adj.* desacreditado, de mala fama o aspecto. *2* deshonroso, vergonzoso.
**disrepute** (-ripiu·t) *s.* descrédito, mala fama, deshonra.
**disrespect** (-rispe·kt) *s.* falta de respeto, desacato.
**disrespect (to)** *tr.* faltar al respeto a, desacatar.
**disrespectful** (-ful) *adj.* irrespetuoso.
**disrobe (to)** (-rou·b) *tr.* desnudar. *2 intr.* desnudarse.
**disrupt (to)** (-rø·pt) *tr.* romper, dividir; desgajar.
**disruption** (-rø·pshøn) *s.* ruptura; desgajamiento.
**disruptive** (-rø·ptiv) *adj.* que rompe. *2* ELECT. disruptivo.
**dissatisfaction** (disætisfæ·kshøn) *s.* descontento, disgusto.
**dissatisfactory** (-tori) *adj.* poco o nada satisfactorio.
**dissatisfy (to)** (-sæ·tisfai) *tr.* descontentar, no satisfacer. ¶ Pret. y p. p.: ~ *fied.*
**dissect (to)** (-se·kt) *tr.* disecar, anatomizar.
**dissector** (-øᶜ) *s.* disector.
**dissemble (to)** (-se·mbøl) *tr.* disimular, disfrazar, ocultar. *2* fingir, fingirse. *3 intr.* fingir.
**dissembler** (-bløᶜ) *s.* disimulador, fingidor, simulador, hipócrita.
**disseminate (to)** (-se·mineit) *tr.* diseminar. *2* difundir, propagar.
**dissension** (-se·nshøn) *s.* disensión, discordia.
**dissent** (-se·nt) *s.* disentimiento. *2* disidencia.
**dissent (to)** *intr.* disentir, diferir. *2* disidir.
**dissenter** (-øᶜ) *s.* discorde [que disiente]. *2* disidente [esp. de la Iglesia anglicana].

**dissentient** (-se·nshiønt)*adj.* disconforme,opuesto. *2 s.* disidente.

**dissert (to)** (-sø·ᵣt), **dissertate (to)** (-teit) *intr.* disertar.

**dissertation** (-ei·shøn) *s.* disertación.

**disserve (to)** (-sø·ᵣv) *tr.* deservir, perjudicar.

**disservice** (-is) *s.* deservicio, perjuicio.

**dissever** (-e·vøᵣ) *tr.* desunir, separar.

**dissidence** (di·sidøns) *s.* disidencia.

**dissident** (-ønt) *adj.-s.* disidente.

**dissimilar** (disi·milaᵣ) *adj.* disímil, desemejante.

**disimilarity** (-similæ·riti) *s.* disimilitud, disparidad.

**dissimilation** (-ei·shøn) *s.* disimilación.

**dissimilitude** (-simi·litiud) *s.* disimilitud.

**dissimulate (to)** (-simiuleit) *tr.-intr.* disimular, fingir.

**dissimulation** (-ei·shøn) *s.* disimulación, disimulo, hipocresía.

**dissipate (to)** (di·sipeit) *tr.* dispersar. *2* esparcir. *3* disipar [desvanecer; malgastar]. *4 intr.* disiparse, desvanecerse. *5* entregarse a los placeres.

**dissipated** (-id) *adj.* disipado, disoluto.

**dissipation** (-ei·shøn) *s.* dispersión, evaporación. *2* disipación. *3* diversión, devaneo. *4* deroche. *5* disolución, vida relajada.

**dissociate (to)** (-shieit) *tr.* disociar. *2 intr.* disociarse.

**dissolubility** (-saliubi·liti) *s.* disolubilidad.

**dissoluble** (-sa·liubøl) *adj.* disoluble.

**dissolute** (di·søliut) *adj.* disoluto, relajado.

**dissoluteness** (-nis) *s.* disolución, relajamiento.

**dissolution** (-søliu·shøn) *s.* disolución [acción de disolver o disolverse]. *2* muerte. *3* licuación, fusión.

**dissolvable** (-ša·lvabøl) *adj.* disoluble.

**dissolve** (-ša·lv) *tr.* disolver. *2* DER. abrogar. *3 intr.* disolverse. *4* deshacerse. *5* desvanecerse, desaparecer, morir. *6* descaecer.

**dissolvent** (-ønt) *adj.-s.* disolvente.

**dissonance, -cy** (di·sønans, -si) *s.* disonancia.

**dissonant** (-ant) *adj.* disonante, discordante.

**dissuade (to)** (disuei·d) *tr.* disuadir.

**dissuasion** (-ei·ÿøn) *s.* disuasión; consejo.

**dissuasive** (-siv) *adj.* disuasivo.

**dissyllabic** (-silæ·bik) *adj.* disílabo, bisílabo·

**dissyllable** (-si·labøl) *s.* disílabo, bisílabo.

**dissymetry** (-metri) *s.* disimetría.

**distaff** (di·stæf) *s.* rueca. *2* fig. la mujer.

**distal** (di·stal) *adj.* BIOL. distal.

**distance** (-tans) *s.* distancia. *2* alejamiento; lejos, lejanía, lontananza: *in the ~,* a lo lejos. *3* trecho, espacio. *4* reserva en el trato: *to keep at ~,* mantener [a uno] a distancia; no permitirle familiaridades.

**distance (to)** *tr.* distanciar. *2* alejar. *3* dejar atrás, adelantar. *4* espaciar.

**distant** (di·stant) *adj.* distante. *2* lejano. *3* diferente. *4* reservado en el trato, esquivo, frío, altivo.

**distaste** (distei·st) *s.* hastío, disgusto, aversión, repugnancia.

**distasteful** (-ful) *adj.* desagradable, repugnante.

**distemper** (-te·mpøᵣ) *s.* mal humor. *2* enfermedad. *3* VET. moquillo. *4* tumulto, disturbio. *5* PINT. templa; pintura al temple.

**distemper (to)** *tr.* perturbar, enfermar. *2* incomodar, irritar. *3* pintar al temple.

**distend (to)** (-te·nd) *tr.* estirar, ensanchar, dilatar, hinchar. *2* MED. distender.

**distension, distention** (-te·nshøn) *s.* dilatación. *2* MED. distensión.

**distich** (di·stik) *s.* dístico.

**distil(l (to)** (disti·l) *tr.* destilar, alambicar. *2 tr.-intr.* destilar [gota a gota].

**distillate** (-eit) *s.* destilado.

**distillation** (-ei·shøn) *s.* destilación. *2* extracto, esencia.

**distillery** (-ti·løri) *s.* destilería.

**distinct** (-ti·nkt) *adj.* distinto, claro; preciso, definido. *2* distinto, diferente.

**distinction** (-nkshøn) *s.* distinción: *in ~ from* o *to,* a distinción de. *2* distingo. *3* diferencia. *4* distintivo, característica.

**distinctive** (-tiv) *adj.-s.* distintivo.

**distinguish (to)** (-ti·ngüish) *tr.* distinguir. *2* discernir. *3* dividir, clasificar. *4 ref.* distinguirse.

**distinguished** (-t) *adj.* distinguido.

**distort (to)** (-to·ᵣt) *tr.* torcer, deformar. *2* desfigurar, falsear, tergiversar.

**distorsion** (-to·ᵣshøn) *s.* torcimiento, distorsión. *2* falseamiento, tergiversación.

**distract (to)** (-træ·kt) *tr.* distraer [apartar la atención]. *2* perturbar, agitar, enloquecer.

**distracted** (-id) *adj.* distraído. *2* trastornado, enloquecido; loco, frenético.

**distraction** (-kshøn) *s.* distracción. *2* perturbación, agitación, enloquecimiento, frenesí, locura. *3* confusión, desorden.

**distrain (to)** (-trei·n) *tr.* DER. embargar, secuestrar.

**distraint** (-t) *s.* DER. embargo, secuestro.

**distraught** (-tro·t) *adj.* DISTRACTED.

**distress** (-tre·s) *s.* dolor, pena, aflicción. *2* infortunio, desgracia. *3* miseria, escasez. *4* apuro, peligro: *ship in ~,* barco en peligro. *5* DER. embargo.

**distress (to)** *tr.* afligir, apenar, angustiar. *2* poner en aprieto. *3* DER. embargar.

**distressful** (-ful) *adj.* doloroso, desdichado, lleno de trabajos o calamidades.

**distressing** (-ing) *adj.* penoso, aflictivo.

**distribute (to)** (-tri·biut) *s.* distribuir.

**distributive** (-iv) *adj.* distributivo.

**district** (di·strikt) *adj.* distrito. *2* partido, comarca, región, territorio.

**distrust** (distrø·st) *s.* desconfianza, recelo, suspicacia.

**distrust (to)** *tr.* desconfiar, sospechar de, no confiar en, recelar.

**distrustful** (-ful) *adj.* desconfiado, que desconfía, receloso, difidente.

**disturb (to)** (-tø·ᵣb) *tr.* turbar, perturbar, alterar, desordenar. *2* inquietar, desasosegar. *3* distraer, estorbar. *4* molestar, incomodar.

**disturbance** (-bans) *s.* perturbación, alteración. *2* disturbio, desorden, alboroto. *3* inquietud. *4* malestar.

**disunion** (-iu·niøn) *s.* desunión.

**disunite (to)** (-iunai·t) *tr.* desunir. *2 intr.* desunirse.

**disuse** (-iu·s) *s.* desuso. *2* falta de práctica o ejercicio.

**disuse (to)** *tr.* desusar. *2* dejar de usar, desechar.

**ditch** (dich) *s.* caz, reguera, zanja, foso, cuneta. *2* BOT. ~ *reed,* carrizo.

**ditch (to)** *tr.* abrir zanjas en.

**dither** (di·døᵣ) *s.* temblor, agitación.

**dither (to)** *intr.* temblar, estar agitado.

**tithyramb** (di·ziræmb) *s.* ditirambo.

**ditone** (dai·toun) *s.* MÚS. dítono.

**dittany** (di·tani) *s.* BOT. díctamo, orégano.

**ditto** (di·tou) *s.-adv.* idem.

**ditty** (-ti) *s.* canción, cantinela.
**diuretic** (daiure·tik) *adj.-s.* MED. diurético.
**diurnal** (daiø·ʰnal) *adj.* diurno. *2* diario, cotidiano.
**diuturnal** (-iutø·ʰnal) *adj.* diuturno.
**diva** (dı·va) *s.* diva, cantante.
**divagate (to)** (dai·vageit) *intr.* divagar.
**divagation** (-ei·shøn) *s.* divagación.
**divan** (divæ·n) *s.* diván.
**divaricate (to)** (daivæ·rikeit) *intr.* bifurcarse.
**dive** (daiv) *s.* zambullida, inmersión. *2* buceo. *3* NAT. salto. *4* AVIA. picado. *5* fam. (E.U.) taberna.
**dive (to)** *intr.* zambullirse. *2* arrojarse de cabeza. *3* sumergirse. *4* AVIA. picar. *5* bucear, profundizar, penetrar, enfrascarse [en]. *6 tr.* zambullir, sumergir. ¶ Pret. y p.p.: *dived* o *dove.*
**diver** (-ø'ʰ) *s.* buzo. *2* zambullidor. *3* ORN. somorgujo.
**diverge (to)** (divø·ʰdȳ) *intr.* divergir.
**divergence** (-øns) *s.* divergencia.
**divergent** (-ønt) *adj.* divergente.
**divers** (daivø·ʰs) *adj.* diversos, varios.
**diverse** (divø·ʰs) *adj.* diverso, diferente. *2* multiforme, variado.
**diversify (to)** (-ifai) *tr.* diversificar. *2* matizar, dar variedad a. ¶ Pret. y p. p.: *diversified.*
**diversion** (-vø·ʰshøn) *s.* diversión.
**diversity** (-siti) *s.* diversidad.
**divert (to)** (-vø·ʰt) *tr.* divertir, desviar, apartar. *2* distraer [de un trabajo, etc.]. *3* divertir, recrear.
**divertisement** (divø·ʰtišmønt) diversión, entretenimiento. *2* intermedio de baile.
**divest (to)** (-ve·st) *tr.* desnudar. *2* despojar, desposeer.
**divestiture** (-ichø'ʰ) *s.* despojo, desposeimiento.
**divide** (-vai·d) *s.* divisoria de aguas.
**divide (to))** *tr.* dividir, partir, repartir; separar. *2* MAT. dividir. *3* compartir. *4 intr.* dividirse. *5* tener una parte, ir a partes.
**dividend** (di·vidønd) *s.* MAT., COM. dividendo.
**divider** (divai·dø'ʰ) *s.* partidor; distribuidor. *2* MAT. divisor. *3 pl.* compás divisor.
**divi-divi** (di·vi·di·vi) *s.* BOT. dividiví.
**divination** (divinei·shøn) *s.* adivinación.
**divinatory** (di·vinatori) *adj.* adivinatorio.
**divine** (divai·n) *adj.* divino. *2* teológico, sagrado. *3 s.* sacerdote; teólogo.
**divine (to)** *tr.-intr.* adivinar. *2* conjeturar.
**diviner** (-ø'ʰ) *s.* adivino. *2* adivinador.
**divineress** (-øris) *s.* adivina. *2* adivinadora.
**diving** (dai·ving) *s.* buceo [trabajo del buzo]: ~ *bell,* campana de buzo; ~ *dress* o *suit,* escafandra. *2* NAT. zambullidura, salto. *3* AVIA. picado.
**divinity** (divi·niti) *s.* vidinidad. *2* deidad. *3* teología.
**divinize (to)** (di·vinaiš) *tr.* divinizar.
**divisibility** (divisibi·liti) *s.* divisibilidad.
**divisible** (-vi·šibøl) *adj.* divisible.
**division** (-ẏøn) *s.* división [acción de dividir]. *2* división, desunión. *3* tabique, etc., que divide. *4* MAT., MIL., MAR. división. *5* ramo, sección, negociado. *6* compartimento; parte, segmento. *7* FERROC. ramal.
**divisional** (-al), **divisionary** (-eri) *adj.* divisional, divisionario. *2* divisorio.
**divisor** (divai·šø'ʰ) *s.* MAT. divisor.
**divorce** (divo·ʰs) *s.* divorcio.
**divorce (to)** *tr.* divorciar. *2* divorciarse de. *3 intr.* divorciarse.
**divorcee** (divo·ʰsı) *s.* persona divorciada.
**divulgation** (-vølgei·shøn) *s.* divulgación, publicación.

**divulge (to)** (-vø·ldȳ) *tr.* divulgar, publicar.
**dizen (to)** (di·šøn) *tr.* ataviar, emperejilar.
**dizzines** (-šinis) *s.* vértigo, mareo, vahído.
**dizzy** (-ši) *adj.* vertiginoso, mareador. *2* desvanecido, mareado. *3* aturdido. *4* caprichoso, alocado.
**dizzy (to)** *tr.* causar vértigo o vahído. *2* aturdir.
**do** (dou) *s.* MÚS. do.
**do (to)** (du) *tr.* hacer [en sentido general o indeterminado]: *what are you going to* ~*?,* ¿qué va usted a hacer? *2* hacer [producir un efecto; infligir, causar]: *that does you credit,* esto le hace honor. *3* hacer [los honores de; justicia, un favor]; rendir, tributar [homenaje]. *4* hacer [efectuar, realizar]; cumplir con: *to* ~ *our duty,* cumplir con nuestro deber. *5* acabar, concluir, terminar, cesar, dejar de [en frases con el part. *done*]: *have done!,* ¡acaba ya! *6* COC. preparar, aderezar, cocer, guisar [convenientemente]: *done to a turn,* en su punto. *7* areglar, ordenar, limpiar, adornar, disponer: *to* ~ *one's hair,* peinarse. *8* hacer [una distancia, una velocidad]. *9* recorrer, visitar [como turista]. *10* verter, traducir. *11* hacer el papel de. *12* engañar, estafar. *13* hacer, cumplir [un tiempo de servicio, de cárcel, etc.]. *14* servir, bastar [al propósito, al objeto]. *15 to* ~ *away with,* deshacerse de; disipar; suprimir; dar al traste con; matar. *16 to* ~ *for,* acabar, arruinar; matar. *17 to* ~ *over,* rehacer; cubrir, untar. *18 to* ~ *up,* atar, envolver; planchar; limpiar, peinar; arreglar; fatigar, cansar.
  *19 intr.* obrar, conducirse, portarse. *20* estar, hallarse, pasarlo: *how* ~ *you* ~*?,* ¿cómo está usted? *21* servir, bastar, ser suficiente: *that will* ~, esto servirá o bastará; ¡basta!, ¡está bien!, ¡no diga más! *22 to* ~ *well,* prosperar, medrar, ir bien. *23 to do without,* prescindir de, pasar sin.
  *25 do* se usa además: a) como verbo auxiliar en las frases negativas e interrogativas y después de ciertos adverbios cuando hay inversión; b) en tono imperativo o deprecativo: *be quiet, do!,* ¡vamos, estáte quieto!; c) para dar más energía a frases afirmativas; d) para sustituir un verbo que no se quiere repetir: *I wanted to see him, and I did so,* quería verle, y le vi.
  ¶ INDIC. Pres. sing.: 1.ª pers., *do;* 2.ª pers., *doest* o *do;* 3.ª pers., *does;* pl., *do.* | Pret.: *did* (2.ª pers. del sing. *didst*). | PART. P: *done.* | GER: *doing.*
**doat (to)** (dout) *intr.* TO DOTE.
**dobbin** (da·bin) *s.* caballo de labor.
**docile** (dou·sil) *s.* dócil.
**docility** (dousi·liti) *s.* docilidad.
**dock** (dak) *s.* maslo [de la cola]; cola cortada. *2* codón. *3* MAR. dique; dársena. *4* desembarcadero; muelle. *5* banquillo [de los acusados], barra. *6* BOT. romaza.
**dock (to)** *tr.* cortar, cercenar. *2* descolar, desrabotar. *3* privar [de]. *4* MAR. hacer entrar en el dique. *5 intr.* MAR. fondear, atracar.
**dockage** (-idȳ) *s.* reducción, rebaja. *2* muellaje. *3* entrada en dique.
**docker** (-ø'ʰ) *s.* trabajador del muelle.
**docket** (da·kit) *s.* minuta, sumario; lista, orden del día. *2* DER. lista de causas pendientes. *3* recibo de la aduana. *4* rótulo, etiqueta.
**docket (to)** *tr.* etiquetar, rotular. *2* extractar. *3* poner en la lista de causas pendientes o en la orden del día.
**dockyard** (-ya'ʰd) *s.* MAR. astillero, arsenal.
**doctor** (da·ktø'ʰ) *m.* doctor. *2* médico, facultativo.

**doctor (to)** *tr.* doctorar. *2* medicinar. *3* reparar, componer. *4* adulterar, amañar. *5 intr.* ejercer la medicina.
**doctoral** (-al) *adj.* doctoral.
**doctorate** (-it) *s.* doctorado.
**doctoress** (-is) *s.* doctora.
**doctorship** (-ship) *s.* doctorado; borla.
**doctrinal** (da·ktrinal) *adj.* doctrinal, didáctico.
**doctrinarian** (daktrine·rian) *adj.-s.* doctrinario.
**doctrine** (ka·ktrin) *s.* doctrina.
**document** (-kiumønt) *s.* documento.
**document (to)** *tr.* documentar.
**documental** (-me·ntal), **documentary** (-me·ntari) *adj.* documental.
**documentation** (-ei·shøn) *s.* documentación.
**dodder** (da·dørʳ) *s.* BOT. cúscuta.
**dodder (to)** *intr.* temblar, temblequear. *2* tambalear.
**doddered** (-d) *adj.* decrépito.
**dodecagon** (dode·kagan) *s.* GEOM. dodecaedro.
**dodge** (-dadȳ) *s.* regate. *2* argucia, artificio, manganilla.
**dodge (to)** *intr.* hurtar el cuerpo, regatear; escabullirse, dar esquinazo. *2* usar de argucias. *3* evitar, eludir, soslayar, burlar. *4* seguir con disimulo.
**dodger** (-ørʳ) *s.* mañero, tramposo.
**dodo** (dou·dou) *s.* ORN. dido. *2* fig. persona anticuada.
**doe** (dou) *s.* ZOOL. gama; coneja; liebre, canguro o antílope hembra.
**doer** (du·øʳ) *s.* hacedor, autor, agente.
**does** (døs) *3.ª pers. sing. del Pres. de Ind.* de TO DO.
**doeskin** (dou·skin) *s.* ante, piel de gama.
**doff (to)** (daf) *tr.* quitarse [el sombrero, la ropa, etc.].
**dog** (dog o dag) *s.* ZOOL. perro, perra, can: *the ~ in the manger*, el perro del hortelano: *to go to the dogs*, arruinarse. *2* macho de algunos animales [zorro, lobo, chacal, etc.]. *3* fig. hombre, sujeto: *sly ~*, astuto, marrullero. *4* ASTR. Can. *5* piel de perro. *6* MEC. garra, grapa, barrilete. *7* morillo. *8* *hot ~*, salchicha caliente. *9* adj. de perro, perruno, canino; *~ days*, canícula; *~ tooth*, colmillo; *~ Latin*, latín macarrónico. *10* BOT. *~ brier*, *~ rose*, agavanzo, zarza perruna. *11* adv. sumamente [esp. en compuestos].
**dog (to)** *tr.* perseguir, seguir, espiar. ¶ Pret. y p. p.: *dogged*; ger.: *dogging*.
**dogaressa** (dogare·sa) *s.* dogaresa.
**dogbane** (dogbei·n) *s.* BOT. acónito.
**dogcart** (-ka·rt) *s.* coche ligero de dos ruedas.
**dog-cheap** (adj.) muy barato, tirado.
**doge** (doudȳ) *s.* dux.
**dogfight** (-fait) *s.* riña de perros.
**dogfish** (-fish) *s.* ICT. cazón, tollo, lija.
**dogged** (do·gid) *adj.* terco, obstinado, tenaz.
**dogger** (do·gøʳ) *s.* MAR. dogre.
**doggerel** (-gørøl) *s.* coplas de ciego, versos malos. *2 adj.* malo, ramplón.
**doggy** (-i) *s.* perrito. *2 adj.* de perro. *3* aficionado a los perros.
**doghouse** (dogjau·š) *s.* caseta de perro.
**dogma** (do·gma) *s.* dogma.
**dogmatic(al** (-mæ·tik(al) *adj.* dogmático.
**dogmatism** (do·gmatišm) *s.* dogmatismo.
**dogmatize (to)** (-mataiš) *intr.* dogmatizar.
**dog's-ear** *s.* esquina doblada en una hoja de libro.
**dogskin** (do·gskin) *s.* piel de perro.
**dog-tired** *adj.* cansadísimo.
**dogwood** (-wud) *s.* BOT. cornejo, sanguiñuelo.

**doily** (doi·li) *s.* tapetito.
**doing** (du·ing) *ger.* de TO DO. *2 s.* acción, obra. *3 pl.* hechos, acciones; acontecimientos.
**doldrums** (da·ldrømš) *s. pl.* MAR. calmas ecuatoriales. *2* fam. murria; aburrimiento.
**dole** (doul) *s.* reparto regular, ración, limosna, subsidio. *2* poét. dolor, aflicción.
**dole (to)** *tr.* dar, distribuir.
**doleful** (dou·lful), **dolesome** (-søm) *adj.* dolorido, lastimero, lúgubre, triste.
**dolichocephalic** (dolikousefæ·lik) *adj.* dolicocéfalo.
**Doll** (dal) *n. pr. f.* dim. de DOROTHY.
**doll** *s.* muñeca, muñeco.
**dollar** (da·laʳ) *s.* dólar. *2* peso [moneda].
**Dolly** (da·li) *n. pr. f.* dim. de DOROTHY.
**dolly** *s.* muñequita [voz infantil]. *2* MEC., MIN. nombre de varios artefactos. *3* FERROC. locomotora auxiliar.
**dolman** (da·lman) *s.* dormán.
**dolmen** (da·lmen) *s.* dolmen.
**dolomite** (da·lomait) *s.* MINER. dolomita.
**dolor** (dou·løʳ) *s.* DOLOUR.
**dolorous** (-øs) *adj.* doloroso, penoso. *2* triste, lastimero.
**dolour** (dou·løʳ) *s.* poét. dolor, duelo.
**dolphin** (da·lfin) *s.* ZOOL., ASTR. delfín. *2* MAR. poste de amarre.
**dolt** (doult) *s.* tonto, zote, zopenco.
**doltish** (-ish) *adj.* tonto, lerdo, estúpido.
**domain** (domei·n) *s.* heredad, finca. *2* dominio [territorio]. *3* dominio, campo, esfera.
**dome** (doum) *s.* ARQ. cúpula, domo, cimborio. *2* poét. edificio majestuoso. *3* AUTO. techo abovedado.
**domesday** (du·mšdei) *s.* DOOMSDAY.
**domestic** (dome·stik) *adj.* doméstico. *2* casero. *3* nacional, interior, del país: *~ commerce*, comercio interior. *4* intestino. *5 s.* doméstico, criado.
**domesticate (to)** (-eit) *tr.* domesticar. *2* civilizar. *3* naturalizar [costumbres, vocablos, etc.].
**domesticity** (-tisiti) *s.* domesticidad. *2 pl.* asuntos domésticos.
**domicile** (da·misil) *s.* domicilio.
**domicile (to)** *tr.* domiciliar. *2 intr.* domiciliarse, morar.
**domiciliary** (domisi·lieri) *adj.* domiciliario.
**domiciliate** (-lieit) *tr.-intr.* TO DOMICILE.
**dominant** (da·minant) *adj.* dominante. *2 s.* MÚS. dominante.
**dominate (to)** (-mineit) *tr.-intr.* dominar. *2 intr.* predominar.
**domination** (-ei·shøn) *s.* dominación. *2* dominio, imperio; tiranía.
**domineer (to)** (damini·r) *intr.-tr.* dominar, tiranizar.
**domineering** (-ing) *adj.* dominante, autoritario.
**Dominic** (da·minik) *n. pr. m.* Domingo.
**dominical** (domi·nikal) *adj.* dominical [del Señor].
**Dominican** (-nikan) *adj.-s.* dominicano. *2* dominico.
**dominie** (da·mini) *s.* dómine.
**dominion** (domi·niøn) *s.* dominio, dominación, señorío, poder. *2* dominio [territorio].
**dominium** (-niøm) *s.* DER. dominio.
**domino** (da·minou), *pl.* **-nos** o **noes** (-nøs) *s.* dominó [traje; pieza del juego]. *2 pl.* dominó [juego].
**Domitian** (domi·shan) *n. pr.* Domiciano.
**Don** (dan) *n. pr. m.* dim. de DONALD.
**don** *s.* don [tratamiento español]. *2* caballero, personaje. *3* profesor de Oxford o Cambridge.

**don (to)** *tr.* vestirse, ponerse. *2* investirse de. ¶ Pret. y p. p.: *donned; ger.: -nning.*
**donate (to)** (dou·neit) *tr.* donar.
**donation** (-ei·shøn) *s.* donación. *2* donativo; dádiva, don.
**donative** (da·nativ) *s.* donativo.
**donator** (dounei·tø*ʳ*) *s.* donador.
**done** (døn)*p. p.* de TO DO: hecho, acabado, fatigado, cocido, arruinado, perdido, muerto, etc.
**donee** (dounı·) *s.* donatario.
**donjon** (dø·ndÿøn) *s.* torre del homenaje.
**donkey** (da·ngki) *s.* asno, burro, borrico, jumento. *2 adj.* MEC. auxiliar.
**donor** (dou·nø*ʳ*) *s.* donador, donante.
**do-nothing** *adj.-s.* inactivo, perezoso.
**don't** (dount) *contr.* de DO NOT.
**doodle (to)** (du·døl) *tr.-intr.* garrapatear.
**doom** (dum) *s.* sentencia, condena. *2* destino, suerte. *3* ruina, perdición. *4* juicio final.
**doom (to)** *tr.* condenar, sentenciar. *2* destinar, predestinar [a la ruina, destrucción, etc.].
**doomsday** (-sdei) *s.* día del juicio final.
**door** (do·ø*ʳ*) *s.* puerta: ~ *bolt,* pasador; ~ *catch,* golpete; ~ *mat,* felpudo; *in* ~, *within doors,* en casa, dentro de la casa; *out of doors, without doors,* fuera de casa, en la calle, al aire libre. *2* portal [de ciudad]. *3* MAR. porta.
**doorcase** (-keis) *s.* marco de la puerta.
**doorhead** (-jed) *s.* dintel.
**doorkeeper** (-kıpø*ʳ*) *s.* portero, conserje.
**doorknob** (-nab) *s.* botón o tirador de puerta.
**doorplate** (-pleit) *s.* placa de puerta.
**doorpost** (-post) *s.* jamba [de puerta]; quicial.
**doorsill** (-sil) *s.* umbral.
**doorstep** (-step) *s.* escalón delante de la puerta; umbral.
**doorway** (-wei) *s.* puerta, entrada, portal.
**dope** (doup) *s.* fam. droga, narcótico, estupefaciente: ~ *fiend,* morfinómano. *2* pop. información confidencial. *3* barniz [para ciertas telas].
**dope (to)** *tr.* drogar, narcotizar.
**dor** (do*ʳ*) *s.* ENT. escarabajo.
**Dorian** (do·rian), **Doric** (-rik) *adj.-s.* dorio; dérico.
**dormancy** (do·*ʳ*mansi) *s.* letargo, inactividad, estado latente.
**dormant** (-mant) *adj.* durmiente, dormido. *2* inactivo, latente, secreto.
**dormer** (-mø*ʳ*) o **dormer window** *s.* buharda.
**dormitive** (-mitiv) *s.* dormitivo, soporífero.
**dormitory** (-tori) *s.* dormitorio [de colegio, etc.].
**dormouse** (-maus) *s.* ZOOL. lirón.
**Dorothy** (do·rozi) *n. pr. f.* Dorotea.
**dorsal** (do·*ʳ*sal) *adj.* dorsal.
**dory** (do·ri) *s.* ICT. gallo, ceo. *2* bote de fondo plano.
**dosage** (dou·sidÿ) *s.* MED. dosificación.
**dose** (dous) *s.* dosis, toma. *2* fig. píldora, mal trago.
**dose (to)** *tr.* medicinar, dar una toma a. *2* dosificar.
**dosimetry** (dosi·metri) *s.* dosimetría.
**dossal** (da·sal) *s.* bancal [tapete]. *2* colgadura [detrás de un altar, etc.].
**dossier** (da·sie*ʳ*) *s.* expediente, papeles; historial.
**dossil** (-sil) *s.* CIR. lechino.
**dost** (døst) *2.ª pers. pres. ind.* de TO DO.
**dot** (dat) *s.* punto, señal, pinta. *2* MÚS. puntillo. *3* *on the* ~, en punto, a la hora exacta.
**dot (to)** *tr.* puntear [marcar con puntos]; poner punto [a la i]. *2* salpicar, esparcir. ¶ Pret. y p. p.: *dotted; ger.: -tting.*
**dotage** (dou·tidÿ) *s.* chochera, chochez.
**dotal** (-tal) *adj.* dotal.
**dotard** (-ta*ʳ*d) *s.* viejo chocho, imbécil.

**dote (to)** (dout) *intr.* chochear, estar chocho: *to* ~ *upon,* estar chocho o loco por.
**doting** (dou·ting) *adj.* chocho.
**dotted line** (da·tid) *s.* línea de puntos.
**dotterel** (-tørøl) *s.* ORN. especie de chorlito.
**dotty** (-ti) *adj.* manchado, punteado.
**double** (dø·bøl) *adj.* doble, duplo, dúplice: ~ *chin,* papada; ~ *entry,* COM. partida doble; ~ *the amount,* el doble. *2* doble, insincero, ambiguo. *3* BOT. doble [flor]. *4 s.* doble, duplo. *5* duplicado, copia. *6* doble [de una pers.]. *7* sombra [aparición]. *8* doblez, pliegue. *9* artificio, engaño. *10 pl.* dobles [en el tenis]. *11 adv.* doblemente, dos veces, de dos en dos.
**double (to)** *tr.* doblar [duplicar; valer el doble de]. *2* redoblar, repetir. *3* doblar, plegar. *4* MAR. doblar [un cabo, etc.]. *5* escapar a [volviendo atrás]. *6* CINE., TEAT. sustituir, doblar. *7* forrar. *8 intr.* doblarse. *9* encorvarse, plegarse. *10* escapar volviendo atrás. *11* obrar con doblez.
**double-acting** *adj.* MEC. de doble efecto.
**double-barrel(l)ed** *adj.* de dos cañones.
**double-breasted** *adj.* cruzado [chaqueta, etc.].
**double-cross** *s.* traición [hecha a un cómplice].
**double-cross (to)** *tr.* traicionar [a un cómplice].
**double-dealing** *s.* doblez, falsía.
**double-edged** *adj.* de dos filos.
**double-faced** *adj.* de dos caras. *2* doble, hipócrita.
**double-hearted** *adj.* falso, traicionero.
**double-minded** *adj.* indeciso. *2* inconsecuente. *3* doble, de dos caras.
**doubleness** (-nis) *s.* duplicidad.
**double-quick** *adj.* redoblado [paso].
**doublet** (dø·blit) *s.* par, pareja. *2* jubón. *3* JOY., FILOL. doblete.
**doubloon** (døblu·n) *s.* doblón [moneda].
**doubt** (daut) *s.* duda: *no* ~, *without* ~, sin duda, indudablemente. *2* incertidumbre. *3* objeción, reparo.
**doubt (to)** *tr.* dudar, dudar de. *2* temer, sospechar. *3 intr.* dudar, vacilar.
**doubtful** (-ful) *adj.* dudoso. *2* dubitativo. *3* indeciso. *4* incierto, problemático. *5* ambiguo.
**doubting** (-ing) *adj.* dudoso, que duda.
**doubtless** (-lis) *adj.* indudable. *2 adv.* indudablemente.
**douche** (dush) *s.* ducha. *2* MED. irrigación. *3* MED. irrigador.
**douche (to)** *tr.* duchar. *2 intr.* ducharse.
**dough** (dou) *s.* masa [del pan]. *2* pasta [masa blanda]. *3* pop. pasta [dinero].
**doughnut** (dou·nøt) *s.* buñuelo, fruta de sartén.
**doughty** (dau·ti) *adj.* fuerte, valiente.
**doughy** (dou·i) *adj.* pastoso, blando, crudo.
**Douro** (dou·ru) *n. pr.* GEOGR. Duero.
**douse (to)** (daus) *tr.* rociar, remojar. *2* chapuzar, zambullir. *3* fam. apagar. *4* MAR. recoger, arriar. *5* TO DOFF. *6* intr. zambullirse.
**dove** (døv) *s.* palomo, paloma: *the Dove,* el Espíritu Santo. *2 p. p.* de TO DIVE.
**dovecot** (-kat) *s.* palomar.
**dovetail** (-teil) *s.* CARP. cola de milano o de pato.
**dovetail (to)** *tr.* ensamblar a cola de milano. *2* unir, enlazar.
**Dover** (dou·vø*ʳ*) *n. pr.* GEOGR. Dóver o Dovres.
**dowager** (dau·adÿø*ʳ*) *s.* viuda [con título que procede del marido]: *queen* ~, reina viuda. *2* fam. matrona respetable.
**dowdy** (dau·di) *adj.* desaliñado, mal vestido.
**dowel** (dau·øl) *s.* CARP. clavija, tarugo, espiga.
**dower** (dau·ø*ʳ*) *s.* DER. bienes asignados a la viuda.

*2 DER.* dote [de la mujer]. *3* don, dote, prenda [de una pers.].

**dower (to)** *tr.* DER. asignar bienes a la viuda. *2* dotar.

**dowery** (dau·ri) *s.* DOWRY.

**down** (daun) *adv.-prep.* abajo, hacia abajo, a lo largo de, por: ~ *the river,* río abajo; ~ *the street,* calle abajo, por la calle. *2* pasando de un tiempo, lugar, etc. a otro posterior: ~ *from,* desde; ~ *to,* hasta; ~ *to date,* hasta la fecha. *3* en o por tierra: ~ *on one's knees,* de rodillas. *4* en sujección. *5* completamente. *6 interj.* ¡abajo!: ~ *with him!,* ¡abajo!, ¡muera! *7 adj.* pendiente, que baja, descendente: ~ *train,* tren descendente. *8* de abajo. *9* bajo, caído, decaído, abatido, enfermo: ~ *in the mouth,* cariacontecido. *10 to be* ~ *on,* tratar con severidad. *11 adj.* y *adv.* al contado. *12 s.* pulmón, flojel: ~ *bed,* edredón. *13* bozo, vello. *14* pelo suave, pelusa. *15* duna. *16* loma. *17* revés de fortuna, caída. *18 pl.* tierra alta ondulada propia para pastos.

**down (to)** *tr.* derribar. *2* vencer, derrotar. *3* tragar. *4* bajar. *5 to* ~ *tools,* declararse en huelga.

**downcast** (dau·nkæst) *adj.* inclinado hacia abajo. *2* bajo [ojos, mirada]. *3* abatido, alicaído.

**downfall** (-fol) *s.* caída [esp. de agua o nieve], chaparrón, nevada. *2* caída, ruina.

**downfallen** (-øn) *adj.* caído, arruinado.

**downhaul** (dau·njol) *s.* MAR. cargadera.

**downhearted** (-je·ʳtid) *adj.* abatido, desanimado.

**downhill** (-jil) *adj.* pendiente, en declive. *2 adv.* hacia abajo, cuesta abajo; de capa caida. *3 s.* declive, bajada.

**downpour** (-poʳ) *s.* aguacero; lluvia fuerte y seguida.

**downright** (-rait) *adj.* claro, categórico. *2* franco, brusco. *3* absoluto, completo. *4* vertical. *5 adv.* francamente. *6* absolutamente, completamente.

**downstairs** (-te·rš) *adj.* de abajo, del piso inferior. *2 adv.* abajo; en el piso inferior, en la planta baja, en los sótanos o hacia ellos.

**downstream** (-strı·m) *s.* aguas abajo.

**downstroke** (-trouk) *s.* MEC. carrera descendente.

**downtown** (-tau·n) *adv.-adj.* hacia el centro o en el centro de la ciudad.

**downward** (-uaʳd) *adj.* descendente; que se dirige o extiende hacia abajo. *2 adv.* DOWNWARDS.

**downwards** (-š) *adv.* hacia abajo. *2* hacia una época posterior.

**downy** (-i) *adj.* velloso, cotudo, felpudo, plumoso. *2* blando, suave, dulce.

**dowry** (dau·ri) *s.* dote.

**doze** (douš) *s.* sueño ligero, adormecimiento, sopor.

**doze (to)** *intr.* dormitar, estar medio dormido.

**dozen** (dø·šn) *s.* docena.

**dozy** (dou·ši) *adj.* soñoliento, amodorrado.

**drab** (dræb) *adj.* pardusco, pardo amarillento. *2* soso, monótono. *3 s.* monotonía. *4* ramera. *5* pazpuerca.

**drabble (to)** (dræ·bøl) *tr.* arrastrar, enlodar.

**drachma** (-kma) *s.* dracma.

**Draconian** (dreikou·nian) *adj.* draconiano.

**draff** (dræf) *s.* heces, desperdicios.

**draffish** (-ish), **draffy**(-i) *adj.* inútil, despreciable.

**draft, draught** (dræft) *s.* acción de sacar; cosa sacada. *2* corriente [de aire]. *3* tiro [de chimenea]. *4* succión, aspiración; inhalación; trago. *5* bebida, pócima. *6* atracción; tracción, tiro: *draft horse,* caballo de tiro. *7* estiramiento, estiraje. *8* redada. *9* traza, trazado. *10* diseño, boceto, dibujo. *11* plan, plano, proyecto. *12* borrador, minuta. *13* giro, libramiento, letra de cambio, orden de pago. *14* MIL. leva, reclutamiento. *15* MIL. destacamento. *16* MAR. calado. *17 pl.* (Ingl.) DRAUGHTS, juego de damas.

¶ En las acepciones 2, 3, 10, 12, 13, 14 y 15, úsase de preferencia *draft;* en las acepciones 4, 5 y 8, úsase de preferencia *draught.*

**draft, draught (to)** *tr.* aspirar [un líquido, etc.]. *2* hacer el borrador de, redactar. *3* trazar, diseñar, bosquejar. *4* destacar [para un servicio]. *5* MIL. reclutar.

**draftsman** (dræ·ftsmæn) *s.* dibujante, delineante.

**drafty** (-fti) *adj.* que tiene o produce corrientes de aire.

**drag** (dræg) *s.* rastra, grada. *2* carro bajo, narria. *3* gancho, etc. para arrastrar. *4* instrumento para rastrear. *6* entorpecimiento; traba, rémora. *7* AVIA. resistencia al avance. *8* ~ *boat,* draga.

**drag (to)** *tr.* arrastrar. *2* rastrear, dragar. *3* AGR. gradar. *4 intr.* arrastrar [ir rozando el suelo]. *5* MAR. garrear. *6* avanzar, lentamente. *7* rezagarse. *8* decaer [la acción o el interés]. *9 to* ~ *on* o *out,* alargarse, durar demasiado. ¶ Pret. y p. p.: *dragged;* ger.: *-gging.*

**draggle (to)** (dræ·gøl) *tr.-intr.* ensuciar o ensuciarse arrastrando. *2 intr.* rezagarse.

**dranet** (-net) *s.* red barredera, jábega.

**dragoman** (dræ·goman) *s.* dragomán, drogmán.

**dragon** (-gøn) *s.* dragón. *2* persona severa o de mal genio. *3* BOT. dragontea. *4* BOT. ~ *tree,* drago.

**dragonfly** (-flai) *s.* ENT. libélula.

**dragonish** (-ish) *adj.* dragontino.

**dragoon** (dragu·n) *s.* MIL. dragón.

**dragoon (to)** *tr.* intimidar, acosar, perseguir.

**drain** (drei·n) *s.* acción de sacar poco a poco; agotamiento. *2* desagüe. *3* cacera, zanja de derivación. *4* albañal, atarjea, sumidero. *5* CIR. tubo de drenaje. *6 pl.* restos [de un líquido], heces.

**drain (to)** *tr.* sacar poco a poco, agotar, apurar; escurrir. *2* vaciar, empobrecer, sangrar. *3* secar, enjugar. *4* desaguar, desecar, avenar [un terreno]. *5* MIN. achicar. *6* MEC. purgar. *7* filtrar. *8 intr.* vaciarse, escurrirse. *9* GEOGR. desaguar.

**drainage** (-idɏ) *s.* acción de sacar, agotamiento. *2* desagüe. *3* avenamiento. *4* drenaje. *5* ~ *basin,* cuenca [de un río].

**drainer** (-øʳ) *s.* palero. *2* colador, filtro. *3* secadero, escurridero.

**drake** (dreik) *s.* dragón [monstruo]. *2* ORN. pato [macho].

**dram** (dræm) *s.* dracma [peso]. *2* trago. *3* poquito, miaja.

**drama** (dra·ma) *s.* drama.

**dramatic (al** (dramæ·tik(al) *adj.* dramático.

**dramatics** (-s) *s. sing.* TEAT. representación de aficionados.

**dramatism** (dræ·matišm) *s.* dramatismo.

**dramatist** (-tist) *s.* dramaturgo.

**dramatize** (-taiš) *tr.* dramatizar.

**dramaturge, -gist** (dræ·matøʳdɏ, -ɏist) *s.* dramaturgo.

**dramaturgy** (-dɏi) *s.* dramática.

**drape (to)** (dreip) *tr.* cubrir con ropajes. *2* colgar, entapizar, adornar. *3* disponer los pliegues de.

**draper** (-øʳ) *s.* pañero.

**drapery** (-i) *s.* pañería, paños. *2* ropaje, colgaduras, tapicería.
**drastic** (dræ·stik) *adj.* drástico. *2* enérgico, riguroso.
**draught** (dræft) *s.* DRAFT.
**draught (to)** *tr.* TO DRAFT.
**draughtboard** (-boʳd) *s.* tablero de damas.
**draughtsman** (-smæn) *s.* peón [del juego de damas]. *2* DRAFTSMAN.
**draw** (dro·) *s.* arrastre, tracción, tiro. *2* atracción. *3* lo que se dice para hacer hablar a uno. *4* BILL. retroceso. *5* NAIPES robo. *6* tablas, empate. *7* sorteo; premio [en la lotería]. *8* TEJ. carrera, pasada.
**draw (to)** *tr.* arrastrar, tirar de. *2* atraer. *3* apartar, distraer. *4* persuadir, inducir, impulsar. *5* hacer hablar, sonsacar. *6* subir [un puente levadizo]. *7* sacar, retirar, extraer, arrancar, obtener. *8* sacar, desenvainar [la pistola, la espada]. *9* correr, descorrer [cortinas, etc.]. *10* hacer salir. *11* batir [un bosque, etc.]. *12* dragar, rastrear. *13* chupar. *14* aspirar, respirar, inhalar. *15* cobrar [un sueldo]; devengar [interés]. *16* retirar [fondos]. *17* COM. librar, girar. *18* echar [suertes]; sortear. *19* estirar. *20* tirar [metales]. *21* tender [un arco]. *22* dibujar, bosquejar, delinear, trazar. *23* redactar, extender. *24* sacar, deducir, inferir. *25* hacer [comparaciones, distinciones]. *26* BILL. picar bajo. *27* MAR. calar. *28* to ~ along, arrastrar. *29* to ~ aside, correr, descorrer [una cortina, etc.]. *30* to ~, breath, respirar, tomar aliento. *31* to ~ forth, hacer salir, sacar. *32* to ~ lots, echar suertes. *33* to ~ out, sacar; extender; sonsacar, hacer hablar. *34* to ~ the long bow, exagerar. *35* to ~ oneself up, erguirse, ponerse tieso. *36* intr. tirar [arrastrando]. *37* atraer público. *38* tirar [una chimenea, etc.]. *39* encogerse, contraerse. *40* estirarse, alargarse. *41* dibujar. *42* echar suertes. *43* MAR. tener calado. *44* NAIPES ir al robo. *45* NAIPES arrastrar. *46* empatar. *47* moverse: to ~ along, arrastrarse; to ~ aside, hacerse a un lado; to ~ away, alejarse; to ~ back, retroceder; to ~ near, acercarse. *48* COM. girar [contra]. *49* sacar la pistola, desenvainar la espada. *50* to ~ to a head, madurar, empezar a supurar.
¶ Pret.: *drew;* p. p.: *drawn.*
**drawback** (-bæk) *s.* inconveniente, desventaja. *2* descuento. *3* reembolso de derechos de aduana.
**drawbridge** (-bridy̆) *s.* puente levadizo o giratorio.
**drawee** (-ɪ·) *s.* COM. librado, girado.
**drawer** (-øʳ) *s.* cajón [de mueble]; gaveta. *2* COM. librador, girador. *3* dibujante. *4* extractor. *5* pl. calzoncillos, pantalones.
**drawing** (-ing) *s.* dibujo: ~ board, tablero de dibujo. *2* trazado, delineación. *3* tracción, arrastre. *4* tirado [de metales]. *5* TEJ. estiramiento, estiraje. *6* extracción, saca. *7* sorteo. *8* ~ room, sala de recibo, salón, estrado.
**drawl** (drol) *s.* enunciación lenta y penosa.
**drawl (to)** *tr.* pronunciar con lentitud. *2* intr. arrastrar las palabras.
**drawn** (dron) *p. p.* de TO DRAW. *2* adj. arrastrado, estirado, dibujado, trazado, etc. *3* de aspecto fatigado, ojeroso [facciones, rostro].
**dray** (drei), **dray-cart** *s.* carretón, carro fuerte, camión.
**drayage** (drei·idy̆) *s.* carretaje, acarreo.
**drayman** (-mæn) *s.* carretero, camionero.
**dread** (dred) *s.* miedo, temor. *2* terror, espanto,

pavor. *3* adj. temible, terrible, espantoso. *2* augusto, venerable.
**dread (to)** *tr.-intr.* temer [a], tener miedo [de].
**dreadful** (-ful) *adj.* terrible, espantoso, horrendo. *2* horrible, desagradable, repugnante.
**dreadless** (-lis) *adj.* intrépido.
**dreadnought, o -naught** (not) *s.* MAR. tipo de acorazado grande.
**dream** (drɪm) *s.* sueño, ensueño. *2* visión, quimera.
**dream (to)** *tr.-intr.* soñar: to ~ of, soñar con o en. *2* tr. imaginar, fantasear. ¶ Pret. y p. p.: *dreamed* o *dreamt.*
**dreamer** (-øʳ) *s.* soñador. *2* visionario, iluso.
**dreamily** (-ili), **dreamingly** (-ingli) *adv.* como en sueños; vagamente.
**dreamt** (dremt) *pret.* y *p. p.* de TO DREAM.
**dreamy** (drɪ·mi) *adj.* soñador. *2* irreal, fantástico. *3* vago, borroso.
**drear** (dri·øʳ) *adj.* poét. DREARY.
**dreary** (-i) *adj.* triste, lúgubre, sombrío. *2* monótono, aburrido.
**dredge** (dredy̆) *s.* draga. *2* MAR. aparato para rastrear.
**dredge (to)** *tr.-intr.* dragar, excavar, limpiar. *2* MAR. rastrear. *3* COC. espolvorear.
**dredger** (-øʳ) *s.* dragador. *2* draga. *3* COC. vaso para espolvorear.
**dredging-machine** *s.* draga.
**dreggy** (dre·gi) *adj.* turbio, zurraposo.
**dregs** (dregy̆) *s. pl.* hez, heces, poso, sedimento. *2* madre [del vino]. *3* hez [lo más vil].
**drench** (drench) *s.* mojadura, remojón. *2* inundación, diluvio. *3* trago, poción.
**drench (to)** *tr.* mojar, remojar, empapar, calar. *2* llenar, saturar. *3* VET. purgar.
**dress** (dres) *s.* vestido, vestuario, indumentaria. *2* traje; hábito; vestido de mujer. *3* atavío, tocado, compostura. *4* aderezo [para una tela, etc.]. *5* adj. de vestir, de etiqueta, de gala: ~ ball, baile de etiqueta; ~ circle, TEAT. galería principal; el gran mundo; ~ coat, frac, casaca; ~ suit, traje de etiqueta.
**dress (to)** *tr.* vestir. *2* vestir de etiqueta o de ceremonia. *3* ataviar, engalanar. *4* peinar, arreglar [el cabello]. *5* almohazar. *6* curar [las heridas]. *7* poner [la mesa]. *8* preparar, disponer, arreglar, aderezar, guisar, aliñar, aprestar, almidonar, engomar. *9* zurrar [pieles]; desbastar [madera]; labrar [piedra]. *10* enlucir, revocar. *11* podar [una planta]. *12* despabilar [una luz]. *13* to ~ down o off, reprender, calentar las orejas. *14* intr. vestirse, ataviarse: to ~ up, vestirse de ceremonia o con lujo. *15* MIL. alinearse.
¶ Pret. y p. p.: *dressed* o *drest.*
**dresser** (dre·søʳ) *s.* el que viste, adereza, prepara, etc. *2* cómoda con espejo. *3* mesa o aparador de cocina.
**dressing** (-ing) *s.* acción de vestir o vestirse. *2* preparación, arreglo, adorno, aderezo. *3* CIR. cura; apósito, vendaje. *4* COC. aderezo, condimento, salsa. *5* TEN. adobo. *6* TEJ. aderezo. *7* AGR. abono. *8* AGR. poda. *9* desbaste, labra. *10* dressing o ~ down, rapapelo, castigo. *11* adj. de vestir, para vestir, etc.: ~ case, neceser; ~ gown, bata, peinador; ~ table, tocador [mueble].
**dressmaker** (-mei·køʳ) *s.* costurera, modista.
**dressmaking** (-king) *s.* modistería.
**dressy** (-i) *adj.* elegante, vistoso, que viste demasiado. *2* demasiado peripuesto.
**drew** (dru) *pret.* de TO DRAW.

**dribble** (dri·bøl) *s.* goteo, chorrillo. *2* llovizna. *3* FÚTBOL. dribling, regate.
**dribble (to)** *intr.* gotear. *2* babear. *3 tr.* dejar caer en gotas. *4* FÚTBOL. driblar, regatear.
**dribblet** (-blit) *s.* gota. *2* pizca.
**dried** (draid) *pret.* y *p. p.* de TO DRY. *2 adj.* seco, desecado: ~ *beef*, cecina, tasajo. *3* pasa [fruta].
**drier** (drai·ø^r) *s.* secador, enjugador.
**drier, driest** *adj.* comp. y superl. de DRY.
**drift** (drift) *s.* lo arrastrado, impulsado o amontonado por una corriente, el mar, el viento, etc. *2* corriente [de agua, de aire]; movimiento, fluctuación [de lo impulsado o arrastrado]; masa que va en una dirección. *3* tendencia, rumbo, dirección, giro. *4* impulso, fuerza, móvil. *5* intención, sentido. *6* MAR., AVIA. deriva. *7* ARQ. empuje. *8* MEC. escariador. *9* MIN. galería.
**drift (to)** *tr.* impeler, llevar, amontonar [como hacen una corriente, el viento, etc.]. *2* MIN. abrir [una galería]. *3* MEC. escariar. *4 intr.* flotar, ir a la deriva; ir a la ventura, sin rumbo. *5* MAR., AVIA. derivar, devalar. *6* correr, amontonarse [al impulso del viento, etcétera].
**driftage** (-idy̆) *s.* MAR. deriva. *2* lo llevado por una corriente, el viento, etc.
**driftwood** (-wud) *s.* madera llevada por el agua.
**drill** (dril) *s.* taladro, broca, perforador. *2* MIN. sonda. *3* AGR. sembradora mecánica. *4* hilera de semillas sembradas. *5* ZOOL. mandril. *6* dril [tela]. *7* adiestramiento. *8* MIL. instrucción, ejercicio.
**drill (to)** *tr.* taladrar, barrenar, perforar. *2* abrir, hacer [un agujero]. *3* MIL. instruir, enseñar el ejercicio. *4 tr.-intr.* AGR. sembrar en surcos o hileras. *5 intr.* MIL. hacer el ejercicio. *6* ejercitarse, adiestrarse.
**drillings** (dri·lings) *s. pl.* material extraído por un taladro.
**drink** (drink) *s.* bebida, poción; bebida alcohólica: *in* ~, borracho. *2* trago: *to take a* ~, echar un trago. *3* bebida [vicio].
**drink (to)** *tr.* beber; beberse: *to* ~ *someone's health*, brindar por uno. *2* aspirar, inhalar. *3* absorber, chupar. *4 to* ~ *in*, absorber, embeber, beber [conocimientos], absorber con placer. *5 intr.* beber, emborracharse. ¶ Pret.: *drank;* p. p.: *drunk.*
**drinkable** (-abøl) *adj.* bebible, potable. *2 s. pl.* bebidas.
**drinker** (-ø^r) *s.* bebedor.
**drinking** (-ing) *s.* acción de beber. *2* bebida [vicio]. *3 adj.* bebedor; de beber, para beber: ~ *place*, ~ *trough*, abrevadero.
**drip** (drip) *s.* goteo, chorreadura; reguero. *2* gotera [del techo]. *3* ARQ. alero, cornisa.
**drip (to)** *tr.* verter o dejar caer a gotas. *2 intr.* gotear, chorrear, destilar, caer gota a gota. ¶ Pret. y p. p.: *dripped;* ger.: *-pping.*
**dripping** (-in) *s.* goteo, chorreo. *2 pl.* líquido o grasa que gotea o chorrea: *dripping pan*, grasera.
**drive** (draiv) *s.* paseo en coche. *2* paseo o avenida para coches. *3* urgencia, presión, exigencia. *4* impulso, empuje. *5* campaña vigorosa, esfuerzo. *6* movimiento rápido, ataque, embestida. *7* tendencia, rumbo. *8* manada de reses. *9* MEC. mando, transmisión. *10* conducción [de un vehículo]: *left* ~, conducción a la izquierda. *11* COM. saldo, liquidación [venta].
**drive (to)** *tr.* impeler, impulsar, mover, llevar. *2* inducir, forzar [a]. *3* guiar, conducir [un vehículo, el ganado]. *4* llevar [en vehículo]. *5* hacer,

realizar. *6* hacer trabajar mucho. *7* meter, clavar, hundir. *8* MEC. mover, accionar. *9* MIN. abrir, prolongar [una galería]. *10* DEP. golpear [la pelota]. *11 to* ~ *away*, ahuyentar, espantar; alejar. *12 to* ~ *in* o *into*, clavar, hacer entrar. *13 to* ~ *mad*, volver loco. *14 to* ~ *out*, echar fuera.
*15 intr.* conducir un vehículo [a]; saber conducir. *16* ir en coche, auto, etc. *17* correr, ser impelido. *18 to* ~ *at*, batir, golpear, aspirar a, proponerse; insinuar, querer decir. *19 to* ~ *away*, trabajar con ahínco. *20 to let* ~, asestar un golpe.
Pret.: *drove;* p. p. *driven.*
**drivel** (dri·vøl) *s.* baba. *2* tonterías, vaciedades.
**drivel (to)** *intr.* babear, babosear. *2* chochear, decir tonterías. ¶ Pret.: y p. p.: *diveled* o ~ lled; ger.: ~ *ling* o ~ *lling.*
**drivel(l)er** (-ø^r) *s.* baboso. *2* simple, tonto, chocho.
**driven** (dri·vøn) *p. p.* de TO DRIVE.
**driver** (drai·vø^r) *s.* conductor [de animales o vehículos], carretero, cochero; chófer, mecánico; maquinista [de tren]. *2* MEC. rueda motriz, pieza impulsora. *3* mazo. *4* persona despótica, cabo de vara.
**driving** (-ing) *s.* acción de impulsar, mover, conducir, etc. *2* impulso. *3* tendencia. *4 adj.* de conducción o conducir. *5* impetuoso, violento. *6* motor, motriz, impulsor. *7* MEC. de mando, de transmisión.
**drizzle** (dri·søl) *s.* llovizna, cernidillo.
**drizzle (to)** *tr.* rociar, salpicar. *2 intr.* lloviznar.
**drizzly** (-šli) *adj.* lloviznoso.
**droll** (droul) *adj.* cómico, chusco, gracioso, raro, estrambótico. *2 s.* bufón, chusco.
**droll (to)** *intr.* bromear, hacer el bufón.
**drollery** (dou·løri) *s.* comicidad, humor. *2* broma, farsa, bufonada; chascarrillo.
**dromedary** (dra·møderi) *s.* ZOOL. dromedario.
**drone** (droun) *s.* ENT. y fig. zángano. *2* zumbido *3* roncón de gaita. *4* ENT. ~ *fly*, moscardón.
**drone (to)** *intr.* holgazanear, zanganear. *2* zumbar.
**droop** (drup) *s.* inclinación, caída, caimiento.
**droop (to)** *tr.* inclinar, bajar. *2 intr.* inclinarse, caer, colgar, pender. *3* declinar, decaer, consumirse, marchitarse, abatirse.
**drooping** (-ing) *adj.* bajo, caído: ~ *lashes*, ojos bajos; medio cerrados. *2* BOT. colgante.
**drop** (drap) *s.* gota [de líquido]. *2* lágrima [adorno]. *3* JOY. pendiente, zarcillo. *4* pastilla, confite. *5* traguito. *6* caída, caimiento. *7* lanzamiento [desde lo alto]. *8* baja, descenso. *9* declive. *10* MAR. caída [de vela]. *11* trampa, escotillón. *12* MEC. pieza que cae. *13* MEC. ~ *hammer*, martinete. *14* MED. ~ *serene*, gota serena.
**drop (to)** *tr.* dejar caer, soltar, verter: *to* ~ *anchor*, echar anclas; *to* ~ *a hint*, soltar una indirecta. *2* parir [un animal]. *3* dejar, abandonar, desprenderse de, suspender, desistir de. *4* omitir, comerse [una letra o palabra]. *5* tumbar, derribar. *6* bajar [una cortina, los ojos, etc.]. *8 to* ~ *a line*, poner unas líneas.
*9 intr.* gotear, chorrear. *10* caer, bajar, descender. *11* caer desmayado o muerto. *12* acabarse, cesar, parar. *13* quedarse atrás. *14 to* ~ *in*, dejarse caer, entrar al pasar. *15 to* ~ *off*, decaer; quedar dormido, morir. *16 to* ~ *out*, retirarse, desaparecer.
¶ Pret. y p. p.: *dropped* o *dropt;* ger.: *dropping.*
**droplet** (-lit) *s.* gotita.
**dropper** (-ø^r) *s.* cuentagotas.
**dropping** (-ing) *s.* caída, goteo, etc. *2 pl.* excremen-

tos de animales. *4* adj. ~ *bottle,* frasco cuentagotas.

**dropsical** (dra·psikal), **dropsied** (-sid) *adj.* MED. hidrópico.

**dropsy** (-si) *s.* MED. hidropesía.

**dropwort** (-uøᵗt) *s.* BOT. filipéndula.

**dross** (drɔs) *s.* escoria [de los metales]. *2* espuma, horrura, borra, desecho, hez.

**drossy** (-i) *adj.* que tiene escoria; feculento, impuro. *2* sin valor.

**drought** (draut) *s.* sequedad, aridez [del suelo]. *2* sequía. *3* fam. sed.

**droughty** (drau·ti) *adj.* árido, seco. *2* fam. sediento.

**drove** (drouv) *s. pret.* de TO DRIVE. *2 s.* manada, hato, rebaño, recua. *3* multitud, gentío.

**drover** (-øᵗ) *s.* ganadero.

**drown** (to) (draun) *tr.* ahogar, anegar. *2* inundar, sumergir. *3* ahogar, apagar [el sonido, etc.]. *4 intr.* ahogarse, anegarse.

**drowse** (draus) *s.* DROWSINESS.

**drowse** (to) *tr.* adormecer, amodorrar. *2 intr.* adormilarse, adormecerse, amodorrarse.

**drowsiness** (-inis) *s.* adormecimiento, somnolencia, modorra, sopor.

**drowsy** (-i) *adj.* soñoliento, adormecido, amodorrado. *2* soporífero.

**drub** (drøb) *s.* golpe, palo, puñada.

**drub** (to) *tr.* abrumar de trabajo. *2 intr.* afanarse, fatigarse, azacanearse.

**drudgery** (-øri) *s.* reventadero, trabajo penoso.

**drug** (drøg) *s.* droga, medicamento. *2* estupefaciente. *3* COM. macana, artículo invendible.

**drug** (to) *tr.* medicinar con exceso. *2* narcotizar. *3* mezclar con drogas. *4 intr.* tomar estupefacientes. ¶ Pret. y p. p.: *drugged;* ger.: *-gging.*

**druggist** (-gist) *s.* droguero. *2* boticario.

**drugstore** (-tøᵗ) *s.* (E.U.) farmacia, botica, droguería.

**druid** (dru·id) *s.* druida.

**Druidism** (drui·dišm) *s.* druidismo.

**drum** (drom) *s.* MÚS. tambor, caja. *2* sonido del tambor. *3* MEC. tambor, cilindro; cuerpo [de caldera, etc.]. *4* COM. bidón, cuñete, barril. *5* ~ *major,* tambor mayor.

**drum** (to) *intr.* tocar el tambor. *2* tabalear, tamborilear, teclear. *3 tr.* tocar [en el tambor]. *4* meter en la cabeza [una lección, etc.].

**drumbeat** (-bɪt) *s.* toque de tambor.

**drumfire** (-fai·øᵗ) *s.* MIL. fuego graneado.

**drumhead** (-jed) *s.* parche [del tambor]. *2* ANAT. membrana del tímpano.

**drummer** (-møᵗ) *s.* tambor, bombo [músico]. *2* (E.U.) COM. viajante.

**drumstick** (-stik) *s.* baquetá, palillo [de tambor].

**drunk** (drønk) *p. p.* de TO DRINK. *2 adj.* bebido, ebrio, borracho. *3 s.* borracho. *4* borrachera.

**drunkard** (-aᵗd) *s.* borrachín.

**drunken** (-øn) *adj.* ebrio, borracho, beodo. *2* ~ *fit,* borrachera.

**drunkenness** (-is) *s.* embriaguez, borrachera.

**drupe** (drup) *s.* BOT. drupa.

**dry** (drai) *adj.* seco: ~ *beef,* cecina, *charqui; ~ pile,* ELECT. pila seca; ~ *cleaning,* lavado en seco; ~ *goods,* COM. tejidos, lencería, mercería, etc.; ~ *law,* ley seca; ~ *nurse,* ama seca, niñera; ~ *wall,* pared de piedra seca. *2* enjuto. *3* árido. *4* sequeroso. *5* pasa [fruta]. *6* para áridos [medida]. *7* insulso, insubstancial. *8* frío, pobre. *9* satírico, mordaz. *10* B. ART. duro, sin matices.

**dry** (to) *tr.* secar, desecar, enjugar. *2* pasar [fruta].

*3* acecinar. *4* dar sed. *5 intr.* secarse, desecarse, enjugarse. | Gralte. con *up.* ¶ Pret. y p. p.: *dried.*

**dryad** (drai·æd) *s.* dríada.

**dryer** (-øᵗ) *s.* DRIER.

**dryness** (-nis) *s.* sequedad. *2* aridez.

**dry-salt** (to) *tr.* salar y secar [carnes, pescado].

**drysalter** (-søltøᵗ) *s.* vendedor de drogas, salazones, etc.

**dry-shod** *adj.* a pie enjuto.

**dual** (diu·al) *adj.* dual, doble.

**dualism** (-išm) *s.* dualismo.

**duality** (diuæ·liti) *s.* dualidad.

**dub** (to) (døb) *tr.* armar [caballero]. *2* titular, apellidar, apodar. *3* alisar, aparar. *4* engrasar [las pieles]. *5* CINEM. doblar. *6 intr.* sonar como un tambor. ¶ Pret. y p. p.: *dubbed;* ger.: *dubbing.*

**dubiety** (diubai·eti) *s.* lo dudoso, cosa dudosa, incertidumbre.

**dubious** (diu·biøs) *adj.* dudoso. *2* ambiguo, equívoco; sospechoso.

**dubitable** (-bitabøl) *adj.* dubitable, dudable.

**dubitative** (-bitei·tiv) *adj.* dubitativo.

**ducal** (diu·kal) *adj.* ducal.

**ducat** (dø·ka) *s.* ducado [moneda].

**duchess** (-chis) *s.* duquesa.

**duchy** (dø·chi) *s.* ducado [territorio].

**duck** (døk) *s.* ORN. ánade, pato. *2* ORN. pata [hembra]. *3* fam. pichón, pichona, amor mío. *4* acción de agacharse rápidamente, chapuz, zambullida. *5* dril, *loneta. *6 pl.* pantalones de dril. *7 to play ducks and drakes* [*with*], hacer saltar piedras sobre el agua; malgastar, derrochar.

**duck** (to) *tr.* zambullir. *2* bajar rápidamente [la cabeza, etc.]. *3 intr.* zambullirse, chapuzar. *4* agacharse o bajar la cabeza rápidamente. *5 pop. to ~ out,* escaparse.

**duckbill** (dø·kbil) *s.* ZOOL. ornitorrinco.

**duck-legged** *adj.* corto de piernas.

**duckling** (-ling) *s.* patito, patita.

**duct** (døkt) *s.* conducto, tubo. *2* ANAT. conducto. *3* BOT. vaso.

**ductile** (-il) *adj.* dúctil.

**ductility** (døkti·liti) *s.* ductilidad.

**dud** (død) *adj.* flojo, sin energía. *2 s.* granada que no estalla; fracaso, cosa o persona inútil. *3 pl.* trapos, pingajos.

**dude** (diud) *s.* petimetre, lechuguino.

**dudgeon** (dø·dyøn) *s.* resentimiento, enojo: *in* ~ , resentido, enojado.

**due** (diu) *adj.* debido: *in* ~ *time,* a su debido tiempo. *2* vencido, devengado, pagadero: *to become* ~ *fall* ~, vencer. *3* esperado, que tiene su llegada: *the train is* ~ *at two o'clock,* el tren llega a las dos. *4* propio, justo. *5* legal, regular. *6 s.* deuda, obligación. *7* merecido; lo que se debe a uno. *8 pl.* derechos [que se pagan]. *9 adv.* directamente, exactamente.

**duel** (diu·øl) *s.* duelo, desafío.

**duel** (to) *intr.* batirse en duelo.

**dueller** (-øᵗ) *s.* el que se desafía.

**duellist** (-ist) duelista.

**duenna** (diue·na) *s.* dueña, señora de compañía.

**duet** (diue·t) *s.* dúo.

**duff** (to) (døf) *tr.* amañar, falsificar; engañar.

**duffel** (dø·føl) *s.* tela de lana basta. *2* saco o equipo de acampador.

**dug** (døg) *pret.* y *p. p.* de TO DIG. *2 s.* teta, ubre.

**dugong** (du·gan) *s.* ZOOL. vaca marina.

**dugout** (dø·gaut) *s.* canoa, piragua. *2* cueva. *3* MIL. cueva de protección, trinchera cubierta.

**duke** (diuk) *s.* duque.

**dukedom** (-døm) *s.* ducado [título, territorio].
**dulcet** (dø·lsit) *adj.* dulce, agradable, armonioso.
**dulcify (to)** (dø·lsifai) *tr.* dulcificar, ablandar, apaciguar. ¶ Pret. y p. p.: *dulcified.*
**dulcimer** (-simøʳ) *s.* MÚS. dulcémele.
**dulia** (dulai·a) *s.* REL. dulia.
**dull** (døl) *adj.* embotado, obtuso, romo. *2* torpe, lerdo. *3* poco agudo [vista, oído]; que los tiene así: ~ *of hearing,* duro de oído. *4* inservible [cosa]. *5* lento, pesado; soñoliento. *6* débil, mortecino. *7* triste, sombrío. *8* aburrido, insulso, prosaico. *9* apagado, mate, sordo. *10* empañado, deslustrado; obscuro, nebuloso. *11* nublado [tiempo]. *12* COM. encalmado.
**dull (to)** *tr.* embotar. *2* entontecer, entorpecer. *3* hacer pesado, monótono. *4* apagar, amortiguar. *5* mitigar. *6* contristar. *7* ofuscar, ensombrecer. *8* empañar, deslustrar. *9 intr.* embotarse. *10* entorpecerse. *11* apagarse; mitigarse. *12* empañarse.
**dullard** (dø·laʳd) *adj.-s.* estúpido, zoquete.
**dull-head** *s.* zote.
**dullness** (-nis) *s.* embotamiento, etc.
**dull-sighted** *adj.* cegato.
**dull-witted** *adj.* tonto, estúpido.
**dulness** *s.* DULLNESS.
**duly** (-i) *adv.* debidamente. *2* puntualmente, a su tiempo.
**dumb** (døm) *adj.* mudo, callado, sin habla: ~ *show,* pantomima: *to strike* ~, dejar sin habla, asombrar.
**dumbbell** (-bel) *s.* pesa de gimnasia.
**dumbfound (to)** (-faund) *tr.* confundir, dejar atónito, sin habla.
**dumbfounded** (-id) *adj.* confuso, atónito, sin habla.
**dumbness** (-nis) *s.* mudez, mutismo; silencio.
**dumb-waiter** *s.* (Ingl.) estante giratorio para platos, vasos, etc. *2* (E.U.) montaplatos.
**dummy** (dø·mi) *adj.* mudo, silencioso. *2* falso, simulado. *3 s.* mudo. *4* testaferro. *5* personaje que no habla. *6* objeto simulado. *7* maniquí [para vestidos, pelucas, etc.]. *8* maqueta [de libro]. *9* WHIST, BRIDGE muerto.
**dump** (dømp) *s.* baque. *2* vaciadero, vertedero: depósito; vaciamiento: ~ *truck,* camión volquete. *3* ~ *the dumps,* murria, melancolía.
**dump (to)** *tr.* vaciar de golpe, descargar, verter [escombros, etc.]. *2* COM. vender al extranjero a precios inferiores a los corrientes.
**dumping** (døm·ping) *s.* COM. dumping.
**dumpish** (-pish) *adj.* estúpido. *2* murrio.
**dumpling** (-pling) *s.* bollito relleno.
**dumpy** (-pi) *adj.* corto y grueso; rechoncho.
**dun** (døn) *adj.* pardo, castaño. *2 s.* acreedor importuno. *3* apremio.
**dun (to)** *tr.* perseguir, apremiar [esp. a un deudor].
**dunce** (døns) *s.* tonto, zote, ignorante.
**dunderhead** (døndøʳjed) *s.* zopenco, badulaque.
**dune** (diun) *s.* duna, médano.
**dung** (døng) *s.* estiércol, bosta, tullidura. *2* ENT. ~ *beetle,* escarabajo bolero.
**dung (to)** *tr.-intr.* estercolar.
**dungeon** (dø·ndẏøn) *s.* calabozo, mazmorra. *2* DONJON.
**dungeon (to)** *tr.* encalabozar.
**dunghill** (dø·ngjil) *s.* muladar, estercolero, basurero. *2 adj.* bajo, vil.
**dungy** (-i) *adj.* estercolizo.
**dunnage** (dø·nidẏ) *s.* MAR. abarrote.
**duo** (diu·ou) *s.* MÚS. dúo.

**duodecimal** (diuode·simal) *adj.* duodecimal. *2 s.* duodécimo.
**duodenum** (-dɪ·nøm) *s.* ANAT. duodeno.
**dupe** (diup) *s.* víctima [de un engaño], engañado. *2* incauto, primo.
**dupe (to)** *tr.* engañar, embaucar.
**duple** (diu·pøl), **duplex** (-plecs) *adj.* duplo, doble, dúplice.
**duplicate** (-plikit) *adj.* duplicado, doble. *2 s.* duplicado.
**duplicate (to)** (-plikeit) *tr.* duplicar, doblar. *2* hacer un duplicado de.
**duplication** (-ei·shøn) *s.* duplicación.
**duplicator** (diu·plikeitøʳ) *s.* duplicador, copiador.
**duplicity** (diupli·siti) *s.* duplicidad.
**durability** (diurabi·liti) *s.* durabilidad, duración; estabilidad, permanencia.
**durable** (diu·rabøl) *adj.* durable, duradero. *2* resistente, de duración. *3* estable, permanente.
**dura mater** (diu·ra mei·tøʳ) *s.* ANAT. duramadre.
**durance** (diu·rans) *s.* prisión, encierro, cautividad. *2* TEJ. sempiterna.
**duration** (-reishøn) *s.* duración, vida.
**duress** (diure·s) *s.* coacción. *2* prisión, encierro.
**during** (diu·ring) *prep.* durante. *2 adj.* duradero.
**durst** (døʳst) *pret. irreg.* de TO DARE.
**dusk** (døsk) *adj.* oscuro, sombrío. *2 s.* crepúsculo, anochecida: *at* ~, al anochecer. *3* sombra, penumbra, oscuridad.
**dusky** (-i) *adj.* oscuro, moreno, pardo, negruzco. *2* sombrío.
**dust** (døst) *s.* polvo: *gold* ~, oro en polvo; pop. dinero; ~ *coat,* guardapolvo [prenda]. *2* tierra, suelo. *3* oro en polvo. *4* cenizas [restos mortales]. *5* polvareda. *6* trapatiesta, riña, alboroto: *to raise a* ~, armar una trapatiesta. *7* basura, barreduras.
**dust (to)** *tr.* desempolvar, quitar o sacudir el polvo a: *to* ~ *one's jacket,* sacudir el polvo a uno. *3* empolvar, llenar de polvo. *4* espolvorear. *5* pulverizar.
**dustbin** (-bin) *s.* recipiente para barreduras, cenizas, etc.
**dustcloth** (-kloz) *s.* trapo para quitar el polvo.
**duster** (-øʳ) *s.* el o lo que quita el polvo; paño, plumero, zorros. *2* guardapolvo [prenda]. *3* utensilio para espolvorear.
**dustman** (-mæn) *s.* basurero, barrendero.
**dustpan** (-pæn) *s.* recogedor [para las barreduras].
**dusty** (-i) *adj.* polvoriento. *2* del color del polvo. *3* pulverulento.
**Dutch** (dø·ch) *adj.-s.* holandés: ~ *tile,* azulejo.
**Dutchman** (-mæn) *s.* holandés [pers.].
**duteous** (diu·tiøs) *adj.* obediente, respetuoso, obsequioso.
**dutiable** (-tiabøl) *adj.* sujeto al pago de derechos.
**dutiful** (-tiful) *adj.* obediente, respetuoso, solícito.
**duty** (-ti) *s.* deber, obligación, incumbencia. *2* sumisión, obediencia, respeto. *3* quehaceres; funciones [de un cargo, etc.]. *4* servicio, guardia: *on* ~, de servicio, de guardia. *5* impuesto, derecho [de aduanas, consumos, etc.]. *6* MEC. trabajo mecánico, efecto útil.
**duumvir** (diuø·mvøʳ) *s.* duunviro.
**dwarf** (duoʳf) *adj.* enano, diminuto. *2 s.* enano, enana.
**dwarf (to)** *tr.* impedir el crecimiento de. *2* empequeñecer, achicar. *3 intr.* empequeñecerse, achicarse.
**dwarfish** (-ish) *adj.* enano, diminuto.
**dwell (to)** (duel) *intr.* habitar, morar, residir, vivir.

2 permanecer. *3 to ~ on* o *upon*, entretenerse, detenerse, espaciarse en. ¶ Pret. y p. p.: *dwelt* o *dwelled*.

**dweller** (due·lø<sup>r</sup>) *s.* morador, habitante.

**dwelling** (-ing) *s.* morada, vivienda, casa, domicilio.

**dwindle (to)** (dui·ndøl) *intr.* menguar, disminuirse. *2* consumirse. *3* decaer, degenerar.

**dye** (dai) *s.* tintura, tinte, color.

**dye (to)** *tr.-intr.* teñir, tinturar, colorar: *to ~ in grain, to ~ in the wool*, teñir en rama. *2 intr.* teñirse. ¶ Pret. y p.p.: *dyed;* ger.: *dyeing*.

**dyeing** (-ing) *adj.* colorante, tintóreo. *2 s.* tinte, tintura, tintorería.

**dyer** (-ø<sup>r</sup>) *s.* tintorero.

**dyers'-broom** *s.* BOT. retama de tintes.

**dyestuff** (-støf) *s.* materia colorante.

**dying** (-ing) *ger.* de TO DIE. *2 adj.* moribundo, agonizante. *3* de la muerte. *4* mortal, perecedero.

**dynamic (al** (dainæ·mik(al) *adj.* dinámico.

**dynamics** (-miks) *s.* dinámica.

**dynamism** (-mišm) *s.* dinamismo.

**dynamite** (dai·namait) *s.* dinamita.

**dynamite (to)** *tr.* dinamitar.

**dynamiter** (-ø<sup>r</sup>) *s.* dinamitero.

**dynamo** (-namou) *s.* ELECT. dinamo.

**dynamometer** (dainama·metø<sup>r</sup>) *s.* dinamómetro.

**dynast** (dai·næst) *s.* dinasta.

**dynastic(al** (dainæ·stik(al) *adj.* dinástico.

**dynasty** (dai·nasti) *s.* dinastía.

**dyne** (dain) *s.* FÍS. dina.

**dysentery** (di·sønteri) *s.* MED. disentería.

**dyspepsia, dispepsy** (dispe·psia, -si) *s.* MED. dispepsia.

**dyspeptic** (-ptik) *adj.-s.* dispéptico.

**disphasia** (-fei·šia) *s.* MED. disfasia.

**dyspnea, dyspnœa** (dispnɪ·a) *s.* MED. disnea.

**dysuria** (disiu·rias) *s.* MED. disuria.

# E

**E, e** (ı) *s.* E, e, quinta letra del alfabeto inglés. *2* MÚS. mi.

**each** (ıch) *adj.* cada, todo. *2 pron.* cada uno, cada cual, todos: ~ *other*, mutuamente, uno a otro, los unos a los otros. *3 adv.* cada uno, por cabeza.

**eager** (ı·gøʳ) *adj.* ávido, ansioso, afanoso, anheloso. *2* ardiente, vehemente. *3* encarnizado [combate, etc.].

**eagerness** (-nis) *s.* avidez, ansia, afán, anhelo, ahinco. *2* ardor, vehemencia.

**eagle** (ı·gøl) *s.* águila. *2* (E.U.) moneda de oro de diez dólares.

**eagless** (ı·glis) *s.* ORN. águila hembra.

**eaglet** (-glit) *s.* ORN. aguilucho.

**ear** (i·øʳ) *s.* ANAT. oreja: ~ *flap*, orejera; ~ *trumpet*, trompetilla acústica; *to set by the ears*, fig. hacer reñir, enemistar; *up to the ears*, fig. hasta los ojos. *2* oído, oídos: *to give* ~ *to*, prestar oído a; *to have one's* ~, ser escuchado por uno, gozar de su favor; *to play by* ~, tocar de oído. *3* orejuela; asa, asidero. *4* ORN. plumas sobre el oído de un ave. *5* BOT. aurícula. *6* BOT. espiga, mazorca [de cereal].

**ear (to)** *intr.* BOT. espigar, echar espigas.

**earache** (-eik) *s.* otalgia, dolor de oídos.

**eardrop** (-drap) *s.* arracada.

**eardrum** (-drøm) *s.* ANAT. tímpano [del oído].

**eared** (-d) *adj.* que tiene orejas o espigas.

**earl** (øʳl) *s.* conde [título inglés].

**earlap** (i·øʳlæp) *s.* lóbulo de la oreja. *2* orejera [de gorra].

**earldom** (ø·ʳldøm) *s.* condado.

**earless** (i·øʳlis) *adj.* desorejado.

**earlock** (-lak) *s.* aladar.

**early** (ø·ʳli) *adj.* primitivo, antiguo, remoto. *2* próximo [en el futuro]. *3* perteneciente o relativo al principio de la mañana, de la vida, de una época: ~ *riser*, madrugador; ~ *Victorian* del principio de la época victoriana. *4* precoz, temprano, anticipado: ~ *fruit*, fruto temprano. *5 to be* ~, llegar temprano. *6 adv.* temprano, tempranamente; pronto. *7* al principio: ~ *in the morning*, de madrugada.

**earmark** (i·øʳmarʳk) *s.* señal en la oreja. *2* señal característica.

**earmark (to)** marcar [el ganado] en la oreja. *2* destinar, reservar [para un fin determinado].

**earn (to)** (øʳn) *tr.* ganar, merecer, lograr. *2* devengar.

**earnest** (o·ʳnist) *adj.* serio, formal. *2* sincero, ardiente, encarecido. *3* celoso, diligente. *4* ansioso. *5 s.* seriedad, buena fe, veras: *in* ~, en serio, de veras. *7* señal, prenda.

**earnestness** (-nis) *s.* seriedad, buena fe. *2* veras, ahinco, ardor.

**earnings** (ø·nings) *s. pl.* ganancias; sueldo, salario.

**earpiece** (i·øʳpis) *s.* TELEF. auricular, receptor.

**earring** (-ing) *s.* pendiente, zarcillo, arete.

**earshot** (-shat) *s.* alcance del oído.

**earth** (øʳz) *s.* tierra, barro, materia térrea. *2* tierra [mundo; país, región; suelo]. *3* mundo, [cosas terrenales]. *4* madriguera. *5* ELECT. tierra.

**earth (to)** *tr.* AGR. acollar, aporcar. *2* ELECT. conectar con tierra. *3 tr.-intr.* hacer entrar o meterse en la madriguera.

**earthboard** (-boʳd) *s.* orejera [del arado].

**earthen** (-øn) *adj.* terrizo, de barro.

**earthenware** (-ønueʳ) *s.* ollería, vasijas de barro.

**earthly** (-li) *adj.* terreno, terrestre. *2* terrenal, temporal. *3* mundano, carnal. *4 to be of no* ~ *use*, no servir para nada.

**earthnut** (-nøt) *s.* BOT. chufa; cacahuete; tubérculo de ciertas plantas.

**earthquake** (-kueik) *s.* terremoto.

**earthworhm** (-uøʳm) *s.* lombriz de tierra.

**earthy** (-zi) *adj.* terroso, térreo. *2* terrenal. *3* basto, grosero.

**earwax** (i·øʳueks) *s.* cerumen.

**earwig** (-ig) *s.* ENT. tijereta. *2* ZOOL. ciempiés.

**ease** (ıš) *s.* alivio, descanso. *2* tranquilidad. *3* comodidad, holgura, desahogo: *at* ~, con desahogo, a gusto; *ill at* ~, incómodo, violento. *4* facilidad, soltura, desembarazo, naturalidad.

**ease (to)** *tr.* aliviar, moderar, mitigar. *2* descargar, desembarazar. *3* tranquilizar. *4* aflojar. *5* hacer más fácil. *6* MAR. lascar. *7 intr. to* ~ *off* o *up*, moderarse, disminuir; moderar la marcha.

**easel** (ı·šøl) *s.* caballete [de pintor].

**easement** (ı·šmønt) *s.* alivio, aflojamiento. *2* ARQ. descarga. *3* DER. servidumbre.

**easiness** (-šinis) *s.* comodidad, holgura. *2* facilidad. *3* soltura, desembarazo. *4* tranquilidad. *5* indiferencia. *6* indulgencia, condescendencia. *7* credulidad.

**east** (ıst) *s.* este, oriente, levante. *2 adj.* oriental, del este. *3 adv.* hacia el este.
**Easter** (ı·stø<sup>r</sup>) *s.* Pascua de Resurrección o florida.
**easterly** (-li) *adj.* oriental, del este. *2 adv.* al este, hacia el este.
**eastern** (-n) *adj.-s.* oriental.
**eastward** (ı·stua<sup>r</sup>d) *adj.* que va o mira hacia el este. *2 adv.* hacia el este.
**easy** (ı·ši) *adj.* fácil, llano, corriente. *2* sencillo, natural. *3* fluido [estilo]. *4* cómodo, holgado: ~ *chair*, butaca, sillón. *5* acomodado. *6* sociable, condescendiente. *7* asequible. *8* tranquilo. *9* suelto, desembarazado, desenvuelto. *10* manejable, fácil de engañar. *11* lento, moderado. *12* ligero, suave. *13 adv.* fácilmente. *14* con calma; quedo, quedito.
**easy-going** *adj.* comodón, indolente.
**eat (to)** (ıt) *tr.* comer, comerse: *to* ~ *one's heart out*, *fig.* sufrir en silencio; *to* ~ *one's words*, retractarse. *2* devorar, tragar. *3* corroer. *4* roer, consumir, gastar. *5 intr.* comer. ¶ Pret.: *ate*; p. p.: *eaten*.
**eatable** (-abøl) *adj.* comestible, comedero. *2 s. pl.* comestibles, vituallas.
**eaten** (-øn) *p. p.* de TO EAT.
**eating-house** *s.* bodegón, figón, restaurante.
**eaves** (ı·vš) *s. pl.* alero, socarrén.
**eavesdrop (to)** (-drap) *intr.* escuchar detrás de las puertas, fisgonear.
**eavesdropper** (-ø<sup>r</sup>) *s.* el que escucha escondido.
**ebb** (eb) *s.* MAR. menguante, reflujo: ~ *tide*, marea menguante. *2* decadencia: ~ *of life*, vejez.
**ebb (to)** *intr.* menguar [la marea]. *2* decaer, bajar, disminuir.
**ebbing** (e·bing) *s.* reflujo, bajamar.
**ebon** (e·bøn) *adj.* de ébano; negro.
**ebonite** (e·bønait) *s.* ebonita.
**ebony** (e·bøni) *s.* BOT. ébano.
**ebullience, -cy** (ibø·liøns, -si) *s.* bullición, hervor, entusiasmo.
**ebullition** (ebø·lishøn) *s.* ebullición. *2* efervescencia. *3 fig.* explosión, arranque.
**eburnean** (ibø·<sup>r</sup>nian) *adj.* ebúrneo.
**écarté** (eika<sup>r</sup>tei·) *s.* ecarté [juego de naipes].
**Ecce homo** (e·ksijou·mou) *s.* eccehomo.
**eccentric** (ikse·ntrik) *s.* MEC. excéntrica. *2* excéntrico [pers.].
**eccentric(al** (-al) *adj.* excéntrico.
**eccentricity** (iksentri·siti) *s.* excentricidad.
**ecchymosis** (ekimou·sis) *s.* equimosis.
**Ecclesiastes** (iclisiæ·stiš) *s.* Eclesiastés.
**ecclesiastic** (-stik) *s.* eclesiástico.
**ecclesiastic(al** (-al) *adj.* eclesiástico.
**ecclesiology** (iclisia·lodÿi) *s.* eclesiología.
**echelon** (e·shølan) *s.* MIL. escalón.
**echidna** (iki·dna) *s.* ZOOL. equidna.
**echinoderm** (ikai·nodø<sup>r</sup>m) *adj.-s.* ZOOL. equinodermo.
**echinus** (ikai·nøs) *s.* ZOOL. equino, erizo de mar. *2* ARQ. equino. *3* ARQ. gallón.
**echo** (e·kou) *s.* eco.
**echo (to)** *tr.* devolver [el sonido]. *2* hacer eco a, repetir, imitar. *3 intr.* repercutir, resonar.
**echoic** (ekou·ik) *adj.* ecoico.
**éclat** (ekla·) *s.* brillo, magnificencia. *2* aplauso, aprobación. *3* fama, notoriedad.
**eclectic** (ikle·ktik) *adj.-s.* ecléctico.
**eclecticism** (-tisišm) *s.* eclecticismo.
**eclipse** (ikli·ps) *s.* eclipse.
**eclipse (to)** *tr.* eclipsar. *2 intr.* poét. eclipsarse.
**ecliptic** (ikli·ptik) *adj.* eclíptico. *2 s.* ASTR. eclíptica.

**eclogue** (e·klag) *s.* égloga.
**economic** (ikøna·mik) *adj.* económico [de la economía]. *2* que compensa, que paga los gastos.
**economical** (-al) *adj.* económico.
**economics** (-s) *s.* economía [ciencia].
**economist** (ika·nomist) *s.* economista.
**economize (to)** (-nomaiš) *tr.-intr.* economizar.
**economy** (-nomi) *s.* economía [en todas las acepciones].
**ecru** (e·cru) *adj.* crudo [sin blanquear].
**ecstasy** (e·kstasi) *s.* éxtasis, arrobamiento.
**ecstasy (to)** *tr.* extasiar, arrobar.
**ecstatic (al** (ekstæ·tik(al) *adj.* extático.
**ectasis** (e·ktæsis) *s.* éxtasis. *2* MED. ectasia.
**ectoblast** (-toblæst) *s.* BIOL. ectoblasto.
**ectoderm** (-dø<sup>r</sup>m) *s.* BIOL. ectodermo.
**ectropion** (ektrou·piøn) *s.* MED. ectropión.
**ecumenic (al** (ekiume·nik(al) *adj.* ecuménico.
**eczema** (e·kšima) *s.* MED. eczema.
**edacious** (idei·shøs) *adj.* voraz, glotón.
**edaphology** (edafa·lodÿi) *s.* edafología.
**eddy** (e·di) *s.* remanso, regolfo. *2* remolino, torbellino.
**eddy (to)** *tr.* arremolinar, remolinear. *2 intr.* regolfar, arremolinarse, remolinar.
**edelweiss** (ei·dølvais) *s.* BOT. edelweis, pie de león.
**edema** (idı·ma) *s.* MED. edema.
**Eden** (ı·døn) *s.* Edén.
**edentate** (ide·nteit) *adj.-s.* ZOOL. desdentado.
**edge** (edÿ) *s.* filo, corte. *2* canto, borde, esquina. *3* extremo, margen, orilla. *4* ribete, pestaña. *5* fuerza, agudeza. *6* DEP. ventaja. *7 to set the teeth on* ~, dar dentera. *8 on* ~, de canto; *fig.* impaciente, ansioso, nervioso.
**edge (to)** *tr.* afilar, aguzar. *2* ribetear, orlar. *3* limitar, rodear. *4* incitar, aguijonear. *5* mover o empujar poco a poco. *6 intr.* avanzar de lado. *7 tr.-intr. to* ~ *in*, introducir, introducirse.
**edged** (e·dÿid) *adj.* afilado, cortante.
**edgeless** (-lis) *adj.* embotado, romo, sin filo.
**edgeways** (-ueiš), **edgewise** (-uaiš) *adv.* de filo, de canto, de lado.
**edging** (-ing) *s.* orilla, orla, ribete, guarnición.
**edible** (e·dibøl) *adj.-s.* comestible.
**edict** (ı·dikt) *s.* edicto, decreto, orden, bando.
**edification** (edifikei·shøn) *s.* edificación [en sentido moral].
**edificatory** (e·difikatori) *s.* edificante.
**edifice** (e·difis) *s.* edificio.
**edify (to)** (e·difai) *tr.* edificar moralmente. ¶ Pret. y p. p.: *edified*.
**edile** (ı·dail) *s.* edil.
**edit** (e·dit) *tr.* revisar, preparar para la publicación. *2* redactar, dirigir [un periódico].
**edition** (edı·shøn) *s.* edición. | No tiene el sentido de acción de editar.
**editor** (e·ditø<sup>r</sup>) *s.* director, redactor [de una publicación].
**editorial** (edito·rial) *adj.* de la dirección o redacción [de una publicación]: ~ *staff*, redacción, cuerpo de redactores. *2 s.* editorial, artículo de fondo.
**educate (to)** (e·diukeit) *tr.* educar. *2* enseñar, instruir. *3* amaestrar.
**educated** (-id) *adj.* educado, instruido, culto.
**education** (-ei·shøn) *s.* educación. | No tiene el sentido de urbanidad. *2* instrucción, enseñanza. *3* ilustración, cultura.
**educational** (-al) *adj.* educativo. *3* cultural.
**educative** (e·diukeitiv) *adj.* educativo.

**educator** (-tøʳ) *s.* educador, pedagogo.
**educe (to)** (idiu·s) *tr.* educir. *2* desarrollar, hacer aparecer.
**edulcorate (to)** (idø·lkoreit) *tr.* edulcorar, endulzar.
**Edward** (e·duaʳd) *n. pr. m.* Eduardo.
**eel** (il) *s.* ICT. anguila: *electric ~,* gimnoto.
**e'en** (i·n) *adv.* EVEN.
**e'er** (e·øʳ) *adv.* EVER.
**eerie, eery** (i·ri) *adj.* asustadizo [de aparecidos, etc.]. *2* temeroso, misterioso, fantástico, sobrenatural.
**efface (to)** (efei·s) *tr.* borrar, hacer desaparecer.
**effect** (ife·kt) *s.* efecto. | No tiene el sentido de efecto mercantil ni del que se da a una pelota o bola: *of no ~,* ineficaz, vano. *2* consecuencia, resultado. *3* cumplimiento; vigencia, vigor: *to take ~,* producir su efecto; tener cumplimiento, ponerse en vigor. *4* realidad: *in ~,* de hecho, en realidad. *5 pl.* efectos, bienes.
**effect (to)** *tr.* efectuar, realizar, llevar a cabo.
**effective** (-iv) *adj.* efectivo, real. *2* eficaz. *3* que hace o produce. *4* impresionante, de efecto. *5* vigente. *6 s.* MIL., COM. efectivo.
**effectless** (-lis) *adj.* ineficaz, sin resultado.
**effectual** (-chual) *adj.* eficaz. *2* DER. válido.
**effectuate (to)** (-chueit) *tr.* efectuar, realizar.
**effeminacy** (efe·minasi) *s.* afeminamiento, molicie.
**effeminate** (-minit) *adj.* afeminado.
**effeminate (to)** (-mineit) *tr.* afeminar, enervar. *2 intr.* afeminarse.
**efferent** (e·førønt) *s.* FISIOL. eferente.
**effervesce (to)** (eføʳve·s) *intr.* hervir, estar en efervescencia.
**effervescence** (-øns) *s.* efervescencia, hervor.
**effervescent** (-ønt) *adj.* efervescente.
**effete** (efi·t) *adj.* estéril, infructuoso. *2* gastado, agotado.
**efficacious** (efikei·shøs) *adj.* eficaz.
**efficacy** (e·fikasi) *s.* eficacia. *2* virtud, poder.
**efficiency** (efi·shønsi) *s.* eficiencia. *2* fuerza, virtud. *3* rendimiento, efecto útil.
**efficient** (-shønt) *adj.* eficiente. *2* MEC. de buen rendimiento. *3 s.* causa eficiente.
**effigy** (e·fidʒi) *s.* efigie.
**effloresce (to)** (eflore·s) *intr.* QUÍM. eflorescerse. *2* BOT. florecer.
**efflorescence** (-øns) *s.* BOT. florescencia. *2* QUÍM., MED. eflorescencia.
**effluence** (e·fluøns) *s.* emanación. *2* efusión, flujo.
**effluent** (-ønt) *adj.* efluente.
**effluvium** (eflu·viøm) *s.* efluvio, emanación.
**effort** (e·føʳt) *s.* esfuerzo, conato, empeño.
**effrontery** (efrø·ntøri) *s.* descaro, desfachatez.
**effulgence** (efø·ldʒøns) *s.* brillantez, resplandor, esplendor, fulgor.
**effulgent** (-ønt) *adj.* brillante, resplandeciente.
**effuse (to)** (efiu·š) *tr.* efundir. *2* esparcir. *3 intr.* emanar, fluir.
**effusion** (efiu·ʒøn) *s.* efusión. *2* expansión, desahogo.
**effusive** (-siv) *adj.* efusivo, expansivo.
**eft** (eft) *s.* ZOOL. tritón, salamandra acuática.
**egg** (eg) *s.* huevo: *~ laying,* postura.
**egg (to)** *tr.* cubrir o mezclar con huevo. *2 to ~ on,* incitar, instigar.
**eggcup** (e·gkøp) *s.* huevera [utensilio].
**eggnog** (-nag) *s.* yema mejida; ponche de huevo.
**eggplant** (-plænt) *s.* BOT. berenjena.
**eggshell** (-shel) *s.* cáscara de huevo, cascarón.

**egis** (i·dʒis) *s.* égida, escudo.
**eglantine** (e·glantain) *s.* BOT. zarzarrosa.
**egoism** (i·goušm) *s.* egoísmo.
**egoist** (-ist) *s.* egoísta.
**egoistic** (igoui·stik) *adj.* egoísta.
**egotism** (i·goutišm) *s.* egotismo.
**egotize** (-taiš) *intr.* hablar mucho de sí mismo.
**egregious** (igri·dʒøs) *adj.* egregio. *2* insigne, notable [por una mala cualidad].
**egress** (i·gress) *s.* salida [acción, lugar].
**egression** (igre·shøn) *s.* salida [acción].
**egret** (e- o i·gret) *s.* ORN. garceta. *2* ORN. garzota. *3* airón, penacho.
**Egypt** (i·dʒipt) *n. pr.* GEOGR. Egipto.
**Egyptian** (idʒi·pshan) *adj.-s.* egipcio, egipcíaco.
**Egyptology** (-ta·lodʒi) *s.* egiptología.
**eh** (e) *interj.* ¿eh?, ¿qué?
**eider, eider-duck** (ai·døʳ) *s.* ORN. . eider, pato de flojel: *~ down,* plumón; edredón.
**eight** (eit) *adj.-s.* ocho: *~ o'clock,* las ocho.
**eighteen** (-i·n) *adj.-s.* diez y ocho, dieciocho.
**eighteenth** (-i·nz) *adj.* decimoctavo. *2 adj.-s.* dieciochavo.
**eighth** (eitz) *adj.-s.* octavo. *2 s.* MÚS. octavo.
**eightieth** (ei·tiez) *adj.-s.* octogésimo.
**eight-sided** *adj.* octogonal. *2* ochavado.
**eighty** (ei·ti) *adj.-s.* ochenta.
**either** (ai·dør) *adj.* uno y otro, ambos, entrambos. *2* uno a otro. *3* cada [de dos]. *4 pron.* uno o cualquiera de los dos; el uno o el otro. *5 conj.* o, ya. *6 adv.* también; [con negación] tampoco.
**ejaculate (to)** (idʒæ·kiuleit) *tr.* eyacular. *2* exclamar, proferir.
**ejaculation** (-ei·shøn) *s.* eyaculación. *2* exclamación, jaculatoria.
**eject (to)** (idʒe·kt) *tr.* arrojar, expeler, vomitar. *2* echar fuera, expulsar. *3* DER. lanzar.
**ejection** (-shøn) *s.* eyección, evacuación. *2* expulsión [de un sitio]; desahucio.
**ejector** (-tøʳ) *s.* MEC. eyector, expulsor.
**eke out (to)** (ik) *tr.* reunir [poco a poco]. *2* ganarse [el sustento] con dificultad.
**elaborate** (ilæ·børit) *adj.* trabajado, primoroso, detallado. *2* complicado, recargado. *3* suntuoso.
**elaborate (to)** (ilæ·børeit) *tr.* elaborar. *2* laborar, trabajar con primor. *3 intr.* extenderse, detallar.
**elaboration** (-ei·shøn) *s.* elaboración. *2* obra acabada.
**eland** (ilæ·nd) *s.* ZOOL. antílope africano.
**elapse (to)** (ilæ·ps) *intr.* pasar, transcurrir [un tiempo].
**elastic** (ilæ·stik) *adj.* elástico. *2* cinta o tejido elástico. *3 pl.* ligas.
**elasticity** (-ti·siti) *s.* elasticidad, resorte.
**elate (to)** (ilei·t) *tr.* exaltar, alborozar. *2* engreir.
**elate (d)** (-t(id) *adj.* triunfante, gozoso. *2* engreído.
**elation** (-ei·shøn) *s.* elación. *2* júbilo, alborozo.
**elbow** (e·lbou) *s.* ANAT. codo: *at one's ~,* al lado, a mano; *out at elbows,* roto, desharrapado. *2* codo, recodo, ángulo; codillo, tubo acodado. *3* brazo [de sillón].
**elbow (to)** *tr.* empujar o dar con el codo. *2 to ~ one's way,* abrirse paso a codazos. *3* codear. *4* formar ángulo o codo.
**elbowpiece** (-pis) *s.* codal [de armadura].
**elbowroom** (-rum) *s.* espacio para moverse. *2* libertad de acción.
**elder** (e·ldøʳ) *adj.* mayor, de más edad, más antiguo, viejo. *2* superior [en categoría, etc.]. *3 s.* mayor [antepasado]; superior; persona mayor

[que uno]. *4* persona de edad. *5* anciano [de una tribu o familia]. *6* BOT. saúco.
**elderberry** (-beri) *s.* BOT. baya del saúco.
**elderly** (-li) *adj.* mayor, de alguna edad, anciano.
**elderwort** (-wø�posᵗ) *s.* BOT. yezgo.
**eldest** (e·ldist) *adj. superl.* mayor; más antiguo. *2* primogénito.
**Eleanor, Elinor** (e·linøᵣ) *n. pr. f.* Leonor.
**elecampane** (elikømpei·n) *s.* BOT. helenio.
**elect** (ile·kt) *adj.* elegido, escogido. *2* electo. *3 s.* TEOL. elegido.
**elect (to)** *tr.* elegir, escoger. *2* elegir [para un cargo].
**election** (ile·kshøn) *s.* elección.
**electioneer (to)** (-i·øᵣ) *intr.* POL. hacer propaganda o trabajar para una elección.
**elective** (ile·ktiv) *adj.* electivo. *2* facultativo.
**elector** (ile·ktøᵣ) *s.* elector.
**electoral** (-ral) *adj.* electoral.
**electorate** (-rit) *s.* electorado.
**electric(al** (-trik(al) *adj.* eléctrico: ~ *chair*, silla eléctrica; ~ *eel*, ICT. gimnoto: ~ *tape*, cinta aislante; ~ *wave*, onda hertziana. *2* electricista: ~ *engineer*, ingeniero electricista. *3* fig. vivo, fogoso, electrizante.
**electrically** (-li) *adv.* eléctricamente.
**electrician** (ilektri·shan) *s.* electricista.
**electricity** (-tri·siti) *s.* electricidad.
**electrification** (-trifikei·shøn) *s.* electrización. *2* electrificación.
**electrify (to)** (-trifai) *tr.* electrizar. *2* electrificar. ¶ Pret. y p. p.: *electrified*.
**electrization** (-triše·shøn) *s.* electrización.
**electrize (to)** (ile·ktraiš) *intr.* electrizar.
**electroanalysis** (ilektroanæ·lisis) *s.* electroanálisis.
**electrocardiogram** (-ka·ᵣdiogræm) *s.* MED. electrocardiograma.
**electrocardiography** (-ka·ᵣdia·grafi) *s.* electrocardiografía.
**electrochemistry** (-ke·mistri) *s.* electroquímica.
**electrocute (to)** (ile·ktrokiut) *tr.* electrocutar.
**electrocution** (-kiu·shøn) *s.* electrocución.
**electrode** (ile·ktroud) *s.* electrodo.
**electrodynamics** (ilektrodainæ·miks) *s.* electrodinámica.
**electro-encephalogram** *s.* MED. electroencefalograma.
**electrokinetics** (-kine·tiks) *s.* electrocinética.
**electrolier** (li·øᵣ) *s.* araña de lámparas eléctricas.
**electrolysis** (-tra·lisis) *s.* electrólisis.
**electrolyte** (ile·ktrolait) *s.* electrólito.
**electrolyze (to)** (-laiš) *tr.* electrolizar.
**electromagnet** (-mæ·gnit) *s.* electroimán.
**electromagnetism** (-mæ·gnetišm) *s.* electromagnetismo.
**electromechanical** (-mikæ·nikal) *adj.* electromecánico.
**electrometer** (ilektra·mitøᵣ) *s.* electrómetro.
**electrometry** (-metri) *s.* electrometría.
**electromotive** (ilektromou·tiv) *adj.* electromotor, electromotriz.
**electron** (ile·ktran) *s.* FÍS., QUÍM. electrón. *2 adj.* electrónico; de vacío, termiónico.
**electronic** (ilektra·nik) *adj.* electrónico.
**electronics** (-s) *s.* electrónica.
**electrophorus** (-tra·førøs) *s.* electróforo.
**electroplate (to)** (ile·ktropleit) *tr.* galvanizar [recubrir de metal].
**electroplating** (-ing) *s.* galvanoplastia.
**electroscope** (ile·ktroskoup) *s.* electroscopio.

**electrostatics** (ilektrostæ·tiks) *s.* electrostática.
**electrotechnics** (-te·kniks) *s.* electrotecnia.
**electrotherapy** (-ze·rapi) *s.* electroterapia.
**electrothermancy** (-ze·ᵣmansi), **electrothermics** (-ze·ᵣmiks) *s.* electrotermia.
**electrotype** (ile·ktrotaip) *s.* electrotipo. *2* electrotipia [estampa].
**electrotype (to)** *tr.* electrotipar, reproducir por electrotipia.
**electrotypy** (-i) *s.* electrotipia.
**electrum** (ile·ktrøm) *s.* electro. *2* plata alemana.
**elegance** (e·ligans) *s.* elegancia. *2* refinamiento.
**elegant** (-ant) *adj.* elegante. *2* refinado, delicado.
**elegiac** (elidÿai·æk) *adj.* elegíaco.
**elegize (to)** (e·lidÿaiš) *intr.* escribir una elegía. *2 tr.* llorar o alabar [a uno] en una elegía.
**elegy** (e·lidÿi) *s.* elegía.
**element** (e·limønt) *s.* elemento [en todas sus acepciones]: *the four elements*, los cuatro elementos; *to be in one's ~*, estar en su elemento. *2 pl.* elementos [rudimentos; fuerzas naturales]. *3* el pan y el vino en la Eucaristía.
**elemental** (elime·ntal) *adj.* elemental, esencial. *2* simple [no compuesto]. *3* de los elementos o fuerzas de la naturaleza; comparable a ellos.
**elementary** (-ari) *adj.* elemental [relativo a los elementos o rudimentos], primario: ~ *school*, escuela elemental o primaria. *2* QUÍM. simple.
**elephant** (e·lifant) *s.* ZOOL. elefante.
**elephantiasis** (elifantai·asis) *s.* MED. elefantiasis, elefancía.
**elephantine** (elifæ·ntin) *adj.* elefantino.
**elevate (to)** (e·liveit) *tr.* elevar, levantar, alzar. *2* elevar, encumbrar, engrandecer. *3* levantar los ánimos, alegrar, excitar.
**elevated** (-id) *adj.* elevado: ~ *railroad*, (E.U.) ferrocarril aéreo o elevado. *2* exaltado, encumbrado. *3* animado, gozoso.
**elevation** (-ei·shøn) *s.* elevación [acción, estado]. *2* encumbramiento, exaltación. *3* alteza, altura. *4* GEOGR. altitud. *5* ARQ., DIB. alzado. *6* TOP. cota. *7* LITURG. elevación.
**elevator** (e·liveitøᵣ) *s.* elevador [el o lo que eleva]. *2* montacargas. *3* (E.U.) ascensor. *4* (Ingl.) escalera mecánica. *5* edificio para almacenar granos. *6* AVIA. timón de profundidad.
**eleven** (ile·vøn) *adj.-s.* once: ~ *o'clock*, las once.
**eleventh** (-z) *adj.* onceno, undécimo. *2 adj.-s.* onceavo.
**elf** (elf) *s.* elfo, duende. *2* enano. *3* diablillo [niño travieso].
**elfish** (-ish) *adj.* de elfo o duende. *2* mágico, fantástico. *3* travieso.
**elicit (to)** (i·lisit) *tr.* sacar, sonsacar, arrancar, producir, despertar.
**elide (to)** (ilai·d) *tr.* elidir.
**eligibility** (elidÿibi·liti) *s.* elegibilidad.
**eligible** (e·lidÿibøl) *adj.* elegible. *2* deseable, conveniente.
**Elijah** (ilai·dÿa) *n. pr. m.* Elías.
**eliminate (to)** (ili·mineit) *tr.* eliminar.
**elimination** (-ei·shøn) *s.* eliminación.
**Eliot** (e·liøt) *n. pr. m.* Elías.
**Elisha** (ilai·sha) *n. pr. m.* Eliseo.
**elision** (ili·ÿøn) *s.* elisión.
**elite** (eli·t) *s.* the ~, la flor y nata.
**elixir** (ili·ksøᵣ) *s.* elixir.
**Eliza** (ilai·ša) *n. pr. f.* Elisa. *2* Isabel.
**Elizabeth** (ili·šabez) *n. pr. f.* Isabel.
**elk** (elk) *s.* ZOOL. anta, alce.
**ell** (el) *s.* ana [medida].

**Ellen** (e·løn) *n. pr. f.* Elena.
**ellipse** (eli·ps) *s.* GEOM. elipse.
**ellipsis** (-is) *s.* GRAM. elipsis.
**ellipsoid** (-oid) *s.* GEOM. elipsoide.
**elliptic(al** (-tik(al) *adj.* elíptico.
**elm** (elm) *s.* BOT. olmo, negrillo.
**elocution** (elokiu·shøn) *s.* elocución, declamación.
**éloge** (e·loudŷ) *s.* elogio, oración fúnebre.
**elongate** (ila·ngeit) *adj.* alargado.
**elongate (to)** *tr.* alargar, prolongar. *2 intr.* alargarse, prolongarse.
**elongation** (-ei·shøn) *s.* alargamiento, prolongación, extensión. *2* ASTR. elongación.
**elope (to)** (ilou·p) *intr.* fugarse [con un amante]. *2* escapar, huir, evadirse.
**elopement** (-mønt) *s.* fuga, rapto.
**eloquence** (e·løkuøns) *s.* elocuencia. *2* retórica. *3* prosa literaria.
**eloquent** (-ønt) *adj.* elocuente.
**else** (els) *adj.* más, otro: *nobody ~*, nadie más; *what ~?*, ¿qué más?, ¿qué otra cosa? *2 adv.* de otro modo; en otro tiempo, lugar, dirección, etc.: *how ~?*, ¿de qué otro modo? *3 conj.* si no, de otro modo, en otro caso.
**elsewhere** (-jue·ø<sup>r</sup>) *adv.* en o a otra parte.
**elucidate (to)** (iliu·sideit) *tr.* elucidir, dilucidar, aclarar.
**elucidation** (-ei·shøn) *s.* elucidación, dilucidación, aclaración.
**elude (to)** (i·liud) *tr.* eludir, evadir, evitar, esquivar. *2* escapar [a la observación, etc.].
**elusión** (iliu·ŷøn) *s.* acción de eludir, evasión.
**elusive** (-siv) *adj.* huidizo; que escapa [esp. al entendimiento], vago, impalpable.
**elusory** (-sori) *adj.* ELUSIVE.
**elves** (e·lṽs) *s. pl.* de ELF.
**Elysian** (ili·ŷan) *adj.* elisio, elíseo.
**Elysium** (-ŷøm) *n. pr.* MIT. Elíseo, Elisio.
**elytron** (e·litrøn) *s.* ENT. élitro.
**em** (em) *s.* eme [letra]. *2* cosa en forma de M.
**'em** *pron.* elisión de THEM.
**emaciate (to)** (imei·shieit) *tr.* enflaquecer, demacrar. *2 intr.* demacrarse.
**emaciate(d** (-id) *adj.* flaco, demacrado.
**emaciation** (-ei·shøn) *s.* demacración, emaciación.
**emanate (to)** (e·maneit) *intr.* emanar, brotar, proceder. *2* radiar [estar radiante].
**emanation** (-ei·shøn) *s.* emanación. *2* efluvio.
**emancipate (to)** (imæ·nsipeit) *tr.* emancipar. *2* libertar.
**emancipation** (-ei·shøn) *s.* emancipación.
**emasculate (to)** (imæ·skiuleit) *tr.* castrar, capar. *2* afeminar. *3* debilitar.
**embalm (to)** (emba·m) *tr.* embalsamar [un cadáver]. *2* embalsamar, perfumar.
**embalmment** (-mønt) *s.* embalsamamiento.
**embank (to)** (embæ·nk) *tr.* limitar o proteger con dique o terraplén; represar.
**embankment** (-mønt) *s.* terraplén, dique, malecón, presa.
**embargo** (emba·<sup>r</sup>gou) *s.* embargo o detención [de buques o mercancías, decretado por el gobierno].
**embargo (to)** *tr.* embargar, prohibir [la entrada o salida de buques o mercancías].
**embark (to)** (emba·<sup>r</sup>k) *tr.* embarcar. *2* invertir [dinero en una empresa]. *3 intr.* embarcarse.
**embarkation** (-ei·shøn) *s.* embarco, embarque.
**embarrass (to)** (embæ·ras) *tr.* turbar, confundir, desconcertar. *2* embarazar, estorbar. *3* enredar, embrollar. *4* poner en apuros [de dinero].

**embarrassment** (-mønt) *s.* turbación, perplejidad, compromiso. *2* embarazo, estorbo. *3* complicación, enredo. *4* apuros, dificultades.
**embassador** (embæ·sadø<sup>r</sup>) *s.* AMBASSADOR.
**embassy** (e·mbasi) *s.* embajada.
**embattle (to)** (embæ·tøl) *tr.* MIL. formar en batalla. *2* fortificar, almenar.
**embay (to)** (embei·) *tr.* abrigar o encerrar [buques] en una bahía. *2* cercar, rodear.
**embed (to)** (embe·d) *tr.* encajar, empotrar, incrustrar. ¶ Pret. y p. p.: *embedded;* p. a.: *embedding.*
**embellish (to)** (embe·lish) *tr.* embellecer, hermosear, adornar.
**embellishment** (-mønt) *s.* embellecimiento. *2* adorno.
**ember** (e·mbø<sup>r</sup>) *s.* ascua, pavesa. *2 pl.* rescoldo, brasas. *3* ECLES. *~ days,* témporas.
**embezzle (to)** (embe·šøl) *tr.* desfalcar [apropiarse].
**embezzlement** (-mønt) *s.* desfalco, peculado.
**embitter (to)** (embi·tø<sup>r</sup>) *tr.* amargar, acibarar; agriar. *2* excitar la animosidad de.
**emblazon (to)** (emblei·šøn) *tr.* blasonar. *2* adornar o esmaltar con colores brillantes. *3* celebrar, ensalzar.
**emblazonry** (-ri) *s.* blasón, figuras del blasón.
**emblem** (emble·m) *s.* emblema. *2* símbolo, signo.
**emblem (to)** *tr.* simbolizar.
**emblematic (al** (-æ·tik(al) *adj.* emblemático.
**embodiment** (emba·dimønt) *s.* encarnación, personificación. *2* incorporación, inclusión.
**embody (to)** (emba·di) *tr.* encarnar, personificar. *2* dar forma perceptible [a una idea, etc.]. *3* incorporar, incluir, englobar. *4* organizar en cuerpo. ¶ CONJUG. Pret. y p. p.: *embodied.*
**embolden (to)** (embou·ldøn) *tr.* animar, envalentonar.
**embolism** (e·mbolišm) *s.* ASTR. embolismo. *2* MED. embolia.
**embolus** (e·mboløs) *s.* MED. émbolo.
**embosom (to)** (embu·šøm) *tr.* abrigar o guardar en el seno; abrazar. *2* envolver, encerrar.
**emboss (to)** (embo·s) *tr.* abollonar, realzar, estampar en relieve.
**embossment** (-mønt) *s.* abollonadura, realce, figura en relieve.
**embowel (to)** (embau·øl) *tr.* desentrañar, destripar.
**embower (to)** (-ø<sup>r</sup>) *tr.* emparrar, enramar.
**embrace** (embrei·s) *s.* abrazo.
**embrace (to)** *tr.* abrazar [en todos sus sentidos]. *2* adoptar, seguir. *3* aceptar [una suerte, etc.]; aprovechar [una oportunidad, etc.]. *4 intr.* abrazarse.
**embracing** (-ing) *adj.* abrazador, comprensivo [que incluye]. *2 s.* abrazamiento.
**embrasure** (-ŷø<sup>r</sup>) *s.* ARQ. alféizar. *2* FORT. cañonera, tronera.
**embrocation** (embrokei·shøn) *s.* embrocación.
**embroider (to)** (embroi·dø<sup>r</sup>) *tr.* bordar, recamar. *2* adornar, embellecer.
**embroidery** (-i) *s.* bordado, bordadura; recamado.
**embroil (to)** (embroi·l) *tr.* embrollar, enredar.
**embroilment** (-mønt) *s.* embrollo, enredo, confusión. *2* intriga. *3* alboroto.
**embryo** (e·mbriou) *s.* embrión. *2 adj.* incipiente.
**embryology** (-bria·lodŷi) *s.* embriología.
**embryonic** (-nik) *adj.* embrionario.
**emend (to)** (ime·nd) *tr.* enmendar, corregir.
**emendation** (-ei·shøn) *s.* enmienda, corrección.
**emerald** (e·mørøld) *s.* esmeralda.
**emerge (to)** (imø·<sup>r</sup>dŷ) *intr.* emerger. *2* salir, aparecer, surgir. *3* salir [de una situación, etc.].

**emergence** (-øns) *s.* emergencia. *2* salida, aparición. *3* BOT. prominencia.
**emergency** (-i) *s.* emergencia, apuro, caso de necesidad; urgencia: ~ *exit,* salida de auxilio; ~ *hospital,* hospital de urgencia; ~ *landing,* aterrizaje forzoso.
**emergent** (ime·ʳdȳønt) *adj.* emergente. *2* urgente. *3* súbito.
**emeritus** (ime·ritøs) *adj.* emérito.
**emersion** (ime·ʳshøn) *s.* emergencia, emersión.
**emery** (e·møri) *s.* esmeril.
**emery (to)** *tr.* cubrir de esmeril. *2* esmerilar. ¶ Pret. y p. p.: *emeried.*
**emetic** (eme·tik) *adj.-s.* emético.
**emigrant** (e·migrant) *adj.* emigrante. *2 s.* emigrante, emigrado.
**emigrate (to)** (-greit) *intr.* emigrar.
**emigration** (emigrei·shøn) *s.* emigración.
**Emily** (e·mili) *n. pr. f.* Emilia.
**eminence** (e·minøns) *s.* eminencia, altura. *2* eminencia, distinción. *3* eminencia [título].
**eminent** (e·minønt) *adj.* eminente. *2* relevante; manifiesto; notable.
**emir** (emi·øʳ) *s.* emir.
**emissary** (emi·seri) *s.* emisario, agente secreto, espía. *2* canal, conducto, orificio de salida.
**emission** (-shøn) *s.* emisión. | No tiene el sentido de emisión de radio.
**emit (to)** (emi·t) *tr.* emitir. *2* dar [una orden o decreto].
**emitter** (-øʳ) *s.* emisor.
**Emma** (e·ma) *n. pr. f.* Ema, Manuela.
**Emmanuel** (imæ·niuøl) *n. pr. m.* Manuel.
**emollient** (ima·liønt) *adj.-s.* emoliente.
**emolument** (ima·liumønt) *s.* emolumento.
**emotion** (imou·shøn) *s.* emoción. *2* afecto del ánimo. *3* agitación, perturbación.
**emotional** (-al) *adj.* emocional. *2* emotivo, impresionable.
**empanel (to)** (empa·nøl) *tr.* TO IMPANEL.
**emperor** (e·mpørøʳ) *s.* emperador.
**emperorship** (-ship) *s.* imperio, dignidad imperial.
**emphasis** (e·mfasis) *s.* énfasis. *2* insistencia, intensidad, fuerza, relieve. *3* recancanilla.
**emphasize (to)** (saiš) *tr.* dar énfasis a. *2* recalcar, acentuar, subrayar, poner de relieve, hacer hincapié en.
**emphatic (al** (emfæ·tik) *adj.* enfático. *2* categórico, enérgico, fuerte, acentuado, marcado.
**emphysema** (emfisi·ma) *s.* MED. enfisema.
**emphyteusis** (-tiu·sis) *s.* DER. enfiteusis.
**empire** (e·mpair) *s.* imperio. *2* (E.U.) *Empire State,* estado de Nueva York.
**empiric** (empi·rik) *adj.-s.* empírico. *2 s.* curandero, charlatán.
**empiricism** (-risiøm) *s.* empirismo. *2* curanderismo, charlatanismo.
**emplacement** (emplei·smønt) *s.* emplazamiento, situación.
**employ** (emploi·) *s.* empleo, puesto, servicio: *to be in one's ~,* estar al servicio de uno.
**employ (to)** *tr.* emplear. *2* ocupar [dar trabajo].
**employee** (emploiˑ) *s.* empleado, dependiente.
**employer** (emploi·ør) *s.* dueño, patrón, principal, el que emplea.
**employment** (-mønt) *s.* empleo. *2* ocupación, trabajo, colocación. *3* profesión, oficio.
**empoison (to)** (empoi·šøn) *tr.* envenenar, corromper, inficionar.

**emporium** (empo·riøm) *s.* emporio. *2* almacén, bazar.
**empower (to)** (empou·øʳ) *tr.* autorizar, facultar, comisionar, dar poder, habilitar.
**empress** (e·mpris) *f.* emperatriz.
**emptiness** (e·mptinis) *s.* vacío, vacuidad. *2* futilidad, vanidad.
**empty** (e·mpti) *adj.* vacío. *2* vacante. *3* vacuo, vano. *4* ignorante. *5* frívolo. *6* desprovisto [de]. *7* fam. hambriento.
**empty (to)** *tr.* vaciar, evacuar, desocupar. *2* descargar, verter. *3* *intr.* vaciarse. *4* GEOGR. desaguar.
**empty-handed** *adj.* manivacío.
**empty-headed** (adj.) tonto, de cabeza vacía.
**empurple (to)** (empø·ʳpøl) *tr.* purpurar.
**empyrean** (empi·rian) *adj.-s.* empíreo.
**emu** (ɪ·miu) *s.* ORN. emeu.
**emulate (to)** (e·miuleit) *tr.* emular. *2* rivalizar con.
**emulation** (-ei·shøn) *s.* emulación. *2* rivalidad.
**emulous** (e·miuløs) *adj.* émulo, competidor.
**emulsify (to)** (imø·lsifai) *tr.* emulsionar.
**emulsion** (imø·lshøn) *s.* emulsión.
**en** (en) *s.* ene [letra].
**enable (to)** (enei·bøl) *tr.* habilitar, capacitar, facultar. *2* hacer posible, permitir, facilitar.
**enact (to)** (e·nækt) *tr.* aprobar y sancionar [una ley]. *2* establecer, estatuir, decretar. *3* TEAT. representar [una escena]; desempeñar [un papel o el papel de].
**enactment** (-mønt) *s.* aprobación y sanción [de una ley]. *2* ley, norma, decreto.
**enallage** (enæ·ladȳi) *s.* GRAM. enálage.
**enamel** (-møl) *s.* esmalte.
**enamel (to)** *tr.* esmaltar. *2* charolar [papel, cuero, etc.]. ¶ Pret. y p. p.: *enameled* o *-lled;* ger.: *enameling* o *-lling.*
**enamo(u)r (to)** (enæ·møʳ) *tr.* enamorar.
**enamo(u)red** (-d) *adj.* enamorado, prendado.
**encamp (to)** (enkæ·mp) *tr.-intr.* acampar.
**encampment** (-mønt) *s.* acampamento. *2* campamento.
**encage (to)** (enkei·dȳ) *tr.* enjaular.
**encase (to)** (enkei·s) *tr.* TO INCASE.
**encash (to)** (enka·sh) *tr.* (Ingl.) convertir en dinero, hacer efectivo.
**encaustic** (enko·stik) *adj.* PINT. encáustico. *2 s.* PINT. encauste, encausto.
**encave (to)** (enkei·v) *tr.* encovar. *2* embodegar.
**enceinte** (ansæ·nt) *s.* ARQ., FORT. recinto. *2 adj.* gal. encinta, embarazada [mujer].
**encephalic** (ensefæ·lik) *adj.* ANAT. encefálico.
**encephalon** (ense·falan) *s.* ANAT. encéfalo.
**enchain (to)** (enchei·n) *tr.* encadenar.
**enchainment** (-mønt) *s.* encadenamiento.
**enchant (to)** (encha·nt) *tr.* encantar, hechizar.
**enchanting** (-ing) *adj.* encantador, embelesador.
**enchantment** (-mønt) *s.* encantamiento, hechicería. *2* encanto, hechizo, embeleso.
**enchantress** (-tris) *s.* encantadora, hechicera.
**enchase (to)** (enchei·s) *tr.* engastar, embutir, incrustar.
**encircle (to)** (ensø·ʳkøl) *tr.* abrazar, ceñir. *2* rodear; cercar, circundar, circunvalar.
**encirclement** (-mønt) *s.* cerco, rodeo, circunvalación.
**enclave** (e·nkleiv) *s.* enclavado.
**enclitic** (enkli·tik) *adj.-s.* enclítico.
**encloister (to)** (enkloi·støʳ) *tr.* enclaustrar.
**enclose (to)** (enklou·š) *tr.* encerrar, cercar, rodear. *2* incluir, englobar; acompañar, enviar adjunto.
**enclosure** (enklou·ȳøʳ) *s.* cercamiento, encerra-

miento. *2* cerca, vallado, reja. *3* cercado, recinto, coto. *4* documento que acompaña a una carta; anexo.

**encomium** (enkou·miøn) *s.* encomio, elogio.

**encompass (to)** (enkø·mpas) *tr.* cercar, rodear, ceñir, circundar. *2* abarcar, comprender.

**encore** (angko·ʳ) *interj.* ¡que se repita! *2 s.* TEAT. repetición [pedida por el público].

**encounter** (enkau·ntøʳ) *s.* encuentro, choque, combate. *2* encuentro [cara a cara].

**encounter (to)** *tr.* encontrar, tropezar con. *2* combatir, luchar con. *3 intr.* encontrarse, entrevistarse. *4* luchar.

**encourage (to)** (enkø·ridy̆) *tr.* alentar, animar, dar alas a. *2* incitar. *3* estimular, fomentar. *4* dar pábulo a.

**encouragement** (-mønt) *s.* aliento, ánimo. *2* estímulo, fomento, pábulo.

**encouraging** (-ing) *adj.* alentador.

**encroach (to)** (enkrou·ch) *intr.* pasar los límites de, usurpar, invadir, intrusarse, abusar. | Gralte. con *on* o *upon.*

**encroachment** (-mønt) *s.* usurpación, intrusión, abuso, intromisión.

**encumber (to)** (enkø·mbøʳ) *tr.* embarazar, estorbar.' *2* cargar, abrumar, gravar.

**encumbrance** (-brans) *s.* embarazo, estorbo. *2* carga, gravamen.

**encyclical** (ensi·klikal) *s.* encíclica.

**encyclopaedia, encyclopedia** (ensaiklopi·dia) *s.* enciclopedia.

**encyst (to)** (ensi·st) *tr.* enquistar. *2 intr.* enquistarse.

**end** (end) *s.* fin, cabo, extremo, punta, cola, remate: *at loose ends*, en desorden, desarreglado; *on* ~, derecho, de pie, de canto; de punta, erizado; seguido, consecutivo. *2* cabo, trozo, retazo, colilla. *3* fin, cabo, término, conclusión, muerte: *to come to an* ~, acabarse; terminarse; *to make an* ~ *of*, acabar con; *at the* ~ *of*, al final, a fines de; *in the* ~, al fin, a la larga; *no* ~ *of*, un sinfín de, la mar de. *4* fin, objeto, mira: *to the* ~ *that*, a fin de que. *5* consecuencia, resultado: *to no* ~, sin efecto, en vano. *6* FÚTBOL extremo.

**end (to)** *tr.* acabar, terminar, concluir, poner fin a. *2 intr.* acabar, terminar, finalizar: *to* ~ *in*, acabar en. *3* cesar, morir. *4 to* ~ *by*, acabar por.

**endanger (to)** (endei·ndy̆øʳ) *tr.* poner en peligro, comprometer, arriesgar.

**endear (to)** (endr·øʳ) *tr.* hacer amar, hacer querido o amado.

**endearing** (-ing) *adj.* cariñoso.

**endearment** (-mønt) *s.* acción de hacer querer. *2* lo que excita el afecto. *3* fiesta, caricia.

**endeavo(u)r** (ende·vøʳ) *s.* esfuerzo, empeño, tentativa.

**endeavo(u)r (to)** *intr.* esforzarse, empeñarse, hacer lo posible, tratar, procurar.

**endemic** (ende·mic) *adj.* endémico. *2 s.* endemia.

**ending** (e·nding) *s.* fin, final, parte final; conclusión, desenlace. *2* acabamiento; muerte. *3* GRAM. terminación, desinencia. *4* MÚS. coda.

**endive** (-iv) *s.* BOT. endibia, escarola.

**endless** (-lis) *adj.* inacabable, interminable, sin fin. *2* continuo, incesante, perpetuo, eterno. *3* infinito.

**endmost** (-moust) *adj.* más remoto, extremo.

**endocardium** (endoka·ʳdiøm) *s.* ANAT. endocardio.

**endocarp** (e·ndoka·ʳp) *s.* BOT. endocarpio.

**endocrine** (-krain) *adj.* FISIOL. endocrino.

**endoderm** (-døʳm) *s.* BIOL. endodermo.

**endogenous** (enda·dy̆inøs) *adj.* H. NAT. endógeno.

**endolymph** (e·ndolimf) *s.* ANAT. endolinfa.

**endorse (to)** (endo·ʳs) *tr.* COM. endosar. *2* respaldar [un documento]. *3* aprobar, sancionar.

**endorsee** (-ı) *s.* endosado, endosatario.

**endorsement** (-mønt) *s.* endoso. *2* aval, garantía, aprobación.

**endorser** (-øʳ) *s.* endosante.

**endosmosis** (endosmou·sis) *s.* FÍS. endósmosis.

**endosperm** (e·ndospøʳm) *s.* BOT. endospermo.

**endow (to)** (endau·) *tr.* dotar [una fundación, instituto, etc.]. *2* dotar [de una cualidad, etc.].

**endowment** (-mønt) *s.* dotación [acción; cantidad con que se dota], fundación. *2* dote, don, prenda personal.

**endue (to)** (endiu·) *tr.* dotar, proveer [de cualidades, etc.]. *2* investir. *3* vestir.

**endurance** (-rans) *s.* sufrimiento. *2* paciencia, resistencia, aguante: *to be beyond* ~, ser insoportable. *3* duración, continuación.

**endure (to)** (-øʳ) *tr.* soportar, sufrir, aguantar, resistir. *2* durar, perdurar.

**enduring** (-ring) *adj.* paciente, sufrido, resistente. *2* constante. *3* durable, permanente.

**endways** (e·ndweiš), **endwise** (e·ndwaiš) *adv.* de punta, de pie, derecho. *2* longitudinalmente.

**enema** (eni·ma) *s.* MED. enema.

**enemy** (e·nømi) *adj.-s.* enemigo.

**energetic (al** (enøʳdy̆e·tik(al) *adj.* enérgico, vigoroso.

**energize (to)** (e·nøʳdy̆aiš) *tr.* dar energía, vigorizar. *2 intr.* obrar con energía.

**energumen** (enøʳ·giu·men) *s.* energúmeno.

**energy** (e·nøʳdy̆i) *s.* energía.

**enervate** (e·nøʳveit) *adj.* enervado, debilitado.

**enervate (to)** *tr.* enervar, debilitar.

**enervating** (-ting) *adj.* enervante, enervador.

**enfeeble (to)** (enfı·bøl) *tr.* debilitar, enervar.

**enfeoff (to)** (enfe·f) *tr.* enfeudar, infeudar. *2* investir con un feudo.

**enfilade** (enfilei·d) *s.* MIL. enfilada.

**enfilade (to)** *tr.* MIL. enfilar.

**enfold (to)** (enfou·ld) *tr.* envolver. *2* abrazar.

**enforce (to)** (enfo·ʳs) *tr.* dar fuerza a. *2* poner en vigor, hacer cumplir [una ley, etc.]. *3* obtener por la fuerza, imponer [obediencia, etc.]. *4* forzar [un paso]. *5* hacer valer [argumentos, razones].

**enfranchise (to)** (enfræ·nchaiš) *tr.* franquear, manumitir. *2* conceder privilegios o derechos políticos. *3* dar carta de naturaleza.

**engage (to)** (engei·dy̆) *tr.* comprometer, empeñar. *2* ajustar, tomar, contratar; alistar; alquilar; hacerse reservar [una habitación, etc.]. *3* ocupar, absorber, atraer, cautivar. *4* trabar batalla, conversación, etc.]. *5* MEC., ARQ. endentar, encajar, empotrar. *6 intr.* comprometerse, obligarse. *7* prometerse: *engaged couple*, novios. *8* entrar [en batalla, conversación, etc.]. *9* ocuparse. *10* MEC. engranar, encajar.

**engagement** (-mønt) *s.* compromiso, obligación; cita. *2* palabra de casamiento; esponsales; noviazgo. *3* ajuste, contrato. *4* TEAT. contrata. *5* colocación, acomodo. *6* MIL. encuentro, combate. *7* MEC. engranaje; acoplamiento.

**engaging** (-ing) *adj.* atractivo, simpático.

**engender (to)** (endy̆e·ndøʳ) *tr.* engendrar. *2 intr.* engendrarse, nacer, formarse.

**engine** (e·ndy̆in) *s.* ingenio, artefacto, mecánico, máquina, motor; locomotora: ~ *driver*, FERROC.

maquinista; ~ *fitter*, montador; ~ *trouble*, ~ *failure*, avería del motor.

**engineer** (endŷinɪˑʳ) *s.* ingeniero. *2* maquinista.

**engineer (to)** *tr.* proyectar, dirigir [como ingeniero]. *2* gestionar, manejar, conducir. *3 intr.* hacer de ingeniero o maquinista. *4* darse maña.

**engineering** (-ring) *s.* ingeniería. *2* dirección, manejo

**enginery** (eˑndŷinri) *s.* maquinaria. *2* ingenios o máquinas de guerra. *3* astucias, tretas.

**England** (iˑngland) *n. pr.* GEOGR. Inglaterra.

**Englander** (-øʳ) *s.* inglés [natural de Inglaterra].

**English** (iˑnglish) *adj.* y *s.* inglés: ~ *Channel*, GEOGR. Canal de la Mancha. *2 s.* efecto [en el billar].

**Englishman** (-mæn) *s.* inglés [hombre]. *2* MAR. buque inglés.

**Englishwoman** (-wumæn) *s.* inglesa.

**englut (to)** (engløˑt) *tr.* engullir.

**engorge (to)** (engoˑʳdŷ) *tr.* engullir, devorar. *2* atracar [de comida]. *3 intr.* comer con voracidad.

**engraft (to)** (engræˑft) *tr.* injertar, enjertar.

**engrailed** (engreiˑid) *adj.* angrelado.

**engrain (to)** (engreiˑn) *tr.* teñir en rama. *2* imbuir, inculcar.

**engrave (to)** (engreiˑv) *tr.* grabar, cincelar. *2* grabar [en la memoria, etc.]. *3* imprimir [un grabado].

**engraver** (-øʳ) *s.* grabador.

**engraving** (-ing) *s.* grabado. *2* lámina, estampa.

**engross (to)** (engrouˑs) *tr.* poner en limpio, copiar o transcribir caligráficamente. *2* absorber, acaparar, monopolizar.

**engrossing** (-ing) *adj.* monopolizador, acaparador, absorbente.

**engulf (to)** (engøˑlf) *tr.* engolfar, sumergir, sumir.

**enhance (to)** (enjaˑns) *tr.* acrecentar, intensificar, engrandecer. *2* realzar, dar mayor valor. *3* exaltar, elevar. *4* ensalzar, encarecer.

**enharmonic** (enjaˑrmoˑnik) *adj.* MÚS. enarmónico.

**enhearten (to)** (enjaˑrtøn) *tr.* alentar, animar.

**enigma** (iniˑgma) *s.* enigma.

**enigmatic (al** (inigmæˑtik(al) *adj.* enigmático.

**enjoin (to)** (endŷoiˑn) *tr.* mandar, ordenar, prescribir, encargar. *2 to* ~ *from*, prohibir, vedar.

**enjoy (to)** (endŷoiˑ) *tr.* gozar o disfrutar de, tener, poseer. *2* gozar con o en; gustar, saborear; gustar de. *3 to* ~ *oneself*, divertirse, deleitarse.

**enjoyable** (-abøl) *adj.* agradable, deleitable.

**enjoyment** (-mønt) *s.* goce, disfrute; uso, usufructo. *2* fruición. *3* gusto, placer, solaz.

**enkindle (to)** (enkiˑndøl) *tr.* encender, inflamar.

**enlace (to)** (enleiˑs) *tr.* enlazar, entrelazar. *2* rodear, ceñir.

**enlarge (to)** (enlaˑʳdŷ) *tr.* agrandar. *2* engrosar, aumentar. *3* ensanchar, ampliar, extender. *4* amplificar. *5 intr.* agrandarse, ensancharse, extenderse. *6 to* ~ *upon*, extenderse sobre [un tema, etc.].

**enlargement** (-mønt) *s.* agrandamiento, ensanchamiento, extensión, etc. *2* FOT. ampliación.

**enlarger** (-øʳ) *s.* ampliador, amplificador. *2* FOT. ampliadora.

**enlighten (to)** (enlaiˑtøn) *tr.* iluminar, alumbrar. *2* ilustrar, instruir. *3* aclarar, esclarecer.

**enlightened** (-d) *adj.* ilustrado, culto.

**enlightenment** (-mønt) *s.* ilustración, luces, instrucción, cultura. *2* esclarecimiento. *3 the Enlightenment*, movimiento filosófico del siglo XVIII.

**enlist (to)** (enliˑst) *tr.* alistar, enrolar. *2* enganchar, reclutar. *3 intr.* alistarse, sentar plaza.

**enliven (to)** (enlaiˑvøn) *tr.* avivar, vivificar. *2* animar, alegrar, alentar.

**enmesh (to)** (enmeˑsh) *tr.* coger, enredar [en mallas o redes]. *2 tr.-intr.* endentar, engranar.

**enmity** (eˑnmiti) *s.* enemistad, hostilidad.

**ennoble (to)** (enouˑbøl) *tr.* ennoblecer.

**ennui** (anuiˑ) *s.* tedio, fastidio, aburrimiento.

**enology** (inaˑlodŷi) *s.* OENOLOGY.

**enormity** (inoˑʳmiti) *s.* enormidad, exceso, demasía, atrocidad.

**enormous** (inoˑʳmøs) *adj.* enorme, descomunal. *2* perverso, atroz.

**enough** (inøˑf) *adj.* bastante, suficiente. *2 s.* lo bastante, lo suficiente. *3 interj.* ¡basta!, ¡bueno! *4 adv.* bastante, suficientemente.

**enounce (to)** (inauˑns) *tr.* enunciar. *2* presentar, aducir [un argumento, etc.]. *3* pronunciar [palabras]. *4* declarar, anunciar.

**enquire (to)** = TO INQUIRE.

**enrage (to)** (enreiˑdŷ) *tr.* enfurecer, encolerizar, exasperar, llenar de rabia.

**enrapt** (enræˑpt) *adj.* arrobado, extasiado.

**enrapture (to)** (enræˑpchøʳ) *tr.* arrebatar, arrobar, extasiar, transportar, enajenar.

**enrich (to)** (enriˑch) *tr.* enriquecer. *2* AGR. fertilizar. *3* realzar el gusto, el olor, el color de.

**enrobe (to)** (enrouˑb) *tr.* vestir, adornar.

**enrol(l (to)** (enrouˑl) *tr.* alistar, matricular, empadronar, inscribir, registrar. *2* enrollar, envolver. *3 intr.* alistarse, inscribirse, sentar plaza.

**enrol(l)ment** (enrouˑlmønt) *s.* alistamiento, empadronamiento, inscripción. *2* registro, padrón.

**ensanguine (to)** (ensæˑngüin) *tr.* ensangrentar.

**ensconce (to)** (enskaˑns) *tr.* esconder. *2* acomodar, situar, poner en sitio cómodo o seguro.

**ensemble** (angsaˑmbøl) *s.* conjunto, totalidad. *2* conjunto [vestido de mujer].

**enshrine (to)** (enshraiˑn) *tr.* envolver, encerrar, guardar [como una cosa preciosa, sagrada].

**enshroud (to)** (enshrauˑd) *tr.* amortajar. *2* envolver, ocultar.

**ensign** (eˑnsain) *s.* bandera, pabellón, enseña. *2* insignia, divisa. *3* (E.U.) alférez [de marina].

**ensign-bearer** *s.* abanderado.

**ensilage** (eˑnsilidŷ) *s.* ensilaje.

**ensilage (to)** *tr.* ensilar.

**enslave (to)** (ensleiˑv) *tr.* esclavizar.

**enslavement** (ensleiˑvmønt) *s.* avasallamiento. *2* esclavitud, servidumbre.

**ensnare (to)** (ensneˑøʳ) *tr.* entrampar, coger en una trampa. *2* tender un lazo a, atraer, seducir.

**ensue (to)** (ensiuˑ) *intr.* seguir, suceder, sobrevenir. *2* seguirse, resultar.

**ensuing** (ensiuˑing) *adj.* siguiente. *2* resultante.

**ensure (to)** (enshuˑʳ) *tr.* asegurar, garantizar.

**entablature** (entæˑblachuʳ) *s.* ARQ. entablamento, cornisamiento.

**entail** (enteiˑl) *s.* DER. vinculación, vínculo. *2* bienes vinculados, mayorazgo.

**entail (to)** *tr.* vincular [bienes]. *2* suponer, traer consigo, ocasionar, acarrear.

**entangle (to)** (entæˑngøl) *tr.* enredar, enmarañar, intrincar. *2* enredar [a uno].

**entanglement** (-mønt) *s.* enredo, maraña, enmarañamiento, complicación.

**enter (to)** (eˑntøʳ) *tr.* entrar en o por: *to* ~ *a room*, entrar en una habitación. *2* ingresar en, afiliarse a, hacerse socio de. *3* inscribir o inscribirse para. *4* entrar, meter, introducir. *5* anotar, inscribir, registrar. *6* DER. *to* ~ *an action*, entablar una acción. *7 intr.* entrar. *8* ingresar. *9* penetrar, introducirse. *10* TEAT. salir, entrar en escena. *11 to* ~ *into*, entrar en, formar parte de. *12 to* ~ *on* o *upon*, comenzar, emprender.

**enteric** (ente·rik) *adj.* ANAT. entérico.

**enteritis** (entørai·tis o -itis) *s.* MED. enteritis.

**enterprise** (e·ntø<sup>r</sup>praiš) *s.* empresa, demanda [acción u obra que se emprende]. *2* energía, resolución. *3* carácter emprendedor.

**enterprising** (-ing) *adj.* emprendedor, atrevido, activo.

**entertain (to)** (entø<sup>r</sup>tei·n) *tr.* entretener, divertir. *2* tener [como huésped o invitado]; hospedar, agasajar. *3* tomar en consideración. *4* tener, acariciar, abrigar, [ideas, sentimientos]. *5 intr.* recibir huéspedes, dar comidas o fiestas.

**entertainer** (-ø<sup>r</sup>) *s.* anfitrión. *2* entretenedor. *3* actor, músico [esp. de variedades].

**entertaining** (-ing) *adj.* entretenido, divertido.

**entertainment** (-mønt) *s.* acogida, hospitalidad; convite, agasajo, fiesta. *2* entretenimiento, diversión; función, espectáculo.

**enthrall (to)** (enzro·l) *tr.* esclavizar, sojuzgar. *2* hechizar, cautivar.

**enthrone (to)** (enzrou·n) *tr.* entronizar.

**enthronement** (-mønt) *s.* entronización.

**enthuse (to)** (enzu·š) *intr.* fam. entusiasmarse.

**enthusiasm** (enzu·šiæšm) *s.* entusiasmo.

**enthusiastic(al** (en·iušsiæ·stik(al) *adj.* entusiástico, entusiasta, caluroso. *2* entusiasmado.

**enthymeme** (e·nzimɪm) *s.* LÓG. entimema.

**entice (to)** (entai·s) *tr.* atraer, tentar, incitar.

**enticement** (-mønt) *s.* tentación, incitación. *2* atractivo, cebo.

**entire** (entai·ø<sup>r</sup>) *adj.* entero, completo, cabal, íntegro, total. *2* VET., BOT. entero.

**entirely** (-li) *adv.* enteramente, íntegramente, completamente, del todo, por completo.

**entirety** (-ti) *s.* integridad, entereza, totalidad.

**entitle (to)** (entai·tøl) *tr.* titular, intitular. *2* dar derecho a; autorizar.

**entity** (e·ntiti) *s.* FILOS. entidad.

**entomb (to)** (entu·m) *tr.* enterrar, sepultar. *2* servir de tumba a.

**entomology** (entoma·lodŷi) *s.* entomología.

**entourage** (angtura·dŷ) *s.* gal. medio ambiente, gente que rodea a uno.

**entozoan** (entošou·an) *adj.-s.* entozoario.

**entr'acte** (angtra·kt) *s.* gal. entreacto.

**entrails** (e·ntreilš) *s. pl.* entrañas, vísceras. *2* entrañas [interior].

**entrance** (e·ntrans) *s.* entrada, acceso, ingreso: *no* ~, *se prohíbe la entrada. *2* entrada [por donde se entra], puerta, zaguán. *3* boca, embocadura. *4* MÚS. entrada.

**entrance (to)** (entræ·ns) *tr.* extasiar, arrebatar, hechizar.

**entranceway** (e·ntranswei) *s.* entrada, portal.

**entrant** (e·ntrant) *adj.* entrante. *2 s.* socio nuevo. *3* principiante. *4* DEP. participante.

**entrap (to)** (entræ·p) *tr.* entrampar [coger o hacer caer en una trampa], atrapar, engañar. ¶ Pret. y p. p.: *entrapped;* ger.: *entrapping*.

**entreat (to)** (entrɪ·t) *tr.-intr.* suplicar, rogar, solicitar, instar, implorar, conjurar.

**entreaty** (-i) *s.* súplica, ruego, instancia.

**entrechat** (antrøcha·) *s.* trenzado [en el baile].

**entrée** (angtrei·) *s.* gal. entrada [derecho de entrar]. *2* COC. principio, entrada.

**entrench (to)** (entre·nch) *tr.* atrincherar. *2 intr. to* ~ *on* o *upon*, invadir, transgredir, infringir.

**entrenchment** (-mønt) *s.* atrincheramiento.

**entrepreneur** (antrøprønø·<sup>r</sup>) *s.* empresario [esp. de teatro]; contratista.

**entresol** (a·ntrøsol) *s.* gal. entresuelo.

**entrust (to)** (entrø·st) *tr.* confiar, dejar al cuidado de. *2 to* ~ *one with*, confiar a uno [una cosa].

**entry** (e·ntri) *s.* entrada, ingreso. *2* puerta, portal, vestíbulo, zaguán. *4* asiento, anotación. *5* artículo [de diccionario]. *6* COM. partida: *double* ~, partida doble. *7* DEP. lista de participantes. *8* MÚS. entrada.

**entwine (to)** (entwai·n) *tr.* entrelazar, entretejer. *2* enroscar [alrededor de], enlazar, abrazar.

**entwist (to)** (entwi·st) *tr.* torcer, retorcer. *2* enroscar [alrededor de].

**enucleate (to)** (iniu·klieit) *tr.* explicar, aclarar. *2* CIR. enuclear.

**enumerate (to)** (iniu·møreit) *tr.* enumerar. *2* contar, numerar.

**enumeration** (-ei·shøn) *s.* enumeración. *2* recuento, censo.

**enunciate (to)** (inø·nshieit) *tr.* enunciar. *2* articular, pronunciar.

**enunciation** (-ei·shøn) *s.* enunciación. *2* pronunciación.

**envelop (to)** (enve·løp) *tr.* envolver, cubrir, forrar.

**envelope** (e·nvøloup) *s.* envoltura, cubierta. *2* funda, carpeta. *3* sobre, sobrecarta.

**envelopment** (mønt) *s.* envolvimiento. *2* envoltura, cubierta.

**envenom (to)** (enve·nøm) *tr.* envenenar, emponzoñar [hacer venenoso]. *2* viciar, corromper.

**enviable** (e·nviabøl) *adj.* envidiable.

**envious** (e·nviøs) *adj.* envidioso.

**environ (to)** (envai·røn) *tr.* rodear, cercar.

**environment** (-mønt) *s.* ambiente, medio ambiente. *2* alrededores.

**environs** (envai·rønš) *s. pl.* contornos, alrededores, cercanías, inmediaciones, afueras.

**envisage (to)** (envi·šidŷ) *tr.* mirar a la cara. *2* encararse con, afrontar. *3* mirar, considerar. *4* representar, imaginarse.

**envoy** (e·nvoi) *s.* enviado, mensajero. *2* LIT. envío.

**envy** (e·nvi) *s,* envidia.

**envy (to)** (e·nvi) *tr.* envidiar. *2* anhelar, codiciar.

**enwrap (to)** (enræ·p) *tr.* envolver, cubrir, abrigar. *2* absorber, embargar.

**enwreathe (to)** (enrɪ·d) *tr.* enguirnaldar. *2* envolver, rodear.

**enzyme** (e·nšaim o -šim) *s.* BIOQUÍM. enzima.

**Eocene** (i·osin) *adj.-s.* GEOL. eoceno.

**Eolian** (iou·lian) *adj.-s.* AEOLIAN.

**eolithic** (ioli·zik) *adj.* PREHIST. eolítico.

**eon** (i·øn) *s.* eón, evo.

**epact** (i·pæct) *s.* epacta.

**epaulet** (e·polet) *s.* MIL. charretera, capona.

**ephebe** (e·fib) *s.* efebo.

**ephemera** (efe·møra) *s.* EPHEMERON.

**ephemeral** (efe·møral) *adj.* efímero.

**ephemeris** (efe·møris) *s.* efemérides astronómicas.

**ephemeron** (efe·møran) *s.* ENT. efímera, cachipolla.

**Ephesus** (e·føsøs) *n. pr.* GEOGR. Éfeso.

**ephod** (e·fad) *s.* efod.

**epic** (e·pic) *adj.* épico. *2 s.* epopeya. *3* épica.

**epical** (e·pikal) *adj.* épico.

**epicarp** (e·pika<sup>r</sup>p) *s.* BOT. epicarpio.

**epicedium** (episɪ·diøm) *s.* epicedio, elegía.

**epicene** (e·pisin) *adj.* GRAM. epiceno.

**epicentra, epicenter** (e·pisentø<sup>r</sup>) *s.* GEOL. epicentro.

**epicure** (e·pikiu<sup>r</sup>) *s.* epicúreo, gastrónomo, sibarita.

**Epicurean** (epikiurŕan) *adj.-s.* FIL. epicúreo. *2* (con min.) epicúreo, sibarita.
**Epicureanism** (-išm) *s.* epicureismo.
**epicycloid** (episai·kloid) *s.* GEOM. epicicloide.
**epidemic** (epide·mik) *adj.* epidémico. *2 s.* epidemia.
**epidermis** (-dø·ŕmis) *s.* epidermis, cutícula.
**epigastrium** (epigæ·striøm) *s.* ANAT. epigastrio.
**epiglottis** (-glo·tis) *s.* ANAT. epiglotis.
**epigram** (e·pigræm) *s.* epigrama.
**epigrammatic** (al (epigramæ·tik(al) *adj.* epigramático.
**epigraph** (e·pigræf) *s.* epígrafe.
**epigraphy** (epi·grafi) *s.* epigrafía.
**epilepsy** (e·pilepsi) *s.* MED. epilepsia.
**epileptic** (epile·ptik) *adj.-s.* epiléptico.
**epilogize** (to) (epi·lodÿaiš) *tr.* poner epílogo a. *2 intr.* recitar o pronunciar un epílogo.
**epilogue** (e·pilog) *s.* epílogo.
**epinicion** (-ni·shøn) *s.* epinicio, himno triunfal.
**Epiphany** (ipi·fani) *n. pr.* Epifanía.
**epiphonema** (epifoni·ma) *s.* RET. epifonema.
**epiphysis** (epi·fisis) *s.* ANAT. epífisis.
**epiphyte** (e·pifait) *s.* BOT. epifito.
**Epirus** (ipai·røs) *n. pr.* GEOGR. El Epiro.
**episcopacy** (ipi·skopasi) *s.* episcopado.
**episcopal** (ipi·skopal) *adj.* episcopal.
**Episcopalian** (ipiskopei·lian) *adj.-s.* de la iglesia episcopal protestante.
**episcopate** (ipi·skopeit) *s.* episcopado.
**episode** (e·pisoud) *s.* episodio.
**episodic** (al (episa·dik(al) *adj.* episódico. *2* esporádico, ocasional.
**epistle** (ipi·søl) *s.* epístola, carta, misiva. *2* (con may.) Epístola [de la misa].
**epistolary** (ipi·stoleri) *adj.* epistolar. *2 s.* ECLES. epistolario.
**epitaph** (e·pitæf) *s.* epitafio.
**epithalamium** (epizalei·miøm) *s.* epitalamio.
**epithelium** (epizi·lium) *s.* ANAT. epitelio.
**epithet** (e·pizet) *s.* epíteto.
**epitome** (epi·tomi) *s.* epítome.
**epitomize** (to) (-aiš) *tr.* epitomar, compendiar.
**epizooty** (epišo·ati) *s.*VET. epizootia.
**epoch** (e·pok) *s.* época, edad, período.
**epoch-making** *adj.* trascendental, memorable, que hace época.
**epode** (e·poud) *s.* epodo.
**eponym** (e·ponim) *s.* personaje o héroe epónimo.
**eponymous** (epa·nimøs) *adj.* epónimo.
**epopee** (e·popi) *s.* epopeya. *2* épica.
**Epsom-salt** (e·psømsolt) *s.* QUÍM. sal de la Higuera.
**equable** (e·kuabøl) *adj.* igual, uniforme. *2* tranquilo, ecuánime.
**equal** (ı·kual) *adj.* igual. *2* distribuido o formado con igualdad. *3* justo, equitativo, imparcial. *4* adecuado, suficiente. *5 to be ~ to*, servir para, poder con, estar a la altura de. *6 s.* igual.
**equal** (to) *tr.* igualar, ser igual a, igualarse con, emparejar. *2* corresponder [al afecto, etc.]. ¶ Pret. y p. p.: *equaled* o -*lled;* ger.: *equaling* o -*lling.*
**equalitarian** (ikualite·rian) *adj.-s.* igualitario.
**equality** (ikua·liti) *s.* igualdad. *2* paridad. *3* uniformidad, lisura.
**equalize** (to) (i·kualaiš) *tr.* igualar. *2* compensar, equilibrar, regularizar.
**equalizer** (ikualai·šøŕ) *s.* igualador.
**equanimity** (ikuani·miti) *s.* ecuanimidad.
**equanimous** (ikua·nimøs) *adj.* ecuánime.
**equate** (to) (i·kueit) *tr.* igualar; poner en ecuación.

**equation** (ikuei·shøn) *s.* MAT. ecuación.
**equator** (ikuei·tøŕ) *s.* GEOM., GEOGR., ASTR. ecuador.
**equatorial** (ikueito·rial) *adj.-s.* ecuatorial.
**equerry** (e·kueri) *s.* caballerizo.
**equestrian** (ikue·strian) *adj.* ecuestre. *2 s.* jinete.
**equid** (e·kuid) *s.* ZOOL. équido.
**equidistant** (ikuidi·stant) *adj.* equidistante.
**equilateral** (-læ·tøral) *adj.-s.* GEOM. equilátero.
**equilibrate** (to) (-lai·breit) *tr.* equilibrar, compensar. *2 intr.* estar en equilibrio.
**equilibration** (-brei·shøn) *s.* equilibrio [acción de equilibrar].
**equilibrium** (-li·briøm) *s.* equilibrio.
**equine** (i·kuain) *adj.* equino, caballar. *2 s.* caballo.
**equinoctial** (ikuina·kshal) *adj.* equinoccial. *2 s.* línea equinoccial. *3* tempestad equinoccial.
**equinox** (i·kuinoks) *s.* ASTR. equinoccio.
**equip** (to) (ikui·p) *tr.* equipar, pertrechar, proveer, municionar. *2* MAR. armar, aparejar.
**equipage** (e·kuipidÿ) *s.* equipo, avíos, pertrechos. *2* tren, séquito, carroza, carruaje.
**equipment** (ikui·pmønt) *s.* equipo, aparejamiento, habilitación. *2* equipo, material, avíos, vestuario, armamento. *3* MEC. equipo, tren, juego.
**equipoise** (i·kuipoiš) *s.* equilibrio. *2* contrapeso.
**equipoise** (to) *tr.* equilibrar. *2* contrapesar.
**equiponderate** (to) (ikuipo·ndereit) *intr.* equiponderar. *2 tr.* hacer de igual peso. *3* contrapesar.
**equisetaceous** (equisitei·shøs) *adj.* BOT. equisetáceo.
**equitable** (e·kuitabøl) *adj.* justo, equitativo, imparcial.
**equitation** (-ei·shøn) *s.* equitación.
**equity** (e·kuiti) *s.* equidad, rectitud, imparcialidad. *2* DER. derecho que se aplica en ciertos tribunales.
**equivalence, equivalency** (ikui·valøns, -si) *s.* equivalencia.
**equivalent** (-valønt) *adj.* equivalente.
**equivocal** (-vokal) *adj.* equívoco, ambiguo. *2* incierto, dudoso, sospechoso.
**equivocate** (to) (vokeit) *tr.* hacer equívoco. *2 intr.* usar de equívocos, mentir.
**equivocation** (-vokei·shøn) *s.* equívoco, anfibología. *2* engaño por medio de frases equívocas.
**era** (i·ra) *s.* era [de tiempo].
**eradicate** (to) (iræ·dikeit) *tr.* erradicar, desarraigar, extirpar.
**erase** (to) (irei·š) *tr.* borrar. *2* tachar, rayar, raspar.
**eraser** (irei·šøŕ) *s.* raspador, goma de borrar, borrador, etc.
**erasion** (irei·ÿøn) *s.* ERASURE. *2* CIR. raspado.
**erasure** (irei·ÿøŕ) *s.* raspadura, borradura, tachón, etc.
**ere** (e·øŕ) *prep.* antes de o de que. *2 conj.* antes que [indicando preferencia].
**erect** (ire·kt) *adj.* derecho, levantado, erguido, enhiesto. *2* vertical. *3* erizado [púa, etc.].
**erect** (to) *tr.* erigir [levantar; edificar; instituir]. *2* levantar, elevar. *3* poner derecho, erguir, enhestar, erizar. *4* GEOM. levantar. *5* MEC. montar, instalar.
**erectile** (-il) *adj.* eréctil.
**erection** (ire·kshøn) *s.* erección. *2* erguimiento, enhestadur. *3* MEC. montaje, instalación.
**erector** (-tøŕ) *s.* erector. *2* MEC. montador.
**erelong** (eøŕlo·ng) *adv.* antes de mucho, dentro de poco, a no tardar.
**eremite** (e·rimait) *s.* eremita, ermitaño.
**erenow** (eøŕnau·) *adv.* antes de ahora; hasta aquí.
**erg** (øŕg) *s.* FÍS. ergio.
**ergot** (øŕgøt) *s.* BOT. cornezuelo del centeno.

**ergotism** (-išm) *s.* MED., LÓG. ergotismo.
**ergotize (to)** (-aiš) *intr.* ergotizar. *2 tr.* infestar de cornezuelo.
**ericaceous** (erikei·shøs) *adj.* BOT. ericáceo.
**Erin** (e·rin) *n. pr.* poét. Erin, Irlanda.
**ermine** (ø·ʳmin) *s.* ZOOL., BLAS. armiño. *2* armiño [piel]. *3* fig. toga, judicatura.
**ern, erne** (øʳn) *s.* ORN. halieto.
**Ernest** (ø·ʳnist) *n. pr. m.* Ernesto.
**erode (to)** (irou·d) *tr.* corroer, roer, desgastar. *2* causar erosión. *3 intr.* sufrir erosión.
**erosion** (irou·ȳon) *s.* corrosión. *2* desgaste, erosión.
**erotic (al** (era·tik(al) *adj.* erótico.
**err (to)** (øʳ) *intr.* errar, equivocarse, pecar, descarriarse. *2* errar, vagar.
**errable** (ø·rabøl) *adj.* falible.
**errand** (e·rand) *s.* misión, encargo, recado, mandado, diligencia; ~ *boy*, botones.
**errant** (e·rant) *adj.* errante, errabundo. *2* andante [caballero]. *3* errático. *4* erróneo. *5* falible.
**errantry** (-ri) *s.* vida errante, aventurera. *2* caballería andante.
**errata** (irei·tæ) *s. pl.* de ERRATUM. *2* fe de erratas.
**erratic** (iræ·tic) *adj.* errático. *2* irregular, variable, inconstante. *3* excéntrico, raro.
**erratum** (irei·tøm) *s.* IMPR. errata.
**erroneous** (erou·niøs) *adj.* erróneo, falso, equivocado.
**error** (e·røʳ) *s.* error. *2* yerro, equivocación. *3* pecado.
**ersatz** (eʳsa·ts) *adj.* sintético, artificial. *2 s.* substitutivo.
**Erse** (øʳs) *s.* lenguaje gaélico de los escoceses.
**erst** (øʳst) *adv.* antiguamente, anteriormente. *2 adj.* de otro tiempo.
**erstwhile** (ø·ʳstjuail) *adj.* antiguamente, antaño, antes, al principio.
**erubescence** (erube·søns) *s.* erubescencia, rubor.
**eruct (to)** (irøkt), **eructate (to)** (irø·kteit) *intr. y tr.* eructar.
**eructation** (irøktei·shøn) *s.* eructación, eructo.
**erudite** (e·rudait) *adj.-s.* erudito.
**erudition** (erudi·shøn) *s.* erudición, conocimientos.
**erupt (to)** (irø·pt) *intr.* hacer erupción. *2* salir [las lavas]. *3 tr.* arrojar [lavas, etc.].
**eruption** (irø·pshøn) *s.* GEOL., MED. erupción. *2* estallido, explosión [de una pasión, de risa, etc.].
**eruptive** (irø·ptiv) *adj.* eruptivo.
**erysipelas** (erisi·pelas) *s.* MED. erisipela.
**Erythraen** (erizri·an) *adj.-s.* eritreo.
**escadrille** (eskadri·l) *s.* escuadrilla aérea o naval.
**escalade** (eskalei·d) *s.* MIL. escalada.
**escalade (to)** *tr.* escalar [una pared, etc.].
**escalator** (eskæle·tøʳ) *s.* escalera mecánica.
**escalop, escallop** (eska·lop) *s.* venera, pechina.
**escapade** (eskapei·d) *s.* evasión, fuga. *2* travesura, correría, aventura.
**escape** (eskei·p) *s.* escape, evasión, fuga, escapatoria. *2* escape [de un fluido; de un reloj]. *3* desagüadero.
**escape (to)** *intr.* escapar, escaparse; fugarse, huir. *2* escaparse [un fluido]. *3 tr.* escapar a, evitar, eludir, rehuir.
**escapement** (-mønt) *s.* escape [de reloj, etc.].
**escarp (to)** (eska·ʳp) *tr.* MIL. escarpar.
**escarpment** (-mønts. escarpa, acantilado.
**eschalot** (e·shalot) *s.* BOT. chalote, escaloña.
**eschar** (e·skaʳ) *s.* CIR. escara.
**eschatology** (eskæta·lodȳi) *s.* TEOL. escatología.

**escheat (to)** (eschɪ·t) *intr.-tr.* revertir [los bienes] o hacer revertir [bienes] al estado.
**eschew (to)** (eschu·) *tr.* evitar, rehuir.
**escort** (e·scoʳt) *s.* escolta, convoy; acompañante.
**escort (to)** (esco·ʳt) *tr.* escoltar, convoyar, acompañar.
**escritoire** (escritua·ʳ) *s.* escritorio, escribanía [mueble].
**Escurial** (eskiu·rial) *n. pr.* Escorial.
**escutcheon** (escø·chøn) *s.* escudo de armas. *2* escudo [de cerradura]. *3* MAR. espejo de popa.
**Eskimo** (e·skimou) *adj.-s.* esquimal.
**esophagus** (isa·fagøs) *s.* ANAT., ZOOL. esófago.
**esoteric** (esote·rik) *adj.* esotérico.
**espalier** (espæ·lioʳ) *AGR.* espaldar, espaldera.
**esparto o esparto grass** (espa·ʳtou) *s.* BOT. esparto.
**especial** (espe·shal) *adj.* especial, peculiar, particular. *2* notable.
**especially** (espe·shali) *adv.* especialmente, sobre todo, máxime. *2* especialmente, señaladamente.
**Esperanto** (espøra·ntou) *s.* esperanto.
**espionage** (e·spionidȳ) *s.* espionaje. *2* acecho.
**esplanade** (esplanei·d) *s.* explanada.
**espousal** (espau·šal) *s.* desposorio, esponsales. *2* adhesión a una causa.
**espouse (to)** (espau·š) *tr.* desposarse, casarse con. *2* adoptar, abrazar, defender [una idea, causa, etc.].
**esprit** (esprɪ·) *s.* ingenio, agudeza, gracejo. *2* ~ *de corps*, compañerismo, espíritu de cuerpo.
**espy (to)** (espai·) *tr.* divisar, columbrar.
**esquire** (eskuai·øʳ) *s.* escudero. *2* caballero [de una dama]. *3* título de cortesía que se pospone al apellido, gralte. en la forma abreviada. *Esq.* y sin anteponer *Mr.* *4* (Ingl.) hacendado.
**essay** (e·sei) *s.* tentativa, esfuerzo, probatura. *2* ensayo [literario].
**essay (to)** (esei·) *tr.* ensayar, probar, examinar. *2* intentar, tentar.
**essayist** (e·seist) *s.* ensayista.
**essence** (e·søns) *s.* FIL. esencia. *2* ser, entidad. *3* substancia, médula [de una cosa]. *4* esencia, extracto, perfume.
**essential** (ese·nshal) *adj.* esencial. *2* substancial, capital, vital, indispensable. *3 s.* esencia, lo esencial.
**establish (to)** (estæ·blish) *tr.* establecer. *2* afirmar, consolidar. *3* sentar, probar, demostrar. *4* hacer oficial [una iglesia o religión].
**establishment** (-mønt) *s.* establecimiento. *2* acción de hacer oficial una iglesia o religión. *3* casa [residencia, muebles, criados]. *4* renta vitalicia.
**estate** (estei·t) *s.* estado [orden, clase de pers.]: *third* ~, estado llano. *2* bienes, propiedades: *personal* ~, bienes muebles; *real* ~, bienes raíces. *3* hacienda, heredad, finca. *4* herencia [bienes].
**esteem** (estɪ·m) *s.* estima, estimación, aprecio.
**esteem (to)** *tr.* estimar, apreciar, tener en mucho. *2* estimar, juzgar, considerar.
**ester** (e·støʳ) *s.* QUÍM. éster.
**Esther** *n. pr. f.* Ester.
**esthetic** (esze·tik) *adj.* estético.
**esthetics** (-s) *s.* estética.
**Esthonia** (eszou·nia) *n. pr.* GEOGR. Estonia.
**estimable** (e·stimabøl) *adj.* estimable, apreciable.
**estimate** (e·stimeit) *s.* estimación, cálculo, avalúo. *2* opinión. *3* presupuesto [de un trabajo].
**estimate (to)** *tr.* estimar, apreciar, evaluar, calcular, juzgar. *2* hacer el presupuesto de.

**estimation** (estimei·shøn) *s.* estima, estimación, aprecio. *2* estimación, evaluación.
**estimator** (e·stimeitø[r]) *s.* estimador, tasador.
**estival** (e·stival) *adj.* estival, estivo, veraniego.
**estop (to)** (esta·p) *tr.* rellenar, tapar. *2* prohibir, impedir.
**estrade** (estrei·d) *s.* estrado, tarima.
**estrange (to)** (estrei·ndӯ) *tr.* extrañar, alejar, enajenar, hacer perder la amistad.
**estrangement** (-mønt) *s.* extrañamiento, alejamiento, desvío, enajenamiento.
**estuary** (e·schueri) *s.* GEOGR. estuario, ría.
**et cetera, &c.** (et se·tera) *s.* etcétera, etc.
**etch (to)** (ech) *tr.* grabar al aguafuerte. *2* atacar con un ácido, etc.
**etching** (e·ching) *s.* grabado al aguafuerte, aguafuerte.
**eternal** (itø·[r]nal) *adj.* eterno, eternal, sempiterno: ~ *flower*, BOT. perpetua. *2* perpetuo, incesante. *3 s. the Eternal*, al Eterno, Dios.
**eternity** (-iti) *s.* eternidad.
**eternize (to)** (itø·[r]naiš) *tr.* eternizar. *2* perpetuar, inmortalizar.
**etesian** (iti·ӯan) *adj.* METEOR. etesio.
**ether** (i·zø[r]) *s.* éter.
**ethereal** (izi·rial) *adj.* etéreo. *2* aéreo, vaporoso, sutil.
**etherealize (to)** (iz·rialais) *tr.* hacer etéreo, aéreo; espiritualizar. *2* QUÍM. convertir en éter.
**etherize (to)** (i·zøraiš) *tr.* MED. eterizar. *2* QUÍM. convertir en éter.
**ethic (al** (e·zik(al) *adj.* ético, moral.
**ethics** (e·ziks) *s.* ética.
**Ethiopian** (iziou·pian) *adj.* etíope; negro. *2 s.* etíope.
**ethmoid** (e·zmoid) *adj.-s.* ANAT. etmoides.
**ethnic (al** (e·znik(al) *adj.* étnico.
**ethnography** (ezna·grafi) *s.* etnografía.
**ethnologist** (ezna·lodӯist) *s.* etnólogo.
**ethnology** (ezna·lodӯi) *s.* etnología.
**ethos** (i·zos) *s.* carácter, genio, rasgo distintivo [de un pueblo o colectividad].
**ethyl** (e·zil) *s.* QUÍM. etilo. *2 adj.* etílico.
**ethylic** (ezi·lik) *adj.* QUÍM. etílico.
**etiolate (to)** (i·tioleit) *tr.* descolorarse [esp. las plantas] por falta de luz; ahilarse.
**etiology** (itia·lodӯi) *s.* etiología.
**etiquette** (e·tiket) *s.* etiqueta, ceremonia. *2* normas de conducta profesional [esp. de abogados y médicos].
**Etruscan** (etrø·skan) *adj.-s.* etrusco.
**etude** (etiu·d) *s.* gal. estudio [de música].
**etymologist** (etima·lodӯist) *s.* etimólogo.
**etymology** (etima·lodӯi) *s.* etimología.
**eucalypt** (yu·kalipt), **eucalyptus** (yu·kaliptøs) *s.* BOT. eucalipto. *2 adj.* de eucalipto.
**Eucharist** (yu·karist) *s.* Eucaristía.
**euchology** (yuka·lodӯi) *s.* eucologio.
**euchre** (yu·kø[r]) *s.* juego de naipes.
**Euclid** (yu·klid) *n. pr. m.* Euclides.
**eudiometer** (yudia·mitø[r]) *s.* FÍS. eudiómetro.
**Eugene** (yu·dӯin) *n. pr. m.* Eugenio.
**Eugenia** (yudӯi·nia) *n. pr. f.* Eugenia.
**eugenics** (yudӯe·nics) *s.* eugenesia.
**eulogist** (yu·lodӯist) *s.* elogiador, panegirista.
**eulogistic** (-ic) *adj.* laudatorio, panegírico.
**eulogium** (yu·loudӯiøm) *s.* EULOGY.
**eulogize (to)** (yu·lodӯais) *tr.* elogiar, loar, alabar.
**eulogy** (yu·lodӯi) *s.* elogio, panegírico, encomio.
**eunuch** (yu·nøk) *s.* eunuco.
**euphemism** (yu·fimišm) *s.* eufemismo.

**euphemize (to)** (yu·fimaiš) *intr.* usar de eufemismos.
**euphonic(al** (yufa·nik(al), **euphonious** (yufou·niøs) *adj.* eufónico.
**euphony** (yu·føni) *s.* eufonía.
**Euphorbiaceae** (yufø[r]biei·sii) *s. pl.* BOT. euforbiáceas.
**euphoria** (yufo·ria), **euphory** (yu·fori) *s.* euforia.
**euphuism** (yu·fiuišm) *s.* eufuismo, culteranismo.
**Eurasian** (yurei·shan) *adj.-s.* eurasiático.
**eureka** (yurı·ka) *interj.* ¡eureka!
**Europe** (yu·rop) *n. pr.* GEOGR. Europa.
**European** (yuropi·an) *adj.-s.* europeo. *2* ~ *plan* (E.U.), cuarto sin comida [en los hoteles].
**Europeanize (to)** (yuropi·anaiš) *tr.* europeizar.
**eurythmy** (yuri·dmi) *s.* euritmia.
**Eustace** (yu·stis) *n. pr. m.* Eustaquio.
**Eustachian tube** (yustei·kian) *adj.* ANAT. trompa de Eustaquio.
**euthanasia** (yuzanei·šia) *s.* eutanasia.
**evacuate (to)** (ivæ·kiueit) *tr.* evacuar. *2* desocupar, vaciar. *3 intr.* evacuar una ciudad, etc.
**evacuation** (ivækiuei·shøn) *s.* evacuación.
**evacuee** (ivækiu·) *s.* gal. evacuado [pers.].
**evade** (ivei·d) *tr.* evadir, eludir, evitar, rehuir, escapar a. *2 intr.* usar de evasivas. *3* escabullirse.
**evaginate** (ivæ·dӯineit) *tr.* volver de dentro a fuera.
**evaluate (to)** (-liueit) *tr.* evaluar, valorar, valuar, tasar.
**evaluation** (-shøn) *s.* evaluación, valoración, avalúo.
**evanesce (to)** (evane·s) *intr.* desvanecerse, disiparse, esfumarse, desaparecer, evaporarse.
**evanescence** (-søns) *s.* desvanecimiento, disipación. *2* fugacidad.
**evanescent** (-nt) *adj.* evanescente; fugaz.
**evangel** (ivæ·ndӯøl) *s.* evangelio. *2* buena nueva.
**evangelic(al** (ivandӯe·lik(al) *adj.* evangélico.
**evangelism** (evæ·ndӯølišm) *s.* predicación del evangelio.
**evangelist** (-list) *s.* evangelista. *2* predicador protestante.
**evangelize (to)** (-laiš) *tr.* evangelizar.
**evaporate (to)** (ivæ·poreit) *tr.* evaporar; vaporizar. *2* secar, desecar. *3* desvanecer, disipar. *4 intr.* evaporarse. *5* disiparse. *6* exhalar vapor.
**evaporation** (-ei·shøn) *s.* evaporación, vaporización.
**evaporator** (ivæ·poreitø[r]) *s.* evaporador, desecador.
**evasion** (ivei·ӯøn) *s.* evasión, evasiva, efugio, subterfugio, escapatoria.
**evasive** (ivei·siv) *adj.* evasivo, ambiguo.
**eve** (iv) *s.* víspera, vigilia: *on the* ~ *of*, en vísperas de.
**Eve** *n. pr. f.* Eva.
**even** (i·vn) *adj.* igual, llano, liso, nivelado, parejo. *2* uniforme, regular, constante, invariable. *3* ecuánime, sereno. *4* justo, imparcial. *5* igualado, equilibrado. *6* igual [del mismo valor, etc.]. *7* en línea [con]; situado al mismo nivel [que], paralelo, coincidente. *8* exacto. cabal. *9* par [divisible por dos]. *10* en paz, desquitado: *to be* ~ *with*, estar en paz con, haber ajustado cuentas con.
*11 adv.* aún, hasta, también, incluso: *if*, ~ *though*, aun cuando, aunque: ~ *so*, aun así. *12* siquiera: *not* ~, ni siquiera. *13* de un modo igual, con uniformidad, con suavidad.
**even (to)** *tr.* igualar, allanar, nivelar, enrasar. *2*

igualar, igualarse con. *3* liquidar [cuentas]; desquitar.

**even-handed** *adj.* justo, imparcial.

**evening** (í·vning) *s.* tarde, anochecer: *prima noche, noche* [hasta que uno se acuesta]; velada: ~ *dress,* traje de noche, traje de etiqueta; ~ *party,* tertulia, velada, sarao; ~ *star,* estrella vespertina. *2* atardecer [de la vida].

**evenness** (í·vønnis) *s.* igualdad, uniformidad, llanura, lisura. *2* constancia. *3* serenidad. *4* imparcialidad. *5* exactitud.

**evensong** (-song) *s.* LITURG. vísperas.

**event** (ive·nt) *s.* caso, hecho, suceso, evento, acontecimiento; consecuencia, resultado: *at all events, in any* ~, en todo caso: *in the* ~ *of,* en caso de.

**even-tempered** *adj.* ecuánime, sereno, tranquilo.

**eventful** (-ful) *adj.* lleno de acontecimientos. *2* importante, memorable.

**eventide** (í·vøntaid) *s.* atardecer, anochecer.

**eventual** (ive·nchual) *adj.* eventual, contingente, fortuito. *2* final, consiguiente.

**eventuality** (ivenchuæ·liti) *s.* eventualidad, contingencia. *2* consecuencia, resultado.

**eventually** (ive·nchuali) *adv.* eventualmente. *2* finalmente, con el tiempo.

**eventuate** (ive·nchueit) *intr.* acontecer, acaecer, ocurrir. *2* resultar.

**ever** (e·vø*r*) *adv.* siempre: *for* ~, para siempre; *for* ~ *and* ~, para siempre jamás; continuamente. *2* alguna vez: *have you* ~ *heard him sing?,* ¿le ha oído usted cantar alguna vez? *3* nunca, jamás: *hardly* ~, casi nunca; *more than* ~, más que nunca: *the best book* ~ *writen,* el mejor libro que jamás se haya escrito. *4* ~ *after,* ~ *since,* desde entonces, después; desde que. *5* ~ *and anon,* de vez en cuando. *6* ~ *so,* ~ *so much,* muy, mucho, muchísimo. *7* ~ *so little,* muy poco, un poquitín. *8* A veces *ever* no es más que un expletivo que sirve para dar mayor energía a la frase. En este caso no se traduce o se traduce libremente: *where* ~ *did I drop it?,* ¿dónde demonio se habrá caído?; *did you* ~*?,* ¿ha visto, o ha oído usted cosa igual?

**everglade** (-gleid) *s.* paúl, terreno pantanoso cubierto de yerbas altas.

**evergreen** (-grɪn) *adj.* BOT. de hojas persistentes. *2 s.* árbol o planta de hojas persistentes. *3 pl.* ramas que se ponen como adorno.

**everlasting** (-la·sting) *adj.* eterno, sempiterno, perpetuo, perdurable, perenne. *2* fastidioso, pesado. *3 s.* eternidad. *4* BOT. siempreviva. *5 the Everlasting,* el Eterno, Dios.

**evermore** (-mø*r*) *adv.* eternamente, siempre; *for* ~, para siempre jamás.

**every** (e·vri) *adj.* cada, todo, todos, todas, todos los, todas las; ~ *day,* cada día, todos los días; ~ *one,* cada uno, cada cual; ~ *one of them,* todos, todos sin excepción; ~ *other day,* cada dos días; *his* ~ *word,* todas sus palabras, cada palabra suya. *2* completo, entero; *I have* ~ *confidence in him,* tengo entera confianza en él. *3* Forma modos adverbiales, como: ~ *bit,* enteramente, en todo: ~ *now and then,* ~ *now and again,* de vez en cuando.

**everybody** (e·vribadi) *pron.* todos, todo el mundo; cada uno, cada cual.

**everyday** (evridei·) *adj.* diario, cotidiano, de todos los días, ordinario.

**everyone** (evriuon) *pron.* todos, todo el mundo: cada uno.

**everything** (e·vrizing) *pron.* todo, cada cosa.

**everywhere** (e·vrijue*r*) *adv.* por o en todas partes; a todas partes. *2* dondequiera, por dondequiera.

**evict (to)** (evi·kt) *tr.* DER. desahuciar, expulsar. *2* DER. recobrar por evicción.

**eviction** (evi·kshøn) *s.* DER. evicción; desahucio.

**evidence** (e·vidøns) *s.* evidencia. *2* señal, prueba, demostración: *circunstantial* ~, DER. prueba indiciaria. *3* testimonio; deposición, declaración [testifical]: *to give* ~, deponer, declarar.

**evidence (to)** *tr.* evidenciar, patentizar, revelar.

**evident** (e·vidønt) *adj.* evidente, claro, patente, manifiesto, visible, notorio.

**evidential** (evide·nshal) *adj.* indicativo, indicador. *2* basado en testimonios o pruebas, probatorio.

**evil** (í·vøl) *adj.* malo [no bueno; nocivo; malvado, maligno; desagradable, ofensivo]; aciago, funesto: ~ *eye,* mal de ojo, aojadura: *the Evil One,* el Malo, Satanás. *2 s.* mal. *3 adv.* mal, malignamente.

**evildoer** (-duø*r*) *s.* malhechor; persona que obra mal.

**evil-favo (u) red** *adj.* feo.

**evil-minded** *adj.* mal intencionado. *2* malicioso, mal pensado.

**evince (to)** (ivi·ns) *tr.* demostrar, hacer patente. *2* mostrar, revelar, indicar.

**eviscerate (to)** (ivi·søreit) *tr.* desentrañar, destripar.

**evisceration** (-shøn) *s.* destripamiento.

**evitable** (e·vitabøl) *adj.* evitable.

**evocation** (evokei·shøn) *s.* evocación. *2* DER. avocación.

**evoke (to)** (ivou·k) *tr.* evocar, llamar.

**evolution** (evoliu·shøn) *s.* evolución, desarrollo, crecimiento. *2* MIL., MAR., FIL., BIOL. evolución. *3* MAT. extracción de raíces.

**evolutional** (-al), **evolutionary** (-eri) *adj.* evolutivo.

**evolutionism** (-ism) *s.* evolucionismo.

**evolve (to)** (iva·lv) *tr.* desenvolver, desarrollar, desplegar, producir. *2* convertir, transformar. *3* despedir [gases, etc.]. *4 intr.* evolucionar, desarrollarse, abrirse, desplegarse.

**ewe** (yu) *f.* ZOOL. oveja: ~ *lamb,* cordera.

**ewer** (yu·ø*r*) *s.* jarro, aguamanil.

**ex** (eks) *prep.* COM. ex [sin incluir]: ~ *coupon,* ex cupón.

**exacerbate (to)** (egšæ·sø*r*beit) *tr.* exacerbar. *2* irritar.

**exact** (egšæ·kt) *adj.* exacto. *2* preciso, estricto, riguroso.

**exact (to)** *tr.* exigir, imponer [tributos, etc.]; obtener por exacción. *2* exigir, requerir [hacer necesario].

**exacting** (-ing) *adj.* exigente.

**exaction** (-shøn) *s.* exacción.

**exactitude** (-itiud) *s.* exactitud. *2* precisión. *3* puntualidad.

**exaggerate (to)** (egšæ·dyøreit) *tr.* exagerar. *2* abultar, ponderar.

**exaggeration** (-ei·shøn) *s.* exageración; abultamiento.

**exalt (to)** (egšo·lt) *tr.* exaltar, ensalzar; elevar, engrandecer. *2* enorgullecer, alegrar. *3* exaltar [la imaginación, etc.].

**exaltation** (-ei·shøn) *s.* exaltación, ensalzamiento. *2* elevación, engrandecimiento, promoción. *3* contento, alborozo. *4* exaltación [de la imaginación, etc.].

**exam** (egšæ·m) *s.* fam. examen.

**examination** (egšæminei·shøn) *s.* examen. *2* inspección, reconocimiento. *3* DER. interrogatorio.
**examine (to)** (egšæ·min) *tr.* examinar. *2* inspeccionar, reconocer, explorar. *3* DER. interrogar.
**example** (egšæ·mpøl) *s.* ejemplo: *for ~*, por ejemplo. *2* modelo, dechado. *3* muestra, ejemplar. *4* escarmiento, lección.
**exanimate** (egšæ·nimit) *adj.* exánime, inanimado, muerto. *2* abatido, sin ánimo.
**exasperate (to)** (egšæ·spøreit) *tr.* exasperar, irritar, encolerizar. *2* agravar, enconar, encrudecer.
**exasperation** (-ei·shøn) *s.* exasperación, irritación, encono.
**excavate (to)** (e·kskaveit) *tr.* excavar. *2* extraer cavando.
**excavation** (-ei·shøn) *s.* excavación. *2* material extraído por excavación.
**excavator** (e·kskaveitø$^r$) *s.* excavador. *2* excavadora [máquina].
**exceed (to)** (eksɪ·d) *tr.* exceder, sobrepujar. *2* ser superior a [las fuerzas, etc., de]. *3 intr.* exceder. *4* descollar.
**exceedingly** (-ingli) *adv.* extremamente, sumamente, por demás, muy.
**excel (to)** (ekse·l) *tr.* aventajar, sobrepujar, superar. *2* descollar, distinguirse, sobresalir.
**excellence, excellency** (e·ksøløns, -si) *s.* excelencia.
**excellent** (e·ksølønt) *adj.* excelente. *2* sobresaliente, relevante. *3* primoroso; magnífico.
**except** (ekse·pt) *prep.* excepto, salvo, menos, a excepción de, fuera de.
**except (to)** *tr.* exceptuar. *2 intr.* poner reparos, oponerse, objetar.
**excepting** (-ing) *prep.* exceptuando, excepto, salvo, a excepción de.
**exception** (ekse·pshøn) *s.* excepción. *2* salvedad. *3* objeción, reparo: *to take ~*, objetar, desaprobar. *4* DER. excepción.
**exceptionable** (-abøl) *adj.* recusable. *2* reprochable, tachable.
**exceptional** (-al) *adj.* excepcional.
**excerpt** (e·ksø$^r$pt) *s.* cita, pasaje, fragmento [escogido de un texto]. *2* excerpta.
**excerpt (to)** (eksø·$^r$pt) *tr.* escoger, sacar, citar [un pasaje o fragmento].
**excess** (ekse·s) *s.* exceso, demasía, sobra: *in ~ of*, más de; *to ~*, en exceso, con demasía, inmoderadamente. *2* exceso, abuso. *3* superfluidad, abundancia. *4* excelente, sobrante. *5 pl.* excesos.
**excess (to)** *tr.* (Ingl.) pagar, exigir o cobrar un suplemento por exceso de peso, etc.
**excessive** (-iv) *adj.* excesivo, desmedido. *2* sumo, extremo.
**excessively** (-li) *adv.* excesivamente. *2* sumamente, extremadamente.
**exchange** (ekschei·ndÿ) *s.* cambio, trueque, permuta: *in ~ for*, a cambio de. *2* cambio [de saludos, cumplidos, golpes, etc.]. *3* canje. *4* COM. bolsa, lonja. *5* COM. cambio; premio del cambio: *~ rate*, tipo del cambio. *6* central [de teléfonos].
**exchange (to)** *tr.* cambiar, canjear, trocar, permutar, conmutar. *2* cambiar, cambiarse, hacerse, etc. [mutuamente]: *to ~ greetings*, saludarse, mandarse felicitaciones. *3 intr.* cambiar, hacer un cambio.
**exchangeable** (-abøl) *adj.* cambiable.
**exchequer** (eks·cheko$^r$) *s.* (Ingl.) hacienda pública, erario, fisco, tesorería del Estado. *2* bolsa, fondos, recursos pecuniarios.
**excise** (eksai·š) *s.* sisa, alcabala, impuesto sobre ciertos artículos de comercio interior.

**excise (to)** *tr.* gravar con el impuesto llamado EXCISE. *2* cortar, separar cortando. *3* quitar, borrar.
**excision** (eksi·ÿøn) *s.* excisión. *2* corte [en un texto].
**excitable** (eksai·tabøl) *adj.* excitable.
**excitant** (-tant) *adj.*-*s.* excitante.
**excitation** (eksitei·shøn) *s.* excitación [acción y efectode excitar]. *2* FÍS., FISIOL. excitación.
**excite (to)** (eksai·t) *tr.* excitar. *2* acalorar, animar.
**excitement** (-mønt) *s.* excitación, agitación, acaloramiento. *2* animación, estímulo. *3* interés, emoción. *4* FISIOL. excitación.
**exciter** (-ø$^r$) *s.* excitador.
**exciting** (-ing) *adj.* excitante, excitador. *2* estimulante, animador. *3* interesante, emocionante.
**exclaim (to)** (eksklei·m) *tr.*-*intr.* exclamar, clamar: *to ~ against*, clamar contra.
**exclamation** (eksklamei·shøn) *s.* exclamación, grito, clamor. *2* GRAM. *~ point*, punto de admiración.
**exclude (to)** (eksklu·d) *tr.* excluir. *2* dejar fuera, impedir la entrada.
**exclusion** (-ÿøn) *s.* exclusión. *2* acción de impedir la entrada.
**exclusive** (-siv) *adj.* exclusivo. *2* privativo. *3* que sólo admite cierta clase de clientes [establecimiento, hotel, etc.], o de personas [grupo, sociedad, etc.]; selecto, distinguido, a la moda. *4* que rehuye el trato social con los que no son de su clase o gusto [pers.]. *5 ~ of*, con exclusión de.
**exclusiveness** (-nis) *s.* exclusividad. *2* calidad de selecto, único.
**excluvivism** (-išm) *s.* exclusivismo. *2* tendencia a excluir.
**excogitate (to)** (ekska·dÿiteit) *tr.* excogitar.
**excommunicate (to)** (ekskømiu·nikeit) *tr.* excomulgar.
**excommunication** (-ei·shøn) *s.* excomunión.
**excoriate (to)** (eksko·rieit) *tr.* excoriar, desollar.
**excoriation** (-ei·shøn) *s.* excoriación.
**excorticate (to)** (eksko·$^r$tikeit) *tr.* descortezar.
**excrement** (e·kskrimønt) *s.* excremento.
**excrescence** (ekskre·søns) *s.* excrecencia.
**excrete (to)** (ekskrɪ·t) *tr.* FISIOL. excretar.
**excretion** (ekskri·shøn) *s.* excreción.
**excretory** (e·kskritori) *adj.* excretorio. *2 s.* FISIOL. emuntorio.
**excruciate (to)** (ekskru·shieit) *tr.* atormentar, torturar.
**excruciating** (-ing) *adj.* torturador, angustioso. *2* agudísimo, vivísimo, atroz [dolor].
**exculpate (to)** (ekskø·lpeit) *tr.* exculpar, justificar, disculpar.
**exculpation** (-ei·shøn) *s.* exculpación, justificación, disculpa.
**excursion** (ekskø·$^r$shøn) *s.* excursión. *2* divagación, digresión.
**excursionist** (-ist) *s.* excursionista.
**excursive** (ekskø·$^r$siv) *adj.* errante, errático. *2* digresivo; dado a la digresión.
**excusable** (ekskiu·šabøl) *adj.* excusable, disculpable.
**excuse** (ekskiu·š) *s.* excusa, disculpa. *2* justificación, exculpación. *3* excusa, exención.
**excuse (to)** *tr.* excusar, disculpar. *2* justificar, exculpar. *3* perdonar, dispensar: *excuse me!*, ¡dispense usted! *4* excusar, eximir.
**execrable** (e·ksikrabøl) *adj.* execrable, abominable.
**execrate (to)** (e·ksikreit) *tr.* execrar, abominar, maldecir.

**execration** (-ei·shøn) *s.* execración.
**executant** (egše·kiutant) *s.* MÚS. ejecutante.
**execute (to)** (e·ksikiut) *tr.* ejecutar, cumplir, realizar, llevar a cabo. *2* TEAT. desempeñar. *3* formalizar, otorgar [un documento]. *4* ejecutar, ajusticiar.
**execution** (eksikiu·shøn) *s.* ejecución. *2* DER. embargo; mandamiento judicial. *3* DER. otorgamiento.
**executioner** (eksikiu·shønø$^r$) *s.* ejecutor de la justicia, verdugo.
**executive** (ekše·kiutiv) *adj.* ejecutivo. *2* que gobierna o dirige. *3 m.* poder ejecutivo. *4* (E.U.) presidente, jefe del Estado; gobernador de un Estado. *5* director, gerente; junta directiva.
**executor** (egše·kiutø$^r$) *s.* ejecutor. *2* albacea.
**executory** (egše·kiutori) *adj.* ejecutorio. *2* ejecutivo, administrativo.
**exedra** (eksi·dra) *s.* ARQ. exedra.
**exegesis** (eksidȳi·sis) *s.* exégesis.
**exemplar** (egše·mpla$^r$) *s.* modelo, dechado, prototipo. *2* ejemplar, espécimen, caso, ejemplo.
**exemplary** (-mpleri) *adj.* ejemplar. *2* ilustrativo.
**exemplification** (egšemplifikei·shøn) *s.* ejemplificación. *2* DER. copia certificada.
**exemplify (to)** (egše·mplifai) *tr.* ejemplificar. *2* DER. copiar, trasladar. ¶ Pret. y p. p.: *exemplified.*
**exempt** (egše·mpt) *adj.* exento, libre, franco.
**exempt (to)** *tr.* exentar, eximir, exceptuar, dispensar.
**exemption** (-mpshøn) *s.* exención.
**exequatur** (eksekuei·tø$^r$) *s.* exequátur.
**exercise** (e·ksø$^r$saiš) *s.* ejercicio [en todos sus sentidos menos en el de tiempo durante el cual rige una ley de presupuestos]. *2 pl.* ejercicios [de examen, etc.]. *3* MIL. ejercicios.
**exercise (to)** *tr.* ejercer, practicar. *2* ejercitar, adiestrar. *3* emplear, poner en ejercicio. *4* preocupar, inquietar. *5* fatigar, poner a prueba. *6 intr.-ref.* ejercitarse, practicarse.
**exercitation** (egsø$^r$sitei·shøn) *s.* ejercicio, ejercitación. *2* discurso, ensayo.
**exergue** (eksø·$^r$g) *s.* exergo.
**exert (to)** (egšø·$^r$t) *tr.* ejercer [influencia]; poner en acción [fuerza, facultades, etc.], esforzar. *2 ref.* esforzarse, empeñarse.
**exertion** (egšø·$^r$shøn) *s.* ejercicio, uso [de una facultad, fuerza, etc.]. *2* esfuerzo, empeño. *3 pl.* esfuerzos, pasos, diligencias.
**exfoliate (to)** (eksfou·lieit) *tr.* exfoliar. *2 intr.* exfoliarse.
**exfoliation** (ei·shøn) *s.* exfoliación.
**exhalation** (eksjalei·shøn) *s.* exhalación [acción]. *2* exhalación, efluvio, vaho, vapor. *3* explosión [de ira, etc.].
**exhale (to)** (eksjei·l) *tr.* exhalar, despedir. *2* espirar [el aire]. *3* evaporar. *4 intr.* evaporarse, escaparse, disiparse.
**exhaust** (egšo·st) *s.* MEC. escape, descarga, salida [de gases, vapor, etc.]: ~ *valve*, válvula de escape o de salida. *2* tubo de escape. *3* FÍS., MEC. vacío, succión, aspiración. *4* aire, vapor, etc., aspirado o de escape.
**exhaust (to)** *tr.* agotar, apurar, consumir. *2* agotar, fatigar, postrar. *3* FÍS., MEC. practicar el vacío en; dar salida o escape a [gases, vapor]; aspirar [el aire, el polvo]. *4 intr.* escapar, salir [los gases, el vapor].
**exhausted** (-id) *adj.* exhausto, agotado. *2* agotado, fatigado, rendido.

**exhauster** (-ø$^r$) *s.* MEC. bomba; aspirador, ventilador aspirante.
**exhausting** (-ing) *adj.* agotador.
**exhaustion** (egšo·schøn) *s.* agotamiento. *2* FÍS., MEC. aspiración. *3* MEC. vaciamiento, descarga.
**exhaustive** (egšo·stiv) *adj.* exhaustivo.
**exhibit** (egši·bit) *s.* objeto (s expuesto (s en una exposición; instalación. *2* exhibición, ostentación.
**exhibit (to)** *tr.* exhibir. *2* exponer [a la vista, al público]. *3* mostrar, dar muestras de. *4* lucir, ostentar.
**exhibiter** (-ø$^r$) *s.* expositor [en una exposición].
**exhibition** (egšibi·shøn) *s.* exhibición. *2* exposición [de productos, cuadros, etc.]. *3* (Ingl.) beca, pensión. *4 to make an ~ of oneself,* ponerse en ridículo.
**exhibitioner** (-ø$^r$) *s.* (Ingl.) estudiante pensionado. *2* expositor.
**exhibitionist** (-ist) *s.* exhibicionista.
**exhibitor** (egši·bitø$^r$) *s.* expositor [en una exposición].
**exhilarant** (egši·larant) *adj.* alegrador, estimulante.
**exhilarate** (-reit) *tr.* alegrar, regocijar, animar, estimular, excitar.
**exhilaration** (-ei·shøn) *s.* alegría, regocijo, animación, excitación.
**exhort (to)** (egšo·$^r$t) *tr.-intr.* exhortar.
**exhortation** (-ei·shøn) *s.* exhortación.
**exhumation** (eksjiumei·shøn) *s.* exhumación.
**exhume (to)** (eksjiu·m) *tr.* exhumar, desenterrar.
**exigence, exigency** (e·ksidÿøns, -si) *s.* exigencia, necesidad, urgencia.
**exigent** (e·ksidÿønt) *adj.* exigente [que requiere mucho]. *2* apremiante.
**exiguity** (eksi·guiti) *f.* exigüidad.
**exiguous** (-giuøs) *adj.* exiguo.
**exile** (e·ksail) *s.* destierro, expatriación, exilio. *2* desterrado, expatriado, exilado.
**exile (to)** *tr.* desterrar, proscribir, extrañar.
**exist (to)** (egš·ist) *intr.* existir. *2* vivir. *3* subsistir.
**existence** (-øns) *s.* existencia.
**existentialism** (egšiste·nshališm) *s.* existencialismo.
**exit** (e·ksit) *s.* salida [acción; sitio]. *2* partida, muerte. *3* TEAT. mutis.
**exit (to)** *intr.* TEAT. irse. | Ús. sólo en el presente: ~ *Joan,* vase Juana.
**exodus** (e·ksødøs) *s.* éxodo.
**exonerate (to)** (egša·nøreit) *tr.* exonerar, descargar, aliviar. *2* exculpar.
**exoneration** (-ei·shøn) *s.* exoneración, descargo; exculpación.
**exorbitance, exorbitancy** (egšo·$^r$bitans, -si) *s.* exorbitancia.
**exorbitant** (egšo·$^r$bitant) *adj.* exorbitante.
**exorcise (to)** (e·kso$^r$saiš) *tr.* exorcizar.
**exorcism** (e·kso$^r$sišm) *s.* exorcismo, conjuro.
**exorcist** (e·kso$^r$sišt) *s.* exorcista.
**exordium** (egšo·$^r$diøm) *s.* exordio.
**exosmose** (e·ksasmous), **exosmosis** (eksasmou·sis) *s.* FÍS. exósmosis.
**exoteric (al** (eksote·rik(al) *adj.* exotérico.
**exotic (al** (eksa·tik(al) *adj.* exótico. *2* extranjero, forastero. *3* planta o palabra exótica.
**exoticism** (eksa·tisišm), **exotism** (eksa·tišm) *s.* exotiquez, exotismo.
**expand (to)** (ekspæ·nd) *tr.* extender, dilatar, ensanchar, alargar. *2* abrir, desplegar. *3* tender, esparcir. *4* desarrollar [una idea, una ecuación,

etc.]. *5 intr.* extenderse, dilatarse. *6* abrirse, desplegarse.

**expanding** (-ing) *adj.* que extiende o ensancha. *2* que se extiende o ensancha. *3* de expansión, de dilatación.

**expanse** (ekspæ·ns) *s.* extensión, espacio.

**expansion** (-shøn) *s.* expansión, dilatación. *2* extensión, ensanchamiento, aumento. *3* expansión [parte ensanchada]. *4* desarrollo [de una idea, ecuación, etc.].

**expansive** (-iv) *adj.* expansivo. *2* ancho, extenso.

**expatiate (to)** (ekspei·shieit) *intr.* espaciarse, explayarse, dilatarse [en el discurso, etc.].

**expatiation** (-ei·shøn) *s.* acción de explayarse, extenderse.

**expatiatory** (ekspei·shiatori) *adj.* extenso, difuso.

**expatriate (to)** (ekspæ·trieit) *tr.* expatriar, desterrar. *2 intr.* expatriarse.

**expatriation** (-ei··shøn) *s.* expatriación.

**expect (to)** (ekspe·kt) *tr.* esperar [contar con, creer que ha de suceder alguna cosa]: *I ~ to see him*, espero verle. *2* esperar [a uno]: *don't ~ me*, no me esperen. *3* esperar que [uno] hará alguna cosa: *I ~ him to come*, espero que vendrá. *4 fam.* pensar, creer, suponer.

**expectable** (-abøl) *adj.* esperable.

**expectance, expectancy** (-ans, -si) *s.* espera, expectación. *2* esperanza, expectativa.

**expectant** (-ant) *adj.* expectante; que espera. *2* que puede o espera ser, futuro, en perspectiva. *3 s.* candidato o aspirante a un cargo.

**expectation** (-ei·shøn) *s.* espera, expectación, lo que se espera. *2* expectativa, perspectiva, esperanza, probabilidad: *~ of life*, índice de longevidad. *3 pl.* perspectivas de heredar.

**expectorate (to)** (ekspe·ctøreit) *tr.-intr.* expectorar, esputar.

**expectoration** (-ei·shøn) *s.* expectoración. *2* esputo.

**expedience, expediency** (ekspi·diøns, -si) *s.* conveniencia, oportunidad, utilidad. *2* oportunismo.

**expedient** (-dient) *adj.* conveniente, propio, oportuno, ventajoso. *2* oportunista. *3 s.* expediente, arbitrio, recurso.

**expedite** (e·kspidait) *adj.* expedito. *2* rápido, pronto.

**expedite (to)** *tr.* apresurar; facilitar. *2* despachar, dar curso a.

**expedition** (ekspidi·shøn) *s.* expedición [militar, científica, etc.]. *2* expedición, prontitud. *3* apresuramiento.

**expeditionary** (-eri) *adj.* expedicionario.

**expeditious** (ekspidi·shøs) *adj.* expeditivo, pronto.

**expel (to)** (ekspe·l) *tr.* expeler. *2* echar, expulsar. ¶ Pret. y p. p.: *expelled*; ger.: *expelling*.

**expend (to)** (ekspe·nd) *tr.* expender, gastar.

**expenditure** (-ichø<sup>r</sup>) *s.* gasto, desembolso.

**expense** (ekspe·ns) *s.* gasto, desembolso. *2* expensas, costa: *at the ~ of*, a expensas de. *3 pl.* gastos, coste, costo: *to cover expenses*, cubrir gastos.

**expensive** (-iv) *adj.* costoso, caro, dispendioso.

**experience** (ekspi·riøns) *s.* experiencia: *by ~*, por experiencia. *2* experimento. *3* paso, lance, aventura, goce, sufrimiento.

**experience (to)** *tr.* experimentar. *2* probar, pasar, sufrir, vivir. *3* aprender o enseñar por experiencia.

**experienced** (-d) *adj.* experimentado. *2* experto, práctico. *3* aleccionado. *4* vivido.

**experiment** (ekspe·rimønt) *s.* experimento, experiencia [prueba, ensayo].

**experiment (to)** *tr.-intr.* experimentar [probar, ensayar].

**experimental** (eksperime·ntal) *adj.* experimental.

**experimentation** (-ei·shøn) *s.* experimentación.

**expert** (ekspø·<sup>r</sup>t) *adj.* experimentado, experto, perito, práctico, diestro. *2* pericial, de perito. *3 s.* experto, perito, especialista.

**expertise** (ekspø·<sup>r</sup>ti·s) *s.* pericia. *2* dictamen pericial.

**expertness** (ekspø·<sup>r</sup>tnis) *s.* pericia, habilidad.

**expiate (to)** (e·kspieit) *tr.* expiar, purgar.

**expiation** (-ei·shøn) *s.* expiación.

**expiration** (ekspirei·shøn) *s.* expiración, término, vencimiento. *2* FISIOL. espiración. *3* muerte.

**expire (to)** (ekspai·ø<sup>r</sup>) *tr.-intr.* FISIOL. espirar. *2 intr.* expirar, vencer, caducar. *3* expirar, morir.

**expiry** (-ri) *s.* expiración, vencimiento.

**explain (to)** (eksplei·n) *tr.* explicar, exponer, aclarar: *to ~ oneself*, explicarse. *2 intr.* dar una explicación.

**explanation** (eksplanei·shøn) *s.* explicación. *2* explanación [de un texto, etc.].

**expletive** (e·ksplitiv) *adj.* expletivo. *2 s.* voz expletiva. *3* exclamación.

**explicate (to)** (e·ksplikeit) *tr.* explicar, explanar, interpretar. *2* desarrollar [una idea].

**explication** (-ei·shøn) *s.* explicación, explanación, exposición. *2* descripción detallada.

**explicit** (ekspli·sit) *adj.* explícito.

**explode (to)** (eksplou·d) *tr.* volar, hacer estallar. *2* desacreditar [una moda, etc.]; refutar [una teoría]. *3* expeler por explosión. *4 intr.* estallar, hacer explosión, volar, reventar: fig. *to ~ with laughter*, soltar la carcajada.

**exploit** (e·ksploit) *s.* hazaña, proeza.

**exploit (to)** (e·ksploi·t) *tr.* explotar [una mina, etc.]. *2* explotar [aprovecharse de].

**exploitation** (-eishøn) *s.* explotación.

**exploiter** (e·ksploitø<sup>r</sup>) *s.* explotador.

**exploration** (eksplorei·shøn) *s.* exploración.

**explore** (eksplo·<sup>r</sup>) *tr.* explorar. *2* examinar, sondear.

**explorer** (-ø<sup>r</sup>) *s.* explorador.

**explosion** (eksplou·ẏøn) *s.* explosión, estallido. *2* acción de hacer estallar, voladura. *3* refutación [de una teoría]. *4* FONÉT. explosión.

**explosive** (-siv) *adj.* explosivo. *2* de explosión. *3 s.* explosivo. *4* FONÉT. consonante explosiva.

**exponent** (ekspou·nønt) *s.* expositor [que interpreta o declara]. *2* exponente [que es representación o ejemplo]. *3* MAT. exponente.

**export** (e·kspo<sup>r</sup>t) *s.* exportación. *2 pl.* exportaciones; artículos de exportación.

**export (to)** (ekspo·<sup>r</sup>t) *tr.* exportar.

**exportation** (-ei·shøn) *s.* exportación.

**exporter** (ekspo·<sup>r</sup>tø<sup>r</sup>) *s.* exportador.

**expose (to)** (ekspou·s) *tr.* exponer [a la vista, a la intemperie, a un riesgo, a una acción, etc.]. *2* exponer, poner en peligro, comprometer. *3* FOT. exponer. *4* descubrir [poner al descubierto]; revelar. *5* desenmascarar; divulgar las faltas o algo deshonroso de [uno]. *6* abandonar, exponer [a un niño].

**exposed** (-d) *adj.* expuesto, a la vista. *2* expuesto, en peligro, descubierto, desabrigado.

**exposition** (eksposhi·shøn) *s.* exposición [acción de exponer, estado de lo expuesto]. *2* exposición, explicación, interpretación. *3* LIT., MÚS. exposición. *4* exposición, situación [de un lugar]. *5* exposición [artística, industrial, etc.].

**expository** (ekspa·sitori) *adj.* explicativo.

**expostulate (to)** (ekspa·schuleit) *intr.* hacer reconvenciones, discutir; tratar de disuadir.

**expostulation** (-ei·shøn) *s.* reconvención, disuasión, protesta, razones.

**exposure** (ekspou·ȳøʳ) *s.* exposición a la intemperie, al peligro, etc.]; desabrigo, falta de protección. *2* exposición, orientación. *3* FOT. exposición. *4* desenmascaramiento; acción de exponer a la vergüenza, al escándalo.

**expound (to)** (ekspau·nd) *tr.* exponer, explicar, comentar.

**express** (ekspre·s) *adj.* expreso, claro, explícito. *2* expreso, especial. *3* exacto, parecido. *4* expreso [tren, mensajero]. *5* de transportes rápidos. *6* (Ingl.) ~ *delivery*, correo urgente. *7 adv.* expresamente, especialmente. *8* de modo expreso. *9 s.* expreso, mensajero, propio. *10* expreso [tren, autobús, etc.]. *11* (Ingl.) correo urgente.

**express (to)** *tr.* expresar. *2* describir, designar. *3* exprimir, prensar, estrujar. *4* extraer el juego. *5 ref.* expresarse, producirse, explicarse.

**expression** (ekspre·shøn) *s.* expresión. *2* acción de exprimir.

**expressionism** (-išm) *s.* expresionismo.

**expressive** (ekspre·siv) *adj.* expresivo. *2* que expresa.

**expressiveness** (-nis) *s.* expresión, energía, fuerza expresiva.

**expressly** (ekspre·sli) *adv.* expresamente, especialmente. *2* clara, explícitamente.

**expropriate (to)** (eksprou·prieit) *tr.* desposeer, expropiar.

**expropriation** (-ei·shøn) *s.* expropiación.

**expugnable** (ekspø·gnabøl) *adj.* expugnable.

**expulse (to)** (e·kspøls) *tr.* expulsar.

**expulsion** (ekspø·lshøn) *s.* expulsión.

**expunge (to)** (ekspø·ndȳ) *tr.* borrar, rayar, tachar.

**expurgate (to)** (e·kspøʳgueit) *tr.* expurgar.

**expurgation** (-ei·shøn) *ts.* expurgación, expurgo; purificación.

**exquisite** (e·kskuišit) *adj.* exquisitez. *2* delicadeza, refinamiento. *3* intensidad, agudeza.

**exquisitness** (-nis) *s.* exquisitez. *2* delicadeza, refinamiento. *3* intensidad, agudeza.

**exsanguine** (eksæ·ngwin) *adj.* exangüe; anémico.

**exsiccate (to)** (e·ksikeit) *tr.* secar, desecar.

**extant** (e·kstənt) *adj.* existente, en existencia.

**extemporaneous** (ekstempørei·niøs) *adj.* improvisado [hecho sin preparación]. *2* improvisado, provisional [hecho para la ocasión].

**extemporary** (ekste·mpøreri) *adj.* improvisado [discurso, orador, etc.]. *2* repentino, inesperado.

**extempore** (ekste·mpøri) *adv.* improvisadamente. *2* improvisante, de improviso. *3 adj.* improvisado. *4 s.* improvisación.

**extemporize (to)** (ekste·mpøraiš) *tr.* improvisar.

**extend (to)** (ekste·nd) *tr.* extender. *2* explayar, ensanchar, prolongar. *3* alargar [el brazo, la mano]. *4* dar, conceder, ofrecer. *5* MIL. desplegar. *6* aguar, rebajar [un líquido]. *7* prorrogar, dar prórroga. *8* agotar las fuerzas de. *9 intr.* extenderse. *10* prolongarse. *11* estirarse, dar de sí.

**extended** (ekste·ndid) *adj.* extendido, estirado. *2* prolongado. *3* diferido.

**extensible** (ekste·nsibøl) *adj.* extensible, extensivo.

**extensile** (-sil) *adj.* extensible. *2* extensor.

**extension** (-shøn) *s.* extensión. *2* prolongación, dilatación, expansión. *3* adición, anexo. *4* MEC. alargadera. *5* prórroga, espera, moratoria.

**extensity** (-siti) *s.* extensión [calidad de extenso].

**extensive** (-siv) *adj.* relativo a la extensión. *2* extensivo. *3* extenso, ancho, vasto, dilatado.

**extensively** (-li) *adv.* extensivamente. *2* extensamente, por extenso: ~ *used*, de uso general o común.

**extent** (ekste·nt) *s.* extensión [de una cosa]; superficie, anchura, longitud, perímetro; magnitud, grado: *to a certain* ~, hasta cierto punto; *to a great* ~, en grado sumo; *to the full* ~, en toda su extensión, completamente. *2* extensión [de terreno]. *3* GEOM. extensión.

**extenuate (to)** (ekste·niueit) *tr.* minorar, atenuar, paliar, excusar. *2* extenuar, enflaquecer.

**extenuating** (-ing) *adj.* atenuante, paliativo.

**exterior** (eksti·riøʳ) *adj.* exterior, externo: ~ *angle*, GEOM. ángulo externo. *2* extrínseco. *3 s.* exterior. *4* exterioridad, conducta.

**exteriority** (ekstiria·riti) *s.* exterioridad [calidad].

**exteriorize (to)** (eksti·riøraiš) *tr.* exteriorizar. *2* dar forma objetiva a.

**exterminate (to)** (ekstø·ʳineit) *tr.* exterminar. *2* desarraigar, extirpar.

**extermination** (-ei·shøn) *s.* exterminio. *2* extirpación, destrucción.

**extern** (ekstø·ʳn) *s.* externo [alumno, médico].

**external** (-al) *adj.* externo, exterior: ~ *angle*, GEOM. ángulo externo; ~ *remedy*, remedio externo; ~ *trade*, comercio exterior. *2 s. pl.* exterior, exterioridad, apariencia [de las cosas].

**externality** (ekstøʳnæ·liti) *s.* exterioridad.

**externalize (to)** (ekstø·ʳnalaiš) *tr.* exteriorizar. *2* dar forma o cuerpo.

**exterritorial** (eksterito·rial) *adj.* extraterritorial.

**extinct** (eksti·nkt) *adj.* extinto, extinguido. *2* apagado [fuego, etc.].

**extinction** (eksti·nkshøn) *s.* extinción.

**extinguish (to)** (eksti·ngwish) *tr.* extinguir. *2* apagar. *3* eclipsar, oscurecer.

**extinguisher** (-øʳ) *s.* el o lo que extingue o apaga. *2* apagador, matacandelas.

**extinguishment** (-mønt) *s.* extinción.

**extirpate (to)** (e·cstøʳpeit) *tr.* extirpar, *2* desarraigar. *3* destruir, exterminar.

**extirpation** (-ei·shøn) *s.* extirpación. *2* erradicación. *3* exterminio.

**extol, extoll (to)** (ekstou·l) *tr.* exaltar, ensalzar, alabar. ¶ Pret. y p. p.: *extolled*; ger.: *extolling*.

**extort (to)** (eksto·ʳt) *tr.* arrancar, obtener, sacar [algo] por la fuerza, la importunación, etc.

**extortion** (exto·ʳshøn) *s.* extorsión. *2* exacción, concusión, violencia.

**extortionate** (-it) *adj.* opresivo, injusto; excesivo, exorbitante.

**extra** (e·kstra) *adj.* extra. *2* extraordinario, adicional, suplementario. *3* de repuesto. *4 s.* extra. *5* pieza de repuesto. *6 adv.* mucho, muy: *extra-fine*, extrafino.

**extract** (e·kstrækt) *s.* QUÍM., FARM. extracto. *2* extracto, cita, fragmento [de un libro, etc.].

**extract (to)** (ekstræ·kt) *tr.* extraer, sacar, obtener. *2* entresacar, seleccionar, citar [fragmentos, pasajes, etc.]. *3* QUÍM. extraer. *4* MAT. extraer [raíces].

**extraction** (-shøn) *s.* extracción [acción de extraer]. *2* extracto, esencia. *3* extracción, origen, alcurnia.

**extractive** (-tiv) *adj.* extractivo.

**extractor** (-tøʳ) *s.* extractor [pers., aparato, pieza, mecanismo]. *2* CIR. fórceps.

**extradite (to)** (e·kstradait) *tr.* conceder o pedir la extradición de.

**extradition** (ekstradi·shøn) s. extradición.
**extrados** (ekstræ·das) s. ARQ. extradós, trasdós.
**extrajudicial** (ekstradỹudi·shal) adj. extrajudicial.
**extramural** (ekstramiu·ral) adj. situado extramuros. 2 fuera del recinto de una institución.
**extraneous** (ekstrei·niøs) adj. extraño, ajeno [a una cosa]: ~ matter, materia extraña. 2 extrínseco.
**extraordinary** (ekstro·ʳdineri) adj. extraordinario.
**extraterritorial** (ekstraterito·rial) adj. extraterritorial.
**extravagance, -cy** (ekstræ·vagans, -si) s. prodigalidad, derroche, despilfarro, profusión, exceso. 2 extravagancia, desarreglo, exageración.
**extravagant** (ekstræ·vagant) adj. pródigo, derrochador, despilfarrador. 2 excesivo, exorbitante. 3 extravagante, disparatado. 4 s. extravagante, excéntrico.
**extravaganza** (ekstrævagæ·nša) s. TEAT. obra extravagante y fantástica.
**extravasate (to)** (ekstræ·vaseit) tr. extravenar. 2 intr. MED. extravasarse, extravenarse.
**extreme** (ekstrı·m) adj. extremo: ~ unction, extremaunción. 2 extremado, riguroso. 3 s. extremo [parte extrema; punto último], extremidad: to go to extremes, extremar las cosas; in the ~, en extremo, con extremo. 4 LÓG., MAT. extremo.
**extremely** (-li) adv. extremadamente, extremamente, sumamente, con o en extremo.
**extremism** (-išm) s. extremismo.
**extremity** (ekstre·miti) s. extremidad, fin. 2 extremo, exceso. 3 situación extrema, necesidad, apuro. 4 pl. medidas extremas. 5 ANAT. extremidades.
**extricate (to)** (e·kstrikeit) tr. desembarazar, desenredar, desembrollar, zafar, librar, sacar de.
**extrication** (-ei·shøn) s. desembarazo, desembrollo, desenredo.
**extrinsic (al** (ekstri·nsik(al)) adj. extrínseco.
**extroversion** (ekstrovø·ʳshøn) s. MED. extroversión. 2 PSIC. extraversión.
**extrovert** (e·kstrovøʳt) s. PSIC. extrovertido.
**extrude (to)** (ekstru·d) tr. empujar fuera, hacer salir.
**extrusión** (ekstru·ỹøn) s. acción de hacer salir; expulsión. 2 operación de hacer pasar [un metal calentado, un plástico, etc.], mediante presión, por los orificios de un molde, hilera, etc.
**exuberance** (egšiu·børans) s. exuberancia. 2 exceso, profusión.
**exuberant** (egšiu·børant) adj. exuberante, lujuriante, profuso. 2 extremado. 3 contento, radiante.
**exudate** (e·ksiudeit) s. exudado.
**exudation** (eksiudei·shøn) s. exudación. 2 exudado.
**exude (to)** (eksiu·d) tr.-intr. exudar, rezumar.

**exult (to)** (egšø·lt) intr. exultar, alegrarse; gozarse en el propio triunfo.
**exultant** (egšsø·ltant) adj. exultante, ufano.
**exultation** (-ei·shøn) s. exultación, alborozo, sentimiento gozoso del propio triunfo.
**eyas** (a·ias) s. halcón niego.
**eye** (ai) s. ojo [órgano de la visión; atención, vigilancia], ojo, vista, mirada: black ~, ojo negro, amoratado; mind your ~, pop. ¡cuidado!, ¡ojo!; my eyes!, exclamación de asombro; to catch the ~, llamar la atención, atraer la mirada; to have a cast in the ~, ser ligeramente bizco; to keep an ~ on, vigilar, mirar con sospecha o deseo; to make eyes at, poner los ojos tiernos a; to see ~ to ~, estar completamente de acuerdo; before one's eyes, a la vista, en presencia de uno; in the ~ of, a los ojos de; up to the eyes, hasta los ojos; completamente metido o enfrascado; with an ~ to, con vistas a, con la intención de. 2 ojo [de una aguja, de una herramienta, del pan, del queso, etc.]. 3 COST. cocheta, presilla. 4 ARQ. abertura superior de una cúpula. 5 ocelo [en una pluma]. 6 centro [de una flor]. 7 BOT. yema, grillo.
**eye (to)** tr. mirar, clavar la mirada en. 2 hacer ojos o agujeros en.
**eyeball** (ai·bol) s. ANAT. globo del ojo.
**eyebolt** (ai·boult) s. armella. 2 perno de ojo.
**eyebright** (ai·brait) s. BOT. eufrasia.
**eyebrow** (ai·brau) s. ANAT. ceja.
**eyecup** (ai·køp) s. ojera [para bañar el ojo].
**eyed** (aid) adj. de ojos: blue-eyed, de ojos azules.
**eyeglass** (ai·glæs) s. ÓPT. ocular; anteojo. 2 pl. anteojos, gafas, lentes, quevedos.
**eyehole** (ai·joul) s. COST. ojete. 2 atisbadero.
**eyelash** (ai·læsh) s. ANAT. pestaña.
**eyeless** (ai·lis) adj. ciego. 2 sin ojos.
**eyelet** (ai·lit) s. COST. ojete. 2 MAR. ollao. 3 resquicio, abertura.
**eyelet (to)** tr. ojetear.
**eyelid** (ai·lid) s. ANAT. párpado.
**eyepiece** (ai·pıs) s. ÓPT. ocular.
**eyeshot** (ai·shat) s. mirada, vista, alcance de la vista.
**eyesight** (ai·sait) s. vista [sentido]. 2 vista, observación. 3 vista, paisaje.
**eyesore** (ai·soʳ) s. cosa que ofende la vista.
**eyestrain** (ai·strein) s. vista fatigada.
**eyetooth** (ai·tuz) s. colmillo.
**eyewash** (ai·uash) s. colirio. 2 fam. jarabe de pico.
**eyewater** (ai·uotøʳ) s. colirio.
**eyewinker** (ai·unkøʳ) s. ANAT. pestaña.
**eyewitness** (aiui·tnis) s. testigo ocular o presencial.
**eyey** (ai·i) adj. ojoso.
**eyrie, eyry** (e·øri) s. nido de águilas, nido de ave de rapiña.
**Ezechias** (eši·kias) n. pr. m. Ezequías.
**Ezekiel** (eši·kiøl) n. pr. m. Ezequiel.

# F

**F, f** (ef) *s*. F, f, sexta letra del alfabeto inglés. *2* MÚS. fa.

**fa** (fa) *s*. MÚS. fa.

**fabaceous** (fabei·shøs) *adj*. BOT. papilionáceo.

**Fabian** (fæbian) *adj*. fabiano.

**fable** (fei·bøl) *s*. fábula.

**fable (to)** *intr*. contar fábulas, fingir, mentir. *2 tr*. inventar, contar falsamente.

**fabled** (-d) *adj*. legendario, ficticio, fabuloso.

**fabric** (fæ·brik) *s*. tejido, tela, género. *2* manufactura, textura. *3* fábrica, edificio.

**fabricate (to)** (fæ·brikeit) *tr*. fabricar, hacer, construir. *2* inventar, forjar.

**fabrication** (ei·shøn) *s*. fabricación, construcción. *2* invención, fábula, mentira.

**fabulist** (fæ·biulist) *s*. fabulista, fabulador.

**fabulous** (fæ·biuløs) *adj*. fabuloso.

**façade** (fasa·d) *s*. ARQ. fachada, frontispicio. *2* cara, frente [de una cosa].

**face** (feis) *s*. cara, faz, rostro, gesto, semblante; *to make a wry ~*, torcer el rostro; *to pull a long ~*, poner cara larga; *to save one's ~*, salvar el prestigio; *to set one's ~ against*, oponerse a, ponerse contra; *~ to ~*, cara a cara; *in the ~ of*, ante, en presencia de; luchando contra, a despecho de. *2* valor, osadía, descaro. *3* mueca, gesto: *to make faces*, hacer muecas. *4* aspecto, apariencia: *on the ~ of it*, según las apariencias. *5* cara, faz, haz, superficie [de una cosa]; frente, fachada. *6* CRISTAL., GEOM. cara. *7* IMPR. ojo [de letra]. *8* IMPR. tipo [de letra]. *9* esfera [de reloj]. *10* boca [de herramienta]; cotillo [de martillo]. *11* paramento [de un muro].
*12 adj*. de cara, etc.: *~ card*, figura [de la baraja]; *~ value*, COM. valor nominal; fig. valor aparente; sentido literal.

**face (to)** *tr*. volverse o mirar hacia. *2* hacer cara o frente a, enfrentarse con; afrontar, arrostrar: *to ~ the music*, afrontar una situación. *3* dar a, mirar a, estar encarado a. *4* carear con, enfrentar con. *5* cubrir, revestir. *6* forrar, guarnecer [un vestido]. *7* pulir, labrar, etc., la superficie de. *8 to ~ out*, persistir audazmente en, sostener con descaro. *9 intr*. volver la cara, dar frente [a]. *10 to ~ about*, volver el rostro, dar media vuelta, cambiar de frente. *11 to ~ up to*, encararse con.

**faced** (fei·st) *adj*. de cara: *pale-faced*, de rostro pálido.

**facer** (fei·sø<sup>r</sup>) *s*. el o lo que pule, labra, etc., la superficie de una cosa. *2* fam. puñetazo en la cara. *3* fam. percance, revés.

**face-saving** *adj*. que salva las apariencias.

**facet** (fæ·sit) *s*. faceta.

**facet (to)** *tr*. labrar facetas en; labrar en facetas.

**facetious** (fasi·shøs) *adj*. jocoso, humorístico. *2* bromista, chancero.

**facial** (fe·shial) *adj*. facial: *~ eagle*, ángulo facial. *2 s*. fam. masaje facial.

**facile** (fæ·sil) *adj*. fácil [de hacer u obtener]. *2* complaciente, dócil. *3* listo, diestro, hábil.

**facilitate (to)** (fasili·liteit) *tr*. facilitar, posibilitar.

**facilitation** (-shøn) *s*. facilitación.

**facility** (fasi·liti) *s*. facilidad. *2* destreza. *3* propensión a complacer o a dejarse persuadir.

**facing** (fei·sing) *s*. paramento, revestimento. *2* COST. vuelta, vistas. *3* encaramento. *4 pl*. MIL. cuello, puños y franjas [de un uniforme].

**facsimile** (faksi·mili) *s*. facsímil, facsímile.

**fact** (fækt) *s*. hecho; verdad, realidad: *the ~ is that*, ello es que; *in ~*, de hecho, en realidad. *2* dato.

**faction** (fæ·kshøn) *s*. facción, bando, parcialidad. *2* discordia, disensión.

**factious** (fæ·kshøs) *adj*. faccioso. *2* partidista.

**factitious** (fæ·ktishøs) *adj*. facticio, artificial.

**factitive** (fæ·ktitiv) *adj*. GRAM. factitivo.

**factor** (fæ·ktø<sup>r</sup>) *s*. factor [elemento, concausa, lo que contribuye a un resultado]. *2* MAT. factor. *3* COM. factor, agente.

**factor (to)** *tr*. MAT. descomponer en factores.

**factorage** (fæ·ktøridŷ) *s*. factoraje. *2* comisión o sueldo del factor o agente.

**factory** (fæ·ktøri) *s*. factoría. *2* fábrica, manufactura.

**factotum** (fæktou·tøm) *s*. factótum.

**facture** (fæ·ksho<sup>r</sup>) *s*. B. ART. factura.

**facula** (fæ·kiula) *s*. ASTR. fácula.

**facultative** (fæ·kølteitiv) *adj*. facultativo [de una facultad]. *2* facultativo, potestativo.

**faculty** (fæ·kølti) *s*. facultad [en todos sus sentidos].

**fad** (fæd) *s*. novedad, moda. *2* marca, chifladura, afición pasajera.

**fade (to)** (feid) *intr*. marchitarse; *2* debilitarse, decaer. *3* palidecer, descolorirse; perder [un color]. *4* apagarse, desvanecerse, desaparecer

[gradualmente]. *5 tr.* marchitar. *6* debilitar. *7* descolorir; poner pálido.
**fade-in** *s.* CINEM. fundido.
**fading** (fei·ding) *s.* marchitamiento. *2* desvanecimiento, pérdida gradual de color, intensidad, etc. *3* RADIO. fading.
**fæcal** (fe·kal) *adj.* fecal.
**fæces** (fi·seš) *s. pl.* heces, excrementos. *2* hez, poso.
**faerie, faery** (fe·øri) *s.* ant. hada, duende. *2* reino de las hadas. *3 adj.* de hadas, maravilloso.
**fag** (fæg) *s.* (Ingl.) estudiante que sirve a otro mayor. *2* azacán. *3* tarea penosa. *4* fatiga: *brain* ~, fatiga mental. *5* fam. (Ingl.) pitillo. *6* ~ *end*, extremo deshilachado; pezolada; cabo, desperdicio, cola, última parte.
**fag (to)** *tr.* fatigar, reventar, hacer trabajar como un negro. *2 intr.* fatigarse, trabajar como un negro. *3* deshilacharse, destorcerse. ¶ Pret. y p. p.: *fagged;* ger.: *fagging.*
**faggot, fagot** (fæ·gøt) *s.* haz de leña, fajina. *2* haz de barras de hierro. *3* (Ingl.) vieja, bruja.
**faggot, fagot (to)** *tr.* atar en haces.
**fail** (feil) *s.* falta, esp. en *without* ~, sin falta.
**fail (to)** *intr.* faltar [no existir, ser insuficiente]. *2* menguar, decaer, debilitarse, consumirse, acabarse. *3* faltar, fallar, ceder, inutilizarse. *4* fracasar. *5* salir mal [en un examen]. *6* fallar, frustrarse, malograrse. *7* errar, equivocarse. *8* COM. quebrar. *9 to* ~ *in*, estar falto o insuficientemente dotado de. *10 to* ~ *to*, no poder, no lograr, dejar de [hacer algo]. *11 tr.-intr.* faltar [dejar de asistir], abandonar; no cumplir sus compromisos, deberes, etc., con [uno]. *12 tr.* errar, marrar. *13* suspender [en un examen].
**failing** (fei·ling) *s.* falta, defecto. *2* decadencia. *3* fracaso, malogro. *4 prep.* faltando, a falta de.
**failure** (fei·liø<sup>r</sup>) *s.* fracaso, fiasco, malogro. *2* persona que ha fracasado. *3* falta, escasez. *4* falta, no ocurrencia, el no hacer o dejar de hacer [algo]. *5* paro [de un motor, etc.]. *6* COM. quiebra.
**fain** (fein) *adj.* contento. *2* dispuesto, resignado. *3* obligado. *4 adv.* de buena gana.
**faint** (feint) *adj.* débil. *2* desfallecido, desmayado. *3* lánguido, abatido. *4* tímido, cobarde. *5* apagado, tenue, leve, imperceptible. *6 s.* FAINTING.
**faint (to)** *intr.* desmayarse. *2* desfallecer. *3* desalentarse.
**faint-hearted** *adj.* tímido, cobarde, medroso, pusilánime, apocado.
**fainting** (fei·inting) *s.* desmayo; desfallecimiento: ~ *fit*, desmayo, síncope.
**faintly** (fei·ntli) *adv.* débilmente. *2* desmayadamente. *3* vagamente, indistintamente.
**fair** (fe·ø<sup>r</sup>) *adj.* hermoso, bello: *the* ~ *sex*, el bello sexo. *2* bueno, regular, mediano, bastante grande: ~ *chance*, buenas probabilidades; ~ *to middling*, fam. mediano, bastante bueno. *3* bueno, favorable, propicio: *to be in a* ~ *way to*, estar en buen camino de. *4* sereno, despejado [cielo]; bueno, bonancible [tiempo]. *5* limpio, terso, sin defecto, sin tacha: ~ *copy*, copia en limpio. *6* justo, recto, honrado, lícito, sincero, leal: ~ *and square*, honrado, leal; ~ *play*, juego limpio. *7* equitativo, razonable. *8* imparcial; sin ventajas por ninguna parte. *9* afable, franco, cortés. *10* blanco [tez], rubio [cabello, pers.]. *11* legible, bien formada [letra]. *12* suave [línea; curva]. *13* libre, expedito.
*14 adv.* favorablemente. *15* bondadosamente, cortésmente. *16* lealmente, imparcialmente: *to*

*play* ~, jugar limpio. *17* clara, distintamente. *18* exactamente, de lleno.
*19 s.* mercado, feria, exposición. *20* poét. bella [mujer]. *21 the* ~, el bello sexo.
**fair (to)** *intr.* aclararse [el tiempo].
**fairground** (-graund) *s.* (E.U.) cercado al aire libre para una feria.
**fairish** (-ish) *adv.* bastante bueno o grande, regular.
**fairly** (-li) *adv.* completamente. *2* bastante, medianamente. *3* favorablemente. *4* razonablemente. *5* justamente, imparcialmente. *6* lealmente, honradamente. *7* claramente, distintamente.
**fair-minded** *adj.* justo, imparcial.
**fairness** (-nis) *s.* limpieza, pureza. *2* honradez. *3* imparcialidad, justicia. *4* hermosura. *5* blancura [de la tez]. *6* serenidad [del cielo]. *7* color rubio.
**fair-spoken** *adj.* cortés, bien hablado.
**fairway** (-uei) *s.* espacio o camino abierto. *2* parte navegable [de un río, etc.]. *3* canal [de un puerto]. *4* cierta parte del campo de golf.
**fairy** (-i) *s.* hada, duende: ~ *tale*, cuento de hadas.
**faith** (fei·z) *s.* fe [en todos sus sentidos]: *in good* ~, de buena fe; *upon my* ~, a fe mía. *2* palabra dada: *to break* ~ *with*, faltar a la palabra dada a. *3 in* ~, a la verdad. *4 interj.* en verdad.
**faithful** (-ful) *adj.* fiel. *2* leal, creyente. *4* solemne [promesa]. *5 s.* fiel [de una iglesia]. *6* creyente.
**faithfully** (-i) *adv.* fielmente. *2* firmemente.
**faithless** (-lis) *adj.* infiel. *2* desleal, pérfido. *3* sin fe.
**fake** (feik) *s.* MAR. aduja [de cable]. *2* imitación, falsificación, filfa, amaño. *3* impostor. *4 adj.* falso, fingido, amañado.
**fake (to)** *tr.* MAR. adujar. *2* falsificar, imitar, fingir, falsear, amañar.
**fakir** (fæ·ki<sup>r</sup>) *s.* faquir.
**Falange** (fei·lændÿ) *s.* POL. Falange.
**Falangist** (falæ·ndÿist) *adj.-s.* POL. falangista.
**falcate(d** (fæ·lkit(id) *adj.* falcado.
**falchion** (fo·lchøn) *s.* cimitarra.
**falciform** (fæ·lsifo<sup>r</sup>m) *adj.* falciforme.
**falcon** (fo·lcøn) *s.* ORN. halcón. *2* ARTILL. falcón.
**falconry** (-ri) *s.* halconería, cetrería.
**falderal** (fæ·ldøræl), **falderol** (fæ·ldørol) *s.* chuchería, fruslería. *2* perendengue.
**faldstool** (fo·ldstul) *s.* faldistorio. *2* facistol.
**fall** (fol) *s.* caída: ~ *of snow*, nevada; *the Fall*, la caída [del primer hombre]. *2* decadencia, ruina. *3* baja, bajada, descenso. *4* declive, pendiente. *5* cascada, catarata, salto de agua. *6* (E.U.) otoño. *7* corta [de árboles]. *8* desembocadura [de un río]. *9* MÚS. cadencia, disminución del sonido. *10* MAR. beta, tira, cinta, etc., colgante.
**fall (to)** *intr.* caer. *2* caerse. *3* bajar, descender. *4* menguar, decrecer, disminuir. *5* decaer. *6* calmarse [el mar, el viento]. *7* venirse abajo, desplomarse. *8* desembocar [un río]. *9* ponerse: *to* ~ *to work*, ponerse a trabajar. *10* tocar, corresponderle [a uno una cosa]; pasar a manos de. *11* MAR. *to* ~ *aboard*, abordar. *12 to* ~ *across*, topar con, encontrar. *13 to* ~ *asleep*, dormirse. *14 to* ~ *a prey to*, ser presa o víctima de. *15 to* ~ *away*, enflaquecer, marchitarse; desvanecerse; rebelarse; apostatar. *16 to* ~ *back*, retroceder; hacerse atrás, no cumplir lo prometido. *17 to* ~ *back on* o *upon*, recurrir a, echar mano de; MIL. replegarse hacia. *18 to* ~ *behind*, rezagarse, atrasarse. *19 to* ~ *down*, caer, caer al suelo, desprenderse; postrarse; hundirse, fracasar. *20 to*

~ *due*, caer, vencer [una letra, etc.]. *21 to ~ flat,* caer tendido; no producir efecto, no tener éxito. *22 to ~ foul of*, reñir con; atacar; MAR. abordar; enredarse con. *23 to ~ in*, desplomarse, hundirse; expirar, caducar; MIL. alinearse. *24 to ~ in love*, enamorarse. *25 to ~ in with*, encontrarse con; ponerse o estar de acuerdo con, coincidir; armonizar con. *26 to ~ into*, trabar [conversación]; adquirir [un hábito]; acceder a. *27 to ~ off*, caer, desprenderse; apartarse; desamistarse; rebelarse; disminuir, decaer; MAR. abatir. *28 to ~ on*, caer sobre; echarse sobre; encontrarse con; empezar; recurrir a, echar mano de. *29 to ~ out*, caerse; reñir, desavenirse; acontecer; resultar. *30 to ~ over*, caer por; desertar, pasarse; pop. adular. *31 to ~ short*, faltar, escasear; quedar corto, no alcanzar; fracasar. *32 to ~ through*, fracasar, malograrse. *33 to ~ to*, empezar a; ponerse a comer; reñir, cerrarse [una puerta]. *34 to ~ to one's lot*, caber o caerle en suerte a uno, tocarle. *35 to.~ upon*, atacar, embestir; recurrir a, echar mano de; tocar, incumbir. ¶ Pret.: *fell*; p. p.: *fallen.*

**fallacious** (fælei·shøs) *adj.* falaz, engañoso, sofístico.

**fallacy** (fæ·lasi) *s.* falacia, apariencia engañosa, sofisma. *2* error.

**fallen** (fo·løn) *p. p.* de TO FALL. *2 s.* pl. *the fallen*, los caídos [en la lucha].

**fallibility** (fælibi·liti) *s.* falibilidad.

**fallible** (fæ·libøl) *adj.* falible.

**falling** (fo·ling) *adj.* cayente. *2* en baja, que disminuye. *3* decreciente [diptongo]. *4* MED. ~ *sickness*, epilepsia. *5* ASTR. ~ *star*, estrella fugaz. *6 s.* caída, bajada, baja, descenso.

**fallow** (fæ·lou) *s.* AGR. barbecho [tierra que descansa]. *2 adj.* en barbecho, baldío. *3 adj.-s.* flavo [color]. *4* ZOOL. ~ *deer*, gamo.

**false** (fols) *adj.* falso: ~ *face*, máscara, careta; ~ *keel*, falsa quilla; ~ *note*, MÚS. nota falsa; ~ *pretences*, dolo, engaño; ~ *rib*, ANAT. costilla falsa; ~ *step*, tropiezo; paso en falso; *to place in a* ~ *light*, poner mal, desacreditar. *2* simulado. *3* postizo: ~ *hair*, cabello postizo. *4* MEC. provisional, de quita y pon. *5* irregular: ~ *imprisonment*, detención ilegal. *6* ~ *bottom*, doble fondo. *7 adv.* falsamente: *to play* ~, engañar.

**false-faced** *adj.* hipócrita, falso.

**false-hearted** *adj.* falso, pérfido, traidor.

**falsehood** (-jud) *s.* falsedad. *2* falsía, perfidia. *3* mentira, inexactitud. *4* mendacidad.

**falsely** (-li) *adv.* falsamente. *2* erróneamente. *3* mentirosamente. *4* pérfidamente.

**falsetto** (folse·tou) *s.* MÚS. falsete.

**falsification** (folsifikei·shøn) *s.* falseamiento, falsificación. *2* confutación.

**falsify** (fo·lsifai) *tr.* falsear, falsificar. *2* faltar [a la fe o a la palabra dada]. *3* confutar, desmentir. *4 intr.* mentir. ¶ Pret. y p. p.: *falsified.*

**falter** (fo·ltø^r) *s.* vacilación, temblor.

**falter (to)** *intr.* vacilar, titubear. *2* tambalearse, temblar. *34 intr.-tr.* balbucir.

**fame** (feim) *s.* fama, reputación. *2* renombre.

**fame (to)** *tr.* afamar, celebrar.

**famed** (-d) *adj.* afamado.

**familiar** (fami·lia^r) *adj.* familiar. | En el sentido de perteneciente a la familia es arcaico. *2* íntimo [amigo, compañero]. *3* ~ *with*, familiarizado con, versado en. *4 s.* amigo íntimo. *5* demonio familiar. *6* ECLES. familiar.

**familiarity** (familiæ·riti) *s.* familiaridad. *2* intimidad. *3* ~ *with*, conocimiento de.

**familiarize (to)** (fami·liaraiš) *tr.* familiarizar. *2* acostumbrar, avezar.

**family** (fæ·mili) *s.* familia. *2* alcurnia, sangre, linaje. *3 adj.* familiar, de familia: ~ *allowance*, subsidio familiar; ~ *circle*, TEAT. galería, ~ *name*, apellido; ~ *tree*, árbol genealógico; *in a* ~ *way*, sin ceremonia; *in the* ~ *way*, encinta, en estado interesante.

**famine** (fæ·min) *s.* hambre, carestía.

**famish (to)** (fæ·mish) *tr.-intr.* hambrear; matar o morirse de hambre.

**famished** (-d) *adj.* hambriento.

**famous** (fei·møs) *adj.* famoso, afamado, célebre, señalado. *2* fam. excelente, de primera.

**fan** (fæn) *s.* abanico, ventalle. *2* AGR. aventador. *3* MEC. ventilador. *4* paleta [de hélice]. *5* aficionado [a un deporte], hincha. *6* entusiasta, admirador.

**fan (to)** *tr.* abanicar. *2* aventar. *3* ventilar. *4* soplar [el fuego, etc.]. *5 tr.-intr. to ~ out*, extender o extenderse como un abanico.

**fanatic(al** (fanæ·tik(al) *adj.* fanático.

**fanaticism** (fanæ·tisišm) *s.* fanatismo.

**fancied** (fæ·nsid) *adj.* imaginario. *2* preferido.

**fancier** (fæ·nsiø^r) *s.* fantaseador. *2* aficionado. *3* criador de aves y animales.

**fanciful** (fæ·nsiful) *adj.* imaginativo, quimérico. *2* antojadizo. *3* caprichoso, fantástico.

**fancy** (fæ·nsi) *s.* fantasía, imaginación. *2* magín. *3* antojo, capricho. *4* imagen, idea, concepción. *5* inclinación, afición, amor. *6* gusto [en materia de vestidos, etc.]. *7* afición [los aficionados]. *8 adj.* fantástico, caprichoso. *9* de capricho, de fantasía: ~ *dress*, disfraz, traje de capricho; ~ *goods*, artículos de fantasía; ~ *skating*, patinaje artístico. *10* de gusto, elegante, precioso.

**fancy (to)** *'tr.* imaginar, fantasear, pensar, figurarse. *2* apetecerle, gustarle a uno [una cosa]; aficionarse a, encapricharse por. *3* criar [animales de raza]. *4 intr.* fantasear. ¶ Pret. y p. p.: *fancied.*

**fancy-free** *adj.* libre del poder del amor.

**fancywork** (-uø^rk) *s.* labor [de aguja, ganchillo, etc.].

**fanfare** (fæ·nfeø^r) *s.* son de trompetas.

**fanfaronade** (fænfarønei·d) *s.* fanfarronada.

**fanfaronade (to)** *intr.* fanfarronear.

**fang** (fæng) *s.* colmillo, navaja [de animal]. *2* diente [de serpiente, venenosa]. *3* raíz [de un diente].

**fang (to)** *tr.* clavar los dientes o colmillos.

**fanion** (fæ·niøn) *s.* banderola.

**fanlight** (fæ·nlait) *s.* ARQ. abanico.

**Fanny** (fæ·ni) *n. pr. f. dim.* de FRANCES.

**fantail** (fæ·nteil) *s.* cola en forma de abanico. *2* CARP. cola de milano. *3* ORN. colipava [paloma].

**fantasía** (fantei·šia) *s.* MÚS. fantasía.

**fantast** (fæ·ntast) *s.* visionario, soñador.

**fantastic(al** (fæntæ·stik(al) *adj.* fantástico, grotesco. *2* excéntrico, extravagante, caprichoso. *3* imaginario.

**fantasy** (fæ·ntasi) *s.* fantasía. *2* ensueño. *3* humor, capricho. *4* dibujo o trabajo fantástico.

**far** (fa^r) *adv.* lejos, a lo lejos, a distancia, en lontananza, remotamente: ~ *from*, lejos de; ~ *be it from me*, lejos de mí, no permita Dios; *how* ~, cuán lejos, hasta donde; *how* ~ *is it?*, ¿cuánto hay de aquí allá?; *to go* ~, ir lejos; alcanzar para mucho, durar mucho; ~ *and near*, ~ *and wide*,

por todas partes; *as ~ as,* tan lejos como, hasta, hasta donde; en cuanto, por lo que a mí toca; *as ~ as I know,* que yo sepa; *in so ~ as,* en cuanto, en lo que, hasta donde; *so ~, thus ~,* hasta ahora, hasta aquí; *so ~ so good,* mientras siga así, todo va bien. *2* muy, mucho, en alto grado, en gran parte, con mucho: *~ away,* muy lejos; *~ better,* mucho mejor; *~ into,* hasta muy adentro; hasta muy tarde de [la noche, etc.]; hasta muy avanzado [el invierno, etc.]; *~ off,* remoto, lejano; a gran distancia, a lo lejos; *by ~,* con mucho; *to go ~ to,* o *toward,* contribuir en mucho a.
*3 adj.* lejano, distante, remoto; hecho a una larga distancia: *the ~ past,* el pasado lejano; *Far East,* el lejano Oriente; *Far West,* el Oeste [de los E.U.]; *it is a ~ cry from,* dista mucho de.
**faraway** (-auei) *adj.* lejano, alejado. *2* distraído.
**farad** (fa'ræd) *s.* ELECT. faradio.
**farce** (fa'rs) *s.* farsa. *2* comicidad, humor grotesco. *4* coc. relleno; albóndiga.
**farce (to)** *tr.* henchir o salpimentar [un libro, etc.] con citas o con pasajes graciosos.
**farcical** (fa·'sikal) *adj.* burlesco, bufo.
**fare** (fe·ø') *s.* pasajero, pasaje; precio del pasaje [en un vehículo público]. *2* comida, alimento, mesa, plato.
**fare (to)** *intr.* pasarlo, irle a uno [bien o mal]: *how did you ~?,* ¿cómo le ha ido? *2* pasar, ocurrir. *3* comer, alimentarse, tratarse. *4 to ~ forth,* ponerse en camino.
**farewell** (-uel) *interj.* ¡adiós! *2* despedida, adiós: *to bid ~ to,* o *take ~ of,* despedir a, despedirse de.
**far-fetched** *adj.* rebuscado, forzado, traido por los cabellos.
**far-flung** (adj. vasto, extenso.
**farina** (farı·na) *s.* harina de cereales, raíces, etc. *2* fécula, almidón. *3* BOT. polen.
**farinaceous** (færinei·shøs) *adj.* farináceo.
**farm** (fa'rm) *s.* granja, cortijo, hacienda, labranza, estancia, finca agrícola. *2* arrendamiento de rentas o impuestos.
**farm (to)** *tr.* cultivar, labrar, explotar [la tierra]. *2* arrendar o tomar en arriendo [impuestos, rentas, trabajos].
**farmer** (-ø') *s.* granjero, labrador, hacendado, colono, *estanciero.
**farmhand** (-jænd) *s.* mozo de labranza, gañán.
**farmhouse** (-jaus) *s.* granja, alquería, casa de labor.
**farming** (-ing) *s.* cultivo, labranza. *2* arrendamiento de rentas o impuestos.
**farmstead** (-sted) *s.* granja, cortijada.
**farmyard** (-ya'd) *s.* corral [de una granja].
**farness** (fa·'nis) *s.* distancia, lejanía.
**faro** (fe·rou o fa·rou) *s.* faraón [juego].
**farrago** (farei·gou) *s.* mezcla, fárrago.
**far-reaching** *adj.* de mucho alcance o trascendencia.
**farrier** (fæ·riø') *s.* herrador, albéitar.
**farriery** (fæ·riøri) *s.* albeitería, herrería.
**farrow** (fe·rou) *s.* lechigada [de cerdos].
**farrow (to)** *tr.-intr.* parir [la cerda].
**farseeing** (fa'sı·ing) *adj.* perspicaz. *2* previsor, precavido.
**farsighted** (fa'sai·tid) *adj.* perspicaz. *2* sagaz. *3* présbita.
**farther** (fa·'dø') *adv.* más lejos, a mayor distancia, más allá. *2* ulteriormente. *3* más, además. *4 adj.* más distante. *5* ulterior. *6* más extenso.

**farthermost** (-moust) *adj.* [el] más lejano o distante.
**farthest** (-est) *adj. superl.* [el] más lejano o extremo. *2 adv.* más lejos, a la mayor distancia; más. *4 at (the) ~,* a lo más o lo sumo.
**fascicle** (fæ·sikøl) *s.* fascículo, hacecillo. *2* BOT. glomérulo. *3* fascículo, entrega [de una obra].
**fascinate (to)** (fæ·sineit) *tr.* fascinar.
**fascination** (fæsine·shøn) *s.* fascinación.
**fascine** (fæsı·n) *s.* FORT. fajina.
**Fascism** (fæ·sišm) *s.* fascismo.
**Fascist** (fæ·sist) *adj.-s.* fascista.
**fashion** (fæ·shøn) *s.* forma, hechura. *2* modo, manera: *in a ~, after a ~,* en cierto modo, hasta cierto punto, así así. *3* clase, uso, estilo: *in ~,* de moda; *out of ~,* pasado de moda, anticuado; *to set the ~,* dictar la moda. *5* elegancia, buen tono, el gran mundo. *6 ~ plate,* figurín.
**fashion (to)** *tr.* formar, hacer, labrar. *2* amoldar.
**fashionable** (-abøl) *adj.* a la moda, de moda, que está en boga. *2* elegante, de buen tono.
**fast** (fast) *adj.* firme, fuerte, seguro; constante, fiel; sólido, duradero. *2* sujeto, atado, fijo, apretado, estrecho, íntimo: *to make ~,* fijar, amarrar, asegurar, cerrar. *3* atascado. *4* rápido, veloz. *5* adelantado [reloj]. *6* profundo [sueño]. *7* disipado, disoluto. *8* BIOL. resistente: *acid ~,* ácido-resistente.
*9 adv.* firmemente, fuertemente. *10* estrechamente. *11* duraderamente. *12* rápidamente, aprisa. *13* profundamente [dormido].
*14 s.* amarra, cable, lo que sujeta. *15* ayuno, abstinencia: *to break one's ~,* desayunarse.
**fast (to)** *intr.* ayunar. *2* hacer abstinencia.
**fasten (to)** (fa·søn) *tr.* afirmar, fijar, atar, amarrar, trincar, sujetar. *2* unir, pegar. *3* cerrar [con cerrojo, aldaba, cierre, etc.]. *4* abrochar. *5* fijar [los ojos, el pensamiento, etc.]. *6* atribuir, echar [la culpa]; poner [un mote]. *7* clavar [los dientes, etc.]. *8 intr.* agarrarse, fijarse, pegarse. *9* fraguar [la argamasa, etc.]. *10* cerrarse, abrocharse.
**fastener** (fa·snø') *s.* lo que sirve para sujetar o asegurar; broche, fiador, pasador, falleba, etc.
**fastening** (-ing) *s.* atadura, amarradura. *2* lo que sirve para sujetar, unir o cerrar; cerradura, cierre, broche, corchete, etc.
**faster** (fa·stø') *s.* ayunador.
**fastidious** (fæsti·diøs) *adj.* descontentadizo, exigente, delicado, esquilimoso. *2* desdeñoso.
**fastigium** (fæsti·yiøm) *s.* fastigio.
**fasting** (fa·sting) *s.* ayuno; abstinencia.
**fastness** (fa·stnis) *s.* firmeza, fijeza, solidez. *2* rapidez. *3* fortaleza, plaza fuerte. *4* disipación, libertinaje. *5 pl.* fragosidades.
**fat** (fæt) *adj.* gordo, obeso; grueso. *2* lleno, repleto. *3* graso, pingüe. *4* fértil, productivo. *5* lucrativo, provechoso. *6* rico, opulento. *7* grosero, tonto, estúpido. *8 s.* gordura, grasa, manteca. *9* lo mejor, lo más rico o provechoso [de una cosa].
**fat (to)** *tr.-intr.* engordar. ¶ Pret. y p. p.: *fatted;* ger.: *fatting.*
**fatal** (fei·tal) *adj.* fatal. *2* mortífero, letal. *3* profético, ominoso. *4 the ~ sisters,* las Parcas.
**fatalism** (-išm) *s.* fatalismo.
**fatality** (fatæ·liti) *s.* fatalidad. *2* desgracia, desastre; muerte.
**fate** (feit) *s.* hado, destino. *2* sino, suerte. *3 pl.* MIT. *the Fates,* las Parcas.
**fated** (-id) *adj.* predestinado. *2* hadado.

**fateful** (-ful) *adj.* fatal, funesto. *2* crítico, trascendental. *3* fatídico.
**fatheaded** (fæ·tjedid) *adj.* fam. torpe, estúpido.
**father** (-fa·ðøʳ) *s.* padre. *2* Dios Padre. *3* tío [tratamiento que se da a un hombre de edad].
**father** (to) *tr.* engendrar, producir, inventar. *2* servir de padre a, tratar como hijo. *3* prohijar, adoptar como suyo. *4* atribuir, achacar.
**fatherhood** (-jud) *s.* paternidad.
**father-in-law** *s.* padre político, suegro.
**fatherland** (-lænd) *s.* patria, madre patria.
**fatherliness** (-linis) *s.* ternura paternal.
**fatherly** (-li) *adj.* paternal. *2 adv.* paternalmente.
**fathom** (fæ·ðøm) *s.* braza [medida].
**fathom** (to) *tr.* MAR. sondar. *2* penetrar, profundizar, comprender.
**fathomless** (fa·ðømlis) *adj.* insondable, impenetrable.
**fatidical** (fati·dikal) *adj.* fatídico.
**fatigue** (to) *tr.* fatigar, cansar, rendir.
**fatigue** (fatı·g) *s.* fatiga, cansancio. *2* trabajo, ajetreo. *3* MIL. ~ *duty*, mecánica.
**fatling** (fæ·tling) *s.* ceboncillo.
**fatness** (-nis) *s.* gordura, obesidad. *2* crasitud, pinguosidad. *3* fertilidad.
**fatten** (to) (-øn) *tr.* engordar, cebar. *2* fertilizar, engrasar. *3 intr.* engordar.
**fattish** (-ish) *adj.* regordete. *2* grasoso.
**fatty** (-i) *adj.* graso, adiposo: ~ *tissue*, ANAT. tejido adiposo. *2* gordo, gordinflón. *3* grasiento, untuoso. *4* QUÍM. graso.
**fatuity** (fatiu·iti) *s.* fatuidad, necedad.
**fatuous** (fæ·chuøs) *adj.* fatuo, necio. *2* ilusorio.
**fauces** (fo·siš) *s. pl.* ANAT. fauces.
**faucet** (fo·sit) *s.* grito, espita, canilla.
**fault** (folt) *s.* falta, defecto, tacha, imperfección; error, equivocación; culpa, desliz: *it is my* ~, yo tengo la culpa; *to find* ~ *with*, hallar defectos en, censurar, criticar. *2* GEOL., MIN. falla. *3* pérdida del rastro por los perros: *at* ~, perplejo, desorientado; fam. en falta.
**fault** (to) *tr.* GEOL. producir falla en.
**faultfinder** (-fai·ndøʳ) *s.* reparón, criticón.
**faultfinding** (-fai·nding) *adj.* reparón, criticón. *2 s.* crítica; manía de criticar.
**faultless** (-lis) *adj.* impecable, perfecto, irreprochable, sin defecto, sin tacha, sin culpa.
**faulty** (-i) *adj.* defectuoso, imperfecto, incorrecto, vicioso, deficiente.
**faun** (fon) *s.* fauno.
**fauna** (fo·na) *s.* fauna.
**Faust** (faust) *n. pr. m.* Fausto.
**favo(u)r** (fei·vøʳ) *s.* favor [privanza; protección; ayuda, preferencia; beneficio, utilidad]: *to be in* ~ *with*, gozar del favor de; *to be in* ~ *of*, estar por, ser partidario de; *in* ~ *of*, en pro de; COM. a favor de. *2* favor [merced, beneficio, fineza]: *do me the* ~ *of*, hágame el favor de. *3* permiso: *by your* ~, con su permiso. *4* favor [cinta, etc.]. *5* grata, atenta [carta]. *6 pl.* favores [de una mujer].
**favo(u)r** (to) *tr.* favorecer. *2* fomentar. *3* agraciar, obsequiar [con]. *4* preferir, apoyar, estar de parte de. *5* apoyar, confirmar [una teoría, etc.]. *6* parecerse, salir a.
**favo(u)rable** (-abøl) *adj.* favorable, propicio. *2* benévolo, benigno.
**favo(u)red** (-d) *adj.* favorecido. *2* querido, preferido.
**favo(u)rite** (-it) *adj.* favorito, predilecto, preferido. *2 s.* favorito, privado, valido, protegido.

**favo(u)ritism** (-itišm) *s.* favoritismo.
**fawn** (fon) *s.* ZOOL. cervato. *2* color del cervato.
**fawn** (to) *tr.-intr.* parir [la cierva]. *2 intr. to* ~ *on* o *upon*, hacer fiestas [el perro]; fig. adular, halagar servilmente.
**fay** (fei) *s.* hada, duende.
**fealty** (fi·alti) *s.* homenaje, fe [feudal]. *2* fidelidad, lealtad.
**fear** (fi·øʳ) *s.* miedo, temor, cuidado. *2* temor, veneración: ~ *of God*, temor de Dios.
**fear** (to) *tr.* temer, recelar, tener miedo de. *2* temer [tener temor o reverencia a]. *3 intr.* temer, tener miedo.
**fearful** (-ful) *adj.* temeroso, espantoso, pavoroso. *2* terrible, tremendo, imponente. *3* grande, enorme. *4* temeroso, medroso, que teme. *5* de miedo.
**fearless** (-lis) *adj.* impávido, intrépido, impertérrito, bravo, osado; que no teme.
**fearsome** (-søm) *adj.* temeroso, espantoso. *2* temeroso, tímido, miedoso.
**feasibility** (fišibi·liti) *s.* calidad de factible, posibilidad.
**feasible** (fi·šibøl) *adj.* factible, hacedero, practicable, posible, viable. *2* a propósito, apropiado.
**feast** (fist) *s.* fiesta [día; solemnidad; regocijo]: ~ *day*, día de fiesta. *2* festejo. *3* festín, banquete.
**feast** (to) *intr.* banquetearse, comer opíparamente. *2* regalarse, deleitarse. *3 tr.* festejar. *4* agasajar, banquetear. *5* recrear, deleitar.
**feat** (fit) *s.* hecho, acción. *2* proeza, hazaña. *3* acto de destreza; juego de manos.
**feather** (fe·ðøʳ) *s.* pluma [de ave]: *a* ~ *in one's cap*, fig. honor, triunfo para uno; *to show the white* ~, mostrar cobardía, volver las espaldas. *2* penacho, vanidad. *3* estado de espíritu, de salud, etc.; *in high* o *full* ~, alegre, animado. *4* mechón de pelos. *5* clase, calaña: *birds of a* ~, gente de la misma calaña. *6* MEC. proyección estrecha; nervio, pestaña, aleta. *7* CARP. lengüeta. *8* defecto [en una piedra preciosa]. *9* MAR. espuma que levanta el tajamar: *to cut a* ~, levantar espuma [el buque]; navegar con pluma del remo; fig. estar hecho un brazo de mar. *10 pl.* plumaje.
*11 adj.* de pluma o plumas: ~ *bed*, colchón de plumas; lecho de plumas. *12* leve, suave.
**feather** (to) *tr.* emplumar. *2* cubrir con plumas: *to* ~ *one's nest*, hacer su agosto, sacar tajada. *3* adelgazar [un borde o filo]. *4* CARP. machihembrar. *5* cortar [el aire] volando. *6* volver [la pala del remo], poniéndola casi horizontal. *7 intr.* emplumecer. *8* tener o tomar aspecto de plumas. *9* correrse [la tinta].
**feathered** (-d) *adj.* cubierto de plumas, emplumado. *2* de pluma [caza]. *3* fig. alado, ligero, veloz.
**featherstitch** (-tich) *s.* COST. punto de espina.
**featherweight** (-ueit) *s.* persona o cosa de poco peso o importancia. *2* BOX. peso pluma.
**feathery** (-ri) *adj.* plúmeo, plumoso.
**feature** (fi·chøʳ) *s.* rasgo, facción [del rostro]. *2* forma, figura. *3* característica, rasgo distintivo. *4* lo más notable o principal: ~ *film*, ~ *picture*, película principal, de largo metraje.
**feature** (to) *tr.* parecerse, asemejarse. *2* destacar, hacer resaltar, dar importancia.
**featured** (-d) *adj.* formado, cincelado. *2* encarado [bien o mal]. *3* (E.U.) anunciado de un modo destacado.
**featureless** (-lis) *adj.* sin rasgos distintivos. *2* poco interesante.

**febrifuge** (fe·brifiudȳ) *adj.-s.* MED. febrífugo.
**febrile** (fí·bril o fe·bril) *adj.* febril.
**February** (fe·brueri) *s.* febrero.
**fecal** (fí·kal) *adj.* fecal.
**feces** (fí·sis̆) *s. pl.* heces.
**fecula** (fe·kiula) *s.* fécula, almidón.
**feculent** (fe·kiulønt) *adj.* feculento [que contiene heces].
**fecund** (fe·kønd) *adj.* fecundo.
**fecundate (to)** (fe·køndeit) *tr.* fecundar, fecundizar.
**fecundation** (-shøn) *s.* fecundación.
**fecundity** (fekø·nditi) *s.* fecundidad. 2 fertilidad.
**fed** (fed) *pret.-p. p.* de TO FEED. 2 ~ up, harto, hastiado, cansado: ~ *up with*, harto de.
**federal** (fe·døral) *adj.* federal.
**federalism** (-iš̆m) *s.* federalismo.
**federalize (to)** (-aiš̆) *tr.* federar.
**federate (to)** (fe·døreit) *tr.* federar, confederar. 2 aliar. 3 *ref.* federarse, confederarse, aliarse.
**federation** (fedørei·shøn) *s.* federación, confederación, liga.
**fee** (fí) *s.* honorarios, derechos; cuota. 2 propina, gratificación. 3 feudo. 4 DER. herencia, propiedad, dominio.
**fee (to)** *tr.* retribuir, pagar. 2 gratificar.
**feeable** (fí·abøl) *adj.* retribuible.
**feeble** (fí·bøl) *adj.* débil. 2 flaco, flojo, endeble. 3 enclenque, enfermizo.
**feeble-minded** *adj.* imbécil, débil mental. 2 irresoluto, vacilante.
**feed** (fíd) *s.* alimento, comida [esp. de los animales]; forraje, pienso: ~ *bag*, cebadera, morral. 2 MEC. alimentación, dispositivo de alimentación.
**feed (to)** *tr.* alimentar, mantener. 2 nutrir, sustentar. 3 dar de comer. 4 dar [como comida]. 5 MEC. alimentar, cebar. 6 *intr.* comer, alimentarse de. ¶ Pret. y p. p.: *fed.*
**feeder** (-ø') *s.* alimentador. 2 engordador [de ganado]. 3 ELECT. conductor principal. 4 afluente [de un río]. 5 FERROC. ramal. 6 tolva. 7 babero [de niño].
**feedback** (-bæk) *s.* ELECT. regeneración, realimentación.
**feeding** (-ing) *s.* alimento [acción de alimentar]. 2 acción de comer o pastar. 3 pasto, forraje.
**feel** (fíl) *s.* tacto [sentido; acción]; palpamiento. 2 sensación, percepción.
**feel (to)** *tr.* tocar, tentar, palpar, manosear. 2 tomar [el pulso]. 3 examinar, explorar, sondear. 4 sentir, experimentar. 5 creer, pensar. 6 *to* ~ *in one's bones*, presentir, decirle a uno [algo] el corazón. 7 *to* ~ *one's way*, ir a tientas, proceder con tiento. 8 *to* ~ *out*, dar un toque a; tantear, sondear. 9 MAR. *to* ~ *the helm*, obedecer al timón.
    10 *intr.* sentirse, estar, tener: *to* ~ *angry*, estar enojado; *to* ~ *happy*, sentirse feliz, estar contento; *I* ~ *cold*, tengo frío. 11 ser suave o áspero al tacto. 12 producir cierta sensación, dolor, etc.: *it feels cold to me*, lo encuentro frío. 13 ser sensible, sentir. 14 *to* ~ *bad*, sentirse mal. 15 *to* ~ *cheap*, avergonzarse, sentirse humillado. 16 *to* ~ *for*, buscar a tientas; dolerse de, compadecer. 17 *to* ~ *like*, tener ganas de, querer. 18 *to* ~ *(like) oneself*, tener la salud, el vigor, el ánimo, etc., acostumbrados. ¶ Pret. y p. p.: *felt.*
**feeler** (-ø') *s.* palpador. 2 el que siente. 3 antena, tentáculo, palpo. 4 lo que se dice para explorar la opinión de los demás. 5 TEJ. pulsador.
**feeling** (-ing) *s.* tacto [sentido]. 2 tocamiento, tiento, palpadura. 3 sensación, percepción. 4

sentimiento: *to hurt one's feelings*, herir los sentimientos de uno. 5 calor, pasión, emoción, ternura, compasión. 6 atmósfera [de una cosa]. 7 presentimiento. 8 *adj.* sensible, tierno. 9 sentido, conmovedor.
**feelingly** (-li) *adv.* con sentimiento; vivamente. 2 con compasión. 3 tiernamente.
**feet** (fít) *s. pl.* de FOOT. pies.
**feign (to)** (fein) *tr.* fingir, inventar, aparentar, simular. 2 *intr.* fingir, disimular.
**feigning** (-ing) *s.* fingimiento.
**feint** (feint) *s.* ficción, treta. 2 ESGR. finta.
**feldspar** (de·ldspa') *s.* MINER. feldespato.
**Felicia** (feli·shia) *n. pr.* Felisa, Felicia.
**felicitate (to)** (feli·siteit) *tr.* felicitar.
**felicitation** (-ei·shøn) *s.* felicitación.
**felicitous** (feli·sitøs) *adj.* feliz [idea, expresión]. 2 que es feliz en sus expresiones.
**felicity** (feli·siti) *s.* felicidad. 2 B. ART. acierto, expresión feliz.
**Felidæ** (fí·lidi) *s. pl.* ZOOL. félidos.
**feline** (fí·lain) *adj.-s.* felino.
**1) fell** (fel) *pret.* de TO FALL.
**2) fell** *s.* cuero, pellejo. 2 páramo elevado. 3 corta [de árboles]. 4 COST. sobrecostura. 5 *adj.* fiero, bárbaro, cruel. 6 mortal, destructivo.
**fell (to)** *tr.* derribar, tumbar. 2 cortar [árboles]. 3 acogotar [reses]. 4 COST. sobrecargar.
**felloe** (fe·lou) *s.* pina [de rueda].
**fellow** (fe·lou) *s.* compañero. 2 individuo, sujeto, prójimo, muchacho. 3 igual, pareja. 4 socio, miembro [de una academia o corporación]. 5 el que goza de pensión para ampliar estudios en una universidad.
    6 *adj.* indica igualdad o asociación en expresiones como: ~ *being*, ~ *creature*, prójimo, semejante; ~ *student*, condiscípulo; ~ *traveller*, compañero de viaje.
**fellowship** (-ship) *s.* compañerismo, confraternidad. 2 comunión, asociación, mancomunidad, participación. 3 compañía, cuerpo, sociedad. 4 plaza pensionada [para ampliar estudios en una universidad]. 5 ARIT. regla de compañía.
**felon** (fe·løn) *adj.* fiero, asesino. 2 malvado, traidor. 3 *s.* felón, criminal. 4 MED. panadizo.
**felonious** (felou·niøs) *adj.* malvado, felón, criminal.
**felony** (fe·løni) *s.* felonía, crimen, delito grave.
**felt** (felt) *pret.* y *p. p.* de TO FEEL. 2 *s.* fieltro.
**felt (to)** *tr.* enfieltrar. 2 cubrir de fieltro.
**felucca** (filø·ka) *s.* MAR. falucho.
**female** (fí·meil) *s.* hembra [mujer, animal o planta]. 2 mujer. 3 *adj.* femenino, hembra: ~ *writer*, escritora; ~ *snake*, serpiente hembra.
**feminine** (fe·minin) *adj.* femenino. 2 mujeril. 3 *s.* GRAM. femenino.
**femininity** (femini·niti) *s.* feminidad, femidad. 2 las mujeres, el bello sexo.
**feminism** (fe·minišm̆) *s.* carácter femenino. 2 POL. feminismo.
**feminist** (-ist) *adj.-s.* feminista.
**femoral** (fe·moral) *adj.* ANAT. femoral.
**femur** (fí·mø') *s.* ANAT. fémur.
**fen** (fen) *s.* marjal, pantano, paúl.
**fence** (fens) *s.* empalizada, valla, vallado, cerca, cercado, seto, barrera; defensa, reparo: *to sit on the* ~, permanecer neutral, no comprometerse. 2 esgrima. 3 fig. habilidad en la discusión. 4 MEC. guarda, guía, resguardo. 5 perista. 6 ~ *season*, tiempo de veda.
**fence (to)** *tr.* cercar, vallar. 2 defender, proteger. 3

negociar con efectos robados. *4 intr.* esgrimir, luchar. *5* defenderse hábilmente [en una discusión, interrogatorio, etc.]. *6* saltar vallas [el caballo].

**fenceless** (-lis) *adj.* abierto, no cercado.

**fencing** (-ing) *s.* esgrima: ~ *bout*, asalto de armas; ~ *foil*, florete. *2* habilidad polemística. *3* material para cercas; valladar.

**fend (to)** (fend) *tr.* poét. defender. *2 to* ~ *off*, resguardar de; rechazar, parar. *3 intr.* esgrimir, defenderse. *4 to* ~ *for oneself*, ganarse la vida.

**fender** (-øⁿ) *s.* guardafuegos [de chimenea]. *2* guardabarros [de coche, etc.]. *3* salvavidas [de tranvía]. *4* MAR. defensas, pallete.

**fenestration** (fenestrei·shøn) *adj.* ARQ. ventanaje.

**Fenian** (fi·nian) *adj.-s.* feniano.

**Fenianism** (fi·nianism) *s.* fenianismo.

**fennel** (fe·nøl) *s.* BOT. hinojo. *2* BOT. *giant* ~, cañaheja.

**fenny** (fe·ni) *adj.* pantanoso, palustre.

**fenugreek** (fe·niugrɪk) *s.* BOT. alholva

**feoff** (fef o fɪf) *s.* FIEF.

**feracious** (førei·shøs) *adj.* feraz.

**feracity** (føræ·siti) *s.* feracidad.

**feral** (fi·ral) *adj.* salvaje, silvestre, montaraz. *2* cruel.

**Ferdinand** (fø·ⁿdinænd) *n. pr. m.* Fernando.

**ferine** (fi·rain) *adj.* FERAL.

**ferment** (fø·ⁿment) *s.* fermento. *2* fermentación, agitación.

**ferment (to)** (fø·ⁿme·nt) *intr.-tr.* fermentar. *2 intr.* bullir, agitarse. *3 tr.* agitar, excitar.

**fermentation** (-ei·shøn) *s.* fermentación. *3* efervescencia, agitación.

**fern** (fø·ⁿn) *s.* BOT. helecho.

**fernery** (-øri) *s.* helechal.

**ferny** (-i) *adj.* de helecho; abundante en helechos.

**ferocious** (firou·shøs) *adj.* fiero, feroz, terrible.

**ferocity** (fira·siti) *s.* fiereza, ferocidad.

**ferreous** (fe·riøs) *adj.* férreo; ferrizo.

**ferret** (fe·rit) *s.* ZOOL. hurón. *2* fig. hurón, buscador, detective.

**ferret (to)** *intr.-tr.* cazar con hurón. *2* buscar, huronear. *3 tr.* perseguir, acosar. *4 to* ~ *out*, buscar, averiguar.

**ferriage** (fe·riidẏ) *s.* barcaje, lo que se paga por pasar un río.

**ferric** (fe·rik) *adj.* QUÍM. férrico.

**ferriferous** (feri·førøs) *adj.* ferrífero.

**ferroconcrete** (feroka·ncrit) *s.* hormigón armado.

**ferrotype** (fe·rotaip) *s.* FOT. ferrotipo. *2* FOT. ferrotipia.

**ferrous** (fe·røs) *adj.* QUÍM. ferroso.

**ferruginous** (feru·dẏinøs) *adj.* ferruginoso. *2* de color de herrumbre.

**ferrule** (fe·rul) *s.* regatón, contera, virola, zuncho; casquillo.

**ferry** (fe·ri) *s.* balsadero, lugar donde se cruza un río, canal, etc. *2* barca, balsa, transbordador, para cruzar un río, etc. *3* FERRYBOAT.

**ferry (to)** *tr.* transportar de una a otra orilla, balsear. *2 tr.-intr.* cruzar [un río, etc.] en barca. ¶ Pret. y p. p.: *ferried.*

**ferryage** (-idẏ) *s.* FERRIAGE.

**ferryboat** (-bout) *s.* barca de pasaje. *2* embarcación para transbordar trenes.

**ferryman** (-mæn) *s.* balsero, barquero; dueño o empleado de un paso de río.

**fertile** (fø·ⁿtil) *adj.* fértil. *2* fecundo.

**fertility** (fø·ⁿti·liti) *s.* fertilidad. *2* fecundidad.

**fertilization** (fø·ⁿtiliše·shøn) *s.* fertilización. *2* fecundación.

**fertilize (to)** (fø·ⁿtilaiš) *tr.* fertilizar. *2* fecundar.

**fertilizer** (fø·ⁿtilaišøⁿ) *s.* AGR. fertilizante, abono. *2* BOT. agente polinizador.

**ferula** (fe·rula) *s.* BOT. férula, cañaheja. *2* férula [palmeta].

**ferule** (fe·rul) *s.* FERULA 2.

**fervency** (fø·ⁿvønsi) *s.* calor, ardor. *2* fervor.

**fervent** (fø·ⁿvønt) *adj.* hirviente, ardiente. *2* ferviente, fervoroso, vehemente, ardoroso.

**fervid** (fø·ⁿvid) *adj.* férvido, ardiente.

**fervo (u) r** (fø·ⁿvøⁿ) *s.* ardor, calor, hervor. *2* fervor, celo, devoción.

**fescue** (fe·skiu) *s.* puntero [para señalar]. *2* BOT. cañuela.

**festal** (fe·stal) *adj.* festivo, de fiesta.

**fester** (fe·støⁿ) *s.* llaga, úlcera.

**fester (to)** *intr.* supurar. *2* enconarse, ulcerarse. *3* pudrirse. *4* fig. enconarse. *5 tr.* enconar, emponzoñar.

**festival** (fe·stival) *adj.* festivo [de fiesta]. *2 s.* fiesta, festividad. *3* festival.

**festive** (fe·stiv) *adj.* festivo, alegre, convival.

**festivity** (fe·sti·viti) *s.* alegría, alborozo, animación. *2* fiesta, festividad.

**festoon** (festu·n) *s.* festón [guirnalda].

**festoon (to)** (festu·n) *tr.* festonear, adornar con festones y guirnaldas.

**fetal** (fi·tal) *adj.* fetal.

**fetch** (fech) *s.* acto de ir a buscar, traer o alcanzar. *2* tirada [distancia], alcance. *3* estratagema, treta, artificio. *4* espectro o fantasma de una persona viva.

**fetch (to)** *tr.* ir por, ir a buscar, traer. *2* cobrar [la caza]. *3* alcanzar. *4* hacer salir [sangre, etc.]; arrancar [lágrimas]. *5* exhalar [un gemido, un suspiro]. *6* producir. *7* venderse [a un precio]. *8* derivar, sacar. *9* fam. interesar, atraer, conmover, encantar. *10* fam. dar, arrear [un golpe]. *11* cebar [una bomba]. *12 to* ~ *down*, derribar; hacer bajar. *13 to* ~ *in*, rodear, encerrar. *14 to* ~ *out*, hacer resaltar. *15 to* ~ *up*, levantar, elevar; traer [a la memoria]; descubrir, recuperar. *16 intr.* ir, moverse, traer y llevar cosas. *17* MAR. ir, seguir, arribar, virar. *18 to* ~ *and carry*, servir como un perro, traer y llevar chismes. *19 to* ~ *up*, detenerse, pararse.

**fetching** (-ing) *adj.* atractivo, encantador.

**fete, fête** (fet) *s.* fiesta, celebración. *2* ~ *day*, día de fiesta; santo, días [de una pers.].

**fete, fête (to)** *tr.* festejar.

**fetid** (fe·tid) *adj.* fétido, hediondo.

**fetish** (fi·tish) *s.* fetiche.

**fetishism** (fi·tishišm) *s.* fetichismo.

**fetlock** (fe·tlak) *s.* cerneja. *2* espolón [del caballo]: ~ *joint*, menudillo.

**fetor** (fi·tøⁿ) *s.* hedor.

**fetter** (fe·tøⁿ) *s.* grillete, prisión. *2* traba. *3 pl.* grillos, hierros, prisiones.

**fetter (to)** *tr.* engrillar, encadenar, trabar.

**fetterlock** (-lak) *s.* traba, maniota.

**fettle** (fe·tøl) *s.* estado, condición: *in fine* ~, en buen estado; de buen humor; bien preparado.

**fetus** (fi·tøs) *s.* feto.

**feud** (fiud) *s.* disputa o enemistad duradera entre familias, grupos o personas. *2* feudo.

**feudal** (fiu·dal) *adj.* feudal.

**feudalism** (-išm) *s.* feudalismo.

**feudatory** (fiu·datori) *adj.-s.* feudatario.

**fever** (fiˑvøʳ) *s.* MED. fiebre, calentura. *2* fiebre, agitación.

**fever (to)** *tr.* causar o dar fiebre.

**feverfew** (-fiu) *s.* BOT. matricaria.

**feverish** (-ish) *adj.* febricitante, calenturiento. *2* febril. *3* infestado con fiebre.

**few** (fiu) *adj.-pron.* pocos: *a* ~, unos cuantos, algunos; *not a* ~, no pocos; *the* ~, los menos, la minoría.

**fewer** (-øʳ) *adj.-pron. compar.* de FEW; menos: *the* ~ *the better*, cuantos menos, mejor.

**fewest** (-ist) *adj.-pron. superl.* de FEW.

**fey** (fei) *adj.* (Esc.) que ha de morir; moribundo.

**fez** (feš), **fezzes** (feˑšiš) *s.* fez.

**fiancé** (fianseiˑ) *s.* novio, prometido.

**fiasco** (fiæˑskou) *s.* fiasco, fracaso.

**fiat** (faˑiat) *s.* fiat, orden, mandato, decisión.

**fib** (fib) *s.* bola, mentirilla, papa, \*macana.

**fib (to)** *intr.* mentir, echar papas. ¶ Pret. y p. p.: *fibbed;* ger.: *fibbing.*

**fibber** (-øʳ) *s.* mentiroso, bolero.

**fiber, fibre** (faiˑbøʳ) *s.* fibra: ~ *plant*, planta textil. *2* fig. carácter, índole.

**fibril** (faiˑbril) *s.* fibrilla.

**fibrin(e** (faiˑbrin) *s.* fibrina.

**fibroma** (fibrouˑma) *s.* MED. fibroma.

**fibrose** (faiˑbrous), **fibrous** (faiˑbrøs) *adj.* fibroso.

**fibula** (fiˑbiula) *s.* fíbula. *2* ANAT. peroné.

**fickle** (fiˑkøl) *adj.* mudable, variable, inconstante, voluble, vleidoso.

**fictile** (fiˑktil) *adj.* plástico, moldeable.

**fiction** (fikshøn) *s.* ficción. *2* literatura de imaginación: cuento, novela, fábula. *3* mentira.

**fictitious** (fiktiˑshøs) *adj.* ficticio.

**fictive** (fiˑktiv) *adj.* fingido, imaginario. *2* de la imaginación creadora; creador [arte].

**fid** (fid) *s.* tarugo, cuña.

**fiddle** (fiˑdøl) *s.* MÚS. fam. violín: *fit as a* ~, en buena condición física, animado; *to play second* ~, hacer un papel secundario.

**fiddle (to)** *intr.* tocar el violín. *2* mover viva o nerviosamente los dedos o las manos; enredar con; ocuparse en tonterías. *3 tr.* tocar [un aire, etc.] con el violín. *4 to* ~ *away*, malgastar [el tiempo, el dinero, etc.].

**fiddle-de-dee** (-didiˑ) *s. fam.* disparate, tontería.

**fiddle-faddle** (-fædøl) *s. fam.* tontería, simpleza. *2* fruslería. *3 interj.* ¡tonterías!

**fiddle-faddle (to)** *intr.* ocuparse en tonterías.

**fiddler** (fiˑdløʳ) *s. fam.* violinista. *2* ZOOL. ~ *crab*, barrilete [cangrejo].

**fiddlestick** (fiˑdølstik) *s.* arco de violín. *2* tontería, nadería. *3 interj. fiddlesticks!,* ¡qué tontería!

**fiddling** (fiˑdling) *adj.* fútil, insignificante.

**fideicommissum** (faidiaikomiˑsøm) *s.* DER. fideicomiso.

**fidelity** (fideˑliti) *s.* fidelidad.

**fidget** (fiˑdẏit) *s.* persona agitada, inquieta. *2* agitación, movimiento. *3 pl. the fidgets,* desasosiego, impaciencia, nerviosidad.

**fidget (to)** *intr.* estar inquieto, agitarse, menearse nerviosamente. *2 to* ~ *with*, jugar o enredar con, manosear. *3 tr.* molestar, poner nervioso.

**fidgety** (-ti) *adj.* inquieto, nervioso, impaciente.

**fiduciary** (fidiuˑshieri) *adj.-s.* fiduciario.

**fie!** (fai) *interj.* ¡uf!, ¡abrenuncio!

**fief** (fif) *s.* feudo.

**field** (fild) *s.* campo, sembrado, tierra laborable. *2* campo, campiña. *3* DEP. campo. *4* BÉISBOL porción de campo que queda fuera del cuadro. *5* FÍS., ELECT. campo: *magnetic* ~, campo magnético. *6* BLAS. campo. *7* campo [de una ciencia, actividad, etc.]. *8* campo [de una lucha]; campo de batalla; la batalla misma; ~ *of honour*, campo del honor; *to take the* ~, entrar en campaña, salir a campaña. *9* campaña [campo llano]. *10* extensión de cielo, mar, hielo, nieve, etc.: ~ *of ice*, banco de hielo. *11* DEP. jugadores [en un partido]; participantes [en una carrera]. *12 adj.* de campo, de campaña; del campo; ~ *artillery*, artillería de campaña; ~ *day*, día de campo, día de ejercicios militares o atléticos; ~ *glass*, gemelos de campaña; ~ *marshal*, mariscal de campo, capitán general; ~ *mouse*, ratón de campo; ~ *officer*, MIL. jefe. *13* ELECT. conductor: ~ *winding*, arrollamiento inductor.

**field (to)** *tr.* DEP. parar y devolver la pelota. *2 intr.* DEP. actuar como *fielder.*

**fielder** (fiˑldøʳ) *s.* en el béisbol o en el cricquet, jugador situado para parar la pelota.

**fieldfare** (fildfeˑøʳ) *s.* ORN. zorzal.

**fiend** (find) *s.* demonio, espíritu malo. *2* persona malvada o cruel.

**fiendish** (fiˑindish) *adj.* diabólico, infernal; malvado, cruel.

**fierce** (fiʳs) *adj.* fiero, feroz, bárbaro, cruel. *2* terrible, espantoso. *3* furioso, violento, impetuoso, vigoroso. *4* vivo, intenso.

**fiery** (faiˑøri) *adj.* ígneo, de fuego. *2* ardiente, abrasador; ardoroso, inflamado, encendido. *3* vehemente, fogoso. *4* violento, irascible, soberbio. *5* furibundo. *6* colorado [tez, etc.]. *7* inflamable.

**fife** (faif) *s.* MÚS. pífano.

**fife (to)** *intr.* tocar el pífano.

**fifer** (faiˑføʳ) *s.* pífano [músico].

**fifteen** (fiftrˑn) *adj.-s.* quince.

**fifteenth** (-z) *adj.* decimoquinto. *2* quince [siglo]. *3 adj.-s.* quinzavo. *4 s.* quince [día].

**fifth** (fifz) *adj.-s. num.* quinto. *2 s.* MÚS. quinta. *3* cinco [día].

**fifthly** (fiˑfzli) *adv.* en quinto lugar.

**fiftieth** (fiˑftiez) *adj.-s.* quincuagésimo, cincuenteno, cincuentavo.

**fifty** (fiˑfti) *adj.-s.* cincuenta.

**fig** (fig) *s.* BOT. higo; higuera: ~ *tree*, higuera. *2* fam. higa [signo de desprecio]. *3* fam. ardite, bledo. *4* fam. *in full*, ~, de veinticinco alfileres.

**fig (to)** *tr.* ataviar, adornar, preparar.

**fig-leaf** *s.* hoja de higuera. *2* fig. hoja de parra.

**fight** (fait) *s.* lucha, combate, duelo, riña, pelea, contienda. *2* fuerza o ánimo para lucha: *to show* ~, no acoquinarse, luchar con denuedo.

**fight (to)** *intr.* luchar, pelear, combatir, contender, lidiar, batirse: *to* ~ *for*, luchar por; *to* ~ *shy of*, fig. rehuir, evitar. *2 tr.* luchar con o contra. *3* lidiar [un toro]. *4* librar [una batalla]; sostener [una lucha]: *to* ~ *another's battles*, tomar la defensa de otro. *5 to* ~ *one's way*, abrirse paso luchando. *6 to* ~ *out*, decidir, resolver en una lucha. ¶ Pret. y p. p.: *fought.*

**fighter** (faiˑtøʳ) *s.* luchador. *2* combatiente, contendiente. *3* de combate o de caza [avión].

**fighting** (-ing) *adj.* luchador, batallador, combativo. *2* de pelea, de guerra: ~ *cock*, gallo de pelea. *3 s.* lucha, pelea, combate, riña.

**figment** (fiˑgmønt) *s.* ficción, invención.

**figpecker** (fiˑgpekøʳ) *s.* ORN. becafigo.

**figuline** (fiˑgiulin) *s.* figulino.

**figurant** (fiˑgiurant) *s.* figurante [de ópera].

**figurante** (figiuraˑnt) *s.* figuranta, bailarina del conjunto.

**figurate** (fiˑgiureit) *adj.* figurado. *2* MÚS. floreado, adornado.

**figuration** (-ei·shøn) s. figuración; forma, figura. 2 MÚS. figuración.

**figurative** (fi·giurativ) adj. figurativo. 2 florido [lenguaje, estilo]. 3 GRAM. figurado, translaticio. 4 plástico, pictórico.

**figure** (fi·giø^r) s. figura [forma, hechura; representación; dibujo, estatua, pintura; persona, personaje]. 2 GEOM., GRAM., RET. figura: ~ of speech, tropo. 3 figura, cuerpo, talle, tipo [de una pers.]. 4 dibujo, muestra [de un papel, tejido, etc.]. 5 papel, viso; distinción. 6 figura [en el baile, en el patinaje]: ~ skating, patinaje artístico. 7 horóscopo. 8 ARIT. cifra, guarismo, número: to be good at figures, estar fuerte en aritmética. 9 precio, valor.

**figure (to)** tr. figurar, delinear, formar, amoldar. 2 representar, simbolizar. 3 adornar con dibujos o figuras. 4 imaginar, figurarse. 5 indicar con números. 6 calcular, computar. 7 to ~ out, resolver, hallar por cálculo; descifrar, entender. 8 to ~ up, sumar. 9 intr. figurar, hacer viso. 10 calcular, planear.

**figured** (-d) adj. figurado. 2 adornado, labrado, floreado.

**figurehead** (-jed) s. MAR. mascarón de proa. 2 fig. figura decorativa; testaferro.

**figurine** (figiuri·n) s. estatuilla, figurita.

**figuring** (fi·giuring) s. cálculo, computación.

**figwort** (fi·gwørt) s. BOT. escrofularia.

**filament** (fi·lamønt) s. filamento.

**filamentous** (filame·ntøs) adj. filamentoso.

**filander** (filæ·ndø^r) s. ZOOL. filandria.

**filaria** (filei·ria) s. ZOOL. filaria.

**filature** (fi·lachø^r) s. hilandería [de seda].

**filbert** (fi·lbø^rt) s. BOT. avellano. 2 avellana.

**filch (to)** (filch) tr. hurtar, ratear, birlar.

**filcher** (fil·chø^r) s. ratero, garduño.

**file** (fail) s. lima, escofina. 2 fig. persona astuta. 3 ensartapapeles. 4 carpeta, archivador. 5 legajo o colección de papeles; archivo; ~ case, fichero. 6 fila, cola, hilera.

**file (to)** tr. limar, pulir [con la lima]. 2 fig. limar, perfeccionar. 3 archivar, guardar; ensartar [en el ensartapapeles]. 4 registrar [un documento]. 5 intr. marchar en fila: to ~ off, MIL. desfilar.

**filefish** (fai·lfish) s. ICT. lija.

**filer** (fai·lø^r) s. limador.

**filial** (fi·lial) adj. filial.

**filiation** (ffiliei·shøn) s. filiación [lazo de parentesco, procedencia, dependencia].

**filibuster** (filibø·stø^r) s. filibustero, pirata. 2 (E.U.) POL. obstruccionista.

**filibuster (to)** s. filibustero, pirata. 2 (E.U.) POL. obstruccionista.

**filibuster (to)** intr. actuar de filibustero. tr.-intr. POL. (E.U.) obstruccionar.

**filibusterism** (fi·libøstørišm) s. filibusterismo.

**filiform** (fi·lifo^rm) adj. filiforme.

**filigree** (fi·ligrı) s. filigrana [obra, adorno].

**filigreed** (-d) adj. afiligranado.

**filing** (fai·ling) s. limadura [acción]. 2 acción de archivar: ~ card, ficha [de fichero]. 3 pl. limaduras, limalla.

**fill** (fil) s. hartura, hartazgo. 2 henchidura, colmo, abundancia. 3 terraplén.

**fill (to)** tr. llenar. 2 completar, rellenar, henchir. 3 hinchar. 4 tapar, obstruir. 5 macizar, terraplenar. 6 empastar [un diente]. 7 satisfacer, saciar, hartar. 8 ocupar [un puesto]. 9 proveer [un cargo]. 10 COM. servir, despachar [un pedido]. 11 ELECT. cargar [un acumulador]. 12 envasar.

13 to ~ in, insertar; llenar [un hueco]; rellenar, terraplenar. 14 to ~ out, ensanchar, redondear, completar; llenar [un formulario]. 15 to ~ up, llenar, ocupar; tapar [un agujero].
16 intr. llenarse, henchirse. 17 llenarse de lágrimas [los ojos]. 18 his heart filled, le ahogaba la emoción. 19 to ~ in, llenarse; hacer de suplente. 20 to ~ out, ensancharse, redondearse; ahuecarse, henchirse.

**filler** (fi·lø^r) s. llenador, envasador. 2 henchidor. 3 embudo. 4 tripa [del cigarro].

**fillet** (-et) s. cinta [para el cabello]. 2 lista, faja, tira. 3 ARQ., ENCUAD. filete. 4 COC. filete; lonja.

**fillet (to)** tr. adornar, atar [con cinta]. 2 ARQ. filetear. 3 COC. cortar en lonjas.

**filling** (-ing) s. relleno. 2 henchimiento. 3 envase [acción]. 4 DENT. empastadura, orificación. 5 llenado.

**fillip** (-ip) s. capirotazo, papirotazo. 2 estímulo, aguijón.

**fillip (to)** tr. dar un papirotazo. 2 estimular, aguijar.

**filly** (fi·li) s. potranca. 2 pop. muchacha retozona.

**film** (film) s. película. 2 membrana, telilla. 3 tela, nata, flor [en un líquido]. 4 nube [en el ojo]. 5 niebla. 6 CINEM. película, filme, cinta: ~ star, estrella de cine. 7 FOT. película.

**film (to)** tr. cubrir con película o telilla. 2 cinematografiar, filmar. 3 llevar al cine [una novela, tema, etc.]. 4 intr. cubrirse de una película, tela, etc.

**filming** (fil·ming) s. filmación.

**filmy** (-i) adj. membranoso; finísimo, delgadísimo. 2 cubierto de película, empañado, nublado.

**filose** (fai·lous) adj. filiforme.

**filter** (fi·ltø^r) s. filtro [para filtrar líquidos]. 2 ELECT., FOT., ÓPT. filtro.

**filter (to)** tr. filtrar. 2 purificar, refinar. 3 intr. filtrarse. 5 MIL. infiltrarse.

**filth** (filz) s. suciedad, inmundicia, porquería, mugre. 2 corrupción, infección, obscenidad.

**filthiness** (fi·lzinis) s. suciedad, inmundicia, porquería, asquerosidad.

**filthy** (-i) adj. sucio, inmundo, cochino, asqueroso, mugriento. 2 corrompido, impuro.

**filtrate** (fi·ltreit) s. líquido filtrado.

**filtrate (to)** tr. filtrar. 2 intr. filtrarse.

**filtration** (-ei·shøn) s. filtración.

**fin** (fin) s. aleta [de pez]. 2 barba [de ballena]. 3 MEC. rebaba, apéndice en forma de aleta. 4 pop. fig. mano, brazo.

**final** (fai·inal) adj. final. 2 conclusivo. 3 definitivo, decisivo; terminante. 4 s. DEP. final. 5 examen final.

**finale** (fina·li) s. MÚS. final.

**finalist** (fai·nalist) s. DEP. finalista.

**finality** (fainæ·liti) s. calidad de decisivo o terminante. 2 lo que es final o conclusivo.

**finally** (fai·nali) adv. finalmente, por último, en fin, por fin, al cabo. 2 definitivamente.

**finance** (finæ·ns) s. ciencia y práctica financiera. 2 pl. finanzas. 3 hacienda, rentas, fondos.

**finance (to)** tr. financiar. 2 manejar los fondos de. 3 intr. ocuparse en operaciones financieras.

**financial** (finæ·nshal) adj. financiero, rentístico, bancario. 2 económico [año].

**financier** (finænsı·^r) s. financiero. 2 hacendista.

**financier (to)** intr.-tr. desp. hacer operaciones financieras. 2 tr. (E.U.) estafar.

**finback** (fi·nbæk) s. ZOOL. rorcual; yubarta.

**finch** (finch) *s.* ORN. cualquiera de los pájaros fringílidos; pinzón.

**find** (faind) *s.* hallazgo, descubrimiento.

**find (to)** *tr.* encontrar, hallar: *to ~ fault with*, hallar defectos, poner tachas, censurar; *to ~ in one's heart*, estar dispuesto o decidido, decidirse [a]. *2* descubrir; buscar, averiguar. *3* procurar, proveer de; mantener. *4* recobrar el uso de. *5* DER. declarar, pronunciar: *to ~ guilty*, declarar culpable. *6 to ~ out*, hallar; descifrar, adivinar; coger [en falta, etc.]; descubrir [un ladrón, un secreto, el verdadero carácter de]. *7 intr.* DER. pronunciar sentencia. ¶ Pret. y p. p.: *found*.

**finder** (-ø<sup>r</sup>) *s.* hallador, descubridor. *2* ÓPT. buscador. *3* FOT. visor.

**finding** (fai·nding) *s.* hallazgo, descubrimiento. *2* DER. fallo, decisión.

**fine** (fain) *s.* multa. *2 adj.* fino [delicado; de buena calidad; puro, precioso; delgado, sutil; no grueso]. *3* de ley [oro, plata]. *4* hermoso, lindo. *5* bueno, excelente, agradable, magnífico. *6* divertido [rato]. *7* guapo, gallardo, distinguido. *8* elegante, primoroso. *9* bueno [tiempo, día]. *10* generoso [vino]. *11 ~ arts*, bellas artes. *12 adv.* fam. finamente. *13* fam. *to feel ~*, sentirse bien de salud.

**fine (to)** *tr.* multar. *2* afinar. *3* refinar, purificar, clarificar. *4 intr.* refinarse, purificarse. *5* aclararse [el tiempo]. *6* adelgazarse.

**fine-drawn** *adj.* estirado en hilos muy finos. *2* muy fino o sutil.

**fine-grained** *adj.* de grano muy fino, compacto.

**fineness** (-nis) *s.* fineza, finura, delicadeza, primor, excelencia. *2* pureza, perfección. *3* agudeza, sutileza. *4* ley [del metal, la moneda].

**finery** (fai·nøri) *s.* galas, adornos, atavíos.

**finespun** (-spøn) *adj.* sutil, alambicado.

**finesse** (fine·s) *s.* sutileza, astucia, estratagema. *2* tacto, diplomacia.

**finesse (to)** *intr.* valerse de artificios o subterfugios.

**fin-footed** *adj.* ORN. palmeado.

**finger** (fi·ngø<sup>r</sup>) *s.* dedo [de la mano o de un guante]: *index ~*, dedo índice; *middle ~*, dedo del corazón; *ring ~*, dedo anular; *little ~*, dedo meñique; *~ board*, MÚS. teclado; diapasón [del violín, etc.]; *~ post*, poste indicador; *~ tip*, punta, yema del dedo; *to have at one's ~ tips*, saber al dedillo. *2* dedo [medida]. *3* aguja indicadora, saetilla, manecilla.

**finger (to)** *tr.* tocar, manosear. *2* sisar, hurtar. *3* MÚS. tocar, tañer [con los dedos], pulsar, teclear. *4* hacer [con los dedos].

**fingerbreadth** (-bredz) *s.* dedo [ancho de un dedo].

**fingering** (-ing) *s.* manoseo, tecleo. *2* MÚS. digitación, dedeo. *3* lana para medias.

**fingernail** (-neil) *s.* uña [del dedo].

**fingerprint** (-print) *s.* huella o impresión digital o dactilar.

**fingerstall** (-stol) *s.* dedil.

**finial** (fi·nial) *s.* ARQ. florón de gablete, pináculo, etc.

**finical** (fi·nikal), **finicking** (-ing), **finicky** (-i) *adj.* melindroso, remilgado, afectado, meticuloso, remirado.

**finish** (fi·nish) *s.* fin, final, término, remate, conclusión, acabamiento. *2* DEP. línea de llegada. *3* DEP. carrera final. *4* finura de ejecución. *5* última mano, acabado, perfección.

**finish (to)** *tr.* acabar, terminar, rematar, concluir, consumar. *2* dar la última mano o el acabado a,

retocar, pulir, perfeccionar. *3* completar la educación de. *4* fam. vencer, matar, aniquilar. *5 intr.* acabar, finalizar; fenecer, cesar, morir: *to ~ by*, acabar por; *to ~ with*, terminar, reñir con.

**finisher** (-ø<sup>r</sup>) *s.* acabador. *2* máquina acabadora. *3* golpe que acaba.

**finishing** (-ing) *s.* acabamiento. *2* perfeccionamiento. *3* acabado. *4 adj.* que acaba, de acabado: *~ blow*, golpe de gracia; *~ touch*, retoque, última mano.

**finite** (fai·nait) *adj.* finito, limitado. *2* GRAM. personal [forma del verbo].

**Finland** (fi·nland) *n. pr.* GEOGR. Finlandia.

**Finlander** (-ø<sup>r</sup>) *s.* finlandés.

**finless** (fi·nlis) *adj.* sin aletas.

**Finn** (fin) *s.* finés. *2* finlandés.

**Finnic** (fi·nik) *adj.* finés. *2 s.* lengua finesa.

**Finnish** (fi·nish) *adj.-s.* finlandés.

**finny** (fi·ni) *adj.* provisto de aletas. *2* abundante en peces.

**fiord** (fiø<sup>r</sup>d) *s.* GEOGR. fiord, fiordo.

**fir** (fø<sup>r</sup>) *s.* BOT. abeto.

**fire** (fai·ø<sup>r</sup>) *s.* fuego [producido por la combustión; materia que arde], lumbre: *~ clay*, arcilla refractaria; *~ pan*, brasero, chofeta; *to be on ~*, estar ardiendo; *to catch ~*, encenderse, inflamarse; *to set ~ on*, to set on ~, pegar fuego a, encender, inflamar; *with ~ and sword*, a sangre y fuego. *2* llama. *3* fuego, incendio: *~ alarm*, avisador de incendios; *~ brigade, ~ company*, cuerpo de bomberos, los bomberos; *~ escape*, escalera de incendios. *4* fuego [disparos con un arma]: *to miss ~*, dar higa; fallar el tiro; fig. fracasar; *under ~*, expuesto al fuego del enemigo. *5* fuego, ardor, pasión, viveza de la imaginación, inspiración. *6* fogosidad. *7* brillo, luminosidad: *~ beetle*, cocuyo. *8* MED. fuego. *9* martirio, aflicción, prueba.

**fire (to)** *tr.* encender, pegar fuego a. *2* iluminar [dar luz a]. *3* calentar [el horno]; cargar [el hogar]; encender [la caldera]. *4* cocer [ladrillos, el esmalte, etc.]. *5* disparar [un arma de fuego]; lanzar [un torpedo]; hacer estallar [una mina]. *6* inflamar, enardecer. *7* despedir [a un empleado]. *8 intr.* encenderse. *9* enardecerse. *10* disparar, hacer fuego. *11* dar explosiones [un motor]. *12 to ~ away*, empezar, continuar, decir deprisa. *13 to ~ up*, enojarse, encolerizarse.

**firearm** (-a<sup>r</sup>m) *n. pr.* arma de fuego.

**fireback** (-bæc) *s.* trashoguero.

**fireball** (-bol) *s.* METEOR. globo de fuego.

**firebox** (-bacs) *s.* caja de fuegos.

**firebrand** (-brænd) *s.* tea, tizón. *2* el que enciende la discordia.

**firecracker** (-krækø<sup>r</sup>) *s.* carretilla, petardo.

**firedamp** (-dæmp) *s.* MIN. grisú, mofeta.

**firedog** (-dog) *s.* morillo.

**fire-eater** (-i·tø<sup>r</sup>) *s.* titiritero que finge comer fuego. *2* jaque, matamoros.

**firefly** (-flai) *s.* ENT. luciérnaga.

**firehouse** (-jaus) *s.* cuartelillo de bomberos.

**firelight** (-lait) *s.* luz de un fuego.

**firelock** (-lak) *s.* fusil de chispa.

**fireman** (-mæn) *s.* bombero. *2* fogonero.

**fireplace** (-pleis) *s.* hogar [de chimenea]; chimenea francesa.

**fireproof** (-pruf) *adj.* incombustible; refractario.

**fireside** (-said) *s.* sitio junto a la lumbre; fig. hogar, vida doméstica.

**firestone** (-stoun) *s.* pedernal.

**firewater** (-uøtø<sup>r</sup>) *s.* aguardiente.

**firewood** (-wud) *s.* leña [para el fuego].

**fireworks** (-uøᵲks) *s. pl.* fuegos artificiales.

**firing** (fai·ring) *s.* encendimiento, disparo, etc. V. TO FIRE. *2* encendido [de un motor]. *3 adj.* de encender, de disparar, de tiro, etc.: ~ *line*, MIL. línea de fuego; ~ *order*, AUTO. orden del encendido: ~ *pin*, percutor.

**firkin** (føᵲkin) *s.* cuñete, barrilillo.

**firm** (føᵲm) *adj.* firme. *2* duro, compacto, consistente. *3* fiel, leal. *4 s.* firma, razón social.

**firmament** (føᵲrmament) *s.* firmamento, cielo.

**firman** (føᵲman) *s.* firmán.

**firmly** (føᵲmli) *adv.* firmemente, fuertemente.

**firmness** (føᵲmnis) *s.* firmeza. *2* dureza, consistencia. *3* fidelidad, lealtad.

**first** (føᵲst) *adj.* primero: ~ *aid*, primeros auxilios, cura de urgencia; ~ *cousin*, primo hermano, prima hermana; ~ *floor* (Ingl.), primer piso; principal, (E.U.) bajos, planta baja; ~ *fruits*, primicias; ~ *name*, nombre de pila; ~ *night*, TEAT. noche de estreno; ~ *person*, GRAM. primera persona; ~ *quarter*, cuarto creciente [de la luna]; *at* ~ *blush* o *wiew*, a primera vista. *2* pristino, primitivo. *3* anterior, original. *4* temprano.
*5 adv.* primero, primeramente: ~ *or last*, tarde o temprano. *6* antes, al principio. *7* por primera vez. *8 s.* primero. *9* principio: *at* ~, al principio; al pronto; *from the* ~, desde el principio. *10* AUTO. primera.

**first-aid** *adj.* de primeros auxilios: *first-aid kit*, botiquín.

**first-begotten, first-born** *adj.-s.* primogénito.

**first-class** *adj.* de primera clase. *2 adv.* en primera clase.

**first-hand** *adj.-adv.* de primera mano.

**firstling** (-ling) *s.* primicias, primer producto, primer nacido.

**firstly** (-li) *adv.* primero, primeramente, en primer lugar.

**first-rate** *adj.* excelente, de primera.

**firth** (føᵲth) *s.* brazo de mar. *2* ría, estuario.

**fisc** (fisk) *s.* físico, erario, hacienda pública.

**fiscal** (-al) *adj.* fiscal [del fisco]; rentístico.

**fish** (fish) *s.* ICT. pez: ~ *bowl*, pecera; ~ *day*, día de vigilia; ~ *hawk*, halieto; ~ *market*, pescadería; ~ *trap*, garlito, nasa; *a queer* ~, fig. un tipo raro. *2* pescado: *to be neither* ~ *nor fowl*, no ser carne ni pescado; *to have another*, o *other*, ~ *to fry*, tener otras cosas que hacer, o en que pensar. *3* MEC. refuerzo. *4* FERROC. eclisa. *5* MAR. jimelga.

**fish (to)** *tr.* pescar [peces u otras cosas]. *2* pescar en [un río, etc.]. *3* buscar, coger, sacar. *4* FERROC. empalmar con eclisa. *5 intr.* pescar: *to* ~ *in troubled waters*, pescar en río revuelto.

**fishbone** (fi·shboun) *s.* espina de pez.

**fisher** (-øᵲ) *s.* pescador. *2* animal pescador. *3* embarcación de pesca. *4* ZOOL. marta del Canadá.

**fisherman** (-øᵲmæn) *s.* pescador. *2* barco pesquero. *3* fig. el Papa.

**fishery** (-øri) *s.* pesca [acción]. *2* pesquería.

**fishhook** (-juk) *s.* anzuelo.

**fishiness** (-inis) *s.* olor o sabor a pescado. *2* calidad de sospechoso o raro.

**fishing** (-ing) *s.* pesca [acción]. *2* pesquería. *3 adj.* de pesca, pescador, pesquero: ~ *fly*, mosca artificial; ~ *eagle*, ORN. halieto; ~ *grounds*, pesquería, pesquera; ~ *rod*, caña de pescar; ~ *tackle*, avíos de pescar.

**fishmonger** (-mongøᵲ) *s.* pescadero.

**fishplate** (-pleit) *s.* FERROC. eclisa.

**fishpond** (-pond) *s.* estanque, vivero.

**fishtail** (-teil) *s.* cola de pez o cosa que se le parece. *2* AVIA. coleadura.

**fishtail (to)** *intr.* AVIA. colear.

**fishwife** (-uaif) *s.* pescadera. *2* fig. verdulera [mujer desvergonzada].

**fishy** (-i) *adj.* de pez, o que lo parece. *2* que sabe o huele a pescado. *3* abundante en peces. *4* sospechoso, raro. *5* apagado, sin brillo.

**fission** (fi·shøn) *s.* hendimiento. *2* BIOL. escisión. *3* FÍS., QUÍM. fisión.

**fissipedal** (fisi·pedal) *adj.* ZOOL. fisípedo.

**fissirostral** (fi·sirostral) *adj.* ORN. fisirrostro.

**fissure** (fi·shøᵲ) *s.* hendidura, grieta. *2* ANAT., CIR., MINER. fisura.

**fissure (to)** *tr.* hender. *2 intr.* henderse.

**fist** (fist) *s.* puño [mano cerrada]: *to shake one's* ~ *at*, amenazar con el puño. *2* fam. mano [del hombre]. *3* fam. letra, escritura.

**fist (to)** *tr.* apuñear, dar de puñetazos. *2* empuñar.

**fistic** (fi·stik) *adj.* pugilístico.

**fisticuff** (fi·stikøf) *s.* puñetazo, puñada. *2 pl.* riña a puñetazos.

**fistula** (fi·schøla) *s.* caña, tubo. *2* CIR. fístula. *3* BOT. cañaheja.

**fistulous** (fi·schøløs) *adj.* fistuloso.

**fit** (fit) *s.* ataque, acceso, paroxismo, convulsión. *2* arranque, arrebato. *3* capricho, antojo. *4* rato, intervalo: *by fits (and starts)*, a empujones, intermitentemente. *5* ajuste, encaje. *6* corte, talle [de un traje]. *7* conveniencia, conformidad. *8* preparación. *9 adj.* apto, capaz, digno, apropiado, conveniente, a propósito, pintiparado. *10* en buena forma, bien; bien de salud. *11* listo, preparado. *12 to see* ~, tener por conveniente.

**fit (to)** *tr.-intr.* adaptarse, ajustarse [a], encajar, concordar, corresponder, convenir, cuadrar, compaginarse [con]; ser propio, a propósito, o adecuado [de o para]. *3* caer, ir, venir [bien o mal]. *4 to* ~ *in with*, concordar, armonizar con. *5 tr.* ajustar, encajar, acomodar, adaptar, adecuar. *6* entallar [un vestido]. *7* surtir, proveer, equipar. *8* disponer, preparar. *9 to* ~ *out*, surtir, equipar, habilitar; tripular, armar. *10 to* ~ *up*, disponer [para un uso]; amueblar; ataviar.

**fitch** (-ch) *s.* ZOOL. turón, veso. *2* pincel de pelo de turón.

**fitful** (-ful) *adj.* incierto, vacilante, intermitente. *2* caprichoso, impulsivo.

**fitness** (-nis) *s.* propiedad, adecuación. *2* conveniencia, pertinencia, oportunidad.

**fitter** (-øᵲ) *s.* ajustador. *2* proveedor. *3* MEC. montador. *4* cortador, probador [sastre].

**fitting** (-ing) *s.* propio, adecuado, conveniente, ajustado. *2 s.* ajuste, encaje. *3* MEC. montaje. *4* SASTR. prueba, entalladura. *5 pl.* accesorios, guarniciones, herrajes; muebles.

**five** (faiv) *adj.-s.* cinco: ~ *o'clock*, las cinco.

**livefold** (-fould) *adj.-s.* quíntuplo.

**five-year** *adj.* quinquenal.

**fix** (fiks) *s.* apuro, aprieto: *to be in a* ~, hallarse en un aprieto.

**fix (to)** *tr.* fijar [un objeto, la atención, la mirada, una fecha, etc.]; poner, establecer. *2* FOT., QUÍM. fijar. *3* grabar [en la mente]. *4* atraer [la atención, la mirada]. *5* arreglar, disponer; componer, reparar. *6* fam. amañar. *7* fam. sobornar; convencer. *8* ajustarle las cuentas [a uno]. *9 to* ~ *up*, componer, arreglar; equipar. *10 intr.* fijar su domicilio, establecerse. *11* fijarse, solidificarse. *12 to* ~ *on*, decidirse por, escoger.

**fixation** (fiksei·shøn) *s.* fijación.

**fixative** (fi·ksativ) *adj.* que fija. *2 s.* TINT. mordiente. *3* DIB. fijador, fijativo.

**fixed** (-t) *adj.* fijo, firme, estable, permanente: ~ *idea*, idea fija, obsesión. *2* decidido, determinado. *3* arraigado.

**fixer** (-ǿ^r) *s.* FOT. fijador. *2* reparador, componedor.

**fixings** (-ings) *s. pl.* accesorios, adornos, enseres.

**fixity** (-iti) *s.* fijeza. *2* cosa fija.

**fixture** (-chǿ^r) *s.* fijación. *2* cosa, accesorio, adorno, mueble, fijos en un lugar. *3* persona permanentemente establecida en un lugar o empleo. *4* fecha fija [para ciertos actos]. *5 pl.* instalación [de una tienda; de gas, electricidad, etc.].

**fizgig** (fi·šgig) *s.* muchacha desenvuelta. *2* buscapiés.

**fizz** (fiš) *s.* ruido como el de un gas que se escapa. *2* efervescencia. *3* fam. champaña, bebida gaseosa.

**fizz (to)** *intr.* hacer un ruido como el de un gas que se escapa.

**fizzle** (fi·šøl) *s.* FIZZ 1 y 2. *2* fam. fiasco.

**fizzle (to)** *intr.* TO FIZZ. *2 to ~ out*, chisporrotear [al apagarse]; hacer fiasco.

**flabbergast (to)** (flæ·bø^r gast) *tr.* asombrar, dejar estupefacto.

**flabby** (flæ·bi) *adj.* fláccido, lacio, flojo.

**flabellum** (flabe·løm) *s.* flabelo.

**flaccid** (flæ·ksid) *adj.* fláccido, flojo.

**flag** (flæg) *s.* bandera, estandarte, banderola. *2* MAR. pabellón, insignia: ~ *officer*, jefe de escuadra; oficial general de la armada. *3* losa, lancha, lastra. *4* BOT. espadaña. *5* BOT. ácoro falso.

**flag (to)** *tr.* embanderar. *2* marcar, señalar, hacer señal [con una bandera]: *to ~ down a train*, hacer señal de parada a un tren. *3* enlosar, pavimentar con lajas. *4 intr.* colgar, pender, estar flojo o lacio. *5* desanimarse. *6* aflojar, flaquear, debilitarse. *7* vacilar. ¶ Pret. y p. p.: *flagged;* ger.: *-gging.*

**flagellant** (flæ·dẏelant) *s.* flagelante; disciplinante.

**flagellate** (-leit) *adj.-s.* BOT., ZOOL. flagelado.

**flagellate (to)** *intr.* flagelar, azotar.

**flagellation** (-ei·shøn) *s.* flagelación.

**flagellum** (fladẏe·løm) *s.* flagelo, azote. *2* BOT., ZOOL. flagelo.

**flageolet** (flædẏole·t) *s.* MÚS. caramillo; chirimía.

**flagging** (flæ·ging) *adj.* lánguido, flojo, desanimado.

**flagitious** (fladẏi·shøs) *adj.* malvado, criminal, atroz.

**flagman** (flæ·gmæn) *s.* el que hace señales con bandera. *2* FERROC. guardavía.

**flagon** (flæ·gøn) *s.* garrafa, jarro, botella.

**flagpole** (flæ·gpoul) *s.* asta de bandera. *2* TOP. banderola, jalón.

**flagrance, -cy** (flei·grans, -si) *s.* notoriedad, escándalo, atrocidad.

**flagrant** (flei·grant) *adj.* flagrante, ardiente. *2* notorio, escandaloso, insigne, atroz.

**flagship** (flæ·gship) *s.* MAR. buque insignia.

**flagstaff** (-staf) *s.* asta de bandera.

**flagstone** (-stoun) *s.* losa, laja.

**flail** (fleil) *s.* mayal [para desgranar]. *2* mangual.

**flail (to)** *tr.* desgranar con mayal. *2* azotar, pegar.

**flair** (fle·ǿ^r) *s.* olfato, instinto, penetración.

**flake** (fleik) *s.* copo [de nieve]. *2* escama, pedacito, hojuela: ~ *of fire*, chispa, centella. *3* BOT. clavel rayado.

**flake (to)** *tr.* dividir en hojuelas o escamas. *2* cubrir de copos [de nieve]. *3 intr.* formar hojuelas o escamas. *4* descascararse.

**flam** (flæm) *s.* falsedad, mentira, embuste.

**flambeau** (flæ·mbou) *s.* hachón, antorcha.

**flamboyant** (flæmbo·iant) *adj.* flamígero. *2* vistoso, llamativo. *3* resplandeciente.

**flame** (fleim) *s.* llama. *2* llamarada. *3* fuego, ardor, pasión, amor. *4* ser amado.

**flame (to)** *intr.* llamear, flamear, arder, encenderse, brillar. *2* fig. exaltarse, inflamarse. *3 tr.* flamear. *4* encender, inflamar.

**flamen** (flei·men) *s.* flamen.

**flaming** (-ming) *adj.* llameante, encendido. *2* inflamado, apasionado. *3* llamativo, fastuoso.

**flamingo** (flami·ngou) *s.* ORN. flamenco.

**flan** (flæ·ɹ o flan) *s.* cospel. *2* flan; tarta de crema.

**Flanders** (flæ·ndø^r š) *n. pr.* GEOGR. Flandes.

**flange** (flæ·ndẏ) *s.* MEC. brida, pestaña, reborde, chapa de cierre.

**flange (to)** *tr.* hacer o poner brida, pestaña o reborde. *2 intr.* proyectarse, salir, extenderse.

**flank** (klænk) *s.* ijar, ijada, delgado, vacío. *2* costado, lado. *3* MIL., FORT. flanco.

**flank (to)** *tr.* flanquear; estar a cada lado de.

**flannel** (flæ·nøl) *s.* TEJ. franela. *2 pl.* ropa, vestido de franela.

**flap** (flæp) *s.* SASTR. cartera, golpe, pata; haldeta, faldón. *2* ala flexible [de sombrero]. *3* hoja plegadiza [de mesa]. *4* trampa [tablero]: ~ *door*, trampa [puerta]. *5* oreja [de zapato]. *6* disco [de válvula]: ~ *valve*, chapaleta. *7* CIR. colgajo. *8* mosqueador. *9* revés, cachete. *10* aletazo. *11* gualdrapazo. *12* golpeteo.

**flap (to)** *tr.* golpear, sacudir [con algo plano]. *2* mosquear. *3* batir, agitar [las alas]. *4* intr. colgar, pender. *5* gualdrapear; batir. *6* aletear, volar. *7* agitarse. ¶ Pret. y p. p.: *flapped;* ger.: -*pping.*

**flapper** (flæ·pø^r) *tr.* el o lo que golpea. *2* CAZA patito. *3* fam. jovencita, tobillera. *4* fam. mano.

**flare** (fle·ǿ^r) *s.* llamarada, destello. *2* señal luminosa, cohete de señales. *3* arrebato [de cólera, etc.]. *4* vuelo [de una falda]. *5* ensanchamiento, abocinamiento.

**flare (to)** *tr.* señalar con luz o fuego. *2* ostentar. *3* dar forma acampanada, abocinar. *4 intr.* llamear, brillar, fulgurar. *5* tener vuelo [una falda]. *6* tener forma acampanada. *7 to ~ up*, encenderse, encolerizarse.

**flare-up** *s.* llamarada, encendimiento. *2* llamarada, explosión [de cólera, etc.].

**flash** (flæsh) *s.* llamarada, resplandor, destello; rayo, ráfaga de luz; fogonazo: ~ *of lightning*, relámpago; ~ *in the pan*, fig. esfuerzo súbito y aparatoso que no logra nada. *2* momento, instante: *in a ~*, en un instante. *3* acción rápida. *4* telegrama breve [en un periódico]. *5* descarga [de esclusa]. *6* CINEM. breve proyección explicativa. *7* ostentación, relumbrón; persona ostentosa; cosa de relumbrón. *8* corredor veloz. *9 adj.* vulgar, charro, chillón. *10* ladronesco, de germanía.

**flash (to)** *tr.* encender, inflamar. *2* hacer brillar. *3* despedir, enviar [luz, destellos]; echar [llamas]. *4* transmitir rápidamente, telegrafiar, radiar. *5* hacer ostentación de. *6 intr.* relampaguear, centellear, llamear, brillar; inflamar. *7* pasar como un relámpago. *8* obrar con ímpetu. *9* pop. lucir, fachendear. '

**flashback** (-bæk) *s.* CINEM. escena retrospectiva.

**flashing** (-ing) *m.* centelleo, relampagueo, fulguración. *2* vierteaguas, despidiente de agua.

**flashlight** (-lait) *s.* linterna eléctrica. *2* fanal de destellos; luz intermitente [de un faro]. *3* FOT. luz instantánea [de magnesio, etc.].

**flashy** (-i) *adj.* relumbrante. *2* llamativo, chillón, ostentoso, de relumbrón; superficial.

**flask** (flæsk) *s.* frasco, redoma.

**flat** (flæt) *adj.* plano, llano, liso, raso, arrasado. *2* chato, aplastado. *3* tendido, extendido. *4* positivo, categórico. *5* insulso, insípido. *6* desbravado [champán, cerveza]. *7* apagado, sin brillo; monótono, sin interés. *8* desanimado. *9* MÚS. desentonado. *10* MÚS. bemol. *11* desinflado [neumático]. *12 adv.* completamente. *13* exactamente; decididamente. *14* desafinadamente. *15 s.* llanura, planicie, plano. *16* banco, bajío. *17* parte o cosa plana; palma [de la mano]; pala [de remo]; barca chata; carro de plataforma. *18* piso, apartamento. *19* simple, mentecato.

**flat (to)** *tr.* aplastar, achatar. *2* hacer insípido. *3* MÚS. abemolar. ¶ Pret. y p. p.: *flatted;* ger.: ~ tting.

**flatcar** (-ka$^r$) *s.* FERROC. vagón de plataforma.

**flat-footed** *adj.* de pies planos. *2* fam. (E.U.) resuelto, determinado; tonto.

**flatiron** (-aiø$^r$n) *s.* plancha [para planchar].

**flatland** (-lænd) *s.* llano, llanada, llanura.

**flat-nosed** *adj.* chato [de nariz chata].

**flatten (to)** (-øn) *tr.* allanar, aplanar, aplastar, achatar. *2* postrar, abatir. *3* desazonar, hacer insípido. *4 to* ~ *out,* extender horizontalmente; enderezar [un avión]. *5 intr.* aplanarse, aplastarse, achatarse. *6* abatirse, desalentarse. *7* perder el sabor. *8 to* ~ *out,* enderezarse [un avión].

**flatter (to)** (flæ·tø$^r$) *tr.* adular, lisonjear: *to* ~ *oneself,* lisonjearse, hacerse una ilusión. *2* halagar. *3* favorecer [un retrato].

**flatterer** (-ø$^r$) *s.* adulador, lisonjero.

**flattery** (-i) *s.* adulación, lisonja. *2* halago.

**flatulence, flatulency** (flæ·tiuløns, -si) *s.* flatulencia. *2* hinchazón, presunción.

**flatulent** (flæ·tiulønt), **flatuous** (flei·tiuøs) *adj.* flatulento, flatoso. *2* hinchado, pomposo, vano.

**flatus** (flei·tøs) *s.* flato. *2* hinchazón.

**flatways** (flæ·tueiš), **flatwise** (flæ·tuaiš) *adv.* de plano, horizontalmente.

**flaunt** (flont) *s.* ostentación, alarde.

**flaunt (to)** *tr.* hacer ondear. *2* lucir, ostentar. *3 intr.* ondear, flotar [al viento]. *4* pavonearse.

**flautist** (flo·tist) *s.* flautista.

**flavo (u) r** (flei·vø$^r$) *s.* sabor, gusto. *2* aroma, perfume. *3* COC. sazón, sainete.

**flavo (u) r (to)** *tr.* saborear, dar sabor. *2* sazonar, condimentar. *3* aromatizar. *4* fig. dar cualidad distintiva [a una cosa]. *5 intr.* saber a, oler a.

**flavo (u) ring** (-ing) *s.* sainete, condimento.

**flaw** (flo) *s.* grieta, raja. *2* falla, falta, defecto, imperfección. *3* pelo [en una piedra o metal]. *4* MAR. ráfaga, racha.

**flaw (to)** *tr.* agrietar, romper. *2* causar defecto, afear, estropear.

**flawless** (-lis) *adj.* entero, sano. *2* sin defecto, sin tacha.

**flax** (flæks) *s.* lino [planta, fibra].

**flaxen** (-øn) *adj.* de lino; parecido al lino.

**flaxseed** (flæ·ksid) *s.* linaza, semilla del lino.

**flay (to)** (flei) *tr.* desollar, despellejar. *2* fig. desollar vivo, robar. *3* fig. reprender, fustigar.

**flea** (flɪ) *s.* ENT. pulga: *a* ~ *in one's ear,* fig. reprensión; repulsa.

**fleabite** (-bait) *s.* picadura de pulga. *2* fig. pequeña molestia.

**fleawort** (-uø$^r$t) *s.* BOT. pulguera, zaragatona.

**fleck** (flek) *s.* punto, mancha [de color o de luz]; pinta, lunar, peca. *2* copo, vedija.

**fleck(er (to)** *tr.* manchar, abigarrar.

**flection** (fle·kshøn) *s.* FLEXIÓN.

**fled** (fled) *pret.* y *p. p.* de TO FLEE.

**fledge (to)** (fle·dŷ) *tr.* emplumar. *2* criar plumas en. *3 intr.* emplumecer, pelechar.

**fledged** (fle·dŷd) *adj.* plumado, con plumas.

**fledg(e)ling** (fle·dŷling) *adj.-s.* volantón. *2* joven, novel, inexperto.

**flee (to)** (flɪ) *tr.* huir de, escapar de, evitar. *2 intr.* huir, escapar, desaparecer. ¶ Pret. y p. p.: *fled.*

**fleece** (flɪ·s) *s.* vellón, vellocino, lana: *the Golden Fleece,* el Vellocino de oro; el Toisón [de oro].

**fleece (to)** *tr.* esquilar [el ganado]. *2* fig. desplumar, pelar. *3* cubrir de lana o nieve.

**fleecy** (-i) *adj.* lanudo. *2* blanco y blando. *3* aborregado [cielo].

**fleer** (flɪ·ø$^r$) *s.* mueca, burla, risa falsa.

**fleer (to)** (tr. burlarse, mofarse de. *2 intr.* reírse o sonreírse con burla o desprecio.

**fleet** (flit) *s.* armada, marina de guerra. *2* MAR., AVIA. flota, escuadra, escuadrilla. *3* conjunto de vehículos pertenecientes a una empresa. *4 adj.* veloz, rápido, ligero.

**fleet (to)** *tr.* rozar, pasar rápidamente sobre. *2 intr.* pasar velozmente, volar, desvanecerse.

**fleeting** (-ing) *adj.* fugaz, pasajero, efímero, transitorio.

**Fleming** (fle·ming) *s.* flamenco [de Flandes].

**Flemish** (fle·miš) *adj.-s.* flamenco [de Flandes]. *2 s.* flamenco [idioma].

**flesh** (flesh) *s.* carne [de una pers. o animal vivos; de una fruta; cuerpo, naturaleza humana; sensualidad]: ~ *and blood,* carne y hueso; fig. sangre, familia; *in the* ~, vivo; en persona. *2* carne [por oposición a pescado]. *3* género humano. *4* sangre, linaje. *5* piel, cutis.

**flesh (to)** *tr.* acostumbrar, avezar. *2* cebar, encarnizar. *3* hundir [un arma] en la carne.

**fleshings** (fle·shingš) *s. pl.* TEAT. mallas de color de carne.

**fleshly** (-li) *adj.* carnoso. *2* corporal. *3* carnal, sensual, mundano.

**fleshy** (-li) *adj.* carnoso, pulposo. *2* suculento. *3* gordo, grueso, corpulento.

**fleur-de-lis** (flø·døli·(s) *s.* BLAS., BOT. flor de lis.

**flew** (flu) *pret.* de TO FLY.

**flex (to)** (fleks) *tr.* doblar, encorvar. *2 intr.* doblarse.

**flexibility** (fleksibi·liti) *s.* flexibilidad.

**flexible** (fle·ksibøl) *adj.* flexible: ~ *cord,* ELECT. flexible. *2* cimbreño, juncal. *3* dócil, manejable.

**flexile** (-il) *adj.* FLEXIBLE.

**flexion** (fle·kshøn) *s.* flexión, doblamiento. *2* codo, curvatura. *3* GRAM. flexión.

**flexor** (-sø$^r$) *s.* ANAT. flexor [músculo].

**flexuose** (-shuous), **flexuous** (-øs) *adj.* flexuoso, tortuoso, sinuoso. *2* vario, inconstante.

**flibbertigibbet** (flibø$^r$tidŷi·bet) *s.* persona frívola, voluble o chismosa.

**flick** (flik) *s.* golpecito [con el dedo, el látigo, etc.]. *2* mancha pequeña. *3 pl.* fam. cine.

**flick (to)** *tr.* dar un golpecito [con el dedo, etc.]. *2* sacudir [la ceniza a un cigarro]. *3* chasquear [un látigo]. *4 intr.* corretear, revolotear.

**flicker** (-ø$^r$) s. vacilación, titilación, luz trémula. 2 parpadeo. 3 aleteo. 4 estremecimiento. 5 ORN. picamaderos norteamericano.

**flicker (to)** intr. fluctuar, vacilar, temblar. 2 entremorir. 3 aletear.

**flier** (flai·ø$^r$) s. animal volador. 2 aviador. 3 avión. 4 cosa veloz [coche, tren, caballo, etc.]. 5 IMPR. sacapliegos. 6 fam. empresa u operación arriesgada.

**flight** (flait) s. vuelo [acción, manera de volar; espacio recorrido volando]; volada: to take ~, alzar el vuelo; ~ path, AVIA. línea de vuelo. 2 viaje aéreo. 3 trayectoria [de un proyectil]. 4 paso rápido [del tiempo]. 5 bandada [de pájaros]. 6 lluvia [de flechas]. 7 escuadrilla [de aviones]. 8 ímpetu, arrebato, exaltación; vuelo [de la fantasía]. 9 fuga, huida, escape, evasión. 10 tramo [de escalera].

**flighty** (-i) adj. fugaz, pasajero. 2 caprichoso, inconstante. 3 alocado. 4 chiflado.

**flimflam** (fli·mflæm) s. necedad, bagatela. 2 soflama, engaño.

**flimsy** (fli·mši) adj. débil, endeble. 2 flaco, futil, trivial, baladí.

**flinch** (flinch) s. vacilación, titubeo.

**flinch (to)** intr. vacilar, desistir, echarse atrás, retroceder [ante lo peligroso, etc.], arredrarse.

**fling** (fling) s. tiro, echada, echamiento. 2 fam. prueba, tentativa: to take o have a ~ at, probar, ensayar. 3 fam. pulla, sarcasmo, burla. 4 brinco, coz. 5 valor, atrevimiento. 6 baile escocés. 7 to go on a ~, echar una cana al aire.

**fling (to)** tr. echar, arrojar, tirar, lanzar; despedir. 2 derribar, echar al suelo. 3 derrotar, vencer. 4 to ~ about, esparcir. 5 to ~ off, desechar, sacudirse; despistar [al que persigue]. 6 to ~ open, abrir de golpe. 7 to ~ out, arrojar con fuerza; hacer ondear [una bandera]. 8 intr. arrojarse, lanzarse, abalanzarse. 9 saltar, brincar. 10 burlarse, mofarse. 11 to ~ out, lanzarse fuera. ¶ Pret. y p. p.: flung.

**flint** (flint) s. pedernal. 2 cosa muy dura. 3 adj. ~ glass, cristal [vidrio pesado].

**flint-hearted** adj. empedernido.

**flintlock** (fli·ntlak) s. llave o fusil de chispa.

**flinty** (-i) adj. pedernalino. 2 duro, cruel.

**flip** (flip) s. golpe vivo, capirotazo. 2 especie de ponche.

**flip (to)** tr. arrojar, lanzar al aire. 2 echar [una moneda sobre el mostrador]. 3 tirar con un movimiento del pulgar y otro dedo. 4 dar un golpe vivo. 5 quitar de golpe.

**flippancy** (-ansi) s. ligereza impropia, impertinencia, petulancia.

**flippant** (-ant) adj. ligero, impertinente, petulante.

**flipper** (-ø$^r$) s. ZOOL. pata [de foca, de tortuga marina, etc.]. 2 pop. mano.

**flirt** (flØ$^r$t) s. flirteador, galanteador. 2 coqueta [mujer]. 3 sacudida, tirón.

**flirt (to)** intr. flirtear, coquetear. 2 juguetear, mariposear. 3 acariciar, dejarse tentar por [una idea, etc.].

**flirtation** (-ei·shØn) s. flirteo, coqueteo, galanteo.

**flit** (flit) s. movimiento rápido y ligero.

**flit (to)** intr. pasar [de un sitio a otro]. 2 moverse rápidamente, volar, revolotear. ¶ Pret. y p. p.: flitted; ger.: flitting.

**flitch** (flich) s. témpano [de tocino]. 2 lonja [de carne o pescado].

**flitter (to)** (fli·tØ$^r$) tr.-intr. TO FLUTTER.

**flittermouse** (-ma·us) s. ZOOL. murciélago.

**flitting** (fli·ting) adj. fugaz.

**float** (flout) s. flotador; cosa que flota. 2 corcho [de caña de pescar]. 3 boya. 4 salvavidas. 5 balsa; armadía. 6 carromato, carroza, carro alegórico [para procesiones, etc.]. 7 paleta [de rueda].

**float (to)** intr. flotar. 2 sobrenadar, boyar, nadar; hacer la plancha [en la natación]. 3 cernerse. 4 fluctuar. 5 tr. hacer flotar, poner o llevar a flote. 6 inundar. 7 COM. emitir, poner en circulación.

**floater** (flou·tø$^r$) s. flotador. 2 el que cambia frecuentemente de residencia, ocupación, etc.

**floating** (-ing) adj. flotante. 2 boyante, a flote. 3 fluctuante, variable. 4 COM. en circulación.

**floculent** (fla·kiulØnt) adj. coposo, lanoso.

**flock** (flak) s. bandada [de aves]; manada; rebaño. 2 grey, congregación. 3 muchedumbre, grupo. 4 hatajo. 5 copo, vedija. 6 borra.

**flock (to)** intr. reunirse, congregarse, atroparse, juntarse. 2 llegar en tropel.

**floe** (flou) s. masa de hielo flotante.

**flog (to)** (flag) tr. azotar, vapulear, fustigar. ‖ Pret. y p. p.: flogged; ger.: flogging.

**flogging** (-ing) s. azotes, azotamiento.

**flood** (flØd) s. riada, avenida, crecida, desbordamiento. 2 diluvio, inundación: the Flood, el Diluvio. 3 torrente, abundancia. 4 flujo [del mar]: ~ tide, marea montante, pleamar. 5 aguas, mar.

**flood (to)** tr. inundar. 2 sumergir, anegar, diluviar. 3 intr. desbordarse; entrar o salir a raudales.

**floodgate** (-geit) s. compuerta; puerta de esclusa.

**floodlight** (-lait) s. reflector, proyector de luz.

**floor** (flo·ø$^r$) s. suelo, piso, pavimento, entarimado: ~ tile, baldosa, baldosín. 2 fondo [del mar, de una piscina, etc.]. 3 plan [de un buque]. 4 piso, alto [de una casa]. 5 hemiciclo [de una asamblea]. 6 to have the ~, tener la palabra.

**floor (to)** tr. solar, enlosar, embaldosar, enladrillar, entarimar. 2 derribar, echar al suelo. 3 apabullar, revolcar, vencer [en una discusión].

**flooring** (-ing) s. suelo, piso. 2 embaldosado, entarimado. 3 material para solar.

**flop** (flap) s. fam. sonido como el del choque de un cuerpo blando. 2 fam. fracaso.

**flop (to)** tr. echar, dejar caer con descuido o con ruido. 2 intr. hacer un ruido como el del choque de un cuerpo blando. 3 menearse [una cosa] de un lado a otro. 4 fracasar, hacer fiasco. 5 to ~ down, dejarse caer, tumbarse. ‖ Pret. y p. p.: flopped; ger.: flopping.

**flora** (flo·ra) s. BOT. flora. 2 (con may.). MIT. Flora.

**floral** (-al) adj. floral.

**Florence** (flo·rØns) n. pr. f. Florencia.

**Florentine** (flo·rØntin) adj.-s. florentino.

**florescence** (flore·sØns) s. BOT. florescencia.

**floret** (flo·ret) s. BOT. flósculo. 2 florecilla.

**floriculture** (floricø·lchØ$^r$) s. floricultura.

**florid** (flo·rid) adj. florido [estilo]. 2 colorado [rostro]. 3 vigoroso, lozano, fresco. 4 vistoso, llamativo.

**floriferous** (flo·riforØs) adj. florífero.

**florin** (flo·rin) s. florín.

**florist** (flo·rist) s. floricultor. 2 florista.

**floscule** (flo·skiul) s. BOT. flósculo.

**floss** (flos) s. seda floja. 2 cadarzo. 3 fibra sedosa. 4 penacho [del maíz].

**flossy** (-i) adj. ligero, suave. 3 pop. llamativo.

**flotation** (flotei·shØn) s. flotación, flotadura. 2 COM. lanzamiento [de un empréstito, de una empresa].

**flotilla** (floti·la) s. flotilla.

**flotsam** (flo·tsam) *s.* pecios.

**flounce** (flauns) *s.* faralá, volante, guarnición. *2* sacudida, movimiento rápido.

**flounce (to)** *tr.* guarnecer con volantes. *2 intr.* andar o moverse violentamente, mostrando enojo.

**flounder** (flau·ndø<sup>r</sup>) *s.* forcejeo, esfuerzo torpe. *2* ICT. nombre de la platija, el lenguado, el rodaballo, etc.

**flounder (to)** *intr.* debatirse, patullar. *2* avanzar o proceder torpemente; equivocarse.

**flour** (flau<sup>r</sup>) *s.* harina.

**flour (to)** *tr.* moler, pulverizar. *2* enharinar.

**flourish** (flø·rish) *s.* molinete o movimiento ostentoso, de saludo, etc., que se hace con un bastón, espada, etc. *2* adorno, rasgo caprichoso. *3* MÚS. adición o preludio improvisado. *5* toque de trompetas. *6* florecimiento, prosperidad, vigor.

**flourish (to)** *intr.* crecer, florecer, prosperar. *2* MÚS. improvisar un preludio. *3* rasguear, hacer dibujos caprichosos. *4 tr.* ornamentar. *5* blandir, hacer molinetes con; mover con gracia u ostentación.

**flourishing** (flø·rishing) *adj.* floreciente, próspero.

**floury** (fla·uri) *adj.* harinoso. *2* enharinado.

**flout** (flaut) *s.* mofa, escarnio, insulto.

**flout (to)** *tr.* mofarse de, escarnecer, insultar.

**flow** (flou) *s.* flujo, corriente. *2* acción de fluir o manar. *3* torrente, chorro, abundancia. *4* afluencia. *5* desagüe. *6* flujo [de la marea]. *7* desbordamiento, inundación. *8* movimiento suave y gradual. *9* FÍS. gasto. *10* ~ *of spirits*, animación habitual.

**flow (to)** *intr.* fluir, manar, correr. *2* salir, proceder, dimanar. *3* afluir. *4* subir [la marea]. *5* abundar, rebosar. *6* deslizarse, correr fácilmente, ser fluido [el estilo, etc.]. *7* caer en ondas o pliegues; ondear. *8 to* ~ *into*, desaguar en. *9 to* ~ *over*, rebosar. *10 tr.* inundar. *11* derramar.

**flower** (flau·ø<sup>r</sup>) *s.* BOT. flor: ~ *garden*, jardín; ~ *girl*, florista; ~ *vase*, jarrón, florero; ~ *of lice*, flor de lis. *2* flor y nata. *3* adorno, ornamento [esp. del estilo] *4 pl.* QUÍM. flor.

**flower (to)** *intr.* florecer. *2* florear [adornar con flores].

**flowered** (-d) *adj.* florido [que tiene flores]. *2* floreado [adornado con flores], espolinado.

**floweret** (-et) *s.* florecilla, florecita.

**flowering** (-ing) *adj.* FLOWERY. *2* florido, en flor. *3* BOT. ~ *rush*, junco florido.

**flowerpot** (-pat) *s.* maceta, tiesto.

**flowery** (-i) *adj.* de flores o que lo parece. *2* cubierto de flores. *3* florido, poético [estilo].

**flowing** (flou·ing) *adj.* fluido, fluente, corriente, manantío. *2* fluido, fácil [estilo]. *3* ondeante.

**flown** (floun) *p. p.* de TO FLY.

**flu** (flu) *s.* MED. fam. trancazo, gripe.

**fluctuant** (fløkchuant) *adj.* fluctuante, fluctuoso.

**fluctuate (to)** (flø·kchueit) *intr.* fluctuar.

**fluctuation** (-ei·shøn) *s.* fluctuación. *2* agitación, incertidumbre.

**flue** (flu) *s.* cañón [de chimenea], humero. *2* conducto o tubo [de ventilación, de humos]. *3* pelusa, tamo. *4* MÚS. *flue* o ~ *pipe*, cañón de planta [del órgano].

**fluency** (-ønsi) *s.* fluidez. *2* afluencia, facundia, soltura, facilidad [de palabra].

**fluent** (-ønt) *adj.* fluido, fluente. *2* facundo. *3* fácil, abundante, fluido [lenguaje, estilo].

**fluff** (fløf) *s.* pelusa, vello, lanilla, tamo. *2* copo [de lana]. *3* masa esponjosa. *4* plumón.

**fluff (to)** *tr.* mullir, esponjar, ahuecar.

**fluffy** (-i) *adj.* cubierto de pelusa o plumón. *2* blando, suave, mullido, esponjado, sedoso.

**fluid** (flu·id) *adj.-s.* fluido.

**fluidity** (-iti), **fluidness** (-inis) *s.* fluidez.

**fluke** (fluk) *s.* uña [de ancla, de arpón]; lengüeta [de flecha]. *2* ICT. platija. *3* duela [gusano]. *4* chiripa. *5 pl.* cola [de la ballena].

**fluke (to)** *tr.* fam. chiripear. *2 intr.* fam. ganar por chiripa. *3* fracasar.

**flume** (flum) *s.* (E.U.) caz, reguera. *2* canal de madera. *3* garganta por cuyo fondo pasa un torrente.

**flummery** (flø·møri) *s.* especie de manjar blanco. *2* patarata, pamplina; alabanza insincera.

**flung** (fløng) *pret.* y *p. p.* de TO FLING.

**flunk** (flønk) *s.* (E.U.) fam. fracaso. *2* fam. suspenso [en un examen].

**flunk (to)** *tr.* (E.U.) fam. fracaso. *2* fam. suspenso [en un examen].

**flunk (to)** *tr.* (E.U.) suspender [en un examen]. *2 intr.* fam. quedar mal, fracasar [en un examen, etc.].

**flunkey, flunky** (flø·nki) *s.* lacayo. *2* adulador, persona servil.

**fluor** (flu·ø<sup>r</sup>) *s.* QUÍM. flúor.

**fluorescent** (fluøre·sønt) *adj.* fluorescente.

**flurry** (flø·ri) *s.* agitación, excitación, prisa. *2* barullo, conmoción. *3* ráfaga, chubasco.

**flurry (to)** *tr.* agitar, excitar, turbar, aturrullar.

**flush** (fløsh) *adj.* lleno, bien provisto, rico. *2* robusto, lleno de vida. *3* rojo, encendido. *4* abundante. *5* pródigo, generoso. *6* próspero. *7* igual, parejo, raso, nivelado, enrasado, al mismo nivel, embutido: ~ *with*, enrasado, ras con ras con. *8* ~ *tank*, depósito de agua para limpia [de inodoros, etc.].

*9 s.* descarga, flujo rápido y copioso. *10* aumento súbito; floración abundante. *11* vuelo súbito [de un pájaro o bandada]. *12* oleada [de un sentimiento]; emoción, agitación, animación. *13* rubor, encendimiento. *14* flux [de naipes].

**flush (to)** *intr.* afluir [la sangre, etc.]. *2* salirse, derramarse. *3* llenarse de agua. *4* encenderse; ruborizarse, sonrojarse. *5* echar a volar [las aves]. *6 tr.* animar, excitar. *7* encender, ruborizar. *8* limpiar con un chorro de agua, inundar. *9* igualar, nivelar, emparejar. *10* levantar [las aves de caza].

**fluster** (flø·stø) *s.* agitación, confusión, aturdimiento.

**fluster (to)** *tr.* agitar, confundir, aturdir; achispar. *2* encender [el rostro]. *3 intr.* agitarse, aturdirse.

**flute** (flut) *s.* MÚS. flauta. *2* MÚS. flautado [del órgano]. *3* ARQ. estría. *4* cañón [pliegue].

**flute (to)** *tr.* estriar, acanalar. *2* alechugar, encañonar. *3 intr.-tr.* tocar la flauta.

**fluting** (flu·ting) *s.* estría, estriadura, acanaladura.

**fluting-iron** *s.* hierros o tenacillas de rizar.

**flutist** (-ist) *s.* flautista.

**flutter** (flø·tø<sup>r</sup>) *s.* vibración, aleteo, ondulación. *2* vuelco [del corazón]. *3* agitación, confusión, alboroto; actividad sin objeto.

**flutter (to)** *intr.* temblar, aletear, revolotear, palpitar. *2* tremolar, flamear, ondear. *3* agitarse, alterarse. *4 tr.* batir [las alas]; tremolar, agitar. *5* agitar, turbar.

**fluvial** (flu·vial) *adj.* fluvial.

**fluviatile** (flu·viatil) *adj.* fluviatil. *2* fluvial.

**flux** (fløks) *s.* flujo. *2* derretimiento, fusión. *3* mudanza o alteración continua. *4* METAL. fundente.

**flux (to)** *tr.* fundir; unir por medio de la fusión. *2* mezclar con fundente. *3 intr.* fluir. *4* fundirse, derretirse.

**fluxion** (flø·kshøn) *s.* flujo; cambio continuo. *2* fusión. *3* MED. fluxión.

**fly** (flai) *s.* ENT. mosca: ~ *net*, mosquitero. *2* mosca artificial [para pescar]. *3* calesín. *4* vuelo [de una bandera; de lo que va por el aire]: *on the* ~, al vuelo. *5* bragueta. *6* lona que tapa la puerta [de una tienda de campaña]. *7* MEC. volante. *8 pl.* TEAT. bambalinas.

**fly (to)** *intr.* volar [moverse en el aire]. *2* huir, escaparse; desaparecer. *3* correr, pasar rápidamente. *4* volar [el tiempo]. *5* lanzarse, precipitarse: *to* ~ *at*, lanzarse sobre. *6* dispararse [un muelle]; saltar, estallar. *7* flotar, ondear [en el aire]. *8 to* ~ *in the face of*, desobedecer abiertamente, desafiar. *9 to* ~ *into a passion, a rage*, montar en clera. *10 to* ~ *off at a tangent*, cambiar de repente, tomar de repente un nuevo rumbo. *11 to* ~ *open, to* ~ *shut*, abrirse o cerrarse de repente.
*12 tr.* hacer volar. *13* dirigir [un avión]. *14* transportar [en avión]. *15* atravesar [en avión]. *16* desplegar, enarbolar [banderas]. *17* evitar; huir de. ¶ Pret.: *flew*; p. p.: *flown*.

**flyaway** (-auei) *adj.* suelto, ondeante. *2* inconstante. *3* casquivano.

**flyblow** (-blou) *s.* huevo de mosca, cresa.

**flyblow (to)** *tr.* depositar la mosca sus huevos en. *2* fig. contaminar, inficionar.

**flyboat** (-bout) *s.* MAR. filibote.

**flyer** (-ø<sup>r</sup>) *s.* FLIER.

**fly-fishing** *s.* pesca con mosca artificial.

**flyflap** (-flæp) *s.* mosqueador, espantamoscas.

**flying** (-ing) *s.* vuelo [acción de volar]. *2 adj.* volador, volante, para volar: ~ *bomb*, bomba volante; ~ *field*, campo de aviación; ~ *fortress*, AVIA. fortaleza volante; ~ *gurnard*, ICT. milano: ~ *saucer*, platillo volante; ~ *sickness*, mal de altura. *3* volante [que va de un lado a otro; que vuela o sobresale]: ~ *buttress*, ARQ. botarel, arbotante; ~ *column*, columna volante. *4* fugitivo. *5* rápido, veloz. *6* ondeante, desplegado [bandera, etc.]: *to come off with* ~ *colours*, salir triunfante. *7* MAR. ~ *jib*, petifoque.

**flyleaf** (-lif) *s.* ENCUAD. guarda.

**flypaper** (-peipø<sup>r</sup>) *s.* papel atrapamoscas.

**flyspeck** (-spek) *s.* mancha de mosca.

**flytrap** (-træp) *s.* atrapamoscas.

**flyweight** (-ueit) *s.* DEP. peso mosca.

**flywheel** (-juil) *s.* MEC. volante.

**foal** (foul) *s.* potro, potra; buche [cría de la yegua o de la burra].

**foal (to)** *tr.-intr.* parir la yegua o la burra.

**foam** (foum) *s.* espuma.

**foam (to)** *intr.* espumar, llenarse de espuma. *2* espumajear. *3 tr.* llenar de espuma.

**foamy** (-i) *adj.* espumante, espumajoso. *2* espumoso.

**fob** (fab) *s.* bolsillo del reloj. *2* engaño.

**fob (to)** *tr.* engañar, estafar, pegársela [a uno]. ¶ Pret. y p. p.: *fobbed*; ger.: *fobbing*.

**focal** (fou·kal) *adj.* focal.

**focus** (fou·køs) *s.* foco; distancia focal; enfoque: *in* ~, enfocado; *out of* ~, desenfocado.

**focus (to)** *tr.* enfocar; concentrar [en un foco]. *2 intr.* quedar enfocado. ¶ Pret. y p. p.: *focused* o -*ssed*; ger.: *focusing* o -*ssing*.

**fodder** (fa·dø<sup>r</sup>) *s.* forraje, pienso.

**fodder (to)** *tr.* pensar, dar pienso a.

**foe** (fou) *s.* enemigo. *2* adversario.

**foeman** (-mæn) *s.* enemigo [en la guerra].

**foetal** (fi·tal) *adj.* fetal.

**foetus** (fi·tos) *s.* feto.

**fog** (fog) *s.* niebla, neblina, bruma: ~ *bell*, ~ *whistle*, campana, silbato, de nieblas. *2* confusión, perplejidad. *3* FOT. velo.

**fog (to)** *tr.* envolver en niebla. *2* empañar; obscurecer. *3* FOT. velar. *4 intr.* ponerse brumoso. *5* hacerse confuso. *6* FOT. velarse. ¶ Pret. y p. p.: *fogged*; ger.: *fogging*.

**fogbound** (-baund) *adj.* inmovilizado por la niebla.

**fogey** *s.* FOGY.

**foggy** (-i) *adj.* de niebla. *2* neblinoso, brumoso. *3* nebuloso, confuso. *4* FOT. velado.

**foghorn** (-jo<sup>r</sup>n) *s.* MAR. bocina, sirena.

**fogy** (fou·gi) *s.* persona chapada a la antigua, obscurantista.

**foible** (foi·bøl) *s.* punto flaco, debilidad, flaqueza.

**foil** (foil) *s.* ESGR. florete. *2* hojuela, laminilla, chapa, pan [de metal]; oropel. *3* azogado [de un espejo]. *4* realce, conraste. *5* ARQ. lóbulo. *6* CAZA rastro.

**foil (to)** *tr.* anular, frustrar. *2* chasquear, desconcertar. *3* cubrir con laminilla. *4* realzar, hacer contrastar. *5* ARQ. adornar con lóbulos.

**foist (to)** (foist) *tr.* introducir, encajar, endosar [algo] subrepticiamente o con engaño.

**fold** (fould) *s.* doblez, pliegue, repliegue, arruga, recogido. *2* hoja [de puerta]. *3* abrazo. *4* IMPR. pliego. *5* envoltorio. *6* redil, aprisco. *7* hato, rebaño. *8* grey. *9* usado como sufijo, veces: *tenfold*, diez veces.

**fold (to)** *tr.* plegar, doblar. *2* enlazar, abrazar. *3* incluir, envolver. *4* cerrar [una puerta]. *5* cruzar [los brazos]; plegar [las alas]. *6* apriscar, meter en redil. *7 intr.* doblarse, plegarse, cerrarse.

**folder** (-ø<sup>r</sup>) *s.* plegador. *2* plegadera. *3* carpeta. *4* programa, prospecto.

**folderol** (fa·lderol) *s.* FALDEROL.

**folding** (fou·lding) *s.* plegado, plegadura. *2 adj.* plegadizo, plegable, que se cierra: ~ *bed*, cama plegable; ~ *chair*, silla plegable o de tijera; ~ *door*, puerta de dos hojas; ~ *screen*, biombo; ~ *seat*, asiento levadizo.

**foliaceous** (fouliei·shøs) *adj.* foliáceo.

**foliage** (fou·liidў) *s.* follaje.

**foliate** (fou·lieit) *s.* provisto de hojas, frondoso.

**foliate (to)** *tr.* foliar. *2* batir, reducir a hojas. *3* azogar [un espejo]. *4* ARQ. adornar con follaje. *5 intr.* BOT. echar hojas.

**foliation** (-ei·shøn) *s.* foliación. *2* ARQ. follaje.

**folio** (fou·liou) *s.* folio. *2* IMPR. pliego. *3* infolio. *4* cartera [para papeles]. *5 adj.* en folio.

**folio (to)** *tr.* foliar.

**foliole** (-l) *s.* BOT. foliolo.

**folk** (fouk) *s.* gente, pueblo, nación, tribu. *2 pl.* gente, personas. *3* gente, familia, parientes. *4 adj.* del pueblo, popular: ~ *dance*, baile popular; ~ *music*, música popular.

**folklore** (fou·klo<sup>r</sup>) *s.* folklore.

**folkloric** (-ik) *s.* folklórico.

**folklorist** (-ist) *s.* folklorista.

**follicle** (fa·likøl) *s.* BOT., ANAT. folículo.

**follicular** (foli·kiula<sup>r</sup>) *adj.* folicular.

**follow (to)** (fa·lou) *tr.* seguir [en todas sus acepciones, menos en la de continuar]. *2* perseguir, tratar de obtener. *3 to* ~ *out*, llevar hasta el fin, llevar a cabo. *4 to* ~ *suit*, servir [en el juego de naipes]; fig. seguir el ejemplo. *5 to* ~ *up*, perseguir infatigablemente; continuar, hacer algo que completa. *6 intr.* seguir: *as follows*, como sigue. *7 seguirse: it follows*, síguese. *8 to* ~ *on*, continuar, proseguir.

**follower** (-øʳ) *s.* seguidor. *2* criado. *3* imitador, discípulo. *4* partidario, secuaz. *5 pl.* séquito, comitiva.

**following** (-ing) *adj.* siguiente. *2* resultante; consiguiente. *3 s.* séquito, acompañamiento. *4* partidarios, secuaces. *5* profesión, carrera.

**folly** (fa·li) *s.* tontería, necedad. *2* locura, insensatez, disparate, desatino. *3* falta de juicio.

**foment (to)** (fome·nt) *tr.* fomentar.

**fomentation** (ei·shøn) *s.* fomentación, fomento.

**fond** (fand) *adj.* aficionado [a]; amigo, amante [de], encariñado [con]: *to be* ~ *of*, querer a [una pers.] tener afición a [una cosa]. *2* afectuoso, tierno. *3* querido, acariciado.

**fondle (to)** (fa·ndøl) *tr.* tratar con amor; agasajar, mimar, acariciar.

**fondling** (-ling) *s.* niño mimado. *2* caricia, mimo. *3 adj.* acariciador.

**fondness** (-nis) *s.* afición. *2* cariño, ternura.

**font** (fant) *s.* pila bautismal o de agua bendita. *2* fuente, manantial. *3* IMPR. fundición.

**fontanel** (fantane·l) *s.* ANAT. fontanela.

**food** (fud) *s.* alimento, nutrimento. *2* comida, sustento. *3* vitualla. *4* fig. materia, pábulo.

**foodstuff** (fu·dstøf) *s.* comestible, producto alimenticio.

**fool** (ful) *s.* necio, tonto, simple, bobo: *to play the* ~, hacer el tonto. *2* loco, insensato. *3* bufón. *4* hazmerreír; primo, víctima [de un engaño]: *fool's errand*, empresa tonta o inútil; *to make a* ~ *of*, poner en ridículo.

**fool (to)** *tr.* chasquear, engañar; estafar. *2* embromar. *3 to* ~ *away*, gastar tontamente. *4 intr.* bromear, tontear, pasar el tiempo en tonterías.

**foolery** (fu·løri) *s.* tontería, locura, absurdidad.

**foolhardy** (-jaʳdi) *adj.* loco, temerario.

**foolish** (-ish) *adj.* tonto, simple, necio, bobo. *2* disparatado. *3* imprudente, desatinado. *4* absurdo, ridículo.

**foolishness** (-nis) *s.* tontería, simpleza, necedad. *2* imprudencia. *3* absurdidad.

**foolscap** (-skæp) *s.* gorro de bufón. *2* papel de escribir [33 × 43 cm].

**fooltrap** (-træp) *s.* engañabobos.

**foot** (fut), *pl.* **feet** (fit) *s.* pie [de pers.]: *to carry someone off is feet*, arrebatar, entusiasmar a uno; *to keep one's feet*, sostenerse, no caer; *to put one's* ~ *down*, mostrarse firme, proceder con energía; *to set on* ~, poner en marcha, en actividad; iniciar, promover; *on* ~, a pie, en marcha, en actividad; *on one's feet*, de pie, en pie; en buena salud; ganándose la vida; *under* ~, bajo los pies; sujeto. *2* pata, pie [de animal, mueble, objeto]. *3* peal, pie [de media]. *4* pie, parte cercana a la base. *5* pie [medida lineal]: ~ *by* ~, palmo a palmo. *6* MÉTR. pie. *7* pierna [de compás]. *8* MAR. pujamen.

*9 adj.* de pie, del pie o los pies, para el pie o los pies; etc.: ~ *bath*, pediluvio; ~ *brake*, freno de pedal; ~ *race*, carrera a pie; ~ *warmer*, calientapiés.

**foot (to)** *intr.* andar, caminar. *2* bailar, saltar. *3* sumar. *4 tr.* pisar, hollar, recorrer [andando]: *to* ~ *it*, andar a pie; bailar. *5* poner pie o pies a. *6* sumar [una columna]. *7* pagar [la cuenta].

**footage** (fu·tidў) *s.* longitud o distancia en pies.

**football** (-bol) *s.* DEP. fútbol, balompié: ~ *player*, futbolista.

**footboard** (-boʳd) *s.* estribo [de coche]. *2* tabla en que se apoyan los pies. *3* pie [de cama].

**footboy** (-boi) *s.* criadito de librea.

**footbridge** (-bridў) *s.* puente para peatones.

**footcloth** (-cloz) *s.* alfombrilla. *2* gualdrapa.

**footed** (fu·tid) *adj.* sumado. *2* de pies o patas: *four-footed*, de cuatro patas.

**footfall** (-fol) *s.* paso, pisada; ruido de un paso.

**footgear** (-giøʳ) *s.* calzado; medias, calcetines.

**foothill** (-jil) *s.* colina al pie de una montña.

**foothold** (-jould) *s.* sitio donde asentar o afirmar el pie. *2* pie firme. *3* posición establecida.

**footing** (-ing) *s.* pie, base, fundamento. *2* sitio donde asentar el pie; posición segura, estable. *3* paso, marcha; baile. *4* entrada [en una sociedad, etc.]. *5* suma, total [de una columna]. *6* pie, relaciones, términos: *on an equal* ~, en pie de igualdad; *on a friendly* ~, en relaciones amistosas.

**footlights** (-laits) *s. pl.* TEAT. candilejas. *2* fig. tablas, profesión teatral.

**footman** (-mæn) *s.* lacayo.

**footmark** (-maʳk) *s.* huella, pisada.

**footpace** (-peis) *s.* paso normal o regular. *2* descansillo [de escalera]. *3* tarima, estrado.

**footpad** (-pæd) *s.* salteador de caminos.

**footpath** (-pæz) *s.* senda, camino para peatones.

**footprint** (-print) *s.* FOOTMARK.

**foots** (-s) *s. pl.* sedimento, heces.

**footscraper** (-screipøʳ) *s.* limpiabarros.

**footsore** (-soʳ) *adj.* despeado.

**footstalk** (stok) *s.* BOT. pedúnculo, pezón.

**footstep** (-step) *s.* paso, pisada.

**footstool** (-stul) *s.* escabel, banqueta.

**footwalk** (-uoc), **footway** (-uei) *s.* senda, camino para peatones. *2* (Ingl.) acera.

**footwear** (-ueøʳ) *s.* FOOTGEAR.

**foozle** (fu·søl) *s.* chapucería, chambonada.

**fozzle (to)** *tr.-intr.* chafallar; jugar mal.

**fop** (fap) *s.* petimetre, pisaverde, lechuguino, currutaco; hombre vano, presumido.

**foppish** (-ish) *adj.* vanidoso, presumido, currutaco, leghuchino, afectado en el vestir.

**for** (foʳ) *prep.* por [indicando: a causa de; en favor de; con respecto a; en nombre de; a favor de, de parte de, etc.]. *2* para [indicando: destino, uso, aplicación; tiempo; fin, provecho, beneficio]: *what for?* para qué? *3* durante, por espacio de. *4* como: ~ *a reward*, como premio. *5* otros empleos: *a cheque* ~ *10 £*, un cheque de diez libras; *tall* ~ *his age*, alto para la edad que tiene; *time* ~ *dinner*, hora de comer; *it is for you to decide*, usted ha de decidir; ~ *all I know*, que yo sepa; ~ *the future*, en lo venidero. *6* ~ *all that*, no obstante, a pesar de todo. *7* ~ *all the world*, por nada del mundo; en todo, exactamente. *8* ~ *good*, de fijo; para no volver. *9* ~ *short*, para abreviar. *10 conj.* porque, puesto que, pues.

**forage** (fa·ridў) *s.* forraje, pasto.

**forage (to)** *tr.* forrajear. *2* dar forraje a. *3* saquear, pillar.

**foramen** (forei·møn) *s.* foramen.

**forasmuch** (forašmø·ch) *conj.* ~ *as*, puesto que, ya que, visto que, por cuanto.

**foray** (fo·rei) *s.* correría, incursión. *2* saqueo.

**foray (to)** *tr.* saquear, pillar. *2 intr.* hacer correrías.

**forbade** (foʳbeid) *pret.* de TO FORBID.

**forbear** (fo·ʳbeøʳ) *s.* antepasado.

**forbear (to)** (foʳbe·øʳ) *tr.* dejar de, abstenerse de.

*2* sufrir con paciencia. *3 intr.* tener paciencia. ¶ Pret.: *forbore;* p. p.: *forborne.*
**forbearance** (foˈbe·ørans) *s.* abstención, contención. *2* paciencia, indulgencia, lenidad.
**forbearing** (-ing) *adj.* paciente, indulgente.
**forbid (to)** (foˈbi·d) *tr.* prohibir, vedar, negar. *2* impedir. ¶ Pret.: *forbad* o *-bade;* p. p.: *forbidden;* ger.: *forbidding.*
**forbidden** (foˈbi·døn) *adj.* prohibido, vedado.
**forbidding** (-ing) *adj.* prohibitivo. *2* repulsivo. *3* inabordable. *4* formidable, adusto.
**forbore** (foˈbo·ʳ) *pret.* de TO FORBEAR.
**forborne** (foˈbo·ʳn) *p. p.* de TO FORBEAR.
**force** (foʳs) *s.* fuerza [en todas sus acepciones]: *by* ~, a la fuerza, por fuerza; *by* ~ *of,* a fuerza de; ~ *pump,* FÍS. bomba impelente. *2* fig. brío, fuego, animación. *3* peso, importancia. *4* poder, virtud, eficacia. *5* validez, vigencia. *6 in* ~, en vigor, envigencia; en gran número, en masa. *7* MIL. fuerza, cuerpo: *armed forces,* fuerzas armadas.
**force (to)** *tr.* forzar. *2* obligar, constreñir: *to* ~ *away,* obligar a alejarse; *to* ~ *back,* obligar a retroceder. *3* esforzar [la voz]. *4* imponer, obligar a aceptar o soportar. *5* obtener, arrancar [por fuerza o violencia]. *6* meter a la fuerza, clavar, encajar. *7* COC. rellenar. *8* AGR. hacer crecer o madurar de prisa. *9* MEC. impulsar. *10 to* ~ *one's way,* abrirse paso. *11 to* ~ *the issue,* hacer que algo se discuta o resuelva pronto.
**forced** (-t) *adj.* forzado. *2* forzoso.
**forceful** (-ful) *adj.* fuerte, poderoso, eficaz; violento.
**forcemeat** (-mɪt) *s.* COC. relleno, picadillo.
**forceps** (-eps) *s.* CIR. fórceps.
**forcible** (-ibøl) *adj.* fuerte, potente, enérgico, eficaz. *2* poderoso, concluyente, de mucho peso. *3* violento.
**forcibly** (-ibli) *adv.* fuertemente, poderosamente. *2* violentamente, a la fuerza.
**forcing** (-ing) *s.* forzamiento, compulsión. *2* acción de hacer crecer, madurar, etc., de prisa.
**ford** (foʳd) *s.* vado. *2* poét. río, riachuelo.
**ford (to)** *tr.* vadear, esguazar.
**fore** (fo·øʳ) *adj.* anterior, delantero. *2* MAR. de proa. *3 adv.* MAR. en la proa o hacia ella. *4 s.* frente, parte delantera: *to the* ~, presente, a la vista. *5* MAR. proa.
**fore-and-aft** *adj.* MAR. de cuchillo [vela].
**forearm** (fo·øraʳm) *s.* antebrazo.
**forebode (to)** (foøˈbou·d) *tr.-intr.* pronosticar, presagiar. *2 tr.* prever, presentir.
**foreboding** (-ing) *s.* presagio, augurio. *2* presentimiento.
**forecast** (fo·øʳkæst) *s.* pronóstico, previsión, proyecto, plan.
**forecast (to)** (foøʳkæ·st) *tr.* pronosticar, prever, calcular. *2* anunciar [ser signo de]. ¶ Pret. y p. p.: *forecast* o *-ted.*
**forecastle** (fo·øʳkæsøl) *s.* MAR. castillo [de proa].
**foreclose (to)** (foøʳclou·š) *tr.* excluir. *2* privar, impedir. *3* cerrar de antemano.
**foredoom (to)** (-du·m) *tr.* destinar, predestinar, condenar de antemano.
**forefather** (fo·øʳfadøʳ) *s.* abuelo, antepasado.
**forefinger** (-fingøʳ) *s.* dedo índice.
**forefoot** (-fut) *s.* pata delantera, mano.
**forefront** (-frønt) *s.* delantera, primera fila, vanguardia.
**forego (to)** (-gou·) *tr.* preceder, ir delante. *2 tr.-intr.* TO FORGO. ¶ Pret.: *forewent;* p. p.: *foregone.*
**foregoing** (-ing) *adj.* anterior, precedente.

**foregone** (-gon) *p. p.* de TO FOREGO. *2 adj.* ~ *conclusion,* prejuicio; resultado seguro, previsible.
**foreground** (-graund) *s.* PERSP. primer plano o término.
**forehand** (-jænd) *s.* ventja. *2* cuartos delanteros [del caballo]. *3 adj.* delantero. *4* adelantado, anticipado. *5* dado con la mano vuelta hacia adelante.
**forehead** (-jed) *s.* ANAT. frente.
**foreign** (fa·rin) *adj.* extranjero, exterior: ~ *trade,* comercio exterior; *Foreign Office* (Ingl.), ministerio de asuntos exteriores; *Foreign Service* (E.U.), servicio diplomático y consular. *2* forastero, extraño. *3* extraño, ajeno.
**foreigner** (-øʳ) *s.* extranjero [pers.].
**forejudge (to)** (foøʳdŷø·dŷ) *tr.* prejuzgar.
**foreknow (to)** (-nou·) *tr.* preconocer, prever.
**foreknowledge** (-lidŷ) *s.* presciencia.
**foreland** (fo·øʳlænd) *s.* GEOGR. cabo, promontorio. *2* tierra de enfrente.
**foreleg** (-leg) *s.* brazo, pata delantera.
**forelock** (-lɑk) *s.* mechón de pelo que cae sobre la frente; copete [del caballo]. *2* MEC. chaveta.
**foreman** (-mæn) *s.* capataz, encargado, mayoral. *2* IMPR. regente. *3* DER. presidente del jurado.
**foremast** (-mast) *s.* MAR. trinquete [palo].
**foremost** (-moust) *adj.* delantero. *2* primero, principal.
**forename** (-neim) *s.* nombre de pila.
**forenoon** (-nun) *s.* la mañana.
**forensic** (fore·nsik) *adj.* forense: ~ *medicine,* medicina legal.
**foreordain (to)** (foøroʳdei·n) *tr.* preordinar.
**forereach (to)** (fo·ørɪch) *tr.* alcanzar, dejar atrás.
**forreun (to)** (fo·ʳrø·n) *tr.* preceder. *2* anunciar, presagiar.
**forerunner** (-øʳ) *s.* predecesor. *2* precursor. *3* anuncio, presagio. *4* mensajero, heraldo.
**foresail** (fo·øʳseil) *s.* trinquete [vela].
**foresee (to)** (foøʳsɪ·) *tr.* prever, antever.
**foreseer** (-øʳ) *s.* previsor.
**foreshadow (to)** (foøʳshæ·dou) *tr.* prefigurar, simbolizar.
**foreshorten (to)** (foøʳsho·ʳtøn) *tr.* B. ART. escorzar.
**foreshortening** (-ning) *s.* B. ART. escorzo.
**foresight** (fo·øʳsait) *s.* previsión, presciencia, perspicacia. *2* providencia, prudencia.
**foreskin** (-kin) *s.* ANAT. prepucio.
**forest** (fo·rist) *s.* bosque, selva, monte: ~ *ranger* (E.U.), guarda forestal.
**forest (to)** *tr.* arbolar.
**forestal** (-al) *adj.* forestal.
**forestall (to)** (foøʳsto·l) *tr.* anticiparse a; prevenir; impedir. *2* anticipar.
**forester** (fo·risteʳ) *s.* guardabosque. *2* silvicultor. *3* habitante del bosque [pers. o animal].
**forestry** (-ri) *s.* silvicultura.
**foretaste** (foøʳtei·st) *s.* anticipo, gusto, goce o conocimiento anticipado.
**foretaste (to)** *tr.* gustar o conocer de antemano.
**foretell (to)** (-te·l) *tr.* predecir, pronosticar.
**foreteller** (-øʳ) *s.* vaticinador, profeta.
**forethought** (-zot) *s.* providencia, previsión. *2* premeditación.
**foretoken** (-tou·køn) *s.* presagio; señal anunciadora.
**foretoken (to)** *tr.* anunciar, prefigurar.
**foretop** (fo·øʳtap) *s.* MAR. cofa del trinquete.
**forever** (fore·vøʳ) *adv.* siempre, para siempre, por siempre.

**forewarn (to)** (foøᵗuo·ᵗn) *tr.* prevenir, advertir, avisar.

**forewoman** (fo·øᵗwumæn) *s.* encargada, primera oficiala.

**foreword** (-uøᵗd) *s.* prefacio, prólogo.

**forfeit** (foᵗfit) *s.* pena, multa, comiso. *2* pérdida legal de una cosa por incumplimiento de un contrato, etc. *3* prenda [en los juegos]: *game of forfeits*, juego de prendas.

**forfeit (to)** *tr.* perder [algo] como pena o castigo.

**forfeiture** (fo·ᵗfichuᵗ) *s.* pérdida de derechos, confiscación, multa.

**forgather** (foᵗgæ·døᵗ) *intr.* reunirse.

**forge** (oᵗdÿ) *s.* forja, fragua; herrería.

**forge (to)** *tr.* forjar, fraguar [metal]. *2* forjar, inventar [mentiras, etc.]. *3* falsificar [documentos, una firma]. *4 intr. to ~ ahead*, avanzar despacio y con esfuerzo.

**forger** (-øᵗ) *s.* forjador. *2* falsificador, falsario.

**forgery** (-ri) *s.* falsificación.

**forget (to)** (foᵗge·t) *tr.-intr.* olvidar, olvidarse de, olvidársele a uno; descuidar: *~ it*, déjelo, no se preocupe. *2 ref. to ~ oneself*, olvidarse de sí mismo; abstraerse; perder la dignidad, el dominio de sí mismo; desmedirse, propasarse. ¶ Pret.: *forgot;* p. p.: *forgotten.*

**forgetful** (-ful) *adj.* olvidado [de algo]. *2* olvidadizo.

**forgetfulness** (-nis) *s.* olvido, descuido.

**forget-me-not** *s.* BOT. nomeolvides, miosotis.

**forgive (to)** (foᵗgi·v) *tr.* perdonar; dispensar. *2* condonar, remitir, indultar.

**forgiveness** (-nis) *s.* perdón, remisión. *2* misericordia, clemencia.

**forgo (to)** (foᵗgou·) *tr.* abandonar; renunciar a, privarse de. ¶ Pret.: *forwent;* p.p.: *forgone.*

**forgot** (foᵗga·t) *pret.* de TO FORGET.

**forgotten** (foᵗga·tøn) *p. p.* de TO FORGET.

**fork** (foᵗk) *s.* tenedor [utensilio]. *2* horca, horcón, horqueta, horquilla. *3* bifurcación. *4* confluencia [de ríos]. *5* horcadura.

**fork (to)** *tr.* ahorquillar. *2 fam. to ~ out* o *over*, entregar, pagar. *3 intr.* ahorquillarse, bifurcarse.

**forked** (fo·ᵗkt) *adj.* ahorquillado, bifurcado.

**forlorn** (foᵗlo·ᵗn) *adj.* abandonado, desamparado. *2* triste. *3* desesperado. *4 ~ hope*, empresa desesperada.

**form** (foᵗm) *s.* forma [en sus principales acepciones]: *in due ~*, en debida forma; *to be in ~*, estar en forma. *2* proceder: *bad ~*, mala educación. *3* fórmula, formalidad, etiqueta: *for form's sake*, por pura fórmula. *4* modelo, patrón, horma, molde. *5* formulario, impreso [para llenar]. *6* banco [asiento largo]; sección de una clase [en una escuela].

**form (to)** *tr.* formar. *2 intr.* formarse. *3* MIL. formar.

**formal** (-al) *adj.* formal [rel. a la forma]. *2* solemne; de cumplido, de etiqueta: *~ attire*, vestido de etiqueta; *~ call*, visita de cumplido. *3* rígido, metódico. *4* ceremonioso, etiquetero. *5* formulario.

**formalism** (-išm) *s.* formalismo.

**formalist** (-ist) *s.* formalista.

**formality** (-iti) *s.* formalidad, requisito. *2* ceremonia, etiqueta, cumplido. *3* solemnidad; formalismo.

**formalize (to)** (-aiš) *tr.* formalizar. *2 intr.* mostrarse ceremonioso.

**format** (fo·ᵗmat) *s.* formato, forma [de un libro].

**formation** (foᵗmei·shøn) *s.* formación. *2* disposición, estructura.

**former** (fo·ᵗmøᵗ) *adj.* anterior, pasado, precedente. *2* antiguo, que fue, ex: *his ~ teacher*, su antiguo maestro. *3 pron. the ~*, aquél, el primero [de dos]. *4 s.* creador, formador. *5* horma, molde.

**formerly** (-li) *adv.* anteriormente, antes. *2* antiguamente, en otros tiempos.

**formic** (fo·ᵗmik) *adj.* QUÍM. fórmico.

**formication** (foᵗmikei·shøn) *s.* MED. formicación.

**formidable** (fo·ᵗmidabøl) *adj.* formidable, terrible.

**formless** (fo·ᵗmlis) *adj.* informe caótico.

**formula** (fo·ᵗmiula) *s.* fórmula.

**formulary** (-eri) *adj.s.* formulario.

**formulate (to)** (-eit) *tr.* formular.

**formulism** (-išm) *s.* formulismo.

**fornicate (to)** (fo·ᵗnikeit) *intr.* fornicar.

**fornicate(d** (fo·ᵗnikeit(id) *adj.* ARQ. abovedado.

**fornication** (foᵗnikei·shøn) *s.* fornicación.

**forsake (to)** (foᵗsei·k) *tr.* abandonar, desamparar. *2* apostatar, renegar de. *3* desechar, renunciar, dejar. ¶ Pret.: *forsook;* p. p.: *forsaken.*

**forsaken** (-øn) *p. p.* de TO FORSAKE.

**forsook** (foᵗsu·k) *pret.* de TO FORSAKE.

**forsooth** (foᵗsu·z) *adv.* ciertamente, en verdad.

**forswear (to)** (foᵗsue·øᵗ) *tr.* abjurar, renunciar. *2 to ~ oneself*, perjurarse. ¶ Pret.: *forswore;* p. p.: *forsworn.*

**fort** (foᵗt) *s.* fuerte, fortaleza.

**forte** (fo·ᵗtei) *adj.-s.* MÚS. forte. *2. s.* fuerte [aquello en ue sobresale uno].

**forth** (foᵗz) *adv.* delante, adelante. *2* en adelante: *from that day ~*, de aquel día en adelante. *3* fuera, afuera, a la vista: *to go ~*, salir. *4 and so ~*, y así sucesivamente, etcétera.

**forthcoming** (-kø·ming) *adj.* venidero, próximo, que viene. *2* disponible.

**forthwith** (-uid) *adv.* inmediatamente.

**fortieth** (fo·ᵗtiiz) *adj.-s.* cuadragésimo. *2* cuarentavo. *3 adj.* cuarenta [ordinal].

**fortification** (foᵗtifikei·shøn). *s.* fortificación, fortalecimiento. *2* MIL. fortificación.

**fortify (to)** (-fai) *tr.* fortificar. *2* fortalecer. *3* reforzar. *4* confirmar, corroborar. *5 intr.* MIL. hacer fortificaciones. ¶ Pret. y p. p.: *fortified.*

**fortitude** (-tiud) *s.* fortaleza [de ánimo], firmeza, valor.

**fortnight** (fo·ᵗtnait) *s.* quincena, dos semanas.

**fortress** (fo·ᵗtris) *s.* fortaleza, fuerte, ciudadela.

**fortuitous** (foᵗtiu·itøs) *adj.* fortuito, casual.

**fortuity** (foᵗtiu·iti) *s.* calidad de fortuito. *2* caso fortuito.

**fortunate** (fo·ᵗchunit) *adj.* afortunado, feliz.

**fortune** (fo·ᵗchun) *s.* fortuna, suerte, destino: *to tell one's ~*, decirle a uno la buenaventura. *2* fortuna, caudal: *~ hunter*, cazador de dotes.

**fortuneteller** (-teløᵗ) *s.* adivino.

**forty** (fo·ᵗti) *adj.-s.* cuarenta.

**forum** (fo·røm) *s.* foro [plaza pública, tribunal].

**forward** (foᵗuøᵗd) *adj.* delantero. *2* precoz, adelantado. *3* que se hace hacia adelante. *4* POL. avanzado. *5* dispuesto, ansioso. *6* atrevido, descarado. *7* COM. futuro. *8 adv.* adelante; en adelante; más allá: *from this time ~*, de aquí en adelante. *9* FÚTBOL. *centre ~*, delantero centro.

**forward (to)** *tr.* enviar, remitir, expedir; reexpedir; hacer seguir. *2* apresurar, activar. *3* adelantar, promover, patrocinar.

**forwarder** (-døᵗ) *s.* COM. agente expedidor.

**forwardness** (-nis) *s.* adelantamiento, progreso. *2*

prontitud, ansia. *3* precocidad. *4* audacia. *5* descaro, impertinencia.

**forwards** (-s) *adv.* adelante, hacia adelante.

**fossa** (fa·ssa) *s.* ANAT. fosa.

**fosse** (fos) *s.* foso.

**fossil** (fa·sil) *adj.-s.* fósil. *2 pers.* anticuada.

**fossilization** (-išei·shøn) *s.* fosilización.

**fossilize (to)** (-aiš) *tr.* convertir en fósil, petrificar. *2 intr.* fosilizarse.

**fossorial** (foso·rial) *adj.* ZOOL. cavador.

**foster** (fo·stø[r]) *adj.* de leche; adoptivo, de adopción; ~ *child*, hijo de leche, hijo adoptivo; ~ *home*, hogar de adopción.

**foster (to)** *tr.* criar, nutrir. *2* alentar, sostener, fomentar.

**fosterling** (-ling) *s.* hijo de leche, hijo adoptivo.

**fought** (fot) *pret.* y *p. p.* de TO FIGHT.

**foul** (faul) *adj.* sucio, asqueroso, inmundo, repugnante. *2* fétido, mal oliente. *3* viciado [aire]. *4* malo [tiempo]. *5* contrario [viento]. *6* malo, injusto, engañoso, obsceno. *7* enredado, atascado, obstruido. *8* sucio, no conforme a las reglas del juego: ~ *play*, juego sucio; fig. dolo, traición. *9* ~ *copy*, borrador. *10 s.* acción de ensuciar; de chocar o enredarse: *to fall* ~ o *run* ~ *of*, MAR. abordar [un buque a otro]; enredarse en. *11* DEP. falta, juego sucio.

**foul (to)** *tr.* ensuciar, emporcar, manchar. *2* atascar, obstruir. *3* MAR. abordar, chocar con, enredarse en. *4* DEP. jugar sucio contra. *5 intr.* ensuciarse. *6* MAR. enredarse; abordarse. *7* DEP. infringir las reglas.

**foulard** (fula·[r]d) *s.* fular.

**foul-mouthed** *adj.* malhablado.

**found** (faund) *pret.* y *p. p.* de TO FIND.

**found (to)** *tr.* fundar. *2* METAL., VID. fundir.

**foundation** (-ei·shøn) *s.* fundación [acción; institución]. *2* fundación, base, cimiento: ~ *stone*, primera piedra. *3* MEC. asiento, pie. *4* ING. firme. *5* COST. forro, refuerzo.

**founder** (fau·ndø[r]) *s.* fundador. *2* fundidor.

**founder (to)** *tr.* MAR. hundir, echar a pique. *2 intr.* hundirse, desplomarse. *3* MAR. irse a pique. *4* tropezar, caer; desparearse [el caballo]. *5* fracasar.

**foundling** (-ling) *s.* expósito, inclusero.

**foundress** (-res) *s.* fundadora.

**foundry** (-ri) *s.* fundición [de metales]. *2* fundición, fundería.

**fount** (faunt) *s.* fuente, manantial.

**fountain** (fa·untin) *s.* fuente, manantial. *2* origen, principio. *3* ~ *pen*, estilográfica.

**four** (fo·ø[r]) *adj.-s.* cuatro; ~ *o'clock*, las cuatro; *on all fours*, a gatas.

**four-cycle** *adj.* MEC. de cuatro tiempos.

**four-flush (to)** *intr.* pop. fanfarronear, fachendear.

**fourfold** (-fould) *adj.* cuádruple, cuádruplo.

**four-handed** *adj.* cuadrúmano. *2* para cuatro jugadores. *3* MÚS. a cuatro manos.

**four-in-hand** *s.* carruaje tirado por cuatro caballos.

**fouur-motor** *adj.* AVIA. cuadrimotor.

**four-o'clock** *s.* BOT. arrebolera, dondiego de noche.

**fourposter** (-poustø[r]) *s.* cama imperial.

**fourscore** (-sko[r]) *adj.* ochenta.

**foursome** (-søm) *s.* DEP. partida de dos contra dos. *2* DEP. conjunto de cuatro jugadores.

**foursquare** (-skue[r]) *adj.* cuadrado. *2* franco, sincero. *3* firme, constante.

**fourteen** (fo[r]ti·n) *adj.-s.* catorce.

**fourteenth** (-z) *adj.* catorceno, decimocuarto, catorce. *2 adj.-s.* catorzavo.

**fourth** (-fo[r]z) *adj.-s.* cuarto. *2* cuatro [en las fechas]. *3* MÚS. cuarta.

**fourthly** (-li) *adv.* en cuarto lugar.

**fowl** (faul) *s.* gallo, gallina, pollo. *2* ave [en general]. *3* carne de ave.

**fowl (to)** *intr.* cazar aves.

**fowler** (fau·lø[r]) *s.* cazador [de aves].

**fowling** (-ing) *s.* caza de aves: ~ *piece*, escopeta.

**fox** (faks) *s.* ZOOL. zorro, zorra, raposo, raposa: ~ *terrier*, foxterrier [perro]; ~ *trot*, trote corto; foxtrot [baile]. *2* piel de zorro. *3* zorro, taimado.

**fox (to)** *intr.* (E.U.) cazar zorras. *2* fingir, raposear. *4* ponerse rojizo, mancharse [el papel]. *5 tr.* engañar con astucia.

**foxglove** (-glouv) *s.* BOT. digital, dedalera.

**foxhole** (-joul) *s.* zorrera. *2* MIL. trinchera individual.

**foxhound** (-jaund) *s.* perro raposero.

**foxiness** (-inis) *s.* astucia, zorrería.

**foxish** (-ish) *adj.* zorruno. *2* astuto.

**foxtail** (-teil) *s.* BOT. rabo de zorra.

**foxy** (-i) *adj.* zorruno. *2* del color del zorro. *3* taimado. *4* descolorido, manchado.

**foyer** (fuaye·) *s.* salón de entrada [de un hotel, etc.]. *2* TEAT. salón de descanso.

**fracas** (frei·kas) *s.* alboroto, riña, zacapela.

**fraction** (fræ·kshøn) *s.* fragmento, porción. *2* fam. poquito. *3* LITURG. fracción [del pan]. *4* MAT. fracción, quebrado. *5* QUÍM. fracción.

**fraction (to)** *tr.* fraccionar.

**fractional** (-al) *adj.* fraccionario. *2* QUÍM. fraccionado.

**fractionate** (-neit) *tr.* fraccionar. *2* QUÍM. separar por destilación fraccionada.

**fractious** (fræ·kshøs) *adj.* quisquilloso, enojado. *2* rebelón.

**fracture** (fræ·kchø[r]) *s.* fractura, rompimiento. *2* CIR., GEOL. fractura.

**fracture (to)** *tr.* fracturar. *2 intr.* fracturarse.

**fragile** (fræ·dŷil) *adj.* frágil. *2* quebradizo, delicado.

**fragility** (fradŷi·liti) *s.* fragilidad.

**fragment** (fræ·gmønt) *s.* fragmento, trozo.

**fragment (to)** *intr.* fragmentarse.

**fragrance, cy** (frei·grans, -i) *s.* fragancia.

**fragrant** (-grant) *adj.* fragante, oloroso.

**frail** (freil) *adj.* frágil. *2* deleznable, endeble. *3* débil [física o moralmente].

**frailty** (-ti) *s.* fragilidad. *2* debilidad, flaqueza.

**fraise** (freš) *s.* FORT. frisa.

**frame** (freim) *s.* armazón, armadura, esqueleto. *2* cuerpo [del hombre o del animal]. *3* bastidor, marco, cerco, cuadro: ~ *saw*, sierra del bastidor. *4* entramado. *5* bastidor [para bordar]. *6* montura [de unas gafas]. *7* MEC. bancada. *8* MAR. cuaderna. *9* MAR. costillaje. *10* HORT. abrigo encristalado. *11* IMPR. chibalete. *12* MEC., TEJ., HIL. nombre de varias máquinas. *13* constitución, estructura. *14* sistema [de gobierno]. *15* ~ *of mind*, humor, estado de ánimo.

**frame (to)** *tr.* fabricar, formar, construir. *2* encuadrar, enmarcar. *3* armar, montar. *4* ajustar, adaptar. *5* idear, trazar, forjar, tramar. *6* expresar, formular, redactar. *7 to* ~ *up*, amañar, preparar fraudulentamente [esp. las pruebas para incriminar a un inocente].

**frame-up** *s.* cosa preparada fraudulentamente, amaño. *2* arreglo, trama [para incriminar a un inocente].

**framework** (-uøᵏk) *s.* armazón, esqueleto. *2* CARP. entramado. *3* sistema [de gobierno, etc.].
**franc** (frænk) *s.* franco [moneda].
**France** (fra·ns) *n. pr.* GEOGR. Francia.
**Frances** (fræ·nsis) *n. pr. f.* Francisca.
**franchise** (fræ·nchaiš) *s.* franqueza, exención, privilegio. *2* asilo, refugio. *3* derecho político.
**Francis** (fræ·nsis) *n. pr. m.* Francisco.
**Franciscan** (fransi·skan) *adj.-s.* franciscano.
**francolin** (fræ·nkolin) *s.* ORN. francolín.
**Francophile** (fræ·nkofail) *adj.-s.* francófilo.
**Frank** (frænk) *s.* franco [del pueblo franco]. *2 n. pr. dim.* de FRANCIS.
**frank** *adj.* franco [sincero, claro, no disimulado]. *2 s.* franquicia postal.
**frank (to)** *tr.* franquear, exceptuar de pago.
**frankfurter** (-føᵗtøʳ) *s.* salchicha de Francfort.
**frankincense** (-insens) *s.* incienso, olíbano.
**frankness** (-nis) *adj.* franqueza, sinceridad.
**frantic** (fræ·ntik) *adj.* frenético, furioso, desesperado.
**frappé** (fræpei·) *s.* helado de zumo de frutas.
**fraternal** (fratø·ʳnal) *adj.* fraternal, fraterno.
**fraternity** (-iti) *s.* fraternidad. *2* gremio, congregación, hermandad. *3* (E.U.) club de estudiantes.
**fraternize (to)** (fræ·tøʳnaiš) *intr.* fraternizar.
**fratricidal** (frætrisai·dal) *adj.* fratricida.
**fratricide** (fræ·trisaid) *s.* fratricidio. *2* fratricida.
**fraud** (frod) *s.* fraude, dolo, engaño. *2* farsante, impostor, timador.
**fraudulence, cy** (fro·diuløns, -si) *s.* fraudulencia, mala fe.
**fraudulent** (-ont) *adj.* fraudulento, engañoso.
**fraught** (frot) *adj.* lleno, cargado, preñado, grávido.
**fraxinella** (fræksine·la) *s.* BOT. fresnillo.
**fray** (frei) *s.* riña, pelea. *2* raedura, deshilachado.
**fray (to)** *tr.* rozar, raer, desgastar. *2 intr.* deshilacharse.
**frayed** (-d) *adj.* raído, deshilachado.
**freak** (frik) *s.* capricho, antojo, rareza. *2* fenómeno, monstruosidad: ~ *of nature,* aborto de la naturaleza.
**freakish** (-ish) *adj.* caprichoso, antojadizo. *2* fantástico, raro, extravagante.
**freckle** (fre·køl) *s.* peca. *2* mota, pinta.
**freckle (to)** *tr.* motear. *2 intr.* llenarse de pecas.
**freckled** (fre·køld) *adj.* pecoso. *2* moteado.
**Fred** (fred), **Freddy** (-i) *n. pr. dim.* Federiquito.
**Frederica** (fre·dørika) *n. pr. f.* Federica.
**Frederick** (fre·dørik) *n. pr. m.* Federico.
**free** (frī) *adj.* libre: ~ *and easy,* campechano; despreocupado; ~ *hand,* carta blanca; ~ *lance,* condotiero; franco, tirador, hombre independiente; ~ *love,* amor libre; ~ *thought,* librepensamiento; ~ *trade,* librecambio; ~ *will,* libre albedrío; propia voluntad. *2* en libertad. *3* franco, exento: ~ *port,* puerto franco; ~ *on board,* COM. franco a bordo. *4* gratuito, de balde. *5* espontáneo, voluntario, discrecional. *6* permitido. *7* liberal, generoso: *to be* ~ *with,* dar abundantemente. *8* franco, comunicativo. *9* suelto, desembarazado; atrevido, desenvuelto. *10* desocupado, vacante. *11* flojo, suelto, desatado. *12 adv.* libremente. *13* gratis.
**free (to)** *tr.* libertar, librar. *2* manumitir. *3* rescatar. *4* eximir. *5* desembarazar; zafar, soltar.
**freebooter** (-butøʳ) *s.* filibustero, pirata.
**freedman** (-dmæn) *pl. s.* liberto.
**freedom** (-døm) *s.* libertad; ~ *of the press,* libertad

de imprenta; ~ *of worship,* libertad de cultos. *2* independencia. *3* exención, inmunidad, privilegio. *4* familiaridad atrevida. *5* facilidad, soltura. *6* libertad de usar de una cosa.
**freehand** (-jænd) *adj.* hecho a pulso [dibujo].
**freehanded** (-jændid) *adj.* liberal, dadivoso.
**freehearted** (-jaʳtid) *adj.* franco, abierto. *2* generoso.
**freehold** (-jould) *s.* DER. dominio absoluto.
**freely** (-li) *adv.* libremente. *2* espontáneamente. *3* profusamente, generosamente.
**freeman** (-mæn) *s.* hombre libre, ciudadano.
**Freemason** (-meisøn) *s.* francmasón.
**Freemasonry** (-meisønri) *s.* francmasonería.
**freer** (-øʳ) *s.* libertador.
**free-spoken** (-øʳ) *adj.* franco, sin reserva.
**freestone** (-stoun) *adj.-s.* BOT. abridero [fruto].
**freethinker** (-zinkøʳ) *s.* librepensador.
**freeze** (frīš) *s.* helada.
**freeze (to)** *tr.* helar, congelar. *2* aterrar, dejar frío. *3* COM. congelar [créditos, etc.]. *4 to* ~ *out,* excluir, deshacerse [de uno], tratándole con frialdad, quitándole la clientela, etc. *5 impers.* helar. *6 intr.* helarse, congelarse. *7 fig.* quedarse helado [de susto, etc.]. ¶ *Pret.: froze;* p. p.: *frozen.*
**freezer** (-øʳ) *s.* helador. *2* heladora, sorbetera; congelador.
**freezing** (-ing) *adj.* glacial. *2* frigorífico. *3* ~ *point,* punto de congelación.
**freight** (freit) *s.* COM. carga [que se transporta]; porte: ~ *train,* tren de carga o de mercancías; *by* ~ FERROC. a pequeña velocidad. *2* flete.
**freight (to)** *tr.* cargar [un buque, etc.]. *2* MAR. fletar. *3* alquilar [para el transporte]. *4* transportar [por buque, tren, etc.].
**freightage** (-idÿ) *s.* cargamento. *2* flete. *3* transporte, porte.
**freighter** (-øʳ) *s.* fletador, cargador. *2* buque de carga.
**French** (french) *adj.-s.* francés: ~ *bean,* alubia, judía; ~ *horn,* MÚS. trompa; ~ *roof,* mansarda; ~ *window,* puerta vidriera de dos hojas; *to take* ~ *leave,* despedirse a la francesa.
**Frenchify (to)** (-ifai) *tr.* afrancesar.
**Frenchman** (-mæn) *s.* francés [hombre].
**Frenchwoman** (-wumæn) *f.* francesa [mujer].
**frenetic** (frine·tik) *adj.* frenético.
**frenzied** (fre·nšid) *adj.* frenético. *2* enloquecido.
**frenzy** (fre·nši) *s.* frenesí, locura, desvarío.
**frequency** (frī·kuønsi) *s.* frecuencia.
**frequent** (frī·kuønt) *adj.* frecuente. *2* habitual, regular, persistente.
**frequent (to)** (frikue·nt) *tr.* frecuentar. *2* tratarse, relacionarse con.
**frequentation** (-ei·shøn) *s.* frecuentación. *2* trato, relación.
**fresco** (fre·skou) *s.* PINT. fresco.
**fresco (to)** *tr.* pintar al fresco.
**fresh** (fre·sh) *adj.* fresco, nuevo, reciente: ~ *from,* recién salido, llegado, etc., de. *2* fresco [flor, fruta, carne, etc.; tez color]. *3* fresco [viento]. *4* fresco [algo frío]. *5* puro [aire]. *6* tierno [pan]. *7* nuevo [otro]. *8* descansado, con nuevas fuerzas. *9* inexperto, bisoño. *10* fresco, descarado. *11* ~ *water,* agua dulce. *12 s.* avenida, riada.
**freshen (to)** (-øn) *tr.* refrescar. *2 intr.* refrescarse. *3* refrescar [el viento]. *4* adquirir frescura, lozanía.
**freshet** (-it) *s.* avenida, riada, inundación.
**freshman** (-mæn) *s.* novato.
**freshness** (-nis) *s.* frescura, frescor. *2* lozanía, ver-

dor. *3* pureza [del aire]. *4* novedad. *5* frescura, descaro.

**fres-water** *adj.* de agua dulce.

**fret** (fret) *s.* roce, rozamiento. *2* raedura, desgaste. *3* impaciencia, irritación, preocupación. *4* greca. *5* B. ART. relieve; calado: ~ *saw*, segueta. *6* MÚS. traste.

**fret (to)** *tr.* rozar, raer, roer, desgastar. *2* agitar [las aguas]. *3* impacientar, irritar, preocupar. *4* adornar con grecas, relieves o calados. *5 intr.* rozarse, desgastarse. *6* irritarse, impacientarse, lamentarse. *7* agitarse [las aguas]. ¶ Pret. y p. p.: *fretted;* ger.: *fretting.*

**fretful** (-ful) *adj.* irritable, enojadizo; malhumorado, nervioso, impaciente.

**fretwork** (-uøᵣk) *s.* grecas. *2* entrelazado, calado.

**Freudian** (froi·dian) *adj.-s.* freudiano.

**friable** (frai·abøl) *adj.* friable.

**friar** (frai·øᵣ) *s.* fraile, monje.

**friary** (-i) *s.* convento de frailes. *2 adj.* frailesco.

**fribble** (-fri·bøl) *adj.* frívolo, vano.

**fribble (to)** *intr.* tontear, bobear.

**fricassee** (frikasɪ·) *s.* COC. fricasé.

**fricative** (fri·kativ) *adj.* FONÉT. fricativo.

**friction** (fri·kshøn) *s.* fricción, rozamiento, roce, frote. *2* MEC. fricción. *3* fig. rozamiento, desavenencia. *4* ELECT. ~ *tape*, cinta aislante.

**Friday** (frai·di) *s.* viernes.

**fried** (fraid) *p. p.* de TO FRY, freído. *2 adj.* frito: ~ *egg*, huevo frito o estrellado.

**friend** (frend) *s.* amigo, amiga: *to be friends with*, ser amigo de; *to make friends with*, trabar amistad con, hacerse amigo de; reconciliarse. *2* partidario; aliado. *3* allegado. *4* (con may.) cuáquero.

**friendless** (fre·ndlis) *adj.* desvalido, sin amigos.

**friendliness** (fre·ndlinis) *s.* amigabilidad, afabilidad, cordialidad; disposición favorable.

**friendly** (fre·ndli) *adj.* amistoso, amigable. *2* benévolo, favorable, propicio.

**friendship** (fre·ndship) *s.* amistad.

**Friesland** (fri·slænd) *n. pr.* GEOGR. Frisia.

**frieze** (friš) *s.* TEJ. risa. *2* ARQ. friso.

**frieze (to)** *tr.* TEJ. frisar.

**frigate** (fri·git) *s.* MAR. fragata. *2* ORN. ~ *bird*, rabihorcado.

**fright** (frait) *s.* miedo, terror; susto, espanto. *2* esperpento, adefesio, espantajo.

**frighten (to)** (frai·tøn) *tr.* asustar, espantar: *to* ~ *away*, ahuyentar. *2 intr.* asustarse.

**frightful** (frai·tful) *adj.* espantoso, terrible. *2* horroroso, feísimo. *3* fam. tremendo, enorme.

**frigid** (fri·dẏid) *adj.* frígido, helado, glacial. *2* frío [sin animación, sin vivacidad; sin cordialidad].

**frigidity** (friẏi·diti) *s.* frigidez, frialdad. *2* fig. frialdad [falta de ardor, de cordialidad].

**frigorific** (frigori·fik) *adj.* frigorífico.

**frill** (fril) *s.* COST. adorno alechugado; chorrera, faralá. *2 pl.* fam. arrequives, ringorrangos.

**frill (to)** *tr.* alechugar. *2* adornar con chorreras, faralaes, etc. *3 intr.* escarolarse.

**fringe** (frindẏ) *s.* franja, fleco, orla, cairel. *2* flequillo. *3* borde, margen, orilla.

**fringe (to)** *tr.* orlar, adornar con flecos o franjas; estar en el borde u orilla de.

**fringillid** (frindẏi·lid) *s.* ORN. fringílido.

**frippery** (fri·pøri) *s.* perifollos. *2* elegancia afectada, cursilería. *3 adj.* despreciable, frívolo.

**frisk** (frisk) *s.* retozo, brinco. *2* pop. cacheo.

**frisk (to)** *intr.* retozar, triscar, cabriolar, brincar. *2 tr.* pop. cachear.

**frisky** (fri·ski) *adj.* juguetón, alegre, vivaracho.

**fritter** (fri·tøᵣ) *s.* frisuelo, buñuelo.

**fritter (to)** *tr.* hacer trizas, desmenuzar. *3 to* ~ *away*, malgastar, desperdiciar poco a poco.

**frivolity** (friva·liti) *s.* frivolidad.

**frivolous** (fri·vøløs) *adj.* frívolo. *2* vano, baladí.

**frizz, frizzle** (friš, fri·šøl) *s.* rizo, cosa rizada.

**frizz, frizzle (to)** *tr.* rizar. *2* encrespar, frisar.

**fro** (frou) *adv.* hacia atrás: *to and* ~, de un lado a otro; *to go to and* ~, ir y venir.

**frock** (frak) *s.* hábito [monacal]. *2* blusa [de pintor, etc.]. *3* vestido [de mujer o niño].

**frock-coat** *s.* levita [prenda].

**frog** (frag) *s.* ZOOL. rana. *2* ranilla [del caballo]. *3* ~ *in the throat*, ronquera. *4 t.* alarmar.

**frolic** (fra·lik) *s.* juego, retozo, travesura. *2* holgorio, diversión.

**frolic (to)** *intr.* juguetear, retozar, travesear; divertirse. ¶ Pret. y p. p.: *frolicked;* ger.: *-king.*

**frolicsome** (-søm) *adj.* juguetón, travieso, retozón.

**from** (frøm) *prep.* de, desde: ~ *afar*, de lejos, desde lejos. *2* de [indicando: origen; estado; separación, exclusión, disentimiento; modelo, modo]: *away* ~ *home*, lejos o fuera del hogar; ~ *nature*, del natural; ~ *now on*, de ahora en adelante. *3* de parte de. *4* a contar de. *5* según. *6* por, a causa de: ~ *kindness*, por bondad. *7* a: *to take something away* ~, quitar algo a.

**frond** (frand) *s.* BOT. fronda, fronde.

**frondescence** (frønde·søns) *s.* BOT. foliación.

**front** (frønt) *s.* ANAT. frente. *2* rostro, semblante. *3* audacia, descaro. *4* apariencia [de riqueza, etc.]: *to put on a* ~, aparentar, hacer ostentación. *5* frente, fachada. *6* delantera. *7* MIL., POL. frente. *5* pechera [de camisa]. *9* paseo frente al mar. *10* frontalera [de la brida]. *11 in* ~, delante, en frente; de enfrente, frontero.

*12 adj.* delantero, anterior; frontero, frontal; ~ *door*, puerta principal; ~ *row*, delantera, primera fila.

**front (to)** *tr.* afrontar, hacer frente a, arrostrar. *2* mirar a, dar a. *3* aparecer delante de. *4* poner fachada a. *5 intr.* estar enfrente de; oponerse. *6 to* ~ *on*, dar a. *7 to* ~ *towards*, mirar hacia.

**frontage** (-frøntidẏ) *s.* terreno que da al mar, un camino, etc.

**frontal** (-al) *adj.* frontal. *2 s.* ANAT., ECLES. frontal. *3* ARQ. fachada.

**frontier** (frønti·øᵣ) *s.* frontera, raya, confín. *2* fronteras de la civilización. *3 adj.* fronterizo.

**frontiersman** (frønti·øᵣšᴴæn) *s.* hombre de la frontera; colonizador, explorador.

**frontispiece** (frø·ntispɪs) *s.* ARQ. frontispicio. *2* frontispicio, portada [de un libro].

**frost** (frost) *s.* helamiento. *2* escarcha, helada. *3* fig. indiferencia. *4* fam. fracaso.

**frost (to)** *tr.* helar, congelar. *2* cubrir de escarcha. *3* quemar [el frío las plantas]. *4* escarchar [frutas], alcorzar [pasteles]. *5* deslustrar [vidrio]. *6 intr.* helarse, cubrirse de escarcha.

**frostbite (to)** (fro·stbait) *tr.* helar, quemar, dañar [el frío, la helada]. ¶ Pret.: *frostbit;* p. p.: *-bitten.*

**frostbitten** (-bitøn) *adj.* helado; quemado, dañado [por la helada].

**frosted** (-id) *adj.* escarchado, alcorzado. *2* deslustrado, mate.

**frosty** (-i) *adj.* helado, glacial. *2* escarchado [cubierto de escarcha]. *3* canoso.

**froth** (froᴢ) *s.* espuma. *2* espumajo. *3* bambolla.

**froth (to)** *tr.* producir espuma en. *2* cubrir de espuma. *3 intr.* espumar, espumajear.

**frothy** (-i) *adj.* espumoso, espumajoso. 2 vano, sin substancia.
**froward** (frou·waᵣd) *adj.* díscolo, indócil.
**frowardness** (-nis) *s.* indocilidad.
**frown** (fraun) *s.* ceño, entrecejo; enojo, rigor.
**frown (to)** *intr.* fruncir el entrecejo: *to ~ at*, on o *upon*, mirar con ceño, desaprobar.
**frowning** (-ing) *adj.* ceñudo, torvo, hosco.
**frowzy** (frau·ši) *adj.* sucio, desaliñado. 2 maloliente.
**froze** (frouš) *pret.* de TO FREEZE.
**frozen** (-n) *p. p.* de TO FREEZE.
**fructiferous** (frøkti·førøs) *adj.* fructífero.
**fructification** (frøktifikei·shøn) *s.* fructificación.
**fructify (to)** (frø·ktifai) *intr.* fructificar. 2 hacer fructífero; fertilizar. ¶ Pret. y p. p.: *fructified*.
**fructose** (frø·ktous) *s.* QUÍM. fructosa.
**fructuous** (frø·kshiuøs) *adj.* fructuoso.
**frugal** (fru·gal) *adj.* frugal.
**frugality** (frugæ·liti) *s.* frugalidad.
**frugivorous** (frudŷi·vørøs) *adj.* frugívoro.
**fruit** (frut) *s.* BOT. fruto. 2 fig. fruto [producto, consecuencia, resultado]. 3 fruta, frutas: ~ *tree*, árbol frutal; ~ *salad*, macedonia de frutas.
**fruit (to)** *intr.* fructificar, frutar.
**fruitage** (fru·tidŷ) *s.* fruta. 2 fruto, resultado, efecto.
**fruit-bearing** *adj.* frutal. 2 fructífero.
**fruiter** (-øᵣ) *s.* frutal. 2 buque frutero.
**fruiterer** (-ørøᵣ) *s.* frutero [vendedor].
**fruitful** (-ful) *adj.* fructífero, fructuoso. 2 prolífico. 3 fértil, abundante.
**fruition** (frui·shøn) *s.* fruición. 2 goce, posesión.
**fruit-piece** *s.* PINT. frutaje, frutero.
**fruitless** (fru·tlis) *adj.* infructuoso, estéril, vano.
**frump** (frømp) *s.* vieja anticuada, regañona. 2 mujer desaliñada.
**frustrate (to)** (frø·streit) *tr.* frustrar, desinflar. 2 burlar, hacer fracasar, molestar [a uno].
**frustration** (-ei·shøn) *s.* frustración, desbaratamiento, desconcierto. 2 fracaso, desenfado.
**frustum** (frø·støm) *s.* GEOM. tronco [de cono o pirámide].
**frutescent** (frute·sønt), **fruticose** (fru·tikous) *adj.* FOT. fruticoso.
**fry** (frai) *s.* freza, morralla, boliche [pececillos, pescado, menudo]: *small ~*, gente menuda.
**fry (to)** *tr.* COC. freír, saltear. 2 *intr.* freírse, asarse. 3 fig. estar agitado, hervir.
**frying** (frai·ing) *s.* freidura: ~ *pan*, sartén.
**fuchsia** (fiu·shia) *s.* BOT. fucsia.
**fuddle (to)** (fø·døl) *tr.* achispar; confundir, atontar [con la bebida]. 2 *intr.* achisparse.
**fudge** (fødŷ) *s.* embuste. 2 dulce de chocolate.
**fudge (to)** *tr.* arreglar, amañar, inventar. 2 hacer chapuceramente. 3 *intr.* TO HEDGE 5.
**fuel** (fiu·øl) *s.* combustible: ~ *oil*, acero pesado, fuel oil. 2 pábulo. 3 incentivo.
**fugacious** (fiugei·shøs) *adj.* fugaz. 2 evanescente.
**fugacity** (fiugæ·siti) *s.* fugacidad.
**fugitive** (fiu·dŷitiv) *adj.* fugitivo. 2 errante, vagabundo. 3 fugaz, pasajero; de intenso pasajero. 4 *s.* fugitivo. 5 exilado.
**fugue** (fiug) *s.* MÚS. fuga.
**fulcrum** (fø·lkrøm) *s.* fulcro.
**fulfil(l (to)** (fulfi·l) *tr.* cumplir, realizar, verificar, efectuar. 2 llenar, colmar.
**fulfil(l)ment** (-mønt) *s.* cumplimiento, desempeño, ejecución, realización. 2 colmo.
**fulgent** (fø·ldŷent) *adj.* fulgente, fúlguro.
**fulgurate (to)** (fø·lgiureit) *tr.* fulgurar.

**fulgurite** (-rait) *s.* fulgurita.
**full** (ful) *adj.* lleno, colmado, repleto, atascado: ~ *house*, lleno [en un espectáculo]: ~ *moon*, luna llena; ~ *of fun*, chistoso, amigo de bromear. 2 cumplido, pleno, entero, completo, todo: ~ *powers*, plenos poderes; ~ *stop*, parada completa; GRAM. punto final; ~ *time*, jornada completa; *at*, o *in*, ~ *blast*, a pelno tiro; en plena actividad; *at* ~ *speed*, a toda velocidad; *in* ~ *swing*, en plena operación; *under* ~ *sail*, a toda vela. 3 plenario. 4 amplio, holgado. 5 absorto, embebido. 6 copioso, abundante. 7 detallado, extenso. 8 carnal [hermano]. 9 bravío [mar]. 10 tendido [galope]. 11 borracho. 12 ~ *age*, mayoría de edad. 13 ~ *dress*, traje de etiqueta, uniforme de gala.
   14 *adv.* enteramente, del todo, plenamente: ~ *nine years*, nueve años cumplidos. 15 detalladamente. 16 de lleno, derechamente.
   17 *s.* lleno, colmo, plenitud; total, totalidad: *in* ~, por completo, detalladamente, sin abreviar.
**full (to)** *tr.* TEJ. abatanar, enfurtir.
**full-blooded** *adj.* de pura raza. 2 pletórico, rubicundo; vigoroso.
**full-bodied** *adj.* fuerte, espeso, aromático [vino].
**fuller** (-øᵣ) *s.* batanero: *fuller's earth*, tierra de batán, greda.
**fullery** (-i) *s.* batán [sitio donde se abatana].
**full-faced** *adj.* carilleno. 2 de rostro entero [retrato].
**full-grown** *adj.* crecido, hecho.
**full-length** *adj.* de cuerpo entero.
**fulling** (-fu·ling) *s.* batanado: ~ *mill*, batán.
**fullish** (-ish) *adj.* llenito, algo lleno.
**fullness** (-nis) *s.* llenura, plenitud, colmo. 2 copia, abundancia. 3 hartura, saciedad.
**full-sized** *adj.* de tamaño natural.
**fully** (-i) *adv.* plenamente, enteramente, completamente. 2 de lleno.
**fulminant** (-fø·lminant) *adj.* fulminante.
**fulminate** (-fø·lmineit) *s.* QUÍM. fulminato.
**fulminate (to)** (tr. fulminar. 2 hacer estallar. 3 *intr.* estallar, denotar. 4 *to* ~ *against*, tronar contra.
**fulminating** (-ing) *adj.* fulminante.
**fulmination** (-shøn) *s.* fulminación.
**fulmine (to)** (fø·lmin) *tr.* lanzar, fulminar.
**fulsome** (fu·lsøm) *adj.* insincero, bajo, vil, empalagoso [adulación, demostraciones de afecto].
**fulvous** (fø·lvøs) *adj.* leonado, amarillo rojizo.
**fumarole** (fiu·maroul) *s.* GEOL. fumarola.
**fumble (to)** (fø·mbøl) *intr.* buscar a tientas, revolver [buscando]. 2 *to* ~ *along*, andar a tientas. 3 *intr.-tr.* balbucear. 4 *tr.* manosear, enredar con. 5 DEP. dejar caer [la pelota].
**fume** (fium) *s.* humo [esp. aromático]. 2 vaho, tufo, gas, vapor: *fumes of wine*, vapores del vino. 3 cólera, acaloramiento.
**fume (to)** *tr.* sahumar. 2 ahumar, fumigar. 3 exhalar [vapor, etc.]. 4 *intr.* avahar, vahear, exhalar gases. 5 humear. 6 rabiar, encolerizarse, echar pestes.
**fumigate (to)** (fiu·migeit) *tr.* fumigar. 2 sahumar.
**fumigation** (-ei·shøn) *s.* fumigación. 2 sahumerio.
**fumitory** (fiu·mitori) *s.* BOT. fumaria, palomina.
**fun** (føn) *s.* broma, chacota, juego, diversión: *for* ~, en broma: *to have* ~, divertirse. 2 chiste, chanza. 3 cosa que divierte: *to be great* ~, ser muy divertido. 4 burla: *to make* ~ *of*, *to poke* ~ *at*, burlarse de, reírse de.
**funambulist** (fiunæ·mbiulist) *s.* funámbulo, volatinero.
**function** (føn·kshøn) *s.* función. | No tiene el sen-

tido de función de teatro o de guerra. 2 fiesta, reunión, acto. 3 ocupación, profesión.
**function (to)** *intr.* funcionar.
**functional** (-al) *adj.* funcional.
**functionary** (-eri) *s.* funcionario.
**functionate (to)** (-eit) *intr.* TO FUNCTION.
**fund** (fønd) *s.* fondo, caudal, capital. 2 acopio, reserva. 3 *pl.* fondos [dinero].
**fund (to)** *tr.* consolidar [una deuda].
**fundament** (fø·ndamønt) *s.* fundamento, base. 2 *fam.* ano; trasero.
**fundamental** (føndame·ntal) *adj.* fundamental. 2 *s.* fundamento, principio, parte esencial.
**funded** (føn·did) *adj.* consolidada [deuda].
**funeral** (fiu·nøral) *s.* entierro, sepelio; cortejo fúnebre. 2 *adj.* funeral, fúnebre, mortuorio: ~ *service*, exequias.
**funereal** (fiuni·rial) *adj.* funerario. 2 fúnebre, triste.
**fungi** (fø·ndẏai) *pl.* BOT. hongos.
**fungosity** (fønga·siti) *s.* fungosidad.
**fungous** (fø·ngøs) *adj.* fungoso.
**fungus** *s.* BOT. hongo. 2 MED. fungosidad.
**funicle** (fiu·nikøl) *s.* funículo.
**funicular** (fiuni·kiular) *adj.* funicular.
**funk** (fønk) *s.* miedo, cobardía. 2 cobarde.
**funk (to)** *intr.* encogerse, arredrarse. 2 *tr.* asustar, arredrar.
**funnel** (fø·nøl) *s.* cañón [de chimenea]; chimenea [de vapor]. 2 embudo. 3 FUND. boca de carga.
**funnies (the)** (fø·nis) *m. pl.* la sección humorística [de un periódico].
**funny** (fø·ni) *adj.* cómico, gracioso, chistoso, divertido. 2 extraño, raro, curioso. 3 *fam.* ~ *bone*, punto sensible del codo.
**fur** (før) *s.* piel [para abrigo o adorno]. 2 pelo espeso de un animal. 3 saburra, sarro. 4 incrustación [en las calderas].
**fur (to)** *tr.* cubrir, forrar o adornar con pieles. 2 cubrir de saburra. 3 *intr.* cubrirse de saburra. 4 formarse incrustaciones. ¶ Pret. y p. p.: *furred;* ger.: *furring.*
**furbelow** (-belou) *s.* COST. faralá, volante.
**furbish (to)** (-bish) *tr.* bruñir, acicalar, limpiar.
**furcate** (-keit) *adj.* ahorquillado.
**furcation** (-ei·shøn) *s.* bifurcación.
**furious** (fiu·riøs) *adj.* furioso, furibundo, airado.
**furl (to)** (fø·rl) *tr.* enrollar, plegar [banderas]. 2 MAR. aferrar [velas].
**furlong** (-long) *s.* estadio [medida].
**furlough** (-lou) *s.* MIL. licencia, permiso.
**furnace** (-nis) *s.* horno, hornillo: *blast* ~, alto horno. 2 hogar [de caldera]; caldera [de calefacción].
**furnish (to)** (fø·rnish) *tr.* surtir, proveer. 2 equipar, aviar, amueblar. 3 suministrar, proporcionar.
**furnished** (-t) *adj.* amueblado.
**furnisher** (-ør) *s.* proveedor, suministrador. 2 mueblista, decorador.
**furnishing** (-ing) *s.* habilitación, equipo, suministro. 2 *pl.* útiles, avíos, adminículos; mobiliario; artículos para caballero.
**furniture** (fø·rnichør) *s.* ajuar, mobiliario, muebles: *piece of* ~, mueble; ~ *van*, carro de mudanzas. 2 equipo, avíos, guarnición; adornos, decoraciones.
**furor** (fiu·ror) *s.* furor, furia. 2 frenesí, locura.
**furred** (fø·rd) *pret.* y *p. p.* de TO FUR.
**furrier** (fø·riør) *s.* peletero.
**furriery** (-ri) *s.* peletería.
**furrow** (fø·rou) *s.* surco. 2 carril, rodada. 3 gárgol, ranura. 4 arruga [en el rostro].

**furrow (to)** *tr.* surcar. 2 abrir ranuras en. 3 arrugar [el rostro]. 4 AGR. arar.
**furry** (fø·ri) *adj.* cubierto o vestido de pieles; peludo. 2 saburroso.
**further** (fø·rdør) *adj. compar.* adicional, ulterior, nuevo, otro; más amplio, más: *till* ~ *orders*, hasta nueva orden. 2 más lejano, más distante, más adelantado: *the* ~ *end*, el extremo más lejano. 3 *adv.* más lejos, más allá, en mayor grado, con mayor extensión. 4 además; aún.
**further (to)** *tr.* adelantar, fomentar, promover, apoyar.
**furtherance** (-ans) *s.* adelantamiento, fomento, promoción, apoyo.
**furtherer** (-ør) *s.* promotor, fomentador.
**furthermore** (-mor) *adv.* además.
**furthermost** (-moust) *adj. superl.* más lejano, más remoto.
**furthest** (fø·rdest) *adj.-adv. superl.* FARTHEST.
**furtive** (fø·rtiv) *adj.* furtivo, oculto, secreto.
**furuncle** (fiu·rønkøl) *s.* MED. furúnculo, divieso.
**fury** (fiu·ri) *s.* furia. 2 entusiasmo, frenesí.
**furze** (fø·rš) *s.* BOT. aulaga, aliaga; hiniesta.
**fuscous** (fø·skøs) *adj.* fusco.
**fuse** (fiuš) *s.* espoleta, cebo, mecha [para dar fuego a una carga]. 2 ELECT. fusible, cortacircuitos: ~ *plug*, tapón fusible.
**fuse (to)** *tr.* fundir, derretir. 2 mezclar, unir. 3 *intr.* fundirse, derretirse.
**fusee** (fiuši·) *s.* caracol [de reloj]. 2 FUSE 1. 3 fósforo grande. 4 FERROC. señal luminosa.
**fuselage** (fiu·šølidẏ) *s.* fuselaje.
**fusible** (fiu·šibøl) *adj.* fusible.
**fusiform** (-fo·rm) *adj.* fusiforme.
**fusil** (fiu·šil) *s.* fusil de chispa.
**fusileer, fusilier** (fiušli·r) *s.* MIL. fusilero.
**fusillade** (fiu·šilei·d) *s.* descarga cerrada, tiroteo.
**fusillade (to)** *tr.* tirotear, fusilar.
**fusion** (fiu·ẏøn) *s.* fusión.
**fuss** (føs) *s.* alboroto, alharaca; ajetreo o inquietud innecesarios: *to make a* ~, hacer alharacas, alborotarse.
**fuss (to)** *intr.* enredar, bullir, ajetrearse; preocuparse o alborotarse por cosas de poco momento: *to* ~ *with*, enredar con, manosear. 2 *tr.* encororar, molestar con tonterías.
**fussy** (-i) *adj.* bullidor, inquieto; minucioso, exigente.
**fust** (føst) *s.* fuste [de columna].
**fustian** (fø·schan) *s.* TEJ. fustán. 2 TEJ. pana. 3 hinchazón [del estilo].
**fustic** (fø·stik) *s.* LOT. fustete.
**fustigate (to)** (-tigeit) *tr.* fustigar, apalear.
**fusty** (-ti) *adj.* mohoso, rancio. 2 que huele a cerrado. 3 pasado de moda; anticuado.
**futile** (fiu·til) *adj.* fútil. 2 frívolo. 3 vano, inútil.
**futility** (fiuti·liti) *s.* futilidad. 2 frivolidad. 3 inutilidad.
**future** (fiu·chør) *adj.* futuro, venidero. 2 *adj.-s.* GRAM. futuro. 3 *m.* futuro, porvenir: *in the* ~, en el futuro, en lo sucesivo. 4 *pl.* COM. futuros.
**futurism** (-rišm) *s.* futurismo.
**futurity** (fiutiu·riti) *s.* futuro, porvenir. 2 lo futuro.
**fuzz** (føš) *s.* vello, pelusa, borra, tamo.
**fuzz (to)** *intr.* soltar pelusa o borra.
**fuzziness** (-inis) *s.* vellosidad.
**fuzzy** (-i) *adj.* velloso, cubierto de pelusa. 2 indistinto, borroso. 3 crespo, rizado [cabello].
**fy!** (fai) *interj.* FIE.
**fylfot** (fi·lføt) *s.* svástica.

# G

**G, g** (dỹi) *s.* G, g, séptima letra del alfabeto inglés. *2* MÚS. sol.
**gab** (gæb) *s.* MEC. gancho, horquilla. *2* fam. cháchara, locuacidad.
**gab (to)** *intr.* charlar, parlotear.
**gabardine** (gæbaʳdɪ·n) *s.* gabardina [tela].
**gabarit** (gabari) *s.* gálibo.
**gabble** (gæ·bøl) *s.* charla, parloteo. *2* cloqueo, graznido.
**gabble (to)** *tr.* charlar, parlotear. *2* cloquear, graznar. *3* decir o leer precipitadamente.
**gabbler** (gæ·bløʳ) *s.* charlatán, picotero.
**gaberdine** (gæbøʳdi·n) *s.* gabardina [tabardo].
**gabion** (gei·biøn) *s.* FORT. gavión, cestón.
**gable** (gei·bøl) *s.* ARQ. aguilón, hastial: ~ *end*, hastial. *2* ARQ. gablete, frontón [sobre puerta o ventana].
**gablet** (gei·blit) *s.* ARQ. gablete.
**gad** (gæd) *s.* aguijada; chuzo. *2* interj. ¡pardiez!
**gad (to)** *intr.* vagar, callejear, andorrear. ¶ Pret. y p. p.: *gadded;* ger.: *gadding.*
**gadabout** (-abaut) *adj.* callejero, vagabundo. *2 s.* persona callejera. *3* pindonga.
**gadder** (-øʳ) *s.* andorrero, haragán, pindonga.
**gadfly** (-flai) *s.* ENT. tábano.
**gadget** (gæ·dẏit) *s.* fam chisme, cosa, mecanismo.
**Gael** (geil) *s.* escocés, celta.
**Gaelic** (gei·lik) *adj.-s.* gaélico, céltico.
**gaff** (gaf) *s.* arpón, garfio. *2* esplón de acero [para un gallo de pelea]. *3* MAR. cangrejo: ~ *sail*, cangreja.
**gaff (to)** *tr.* enganchar con garfio.
**gag** (gæg) *s.* mordaza [para la boca; lo que hace callar]. *2* bocado que produce náuseas. *3* burla, engaño. *4* TEAT. morcilla; episodio cómico.
**gag (to)** *tr.* amordazar. *2* dar náuseas a. *3* TEAT. meter morcillas en. *4* engañar, burlar. *5* MEC. obstruir [una válvula]. ¶ Pret. y p. p.: *gagged;* ger.: *gagging.*
**gage** (geidẏ) *s.* prenda, caución. *2* guante, reto; gaje. *3* GAUGE. *4* BOT. variedad de ciruela.
**gage (to)** *tr.* empeñar, dar en prenda. *2* apostar. *3* TO GAUGE.
**gagger** (gæ·gøʳ) *s.* el que amordaza. *2* bromista.
**gaggle (to)** (gæ·gøl) *tr.* graznar.
**gaiety** (gei·iti) *s.* alegría, jovialidad, algazara, diversión. *2* viveza [de los colores]; lujo [del vestir]; fausto, pompa.

**gaily** (gei·li) *adv.* alegremente. *2* jovialmente.
**gain** (gein) *s.* ganancia, beneficio, lucro. *2* aumento, adquisición. *3* CARP. gárgol, ranura.
**gain (to)** *tr.* ganar [en todas las acepciones, menos en la de vencer o aventajar a uno]: *to* ~ *over,* conquistar; persuadir. *2 intr.* ganar, progresar, mejorarse. *3 to* ~ *on* o *upon,* avanzar, acercarse a, ir alcanzando; ganar ventaja, espacio o terreno a.
**gainer** (-øʳ) *s.* ganador [el que sale ganando].
**gainful** (-ful) *adj.* ganancioso, provechoso, lucrativo.
**gainless** (-lis) *adj.* improductivo, infructuoso.
**gainsaid** (geinse·d) *pret. y p. p.* de TO GAINSAY.
**gainsay (to)** (geinsei·) *tr.* contradecir, negar, discutir. *2* oponerse a, contrariar. ¶ Pret y p. p.: *gainsaid* o *-sayed.*
**gait** (geit) *s.* andar, paso, marcha. *2* porte, continente. *3* TEAT. varia.
**gaiter** (-øʳ) *s.* polaina, botín. *2* botina.
**gala** (gei·la) *s.* fiesta, función lucida: ~ *day,* día de gala, de gran fiesta.
**galactic** (galæ·ktik) *adj.* láctico. *2* ASTR. galáctico.
**galactite** (galæ·ktait) *s.* MINER. galactita.
**galantine** (galæ·ntin) *s.* galantina.
**Galatian** (galei·shian) *adj.-s.* gálata.
**Galaxy** (gæ·læksi) *s.* ASTR. Galaxia. *2* (con min.) pléyade [de artistas, etc.].
**galbanum** (gæ·lbanøm) *s.* gálbano.
**gale** (geil) *s.* viento, ventarrón; temporal. *2* pop. algazara. *3* pago periódico del alquiler.
**galea** (gei·lia) *s.* gálea.
**Galen** (gei·len) *n. pr.* Galeno. *2* fig. galeno [médico].
**galena** (gali·na) *s.* MINER. galena.
**Galicia** (gæli·sha) *n. pr.* GEOGR. Galicia [de Polonia y de España].
**Galician** (gæli·shan) *adj.-s.* gallego. *2* galiciano.
**Galilean** (galili·an) *s.* galileo.
**galiot** (gæ·liøt) *s.* MAR. galeota. *2* galeote.
**gall** (gol) *s.* bilis, hiel: ~ *bladder,* vejiga de la hiel. *2* hiel, amargura, inquina. *3* (E.U.) descaro. *4* rozadura. *5* VET. matadura. *6* BOT. agalla: ~ *oak,* quejigo.
**gall (to)** *tr.* rozar, desollar. *2* irritar, mortificar, molestar. *3* anhelar. *4 intr.* rozarse, escoriarse.
**1) gallant** (gæ·lant) *adj.* magnífico, galano. *2* bizarro, gallardo, valiente. *3* caballeroso.

**2) gallant** (gælæ·nt) *adj.* galante [con las damas]. *2* amatorio. *3 s.* galán. *4* cortejador.
**gallant (to)** *tr.* galantear. *2* escoltar [a una dama].
**gallantry** (gæ·lantri) *s.* gallardía, bizarría, valor, nobleza. *2* galantería [para con las damas]. *3* galanteo.
**galleass** (gæ·liæs) *s.* MAR. galeaza.
**galleon** (gæ·liøn) *s.* MAR. galeón.
**gallery** (gæ·løri) *s.* ARQ. galería; pórtico, columnata. *2* pasadizo. *3* balcón corrido. *4* galería [de pinturas, etc.]. *5* tribuna [en una iglesia]. *6* FORT., MIN., TEAT. galería. *7* galería [público].
**galley** (gæ·li) *s.* MAR. galera: ~ *slave*, galeote. *2* MAR. cocina, fogón. *3* (Ingl.) falúa. *4* IMPR. galera.
**gallfly** (go·lflai) *s.* ENT. cinípedo.
**Gallia** (gæ·lia) *n. pr.* GEOGR. Galia.
**Gallican** (gæ·likan) *adj.-s.* galicano.
**Gallicanism** (-išm) *m.* galicanismo.
**Gallicism** (gæ·lisišm) *s.* galicismo.
**galligaskins** (gæligæ·skinš) *s.* fam. calzones.
**gallinaceous** (galinei·shøs) *adj.* ORN. gallináceo.
**galling** (go·ling) *adj.* irritante, mortificante.
**gallinule** (gæ·liniul) *s.* ORN. gallineta.
**galliot** (gæ·liøt) *s.* GALIOT.
**gallipot** (gæ·lipat) *s.* orza, bote.
**gallium** (gæ·liøm) *s.* QUÍM. galio.
**gallivant (to)** (gælivæ·nt) *intr.* vagar, callejear.
**gallnut** (go·lnøt) *s.* BOT. agalla.
**gallon** (gæ·løn) *s.* galón [medida: *Ingl.*, 4.543 l.; E. U., 3785 l.].
**galloon** (gælu·n) *s.* TEJ. galón, trencilla.
**gallop** (gæ·løp) *s.* galope.
**gallop (to)** *intr.* galopar. *2* hacer galopar.
**galloping** (-ing) *adj.* galopante: ~ *consumption*, tisis galopante.
**gallows** (gæ·louš) *s.* horca, patíbulo: ~ *bird*, carne de horca. *2* armazón en forma de horca.
**gall-stone** *s.* MED. cálculo biliar.
**gally** (fo·li) *adj.* amargo.
**galop** (gæ·løp) *s.* galop [danza].
**galore** (galo·r) *adj.* muchísimos. *2 adv.* abundantemente. *3 s.* abundancia.
**galosh(e** (gala·sh) *s.* chanclo. *2* ant. galocha.
**galvanic** (gælvæ·nik) *adj.* galvánico.
**galvanism** (gæ·lvanišm) *s.* galvanismo.
**galvanize (to)** (gæ·lvanaiš) *tr.* galvanizar. *2* MED. aplicar corrientes eléctricas.
**galvanometer** (gælvano·mete·r) *s.* galvanómetro.
**galvanoplasty** (gæ·lvanoplæsti) *s.* galvanoplastia.
**gama grass** (ga·ma) *s.* BOT. maicillo.
**gambit** (gæ·mbit) *s.* gambito.
**gamble** (gæ·mbøl) *s.* juego [en que se arriesga dinero]. *2* jugada, empresa arriesgada.
**gamble (to)** *intr.* jugar [por dinero]. *2* especular, aventurarse [en la Bolsa, etc.]. *3 tr.* jugar [dinero]. *4* aventurar, perder [en el juego].
**gambler** (gæ·mblø·r) *s.* jugador, tahur.
**gambling** (gæ·mbling) *s.* juego [por dinero]; ~ *house*, garito.
**gambol** (gæ·mbøl) *s.* brinco, cabriola, retozo.
**gambol (to)** *intr.* brincar, cabriolar, retozar, travesar. ¶ Pret. y p. p.: *gamboled* o *-bolled*; ger.: *gamboling* o *-bolling.*
**gambrel** (gæ·mbrøl) *s.* jarrete, corvejón. *2* gancho, garabato. *3* ARQ. ~ *roof*, techo a la holandesa.
**game** (geim) *s.* juego, entretenimiento, diversión: ~ *of chance*, juego de azar: *to play the* ~, jugar limpio. *2* partida [de juego]. *3* DEP. partido. *4* juego, manejo, asunto, plan: *the* ~ *is up*, la cosa ha fracasado. *5* burla, broma. *6* caza [animales]: *big* ~, caza mayor. *7* valentía.

*8 adj.* de juego. *9* de caza: ~ *bag*, zurrón, morral. *10* valiente, animoso, luchador, peleón: *to die* ~, morir peleando. *11* estropeado [brazo, pierna].
**game (to)** *tr.* jugar [dinero]. *2 intr.* jugar [por dinero].
**gamecock** (gei·mkak) *s.* gallo de pelea.
**gamekeeper** (-kipø·r) *s.* guardabosque, guarda de coto.
**gamesome** (-søm) *adj.* alegre, juguetón.
**gamester** (-stø·r) *s.* jugador, tahur.
**gamete** (gæ·mit) *s.* BIOL. gameto.
**gaming** (gei·ming) *s.* GAMBLING.
**gamma** (gæ·ma) *s.* gamma [letra griega].
**gammon** (gæ·møn) *s.* jamón curado. *2* partida doble [en el chaquete]. *3* fam. embuste. faramalla.
**gammon (to)** *tr.* curar [jamón]. *2* ganar partida doble [al chaquete]. *3* fam. enlabiar, embaucar.
**gamopetalous** (gæmope·taløs) *adj.* BOT. gamopétalo.
**gamut** (gæ·møt) *s.* escala, gama.
**gamy** (gei·mi) *adj.* manido. *2* abundante en caza.
**gander** (gæ·ndø·r) *s.* ZOOL. ganso.
**gang** (gæng) *s.* pelotón, cuadrilla, brigada; pandilla, banda. *2* juego [de herramientas, etc.]. *4 adj.* múltiple: ~ *condenser*, RADIO. condensador múltiple.
**gang (to)** *intr.* juntarse, formar cuadrilla.
**ganglion** (gæ·ngliøn) *s.* ANAT., MED. ganglio.
**ganglionic** (gænglia·nik) *adj.* ganglionar.
**gangplank** (gæ·ngplænk) *s.* plancha, pasarela.
**gangrene** (gæ·ngrin) *s.* MED. gangrena.
**gangrene (to)** *tr.* gangrenar. *2* gangrenarse.
**gangrenous** (-øs) *adj.* gangrenoso.
**gangster** (gæ·ngstø·r) *s.* gangster, pistolero.
**gangue** (gæng) *s.* MIN. ganga.
**gangway** (gæ·ngwei) *s.* pasillo. *2* pasarela. *3* MAR. portalón; plancha de atraque.
**gannet** (gæ·nit) *s.* ORN. planga.
**gantlet** (ga·ntlit) *s.* GAUNTLET.
**gantry** (gæ·ntri) *s.* poíno, caballete. *2* puente para grúa corrediza, señales de ferrocarril, etc.
**Ganymede** (gænimi·d) *n. pr.* Ganimedes.
**gaol** (dÿeil) *s.* (Ingl.) cárcel.
**gaoler** (-ø·r) *s.* (Ingl.) carcelero.
**gap** (gæp) *s.* boquete, portillo, brecha, abertura, resquicio. *3* quebrada, barranca. *4* hueco, claro, espacio, laguna.
**gap (to)** *tr.* abrir boquete o brecha en.
**gape** (geip) *s.* bostezo. *2* asombro, embobamiento. *3* abertura, boquete. *4 pl. the gapes*, ganas de bostezar.
**gape (to)** *intr.* bostezar. *2* abrir la boca: *to* ~ *after*, desear, codiciar. *3* estar o quedar boquiabierto: *to* ~ *at*, mirar embobado. *4* abrirse, estar abierto.
**gaper** (-ø·r) *s.* bostezador. *2* bobalicón.
**gar** (ga·r) *s.* ICT. nombre de la aguja, el sollo, etc.
**garage** (gara·ÿ) *s.* garaje. *2* AER. hangar.
**garage (to)** *tr.* dejar o encerrar en el garaje.
**garb** (gæ·rb) *s.* vestido, traje.
**garb (to)** *tr.* vestir, ataviar.
**garbage** (ga·rbidÿ) *s.* desperdicios, basura.
**garble** (ga·rbøl) *s.* alteración, amaño [de un texto, etc.].
**garble (to)** *tr.* alterar, amañar [un texto, etc.].
**garden** (ga·rdøn) *s.* jardín [de flores, etc.]: ~ *balm*, BOT. melisa, toronjil; ~ *city*, ciudad jardín; ~ *party*, fiesta en un jardín. *2* huerto: ~ *stuff*, hortalizas.
**garden (to)** *tr.-intr.* cultivar un huerto o jardín.

**gardener** (ga·ʳdnøʳ) s. jardinero. 2 hortelano.
**gardenia** (gaʳdɪ·nia) s. BOT. gardenia.
**gardening** (ga·ʳdning) s. jardinería; horticultura.
**garfish** (ga·ʳfish) s. GAR.
**garganey** (gæ·ʳgani) s. ORN. cerceta.
**gargle** (ga·ʳgøl) s. gargarismo [licor].
**gargle (to)** tr.-intr. gargarizar.
**gargoyle** (ga·ʳgoil) s. ARQ. gárgola.
**garish** (ge·rish) adj. deslumbrante, llamativo, charro; ostentoso.
**garland** (ga·ʳland) s. guirnalda.
**garland (to)** tr. enguirnaldar.
**garlic** (ga·ʳlik) s. BOT. ajo.
**garlicky** (-i) adj. aliáceo. 2 que huele o sabe a ajo.
**garment** (ga·ʳmønt) s. vestido, prenda.
**garner** (ga·ʳnøʳ) s. granero, hórreo. 2 acopio.
**garner (to)** tr. entrojar, acopiar, almacenar.
**garnet** (ga·ʳnit) s. granate [piedra, color].
**garnish** (ga·ʳnish) s. adorno, guarnición. 2 atavío. 3 COC. aderezo.
**garnish (to)** tr. adornar, guarnecer, ataviar. 2 COC. aderezar [un guiso]. 3 DER. notificar un embargo.
**garniture** (ga·ʳnichuʳ) s. adorno, guarnición.
**Garonne** (garo·n) n. pr. GEOGR. Garona.
**garret** (gæ·rit) s. desván, buhardilla, sotabanco.
**garrison** (gæ·risøn) s. MIL. guarnición, presidio.
**garrison (to)** tr. MIL. guarnicionar. 2 MIL. guarnecer.
**garrot** (gæ·røt) s. CIR. torniquete.
**garrote** (garou·t) s. garrote.
**garrot (to)** tr. agarrotar, dar garrote.
**garrulity** (gæ·riuliti) s. garrulidad, locuacidad.
**garrulous** (gæ·riuløs) adj. gárrulo, locuaz.
**garter** (ga·ʳtøʳ) s. liga, jarretera: *the Garter*, la Orden de la Jarretera.
**garter (to)** tr. sujetar con ligas. 2 investir con la orden de la Jarretera.
**gas** (gæs) s. gas: ~ *burner*, mechero de gas; ~ *chamber*, cámara de gases; ~ *generator*, gasógeno; ~ *mask*, careta antigás; ~ *range*, cocina de gas; ~ *works*, fábrica de gas. 2 fam. gasolina: *to cut off the* ~, AUTO. cerrar el carburador. 3 fam. palabrería, jactancia.
**gas (to)** tr. proveer de gas o gasolina. 2 gasear. 3 intr. despedir gas. 4 fam. charlar, fanfarronear.
**Gascon** (gæ·skøn) adj.-s. gascón.
**gasconade** (gæskønei·d) s. fanfarronada.
**gasconade (to)** intr. jactarse, fanfarronear.
**Gascony** (gæ·skøni) n. pr. GEOGR. Gascuña.
**gaseous** (gæ·siøs) adj. gaseoso. 2 vago, sin consistencia.
**gash** (gæsh) s. cuchillada, herida, incisión.
**gash (to)** tr. acuchillar, herir, cortar.
**gasiform** (gæ·sifoʳm) adj. gaseiforme.
**gasify (to)** (gæ·sifai) tr. gasificar.
**gasket** (gæ·skit) s. MAR. tomador. 2 MEC. relleno, empaquetadura.
**gaslight** (gæ·slait) s. mechero de gas. 2 luz de gas.
**gasogen(e** (gæ·sodỹin) s. GAZOGENE.
**gasoline** (gæ·solin) s. gasolina: ~ *pump*, surtidor de gasolina.
**gasometer** (gæsa·mitøʳ) s. gasómetro.
**gasp** (gasp) s. boqueada; respiración entrecortada; grito sofocado.
**gasp (to)** intr. boquear, abrir la boca [con asombro o jadeando], anhelar: *to* ~ *for breath*, jadear. 2 tr. decir de manera entrecortada.
**gassy** (gæ·si) adj. gaseoso. 2 fig. ampuloso.
**gasteropod** (gæ·støropoud) adj.-s. GASTROPOD.
**gastralgia** (gæstræ·ldỹia) s. gastralgia.

**gastric** (gæ·strik) adj. gástrico.
**gastritis** (gæstrai·tis) s. MED. gastritis.
**gastronomer** (gæstra·nomøʳ) s. gastrónomo.
**gastronomy** (gæstra·nomi) s. gastronomía.
**gastropod** (gæ·stropoud) adj.-s. ZOOL. gasterópodo.
**gastrula** (gæ·strula) s. BIOL. gástrula.
**gate** (geit) s. puerta [de entrada; de una ciudad; en un muro], portal, verja, cancilla, portilla, tranquera, barrera. 2 DEP. entrada [dinero]. 3 compuerta [de esclusa, etc.].
**gatekeeper** (-kɪpøʳ) s. portero. 2 guardabarrera.
**gateway** (-wei) s. entrada, puerta. 2 paso [con portillo]; arco [de entrada].
**gather** (gæ·døʳ) s. frunce, pliegue, plegado.
**gather (to)** tr. recoger, juntar, allegar, reunir, amontonar. 2 recolectar, coger, cosechar. 3 congregar, juntar. 4 recaudar. 5 COST. recoger, fruncir. 6 IMPR. alzar. 7 colegir, deducir, inferir. 8 cobrar [fuerzas]. 9 tomar [aliento; color]. 10 cubrirse de [polvo, musgo, etc.]. 11 ganar [terreno]. 12 to ~ *flesh*, criar carnes. 13 to ~ *speed*, ir aumentando su velocidad.
    14 intr. amontonarse, acumularse. 15 juntarse, congregarse. 16 concentrarse, aumentar. 17 MED. madurar.
**gathering** (-ing) s. recolección. 2 acumulación, hacinamiento. 3 reunión [de gente]. 4 recaudación; colecta [caritativa]. 5 IMPR. alzado. 6 contracción, fruncimiento. 7 MED. maduración, supuración; absceso. 8 COST. fruncido.
**gauche** (goush) adj. torpe, falto de tacto.
**gaud** (god) s. adorno ostentoso o charro.
**gaudery** (-øʳi) s. ostentación, charrería.
**gaudiness** (-inis) s. pompa, boato, charrería.
**gaudish** (-ish), **gaudy** (-i) adj. ostentoso, llamativo, chillón, charro.
**gauge** (geidỹ) s. medida, norma. 2 dimensión, calibre, capacidad. 3 instrumento parar medir ciertas cosas: regla de medir, manómetro, indicador, calibrador, etc. 4 gramil. 5 FERROC. ancho de vía. 6 MAR. calado.
**gauge (to)** tr. medir, graduar, calibrar, aforar. 2 MAR. arquear. 3 estimar, apreciar, juzgar, calcular.
**Gaul** (gol) n. pr. GEOGR. Galia. 2 s. galo.
**Gaulish** (go·lish) adj. galo [de los galos]
**gaunt** (gont) adj. flaco, desvaído; demacrado. 2 tétrico, desolado.
**gauntlet** (go·ntlit) s. guantelete, manopla: *to fling down the* ~, arrojar el guante, retar. 2 MIL. baquetas: *ton run the* ~, pasar por las baquetas; pasar entre dos peligros.
**gauntry** (go·ntri) s. GANTRY.
**gauze** (goš) s. gasa, cendal.
**gauziness** (go·šinis) s. ligereza, transparencia.
**gauzy** (go·ši) adj. ligero, transparente.
**gave** (geiv) pret. de TO GIVE.
**gavel** (gæ·vøl) s. martillo o mazo [de presidente]. 2 ALBAÑ. maceta. 3 gavilla.
**gavial** (gei·vial) s. ZOOL. gavial.
**gavot gavotte** (gævo·t) s. gavota.
**gawk** (gok) s. lerdo, torpe. 2 bobo, papanatas.
**gawky** (go·ki) adj. torpe, encogido, desmañado. 2 m.-f. torpe, bobo.
**gay** (gei) adj. alegre, animado, festivo. 2 alegre, vivo, vistoso, elegante. 3 alegre, ligero de cascos, calavera. 4 ~ *science*, gaya ciencia.
**gaze** (geiš) s. mirada fija, atenta; contemplación.
**gaze (to)** intr. mirar fijamente; contemplar.
**gazelle** (gaše·l) s. ZOOL. gacela; gacel.
**gazer** (gei·šøʳ) s. contemplador, mirón.

**gazette** (gašeˑt) *s.* gaceta [periódico].
**gazette (to)** *tr.* anunciar en un periódico oficial.
**gazetteer** (gæšeˑtɪʳ) *s.* gacetero. *2* nomenclator o diccionario geográfico.
**gazingstock** (geiˑšingstak) *s.* hazmerreír.
**gazogene** (gæˑsodȳin) *s.* gasógeno.
**gear** (gɪˑøʳ) *s.* vestidos, atavíos, prendas de uso. *2* guarniciones [del caballo]. *3* equipo, herramientas, utensilios. *4* MAR. aparejo, maniobra. *5* MEC. rueda, engranaje, juego; mecanismo [de transmisión, de gobierno, etc.]: ~ *box*, . caja de engranajes o de velocidades; ~ *shift*, cambio de marcha; *to throw into* ~, engranar, embragar; *to throw out of* ~, desengranar, desembragar; fig. trastornar.
**gear (to)** *tr.* vestir, ataviar. *2* enjaezar. *3* montar, armar, pertrechar. *4* conectar, hacer engranar. *5 intr.* engranar, estar en juego.
**gearing** (-ing) *s.* MEC. engranaje; mecanismo o tren de engranaje. *2* MAR. drizas y aparejos.
**gearshift** (-shift) *s.* AUTO. cambio de marchas.
**gearwheel** (-juil) *s.* MEC. rueda dentada.
**gee** (dȳi) *interj.* ¡arre!
**gee (to)** *tr.* arrear hacia la derecha. *2 intr.* torcer hacia la derecha.
**geese** (gɪs) *s. pl.* de GOOSE.
**Gehenna** (gijeˑna) *s.* gehena. *2* infierno.
**gel** (dȳel) *s.* QUÍM. gel.
**gelatine** (dȳeˑlætin) *s.* gelatina.
**gelatinize (to)** (dȳilæˑtinais) *tr.-intr.* gelatinar.
**gelaitnous** (-øs) *adj.* gelatinoso.
**gelation** (dȳileiˑshøn) *s.* congelación.
**geld (to)** (geld) *tr.* castrar, capar. *2* castrar [la colmena].
**gelder** (-ør) *s.* castrador, capador.
**gelding** (-ing) *s.* capón; caballo capado.
**gelid** (dȳeˑlid) *adj.* gélido, helado.
**gelidity** (dȳeliˑditi) *s.* frío o frialdad extremos.
**gem** (dȳem) *s.* gema, piedra preciosa. *2* fig. perla, joyel, joya.
**gem (to)** *tr.* adornar con piedras preciosas. ¶ Pret. y p. p.: *gemmed;* ger.: *gemming.*
**geminate** (dȳeˑmineit) *adj.* geminado.
**geminate (to)** *tr.* geminar.
**Gemini** (dȳeˑminai) *s.* ASTR. Géminis.
**gemma** (dȳeˑma) *s.* H. NAT. gema, yema,botón.
**gemmule** (dȳeˑmiul) *s.* H. NAT. yemecilla.
**gender** (dȳeˑndøʳ) *s.* GRAM. género.
**gene** (dȳin) *s.* BIOL. gen.
**genealogical** (dȳeniala·dȳikal) *adj.* genealógico.
**genealogy** (dȳenia·lodȳi) *s.* genealogía.
**generable** (dȳeˑnørabøl) *adj.* generable.
**general** (dȳeˑnøral) *adj.* general: ~ *delinery*, lista de correos. *2 m.* MIL., ECL. general. *3* lo general: *in* ~, en general, por lo común. *4* el público, el vulgo. *5* MIL. generala [toque].
**generalissimo** (dȳenørali·simou) *s.* generalísimo.
**generality** (dȳenøræ·liti) *s.* generalidad.
**generalization** (dȳenørališei·shøn) *s.* generalización.
**generalize (to)** (dȳe·nøralaiš) *tr.* generalizar. *2 intr.* MED. generalizarse.
**generally** (-i) *adv.* generalmente.
**generalship** (-ship) *s.* generalato. *2* don de mando.
**generate (to)** (dȳe·nøreit) *tr.* generar, engendrar, originar. *2* GEOM. generar.
**generating** (dȳenørei·ting) *adj.* generador: ~ *station*, ELECT. central.
**generation** (-shøn) *s.* generación.
**generative** (dȳe·nørativ) *adj.* generativo. *2* generador.

**generator** (dȳe·nøreitøʳ) *s.* generador, engendrador. *2* ELECT., MEC. generador.
**generatrix** (dȳe·nøratriks) *s.* madre. *2* ELECT. generador, dinamo. *3* GEOM. generatriz.
**generic(al** (dȳene·rik(al) *adj.* genérico.
**generosity** (dȳenøra·siti) *s.* generosidad.
**generous** (dȳe·nørøs) *adj.* generoso. *2* noble, magnánimo. *3* valeroso. *4* abundante, amplio, holgado.
**genesial** (dȳini·sial) *adj.* genésico.
**genesis** (dȳe·nesis) *s.* génesis. *2* (con may.) Génesis [libro de la Biblia].
**genet** (dȳe·nit) *s.* ZOOL. jineta. *2* jaca española.
**genetic** (dȳine·tik) *adj.* genético.
**geneticist** (dȳine·tisist) *s.* genetista.
**genetics** (dȳine·tiks) *s.* genética.
**Geneva** (dȳeni·va) *n. pr.* GEOGR. Ginebra.
**Genevan** (dȳeni·van) *adj.-s.* ginebrino.
**genial** (dȳi·nial) *adj.* genial. *2* cordial, afable. *3* alegre, jovial. *4* confortante, agradable. *5* ANAT., ZOOL. geniano.
**geniality** (dȳiniæ·liti) *s.* cordialidad, afabilidad. *2* jovialidad.
**genii** (dȳɪ·niai) *s. pl.* de GENIUS 2.
**genista** (dȳini·sta) *s.* BOT. genista, retama.
**genital** (dȳe·nital) *adj.* genital. *2 s. pl.* partes genitales.
**genitive** (dȳe·nitiv) *adj.-s.* GRAM. genitivo.
**genitor** (dȳe·nitøʳ) *s.* genitor, progenitor.
**1) genius** (dȳɪ·niøs), *pl.* **geniuses** (-iš) *s.* genio [fuerza creadora; pers. que la tiene]. *2* genio, carácter particular [de una nación, época, lugar, etc.].
**2) genius** (dȳɪ·niøs), *pl.* **genii** (dȳ·niai) *s.* genio [deidad]; demonio, espíritu elemental.
**Genoa** (dȳe·noa) *n. pr.* GEOGR. Génova.
**genocide** (dȳ·nøssaid) *s.* genocidio.
**Genoese** (dȳenoi·š) *adj.-s.* genovés.
**genre** (dȳa·nʳ) *s.* LIT., B. ART. género, estilo costumbrista.
**genteel** (dȳentɪ·l) *adj.* urbano, cortés. *2* señoril, elegante, refinado, distinguido. *3* gentil, gallardo.
**genteelness** (-nis) *s.* urbanidad, cortesía. *2* elegancia, distinción. *3* garbo, gentileza.
**gentian** (dȳe·nshan) *s.* BOT. genciana.
**gentile, Gentile** (dȳe·ntail) *adj.-s.* gentil [pagano]. *2 adj.* GRAM. gentilicio.
**gentilic** (dȳenti·lik) *adj.* gentílico. *2* tribal, nacional, racial. *3* GRAM. gentilicio.
**gentilitious** (dȳentili·shøs) *adj.* gentilicio.
**gentility** (dȳenti·liti) *s.* calidad del nacido de buena familia aunque no noble. *2* buena educación, dignidad, valor, gracia, gentileza.
**gentle** (dȳe·ntøl) *adj.* de buena familia, de clase rica, aunque no noble; distinguido. *2* manso, dócil. *3* afable, apacible, dulce, benigno. *4* suave, ligero, moderado. *5 the* ~ *sex*, el bello sexo.
**gentlefolk** (-fouk) *s.* señores, gente distinguida.
**gentleman** (-mæn) *s.* caballero, señor; hombre correcto, bien educado. *2* gentilhombre: ~ *in waiting*, gentilhombre de cámara. *3* ~ *of fortune*, aventurero.
**gentlemanly** (-mænli) *adj.* caballeroso, civil, urbano, correcto.
**gentlemen** (-men) *s. pl.* de GENTLEEMAN, señores. *2* muy señores míos o nuestros [en las cartas]. *3* *gentlemen's agreement*, pacto de caballeros, acuerdo verbal entre naciones.
**gentleness** (-nis) *s.* apacibilidad, mansedumbre. *2*

afabilidad. 3 delicadeza, dulzura, suavidad. 4 distinción, buen tono.

**gentlewoman** (-wumæn) *f.* señora, dama. 2 dama de honor.

**gently** (dẙe·ntli) *adv.* mansamente, suavemente, dulcemente. 2 despacio, quedo, con tiento.

**gentry** (dẙe·ntri) *s.* señorío, gente bien educada, rica, pero no noble. 2 gente, personas.

**genuflect (to)** (dẙe·niuflekt) *intr.* doblar la rodilla.

**genuflection** (dẙeniufle·kshøn) *s.* genuflexión.

**genuine** (dẙe·niuin) *adj.* genuino, auténtico, legítimo, verdadero. 2 franco, sincero.

**genuineness** (dẙe·niuinnis) *s.* autenticidad, legitimidad, pureza. 2 sinceridad.

**genus** (dẙi·nøs) *s.* H. NAT., LÓG. género. 2 género, clase, índole.

**geocentric** (dẙiose·ntrik) *adj.* geocéntrico.

**geode** (dẙi·oud) *s.* GEOL. geoda.

**geodesy** (dẙia·døsi) *s.* geodesia.

**Geoffrey** (dẙe·fri) *n. pr.* Godofredo.

**geogeny** (dẙia·dẙeni) *s.* GEOL. geogenia.

**geognosy** (dẙia·gnosi) *s.* GEOL. geognosia.

**geographer** (dẙia·graføʳ) *s.* geógrafo.

**geographic(al** (dẙiogræ·fik(al) *adj.* geográfico.

**geography** (dẙia·grafi) *s.* geografía.

**geologic(al** (dẙiola·yik(al) *adj.* geológico.

**geologist** (dẙia·lodẙist) *s.* geólogo.

**geology** (dẙia·lodẙi) *s.* geología.

**geometer** (dẙia·mitøʳ) *s.* geómetra.

**geometric(al** (dẙiome·trik(al) *adj.* geométrico.

**geometrician** (dẙiame·trishan) *s.* geómetra.

**geometry** (dẙia·metri) *s.* geometría.

**geophysics** (dẙiofi·šiks) *s.* geofísica.

**geopolitics** (dẙiopa·litiks) *s.* geopolítica.

**George** (dẙoʳdẙ) *n. pr.* Jorge.

**georgete** (dẙo·ʳdẙet) *s.* crespón de seda muy fino.

**georgic** (dẙo·ʳdẙik) *s.* geórgica.

**geotropism** (dẙia·tropišm) *s.* BOT. geotropismo.

**geraniaceous** (dẙøreiniei·shøs) *adj.* geraniáceo.

**geranium** (dẙørei·niøm) *s.* BOT. geranio.

**Gerald** (dẙe·rald) *n. pr. m.* Gerardo.

**gerent** (dẙe·rønt) *s.* director, gerente.

**gerfalcon** (dẙøʳfo·lkøn) *s.* ORN. gerifalte.

**germ** (dẙøʳm) *s.* germen. 2 BOT. yema. 3 BOT. semilla. 4 pop. microbio.

**german** (dẙøʳman) *adj.* carnal [hermano, primo].

**German** *adj.-s.* alemán: ~ *measles*, MED. rubéola; ~ *silver*, alpaca, metal blanco. 2 germano, tudesco. 3 *adj.* germánico.

**germander** (dẙøʳmæ·ndøʳ) *s.* BOT. camedrio; maro.

**germane** (dẙøʳma·n) *adj.* afín. 2 propio, adecuado, pertinente.

**Germanic** (dẙøʳmænik) *adj.* alemán; germánico.

**Germanism** (dẙøʳmanišm) *s.* germanismo.

**germanium** (dẙøʳmei·niøm) *s.* QUÍM. germanio.

**Germanophile** (dẙøʳmæ·nofail) *adj.-s.* germanófilo.

**Germany** (dẙøʳmani) *n. pr.* Alemania.

**germicidal** (dẙøʳmisi·dal) *adj.* bactericida.

**germicide** (dẙøʳmisaid) *s.* bactericida.

**germinal** (dẙøʳminal) *adj.* germinal. 2 en embrión.

**germinate (to)** (dẙø·ʳmineit) *intr.* germinar. 2 brotar, desarrollarse. 3 *tr.* hacer germinar o brotar.

**germination** (dẙøʳmei·shøn) *s.* germinación.

**gerontology** (dẙeranta·lødẙi) *s.* gerontología.

**Gertrude** (gø·ʳtrud) *n. pr. f.* Gertrudis.

**gerund** (dẙø·rønd) *s.* GRAM. gerundio.

**gerundial** (dẙirø·ndial) *adj.* GRAM. del gerundio.

**Gervas** (dẙøʳvas) *n. pr. m.* Gervasio.

**gest, geste** (dẙest) *s.* gesta, romance.

**gestation** (dẙestei·shøn) *s.* gestación. 2 incubación.

**gestatorial** (dẙestato·rial) *adj.* gestatorio.

**gesticulate (to)** (dẙesti·kiuleit) *intr.* accionar, manotear, hacer ademanes.

**gesticulation** (dẙestikiulei·shøn) *s.* acción, manoteo, ademanes.

**gesticulator** (dẙesti·kiuleitøʳ) *s.* el que acciona o hace ademanes.

**gesture** (dẙe·schøʳ) *s.* acción, ademán, signo. 2 cosa dicha o hecha por cortesía o diplomacia.

**gesture (to)** *intr.* accionar, hacer ademanes.

**get** (get) *s.* engendro, engendramiento. 2 producto, progenie, casta.

**get (to)** *tr.* obtener, conseguir, lograr, ganar, sacar, llevarse, recibir, tener. 2 hallar; ir a buscar, traer. 3 coger, capturar, atrapar. 4 vencer, dominar. 5 coger [una enfermedad]. 6 inducir, persuadir; mandar, hacer que: *to ~ one's hair cut*, hacerse cortar el pelo. 7 poner [en un estado, situación, etc.]: *to ~ ready*, preparar; *to ~ going*, poner en marcha; *to ~ together*, juntar, reunir. 8 alcanzar. 9 RADIO. captar, sintonizar con. 10 comunicar con [por teléfono, etc.]. 11 hacer [la comida]; disponer, preparar. 12 proporcionar, suministrar. 13 engendrar, procrear. 14 pop. dar [un puñetazo, etc.]. 15 comprender, entender. 16 aprender [de memoria]. 17 pasar, llevar, hacer llegar o pasar. 18 *to ~ air* o *wind*, divulgarse; enterarse, tener noticia [de]. 19 *to ~ back*, recobrar. 20 *to ~ down*, bajar, descolgar; tragar. 21 *to ~ hold of*, asir; apoderarse de. 22 *to ~ into*, meter en. 23 *to ~ it*, cargársela; recibir un castigo. 24 *to ~ off*, quitar, quitarse; librar, hacer salir de. 25 *to ~ out*, sacar, quitar; ayudar a salir; publicar. 26 *to ~ over*, hacer pasar por encima o más allá de; ganar [a una causa]; acabar. 27 *to ~ the better of*, llevar ventaja a, ganar. 28 *to ~ the worse*, llevar la peor parte; salir mal parado. 29 *to have got*, tener, poseer.

30 *intr.* ganar dinero, etc. 31 llegar [a un punto, estado, etc.]. 32 estar, hallarse. 33 meterse, introducirse, pasar. 34 hacerse, volverse, ponerse: *to ~ old*, hacerse viejo. 35 *to ~ about*, levantarse [un convaleciente]; circular, divulgarse. 36 *to ~ abroad*, divulgarse. 37 *to ~ along*, marcharse, irse; seguir andando; apresurarse; pasarlo. 38 *to ~ along with*, avenirse con. 39 *to ~ around*, ir a todas partes; manejar a [una pers.]; eludir [una ley]; TO GET ABOUT. 40 *to ~ at*, llegar a, ir a; alcanzar; averiguar, descubrir. 41 *to ~ away*, irse, escapar. 42 *to ~ away with*, llevarse, escaparse con. 43 *to ~ back*, volver. 44 *to ~ behind*, quedarse atrás. 45 *to ~ better*, mejorar. 46 *to ~ down*, bajar, bajarse, descender. 47 *to ~ in*, meterse; llegar. 48 *to ~ in with*, lograr la amistad o el favor de. 49 *to ~ into*, entrar en, meterse en. 50 *to ~ near*, acercarse. 51 *to ~ off*, partir, marchar; salir de; apearse de; salir bien librado. 52 *to ~ on*, montar, subir, ponerse sobre; armonizar; adelantar, medrar. 53 *to ~ on one's nerves*, irritar, poner nervioso. 54 *to ~ out*, salir; apartarse; divulgarse. 55 *to ~ over*, reponerse, recobrarse de; olvidar [un disgusto, etc.]; superar un obstáculo; pasar al otro lado. 56 *to ~ through*, pasar por o entre; llegar a su destino; terminar. 57 *to ~ under*, ponerse debajo de. 58 *to ~ under way*, MAR. zarpar. 59 *to ~ up*, levantarse, ponerse en pie; subir. 60 *to have got to*, haber de, tener que. 61 *~ out!*, ¡largo de aquí!;

fam. ¡aprieta! [expresando incredulidad].
¶ Pret.: *got;* p. p.: *got* o *gotten;* ger.: *getting.*
**getaway** (ge·tauei) *s.* partida, escape. *2* DEP. salida [de una carrera]. *3* AUTO. arranque.
**Gethsemane** (gezse·mani) *n. pr.* BIB. Getsemaní.
**get-up** (ge·tøp) *s.* fam. arreglo, disposición, presentación. *2* fam. atavío, traje.
**gewgaw** (giu·go) *s.* chuchería. *2* adorno cursi. *3 adj.* cursi, charro.
**geyser** (gai·$ø$$^r$) *s.* géiser. *2* calentador de baño.
**ghastly** (ga·stli) *adj.* horrible, espantoso. *2* espectral, fantasmal. *3* pálido, lívido, cadavérico. *4 adv.* horriblemente. *5* lívidamente.
**Ghent** (gent) *n. pr.* GEOGR. Gante.
**gherkin** (gø·$^r$kin) *s.* BOT. pepinillo, cohombrillo.
**ghetto** (ge·tou) *s.* judería, barrio judío.
**Ghibelline** (gi·bølin) *adj.-s.* gibelino.
**ghost** (goust) *s.* espíritu, alma: *the Holy Ghost,* el Espíritu Santo: *to give up the* ∼, dar el alma a Dios, morir. *2* espectro, fantasma, sombra, alma en pena. *3* fig. sombra, asomo: *not a* ∼ *of,* ni una sombra de. *4* TELEV. fantasma.
**ghostly** (gou·stli) *adj.* espiritual. *2* espectral, fantasmal. *3* de aparecidos o fantasmas.
**ghoul** (gul) *s.* demonio, vampiro. *2* ladrón de tumbas. *3* persona que se deleita en cosas horribles.
**ghoulish** (gu·lish) *adj.* horrible, brutal, asqueroso.
**giant** (dÿai·ant) *adj* gigante, gigantesco. *2 m.* gigante.
**giantness** (-is) *s.* giganta.
**gib** (gib) *s.* chaveta, cuña, contraclavija. *3* aguilón, brazo de grúa.
**gibber** (gi·bø$^r$) *s.* farfulla, charla.
**gibber (to))** *intr.* farfullar, charlar.
**gibberish** (-ish) *s.* charla incoherente. *2* jerga, jerigonza. *3 adj.* incoherente [charla].
**gibbet** (dÿi·bit) *s.* horca, patíbulo.
**gibbet (to)** *tr.* ahorcar. *2* fig. poner en la picota.
**gibbon** (gi·bøn) *s.* ZOOL. mono de Asia.
**gibbosity** (giba·siti) *s.* gibosidad, giba.
**gibbous** (gi·bøs) *adj.* giboso. *2* jorobado, corcovado. *3* convexo.
**gibe** (dÿaib) *s.* burla, mofa, escarnio, pulla.
**gibe (to)** *tr.* mofarse, escarnecer, ridiculizar. *2 intr.* burlarse, hacer mofa.
**giblets** (dÿi·blits) *s. pl.* menudillos [de ave, etc.].
**gid** (gid) *s.* VET. torneo, modorra.
**giddiness** (gi·dinis) *s.* vértigo, vahído. *2* atolondramiento, aturdimiento, falta de juicio. *3* inconstancia, ligereza.
**giddy** (gi·di) *adj.* vertiginoso. *2* mareado, aturdido, que sufre vértigo. *3* atolondrado, ligero de cascos. *4* inconstante, veleidoso.
**Gideon** (gi·diøn) *n. pr. m.* Gedeón.
**gift** (gift) *s.* donación. *2* donativo, dádiva, don, regalo, obsequio, presente. *3* dación. *4* don, dote, prenda: ∼ *of tongues,* don de lenguas.
**gift (to)** *tr.* regalar, hacer don de. *2* dotar, agraciar.
**gifted** (-id) *adj.* dotado, talentoso, inspirado.
**gig** (gig) *s.* carruaje ligero de dos ruedas. *2* MAR. bote, lancha, falúa. *3* fisga, arpón.
**gig (to)** *tr.-intr.* pescar con fisga o arpón.
**gigantic** (dÿigæ·ntik) *adj.* gigantesco.
**giggle** (gi·gøl) *s.* risita, risa ahogada.
**giggle (to)** *intr.* reírse tratando de contener la risa. *2* reír tontamente o con risa afectada.
**giggler** (gi·glø$^r$) *s.* el que ríe tontamente.
**Gilbert** (gi·lbø$^r$t) *n. pr. m.* Gilberto.
**gild** (gild) *s.* GUILD.
**gild (to)** *tr.* dorar. ¶ Pret. y p. p.: *gilded* o *gilt.*
**gilder** (gi·ldø$^r$) *s.* dorador.

**gilding** (-ing) *s.* duradura. *2* dorado.
**Giles** (dÿails) *n. pr. m.* Giles.
**gill** (gil) *s.* agalla [de pez]; branquia. *2* barba [de gallo]. *3* papada. *4* torrentera.
**gillie** (dÿi·li) *s.* (Esc.) servidor, criado.
**gillyflower** (dÿi·liflauø$^r$) *s.* BOT. alhelí.
**gilt** (gilt) *adj.* dorado; áureo. *2 s.* doradura; dorado. *3* falso brillo, oropel.
**gilt-edged** *adj.* ENCUAD. de cantos dorados. *2* fig. de lo mejor que hay.
**gimcrack** (dÿi·mkræk) *s.* chuchería. *2 adj.* de baratillo, de oropel.
**gimlet** (gi·mlit) *s.* barrena de mano.
**gin** (dÿin) *s.* ginebra [licor]. *2* trampa, armadijo [para cazar]. *3* cabria, malacate. *4* máquina para alijar el algodón.
**gin (to)** *tr.* coger con trampa. *2* alijar [el algodón]. ¶ Pret. y p. p.: *ginned;* ger.: *ginning.*
**ginger** (dÿi·ndÿø$^r$) *s.* BOT. jengibre: ∼ *ale,* gaseosa aromatizada con jengibre. *2* color rubio rojizo. *3* fam. viveza, energía.
**ginger (to)** *tr.* animar; estimular.
**gingerbread** (-bred) *s.* galleta o bollo de jengibre.
**gingerly** (-li) *adv.* cautelosamente, con precaución. *2 adj.* cauteloso, escrupuloso.
**gingerness** (-nis) *s.* cautela; escrupulosidad.
**gingham** (gi·ngam) *s.* TEJ. guinga.
**gipsy** (dÿi·psi) *s.* GYPSY.
**giraffe** (dÿiræ·f) *s.* ZOOL. jirafa.
**girandole** (dÿi·randoul) *s.* girándula. *2* araña, candelabro. *3* JOY. pendiente, arracada.
**gird** (gø$^r$d) *s.* pulla, sarcasmo, escarnio.
**gird (to)** *tr.* ceñir, cercar, rodear; ceñir [llevar ceñido]: *to* ∼ *sword,* ceñir espada. *2* investir [de]. *3* mofarse, burlarse. ¶ Pret. y p. p.: *girded* o *girt.*
**girder** (-ø$^r$) *s.* ARQ. viga, jácena. *2* burlón, reparón.
**girdle** (gø·$^r$døl) *s.* cinto, faja, ceñidor. *2* circunferencia, cerco, zona. *3* zodíaco.
**girdle (to)** *tr.* ceñir, circundar, rodear. *2* hacer una incisión circular [en un árbol].
**girl** (gø$^r$l) *s. f.* niña, muchacha, joven: *best* ∼, novia. *2* chica, doncella, criada.
**girlhood** (-ud) *s.* niñez, juventud [en la mujer].
**girlish** (-ish) *adj.* juvenil; de niña o muchacha.
**girt** (gø$^r$t) *pret.* y *p. p.* de TO GIRD. *2 adj.* ∼ *up,* preparado, animoso.
**girt (to)** *tr.* ceñir, rodear. *2* sitiar. *3* investir [de].
**girth** (gø$^r$z) *s.* cincha. *2* cinturón, faja. *3* periferia, contorno.
**girth (to)** *tr.* cinchar. *2* ceñir, rodear.
**gist** (dÿist) *s.* quid, busilis, punto esencial.
**give** (giv) *s.* elasticidad.
**give (to)** *tr.* dar [donar, ofrecer; causar, ocasionar; comunicar]. *2* dar [un golpe, un consejo, etc.]. *3* entregar, confiar. *4* conceder, otorgar. *5* aplicar, dedicar, consagrar. *6* proferir, emitir, lanzar. *7* describir, referir. *8* presentar, exponer. *9* cantar [una canción]; pronunciar [un discurso]; representar [una obra]. *10* brindar por. *11* asignar, atribuir. *12 to* ∼ *away,* dar, regalar; vender regalado; revelar [un secreto]; vender, traicionar. *13 to* ∼ *back,* devolver, restituir. *14 to* ∼ *birth to,* dar a luz; dar origen a. *15 to* ∼ *forth,* publicar; divulgar; producir; despedir [olores, etc.]. *16 to* ∼ *ground,* ceder terreno. *17 to* ∼ *it to one,* dar dè palos a uno; regañarle. *18 to* ∼ *off,* despedir [olores, etc.]. *19 to* ∼ *oneself up,* entregarse, rendirse. *20 to* ∼ *oneself up to,* entregarse a; darse a. *21 to* ∼ *out,* publicar, declarar; emitir; repartir. *22 to* ∼ *over,* entregar; desistir de. *23 to* ∼ *rise to,* originar, ocasionar. *24 to* ∼ *the lie to,* dar

un mentís, desmentir. *25 to ~ the sack*, dar calabazas, despedir. *26 to ~ the slip*, dar esquinazo, burlar la vigilancia de. *27 to ~ up*, renunciar a, abandonar; entregarse, ceder, rendir; dar por perdido; desahuciar [a un enfermo]; dedicar. *28 to ~ way*, ceder; cejar; hundirse; aflojarse, romperse [una cuerda]; ponerse a remar. *29 to ~ way to*, ser reemplazado por; ceder a, abandonarse a. *30 intr.* dar, ser dadivoso. *31* aflojarse, ablandarse, dar de sí; ceder, romperse. *32* [hablando de puertas, ventanas, etc.] dar, salir [a]. *33 to ~ in*, ceder, consentir; darse por vencido. *34 to ~ out*, acabarse, agotarse; no poder más. *35 to ~ over*, cesar, discontinuar. *36 to ~ up*, desistir, cejar; darse por vencido.
¶ Pret.: *gave;* p. p.: *given.*

**giveaway** (gi·va̯uei) *s.* pop. traición, denuncia. *2* revelación involuntaria. *3* ganapierde.

**given** (gi·vn) *p. p.* de TO GIVE. *2 adj.* dado. *3* MAT. conocido. *4 ~ name*, nombre de pila. *5 conj. ~ that*, suponiendo que.

**giver** (gi·və̯r) *s.* dador, donador, donante. *2* distribuidor, dispensador.

**guizzard** (gi·ša̯rd) *s.* molleja [de ave].

**glabrous** (glei·brø̯s) *adj.* BOT., ZOOL. glabro.

**glacé** (glæsei·) *adj.* glaseado. *2* cubierto de una capa de azúcar.

**glacial** (glei·shia̯l) *adj.* glacial.

**glacier** (-shiø̯r) *s.* glaciar, helero, ventisquero.

**glacis** (glæ·sis) *s.* FORT. glacis.

**glad** (glæd) *adj.* alegre, contento, gozoso: *to be ~ of, that, to*, etc., alegrarse de o de que; tener mucho gusto en. *2* alegre, brillante, hermoso.

**gladden (to)** (glæ·dø̯n) *tr.* alegrar, regocijar, recrear, agradar. *2* animar, hermosear.

**gladdon** (glæ·don) *s.* BOT. íride. *2* GLADIOLUS.

**glade** (gleid) *s.* claro herboso [en un bosque].

**gladiator** (glæ·dieitø̯r) *s.* gladiador.

**gladiolus** (glædai·olø̯s) *s.* BOT. gladiolo, estoque.

**gladly** (glæ·dli) *adv.* alegremente. *2* gustosamente, de buen grado; de buena gana.

**gladness** (-nis) *s.* alegría, contento.

**gladsome** (-sø̯m) *adj.* alegre, placentero.

**glair** (gle·ø̯r) *s.* clara de huevo. *2* cualquier substancia viscosa y transparente.

**glair (to)** *tr.* untar con clara de huevo.

**glairy** (-i) *adj.* viscoso, pegajoso.

**glamorous** (glæ·mørø̯s) *adj.* fascinador.

**glamo(u)r** (glæ·mø̯r) *s.* fascinación, encanto, hechizo.

**glance** (glæns) *s.* mirada, ojeada, vistazo: *at a ~*, de una ojeada. *2* vislumbre. *3* destello, relámpago. *4* golpe dado oblicuamente; desviación [por choque].

**glance (to)** *intr.-tr.* dar o lanzar una mirada, dar una ojeada, un vistazo; mirar al soslayo; *to ~ over*, hojear [un libro]. *2 intr.* destellar, fulgurar. *3* rebotar y desviarse [una bala, etc.]. *4* aludir o referirse de paso. *5 tr.* dirigir súbitamente u oblicuamente [la mirada, un tiro, etc.].

**glancing** (-ing) *adj.* oblicuo, de refilón [golpe]. *2* hecho o dicho de paso.

**gland** (glænd) *s.* ZOOL., BOT. glándula. *2* ANAT. ganglio.

**glanders** (glæ·ndø̯rs) *s.* VET. muermo.

**glandula** (-ȳula) *s.* glándula.

**glandular** (-ȳula̯r) *adj.* glandular.

**glandulous** (-ȳulø̯s) *adj.* glanduloso.

**glans** (glæns) *s.* ANAT. glande. *2* BOT. bellota.

**glare** (gle·ø̯r) *s.* luz intensa, vivo resplandor. *2* re-

sol. *3* viso, destello. *4* aspecto deslumbrante. *5* mirada feroz, penetrante. *6* superficie lisa y brillante.

**glare (to)** *intr.* brillar, resplandecer, relumbrar, deslumbrar. *2* ser vivo [un color]. *3* mirar con fiereza o enojo.

**glaring** (-gle·ø̯ring) *adj.* brillante, deslumbrador. *2* evidente, notorio, que salta a la vista. *3* de mirada feroz, penetrante [ojos].

**glass** (glas) *s.* vidrio, cristal [materia]: *~ blower*, vidriero; *~ case*, escaparate,vitrina. *2* vaso, copa. *3* cristalería [de mesa]. *4* cristal [de ventana, de reloj, etc.]. *5* espejo. *6* ÓPT. lente; anteojo, catalejo, telescopio, etc. *7* reloj de arena. *8* termómetro o barómetro. *9 pl.* lentes, anteojos, gafas; gemelos.

**glassful** (-ful) *s.* vaso, copa [contenido].

**glasshouse** (-jaus) *s.* fábrica de vidrio o cristal. *2* invernáculo. *3* galería de fotógrafo.

**glassmaker** (-meikø̯r) *s.* vidriero.

**glassware** (-ue̯r) *s.* cristalería, vajilla de cristal; objetos de vidrio.

**glasswork** (-uø̯rk) *s.* fabricación del vidrio. *2* artículos de vidrio. *3 sing.* o *pl.* fábrica de vidrio o cristal.

**glasswort** (-uø̯rt) *s.* BOT. sosa, barrilla.

**glassy** (-i) *adj.* cristalino. *2* vítreo; vidrioso.

**glaucoma** (glokou·ma) *s.* MED. glaucoma.

**glaucous** (glo·kø̯s) *adj.* glauco.

**glaze** (gleiš) *s.* vidriado. *2* glaseado, satinado, lustre. *3* velo [de los ojos vidriosos]. *4* capa muy fina de hielo. *5* PINT. veladura.

**glaze (to)** *tr.* vidriar, barnizar. *2* glasear, satinar, velar [los ojos]. *3* PINT. velar. *4* poner vidrios o cristales a.

**glazed** (-d) *adj.* vidriado; glaseado, satinado: *~ tile*, azulejo.

**glazing** (-ing) *s.* vidriado; satinado, glaseado. *2* lustre, barniz. *3* colocación de cristales. *4* cristalería [de puertas, ventanas, etc.].

**gleam** (glim) *s.* destello. *2* resplandor, brillo tenue o pasajero. *3* rayo [de luz, de esperanza].

**gleam (to)** *intr.* destellar, fulgurar, brillar [con luz tenue o pasajera]. *2* aparecer [una luz].

**glean (to)** (glin) *tr.* espigar, rebuscar.

**gleaner** (ø̯r) *s.* espigador, espigadera.

**gleaning** (-ing) *s.* espigueo, rebusca.

**glebe** (glib) *s.* poét. suelo, tierra [laborable]. *2* ECLES. (Ingl.) tierras beneficiales.

**glee** (gli) *s.* alegría, gozo, júbilo, regocijo. *2* MÚS. canción para voces solas.

**gleeful** (-ful), **gleesome** (-sø̯m) *adj.* alegre, gozoso, jubiloso.

**glen** (glen) *s.* cañada, hondonada, valle angosto.

**glengarry** (glengæ·ri) *s.* gorra escocesa.

**glenoid** (gli·noid) *adj.* ANAT. glenoideo.

**glib** (glib) *adj.* locuaz, suelto de lengua.

**glibness** (-nis) *s.* facundia, labia, locuacidad.

**glide** (glaid) *s.* deslizamiento, escurrimiento. *2* AVIA. planeo.

**glide (to)** *intr.* deslizarse, escurrirse, resbalar. *2* correr suavemente. *3* AVIA. planear.

**glider** (-o̯r) *s.* AVIA. planeador.

**glimmer** (gli·mø̯r) *s.* vislumbre, resplandor, viso, luz débil. *2* MINER. mica.

**glimmer (to)** *intr.* brillar, lucir [débilmente]; rielar; alborear; titilar.

**glimmering** (-ing) *s.* luz débil o trémula. *2* vislumbre, atisbo, vaga idea.

**glimpse** (glimps) *s.* resplandor fugaz; visión rápida, breve; vislumbre: *to catch a ~ of*, vislumbrar, entrever.

**glimpse (to)** *intr.* echar una ojeada. *2* brillar con luz débil o trémula; destellar. *3 tr.* vislumbrar, entrever.

**glint** (glint) *s.* brillo, fulgor, rayo, destello.

**glint (to)** *intr.* brillar, lucir, destellar. *2* rebotar. *3 tr.* reflejar [la luz]; hacer brillar.

**glisten** (gli·søn) *s.* brillo, centelleo.

**glisten (to)** *intr.* brillar, centellear, relucir.

**glitter** (gli·tøʳ) *s.* luz brillante, resplandor. *2* brillo, resplandor, lustre.

**glitter (to)** *intr.* brillar, relucir, chispear, rutilar. *2* brillar, resplandecer, ser espléndido.

**gloaming** (glou·ming) *s.* anochecer, anochecida.

**gloat (to)** (glout) *intr.* gozarse en; mirar con satisfacción maligna; con avaricia.

**globate (d** (glou·beit(id) *adj.* esférico, globular.

**globe** (gloub) *s.* globo, esfera, bola. *2* GEOGR., ASTR.. globo, esfera [terrestre o celeste]. *3* globo [de lámpara]. *4* pecera globular. *5* BOT. *~ amaranth*, perpetua.

**globefish** (-fish) *s.* ICT. orbe.

**globetrotter** (-ratøʳ) *s.* trotamundos.

**globose** (-ous) *adj.* globoso, redondo.

**globular** (glo·biulaʳ) *adj.* globular. *2* esférico.

**globule** (glo·biul) *s.* glóbulo.

**globulin** (-in) *s.* QUÍM. globulina.

**glomerate** (glo·mørit) *adj.* aglomerado [en forma de bola], conglobado.

**glomerule** (glo·mørul) *s.* BOT. glomérulo.

**gloom** (glum) *s.* oscuridad, lobreguez, tinieblas. *3* tristeza, melancolía.

**gloom (to)** *tr.* oscurecer, entenebrecer. *2* entristecer. *3 intr.* oscurecerse, entenebrecerse. *4* aparecer sombrío, destacarse sombríamente. *5* entristecerse.

**gloomy** (-i) *adj.* oscuro, lóbrego, tenebroso. *2* sombrío, triste, melancólico, tétrico; abatido. *3* adusto, hosco.

**Gloria** (glo·riæ) *s.* LITURG. Gloria.

**glorification** (glorifikei·shøn) *s.* glorificación. *2* fam. celebración, fiesta, holgorio.

**glorify (to)** (glo·rifai) *tr.* glorificar. *2* ensalzar, magnificar. ¶ Pret. y p. p.: *glorified.*

**gloriole** (glo·rioul) *s.* aureola, halo.

**glorious** (glo·riøs) *adj.* glorioso. *2* magnífico, espléndido. *3* fam. achispado.

**glory** (glo·ri) *s.* gloria [bienaventuranza, cielo; fama, celebridad; esplendor, magnificencia]: *to go to ~*, fig. morir. *2* grandeza, brillantez, lustre, belleza radiante. *3* aureola, halo.

**glory (to)** *intr.* exultar; gloriarse: *to ~ in*, gloriarse de; gloriarse en. ¶ Pret. y p. p.: *gloried.*

**gloss** (glos) *s.* lustre, brillo, pulimento. *2* falsa apariencia, oropel. *3* colorido, paliativo. *4* glosa.

**gloss (to)** *tr.* lustrar, glasear, satinar, pulir. *2* colorear, cohonestar, paliar. *3 tr.-intr.* glosar.

**glossarist** (gla·sarist) *s.* glosador, escoliasta.

**glossary** (gla·sari) *s.* glosario.

**glossiness** (gla·sinis) *s.* lustre, pulimento.

**glossy** (glo·si) *adj.* lustroso, brillante, glaseado, satinado. *2* especioso, de apariencia plausible.

**glottis** (gla·tis) *s.* ANAT. glotis.

**glove** (gløv) *s.* guante: *~ stretcher*, abridor de guantes.

**glove (to)** *tr.* enguantar. *2* proveer de guantes.

**glover** (glø·vøʳ) *s.* guantero.

**glow** (glou) *s.* luz, resplandor [de un ascua, de un cuerpo candente], soflama. *2* resplandor rojo en el cielo, arrebol. *3* viveza de color. *4* color [en las mejillas, en el cuerpo]. *5* ardor, vehemencia; animación. *6* calor [en el cuerpo].

**glow (to)** *intr.* dar luz o calor vivos; estar candente, arder sin llama. *2* brillar, resplandecer; estar encendido [el rostro, el cielo, etc.]; mostrar interés, animación. *3* tener colores vivos. *4* arder [de pasión, ira, etc.]. *5* sentir calor.

**glower** (gla·uøʳ) *s.* mirada ceñuda, amenazadora.

**glower (to)** *intr.* mirar ceñudo.

**glowing** (glou·ing) *adj.* resplandeciente. *2* ardiente, encendido. *3* brillante [color]. *4* entusiasta.

**glowworm** (glou·uøʳm) *s.* ENT. luciérnaga; cocuyo.

**gloze (to)** (glouš) *tr.-intr.* colorear, paliar. *3* adular. *3* abrillantar.

**glucemia** (glusi·mia) *s.* MED. glucemia.

**glucinium** (glusi·niøm), **glucinum** (glusai·nøm) *s.* QUÍM. glucinio.

**glucose** (glu·kous) *s.* QUÍM. glucosa.

**glue** (glu o gliu) *s.* cola [para pegar]; gluten. *2* liga, visco.

**glue (to)** *tr.* encolar, pegar, conglutinar, unir.

**gluepot** (glu·pot) *s.* cazo para la cola.

**gluey** (glu·i) *adj.* viscoso, pegajoso, glutinoso.

**glum** (gløm) *adj.* malhumorado, hosco, sombrío.

**glume** (glum) *s.* BOT. gluma.

**glut** (gløt) *s.* hartura, hartazgo. *2* plétora, exceso, saturación.

**glut (to)** *tr.* hartar. *2* colmar, saturar; atascar. *3* COM. inundar [el mercado]. *4 intr.* tragar, atracarse. ¶ Pret. y p. p.: *glutted*; ger.: *glutting.*

**gluteal** (gluti·al) *adj.* glúteo.

**gluten** (glu·tøn) *s.* gluten.

**gluteus** (glu·tiøs) *s.* ANAT. músculo glúteo.

**glutinous** (glu·tinøs) *adj.* glutinoso.

**glutton** (glø·tøn) *adj.-s.* glotón, tragón. *2 s.* ZOOL. glotón.

**gluttonize (to)** (-aiš) *intr.* glotonear.

**gluttonous** (-øs) *adj.* glotón, tragón.

**gluttony** (-i) *s.* glotonería, gula.

**glycerin (e** (gli·serin) *s.* glicerina.

**glycine** (glai·sin) *s.* BOT., QUÍM. glicina.

**glycogen** (glaiko·dýin) *s.* gicógeno.

**gliptics** (gli·ptiks) *s.* glíptica.

**gliptography** (glipta·grafi) *s.* gliptografía.

**gnarl** (naʳl) *s.* nudo [en el árbol o la madera].

**gnarl (to)** *tr.* torcer, retorcer.

**gnarled** (-d), **gnarly** (-i) *adj.* nudoso, retorcido. *2* pendenciero, terco.

**gnash (to)** (næsh) *intr.* hacer rechinar los dientes. *2* rechinar [los dientes]. *3 tr.* hacer rechinar [los dientes].

**gnashing** (-ing) *s.* rechinamiento de dientes.

**gnat** (næt) *s.* ENT. mosquito, cinife.

**gnaw (to)** (no) *tr.* roer. *2* morder, mordicar.

**gnawer** (-øʳ) *s.* roedor.

**gneiss** (nais) *s.* GEOL. gneis.

**gnome** (noum) *s.* gnomo. *2* máxima, aforismo.

**gnomon** (nou·møn) *s.* gnomon.

**gnomonics** (noma·niks) *s.* gnomónica.

**Gnostic** (na·stik) *adj.-s.* gnóstico.

**Gnosticism** (-tišism) *s.* gonosticismo.

**gnu** (nu) *s.* ZOOL. gnu, ñu.

**go** (gou) *s.* ida, ir. *2* marcha, curso, movimiento. *3* energía, empuje, brío. *4* incidente, situación; *this is a pretty ~*, estamos frescos. *5* tentativa: *to have a ~ at*, probar a, tratar de. *6* breve período. *7* convenio, trato: *is it a ~?*, ¿convenido? *8* moda, boga: *it is all the ~*, es la gran moda. *9* éxito. *10* paso libre [a los automóviles].

**go (to)** *intr.* ir [en casi todos sus sentidos]. *2* caminar, andar. *3* andar, marchar, funcionar. *4* irse. *5* morir. *6* pasar, desaparecer. *7* acabarse. *8* debilitarse, decaer. *9* dirigirse, acudir, recurrir. *10* correr, circular, tener curso. *11* armonizar, adaptarse. *12* alcanzar, llegar [a un límite, cantidad, etc.]. *13* ponerse, volverse, hacerse: *to ~ mad,* volverse loco. *14* contribuir, conducir, tender. *15* salir, resultar. *16* tener éxito, surtir efecto. *17* gobernarse, guiarse, regularse [por]. *18* ceder, soltarse, romperse. *19* rezar, decir [hablando de un texto, una frase, etc.]. *20* hacer [cierto ruido]: *bang went the door,* la puerta hizo ¡pan! *21* entrar, caber *22 to ~ about,* ir por ahí, ir de un lado a otro; ocuparse en; MAR. virar de bordo. *23 to ~ across,* atravesar, cruzar. *24 to ~ after,* seguir; ir en busca de. *25 to ~ against,* ir en contra, oponerse. *26 to ~ ahead,* avanzar; proseguir; adelantar, progresar. *27 to ~ along,* seguir, continuar. *28 to ~ along with,* acompañar. *29 to ~ around,* ir de un lado a otro; dar vueltas, contornar, rodear; alcanzar para todos. *30 to ~ astray,* extraviarse; descarriarse. *31 to ~ at,* atacar, acometer. *32 to ~ away,* irse, ausentarse; pasar [un dolor, etc.]. *33 to ~ back,* retroceder; volverse atrás; *to ~ back on one's word,* desdecirse, faltar uno a su palabra. *34 to ~ bad,* echarse a perder; ir mal. *35 to ~ between,* interponerse, mediar, terciar. *36 to ~ by,* pasar por, junto a; regirse por, atenerse a; ser conocido por, tener, usar [un nombre o apodo]. *37 to ~ down,* bajar, descender; caer; irse a pique; llegar, continuarse [hasta un punto]; ser anotado o registrado. *38 to ~ far,* ir lejos; durar mucho; servir de mucho; alcanzar para mucho. *39 to ~ for,* ser partidario de; representar; ser tenido por; ir en busca de; embestir. *40 to ~ forth,* salir; divulgarse, publicarse. *41 to ~ in,* entrar, encajar. *42 to ~ in for,* favorecer, apoyar; participar en; competir por [un premio, etc.]; dedicarse a; buscar, perseguir. *43 to ~ into,* entrar en; tomar parte en, emprender, dedicarse a; investigar; discutir, tratar de. *44 to ~ near,* acercarse. *45 to ~ off,* irse, largarse; dispararse, estallar, hacer explosión; dormirse, desmayarse; morir; desaparecer; salir, quedar [bien o mal]; fracasar. *46 to ~ off one's head,* volverse loco. *47 to ~ on,* obrar, portarse; continuar, proseguir; durar; progresar; pasar [a hacer algo]; TEAT. salir a la escena. *48 to ~ out,* salir; apagarse, extinguirse; morir; desafiarse; divulgarse. *49 to ~ out of fashion,* pasar de moda. *50 to ~ out of the way,* apartarse, descarriarse, molestarse [en hacer algo]. *51 to ~ over,* pasar [por encima de], atravesar, salvar; pasarse [a otro partido]; releer, repasar, revisar, examinar. *52 to ~ through,* pasar por; traspasar, hender; recorrer, examinar; sufrir, pasar; llevar a cabo; derrochar. *53 to ~ to sleep,* dormirse. *54 to ~ under,* ser conocido por el nombre, título, etc., de; irse a pique; arruinarse; sucumbir, ser vencido. *55 to ~ up,* subir. *56 to ~ with,* acompañar, ir con; cortejar; armonizar con. *57 to ~ without,* pasar o pasarse sin. *58 to ~ wrong,* salir mal, fracasar; ir por mal camino, darse a la mala vida. *59 tr.* ir o llegar hasta. *60* llevar, seguir [un camino]. *61* soportar, tolerar. *62* apostar [en el juego]. *63 to ~ bail,* salir fiador. *64 to ~ halves,* ir a medias. *65 to ~ it,* obrar, avanzar, etc. impetuosamente; pop. obrar, proceder. *66 to ~ one's way,* seguir uno su camino. *67 to ~ shares,*

ir a la parte.

¶ Pret.: *went;* p. p. *gone;* 3.ª pers. del sing.: *goes.*

**goad** (goud) *s.* aguijada, focino, pincho, aguijón. *2* acicate [estímulo].

**goad (to)** *tr.* aguijar, aguijonear, picar.

**go-ahead** *adj.* emprendedor, activo.

**goal** (goul) *s.* DEP. meta; puerta, portería. *2* DEP. gol. *3* meta, fin, objeto.

**goalkeeper** (-kɪpər) *s.* DEP. guardameta, portero.

**goat** (gout) *s.* ZOOL. cabra; *~ buck,* macho cabrío; *wild ~,* cabra montés; *to be the ~,* fig. pagar el pato.

**goatee** (goutɪˑ) *s.* perilla [barba].

**goatherd** (-hərd) *s.* cabrero, cabrerizo.

**goatish** (-ish) *adj.* cabruno, hircino. *2* lascivo.

**goatskin** (-skin) *s.* piel de cabra.

**goatsucker** (-søkər) *s.* ORN. chotacabras.

**gob** (gab) *s.* pedazo, masa informe y pequeña.

**gobbet** (ga·bit) *s.* bocado, pedacito. *2* grumo, pella.

**gobble** (ga·bøl) *s.* voz del pavo.

**gobble (to)** *tr.* engullir, tragar. *2 intr.* hacer ruido en la garganta como los pavos.

**gobbler** (ga·blør) *s.* engullidor, tragón, glotón. *2* ORN. pavo.

**go-between** *s.* correveidile. *2* alcahuete. *3* intermediario, corredor.

**goblet** (ga·blit) *s.* copa [para beber].

**goblin** (ga·blin) *s.* duende, trasgo.

**go-by** *s.* fam. desaire, esquinazo.

**go-cart** *s.* carretilla. *2* carruaje ligero. *3* cochecito de niño. *4* andadiño, pollera.

**God** (gad) *n. pr.* Dios: *act of ~,* fuerza mayor; *~ forbid,* no lo quiera Dios; *~ willing,* Dios mediante; *God's acre,* camposanto. *2 m.* (con min.) dios, deidad [pagana].

**godchild** (-chaild) *s.* ahijado, ahijada.

**goddaughter** (-dotør) *s.* ahijada.

**goddess** (-is) *s.* diosa, deidad, diva.

**godfather** (-fadør) *s.* padrino [de bautismo].

**God-fearing** *adj.* temeroso de Dios.

**God-forsaken** *adj.* abandonado. *2* triste, desierto, desolado.

**Godfrey** (-fri) *n. pr. m.* Godofredo.

**Godhead** (-jed) *n. pr.* y *s.* Deidad, Divinidad.

**godless** (-lis) *adj.* sin Dios, ateo, impío. *2* malvado.

**godlike** (-laik) *adj.* divino, deiforme.

**godliness** (-linis) *s.* piedad, devoción, santidad.

**godly** (-li) *adj.* piadoso, religioso, devoto.

**godmother** (-møðør) *f.* madrina [de bautismo].

**godsend** (-send) *s.* merced divina; ganga, suerte inesperada.

**godship** (-ship) *s.* divinidad.

**godson** (-søn) *s.* ahijado.

**Godspeed** (-spid) *s.-interj.* buena suerte, buen viaje.

**godwit** (-uit) *s.* ORN. especie de chorlito.

**goffer (to)** (ga·før) *tr.* plegar, rizar, encrespar. *2* estampar [el cuero].

**go-getter** *s.* fam. (E.U.) buscavidas, persona emprendedora.

**goggle** (ga·gøl) *adj.* saltón [ojo]. *2 pl.* gafas ahumadas o protectoras.

**goggle (to)** *intr.* torcer los ojos o abrirlos desmesuradamente.

**goggle-eyed** *adj.* de ojos saltones.

**going** (gou·ing) *p. a. de* TO GO. *2 s.* paso, andar, andadura. *3* ida, marcha, partida. *4* estado del camino. *5 pl.* idas y venidas. *6 goings on,* ocurrencias, sucesos; acciones, conducta.

**goiter, goitre** (goi·tør) *s.* MED. bocio, papera.

goitrous

**goitrous** (goi·trøs) *adj.* que tiene bocio.
**gold** (gould) *s.* oro [metal]. *2* fig. oro [dinero, riqueza]. *3* color del oro. *4 adj.* de oro; áureo, dorado: *Gold Coast,* GEOGR. Costa de Oro; ~ *lace,* galón o encaje de oro; ~ *leaf,* pan de oro; ~ *standard,* patrón oro.
**gold-bearing** *adj.* aurífero.
**goldbeater** (gou·ldbɪtøʳ) *s.* batidor de oro, batihoja.
**goldcrest** (gou·ldcrest) *s.* ORN. reyezuelo.
**golden** (-øn) *adj.* de oro, áureo, dorado: ~ *calf,* becerro de oro; ~ *eagle,* águila caudal; *golden Fleece,* MIT. Vellocino de oro, Toisón de oro; ~ *mean,* justo medio, ~ *number,* número áureo; ~ *wedding,* bodas de oro.
**goldfinch** (-finch) *s.* ORN. jilguero, pintacilgo.
**goldfish** (-fish) *s.* ICT. carpa dorada. *2* pececillo de color.
**gold-laced** *adj.* galoneado de oro.
**goldsmith** (-smiz) *s.* orifice, orfebre.
**golf** (galf) *s.* DEP. golf: ~ *course,* ~ *links,* campo de golf.
**golf (to)** *intr.* jugar al golf.
**golfer** (-øʳ) *s.* jugador de golf.
**Golgotha** (ga·lgoza) *s.* Gólgota.
**Goliath** (goulai·az) *n. pr.* BIB. Goliat.
**golliwog** (ga·liuag) *s.* muñeca grotesca.
**gondola** (ga·ndola) *s.* góndola. *2* barquilla [de dirigible]. *3* FERROC. batea.
**gondolier** (gandøli·øʳ) *s.* gondolero.
**gone** (gon) *p. p.* de TO GO. *2* ido, pasado. *3* muerto. *4* desaparecido. *5* agotado. *6* débil, desfallecido. *7* perdido, arruinado.
**gonfalon** (ga·nfaløn) *s.* confalón, gonfalón.
**gonfalonier** (ganfaløni·øʳ) *s.* confalonier, confaloniero.
**gong** (gong) *s.* gong, batintín.
**Gongorism** (ga·ngørišm) *s.* gongorismo.
**goniometer** (gounia·mitøʳ) *s.* goniómetro.
**goniometry** (gounia·metri) *s.* goniometría.
**good** (gud) *adj.* bueno: ~ *afternoon,* buenas tardes; ~ *books,* fig. favor, bienquerencia; ~ *cheer,* ánimo, confianza, alegría; festín, buena mesa; ~ *day,* buenos días; ~ *evening,* buenas noches; ~ *for nothing,* inútil; perdido, haragán; ~ *form,* buena educación; *Good Friday,* Viernes Santo; ~ *looks,* buen aspecto; hermosura; ~ *morn,* ~ *morning,* buenos días; ~ *nature,* bondad buen corazón, benevolencia; ~ *night,* buenas noches; ~ *sense,* buen sentido, sensatez; ~ *time,* buen rato, día, etc.; diversión: ~ *turn,* favor, servicio; ~ *will,* buena voluntad; *a ~ deal,* bastantes, mucho; *a ~ while,* un buen rato, bastante tiempo; *as ~ as,* prácticamente, como sí; *as ~ as done,* cosa hecha, como si estuviera hecho; *to be as ~ as one's word,* ser hombre de palabra; *in ~ earnest,* de veras, seriamente; *in ~ order,* en buen estado. *2* valiente, animoso. *3* solvente, responsable; que dispone de o responde por [cierta cantidad].
   *4 interj.* ¡bueno!, ¡bien!, ¡magnífico!
   *5 s.* bien; beneficio, provecho, ventaja: *to do* ~, hacer el bien; aprovechar; ir bien para la salud; *much* ~ *may it do you,* buen provecho le haga; *what is the* ~ *of it?,* ¿para qué sirve? *6 for* ~, para siempre, definitivamente. *7 for* ~ *and all,* de una vez para siempre. *8 the* ~, el bien; lo bueno; los buenos.
**good-by, good-bye** (-bai·) *s.* adiós, despedida. *2 interj.* ¡adiós!, ¡hasta la vista!
**good-fellowship** *s.* compañerismo, camaradería.

**good-hearted** *adj.* de buen corazón.
**good-humoured** *adj.* jovial; afable.
**goodish** (-ish) *adj.* bastante bueno; bastante grande, regular, considerable.
**goodlines** (-linis) *s.* belleza, hermosura, gracia, elegancia.
**good-looking** *adj.* guapo, bien parecido.
**goodly** (-li) *adj.* bello, hermoso, gracioso. *2* guapo, bien parecido. *3* agradable, vistoso. *4* excelente. *5* bueno, bastante grande, considerable.
**good-natured** *adj.* bonachón, afable.
**goodness** (-nis) *s.* bondad. *2* virtud. *3* fineza, favor. *4 interj.* ¡válgame Dios!; ~ *gracious!,* ¡Santo Dios!, *for* ~ *sake,* ¡por Dios!
**goods** (-s) *s. pl.* géneros, mercancías, efectos: ~ *train,* ~ *wagon,* (Ingl.) tren, vagón, de carga o mercancías.
**goodwife** (-uaif) *s.* ant. ama de casa, señora.
**goody** (-i) *adj.* bonachón. *2* sensiblero. *3* mojigato. *4 s.* tía, mujer del pueblo. *5* golosina.
**goosander** (gusæ·ndøʳ) *s.* ORN. mergánsar, mergo.
**goose** (gus), *pl.* **geese** (gis) *s.* ORN. ganso, ánsar, oca: ~ *flesh,* fig. carne de gallina; ~ *step,* paso de la oca; *to kill the* ~ *that lays the golden eggs,* matar la gallina de los huevos de oro. *2* fig. ganso, bobo.
**gooseberry** (-beri) *s.* BOT. grosellero silvestre, uva espina o crespa.
**foosefoot** (-fut) *s.* BOT. quenopodio.
**gooseherd** (-smiz) *s.* ansarero.
**gooseneck** (-nek) *s.* cuello de cisne. *2* MAR. pescante de bote. *3* barra, tubo, etc., curvos.
**Gordian** (go·ʳdian) *adj.* gordiano: ~ *knot,* nudo gordiano.
**gore** (gouʳ) *s.* sangre. *2* sangre espesa o cuajada. *3* COST. cuchillo, nesga. *4* pieza triangular.
**gore (to)** *tr.* poner cuchillo o nesga a. *2* acornear. *3* herir con los colmillos.
**gorge** (go·ʳdў) *s.* garganta, gaznate. *2* desfiladero, garganta, barranca. *3* contenido del estómago: *my* ~ *rises at,* me revuelve el estómago. *4* masa que obstruye. *5* FORT. golà.
**gorge (to)** *tr.* engullir, tragar. *2* hartar, atiborrar. *3* obstruir. *4 intr.* hartarse, atracarse.
**gorgeous** (go·ʳdўøs) *adj.* brillante, vistoso, magnífico, suntuoso.
**gorget** (go·ʳdўit) *s.* gorguera, gorjal [de la armadura]. *2* MIL. gola. *3* collar, adorno para el cuello.
**Gorgon** (gø·ʳgøn) *s.* MIT. Gorgona. *2* fam. esperpento; mujer muy fea.
**gorilla** (gøri·la) *s.* ZOOL. gorila.
**gormand** (go·ʳmnd) *s.* glotón, goloso.
**gormandize** (-aiš) *s.* gastronomía.
**gormandize (to)** *tr.-intr.* comer con gula.
**gormandizer** (-aisøʳ) *s.* goloso, glotón.
**gorse** (go·ʳs) *s.* BOT. aulaga. *2* BOT. enebro.
**gory** (gou·ri) *adj.* ensangrentado, sangriento.
**goshawk** (ga·sjok) *s.* ORN. azor.
**gosling** (ga·sling) *s.* ORN. ansarino, gansarón.
**gospel** (ga·spøl) *s.* evangelio: *the* ~ *truth,* la pura verdad, el evangelio.
**gospel (to)** *intr.* predicar el evangelio.
**gossamer** (ga·samøʳ) *s.* hilo de araña o telaraña flotante. *2* TEJ. gasa. *3* cosa muy fina o sutil.
**gossamer(y** (-i) *adj.* sutil, delgado.
**gossip** (ga·sip) *s.* chismografía, comadreo, murmuración. *2* charla. *3* habladuría, chisme. *4* chismoso, murmurador. *5* compadre, comadre.
**gossip (to)** *intr.* chismear, murmurar, charlar.
**gossipy** (-i) *adj.* chismoso, murmurador.
**got** (gat) *pret.* y *p. p.* de TO GET.

**Goth** (goz) *s.* godo. *2* bárbaro, rudo.
**Gothic** (-ik) *adj.* gótico. *2 s.* lengua goda.
**Gothicism** (-isìsm) *s.* estilo gótico. *2* (con min.) barbarie, rudeza.
**gotten** (ga·tøn) (E.U.) *p. p.* de TO GET.
**gouge** (gaudȳ) *s.* gubia, mediacaña. *2* acanaladura, estría. *4* (E.U.) estafa.
**gouge (to)** *tr.* estropear, acanalar. *2 to ~ out,* sacar [un ojo, esp. con el pulgar]; (E.U.) engañar, estafar.
**gourd** (gøʳd o guʳd) *s.* BOT. calabaza; calabacera: *bottle ~,* calabaza vinatera. *2* calabacino.
**gourmand** (gu·ʳmand) *s.* gastrónomo, goloso; glotón.
**gourmet** (guʳmei·) *s.* gastrónomo.
**gout** (gaut) *s.* MED. gota.
**goutiness** (-inis) *s.* afección gotosa.
**gouty** (-i) *adj.* gotoso.
**govern (to)** (gø·vøʳn) *tr.* gobernar, regir, dirigir, manejar, regular. *2* dominar, refrenar. *3* GRAM. regir. *4* MAR. gobernar.
**governable** (-abøl) *adj.* dócil, manejable.
**governance** (-ans) *s.* gobierno, gobernación.
**governess** (-is) *s.* aya, institutriz. *2* ant. gobernadora.
**government** (-mønt) *s.* gobierno, gobernación, dirección, manejo, administración; mando, autoridad: *for your ~,* para su gobierno. *2* gobierno [forma política; ministerio]. *3* GRAM. régimen.
**governmental** (-mental) *adj.* gubernamental, gubernativo.
**governor** (-øʳ) *s.* gobernador. *2* director, administrador. *3* ayo, preceptor. *4* pop. padre, tutor; amo, principal. *5* MEC. regulador.
**gowan** (gau·an) *s.* DAISY 1.
**gown** (gaun) *s.* vestido [de mujer]. *2* bata; túnica; toga, vestido talar: *dressing ~,* bata.
**gownsman** (-smæn) *s.* togado. *2* civil, paisano.
**grab** (græb) *s.* agarro, asimiento, presa. *2* arrebatiña. *3* robo, sisa. *4* MEC. garfio, grapa. *5* MEC. *~ bucket,* cucharón de quijadas.
**grab (to)** *tr.* agarrar, asir, coger, arrebatar. *2* apropiarse indebidamente. *3* intr. *to ~ at,* tratar de coger, de arrebatar. ¶ Pret. y p. p.: *grabbed;* ger.: *-bbing.*
**grabble (to)** (græ·bøl) *intr.* ir o hacer a tientas. *2* estar postrado.
**Grace** (greis) *n. pr. f.* Gracia.
**grace** *s.* gracia [en todos sus sentidos menos en el de chiste y en el de nombre de cada uno]: *~ stroke,* golpe de gracia; *to be in one's good graces,* estar en gracia cerca de uno. *2* dignación, amabilidad. *3* garbo, donaire. *4* disposición, talante: *with a bad ~,* de mala gana, con aspereza. *5* tratamiento que se da a un duque, un arzobispo, etc. *6* MÚS. adorno: *~ note,* nota de adorno. *7 to say ~,* dar gracias o bendecir la mesa. *8 pl.* MIT. *The Graces,* las gracias.
**grace (to)** *tr.* adornar. *2* agraciar, favorecer. *3* honrar, elevar.
**graceful** (-ful) *adj.* gracioso, airoso, agraciado, elegante; fácil, natural.
**gracefulness** (-fulnis) *s.* gracia, donosura, garbo, donaire, gentileza, elegancia.
**graceless** (-lis) *adj.* desgraciado, falto de gracia, feo, desgarbado. *2* malvado, depravado.
**gracile** (græ·sil) *adj.* grácil.
**gracious** (grei·shøs) *adj.* gracioso, atractivo. *2* afable, cortés. *3* benigno, bondadoso. *4* de afable superioridad [aire, maneras]. *5* interj. *gracious!* ¡válgame Dios!

**graciously** (-i) *adv.* graciosamente, afablemente, cortesmente, benignamente.
**grackle** (græ·køl) *s.* ORN. especie de mirlo.
**gradate (to)** (grei·deit) *intr.* ir en gradación. *2 tr.* graduar [disponer en grados]. *3* PINT. degradar.
**gradation** (greidei·shøn) *s.* gradación; paso gradual. *2* grado [en una serie, etc.]. *3* rango. *4* graduación [disposición en grados]. *5* PINT. degradación.
**grade** (grei·d) *s.* grado [que puede tener una cosa]. *2* clase, calidad. *3* MIL. graduación. *4* GEOM. centésima parte del ángulo recto. *5* (E.U.) grado, curso [de una escuela]. *6* ING. pendiente, desnivel; grado de pendiente: *down ~,* cuesta abajo; *up ~,* cuesta arriba. *7* (E.U.) *~ crossing,* paso a nivel.
**grade (to)** *tr.* graduar [disponer por grados]. *2* clasificar [por grados o clases]. *3* matizar [un color, etc.]. *4* ING. nivelar, explanar [un camino, etc.].
**grader** (-øʳ) *s.* el o lo que gradúa, clasifica, etc. *2* ING. nivelador.
**gradient** (grei·diønt) *s.* ING. pendiente, inclinación, desnivel. *2* METEOR. gradiente. *3* grado de aumento o disminución de una magnitud variable.
**gradin** (grei·din) *s.* grada, escalón. *2* gradilla [de altar]. *3 pl.* gradería.
**gradine** (gra·din) *s.* GRADIN. *2* gradina [de escultor].
**gradual** (græ·diual) *adj.* gradual; graduado. *2 m.* LITURG. Gradual.
**gradualness** (-nis) *s.* calidad de gradual.
**graduate** (græ·diuit) *adj.* graduado [en universidad]. *2 s.* el que tiene grado académico. *3* QUÍM. graduador, probeta.
**graduate (to)** (græ·diueit) *tr.* graduar [dividir por grados]. *2* aumentar, disminuir, etc., gradualmente. *3* graduar [conferir un grado]. *4 intr.* variar gradualmente. *5* graduarse [recibir un grado académico].
**graduation** (grædiuei·shøn) *s.* graduación. | No tiene el sentido de categoría de un militar.
**graduator** (græ·diueitøʳ) *s.* graduador.
**Gr(a)ecism** (gri·sìsm) *s.* grecismo, helenismo.
**graffito** (grafi·tou), *pl.* -ti (tai) *s.* ARQUEOL. grafito. *2* esgrafiado.
**graft** (graft) *s.* AGR., CIR. injerto. *2* fam. (E.U.) ganancia ilícita, malversación, chanchullo.
**graft (to)** *tr.* injertar. *2* injerir, inserir, unir. *3* fam. (E.U.) adquirir ilícitamente. *4 intr.* hacer injertos. *5* fam. (E.U.) hacer chanchullos.
**grafter** (-øʳ) *s.* injertador. *2* (E.U.) ladrón, chanchullero.
**grafting** (-ing) *s.* injerto [acción].
**grail** (greil) *s.* grial: *the Holy Grail,* el Santo Grial.
**grain** (grein) *s.* grano [de los cereales, de la uva, etc.; semilla, partícula]: *~ weevil,* gorgojo del grano; *with a ~ of salt,* fig. con cierto escepticismo. *2* plantas que dan grano, cereales. *3* grano [peso]. *4* átomo, pizca, pequeña cantidad. *5* cuenta, perla. *6* grana, quermes, color rojo. *7* grano [de una superficie, de la piedra]; flor [del cuero]; granilla [del paño]; fibra, veta [de la madera]. *8* índole, disposición, inclinación: *against the ~,* contra la inclinación de uno, cuesta arriba, a contrapelo. *9 to dye in the ~,* teñir en rama. *10* BOT. *grains of Paradise,* granos del Paraíso.
**grain (to)** *intr.* formar grano. *2 tr.* teñir en rama. *3*

granular. *4* granear. *5* granelar [el cuero]. *6* vetear.

**grainfield** (-fıld) *s.* mies, sembrado.

**grainy** (-i) *adj.* granular, granoso. *2* lleno de granos.

**gram** (græm) *s.* GRAMME.

**gramercy** (gramø·ʳsi) *interj.* ¡gracias! *2* ¡Dios mío!

**graminaceous** (graminei·shiøs) *adj.* gramináceo.

**grammar** (græ·maʳ) *s.* gramática. *2* principios, elementos [de una ciencia o arte]. *3* ~ *school*, colegio de segunda enseñanza; (E.U.) escuela elemental.

**grammarian** (græme·rian) *s.* gramático.

**grammatic (al** (gr-aemæ·tik(al) *adj.* gramatical, gramático.

**grammaticalness** (-nis) *s.* corrección gramatical.

**gramme** (græm) *s.* gramo.

**gramophone** (græ·mofoun) *s.* gramófono.

**grampus** (græ·mpøs) *s.* ZOOL. orca, orco.

**granadilla** (grændi·l) *s.* BOT. granadilla. *2* ~ *tree*, ~ *wood*, granadillo [árbol; madera].

**granary** (græ·nari) *s.* granero.

**grand** (grænd) *adj.* grande, gran [en ciertos sentidos]: *Grand Canyon*, Gran Cañón [del Colorado]; ~ *duke*, gran duque; ~ *jury*, DER. jurado que investiga y decide si hay motivo para procesar; ~ *master*, gran maestre; ~ *piano*, piano de cola. *2* grandioso. *3* admirable, magnífico, espléndido, soberbio. *4* solemne, majestuoso. *5* completo, comprensivo.

**grandam** (-æm) *s.* abuela. *2* anciana.

**grandaunt** (-ænt) *s.* tía abuela.

**grandchild** (-chaild) *s.* nieto, nieta.

**granddaughter** (-døtøʳ) *s.* nieta.

**grandee** (-ı·) *s.* grande [de un reino]; prócer, magnate.

**grandeur** (-ŷøʳ) *s.* grandeza, magnificencia.

**grandfather** (-fadøʳ) *s.* abuelo: *grandfather's clock*, reloj de caja.

**grandiloquence** (grændi·lokuøns) *s.* grandilocuencia.

**grandiloquent** (grændi·lokuønt), **grandiloquous** (grændi·lokuøs) *adj.* grandilocuente, grandilocuo.

**grandiose** (græ·ndiouš) *adj.* grandioso, imponente. *2* pomposo, hinchado, bombástico.

**grandma** (-ma) *s.* fam. abuela, abuelita.

**grandmother** (-mødøʳ) *s.* abuela.

**grandnephew** (-nefiu) *s.* resobrino.

**grandness** (-nis) *s.* grandeza, grandiosidad, magnificencia.

**grandniece** (-nıs) *s.* resobrina.

**grandpa** (-pa) *s.* fam. abuelo, abuelito.

**grndparent** (-perøn) *s.* abuelo o abuela. *2 pl.* abuelos [el abuelo y la abuela].

**grandson** (-søn) *s.* nieto.

**grandstand** (-stænd) *s.* gradería cubierta, tribuna.

**granduncle** (-ønkøl) *s.* tío abuelo.

**grange** (greindŷ) *s.* granja, hacienda, cortijo, alquería.

**granger** (-øʳ) *s.* granjero, cortijero.

**granite** (græ·nit) *s.* MINER. granito.

**granitic(al** (græni·tik(al) *adj.* granítico.

**granivorous** (græni·vørøs) *adj.* granívoro.

**granny** (græ·ni) *s.* fam. abuela, abuelita.

**grant** (grant) *s.* concesión, otorgamiento, donación. *2* don, merced, subvención, privilegio; cosa concedida. *3* DER. cesión por escritura. *4* asentimiento, asenso.

**grant (to)** *tr.* conceder, otorgar, dispensar, dar. *2*

conceder, dar de barato: *to take for granted*, dar por supuesto. *3* DER. ceder, transferir.

**grantee** (-ı·) *s.* cesionario.

**grantor** (-øʳ) *s.* otorgador, dispensador, el que concede. *2* cesionista.

**granular** (græ·niulaʳ), **granulary** (græ·niuleri) *adj.* granular. *2* granuloso, granilloso.

**granulate (to)** (græ·niuleit) *tr.* granular. *2* granear. *3 intr.* formar gránulos. *4* MED. granular.

**granulated** (-id) *adj.* granulado, graneado. *2* en grano.

**granulation** (-ei·shøn) *s.* granulación.

**granule** (græ·niul) *s.* gránulo.

**granulous** (-øs) *adj.* granular, granuloso.

**grape** (greip) *s.* BOT. uva: *sour grapes*, ¡están verdes! *2* BOT. baya de ciertas plantas. *3* vid, parra.

**grapefruit** (-frut) *s.* BOT. toronja, pomelo.

**grapery** (-øri) *s.* invernadero o criadero de uvas.

**grapeshot** (-shat) *s.* ARTILL. metralla.

**grapeskin** (-kin) *s.* hollejo de uva.

**grapestone** (-stoun) *s.* semilla de uva.

**grapevine** (-vain) *s.* vid, parra.

**graph** (græf) *s.* gráfica, curva, diagrama. *2* GRAM. grafía.

**graph (to)** *tr.* representar con una gráfica.

**graphic (al** (-ik(al) *adj.* gráfico.

**graphite** (græ·fait) *s.* MINER. grafito, plombagina.

**graphology** (græfa·lodŷi) *s.* grafología.

**graphometer** (grafa·metøʳ) *s.* grafómetro.

**grapnel** (græ·pnel) *s.* MAR. rezón, rizón. *2* arpeo, rebañadera, garabato, garfio.

**grapple** (græ·pøl) *s.* presa, agarro, engarro. *2* lucha cuerpo a cuerpo. *3* GRAPNEL.

**grapple (to)** *tr.* asir, aferrar, agarrar, sujetar. *2 intr.* agarrarse, cogerse; luchar cuerpo a cuerpo. *3 to* ~ *with*, luchar con; tratar de comprender, resolver, etc.

**grappling hook** o **iron** (græ·pling) *s.* arpeo, garfio.

**grasp** (grasp) *s.* asimiento, agarro. *2* apretón de manos. *3* abrazo. *4* dominio, poder, alcance: *within the* ~ *of*, al alcance de. *5* comprensión.

**grasp (to)** *tr.* asir, coger, empuñar. *2* abrazar, abarcar; apoderarse de. *3* comprender, entender. *4* intr. *to* ~ *at*, tratar de asir o coger; aceptar con avidez.

**grasping** (-ing) *adj.* codicioso, avaro.

**grass** (græs) *s.* hierba, yerba, herbaje, césped, pasto: *to let the* ~ *grow under one's fett*, perder el tiempo, dormirse en las pajas. *2* BOT. ~ *pink*, clavel coronado.

**grass (to)** *tr.* apacentar. *2* cubrir de hierba. *3 intr.* pacer.

**grass-green** *adj.* verde como la hierba.

**grass-grown** *adj.* cubierto de hierba.

**grasshopper** (-japøʳ) *s.* ENT. langosta, saltamontes.

**grassland** (-lænd) *s.* prado, tierra de pasto.

**grassplot** (-plat) *s.* prado, cuadro de césped.

**grassy** (-i) *adj.* herboso. *2* herbáceo.

**grate** (greit) *s.* reja, verja, enrejado. *2* emparrillado. *3* parrilla, rejilla [de hogar].

**grate (to)** *tr.* coc. rallar. *2* raspar. *3* hacer rechinar. *4* molestar, irritar. *5* enrejar. *6 intr.* rechinar.

**grateful** (grei·tful) *adj.* agradecido, reconocido. *2* grato, agradable.

**grater** (grei·tøʳ) *s.* rallador, rallo, raspador.

**graticulate (to)** (græti·kiuleit) *tr.* DIB. cuadricular.

**gratification** (grætifikei·shøn) *s.* satisfacción, contento, complacencia, gusto, placer. *2* gratificación, recompensa.

**gratify (to)** (græ·tifai) *tr.* satisfacer, dar gusto, con-

tentar, complacer, agradar. *2* gratificar. ¶ Pret. y p. p.: *gratified.*
**grating** (grei·ting) *adj.* que raspa. *2* rechinante, chirriante. *3* discordante [sonido]. *4* áspero, irritante. *5 s.* rechinamiento, chirrido. *6* reja, rejilla. *7* verja, enrejado. *8* MAR. enjaretado. *9* ÓPT. retícula. *10 pl.* COC. ralladuras.
**gratis** (grei·tis) *adv.* gratis, de balde.
**gratitude** (græ·titiud) *s.* gratitud, reconocimiento.
**gratuitous** (gratiu·tøs) *adj.* gratuito.
**gratuity** (gratiu·ti) *s.* don, gratificación, propina.
**gratulation** (græchulei·shøn) *s.* gratulación.
**gratulatory** (græ·chulatori) *adj.* gratulatorio.
**grave** (greiv) *adj.* grave [importante, arduo]. *2* grave, serio, digno, solemne. *3* serio [color]. *4* MÚS., GRAM. grave. *6 s.* tumba, sepultura, sepulcro, fosa, hoya. *7* GRAM. acento grave.
**grave (to)** *tr.* grabar. *2* cincelar, esculpir. ¶ Pret.: *graved;* p. p.: *graved* o *graven.*
**gravedigger** (-digøʳ) *s.* sepulturero, enterrador.
**gravel** (græ·vøl) *s.* arena gruesa, guijo, grava. *2* MED. cálculos, arenas.
**gravel (to)** *tr.* enarenar [una superficie], confundir, embarazar. *3* fam. irritar.
**graveless** (-i·vlis) *adj.* insepulto.
**gravelly** (græ·vøli) *adj.* arenoso, guijoso.
**gravely** (grei·vli) *adv.* gravemente.
**graven** (-n) *p. p.* de TO GRAVE. *2 adj.* grabado, esculpido.
**graveness** (-nis) *s.* gravedad; seriedad.
**graver** (-øʳ) *s.* grabador, cincelador, escultor. *2* buril, punzón, cincel.
**gravestone** (-stoun) *s.* lápida sepulcral.
**graveyard** (-iaʳd) *s.* cementerio, camposanto.
**gravid** (græ·vid) *adj.* grávido, preñado, fecundo.
**gravimeter** (græ·vi·metøʳ) *s.* gravímetro.
**gravitate (to)** (græ·viteit) *intr.* gravitar. *2* gravear.
**gravitation** (grævitei·shøn) *s.* gravitación.
**gravity** (græ·viti) *s.* gravedad [importancia; solemnidad, seriedad]. *2* FÍS. gravedad, pesantez.
**gravy** (grei·vi) *s.* COC. salsa, jugo [de la carne]: ~ *boat,* salsera.
**gray** (grei) *adj.* gris, pardo: ~ *matter,* ANAT. substancia gris; ~ *friars,* franciscanos. *2* cano, encanecido. *3 adj.-s.* rucio, tordo. *4 s.* color gris o pardo.
**gray (to)** *tr.* poner gris o cano. *2 intr.* volverse gris; encanecer.
**gray-haired, gray-headed** *adj.* cano, canoso [pers.].
**grayish** (-ish) *adj.* grisáceo, agrisado. *2* pardusco. *3* entrecano.
**graylag** (-læg) *s.* ORN. ánsar, bravo.
**grayling** (-ling) *s.* ICT. tímalo.
**graze** (greiš) *s.* rozamiento, roce, rozadura. *2* pasto, apacentamiento.
**graze (to)** *tr.* rozar [pasar, herir o desgastar rozando]; arañar, rasguñar; raspar. *2* pacer [la hierba]. *3* apacentar. *4 intr.* pacer, pastar.
**grazier** (-øʳ) *s.* ganadero.
**grease** (grís) *s.* grasa; ~ *cup,* MEC. vaso de engrase; ~ *lift,* AUTO. puente de engrase. *2* manteca, unto, sebo, pringue. *3* pop. lisonja; soborno.
**grease (to)** *tr.* engrasar, untar, lubricar, pringar. *2* fig. untar, sobornar.
**greaser** (-øʳ) *s.* engrasador.
**greasy** (-i) *adj.* grasiento, pringoso, aceitoso, mugriento. *2* graso. *3* untuoso.
**great** (greit) *adj.* grande, gran, magno, mayor: ~ *age,* edad avanzada; *Great Bear,* ASTR. Osa Mayor; *Great Britain,* la Gran Bretaña; ~ *gun,* ant.

cañón pesado; fig. personaje; *Alexander the Great,* Alejandro Magno. *2* largo, dilatado. *3* crecido. *4* favorito, preferido. *5* magnífico, estupendo. *6* ASTR. máximo [círculo]. *7* mayúscula [letra]. *8* fam. *to be ~ at,* ser muy hábil o fuerte en. *9* fam. *to be ~ on,* dar mucha importancia a. *10* en nombres de parentesco, indica una generación más, como en *great-grandfather,* bisabuelo. *11 s. the ~,* lo grande, los grandes.
**great-aunt** *s.* tía abuela.
**great-bellied** *adj.* barrigudo. *2* preñada.
**greatcoat** (grei·tkout) *s.* gabán. *2* levitón. *3* capote.
**greater** (-øʳ) *adj. comp.* de GREAT; mayor, más grande: *the ~ part,* la mayoría. *2 Greater Britain,* Imperio Británico.
**greatest** (-ist) *adj. superl.* de GREAT; máximo, sumo, el mayor; ~ *common divisor,* ART. máximo común divisor.
**great-hearted** *adj.* animoso, valiente. *2* generoso, noble, magnánimo.
**greatly** (-li) *adv.* muy, mucho, grandemente. *2* grandiosamente. *3* en gran parte.
**greatness** (-nis) *s.* grandeza. *2* magnitud, amplitud, extensión. *3* pompa, esplendor.
**greave** (grív) *s.* ARM. greba. *2 pl.* COC. chicharrones.
**grebe** (grib) *s.* ORN. colimbo.
**Grecian** (grí·shan) *adj.* griego, greco. *2 s.* griego. *3* helenista.
**Grecianize (to)** (-aiš) *tr.-intr.* TO GRECIZE.
**Grecism** (grí·sišm) *s.* grecismo, helenismo.
**Grecize (to)** (grísai·š) *tr.-intr.* grecizar, greguizar.
**Greco-Latin** (grí·kou-) *adj.* grecolatino.
**Greco-Roman** *adj.* grecorromano.
**Greece** (grís) *n. pr.* GEOGR. Grecia.
**greed** (grid), **greediness** (-nis) *s.* ansia, avidez, codicia. *2* avaricia. *3* voracidad, gula.
**greedy** (grí·di) *adj.* ávido, ansioso, codicioso, hambriento. *2* avaro. *3* voraz, glotón.
**Greek** (grík) *adj.* griego. *2 s.* griego [persona, lengua griega; lenguaje ininteligible]. *3* (con min.) fullero.
**green** (grín) *adj.* verde [de color, de sazón]: ~ *barley,* alcacer; ~ *cloth,* o *greencloth,* tapete verde; ~ *fly,* pulgón; ~ *vitriol,* caparrosa verde. *2* lozano, lleno de vigor. *3* crudo [ladrillo, loza, etc.]. *4* fresco, reciente. *5* bisoño, inexperto: ~ *hand,* novicio, principiante. *6* verde, lívido, pálido [de miedo, celos, etc.]. *7 s.* verde [color; follaje, hierba]. *8* verdor, verdura. *9* prado, pradera. *10 pl.* verduras, hortalizas.
**green (to)** *tr.* poner o volver verde; pintar o teñir de verde. *2 intr.* verdear.
**greenback** (grí·nbæk) *s.* (E.U.) billete de banco.
**greenfinch** (-finch) *s.* ORN. verderón.
**greengage** (-gidÿ) *s.* ciruela verdal.
**greengrocer** (-grousøʳ) *s.* verdulero.
**greengrocery** (-grousøri) *s.* verdulería.
**greenhorn** (-joʳn) *s.* pipiolo, novato. *2* palurdo. *3* bobo, primo, incauto.
**greenhouse** (-jaus) *s.* invernáculo.
**greening** (-ing) *s.* BOT. variedad de manzana de color verdoso.
**greenish** (-ish) *adj.* verdoso, verdusco.
**Greenland** (-lænd) *n. pr.* GEOGR. Groenlandia.
**Greenlander** (-lændøʳ) *s.* groenlandés.
**greenness** (-nis) *s.* verdura, verdor. *2* lozanía, vigor, frescura. *3* falta de experiencia. *4* novedad.
**greenroom** (-rum) *s.* TEAT. sala de espera de los actores.
**greensand** (-sænd) *s.* GEOL. arenisca verde.
**greenstall** (-stol) *s.* puesto de verduras.

**greensward** (-suoᵗd) s. césped.
**greenwood** (-wud) s. bosque verde. 2 BOT. retama de tintes.
**greet (to)** (grıt) tr. saludar, acoger, dar la bienvenida. 2 intr. saludarse.
**greeter** (grı·tøᵗ) s. el que saluda.
**greeting** (-ing) s. saludo, salutación, recibimiento. 2 greetings!, ¡salud!
**gregarious** (grigei·riøs) adj. que vive en grey o compañía, gregal. 2 sociable, que gusta de la compañía.
**Gregorian** (grigo·rian) adj. gregoriano.
**Gregory** (gre·gori) n. pr. m. Gregorio.
**gremial** (gri·mial) s. ECLES. gremial.
**grenade** (grinei·d) s. granada [proyectil].
**grenadier** (grenɑdi·øᵗ) s. MIL. granadero.
**grenadine** (gre·nadin) s. granadina.
**grew** (gru) pret. de TO GROW.
**grey** (grei) adj. GRAY.
**greyhound** (-jaund) s. ZOOL. galgo.
**greyish** (-ish) adj. GRAYISH.
**grid** (grid) s. reja, rejilla, parrilla. 2 RADIO. rejilla. 3 ELECT. red.
**griddle** (gri·døl) s. tartera, tortera. 2 plancha [para tapar el hornillo; para asar].
**gridiron** (gri·daiøᵗn) s. COC. parrillas. 2 MAR. andamiada. 3 TEAT. telar. 4 red [de vigas, tubos, etc.].
**grief** (grıf) s. dolor, pesar, pesadumbre, duelo, aflicción, congoja. 2 daño, quebranto, fracaso: to come to ~, sufrir algún daño o fracaso; arruinarse.
**grievance** (grı·vans) s. agravio, ofensa, injusticia, motivo de queja, queja.
**grieve (to)** (grıv) tr. afligir, apesadumbrar, oprimir. 2 llorar, lamentar. 3 intr. afligirse, dolerse.
**grievingly** (-ingli) adj. apesaradamente.
**grievous** (-øs) adj. doloroso, aflictivo, penoso, sensible. 2 lastimoso, lastimero. 3 gravoso, oneroso. 4 fiero, cruel, atroz.
**griffin** (gri·fin) s. MIT. grifo.
**griffon** (gri·føn) s. GRIFFIN. 2 perro de cierta raza.
**grig** (grig) s. ENT. grillo; saltamontes. 2 ICT. anguila pequeña. 3 persona vivaracha.
**grill** (gril) s. COC. parrillas. 2 asado hecho en parrillas. 3 GRILLROOM.
**grill (to)** tr. asar en parrillas. 2 fig. atormentar. 3 intr. asarse.
**grillade** (grilei·d) s. manjar asado en parrillas.
**grillage** (gri·lidǳ) s. emparrillado, zampeado.
**grille** (gril) s. verja, reja.
**grillroom** (gri·lrum) s. restaurante o comedor de hotel especializado en los asados a la parrilla.
**grilse** (grils) s. salmón joven.
**grim** (grim) adj. torvo, ceñudo. 2 feo, horrendo. 3 horrible, siniestro. 4 inflexible, implacable.
**grimace** (grimei·s) s. mueca, mohín, visaje, gesto.
**grimace (to)** intr. hacer muecas o visajes.
**grimalkin** (grimæ·lkin) s. gatazo; gata vieja. 2 vieja malévola.
**grime** (graim) s. tizne, mugre, porquería.
**grime (to)** tr. tiznar, ensuciar.
**grimy** (-i) adj. tiznado, sucio, mugriento.
**grin** (grin) s. mueca de dolor o de cólera. 2 sonrisa burlona, forzada o estúpida.
**grin (to)** intr. hacer muecas mostrando los dientes. 2 sonreír con toda la boca; con complacencia, burla o sarcasmo.
**grind** (graind) s. molienda, trituración. 2 fam. trabajo o estudio continuado. 3 fam. empollón.
**grind (to)** tr. moler, pulverizar, triturar. 2 afilar, amolar. 3 gastar [con el roce]; bruñir, deslus-

trar, esmerilar. 4 hacer rechinar [los dientes]. 5 molestar, oprimir, agobiar. 6 mover [con manubrio]. 7 intr. moler. 8 ser molido o afilado. 9 pulirse [con el roce]. 10 trabajar duramente; estudiar con ahinco. ¶ Pret. y p. p.: ground.
**grinder** (-øᵗ) s. molendero, moledor. 2 amolador. 3 pulidor, esmerilador. 4 molino, molinillo. 5 muela [de amolar]. 6 torno de pulir. 7 ANAT. muela.
**grindstone** (-stoun) s. muela, amoladera, piedra de afilar.
**gringo** (gri·ngou) s. desp. gringo.
**grip** (grip) s. empuñamiento, agarro, presa. 2 capacidad de agarrar y retener; de comprender. 3 poder, dominio. 4 asidero, puño, mango. 5 (E.U.) maletín. 6 MED. gripe. 7 to come to grips, luchar a brazo partido.
**grip (to)** tr. agarrar, asir, apretar, empuñar, sujetar. 2 intr. agarrarse. 3 absorber la atención. ¶ Pret. y p. p.: gripped o gript; ger.: gripping.
**gripe** (graip) s. agarro, asimiento. 2 garras, poder, sujeción. 3 mango, puño, manija. 4 MEC. grapa, mordaza. 5 pl. dolor, cólico, retortijones. 6 VET. torozón.
**gripe (to)** tr. TO GRIP 1. 2 punzar; afligir, oprimir. 3 pop. fastidiar, molestar. 4 dar retortijones. 5 MEC. morder. 6 intr. padecer retortijones. 7 sacar dinero. 8 pop. refunfuñar.
**griper** (grai·pøᵗ) s. fam. usurero.
**grippe** (grip) s. MED. gripe.
**gripping** (gri·ping) adj. muy conmovedor o interesante [drama, novela, etc.].
**gripsack** (gri·psæk) s. (E.U.) maletín.
**gript** (gript) p. p. de TO GRIP.
**grisly** (gri·ṡli) adj. espantoso, horroroso, terrible. 2 torvo.
**grist** (grist) s. molienda [cantidad de grano]. 2 provisión [para una ocasión].
**gristle** (gri·søl) s. cartílago, ternilla.
**gristly** (gri·sli) s. cartilaginoso.
**grit** (grit) s. arena, guijo fino. 2 arenisca silícea, asperón. 3 firmeza, entereza, tesón; ánimo, valentía. 4 pl. sémola, farro.
**gritty** (gri·ti) adj. arenisco. 2 animoso, esforzado.
**grizzle** (gri·ṡøl) s. color gris. 2 cabellos grises.
**grizzle (to)** tr.-intr. poner o volverse gris.
**grizzled** (gri·ṡøld) adj. canoso. 2 tordillo.
**grizzly** (gri·ṡli) adj. grisáceo, pardusco: ~ bear, oso pardo.
**groan** (groun) s. gemido, quejido.
**groan (to)** intr. gemir, quejarse, ayear.
**groaning** (-ing) s. GROAN.
**groat** (grout) s. ant. moneda de cuatro peniques. 2 pl. grano quebrantado; farro, sémola.
**grocer** (grou·søᵗ) s. especiero, abacero; *pulpero, *bodeguero: grocer's shop, abacería, tienda de comestibles o ultramarinos; *pulpería, *bodega.
**grocery** (-ri) s. comestibles, ultramarinos; comercio de ellos. 2 (E.U.) abacería, *pulpería.
**grog** (grag) s. grog. 2 bebida alcohólica.
**groggy** (gra·gi) adj. calamocano. 2 DEP. vacilante, atontado.
**groin** (groin) s. ANAT. ingle. 2 ARQ. arista de encuentro. 3 espolón, malecón.
**groin (to)** tr. ARQ. formar aristas de encuentro.
**groined** (groind) adj. de arista [arco, etc.].
**grommet** (gra·mit) s. anillo de cuerda. 2 ojete metálico.
**groom** (grum) s. novio, desposado. 2 caballerizo, mozo de cuadra, palafrenero; lacayo.

**groom (to)** *tr.* cuidar, almohazar [caballos]. *2* fam. vestir, componer, asear.

**groomsman** (-smæn) *s.* padrino de boda.

**groove** (gruv) *s.* ranura, gárgol, rebajo. *2* estría, surco. *3* carril, rodera. *4* fig. rutina, hábito arraigado.

**groove (to)** *tr.* acanalar, estriar, hacer ranuras o surcos en.

**grooved** (gru·vd) *adj.* acanalado, estriado.

**grope (to)** (group) *tr.-intr.* tentar; andar a tientas: *to ~ for,* buscar a tientas, tentando.

**gros** (grous) *s.* TEJ. gro.

**grosbeak** (grou·sbɪk) *s.* nombre de varios pájaros.

**grosgrain** (grou·grein) *s.* GROS.

**gross** (grous) *adj.* grueso. *2* denso, espeso. *3* grosero, tosco, basto, vulgar. *4* obsceno. *5* craso, enorme: ~ *error,* error craso. *6* lerdo, estúpido. *7* COM. total; bruto [sin deducciones]. *8* ~ *ton,* tonelada de 2.240 libras (1.016,06 kg.). *9* *s.* gruesa [doce docenas]. *10* grueso [la mayor parte], totalidad, conjunto: *in ~, in the ~,* en grueso, por junto.

**grossly** (grou·sly) *adv.* en bruto. *2* crasamente; toscamente, groseramente. *3* aproximadamente.

**grot** (grat) *s.* gruta.

**grotesque** (grote·sk) *adj.* grotesco, extravagante. *2* *adj.-s.* B. ART. grotesco, grutesco.

**grotto** (gra·tou) *s.* gruta, cueva.

**grouch** (grauch) *s.* fam. enojo, mal humor. *2* fam. gruñón, cascarrabias.

**grouch (to)** *intr.* fam. gruñir, refunfuñar.

**ground** (graund) *s.* tierra, suelo, piso: *to fall to the ~,* caer al suelo; venirse abajo, fracasar. *2* terreno: *to stand,* o *hold one's ground,* mantenerse firme. *3* MAR. tierra, fondo: *to take the ~,* encallar. *4* campo, región, territorio. *5* B. ART. campo, fondo. *6* PERSP. término. *7* tema, materia, base, fundamento, pie, razón, motivo: *on the ~ of,* con motivo de, por razón de. *8* campo de batalla. *9* ELECT. tierra. *10* *pl.* terrenos, recinto [de una finca o edificio]. *11* campo, cancha [de juego]. *12* poso, sedimento.

*13 adj.* de tierra, del suelo, etc.: ~ *floor,* bajos, piso bajo; ~ *lead,* ELECT. hilo de tierra; ~ *plot,* solar, parcela; ~ *rent,* censo; ~ *sea,* ~ *swell,* MAR. mar de fondo. *14* BOT. ~ *cherry,* alquequenje; ~ *pine,* pinillo. *Pret. y p. p.* de TO GRIND.

**ground (to)** *tr.* fundamentar, cimentar, establecer, basar, apoyar, vincular. *2* poner en tierra. *3* ELECT. conectar con tierra. *4* *intr.* basarse, fundamentarse. *5* descender al suelo. *6* MAR. encallar, varar.

**groundless** (-lis) *adj.* infundado, inmotivado, gratuito.

**groundling** (-ling) *s.* persona de poca cultura. *2* planta enana o rastrera.

**groundnut** (-nøt) *s.* BOT. chufa. *2* BOT. cacahuete.

**groundsel** (-sel) *s.* BOT. hierba cana, zuzón. *2* GROUNDSILL.

**groundwork** (-uøᵏk) *s.* cimiento, fundamento; base. *2* firme [de carretera].

**group** (grup) *s.* grupo, agrupación, conjunto.

**group (to)** *tr.* agrupar. *2* *intr.* agruparse.

**grouper** (gru·pøᵣ) *s.* ICT. mero.

**grouse** (graus) *s.* ORN. nombre de varias gallináceas silvestres, como el urogallo, el lagópodo o perdiz blanca, -la ortega, etc. *2* fam. queja, refunfuño.

**grouse (to)** *intr.* fam. (Ingl.) quejarse, refunfuñar.

**grout** (graut) *s.* farro. *2* lechada. *3* *pl.* poso, heces.

**grove** (grouv) *s.* bosquecillo, soto, arboleda.

**grovel (to)** (grø·vøl) *intr.* arrastrarse. *2* rebajarse servilmente. *3* hundirse [en lo vil o bajo].

**grovel (l) er** (grø·vløᵣ) *s.* persona servil, rastrera.

**grovel(l)ing** (-ling) *adj.* servil, rastrero.

**grow (to)** (grou) *intr.* crecer, desarrollarse, formarse, producirse. *2* nacer, salir [el pelo, las plantas, etc.]. *3* nacer, proceder, provenir. *4* aumentar, progresar, extenderse. *5* ponerse, volverse, convertirse en: *to ~ better,* ponerse mejor, mejorar; *to ~ dark,* oscurecer, anochecer; *to ~ fat,* engordar; *to ~ late,* hacerse tarde; *to ~ old,* envejecer. *6 to ~ into fashion,* ponerse de moda; *to ~ out of fashion,* pasar de moda, caer en desuso. *7 to ~ on* o *upon,* hacerse más fuerte en uno [un hábito, pasión, sensación, etc.]. *8 to ~ out of,* nacer de; perder, pasársele a uno [un hábito, un sentimiento, etc.]. *9 to ~ to,* llegar a [amar, odiar, etc.]; arraigarse en.

*10 tr.* cultivar, criar, producir. *11* salirle a uno o dejarse uno [la barba, el bigote]. ¶ *Pret.: grew;* *p. p.: grown.*

**grower** (-øᵣ) *adj.* cultivador, criador.

**growing** (-ing) *adj.* creciente. *2* que crece, que está en la edad de crecer. *3* de crecimiento. *4* *s.* crecimiento, desarrollo. *5* cría, cultivo.

**growl** (graul) *s.* gruñido. *2* refunfuño. *3* RUMBLE 1.

**growl (to)** *intr.* gruñir. *2* refunfuñar. *3* TO RUMBLE 1.

**growler** (-øᵣ) *s.* perro gruñidor. *2* gruñón, regañón.

**grown** (groun) *p. p.* de TO GROW. *2* *adj.* crecido, espigado, desarrollado; adulto. *3* cubierto [de hierba, maleza, etc.].

**grown-up** *adj.-s.* adulto, mayor [persona].

**growth** (grouz) *s.* crecimiento, desarrollo. *2* producción, cultivo. *3* vegetación, lo que crece o ha crecido. *4* acrecentamiento, aumento. *5* producto, resultado. *6* tumor, excrecencia. *7* estatura completa.

**grub** (grøb) *s.* larva, gusano, coco. *2* azacán. *3* persona desaliñada. *4* pop. comida, alimento.

**grub (to)** *tr.* rozar, desyerbar, desmalezar; cavar. *2* arrancar, descuajar. *3* limpiar de gusanos; descocar. *4* pop. alimentar. *5* *intr.* alimentarse. *6* trabajar en oficios bajos. ¶ *Pret. y p. p.: grubbed;* p. a.: *-bbing.*

**grubby** (-bi) *adj.* gusaniento. *2* sucio, roñoso.

**grudge** (grødy) *s.* resentimiento, rencor, inquina, mala voluntad.

**grudge (to)** *tr.* regatear, escatimar, dar de mala gana. *2* envidiar [una cosa].

**grudgingly** (-ingli) *adv.* de mala gana.

**gruel** (gru·øl) *s.* gachas o puches claros.

**gruesome** (gru·søm) *adj.* horrible, horripilante. *2* repugnante.

**gruff** (grøf) *adj.* rudo, brusco, áspero, malhumorado. *2* bronca [voz].

**grumble** (grø·mbøl) *s.* refunfuño, rezongo, queja. *2* ruido sordo.

**grumble (to)** *intr.* refunfuñar, rezongar, quejarse. *2* roncar [un animal]. *3* producir un ruido sordo.

**grumbler** (grø·mbløᵣ) *s.* refunfuñón, rezongador, descontento.

**grume** (grum) *s.* grumo, cuajarón; masa viscosa.

**grumous** (gru·møs) *adj.* grumoso.

**grumpy** (grø·mpi) *adj.* gruñón, malhumorado.

**grunt** (grønt) *s.* gruñido. *2* ICT. nombre de un pez americano.

**grunt (to)** *intr.* gruñir.

**grunter** (-øᵣ) *s.* gruñón. *2* ZOOL. cerdo.

**gruntling** (-ling) *s.* lechón, cochinillo.

**guaco** (gua·kou) *s.* BOT. guaco.

**Guadeloupe** (guadølu·p) *n. pr.* Guadalupe.

**guaiac** (gua·iæk), **guaiacum** (-iakøm) s. BOT. guacayo, guacayán. 2 resina de guacayo.
**guanaco** (guana·kou) s. ZOOL. guanaco.
**guano** (gua·nou) s. guano.
**guarantee** (gærantı·) s. persona de quien otra sale fiadora. 2 garantía, fianza. 3 garante, fiador.
**guarantee (to)** tr. garantizar, garantir. 2 salir fiador, responder o dar fianza por.
**guarantor** (gæ·rantø^r) s. garante, fiador.
**guaranty** (-ti) s. garantía [acción]. 2 garantía, fianza, prenda. 3 garante, fiador.
**guaranty (to)** tr. TO GUARANTEE.
**guard** (ga^rd) s. guardia [estado de defensa o precaución]: on ~, on one's ~, alerta, sobre aviso; en guardia; off one's ~, desprevenido. 2 guardia, guardia, vigilancia, custodia, protección. 3 guarda, gurrdián, custodio, vigilante, centinela. 4 guardia [cuerpo; individuo de él]. 5 MIL., ESGR. guardia. 6 guarnición de una espada, un vestido]. 7 arandela [de lanza]. 8 cadena [de reloj]. 9 guardamonte [de fusil]. 10 salvavidas [de tranvía]. 11 FERROC. (Ingl.) revisor; (E.U.) guardafrenos.
**guard (to)** tr. guardar, proteger, defender, resguardar. 2 custodiar, vigilar. 3 intr. guardarse, estar prevenido.
**guarded** (-id) adj. defendido, protegido. 2 cauteloso, cauto, precavido.
**guardedness** (-nis) s. cautela, precaución, circunspección.
**guardian** (ga·^rdian) s. guardián, guarda, custodio. 2 DER. tutor o curador. 3 adj. ~ angel, ángel custodio o de la guarda.
**guardianship** (-ship) s. protección, amparo, guarda, custodia. 2 DER. tutela, curadoría.
**guardrail** (ga·^rdreil) s. barandilla. 3 FERROC. contracarril.
**guardroom** (-rum) s. MIL. cuerpo de guardia. 2 MIL. prevención.
**guardsman** (-śmæn) s. militar de uno de los cuerpos llamados guardia.
**guava** (gua·va) s. BOT. guayabo; guayaba.
**gubernatorial** (giubø^rnato·rial) adj. gubernativo. 2 del gobernador.
**gudgeon** (gø·dɥøn) s. ICT. gobio. 2 bobo, fácil de engañar. 3 ganga, chiripa. 4 MEC. gorrón, muñón, cuello de eje. 6 MAR. hembra del timón.
**gudgeon (to)** tr. engañar, estafar.
**Guelf, Guelph** (gwelf) s. güelfo.
**guerdon** (gø·^rdøn) s. galardón, premio.
**guer(r)illa** (gueri·l) s. guerrillero. 2 guerrilla, guerra de guerrillas.
**guess** (ges) s. conjetura, suposición; cosa que se piensa o dice tratando de adivinar.
**guess (to)** tr. conjeturar, barruntar, suponer; adivinar o tratar de adivinar. 2 fam. pensar, creer.
**guesser** (ge·sø^r) s. conjeturador, adivinador.
**guesswork** (-uø^rk) s. conjetura: by ~, por conjeturas.
**guest** (gest) s. huésped [pers. alojada]; forastero, visita, invitado. 2 pensionista, inquilino. 3 ZOOL. huésped.
**guffaw** (gøfo) s. risotada, carcajada.
**guffaw (to)** intr. reír a carcajadas o groseramente.
**Guiana** (gaiæø) n. pr. GEOGR. Guayana.
**guidance** (gai·dans) s. guía, gobierno, dirección: for your ~, para su gobierno.
**guide** (gaid) s. guía [pers. o cosa que guía], norte. 2 guía [libro]. 3 MEC. guía, guiadera. 4 MIL. guía. 5 pauta, patrón.

**guide (to)** tr. guiar. | No tiene el sentido de guiar un coche. 2 dirigir, gobernar. 3 encaminar.
**guideboard** (gai·dbo^rd) s. letrero indicador.
**guidebook** (gai·dbuk) s. guía de turismo.
**guideless** (gai·dlis) adj. sin guía. 2 sin gobierno.
**guidepost** (gai·dpoust) s. guía, poste indicador.
**guidon** (gai·døn) s. MIL. banderín.
**guild** (gild) s. gremio, cofradía, asociación.
**guilder** (gi·ldø^r) s. GULDEN.
**guildhall** (gi·dljol) s. casa de un gremio. 2 casa del Ayuntamiento.
**guile** (gail) s. astucia, artificio, dolo, maña.
**guileful** (gai·lful) adj. artificioso, doloso, engañoso.
**guileless** (gai·lis) adj. sencillo, cándido, sincero.
**guillemot** (gi·limot) s. ORN. pájaro niño.
**guillotine** (gi·lotin) s. guillotina.
**guillotine (to)** tr. guillotinar.
**guilt** (gilt) s. culpa, delito, crimen, pecado. 2 culpabilidad.
**guiltless** (gi·ltlis) adj. inocente, libre de culpa; puro, sin mancha. 2 ignorante [de algo].
**guilty** (-i) adj. culpable, reo; delincuente.
**guimpe** (gimp) s. COST. canesú.
**Guinea** (gi·ni) n. pr. GEOGR. Guinea.
**guinea** s. guinea [moneda]. 2 ORN. ~ fowl, ~ hen, gallina de Guinea. 3 ZOOL. ~ pig, conejillo de Indias, cobayo.
**guise** (gaiš) s. guisa, modo, manera. 2 apariencia, disfraz; capa, pretexto: under the ~ of, so capa de.
**guitar** (gita·^r) s. MÚS. guitarra.
**gulch** (gølch) s. (E.U.) quebrada, barranca.
**gulden** (gu·ldøn) s. guilden.
**gules** (giulš) s. BLAS. gules.
**gulf** (gølf) s. GEOGR. golfo: Gulf Stream, corriente del Golfo de Méjico. 2 sima, abismo, vorágine.
**gulfweed** (-uid) s. BOT. sargazo.
**gull** (gøl) s. ORN. gaviota. 2 incauto, primo. 3 engaño, timo.
**gull (to)** tr. engañar, estafar, timar.
**gullet** (gø·lit) s. gaznate. 2 esófago. 3 zanja.
**gullibility** (gølibi·liti) s. tragaderas, credulidad.
**gullible** (gø·libøl) adj. incauto, bobo, crédulo.
**gully** (gø·li) s. cárcava, barranca, hondonada.
**gully (to)** tr. excavar, formar canal.
**gulp** (gølp) s. acción de tragar, contracción de la garganta. 2 trago, engullida.
**gulp (to)** tr. [gralte. con down] tragar, engullir. 2 reprimir [las lágrimas], ahogar [un sollozo].
**gum** (gøm) s. ANAT. encía. 2 goma [substancia]: ~ arabic, goma arábiga; ~ elastic, goma elástica; ~ resin, gomorresina. 3 árbol que da goma. 4 (E.U.) chanclo de goma.
**gun (to)** tr. engomar. ¶ Pret. y p. p.: gummed; ger.: gumming.
**gumboil** (-boil) s. flemón, párulis.
**gumdrop** (-drap) s. pastilla de goma.
**gummiferous** (gømi·førøs) adj. gomífero.
**gummous** (gø·møs), **gummy** (-i) adj. gomoso, viscoso.
**gump** (gømp) s. pop. tonto, majadero.
**gumption** (gø·mshøn) s. fam. perspicacia, sentido común. 2 fam. empuje, iniciativa.
**gun** (gøn) s. ARTILL. cañón: ~ carriage, cureña, afuste. 2 fusil, escopeta, carabina, tercerola: ~ barrel, cañón de fusil, escopeta, etc. 3 (E.U.) pistola revólver. 4 cañonazo [de salva o señal]. 5 tubo o jeringa. 6 tirador [pers.].
**gun (to)** tr. fam. hacer fuego sobre. 2 intr. cazar

con escopeta o fusil: *to ~ for*, ir a la caza de. ¶
Pret. y p. p.: *gunned;* ger.: *gunning.*
**gunboat** (-bout) *s.* cañonero [embarcación].
**guncotton** (-katøn) *s.* algodón pólvora.
**gunlock** (-lak) *s.* llave de fusil.
**gunman** (-mæn) *s.* (E.U.) pistolero.
**gunnel** (-nøl) *s.* MAR. GUNWALE.
**gunner** (-ø$^r$) *s.* artillero. *2* MAR. condestable. *3* cazador.
**gunnery** (-øri) *s.* artillería.
**gunning** (-ing) *s.* caza con escopeta.
**gunny** (-i) *s.* yute; saco de yute.
**gunpowder** (-paudø$^r$) *s.* pólvora.
**gunshot** (-shat) *s.* tiro de fusil, balazo, escopetazo. *2* tiro, alcance del fusil: *within ~*, a tiro de fusil.
**gunsmith** (-smiz) *s.* armero [pers.].
**gunwale** (-ueil) *s.* MAR. borda, regala.
**gurgitation** (gø$^r$ÿite·shøn) *s.* hervor, agitación.
**gurgle** (gø·$^r$gøl) *s.* borboteo; gorgoteo. *2* gorjeo [del niño].
**gurgle (to)** *intr.* borbotar; gorgotear. *2* gorjear [el niño].
**gurnard** (gø·$^r$na$^r$d), **gurnet** (gø·$^r$nit) *s.* ICT. rubio, escarcho; golondrina: *flying ~*, milano.
**gush** (gøsh) *s.* chorro, borbollón, borbotón. *2* efusión, extremo.
**gush (to)** *tr.* echar, derramar a chorros. *2 intr.* brotar, manar a borbotones. *3* hacer extremos, ser extremoso.
**gushing** (-ing) *adj.* extremoso.
**gusset** (gø·sit) *s.* COST. escudete, cuchillo. *2* ARM. gocete. *3* MEC. palomilla de refuerzo.
**gust** (gøst) *s.* ráfaga, racha. *2* chubasco. *3* explosión, acceso, arrebato.
**gustative** (-ativ), **gustatory** (gø·statori) *adj.* gustativo.
**gusto** (-ou) *s.* gusto, placer, afición [con que se hace una cosa].
**gusty** (-ti) *adj.* borrascoso. *2* impetuoso, explosivo.
**gut** (gøt) *s.* vulg. intestino, tripa. *2* cuerda de tripa. *3* estrecho, desfiladero. *4 pl.* pop. tripas, bandullo. *5* pop. valor, agallas.
**gut (to)** *tr.* destripar, desentrañar.
**gutta-percha** (gø·ta-pø$^r$cha) *s.* gutapercha.

**gutter** (gø·tø$^r$) *s.* arroyo [de la calle]. *2* albollón. *3* canal, canalón [de un tejado]. *4* surco que hacen las aguas llovedizas. *5* badén, cuneta. *6* zanja. *7* surco, acanaladura.
**gutter·(to)** *tr.* acanalar. *2* poner canalones, etc. *3 intr.* correr, gotear. *4* correrse [una vela].
**guttersnipe** (-snaip) *s.* pilluelo, golfillo.
**guttiferous** (gøti·førøs) *adj.* BOT. gutífero.
**guttle (to)** (gø·tøl) *tr.-intr.* comer, engullir.
**guttural** (gø·tøral) *adj.* gutural.
**Guy** (gai) *n. pr. m.* Guido.
**guy** *s.* tirante, viento; retenida. *2* desp. tipo, individuo. *3* fam. adefesio, mamarracho.
**guy (to)** *tr.* sujetar con vientos o retenida. *2* fam. burlarse, hacer mofa de.
**guzzle (to)** (gø·šøl) *tr.-intr.* beber mucho. *2 intr.* ser muy bebedor.
**guzzler** (gø·šlø$^r$) *s.* bebedor, borrachín.
**gymnasium** (dÿimnei·ÿøm) *s.* gimnasio.
**gymnast** (dÿi·mnæst) *s.* gimnasta.
**gymnastic(al** (dÿimnæ·stik(al) *adj.* gimnástico.
**gymnastics** (dÿimnæ·stiks) *s.* gimnasia, gimnástica.
**gymnosperm** (dÿi·mnospø$^r$m) *s.* BOT. gimnosperma.
**gymnospermous** (dÿi·mnospø$^r$møs) *adj.* BOT. gimnospermo.
**gynaeceum, gynaecium** (dÿainisi·øm) *s.* gineceo.
**gynaecologist, gynecologist** (dÿainika·lodÿist) *s.* ginecólogo.
**gynaecology, gynecology** (-dÿi) *s.* ginecología.
**gypseous** (dÿi·psiøs), **gypsine** (-sin) *adj.* yesoso.
**gypsum** (dÿi·psøm) *s.* yeso, aljez.
**gypsy** (dÿi·psi) *adj.-s.* gitano, bohemio, cíngaro.
**gyrate (to)** (dÿai·reit) *intr.* girar [dar vueltas].
**gyration** (-ei·shøn) *s.* giro, vuelta, rotación, revolución.
**gyratory** (dÿai·ratori) *s.* giratorio, de rotación.
**gyre** (dÿai·ø$^r$) *s.* GYRATION.
**gyrfalcon** (dÿø·$^r$folkøn) *s.* GERFALCON.
**gyroscope** (dÿai·roskoup) *s.* giroscopio.
**gyrostat** (dÿai·rostæt) *s.* giróstato.
**gyrostatics** (dÿairostæ·tiks) *s.* girostática.
**gyve (to)** (dÿaiv) *tr.* encadenar, apiolar.
**gyves** (-s) *s. pl.* grillos.

**H, h** (eich) *s.* H, h, octava letra del alfabeto inglés.
**ha** (ja) *interj.* ¡ah! *2 ha, ha!,* ¡ja, ja!
**haberdasher** (jæ·bøʳdæshøʳ) *s.* mercero, camisero; comerciante que vende artículos para caballero.
**haberdashery** (-i) *s.* mercería; camisería; tienda de artículos para caballero.
**habergeon** (jæ·bøʳdȳøn) *s.* cota de malla.
**habiliment** (jabi·limønt) *s.* vestido, traje, ropa.
**habit** (jæ·bit) *s.* hábito, vestido: *riding ~,* traje de amazona. *2* hábito, costumbre, uso, vicio: *to be in the ~ of,* soler, acostumbrar. *4* condición, constitución, complexión. *5* H. NAT. hábito.
**habit (to)** *tr.* vestir, ataviar.
**habitable** (-abøl) *adj.* habitable.
**habitant** (-ant) *s.* habitante, morador.
**habitat** (jæ·bitat) *s.* H. NAT. habitación.
**habitation** (-ei·shøn) *s.* habitación, morada.
**habitual** (jabi·chual) *adj.* habitual; acostumbrado.
**habituate (to)** (-cheuit) *tr.* habituar, acostumbrar.
**habitude** (jæ·bitiud) *s.* hábito, costumbre. *2* disposición, actitud habitual.
**habitué** (jabichuei·) *s.* concurrente, habitual.
**hack** (jæk) *s.* caballo de alquiler. *2* rocín, jamelgo. *3* coche de alquiler, simón. *4* alquilón; escritor o literato a sueldo. *5* azacán, peón. *6* hacha, cuchilla, pico. *7* corte, tajo, muesca. *8* tos seca. *9 adj.* alquiladizo. *10* trillado, gastado. *11* de cortar o picar.
**hack (to)** *tr.* tajar, cortar, picar. *2* alquilar [un coche, etc.]. *3* toser con tos seca. *4* alquilarse, venderse. *6* escribir artículos, etc., mal pagados. *7* ir a caballo.
**hackberry** (-beri) *s.* almez. *2* BOT. almeza.
**hackle** (-øl) *s.* rastrillo [para el lino, etc.]. *2* pluma del cuello de un ave. *3* mosca para pescar.
**hackle (to)** *tr.* rastrillar [lino, cáñamo]. *2* tajar, cortar, estropear a tajos.
**hackman** (-mæn) *s.* cochero de punto.
**hackney** (-ni) *s.* caballo corriente, jaca, cuartago. *2* coche de alquiler. *3* alquilón, azacán. *4 adj.* alquilado, de alquiler: *~ coach,* coche de punto; *~ writer,* escritor a sueldo. *3* común, trillado.
**hackney (to)** *tr.* gastar, hacer común, trillado.
**hackneyed** (-nid) *adj.* gastado, trillado, manoseado.
**had** (jæd) *pret.* y *p. p.* de TO HAVE.
**haddock** (jæ·døk) *s.* ICT. pez semejante al bacalao.

**hade** (jeid) *s.* GEOL., MIN. buzamiento.
**Hades** (jei·diš) *s.* MIT. Hades.
**Hadrian** (jei·drian) *n. pr. m.* Adriano.
**hae-,** HE-.
**haft** (jaft) *s.* mango, puño.
**haft (to)** *tr.* poner mango o puño a.
**hag** (jæg) *s.* bruja vieja. *2* bruja, hechicera.
**haggard** (jæ·gaʳd) *adj.* macilento, ojeroso, trasnochado, demacrado; fatigado, angustiado. *2* arañero [halcón].
**haggish** (jæ·gish) *adj.* de bruja.
**haggle** (jæ·gøl) *s.* altercado, disputa. *2* regateo.
**haggle (to)** *tr.* tajar, cortar toscamente. *2 intr.* altercar, disputar. *3* regatear [discutir un precio].
**hagiographer** (jædȳia·graføʳ) *s.* hagiógrafo.
**hagiography** (-grafi) *s.* hagiografía.
**hagiolatry** (-latri) *s.* culto de los santos.
**Hague (The)** (jeg) *n. pr.* GEOGR. La Haya.
**hah** (ja) *interj.* HA.
**haik** (jeik) *s.* jaique.
**hail** (jeil) *s.* granizo, pedrisco, piedra. *2* granizada. *3* saludo; grito, llamada: *within ~,* al alcance de la voz; MAR. al habla. *4 interj.* ¡ave!, ¡salve!, ¡salud!: *Hail Mary,* Ave María.
**hail (to)** *intr.-tr.* granizar. *2 tr.* saludar, aclamar. *3* llamar, vocear. *4 intr. to ~ from,* venir, proceder de.
**hail-fellow** o **hail fellow** *adj.-s.* amigo, compañero íntimo.
**hailstone** (-stoun) *s.* piedra de granizo.
**hailstorm** (-stoʳm) *s.* granizada, pedrisco.
**hair** (je·øʳ) *s.* cabello, pelo, vello; cabellos, cabellera; *~ dye,* tintura para el pelo; *~ net,* redecilla, albanega; *~ shirt,* cilicio; *head of ~,* cabellera, mata de pelo; *to split hairs,* sutilizar demasiado; pararse en quisquillas; *not to turn a ~,* no inmutarse; quedarse tan fresco; *against the ~,* a contrapelo; *to a ~,* con la mayor exactitud. *2* pelo, hebra, filamento. *3* tejido de pelo. *4* pelo [de un arma de fuego].
**hairbreadth** (-bredz) grueso de un cabello; casi nada: *to have a ~ escape,* escapar por un pelo, librarse de milagro.
**hairbrush** (-brøsh) *s.* cepillo para el pelo.
**haircloth** (-cloz) *s.* tela de crin. *2* cilicio.
**haircut** (-cøt) *s.* corte de pelo.
**hairdo** (-du) *s.* peinado, tocado.

**hairdresser** (-dresǿ<sup>r</sup>) s. peluquero. 2 peluquera, peinadora.

**haired** (-d) adj. cabelludo, peludo. 2 de pelo: *curly-haired*, de pelo rizado o crespo.

**hairless** (-lis) adj. pelón, calvo, lampiño.

**hairpin** (-pin) s. horquilla [para el pelo].

**hair-raising** adj. espeluznante, horripilante.

**hairsplitting** (-pliting) adj. demasiado sutil, que sutiliza demasiado. 2 s. sutileza excesiva.

**hairspring** (-spring) s. espiral [de un reloj].

**hairy** (-i) adj. cabelludo, peludo, velloso, velludo, hirsuto.

**Haiti** (jei·ti) n. pr. GEOGR. Haití.

**Haitian** (jei·tian) adj.-s. haitiano.

**hake** (jeik) s. ICT. merluza, pescada.

**halation** (jeilei·shøn) s. FOT. halo.

**halberd** (jæ·lbø<sup>r</sup>d) s. alabarda.

**halberdier** (jælbø<sup>r</sup>di·ø<sup>r</sup>) s. alabardero [soldado].

**halcyon** (jæ·lsiøn) adj. apacible, sereno, tranquilo. 2 s. ORN. alción, martín pescador.

**hale** (jeil) adj. sano, fuerte, robusto.

**hale (to)** tr. halar, tirar de, arrastrar.

**half** (jæf o jaf) s. mitad: *(the) ~ of*, la mitad de; *by ~*, con mucho; *in ~*, por la mitad. 2 ARIT. medio [quebrado]. 3 DEP. parte [de un partido de fútbol]. 4 V. HALVES.
5 adj.-adv. medio, semi, casi; a medias: *a ~, ~a*, medio; *~ after* o *~ past*, [hablando de horas] y media: *~ after two*, las dos y media; *~ binding, ~ leather*, ENCUAD. media pasta; *~ brother*, medio hermano; *~ done*, medio hecho; medio cocido; *~ light*, media luz; *~ mesures*, medias tintas, paños calientes; *~ note*, MÚS. blanca; *~ time*, media jornada; media parte [en el fútbol]; *~ tone*, MÚS. semitono; B. ART. media tinta; fotograbado.

**half-and-half** adj. mitad y mitad. 2 adv. a medias, en partes iguales.

**half-back** (-bæk) s. FÚTBOL. *centre ~*, medio centro.

**half-baked** adj. a medio cocer, asar, hacer, etc. 2 incompleto. 3 poco juicioso, inexperto, tonto.

**half-blood** s. mestizo. 2 medio hermano o media hermana.

**half-bound** adj. encuadernado en pasta.

**half-breed** adj.-s. mestizo.

**half-caste** adj.-s. mestizo.

**halfcocked** (-kakt) adj. amartillado a medias.

**half-dead** adj. medio muerto.

**half-full** adj. mediado, lleno a medias.

**half-hearted** adj. frío, indiferente. 2 sin ánimo.

**half-length** adj. de medio cuerpo [retrato].

**half-mast** s. media asta: *at ~*, a media asta.

**half-mast (to)** tr. poner a media asta.

**half-moon** s. media luna. 2 adj. en figura de media luna.

**half-opened** adj. entreabierto.

**halfpence** (-pøns) s. pl. medios peniques.

**halfpenny** (-pøni) s. medio penique.

**half-seas over** adj. pop. achispado, entre dos velas.

**halftone** (-toun) s. media tinta. 2 fotograbado. 3 adj. a media tinta.

**half-truth** s. media verdad, verdad a medias.

**halfway** (-uei) adj. situado a mitad del camino, equidistante. 2 medio, incompleto, parcial. 3 adv. a medio camino, parcialmente [en parte]: *to meet ~*, partir la diferencia con; hacer o hacerse concesiones.

**half-witted** adj. tonto, simple, imbécil. 2 alocado.

**halibut** (jæ·libøt) s. ICT. especie de lenguado.

**hall** (jol) s. vestíbulo, zaguán, recibimiento, antecámara. 2 pasadizo, corredor. 3 salón, sala

[para reuniones, etc.]. 4 paraninfo [de universidad]. 5 edificio público. 6 casa señorial en el campo.

**hallelluia, hallelujah** (jælilu·ia) s. e interj. aleluya.

**halliard** (jæ·lia<sup>r</sup>d) s. HALYARD.

**hallmark** (jo·lma<sup>r</sup>k) s. marca del contraste.

**hallo, halloa** (jalou·) interj. ¡eh!, ¡hola!, ¡oiga!. 2 s. grito llamada.

**hallo, hallos (to)** intr. gritar *hallo* o *halloa*.

**halloo** (jalu) interj. voz para llamar la atención. 2 ¡sus!, ¡busca! [para azuzar a los perros].

**halloo (to)** tr. gritar, llamar. 2 perseguir o incitar a gritos, azuzar.

**hallooing** (-ing) s. grita, vocerío.

**hallow (to)** (jæ·lou) tr. santificar, consagrar, reverenciar.

**hallowed** (-d) adj. bendito, santo, sagrado.

**Hallowmas** (-mas) s. día de Todos los Santos.

**hallucinate (to)** (jæliu·sineit) tr. alucinar.

**hallucination** (-ei·shøn) s. alucinación.

**hallway** (jo·luei) s. (E.U.) vestíbulo; corredor.

**halo** (jei·lou) s. METEOR. halo. 2 halo, aureola, nimbo.

**halogen** (jæ·lodyøn) s. QUÍM. halógeno.

**haloid** (jæ·loid) adj. QUÍM. haloideo. 2 s. QUÍM. sal haloidea.

**halt** (jolt) s. alto, detención, parada. 2 cojera. 3 vacilación. 4 adj. cojo.

**halt (to)** intr. detenerse, parar, hacer alto. 2 cojear, renquear. 3 vacilar; tartamudear. 4 tr. detener, mandar hacer alto.

**1) halter** (-ø<sup>r</sup>) s. cabestro, ronzal, jáquima. 2 cuerda para ahorcar, dogal. 3 muerte en la horca.

**2) halter**, pl. **-teres** ENT. balancín [de díptero].

**halter (to)** tr. poner el cabestro, echar el ronzal a.

**halting** (-ing) adj. cojo, renqueante. 2 defectuoso. 3 vacilante.

**halve (to)** (jav) tr. partir en dos. 2 reducir a la mitad. 3 ser la mitad de.

**halves** (-š) s. pl. de HALF. 2 *to go halves*, ir a medias.

**halyard** (jæ·lia<sup>r</sup>d) s. MAR. driza.

**ham** (jæm) s. pernil, jamón. 2 ANAT. corva. 3 fam. (E.U.) aficionado [a la radio, etc.]. 4 fam. (E.U.) comicastro. 5 pl. fam. nalgas.

**hamadryad** (jæ·madraiæd) s. MIT. hamadríada.

**hamburger** (jæ·mbø<sup>r</sup>gø<sup>r</sup>) s. bocadillo de carne picada y frita.

**Hamburg steak** s. COC. biftec ruso.

**hames** (jeims) s. pl. horcate.

**Hamilcar** (jami·lka<sup>r</sup>) n. pr. m. Amílcar.

**Hamite** (jæ·mait) s. camita [descendiente de Cam].

**hamlet** (jæ·mlit) s. aldea, caserío.

**hammer** (jæ·mø<sup>r</sup>) s. martillo [herramienta]: *wood ~*, mazo. 2 macillo [del piano]. 3 pilón o maza [de martinete]. 4 gatillo, percutor [de arma de fuego]. 5 ANAT. martillo.

**hammer (to)** tr. martillar, golpear, batir. 2 forjar, repujar [metales]. 3 clavar [con martillo]. 4 meter, encajar [a golpes, a martillazos]. 5 *to ~ one's brains*, devanarse los sesos. 7 intr. martillar, dar golpes. 8 fig. trabajar, hacer esfuerzos reiterados; insistir.

**hammerhead** (-jed) s. ICT. pez martillo.

**hammering** (-ing) s. martilleo. 2 repujado.

**hammerless** (-lis) adj. sin martillo. 2 de percutor interior [arma].

**hammock** (jæ·møk) s. hamaca. 2 MAR. coy.

**hamper** (jæ·mpø<sup>r</sup>) s. cesta [con tapa]; cuevano, canasta. 2 traba, impedimento. 3 MAR. aparejo.

**hamper (to)** *tr.* estorbar, embarazar, enredar. *2* estropear [una cerradura, etc.].

**hamstring** (jæ·mstring) *s.* tendón de la corva.

**hamstring (to)** *tr.* desjarretar. *2* fig. debilitar. ¶ Pret. y p. p.: *hamstrung.*

**hanaper** (jæ·napøʳ) *s.* cestita para documentos, etc.

**hand** (jænd) *s.* mano [de pers.; posesión, poder, dominio, dirección; pers. que ejecuta una cosa]: *clean hands,* manos limpias, honradez; *to be ~ and glove* o *~ in glove,* ser uña y carne; *to get the upper ~,* llevar ventaja; dominar; *to have in ~,* tener o traer entre manos; *to have one's hands full,* estar muy ocupado; *to keep one's hands off,* no tocar; no intervenir en; *to put* o *set the ~ to* o *into,* meter mano a; principiar, emprender; *at ~, near at ~,* a mano, cerca; próximo a ocurrir, al llegar; *at the ~ of,* a manos de; de manos de [por obra de]; *by ~,* a mano, manualmente; *by the ~,* de la mano; *in ~,* asidos de la mano; juntos; *~ over head,* precipitadamente, inconsideradamente; *hands off,* ¡manos quedas!, ¡no tocar!; *hands up!,* ¡manos arriba!; *~ to ~,* cuerpo a cuerpo; *in ~,* contante [dinero]; en mano; *off ~,* sin preparación, en el acto; *on ~,* a mano, disponible; presente; *out of ~,* inmediatamente; terminado; desbocado; incontenible; *to ~,* en poder [de uno]; a la mano; *with a heavy ~,* con mano dura; *with a high ~,* sin miramientos; con arrogancia. *2* mano, parte, participación: *to have a ~ in,* tener mano o parte en. *3* mano, lado, parte: *right ~,* mano derecha, la derecha; *on all hands, on every ~,* por todas partes, por todos lados. *4* mano, habilidad, destreza: *to have a ~ for,* tener mano para. *5* persona hábil o diestra: *to be a good ~ at,* ser hábil o diestro en. *6* mano, auxilio, ayuda: *to bear* o *lend a ~,* echar una mano, dar la mano, ayudar. *7* letra [carácter de letra]. *8* letra, escritura [de una pers.], letra y puño. *9* firma: *under the ~ of,* firmado por. *10* aplauso. *11* mano [origen, fuente]: *at first ~,* de primera mano. *12* ZOOL. mano [de mono]; pinza [de crustáceo]. *13* manecilla, aguja [de reloj]. *14* IMPR. manecilla. *15* palmo menor. *16* NAIPES mano [lance entero]; juego [naipes de un jugador]; jugador; *to show one's ~,* fig. descubrir uno su juego. *17* obrero, peón. *18* MAR. marinero, tripulante: *all hands,* toda la tripulación; todo el mundo.

*19 adj.* de mano, manual, para la mano, etc.: *~ glass,* espejo de mano; lupa; *~ mill,* molinillo; *~ organ,* organillo, aristón.

**hand (to)** *tr.* dar, entregar, poner en manos de, pasar. *2* conducir, guiar por la mano. *3 to ~ down,* transmitir; pasar [de arriba abajo]. *4 to ~ in,* entregar, presentar. *5 to ~ out,* dar, distribuir. *6 to ~ over,* entregar, resignar. *7 to ~ up,* pasar [de abajo arriba].

**handbag** (-bæg) *s.* maletín. *2* bolso [de señora].

**handball** (-bol) *s.* pelota; juego de pelota a mano.

**handbarrow** (-bærou) *s.* angarillas, parihuelas. *2* carretilla de mano.

**handbill** (-bil) *s.* hoja suelta, anuncio [que se entrega a mano].

**handbook** (-buk) *s.* manual, guía [libro].

**handbreadth** (-bredz) *s.* palmo menor.

**handcart** (-kaʳt) *s.* carrito de mano.

**handcuff** (-køf) *s.* manilla. *2 pl.* manillas, esposas.

**handcuff (to)** *tr.* esposar, poner manillas a.

**handed** (-id) *adj.* que tiene mano; de mano, etc.: *left-handed,* zurdo; dado con la izquierda.

**handful** (-ful) *s.* manojo, puñado.

**handhold** (-jould) *s.* asidero.

**handicap** (-ikæp) *s.* DEP. handicap.

**handicap (to)** *tr.* DEP. handicapar. *2* estorbar, poner trabas a. ¶ Pret. y p. p.: *handicapped;* ger.: *handicapping.*

**handicraft** (-ikræft) *s.* oficio, arte mecánica. *2* ocupación o habilidad manual.

**handicraftsman** (-mæn) *s.* artesano, artífice.

**handily** (-ili) *adv.* diestramente. *2* cómodamente.

**handiwork** (-uøʳk) *s.* obra manual. *2* obra de las manos [de uno]. *3* labor, obra, hechura.

**handkerchief** (-køʳchif) *s.* pañuelo.

**handle** (jæ·ndøl) *s.* asa; asidero; astil, mango, manija; manubrio; puño [de bastón, paraguas, etc.]; tirador [de cajón, puerta, etc.]; *~ bar,* manillar, guía [de bicicleta]. *2* tacto [de una cosa].

**handle (to)** *tr.* tocar, manosear. *2* manejar, manipular, tratar. *3* gobernar, dirigir. *4* tratar, comerciar en. *5* poner mango a. *6 intr.* usar las manos. *7* manejarse, ser manejado [con facilidad, etc.].

**handless** (-lis) *adj.* manco, sin manos.

**handling** (-ling) *s.* toque, manoseo. *2* manejo, manipulación, trato. *3* gobierno, dirección.

**handmade** (jændmei·d) *adj.* hecho a mano.

**handmaid** (jæ·ndmeid), **handmaiden** (-meidøn) *s.* criada, sirvienta.

**hand-me-down** *adj.* fam. hecho, de confección; barato; poco elegante [ropa, vestido, etc.].

**handrail** (jæ·ndreil) *s.* barandal, pasamano.

**handsaw** (jæ·ndso) *s.* serrucho, sierra de mano.

**handsel** (jæ·ndsøl) *s.* estreno. *2* aguinaldo. *3* prenda, señal, arras.

**handsel (to)** *tr.* estrenar. *2* dar aguinaldo. *3* ser el primero en probar o tener conocimiento de [una cosa]. ¶ Pret. y p. p.: *handseled* o *-selled;* ger.: *-seling* o *-selling.*

**handset** (jæ·ndset) *s.* TELEF. microteléfono.

**handshake** (jæ·ndsheik) *s.* apretón de manos.

**handsome** (jæ·nsøm) *adj.* hermoso, elegante, primoroso. *2* guapo, bien parecido. *3* noble, excelente. *4* liberal, generoso. *5* bonito, considerable.

**handsomeness** (-nis) *s.* hermosura, elegancia, apostura. *2* generosidad.

**handspike** (jæ·ndspaik) *s.* espeque.

**handspring** (jæ·ndspring) *s.* voltereta sobre las manos.

**hand-to-hand** *adj.* cuerpo a cuerpo.

**hand-to-mouth** *adj.* precario, inseguro.

**handwork** (jæ·nduøʳk) *s.* obra hecha a mano.

**handwriting** (jændrai·ting) *s.* carácter de letra, letra, escritura [de una pers.].

**handy** (jæ·ndi) *adj.* diestro, hábil, mañoso. *2* manual, manuable, fácil de manejar. *3* a la mano, próximo. *4* cómodo, conveniente, útil. *5 ~ man,* mozo para todo.

**hang** (jæng) *s.* manera que tiene de colgar o inclinarse [una cosa]; caída [de un vestido]. *2* inclinación, declive. *4* sentido, intención [de un discurso, etc.]. *5* modo, manera, tranquilo: *to get the ~ of,* cogerle el tranquillo a. *6* detención, vacilación. *7* fig. nada, un bledo.

**hang (to)** *tr.* colgar, suspender. *2* colgar, ahorcar. *3* adornar con colgaduras, cuadros, etc., colgar, entapizar, tapizar, empapelar [paredes, habitaciones]; pegar, o fijar en, la pared. *4* tender [la ropa]. *5* bajar [la cabeza]. *6* engoznar [una puerta]. *7 to ~ fire,* fallar [un arma de fuego]; vacilar; alargarse, retardarse [una cosa]. *8 to ~*

*out*, colgar al exterior. *9 to* ~ *up*, colgar [el sombrero, el teléfono, etc.]; suspender, dejar en suspenso. *10* ~ *it!*, ~ *it all!*, ¡demonio! *11 intr.* colgar, pender, caer. *12* ser ahorcado. *13* hacer pendiente. *14* estar engoznado. *15* estar adornado con colgaduras. *16* depender, descansar. *17* asirse [a], colgarse [de], abrazarse [a]. *18* adherirse, pegarse. *19* ser inminente, amenazar. *20* estar en suspenso. *21* detenerse, estar [en un sitio]. *22 to* ~ *around*, rondar, andar holgazaneando; esperar sin hacer nada. *23 to* ~ *back*, vacilar, titubear; quedarse atrás. *24 to* ~ *down*, colgar, estar pendiente. *25 to* ~ *on*, colgar de; abrazarse [al cuello] de; pegarse a [uno]; depender, estar pendiente de; continuar, persistir, insistir. *26 to* ~ *out*, estar colgado al exterior; asomarse [a una ventana, etc.] sacando fuera el busto; fam. vivir, residir. *27 to* ~ *over*, amenazar, cernerse sobre; quedar. *28 to* ~ *up*, TELEF. colgar.

¶ Pret. y p. p.: *hung* o *hanged*. | En la acep. *2* se prefiere *hanged*.

**hangar** (jæ·nga·) *s.* hangar. *2* cobertizo.

**hangdog** (-dog) *adj.* avergonzado. *2* bajo, rastrero.

**hanger** (-ø·) *s.* soporte colgante, barra de suspensión. *2* colgadero, percha. *3* el que cuelga o coloca.

**hanger-on**, *pl.* **hangers-on** *s.* pegote, parásito. *2* el que frecuenta un paraje.

**hanging** (-ing) *adj.* colgante, pendiente, suspendido. *2* de suspensión. *3* merecedor de la horca. *4 s.* colgamiento. *5* ejecución en la horca. *6 pl.* colgaduras.

**hangman** (-mæn) *s.* verdugo.

**hangnail** (-neil) *s.* padrastro, respigón.

**hank** (jænk) *s.* madeja, cadejo. *2* MAR. anillo [de vela].

**hank (to)** *intr.* hacer madejas. *2* adujar.

**hanker (to)** (jæ·nko·) *intr.* ansiar, anhelar, apetecer. Gralte. con *for* o *after*.

**hankering** (jæ·nkøring) *s.* ansia, anhelo, deseo.

**Hannah** (jæ·na) *n. pr. f.* Ana.

**Hannibal** (jæ·nibal) *n. pr. m.* Aníbal.

**Hanover** (jæ·novø·) *n. pr.* GEOGR. Hannover.

**Hanse** (jæns) Ansa, Hansa.

**hanseatic** (jænsiæ·tik) *adj.* anseático, hanseático.

**hansel** (jæ·nsel) *s.* HANDSEL.

**hansel (to)** *tr.* TO HANDSEL.

**hansom** o **hansom cab** (jæ·nsøm) *s.* cabriolé con el pescante en la parte alta de la zaga.

**hap** (jæp) *s.* ant. acaso, ocurrencia; suerte, casualidad.

**hap (to)** *intr.* ant. acontecer, acaecer.

**haphazard** (-jæ·ša·d) *s.* casualidad, azar. *2 adj.* casual, fortuito, impensado. *3* descuidado, hecho a bulto. *4 adv.* al azar, al buen tuntún.

**hapless** (-lis) *adj.* desgraciado, desventurado.

**haply** (-li) *adv.* quizás. *2* acaso, por casualidad.

**happen (to)** (jæ·pøn) *intr.* acontecer, acaecer, suceder, ocurrir, pasar: *no matter what happens*, pase lo que pase. *2* dar la casualidad de que, ser el caso que, resultar que; acertar a: *it happens that I know it*, el caso es que yo lo sé; *he happened to be there*, él acertaba a estar allí. *3 to* ~ *in* o *into*, entrar un momento, al pasar. *4 to* ~ *on*, encontrar, tropezar con.

**happening** (-øning) *s.* acontecimiento, suceso, sucedido.

**happiness** (-inis) *s.* felicidad, dicha, ventura. *2* contento.

**happy** (-i) *adj.* feliz, dichoso, afortunado, fausto. *2*
alegre, contento. *3* hábil, pronto, oportuno. *4 to be* ~, alegrarse de, celebrar, tener gusto en.

**happy-go-lucky** *adj.-s.* descuidado, impróvido. *2 adv.* a la buena ventura.

**harangue** (jaræ·ng) *s.* arenga, perorata.

**harangue (to)** *tr.* arengar. *2 intr.* discursear.

**harass (to)** (jæ·ras) *tr.* cansar, fatigar, agotar; atormentar; acosar, importunar. *2* MIL. hostigar, hostilizar.

**harassment** (-mønt) *s.* fatiga. *2* hostigamiento.

**harbinger** (-ja··bindȳø·) *s.* heraldo, nuncio, precursor. *2* anuncio, presagio.

**harbinger (to)** *tr.* anunciar, presagiar.

**harbo (u) r** (ja··bø·) *s.* puerto [de mar o de río]: ~ *master*, capitán de puerto. *2* puerto seguro. *3* asilo, refugio, abrigo.

**harbo (u) r (to)** *tr.* abrigar, resguardar. *2* acoger, dar asilo. *3* hospedar, albergar. *4* abrigar [ideas, sentimientos]. *5* contener, guardar. *6 intr.* albergarse. *7* refugiarse.

**harbo (u) rage** (-idȳ) *s.* puerto, refugio, amparo, abrigo. *2* hospedaje, albergue.

**hard** (ja·d) *adj.* duro [en todas sus acepciones]. *2* endurecido. *3* firme, fuerte, enérgico, persistente. *4* arduo, difícil: ~ *to please*, descontentadizo, difícil de contentar. *5* inclemente [tiempo]. *6* perverso, incorregible. *7* áspero, agrio [vino, etc.]. *8* cruda, gorda [agua]. *9* COM. sostenido [precio]. *10* apretado [nudo]. *11* FONÉT. gutural, velar. *12* ~ *and fast*, rígido, inflexible [regla, etc.]. ~ *cash*, dinero efectivo; metálico. *13* ~ *facts*, hechos indiscutibles. *14* ~ *lines*, apuro, situación angustiosa. *15* ~ *of hearing*, duro de oído. *16* ~ *usage*, mal trato. *17 to be* ~ *on*, tratar con dureza; gastar, estropear. *18 adv.* duramente, duro, fuerte, firmemente, de firme, recio, vigorosamente, con ahinco, con violencia. *19* difícilmente. *20* ~ *by*, al lado, junto, muy cerca. *21* ~ *labour*, trabajos forzados. *22* ~ *pressed*, *pushed* o *run*, acosado; apremiado, apurado. *23* ~ *up*, apurado, falto [de dinero, etc.]. *24 to drink* ~, beber fuerte, con exceso.

*25 s.* suelo o piso duro.

**hard-bitten** *adj.* duro, resistente [en la lucha]. *2* terco, tenaz.

**hard-boiled** *adj.* duro [huevo].

**hard-earned** *adj.* ganado con dificultad.

**harden (to)** (ja··døn) *tr.* endurecer. *2* encallecer, curtir, hacer insensible. *3* consolidar, solidar. *4* robustecer. *5* fortalecer [en un sentimiento, etc.]. *6 intr.* endurecerse. *7* encallecerse, empedernirse, curtirse. *8* fortalecerse.

**hard-favoured, hard-featured** *adj.* cariagrio, de facciones duras.

**hard-fought** *adj.* empeñado, reñido.

**hard-headed** *adj.* testarudo. *2* astuto, sagaz.

**hard-hearted** *adj.* duro de corazón, insensible, cruel.

**hard-mouthed** *adj.* boquiduro [caballo].

**hardihood** (ja··dijud) *s.* valor, intrepidez, resolución. *2* audacia, osadía. *3* descaro.

**hardiness** (-nis) *s.* vigor, robustez, resistencia. *2* HARDIHOOD.

**hardly** (ja··dli) *adv.* difícilmente. *2* apenas, escasamente. *3* duramente, ásperamente.

**hardness** (-nis) *s.* dureza. *2* firmeza, solidez. *3* penalidad, trabajo. *4* crueldad, rigor, aspereza.

**hardship** (-ship) *s.* penalidad, fatiga, privación, estrechez. *2* opresión, injusticia.

**hardtack** (-tæk) *s.* galleta [de munición].

**hardware** (-ue^r) *s.* quincalla, ferretería.
**hardwood** (-wud) *s.* madera dura o noble.
**hardy** (-i) *adj.* robusto, fuerte. 2 bravo, intrépido. 3 audaz, temerario. 4 BOT. resistente.
**hare** (je·ø·) *s.* ZOOL., ASTR. liebre: ~ *and hounds,* juego en que se imita la caza de la liebre.
**harebell** (-bel) *s.* BOT. campanilla.
**harebrained** (-breind) *adj.* aturdido, casquivano, ligero de cascos.
**harefoot** (-fut) *s.* BOT. pie de liebre.
**harehearted** (-ha·tid) *adj.* medroso, tímido.
**harehound** (-jaund) *s.* lebrel.
**harelip** (-lip) *s.* labio leporino.
**harelipped** (-lipt) *adj.* labihendido.
**harem** (je·røm) *s.* harén, harem, serrallo.
**hare's-ear** *s.* BOT. perfoliada.
**hark** (ja^rk) *interj.* ¡eh!, ¡oye!, ¡oigan!, ¡oíd!
**hark (to)** *tr.-intr.* escuchar, oir con atención, atender.
**harken (to)** (ja··køn) *tr.* TO HEARKEN.
**harl** (ja·l) *s.* filamento, hebra.
**harlequin** (ja··lekuin) *s.* arlequín. 2 *adj.* arlequinesco, abigarrado.
**harlequin (to)** *tr.-intr.* hacer el bufón, embromar.
**harlequinade** (ja·lekuinei·d) *s.* arlequinada.
**harlot** (ja·^rløt) *s.* ramera, prostituta. 2 *adj.* lascivo, soez.
**harlotry** (-ri) *s.* prostitución.
**harm** (ja^rm) *s.* mal, daño, detrimento, perjuicio.
**harm (to)** *tr.* dañar, hacer mal, perjudicar.
**harmful** (-ful) *adj.* dañoso, dañino, nocivo, perjudicial, pernicioso.
**harmless** (-lis) *adj.* indemne. 2 inofensivo, inocuo, inocente.
**harmonic** (ja·ma·nik) *adj.-s.* armónico. 2 *s. pl.* armonía [teoría musical].
**harmonica** (-a) *s.* MÚS. armónica.
**harmonical** (-al) *adj.* armónico.
**harmonious** (ja^rmou·niøs) *adj.* armonioso.
**harmonist** (ja·^rmonist) *s.* armonista.
**harmonium** (ja^rmou·niøm) *s.* MÚS. armonio.
**harmonize (to)** (ja·^rmønaiš) *tr.-intr.* armonizar. 2 *intr.* armonizarse, concordar; congeniar.
**harmony** (ja·^rmøni) *s.* armonía.
**harness** (ja·^rnis) *s.* arneses, arreos, guarniciones: ~ *maker,* guarnicionero, talabartero; ~ *room,* guardarnés. 2 ARM. arnés. 3 fig. *in* ~, trabajando, en servicio activo. 4 MEC. equipo. 5 TEJ. montura, lizos.
**harness (to)** *tr.* poner las guarniciones a; enjaezar, aparejar. 2 armar con arnés. 3 represar [las aguas de un río].
**harp** (ja^rp) *s.* MÚS. arpa. 2 ASTR. Lira.
**harp (to)** *intr.* tocar el arpa. 2 *to* ~ *on* o *upon,* machacar, repetir porfiadamente.
**harper** (-ø·), **harpist** (-ist) *s.* arpista.
**harpoon** (ja^rpu·n) *s.* arpón.
**harpoon (to)** *tr.* arponear.
**harpooner** (-ø·) *s.* arponero.
**harpsichord** (ja·^rpsico·d) *s.* MÚS. clavicordio.
**harpy** (ja·^rpi) *s.* MIT., ORN. arpía. 2 fig. arpía [pers. rapaz y codiciosa].
**harquebus** (ja·^rkuibøs) *s.* arcabuz.
**harquebusier** (ja^rkuibøsi·^r) *s.* arcabucero.
**harridan** (jæ·ridan) *s.* vieja bruja, arpía.
**harrier** (jæ·riø^r) *s.* lebrel. 2 pillador, asolador. 3 molestador. 4 ORN. nombre de algunas aves falcónidas.
**Harriet** (jæ·riet) *n. pr. f.* HENRIETTA.
**harrow** (jæ·rou) *s.* AGR. grada de dientes; escarificador. 2 instrumento de tortura.

**harrow (to)** *tr.* AGR. gradar, escarificar. 2 desgarrar, atormentar.
**harrowing** (-ing) *adj.* agudo, desgarrador; horripilante.
**Harry** (jæ·ri) *n. pr. m. dim.* de HENRY.
**harry (to)** *tr.* pillar, asolar, devastar. 2 perseguir, acosar, atormentar.
**harsh** (ja^rsh) *adj.* áspero. 2 rudo, tosco, bronco. 3 discordante, desagradable, chillón. 4 brusco, desabrido, acerbo, duro, riguroso, cruel, injusto.
**hart** (ja^rt) *s.* ZOOL. ciervo [macho], venado.
**hartshorn** (-sjo^rn) *s.* cuerna de ciervo. 2 QUÍM. sal amoníaco. 3 BOT. estrellamar.
**hart's-tongue** (-støng) *s.* BOT. lengua de ciervo.
**harum-scarum** (je·røm-ske·røm) *adj.-s.* atolondrado, aturdido, tarambana. 2 *adv.* atolondradamente, al tuntún.
**haruspex** (jarø·speks), **haruspice** (-pis) *s.* arúspice.
**harvest** (ja·^rvist) *s.* cosecha, recolección, siega, agosto. 2 fig. fruto, premio [de un trabajo, esfuerzo, conducta, etc.]. 3 ENT. ~ *fly,* cigarra.
**harvest (to)** *tr.* cosechar, recoger, recolectar; segar [la mies]. 2 *intr.* cosechar, segar [hacer la cosecha, la siega].
**harvester** (-ø^r) *s.* cogedor de frutos, segador, agostero. 2 segadora, máquina de segar.
**harvestman** (-mæn) *s.* HARVESTER 1. 2 ZOOL. segador.
**harvester-thresther** *s.* AGR. segadora-trilladora.
**has** (jæš) *3.ª pers. pres. ind.* de TO HAVE.
**hash** (jæsh) *s.* picadillo, jigote. 2 revoltillo, enredo: *to make a* ~ *of,* enredar, estropear [un asunto o trabajo].
**hash (to)** *tr.* picar, desmenuzar. 2 enredar, estropear.
**hasheesh, hashish** (jæ·shish) *s.* haxix.
**haslet** (jæ·slit) *s.* COC. asadura de cerdo.
**hasn't** (jæ·sønt) contracción de HAS NOT.
**hasp** (jasp) *s.* manecilla [de libro]; cierre [de baúl].
**hasp (to)** *tr.* cerrar con broche o cierre.
**hassock** (jæ·søk) *s.* almohadón, cojín.
**hastate** (jæ·steit) *adj.* BOT. alabardado.
**haste** (jeist) *s.* prisa, presteza, celeridad, apresuramiento; precipitación, aturdimiento: *to be in* ~, tener prisa; *to make* ~, darse prisa.
**hasten (to)** (jei·søn) *tr.* acelerar, apresurar, avivar. 2 dar prisa. 3 *intr.* apresurarse, darse prisa.
**hasty** (jei·sti) *adj.* apresurado. 2 pronto, vivo; de genio vivo; colérico. 3 precipitado, atropellado, inconsiderado, temerario.
**hat** (jæt) *s.* sombrero: ~ *factory,* ~ *shop,* sombrerería; *to pass round the* ~, hacer una colecta, echar un guante. 2 capelo. 3 MAR. ~ *money,* capa [que percibe el capitán].
**hatband** (-bænd) *s.* cinta del sombrero.
**hatbox** (-baks), **hatcase** (-keis) *s.* sombrerera.
**hatch** (jæch) *s.* compuerta, media puerta. 2 trampa, escotillón. 3 MAR. escotilla. 4 MAR. cuartel [de escotilla]. 5 HIDR. paradera, compuerta. 6 echadura, incubación. 7 salida del cascarón. 8 nidada, pollada. 9 B. ART. línea de sombreado.
**hatch (to)** *tr.* empollar, incubar. 2 producir, idear, tramar, maquinar. 3 rayar, sombrear con líneas. 4 *intr.* encobar. 5 salir del cascarón. 6 incubarse, formarse.
**hatchel** (jæ·chøl) *s.* rastrillo [para el lino, etc.].
**hatchel (to)** *tr.* rastrillar [lino, etc.]. 2 molestar,

inquietar. ¶ Pret. y p. p.: *hatcheled* o *-lled;* p. a.: *-ling* o *-lling.*

**hatchery** (jæ·chøri) *s.* vivero, criadero [de peces].

**hatchet** (jæ·chit) *s.* destral. *2* hacha [de los indios]: *to bury the ~,* hacer la paz, olvidar rencores; *to dig up the ~,* hacer la guerra.

**hatched-faced** *adj.* de facciones enjutas.

**hatching** (jæ·ching) *s.* B. ART. sombreado, plumeado.

**hatchway** (jæ·chuei) *s.* MAR. escotilla.

**hate** (jeit) *s.* odio, aborrecimiento, aversión.

**hate (to)** *tr.* odiar, aborrecer, detestar.

**hateful** (-ful) *adj.* odioso, aborrecible. *2* malévolo, rencoroso.

**hatefulness** (-nis) *s.* odiosidad.

**hater** (jei·tøʳ) *s.* aborrecedor, enemigo.

**hath** (jæz) ant. *3.ª pers. pres. ind.* de TO HAVE.

**hatpin** (jæ·tpin) *s.* aguja para el sombrero.

**hatrack** (-ræk) *s.* perchero [para sombreros].

**hatred** (jei·trid) *s.* odio, aborrecimiento.

**hatted** (jæ·tid) *adj.* cubierto con sombrero.

**hatter** (-øʳ) *s.* sombrerero.

**Hatty** (jæ·ti) *n. pr. f. dim.* de HENRIETTA.

**hauberk** (jo·bøʳk) *s.* camisote, cota de mallas.

**haughtiness** (jo·tinis) *s.* orgullo, altivez, altanería.

**haughty** (jo·ti) *adj.* orgulloso, altivo, altanero.

**haul** (jol) *s.* tirón, estirón. *2* acción de halar o tirar de, tiro, arrastre. *3* redada.

**haul (to)** *tr.-intr.* tirar de, arrastrar. *2 tr.* MAR. halar, cazar. *3* acarrear, transportar. *4* sacar [con red]. *5 to ~ down,* arriar. *6 to ~ up,* pedir cuentas a, reprender. *7 intr.* mudarse [el viento]. *8* MAR. virar [la nave]; *to ~ upon the wind,* ceñir el viento.

**haulage** (-idẏ) *s.* arrastre, acarreo, transporte.

**haulm, haum** (jom) *s.* paja, rastrojo.

**haunch** (jonch) *s.* cadera. *2* anca, grupa. *3* COC. pierna [de venado, etc.].

**haunt** (jo·nt) *s.* lugar que se frecuenta; querencia; guarida. *2* morada.

**haunt (to)** *tr.* frecuentar, rondar. *2* aparecerse en [hablando de fantasmas]. *3* perseguir, obsesionar [a uno una idea, un recuerdo].

**haunting** (-ing) *adj.* persistente, obsesionante.

**hautboy** (jou·boi) *s.* MÚS. óboe.

**Havana** (javæ·na) *n. pr.* GEOGR. Habana. *2 s.* habano [cigarro].

**have (to)** (jæv) *aux.* haber: *I ~ worked,* he trabajado; *had he read the letter,* si él hubiera leído la carta; *I had as soon, I had rather,* preferiría, más quisiera; *we had better,* vale más que, es mejor que.

*2 tr.* haber, tener, poseer. *3* tener [duda, cuidado, asuntos, un dolor, un niño, etc.]. *4* sufrir [cierto accidente]: *I had my leg broken,* me rompí la pierna. *5* tener, recibir [una carta, una noticia, etc.]. *6* sostener, afirmar, decir: *he will ~ it that,* él sostiene que. *7* conocer, saber: *he has no Latin,* no sabe latín. *8* jugar [una partida]. *9* tomar, comer, beber; aceptar: *~ a cigar,* tome un cigarro. *10* permitir, consentir. *11* desear, querer, mandar, hacer [que se haga una cosa]: *he had his shoes repaired,* se hizo componer los zapatos. *12* coger, atrapar, engañar. *13* obtener, adquirir: *to be had of,* pídase en, de venta en. *14* echar, dar [una mirada]. *15 to ~ a mind to,* tener ganas de, estar tentado de. *16 to ~ at,* atacar, acometer. *17 to ~ at heart,* desear vivamente. *18 to ~ it out,* liquidar un asunto con explicaciones o peleándose. *19 to ~ recourse,* recurrir. *20 to ~ to* o *to ~ got to,* tener que, haber

de, deber. *21 to ~ to do with,* tener que ver con. ¶ *3.ª pers. pres. ind.: had.*

**havelock** (jæ·vlak) *s.* MIL. cogotera.

**haven** (jei·vn) *s.* puerto, abra. *2* asilo, abrigo.

**haven't** (jæ·vønt) contracción de HAVE NOT.

**haversack** (jæ·vø·sæk) *s.* mochila, barjuleta.

**having** (jæ·ving) *s.* bienes, hacienda, haber.

**havoc** (jæ·vøk) *s.* estrago, destrucción, asolamiento: *to play ~,* hacer estragos.

**havoc (to)** *tr.* asolar, causar estrago en.

**haw** (jo) *s.* BOT. majuela. *2* especie de tartamudeo. *3* voz para guiar a una caballería.

**haw (to)** *3 tr.-intr.* hacer volver o volver [una caballería] a la izquierda. *2 intr.* hacer una especie de tartamudeo.

**Hawaiian** (jauai·ian) *adj.-s.* hawaiano.

**haw-haw** *s.* risotada, carcajada.

**hawk** (jok) *s.* ORN. nombre que se da al halcón, al cernícalo, al gavilán, al azor y a otras aves falcónidas. *2* ORN. *~ owl,* autillo, úlula. *3* fig. ave de presa [pers.].

**hawk (to)** *tr.* cazar con halcón. *2* pregonar [mercancías, una noticia, un secreto]. *3 intr.* carraspear, gargajear.

**hawker** (-øʳ) *s.* halconero, cetrero. *2* vendedor ambulante, buhonero.

**hawk-eyed** *adj.* lince, de mirada perspicaz.

**hawking** (-ing) *s.* cetrería. *2* buhonería.

**hawkweed** (-wid) *s.* BOT. vellosilla.

**hawse** (jo·š) *s.* MAR. frente a los escobenes. *2* MAR. escobén. *3* MAR. longitud de cadenas.

**hawsehole** (-joul) *s.* MAR. escobén.

**hawser** (-øʳ) *s.* MAR. guindaleza, estacha.

**hawthorn** (jo·zoʳn) *s.* BOT. majuelo o espino blanco.

**hay** (jei) *s.* heno, forraje; *~ fever,* MED. fiebre del heno.

**hay (to)** *intr.* hacer heno. *2 tr.* dar heno a.

**haycock** (-kak) *s.* almiar, niara.

**hayfield** (-fild) *s.* henar.

**hayfork** (-foʳk) *s.* AGR. horca, horcón, bieldo.

**hayloft** (-loft) *s.* henil, pajar.

**hayrack** (-ræk) *s.* pesebre.

**hayrik** (-rik), **haystack** (-tæk) *s.* almiar, niara, montón de heno.

**hazard** (jæ·šaʳd) *s.* azar, suerte, casualidad. *2* albur, riesgo: *at all hazards,* por grande que sea el riesgo. *3* BILLAR. billa. *4* GOLF. obstáculo.

**hazard (to)** *tr.* arriesgar, aventurar. *2 intr.* correr riesgo.

**hazardous** (-øs) *adj.* arriesgado, peligroso.

**haze** (jeiš) *s.* niebla, calina. *2* confusión, vaguedad.

**haze (to)** *intr.* aneblarse [la atmósfera]. *2 tr.* dar la novatada a.

**hazel** (jei·šøl) *s.* avellano. *2 adj.* de color de avellana.

**hazelnut** (-nøt) *s.* BOT. avellana.

**hazing** (jei·šing) *s.* novatada.

**hazy** (jei·ši) *adj.* aneblado, nebuloso, brumoso, caliginoso. *2* confuso, vago.

**H-bomb** *s.* bomba de hidrógeno.

**he** (ji) *pron. pers.* él. | Se emplea en composición, para designar al macho o varón: *~ bear,* oso [macho]. *2 pron. indef.* el, aquel: *~ who, ~ that,* el que, aquel que, quien.

**head** (jed) *s.* cabeza [del hombre, del animal, de una cosa; intelecto, talento, capacidad]: *~ of hair,* cabellera, mata de pelo; *to be off one's ~,* delirar, estar loco; *to come into one's ~,* pasarle por la cabeza a uno; *I cannot make ~ or tail of it,* no puedo entenderlo o descifrarlo; *to lose one's ~,* perder la cabeza; *from ~ to foot,* de pies a cabeza; ~ *on*, de cabeza; *out of one's* ~, de la cabeza de uno, de su cosecha; *over* ~ *and ears*, hasta los ojos; *over one's* ~, por encima de uno; fuera del alcance o comprensión de uno. *2* cabeza, jefe, director, primer puesto, dirección: *at the* ~ *of*, a la cabeza de, al frente de. *3* cabeza [de ganado; pers. unidad]. *4* cima, cumbre. *5* cabecera [de la mesa, de la cama, de un río]. *6* título, encabezamiento. *7* sección [de un escrito]. *8* punto, tema particular, concepto: *on this* ~, sobre este punto, por este concepto. *9* punta, extremo. *10* puño [de bastón]. *11* cuerna [de ciervo]. *12* MAR. proa. *13* témpano [de tonel]; tapa [de cilindro]; parche [de tambor]; montera [de alambique]. *14* grátil [de vela]. *15* promontorio. *16* BOT. cabezuela. *17* repollo, pella [de col, etc.]. *18* presa, embalse [de molino, etc.]. *19* espuma [de un líquido]. *20* avance, progreso: *to make* ~, avanzar, progresar. *21* punta [de un divieso]. *22* MED. maduración; fig. crisis, punto culminante o decisivo. *23 heads or tails*, cara o cruz.

*24 adj.* de cabeza, cabecera, proa, etc. *25* principal, primero, jefe: ~ *cook*, primer cocinero.

**head (to)** *tr.* encabezar. *2* ser el primero de; mandar, acaudillar. *3* poner cabeza, título, etc., a. *4* adelantar [a uno]. *5* conducir [un coche, etc.] en cierta dirección. *5* descabezar; desmochar. *6 to*~ *off*, cortar el paso a; atajar. *7 intr.* ir, dirigirse. *8* nacer [un río]. *9* repollar [una planta]. *10* supurar [un absceso].

**headache** (-eik) *s.* dolor de cabeza, jaqueca.

**headband** (-bænd) *s.* cinta para la cabeza. *2* cabezada [de libro].

**headboard** (-bord) *s.* cabecera [de cama].

**headdress** (-dres) *s.* prenda para la cabeza; tocado.

**header** (-ø^r) *s.* cabecilla, director. *2* descabezador. *3* ARQ. brochal. *4* ALBAÑ. ladrillo puesto a tizón. *5* caída o salto de cabeza; zambullida.

**headfirst** (-først), **headforemost** (-formoust) *adv.* de cabeza.

**headgear** (-gir) *s.* prenda para la cabeza. *2* cabezada [de caballería].

**heading** (je·ding) *s.* título, encabezamiento; membrete. *2* MIN. galería de avance.

**headland** (-land) *s.* GEOGR. cabo, punta, promontorio.

**headless** (-lis) *adj.* acéfalo. *2* decapitado. *3* sin seso, estúpido. *4* sin jefe o caudillo.

**headlight** (-lait) *s.* faro [de locomotora o automóvil]. *2* MAR. farol de tope.

**headline** (-lain) *s.* titulares [de un periódico]. *2* título de página, titulillo.

**headlong** (-long) *adj.* precipitado, impetuoso, temerario. *2* de cabeza [zambullida, etc.]. *3 adv.* precipitadamente, temerariamente. *4* de cabeza.

**headman** (-mæn) *s.* jefe, caudillo.

**headmaster** (-mæ·sto^r) *s.* director [de un colegio].

**headmistress** (-mi·stris) *s.* directora [de un colegio].

**headmost** (je·dmoust) *adj.* más avanzado; delantero, primero, que va en cabeza.

**headphone** (-foun) *s.* TELÉF. auricular de casco.

**headpiece** (-pis) *s.* casco, yelmo. *2* IMPR. viñeta, cabecera. *3* fam. chola, mollera.

**headquarters** (-kuortørs) *s.* MIL. cuartel general. *2* jefatura [de policía]. *3* sede [de una entidad]. *4* dirección, oficina principal.

**headrace** (-reis) *s.* caz, saetín [de molino].

**headrest** (-rest) *s.* apoyo para la cabeza.

**headsail** (-seil) *s.* MAR. vela delantera.

**headset** (-set) *s.* juego de auriculares con casco.

**headsman** (-smæn) *s.* verdugo [que decapita].

**headstall** (-stol) *s.* cabezada [de freno], testera.

**headstone** (-stoun) *s.* lápida mortuoria. *2* ARQ. piedra angular.

**headstream** (-strim) *s.* afluente principal [de un río].

**headstrong** (-strong) *adj.* cabezudo, testarudo, terco, obstinado. *2* ingobernable.

**headwaters** (-uotø^rs) *s.* fuentes [de un río].

**headway** (-uei) *s.* marcha [de un buque]. *2* avance, progreso; ímpetu: *to make* ~, avanzar, adelantar, progresar. *3* FERROC. distancia [entre dos trenes en una misma vía].

**headwork** (-uø^rk) *s.* trabajo intelectual.

**heady** (-i) *adj.* temerario, arrojado. *2* violento, impetuoso. *3* obstinado. *4* fuerte [vino, licor].

**heal (to)** (ji·l) *tr.* curar, sanar. *2* remediar, reparar. *3* limpiar [del pecado, etc.]. *4 intr.* curar, curarse, sanar: *to* ~ *up*, cicatrizarse. *5* remediarse.

**heald** (-d) *s.* TEJ. lizo.

**healer** (-ø^r) *s.* curador, sanador.

**healing** (-ing) *s.* cura, curación, cicatrización. *2 adj.* curativo, cicatrizante.

**health** (jelz) *s.* salud, sanidad: *to be in good (poor o bad)* ~, estar bien (mal) de salud; *your* ~*!*, ¡a la salud de usted!; ~ *officer*, inspector de sanidad.

**healthful** (-ful) *adj.* sano, saludable, salubre.

**health-giving** *adj.* saludable, que da salud.

**healthiness** (-inis) *s.* buena salud, sanidad.

**healthy** (-i) *adj.* sano [en buena salud]. *2* vigoroso, robusto. *3* sano, saludable.

**heap** (jip) *s.* montón, pila, rimero, cúmulo. *2* fam. [a veces en pl.] gran cantidad, multitud, gentío: *in heaps*, a montones.

**heap (to)** *tr.* amontonar, apilar, juntar, acumular. *2* cargar, colmar, llenar.

**hear (to)** (ji·ø^r) *tr.* oír [los sonidos, etc.], escuchar: *to* ~ *it said*, oírlo decir; *to* ~ *someone out*, escuchar a uno hasta el fin. *2* oír decir: *I heard that*, oí decir que. *3* oír [misa]. *4* oír, escuchar, atender [ruegos, etc.]. *5 intr.* oír: *to* ~ *about, from* o *of*, oír hablar de, tener noticias de, enterarse de. ¶ Pret. y p. p.: *heard*.

**heard** (jø·d) *pret.* y *p. p.* de TO HEAR.

**hearer** (ji·ørø^r) *s.* oyente.

**hearing** (-ing) *s.* oído [sentido]; audición [acción de oír]. *2* oportunidad para ser oído, audiencia. *3* DER. examen de testigos. *4* alcance del oído: *within* ~, al alcance del oído.

**hearken (to)** (ja·^rkøn) *intr.* escuchar.

**hearsay** (ji·ø^rsei) *s.* rumor, voz común: *by* ~, de oídas.

**hearse** (jø^rs) *s.* coche o carroza fúnebre. *2* tenebrario.

**heart** (ja·t) *s.* corazón [órgano; parte central; sentimiento interior; ánimo, valor, etc.]: *to be of good* ~, tener ánimo; *to die of broken* ~, morir de pena; *to get to the* ~ *of*, llegar al fondo o al corazón de; *to have at* ~, desear vivamente; *to have one's* ~ *in one's boots*, o *mouth*, estar con el alma en un hilo; estar muerto de miedo; *to take to* ~, tomar en serio, a pecho; *after one's own* ~, a gusto de uno, como uno desea; *at* ~, en el fondo, en realidad; *by* ~, de memoria; ~ *and soul*, en cuerpo y alma; *to one's* ~ *content*, a placer, sin restricción; *with all one's* ~, con toda el alma, de todo corazón. *2* cogollo [de lechuga, etc.]. *3 pl.* copas [de la baraja].

*4 adj.* del corazón, cardíaco: ~ *failure,* colapso cardíaco; ~ *trouble,* enfermedad del corazón.

**heartache** (-eik) *s.* dolor de corazón, congoja, pesar, aflicción.

**heartbeat** (-bɪt) *s.* latido del corazón. *2* emoción profunda.

**heartbreak** (-breik) *s.* angustia, aflicción grande.

**heartbreaking** (-ing) *adj.* doloroso, desgarrador.

**heartbroken** (-broukøn) *adj.* acongojado, transido de dolor.

**heartburn** (-bøʳn) *s.* acedía.

**heartburning** (-ning) *s.* envidia, animosidad.

**hearten (to)** (-øn) *tr.* animar, alentar.

**heartfelt** (-felt) *adj.* cordial, sincero; sentido.

**heartgrief** (-grɪf) *s.* congoja, angustia.

**hearth** (-jaʳz) *s.* hogar; chimenea. *2* hogar [doméstico]. *3* solera, suelo, crisol [de horno].

**heartily** (ja·ʳtili) *adv.* sinceramente, cordialmmente. *2* vigorosamente. *3* copiosamente, con buen apetito.

**heartiness** (-inis) *s.* sinceridad, cordialidad, calor. *2* ganas, apetito.

**heartless** (-lis) *adj.* sin corazón, cruel, insensible. *2* tímido, pusilánime, abatido.

**heart-rending** *adj.* agudo, desgarrador, que parte el corazón.

**heartsease** o **heart's-ease** (sɪš) *s.* serenidad de ánimo. *2* BOT. pensamiento, trinitaria.

**heartseed** (-sɪd) *s.* BOT. farolillo.

**heartsick** (-sik) *adj.* dolorido, desconsolado.

**heartstricken** (-strikøn) *adj.* afligido, angustiado.

**heartstrings** (-strings) *s. pl.* fibras del corazón, entretelas.

**heart-to-heart** *adj.* sincero, franco.

**hearty** (-i) *adj.* cordial, caluroso, sincero. *2* fuerte, vigoroso. *3* robusto, sano. *4* nutritivo, abundante. *5* que se hace con gusto. *6* ~ *eater,* gran tragón.

**heat** (jɪt) *s.* calor: ~ *wave,* ola de calor. *2* calórico. *3* calefacción. *4* acaloramiento. *5* ardor, fogosidad. *6* lo más fuerte o recio [de una acción, etc.]. *7* celo [de la hembra]. *8* DEP. carrera [en una serie de ellas], carrera de prueba o eliminatoria.

**heat (to)** *tr.* calentar, caldear. *2* acalorar, excitar. *3 intr.* calentarse. *4* acalorarse, excitarse.

**heater** (-ø') *s.* calentador. *2* aparato de calefacción.

**heath** (jɪz) *s.* BOT. brezo, urce. *2* brezal, matorral: ~ *cock,* especie de urogallo.

**heathen** (jɪ·ɖøn) *adj.-s.* pagano, gentil. *2* irreligioso. *3* fig. salvaje.

**heathenism** (-išm) *s.* paganismo, gentilidad.

**heather** (je·ɖøʳ) *s.* BOT. brezo, urce.

**heathery** (-i) *adj.* cubierto de brezos, matoso.

**heating** (jɪ·ting) *s.* calefacción, calentamiento, caldeo, calda. *2 adj.* calefaciente, calorífico; de calefacción: ~ *pad,* almohadilla eléctrica.

**heave** (jɪv) *s.* esfuerzo para levantar, solevar o levantarse. *2* movimiento de lo que se levanta [como el de una ola]. *3* jadeo. *4* náusea, arcada. *5* lanzamiento, echada.

**heave (to)** *tr.* levantar, solevar; mover con esfuerzo. *2* lanzar, arrojar, echar. *3* exhalar [un suspiro, etc.]. *4* hinchar [el pecho]. *5* MAR. halar [un cable]. *6* MAR. *to* ~ *to,* poner al pairo o en facha. *7 intr.* levantarse, combarse. *8* levantarse y bajar alternativamente, agitarse [el pecho]. *9* arquear, basquear. *10* esforzarse. *11 to* ~ *in sight,* aparecer, asomar en el horizonte. ¶ Pret. y p. p.: *heaved* o *hove.*

**heaven** (je·vøn) *s.* cielo [de los bienaventurados], gloria, paraíso: *for heaven's sake,* ¡por Dios!;

*good heavens!* ¡válgame Dios! *2* cielo, firmamento.

**heavenliness** (je·vønlinis) *s.* calidad de celestial.

**heavenly** (-li) *adj.* celestial, divino. *2* celeste.

**heavenward** (-uøʳd) *adv.* hacia el cielo.

**heaver** (jɪ·vøʳ) *s.* cargador [obrero]. *2* MAR. tortor.

**heaves** (jɪvs) *s. pl.* VET. huélfago.

**heavily** (je·vili) *adv.* pesadamente. *2* lentamente. *3* fuertemente, duramente. *4* sumamente.

**heaviness** (-nis) *s.* pesadez, pesantez, peso, gravedad. *2* pesadez, torpeza, lentitud. *3* languidez, modorra. *4* peso, importancia. *5* opresión. *6* abatimiento.

**heavy** (je·vi) *adj.* pesado, ponderoso: ~ *industry,* industria pesada. *2* pesado, opresivo, gravoso, aflictivo, severo. *3* fuerte, grande, serio, grave, recio, violento: ~ *losses,* fuertes pérdidas; ~ *shower,* chaparrón. *4* profundo, intenso. *5* pesado, lento, tardo. *6* amodorrado, soñoliento. *7* pesado [estilo]. *8* cargado, agobiado. *9* oprimido [corazón, etc.]. *10* cansado. *11* grueso, denso, tupido; macizo, tosco. *12* laborioso, difícil. *13* indigesto. *14* fragoroso [cañoneo]. *15* triste, abatido. *16* encapotado, sombrío. *17* malo [camino]; empinada [cuesta]. *18* desanimado [mercado]. *19* ~ *drinker,* gran bebedor. *20 adv.* fuerte, pesadamente.

*21 s.* TEAT. personaje solemne o perverso.

**heavy-handed** *adj.* torpe. *2* de mano dura, opresivo.

**heavy-footed** *adj.* de andar torpe. *2* despeado.

**heavy-eyed** *adj.* de ojos soñolientos.

**heavy-set** *adj.* costilludo, espaldudo.

**heavyweight** (-ueit) *s.* boxeador o luchador de peso pesado.

**hebdomadal** (jebda·madal) *adj.* hebdomadario, semanal.

**hebetude** (je·bitiud) *s.* estupidez, embotamiento.

**Hebraic** (jibrei·ik) *adj.* hebraico.

**Hebraism** (ji·briišm) *s.* hebraísmo.

**hebraist** (-ist) *s.* hebraísta. *2* hebraizante.

**Hebraize (to)** (ji·briaiš) *tr.-intr.* hebraizar.

**Hebrew** (ji·bru) *adj.-s.* hebreo, israelita, judío.

**hecatomb** (je·katum) *s.* hecatombe.

**heckle (to)** (je·køl) *tr.* interrumpir [a un orador] con preguntas intencionadas o molestas.

**hectare** (je·kteʳ) *s.* hectárea.

**hectic** (je·ktik) *adj.-s.* héctico, hético. *2 adj.* fam. febril, excitado, agitado.

**hectogram, -gramme** (je·ktøgræm) *s.* hectogramo.

**hectoliter, -litre** (-litøʳ) *s.* hectolitro.

**hectometer, -metre** (-mitøʳ) *s.* hectómetro.

**hector** (je·ktøʳ) *s.* matón, fanfarrón.

**hector (to)** *tr.* atropellar, intimidar, con palabras, amenazas, etc. *2 intr.* bravear, baladronear.

**he'd** (jid) contracción de HE HAD y de HE WOULD.

**heddle** (je·døl) *s.* TEJ. lizo, malla.

**hedge** (jedɣ) *s.* seto vivo; cerca, vallado. *2* fig. límite, valla.

**hedge (to)** *tr.* cercar con seto, vallar. *2* defender, circundar. *3* rodear, encerrar. *4 intr.* abrigarse, escudarse. *5* no comprometerse [al hablar].

**hedgehog** (-jag) *s.* ZOOL. erizo. *2* BOT. ~ *grass,* guizacillo.

**hedgehop (to)** (-jap) *intr.* AVIA. volar a ras de los árboles o setos.

**hedger** (-ø') *s.* el que hace o cuida setos. *2* el que usa de evasivas.

**hedgerow** (-rou) *s.* seto vivo.

**hedonism** (ji·dønišm) *s.* hedonismo.

**hedonist** (-ist) *adj.-s.* hedonista.

**heed** (jɪd) *s.* atención, cuidado; caso: *to take* ~, poner atención, ir con cuidado.

**heed (to)** *tr.* atender, prestar atención a, considerar, hacer caso de. *2* notar, observar, reparar. *3 intr.* poner atención o cuidado.

**heedful** (-ful) *adj.* atento, cuidadoso, cauto.

**heedless** (-lis) *adj.* desatento, distraído, descuidado, atolondrado.

**heel** (jɪl) *s.* talón [de pie, media o zapato]; tacón [de zapato]: *at, on,* o *upon, one's heels,* pisando los talones a uno; *down at (the)* ~, con los tacones gastados; en chancletas; desaliñado; apurado, en mala situación; *heels over head,* patas arriba; precipitadamente, irreflexivamente; *out at the heels,* con las medias rotas, desharrapado. *2* calcañar, zancajo. *3* parte inferior o trasera [de ciertas cosas]. *4* MAR. coz [de mástil]; talón [de quilla]. *5* MÚS. talón [de arco]. *6* cantero, cuscurro [de pan, queso, etc.]. *7* fin, conclusión. *8 pl.* cascos traseros [del caballo].

**heel (to)** *tr.* poner talón o tacón a. *2* armar con espolones [un gallo de pelea]. *3* seguir de cerca. *4 intr.* taconear [al bailar]. *5* MAR. inclinarse, escorar.

**heeltap** (-tap) *s.* tapa [de tacón]. *2* escurriduras [de un vaso].

**heft** (jeft) *s.* fam. peso. *2* fam. influencia. *3* (E.U.) la mayor parte.

**heft (to)** *tr.* fam. levantar en alto. *2* fam. sopesar.

**hefty** (-ti) *adj.* pesado. *2* fam. fornido, recio.

**Hegelian** (jidỹi·lian) *adj.* hegeliano.

**hegemony** (jedỹi·moni) *s.* hegemonía.

**hegira** (jidỹai·ra) *s.* hégira, hejira.

**heifer** (je·føʳ) *s.* novilla, vaquilla.

**height** (jait) *s.* altura, altitud, elevación. *2* alto, altura [dimensión]; talla, estatura, alzada. *3* alto, altura, elevación [del terreno], cerro, colina, cumbre, punto elevado. *4* extremo, colmo; lo más fuerte de: *at the* ~ *of winter,* en pleno invierno. *5* ARQ. montea [de un arco].

**heighten (to)** (-øn) *tr.* levantar, elevar [hacer más alto]. *2* exaltar, sublimar. *3* avivar, aumentar, realzar. *4 intr.* elevarse. *5* aumentar.

**heinous** (jei·nøs) *adj.* odioso, horrible, atroz.

**heir** (e·øʳ) *s.* heredero.

**heirdom** (-døm) *s.* condición de heredero.

**heiress** (-is) *f.* heredera.

**heirloom** (-lum) *s.* DER. bienes muebles unidos a la herencia. *2* herencia de familia.

**held** (jeld) *pret.* y *p. p.* de TO HOLD.

**Helen** (je·løn) *n. pr. f.* Elena.

**heliac(al** (jilai·ak(al) *adj.* ASTR. helíaco.

**helianthus** (jilia·nzøs) *s.* BOT. helianto.

**helical** (je·likal) *adj.* espiral; helicoidal.

**helicopter** (jelika·ptøʳ) *s.* helicóptero.

**heliocentric(al** (jiliose·ntrik(al) *adj.* heliocéntrico.

**helioengraving** (ji·lioengreiving) *s.* heliograbado.

**heliograph** (-græf) *s.* heliógrafo.

**heliostat** (-stæt) *s.* helióstato.

**heliotherapy** (jilioze·rapi) *s.* MED. helioterapia.

**heliotrope** (ji·liotroup) BOT., MINER. heliotropo.

**helium** (ji·liøm) *s.* QUÍM. helio.

**helix** (jɪ·liks) *s.* GEOM., ANAT. hélice. *2* ELECT. arrollamiento en hélice. *3* espira; voluta.

**he'll** (jɪl) contracción de HE SHALL y de HE WILL.

**hell** (jel) *s.* infierno [de los condenados; averno; lugar de sufrimiento, etc.]. *2* fig. garito. *3* fig. cajón de sastre.

**Hellas** (je·las) *s.* Hélade [Grecia].

**hellbroth** (-broz) *s.* caldo mágico maligno.

**hellcat** (-kæt) *s.* bruja. *2* arpía, mujer perversa.

**hell-doomed** *adj.* réprobo, condenado.

**hellebore** (je·liboʳ) *s.* BOT. eléboro. *2* BOT. vedegambre, veratro.

**Hellenic** (jele·nik) *adj.* helénico.

**Hellenism** (je·lønišm) *s.* helenismo.

**Hellenist** (-ist) *s.* helenista.

**Hellenistic** (jeløni·stik) *adj.* helenístico.

**Hellespont** (je·lispønt) *n. pr.* GEOGR. Helesponto.

**hellish** (-ish) *adj.* infernal, diabólico.

**hellishness** (-nis) *s.* malicia diabólica.

**hello** (je·lou) *interj.* ¡hola! *2* ¡ah!, ¡eh! *3* ¡diga! [en el teléfono].

**helm** (jelm) *s.* MAR. timón; rueda o caña del timón. *2* timón, dirección, gobierno. *3* HELMET 1.

**helm (to)** *tr.* dirigir, gobernar.

**helmet** (je·lmit) *s.* yelmo, casco, celada, morrión. *2* casco [de soldado, bombero, etc.].

**helmeted** (-id) *adj.* cubierto con casco.

**helminth** (je·lminz) *s.* ZOOL. helminto.

**helmless** (je·lmlis) *adj.* sin timón.

**helmsman** (-šmæn) *s.* timonero, timonel.

**helot** (je·løt) *s.* ilota.

**helotism** (-išm) *s.* ilotismo.

**help** (jelp) *s.* ayuda, auxilio, asistencia; socorro, favor, apoyo: *to cry out for* ~, pedir auxilio; *by the* ~ *of,* con ayuda de; *help!,* ¡socorro! *2* remedio, recurso: *there is no* ~ *for it,* no tiene remedio. *3* (E.U.) criado, mozo; criada. *4* fam. HELPING.

**help (to)** *tr.* ayudar, coadyuvar a, apoyar, secundar, contribuir a, fomentar. *2* ayudar, socorrer, amparar, valer: *so* ~ *me God,* así Dios me valga. *3* remediar, evitar: *I cannot* ~ *it,* no puedo remediarlo; *he cannot* ~ *but,* no puede menos de; no puede dejar de. *4* servir [comida, bebida]: *to* ~ *oneself to,* servirse [algo de comer o beber]. *5 to* ~ *down,* ayudar a caer o a bajar; *to* ~ *forward,* adelantar, activar. *6 to* ~ *out,* ayudar a salir [de una dificultad, etc.]. *7 intr.* ayudar, servir.

**helper** (-øʳ) *s.* auxiliador. *2* ayudante, peón.

**helpful** (je·lpful) *adj.* que ayuda; útil. *2* saludable.

**helping** (-ing) *s.* porción de comida o bebida que se sirve a uno de una vez.

**helpless** (-lis) *adj.* desvalido. *2* impotente, imposibilitado, incapaz; inútil. *3* perplejo. *4* irremediable.

**helpmate** (-meit) *s.* compañero. *2* esposa, ¡mujer.

**helter-skelter** (je·ltø-ske·ltøʳ) *adv.* atropelladamente, precipitadamente, en confusión, en desorden.

**helve** (jelv) *s.* ástil, mango [de hacha, etc.].

**helve (to)** *tr.* poner ástil o mango, enmangar.

**Helvetia** (jelvi·shia) *n. pr.* GEOGR. Helvecia.

**Helvetian** (-shan), **Helvetic** (jelve·tik) *adj.-s.* helvético, helvecio.

**hem** (jem) *s.* COST. dobladillo, bastilla, repulgo. *2* borde, orilla. *3 interj.* ¡ejem!

**hem (to)** *tr.* COST. dobladillar, bastillar, repulgar. *2 to* ~ *in,* cercar, rodear, encerrar. *3 intr.* fingir tos. *4* vacilar [al hablar].

**hemal** (jɪ·mal) *s.* de la sangre.

**hematin** (je·matin) *s.* QUÍM. hematina.

**hematite** (-tait) *s.* MINER. hematites.

**hematoma** (-tou·ma) *s.* hematoma.

**hematuria** (-tiu·ria) *s.* MED. hematuria.

**hemelytron** (jeme·litran) *s.* hemélitro.

**hemi-** (je·mi) *pref.* hemi-.

**hemicrania** (jemikrei·nia) *s.* MED. hemicránea.

**hemicycle** (je·misaikøl) *s.* hemiciclo.

**hemihedral** (jemihi·dral) *adj.* CRISTAL. hemiédrico.

**hemihedron** (-drøn) *s.* CRISTAL. hemiedro.

**hemiplegia** (jemipli·dẏia), **hemiplegy** (-dẏi) *s*. MED. hemiplejía.
**hemipterous** (jimi·ptørøs) *adj*. ENT. hemíptero.
**hemisphere** (jemi·sfiøʳ) *s*. hemisferio.
**hemispheric** (al (jemisfe·rik(al) *adj*. hemisférico.
**hemistich** (je·mistik) *s*. hemistiquio.
**hemlock** (je·mlak) *s*. BOT. cicuta. *2* BOT. abeto del Canadá.
**hemoglobin** (jimøglou·bin) *s*. BIOQUÍM. hemoglobina.
**hemophilia** (jimøfi·lia) *s*. MED. hemofilia.
**hemoptysis** (jima·ptisis) *s*. MED. hemoptisis.
**hemorrhage** (je·møridẏ) *s*. MED. hemorragia.
**hemorrhoids** (je·møroids) *s*. MED. hemorroides.
**hemostatic** (jemøstæ·tik) *adj*. MED. hemostático.
**hemp** (jemp) *s*. cáñamo [planta, fibra]. *2* dogal.
**hempen** (-øn) *adj*. cañameño.
**hempseed** (-sid) *s*. cañamón.
**hemstitch** (je·mstich) *s*. COST. vainica.
**hemstitch (to)** *tr*. COST. hacer vainica en.
**hen** (jen) *f*. ORN. gallina. *2* hembra de ave [esp. de gallinácea]: ~ *turkey*, pava.
**henbane** (-bein) *s*. BOT. beleño.
**hence** (jens) *adv*. de, o desde, aquí o ahora. *2* de aquí a, dentro de: *two months* ~, de aquí a dos meses. *3* por tanto, por consiguiente, luego, de aquí que. *4 interj*. ¡largo de aquí!
**henceforth** (-foʳz), **henceforward** (-foʳuøʳd) *adv*. de aquí en adelante; desde ahora, en lo sucesivo.
**henchman** (je·nchmæn) *s*. secuaz, servidor, paniaguado.
**hencoop** (je·ncup) *s*. gallinero.
**hendecagon** (jende·kagan) *s*. endecágono.
**hendecasyllable** (jendekasi·labøl) *s*. endecasílabo.
**henhouse** (je·njaus) *s*. gallinero.
**henna** (je·na) *s*. BOT. alheña. *2* henné.
**hennery** (je·nøri) *s*. gallinero.
**henpeck (to)** (je·npek) *tr*. dominar e importunar [la mujer al marido].
**henpecked** (-t) *adj*. dominado por la mujer.
**Henrietta** (jenrie·ta) *n. pr. f*. Enriqueta.
**henroost** (je·nrust) *s*. gallinero.
**Henry** (je·nri) *n. pr*. Enrique.
**henry** (je·nri) *s*. ELECT. henrio.
**hepatic** (jipæ·tik) *adj*. hepático. *2* del color del hígado.
**hepatica** (jipæ·tika) *s*. BOT. hepática.
**hepatite** (je·patait) *s*. MINER. hepatita.
**hepatitis** (jepatai·tis) *s*. MED. hepatitis.
**heptachord** (je·ptakoʳd) *s*. MÚS. heptacordio.
**heptad** (je·ptad) *s*. setena.
**heptagon** (je·ptagon) *s*. GEOM. heptágono.
**heptagonal** (jeptæ·gonal) *adj*. heptagonal.
**heptameter** (jeptæ·mitø·) *s*. heptámetro.
**heptarchy** (je·ptaʳki) *s*. heptarquía.
**Heptateuch** (je·ptatiuk) *s*. Heptateuco.
**her** (jøʳ) *pron. pers. f*. de *3. pers. sing*. (ac. o dat.) la, le. *2* [con prep.] ella: *to* ~, a ella; *for* ~, para ella. *3 adj. pos. f*. de *3.ª pers*. [indicando una sola poseedora] su, sus [de ella].
**herald** (je·rald) *s*. heraldo. *2* nuncio, precursor.
**herald (to)** *tr*. anunciar, ser nuncio de.
**heraldic** (jeræ·ldik) *adj*. heráldico.
**heraldry** (je·raldri) *s*. heráldica, blasón. *2* armas, blasones. *3* pompa heráldica.
**herb** (øʳb o jøʳb) *s*. BOT. hierba, yerba: ~ *Louisa*, luisa, hierba luisa; ~ *trinity*, trinitaria, pensamiento.
**herbaceous** (jøʳbei·shøs) *adj*. herbáceo.
**herbage** (jø·ʳbidẏ) *s*. hierba, herbaje.
**herbal** (jø·ʳbal) *adj*. herbario.

**herbalist** (-ist) *s*. botánico, herbario. *2* herbolario.
**herbarium** (jøʳbe·riøm) *s*. herbario [colección].
**Herbert** (jø·ʳbøʳt) *n. pr. m*. Heriberto.
**herbivore** (jø·ʳbivoʳ) *s*. ZOOL. herbívoro.
**herbivorous** (jø·biʳvørøs) *adj*. herbívoro.
**herborist** (jø·ʳbørist) *s*. HERBALIST.
**herborization** (jøʳbørisei·shøn) *s*. herborización.
**herborize (to)** (jø·ʳbøraiš) *intr*. herborizar.
**herbose** (jø·ʳbous), **herbous** (-bøs), **herby** (-bi) *adj*. herboso. *2* herbáceo.
**Herculean** (jøʳkiu·lian) *adj*. hercúleo.
**herd** (jøʳd) *s*. rebaño, grey, manada, piara. *2* hato, pandilla. *3* multitud, chusma. *4* pastor [esp. en composición]: *cowherd*, vaquero.
**herd (to)** *intr*. ir en manadas o rebaños. *2* juntarse, asociarse. *3 tr*. reunir o juntar en rebaño.
**herdsman** (-smæn) *s*. pastor, manadero.
**here** (ji·ø·) *adv*. aquí, ahí, acá; ahora, en este momento; en este mundo, en esta vida: ~ *goes!*, ¡ahí va!; ~ *it is*, aquí está, helo aquí; ~ *below*, aquí abajo, en la tierra. *2* ~ *is to you*, a la salud de usted.
**hereabouts** (-abauts) *adv*. por aquí cerca.
**hereafter** (-aftøʳ) *adv*. de aquí en adelante, en lo futuro. *2 s*. *the* ~, el futuro; la otra vida.
**hereat** (-æt) *adv*. a esto, en esto, por eso.
**hereby** (-bai) *adv*. por este medio, por este acto. *2* por la presente.
**hereditary** (jire·diteri) *adj*. hereditario.
**heredity** (-iti) *s*. BIOL. herencia.
**herefrom** (ji·øʳfrom) *adv*. de aquí, desde aquí. *2* a causa de esto.
**herein** (-i·n), **hereinto** (i·ntu) *adv*. aquí dentro, incluso; en esto.
**hereinafter** (-ina·ftøʳ) *adv*. después, más abajo, más adelante [en un libro o escrito].
**hereof** (jiøra·v) *adv*. de esto, acerca de esto; de aquí.
**hereon** (jiøra·n) *adv*. sobre esto, sobre este punto.
**heresiarch** (jiri·sia·ʳk) *s*. heresiarca.
**heresy** (je·røsi) *s*. herejía.
**heretic** (je·retik) *s*. hereje.
**heretic(al** (jire·tik(al) *adj*. herético.
**hereto** (jiø·ʳtu·) *adv*. a esto, a este fin.
**heretofore** (-fo·ʳ) *adv*. hasta aquí, hasta ahora. *2* en el pasado, en otro tiempo. *3 s*. *the* ~, el tiempo pasado, el pasado.
**hereunder** (-ø·ndøʳ) *adv*. bajo esto, abajo, al pie. *2* en virtud de esto.
**hereunto** (-øntu·) *adv*. a esto, a eso.
**hereupon** (-øpa·n) *adv*. a esto. *2* sobre esto, acerca de esto.
**herewith** (-uiz) *adv*. con esto, adjunto.
**heritage** (je·ritidẏ) *s*. herencia.
**hermaphrodite** (jøʳmæ·frødait) *adj.,-s*. hermafrodita.
**hermeneutic(al** (jøʳminiu·tik(al) *adj*. hermenéutico.
**hermeneutics** (-tiks) *s*. hermenéutica.
**hermetic(al** (jøʳme·tik(al) *adj*. hermético.
**hermit** (jø·ʳmit) *s*. ermitaño, eremita, anacoreta. *2* ZOOL. ~ *crab*, ermitaño, paguro.
**hermitage** (jø·ʳmitidẏ) *s*. ermita.
**hermitical** (jøʳmi·tikal) *adj*. eremítico.
**hernia** (jø·ʳnia) *s*. MED. hernia.
**hernial** (jø·ʳnial) *adj*. herniario.
**hero** (ji·rou) *s*. héroe.
**Herod** (je·rød) *n. pr. m*. Herodes.
**Herodian** (jira·dian) *adj.-s*. herodiano.
**heroic(al** (jirou·ik(al) *adj*. heroico. *2 s*. poema heroico.

**heroicomic** (jirouika·mik) *adj.* comicoheroico.
**heroics** (jirou·iks) *s.* verso heroico. *2* lenguaje rimbombante.
**heroin** (je·roin) *s.* QUÍM. heroína.
**heroine** *f.* heroína [mujer].
**heroism** (je·roišm) *s.* heroísmo.
**heron** (je·røn) *s.* ORN. garza, airón.
**heronry** (-ri) *s.* lugar donde anidan las garzas.
**heron's-bill** *s.* BOT. pico de cigüeña.
**herpes** (jø·rpiš) *s.* MED. herpe.
**herpetic** (jø<sup>r</sup>pe·tik) *adj.* herpético.
**herpetology** (jø<sup>r</sup>pita·lødŷi) *s.* herpetología.
**herring** (je·ring) *s.* ICT. arenque.
**herringbone** (-bou·n) *s.* espinapez. *2* espiga, punto espigado.
**hers** (jø<sup>r</sup>š) *pron. pos. f. de 3.ª pers.* [indicando una sola poseedora] suyo, suya, suyos, suyas; el suyo, la suya, los suyos, las suyas; el, la, lo, las, de ella. *2 a friend of* ~, un amigo suyo [de ella].
**herself** (jø<sup>r</sup>se·lf) *pron. pers. f. de 3.ª pers. sing.* ella, ella misma, se, sí, si misma.
**Hertzian** (jø·<sup>r</sup>tsian) *adj.* FÍS. hertziano.
**he's** (jīš) contracción de HE IS y de HE HAS.
**Hesiod** (jī·siød) *n. pr. m.* Hesiodo.
**hesitancy** (je·šitansi) *s.* vacilación, duda.
**hesitant** (-tant) *adj.* vacilante, indeciso, irresoluto, titubeante.
**hesitate (to)** (-eit) *intr.* vacilar, dudar, titubear. *2* tartamudear, balbucear.
**hesitation** (-ei·shøn) *s.* vacilación, duda, titubeo. *2* tartamudeo, balbucencia.
**Hesper** (je·spø<sup>r</sup>) *s.* véspero, estrella vespertina.
**Hesperides** (jespe·ridis) *s. pl.* MIT. Hespérides. *2* MIT. jardín de las Hespérides.
**hesperidium** (jespøri·diøm) *s.* BOT. hesperidio.
**hessian** (je·shan) *s.* arpillera.
**Hester** (je·stø<sup>r</sup>) *n. pr. f.* Ester.
**heterocercal** (je·tørøse<sup>r</sup>kal) *adj.* ICT. heterocerca.
**heteroclite** (-clait) *adj.* heteróclito.
**heterodox** (-daks) *adj.-s.* heterodoxo.
**heterodoxy** (-daksi) *s.* heterodoxia.
**heterodyne** (-dain) *adj.* RADIO. heterodino. *2 s.* RADIO. heterodino [oscilador].
**heterogeneity** (-dŷna·iti) *s.* heterogeneidad.
**heterogeneous** (-dŷi·niøs) *adj.* heterogéneo.
**heteronomous** (jetøra·nomøs) *adj.* heterónomo.
**heteroscians** (-shans) *adj.-s. pl.* GEOGR. heteroscios.
**hew (to)** (jiu) *tr.* tajar, cortar, picar, hachear, desbastar; labrar [madera, piedra]. *2* formar, hacer [a golpes de un instrumento cortante]; abrir, esculpir. *3 intr.* dar golpes o hachazos. *4 to* ~ *close to the line,* fig. hilar delgado. ¶ Pret.: *hewed*; p. p.: *hewn.*
**hewer** (-ø<sup>r</sup>) *s.* picapedrero. *2* desbastador.
**hewn** (-n) *p. p.* de TO HEW.
**hexachord** (je·ksako<sup>r</sup>d) *s.* MÚS. hexacordo.
**hexagon** (-gan) *s.* GEOM. hexágono.
**hexagonal** (jeksæ·gønal) *adj.* hexagonal.
**hexahedron** (jeksaji·drøn) *s.* GEOM. hexaedro.
**hexameter** (jeksæ·mitø<sup>r</sup>) *s.* hexámetro.
**hexapod** (je·ksapad) *adj.-s.* ZOOL. hexápodo.
**hexastyle** (-stail) *s.* ARQ. hexástilo.
**hey** (jei) *interj.* ¡eh!, ¡oiga!, ¡digo! *2* ¡ea!
**heyday** (jei·dei) *s.* apogeo, colmo [de vitalidad, fuerza, etc.]. *2 interj.* ¡hola!
**Hezekiah** (jesikai·a) *n. pr. m.* Ezequías.
**hiatus** (jaiei·tøs) *s.* blanco, laguna, espacio, vacío, salto. *2* hiato.
**hibernal** (jaibø·<sup>r</sup>nal) *adj.* ibernal, hiemal.
**hibernate (to)** (jai·bø<sup>r</sup>neit) *intr.* estar en hibernación.

**hibernation** (-ei·shøn) *s.* hibernación, hiemación.
**Hibernian** (jaibø·<sup>r</sup>nian) *s.* hibernés.
**hibiscus** (jaibi·skøs) *s.* BOT. hibisco.
**hiccough** (ji·kof), **hiccup** (ji·køp) *s.* hipo.
**hiccough, hiccup (to)** *intr.* hipar [tener hipo].
**hickory** (ji·køri) *s.* nogal americano.
**hickup** (ji·køp) *s.* HICCUP.
**hid** (jid) *pret.* y *p. p.* de TO HIDE.
**hidden** (-øn) *p. p.* de TO HIDE. *2 adj.* oculto, escondido, recóndito, secreto, latente.
**hide** (jaid) *s.* cuero, piel, pellejo [de animal]. *2* fig. pellejo [de persona].
**hide (to)** *tr.* esconder, ocultar, cubrir, tapar, disimular. *2* azotar. *3 intr.* esconderse, ocultarse: *to* ~ *out,* estarse escondido. ¶ Pret.: *hid*; p. p.: *hidden* o *hid.*
**hide-and-seek** *s.* juego del escondite.
**hidebound** (-baund) *adj.* de piel pegada a los huesos. *2* fanático, dogmático, de ideas mezquinas.
**hideous** (ji·diøs) *adj.* horrible, horrendo. *2* feo, horroroso. *3* odioso, repugnante.
**hiding** (jai·ding) *s.* ocultamiento, escondimiento. *2* retiro. *3* paliza, zurra. *4* ~ *place,* escondite, escondrijo.
**hie (to)** (jai) *intr.* apresurarse; correr, volar. *2* apresurar, aguijar; ~ *thee,* date prisa.
**hierarch** (jai·øra<sup>r</sup>k) *s.* jerarca.
**hierarchical** (jaiøra·<sup>r</sup>kikal) *adj.* jerárquico.
**hierarchy** (jai·øra<sup>r</sup>ki) *s.* jerarquía.
**hieratic(al** (jaiørø·tik(al) *adj.* hierático.
**hieroglyph** (jaiørøgli·f), **hieroglyphic** (-ik) *s.* jeroglífico, hieroglífico.
**hieroglyphic(al** (-fik(al) *adj.* jeroglífico, hieroglífico.
**Hieronymite** (jaiøra·nimait) *adj.-s.* jerónimo [religioso].
**hierophant** (jai·ørøfant) *s.* hierofanta, hierofante.
**high** (jai) *adj.* alto [que tiene altura]. *2* de alto: *a wall twelve feet* ~, una pared de doce pies de alto. *3* alto, elevado, encumbrado; noble, ilustre; grande; sublime; superior, principal, sumo: *High Chancellor,* Gran Canciller; ~ *command,* alto mando; ~ *priest,* sumo sacerdote. *4* altivo, altanero. *5* intenso, vivo, fuerte. *6* alborotada, gruesa [mar]. *7* alta [calidad, traición, comedia, frecuencia, presión, tensión]. *8* MÚS. alto, agudo. *9* B. ART. alto [relieve]. *10* subido [precio]; caro: ~ *cost of living,* carestía de la vida. *11* mayor [calle, altar, misa]. *12* remota [antigüedad]. *13* pleno [día, etc.]. *14* pasada, manida [carne]. *15* COC. fuerte, picante. *16* fam. achispado. *17* rico en. *18* Otros sentidos: ~ *and mighty,* fam. orgulloso, altanero; dominador; ~ *colour,* color encendido, rubicundez, rubor; ~ *gear,* AUTO. directa; *High German,* alto alemán; ~ *hand,* despotismo; altanería; ~ *hat,* sombrero de copa, chistera; ~ *life,* alta sociedad, gran mundo; ~ *school,* escuela de segunda enseñanza; ~ *seas,* alta mar, piélago; ~ *spirits,* alegría, buen humor, animación; ~ *tide,* marea alta, pleamar; apogeo; ~ *words,* palabras fuertes, ofensivas; *the Most High,* el Altísimo; *in* ~ *terms,* en términos lisonjeros; *it is* ~ *time to,* ya es hora de que de que.
*19 adv.* arriba: ~ *and low,* arriba y abajo, por todas partes. *20* alto, a gran altura. *21* altamente. *22* profundamente. *23* en grande. *24* caro.
*25 s.* lo alto, las alturas, el cielo: *from on* ~, de lo alto. *26* [el] colmo. *27* [el] precio más alto. *28* AUTO. directa; marcha directa.

**highborn** (-bo<sup>r</sup>n) *adj.* noble, linajudo.
**highboy** (-boi) *s.* especie de cómoda con patas altas.
**high-brow** *s.* (E.U.) intelectual, sabio; el que se da aires de superioridad intelectual.
**high-coloured** *adj.* subido de color.
**high-duty** *adj.* de alto rendimiento [máquina].
**higher** (-ø<sup>r</sup>) *adj. comp.* de HIGH; más alto; alto, superior: ~ *classes*, clases altas; ~ *mathematics*, matemáticas superiores.
**highest** (-est) *adj. superl.* de HIGH; el más alto; sumo, supremo, mayor, máximo: ~ *common divisor* o *factor*, ARIT. máximo común divisor.
**highfalutin** (jaifælu·tin) *adj.* fam. hinchado, ampuloso, retumbante.
**high-fidelity** *adj.* RADIO. de alta fidelidad.
**high-flown** (jai·floun) *adj.* de alto vuelo. *2* orgulloso, presuntuoso. *3* hinchado, campanudo.
**high-grade** *adj.* fino, de calidad superior.
**high-handed** *adj.* despótico, arbitrario.
**high-hearted** *adj.* noble, valeroso.
**highjack (to)** *tr.* TO HIJACK.
**high-keyed** *adj.* impresionable, sensible. *2* MÚS. agudo.
**highland** (-land) *s.* montaña, región montañosa. *2* pl. *the Highlands*, región montañosa de Escocia. *3 adj.* de las tierras altas.
**highlander** (-ø<sup>r</sup>) *s.* montañés [esp. de Escocia].
**highly** (-li) *adv.* altamente, sumamente, en sumo grado. *2* elevadamente. *3* a un alto precio. *4* bien, favorablemente.
**high-minded** *adj.* magnánimo, de nobles o elevados sentimientos; orgulloso, altivo.
**highness** (-nis) *s.* altura, alteza, elevación, celsitud. *2* alteza [tratamiento].
**high-pitched** *adj.* MÚS. agudo. *2* chillona [voz]. *3* de mucha pendiente. *4* HIGHSTRUNG 2.
**high-priced** *adj.* caro, de subido precio.
**highroad** (-roud) *s.* carretera, camino real.
**high-seasoned** *adj.* picante, fuerte de especias.
**high-sounding** *adj.* pomposo, altisonante.
**high-spirited** *adj.* gallardo, animoso, valiente. *2* fogoso [caballo]. *3* orgulloso.
**high-strung** *adj.* tenso, vigoroso. *2* en estado de aguda sensibilidad, excitable, nervioso.
**high-test** adj. ~ *fuel*, supercarburante.
**high-toned** (jai·tound) *adj.* MÚS. agudo. *2* digno, caballeroso. *3* fam. (E. U.) elegante, distinguido.
**highty-tighty** *adj.* HOITY-TOITY.
**high-water mark** *s.* nivel más alto a que llega la marea. *2* fig. colmo, apogeo.
**highway** (-uei) *s.* camino real, carretera.
**highwayman** (-mæn) *s.* bandolero, salteador [de caminos].
**high-wrought** *adj.* primorosamente labrado o trabajado. *2* muy excitado.
**hijack (to)** (jai·dÿæk) *tr.* fam. (E.U.) robar [a un contrabandista de licores].
**hike** (jaik) *s.* fam. marcha, caminata, viaje a pie.
**hike (to)** *intr.* fam. hacer una caminata.
**hilarious** (jaile·riøs) *adj.* alegre, bullicioso.
**hilarity** (jailæ·riti) *s.* hilaridad, regocijo, bullicioso.
**Hilary** (ji·lari) *n. pr. m.* Hilario.
**hill** (jil) *s.* colina, collado, cerro, altozano, cuesta. | A veces se usa por montaña. *2* montón, montículo.
**hill (to)** *tr.* amontonar. *2* AGR. aporcar. *3 intr.* amontonarse.
**hillock** (-øk) *s.* montículo, altillo, altozano.
**hillside** (-said) *s.* ladera [de una colina].

**hilly** (-i) *adj.* montuoso. *2* pendiente [en cuesta].
**hilt** (jilt) *s.* puño, empuñadura [de un arma]: *up to the* ~, hasta el puño, completamente.
**him** (jim) *pron. pers. m. de 3.ª pers. sing.* [ac. o dat.] lo, le. *2* [con prep. o como atributo] él: *to* ~, a él.
**himself** (jimse·lf) *pron. pers. m. de 3.ª pers. sing.* él, él mismo, se, sí, sí mismo.
**hind** (jaind) *adj.* trasero, zaguero, posterior. *2 s.* ZOOL. cierva. *3* mozo de labranza.
**hinder** (-ø<sup>r</sup>) *adj.* posterior, trasero.
**hinder (to)** (ji·ndø<sup>r</sup>) *tr.* impedir, estorbar, dificultar. *2 intr.* ser obstáculo, oponerse, obstar.
**hindermost** (jai·ndø·moust), **hindmost** (hai·ndmoust) *adj.* postrero, último.
**Hindoo** (ji·ndu) *s.* HINDU.
**hindquarter** (jai·ndkuø<sup>r</sup>tø<sup>r</sup>) *s.* cuarto trasero [de res].
**hindrance** (ji·ndrans) *s.* estorbo, impedimento, embarazo, obstáculo. *2* traba, cortapisa.
**Hindu** (ji·ndu) *adj.-s.* hindú, indio.
**Hinduism** (-išm) *s.* hinduismo.
**Hindustan** (jindusta·n) *n. pr.* GEOGR. Indostán.
**Hindustani** (-ni) *adj.* indostánico. *2 s.* indostani, hindustani [lenguaje].
**hinge** (ji·ndÿ) *s.* gozne, bisagra, pernio, charnela. *2* fig. eje, principio rector, punto capital. *3* ENCUAD. cartivana.
**hinge (to)** *tr.* engoznar, poner goznes o bisagras a. *2 intr. to* ~ *on*, girar sobre, depender de.
**hinny** (ji·ni) *s.* ZOOL. burdégano.
**hint** (jint) *s.* indicación, insinuación, sugestión, indirecta, alusión.
**hint (to)** *tr.-intr.* indicar, insinuar, sugerir, aludir vagamente.
**hinterland** (ji·ntø<sup>r</sup>land) *s.* hinterland.
**hip** (jip) *s.* ANAT. cadera. *2* ARQ. lima tesa. *3* BOT. hip o ~ *rose*, tapaculo, escaramujo. *4 interj.* VOZ para llamar o aclamar. *5 adv.* ~ *and thigh*, duramente, sin piedad.
**hip (to)** *tr.* descaderar, derrengar. *2* echar sobre la cadera. ¶ Pret. y p. p.: *hipped*; p. a.: *hipping*.
**hipbone** (ji·pboun) *s.* ANAT. cía, hueso de la cadera.
**hipped** (jipt) *adj.* renco. *2* melancólico, abatido. *3* obsesionado.
**hippocampus** (jipokæ·mpøs) *s.* MIT., ICT., ANAT. hipocampo.
**hippocras** (ji·pokras) *s.* hipocrás.
**Hippocrates** (ji·pokratiš) *n. pr. m.* Hipócrates.
**hippodrome** (ji·pødroum) *s.* hipódromo, circo.
**hippogriff** (ji·pøgrif) MIT. hipogrifo.
**hippopotamus** (jipøpa·tamøs) *s.* ZOOL. hipopótamo.
**hipshot** (ji·pshat) *adj.* renco.
**hircine** (jø·<sup>r</sup>sin) *adj.* hircino.
**hircocervus** (jø<sup>r</sup>cosø·<sup>r</sup>vøs) *s.* MIT. hircocervo.
**hire** (jai<sup>r</sup>) *s.* alquiler, arrendar. *2* contratar, asoldar, asalariar. *3 intr.* alquilarse, ajustarse.
**hireling** (jai·<sup>r</sup>ling) *adj.-s.* asalariado. *2* alquilón, mercenario.
**hirer** (jai·rø<sup>r</sup>) *s.* alquilador, arrendador.
**hirsute** (jø·<sup>r</sup>siut) *adj.* hirsuto, híspido.
**his** (jiš) *adj. y pron. pos. m. de 3.ª pers.* [indicando un solo poseedor] suyo, suya, suyos, suyas, de él; el suyo, la suya, los suyos, las suyas; el, la, los, las de él. *2 a friend of* ~, un amigo suyo [de él].
**Hispanic** (jispæ·nik) *adj.* hispánico, hispano.
**Hispanist** (ji·spænist) *s.* hispanista.
**hispid** (ji·spid) *adj.* híspido.

**hiss** (jis) *s.* siseo. *2* silbido, sonido sibilante, chirrido.

**hiss (to)** *intr.* silbar, sisear, chirriar. *2 tr.* silbar, sisear [mostrar desaprobación].

**hissing** (-ing) *s.* siseo, silba, sonido sibilante.

**hist** (jist) *interj.* ¡atención!; ¡psit! *2* ¡chitón!

**histologist** (jista·lødÿist) *s.* histólogo.

**histology** (jista·lødÿi) *s.* histología.

**historian** (jisto·rian) *s.* historiador.

**historic(al** (-rik(al) *adj.* histórico.

**historiographer** (jistoria·grafø^r) *s.* historiógrafo.

**historiography** (-grafi) *s.* historiografía.

**history** (ji·stori) *s.* historia. | No tiene el sentido de chisme, cuento.

**histrion** (ji·striøn) *s.* histrión.

**histrionic (al** (jistria·nik(al) *adj.* histriónico.

**histrionism** (ji·striønišm) *s.* histrionismo.

**hit** (jit) *s.* golpe, choque. *2* golpe de fortuna. *3* golpe certero, acierto, éxito: *to make a ~,* tener gran éxito. *4* agudeza, sarcasmo.

**hit (to)** *tr.* dar, pegar, golpear, chocar con. *2* dar [un golpe]. *3* afectar, herir [una cosa a uno]. *4* atinar, acertar: *to ~ the nail on the head,* dar en el clavo; *~ or miss,* salga lo que saliere. *5* encontrar, dar con. *6* convenir, adaptarse a. *7 to ~ it off,* avenirse, congeniar. *8 to ~ off,* imitar, describir o expresar con acierto. *9 to ~ the spot,* llenar, satisfacer. *10 to ~ the trail,* ponerse en camino. *11 intr.* tocar, chocar. *12 to ~ on* o *upon,* dar con; acordarse de; ocurrírsele a uno. ¶ Pret. y p. p.: *hit;* ger.: *hitting.*

**hitch** (ji·ch) *s.* tirón, sacudida. *2* cojera. *3* obstáculo, impedimento, tropiezo, dificultad. *4* alto, parada. *5* MAR. nombre de varios nudos.

**hitch (to)** *tr.* mover [a tirones o poquito a poco]. *2* enganchar, unir, atar, sujetar, amarrar. *3 intr.* moverse [a sacudidas, a saltos]. *4* enredarse, engancharse. *5* avenirse, congeniar.

**hitchhike (to)** (-jaik) *intr.* hacer autostop.

**hitchhiking** (-ing) *s.* autostop.

**hither** (-ji·dø^r) *adv.* acá, hacia acá: *~ and thither,* acá y acullá. *2 adj.* citerior, de este lado.

**hithermost** (-moust) *adj.* más cercano.

**hitherto** (-tu·) *adv.* hasta aquí, hasta ahora.

**Hitlerism** (ji·tlørišm) *s.* hitlerismo.

**hit-run** *adj.* que atropella y se da a la fuga.

**Hittite** (ji·tait) *adj.-s.* HIST. heteo, hitita.

**hive** (jaiv) *s.* colmena. *2* enjambre.

**hive (to)** *tr.* API. enjambrar. *2 intr.* vivir como en colmena.

**hives** (-øs) *s.* MED. urticaria.

**ho, hoa** (jo) *interj.* ¡eh!, ¡ah!; ¡oiga!; ¡alto!

**hoar** (jo^r) *adj.* blanco, cano, canoso, gris. *2 s.* blancura, canicie. *4* HOARFROST.

**hoard** (jø^rd) *s.* depósito, acumulamiento, tesoro, repuesto; dinero guardado.

**hoard (to)** *tr.* acumular, guardar, atesorar.

**hoarder** (-ø^r) *s.* atesorador.

**hoarding** (-ing) *s.* amontonamiento, atesoramiento. *2* cerca de construcción. *3* cartelera.

**hoarfrost** (jo·^rfrost) *s.* escarcha, helada blanca.

**hoarhound** (-jaund) *s.* BOT. marrubio.

**hoariness** (-inis) *s.* blancura, canicie.

**hoarse** (jo^rs) *adj.* ronco, rauco, áspero, bronco.

**hoarseness** (-nis) *s.* ronquera, bronquedad.

**hoary** (jo·ri) *adj.* cano, canoso. *2* blanco. *3* venerable, vetusto.

**hoax** (jouks) *s.* broma, engaño; bulo, pajarota.

**hoax (to)** *tr.* embromar, engañar.

**hob** (jab) *s.* repisa, interior del hogar. *2* cubo [de

rueda]. *3* chito, tángano. *4* fam. to play *~* with, trastornar.

**hobble** (ja·bøl) *s.* cojera. *2* traba, manea, maniota. *3* fam. dificultad, atolladero.

**hobble (to)** *intr.* cojear. *2* bailar [un pendiente, etc.]. *3 tr.* manear. *9* hacer cojear.

**hobby** (ja·bi) *s.* afición [trabajo, estudio, etc., hecho por afición o pasatiempo].

**hobbyhorse** (-jo^rs) *s.* caballito, caballo mecedor [juguete]. *2* fig. manía, tema.

**hobgoblin** (ja·bgablin) *s.* duende, trasgo.

**hobnail** (-neil) *s.* clavo de cabeza gruesa para zapatos. *2* rústico, patán.

**hobnail (to)** *tr.* clavetear [zapatos].

**hobnob (to)** (-nab) *intr.* beber juntos. *2* codearse, rozarse. ¶ Pret. y p. p.: *hobnobbed;* ger.: *-bbing.*

**hobo** (jou·bou) *s.* fam. (E. U.) vagabundo.

**hock** (jak) *s.* corvejón, jarrete. *2* COC. garrón [de cerdo]. *3* vino del Rin.

**hock (to)** *tr.* desjarretar.

**hockey** (ja·ki) *s.* hockey [juego de pelota].

**hocus** (jou·køs) *tr.* burlar, engañar. *2* narcotizar, atontar, con drogas. ¶ Pret. y p. p.: *hocused* o *-ssed;* ger.: *hocusing* o *-ssing.*

**hocus-pocus** (-pou·køs) *s.* fórmula de prestidigitador. *2* pasapasa. *4* treta, engaño.

**hod** (jad) *s.* ALBAÑ. cuezo. *2* cubo para carbón.

**hodgepodge** (ja·dÿpadÿ) *s.* almodrote, baturrillo, mezcolanza.

**hodman** (ja·dmæn) *s.* peón de albañil; bracero.

**hoe** (jou) *s.* azada, azadón, almocafre, escardillo.

**hoe (to)** *tr.* cavar, azadonar, sachar.

**hog** (jog) *s.* cerdo, cochino [animal, persona sucia]. *2* egoísta. *3* glotón. *4* pop. to go the whole *~,* llegar hasta el último límite. *5 ~ Latin,* latín de cocina.

**hog (to)** *tr.* recortar [la crin de un caballo]. *2* arquear, combar. *3 intr.* arquearse, combarse. ¶ Pret. y p. p.: *hogged;* ger.: *hogging.*

**hogback** (-bæk) *s.* cuchilla, cerro escarpado.

**hoggish** (-ish) *adj.* puerco. *2* glotón. *3* egoísta.

**hogherd** (-jø^rd) *s.* porquero, porquerizo.

**hogshead** (-šjed) *s.* pipa, bocoy.

**hog's-fennel** *s.* BOT. servato.

**hogskin** (-skin) *s.* piel de cerdo.

**hogsty** (-stai) *s.* pocilga.

**hogwash** (-uøsh) *s.* bazofia.

**hoiden** (joi·døn) *s.* HOYDEN.

**hoist** (joist) *s.* cabría, grúa, montacargas. *2* lo que se iza o eleva. *3* elevación; enarbolamiento; empujón hacia arriba.

**hoist (to)** *tr.* izar, subir, elevar. *2* enarbolar.

**hoity-toity** (joiti-toi·ti) *adj.* frívolo, veleidoso. *2* engreído. *3 s.* frivolidad, veleidad. *4* engreimiento. *5 interj.* ¡hombre!, ¡tate!

**hokey-pokey** (jou·ki-pou·ki) *s.* HOCUS-POCUS.

**hold** (jould) *s.* presa, agarro, sostenimiento. *2* presa [en la lucha]. *3* asidero, agarradero, sostén. *4* poder, influencia, dominio. *5* custodia, prisión. *6* MAR. bodega, cala. *7* AVIA. cabina de carga. *8* MÚS. calderón. *9* fortaleza, refugio. *10* guarida. *11* receptáculo. *12 to get, lay* o *take ~ of,* agarrar, agarrarse a; apoderarse de.

**hold (to)** *tr.* tener, poseer. *2* ocupar [un cargo, etc.]. *3* sujetar, asir, tener asido. *4* aguantar, apoyar, sostener. *5* defender [una posición, etc.]. *6* retener, mantener, tener [en un lugar, situación o estado]. *7* contener, detener, refrenar. *8* tener [en estima, etc.]. *9* juzgar, considerar, tener por. *10* absorber, ocupar [la atención, etc.]. *11* contener; coger, tener cabida para. *12* celebrar

[una reunión]; sostener [una conversación]. *13* guardar, observar. *14* hacer [compañía]. *15* usar [cierto lenguaje]. *16 to ~ back*, contener, detener, refrenar. *17 to ~ down*, tener sujeto, oprimir; mantenerse en [un cargo]. *18 to ~ forth*, presentar; expresar. *19 to ~ in*, refrenar. *20 to ~ off*, mantener alejado. *21 to ~ one's own*, mantenerse firme, resistir. *22 to ~ one's peace*, callar. *23 to ~ on*, ofrecer, tender; presentar, proponer. *24 to ~ over*, aplazar, diferir. *25 to ~ up*, levantar, alzar; sostener; mostrar; refrenar; atracar, saltear, detener para robar. *26 to ~ up to*, exponer [al desprecio, etc.]. *27 intr.* agarrarse, asirse. *28* pegarse, adherirse. *29* valer, ser válido, estar o seguir en vigor. *30* mantenerse, sostenerse. *31* mantenerse firme o fiel. *32* durar, continuar. *33 to ~ back*, detenerse, contenerse; abstenerse; recular. *34 to ~ forth*, predicar, perorar. *35 to ~ good*, subsistir. *36 to ~ in*, contenerse. *37 to ~ off*, esperar; mantenerse a distancia; mostrarse frío. *38 to ~ on*, agarrarse; aguantar; seguir, continuar; detenerse. *39 to ~ out*, mantenerse firme; durar, continuar, resistir. *40 to ~ up*, cesar de llover; continuar, durar; no recular.
¶ *Pret.* y *p. p.: held*.

**holdback** (-bæk) *s.* restricción, freno. *2* cejadero.

**holder** (-ø<sup>r</sup>) *s.* sostenedor, sostén, sustentáculo, agarrador, mango, asa. *2* receptáculo. *3* FOT. chasis. *4* tenedor, poseedor, propietario. *5* arrendatario [de tierras]. *6* COM. tenedor. *7* titular [de un cargo, un pasaporte, etc.].

**holdfast** (-fast) *s.* grapón, grapa, laña; barrilete. *2* agarradero, sostén. *3* hombre muy avaro.

**holding** (-ing) *s.* tenencia, pertenencia, posesión. *2* arriendo. *3* tierra arrendada. *4* celebración [de una sesión, reunión, etc.]. *5* opinión, creencia. *6 pl.* COM. valores, títulos. *7 adj.* COM. ~ *company*, compañía tenedora de acciones de otras compañías.

**holdup** (-øp) *s.* fam. atraco, salteamiento.

**hole** (joul) *s.* agujero, orificio, abertura, boquete. *2* hoyo, hueco, cavidad. *3* ojo [del pan o el queso]. *4* olla, remanso [en un río]. *5* bache. *6* cueva, madriguera. *7* rincón [lugar apartado]. *8* tabuco, cochitril. *9* calabozo. *10* defecto, falla, tacha. *11* aprieto, atolladero. *12* GOLF. hoyo.

**hole (to)** *tr.* agujerear, horadar. *2* BILLAR entronerar. *3* GOLF meter [la pelota] en el hoyo. *4 intr.* encovarse ~ *up*, encovarse; buscar un escondrijo o un rincón cómodo.

**holiday** (ja·lidei) *s.* fiesta, festividad, día festivo. *2* vacación, asueto. *3 pl.* vacaciones. *4 adj.* de fiesta, festivo.

**holiness** (jou·linis) *s.* santidad, beatitud. *2 His Holiness*, Su Santidad.

**Holland** (ja·land) *n. pr.* GEOGR. Holanda. *2 s.* holanda [lienzo].

**Hollander** (-ø<sup>r</sup>) *s.* holandés.

**Hollands** (-s) *s.* ginebra holandesa.

**hollo, holloa** (jølou·) *interj.* ¡eh!, ¡hola!; ¡vítor! *2 s.* grito, saludo; grito de triunfo.

**hollo, holloa (to)** *tr.* decir a gritos. *2 intr.* gritar.

**hollow** (ja·lou) *adj.* hueco, cóncavo, vacío. *2* hundido [ojos, mejillas]. *3* flaco, hambriento. *4* profundo, cavernoso [sonido, voz]. *5* falso, insincero. *6* vano, sin substancia. *7 s.* hueco. *8* depresión, hondonada, valle.

**hollow (to)** *tr.* ahuecar, ahondar, acopar, excavar, hundir.

**hollow-hearted** *adj.* insincero, solapado.

**hollowness** (-nis) *s.* cavidad, hueco, vacío. *2* doblez, falsía.

**holly** (ja<sup>r</sup>li) *s.* BOT. acebo, agrifolio.

**hollyhock** (-jak) *s.* BOT. malvarrosa, malvaloca.

**holm** (jou·lm) *s.* mejana, isleta. *2* vega ribereña. *3* BOT. holm o ~ *oak*, encina.

**holocaust** (ja·løkost) *s.* holocausto.

**holograph** (ja·løgræf) *s.* hológrafo, ológrafo.

**holographic** (jaløgræ·fik) *adj.* hológrafo, ológrafo.

**holohedron** (-ji·drøn) *s.* CRIST. holoedro.

**holothurian** (-ziu·rian) *s.* ZOOL. holoturia.

**holster** (jou·lstø<sup>r</sup>) *s.* pistolera.

**holy** (jou·li) *adj.* santo: ~ *Cross*, Santa Cruz; *Holy Father*, Santo Padre; ~ *Office*, Santo Oficio; ~ *of holies*, santo de los santos; *Holy See*, Santa Sede; *Holy Week*, semana santa. *2* sacro, sagrado, bendito: *Holy Communion*, sagrada comunión; ~ *water*, agua bendita; *Holy Writ*, Sagradas Escrituras. *3* divino: ~ *lamb*, divino cordero. *4* dedicado a Dios: ~ *day* o *holiday*, día de fiesta; fiesta [de la Iglesia].

**homage** (ja·midy) *s.* homenaje [feudal]. *2* homenaje, deferencia, respeto.

**homard** (oma·<sup>r</sup>) *s.* ZOOL. bogavante.

**home** (joum) *s.* hogar, lares, casa, morada, domicilio. *2* asilo, albergue, hospicio. *3* país natal, patria, patria chica. *4* [para los coloniales] Inglaterra. *5* BIOL. habitación. *6* DEP. meta, límite, término. *7 at ~*, en casa; en su país; a gusto, con comodidad: *make yourself at ~*, haga como si estuviera en su casa; póngase cómodo. *8 adj.* doméstico, hogareño, casero. *9* nativo, natal. *10* nacional, del país; del interior: ~ *products*, productos nacionales; *Home office*, (Ingl.) ministerio de la Gobernación. *11* regional: ~ *rule*, autonomía. *12* de regreso [que regresa o acaba de regresar]. *13* eficaz, que da en el clavo. *14 adv.* en, o a casa; en, o al país de uno. *15 to bring*, o *drive ~*, hacer que convenza; *to hit*, o *strike ~*, herir en lo vivo; llegar al alma; dar en el blanco.

**home (to)** *tr.* mandar a casa. *2* dar morada o domicilio a. *3 intr.* habitar. *4* volver a casa.

**homebred** (-bred) *adj.* nativo, doméstico, casero; criado en casa. *2* sencillo, inculto, tosco.

**homefelt** (-felt) *adj.* íntimo, cordial.

**homekeeping** (-kiping) *adj.* de gustos caseros.

**homeless** (-lis) *adj.* sin casa ni hogar. *2* inhabitable, inhóspito.

**homelike** (-laik) *adj.* como de casa; cómodo, acogedor; familiar. *2* sosegado.

**homeliness** (-linis) *s.* sencillez, simplicidad. *2* falta de elegancia o refinamiento. *3* fealdad.

**homely** (-li) *adj.* llano, sencillo, casero. *2* feo, vulgar, ordinario. *3* rústico, inculto.

**homemade** (-meid) *adj.* casero, hecho en casa. *2* fabricado en el país.

**homeopath** (jou·miopaz), **homeopathist** (-pæ·zist) *s.* homeópata.

**homeopathy** (joumio·pæzi) *s.* homeopatía.

**Homer** (jou·mø<sup>r</sup>) *n. pr. m.* Homero.

**homer** *s.* fam. paloma mensajera.

**Homeric** (joume·rik) *adj.* homérico.

**homesick** (jou·msik) *adj.* nostálgico.

**homesickness** (-nis) *s.* nostalgia, añoranza.

**homespun** (-spøn) *adj.* hilado o hecho en casa. *2* basto, sin elegancia.

**homestead** (-sted) *s.* casa y tierras adyacentes, heredad. *2* fig. casa, hogar.

**homesteader** (-stedø<sup>r</sup>) *s.* dueño de una heredad que habita en ella y la cultiva. *2* (E. U.) colono que ha recibido sus tierras del Gobierno.

**homeward** (-uaᵣd) *adv.* hacia casa, hacia su país. *2 adj.* de regreso, de vuelta.
**homewards** (-s) *adv.* HOMEWARD.
**homicidal** (jamisai·dal) *adj.* homicida.
**homicide** (ja·misaid) *s.* homicidio. *2* homicida.
**homiletics** (jamile·tiks) *s.* homilética.
**homily** (ja·mili) *s.* homilía, sermón.
**homing** (jou·ming) *adj.* mensajera [paloma].
**hominy** (ja·mini) *s.* maíz molido o machacado.
**homo-** (joumo-) *pref.* homo-.
**homocerc (al** (-sø·ᵣk(al) *adj.* ICT. homocerco.
**homogeneity** (-dȳi·nıiti) *s.* homogeneidad.
**homogeneous** (-dȳi·niøs) *adj.* homogéneo.
**homogenize (to)** (-dȳinaiš) *tr.* hacer homogéneo, homogeneizar.
**homologate (to)** (-logeit) *tr.* homologar.
**homologation** (-ei·shøn) *s.* homologación.
**homologous** (jouma·løgøs) *adj.* homólogo.
**homolog(ue** (ja·mølog) *s.* cosa homóloga de otra.
**homonym** (-nim) *s.* homónimo.
**homonymous** (jouma·nimøs) *adj.* homónimo.
**homophonous** (-fønøs) *adj.* homófono.
**homophony** (-føni) *s.* homofonía.
**homopterous** (-ptørøs) *adj.* homóptero.
**homosexual** (joumøse·kshual) *adj.-s.* homosexual.
**homunculus** (joumø·nkiuløs) *s.* homúnculo.
**hone** (joun) *s.* piedra de afilar.
**hone (to)** *tr.* afilar, vaciar, asentar [navajas, etcétera].
**honest** (a·nist) *adj.* honrado, probo, íntegro. *2* justo, recto. *3* leal, sincero. *4* honesta [mujer]. *5* bien adquirido [dinero].
**honesty** (-i) *s.* honradez, probidad, rectitud. *2* sinceridad, lealtad. *4* honestidad.
**honey** (jø·ni) *s.* miel [de abejas]. *2* dulzura, melosidad. *3* fam. cariño, vida mía.
**honey (to)** *tr.* enmelar. *2* adular, halagar. *3 intr.* hablar con melosidad.
**honeybee** (jø·nibı) *s.* ENT. abeja melífera.
**honeycomb** (jø·nicoum) *s.* panal de miel. *2* cosa parecida a un panal. *3 adj.* apanalado, de panal, de nido de abeja.
**honeycomb (to)** *tr.* llenar de hoyos o agujeros.
**honeyed** (jø·nid) *adj.* enmelado. *2* dulce, meloso, melifluo, adulador.
**honeymoon** (-mun) *s.* luna de miel.
**honeymoon (to)** *intr.* pasar la luna de miel.
**honeysuckle** (-søkøl) *s.* BOT. madreselva.
**honeysweet** (-suıt) *adj.* dulce como la miel.
**honk** (jonk) *s.* graznido del ganso. *2* bocinazo.
**honk (to)** *tr.* tocar [la bocina]. *2 intr.* graznar [el ganso]. *3* dar bocinazos.
**honor, honorability, honorable,** etc. HONOUR, HONOURABILITY, HONOURABLE, etc.
**honorarium** (anøre·riøm) *s.* honorarios.
**honorary** (a·nøreri) *adj.* honorario, honorífico. *2* de honor.
**Honorius** (ano·riøs) *n. pr. m.* Honorio.
**honour** (a·nøᵣ) *s.* honor, honra: *court of* ~, tribunal de honor; *point of* ~, punto de honra; *to do* ~ *to*, hacer honor a, honrar; *on my* ~, por mi honor; ~ *bright*, fam. de veras, a fe de caballero. *2* honradez. *3* prez. *4* lauro, condecoración. *5 your Honour,* usía, su señoría. *6 pl.* honores: *to do the honours of,* hacer los honores de. *7* honras: *funeral honours,* honras fúnebres. *8* nota sobresaliente [en los estudios].
**honour (to)** *tr.* honrar. *2* reverenciar, respetar. *3* enaltecer. *4* glorificar. *5* laurear, condecorar. *6* COM. hacer honor a [su firma]; aceptar, pagar.

**honourable** (a·nørabøl) *adj.* honorable. *2* honrado. *3* honroso, meritorio, estimable.
**hood** (juf) *s.* capucha, capucho, capilla, capirote, caperuza. *2* capirote [de ave]. *3* distintivo que se lleva sobre una toga académica para indicar el grado. *4* cosa que cubre: capota [de coche]; capó [de auto]; campana [de hogar]; sombrerete [de chimenea]. *5* MAR. tambucho.
**hood (to)** *tr.* encapuchar, encapirotar, cubrir con caperuza, capucho, etc. *2* tapar, ocultar.
**hoodlum** (-løm) *s.* (E.U.) fam. golfo, matón.
**hoodoo** (-u) *s.* VOODOO. *2* (E. U.) cenizo; lo que trae mala suerte.
**hoodoo (to)** *tr.* (E. U.) traer mala suerte a.
**hoodwink (to)** (-uink) *tr.* vendar los ojos a. *2* engañar, embaucar, burlar.
**hoof** (juf) *s.* ZOOL. casco, pezuña, uña [de solípedo]; pesuña, pezuña; pata, pie [de animal ungulado]. *2* pesuño. *3* animal ungulado.
**hoof (to)** *tr.-intr.* andar, hollar. *2 to* ~ *it,* andar, ir a pie; bailar.
**hoofbeat** (-bıt) *s.* pisada, ruido de la pisada [de un animal ungulado].
**hoofed** (-t) *adj.* ungulado.
**hook** (juk) *s.* gancho, garfio, garabato: *to get the* ~, fam. ser despedido; *by* ~ *or by crook,* a tuertas o a derechas. *2* aldabilla. *3* escarpia, alcayata. *4* anzuelo; lazo, trampa. *5* pernio [de gozne]. *6* hoz, hocino. *7* recodo [de camino, etc.]. *8* rasgo [de letra]. *9* MÚS. rabo [de nota]. *10* corchete, gafete: ~ *and eye,* corchete [macho y hembra]. *11* BOXEO golpe de gancho.
**hook (to)** *tr.* encorvar, dar forma de gancho. *2* engarabatar. *3* enganchar [con gancho]; unir, conectar. *4* pescar, coger, atrapar. *5* cornear, herir con los cuernos. *6* encorchetar, abrochar. *7* birlar, hurtar. *8* fam. *to* ~ *it,* irse, huir. *9* BOXEO dar un golpe de gancho a.
**hooked** (-t) *adj.* encorvado, corvo, ganchudo. *2* enganchado.
**hooknose** (-nouš) *s.* nariz aguileña.
**hookup** (-øp) *s.* RADIO. montaje. *2* RADIO. esquema.
**hooky** (-i) *adj.* ganchudo. *2* que tiene ganchos. *3 to play* ~, hacer novillos, fumarse la clase.
**hooligan** (ju·ligan) *s.* golfo, gamberro.
**hoop** (jup) *s.* aro, cerco, arco, ceño, fleje, virola: ~ *skirt,* miriñaque. *2* aro [juguete]. *3* anilla, anillo, sortija, argolla.
**hoop (to)** *tr.* encarcar [un tonel]. *2* zunchar. *3* cercar, ceñir. *4 intr.* TO WHOOP.
**hooping-cough** *s.* WHOOPING-COUGH.
**hoopoe** (ju·pu) *s.* ORN. abubilla, upupa.
**hoot** (jut) *s.* grito; grita. *2* silbo [del mochuelo]. *3* pitido [de locomotora, etc.]; bocinazo.
**hoot (to)** *intr.-tr.* gritar, huchear, abuchear, dar grita. *2 intr.* silbar [el mochuelo]. *3* dar pitidos o bocinazos.
**hooter** (-øᵣ) *s.* bocina, sirena, pito.
**hop** (jap) *s.* salto, brinco. *2* fam. baile [reunión]. *3* pop. vuelo [en avión]. *4* BOT. lúpulo, hombrecillo. *5 pl.* lúpulo [frutos del lúpulo].
**hop (to)** *intr.* brincar, saltar; andar a saltitos o a la pata coja. *2* fam. bailar. *3* recoger el lúpulo. *4* AVIA. *to* ~ *off,* despegar, alzar el vuelo. *5 tr.* cruzar o salvar saltando o volando. *6* aromatizar con lúpulo. ¶ Pret. y p. p.: *hopped;* ger. *-pping.*
**hope** (joup) *s.* esperanza, confianza.
**hope (to)** *tr.* esperar [tener esperanza de]. *2 intr.* esperar [tener esperanza]; esperar, confiar en. *3 to* ~ *for,* esperar, desear [una cosa].

**hopeful** (-ful) *adj.* esperanzado, lleno de esperanzas. *2* risueño, prometedor, que promete.
**hopefulness** (-nis) *s.* esperanza. *2* buenas perspectivas, aspecto prometedor.
**hopeless** (-lis) *adj.* desesperado, desesperanzado, sin esperanza. *2* incurable, irremediable; perdido, imposible, inútil.
**hoper** (-ø<sup>r</sup>) *s.* el que espera o tiene esperanza.
**hoplite** (ja·plait) *s.* hoplita.
**hopper** (ja·pø<sup>r</sup>) *s.* saltador. *2* saltamontes. *3* tolva.
**hopple** (ja·pøl) *s.* traba, manea, maniota.
**hopple (to)** *tr.* trabar, manear.
**hopscotch** (ja·pska·ch) *s.* coxcojita, infernáculo.
**Horace** (jo·ris), *n. pr. m.* Horacio.
**Horatian** (jorei·shian) *adj.* horaciano.
**horde** (jo<sup>r</sup>d) *s.* horda.
**horehound** (jo·<sup>r</sup>jaund) *s.* BOT. marrubio.
**horizon** (jørai·šøn) *s.* horizonte.
**horizontal** (jariša·ntal) *adj.* horizontal.
**horizontality** (-tæ·liti) *s.* horizontalidad.
**hormone** (jo·<sup>r</sup>moun) *s.* FISIOL. hormón, hormona.
**horn** (jo<sup>r</sup>n) *s.* asta, cuerno [de animal]. *2* cuerno [de caracol, de insecto, de la luna, etc.]. *3* cuerno [materia, vaso]: ~ *of plenty,* cuerno de la abundancia, cornucopia. *4* callosidad, dureza. *5* ZOOL. excrecencia córnea. *6* bocina [de automóvil o fonógrafo]. *7* MÚS. cuerno, trompa, cuerno de caza.
**horn (to)** *tr.* poner cuernos. *2* acornear. *3 intr.* MÚS. tocar el cuerno.
**hornbeam** (-bɪm) *s.* BOT. carpe, ojaranzo.
**hornbil** (-bil) *s.* ORN. cálao.
**hornblende** (-blend) *s.* MINER. hornablenda.
**horned** (-d) *adj.* astado, cornudo, cornígero. *2* encornado. *3* en forma de cuerno.
**hornet** (-it) ENT. avispón: *hornet's nest,* panal el avispón; fig. avispero.
**horning** (-ing) *s.* cencerrada.
**hornish** (-ish) *adj.* córneo.
**hornless** (-lis) *adj.* sin cuernos.
**hornpipe** (-paip) *s.* baile inglés que ejecuta una sola persona. *2* MÚS. gaita, chirimía.
**horn-rimmed** *adj.* con montura de concha [gafas].
**horny** (-ni) *adj.* córneo. *2* de cuerno. *3* calloso.
**hologe** (ja·røloudỹ) *s.* reloj.
**horologer** (joura·lodỹø<sup>r</sup>), **horologist** (-dỹist) *s.* relojero; el que se dedica a la horología.
**horology** (-lodỹi) *s.* horología.
**horometry** (-metri) *s.* medición del tiempo.
**horopter** (-ptø<sup>r</sup>) *s.* ÓPT. horópter, horóptero.
**horoscope** (ja·røscoup) *s.* horóscopo.
**horrendous** (jare·ndøs) *adj.* horrendo, espantoso.
**horrible** (ja·<sup>r</sup>ibøl) *adj.* horrible, horrendo, terrible.
**horrid** (ja·rid) *adj.* hórrido. *2* muy desagradable.
**horrific** (ja·rific) *adj.* horrífico.
**horrify (to)** (-fai) *tr.* horrorizar. ¶ Pret. y p. p.: *horrified.*
**horripilation** (jaripilei·shøn) *s.* MED. horripilación.
**horripilate (to)** (jari·pileit) *tr.* horripilar. *2 intr.* horripilarse.
**horrisonant** (jari·sonant) *adj.* horrísono.
**horror** (ja·rø<sup>r</sup>) *s.* horror. *2* pl. *the horrors,* melancolía, murria; estremecimiento de horror.
**horrorous** (-øs) *adj.* horroroso.
**horse** (jo<sup>r</sup>s) *s.* ZOOL. caballo: *to get on the high ~,* fig. darse tono, tomar una actitud orgullosa; *hold your horses,* fig. pare usted el carro, modérese; *to horse!,* ¡a caballo! *2* bridón, corcel. *3* MIL. caballería, caballos. *4* caballete, asnilla, borriquete. *5* potro [para gimnasia]. *6* fam. manía, chifladura. *7 adj.* de caballo o caballos; para ca-

ballos; montado; hípico: ~ *artillery,* artillería montada; ~ *block,* apeadero, montadero; ~ *doctor,* fam. albéitar; ~ *nail,* clavo de herradura; ~ *pistol,* pistola de arzón; ~ *race,* carrera de caballos; ~ *sense,* sentido práctico, sentido común. *8* grande; ordinario. *9* BOT. ~ *chestnut,* castaño de Indias; su fruto.
**horse (to)** *tr.* montar [proveer de caballo; poner a caballo]. *2* cargar con, llevar a cuestas. *3* azotar. *4 intr.* montar, cabalgar, andar a caballo.
**horseback** (-bæk) *s.* lomo de caballo: *on ~,* a caballo, montado. *2 adv.* a caballo.
**horsebreaker** (-brei·kø<sup>r</sup>) *s.* picador, domador de caballos.
**horseflesh** (-flesh) *s.* carne de caballo. *2* caballos [colectivamente]. *3* variedad de caoba de las Bahamas.
**horsefly** (-flai) *s.* ENT. tábano. *2* ENT. mosca de burro.
**horsehair** (-jeø<sup>r</sup>) *s.* crin de caballo. *2* tela de crin.
**horsekeeper** (-kɪpø<sup>r</sup>) *s.* establero, mozo de cuadra.
**horselaugh** (-læf) *s.* risotada, risa grosera.
**horseless** (-lis) *adj.* sin caballo.
**horseman** (-mæn) *s.* jinete, caballista. *2* el que guía un caballo.
**horsemanship** (-ship) *s.* manejo, equitación.
**horsemint** (-mint) *s.* BOT. hierbabuena rizada.
**horseplay** (-plei) *s.* payasada, chanza pesada.
**horsepower** (-pauø<sup>r</sup>) *s.* caballo de fuerza o de vapor.
**horseradish** (-rædish) *s.* BOT. rábano picante.
**horseshoe** (-shu) *s.* herradura; cosa en forma de herradura: ~ *arch,* ARQ. arco de herradura. *2* ZOOL. cangrejo de las Molucas.
**horsetail** (-teil) *s.* cola de caballo. *2* BOT. cola de caballo, equiseto.
**horseway** (-uei) *s.* camino de herradura.
**horsewhip** (-juip) *s.* látigo.
**horsewhip (to)** *tr.* azotar, dar latigazos. ¶ Pret. y p. p.: *whipped;* ger.: *-pping.*
**horsewoman** (-wumæn) *s.* amazona [mujer que monta a caballo].
**horsey** (jo·<sup>r</sup>si) *adj.* HORSY.
**horsy** (-si) *adj.* caballar, caballuno. *2* hípico. *3* aficionado a los caballos.
**hortation** (jo<sup>r</sup>tei·shøn) *s.* exhortación.
**hortative** (jo·<sup>r</sup>tativ), **hortatory** (jo·<sup>r</sup>tatori) *adj.* exhortatorio.
**hortensial** (jo<sup>r</sup>te·nshal) *adj.* hortense.
**horticultural** (jo<sup>r</sup>tikø·lchural) *adj.* hortícola.
**horticulture** (jo<sup>r</sup>tikø·lchø·) *s.* horticultura.
**horticulturist** (jo<sup>r</sup>tikø·lchurist) *s.* horticultor.
**hosanna** (jo<sup>r</sup>tei·shøn) *s.-interj.* hosanna.
**1) hose** (jouš), *pl.* **hose** *s.* calza, media. *2 pl.* calzas, medias calzas.
**2) hose,** *pl.* **hose** o **hoses** *s.* manga, manguera [de bomba o riego].
**Hosea** (joši·æ) *n. pr.* Oseas.
**hosier** (jou·ỹo<sup>r</sup>) *s.* mediero, calcetero.
**hosiery** (-ri) *s.* calcetería, géneros de punto.
**hospice** (ja·spis) *s.* hospicio; hospedería.
**hospitable** (ja·spitabøl) *adj.* hospitalario, acogedor.
**hospital** (ja·spital) *s.* hospital. *2* clínica. *3* asilo [institución].
**hospitality** (-tæ·liti) *s.* hospitalidad.
**hospitalize (to)** (jaspi·talaiš) *tr.* hospitalizar.
**hospital(l)er** (-ø<sup>r</sup>) *s.* hospitalero. *2* caballero de una orden hospitalaria. *3* hospiciano.
**host** (joust) *s.* hospedero, posadero, mesonero, pa-

trón. 2 huésped [que hospeda]; anfitrión. 3 BIOL. huésped. 4 hueste. 5 multitud. 6 hostia.
**hostage** (ja·stidў) s. rehén.
**hostel** (ja·støl) s. hostería. 2 residencia para estudiantes.
**hostelry** (-ri) s. posada, hostelería, mesón, parador.
**hostess** (jou·stis) s. posadera, mesonera. 2 huéspeda, señora de la casa. 3 avia. azafata.
**hostile** (ja·stil) adj. hostil.
**hostility** (jasti·liti) s. hostilidad. 2 pl. hostilidades [actos de guerra].
**hostilize (to)** (ja·stilaiš) tr. hostilizar.
**hostler** (ja·sløʳ) s. establero, palafrenero.
**hot** (jat) adj. caliente: ~ baths, termas, baños termales; ~ dog, salchicha caliente; bocadillo de salchicha caliente; ~ pad, almohadilla eléctrica; ~ springs, fuentes de aguas termales; ~ wave, ola de calor; it is ~ today, hace calor; to get o grow ~, calentarse; empezar a hacer calor. 2 cálido, caluroso, tórrido. 3 acalorado, ardoroso. 4 acre, picante, ardiente: ~ pepper, pimiento picante. 5 ardiente, fogoso, vehemente, fervoroso. 6 violento, furioso, enérgico, activo: ~ chase, ~ pursuit, activa persecución. 7 vivo [genio]. 8 ávido, ansioso. 9 fam. incómodo, peligroso: to make it ~ for someone, perseguir, poner en peligro a uno. 10 empeñado [disputa, etc.]. 11 fresco, reciente [noticia, rastro]. 12 en celo [animal].
13 adv. HOTLY.
**hotbed** (-bed) s. AGR. almajara cubierta, estufa. 2 fig. foco, plantel.
**hot-blooded** adj. fogoso, irascible, de genio vivo. 2 de pura raza [animal].
**hotbox** (-baks) s. MEC. cojinete recalentado.
**hot-brained** adj. impetuoso, exaltado.
**hotch-potch** (ja·ch-pa·ch) s. HODGEPODGE.
**hotel** (joute·l) s. hotel.
**hotelkeeper** (-kıpøʳ) s. hotelero.
**hotfoot** (ja·tfut) adv. fam. a toda prisa.
**hothead** (-jed) s. persona impetuosa, exaltada. 2 agitador, alborotador.
**hotheaded** (-jedid) adj. impetuoso, exaltado.
**hothouse** (-jaus) s. invernáculo, estufa [para plantas].
**hotly** (-li) adv. calurosamente. 2 ardientemente, vehementemente.
**hotspur** (-spøʳ) adj.-s. temerario, impetuoso.
**hottentot** (ja·tønt at) adj.-s. hotentote.
**hough** (jak) s. corvejón [de cuadrúpedo].
**hough (to)** tr. desjarretar.
**hound** (jaund) s. lebrel, galgo, sabueso, podenco, perro de caza o de busca. 2 fig. canalla, villano. 3 pl. MAR. cacholas.
**hound (to)** tr. cazar con perros. 2 azuzar. 3 acosar, perseguir, seguir la pista.
**hound's-tongue** s. BOT. cinoglosa, viniebla.
**houppelande** (ju·plænd) s. hopalanda.
**hour** (auʳ) s. hora: ~ circle, ASTR. círculo horario; ~ hand, horario [saetilla]; small hours, primeras horas de madrugada; to keep late hours, recogerse a deshora, trasnochar; by the ~, por horas; hours on end, horas enteras; in evil ~, en mala hora; in good ~, en buena hora. 2 momento, trance. 3 pl. ECLES. horas [rezo].
**hourglass** (-glæs) s. reloj de arena.
**houri** (ju·ri) s. hurí.
**hourly** (au·ʳli) adj. de la hora; de cada hora, continuo. 2 adv. a cada hora; continuamente.
**house** (jaus) s. casa [habitación; hogar; edificio;

familia, linaje]; ~ of God, casa de Dios, iglesia; to clean ~, hacer limpieza; to put o set one's ~ in order, fig. arreglar uno sus asuntos. 2 lugar donde se aloja, o guarda, una cosa. 3 cámara legislativa o deliberante: House of Commons, Cámara de los Comunes. 4 TEAT. sala, público, entrada: good ~, buena entrada; to bring down the ~, fig. provocar una tempestad de aplausos. 5 escaque, casilla [de ajedrez]. 6 ~ of cards, castillo de naipes.
7 adj. de casa o casas; casero, doméstico: ~ agent, corredor o administrador de fincas; ~ dove, paloma doméstica; ~ painter, pintor de brocha gorda; ~ rent, alquiler de la casa.
**house (to)** tr. albergar, alojar. 2 dar casa o habitación a. 3 entrojar, almacenar o guardar. 4 encajar, empotrar. 5 intr. alojarse, residir.
**houseboat** (-bout) s. barco vivienda, casa flotante.
**housebreaker** (-breikøʳ) s. ladrón que roba con escalo.
**housebreaking** (-breiking) s. robo con escalo.
**housefather** (-fadøʳ) s. cabeza de familia.
**housefly** (-flai) s. ENT. mosca común.
**household** (-hould) s. casa, familia [los que viven juntos]. 2 The Household, la Real Casa. 3 adj. doméstico, casero: ~ bread, pan casero; ~ furniture, menaje de casa.
**householder** (-øʳ) s. amo de casa; padre de familia.
**housekeeper** (-kıpøʳ) s. guardián de una casa. 2 ama de casa. 3 ama de llaves o de gobierno.
**housekeeping** (-ing) s. gobierno de la casa; quehaceres domésticos. 2 adj. doméstico, casero.
**houseleek** (-lik) s. BOT. siempreviva mayor.
**housemaid** (-meid) s. criada.
**housemother** (-modøʳ) s. mujer encargada de una residencia de estudiantes.
**housetop** (-tap) s. techo, tejado, azotea; to shout from the housetops, pregonar a los cuatro vientos.
**housewarming** (uøʳming) s. fiesta para celebrar el estreno de una casa.
**housewife** (-uaif) s. madre de familia, ama de casa. 2 (jø·sif) agujetero, neceser de costura.
**housewifery** (-ori) s. gobierno de una casa, economía doméstica.
**housework** (-uøʳk) s. quehaceres domésticos.
**housing** (-ing) s. abrigo, albergue. 2 alojamiento, vivienda: ~ problem, problema de la vivienda. 3 almacenaje. 4 muesca, encaje. 5 MEC. chumacera. 6 MEC. caja, cárter. 7 ARQ. nicho. 8 mantilla, gualdrapa.
**hove** (jouv) pret. y p. p. de TO HEAVE.
**hovel** (jø·vøl) s. cobertizo. 2 cabaña, choza, tabuco.
**hover (to)** (jø·vøʳ) tr. cubrir con las alas. 2 intr. flotar, cernerse [en el aire], revolotear. 3 rondar, andar alrededor. 4 asomar [una sonrisa, expresión, etc.]. 5 dudar, vacilar.
**how** (jau) adv. cómo, de qué modo, por qué: ~ do you do?, ¿cómo está usted?; ~ so?, ¿cómo es eso?, ¿por qué? 2 a cómo: ~ do you sell it?, ¿a cómo lo vende usted? 3 En ciertas locuciones tiene los sentidos de cuán, cuánto, hasta qué punto, qué, lo que, si, etc.: ~ about it?, ¿qué le parece?, ¿qué hacemos?; ~ far?, ¿a qué distancia? ¿hasta dónde?; ~ if I could not go?, ¿y si yo no pudiese ir?; ~ long?, ¿cuánto tiempo?; ~ many, cuántos, cuántas; ~ much, cuánto, lo mucho que. 4 qué, cuán [admirativos]: ~ little!, ¡qué poco!, ¡cuán poco!
5 s. como [modo, manera].

**howbeit** (-bɪ·it) *adv.* sea como fuere; no obstante.
**howdah** (-da) *s.* castillo [sobre el elefante].
**howel** (-øl) *s.* argallera.
**however** (-e·vø<sup>r</sup>) *adv.* de cualquier modo que, como quiera que, por muy... que, por mucho que. *2 conj.* sin embargo, no obstante, con todo.
**howitzer** (-itšø<sup>r</sup>) *s.* ARTILL. obús.
**howl** (jaul) *s.* aullido. *2* grito, ululato, alarido, chillido. *3* lamento.
**howl (to)** *intr.* aullar. *2* gritar, dar alaridos; chillar. *3* lamentarse [a gritos]. *4 tr.* gritar.
**howler** (-ø<sup>r</sup>) *s.* aullador. *2* gritador. *3* ZOOL. mono aullador, araguato. *4* plañidera. *5* fam. adefesio, desacierto, disparate grande.
**howling** (-ing) *adj.* aullador; ~ *monkey*, HOWLER 2. *2* clamoroso, ruidoso.
**howsoever** (-soue·vø·) *adv.* como quiera que, de cualquier modo que, por muy... que.
**hoyden** (joi·døn) *s.* muchacha traviesa, tunantuela.
**hub** (jøb) *s.* cubo [de rueda]: ~ *cap*, AUTO. tapacubo. *2* fig. centro, eje. *3* centro de actividad.
**Hubert** (jiu·bø<sup>r</sup>t) *n. pr. m.* Huberto.
**hubbub** (jø·bøb) *s.* griterío, batahola, algazara, barullo, tumulto.
**huckleberry** (jø·kølberi) *s.* BOT. variedad de gayuba.
**hucklebone** (-boun) *s.* taba [hueso; juego].
**huckster** (jø·kstø<sup>r</sup>) *s.* buhonero; vendedor ambulante.
**huckster (to)** *intr.* vender por las calles.
**huddle** (jø·døl) *s.* montón, tropel, confusión. *2* fam. reunión secreta.
**huddle (to)** *tr.* amontonar sin orden, confundir. *2* empujar, hacer salir, etc., en tropel. *3* hacer [algo] atropelladamente. *4 to* ~ *oneself*, acurrucarse. *5 intr.* amontonarse, apiñarse. *6* acurrucarse. *7* FÚTBOL reunirse para recibir órdenes.
**hue** (jiu) *s.* color, matiz, tinte. *2* griterío, clamor: ~ *and cry*, alarma, grito para perseguir a un ladrón, etc.; gritos de indignación.
**huff** (jøf) *s.* enojo, enfado: *in a* ~, enojado, ofendido.
**huff (to)** *tr.* inflar, hinchar. *2* tratar con arrogancia, maltratar. *3* ofender, enojar. *4* soplar [un peón]. *5 intr.* enojarse, ofenderse.
**huffish** (-ish) *adj.* enojadizo, irritable. *2* arrogante, insolente.
**huffy** (-i) *adj.* HUFFISH.
**hug** (jøg) *s.* abrazo estrecho; abrazo [de cariño, de luchador].
**hug (to)** *tr.* abrazar; estrechar contra su pecho. *2* abrazarse a. *3* acariciar. *4* MAR. navegar muy cerca de [la costa]. *5 to* ~ *oneself*, felicitarse. ¶ Pret. y p. p.: *hugged;* ger.: *hugging.*
**huge** (jiudỹ) *adj.* grande, enorme, colosal, vasto, inmenso.
**hugeness** (-nis) *s.* magnitud, enormidad, inmensidad.
**Hugh** (jiu·) *n. pr. m.* Hugo.
**Huguenot** (jiu·gønat) *s.* hugonote.
**huisache** (juisa·chæ) *s.* BOT. aromo.
**hulk** (jølk) *s.* MAR. casco arrumbado, pontón [que sirve de cárcel], carraca. *2* fig. armatoste.
**hulking** (-ing) *adj.* tosco, grueso, pesado.
**hull** (jøl) *s.* cáscara, corteza, hollejo [de fruta]; vaina [de legumbre]. *2* casco [de buque]. *3* armazón [de dirigible]. *4* flotador [de hidroavión].
**hull (to)** *tr.* pelar, mondar, deshollejar, desvainar.

*2* MAR. dar un proyectil en el casco de [un buque].
**hullabaloo** (jølabalu·) *s.* batahola, barahúnda.
**hullo** (jølou·) *interj.-s.* HELLO; HOLLO.
**hum** (jøm) *s.* zumbido; ronroneo [de un motor, etc.]; rumor. *2* canturreo, tarareo.
**hum (to)** *intr.* zumbar, ronronear; rumorear; fig. *to make things hum,* desplegar actividad. *2 tr.-intr.* canturrear, tararear.
**human** (jiu·man) *adj.* humano. *2 s.* humano, mortal [ser humano].
**humane** (jiumei·n) *adj.* humano, humanitario, benigno, compasivo.
**humanism** (jiu·manišm) *s.* humanismo.
**humanist** (-ist) *s.* humanista.
**humanitarian** (jiumænite·rian) *adj.* humanitario. *2 s.* filántropo.
**humanity** (jiumæ·niti) *s.* humanidad. *2 pl.* humanidades.
**humble** (jø·mbøl) *adj.* humilde. *2* modesto, sencillo. *3 to eat* ~ *pie,* humillarse, dar excusas, pedir perdón.
**humble (to)** *tr.* humillar. *2* abatir [el poder, el orgullo, etc.]. *3 ref.* humillarse.
**humbleness** (-nis) *s.* humildad.
**humbug** (jø·mbøg) *s.* farsa, engaño, embeleco. *2* charlatanería, charlatanismo. *3* farsante, charlatán, embaucador, embustero.
**humbug (to)** *tr.* engañar, embaucar, embelecar. *2* timar, sacar [dinero]. ¶ Pret. y p. p.: *humbugged;* ger.: *-gging.*
**humbuggery** (-ri) *s.* engaño, embeleco.
**humdrum** (jø·ndrøm) *adj.* monótono, pesado, aburrido, trivial. *2 s.* lata, cosa aburrida. *3* latoso.
**humectate (to)** (jøme·kteit) *tr.* humedecer.
**humectation** (jømektei·shøn) *s.* humectación.
**humeral** (jiu·møral) *adj.* humeral.
**humerus** (-øs) *s.* ANAT. húmero.
**humid** (jiu·mid) *adj.* húmedo.
**humidify (to)** (jiumi·difai) *tr.* humedecer. ¶ Pret. y p. p.: *humidified.*
**humidity** (jiumi·diti) *s.* humedad.
**humiliate (to)** (jiumi·lieit) *tr.* humillar.
**humiliation** (-ei·shøn) *s.* humillación.
**humility** (jiumi·liti) *s.* humildad, sumisión.
**humming** (jø·ming) *adj.* zumbador. *2* muy activo, intenso, grande.
**hummingbird** (-børd) *s.* ORN. colibrí, pájaro mosca, tominejo.
**hummock** (jø·mok) *s.* montecillo, mota, colina.
**humor, humorous,** etc. HUMOUR, HUMOUROUS, etc.
**humoresque** (jiumøre·sk) *s.* capricho musical.
**humorism** (jiu·morišm) *s.* MED. humorismo. *2* humor, gracia, ingenio.
**humorist** (-ist) *s.* humorista. *2* chistoso, chancero [pers.].
**humour** (jiu·mø<sup>r</sup>) *s.* ANAT., MED. humor. *2* humor, disposición del ánimo, inclinación: *to be out of* ~, estar de mal humor; *to be in the* ~ *for,* tener ganas de. *3* genio, temperamento. *4* humor [facultad del humorista]. *5* humorada, capricho. *6* lo cómico [de una situación, etc.].
**humour (to)** *tr.* complacer, dar gusto. *2* mimar, consentir. *3* adaptarse, acomodarse a.
**humourous** (-øs) *adj.* cómico, gracioso, humorístico. *2* caprichoso, antojadizo.
**hump** (jø·mp) *s.* giba, joroba, corcova. *2* pop. murria, mal humor.
**hump (to)** *tr.* encorvar, hacer jorobado. *2* fam. *to* ~ *it,* hacer un esfuerzo, esforzarse.
**humpback** (-bæk) *s.* giba, joroba. *2* jorobado.

**humpbacked** (-bækt) *adj.* jorobado.
**humped** (-t), **humpy** (-i) *adj.* giboso, corcovado.
**hunch** (jø·nch) *s.* joroba, giba. *2* pedazo [de pan, etc.]. *3* fam. corazonada, presentimiento.
**hunch (to)** *tr.* sacar [formando protuberancia]. *2* encorvar [la espalda]. *3 intr.* encorvarse.
**hunchback** (-bæk) *s.* HUMPBACK.
**hundred** (jø·ndrød) *adj.* [precedido de *a* o *one*] cien, ciento. *2 s.* ciento, centena, centenar: *by the ~*, por centenares.
**hundred-per-cent** (-pø^rse·nt) *adj.* cien por cien, cabal, perfecto, puro.
**hundredth** (jø·ndrøz) *adj.* centésimo. *2* centeno. *3* ciento [ordinal]. *4 s.* cento, centena [cifra de las centenas]. *5* centésimo, centésima.
**hundredweight** (jø·ndrødueit) *s.* quintal: (Ingl.) 112 lbs. (50.8 kg.); (E.U.) 100 lbs. (45.36 kg.).
**hung** (jøng) *pret.* y *p. p.* de TO HANG.
**Hungarian** (jønge·rian) *adj.-s.* húngaro.
**Hungary** (jø·ngari) *n. pr.* GEOGR. Hungría.
**hunger** (jø·ngø^r) *s.* hambre. *2* gana, apetito. *3* ansia, anhelo.
**hunger (to)** *intr.* tener hambre: *to ~ for*, tener hambre o sed de, anhelar. *2 tr.* hambrear, matar de hambre.
**hungry** (jø·ngri) *adj.* hambriento: *to be ~*, *to feel ~*, tener hambre o apetito. *2* famélico. *3* ganoso, deseoso. *4* pobre, estéril [suelo].
**hunk** (jønk) *s.* fam. trozo, buen pedazo, pedazo grande.
**Huns** (jøns) *s. pl.* HIST. hunos.
**hunt** (jønt) *s.* caza [acción]; montería. *2* cacería. *3* conjunto de cazadores. *4* sociedad de cazadores. *5* búsqueda. *6* perseguimiento, acosamiento. *7* *on the ~ for*, a caza de.
**hunt (to)** *tr.* cazar; buscar, perseguir. *2* recorrer buscando, registrar. *3* emplear en la caza [perros, caballos]; cazar y matar, perseguir y destruir; buscar [una cosa]. *4 intr.* cazar, ir de caza: *to ~ for* o *after*, buscar, perseguir, ir tras de. *9* MEC. oscilar.
**hunter** (-ø^r) *s.* cazador. *2* perro o caballo de caza. *3* buscador. *4* saboneta.
**hunting** (-ing) *s.* caza, ejercicio de la caza, montería: *~ ground*, cazadero; *~ knife*, cuchillo de monte; *~ party*, cacería; partida de caza.
**huntress** (-ris) *f.* cazadora [mujer].
**huntsman** (-smæn) *s.* cazador; montero.
**hurdle** (jø·^rdøl) *s.* zarzo, cañizo. *2* adral. *3* valla [que se salta en las carreras]; fig. obstáculo, dificultad: *~ race*, carrera de saltos o de obstáculos.
**hurdle (to)** *tr.* cubrir o cercar con zarzos. *2* DEP. saltar [un obstáculo].
**hurdy-gurdy** (-i-gø·^rdi) *s.* MÚS. zanfonia, organillo.
**hurl** (jø^rl) *s.* tiro, lanzamiento.
**hurl (to)** *tr.* lanzar, tirar, arrojar con fuerza: *to ~ oneself*, lanzarse, arrojarse. *2* derribar. *3* lanzar [gritos, invectivas, etc.].
**hurly-burly** (-ibø^rli) *s.* gritería, batahola.
**hurra(h** (jura·) *interj.* ¡viva!, ¡hurra!
**hurra(h (to)** *tr.* aclamar, vitorear.
**hurricane** (jø·rikein) *s.* huracán, ciclón: *~ lamp*, linterna construida a prueba de viento.
**hurried** (jø·rid) *p. p.* de TO HURRY. *2 adj.* precipitado, apresurado, hecho de prisa.
**hurry** (jø·ri) *s.* prisa, premura, precipitación; paso o movimiento rápido: *to be in a ~*, tener prisa, ir de prisa; *in a ~*, de prisa, precipitadamente.
**hurry (to)** *tr.* dar prisa, apresurar, acuciar. *2* acelerar, avivar. *3* atropellar, precipitar. *4* llevar corriendo, con prisa. *5 to ~ on* o *up*, apresurar. *6 intr.* correr, apresurarse, darse prisa, precipitarse. *7 to ~ after*, correr en pos de. *8 to ~ away*, marcharse o salir precipitadamente. *9 to ~ back*, apresurarse a volver. *10 to ~ up*, apresurarse, darse prisa. ¶ Pret. y p. p.: *hurried*.
**hurry-scurry** (-skø·ri) *s.* precipitación, confusión. *2 adv.* atropelladamente, precipitadamente.
**hurt** (jø^rt) *s.* herida, lesión, lastimadura. *2* daño, dolor. *3* daño, perjuicio. *4 adj.* herido, lastimado. *5* ofendido. *6* perjudicado.
**hurt (to)** *tr.* herir, lastimar: *to ~ one's feelings*, herir los sentimientos de uno, ofenderle. *2* dañar, perjudicar. *3* hacer daño, causar dolor. *4* apenar, afligir. *5 intr.* doler. ¶ Pret. y p. p.: *hurt*.
**hurtful** (-ful) *adj.* perjudicial, dañino, nocivo, pernicioso.
**hurtle (to)** (-øl) *tr.* lanzar, arrojar; hacer chocar. *2 intr.* lanzarse, arrojarse. *3* chocar [con]; moverse con estruendo.
**hurtless** (-lis) *adj.* inofensivo. *2* ileso.
**husband** (jø·sband) *s.* marido, esposo.
**husband (to)** *tr.* administrar con prudencia, ahorrar, economizar.
**husbandman** (-mæn) *s.* agricultor, labrador.
**husbandry** (-ri) *s.* agricultura, labranza. *2* frugalidad, economía; buen gobierno.
**hush** (jøsh) *interj.* ¡chitón!, ¡silencio! *2 s.* quietud, silencio.
**hush (to)** *tr.* callar. *2* acallar, aquietar. *3 to ~ up*, ocultar, echar tierra a. *4 intr.* callar, enmudecer.
**husk** (jøsk) *s.* cáscara, vaina, cascabillo, bagazo, zurrón o cubierta seca [de fruto]. *2* perfolla [del maíz].
**husk (to)** *tr.* descascarar, desvainar, desgranar, quitar la cubierta seca de [ciertos frutos].
**huskiness** (-inis) *s.* calidad de lo que tiene mucha cáscara o cubierta seca. *2* ronquera, bronquedad de la voz. *3* sequedad en la garganta.
**husky** (-i) *adj.* que tiene perfolla, cáscara, vaina, zurrón o cubierta seca. *2* seco. *3* con la garganta seca. *4* ronco, rauco. *5* fam. robusto, fornido. *6 s.* fam. persona robusta, fornida. *7* perro esquimal.
**hussar** (jø^rša·) *s.* húsar.
**hussy** (jø·si) *s.* pícara, buena pieza. *2* mujer perdida.
**hustings** (jø·stingš) *s. pl.* tribuna para discursos electorales. *2* elecciones.
**hustle** (jø·søl) *s.* empujón, sacudida. *2* energía, vigor. *3* apresuramiento, actividad febril.
**hustle (to)** *tr.* empujar, atropellar; echar a empellones. *2* mezclar, confundir. *3* fam. apresurar. *4 intr.* andar empujando. *5* menearse, apresurarse, bullir, mostrar gran actividad.
**hustler** (jø·sle^r) *s.* trafagón, bullebulle; trabajador enérgico.
**hut** (jøt) *s.* choza, cabaña. *2* caseta, garita.
**hut (to)** *tr.-intr.* alojar o vivir en una choza, cabaña, etc.
**hutch** (jøch) *s.* arca, cofre. *2* conejera. *3* amasadera. *4* MIN. cuba. *5* fam. choza, tugurio.
**Hyacinth** (jai·asinz) *n. pr.* Jacinto. *2* Jacinta.
**hyacinth** (-s. BOT., MINER. jacinto.
**hyaena** (jai·ina) *s.* ZOOL. hiena.
**hyaline** (jai·alin) *adj.* hialino.
**hybrid** (jai·brid) *adj.* híbrido.
**hybridization** (jaibridiše·shøn) *s.* hibridación.
**hybridize (to)** (jai·bridaiš) *tr.-intr.* hacer híbrido, producir o engendrar híbridos.

**hydra** (jai·dra) s. ZOOL., ASTR., MIT. hidra. 2 fig. mal difícil de extirpar.
**hydracid** (jaidræ·sid) s. hidrácido.
**hydrangea** (-ndÿiæ) s. BOT. hortensia.
**hydrant** (jai·draant) s. boca de agua, boca de riego.
**hydrate** (jai·dreit) s. QUÍM. hidrato.
**hydrate (to)** tr. QUÍM. hidratación.
**hydraulic** (jaidro·lik) adj. hidráulico.
**hydraulics** (-s) s. hidráulica.
**hydric** (jai·drik) adj. QUÍM. hídrico.
**hydrocarbon** (jaidrøka·ʳbøn) s. QUÍM. hidrocarburo.
**hydrochloric** (-clou·rik) adj. QUÍM. clorhídrico.
**hydrocyanic** (-saiæ·nik) adj. QUÍM. cianhídrico.
**hydrodynamic** (-dainæ·mik) adj. hidrodinámico.
**hydrodynamics** (-s) s. hidrodinámica.
**hydroelectric** (-ile·ktrik) adj. hidroeléctrico.
**hydroelectricity** (-ilektri·siti) s. hidroelectricidad.
**hydrogen** (jai·drødÿin) s. QUÍM. hidrógeno.
**hydrogenate (to)** (jaidra·dÿøneit) tr. QUÍM. hidrogenar.
**hydrography** (-grafi) s. hidrografía.
**hydrology** (-lødÿ) s. hidrología.
**hydrolysis** (-lisis) s. QUÍM. hidrólisis.
**hydrolyze (to)** (jai·drølaiš) tr. QUÍM. hidrolizar.
**hydromel** (-mel) s. hidromel.
**hydrometer** (jaidra·metøʳ) s. hidrómetro.
**hydrometry** (-metri) s. hidrometría.
**hydropathy** (-pazi) s. hidropatía.
**hydrophobe** (-foub) s. MED. hidrófobo.
**hydrophobia** (jaidrøfou·bia) s. MED. hidrofobia.
**hydropic(al** (jaidra·pik(al) adj. hidrópico.
**hydroplane** (jai·droplein) s. hidroavión.
**hydrosphere** (-sfiʳ) s. hidrosfera.
**hydrostat** (-stæt) s. hidrostato.
**hydrostatics** (-stæ·tiks) s. hidrostática.
**hydrosulphide** (jaidrøsø·lfaid) s. QUÍM. sulfhidrato, hidrosulfuro.
**hydrotherapy** (-ze·rapi) s. hidroterapia.
**hydrous** (jai·drøs) adj. hidratado.
**hydroxid(e** (jaidra·ksid) s. QUÍM. hidróxido.
**hydroxyl** (jaidra·ksil) s. QUÍM. hidroxilo, oxhidrilo.
**hyena** (jaiɪ·na) s. ZOOL. hiena.
**hygiene** (jai·dÿiin) s. higiene, profiláctica.
**hygienic** (jai·dÿie·nik) adj. higiénico.
**hygienist** (jai·dÿienist) s. higienista.
**hygrometer** (jaigra·metøʳ) s. higrómetro.
**hygrometry** (jaigra·metri) s. higrometría.
**hygroscope** (jai·grøskoup) s. higroscopio.
**hymen** (jai·men) s. ANAT. himen. 2 himeneo.
**hymeneal** (jaimeni·al) adj. nupcial. 2 s. epitalamio.
**hymenopter** (-a·ptøʳ) s. ENT. himenóptero.
**hymenopterous** (-a·ptørøs) adj. ENT. himenóptero.
**hymn** (jim) s. himno.
**hymn (to)** tr. alabar con himnos. 2 intr. cantar himnos.
**hymnal** (ji·mnal) s. himnario.

**hymnology** (jimna·lodÿi) s. tratado, estudio o composición de himnos. 2 himnos [colect.].
**hyoid** (jai·oid) s. ANAT. hioideo; hioides.
**hyperaesthesia** (jaipøreszɪ·šia) s. MED. hiperestesia.
**hyperbaton** (jaipø·ʳbaton) s. GRAM. hipérbaton.
**hyperbola** (-bola) s. GEOM. hipérbola.
**hyperbole** (-boli) s. RET. hipérbole.
**hyperbolic (al** (jaipøʳbø·lik(al) adj. hiperbólico.
**hyperbolist** (jaipø·ʳbolist) s. exagerador.
**hyperborean** (jaipøʳbou·rian) adj.-s. hiperbóreo.
**hyperchlorhydria** (-klori·dia) s. hiperclorhidria.
**hypercritical** (-kri·tikal) adj. hipercrítico.
**hyperdulia** (-diulai·a) s. TEOL. hiperdulía.
**hypericum** (jaipø·rikøm) s. BOT. hipérico.
**hypermetropia** (jaipøʳmitrou·pia) f. MED. hiper-·metropía.
**hypersensitive** (-se·nsitiv) adj. extremadamente sensible. 2 MED. hipersensible.
**hypertension** (-te·nshøn) s. MED. hipertensión.
**hypertrophy** (-trøfi) s. hipertrofia.
**hypertrophy (to)** intr. hipertrofiarse.
**hypha** (jai·fa) s. BOT. hifa.
**hyphen** (jai·føn) s. ORTOG. división, guión.
**hyphen, hyphenate (to)** (jai·føneit) tr. unir con guión. 2 separar con guión.
**hypnosis** (jipnou·sis) s. hipnosis.
**hypnotic** (jipna·tik) adj.-s. hipnótico.
**hypnotism** (ji·pnøtišm) s. hipnotismo.
**hypnotize (to)** (ji·pnøtaiš) tr. hipnotizar.
**hypo** (jai·pou) s. FOT. hiposulfito sódico. 2 pop. aguja hipodérmica, inyección hipodérmica.
**hypocaust** (jai·pøkøst) s. hipocausto.
**hypochlorite** (jaipøklo·rait) s. QUÍM. hipoclorito.
**hypochondria** (-ka·ndria) s. hipocondria.
**hypochondriac** (-ndriak) adj.-s. hipocondríaco.
**hypochondrium** (-ndriøm) s. ANAT. hipocondrio.
**hypocrisy** (jipa·krisi) s. hipocresía.
**hypocrite** (ji·pøkrit) s. hipócrita.
**hypocritical** (jipøkri·tikal) adj. hipócrita.
**hypodermic** (jaipødø·ʳmik) adj. hipodérmico.
**hypogastrium** (-gæ·striøm) s. ANAT. hipogastrio.
**hypogeum** (-dÿɪ·øm) s. ARQ. hipogeo.
**hypophysis** (jaipa·fisis) ANAT. hipófisis.
**hypophosphite** (jaipøfa·sfait) s. QUÍM. hipofosfito.
**hypostasis** (jaipa·stasis) s. FIL., TEOL. hipóstasis.
**hypostatic(al** (jaipøstæ·tik(al) adj. hipostático.
**hypotenuse** (jai·pøtinius) s. GEOM. hipotenusa.
**hypothec** (-zik) s. DER. hipoteca.
**hypothecary** (-zikeri) adj. hipotecario.
**hypothecate (to)** (-zikeit) tr. hipotecar.
**hypothesis** (-zisis) s. hipótesis.
**hypothetic (al** (jaipøze·tik(al) adj. hipotético.
**hypsometer** (jipsa·mitøʳ) s. hipsómetro.
**hypsometry** (-metri) s. hipsometría.
**hyson** (jai·søn) s. té verde de China.
**hyssop** (ji·søp) s. BOT. hisopo, aspersorio.
**hysteresis** (jistørɪ·sis) s. FÍS. histérisis.
**hysteria** (jisti·ria) s. histeria, histerismo.
**hysterics** (jiste·riks) s. ataque de nervios, de histerismo.

# I

**I, I** (ai) *s.* I, i, novena letra del alfabeto inglés.
**I** *pron. pers.* y *s.* yo. | Se escribe siempre con mayúscula.
**iamb** (ai·æm) *s.* IAMBUS.
**iambic** (aiæ·mbik) *adj.* yámbico. *2 s.* yambo.
**iambus** (aiæ·mbøs) *s.* yambo.
**Iberia** (aibi·ria) *n. pr.* GEOGR. Iberia.
**Iberian** (aibi·rian) *adj.* ibérico. *2 adj.-s.* ibero.
**ibex** (ai·beks) *s.* ZOOL. íbice, bicerra.
**ibis** (ai·bis) *s.* ORN. ibis.
**Icarian** (aike·rian) *adj.* icario. *2* arriesgado.
**ice** (ais) *s.* hielo. *2* helado, sorbete, granizado. *3* capa de azúcar, alcorza [en pastelería]. *4 adj.* de hielo, glacial; para el hielo; helado, garapiñado: ~ *age*, GEOL. época glacial; ~ *cream*, helado de crema, mantecado; ~ *drift*, ~ *float*, témpano, banco de hielo; ~ *hockey*, hockey sobre hielo; ~ *plant*, fábrica de hielo.
**ice (to)** *tr.* helar, congelar, garapiñar. *2* refrigerar, enfriar con hielo. *3* alcorzar, cubrir con capa de azúcar.
**iceberg** (-bø<sup>r</sup>g) *s.* iceberg.
**iceboat** (-bout) *s.* buque rompehielos. *2* trineo con vela para deslizarse sobre el hielo.
**icebound** (-baund) *adj.* rodeado de hielo. *2* detenido o aprisionado por el hielo.
**icebox** (-baks) *s.* nevera.
**icebreaker** (-breikø<sup>r</sup>) *s.* buque rompehielos.
**ice-cream** *adj.* de helado o mantecado: ~ *freezer*, heladora, sorbetera; ~ *soda*, agua carbónica con helado.
**icehouse** (-jaus) *s.* depósito de hielo.
**Iceland** (-lænd) *n. pr.* GEOGR. Islandia.
**Icelander** (-landø<sup>r</sup>) *adj.-s.* islandés.
**Icelandic** (-lændik) *adj.* islandés. *2 m.* islandés [idioma].
**ichneumon** (ikniu·møn) *s.* ZOOL., ENT. icneumón.
**ichnography** (ikna·grafi) *s.* ARQ. icnografía.
**ichor** (ai·kø<sup>r</sup>) *s.* MED. icor.
**ichthyol** (ikzia·l) *s.* FARM. ictiol.
**ichthyology** (-lodӯi) *s.* ictiología.
**ichthyophagous** (-fagøs) *adj.* ictiófago.
**ichthyosaurus** (ikziøso·røs) *s.* ZOOL. ictiosauro.
**icicle** (ai·sikøl) *s.* carámbano, candelizo, canelón.
**icily** (ai·sili) *adv.* fríamente, frígidamente.
**icing** (ai·sing) *s.* alcorza, capa de azúcar. *2* AVIA. formación de hielo.
**icon** (ai·kan) *s.* icono. *2* imagen, retrato.

**iconoclasm** (aika·nøklæšm) *s.* iconoclasia.
**iconoclast** (-klæst) *s.* iconoclasta.
**iconography** (aikøna·grafi) *s.* iconografía.
**iconology** (-lodӯ) *s.* iconología.
**iconostasis** (-stasis) *s.* iconostasio.
**icosahedron** (aikøsaji·drøn) *s.* GEOM. icosaedro.
**icteric** (ikte·rik) *adj.-s.* MED. ictérico.
**ictus** (i·ktøs) *s.* ictus.
**icy** (ai·si) *adj.* frígido, helado, glacial. *2* cubierto de hielo.
**I'd** (aid) contracción de *I would, I had* y *I shoud.*
**idea** (aidi·a) *s.* idea [en todos los sentidos menos en el de ingenio para disponer o inventar].
**ideal** (aidi·al) *adj.-s.* ideal.
**idealism** (aidi·ališm) *s.* idealismo.
**idealist** (aidi·alist) *s.* idealista.
**idealistic** (aidiali·stik) *adj.* idealista.
**idealize (to)** (aidi·alaiš) *tr.* idealizar.
**ideation** (aidiei·shøn) *s.* ideación.
**idem** (ai·dem) *adj.-pr.* lat. ídem.
**identic(al** (aide·ntik(al) *adj.* idéntico.
**identification** (aidentifikei·shøn) *s.* identificación.
**identify (to)** (aide·ntifai) *tr.* identificar. ¶ Pret. y p. p.: *identified.*
**identify** (-ti) *s.* identidad.
**ideogram** (ai·diogræm), **ideograph** (-græf) *s.* ideograma.
**ideographic** (aidiogræ·fik) *adj.* ideográfico.
**ideology** (-a·lodӯi) *s.* ideología. *2* teorización; especulación visionaria.
**ides** (aidš) *s.* idus.
**idiocy** (i·diøsi) *s.* idiotez. *2* necedad, tontería.
**idiom** (i·diøm) *s.* idioma, habla, lenguaje. *2* genio, índole [de una lengua]. *3* modismo, locución, idiotismo.
**idiomatic(al** (idiomæ·tik(al) *adj.* idiomático. *2* relativo a las locuciones o idiotismos.
**idiosyncrasy** (idiosi·nkrasi) *s.* idiosincrasia. *2* peculiaridad, excentricidad.
**idiosyncratic** (idiosinkræ·tik) *adj.* idiosincrásico.
**idiot** (i·diat) *s.* idiota. *2* necio, tonto, bobo.
**idiotic(al** (idia·tik(al) *adj.* idiota, tonto, estúpido.
**idle** (ai·døl) *adj.* ocioso, desocupado; inactivo. *2* de ocio: ~ *hours*, horas de ocio, ratos perdidos. *3* ocioso, inútil, vano. *4* infundado, futil: ~ *tale*, cuento, patraña. *5* perezoso, holgazán. *6* loca [rueda].
**idle (to)** *intr.* holgar, estar ocioso. *2* holgazanear.

**3** *intr.-tr.* MEC., AUTO. marchar, o hacer marchar [un motor] en vacío, al ralentí. **4** *tr.* gastar ociosamente: *to ~ away one's time,* pasar o perder el tiempo.
**idleness** (-nis) *s.* ocio, ociosidad, inactividad. *2* futilidad, inutilidad. *3* pereza, holgazanería.
**idler** (ai·dlø<sup>r</sup>) *s.* ocioso, holgazán. *2* MEC. rueda loca
**idol** (ai·døl) *s.* ídolo. *2* LÓG. falsa idea o concepto.
**idolater** (aida·latø<sup>r</sup>) *s.* idólatra.
**idolatress** (-tris) *f.* idólatra [mujer].
**idolatrous** (-trøs) *adj.* idolátrico. *2* idólatra.
**idolatry** (-tri) *s.* idolatría.
**idolize (to)** (ai·dølaiš) *tr.* convertir en ídolo. *2 tr.-intr.* idolatrar.
**idyll, idyl** (ai·døl) *s.* LIT. idilio.
**idyllic** (aidi·lik) *adj.* idílico; pastoral, bucólico.
**if** (if) *conj.* si; en caso que, con tal que; aunque, aun cuando: *as ~,* como si; *~ only,* si, si al menos [expresando deseo]. *2* Úsase elípticamente en vez de *if it is, if they are,* etc.: *~ so,* si es así; *~ true,* si es verdad. *3 s.* condición, suposición.
**igloo** (i·glu) *s.* iglú.
**Ignatius** (ignei·shøs) *n. pr. m.* Ignacio.
**igneous** (i·gniøs) *adj.* ígneo.
**ignifuge** (ig·nifiudỹ) *adj.* ignífugo.
**ignis fatuus** (i·gnis fæ·chøs) *s.* fuego fatuo.
**ignite (to)** (ignai·t) *tr.* encender, pegar fuego a. *2 intr.* encenderse, inflamarse, arder.
**ignition** (igni·shøn) *s.* ignición, inflamación. *2* encendido [de un motor]: *~ switch,* interruptor del encendido, contacto.
**ignoble** (ignou·bøl) *adj.* innoble, indigno, vil. *2* villano, plebeyo.
**ignominious** (ignømi·niøs) *adj.* ignominioso.
**ignominy** (i·gnømini) *s.* ignominia.
**ignoramus** (ignørei·møs) *s.* ignorante; pedante.
**ignorance** (i·gnørans) *s.* ignorancia, desconocimiento. *2* ignorancia, falta de cultura.
**ignorant** (-t) *adj.* ignorante, desconocedor: *to be ~ of,* ignorar [una cosa]. *2* ignorante, ignaro, indocto, inculto.
**ignore (to)** (igno·<sup>r</sup>) *tr.* desconocer, cerrar los ojos a una cosa. *2* hacer caso omiso [de uno]; desairarle. *3* DER. desestimar.
**iguana** (igua·na) *s.* ZOOL. iguana.
**ileum** (i·liøm) *s.* ANAT. íleon [intestino].
**ileus** (i·liøs) *s.* MED. íleo.
**ilex** (ai·leks) *s.* BOT. encina. *2* BOT. coscoja. *3* BOT. acebo.
**iliac** (i·liæk) *adj.* ANAT. ilíaco.
**Iliad** (i·liæd) *s.* Ilíada.
**ilium** (i·liøm) *s.* ANAT. íleon, ílion [hueso].
**ilk** (ilk) *s.* fam. raza, clase, especie, jaez:
**I'll** (ail) *contr.* de I SHALL y I WILL.
**ill** (il) *adj.* enfermo, malo, doliente: *to fall ~,* caer enfermo. *2* mareado. *3* malo, mal [no bueno, desfavorable; perjudicial; insalubre; infortunado; desagradable; difícil; malévolo, perverso]: *~ breeding,* mala crianza, mala educación, grosería; *~ health,* mala salud; *~ repute,* mala reputación, mala fama; *~ temper,* mal genio, mal humor; *~ will,* mala voluntad, ojeriza; *in ~ part,* en mala parte. *4 s.* mal, desgracia, infortunio. *5 adv.* mal, malamente: *to think ~,* pensar mal; *~ at ease,* molesto; inquieto, intranquilo.
**ill-advised** *adj.* malaconsejado. *2* desacertado, imprudente.
**illation** (ilei·shøn) *s.* ilación, inferencia.
**illative** (i·lativ) *adj.* ilativo.
**ill-bred** *adj.* malcriado, grosero, descortés.

**ill-conditioned** *adj.* de mala inclinación; de mal genio. *2* malparado.
**illegal** (il·gal) *adj.* ilegal.
**illegality** (ilɪgæ·liti) *s.* ilegalidad. *2* desaguisado.
**illegibility** (iledỹibi·liti) *s.* calidad de ilegible.
**illegible** (ile·dỹibøl) *adj.* ilegible.
**illegitimacy** (ilidỹi·timasi) *s.* ilegitimidad.
**illegitimate** (-timit) *adj.* ilegítimo. *2* bastardo. *3* ilógico; erróneo.
**illegitimate (to)** (-meit) *tr.* ilegitimar.
**ill-fated** *adj.* malhadado, desgraciado. *2* aciago.
**ill-favoured** *adj.* mal parecido, feo, repulsivo.
**ill-gotten** *adj.* mal habido, mal adquirido.
**ill-humo (u) red** (-jiu·mø<sup>r</sup>d) *adj.* malhumorado.
**illiberal** (ili·børal) *adj.* iliberal. *2* inculto, rústico. *3* mezquino, tacaño. *4* estrecho de miras.
**illiberality** (ilibøræ·liti) *s.* falta de liberalidad. *2* mezquindad, tacañería. *3* estrechez de miras.
**illicit** (-sit) *adj.* ilícito.
**illicitness** (-nis) *s.* ilicitud.
**illimitable** (-mitabøl) *adj.* ilimitado.
**illiquid** (-kuid) *adj.* COM. no realizable.
**illiteracy** (-torasi) *s.* falta de cultura, ignorancia. *2* analfabetismo.
**illiterate** (-tørit) *adj.* iletrado, analfabeto.
**ill-mannered** *adj.* mal educado, de malos modales.
**illness** (i·lnis) *s.* enfermedad, dolencia.
**illogical** (ila·dỹikal) *adj.* ilógico. *2* que no razona con lógica.
**ill-pleased** *adj.* descontento.
**ill-starred** *adj.* desdichado, malaventurado.
**ill-suited** *adj.* inadecuado; poco a propósito.
**ill-timed** *adj.* intempestivo, inoportuno.
**ill-treat (to)** *tr.* maltratar.
**illuminant** (iliu·minant) *adj.-s.* iluminante.
**illuminate (to)** (iliu·mineit) *tr.* iluminar, alumbrar. *2* esclarecer, aclarar. *3* hacer resplandeciente. *4* B. ART. iluminar.
**illuminati** (iliuminei·tai) *s. pl.* iluminados [secta].
**illumination** (-shøn) *s.* iluminación; alumbrado. *2* esclarecimiento. *3* ilustración, saber. *4* B. ART. iluminación [en colores]. *5 pl.* luminarias.
**illumine (to)** (iliu·min) *tr.* iluminar.
**illusion** (iliu·ỹøn) *s.* ilusión; espejismo, engaño. *2* aparición.
**illusionist** (-ist) *s.* ilusionista.
**illusive** (iliu·siv) *adj.* ilusivo, ilusorio, irreal.
**illusory** (-sori) *adj.* ilusorio, engañoso.
**illustrate (to)** (i·løstreit) *tr.* ilustrar [con explicaciones, dibujos, etc.].
**illustration** (-ei·shøn) *s.* ilustración. | No tiene el sentido de cultura, luces.
**illustrator** (-tø<sup>r</sup>) *s.* ilustrador.
**illustrious** (ilø·striøs) *adj.* ilustre, preclaro, famoso.
**I'm** (aim) contracción de I AM.
**image** (i·midỹ) *s.* imagen: *in his own ~,* a su imagen. *2* símbolo, representación. *3* retrato, efigie. *4* parecido, semejanza.
**image (to)** *tr.* figurar, retratar, reproducir, reflejar. *2* concebir, imaginar, representarse. *3* representar, simbolizar.
**imagery** (-ri) *s.* B. ART. imaginería. *2* imágenes retóricas. *3* fantasías, recuerdos. *4* detalles pintorescos de un paisaje, etc.
**imaginary** (imæ·dỹineri) *adj.* imaginario.
**imagination** (imædỹinei·shøn) *s.* imaginación. *2* creación poética o de la imaginación.
**imaginative** (imæ·dỹineitiv) *adj.* imaginativo.
**imagine (to)** (imæ·dỹin) *tr.* imaginar, concebir, idear. *2* imaginarse, figurarse.

**imago** (imei·gou) *s.* ENT. imago.
**imam** (ima·m) *s.* imán [título mahometano].
**imbecile** (i·mbisil) *adj.-s.* imbécil, estúpido. 2 débil, sin fuerzas.
**imbecility** (imbisi·liti) *s.* imbecilidad, tontería, absurdidad.
**imbibe (to)** (imbai·b) *tr.* embeber, absorber, chupar. 2 fig. empaparse de, asimilar. 3 *intr.* fam. beber, empinar el codo.
**imbricate (to)** (i·mbrikeit) *tr.* disponer como las tejas de un tejado.
**imbrication** (-ei·shøn) *s.* imbricación.
**imbroglio** (imbrou·liou) *s.* enredo, embrollo, lío.
**imbrue (to)** (imbru·) *tr.* ensangrentar, teñir en sangre, manchar de sangre.
**imbue (to)** (imbiu·) *tr.* saturar, empapar, impregnar, teñir. 2 imbuir, infundir.
**imitable** (i·mitabøl) *adj.* imitable.
**imitate (to)** (i·miteit) *tr.* imitar. 3 contrahacer, remedar.
**imitation** (-shøn) *s.* imitación. 2 remedo. 3 *adj.* de imitación.
**immaculate** (imæ·kiulit) *adj.* inmaculado: *Immaculate Conception*, Inmaculada Concepción.
**immanence, -cy** (i·manøns, -si) *s.* inmanencia.
**immanent** (i·manønt) *adj.* inmanente.
**Immanuel** (imæ·niuel) *n. pr.* Emanuel.
**Immaterial** (imati·rial) *adj.* inmaterial, incorpóreo. 2 indiferente, que no importa, sin importancia: *it is* ~, es indiferente, lo mismo da.
**immaterialism** (-išm) *s.* FIL. idealismo.
**immateriality** (imatiriæ·liti) *s.* inmaterialidad, incorporeidad. 2 cualidad de lo que no importa.
**immature** (imatiu·ø^r) *adj.* inmaturo, sin madurar, joven. 2 inacabado, imperfecto. 3 verde [fruta].
**immaturity** (-riti) *s.* calidad de inmaturo, falta de madurez, de sazón.
**inmmeasurable** (ime·ȳurabøl) *adj.* inconmensurable, desmesurado.
**immediacy** (imi·diasi) *s.* inmediación, proximidad.
**immediate** (-diit) *adj.* inmediato. 2 directo, intuitivo, intuido, conocido por intuición.
**immediately** (-li) *adv.* inmediatamente. 2 directamente, intuitivamente. 3 *conj.* tan pronto como, en cuanto.
**immemorial** (imimo·rial) *adj.* inmemorial, inmemorable.
**immense** (ime·ns) *adj.* inmenso, infinito, vasto. 2 pop. estupendo, magnífico.
**immensity** (ime·nsiti) *s.* inmensidad. 2 infinidad, vastedad.
**immensurable** (ime·nshurabøl) *adj.* inmensurable; inconmensurable.
**immerge (to)** (imø·^rdȳ) *tr.* hundir, sumergir. 2 *intr.* hundirse, sumergirse.
**immerse (to)** (imø·^rs) *tr.* sumergir, hundir, sumir. 2 bautizar por inmersión. 3 absorber [la atención, el pensamiento, etc.].
**immersion** (imø·^rshøn) *s.* inmersión. 2 sumersión. 3 bautismo por inmersión.
**immess (to)** (ime·sh) *tr.* enredar, enmallar.
**immigrant** (i·migrant) *adj.-s.* inmigrante.
**immigrate (to)** (i·migreit) *intr.* inmigrar.
**immigration** (imigre·shøn) *s.* inmigración.
**imminence** (i·minøns) *s.* inminencia. 2 cosa inminente, que amenaza.
**imminent** (-t) *adj.* inminente.
**immiscible** (imi·sibøl) *adj.* FÍS., QUÍM. inmiscible.
**immobile** (imou·bil) *adj.* inmóvil, inmoble.
**imobility** (imoubi·liti) *s.* inmovilidad.

**immobilize (to)** (imou·bilaiš) *tr.* inmovilizar.
**immoderate** (ima·dørit) *adj.* inmoderado, desmedido. 2 irrazonable, exagerado.
**immoderation** (imadørei·shøn) *s.* inmoderación.
**immodest** (ima·dıst) *adj.* inmodesto. 2 deshonesto, indecente. 3 atrevido, insolente.
**immodesty** (-i) *s.* inmodestia. 2 indecoro, indecencia. 3 descaro.
**immolate (to)** (i·moleit) *tr.* inmolar.
**immolation** (-ei·shøn) *s.* inmolación.
**immoral** (ima·ral) *adj.* inmoral.
**immorality** (imøræ·liti) *s.* inmoralidad.
**immortal** (imo·^rtal) *adj.* inmortal, imperecedero. 2 *s.* inmortal.
**immortality** (imo·^rtæ·liti) *s.* inmortalidad.
**immortalize (to)** (imo·^rtalaiš) *tr.* inmortalizar.
**immortelle** (imo·^rte·l) *s.* BOT. siempreviva.
**immovability** (inmuvabi·liti) *s.* inamovilidad, inmovilidad, fijeza. 2 inalterabilidad. 3 insensibilidad.
**immovable** (imu·vabøl) *adj.* inamovible, inmóvil, fijo. 2 inalterable, inflexible. 3 impasible. 4 DER. inmueble. 5 *s. pl.* bienes raíces.
**immune** (imiu·n) *adj.-s.* inmune.
**immunity** (imiu·niti) *s.* inmunidad. 2 libertad, privilegio, exención.
**immunization** (ei·shøn) *s.* inmunización.
**immunize (to)** (i·miunaiš) *tr.* inmunizar.
**immunology** (imiuna·lodȳi) *s.* inmunología.
**immure** (to) (imiu·ø^r) *tr.* emparedar. 2 amurallar.
**immutability** (imiutabi·liti) *s.* inmutabilidad. 2 constancia, firmeza.
**immutable** (imiu·tabøl) *adj.* inmutable.
**imp** (imp) *s.* diablillo, duende. 2 diablillo [niño travieso].
**impact** (i·mpækt) *s.* golpe, choque, impacto.
**impaction** (impæ·kshøn) *s.* MED. impacción.
**impair (to)** (impe·ø^r) *tr.* dañar, perjudicar, estropear, deteriorar, disminuir, debilitar.
**impairment** (-mønt) *s.* deterioro, menoscabo, mengua, debilitación.
**impale** (impei·l) *tr.* empalar. 3 empalizar, cercar.
**impalpable** (impæ·lpabøl) *adj.* impalpable.
**impanel** (to) (impæ·nøl) *tr.* DER. elegir o designar [un jurado]; incluir en él.
**imparity** (impæ·riti) *s.* disparidad, desigualdad.
**impart (to)** (impa·^rt) *tr.* impartir, dar, comunicar. 2 declarar, dar a conocer.
**impartial** (impa·^rshal) *adj.* imparcial.
**impartiality** (impa·shiæ·liti) *s.* imparcialidad.
**impartment** (impa·^rtmønt) *s.* acción de impartir.
**impassable** (impæ·sabøl) *adj.* impracticable, intransitable.
**impasse** (impæ·s) *s.* callejón sin salida. 2 atolladero, dificultad insuperable.
**impassibility** (-sibi·liti) *s.* impasibilidad.
**impassible** (-bøl) *adj.* impasible.
**impassion (to)** (-shøn) *tr.* apasionar, conmover.
**impasioned** (-d) *adj.* apasionado, vehemente, ardiente. 2 extremoso.
**impassive** (impæ·siv) *adj.* impasible. 2 insensible, inanimado.
**impassiveness** (-nis) *s.* impasibilidad.
**impaste (to)** (impei·st) *tr.* PINT. empastar.
**impatience** (impei·shøns) *s.* impaciencia.
**impatient** (impei·shønt) *adj.* impaciente. 2 que no puede sufrir una cosa.
**impeach (to)** (impı·ch) *tr.* discutir, poner en tela de juicio. 2 acusar [esp. a un funcionario público]; residenciar. 3 acriminar, culpar.
**impeachable** (-abøl) *adj.* censurable. 2 discutible.

**impeachment** (-mønt) s. acción de poner en tela de juicio. *2* acusación; residencia [acción de residenciar].
**impeccability** (impekabi·liti) s. impecabilidad.
**impeccable** (impe·kabøl) adj. impecable.
**impecuniosity** (-kiunia·siti) s. inopia, pobreza.
**impecunious** (-kiu·niøs) adj. pobre, sin dinero.
**impedance** (impɪ·dans) s. ELECT. impedancia.
**impede (to)** (impɪ·d) tr. impedir, estorbar, obstruir.
**impediment** (impe·dimønt) s. impedimento, estorbo, obstáculo, traba. *2 pl.* impedimenta.
**impedimenta** (impedime·nta) s. *pl.* impedimenta.
**impel (to)** (impe·l) tr. impeler, impulsar. *2* mover, obligar. ¶ Pret. y p. p.: *impelled;* p. a.: *-lling.*
**impellent** (impe·lønt) adj. impelente. *2* impulsor. *3 s.* impulsor, motor, móvil; empuje.
**impend (to)** (impe·nd) intr. pender [sobre]; amenazar, amagar, ser inminente.
**impenetrability** (impenitrabi·liti) s. impenetrabilidad.
**impenetrable** (impe·nitrabøl) adj. impenetrable. *2* duro, inconmovible.
**impenitence** (impe·nitøns) s. impenitencia.
**impenitent** (impe·nitønt) adj.-s. impenitente.
**imperative** (impe·rativ) adj. imperativo, imperioso. *2* perentorio, indispensable. *3 adj.-s.* GRAM. imperativo. *4 s.* imperativo, necesidad imperiosa.
**imperceptibility** (impøʳseptibi·liti) s. imperceptibilidad.
**imperceptible** (impøʳse·ptibøl) adj. imperceptible.
**imperfect** (impø·ʳfikt) adj. imperfecto, incompleto, defectuoso. *2 s.* GRAM. pretérito imperfecto.
**imperfection** (impøʳfe·kshøn) s. imperfección. *2* falta, defecto.
**imperfective** (-tiv) adj. GRAM. imperfectivo.
**imperial** (impi·rial) adj. imperial. *2 s.* perilla, para [barba]. *3* imperial [de un vehículo].
**imperialism** (impi·rialism) s. imperialismo.
**imperialist** (impi·rialist) s. imperialista.
**imperil (to)** (impe·ril) tr. poner en peligro. ¶ Pret. y p. p. *-iled* o *-illed;* p. a.: *-iling* o *-illing.*
**imperious** (impi·riøs) adj. imperioso, arrogante, autoritario. *2* imperioso, urgente.
**imperiousness** (-nis) s. autoridad, mando. *2* imperio, arrogancia.
**imperishable** (impe·rishabøl) adj. imperecedero. *2* indestructible.
**impermanence** (impø·ʳmanøns) s. instabilidad.
**impermanent** (-nt) adj. no permanente, instable.
**impermeable** (impø·ʳmiabøl) adj. impermeable, impenetrable.
**impersonal** (impø·ʳsønal) adj. impersonal.
**impersonate (to)** (impø·ʳsøneit) tr. personificar. *2* TEAT. representar [a un personaje]. *3* imitar, fingirse, hacerse pasar por [una pers.].
**impersonation** (-shøn) s. personificación. *2* TEAT. representación [de un personaje], papel.
**impersonator** (-ø·ʳ) s. personificador. *2* TEAT. intérprete [de un papel]. *3* TEAT. artista que imita personajes conocidos. *4* el que se hace pasar por otro.
**impertinence, -cy** (-tinøns, -si) s. impertinencia. *2* falta de pertinencia.
**impertinent** (-tinønt) adj. impertinente.
**imperturbable** (impøʳtø·ʳbabøl) adj. imperturbable.
**imperturbed** (-tø·ʳbd) adj. tranquilo, sereno.

**impervious** (impø·ʳviøs) adj. impenetrable, impermeable. *2* que no atiende a [razones, etc.].
**impetigo** (impi·taigou) s. MED. impétigo.
**impetrate (to)** (i·mpetreit) tr. impetrar.
**impetratory** (i·mpetratori) adj. impetratorio.
**impetuosity** (impechua·siti) s. impetuosidad, ímpetu, vehemencia.
**impetuous** (impe·chuøs) adj. impetuoso.
**impetus** (i·mpitøs) s. ímpetu. *2* impulso, estímulo.
**impiety** (impai·øti) s. impiedad, irreligiosidad.
**impinge (to)** (impi·ndy) tr. dar en o contra, chocar con. *2* intr. *to ~ on* o *upon,* tocar, golpear contra, herir; invadir [derechos, etc.].
**impious** (i·mpiøs) adj. impío, irreverente, profano. *2* malvado.
**impiousness** (-nis) s. impiedad.
**impish** (i·mpish) adj. travieso, endiablado.
**implacability** (implækabi·liti) s. implacabilidad.
**implacable** (implæ·cabøl) adj. implacable.
**implant (to)** (implæ·nt) tr. implantar, fijar. *2* inculcar. *3* plantar, injerir.
**implantation** (-ei·shøn) s. implantación, fijación. *2* inculcación.
**implement** (i·mplimønt) s. instrumento, herramienta, utensilio. *2 pl.* enseres, avíos.
**implement (to)** tr. llevar a cabo, ejecutar, cumplir.
**implicate (to)** (i·mplikeit) tr. implicar. *2* enredar, entrelazar. *3* complicar, comprometer [a uno].
**implication** (-ei·shøn) s. implicación, enredo. *2* deducción, inferencia. *3* complicación, complicidad.
**implicative** (i·mplikativ) adj. implicatorio.
**implicit** (impli·sit) adj. implícito. *2* virtual, potencial. *3* absoluto, ciego, sin duda ni reserva.
**implicitness** (-nis) s. calidad de implícito.
**implied** (implai·d) adj. implícito, sobreentendido. *2* significado, denotado.
**imploration** (implorei·shøn) s. imploración.
**implore (to)** (implo·ʳ) tr. implorar.
**impluvium** (implu·viøm) s. impluvio.
**imply (to)** (implai·) tr. implicar, entrañar, argüir, incluir en esencia. *2* dar a entender; significar, denotar. ¶ Pret. y p. p.: *implied.*
**impolicy** (impa·lisi) s. inoportunidad, torpeza, inhabilidad.
**impolite** (impølai·t) adj. impolítico, descortés.
**impoliteness** (-nis) s. impolítica, descortesía.
**impolitic** (impa·litik) adj. impolítico, poco hábil, imprudente.
**imponderable** (impa·ndørabøl) adj.-s. imponderable.
**imporous** (impo·røs) adj. no poroso.
**import** (i·mpoʳt) s. importancia, peso, entidad. *2* significado, sentido; intención. *3* importación. *4 pl.* géneros importados.
**import (to)** (impo·ʳt) tr.-intr. importar [ser de importancia]. *2* tr. importar, implicar, significar. *3* importar, introducir.
**importance** (-ans) s. importancia. *2* cuantía. *3* vanidad, presunción, engreimiento.
**important** (-ant) adj. importante, considerable. *2* pomposo, presuntuoso, engreído.
**importation** (-ei·shøn) s. importación.
**importer** (impo·ʳtøʳ) s. importador.
**importunacy** (impo·ʳtiunasi) s. importunidad.
**importunate** (-nit) adj. importuno, pesado, insistente.
**importune (to)** (impo·ʳtiun) tr.-intr. importunar.
**importunity** (-tiu·niti) s. importunidad, machaquería. *2* importunación.
**impose (to)** (impou·s) tr. imponer [tributos, silen-

cio, las manos, etc.]. *2* hacer aceptar. *3* IMPR. imponer. *4* intr. *to ~ on* o *upon,* engañar, abusar de la buena fe de.

**imposing** (-ing) *adj.* imponente, impresionante.

**imposition** (impøši·shøn) *s.* imposición. *2* carga, tributo, impuesto. *3* engaño, ficción, impostura.

**impossibility** (impasibi·liti) *s.* imposibilidad. *2* imposible.

**impossible** (impa·sibøl) *adj.* imposible, irrealizable, impracticable. *2* estrafalario. *3 s.* imposible.

**impost** (i·mpoust) *s.* impuesto, tributo, contribución. *2* ARQ. imposta [de un arco].

**impostor** (impa·stør) *s.* impostor, engañador, estafador.

**imposture** (impa·schør) *s.* impostura, engaño.

**impotence, -cy** (i·mpatøns, -si) *s.* impotencia.

**impotent** (-tønt) *adj.* impotente. *2* débil [sin fuerzas].

**impound (to)** (impau·nd) *tr.* encerrar, acorralar. *2* embalsar, represar. *3* DER. depositar.

**impoverish (to)** (impa·vørish) *tr.* empobrecer, depauperar.

**impracticability** (impræktikabi·liti) *s.* impracticabilidad.

**impracticable** (impræ·ktikabøl) *adj.* impracticable. *2* intransitable.

**imprecate (to)** (i·mprikeit) *tr.* imprecar. *2 intr.* proferir imprecaciones.

**imprecation** (-ei·shøn) *s.* imprecación.

**impregnable** (impre·gnabøl) *adj.* inexpugnable.

**impregnate** (impre·gneit) *adj.* preñado; fecundado. *2* impregnado, empapado, lleno.

**impregnate (to)** *tr.* empreñar, fecundar. *2* impregnar, empapar, saturar.

**impregnation** (-ei·shøn) *s.* fecundación. *2* impregnación, empapamiento.

**impresario** (imprisa·riou) *s.* TEAT. empresario.

**imprescriptible** (impriskri·ptibøl) *adj.* imprescriptible.

**impress** (i·mpres) *s.* impresión, señal, marca, huella. *2* sello [carácter distintivo].

**impress (to)** (impre·s) *tr.* imprimir, estampar, grabar. *2* inculcar. *3* imprimir [un carácter, movimiento, etc.]. *4* impresionar, causar impresión en.

**impressible** (-ibøl) *adj.* impresionable. *2* imprimible, estampable.

**impression** (impre·shøn) *s.* impresión [en todos sus sentidos]. *2* estampa, sigilación. *3* marca, señal, huella. *4* edición [ejemplares que se publican de una vez].

**impressionable** (-abøl) *adj.* impresionable.

**impressionism** (-išm) *s.* B. ART. impresionismo.

**impressive** (impre·siv) *adj.* impresionante, que causa impresión, emocionante, grandioso, solemne.

**imprevision** (imprevi·ẏøn) *s.* imprevisión.

**imprimatur** (imprimei·tør) *s.* imprimátur. *2* sanción, aprobación.

**imprint** (i·mprint) *s.* impresión, marca, señal, huella. *2* pie de imprenta.

**imprint (to)** (impri·nt) *tr.* imprimir, estampar. *2* imprimir, grabar [en el ánimo].

**imprison (to)** (impri·søn) *tr.* encarcelar, poner preso, encerrar, aprisionar.

**imprisonment** (-mønt) *s.* encarcelamiento. *2* encierro, prisión.

**improbability** (imprababi·liti) *s.* improbabilidad. *2* inverosimilitud.

**improbable** (impra·babøl) *adj.* improbable. *2* inverosímil.

**improbity** (improu·biti) *s.* improbidad.

**impromptu** (impro·mptiu) *adj.* impremeditado, improvisado. *2 adv.* de repente, en el acto. *3 s.* improvisación. *4* MÚS. impromptu.

**improper** (impro·pør) *adj.* impropio. *2* incorrecto, inexacto. *3* inconveniente, indecoroso.

**impropriety** (imprøprai·eti) *s.* impropiedad. *2* inconveniencia, indecoro.

**improvable** (-abøl) *adj.* mejorable. *2* cultivable. *3* útil.

**improve (to)** (impru·v) *tr.* mejorar, perfecionar, desarrollar. *2* aprovechar, sacar partido de. *3* beneficiar, explotar, urbanizar. *4 intr.* mejorar, mejorarse. *5* adelantar, progresar. *6 to ~ on* o *upon,* mejorar, perfeccionar.

**improvement** (-mønt) *s.* mejoramiento, perfeccionamiento. *2* mejora, adelanto, progreso. *3* MED. mejoría. *4* aprovechamiento. *5* explotación, urbanización.

**improvidence** (impra·vidøns) *s.* imprevisión, descuido.

**improvident** (-nt) *adj.* impróvido, imprevisor, descuidado.

**improvisation** (impravišei·shøn) *s.* improvisación.

**improvisator** (-tø ) *s.* improvisador.

**improvise (to)** (imprøvai·š) *tr.-intr.* improvisar.

**imprudence** (impru·døns) *s.* imprudencia.

**imprudent** (-nt) *adj.* imprudente.

**impuberate** (impiu·børeit) *adj.* impúber.

**impudence** (-døns) *s.* aplomo, atrevimiento, impudencia, descaro, desfachatez, insolencia.

**impudent** (-dønt) *adj.* atrevido, impudente, descarado, insolente.

**impudicity** (impiudi·siti) *s.* impudicicia, impudicia.

**impugn (to)** (impiu·n) *tr.* impugnar; poner en tela de juicio.

**impugnment** (-mønt) *s.* impugnación.

**impuissant** (impui·sant) *adj.* impotente.

**impulse** (i·mpøls) *s.* impulso. *2* impulsión; ímpetu.

**impulsion** (impø·lshøn) *s.* impulsión, impulso.

**impulsive** (impø·lsiv) *adj.-s.* impulsivo.

**impunity** (impiu·niti) *s.* impunidad.

**impure** (impiu·ø ) *adj.* impuro.

**impurity** (-riti) *s.* impureza.

**imputable** (-tabøl) *adj.* adj. imputable, achacable.

**impute (to)** (impiu·t) *tr.* imputar.

**in** (in) *prep.* en, con, de, dentro de, durante, mientras, entre, por: *~ a drawer,* en un cajón; *~ April,* en abril; *cut ~ two,* partido en dos; *~ a husky voice,* con voz ronca, *dressed ~ black,* vestido de negro; *~ an instant,* en un instante, dentro de un instante; *~ deference to him,* por deferencia hacia él; *~ the morning,* por la mañana; *~ the meantime,* mientras, entre tanto; *one ~ a thousand,* uno entre mil. *2 ~ so far as,* en lo que, hasta donde. *3 ~ that,* en que; por cuanto.

*4 adj.* interior, entrante; de dentro. *5* encendido [luz, etc.]. *6 to be ~ with,* tener influencia con.

*7 adv.* dentro, adentro; en casa; en el poder; en su turno: *to be ~,* estar en casa, en la oficina, etc.; *~ here,* aquí dentro; *~ there,* allí dentro. *8 to be ~ for,* estar comprometido, destinado o expuesto a.

*9 s.* rincón, recodo, recoveco: *ins and outs,* recovecos, interioridades, pormenores.

**in** abreviatura de INCH o INCHES.

**inability** (inabi·liti) *s.* incapacidad, impotencia. *2* inhabilidad, incompetencia.

**inaccessibility** (inæksesibi·liti) *s.* inaccesibilidad.

**inaccessible** (inækse·sibøl) *adj.* inaccesible.

**inaccuracy** (inæ·kiurasi) *s.* inexactitud, incorrección, error.

**inaction** (inæ·kshøn) *s.* inacción.

**inactive** (-tiv) *adj.* inactivo. *2* ocioso. *3* indolente, perezoso.

**inactivity** (inækti·viti) *s.* inactividad. *2* ociosidad.

**inadaptable** (inadæ·ptabøl) *adj.* inadaptable.

**inadequacy** (inæ·dikuisi) *s.* falta de adecuación. *2* desproporción. *3* insuficiencia.

**inadequate** (-kuit) *adj.* inadecuado. *2* insuficiente.

**inadmissible** (inædmi·sibøl) *adj.* inadmisible.

**inadvertence, -cy** (inædvø·ʳtøns, -si) *s.* inadvertencia. *2* distracción, falta de atención.

**inadvertent** (-ønt) *adj.* inadvertido [que no advierte]. *2* distraído, negligente, descuidado. *3* dicho o hecho sin poner atención, al descuido.

**inadvisable** (inædvai·šabøl) *adj.* poco aconsejable o prudente.

**inalienable** (inei·liønabøl) *adj.* inalienable.

**inalterable** (ino·lterabøl) *adj.* inalterable.

**inamorata** (inæmora·tæ) *s.* enamorada, novia.

**inane** (inei·n) *adj.* inane. *2* mentecato, sandio. *3 s.* el vacío, el espacio infinito.

**inanimate (d** (inæ·nimit(id) *adj.* inanimado. *2* exánime.

**inanition** (inani·shøn) *s.* inanición.

**inanity** (inæ·niti) *s.* inanidad, vaciedad, sandez.

**inappetence** (inæ·pitens) *s.* inapetencia.

**inapplicable** (inæ·plicabøl) *adj.* inaplicable; inadecuado.

**inapposite** (inæ·pošit) *adj.* inadecuado, poco apropiado.

**inappreciable** (inæpri·shiabøl) *adj.* inapreciable, inestimable. *2* inapreciable, imperceptible.

**inapproachable** (inæprou·chabøl) *adj.* inabordable, inaccesible. *2* sin rival, sin par.

**inappropriate** (inæprou·priit) *adj.* impropio, inadecuado, no apropiado.

**inapt** (inæ·pt) *s.* no apto. *2* inepto.

**inaptitude** (-itiud) *s.* ineptitud. *2* insuficiencia.

**inarticulate** (inaʳti·kiulit) *adj.* inarticulado.

**inartistic** (inaʳti·stik) *adj.* no artístico. *2* falto de gusto artístico.

**inasmuch as** (inašmø·ch aš) *loc.* considerando que, visto que, puesto que. *2* tanto como, hasta donde.

**inattention** (inate·nshøn) *s.* desatención. *2* distracción, inadvertencia.

**inattentive** (-tiv) *adj.* desatento. *2* distraído, descuidado.

**inaudible** (ino·dibøl) *adj.* inaudible.

**inaugural** (ino·giural) *adj.* inaugural.

**inaugurate (to)** (ino·giureit) *tr.* inaugurar. *2* instalar, dar posesión solemnemente.

**inauguration** (inogiurei·shøn) *s.* inauguración. *2* toma de posesión solemne.

**inauspicious** (inospi·shøs) *adj.* poco propicio, desfavorable, siniestro, infeliz.

**inborn** (i·nboʳn) *adj.* innato, ingénito, connatural.

**inbred** (i·nbred) *p. p.* de INBREED. *2 adj.* innato, ingénito. *3* nacido de padres de una misma raza.

**inbreed (to)** (inbrı·d) *tr.* producir, crear [en]. *2* criar o engendrar sin mezcla de razas. ¶ Pret. y p. p.: *inbred*.

**Inca** (i·nka) *adj.* incaico. *2 s.* inca.

**incalculable** (inkæ·kiulabøl) *adj.* incalculable. *2* imprevisible. *3* incierto.

**incandescence, -cy** (inkænde·søns, -si) *s.* incandescencia.

**incandescent** (-ønt) *adj.* incandescente.

**incantation** (inkantei·shøn) *s.* encantamiento, conjuro, sortilegio.

**incapability** (inkeipabi·liti) *s.* incapacidad.

**incapable** (inkei·pabøl) *adj.* incapaz. | No tiene el sentido de falto de cabida.

**incapacitate (to)** (inkapæ·siteit) *tr.* incapacitar, inhabilitar.

**incapacitation** (-ei·shøn) *s.* incapacitación.

**incapacity** (-siti) *s.* incapacidad, inhabilidad; simpleza. *2* DER. incapacidad.

**incarcerate (to)** (inka·ʳsøreit) *tr.* encarcelar, encerrar.

**incarceration** (-ei·shøn) *s.* encarcelamiento, encierro, prisión.

**incarnadine** (inka·ʳnadin) *adj.* encarnado [de color de carne]; encarnadino.

**incarnate** (inka·ʳnit) *adj.* encarnado, personificado: ~ *devil*, demonio encarnado.

**incarnate (to)** (inca·ʳneit) *tr.* tomar la forma o el cuerpo de. *2* encarnar, personificar.

**incarnation** (-ei·shøn) *s.* encarnación [del Verbo]. *2* encarnación, personificación.

**incautious** (inco·shøs) *adj.* incauto, imprudente.

**incautiousness** (-nis) *s.* falta de cautela, descuido, imprudencia.

**incendiarism** (inse·ndiarišm) *s.* incendio intencionado [delito].

**incendiary** (inse·ndieri) *s.* incendiario. *2* agitador.

**incense** (i·nsens) *s.* incienso: ~ *boat*, naveta.

**incense (to)** (inse·ns) *tr.* incensar. *2* exasperar, irritar, enfurecer, encolerizar.

**incensory** (-ori) *s.* incensario.

**incentive** (-tiv) *adj.* incitativo. *2 s.* incentivo, aliciente.

**inception** (inse·pshøn) *s.* principio, comienzo.

**inceptive** (-tiv) *adj.* incipiente. *2* incoativo.

**incertitude** (insø·ʳtitiud) *s.* incertidumbre.

**incessant** (inse·sant) *adj.* incesante, continuo.

**incest** (i·nsest) *s.* incesto.

**incestuous** (inse·schuøs) *adj.* incestuoso.

**inch** (inch) *s.* pulgada [2,54 cm.]; fig. pequeña cantidad: *by inches*, gradualmente; a poquitos; *every ~ a man*, todo un hombre; ~ *by ~*, pulgada por pulgada, palmo a palmo.

**inch (to)** *intr.* moverse poco a poco: *to ~ ahead*, avanzar poco a poco.

**inchmeal** (-mıl) *s. adv.* poco a poco.

**inchoate** (i·nkouit) *adj.* incipiente, en embrión.

**inchoate (to)** (i·nkoueit) *tr.* incoar, principiar.

**inchoative** (inkou·ativ) *adj.* incipiente. *2* GRAM. incoativo.

**inchworm** (i·nchuøʳm) *s.* ENT. geómetra.

**incidence** (i·nsidøns) *s.* GEOM., FÍS. incidencia. *2* acto o manera de afectar o modificar.

**incident** (-t) *adj.* incidente. *2* concomitante. *3* incidental, fortuito. *4 s.* incidente. *5* casualidad. *6* suceso, ocurrencia.

**incidental** (inside·ntal) *adj.* incidental, accidental. *2* casual, contingente. *3* inherente, concomitante. *4 s. pl.* imprevisto.

**incinerate (to)** (insi·nøreit) *tr.* incinerar.

**incineration** (-ei·shøn) *s.* incineración.

**incipience** (insi·piøns) *s.* principio, comienzo.

**incipient** (-ønt) *adj.* incipiente.

**incise (to)** (insai·š) *tr.* cortar, hacer incisión; grabar, tallar.

**incision** (insi·ɏøn) *s.* incisión.

**incisive** (insai·siv) *adj.* incisivo. 2 agudo, penetrante.
**incisor** (insai·ṣøʳ) *adj.-s.* ANAT. incisivo [diente].
**incitation** (insitei·shøn) *s.* incitación; instigación.
**incite (to)** (insai·t) *tr.* incitar, aguijonear, estimular.
**incitement** (-mønt) *s.* incitación, incitamiento. 2 incentivo, estímulo.
**incivility** (insivi·liti) *s.* incivilidad, descortesía.
**inclemency** (inkle·mønsi) *s.* inclemencia. 2 intemperie. 3 desgracia.
**inclement** (-ønt) *adj.* inclemente. 2 tempestuoso. 3 contrario, adverso. 4 severo, cruel.
**inclination** (inklinei·shøn) *s.* inclinación [en todas sus acepciones]. 2 declive, pendiente. 3 disposición, estado, afecto.
**incline** (i·nklain) *s.* declive, pendiente, cuesta.
**incline (to)** (inklai·n) *tr.* inclinar. 2 bajar, doblar [la cabeza, etc.]. 3 *intr.* inclinarse. 4 bajar, hacer pendiente. 5 propender, tender. 6 tirar [a un color].
**inclined** (-d) *adj.* inclinado. 2 propenso.
**inclose (to)** (inklou·ṣ) *tr.* ENCLOSE.
**inclosure** (-ȳøʳ) *s.* ENCLOSURE.
**include (to)** (inklu·d) *tr.* incluir.
**inclusion** (-ȳøn) *s.* inclusión. 2 cosa incluida. 3 carta que acompaña a otra.
**inclusive** (-siv) *adj.* inclusivo, que incluye o contiene. 2 *adv.* inclusive.
**incoercible** (inkou·ʳsibøl) *adj.* incoercible.
**incognito** (inka·gnitou) *adj.-s.* incógnito. 2 *adv.* de incógnito.
**incognizable** (-nišabøl) *adj.* incognoscible; no reconocible.
**incoherence, -cy** (inkouji·røns, -si) *s.* incoherencia, inconexión, incongruencia.
**incoherent** (-ønt) *adj.* incoherente, inconexo.
**incombustibility** (inkømbøstibi·liti) *s.* incombustibilidad.
**incombustible** (inkømbø·stibøl) *adj.* incombustible.
**income** (i·nkøm) *s.* entrada, ingreso. 2 ingresos, renta, utilidades: ~ *tax*, impuesto sobre la renta.
**incoming** (-ing) *adj.* entrante, que está por llegar. 3 que aumenta [beneficio]; que empieza [año, etc.].
**incommensurable** (inkøme·nshurabøl) *adj.* inconmensurable.
**incommensurate** (-it) *adj.* inconmensurable. 2 inadecuado, desproporcionado.
**incommode (to)** (inkømou·d) *tr.* incomodar, molestar, desacomodar.
**incommodious** (-iøs) *adj.* incómodo, inconveniente, molesto.
**incommodity** (-iti) *s.* incomodidad, inconveniencia.
**incommunicable** (inkømiu·nikabøl) *adj.* incomunicable; indecible.
**incommunicative** (inkømiu·nikativ) *adj.* reservado, poco comunicativo; insociable.
**incommutable** (inkømiu·tabøl) *adj.* inconmutable.
**incomparable** (inka·mparabøl) *adj.* incomparable, sin igual, sin par.
**incompatibility** (inkømpætibi·liti) *s.* incompatibilidad, contrariedad.
**incompatible** (inkømpæ·tibøl) *adj.* incompatible, contrario.
**incompetence, -cy** (inka·mpitøns, -si) *s.* incompetencia, inhabilidad. 2 DER. incapacidad.

**incompetent** (-t) *adj.* incompetente, inhábil, inepto. 2 DER. incapaz.
**incomplete** (inkømplı·t) *adj.* incompleto.
**incomprehensibility** (inkamprijensibi·liti) *s.* incomprensibilidad.
**incomprehensible** (inkamprije·nsibøl) *adj.* incomprensible, impenetrable.
**incomprehension** (-shøn) *s.* falta de comprensión.
**incomprehensive** (-siv) *adj.* no comprensivo, limitado, de poco alcance.
**incompressible** (inkømpre·sibøl) *adj.* incompresible.
**inconceivable** (inkønsı·vabøl) *adj.* inconcebible. 2 increíble, inimaginable.
**inconclusive** (inkønklu·siv) *adj.* no concluyente o decisivo; que no convence.
**incondite** (inkø·ndit) *adj.* tosco, mal acabado.
**incongruent** (inka·ngruønt) *adj.* incongruente, incongruo. 2 incoherente. 3 inadecuado.
**incongruity** (inkøngru·iti) *s.* incongruencia, inconexión, incoherencia.
**incongruous** (inka·ngruøs) *adj.* incongruente, incongruo, inconexo, incoherente. 2 disconforme. 3 impropio, inadecuado.
**inconsequence** (sikuøns) *s.* inconsecuencia, falta de lógica.
**inconsequent** (-t) *adj.* inconsecuente, inconsiguiente, ilógico.
**inconsequential** (inkansikuen·shal) *adj.* inconsiguiente. 2 de poca importancia, sin importancia.
**inconsiderable** (inkønsi·dørabøl) *adj.* insignificante.
**inconsiderate** (-it) *adj.* inconsiderado, irreflexivo, precipitado. 2 desconsiderado.
**inconsideration** (inkønsidøre·shøn) *s.* inconsideración. 2 falta de consideración.
**inconsistency** (inkønsi·stønsi) *s.* incompatibilidad, contradicción, disconformidad, incoherencia. 2 inconsecuencia. 3 inconsistencia.
**inconsistent** (-nt) *adj.* incompatible, contradictorio, disconforme, incoherente. 2 inconsecuente. 3 inconsistente.
**inconsolable** (inkønsou·labøl) *adj.* inconsolable.
**inconsonance** (inka·nsønans) *s.* discordancia, disconformidad.
**inconspicuous** (inkønspi·kuøs) *adj.* poco visible o notable.
**inconstancy** (inka·nstansi) *s.* inconstancia.
**inconstant** (inka·nstant) *adj.* inconstante.
**incontestable** (inkønte·stabøl) *adj.* incontestable, inconcuso, indiscutible, incontrovertible.
**incontinence** (inka·ntinøns) *s.* incontinencia.
**incontinent** (-t) *adj.* incontinente.
**incontrollable** (inkøntrou·labøl) *adj.* ingobernable, irrefrenable. 2 incontrolable.
**incontrovertible** (inkøntrøvø·ʳtibøl) *adj.* incontrovertible, indisputable.
**inconvenience** (inkønvi·niøns) *s.* inconveniencia; inoportunidad. 2 incomodidad, molestia, engorro, inconveniente.
**inconvenience (to)** *tr.* incomodar, molestar, estorbar.
**inconvenient** (-t) *adj.* inconveniente, impropio, inoportuno. 2 incómodo, molesto.
**inconvincible** (inkønvi·nsibøl) *adj.* inconvencible.
**incorporate** (inkoʳpørit) *adj.* incorporado, unido íntimamente. 2 constituido en cuerpo, corporación o sociedad. 3 incorpóreo.
**incorporate (to)** (-reit) *tr.* dar cuerpo o forma material. 2 incorporar, unir íntimamente; combi-

nar, reunir en un todo. *3* comprender, incluir. *4* constituir en corporación o sociedad. *5 intr.* incorporarse, unirse, mezclarse. *6* constituirse en corporación o sociedad.

**incorporation** (inkoᵣpøreiˑshøn) *s.* incorporación, unión. *2* asociación; formación de un cuerpo, gremio, corporación, etc. *3* acción de dar forma corpórea.

**incorporeal** (inkoᵣpouˑrial) *adj.* incorpóreo.

**incorrect** (inkøreˑkt) *adj.* incorrecto. *2* inexacto.

**incorrectness** (-nis) *s.* incorrección. *2* inexactitud.

**incorrigible** (inkaˑridŷibøl) *adj.* incorregible.

**incorrupt** (inkørøˑpt) *adj.* incorrupto. *2* honrado, íntegro.

**incorruptibility** (ibiˑliti) *s.* incorruptibilidad.

**incorruptible** (-ibøl) *adj.* incorruptible.

**incorruption** (-shøn) *s.* incorrupción.

**incrassate (to)** (inkraˑseit) *tr.* espesar, encrasar.

**incrassation** (-seiˑshøn) *s.* espesamiento.

**increase** (inkrɪˑs) *s.* aumento, acrecentamiento, incremento: *to be on the* ~, ir en aumento. *2* progenie. *3* productos [de la tierra]. *4* ganancia, interés. *5* creciente [de la luna].

**increase (to)** *tr.* aumentar, acrecentar, incrementar. *2* abultar, agrandar. *3 intr.* aumentarse, acrecentarse, crecer, multiplicarse.

**increasingly** (-ingli) *adv.* en aumento, crecientemente.

**incredibility** (inkredibiˑliti) *s.* incredibilidad.

**incredible** (inkreˑdibøl) *adj.* increíble.

**indredulity** (inkridiuˑliti) *s.* incredulidad.

**incredulous** (inkreˑdiuløs) *adj.* incrédulo.

**increment** (iˑnkrimøn) *s.* incremento, aumento: *unearned* ~, plusvalía. *2 MAT.* incremento.

**incriminate (to)** (inkriˑmineit) *tr.* incriminar, acriminar.

**incrimination** (-eiˑshøn) *s.* incriminación, acriminación.

**incrust (to)** (inkrøˑst) *tr.* incrustar. *2* encostrar.

**incrustation** (inkrøsteiˑshøn) *s.* incrustación. *2* encostradura, costra.

**incubate (to)** (iˑnkiubeit) *tr.* incubar. *2* empollar. *3 intr.* estar en incubación.

**incubation** (-eiˑshøn) *s.* incubación.

**incubator** (iˑnkiubeitøᵣ) *s.* incubador. *2* incubadora.

**incubus** (iˑnkiubøs) *s.* incubo. *2 MED.* pesadilla.

**inculcate (to)** (inkøˑlkeit) *tr.* inculcar.

**inculcation** (-eiˑshøn) *s.* inculcación.

**inculpability** (inkølpabiˑliti) *s.* inculpabilidad.

**inculpable** (inkøˑlpabøl) *adj.* inculpable, inocente.

**inculpate (to)** (inkøˑlpeit) *tr.* inculpar, acriminar.

**inculpation** (-eiˑshøn) *s.* inculpación.

**incult** (inkøˑlt) *adj.* inculto.

**incumbency** (inkøˑmbønsi) *s.* incumbencia. *2* goce de un empleo o de un beneficio eclesiástico.

**incumbent** (-ønt) *adj.* extendido o reclinado. *2* que incumbe: *to be* ~ *on* o *upon one*, incumbir a uno. *3 s.* titular de un cargo eclesiástico [párroco, etc.].

**incunabula** (inkiunæˑbiula) *s. pl.* orígenes, cuna. *2* incunables.

**incur (to)** (inkøˑ ᵣ) *tr.* incurrir en, atraerse. *2* contraer [una deuda]. ¶ Pret. y p. p.: *incurred*; ger.: *-rring*.

**incurable** (inkiuˑrabøl) *adj.* incurable.

**incurious** (inkiuˑriøs) *adj.* poco curioso, que no se interesa, indiferente. *2* poco interesante.

**incursión** (inkøˑᵣshøn) *s.* incursión, correría.

**incurvate** (inkøˑᵣveit) *adj.* encorvado, torcido.

**incurvate (to)** *tr.* encorvar, torcer.

**incus** (iˑnkøs) *s.* ANAT. yunque [del oído].

**incuse** (inkiuˑš) *adj.* incuso.

**indebted** (indeˑtid) *adj.* endeudado. *2* deudor [de un favor, etc.], obligado, reconocido.

**indebtedness** (-nis) *s.* deuda; obligación, agradecimiento.

**indecency** (indiˑsønsi) *s.* indecencia. *2* indecoro.

**indecent** (-nt) *adj.* indecente. *2* indecoroso.

**indecipherable** (-saiˑførabøl) *adj.* indescifrable.

**indecision** (-siˑ ẏøn) *s.* indecisión, irresolución.

**indecisive** (-saiˑšiv) *adj.* no decisivo. *2* indeciso, irresoluto. *3* incierto, dudoso.

**indeclinable** (-klaiˑnabøl) *adj.* indeclinable.

**indecorous** (indeˑkørøs) *adj.* indecoroso. *2* contrario a la etiqueta, inconveniente.

**indecorum** (indikoˑrøm) *s.* indecoro. *2* inconveniencia, mala educación.

**indeed** (indɪˑd) *adv.* realmente, verdaderamente, de veras, en verdad. *2* si tal, claro está.

**indefatigable** (indifæˑtigabøl) *adj.* infatigable, incansable.

**indefeasible** (-fɪˑsibøl) *adj.* DER. inabrogable, irrevocable.

**indefectible** (-feˑktibøl) *adj.* indefectible, indeficiente. *2* sin defecto, sin tacha.

**indefensible** (-feˑnsibøl) *adj.* indefendible, insostenible.

**indefinable** (-faiˑnabøl) *adj.* indefinible.

**indefinite** (indeˑfinit) *adj.* indefinido. *2* indeterminado, impreciso. *3 GRAM.* indefinido.

**indehiscence** (indijiˑsøns) *s.* BOT. indehiscencia.

**indehiscent** (-nt) *adj.* BOT. indehiscente.

**indeliberate(d** (-liˑbørit(id) *adj.* indeliberado, impremeditado.

**indelible** (indiˑlibøl) *adj.* indeleble.

**indelicacy** (indeˑlikasi) *s.* falta de delicadeza. *2* indecoro, grosería.

**indelicate** (-likit) *adj.* indelicado, falta de delicadeza. *2* indecoroso. *3* grosero.

**indemnification** (indemnifikeiˑshøn) *s.* indemnización, resarcimiento, reparación.

**indemnify (to)** (indeˑmnifai) *tr.* indemnizar, resarcir, compensar. *2* preservar de pérdida o daño. ¶ Pret. y p. p.: *indemnified*.

**indemnity** (-ti) *s.* indemnidad, seguridad contra pérdida o daño. *2* indemnización.

**indent** (indeˑnt) *s.* mella, muesca, dieˑite, entalladura; depresión, surco. *2 IMPR.* sangría. *3 COM.* pedido del extranjero. *4 INDENTURE.*

**indent (to)** (indeˑnt) *tr.* mellar, dentar, hacer muescas en. *2* estampar, hacer depresiones en. IMPR. sangrar.

**indentation** (indenteiˑshøn) *s.* mella, muesca, diente, entrada [en el borde de una cosa]. *2* hundimiento, depresión [en una superficie]. *3 IMPR.* sangría.

**indented** (indeˑntid) *adj.* mellado, dentado, etc. *2* BOT. dentado. *3* BLAS. endentado.

**indention** (-shøn) *s.* mella, muesca, diente, hundimiento, depresión. *2 IMPR.* sangría.

**indenture** (-chøᵣ) *s.* carta partida por a, b, c. *2* escritura, documento [esp. por duplicado]. *3* contrato de aprendizaje.

**indenture (to)** *tr.* escriturar.

**independence** (indipeˑndøns) *s.* independencia. *2* estado del que se mantiene a sí mismo. *3* holgura, posición acomodada.

**independent** (-nt) *adj.* independiente. *2* que se mantiene a sí mismo. *3* altivo. *4* acomodado, que tiene medios suficientes.

**indescribable** (indiskrai·babøl) *adj.* indescriptible.
**indestructibility** (indistrøktibi·liti) *s.* indestructibilidad.
**indestructible** (indistrø·ktibøl) *adj.* indestructible.
**indeterminate** (inditø·ʳminit) *adj.* indeterminado.
**indetermination** (inditø·ʳminei·shøn) *s.* indeterminación. 2 duda, suspensión, indecisión, fluctuación.
**index** (i·ndeks), *pl.* **indexes** o **indices** *s.* índice [lista; aguja indicadora; relación entre valores]. 2 MAT. índice, exponente. 3 indicio, señal. 4 IMPR. manecilla. 5 *adj.*-*s.* ANAT. índice [dedo].
**index (to)** *tr.* poner en un índice. 2 proveer de índice [lista].
**India** (i·ndia) *n. pr.* GEOGR. India. 2 ~ *ink*, tinta china. 3 ~ *rubber*, caucho, goma elástica, goma de borrar.
**indiaman** (-mæn) *s.* buque que hace el comercio con la India.
**Indian** (i·ndian) *s.* indio [de Asia o América]. 2 *adj.* indio, indiano, índico: ~ *file*, fila india; ~ *Ocean*, Océano Índico; ~ *summer* (E.U.), veranillo de San Martín. 3 ~ *corn*, maíz; ~ *meal*, harina de maíz.
**indicant** (i·ndikønt) *adj.*-*s.* indicador.
**indicate** (i·ndikeit) *tr.* indicar.
**indication** (-ei·shøn) *s.* indicación. 2 indicio, señal.
**indicative** (indi·kativ) *adj.* indicativo, indicador. 2 GRAM. *adj.*-*s.* indicativo.
**indicator** (i·ndikeitøʳ) *s.* indicador, señalador. 2 índice, aguja. 3 QUÍM. indicador.
**indicatory** (i·ndikatori) *adj.* indicativo, demostrativo.
**indicia** (indi·sia) *s. pl.* indicios, señales.
**indict (to)** (indai·t) *tr.* acusar [ante el juez]. 2 procesar, encausar, enjuiciar.
**indictable** (-abøl) *adj.* procesable, enjuiciable.
**indictment** (-mønt) *s.* acusación, procesamiento. 2 auto de acusación formulado por el Gran Jurado.
**Indies** (i·ndiš) *s. pl.* GEOGR. Indias: *West* ~, Indias Occidentales, Antillas.
**indifference** (indi·førøns) *s.* indiferencia. 2 desinterés, desapego. 3 mediocridad. 4 poca importancia, insignificancia.
**indifferent** (-nt) *adj.* indiferente. 2 imparcial, neutral. 3 mediocre, ordinario: ni bueno ni malo. 4 sin importancia.
**indifferentism** (-išm) *s.* indiferentismo.
**indigence** (i·ndiÿøns) *s.* indigencia.
**indigenous** (indi·ÿinøs) *adj.* indígena. 2 autóctono. 3 innato, nativo, natural.
**indigent** (i·ndidÿønt) *adj.* indigente.
**indigested** (indidÿe·stid) *adj.* mal digerido. 2 mal ordenado, confuso.
**indigestible** (-ibøl) *adj.* indigesto.
**indigestion** (-chøn) *s.* indigestión.
**indignant** (indi·gnant) *adj.* indignado.
**indignation** (indignei·shøn) *s.* indignación.
**indignity** (indi·gniti) *s.* indignidad. 2 ultraje, afrenta.
**indigo** (i·ndigou) *adj.* índigo; de añil. 2 añil, índigo [planta y color].
**indirect** (indire·kt) *adj.* indirecto. 2 oblicuo, torcido. 3 desleal, engañoso.
**indirection** (-shøn) *s.* rodeo, tortuosidad. 2 medio indirecto. 3 conducta torcida.
**indiscernible** (indisø·ʳnibøl) *adj.* no discernible, imperceptible.

**indiscreet** (indiskrı·t) *adj.* indiscreto. 2 imprudente, torpe; impolítico, poco hábil u oportuno.
**indiscrete** (-kri·t) *adj.* compacto, continuo, no dividido o separado.
**indiscretion** (-kre·shøn) *s.* indiscreción. 2 imprudencia, torpeza.
**indiscriminate** (kri·minit) *adj.* que no hace distinción, indistinto, confuso; promiscuo.
**indiscrimination** (-ei·shøn) *s.* indistinción, falta de distinción o separación.
**indispensable** (-pe·nsabøl) *adj.* indispensable, imprescindible, forzoso.
**indispose (to)** (-pou·š) *tr.* indisponer. 2 disponer en contra, desinclinar.
**indisposition** (-pøši·shøn) *s.* indisposición, enfermedad. 2 aversión, repugnancia, falta de inclinación.
**indisputable** (indi·spiutabøl) *adj.* indisputable, indiscutible, incontestable.
**indissolubility** (-saliubi·liti) *s.* indisolubilidad. 2 insolubilidad.
**indissoluble** (-sa·liubøl) *adj.* indisoluble. 2 insoluble; infusible.
**indisolvable** (-sa·lvabøl) *adj.* indisoluble.
**indistinct** (indisti·nkt) *adj.* indistinto. 2 confuso, borroso. 3 vago, obscuro.
**indistinction** (-kshøn) *s.* indistinción. 2 confusión, vaguedad, obscuridad.
**indistinguishable** (-gwishabøl) *adj.* indistinguible.
**indite (to)** (indai·t) *tr.* redactar, componer, escribir.
**indium** (i·ndiøm) *s.* QUÍM. indio.
**individual** (indivi·dÿual) *adj.* invidiaul, individuo, particular, peculiar. 2 *s.* individuo.
**individualism** (-išm) *s.* individualismo.
**individuality** (individÿuæ·liti) *s.* individualidad.
**individualize (to)** (indivi·dÿualaiš) *tr.* individualizar.
**individuate** (-dÿueit) *adj.* individuado.
**individuate (to)** *tr.* individuar.
**indivisibility** (indivišibi·liti) *s.* indivisibilidad.
**indivisible** (indivi·šibøl) *adj.* indivisible.
**indivision** (-shøn) *s.* indivisión.
**Indo-Chinese** (i·ndou-chaini·š) *adj.*-*s.* indochino.
**indocil(e** (inda·sil) *adj.* indócil.
**indocility** (indøsi·liti) *s.* indocilidad.
**indoctrinate (to)** (inda·ktrineit) *tr.* adoctrinar.
**Indo-European** *adj.*-*s.* indoeuropeo.
**indolence** (i·ndøløns) *s.* indolencia.
**indolent** (-nt) *adj.* indolente.
**indomitable** (inda·mitabøl) *adj.* indomable, indómito.
**indomitably** (-bli) *adv.* indomablemente.
**indoor** (indo·ʳ) *adj.* interior, interno, de puertas adentro.
**indoors** (indo·ʳš) *adv.* en, o dentro de, la casa o edificio; en local cerrado.
**indorse (to), indorsee, indorsement, indorser** ENDORSE (TO), ENDORSEE, ENDORSEMENT, ENDORSER.
**indraft, indraught** (i·ndraft) *s.* atracción o corriente hacia el interior; absorción, aspiración.
**indrawn** (i·ndron) *adj.* sorbido, aspirado. 2 abstraido, introspectivo.
**indubitable** (indiu·bitabøl) *adj.* indubitable, indudable, indiscutible.
**induce (to)** (indiu·s) *tr.* inducir, instigar. 2 LÓG., ELECT. inducir. 3 producir, causar.
**inducement** (-mønt) *s.* inducimiento. 2 móvil, incentivo, aliciente.
**induct (to)** (indø·kt) *tr.* instalar [en un cargo]. 2 introducir. 3 iniciar [en]. 4 MIL. alistar.

**inductance** (-ans) *s.* ELECT. inductancia.
**induction** (-shøn) *s.* instalación [en un cargo]. *2* aducción [de pruebas, etc.]. *3* LÓG., ELECT. inducción. *4* MIL. alistamiento.
**inductive** (-iv) *adj.* inductivo, ilativo. *2* introductor. *3* ELECT. inductivo, inductor.
**inductor** (-oʳ) *s.* ECLES. instalador. *2* ELECT. inductor.
**indue (to)** (indiu·) *tr.* ponerse, vestirse. *2* vestir, investir, dotar.
**indulge (to)** (indø·ldỹ) *tr.* satisfacer [pasiones, gustos, etc.]. *2* complacer; dar gusto a; mimar,consentir. *3* COM. dar prórroga a. *4 intr. to ~ in,* entregarse, abandonarse a, permitirse.
**indulgence, -cy** (-øns, -si) *s.* satisfacción [de las pasiones, gustos, etc.], exceso, intemperancia. *2* indulgencia, lenidad; mimo. *3* COM. prórroga. *4* ECLES. indulgencia.
**indulgent** (-ønt) *adj.* indulgente.
**indult** (indø·lt) *s.* ECLES. indulto, dispensa.
**indurate** (i·ndiurit) *adj.* endurecido. *2* empedernido.
**indurate (to)** (-reit) *tr.* endurecer. *2* empedernir. *3 intr.* endurecerse, empedernirse.
**induration** (-ei·shøn) *s.* endurecimiento. *2* dureza de corazón. *3* MED. induración.
**Indus** (i·ndøs) *n. pr.* GEOGR. Indo.
**industrial** (indø·strial) *adj.* industrial. *2 s.* industrial; artesano.
**industrialism** (-išm) *s.* industrialismo.
**industrialize (to)** (-laiš) *tr.* industrializar.
**industrious** (-triøs) *adj.* industrioso, hacendoso, laborioso, aplicado.
**industry** (i·ndøstri) *s.* industria. *2* diligencia, laboriosidad, aplicación.
**indwell (to)** (indue·l) *tr.* residir, morar en.
**inebriate** (ini·briit) *adj.* ebrio. *2 s.* borracho, beodo.
**inebriate (to)** (ini·brieit) *tr.* embriagar, emborrachar.
**inedited** (ine·ditid) *adj.* inédito.
**ineffable** (ine·fabøl) *adj.* inefable, indecible.
**ineffaceable** (inefei·sabøl) *adj.* imborrable, indeleble.
**ineffective** (inefe·ktiv) *adj.* ineficaz, sin efecto. *2* inútil, incapaz.
**ineffectual** (-chual) *adj.* ineficaz. *2* inútil, vano, infructuoso.
**inefficacious** (inefikei·shøs) *adj.* ineficaz.
**inefficacy** (ine·fikasi) *s.* ineficacia.
**inefficiency** (inefi·shønsi) *s.* ineficacia. *2* falta de aptitud o capacidad. *3* mal rendimiento.
**inefficient** (inefi·shønt) *adj.* ineficaz. *2* incapaz. *3* de mal rendimiento.
**inelastic** (inilæ·stik) *adj.* falto de elasticidad.
**inelegance, -cy** (ine·ligans, -si) *s.* falta de elegancia.
**inelegant** (-t) *adj.* inelegante.
**ineligible** (ine·lidỹibøl) *adj.* inelegible. *2* poco deseable o ventajoso.
**ineluctable** (inilø·ktabøl) *adj.* ineluctable.
**inept** (ine·pt) inepto, no apto. *2* inadecuado, impropio. *3* absurdo.
**ineptitude** (-titiud) *s.* ineptitud, incapacidad. *2* absurdidad.
**inequality** (inikua·liti) *s.* desigualdad. *2* disparidad, desproporción. *3* insuficiencia.
**inequitable** (ine·kuitabøl) *adj.* injusto.
**ineradicable** (iniræ·dikabøl) *adj.* que no se puede desarraigar, indeleble, permanente.
**inerrable** (ine·rabøl) *adj.* infalible, seguro.
**inert** (inø·ʳt) *adj.* inerte.

**inertia** (inø·ʳshia) *s.* inercia.
**inertness** (inø·ʳtnis) *s.* flojedad, falta de actividad.
**inescapable** (ineskei·pabøl) *adj.* ineludible.
**inestimable** (ine·stimabøl) *adj.* inestimable, inapreciable.
**inevitable** (ine·vitabøl) *adj.* inevitable, ineludible.
**inexact** (inegšæ·kt) *adj.* inexacto.
**inexactitude** (-titiud) *s.* inexactitud.
**inexcusable** (inekskiu·šabøl) *adj.* inexcusable, imperdonable.
**inexhausted** (inegšo·stid) *adj.* inexhausto.
**inexhaustible** (inegšo·stibøl) *adj.* inagotable.
**inexistence** (inegši·støns) *s.* inexistencia.
**inexistent** (-tønt) *adj.* inexistente.
**inexorability** (ineksørabi·liti) *s.* inexorabilidad.
**inexorable** (ine·ksørabøl) *adj.* inexorable; inflexible.
**inexpedience, -cy** (inekspi·diøns, -si) *s.* inoportunidad, improcedencia, impropiedad.
**inexpedient** (-iønt) *adj.* inoportuno, improcedente, impropio.
**inexpensive** (inekspe·nsiv) *adj.* barato, poco costoso.
**inexperience** (-pi·riøns) *s.* inexperiencia, impericia.
**inexperienced** (-pi·riønst) *adj.* inexperto.
**inexpert** (-pø·ʳt) *adj.* inexperto, imperito.
**inexplicable** (ine·ksplikabøl) *adj.* inexplicable.
**inexplicably** (-plikabli) *adv.* inexplicablemente.
**inexpressible** (inekspre·sibøl) *adj.* inexpresable, indecible.
**inexpressibly** (-bli) *adv.* indeciblemente.
**inexpressive** (-iv) *adj.* inexpresivo.
**inexpugnable** (-pø·gnabøl) *adj.* inexpugnable.
**inextensible** (-te·nsibøl) *adj.* inextensible.
**inextensive** (-te·nsiv) *adj.* inextenso.
**inextinguishable** (-ti·ngwishabøl) *adj.* inextinguible, inapagable.
**inextricable** (ine·kstrikabøl) *adj.* inextricable.
**infallibility** (infælibi·liti) *s.* infalibilidad.
**infallible** (infæ·libøl) *adj.* infalible.
**infamous** (i·nfamøs) *adj.* infame.
**infamy** (i·nfami) *s.* infamia, ignominia, deshonor.
**infancy** (i·nfansi) *s.* infancia, niñez. *2* DER. menor edad.
**infant** (i·nfant) *s.* infante, criatura, niño. *2 adj.-s.* DER. menor [de edad]. *3 adj.* infantil; pequeño, no desarrollado.
**infanta** (infa·nta) *s.* infanta [de España o Portugal].
**infante** (-ei) *s.* infante [de España o Portugal].
**infanticidal** (infæntisai·dal) *adj.* infanticida.
**infanticide** (infæ·ntisaid) *s.* infanticidio. *2* infanticida.
**infantile** (i·nfantil) *adj.* infantil. *2* aniñado, pueril.
**infantilism** (infa·ntilišm) *s.* infantilismo.
**infantine** (i·nfantin) *adj.* infantil, pueril.
**infantry** (-tri) *s.* MIL. infantería.
**infarct** (infa·ʳkt) *s.* MED. infarto.
**infatuate (to)** (infæ·chueit) *tr.* entontecer. *2* enamorar o apasionar locamente.
**infatuate(d** (-it(id) *adj.* simple, bobo. *2* locamente enamorado o apasionado.
**infatuation** (-shøn) *s.* tontería, simpleza. *2* enamoramiento, apasionamiento.
**infect (to)** (infe·kt) *tr.* infectar. *2* inficionar, contaminar. *3* contagiar. *4* comunicar, llenar de [fe, entusiasmo, etc.].
**infection** (-shøn) *s.* infección. *2* contaminación. *3* contagio.

**infectious** (-shøs) *adj.* infeccioso. 2 contagioso; pedadizo.
**infective** (-tiv) *adj.* infectivo, infeccioso.
**infelicitous** (infili·sitøs) *adj.* desgraciado. 2 poco feliz o acertado; desatinado.
**infelicity** (-ti) *s.* infelicidad. 2 calidad de poco feliz o acertado; tontería, desatino.
**infer (to)** (infø·ʳ) *tr.* inferir, deducir, colegir. 2 argüir, probar, indicar. 3 *intr.* hacer deducciones. ¶ Pret. y p. p.: *inferred;* ger.: *-rring.*
**inference** (i·nførøns) *s.* inferencia, ilación, deducción, conclusión.
**inferior** (infi·riøʳ) *adj.-s.* inferior.
**inferiority** (infiria·riti) *s.* inferioridad.
**infernal** (infø·ʳnal) *adj.* infernal.
**inferno** (infø·ʳnou) *s.* infierno.
**infertile** (infø·ʳtil) *adj.* infecundo, estéril.
**infest (to)** (infe·st) *tr.* infestar, plagar.
**infestation** (-ei·shøn) *s.* infestación.
**infeudation** (infiudei·shøn) *s.* infeudación.
**infidel** (i·nfidøl) *adj.-s.* infiel, gentil. 2 descreído.
**infidelity** (infide·liti) *s.* infidelidad. 2 descreimiento.
**infield** (i·nfild) *s.* terrenos de una finca rústica más inmediatos a los edificios. 2 BÉISBOL. losange.
**infighting** (i·nfaiting) *s.* BOX. cuerpo a cuerpo.
**infiltrate (to)** (infi·ltreit) *tr.* infiltrar. 2 infiltrarse en. 3 *intr.* infiltrarse.
**infiltration** (-ei·shøn) *s.* infiltración.
**infinite** (i·nfinit) *adj.-s.* infinito: *the Infinite,* el Ser infinito, Dios.
**infinitesimal** (infinite·simal) *adj.* infinitesimal.
**infinitive** (infi·nitiv) *adj.-s.* GRAM. infinitivo.
**infinitude** (-iud) *s.* infinitud.
**infinity** (-i) *s.* infinidad, sin fin. 2 infinito.
**infirm** (infø·ʳm) *adj.* débil, vacilante. 3 inseguro, inestable. 4 enfermizo, achacoso.
**infirmary** (-ri) *s.* enfermería.
**infirmity** (-iti) *s.* enfermedad, dolencia, achaque. 2 flaqueza, debilidad. 3 defecto, imperfección.
**infix (to)** (infi·ks) *tr.* clavar, encajar. 2 imprimir, inculcar.
**inflame (to)** (inflei·m) *tr.* inflamar. 2 encolerizar. 3 *intr.* inflamarse. 4 encolerizarse.
**inflamed** (-d) *adj.* inflamado, encolerizado.
**inflammable** (inflæ·mabøl) *adj.* inflamable. 2 irascible.
**inflammation** (inflamei·shøn) *s.* inflamación. 2 irritación, cólera.
**inflammatory** (inflæ·matori) *adj.* inflamatorio.
**inflate (to)** (inflei·t) *tr.* inflar, hinchar.
**inflated** (-id) *adj.* inflado, hinchado, túmido. 2 hinchado [estilo].
**inflating** (-ing) *adj.* inflativo.
**inflation** (-ei·shøn) *s.* inflación, hinchazón. 2 ECON. inflación.
**inflect (to)** (infle·kt) *tr.* torcer, doblar, curvar. 2 modular [la voz]. 3 GRAM. modificar [una palabra] por inflexión.
**inflection** (-shøn) *s.* inflexión.
**inflectional** (-al) *adj.* flexional.
**inflexibility** (infleksibi·liti) *s.* inflexibilidad.
**inflexible** (infle·ksibøl) *adj.* inflexible.
**inflexion** *s.* INFLECTION.
**inflexional** *s.* INFLECTIONAL.
**inflict (to)** (infli·kt) *tr.* infligir, imponer.
**infliction** (-shøn) *s.* acción de infligir. 2 pena, castigo, sufrimiento.
**inflictive** (-tiv) *adj.* que inflige, punitivo.
**inflorescence** (inflore·søns) *s.* BOT. inflorescencia. 2 BOT. florescencia [época].

**inflow** (inflou·) *s.* afluencia, flujo; entrada.
**inflow (to)** *intr.* afluir, entrar.
**influence** (i·nfluøns) *s.* influencia, influjo. 2 ELECT. inducción.
**influence (to)** *tr.* influir en o sobre.
**influential** (influe·nshal) *adj.* influente, influyente.
**influenza** (influe·nša) *s.* MED. influenza.
**influx** (i·nfløks) *s.* flujo, entrada, afluencia.
**infold (to)** (infou·ld) *tr.* envolver, rodear, incluir. 2 abrazar. 3 plegar.
**inform** (info·ʳm) *adj.* informe.
**inform (to)** *tr.* informar. 2 participar, comunicar. 3 *intr. to ~ against,* delatar, declarar contra [uno].
**informal** (-al) *adj.* que no se ajusta a formalidades o ceremonias; sin solemnidad, casero, de confianza, familiar.
**informality** (info·ʳmæ·liti) *s.* calidad o estado de lo que no se ajusta a formalidades o ceremonias; sencillez. 2 acto sencillo o de confianza.
**informant** (info·ʳmant) *s.* informador.
**information** (-shøn) *s.* información. 2 informes, noticias, avisos. 3 conocimientos, saber, instrucción. 4 DER. delación.
**informative** (info·ʳmativ) *adj.* informativo.
**informed** (info·ʳmd) *adj.* informado. 2 culto, instruido.
**informer** (info·ʳmøʳ) *s.* informador, informante. 2 DER. delator [esp. el profesional].
**infraction** (infræ·kshøn) *s.* infracción.
**infractor** (-tøʳ) *s.* infractor.
**infrangible** (infræ·ndÿibøl) *adj.* infrangible, inquebrantable.
**infrared** (infrare·d) *adj.* FÍS. infrarrojo.
**infrequent** (infri·kuønt) *adj.* infrecuente, raro.
**infringe (to)** (infri·ndÿ) *tr.* infringir. 2 *intr. to ~ on* o *upon,* usurpar, invadir [derechos, etc.].
**infringement** (-mønt) *s.* infracción.
**infringer** (-øʳ) *s.* infractor.
**infuriate (to)** (infiu·rieit) *tr.* enfurecer, encolerizar, poner furioso.
**infuriated** (-id) *adj.* enfurecido, furioso.
**infuse (to)** (infiu·š) *tr.* infundir. 2 *to ~ with,* imbuir de, llenar de.
**infusible** (infiu·šibøl) *adj.* infusible.
**infusion** (infiu·ÿøn) *s.* infusión.
**infusive** (-šiv) *adj.* infusor.
**infusory** (infiu·sori) *adj.-s.* ZOOL. infusorio.
**ingenerate** (indÿe·nøreit) *adj.* innato, ingénito.
**ingenious** (indÿi·niøs) *adj.* ingenioso, hábil, sutil.
**ingeniousness** (-nis) *s.* ingeniosidad.
**ingenuity** (indÿiniu·iti) *s.* ingenio, habilidad, inventiva. 2 ingeniosidad, artificio.
**ingenuous** (indÿe·niuøs) *adj.* ingenuo, sincero, franco.
**ingenuousness** (-nis) *s.* ingenuidad, sinceridad.
**ingest (to)** (indÿe·st) *tr.* ingerir, injerir [en el estómago].
**ingestion** (-chøn) *s.* ingestión.
**ingle** (i·ngøl) *s.* llama, fuego. 2 chimenea, hogar.
**inglenook** (-nuk) *s.* rincón de la chimenea.
**inglorious** (inglo·riøs) *adj.* nada glorioso, obscuro. 2 vergonzoso, ignominioso.
**ingoing** (i·ngouing) *adj.* entrante, que entra. 2 entrada, ingreso.
**ingot** (i·ngøt) *s.* lingote.
**ingrain** (ingrei·n) *adj.* teñido en rama. 2 fijado, inculcado, arraigado profundamente; innato.
**ingrain (to)** *tr.* teñir con grana. 2 teñir en rama. 3 fijar, arraigar, inculcar.
**ingrained** (i·ngreind) *adj.* INGRAIN.

**ingrate** (i·ngreit) *adj.-s.* ingrato.
**ingratiate (to)** (ingrei·shieit) *tr.* congraciar: *to ~ oneself with*, congraciarse con.
**ingratiating** (-ing) *adj.* congraciador, obsequioso.
**ingratitude** (ingræ·titiud) *s.* ingratitud, desagradecimiento.
**ingredient** (ingrɪ·diønt) *s.* ingrediente.
**ingress** (i·ngres) *s.* ingreso, entrada, acceso.
**ingression** (ingre·shøn) *s.* ingreso, entrada [acción].
**ingrowing** (i·ngrouing) *adj.* que crece hacia dentro; ~ *nail*, uñero.
**inguinal** (i·ngwinal) *adj.* ANAT. inguinal.
**ingulf (to)** (ingø·lf) *tr.* TO ENGULF.
**ingurgitate (to)** (ingø·ʳdÿiteit) *tr.* ingurgitar, engullir, tragar.
**inhabit (to)** (injæ·bit) *tr.* habitar, morar en.
**inhabitable** (-abøl) *adj.* habitable.
**inhabitant** (-ant) *s.* habitante, morador, vecino.
**inhabited** (-id) *adj.* habitado.
**inhalation** (injalei·shøn) *s.* inhalación.
**inhale (to)** (injei·l) *tr.* inhalar, tragar [el humo].
**inharmonic (al** (injaʳma·nik(al) *adj.* inarmónico, disonante.
**inharmonious** (-ou·niøs) *adj.* inarmónico, discordante.
**inhere (to)** (inji·ø·ʳ) *intr.* ser inherente, pertenecer [como atributo, cualidad, etc.].
**inherence, -cy** (inji·røns, -si) *s.* inherencia.
**inherent** (-t) *adj.* inherente. *2* innato.
**inherit (to)** (inje·rit) *tr.-intr.* heredar.
**inheritance** (-ans) *s.* herencia.
**inheritor** (inje·ritøʳ) *s.* heredero.
**inheritress, -trix** (inje·ritris, -triks) *s.* heredera.
**inhesion** (inji·ÿon) *s.* inherencia.
**inhibit (to)** (inji·bit) *tr.* prohibir. *2* detener, suprimir. *3* inhibir [causar inhibición].
**inhibition** (injibi·shøn) *s.* prohibición, restricción. *2* inhibición.
**inhibitive, -tori** (inji·bitiv, -tori) *adj.* prohibitivo. *2* inhibitorio.
**inhospitable** (inja·spitabøl) *adj.* inhospitalario. *2* inhospitable, inhóspito.
**inhospitality** (injaspitæ·liti) *s.* inhospitalidad.
**inhuman** (injiu·man) *adj.* inhumano.
**inhumane** (-mein) *adj.* inhumano, inhumanitario.
**inhumanity** (injiumæ·niti) *s.* inhumanidad.
**inhumate (to)** (injiu·meit) *tr.* TO INHUME.
**inhumation** (-ei·shøn) *s.* inhumación.
**inhume (to)** (injiu·m) *tr.* inhumar.
**inimical** (ini·mikal) *adj.* de enemigo, hostil. *2* adverso, enemigo.
**inimitable** (ini·mitabøl) *adj.* inimitable.
**iniquitous** (ini·kuitøs) *adj.* inicuo.
**iniquity** (-ti) *s.* iniquidad.
**initial** (ini·shal) *adj.* inicial. *2 s.* inicial [letra].
**initial (to)** *tr.* firmar o marcar con iniciales. ¶ Pret. y p. p.: *initialed* o *-lled*; ger.: *-ling* o *-lling*.
**initiate** (ini·shieit) *adj.-s.* iniciado.
**initiate (to))** *tr.* iniciar [a uno]. *2* iniciar, comenzar.
**initiation** (-ei·shøn) *s.* iniciación. *2* principio, comienzo.
**initiative** (ini·shiativ) *adj.* iniciativo, inicial. *2 s.* iniciativa.
**initiator** (-eitøʳ) *s.* iniciador.
**inject (to)** (indÿe·kt) *tr.* inyectar. *2* jeringar. *3* introducir.
**injectable** (-abøl) *adj.* inyectable.
**injection** (-shøn) *s.* inyección. *2* lavativa.
**injector** (-tøʳ) *s.* MEC., MED. inyector.

**injudicious** (indÿudi·shøs) *adj.* torpe, imprudente.
**injunction** (indÿo·nkshøn) *s.* orden, mandato, requerimiento. *2* DER. entredicho.
**injure (to)** (i·ndÿøʳ) *tr.* dañar, perjudicar, injuriar. *2* herir, lastimar. *3* ofender, agraviar.
**injurious** (indÿu·riøs) *adj.* dañoso, perjudicial, nocivo. *2* lesivo. *3* injurioso, ofensivo.
**injury** (i·ndÿuri) *s.* daño, perjuicio, deterioro, menoscabo. *3* herida, lesión. *4* injuria, ofensa, agravio.
**injustice** (indÿø·stis) *s.* injusticia.
**ink** (ink) *s.* tinta [para escribir, etc.]. *2* ZOOL. tinta [del calamar].
**ink (to)** *tr.* entintar, dar tinta. *2* pasar en tinta.
**inkhorn** (-joʳn) *s.* tintero de cuerno.
**inking** (-ing) *s.* entintado.
**inkling** (-ling) *s.* insinuación. *2* indicio. *3* leve conocimiento o idea, vislumbre, sospecha.
**inkstand** (-tænd) *s.* tintero; escribaní.
**inkwell** (-wel) *s.* tintero; frasco de tintero.
**inky** (-i) *adj.* de tinta; manchado de tinta; negro.
**inlaid** (inlei·d) *pret.* y *p. p.* DE TO INLAY.
**inland** (i·nland) *adj.* interior, del interior, de tierra adentro, del país. *2 adv.* tierra adentro.
**in-law** *adj.* político [pariente]: *father in-law*, padre político, suegro.
**inlay** (inlei·) *s.* embutido, incrustación, taracea.
**inlay (to)** *tr.* embutir, incrustar. *2* taracear, hacer ataujía o mosaico. ¶ Pret. y p. p.: *inlaid*.
**inlet** (i·nlet) *s.* abra, caleta, ría pequeña. *2* acceso, entrada. *3* material embutido.
**inly** (-i) *adj.* interno, interior, íntimo. *2 adv.* interiormente, íntimamente.
**inmate** (-meit) *s.* asilado, preso, residente, etc. [de un asilo, cárcel, etc.].
**inmost** (-moust) *adj.* más interior, íntimo, recóndito o profundo.
**inn** (in) *s.* posada, fonda, mesón.
**innate** (inei·t) *adj.* innato, ingénito, connatural.
**innateness** (-nis) *s.* calidad de innato.
**inner** (i·nøʳ) *adj.* interior, interno, íntimo: ~ *tube*, cámara [de neumático].
**innermost** (-moust) *adj.* INMOST.
**innervate (to)** (inø·ʳveit) *tr.* FISIOL. inervar.
**innervation** (-ei·shøn) *s.* FISIOL. inervación.
**innings** (i·nings) *s.* y *pl.* en béisbol, criquet, etc., turno, entrada.
**innkeeper** (i·nkɪpøʳ) *s.* posadero, fondista.
**innocence** (i·nøsøns) *s.* inocencia. *2* candor, sencillez. *3* inocuidad.
**innocent** (-nt) *adj.-s.* inocente. *2 adj.* MED. benigno. *3* fam. desprovisto [de].
**innocuity** (ina·kuiti) *s.* inocuidad.
**innocuous** (-kiuøs) *adj.* inocuo, inofensivo.
**innovate (to)** (i·noveit) *tr.* innovar. *2* introducir [algo nuevo].
**innovation** (-ei·shøn) *s.* innovación, novedad.
**innoxious** (ina·kshøs) *adj.* inocuo.
**innuendo** (iniue·ndou) *s.* indirecta, insinuación, pulla.
**innumerable** (iniu·mørabøl) *adj.* innumerable, incontable.
**innumerous** (-røs) *adj.* innúmero, innumerable.
**inobedience** (inøbi·diøns) *s.* inobediencia, desobediencia.
**inobedient** (-nt) *adj.* inobediente, desobediente.
**inobservance** (inobšø·ʳvans) *s.* inobservancia. *2* inadvertencia.
**inoculate (to)** (ina·kiuleit) *tr.* inocular.
**inoculation** (-ei·shøn) *s.* inoculación.
**inodorous** (inou·dørøs) *adj.* inodoro.

**inoffensive** (inøfe·nsiv) *adj.* inofensivo. *2* pacífico.
**inofficious** (inøfi·shøs) *adj.* DER. inoficioso.
**inoperable** (ina·pørabøl) *adj.* CIR. inoperable.
**inoperative** (-tiv) *adj.* inoperante, ineficaz.
**inopportune** (inapø$^r$tiu·n) *adj.* inoportuno.
**inordinate** (ino·$^r$dinit) *adj.* inmoderado, excesivo.
**inorganic** (ino$^r$gæ·nik) *adj.* inorgánico.
**inosculate (to)** (ina·skiuleit) *tr.* unir por anastomosis. *2* fig. unir íntimamente. *3 intr.* anastomizarse.
**input** (i·nput) *s.* MEC. fuerza consumida, energía absorbida [por una máquina], gasto, consumo.
**inquest** (i·nkuest) *s.* información o pesquisa judicial con ayuda de un jurado: *coroner's* ~, encuesta judicial que preside el CORONER.
**inquietude** (inkuai·itiud) *s.* inquietud, desasosiego, descontento.
**inquire (to)** (inkuai·ø$^r$) *tr.* inquirir, averiguar, investigar. *2* preguntar. *3 intr. to* ~ *about, after* o *for*, preguntar por: *to* ~ *into*, averiguar, investigar, examinar, informarse de.
**inquiry** (-ri) *s.* indagación, investigación, información, averiguación. *2* pregunta, interrogatorio.
**inquisition** (inkuiši·shøn) *s.* inquisición, investigación, pesquisa, examen. *2* (con may.) Inquisición.
**inquisitive** (inkui·šitiv) *adj.* inquisitivo. *2* dado a la investigación. *3* curioso, preguntón.
**inquisitor** (-ø$^r$) *s.* inquiridor, investigador. *2* inquisidor.
**inroad** (i·nroud) *s.* incursión, invasión, ataque.
**inrush** (i·røsh) *s.* empuje, corriente hacia dentro; invasión.
**insalivate (to)** (insæ·liveit) *tr.* insalivar.
**insalubrious** (insaliu·briøs) *adj.* insalubre, malsano.
**insalubrity** (-briti) *s.* insalubridad.
**insane** (insei·n) *adj.* insano, demente, loco, insensato: ~ *asylum*, manicomio, casa de locos.
**insanity** (insæ·niti) *s.* locura, demencia, insania, enajenación mental.
**insatiable** (insei·shiabøl) *adj.* insaciable.
**insatiate** (-shiet) *adj.* no saciado. *2* insaciable.
**inscribe (to)** (inskrai·b) *tr.* inscribir, grabar. *2* inscribir, apuntar [en un registro, etc.]. *3* GEOM. inscribir. *4* dedicar [un verso, etc.].
**inscription** (inskri·pshøn) *s.* inscripción. *2* título, epígrafe, rótulo, leyenda. *3* dedicatoria.
**inscrutability** (inskrutabi·liti) *s.* inescrutabilidad.
**inscrutable** (inskru·tabøl) *adj.* inescrutable.
**insect** (i·nsekt) *s.* ZOOL. insecto. *2* bicho [animal pequeño].
**insecta** (-tæ) *s. pl.* ZOOL. insectos.
**insecticide** (-isaid) *adj.-s.* insecticida.
**insectile** (-il) *adj.* insectil.
**insection** (inse·kshøn) *s.* incisión; segmentación.
**insectivorous** (insekti·vørøs) *adj.* insectívoro.
**insecure** (insikiu·ø$^r$) *adj.* inseguro.
**insecurity** (-riti) *s.* inseguridad. *2* peligro, riesgo.
**inseminate (to)** (inse·mineit) *tr.* sembrar. *2* inseminar.
**insemination** (-ei·shøn) *s.* siembra. *2* inseminación.
**insensate** (inse·nseit) *adj.* insensato. *2* insensible.
**insensibility** (insensibi·liti) *s.* insensibilidad.
**insensible** (inse·nsibøl) *adj.* insensible. *2* imperceptible. *3* inanimado. *4* sordo, indiferente.
**insensitive** (-sitiv) *adj.* insensible, no sensitivo. *2* falto de sensibilidad moral o mental.
**insentient** (-shønt) *adj.* insensible, inanimado.

**inseparable** (inse·parabøl) *adj.* inseparable.
**insert** (i·nsø$^r$t) *s.* cosa inserida, intercalada, etc.; inserción.
**insert (to)** (insø·$^r$t) *tr.* inserir, insertar, ingerir, introducir, intercalar, encajar.
**insertion** (insø·$^r$shøn) *s.* inserción, metimiento. *2* COST. entredós. *3* ZOOL., BOT. inserción.
**inserviceable** (insø·$^r$visabøl) *adj.* inservible, inútil.
**inset** (i·nset) *s.* intercalación. *2* hoja u hojas encajadas en un libro, folleto, mapa, etc.
**inshore** (i·nsho$^r$) cercano a la orilla. *2 adv.* cerca de, o hacia la, orilla.
**inside** (i·nsaid) *s.* interior [de una cosa; del hombre]. *2* forro [de un vestido]. *3* contenido. *4 pl.* entrañas; interioridades. *5 adj.* interior, interno; íntimo, secreto. *6 adv.* dentro, adentro, en el interior: ~ *out*, de dentro afuera, al revés. *7 prep.* dentro de [en el interior de].
**insider** (-ø$^r$) *s.* persona de dentro [de un grupo, sociedad, etc.]; persona enterada, que está en el secreto.
**insidious** (insi·diøs) *adj.* insidioso, engañoso, solapado.
**insight** (i·nsait) *s.* discernimiento, penetración, perspicacia, comprensión, intuición.
**insignia** (insi·gnia) *s. pl.* insignias, distintivos.
**insignificance** (insigni·fikans) *s.* insignificancia.
**insignificant** (-ant) *adj.* insignificante.
**insincere** (insinsi·ø$^r$) *adj.* insincero, hipócrita.
**insincerity** (insinse·riti) *s.* insinceridad, hipocresía.
**insinuate (to)** (insi·niueit) *tr.* insinuar. *2* introducir, deslizar, hacer penetrar, instilar.
**insinuation** (-shøn) *s.* insinuación, sugestión, indirecta. *2* acción de insinuarse.
**insipid** (insi·pid) *adj.* insípido, insulso, soso.
**insipidity** (-iti) *s.* insipidez, insulsez, sosería.
**insist (to)** (insi·st) *intr.* insistir, persistir, empeñarse en, porfiar; hacer hincapié en.
**insistence, -cy** (insi·støns, -si) *s.* insistencia, persistencia.
**insistent** (-nt) *adj.* insistente, persistente.
**insobriety** (insoubrai·eti) *s.* intemperancia.
**insofar as** (insoufa·$^r$ æš) *adv.* en lo que, hasta donde.
**insolate (to)** (i·nsouleit) *tr.* insolar.
**insolation** (-ei·shøn) *s.* MED., METEOR. insolación.
**insole** (i·nsoul) *s.* plantilla [de zapato].
**insolence** (i·nsøløns) *s.* insolencia. *2* altanería.
**insolent** (-nt) *adj.* insolente. *2* altanero.
**insolubility** (insaliubi·liti) *s.* insolubilidad.
**insoluble** (insa·liubøl) *adj.* insoluble. *2* impagable [deuda].
**insolvable** (insa·lvabøl) *adj.* insoluble. *2* indisoluble. *3* que no se puede saldar.
**insolvency** (insa·lvønsi) *s.* insolvencia.
**insolvent** (-vønt) *adj.* insolvente.
**insomnia** (insa·mnia) *s.* insomnio.
**insomuch** (insoumø·ch) *conj.* de manera, hasta el punto: ~ *that*, de manera que, hasta el punto que. *2* ~ *as*, ya que, puesto que.
**insouciance** (insu·sians) *s.* despreocupación.
**insouciant** (-nt) *adj.* despreocupado.
**inspect (to)** (inspe·kt) *tr.* inspeccionar, examinar, registrar, reconocer.
**inspection** (-shøn) *s.* inspección, examen, registro, reconocimiento.
**inspector** (-ø$^r$) *s.* inspector, interventor, controlador.
**inspiration** (inspirei·shøn) *s.* inspiración.
**inspiratory** (inspai·ratori) *adj.* inspirador.

**inspire (to)** (inspai·ø$^r$) *tr.* inspirar. *2* infundir, comunicar. *3* sugerir. *4 intr.* FISIOL. inspirar.
**inspiring** (inspai·ring) *adj.* inspirador, animador.
**inspirit (to)** (inspi·rit) *tr.* animar, vigorizar, alentar, estimular.
**inspissate (to)** (inspi·seit) *tr.* espesar, condensar, trabar.
**instability** (instabi·liti) *s.* inestabilidad, mutabilidad, inconstancia.
**instable** (instei·bøl) *adj.* instable, inestable, mudable, inconstante.
**install (to)** (insto·l) *tr.* instalar en, dar posesión oficialmente de [un cargo o dignidad]. *2* instalar, colocar [un aparato, etc.].
**installation** (-ei·shion) *s.* instalación.
**installment, instalment** (-mønt) *s.* instalación [acción]. *2* plazo [pago o entrega parcial]: *on the ~ plan*, a plazos, con facilidades de pago. *3* entrega, fascículo [de una publicación].
**instance** (i·nst*ə*ns) *s.* ejemplo, caso: *for ~*, por ejemplo. *2* vez, ocasión. *3* ruego, petición, instancia. *4* DER. instancia. *5 in the first ~*, en primer lugar, desde el principio.
**instance (to)** *tr.* poner por caso o por ejemplo, citar.
**instancy** (i·nst*ə*nsi) *s.* insistencia, instancia. *2* prontitud, instantaneidad.
**instant** (i·nst*ə*nt) *adj.* instante, insistente. *2* inminente, inmediato. *3* apremiante, urgente. *4* presente, corriente, actual: *the 10th ~*, el diez del corriente [mes]. *5 s.* instante, momento.
**instantaneous** (instantei·ni*ə*s) *adj.* instantáneo. *2* inmediato [hecho en seguida].
**instanter** (inst*æ*·nt*ø*$^r$) *adv.* inmediatamente.
**instantly** (i·nst*ə*ntli) *adv.* al instante, inmediatamente.
**instead** (inste·d) *adv.* en cambio, en lugar. *2 ~ of*, en lugar de, en vez de.
**instep** (i·nstep) *s.* empeine [del pie, del zapato].
**instigate (to)** (i·nstigeit) *tr.* instigar. *2* promover, fomentar.
**instigation** (-ei·shøn) *s.* instigación.
**instil, instill (to)** (insti·l) *tr.* instilar.
**instillation** (instilei·shøn) *s.* instilación.
**1) instinct** (i·nstinkt) *s.* instinto.
**2) instinct** (insti·nkt) *adj.* *~ with*, animado por; lleno, rebosante de [vida, fuerza, etc.].
**instinctive** (insti·nktiv) *adj.* instintivo.
**institute** (i·nstitiut) *s.* instituto, institución. *2* principio, regla, precepto. *3 pl.* instituta, instituciones.
**institute (to)** *tr.* instituir. *2* abrir, incoar, iniciar.
**institution** (institu·shøn) *s.* institución [acción de instituir; cosa instituida, organización, fundación]. *2* iniciación, comienzo. *3* costumbre establecida. *4* fig. institución [persona o cosa muy conocida].
**instruct (to)** (instrø·kt) *tr.* instruir, enseñar. *2* instruir, informar, enterar. *3* ordenar, mandar.
**instruction** (-shøn) *s.* instrucción, enseñanza. *2* instrucción, saber. *3 pl.* instrucciones, indicaciones.
**instructive** (-tiv) *adj.* instructivo.
**instructor** (-t*ø*$^r$) *m.* instructor, maestro.
**instructress** (-tris) *f.* instructora, maestra.
**instrument** (i·nstrumønt) *s.* instrumento [utensilio, máquina, etc.]. *2* DER., MÚS. instrumento.
**instrument (to)** *tr.* MÚS. instrumentar.
**instrumental** (instrume·ntal) *adj.* MÚS. instrumental. *2 to be ~ in*, contribuir a. *3 s.* GRAM. caso instrumental.

**instrumentalist** (-ist) *s.* MÚS. instrumentista.
**instrumentation** (-ei·shøn) *s.* MÚS. instrumentación. *2* MÚS. ejecución.
**insubordinate** (ins*ø*bo·$^r$dineit) *adj.* insubordinado.
**insubordination** (-ei·shøn) *s.* insubordinación, indisciplina.
**insubstantial** (ins*ø*bst*æ*·nsh*ə*l) *adj.* insubstancial, poco sólido, ligero, tenue, frágil. *2* sin substancia corpórea, irreal.
**insufferable** (ins*ø*·f*ø*rab*ø*l) *adj.* insufrible.
**insufficience, -cy** (ins*ø*fi·shøns, -si) *s.* insuficiencia. *2* incapacidad, incompetencia.
**insufficient** (ins*ø*fi·shent) *adj.* insuficiente. *2* incapaz, incompetente.
**insufflate (to)** (ins*ø*·fleit) *tr.* insuflar.
**insufflation** (-ei·shøn) *s.* insuflación, soplo.
**insular** (i·nsiula$^r$) *adj.* insular, isleño. *2* fig. limitado, de miras estrechas.
**insularity** (insiul*æ*·riti) *s.* insularidad. *2* estrechez de miras.
**insulate (to)** (i·nsiuleit) *tr.* aislar.
**insulating** (-ing) *adj.* aislador, aislante.
**insulation** (-ei·shøn) *s.* aislamiento. *2* material aislante.
**insulator** (i·nsiuleit*ø*$^r$) *s.* aislador.
**insulin** (i·nsiulin) *s.* QUÍM. insulina.
**insult** (i·ns*ø*lt) *s.* insulto, denuesto, ultraje, afrenta.
**insult (to)** (ins*ø*·lt) *tr.* insultar, ultrajar.
**insulting** (-ing) *adj.* insultante.
**insuperable** (insiu·p*ø*rab*ø*l) *adj.* insuperable, invencible.
**insupportable** (ins*ø*po·$^r$tab*ø*l) *adj.* insoportable, inaguantable, insufrible.
**insurance** (inshu·r*ə*ns) *s.* COM. seguro, aseguración: *life ~*, seguro de vida; *~ broker*, corredor de seguros; *~ policy*, póliza de seguro. *2* prima o premio del seguro. *3* garantía, seguridad.
**insurant** (-*ə*nt) *s.* COM. asegurado.
**insure (to)** (inshu·ø$^r$) *tr.* COM. asegurar. *2* asegurar, garantizar.
**insured** (inshu·$^r$d) *adj.-s.* COM. asegurado.
**insurer** (inshu·r*ø*$^r$) *s.* COM. asegurador.
**insurgence, -cy** (ins*ø*·$^r$dÿøns, -si) *s.* insurrección, sublevación.
**insurgent** (-ønt) *adj.-s.* insurgente, insurrecto.
**insurmountable** (ins*ø*$^r$mau·ntab*ø*l) *adj.* insuperable, invencible. *2* que no se puede pasar o transponer.
**insurrection** (ins*ø*re·kshøn) *s.* insurrección, rebelión.
**insurrectionist** (-ist) *s.* insurrecto, rebelde.
**insusceptible** (ins*ø*se·ptib*ø*l) *adj.* no susceptible. *2* insensible.
**intact** (int*æ*·kt) *adj.* intacto, íntegro, entero.
**intaglio** (int*æ*·liou) *s.* obra de talla, grabado.
**intake** (i·nteik) *s.* succión, aspiración, toma, entrada. *2* cantidad de aire, etc., que se aspira o que entra de una vez. *3* contracción, estrechamiento. *4* MEC. válvula de admisión, orificio de entrada. *5* acometida [de una conducción]. *6* producto de una finca.
**intangibility** (int*æ*ndÿibi·liti) *s.* intangibilidad.
**intangible** (int*æ*·ndÿib*ø*l) *adj.* intangible; impalpable.
**integer** (i·ntidÿø$^r$) *s.* número entero. *2* entidad completa.
**integral** (i·ntigr*ə*l) *adj.* integrante, esencial. *2* íntegro, entero. *3 adj.-s.* MAT. integral. *4 s.* totalidad.
**integrality** (intigr*æ*·liti) *s.* integridad.

**integrate (to)** (i·ntigreit) *tr.* integrar, formar un todo. *2* indicar el total. *3* MAT. integrar.
**integration** (-ei·shøn) *s.* integración.
**integrity** (inte·griti) *s.* integridad.
**integument** (inte·giumønt) *s.* integumento.
**intellect** (i·ntølekt) *s.* intelecto, inteligencia. *2* persona, o gente, de talento.
**intellection** (intøle·kshøn) *s.* intelección.
**intellectual** (-chual) *adj.-s.* intelectual.
**intellectuality** (intølekchuæ·liti) *s.* intelectualidad.
**intelligence** (inte·lidÿøns) *s.* inteligencia, entendimiento, penetración, talento. *2* información, conocimiento, noticia: *piece of* ~, informe, noticia, aviso. *3* información secreta: ~ *department* o *service*, servicio de información secreta o de espionaje. *4* inteligencia, armonía [entre personas].
**intelligencer** (-ør) *s.* noticiero. *2* espía.
**intelligent** (-nt) *adj.* inteligente.
**intelligibility** (intelidÿibi·liti) *s.* inteligibilidad.
**intelligible** (inte·lidÿibøl) *adj.* inteligible.
**intemperance** (inte·mpørans) *s.* intemperancia. *2* inclemencia [del tiempo].
**intemperate** (-ørit) *adj.* inmoderado, excesivo, extremado. *2* intemperante, desordenado. *3* bebedor.
**intend (to)** (inte·nd) *tr.* tener la intención de, proponerse, proyectar, pensar, querer. *2* destinar, hacer [para un fin]. *3* entender, querer decir.
**intendance** (inte·ndans) *s.* intendencia.
**intendant** (-dant) *s.* intendente.
**intended** (inte·ndid) *adj.* propuesto, deseado, que se tiene como objeto; hecho [para], destinado [a]. *2 adj.-s.* fam. prometido, futuro.
**intendedly** (-li) *adv.* adrede, de intento.
**intense** (inte·ns) *adj.* intenso. *2* grande, fuerte, vivo, profundo, ardiente. *3* sumo, extremado. *4* que siente profundamente. *5* FOT. duro [negativo].
**intensify (to)** (-sifai) *tr.* intensificar. *2* FOT. reforzar. *3 intr.* intensificarse. ¶ Pret y p. p.: *intensified*.
**intension** (-shøn) *s.* intensión. *2* intensificación. *3* fuerza, profundidad, ardor, energía.
**intensity** (-siti) *s.* intensidad.
**intensive** (-siv) *adj.* intenso. *2* intensivo.
**intensively** (-li) *adj.* intensamente. *2* intensivamente.
**intent** (inte·nt) *adj.* profundo, detenido; fijo [pensamiento, mirada]. *2* ~ *on*, atento, dedicado a, absorto, concentrado en; resuelto a, empeñado en. *3 s.* intento, designio, ánimo, intención, propósito. *4 to all intents*, en todos los casos o sentidos, prácticamente.
**intention** (-shøn) *s.* intención.
**intentional** (-al) *adj.* intencional.
**intentness** (inte·ntnis) *s.* aplicación asidua, atención, empeño. *2* fijeza [de la mirada, etc.].
**inter (to)** (intø·r) *tr.* enterrar, sepultar, inhumar.
**interact (to)** (intøræ·kt) *tr.* obrar recíprocamente.
**interaction** (-æ·kshøn) *s.* acción recíproca.
**intercalary** (intø·rkaleri) *adj.* intercalar.
**intercalation** (-ei·shøn) *s.* intercalación.
**intercede (to)** (intø·rsi·d) *intr.* interceder; mediar.
**intercellular** (-se·liular) *adj.* BIOL. intercelular.
**intercept (to)** (-se·pt) *tr.* interceptar.
**interception** (-shøn) *s.* interceptación.
**intercession** (-se·shøn) *s.* intercesión.
**intercessor** (-se·sør) *s.* intercesor; medianero.
**interchange** (i·ntørcheindÿ) *s.* intercambio, cam-

bio, trueque. *2* comercio, tráfico. *3* alternación, sucesión alternada.
**interchange (to)** (intør·chei·ndÿ) *tr.* cambiar, trocar. *2* alternar, variar. *3 intr.* alternarse.
**interchangeable** (-abøl) *adj.* intercambiable. *2* de recambio. *3* mutuo, recíproco.
**intercollegiate** (intørkøli·dÿiit) *adj.* interescolar, interuniversitario.
**intercom** (i·ntørkam) *s.* teléfono interior.
**intercolumniation** (intørkølømniei·shøn) *s.* ARQ. intercolumnio.
**intercommunicate (to)** (-kømiu·nikeit) *intr.* comunicarse con otro.
**intercontinental** (-kantine·ntal) *adj.* intercontinental.
**intercostal** (-ka·stal) *adj.* ANAT. intercostal.
**intercourse** (i·ntørko·rs) *s.* trato, comunicación; correspondencia, conversación: *sexual* ~, trato carnal, cópula. *2* intercambio, comercio, tráfico.
**interdental** (-de·ntal) *adj.* interdental.
**interdependence** (-dipe·ndøns) *s.* interdependencia.
**interdict** (i·ntø·rdikt) *s.* interdicto, entredicho.
**interdict (to)** (intø·rdi·kt) *tr.* entredecir. *2* interdecir, prohibir, vedar.
**interdiction** (-shøn) *s.* interdicción. *2* prohibición.
**interest** (i·ntørest) *s.* interés: *to one's interest*, en interés o provecho de uno; *to put out at* ~, poner a interés, a rédito. *2* participación [en un negocio]. *3* influencia [de una persona]. *4* creces: *with* ~, con creces.
**interest (to)** *tr.* interesar.
**interfere (to)** (intø·rfi·ør) *intr.* FÍS. interferir, interferirse. *2* interponerse, meterse, entrometerse, inmiscuirse. *3* oponerse, chocar. *4* VET. tropezarse [los caballos]. *5 to* ~ *with*, estorbar, dificultar.
**interference** (-røns) *s.* FÍS., RADIO, interferencia. *2* interposición, intervención, intromisión. *3* estorbo.
**interfuse (to)** (-fiu·š) *tr.* combinar, mezclar. *2* difundir. *3* penetrar, saturar. *4 intr.* mezclarse, fundirse.
**interfusion** (-dÿøn) *s.* combinación, mezcla. *2* difusión. *3* saturación.
**interim** (i·ntørim) *adj.* interino, provisional. *2 s.* entretanto, ínterin: *in the* ~, entretanto, en el interín.
**interior** (inti·riør) *adj.* interior, interno. *2 s.* interior.
**interjacent** (intø·rdÿei·šønt) *adj.* interyacente.
**interject (to)** (intø·rdÿe·kt) *tr.* interponer, insertar. *2 intr.* interponerse.
**interjection** (-shøn) *s.* interposición. *2* GRAM. interjección.
**interlace (to)** (-lei·s) *tr.* entrelazar. *2* entremezclar.
**interlapse** (-læ·ps) *s.* intervalo [de tiempo].
**interlard (to)** (-li·v) *tr.* interfoliar.
**interline (to)** (-lain) *tr.* interlinear, entrerrenglonar. *2* COST. entretelar.
**interlineation** (-ei·shøn) *s.* interlineación.
**interlink (to)** (-li·nk) *tr.* eslabonar.
**interlock** (i·ntørlak) *s.* traba, trabazón.
**interlock (to)** (-la·k) *tr.* unir, trabar o entrelazar fuertemente, enclavijar. *2* engranar, engargantar. *3 intr.* trabarse, enclavijarse.
**interlocution** (-la·kiutør) *s.* interlocutor.
**interloper** (-lou·pør) *s.* entrometido, intruso.
**interlude** (-lud) *s.* TEATR. intermedio. *2* MÚS. interludio. *3* intervalo.

**interlunar** (intø^r liu·na^r) *adj.* del interlunio.
**intermarriage** (-mæ·ridÿ) *s.* casamiento entre personas de distintas tribus, castas, etc. *2* casamiento entre parientes.
**intermarry** (-mæ·ri) *intr.* unirse por casamientos diferentes familias, tribus, castas, etc.
**intermediary** (-mɪ·diæri) *adj.* intermedio. *2 s.* medio, conducto.
**intermediate** (-dieit) *adj.* intermedio. *2 s.* cosa intermedia. *4* intermediario, mediador.
**intermediate (to)** *intr.* interponerse, intermediar. *2* intervenir, mediar.
**intermediation** (-shøn) *s.* interposición, intervención, mediación.
**interment** (intø·^r mønt) *s.* entierro, enterramiento.
**intermezzo** (-me·dšou) *s.* MÚS. intermedio.
**interminable** (intø·^r minabøl) *adj.* interminable.
**intermingle (to)** (intø^r mi·ngøl) *tr.* entremezclar. *2 intr.* entremezclarse.
**intermission** (intø^r mi·shøn) *s.* intermisión, interrupción, tregua. *2* TEAT. intermedio, entreacto.
**intermit (to)** (-mi·t) *tr.* intermitir. *2 intr.* ser intermitente. ¶ Pret. y p. p.: *-tted;* ger.: *-tting.*
**intermittence** (-øns) *s.* intermitencia.
**intermittent** (-ønt) *adj.* intermitente.
**intermix (to)** (-mi·ks) *tr.* entremezclar. *2 intr.* entremezclarse.
**intermixture** (-chu^r) *s.* entremezcladura.
**intern** (i·ntø^r n) *s.* interno [de un hospital]. *2* persona internada.
**intern (to)** (intø·^r n) *tr.* internar.
**internal** (-nal) *adj.* interior, interno, intestino: *internal-combustion engine,* motor de explosión, de combustión interna.
**international** (intø^r næ·shønal) *adj.* internacional.
**internationalism** (intø^r næ·shønaliśm) *s.* internacionalismo.
**internationalize (to)** (-laiś) *tr.* internacionalizar.
**internecine** (-ni·sin) *adj.* mortífero, sanguinario.
**internist** (intø·^r nist) *s.* MED. internista.
**internment** (-mønt) *s.* internación.
**internode** (intø^r nou·d) *s.* BOT. entrenudo.
**internuncio** (intø^r nø·nshiou) *s.* internuncio.
**interparliamentary** (-pa^r lime·ntari) *adj.* interparlamentario.
**interpellate (to)** (-pe·leit) *tr.* interpelar.
**interpellation** (-ei·shøn) *s.* interpretación.
**interpenetrate (to)** (-pe·nitreit) *tr.-intr.* penetrar entre, dentro o a través. *2* penetrarse mutuamente.
**interphone** (i·ntø^r foun) *s.* INTERCOM.
**interplanetary** (intø^r plæ·niteri) *adj.* interplanetario.
**interpolate (to)** (intø^r poleit) *tr.* interpolar.
**interpose (to)** (intø^r pou·ś) *tr.* interponer. *2 intr.* interponerse, mediar, intervenir. *3* interrumpir [con una observación, etc.].
**interposition** (-poši·shøn) *s.* interposición, intervención, mediación.
**interpret (to)** (intø·^r prit) *tr.* interpretar.
**interpretation** (-ei·shøn) *s.* interpretación.
**interpreter** (intø·^r pritø^r) *s.* intérprete.
**interregnum** (intø^r re·gnøm) *s.* interregno.
**interrogate (to)** (inte·røgeit) *tr.* interrogar [a un testigo, etc.]. *2 intr.* hacer preguntas.
**interrogation** (-ei·shøn) *s.* interrogación; pregunta. *2* ORT. ~ *mark* o *point,* interrogante, signo de interrogación.
**interrogative** (intøra·gativ) *adj.* interrogativo. *2 s.* palabra interrogativa.

**interrogator** (inte·røgeitø^r) *s.* interrogante, preguntador.
**interrogatory** (intøra·gatori) *adj.* interrogativo. *2 s.* interrogatorio.
**interrupt (to)** (intørø·pt) *tr.-intr.* interrumpir.
**interruptedly** (-tidli) *adv.* interrumpidamente, de un modo discontinuo.
**interruption** (-shøn) *s.* interrupción. *2* solución de continuidad. *3* estorbo, obstáculo.
**intersect (to)** (intø^r se·kt) *tr.* cortar, cruzar [una línea, etc., a otra]. *2 intr.* intersecarse, cortarse.
**intersection** (-shøn) *s.* intersección. *2* cruce [de calles, etc.].
**interspace (to)** (-pei·s) *tr.* espaciar.
**intersperse (to)** (-pø·^r s) *tr.* esparcir, entremezclar, sembrar, salpicar.
**interstate** (-teit) *adj.* interestatal.
**interstellar** (-te·la^r) *adj.* interestelar.
**interstice** (intø·^r stis) *s.* intersticio. *2* resquicio, hendedura.
**intertwine, intertwist (to)** (-tuai·n, -tui·st) *tr.* entretejer, entrelazar. *2 intr.* entrelazarse.
**interval** (i·ntø^r val) *s.* intervalo, espacio, claro. *2* intermedio, descanso. *3* MÚS. intervalo.
**intervene (to)** (intø^r vi·n) *intr.* intervenir, mediar. *2* interponerse, atravesarse. *3* sobrevenir, ocurrir [entre dos momentos o hechos].
**intervening** (intø·vi·ning) *adj.* que interviene. *2* intermedio, que media.
**intervention** (intø^r ve·nshøn) *s.* intervención [acción de tomar parte o mediar]; mediación. *2* interposición.
**interview** (i·ntø^r viu) *s.* entrevista, conferencia. *2* interviev, interviu [periodística].
**interview (to)** *tr.* entrevistarse con. *2* intervievar.
**interweave (to)** (intø·^r uiv) *tr.* entretejer, entrelazar. *2 intr.* entretejerse, entrelazarse. ¶ Pret.: *interwove* o *-weaved;* p. p.: *interwove, -woven* o *-weaved.*
**intestate** (inte·steit) *adj.-s.* intestado. *2 adj.* no dejado en testamento.
**intestinal** (-tinal) *adj.* ANAT., ZOOL. intestinal.
**intestine** (-tin) *adj.* intestino. *2* interno. *3 s.* ANAT. intestino.
**intimacy** (i·ntimasi) *s.* intimidad, familiaridad, amistad íntima.
**intimate** (i·ntimit) *adj.* íntimo. *2* de confianza, casero. *3 s.* amigo íntimo.
**intimate (to)** (i·ntimeit) *tr.* anunciar, notificar, intimar. *2* indicar, insinuar, dar a entender.
**intimation** (intimei·shøn) *s.* notificación, intimación. *2* insinuación, indicación.
**intimidate (to)** (inti·mideit) *tr.* intimidar.
**intimidation** (-ei·shøn) *s.* intimidación.
**into** (i·ntu) *prep.* en, dentro, adentro, hacia el interior, a [indicando movimiento o dirección de fuera a dentro; tránsito de un estado a otro; transformación; penetración, inclusión]: *to go* ~, entrar en; *translated* ~ *many languages,* traducido a muchas lenguas.
**intolerable** (inta·lørabøl) *adj.* intolerable, insoportable, insufrible.
**intolerance** (inta·løraņs) *s.* intolerancia.
**intolerant** (-nt) *adj.-s.* intolerante. *2 adj.* que no puede resistir o sufrir.
**intonation** (intounei·shøn) *s.* entonación.
**intone (to)** (intou·n) *tr.* entonar [una canción, etc.]. *2* salmear, salmodiar.
**intoxicant** (inta·ksikant) *adj.* embriagador. *2 s.* bebida alcohólica.

**intoxicate (to)** (-keit) *tr.* embriagar. *2* MED. intoxicar.
**intoxication** (-ei·shøn) *s.* MED. intoxicación. *2* embriaguez, borrachera.
**intractability** (intræktabi·liti) *s.* indocilidad, obstinación.
**intractable** (intræ·ktabøl) *adj.* indócil, rebelde, obstinado. *2* difícil de trabajar [material].
**intrados** (intrei·das) *s.* ARQ. intradós.
**intranquility** (intrænkui·liti) *s.* intranquilidad, desasosiego.
**intransigence** (intræ·nšidÿøns) *s.* intransigencia.
**intransigent** (-ønt) *adj.-s.* intransigente.
**intransitive** (intræ·nsitiv) *adj.* GRAM. intransitivo.
**intravenous** (intravi·nøs) *adj.* intravenoso.
**intrench (to)** (intre·nch) *tr.* TO ENTRENCH.
**intrepid** (intre·pid) *adj.* intrépido, denodado.
**intrepidity** (intripi·diti) *s.* intrepidez.
**intricacy** (i·ntrikasi) *s.* intrincación, enredo, complicación.
**intricate** (i·ntrikit) *adj.* intrincado, complicado, confuso.
**intrigue** (intri·g) *s.* intriga, conspiración. *2* enredo amoroso, lío. *3* LIT. enredo.
**intrigue (to)** *intr.* intrigar. *2* tener intrigas amorosas. *3 tr.* intrigar [despertar curiosidad].
**intriguer** (-ø<sup>r</sup>) *s.* intrigante.
**intrinsic(al** (intri·nsik(al) *adj.* intrínseco.
**introduce (to)** (intrødiu·s) *tr.* introducir. *2* presentar [un proyecto de ley, etc.; una persona a otra].
**introduction** (-dø·kshøn) *s.* introducción. *2* presentación.
**introductory** (-tori) *adj.* introductorio, de introducción, preliminar. *2* de presentación.
**introit** (introu·it) *s.* LITURG. introito.
**introrse** (intrø·<sup>r</sup>s) *adj.* BOT. introrso.
**introspection** (intrøspe·kshøn) *s.* introspección.
**introspective** (-tiv) *adj.* introspectivo.
**introversion** (-vø·<sup>r</sup>shøn) *s.* introversión.
**introvert** (i·ntrøvø<sup>r</sup>t) *adj.-s.* introverso, introvertido.
**introvert (to)** *tr.* volver [el pensamiento, etc.] hacia el propio interior de uno. *2* volver hacia adentro. *3* ZOOL. invaginar.
**intrude (to)** (intru·d) *tr.* imponer uno [su presencia, sus opiniones, etc.]. *2 intr.* entrometerse, imponer uno su presencia [donde no es llamado]; estorbar. *3* intrusarse.
**intruder** (-ø<sup>r</sup>) *s.* intruso. *2* entremetido.
**intrusion** (intru·ÿøn) *s.* intrusión, entremetimiento. *2* GEOL. intrusión.
**intrusiveness** (-sivnis) *s.* tendencia a intrusarse o entremeterse.
**intubate** (i·ntiubeit) *tr.* MED. intubar.
**intuit (to)** (i·ntiuit) *tr.-intr.* intuir.
**intuition** (intiui·shøn) *s.* intuición.
**intuitive** (intiu·itiv) *adj.* intuitivo.
**intumesce (to)** (intiume·s) *intr.* hinchar, dilatar.
**intumescence, -cy** (-øns, -si) *s.* intumescencia; hinchazón.
**inunction** (inø·nkshøn) *s.* untura, friega.
**inundate (to)** (-deit) *tr.* inundar, anegar.
**inundation** (-ei·shøn) *s.* inundación.
**inurbane** (inø<sup>r</sup>bei·n) *adj.* inurbano, descortés.
**inure (to)** (iniu·ø<sup>r</sup>) *tr.* habituar, avezar, hacer, curtir.
**inured** (-d) *adj.* avezado, hecho [a], curtido [en].
**inurement** (-mønt) *s.* hábito, práctica, costumbre.
**inutility** (iniuti·liti) *s.* inutilidad.

**invade (to)** (invei·d) *tr.* invadir. *2* usurpar, violar [derechos, etc.].
**invader** (invei·dø<sup>r</sup>) *s.* invasor.
**invaginate (to)** (invæ·dÿineit) *tr.* invaginar.
**invagination** (invædÿine·shøn) *s.* invaginación.
**1) invalid** (invæ·lid) *adj.* inválido, irrito, nulo.
**2) invalid** (i·nvalid) *adj.* inválido, tullido, enfermo, achacoso. *2 s.* inválido. *3* persona achacosa, valetudinario.
**invalid (to)** (invali·d) *tr.* convertir en un inválido. *2* licenciar como inválido.
**invalidate (to)** (invæ·lideit) *tr.* invalidar, anular.
**invalidation** (-shøn) *s.* invalidación.
**invalidity** (invæli·diti) *s.* invalidez.
**invaluable** (invæ·liuabøl) *adj.* inestimable, inapreciable, precioso. *2* sin valor.
**invariability** (inveriabi·liti) *s.* invariabilidad, invariación.
**invariable** (inve·riabøl) *adj.* invariable.
**invasion** (invei·ÿøn) *s.* invasión. *2* usurpación, violación [de derechos, etc.].
**invective** (inve·ktiv) *s.* invectiva.
**inveigh (to)** (invei·) *intr.* lanzar o decir invectivas [contra].
**inveigle (to)** (invi·gøl) *tr.* engañar, seducir, engatusar. *2* atraer u obtener con engaño.
**invent (to)** (inve·nt) *tr.* inventar.
**invention** (inve·nshøn) *s.* invención. *2* invento. *3* ingenio, mecanismo. *4* inventiva.
**inventor** (-tø<sup>r</sup>) *s.* inventor. *2* invencionero.
**inventory** (i·nventori) *s.* inventario.
**inventory (to)** *tr.* inventariar.
**inventress** (inve·ntris) *s.* inventora.
**inverness** (invø<sup>r</sup>ne·s) *s.* macferlán.
**inverse** (invø·<sup>r</sup>s) *adj.* inverso. *2 s.* lo inverso.
**inversion** (-shøn) *s.* inversión.
**invert** (i·nvø<sup>r</sup>t) *s.* COM. invertosa. *3* PSIC. invertido.
**invert (to)** (invø·<sup>r</sup>t) *tr.* invertir [alterar el orden de; volver de arriba abajo, de fuera a adentro, etc.]. *2* MAT., QUÍM. invertir.
**invertebrata** (-tøbreita) *s. pl.* ZOOL. invertebrados.
**invertebrate** (-tøbreit) *s. pl.* ZOOL. invertebrado.
**inverted** (-tid) *adj.* invertido: ~ *commas*, comillas.
**invest (to)** (inve·st) *tr.* investir [de una dignidad, etc.]. *2* vestir, envolver, cubrir. *3* invertir, emplear [dinero]. *6* MIL. cercar, sitiar.
**investigate (to)** (inve·stigeit) *tr.* investigar. *2* averiguar, indagar.
**investigation** (-ei·shøn) *s.* investigación, averiguación, indagación, pesquisa.
**investigator** (inve·stigeitø<sup>r</sup>) *s.* investigador. *2* averiguador, indagador.
**investiture** (-ichø<sup>r</sup>) *s.* investidura. *2* vestidura, envoltura.
**investment** (-mønt) *s.* INVESTITURE. *2* inversión [de dinero]. *3* MIL. cerco, sitio.
**investor** (-ø<sup>r</sup>) *s.* persona que invierte dinero.
**inveteracy** (inve·tørasi) *s.* calidad de inveterado.
**inveterate** (invæ·tørit) *adj.* inveterado, arraigado. *2* empedernido, pertinaz.
**invidious** (invi·diøs) *adj.* injusto, irritante, odioso.
**invigorate (to)** (invi·gøreit) *tr.* vigorizar, fortalecer, animar.
**invigoration** (invigøre·shøn) *s.* fortalecimiento.
**invincibility** (invinsibi·liti) *s.* invencibilidad.
**invincible** (invi·nsibøl) *adj.* invencible.
**inviolability** (invaiølabi·liti) *s.* inviolabilidad.
**inviolable** (invai·ølabøl) *adj.* inviolable; sagrado. *2* inquebrantable, infrangible.
**invisibility** (invišibi·liti) *s.* invisibilidad.

**invisible** (invi·šibøl) *adj.* invisible: ~ *ink*, tinta simpática.
**invitation** (invitei·shøn) *s.* invitación. *2* llamada, atractivo.
**invite (to)** (invai·t) *tr.* invitar, convidar. *2* rogar, inducir, tentar.
**inviting** (invai·ting) *adj.* que invita. *2* atractivo, seductor, tentador, provocativo. *3* apetitoso.
**invocation** (invokei·shøn) *s.* invocación. *2* evocación [de los espíritus, etc.].
**invoice** (i·nvois) *s.* COM. factura: *as per* ~, según factura.
**invoice (to)** *tr.-intr.* COM. facturar.
**invoke (to)** (invou·k) *tr.* invocar. *2* evocar [a los espíritus, etc.].
**involucre** (invøliu·kø<sup>r</sup>) *s.* BOT. involucro.
**involuntary** (inva·lønteri) *adj.* involuntario.
**involute** (i·nvøliut) *adj.* intrincado. *2* involuto. *3* s. GEOM. involuta.
**involution** (invøliu·shøn) *s.* envolvimiento. *2* complicación, enredo. *3* MAT. potenciación. *4* MAT., BIOL., MED. involución.
**involve (to)** (inva·lv) *tr.* envolver, enrollar. *2* envolver, complicar, comprometer. *3* enredar, complicar, oscurecer. *4* comprender, incluir.
**involved** (-d) *adj.* envuelto, enredado; complicado, comprometido. *2* intrincado, obscuro. *3* absorto, engolfado.
**involvement** (-mønt) *s.* envolvimiento. *2* complicación, intrincación.
**invulnerability** (invølnørabi·liti) *s.* invulnerabilidad.
**invulnerable** (invø·lnørabøl) *adj.* invulnerable. *2* inatacable, irrebatible.
**inward** (i·nua<sup>r</sup>d) *adj.* interior, interno, íntimo. *2* dirigido hacia el centro o el interior. *3* adv. INWARDS.
**inwardness** (-nis) *s.* interioridad. *2* interior, fondo, esencia.
**inwards** (-s) *adv.* hacia el centro, hacia adentro. *2* interiormente, mentalmente.
**inweave (to)** (inuı·v) *tr.* entretejer, enlazar.
**inwrought** (inro·t) *adj.* labrado, tejido en; embutido, incrustado.
**iodid(e** (ai·ødid) . QUÍM. yoduro.
**iodin(e** (-in) *s.* QUÍM. yodo.
**iodize (to)** (-aiš) *tr.* yodurar.
**iodoform** (aiou·døfo<sup>r</sup>m) *s.* QUÍM. yodoformo.
**ion** (ai·øn) *s.* FÍS., QUÍM. ion.
**ionian** (aiou·nian) *adj.-s.* jonio: ~ *Sea*, Mar Jonio.
**Ionic** (aia·nik) *adj.* jónico.
**ionization** (aiønišei·shøn) *s.* ionización.
**ionize (to)** (ai·ønaiš) *tr.* ionizar. *2* intr. ionizarse.
**iota** (aiou·ta) *s.* iota [letra griega]. *2* fig. ápice, jota.
**I.O.U.** (ai ou you) (abreviatura de *I owe you*) *s.* pagaré, vale.
**Irak** (i·rak) *n. pr.* GEOGR. Irak.
**Iran** (i·ran o ai·ræn) *n. pr.* GEOGR. Irán, Persia.
**Iranian** (airei·nian) *adj.-s.* iranio, persa.
**irascible** (airæ·sibøl) *adj.* irascible.
**irate** (airei·t) *adj.* encolerizado, airado.
**ire** (ai·ø<sup>r</sup>) *s.* ira, iracundia, cólera.
**ireful** (ai·ø<sup>r</sup>ful) *adj.* iracundo, colérico, airado.
**Ireland** (ai·<sup>r</sup>land) *n. pr.* GEOGR. Irlanda.
**iridaceous** (airidei·shiøs) *adj.* BOT. iridáceo.
**iridescence** (iride·søns) *s.* cambiante, tornasol.
**iridescent** (iride·sønt) *adj.* iridescente, irisado.
**iridium** (iri·diøm) *s.* QUÍM. iridio.
**iris** (ai·ris) *s.* ANAT., ÓPT. iris. *2* arco iris. *3* BOT. lirio.
**irisation** (-rišei·shøn) *s.* irisación.

**Irish** (ai·rish) *adj.* irlandés, de Irlanda. *2 m.* irlandés [idioma]. *3* pl. *the Irish*, los irlandeses.
**Irishman** (ai·rishmæn) *s.* irlandés [hombre].
**Irishwoman** (ai·rishwumæn) *s.* irlandesa [mujer].
**iritis** (airai·tis) *s.* MED. iritis.
**irk (to)** (ø<sup>r</sup>k) *tr.* fastidiar, cansar, encocorar.
**irksome** (ø·<sup>r</sup>ksøm) *adj.* fastidioso, tedioso, pesado, cargante.
**iron** (ai·ø<sup>r</sup>n) *s.* hierro, [metal; arma, instrumento, etc., de hierro]: *to have many irons in the fire*, tener muchos asuntos entre manos; *to strike while the ~ is hot*, aprovechar la ocasión. *2* hierro [para marcar]. *3* plancha [para la ropa]. *4 pl.* hierros, cadenas, grilletes. *5* adj. de hierro, férreo, férrico: *Iron Age*, Edad de Hierro; ~ *curtain*, cortina de hierro; fig. telón de acero; ~ *lung*, MED. pulmón de acero; ~ *scrap*, chatarra; ~ *will*, voluntad de hierro.
**iron (to)** *tr.* guarnecer de hierro, herrar. *2* aherrojar, poner grilletes a. *3* planchar [la ropa]: *to ~ out*, fig. allanar.
**iron-bound** *adj.* unido o sujeto con hierro. *2* escabroso, rocoso. *3* férreo, inflexible, duro.
**ironclad** (-klæd) *adj.* acorazado, blindado. *2* fig. riguroso, severo. *3 s.* MAR. acorazado.
**ironic** (al (aira·nik(al) *adj.* irónico.
**ironing** (ai·ø<sup>r</sup>ning) *s.* planchado; ~ *board*, tabla de planchar.
**ironmaster** (-mæstø<sup>r</sup>) *s.* dueño de una herrería.
**ironmonger** (-møngø<sup>r</sup>) *s.* ferretero, quincallero.
**ironsides** (-saidš) *s.* hombre fuerte. *2* MAR. acorazado. *3 pl.* caballería de Oliverio Cromwell.
**ironware** (-ue<sup>r</sup>) *s.* ferretería [artículos].
**ironwork** (-uø<sup>r</sup>k) *s.* herraje.
**ironworks** (-uo<sup>r</sup>ks) *s.* fundición de hierro, herrería, ferrería.
**ironwort** (-uø<sup>r</sup>t) *s.* BOT. siderita.
**1) irony** (-i) *adj.* férreo; ferrugiento.
**2) irony** (ai·røni) *s.* ironía.
**iroquois** (i·rokua) *s.* iroqués.
**irradiance, -cy** (irei·dians, -si) *s.* irradiación. *2* lustre, esplendor.
**irradiate (to)** (irei·dieit) *tr.* irradiar, esparcir. *2* iluminar. *3* MED., QUÍM. someter a una radiación. *4* intr. lucir, brillar.
**irradiation** (-ei·shøn) *s.* irradiación. *2* iluminación. *3* brillo, esplendor.
**irrational** (iræ·shønal) *adj.* irracional [que carece de razón; opuesto a la razón]. *2* absurdo, ilógico. *3* MAT. irracional.
**irrationality** (iræshonæ·liti) *s.* irracionalidad.
**irreclaimable** (iriklei·mabøl) *adj.* incorregible. *2* irredimible.
**irreconcilable** (irecønsai·labøl) *adj.* irreconciliable. *2* inconciliable, incompatible. *3 s.* POL. intransigente.
**irrecoverable** (irikø·vørabøl) *adj.* irreparable. *2* irrecuperable. *3* incobrable.
**irrecusable** (irikiu·šabøl) *adj.* irrecusable.
**irredeemable** (iridı·mabøl) *adj.* irredimible. *2* no convertible en metálico [papel moneda].
**irredentism** (iride·ntism) *s.* irredentismo.
**irreducible** (iridiu·sibøl) *adj.* irreducible, irreductible.
**irrefragable** (ire·fragabøl) *adj.* irrefragable. *2* innegable, incontestable.
**irrefutable** (irefiu·tabøl) *adj.* irrefutable.
**irregular** (ire·giula<sup>r</sup>) *adj.* irregular. *2* anormal, anómalo. *3* desarreglado, desordenado.
**irregularity** (iregiulæ·riti) *s.* irregularidad. *2* anomalía. *3* desarreglo, desorden.

**irrelative** (ire·lativ) *adj.* inconexo, que no guarda relación.

**irrelevance, -cy** (ire·livans, -si) *s.* impertinencia [falta de pertinencia], calidad de lo que no es aplicable o que no viene al caso. *2* cosa que no viene a propósito o al caso.

**irrelevant** (-nt) *adj.* impertinente [no pertinente], fuera de propósito, que no es aplicable o que no viene al caso, ajeno [a la cuestión].

**irreligion** (irili·dŷøn) *s.* irreligión, impiedad.

**irreligious** (-øs) *adj.* irreligioso.

**irremediable** (irimı·diabøl) *adj.* irremediable, irreparable. *2* incurable.

**irremissible** (irimi·sibøl) *adj.* irremisible.

**irremovable** (irimu·vabøl) *adj.* inamovible. *2* que no se puede quitar.

**irreparable** (ire·parabøl) *adj.* irreparable.

**irrepealable** (iripı·labøl) *adj.* irrevocable.

**irreplaceable** (iriplei·sabøl) *adj.* irreemplazable, insustituible.

**irreprehensible** (ireprije·nsibøl) *adj.* irreprensible.

**irrepressible** (iripre·sibøl) *adj.* irreprimible, incontenible.

**irreproachable** (iriprou·chabøl) *adj.* irreprochable.

**irresistible** (iriši·stibøl) *adj.* irresistible, incontrastable.

**irresolute** (ire·šøliut) *adj.* irresoluto, indeciso.

**irresolution** (irešøliu·shøn) *s.* irresolución, indecisión, vacilación.

**irresolvable** (ireša·lvabøl) *adj.* que no se puede resolver o descomponer.

**irrespective** (irispe·ktiv) *adj.-adv.* ~ *of*, que no toma en cuenta, que prescinde de, independiente de; prescindiendo de, independientemente de.

**irrespirable** (irispai·rabøl) *adj.* irrespirable.

**irresponsibility** (irispansibi·liti) *s.* irresponsabilidad.

**irresponsible** (irispa·nsibøl) *adj.* irresponsable.

**irresponsive** (-siv) *adj.* que no responde [a una influencia, acción o afecto].

**irretrievable** (iritrı·vabøl) *adj.* irreparable, irrevocable. *2* irrecuperable. *3* incobrable.

**irreverence** (ire·vørøns) *s.* irreverencia; falta de respeto.

**irreverent** (-nt) *adj.* irreverente; irrespetuoso.

**irreversibility** (irivøᵣsibi·liti) *s.* irreversibilidad.

**irreversible** (irivø·ᵣsibøl) *adj.* irreversible.

**irrevocability** (irevøkabi·liti) *s.* irrevocabilidad.

**irrevocable** (ire·vøkabøl) *adj.* irrevocable. *2* inalterable, inquebrantable.

**irrigable** (i·rigabøl) *adj.* irrigable. *2* regadío, regadizo.

**irrigate (to)** (i·rigeit) *tr.* irrigar, regar. *2* MED. irrigar.

**irrigation** (-ei·shøn) *s.* irrigación, riego. *2* MED. irrigación.

**irritability** (iritabi·liti) *s.* irritabilidad.

**irritable** (i·ritabøl) *adj.* irritable.

**irritant** (i·ritant) *adj.-s.* irritante. *2* irritador.

**irritate (to)** (i·riteit) *tr.* irritar. *2* FISIOL. excitar.

**irritation** (-ei·shøn) *s.* irritación. *2* FISIOL. excitación.

**irruption** (irø·pshøn) *s.* irrupción.

**is** (iš) *3.ᵃ pers. sing. pres. ind.* de TO BE.

**Isaac** (ai·šæk) *n. pr.* Isac.

**Isabella** (išabe·la) *n. pr.* Isabel.

**Isaiah** (aišei·æ o aišai·æ) *n. pr.* BIB. Isaías.

**Iscariot** (iskæ·riøt) *n. pr.* BIB. Iscariote.

**ischiatic** (iskiæ·tik) *adj.* ANAT. isquiático.

**ischium** (i·skiøm) *s.* ANAT. isquión.

**Ishmael** (i·shmiøl) *n. pr.* BIB. Ismael.

**Ishmaelite** (i·shmiølait) *s.* ismaelita. *2* fig. paria.

**Isidore** (i·šidoᵣ) *n. pr.* Isidoro, Isidro.

**isinglass** (ai·šinglas) *s.* colapez, cola de pescado. *2* MINER. mica.

**Islam** (i·slæm) *s.* Islam.

**Islamism** (i·slamišm) *s.* islamismo.

**island** (ai·lạnd) *s.* isla, ínsula.

**islander** (-øᵣ) *s.* isleño, insular.

**isle** (ail) *s.* isla, insula. *2* isleta.

**islet** (ai·let) *s.* isleta, cayo.

**ism** (išm) *s.* ismo [doctrina, sistema, etc.].

**isobar** (ai·sobaᵣ) *s.* METEOR. línea isobárica, isobara.

**Isochronous** (aisa·krønøs) *adj.* isócrono.

**isoclinal** (aisoclai·nal) *adj.* isoclino. *2 s.* isoclina [línea].

**isodactylous** (aisodæ·ktiløs) *adj.* isodáctilo.

**isogonal** (aisa·gonal) *adj.* CRISTAL. isógono.

**isogonic** (aisoga·nik) *adj.* isogónico.

**isolate (to)** (ai·søleit) *tr.* aislar. *2* separar, incomunicar.

**isolation** (-ei·shøn) *s.* aislamiento. *2* soledad, incomunicación.

**isolationism** (-išm) *s.* aislacionismo.

**isomeric** (aisome·rik) *adj.* QUÍM. isómero.

**isomerous** (aisa·mørøs) *adj.* BIOL., QUÍM. isómero.

**isomorphic, -phous** (aisomo·ᵣfik, -føs) *adj.* isomorfo.

**Isopoda** (aisa·podæ) *s. pl.* ZOOL. isópodos.

**isosceles** (aisa·søliz) *adj.* GEOM. isósceles.

**isotherm** (ai·sozøᵣm) *s.* isoterma, línea isoterma.

**isotope** (-toup) *s.* QUÍM. isótopo.

**isotropic** (aisotra·pik) *adj.* isótropo.

**Israel** (i·šriøl) *n. pr.* Israel.

**israeli** (išrai·li) *adj.-s.* israelí.

**Israelite** (i·šrialait) *s.* israelita.

**issuance** (i·shuans) *s.* emisión. *2* publicción.

**issue** (i·shu) *s.* salida, egreso. *2* fuente, principio. *3* conclusión, solución, fin, decisión; consecuencias, resultado. *4* prole, hijos, sucesión. *5* producto, beneficios, rentas. *6* emisión [de valores]; expedición [de una orden, etc.]. *7* punto [que se debate o ha de decidir]: *to join* ~, ponerse a debatir; *to take* ~ *with*, llevar la contraria a, oponerse a; *at* ~, en disputa. *8* edición, tirada, número [de una publicación]. *9* MED. fuente, exutorio.

**issue (to)** *tr.* arrojar, verter. *2* expedir, dar [una orden, decreto, etc.]. *3* emitir, poner en circulación. *4* publicar, dar a luz. *5 intr.* salir, nacer, manar. *6* provenir, descender. *7* acabar, resolverse. *8* salir, ser publicado o emitido.

**Istambul** (istanbu·l) *n. pr.* GEOGR. Estambul.

**isthmian** (i·smian) *adj.-s.* istmeño. *2 adj.* (con may.) ístmico.

**isthmus** (i·smøs) *s.* GEOGR., ANAT. istmo.

**it** (it) *pron. neutro* él, ella, ello, eso, lo, la, le. | Se aplica a cosas inanimadas, a niños de teta y a animales cuyo sexo no se determina. *2* Se emplea como sujeto gramatical de los verbos impersonales, como sujeto expletivo y como atributo indeterminado. En todos estos casos no se traduce: ~ *rains*, llueve; ~ *is easy to say*, es fácil decir; *that is* ~, eso es; *who is* ~?, ¿quién es?

**Italian** (itæ·lian) *adj.-s.* italiano.

**Italic** (itæ·lik) *adj.* itálico. *2 pl.* IMPR. letra itálica, bastardilla o cursiva.

**italicize (to)** (itæ·lisaiš) *tr.* poner en bastardilla. *2* subrayar, recalcar.

**Italy** (i·tali) *n. pr.* GEOGR. Italia.
**itch** (ich) *s.* MED. sarna. *2* picazón, picor, comezón, prurito. *3* comezón, deseo. *4* ZOOL. ~ *mite*, arador de la sarna.
**itch (to)** *intr.* sentir picor, picazón, comezón, prurito. *2* tener comezón o deseo [de], rabiar [por]. *3 tr.* picar, producir picazón o comezón.
**itching** (i·ching) *adj.* que siente o da comezón. *2 s.* ITCH. 2 y 3.
**itchy** (i·chi) *adj.* sarnoso. *2* que siente o da comezón.
**item** (ai·tøm) *adv.* item. *2 s.* partida [de una cuenta] artículo, elemento [de una enumeración]. *3* fam. punto, detalle, particular. *4* noticia, suelto.
**itemize (to)** (-aiš) *tr.* detallar, especificar, pormenorizar.
**iterate (to)** (i·tøreit) *tr.* iterar, repetir, reiterar.
**iteration** (-ei·shøn) *s.* iteración.
**iterative** (i·tørativ) *adj.* iterativo. *2* GRAM. frecuentativo.

**itinerant** (aiti·nørant) *adj.* que viaja, ambulante, errante. *2 s.* viandante.
**itinerary** (-reri) *adj.-s.* itinerario. *2 s.* relación de un viaje. *3* guía [de viajeros].
**itinerate (to)** (-reit) *intr.* viajar.
**its** (its) *adj.-pron. pos.* su, sus, suyo, suyos [de él, de ella, de ello, cuando les corresponde estar representados por el pron. neutro IT. ].
**it's** contracción de IT IS.
**itself** (itse·lf) *pron.* él mismo, ella misma, ello mismo, sí, sí mismo, mismo [aplicado a cosas inanimadas, a niños de teta y a animales cuyo sexo no se determina].
**I've** (aiv) contracción de I HAVE.
**ivied** (ai·vid) *adj.* cubierto de hiedra.
**ivory** (ai·vøri) *s.* marfil. *2* objeto de marfil. *3 pl.* teclas del piano. *4* bolas de billar. *5* dados [para jugar]. *6* fam. dientes. *7 adj.* de marfil, ebúrneo.
**ivy** (ai·vi) *s.* BOT. hiedra, yedra.
**izard** (i·šø<sup>r</sup>d) *s.* ZOOL. gamuza de los Pirineos.

# J

**J, j** (dȳei) s. J, j, décima letra del alfabeto inglés.
**jab** (dȳæb) s. pinchazo, hurgonazo.
**jab (to)** tr. pinchar, picar, hurgonear. ¶ Pret. y p.
p.: *jabbed;* ger.: *-bbing.*
**jabber** (dȳæ·bø^r) s. cháchara, charla. 2 chapurreo.
**jabber (to)** intr. charlar, parlotear. 2 tr. farfullar.
3 chapurrear.
**jabot** (dȳæbo·) s. VEST. chorrera.
**jacaranda** (dȳækaræ·nda) s. BOT. jacaranda.
**jacinth** (dȳei·sinz) s. MINER. jacinto, circón.
**Jack** (dȳæk) n. pr. fam. Juan, Juanito.
**jack** s. hombre; mozo; marinero. 2 sota [naipe]. 3
macho de algunos animales; asno, burro. 4 MEC.
gato, cric. 5 boliche [bola pequeña]. 6 torno [de
asador]. 7 sacabotas. 8 jaquemar. 9 RADIO., TE-
LEF. clavija de conexión. 10 MAR. bandera de
proa. 11 fam. ~ tar, marinero. 12 ~ towel, toalla
sin fin colgada de un rodillo. 13 every man ~,
todos sin excepción. 14 pl. juego de los cantillos.
**jack (to)** tr. [con up] alzar [con gato o cric]. 2 subir
[precios, salarios, etc.].
**jackal** (dȳæ·kal) s. ZOOL. chacal.
**jackanapes** (-aneips) s. mequetrefe.
**jackass** (-æs) s. ZOOL. y fig. asno, burro.
**jackboots** (-buts) s. botas altas y fuertes.
**jackdaw** (-do) s. ORN. chova.
**jacket** (-it) s. chaqueta; americana; cazadora
[prenda]. 2 camisa, cubierta, envoltura. 3 sobrecubierta [de libro].
**jacket (to)** tr. poner chaqueta, cubierta, etc., a.
**jackhammer** (-jæmø^r) s. MEC. martillo perforador.
**jack-in-the-box** s. muñeco en una caja de resorte.
**jackknife** (-naif) s. navaja de bolsillo. 2 NAT. salto
de carpa.
**Jack-of-all-trades** s. persona que sirve para muchos oficios.
**jack-o'-lantern** s. fuego fatuo.
**jackscrew** (-skru) s. MEC. cric o gato de tornillo.
**jackstraw** (-stro) s. efigie de paja. 2 pelagatos. 3
pajita [para jugar]. 4 pl. juego de las pajitas.
**Jacob** (dȳei·køb) n. pr. Jaime, Jacobo. 2 Jacob.
**Jacobean** (dȳeikøbi·an) adj. de Jacobo I de Inglaterra o de su reinado.
**Jacobin** (dȳæ·købin) s. jacobino. 2 (con min.) pichón capuchino.
**Jacobite** (-bait) adj.-s. jacobita.
**Jacob's ladder** s. BIB. escalera de Jacob. 2 MAR. escala de jarcia.

**Jacob's-ladder** s. BOT. polemonio. 2 BOT. sello de
Salomón.
**jaconet** (dȳæ·konet) s. chaconá [tela].
**jade** (dȳeid) s. MINER. jade. 2 rocín, jamelgo. 3 mala
pécora; mujerzuela. adj. verde.
**jade (to)** tr. cansar, agotar. 2 estragar, hastiar. 3
intr. cansarse, desalentarse.
**jag** (dȳæg) s. diente, punta, mella, corte irregular
[esp. en el borde de una cosa]. 2 onda o punta
colgante; cuchillada [en un vestido].
**jag (to)** tr. dentar, mellar, hacer cortes irregulares
[esp. en el borde]; 2 hacer cuchilladas [en un
vestido]. ¶ Pret. y p. p.: *jagged;* ger.: *-gging.*
**jagged** (-id) adj. dentado, mellado, cortado irregularmente en el borde.
**jaguar** (dȳa·gua^r) s. ZOOL. jaguar.
**jail** (dȳeil) s. cárcel, prisión, calabozo: *fever,* MED.
tifus.
**jail (to)** tr. encarcelar, meter en la cárcel.
**jailbird** (-bø^rd) s. fam. preso. 2 delincuente habitual.
**jailer** (-ø^r) s. carcelero.
**jalap** (dȳæ·lap) s. BOT., FARM. jalapa.
**jalopy** (dȳala·pi) s. fam. carraca, fotingo [auto-
móvil o avión viejo].
**jalousie** (dȳæluši·) s. persiana.
**jam** (dȳæm) s. compota, confitura, mermelada. 2
apretura, apiñamiento. 3 atasco; obstrucción;
embotellamiento [del tráfico]. 4 (E.U.) aprieto,
situación difícil.
**jam (to)** tr. apretar, estrechar, apiñar. 2 estrujar,
machucar. 3 atascar, obstruir. 4 meter o introducir apretando, a la fuerza. 5 RADIO. perturbar
con interferencias. 6 to ~ on the brakes, frenar
de golpe. 7 intr. agolparse, apiñarse. 8 atascarse. ¶ Pret. y p. p.: *jammed;* ger.: *-mming.*
**Jamaica** (dȳamei·ka) n. pr. GEOGR. Jamaica.
**jamb, jambe** (dȳæm) s. jamba. 2 ARM. espinillera.
**jamboree** (dȳæmbøri·) s. pop. jolgorio, fiesta. 2
reunión de muchachos exploradores.
**James** (dȳeims) n. pr. Jaime.
**Jane** (dȳein) n. pr. Juana.
**jangle** (dȳæ·ngøl) s. charla, parloteo. 2 sonido discordante, cencerreo.
**jangle (to)** intr. charlar, parlotear. 2 altercar, disputar. 3 sonar de un modo discordante, cencerrear.
**janitor** (dȳæ·nitø^r) s. portero, conserje.

**janizary** (dӯæ·nišæri) s. jenízaro.
**Jansenism** (dӯæ·nsønišm) s. jansenismo.
**January** (dӯæ·niueri) s. enero.
**Janus** (dӯæ·nøs) n. pr. MIT. Jano.
**Jap** (dӯæp) abrev. de JAPAN y JAPANESE.
**Japan** (dӯapæ·n) n. pr. GEOGR. Japón.
**japan** s. barniz, laca, charol; laca japonesa.
**japan (to)** tr. barnizar [esp. con laca]. 2 charolar. ¶ Pret. y p. p.: *japanned*; ger.: *-nning*.
**Japanese** (dӯæpanı·š) adj.-s. japonés: ~ *lantern*, farolillo a la veneciana.
**jape** (dӯeip) s. broma, burla.
**jape (to)** tr. embromar, burlar.
**Japheth** (dӯæ·fez) n. pr. Jafet.
**japonica** (dӯæpa·nika) s. BOT. camelia japonesa. 2 BOT. membrillo japonés.
**jar** (dӯaʳ) s. jarra, tarro. 2 sonido áspero, discordante; chirrido. 3 vibración, choque, sacudida. 4 efecto desagradable, irritante. 5 desacuerdo, desavenencia. 6 *on the* ~, entreabierto, entornado.
**jar (to)** intr. sonar de un modo áspero o discordante. 2 vibrar, trepidar, chocar [con sonido áspero]. 3 producir un efecto desagradable, irritante. 4 discordar, chocar, no armonizar. 5 reñir, disputar. 6 tr. poner en tarro. 7 hacer sonar de un modo áspero; sacudir, hacer vibrar o trepidar. ¶ Pret. y p. p.: *jarred*; ger.: *rring*.
**jardiniere** (dӯa·dini·øʳ) s. jardinera [para plantas]. 2 jarrón [pará flores].
**jargon** (dӯa·ʳgøn) s. jerga, jerigonza. 2 monserga.
**jasmine** (dӯæ·smin) s. BOT. jazmín.
**Jasper** (dӯæ·spøʳ) n. pr. Gaspar.
**jasper** s. MINER. jaspe.
**jaundice** (dӯo·ndis) s. MED. ictericia. 2 mal humor, envidia, celos.
**jaundice (to)** tr. MED. causar ictericia. 2 amargar, predisponer, ofuscar.
**jaunt** (dӯont) s. paseo, excursión, caminata.
**jaunt (to)** intr. pasear, hacer una excursión.
**jaunty** (-i) adj. vivo, garboso, airoso. 2 elegante, vistoso.
**javelin** (dӯæ·vlin) s. jabalina, venablo.
**jaw** (dӯo) s. ZOOL. mandíbula, quijada. 2 MEC. quijada, mordaza; horquilla, boca. 3 palabrería; disputa: *hold your* ~*!*, ¡cállese ya! 4 *pl*. boca, entrada [de un valle, desfiladero, etc.]. 5 fig. garras, poder. 6 pop. la boca.
**jaw (to)** tr. reñir, regañar, sermonear. 2 intr. charlar, dar la lata.
**jawbone** (-boun) s. quijada, mandíbula.
**jawbreaker** (-breikøʳ) s. fam. palabra de difícil pronunciación, trabalenguas.
**jay** (dӯei) s. ORN. arrendajo.
**jaywalker** (-uokoʳ) s. peatón imprudente que no obedece las reglas de la circulación.
**jazz** (dӯæš) s. jazz: ~ *band*, orquesta de jazz. 2 pop. viveza, animación.
**jazz (to)** tr. transformar en jazz, poner en música de jazz.
**jealous** (dӯe·løs) adj. celoso [de sus derechos, etc.]. 2 celoso [que tiene celos]; envidioso. 3 receloso.
**jealousy** (-i) s. celos. 2 envidia. 3 recelo, desconfianza, vigilancia.
**Jean** (dӯın) n. pr. Juana.
**jean** (dӯın o dӯen) s. TEJ. dril. 2 *pl*. pantalones de dril, guardapolvo de dril.
**jeep** (dӯıp) s. jip, pequeño automóvil militar.
**jeer** (dӯi·øʳ) s. burla, pitorreo, mofa, befa.
**jeer (to)** tr.-intr. burlarse, mofarse de, befar.
**Jeff** (dӯef) n. pr. abrev. de GEOFFREY.

**Jehovah** (dӯijou·va) n. pr. Jehová.
**jejune** (dӯi·dӯun) adj. falto, escaso. 2 seco, árido. 3 insípido, insustancial.
**jejunum** (dӯidӯu·røm) s. ANAT. yeyuno.
**jellied** (dӯe·lid) adj. gelatinoso.
**jelly** (dӯe·li) s. jalea. 2 gelatina; substancia gelatinosa.
**jelly (to)** intr. convertirse en jalea o gelatina.
**jellyfish** (-fish) s. ZOOL. medusa, aguamar.
**jennet** (dӯe·nit) s. jaca española. 2 burra, jumenta.
**Jennie, Jenny** (dӯe·ni) n. pr. dim. de JANE.
**jenny** s. ant. máquina de hilar. 2 MEC. grúa locomóvil. 3 *jenny* o ~ *ass*, asna, burra.
**jeopardize (to)** (dӯe·paʳdaiš) tr. arriesgar, exponer, comprometer, poner en peligro.
**jeopardy** (-i) s. riesgo, peligro, exposición.
**jerboa** (dӯøʳbou·a) s. ZOOL. gerbo, jerbo.
**jeremiad** (dӯerimai·æd) s. jeremiada.
**Jeremiah** (dӯerimai·a) n. pr. Jeremías.
**Jericho** (dӯe·rikou) n. pr. GEOGR. HIST. Jericó.
**jerk** (dӯøʳk) s. tirón, sacudida, movimiento brusco: *by jerks*, a sacudidas. 2 salto, repullo, respingo. 3 tic, espasmo muscular.
**jerk (to)** tr. sacudir, traquetear, dar tirones o sacudidas a; mover bruscamente, a tirones o sacudidas. 2 atasajar [la carne]: *jerked beef*, tasajo, *charqui. 3 intr. moverse a sacudidas; avanzar dando tumbos.
**jerkin** (-in) s. justillo, jubón.
**jerky** (-i) adj. accidentado [camino]. 2 desigual [estilo]. 3 que marcha dando sacudidas.
**Jerome** (dӯirou·m o dӯe·rom) n. pr. m. Jerónimo.
**Jerry** (dӯe·ri) n. pr. dim de JEREMIAH.
**jerry** s. fam. vaso de noche.
**jerry-build** adj. mal construido, hecho con malos materiales.
**Jersey** (dӯøʳsi) n. pr. GEOGR. Jersey. 2 (con min.) estambre fino. 3 jersey.
**Jerusalem** (dӯiru·salem) n. pr. GEOGR., HIST. Jerusalén. 2 BOT. ~ *artichoke*, aguaturma, cotufa.
**jess** (dӯes) s. CETR. pihuela.
**jessamine** (dӯe·samin) s. BOT. jazmín.
**jest** (dӯest) s. broma, burla, chanza, chiste: *in* ~, en broma. 2 cosa de risa.
**jest (to)** intr. bromear, burlarse, chancearse.
**jester** (-øʳ) s. bromista. 2 gracioso, bufón.
**Jesuit** (dӯe·šuit) s. jesuita.
**Jesus** (dӯi·šøs) n. pr. Jesús. 2 *Jesus Christ*, Jesucristo.
**jet** (dӯet) s. MINER. azabache. 2 chorro, vena, surtidor: ~ *propulsion*, propulsión a chorro; ~ *plane*, avión de reacción. 3 chorretada. 4 caño, boquilla, mechero: *gas* ~, mechero de gas.
**jet (to)** intr. salir, brotar o manar en chorro. 2 tr. lanzar o arrojar en chorro. ¶ Pret. y p. p.: *jetted*; ger.: *-tting*.
**jet-black** adj. negro como el azabache.
**jetsam** (-sam) s. DER. MAR. echazón. 2 pecio. 3 fig. cosa desechada por inútil.
**jettison (to)** (dӯe·tisøn) tr. DER. MAR. hacer echazón de. 2 echar, desechar [lo que estorba].
**jetton** (dӯe·tøn) s. ficha [de juego, etc.].
**jetty** (dӯe·ti) s. malecón, escollera, rompeolas, dique. 2 muelle, desembarcadero. 3 adj. JETBLACK.
**Jew** (dӯu) adj.-s. judío, israelita.
**jewel** (-øl) s. joya, alhaja, joyel. 2 gema, piedra preciosa. 3 rubí [de reloj].
**jewel (to)** tr. enjoyar. 2 adornar con piedras preciosas. ¶ Pret. y p. p.: *jeweled* o *-lled*; p. a.: *-ling* o *-lling*.

**jewel (l) er** (-øʳ) *s.* joyero, platero: *jeweler's shop*, joyería, platería.
**jewellery, jewelry** (-ri) *s.* joyas, pedrería; aderezo.
**Jewess** (dÿu·is) *s.* judía, israelita.
**Jewish** (dÿu·ish) *adj.* judaico, judío. *2* ajudiado.
**Jewry** (dÿu·ri) *n. pr.* GEOGR. Judea. *2 s.* judería, barrio judío.
**Jews'-harp** *s.* MÚS. birimbao.
**jib** (dÿib) *s.* MAR. foque: ~ *boom*, botalón de foque. *2* brazo, aguilón [de grúa].
**jib (to)** *intr.* MAR. moverse bruscamente una vela de cuchillo cuando se vira. *2* repropiarse [el caballo]. ¶ Pret. y p. p.: *jibbed;* ger.: *-bbing.*
**jibe (to)** (dÿaib) *tr.-intr.* TO JIB. *2* TO GIBE. *3 intr.* (E.U.) concordar, pegar [dos cosas].
**jiffy** (dÿi·fi) *s.* fam. instante, periquete, santiamén.
**jig** (dÿig) *s.* MÚS., DANZA giga, jiga. *2* anzuelo de cuchara. *3* plantilla [para taladrar, etc.]. *4* MIN. criba hidráulica. *5* ~ *saw*, segueta, sierra de vaivén. *6 the* ~ *is up*, se acabó todo, no hay más esperanza.
**jig (to)** *tr.-intr.* bailar una jiga. *2* mover o moverse de arriba a abajo y de abajo arriba, rítmicamente, con sacudidas. *3* cortar con segueta. *4* pescar con anzuelo de cuchara.
**jigger** (-øʳ) *s.* bailador de jiga. *2* MEC. cualquier aparato o utensilio con movimiento rápido de vaivén. *3* ELECT. transformador de oscilaciones. *4* anzuelo de cuchara. *5* MAR. contramesana. *6* MAR. pequeña embarcación. *7* ENT. nigua. *8* ZOOL. garrapata. *9* fam. cosa, chisme.
**jiggle** (dÿi·gøl) *tr.-intr.* mover o moverse a sacudidas o tirones, moverse de un lado a otro.
**jigsaw puzzle** (dÿi·gso) *s.* rompecabezas.
**jilt (to)** (dÿilt) *tr.* despedir o dejar plantado [a un novio]. *2 intr.* coquetear.
**Jim** (dÿim) *n. pr. dim.* de JAMES. *2* ~ *Crow*, fam. y desp. (E.U.) negro.
**Jimmy** (-i) *n. pr. dim.* de JAMES.
**jimmy** *s.* palanqueta [de ladrón].
**jingle** (dÿi·ngøl) *s.* tintineo, cascabeleo, sonido metálico. *2* rima o verso pueril. *3* sonaja [del pandero]; cascabel.
**jingle (to)** *intr.* tintinear, cascabelear; sonar [las monedas, llaves, etc.]. *2* rimar. *3 tr.* hacer sonar o tintinear.
**jingo** (dÿi·ngou) *adj.-s.* jingoísta. *3* interj. *by* ~*!*, ¡caramba!, ¡por Dios!
**jingoism** (-išm) *s.* jingoísmo, patriotería.
**jinnee** (dÿini) *s.* genio [en la mitología mahometana].
**jitters** (dÿi·tøʳš) *s. pl.* fam. (E.U.) agitación, inquietud, nerviosismo: *to give the* ~, poner nervioso, volver loco.
**jiujitsu** (dÿudÿi·tsu) *s.* JUJITSU.
**Joan** (dÿou·n o dÿo·an) *n. pr. f.* Juana.
**job** (dÿab) *s.* obra, trabajo, tarea, quehacer, cometido: *on the* ~, fam. en su puesto, atendiendo a sus obligaciones. *2* empleo, ocupación: *to be out of* ~, estar sin trabajo. *3* asunto, negocio: *bad* ~, mal asunto, mal negocio. *5* destajo: *by the* ~, a destajo. *6* agiotaje. *7* chanchullo. *8* IMPR. remiendo.
**job (to)** *tr.-intr.* negociar como corredor o intermediario. *2* especular en fondos públicos. *3* hacer o trabajar a destajo. *4* hacer chapuzas. *5* hacer chanchullos. *6 tr.* subarrendar [un trabajo]. *7* pinchar, picar, herir ligeramente. ¶ Pret. y p. p.: *jobbed;* ger.: *-bbing.*
**jobber** (-bøʳ) *s.* COM. intermediario, corredor. *2*

destajista. *3* (Ingl.) agiotista. *4* chanchullero, traficante político.
**jobholder** (-jouldøʳ) *s.* empleado, burócrata.
**jobless** (-lis) *adj.* desocupado, sin empleo.
**Job's-tears** *s.* BOT. lágrimas de David o de Job.
**jockey** (dÿa·ki) *s.* DEP. jockey. *2* (E.U.) chalán. *3* maulero, tramposo, engañador.
**jockey (to)** *tr.-intr.* engañar, embaucar. *2 intr.* maniobrar [para obtener una ventaja].
**jocose** (dÿoukou·s) *adj.* jocoso. *2* bromista, chancero.
**jocosity** (dÿouka·siti) *s.* jocosidad. *2* broma, chanza.
**jocular** (dÿa·kiulaʳ) *adj.* jocoso. *2* chancero. *3* alegre, jovial.
**jocularity** (dÿakiulæ·riti) *s.* jocosidad. *2* jovialidad.
**jocund** (dÿa·kønd) *adj.* jocundo. *2* animado, jovial.
**jocundity** (dÿakø·nditi) *s.* jocundidad, jovialidad.
**jodhpurs** (dÿa·dpøʳs) *s. pl.* pantalón de montar.
**Joe** (dÿou) *n. pr. dim.* de JOSEPH.
**jog** (dÿag) *s.* empujoncito, golpecito, sacudida ligera. *2* estímulo [para la memoria]. *3* trote o paso corto.
**jog (to)** *tr.* empujar. *2* dar un golpecito, tocar con el codo. *3* excitar suavemente; estimular [la memoria]. *4* mover poco a poco. *5 intr. to* ~ *on* o *along*, andar despacio o al trote corto. ¶ Pret. y p. p.: *jogged;* ger.: *-gging.*
**joggle** (dÿa·gøl) *s.* diente, muesca. *2* sacudida.
**joggle (to)** *tr.* unir o asegurar con diente y muesca. *2* dar una sacudida ligera. *3 intr.* avanzar o moverse a sacudidas, vacilar.
**John** (dÿan) *n. pr.* Juan. *2* ~ *Bull*, el inglés típico; el pueblo inglés. *3* ~ *Doe*, fulano de tal. *4* ICT. ~ *Dory*, gallo, pez de San Pedro.
**Johnny, Johnnie** (dÿa·ni) *n. pr. dim.* de JOHN.
**join** (dÿoin) *s.* punto de unión o encuentro.
**join (to)** *tr.* unir, juntar. *2* acoplar, ensamblar. *3* añadir, agregar. *4* asociar. *5* unirse, agregarse, incorporarse a; ingresar en; abrazar [una causa]. *6* aunarse. *7* trabar [batalla]. *8* desaguar en. *9* tocar o lindar con. *10 intr.* unirse, juntarse, asociarse. *11* confluir [dos ríos]. *12 to* ~ *in*, tomar parte en.
**joiner** (-øʳ) *s.* el que une o junta. *2* ensamblador, montador. *3* ebanista, carpintero.
**joinery** (-i) *s.* ebanistería; carpintería de taller.
**joint** (dÿoint) *s.* ANAT. coyuntura, articulación, nudillo: *out of* ~, dislocado; fig. desbarajustado. *2* junta, juntura, unión, articulación, empalme, ensambladura. *3* ALB. llaga. *4* BOT. nudo, axila; entrenudo. *5* ZOOL. artejo, artículo. *6* CARN. trozo de carne. *7* ENCUD. cartivana. *8* fam. casa, establecimiento.
*9 adj.* unido, mixto, común, mancomunado, solidario, indiviso: ~ *committee*, comisión mixta; ~ *consent*, común acuerdo; ~ *stock*, capital social; fondo en común. *10* copartícipe, co-: ~ *heir*, coheredero. *11* de articulación, empalme, etc.: ~ *box*, ELECT. caja de empalmes. *12* BOT. ~ *fir*, belcho.
**joint (to)** *tr.* unir, articular, ajustar, ensamblar. *2* descoyuntar, cortar por las coyunturas. *3* CARN. destazar. *4 intr.* articularse.
**jointed** (-id) *adj.* articulado [que tiene articulaciones]. *2* nudoso.
**jointly** (-li) *adv.* juntamente, conjuntamente.
**joint-stock company** *s.* compañía por acciones, sociedad anónima.
**joist** (dÿoist) *s.* ARQ. viga, vigueta.

**joke** (dȳouk) *s.* chiste, chascarrillo; chanza, broma: *to play a ~ on,* gastar una broma a; *in ~,* de broma, por chanza.

**joke (to)** *intr.* bromear, hablar en broma, chancearse. *2 fam.* gastar bromas: *joking aside, no joking,* bromas aparte, hablando en serio.

**joker** (dȳou·kø<sup>r</sup>) *s.* bromista, chancero, guasón. *2* comodín [naipe].

**jollity** (dȳa·lɪtɪ) *s.* alegría, animación, regocijo. *2* diversión, fiesta.

**jolly** (dȳa·lɪ) *adj.* alegre, animado, divertido, jovial. *2 fam.* estupendo; bueno, grande. *3 MAR. ~ boat,* chinchorro. *4 adv.* muy, sumamente.

**jolly (to)** *tr.* animar, alegrar. *2* candonguear, dar coba a, seguir el humor a.

**jolt** (dȳoult) *s.* traqueteo, tumbo, sacudida. *2* golpe, choque.

**jolt (to)** *intr.* dar tumbos o sacudidas. *2 tr.* traquetear, sacudir.

**Jonah** (ȳou·na) *n. pr.* Jonás. *2 m.* fig. cenizo.

**Jonathan** (dȳa·nazan) *n. pr.* Jonatán.

**jongleur** (dȳa·nglø<sup>r</sup>) *s.* juglar, trovador.

**jonquil** (dȳa·nkuil) *s. BOT.* junquillo.

**Jordan** (dȳo·<sup>r</sup>dan) *n. pr. GEOGR.* Jordán [río]. *2 GEOG.* Jordania.

**Joseph** (dȳou·šef) *n. pr.* José.

**Josephine** (-šøfin) *n. pr.* Josefina.

**josh (to)** (dȳash) *tr.* fam. (E.U.) embromar, burlarse de. *2 intr.* fam. (E.U.) chancearse.

**Joshua** (dȳa·shua) *n. pr.* Josué.

**joss** (dȳas) *s.* ídolo chino.

**jostle** (dȳa·søl) *s.* empujones, empellones. *2* choque.

**jostle (to)** *tr.* empujar, empellar, dar codazos a. *2* meter a empellones. *3* hacer chocar. *4 intr.* empujarse, atropellarse. *5* avanzar a fuerza de empujones o codazos. *6* chocar, encontrarse.

**jot** (dȳat) *s.* jota, ápice, pizca, tilde.

**jot (to)** escribir de prisa. *2 to ~ down,* apuntar, anotar. ¶ Pret. y p. p.: *jotted;* ger.: *-tting.*

**joule** (dȳaul o dȳul) *s. ELECT.* julio.

**jounce** (dȳauns) *s.* sacudida, traqueteo.

**jounce (to)** *tr.* sacudir, traquetear. *2 intr.* botar, dar tumbos.

**journal** (dȳø·<sup>r</sup>nal) *s.* diario, periódico. *2* diario [relación día por día]. *3 COM.* diario. *4 MEC.* gorrón, espiga.

**journalese** (dȳø<sup>r</sup>nali·š) *s.* lenguaje periodístico.

**journalism** (dȳø·<sup>r</sup>nališm) *s.* periodismo.

**journey** (dȳø·<sup>r</sup>ni) *s.* viaje; camino, jornada. *2* tránsito, pasaje.

**journey (to)** *intr.* viajar. *2 tr.* viajar por; recorrer en viaje.

**journeyman** (-mæn) *s.* jornalero. *2* oficial [de un oficio].

**joust** (dȳøst o dȳaust) *s.* justa. *2 pl.* torneo.

**joust (to)** *intr.* justar.

**Jove** (dȳouv) *n. pr. MIT.* Jove: *by ~!,* ¡por Dios!

**jovial** (dȳou·vial) *adj.* jovial, alegre, fetivo.

**joviality** (dȳouviæ·liti) *s.* jovialidad, alegría.

**jowl** (dȳaul) *s.* carrillo. *2* quijada. *3* papada [de res].

**joy** (dȳoi) *s.* gozo, júbilo, regocijo, alegría.

**joy (to)** *tr.* alegrar. *2 intr.* alegrarse, regocijarse.

**joyful** (-ful) *adj.* jubiloso, gozoso, alegre.

**joyless** (-lis) *adj.* triste, sin alegría.

**joyous** (-øs) *adj.* alegre, gozoso.

**jubilant** (dȳu·bilant) *adj.* jubiloso, alborozado.

**jubilate (to)** (-eit) *intr.* jubilar, alegrarse.

**jubilation** (-ei·šøn) *s.* jubilación, exultación, exclamación de júbilo.

**jubilee** (dȳu·bilɪ) *s.* júbilo. *2* jubileo. *3* aniversario, quincuagésimo aniversario.

**Judaic (al** (dȳudei·k(al) *adj.* judaico, judío.

**Judaism** (dȳu·diišm) *s.* judaísmo.

**Judaize (to)** (dȳu·diaiš) *s.* judaizar.

**Judas** (dȳu·das) *n. pr.* y fig. Judas; *~ tree,* BOT. ciclamor, árbol de Judas. *2* (con min.). mirilla de puerta.

**Judea** (dȳudi·a) *n. pr. GEOGR. HIST.* Judea.

**judge** (dȳødȳ) *s.* juez, magistrado: *~ advocate,* auditor de guerra o de marina. *2* juez, perito, conocedor.

**judge (to)** *tr.-intr. DER., FIL.* juzgar. *2* juzgar, creer, estimar, deducir, suponer: *judging by,* o *from,* a juzgar por.

**judgement, judgment** (-mønt) *s.* decisión, fallo, sentencia. *2* juicio, opinión, dictamen. *3* juicio, criterio, discernimiento. *4* castigo de Dios. *5 LÓG., FIL., TEOL.* juicio: *the (Last) Judgment,* el juicio final.

**judicature** (dȳu·dikachu<sup>r</sup>) *s.* judicatura.

**judicial** (dȳudi·šal) *adj.* judicial. *2* judiciario. *3* crítico, apto para juzgar.

**judiciary** (-shiæri) *adj.* judicial. *2 s.* administración de justicia, judicatura.

**judicious** (-shøs) *adj.* juicioso, de buen sentido, discreto, atinado.

**judiciousness** (-nis) *s.* juicio, cordura, buen sentido, discernimiento.

**Judith** (dȳu·diz) *n. pr.* Judit.

**jug** (dȳøg) *s.* jarro, cántaro. *2* [E.U.] botija. *3* pop. cárcel, chirona.

**jug (to)** *tr.* coc. estofar. *2 fam.* encarcelar. ¶ Pret. y p. p.: *jugged;* ger.: *-gging.*

**juggle** (dȳø·gøl) *s.* juego de manos, escamoteo. *2* engaño, trampa.

**juggle (to)** *intr.* hacer juegos de manos o juegos malabares. *2* hacer trampas, engañar. *3 to ~ away,* escamotear.

**juggler** (dȳø·glø<sup>r</sup>) *s.* juglar, prestidigitador, malabarista. *2* tramposo, escamoteador.

**jugular** (dȳø·giula<sup>r</sup>) *adj.-s. ANAT.* yugular.

**jugulate (to)** (-leit) *tr.* cortar, detener una enfermedad, etc.

**juice** (dȳu·s) *s.* zumo; jugo. *2 fig.* jugo, substancia. *3 pop.* electricidad, gasolina, etc., como fuerza motriz.

**juicy** (dȳu·si) *adj.* jugoso, zumoso. *2* picante, divertido.

**jujitsu** (dȳudȳi·tsu) *s.* jiu-jitsu.

**jujube** (dȳu·dȳub) *s. BOT.* yuyuba, azufaifa.

**juke box** (dȳuk) *s.* gramófono, tragaperras.

**julep** (dȳu·lip) *s. FARM.* julepe. *2 mint ~,* refresco alcohólico con hojas de hierbabuena.

**Julian** (dȳu·lian) *n. pr.* Julián. *2* Juliano.

**julienne** (dȳulie·n) *s.* sopa Juliana.

**Julius** (dȳu·liøs) *n. pr.* Julio.

**July** (dȳulai·) *s.* julio [mes].

**jumble** (dȳø·mbøl) *s.* mezcla, revoltillo, confusión. *2* especie de rosquilla [dulce].

**jumble (to)** *tr.* emburujar, amontonar o mezclar confusamente. *2 intr.* mezclarse, juntarse, moverse de un modo confuso o agitado.

**jumbo** (dȳø·mbou) *adj.* enorme, grande [en su línea]. *2 s.* fam. elefante.

**jump** (dȳømp) *s.* salto, brinco. *2* lanzamiento [en paracaídas]. *3* sacudida, movimiento convulsivo. *4* transición brusca, salto, omisión. *5 to be on the ~,* andar de aquí para allá, trafagar.

**jump (to)** *intr.* saltar, brincar, dar saltos; dar un salto, una sacudida: *to ~ for joy,* brincar de gozo. *2* lanzarse [en paracaídas]. *3* subir repentinamente [los precios]. *4* concordar, coincidir. *5 to ~ at,* apresurarse a aprovechar o aceptar. *6 to ~ on one,* regañar, criticar, poner como nuevo. *7 to ~ to a conclusion,* hacer una deducción precipitada. *8 tr.* saltar [salvar de un salto]. *9* hacer saltar [a un niño, un caballo, etc.]. *10* sobresaltar, hacer dar un salto, un repullo. *11* FERROC. *to ~ the track,* descarrilar.

**jumper** (-øʳ) *s.* saltador. *2* blusa [de obrero, de marinero]. *3* jersey. *4* ELECT. alambre de cierre. *5 pl.* mono [para niños].

**jumpy** (dÿø·mpi) *adj.* saltón, que salta. *2* nervioso, excitable en extremo.

**junction** (dÿø·nkshøn) *s.* unión, reunión. *2* punto de unión o reunión; confluencia. *3* FERROC. empalme. *4* cosa que une.

**juncture** (dÿø·nkchøʳ) *s.* junta, juntura. *2* articulación, conexión. *3* coyuntura, sazón, estado de cosas, momento crítico, ocasión.

**June** (dÿun) *s.* junio.

**jungle** (dÿø·ngøl) *s.* selva virgen, manigua. *2* matorral, espesura, maraña.

**junior** (dÿu·niøʳ) *adj.* menor, más joven, menos antiguo, hijo: *X. X. ~, X. X.* hijo; *the ~ partner,* el socio menos antiguo. *2* para jóvenes. *3 s.* joven. *4* junior [religioso].

**juniper** (dÿu·nipøʳ) *s.* BOT. junípero, enebro.

**junk** (dÿønk) *s.* junco [embarcación]. *2* desechos, desperdicios de vidrio, papel, cuerda, etc.; chatarra. *3* MAR. trozos de cabo viejo para hacer estopa, etc. *4* fig. desecho, borra, basura. *5 ~ room,* trastera, leonera.

**junket** (dÿø·nkit) *s.* COC. manjar de leche, cuajo y azúcar. *2* banquete, francachela; jira.

**junket (to)** *intr.* ir de jira o de jolgorio.

**junkman** (dÿø·nkmæn) *s.* comerciante en desperdicios; chatarrero.

**Juno** (dÿu·nou) *n. pr.* MIT. Juno.

**junto** (dÿø·ntou) *s.* camarilla.

**Jupiter** (dÿu·pitøʳ) *n. pr.* MIT., ASTR. Júpiter.

**Jurassic** (dÿuræ·sik) *adj.-s.* GEOL. jurásico.

**jurel** (dÿure·l) *s.* ICT. jurel.

**juridic(al** (dÿuri·dik(al) *adj.* jurídico. *2* judicial.

**jurisconsult** (dÿuriska·nsølt) *s.* jurisconsulto.

**jurisdicción** (-di·kshøn) *s.* jurisdicción.

**jurisprudence** (-pru·døns) *s.* jurisprudencia.

**jurisprudent** (-prudønt) *s.* jurisperito.

**jurist** (dÿu·rist) *s.* jurista, legista.

**juror** (dÿu·røʳ) *s.* jurado [individuo].

**jury** (dÿu·ri) *s.* DER. jurado [cuerpo e institución]. *2* jurado [de un concurso, etc.].

**juryman** (-møn) *s.* jurado [individuo].

**just** (dÿøst) *adj.* justo, recto, honrado. *2* justiciero, imparcial. *3* justo [arreglado a justicia y razón; merecido]. *4* justo, fiel, exacto, preciso. *5* verdadero, bien fundado. *6 adv.* justamente, cabalmente, precisamente: *~ so,* eso mismo. *7* no más que, sólo, nada más; *he is ~ a child,* no es más que un niño. *8* en el mismo instante, poco ha, recién; dentro de un momento; *~ now,* ahora mismo, hace poco; *he has ~ arrived,* acaba de llegar. *9* fam. verdaderamente, muy. *10 ~ about,* casi, bastante, poco más o menos; *11 ~ as,* al tiempo que, en el momento que, cuando, no bien; lo mismo que; semejante a. *12 ~ beyond,* un poco más allá de.

**justice** (dÿø·stis) *s.* justicia: *to do oneself ~,* hacerlo uno lo mejor que pueda, quedar bien. *2* verdad, exactitud. *3* DER. Juez, magistrado: *~ of the peace,* juez de paz.

**justiciary** (dÿø·stisheri) *adj.* judicial. *2 s.* juez, magistrado.

**justifiable** (dÿø·stifaiabøl) *adj.* justificable.

**justification** (dÿøstifikei·shøn) *s.* justificación. *2* descargo, defensa. *3* razón de ser.

**justify (to)** (dÿø·stifai) *tr.* justificar. *2* defender, sincerar. *3* demostrar ser justo o exacto. *4 intr.* DER. justificarse. ¶ Pret. y p. p.: *justified.*

**justly** (dÿø·stli) *adv.* justamente, rectamente. *2* justamente [con justicia o razón; merecidamente]. *3* exactamente, precisamente.

**justness** (-nis) *s.* justicia, equidad. *2* exactitud, propiedad, precisión, corrección.

**jut** (dÿøt) *s.* salidizo, proyección, vuelo, resalto.

**jut (to)** *intr.* [a veces con *out*] salir, sobresalir; proyectarse, extenderse. ¶ Pret. y p. p.: *jutted;* ger.: *-tting.*

**jute** (dÿut) *s.* yute, cáñamo de Indias.

**juvenescence** (dÿuvøne·søns) *s.* rejuvenecimiento.

**juvenile** (dÿu·vønil) *adj.* juvenil, joven. *2* de o para jóvenes o menores. *3 s.* joven, mocito, mocita. *4* TEAT. galancete. *5* libro para niños.

**juvenility** (dÿuvøni·liti) *s.* juventud, carácter juvenil.

**juxtapose (to)** (dÿøkstapou·s) *tr.* yuxtaponer.

**juxtaposition** (-si·shøn) *s.* yuxtaposición, contigüidad.

# K

**K, k** *s.* K, k, undécima letra del alfabeto inglés.
**Kabyle** (*k*abai·l) *s.* cabila.
**Kaffir, Kafir** (kæ·fø<sup>r</sup>) *s.* cafre [de Cafrería].
**kail** (keil) *s.* KALE.
**Kaiser** (kai·šø<sup>r</sup>) *s.* kaiser.
**kaki** (ka·ki) *s.* BOT. caqui, níspero del Japón.
**kale** (keil) *s.* BOT. col, col rizada.
**kaleidoscope** (kalai·døskoup) *s.* calidoscopio.
**kaleidoscopic** (-ka·pik) *adj.* calidoscópico.
**kalends** (kæ·lindš) *s. pl.* CALENDS.
**Kalmuck** (kæ·lmøk) *adj.-s.* calmuco.
**Kanaka** (kæ·naka) *s.* canaco.
**kangaroo** (kængaru·) *s.* ZOOL. canguro.
**Kantian** (kæ·ntian) *adj.* kantiano.
**Kantism** (kæ·ntišm) *s.* kantismo.
**kaolin** (kei·ølin) *s.* caolín.
**kapok** (kei·pak) *s.* capoc, lana de ceiba.
**kappa** (kæ·pa) *s.* kappa [letra griega].
**karakul** (kæ·rakul) *s.* caracul, astracán [piel].
**karat** (kæ·rat) *s.* JOY. quilate.
**karyokinesis** (kærioukinɪ·sis) *s.* BIOL. cariocinesis.
**Kate** (kei·t) *n. pr. f. dim.* de CATHERINE.
**Katherine** (kæ·zørin) *n. pr. f.* CATHERINE.
**kation** (kæ·taion) *s.* CATION.
**katydid** (kei·tidid) *s.* ENT. especie de saltamontes americano.
**kay** (kei) *s.* nombre de la letra *k*.
**kayak** (kai·æk) *s.* canoa de los esquimales.
**keck (to)** (kek) *intr.* arquear; vomitar.
**kedge** (kedɣ) *s.* MAR. anclote.
**keel** (kɪl) *s.* MAR., BOT., ZOOL. quilla.
**keel (to)** *tr.* poner quilla. *2* surcar [el mar]. *3* dar de quilla, voltear. *4 intr. to ~ over*, volcarse; desplomarse, desmayarse.
**keelhaul (to)** (kɪ·ljol) *tr.* MAR. pasar por debajo de la quilla [castigo].
**keelson** (ke·lsøn) *s.* MAR. sobrequilla.
**keen** (kɪn) *adj.* agudo, afilado. *2* agudo, vivo, intenso, fuerte. *3* agudo, sutil, perspicaz. *4* mordaz, incisivo. *5* vehemente. *6* ansioso, deseoso. *7* muy interesado [por]; entusiasta. *8* (E.U.) lindo, agradable.
**keenness** (kɪ·nnis) *s.* agudeza, viveza. *2* sutileza, perspicacia. *3* aspereza. *4* ansia, vehemencia, entusiasmo.
**keep** (kɪp) *s.* mantenimiento, subsistencia. *2* fortaleza, torreón. *3* fam. (E.U.) *for keeps*, para siempre, para quedarse con ello.

**keep (to)** *tr.* guardar, tener guardado. *2* tener, mantener [en un lugar, situación o estado]. *3* cuidar, custodiar, guardar. *4* dirigir, tener [un establecimiento, etc.]. *5* llevar [los libros, una cuenta, un diario, etc.]. *6* mantener, conservar, preservar, defender. *7* mantener, sustentar. *8* tener [criados, caballos, huéspedes, etc.]. *9* detener, impedir. *10* retener, guardar [para sí], quedarse con. *11* callar, ocultar. *12* guardar [silencio, etc.]. *13* observar, cumplir, guardar. *14* atenerse a, seguir, no apartarse de. *15* no moverse de, no salir de: *to ~ one's bed*, guardar cama. *16* celebrar, tener [reunión, sesión, consejo]. *17* hacer [guerra]. *18 to ~ away*, tener alejado, no dejar entrar, venir, etc. *19 to ~ back*, tener a raya; refrenar, reprimir, impedir; retener, reservar [no divulgar]. *20 to ~ company*, acompañar, salir juntos [como novios]. *21 to ~ down*, sujetar, oprimir; reprimir. *22 to ~ from*, guardar de, impedir, no dejar. *23 to ~ in*, no dejar salir; hacer quedar [en la escuela]. *24 to ~ off*, mantener a distancia; no dejar entrar o penetrar. *25 to ~ on*, conservar puesta [una prenda]. *26 to ~ one's head*, no perder la cabeza. *27 to ~ out*, no dejar entrar; excluir. *28 to ~ step*, llevar el paso. *29 to ~ time*, seguir o llevar el compás. *30 to ~ under*, tener sujeto, oprimir. *31 to ~ up*, mantener, sostener; tener levantado [sin irse a la cama].
*32 intr.* mantenerse, sostenerse, conservarse. *33* seguir, continuar, permanecer, quedarse. *34* estar, ir, venir [haciendo una cosa]. *35* residir, vivir. *36 to ~ at it*, fam. perseverar, persistir. *37 to ~ away*, mantenerse apartado, no acercarse. *38 to ~ from*, abstenerse de. *39 to ~ off*, no acercarse a; no tocar; no andar por, no pisar. *40 to ~ on*, ir adelante, proseguir. *41 to ~ out of*, evitar, no meterse en. *42 to ~ to*, atenerse a; seguir por; llevar [la derecha, la izquierda]. *43 to ~ up*, seguir, persistir; seguir, no quedarse atrás.
¶ Pret. y p. p.: *kept*.
**keeper** (-ø<sup>r</sup>) *s.* guardián, guardia, custodio, velador, defensor. *2* alcaide. *3* portero, conserje. *4* carcelero. *5* loquero. *6* guardabosques. *7* el que lleva [una cuenta, registro, etc.]. *8* tenedor [pers.]. *9* propietario o director [de ciertos establecimientos]. *10* armadura [de imán].
**keeping** (-ing) *s.* guarda, custodia, cargo, cuidado, conservación, defensa: *in safe ~*, a buen re-

caudo, en buenas manos. 2 mantenimiento. 3 tenencia, posesión. 4 observancia, cumplimiento. 5 concordancia, armonía. 6 acción de llevar [los libros, una cuenta, un diario, etc.].

**keepsake** (-seik) s. recuerdo, regalo.

**keg** (keg) s. cuñete, barril, barrilete.

**kelson** (ke·lsøn) s. KEELSON.

**Kelt** (kelt) s. celta.

**kelter** (-ø$^r$) s. KILTER.

**Keltic** (-ik) adj. céltico.

**ken** (ken) s. (ant. y Esc.) alcance de la vista, de la comprensión.

**ken (to)** tr. (ant. y Esc.) conocer, comprender, ver, saber. ¶ Pret. y p. p.: kenned; ger.: -nning.

**kennel** (-øl) s. perrera. 2 jauría. 3 fig. cuchitril. 4 arroyo [de la calle]; reguera.

**kennel** tr. poner o tener en una perrera. 2 intr. estar en una perrera. ¶ Pret. y p. p.: keneled o -lied; ger.: -ling o -lling.

**keno** (ki·nou) s. quinterno [en la lotería].

**kepi** (ke·pi) s. kepis, quepis.

**kept** (kept) pret. y p. p. de TO KEEP.

**keramic** (kiræ·mik) adj. CERAMIC.

**keramics** (-s) s. CERAMICS.

**keratin** (ke·ratin) s. BIOQUÍM. queratina.

**kerb** (kø$^r$b) s. encintado [de las aceras].

**kerchief** (kø·$^r$chif) s. pañuelo, pañolón.

**kerf** (kø$^r$f) s. corte, muesca, entalladura.

**kermes** (kø·$^r$miš) s. quermes, alquermes, grana: 2 BOT. kermes o ~ oak, coscoja. 3 ~ berry, coscojo.

**kermess** (-mes o -mis) s. (E.U.) feria, tómbola, bazar.

**kernel** (-nøl) s. grano [de trigo o maíz]. 2 almendra, núcleo [de fruto]. 3 fig. corazón [parte esencial].

**kerosene** (ke·røsin) s. petróleo para lámparas.

**kestrel** (ke·strøl) s. ORN. cernícalo.

**ketch** (kech) s. MAR. queche.

**ketchup** (ke·chøp) s. CATCHUP.

**ketone** (kɪ·toun) s. QUÍM. cetona.

**kettle** (ke·tøl) s. caldero, perol, olla, marmita. 2 tetera, pava. 3 MAR. caja [de brújula].

**kettledrum** (-drøm) s. MÚS. timbal, atabal.

**kettleful** (-ful) s. calderada.

**key** (kɪ) s. llave [para abrir o cerrar, dar cuerda, etc.]. 2 llave [en sentido figurado]. 3 clave [de un enigma, una traducción, etc.; principio fundamental]. 4 clave, contracifra. 5 llave de tuerca. 6 templador, afinador [instrumento]. 7 MEC. llave, cuña de ajuste; clavija, chaveta. 8 ARQ. clave. 9 MÚS. llave, pistón. 10 TELEG. manipulador. 11 tecla [de piano, etc.]. 12 MÚS. tono: in ~, templado; fig. a tono, en armonía. 13 fig. tono, estilo, tenor. 14 cayo, isleta. 15 BOT. sámara.

**key (to)** tr. poner a tono, armonizar. 2 MÚS. afinar, templar. 3 cerrar [con llave]; asegurar [con clavijas, chavetas, etc.]. 4 ARQ. poner la clave. 5 to ~ up, elevar el tono, el nivel de, excitar.

**keyboard** (kɪ·bø$^r$d) s. teclado.

**keyhole** (-joul) s. ojo de la cerradura.

**keynote** (-nout) s. MÚS. nota tónica. 2 hecho, idea, etc., principal o fundamental.

**keystone** (-stoun) s. ARQ. clave. 2 base, fundamento principal, piedra angular.

**khaki** (ka·ki) s. caqui [tela y color]. 2 pl. uniforme caqui.

**khan** (kan) s. kan, can [título]. 2 caravasar.

**khedive** (kedɪ·v) s. jedive.

**kibe** (kai·b) s. grieta [en la piel]; sabañón ulcerado.

**kibed** (-d) adj. agrietado, lleno de sabañones.

**kiblah** (ki·bla) s. alquibla.

**kick** (kik) s. puntapié, patada, coz: free ~, FÚTBOL golpe franco. 2 coz [de un animal]. 3 coz, retroceso [de un arma]. 4 fam. oposición, protesta, queja. 5 fam. fuerza, efecto estimulante [de una bebida]. 6 fam. placer, gusto. 7 fam. capacidad para reaccionar, elasticidad; vida, animación. 8 fondo entrante [de una botella].

**kick (to)** tr. dar de puntapiés o un puntapié a, dar patadas o una patada a; acocear; mover o sacudir [los pies]; hacer, echar, etc., de un puntapié o a puntapiés: to ~ down, echar abajo de un puntapié; to ~ one's heels, estar esperando; to ~ out, echar a puntapiés, echar fuera; to ~ the bucket, fam. estirar la pata, morir. 2 to ~ up, levantar, armar, promover. 3 intr. patear, pernear, dar puntapiés, dar coces: to ~ against the pricks, dar coces contra el aguijón. 4 dar coz [un arma]. 5 fam. oponerse, protestar, quejarse. 6 FÚTBOL . poner la pelota en juego.

**kicker** (ki·kø$^r$) s. acoceador, pateador. 2 reparón, gruñón.

**kickoff** (ki·kof) s. FÚTBOL golpe de salida, acción de poner la pelota en juego.

**kickshaw** (ki·ksho) s. plato de fantasía; golosina. 2 chuchería, fruslería.

**kickup** (ki·køp) s. pop. riña, alboroto, trapatiesta.

**kid** (kid) s. ZOOL. cabrito, chivo. 2 cabritilla. 3 fam. niño, niña, chico, chica. 4 pl. guantes o zapatos de cabritilla.

**kid (to)** intr. parir [la cabra]. 2 tr. embromar, tomar el pelo a. ¶ Pret. y p. p.: kidded; ger.: -dding.

**kidder** (ki·dø$^r$) s. fam. bromista, chancero.

**kidling** (ki·dling) s. choto, cabritillo.

**kidnap (to)** (ki·dnæp) tr. secuestrar, raptar. ¶ Pret. y p. p.: kidnaped o -pped; ger.: kidnaping o -pping.

**kidnaper** (ki·dnæpø$^r$) s. secuestrador, raptor.

**kidnapping** (ki·dnæping) s. secuestro, rapto.

**kidney** (ki·dni) s. ANAT. riñón. 2 COC. riñones. 3 fig. temperamento; índole, clase. 4 ~ bean, alubia, judía, judía colorada.

**kidney-shaped** adj. arriñonado.

**kidskin** (ki·dskin) s. cabritilla.

**kill** (kil) s. muerte, matanza [acción]. 2 pieza, caza, cacería [animal o animales muertos]. 3 (E.U.) arroyo, riachuelo.

**kill (to)** tr. matar [dar muerte a, causar la muerte a; fatigar, alterar la salud de]: to ~ two birds with one stone, matar dos pájaros de un tiro. 2 matar, apagar, destruir, suprimir, neutralizar. 3 matar [el tiempo]. 4 producir una impresión irresistible en.

**killdee(r** (ki·ldɪ$^r$) s. ORN. tildío.

**killer** (ki·lø$^r$) s. matador. 2 ZOOL. killer o ~ wale, orca.

**killing** (ki·ling) s. muerte, matanza [acción]. 2 fam. éxito sensacional; gran ganancia. 3 adj. matador. 4 destructivo. 5 fam. irresistible. 6 muy divertido o ridículo.

**kill-joy** s. aguafiestas.

**kiln** (kilo klin) s. horno [para secar, calcinar, etc.].

**kilo** (ki·lou) s. kilo, quilo, kilogramo.

**kilocycle** (ki·løsaikøl) s. kilociclo.

**kilogram, -gramme** (ki·løgræm) s. kilogramo, quilogramo.

**kilogrammeter** (-ɪ·tø$^r$) s. kilográmetro.

**kilolitre, -liter** (-litø$^r$) s. kilolitro, quilolitro.

**kilometre, -meter** (-mɪtø$^r$) s. kilómetro, quilómetro.

**kilometric** (kiløme·trik) *adj.* kilométrico, quilométrico.

**kilowatt** (ki·løuot) *s.* ELECT. kilovatio.

**kilt** (kilt) *s.* falda corta del traje masculino escocés.

**kilt (to)** *tr.* (Esc.) arremangar. *2* plegar, hacer pliegues anchos y planos.

**kilter** (ki·ltøʳ) *s.* fam. buen estado.

**kimono** (kimou·nou) *s.* kimono, quimono.

**kin** (kin) *s.* parientes, parentela, familia: *of ~,* AKIN; *near of ~,* próximo pariente; *the next of ~,* el pariente o los parientes más próximos. *2 adj.* pariente, allegado.

**kind** (kaind) *adj.* bueno, benigno, bondadoso, benévolo. *2* amable. *3* afectuoso, cariñoso. *4* manso, dócil. *5 s.* género, especie, clase, naturaleza, linaje, suerte, calaña: *a ~ of,* una especie de; *of a ~,* de una misma especie; malo, de poco valor; *of the ~,* parecido, por el estilo. *6* TEOL., COM. especie: *in ~,* en especie; fig. en la misma moneda. *7 ~ of,* un poco, algo, casi, en cierto modo.

**kind-hearted** *adj.* bondadoso, de buen corazón.

**kindle (to)** (ki·ndøl) *tr.* encender. *2* inflamar, enardecer. *3 intr.* encenderse, arder. *4* inflamarse, enardecerse. *5* prender [el fuego].

**kindliness** (kai·ndlinis) *s.* bondad, benevolencia, benignidad. *2* favor, amabilidad.

**kindling** (ki·ndling) *s.* encendimiento; ignición. *2* leña menuda, hornija, encendajas.

**kindly** (kai·ndli) *adj.* bondadoso, amable, afectuoso. *2* apacible, benigno; favorable. *4 adv.* bondadosamente, amablemente, afectuosamente.

**kindness** (kai·ndnis) *s.* bondad, benevolencia, benignidad, humanidad, generosidad, amabilidad, afectuosidad. *2* favor, fineza.

**kindred** (ki·ndrid) *adj.* pariente. *2* parecido, afín. *3 s.* parentesco. *4* parentela, familia.

**kine** (kain) *s. pl.* ant. o dial, vacas, ganado.

**kinematics** (kinimæ·tics) *s.* FÍS. cinemática.

**kinescope** (ki·niscoup) *s.* TELEV. cinescopio.

**kinetics** (kine·tiks) *s.* FÍS. cinética.

**kinfolk** (ki·nfouk) *s.* KINSFOLK.

**king** (king) *s.* rey [monarca; el primero entre los de su clase]: *King's speech,* discurso de la Corona. *2* rey [pieza del ajedrez]; dama [en el juego de damas]. *3* ZOOL. *~ crab,* cangrejo de las Molucas. *4* ARQ. *~ post,* pendolón.

**kingbird** (-bø·d) *s.* cierto pájaro americano.

**kingbolt** (-boult) *s.* perno central o principal.

**kingcraft** (-kræft) *s.* arte de reinar o gobernar.

**kingcup** (-øp) *s.* BOT. botón de oro.

**kingdom** (-døm) *s.* reino.

**kingfisher** (-fishøʳ) *s.* ORN. martín pescador.

**kinglet** (-lit) *s.* reyezuelo, régulo. *2* ORN. reyezuelo.

**king-size** *adj.* de tamaño largo [cigarrillo].

**kingly** (-li) *adj.* real, regio. *2 adv.* regiamente.

**kingship** (-ship) *s.* majestad. *2* realeza. *3* reino, monarquía.

**kink** (kink) *s.* anilla, rizo, coca [que forma un hilo, etc., cuando se encarruja]. *2* tortícolis. *3* capricho, chifladura.

**kink (to)** *tr.* ensortijar, encarrujar. *2 intr.* retorcerse, encarrujarse, formar cocas.

**kinky** (-i) *adj.* encarrujado; ensortijado, crespo. *2* fam. excéntrico, chiflado.

**kinsfolk** (ki·nšfouk) *s.* parientes, parentela.

**kinship** (-ship) *s.* parentesco. *2* afinidad.

**kinsman** (-šmæn) *s.* pariente, deudo.

**kinswoman** (-šwumæn) *f.* parienta.

**kiosk** (kia·sk) *s.* kiosco, quiosco.

**kipper** (ki·pøʳ) *s.* salmón o arenque curado. *2* salmón macho en la época de la cría.

**kipper (to)** *tr.* curar, salar, ahumar.

**kirk** (køʳk) *s.* [Esc. y dial. ingl.] iglesia.

**kismet** (ki·šmet) *s.* hado, destino.

**kiss** (kis) *s.* beso, ósculo. *2* ligero contacto. *3* dulce, merengue.

**kiss (to)** *tr.* besar. *2 to ~ away,* borrar, curar, con bèsos [las penas, etc., de otro]. *3 intr.* besar. *4* besarse. *5* tocarse ligeramente.

**kit** (kit) *s.* equipo, avíos; juego, cartera o caja de herramientas, instrumentos, etc. *2* fam. juego, colección, grupo. *3* colodra, cubo. *4* FOT. adaptador. *5* violín pequeño. *6* gatito, gatita.

**kit-bag** *s.* mochila.

**kitchen** (ki·chøn) *s.* cocina: *~ garden,* huerto [de hortalizas]; *~ range,* cocina económica; *~ sink,* fregadero. *2* fogón portátil.

**kitchenette** (kichøne·t) *s.* cocinilla.

**kitchenmaid** (ki·chønmeid) *s.* pincha, ayudanta de cocina.

**kitchenware** (-ueʳ) *s.* utensilios de cocina.

**kite** (kait) *s.* cometa, pájara [juguete]. *2* ORN. milano. *3* fig. bribón, fullero. *4* COM. pelota, letra de favor.

**kith and kin** (kiz) *s. pl.* parientes y amigos.

**kitten** (ki·tøn) *s.* gatito, minino. *2* conejito.

**kitten (to)** *intr.* parir [la gata].

**kittenish** (-ish) *adj.* juguetón, retozón. *2* coquetón.

**kittiwake** (ki·tiueik) *s.* ORN. especie de gaviota.

**Kitty** (ki·ti) *n. pr.* dim. de KATHARINE.

**kitty** *s.* gatito minino.

**kleptomania** (kleptomei·nia) *s.* cleptomanía.

**kleptomaniac** (-iæk) *adj.-s.* cleptómano.

**knack** (næk) *s.* maña, don, arte [para hacer una cosa]; tranquillo. *2* hábito, costumbre. *3* artificio, truco.

**knag** (næg) *s.* nudo [en la madera].

**knaggy** (-i) *adj.* nudoso, rugoso.

**knapsack** (næ·psæk) *s.* mochila, morral, barjuleta.

**knapweed** (-wid) *s.* BOT. centaura, centaurea.

**knave** (neiv) *s.* bribón, granuja, pícaro, bellaco. *2* sota [naipe].

**knavery** (-øri) *s.* bribonada, granujada.

**knavish** (-ish) *adj.* bribón, bellaco. *2* bribonesco, doloso. *3* travieso.

**knead (to)** (nɪd) *tr.* amasar, heñir, sobar.

**kneader** (-øʳ) *s.* amasador, heñidor.

**kneading** (-ing) *s.* amasadura, soba: *~ trough,* amasadera.

**knee** (nɪ) *s.* ANAT. rodilla, hinojo: *~ breeches,* calzón corto; *to be on the knees of the goods,* ser incierto, depender de la voluntad divina; *to go down on one's knees,* arrodillarse, caer de rodillas. *2* rodilla [en los cuadrúpedos]. *3* MEC. codo, codillo, ángulo, escuadra. *4* MAR. curva.

**kneecap** (-kæp) *s.* rótula, choquezuela. *2* rodillera [abrigo de la rodilla].

**knee-deep** *adj.-adv.* metido hasta las rodillas.

**kneed** (nɪd) *adj.* articulado, acodillado.

**knee-high** *adj.* que llega hasta la rodilla.

**kneel (to)** (nɪl) *intr.* arrodillarse, hincar o doblar la rodilla. *2* estar de rodillas. ¶ Pret. y p. p.: *knelt* o *kneeled.*

**kneepad** (nɪ·pæd) *s.* rodillera [abrigo de la rodilla].

**kneepan** (-pæn) *s.* rótula, choquezuela.

**knell** (nel) *s.* doble, toque de difuntos: *to toll the ~ of,* anunciar el fin de.

**knell (to)** *intr.* doblar, tocar a muerto; sonar tristemente. *2 tr.* anunciar o llamar a toque de campana.

**knew** (niu·) *pret.* de TO KNOW.

**knickerbockers** (ni·køʳba·køʳs), **knickers** [ni·køʳs] *s. pl.* calzón ancho, bragas.

**knick-knack** (ni·knæk) *s.* chuchería, bujería, chisme.

**knife** (naif) *s.* cuchillo [para cortar]; cuchilla; navaja: ~ *grinder*, afilador; ~ *switch*, ELECT. interruptor de cuchillo.

**knife (to)** *tr.* cortar o herir con cuchillo, acuchillar. *2* fig. perjudicar secretamente.

**knight** (nait) *s.* caballero [de una orden o de la orden de caballería; dignidad nobiliaria]: ~ *Templar* o *of the Temple*, templario. *2* caballero [de una dama]. *3* caballo [de ajedrez].

**knight (to)** *tr.* armar caballero.

**knight-errant** *s.* caballero andante.

**knight-errantry** *s.* caballería andante.

**knighthood** (-jud) *s.* caballería [institución; conjunto de caballeros].

**knighthood-errant** *s.* caballería andante.

**knightly** (-li) *adj.* caballeresco, caballeroso. *2 adv.* caballerescamente, caballerosamente.

**knit (to)** (nit) *tr.* hacer, tejer [a punto de aguja o de malla]. *2* unir, trabar, enlazar. *3 to ~ one's brow*, fruncir las cejas. *3 intr.* hacer calceta o tejido de punto; hacer malla. *4* unirse, enlazarse, trabarse. *5* contraerse, fruncirse. ¶ Pret. y p. p.: *knit* o *knitted;* ger.; *knitting.*

**knit, knitted** (-id) *pret.* y *p. p.* de TO KNIT. *2 adj.* de punto: *knit goods,* géneros de punto.

**knitting** (-ing) *s.* acción de hacer calceta; labor o tejido de punto: ~ *needle,* aguja de hacer media. *2* unión, trabamiento. *3* fruncimiento.

**knittle** (ni·təl) *s.* hilo fino para pescar.

**knives** (nai·vš) *s. pl.* de KNIFE.

**knob** (nab) *s.* bulto, protuberancia redondeada. *2* perilla, botón, tirador [de puerta, cajón, etc.]. *3* nudo [en la madera]. *4* terrón, pedacito [de azúcar, carbón, etc.]. *5* colina o eminencia redondeada.

**knobby** (na·bi) *adj.* lleno de protuberancias, nudoso. *2* (E.U.) montuoso.

**knock** (nak) *s.* golpe, choque, porrazo. *2* golpe, llamada [a una puerta], aldabonazo. *3* pistoneo [del motor]. *4* fam. (E.U.) censura, crítica.

**knock (to)** *tr.* golpear, aporrear. *2* hacer chocar o topar. *3* despertar, llamar [golpeando en la puerta]. *4* fam. asombrar, admirar. *5* fam. (E.U.) censurar, criticar. *6 to ~ down,* derribar, tumbar, hacer sucumbir; atropellar [con un coche, etc.]; desarmar, desmontar; rebajar [los precios]; adjudicar [en una subasta]. *7 to ~ off,* quitar, hacer saltar [a golpes]; dejar [el trabajo]; hacer [algo] rápidamente; deducir, rebajar. *8 to ~ out,* hacer salir [golpeando]; poner fuera de combate. *9 to ~ together,* hacer chocar; juntar o construir precipitadamente.
*10 intr.* golpear, llamar [a una puerta]. *11* chocar, topar [con], topetar. *12* pistonear [un motor]. *13 to ~ about,* viajar, andar de un lado para otro. *14 to ~ off,* dejar el trabajo; desistir, morir. *15 to ~ under,* sucumbir.

**knockabout** (-abaut) *adj.* de vagabundeo. *2* de trabajo, resistente [ropa, vestido]. *3* ruidoso, tumultuoso. *4 s.* MAR. yate pequeño.

**knockdown** (-daun) *adj.* tremendo, que derriba [golpe]. *2* en piezas; desarmable, desmontable. *3 s.* golpe irresistible; cosa que tumba o derriba. *4* cosa desarmable o desmontable.

**knocker** (-øʳ) *s.* golpeador. *2* llamador, aldaba, aldabón.

**knock-kneed** (-nıd) *adj.* zambo, patizambo.

**knockout** (-aut) *adj.* irresistible, que pone fuera de combate. *2 s.* BOXEO acto de poner fuera de combate.

**knoll** (noul) *s.* loma, otero. *2* MAR. cima de un bajo.

**knot** (nat) *s.* nudo, lazo. *2* nudo [de montañas; de la madera; de una cuestión, de una obra dramática, etc.]. *3* BOT., ANAT. nudo. *4* MAR. nudo, milla náutica. *5* grupo, colección, hato.

**knot (to)** *tr.* anudar; hacer nudo en. *2* atar, unir, enlazar, enredar. *3* fruncir [las cejas]. *4 intr.* anudarse, enredarse. ¶ Pret. y p. p.: *knotted;* ger.: *-tting.*

**knotgrass** (-græs) *s.* BOT. centinodia, sanguinaria mayor.

**knotted** (-id) *adj.* anudado. *2* nudoso. *3* enredado, intrincado.

**knotty** (-i) *adj.* anudado. *2* difícil, espinoso, intrincado. *3* áspero, rugoso.

**knout** (naut) *s.* knut [azote ruso].

**know (to)** (nou) *tr.* conocer: *to ~ by sight,* conocer de vista. *2* saber: *to ~ a thing,* or *two, to ~ what is what,* estar enterado; no ser tonto; *to ~ how to, to ~ to [do,* etc.], saber [hacer, etc.]; *for all I ~,* a mi ver, a mi juicio. *3* comprender, hacerse cargo, caer en la cuenta, ver. *4* distinguir, discernir.
*6 intr.* saber: *to ~ best,* saber mejor lo que conviene; *to ~ better,* saber que no es así; saber uno como debe portarse, lo que debe hacer; *to ~ of,* tener noticias o conocimiento de. ¶ Pret.: *knew;* p. p.: *known.*

**knowable** (-abøl) *adj.* conocible.

**know-how** *s.* destreza, habilidad, pericia.

**knowing** (-ing) *adj.* inteligente; astuto; entendido, enterado. *2* de inteligente. *3* de inteligencia, de complicidad.

**knowingly** (-li) *adv.* a sabiendas. *2* hábilmente. *3* con aire de inteligencia.

**know-it-all** *adj.-s.* sabidillo, sabihondo, sábelotodo.

**knowledge** (na·lidỹ) *s.* conocimiento, cognición, noticia: *to my ~,* a mi conocimiento; que yo sepa. *2* conocimientos, saber: *to the best of my ~,* según mi leal saber y entender.

**knowledgeable** (-abøl) *adj.* fam. conocedor, inteligente.

**known** (noun) *p. p.* de TO KNOW.

**know-nothing** *s.* ignorante. *2* agnóstico.

**knuckle** (nø·køl) *s.* ANAT. nudillo. *2* jarrete [de la res]. *3* MEC. *knucke* o ~ *joint,* articulación, junta articulada.

**knuckle (to)** *intr.* apoyar los nudillos en el suelo [en el juego de las canicas]. *2* someterse, rendirse, ceder. | Gralte. con *down* o *under. 3 tr.* golpear, apretar, etc., con los nudillos.

**knucklebone** (-boun) *s.* taba [hueso]. *2 pl.* taba [juego].

**knuckled** (-d) *adj.* nudoso.

**knurl** (nøʳl) *s.* protuberancia. *2* botón, asidero. *3* moleteado [de una pieza metálica].

**knuried** (-d) *adj.* nudoso. *2* MEC. moleteado.

**koala** (koa·la) *s.* ZOOL. oso marsupial.

**kodak** (kou·dæk) *s.* FOT. kodak.

**kohl** (koul) *s.* alcohol [afeite].

**kola** (kou·la) *s.* COLA.

**kopeck** (kou·pek) *s.* copec [moneda rusa].

**Koran** (kora·n) *s.* Alcorán, Corán.

**Korea** (korı·a) *n. pr.* GEOGR. Corea.

**Korean** (korɪ·an) *adj.-s.* coreano.
**kotow** (koutau·), **kowtow** [kau·tau] *s.* saludo chino de reverencia y sumisión.
**kotow, kowtow (to)** *intr.* hacer el saludo. *2* humillarse servilmente.
**kraal** (kral) *s.* poblado de hotentotes. *2* (Áfr. del S.) corral, redil.
**Krausism** (krau·sišm) *s.* FIL. krausismo.

**Kuklux, Ku-Klux, Ku-Klux-Klan** (kiu-kløks-klæn) *s.* (E.U.), organización secreta que dirige sus actividades contra los negros, los judíos, los católicos y los extranjeros.
**kummel** (ki·møl) *s.* cúmel [licor].
**Kurd** (køʳd) *s.* kurdo, curdo.
**kurdish** (-ish) *adj.* kurdo, curdo.
**kyphosis** (kaifou·sis) *s.* MED. cifosis.
**Kyrie** (ki·riı) *s.* LITURG. kirie: ~ *eleison*, kirieleison.

# L

**L, l** (el) *s*. L, l, duodécima letra del alfabeto inglés.
**la** (la) *s*. MÚS. la. *2 interj*. para indicar sorpresa.
**lab** (læb) *s*. fam. laboratorio.
**labarum** (læ·barøm) *s*. lábaro.
**labdanum** (læ·bdanøm) *s*. ládano.
**label** (lei·bøl) *s*. marbete, rótulo, etiqueta; designación, calificación. *2* BLAS. lambel.
**label (to)** *tr*. rotular, marcar, poner etiqueta. *2* designar, clasificar como. ¶ Pret. y p. p.: *labeled* o *-lled*; ger.: *-ling* o *lling*.
**labellum** (labe·løm) *s*. BOT., ENT. labelo.
**labial** (lei·bial) *adj*. labial. *2 s*. letra labial.
**labiate(d** (lei·bieiti(d) *adj.-s*. BOT. labiado.
**labile** (lei·bil) *adj*. QUÍM. lábil.
**labiodental** (leibiode·ntal) *adj.-s*. labiodental.
**labium** (lei·bøʳ) *s*. ANAT., BOT., ZOOL. labio.
**labor** (lei·boʳ) *s*. LABOUR. *2* (E.U.) *Labor Day*, fiesta del trabajo.
**labor (to)** *tr.-intr*. TO LABOUR.
**laboratory** (læ·boratori) *s*. laboratorio.
**labored** (-d) *adj*. LABOURED.
**laborer** (-øʳ) *s*. LABOURER.
**laborious** (labou·riøs) *adj*. trabajador, laborioso. *2* laborioso, trabajoso, arduo, ímprobo.
**labour** (lei·bøʳ) *s*. trabajo, labor; pena, fatiga: *lost ~*, trabajo perdido. *2* tarea, faena, quehacer, obra. *3* mano de obra. *4* la clase obrera; trabajo [en oposición a capital]: *Labour Party*, partido laborista. *5* MAR. balanceo, cabeceo. *6* dolores del parto: *to be in ~*, estar de parto.
**labour (to)** *intr*. trabajar, esforzarse, forcejear. *2* estar de parto. *3* MAR. trabajar [un buque] contra las olas y el viento. *4* moverse, avanzar con dificultad. *5 to ~ under*, estar padeciendo [una enfermedad, error, etc.]; estar luchando [con dificultades]. *6 tr*. trabajar; arar, cultivar. *7* pulir, perfilar, exponer en detalle.
**laboured** (-d) *adj*. trabajado, complicado. *2* forzado, poco natural.
**labourer** (-øʳ) *s*. trabajador, obrero, jornalero, bracero.
**labouring** (-ing) *s*. trabajo, esfuerzo. *2 adj*. trabajador, obrero: *~ classes*, clase obrera.
**labourism** (-išm) *s*. laborismo, trabajismo.
**Labourite** (-ait) *s*. (Ingl.) laborista.
**labour-saving** *adj*. que ahorra trabajo.
**laboursome** (-øm) *adj*. trabajador, industrioso. *2* arduo, penoso, ímprobo.

**labradorite** (læ·bradorait) *s*. MINER. labradorita.
**labrum** (le·brøm) *s*. ENT. labro.
**laburnum** (labø·ʳnøm) *s*. BOT. laburno.
**labyrinth** (læ·birinz) *s*. laberinto, dédalo. *2* ANAT. laberinto.
**labyrinthine** (læbiri·nzin) *adj*. laberíntico.
**lac** (læk) *s*. laca, goma laca.
**lace** (leis) *s*. cordón, cinta [de zapatos, corsé, etc.], agujeta. *2* galón [de oro o plata]. *3* encaje, blonda, randa: *~ pillow*, mundillo [para hacer encaje]. *4* gotas [que se echan al café, etc.].
**lace (to)** *tr*. atar, ajustar [zapatos, el corsé, etc.] con cordones o cintas; apretar, encorsetar. *2* pasar [un cordón]. *3* galonear. *4* guarnecer con encajes. *5* rayar, adornar con rayas. *6* enlazar, entrelazar. *7* azotar, dar una paliza. *8* aromatizar [con gotas de licor]. *9 intr*. apretarse, encorsetarse. *10 to ~ into*, arremeter contra, pegar [a uno].
**Lacedaemon** (læsidi·møn) *n. pr*. GEOGR., HIST. Lacedemonia.
**lacerate (to)** (læ·søreit) *tr*. lacerar. *2* rasgar, desgarrar, despedazar.
**laceration** (-ei·shøn) *s*. laceración, desgarradura.
**lace-winged** *adj*. de alas membranosas y reticuladas [insecto].
**lacewoman** (lei·swumæn) *s*. encajera.
**lacework** (-uøʳk) *s*. obra de encaje.
**lachrymal** (læ·krimal) *adj*. lacrimal. *2 adj.-s*. ANAT. lagrimal.
**lachrymation** (-ei·shøn) *s*. secreción de lágrimas. *2* llanto, lloro.
**lachrymatory** (læ·crimatori) *s*. lacrimatorio.
**lachrymose** (-mouš) *adj*. lacrimoso.
**lacing** (lei·sing) *s*. acción de TO LACE. *2* cordones [para zapatos, corsés, etc.], agujetas. *3* borde coloreado [en una flor, pluma, etc.]. *4* zurra, tunda.
**lacinia** (lasi·nia) *s*. BOT. lacinia.
**lack** (læk) *s*. falta, carencia. *2* privación, necesidad.
**lack (to)** *intr*. faltar [no existir]. *2 intr.-tr*. carecer de, faltarle [a uno o a algo una cosa]; necesitar.
**lackadaisical** (lækadei·šikal) *adj*. afectado; afectadamente lánguido o indiferente. *2* sensiblero.
**lackey** (læ·ki) *s*. lacayo.
**lackey (to)** *tr.-intr*. servir como lacayo o criado.

**lacking** (læ·king) *adj.* carente, falto, deficiente: *he is ~ in courage,* le falta valor. *2* faltante.
**lacklustre, lackluster** (læ·kløstø) *adj.* deslustrado.
**laconic** (laka·nik) *adj.* lacónico.
**lacquer** (læ·kø) *s.* laca, barniz.
**lacquer (to)** *tr.* barnizar, dar laca, laquear.
**lacquering** (-ing) *s.* barnizado de laca.
**lacrimal, lacrimatory,** etc. LACHRYMAL, LACHRYMA-TORY, etc.
**lacrosse** (lakro·s) *s.* juego de pelota.
**lactase** (læ·kteis) *s.* BIOQUÍM. lactasa.
**lactate (to)** (læ·kteit) *intr.* lactar, amamantar. *2* dar leche.
**lactation** (-ei·shøn) *s.* segregación de leche. *2* lactación.
**lacteal** (læ·ktial) *adj.* lácteo. *2* ANAT. quilífero. *3 s.* ANAT. vaso quilífero.
**lactescent** (lækte·sønt) *adj.* lactescente.
**lactic** (læ·ktik) *adj.* láctico.
**lactiferous** (lækti·førøs) *adj.* lactífero. *2* BOT. lechoso, lechal.
**lactose** (læ·ktous) *s.* QUÍM. lactosa, lactina.
**lacuna** (lakiu·na) *s.* laguna, blanco, claro, espacio. *2* hoyo, hueco.
**lacunar** (-na) *adj.-s.* ARQ. lagunar.
**lacustrine** (lakø·strin) *adj.* lacustre.
**lacy** (lei·si) *adj.* de encaje o parecido a él.
**lad** (læd) *s.* muchacho, chico, mozo, chaval.
**ladder** (læ·dø) *s.* escalera [hecha de dos banzos y escalones]; escalera de mano, escala. *2* fig. escabel [lo que sirve para subir o medrar]. *3* carrera [en las medias].
**laddie** (læ·di) *s. dim.* de LAD.
**lade (to)** (leid) *tr.* cargar [poner o echar carga en o sobre]. *2* cargar, embarcar [mercancías, etc.]. *3* echar o sacar [con cucharón, etc.]. *4 intr.* tomar cargamento. ¶ Pret.: *laded;* p. p.: *laded* o *laden.*
**laden** (-øn) *p. p. irreg.* de TO LADE. *2 adj.* cargado. *3* abrumado, oprimido.
**lading** (-ing) *s.* carga, embarque [de mercancías]: *bill of ~,* conocimiento de embarque.
**ladle** (-øl) *s.* cucharón, cazo, cacillo.
**ladle (to)** *tr.* servir, verter o sacar con cucharón.
**lady** (lei·di) *s.* señora, señorita, dama: *ladies and gentlemen,* señoras y caballeros; *~ of waiting,* dama [de una reina o princesa]; *~ of the house,* señora de la casa. *2* señora [esposa]. *3* novia, dulcinea. *4* (con may.) Señora [la Virgen]: *Our Lady,* Nuestra Señora. *5* (Ingl.) título que se antepone al nombre de las señoras de la nobleza.
**ladybird** (-bø·d), **ladybug** (-bøg) *s.* ENT. mariquita, vaca de san Antón.
**ladyfinger** (-fingø) *s.* melindre, bizcocho.
**lady-killer** *s.* don Juan Tenorio, hombre irresistible.
**ladylike** (-laik) *adj.* delicado, elegante. *2* afeminado, amujerado.
**ladylove** (-løv) *s.* amada, mujer querida.
**ladyship** (-ship) *s.* señoría [refiriéndose a una señora a quien se da el título de lady].
**lady's-mantle** *s.* BOT. alquimila, pie de león.
**lady's-thumb** *s.* BOT. duraznillo, persicaria.
**lag** (læg) *s.* retardo, retraso. *2* FÍS. retardación.
**lag (to)** *intr.* andar o moverse lentamente, retrasarse: *to ~ behind,* rezagarse, quedarse atrás. *2* roncear. ¶ Pret. y p. p.: *lagged;* ger.: *-gging.*
**lager** (la·gø) *s.* especie de cerveza.
**laggard** (læ·gø·d) *adj.-s.* rezagado; perezoso, holgazán.
**lagoon** (lagu·n) *s.* albufera; laguna junto al mar o en una isla de coral.

**laic** (lei·ik) *adj.* laico, secular. *2 s.* lego, seglar.
**laicism** (-isiš·m) *s.* laicismo.
**laicize** (-isaiš) *tr.* laicizar, secularizar.
**laid** (leid) *pret.* y *p. p.* de TO LAY.
**lain** (lein) *p. p.* de TO LIE [reclinar].
**lair** (le·ø) *s.* yacija. *2* cubil, cueva de fieras.
**laird** (le·ø·d) *s.* (esp. Esc.) señor; hacendado.
**laity** (lei·iti) *s.* estado seglar o laico. *2* los laicos, los legos.
**lake** (leik) *s.* lago, laguna, estanque. *2* laca, carmín [color].
**lama** (la·ma) *s.* lama [sacerdote]. *2* ZOOL. llama.
**Lamaism** (-išm) *s.* lamaísmo.
**lamasery** (-søri) *s.* lamasería.
**lamb** (læm) *s.* cordero [animal; carne; pers. dócil, inocente]: *Lamb of God,* Divino Cordero. *2* piel de cordero.
**lambaste (to)** (læmbei·st) *tr.* apalear, dar una paliza a. *2* reprender o criticar duramente.
**lambent** (læ·mbønt) *adj.* ondulante, lamiente [llama]. *2* suave [luz]. *3* brillante, radiante [cielo, ojos, etc.]. *4* centelleante [ingenio].
**lambkin** (læ·mkin) *s.* corderito, corderillo.
**lambrequin** (læ·mbø·kin) *s.* BLAS. lambrequín. *2* guardamalleta, sobrepuerta.
**lambskin** (læ·mskin) *s.* corderina, corderillo [piel].
**lame** (leim) *adj.* cojo, renco, lisiado. *2* fig. cojo, defectuoso, imperfecto. *3* fig. pobre, vano, frívolo: *~ excuse,* excusa pobre o frívola.
**lame (to)** *tr.* encojar, derrengar, lisiar.
**lamella** (lame·la) *s.* ANAT., ZOOL., BOT. laminilla.
**lamellar** (læ·mølø) *adj.* ANAT., ZOOL., BOT. laminar.
**lamellibranch** (lame·librænk) *adj.-s.* ZOOL. lamelibranquio.
**lamellicorn** (-ko·n) *adj.* ENT. lamelicornio.
**lameness** (lei·mnis) *s.* cojera. *2* imperfección, debilidad, ineficacia.
**lament** (lame·nt) *s.* lamento, queja. *2* elegía, endecha.
**lament (to)** *intr.* lamentarse, plañir. *2 tr.* lamentar, llorar, deplorar.
**lamentable** (-abøl) *adj.* lamentable, deplorable. *2* lastimoso, lastimero, dolorido.
**lamentation** (-ei·shøn) *s.* lamentación, lamento.
**lamented** (lame·ntid) *adj.* lamentado. *2* llorado.
**lamia** (læ·mia) *s.* MIT., ICT. lamia. *2* bruja.
**lamina** (læ·mina) *s.* lámina, planchita, hoja.
**laminar** (-a) *adj.* laminar.
**laminate (to)** (-eit) *tr.* laminar. *2 tr.-intr.* dividir o dividirse en láminas.
**lammergeier** (læ·mø·gaiø) *s.* ORN. quebrantahuesos, águila barbuda.
**lamp** (læmp) *s.* lámpara, lustro, candil, farol, luz. *2* bombilla eléctrica: *~ holder,* portalámparas. *3* fig. luminar, astro.
**lampblack** (-blæk) *s.* negro de humo.
**lamplight** (-lait) *s.* luz artificial.
**lamplighter** (-laitø) *s.* farolero.
**lampoon** (læmpu·n) *s.* sátira virulenta o grosera, libelo.
**lampoon (to)** *tr.* satirizar, ridiculizar virulenta o groseramente.
**lamp-post** *s.* poste o pie de farol [de la calle].
**lamprey** (læ·mpri) *s.* ICT. lamprea.
**lanate (d** (lei·neit(id) *adj.* lanoso. *2* lanudo.
**lance** (læns) *s.* lanza [arma; hombre de armas]. *2* lanceta.
**lance (to)** *tr.* alancear. *2* CIR. abrir con lanceta.
**Lancelot** (-ølat) *n. pr.* Lanzarote.
**lanceolate** (-ioleit) *adj.* lanceolado.

**lancer** (-ø$^r$) *s.* lancero. *2 pl.* lanceros [baile].
**lancet** (-it) *s.* CIR. lanceta. *2* ARQ. ojiva aguda.
**lancinate (to)** (-ineit) *tr.* lancinar, desgarrar.
**land** (lænd) *s.* tierra [parte sólida de la superficie del globo]; tierra firme: *to see how the ~ lies,* fig. sondear el terreno; *by ~,* por tierra. *2* terreno, suelo. *3* tierra [cultivada], finca rústica. *4* tierra, país, nación, región; *Land of Promise,* tierra prometida, de promisión; *the ~ of the leal,* la Gloria. *5* reino, dominio. *6 adj.* de tierra; del suelo; de fincas rústicas: *~ forces,* MIL. fuerzas de tierra; *~ gent,* administrador o corredor de fincas rústicas; *~ surveying,* agrimensura, topografía.
**land (to)** *tr.* desembarcar [a una pers. o cosa]. *2* dejar, echar, hacer llegar, poner [en un punto, situación, estado]. *3* fam. arrear, atizar [un golpe, etc.]. *4* coger, sacar [un pez]. *5* lograr, conseguir [un empleo, etc.]. *6 intr.* desembarcar. *7* apearse. *8* tomar tierra [un buque]. *9* aterrizar o amarrar [un avión]. *10* ir a parar, llegar, caer: *to ~ on one's feet,* caer de pies.
**landau** (læ·ndo) *s.* landó.
**landed** (læ·ndid) *adj.* hacendado. *2* consistente en tierras: *~ property,* propiedad rústica.
**landfall** (-fol) *s.* herencia de tierras. *2* desprendimiento de tierras. *3* MAR. recalada. *4* AVIA. aterrizaje.
**landgrave** (-greiv) *s.* landgrave.
**landholder** (-jouldø$^r$) *s.* hacendado, terrateniente.
**landing** (-ing) *s.* desembarco, desembarque. *2* desembarcadero, apeadero. *3* descansillo, meseta, rellano [de escalera]. *4* AVIA. aterrizaje: *~ gear,* tren de aterrizaje.
**landlady** (-leidi) *s.* propietaria, dueña [de tierras o casas], casera. *2* mesonera, posadera, huéspeda; patrona [de casa de huéspedes].
**landlocked** (-lakt) *adj.* rodeado de tierra.
**landlord** (-lo$^r$d) *s.* propietario, dueño [de tierras o casas], casero. *2* mesonero, posadero, huésped; patrón [de casa de huéspedes].
**landlubber** (-løbø$^r$) *s.* fam. marinero torpe. *2* marinero de agua dulce.
**landmark** (-ma$^r$k) *s.* hito, mojón. *2* señal, edificio, etc., que sirve de guía o para reconocer un sitio. *3* MAR. marca. *4* suceso que hace época.
**landowner** (-ounø$^r$) *s.* hacendado, terrateniente.
**landscape** (-skeip) *s.* paisaje, vista. *2* PINT. paisaje: *~ painter,* paisajista.
**landscape (to)** *tr.* modificar un terreno hermoseándolo.
**landscapist** (-ist) *s.* PINT. paisajista.
**landslide** (læ·ndslaid) *s.* derrubamiento o deslizamiento de tierras; argayo. *2* POL. mayoría de votos abrumadora.
**landward** (-uø$^r$d) *adj.* de hacia la tierra, de la parte de tierra. *2 adv.* hacia la tierra.
**landwards** (-uø$^r$ds) *adv.* hacia tierra.
**lane** (lein) *s.* senda, vereda, camino estrecho. *2* faja o división longitudinal [en una carretera, etc.]. *3* callejuela, callejón. *4* ruta [de vapores o aviones].
**language** (læ·ngwidy̆) *s.* lenguaje, lengua, habla, idioma, vocabulario.
**languid** (læ·ngwid) *adj.* lánguido. *2* débil, mustio, lacio. *3* flojo, tibio.
**languish (to)** (-sh) *intr.* languidecer. *2* debilitarse, decaer. *3* consumirse. *4* tomar una expresión lánguida. *5* *to ~ for,* penar o suspirar por.
**languishing** (-ing) *adj.* que languidece. *2* lánguido, tierno. *3* lento, aburrido.

**languor** (læ·ngø$^r$) *s.* languidez, desfallecimiento, desaliento. *2* flojedad, indolencia, dejamiento.
**languorous** (-øs) *adj.* lánguido, flojo.
**lank** (lænk) *adj.* alto y delgado, enjuto, seco, flaco, cenceño. *2* lacio, colgante [cabello, etc.].
**lanky** (-i) *adj.* larguirucho, desgarbado.
**lanner** (læ·nø$^r$) *s.* ORN. alcotán.
**lanolin(e** (læ·nolin) *s.* FARM. lanolina.
**lansquenet** (læ·nskønet) *s.* lansquenete. *2* sacanete.
**lantern** (læ·ntø$^r$n) *s.* linterna, farol, fanal: *~ slide,* diapositiva, tira de vidrio para la linterna mágica. *2* fanal [de faro]. *3* ARQ., MEC. linterna.
**lantern-jawed** *adj.* carilargo, carienjuto, chupado de cara.
**lanyard** (læ·nya$^r$d) *s.* MAR. acollador.
**Laoco-on** (lei·økouan) *n. pr.* MIT. Laoconte.
**lap** (læp) *s.* falda, faldón, enfaldo. *2* falda, regazo; *~ dog,* perro faldero; *to live in the ~ of luxury,* fig. llevar una vida regalada. *3* parte de una cosa que cae o se extiende sobre otra. *4* traslapo, solapo. *5* DEP. vuelta [en una carrera]. *6* lamedura. *7* chapaleteo [de las olas].
**lap (to)** *tr.* sobreponer, encaballar, cruzar. *2* traslapar, solapar; juntar a traslapo. *3* plegar, arrollar [sobre algo]. *4* envolver, rodear. *5* tener o reclinar en el regazo. *6* DEP. llevar una o más vueltas de ventaja [a uno]. *7* lamer, besar [dicho de las olas, el agua]. *8 tr.-intr.* lamer, beber lamiendo. *9 intr.* sobresalir, solapar, cruzar. *10* caer, estar doblado o plegado. *11* susurrar [el agua]. ¶ Pret. y p. p.: *lapped;* ger.: *-pping.*
**lapel** (lape·l) *s.* solapa [de vestido].
**lapidary** (læ·pideri) *adj.* lapidario. *2* de piedra, grabado en la piedra. *3 s.* lapidario.
**lapidate (to)** (-eit) *tr.* lapidar.
**lapidation** (-ei·shøn) *s.* lapidación.
**lapidify (to)** (lapi·difai) *tr.* lapidificar. *2 intr.* lapidificarse. ¶ Pret. y p. p.: *lapidified.*
**lapislazuli** (lei·pislašu·li) *s.* MINER. lapislázuli.
**Lapland** (læ·plønd) *n. pr.* GEOGR. Laponia.
**Lapp** (læp) *s.* lapón [pers.; idioma].
**lappet** (læ·pit) *s.* caída, cinta o pliegue colgante [de toca, cofia, vestido, etc.]. *2* pliegue [de una membrana, etc.]. *3* carúnculas [de gallo u otras aves].
**lapse** (læps) *s.* lapso, error, equivocación, desliz. *2* caída en la herejía, apostasía. *3* caída [en un estado, condición, etc.]. *4* lapso, transcurso [del tiempo]. *5* DER. prescripción, caducidad.
**lapse (to)** *intr.* deslizarse, pasar, transcurrir. *2* decaer [el interés, etc.]. *3* caer [en un estado o condición]. *4* caer en error, falta o defecto. *6* DER. prescribir, caducar.
**lapwing** (læ·puing) *s.* ORN. avefría.
**lar** (la$^r$) *s.* lar [dios doméstico].
**larboard** (la·$^r$bo$^r$d) *s.* MAR. ant. babor.
**larceny** (la·$^r$søni) *s.* robo, hurto, latrocinio: *petty ~,* hurto, ratería; *grand ~,* robo.
**larch** (la$^r$ch) *s.* BOT. alerce, pino alerce. *2* BOT. pino cascalbo o negral.
**lard** (la$^r$d) *s.* tocino gordo, lardo. *2* manteca de cerdo.
**lard (to)** *tr.* COC. mechar. *2* COC. lardear. *3* guarnecer, entreverar.
**lardaceous** (la·$^r$dei·shøs) *adj.* lardáceo. *2* MED. graso.
**larder** (la·$^r$dø$^r$) *s.* despensa.
**lardy** (-i) *adj.* lardoso, mantecoso.
**large** (la·$^r$dy̆) *adj.* grande, grueso, cuantioso, copioso; *~ intestine,* ANAT. intestino grueso; *on a*

~ *scale*, en gran escala. *2* amplio, vasto, dilatado: ~ *powers*, amplios poderes. *3* extenso, lato. *4* ant. generoso, comprensivo. *5* MAR. favorable [viento]. *6 s. at* ~ extensamente, detalladamente; en general; sin limitación; suelto, en libertad.

**large-hearted** *adj.* magnánimo, desprendido, generoso.

**large-minded** *adj.* de ideas liberales; comprensivo, de espíritu abierto.

**largeness** (-nis) *s.* grandor, extensión, amplitud. *2* magnanimidad.

**larger** (-oʳ) *adj. compar.* de LARGE.

**largess** (-is) *s.* don, dádiva, regalo.

**largest** (-est) *adj. superl.* de LARGE.

**largo** (laʳgou) *adj.-s.* MÚS. largo.

**lariat** (læ·riat) *s.* lazo, mangana; *boleadoras.

**lark** (laʳk) *s.* ORN. alondra, calandria. *2* diversión, retozo, holgorio: *to have a* ~, divertirse, echar una cana al aire.

**lark (to)** *intr.* bromear, divertirse.

**larkspur** (-spøʳ) *s.* BOT. espuela de caballero.

**Larry** (la·ri) *n. pr. dim.* de LAWRENCE.

**larva** (la·ʳva) *s.* ZOOL. larva.

**larvate(d** (la·ʳveit(id) *adj.* MED. larvado.

**laryngeal** (lari·ndȳial) *adj.* laríngeo.

**laryngitis** (lærindȳai·tis) *s.* MED. laringitis.

**laryngoscope** (læri·ngoscoup) *s.* laringoscopio.

**larynx** (læ·rinks) *s.* ANAT. laringe.

**lascivious** (læsi·viøs) *adj.* lascivo, torpe.

**lasciviousness** (-nis) *s.* lascivia.

**lash** (læsh) *s.* pestaña [del ojo]. *2* trallazo, latigazo, zurriagazo. *3* tralla [del látigo]; látigo, azote. *4* TEJ. tirataco.

**lash (to)** *tr.* azotar, fustigar, dar latigazos a. *2* romper contra [dicho de las olas]. *3* atar, trincar. *4* fustigar, vituperar. *5* mover vivamente. *6* excitar. *7 intr.* chasquear [el látigo]. *8* caer con fuerza [la lluvia]. *9* relampaguear. *10 to* ~ *out*, cocear; desatarse; desenfrenarse.

**lashing** (-ing) *s.* zurra, castigo de azotes. *2* fustigación. *3* atadura, cuerda, trinca.

**lass** (læs) *f.* chica, moza, zagala.

**lassie** (læ·si) *f.* muchachita.

**lassitude** (-itiud) *s.* lasitud, dejamiento, flojedad.

**lasso** (-ou) *s.* lazo, mangana.

**lasso (to)** *tr.* lazar, echar el lazo a.

**last** (læst) *adj.* último, postrero, final: ~ *but one*, *next to the* ~, penúltimo; ~ *Judgment*, juicio final; *Last Supper*, Cena [de Jesucristo]; ~ *will and testament*, DER. última voluntad; *the* ~ *straw*, el colmo, lo que faltaba. *2* pasado [más próximo en el pasado]: ~ *night*, anoche; ~ *year*, el año pasado. *3 s.* fin, final, término; lo último: *to see the* ~ *of one*, no volver a ver a uno, librarse de él; *at* ~, al fin, por fin; *to the* ~, hasta el fin. *4* duración, resistencia. *5* horma [de zapato]. *6 adv.* últimamente, finalmente. *7* la última vez, por última vez.

**last (to)** *intr.* durar. *2* perdurar, permanecer, continuar, conservarse.

**lasting** (-ing) *adj.* duradero, durable, perdurable. *2* sólido, permanente.

**lastly** (-li) *adv.* en último lugar, finalmente.

**last-minute** *adj.* de última hora.

**latch** (læch) *s.* picaporte, pestillo de golpe.

**latch (to)** *tr.* cerrar con picaporte o pestillo de golpe.

**latchkey** (-ki) *s.* llavín, picaporte [llave].

**late** (leit) *adj.* que llega, ocurre, hace o se hace tarde; retrasado, tardío, avanzado; de fines de:

*to be* ~, llegar tarde, retrasarse; ~ *fruits*, frutos tardíos; ~ *hour*, hora avanzada. *2* interior, último. *3* difunto: *the Mr. X*, el difunto señor **X**. *4* reciente. *5 adv.* tarde. *6* hasta una hora avanzada. *7* recientemente. *8 of* ~, últimamente. *9* ~ *in*, hacia fines de.

**late-comer** *s.* rezagado. *2* recién llegado.

**lateen´** (lætiˑn) *adj.* MAR. ~ *sail*, vela latina; ~ *yard*, entena.

**lately** (leiˑtli) *adv.* últimamente, recientemente.

**latency** (-ønsi) *s.* estado latente.

**latent** (-ønt) *adj.* latente. *2* oculto, disimulado.

**later** (-øʳ) *adj.-adv. compar.* de LATE: ~ *on*, más adelante.

**lateral** (læ·tøral) *adj.* lateral, ladero.

**Lateran** (læ·tøran) *adj.* lateranense. *2 s.* San Juan de Letrán (basílica). *3* palacio de Letrán.

**latest** (leiˑtist) *adj.-adv. superl.* de LATE: *the* ~ *fashion*, la última moda; *at the* ~, a más tardar.

**lath** (laz) *s.* CARP., ALBAÑ. listón, lata.

**lath (to)** *tr.* ALBAÑ. listonar, enlatar.

**lathe** (leid) *s.* MEC. torno [de tornear; de taladrar; de alfarero]. *2* TEJ. batán [del telar].

**lathe (to)** *tr.* tornear.

**lather** (læ·ðøʳ) *s.* jabonadura, espuma de jabón. *2* espuma de sudor.

**lather (to)** *tr.* enjabonar, jabonar. *2* fam. azotar, zurrar. *3 intr.* espumar, hacer espuma. *4* cubrirse de espuma [un caballo, etc.].

**lathery** (-i) *adj.* espumoso; cubierto de espuma.

**lathing** (læ·zing) *s.* enlatado, enlistonado.

**Latin** (læ·tin) *adj.* latino. *2 s.* latín [lengua], latino [pers.].

**Latinism** (-išm) *s.* latinismo.

**Latinist** (-ist) *s.* latinista.

**Latinity** (-iti) *s.* latinidad.

**Latinize (to)** (-aiš) *tr.* latinizar.

**latitude** (læ·titiud) *s.* GEOGR., ASTR. latitud. *2* latitud, amplitud, libertad.

**Latium** (læ·siøm) *n. pr.* GEOGR., HIST. Lacio.

**latria** (latrai·a) *s.* latria, culto de latría.

**latrine** (latriˑn) *s.* letrina.

**latten** (læ·tøn) *s.* latón en láminas.

**latter** (læ·tøʳ) *adj.* más reciente, moderno. *2* último. *3 the* ~, éste, esto, el segundo, este último.

**latter-day** *adj.* de nuestros días, moderno.

**Latter-Day Saints (the)** *s. pl.* los mormones.

**lattice** (læ·tis) *s.* celosía, enrejado, rejilla: ~ *window*, ventana con celosía.

**lattice (to)** (læ·tis) *tr.* enrejar, poner celosías en.

**latticework** (-wøʳk) *s.* enrejado, celosía.

**Latvia** (læ·tvia) *n. pr.* GEOGR. Letonia.

**laud** (lod) *s.* alabanza, loor. *2 pl.* LITURG. laudes.

**laud (to)** *tr.* loar, alabar, encomiar, elogiar.

**laudable** (-øbøl) *adj.* laudable, loable.

**laudanum** (-anøm) *s.* láudano.

**laudatory** (lo·datori) *adj.* laudatorio.

**laugh** (laf o læf) *s.* risa.

**laugh (to)** *intr.* reír, reírse: *to* ~ *at*, reírse de, burlarse de; *to* ~ *in one's sleeve*, reír para sus adentros. *2 tr.* expresar riendo. *3 to* ~ *away*, echar a broma; *to* ~ *off*, tomar a risa; hacer desaparecer riendo.

**laughable** (-øbøl) *adj.* risible, ridículo, divertido.

**laughing** (-ing) *adj.* riente, risueño, reidor. *2* risible: ~ *matter*, cosa de risa. *3* ~ *gas*, gas hilarante.

**laughingstock** (la·fing- o læ·fingstak) *s.* hazmerreír.

**laughter** (-tøʳ) *s.* risa, hilaridad.

**launch** (lonch) s. MAR. lanzamiento, botadura. *2* MAR. lancha, chalupa.

**launch (to)** *tr.* lanzar, arrojar. *2* MAR. lanzar, botar. *3* emprender. *4* lanzar [un producto, una ofensiva]. *5 intr.* lanzarse, arrojarse. *6 to ~ forth* o *out,* salir, ponerse en marcha.

**launder (to)** (lo·ndøʳ) *tr.-intr.* lavar y planchar [la ropa].

**laundress** (-ris) s. lavandera.

**laundry** (-ri) s. lavadero [cuarto]. *2* lavandería. *3* lavado [de la ropa]. *4* ropa lavada o para lavar.

**Laura** (lo·ra) *n. pr.* Laura.

**lauraceous** (lorei·shøs) *adj.* BOT. lauráceo.

**laureate** (lo·rieit o lo·riit) *adj.* laureado. *2* láureo. *3 s.* poeta laureado.

**laurel** (lo·røl) s. BOT. laurel. *2* fig. laurel, lauro.

**Laurence** (lo·røns) *n. pr.* Lorenzo.

**laurustine** (lo·røstin) s. BOT. durillo.

**lava** (la·va) s. lava [de volcán].

**lavabo** (lævei·bo) s. LITURG. lavabo.

**lavaret** (la·varet) s. ICT. farra.

**lavatory** (læ·vatori) s. lavabo; lavamanos; retrete. *2* LITURG. lavatorio.

**lave (to)** (lei·v) *tr.* poét. lavar, bañar.

**lavement** (-mønt) s. lavado, baño. *2* lavativa.

**lavender** (læ·vøndøʳ) s. BOT. lavándula, espliego, alhucema. *2* color de la flor de lavándula.

**lavish** (læ·vish) *adj.* pródigo, dadivoso; despilfarrado. *2* abundante, copioso, profuso.

**lavish (to)** *tr.* prodigar. *2* despilfarrar.

**lavishness** (-nis) s. prodigalidad, profusión, derroche, despilfarro.

**law** (lo) s. ley, regla, precepto, norma: fig. *to lay down the ~,* dictar la ley, hablar dogmáticamente. *2* ley [de Dios, de la natura, de la ciencia]. *3* derecho, jurisprudencia: *to study ~,* estudiar derecho [en el bufete de un abogado]. *4* ley, derecho [conjunto de leyes]; código, legislación, fuero: *commercial ~,* derecho mercantil, código de comercio: *civil ~,* derecho civil; *roman ~,* derecho romano. *5* foro, abogacía: *to enter the ~,* hacerse abogado. *6* justicia, administración de la justicia: *to take the ~ into one's own hands,* tomarse uno la justicia por su mano. *7* BIB. *the ~ of Moses,* la ley de Moisés.

**law-abiding** *adj.* observante de la ley.

**lawbreaker** (-breikøʳ) s. transgresor de la ley.

**lawful** (-ful) *adj.* legal, legítimo. *2* conforme a la ley, según derecho. *3* justo, válido; lícito. *4* DER. hábil [día]. *5 ~ age,* mayoría de edad.

**lawgiver** (-givøʳ) s. legislador.

**lawless** (-lis) *adj.* sin ley. *2* ilegal, ilícito. *3* desenfrenado, revoltoso; licencioso.

**lawmaker** (-meikøʳ) s. legislador.

**lawn** (lon) s. césped [terreno cubierto de], prado: *~ tennis,* lawn tennis, tenis. *2* linón. *3* fig. dignidad de obispo [anglicano].

**Lawrence** (lo·røns) *n. pr.* Lorenzo.

**lawsuit** (lo·siut) s. DER. proceso, pleito, litigio.

**lawyer** (lo·yøʳ) s. letrado, abogado, procurador, hombre de leyes.

**lax** (læks) *adj.* laxo, relajado, flojo, suelto. *2* flojo, negligente. *3* vago, impreciso.

**laxation** (-ei·shøn) s. laxación, laxamiento.

**laxative** (læ·ksativ) *adj.-s.* laxativo, laxante.

**laxity** (-iti) s. laxitud, flojedad. *2* relajamiento. *3* negligencia, descuido. *4* imprecisión.

**laxly** (-li) *adv.* flojamente, sueltamente.

**laxness** (-nis) s. LAXITY.

**1) lay** (lei) *pret.* de TO LIE [yacer, estar acostado, situado, etc.].

**2) lay** *adj.* laico, lego, secular, seglar: *~ brother,* converso; *~ sister,* lega. *2* lego, profano, no profesional. *3* MAR. *~ days,* estadía. *4 ~ figure,* maniquí articulado; fig. maniquí, persona manejada por otros. *5 s.* disposición, situación, orientación, caída, inclinación; sesgo, cariz: *~ of the land,* LIE OF THE LAND. *6* grado de torsión de una cuerda o cable. *7* pop. campo de operaciones; género de actividad, ocupación. *8* LIT. lay, balada, canción.

**lay (to)** *tr.* derribar, tumbar, acostar, tender. *2* poner, depositar, dejar; colocar, instalar. *3* enterrar. *4* poner, dejar [en cierto estado, situación, etc.]. *5* tender [un cable, etc.]. *6* extender, aplicar [sobre]. *7* cubrir, tapizar, adornar. *8* disponer, preparar, trazar, urdir. *9* poner [huevos; la mesa]. *10* imponer [cargas, etc.]. *11* calmar, aquietar, sosegar. *12* hacer huir [a un fantasma o aparecido]. *13* echar [la culpa], atribuir. *14* presentar, exponer. *15* apostar [dinero]; hacer [una apuesta]. *16* situar [la acción de un drama, etc.]. *17* torcer [cabos], hacer [una cuerda]. *18* MAR. alejarse de. *19* apuntar [un cañón]. *20* matar [el polvo]. *21 to ~ aside,* poner a un lado; desechar; guardar, ahorrar. *22 to ~ bare,* desnudar; descubrir; poner al descubierto. *23 to ~ by,* guardar, ahorrar. *24 to ~ claim to,* reclamar, pretender. *25 to ~ down,* acostar, derribar; entregar, rendir; abandonar; dimitir; apostar [dinero]; urdir, tramar, delinear, proyectar; formular, establecer; dictar [la ley]. *26 to ~ hands on,* poner las manos encima a; tomar, coger; ECLES. imponer las manos. *27 to ~ hold of,* asir, tomar, apoderarse de. *28 to ~ in,* hacer provisión de; almacenar; PINT. bosquejar. *29 to ~ low,* derribar, matar. *30 to ~ on,* aplicar, dar [pintura, etc.]; pegar, atacar; distribuir, instalar [gas, agua, electricidad]. *31 to ~ out,* extender, desplegar; disponer, arreglar, trazar, proyectar; amortajar; invertir [dinero]. *32 to ~ siege to,* poner sitio a. *33 to ~ stress on,* insistir, hacer hincapié en. *34* MAR. *to ~ to,* poner al pairo. *35 to ~ to heart,* tomar a pecho. *36 to ~ up,* guardar, amontonar; hacer guardar cama; MAR. desarmar. *37 to ~ waste,* asolar, devastar. *38 intr.* poner [las gallinas]. *39* aplicarse vigorosamente. *40* MAR. situarse. *41 to ~ about,* dar palos en todas direcciones. *42* MAR. *to ~ to,* estar al pairo. ¶ Pret. y p. p.: *laid.*

**layer** (lei·øʳ) s. colocador, instalador. *2* gallina ponedora. *3* capa, lecho, estrato. *4* ALBAÑ. hilada. *5* AGR. acodo.

**layer (to)** *tr.* AGR. acodar.

**layette** (leiye·t) s. canastilla [de recién nacido].

**laying** (lei·ing) s. colocación, instalación. *2* tendido [de un cable, etc.]. *3* primera capa [de un enlucido]. *4* estrato. *5* postura [de huevos]. *7 ~ on of hands,* imposición de manos.

**layman** (-mæn) s. lego, laico, seglar. *2* lego, profano [en una materia].

**layoff** (-of) s. despido [de obreros].

**layout** (-aut) s. arreglo, disposición, plan, esquema. *2* equipo [de útiles, etc.].

**layover** (-ouvøʳ) s. detención [en un viaje].

**lazar** (læ·šaʳ) s. apestado. *2* leproso, lazarino.

**lazaret** (læ·šaret), **lazaretto** (-ou) s. lazareto. *2* leprosería. *3* MAR. pañol.

**Lazarist** (læ·šarist) s. lazarista.

**Lazarous** (læ·šarøs) *n. pr.* Lázaro.

**laze (to)** (leiš) *intr.* holgazanear, estar ocioso.

**laziness** (lei·šinis) *s.* pereza, holgazanería, indolencia, ociosidad.

**lazuli** (læ·šiuli) *s.* lapislázuli.

**lazulite** (læ·šiulait) *s.* MINER. lazulita.

**lazy** (lei·ši) *adj.* perezoso, holgazán, indolente, ocioso. *2* lento, pesado.

**lea** (lɪ) *s.* pasto, prado.

**leach** (lɪch) *s.* cenizas de lejía. *2* colada [de la ropa]. *3* lixiviación.

**leach (to)** *tr.* colar [la ropa]. *2* lixiviar.

**leachy** (lɪ·chi) *adj.* permeable, poroso.

**1) lead** (led) *s.* plomo [metal]; objeto de plomo. *2* MAR. plomada, sonda: ~ *line*, sondaleza. *3* IMPR. interlínea, regleta. *4* MINER. grafito, plombagina. *5* mina. *6 pl.* emplomaduras [de las vidrieras].

**2) lead** (lɪd) *s.* primacía, primer lugar. *2* dirección, mando, guía. *3* delantera, ventaja [en una carrera]. *4* ejemplo, indicación, etc. [con que se guía a otro o se le sugiere algo]. *5* salida [en el juego]; palo o ficha con que se sale. *6* MEC., ELECT. avance. *7* ELECT. conductor; hilo de entrada. *8* traílla, correa [de perro]. *9* TEAT. primer papel; primer actor; primera actriz. *10* BOX. primer golpe. *11* MÚS. guía.

**1) lead (to)** (led) *tr.* emplomar, guarnecer de plomo. *2* IMPR. interlinear, regletear. ¶ Pret. y p. p.: *leaded.*

**2) lead (to)** (lɪd) *tr.* llevar, conducir, guiar; mover, impulsar, inducir; atraer. *2* dirigir, llevar la batuta; acaudillar. *3* hacer pasar [una cuerda, un hilo, etc.]. *4* conducir [agua, vapor, etc.]. *5* llevar [un género de vida]. *6* ir delante o a la cabeza; ser el primero entre. *7* salir [de un palo o ficha]. *8 to* ~ *astray*, descarriar, seducir. *9 to* ~ *off*, iniciar, abrir [el baile, etc.]. *10 to* ~ *out*, sacar a bailar. *11 to* ~ *the way*, ir delante, mostrar el camino. *12 intr.* mandar en jefe, guiar, dirigir. *13* ser el primero. *14* ir delante. *15* ser mano, salir [en el juego]. *16* conducir, llevar [ser camino de]. *17* dar, salir [una puerta, un pasadizo]. *18* BOX. pasar al ataque. *19 to* ~ *up to*, conducir o llevar a; llevar la conversación a. ¶ Pret. y p. p.: *led.*

**leaded** (le·did) *adj.* emplomado, guarnecido de plomo.

**leaden** (-øn) *adj.* de plomo. *2* plomizo, plúmbeo. *3* pesado, lento. *4* cargado [de sueño, etc.].

**leaden-eyed** *adj.* soñoliento, de ojos soñolientos.

**leaden-footed** *adj.* lento, tardo.

**leader** (lɪ·døʳ) *s.* conductor, guía. *2* jefe, caudillo, adalid, cabecilla. *3* director [de orquesta]. *4* primer violín. *5* el que va delante. *6* guía, caballo delantero. *7* editorial, artículo de fondo. *8* ALBAÑ. condutal. *9* MEC. rueda motriz. *10* MEC., MIN. guía. *11* guía [de un árbol o planta]. *12 pl.* IMPR. línea de puntos para guiar la vista.

**leadership** (-ship) *s.* dirección, jefatura, caudillaje. *2* dotes de mando.

**1) leading** (le·ding) *s.* objetos de plomo. *2* IMPR. interlineación.

**2) leading** (lɪ·ding) *adj.* que va delante; que guía o conduce; primero, principal, capital: ~ *article*, artículo de fondo; ~ *question*, pregunta que sugiere la respuesta. *2 s.* guía, conducción, dirección.

**leadwort** (le·duøʳt) *s.* BOT. belesa.

**leady** (le·di) *adj.* plomizo.

**leaf** (lɪf) *pl.* **leaves** (-vš) *s.* BOT. hoja; pétalo. *2* hoja [de libro, puerta, etc.]: *to turn a new* ~, mudar

de vida; enmendarse; *over the* ~, a la vuelta. *3* ala [de mesa]. *4* hoja [lámina delgada].

**leaf (to)** *intr.* BOT. echar hojas. *2 tr.* hojear [un libro].

**leafage** (-idy̆) *s.* follaje, frondas.

**leafed** (-t) *adj.* que tiene hojas; de hojas: *broad-leafed*, de hojas anchas.

**leaflet** (-lit) *s.* hojita, hojuela. *2* BOT. folíolo. *3* hoja impresa, papel volante.

**leafstalk** (-stok) *s.* BOT. pecíolo, rabillo de hoja.

**leafy** (-i) *adj.* frondoso. *2* hojoso, hojudo.

**league** (lɪg) *s.* liga, unión, alianza, confederación. *2* legua. *3* DEP. liga.

**league (to)** *tr.* ligar, unir, confederar. *2 intr.* ligarse, unirse, aliarse, confederarse.

**leaguer** (-øʳ) *s.* miembro de una liga.

**Leah** (lɪ·a) *n. pr.* BIB. Lía.

**leak** (lɪk) *s.* escape, fuga [de un fluido]; goteo, filtración [de un líquido]. *2* fig. filtración [de dinero, noticias, etc.]. *3* ELECT. pérdida de corriente. *4* grieta, raja, gotera. *5* MAR. vía de agua.

**leak (to)** *intr.* salirse, tener escapes o pérdidas [un recipiente, etc.] hacer agua [un buque]. *2* salirse, escapar, perderse [un fluido]. *3* gotear [un techo]. *4* filtrarse [dinero, noticias].

**leakage** (-idy̆) *s.* goteo, derrame, fuga, escape, filtración. *2* ELECT. pérdida [de corriente]; dispersión. *3* COM. pérdida, merma, derrame [avería].

**leaky** (-i) *adj.* resquebrajado, que se sale, que tiene escapes, que hace agua. *2* llovedizo [techo]. *3* fam. hablador, indiscreto [persona].

**leal** (lɪ·øl) (Esc.) *adj.* leal, honrado.

**lean** (lɪn) *adj.* delgado, flaco, enjuto, cenceño, seco. *2* magro. *3* pobre, escaso; deficiente. *4* estéril, improductivo. *5* de carestía, de escasez. *6 s.* carne magra o mollar. *7* LEANING 2.

**lean (to)** *intr.* apoyarse; reclinarse, recostarse: *to* ~ *back*, retreparse. *2* inclinarse, ladearse, torcerse. *3* inclinarse [en opinión, deseo, etc.]. *4 tr.* apoyar, recostar, reclinar, descansar.

**Leander** (lɪæ·ndøʳ) *n. pr.* Leandro.

**leaning** (lɪ·ning) *s.* inclinación, ladeo. *2* inclinación, propensión, tendencia, preferencia. *3 adj.* inclinado.

**leanness** (-nis) *s.* delgadez, flacura, magrura. *2* pobreza, escasez, esterilidad.

**lean-to** (-tu) *s.* alpende, cobertizo.

**lean-witted** *adj.* necio, tonto.

**leap** (lɪp) *s.* salto, brinco; cabriola, zapateta: *by leaps and bounds*, rápidamente. *2 adj.* ~ *year*, año bisiesto.

**leap (to)** *intr.* saltar, brincar, dar un salto. *2* saltar [de un sitio, etc. a otro]. *3* latir fuertemente. *4 tr.* saltar [salvar de un salto]. *5* hacer saltar. ¶ Pret. y p. p.: *leaped* o *leapt.*

**leaper** (-øʳ) *s.* saltador, brincador.

**leapfrog** (-frag) *s.* fil derecho, salto [juego].

**learn (to)** (løʳn) *tr.-intr.* aprender, instruirse. *2 tr.* enterarse de, tener noticia de, oír decir. ¶ Pret. y p. p.: *learned* o *learnt.*

**learned** (-id) *adj.* ilustrado, docto, sabio, erudito, versado.

**learning** (-ing) *s.* instrucción, ilustración, saber, ciencia, erudición. *2* aprendizaje, estudio.

**learnt** (-t) *pret.* y *p. p.* de TO LEARN.

**lease** (lɪs) *s.* arriendo, arrendamiento.

**lease (to)** *tr.* arrendar, dar o tomar en arriendo.

**leash** (lɪsh) *s.* traílla, correa. *2* pihuela. *3* grupo de tres. *4* TEJ. lizo.

**leash (to)** *tr.* atraillar, atar.

**least** (lɪst) *adj. superl.* de LITTLE. *2* mínimo, menor,

más pequeño: ~ *common multiple*, mínimo común múltiplo. *3 s. the* ~, lo más pequeño, lo menos; *at* ~, *at the* ~, al menos, a lo menos, por lo menos; *not in the* ~, de ningún modo. *4 adv.* en el menor grado.
**leastways** (-ueiš), **leastwise** (-uaiš) *adv.* al menos, por lo menos.
**leather** (-le·ðøʳ) *s.* cuero, piel [curtida]: ~ *dresser*, curtidor; ~ *strap*, correa. *2* fam. pellejo [de persona]. *3* objeto de cuero; suela [de taco].
**leather (to)** *tr.* forrar o guarnecer de cuero. *2* hacer cuero. *3* fam. pegar, zurrar.
**leatherback** (-bæk) *s.* ZOOL. laúd [tortuga].
**leather-bound** *adj.* encuadernado en piel.
**leatherette** (-e·t) *s.* papel o tela que imita el cuero.
**leathern** (-n) *adj.* de cuero. *2* coriáceo.
**leatheroid** (-oid) *s.* cuero artificial.
**leathery** (-i) *adj.* coriáceo, correoso.
**leave** (lɪv) *s.* licencia, permiso, venia: ~ *of absence*, MIL. licencia, permiso; *by your* ~, *with your* ~, con su permiso. *2* despedida: *to take* ~, despedirse.
**1) leave (to)** *tr.* dejar [no tocar, no ocuparse de, etc.]. *2* dejar [algo tras de sí, hacer que quede algo]; dejar [en un lugar, estado, etc.]: *to* ~ *behind*, dejar atrás; dejar, dejarse olvidado; *to* ~ *in the lurch*, dejar en la estacada; *to* ~ *out*, dejar fuera, omitir; ~ *to word*, dejar dicho, dejar recado. *3* dejar, abandonar, separarse de, salir de. *4* dejar de, cesar de. *5* dejar [al morir]; legar. *6* ARIT. *four from five leaves one*, de cuatro a cinco va uno. *7 to* ~ *off*, dejar de [hacer una cosa]; dejar [el trabajo, una hábito]; dejar de usar [una prenda]. *8 intr.* partir, salir, irse, marcharse. *9* acabar, cesar. ¶ Pret. y p. p.: *left*.
**2) leave (to)** *intr.* echar hojas [las plantas]. ¶ Pret. y p. p.: *leaved*.
**leaved** (-d) *adj.* BOT. de hojas: *entire-leaved*, de hojas enteras.
**leaven** (le·vøn) *s.* levadura, fermento.
**leaven (to)** *tr.* leudar, hacer fermentar. *2* fig. penetrar, impregnar, imbuir, viciar.
**leavening** (-ning) *s.* levadura.
**leaves** (lɪvš) *s. pl.* de LEAF. *2* ENCUAD. cantos [de un libro]: *gilt* ~, cantos dorados.
**leave-taking** *s.* despedida.
**leavings** (lɪ·vings) *s. pl.* restos, sobras, desperdicios.
**Lebanese** (le·bøniš) *adj.-s.* libanés.
**Lebanon** (le·bønøn) *n. pr.* GEOGR. Líbano.
**lecher** (le·chøʳ) *s.* libertino, disoluto.
**lecherous** (-øs) *adj.* lujurioso, lascivo, salaz.
**lechery** (-i) *s.* libertinaje, lujuria.
**lecithin** (le·sizin) *s.* QUÍM. lecitina.
**lectern** (le·ktøʳn) *s.* facistol.
**lection** (-shøn) *s.* LITURG. lección.
**lectionary** (-eri) *s.* leccionario.
**lector** (-tøʳ) *s.* ECLES. lector.
**lectorate** (-it) *s.* ECLES. lectorado.
**lecture** (-chøʳ) *s.* conferencia, disertación, lección, plática. *2* represión, sermón.
**lecture (to)** *intr.* disertar, dar una conferencia. *2 tr.* enseñar, sermonear, reprender.
**lecturer** (-øʳ) *s.* disertante, conferenciante. *2* lector.
**lectureship** (-ship) *s.* lectoría; cátedra.
**led** (led) *pret.* y *p. p.* de TO LEAD.
**ledge** (ledÿ) *s.* anaquel, repisa. *2* saliente o rellano estrecho. *3* arrecife. *4* MIN. vena.
**ledger** (-øʳ) *s.* COM. mayor [libro]. *2* losa [piedra]. *3* traviesa [de andamio].

**lee** (lɪ) *s.* abrigo, socaire. *2* MAR. sotavento.
**leeboard** (lɪ·boʳd) *s.* MAR. orza de deriva.
**leech** (lɪch) *s.* MED. ventosa. *3* ant. médico. *4* MAR. caída [de vela].
**leech (to)** *tr.* poner sanguijuelas a.
**leek** (lɪk) *s.* BOT. puerro.
**leer** (liøʳ) *s.* mirada de soslayo [con expresión maligna, astuta o lujuriosa].
**leer (to)** *tr.* atraer [con miradas]. *2 intr.* mirar de soslayo [con expresión maligna, astuta o lujuriosa].
**leery** (-ri) *adj.* fam. astuto, suspicaz, receloso.
**lees** (lɪš) *s. pl.* heces, poso.
**leeward** (lɪuøʳd o lu·øʳd) *s.* sotavento. *3 adv.* a sotavento, hacia sotavento.
**leeway** (-uei) *s.* MAR. deriva, abatimiento. *2* margen de tiempo, etc.; plazo, respiro.
**left** (left) *pret.* y *p. p.* de TO LEAVE: *to be* ~ *over*, ser dejado, quedar, sobrar. *2 adj.* izquierdo, siniestro. *3 s.* izquierda.
**left-hand** *adj.* izquierdo; de la izquierda; hecho con la izquierda o hacia la izquierda; ~ *drive*, AUTO. conducción a la izquierda.
**left-handed** *adj.* zurdo. *2* de la mano izquierda. *3* torpe, desmañado. *4* insincero. *5* que gira hacia la izquierda.
**leftist** (-ist) *adj.-s.* POL. izquierdista.
**leftover** (-ouvøʳ) *adj.* que queda, sobrante. *2 s.* sobrante, resto. *4 pl.* sobras.
**leg** (leg) *s.* ANAT. pierna: *to give a* ~ *up*, ayudar a subir; *on one's last legs*, agonizante; en las últimas; sin recursos; *on one's legs*, en pie; restablecido; en próspero estado. *2* pata [de animal]. *3* pie, pata [de un mueble, etc.]. *4* puntal, apoyo: *not to have a* ~ *to stand on*, no tener una razón en que apoyarse. *5* COC. pierna [de cordero, etc.]. *6* pierna [de media, de compás]. *7* pernera, pernil [de pantalón], caña [de bota]. *8* GEOM. cateto. *9* etapa, trecho. *10* MAR. bordada.
**leg (to)** *tr.* hacer con la pierna; tirar de la pierna; dar en la pierna. *2 to* ~ *it*, andar, correr.
**legacy** (le·gasi) *s.* legado, manda, herencia.
**legal** (lɪ·gal) *adj.* legal: ~ *tender*, curso legal, moneda de curso legal. *2* legítimo, lícito. *3* jurídico.
**legalism** (lɪ·gališm) *s.* legalismo.
**legality** (ligæ·liti) *s.* legalidad; legitimidad.
**legalize (to)** (lɪ·galaiš) *tr.* legalizar [dar estado o validez legal]. *2* refrendar, autorizar.
**legate** (le·git) *s.* legado [pers.].
**legate (to)** (li·geit) *tr.* DER. legar.
**legatee** (le·gætɪ) *s.* legatario.
**legateship** (le·gitship) *s.* legacía.
**legation** (ligei·shøn) *s.* legación. *2* misión, embajada.
**legend** (le·dÿønd) *s.* leyenda. *2* legenda.
**legendary** (-eri) *adj.* legendario.
**leger** (le·dÿøʳ) *adj.* MÚS. suplementario [espacio, línea].
**legerdemain** (ledÿøʳdimei·n) *s.* juego de manos, prestidigitación.
**legged** (le·gd o le·gid) *adj.* de piernas o patas: *bandy-legged*, estevado.
**legging** (-ing) *s.* polaina, sobrecalza.
**Leghorn** (-joʳn) *n. pr.* GEOGR. Liorna.
**legibility** (ledÿibi·liti) *s.* legibilidad.
**legible** (le·dÿibøl) *adj.* legible.
**legion** (lɪ·dÿøn) *s.* legión.
**legionary** (-eri) *adj.-s.* legionario.
**legislate (to)** (le·dÿisleit) *intr.* legislar.
**legislation** (-ei·shøn) *s.* legislación.

**legislative** (le·dẏisleitiv) *adj.* legislativo. *2 s.* poder o cuerpo legislativo.
**legislator** (-ø$^r$) *m.* legislador.
**legislatress** (-ris) *f.* legisladora.
**legislature** (le·dẏislechø$^r$) *s.* cuerpo o cuerpos legisladores. *2* función legislativa: *term of* ~, legislatura.
**legist** (lı·dẏist) *s.* legista.
**legitim** (le·dẏitim) *s.* DER. legítima.
**legitimacy** (lidẏi·timasi) *adj.* legitimidad.
**legitimate** (-it) *adj.* legítimo. *2* lógico, razonable. *3 the* ~ *drama*, el teatro serio o clásico.
**legitimate (to)** (-eit) *tr.* legitimar. *2* justificar, aprobar. *3* dar fuerza legal.
**legitimation** (-ei·shøn) *s.* legitimación.
**legitime** (le·dẏitim) *s.* LEGITIM.
**legitimist** (lidẏi·timist) *s.* POL. legitimista.
**legitimize (to)** (-aiš) *tr.* legitimar.
**leg-of-mutton** *adj.* triangular [vela]; de pernil [manga].
**legume** (le·gium), **legumen** (legiu·møn) *s.* BOT. legumbre. *2* COC. verdura.
**legumin** (legiu·min) *s.* QUÍM. legúmina.
**leguminous** (-øs) *adj.* leguminoso.
**leisure** (le·ẏø$^r$) *s.* ocio, vagar, desocupación; tiempo libre: ~ *hours*, horas de ocio, ratos perdidos; *at one's* ~, a la conveniencia de uno, cuando uno pueda.
**leisurely** (-li) *adj.* lento, pausado, sosegado. *2* desocupado. *3 adv.* despacio, sin prisas.
**lemma** (le·ma) *s.* lema.
**lemniscate** (le·mniskeit) *s.* GEOM. lemniscata.
**lemniscus** (le·mniscøs) *s.* lemnisco.
**lemon** (le·møn) *s.* BOT. limón: ~ *tree*, limonero. *2* BOT. ~ *balm*, toronjil. *3* ~ *verbena*, luisa, hierba luisa.
**lemonade** (lemønei·d) *s.* limonada.
**lemur** (lı·mø$^r$) *s.* ZOOL. lémur, lemúrido.
**lemures** (le·miuriš) *s. pl.* MIT. lémures.
**lend (to)** (lend) *tr.* prestar [dar prestado; dar, comunicar, proporcionar]: *to* ~ *oneself*, o *itself*, *to*, entregarse, acomodarse, prestarse a. ¶ Pret. y p. p.: *lent*.
**lender** (-ø$^r$) *s.* prestador, prestamista.
**lending library** (-ing) *s.* biblioteca circulante.
**length** (lengz) *s.* longitud; largo; extensión, duración: *at full* ~, por extenso; tendido, cuan largo es uno; *at* ~, por extenso; al fin, a la larga. *2* espacio, trecho, trozo. *3* grado, punto, extremo [en una acción, esfuerzo, etc.]: *to go any* ~, hacer uno todo lo posible.
**lengthen (to)** (-øn) *tr.* alargar, prolongar. *2* aguar, diluir. *3 intr.* alargarse, prolongarse.
**lengthways** (-ueiš), **lengthwise** (-uaiš) *adv.* longitudinalmente, a la larga.
**lengthy** (-i) *adj.* largo; difuso, prolijo.
**leniency** (lı·niønsi) *s.* lenidad, indulgencia; suavidad.
**lenient** (-ønt) *adj.* indulgente, clemente; suave.
**lenify (to)** (le·nifai) *tr.* lenificar.
**lenitive** (-tiv) *adj.-s.* lenitivo.
**lenity** (-i) *s.* lenidad, blandura, suavidad.
**lens** (lenš) *s.* ÓPT. lente. *2* ANAT. cristalino.
**Lent** (lent) *s.* cuaresma, cuadragésima.
**lent** *pret.* y *p. p.* de TO LEND.
**lenten** (-øn) *adj.* cuaresmal.
**lenticular** (lenti·kiula$^r$) *adj.* lenticular.
**lentil** (le·ntil) *s.* BOT. lenteja.
**lentiscus** (lenti·skøs), **lentisk** (le·ntisk) *s.* BOT. lentisco.
**Leo** (lı·ou) *s.* ASTR. leo, león. *2 n. pr.* León.

**Leonard** (le·na$^r$d) *n. pr.* Leonardo.
**Leonese** (liøni·š), *pl.* **-nese** (-ši) *adj.-s.* leonés.
**leonine** (lı·ønain) *adj.* leonino.
**Leonora** (li·ønora), **Leonore** (li·ønou$^r$) *n. pr.* Leonor.
**leopard** (le·pa$^r$d) *s.* ZOOL. leopardo.
**Leopold** (lı·øpould) *n. pr.* Leopoldo.
**leper** (le·pø$^r$) *s.* leproso.
**Lepidoptera** (lepida·ptøra) *s. pl.* ENT. lepidópteros.
**lepidopteran** (-n) *adj.-s.* ENT. lepidóptero.
**leporine** (le·pørin o le·pørain) *adj.* leporino.
**leprosarium** (leprøse·riøm) *s.* leprosería.
**leprosy** (le·prøsi) *s.* MED. lepra.
**leprous** (le·prøs) *adj.* leproso. *2* HIST. NAT. escamoso.
**Lesbian** (le·šbian) *adj.-s.* lesbiano, lesbio.
**lese-majesty** (lı·šmæ·dẏesti) *s.* lesa majestad.
**lesien** (lı·ẏøn) *s.* lesión.
**less** (les) *adj.-adv.-prep.* menos: ~ *and* ~, cada vez menos; *the* ~ ..., *the* ... *(the more)*, cuanto menos..., menos (o más). *2 adj.* menor: *to grow* ~, disminuir.
**lessee** (lesı·) *adj.* DER. arrendatario.
**lessen (to)** (le·søn) *tr.* minorar, disminuir, achicar, reducir. *2* rebajar, quitar importancia a. *3 intr.* disminuirse, menguar, decrecer.
**lesser** (le·sø$^r$) *adj. compar.* de LITTLE: menor, más pequeño. *2* BOT., ZOOL. menor.
**lesson** (le·søn) *s.* lección. *2* enseñanza, ejemplo.
**lesson (to)** *tr.* enseñar; amonestar, reprender.
**lessor** (le·sø$^r$) *s.* DER. arrendador.
**lest** (lest) *conj.* para que no, de miedo de que, por miedo de que, no sea que.
**let** (let) *s.* estorbo, obstáculo, impedimento.
**let (to)** *tr.* arrendar, alquilar [dar en arriendo o alquiler]: *to* ~, se alquila, por o para alquilar. *2* dejar, permitir. *3* dejar o hacer entrar, pasar o salir [por una puerta, etc.]. *4* sacar [sangre a un enfermo]. *5* Como auxiliar sirve para formar imperativos y subjuntivos de otros verbos: *let's run*, corramos: ~ *him come*, que venga. *6 to* ~ *alone*, dejar en paz; no tocar; ~ *alone* [usado adverbialmente], por no decir, por no hablar de, y mucho menos. *7 to* ~ *down*, dejar caer, bajar, descolgar; abandonar, traicionar, dejar colgado; chasquear; humillar. *8 to* ~ *go*, dejar ir; soltar, aflojar. *9 to* ~ *in*, dejar o hacer entrar, meter; embutir. *10 to* ~ *know*, hacer saber. *11 to* ~ *loose*, soltar, desatar; desencadenar, aflojar. *12 to* ~ *off*, disparar [un arma]; soltar, dejar salir. *13 to* ~ *out*, dejar o hacer salir; dejar escapar; soltar; aflojar; largar [un cabo]; ensanchar [un vestido]; arrendar, alquilar.
   *14 intr.* arrendarse o alquilarse. *15 to* ~ *up*, cesar, desistir; disminuir, moderarse. ¶ Pret. y p. p.: *let*; ger.: *letting*.
**letdown** (-daun) *s.* aflojamiento, disminución. *2* chasco, desilusión. *3* humillación.
**lethal** (lı·zal) *adj.* letal.
**lethargic (al** (liza$^r$dẏik(al) *adj.* letárgico.
**lethargy** (le·za$^r$dẏi) *s.* letargo.
**Lethe** (le·z) *n. pr.* MIT. Leteo [río]. *2* fig. olvido.
**Lethean** (lizı·an) *adj.* leteo.
**Letitia** (leti·shia) *n. pr.* Leticia.
**let's** (le·ts) *contr.* de LET US.
**Lett** (let) *s.* letón.
**letter** (le·tø$^r$) *s.* letra [del alfabeto]. *2* IMPR. letra, tipo, carácter. *3* letra [sentido literal]: *to the* ~, al pie de la letra. *4* carta, epístola, documento: ~ *of credit*, carta de crédito; *letters patent*, patente, privilegio; ejecutoria [de nobleza]; *letters*

*rogatory*, DER. exhorto; ~ *book*, copiador [libro]; ~ *box*, buzón [para cartas]; ~ *opener*, plegadera; ~ *press*, prensa de copiar cartas. *5 pl.* letras, literatura.
**letter (to)** *tr.* rotular, estampar o marcar con letras.
**lettered** (-d) *adj.* rotulado, marcado con letras. *2* culto, instruido, docto, letrado.
**letterhead** (-jed) *s.* membrete [de carta]. *2* hoja o pliego de papel con membrete.
**lettering** (-ing) *s.* inscripción, letrero. *2* acción de poner letras o letreros.
**letterless** (-lis) *adj.* iletrado.
**letterpress** (-pres) *s.* IMPR. letra impresa, texto [a distinción de las ilustraciones y grabados].
**lettues** (le·tis) *s.* BOT. lechuga.
**letup** (le·tøp) *s.* fam. calma, disminución.
**leucocyte** (liu·kouseit) *s.* FISIOL. leucocito.
**leucoma** (liukou·ma) *s.* MED. leucoma.
**leukemia** (liuki·mia) *s.* MED. leucemia.
**Levant** (livæ·nt) *n. pr.* Levante [parte oriental del Mediterráneo].
**levant (to)** *intr.* (Ingl.) marcharse [esp. sin pagar las deudas de juego].
**levanter** (-øᵣ) *s.* viento de levante.
**Levantine** (-in) *adj.-s.* levantino [del Levante].
1) **levee** (le·vi o levi·) *s.* besamanos, recepción.
2) **levee** (le·vi) *s.* (E.U.) dique para contener las aguas. *2* (E.U.) desembarcadero.
**level** (-øl) *adj.* llano, liso, igualado, nivelado, horizontal; ~ *crossing*, FERROC. paso a nivel. *2* igual, que está al mismo nivel: ~ *with*, al nivel de; igual que. *3* igual, uniforme, poco accidentado. *4* equilibrado; imparcial. *5* juicioso, discreto. *6 to do one's* ~ *best*, esforzarse, esmerarse. *7 s.* nivel [aparato; grado de elevación; altura, categoría]: *on a* ~ *with*, al mismo nivel que. *8* plano horizontal, llano, llanura. *9 adv.* a nivel. *10* en línea recta; directamente.
**level (to)** *tr.* nivelar. *2* enrasar. *3* allanar, igualar. *4* derribar; arrasar. *5* apuntar, asestar [un arma]; dirigir [la mirada, etc.]. *6* poner al nivel o al alcance [de]. *7 to* ~ *off*, aplanar, nivelar. ¶ Pret. y p. p.: *leveled* o *-lled;* ger.: *leveling* o *-lling.*
**level-headed** *adj.* juicioso, sensato, de buen sentido.
**lever** (le·vøᵣ) *s.* FÍS., MEC. palanca. *2* fig. palanca [medio, influencia].
**lever (to)** *tr.* apalancar.
**leverage** (le·vørid̯) *s.* acción o poder de una palanca. *2* sistema de palancas. *3* fig. medios o influencia para conseguir una cosa.
**leveret** (le·vøret) *s.* ZOOL. lebrato.
**leviathan** (livai·azan) *s.* leviatán.
**levigate (to)** (le·vigeit) *tr.* levigar. *2* pulverizar.
**levirate** (le·virit) *s.* levirato.
**levitation** (levitei·shøn) *s.* levitación.
**Levite** (li·vait) *s.* levita [pers.].
**Levitic (al** (livi·tik(al) *adj.* levítico.
**Leviticus** (-øs) *s.* Levítico [libro de la Biblia].
**levity** (le·viti) *s.* levedad. *2* frivolidad. *3* veleidad.
**levulose** (le·viulous) *s.* QUÍM. levulosa.
**levy** (le·vi) *s.* leva, recluta, enganche. *2* exacción, imposición, recaudación [de tributos, etc.]. *3* DER. embargo.
**levy (to)** *tr.* reclutar, hacer leva de. *2* hacer [guerra]. *3* exigir, recaudar [tributos, etc.]. *4* DER. embargar.
**lewd** (liu·d) *adv.* lujurioso, lascivo, lúbrico, obsceno. *2* libertino, disoluto.
**Lewis** (lu·is) *n. pr.* Luis.

**lexicographer** (leksika·graføᵣ) *s.* lexicógrafo.
**lexicography** (-i) *s.* lexicografía.
**lexicon** (le·ksikøn) *s.* léxico, diccionario.
**Leyden jar** (lai·døn) *s.* FÍS. botella de Leiden.
**liability** (lalabi·liti) *s.* riesgo, exposición, posibilidad de incurrir [en]. *2* responsabilidad, obligación [pecuniaria]. *3 pl.* COM. deudas, obligaciones, pasivo.
**liable** (lai·abøl) *adj.* expuesto, sujeto, propenso. *2* obligado, responsable [pecuniariamente].
**liaison** (lieʃo·n o liei·ʃøn) *s.* lazo, unión. *2* enlace, coordinación: ~ *officer*, MIL. oficial de enlace. *3* FONÉT. enlace. *4* enredo [relación ilícita].
**liana** (liæ·na), **liane** (lia·n) *s.* BOT. bejuco, liana.
**liar** (lai·aᵣ) *s.* embustero, mentiroso.
**Liassic** (laiæ·sik) *adj.-s.* GEOL. liásico.
**libation** (laibei·ʃøn) *s.* libación.
**libel** (lai·bøl) *s.* libelo; calumnia, difamación.
**libel(l)ous** (-øs) *adj.* difamatorio, calumniador.
**libellula** (laibe·liula) *s.* ENT. libélula.
**liber** (lai·bøᵣ) *s.* BOT. líber. *2* libro registro.
**liberal** (li·børal) *adj.* liberal, generoso. *2* abundante. *3* noble, caballeroso. *4* latitudinario, despreocupado. *5* libre [traducción, etc.]. *6* ~ *arts*, artes liberales. *7 adj.-s.* POL. liberal.
**liberalism** (-iʃm) *s.* liberalismo.
**liberality** (libøræ·liti) *s.* liberalidad. *2* don, dádiva.
**liberalize (to)** (li·børalaiʃ) *tr.* liberalizar.
**liberate (to)** (li·børeit) *tr.* libertar, liberar.
**liberation** (libørei·ʃøn) *s.* liberación. *2* redención [de cautivos].
**liberator** (libørei·tøᵣ) *s.* liberador, libertador.
**Liberia** (laibi·ria) *s.* GEOGR. Liberia.
**liberticidal** (libøᵣtisai·dal) *adj.* liberticida.
**libertine** (li·bøᵣtin) *adj.-s.* libertino; disoluto. *2* librepensador.
**libertinism** (-iʃm) *s.* libertinaje.
**liberty** (li·bøᵣti) *s.* libertad: ~ *of press*, libertad de imprenta; ~ *cap*, gorro frigio; *to be at* ~ *to*, ser libre de; tener permiso para [hacer algo]; *to take liberties*, tomarse libertades; *at* ~, en libertad, libre. *2* exención, franqueza, privilegio.
**libidinous** (libi·dinøs) *adj.* libidinoso.
**libido** (-ou o libai·dou) *s.* libido.
**Libra** (lai·bra) *n. pr.* ASTR. Libra.
**librarian** (laibre·rian) *s.* bibliotecario.
**library** (lai·breri) *s.* biblioteca. *2* estudio, despacho, gabinete.
**libration** (laibrei·ʃøn) *s.* libración.
**librettist** (libre·tist) *s.* libretista.
**libretto** (-ou) *s.* libreto.
**Libya** (li·biæ) *n. pr.* GEOGR. Libia.
**Lybyan** (-n) *adj.-s.* líbico.
**lice** (lais) *s. pl.* de LOUSE.
**license, licence** (lai·søns) *s.* licencia [libertad abusiva], libertinaje. *2* licencia [poética]. *3* libertad de acción. *4* licencia, permiso, venia. *5* autorización, permiso, matrícula, patente, título, concesión: ~ *number*, número de matrícula.
**license, licence (to)** *tr.* autorizar, dar permiso, título o patente.
**licensee** (laisensɪ·) *s.* titular de permiso o concesión.
**licentiate** (laise·nshiit) *s.* licenciado, persona que tiene título de una facultad.
**licentious** (-øs) *adj.* licencioso.
**licentiousness** (-nis) *s.* licencia, libertinaje.
**lichen** (lai·køn) *s.* BOT., MED. liquen.
**lich-gate** (lich-geit) *s.* entrada cubierta de un cementerio.
**licit** (li·sit) *adj.* lícito.

**lick** (lik) *s.* lamedura, lengüetada. *2* fam. ligera aplicación de algo; pincelada: *to give a ~ and promise to*, fig. hacer de prisa y mal. *3* fam. esfuerzo. *4* pop. paso, velocidad. *5* salegar.
**lick (to)** *tr.* lamer: *to ~ one's shoes*, fig. adular servilmente; *to ~ the dust*, morder el polvo. *2* fam. pegar, apalizar. *3* fam. vencer, ganar [a uno]. *4* fam. sobrepujar. *5* fam. *that licks me*, no lo entiendo, no puedo entenderlo. *6* fig. *to ~ into shape*, dar forma a, hacer presentable.
**licking** (-ing) *s.* lengüetada. *2* paliza, tunda; derrota.
**lickspittle** (-spitøl) *s.* adulón.
**licorice** (-øris) *s.* BOT. regaliz.
**lictor** (-tø^r) *s.* lictor.
**lid** (lid) *s.* tapa, tapadera. *2* tapa [de un libro]. *3* ANAT. párpado.
**lie** (lai) *s.* mentira, embuste, falsedad. *2* mentis: *to give the ~ to*, dar un mentis a, desmentir. *3* disposición, situación, orientación: *the ~ of the land*, disposición del terreno; fig. estado de las cosas.
**1) lie (to)** *intr.* mentir. ¶ Pret. y p. p.: *lied;* ger.: *lying.*
**2) lie (to)** *intr.* tenderse, acostarse, recostarse, apoyarse. *2* estar tendido o acostado, yacer. *3* estar, permanecer: *to ~ in wait*, estar al acecho; *to ~ in state*, estar [un difunto] en la capilla ardiente. *4* yacer, estar enterrado. *5* consistir, estribar. *6* estar, hallarse, extenderse. *7* MAR. *to ~ at anchor*, estar anclado. *8 to ~ about*, estar esparcido. *9 to ~ down*, acostarse, echarse. *10 to ~ hard on*, pesar sobre; afligir. *11 to ~ in*, estar de parto. *12 to ~ low*, estar postrado o muerto; agazaparse, estar quieto, escondido. *13 to ~ on*, depender de; pesar, cargar sobre. *14 to ~ over*, aplazarse, quedar aplazado. *15 to ~ to*, MAR. pairar, ponerse en facha. *16 to ~ under*, estar bajo el peso de. *17 to ~ up*, retirarse; irse a la cama. *18 to ~ with*, tocar, incumbir a. ¶ Pret.: *lay;* p. p.: *lain;* ger.: *lying.*
**lief** (lɪf) *adv.* de buen grado: *I would as ~ go as not*, tanto me da ir como no ir.
**liege** (lidȳ) *adj.* ligio, feudatario. *2* adj.-s. *liege* o ~ *lord*, señor feudal. *3 s.* vasallo.
**Liege** (liedȳ) *n. pr.* GEOGR. Lieja.
**liegeman** (lɪ·dȳmæn) *s.* vasallo. *2* seguidor leal.
**lien** (lien o lɪn) *s.* DER. embargo preventivo.
**lieu** (liu·) *s. in ~ of*, en lugar de, en vez de.
**lieutenancy** (liute·nansi) *s.* lugartenencia. *2* tenencia, tenientazgo.
**lieutenant** (-nant) *s.* teniente, lugarteniente. *2* MIL. teniente: *~ colonel*, teniente coronel; *~ general*, teniente general. *3* MAR. teniente de navío; ~ *commander*, capitán de corbeta.
**life** (laif), *pl.* **lives** [-vš] *s.* vida: *the other ~*, la otra vida; *~ belt*, cinturón salvavidas; *~ expectancy*, índice de longevidad, promedio vital; *~ preserver*, MAR. salvavidas; (Ingl.) cachiporra flexible; *~ sentence*, cadena perpetua; *to be the ~ and soul of*, ser el alma de; *to come to ~*, volver a la vida, volver en sí; *to have the time of one's ~*, divertirse o gozar como nunca; *to take one's ~ in one's hand*, jugarse la vida; *as big as ~*, de tamaño natural; *for ~*, para toda la vida; *for ~, for one's ~, for dear ~*, desesperadamente, para salvar la vida; *for the ~ of me*, a fe mía; aunque me maten; *to the ~*, al vivo, fielmente. *2* animación, alegría, movimiento. B. ART. natural: *from ~*, del natural.
**lifeblood** (-bløɗ) *s.* sangre vital. *2* alma, nervio.

**lifeboat** (-bout) *s.* bote salvavidas.
**lifeless** (-lis) *adj.* sin vida, muerto, inanimado, inerte. *2* falto de animación. *3* desierto, inhabitado.
**lifelike** (-laik) *adj.* que parece vivo, natural.
**lifelong** (-long) *adj.* de toda la vida.
**lifesaver** (-seivø^r) *s.* salvador, el que salva la vida. *2* miembro de una estación de salvamento.
**lifesaving** (-seiving) *adj.* de salvamento: ~ *gun*, cañón lanzacabos. *2 m.* acción de salvar vidas. *3* servicio de salvavidas.
**life-size** *adj.* de tamaño natural.
**lifetime** (-taim) *s.* vida, curso de la vida. *2* fig. eternidad [largo tiempo]. *3 adj.* perpetuo, vitalicio.
**lift** (lift) *s.* alzamiento, elevación, levantamiento; esfuerzo para levantar. *2* altura, grado de elevación. *3* fuerza o influencia elevadora; AVIA. fuerza ascensional o de sustentación. *4* ayuda [para levantar]. *5* alza, aumento, ascenso. *6* mecanismo elevador; (Ingl.) ascensor. *7* elevación [del terreno], repecho. *8* tapa [de un tacón de zapato]. *9 to give someone a ~*, llevar uno en su coche a otro; ayudar a uno. *10 adj.* ~ *force* o *power*, fuerza ascensional o elevadora; ~ *pump*, bomba aspirante.
**lift (to)** *tr.* alzar, levantar, elevar, izar, solevantar. | A veces con *up, off* o *out*. *2* quitar [un peso de encima]. *3* quitarse [el sombrero]. *4* (E.U.) cancelar [una hipoteca]. *5* elevar, exaltar; engreír. | Gralte. con *up*. *6* fam. hurtar, robar; plagiar. *7* levantar [las tiendas]. *8 intr.* levantarse, subir, elevarse. *9* disiparse [las nubes, la niebla, la obscuridad].
**lifter** (-ø^r) *s.* levantador, alzador, elevador. *2* MEC. leva.
**liftman** (-mæn) *s.* (Ingl.) ascensorista.
**ligament** (li·gamønt) *s.* ligadura, atadura. *2* ANAT. ligamento.
**ligate (to)** (lai·geit) *tr.* CIR. ligar, atar.
**ligation** (-ei·shøn) *s.* ligación, ligadura.
**ligature** (li·gæchu^r) *s.* ligación, ligadura. *2* MÚS. ligado. *3* IMPR. letras unidas [œ, fi, etc.].
**light** (lait) *s.* luz [agente físico; claridad, resplandor; día; lo que ilumina]: *to bring to ~*, sacar a luz; *to come to ~*, salir a luz; *to see the ~*, ver la luz; ver luz, empezar a comprender; ver la solución; *to throw o shed ~ upon*, arrojar luz sobre; *against the ~*, a contraluz; al trasluz; *in the ~ of*, a la luz de [unos hechos, etc.]. *2* luz, lámpara, vela, etc.; farol, faro; luz, señal [de tráfico]. *3* pop. ojos. *4* fuego, cerilla, etc. [para encender]. *5* lumbrera [pers. notable]. *6* ARQ., PINT. luz. *7* aspecto, punto de vista: *to place in a good ~*, presentar bajo un aspecto favorable. *8 pl.* luces, alumbrado. *9* luces, ilustración; entendimiento: *according to his lights*, según Dios le da a entender. *10* bofes, livianos.
*11 adj.* de luz; de farol, faro, etc.; luminoso, claro: ~ *wave*, onda luminosa; *to be ~*, ser de día. *12* blondo, rubio; blanca [tez]; claro, alegre [color]. *13* ligero, leve, liviano, suave. *14* ligero [comida, sueño]. *15* ligero, ágil, pronto. *16* ligero, inconstante; frívolo, no serio; licencioso. *17* MIL. ligero: ~ *horse*, caballería ligera. *18* ligero, libre de penas, confiado. *19* boyante [buque]. *20* flojo [vino, cerveza]. *21* arijo [suelo]. *22 ~ in the head*, atolondrado; mareado; delirante. *23 to make ~ of*, no dar importancia a. *24 adv.* ligeramente. *25* fácilmente.
**light (to)** *tr.* encender [el fuego, el cigarro, una luz, etc.]. *2* alumbrar, iluminar. *3 intr.* encenderse.

*4* iluminarse. | Gralte. con *up*. *5* apearse. *6* posarse, descender, caer [en o sobre]. *7 to ~ on* o *upon*, tropezar o topar con, encontrar por casualidad. ¶ Pret. y p. p.: *lighted* o *lit*.

**light-complexioned** *adj*. de tez blanca.

**lighten (to)** *tr*. iluminar, alumbrar; hacer brillar o resplandecer. *2* aclarar, avivar [un color]. *3* alegrar. *4* aligerar, aliviar. *5* alijar, descargar [un buque]. *6 intr*. iluminarse. *7* aclararse [hacerse menos obscuro]. *8* relampaguear. *9* aligerarse.

**lighter** (-ø<sup>r</sup>) *adj*. comp. de LIGHT. *2 s*. encendedor [pers.]. *3* encendedor, mechero. *4* MAR. alijador, gabarra.

**lighter (to)** *tr*. cargar o descargar por medio de alijadores o gabarras.

**lighterman** (-mæn) *s*. gabarrero.

**light-fingered** *adj*. ligero de dedos, largo de uñas.

**light-footed** *adj*. ligero de pies.

**light-headed** *adj*. ligero de cascos, atolondrado. *2* aturdido, mareado. *3* delirante.

**light-hearted** *adj*. alegre; libre de cuidados.

**lighthouse** (lai·tjaus) *s*. MAR. faro, farola.

**lighthouseman** (-mæn) *s*. torrero [de faro].

**lighting** (-ing) *s*. iluminación. *2* alumbrado: luz [eléctrica, de gas, etc.]: *~ fixtures*, aparatos de alumbrado. *3* encendido.

**lightly** (-li) *adv*. ligeramente. *2* alegremente. *3* a la ligera, de ligero. *4* sin seriedad.

**light-minded** *adj*. voluble, atolondrado.

**lightness** (-nis) *s*. claridad, luminosidad. *2* lo claro [de un color]. *3* ligereza. *4* delicadeza, suavidad.

**lightning** (-ning) *s*. METEOR. relámpago, fucilazo; rayo, centella: *~ arrester, ~ rod*, pararrayos. *2* ENT. *~ bug*, luciérnaga; cocuyo. *3 like ~*, fig. como el rayo.

**lightsome** (-søm) *adj*. claro, luminoso. *2* alegre, festivo. *3* ligero [ágil; frívolo].

**lightweight** (-ueit) *adj*. ligero, de poco peso. *2* ligero, de entretiempo [vestido]. *3 s*. DEP. peso ligero [boxeador]. *6* fig. pelele.

**light-year** *s*. ASTR. año de luz.

**ligneous** (li·gniøs) *adj*. leñoso.

**lignify (to)** (-ifai) *tr*. lignificar. *2 intr*. lignificarse. ¶ Pret. y p. p.: *lignified*.

**lignin** (-in) *s*. BOT., QUÍM. lignina.

**lignite** (-ait) *s*. MINER. lignito.

**lignum-vitæ** (-øm-vai·ti) *s*. BOT. guayacán, palo santo.

**ligule** (li·giul) *s*. BOT. lígula.

**Ligurian** (ligiu·rian) *adj.-s*. ligur, ligurino.

**likable** (lai·kabøl) *adj*. agradable, simpático.

**like** (laik) *adj*. igual, parecido, zemejante, tal, como: *~ father, ~ son*, de tal palo, tal astilla; *something ~*, algo así como; *to be ~*, parecerse, ser parecido; *what is he ~?*, ¿cómo es él? *2* propio, característico de: *it is just ~ him*, es muy propio de él. *3* probable: *he is ~ to come*, es probable que venga. *4 adv., prep., conj.* como, del mismo modo que: *~ mad*, como un loco; *~ this*, así, de este modo; *nothing ~*, ni con mucho. *4 ~ enough, very ~*, probablemente.

*6 s*. igual, pers. o cosa igual o semejante: *and the ~*, y cosas así; *the ~ of*, otro igual o que se parezca a. *7 pl*. gustos, simpatías.

**like (to)** *tr*. querer, tener simpatía a; gustar de, gustarle a uno; querer, desear: *I ~ him*, le quiero, me gusta; *do you ~ tea?*, ¿le gusta el té?; *how do you ~ it?*, ¿qué le parece?, ¿le gusta?; *I should ~ to see it*, quisiera verlo; *as you ~ [it]*, como quiera, como guste; *to ~ better* o *best*, preferir. *2* sentar [una comida o bebida].

**likeable** (-abøl) *adj*. LIKABLE.

**likelihood** (-lijud) *s*. probabilidad, posibilidad; verosimilitud.

**likely** (-li) *adj*. probable: *he is ~ to come*, es probable que venga. *2* verosímil, creíble. *3* apropiado. *4* prometedor. *5 adv*. probablemente.

**liken (to)** (lai·køn) *tr*. asemejar, comparar.

**likeness** (-nis) *s*. semejanza, parecido, aire. *2* apariencia, forma. *3* efigie, retrato.

**likewise** (-uaiŝ) *adv*. igualmente, lo mismo. *2* asimismo, también, además.

**liking** (-ing) *s*. inclinación, afición, simpatía. *2* agrado, gusto, preferencia.

**lilac** (lai·lak) *s*. BOT. lilac, lila.

**liliaceous** (liliei·shøs) *adj*. liliáceo.

**lilied** (li·lid) *adj*. parecido a un lirio.

**Lille** (li·l) *n. pr.* GEOGR. Lila.

**liliputian** (lilipiu·shan) *adj.-s*. liliputiense.

**lilt** (lilt) *s*. canción de movimiento vivo, alegre. *2* ritmo, cadencia.

**lilt (to)** *tr*. cantar con movimiento vivo, alegre.

**lily** (li·li) *pl. s*. BOT. lirio; azucena, lis: *~ of the valley*, lirio de los valles, muguete. *2* flor de lis. *3 water ~*, nenúfar.

**lily-livered** *adj*. fig. cobarde.

**limb** (lim) *s*. miembro [del cuerpo del hombre o del animal]. *2* brazo o rama [de una cosa]. *3* rama [de árbol]. *4* limbo, borde graduado. *5* ASTR., BOT. limbo. *6 ~ of the devil*, muchacho travieso.

**limb (to)** *tr*. lisiar. *2* desmembrar, despedazar.

**limber** (-bø<sup>r</sup>) *adj*. flexible, cimbreño, ágil. *2 s*. ARTILL. armón, avantrén.

**limber (to)** *tr*. hacer flexible o ágil. *2* ARTILL. enganchar el armón a.

**limbo** (-bou) *s*. limbo [de las almas]. *2* fig. prisión, encierro; olvido.

**lime** (laim) *s*. cal: *~ pit*, calera; TEN. encalador. *2* caliza. *3* liga [para cazar pájaros]: *~ twig*, vareta. *4* BOT. tilo. *5* BOT. lima agria; limero agrio.

**lime (to)** *tr*. encalar. *2* AGR. abonar con cal. *3* untar con liga; cazar con liga.

**limekiln** (-kiln) *s*. calera [horno de cal].

**limelight** (-lait) *s*. TEAT. foco, reflector; haz luminoso del reflector. *2* fig.: *to be in the ~*, estar a la vista del público, ser objeto de la curiosidad del público, ser de actualidad, ser notable.

**limerick** (li·mørik) *s*. quintilla jocosa.

**limestone** (lai·mstoun) *s*. caliza, piedra caliza.

**limit** (li·mit) *s*. límite: *without ~*, ilimitado, sin límites. *2* fam. colmo: *to be the ~*, ser el colmo, ser intolerable.

**limit (to)** *tr*. limitar [poner límite o límites]. *2* DER. fijar, determinar.

**limitary** (-eri) *adj*. sujeto a restricción, limitado. *2* de límite. *3* limitador, restrictivo.

**limitation** (-i·shøn) *s*. limitación. *2* restricción.

**limited** (li·mitid) *adj*. limitado: *~ company*, COM. sociedad limitada. *2* constitucional [monarquía]. *3* (E.U.) expreso, de lujo [tren].

**limitless** (-lis) *adj*. sin límites, ilimitado.

**limitrophe** (-traf) *adj*. limítrofe.

**limonite** (li·monait) *s*. MINER. limonita.

**limousine** (limuŝi·n) AUT. limousine.

**limp** (limp) *s*. cojera, claudicación. *2 adj*. flojo, flexible, flácido, lacio. *3* débil, sin energía.

**limp (to)** *intr*. cojear. *2* MEC. marchar irregularmente.

**limpet** (-et) *s*. ZOOL. lapa, lápade [molusco].

**limpid** (-id) *adj*. límpido, claro, transparente.

**limpidity** (limpi·diti) *s*. limpidez.

**list**

**limy** (lai·mi) *adj.* viscoso, pegajoso, untado con liga. *2* calizo.
**linaceous** (lainei·shøs) *adj.* lináceo.
**linchpin** (li·nchpin) *s.* pezonera [de carruaje].
**linden** (li·ndøn) *s.* BOT. tilo. *2* madera de tilo.
**line** (lain) *s.* cuerda, cabo, cable [relativamente delgados], cordel, hilo. *2* sedal [para pescar]. *3* cordel o cinta [para medir o nivelar]. *4* hilo [de la plomada]. *5* línea [en geometría, topografía, etc.]; línea, raya, trazo, rasgo: ~ *of force*, FÍS. línea de fuerza; ~ *of sight*, línea de mira; *the* ~, GEOGR. la línea, el ecuador. *6* línea recta; línea, fila, hilera: *to bring into* ~, alinear; fig. hacer que uno siga una opinión, partido, etc.; *in* ~, alineado; fig. de acuerdo, dispuesto; *out of* ~, desalineado; fig. en desacuerdo. *7* línea, raya, término, límite: *to draw the* ~ *at*, no ir más allá de; *on the* ~, en la línea divisoria. *8* MIL., FORT. línea: ~ *of battle*, línea de combate; *all along the* ~, fig. en toda la línea. *9* línea [aérea, férrea, marítima, telegráfica, etc.]. *10* conducción, cañería, tubería. *11* línea, renglón: *a* ~, fig. unas líneas [breve misiva]. *12* verso [línea]. *13* arruga [en el rostro, etc.], raya [de las manos]. *14* línea [medida]. *15* línea [de parentesco], linaje. *16* línea [de conducta, acción o pensamiento]: ~ *of least resistance*, línea del menor esfuerzo. *17* ramo de negocios, género de actividad, especialidad, estilo. *18* COM. clase de artículos; surtido. *19 pl.* líneas, contornos, rasgos. *20* verso, versos. *21* TEAT. papel, parte. *22* riendas [del caballo].
**line** (to) *tr.* linear, rayar, reglar. *2* marcar con rayas. *3* delinear, dibujar. *4* arrugar [el rostro, etc.]. *5* formar fila o hilera a lo largo de. *6* forrar, guarnecer, revestir; llenar. *7 to* ~ *up*, alinear; MEC. ajustar. *8 intr.* alinearse. *9 to* ~ *up*, ponerse en fila.
**lineage** (li·niidȳ) *s.* linaje, bolengo, prosapia.
**lineal** (-al) *adj.* lineal. *2* que viene por línea directa; hereditario.
**lineament** (-amønt) *s.* lineamento. *2* facción [del rostro]. *3 pl.* facciones; fisonomía.
**linear** (-iaʳ) *adj.* lineal: ~ *drawing*, dibujo lineal; ~ *measure*, medida de longitud. *3* BOT., ZOOL. linear.
**lineation** (-shøn) *s.* delineación. *2* disposición por líneas.
**lined** (laind) *adj.* rayado: ~ *paper*, papel rayado. *2* arrugado [rostro, manos]. *3* forrado, revestido.
**lineman** (-mæn) *s.* FERROC., ELECT., TELEF., TELEGR. operario o empleado que repara la línea.
**linen** (li·nøn) *s.* hilo de lino. *2* lienzo, lino [tela]. *3* ropa blanca: *bed* ~, ropas de cama; *table* ~, mantelería.
**liner** (lai·nøʳ) *s.* vapor o avión de una línea.
**linesman** (-šmæn) *s.* LINEMAN. *2* DEP. juez de línea. *3* soldado de línea.
**line-up** *s.* formación, fila. *2* rueda de presos.
**ling** (ling) *s.* ICT. bacalao. *2* BOT. brezo.
**linger** (to) (li·ngøʳ) *intr.* demorar, tardarse, ir despacio, quedarse, entretenerse, estar ocioso, vacilar. *2* durar, prolongarse [aunque apagándose, amainando, etc.]; consumirse.
**lingerie** (læ·nȳøri) *s.* ropa interior [de mujer].
**lingering** (lı·ngøring) *adj.* lento, prolongado. *2* tardo, moroso. *3* que dura, que subsiste.
**lingo** (li·ngou) *s.* lenguaje, jerga.
**lingua franca** (li·ngua fræ·nka) *s.* lengua franca.
**lingual** (li·ngual) *adj.* lingual.
**linguist** (-ist) *s.* lingüista. *2* poligloto.

**linguistics** (lingüi·stiks) *s.* lingüística.
**liniment** (li·nimønt) *s.* linimento.
**lining** (lai·ning) *s.* forro, aforro, revestimiento. *2* AUTO. guarnición de freno.
**link** (link) *s.* eslabón [de cadena]. *2* vínculo, enlace, lo que une o enlaza. *3* gemelo [de puño]. *4* MEC. articulación: varilla de conexión. *4* hacha de viento. *6 pl.* campo de golf.
**link** (to) *tr.* eslabonar, unir, enlazar, encadenar, engarzar. *2 intr.* eslabonarse, unirse, enlazarse.
**linkage** (-idȳ) *s.* eslabonamiento. *2* MEC. varillaje. *3* QUÍM. enlace. *4* ELECT. acoplamiento inductivo.
**linkboy** (-boi) *s.* paje de hacha.
**linnet** (li·nit) *s.* ORN. pardillo. *2* ORN. jilguero.
**linoleum** (linou·liøm) *s.* linóleo.
**linotype** (lei·notaip) *s.* IMPR. linotipia. *2* IMPR. linotipo.
**linseed** (-nsid) *s.* linaza.
**linstock** (-tak) *s.* ARTILL. botafuego.
**lint** (lint) *s.* CIR. hilar. *2* borra de algodón.
**lintel** (-øl) *s.* ARQ. dintel.
**lion** (lai·øn) *s.* ZOOL. león: *lion's share*, parte del león. *2* fig. león [hombre valiente]. *3* fig. pers. célebre, muy solicitada en la vida de sociedad. *4* ASTR. Leo. *5* ENT. ~ *ant*, hormiga león.
**lioness** (-is) *s.* leona.
**lion-hearted** *adj.* valiente.
**lionize** (-aiš) *tr.* agasajar mucho [a uno] en la vida de sociedad.
**lip** (lip) *s.* ANAT. y fig. labio: *stiff upper* ~, fig. firmeza, obstinación; ~ *service*, jarabe de pico; alabanza, apoyo, etc., insinceros. *2* fam. lenguaje insolente. *3* labio [de una herida, una flor, un vaso]; pico [de jarro].
**lip** (to) *tr.* tocar con los labios; besar. *2* besar, lamer [dicho del agua, etc.]. *3* susurrar, murmurar. ¶ Pret. y p. p.: *lipped;* ger.: *-pping*.
**lipoma** (lipou·ma) *s.* MED. lipoma.
**lipstick** (li·pstik) *s.* lápiz para los labios.
**liquate** (to) (lai·kueit) *tr.* METAL. licuar.
**liquefaction** (likuifæ·kshøn) *s.* licuación, licuefacción, liquidación.
**liquefy** (to) (li·kuifai) *tr.* liquidar, licuar, licuefacer. *2 intr.* liquidarse, licuarse. ¶ Pret. y p. p.: *liquefied*.
**liquescent** (likue·sønt) *adj.* licuescente.
**liqueur** (likø·ʳ) *s.* licor [bebida].
**liquid** (li·kuid) *adj.* FÍS., FONÉT. líquido. *2* para líquidos [medida o medidas]. *3* claro, cristalino. *4* puro, suave [sonido]. *5* COM. realizable. *6 s.* líquido. *7* FONÉT. líquida.
**liquidambar** (li·kuidæmbaʳ) *s.* liquidámbar.
**liquidate** (to) (-deit) *tr.* liquidar, saldar [cuentas]. *2* pop. liquidar, acabar con, matar. *3 intr.* COM. liquidar.
**liquidation** (-ei·shøn) *s.* COM. liquidación.
**liquidity** (likui·diti) *s.* liquidez. *2* claridad, transparencia, brillo. *3* pureza [de un sonido].
**liquidize** (to) (li·kuidaiš) *tr.* liquidar, licuar.
**liquor** (li·køʳ) *s.* licor, líquido. *2* licor, bebida alcohólica: *in* ~, embriagado.
**liquorice** (li·køris) *s.* LICORICE.
**lira** (li·ra) *s.* lira [moneda].
**Lisbon** (li·šbøn) *n. pr.* GEOGR. Lisboa.
**lisp** (lisp) *s.* ceceo. *2* balbuceo [de los niños].
**lisp** (to) *intr.* cecear. *2* balbucir.
**lisper** (-øʳ) *s.* ceceoso, zopas.
**lissom(e** (li·søm) *adj.* flexible, elástico. *2* ágil.
**list** (list) *s.* lista, catálogo, minuta, rol, matrícula. *2* orillo. *3* lista, faja, raya, cenefa. *4* orilla [de una tela]. *5* poét. límite, lindero. *6* ARQ. listel,

filete. 7 CARP. listón. 8 CARP. barandal. 9 MAR. *to have a ~*, irse a la banda, escorar. *10 pl.* liza, palenque.

**list (to)** *tr.* poner en [una] lista; registrar, catalogar. 2 alistar. 3 COM. cotizar, facturar. 4 guarnecer con cenefa, etc.; listar, rayar. 5 cercar con palenque. 6 MAR. hacer escorar. 7 *intr.* alistarse. 8 MAR. escorar.

**listel** (-øl) *s.* ARQ. listel.

**listen (to)** (li·søn) *intr.-tr.* escuchar: *to ~ to*, escuchar, oír, atender, prestar atención a. 2 *to ~ in*, escuchar subrepticiamente una conversación telefónica; escuchar por radio.

**listener** (li·snø[r]) *s.* oyente, escucha, radioyente.

**listening post** (-ning) *s.* puesto de escucha.

**listless** (li·stlis) *adj.* distraído, indiferente, que no siente interés, apático, abatido.

**lit** (lit) *pret. y p. p.* de TO LIGHT.

**litany** (li·tani) *s.* letanía.

**liter** (li·tø[r]) *s.* litro.

**literacy** (li·tørasi) *s.* condición del que sabe leer y escribir.

**literal** (-al) *adj.* literal. 2 formado o expresado por letras. 3 prosaico, positivista.

**literalness** (-nis) *s.* exactitud literal. 2 prosaísmo, positivismo.

**literary** (-eri) *adj.* literario: *~ man*, literato, hombre de letras.

**literate** (-it) *adj.* instruido; que sabe leer y escribir [pers.].

**literati** (litørei·tai) *s. pl.* literatos. 2 personas ocultas.

**literatim** (-tim) *adv.* letra por letra, a la letra, literalmente.

**literature** (li·tøræchø[r]) *s.* literatura.

**lithe** (laið), **lithesome** (-søm) *adj.* flexible, elástico, cimbreño, ágil.

**lithiasis** (lizai·asis) *s.* MED. litiasis.

**lithium** (li·ziøm) *s.* QUÍM. litio.

**lithograph** (li·zøgræf) *s.* litografía [impresión].

**lithograph (to)** *tr.* litografiar.

**lithographer** (liza·grafø[r]) *s.* litógrafo.

**lithography** (liza·grafi) *s.* litografía [arte].

**lithophagous** (-fagøs) *adj.* ZOOL. litófago.

**Lithuania** (li·zyueinia) *n. pr.* GEOGR. Lituania.

**Lithuanian** (lizyuei·nian) *adj.-s.* lituano.

**litigant** (li·tigant) *adj.-s.* litigante; contendiente.

**litigate (to)** (-eit) *tr.-intr.* litigar, contender.

**litigation** (-ei·shøn) *s.* litigación, litigio, pleito.

**litigious** (liti·dyøs) *adj.* litigioso.

**litmus** (li·tmøs) *s.* QUÍM. tornasol.

**litre** (li·tø[r]) *s.* litro.

**litter** (li·tø[r]) *s.* litera [vehículo]. 2 camilla, parihuelas. 3 camada, lechigada. 4 cama [de paja para las caballerías]. 5 fig. tendalera; escombros, basura; desorden.

**litter (to)** *tr.-intr.* parir [un animal]. 2 *tr.* esparcir, desordenar. 3 cubrir [de cosas en desorden]; cubrir [el suelo] de paja.

**little** (-øl) *adj.* pequeño, chico, menudo, menor, parvo: *a ~ one*, un pequeñuelo; *Little Bear*, ASTR. Osa menor; *~ finger*, dedo meñique; *~ hours*, ECLES. horas menores; *~ office*, ECLES. oficio parvo; *Little Red Ridinghood*, caperucita encarnada. Muchas veces se traduce por un diminutivo: *~ house*, casita. 2 *adj.-adv.-s.* poco: *~ hope*, poca esperanza; *a ~*, un poco de; algo; *~ more than*, poco más que; *after a ~*, al cabo de un poco; *~ by ~*, poco a poco; *not a ~*, no poco. 3 *in ~*, en pequeño, en pequeña escala.

**littleness** (-nis) *s.* pequeñez, poquedad, cortedad. 2 mezquindad, ruindad.

**littoral** (li·tøral) *adj.-s.* litoral.

**liturgic(al** (litø·[r]dyik(al) *adj.* litúrgico.

**liturgy** (li·tø[r]dyi) *s.* liturgia, ritual.

**livable** (li·vabøl) *adj.* habitable. 2 llevadero. 3 agradable, simpático.

**live** (laiv) *adj.* vivo [que vive, con vida]. 2 fam. real, verdadero. 3 ardiente, encendido: *~ coals*, ascuas, carbón encendido. 4 vivo, enérgico, activo. 5 palpitante, de actualidad. 6 viva [peña, roca]. 7 cargado [cartucho, granada]. 8 ELECT. que lleva corriente [conductor]. 9 MEC. vivo. *10* IMPR. útil. *11* BOT. *~ oak*, encina norteamericana.

**live (to)** (li·v) *intr.* vivir [tener vida, existir; durar, subsistir; conducirse; habitar, morar]: *to ~ and learn*, vivir para ver; *to ~ by one's wits*, vivir de la trampa, ser caballero de industria; *to ~ from hand to mouth*, vivir al día; *to ~ high*, darse buena vida; *to ~ on o upon*, vivir a costa de; vivir o sustentarse de; *to ~ up to*, vivir con arreglo a; cumplir [lo prometido]. 3 *tr.* llevar, pasar [tal o cual vida]. 4 vivir, pasar, experimentar, practicar. 5 *to ~ down*, olvidar, ver desaparecer [con el tiempo]; borrar uno con su vida [una falta, etc.].

**liveable** (li·vabøl) *adj.* LIVABLE.

**livelihood** (lai·vlijud) *s.* vida, medios de vida.

**liveliness** (-nis) *s.* vida, vivacidad, animación.

**livelong** (li·vlong) *adj.* todo, largo [que tarda en pasar]: *all the ~ night*, toda la santa noche.

**lively** (lai·vli) *adj.* vivo, vivaz, vivaracho. 2 animado. 3 vivo, brioso, airoso, rápido. 4 vivo, alegre, brillante. 5 vivo, intenso. 6 vivo, pronto. 7 animador. 8 gráfica [descripción, etc.]. 9 *adv.* vivamente. *10* airosamente.

**liver** (li·vø[r]) *s.* viviente. 2 el que vive de cierto modo. 3 ANAT., ZOOL. hígado.

**liveried** (-id) *adj.* que lleva librea.

**liverwort** (-uø[r]t) *s.* BOT. hepática.

**liverwurst** (-uø[r]st) *s.* embutido de hígado.

**livery** (li·vøri) *s.* librea. 2 uniforme [de un gremio, etc.]. 3 fig. plumaje, ropaje, aspecto característico. 4 pensión o pupilaje de caballos; alquiler de caballos, coches, botes, etc.: *~ horse*, caballo de alquiler; *~ stable*, cuadra o cochería de alquiler.

**liveryman** (-mæn) *s.* dueño de una cuadra o cochería de alquiler. 2 criado de librea. 3 (Ingl.) individuo de un gremio.

**lives** (lai·vš) *s. pl.* de LIFE.

**livestock** (lai·vstak) *s.* ganado, animales que se crían.

**livid** (li·vid) *adj.* lívido. 2 pálido.

**lividity** (livi·diti) *s.* lividez.

**living** (li·ving) *adj.* vivo, viviente. 2 de vivientes. 3 en vivo. 4 vivo, activo. 5 vivaz, animado. 6 donde se está o se vive: *~ room*, cuarto de estar. 7 viva [agua, roca, lengua]. 8 vital [salario]. 9 *s.* vida [estado del que vive; modo de vivir]. *10* vida, sustento, medios de vida. *11* (Ingl.) beneficio [eclesiástico]. *12 pl. the living*, los vivientes.

**lizard** (li·ša[r]d) *s.* ZOOL. lagarto: *green ~*, *wall ~*, lagartija. 2 reptil saurio.

**Lizzie** (li·ši) *n. pr. dim.* de ELIZABETH.

**llama** (la·ma) *s.* ZOOL. llama.

**lo** (lou) *interj.* he aquí, ved aquí, cata; ¡mirad!

**loach** (louch) *s.* ICT. locha, lobo.

**load** (loud) *s.* carga [lo que se lleva o soporta]. 2 fig. carga, peso, agobio. 3 ELECT., MEC. carga. 4

carga [de un arma]. *5* pl. *loads of,* la mar de, montones de.
**load (to)** *tr.* cargar [un buque, mercancías, un arma, un dado, etc.]. *2* oprimir, agobiar. *3* cargar, colmar [de honores, etc.]. *4 intr.* cargar; tomar carga.
**loader** (-ø^r) *s.* cargador, embarcador.
**loading** (-ing) *s.* carga [acción de cargar]. *2 adj.* que carga, de cargar.
**loadstar** (-ta^r) *s.* LODESTAR.
**loadstone** (-stoun) *s.* magnetita; imán.
**loaf** (louf) *s.* barra de pan, hogaza. *2* pilón [de azúcar]: ~ *sugar,* azúcar de pilón.
**loaf (to)** *intr.* holgazanear, haraganear; pasearse.
**loafer** (-ø^r) *s.* holgazán, vago, callejero.
**loam** (loum) *s.* marga, tierra o suelo margoso. *2* mezcla de arcilla, arena, etc., para hacer ladrillos, moldes, etc.
**loam (to)** *tr.* tapar o cubrir con barro o arcilla.
**loan** (loun) *s.* préstamo: *on* ~, a préstamo. *2* empréstito. *3* cosa prestada.
**loan (to)** *tr.-intr.* prestar [dinero].
**loath** (louz) *adj.* renuente, poco dispuesto, reacio: *nothing* ~, dispuesto, de buena gana.
**loathe (to)** (loud) *tr.* aborrecer, abominar, detestar, repugnarle a uno [una cosa].
**loathing** (-ing) *s.* aborrecimiento, aversión, asco, repugnancia, hastío.
**loathsome** (-šøm) *adj.* aborrecible, odioso, asqueroso, repugnante, nauseabundo.
**loaves** (lou·vs) *s.* pl. de LOAF.
**lob** (lab) *s.* lombriz para cebo. *2* DEP. en el tenis, voleo alto y tendido de la pelota; en el criquet, voleo bajo de la pelota.
**lob (to)** *tr.* lanzar lenta o pesadamente. *2* DEP. hacer un LOB con la pelota. ¶ Pret. y p. p.: *lobbed;* p. a.: *-bbing.*
**lobate(d** (lou·beit(id) *adj.* lobulado.
**lobby** (la·bi) *s.* pasillo [esp. de una Cámara legislativa]; galería, antecámara, vestíbulo. *2* salón de entrada [de un hotel]. *2* (E.U.) camarilla política, grupo de cabilderos.
**lobby (to)** *intr.* (E.U.) cabildear.
**lobbyist** (-ist) *s.* cabildero.
**lobe** (loub) *s.* lóbulo, lobo.
**lobed** (-d) *adj.* lobulado, lobado.
**lobelia** (loub·lia) *s.* BOT. lobelia.
**lobeliaceous** (loubiliei·shøs) *adj.* BOT. lobeliáceo.
**loblolly** (la·blali) *s.* gachas. *2* MAR. medicina.
**lobster** (la·bstø^r) *s.* ZOOL. langosta [crustáceo]; bogavante; *spiny* ~, langosta.
**lobule** (la·biul) *s.* lobulillo.
**local** (lou·kal) *adj.* local: ~ *anaesthesia,* anestesia local; ~ *call,* TELEF. llamada urbana; ~ *colour,* LIT. PINT. color local. *2* municipal, regional, de un distrito, etc.: ~ *government,* autonomía, descentralización. *3* localizado, no general. *4* FERROC. ~ *train,* tren suburbano. *5 s.* persona de una localidad. *6* sección local [de un sindicato, etc.]. *7* noticias de interés local..
**locale** (loukæ·l) *s.* sitio, lugar [esp. como escena de ciertos acontecimientos]; ambiente.
**localism** (lou·kališm) *s.* localismo. *2* costumbre local. *3* limitación de ideas.
**locality** (loukæ·liti) *s.* situación, lugar [donde se encuentra una cosa]. *2* lugar o escena [de algo]. *3* facultad de recordar y reconocer los lugares.
**localization** (lou·kališei·shøn) *s.* localización [limitación a un punto o lugar].
**localize (to)** (-aiš) *tr.* localizar [limitar a un punto

o lugar]. *2* dar carácter local. *3* descentralizar. *4* concentrar [la atención en].
**locate (to)** (lou·keit) *tr.* localizar [descubrir la situación de]. *2* establecer, situar, poner, colocar.
**location** (loukei·shøn) *s.* localización [acción y efecto de descubrir la situación de]. *2* establecimiento, situación, ubicación. *3* CINEM. lugar fuera del estudio donde se rueda una película o parte de ella.
**locative** (la·kativ) *adj.* GRAM. locativo.
**loch** (lak) *s.* (Esc.) lago. *2* (Esc.) ensenada, brazo de mar.
**lock** (lak) *s.* rizo, bucle, mechón, guedeja. *2* vellón, vedija [de lana]. *3* cerradura, cerraja: *under* ~ *and key,* debajo de llave. *4* llave [de arma de fuego]. *5* esclusa [de canal]. *6* lo que sujeta o traba; acción y resultado de sujetar, trabar o inmovilizar apretando o enlazando unas cosas con otras. *7* presa, llave [en la lucha]; abrazo estrecho. *8* embotellamiento [del tráfico]. *9 pl.* cabellos.
**lock (to)** *tr.* cerrar [con llave o cerradura], echar la llave a, acerrojar; encerrar: *to* ~ *in,* encerrar, poner debajo de llave; *to* ~ *out,* cerrar la puerta [a uno]; *to* ~ *up,* encerrar; encarcelar. *2* apretar [entre los brazos], abrazar. *3* juntar, sujetar, - trabar, inmovilizar [apretando o entrelazando]; enclavijar. *4* hacer pasar [una embarcación] por una esclusa. *5 intr.* cerrarse con llave. *6* unirse, entrelazarse, enclavijarse. *7* pasar por una esclusa.
**locker** (-ø^r) *s.* el que cierra. *2* cajón, gaveta, cofre, armario [que se cierra con llave].
**locket** (-it) *s.* guardapelo, medallón, relicario.
**lockjaw** (-dYo) *s.* MED. trismo, tétano.
**locknut** (-nøt) *s.* MEC. fiador, contratuerca.
**lockout** (-aut) *s.* lockout [cierre de una fábrica, etc., por los patronos].
**locksmith** (-smiz) *s.* cerrajero.
**lockup** (-øp) *s.* encierro. *2* cárcel, calabozo.
**locomotion** (loukømou·shøn) *s.* locomoción.
**locomotive** (-tiv) *adj.* locomotor, triz. *2* locomóvil. *3 s.* locomotora.
**locomotor** (-tø^r) *adj.* locomotor, triz.
**loculicidal** (lakiulisa·dal) *adj.* BOT. loculicida.
**loculus** (la·kiuløs) *s.* ARQ., BOT. lóculo.
**locust** (lou·køst) *s.* ENT. langosta. *2* ENT. (E.U.) cigarra. *3* BOT. *locust* o ~ *tree,* algarrobo; acacia falsa.
**locution** (lokiu·shøn) *s.* locución.
**locutory** (la·kiutori) *s.* locutorio [de convento].
**lode** (loud) *s.* MIN. vena, veta, filón.·
**lodestar** (-sta^r) *s.* Estrella del Norte o Polar. *2* fig. norte, guía.
**lodestone** (-stoun) *s.* LOADSTONE.
**lodge** (ladY) *s.* casita, pabellón [de caza, etc.]. *2* casa del guarda, el portero, etc. [en una finca]; portería. *3* logia [masónica].
**lodge (to)** *tr.* alojar, hospedar, albergar. *2* alojar, introducir, colocar. *3* depositar, dar a guardar. *4* conferir [poderes]. *5* presentar [una denuncia, etc.]. *6 intr.* alojarse, hospedarse, residir.
**lodgement** (-mønt) *s.* alojamiento. *2* depósito; acumulación. *3* MIL. ocupación de una posición.
**lodger** (-ø^r) *s.* huésped, inquilino.
**lodging** (-ing) *s.* alojamiento, posada, hospedaje [sin manutención]. *2* morada, vivienda. *3 pl. to take lodgings in,* alojarse, hospedarse en.
**lodginghouse** (-jaus) *s.* casa de huéspedes.
**lodgment** (-mønt) *s.* LODGEMENT.
**loft** (loft) *s.* desván, sobrado. *2* (E.U.) piso alto de

un almacén, etc. *3* GOLF golpe que lanza la pelota en alto.
**loft (to)** *tr.* GOLF lanzar [la pelota] en alto.
**loftiness** (-inis) *s.* altura, elevación. *2* excelsitud, sublimidad. *3* altanería, altivez.
**lofty** (-i) *adj.* alto, elevado [de gran altura]. *2* excelso, sublime, elevado, noble, majestuoso. *3* altanero, altivo, orgulloso.
**log** (log) *s.* leño, troza, tronco: ~ *cabin*, cabaña de troncos; *like a* ~, como un tronco. *2* MAR. corredera: ~ *chip*, ~ *line*, barquilla, cordel, de la corredera. *3* MAR. cuaderno de bitácora, diario de navegación. *4* AVIA. diario de vuelo.
**loganberry** (lou·ganberi) *s.* BOT. especie de frambueso; su fruto.
**logarithm** (lo·gariðm) *s.* MAT. logaritmo.
**logbook** (lo·gbuk) *s.* LOG 3 y 4.
**logger** (lo·gø<sup>r</sup>) *s.* hachero, cortador de árboles.
**loggerhead** (-jed) *s.* cabezota. *2* ZOOL. variedad de tortuga marina. *3 to be at loggerheads*, estar en desacuerdo.
**loggia** (la·dỹa) *s.* ARQ. pórtico, galería abierta.
**logic** (la·dỹik) *s.* lógica, dialéctica.
**logical** (-al) *adj.* lógico.
**logician** (lodỹi·shan) *s.* lógico, dialéctico.
**logistics** (-stiks) *s. pl.* MIL. logística.
**logogriph** (lo·gøgrif) *s.* logogrifo.
**logomachy** (louga·maki) *s.* logomaquia.
**logos** (la·gas) *s.* FIL. logos. *2* TEOL. (con may.) El Verbo.
**logroll (to)** (lo·groul) *tr.* (E.U., Can.) hacer rodar troncos [hasta el agua o dentro del río]. *2* (E.U.) en una Cámara legislativa estorbar o favorecer la aprobación de [un proyecto, etc.] entrando en contubernio individuos de diferentes partidos.
**logwood** (lo·gwud) *s.* palo de campeche.
**loin** (loin) *s.* ijada, ijar. *2* CARN. lomo, solomillo. *3 pl.* lomos, riñones: fig. *to gird up one's loins*, apercibirse para la acción.
**loincloth** (-kloz) *s.* taparrabo, pampanilla.
**Loire** (lua·<sup>r</sup>) *n. pr.* GEOGR. Loira.
**loiter (to)** (loi·tø<sup>r</sup>) *intr.* rezagarse, entretenerse; pasear, holgazanear, vagar. *2 tr. to* ~ *away*, malgastar [un tiempo].
**loiterer** (-ø<sup>r</sup>) *s.* rezagado, vago.
**loll (to)** (lal) *intr.* colgar, pender [flojo o lacio]. *2* reclinarse indolentemente; repantigarse. *3 tr.* sacar [la lengua] el animal cansado.
**lollypop** (la·lipap) *s.* dulce, caramelo.
**London** (lø·ndøn) *n. pr.* GEOGR. Londres.
**Londoner** (-ø<sup>r</sup>) *s.* londinense.
**lone** (loun) *adj.* solo, solitario [sin compañía]. *2* solo, único. *3* solitario [lugar].
**loneliness** (-linis) *s.* soledad. *2* tristeza del que está solo.
**lonely** (-li) *adj.* solo, solitario [sin compañía]. *2* solitario, desolado, triste [lugar]. *3* solo, soledoso [que siente soledad].
**lonesome** (-søm) *s.* LONELY 2 y 3.
**long** (long) *adj.* largo [en sus principales acepciones], luengo, extenso, prolongado, tedioso: ~ *dozen*, docena de fraile; ~ *ton*, tonelada de 2.240 libras inglesas. *2* de largo, de longitud: *a mile* ~, de una milla de largo; ~ *measure*, medida o medidas de longitud. *3* que llega o alcanza lejos. *4* que tarda: *to be* ~ *in coming*, tardar en venir.
*5 adv.* durante [un tiempo]; mucho, mucho tiempo: *all the day* ~, todo el santo día; *as* ~ *as*, mientras; *con tal que*, puesto que; *how* ~ *is it since...?*, ¿cuánto hace que...?; *before* ~, dentro de poco; ~ *ago*, hace mucho tiempo; ~ *live!*,

¡viva! *6* lejos, a distancia; *so* ~, hasta la vista. *7 s.* largo, longitud: *the* ~ *and the short of*, la substancia, el resumen de. *8* letra o sílaba larga. *9* MÚS. longa.
**long (to)** *intr.* [con *for*, *after* o *to*] ansiar, anhelar; añorar.
**longboat** (-bout) *s.* lancha, chalupa.
**longbow** (-bou) *s.* arco [arma]; *to draw the* ~, fig. exagerar, contar cosas increíbles.
**long-cut** *adj.* en hebra [tabaco].
**long-distance** *adj.* TELÉF. de larga distancia, interurbano: *long-distance call*, conferencia interurbana. *2* DEP. de fondo [carrera].
**longer** (-ø<sup>r</sup>) *adj.-adv. compar.* de LONG: más largo; más, más tiempo: *no* ~, ya no, no más.
**longeron** (lo·ndỹørøn) *s.* AVIA. larguero.
**longest** (lo·ngist) *adj. y superl.* de LONG: *at the* ~, todo lo más, a más tardar.
**longevity** (londỹe·viti) *s.* longevidad.
**longevous** (londỹe·vøs) *adj.* longevo.
**longhand** (lo·ngjænd) *s.* escritura corriente [no taquigráfica].
**long-headed** *adj.* dolicocéfalo. *2* fam. listo, sagaz.
**longing** (-ing) *s.* ansia, anhelo. *2* añoranza, nostalgia. *3 adj.* anhelante, ansioso; nostálgico.
**longish** (-ish) *adj.* algo largo.
**longitude** (la·ndỹitiud) *s.* GEOGR., ASTR. longitud.
**longitudinal** (landỹitiu·dinal) *adj.* longitudinal.
**long-legged** *adj.* zanquilargo.
**long-lived** (longlai·vd o -li·vd) *adj.* longevo, de larga vida.
**long-necked** *adj.* cuellilargo.
**long-range** *adj.* de largo alcance.
**longshoreman** (-sho<sup>r</sup>mæn) *s.* (E.U.) obrero portuario.
**long-sighted** *adj.* présbita. *2* perspicaz, sagaz. *3* previsor, precavido.
**long-standing** *adj.* antiguo, que existe desde hace mucho tiempo.
**long-suffering** *adj.* sufrido, paciente.
**long-term** *adj.* COM. a largo plazo.
**longways** (-weiß) *adv.* a lo largo, longitudinalmente.
**long-winded** *adj.* de buenos pulmones. *2* pesado, latoso.
**loo** (lu) *s.* cierto juego de naipes.
**look** (luk) *s.* mirada, vistazo, ojeada. *2* semblante, cara. *3* aspecto, apariencia, aire, traza, cariz. *4 pl. good looks*, buen parecer, hermosura.
**look (to)** *intr.* mirar [dirigir la mirada; considerar]. | Gralte. con *at*, etc. *2* mirar, dar, caer; estar situado. *3* parecer: *he looked tired*, parecía cansado. *4* parecer, manifestarse. *5* sentar, caer [bien o mal]. *6* buscar, inquirir. | Gralte. con *after* o *for*. *7* cuidar, atender. | Gralte. con *after*. *8 to* ~ *about*, mirar alrededor, observar. *9 to* ~ *after*, seguir con la vista; buscar; inquirir; cuidar de, atender, mirar por. *10 to* ~ *alike*, parecerse. *11 to* ~ *alive*, darse prisa. *12 to* ~ *back*, volver la vista atrás. *13 to* ~ *down* on o *upon*, mirar por encima del hombro, despreciar. *14 to* ~ *for*, buscar, esperar. *15 to* ~ *forward to*, esperar con placer. *16 to* ~ *in*, entrar, hacer una corta visita. *17 to* ~ *into*, mirar, examinar, investigar. *18 to* ~ *like*, parecer; parecer que, tener trazas de: *it looks like rain*, parece que va a llover. *19 to* ~ *on* o *upon*, considerar; tener en aprecio. *20 to* ~ *out*, mirar afuera; asomarse; tener cuidado; ~ *out!*, ¡cuidado! *21 to* ~ *out for*, esperar, vigilar [si llega alguien o algo]; guardarse de; mirar por. *22 to* ~ *sharp*, vigilar, estar

ojo avizor. *23 to* ~ *to*, cuidar de, velar por; esperar de [una pers.]. *24 to* ~ *up to*, respetar, tratar con respeto. *25 tr.* mirar [dirigir la vista a; considerar]: ~ *how you behave*, mira como te portas. *26* expresar con la mirada. *27 to* ~ *daggers* [*at*], mirar airadamente o amenazadoramente. *28 to* ~ *one's age*, representar uno los años que tiene. *29 to* ~ *over*, repasar, dar una ojeada; hojear [un libro]. *30 to* ~ *up*, buscar [esp. en un diccionario, guía, etc.]; visitar [a una pers.].

**looker, looker-on** (-ǿr) *s.* mirón, espectador.

**looking** (-ing) *adj.* de mirar, para mirar: ~ *glass*, espejo. *2* que tiene cierto aspecto: *good-looking*, guapo, bien parecido.

**lockout** (-aut) *s.* vigía, atalaya, vigilante. *2* atalaya, miradero. *3* vigilancia, observación, espera: *to be on the* ~ *for*, estar a la mira de. *4* vista, perspectiva. *5* perspectivas. *6 fam. that is your* ~, allá usted.

**loom** (lum) *s.* TEJ. telar. *2* guión [del remo]. *3* aparición, presencia [de algo voluminoso, de una sombra o reflejo].

**loom (to)** *tr.* tejer [en el telar]. *2 intr.* aparecer, asomar [de una manera confusa o impresionante]; destacar, descollar. *5* vislumbrarse, amenazar.

**loon** (lun) *s.* (Esc. y ant.) bribón; patán; muchacho. *2* ORN. colimbo.

**loop** (lup) *s.* curva, vuelta muy pronunciada o de algo que cruza sobre sí mismo. *2* gaza, lazo; presilla, alamar. *3* asa, anilla, armella. *4* ELECT. circuito cerrado. *5* AVIA. rizo.

**loop (to)** *tr.* doblar formando gaza; formar ondas o curvas en. *2* asegurar con presilla, gaza, etc. *3* AVIA. *to* ~ *the loop*, hacer o rizar el rizo. *4 intr.* formar vuelta, gaza o lazo. *5* arrastrarse encorvándose [como ciertas orugas].

**loophole** (-joul) *s.* aspillera, saetera, tronera; abertura estrecha. *2 fig.* salida, escapatoria.

**loose** (lus) *adj.* suelto, flojo, laxo, desatado, desenredado, desprendido: *to hang* ~, caer suelto, colgar, flotar. *2* flojo [tornillo, diente]. *3* suelto, poco compacto, disgregado. *4* sueltas, sin encuadernar [hojas]. *5* loca [polea]. *6* desgarbado. *7* holgado, ancho [vestido]. *8* suelto, en libertad, no sujeto: *to break* ~, escaparse, soltarse, zafarse; desatarse, desencadenarse. *9* QUÍM. libre. *10* vago, indeterminado; poco exacto, lato; libre [traducción, interpretación, etc.]. *11* libre, relajado, licencioso, disoluto. *12* ~ *end*, cabo suelto; *at* ~ *end*, sin empleo; *at* ~ *ends*, desarreglado. *13 s.* libertad, soltura: *to give* ~ *to*, dar rienda suelta a.

**loose (to)** *tr.* soltar, desatar, deshacer, desliar, aflojar, desapretar, desprender. *2* soltar, dejar en libertad. *3* lanzar [flechas, etc.].

**loose-leaf** *adj.* de hojas sueltas [cuaderno, etc.].

**loosen (to)** (-øn) *tr.* soltar, desatar, libertar. *2* aflojar, desceñir, desasir. *3* ahuecar, mullir. *4* relajar. *5* soltar [el vientre]. *6* ablandar [la tos]. *7 intr.* aflojarse, relajarse. *8* soltarse, desatarse.

**looseness** (-nis) *s.* flojedad. *2* holgura [de un vestido]. *3* soltura. *4* relajación, relajamiento. *5* flujo [de vientre]. *6* vaguedad, poca exactitud.

**loosestrife** (-traif) *s.* BOT. lisimaquia. *2* BOT. salicaria.

**loot** (lut) *s.* botín, presa. *2* pillaje, saqueo.

**loot (to)** *tr.-intr.* pillar, saquear, robar.

**looting** (-ing) *s.* saqueo, saqueamiento.

**lop** (lap) *s.* chapodo, desmocho. *2 adj.* colgante, gacho [orejas, etc.].

**lop (to)** *tr.* podar, desmochar, cortar. *2 intr.* colgar, pender flojamente. *3* picarse [el mar].

**lope** (loup) *s.* medio galope, paso largo.

**lope (to)** *intr.* ir a medio galope, a paso largo.

**lop-eared** *adj.* de orejas caídas.

**lophobranch** (lou·føbrænch) *adj.-s.* lofobranquio.

**lopsided** (la·psaidid) *adj.* torcido, inclinado, con un lado más bajo o pequeño que otro; asimétrico, desproporcionado. *2* desequilibrado.

**loquacious** (loukuei·shøs) *adj.* locuaz, gárrulo.

**loquacity** (-siti) *s.* locuacidad.

**lord** (loʳd) *s.* señor, dueño, amo. *2 poét.* y *fam.* marido. *3* lord [título]: *Lord Chamberlain*, camarero mayor; *Lord Mayor*, alcalde de Londres, de York, de Dublín, etc.; *the Lords*, la Cámara de los lores. *4 the Lord*, el Señor, Dios: *Our Lord*, Nuestro Señor, Jesucristo; *the Lord's Prayer*, el padrenuestro; *the Lord's Supper*, la Santa Cena, la Eucaristía; *to die in the Lord*, morir en la paz del Señor.

**lord (to)** *intr.-tr. to* ~ *over* o *to* ~ *it over*, señorear, mandar despóticamente. *2 tr.* hacer lord; dar título de lord.

**lordliness** (-linis) *s.* señorío, dignidad. *2* altivez, orgullo.

**lord(l)ing** (-(l)ing) *s.* desp. pequeño señor.

**lordly** (-li) *adj.* señorial, señoril, noble; espléndido, magnífico. *2* altanero, imperioso.

**lordosis** (loʳdou·sis) *s.* MED. lordosis.

**lordship** (loʳdship) *s.* señoría, dominio. *2 his* ~, *your* ~, su señoría, su excelencia.

**lore** (louʳ) *s.* saber. *2* ciencia o saber popular.

**lorgnette** (loʳñe·t) *s.* impertinentes. *2* gemelos de teatro con mango.

**lorica** (lorai·ka) *s.* ARM., ZOOL. loriga.

**loricate(d** (la·rikeit(id) *adj.* ZOOL. loricado.

**loriot** (la·riat) *s.* ORN. oropéndola.

**lorn** (loʳn) *adj.* abandonado, solo, sin parientes ni amigos.

**Lorrain(e** (lore·n) *n. pr.* GEOGR. Lorena.

**Lorrainer** (lore·nøʳ) *s.* lorenés.

**lorry** (lo·ri) *s.* ORN. especie de loro o perico.

**lose (to)** (luš) *tr.* perder: *to* ~ *heart*, desalentarse; *to* ~ *one's temper*, perder la calma, encolerizarse; *to* ~ *one's way*, perderse, extraviarse; *to* ~ [*something*] *to*, perder [algo] en beneficio de. *2* hacer perder: *that lost him his place*, esto le hizo perder su empleo. *3 intr.* perder, tener una pérdida. *4 ref.* perderse; extraviarse; engolfarse, ensimismarse. ¶ Pret. y p. p.: *lost*.

**loser** (-øʳ) *s.* perdedor, el que pierde.

**losing** (-ing) *s.* pérdida. *2 adj.* perdedor, perdidoso.

**loss** (los) *s.* pérdida: *to be at a* ~, no saber qué hacer: *to sell at a* ~, vender con pérdida. *2* perdición. *3* COM. daño, quebranto; siniestro.

**lost** (lost) *pret.* y *p. p.* de TO LOSE. *2 adj.* perdido. *3* arruinado. *4* olvidado. *5* extraviado. *6* desorientado, perplejo. *7* ~ *in thought*, abstraído, pensativo. *8* ~ *to*, perdido para; insensible a, que ha perdido [el sentimiento] de.

**lost-and-found department** *s.* oficina de objetos perdidos.

**Lot** (lat) *n. pr. m.* BIB. Lot.

**lot** *s.* lote, parte, porción. *2* porción de terreno, solar. *3* suerte [para decidir]: *to draw*, *o cast*, *lots*, echar suertes; *to fall to one's* ~, caerle a uno en suerte. *4* suerte, sino. *5* colección, hato, partida. *6 fig.* sujeto, persona: *a bad* ~, una mala persona. 7 *a* ~ *of, lots of,* la mar de. 8 adv. *a* ~, mucho.

**lot (to)** *tr.* dividir en lotes. 2 repartir o asignar echando suertes. ¶ Pret. y p. p.: *lotted;* ger.: - *tting.*

**loth** (louz) *adj.* LOATH.

**lotos** *s.* LOTUS.

**lottery** (la·tøri) *s.* lotería, rifa.

**lotto** (la·tou) *s.* lotería [juego casero].

**lotus** (lou·tøs) *s.* BOT. loto.

**lotus-eater** *s.* lotófago.

**loud** (laud) *adj.* fuerte [sonido]. 2 alta [voz]. 3 recio, clamoroso, ruidoso, estrepitoso. 4 chillón, llamativo. 5 vulgar, ordinario. 6 adv. en voz alta. 7 ruidosamente.

**loud-speaker** *s.* RADIO. altavoz.

**lough** (lak) *s.* (Irl.) lago; ría.

**Louis** (lu·is) *n. pr.* Luis.

**Louisa** (lui·sa), **Louise** (luis) *n. pr.* Luisa.

**lounge** (lau·ndӯ) *s.* paseo; acción de pasear o de pasar el rato. 2 salón de descanso, de tertulia. 3 sofá, diván.

**lounge (to)** *intr.* pasear, callejear, pasar el rato. 2 estar sentado o reclinado indolentemente.

**lounger** (lau·ndӯøʳ) *s.* ocioso. 2 paseante, azotacalles.

**lour (to)** (lauʳ) *s.* TO LOWER.

**louse** (laus), *pl.* **lice** (-lais) *s.* ENT. piojo.

**lousewort** (-wøʳt) *s.* BOT. estafisagria.

**lousiness** (-inis) *s.* piojería.

**lousy** (lau·ši) *adj.* piojoso. 2 astroso, asqueroso.

**lout** (laut) *s.* patán, rústico, zafio.

**loutish** (lau·tish) *adj.* rudo, rústico, tosco, zafio.

**Louvain** (luve·n) *n. pr.* GEOGR. Lovaina.

**louver** (lu·vøʳ) *s.* ARQ. lumbrera. 2 juego de tablillas a manera de persiana. 3 persiana de automóvil.

**lovable** (lø·vabøl) *adj.* amable [digno de ser amado].

**lovage** (lø·vidӯ) *s.* BOT. lingüístico.

**love** (løv) *s.* amor, cariño afecto, afición: ~ *affair,* amores, amorío; ~ *feast,* ágape; ~ *knot,* lazo, nudo de cinta; *to be in* ~, estar enamorado; *to make* ~ *to,* enamorar, cortejar; *to send one's* ~, mandar afectuosos recuerdos; *for* ~, sin interés, de balde; *not for* ~ *or money,* ni a tiros, por nada del mundo. 2 amor [pers. amada]. 3 fam. preciosidad. 4 B. ART. amorcillo. 5 (con may.) Amor, Cupido. 6 DEP. cero, nada [en el tenis y oros juegos].

**love (to)** *tr.* amar, querer, adorar; tener cariño a. 2 gustar de, tener afición a. 3 *intr.* amar.

**lovebird** (-bøʳd) *s.* ORN. periquito.

**love-in-a-mist** *s.* BOT. ajenuz, arañuela, neguilla.

**Lovelace** (-leis) *s.* seductor, libertino.

**loveless** (-lis) *adj.* sin amor. 2 desamado. 3 desamorado.

**loveliness** (-linis) *s.* amabilidad, encanto, belleza, exquisitez.

**lovelock** (-lak) *s.* ant. rizo sobre las sienes o la frente.

**lovelorn** (-loʳn) *adj.* abandonado por su amor; que suspira de amor.

**lovely** (-li) *adj.* amable, adorable, encantador, hermoso, exquisito. 2 deleitoso, ameno.

**love-maker** *s.* cortejante, enamorado.

**love-making** *s.* cortejo, galanteo.

**lover** (-øʳ) *s.* enamorado. 2 amante, amador, galán. 3 amigo, aficionado.

**lovesick** (-sik) *adj.* enamorado, enfermo de amor.

**lovesickness** (-nis) *s.* mal de amor.

**loving** (-ing) *adj.* amante. 2 amoroso, afectuoso, cariñoso. 3 bondadoso.

**low** (lou) *adj.* bajo: *Low Countries,* Países Bajos; *Low Latin,* bajo latín; *Low Mass,* misa baja o rezada; ~ *relief,* B. ART. bajo relieve; ~ *shoe,* zapato bajo; ~ *trick,* cochinada, mala pasada; ~ *water,* bajamar, marea baja; estiaje. | Hablando de una pers. de baja estatura, se dice *short.* 2 profunda [inclinación, reverencia]. 3 escotado [vestido]. 4 pobre, humilde. 5 inferior [organismo, mentalidad, etc.]. 6 pobre, escaso, insuficiente. 7 pobre [concepto, opinión]. 8 débil, enfermo; abatido, desalentado: ~ *spirits,* abatimiento, desánimo. 9 muerto. 10 ~ *comedy,* farsa, sainete. 11 AUTO. ~ *gear,* primera. 12 adv. bajo. 13 bajamente. 14 barato, a bajo precio. 15 sumisamente. 16 *s.* mugido, berrido. 17 lo bajo; punto o lugar bajo, tierra baja. 18 AUTO. primera.

**low (to)** *intr.* mugir, berrear.

**lowbell** (-bel) *s.* cencerro.

**lowborn** (-bo·ʳn) *adj.* de humilde cuna.

**lowbred** (-bred) *adj.* zafio, grosero.

**low-brow** *s.* fam. persona inculta.

**Low-Church** *adj.* perteneciente a la secta anglicana opuesta al ritualismo.

**low-down** *adj.* fam. bajo, vil. 2 *s.* pop (E. U.) información confidencial o de primera mano.

**1) lower** (-øʳ) *adj.* y *adv. compar.* de LOW: más bajo, etc.; bajo; ~ *case,* IMPR. caja baja; *Lower Empire,* Bajo Imperio; ~ *floor,* piso bajo; *Lower House,* Cámara baja; *the* ~ *orders* o *classes,* la clase baja, el pueblo.

**2) lower (to)** (lau·øʳ) *s.* ceño; aspecto amenazador.

**1) lower (to)** (lou·øʳ) *tr.* bajar [poner más bajo, inclinar hacia abajo]. 2 arriar. 3 agachar. 4 bajar, rebajar, reducir. 5 abatir, humillar. 6 *intr.* bajar, reducirse, disminuir.

**2) lower (to)** (lau·øʳ) *intr.* mirar ceñudo, fruncir el ceño. 2 amenazar [la tempestad]; encapotarse [el cielo].

**lower-case** (lou·øʳ) *adj.* IMPR. de caja baja.

**lowering** (lau·øring) *adj.* ceñudo, amenazador, sombrío. 2 encapotado [cielo].

**lowermost** (lou·øʳmout), **lowest** (-it) *adj. superl.* de LOW: (el) más bajo.

**lowing** (-ing) *s.* mugido, berrido.

**lowland** (-lænd) *s.* tierra baja: *the Lowlands,* las tierras bajas de Escocia.

**Lowlander** (-øʳ) *s.* natural o habitante de las tierras bajas de Escocia.

**lowly** (lou·li) *adj.* humilde, modesto, sencillo. 2 bajo [tierras, etc.]. 3 adv. humildemente.

**low-necked** *adj.* escotado, de cuello bajo [vestido].

**low-pitched** *adj.* de poca inclinación o pendiente [tejado]. 2 grave [sonido].

**low-pressure** *adj.* de baja presión.

**low-spirited** *adj.* abatido, desanimado, triste.

**low-tension** *adj.* ELECT. de baja tensión.

**low-water line** o **mark** *s.* línea de nivel mínimo de las aguas. 2 fig. punto más bajo.

**loyal** (loi·al) *adj.* leal, fiel.

**loyalist** (loi·alist) *s.* POL. realista. 2 POL. fiel al príncipe o al gobierno establecido, leal.

**loyalty** (loi·alti) *s.* lealtad, fidelidad.

**lozenge** (la·šendӯ) *s.* GEOM. rombo. 2 BLAS. losange. 3 pastilla [de menta, etc.].

**lozenged** (-d) *adj.* rombal.

**lubber** (lø·bøʳ) *s.* patán, bobalicón. 2 marinero torpe.

**lubberly** (-li) *adj.* torpe, desmañado. 2 *adv.* torpemente, desmañadamente.
**lubricant** (liu·bricant) *s.* lubrificante.
**lubricate (to)** (-keit) *tr.* lubrificar.
**lubrication** (-ei·shøn) *s.* lubrificación.
**lubricious** (liubri·søs) *adj.* LUBRICOUS.
**lubricity** (-siti) *s.* lubricidad. 2 inestabilidad.
**lubricous** (liu·bricøs) *adj.* lúbrico.
**luce** (lius) *s.* ICT. lucio.
**lucent** (liu·šønt) *adj.* luciente. 2 claro, transparente.
**lucern(e** (lusø·ᵣn) *s.* BOT. mielga, alfalfa.
**Lucerne** *n. pr.* GEOGR. Lucerna.
**Lucia** (lu·shia) *n. pr. f.* Lucía.
**lucid** (liu·sid) *adj.* lúcido. 2 luciente.
**lucidity** (liusi·diti) *s.* lucidez.
**lucidly** (liu·sidli) *adj.* lúcidamente.
**Lucifer** (-siføᵣ) *n. pr.* Lucifer. 2 ASTR. lucífero.
**luciferous** (liusi·førøs) *adj.* luminoso, lucífero.
**lucifugous** (-fiugøs) *adj.* lucífugo.
**luck** (løk) *s.* suerte, fortuna [buena o mala]; buena suerte: *down on one's ~*, fam. de mala suerte, de malas; *for ~*, para que traiga suerte; *worse ~*, desgraciadamente.
**luckily** (-ili) *adv.* afortunadamente.
**luckiness** (-inis) *s.* suerte, buena fortuna, dicha.
**luckless** (-lis) *adj.* desafortunado. 2 desdichado.
**lucky** (-i) *adj.* afortunado; de suerte: *~ hit*, golpe de fortuna; *to be ~*, tener suerte. 2 feliz, oportuno. 3 feliz, dichoso, venturoso.
**lucrative** (liu·krativ) *adj.* lucrativo.
**lucre** (liu·køᵣ) *s.* lucro.
**Lucretia** (lukri·shia) *n. pr. f.* Lucrecia.
**lucubrate (to)** (liu·kiubreit) *tr.-intr.* lucubrar.
**lucubration** (-ei·shøn) *s.* lucubración.
**Lucy** (lu·si) *n. pr. f.* Lucía.
**ludicrous** (liu·dicrøs) *adj.* cómico, ridículo, absurdo.
**luff** (løf) *s.* MAR. orza, orzada. 2 MAR. caída de proa [de una vela]. 3 MAR. aparejo de bolinear.
**luff (to)** *tr.* MAR. orzar, ceñir el viento, bolinear.
**lug** (løg) *s.* oreja, asa, etc., por donde se ase o sujeta una cosa. 2 tirón; tiro, arrastre. 3 lo que se arrastra; peso, carga. 4 MAR. vela al tercio.
**lug (to)** *tr.* tirar de, halar; arrastrar. 2 introducir forzadamente [una especie] en la conversación. 3 *intr.* tirar [de]. ¶ Pret. y p. p.: *lugged;* ger.: *lugging.*
**luggage** (-idẏ) *s.* equipaje [de viajero].
**lugger** (-øᵣ) *s.* MAR. lugre.
**lugubrious** (liugiu·briøs) *adj.* lúgubre, fúnebre.
**lugworm** (lø·gwøᵣm) *s.* lombriz usada como cebo.
**Luke** (luk) *n. pr.* Lucas.
**lukewarm** (liu·kwøᵣm) *adj.* tibio, templado. 2 fig. tibio.
**lukewarmness** (-nis) *s.* tibieza.
**lull** (løl) *s.* momento de calma o de silencio.
**lull (to)** *tr.* adormecer, arrullar. 2 calmar, aquietar, sosegar. 3 *intr.* calmarse, amainar.
**lullaby** (lø·labai) *s.* arrullo, canción de cuna.
**Lullian** (lø·lian) *adj.* luliano.
**lumbago** (lømbei·gou) *s.* MED. lumbago.
**lumbar** (lø·mbaᵣ) *adj.* ANAT. lumbar.
**lumber** (lø·mbøᵣ) *s.* madera [aserrada], madera de construcción. 2 trastos viejos: *~ room*, trastera. 3 fig. balumba, cosa que estorba.
**lumber (to)** *tr.* cortar [árboles], aserrar [troncos]. 2 amontonar en; llenar, atestar. 3 moverse pesadamente. 4 avanzar con ruido sordo.
**lumbering** (-ing) *s.* explotación de bosques maderables. 2 *adj.* pesado, que se mueve pesadamente.
**lumberman** (-mæn) *s.* hachero. 2 maderero.
**lumberyard** (-yaᵣd) *s.* almacén de maderas.
**lumen** (liu·min) *s.* FÍS. lumen.
**luminary** (liu·mineri) *s.* luminar, astro. 2 fig. luminar, lumbrera.
**luminiscence** (liumine·søns) *s.* luminescencia.
**luminescent** (-t) *adj.* luminescente.
**luminosity** (liumina·siti) *s.* luminosidad.
**luminous** (liu·minøs) *s.* luminoso.
**lummox** (lø·maks) *s.* fam. porro [sujeto torpe].
**lump** (lømp) *s.* trozo, pedazo, terrón, pella, burujo. 2 bulto, protuberancia, chichón. 3 nudo [en la garganta]. 5 TEJ. mota. 6 sujeto torpe. 7 fig. persona rehecha. 9 conjunto, totalidad: *in the ~*, en junto, por junto; *~ sum*, suma global o total, tanto alzado.
**lump (to)** *tr.* aburujar. 2 levantar bultos en. 3 tomar en junto, en globo. 4 fam. aguantar, tragar, apechugar con. 5 *intr.* aterronarse, aburujarse. 6 abultarse, crecer. 7 moverse pesadamente.
**lumpish** (-ish) *adj.* parecido a una pella o terrón. 2 pesado, macizo, tosco. 3 torpe, estúpido.
**lumpy** (lø·mpi) *adj.* lleno de bultos o protuberancias. 2 aterronado, aburujado. 3 agitado [mar].
**lunacy** (liu·nasi) *s.* locura, demencia.
**lunar** (-naᵣ) *adj.* lunar. 2 lunado.
**lunate(d** (-neit)id] *adj.* lunado.
**lunatic** (-natik) *adj.-s.* loco, demente: *~ asylum*, manicomio.
**lunation** (-ei·shøn) *s.* lunación.
**lunch** (lønch) *s.* almuerzo, comida ligera: *~ basket*, fiambrera.
**lunch (to)** *intr.* almorzar, tomar una comida ligera.
**luncheon** (-øn) *s.* refacción, tentempié. 2 LUNCH.
**luncheon (to)** *intr.* tomar un LUNCHEON.
**lune** (lu·n) *s.* GEOM. lúnula.
**lunette** (lune·t) *s.* luneta [adorno]. 2 ARQ., FORT. luneta. 3 LITURG. lúnula, viril.
**lung** (løng) *s.* pulmón.
**lunge** (løndẏ) *s.* estocada, hurgonazo. 2 arremetida, embestida. 3 LONGE.
**lunge (to)** *intr.* ESGR. tirar una estocada. 2 abalanzarse, arremeter.
**lungwort** (lø·ngwøᵣ) *s.* BOT. pulmonaria.
**lunule** (liu·niul) *s.* lúnula, blanco de la uña.
**Lupercalia** (liu·pøᵣkeilia) *s. pl.* lupercales.
**lupine** (liu·pin) *s.* BOT. altramuz. 2 *adj.* lupino.
**lupus** (-øs) *s.* MED. lupus.
**lurch** (løᵣch) *s.* sacudida, tumbo, balance brusco. 2 bandazo. 3 *to leave in the ~*, dejar en la estacada.
**lurch (to)** *intr.* andar tambaleándose, dar tumbos, dar un tumbo. 2 MAR. dar bandazos.
**lurcher** (-øᵣ) *s.* acechador. 2 cierto perro de caza.
**lure** (liuᵣ) *s.* señuelo, añagaza, reclamo. 2 cebo, atractivo, tentación.
**lure (to)** *tr.* atraer [con señuelo o engaño]; seducir, inducir, tentar.
**lurid** (liu·rid) *adj.* rojo, cárdeno, tempestuoso [cielo, nubes, etc.]. 2 fantasmal, pavoroso, espeluznante.
**lurk** (løᵣk) *s. on the ~*, en acecho.
**lurk (to)** *intr.* acechar, esconderse; estar escondido, estar latente. 2 moverse furtivamente.
**lurking** (-ing) *adj.* escondido, en acecho. 2 *~ place*, escondite, emboscada.
**luscious** (lø·shøs) *adj.* delicioso, exquisito. 2 dulce, sabroso. 3 meloso, empalagoso.

**lush** (løsh) *adj.* lujuriante, fresco, lozano. *2* rico, profuso. *3 s.* pop. licor, bebida.
**Lusitanian** (liusitei·nian) *adj.-s.* lusitano.
**lust** (løst) *s.* avidez. *2* concupiscencia, lujuria.
**lust (to)** *intr.* codiciar. *2* desear [con lujuria]. Gralte. con *for* o *after.*
**luster** (-øʳ) *s.* LUSTRE.
**luster (to)** *tr.* lustrar, abrillantar.
**lustful** (-ful) *adj.* sensual, carnal, lujurioso.
**lustfulness** (-nis) *s.* sensualidad, lujuria.
**lustily** (-ili) *adv.* fuertemente, vigorosamente.
**lustral** (lø·stral) *adj.* lustral.
**lustration** (-ei·shøn) *s.* lustración.
**lustre** (lø·støʳ) *s.* lustre, brillo. *2* reflejo, viso. *3* lustre, esplendor. *4* araña [lámpara]. *5* lustro.
**lustrine** (lø·strin) *s.* lustrina.
**lustrous** (-øs) *adj.* lustroso, brillante.
**lustrum** (-øm) *s.* lustro.
**lusty** (lø·sti) *adj.* lozano, fuerte, robusto. *2* vigoroso, enérgico.
**lute** (liut) *s.* MÚS. laúd. *2* luten; pasta para tapar junturas.
**lutecium** (liuti·shiøm) *s.* QUÍM. lutecio.
**Luther** (lu·zøʳ) *n. pr.* Lutero.
**Lutheran** (lu·zøran) *adj.-s.* luterano.
**Lutheranism** (lu·zøranišm) *s.* luteranismo.
**luthier** (liutie·ʳ) *m.* guitarrero.
**lux** (løks), *pl.* **luces** (liu·siš) *s.* FÍS. lux.
**luxate (to)** (lø·kseit) *tr.* dislocar, descoyuntar.
**luxation** (løkse·shøn) *s.* luxación, dislocación.
**Luxemburg** (lø·ksembøʳg) *n. pr.* GEOGR. Luxemburgo.
**luxuriance, -cy** (løgshu·rians, -si) *s.* demasía, exuberancia, frondosidad, lozanía.
**luxuriant** (-riant) *adj.* lujuriante, exuberante, lozano, frondoso.
**luxuriate (to)** (-rieit) *intr.* crecer con lozanía. *2* vivir con lujo. *3* gozarse, complacerse.

**luxurious** (-riøs) *adj.* lujoso. *2* dado al lujo. *3* muelle, sibarítico.
**luxuriousness** (-nis) *s.* lujo, fausto.
**luxury** (lø·gshuri) *s.* lujo, fausto. *2* regalo, molicie. *3* placer.
**lycanthrope** (lai·kænzroup) *s.* licántropo.
**lyceum** (laisi·øm) *s.* liceo, ateneo.
**Lycian** (li·sian) *adj.-s.* licio.
**lycopodium** (laicopou·diøm) *s.* BOT. licopodio.
**Lycurgus** (laicø·ʳgøs) *n. pr.* Licurgo.
**Lydia** (li·dia) *n. pr.* GEOGR. Lidia.
**Lydian** (li·dian) *adj.-s.* lidio. *2 adj.* blando, voluptuoso.
**lye** (lai) *s.* lejía. *2* (Ingl.) FERROC. desviadero.
**lying** (lai·ing) *ger.* de TO LIE. *2 adj.* mentiroso. *3* tendido, echado, yacente: ~ *down,* acostado. *4* sito, situado.
**lying-in** *s.* parto: ~ *hospital,* clínica maternal.
**lymph** (limf) *s.* FISIOL. linfa. *2* poét. linfa, agua.
**lymphatic** (limfæ·tik) *adj.* linfático. *2 s.* ANAT. vaso linfático.
**lymphatism** (li·mfatišm) *s.* MED. linfatismo.
**lymphocyte** (li·mfosait) *s.* ANAT. linfocito.
**lyncean** (li·nsian) *adj.* línceo.
**lynch (to)** (linch) *tr.* linchar.
**lynching** (li·nching) *s.* linchamiento.
**lynx** (links) *s.* ZOOL. lince.
**lynx-eyed** *adj.* de ojos linces, perspicaz.
**Lyon** (lai·øn), **Lyons** (lai·ønš) *n. pr.* GEOGR. Lión.
**Lyonese** (laiøni·š) *adj.-s.* lionés.
**lyrate** (lai·reit) *adj.* BOT., ORN. lirado.
**lyre** (laiʳ) *s.* MÚS. lira. *2* ASTR. (con may.) Lira.
**lyrebird** (-bøʳd) *s.* ORN. ave lira.
**lyric** (li·rik) *adj.* lírico. *2 s.* poema lírico. *3* fam. letra de una canción.
**lyrical** (-al) *adj.* lírico.
**lyricism** (li·risišm) *s.* lirismo.
**Lysander** (laisæ·ndøʳ) *n. pr.* Lisandro.
**Lysippus** (laisi·pøs) *n. pr.* Lisipo.
**lysis** (lai·sis) *s.* MED. lisis.
**lythraceous** (litrei·šøs) *adj.* litráceo.

**M, m** (em) *s.* M, m, decimotercera letra del alfabeto inglés.
**ma** (ma) *s.* fam. madre, mamá.
**ma'am** (mam o mæm) *s.* contr. de MADAM, señora.
**macaber, macabre** (maka·bø<sup>r</sup>) *adj.* macabro.
**macadam** (makæ·dam) *s.* macadam, macadán.
**macadamize (to)** (-aiš) *tr.* macadamizar.
**macaque** (maka·k) *s.* ZOOL. macaco.
**macaroni** (mækarou·ni) *s.* macarrones. 2 pisaverde.
**macaronic** (mækara·nik) *adj.* macarrónico. 2 *s. pl.* macarronea.
**macaroon** (mækaru·n) *s.* macarrón, mostachón, bollo de almendra, coco, etc.
**Macassar** (makæ·sa<sup>r</sup>) *n. pr.* GEOGR. Macasar.
**macaw** (maco·) *s.* ORN. ara, guacamayo.
**Maccabees** (mæ·købıš) *n. pr.* BIB. Macabeos.
**mace** (meis) *s.* maza [arma, insignia]: ~ *bearer,* macero. 2 macia, macis [especia].
**Macedon** (mæ·sidan), **Macedonia** (mæsidou·nia) *n. pr.* GEOGR., HIST. Macedonia.
**Macedonian** (-*n*) *adj.-s.* macedonio.
**macer** (mei·sø<sup>r</sup>) *s.* macero.
**macerate (to)** (mæ·søreit) *tr.* macerar.
**maceration** (mæsørei·shøn) *s.* maceración.
**machete** (mashe·t o machei·ti) *s.* MATCHET.
**Machiavel** (Mæ·kiavel) *n. pr.* Maquiavelo.
**Machiavel(l)ian** (mækiave·lian) *adj.-s.* maquiavelista. 2 maquiavélico.
**Machiavellism** (mæ·kiaveliš*m*) *s.* maquiavelismo.
**machicolation** (mæchikole·shøn) *s.* FORT. matacán.
**machinate (to)** (mæ·kineit) *intr.-tr.* maquinar.
**machination** (mækinei·shøn) *s.* maquinación.
**machinator** (mæ·kineitø<sup>r</sup>) *s.* maquinador.
**machine** (mashı·n) *s.* máquina, ingenio. 2 bicicleta, automóvil, aeroplano, etc. 3 TEAT., LIT. máquina. 4 máquina [política, social, etc.]; (E.U.) camarilla. 5 *adj.* ~ *gun,* ametralladora; ~ *tool,* máquina herramienta.
**machine (to)** *tr.* trabajar a máquina.
**machine-gun (to)** *tr.* ametrallar.
**machinery** (-øri) *s.* maquinaria. 2 fig. máquina, organización. 3 LIT. máquina.
**machinist** (-ist) *s.* maquinista; mecánico. 2 TEAT. tramoyista.
**mackerel** (mæ·kørøl) *s.* ICT. escombro, caballa. 2 ~ *sky,* cielo aborregado.

**mackinaw** (mæ·kino) *s.* tela de lana de dos caras para abrigos.
**mackintosh** (mæ·kintash) *s.* impermeable. 2 tela impermeabilizada.
**macle** (mæ·køl) *s.* MINER. macla.
**macrobian** (mækrou·bian) *s.* que vive muchos años.
**macrobiotics** (mækrøbaia·tiks) *s.* macrobiótica.
**macrocephalous** (-se·faløs) *adj.* macrocéfalo.
**macrocosm** (mæ·krøkošm) *s.* macrocosmo.
**macrogamete** (mækrøgami·t) *s.* BIOL. macrogameto.
**macron** (me·kran) *s.* IMPR. signo de vocal larga.
**Macrura** (mækru·ræ) *s. pl.* ZOOL. macruros.
**macula** (mæ·kiul*a*), *pl.* **-lae** (-li) *s.* ASTR., ANAT., MED. mácula.
**maculate** (mæ·kiuleit) *adj.* maculado.
**maculate (to)** *tr.* macular.
**maculation** (mækiulei·shøn) *s.* mácula, mancha.
**mad** (mæd) *adj.* loco: *like* ~, como un loco; *to be* ~ *about,* tener una locura por. 2 insensato, desesperado. 3 encolerizado, furioso. 4 disparatado. 5 rabioso [animal].
**madam** (mæ·dam) *s.* señora [tratamiento de respeto].
**madapollam** (mædapa·lam) *s.* madapolán.
**madcap** (mæ·dkæp) *adj.-s.* alocado, alborotado, atolondrado.
**madden (to)** (mæ·døn) *tr.* enloquecer. 2 exasperar. 3 *intr.* enloquecer, volverse loco.
**maddening** (mæ·dning) *adj.* enloquecedor, exasperante.
**madder** (mæ·dø<sup>r</sup>) *s.* BOT., TINT. rubia, granza.
**made** (meid) *pret.* y *p. p.* de TO MAKE. 2 *adj.* hecho, compuesto, confeccionado, fabricado: ~ *man,* hombre que ha triunfado en la vida.
**Madeira** (mædi·ra) *s.* vino de Madera.
**made-to-order** *adj.* hecho de encargo. 2 hecho a la medida.
**made-up** *adj.* completo, acabado. 2 hecho [vestido, ropa]. 3 maquillado, pintado [rostro]. 4 artificial, ficticio, inventado.
**Madge** (mæ·dỹ) *n. pr. abrev.* de MARGARET.
**madhouse** (mæ·djaus) *s.* manicomio, casa de orates.
**madly** (mæ·dli) *adv.* locamente, furiosamente, desesperadamente, insensatamente.
**madman** (mæ·dmæn) *s.* loco, orate.

**madness** (mæ·dnis) *s.* locura. *2* furia, frenesí.
**Madonna** (mada·na) *s.* madona: ~ *lily*, azucena.
**madrepore** (mæ·dripøʳ) *s.* ZOOL. madrépora.
**madrigal** (mæ·drigal) *s.* LIT., MÚS. madrigal.
**Madrilene** (mæ·drilin), **Madrilenian** (-li·nian) *adj.-s.* madrileño.
**madwort** (mæ·duøʳt) *s.* BOT. raspilla.
**Maecenas** (misɪ·nas) *s.* mecenas.
**maelstrom** (mei·lstrøm) *s.* remolino, vorágine.
**maenad** (mɪ·næd) *s.* ménade.
**magazine** (mægaʃɪ·n) *s.* almacén, depósito. *2* polvorín; santabárbara. *3* revista [periódico].
**Magdalen** (mæ·gdaløn) *n. pr.* Magdalena. *2 s.* (con min.) ramera arrepentida.
**Magdalene** (mæ·gdalin o -li·ni) *n. pr.* Magdalena.
**Magdalenian** (-nian) *adj.* GEOL. magdaleniense.
**Magellan (Strait of)** (madỹe·lan) *n. pr.* GEOGR. Estrecho de Magallanes.
**Magellanic** (mædỹølæ·nik) *adj.* magallánico.
**magenta** (madỹe·nta) *s.* color magenta.
**maggot** (mæ·gøt) *s.* cresa [larva]. *2* capricho, antojo.
**maggoty** (mæ·gøti) *adj.* gusaniento. *2* caprichoso.
**Magi** (mei·dỹai) *s. pl.* magos o sabios del Oriente.
**Magian** (mei·dỹian) *adj.-s.* mago [del Oriente].
**magic** (mæ·dỹik) *s.* magia, mágica: *as if by* ~, como por ensalmo. *2 adj.* mágico: ~ *lantern*, linterna mágica.
**magical** (-al) *adj.* mágico; encantado.
**magician** (madỹi·shan) *s.* mágico, mago.
**magisterial** (mædỹisti·rial) *adj.* de magistrado. *2* magistral, autoritario, dogmático.
**magistery** (mæ·dỹisteri) *s.* QUÍM. magisterio.
**magistracy** (mæ·dỹistrasi) *s.* magistratura.
**magistral** (-tral) *adj.* de maestro o profesores. *2* MAGISTERIAL *2. 3 adj.-s.* FARM. magistral.
**magistrate** (-treit) *s.* magistrado. *2* juez de paz.
**magma** (mæ·gma) *s.* GEOL. magma.
**Magna Charta** (mæ·gn·ka·ʳta) *s.* Carta Magna.
**magnanimity** (mægnani·miti) *s.* magnanimidad.
**magnanimous** (mægnæ·nimøs) *adj.* magnánimo.
**magnate** (mæ·gneit) *s.* magnate.
**magnesia** (mægnɪ·shia) *s.* magnesia.
**magnesian** (-an) *adj.* magnesiano.
**magnesic** (-sik) *adj.* magnésico.
**magnesite** (mæ·gnisait) *s.* MINER. magnesita.
**magnesium** (mægnɪ·shiøm) *s.* QUÍM. magnesio.
**magnet** (mæ·gnit) *s.* ELECT. imán. *2* piedra imán. *3* fig. imán [lo que atrae].
**magnetic** (mægne·tik) *adj.* magnético: ~ *needle*, aguja magnética, brújula; ~ *recorder*, aparato magnetofónico. *2* atrayente, cautivador.
**magnetical** (mægne·tikal) *adj.* magnético. *2* atrayente, cautivador.
**magnetism** (mæ·gnitiẑm) *s.* magnetismo.
**magnetite** (-tait) *s.* MINER. magnetita.
**magnetization** (-ei·shøn) *s.* magnetización.
**magnetize (to)** (mæ·gnitaiẑ) *tr.* magnetizar. *2* atraer, cautivar, fascinar. *3 intr.* imanarse.
**magnetizer** (-øʳ) *s.* magnetizador.
**magneto** (mægnɪ·tou) *s.* AUTO., ELECT. magneto.
**magnetoelectricity** (-ile·ctrisiti) *s.* electromagnetismo.
**magnetometer** (mægnøta·metøʳ) *s.* magnetómetro.
**magneton** (mæ·gnøtan) *s.* FÍS. magnetón.
**Magnificat** (mægni·fikat) *s.* Magnificat [cántico a la Virgen]. *2* canto de alabanza.
**magnification** (-ei·shøn) *s.* ÓPT. aumento, amplificación. *2* exageración.
**magnificence** (mægni·fisøns) *s.* magnificencia.

**magnificent** (-t) *adj.* magnífico, espléndido, suntuoso. *2* noble, elevado.
**magnifier** (mægnifaiøʳ) *s.* ÓPT. amplificador, lente de aumento. *2* exagerador.
**magnify (to)** (mæ·gnifai) *tr.* agrandar, aumentar, amplificar. *2* abultar, exagerar. ¶ Pret. y p. p.: *magnified.*
**magnifying glass** (-ing) *s.* lente de aumento, lupa.
**magniloquence** (mægni·løkuøns) *s.* grandilocuencia.
**magniloquent** (-t) *s.* grandílocuo.
**magnitude** (mæ·gnitiud) *s.* magnitud.
**magnolia** (mægnou·lia) *s.* BOT. magnolia.
**magnum** (mæ·gnøm) *s.* botella de dos litros.
**magpie** (mæ·gpai) *s.* ORN. urraca, picaza. *2* fig. charlatán, cotorra. *3* fig. regañón.
**Magus** (mei·gøs), *pl.*, **Magi** (-dỹai) *s.* mago [de oriente].
**Magyar** (mæ·gyaʳ) *adj.-s.* magiar.
**maharaja(h** (majara·dỹa) *s.* maharajá.
**Maharanee** (majarani·) *f.* esposa del maharajá.
**mahistick** (ma·lstik) *s.* PINT. tiento.
**mahogany** (maja·gani) *s.* BOT. caoba, caobo. *2* caoba [madera; color].
**Mahomet, Mahometan,** etc. MOHAMMED, MOHAMMEDAN, etc.
**mahout** (mæjau·t) *s.* cornaca, naire.
**maid** (meid) *s.* doncella [soltera, virgen]: ~ *of honour*, doncella o dama de honor. *2* doncella, criada: ~ *of all work*, criada para todo.
**maiden** (-øn) *s.* doncella, virgen, joven soltera. *2 adj.* soltera; de soltera: ~ *name*, nombre de soltera. *3* virginal. *4* virgen, nuevo. *5* primero, inicial.
**maidenhair** (-jeʳ) *s.* BOT. adianto, culantrillo.
**maidenhood** (-jud) *s. f.* doncellez.
**maidenly** (-li) *adj.* virginal, modesto, candoroso.
**maidservant** (mei·dsøʳvant) *s.* criada, doméstica.
**mail** (meil) *s.* malla [tejido de anillos, etc., de metal]; cota de malla. *2* correo, correspondencia, saco de la correspondencia, mala, valija. *3* correo, servicio postal [en Ingl., esp. con el extranjero]: ~ *boat*, buque correo; *air* ~, correo aéreo. *4* TEJ. malla [de lizo].
**mail (to)** *tr.* echar al correo; enviar por correo. *2* armar con malla o cota de malla.
**mailbox** (-baks) *s.* buzón; apartado.
**mailman** (-mæn) *s.* cartero.
**mailplane** (-plein) *s.* avión correo.
**maim** (meim) *s.* mutilación, estropeo.
**maim (to)** *tr.* mutilar, estropear, mancar, lisiar.
**main** (mein) *adj.* primero, principal, esencial, mayor, maestro: ~ *body*, grueso [del ejército]; ~ *office*, oficina central, casa matriz; ~ *road*, carretera principal. *2* grande, fuerte. *3 by* ~ *force*, a pura fuerza, por la fuerza. *4 s.* lo principal, lo esencial, la mayor parte: *in the* ~, en su mayor parte, principalmente. *5* poét. alta mar. *6* línea, tubería, conducto principal [de gas, agua, electricidad, etc.].
**mainland** (-lønd) *s.* continente, tierra firme.
**mainly** (-li) *adv.* principalmente, en su mayor parte. *2* poderosamente.
**mainmast** (-mæst) *s.* MAR. palo mayor.
**mainsail** (-seil) *s.* MAR. vela mayor.
**mainspring** (-spring) *s.* muelle principal o real. *2* móvil, causa principal.
**mainstay** (-stei) *s.* MAR. estay del palo mayor. *2* soporte principal.
**maintain (to)** (-tei·n) *tr.* mantener.

**maintainer** (-tei·nøʳ) *s.* mantenedor, defensor, partidario.

**maintenance** (mei·ntønans) *s.* mantenimiento, sostenimiento. 2 apoyo, sostén. 3 manutención, sustento. 4 IND. mantenimiento, conservación.

**maintop** (-tap) *s.* MAR. cofa mayor.

**main-topgallant** *s.* MAR. juanete mayor.

**main-topmast** *s.* MAR. mastelero mayor.

**main-topsail** *s.* MAR. gavia [vela].

**Mainz** (mai·nts) *n. pr.* Maguncia.

**maize** (meiš) *s.* BOT. maíz.

**maizena** (meiši·na) *s.* maicena.

**majestic** (madÿe·stik) *adj.* majestuoso.

**majestically** (-ali) *adj.* majestuosamente.

**majesty** (mæ·dÿisti) *s.* majestad; majestuosidad. 2 (con may.) Majestad [tratamiento].

**majolica** (madÿa·lika) *s.* mayólica.

**major** (mei·dÿøʳ) *adj.* mayor, más grande, principal. 2 MÚS. mayor. 3 *s.* DER. mayor de edad. 4 LÓG. mayor. 5 MIL. comandante. 6 MIL. ~ *general*, general de división.

**Majorca** (madÿo·ʳka) *n. pr.* GEOGR. Mallorca.

**Majorcan** (madÿo·ʳkan) *adj.-s.* mallorquín.

**major-domo** (meidÿøʳ-dou·mou) *s.* mayordomo.

**majority** (madÿa·riti) *s.* mayoría. 2 mayor de edad. 3 MIL. comandancia [empleo de comandante].

**majuscule** (madÿu·skiul) *s.* PALEOGR. mayúscula.

**make** (meik) *s.* hechura, forma; estructura; constitución, manera de ser. 2 hechura [acción de hacer], obra, fabricación, producción. 3 marca, modelo.

**make (to)** *tr.* hacer [crear, confeccionar, elaborar, fabricar; componer, formar; causar, ocasionar; producir, preparar, disponer; efectuar, ejecutar]: *to ~ bread*, hacer pan; *to ~ fun*, hacer burla, burlarse; *to ~ a mistake*, cometer un error, equivocarse; *to ~ a noise*, hacer ruido; *to ~ a stop*, hacer alto, detenerse; *to ~ a will*, hacer u otorgar testamento. 2 hacer [obligar, inducir a]: *he was made to dance*, le hicieron bailar. 3 poner en el estado o dar la cualidad que expresa un adjetivo: *to ~ angry*, enfadar, enojar; *to ~ clear*, hacer claro, aclarar; *to ~ fast*, fijar, amarrar, asegurar; cerrar; *to ~ level*, allanar, nivelar; *to ~ ready*, preparar, disponer; prepararse, disponerse, aprestarse. 4 hacer, convertir en, nombrar. 5 elevar, hacer llegar [a una cifra o cantidad]. 6 tener por, considerar como, creer, suponer. 7 entender, deducir, inferir: *what do you ~ of this?*, ¿qué deduce usted de esto? 8 hacer, ganar: *to ~ money*, hacer dinero; *to ~ a living*, ganarse la vida. 9 recorrer, hacer el trayecto o recorrido de; pasar, cruzar; llegar a, visitar [un lugar]. 10 hacer, andar [tantos nudos, kilómetros, etc., por hora, etc.]. 11 determinar, fijar, calcular. 12 MAR. descubrir, divisar, avistar. 13 ELECT. cerrar [un circuito]; establecer [un contacto]. 14 *to ~ a clean breast of it*, desembuchar, confesarlo todo. 15 *to ~ a great deal of*, TO ~ MUCH OF. 16 *to ~ believe*, hacer creer, fingir. 17 *to ~ both ends meet*, pasar o vivir con lo que se tiene o gana. 18 *to ~ friends with*, hacerse amigo de, reconciliarse con. 19 *to ~ good*, cumplir, llevar a cabo, probar; mantener, defender; justificar [con el éxito o resultado]; compensar, indemnizar. 20 *to ~ haste*, apresurarse, darse prisa. 21 *to ~ known*, hacer saber, dar a conocer. 22 *to ~ much of*, dar mucha importancia a, hacer mucho caso de; apreciar; mimar. 23 *to ~ neither head or tail of*, no comprender nada de.

24 *to ~ no difference* o *no matter*, no importar, ser lo mismo. 25 *to ~ one's mark*, firmar con una cruz; distinguirse, señalarse. 26 *to ~ one's mouth water*, hacer que se le haga a uno la boca agua. 27 *to ~ one's way*, avanzar; abrirse paso. 28 *to ~ out*, hacer, escribir, extender [una lista, un documento, etc.]; hacer, componer; comprender, descifrar, descubrir; divisar; probar, justificar; completar; conseguir. 29 *to ~ over*, rehacer; ceder, traspasar. 30 MAR. *to ~ sail*, largar velas. 31 *to ~ (a) shift*, arreglárselas, componérselas. 32 *to ~ the most of*, sacar el mejor partido de. 33 *to ~ up*, hacer, componer, formar; envolver, atar; confeccionar, preparar; componer, pintar [el rostro], TEAT. caracterizar, maquillar; completar; sumar; compensar; arreglar, reconciliar; inventar, forjar; IMPR. compaginar. 34 *to ~ up one's mind*, decidirse, resolverse, hacer ánimo [de]. 35 *to ~ water*, orinar; MAR. hacer aguas.

36 *intr.* dirigirse, encaminarse a; abalanzarse a. | Con *for*, *toward* o *at*, 37 contribuir a, servir para, tender a. | Con *for* o *to*. 38 hacerse, crecer, aumentar. 39 *to ~ after*, perseguir. 40 *to ~ away*, largarse, huir. 41 *to ~ away with*, llevarse; derrochar; destruir, matar. 42 *to ~ bold to*, atreverse a. 43 *to ~ free with*, tomarse libertades con. 44 *to ~ merry*, divertirse. 45 *to ~ off*, largarse, marcharse, huir. 46 *to ~ sure*, cerciorarse, asegurarse. 47 *to ~ up*, hacer las paces; componerse, pintarse; TEAT. caracterizarse, maquillarse. 48 *to ~ up for*, suplir, compensar. 49 *to ~ up to*, tratar de congraciarse con. ¶ Pret. y p. p.: made.

**make-believe** *adj.* fingido, simulado. 2 *s.* ficción, simulación, pretexto. 3 simulador.

**make-fast** *s.* MAR. amarradero.

**makepeace** (mei·kpis) *s.* PEACEMAKER.

**maker** (mei·køʳ) *s.* hacedor, autor, artífice: *the Maker*, el Hacedor, Dios. 2 fabricante, confeccionador.

**makeshift** (-shift) *adj.* provisional, de fortuna. 2 *s.* recurso, sustitutivo, sustituto.

**make-up** (-øp) *s.* composición, constitución, modo de ser. 2 afeite [del rostro]; TEAT. caracterización, maquillaje. 3 IMPR. compaginación.

**makeweight** (-ueit) *s.* añadidura [para completar el peso]. 2 suplente.

**making** (-ing) *s.* hechura, confección, fabricación: *in the ~*, haciéndose; sin terminar. 2 causa del éxito o la fortuna de uno. 3 (a veces *pl.*) cualidades [para ser algo]. 4 ganancias.

**Malabar** (mæ·labaʳ) *adj.* malabar, malabárico.

**Malacca** (malæ·ka) *n. pr.* GEOGR. Malaca: ~ *cane*, malaca, roten.

**Malachi** (mæ·lakai), **Malachias** (mælaka·ias) *n. pr.* BIB. Malaquías.

**malachite** (mæ·lakait) *s.* MINER. malaquita.

**malacia** (malei·shia) *s.* MED. malacia.

**malacology** (mælaka·lodÿi) *s.* malacología.

**malacopterygian** (-kaptøri·dÿian) *adj.* ICT. malacopterigio.

**malacostracan** (-ka·strakan) *adj.-s.* ZOOL. malacostráceo.

**maladdress** (-dre·s) *s.* torpeza, falta de tacto, descortesía.

**maladjusted** (-dÿø·stid) *adj.* de mal ajuste, mal ajustado. 2 inadaptado.

**maladministration** (-dministrei·shøn) *s.* mal gobierno, desgobierno.

**maladroit** (-droi·t) *adj.* torpe; falto de tacto.

malady (mæ·ladi) s. enfermedad.
Malagasy (malei·gasi) adj.-s. malgache.
malaise (mælei·š) s. malestar, indisposición.
malapert (mæ·lapø$^r$t) adj.-s. descarado, insolente.
malapropos (mælapropou) adj. impropio, inoportuno, fuera de propósito.
malar (mei·la$^r$) adj. ANAT. malar.
malaria (male·ria) s. MED. malaria.
malarial (-l) adj. palúdico.
Malayan (mælei·sha) s. GEOGR. Malasia.
Malaysian (mælei·sha) adj.-s. malasio.
malcontent (mæ·lkøntent) adj.-s. malcontento.
Maldives (mæ·ldaivs) n. pr. pl. GEOGR. Maldivas.
male (meil) adj. ZOOL., BOT., MEC. macho. 2 masculino: ~ flower, flor masculina. 3 varón: ~ child, hijo varón. 4 varonil, viril. 5 s. varón. 6 animal macho.
malediction (mælidi·kshøn) s. maldición.
malefaction (-fæ·kshøn) s. delito, fechoría.
malefactor (-fæ·ktø$^r$) s. malhechor.
malefic (male·fik) adj. maléfico.
maleficence (-fisøns) s. maleficencia.
maleficent (-fisønt) adj. maléfico.
malevolence (-vøløns) s. malevolencia, malquerencia, mala voluntad.
malevolent (-t) adj. malévolo.
malfeasance (mælfı·šans) s. proceder ilegal, desaguisado [esp. de un funcionario].
malformation (mælfo$^r$mei·shon) s. malformación.
malic (mei·lik) adj. QUÍM. málico.
malice (mæ·lis) s. mala voluntad, rencor. 2 malicia, malignidad, mala intención.
malicious (mali·shøs) adv. malévolo, rencoroso, maligno. 2 pícaro, travieso. 3 DER. culpable.
maling (malai·n) adj. maligno. 2 dañino, pernicioso.
maling (to) tr. detraer, difamar, calumniar.
malignancy (mali·gnansi) s. malignidad. 2 malevolencia, encono.
malignant (mali·gnant) adj. maligno. 2 maléfico. 3 malévolo.
malignity (-iti) s. malignidad.
malinger (to) (mali·ngø$^r$) intr. hacerse el enfermo, fingirse enfermo.
malingerer (-ø$^r$) s. maula, el que se finge enfermo para evitarse un trabajo.
malison (mæ·lišøn) s. poét. maldición.
mall (mol) s. mallo [mazo; juego]. 2 the Mall, paseo público.
mallard (mæ·la$^r$d) s. ORN. pato silvestre [macho].
malleability (mæliabi·liti) s. maleabilidad.
malleable (mæ·liabøl) adj. maleable.
malleolous (mæli·øløs) s. ANAT. maléolo.
mallet (mæ·lit) s. mazo, mallete.
malleus (mæ·liøs) s. ANAT. martillo.
mallow (mæ·lou) s. BOT. malva.
malmsey (ma·mši) s. malvasía.
malnutrition (mælniutri·shøn) s. desnutrición.
malodour (mælou·dø$^r$) s. mal olor, fetidez, hedor.
malpractice (mælpræ·ktis) s. MED., DER. tratamiento o proceder erróneo o ilegal.
malt (molt) s. malta. 2 cerveza.
malt (to) tr. convertir [là cebada] en malta.
Malta (mo·lta) n. pr. GEOGR. Malta.
Maltese (-iš), pl. -tese adj.-s. maltés.
Malthusian (mælziu·šian) adj. maltusiano.
malthusianism (-išm) s. maltusianismo.
maltose (mo·ltous) s. QUÍM. maltosa.
maltreat (to) (mæltrı·t) s. maltratar.

maltreatment (-mønt) s. maltratamiento, maltrato.
malvaceous (mælvei·shøs) adj. BOT. malvácea.
malversation (-ø$^r$se·shøn) s. malversación.
malvoise (mæ·lvoiši) s. MALMSEY.
mama (ma·ma o møma) s. mamá, madre.
Mameluke (mæ·meliuk) s. mameluco.
mamma (mæ·ma) s. MAMA. 2 (pl. -mae) mama, teta.
mammal (-al) s. ZOOL. mamífero.
Mammalia (mæmei·lia) s. pl. ZOOL. mamíferos.
mammary (mæ·mari) adj. mamario.
mammee (mamei o mamı·) s. BOT. mamey.
mammiferous (mæmi·førøs) adj. mamífero.
mammilla (mami·la), pl. -lae (-li) s. ANAT. mamila.
mammiliary (mæ·mileri) adj. mamilar.
mammoth (mæ·møz) s. ZOOL. mamut. 2 adj. gigantesco.
mammy (mæ·mi) s. mamá, mamita. 2 (Ingl.) abuela. 3 (E.U.) negra vieja, ama o criada negra.
man (mæn), pl. men (men) s. hombre [pers. humana; varón]: ~ about town, hombre desocupado, que hace vida de sociedad; ~ and wife, marido y mujer; Man of Sorrows, Jesucristo; ~ of straw, testaferro; ~ overboard!, MAR. ¡hombre al agua!; the ~ in the street, el hombre corriente; a ~, uno, un hombre; to a ~, todos sin excepción. 2 hombre, soldado, criado, seguidor, vasallo: to be one's own ~, no depender de nadie; ser dueño de sí mismo. 3 [usado sin artículo], el hombre, el género humano. 4 pieza [de ajedrez]; peón [de damas]. 5 [en composición] buque, navío: merchantman, buque mercante.
man (to) tr. MAR. tripular, dotar, amarinar. 2 MIL. guarnecer [un fuerte, etc.]. ¶ Pret. y p. p.: manned; ger.: -nning.
manacle (mæ·nakøl) s. manilla [grillete]. 2 pl. manillas, esposas.
manacle (to) tr. esposar, poner las manillas a.
manage (to) (mæ·nidý) tr. manejar. 2 dirigir, regir, gobernar, administrar. 3 tratar con cuidado. 4 adiestrar [el caballo]. 5 tr.-intr. ingeniarse, componérselas; lograr, conseguir.
manageable (-abøl) adj. manejable, dócil.
management (-mønt) s. manejo, dirección, gobierno, gestión, administración. 2 gerencia, consejo de administración. 3 habilidad, trastienda; aptitud para dirigir.
manager (-ø$^r$) s. director, administrador, gerente. 2 empresario. 3 buen administrador.
managerial (mænadýi·rial) adj. directivo, administrativo.
Manasseh (manæ·sø) n. pr. m. BIB. Manasés.
man-at-arms, pl. men-at-arms s. hombre de armas.
manatee (mænatı·) s. ZOOL. manatí.
manchineel (mænchinı·l) s. BOT. manzanillo.
Mancunian (mankiu·nian) adj.-s. manchesteriano.
mandarin (mændari·n) s. mandarín. 2 BOT. mandarina. 3 (con may.) lengua mandarina.
mandatary (mæ·ndateri) s. mandatario.
mandate (mæ·ndeit) s. mandato, orden, precepto. 2 DER., POL. mandato.
mandate (to) tr. asignar o conferir por mandato.
mandator (mændei·tø$^r$) s. mandante.
mandatory (mæ·ndatori) adj. obligatorio. 2 conferido por mandato. 3 s. mandatario.
mandible (mæ·ndibøl) s. ANAT., ZOOL. mandíbula.
mandolin (mæ·ndølin) s. MÚS. mandolina.
mandragora (mændræ·gora), mandrake (mæ·ndreik) s. BOT. mandrágora.
mandrel, mandril (mæ·ndrøl) s. MEC. mandril.

**mandrill** (-dril) s. zool. mandril.
**mane** (mein) s. crin [de caballo]; melena [de león, de pers.].
**maned** (-d) adj. crinado, crinito.
**manege** (mane·ȳ) s. EQUIT. picadero. 2 equitación. 3 marcha, aire [del caballo adiestrado].
**manes** (mei·niš) s. pl. manes.
**maneuver, to maneuver, maneuverer** = MANOEUVRE, TO MANOEUVRE, MANOEUVRER.
**manful** (mæ·nful) adj. viril, varonil. 2 bravo, esforzado, noble.
**manganate** (mænganei·t) s. QUÍM. manganato.
**manganese** (mænganı·s) s. QUÍM. manganeso.
**mange** (meindȳ) s. roña, sarna.
**manger** (mei·ndȳøʳ) s. pesebre.
**mangle** (mæ·ngøl) s. máquina de planchar, mangle.
**mangle (to)** tr. planchar con máquina. 2 magullar, desgarrar, destrozar, mutilar, estropear.
**mango** (-gou) s. BOT. mango.
**mangonel** (-gonel) s. maganel, almajaneque.
**mangosteen** (-gøstın) s. BOT. mangosto.
**mangrove** (-grouv) s. BOT. mangle.
**mangy** (mei·ndȳi) adj. sarnoso. 2 desastrado, mugriento.
**manhole** (mæ·njoul) s. boca de inspección o acceso a calderas, etc. 2 refugio en un túnel.
**manhood** (-jud) s. condición de hombre. 2 los hombres. 3 virilidad, valor.
**mania** (mei·nia) s. MED. manía. 2 manía, afición.
**maniac** (-k) adj.-s. maníaco, loco furioso.
**maniacal** (-al) adj. MANIAC.
**Manichean** (mæniki·an) s. maniqueo.
**Manicheism** (-išm) s. maniqueísmo.
**manichord** (mæ·nikoʳd) s. MÚS. manicordio.
**manicure** (-kiuʳ) s. manicura [cuidado de las manos]. 2 manicuro, ra [pers.].
**manicure (to)** tr. hacer la manicura a.
**manicurist** (-kiurist) s. manicuro, ra [pers.].
**manifest** (-fest) adj. manifiesto. 2 s. COM. manifiesto.
**manifest (to)** tr. manifestar; demostrar, revelar. 2 intr. hacer una manifestación pública, tomar parte en ella.
**manifestant** (mænife·stant) s. manifestador. 2 manifestante.
**manifestation** (-ei·shøn) s. manifestación; demostración, revelación. 2 manifestación [pública].
**manifesto** (mænife·stou) s. manifiesto; proclama.
**manifold** (-fould) adj. múltiple, multíplice, vario, diverso, numeroso. 2 s. copia [de una carta, etc.]. 3 MEC. tubo de unión múltiple.
**manifold (to)** tr. sacar varias copias a la vez.
**manikin** (-kin) s. enano. 2 maniquí [figura]. 3 hombre clástico.
**Manil(l)a** (mani·la) n. pr. GEOGR. Manila: ~ hemp, abacá; ~ paper, papel de manila.
**manille** (mani·l) s. mala, malilla [naipe].
**manioc** (mæ·niak) s. BOT. mandioca.
**maniple** (-pøl) s. manípulo.
**manipulate (to)** (maani·piuleit) tr. manipular, manejar.
**manipulation** (-ei·shøn) s. manipulación, manipuleo; manejo.
**manipulator** (mani·piuleitøʳ) s. manipulador.
**mankind** (mænkai·nd) s. género humano. 2 [mæ·nkaind] los hombres, el sexo masculino.
**manlike** (-laik) adj. varonil. 2 hombruno. 3 esforzado, noble.
**manliness** (-linis) s. virilidad, hombradía, valor, nobleza.

**manly** (-li) adj. varonil, viril, valeroso, noble.
**manna** (mæ·na) s. BIB., BOT. maná.
**mannequin** (mæ·nikin) s. maniquí [figura]. 2 modelo [de una casa de modas].
**manned** (mæ·nd) pret. y p. p. de TO MAN.
**manner** (mæ·nøʳ) s. manera, modo: adverb of ~, adverbio de modo; after, o in, the ~ of, a la manera de, a la, a lo; by no ~ of means, de ningún modo; in a ~, en cierto modo, hasta cierto punto; in this ~, así, de este modo. 2 B. ART., LIT. manera; amaneramiento. 3 hábito, costumbre. 4 clase, género, suerte. 5 aire, porte, conducta. 6 pl. maneras, modales, educación.
**mannerism** (-išm) s. amaneramiento.
**mannerist** (-ist) s. artista amanerado.
**mannerliness** (-linis) s. cortesía, urbanidad.
**mannerly** (-li) adj. cortés, urbano, atento. 2 adv. urbanamente.
**mannish** (mæ·nish) adj. varonil, hombruno.
**manoeuvre** (manu·vøʳ) s. MIL., MAR. maniobra [evolución]. 2 maniobra, manejo; artificio.
**manoeuvre (to)** tr. hacer maniobrar [las tropas, etc.]. 2 inducir, obligar, etc., con maniobras o manejos.
**manoeuvrer** (manu·vrøʳ) s. maniobrero.
**man-of-war** pl., **men-of-war** s. buque de guerra.
**manometer** (mana·metøʳ) s. manómetro.
**manor** (ma·nøʳ) s. feudo, señorío, hacienda de un señor: ~ house, casa señorial en el campo.
**manorial** (mano·rial) adj. señorial.
**mansard roof** (mæ·nsaʳd) s. ARQ. mansarda.
**manse** (mæ·ns) s. (Esc.) rectoría.
**manservant** (mæ·nsøʳvant) s. criado.
**mansion** (-shøn) s. hotel, palacio, casa grande. pl. edificio grande dividido en pisos.
**mansion-house** s. MANOR HOUSE. 2 (con may.) residencia del Lord Mayor de Londres.
**manslaughter** (-slotøʳ) s. homicidio.
**manslayer** (-leiøʳ) s. homicida.
**manteau** (-tou) s. capa, manto.
**mantel** (-tøl) s. manto [de chimenea]. 2 repisa [de chimenea].
**mantelet** (-tølet) s. capotillo; manteleta. 2 MIL. mantelete.
**mantelletta** (mæntøle·ta) s. ECLES. mantelete.
**mantelpiece** (-tølpıs) s. repisa de chimenea.
**mantilla** (mænti·la) s. mantilla, mantón.
**mantis** (mæ·ntis) s. ENT. campanero.
**mantissa** (mænti·sa) s. MAT. mantisa.
**mantle** (mæ·ntøl) s. manto [prenda]. 2 fig. manto, capa [lo que cubre]. 3 zool. manto. 4 camisa, manguito [de luz de gas].
**mantle (to)** tr. cubrir [con manto], tapar, envolver. 2 intr. extenderse [como un manto]. 3 cubrirse de espuma, etc. 4 encenderse [el rostro].
**mantling** (-ling) s. BLAS. mantelete.
**manual** (mæ·niual) adj. manual: ~ arts, artes mecánicas. 2 s. manual [libro]. 3 MÚS. teclado de mano. 4 MIL. ejercicio [de armas].
**manubrium** (maniu·briøm) s. ANAT., ZOOL. manubrio.
**manufactory** (mæniufæ·ktori) s. manufactura, fábrica, taller.
**manufacture** (-chøʳ) s. manufactura [fabricación; producto fabricado].
**manufacture (to)** tr. manufacturar, fabricar.
**manufacturer** (-chørøʳ) s. fabricante.
**manufacturing** (-chøring) adj. manufacturero, industrial, fabril.
**manumission** (mæniumi·shøn) s. manumisión.

**manumit (to)** (mæniumi·t) *tr.* manumitir. ¶ Pret. y p. p.: *mitted;* ger.: *-tting.*
**manumitter** (-tø<sup>r</sup>) *s.* manumisor.
**manure** (maniu·ø<sup>r</sup>) *s.* AGR. abono, estiércol.
**manure (to)** *tr.* AGR. abonar, estercolar.
**manuscript** (mæ·niuskript) *adj.-s.* manuscrito.
**Manx** (mæ·nks) *adj.-s.* de la isla de Man.
**many** (me·ni) *adj.* muchos, chas: ~ *times*, ~ *a time*, muchas veces, frecuentemente; *as* ~, otros tantos; *as* ~ *as*, tantos como; hasta [cierto número]; *how* ~?, ¿cuántos?; *so* ~, tantos; *too* ~, demasiados; de más, de sobra; *too* ~ *for* o *one too* ~ *for*, más listo, más fuerte, etc., que; *twice as* ~, el doble, dos veces más. 2 [en composición] multi-, poli-, de muchos: *many-coloured*, multicolor, policromo. 3 *pron.* muchos. 4 *s.* número [de]: *a great* ~, un gran número, muchos, muchísimos.
**many-flowered** *adj.* multifloro.
**manyplies** (-plaiš) *s.* ZOOL. libro [de los rumiantes].
**many-sided** *adj.* multilátero; apto para muchas cosas, de gran curiosidad intelectual.
**Maori** (ma·ori) *adj.-s.* maorí.
**map** (mæp) *s.* mapa.
**map (to)** trazar el mapa de. 2 indicar en el mapa. 3 fig. *to* ~ *out*, planear, trazar el plan de. ¶ Pret. y p. p.: *mapped;* ger.: *-pping.*
**maple** (mei·pøl) *s.* BOT. arce,\* meple.
**mar (to)** (ma<sup>r</sup>) *tr.* estropear, echar a perder, destruir. ¶ Pret. y p. p.: *marred;* ger.: *-rring.*
**marabou** (mæ·rabu) *s.* marabú [ave y adorno].
**marabout** (-t) *s.* morabito.
**maraca** (mara·ka) *s.* MÚS. maraca.
**maraschino** (mæraski·nou) *s.* marrasquino.
**marasmus** (mæræ·smøs) *s.* MED. marasmo.
**Marathon** (mæ·razan) *n. pr.* GEOGR., DEP. Maratón.
**maraud (to)** (maro·d) *intr.* merodear, pecorear. 2 *tr.* saquear, merodear en.
**marauder** (-ø<sup>r</sup>) *s.* merodeador, pecoreador.
**marauding** (-ing) *s.* merodeo, pillaje.
**maravedi** (mæravei·di) *s.* maravedí.
**marble** (ma·rbøl) *s.* mármol. 2 canica, pita [bolita]. 3 IMPR. platina. 4 jaspeado. 5 *pl.* canicas [juego].
**marble (to)** *tr.* jaspear.
**marbler** (ma·rblø<sup>r</sup>) *s.* marmolista. 2 jaspeador.
**marbly** (-i) *adj.* marmóreo, marmoleño.
**marc** (ma·rk) *s.* orujo.
**marcasite** (ma·rkašait) *s.* MINER. marcasita.
**marcel** (ma·rse·l) o **marcel wave** *s.* ondulación marcel.
**marcescent** (ma·rse·sønt) *adj.* BOT. marcescente.
**March** (ma·rch) *s.* marzo [mes].
**march** *s.* marcha [acción de caminar, camino; curso, progreso]. 2 MIL., MÚS. marcha. 3 MIL. paso. 4 marca [distrito fronterizo].
**march (to)** *intr.* marchar, andar, caminar. 2 marchar, progresar. 3 *to* ~ *with*, limitar, lindar con. 4 *tr.* hacer marchar [las tropas]; hacer ir [a un sitio].
**marchioness** (ma·rshønis) *f.* marquesa [título].
**marchpane** (-pein) *s.* mazapán.
**marconigram** (markou·nigræm) *s.* marconigrama.
**Marcus** (mæ·rkøs) *n. pr. m.* Marcos.
**mare** (me<sup>r</sup>) *s.* yegua. 2 mula, asna.
**mareograph** (mæ·riogræf) *s.* mareógrafo.
**mare's-nest** *s.* fam. descubrimiento ilusorio.
**mare's-tail** *s.* BOT. cola de caballo. 2 METEOR. cirro.
**Margaret** (ma·rgarit) *n. pr.* Margarita.

**margarine** (-in) *s.* margarina.
**margarite** (-ait) *s.* MINER. margarita.
**margay** (ma·rgei) *s.* ZOOL. maracayá, tigrillo.
**marge** (ma·rdŷ) *s.* poét. margen, orilla.
**Margery** (-øri) *n. pr.* Margarita.
**margin** (-in) *s.* margen, borde, orilla. 2 margen [de una página]. 3 límite [del que una cosa no puede pasar]. 4 COM., ECON. margen. 5 sobrante, exceso, reserva.
**margin (to)** *tr.* marginar, margenar, apostillar.
**marginal** (-al) *s. pl.* notas marginales.
**marginate (to)** (-eit) *tr.* marginar.
**margrave** (ma·rgreiv) *s.* margrave.
**marguerite** (ma·rgørit) *s.* BOT. margarita.
**Marian** (mæ·rian o me·rian) *adj.* mariano. 2 *n. pr. f.* Mariana.
**Marianne** (meriæ·n) *n. pr. f.* Mariana.
**Marie** (mari·) *n. pr. f.* María.
**marigold** (mæ·rigould) *s.* BOT. maravilla, caléndula, flamenquilla. 2 BOT. clavelón.
**marigraph** (-græf) *s.* mareógrafo.
**marihuana, marijuana** (marijua·na) *s.* BOT. marihuana.
**marimba** (mari·mba) *s.* MÚS. marimba.
**marinade** (mærinei·d) *s.* escabeche.
**marine** (marı·n) *adj.* marino, marítimo. 2 oceánico. 3 náutico, naval, de marina: *Marine Corps* (E.U.) infantería de marina. 4 *s.* soldado de marina. 5 marina [buques]. 6 PINT. marina.
**mariner** (ma·rinø<sup>r</sup>) *s.* marinero, marino.
**Marion** (mæ·riøn) *n. pr. m.* Mariano. 2 *n. pr. f.* Mariana.
**marionette** (mærione·t) *s.* marioneta, títere.
**Marist** (me·rist) *s.* ECLES. marista.
**marital** (mæ·rital) *adj.* marital, matrimonial.
**maritime** (-tim o -taim) *adj.* marítimo.
**Marius** (me·riøs) *n. pr. m.* Mario.
**marjoram** (ma·rdŷøram) *s.* BOT. mejorana.
**Mark** (ma·rk) *n. pr. m.* Marcos.
**mark** *s.* marca, señal. 2 mancha, pinta. 3 impresión, huella. 4 signo, indicio, prueba. 5 signo, símbolo. 6 cruz [para firmar]. 7 rótulo, marbete. 8 DEP. línea de salida. 9 importancia, nota, distinción: *of mark*, de nota [pers.]. 10 tipo, límite, altura, etc., requeridos. 11 punto, nota, calificación [en exámenes, etc.]. 12 blanco, hito, fin, propósito: *to miss the* ~, errar el tiro; *beside the* ~, errado; que no viene al caso. 13 marco [moneda]. 14 marca [territorio].
**mark (to)** *tr.* marcar, señalar. 2 indicar [ser señal o indicio de]. 3 delimitar, señalar los límites de. 4 notar, observar, advertir, fijarse en: ~ *my words!*, ¡advierte lo que te digo! 5 caracterizar. 6 mostrar, manifestar. 7 puntuar, calificar [en un examen]. 8 FÚTBOL. marcar [un jugador a otro]. 9 *to* ~ *down*, apuntar, poner por escrito; rebajar el precio de. 10 *to* ~ *out*, indicar, señalar; designar, elegir; separar con un guión o una raya. 11 *to* ~ *time*, MIL. marcar el paso.
**markdown** (-kdaun) *s.* precio rebajado.
**marked** (-t) *adj.* marcado, notable. 2 ~ *man*, hombre sospechoso; futura víctima.
**marker** (-ø<sup>r</sup>) *s.* marcador. 2 ficha [de juego]. 3 mojón.
**market** (-it) *s.* mercado [en todas sus acepciones]; bolsa, mercado de valores: ~ *garden*, huerto [de hortalizas]; ~ *price*, precio corriente; ~ *town*, población con mercado, villa.
**market (to)** *tr.* negociar, comprar o vender [en el mercado]. 2 llevar al mercado. 3 *intr.* hacer la compra. 4 comerciar.

**marketable** (-abøl) *adj.* comerciable, vendible.
**marketing** (-ing) *s.* compra o venta en el mercado.
**marksman** (-smæn) *s.* tirador [que tiene buena puntería].
**marksmanship** (-ship) *s.* puntería.
**marl** (ma$^r$l) *s.* marga.
**marl (to)** *tr.* AGR. margar. *2* MAR. cubrir o atar con vueltas de cordel.
**marlin** (-in) *s.* ICT. especie de aguja.
**marline** *s.* MAR. merlín.
**marlpit** (-pit) *s.* margal, marguera.
**marly** (-i) *adj.* margoso.
**marmalade** (ma$^r$maleid) *s.* mermelada.
**marmit** (-mit) *s.* marmita.
**marmoration** (-mørei·shøn) *s.* marmoración.
**marmoreal** (-mou·rial) *adj.* marmóreo.
**marmoset** (-mošet) *s.* ZOOL. tití.
**marmot** (-møt) *s.* ZOOL. marmota.
**Maronite** (ma·ronait) *s.* maronita.
**maroon** (maru·n) *adj.* castaño. *2 s.* BOT. castaña. *3* color castaño. *4* cimarrón.
**maroon (to)** *tr.* dejar abandonado, aislado, en un lugar desierto.
**marplot** (ma$^r$plat) *s.* entrometido, aguafiestas.
**marquee** (-i·) *s.* gran tienda de campaña. *2* marquesina.
**marquetry** (-øtri) *s.* marquetería, taracea.
**marquis** (-uis) *s.* marqués.
**marquisate** (-uisit) *s.* marquesado.
**marquise** (-iš) *s.* marquesa [mujer]. *2* MARQUEE.
**marriage** (mæ·ridỹ) *s.* matrimonio: ~ *articles*, capitulaciones; ~ *lines*, partida de matrimonio; *by* ~, político [pariente]. *2* casamiento, boda. *3* maridaje.
**marriageable** (-abøl) *adj.* casadero, núbil.
**married** (mæ·rid) *adj.* casado; ~ *couple*, matrimonio [marido y mujer]. *2* maridado. *3* matrimonial, conyugal.
**marrow** (-ou) *s.* ANAT. médula, tuétano. *2* médula, meollo, substancia. *3* BOT. *marrow* o *vegetable* ~, calabacín.
**marrowbone** (-boun) *s.* canilla, hueso largo. *2 pl.* fam. rodillas.
**marrowy** (-i) *adj.* medular. *2* meolludo.
**marry (to)** (mæ·ri) *tr.* casar, desposar. *2* casarse con. *3* unir, juntar, maridar. *4 intr.* casarse.
**Mars** (ma$^r$s) *s.* MIT., ASTR. Marte.
**Marseillais** (ma$^r$seye·) *adj.-s.* marsellés.
**marseillaise** (ma$^r$seye·š) *s.* Marsellesa [himno].
**Marseilles** (ma$^r$sei·lš) *n. pr.* GEOGR. Marsella.
**marsh** (ma$^r$sh) *s.* marjal, paúl, pantano, humedal: ~ *harrier*, ORN. arpella; ~ *warbler*, ORN. arandillo.
**marshal** (ma·$^r$shal) *s.* MIL. mariscal. *2* maestro de ceremonias, bastonero. *3* (E.U.) alguacil; jefe de policía.
**marshal (to)** *tr.* ordenar, poner en orden. *2* formar [tropas]. *3* conducir con solemnidad o ceremonia. *4* guiar, dirigir, disciplinar. *5 intr.* formar, ponerse en orden. ¶ Pret. y p. p.: *marshaled* o *-lled*; ger.: *-ling* o *-lling*.
**marshalship** (-ship) *s.* mariscalía, mariscalato.
**marshmallow** (-mælou) *s.* BOT. malvavisco. *2* pastilla o bombón de malvavisco.
**marshy** (-i) *adj.* pantanoso. *2* palustre.
**marsupial** (ma$^r$siu·pial) *adj.-s.* ZOOL. marsupial.
**mart** (ma$^r$t) *s.* emporio, centro comercial.
**marteline** (-ølin) *s.* martellina.
**marten** (-øn) *s.* ZOOL. marta. *2* ZOOL. garduña.
**Martha** (ma·$^r$za) *n. pr. f.* Marta.
**Martial** (ma·$^r$shal) *n. pr. m.* Marcial.

**martial** *adj.* marcial, militar, bélico: ~ *law*, ley marcial, estado de guerra. *2* QUÍM. marcial.
**Martian** (-ian) *adj.-s.* marciano.
**Martin** (ma·$^r$tin) *n. pr.* Martín.
**martin** *s.* ORN. vencejo, avión.
**martinet** (ma$^r$tine·t) *s.* ordenancista.
**martingale** (ma·$^r$tingeil) *s.* gamarra. *2* MAR. moco de bauprés.
**Martinique** (ma$^r$tini·k) *n. pr.* GEOGR. Martinica.
**Martinmas** (ma·$^r$tinmas) *s.* día de San Martín.
**martlet** (map$^r$tlet) *s.* MARTIN.
**martyr** (-ø$^r$) *s.* mártir.
**martyr to** *tr.* martirizar.
**martyrdom** (-døm) *s.* martirio.
**martyrize (to)** (-aiš) *tr.* hacer mártir.
**martyrology** (ma$^r$tøra·lodỹi) *s.* martirologio.
**marvel** (ma·$^r$vøl) *s.* maravilla, prodigio.
**marvel (to)** *intr.* maravillarse, admirarse. *2* preguntarse.
**Marvel-of-Peru** *s.* BOT. dondiego [de noche].
**marvel(l)ous** (-løs) *adj.* maravilloso, prodigioso. *2* asombroso.
**Marxian** (ma·$^r$ksian) *adj.-s.* marxista.
**Marxism** (-sišm) *s.* marxismo.
**Marxist** (-sist) *adj.-s.* marxista.
**Mary** (me·ri) *n. pr. f.* María.
**marzipan** (ma·$^r$šipæn) *s.* mazapán.
**mascot** (mæ·skat) *s.* mascota.
**masculine** (mæ·skiulin) *adj.* masculino, varonil. *2* hombruno. *3 adj.-s.* GRAM. masculino.
**masculinity** (mæskiuli·niti) *s.* masculinidad.
**mash** (mæsh) *s.* masa, pasta [de cosas mojadas]. *2* malta remojado. *3* farro [para el ganado]. *4* fig. revoltijo, embrollo.
**mash (to)** *tr.* majar, machacar, hacer pasta. *2* macerar [el malta].
**mashy** (-i) *adj.* majado, pastoso.
**mask** (mæsk) *s.* máscara, antifaz, careta, carátula. *2* máscara [pers.; disfraz; lo que oculta]. *3* mascarilla [vaciado]. *4* FOT. desvanecedor. *5* ARQ. mascarón. *6* mascarada.
**mask (to)** *tr.* enmascarar. *2 intr.* ponerse careta. *3* disfrazarse, ir disfrazado.
**masked ball** (-d) *s.* baile de máscaras.
**masker** (-ø$^r$) *s.* máscara [pers.].
**masochism** (mæ·šøkišm) *s.* masoquismo.
**masochist** (-ist) *s.* masoquista.
**masochistic** (mæšøki·stik) *adj.* masoquista.
**mason** (mei·søn) *s.* albañil. *2* masón, francmasón.
**masonic** (meisa·nik) *adj.* masónico.
**masonry** (mei·sønri) *s.* albañilería. *2* mazonería. *3* (con may.) masonería.
**masque** (mæsk) *s.* mascarada; baile de máscaras.
**masquerade** (mæskørei·d) *s.* mascarada: ~ *ball*, baile de máscaras. *2* máscara [disfraz]. *3* fig. farsa.
**masquerade (to)** *intr.* tomar parte en una mascarada. *2* disfrazarse.
**masquerader** (-ø$^r$) *s.* máscara [pers.].
**mass** (mæs) *s.* masa [agregado, conjunto], bulto, mole. *2* montón, gran cantidad: ~ *production*, fabricación en serie. *3* FÍS. masa. *4 pl. the masses*, las masas.
**Mass** o **mass** *s.* LITURG., MÚS. misa.
**mass (to)** *tr.* amasar, juntar, reunir en masa. *2 intr.* juntarse, reunirse, formar masa.
**massacre (to)** (mæ·sakør) *tr.* hacer una matanza de. *2* asesinar.
**massage** (masa·ỹ) *s.* amasamiento, masaje.
**massage (to)** *tr.* amasar, dar masaje a.
**masseter** (mæsi·tø$^r$) *s.* ANAT. masetero.

**masseur** (mæsø.ʳ) *s*. masajista [hombre].
**masseuse** (-š) *s*. masajista [mujer].
**massicot** (mæ·sikat) *s*. masicote.
**massif** (masi·f) *s*. GEOGR. macizo.
**massive** (mæ·siv) *adj*. macizo. *2* voluminoso, imponente. *3* pesadas, gruesas [facciones].
**massy** (mæ·si) *adj*. macizo, voluminoso, pesado.
**mast** (mæst) *s*. MAR. mástil, palo, árbol: *before the* ~, como simple marinero. *2* asta, mástil, poste. *3* RADIO. torre. *4* AGR. bellotas, hayucos, etc. [para los cerdos].
**mast (to)** *tr*. MAR. arbolar.
**mastaba(h** (mæ·staba) *s*. mastaba.
**master** (mæ·stø.ʳ) *s*. amo, patrón, dueño, señor. *2* señor, señorito [dicho por un criado]. *3* MAR. patrón, capitán. *4* maestro: ~ *of ceremonies*, maestro de ceremonias; *the Master*, el Maestro (Jesucristo). *5* jefe, director, rector. *6* título de ciertos cargos: *Master of the horse*, caballerizo mayor. *7 adj*. maestro; magistral, superior, de maestro: ~ *hand*, mano maestra, maestría; ~ *key*, llave maestra.
**master (to)** *tr*. dominar, vencer, subyugar, sobreponerse a. *2* dominar [una ciencia, arte, etc.].
**masterful** (-ful) *adj*. dominante, autoritario. *2* fuerte, hábil, diestro; de maestro.
**masterless** (-lis) *adj*. ingobernable. *2* sin amo.
**masterly** (-li) *adj*. magistral, hábil, de maestro. *2 adv*. magistralmente.
**mastermind** (-maind) *s*. mente directora.
**masterpiece** (-pis) *s*. obra maestra.
**mastership** (-ship) *s*. dominio, superioridad. *2* magisterio. *3* maestría.
**masterwork** (-uø.ʳk) *s*. obra maestra.
**mastery** (-i) *s*. dominio [poder; conocimiento]. *2* maestría. *3* superioridad, ventaja.
**masthead** (mæ·stjed) *s*. MAR. tope. *2* cabecera [de un periódico].
**mastic** (mæ·stik) *s*. almáciga, mástique. *2* BOT. almácigo, lentisco. *3* masilla.
**masticate (to)** (mæ·stikeit) *tr*. masticar.
**mastication** (-ei·shøn) *s*. masticación.
**mastiff** (mæ·stif) *s*. mastín.
**mastodon** (mæ·stødan) *s*. mastodonte.
**masturbate (to)** (mæ·stø.ʳbeit) *intr*. masturbarse.
**mat** (mæt) *s*. estera. *2* esterilla, ruedo, felpudo; petate. *3* tapetito. *4* enredijo, greña. *5* MAR. pallete, empalletado. *6* orla de cartón, paspartú. *7* superficie mate. *8 adj*. mate, sin lustre.
**mat (to)** *tr*. esterar. *2* enredar, enmarañar apelmazar. *3* matar el brillo [un metal]. *4 intr*. enredarse, enmarañarse, apelmazarse. ¶ Pret. y p. p.: *matted*; ger.: -*tting*.
**matador** (mætædo·ʳ) *s*. espada, diestro [torero]. *2* matador [naipe].
**match** (mæch) *s*. fósforo, cerilla. *2* pajuela, mecha. *3* pareja [cosa que hace juego]; igual [pers. o cosa igual]. *4* contrincante temible, persona capaz de competir o entendérselas con otra: *to meet one's* ~, hallar la horma de su zapato. *5* juego [de dos cosas]. *6* lucha deportiva; partido, partida. *7* casamiento; partido: *good* ~, buen partido.
**match (to)** *tr*. casar, hermanar, aparear, emparejar. *2* oponer [a otra una pers. o cosa igual]. *3* igualar a, poder competir con. *4* igualar, proporcionar, adaptar, ajustar. *5* hacer juego con. *6 intr*. casarse. *7* casar, hacer juego.
**matchbox** (-baks) *s*. fosforera, cerillera.
**matchet** (-øt) *s*. machete.
**matchless** (-lis) *adj*. sin igual, incomparable.

**matchlock** (-lak) *s*. llave de mosquete. *2* mosquete.
**matchmaker** (mæ·chmeikø.ʳ) *s*. casamentero. *2* organizador de luchas deportivas. *3* fabricante de fósforos.
**mate** (meit) *s*. compañero, compañera. *2* consorte, cónyuge. *3* macho [de una hembra]; hembra [de un macho]. *4* MAR. segundo de a bordo, piloto, oficial. *5* ayudante. *6* AJED. mate.
**mate (to)** *tr*. casar, desposar. *2* aparear. *3* hermanar. *4* dar jaque mate. *5* fig. contrarrestar, hacer imponente. *6 intr*. aparearse. *7* casar, hermanarse. *8* MEC. engranar.
**maté** (ma·tei) *s*. BOT. mate, té del Paraguay.
**mateless** (mei·tlis) *adj*. solo; desparejado.
**mater** (ma·tø.ʳ) *s*. fam. madre.
**material** (mati·rial) *adj*. material. *2* físico, corpóreo. *3* materialista. *4* importante, esencial. *5 s*. material. *6* materia, ingrediente. *7* tela, género. *8 pl*. avíos, recado.
**materialism** (mati·riališm) *s*. materialismo.
**materialist** (-ist) *m*. materialista.
**materialistic** (matiriali·stik) *adj*. materialista.
**materiality** (-æ·liti) *s*. materialidad. *2* importancia.
**materialize (to)** (mati·rialaiš) *tr*. materializar. *2* hacer sensible, perceptible. *3* convertir en realidad. *4 intr*. materializarse. *5* hacerse visible o corpóreo, tomar forma, aparecer.
**materially** (-li) *adv*. materialmente. *2* esencialmente.
**materiel** (matirie·l) *s*. materiales, pertrechos. *2* MIL. material.
**maternal** (matø·ʳnal) *adj*. maternal. *2* materno.
**maternity** (-iti) *s*. maternidad: ~ *hospital*, casa de maternidad, clínica maternal.
**maternize (to)** (ma·tø.ʳnaiš) *tr*. maternizar.
**mathematic(al** (mæzimæ·tik(al) *adj*. matemático.
**mathematician** (mæzimati·shan) *s*. matemático.
**mathematics** (mæzimæ·tiks) *s*. matemáticas.
**Matilda** (mati·lda) *n. pr*. Matilde.
**matinal** (mæ·tinal) *adj*. matinal, matutino.
**matinée** (mæ·tinei·) *s*. TEAT. matiné.
**matins** (mæ·tinš) *s. pl*. LITURG. maitines.
**matrass** (mæ·tras) *s*. QUÍM. matraz.
**matriarch** (mei·tria.ʳk) *s*. matriarca.
**matriarchal** (meitria·ʳkal) *adj*. matriarcal.
**matrices** (mei·trisiš) *s. pl*. de MATRIX.
**matricidal** (meitrisai·dal) *adj*. matricida.
**matricide** (mei·trisaid) *s*. matricida. *2* matricidio.
**matriculate (to)** (matri·kiuleit) *tr*. matricular [esp. en una universidad]. *2 intr*. matricularse.
**matrimonial** (mætrimou·nial) *adj*. matrimonial, conyugal, marital.
**matrimony** (-i) *s*. matrimonio [casamiento, sacramento; estado]. *2* juego de naipes.
**matrix** (mei·triks) *s*. ANAT., MAT., MINER. matriz. *2* matriz, molde.
**matron** (mei·trøn) *s*. matrona [mujer respetable]. *2* ama de llaves [de un hospicio, etc.]. *3* matrona [de un puesto de policía, etc.].
**matronly** (-li) *adj*. matronal. *2* de alguna edad. *3* digna, respetable. *4* maternal.
**Matt** (mæt) *n. pr. abrev*. de MATTHEW.
**matted** (mæ·tid) *pret. y p. p*. de TO MAT.
**matter** (mæ·tø.ʳ) *s*. materia, substancia. *2* materia, pus. *3* cosa escrita o impresa. *4* materia, asunto, tema, cuestión, cosa: ~ *of course*, cosa lógica, natural, de cajón; ~ *of fact*, hecho cierto o positivo; *as a* ~ *of fact*, de hecho, en realidad; a decir verdad; *for that* ~, en cuanto a eso; *in the* ~, al respecto; *in the* ~ *of*, en materia de. *5* mo-

tivo, ocasión. *6* cosa, obra [cantidad, tiempo, etc., aproximados]: *a ~ of ten years*, cosa de diez años. *7* cosa que ocurre, mal, defecto, inconveniente, etc.: *what is the ~?*, ¿qué ocurre?; *what is the ~ with you?*, ¿qué le pasa a usted?, ¿qué tiene usted? *8* importancia: *no ~*, no importa; *no ~ how*, de cualquier modo [que]; *no ~ how [far, much*, etc.], por lejos, mucho, etc., que; *no ~ where*, dondequiera que. *9 pl.* el estado de cosas, las cosas.

**matter (to)** *intr.* importar, ser de importancia. *2* MED. supurar.

**matterless** (-lis) *adj.* fútil.

**matter-of-fact** *adj.* material, positivo. *2* positivista. *3* prosaico.

**mattery** (-i) *s.* importante. *2* purulento.

**Matthew** (mæ·ziu) *n. pr.* Mateo.

**Mathias** (mætza·ias) *n. pr.* Matías.

**matting** (mæ·ting) *s.* estera; esterado. *2* MAT 5, 6 y 7.

**mattock** (-øk) *s.* AGR. zapapico, azadón de pico.

**mattress** (-res) *s.* colchón.

**maturate (to)** (mæ·chureit) *tr.-intr.* madurar [esp. un tumor].

**maturation** (-ei·shøn) *s.* maduración.

**maturative** (mæ·chørativ) *adj.-s.* madurativo.

**mature** (matiu·ø<sup>r</sup>) *adj.* maduro. *2* adulto; juicioso. *3* perfecto, acabado. *4* COM. vencido, pagadero.

**mature (to)** *tr.* madurar. *2* llevar a la perfección. *3 intr.* madurar. *4* vencer [una deuda, plazo, etc.].

**maturity** (matiu·riti) *s.* madurez. *2* perfección. *3* vencimiento [de una deuda, plazo, etc.].

**matutinal** (-tinəl) *adj.* matutinal, matutino.

**matweed** (mæ·twid) *s.* BOT. esparto, albardín.

**maudlin** (mo·dlin) *adj.* lacrimoso, sentimental, sensiblero. *2* chisposo y lloroso.

**maugre** (mo·gø<sup>r</sup>) *prep.* ant. a pesar de.

**maul** (mol) *s.* mazo, machota.

**maul (to)** *tr.* aporrear, magullar; maltratar.

**maulstick** (-tik) *s.* tiento [de pintor].

**maunder (to)** (mo·ndø<sup>r</sup>) *intr.-tr.* mascullar, refunfuñar. *2 intr.* obrar o moverse como atontado. *3* divagar.

**Maundy** (-i) *s.* mandato, lavatorio [del jueves santo]. *2 ~ Thursday*, jueves santo.

**Maurice** (mo·ris) *n. pr.* Mauricio.

**Mauritius** (mori·shiøs) *n. pr.* GEOGR. Mauricio [Isla].

**Mauser, mauser** (mau·šø<sup>r</sup>) *s.* máuser.

**mausoleum** (mosøl·røm) *s.* mausoleo.

**mavis** (mei·vis) *s.* ORN. malvís. *2* ORN. cagaceite.

**maw** (mo) *s.* estómago. *2* cuajar [de los rumiantes]. *3* buche [de las aves]. *4* fauces; tragadero.

**mawkish** (-kish) *adj.* sensiblero, empalagoso. *2* nauseoso.

**maxilla** (mæksi·la) *s.* ANAT., ZOOL. hueso maxilar.

**maxillar** (mæ·ksila<sup>r</sup>), **maxillary** (mæ·ksileri) *adj.-s.* maxilar [hueso].

**maxim** (mæ·ksim) *s.* máxima, sentencia.

**maximal** (-əl) *adj.* máximo.

**maximize (to)** (-aiš) *tr.* llevar hasta el máximo; abultar, exagerar.

**maximum** (-øm), *pl.* **-mums** o **-ma** (-ma) *s.* máximum, máximo.

**May** (mei) *s.* mayo [mes]: *~ Day*, primero de mayo; *~ fly*, ENT. efímera, cachipolla. *2* fig. primavera [de la vida].

**1) may** *s.* BOT. acerolo, espino albar. *2* BOT. viburno.

**2) may** *v. aux.* poder [tener facultad, libertad, oportunidad o permiso; ser lícito, permitido, posible o contingente]: *may I go?*, ¿puedo mar-

charme?; *it ~ be, ~ be*, puede ser, acaso. *2* A veces indica deseo vivo y se traduce por «ojalá», «que», etc., o se omite y se pone el verbo en subjuntivo: *~ it be so*, ojalá sea así; *~ you live happily*, viva usted feliz. *3* A veces se usa con elipsis del segundo verbo: *come what ~*, venga lo que viniere. ¶ Pret.: *might.* | Carece de infinitivo, de participios y de gerundio.

**Maya** (ma·ia), **Mayan** (-n) *adj.-s.* maya [de los mayas].

**maybe** (mei·bi) *adv.* acaso, quizá, tal vez.

**Mayflower** (mei·flauø<sup>r</sup>) *s.* BOT. (Ingl.) espino blanco; calta, hierba centella. *2* BOT. (E.U.) anémona; epígea rastrera.

**mayhap** (mei·jæp) *adv.* acaso, quizá, tal vez.

**mayonnaise** (meiønei·š) *s.* salsa mahonesa.

**mayor** (mei·iø<sup>r</sup>) *s.* alcalde, corregidor.

**mayoralty** (-alti) *s.* alcaldía, corregimiento.

**mayoress** (-is) *f.* alcaldesa.

**Maypole** (mei·poul) *s.* mayo, árbol de mayo.

**Maytide** (-taid), **Maytime** (mei·taim) *s.* mes de mayo.

**mayweed** (-uid) *s.* BOT. manzanilla loca.

**mazard** (mæ·ša<sup>r</sup>d) *s.* BOT. cerezo silvestre.

**Mazdaism** (mæ·šdaism), **Mazdeism** (-diišm) *s.* mazdeismo.

**maze** (meiš) *s.* laberinto, dédalo. *2* confusión, perplejidad.

**maze (to)** *tr.* enredar, intrincar. *2* aturdir, confundir.

**mazurka** (mašu·<sup>r</sup>ka) *s.* mazurca.

**mazy** (mei·ši) *adj.* laberíntico, intrincado.

**me** (mı) *pron. pers.* me, mi: *with ~*, conmigo.

**mead** (mıd) *s.* licor de aguamiel.

**meadow** (me·dou) *s.* prado, pradera.

**meadowsweet** (-suit) *s.* BOT. ulmaria, reina de los prados.

**meadowy** (-i) *adj.* pradeño; praderoso.

**meager, meagre** (mı·gø<sup>r</sup>) *adj.* magro, flaco. *2* pobre, estéril, escaso, mezquino. *3* de vigilia.

**meal** (mıl) *s.* harina [de ciertos granos y semillas]. *2* (E.U.) harina de maíz. *3* comida [que se toma a ciertas horas del día].

**mealtime** (-taim) *s.* hora de comer.

**mealy** (-i) *adj.* harinoso, farináceo. *2* polvoriento. *3* meloso [en el hablar].

**mean** (mın) *s.* bajo, humilde. *2* ordinario, inferior, pobre, mezquino: *no ~*, bueno, excelente. *3* ruin, bajo, vil. *4* mezquino, tacaño, sórdido. *5* (E.U.) avergonzado; indispuesto. *6* medio, mediano, intermedio. ~ *term*, LÓG. término medio; ~ *time*, ASTR. tiempo medio. *7* medio [punto medio]. *8* MAT. medio [de una proporción], media: ~ *proportional*, media proporcional. *9* justo medio, moderación. *10 pl.* [ús. como sing. o pl.] medio, medios [de hacer, obtener, etc.]: *by all means*, de todos modos, a toda costa; sin falta; si, por cierto; *by means of*, por medio de; *by no means*, de ningún modo. *11 pl.* medios, recursos, posibles, bienes de fortuna: *man of means*, hombre rico, de posibles.

**mean (to)** *tr.* significar, denotar, querer decir. *2* pensar, proponerse, tener intención de: *what do you ~ to do?*, ¿qué piensa usted hacer?; *to ~ business*, ir en serio, estar resuelto a hacer algo. *3* destinar: *his criticism was not meant for me*, su crítica no se dirigía a mí; *clothers are meant for use*, los vestidos se hacen para usarlos. *4* tener intención [buena o mala]: *he means well*, tiene buena intención. ¶ Pret. y p. p.: *meant.*

**mean-born** *adj.* de humilde cuna.

**meander** (miæ·ndø<sup>r</sup>) *s*. meandro. *2* laberinto, camino tortuoso.
**meander (to)** *intr*. serpentear. *2* errar, vagar.
**meandrous** (-røs) *adj*. sinuoso.
**meaning** (mɪ·ning) *s*. significación, significado, sentido, acepción. *2* intención, designio.
**meaningful** (-ful) *adj*. significante.
**meaningless** (-lis) *adj*. sin sentido.
**meanness** (mɪ·nnis) *s*. humildad, pobreza. *2* ordinariez, mala calidad. *3* ruindaz, bajeza. *4* mezquindad, tacañería.
**mean-spirited** *adj*. bajo, ruin.
**meant** (ment) *pret*. y *p*. *p*. de TO MEAN.
**meantime** (mɪ·ntaim), **meanwhile** (-juail) *adv*. entretanto, mientras tanto. *2 m*. ínterin: *in the meantime*, en el ínterin, mientras tanto.
**measles** (mɪ·šølš) *s*. *pl*. MED. sarampión: *German ~*, rubéola. *2* VET. cisticercosis.
**measurable** (me·ȳørabøl) *adj*. mensurable.
**measure** (me·ȳø<sup>r</sup>) *s*. medida [de una cosa; lo que sirve para medir; unidad de medida; acción de medir]: *made to ~*, hecho a medida. *2* sistema de medidas. *3* medida; tasa, moderación: *beyond ~*, sobremanera; *without ~*, sin medida, sin tasa. *4* cantidad, grado, extensión: *in some ~*, en cierto grado, en cierto modo. *5* medida, disposición: *to take measures*, tomar las medidas necesarias. *6* ritmo, cadencia. *7* MÚS. compás. *8* fig. baile: *to tread a ~*, bailar. *9* MÉTR. metro, pie.
**measure (to)** *tr.-intr*. medir: *to ~ one's length*, medir el suelo, caerse a la larga. *2 tr*. ajustar, proporcionar. *3* recorrer [un país, una distancia]. *4 to ~ off*, medir, señalar una medida. *5 to ~ out*, medir, dar o distribuir según medida.
**measured** (me·ȳø<sup>r</sup>d) *adj*. medido. *2* mesurado, lento, rítmico, acompasado. *3* moderado.
**measureless** (me·ȳø<sup>r</sup>lis) *adj*. inconmensurable, ilimitado, infinito.
**measurement** (me·ȳø<sup>r</sup>mønt) *s*. medición. *2* medida.
**measuring worm** (-ing) *s*. ENT. geómetra [oruga].
**meat** (mɪt) *s*. carne [como alimento]: *~ ball*, albóndiga; *~ fly*, mosca de la carne; *~ safe*, fresquera. *2* vianda, comida. *3* materia [para reflexión, etc.].
**meathook** (-uk) *s*. garabato de carnicero.
**meatus** (miei·tøs) *s*. ANAT. meato.
**meaty** (mɪ·ti) *adj*. carnoso. *2* jugoso, sustancioso.
**mechanic** (mikæ·nik) *adj*. mecánico [de los oficios; de las máquinas]. *2 s*. obrero, artesano, mecánico.
**mechanical** (-al) *adj*. mecánico, de máquinas. *2* maquinal, rutinario. *3* automático.
**mechanician** (mecani·shan) *s*. mecánico. *2* maquinista [que hace máquinas].
**mechanics** (mikæ·niks) *s*. mecánica [ciencia, arte]. *2* maquinaria. *3* detalles prácticos, técnica.
**mechanism** (me·kanišm) *s*. mecanismo. *2* mecanicismo.
**mechanist** (-st) *s*. mecanicista. *2* mecánico.
**mechanistic** (-ik) *s*. mecanicista.
**mechanization** (-ei·shøn) *s*. mecanización. *2* MIL. motorización. *3* maquinismo.
**mechanize (to)** (me·kanaiš) *tr*. mecanizar. *2* MIL. motorizar.
**mechanotherapy** (mekanoze·rapi) *s*. mecanoterapia.
**Mechlin** (me·klin) *n*. *pr*. GEOGR. Malinas.
**meconium** (meko·niøm) *s*. meconio, alhorre.
**medal** (me·dal) *s*. medalla.

**medallion** (midæ·liøn) *s*. medallón.
**medal(l)ist** (me·dalist) *s*. numismático. *2* medallista. *3* el que ha ganado una medalla.
**meddle (to)** (me·døl) *intr*. entrometerse, injerirse, meterse [en]. | Gralte. con *with* o *in*.
**meddlesome** (me·dølsøm) *adj*. entremetido.
**meddling** (-ling) *s*. entretenimiento, intromisión.
**Mede** (mɪd) *adj*.-*s*. medo.
**mediaeval** (mɪdiɪ·val) *adj*. medieval. *2* medioeval.
**mediaevalism** (-išm) *s*. medievalismo.
**medial** (mɪ·dial) *adj*. medio [que está entre los extremos].
**Median** (-an) *adj*. meda, médico. *2 s*. meda.
**median** *adj*. medio [que está en medio; que es el término medio de]. *2 s*. GEOM. mediana.
**mediastinum** (mɪdiæstai·nøm) *s*. ANAT. mediastino.
**mediate** (mɪ·dieit) *adj*. mediato. *2* intermedio.
**mediate (to)** *intr*. mediar, intermediar. *2* mediar, intervenir. *3 tr*. ser el medio o conducto para [algo]; arreglar, procurar, comunicar.
**mediation** (-ei·shøn) *s*. mediación.
**mediatize (to)** (mɪ·diætaiš) *tr*. mediatizar.
**mediator** (mɪ·dieitøš) *s*. mediador, medianero.
**mediatrix** (-triks) *f*. medidora, medianera.
**Medic** (mɪ·dik) *adj*. médico, medo [de Media].
**medic** (me·dik) *s*. BOT. alfalfa, mielga. *2* fam. estudiante de medicina.
**medicable** (me·dikabøl) *adj*. medicable.
**medical** (-al) *adj*. médico, de medicina: *~ student*, estudiante de medicina; *~ treatment*, tratamiento médico.
**medicament** (medi·kamønt) *s*. medicamento.
**medicamental** (medikame·ntal) *adj*. medicamentoso.
**medicaster** (me·dikæstøš) *s*. medicastro.
**medicate (to)** (-eit) *tr*. tratar [a un enfermo]. *2* impregnar con una sustancia medicinal.
**medication** (-ei·shøn) *s*. medicación. *2* medicamento.
**medicinal** (medi·sinal) *adj*. medicinal.
**medicine** (me·disin) *s*. medicina, medicamento: *to take one's ~*, fam. echar el pecho al agua; hacer uno a la fuerza lo que no quisiera hacer. *2* medicina [ciencia y arte].
**medieval** (mɪdiɪ·val) *adj*. MEDIAEVAL.
**medievalism** (-išm) *s*. MEDIAEVALISM.
**mediocre** (mɪ·diokøš) *adj*. mediocre, mediano.
**mediocrity** (mɪdia·kriti) *s*. mediocridad, medianía.
**meditate (to)** (me·diteit) *tr*. proyectar, proponerse. *2 intr*. meditar, reflexionar.
**meditation** (-ei·shøn) *s*. meditación, reflexión.
**meditative** (me·diteitiv) *adj*. meditativo, contemplativo. *2* meditabundo.
**Mediterranean** (meditørei·nian) *adj*.-*s*. Mediterránea: *~ Sea*, mar Mediterráneo.
**medium** (mɪ·diøm) *s*. medio, punto o grado medio. *3* medio, conducto. *4* médium [en espiritismo]. *5* BIOL., BACT. medio, elemento. *6 adj*. mediano, medio, intermedio.
**medlar** (me·dlaš) *s*. BOT. níspero. *2* níspola.
**medley** (me·dli) *s*. mezcla, mezcolanza, batiburrillo. *2* MÚS. popurrí. *3 adj*. mezclado, confuso.
**medulla** (medø·la), *pl*. **-lae** (-li) *s*. ANAT., BOT. médula.
**medullary** (me·døleri) *adj*. medular.
**medusa** (medi·sa) *s*. ZOOL. medusa. *2* (con may.) MIT. Medusa.
**meed** (mɪd) *s*. poét. premio, galardón.
**meek** (mɪk) *adj*. manso, suave, humilde, dócil.

**meekness** (-nis) *s.* mansedumbre, suavidad, humildad, docilidad.

**meerschaum** (mɪ·øšshom) *s.* espuma de mar.

**meet** (mɪt) *adj.* apropiado, conveniente, idóneo. *2 s.* reunión o concurso deportivo.

**meet (to)** *tr.* encontrar, hallar, encontrarse con, topar; tropezar, chocar con; enfrentarse con; batirse con. *2* conocer, ser presentado a: *pleased to ~ you*, mucho gusto en conocerle. *3* reunirse, entrevistarse con. *4* hacer frente a [gastos, etc.]; satisfacer, llenar [necesidades, requisitos, etc.]; cumplir [obligaciones]; cumplimentar [un pedido]. *5* refutar, responder [a una acusación, una objeción]. *6* enlazar [con otro tren, ómnibus, etc.]. *7 to go to ~*, ir a esperar o recibir a [uno]. *8 to ~ half way*, partir la diferencia. *9 intr.* reunirse, juntarse. *10* encontrarse, entrevistarse. *11* chocar, oponerse, pelear. *12* confluir. *13* enlazar [dos trenes, etc.]. *14 to ~ with*, encontrar, encontrarse con; tener, sufrir [contrariedades, una desgracia, etc.]. ¶ Pret. y p. p.: *met.*

**meeting** (mɪ·ting) *s.* reunión, junta, sesión. *2* asamblea, mitin. *3* conferencia, entrevista. *4* encuentro. *5* duelo, desafío. *6* confluencia [de ríos]. *7* cruce, empalme [de caminos, etc.].

**meetly** (mɪ·tli) *adv.* convenientemente.

**Meg** (meg) *n. pr. dim.* de MARGARET.

**megacycle** (me·gasaikøl) *s.* RADIO. megaciclo.

**megalith** (-liz) *s.* megalito.

**megalithic** (megali·zik) *adj.* megalítico.

**megalomania** (megalomei·nia) *s.* megalomanía.

**megaphone** (me·gafoun) *s.* megáfono, bocina, portavoz.

**megatherium** (megazi·riøn) *s.* PALEONT. megaterio.

**megaton** (me·gatøn) *s.* megatón.

**megohm** (-oum) *s.* megohmio.

**megrim** (mɪ·grim) *s.* jaqueca, migraña. *2 pl.* malhumor, hipocondria.

**melancholia** (melankou·lia) *s.* MED. melancolía.

**melancholic** (-a·lik) *adj.-s.* MED. melancólico.

**melancholy** (me·lankali) *s.* melancolía, tristeza, hipocondría. *2 adj.* melancólico.

**Melanesia** (melanɪ·sia) *n. pr.* GEOGR. Melanesia.

**mélange** (meila·ndÿ) *s.* mezcla.

**melanite** (me·lanait) *s.* MINER. melanita.

**melaphyre** (-faiʳ) *s.* GEOL. meláfido.

**Melchior** (me·lkiøʳ) *n. pr.* Melchor.

**Melchisedec** (melki·sedek) *n. pr.* Melquisedec.

**melee, mêlée** (mei·lei) *s.* refriega, reyerta.

**meliaceous** (miliei·shøs) *adj.* BOT. meliáceo.

**melilot** (me·lilat) *s.* BOT. meliloto, trébol oloroso.

**melinite** (me·linait) *s.* melinita.

**meliorate (to)** (mɪ·liøreit) *tr.* mejorar [hacer mejor]. *2 intr.* mejorar, mejorarse.

**melioration** (-ei·shøn) *s.* mejoramiento, mejora.

**melissa** (møli·sa) *s.* BOT. melisa.

**melliferous** (meli·førøs) *adj.* melífero.

**mellifluence** (-fluøns) *s.* melifluidad.

**mellifluous** (-fluøs) *adj.* melifluo.

**mellow** (me·lou) *adj.* maduro, sazonado [fruto]. *2* tierno, blando, suave, pastoso, meloso. *3* suave [vino]. *4* AGR. blando, margoso [suelo]. *5* lleno, puro, suave [voz, sonido, color, luz]; melodioso. *6* calamocano.

**mellow (to)** *tr.* madurar, sazonar. *2* ablandar, suavizar. *3 intr.* madurar, sazonarse. *4* suavizarse.

**mellowy** (-i) *adj.* MELLOW.

**melodic** (mela·dik) *adj.* melódico.

**melodics** (-s) *s.* melódica.

**melodious** (melou·diøs) *adj.* melodioso.

**melodrama** (me·lødrama) *s.* melodrama.

**melodramatic** (melodramæ·tik) *adj.* melodramático.

**melody** (me·lødi) *s.* melodía.

**melomane** (me·lømein) *s.* melómano.

**melon** (me·løn) *s.* BOT. melón. *2* BOT. sandía, melón de agua.

**melonry** (-ri) *s.* melonar.

**melopoeia** (melopɪ·ya) *s.* MÚS. melopeya.

**Melpomene** (melpa·mini) *n. pr.* MIT. Melpómene.

**melroze** (me·lrouš) *s.* miel rosada.

**melt** (melt) *s.* fusión, derretimiento. *2* METAL. hornada.

**melt (to)** *tr.* fundir, derretir. *2* disolver [una sustancia]. *3* disipar, desvanecer. *4* ablandar, aplacar, enternecer. *5* mezclar, confundir. *6 intr.* fundirse, derretirse. *7* deshacerse, disolverse. *8* disiparse, desvanecerse. *9* ablandarse, enternecerse. *10* mezclarse, confundirse. *11 to ~ into tears*, deshacerse en lágrimas.

**melting point** (-ing) *s.* punto de fusión.

**melting pot** *s.* crisol.

**melton** (-øn) *s.* TEJ. melton.

**member** (me·mbøʳ) *s.* miembro. *2* socio, individuo. *3* diputado [de una Cámara].

**membership** (-ship) *s.* calidad de miembro o socio. *2* sociedad, conjunto de socios.

**membrane** (me·mbrein) *s.* membrana.

**membranous** (-brønøs) *adj.* membranoso.

**memento** (meme·ntou) *s.* memento. *2* recuerdo, memoria, recordatorio.

**memo** (me·mou) *s. abrev.* de MEMORANDUM.

**memoir** (me·muar) *s.* memoria, informe, nota. *2* memoria [disertación, relación]. *3 pl.* memorias [relación escrita].

**memorable** (me·mørabøl) *adj.* memorable, memorando.

**memorandum** (memøræ·ndøm), *pl.* **dums** o **da** *s.* memorándum. *2* nota, apuntación, apunte.

**memorial** (mimo·rial) *adj.* conmemorativo: *~ arch*, arco de triunfo. *2 s.* monumento conmemorativo. *3* recuerdo, memoria. *4* memorial, petición. *5* nota, apuntamiento. *6 pl.* memorias.

**memorialize (to)** (-aiš) *tr.* dirigir o presentar un memorial a. *2* conmemorar.

**memorize (to)** (me·møraiš) *tr.* aprender de memoria.

**memory** (-i) *s.* memoria, retentiva [facultad]. *2* memoria, recuerdo, recordación: *within ~ of man*, que registra la historia.

**Memphis** (me·mfis) *n. pr.* GEOGR. Menfis.

**men** (men) *s. pl.* de MAN: hombres.

**menace** (me·nis) *s.* amenaza.

**menace (to)** *tr.-intr.* amenazar.

**menad** *s.* MAENAD.

**menage** (me·naÿ) *s.* casa, hogar. *2* economía doméstica, gobierno de la casa.

**menagerie** (mønæ·dÿøri) *s.* colección de animales; casa de fieras.

**mend** (mend) *s.* mejoría; reforma. *2* remiendo, reparación.

**mend (to)** *tr.* componer, reparar, remendar. *2* repasar, zurcir [la ropa]. *3* corregir, enmendar. *4* mejorar. *5 intr.* corregirse, enmendarse. *6* mejorar, mejorarse; restablecerse.

**mendacious** (mendei·shøs) *adj.* mendaz, mentiroso; falso.

**mendacity** (mendæ·siti) *s.* mendacidad. *2* mentira, embuste.

**mender** (me·ndø[r]) s. componedor, reparador; enmendador: ~ of roads, peón caminero.
**mendicant** (-ikant) adj.-s. mendicante. 2 mendigo.
**mendicity** (mendi·siti) s. mendicidad.
**menfolk** (me·nfouk) s. pl. hombres.
**menhir** (-ji[r]) s. menhir.
**menial** (mɪ·nial) adj. doméstico, servil. 2 s. criado, lacayo.
**meningeal** (meni·ndŷial) adj. meníngeo.
**meninges** (-iš) s. pl. ANAT. meninges.
**meningitis** (meninŷai·tis) s. MED. meningitis.
**meniscus** (meni·skøs) s. ANAT., FÍS., ÓPT. menisco. 2 lúnula.
**menisperm** (me·nispø[r]m) s. BOT. menisperma.
**menispermaceous** (menispø[r]mei·shøs) adj. BOT. menispermáceo.
**menopause** (me·nøupoš) s. FISIOL. menopausia.
**menses** (me·nsiš) s. pl. menstruo, regla.
**Menshevik** (me·nshøvik) s. menchevique.
**menstruate (to)** (me·nstrueit) intr. menstruar.
**menstruation** (-ei·shøn) s. menstruación.
**menstruum** (me·nstruøm) s. QUÍM. menstruo.
**mensurability** (menshurabi·liti) s. mensurabilidad.
**mensurable** (me·nshurabøl) adj. mensurable.
**mensuration** (-ei·shøn) s. medición, medida, mensura.
**mental** (me·ntal) adj. mental, intelectual; ~ reservation, reserva o restricción mental.
**mentality** (mentæ·liti) s. mentalidad.
**menthol** (me·nzal) s. QUÍM. menthol.
**mention** (me·nshøn) s. mención.
**mention (to)** tr. mencionar, mentar, nombrar: don't ~ it, no hay de qué; not to ~, sin contar, además de.
**mentor** (me·ntø[r]) s. mentor, guía.
**menu** (me·niu) s. lista de platos, minuta. 2 comida.
**Mentz** (ments) n. pr. Maguncia.
**meow** (mi·au) s. maullido, miau.
**meow (to)** intr. maullar.
**Mephistopheles** (mefista·filis) n. pr. Mefistófeles.
**Mephistophelian** (mefistøfi·lian) adj. mefistofélico.
**mephitic(al** (mifi·tik(al) adj. mefítico.
**mercantile** (mø[r]kantil) adj. mercantil, mercante.
**mercantilism** (mø[r]kantilišm) s. mercantilismo.
**Mercedarian** (mø[r]sidæ·rian) s. mercedario.
**mercenary** (mø[r]søneri) adj. mercenario; venal, interesado. 2 s. MIL. mercenario.
**mercer** (mø[r]sø[r]) s. (Ingl.) sedero [comerciante].
**mercerize (to)** (-aiš) tr. mercerizar.
**mercery** (-i) s. sedería [comercio].
**merchandise** (mø[r]chandaiš) s. mercadería, mercancía, géneros.
**merchandise (to)** intr.-tr. comerciar, traficar.
**merchant** (-t) s. mercader, comerciante. 2 tendero. 3 adj. mercante, mercantil; ~ marine, marina mercante.
**merchantable** (-abøl) adj. comerciable, vendible; corriente.
**merchantman** (-mæn) s. buque mercante.
**merciful** (mø[r]siful) adj. misericordioso, clemente, piadoso, compasivo, humano, benigno.
**mercifulness** (-nis) s. misericordia, clemencia, piedad, compasión.
**merciless** (mø[r]silis) adj. implacable, despiadado, cruel, inhumano.
**mercurial** (mø[r]kiu·rial) adj. mercurial, mercúrico. 2 activo, vivo, despierto. 3 veleidoso, volátil. 4 s. FARM. preparado mercurial.
**mercuric** (mø[r]kiu·rik) adj. QUÍ. mercúrico.

**Mercury** (mø·[r]kiuri) n. pr. ASTR., MIT. Mercurio: Mercury's wand, caduceo.
**mercury** s. QUÍM. mercurio, azogue. 2 BOT. mercurial.
**mercy** (mø·[r]si) s. misericordia, clemencia, piedad, compasión: to cry for ~, pedir misericordia. 2 merced, gracia. 3 merced [voluntad, arbitrio]: at the ~ of, a la merced de.
**mere** (mi·ø[r]) adj. mero, solo, no más que. 2 s. (Ingl.) lago, estanque.
**merely** (-li) adv. meramente.
**meretricious** (meritri·shøs) adj. meretricio. 2 fig. llamativo, de oropel; de mal gusto.
**merganser** (mø[r]gæ·nsø[r]) s. ORN. mergo, mergánsar.
**merge (to)** (mø[r]dŷ) tr. unir, combinar, fusionar. 2 intr. sumergirse, fundirse, unirse, fusionarse. 3 to ~ into, convertirse gradualmente en.
**merger** (-ø[r]) s. unión, fusión [esp. de sociedades anónimas].
**mericarp** (me·rikæ[r]p) s. BOT. mericarpio.
**meridian** (miri·dian) adj. ASTR., GEOGR., GEOM. meridiano. 2 fig. culminante, supremo. 3 s. ASTR., GEOGR., GEOM. meridiano. 4 altura meridiana. 5 fig. apogeo.
**meridional** (miri·diønal) adj.-s. meridional.
**meringue** (meræ·ng) s. merengue.
**merino** (møri·nou) adj.-s. merino [carnero, lana, paño].
**meristem** (me·ristem) s. BOT. meristemo.
**merit** (me·rit) s. mérito. 2 merecimiento.
**merit (to)** tr. merecer; ser digno de.
**meritorius** (merito·riøs) adj. meritorio, benemérito.
**merle** (mø[r]l) s. ORN. poét. mirlo.
**merlin** (mø·[r]lin) s. ORN. esmerejón.
**merlon** (mø·[r]løn) s. FORT. merlón.
**mermaid** (mø·[r]meid) s. MIT. sirena.
**merman** (mø·[r]mæn) s. MIT. tritón.
**Merovingian** (merovi·nŷian) adj.-s. merovingio.
**merrily** (me·rili) adv. alegremente, regocijadamente, jovialmente.
**merriment** (-mønt) s. alegría, regocijo. 2 fiesta, diversión.
**merry** (me·ri) adj. alegre, gozoso, regocijado, divertido, jovial, festivo: to make ~, divertirse. 2 risueño, placentero.
**merry-andrew** s. bufón, truán, payaso.
**merry-go-round** s. tiovivo, caballitos.
**merrymaker** (-meikø[r]) s. persona que se divierte; fiestero, jaranero.
**merrymaking** (-meiking) s. alegría, diversión, fiesta, holgorio.
**merrythought** (-zot) s. espoleta [de ave].
**mescal** (meskæl) s. mezcal.
**mesencephalon** (mesønse·falan) s. ANAT. mesencéfalo.
**mesentery** (me·sønteri) s. ANAT. mesenterio.
**mesh** (mesh) s. malla [de red]. 2 red, tejido de malla. 3 MEC. engranaje [acción]: in ~, engranado. 4 pl. red, lazos, trampa.
**mesh (to)** tr. coger con red, enredar. 2 intr. enredarse, enmallarse. 4 MEC. endentar, engranar.
**mesmeric** (mešme·rik) adj. mesmeriano.
**mesmerism** (me·smørišm) s. mesmerismo.
**mesmerize (to)** (-aiš) tr. magnetizar, hipnotizar.
**mesocarp** (me·søka[r]p) s. BOT. mesocarpio.
**mesothorax** (mesøzo·ræks) s. ZOOL. mesotórax.
**Mesozoic** (-šou·ik) adj.-s. GEOL. mesozoico.
**mesquite** (meskɪ·t) s. BOT. mezquite.
**mess** (mes) s. plato [cantidad de vianda]. 2 bazo-

fia, comistrajo. *3* enredo, lío, revoltijo; asco, suciedad: *to get into a* ~, meterse en un lío; *to make a* ~ *of*, desarreglar, enredar, ensuciar, echar a perder. *4* grupo de personas que regularmente comen juntos [esp. en el ejército o en la armada; mesa donde comen; mesa de oficiales].
**mess (to)** *tr.* desarreglar, enredar, ensuciar, echar a perder. | A veces con *up. 2 intr.* comer regularmente con. *3 to* ~ *about in*, meterse en, enredar en.
**message** (me·sidÿ) *s.* mensaje. *2* recado, mandado, parte, aviso.
**Messalina** (misælai·na) *n. pr.* Mesalina.
**messenger** (me·søndÿøʳ) *s.* mensajero. *2* mandadero. *3* heraldo, nuncio.
**Messiah** (mesai·a) *s.* mesías.
**Messianic** (mesiæ·nik) *adj.* mesiánico.
**Messianism** (mesai·anišm) *s.* mesianismo.
**messieurs** (me·søʳš) *s. pl.* de MISTER, señores.
**messmate** (me·smeit) *s.* compañero de mesa [esp. en la marina].
**messy** (me·si) *adj.* desarreglado, enredado; sucio.
**mestizo** (mesti·šou) *s.* mestizo.
**met** (met) *pret.* y *p. p.* de TO MEET.
**metabolism** (metæ·bølišm) *s.* BIOL. metabolismo.
**metarcapal** (metaka·ʳpal) *adj.* metarcapiano.
**metacarpus** (-øs) *s.* ANAT. metacarpo.
**metal** (me·tal) *s.* QUÍM., IMPR., BLAS. metal. *2* metal [aleación]. *3* materia [de que una cosa está hecha]; cualidad esencial; ánimo, temple. *4* vidrio en fusión. *5* material [grava, etc.] para firmes de carretera.
**metalepsis** (metale·psis) *s.* RET. metalepsis.
**metallic** (metæ·lik) *adj.* metálico. *2* puro [metal].
**metalliferous** (metali·førøs) *adj.* metalífero.
**metalline** (me·talin) *adj.* metálico. *2* que tiene metal en disolución.
**metallist** (me·talist) *s.* metalario, metalista.
**metallize (to)** (-aiš) *tr.* metalizar.
**metallography** (metala·grafi) *s.* metalografía.
**metalloid** (me·taloid) *adj.-s.* QUÍM. metaloide.
**metallurgic(al** (metaløʳdÿik(al) *adj.* metalúrgico.
**metallurgist** (me·taløʳdÿist) *s.* metalúrgico.
**metallurgy** (-i) *s.* metalurgia.
**metamere** (me·tamiʳ) *s.* ZOOL. metámero.
**metamorphic** (metamo·ʳfik) *adj.* metamórfico.
**metamorphism** (-fišm) *s.* GEOL. metamorfismo.
**metamorphize** (-faiš), **metamorphose (to)** (-fouš) *tr.* metamorfosear.
**metamorphosis** (-føsis) *s.* metamórfosis.
**metaphase** (me·tafeiš) *s.* BIOL. metafase.
**metaphor** (-føʳ) *s.* RET. metáfora.
**metaphoric(al** (me·taforik(al) *adj.* metafórico.
**metaphysic(al** (metafi·šik(al) *adj.* metafísico.
**metaphysician** (metafiši·shan) *s.* metafísico.
**metaphysics** (metafi·šiks) *s.* metafísica.
**metaplasm** (me·taplæšm) *s.* GRAM. metaplasmo. *2* BIOL. metaplasma.
**metastasis** (metæ·stasis) *s.* MED. metástasis.
**metatarsus** (metata·ʳsøs) *s.* ANAT. metatarso.
**metathesis** (metæ·zøsis) *s.* GRAM. metátesis.
**metazoan** (metašou·an) *s.* ZOOL. metazoo.
**mete (to)** (mıt) *tr.* medir. *2 to* ~ *out*, distribuir.
**metempsychosis** (mitempsikou·sis) *s.* metempsicosis.
**meteor** (mı·tiøʳ) *s.* meteoro. *2* bólido, estrella fugaz.
**meteoric** (mıtio·rik) *adj.* meteórico.
**meteorism** (mı·tiørism) *s.* MED. meteorismo.
**meteorite** (-ait) *s.* meteorito.

**meteorological** (mıtiørøla·dÿikal) *adj.* meteorológico.
**meteorologist** (mıtiøra·lødÿist) *adj.* meteorológico.
**meteorologist** (mıtiøra·lødÿist) *s.* meteorologista.
**meteorology** (-i) *s.* meteorología.
**meteorous** (mı·tiørøs) *adj.* meteórico.
**meter** (mı·tøʳ) *s.* medidor. *2* contador [de agua, gas, etc.]. *3* METRE.
**methane** (me·zein) *s.* QUÍM. metano.
**methinks** (mizi·nks) *impers.* poét. me parece, pienso. ¶ Pret.: *methought.*
**method** (me·zød) *s.* método. *2* técnica.
**methodic(al** (meza·dik(al) *adj.* metódico.
**Methodism** (me·zødišm) *s.* metodismo.
**Methodist** (-t) *s.* metodista.
**methodize (to)** (-aiš) *tr.* metodizar.
**methodology** (mezøda·lodÿi) *s.* metodología.
**methought** (mizo·t) *pret.* de TO METHINKS.
**methyl** (me·zil) *s.* QUÍM. metilo.
**methylene** (-in) *s.* QUÍM. metileno.
**methylic** (mezi·lik) *adj.* metílico.
**meticulous** (miti·kiuløs) *adj.* meticuloso, minucioso, escrupuloso.
**metonymy** (mita·nimi) *s.* RET. metonimia.
**metope** (me·topi) *s.* ARQ. métopa.
**metre** (mı·tøʳ) *s.* metro [medida de longitud]. *2* metro [del verso]. *3* MÚS. ritmo.
**metric (al** (me·trik(al) *adj.* métrico.
**metrify (to)** (me·trifai) *tr.* metrificar, versificar.
**metronome** (me·tronoum) *s.* metrónomo.
**metropolis** (mitra·polis) *s.* metrópoli.
**metropolitan** (metropa·litan) *adj.-s.* metropolitano.
**mettle** (me·tøl) *s.* temple, brío, ánimo, valor, fuego: *on one's* ~, en estado de hacer todo el esfuerzo posible.
**mettlesome** (-søm) *adj.* brioso, vivo, fogoso, ardiente.
**mew** (miu·) *s.* maullido. *2* ORN. gaviota. *3* jaula, muda [para las aves de caza]. *4 pl.* grupo de establos, caballerizas o garajes.
**mew (to)** *tr.* enjaular, encerrar. *2 intr.* maullar, mayar.
**mewl (to)** (miul) *intr.* llorar, gimotear [como un niño]. *2* maullar.
**Mexican** (me·ksikan) *adj.-s.* mejicano.
**Mexico** (me·ksikou) *n. pr.* GEOGR. Méjico.
**mezereon** (meši·rion) *s.* BOT. laureola hembra.
**mezzanine** (me·šanin) *s.* ARQ. entresuelo.
**mezzo-rilievo** (me·dšou-rilie·vou) *s.* medio relieve.
**mezzo-soprano** (-sopræ·nou) *s.* MÚS. mezzo soprano.
**mi** (mi) *s.* MÚS. mi.
**miaow** (miau·) *s.* miau, maullido.
**miaow (to)** *intr.* maullar, mayar.
**miasm(a** (maiæ·šm(a) *s.* miasma.
**miasmal** (-al), **miasmatic** (maiæšmæ·tik) *adj.* miasmático.
**mica** (mai·ka) *s.* MINER. mica: ~ *schist*, micacita.
**mice** (mais) *s. pl.* de MOUSE.
**Michael** (mai·køl) *n. pr.* Miguel.
**Michaelmas** (mi·kolmas) *s.* día de San Miguel.
**mickle** (mi·køl) *adj.-adv.* grande, mucho.
**microbe** (mai·kroub) *s.* microbio.
**microbial** (maikrou·bial) *adj.-s.* microbicida.
**microbiology** (maikroubaia·lødÿi) *s.* microbiología.
**microcephalic** (-sifæ·lik) *adj.* microcéfalo.
**micrococcus** (-ka·køs) *s.* BACT. micrococo.
**microcosm** (-kašm) *s.* microcosmo.

microfilm (-film) s. microfilm.
microgamete (-gæ·mit) s. BIOL. microgameto.
micrography (maikra·grafi) s. micrografía.
microgroove (mai·krogruv) s. microsurso.
micrometer (-mitøᶜ) s. micrómetro.
micrometric (al (maikroume·trik(al) adj. micrométrico.
micron (mai·kran) s. micra, micrón.
Micronesia (maikrouni·sha) n. pr. GEOGR. Micronesia.
micro-organism s. microorganismo.
microphone (mai·kroufoun) s. micrófono.
microphotograph (maikroufou·tøgræf), microphotography (-føta·grafi) s. microfotografía.
micropyle (-pail) s. BOT., ZOOL. micrópilo.
microscope (-skoup) s. microscopio.
microscopic (al (-ska·pik(al) adj. microscópico.
microtome (mai·kroutoum) s. micrótomo.
micturition (miktiuri·shøn) s. micción.
mid (mid) adj. medio, mitad [punto medio]: in ~ ocean, en mitad del océano.
midday (mi·ddei) s. mediodía [las doce]. 2 adj. del mediodía.
middle (mi·døl) adj. medio, de en medio, mediano, intermedio: ~ age, mediana edad; Middle Ages, Edad Media; ~ class, clase media; ~ ear; ANAT. oído medio; Middle East, GEOGR. Oriente medio; ~ finger, dedo de un medio o del corazón; ~ term, LÓG. término medio. 2 m. medio, mediados, mitad, centro: in the ~ of, en medio de, a medio, a mediados de, a la mitad de. 3 cintura [del cuerpo humano]. 4 promedio.
Middle-Age adj. medieval.
middle-aged adj. de mediana edad.
middle-class adj. de la clase media.
middleman (-mæn) s. intermediario.
middleweight (-ueit) adj. DEP. de peso medio. 2 s. DEP. peso medio.
middling (mi·dling) adj. mediano, regular. 2 adv. fam. medianamente: fairly ~, así, así. 3 s. pl. acemite. 4 artículos de calidad o precio mediano.
middy (mi·di) s. (fam.) guardia marina. 2 ~ blouse, marinera [blusa para mujeres y niños].
midge (midŷ) s. ENT. cagachín; mosca de agua. 2 enano.
midget (mi·dŷit) s. enano, liliputiense.
Midianite (mi·diænait) s. BIBL. madianita.
midland (mi·dland) adj. de tierra adentro, interior. 2 s. interior, corazón [de un país].
midnight (-nait) s. medianoche. 2 adj. de la media noche, oscuro: ~ Mass, misa del gallo; ~ sun, sol de medianoche.
midrib (-rib) s. BOT. nervio central.
midriff (-rif) s. ANAT. diafragma.
mid-sea s. alta mar.
midship (-ship) adj. MAR. del medio o en medio del buque.
midshipman (-mæn) s. MAR. alférez alumno, guardia marina.
midships (-s) adv. MAR. en la parte media del buque. 2 s. pl. parte media del buque.
midst (midst) s. centro, medio: in the ~ of, en medio de, entre; en lo más recio de.
midstream (-strim) s. el medio de una corriente o río.
midsummer (-sømøᶜ) s. canícula, solsticio estival; pleno verano: Midsummer Day, día de San Juan.
midway (-wei) s. mitad del camino. 2 avenida central [de una exposición, etc.]. 3 adj. situado a mitad del camino. 4 adv. a mitad del camino.

midweek (-wik) s. mediados de la semana.
midwife (-waif) s. partera, comadrona.
midwife (to) tr.-intr. partear.
midwifery (-waifri) s. partería, obstetricia.
midwinter (-wintøᶜ) s. solsticio hiemal; pleno invierno.
mien (min) s. semblante, aire, continente.
miff (mif) s. desavenencia, disgusto, enojo.
miff (to) tr. disgustar, ofender. 2 intr. ofenderse.
might (mait) pretérito de MAY. 2 s. poderío, fuerza, energía: with ~ and main, con todas sus fuerzas, a más no poder.
mightily (-ili) adv. poderosamente. 2 muchísimo.
mightiness (-inis) s. poder, poderío. 2 fuerza, potencia. 3 grandeza.
mighty (-i) adj. poderoso. 2 potente, vigoroso. 3 importante, grande, enorme, violento. 5 adv. fam. muy, sumamente.
mignonette (miñøne·t) s. BOT. reseda.
migraine (maigrei·n) s. migraña, jaqueca.
migrant (mai·grant) adj.-s. que efectúa una migración. 2 de paso [ave].
migrate (to) (mai·greit) intr. pasar de un lugar o país a otro; emigrar.
migration (maigre·shøn) s. migración.
migratory (mai·gratori) adj. migratorio.
mihrab (mira·b) s. mihrab.
Mikado (mika·dou) s. micado.
Mike (maik) n. pr. dim. de MICHAEL.
mil (mil) s. milésima de pulgada.
milady (milei·di) s. miladi.
Milanese (milani·š) n. pr. milanés.
milch (milch) adj. que da leche: ~ cow, vaca lechera.
mild (maild) adj. apacible, blando, suave. 2 manso, dócil. 3 leve, ligero, moderado, templado. 4 dúctil, maleable.
mildew (mi·ldiu) s. AGR. mildin; añublo. 2 moho [orgánico].
mildew (to) tr.-intr. AGR. atacar o ser atacado de mildiu; añublar (se; enmohecer (se.
mildly (mai·ldli) adv. suavemente, dócilmente. 2 con lenidad. 3 ligeramente, moderadamente.
mildness (mai·ldnis) s. suavidad, benignidad. 2 lenidad, indulgencia. 3 mansedumbre. 4 levedad, moderación. 5 templanza [del clima].
mile (mail) s. milla [1.609 m.]: ~ stone, piedra miliaria.
mileage (-idŷ) s. longitud o recorrido en millas. 2 gastos de viaje que se abonan por millas: ~ book, carnet kilométrico.
Milesian (mili·shian) adj. milesio.
milfoil (mi·lfoil) s. BOT. milenrama, aquilea.
miliary (-ieri) adj. ANAT., MED. miliar.
militancy (-itansi) s. belicosidad, combatividad.
militant (-itant) adj. militante. 2 combativo.
militarism (-itarišm) s. militarismo.
militarist (-t) s. militarista.
militarize (to) (-ais) tr. militarizar.
military (-iteri) adj. militar. 2 castrense. 3 s. the ~, los militares, las tropas.
militate (to) (-iteit) intr. militar: to ~ against, militar contra.
militia (mili·sha) s. milicia, guardia nacional.
militiaman (-mæn) s. miliciano.
milk (milk) s. leche: ~ can, lechera [vasija]; ~ food, lactinio; ~ sugar, lactosa; ~ thistle, cardo lechero; ~ tooth, diente de leche. 2 lechada [de cal]. 3 BOT. látex. 4 jugo lechoso.
milk (to) tr. ordeñar. 2 fig. chupar, extraer. 3 intr. dar leche.

**milk-and-water** adj. débil [de carácter]. 2 ñoño.
**milker** (-ø<sup>r</sup>) s. ordeñador, ordeñadora. 2 animal que da leche.
**milking** (-ing) s. ordeño.
**milkmaid** (-meid) s. lechera; criada de vaquería.
**milkman** (-mæn) s. lechero.
**milksop** (-sap) s. mantecón, marica.
**milkwort** (-uø<sup>r</sup>t) s. BOT. polígala.
**milky** (-i) adj. lechoso, lácteo: Milky Way, Vía Láctea. 2 fig. tímido, apocado.
**mill** (mil) s. molino: to go through the ~, to put through the ~, fig. aprender, hacer aprender por experiencia; entrenarse o entrenar rigurosamente. 2 fábrica, taller. 3 hilandería, fábrica de hilados; fábrica de tejidos. 4 ingenio [de azúcar]. 5 MEC. fresadora. 7 prensa [para estrujar]. 8 volante [para acuñar]. 9 nombre de varias máquinas. 10 pop. pugilato. 11 (E.U.) milésima de dólar.
**mill** (to) tr. moler, triturar. 2 acordonar [monedas]. 3 batanar. 4 aserrar. 5 MEC. fresar. 6 producir, transformar [en fábrica]. 7 batir. [hacer espumoso]. 8 pegar, dar una paliza a. 9 intr. arremolinarse. 10 dar vueltas en círculo [el ganado]. 11 pop. luchar a puñetazos.
**millboard** (-bo<sup>r</sup>d) s. cartón para encuadernar.
**millclapper** (-klæpø<sup>r</sup>) s. cítola, tarabilla.
**milldam** (-dæm) s. presa, represa.
**millenarian** (miløne·rian) adj. milenario.
**millenary** (mi·løneri) adj.-s. milenario.
**millennial** (mile·nial) adj. del milenio.
**millennium** (-iøm) s. milenio.
**millepede** (mi·lipid) s. ZOOL. cardador [miriápodo].
**miller** (mi·lø<sup>r</sup>) s. molinero. 2 pop. boxeador, púgil. 3 ENT. polilla blanca.
**millesimal** (mile·simal) adj.-s. milésimo, -ma.
**millet** (mi·lit) s. BOT. mijo.
**milliard** (mi·lia<sup>r</sup>d) s. mil millones.
**milliary** (-eri) adj. miliar [piedra, columna].
**milligram, milligramme** (-græm) s. miligramo.
**milliliter, millilitre** (-litø<sup>r</sup>) s. mililitro.
**millimeter, millimetre** (-mitø<sup>r</sup>) s. milímetro.
**milliner** (-nø<sup>r</sup>) s. modista de sombreros.
**millinery** (-neri) s. sombreros de señora. 2 ocupación o tienda de la modista de sombreros.
**milling** (-ing) s. molienda, moltura. 2 fabricación. 3 batanado. 4 MEC. fresado: ~ machine, fresadora.
**million** (mi·liøn) s. millón.
**millionaire** (-eø<sup>r</sup>) s. millonario.
**millionth** (-z) adj.-s. millonésimo.
**millipede** (-pid) s. MILLEPEDE.
**millpond** (mi·lpand) s. alberca o represa de molino.
**millrace** (-reis) s. caz, saetín [de molino].
**millstone** (-stoun) s. muela de molino.
**millwork** (-uø<sup>r</sup>k) s. obra de molino, fábrica o taller. 2 carpintería mecánica.
**milord** (milo·<sup>r</sup>d) s. milord.
**milreis** (-reis) s. milreis.
**milt** (milt) s. ANAT. bazo. 2 lecha [de los peces].
**Miltiades** (miltai·ædiš) n. pr. Milcíades.
**mimbar** (mi·mba<sup>r</sup>) s. mimbar.
**mime** (maim) s. TEAT. mimo. 2 payaso, bufón.
**mimesis** (mimi·sis) s. RET., BIOL. mimesis.
**mimetic (al** (mime·tik(al) adj. mímico, imitativo.
**mimetism** (mi·mitišm) s. BIOL. mimetismo.
**mimic** (mi·mik) adj. mímico. 3 s. pantomimo; imitador.
**mimic** (to) tr. imitar, parecer. 2 imitar, remedar

[esp. por burla]. ¶ Pret. y p. p.: mimicked; ger.: -cking.
**mimicry** (-ri) s. imitación, remedo, monería. 2 ZOOL. mimetismo.
**mimographer** (mima·grafø<sup>r</sup>) s. mimógrafo.
**mimosa** (mimou·sa) s. BOT. mimosa, sensitiva.
**mimosaceous** (mimøsei·shøs) adj. BOT. mimosáceo.
**minacious** (minei·shøs) adj. amenazador.
**minaret** (minare·t) s. alminar.
**minatory** (mi·natori) adj. amenazador.
**mince** (mins) s. cosa picada o desmenuzada; picadillo: ~ pie, pastel de carne picada y frutas. 2 afectación.
**mince** (to) tr. desmenuzar; picar [carne]. 2 medir [las palabras]; andar con rodeos [al hablar de]: without mincing words, sin rodeos, sin morderse la lengua. 3 atenuar, suavizar. 4 hacer o decir [algo] remilgadamente. 5 intr. andar, hablar, etc., de un modo afectado o remilgado.
**mincemeat** (-mit) s. picadillo; carne picada con frutas, etc.
**mincing** (-ing) adj. afectado, remilgado.
**mincingly** (-i) adj. con afectación. 2 a pedacitos, a pasitos.
**mind** (maind) s. mente, espíritu, entendimiento, juicio: to be in one's right ~, estar en sus cabales, estar en su juicio; to go out of one's ~, to lose one's ~, perder el juicio. 2 mentalidad. 3 espíritu, ánimo, estado de ánimo. 4 intención, propósito, deseo, inclinación, gusto: to be in two minds, dudar, vacilar, estar indeciso; to have a ~, tener ganas de, estar por [hacer una cosa]; to know one's ~, a gusto de uno. 5 pensamiento, mientes, memoria, recuerdo: to bear, o keep, in ~, tener presente, tener en cuenta; to come to ~, venir a las mientes; to pass out of ~, caer en el olvido; to put in ~, recordar [hacer recordar]; out of ~, olvidado; inmemorial. 6 pensamiento, opinión, parecer: to be of one ~, estar de acuerdo, pensar igual; to change one's ~, mudar de opinión, de parecer; of one ~, unánimes; with one ~, unánimemente.
**mind** (to) tr. notar, observar. 2 considerar, tener en cuenta; mirar, fijarse en. 3 dar importancia a, hacer caso, preocuparse de; tener inconveniente en; molestarle a uno [una cosa]: do you ~ the smoke?, ¿le molesta el humo? 4 obedecer, escuchar. 5 cuidar de, atender, ocuparse de: ~ your own business, métase en lo que le importa. 6 tener cuidado con: ~ the step!, ¡cuidado con el escalón! 7 recordar, acordarse de. 8 intr. never ~, no importa, no haga caso, no se preocupe. 9 mind!, ¡cuidado!
**minded** (-id) adj. dispuesto, inclinado, intencionado [esp. en composición].
**mindful** (-ful) adj. atento, cuidadoso. 2 ~ of, atento a, que tiene presente.
**midfulness** (-fulnis) s. atención, cuidado.
**mindless** (-lis) s. tonto, necio. 2 descuidado; que no recuerda o no tiene en cuenta.
**1) mine** (main) pron. pos. mío, mía, míos, mías: this hat is ~, este sombrero es mío o el mío; a friend of ~, un amigo mío. 2 adj.-pos. poét. mi, mis, mío, mía, míos, mías.
**2) mine** s. MIN., FORT., MIL. mina. 2 MAR. mina submarina: ~ sweeper, dragaminas. 3 fig. mina [de noticias, etc.].
**mine** (to) tr. minar. 2 extraer [mineral]; beneficiar [un filón]. 3 intr. hacer minas. 4 dedicarse a la minería.

**miner** (-ø<sup>r</sup>) s. minero. 2 minador, zapador. 3 ZOOL. cavador.

**mineral** (mi·nøral) adj. mineral: ~ *kingdom*, reino mineral; ~ *water*, agua mineral. 2 s. mineral [substancia inorgánica]. 3 MIN. mineral.

**mineralize (to)** (mi·nøralaiš) tr. mineralizar.

**mineralogist** (minøræ·lodÿist) s. mineralogista.

**mineralogy** (minøræ·lodÿi) s. mineralogía.

**minever** (mi·nivø<sup>r</sup>) s. MINIVER.

**mingle (to)** (mi·ngøl) tr. mezclar; entremezclar. 2 preparar [mezclando]. 3 intr. mezclarse, confundirse; juntarse.

**Minho** (mai·ñou) n. pr. GEOGR. Miño.

**miniate (to)** (mi·nieit) tr. pintar con minio, miniar.

**miniature** (-achø<sup>r</sup>) s. miniatura: ~ *painter*, miniaturista.

**minify (to)** (-fai) tr. empequeñecer, disminuir.

**minim** (mi·nim) m. cosa o pers. pequeña, insignificante. 2 pizca. 3 MÚS. mínima. 4 (con may.) mínimo [religioso].

**minimal** (-al) adj. mínimo.

**minimize (to)** (-aiš) tr. reducir al mínimo. 2 menospreciar, tener en poco.

**minimum** (-øm) s. mínimo, minimum. 2 adj. mínimo.

**mining** (-øm) s. minería, mineraje. 2 acción de minar. 3 adj. minero; de minas.

**minion** (mi·niøn) s. favorito, paniaguado, seguidor servil. 2 esbirro. 3 IMPR. miñona [tipo]. 4 adj. lindo, delicado.

**minister** (mi·nistø<sup>r</sup>) s. ministro [en todas sus acepciones]: ~ *plenipotentiary*, ministro plenipotenciario. 2 pastor protestante.

**minister (to)** tr. dar, suministrar. 2 intr. oficiar, ministrar. 3 asistir, auxiliar. 4 tender, contribuir.

**ministerial** (ministi·rial) adj. ministerial. 2 sacerdotal. 3 gubernativo. 4 que obra como agente, instrumento o medio.

**ministerialism** (-ism) s. ministerialismo.

**ministrant** (mini·strant) s. ministrante. 2 oficiante.

**ministration** (-ei·shøn) s. suministración. 2 ayuda, agencia, solicitud, cuidado. 3 ECLES. ministerio.

**ministry** (mi·nistri) s. ministerio, oficio, ayuda, intervención. 2 POL. ministerio. 3 ECLES. ministerio. 4 clero, conjunto de ministros.

**minium** (mi·niøm) s. QUÍM. minio.

**mink** (mink) s. ZOOL. visón. 2 piel de visón.

**minnow** (mi·nou) s. cierto pez de agua dulce.

**minor** (mai·nø<sup>r</sup>) adj. menor [menos importante, de poca importancia], secundario, inferior: ~ *orders*, órdenes menores. 2 de menor de edad. 3 MÚS. menor; ~ *key*, tono menor. 4 adj.-s. LÓG. menor. 5 s. menor [de edad]. 6 menor, minorita [religioso]. 7 (E.U.) asignatura de importancia secundaria.

**Minorca** (mino·<sup>r</sup>ka) n. pr. GEOGR. Menorca.

**minority** (maina·riti) s. minoridad, minoría, menor edad. 2 minoría [los menos]. 3 adj. minoritario.

**minotaur** (mi·notø<sup>r</sup>) n. pr. MIT. Minotauro.

**minster** (mi·nstø<sup>r</sup>) s. iglesia de monasterio. 2 basílica, catedral.

**minstrel** (-trøl) s. trovador, juglar, ministril. 2 (E.U.) cantor cómico.

**mint** (mint) s. casa de moneda, ceca. 2 fig. mina, fuente inagotable, gran cantidad: a ~ *of money*, un dineral. 3 BOT. menta. 4 pastilla de menta.

**mint (to)** tr. acuñar [moneda]. 2 fig. fabricar, inventar [una palabra, una frase, etc.].

**mintage** (-idÿ) s. acuñación. 2 monedaje. 3 BOT. menta. 4 pastilla de menta.

**mint (to)** tr. acuñar [moneda]. 2 fig. fabricar, inventar [una palabra, una frase, etc.].

**mintage** (-idÿ) s. acuñación. 2 monedaje. 3 moneda acuñada.

**minuend** (mi·niuend) s. ARIT. minuendo.

**minuet** (miniue·t) s. minué, minuete.

**minus** (mai·nøs) prep.-adj. menos: ~ *sign*, signo menos. 2 falto de, sin. 3 adj. MAT., ELECT. negativo. 4 s. MAT. signo menos. 5 cantidad negativa.

**1) minute** (mainiu·t) adj. menudo, pequeño, diminuto. 2 nimio, minucioso.

**2) minute** (mi·nit) s. minuto [división de la hora o del grado]: ~ *hand*, minutero; *up to the* ~, al corriente; de última hora. 2 momento, instante. 3 minuta, nota, apuntamiento. 4 pl. acta [de una junta, etc.].

**minute (to)** tr. cronometrar. 2 minutar, anotar; poner en el acta.

**minutely** (mainiu·tli) adv. minuciosamente; detalladamente. 2 (mi·nitli) de minuto en minuto.

**minuteman** (mi·nitmæn) s. (E.U.) HIST. miliciano de la Revolución.

**minutiae** (miniu·shi) s. pl. minucias.

**minx** (minks) s. moza descarada, bribona. 2 ZOOL. marta.

**Miocene** (mai·øsin) adj.-s. GEOL. mioceno.

**miracle** (mi·rakøl) s. milagro: *to a* ~, perfectamente. 2 TEAT. miracle o ~ *play* auto [drama religioso].

**miraculous** (miræ·kiuløs) adj. milagroso. 2 maravilloso, prodigioso.

**mirage** (mi·radÿ) s. espejismo, miraje.

**mire** (mai·ø<sup>r</sup>) s. cieno, lodo, fango. 2 cenagal.

**mire (to)** tr. enlodar. 2 hundir en el cieno; atascar, atollar.

**Miriam** (mi·riam) n. pr. María.

**mirific** (miri·fic) adj. mirífico.

**mirk** (mø<sup>r</sup>k) s. MURK.

**mirky** (-i) adj. MURKY.

**mirror** (mi·rø<sup>r</sup>) s. espejo.

**mirror (to)** tr. reflejar [una imagen]. 2 intr. reflejarse, retratarse; mirarse [en un espejo].

**mirth** (mø<sup>r</sup>z) s. alegría, regocijo, hilaridad.

**mirthful** (-ful) adj. alegre, regocijado, jovial.

**mirthless** (-lis) adj. triste, melancólico.

**miry** (mai·ri) adj. cenagoso, lodoso, fangoso.

**misadventure** (misadve·nchø<sup>r</sup>) s. desgracia, percance.

**misadvised** (-vai·šd) adj. mal aconsejado.

**misalliance** (misalai·ans) s. casamiento desigual.

**misanthrope** (mi·sanzroup) s. misántropo.

**misanthropic (al** (misanzra·pik(al) adj. misantrópico.

**misanthropy** (misæ·nzrøpi) s. misantropía.

**misapply (to)** (misaplai·) tr. usar o emplear mal; hacer mal uso de.

**misapprehend (to)** (-prije·nd) tr. entender mal.

**misapprehension** (-prije·nshøn) s. equivocación; mala inteligencia, concepto erróneo.

**misappropriate (to)** (-prou·prieit) tr. malversar. 2 distraer [fondos].

**misbecoming** (-bikø·ming) adj. impropio, indigno; que sienta o cae mal.

**misbegot(ten** (-biga·t(øn) adj. bastardo.

**misbehave (to)** (-bijei·v) intr. portarse mal.

**misbehaved** (-d) adj. malcriado, descortés.

**misbehaviour** (-iø<sup>r</sup>) s. mal comportamiento. 2 descortesía.

**misbelief** (misbili·f) s. error, herejía, falsa creencia.

**misbelieve (to)** (-v) *intr.* tener creencias erróneas. *2 tr.* no creer, no dar crédito a.

**misbeliever** (-øʳ) *s.* hereje, infiel. *2* incrédulo.

**misbirth** (-bøˑʳz) *s.* aborto, parto prematuro.

**miscalculate (to)** (-kæˑlkiuleit) *tr.* calcular mal.

**miscall (to)** (-koˑl) *tr.* nombrar impropiamente.

**miscarriage** (-kæˑridỹ) *s.* aborto. *2* malogro. *3* extravío. *4* desmán.

**miscarry (to)** (-kæˑri) *intr.* abortar, malparir. *2* malograrse. *3* extraviarse [una carta].

**miscellanea** (miseleiˑnia) *s. pl.* miscelánea.

**miscellaneous** (miseleiˑniøs) *adj.* misceláneo.

**miscellany** (miˑseleini) *s.* miscelánea.

**mischance** (mischæˑns) *s.* desgracia, mala suerte, fatalidad, percance.

**mischarge (to)** (-chaˑʳdỹ) *tr.* cargar en cuenta indebidamente.

**mischief** (-chif) *s.* mal, daño, perjuicio: *to make* ~, enredar, meter cizaña. *2* travesura, diablura. *3* persona molesta; diablillo.

**mischief-maker** *s.* enredador, cizañero.

**mischievous** (-vøs) *adj.* malo, dañino. *2* enredador, chismoso. *3* travieso, malicioso, juguetón.

**miscible** (miˑsibøl) *adj.* miscible.

**misconceive (to)** (miscønsiˑv) *intr.* entender mal.

**misconception** (-kønseˑpshøn) *s.* concepto erróneo, mala interpretación.

**misconduct** (-kaˑndøkt) *s.* mala conducta. *2* dirección o administración.

**misconduct (to)** (miskøndøˑkt) *tr.* dirigir o administrar mal. *2 to* ~ *oneself,* conducirse mal.

**misconstruction** (-kønstrøˑkshøn) *s.* error, mala interpretación.

**misconstrue (to)** (-kønstruˑ) *tr.* interpretar equivocadamente. *2* torcer el sentido de.

**miscount** (-kauˑnt) *s.* error de cuenta.

**miscreant** (miˑskriant) *s.* malandrín, bribón.

**miscue** (miskiuˑ) *s.* BILLAR pifia. *2 fam.* error, desacierto.

**miscue (to)** *intr.* BILLAR pifiar.

**misdate (to)** (-deˑt) *tr.* poner fecha equivocada; fechar falsamente.

**misdeed** (-dɪˑd) *s.* fechoría, mala acción.

**misdemeanour** (-dimiˑnøʳ) *s.* mala conducta. *2* fechoría, mala acción. *3* DER. delito menos grave.

**misdirect (to)** (-direˑkt) *tr.* dirigir erradamente.

**misdoer** (misduˑøʳ) *s.* malhechor, delincuente, el que obra mal.

**misdoing** (-duˑing) *s.* yerro. *2* mal obrar; mala acción, delito.

**misemploy (to)** (-emploˑi) *tr.* emplear mal.

**miser** (maiˑsøʳ) *adj.-s.* mísero, avaro, roñoso.

**miserable** (miˑsørabøl) *adj.* miserable, mísero. *2* desdichado, infeliz. *3* que causa molestia o infelicidad. *4* lastimoso.

**Miserere** (mišørɪˑri) *s.* LITURG. Miserere.

**misericorde** (-rikoˑʳd) *s.* misericordia [puñal]. *2* misericordia, coma [de silla de coro].

**miserly** (maiˑsøʳli) *adj.* avaro, tacaño, roñoso.

**misery** (miˑsøri) *s.* miseria, laceria. *2* desdicha, infelicidad. *3* aflicción, pena, angustia, dolor, sufrimiento.

**misfeasance** (misfiˑsans) *s.* abuso de autoridad.

**misfire** (-faiˑøʳ) *s.* acción de fallar [un arma de fuego, el encendido de un motor, etc.].

**misfire (to)** *intr.* fallar [un arma de fuego, el encendido de un motor, etc.].

**misfit (to)** (misfiˑt) *tr.-intr.* no sentar o ajustar bien, no ser propio o a propósito. *2* no encajar.

**misfortune** (-foˑʳchøn) *s.* infortunio, desdicha, desgracia.

**misgive (to)** (-giˑv) *tr.* dar dudas o temores [dic. del pensamiento o el corazón]. *2 intr.* recelar, temer.

**misgiving** (-ing) *s.* presentimiento, recelo, temor.

**misgotten** (-gaˑtøn) *adj.* mal adquirido.

**misgovernment** (-gøˑvøʳmøn) *s.* desgobierno, desbarajuste, mala administración.

**misguide (to)** (-gaiˑd) *tr.* dirigir mal; aconsejar mal, desencaminar, descarriar, engañar.

**mishandle (to)** (-jæˑndøl) *tr.* manejar mal; maltratar.

**mishap** (-jæˑp) *s.* mala suerte, desgracia. *2* percance, contratiempo. *3* desliz, tropiezo.

**mishear (to)** (-jiˑøʳ) *tr.* oír mal, trasoír.

**misinform (to)** (-infoˑʳm) *intr.* informar o enterar mal.

**misinformation** (-eiˑshøn) *s.* noticia o informes falsos.

**misinterpret (to)** (intøˑrprit) *tr.* interpretar mal.

**misjudge (to)** (-ỹøˑdỹ) *tr.* juzgar mal, erróneamente o injustamente.

**mislay (to)** (-lei) *tr.* colocar fuera de su sitio; extraviar, perder; traspapelar.

**mislead (to)** (-lɪd) *tr.* desencaminar, descarriar, despistar. *2* inducir a error, engañar; seducir.

**mismanage (to)** (mæˑnidỹ) *tr.* manejar o administrar mal.

**mismanagement** (-møn) *s.* mala administración, desgobierno.

**misname (to)** (-neiˑm) *tr.* nombrar equivocadamente.

**misnomer** (-ouˑmøʳ) *s.* nombre equivocado.

**misogynist** (misaˑdỹinist) *s.* misógino.

**misogynous** (-øs) *adj.* misógino.

**misoneism** (misonɪˑism) *s.* misoneísmo.

**misplace (to)** (mispleiˑs) *tr.* poner fuera de su sitio; colocar mal. *2* extraviar, traspapelar.

**misprint** (-prɪˑnt) *s.* errata, error de imprenta.

**misprint (to)** *tr.* imprimir con erratas.

**misprize (to)** (-praiˑš) *tr.* menospreciar.

**mispronounce (to)** (-prønauˑns) *tr.* pronunciar mal.

**misquotation** (-kuoteiˑshøn) *s.* cita falsa o equivocada.

**misrate (to)** (-reiˑt) *tr.* valuar, tasar mal.

**misread (to)** (-rɪˑd) *tr.* leer mal.

**misrepresent (to)** (-reprišeˑnt) *tr.* desfigurar, tergiversar, falsear.

**misrepresentation** (-eiˑshøn) *s.* noticia o relación falsa; tergiversación; falsedad.

**misrule** (-ruˑl) *s.* desgobierno, mal gobierno.

**misrule (to)** *tr.* desgobernar, gobernar mal.

**Miss** (mis) *s.* señorita [antepuesto al nombre]. *2* (con min.) señorita, joven.

**miss** (mis) *s.* acción de errar el tiro, el golpe, etc.; errada; fracaso, malogro. *2* falta, pérdida.

**miss (to)** *tr.* errar [el blanco, la vocación, etc.]. *2* no dar con, no hallar; no coger, no obtener. *3* no ver, no oír, no comprender: *to* ~ *the point,* no ver la intención. *4* perder [un tren, la ocasión, etc.]. *5* omitir. *6* escapar, evitar: *he barely missed being killed,* por poco se mata o lo matan. *7* echar de menos, sentir o advertir la falta de. *8 to* ~ *fire,* fallar [un arma]. *9 intr.* errar el blanco. *10* fallar, no surtir efecto.

**missal** (miˑsal) *s.* LITURG. misal. *2* devocionario.

**missel thrush** (miˑsøl) *s.* ORN. cagaceite.

**misshape (to)** (-sheiˑp) *tr.* deformar, afear.

**misshapen** (-øn) *adj.* deformado, deforme, monstruoso.

**missile** (mi·sil) *adj.* arrojadizo. *2 s.* proyectil. *3* arma arrojadiza.

**missing** (mi·sing) *adj.* extraviado, perdido, que falta: *to be ~*, faltar, estar extraviado o perdido.

**mission** (mi·shøn) *s.* misión. *2* organización religiosa y benéfica.

**missionary** (-eri) *adj.* misional. *2 s.* misionero. *3* misionario.

**missis** (mi·sis) *s.* fam. señora. *2* ama de casa. *3* esposa.

**Mississipi** (misisi·pi) *n. pr.* GEOGR. Misisipí.

**missive** (mi·siv) *adj.* misivo. *2 s.* carta, misiva.

**Missouri** (mišu·ri) *n. pr.* GEOGR. Misuri.

**misspell (to)** (misspe·l) *tr.* deletrear mal. *2* escribir con mala ortografía.

**misspend (to)** (-spend) *tr.* malgastar.

**misstate (to)** (-stei·t) *tr.* relatar o afirmar falsamente; desfigurar [un hecho].

**misstatement** (-mønt) *s.* relación o aserción falsa o equivocada; error.

**misstep** (-ste·p) *s.* paso en falso; desliz, tropiezo.

**missus** (mi·søš) *s.* MISSIS.

**missy** (mi·si) *s.* fam. señorita.

**mist** (mist) *s.* niebla, vapor, calígine, vaho, llovizna. *2* nube, confusión, obscurecimiento.

**mist (to)** *intr.* anublarse [el tiempo]; lloviznar. *2* anublarse; empañarse [los ojos]. *3 tr.* nublar, empañar.

**mistake** (mistei·k) *s.* equivocación, error, confusión: *to make a ~*, equivocarse; *and no ~*, fam. sin duda alguna; *by ~*, por equivocación, por descuido.

**mistake (to)** *tr.* equivocar; confundir, tomar [una pers. o cosa] por otra; entender mal. ¶ Pret.: *mistook*; p. p.: *-taken*.

**mistaken** (-øn) *p. p.* de TO MISTAKE. *2 adj.* equivocado, errado, engañado. *3* erróneo, incorrecto.

**Mister** (mi·stø) *s.* Señor [tratamiento de cortesía usado delante del nombre].

**mistimed** (mistai·md) *adj.* inoportuno; extemporáneo, intempestivo.

**mistiness** (mi·stinis) *s.* calígine, oscuridad.

**mistletoe** (mi·søltou) *s.* BOT. muérdago, liga.

**mistook** (mistu·k) *pret. p. p.* de TO MISTAKE.

**mistral** (mi·stral) *s.* mistral [viento].

**mistreat (to)** (mistri·t) *tr.* maltratar.

**mistress** (mi·stris) *s.* ama, dueña, señora. *2* señora de la casa. *3* directora [de una escuela]. *4* maestra. *5* querida, manceba. *6* cortejo, novia. *7* fam. señora, esposa. *8* (con may.) Señora [tratamiento de cortesía].

**mistrust** (mistrø·st) *s.* desconfianza, suspicacia.

**mistrust (to)** *tr.* desconfiar de, recelar.

**mistrustful** (-ful) *adj.* desconfiado, que desconfía, receloso.

**misty** (mi·sti) *adj.* brumoso, nublado, caliginoso. *2* empañado. *3* confuso, vago, distinto.

**misunderstand (to)** (misøndø·rstæ·nd) *tr.* entender o interpretar mal.

**misunderstanding** (-ing) *s.* equivocación, error, mala inteligencia, mala interpretación. *2* desavenencia.

**misusage** (misiu·sidÿ) *s.* maltrato. *2* MISUSE.

**misuse** (misyu·s) *s.* mal uso, uso impropio; malversación [de fondos].

**misuse (to)** (misyu·š) *tr.* maltratar, tratar mal. *2* usar o emplear mal. *3* malversar [fondos].

**mite** (mait) *s.* ZOOL. ácaro. *2* pizca; pequeñez. *3* criatura, enano. *4 one's ~*, su óbolo.

**miter** (-ø) *s.* MITRE.

**miter (to)** *tr.* TO MITRE.

**mitigate (to)** (mi·tigeit) *tr.* mitigar, disminuir, atenuar, suavizar, paliar.

**mitigation** (-ei·shøn) *s.* mitigación.

**mitigative** (mi·tigeitiv) *adj.-s.* mitigativo, lenitivo, paliativo.

**mitosis** (mitou·sis) *s.* BIOL. mitosis.

**mitral** (mai·tral) *adj.* mitral.

**mitre** (mai·tø) *s.* mitra. *2* CARP. inglete. *3 ~ sill*, busco [de la esclusa].

**mitre (to)** *tr.* conferir una mitra a. *2* CARP. ingletear.

**mitred** (-d) *adj.* mitrado.

**mitt** (mit) *s.* mitón, confortante. *2* guante sin división para los dedos, excepto para el pulgar. *3* guante de béisbol.

**mitten** (-øn) *s.* MITT 1 y 2. *2 to get*, o *give, the ~*, recibir o dar calabazas. *3 pl.* guantes de boxeo.

**mix** (miks) *s.* mezcla [de ingredientes]. *2* fam. *~ up*, lío, embrollo, confusión.

**mix (to)** *tr.* mezclar, mixturar, barajar. *2* preparar, hacer, amasar [mezclando]. *3* aderezar [ensalada]. *4 to ~ up*, mezclar; confundir; *to be mixed up in* o *with*, tener que ver con [un asunto feo]. *5 intr.* mezclarse. *6* juntarse, tratarse, alternar. *7* tomar parte. ¶ Pret. y p. p.: *mixed* o *mixt*.

**mixed** (-t) *adj.* mezclado, barajado. *2* mixto: *~ number*, número mixto; *~ train*, tren mixto. *3* misceláneo, variado. *4* formado de gente muy distinta; poco selecto. *5 ~ up*, confundido, aturdido.

**mixer** (-ø) *s.* mezclador. *2* fam. (E.U.) persona sociable.

**mixtilineal, mixtilinear** (mikstili·nial, -nia) *adj.* GEOM. mixtilíneo.

**mixture** (mi·kschø) *s.* mezcla, mixtura.

**mizen, mizzen** (mi·søn) *s.* MAR. mesana.

**mizzenmast** (-mæst) *s.* MAR. palo de mesana.

**mnemonic(al** (nima·nik(al) *adj.* mnemotécnico.

**mnemonics** (-s) *s.* mnemónica, mnemotecnia.

**Moabite** (mou·abait) *adj.-m.* moabita.

**moan** (moun) *s.* gemido, quejido, lamento. *2* murmullo [de las olas].

**moan (to)** *intr.* gemir, quejarse, lamentarse. *2 tr.* llorar, deplorar.

**moanful** (-ful) *adj.* plañidero.

**moat** (mout) *s.* FORT. foso.

**moat (to)** *tr.* rodear con fosos.

**mob** (mab) *s.* populacho, chusma; turba, turbamulta. *2* gentío, tropel.

**mob (to)** *tr.* atacar, rodear tumultuosamente. *2 intr.* tumultuarse. ¶ Pret. y p. p.: *mobbed*; ger.: *-bbing*.

**mobcap** (-kæp) *s.* toca o cofia de mujer.

**mobile** (mou·bil) *adj.* móvil. *2* inconstante, variable.

**mobility** (moubi·liti) *s.* movilidad. *2* inconstancia.

**mobilization** (moubiliši·shøn) *s.* movilización.

**mobilize (to)** (mou·bilaiš) *tr.* movilizar.

**moccasin** (ma·kasin) *s.* mocasín [calzado, serpiente].

**Mocha** (mou·ka) *n. pr.* GEOGR. Moca. *2 s.* (con min.) moca [café].

**mock** (mak) *adj.* ficticio, falso, imitado. *2* fingido, burlesco. *3* BOT. *~ cypress*, mirabel; *~ orange*, jeringuilla. *4 s.* burla, mofa, irrisión. *5* remedo.

**mock (to)** *tr.* mofarse de, burlarse de, escarnecer; reírse [de]; engañar. *2* imitar, remedar. *3 intr. to ~ at*, burlarse de.

**mockery** (-øri) *s.* burla, mofa, escarnio. *2* remedo, imitación.

**mock-heroic** *adj.* épico-burlesco.

**moking** (-ing) *adj.* burlón, mofador.
**mockingbird** (-bø·ʳd) *s.* ORN. sinsonte.
**modal** (mou·dal) *adj.* modal.
**modality** (modæ·liti) *s.* modalidad.
**mode** (moud) *s.* modo, manera. *2* GRAM., LÓG., ME-
TAL., MÚS. modo. *3* moda, estilo, uso.
**model** (ma·døl) *s.* modelo. *2* patrón, plantilla. *3*
diseño, muestra. *4* figurín. *5* dechado, ejemplo.
*6 adj.* modelo: ~ *school*, escuela modelo.
**model (to)** *tr.* modelar, formar, moldear. *2 intr.* posar como modelo. ¶ Pret. y p. p.: *model(l)ed;* ger.:
*-l(l)ing.*
**model(l)er** (-øʳ) *s.* modelador. *2* diseñador.
**model(l)ling** (-ing) *s.* B. ART. modelado.
**model(l)ist** (-ist) *s.* modelista.
**moderate** (ma·dørit) *adj.* moderado; templado. *2*
morigerado. *3* mesurado. *4* módico. *5* mediano,
regular. *6 s.* POL. moderado.
**moderate (to)** (ma·døreit) *tr.* moderar; templar;
reprimir; morigerar. *2 tr.-intr.* presidir [una
reunión, etc.]. *3 intr.* moderarse.
**moderation** (-ei·shøn) *s.* moderación: *in* ~, con
moderación. *2* sobriedad, templanza. *3* mesura,
comedimiento.
**moderator** (-eitøʳ) *s.* moderador. *2* concordador,
árbitro. *3* MEC. regulador.
**modern** (ma·døʳn) *adj.* moderno.
**modernism** (-išm) *s.* modernismo.
**modernist** (-ist) *s.* modernista.
**modernistic** (-i·stik) *adj.* modernista.
**modernity** (mødø·ʳniti) *s.* modernidad.
**modernize (to)** (ma·døʳnaiš) *tr.* modernizar. *2 intr.*
modernizarse.
**modest** (ma·dist) *adj.* modesto, recatado, decente.
*2* modesto, humilde. *3* moderado [no excesivo].
**modesty** (-i) *s.* modestia. *2* pudor, recato, decencia.
**modicum** (ma·dikøm) *s.* poco, pequeña cantidad.
**modification** (madifikei·shøn) *s.* modificación.
**modifier** (ma·difaiøʳ) *s.* modificador. *2* GRAM. palabra modificativa.
**modify (to)** (-fai) *tr.* modificar. *2* moderar, templar, suavizar. *3 intr.* modificarse, variar. ¶ Pret.
y p. p.: *modified.*
**modillion** (modi·liøn) *s.* ARQ. modillón.
**modish** (mou·dish) *adj.* a la moda, hecho a la
moda.
**modulate (to)** (ma·diuleit) *tr.* modular. *2* regular,
ajustar. *3 intr.* MÚS. modular.
**modulation** (madiulei·shøn) *s.* modulación.
**modulator** (ma·diuleitøʳ) *s.* modulador.
**module** (ma·dÿul) *s.* ARQ., HIDR., NUM. módulo.
**modulus** (ma·diuløs) *s.* MAT. módulo.
**mof(f)ette** (mofe·t) *s.* mofeta [gas].
**Mogul** (mogø·l) *s.* mogol: *the Great* ~, el Gran Mogol. *2 pl.* naipes de superior calidad.
**mohair** (mou·jeøʳ) *s.* mohair.
**Mohammed** (moujæ·mid) *n. pr.* Mahoma.
**Mohammedan** (moujæ·midan) *s.* mahometano.
**Mohammedanism** (-išm) *s.* mahometismo.
**moiety** (mo·ieti) *s.* mitad.
**moil (to)** (moul) *intr.* afanarse, trabajar sin descanso.
**moire, moiré** (muaʳ, muarei·) *s.* muaré.
**moist** (moist) *adj.* húmedo, mojado. *2* guanoso.
**moisten (to)** (moi·søn) *tr.* humedecer, humectar,
mojar ligeramente. *2 intr.* humedecerse.
**moisture** (moi·schøʳ) *s.* humedad. *2* sudor.
**molar** (mou·laʳ) *adj.* ANAT., FÍS. molar. *2 s.* molar
[diente].
**molary** (mou·lari) *adj.* molar.

**molasses** (mølæ·siš) *s.* melaza, melote.
**mold, to mold,** etc., MOULD, TO MOULD, etc.
**Moldavian** (maldæ·vian) *adj.-s.* moldavo.
**mole** (moul) *s.* MED. mola. *2* lunar. *3* rompeolas;
dársena. *4* ZOOL. topo. *5* ENT. ~ *cricket*, cortón,
grillotalpa.
**molecular** (møle·kiulaʳ) *adj.* molecular.
**molecule** (ma·likiul) *s.* molécula.
**molehill** (mou·ljil) *s.* topera, topinera. *2* (fig.) pequeño obstáculo, dificultad, etc.
**moleskin** (-skin) *s.* piel de topo. *2* especie de fustán. *3 pl.* pantalón de esta tela.
**molest (to)** (mole·st) *tr.* molestar, inquietar, vejar.
*2* faltar al respeto [a una mujer].
**molestation** (molestei·shøn) *s.* molestia, vejación.
**mollification** (malifikei·shøn) *s.* molificación. *2*
mitigación. *3* apaciguamiento.
**mollify (to)** (ma·lifai) *tr.* molificar. *2* mitigar. *3* calmar, aplacar, apaciguar. ¶ Pret. y p. p.: *mol-
lified.*
**mollusc** (ma·løsk) *s.* ZOOL. molusco.
**Molly** (ma·li) *n. pr. dim.* de MARY, Mariquita.
**mollycoddle** (-kadøl) *s.* marica, mantecón.
**mollycoddle (to)** *tr.* consentir, mimar.
**Moloch** (mou·lak) *n. pr.* MIT. Moloc. *2 s.* (con min.)
ZOOL. moloc.
**molt, to molt,** MOULT, TO MOULT.
**molten** (mou·ltøn) *p. p. irreg.* de TO MELT. *2 adj.* fundido [metal].
**molybdenum** (moli·bdønøm) *s.* QUÍM. molibdeno.
**moment** (mou·mønt) *s.* momento, instante, coyuntura: *at any* ~, de un momento a otro; *for the* ~,
de momento, por el momento. *2* momento, importancia. *3* MEC. momento.
**momentarily** (-erili) *adv.* momentáneamente. *2*
instantáneamente.
**momentary** (-eri) *adj.* momentáneo. *2* que ocurre
a cada momento.
**momently** (mou·møntli) *adv.* a cada momento. *2*
por momentos. *3* por un momento.
**momentous** (moume·ntøs) *adj.* importante, grave,
trascendental.
**momentum** (-øm) *s.* ímpetu, impulso, velocidad
adquirida. *2* MEC. cantidad de movimiento.
**Momus** (mou·møs) *n. pr.* MIT. Momo.
**monachal** (ma·nakal) *adj.* monacal.
**monachism** (ma·nakišm) *s.* monaquismo, monacato.
**monad** (ma·næd) *s.* mónada.
**monadelphous** (manade·lføs) *adj.* BOT. monadelfo.
**monadism** (ma·nædišm) *s.* monadismo.
**monarch** (ma·naʳk) *s.* monarca.
**monarchic (al** (møna·ʳkik(al) *adj.* monárquico.
**monarchism** (ma·naʳkišm) *s.* monarquismo.
**monarchist** (-ist) *s.* monárquico.
**monarchy** (-i) *s.* monarquía.
**monastery** (ma·nasteri) *s.* monasterio, convento.
**monastic(al** (mønæ·stik(al) *adj.* monástico.
**Monday** (mø·ndi) *s.* lunes.
**monetary** (mø·niteri) *adj.* monetario. *2* pecuniario.
**monetize (to)** (-aiš) *tr.* monetizar.
**money** (mø·ni) *s.* moneda, dinero: ~ *of account*,
moneda de cuenta; *hard* ~, metálico; *ready* ~,
dinero contante; ~ *changing*, cambio de moneda; ~ *order*, giro postal.
**moneyage** (-idÿ) *s.* monedaje.
**moneybag** (-bæg) *s.* talega, bolsa. *2 pl. fam.* tale-
gas, riqueza. *3 fam.* ricacho.
**money-changer** *s.* cambista.
**moneyed** (-d) *adj.* adinerado, acaudalado.

**money-lender** s. prestamista.
**money-making** s. lucro, ganancia. 2 prosperidad. 3 adj. lucrativo, provechoso.
**monger** (mø·ngø<sup>r</sup>) s. tratante, traficante.
**Mongol** (ma·ngøl) adj.-s. mogol, mongol.
**Mongolia** (mangou·lia) n. pr. GEOGR. Mogolia.
**Mongolian** (-n) adj.-s. mogol, mongol, mongólico.
**mongoose** (ma·ngus) s. ZOOL. mangosta.
**mongrel** (møn·grøl) adj.-s. mestizo. 2 s. animal o planta cruzados; perro de raza indefinida.
**monism** (ma·nišm) s. monismo.
**monition** (mouni·shøn) s. aviso, consejo, advertencia, amonestación.
**monitor** (ma·nito<sup>r</sup>) s. amonestador, admonitor. 2 instructor. 3 MAR., ZOOL. monitor.
**monitor (to)** tr. amonestar, advertir. 2 RADIO. controlar.
**monk** (mønk) s. monje, fraile.
**monkery** (-øri) s. monasterio. 2 vida monástica, frailía. 3 cosa de fraile.
**monkey** (-i) s. ZOOL. mono, mona, mico, simio. 2 fig. mono, mona [pers.]. 3 *to make a ~ of*, tomar el pelo a uno. 4 *to get one's ~ up*, montar en cólera. 5 adj. de mono: *~ trick*, monería. 6 MEC. *~ wrench*, llave inglesa.
**monkey (to)** tr. imitar, remedar. 2 intr. *to ~ about*, hacer payasadas. 3 *to ~ with*, enredar con.
**monkeyshine** (-shain) s. fam. (E.U.) monería, payasada.
**monkhood** (mø·nkjud) s. monacato. 2 los monjes.
**monkish** (mø·nkish) adj. monacal; frailesco.
**monk's-hood** s. BOT. acónito, anapelo.
**monobasic** (manøbei·sik) adj. QUÍM. monobásico.
**monochord** (ma·nøko<sup>r</sup>d) s. MÚS. monocordio.
**monochrome** (-kroum) adj. monocromo.
**monocle** (-køl) s. monóculo.
**monocled** (-køld) adj. con monóculo.
**monoclinic** (manøkli·nik) adj. CRISTAL. monoclínico.
**monocotyledon** (manøkatil·døn) s. BOT. monocotiledónea.
**monocular** (mønə·kiula<sup>r</sup>) adj. monóculo. 2 para un solo ojo.
**monody** (ma·nødi) s. MÚS. monodia. 2 elegía.
**monoecious** (moni·shøs) adj. BOT. monoico.
**monogamous** (mønə·gamøs) adj. monógamo.
**monogamy** (-i) s. monogamia.
**monogram** (ma·nøgræm) s. monograma.
**monograph** (-f) s. monografía.
**monolith** (-liz) s. monolito.
**monolithic** (manøli·zik) adj. monolítico.
**monologist** (ma·nolodgist) s. monologador.
**monologize (to)** (mønə·lodỹaiš) intr. monologar.
**monologue** (ma·nølag) s. monólogo; soliloquio.
**monomania** (manømei·nia) s. monomanía.
**monometallism** (-e·tališm) s. monometalismo.
**monomial** (manou·mial) adj. MAT. de un solo término. 2 s. monomio.
**monopetalous** (manøpe·taløs) adj. BOT. monopétalo.
**monophase** (ma·nøfeiš) adj. ELECT. monofásico.
**monoplane** (-plein) s. monoplano.
**monopolist** (mønə·polist) s. monopolista.
**monopolize (to)** (-aiš) tr. monopolizar.
**monopolizer** (-šø<sup>r</sup>) s. monopolizador.
**monopoly** (-i) s. monopolio.
**monopteral** (-ptøral) adj. ARQ. monóptero.
**monorail** (ma·nøreil) s. vía de un solo riel.
**monosepalous** (manøse·paløs) adj. BOT. monosépalo.
**monospermous** (-spø·<sup>r</sup>møs) adj. BOT. monospermo.

**monosyllable** (manøsi·labøl) s. monosílabo.
**monotheism** (ma·nøziišm) s. monoteísmo.
**monotheist** (-st) s. monoteísta.
**monotone** (-toun) s. monotonía; unisonancia.
**monotone (to)** tr. cantar, recitar, etc., en un tono uniforme.
**monotonous** (møna·tønøs) adj. monótono.
**monotony** (møna·tøni) s. monotonía. 2 unisonancia.
**monotreme** (ma·nøtrim) s. ZOOL. monotrema.
**monotype** (-taip) s. BIOL. representante único de un género, familia, etc. 2 IMPR. monotipia.
**monovalent** (-vei·lønt) adj. QUÍM. monovalente.
**monoxide** (møna·ksaid) s. QUÍM. monovalente.
**Monseigneur** (monseñø·<sup>r</sup>) s. monseñor.
**monsoon** (mansu·n) s. monzón.
**monster** (ma·nstø<sup>r</sup>) s. monstruo. 2 adj. monstruo, enorme.
**monstrance** (-trans) s. LITURG. custodia, ostensorio.
**monstrosity** (manstra·siti) s. monstruosidad.
**monstrous** (ma·nstrøs) adj. monstruoso.
**monte** (ma·nti) s. monte [juego de naipes].
**month** (mønz) s. mes.
**monthly** (-li) adj. mensual: *~ allowance, pay*, etc., mensualidad, mesada. 2 menstrual. 3 s. publicación mensual.
**monument** (ma·niumønt) s. monumento.
**monumental** (-e·ntal) adj. monumental. 2 conmemorativo.
**moo** (mu) s. mugido.
**moo (to)** intr. mugir.
**modd** (mud) s. genio, talante. 2 humor, disposición: *to be in no ~ for o to*, no tener ganas de. 3 capricho. 4 GRAM., LÓG., MÚS. modo. 5 pl. mal humor.
**moody** (-i) adj. malhumorado, mohíno, irritable, triste, caviloso. 2 raro, caprichoso, variable, veleidoso.
**moon** (mun) s. luna [satélite; lunación]: *new ~*, luna nueva; *full ~*, luna llena; *once in a blue ~*, fig. muy raras veces. 2 luz de la luna. 3 ASTR. satélite.
**moon (to)** intr. andar absorto y distraído.
**moonbeam** (-bim) s. rayo de luna.
**moon-calf** s. bobo, tonto.
**moonfish** (-fish) s. ICT. pez luna.
**moonlight** (-lait) s. luz de la luna. 2 escena iluminada por la luna.
**moonlit** (-lit) adj. iluminado por la luna.
**moonrise** (-raiš) s. salida de la luna.
**moonshine** (-shain) s. claridad de la luna. 2 cosa sin substancia; vana fantasía. 3 (E.U.) licor, whisky, destilado clandestinamente.
**moonshiner** (-ø<sup>r</sup>) s. (E.U.) destilador clandestino.
**moonstruck** (-strøk) adj. lunático.
**moony** (-i) adj. lunado. 2 alelado, bobo.
**moor** (mu<sup>r</sup>) s. páramo, brezal, marjal: *~ cock*, lagópodo.
**Moor** s. moro. 2 sarraceno.
**moor (to)** tr. MAR. amarrar, anclar [un buque]. 2 aferrar, arraigar, fijar en un sitio. 3 intr. MAR. anclar, estar amarrado o anclado [un buque].
**moorage** (mu·ridỹ) s. MAR. amarraje.
**mooring** (mu·ring) s. MAR. amarre: *~ berth*, amarradero. 2 MAR. amarra. 3 pl. MAR. amarradero, anclaje.
**Moorish** adj. moro, morisco. 2 ARQ. árabe.
**moorland** (mu·<sup>r</sup>lænd) s. paramera, marjal, brezal.
**moose** (mus) s. ZOOL. anta, alce americano.

**moot** (mut) *adj.* discutible, en discusión. *2* que se discute como ejercicio.

**moot (to)** *tr.* discutir, debatir [esp. como ejercicio].

**mop** (map) *s.* aljofifa, rodilla. *2* greña, cabello revuelto. *3* mueca.

**mop (to)** *tr.* aljofifar, fregar. *2* enjugar, limpiar [el sudor, etc.]. *3* MIL. *to ~ up*, limpiar de enemigos. *4 intr.* hacer muecas. ¶ Pret. y p. p.: *mopped*; ger.: *-pping.*

**mope** (moup) *s.* persona abatida, desanimada, apática. *2 pl.* murria, melancolía, aburrimiento.

**mope (to)** *intr.* andar abatido y melancólico; aburrirse.

**mopish** (-ish) *adj.* abatido, melancólico.

**mopping-up** *s.* MIL. operación de limpieza.

**moquete** (moke·t) *s.* moqueta.

**mora** (mou·ra) *s.* morra [juego].

**moraine** (morei·n) *s.* GEOL. morena.

**moral** (ma·ral) *adj.* moral: *~ support*, apoyo moral. *2* virtuoso. *3* que tiene sentido moral. *4 s.* moraleja, moralidad, enseñanza. *5 pl.* moral, ética. *6* moral [costumbres, conducta].

**morale** (moræ·l) *s.* moral [estado de ánimo].

**moralist** (ma·ralist) *s.* moralista. *2* moralizador. *3* el que lleva una vida moral.

**morality** (moræ·liti) *s.* moralidad. *2* moraleja. *3* moral [ciencia]. *4* principios éticos [de un hombre, etc.]. *5* TEAT. antiguo drama moral.

**moralize (to)** (ma·ralaiš) *tr.* moralizar. *2* deducir una moraleja de. *3 intr.* moralizar.

**moralizer** (-ø<sup>r</sup>) *s.* moralizador.

**morass** (møra·s) *s.* pantano, cenagal. *2* fig. atolladero.

**moratorium** (morato·riøm) *s.* moratoria.

**moray** (mourei·) *s.* ICT. morena.

**morbid** (mo·<sup>r</sup>bid) *adj.* mórbido, morboso. *2* horrible, espantoso.

**morbidity** (mo<sup>r</sup>bi·diti) *s.* morbosidad. *2* morbididad.

**mordacious** (mo·dei·shøs) *adj.* mordaz, cáustico.

**mordacity** (mo<sup>r</sup>dæ·siti) *s.* mordacidad.

**mordant** (mo·<sup>r</sup>dant) *adj.* mordiente, corrosivo. *2* acre, mordaz. *3 s.* mordente, mordiente.

**mordent** (-ønt) *s.* MÚS. mordente.

**more** (mo<sup>r</sup>) *adj.-adv.* más: *any ~*, ya no; *~ and ~*, más y más, cada vez más; *~ or less*, (poco) más o menos; *neither*, o *no, ~ nor less*, ni más ni menos, exactamente; *no ~*, no más; ya no; se acabó; *once ~*, otra vez; *so much the ~*, tanto más; *the ~* ... *the better*, cuanto más... mejor; *the ~ the merrier*, cuantos más mejor; *the ~* ...*the more*, cuanto más... más.

**morel** (møre·l) *s.* BOT. colmenilla, cagarria.

**moreover** (morou·vø<sup>r</sup>) *adv.* además, por otra parte, también.

**Moresque** (more·sk) *adj.* moro, morisco. *2* B. ART. árabe. *3 s.* B. ART. estilo árabe.

**morganatic** (mø<sup>r</sup>ganæ·tik) *adj.* morganático.

**morgue** (mo·<sup>r</sup>g) *s.* depósito de cadáveres.

**moribund** (mo·ribønd) *adj.* moribundo.

**morion** (mou·riøn) *s.* morrión [casco].

**Morisco** (møri·skou) *adj.-s.* morisco.

**Mormon** (mo·<sup>r</sup>møn) *s.* mormón.

**morn** (mo<sup>r</sup>n) poét. mañana.

**morning** (mo·<sup>r</sup>ning) *s.* mañana [primera parte del día; de la vida]: *good ~*, buenos días; *tomorrow ~*, mañana por la mañana. *2* alba, aurora, albores. *3 adj.* de la mañana, del alba, matinal, matutino: *~ coat*, chaqué; *~ gown*, bata; *~ star*, lucero del alba.

**morning-glory** *s.* BOT. dondiego de día.

**Moroccan** (møra·kan) *adj.-s.* marroquí, marrueco.

**morocco** (møra·kou) *s.* marroquí, tafilete.

**Morocco** *n. pr.* GEOGR. Marruecos.

**moron** (mou·ran) *s.* atrasado mental.

**morose** (mørou·s) *adj.* malhumorado, hosco, displicente, arisco. *2* moroso.

**morosity** (-a·siti) *s.* mal humor, displicencia.

**Morpheus** (mo·<sup>r</sup>fius) *n. pr.* MIT. Morfeo.

**morphia** (mo·<sup>r</sup>fia), **morphine** (mo·<sup>r</sup>fin) *s.* morfina.

**morphinism** (-išm) *s.* MED. morfinismo.

**morphology** (mo<sup>r</sup>fa·lodŷi) *s.* morfología.

**Morris** (ma·ris) *n. pr.* Mauricio.

**morris dance** *s.* danza grotesca, mojiganga.

**morrow** (mo·rou) *s.* mañana, día siguiente: *on the ~*, en el día de mañana, el día siguiente. *2* ant. mañana [primera parte del día].

**morse** (mo·<sup>r</sup>s) *s.* ZOOL. morsa.

**Morse code** *s.* TELEGR. alfabeto Morse.

**morsel** (mo·rsøl) *s.* bocado [comida]. *2* pedacito.

**mortal** (mo·<sup>r</sup>tal) *adj.* mortal: *~ sin*, pecado mortal. *2* de la muerte. *3* a muerte. *4* letal, fatal. *5 s.* mortal.

**mortality** (mo<sup>r</sup>tæ·liti) *s.* mortalidad. *2* humanidad, género humano; naturaleza humana.

**mortalize (to)** (mo·<sup>r</sup>talaiš) *tr.* hacer mortal.

**mortar** (mo·<sup>r</sup>ta<sup>r</sup>) *s.* mortero, almirez. *2* ARTILL. mortero. *3* PIROT. morterete. *4* mortero, argamasa.

**mortarboard** (-bo<sup>r</sup>d) *s.* ALBAÑ. esparavel. *2* birrete académico cuadrado.

**mortgage** (mo·<sup>r</sup>gidŷ) *s.* hipoteca.

**mortgage (to)** *tr.* hipotecar.

**mortician** (mo<sup>r</sup>ti·shan) *s.* UNDERTAKER 2.

**mortiferous** (mo<sup>r</sup>ti·førøs) *adj.* mortífero.

**mortification** (mo<sup>r</sup>tifike·shøn) *s.* mortificación.

**mortify (to)** (mo·<sup>r</sup>tifai) *tr.* mortificar, humillar, herir los sentimientos de. *2* mortificar [el cuerpo]. *3* MED. mortificar. *4 intr.* mortificarse. ¶ Pret. y p. p.: *mortifiea.*

**mortise** (mo·<sup>r</sup>tis) *s.* mortaja, muesca, caja, entalladura.

**mortise (to)** *tr.* hacer muescas o mortajas en.

**mortmain** (mo·<sup>r</sup>tmein) *s.* DER. manos muertas.

**mortuary** (mo·<sup>r</sup>chuæri) *adj.* mortuorio, funerario. *2 s.* depósito de cadáveres.

**Mosaic** (mošei·ik) *adj.* mosaico [de Moisés].

**mosaic** *s.* mosaico [obra taraceada].

**mosaicist** (mošei·isist) *s.* el que hace o vende mosaicos.

**Mosaism** (mo·šeiišm) *s.* mosaísmo.

**Moscow** (ma·skau) *n. pr.* GEOGR. Moscú.

**Moses** (mou·šiš) *n. pr.* Moisés.

**Moslem** (ma·šlem) *adj.-s.* muslime, musulmán.

**mosque** (mask) *s.* mezquita.

**mosquito** (møski·tou) *s.* ENT. mosquito: *~ net*, mosquitero.

**moss** (mos) *s.* BOT. musgo, musco; moho, verdín. *2 adj.* musgoso: *~ rose*, BOT. rosa musgosa.

**moss-grown** *adj.* musgoso [cubierto de musgo].

**mossy** (-i) *adj.* musgoso, mohoso.

**most** (moust) *adj.* (superl. de MORE, MUCH, MANY). *2* muchos, los más de, la mayoría de. *3* mayor: *for the ~ part*, en su mayor parte. *4* casi: *~ every body*, casi todos. *5 adv.* sumamente, muy; más: *Most Reverend*, reverendísimo; *the ~ courageous men*, los hombres más valientes. *6 s.* lo más, lo sumo: *at the ~*, a lo más, cuando más, a lo sumo.

**mostly** (-li) *adv.* en su mayor parte, principalmente; generalmente; casi, casi todo o todos.

**mote** (mout) *s.* mota de polvo: ~ *in another's eye,* fig. paja en el ojo ajeno.
**motel** (mou·tel) *s.* motel.
**motet** (mote·t) *s.* mús. motete.
**moth** (moz) *s.* polilla. *2* ent. pequeña mariposa nocturna.
**moth-eaten** *adj.* apolillado. *2 fig.* anticuado.
**mother** (mø·dø<sup>r</sup>) *s.* madre. *2* tía [mujer de edad]. *3 adj.* madre; materno; natal: ~ *country,* madre patria, país natal; ~ *tongue,* lengua madre; lengua materna. *4* natural, ingénito: ~ *wit,* inteligencia natural; chispa, ingenio.
**mother (to)** *tr.* servir de madre a. *2* reconocer por hijo. *3* ser causa u origen de.
**mother-in-law** *s.* madre política, suegra.
**motherhood** (-jud) *s.* maternidad. *2* madres.
**motherless** (-lis) *adj.* huérfano de madre.
**motherly** (-li) *adj.* maternal, materno.
**mother-of-pearl** *s.* nácar, madreperla.
**mothy** (mo·zi) *adj.* apolillado.
**motif** (mouti·f) *s.* mús., b. art. motivo, tema.
**motility** (mouti·liti) *s.* motilidad.
**motion** (mou·shøn) *s.* movimiento, moción. *2* impulso: *of his own* ~, de su propio impulso. *3* meneo. *4* seña, signo, ademán. *5* mec. juego, marcha; mecanismo. *6* mús. movimiento. *7* moción, proposición.
**motion (to)** *intr.-tr.* hacer seña o ademán [a uno].
**motionless** (-lis) *adj.* inmóvil, inmoble.
**motion picture** *s.* película [cinematográfica]. *2 pl.* cine, cinematógrafo.
**motivate (to)** (mou·tiveit) *tr.* motivar. *2* mover, impulsar.
**motive** (mou·tiv) *s.* motivo, causa, razón. *2* b. art., mús. motivo. *3 adj.* motor, motriz: ~ *power,* fuerza motriz.
**motley** (ma·tli) *adj.* abigarrado. *2 s.* abigarramiento, mezcolanza. *3* traje de bufón.
**motor** (mou·tø<sup>r</sup>) *s.* motor [lo que mueve]. *2* mec. motor. *3* automóvil. *4 adj.* motor, motriz. *5* de motor: automóvil. ~ *oil,* aceite lubricante de motores; ~ *ship,* motonave; ~ *truck,* autocamión.
**motor (to)** *tr.-intr.* llevar o ir en automóvil.
**motorboat** (-bout) *s.* canoa, automóvil.
**motorcade** (-keid) *s.* caravana o desfile de automóviles.
**motorcar** (-ka<sup>r</sup>) *s.* automóvil. *2* autocar. *3* (E.U.) coche motor.
**motorcycle** (-saikøl) *s.* motocicleta.
**motoring** (-ing) *s.* automovilismo.
**motorist** (-ist) *s.* motorista, automovilista.
**motorize (to)** (-aiš) *tr.* motorizar.
**motorman** (-mæn) *s.* conductor de tranvía o locomotora eléctrica.
**motorway** (mou·tø<sup>r</sup>uei) *s.* autopista.
**mottle** (ma·tøl) *s.* pinta, mancha, veta [de color].
**mottle (to)** *tr.* motear, jaspear, vetear, abigarrar.
**motto** (ma·tou), *pl.* **-toes** o **-tos** *s.* mote, lema, divisa. *2* máxima.
**mouf(f)lon** (mu·flan) *s.* zool. musmón.
**mould** (mould) *s.* moho [orgánico], verdín. *2* tierra vegetal, mantillo, barro. *3* molde, matriz, modelo. *4* forma, hechura. *5* carácter, índole. *6* arq. moldura.
**mould (to)** *tr.* amoldar. *2* moldear. *3* modelar. *4* moldurar. *5* agr. cubrir con mantillo. *6 intr.* enmohecerse, florecerse.
**mouldboard** (-bo<sup>r</sup>d) *s.* vertedera [del arado].
**moulder** (-ø<sup>r</sup>) *s.* moldeador.

**moulder (to)** *tr.* consumir, convertir en polvo. *2 intr.* consumirse, convertirse en polvo.
**moulding** (-ing) *s.* carp., arq. moldura. *2* amoldamiento, moldeado. *3* vaciado.
**mouldy** (-i) *adj.* mohoso, florecido.
**moult** (moult) *s.* moulting.
**moult (to)** *tr.* mudar [la pluma, la piel, etc.]. *2 intr.* mudar, hacer la muda [un animal].
**moulting** (-ing) *s.* muda [de los animales].
**mound** (maund) *s.* montón de tierra, montículo, túmulo. *2* terraplén, atrincheramiento.
**mound (to)** *tr.* amontonar. *2* cercar, atrincherar.
**mount** (maunt) *s.* monte, montaña. *2* manera de montar [a caballo, en bicicleta, etc.]. *3* montura, cabalgadura. *4* mil. monta [toque]. *5* montura [de un objeto]. *7* varillaje [de abanico]. *8* ~ *of piety,* monte de piedad.
**mount (to)** *tr.* subir [una cuesta, etc.]. *2* subir, elevarse por. *3* subir, levantar, alzar. *4* montar o montarse en o sobre. *5* montar [poner a caballo, dar caballo]. *6* montar, armar, engastar, engarzar. *7* teat. poner en escena. *8* mar. montar [tantos cañones]. *9* mil. montar [la guardia]. *10 intr.* subir, elevarse. *11* remontarse. *12* subir, aumentar. *13* subirse, montarse [en o sobre]. *14* ascender [una cuenta].
**mountain** (mau·ntin) *s.* montaña, monte. *2 adj.* montañés, montés, de montaña, montañoso; ~ *ash,* bot. especie de serbal; ~ *chain,* cadena de montañas; ~ *climber,* montañero; ~ *dew,* whisky de contrabando; ~ *lion,* puma; ~ *range,* cordillera, sierra.
**mountaineer** (-i-<sup>r</sup>) *s.* montañés. *2* alpinista, montañero.
**mountaineer (to)** *intr.* practicar el alpinismo.
**mountaineering** (-ing) *s.* alpinismo, montañismo.
**mountainous** (mau·ntinøs) *adj.* montañoso, montuoso. *2* enorme.
**mountebank** (mou·ntibænk) *s.* charlatán, truhán.
**mounted** (-id) *adj.* montado.
**mounting** (-ing) *s.* subida, ascensión. *2* monta [acción]. *3* montaje. *4* montura, engaste, marco.
**mourn (to)** (mou<sup>r</sup>n) *tr.* deplorar, lamentar, llorar. *2 intr.* lamentarse, dolerse. *3 to ~ for,* llevar luto por; llorar a.
**mourner** (-ø<sup>r</sup>) *s.* afligido, el que llora una pérdida. *2* enlutado. *3* plañidera.
**mournful** (-ful) *adj.* triste, lúgubre, lastimero, fúnebre. *2* apesadumbrado, dolorido. *3* entristecedor.
**mourning** (-ing) *s.* aflicción, dolor, pesar, duelo. *2* lamento, llanto. *3* luto; *to be in* ~, estar de luto. *4 adj.* triste, dolorido, lamentoso. *5* de luto. *6* bot. ~ *bride,* o *widow,* viuda.
**mouse** (mous), *pl.* **mice** (mais) *s.* zool. ratón.
**mouse (to)** *intr.* cazar razones. *2* andar a la caza o al acecho; husmear.
**mouse-ear** *s.* bot. miosotis. *2* bot. vellosilla.
**mousehole** (-joul) *s.* ratonera [agujero].
**mouser** (-ø<sup>r</sup>) *s.* perro o gato ratonero.
**mousetrap** (-træp) *s.* ratonera [trampa].
**mousse** (mus) *s.* coc. especie de crema batida.
**moustache** (møstæ·sh) *s.* mustache.
**mouth** (mouz) *s.* anat. boca: ~ *organ,* mús. armónica; zampoña; *down in the* ~, alicaído, cariacontecido; *to keep one's* ~ *shut,* guardar silencio. *2* boca [entrada, abertura, orificio]. *3* bocas, desembocadura [de un río].
**mouth (to)** *tr.* decir, proferir, vocear, declamar. *2* coger con la boca; tomar en la boca. *3 intr.* ha-

blar [con voz hueca], gritar, declamar. *4* hacer una mueca.

**mouther** (-øʳ) *s.* declamador.

**mouthful** (-ful) *s.* bocado [de comida]. *2* pizca.

**mouthpiece** (-pɪs) *s.* MÚS. boquilla, embocadura, estrangul, tudel. *2* bocado [del freno]. *3* bocal [de bota]. *4* portavoz, vocero.

**mouthwash** (-uash) *s.* enjuague, colutorio.

**mouthy** (-i) *adj.* gritón. *2* ampuloso, pomposo.

**movable** (muˑvabøl) *adj.* movible, móvil; locomovible. *2 s. pl.* muebles, mobiliario, efectos.

**move** (muv) *s.* movimiento [acción de moverse]: *to get a ~ on,* menearse, darse prisa; *on the ~,* en movimiento. *2* cambio de sitio. *3* jugada [de damas, ajedrez, etc.]. *4* paso, diligencia. *5* moción, propuesta.

**move (to)** *tr.* mover. *2* inducir, persuadir, inclinar. *3* menear. *4* remover, trasladar, mudar. *5* conmover, enternecer. *6* excitar [un sentimiento]. *7* proponer [en una asamblea]. *8* jugar [una pieza, un peón]. *9* exonerar [el vientre]. *10 intr.* moverse; andar: *to ~ about,* moverse, ir de un lado a otro; *to ~ away,* irse, alejarse, apartarse; *to ~ forward,* adelantarse, avanzar; *to ~ round,* dar vueltas. *11* irse, partir, ponerse en marcha. *12* trasladarse, mudarse. *13* marchar, progresar. *14* jugar [hacer una jugada].

**movement** (-mønt) *s.* movimiento [en todos sus sentidos]. *2* MEC. mecanismo, máquina [de reloj, etc.]. *3* MÚS. tiempo [división de una obra].

**mover** (-øʳ) *s.* movedor, motor. *2* promovedor. *3* autor de una moción. *4* el que se ocupa del traslado de muebles.

**movie** (-i) *s.* película [de cine]. *2 pl. the movies,* el cine.

**movie-goer** *s.* fam. aficionado al cine.

**moving** (-ing) *s.* movimiento, moción. *2* traslado, mudanza. *3 adj.* móvil, que se mueva: *~ picture,* MOTION PICTURE; *~ staircase* o *stairway,* escalera mecánica. *4* motor, motriz, que mueve: *~ spirit,* alma [de una empresa]. *5* conmovedor. *6* de mudanzas: *~ van,* carro de mudanzas.

**mow** (mau) *s.* almiar; granero, henil.

**mow (to)** (mou) *tr.* segar, guadañar, dallar. ¶ P. P.: *mowed* o *mown.*

**mower** (-øʳ) *s.* segador, guadañador, dallador. *2* segadora o guadañadora mecánica; máquina para cortar el césped.

**mown** (-n) *p. p. irr.* de TO MOW.

**Mozarab** (mouˑšæˑrab) *adj.-s.* mozárabe.

**mozetta** (mošeˑta) *s.* ECLES. muceta.

**much** (møch) *adj.* mucho, mucha: *~ ado about nothing,* mucho ruido para nada. *2 adv.* muy, mucho: *as ~,* tanto; otro tanto; *as ~ as,* tanto como; *how ~?,* ¿cuánto?; *~ the same,* casi lo mismo; *so ~,* tanto; *so ~ the better,* tanto mejor; *very ~,* muchísimo. *3 s.* mucho, gran cosa: *~ of a [gentleman,* etc.]; todo un [caballero, etc.]; *to make ~ of,* tener en mucho, festejar.

**muchness** (-nis) *s.* cantidad, demasía.

**mucilage** (miuˑsilidÿ) *s.* mucílago.

**mucilaginous** (miusilæˑdÿinøs) *adj.* mucilaginoso.

**muck** (møk) *s.* estiércol húmedo. *2* suciedad pegajosa; porquería. *3* desp. dinero.

**muck (to)** *tr.* AGR. estercolar. *2* fam. *to ~ up,* ensuciar.

**muckworm** (-uøʳm) *s.* gusano de muladar. *2* fig. golfo, pillete. *3* fig. avaro.

**mucky** (-i) *adj.* sucio, asqueroso.

**mucosa** (miukouˑsa) *pl.* **-sae** *s.* ANAT. mucosa.

**mucosity** (miukaˑsiti) *s.* mucosidad, viscosidad.

**mucous** (miuˑkøs) *adj.* mucoso: *~ membrane,* membrana mucosa.

**mucus** (miuˑkøs) *s.* moco, mucosidad.

**mud** (mød) *s.* barro, lodo, fango: *~ bath,* baño de lodo; *~ wall,* tapia; *to sling ~ at,* llenar de fango, difamar.

**mud (to)** *tr.* enlodar, embarrar. *2* enturbiar.

**muddle** (-øl) *s.* enredo, embrollo, confusión, lío, desorden.

**muddle (to)** *tr.* enredar, embrollar, confundir. *2* enturbiar. *3* embriagar, entontecer. *4 intr.* hacerse un lío, enredar las cosas: *to ~ through,* hacer algo torpemente, salir del paso a duras penas.

**muddle-head** *s.* estúpido, atontado.

**muddy** (-i) *adj.* barroso, fangoso, lodoso. *2* embarrado, enlodado. *3* turbio, empañado. *4* confuso, obscuro.

**muddy (to)** *tr.* embarrar, enlodar, ensuciar. *2* enturbiar. *3* obscurecer, entontecer, turbar. ¶ Pret. y p. p.: *muddied;* ger.: *-ddying.*

**Mudejar** (muðeiˑjaʳ) *adj.-s.* mudéjar.

**mudguard** (møˑdgaʳd) *s.* guardabarros.

**mudhole** (møˑdjoul) *s.* atolladero.

**muezzin** (miuˑšin) *s.* almuecín, almuédano.

**muff** (møf) *s.* manguito [de piel]. *2* MEC. manguito. *3* torpeza, fracaso. *4* fam. torpe, tonto.

**muff (to)** *tr.-intr.* hacer algo torpemente.

**muffin** (møˑfin) *s.* bollo o panecillo redondo.

**muffle** (møˑføl) *s.* mufla. *2* MITTEN. *3* apagador de sonido. *4* cuadernal. *5* hocico, morro.

**muffle (to)** *tr.* envolver, embozar, cubrir, tapar. *2* envolver con ropa la cabeza de [uno] para que no vea, oiga, grite, etc. *3* apagar [un sonido]. *4* *to ~ a drum,* enfundar o destemplar un tambor.

**muffler** (-løʳ) *s.* bufanda, tapaboca, embozo. *2* MEC. silenciador. *3* MÚS. apagador. *4* guante de boxeo.

**mufti** (-ti) *s.* muftí. *2* MIL. (Ingl.) traje de paisano.

**mug** (møg) *s.* jarro [para beber]. *2* pop. cara, jeta. *3* pop. (Ingl.) primo, tonto. *4* fam. (Ingl.) empollón. *5* mueca, visaje.

**mug (to)** *tr.* fam. fotografiar [esp. a los criminales]. *2 intr.* (Ingl.) empollar [para un examen]. *3 tr.-intr.* hacer muecas.

**muggy** (-i) *adj.* húmedo, cargado, bochornoso, sofocante [aire, tiempo].

**mugwort** (-wøʳt) *s.* BOT. artemisa.

**mulatto** (miulæˑtou) *adj.-m.* mulato.

**mulattress** (miulæˑtris) *adj.-f.* mulata.

**mulberry** (møˑlberi) *s.* BOT. moral: *white ~,* morera. *2* mora [fruto]. *3* BOT. (Ingl.) zarza, zarzamora.

**mulct** (mølkt) *s.* multa.

**mulct (to)** *tr.* multar. *2* privar [de].

**mule** (miul) *s.* ZOOL. mulo, macho: *she-mule,* mula. *2* fig. mula [pers. terca y necia]. *3* BIOL. planta o animal híbridos. *4* cierta máquina de hilar.

**mule-jenny** *s.* MULE [máquina de hilar].

**muleteer** (miuletiˑʳ) *s.* mulero, mulatero.

**mull** (møl) *s.* muselina clara. *2* fam. confusión, lío; fracaso.

**mull (to)** *tr.* calentar [vino, etc.] con azúcar y especias. *2* fam. confundir, enredar.

**mullein** (møˑlin) *s.* BOT. verbasco, gordolobo.

**muller** (møˑløʳ) *s.* moleta.

**mullet** (møˑlet) *s.* ICT. mújol, múgil. *2* ICT. *red ~,* salmonete.

**mulligatawny** (møligatoˑni) *s.* sopa de arroz y carne sazonada con *curry.*

**mullion** (møˑliøn) *s.* ARQ. mainel, parteluz.

**mullioned** (-d) *adj.* ARQ. dividido por maineles o parteluces.

**mulse** (møls) *s.* vino mulso.

**multicoloured** (mølticø·løʳd) *adj.* multicolor.

**multifarious** (-fe·riøs) *adj.* múltiple, vario, variado, de varias clases.

**multiflorous** (-flo·røs) *adj.* multifloro.

**multifold** (mø·ltifould) *adj.* múltiple.

**multiform** (-foʳm) *adj.* multiforme.

**multimillionaire** (-milione·ʳ) *s.* multimillonario.

**multipara** (mølti·para) *f.* mujer multípara.

**multiparous** (-parøs) *adj.* multípara.

**multiphase** (mø·ltifeis) *adj.* ELECT. polifásico.

**multiple** (mø·ltipøl) *adj.* múltiple, multiplice. *2 s.* múltiplo. *3* ELECT. *in* ~, en paralelo.

**multiplex** (-plex) *adj.* multíplice.

**multiplicand** (-plikæ·nd) *s.* ARIT. multiplicando.

**multiplication** (-ei·shøn) *s.* multiplicación: ~ *table*, tabla de multiplicar.

**multiply** (tc) (-plai) *tr.* multiplicar. *2 intr.* multiplicarse. ¶ Pret. y p. p.: *multiplied*.

**multipolar** (-pou·laʳ) *adj.* multipolar.

**multitude** (mø·ltitiud) *s.* multitud, muchedumbre. *2* multitud, vulgo.

**multitudinous** (møltitiu·dinøs) *adj.* numeroso, numerosos. *2* multitudinario. *3* de muchos, compuesto o formado por muchos.

**multivalent** (-vei·lønt) *adj.* QUÍM. polivalente.

**multilocular** (-la·kiulaʳ) *adj.* BOT. plurilocular.

**mum** (møm) *s.* fam. mamá. *2 adj.* callado: *to keep* ~, callarse; *mum's the word*, punto en boca. *3 interj.* ¡chitón!, ¡silencio!

**mum (to)** *intr.* disfrazarse, hacer pantomima.

**mumble (to)** (-bøl) *tr.-intr.* mascullar, murmurar, musitar, barbotar. *2* mascujar.

**Mumbo Jumbo** (-bou jø·mbou) *s.* genio tutelar [entre los negros]. *2* fig. (con min.) coco, fetiche. *3* sortilegio ridículo; monserga.

**mummer** (-øʳ) *s.* máscara [pers.]. *2* bufón, histrión.

**mummery** (-øri) *s.* momería, mojiganga, mascarada.

**mummification** (mømifikei·shøn) *s.* momificación.

**mummify (to)** (mø·mifai) *tr.* momificar. *2 intr.* momificarse. ¶ Pret. y p. p.: *mummified*.

**mummy** (-i) *s.* momia. *2* mamá [voz infantil].

**mump (to)** (mømp) *intr.* estar murrio. *2* mendigar.

**mumpish** (-ish) *adj.* malhumorado.

**mumps** (-s) *s.* mal humor. *2* MED. paperas, parótida.

**munch (to)** (mønch) *tr.* mascar, ronzar.

**mundane** (mø·ndein) *adj.* mundano. *2* cósmico.

**mundanity** (miunda·niti) *s.* mundanalidad.

**mundify (to)** (mø·ndifai) *tr.* mundificar.

**municipal** (miuni·sipal) *adj.* municipal. *2* que tiene municipio [población].

**municipality** (miunisipæ·liti) *s.* municipalidad, municipio.

**municipalize (to)** (miuni·sipalaiš) *tr.* municipalizar.

**munificence** (miuni·fisøns) *s.* munificencia.

**munificient** (-t) *adj.* munificiente.

**muniment** (miu·nimønt) *s. pl.* DER. documentos o títulos que acreditan un derecho.

**munition (to)** *tr.* municionar, proveer.

**munitions** (miuni·shøns) *s. pl.* municiones.

**mural** (miu·ral) *adj.* mural. *2 s.* pintura mural; decoración mural.

**murder** (mø·ʳdøʳ) *s.* asesinato, homicidio.

**murder (to)** *tr.* asesinar, matar. *2* asesinar, destrozar, estropear [hacer o ejecutar mal].

**murderer** (-øʳ) *s.* asesino, homicidio, matador.

**murderess** (-is) *s.* asesina, matadora.

**murderous** (-øs) *adj.* asesino, homicida. *2* sanguinario, cruel. *3* mortífero, mortal, fatal.

**murex** (miu·reks), *pl.* **-rexes** o **-rices** (-risiš) *s.* ZOOL. múrice.

**murk(y** (mø·ʳk(i) *adj.* oscuro, lóbrego, sombrío.

**murmur** (mø·ʳmøʳ) *s.* murmullo, murmurio, susurro, rumor. *2* queja, descontento.

**murmur (to)** *intr.-tr.* murmurar, murmullar, susurrar. *2 intr.* quejarse, murmurar, refunfuñar: *to* ~ *at*, quejarse de.

**murmurous** (-øs) *adj.* rumoroso. *2* murmurante. *3* quejoso, murmurador.

**murrain** (mø·rin) *s.* VET. peste, fiebre aftosa.

**musaceous** (miušei·shøs) *adj.* BOT. musáceo.

**muscat** (mø·skæt), **muscatel** (møskate·l) *s.* moscatel [vid, uva, vino]. *2* pasa moscatel.

**muscid** (mø·sid) *adj.-s.* ENT. múscido.

**muscle** (mø·søl) *s.* ANAT. músculo. *2* fuerza muscular.

**muscosity** (møska·siti) *s.* calidad de musgoso.

**Muscovite** (mø·skøvait) *adj.-s.* moscovita.

**Muscovy** (-vi) *n. pr.* GEOGR. Moscovia.

**muscular** (mø·skiulaʳ) *adj.* muscular. *2* musculoso, vigoroso, fornido.

**musculature** (mø·skiu·lachøʳ) *s.* musculatura.

**Muse** (miuš) *s.* MIT. Musa. *2* (con min.) musa [que inspira; numen; poesía]. *3* meditación, abstracción.

**muse (to)** *intr.* meditar, reflexionar, cavilar. *2* estar o mirar absorto, distraído.

**museum** (miuši·øm) *s.* museo.

**mush** (møsh) *s.* gacha, masa blanda y espesa. *2* (E.U.) gachas de maíz. *3* sentimentalismo empalagoso. *4* (E.U.) marcha a pie sobre la nieve [esp. con perros]. *5* fam. paraguas.

**mushroom** (mø·shrum) *s.* BOT. seta, hongo. *2* cosa en forma de hongo.

**mushroom (to)** *intr.* coger setas. *2* tomar forma de hongo. *3* aparecer y desarrollarse rápidamente.

**mushy** (-i) *adj.* blando, mollar, pulposo. *2* empalagosamente efusivo o sentimental.

**music** (miu·šik) *s.* música: ~ *cabinet*, musiquero; ~ *hall*, sala de variedades, café concierto; ~ *rack*, atril; *to set to* ~, poner en música. *2* oído musical. *3* MIL. música, banda.

**musical** (-al) *adj.* musical, músico: ~ *comedy*, comedia musical, opereta. *2* armonioso, melodioso, canoro. *3* aficionado a la música.

**musicale** (miušika·l) *s.* velada musical.

**musician** (miuši·shan) *s.* músico.

**musicologist** (-ka·lodẏist) *s.* musicólogo.

**musk** (møsk) *s.* almizcle. *2* olor o perfume de almizcle. *3* ZOOL. almizclero. *4 adj.* almizclero, almizcleño: ~ *deer*, almizclero; ~ *melon*, melón; ~ *rat*, desmán.

**musket** (-it) *s.* mosquete; fusil.

**musketeer** (møskitı·ʳ) *s.* mosquetero; fusilero.

**musketry** (mø·skitri) *s.* mosquetería, fusilería. *2* tiro con mosquetes o fusiles.

**musky** (-i) *adj.* almizclado, almizcleño.

**Muslim** (mø·slim) *s.* MOSLEM.

**muslin** (mø·šlin) *s.* muselina. *2* percal.

**muss** (møs) *s.* desorden, confusión.

**muss (to)** *tr.* desordenar, desarreglar. *2* desgreñar. *3* arrugar, chafar, ensuciar.

**mussel** (mø·søl) *s.* ZOOL. mejillón.

**Mussulman** (mø·sølmæn) *s.* musulmán.

**must** (møst) *s.* mosto. *2* moho [orgánico]; ranciedad.

**must (to)** *intr.* enmohecerse. *2 aux. def.* [gralte. usado sólo en el presente] deber, haber de, tener que: *I ~ go,* he de irme. *3* deber de: *he ~ be downstairs,* debe de estar abajo. *5* ser preciso, ser necesario, convenir.

**mustache** (møstæ·šh) *s.* bigote, mostacho.

**mustang** (møs·tæng) *s.* mustango.

**mustard** (mø·sta<sup>r</sup>d) *s.* bot., coc. mostaza: *~ seed,* semilla de mostaza; mostacilla [munición]. *2* harina de mostaza: *~ plaster,* sinapismo.

**musteline** (mø·stilin) *adj.-s.* mustélido.

**muster** (mø·stø<sup>r</sup>) *s.* reunión [esp. para recuento, pasar lista, etc.]. *2* mil., mar. lista, revista: *to pass ~,* pasar revista; fig. ser aceptado o aceptable. *3 ~ roll,* rol de la tripulación.

**muster (to)** *tr.* juntar, reunir. *2* mil. reunir [para pasar lista, revista, etc.]. *3 to ~ up one's courage,* revestirse de valor, cobrar ánimo. *4 intr.* reunirse, juntarse.

**musty** (mø·sti) *adj.* mohoso; que huele a cerrado. *2* rancio, trasnochado. *3* mustio, triste.

**mutable** (miu·tabøl) *adj.* mudable, inconstante.

**mutable (to)** (miu·teit) *tr.* mudar, alterar. *2 intr.* mudarse, alterarse. *3* biol. sufrir mutación.

**mutation** (-shøn) *s.* mutación, mudanza, variación', cambio. *2* vicisitud.

**mute** (miut) *adj.* mudo. *2 s.* mudo. *3* mús. sordina. *5* fonét. letra muda.

**mute (to)** *tr.* mús. poner sordina a. *2 intr.-tr.* arrojar el excremento, tullir [las aves].

**mutilate (to)** (miu·tileit) *tr.* mutilar.

**mutilation** (-ei·shøn) *s.* mutilación.

**mutineer** (miutinı·<sup>r</sup>) *s.* amotinado. *2* amotinador.

**mutinous** (miu·tinøs) *adj.* rebelde, indómito. *2* amotinado. *3* subversivo.

**mutinously** (miu·tinøsli) *adv.* amotinadamente, rebeldemente.

**mutiny** (-i) *s.* motín, amotinamiento, insubordinación, sedición.

**mutiny (to)** *intr.* amotinarse, insubordinarse, rebelarse. ¶ Pret. y p. p.: *mutinied.*

**mutism** (miu·tišm) *s.* mutismo. *2* mudez.

**mutter** (mø·tø<sup>r</sup>) *s.* murmullo.

**mutter (to)** *tr.-intr.* murmurar, murmujear, barbotar, musitar, refunfuñar.

**mutton** (mø·tøn) *s.* carnero, carne de carnero: *~ chop,* chuleta de carnero; *~ chops,* fig. chuletas, patillas.

**muttonhead** (-jed) *s.* zopenco.

**mutual** (miu·chual) *adj.* mutual, mutuo; recíproco; respectivo: *~ benefit society,* mutualidad; *by ~ consent,* de común acuerdo.

**mutualism** (-išm) *s.* mutualismo.

**mutuality** (miuchuæ·liti) *s.* mutualidad. *2* reciprocidad. *3* interdependencia.

**mutualize (to)** (miu·chualaiš) *tr.* hacer mutuo.

**muzzle** (mø·šøl) *s.* hocico, morro, jeta [de animal]. *2* bozal, frenillo [para la boca]. *3* boca [de un arma de fuego]. *4* máscara [para gases, etc.].

**muzzle (to)** *tr.* abolazar, embozalar. *2* amordazar, imponer silencio.

**muzzy** (mø·ši) *adj.* abatido, triste. *2* calamocano.

**my** (mai) *adj. pos.* mi, mis: *~ book,* mi libro; *~ shoes,* mis zapatos. *2 interj. oh, my!,* ¡Ave María!, ¡caramba!

**mycelium** (misı·liøm) *s.* bot. micelio.

**Mycenae** (maisı·ni) *pr. n.* hist. Micenas.

**mycology** (maika·lodÿi) *s.* micología.

**myelitis** (mailai·tis) *s.* med. mielitis.

**myocardium** (maioka·<sup>r</sup>diøm) *s.* anat. miocardio.

**myology** (maia·lodÿi) *s.* miología.

**myope** (mai·oup) *s.* miope.

**myopia** (maiou·pia) *s.* miopía.

**myopic** (maia·pik) *adj.* miope, corto de vista.

**myopy** (mai·oupi) *s.* miopía.

**myosotis** (maiø·soutis) *s.* bot. miositis.

**myotic** (maia·tik) *adj.* miótico.

**myriad** (mi·riad) *s.* miríada. *2 adj.* innumerable.

**myriagram** (mi·riagræm) *s.* miriagramo.

**myrialiter, -litre** (-litø<sup>r</sup>) *s.* mirialitro.

**myriameter, -metre** (-mitø<sup>r</sup>) *s.* miriámetro.

**myriapod** (-pad) *s.* zool. miriápodo, miriópodo.

**myrmidon** (mø·<sup>r</sup>midøn) *s.* esbirro.

**myrrh** (mø<sup>r</sup>) *s.* mirra.

**myrrhic** (-ik) *adj.* mirrino.

**myrtaceous** (mø·<sup>r</sup>tei·shøs) *adj.* bot. mirtáceo.

**myrtle** (mø·<sup>r</sup>tøl) *s.* mirto, arrayán.

**myself** (maise·lf) *pron.* yo, yo mismo; a mí, a mí mismo, me.

**mystagogue** (mi·stagag) *s.* mistagogo.

**mysterious** (misti·riøs) *adj.* misterioso.

**mystery** (mi·støri) *s.* misterio. *2* arcano, enigma. *3* teat. auto, drama religioso.

**mystic** (mi·stikt) *adj.* místico. *2* enigmático, misterioso. *3* mágico. *4 s.* místico.

**mystical** (-al) *adj.* místico, simbólico, anagógico. *2* místico [de la mística].

**mysticism** (mi·stisišm) *s.* misticismo.

**mystification** (mistifikei·shøn) *s.* confusión, perplejidad. *2* engaño, superchería.

**mystify (to)** (mi·stifai) *tr.* envolver en misterio, obscurecer. *2* confundir, desconcertar, engañar. ¶ Pret. y p. p.: *mistified.*

**myth** (miz) *s.* mito. *2* fábula, ficción.

**mythical** (-al) *adj.* mítico.

**mythologist** (miza·lodÿist) *s.* mitologista; mitólogo.

**mythology** (-i) *s.* mitología.

**myxomycete** (miksomaisi·t) *s.* bot. mixomiceto.

# N

**N, n** (en) *s.* N, n, decimocuarta letra del alfabeto inglés.

**nab (to)** (næb) *tr.* prender, agazapar, coger.

**nabob** (nei·bab) *s.* nabab.

**nacarat** (næ·kærat) *s.* color nacarado, rosado.

**nacelle** (næse·l) *s.* AER. barquilla.

**nacre** (nei·køᵣ) *s.* nácar.

**nacreaous** (nei·kriøs) *adj.* nacarado, nacarino.

**nadir** (nei·døᵣ) *s.* ASTR. nadir.

**nag** (næg) *s.* jaca, cuartago. *2* jaco, rocín.

**nag (to)** *tr.-intr.* encocorar [con reprensiones, críticas, etc.]; regañar, hallarlo todo mal. ¶ Pret. y p. p.: *nagged;* ger.: *-gging.*

**naiad** (nei·yad) *s.* MIT. náyade.

**nail** (neil) *s.* ANAT.,ZOOL. uña: ~ *clippers,* cortauñas; ~ *polish,* esmalte para las uñas. *2* clavo, punta; tachón: ~ *puller,* arrancaclavos; *on the* ~, en el acto, a toca teja.

**nail (to)** *tr.* clavar, enclavar [fijar, asegurar con clavos]; *to* ~ *down, to* ~ *up,* clavar, sujetar con clavos. *2* clavetear, adornar con clavos. *3* fijar, sujetar, agarrar, atrapar. *4 to* ~ *a lie,* acabar con una mentira.

**nailbrush** (-brøsh) *s.* cepillo para las uñas.

**nailer** (-øᵣ) *s.* fabricante de clavos. *2* el que clava [con clavos].

**nainsook** (nei·nsuk) *s.* nansú.

**naive, naïve** (naɪ·v) *adj.* ingenuo, sencillo, cándido.

**naiveté** (-tei) *s.* ingenuidad, sencillez, candor.

**naked** (nei·kid) *adj.* desnudo: *the* ~ *truth,* la verdad desnuda; *with the* ~ *eye,* a simple vista. *2* puro, sin mezcla. *3* descubierto, sin defensa o protección.

**nakedness** (nei·kidnis) *s.* desnudez.

**namby-pamby** (næ·mbi-pæ·mbi) *adj.* afectado, insípido, ñoño. *2 s.* melindre, pamplina. *3* persona ñoña o sensiblera.

**name** (neim) *s.* nombre: *Christian* ~, nombre de pila; *family* ~, apellido; *what is your* ~*?,* ¿cómo se llama usted?; *by* ~, de nombre; *in the* ~ *of,* en nombre de; ~ *plate,* letrero o placa con el nombre. *2* fama, reputación: *bad* ~, mala reputación. *3* apodo, mote: *to call names,* motejar, insultar.

**name (to)** *tr.* llamar, denominar, apellidar. *2* nombrar [decir el nombre, hacer mención de]. *2* señalar, indicar, fijar.

**nameless** (-lis) *adj.* anónimo; no nombrado: *he*

*shall be* ~, no diremos su nombre. *2* innominado. *3* obscuro, humilde. *4* indescriptible; horrible.

**namely** (-li) *adv.* a saber, esto es, es decir.

**namesake** (-seik) *s.* tocayo, homónimo.

**Nancy** (na·nsi) *n. pr. dim.* de ANN.

**nandu** (næ·ndu) *s.* ORN. ñandú.

**nankeen, nankin** (nænkɪ·n) *s.* TEJ. mahón, manquín. *2 pl.* pantalones de nanquín.

**nanny** (na·ni) *s.* niñera [voz infantil]. *2* ~ *goat,* fam. cabra [animal].

**nap** (næp) *s.* sueñecito, siesta: *to take a* ~, echar un sueñecito. *2* pelo [de un tejido].

**nap (to)** *intr.* dormitar, descabezar el sueño: *to catch someone napping,* coger a uno desprevenido. *2 tr.* cardar, perchar [un tejido].

**nape** (nei·p) *s.* ~ *of the neck,* nuca, cogote.

**napery** (nei·pøri) *s.* mantelería.

**naphtha** (næ·fza) *s.* nafta.

**Naphtali** (-tølai) *n. pr.* Naftalí.

**naphthalene** (-zalin) *s.* naftalina.

**Napierian** (neipi·rian) *adj.* neperiano, de Néper.

**napkin** (næ·pkin) *s.* servilleta: ~ *ring,* servilletero. *2* toalleta.

**Naples** (nei·pøls) *n. pr.* GEOGR. Nápoles.

**napless** (næ·plis) *adj.* raído [paño, etc.].

**Napoleon** (napou·liøn) *n. pr.* Napoleón. *2 s.* (con min.) napoleón [moneda].

**napping** (næ·ping) *s.* TEJ. perchado.

**nappy** (-i) *adj.* peludo, velloso. *2* fuerte, con mucha espuma [bebida].

**narcissism** (naᵣsi·sišm) *s.* narcisismo.

**narcissus** (naᵣsi·søs) *s.* BOT. narciso.

**narcosis** (naᵣkou·sis) *s.* MED. narcotismo [sopor].

**narcotic** (naᵣka·tik) *adj.-s.* narcótico.

**narcotize (to)** (na·ᵣkøtaiš) *tr.* narcotizar.

**nard** (naᵣd) *s.* BOT. espicanardo, nardo. *2* ungüento de nardo.

**narghile** (na·ᵣgili) *s.* narguile.

**narrate (to)** (nærei·t) *tr.* narrar.

**narration** (nærei·shøn) *s.* narración.

**narrative** (næ·rativ) *adj.* narrativo. *2 s.* narración, relato. *3* narrativa.

**narrator** (nærei·tøᵣ) *s.* narrador.

**narrow** (næ·rou) *adj.* estrecho, angosto: ~ *gauge,* FERROC. vía estrecha. *2* limitado, reducido, escaso. *3* mezquino, tacaño. *4* iliberal, intolerante. *5* atento, escrupuloso, riguroso. *6* ~ *es-*

*cape*, escapada difícil, por poco. 7 ~ *circumstances*, pobreza, apuro, estrechez. *8 s. pl.* parte estrecha de un río, estrecho, calle, etc. *9* desfiladero.

**narrow (to)** *tr.* estrechar, angostar. *2* reducir, limitar, encoger. *3 intr.* estrecharse, reducirse.

**narrow-fisted** *adj.* agarrado, tacaño.

**narrowing** (-ing) *s.* estrechamiento. *2* reducción, limitación, mengua, disminución.

**narrow-minded** *adj.* de miras estrechas; mezquino, liberal, mojigato.

**narrow-mindedness** *f.* falta de amplitud en las ideas, intolerancia.

**narthex** (na·ʳzeks) *s.* ARQ. nártex.

**narwhal** (-jual) *s.* ZOOL. narval.

**nasal** (nei·šal) *adj.-s.* nasal: ~ *twang*, gangueo.

**nasalize (to)** (-aiš) *tr.* nasalizar.

**nascent** (næ·sønt) *adj.* naciente.

**nastiness** (næ·stinis) *s.* asquerosidad. *2* indecencia. *3* mal genio. *4* mal gusto u olor. *5* condición de malo, peligroso, desagradable, etc.

**nasturtium** (næstø·ʳshøm) *s.* BOT. capuchina.

**nasty** (næ·sti) *adj.* sucio, asqueroso, nauseabundo. *2* feo, indecente, grosero. *3* desagradable. *4* repugnante. *5* malo, peligroso: *a ~ fall*, una caída peligrosa. *6* avieso, intratable. *7* malo, tempestuoso [tiempo, mar, etc.].

**natal** (nei·tal) *adj.* natal, nativo.

**natality** (neitæ·liti) *s.* natalidad.

**natant** (nei·tant) *adj.* BOT. natátil, flotante.

**natation** (natei·shøn) *s.* natación.

**natatory** (-tori) *adj.* natatorio.

**Nathan** (nei·zan) *n. pr.* Natán.

**Nathaniel** (nazæ·niøl) *n. pr.* Nataniel.

**nation** (nei·shøn) *s.* nación. *2* multitud, hueste.

**national** (næ·shønal) *adj.-s.* nacional.

**nationalism** (-išm) *s.* nacionalismo.

**nationality** (næshønæ·liti) *s.* nacionalidad. *2* nación. *3* sentimiento nacional, patriotismo.

**nationalization** (-išei·shøn) *s.* nacionalización. *2* conversión en nación.

**nationalize (to)** (næ·shønalaiš) *tr.* nacionalizar. *2* naturalizar. *3* convertir en nación.

**native** (nei·tiv) *adj.* nativo, natío [metal]. *2* natal, nativo, patrio; ~ *country*, país natal. *3* natural [de un país], indígena, autóctono; vernáculo. *4* originario. *5* natural, sencillo. *6 s.* natural; indígena.

**native-born** *adj.* natural, indígena.

**nativity** (neiti·viti) *s.* nacimiento, natividad. *2* ASTR. horóscopo. *3* (con may.) Natividad [del Señor, etc.].

**natty** (næ·ti) *adj.* elegante, pulido. *2* diestro, garboso.

**natural** (næ·chøral) *adj.* natural: ~ *history*, ~ *law*, ~ *religion*, ~ *son*, historia, ley, religión, hijo natural. | No tiene el sentido de natural o nativo de un país. *2* innato, nativo. *3* nato, de nacimiento. *4* físico, real. *5* parecido [retrato, etc.]. *6 s.* idiota, simple. *7* MÚS. becuadro; nota natural.

**naturalism** (-išm) *s.* naturalismo.

**naturalist** (-ist) *s.* naturalista.

**naturalization** (næchøralisei·shøn) *s.* naturalización. *2* aclimatación.

**naturalize (to)** (næ·chøralaiš) *tr.* naturalizar. *2* aclimatar. *3* habituar.

**naturalness** (-inis) *s.* naturalidad.

**nature** (ne·chøʳ) *s.* naturaleza, natura. *2* naturaleza, carácter, especie: *in the ~ of*, como, de la naturaleza de. *3* natural, índole, genio. *4* natu-

ralidad, espontaneidad. *5* B. ART. natural: *from ~*, del natural.

**natured** (-d) *adj.* de tal o cual natural, genio, etc.: *good-natured*, afable, bondadoso.

**naught** (not) *s.* cero. *2* nada: *to come to ~*, reducirse a nada, malograrse, frustrarse.

**naughtiness** (-inis) *s.* desobediencia, travesura.

**naughty** (-i) *adj.* malo, desobediente, travieso: ~ *boy*, niño malo, picaruelo.

**nausea** (no·shia) *s.* náusea, asco, basca.

**nauseate (to)** (-ieit) *tr.* dar náuseas. *2* sentir asco. *3 intr.* nausear.

**nauseous** (-øs) *adj.* nauseoso, nauseabundo, repugnante, asqueroso.

**nautic (al** (no·tik(al) *adj.* náutico, marino.

**nautics** (-s) *s.* náutica.

**nautilus** (no·tiløs) *s.* ZOOL. nautilo, argonauta.

**naval** (nei·val) *adj.* naval, de marina, de la armada: ~ *base*, base naval; ~ *vessel*, buque de guerra.

**Navarre** (næva·ʳ) *n. pr.* GEOGR. Navarra.

**nave** (neiv) *s.* ARQ. nave. *2* cubo [de rueda].

**navel** (-øl) *s.* ombligo. *2* centro, medio. *3* BOT. ~ *orange*, naranja de ombligo.

**navicert** (næ·visøʳt) *s.* MAR. navicert.

**navicula** (navi·kiøla) *s.* BOT. navícula. *2* LITURG. naveta.

**navicular** (navi·kiulaʳ) *adj.* ANAT., BOT. navicular.

**navigability** (nævigabi·liti) *s.* navegabilidad.

**navigable** (næ·vigabøl) *adj.* navegable.

**navigate (to)** (næ·vigeit) *intr.-tr.* navegar. *2 tr.* gobernar [un buque o avión].

**navegation** (nævigei·shøn) *s.* navegación.

**navigator** (næ·vigeitøʳ) *s.* navegante, mareante.

**navvy** (næ·vi) *s.* (Ingl.) peón, bracero. *2* máquina excavadora.

**navy** (nei·vi) *s.* armada, flota, marina de guerra: ~ *blue*, azul marino; ~ *yard*, arsenal, astillero.

**nay** (nei) *adv.* no: *to say ~*, decir no. *2* es más; y aún. *3* es negativa, denegación. *4* voto en contra.

**Nazarene** (næšari·n) *adj.-s.* nazareno.

**Nazi** (na·tsi) *s.* naci.

**Nazism** (-išm) *s.* nacismo.

**neap** (nip) *s.* marea muerta.

**Neapolitan** (niapa·litan) *adj.-s.* napolitano.

**near** (niøʳ) *adj.* cercano, próximo, inmediato: ~ *relation*, pariente cercano; *Near East*, próximo Oriente. *2* íntimo, estrecho. *3* corto, directo [camino]. *4* cicatero, tacaño. *5* fiel, muy aproximada [versión, etc.]. *6* izquierdo [caballo, rueda]. *7 adv.* cerca: ~ *at hand*, cerca, a la mano. *8* casi, a punto de. *9* aproximadamente. *10 prep.* cerca de.

**near (to)** *tr.-intr.* acercarse [a].

**nearby** (-bai) *adv.* cerca. *2 adj.* cercano.

**nearly** (-li) *adv.* cerca, cercanamente. *2* de cerca. *3* íntimamente; estrechamente. *4* casi, aproximadamente.

**nearness** (-nis) *s.* proximidad. *2* inminencia. *3* intimidad.

**nearsighted** (-saitid) *adj.* corto de vista, miope.

**neat** (nit) *adj.* aseado, pulcro, ordenado. *2* primoroso. *3* límpido, claro. *4* elegante, de buen gusto, lindo. *5* limpio [ejecutado con limpieza], hábil, diestro. *6* puro, sin mezcla. *7* neto. *8 s.* res vacuna, ganado vacuno.

**neatness** (-nis) *s.* aseo, pulcritud. *2* elegancia, buen gusto, primor. *3* nitidez. *4* limpieza, precisión, destreza.

**neb** (neb) *s.* pico [de ave, tortuga, etc.].

**Nebuchadnezzar** (nebiukødne·ša$^r$) *n. pr. m.* Nabucodonosor.
**nebula** (ne·biul*a*) *s.* ASTR. nebulosa.
**nebulosity** (nebiula·siti) *s.* nebulosidad.
**nebulous** (ne·biuløs) *adj.* nebuloso. 2 vago, indeterminado.
**necessary** (ne·siseri) *adj.* necesario. 2 forzoso, obligado. 3 *s.* cosa necesaria; requisito.
**necessitarian** (nisesite·rian) *adj.-s.* determinista.
**necessitate (to)** (nise·siteit) *tr.* hacer necesario, indispensable. 2 reducir a la necesidad de, obligar.
**necessitous** (-øs) *adj.* necesitado, pobre.
**necessity** (nise·siti) *s.* necesidad: *of* ~, por necesidad. | No tiene el sentido de evacuación corporal.
**neck** (nek) *s.* cuello, pescuezo, garganta: *to break one's* ~, desnucarse; fig. matarse [trabajando]; ~ *and* ~, lado a lado [en una carrera]; ~ *or nothing*, a toda costa. 2 cuello [de una prenda, una vasija, etc.]: *low* ~, escote. 3 gollete [de botella]. 4 GEOGR. istmo; cabo; estrecho; desfiladero. 5 MÚS. mástil.
**neck (to)** *tr.* MEC. estrechar. 2 pop. besar, acariciar. 3 *intr.* pop. besarse, acariciarse.
**neckband** (-bænd) *s.* tirilla [de camisa].
**neckcloth** (-kloz) *s.* pañuelo para el cuello; corbata, corbatín.
**neckerchief** (-ø$^r$chif) *s.* pañuelo para el cuello. 2 especie de pañoleta. 3 corbata, corbatín.
**necklace** (-lis), **necklet** (-lit) *s.* collar, gargantilla.
**necktie** (-tai) *s.* corbata.
**neckwear** (-ue$^r$) *s.* prendas para el cuello.
**necrology** (nekra·lodÿi) *s.* necrología. 2 obituario.
**necromancer** (ne·krømænsø$^r$) *s.* nigromante.
**necromancy** (-i) *s.* necromancia, nigromancia.
**necropolis** (nekra·pølis) *s.* necrópolis.
**necrosis** (nekrou·sis) *s.* MED. necrosis.
**nectar** (ne·kta$^r$) *s.* néctar.
**nectareous** (nekte·riøs) *adj.* nectáreo, nectarino.
**nectarine** (ne·ktarin) *s.* BOT. griñón, briñón.
**nectary** (ne·ktari) *s.* BOT. nectario.
**Ned** (ned) *n. pr.* dim. de EDWARD y EDWIN.
**née** o **nee** (nei) *adj.* gal. nacida.
**need** (nɪd) *s.* necesidad, carencia, falta; momento de apuro: *if* ~ *be*, si fuese menester. 2 necesidad, pobreza: *to be in* ~, estar necesitado.
**need (to)** *tr.* necesitar, haber menester, requerir. 2 *intr.* estar necesitado. 3 *impers.* ser necesario, ser menester, ser preciso.
**needful** (-ful) *adj.* necesario. 2 necesitado. 3 *s.* lo necesario.
**needle** (-øl) *s.* aguja [de coser, de media, de gancho, de gramófono, etc.]: *look for a* ~ *in a haystack*, buscar una aguja en un pajar. 2 aguja [roca puntiaguda]. 3 ARQ. aguja. 4 BOT. hoja acicular. 5 fiel [de balanza]. 6 estilo [de un reloj de sol]. 7 brújula. 8 fig. *the* ~, nerviosismo.
**needlecase** (-keis) *s.* alfiletero.
**needlefish** (-fish) *s.* ICT. aguja.
**needleful** (-ful) *s.* hebra de hilo.
**needles** (-š) *s.* BOT. aguja de pastor.
**needless** (nɪ·dlis) *adj.* innecesario, inútil.
**needlewoman** (nɪ·dølwumæn) *f.* costurera.
**needlework** (-uø$^r$k) *s.* costura. 2 labor o bordado de aguja.
**needn't** (nɪ·dønt) *contr.* de NEED NOT.
**needs** (nɪds) *adv.* necesariamente. | Gralte. con *must*.
**needy** (nɪ·di) *adj.* necesitado, menesteroso.
**ne'er** (ne·ø$^r$) *adv. contr.* de NEVER.

**ne'r-do-well** *adj.-s.* haragán, perdido, inútil.
**nefarious** (nife·riøs) *adj.* nefario, inicuo, atroz.
**negate (to)** (nigei·t) *tr.* negar. 2 anular, invalidar.
**negation** (nigei·shøn) *s.* negación.
**negative** (ne·gativ) *adj.* negativo. 2 *s.* negativa, negación, denegación. 3 GRAM. negación. 4 FOT., ELECT. negativo. 6 MAT. término negativo.
**negative (to)** *tr.* negar, contradecir. 2 rechazar, no aprobar. 3 contrarrestar. 4 poner el veto a.
**negatron** (ne·gatran) *s.* QUÍM. negatón.
**neglect** (nigle·kt) *s.* abandono, descuido, negligencia, olvido. 2 indiferencia, desdén. 3 desuso. 4 inobservancia.
**neglect (to)** *tr.* abandonar, descuidar, olvidar, omitir. 2 no hacer caso de, desdeñar, arrinconar, preterir.
**neglectful** (-ful) *adj.* descuidado, negligente, omiso, desaplicado; que desatiende.
**négligé, negligee** (negliÿei·) *s.* traje de casa; bata de mujer.
**negligence** (ne·glidÿøns) *s.* negligencia. 2 LIT., B. ART. abandono, naturalidad.
**negligent** (-ønt) *adj.* negligente, descuidado.
**negligible** (-ibøl) *adj.* despreciable, insignificante.
**negotiable** (nigou·shiabøl) *adj.* negociable. 2 que puede ser pasado, salvado, superado.
**negotiate (to)** (nigou·shieit) *tr.-intr.* negociar. 2 fam. atravesar, saltar, salvar, superar: *to* ~ *a fence*, saltar una valla.
**negotiation** (nigoushie·shøn) *s.* negociación. 2 negocio, gestión.
**negotiator** (nigou·shietø$^r$) *m.* negociador.
**Negress** (nɪ·gris) *f.* negra [mujer].
**Negro** (nɪ·grou) *adj.-s.* negro [pers.]. 2 *adj.* de negro, de los negros.
**Negroid** (nɪ·groid) *adj.-s.* negroide.
**Negus** (nɪ·gøs) *s.* Negus. 2 (con min.) bebida caliente de vino, agua, azúcar, etc.
**neigh** (nei) *s.* relincho.
**neigh (to)** *intr.* relinchar.
**neighbo(u)r** (nei·bø$^r$) *s.* vecino. 2 amigo. 3 prójimo.
**neighbo(u)r (to)** *tr.-intr.* ser vecino [de]. 2 *intr.* estar en buenas relaciones. 3 vivir o estar situado cerca.
**neighbo(u)rhood** (-jud) *s.* vecindad. 2 cercanías. 3 vecindario. 4 *in the* ~ *of*, alrededor de, aproximadamente.
**neighbo(u)ring** (-ing) *adj.* vecino, adyacente. 2 rayano, cercano.
**neighbo(u)rly** (-li) *adj.* atento; amistoso; buen vecino.
**neither** (nai·ðø$^r$) *adj.* ninguno de los dos; ni uno ni otro; ninguno, ningún. 2 *conj.* ni: ~ ... *nor*, ni ... ni. 3 *adv.* tampoco, ni siquiera. 4 *pron.* ninguno, ni uno ni otro, ni el uno ni el otro: ~ *of them*, ninguno de ellos.
**nemathelminth** (nemazelmi·nz) *s.* ZOOL. nematelminto.
**nematode** (ne·matoud) *adj.-s.* ZOOL. nematodo.
**Nemaean** (nimi·an) *adj.* nemeo.
**Nemesis** (ne·misis) *s.* MIT. Némesis. 2 (con min.) justicia, venganza, justo castigo.
**nenuphar** (ne·niufa$^r$) *s.* BOT. nenúfar.
**neoclassic (al** (nɪoklæ·sik(al) *adj.* neoclásico.
**Neo-Latin** *adj.* neolatino.
**neolithic** (nɪoli·zik) *adj.* neolítico.
**neologism** (nɪa·lodÿism) *s.* neologismo.
**neon** (nɪ·an) *s.* neón: ~ *light*, lámpara de neón.
**neophyte** (nɪ·ofait) *s.* neófito.
**neoplasia** (nɪøplæ·sia) *s.* MED. neoplasia.
**Neoplatonic** (-pleita·nik) *adj.* neoplatónico.

**Neozoic** (-šou·ik) *adj.* GEOL. neozoico.
**nephew** (ne·fiu o ne·viu) *s.* sobrino.
**nephridium** (nefri·diøm) *s.* ZOOL. nefridio.
**nephritic** (-tik) *adj.-s.* MED. nefrítico.
**nephritis** (nefrai·tis) *s.* MED. nefritis.
**nepotism** (ne·potišm) *s.* nepotismo.
**Neptune** (ne·ptiun) *s.* MIT., ASTR. Neptuno.
**Nereid** (ni·riid) *s.* MIT. Nereida.
**nerval** (nø·ʳval) *adj.* ANAT. nérveo.
**nervation** (nø·ʳvei·shøn) *s.* BOT. nervadura.
**nerve** (nøʳv) *s.* ANAT. nervio: ~ *cell*, célula nerviosa; *to strain every* ~, hacer los mayores esfuerzos. 2 BOT. nervio, vena. 3 nervio, fuerza, vigor. 4 sangre fría, resolución. 5 pop. desfachatez. 6 *pl.* nervios, excitabilidad nerviosa: *to get on one's nerves*, crispar los nervios.
**nerve (to)** *tr.* fortalecer. 2 alentar, dar valor.
**nerveless** (-lis) *adj.* enervado, débil. 2 acobardado. 3 sin nervios.
**nerve-racking** (ræ·king) *adj.* irritante, exasperante.
**nervosity** (-va·siti) *s.* nervosidad.
**nervous** (-øs) *adj.* nervudo. 2 nervioso: ~ *breakdown*, crisis nerviosa. 3 vigoroso, enérgico. 4 tímido. 5 de nerviosismo.
**nervousness** (-nis) *s.* nervosidad, nerviosidad. 2 vigor, fuerza.
**nervure** (-iøʳ) *s.* ARQ. nervadura. 2 BOT., ENT. nervio.
**nervy** (-i) *adj.* vigoroso. 2 atrevido, audaz. 3 pop. descarado. 4 (Ingl.) nervioso, excitable.
**nescience** (ne·shiøns) *s.* nesciencia.
**nest** (nest) *s.* nido. 2 nidal, ponedero. 3 nidada [de pajaritos]. 4 guarida, manida: ~ *of thieves*, cueva de ladrones. 5 juego de objetos que encajan uno dentro de otro mayor.
**nest (to)** *intr.* anidar. 2 nidificar. 3 buscar nidos. 4 *tr.* poner como en un nido.
**nest-egg** *s.* nidal [huevo]. 2 gato [dinero]; ahorros.
**nestle (to)** (ne·søl) *tr.* abrigar, proveer de nido. 2 recostar [una parte del cuerpo] como en un nido. 3 cuidar, mimar. 4 *intr.* acurrucarse, recostarse; apretarse [contra]. 5 anidar; establecerse.
**nestling** (-ling) *s.* pollo que aún no ha abandonado el nido. 2 niño pequeño.
**Nestorian** (nesto·rian) *adj.* nestoriano.
**net** (net) *s.* red. 2 malla, redecilla [tejido]. 3 COM. líquido. 4 *adj.* puro, sin mezcla. 5 COM. neto, líquido: ~ *profit*, beneficio líquido; ~ *weight*, peso neto.
**net (to)** *tr.* tejer de malla; hacer malla con. 2 cubrir con red. 3 enredar [coger con red]. 4 COM. producir u obtener [cierto beneficio líquido]. ¶ Pret. y p. p.: *netted;* ger.: *metting.*
**netful** (-ful) *s.* redada.
**nether** (ne·ðøʳ) *adj.* inferior, más bajo, de debajo: ~ *world*, el infierno; el otro mundo.
**Netherlander** (-lændøʳ) *s.* holandés.
**Netherlands (the)** (-lændš) *n. pr.* Países Bajos.
**nethermost** (-moust) *adj.* [el] más bajo.
**netting** (ne·ting) *s.* red, obra de malla. 2 alambrado. 3 MAR. jareta.
**nettle** (-øl) *s.* BOT. ortiga. 2 MED. ~ *rash*, urticaria. 3 BOT. ~ *tree*, almez.
**nettle (to)** *tr.* picar [como una ortiga]. 2 picar, irritar, provocar.
**network** (ne·twøʳk) *s.* red; obra de malla; retículo. 2 FERROC., RADIO., etc. red, cadena.
**neume** (nium) *s.* MÚS. neuma.
**neuralgia** (niuræ·ldỹia) *s.* neuralgia.
**neurasthenia** (niuræszi·nia) *s.* MED. neurastenia.

**neuritis** (niurai·tis) *s.* MED. neuritis.
**neurologist** (niura·lødỹist) *s.* neurólogo.
**neuron** (niu·ran) *s.* ANAT. neurona.
**neuropath** (niu·røpæz) *s.* MED. neurópata.
**neuropathy** (niura·pazi) *f.* neuropatía.
**neuropteran** (-ptøran) *adj.-s.* ENT. neuróptero.
**neurosis** (niurou·sis) *s.* MED. neurosis.
**neurotic** (niura·tik) *adj.-s.* MED. neurótico.
**neuter** (niu·tøʳ) *adj.* GRAM., BIOL. neutro. 2 neutral.
**neutral** (niu·tral) *adj.* neutral. 2 BIOL., QUÍM., ELECT., PINT. neutro. 3 gris, indefinido, medio. 4 *s.* neutral. 5 AUTO. punto muerto.
**neutrality** (niutræ·liti) *s.* neutralidad. 2 calidad de neutro.
**neutralization** (niutrališei·shøn) *s.* neutralización.
**neutralize (to)** (niu·tralaiš) *tr.* neutralizar.
**neutron** (niu·tran) *s.* FÍS. neutrón.
**never** (ne·vøʳ) *adv.* nunca, jamás: ~ *again*, nunca más. 2 de ningún modo, no, ni... siquiera: ~ *fear*, no hay cuidado; ~ *mind*, no importa.
**never-ending** *adj.* perpetuo, eterno, continuo.
**nevermore** (nevøʳmo·ʳ) *adv.* nunca más, jamás, más.
**nevertheless** (nevøʳðøle·s) *adv.-conj.* no obstante, sin embargo, a pesar de eso.
**new** (niu) *adj.* nuevo: *a* ~ *man*, un hombre nuevo, otro hombre; ~ *moon*, luna nueva; *New Testament*, Nuevo Testamento; *New World*, Nuevo Mundo; *New Year*, año nuevo; *what is* ~*?*, ¿qué hay de nuevo? 2 tierno [pan]. 3 moderno. 4 reciente. 5 ~ *arrival*, persona recién llegada. 6 *adv.* recientemente; nuevamente.
**newborn** (niu·bøʳn) *adj.* recién nacido. 2 ᵣenacido.
**newcomer** (-cømøʳ) *s.* recién venido o llegado.
**newel** (niu·øl) *s.* ARQ. nabo, bolo [de escalera]. 2 poste, pilar [con que termina la barandilla de una escalera].
**New England** *n. pr.* GEOGR. Nueva Inglaterra.
**newfangled** (niufæ·ngøld) *adj.* nuevo, recién inventado, de última moda.
**Newfoundland** (-fau·ndlænd) *n. pr.* GEOGR. Terranova. 2 *s.* perro de Terranova.
**New Guinea** *n. pr.* GEOGR. Nueva Guinea.
**newish** (-ish) *adj.* bastante nuevo o reciente.
**new-laid** *adj.* fresco [huevo].
**newness** (-nis) *s.* novedad, calidad de nuevo.
**New Orleans** (-o·ʳliønš) *n. pr.* GEOGR. Nueva Orleans.
**news** (niuš) *s.* noticia, noticias: *a piece of* ~, una noticia; *this is* ~ *to me*, esto me coge de nuevas. | Gralte. se construye en sing.: *what is the* ~*?*, ¿qué noticias hay? 2 prensa, periódicos: ~ *agency*, agencia informativa; ~ *dealer*, vendedor de periódicos.
**newsboy** (-boi) *s.* vendedor de periódicos.
**newscast** (-kæst) *s.* RADIO. noticiario.
**newscaster** (-kæstøʳ) *s.* cronista de radio.
**newsman** (-mæn) *s.* periodista, reportero, noticiero.
**newspaper** (-peipøʳ) *s.* diario, periódico: ~ *clipping*, recorte de periódico.
**newspaperman** (-mæn) *s.* periodista.
**newsprint** (niu·sprint) *s.* papel de periódico.
**newsreel** (-ril) *s.* CINEM. noticiario, actualidades.
**newstand** (-tænd) *s.* quiosco de periódicos.
**newt** (niut) *s.* ZOOL. tritón.
**New York** (-yoʳk) *n. pr.* GEOGR. Nueva York.
**New Yorker** (-yo·ʳkøʳ) *s.* neoyorquino.
**New Zealand** (-zi·land) *n. pr.* GEOGR. Nueva Zelanda.
**New Zealander** (-zi·landøʳ) *s.* neozelandés.

**next** (nekst) *adj.* próximo, inmediato, contiguo; siguiente, sucesivo; futuro, venidero: ~ *door*, la puerta de al lado; ~ *door to*, en la casa de al lado de; rayano en; ~ *month*, el mes que viene; ~ *of kin*, pariente (s más cercano (s; *the* ~ *day*, el día siguiente; *the* ~ *life*, la vida futura. *2 adv.* luego, después, en seguida: ~ *to*, al lado de; después de; casi: ~ *to nothing*, casi nada; *what* ~?, ¿y después qué?, ¿y qué más? *3 prep.* junto a, al lado de; después de.

**nexus** (ne·ksøs) *s.* nexo, lazo, vínculo.

**nib** (nib) *s.* ORN. pico. *2* punta, extremo. *3* punto [de la pluma].

**nibble** (-øl) *s.* mordisco, bocadito.

**nibble (to)** *tr.-intr.* mordiscar, roer, ramonear, comer a bocaditos. *2* picar [como el pez].

**niblick** (-lik) *s.* DEP. uno de los palos de golf.

**nice** (nais) *adj.* fino, sutil; exacto, preciso. *2* concienzudo, escrupuloso, puntilloso. *3* delicado, mirado, exigente. *4* delicado [que exige cuidado, tacto, etc.]. *5* refinado, pulcro, elegante. *6* primoroso. *7* bueno, agradable; delicioso, exquisito. *8* lindo. *9* decoroso, conveniente. *10* bien educado. *11* amable, simpático.

**Nice** (nis) *n. pr.* GEOGR. Niza.

**Nicene** (nai·sin) *adj.* niceno.

**niceness** (-nis) *f.* finura. *2* amabilidad, gentileza. *3* lindeza. *4* delicadeza, exactitud, esmero.

**nicety** (-ti) *s.* finura, sutilidad; sutileza. *2* exactitud, precisión: *to a* ~, con la mayor precisión. *3* delicadeza, cuidado, esmero, primor. *4* refinamiento, atildamiento. *5* amabilidad.

**niche** (nich) *s.* nicho, hornacina.

**Nick** (nik) *n. pr. dim.* Nicolás. *2 Old* ~, el diablo.

**nick** *s.* muesca, entalladura; mella. *2* IMPR. cran. *3 in the* ~ *of time*, en el momento preciso, a tiempo.

**nick (to)** *tr.* hacer muescas en; cortar; mellar. *2* pop. estafar, robar. *3* acertar; llegar a tiempo.

**nickel** (ni·køl) *s.* QUÍM. níquel. *2* fam. (E.U.) moneda de cinco centavos.

**nickel-plate (to)** *tr.* niquelar.

**nicknack** (ni·knæk) *s.* KNICKNACK.

**nickname** (-neim) *s.* apodo; nombre familiar.

**nickname (to)** *tr.* apodar, apellidar.

**nicotin(e** (ni·køtin) *s.* nicotina.

**nictitating** (ni·ktiteiting) *adj.* nictitante.

**nidification** (nidifikei·shøn) *s.* nidificación.

**niece** (nɪs) *f.* sobrina.

**niello** (nie·lou) *s.* niel; nielado.

**niello (to)** *tr.* helar.

**Niger** (nai·dỹø<sup>r</sup>) *n. pr.* GEOGR. Níger.

**niggard** (ni·ga<sup>r</sup>d) *adj.-s.* tacaño, cicatero, avaro.

**niggardly** (-li) *adj.* tacaño. *2 adv.* tacañamente.

**nigger** (ni·gø<sup>r</sup>) *s.*desp. negro, negra [pers.]: ~ *in the woodpile*, fig. gato encerrado.

**niggle (to)** *intr.* ser meticuloso; pasar el tiempo en minucias.

**niggling** (ni·gling) *adj.* demasiado minucioso.

**nigh** (nai·) *adj., adv., prep.* ant NEAR.

**night** (nait) *s.* noche: *by* ~, por la noche; *good* ~, buenas noches; *last* ~, anoche; *to make a* ~ *of it*, pasar toda la noche en una diversión, etc. *2 adj.* de noche, nocturno: ~ *club*, cabaret, club nocturno; ~ *dew*, sereno, relente; ~ *light*, luz que se deja por la noche; mariposa, lamparilla; ~ *owl*, búho, lechuza; noctámbulo; ~ *shool*, escuela nocturna; ~ *watch*, guardia nocturna; sereno; vigilante de noche.

**nightcap** (-kæp) *s.* gorro de dormir. *2 fig.* bebida que se toma antes de acostarse.

**nightfall** (-fol) *s.* anochecer, anochecida, caída de la tarde; *at* ~, al anochecer.

**nightgown** (-gaun) *s.* camisón, bata de noche.

**nighthawk** (-jok) *s.* ORN. chotacabras norteamericana.

**nightingale** (-ingeli) *s.* ORN. ruiseñor.

**nightjar** (-dỹø<sup>r</sup>) *s.* ORN. chotacabras.

**nightly** (-li) *adj.* nocturno, de noche. *2 adv.* por las noches; todas las noches.

**nightmare** (-me<sup>r</sup>) *s.* pesadilla.

**nightmarish** (-merish) *adj.* angustioso [como una pesadilla].

**nightshade** (-sheid) *s.* BOT. hierba mora. *2* BOT. *deadly* ~, belladona.

**nightshirt** (-shø<sup>r</sup>t) *s.* camisa de dormir.

**nighttime** (-taim) *s.* noche: *in the* ~, de noche.

**nigtwalker** (-uokø<sup>r</sup>) *s.* noctámbulo. *2* sonámbulo. *3* ramera; ladrón nocturno.

**night-watchman** *s.* sereno; vigilante nocturno.

**nightwear** (-ue<sup>r</sup>) *s.* camisón, pijama.

**nihilism** (nai·jilišm) *s.* nihilismo.

**nihilist** (nai·jilist) *s.* nihilista.

**nil** (nil) *s.* nada, ninguno.

**Nile** (nail) *n. pr.* GEOGR. Nilo.

**nilgai** (ni·lgai) *s.* ZOOL. antílope de la India.

**Nilotic** (naila·tik) *adj.* nilótico.

**nimble** (ni·mbøl) *adj.* ágil, ligero, vivo, activo.

**nimble-footed** *adj.* ligero de pies, veloz.

**nimbleness** (-nis) *s.* agilidad, ligereza, viveza. *2* expedición, destreza, prontitud.

**nimble-witted** *adj.* listo, despierto, inteligente.

**nimbus** (ni·mbøs) *s.* nimbo. *2* aureola.

**nincompoop** (ninkømpup) *s.* bobo, simple.

**nine** (nain) *adj.-s.* nueve: ~ *o'clock*, las nueve. *2 The Nine*, las Musas.

**ninefold** (-fould) *adj.-s.* nónuplo. *2 adv.* nueve veces.

**ninepins** (-pins) *s.* juego de bolos.

**nineteen** (tɪ·n) *adj.-s.* diez y nueve.

**nineteenth** (-tɪnz) *adj.-s.* decimonono. *2* diecinueve [del mes].

**ninetieth** (-tiez) *adj.-s.* nonagésimo; noventavo.

**ninety** (-ti) *pl. adj.-s.* noventa.

**Nineveh** (ni·nivi) *n. pr.* GEOGR. Nínive.

**ninny** (ni·ni) *s.* bobo, mentecato.

**ninth** (nainz) *adj.-s.* noveno. *2* nueve [del mes].

**niobium** (naiou·biøm) *s.* QUÍM. niobio.

**nip** (nip) *s.* pellizco, mordisco, picotazo. *2* traguito; pedacito. *3* fig. pinchazo, sarcasmo. *4* punzada [del viento frío]. *5* daño del frío [en las plantas].

**nip (to)** *tr.* pellizcar. *2* mordiscar, picotear. *3* helar, marchitar [el frío]. *4* coger, prender. *5* cortar: *to* ~ *in the bud*, cortar en flor. *6 tr.-intr.* beber a tragos. ¶ Pret. y p. p.: *nipped*; ger.: *-pping*.

**nipa** (nai·pa) *s.* BOT. nipa.

**nipper** (ni·pø<sup>r</sup>) *s.* boca, pinzas [de crustáceo]. *2 pl.* pinzas, alicates, cortaalambres.

**nipple** (ni·pøl) *s.* ANAT. pezón, tetilla. *2* pezón de goma. *3* protuberancia.

**Nipponese** (nipanni·š) *s.* nipón, japonés.

**Nirvana, nirvana** (ni<sup>r</sup>va·na) *s.* nirvana.

**nit** (nit) *s.* liendre.

**niter** (nai·tø<sup>r</sup>) *s.* nitro, salitre.

**nitrate** (-treit) *s.* QUÍ. nitrato.

**nitre** (-tø<sup>r</sup>) *s.* NITER.

**nitric** (-trik) *adj.* nítrico.

**nitrocellulose** (naitrøse·liulous) QUÍM. nitrocelulosa.

**nitrogen** (nai·trødỹøn) *s.* QUÍM. nitrógeno, ázoe.

**nitroglicerin** (naitrøgli·sørin) *s.* nitroglicerina.

**nitrous** (nai·trøs) *adj.* nitroso.

**nitty** (ni·ti) *adj.* lendroso.

**nitwit** (ni·twit) *s.* fam. simple, bobo, papanatas.

**no** (nou) *adv.* no: ~ *longer*, ya no; ~ *more*, no más; *are you going? —No, ¿va usted? —No. 2 adj.* ningún, ninguna: *by* ~ *means*, de ningún modo; ~ *one*, nadie; ~ *man's land*, tierra de nadie. | En muchos casos, hay que traducir la frase entera: *there is* ~ *wine*, no hay vino; *with* ~ *money*, sin dinero. *3* prohibido, se prohíbe: *no smoking*, prohibido fumar.

**Noah** (nou·a) *n. pr.* Noé. *2 Noah's ark*, arca de Noé.

**nob** (nab) *s.* fam. cabeza, chola. *2* pop. persona de viso.

**nobby** (na·bi) *adj.* pop. elegante.

**nobiliary** (noubi·lieri) *adj.* nobiliario.

**nobility** (noubi·liti) *s.* nobleza.

**noble** (nou·bøl) *adj.-s.* noble. *2 adj.* magnífico, majestuoso.

**nobleman** (nou·bølmæn) *s.* noble, aristócrata.

**nobleness** (nou·bølnis) *s.* nobleza [cualidad].

**noblewoman** (nou·bølwuman) *s.* mujer noble.

**nobody** (nou·badi) *pron.* nadie, ninguno. *2 s.* nadie [pers. insignificante].

**nocturnal** (naktø·ʳnal) *adj.* nocturno, nocturnal.

**nocturne** (na·ktøʳn) *s.* MÚS. nocturno. *2* PINT. escena nocturna.

**nod** (nad) *s.* inclinación de cabeza [en señal de asentimiento, saludo, etc.]; reverencia. *2* cabeceo, cabezada [del que duerme sentado].

**nod** (to) *intr.-tr.* inclinar la cabeza [en señal de asentimiento, saludo, etc.]. *2 intr.* cabecear, dar cabezadas, dormitar. *3* estar descuidado. ¶ Pret. y p. p.: *nodded;* ger.: *-ding.*

**nodal** (nou·dal) *adj.* nodal. *2* ANAT. nodátil.

**noddle** (na·døl) *s.* mollera, cabeza.

**noddy** (na·di) *s.* bobo, simple.

**node** (noud) *s.* nodo. *2* bulto, protuberancia. *3* BOT. nudo. *4* nudo [punto de convergencia].

**nodose** (-ous) *adj.* nudoso.

**nodosity** (nøda·siti) *s.* nudosidad.

**nodular** (na·diulaʳ) *adj.* nodular.

**nodule** (na·diul) *s.* nódulo.

**nodus** (na·døs) *s.* nudo, enredo, complicación.

**nog** (nag) *s.* taco de madera. *2* cierta cerveza fuerte. *3* EGGNOG.

**noggin** (-in) *s.* tacita, copa. *2* pequeña cantidad [de un licor].

**nohow** (nou·jau) *adv.* fam. de ninguna manera.

**noise** (noiš) *s.* ruido; sonido. *2* ruido, barullo, alboroto, gritería. *3* rumor, fama.

**noise** (to) *tr.* esparcir, divulgar, rumorear.

**noiseless** (-lis) *adj.* silencioso, callado, tranquilo.

**noisily** (-ili) *adv.* ruidosamente.

**noisiness** (-inis) *s.* ruidosidad. *2* ruido.

**noisome** (noi·søm) *adj.* nocivo, pernicioso, malsano. *2* fétido, ofensivo, repugnante.

**noisy** (noi·ši) *adj.* ruidoso, clamoroso, bullicioso.

**nolition** (noli·shøn) *s.* nolición.

**nomad** (nou·mæd) *adj.* y *s.* nómada.

**nomadism** (-išm) *s.* nomadismo.

**nomenclature** (nou·menkleichøʳ) *s.* nomenclatura.

**nominal** (na·minal) *adj.* nominal. *2* GRAM. substantivado, substantivo.

**nominalism** (-išm) *s.* nominalismo.

**nominate** (to) (-eit) *tr.* nombrar. *2* proponer [para un cargo], designar como candidato.

**nomination** (-ei·shøn) *s.* nominación, nombramiento, propuesta.

**nominative** (na·minativ) *s.* nominativo. *2 adj.* propuesto; de propuesta [para un cargo].

**nominator** (-eitøʳ) *s.* nominador.

**nominee** (nmini·) *s.* propuesto, candidato [para un cargo].

**non-** (nan) partícula negativa que forma compuestos con los sentidos de *no, an, dis, falta de*, etc.

**nonacceptance** (nanækse·ptans) *s.* falta de aceptación.

**nonage** (na·nidỹ) *s.* minoridad, menor edad.

**nonagenarian** (nanadỹine·rian) *adj.-s.* nonagenario.

**nonagesimal** (-e·simal) *adj.* nonagésimo.

**nonagon** (na·nagan) *s.* GEOM. eneágono.

**nonaggression** (nanagre·shøn) *s.* no agresión.

**nonappearance** (-pi·rans) *s.* DER. incomparecencia.

**nonce** (nans) *s. for the* ~, por ahora, por el momento. *2 adj.* ~ *word*, palabra para el caso.

**nonchalance** (na·nshalans) *s.* indiferencia, abandono, indolencia.

**non-combatant** *adj.-s.* no combatiente.

**non-commissioned** *adj.* ~ *officer*, cabo, sargento, clase.

**non-committal** *adj.* reservado, evasivo, que no se compromete.

**noncompliance** (nankømplai·ans) *s.* incumplimiento, inobediencia.

**non-conductor** *s.* FÍS., ELECT. cuerpo mal conductor; aislador.

**non-conformist** *adj.-s.* disidente [esp. de la Iglesia Anglicana].

**non-delivery** *s.* falta de entrega.

**nondescript** (na·ndiskript) *adj.* indefinible, difícil de clasificar, raro. *2 s.* objeto o persona difícil de clasificar.

**none** (nøn) *pron.* ninguno; nada: *I have* ~, no tengo ninguno; ~ *of*, ninguno de; nada de. *2* nadie. *3 adv.* no, de ningún modo: ~ *the less*, no menos; no obstante, sin embargo; *he was* ~ *the better* (o *the worse*) *for it*, no por ello se hallaba mejor (o peor); no ganó (o perdió) nada con ello.

**nonentity** (nane·ntiti) *s.* nada; no existencia. *2* cosa no existente. *3* nulidad, cero a la izquierda.

**nones** (nounš) *s. pl.* nonas. *2* LITURG. nona.

**non-essential** *adj.* no esencial.

**nonesuch** (nø·nsøch) *s.* persona o cosa sin igual.

**non-existence** *s.* inexistencia.

**non-existent** *adj.* inexixtente.

**non-intervention** *s.* no intervención.

**nonius** (nou·niøs) *s.* nonio.

**nonpareil** (nanpare·l) *adj.* sin par, sin igual. *2 s.* persona o cosa sin par. *3* IMPR. nomparell.

**nonpartisan** (-pa·ʳtišan) *adj.* POL. independiente.

**nonpayment** (-peimønt) *s.* falta de pago.

**nonplus** (na·npløs) *s.* perplejidad, confusión, estupefacción.

**nonplus** (to) *tr.* confundir, dejar perplejo. *2* aplastar, dejar sin palabra.

**non-resident** *adj.-s.* no residente.

**nonsense** (-sens) *s.* cosa sin sentido, absurdidad. *2* tontería, necedad, desatino. *3* tonterías, pamplinadas. *4 interj.* ¡bah!

**nonsensical** (nanse·nsikal) *adj.* sin sentido, absurdo, disparatado, desatinado.

**non-skid** *adj.* antideslizante.

**nonstriated** (-strai·atid) *adj.* liso [músculo].

**non-transferable** *adj.* intransferible.

**non-union** *adj.* no sindicado [obrero].

**noodle** (nu·døl) *s.* tallarín; fideo. *2* simple, tonto, zote. *3* fam. cabeza.

**nook** (nuk) *s.* rincón. *2* lugar retirado y apacible.

**noon** (nun), **noonday** (-dei), **noontide** (-taid) *s.* mediodía [hora]: *high noon*, las doce en punto. *2* apogeo, punto culminante.

**noose** (nus) *s.* lazo, nudo corredizo, gaza. *2* dogal.

**noose (to)** *tr.* lazar, coger con lazo o trampa. *2* ahorcar. *3* hacer un lazo o nudo corredizo en.

**nopal** (nou·pal) *s.* BOT. nopal, higuera, chumba.

**nor** (no<sup>r</sup>) *conj.* ni: *neither you ~ I*, ni usted ni yo. *2* tampoco, y no: *~ I*, yo tampoco; *~ was it all*, y ello no era todo.

**Nordic** (no·<sup>r</sup>dik) *adj.-s.* nórdico.

**norm** (no<sup>r</sup>m) *s.* norma, pauta, regla, modelo.

**normal** (no·<sup>r</sup>mal) *adj.* normal. *2 s.* estado normal; lo normal. *3* escuela normal. *4* GEOM. normal.

**normalcy** (-si), **normality** (-liti) *s.* normalidad.

**normalize (to)** (-laiš) *tr.* normalizar; regularizar.

**Norman** (no·<sup>r</sup>man) *adj.-s.* normando.

**Normandy** (-di) *n. pr.* GEOGR. Normandía.

**Norse** (no<sup>r</sup>s) *adj.-s.* escandinavo.

**Norseman** (no·<sup>r</sup>smæn) *s.* NORTHMAN.

**north** (no<sup>r</sup>z) *s.* norte, septentrión. *2* norte [región]. *3 adj.* del norte, septentrional: *North America*, Norteamérica, América del Norte; *North Pole*, polo norte; *North Sea*, mar del norte; *North Star*, estrella del norte. *4 adv.* al norte, hacia el norte.

**northeast** (-I·st) *adj.-s.* nordeste.

**northeaster** (no<sup>r</sup>zI·stø<sup>r</sup>) *s.* viento del norte. *2* norteño.

**northerly** (-li) *adj.* septentrional, boreal.

**northern** (-n) *adj.* del norte; septentrional. *2* (E.U.) de los Estados del Norte.

**northerner** (-nø<sup>r</sup>) *s.* norteño, esp. (E.U.) de los Estados del Norte.

**northland** (no·<sup>r</sup>zlænd) *s.* tierra del norte. *2* (con may.) región boreal. *3* Península escandinava.

**Northman** (-mæn) *s.* normando, antiguo escandinavo.

**northward (s** (-wø<sup>r</sup>d (š) *adv.* hacia el norte.

**northwest** (-we·st) *s.* noroeste, norueste.

**Norway** (no·<sup>r</sup>wei) *n. pr.* GEOGR. Noruega.

**Norwegian** (norwI·dÿian) *adj.-s.* noruego.

**nose** (nouš) *s.* ANAT., ZOOL. nariz: *to blow one's ~*, sonarse; *to count noses*, contar personas; *to follow one's ~*, seguir en línea recta; *to lead by the ~*, manejar [a uno] a su antojo; *to poke one's ~ into*, meter las narices en; *to turn up one's ~ at*, desdeñar, mirar con desprecio; *before*, o *under, one's ~*, en las barbas de uno. *2* nariz, olfato. *3* morro, hocico; *~ bag*, morral, cebadera. *4* NOOZLE. *5* MAR. proa. *6* adj. AVIA. *~ dive*, picado.

**nose (to)** *tr.* oler, olfatear, husmear, rastrear; *2* encararse con. *3* oponerse, hacer frente a. *4* restregar la nariz contra.

**noseband** (-bænd) *s.* muserola, sobarba.

**nosebleed** (blid) *s.* hemorragia nasal.

**nose-dive (to)** *intr.* AVIA. picar, descender en picado.

**nosegay** (-gei) *s.* ramillete [de flores].

**nosepiece** (-pIs) *s.* visera [del yelmo]. *2* muserola, sobarba. *3* portaobjetivo [de microscopio].

**nosey** (nou·ši) *adj.* fam. curioso, entremetido.

**nosology** (nøsa·lodÿi) *s.* nosología.

**nostalgia** (nastæ·ldÿia) *s.* nostalgia.

**nostril** (na·stril) *s.* ventana de la nariz. *2* ollar.

**nostrum** (no·strøm) *s.* remedio de curandero; panacea.

**not** (nat) *adv.* no: *he has ~ come*, no ha venido; *I think ~*, no lo creo, creo que no; *~ at all*, nada, de ningún modo; de nada; *~ that*, no es (decir) que; *~ even*, ni siquiera; *~ yet*, todavía no.

**notability** (noutabi·liti) *s.* notabilidad. *2* pers. de nota.

**notable** (nou·tabøl) *adj.* notable. *2* memorable. *3 s.* notable, pers. de nota.

**notableness** (nou·tabølnis) *s.* notabilidad [calidad].

**notably** (-bli) *adv.* notablemente.

**notarial** (noute·rial) *adj.* notarial.

**notarize** (nou·taraiš) *tr.* autorizar ante notario. *2* dar fe notarial de.

**notary (public)** (nou·tari) *s.* notario.

**notation** (notei·shøn) *s.* notación. *2* anotación. *3* acción de notar, observar. *4* sistema de numeración.

**notch** (na·tch) *s.* muesca, entalladura, mella. *2* fam. grado, escalón. *3* MAR. tojino.

**notch (to)** *tr.* hacer muescas en, entallar, escoplear. *2* mellar, dentar. *3* tarjar.

**note** (nout) *s.* nota, marca, señal. *2* mediodía, canción, voz, acento. *3* nota, distinción. *4* nota, apunte, anotación, relación, cuenta. *5* nota [oficial]. *6* billete, esquela: *~ paper*, papel de cartas. *7* billete [de banco]. *8* cédula, vale. *9* MÚS. nota. *10 to take no ~ of*, no hacer caso de.

**note (to)** *tr.* notar, observar, reparar. *2* distinguir, señalar, hacer notar. *3* notar, anotar. *4* asentar, registrar, apuntar. | Gralte. con *down*.

**notebook** (-buk) *s.* agenda, memorándum, libro de memoria; libreta.

**noted** (-id) *adj.* nombrado, conocido, reputado, afamado, prestigioso, célebre, eminente.

**noteworthy** (-wø<sup>r</sup>ði) *adj.* notable; digno de ser notado.

**nothing** (nø·zing) *s.* nada: *~ doing*, imposible, ni por pienso; *~ else*, nada más; *for ~*, inútilmente; *por nada*, de balde; *to come to ~*, reducirse a nada; fracasar, malograrse; *to make ~ of*, no reparar en; no hacer caso de; no entender, no sacar nada de. *2* ARIT. cero. *3* nadería, insignificancia. *4 adv.* nada, de ningún modo, no: *~ daunted*, sin acobardarse; *~ less*, no menos.

**nothingness** (nø·zingnis) *s.* [la] nada. *2* nadería.

**notice** (nou·tis) *s.* informe, aviso, advertencia, anuncio: *on short ~*, con poco tiempo de aviso; *until further ~*, hasta nuevo aviso. *2* conocimiento, observación, atención, caso; mención: *to take ~ of*, notar, observar, hacer caso de; *worthy of ~*, digno de atención, de mención. *3* atención, cortesía. *4* notificación, despido: *to give ~*, dar uno su despido. *6* reseña [literaria, etc.].

**notice (to)** *tr.* notar, observar, advertir, reparar. *2* hacer mención de; reseñar [un libro]. *3* reconocer, hacer caso de.

**noticeable** (-abøl) *adj.* notable, visible, perceptible. *2* digno de atención.

**notification** (-ifikei·shøn) *s.* notificación, aviso.

**notify (to)** (nou·tifai) *tr.* notificar. *2* informar, avisar. *3* requerir, citar. ¶ Pret. y p. p.: *notified*.

**notion** (nou·shøn) *s.* noción. *2* idea, concepto, opinión. *3* idea, intención; capricho. *4 pl.* (E.U.) novedades, mercería.

**notional** (-al) *adj.* nocional. *2* imaginario, ideal. *3* fantaseador. *4* caprichudo.

**notoriety** (noutørai·iti) *s.* notoriedad [esp. la debida a cosas censurables].

**notorious** (nouto·riøs) *adj.* notorio, conocido, famoso. | Ús. gralte. en sentido peyorativo.

**no-trump** (nou·trømp) *adj.-s.* NAIPES. sin triunfo.

**notwithstanding** (natwidstæ·nding) *adv.* no obstante. *2 prep.* a pesar de. *3 conj.* aunque; por más que.

**nougat** (nu·gat) *s.* nuégado, guirlache, turrón.

**nought** (not) *s.* NAUGTH.
**noun** (noun) *s.* GRAM. nombre.
**nourish (to)** (nø·rish) *tr.* nutrir, alimentar; sustentar. *2* alimentar, abrigar [sentimientos, etc.].
**nourishing** (-ing) *adj.* nutritivo, nutricio, alimentoso, substancioso.
**nourishment** (-mønt) *s.* nutrición, nutrimento. *2* alimento, sustento. *3* pábulo, pasto.
**nova** (nou·va) *s.* ASTR. nova.
**novel** (na·vøl) *adj.* nuevo; raro, poco usual. *3 s.* novela; novelística. *4 pl.* DER. novelas.
**novelette** (navøle·t) *s.* novela corta.
**novelist** (na·vølist) *s.* novelista.
**novelize (to)** (-aiš) *tr.* novelar.
**novelty** (-ti) *s.* novedad. *2* innovación. *3 pl.* COM. novedades.
**November** (nove·mbø') *s.* noviembre.
**novena** (novɪ·na) *s.* novena.
**novice** (na·vis) *s.* novicio, principiante. *2* REL. novicio.
**novitiate** (novi·shieit) *s.* noviciado.
**now** (nau) *adv.* ahora; hoy día; actualmente: *from ~ on*, de ahora en adelante; *just ~*, ahora mismo; *~ and again, ~ and then*, de vez en cuando. *2* entonces. *3 conj.* ahora, ahora bien: *~ then*, ahora bien; pues bien. *4* mas, pero. *5 now ... now*, ora... ora, ya... ya. *6 interj.* ¡vamos!, ¡vaya! *7 adj.* de ahora.
**nowadays** (-deiš) *adv.* hoy día, hoy en día.
**noway (s** (nou·wei(š) *adv.* de ningún modo.
**nowhere** (-jue') *adv.* en ninguna parte; a ninguna parte.
**nowise** (-uaiš) *adv.* de ningún modo, nada.
**noxious** (na·kshøs) *adj.* nocivo, dañino, pernicioso.
**noxiousness** (-nis) *s.* nocividad.
**nozzle** (na·šøl) *s.* lanza [de manguera]; punta [de soplete]; pitón [de vasija]. *2* nariz, pico, parte saliente. *3* hocico.
**nuance** (niu·ans) *s.* matiz.
**Nubian** (niu·bian) *adj.* nublo.
**nubile** (niu·bil) *adj.* núbil.
**nubility** (niubi·liti) *s.* nubilidad.
**nuclear** (niu·klia') *adj.* nuclear, nucleario: *~ fission*, fisión nuclear.
**nucleate (to)** (-klieit) *tr.-intr.* formar núcleo.
**nuclein** (-kliin) *s.* BIOQUÍM. nucleína.
**nucleus** (-kliøs) *s.* núcleo.
**nude** (niud) *adj.* nudo, desnudo. *2* escueto. *3 s.* B. ART. desnudo.
**nudge** (nødẏ) *s.* codazo ligero.
**nudge (to)** *tr.* tocar con el codo [como señal, advertencia, etc.].
**nudist** (niu·dist) *s.* nudista.
**nudity** (-diti) *s.* desnudez.
**nugatory** (-gatori) *adj.* ineficaz, nugatorio. *2* fútil, sin valor.
**nugget** (nø·git) *s.* MIN. pepita.
**nuisance** (niu·sans) *s.* daño, molestia, fastidio, lata. *2* pers. o cosa molesta, fastidiosa; chinche.
**null** (nøl) *adj.* nudo. *2* de ningún valor.
**nullification** (nølifikei·shøn) *s.* anulación, invalidación.
**nullify (to)** (nø·lifai) *tr.* anular, invalidar.
**nullity** (nø·liti) *s.* nulidad. *2* acto o documento nulo.
**numb** (nøm) *adj.* entumecido, adormecido, envarado, insensible. *2* entorpecido, torpe.
**number** (nø·mbø') *s.* número [en todas sus acepciones]: *back ~*, número atrasado [de un periódico]; *~ one*, fam. uno mismo; *~ plate*, AUTO. placa de matrícula; *a ~ of*, varios, muchos; *out*

*of ~, without ~*, innumerables. *2 pl.* verso, versos. *3* (con may.) Números [libro de la Biblia].
**number (to)** *tr.* numerar. *2* contar, computar. *3* contar [tener cierto número de años, etc.; incluir en el número de].
**numberless** (-lis) *adj.* innumerable, innúmero, sin fin de.
**numbness** (nø·mnis) *s.* entumecimiento, torpor, adormecimiento.
**numen** (niu·min) *s.* MIT. numen.
**numerable** (niupmørabøl) *adj.* numerable.
**numeral** (-al) *adj.* numeral. *2* numérico. *3 s.* número, cifra: *Arabic ~*, número arábigo.
**numerary** (-eri) *adj.* numerario.
**numerate (to)** (-eit) *tr.* numerar, contar.
**numeration** (niumørei·shøn) *s.* numeración.
**numerator** (niu·møreitø') *s.* numerador.
**numeric (al** (niume·ric(al) *adj.* numérico.
**numerous** (niu·mørøs) *adj.* numeroso, numerosos, muchos. *2* numeroso, armonioso.
**Numidian** (niumi·dian) *adj.-s.* númida.
**numismatics** (niumišmæ·tiks) *s.* numismática.
**numismatist** (niumi·šmatist) *s.* numismático.
**numskull** (nø·mskøl) *s.* bodoque, zopenco.
**nun** (nøn) *s.* monja, religiosa.
**nunciature** (-shiechø') *s.* nunciatura.
**nuncio** (-shiou) *s.* nuncio [apostólico].
**nunnery** (-øri) *s.* convento [de monjas]. *2* monjío.
**nuptial** (nø·pshal) *adj.* nupcial. *2 s. pl.* nupcias, boda.
**nurse** (nø's) *s.* ama [de cría], nodriza; niñera: *wet ~*, nodriza. *2* fomentador. *3* enfermero, enfermera.
**nurse (to)** *tr.* criar, amamantar. *2* alimentar, mantener; abrigar, acariciar; cuidar con esmero; fomentar. *3* cuidar [de un niño, a un enfermo]. *4* curar, cuidar [una enfermedad, una parte enferma]. *5 intr.* amamantarse. *6* ser ama, niñera o enfermera.
**nursemaid** (-meid) *f.* niñera.
**nursery** (-øri) *s.* cuarto o aposento destinado a los niños: *~ rhymes*, cuentos en verso para niños. *2* plantel, semillero. *3* criadero, vivero.
**nurseryman** (nø·'sørimæn) *s.* dueño o empleado de un plantel o criadero.
**nursing** (-ing) *s.* crianza, lactancia. *2* cuidado [de un enfermo]: *~ home*, clínica.
**nursling** (-ling) *s.* niño de teta.
**nurture** (nø·'chø') *s.* nutrimento, alimentación. *2* crianza, educación. *3* fomento. *4* cuidado, tutela.
**nurture (to)** *tr.* nutrir, alimentar. *2* criar, educar, cuidar. *3* fomentar.
**nut** (nøt) *s.* BOT. nuez: *a hard ~ to crack*, fig. hueso duro de roer. *2* pop. cabeza, chola. *4* pop. guillado. *5* petímetre. *6* nuez [del arco del violín]. *7* MÚS. ceja. *8* MEC. tuerca.
**nutation** (niutei·shøn) *s.* nutación.
**nut-brown** *adj.* castaño, tostado.
**nutcracker** (nø·tkrækø') *s.* cascanueces.
**nutgall** (-gol) *s.* BOT. agalla.
**nuthatch** (-jæch) *s.* ORN. trepatroncos.
**nutmeat** (-nɪt) *s.* carne de nuez.
**nutmeg** (-meg) *s.* BOT. mirística. *2* nuez moscada.
**nutria** (niu·tria) *s.* ZOOL. coipo. *2* piel de coipo.
**nurient** (-triønt) *adj.* nutritivo.
**nutriment** (-trimønt) *s.* nutrimento.
**nutrition** (niutri·shøn) *s.* nutrición. *2* alimento.
**nutritious** (-shøs), **nutritive** (niu·tritiv) *adj.* nutritivo, alimenticio.

**nutshell** (nø·tshel) *s.* cáscara de nuez o avellana: (fig.) *in a ~*, en pocas palabras, en resumidas cuentas.

**nutty** (-i) *adj.* abundante en nueces. *2* que sabe a nueces. *3 ~ about*, loco por.

**nux-vomica** (no·ks-va·mika) *s.* nuez vómica.

**nuzzle (to)** (nø·zøl) *intr.* husmear; hocicar, hozar. *2* arrimarse cómodamente, acurrucarse.

*3 tr.* tocar, empujar o restregar con la nariz.

**nyctalopy** (niktæ·lopi) *s.* nictalopia.

**nylon** (nai·lan) *s.* nilón. *2 pl.* medias de nilón.

**nymph** (nimf) *s.* MIT., ZOOL. ninfa. *2* poét. ninfa.

**nympha** (ni·mfa) *s.* ZOOL. ninfa, crisálida.

**nymphaea** (ni·mfia) *s.* BOT. ninfea.

**nymphomania** (nimfomei·nia) *s.* MED. ninfomanía.

# O

**O, o** (ou) *s.* O, o, decimoquinta letra del alfabeto inglés.

**o'** abrev. de OF.

**O!** *interj.* ¡oh! *2 O that!* ¡ojalá [que]!

**oaf** (ouf) *s.* simple, idiota. *2* niño contrahecho.

**oafish** (ou·fish) *adj.* simple, tonto.

**oak** (ouk) *s.* BOT. roble; cualquier árbol o arbusto del gén. *Quercus:* ~ *apple,* ~ *gall,* agalla de roble. *2* roble [madera].

**oaken** (-øn) *adj.* de roble; roblizo.

**oakum** (-øm) *s.* MAR. estopa.

**oaky** (-i) *adj.* roblizo, duro, fuerte.

**oar** (o$^r$) *s.* remo [instrumento]: *to lie, o rest, on the oars,* cesar de remar; descansar; *to put in one's* ~, meter uno su cucharada. *2* remero.

**oar (to)** *intr.* remar, bogar. *2 tr.* mover a remo.

**oared** (-d) *adj.* provisto de remos.

**oarlock** (-lak) *s.* MAR. escálamo, tolete, horquilla.

**oarsman** (-smæn) *m.* remero.

**oasis** (ouei·sis) *s.* oasis.

**oat** (out) *s.* BOT. avena. *2* pipiritaña. *3 pl.* avena preparada como alimento.

**oatcake** (-keik) *s.* torta de avena.

**oaten** (-øn) *adj.* aveníceo, de avena.

**oath** (ouz) *s.* juramento, jura: *to take an* ~, prestar juramento; *on, o upon* ~, bajo juramento. *2* juramento, voto, reniego.

**oatmeal** (ou·tmil) *s.* harina o puches de avena.

**obbligato** (abliga·tou) *s.* MÚS. obligado.

**obduracy** (a·bdiurasi) *s.* dureza [de corazón]; obduración, obstinación, impenitencia.

**obdurate** (a·bdiurit) *adj.* duro, insensible. *2* inexorable, obstinado. *3* impenitente.

**obedience** (obi·diøns) *s.* obediencia.

**obedient** (-t) *adj.* obediente. *2* dócil.

**obeisance** (obei·sans) *s.* reverencia, cortesía [saludo]. *2* respeto, homenaje.

**obelisk** (a·bølisk) *s.* obelisco.

**obese** (obi·s) *adj.* obeso, gordo.

**obesity** (-iti) *s.* obesidad, gordura.

**obey** (to) (obei·) *tr.-intr.* obedecer.

**obfuscate** (to) (abfø·skeit) *tr.* ofuscar, obscurecer. *2* obcecar, cegar.

**obituary** (obi·chueri) *adj.* necrológico. *2 s.* nota necrológica.

**object** (a·bdÿekt) *s.* objeto. *2* espectáculo, cosa que mueve a lástima, risa, etc. *3* GRAM. complemento [directo o indirecto]. *4* BILLAR. ~ *ball,* mingo. *5*

OPT. ~ *glass,* objetivo. *6* ~ *lesson,* lección práctica o de cosas.

**object (to)** (øbdÿe·kt) *tr.* objetar. *2* reprochar. *3 intr.* oponerse, poner objeción, tener inconveniente, no gustarle a uno.

**objectify (to)** (-tifai) *tr.* objetivar.

**objection** (-shøn) *s.* objeción, reparo, tacha, inconveniente.

**objectionable** (-shønabøl) *adj.* inaceptable, poco grato. *2* censurable. *3* molesto, inconveniente.

**objective** (-tiv) *adj.* objetivo. *2* GRAM. ~ *case,* acusativo o dativo. *3 s.* objetivo. *4* objeto, fin, meta, blanco.

**objectivity** (abdÿekti·viti) *s.* objetividad.

**objector** (øbdÿe·ktø$^r$) *s.* objetante.

**objurgate (to)** (a·bdÿø$^r$geit) *tr.* reprender, reconvenir.

**objurgation** (-eishøn) *s.* reprensión, reconvención.

**oblate** (ablei·t) *adj.-s.* oblato. *2 adj.* GEOM. deprimido en sus polos.

**oblation** (ablei·shøn) *s.* oblación. *2* oblata.

**obligate (to)** (a·bligeit) *tr.* obligar, comprometer.

**obligation** (-ei·shøn) *s.* obligación [deber, necesidad, compromiso, etc.]: *of* ~, de precepto. *2* deuda de agradecimiento: *to be under* ~ *to,* deber favores a.

**obligatory** (øbli·gatori) *adj.* obligatorio; forzoso.

**oblige (to)** (øblai·dÿ) *tr.* obligar, compeler, constreñir. *2* complacer, servir, hacer un favor; poner en obligación o deuda [por un favor]: *much obliged,* muchas gracias.

**obliging** (-ing) *adj.* complaciente, servicial, cortés.

**oblique** (øbli·k) *adj.* oblicuo. *2* indirecto. *3* insincero, evasivo, doloso.

**oblique (to)** (øblai·k) *intr.* oblicuar. *2* torcerse.

**obliquity** (øbli·kuiti) *s.* oblicuidad.

**obliterate (to)** (øbli·tøreit) *tr.* borrar [tachar; hacer desaparecer]. *2* matar [un sello]. *3* MED. obliterar.

**obliteration** (-ei·shøn) *s.* borradura, testadura; extinción.

**oblivion** (øbli·viøn) *s.* olvido.

**oblivious** (-viøs) *adj.* desmemoriado. *2* olvidado [que olvida]. *3* abstraído, sin tener conciencia [de].

**oblong** (a·blong) *adj.* oblongo. *2 s.* cuadrilongo.

**obloquy** (a·blokui) *s.* reprobación, difamación, vilipendio.

**obnoxious** (øbnaˑkshøs) *adj.* ofensivo, molesto, detestable, odioso.
**oboe** (ouˑbou) *s.* MÚS. oboe [instrumento].
**oboist** (-ist) *s.* oboe [músico].
**obol** (aˑbøl) *s.* óbolo [peso y moneda].
**obovate** (abouˑveit) *adj.* BOT. trasovado.
**obscene** (absɪˑn) *adj.* obsceno; indecente.
**obscenity** (abseˑniti) *s.* obscenidad.
**obscurantism** (abskiuˑrantišm) *s.* obscurantismo.
**obscuration** (abskiureiˑshøn) *s.* obscurecimiento.
**obscure** (øbskiuˑ[r]) *adj.* oscuro. 2 vago, indistinto.
**obscure (to)** *tr.* oscurecer. 2 ocultar, disimular.
**obscurity** (øbskiuˑriti) *s.* oscuridad. 2 confusión, vaguedad.
**obsecration** (absikreiˑshøn) *s.* obsecración.
**obsequies** (aˑbsɪkuis) *s. pl.* exequias, funerales.
**obsequious** (øbsɪˑkuiøs) *adj.* obsequioso, servil, zalamero.
**observable** (øbšøˑ[r]vabøl) *adj.* observable, notable.
**observance** (-vans) *s.* observancia. 2 ceremonia, rito; práctica, uso.
**observant** (-vant) *adj.* atento, vigilante. 2 observante, obediente. 3 cuidadoso [de].
**observation** (-eiˑshøn) *s.* observación: *to keep under* ~, tener en observación, vigilar.
**observatory** (øbšøˑ[r]vatori) *s.* observatorio. 2 atalaya, mirador, miradero.
**observe (to)** (øbšøˑ[r]v) *tr.* observar. 2 guardar [una fiesta]. 3 decir, hacer notar.
**observer** (-ø[r]) *s.* observador.
**obsess (to)** (øbseˑs) *tr.* obsesionar; causar obsesión.
**obsession** (-shøn) *s.* obsesión.
**obsidian** (absiˑdian) *s.* MINER. obisidiana.
**obsidional** (absiˑdional) *adj.* que se hace anticuado, que cae en desuso.
**obselescent** (aˑbsølit) *adj.* que se hace anticuado, que cae en desuso.
**obselete** (aˑbsølit) *adj.* anticuado, desusado, fuera de uso. 2 BIOL. atrofiado, ausente.
**obstacle** (aˑbstakøl) *s.* obstáculo. 2 embarazo, impedimento, óbice.
**obstetrician** (øbstetriˑshan) *s.* tocólogo.
**obstetrics** (øbsteˑtriks) *s.* obstetricia, tocología.
**obstinacy** (aˑbstinɑsi) *s.* obstinación. 2 pertinacia, persistencia. 3 MED. rebeldía.
**obstinate** (-it) *adj.* obstinado. 2 emperrado. 3 persistente. 4 MED. rebelde.
**obstreperous** (obstreˑpørøs) *adj.* estrepitoso, ruidoso, turbulento.
**obstruct (to)** (øbstrøˑkt) *tr.* obstruir. 2 atorar, atascar. 3 entorpecer, impedir, estorbar.
**obstruction** (-shøn) *s.* obstrucción. 2 obstáculo, embarazo, estorbo, impedimento.
**obstructionism** (-išm) *s.* obstruccionismo.
**obstructive** (øbstrøˑktiv) *adj.* obstructivo. 2 *s.* impedimento, estorbo.
**obstructor** (-tø[r]) *s.* obstructor.
**obstruent** (aˑbstruønt) *adj.* MED. opilativo.
**obtain (to)** (øbteiˑn) *tr.* obtener, alcanzar, conseguir, lograr, adquirir. 2 *intr.* ser general, estar en vigor o en boga.
**obtainment** (-mønt) *s.* obtención, consecución, logro.
**obtrude (to)** (øbtruˑd) *tr.* imponer o introducir quieras que no. 2 *intr.-ref.* entremeterse, intrusarse.
**obtruder** (-dø[r]) *s.* entremetido, intruso.
**obtrusion** (-dȳøn) *s.* entremetimiento, intrusión.
**obtrusive** (-siv) *adj.* entremetido, intruso, importuno, molesto.
**obturate (to)** (aˑbtiureit) *tr.* obturar.

**obturation** (-eiˑshøn) *s.* obturación.
**obturator** (aˑbtiureitø[r]) *adj.-s.* obturador.
**obtuse** (øbtiuˑs) *adj.* obtuso [romo; torpe]. 2 embotado [sentido]; sordo [dolor]. 3 GEOM. obtuso.
**obtuse-angled** *adj.* GEOM. obtusángulo.
**obverse** (aˑbvø[r]s) *s.* anverso, frente. 2 *adj.* del anverso. 3 de base más estrecha que la punta.
**obviate (to)** (aˑbvieit) *tr.* obviar, prevenir, evitar.
**obvious** (aˑbviøs) *adj.* obvio, evidente, palmario. 2 sencillo, fácil de descubrir.
**obviousness** (aˑbviøsnis) *s.* claridad, evidencia.
**ocarina** (acariˑna) *s.* MÚS. ocarina.
**occasion** (økeiˑȳøn) *s.* ocasión, oportunidad, coyuntura, caso, circunstancia: *on* ~, cuando se ofrece, ocasionalmente. 2 causa, motivo, origen, pie: *by* ~ *of,* a consecuencia de. 3 necesidad: *I have no* ~ *for,* no necesito, no me hace falta.
**occasion (to)** *tr.* ocasionar, causar, motivar.
**occasional** (-al) *adj.* ocasional. 2 incidental, fortuito. 3 poco frecuente; alguno que otro.
**occasionally** (-i) *adv.* ocasionalmente, de vez en cuando, a veces.
**occident** (aˑksidønt) *s.* occidente, ocaso, oeste. 2 *n. pr.* (con may.) Occidente [Europa y América].
**occidental** (aksideˑntal) *adj.-s.* occidental.
**occipital** (aksiˑpital) *adj.-s.* ANAT. occipital.
**occiput** (aˑksipøt) *s.* ANAT. occipucio.
**occlude (to)** (økluˑd) *tr.* ocluir. 2 cerrar, tapar.
**occlusion** (-ȳøn) *s.* oclusión.
**occlusive** (-siv) *adj.* oclusivo.
**occult** (økøˑlt) *adj.* oculto, secreto, esotérico, misterioso: ~ *sciences,* ciencias ocultas.
**occultism** (økøˑltišm) *s.* ocultismo.
**occupancy** (aˑkiupansi) *s.* DER. ocupación.
**occupant** (-nt) *s.* ocupante.
**occupation** (-eiˑshøn) *s.* ocupación. 2 posesión, tenencia.
**occupier** (aˑkiupaiø[r]) *s.* ocupante.
**occupy (to)** (aˑkiupai) *tr.* ocupar. 2 emplear, invertir. ¶ Pret. y p. p.: *occupied.*
**occur (to)** (økøˑ[r]) *intr.* hallarse. 2 ocurrir, suceder. 3 ocurrirse [venir a la imaginación].
**occurrence** (-øns) *s.* ocurrencia, incidente, suceso, caso. 2 *to be of frequent* ~, suceder a menudo.
**ocean** (ouˑshan) *s.* océano. 2 *pl.* la mar, mares [de].
**Oceania** (oushiæˑnia) *n. pr.* GEOGR. Oceanía.
**oceanic** (-nik) *adj.* oceánico.
**oceanography** (oushænaˑgrafi) *s.* oceanografía.
**ocellate(d** (ouˑsøleit(id) *adj.* ZOOL. ocelado.
**ocellus** (ouseˑløs), *pl.* **-lli** (-lai) *s.* ZOOL. ocelo.
**ocelot** (ouˑselat) *s.* ZOOL. ocelote.
**ocher, ochre** (ouˑkø[r]) *s.* ocre: *red* ~, almagre.
**o'clock** (øklaˑk) *loc. contr.* de OF THE CLOCK: *what* ~ *is it?,* ¿qué hora es?; *it is three* ~, son las tres.
**octagon** (aˑktægøn) *s.* octágono.
**octahedron** (actaȳˑdrøn) *s.* octaedro.
**octane** (aˑktein) *s.* QUÍ. octano.
**octave** (aˑkteiv) *s.* REL., MÚS., LIT. octava.
**Octavian** (akteiˑvian) *adj.* octaviano.
**Octavius** (-viøs) *n. pr.* Octavio.
**octavo** (-vou) *adj.* IMPR. en octavo. 2 *s.* libro, etc., en octavo.
**octet** (akteˑt) *s.* MÚS. octeto.
**October** (aktouˑbø[r]) *s.* octubre.
**octogenarian** (aktodȳineˑrian) *adj.-s.* octogenario, ochentón.
**octopod** (aˑktopad) *adj.-s.* ZOOL. octópodo.
**octopus** (-øs) *s.* ZOOL. pulpo.
**octosyllable** (-siˑlabøl) *s.* octosílabo.
**octroi** (aktuaˑ) *s.* fielato. 2 consumos [impuesto].
**octuple** (aˑktiupøl) *adj.* óctuplo.

**ocular** (a·kiula^r) *adj.* ocular. *2 s.* ÓPT. ocular.
**oculist** (-ist) *s.* oculista, oftalmólogo.
**odalisk, odalisque** (ou·dalisk) *s.* odalisca.
**odd** (ad) *adj.* impar, non. *2* suelto, solo, desaparado. *3* ocasional, no regular: ~ *job*, trabajo ocasional; *at* ~ *times*, a ratos perdidos. *4* sobrante, de más; y tanto, y pico: *ten pounds* ~, diez libras y pico. *5* singular, raro, curioso, extraño.
**oddity** (-iti) *s.* singularidad, rareza. *2* ente raro.
**oddments** (-mønts) *s. pl.* cosa suelta; pedazos, retales.
**odds** (adš) *s. pl.* y *sing.* desigualdad, disparidad [de condiciones, fuerzas, etc.]; superioridad, exceso [de una cosa sobre otra]: *to fight against* ~, luchar contra fuerzas superiores. *2* ventaja [en el juego]: *to give* ~, dar ventaja. *3* probabilidades [en favor o en contra]. *4* desavenencia: *to be at* ~ *with*, estar reñido con. *5* ~ *and ends*, retazos, trozos, cosas sueltas.
**ode** (oud) *s.* LIT. oda.
**odeum** (odɪ·øm) *s.* odeón.
**odious** (ou·diøs) *adj.* odioso, repugnante.
**odium** (-øm) *s.* odio, odiosidad.
**odontocete** (oda·ntøsit) *adj.-s.* ZOOL. odontoceto.
**odontologist** (odanta·lodÿist) *s.* odontólogo.
**odontology** (-lodÿi) *s.* odontología.
**odoriferous** (oudøri·førøs) *adj.* odorífero, oloroso.
**odorous** (ou·dørøs) *adj.* odorante, oloroso, fragante.
**odour** (ou·dø^r) *s.* olor [bueno o malo]. *2* fragancia. *3* olor, fama, estima: *to be in bad* ~ *with*, tener mala fama entre.
**odourless** (-lis) *adj.* inodoro.
**Odyssey** (a·disi) *s.* Odisea; odisea.
**œcumenical** (ekiume·nikal) *adj.* ecuménico.
**Oedipus** (e·dipøs) *n. pr.* MIT. Edipo.
**oenology** (ina·lodÿi) *s.* enología.
**o'er** (o·ø^r) *contr.* de OVER.
**oesophagus** (isa·fagøs) *s.* ANAT. esófago.
**of** (av) *prep.* En muchos casos se traduce por *de*; en otro, por *a, en, con, por*, etc.: *empty* ~, vacío de; *to smell* ~, oler a; *to think* ~, pensar en; *to dream* ~, soñar en o con; ~ *an evening*, por la noche; *he* ~ *all men*, él precisamente; ~ *myself, himself*, etc., solo; por mí mismo, por sí mismo, etc.; ~ *late*, últimamente; ~ *old*, ~ *yore*, de antaño.
**off** (of) *adv.* lejos, fuera; enteramente, del todo; indica alejamiento, ausencia, separación, disminución, privación, cesación: *a little way* ~, a poca distancia; *to be* ~, irse, partir, salir; *to have the afternoon* ~, tener la tarde libre; *hands* ~!, manos quietas; *hats* ~!, descúbranse; *from* ~, de lejos; ~ *and on*, de vez en cuando, a intervalos.
*2 prep.* lejos de, fuera de; de o desde: ~ *the track*, fam. despistado. *3* MAR. frente a, a la altura de.
*4 adj.* apartado, alejado, ausente. *5* lateral [calle, etc.]. *6* libre, de asueto. *7* suspendido, interrumpido, parado; abandonado: *the wedding is* ~, se ha deshecho la boda. *8* quitado, sin poner. *9* cerrado, cortado [gas, agua, vapor, etc.]. *10* equivocado. *11* chalado. *12* derecho, de la derecha [caballo, rueda, etc., de un vehículo]. *13* FÚTBOL. ~ *side*, fuera de juego.
*14 interj.* ¡fuera!; ¡vamos!
**offal** (o·fal) *s. sing.* y *pl.* despojos de reses muertas; desperdicios, basura.

**off-colo(u)r** (o·fkølø^r) *adj.* verde, atrevido, subido de color.
**offence** (øfe·ns) *s.* ofensa, agravio: *to take* ~, ofenderse. *2* ofensa, ataque. *3* pecado. *4* falta, infracción; delito.
**offenceless** (-lis) *adj.* inofensivo.
**offend** (to) (-d) *tr.* ofender. *2* atacar, acometer. *3 intr.* pecar; delinquir.
**offender** (-dø^r) *s.* ofensor. *2* pecador, delincuente.
**offense** *s.*, **offenseless** *adj.* OFFENCE, OFFENCELESS.
**offensive** (-siv) *adj.* ofensivo. *2* perjudicial. *3 s.* ofensiva: *to take the* ~, tomar la ofensiva.
**offer** (o·fø^r) *s.* oferta, ofrecimiento. *2* promesa. *3* envite. *4* proposición, propuesta. *5* COM. oferta: *on* ~, en venta.
**offer** (to) *tr.* ofrecer. *2* brindar. *3* prometer; amenazar. *4* hacer, inferir. *5 intr.* ofrecerse.
**offering** (-ing) *s.* ofrenda. *2* oblación, sacrificio. *3* ofrecimiento. *4* don, dádiva.
**offertory** (-tori) *s.* LITURG. ofertorio. *2* colecta [durante una función religiosa].
**offhand** (o·fjænd) *adv.* de improviso, de repente, sin detenerse a pensar; al descuido, bruscamente. *2 adj.* dicho o hecho de improviso, al descuido, etc.; brusco.
**offhanded** (ofjæ·ndid) *adj.* OFFHAND 2.
**office** (a·fis) *s.* oficio, función, ejercicio, ministerio. *2* cargo, empleo [esp. público o de autoridad]: *to be in* ~, desempeñar un cargo, estar en el poder. *3* oficina, despacho, bufete, agencia, departamento, negociado: ~ *boy*, meritorio, botones de oficina. *4* oficio [rezo, función de iglesia]. *5* ceremonia, rito. *6 pl.* oficios: *good offices*, buenos oficios, mediación. *7* exequias. *8* cocina y dependencias de servicio.
**officeholder** (-jouldø^r) *s.* funcionario.
**officer** (-ø^r) *s.* persona que tiene cargo público; funcionario; alto empleado; presidente, secretario, etc., de una sociedad. *2* MIL., MAR. oficial; clase. *3* agente de policía, alguacil, etc.
**official** (øfi·shal) *adj.* oficial. *2* autorizado. *3 s.* el que tiene un cargo público o de gobierno; funcionario. *4* (Ingl.) provisor o juez eclesiástico.
**officially** (-shali) *adv.* oficialmente, de oficio.
**officiant** (øfi·shant) *s.* ECLES. oficiante, celebrante.
**officiate** (to) (-ieit) *intr.* oficiar. *2 tr.* celebrar [un rito, etc.]. *3* suministrar.
**officinal** (-sinal) *adj.* oficinal.
**officious** (-shøs) *adj.* DIPL. oficioso. *2* oficioso, entrometido.
**offing** (o·fing) *s.* mar afuera, alta mar; lejanía: *in the* ~, mar afuera; en perspectiva.
**offish** (o·fish) *adj.* reservado, adusto, esquivo.
**offprint** (o·fprint) *s.* IMPR. separata.
**offscourings** (o·fskauringš) *s. pl.* hez, desecho, escoria.
**offset** (o·fset) *s.* compensación, equivalente. *2* cosa que da realce. *3* AGR. vástago lateral, acodo. *4* ARQ. retallo. *5* ELECT. ramal. *6* GEOGR. estribación. *7* TOP. ordenada. *8* IMPR. offset.
**offset** (to) *tr.* compensar, contrapesar, contrabalancear. *2* oponer. *3* ARQ. retallar. *4* imprimir por offset. ¶ Pret. y p. p.: *offset*; ger.: *-setting*.
**offshoot** (-shut) *s.* vástago, renuevo. *2* ramal, estribación.
**offshore** (-sho^r) *adv.* de la costa; a cierta distancia de la costa.
**offside** (o·fsaid) *s.* FÚTBOL. fuera de juego.
**offspring** (-spring) *s.* vástago, hijo, hijos, prole, descendencia. *2* fig. producto, resultado.
**off-stage** (-teidÿ) *adj.* TEAT. de entre bastidores.

**oft** (oft) *adj.-adv.* poét. y dial. OFTEN.

**often** (ọ·føn) *adv.* a menudo, muchas veces, frecuentemente: *as ~ as*, siempre que: *how ~?*, ¿cuántas veces?

**ogee** (oudỹı·) *s.* ARQ. gola, cimacio.

**ogival** (odỹai·val) *adj.* ARQ. ojival.

**ogive** (o·dỹiv) *s.* ARQ. ojiva.

**ogle** (ou·gøl) *s.* mirada de amor o coquetería; mirada provocativa. 2 pop. ojo.

**ogle (to)** *tr.-intr.* mirar con amor o coquetería; echar el ojo, comerse con los ojos.

**ogre** (ou·gøʳ) *s.* ogro.

**ogress** (-ris) *f.* ogro hembra, ogresa.

**oh!** (o) *interj.* ¡oh!

**ohm** (oum) *s.* ELECT. ohm, ohmio.

**oidium** (oi·diøm) *s.* BOT., AGR. oidio.

**oil** (oil) *s.* aceite; óleo: *~ of vitriol*, aceite de vitriolo; *to pour ~ on the flame*, fig. echar leña al fuego; *to pour ~ on the (troubled) waters*, fig. calmar el enojo, poner la paz. 2 petróleo. 3 *sing.* y *pl.* color o pintura al óleo. 4 *adj.* de aceite, oleífero; de petróleo; para aceite o petróleo; *~ beetle*, ENT. carraleja; *~ gauge*, MEC. indicador de nivel de aceite; *~ painting*, pintura o cuadro al óleo; *~ stove*, estufa o fogón de petróleo; *~ tanker*, buque petrolero; *~ well*, pozo de petróleo.

**oil (to)** *tr.* aceitar. 2 engrasar, lubrificar, untar.

**oilbird** (-bøʳd) *s.* ORN. guácharo.

**oilcan** (-kæn) *s.* lata de aceite. 2 alcuza, aceitera.

**oilcloth** (-kloz) *s.* hule, encerado. 2 linóleo.

**oiler** (-øʳ) *s.* engrasador. 2 aceitera [para engrasar]. 3 buque petrolero.

**oiling** (-ing) *s.* aceitado, engrase, lubricación.

**oilskin** (-skin) *s.* encerado, impermeable.

**oilstone** (-stoun) *s.* piedra de amolar al aceite.

**oily** (-i) *adj.* aceitoso, oleaginoso. 2 grasiento; resbaladizo. 3 untuoso. 4 zalamero, hipócrita.

**ointment** (oi·ntmønt) *s.* unto, untura, ungüento.

**O.K., OK., okay** (ou·kei) *adj.* bueno, conforme. 2 *adv.* bien, está bien. 3 *s.* visto bueno, aprobación.

**okra** (ou·kra) *s.* BOT. quimbombó.

**old** (ou·ld) *adj.* viejo, anciano, añoso, añejo; antiguo; inveterado: *~ age*, vejez; *~ bachelor*, soltero; *~ boy*, chico, viejo [expresión de afecto; *Old Boy, Old Nick, Old One*, fam. el diablo; *~ fog(e)y*, persona anticuada; *~ hand*, experto, perro viejo; *~ maid*, solterona; la mona [juego de naipes]; *~ man*, viejo; TEAT. barba; *~ salt*, lobo de mar; *Old Testament*, Antiguo Testamento; *~ wive's tale*, cuento de viejas. 2 *of ~*, de antaño, antiguamente. 3 *how ~ are you?*, ¿qué edad tiene usted?; *the baby is three months ~*, el niño tiene tres meses.

**old-clothesman** *s.* ropavejero.

**olden** (ou·ldøn) *adj.* poét. antiguo.

**old-fashioned** *adj.* anticuado; pasado de moda.

**old-fog(e)yish** (fou·gish) *adj.* atrasado, anticuado, chapado a la antigua.

**oldish** (ou·ldish) *adj.* algo viejo.

**old-looking** *adj.* avejentado.

**old-school** *adj.* a la antigua; de la vieja escuela.

**oldster** (-dstøʳ) *s.* fam. viejo, vieja.

**old-time** *adj.* antiguo, anticuado. 2 de antaño.

**old-timer** *s.* antiguo residente. 2 antiguo concurrente. 3 veterano [en una profesión]. 4 persona chapada a la antigua.

**old-word** *adj.* del antiguo mundo.

**oleaceous** (oliei·shøs) *adj.* BOT. oleáceo.

**oleaginous** (oliæ·dỹinøs) *adj.* oleaginoso, oleoso.

**oleander** (-ndøʳ) *s.* BOT. adelfa.

**oleaster** (-støʳ) *s.* BOT. oleastro, acebuche.

**oleic** (olı·ik) *adj.* QUÍM. oleico.

**oleograph** (ou·liøgræf) *s.* oleografía.

**olfaction** (alfæ·kshøn) *s.* olfacción.

**olfactory** (-tori) *adj.* olfatorio.

**oligarch** (a·ligaʳk) *s.* oligarca.

**oligarchy** (-i) *s.* oligarquía.

**Oligocene** (a·ligosin) *adj.-s.* GEOL. oligoceno.

**olivaceous** (alivei·shøs) *adj.* aceitunado.

**olive** (a·liv) *s.* BOT. olivo: *~ grove*, olivar; *~ branch*, rama de olivo; fig. niño, hijo. 2 oliva, aceituna: *~ oil*, aceite de oliva; *~ tree*, olivo. 3 *adj.* aceitunado.

**Oliver** (a·livøʳ) *n. pr.* Oliverio.

**Olympia** (oli·mpiæ) *n. pr.* Olimpia.

**Olympiad** (-iæd) *s.* olimpiada.

**Olympian** (-ian), **Olympic** (-ik) *adj.* olímpico: *Olimpic games*, juegos olímpicos.

**Olympus** (-øs) *s.* Olimpo.

**omasum** (omei·søm) *s.* ZOOL. omaso.

**omber, ombre** (a·mbøʳ) *s.* tresillo, juego del hombre.

**omega** (amı·ga) *s.* omega. 2 fig. fin.

**omelet, omelette** (a·mlit) *s.* tortilla de huevos.

**omen** (ou·min) *s.* agüero, presagio, pronóstico.

**omen (to)** *tr.* presagiar, augurar, ominar.

**omentum** (ome·ntøm) *s.* ANAT. omento.

**ominous** (a·minøs) *adj.* ominoso. 2 presagioso.

**omission** (omi·shøn) *s.* omisión. 2 olvido, descuido.

**omit (to)** (omi·t) *tr.* omitir. 2 dejar de, olvidar.

**omnibus** (a·mnibøs) *s.* ómnibus. 2 *adj.* general, colecticio.

**omnifarious** (amnifæ·riøs) *adj.* de todo género.

**omnimodous** (amni·mødøs) *adj.* omnímodo.

**omnipotence** (-pøtøns) *s.* omnipotencia.

**omnipotent** (-pøtønt) *adj.* omnipotente. 2 *n. pr. the Omnipotent*, el Omnipotente, Dios.

**omnipresence** (amnipre·søns) *s.* omnipresencia.

**omnipresent** (-t) *adj.* omnipresente, ubicuo.

**omniscience** (amni·shøns) *s.* omnisciencia.

**omniscient** (-t) *adj.* omnisciente.

**omnium-gatherum** (amniømgæ·ðørøm) *s.* fam. miscelánea, maremagnum.

**omnivorous** (amni·vorøs) *adj.* omnívoro.

**omoplate** (ou·mopleit) *s.* ANAT. omóplato.

**on** (an) *prep.* en, sobre, a, de, con, contra, por, bajo, so: *bent ~*, empeñado en; *~ the table*, sobre la mesa; *~ horseback*, a caballo; *~ duty*, de servicio; *~ this condition*, con esta condición; *to draw on*, COM. girar contra; *~ all sides*, por todos lados; *~ pain of*, bajo pena de; *~ seeing him*, en viéndole, al verlo. 2 cuando precede a una fecha, no se traduce: *~ the fourth May*, el cuatro de mayo.

3 *adv.* encima, puesto: *to have one's hat ~*, tener puesto el sombrero. 4 adelante; progresivamente; continuando, sin cesar: *to go ~*, seguir, proseguir, continuar; *farther ~*, más adelante; *later ~*, más tarde; *~ and*, sin parar; *and so ~*, y así sucesivamente. 5 *to turn the water, steam*, etc., *~*, abrir [la llave de] el agua, el vapor, etc.

6 *adj.* puesto: *the lid is ~*, la tapa está puesta. 2 que se está verificando, que ha empezado, que funciona; abierto, encendido, conectado: *the fight is ~*, la lucha ha empezado; *the light is ~*, la luz está encendida.

**onager** (a·nadỹoʳ) *s.* ZOOL., MIL. onagro.

**onanism** (ou·naniŝm) *s.* onanismo.

**once** (uøns) *adv.-s.* vez, una vez: *~ and again*, una

y otra vez; ~ *for all*, de una vez para siempre, definitivamente; ~ *in a while*, de vez en cuando; *all at* ~, de súbito; *at* ~, a la vez, de una vez; en seguida; ~ *upon a time there was*, érase una vez; *this* ~, esta vez. 2 alguna vez. 3 en otro tiempo. 4 *adj.* antiguo, que fue. 5 *conj.* una vez que, en cuanto.

**oncoming** (a·ncøming) *adj.* próximo, venidero. 2 *s.* proximidad, aproximación, llegada.

**ondometer** (anda·metø$^r$) *s.* ELECT. ondómetro.

**one** (uøn) *adj.* uno, una: ~ *half*, una mitad; ~ *hundred*, ciento. 2 primero [capítulo, etc.]. 3 un solo, solo, único: *his* ~ *chance*, su única oportunidad. 4 uno [no dividido]. 5 uno, unido; idéntico, lo mismo; el mismo, un mismo: *with one accord*, unánimemente; *it is all* ~ *to me*, me da lo mismo; *of* ~ *height*, de una misma talla o altura. 6 un, cierto, un tal: ~ *day*, un día; ~ *Mr. Smith*, un tal señor Smith.

7 *pron.* uno, una: *no* ~, nadie; ~ *and all*, todos sin excepción; ~ *another*, el uno al otro, unos a otros; ~ *by* ~, uno a uno; *how is one to know...?*, ¿cómo ha de saber uno...?

8 *s.* uno, el número uno. 9 una persona o cosa: | Gralte. no se traduce: *the little ones*, los pequeñuelos; *the* ~ *who*, el que, la que; *the white* ~, el blanco, la blanca; *this* ~, éste, ésta. 10 *one o'clock*, la una.

**one-act** *adj.* TEAT. en un acto.

**one-armed** *adj.* manco, que sólo tiene un brazo.

**one-horse** *adj.* de un solo caballo. 2 pop. inferior; de poca importancia.

**oneiric** (onai·rik) *adj.* onírico.

**oneiromancy** (-rømænsi) *f.* oniromancía.

**oneness** (uøn·nis) *s.* unicidad, singularidad. 2 identidad, uniformidad. 3 unión, concordia.

**onerous** (a·nørøs) *adj.* oneroso, gravoso, molesto.

**oneself** (uønse·lf) *pron.* se, sí, uno mismo: *with* ~, consigo.

**one-sided** *adj.* de un solo lado; desigual; unilateral; injusto, parcial.

**one's self** *pron.* ONESELF.

**one-step** *s.* cierto baile de salón.

**one-track** *adj.* FERROC. de una sola vía. 2 fig. estrecha [mentalidad].

**one-way** *adj.* de dirección única. 2 de ida [billete].

**onion** (a·nyøn) *s.* BOT. cebolla. 2 pop. cabeza chola.

**onionskin** (-skin) *s.* bizna, tela de cebolla. 2 papel cebolla.

**onlooker** (a·nlukø$^r$) *s.* espectador, observador.

**only** (ou·nli) *adj.* solo, único. 2 singular, preeminente. 3 *adv.* sólo, solamente, únicamente: *not* ~ ... *but also*, no sólo... sino también. 4 *if* ~, ojalá; sí, si al menos. 5 *conj.* solo que, pero, si no fuera que.

**only-begotten** *adj.* unigénito.

**onomastic** (anømæ·stik) *adj.* onomástico.

**onomatopœia** (-mætøpi·a) *s.* onomatopeya.

**onomatopœic** (-ik) *adj.* onomatopéyico.

**onrush** (a·nrøsh) *s.* embestida, arremetida, carga, fuerza impetuosa.

**onset** (-set) *s.* ataque, asalto. 2 principio.

**onshore** (-sho$^r$) *adj.-adv.* de tierra; hacia tierra.

**onslaught** (-slot) *s.* ataque furioso, asalto.

**onto** (-tu) *prep.* hacia, sobre.

**ontogeny** (anta·dyini) *s.* ontogenia.

**ontology** (-lodyi) *s.* ontología.

**onward** (a·nwø$^r$d) *adj.* que se mueve hacia adelante. 2 avanzado, progresivo.

**onward(s** (-(š) *adv.* adelante; hacia adelante.

**onyx** (a·niks) *s.* MINER. ónix, ónice.

**oösphere** (ou·sfi$^r$) *s.* BOT. oosfera.

**ooze** (uš) *s.* fango, légamo, limo, cieno.

**ooze (to)** *intr.* rezumarse, escurrirse. 2 escaparse, manar, fluir suavemente. 3 llenarse [de sudor]. 4 *tr.* exudar, sudar; desprender.

**oozy** (-i) *adj.* legamoso, limoso, cenagoso.

**opacity** (opæ·siti) *s.* opacidad. 2 torpeza del entendimiento.

**opal** (ou·pal) *s.* MINER. ópalo.

**opalescence** (opale·søns) *s.* opalescencia.

**opalescent** (opale·sønt) *adj.* opalescente.

**opaline** (ou·palain) *adj.* opalino.

**opaque** (opei·k) *adj.* opaco. 2 obscuro, ininteligible. 3 torpe, obtuso.

**ope (to)** (oup) *tr.-ref.* poét. abrir.

**open** (ou·pøn) *adj.* abierto: *in the* ~ *air*, a cielo abierto, al aire libre; *with* ~ *arms*, con los brazos abiertos; *to set* o *throw* ~, abrir. 2 raso, descubierto. 3 libre, expedito. 4 descubierto, destapado: ~ *carriage*, coche descubierto. 5 expuesto [a]. 6 visible, manifiesto, público, conocido: ~ *secret*, secreto a voces. 7 franco, sincero. 8 claro, ralo; calado, poroso. 9 pendiente, no resuelto; discutible. 10 accesible [a ideas, ruegos, etc.]. 11 libre de hielos o de heladas [río; tiempo]. 12 MAR. despejado, sin niebla. 13 ~ *season*, temporada de caza o pesca. 14 ~ *water*, mar libre.

15 *s.* claro, raso; lugar abierto: *in the* ~, al raso, al aire libre; en alta mar; al descubierto.

**open (to)** *tr.* abrir. 2 ofrecer a la vista. 3 declarar, descubrir [sus sentimientos, etc.]. 4 iniciar, empezar. 5 MAR. avistar. 6 *to* ~ *up*, descubrir [a la vista, al entendimiento]; abrir, hacer accesible. 7 *intr.* abrir, abrirse. 8 descubrirse, aparecer. 9 confiarse, abrir su corazón; hablar claro, explicarse. 10 empezar, comenzar. 11 TEAT. estrenarse. 12 *to* ~ *into, on, upon, toward*, dar acceso a, salir a, dar a, mirar a. 13 *to* ~ *up*, aparecer a la vista, presentarse; perder la reserva, el encogimiento.

**open-air** *adj.* al aire libre.

**opener** (ou·pønø$^r$) *s.* abridor. 2 TEJ. abridora.

**open-eyed** *adj.* alerta, vigilante. 2 con los ojos abiertos. 3 asombrado.

**open-handed** *adj.* liberal, generoso, dadivoso.

**open-hearted** *adj.* franco, sincero; generoso.

**opening** (ou·pøpning) *s.* abertura, apertura. 2 abertura, entrada, brecha, boquete, portillo. 3 abra, bahía. 4 (E.U.) claro [en un bosque]. 5 comienzo, inauguración. 6 TEAT. estreno: ~ *night*, noche de estreno. 7 AJED. apertura. 8 oportunidad, coyuntura.

**openly** (-li) *adv.* abiertamente, francamente, públicamente.

**open-minded** *adj.* de espíritu abierto, razonable.

**open-mouthed** *adj.* con la boca abierta, boquiabierto. 2 ávido, voraz. 3 clamoroso. 4 ancho de boca.

**openness** (ou·pønnis) *s.* franqueza, sinceridad.

**openwork** (ou·pønuø$^r$k) *s.* calado [obra calada].

**opera** (a·pøra) *s.* MÚS. ópera: ~ *comique*, ópera cómica, zarzuela; ~ *glasses*, gemelos de teatro; ~ *hat*, clac; ~ *house*, teatro de la ópera.

**operate (to)** (a·pøreit) *tr.* hacer funcionar, mover, manejar, dirigir, explotar. 2 producir, efectuar. 3 *intr.* operar, obrar, producir efecto. 4 COM., MIL. operar. 5 CIR. operar: *to* ~ *upon someone for*, operar a uno de.

**operating** (-ing) *adj.* operante. 2 de funciona-

miento, de explotación. *3* operatorio, de operación: ~ *room,* quirófano.
**operation** (apørei·shøn) *s.* operación. *2* función, funcionamiento. *3* manejo; explotación. *4* vigor, vigencia.
**operative** (a·pøreitiv) *adj.* operativo. *2* CIR. operatorio. *3 s.* operario, obrero, artesano.
**operator** (a·pøreitø$^r$) *s.* operador, maquinista: *telephone* ~, telefonista. *2* CIR. operador. *3* especulador [en Bolsa], corredor de Bolsa.
**operculum** (opø·$^r$kuløm) *s.* opérculo.
**operetta** (apøre·ta) *s.* opereta.
**ophicleide** (a·fiklaid) *s.* MÚS. figle.
**ophidian** (ofi·dian) *s.* ZOOL. ofidio.
**ophiuroidean** (afiyuroi·dian) *adj.-s.* ZOOL. ofiuroideo.
**opthalmia** (afzæ·lmia) *s.* MED. olftalmía.
**ophthalmic** (-mik) *adj.* oftálmico.
**ophthalmology** (-ma·lodȳi) *s.* oftalmología.
**opiate** (ou·pieit) *s.* opiato. *2* narcótico. *3 adj.* opiado. *4* narcótico, adormecedor.
**opine** (o·pain) *tr.-intr.* opinar.
**opinion** (øpi·niøn) *s.* opinión: *public* ~, opinión pública. *2* buen concepto: *to have no* ~ *of*, no tener buen concepto de.
**opinionable** (-abøl) *adj.* opinable.
**opinionate(d** (-eit(id) *adj.* obstinado, terco.
**opinionative** (-eitiv) *adj.* doctrinal. *2* pertinaz, porfiado.
**opinioned** (-d) *adj.* presumido, obstinado.
**opium** (o·piøm) *s.* opio: ~ *poppy*, BOT. adormidera.
**opossum** (øpa·søm) *s.* ZOOL. zarigüeya, opósum.
**oppilation** (apilei·shøn) *s.* opilación.
**opponent** (øpou·nønt) *s.* oponente, contrario, adversario, antagonista. *2 adj.* opuesto [situado en frente]. *3* contrario, adverso.
**opportune** (apø$^r$tiu·n) *adj.* oportuno, conveniente, a propósito.
**opportunism** (-išm) *s.* oportunismo.
**opportunist** (-nist) *s.* oportunista.
**opportunity** (-iti) *s.* oportunidad; sazón, lugar, ocasión.
**opposable** (øpou·šabøl) *adj.* oponible. *2* resistible.
**oppose (to)** (øpou·š) *tr.* oponer, contraponer. *2* oponerse a, luchar contra, resistir, contrarrestar.
**opposed** (-d) *adj.* opuesto, contrario.
**opposer** (-ø$^r$) *s.* contrario, el que se opone.
**opposite** (a·pøšit) *adj.* opuesto: ~ *angles*, ángulos opuestos. *2* frontero. *3* contrario; adverso. *4 s. the* ~, lo opuesto, lo contrario. *5 prep.* frente a, en frente de. *6 adv.* enfrente, en situación opuesta.
**opposition** (apoši·shøn) *s.* oposición. | No tiene el sentido de concurso de pretendientes. *2* resistencia [acción]. *3* contrariedad, contradicción.
**oppositionist** (-ist) *s.* oposicionista.
**oppress (to)** (øpre·s) *tr.* oprimir. *2* tiranizar. *3* agobiar, abrumar, abatir.
**oppression** (-shøn) *s.* opresión. *2* tiranía. *3* agobio, abatimiento. *4* ahogo, sofocación, pesadez.
**oppresive** (-siv) *adj.* opresivo, opresor. *2* tiránico. *3* abrumador, agobiador. *4* sofocante.
**oppressor** (-sø$^r$) *s.* opresor, tirano.
**opprobrious** (øprou·briøs) *adj.* oprobioso, infamante. *2* injurioso, ultrajante.
**opprobrium** (-briøm) *s.* oprobio, deshonra.
**oppugn (to)** (øpiu·n) *tr.* opugnar, combatir.
**opt (to)** (apt) *intr.* optar.
**optative** (a·ptativ) *adj.* optativo.
**optic** (a·ptic) *adj.* óptico [de la visión, del ojo].
**optician** (apti·shan) *s.* óptico.

**optics** (a·ptiks) *s.* óptica [ciencia].
**optimist** (-ist) *s.* optimista.
**optimistic** (-istik) *adj.* optimista.
**optimum** (-øm) *adj.* óptimo, más favorable. *2 s.* cantidad, grado, punto, etc., óptimos.
**option** (a·pshøn) *s.* opción. *2* alternativa.
**optional** (-al) *adj.* facultativo, discrecional.
**optometer** (apta·metø$^r$) *s.* ÓPT. optómetro.
**opulence** (a·piuløns) *s.* opulencia.
**opulent** (-ønt) *adj.* opulento.
**opuscle** (øpø·søl), **opuscule** (opø·skiul) *s.* opúsculo.
**or** (o$^r$) *conj.* o, u. *2* si no, de otro modo.
**orach** (a·ræk) *s.* BOT. armuelle; orgaza.
**oracle** (a·rakøl) *s.* oráculo.
**oracular** (oræ·kiula$^r$) *adj.* de oráculo. *2* profético. *3* dogmático, magistral. *4* obscuro, ambiguo.
**oral** (o·ral) *adj.* oral. *2 s.* examen oral.
**orange** (a·røndȳ) *s.* BOT. naranja, naranjo; ~ *blossom*, azahar; ~ *grove*, naranjal; ~ *tree*, naranjo. *2* BOT. ~ *jessamine*, boj de China. *3 adj.-s.* anaranjado [color].
**orangeade** (arøndȳei·d) *s.* naranjada.
**orangery** (a·røndȳri) *s.* invernadero para naranjos.
**orang-outang** (orœ·ngutæn) *s.* ZOOL. orangután.
**orate (to)** (orei·t) *intr.* perorar, discursear.
**oration** (-shøn) *s.* oración, discurso.
**orator** (a·ratø$^r$) *s.* orador.
**oratorical** (arato·rikal) *adj.* oratorio; retórico.
**oratorio** (-riou) *s.* MÚS. oratorio.
**oratory** (a·ratori) *s.* oratoria. *2* oratorio, capilla.
**orb** (orb) *s.* orbe, esfera, globo. *2* astro. *3* círculo.
**orb (to)** *tr.* dar forma de círculo. *2* cercar, rodear, englobar.
**orbicular** (o$^r$bi·kiula$^r$) *adj.* orbicular.
**orbit** (o·$^r$bit) *s.* ANAT., ASTR. órbita.
**orbital** (o·$^r$bital) *adj.* orbital. *2* orbitario.
**orca** (o·$^r$ka) *s.* ZOOL. orca.
**orchard** (o·$^r$cha$^r$d) *s.* huerto [de frutales]; pomar.
**orchestra** (o·$^r$kistra) *s.* orquesta. *2* TEAT. platea.
**orchestrate (to)** (o·$^r$kistreit) *tr.* MÚS. orquestar.
**orchestration** (o$^r$kistre·shøn) *s.* MÚS. orquestación.
**orchid** (o·$^r$kid) *s.* BOT. orquídea.
**orchidaceous** (o$^r$kidei·shøs) *adj.* orquidáceo.
**orchis** (o·$^r$kis) *s.* ORCHID.
**ordain (to)** (o$^r$dei·n) *tr.* ordenar [conferir órdenes]. *2* ordenar, decretar, disponer. *3* destinar, predestinar [Dios, el hado, etc.].
**ordainment** (-mønt) *s.* decreto [de Dios, el destino, etc.].
**ordeal** (o·$^r$dial) *s.* ordalía. *2* prueba [penosa].
**order** (o·$^r$dø$^r$) *s.* orden [disposición o sucesión regular; método, regla; concierto]; condición o estado [de las cosas]; buen estado: ~ *of the day*, orden del día; *in good* ~, en buen estado; *in* ~, en orden; por su orden, en regla; funcionando; *out of* ~, desordenado; descompuesto, estropeado. *2* orden [religiosa, militar, de caballería, etc.]. *3* condecoración o insignia de una orden. *4* orden, clase, grado: *the lower orders*, la clase baja; *on the* ~ *of*, del orden de, a modo de. *5* MAT., H. NAT., ARQ. orden. *6* orden [sacramento]: *to take orders*, ordenarse. *7* orden, mandato, precepto: *by* ~ *of*, por orden de. *8* COM. orden, pedido, encargo: *to the* ~ *of*, a la orden de; *to* ~, a la medida, por encargo. *9* *in* ~ *to*, para, a fin de; *in* ~ *that*, para que, a fin de que.
**order (to)** *tr.* ordenar, poner en orden. *2* ordenar, disponer, mandar: *to* ~ *away*, despedir, decir [a uno] que se vaya; *to* ~ *in*, mandar entrar; mandar traer; *to* ~ *out*, mandar salir. *3* pedir, encargar [mercancías, un coche, la comida, etc.];

mandar hacer. 4 ECLES. ordenar. 5 MIL. *Order arms!*, ¡descansen!
**orderliness** (oˈrdəˈrlinis) s. orden, arreglo, método.
**orderly** (oˈrdəˈrli) *adj.* ordenado, arreglado, metódico. 2 obediente, tranquilo. 3 MIL. ~ *officer*, oficial de día. 4 s. MIL. ordenanza. 2 practicante [de hospital].
**ordinal** (oˈrdinal) *adj.-s.* ordinal. 2 s. ritual [libro].
**ordinance** (-ans) s. ordenación, arreglo. 2 ordenanza, decreto. 3 ECLES. rito, ceremonia.
**ordinarily** (-erili) *adv.* ordinariamente.
**ordinary** (oˈrdineri) *adj.* ordinario. 2 s. ordinario [juez, obispo]. 3 mesa redonda [en una fonda]. 4 ordinario [de la misa]. 5 lo ordinario: *out of the* ~, excepcional, extraordinario. 6 *in* ~, en ejercicio; de cámara.
**ordinate** (-neit) s. GEOM. ordenada.
**ordination** (-eiˈshøn) s. ECLES. ordenación.
**ordinee** (oˈrdiniˑ) s. ordenando.
**ordnance** (oˈrdnɑns) s. MIL. artillería, cañones, máquinas de guerra. 2 MIL. pertrechos, suministros.
**ordure** (oˈrdiur) s. inmundicia, suciedad.
**ore** (ouˈr) s. MIN. mineral, ganga, mena.
**oread** (ouˈriæd) s. MIT. oréade.
**organ** (oˈrgan) s. órgano [de un animal, una planta, un partido, etc.]. 2 MÚS. órgano: *barrel* ~, organillo; ~ *grinder*, organillero.
**organdy** (oˈrgandi) s. organdí.
**organic** (oˈrgæˑnik) *adj.* orgánico; ~ *chemistry*, química orgánica.
**organism** (oˈrganišm) s. BIOL., FIL. organismo.
**organist** (oˈrganist) s. organista.
**organization** (organaiseˑshøn) s. organización.
**organize (to)** (oˈrganaiš) *tr.* organizar. 2 *intr.* organizarse.
**organography** (oˈrganaˑgrafi) s. organografía.
**orgasm** (oˈrgæšm) s. orgasmo.
**orgeat** (oˈrdÿæt) s. horchata; agua de cebada.
**orgiastic** (oˈrdÿiæˑstik) *adj.* orgiástico.
**orgy** (oˈrdÿi) s. orgía.
**oriel** (ouˈriøl) s. ARQ. mirador, cierro de cristales.
**Orient** (ouˈriønt) s. oriente, levante. 2 [con min.] oriente [de una perla]. 3 *adj.* naciente [sol]. 4 brillante, transparente.
**orient (to)** *tr.* orientar.
**oriental** (orieˑntal) *adj.-s.* oriental.
**orientalist** (orieˑntalist) s. orientalista.
**orientate (to)** (ouˈrienteit) *tr.* orientar. 2 *intr.* caer o mirar hacia el este.
**orientation** (orienteiˑshøn) s. orientación.
**orifice** (aˈrifis) s. orificio.
**oriflame** (aˈriflæm) s. oriflama.
**origin** (aˈridÿin) s. origen. 2 linaje, nacimiento.
**original** (oriˑdÿinal) *adj.* original: ~ *sin*, pecado original. 2 primitivo, prístino, primero. 3 s. original. | No tiene sentido de original de imprenta.
**originality** (oridÿinæˑliti) s. originalidad.
**originate (to)** (oriˑdÿineit) *tr.* originar, crear, producir. 2 *intr.* originarse, nacer, dimanar.
**origination** (-eiˑshøn) s. origen; creación, producción.
**originator** (oriˑdÿineitøˈr) s. originador, creador, inventor, autor; causa primera.
**oriole** (ouˈrioul) s. ORN. oropéndola, oriol.
**orison** (aˈrišøn) s. oración, plegaria.
**Orkney Islands** (øˈrkni) *n. pr.* GEOGR. Orcadas.
**orlop** (oˈrlap) s. MAR. sollado.
**ormolu** (oˈrmolu) s. metal dorado, similor. 2 polvo para dorar.

**ornament** (øˈrnamønt) s. ornamento, ornato, adorno. 2 honra, gala [pers. que honra]. 3 MÚS. adorno. 4 *pl.* LITURG. ornamentos.
**ornament (to)** *tr.* ornamentar, adornar, decorar.
**ornamental** (oˈrnameˑntal) *adj.* ornamental, decorativo.
**ornamentation** (-eiˑshøn) s. ornamentación.
**ornate** (oˈrneiˑt) *adj.* adornado en exceso; recargado. 2 florido [estilo].
**ornery** (oˈrnøri) *adj.* (E.U.) fam. malhumorado, difícil.
**ornithologist** (oˈrnizaˑlodÿist) s. ornitólogo.
**ornithology** (oˈrnizaˑlodÿ) s. ornitología.
**orogeny** (oraˑdÿeni) s. orogénesis.
**orographic** (oˈrogræˑfik(al) *adj.* orográfico.
**orography** (oraˑgrafi) s. orografía.
**orology** (oraˑlødÿi) s. orología.
**orotund** (ouˈrotønd) *adj.* rotundo, sonoro.
**orphan** (oˈrfan) *adj.-s.* huérfano.
**orphan (to)** *tr.* dejar huérfano.
**orphanage** (-idÿ) s. orfandad. 2 orfanato.
**orphanhood** (-jud) s. orfandad [estado].
**Orpheus** (oˈrfiøs) *n. pr.* MIT. Orfeo.
**Orphic** (oˈrfik) *adj.* órfico.
**orpiment** (oˈrpimønt) s. oropimente.
**orrery** (oˈrøri) s. planetario.
**orris** (oˈris) s. galón de seda y oro. 2 BOT. lirio de Florencia.
**orthodox** (oˈrzødaks) *adj.-s.* ortodoxo.
**orthodoxy** (-i) s. ortodoxia.
**orthogenesis** (-dÿeˑnisis) s. ortogénesis.
**orthogonal** (oˈrza·gønal) *adj.* ortogonal.
**orthographic (al** (oˈrzogræˑfik(al) *adj.* ortográfico.
**orthography** (oˈrzaˑgrafi) s. ortografía.
**orthop (a) edy** (oˈrzopidi) s. ortopédico.
**orthopterous** (oˈrzaˑptørøs) *adj.* ortóptero.
**ortive** (aˈrtiv) *adj.* ortivo).
**ortolan** (oˈrtølan) s. ORN. hortelano.
**oscillate (to)** (aˈsileit) *tr.* hacer oscilar. 2 *intr.* oscilar. 3 vibrar. 4 fluctuar.
**oscillation** (-eiˑshøn) s. oscilación. 2 vibración. 3 fluctuación.
**oscillator** (aˈsileitøˈr) s. oscilador.
**oscillatory** (asileiˑtori) *adj.* oscilatorio.
**osculate (to)** (aˈskiuleit) *tr.* besar. 2 GEOM. tocar por osculación.
**osculation** (-eiˑshøn) s. GEOM. osculación.
**osier** (ouˈÿøˈr) s. BOT. mimbrera; sarga. 2 mimbre.
**osiery** (ouˈÿøri) s. mimbreral. 2 objetos de mimbre.
**Osmanil** (asmæˑnli) *adj.-s.* osmanlí.
**osmium** (aˈsmiøm) s. QUÍM. osmio.
**osmose** (aˈsmous), **osmosis** (asmouˑsis) s. ósmosis.
**osmotic** (asmaˑtik) *adj.* osmótico.
**osprey** (aˈsprei) s. ORN. halieto, osífraga, quebrantahuesos.
**osseous** (aˈsiøs) *adj.* óseo.
**ossicle** (aˈsikøl) s. huesecillo.
**ossification** (asifikeiˑshøn) s. osificación.
**ossifrage** (aˈsifridÿ) s. OSPREY.
**ossify (to)** (-fai) *tr.* convertir en hueso. 2 *intr.* osificarse. ¶ Pret. y p. p.: *ossified.*
**ossuary** (aˈsiueri) s. osario.
**Ostend** (asteˑnd) *n. pr.* GEOGR. Ostende.
**ostensible** (asteˑnsibøl) *adj.* ostensible. 2 aparente.
**ostensive** (-siv) *adj.* ostensivo. 2 ostensible.
**ostensory** (asteˑnsori) s. ostensorio, custodia.
**ostentation** (astønteiˑshøn) s. ostentación. 2 boato, pompa. 3 gala, alarde.
**ostentatious** (-shøs) *adj.* ostentoso, pomposo.
**osteologist** (astiaˑlødÿist) s. osteólogo.

**osteology** (-i) *s.* osteología.
**osteopath** (a·stiøpæz) *s.* osteópata.
**osteopathy** (astia·pazi) *s.* osteopatía.
**ostiary** (a·stieri) *s.* ostiario.
**ostler** (a·slø$^r$) *s.* mozo de cuadra, palafrenero.
**ostlery** (a·sløri) *s.* hostería.
**ostracism** (a·strasišm) *s.* ostracismo. 2 exclusión del trato social.
**ostracize (to)** (-saiš) *tr.* condenar al ostracismo. 2 excluir del trato social.
**ostrich** (a·strich) *s.* ORN. avestruz.
**Ostrogoth** (a·strogaz) *adj.-s.* ostrogodo.
**other** (ø·ðø$^r$) *adj.* otro, otra, otros, otras: *the ~ world*, el otro mundo. 2 *pron.* (*pl.* **others**) otro, otra, otros, otras: *others would do it*, los otros lo harían. 3 *adv.* [con *than*], más que, otra cosa que.
**otherwise** (-uaiš) *adv.* otramente, de otra manera: *~ called*, alias, por otro nombre. 2 en otro caso, por otra parte, fuera de eso. 3 *conj.* si no, de otro modo, de lo contrario.
**otiose** (ou·shious) *adj.* ocioso.
**otitis** (outai·tis) *s.* MED. otitis.
**otocyst** (ou·tøsist) *s.* ZOOL. otocisto.
**otologist** (ota·lodÿist) *s.* otólogo.
**otology** (-i) *s.* otología.
**otoscope** (ou·tøskoup) *s.* otoscopio.
**otter** (o·tø$^r$) *s.* ZOOL. nutria. 2 piel de nutria.
**Ottoman** (a·tomæn) *adj.-s.* otomano. 2 *s.* [con min.] otomana [mueble]. 3 otomán [tejido].
**ouch** (auch) *s.* broche, joya. 2 *interj.* ¡uy!, ¡ay!
**1) ought** (ot) *s.-adv.* AUGHT.
**2) ought** *def.* y *aux.*, seguido gralte. de un infinitivo con *to*. Sólo se usa en la forma *ought* que se traduce generalmente por el pres. y el condicional de deber, haber de o haber que: *I ~ to write*, debo escribir o debería escribir.
**ounce** (auns) *s.* onza [28.35 gr.]. 2 pizca. 3 ZOOL. onza.
**our** (aur) *adj.* nuestro, nuestra, nuestros, nuestras: *Our Lady*, Nuestra Señora.
**ours** (-š) *pron. pos.* [el] nuestro, [la] nuestra; [los] nuestros, [las] nuestras: *your room is larger than ~*, vuestro cuarto es mayor que el nuestro; *a friend of ~*, un amigo nuestro.
**ourself** (aurse·lf) *pron.* nosotros mismos, nos [cuando se usa el plural para una sola pers.].
**ourselves** (-lvš) *pron.* nosotros mismos. 2 nos, a nosotros mismos.
**oust (to)** (aust) *tr.* desalojar, desahuciar, echar fuera.
**ouster** (au·stø$^r$) *s.* DER. desposeimiento; desahucio.
**out** (aut) *adv.* fuera, afuera, hacia fuera, en el exterior: *~ of*, fuera de; *to go ~*, partir, salir. 2 en sociedad, en escena, en público. 3 distintamente, claro, sin rodeos: *speak ~*, hable claro, sin rodeos. 4 completamente, enteramente, hasta agotarse, hasta el fin. 5 en partes [para distribuir]: *to pass ~*, distribuir, repartir. 6 por, movido por [un sentimiento, etc.]: *~ of pity*, por compasión. 7 de, con [un recipiente]: *~ of the bottle*, de la botella. 8 *adj.* [como predicado o pospuesto al nombre] ausente, fuera de casa. 9 alejado, distante [de un centro, etc.]. 10 fuera de sitio. 11 destituido, cesante. 12 dado, puesto [en arriendo, a préstamo]: *~ at interest*, puesto a interés. 13 expedido, dictado [orden, mandato, etc.]. 14 en huelga. 15 agotado, gastado; acabado; cerrado, apagado; terminado, expirado: *the milk is ~*, se ha acabado la leche; *the lights are ~*, las luces están apagadas; *the time*

*is ~*, ha pasado la hora; ha expirado el plazo. 16 descubierto, publicado, aparecido: *the book is just ~*, el libro acaba de salir. 17 que ya no está en uso o moda. 18 desavenido, reñido. 19 equivocado.
20 Forma gran número de locuciones, muchas de las cuales se encuentran en otros artículos de este Diccionario: *~ and away*, con mucho; *~ and ~*, completamente; *~ for*, en compaña para, en busca de; en favor de; *~ of favour*, en desgracia; *~ of money*, sin dinero; *~ of this world*, extraordinario, del otro jueves; *~ to win*, decidido a vencer; *three ~ of four*, de cada cuatro, tres.
21 *interj.* ¡fuera! 22 *~ with it!*, ¡desembuche usted!
23 *s.* exterior, parte de fuera, esquina, saliente. 24 IMPR. omisión. 25 *at outs*, o *on the outs with*, reñido con.
**out (to)** *tr.* desposeer, echar fuera, expulsar. 2 apagar. 3 *intr.* salir. 4 descubrirse, divulgarse.
**out-and-out** *adj.* acérrimo; consumado. 2 rotundo, categórico.
**outbalance (to)** (autbæ·lans) *tr.* pesar más que; exceder en peso o efecto, sobrepujar, aventajar.
**outbid** (autbi·d) *tr.* mejorar, pujar, ofrecer más que [otro] en subasta, etc.
**outboard** (au·tbo$^r$d) *adv.-adj.* MAR. fuera de borda: *~ motor*, motor fuera de borda.
**outbound** (-baund) *adj.* en viaje de ida, que sale, de salida.
**outbrave (to)** (-breiv) *tr.* resistir, arrostrar, desafiar. 2 sobrepujar en valentía.
**outbreak** (-breik) *s.* erupción, brote. 2 arrebato; explosión, estallido. 3 tumulto, motín, insurrección. 4 principio [de una guerra, una epidemia, etc.]: *at the ~ of the war*, al estallar la guerra.
**outbreathe (to)** (-brez) *tr.* dejar sin aliento, agotar.
**outbuilding** (-bilding) *s.* dependencia, accesoria, anejo [de un edificio].
**outburst** (-bø$^r$st) *s.* arranque, explosión, estallido: *~ of laughter*, explosión de risas, risotada.
**outcast** (-kæst) *adj.-s.* desterrado, proscrito; paria, excluido de la sociedad.
**outclass (to)** (-klæs) *tr.* sobrepujar, ser superior a.
**outcome** (-køm) *s.* resultado, consecuencia, desenlace.
**outcry** (-krai) *s.* grito. 2 gritería, clamor, clamoreo, alboroto.
**outdare (to)** (autde·ø$^r$) *tr.* ser más atrevido [que otro]. 2 dominar por la osadía; desafiar.
**outdate (to)** (-dei·t) *tr.* anticuar.
**outdistance (to)** (-di·stans) *tr.* adelantar, dejar atrás.
**outdo (to)** (-du) *tr.* exceder, sobrepujar, eclipsar, vencer: *to ~ oneself*, excederse a sí mismo.
**outdoor** (au·tdo$^r$) *adj.* de fuera de casa, al aire libre. 2 externo, a domicilio.
**outdoors** (autdo·$^r$š) *adv.* al aire libre, el campo, la calle. 2 *adv.* fuera de casa, al aire libre, al raso.
**outer** (au·tø$^r$) *adj.* exterior, externo. 2 *s.* círculo exterior de un blanco.
**outermost** (-moust) *adj.* extremo, más exterior.
**outface (to)** (autfei·š) *tr.* dominar, intimidar [con la mirada]. 2 arrostrar, desafiar.
**outfall** (au·tfol) *s.* salida, desembocadura.
**outfield** (-fild) *s.* campo abierto.
**outfit** (-fit) *s.* equipo. 2 pertrechos, ajuar, avíos.
**outfit (to)** *tr.* equipar, aviar, habilitar, armar.
**outfitter** (-fitø$^r$) *s.* abastecedor, proveedor, equipador de ropa hecha.

**outflank (to)** (autflæ·nk) *tr.* MIL. flanquear.
**outflow** (au·tflou) *s.* efusión, flujo, salida.
**outflow (to)** *intr.* salir, fluir, manar.
**outgeneral (to)** (autdẏe·nǿrɑl) *tr.* superar en estrategia; ser más listo que.
**outgo** (-gou·) *s.* salida, gasto, desembolso.
**outgo (to)** *tr.* aventajar, adelantarse a.
**outgoing** (-ing) *adj.* saliente, que sale, cesante. *2 s.* salida.
**ougrow (to)** (autgrou·) *tr.* crecer más que; hacerse demasiado grande para: *to ~ one's clothing*, quedársele a uno corta la ropa. *2* curársele, pasársele a uno [algo] con los años, al crecer.
**outgrowth** (ou·tgrouz) *s.* excrecencia, nacencia. *2* resultado, consecuencia, producto, efecto.
**outhouse** (-jaus) *s.* dependencia, anejo [de un edificio]. *2* retrete fuera de la casa.
**outing** (-ing) *s.* salida, paseo, jira, excursión.
**outlander** (-lændǿʳ) *s.* extranjero, forastero.
**outlandish** (autlæ·ndish) *adj.* de aspecto extranjero; exótico. *2* extraño, raro. *3* remoto, salvaje.
**outlast (to)** (-læ·st) *tr.* durar más que.
**outlaw** (aut·tlo) *s.* bandido, forajido. *2* proscrito.
**outlaw (to)** *tr.* proscribir. *2* declarar ilegal.
**outlawry** (-lori) *s.* proscripción, rebeldía.
**outlay** (-lei) *s.* desembolso, gasto, salida.
**outlay (to)** *t.* desembolsar, gastar.
**outlet** (au·tlet) *s.* salida; orificio de salida, desaguadero, desagüe; toma de corriente. *2* corriente que sale [de un río, etc.]. *3* COM. salida, mercado.
**outline** (au·tlain) *s.* contorno, perfil. *2* bosquejo, esbozo, croquis. *3* plan, idea, esquema. *4* resumen, compendio; líneas generales de.
**outline (to)** *tr.* perfilar, contornar, delinear. *2* bosquejar, esbozar; trazar las líneas generales de.
**outlive (to)** (-li·v) *tr.* sobrevivir a; durar más que.
**outlook** (au·tluk) *s.* atalaya. *2* vista, perspectiva. *3* actitud mental, punto de vista. *4* perspectivas, probabilidades.
**outlying** (-laiing) *adj.* remoto; alejado del centro, exterior, circundante. *2* extrínseco.
**outmatch (to)** (autmæ·ch) *tr.* aventajar, mostrarse superior a.
**outmeasure (to)** (-me·ẏǿʳ) *tr.* exceder en medida.
**outmoded** (-mou·did) *adj.* pasado de moda, anticuado.
**outmost** (au·tmoust) *adj.* OUTERMOST.
**outnumber (to)** (autnǿ·mbǿʳ) *tr.* exceder en número, ser más que.
**out-of-date** *adj.* anticuado, pasado de moda.
**out-of-door** *adj.* OUTDOOR.
**out-of-print** *adj.* agotado [libro, edición].
**out-of-the-way** *adj.* apartado, remoto, desviado, inaccesible. *2* poco usual, poco común.
**outpatient** (au·tpeishǿnt) *s.* enfermo ambulatorio.
**outpost** (-poust) *s.* MIL. avanzada; puesto avanzado. *2* fortín [en las fronteras de la civilización].
**outpour** (-poʳ), **outpouring** (-ing) *s.* efusión, derramamiento; chorro. *2* fig. efusión, desahogo.
**output** (-put) *s.* rendimiento, producción. *2* ELECT. salida; circuito de salida. *3* MEC. potencia, capacidad, efecto útil.
**outrage** (au·treidẏ) *s.* ultraje, desafuero, atropello, daño; atrocidad. *2* violación.
**outrage (to)** *tr.* ultrajar, atropellar. *2* violar.
**outrageous** (-rei·dẏøs) *adj.* ultrajante, injurioso. *2* violento, furioso. *3* desaforado, enorme, atroz; desenfrenado.

**outreach (to)** (au·trıch) *tr.* pasar, pasar más allá de, exceder.
**outride (to)** (-rai·d) *tr.* ganar la delantera [yendo a caballo o en coche]. *2 intr.* cabalgar junto a un coche.
**outrider** (-ǿʳ) *s.* criado a caballo que acompaña a un coche.
**outrigger** (-ri·gǿʳ) *s.* MAR. botalón, tangón, pescante. *2* MAR. outrigger. *3* caballo de refuerzo.
**outright** (au·trait) *adj.* sincero, franco, directo. *2* completo, absoluto. *3 adv.* completamente. *4* abiertamente, sin reserva. *5* en seguida.
**outroot (to)** (-ru·t) *tr.* desarraigar.
**outrun (to)** (-rø·n) *tr.* correr más que; aventajar, dejar atrás.
**outsell (to)** (-se·l) *tr.* vender más, más caro o más aprisa que.
**outset** (au·tset) *s.* comienzo, principio, salida.
**outshine (to)** (-shai·n) *intr.* brillar, resplandecer. *2 tr.* eclipsar, exceder en brillantez.
**outside** (au·tsaid) *s.* exterior, parte externa; superficie, haz: *on the ~*, por fuera. *2* apariencia. *3* lo más, lo sumo: *at the ~*, a lo más, a lo sumo. *4 adj.* exterior, externo. *5* superficial, aparente. *6* extraño, ajeno. *7* neutral. *8* extremo. *9* extraño a la ocupación normal de uno. *10 adv.* fuera, afuera, por fuera. *11 prep.* fuera de, más allá de; excepto.
**outsider** (-sai·dǿʳ) *s.* forastero. *2* extraño, profano. *3* intruso. *4* DEP. caballo que no figura entre los favoritos.
**outskirt** (au·tskǿʳt) *s.* borde, orilla. *2 pl.* alrededores.
**outspoken** (-spou·kǿn) *adj.* claro, franco, abierto; boquifresco.
**outspread** (-spre·d) *s.* extensión, despliegue, difusión. *2 adj.* extendido; difundido.
**outspread (to)** *tr.* extender; difundir. *2 intr.* extenderse, difundirse.
**outstanding** (-stæ·nding) *adj.* saledizo, saliente. *2* destacado, descollante, notable, sobresaliente, principal. *3* pendiente, sin pagar, sin cobrar.
**outstay (to)** (-stei·) *tr.* quedarse más tiempo que [uno]. *2* quedarse más tiempo de lo que autoriza [la cortesía, el permiso que uno tiene, etc.].
**outstretch (to)** (-stre·ch) *tr.* extender, alargar.
**outstrip (to)** (-stre·ch) *tr.* extender, alargar.
**outstrip (to)** (-stri·p) *tr.* adelantar, dejarr atrás.
**outtalk** (-to·k) *tr.* hablar más o mejor que.
**outturn** (-tǿʳn) *s.* ECON. producción.
**outward** (au·twǿ·d) *adj.* exterior, externo, visible. *2* dirigido hacia fuera; que sale, de ida [tren, cargamento]. *3* aparente, superficial. *4* corporal, carnal. *5 adv.* afuera, hacia fuera. *6* exteriormente. *7* superficialmente. *8* corporalmente.
**outwardness** (-nis) *s.* exterioridad.
**outwards** (-s) *adv.* OUTWARD.
**outwear (to)** (autwe·ʳ) *tr.* gastar; estropear con el uso. *2* durar más que. *3* pasársele a uno [una pena, etc.], con el tiempo.
**outweigh (to)** (-wei·) *tr.* pesar más que. *2* preponderar sobre. *3* contrapesar.
**outwit (to)** (-wi·t) *tr.* engañar con astucia; ser más listo que. ¶ Pret. y p. p.: *outwitted*; ger.: *-tting*.
**outwork** (au·twǿʳk) *s.* FORT. obra exterior.
**outworn** (autwo·ʳn) *adj.* gastado, usado. *2* anticuado.
**ouzel** (u·šøl) *s.* ORN. mirlo.
**oval** (ou·val) *adj.* oval, ovalado. *2 s.* óvalo.
**ovarian** (ove·riøn) *adj.* ovárico.

**ovary** (ou·vari) *s.* ANAT., ZOOL., BOT. ovario.
**ovate** (ou·veit) *adj.* aovado, ovado.
**ovation** (ovei·shøn) *s.* ovación.
**oven** (ø·vøn) *s.* horno, hornillo.
**over** (ou·vø<sup>r</sup>) *adv.* arriba, por encima. *2* al otro lado; de una mano a otra: *to go ~ to the enemy,* pasarse al enemigo; *to hand ~,* dar, entregar. *3* enfrente. *4* al revés, trastornado. *6* de ancho, a lo ancho; de un extremo a otro. *7* completamente: *all ~,* por todas partes, completamente. *8* más, de más, demasiado. *9* hacia fuera: *to run ~,* salirse, derramarse. *10* en extremo. *11 ~ again,* de nuevo, otra vez. *12 ~ and above,* además de; fam. demasiado.
 *13 prep.* sobre, encima de, por encima de. *14* al otro lado de, allende; a la vuelta de. *15* arriba de, más de: *~ a million,* más de un millón. *16* durante. *17* por todo, a lo largo de [un espacio, camino, etc.]: *all ~ the city,* por toda la ciudad. *18* de, con motivo de, a propósito de.
 *19 adj.* superior, más alto. *20* que cubre. *21* excesivo, de más. *22* que ha llegado al otro lado. *23* acabado, terminado.
**overabundance** (-abø·ndans) *s.* sobreabundancia, superabundancia.
**overact** (-æ·kt) *tr.* exagerar.
**over-all** *adj.* completo, global, de conjunto.
**overalls** (ou·vørolš) *s. pl.* pantalones de trabajo, mono. *2* sobrerropa. *3* polainas impermeables.
**overarch (to)** (ouvøra·<sup>r</sup>ch) *tr.* abovedar.
**overawe (to)** (ouvøro·) *tr.* intimidar, atemorizar.
**overbalance (to)** (-bæ·lans) *tr.* pesar más que, sobrepujar. *2* hacer perder el equilibrio.
**overbear (to)** (-be·<sup>r</sup>) *tr.* agobiar, abrumar, oprimir. *2* dominar, tiranizar, imponerse.
**overbearing** (ouvø<sup>r</sup>be·ring) *adj.* dominador, despótico, imperioso, altanero.
**overblown** (ou·vø<sup>r</sup>blou) *adj.* que ha florecido demasiado; demasiado abierta, marchita, pasada [flor]. *2* cubierto [de cosas traídas por el viento].
**overboard** (-bo<sup>r</sup>d) *adv.* MAR. por la borda. *2* MAR. al mar, al agua: *man ~!,* ¡hombre al agua!
**overbore** (-bo·<sup>r</sup>) *pret.* de TO OVERBEAR.
**overborne** (-bo·<sup>r</sup>n) *p. p.* de TO OVERBEAR.
**overburden** (-bø·<sup>r</sup>døn) *s.* sobrecarga.
**overburden (to)** *tr.* sobrecargar. *2* abrumar.
**overcame** (-kei·m) *pret.* de TO OVERCOME.
**overcast** (ou·vø<sup>r</sup>kæst) *adj.* nublado, cubierto, encapotado. *2* sombrío. *3* COST. sobrehilado.
**overcast (to)** (-kæ·st) *tr.* anublar, obscurecer, entristecer. *2* COST. sobrehilar. *3 intr.* nublarse.
**overcharge** (ou·vø<sup>r</sup>cha<sup>r</sup>dȳ) *s.* sobrescarga. *2* recargo [de precio]; precio exhorbitante.
**overcharge (to)** (-cha·<sup>r</sup>daȳ) *tr.* sobrecargar, recargar. *2* cobrar demasiado.
**overcloud (to)** (-klau·d) *tr.* cubrir de nubes, anublar. *2 intr.* anublarse, nublarse.
**overcoat** (ou·vø<sup>r</sup>kout) *s.* sobretodo, gabán, abrigo.
**overcome (to)** (ouvø<sup>r</sup>kø·m) *tr.* vencer, domar, dominar, triunfar de. *2* vencer, superar, allanar [obstáculos, dificultades, etc.]. *3* sobreponerse, hacerse superior a. *4* rendir, agotar, agobiar.
**overconfident** (-ka·nfidønt) *adj.* presumido; demasiado confiado.
**overcrowd (to)** (-krau·d) *tr.* apiñar, atestar.
**overdevelop (to)** (-dive·løp) *tr.* desarrollar excesivamente. *2* FOT. revelar demasiado.
**overdid** (-di·d) *pret.* de TO OVERDO.
**overdo (to)** (ouvø<sup>r</sup>du·) *tr.* hacer [algo] demasiado, llevar al exceso; exagerar. *2* cocer demasiado. *3*

fatigar, agotar, agobiar de trabajo. *4 intr.* excederse; hacer o trabajar demasiado.
**overdone** (-dø·n) *p. p.* de TO OVERDO.
**overdose** (ou·vø<sup>r</sup>dous) *s.* dosis excesiva.
**overdraft** (-dræft) *s.* COM. sobregiro, giro en descubierto, en exceso.
**overdraw (to)** (ouvø<sup>r</sup>dro·) *intr.-tr.* sobregirar, girar en descubierto.
**overdress (to)** (-dre·s) *tr.-intr.* vestir, ataviar o ataviarse con exceso.
**overdue** (-diu·) *adj.* COM. vencido y no pagado. *2* que lleva retraso [buque, etc.].
**overestimate** (-e·stimeit) *tr.* estimar, tasar, avaluar o presuponer por encima del valor real. *2* atribuir un valor excesivo, exagerar.
**overexcite (to)** (-ksai·t) *tr.* sobreexcitar.
**overexcitement** (-mønt) *s.* sobrexcitación.
**overexposure** (-ekspou·ȳø<sup>r</sup>) *s.* FOT. exceso de exposición.
**overfeed (to)** (-fi·d) *tr.* sobrealimentar.
**overflow** (ou·vø<sup>r</sup>flou) *s.* inundación, avenida. *2* desbordamiento, derrame, rebosamiento. *3* superabundancia. *4* rebosadero, descarga.
**overflow (to)** (-flou·) *tr.* inundar; sobrellenar. *2* salir de [los bordes]. *3 intr.* desbordarse, rebosar.
**overflowing** (-ing) *adj.* desbordante, rebosante. *2 s.* desbordamiento.
**overgrow (to)** (-grou·) *tr.* crecer en, cubrir [díc. de plantas, hierbas, etc.]. *2* crecer más que. *3 intr.* crecer, desarrollarse con exceso. *4* cubrirse de plantas, hierbas, etc.
**overgrown** (-n) *adj.* cubierto de plantas, hierbas. *2* anormalmente crecido o desarrollado.
**overgrowth** (ou·vø<sup>r</sup>grouz) *s.* crecimiento excesivo. *2* vegetación exuberante, maleza.
**overhand** (-jænd) *adj.* DEP. voleado por lo alto; palma abajo. *2* COST. sobrehilado.
**overhang** (-jæng) *s.* proyección, parte que sobresale. *2* ARQ. alero; salidizo; vuelo.
**overhang (to)** (-jæ·ng) *tr.* hacer saliente, volar, colgar sobre; caer a. *2* estar suspendido sobre; amenazar. *3 intr.* hacer saliente.
**overhaul** (ou·vø<sup>r</sup>jol) *s.* MEC. repaso, recorrido.
**overhaul (to)** (ouvø<sup>r</sup>jo·l) *tr.* repasar, recorrer. *2* revisar. *3* registrar, examinar. *4* alcanzar [al que va delante].
**overhead** (-je·d) *adv.* sobre la cabeza de uno, arriba, en lo alto. *2 adj.* (ou·vø<sup>r</sup>jed) situado en lo alto: *~ crossing,* cruce o paso superior; *~ railway,* (Ingl.) ferrocarril aéreo o elevado. *3 ~ expenses,* COM. gastos generales.
**overhear (to)** (-ji·<sup>r</sup>) *tr.* oír por casualidad o espiando, acertar a oir.
**overheat (to)** (-ji·t) *tr.* acalorar. *2* sobrecalentar, recalentar.
**overindulge** (-indø·ldȳ) *tr.* mimar demasiado. *2 intr.* tratarse demasiado bien.
**overindulgence** (-øns) *s.* indulgencia o mimo excesivo. *2* exceso [en el comer, etc.].
**overjoyed** (-dȳoi·d) *adj.* alborozado, jubiloso.
**overladen** (-lei·døn) *adj.* sobrecargado.
**overlaid** (-lei·d) *pret.* y *p. p.* de TO OVERLAY.
**overlain** (-n) *p. p.* de TO OVERLIE.
**overland** (ou·vø<sup>r</sup>læ·nd) *adj.-s.* por tierra, por vía terrestre.
**overlap** (-læp) *s.* parte que traslapa, cubre o cruza; solapo, traslapo.
**overlap (to)** (-læ·p) *tr.-intr.* traslapar, solapar, cruzar sobre, cubrir. *2 tr.* lamer [las olas].
**overlay** (ou·vø<sup>r</sup>lei) *s.* capa [que recubre]. *2 pret.* de TO OVERLIE.

**overlay (to)** (-lei·) *tr.* cubrir, recubrir, dar una capa, dorar, platear, chapear. *2* cubrir, obscurecer. *3* oprimir, abrumar.

**overleaf** (ou·vø$^r$lif) *adv.* al dorso, a la vuelta.

**overlie (to)** (-lai·) *tr.* descansar, estar sobre.

**overload** (ou·vø$^r$loud) *s.* carga excesiva, sobrecarga.

**overload (to)** (-lou·d) *tr.* cargar excesivamente. *2* sobrecargar.

**overlook** (-luk) *s.* altura, atalaya. *2* ojeada, examen general. *3* descuido, inadvertencia.

**overlook (to)** (-lu·k) *tr.* mirar desde lo alto. *2* dominar [estar más elevado]. *3* dar a, tener vista a. *4* examinar, inspeccionar, vigilar. *5* repasar, revisar. *6* no notar, dejar de ver. *7* no hacer caso; pasar por alto, descuidar. *8* tolerar, perdonar.

**overlord (to)** (-lo·$^r$d) *tr.* señorear, dominar despóticamente.

**overly** (ou·vø$^r$li) *adv.* fam. muy, mucho, demasiado.

**overlying** (-lai·ng) *ger.* de TO OVERLIE.

**overmuch** (ou·vø$^r$møch) *adj.-adv.* demasiado.

**overnice** (-nai·s) *adj.* remilgado, dengoso, demasiado escrupuloso o exigente.

**overnight** (-nai·t) *adv.* en la noche anterior. *2* toda la noche: *to stay ~*, pasar la noche. *3* de la noche a la mañana.

**overpass** (ou·vø$^r$pæs) *s.* paso elevado; puente o vía por encima de un ferrocarril, carretera, etc.

**overpay (to)** (-pei·) *tr.* pagar demasiado.

**overpeopled** (-pɪ·pøld) *adj.* excesivamente poblado, superpoblado.

**overpopulation** (-papiule·shøn) *s.* exceso de población.

**overpower (to)** (-pau·ø$^r$) *tr.* predominar, dominar, vencer, subyugar. *2* abrumar, sofocar.

**overpowering** (-ing) *adj.* dominador, dominante. *2* abrumador, arrollador, irresistible.

**overproduction** (-prøda·kshøn) *s.* sobreproducción.

**overran** (-ræ·n) *pret.* de TO OVERRUN.

**overrate (to)** (-rei·t) *tr.* valorar excesivamente.

**overreach (to)** (-rɪ·ch) *tr.* llegar más allá de; exceder, pasar; extenderse sobre. *2* engañar a, ser más listo que. *3* *intr.* VET. alcanzarse. *4* *intr.-ref.* excederse, querer hacer demasiado, pasarse de listo.

**override (to)** (-raid) *tr.* pasar sobre o por encima de. *2* atropellar, pisotear. *3* supeditar, vencer. *4* desechar; anular. *5* reventar [a un caballo].

**overripe** (-rai·p) *adj.* demasiado maduro, papandujo.

**overrule (to)** (-ru·l) *tr.* dominar, señorear, vencer. *2* gobernar, regir. *3* decidir en contra, revocar. *4* predominar.

**overrun (to)** (-rø·n) *tr.* cubrir enteramente, inundar, invadir, infestar. *2* recorrer, pasar corriendo. *3* pasar por encima, atropellar. *4* exceder, traspasar los límites de: *to ~ one's time*, quedarse, hablar, etc., más tiempo del debido. *5* IMPR. recorrer. *6* *intr.* desbordarse, rebosar.

**oversaw** (-so·) *pret.* de TO OVERSEE.

**overscore** (-sko·$^r$) *tr.* poner tilde o raya.

**oversea(s** (-sɪ·(š) *adv.* ultramar, allende los mares. *2* *adj.* de ultramar; (Ingl.) colonial; extranjero.

**oversee (to)** (-sɪ·) *tr.* vigilar, superintender, inspeccionar, revisar.

**overseer** (ou·vø$^r$sɪø$^r$) *s.* inspector, superintendente, veedor. *2* sobrestante, capataz.

**overset (to)** (-$^r$se·t) *tr.* volcar, voltear, tumbar, derribar.

**overshadow (to)** (-shæ·dou) *tr.* sombrear, dar sombra a. *2* oscurecer, eclipsar. *3* fig. cubrir, proteger. *4* dominar [ser más alto].

**overshoe** (ou·vø$^r$shu) *s.* (E.U.) chanclo, zapato de goma.

**overshoot (to)** (-shu·t) *tr.* tirar por encima, más allá de. *2* *to ~ oneself*, *to ~ the mark*, pasar de la raya, excederse; pasarse de listo. *3* pasar rápidamente por encima o más allá de.

**overshot** (ouvø$^r$sha·t) *p. p.* de TO OVERSHOOT.

**oversight** (ou·vø$^r$sait) *s.* descuido, omisión, inadvertencia. *2* vigilancia, atención, cuidado.

**overskirt** (-skø$^r$t) *s.* sobrefalda.

**oversleep (to)** (-slɪ·p) *tr.* dormir hasta pasada [cierta hora]. *2* *intr.* dormir demasiado.

**overspread (to)** (-spre·d) *tr.* desparramar, extender. *2* extenderse sobre, cubrir.

**overstate (to)** (-tei·t) *tr.* exagerar.

**overstatement** (-mønt) *s.* exageración.

**overstep (to)** (-ste·p) *tr.* pasar, transgredir.

**overstock** (ou·vø$^r$stak) *s.* exceso de existencias.

**overstock (to)** (-sta·k) *tr.* abarrotar: *to be overstocked with*, tener demasiada existencia de.

**overstrung** (-strø·ng) *adj.* demasiado tirante. *2* muy sensible, excitable o impresionable. *3* de cuerdas cruzadas [piano].

**overt** (ou·vø$^r$t) *adj.* abierto, visible, manifiesto.

**overtake (to)** (ouvø$^r$tei·k) *tr.* alcanzar, atrapar. *2* pasar, dejar atrás. *3* sorprender, coger.

**overtaken** (-øn) *p. p.* de TO OVERTAKE.

**overtax** (-tæks) *tr.* sobrecargar de impuestos. *2* abrumar, exigir demasiado esfuerzo de.

**overthrew** (-zru) *pret.* de TO OVERTHROW.

**overthrow** (-zrou) *s.* vuelco, derribo. *2* derrocamiento. *3* destrucción. *4* trastorno. *5* subversión.

**overthrow (to)** (-zrou·) *tr.* volcar, tumbar, derribar. *2* derrocar. *3* demoler, destruir. *4* trastornar. *5* subvertir. *6* vencer.

**overthrown** (-n) *p. p.* de TO OVERTHROW.

**overtime** (-taim) *s.* tiempo suplementario; horas extraordinarias de trabajo. *2* *adj.-adv.* en horas extraordinarias.

**overtire (to)** (-tai·ø$^r$) *tr.* fatigar con exceso.

**overtly** (ou·vø$^r$tli) *adv.* abiertamente, públicamente.

**overtone** (ou·vø$^r$toun) *s.* MÚS. armónico.

**overtook** (-tu·k) *pret.* de TO OVERTAKE.)

**overtop (to)** (-ta·p) *tr.* dominar, descollar sobre; sobresalir entre. *2* rebasar, pasar de. *3* cubrir, pasar por encima de.

**overture** (ou·vø$^r$chu$^r$) *s.* insinuación, proposición, propuesta [de paz, de amistad, etc.]; declaración [de amor]. *2* MÚS. obertura.

**overturn** (ou·vø$^r$tø$^r$n) *s.* vuelco. *2* derrocamiento. *3* COM. movimiento de mercancías.

**overturn (to)** (-tø·$^r$n) *tr.* volcar, trabucar. *2* derribar, derrocar. *3* trastornar. *4* *intr.* volcar, trabucarse.

**overweening** (-wɪ·ning) *adj.* presuntuoso, arrogante.

**overweigh (to)** (-wei) *tr.* pesar más que, preponderar sobre; prevalecer contra. *2* oprimir, abrumar.

**overweight** (ou·vø$^r$ueit) *s.* sobrepeso. *2* preponderancia, superioridad.

**overwhelm (to)** (-jue·lm) *tr.* inundar. *2* aplastar, arrollar, abrumar, oprimir. *3* confundir, anonadar.

**overwhelming** (-ing) *adj.* aplastante, arrollador, abrumador, irresistible, poderoso.
**overwork** (ou·vø<sup>r</sup>uø<sup>r</sup>k) *s.* exceso de trabajo.
**overwork (to)** (-uø·<sup>r</sup>k) *tr.* hacer trabajar con exceso; fatigar el espíritu de, excitar. *2* abrumar de trabajo. *3* trabajar demasiado [un objeto, etc.]. *4 intr.* trabajar demasiado.
**overwrought** (-ro·t) *adj.* demasiado trabajado; recargado de adornos. *2* rendido por el trabajo. *3* sobrexcitado.
**Ovid** (a·vid) *n. pr.* Ovidio.
**oviduct** (ou·vidøkt) *s.* ANAT., ZOOL. oviducto.
**ovine** (ou·vain) *adj.-s.* ZOOL. ovino.
**oviparous** (ouvi·parøs) *adj.* ovíparo.
**ovipositor** (ouvipa·šitø<sup>r</sup>) *s.* ENT. oviscapto.
**ovoid** (ou·void) *adj.* ovoide, aovado.
**ovolo** (ou·volou) *s.* ARQ. óvolo, cuarto bocel.
**ovoviviparous** (ouvovaivi·parøs) *adj.* BIOL. ovovivíparo.
**ovule** (ou·viul) *s.* BOT. óvulo. *2* huevecillo.
**owe (to)** (ou) *tr.* deber; adeudar. *2 intr.* deber, tener deudas.
**owing** (-ing) ger. de TO OWE. *2* adj.-adv. ~ *to*, debido a, por causa de.
**owl** (aul) *s.* ORN. búho, mochuelo, lechuza.
**owlet** (-it) *s.* polluelo del búho, de la lechuza.
**own** (oun) *adj.* propio, mismo, de uno. | Acompaña como intensivo a los posesivos: *his* ~ *mother*, su propia madre. *2* carnal, hermano: ~ *cousin*, primo hermano. *3* s. *one's* ~, lo suyo, lo de uno; *to hold one's* ~, mantenerse firme; no cejar; *on one's* ~, solo, independientemente, por su cuenta.
**own (to)** *tr.* poseer, tener. *2* reconocer, confesar. *3 intr. to* ~ *up*, fam. confesar de plano.

**owner** (-ø<sup>r</sup>) *s.* dueño, propietario, poseedor.
**ownership** (-ship) *s.* propiedad, pertenencia.
**ox** (aks), *pl.* **oxen** (-øn) *s.* ZOOL. buey.
**oxalic** (aksæ·lik) *adj.* QUÍM. oxálico.
**oxen** (a·ksøn) *s. pl.* de OX.
**oxeye** (-ai) *s.* MAR., BOT. ojo de buey.
**oxfly** (-flai) *s.* ENT. estro, tábano.
**Oxford** (-fo<sup>r</sup>d) *n. pr.* GEOGR. Oxford. *2* universidad de Oxford.
**oxhide** (-jaid) *s.* cuero de buey.
**oxidation** (aksidei·shøn) *s.* oxidación.
**oxide** (a·ksid) *s.* QUÍM. óxido.
**oxidize (to)** (-aiš) *tr.* oxidar.
**oxidizer** (-ø<sup>r</sup>) *s.* oxidante.
**oxidizing** (-ing) *adj.* oxidante.
**oxlip** (a·kslip) *s.* BOT. planta primulácea.
**oxtail** (a·ksteil) *s.* cola o rabo de buey.
**oxygen** (a·ksidÿen) *s.* QUÍM. oxígeno.
**oxygenate (to)** (-eit) *tr.* oxigenar.
**oxygenation** (-ei·shøn) *s.* oxigenación.
**oxygenize (to)** (a·ksidÿenaiš) *tr.* oxigenar.
**oxygenous** (aksi·dÿenøs) *adj.* de oxígeno, oxigenado.
**oxyhydrogen** (-jai·drodÿin) *adj.-m.* QUÍM. oxhídrico.
**oxymel** (a·ksimel) *s.* oximel, ojimiel.
**oxytone** (a·ksitoun) *adj.-s.* GRAM. oxítono, agudo.
**oyster** (oi·stø<sup>r</sup>) *s.* ostra; ostión, ostrón: ~ *bed*, ostral, ostrero; ~ *fork*, desbullador; ~ *knife*, cuchillo para abrir ostras.
**ozaena** (oši·na) *s.* MED. ocena.
**ozone** (ou·šoun) *s.* QUÍM. ozono. *2* fig. aire puro.
**ozonization** (-ei·shøn) *s.* ozonización.
**ozonize (to)** (ou·šonaiš) *tr.* ozonizar.

# P

**P, p** (pi) *s.* P, p, decimosexta letra del alfabeto inglés.
**pa** (pa) *s.* (fam.) papá.
**pabulum** (pæ·biuløm) *s.* pábulo.
**paca** (pæ·ka) *s.* ZOOL. paca.
**pace** (peis) *s.* paso, marcha, modo de andar: *to keep* ~ *with*, ir al mismo paso que; *to set the* ~, dar el ejemplo. *2* paso, aire; andadura, portante [del caballo]. *3* paso [medida]. *4* estrado, tarima.
**pace (to)** *intr.* andar, pasear. *2* amblar. *3 tr.* recorrer o medir a pasos: *to* ~ *the floor*, pasearse por una habitación. *4* marcar o dirigir el paso de.
**pacer** (pei·søʳ) *s.* amblador. *2* el que mide a pasos.
**pachyderm** (pæ·kidøʳm) *s.* ZOOL. paquidermo.
**pacific** (pasi·fik) *adj.* pacífico. *2* GEOGR. *Pacific Ocean*, océano Pacífico.
**pacification** (pæsifikei·shøn) *s.* pacificación.
**pacifier** (pæ·sifaiøʳ) *s.* pacificador, apaciguador. *2* chupete [para niños].
**pacifism** (pæ·sifišm) *s.* pacifismo.
**pacifist** (pæ·sifist) *adj.-s.* pacifista.
**pacify** (pæ·sifai) *tr.* pacificar, apaciguar, sosegar, calmar. ¶ Pret. y p. p.: *pacified*.
**pack** (pæk) *s.* lío, fardo, bala, paca; paquete, mazo. *2* cantidad empaquetada. *3* baraja [de naipes]. *4* hato, hatajo, sarta. *5* cuadrilla, pandilla. *6* manada, bandada. *7* jauría; equipo de perros. *8* carga [de un animal o pers.]; ~ *animal*, acémila, bestia de carga. *9* extensión de témpanos flotantes.
**pack (to)** *tr.-intr.* empacar, empaquetar, embalar; envasar, enlatar. *2 tr.* hacer [el baúl, la maleta]. *3* amontonar, apiñar. *4* llenar, atestar, apretar. *5* cargar [una acémila, etc.]. *6* MEC. empaquetar [una junta]. *7* reunir, juntar [en jauría, baraja, etc.]. *8* preparar, formar, fraudulentamente [una baraja, un jurado, etc.]. *9 to* ~ *down*, apretar, apisonar. *10 to* ~ *off*, despedir, enviar. *11 to* ~ *up*, empaquetar. *12 intr.* reunirse, juntarse. *13* formar masa compacta, endurecerse. *14 to* ~ *o to* ~ *up*, hacer la maleta, el equipaje.
**package** (pæ·kidỹ) *s.* paquete, fardo, bulto. *2* cajetilla [de cigarrillos]. *3* empaquetadura, embalaje, envase [acción].
**package (to)** *tr.* empacar, empaquetar.
**packer** (pæ·køʳ) *s.* empaquetador, envasador.
**packet** (pæ·kit) *s.* paquete [fardo pequeño]. *2* MAR. *packet o* ~ *boat*, paquete, paquebote.

**packing** (-ing) *s.* empaque, embalaje; envase: ~ *needle*, aguja saquera. *2* MEC. empaquetadura, estopada; guarnición de junta.
**packman** (pæ·kmæn) *s.* buhonero.
**packsack** (pæ·ksæk) *s.* barjuleta.
**packsaddle** (pæ·ksædøl) *s.* albarda, basto.
**packthread** (pæ·kzred) *s.* bramante.
**pact** (pækt) *s.* pacto, convenio, acuerdo.
**pad** (pæd) *s.* cojincillo, almohadilla; postizo, relleno; compresa; hombrera, tontillo. *2* secatintas. *3* tampón [para entintar]. *4* ESGR. pleto, plastrón. *5* taco, bloc [de papel]. *6* sillín [de caballería]. *7* pie [de liebre, zorra, etc.]. *8* paso, pisada [ruido]. *9* jaca. *10* pop. camino.
**pad (to)** *tr.* rellenar, emborrar, acolchar; forrar [de algo blando]. *2* aumentar, hinchar [con elementos superfluos, partidas falsas, etc.]. *3 tr.-intr.* recorrer o andar a pie. ¶ Pret.: *padded*; ger.: ~ *-dding*.
**padding** (-ing) *s.* relleno, acolchado; borra, guata. *2* fig. relleno, paja [en un escrito, etc.].
**paddle** (pæ·døl) *s.* canalete, zagual [remo]. *2* pala [de lavandera], batidor. *3* paleta [de rueda]: ~ *boat*, buque de ruedas; ~ *wheel*, rueda de paletas.
**paddle (to)** *tr.* impulsar con canalete o rueda de paletas. *2* apalear. *3 intr.* remar con canalete o suavemente. *4* chapotear, guachapear.
**paddock** (pæ·døk) *s.* dehesa, prado [junto a una casa o establo]. *2* cercado adjunto a un hipódromo.
**paddy** (pæ·di) *s.* arroz; arroz en cáscara. *2* fam. (con may.) irlandés.
**padlock** (-lak) *s.* candado.
**padlock (to)** *tr.* cerrar con candado, echar el candado a.
**padre** (pa·dri) *s.* MIL., MAR. capellán.
**paean** (pɹ·in) *s.* canto de júbilo o alabanza.
**paederasty** (pe·døræsti) *s.* pederastia.
**pagan** (pei·gan) *adj.-s.* pagano, gentil, infiel.
**paganism** (-išm) *s.* paganismo.
**paganize (to)** (-aiš) *tr.-intr.* paganizar.
**page** (pei·dỹ) *s.* paje. *2* botones; criado joven. *3* página; plana, carilla.
**page (to)** *tr.* buscar [a uno] llamándole [en un hotel, etc.]. *2* paginar, foliar. *3* IMPR. compaginar.
**pageant** (pæ·dỹant) *s.* cabalgata, desfile, espectáculo, etc. [magníficos]. *2* aparato, pompa.

**pageantry** (-tri) *s.* pompa, aparato, espectáculo.
**pager** (pei·dȳøʳ) *s.* IMPR. compaginador, ajustador.
**pagination** (pædȳinei·shøn) *s.* paginación.
**pagoda** (pagou·da) *s.* pagoda.
**paid** (peid) *pret.* y *p. p.* de TO PAY. *2 adj.* pagado, asalariado.
**pail** (peil) *s.* herrada, colodra, cubo. *2* MAR. balde.
**paillasse** (pælia·s) *s.* jergón.
**pain** (pein) *s.* dolor, pena, sufrimiento; aflicción, inquietud. *2* pena [castigo]: *on* o *under ~ of*, bajo pena de. *3* trabajo, molestia: *to take pains to*, esforzarse, esmerarse por. *4 pl.* dolores del parto.
**pain (to)** *tr.* doler, punzar. *2* causar dolor, afligir.
**pained** (-d) *adj.* dolorido, apenado, afligido.
**painful** (-ful) *adj.* doloroso. *2* penoso, aflictivo, angustioso. *3* trabajoso, arduo. *4* dolorido.
**painstaking** (-steiking) *adj.* afanoso, industrioso, cuidadoso, concienzudo, esmerado.
**paint** (peint) *s.* pintura, color. *2* afeite, colorete.
**paint (to)** *tr.* pintar. *2 intr.* pintar, ser pintor. *3* pintarse el rostro.
**paintbox** (-baks) *s.* caja de colores o pinturas.
**paintbrush** (-brøsh) *s.* brocha, pincel.
**painter** (-tøʳ) *s.* pintor. *2* MAR. boza, amarra.
**painting** (-ing) *s.* pintura [acción, arte; color]. *2* pintura, cuadro.
**paintress** (-tris) *f.* pintora.
**pair** (pe·øʳ) *s.* par, pareja. *2* yunta, mancuerna. *3* grupo, serie [de cosas iguales]. *4 a ~ of scissors*, unas tijeras; *a ~ of trousers*, unos pantalones.
**pair (to)** *tr.* aparear, unir en pareja, casar; juntar, asociar; acoplar. *2* parear [poner de dos en dos]. *3 intr.* aparearse, formar pareja; unirse, casarse. *4 to ~ off*, aparearse.
**pajamas** (padȳa·mas) *s. pl.* pijama.
**pal** (pæl) *s.* compañero, camarada. *2* compinche.
**pal (to)** *intr.* hacerse o ser amigo (s o compañero (s.
**palace** (pæ·lis) *s.* palacio.
**paladin** (pæ·ladin) *s.* paladín.
**palaeography** (peilia·grafi) *s.* paleografía.
**palaelogist** (-lodȳist) *s.* paleólogo.
**palaeology** (-lodȳi) *s.* paleología.
**palaeolithic** (peilioli·zik) *adj.-s.* paleolítico.
**palaeontology** (peilianta·lodȳi) *s.* paleontología.
**Palaeozoic** (-ozou·ik) *adj.-s.* paleozoico.
**palaestra** (pale·stra) *s.* palestra.
**palankeen, palanquin** (pælankɪ·n) *s.* palanquín [andas].
**palatable** (pæ·latabøl) *adj.* sabroso, apetitoso. *2* agradable, aceptable.
**palatal** (-tal) *adj.-s.* palatal. *2* ANAT. palatino.
**palate** (pæ·lit) *s.* paladar.
**palatial** (palei·shal) *adj.* magnífico, suntuoso.
**palatinate** (palæ·tinit) *s.* palatinado.
**palatine** (pæ·latain) *adj.* palatino. *2 s.* conde palatino.
**palaver** (palæ·vøʳ) *s.* conferencia, debate [con los indígenas de África]. *2* fig. conversación, palabrería, embuste.
**palaver (to)** *intr.* charlar, discutir.
**pale** (peil) *adj.* pálido. *2* descolorido; apagado, sin brillo. *3 s.* estaca. *4* estacada, palizada. *5* fig. límites, esfera, gremio, seno. *6* BLAS. palo.
**pale (to)** *intr.* palidecer, perder el color. *2 tr.* hacer palidecer, descolorir. *3* empalizar, cercar.
**paleface** (-feis) *s.* rostro pálido.
**paleness** (-nis) *s.* palidez, descolorimiento.
**paleography,** etc. V. PALAEOGRAPHY, etc.
**Palestine** (pæ·listain) *n. pr.* GEOGR. Palestina.

**Palestinian** (pælisti·nian) *adj.* palestino.
**palestra** *s.* PALAESTRA.
**palette** (pæ·let) *s.* PINT. paleta. *2 ~ knife*, espátula.
**palfrey** (po·lfri) *s.* palafrén.
**palimpsest** (pæ·limpsest) *s.* palimpsesto.
**paling** (pei·ling) *s.* palenque, estacada.
**palingenesis** (pælindȳe·nisis) *s.* palingenesia.
**palinode** (pæ·linoud) *s.* palinodia.
**palisade** (pælisei·d) *s.* palizada, estacada.
**palisade (to)** *tr.* empalizar.
**palisander** (pælisæ·ndøʳ) *s.* palisandro.
**palish** (pei·lish) *adj.* algo pálido, paliducho.
**pall** (pol) *s.* paño mortuorio. *2* fig. capa [lo que cubre u oscurece]. *3* palio [insignia]. *4* LITURG. palia.
**pall (to)** *tr.* quitar el sabor a. *2* ahitar, empalagar. *3 intr.* perder la fuerza, el sabel: *to ~ on* o *upon*, cansar, dejar de gustar.
**palladium** (pælei·diøm) *s.* paladión. *2* QUÍM. paladio.
**Pallas** (pæ·las) *n. pr.* MIT. Palas.
**pallbearer** (po·lberøʳ) *s.* el que lleva o acompaña el féretro.
**pallet** (pæ·let) *s.* ALBAÑ., PINT. paleta. *2* pincel plano para dorar. *3* jergón, petate.
**palliate (to)** (pæ·lieit) *tr.* paliar. *2* mitigar. *3* excusar, disimular, encubrir.
**palliative** (pæ·liativ) *adj.-s.* paliativo.
**pallid** (pæ·lid) *adj.* pálido; desvaído.
**pallium** (pæ·liøm) *s.* LITURG., HIST., ANAT. palio.
**pall-mall** (pel·mel) *s.* mallo [juego].
**pallor** (pæ·løʳ) *s.* palidez.
**palm** (pam) *s.* palma [de la mano]. *2* palmo menor. *3* MAR. rempujo. *4* BOT. palma, palmera: *~ tree*, palmera; *Palm Sunday*, Domingo de Ramos. *5* fig. palma, victoria.
**palm (to)** *tr.* tocar, manosear. *2* esconder en la palma de la mano; escamotear. *3* pop. untar la mano. *4 to ~ something off on someone*, encajar, endosar algo a uno.
**palmaceous** (pælmei·shøs) *adj.* BOT. palmáceo.
**palmar** (pæ·lmaʳ) *adj.* ANAT. palmar.
**palmary** (pæ·lmari) *adj.* preeminente, superior.
**palmate (d** (pæ·lmeit(id) *adj.* palmado, palmeado.
**palmer** (pa·møʳ) *s.* palmero, peregrino.
**palmetto** (pælme·tou) *s.* BOT. palmito; palmera enana.
**palmiped** (pæ·lmiped) *adj.* ORN. palmípedo. *2* ZOOL. de pies palmeados.
**palmist (er** (pa·mist(øʳ) *s.* quiromántico.
**palmistry** (-tri) *s.* quiromancía.
**palmy** (pa·mi) *adj.* abundante en palmas. *2* próspero, floreciente, glorioso.
**palp** (pælp) *s.* ZOOL. palpo.
**palpable** (pæ·lpabøl) *adj.* palpable, evidente.
**palpably** (pæ·lpabli) *adv.* palpablemente.
**palpate (to)** (pæ·lpeit) *tr.* palpar, tentar.
**palpebral** (pæ·lpibral) *adj.* palpebral.
**palpitate (to)** (pæ·lpiteit) *intr.* palpitar, latir.
**palpitation** (pælpitei·shøn) *s.* palpitación.
**palsied** (po·lšid) *adj.* paralítico, perlático. *2* vacilante, tembloroso.
**palsy** (po·lši) *s.* MED. parálisis, perlesía.
**palsy (to)** *tr.* paralizar.
**palter (to)** (po·ltøʳ) *intr.* andar con rodeos o subterfugios, engañar. *2* regatear, discutir.
**paltriness** (po·ltrinis) *s.* bajeza, mezquindad, pobreza, fucilidad.
**paltry** (po·ltri) *adj.* vil, ruin, mezquino, despreciable. *2* pobre, fútil, baladí.
**paludal** (paliu·dal) *adj.* palustre, palúdico.

**paludism** (pæ·liudišm) *s.* MED. paludismo.
**pampas** (pæ·mpaš) *s. pl.* pampa.
**pampean** (pæmpɪ·an) *adj.-s.* pampero.
**pamperer** (pæ·mpørøʳ) *s.* mimador.
**pamphlet** (pæ·mfløt) *s.* folleto.
**pamphleteer** (pæmfløtɪ·ʳ) *s.* folletista, foliculario.
**pan** (pæn) *s.* cacerola, cazuela, cazo, caldero; recipiente de poco fondo. *2* MIN. artesa, gamella. *3* platillo [de balanza]. *4* cazoleta [de arma de fuego]: *to flash in the ~,* dar higa [un fusil].
**Pan** *n. pr.* MIT. Pan: *Pan's pipes,* flauta de Pan.
**pan (to)** *tr.* cocer, freír. *2* MIN. lavar en artesa. *3* pop. criticar, poner como nuevo. *4* intr. *to ~ out,* dar oro [la arena], fig. resultar. ¶ Pret. y p. p.: *panned;* ger.: *-nning.*
**panacea** (pænasɪ·a) *s.* panacea, curalotodo.
**panache** (panæ·sh) *s.* penacho. *2* fanfarronería.
**Panama** (pæ·nama o pænama) *n. pr.* GEOGR. Panamá: *~ hat,* sombrero de jipijapa.
**Pan-American** *adj.* panamericano.
**pancake** (pæ·nkeik) *s.* hojuela [fruta de sartén]; torta delgada. *2* AVIA. aterrizaje hecho de plano.
**pancratium** (pænkrei·shiøm) *s.* pancracio.
**pancreas** (pæ·nkrias) *s.* ANAT. páncreas.
**pancreatic** (pænkriæ·tik) *adj.* pancreático.
**panda** (pæ·nda) *s.* ZOOL. panda.
**Pandects** (pæ·ndekts) *s. pl.* Pandectas.
**pandemic** (pænde·mik) *adj.* pandémico. *2 s.* pandemia.
**pandemonium** (-dimou·niøm) *s.* pandemónium.
**pander** (pæ·ndøʳ) *s.* alcahuete, rufián.
**pander (to)** *tr.* alcahuetear, rufianear.
**panderess** (pæ·ndøris) *s.* alcahueta.
**Pandora** (pændou·ra) *n. pr.* Pandora: *Pandora's box,* caja de Pandora.
**pane** (pein) *s.* hoja de vidrio o cristal; cristal, vidrio [de ventana o vidriera]. *2* cara, faceta.
**panegyric** (pænidyi·rik) *adj.-s.* panegírico.
**panegyrist** (-ist) *s.* panegirista.
**panegyrize (to)** (pæ·nidyiraiš) *tr.* panegirizar.
**panel** (pæ·nøl) *s.* CARP., ARQ., ING. panel, cuarterón, entrepaño, artesón; compartimiento, sección. *2* PINT. tabla. *3* COST. adorno de tela. *4* recuadro. *5* AUTO., ELECT. tablero, cuadro. *6* lista [de jurados o de pers. designadas para un servicio, etc.]. *7* DER. jurado.
**panel (to)** *tr.* formar tableros, paneles o artesones; artesonar. *2 to* IMPANEL. ¶ Pret. y p. p.: *panel(l)ed;* ger.: *-l(l)ing.*
**paneless** (-lis) *adj.* sin cristales [ventana, etc.].
**panel(l)ing** (pæ·nøling) *s.* entrepaños, cuarterones; revestimiento de madera. *2* artesonado.
**panetella** (pænøte·la) *s.* panetela [cigarro].
**pang** (pæng) *s.* punzada, dolor agudo, tormento, ansia, congoja.
**pangolin** (pængou·lin) *s.* ZOOL. pangolin.
**pan-handle** *s.* mango de sartén, cacerola, etc.
**pan-handle (to)** *intr.* mendigar por las calles.
**panic** (pæ·nik) *adj.-s.* pánico.
**panic-grass** *s.* BOT. mijo.
**panicky** (-i) *adj.* pánico. *2* asustadizo.
**panicle** (pæ·nikøl) *s.* BOT. panícula.
**panic-stricken** *adj.* aterrorizado, preso de pánico.
**paniculate** (d (pani·kiuleit(id) *adj.* paniculado.
**panification** (panifikei·shøn) *s.* panificación.
**Pan-Islamism** *s.* panislamismo.
**panjandrum** (pændyæ·ndrøm) *s.* joc. personaje. *2* joc. ceremonia exagerada.
**panniculus** (pæni·kiuløs) *s.* BIOL. panículo.
**pannier** (pæ·niøʳ) *s.* cesta grande, cuévano. *2* cestón. *3* tontillo, caderillas.

**pannikin** (-ikin) *s.* cacillo. *2* vaso de metal.
**panoply** (-øpli) *s.* panoplia [armadura]. *2* cosa que protege o que envuelve suntuosamente.
**panorama** (pænøra·ma) *s.* panorama.
**panoramic** (-mik) *a.* panorámico.
**pansy** (pæ·nši) *s.* BOT. pensamiento, trinitaria.
**pant** (pænt) *s.* jadeo, resuello. *2* palpitación.
**pant (to)** *intr.* jadear, resollar. *2* palpitar. *3 to ~ for* o *after,* desear con ansia, suspirar por.
**Pantagruelic** (pæntagrue·lik) *adj.* pantagruélico.
**pantaloon** (pæntælu·n) *s.* bufón, gracioso. *2 pl.* pantalones, calzones.
**pantheism** (pæ·nziišm) *s.* panteísmo.
**pantheist** (-ist) *s.* panteísta.
**Pantheon** (-iøn) *s.* panteón.
**panther** (pæ·nzøʳ) *s.* ZOOL. pantera; (E.U.) puma.
**panties** (-tis) *s. pl.* bragas [de mujer].
**pantile** (-tail) *s.* teja de sección en S.
**panting** (-ting) *adj.* jadeante. *2 s.* jadeo; palpitación.
**pantograph** (-tøgræf) *s.* pantógrafo.
**pantomime** (-tømaim) *s.* pantomima. *2* pantomimo.
**pantomimist** (-mai·mist) *s.* pantomimo. *2* autor de pantomimas.
**pantry** (pæ·ntri) *s.* despensa, repostería.
**pants** (pæ·nts) *s.* fam. pantalones. *2* (fam.) calzoncillos.
**pap** (pæp) *s.* papas, gachas, papilla.
**papa** (pa·pø o pøpa·) *s.* papá.
**papacy** (pei·pasi) *s.* papado. *2* adhesión al Papa.
**papal** (-pal) *adj.* papal; pontificio.
**papaveraceous** (papævørei·shøs) *adj.* papaveráceo.
**papaw** (papo·) *s.* BOT. asimina. *2* PAPAYA.
**papaya** (peipa·ia) *s.* BOT. papayo. *2* papaya.
**paper** (pei·pøʳ) *s.* papel [materia; hoja de papel; escrito, documento]: *~ clip,* sujetapapeles, clip; *~ currency, ~ money,* papel moneda; *~ cutter,* plegadera; guillotina; *~ hanger,* empapelador; *~ knife,* plegadera; *~ mill,* fábrica de papel. *2* COM. papel [valor negociable]. *3* papel, periódico, diario. *4 pl.* papeles, documentos, apuntes, memorias. *5* papillotes.
**paper (to)** *tr.* empapelar. *2* envolver en papel.
**paperback** (-bæk) *s.* libro en rústica.
**paper-bound** *adj.* ENCUAD. en rústica.
**paperweight** (-ueit) *s.* pisapapeles.
**papery** (-i) *adj.* parecido al papel.
**papess** (pei·pis) *s.* papisa.
**papilionaceous** (papilionei·shøs) *adj.* papilionáceo.
**papilla** (papi·la) *s.* ANAT. pezón. *2* ANAT., ZOOL., BOT. papila.
**papillary** (pæ·pilæri) *adj.* papilar.
**papion** (pæ·pian) *s.* ZOOL. papión, zambo.
**papist** (pei·pist) *s.* desp. papista, católico.
**papistry** (-ri) *s.* desp. papismo, catolicismo.
**pap(p)oose** (pæpu·s) *s.* niño indio [de Norteamérica].
**pappus** (pæ·pos) *s.* BOT. vilano.
**pappy** (-i) *s.* fam. papá. *2 adj.* mollar, jugoso.
**papule** (-iul) *s.* pápula.
**papyrus** (papai·ros) *s., pl.* **-ri** (-rai) *s.* papiro.
**par** (paʳ) *s.* equivalencia, paridad, nivel; COM. par: *at ~,* a la par; *above ~,* con premio, sobre la par; *to be on a ~ with,* ser igual a, correr parejas con; *~ value,* valor nominal.
**parable** (pæ·rabøl) *s.* parábola [narración].
**parabola** (paræ·bola) *s.* GEOM. parábola.
**parabolic (al** (paraba·lik(al) *adj.* parabólico.

**paraboloid** (paræ·boloid) *s.* GEOM. paraboloide.
**parachute** (pæ·rashut) *s.* paracaídas.
**parachutist** (-ist) *s.* paracaidista.
**Paraclete** (pæ·raclit) *n. pr.* Paráclito, Paracleto.
**parade** (parei·d) *s.* pompa, ostentación; alarde, gala. *2* MIL. parada, revista: ~ *ground*, plaza de armas. *3* desfile, cabalgata. *4* (Ingl.) paseo público.
**parade (to)** *tr.* ostentar, alardear de. *2 tr.-intr.* MIL. formar en parada, (hacer) desfilar. *3 intr.* exhibirse, pasearse.
**paradigm** (pæ·radaim) *s.* paradigma. *2* ejemplo.
**paradise** (pæ·radais) *s.* paraíso. *2* ORN. ~ *bird*, ave del Paraíso.
**paradisiacal** (pæradisai·akal) *adj.* paradisíaco.
**paradox** (pæ·radaks) *s.* paradoja.
**paradoxical** (-ikal) *adj.* paradójico, paradojo.
**paraffin(e** (pæ·rafin) *s.* parafina.
**paragoge** (-gou·dÿi) *s.* GRAM. paragoge.
**paragon** (-gan) *s.* modelo, ejemplar, dechado; tipo de perfección. *2* IMPR. parangona.
**paragraph** (-græf) *s.* párrafo, aparte. *2* suelto, artículo corto. *3* IMPR. calderón.
**paragraph (to)** *tr.* dividir en párrafos. *2* escribir o comentar en sueltos o artículos cortos.
**Paraguay** (-gwei) *n. pr.* GEOGR. Paraguay.
**parakeet** (-kɪt) *s.* ORN. periquito.
**parallactic (al** (-læ·ktik(al) *adj.* paraláctico.
**parallax** (pæ·ralæks) *s.* ASTR. paralaje.
**parallel** (-el) *adj.* paralelo: ~ *bars*, paralelas [de gimnasia]. *2 s.* línea o superficie paralela. *3* paralelismo, semejanza. *4* par, igual. *5* paralelo [comparación]. *6* GEOGR., ELECT. paralelo. *7* FORT. paralela.
**parallel (to)** *tr.* igualar, parangonar. *2* ser igual a. *3* poner paralelo. *4* ser paralelo a. ¶ Pret. y p. p.: *parallel(l)ed;* ger.: *-l(l)ing.*
**parallelepiped** (-øpai·pid) *s.* GEOM. paralelepípedo.
**parallelism** (pæ·ralelišm) *s.* paralelismo.
**parallelogram** (pærale·løgræm) *s.* GEOM. paralelogramo.
**paralysis** (paræ·lisis) *s.* MED. parálisis, perlesía. *2* paralización, estancamiento.
**paralytic** (pærali·tik) *adj.-s.* paralítico.
**paralyzation** (-šei·shøn) *s.* paralización.
**paralyze (to)** (pæ·ralaiš) *tr.* paralizar.
**paralyzed** (-d) *adj.* paralizado. *2* paralítico.
**parameter** (paræ·metø') *s.* MAT. parámetro.
**paramount** (pæ·ramaunt) *adj.* superior, supremo, máximo, capital, principalísimo.
**paramour** (-mu') *s.* amante; querido; querida.
**paranoia** (pærano·ia) *s.* MED. paranoia.
**paranoiac** (-iæk) *adj.-s.* paranoico.
**parapet** (pæ·rapet) *s.* parapeto. *2* pretil, baranda, antepecho.
**paraph** (pæ·raf) *s.* rúbrica, signo.
**paraphernalia** (pærafø'nei·lia) *s. pl.* avíos, enseres, trastos; atavíos, galas.
**paraphrase** (pæ·rafreiš) *s.* paráfrasis.
**paraphrase (to)** *tr.* parafrasear.
**paraselene** (pæraseli·ni) *s.* METEOR. paraselene.
**parasite** (pæ·rasait) *s.* parásito. *2* gorrón, gorrero.
**parasitic (al** (-si·tik(al) *adj.* parásito, parasitario.
**parasiticide** (-tisaid) *adj.-s.* parasiticida.
**parasitology** (-saita·lodÿi) *s.* parasitología.
**parasol** (pæ·rasol) *s.* sombrilla, parasol, quitasol.
**paratrooper** (-trupø') *s.* MIL. paracaidista.
**paratroops** (-trups) *s. pl.* MIL. tropas paracaidistas.
**paratyphoid** (pæratai·foid) *adj.* MED. paratifoide, paratífico: ~ *fever*, paratifoidea, paratifus.

**parboil (to)** (pa·'boil) *tr.* sancochar, cocer a medias.
**Parcae** (pa·'si) *s. pl.* MIT. Parcas.
**parcel** (-søl) *s.* paquete, bulto, lío, atado: ~ *post*, servicio de paquetes postales. *2* hatajo, cuadrilla. *3* parcela, solar. *4* COM. lote, partida.
**parcel (to)** *tr.* parcelar, dividir: ~ *out*, repartir. *2* empaquetar, envolver. ¶ Pret. y p. p.: *parcel(l)ed;* ger.: *-l(l)ing.*
**parcener** (pa·'sønø') *s.* DER. coheredero.
**parch (to)** (parch) *tr.* tostar. *2* quemar, abrasar [el calor, el frío, la fiebre, la sed]; resecar; agostar: *to be parched with thirst,* morirse de sed. *3 intr.* tostarse, abrasarse, resecarse.
**parchesi** (pa·'chɪ·ši) *s.* parchís [juego].
**parchment** (pa·'chmønt) *s.* pergamino; vitela.
**pard** (pa·'d) *s.* pop. compinche, camarada.
**pardon** (pa·'døn) *s.* perdón: *I beg your* ~, usted perdone. *2* indulto, amnistía.
**pardon (to)** *tr.* perdonar. *2* indultar, amnistiar. *3* excusar, dispensar: ~ *me*, dispense usted.
**pardonable** (-abøl) *adj.* perdonable, excusable, dispensable.
**pardoner** (-ø') *s.* perdonador.
**pare (to)** (pe·ø') *tr.* mondar, pelar [fruta, patatas, etc.]. *2* cortar, recortar, raer, despalmar: *to* ~ *the nails,* cortar las uñas. *3* reducir [gastos, etc.].
**parenchyma** (pare·nkima) *s.* ANAT., BOT. parénquima.
**parent** (pe·rønt) *s.* padre o madre. *2* autor, causa, origen. *3 pl.* padres. *4 adj.* de los padres. *5* madre, matriz, principal.
**parentage** (pe·røntidÿ) *s.* linaje, nacimiento, origen.
**parental** (pare·ntal) *adj.* paternal, maternal.
**parenthesis** (pare·nzesis) *s.* paréntesis.
**parenthetic (al** (pærønze·tik(al) *adj.* parentético.
**paresis** (pærɪsis) *s.* MED. paresia.
**parget** (par·dÿit) *s.* yeso, mortero, enlucido.
**parget (to)** *tr.* ALBAÑ. enyesar, enlucir. *2* adornar con molduras de yeso.
**parhelion** (pa·'jɪ·liøn) *s.* METEOR. parhelio.
**pariah** (pa·ria o parai·a) *s.* paria.
**parietal** (pæ·riøtal) *adj.* parietal. *2* interno. *3 s.* ANAT. parietal [hueso].
**parietary** (pæ·riøteri) *s.* BOT. parietaria.
**pari-mutuel** (peri·miu·chuel) *s.* apuesta mutua.
**paring** (pe·ring) *s.* mondadura, peladura, raedura, corte, despalme: ~ *knife,* chifla; pujavante. *2 pl.* mondaduras, raeduras, recortes.
**paripinnate** (pæripi·neit) *adj.* BOT. paripinado.
**Paris** (pæ·ris) *n. pr.* MIT. Paris; GEOGR. París.
**parish** (pæ·rish) *s.* parroquia, feligresía; pueblo: ~ *church,* iglesia parroquial; ~ *clerk,* sacristán.
**parishioner** (-shønø') *s.* parroquiano, feligrés.
**Parisian** (-šian) *adj.-s.* parisiense.
**park** (pa·'k) *s.* parque.
**park (to)** *tr.* encerrar en un parque. *2* aparcar, estacionar. *3 intr.* aparcar, estacionarse.
**parking** (-ing) *s.* aparcamiento, estacionamiento: *no* ~, prohibido el estacionamiento.
**parkway** (pa·'kuei) *s.* gran vía adornada con árboles. *2* (E.U.) autopista.
**parlance** (pa·'lans) *s.* lenguaje, habla.
**parley** (pa·'li) *s.* conferencia, discusión. *2* MIL. parlamento.
**parley (to)** *intr.* discutir, parlamentar.
**Parliament** (pa·'limønt) *s.* parlamento, cortes.
**parliamentarian** (pa·'limønte·rian) *s.* parlamentario.

**parliamentarism** (paᵣlime·ntarišm) *s.* parlamentarismo.
**parliamentary** (-tari) *adj.-s.* parlamentario.
**parlo (u) r** (pa·ᵣløᵣ) *s.* sala de estar o de recibimiento. *2* (E.U.) salón [de peluquería]; sala [de billares, etc.]. *3* locutorio, parlatorio.
**parlo (u) rmaid** (-meid) *s.* doncella, camarera.
**Parmesan** (pa·ᵣmišan) *adj.-s.* parmesano.
**Parnassus** (paᵣnæ·søs) *n. pr.* GEOGR., MIT., LIT. Parnaso.
**parochial** (parou·kial) *adj.* parroquial. *2* fig. limitado, local; mezquino, estrecho.
**parodist** (pæ·rødist) *s.* parodista.
**parody** (pæ·rødi) *s.* parodia.
**parody (to)** *tr.* parodiar.
**parole** (parou·l) *s.* palabra de honor [esp. la de un prisionero]. *2* MIL. santo y seña.
**parole (to)** *tr.* poner en libertad bajo palabra de honor.
**paronomasia** (pæranomei·ŷia) *s.* paronomasia.
**paronymy** (pæra·nimi) *s.* paronimia.
**paroquet** (pæ·roket) *s.* PARAKEET.
**parotid** (pæra·tid) *adj.* parotídeo. *2 s.* ANAT. parótida.
**paroxysm** (pæ·røksišm) *s.* paroxismo. *2* acceso, arrebato.
**paroxytone** (pæra·ksitoun) *adj.-s.* GRAM. paroxitono.
**parquet** (pa·ᵣkeit) *s.* TEAT. platea. *2* mosaico de madera.
**parquetry** (pa·ᵣkitri) *s.* mosaico de madera.
**parr** (paᵣ) *s.* ICT. esguín, murgón.
**parricide** (pæ·risaid) *s.* parricida. *2* parricidio.
**parrot** (pæ·røt) *s.* ORN. loro, cotorra, papagayo. *2* ICT. ~ *fish*, escaro; papagayo.
**parrot (to)** *tr.* repetir como un papagayo.
**parry** (pæ·ri) *s.* parada, quite.
**parry (to)** *tr.-intr.* parar [un golpe, una estocada, etc.]. *2* evitar, eludir. ¶ Pret. y p. p.: *parried;* ger.: *-rrying.*
**parse (to)** (paᵣs) *tr.* GRAM. analizar.
**Parsee, Parsi** (pa·ᵣsi) *s.* parsi.
**parsimonious** (parsimou·niøš) *adj.* parsimonioso, frugal, parco, mezquino, tacaño.
**parsimony** (pa·ᵣsimouni) *s.* parsimonia, frugalidad, parquedad.
**parsing** (pa·ᵣsing) *s.* GRAM. análisis.
**parsley** (pa·ᵣsli) *s.* BOT. perejil.
**parsnip** (pa·ᵣsnip) *s.* BOT. pastinaca, chirivía.
**parson** (pa·ᵣsøn) *s.* párroco, cura, sacerdote.
**parsonage** (pa·ᵣsønidŷ) *s.* rectoría, rectoral.
**part** (paᵣt) *s.* parte [porción, fracción, división; miembro, elemento; participación]: ~ *and parcel*, parte esencial o inseparable; ~ *of speech*, parte de la oración; *to take* ~ *in*, tomar parte en; *for my* ~, por mi parte; *in* ~, en parte. *2* cuidado, obligación, deber. *3* parte o partido [en una contienda, etc.]: *to take in the* ~ *of*, ponerse de parte de. *4* TEAT. parte, papel. *5* MÚS. parte. *6* MEC. pieza. *7* (E.U.) raya [del cabello]. *8* *to take in good* ~, echar a buena parte. *9 pl.* lugares, países. *10* talento, dotes.
  *11 adj.-adv.* parcial, parcialmente: ~ *owner*, condueño.
**part (to)** *tr.* dividir, partir, separar. *2* repartir. *3 to* ~ *the hair*, hacerse la raya. *4 to* ~ *company*, separarse. *5 intr.* partirse, desunirse; separarse, desprenderse. *6* partir, irse, despedirse. *7* fig. morir. *8 to* ~ *with*, desprenderse de, separarse de.
**partage** (pa·ᵣtidŷ) *s.* repartimiento. *2* parte, porción.

**partake (to)** (paᵣtei·k) *tr.* compartir. *2 intr. to* ~ *in*, participar en. *3 to* ~ *of*, participar de, tener algo de; comer, beber.
**partaker** (-øᵣ) *s.* participante, partícipe.
**parterre** (paᵣte·ᵣ) *s.* parterre, cuadro de jardín.
**parthenogenesis** (paᵣzinodŷe·nesis) *s.* BIOL. partenogénesis.
**Parthenon** (pa·ᵣzinan) *n. pr.* Partenón.
**Parthian** (pa·ᵣzian) *adj.-s.* parto [de Partia].
**partial** (pa·ᵣshal) *adj.* parcial. *2* afecto, aficionado.
**partiality** (paᵣshæ·liti) *s.* parcialidad. *2* inclinación, afición.
**participant** (paᵣti·sipant) *adj.-s.* participante, partícipe.
**participate (to)** (-sipeit) *intr.-tr.* participar [tomar o tener parte].
**participation** (-ei·shøn) *s.* participación, parte.
**participator** (paᵣti·sipeitøᵣ) *adj.-s.* partícipe.
**participial** (paᵣtisi·pial) *adj.* participial.
**participle** (pa·ᵣtisipøl) *s.* GRAM. participio.
**particle** (pa·ᵣtikøl) *s.* partícula. *2* pizca.
**parti-colo (u) red** *adj.* de varios colores, abigarrado.
**particular** (paᵣti·kiulaᵣ) *adj.* particular. *2* exacto, minucioso, detallado, esmerado. *3* escrupuloso, delicado, exigente. *4 s.* particular, particularidad, pormenor, detalle: *to go into particulars*, entrar en detalles. *5 in* ~, en particular.
**particularity** (paᵣtikiulæ·riti) *s.* particularidad. *2* minuciosidad.
**particularize (to)** (paᵣti·kiularaiš) *tr.* particularizar, detallar, especificar.
**parting** (pa·ᵣting) *s.* separación, división. *2* partida, marcha; separación, despedida. *3* raya, línea divisoria. *4* raya [del pelo]. *5* ~ *of ways*, bifurcación, cruce de caminos; momento de separarse.
**partisan** (pa·ᵣtišan) *s.* partidario. *2* guerrillero. *3* partesana. *4 adj.* partidista.
**partisanship** (-ship) *s.* partidismo.
**partition** (paᵣti·shøn) *s.* partición. *2* división, separación. *3* tabique, barandilla, etc., que divide. *4* parte, porción.
**partition (to)** *tr.* dividir, separar. *2* repartir. *3 to* ~ *off*, separar con un tabique.
**partitive** (pa·ᵣtitiv) *adj.-s.* partitivo.
**partizan** (pa·ᵣtišan) *adj.-s.* PARTISAN.
**partly** (pa·ᵣtli) *adv.* en parte, en cierto modo.
**partner** (-nøᵣ) *s.* socio [en un negocio]. *2* compañero [en el juego]. *3* pareja [en el baile]. *4* cónyuge. *5* aparcero.
**partnership** (-ship) *s.* sociedad, compañía, asociación. *2* aparcería.
**partook** (paᵣtu·k) *pret.* de TO PARTAKE.
**partridge** (pa·ᵣtridŷ) *s.* ORN. perdiz.
**parturition** (paᵣtiuri·shøn) *s.* parto, alumbramiento.
**party** (pa·ᵣti) *s.* partido [político], bando, facción. *2* partido, causa. *3* partida, reunión, convite, fiesta; grupo de personas que viajan, cazan, etc., juntas. *4* MIL. destacamento, pelotón. *5* DER. parte. *6* parte [en contrato, contienda, etc.]. *7* individuo, sujeto. *8 to be a* ~ *to*, tener parte en, contribuir a. *9 adj.* de partido; de varios; en común; que divide: ~ *wall*, pared medianera.
**parvis** (pa·ᵣvis) *s.* ARQ. atrio.
**paschal** (pæ·skal) *adj.* pascual.
**pasha** (pasha·) *s.* bajá.
**pashalic** (-lik) *adj.* bajalato.
**pasqueflower** (pæ·skflauøᵣ) *s.* BOT. pulsatila.
**pasquinade** (pæskuinei·d) *s.* pasquinada; pasquín.

**pass** (pas) *s.* paso, pasaje; estrecho, desfiladero; desembocadero. *2* paso [acción o permiso de pasar]; pase, permiso, salvoconducto. *3* aprobación [en un examen]. *4* pase [magnético]. *5* ESGR. estocada. *6* trance, situación.

**pass (to)** *intr.* pasar [en todas sus acepciones]. *2* morir. *3 to* ~ *along,* pasar de largo; pasar por [una calle, etc.]. *4 to* ~ *away,* morir; pasar, desaparecer. *5 to* ~ *by,* pasar de largo, pasar [por el lado o delante de]. *6 to* ~ *for,* pasar, ser tenido por. *7 to* ~ *off,* pasar [una enfermedad, tempestad, etc.]. *8 to* ~ *out,* salir; desmayarse. *9 to* ~ *over,* pasar al otro lado. *10 to come to* ~, suceder, ocurrir.

*11 tr.* pasar [atravesar, cruzar, ir al otro lado de; dejar atrás; trasponer]. *12* pasar por el lado de, cruzarse con. *13* pasar, exceder, pasar de. *14* pasar, sufrir, tolerar. *15* tomar [un acuerdo]; aprobar [a un examinando; un proyecto de ley]. *16* pasar, aprobar [un examen]. *17* pasar, hacer pasar; dar, entregar, transferir. *18* pasar por alto, omitir. *19* no pagar [un dividendo]. *20* emitir [juicios], pronunciar [sentencia]. *21* pasar, colar, cerner. *22 to* ~ *along* o *around,* pasar de uno a otro, hacer circular. *23 to* ~ *by,* perdonar, no hacer caso de; omitir. *24 to* ~ *off,* hacer pasar [moneda falsa, etc.]. *25 to* ~ *on,* pasar [algo] a otro. *26 to* ~ *over,* transferir; omitir; postergar; perdonar.
¶ Part. p.: *passed* o *past.*

**passable** (pæ·sabøl) *adj.* pasadero. *2* transitorio. *3* tolerable, regular, mediano.

**passage** (pæ·sidỹ) *s.* paso, pasaje, tránsito. *2* paso, entrada, pasadizo. *3* MAR. viaje. *4* pasaje [de un buque]. *5* intercambio [de confidencias, golpes, etc.]; lance, encuentro; ~ *at arms,* asalto combate. *6* incidente, episodio. *7* pasaje [de un libro, etc.].

**passageway** (-dỹuei) *s.* pasadizo, pasaje.

**passant** (pæ·sant) *adj.* BLAS. pasante.

**passbook** (pæ·sbuk) *s.* cartilla o libreta de banco.

**passementerie** (pæsme·ntri) *s.* pasamanería.

**passenger** (pæ·sendỹør) *s.* pasajero, viajero.

**passer (-by)** (pæ·søř) *s.* transeúnte, viandante.

**passerine** (pæ·sørin) *adj.* ORN. del orden de los pájaros.

**passible** (pæ·sibøl) *adj.* pasible.

**passing** (pæ·sing) *s.* paso, pasada. *2* transcurso [del tiempo]. *3* tránsito, muerte. *4 adj.* que pasa, de paso. *5* pasajero, transitorio, momentáneo. *6* hecho o dicho de paso.

**passion** (pæ·shøn) *s.* pasión. *2* cólera, ira: *to fly into a* ~, montar en cólera. *3* (con may.) Pasión [de N. S.].

**passionate** (-it) *adj.* apasionado. *2* vivo, ardiente. *3* acalorado, colérico, arrebatado.

**passionflower** (-flauø̌) *s.* BOT. pasionaria.

**passionless** (-lis) *adj.* frío, tranquilo, desapasionado.

**passive** (pæ·siv) *adj.* pasivo. | No tiene el sentido de pasivo [haber] ni el de pasivo [participio]. *2 s.* GRAM. VOZ pasiva.

**passivity** (pæsi·viti) *s.* pasividad.

**passkey** (pæ·ski) *s.* llavín, llave maestra.

**Passover** (-ouvø̌) *s.* pascua de los hebreos.

**passport** (-pǒt) *s.* pasaporte. *2* salvoconducto.

**password** (-uǿd) *s.* santo y seña, contraseña.

**past** (pæst o past) *adj.* pasado, pretérito; último, ex, que fue: *for some years* ~, desde hace algunos años. *2* consumado. *3* GRAM. pasivo [participio]; pretérito [tiempo]. *4 s.* pasado. *5* GRAM. preté-

rito: ~ *perfect,* pluscuamperfecto. *6 prep.* pasado, después de, más allá de; fuera de; sin: ~ *two o'clock,* después de las dos, pasadas las dos; ~ *belief,* increíble; ~ *recovery,* incurable, sin remedio. *7 adv.* más allá, por delante.

**paste** (peist) *s.* pasta, masa. *2* engrudo. *3* imitación de piedra preciosa.

**paste (to)** *tr.* pegar [con engrudo, etc.] engrudar.

**pasteboard** (-bǒd) *s.* cartón.

**pastel** (pæ·stel) *s.* BOT. hierba pastel. *2* PINT. pastel.

**pastel(l)ist** (-ist) *s.* PINT. pastelista.

**paster** (pei·stǿ) *s.* engrudador. *2* papel engomado.

**pastern** (pæ·stǿn) *s.* VET. cuartilla, cerruma.

**pasteurize (to)** (pæ·støraiš) *tr.* pasterizar.

**pastil** (pæ·stil), **pastille** (pæsti·l) *s.* pastilla.

**pastime** (pæ·staim) *s.* pasatiempo, entretenimiento.

**pastor** (pæ·stǿ) *s.* pastor [esp. espiritual]; párroco, clérigo. *2* ORN. variedad de estornino.

**pastoral** (-al) *adj.* pastoril. *2 adj.-s.* pastoral.

**pastry** (pei·stri) *s.* pastelería, pasteles, pastas, repostería: ~ *cook,* pastelero, repostero; ~ *shop,* pastelería [tienda].

**pasturage** (pæ·schuridỹ) *s.* pasto, pastura. *2* apacentamiento.

**pasture** (pæ·schǿ) *s.* pasto, pastura, dehesa.

**pasture (to)** *tr.-intr.* pastar, pacer, apacentarse. *2 tr.* pastar, apacentar, pastorear.

**pasty** (pei·sti) *adj.* pastoso. *2* fofo, pálido, descolorido. *3 s.* (Ingl.) pastel [de carne o pescado].

**pat** (pæt) *adj.* exacto, conveniente, oportuno. *2* fijo, firme. *3 adv.* oportunamente; a punto; perfectamente, al dedillo. *4 s.* golpecito, palmadita. *5* pastilla [de mantequilla, etc.].

**pat (to)** *tr.* dar golpecitos o palmaditas a; acariciar: *to* ~ *on the back,* fig. elogiar, felicitar. ¶ Pret. y p. p.: *patted;* ger.: *-tting.*

**Patagonian** (pætagou·nian) *adj.-s.* patagón.

**patch** (pæch) *s.* remiendo; parche. *2* lunar postizo. *3* trozo, retazo. *4* mancha [de color]. *5* pedazo [de terreno]. *6* MED. placa.

**patch (to)** *tr.* remendar, apedazar, componer. *3* cubrir con manchas de color. *4* chafallar. *5 to* ~ *up,* componer, arreglar; hacer con retazos.

**patchouli** (-uli) *s.* pachulí.

**patchwork** (-uø̌k) *s.* centón, obra de retazos, mezcolanza. *2* chapucería.

**patchy** (-i) *adj.* lleno de remiendos. *2* fig. manchado, abigarrado.

**pate** (peit) *s.* fam. cabeza, sesera, coronilla.

**paten** (pæ·tøn) *s.* LITURG. patena.

**patent** (pæ·tøn) *adj.* patente, manifiesto. *2* abierto. *3* patentado. *4* ~ *leather,* charol. *5* ~ *medicine,* específico. *6* ~ patente, privilegio exclusivo; diploma, título.

**patent (to)** *tr.* patentar.

**pater** (pei·tǿ) *s.* padrenuestro. *2* pop. padre, papá.

**paternal** (patǿ·nal) *adj.* paternal, paterno, patrio.

**paternity** (patǿ·niti) *s.* paternidad. *2* linaje, origen [por parte de padre].

**paternoster** (peitǿna·stǿ) *s.* padrenuestro, paternóster. *2* rosario.

**path** (paz) *s.* camino, senda, vereda. *2* ruta, curso, trayectoria. *3* órbita [de un astro].

**pathetic** (paze·tik) *adj.* patético. *2* lastimoso.

**patheticalness** (-alnis) *s.* patetismo.

**pathless** (pa·zlis) *adj.* sin caminos, no transitado.

**pathogenic** (pæzødỹe·nik) *adj.* patógeno.

**pathologic (al** (pæzøla·dỹik(al) *adj.* patológico.

**pathologist** (paza·lodỹist) *s.* patólogo.

**pathology** (-i) *s.* patología.

**pathos** (pei·zas) *s.* patetismo, sentimiento.
**pathway** (pa·zuei) *s.* camino, senda.
**patience** (pei·shøns) *s.* paciencia: *to have no* ~ *with*, no poder sufrir. *2* solitario [juego].
**patient** (-t) *adj.* paciente. *2* susceptible [de]. *3 s.* FIL., GRAM., MED. paciente.
**patina** (pæ·tina) *s.* pátina.
**patly** (pæ·tli) *adv.* PAT.
**patois** (pæ·tua) *s.* jerga, dialecto.
**patriarch** (pei·tria<sup>r</sup>k) *s.* patriarca.
**patriarchal** (peitria·<sup>r</sup>kal) *adj.* patriarcal.
**patriarchate** (pei·tria<sup>r</sup>keit), **patriarchy** (-ki) *s.* patriarcado.
**patrician** (patri·shan) *adj.-s.* patricio.
**patriciate** (patri·shieit) *s.* patriciado.
**Patrick** (pæ·trik) *n. pr.* Patricio.
**patrimony** (pæ·trimoni) *s.* patrimonio.
**patriot** (pei·triøt) *s.* patriota.
**patriotic** (**al** (peitria·tik(al) *adj.* patriótico.
**patriotism** (pei·triøtišm) *s.* patriotismo.
**patristic** (patri·stik) *adj.* patrístico.
**patristics** (-s) *s.* patrística.
**patrol** (patrou·l) *s.* patrulla; ronda.
**patrol (to)** *intr.-tr.* patrullar, rondar. ¶ Pret. y p. p.: *patrolled;* ger.: *patrolling.*
**patrolman** (patrou·lmæn) *s.* rondador; vigilante de policía, guardia municipal, etc.
**patron** (pei·trøn) *adj.* patrón, tutelar. *2 s.* patrón [santo]. *3* patrono, protector. *4* parroquiano, cliente. *5* ECLES. patrono.
**patronage** (-idȳ) *s.* protección, patrocinio, amparo. *2* clientela. *3* ECLES. patronato.
**patroness** (-is) *f.* protectora, patrocinadora.
**patronize (to)** (-aiš) *tr.* proteger, patrocinar, favorecer. *2* ser cliente de. *3* tratar con aire de protección, de superioridad.
**patronymic** (pætrøni·mik) *adj.-s.* patronímico.
**patten** (pæ·tøn) *s.* galocha, zueco, chanclo.
**patter** (pæ·tø<sup>r</sup>) *s.* jerga, lenguaje. *2* charla, parlería, ruido de pasitos, de gotas de agua, etc.
**patter (to)** *intr.* hacer ruidos ligeros, como los de la lluvia, pasos menudos, etc. *2* rezar de prisa. *3* charlar. *4* hablar en jerga.
**pattern** (pæ·tø<sup>r</sup>n) *s.* modelo, muestra, dechado; ejemplar, tipo. *2* patron, plantilla. *3* dibujo, diseño, motivo.
**pattern (to)** *tr.* servir de ejemplo. *2 to* ~ *after, on* o *upon*, hacer, modelar, a imitación de.
**patty** (pæ·ti) *s.* pastelillo, empanada.
**paucity** (po·siti) *s.* poquedad, exigüidad.
**Paul** (pol) *n. pr.* Pablo.
**Pauline** (po·lin) *adj.* referente a San Pablo.
**paunch** (ponch) *s.* panza, barriga. *2* MAR. pallete.
**pauper** (po·pø<sup>r</sup>) *s.* pobre [pers.].
**pauperism** (-išm) *s.* pauperismo.
**pauperize (to)** (-aiš) *tr.* empobrecer.
**pause** (poš) *s.* pausa, interrupción, paro, descanso. *2* pausa, cesura. *3* MÚS. calderón, fermata. *4* vacilación. *5* respiro, tregua.
**pause (to)** *intr.* pausar, interrumpirse, detenerse. *2* vacilar.
**pavan** (pæ·van) *s.* pavana.
**pave (to)** (peiv) *tr.* pavimentar, solar, adoquinar, empedrar: *to* ~ *the way*, preparar el terreno.
**pavement** (-mønt) *s.* pavimento, suelo, adoquinado. *2* acera, andén.
**pavilion** (pavi·liøn) *s.* pabellón [tienda, dosel]. *2* ANAT., ARQ. pabellón.
**paving** (pei·ving) *s.* pavimento, pavimentación.
**pavis** (pæ·vis) *s.* pavés.
**paw** (po) *s.* garra, zarpa. *2* fig. garra, mano.

**paw (to)** *tr.* manosear, sobar. *2* dar manotazos en. *3 tr.-intr.* arañar. *4* patear, piafar.
**pawl** (pol) *s.* MEC. linguete, trinquete, retén.
**pawn** (pon) *s.* peón [de ajedrez]. *2* empeño; garantía, prenda: ~ *ticket*, papeleta de empeño; *in* ~, en prenda.
**pawn (to)** *tr.* empeñar [dar o dejar en prenda].
**pawnbroker** (-broukø<sup>r</sup>) *s.* prestamista [sobre prendas].
**pawner** (-ø<sup>r</sup>) *s.* prendador.
**pawnshop** (-shap) *s.* casa de empeños.
**pax** (pæks) *s.* LITURG. paz.
**pay** (pei) *s.* paga, sueldo, salario: *in the* ~ *of*, al servicio de. *2* paga, pago [recompensa; acción de pagar]: ~ *list* o *roll*, nómina; *good* ~, *bad* ~, buena paga, mala paga [pers.]. *3* MIN. ~ *dirt*, tierra o arena que da buena cantidad de oro.
**pay (to)** *tr.-intr.* pagar: *to* ~ *back*, devolver; *to* ~ *for*, pagar [lo que se compra]; recompensar; pagar, purgar, expiar; *to* ~ *off*, pagar y despedir; saldar, pagar todo lo adeudado; vengarse de; *to* ~ *out*, desembolsar; *to* ~ *through the nose*, pagar muy caro [comprando]; *to* ~ *up*, saldar. *2 tr.* costear, sufragar. *3* hacer [una visita; la corte]; rendir [homenaje]; ofrecer [sus respetos]; prestar [atención]; dirigir [cumplidos]. *4* MAR. *to* ~ *out* o *away*, largar, lascar, filar. *5 intr.* compensar, ser provechoso. ¶ Pret. y p. p.: *paid*.
**payable** (pei·abøl) *adj.* pagable, pagadero.
**payday** (pei·dei) *s.* día de pago.
**payee** (peii·) *s.* portador, tenedor [de una letra, cheque, etc.].
**payer** (pei·ø<sup>r</sup>) *s.* pagador.
**paying** (-ing) *s.* pago, acción de pagar: ~ *teller*, pagador [de un banco].
**paymaster** (-mæstø<sup>r</sup>) *s.* pagador, contador; habilitado.
**payment** (-mønt) *s.* pago, paga: *on the* ~ *of*, mediante el pago de. *2* pago, recompensa.
**pay-office** *s.* pagaduría.
**pea** (pi) *s.* BOT. guisante, chicharro: ~ *soup*, puré de guisantes; neblina espesa y amarillenta. *2* ~ *jacket*, chaquetón de marinero.
**peace** (pi·s) *s.* paz: ~ *of God*, paz de Dios, tregua de Dios; ~ *offering*, sacrificio propiciatorio; prenda de paz; *at* ~, en paz. *2* orden público: ~ *officer*, policía, guardia municipal. *3* quietud, tranquilidad, silencio: *to hold one's* ~, guardar silencio, callar. *4 interj.* ¡paz!, ¡silencio!
**paceable** (-abøl) *adj.* pacífico, tranquilo.
**peaceful** (-ful) *adj.* pacífico, tranquilo, sosegado.
**peacefulness** (-nis) *s.* paz, tranquilidad, sosiego.
**peacemaker** (-meikø<sup>r</sup>) *s.* pacificador, conciliador.
**peacetime** (-taim) *s.* tiempo o período de paz. *2 adj.* de tiempo de paz.
**peach** (pich) *s.* BOT. pérsico, melocotón, durazno: ~ *tree*, pérsico, melocotonero, duraznero. *2* color de melocotón. *3* pop. persona o cosa excelente.
**peach (to)** *intr.* pop. delatar a un cómplice.
**peachick** (pi·shik) *s.* ORN. pollo del pavo real.
**peachy** (pi·chi) *adj.* amelocotonado. *2* fam. magnífico, estupendo.
**peacock** (pi·kak) *s.* ORN. pavón, pavo real. *2* ENT. ~ *butterfly*, mala paga; ICT. ~ *fish*, budión.
**pea-gun** *s.* cerbatana.
**peahen** (pi·jen) *s.* ORN. pava real.
**peak** (pik) *s.* pico, cumbre, cima. *2* cúspide. *3* punto máximo. *4* pico, punta [de una cosa]. *5* cresta [de onda]. *6 adj.* máximo o de máximo [precio, actividad, velocidad, etc.].

**peak (to)** *tr.* MAR. levantar, poner casi vertical.
**peaked** (pɪ·kt o pɪ·kit) *adj.* puntiagudo, picudo, en punta. *2* enjuto, delgado; afilada [nariz].
**peaky** (-i) *adj.* puntiagudo. *2* que tiene picos.
**peal** (pɪl) *s.* repique [de campanas]. *2* estrépito, estruendo: ~ *of thunder*, trueno.
**peal (to)** *tr.-intr.* repicar [las campanas]. *2* gritar, vocear. *3* sonar, resonar, retronar.
**peanut** (pɪ·nɒt) *s.* BOT. cacahuete; *mani.
**pear** (peˑøʳ) *s.* BOT. pera; peral: ~ *tree*, peral. *2* perilla [adorno].
**pearl** (pøʳl) *s.* perla, margarita: ~ *seed*, aljófar; *to cast pearls before swine*, echar margaritas a cerdos. *2* B. ART., FARM., IMPR. perla. *3* adj. ~ *barley*, cebada perlada.
**pearl (to)** *tr.* perlar; aljofarar. *2* dar color de perla. *3* *intr.* pescar perlas. *4* perlarse.
**pearled** (-d) *adj.* perlado, aljofarado.
**pearly** (-i) *adj.* perlino, nacarado. *2* aljofarado.
**pearmain** (peˑʳmein) *s.* BOT. pero.
**pear-shaped** *adj.* piriforme.
**peasant** (peˑšant) *s.* labriego, campesino.
**peasantry** (-tri) *s.* paisanaje, gente del campo.
**peascod** (pɪ·škad) *s.*vaina de guisante.
**peat** (pɪt) *s.* turba [materia]: ~ *bog*, turbera.
**peaty** (-i) *adj.* turboso.
**pebble** (peˑbøl) *s.* guija, guijarro, china. *2* cristal de roca.
**pebble (to)** *tr.* enguijarrar. *2* granular, abollonar [el cuero, etc.].
**pebbly** (peˑbli) *adj.* guijarroso.
**pecan** (pikæ·n) *s.* BOT. pacana.
**peccadillo** (pekadi·lou) *s.* pecadillo, falta.
**peccancy** (peˑkansi) *s.* vicio, defecto. *2* pecado.
**peccant** (-kant) *adj.* pecante. *2* incorrecto, defectuoso.
**peccary** (-kari) *s.* ZOOL. pécari, báquira.
**peck** (pek) *s.* medida de áridos [9 litros]. *2* fam. montón, la mar. *3* picotazo, picotada.
**peck (to)** *tr.* picar, picotear. *2* picar, labrar [con algo puntiagudo]. *3* intr. *to* ~ *at*, picotear, coger con el pico; comiscar; regañar, censurar.
**pecker** (-øʳ) *s.* picoteador. *2* ORN. pico verde.
**pectin, pectine** (peˑktin) *s.*pectina.
**pectinate(d** (-neit(id) *adj.* pectinado.
**pectoral** (peˑktøral) *adj.-s.* pectoral. *2 s.* ARM. peto.
**peculate (to)** (peˑkiuleit) *tr.-intr.* desfalcar, malversar.
**peculation** (-eiˑshøn) *s.* peculado, desfalco.
**peculiar** (pikiu̥ˑliaʳ) *adj.* peculiar. *2* particular, especial. *3* raro, singular.
**peculiarity** (pikiuliæ·riti) *s.* peculiaridad, particularidad, singularidad. *2* individualidad.
**peculiarize (to)** (pikiu·liaraiš) *tr.* particularizar, individualizar.
**pecuniary** (pikiu·nieri) *adj.* pecuniario.
**pedagogic(al** (pedaga·dȳik(al) *adj.* pedagógico.
**pedagogue** (peˑdagag) *s.* pedagogo. *2* pedante.
**pedagogy** (-goudȳi) *s.* pedagogía.
**pedal** (peˑdal) *s.* pedal. *2* adj. de pie o de pedal: ~ *board*, teclado de pie.
**pedal (to)** *intr.* pedalear. *2* tr. mover con pedal.
**pedant** (peˑdant) *s.* pedante.
**pedantic(al** (pidæ·ntik(al) *adj.* pedantesco.
**pedantry** (peˑdantri) *s.* pedantería.
**peddle (to)** (peˑdøl) *tr.* vender de puerta en puerta. *2* intr. hacer de buhonero.
**peddler** (peˑdløʳ) *s.* buhonero, vendedor ambulante.
**pederasty** (peˑdøræsti) *s.* pederastia.

**pedestal** (peˑdistal) *adj.* pedestal; peana, pie. *2* MÚS. cubeta [del arpa].
**pedestrian** (pideˑstrian) *adj.* pedestre. *2 s.* peatón, caminante; andarín.
**pediatrics** (pidiæ·triks) *s.* pediatría.
**pediatrician** (pidiatri·shan) *s.* pediatra.
**pedicel** (peˑdisel) *s.* BOT., ZOOL. pedicelo.
**pedicle** (peˑdikøl) *s.* ANAT. pedículo.
**pedicular** (pidi·kiulaʳ), **pediculous** (-løs) *adj.* pedicular.
**pedigree** (peˑdigrɪ) *s.* genealogía, linaje, árbol genealógico.
**pediment** (peˑdimønt) *s.* ARQ. frontón.
**pedlar, pedler** (pedløʳ) *s.* PEDDLER.
**pedometer** (pida·mitøʳ) *s.* podómetro, cuentapasos.
**peduncle** (pidø·nkøl) *s.* ANAT., ZOOL., BOT. pedúnculo.
**peek** (pɪk) *s.* atisbo, atisbadura, mirada.
**peek (to)** *intr.* atisbar, espiar, mirar con disimulo.
**peel** (pɪl) *s.* piel, corteza, cáscara, hollejo, telilla. *2* pala [de horno; de remo].
**peel (to)** *tr.* pelar, mondar, descortezar, descascarar. *2* intr. pelarse, descascararse. *3* fam. desnudarse. *4* desprenderse [la piel, la corteza, etc.].
**peeling** (-ing) *s.* peladura, mondadura.
**peen** (pɪn) *s.* boca o punta [del martillo].
**peep** (pɪp) *s.* atisbo, ojeada; atisbo a través de una rendija. *2* rendija por donde se mira. *3* asomo: *at the* ~ *of the day*, al despuntar el día. *4* pío, piada [de ave]; vocecita.
**peep (to)** *intr.* atisbar, fisgar; mirar por una rendija. *2* asomar, mostrarse. *3* piar, pipiar.
**peeper** (-øʳ) *s.* atisbador. *2* fam. ojo.
**peephole** (-joul) *s.* atisbadero, mirilla.
**peer** (pɪʳ) *s.* par, igual, compañero. *2* par [noble].
**peer (to)** *intr.* mirar [atentamente, escrutadoramente]. *2* asomar, salir, aparecer.
**peerage** (-idȳ) *s.* dignidad de par. *2* cuerpo o catálogo de la nobleza.
**peeress** (-is) *f.* paresa.
**peerless** (-lis) *adj.* sin par, incomparable.
**peevish** (pɪ·vish) *adj.* malhumorado, brusco; displicente, quisquilloso, enojadizo.
**peevishness** (-nis) *s.* mal humor, brusquedad, displicencia, quejumbre.
**peewit** (pɪ·uit) *s.* PEWIT.
**peg** (peg) *s.* clavija, estaquilla, espiga, taco, sobina. *2* percha, colgador. *3* pretexto, razón. *4* grado, escalón: *to take down a* ~, rebajar o humillar [a uno]. *5* estaca, jalón. *6* (Ingl.) traguito.
**peg (to)** *tr.* estaquillar, clavar, ataraguar. *2* marcar, jalonar. *3* limitar, fijar, estabilizar [precios, etc.]. *4* lanzar, arrojar. *5* intr. afanarse; andar de prisa. ¶ Pret. y p. p.: *pegged*; ger.: *-gging*.
**Pegasus** (peˑgasøs) *n. pr.* MIT. Pegaso.
**pegbox** (peˑgbaks) *s.* MÚS. clavijero [de violín, etc.].
**Peggy** (peˑgi) *n. pr. dim.* de MARGARET.
**peg-top** *s.* peonza.
**pejorative** (pi·dȳøreitiv) *adj.* peyorativo, despectivo.
**Pekin** (pikɪ·n) *n. pr.* GEOGR. Pequín.
**Pekinese** (pɪ·kinis) *adj.-s.* pequinés.
**pekoe** (pɪ·kou) *s.* té negro de calidad superior.
**pelagic** (pilæ·dȳik) *adj.* pelágico.
**Pelasgic** (pilæ·šdȳik) *adj.* pelásgico.
**pelerine** (peˑlørin) *s.* manteleta, pelerina.
**pelf** (pelf) *s.* desp. bienes, dinero.
**pelican** (peˑlikan) *s.* ORN. pelícano, alcatraz.
**pelisse** (pøliˑs) *s.* pelliza.

**pellagra** (pølæ·gra) *s.* MED. pelagra.
**pellet** (pe·lit) *s.* pelotilla, bolita. *2* píldora. *3* bala, perdigón. *4* bodoque.
**pellicle** (pe·licøl) *s.* película, telilla.
**pellitory** (pe·litori) *s.* BOT. parietaria; pelitre.
**pell-mell** (pelme·l) *adv.* revueltamente, atropelladamente. *2 s.* confusión, desorden.
**pellucid** (pøliu·sid) *adj.* diáfano, transparente.
**Peloponnesus** (pelopøni·søs) *n. pr.* GEOGR. Peloponeso.
**pelt** (pelt) *s.* pellejo, cuero, zalea. *2* golpe [de algo tirado]; golpear [de la lluvia]. *3* velocidad.
**pelt (to)** *tr.* apedrear; tirar, hacer llover [algo] sobre. *2 intr.* caer con fuerza [la lluvia, etc.]. *4* apresurarse.
**peltry** (pe·ltri) *s.* pellejería, corambre. *2* pellejo.
**pelvic** (pe·lvik) *adj.* ANAT. pelviano.
**pelvis** (pe·lvis) *s.* ANAT., ZOOL. pelvis.
**pemmican** (pe·mikan) *s.* penmicán.
**pemphigus** (pe·mfigøs) *s.* MED. pénfigo.
**pen** (pen) *s.* pluma [para escribir]: ~ *name*, seudónimo. *2* corral; departamento [para encerrar ganado o exhibir animales].
**pen (to)** *tr.* escribir, pergeñar. *2* encerrar, acorralar. ¶ Pret. y p. p.: *penned* o *pent*; ger.: *-nning*.
**penal** (pɪ·nal) *adj.* penal: ~ *servitude*, presidio, trabajos forzados. *2* penable.
**penalize (to)** (pɪ·nalaiš) *tr.* penar, castigar.
**penalty** (pe·nalty) *s.* pena, castigo, sanción; multa de. *2* DEP. penalti, castigo.
**penance** (pe·nans) *s.* penitencia.
**Penates** (pinei·tiš) *s. pl.* MIT. Penates.
**pence** (pens) *s. pl.* de PENNY. | Ús. en composición.
**penchant** (pe·nchant) *s.* afición, tendencia.
**pencil** (pe·nsil) *s.* lápiz; lapicero: ~ *sharpener*, afilalápices. *2* pincel fino.
**pencil (to)** *tr.* dibujar o escribir con lápiz. *2* pintar con pincel fino. ¶ Pret. y p. p.: *pencil(l)ed*; ger.: -l(l)ing.
**pendant** (-dant) *s.* cosa que cuelga; colgante, pendiente, zarcillo; medallón. *2* araña [de luces]. *3* ARQ. pinjante.
**pendent** (-dønt) *adj.* pendiente. *2 prep.* durante.
**pendular** (-diulaᵣ) *adj.* pendular.
**pendulous** (-iuløs) *adj.* péndulo, colgante.
**pendulum** (-diuløm) *s.* péndulo; péndola.
**Penelope** (pine·løp) *n. pr.* Penélope.
**penetrable** (pe·nitrabøl) *adj.* penetrable, accesible.
**penetrancy** (-transi) *s.* fuerza de penetración.
**penetrate (to)** (-treit) *tr.-intr.* penetrar. *2 tr.* atravesar, perforar.
**penetrating** (-treiting) *adj.* penetrante. *2* perspicaz.
**penetration** (-ei·shøn) *s.* penetración.
**penguin** (pe·ngüin) *s.* ORN. pingüino.
**penholder** (pe·njouldøᵣ) *s.* portapluma.
**penicillin** (penisi·lin) *s.* penicilina.
**peninsula** (peni·nshiula) *s.* GEOGR. península.
**peninsular** (-laᵣ) *adj.-s.* peninsular.
**penis** (pɪ·nis) *s.* ANAT. pene.
**penitence** (pe·nitøns) *s.* penitencia, contricción.
**penitent** (-ønt) *adj.-s.* penitente, arrepentido.
**penitential** (penite·nshal) *adj.* penitencial.
**penitentiary** (-shari) *adj.* penitencial. *2* penitenciario. *3 s.* penitenciaría.
**penknife** (pe·n-naif) *s.* cortaplumas.
**penman** (-mæn) *s.* pendolista. *2* escritor.
**pennant** (pe·nant) *s.* flámula, gallardete, banderola. *2* MAR. insignia.
**pennies** (pe·nis) *s. pl.* de PENNY.
**penniless** (pe·nilis) *adj.* pobre, sin dinero.

**pennon** (pe·nøn) *s.* pendón, flámula, banderola.
**penninervate** (peninøᵣ·vit) *adj.* BOT. peninervia.
**Pennsylvania** (pensilvei·nia) *n. pr.* GEOGR. Pensilvania.
**penny** (pe·ni), **pennies** o [en composición] **pence** (pens) *s.* penique; centavo de dólar: *to cost a pretty* ~, costar un dineral; *to turn an honest* ~, ganar algún dinero honradamente.
**penny-a-liner** *s.* gacetillero; escritorzuelo.
**pennyroyal** (peniro·ial) *s.* BOT. poleo.
**penny-wise** *adj.* que sólo es prudente o ahorrativo en cosas sin importancia.
**penologist** (pina·lodŷist) *s.* penalista.
**penology** (pina·lodŷi) *s.* ciencia penal.
**pensile** (pe·nsil) *adj.* pensil, péndulo, colgante.
**pension** (pe·nshøn) *s.* pensión, retiro, jubilación. *2* pensión [pupilaje; casa de huéspedes].
**pension (to)** *tr.* pensionar, retirar, jubilar.
**pensioner** (-øᵣ) *s.* pensionado. *2* retirado, jubilado. *3* MIL. inválido. *4* pensionista.
**pensive** (pe·nsiv) *adj.* pensativo; melancólico.
**penstock** (pe·nstak) *s.* compuerta [de esclusa, etc.]. *2* paradera [del caz].
**pent** (pent) *adj.* encerrado, acorralado. *2* contenido, reprimido. | Gralte. con *up* o *in.*
**pentacle** (pe·ntakøl) *s.* pentáculo.
**pentadactyl(e** (pentadæ·ktil) *adj.* pentadáctilo.
**pentagon** (pe·ntagan) *s.* GEOM. pentágono.
**pentagonal** (pentæ·gonal) *adj.* pentagonal.
**pentahedron** (pentaji·drøn) *s.* GEOM. pentaedro.
**pentamerous** (pentæ·mørøs) *s.* H. NAT. pentámero.
**pentameter** (pentæ·mitøᵣ) *s.* MET. pentámetro.
**pentane** (pe·ntein) *s.* QUÍM. pentano.
**pentapolis** (pe·ntapolis) *s.* pentápolis.
**Pentateuch** (-atiuk) *s.* Pentateuco.
**Pentecost** (pe·nticost) *s.* Pentecostés.
**penthouse** (pe·ntjaus) *s.* cobertizo, alpende. *2* tejadillo, colgadizo. *3* (E.U.) piso en la azotea.
**penultimate** (pinø·ltimit) *adj.* penúltimo. *2 s.* penúltima sílaba.
**penumbra** (-mbra) *s.* ASTR., PINT. penumbra.
**penurious** (piniu·riøs) *adj.* pobre. *2* de penuria. *3* cicatero, roñoso.
**penury** (pe·niuri) *s.* penuria, estrechez. *2* escasez.
**peon** (pɪ·an) *s.* [en la India y Ceilán] peón [soldado]; policía indígena; criado.
**peony** (pɪ·øni) *s.* BOT. peonia, saltaojos.
**people** (pɪ·pøl) *s.* pueblo, raza, nación, grey. *2* pueblo [de un país, etc.]: *the common* ~, el pueblo, el vulgo. *3* gente, personas: *two* ~, dos personas; *the young* ~, la gente joven; *my* ~, los míos, mi familia.
**people (to)** *tr.* poblar. *2* colonizar.
**pep** (pep) *s.* pop. (E.U.) energía, estímulo, brío: *to be full of* ~, tener mucha energía.
**pep (to)** *tr.* animar, estimular, vigorizar.
**pepper** (pe·pøᵣ) *s.* pimienta. *2* pimiento, ají, chile. *3 red* ~, pimentón. *4* BOT. ~ *cress*, mastuerzo; ~ *tree*, turbinto.
**pepper (to)** *tr.* sazonar con pimiento. *2* salpimentar. *3* esparcir, salpicar. *4* acribillar.
**pepperbox** (-baks) *s.* pimentero [vasija].
**peppercorn** (-koᵣn) *s.* grano de pimienta.
**peppermint** (-mint) *s.* BOT. menta, piperita. *2* pastilla o licor de menta.
**peppery** (-i) *adj.* picante. *2* mordaz. *3* colérico, de mal genio.
**pepsin(e** (pe·psin) *s.* BIOQUÍM. pepsina.
**peptic** (-tik) *adj.* péptico.
**peptone** (-toun) *s.* BIOQUÍM. peptona.

**per** (p∂ʳ) *prep.* por: ~ *cent*, por ciento. *2 as per*, según.
**peradventure** (-adve·nch∂ʳ) *adv.* acaso, por ventura. *2* duda: *beyond* ~, fuera de duda.
**perambulate (to)** (p∂ræ·mbiuleit) *tr.* recorrer, visitar o inspeccionar andando. *2 intr.* andar, pasear.
**perambulator** (-∂ʳ) *s.* cochecito de niño.
**perborate** (p∂ʳbou·reit) *s.* QUÍM. perborato.
**percale** (p∂ʳkei·l) *s.* percal.
**perceivable** (p∂ʳsɪ·vabøl) *adj.* perceptible, inteligible.
**perceive (to)** (p∂ʳsɪ·v) *tr.* percibir, ver, distinguir, advertir, comprender.
**percentage** (p∂ʳse·ntidÿ) *s.* porcentaje.
**perceptible** (p∂ʳse·ptibøl) *adj.* perceptible, sensible, visible.
**perception** (-shøn) *s.* percepción [con los sentidos, el entendimiento]. *2* DER. perceptivo.
**perch** (p∂ʳch) *s.* ICT. perca. *2* pértica [medida]. *3* percha, alcándara. *4* pértiga, palo.
**perch (to)** *tr.* emperchar. *2* encaramar. *3 intr.* encaramarse, posarse [en percha, rama, etc.]; sentarse [en sitio elevado].
**perchance** (p∂ʳcha·ns) *adv.* acaso, por ventura.
**Percheron** (p∂ʳshøran) *adj.-s.* percherón.
**percipient** (p∂ʳsi·piønt) *adj.-s.* capaz de percepción.
**percolate (to)** (pø·ʳkøleit) *tr.* colar, pasar, filtrar. *2 tr.-intr.* trascolarse o filtrarse [por].
**percolation** (-ei·shøn) *s.* coladura, filtración.
**percolator** (pø·ʳkøleitøʳ) *s.* filtro, colador. *2* cafetera de filtro.
**percuss (to)** (pø·ʳkø·s) *tr.* percutir.
**percussion** (-shøn) *s.* percusión: ~ *cap*, pistón, cápsula fulminante; ~ *instrument*, instrumento de percusión.
**perdition** (p∂ʳdi·shøn) *s.* perdición.
**perdurable** (pø·ʳdiurabøl) *adj.* perdurable.
**peregrinate (to)** (pe·rigrineit) *intr.* viajar.
**peregrination** (-ei·shøn) *s.* peregrinación, viaje.
**peremptory** (pøre·mptori) *adj.* perentorio, terminante, decisivo. *2* autoritario, imperioso.
**perennial** (pøre·nial) *adj.* perennal, perenne. *2* BOT. perenne, vivaz. *3 s.* planta perenne.
**perfect** (pø·ʳfikt) *adj.* perfecto. *2* acabado, completo. *3 s.* GRAM. tiempo perfecto.
**perfect (to)** (pø·ʳfikt) *tr.* perfeccionar, acabar, completar, coronar, redondear.
**perfectible** (-tibøl) *adj.* perfectible.
**perfection** (-shøn) *s.* perfección: *to* ~, a la perfección.
**perfective** (-tiv) *adj.* perfectivo.
**perfervid** (pø·ʳfø·ʳvid) *adj.* muy férvido, ardiente.
**perfidious** (pø·ʳfi·diøs) *adj.* pérfido.
**perfidy** (pø·ʳfidi) *s.* perfidia.
**perfoliate** (pø·ʳfou·lieit) *adj.* BOT. perfoliada.
**perforate (to)** (pø·ʳføreit) *tr.* perforar, horadar. *2* taladrar, trepar.
**perforation** (-ei·shøn) *s.* perforación. *2* línea de agujeros, calado.
**perforator** (-tøʳ) *s.* perforador. *2* perforadora.
**perforce** (pø·ʳfo·ʳs) *adv.* por fuerza, a la fuerza.
**perform (to)** (pø·ʳfo·ʳm) *tr.* hacer, ejecutar, realizar, cumplir, desempeñar, ejercer. *2 intr.* actuar. *3* desempeñar un papel, tocar un instrumento, etc. *4* funcionar [una máquina].
**performance** (-∂ns) *s.* ejecución, cumplimiento, desempeño. *2* obra, acción, hazaña. *3* función, representación, concierto; actuación de un artista, etc.

**performer** (-∂ʳ) *s.* ejecutante, representante, actor, artista, acróbata.
**perfume** (pø·ʳfium o pø·ʳfiu·m) *s.* perfume.
**perfume (to)** *tr.* perfumar, embalsamar.
**perfumer** (pø·ʳfiu·mø·ʳ) *s.* perfumador. *2* perfumista.
**perfumery** (-i) *s.* perfumería.
**perfunctory** (pø·ʳfø·nktori) *adj.* perfunctorio, hecho sin interés, superficial, formulario.
**perfusion** (pø·ʳfiu·dÿøn) *s.* perfusión, baño, aspersión.
**pergola** (pø·ʳgøla) *s.* pérgola.
**perhaps** (pørjæ·ps) *adv.* quizás, tal vez, acaso.
**peri** (pɪ·ri) *s.* peri, hada.
**perianth(ium** (periæ·nz(iøm) *s.* BOT. periantio.
**pericardium** (-ka·ʳdiøm) *s.* ANAT. pericardio.
**pericarp** (-ka·ʳp) *s.* BOT. pericarpo.
**perigee** (-dÿɪ) *s.* ASTR. perigeo.
**perihelion** (-jɪ·liøn) *s.* ASTR. perihelio.
**peril** (pe·ril) *s.* peligro, riesgo, exposición.
**peril (to)** *tr.* poner en peligro. *2 intr.* peligrar.
**perilous** (pe·riløs) *adj.* peligroso; expuesto.
**perimeter** (peri·mitø·ʳ) *s.* perímetro.
**perineum** (-nɪ·øm) *s.* ANAT. perineo.
**period** (pi·riød) *s.* período. *2* hora [de clase]. *3* punto final. *4 pl.* período, menstruación.
**periodic** (piria·dik) *adj.* periódico.
**periodical** (-al) *adj.* periódico. *2 s.* publicación periódica, revista.
**perioeci** (peri·sai) *s. pl.* GEOGR. periecos.
**periosteum** (-a·stiøm) *s.* ANAT. periostio.
**peripatetic** (-pate·tik) *adj.* ambulante. *2 adj.-s.* (con may.) peripatético.
**peripheral** (peri·føral) *adj.* periférico.
**periphery** (-føri) *s.* periferia.
**periphrase (to)** (pe·rifreiš) *tr.-intr.* RET. perifrasear.
**periphrasis** (peri·frasis) *s.* RET. perífrasis.
**periplus** (pe·ripløs) *s.* periplo.
**peripteros** (peri·ptørøs) *s.* ARQ. períptero.
**periscii** (-shiai) *s. pl.* GEOGR. periscios.
**periscope** (pe·riskoup) *s.* periscopio.
**perish (to)** (pe·rish) *intr.* perecer, fenecer, acabar. *2* pasarse, averiarse.
**perishable** (-abøl) *adj.* perecedero. *2* deleznable, marchitable. *3* averiable.
**perissodactyl(e** (pirisødæ·ktil) *s.* ZOOL. perisodáctilo.
**perisperm** (pe·rispø·ʳm) *s.* BOT. perispermo.
**peristaltic** (peristæ·ltik) *adj.* peristáltico.
**peristyle** (pe·ristail) *s.* ARQ. peristilo.
**peritoneum** (peritonɪ·øm) *s.* ANAT. peritoneo.
**peritonitis** (peritønai·tis) *s.* MED. peritonitis.
**periwig** (pe·riuig) *s.* peluquín.
**periwinkle** (pe·riuinkøl) *s.* BOT. vincapervinca. *2* ZOOL. litorina.
**perjure (to)** (pø·ʳdÿøʳ) *intr.* perjurar. *2 tr. to* ~ *oneself*, perjurarse.
**perjurer** (-øʳ) *s.* perjurador, perjuro.
**perjury** (-i) *s.* perjurio.
**perk (to)** (pø·ʳk) *tr.* erguir, levantar [la cabeza, las orejas]. *2* ataviar. *3 intr.* asomar; erguirse, darse tono. *4 to* ~ *up*, reponerse, animarse; despejarse.
**perky** (pø·ʳki) *adj.* gallardo, presumido, desenvuelto.
**permanence** (pø·ʳmanøns) *s.* permanencia.
**permanent** (-nt) *adj.* permanente, estable, fijo, duradero: ~ *wave*, ondulación permanente.
**permeable** (pø·ʳmiabøl) *adj.* permeable, penetrable.

**permeate (to)** (pøˑ'mieit) *tr.* penetrar, atravesar, calar; llenar, impregnar.
**permeation** (-eiˑshøn) *s.* penetración a través de los poros; impregnación.
**Permian** (pøˑ'mian) *adj.-s.* GEOL. pérmico.
**permissible** (pø'miˑsibøl) *adj.* permisible.
**permission** (-shøn) *s.* permiso, permisión, licencia, venia. 2 MIL. permiso.
**permissive** (-siv) *adj.* permisivo. 2 permitido, consentido.
**permit** (pøˑ'mit) *s.* permiso, licencia, pase, guía.
**permit (to)** (pø'miˑt) *tr.* permitir. 2 *intr. to ~ of*, admitir, sufrir. ¶ Pret. y p. p.: *permitted*; ger.: *-tting*.
**permutation** (pø'miuteiˑshøn) *s.* permutación.
**permute (to)** (pø'miuˑt) *tr.* permutar.
**pern** (pø'n) *s.* ORN. buharro.
**pernicious** (pø'niˑshøs) *adj.* pernicioso. 2 malvado.
**pernickety** (pø'niˑkiti) *adj.* fam. quisquilloso, meticuloso, difícil, delicado.
**perorate (to)** (peˑrøreit) *intr.* perorar.
**peroration** (-eiˑshøn) *s.* peroración.
**peroxid(e** (pøraˑksaid) *s.* QUÍM. peróxido: *~ blonde*, rubia oxigenada.
**perpend** (pø'peˑnd) *s.* ALBAÑ. perpiaño.
**perpendicular** (pø'pøndiˑkiulaʳ) *adj.-s.* perpendicular. 2 *adj.* vertical. 3 muy pendiente, escarpado.
**perpetrate (to)** (pøˑ'pitreit) *tr.* perpetrar.
**perpetration** (-eiˑshøn) *s.* perpetración.
**perpetual** (pø'peˑchual) *adj.* perpetuo. 2 continuo, incesante. 3 BOT. perenne.
**perpetuate (to)** (-chueit) *tr.* perpetuar.
**perpetuation** (-eiˑshøn) *s.* perpetuación.
**perpetuity** (pø'pitiuˑiti) *s.* perpetuidad.
**perplex (to)** (pø'pleˑks) *tr.* dejar perplejo; confundir. 2 turbar, aturrullar. 3 complicar, enredar.
**perplexed** (pø'pleˑkst) *adj.* perplejo, confuso. 2 turbado, preocupado. 3 complicado, enredado.
**perplexity** (pø'pleˑksiti) *s.* perplejidad, duda, confusión. 2 complicación, enredo.
**perquisite** (pøˑ'kuišit) *s.* gaje, obvención, propina.
**perron** (peˑrøn) *s.* ARQ. escalinata.
**perry** (peˑri) *s.* sidra de peras.
**persecute (to)** (pøˑ'rsikiut) *tr.* perseguir, molestar, vejar, oprimir. 2 perseguir, acosar.
**persecution** (po'sikiuˑshøn) *s.* persecución.
**persecutor** (pøˑ'sikiutø'ʳ) *s.* perseguidor.
**Perseus** (pøˑ'siøs) *n. pr.* MIT. Perseo.
**perseverance** (pø'siviˑrans) *s.* perseverancia.
**persevere (to)** (-ø'ʳ) *intr.* perseverar.
**persevering** (-ring) *adj.* perseverante.
**Persian** (pø'ʳshan) *adj.* persa, pérsico: *~ blinds*, persianas [celosías]; *~ Gulf*, golfo Pérsico. 2 *s.* persa [pers., lengua].
**Persic** (pø'sik) *adj.* pérsico.
**persicary** (pø'ʳsikeri) *s.* BOT. persicaria, duraznillo.
**persiflage** (pø'ʳsifladẏ) *s.* burla, zumba.
**persimmon** (pø'siˑmøn) *s.* BOT. caqui; su fruto.
**persist (to)** (pø'siˑst) *intr.* persistir; permanecer; continuar. 2 insistir, porfiar.
**persistence, -cy** (-øns, -si) *s.* persistencia, constancia. 2 insistencia, porfía.
**persistent, -ting·** (-ønt, -ting) *adj.* persistente. 2 constante, tenaz. 3 insistente.
**person** (pø'søn) *s.* persona: *first ~*, primera persona; *in ~*, en persona, personalmente.
**personable** (-abøl) *adj.* bien parecido.
**personage** (-idẏ) *s.* personaje.
**personal** (-al) *adj.* personal: *~ pronoun*, pronombre personal. 2 en persona. 3 que incluye per-

sonalismo: *to become ~*, hacer alusiones de carácter personal y ofensivo. 4 *~ estate*, bienes muebles. 5 *s.* nota de sociedad; remitido [en un periódico].
**personalism** (pø'ʳsønališm) *s.* cualidad, carácter o influencia personal. 2 individualidad. 3 FIL. personalismo.
**personality** (pø'ʳsønæˑliti) *s.* personalidad. 2 individualidad. 3 personalismo, alusión personal.
**personalize (to)** (pø'ʳsønalais) *s.* individualizar. 2 personificar. 3 personalizar.
**personate** (pø'ʳsøneit) *adj.* BOT. personada.
**personate (to)** *tr.* TEAT. representar el papel de. 2 fingir, fingirse, hacerse pasar por. 3 personificar.
**personation** (-eiˑshøn) *s.* representación [de un papel]. 2 DER. usurpación de personalidad.
**personator** (pø'ʳsøneitø'ʳ) *s.* intérprete [de un papel]. 2 el que se hace pasar por otro.
**personification** (pø'ʳsaˑnifikeiˑshøn) *s.* personificación. 2 RET. prosopopeya.
**personify (to)** (-nifai) *tr.* personificar. ¶ Pert. y p. p.: *personified*.
**personnel** (pø'ʳsøneˑl) *s.* personal, dependencia.
**perspective** (pø'ʳspeˑktiv) *s.* perspectiva. 2 *adj.* de perspectiva, en perspectiva.
**perspicacious** (pø'ʳspikeiˑshøs) *adj.* perspicaz.
**perspicacity** (pø'ʳspikæˑsiti) *s.* perspicacia, penetración.
**perspicuity** (pø'ʳspikiuˑiti) *s.* perspicuidad.
**perspicuous** (pø'ʳspiˑkiuøs) *adj.* perspicuo.
**perspiration** (pø'ʳspireiˑshøn) *s.* transpiración, sudor.
**perspire (to)** (pø'ʳspaiˑø'ʳ) *tr.-intr.* transpirar, sudar, trasudar. 2 *tr.* exudar.
**persuade (to)** (pø'sueiˑd) *tr.* persuadir, inducir, mover. 2 exhortar, tratar de convencer.
**persuasible** (pø'sueiˑsibøl) *adj.* fácil de persuadir.
**persuasion** (pø'sueiˑẏøn) *s.* persuasión. 2 persuasiva. 3 creencia. 4 credo, fe, religión, secta.
**persuasive** (pø'sueiˑsiv) *adj.* persuasivo. 2 *s.* cosa que persuade; incentivo.
**pert** (pø'ʳt) *adj.* petulante, atrevido, descarado. 2 vivo, alegre, desenvuelto.
**pertain (to)** (pø'teiˑn) *intr.* pertenecer; corresponder, tocar, atañer. 2 hacer relación, referirse.
**pertinacious** (pø'ʳtineiˑshøs) *adj.* pertinaz.
**pertinacity** (pø'ʳtinæˑsiti) *s.* pertinacia.
**pertinence, -cy** (pø'ʳtinøns, -si) *s.* pertinencia, oportunidad.
**pertinent** (-nt) *adj.* pertinente, que viene a propósito, oportuno, atinado.
**pertness** (pø'ʳtnis) *s.* petulancia, descaro.
**perturb (to)** (pø'ʳtø'b) *tr.* perturbar, conturbar, agitar.
**perturbation** (pø'ʳtø'beiˑshøn) *s.* perturbación, conturbación, agitación.
**perturber** (pø'ʳtø'bø'ʳ) *s.* perturbador, agitador.
**Peru** (pøruˑ) *n. pr.* el Perú.
**peruke** (peruˑk) *s.* peluca, peluquín.
**perusal** (peruˑšal) *s.* lectura, lectura atenta.
**peruse (to)** (peruˑš) *tr.* leer, leer con cuidado.
**Peruvian** (peruˑvian) *adj.-s.* peruano.
**pervade (to)** (pø'veiˑd) *tr.* penetrar, llenar, saturar, impregnar, difundirse por.
**pervasion** (pø'ʳveiˑẏøn) *s.* penetración, impregnación, difusión.
**perverse** (pø'vøˑʳs) *adj.* perverso, avieso. 2 pervertido. 3 terco, indócil, que lleva la contraria.
**perverseness** (-nis) *s.* perversidad, malicia. 2 terquedad.

**perversion** (-shøn) *s.* perversión. *2* pervertimiento. *3* corrupción, alteración.
**perversity** (-siti) *s.* PERVERSENESS.
**pervert** (-t) *s.* pervertido. *2* apóstata, hereje.
**pervert (to)** *tr.* pervertir. *2* corromper, tergiversar, falsear, desnaturalizar.
**perverter** (-ø^r) *s.* pervertidor.
**pervious** (pø·^rviøs) *adj.* penetrable, accesible, permeable: ~ *to light,* diáfano.
**pesade** (pisei·d) *s.* empinada [del caballo].
**pesky** (pe·ski) *adj.* fam. (E.U.) molesto, cargante.
**pessary** (pe·sari) *s.* CIR. pesario.
**pessimism** (pe·simišm) *s.* pesimismo.
**pessimist** (-ist) *s.* pesimista.
**pessimistic (al** (pesimi·stik(al) *adj.* pesimista.
**pest** (pest) *s.* peste; plaga. *2* pers. o cosa molesta. *3* insecto nocivo.
**pester (to)** (-ø^r) *tr.* molestar, importunar.
**pesthouse** (-jaus) *s.* lazareto.
**pestiferous** (pesti·førøs) *adj.* pestífero, pestilente.
**pestilence** (pe·stiløns) *s.* peste, pestilencia.
**pestilent** (-t) *adj.* pestilente, pernicioso. *2* molesto, cargante, travieso.
**pestilential** (pestile·nshal) *adj.* pestilencial.
**pestle** (pe·søl) *s.* mano de almirez, majadero.
**pestle (to)** *tr.* majar, machacar, pistar, moler.
**pet** (pet) *adj.* querido, mimado, favorito. *2* ~ *name,* apelativo cariñoso. *3 s.* animal doméstico. *4* pers. o niño querido, mimado. *5* enojo, despecho, berrinche: *to go away in a* ~, irse enojado.
**pet (to)** *tr.* mimar, regalar, acariciar. ¶ Pret. y p. p.: *petted;* ger.: *-tting.*
**petal** (pe·tal) *s.* BOT. pétalo.
**petalism** (-lišm) *s.* petalismo.
**petaloid** (-oid) *adj.* petaloideo.
**petard** (pita·^rd) *s.* petardo.
**Peter** (pɪ·tø^r) *n. pr.* Pedro: *Peter's pence,* dinero de San Pedro.
**peter (to)** *intr.* disminuir, gastarse, agotarse. | Gralte. con *out.*
**petiolate** (pe·tioleit) *adj.* peciolado.
**petiole** (pe·tioul) *s.* BOT. peciolo.
**petition** (piti·shøn) *s.* instancia, solicitud, petición, memorial. *2* ruego, súplica.
**petition (to)** *tr.* solicitar; suplicar, pedir. *2* dirigir una petición o memorial a.
**petitionary** (-eri) *adj.* petitorio.
**petitioner** (-ø^r) *s.* solicitante, peticionario.
**Petrarch** (pɪ·trark) *n. pr.* Petrarca.
**petrel** (pe·trøl) *s.* ORN. petrel.
**petrifaction** (petrifæ·kshøn), **petrification** (-fikei·shøn) *s.* petrificación.
**petrify (to)** (pe·trifai) *tr.* petrificar. *2 intr.* petrificarse, fosilizarse. ¶ Pret. y p. p.: *petrified.*
**petrography** (petra·grafi) *s.* petrografía.
**petrol** (pe·trøl) *s.* (Ingl.) gasolina, bencina.
**petrol (to)** *tr.* proveer de bencina.
**petroleum** (pitrou·liøm) *s.* petróleo.
**petroliferous** (pitrøli·førøs) *adj.* petrolífero.
**petrology** (pitra·lodẏi) *s.* petrología, petrognosia.
**petrous** (pe·trøs) *adj.* pétreo, petroso.
**petticoat** (pe·tikout) *s.* enaguas. *2* falda, basquiña, faldellín. *3* fig. faldas, mujer, muchacha. *4* ELECT. campana de aislador. *5* adj. de mujeres, de faldas.
**pettifogger** (pe·tifagø^r) *s.* leguleyo, picapleitos.
**pettifoggery** (-ri) *s.* triquiñuela, enredo de picapleitos.
**pettiness** (pe·tinis) *s.* pequeñez, insignificancia, mezquindad.

**pettish** (pe·tish) *adj.* enojadizo, malhumorado, regañón.
**pettishness** (-nis) *s.* mal humor, enojo, aspereza.
**petty** (pe·ti) *adj.* pequeño, menor, insignificante, mezquino: ~ *cash,* dinero para gastos menores; ~ *jury,* jurado [de juicio]; ~ *larceny,* ratería; ~ *prince,* principillo. *2* inferior, subalterno.
**petulance, -cy** (pe·chulans, -si) *s.* impaciencia, mal humor, mal genio.
**petulant** (-t) *adj.* enojadizo, malhumorado, impaciente, áspero. *2* poc. us. petulante.
**petunia** (pitiu·nia) *s.* BOT. petunia.
**pew** (piu) *s.* banco de iglesia.
**pewit** (pi·uit) *s.* ORN. avefría. *2* ORN. laro.
**pewter** (piu·tø^r) *s.* peltre. *2* vasijas de peltre.
**Phaedra** (fɪ·dræ) *n. pr.* MIT. Fedra.
**Phaeton** (fei·tan) *n. pr.* MIT. Faetón. *2 s.* (con min.) faetón.
**phagocyte** (fæ·gøsait) *s.* BIOL. fagocito.
**phalange** (fæłæ·ndẏ) *s.* ANAT., ZOOL., POL. falange.
**phalanger** (falæ·ndẏø^r) *s.* ZOOL. falangero.
**phalanstery** (fæ·lansteri) *s.* falansterio.
**phalanx** (fæ·lænks), *pl.* **phalanges** *s.* MIL., ANAT., ZOOL. falange.
**phallus** (fæ·løs) *s.* falo.
**phanerogam** (fæ·nørøgam) *s.* BOT. fanerógama.
**phanerogamous** (fænøra·gamøs) *adj.* BOT. fanerógamo.
**phantasm** (fæ·ntæšm) *s.* fantasma.
**phantasmagoria** (-ago·ria) *s.* fantasmagoría.
**phantasmal** (fæntæ·smal) *adj.* espectral, fantástico, irreal.
**phantasy** (fæ·ntasi) *s.* fantasía, imaginación. *2* fantasía [producto de la imaginación].
**phantom** (fæ·ntøm) *s.* fantasma, aparición. *2* ilusión óptica. *3* imaginación engañosa. *4 adj.* fantasmal, quimérico; fantasma.
**Pharaoh** (fe·ørou) *s.* faraón.
**Pharanoic** (feria·nik) *adj.* faraónico.
**pharisaic (al** (færisei·ik(al) *adj.* farisaico.
**pharisaism** (fæ·riseiišm) *s.* fariseísmo.
**Pharisee** (fæ·risɪ) *s.* fariseo.
**pharmaceutic (al** (fa^rmasiu·tik(al) *adj.* farmacéutico.
**pharmaceutics** (-tiks) *s.* farmacia [ciencia, arte].
**pharmacist** (fa·^rmasist) *s.* farmacéutico, boticario.
**pharmacology** (fa^rmaka·lodẏi) *s.* farmacología.
**pharmacy** (fa·^rmasi) *s.* farmacia.
**pharos** (fei·røs) *s.* MAR. faro.
**pharyngeal** (færi·ndẏial) *adj.* ANAT. faríngeo.
**pharyngitis** (færindẏai·tis) *s.* MED. faringitis.
**pharyngoscope** (fari·ngoskoup) *s.* faringoscopio.
**pharynx** (fæ·rinks) *s.* ANAT. faringe.
**phase** (feiš) *s.* fase: *to be in* ~, estar en fase.
**pheasant** (fe·šant) *s.* ORN. faisán.
**phenic** (fe·nik) *adj.* fénico.
**phenix** (fɪ·niks) *s.* PHOENIX.
**phenol** (fɪ·nol) *s.* QUÍM. fenol.
**phenomenal** (fina·minal) *adj.* fenoménico. *2* fenomenal.
**phenomenon** (-øn), *pl.* **-na** (-na) *s.* fenómeno.
**phew!** (fiu) *interj.* uf!
**phi** (fai o fi) *s.* phi [letra griega].
**phial** (fai·al) *s.* redoma, frasco.
**Phidias** (fi·diæs) *n. pr.* Fidias.
**Philadelphia** (filade·lfia) *n. pr.* GEOGR. Filadelfia.
**philander (to)** (filæ·ndø^r) *intr.* galantear, flirtear.
**philanderer** (-ø^r) *s.* galanteador, flirteador.
**philanthropic (al** (filanzra·pik(al) *adj.* filantrópico.
**philanthropist** (filæ·nzrøpist) *adj.* filántropo.

**philanthropy** (-zrøpi) *s.* filantropía.
**philatelic (al** (filate·lik(*al*) *adj.* filatélico.
**philatelist** (filæ·tølist) *s.* filatelista.
**philately** (-tøli) *s.* filatelia.
**philharmonic** (filjaʳma·nik) *adj.* filarmónico.
**Philip** (fi·lip) *n. pr.* Felipe. *2* Filipo.
**philippic** (fili·pik) *adj.* filípica.
**Philippine** (filipi·n) *adj.* filipino.
**Philippines** (-š) *n. pr.* GEOGR. Filipinas.
**Philistine** (filisti·n) *adj.-s.* filisteo. *2* inculto, prosaico. *3* reaccionario.
**philologic (al** (filøla·dyik(*al*) *adj.* filológico.
**philologist** (fila·lodyist) *s.* filólogo.
**philology** (-lodyi) *s.* filología.
**philomel** (fi·lømel) *s.* poét. filomela, ruiseñor.
**philosopher** (fila·søføʳ) *s.* filósofo: *philosopher's stone,* piedra filosofal.
**philosophic (al** (filøsa·fik(*al*) *adj.* filosófico.
**philosophize (to)** (fila·søfaiš) *intr.* filosofar.
**philosophy** (-søfi) *s.* filosofía.
**philter, philtre** (fi·ltøʳ) *s.* filtro, bebedizo.
**philter** o **philtre (to)** *tr.* hechizar con filtro.
**phimosis** (faimou·sis) *s.* fimosis.
**phiz** (fiš) *s.* pop, cara, facha, fisonomía.
**phlebitis** (flibai·tis) *s.* MED. flebitis.
**phlegm** (fle·m) *s.* flema [mucosidad]. *2* QUÍM. flema. *3* flema, calma.
**phlegmatic (al** (flegmæ·tik(*al*) *adj.* flemático.
**phlegmon** (-man) *s.* MED. flemón.
**phobia** (fou·bia) *s.* fobia.
**Phocian** (fou·shan) *adj.-s.* focense.
**Phocis** (fou·sis) *n. pr.* GEOGR., HIST. La Fócida.
**Phoebe** (fi·bi) *n. pr.* MIT., ASTR. Febe.
**Phoebus** (fi·bøs) *n. pr.* MIT., poét. Febo.
**Phoenicia** (fini·sha) *n. pr.* GEOGR. Fenicia.
**Phoenician** (-an) *adj.-s.* fenicio.
**phoenix** (fi·niks) *s.* fénix.
**phonation** (fonei·shøn) *s.* fonación.
**phone** (fou·n) *s.* fam. teléfono. *2* RADIO. auricular.
**phone (to)** *tr.-intr.* fam. telefonear.
**phoneme** (fou·nim) *s.* fonema.
**phonetic (al** (fone·tik(*al*) *adj.* fonético.
**phonetics** (fone·tiks) *s.* fonética, fonología.
**phoney** (founi) *adj.* PHONY.
**phonic** (fa·nik) *adj.* fónico.
**phonogram** (fou·nøgræm) *s.* fonograma.
**phonograph** (-græf) *s.* fonógrafo.
**phonographic (al** (fonøgræ·fik(*al*) *adj.* fonográfico.
**phonolite** (fou·nølait) *s.* PETROGR. fonolita.
**phonology** (fona·lodyi) *s.* fonología.
**phonoscope** (fou·nøskoup) *s.* Fís. fonoscopio.
**phony** (fou·ni) *s.* fam. (E.U.) farsa, engaño; farsante. *2 adj.* fam. (E.U.) falso, imitado.
**phosphate** (fa·sfeit) *s.* QUÍM. fosfato.
**phosphaturia** (fasfatiu·ria) *s.* MED. fosfaturia.
**Phosphor** (fa·sføʳ) *s.* fósforo, lucero del alba.
**phosphoresce (to)** (fasføre·s) *intr.* fosforecer.
**phosphorescence** (-øns) *s.* fosforescencia.
**phosphorescent** (-ønt) *adj.* fosforescente.
**phosphoric** (fasfo·rik) *adj.* QUÍM. fosfórico.
**phosphorite** (fa·sførait) MINER. fosforita.
**phosphorous** (fa·sførøs) *adj.* QUÍM. fosforoso.
**phosphorus** *s.* QUÍM. fósforo.
**phosphuret** (fa·sfiurit) *adj.* QUÍM. fosfuro.
**phot** (fa·t) *s.* Fís. fotio.
**photo** (fou·tou) *s.* fam. fotografía, retrato.
**photo (to)** *tr.* fam. fotografiar.
**photochemical** (foutouke·mikal) *adj.* fotoquímico.
**photocopy** (fou·toukapi) *s.* fotocopia.
**photoelectric** (foutouile·ktrik) *adj.* fotoeléctrico.
**photoengrave (to)** (-engrei·v) *s.* fotograbar.

**photoengraving** (-ing) *s.* fotograbado.
**photogen** (fou·toudyen) *s.* BIOL. organismo fotógeno.
**photogenic** (-dye·nik) *adj.* fotógeno. *2* fotogénico.
**photograph** (fou·tøgræf) *s.* fotografía, retrato.
**photograph (to)** *tr.-intr.* fotografiar.
**photographer** (føta·graføʳ) *s.* fotógrafo.
**photography** (-fi) *s.* fotografía [arte].
**photogravure** (foutougraviu·ʳ) *s.* fotograbado.
**photolithograph** (-li·zøgræf) *s.* fotolitografía [lámina].
**photolithograph (to)** *tr.* fotolitografiar.
**photolithography** (-liza·grafi) *s.* fotolitografía [arte].
**photometry** (fouta·metri) *s.* fotometría.
**photomicrography** (foutomaikra·grafi) *s.* microfotografía.
**photon** (fou·tan) *s.* Fís. fotón.
**photophobia** (foutofou·bia) *s.* MED. fotofobia.
**photoprint** (-print) *s.* fotocalco, fotocopia.
**photosphere** (-sfiʳ) *s.* ASTR. fotosfera.
**photosynthesis** (-si·nzesis) *s.* BOT. fotosíntesis.
**phototropism** (fouta·trøpišm) *s.* BIOL. fototropismo.
**phototypography** (foutotaipa·grafi) *s.* fototipografía.
**phrase** (frei·š) *s.* frase, expresión, locución, modo, modismo. *2* fraseología, estilo. *3* MÚS. frase.
**phrase (to)** *tr.* expresar [con palabras]. *2* llamar, nombrar. *3* *tr.-intr.* frasear.
**phraseology** (freišia·lodyi) *s.* fraseología.
**phrasing** (frei·šing) *s.* fraseo.
**phrenetic** (frine·tik) *adj.* frenético. *2* delirante. *3* fanático.
**phrenic** (fre·nik) *adj.* ANAT., PSIC. frénico.
**phrenology** (frena·lodyi) *s.* frenología.
**phrenopathy** (-pazi) *s.* frenopatía.
**Phrygia** (fri·dyia) *n. pr.* GEOGR. Frigia.
**Phrygian** (fri·dyian) *adj.-s.* frigio.
**phthisic (al** (ti·šik(*al*) *adj.* tísico, hético. *2* asmático.
**phthisis** (zai·sis) *s.* tisis, hetiquez, consunción.
**phylactery** (filæ·ktøri) *s.* filactería.
**phyllode** (fi·loud) *s.* BOT. filodio.
**phylloxera** (filaksi·ra) *s.* filoxera.
**phylum** (fai·løm) *s.* BIOL. tipo.
**physic** (fi·šik) *s.* medicina, remedio. *2* purga.
**physic (to)** *tr.* medicinar, curar, purgar.
**physical** (-al) *adj.* físico: ~ *training,* educación física.
**physician** (fiši·shan) *s.* médico, doctor, facultativo.
**physicist** (fi·šisist) *s.* físico [versado en física].
**physics** (fi·šiks) *s. pl.* física; filosofía natural.
**physicochemistry** (fišikoke·mistri) *s.* fisicoquímica.
**physiocracy** (ffišia·krasi) *s.* fisiocracia.
**physiocrat** (fi·šiokræt) *s.* fisiócrata.
**physiognomic (al** (fišiagna·mik(*al*) *adj.* fisonómico.
**physiognomist** (fišia·gnomist) *s.* fisonomistsa.
**physiognomy** (-nomi) *s.* fisonomía.
**physiologic (al** (fišiola·dyik(*al*) *adj.* fisiológico.
**physiologist** (fišia·lodyist) *s.* fisiólogo.
**physiology** (-lodyi) *s.* fisiología.
**physiotherapy** (fišioze·rapi) *s.* fisioterapia.
**physique** (fiši·k) *s.* físico, figura, constitución [de una pers.].
**phytography** (faita·grafi) *s.* fitografía.
**phytophagous** (faita·fagøs) *adj.* fitófago.
**pi** (pai) *s.* pi [letra griega; signo]. *2* IMPR. pastel.

**piaffe (to)** (piæ·f) *intr.* EQUIT. piafar.
**pia-mater** (paia-mei·tø<sup>r</sup>) *s.* ANAT. pía-mater.
**pianissimo** (piani·simou) *adv.-adj.* MÚS. pianísimo.
**pianist** (piæ·nist) *s.* MÚS. pianista.
**piano** (-nou) *adj.-adv.* MÚS. piano. *2 s.* piano, pianoforte: *grand* ~, piano de cola; *upright* ~, piano vertical.
**pianoforte** (-noufo<sup>r</sup>t) *s.* MÚS. piano, pianoforte.
**pianola** (piænou·la) *s.* pianola.
**piaster, piastre** (piæ·stø<sup>r</sup>) *s.* piastra.
**piazza** (piæ·śa) *s.* plaza. *2* pórtico, galería.
**pibroch** (pi·brak) *s.* música marcial o plañidera tocada con la gaita escocesa.
**pica** (pai·ka) *s.* MED. pica. *2* IMPR. cícero.
**Picard** (pi·ka<sup>r</sup>d) *adj.-s.* picardo.
**Picardy** (pi·ka<sup>r</sup>di) *n. pr.* GEOGR. Picardía.
**picaresque** (pikare·sk) *adj.* picaresco.
**picaroon** (pikaru·n) *s.* pícaro. *2* ladrón. *3* pirata.
**picayune** (pikayu·n) *s.* (E.U.) moneda o cosa de poco valor. *2 adj.* mezquino, insignificante.
**piccalilli** (pi·kalili) *s.* especie de encurtidos.
**piccolo** (pi·kolou) *s.* MÚS. flautín.
**piceous** (pi·siøs) *adj.* píceo. *2* inflamable.
**pick** (pik) *s.* pico [herramienta], zapapico. *2* MÚS. pua, plectro. *3* pinchazo. *4* cosecha. *5* selección; derecho a escoger. *6* flor, lo más escogido.
**pick (to)** *tr.* picar, agujerear; romper [con pico, punzón, etc.]. *2* hacer [un agujero, etc.]: *to* ~ *a hole in*, hacer un agujero en; hallar un defecto en. *3* coger [flores, frutos, etc.]; recoger. *4* escoger. *5* limpiar [quitando], mondar, pelar, desplumar: *to* ~ *a bone*, roer un hueso; ajustar cuentas; *to* ~ *one's teeth*, mondarse los dientes; *to* ~ *pockets*, limpiar bolsillos, ser ratero. *6* forzar [una cerradura]. *7* MÚS. puntear [un instrumento]. *8* picar, picotear. *9* comer a bocaditos. *10* hallar [defectos]. *11 to* ~ *a quarrel*, buscar pendencia. *12 to* ~ *off*, arrancar, quitar. *13 to* ~ *out*, escoger; ver, descifrar; quitar. *14 to* ~ *to pieces*, desmenuzar, analizar. *15 to* ~ *up*, recoger; coger, adquirir, tomar; captar [una emisión de radio, etc.]; hallar [por casualidad]; aprender [con la práctica]; recobrar [ánimo, vigor, etc.]; entablar conversación con [uno] de un modo casual. *16 to* ~ *up speed*, ganar velocidad.
   *17 intr. to* ~ *at*, tirar de; picar de [un manjar]; tomarla con, criticar, regañar. *18 to* ~ *up*, restablecese; cobrar carnes; ganar velocidad.
**pickaback** (pi·kabæk) *adv.* fam. a cuestas.
**pickaninny** (pi·kanini) *s.* negrito, niño negro. *2* muchacho, muchachito.
**picax, picaxe** (pi·kæks) *s.* piqueta, zapapico.
**picker** (pi·kø<sup>r</sup>) *s.* mondador. *2* escardador. *2* escogedor. *4* recolector. *5* nombre de varios instrumentos.
**pickerel** (pi·kørøl) *s.* ICT. variedad de lucio.
**picket** (pi·kit) *s.* estaca, piquete [palo]. *2* MIL. piquete. *3* huelguista puesto de vigilancia cerca de una fábrica, etc.
**picket (to)** *tr.* cercar con estacas. *2* estacar [un caballo]. *3* MIL. guardar; poner de guardia. *4* vigilar los huelguistas [una fábrica, etc.].
**pickings** (-ings) *s. pl.* desperdicios, desechos. *2* lo pillado o robado. *3* gajes, ganancias.
**pickle** (pi·køl) *s.* salmuera, escabeche, vinagre, adobo: *in* ~, en escabeche, en vinagre; fig. en reserva. *2* apuro, aprieto, lío. *3* niño travieso. *4 pl.* encurtidos.
**pickle (to)** *tr.* encurtir, escabechar, adobar.
**picklock** (pi·klak) *s.* ganzúa [garfio, ladrón].

**pickpocket** (-pakit) *s.* ratero, carterista.
**pickup** (-øp) *s.* recogida. *2* cosa recogida, hallada. *3* AUTO. aceleración. *4* fam. mejoría, recobro. *5* ELECT. fonocaptor, pick-up.
**pickwik** (-wik) *s.* cigarro barato.
**picnic** (-nik) *s.* partida de campo, jira, comida al aire libre.
**picnic (to)** *intr.* ir de jira, comer o merendar en el campo, al aire libre. ¶ Pret. y p. p.: *picnicked;* ger.: *-cking*.
**picot** (pi·kou) *s.* puntilla [encaje].
**picotee** (pikotı·) *s.* BOT. clavel moteado.
**picric** (pi·krik) *adj.* QUÍM. pícrico.
**Pict** (pikt) *s.* picto.
**pictography** (pikta·grafi) *s.* pictografía.
**pictorial** (pikto·rial) *adj.* pictórico. *2* gráfico, ilustrado. *3 s.* revista ilustrada.
**picture** (pi·kchø<sup>r</sup>) *s.* pintura, cuadro: ~ *gallery*, galería de pinturas. *2* retrato, fotografía; dibujo, estampa, lámina, grabado: ~ *page*, página ilustrada [de un periódico]. *3* cuadro, escena, conjunto. *4* pintura, descripción. *5* imagen, semejanza. *6* ÓPT. imagen. *7* cuadro [clínico]. *8* película cinematográfica: ~ *house*, ~ *palace*, cinematógrafo [edificio]; *the pictures*, el cinematógrafo, el cine. *9* ~ *hat*, especie de pamela.
**picture (to)** *tr.* pintar, dibujar, retratar. *2* describir. *3 intr.* imaginarse, representarse.
**picturesque** (pikchøre·sk) *adj.* pintoresco.
**piddle (to)** (pi·døl) *intr.* malgastar el tiempo. *2* hacer pipí [expr. infantil].
**piddling** (pi·dling) *adj.* fútil, baladí.
**pidgin English** (pi·dỹin) *s.* inglés chapurrado que sirve como lengua franca en China.
**pie** (pai) *s.* pastel, empanada. *2* ORN. urraca, marica. *3* IMPR. empastelar.
**piebald** (-bold) *adj.-s.* pío [caballo]. *2 adj.* mezclado, abigarrado.
**piece** (pıs) *s.* pieza, trozo, pedazo, fragmento: *to cut to pieces*, despedazar; destrozar [un ejército]; *to go to pieces*, desvencijarse; fracasar [un negocio]; perder la salud; tener los nervios destrozados; *to take to pieces*, desarmar, desmontar; deshacer. *2* pieza [de tela, de un juego, etc.]; ejemplo, caso, acto: ~ *of furniture*, mueble; ~ *of advice*, consejo; ~ *of news*, noticia; *to give one a* ~ *of one's mind*, decir las verdades a uno; *of a* ~ *with*, lo mismo o de la misma clase que. *3* cañón, arma de fuego. *4* moneda. *5* casco, tonel. *6* PINT. cuadro. *7* MÚS., LIT., TEAT. pieza, obra.
**piece (to)** *tr.* apedazar, remendar. *2* reunir, juntar; formar juntando piezas o partes.
**piecemeal** (-mıl) *adj.* hecho de trozos. *2* hecho por partes. *3 adv.* en pedazos. *4* poco a poco, de trozo en trozo, por partes.
**piecework** (-wø<sup>r</sup>k) *s.* trabajo a destajo.
**pied** (paid) *adj.* de varios colores, moteado, pinto, abigarrado.
**Piedmont** (pi·dmant) *n. pr.* GEOGR. Piamonte.
**pier** (pi·ø<sup>r</sup>) *s.* pilar [para sostener]. *2* ARQ. estribo, machón. *3* muelle, embarcadero. *4* malecón, rompeolas. *5* ARQ. entrepaño: ~ *glass*, espejo de cuerpo entero; ~ *table*, consola.
**pierce (to)** (pı<sup>r</sup>s) *tr.* atravesar, traspasar; taladrar, perforar, agujerear, punzar. *2* penetrar. *3* conmover. *4* abrir [un agujero, paso, etc.]. *5 intr.* penetrar, internarse.
**piercing** (-ing) *s.* agudo, penetrante. *2* punzante. *3* terebrante. *4* lastimero, conmovedor.
**Pierides** (paii·ridiš) *s. pl.* Piérides.
**pietism** (pai·otišm) *s.* pietismo. *2* mojigatería.

**pietist** (-øtist) *s.* pietista. 2 mojigato.
**piety** (-øti) *s.* piedad, devoción.
**piezometer** (paiiša·mitø<sup>r</sup>) *s.* FÍS. piezómetro.
**piffle** (pi·føl) *s.* tontería, despropósito; palabrería.
**piffle (to)** *intr.* disparatar, decir tonterías.
**pig** (pig) *s.* ZOOL. cerdo, puerco, cochino. 2 COC. lechón. 3 fig. cerdo [pers.]. 4 FUND. lingote, barra, tejo.
**pigeon** (pi·dÿøn) *s.* ORN. pichón, palomo, paloma: ~ *breast*, MED. pecho en quilla; ~ *house*, palomar. 2 fig. primo, incauto.
**pigeon-breasted** *adj.* MED. de pecho en quilla.
**pigeonfoot** (-fut) *s.* BOT. pie de milano.
**pigeon-hearted** *adj.* tímido, cobarde.
**pigeonhole** (-joul) *s.* hornilla [de palomar]. 2 casilla [de casillero].
**pigeonhole (to)** *tr.* encasillar. 2 clasificar y guardar en la memoria. 3 relegar al olvido, archivar, dar carpetazo a.
**pigeonry** (-ri) *s.* palomar.
**pigeon-toed** *adj.* de pies torcidos hacia dentro.
**pigeon's-blood** *s.* MINER. granate, piropo.
**piggery** (pi·gøri) *s.* zahurda.
**piggin** (pi·gin) *s.* cubeta, balde.
**piggish** (pi·giš) *adj.* de cerdo. 2 voraz, puerco, cochino.
**pig-headed** *adj.* terco, testarudo.
**pigmean** (pigmı·an) *adj.-s.* PYGMEAN.
**pigment** (pi·gmønt) *s.* pigmento. 2 color, pintura, materia colorante.
**pigmentary** (-teri) *adj.* pigmentario.
**pigmentation** (-ei·shøn) *f.* pigmentación.
**pigmy** (pi·gmi) *adj.-s.* PIGMY.
**pignut** (-nøt) *s.* BOT. pacanero. 2 BOT. pacana. 3 BOT. fruto o tubérculo de varias plantas.
**pigpen** (-pen) *s.* pocilga, zahurda.
**pigskin** (-skin) *s.* piel de cerdo. 2 fam. silla de montar. 3 fam. balón [de fútbol].
**pigsty** (-stai) *s.* pocilga, zahurda.
**pigtail** (-teil) *s.* coleta [de pelo].
**pike** (paik) *s.* pica [arma]; garrocha; chuzo. 2 camino de barrera. 3 ICT. lucio.
**pikeman** (-mæn) *s.* piquero.
**pikestaff** (-stæf) *s.* asta de pica; bastón herrado.
**pilar** (pai·la<sup>r</sup>) *adj.* piloso.
**pilaster** (pilæ·stø<sup>r</sup>) *s.* ARQ. pilastra.
**Pilate** (pai·leit) *n. pr.* Pilatos.
**pilchard** (pi·lchø<sup>r</sup>d) ICT. sardina.
**pile** (pail) *s.* pelo, pelusa, lana. 2 pelo [de ciertos tejidos]. 3 pila, montón, rimero. 4 fortuna, caudal. 5 ELECT. pila, batería. 6 pira. 7 mole, masa de edificios. 8 estaca, pilote. 9 cruz [de una moneda]. *10 pl.* almorranas.
**pile (to)** *tr.* amontonar, apilar. 2 cubrir, llenar, cargar. 3 sostener con pilotes. 4 TEJ. formar pelo en. 5 *intr.* amontonarse, acumularse.
**pileus** (pai·liøs) *s.* píleo.
**pilework** (-uø<sup>r</sup>k) *s.* pilotaje [de pilotes].
**pilfer (to)** (pi·lfø<sup>r</sup>) *tr.-intr.* hurtar, ratear, sisar.
**pilferage** (-idÿ) *s.* ratería, hurto.
**pilferer** (-ø<sup>r</sup>) *s.* ratero, ladrón.
**pilfering** (-ing) *s.* ratería, hurto.
**pilgrim** (pi·lgrim) *s.* peregrino, romero; viajero.
**pilgrim (to)** *intr.* peregrinar.
**pilgrimage** (-idÿ) *s.* peregrinación, peregrinaje, romería.
**piling** (pai·ling) *s.* PILEWORK.
**pill** (pil) *s.* píldora. 2 fig. mal trago. 3 posma, persona cargante. *4 pl.* pop. billar.
**pill (to)** *tr.* medicinar con píldoras.

**pillage** (pi·lidÿ) *s.* pillaje, saqueo, extorsión. 2 botín [de un pillaje].
**pillage (to)** *tr.* pillar, saquear, robar.
**pillar** (pi·la<sup>r</sup>) *s.* pilar, columna, puntal: *from* ~ *to post*, de Herodes a Pilatos. 2 fig. pilar, sostén.
**pillared** (pi·la<sup>r</sup>d) *adj.* sostenido por columnas.
**pillion** (pi·lion) *s.* asiento trasero de motocicleta.
**pillory** (pi·løri) *s.* picota.
**pillory (to)** *tr.* empicotar, poner en la picota.
**pillow** (pi·lou) *s.* almohada, cabezal. 2 almohadón, cojín. 3 mundillo [para hacer encaje]. 4 MEC. cojín, cojinete, dado: ~ *block*, chumacera.
**pillow (to)** *tr.* poner sobre una almohada; sostener con almohadas; servir de almohada a.
**pillowcase** (pi·loukeis) *s.* funda de almohada.
**pilose** (pai·lous) *adj.* piloso.
**pilosity** (paila·siti) *s.* vellosidad.
**pilot** (pai·løt) *m.* MAR. piloto, práctico. 2 AVIA. piloto, aviador. 3 guía, consejero. 4 FERROC. trompa, quitapiedras. 5 *adj.* piloto: ~ *lamp*, lámpara piloto.
**pilot (to)** *t.* pilotar, pilotear. 2 dirigir, gobernar.
**pilotage** (pai·løtidÿ) *s.* MAR. pilotaje, practicaje.
**pilous** (pai·løs) *adj.* piloso, peludo.
**pimento** (pime·ntou) *s.* BOT. pimienta. 2 BOT. pimentero.
**pimiento** (pimie·ntou) *s.* BOT. pimiento.
**pimp** (pimp) *s.* alcahuete.
**pimp (to)** *intr.* alcahuetear.
**pimpernel** (-ø<sup>r</sup>nel) *s.* BOT. murajes. 2 BOT. pimpinela.
**pimping** (-ing) *adj.* pequeño, mezquino. 2 enfermizo.
**pimple** (-øl) *s.* grano, barro [en la piel].
**pimply** (-li) *adj.* granujiento, barroso.
**pin** (pin) *s.* alfiler: *to be on pins and needles*, estar sobre ascuas. 2 prendedor, broche. 3 clavillo, clavija, chaveta, pasador, espiga: *firing* ~, percutor [de un arma]. 4 MEC. gorrón; muñón. 5 bolo [para jugar]. *6 pl.* palos [del billar]. *7 fam.* piernas.
**pin (to)** *tr.* prender [con alfileres]: clavar, fijar, sujetar, pegar: *to* ~ *down*, fijar, inmovilizar; hacer dar una respuesta definitiva; *to* ~ *in*, encerrar; *to* ~ *up*, recoger y prender con alfileres; fijar [un dibujo, etc.] con alfileres o chinchetas. ¶ Pret. y p. p.: *pinned*; ger.: *pinning*.
**pinafore** (pi·nafo<sup>r</sup>) *s.* delantal [de niño].
**pinaster** (pinæ·stø<sup>r</sup>) *s.* BOT. pinastro, pino rodeno.
**pincase** (pi·nkeis) *s.* alfiletero.
**pince-nez** (pæ·nsnei) *s.* lentes [anteojos].
**pincers** (pi·nsørš) *s. pl.* tenazas, mordazas. 2 pinzas, tenacillas. 3 ZOOL. pinza.
**pinch** (pinch) *s.* aprieto, apuro, necesidad: *at a* ~, en caso de apuro. 2 opresión, punzada, dolor, tormento. 3 pellizco; apretón. 4 pulgarada; polvo de rapé.
**pinch (to)** *tr.* pellizcar; apretar [con pinzas, etc.]; cogerse [el dedo en la puerta]. 2 apretar, hacer daño [un zapato, etc.]. 3 oprimir, afligir. 4 robar, estafar. 5 contraer, reducir, limitar, escatimar. 6 adelgazar, demacrar. 7 prender, arrestar. 8 *intr.* apretar. 9 economizar.
**pinchbeck** (-bec) *s.* similor.
**pinchers** (-ø<sup>r</sup>s) *s. pl.* PINCERS.
**pinchfist** (-fist) *s.* avaro, roñoso.
**pincushion** (pi·nkushøn) *s.* acerico.
**Pindar** (pi·nda<sup>r</sup>) *n. pr.* Píndaro.
**Pindaric** (pindæ·rik) *adj.* pindárico.
**pine** (pain) *s.* BOT. pino: ~ *cone*, piña; ~ *needle*, pinocha; ~ *nut*, piñón.

**pine (to)** *intr.* desfallecer, languidecer, descaecer, consumirse. | Gralte. con *away*. *2* afligirse, penar. *3 to ~ for* o *after*, anhelar.

**pineal** (pi·nial) *adj.* pineal.

**pineapple** (pai·næpøl) *s.* BOT. ananás, piña de América.

**pinery** (-ri) *s.* planación de ananás. *2* pinar.

**pinfold** (pi·nfould) *s.* corral o depósito donde se recoge el ganado extraviado.

**ping-pong** (ping-pang) *s.* tenis de salón, ping-pong.

**pinguid** (pi·ngwid) *adj.* pingüe, craso, gordo.

**pinhead** (pi·njed) *s.* cabeza de alfiler. *2* insignificancia. *3* bobo, tonto.

**pinion** (pi·niøn) *s.* ORN. ala; extremo del ala. *2* alón. *3* MEC. piñón.

**pinion (to)** *tr.* cortar las alas a. *2* sujetar los brazos de; atar, maniatar.

**pinioned** (-d) *adj.* alado. *2* atado, maniatado.

**pink** (pink) *s.* BOT. clavel; clavellina. *2* color de rosa. *3* modelo, dechado. *4* estado perfecto. *5 adj.* rosado, rojizo.

**pinkish** (-ish) *adj.* rosáceo, que tira a rosado.

**pinky** (-i) *adj.* rosado, rosáceo.

**pinnace** (pi·nis) *s.* MAR. pinaza.

**pinnacle** (pi·nakøl) *s.* pináculo. *2* cima, cumbre.

**pinnate (d** (pi·neit(id) *adj.* BOT. pinnado.

**pinnatifid** (pinæ·tifid) *adj.* BOT. pinatífido.

**pinniped** (pi·niped) *adj.-s.* ZOOL. pinípedo.

**pinnule** (pi·nul) *s.* pínula.

**pin-oak** (pi·nouk) *s.* BOT. carrasca de América.

**pinocle** (pinø·køl) *s.* pinacle [juego de naipes].

**pint** (paint) *s.* pinta, cuartillo [medida].

**pintail** (pi·nteil) *s.* ORN. ánade de cola larga.

**pintle** (pi·ntøl) *s.* perno [del pernio]. *2* MAR. pinzote.

**pinwheel** (pi·njuil) *s.* rueda [de fuegos artificiales]. *2* molinete [juguete].

**pinworm** (-uøʳm) *s.* ZOOL. lombriz intestinal.

**pioneer** (pai·øniʳ) *s.* MIL. zapador, gastador. *2* primer colonizador. *3* precursor; pionero.

**pioneer (to)** *tr.-intr.* abrir camino; guiar; explorar, colonizar.

**pious** (pai·øs) *adj.* pío, piadoso.

**pip** (pip) *s.* pepita [de las aves]. *2* fam. indisposición. *3* BOT. pepita. *4* punto [de naipe, etc.].

**pip (to)** *intr.* piar. *2 tr.* ORN. romper [el cascarón].

**pipe** (paip) *s.* tubo, caño, cañería, conducto: *~ line*, PIPELINE. *2* cañón [de órgano]. *3* caramillo, flauta, zampoña. *4* MAR. silbato [de contramaestre]. *5* pitido, silbo; voz atiplada o aflautada. *6* pipa [para fumar]. *7* tallo [de lila u otras plantas]. *8* pipa, tonel. *9 pl.* tubería. *10* MÚS. gaita.

**pipe (to)** *tr.* tocar [en el caramillo, etc.]. *2* emitir con voz aguda. *3* conducir por tuberías; proveer de tuberías. *4* MAR. mandar o llamar [con silbato]. *5* COST. adornar con vivos. *6 to ~ one's eye*, fam. soltar el trapo, echarse a llorar. *7 intr.* cantar o hablar con voz aguda, chillar. *8* pitar. *9 to ~ down*, callar. *10 to ~ up*, ponerse a tocar, a cantar, a hablar.

**pipeline** (-lain) *s.* tubería, oleoducto.

**pipeline (to)** *tr.* conducir por medio de un oleoducto. *2* proveer de oleoducto.

**piper** (-øʳ) *s.* gaitero.

**piperaceous** (pipørei·shøs) *adj.* BOT. piperáceo.

**pipette** (pipe·t) *s.* pipeta.

**piping** (pai·ping) *adj.* agudo, aflautado. *2 adv. ~ hot*, muy caliente. *3 s.* voz o sonido agudos, aflauados. *4* lloro; gemido. *5* tubería; canalización. *6* COST. vivo.

**pipit** (pi·pit) *s.* ORN. especie de alondra.

**pipkin** (pi·pkin) *s.* pucherito, ollita.

**pippin** (pi·pin) *s.* BOT. camuesa [manzana].

**piquancy** (pi·kansi) *s.* lo picante [de una cosa].

**piquant** (pi·kant) *adj.* picante. *2* travieso, picaresco.

**pique** (pik) *s.* pique, resentimiento: *in a ~*, resentido.

**pique (to)** *tr.* picar, ofender, irritar. *2* picar, mover, estimular. *3 to ~ oneself on*, picarse, enorgullecerse de. *4 intr.* AVIA. picar.

**piqué** (pikei·) *s.* TEJ. piqué.

**piquet** (pike·t) *s.* juego de los cientos.

**piracy** (pai·rasi) *s.* piratería. *2* robo, plagio.

**pirate** (pai·rit) *s.* pirata. *2* plagiario.

**piratical** (pairæ·tikal) *adj.* pirático.

**pirogue** (pirou·g) *s.* piragua, canoa.

**pirouette** (pirue·t) *s.* pirueta, girada [en la danza].

**pirouette (to)** *intr.* piruetear, girar.

**Pisan** (pi·šan) *adj.-s.* pisano.

**pisciculture** (pisikø·lchøʳ) *s.* piscicultura.

**pisciculturist** (-ist) *s.* piscicultor.

**pisciform** (pi·sifoʳm) *adj.* pisciforme.

**piscina** (pi·sina) *s.* LITURG. piscina.

**piscivorous** (pisi·vørøs) *adj.* piscívoro.

**pish** (pish) *interj.* ¡ba!, ¡quita allá!

**pisiform** (pai·sifoʳm) *adj.-s.* pisiforme.

**piss** (pis) *s.* vulg. orina.

**piss (to)** *intr.* vulg. orinar, mear.

**pistachio** (pista·chiou) *s.* BOT. alfóncigo, pistacho.

**pistil** (pi·stil) *s.* BOT. pistilo.

**pistol** (pi·støl) *s.* doblón de oro.

**pistoleer** (pistølı·ʳ) *s.* pistolero.

**piston** (pi·støn) *s.* MEC. pistón, émbolo: *~ stroke*, embolada. *2* MÚS. pistón.

**pit** (pit) *s.* hoyo; hoya, cárcava; excavación, foso, pozo, abismo. *2* boca [del estómago]. *3* cacaraña. *4* mina o sitio de donde se extrae algo. *5* reñidero [de gallos, perros, etc.]. *6* TEAT. parte posterior del patio. *7* (E.U.) corro [de Bolsa]. *8* hueso [de fruta].

**pit (to)** *tr.* poner en un hoyo. *2* marcar con hoyos, cacarañar. *3* deshuesar [una fruta]. *4 to ~ against*, oponer a, poner en competencia con. ¶ Pret. y p. p.: *pitted*; ger.: *-tting*.

**pitapat** (pi·tapæt) *s.* trip trap; palpitación. *2 adv.* con paso o trotecito ligero; con palpitación.

**pitch** (pich) *s.* pez, brea, alquitrán. *2* echada, lanzamiento, tiro [en ciertos juegos]. *3* grado de inclinación, pendiente, declive. *4* extremo, colmo; grado, punto. *5* MÚS. tono, diapasón. *6* FONÉT. tono. *7* MEC. paso [de rosca; de hélice, etc.]. *8* MAR. cabezada, arfada. *9* ARQ. altura [de un arco].

**pitch (to)** *tr.* empecinar, embrear. *2* tirar, lanzar, arrojar. *3* levantar [el heno, etc.] con el horcón. *4* clavar, fijar en tierra; armar [una tienda]. *5* poner, colocar. *6* MÚS. graduar el tono de. *7* cantear [una piedra]. *8 intr.* echarse o caer de cabeza. *9* inclinarse, bajar en declive. *10* acampar, instalarse. *11* MEC. engranar, endentar. *12* MAR. cabecear, arfar. *13* fam. *to ~ in*, poner manos a la obra. *14 to ~ into*, arremeter contra; reprender.

**pitch and toss** *s.* especie de juego de cara o cruz.

**pitch-dark** *adj.* oscuro como boca de lobo.

**pitched battle** (-t) *s.* batalla campal.

**pitcher** (-øʳ) *s.* jarro, cántaro. *2* lanzador.

**pitchfork** (-foʳk) *s.* AGR. horca, horquilla.

**pitchiness** (-inis) *s.* oscuridad, negrura.

**pitchstone** (-stoun) *s.* PETROGR. vidrio volcánico.

**pitchy** (-i) *adj.* peceño, píceo. *2* empeguntado. *3* negro, oscuro. *4* profunda [oscuridad].
**piteous** (pi·tiøs) *adj.* lastimoso, lastimero.
**pitfall** (pi·tfol) *s.* trampa [para cazar]; hoyo disimulado. *2* añagaza; escollo, peligro insospechado.
**pith** (piz) *s.* BOT., ANAT. meollo, médula. *2* fig. meollo, substancia. *3* fuerza, vigor.
**pithy** (pi·zi) *adj.* meticuloso. *2* vigoroso. *3* expresivo, enérgico y conciso.
**pitiable** (pi·tiabøl) *adj.* lastimoso, compasible, lamentable. *2* pobre, despreciable.
**pitiful** (pi·tiful) *adj.* PITIABLE. *2* compasivo.
**pitiless** (-lis) *adj.* despiadado, cruel, inhumano, duro de corazón.
**pitman** (pi·tmæn) *s.* aserrador de foso. *2* MIN. pocero.
**pitpit** (pi·tpit) *s.* ORN. pitpit.
**piton** (pito·n) *s.* estaca de hierro usada por los montañeros.
**pittance** (pi·tans) *s.* pitanza. *2* miseria, jornal miserable, renta insuficiente.
**pitter-patter** *s.* golpeteo ligero y rápido; chapaleteo [de la lluvia].
**pituita** (pitiuai·ta) *s.* pituita.
**pituitary** (pitiui·teri) *adj.* pituitario: ~ *body*, ~ *gland*, glándula pituitaria.
**pituitous** (pitiu·itøs) *adj.* pituitoso.
**pity** (pi·ti) *s.* piedad, misericordia, compasión: *for pity's sake*, ¡por piedad!, ¡por Dios! *2* lástima: *what a ~!*, ¡qué lástima!
**pity (to)** *tr.* comparecer, tener lástima de, apiadarse de. ¶ Pret. y p. p.: *pitied*.
**pitying** (-ing) *adj.* compasivo.
**pivot** (pi·vøt) *s.* eje, gorrón, pivote. *2* fig. eje, punto fundamental. *3* MIL. guía.
**pivot (to)** *tr.* montar sobre un eje o pivote. *2* proveer de eje o pivote. *3 intr.* pivotar: *to ~ on*, girar sobre.
**pix** (piks) *s.* PYX.
**pixy, pixie** (pi·ksi) *s.* (Ingl.) duende.
**pizzle** (pi·søl) *s.* vergajo.
**placability** (pleikabi·liti) *s.* placabilidad.
**placable** (plei·kabøl) *adj.* placable, clemente.
**placard** (plæ·ka^r d) *s.* cartel, anuncio, letrero.
**placard (to)** *tr.* publicar o anunciar por medio de carteles. *2* fijar [un cartel]; fijar carteles en.
**placate (to)** (plei·keit) *tr.* aplacar, apaciguar.
**place** (pleis) *s.* lugar, sitio, paraje; población; parte, punto; local: *in no ~*, en ninguna parte. *2* lugar, sitio, puesto; rango, dignidad; plaza, espacio, cabida: *in the first ~*, en primer lugar; *in ~ of*, en lugar de, en vez de; *out of ~*, fuera de lugar o de propósito; *to know one's ~*, no tomarse libertades; ser respetuoso; *to take ~*, verificarse, ocurrir. *3* empleo, cargo. *4* MIL. plaza. *5* plazuela; calle corta. *6* mansión, quinta. *7* ARIT. cifra decimal.
**place (to)** *tr.* poner, colocar, situar, instalar, fijar. *2* colocar [a una pers.; dinero; mercancías]. *3 intr.* colocarse [un caballo en las carreras].
**placement** (-mønt) *s.* colocación, situación.
**placenta** (plase·nta) *s.* ANAT., ZOOL., BOT. placenta.
**1) placer** (plei·sø^r) *s.* el que coloca.
**2) placer** (plæ·sø^r) *s.* MIN. placer; lavadero de oro.
**placid** (plæ·sid) *adj.* plácido, apacible.
**placidity** (plasi·diti) *s.* placidez, apacibilidad.
**placard** (plei·gal) *adj.* MÚS. plagal.
**plagiarism** (plei·dýiarišm) *s.* plagio.
**plagiarist** (-ist) *s.* plagiario.
**plagiarize (to)** (-aiš) *tr.-intr.* plagiar.

**plagiary** (-i) *s.* plagiario. *2* plagio.
**plague** (pleig) *s.* plaga. *2* peste, pestilencia. *3* calamidad. *4 a ~ on...*, al demonio...
**plague (to)** *tr.* plagar; infestar. *2* atormentar, molestar, importunar.
**plaguey, plaguy** (plei·gi) *adj.* enojoso, molesto.
**plaice** (pleis) *s.* ICT. platija, acedía.
**plaid** (plæd) *s.* manta escocesa. *2* tartán. *3* diseño a cuadros. *4 adj.* listado a cuadros.
**plain** (plein) *adj.* llano, raso, liso. *2* claro, evidente: ~ *as a pickestaff*, claro como la luz. *3* claro, franco, sincero: ~ *dealing*, sinceridad, buena fe; *in ~ English*, sin eufemismos. *4* simple, sencillo, corriente, común; humilde. *5* feo, sin atractivo. *6* puro, sin mezcla: *the ~ truth*, la pura verdad. *7* MÚS. ~ *song*, canto llano. *8* ~ *clothes*, vestido de paisano. *9 adv.* claro, sin ambigüedad. *10 s.* llano, llanura.
**plain-clothes man** *s.* agente de policía secreta.
**plainness** (plei·nnis) *s.* llanura. *2* sencillez; franqueza, claridad. *3* fealdad; vulgaridad.
**plain-spoken** *adj.* claro, sincero. *2* francote, brusco.
**plaint** (pleint) *s.* queja. *2* DER. querella.
**plaintiff** (-if) *s.* DER. demandante, actor.
**plaintive** (-iv) *adj.* lamentoso, lastimero, triste, elegíaco.
**plait** (plæt, pleit o plit) *s.* pliegue, plegado. *2* trenza; pleita.
**plait (to)** *tr.* plegar, alechugar, encañonar. *2* trenzar.
**plaiting** (-ing) *s.* plegadura, plegado. *2* trenzado.
**plan** (plæn) *s.* plano, planta, diseño, esquema. *2* PERSP., ESC. plano. *3* plan, proyecto.
**plan (to)** *tr.* hacer el plano de. *2* planear, proyectar, idear; planificar. *3 intr.* hacer planes. ¶ Pret. y p. p.: *planned*; ger.: *-nning*.
**planchette** (plønshe·t) *s.* TOP. plancheta. *2* tabla de escritura espiritista.
**plane** (plein) *adj.* plano: ~ *geometry*, geometría plana. *2 s.* plano [superficie plana]. *3* GEOM., MEC. plano. *4* plano, nivel. *5* aeroplano, avión: ~ *sickness*, mareo en el aire. *6* CARP. cepillo, garlopa. *7* BOT. *plane* o ~ *tree*, plátano [árbol].
**plane (to)** *tr.* CARP. acepillar, cepillar. *2 intr.* AVIA. volar; viajar en avión. *3* AVIA. planear.
**planer** (-ø^r) *s.* acepillador. *2* acepilladora mecánica. *3* IMPR. tamborilete.
**planet** (plæ·nit) *s.* ASTR. planeta. *2 adj.* planetario.
**planetarium** (plænøte·riøm) *s.* planetario.
**planetary** (plæ·nøteri) *adj.* planetario. *2* mundano, terrestre. *3* errático, inconstante.
**planimeter** (plæni·metø^r) *s.* planímetro.
**planimetry** (-tri) *s.* planimetría.
**planing** (plei·ning) *s.* acepilladura: ~ *machine*, acepilladora mecánica.
**planish (to)** (plæ·nish) *tr.* allanar, aplanar, alisar, pulir.
**planisphere** (plæ·nisfiø^r) *s.* planisferio.
**plank** (plænk) *s.* tablón, plancha, tabla gruesa. *2 pl.* tablado, entarimado.
**plank (to)** *tr.* entablar, entarimar. *2* MIN. encofrar. *3 fam. to ~ down*, poner firmemente; arrojar con violencia [sobre una mesa, etc.].
**planking** (-ing) *s.* entarimado, tablazón.
**plankton** (-tøn) *s.* BIOL. plancton.
**planner** (plæ·nø^r) *s.* proyectista.
**plant** (plænt) *s.* BOT. planta: ~ *louse*, pulgón. *2* mata, estaca, esqueje. *3* equipo, instalación de fábrica, etc. *4* fábrica, taller.
**plant (to)** *tr.* plantar, sembrar. *2* plantar, colocar,

poner. *3* fundar, establecer. *4* implantar, inculcar.

**plantaginaceous** (plæntadÿine·shøs) *adj.* bot. plantagináceo.

**plantain** (plæ·ntin) *s.* bot. llantén. *2* bot. banano; banana.

**plantar** (plæ·ntaᵣ) *adj.* plantar.

**plantation** (plæntei·shøn) *s.* plantación, plantío. *2* hacienda, ingenio. *3* [en Terranova] pesquería.

**planter** (plæ·ntøᵣ) *s.* plantador; cultivador, hacendado. *2* plantadora [máquina].

**plantigrade** (plæ·ntigreid) *adj.-s.* plantígrado.

**plaque** (plæk) *s.* placa [decorativa; condecoración]. *2* med. placa.

**plaquette** (plæke·t) *s.* anat. plaqueta.

**plash** (plæsh) *s.* chapaleteo. *2* mancha [de color]. *3* charco, lagunajo.

**plash (to)** *tr.-intr.* chapalear. *2* pint. manchar. *3* entretejer [ramas].

**plashy** (plæ·shi) *adj.* pantanoso. *2* manchado.

**plasm** (plæsm), **plasma** (-a) *s.* anat., miner. plasma. *2* biol. protoplasma.

**plaster** (plæ·støᵣ) *s.* yeso; estuco, escayola, argamasa para enlucir: ~ *of Paris*, yeso. *2* farm. parche, emplasto.

**plaster (to)** *tr.* enyesar, enlucir, revocar. *2* embadurnar. *3* emplastar. *4* pegar [un cartel, etc.].

**plasterer** (-øᵣ) *s.* yesero. *2* enlucidor, revocador, estuquista.

**plasterwork** (-uøᵣk) *s.* enlucido, enyesado; yesería.

**plastic** (plæ·stik) *adj.* plástico. *2 s.* plástico. *3* plástica.

**plasticity** (plæsti·siti) *s.* plasticidad.

**plastron** (-trøn) *s.* arm., zool. peto. *2* pechera [de camisa]. *3* esgr. plastrón.

**plat** (plæt) *s.* plano, mapa. *2* pedazo de tierra. *3* trenza.

**plat (to)** *tr.* hacer el plano o mapa de. *2* trenzar. ¶ Pret. y p. p.: *platted;* ger.: *-tting.*

**platanaceous** (plætanei·shøs) *adj.* platanáceo.

**platan(e** (plæ·tan) *s.* bot. plátano [árbol].

**platband** (plæ·tbænd) *s.* arriate. *2^*arq. faja de la cornisa.

**plate** (pleit) *s.* placa, plancha, lámina, hoja, chapa. *2* lámina, grabado, ilustración. *3* elect., fot., bact., zool. placa: ~ *circuit*, circuito de placa. *4* platina [de la máquina neumática]. *5* elect. elemento [de pila]. *6* vajilla [de oro, plata, etc.]. *7* plato, platillo, fuente [vasija]: ~ *rack*, escurreplatos. *8* plato [comida]. *9* dep. copa o placa [premio]. *10* carn. falda.

**plate (to)** *tr.* planchear. *2* dorar, platear, niquelar, chapear [metales]. *3* blindar. *4* impr. clisar.

**plateau** (plætou·) *s.* geogr. mesa, meseta, altiplanicie. *2* plato o bandeja decorativos.

**plateful** (plei·tful) *s.* plato, fuente [su contenido].

**plateholder** (-jouldøᵣ) *s.* fot. chasis, portaplacas.

**platen** (plæ·tøn) *s.* impr., mec. platina. *2* rodillo [de la máquina de escribir].

**plateresque** (plætøre·sk) *adj.* arq. plateresco.

**platform** (plæ·tfoᵣm) *s.* plataforma. *2* tablado, tribuna. *3* cadalso. *4* ferroc. andén. *5* terraplén. *6* (E.U.) programa; declaración de principios.

**plating** (plei·ting) *s.* dorado, plateado, niquelado, chapeado; galvanoplastia. *2* blindaje.

**platinum** (plæ·tinøm) *s.* quím. platino: ~ *blonde*, rubia platinada.

**platitude** (plæ·titiud) *s.* insulsez, perogrullada, lugar común.

**Plato** (plei·tou) *n. pr.* Platón.

**Platonic** (plata·nik) *adj.* platónico.

**Platonism** (plei·tonišm) *s.* platonismo.

**Platonist** (plei·tonist) *s.* platónico.

**platoon** (platu·n) *s.* mil. sección. *2* pelotón, grupo.

**platter** (plæ·tøᵣ) *s.* fuente, platel. *2* (E.U.) plato.

**platyhelminth** (plætije·lminz) *s.* zool. platelminto.

**platyrrhine** (plæ·tirain) *adj.-s.* zool. platirrino.

**plaudit** (plo·dit) *s.* aplauso. *2* aprobación.

**plausibility** (plošibi·liti) *s.* especiosidad; bondad o credibilidad aparentes.

**plausible** (plo·šibøl) *adj.* especioso, aparentemente bueno, creíble.

**play** (plei) *s.* juego [acción de jugar; diversión, entretenimiento, deporte], broma: ~ *upon words*, juego de palabras; *full of* ~, travieso, juguetón. *2* mec. juego; juego, funcionamiento, acción, operación: *to come into* ~, entrar en juego; *full* ~, juego libre, rienda suelta. *3* juego [de luz, de colores, etc.]. *4* teat. representación. *5* teat. obra, comedia, drama, etc.

**play (to)** *tr.* jugar [una partida, una pieza, un naipe, etc.]. *2* jugar a [un juego]. *3* poner en acción, hacer, causar: *to* ~ *a trick on*, hacer una mala jugada a; *to* ~ *havoc with*, hacer estragos en. *4* fingir, hacer o hacerse: *to* ~ *the fool*, hacerse el tonto. *5* teat. representar [una obra]; hacer, desempeñar [un papel]. *6* apostar por [un caballo]. *7* dejar que se canse [el pez cogido en el anzuelo]. *8* mús. tocar, tañer; ejecutar. *9* malgastar, dilapidar. *10 to* ~ *out*, agotar, cansar. *11 to* ~ *truant* o *the truant*, hacer novillos.

*12 intr.* jugar, divertirse; juguetear, retozar; bromear. *13* mús. tocar: *to* ~ *on an instrument*, tocar un instrumento. *14* sonar [el instrumento]. *15* obrar, conducirse: *to* ~ *fair*, jugar limpio. *16* jugar, moverse, funcionar. *17* flotar, ondear. *18 to* ~ *into the hands of*, hacer el caldo gordo a. *19 to* ~ *on* o *upon*, jugar con; aprovecharse de, abusar de. *20 to* ~ *up to*, halagar servilmente.

**playbill** (-bil) *s.* teat. cartel, programa.

**playboy** (-boi) *s.* fam. joven rico y disipado, niño bonito.

**player** (-øᵣ) *s.* jugador. *2* teat. actor, representante, tocador; ejecutante.

**playfellow** (-felou) *s.* compañero de juegos.

**playful** (-ful) *adj.* juguetón, chancero.

**playgoer** (-gouøᵣ) *s.* aficionado al teatro.

**playground** (-graund) *s.* patio de recreo. *2* campo de juego.

**playhouse** (-jaus) *s.* teatro, coliseo.

**playing card** *s.* naipe.

**playmate** (-meit) *s.* playfellow.

**plaything** (-zing) *s.* juguete [cosa, pers., etc., con que se juega].

**playtime** (-taim) *s.* hora o tiempo de recreo.

**playwright** (-rait) *s.* autor dramático.

**plea** (plı) *s.* argumento, argumentación. *2* defensa, alegato. *3* excusa, disculpa, pretexto. *4* súplica, ruego. *5* proceso, litigio.

**pleach (to)** (plich) *tr.* entretejer [ramas, etc.].

**plead (to)** (plıd) *tr.* der. defender en juicio. *2* alegar [en defensa, excusa, etc.]. *3 intr.* pleitear, abogar. *4* der. *to* ~ *guilty*, confesarse culpable; *to* ~ *not guilty*, declararse inocente. *5 to* ~ *with*, rogar, suplicar.

**pleader** (-øᵣ) *s.* abogado; defensor. *2* suplicante.

**pleading** (-ing) *s.* alegación, defensa. *2* súplica, ruegos.

**pleasant** (ple·šant) *adj.* agradable, grato, placentero. *2* simpático, afable.

**pleasantry** (-tri) *s.* broma, chanza, agudeza.
**please (to)** (pliš) *tr.-intr.* agradar, gustar, placer, dar gusto, complacer: *to ~ oneself*, darse gusto; hacer uno lo que le guste. *2 to be pleased*, estar contento; *to be pleased to*, tener gusto en; querer, tener a bien: *to be pleased with*, estar contento de. *3 intr.* gustar, servirse, querer, tener a bien; *~ God*, quiera Dios; *as you ~*, como usted quiera o guste; *if you ~* o simplte. *please*, haga usted el favor de.
**pleasing** (-ing) *adj.* agradable, grato, placentero. *2* afable, cortés.
**pleasurable** (ple·ȳurabøl) *adj.* agradable, grato, deleitoso, festivo.
**pleasurably** (-bli) *adj.* agradablemente.
**pleasure** (ple·ȳøʳ) *s.* placer, deleite, goce, gusto; recreo; gozo, alegría: *~ boat*, embarcación de recreo; *~ trip*, viaje de placer; *with ~*, con mucho gusto. *2* gusto, voluntad, deseo, arbitrio: *what is your ~?*, ¿qué desea usted?
**pleat** (plıt) *s.* pliegue, doblez.
**pleat (to)** *tr.* plegar, hacer pliegues en.
**plebeian** (plibɪ·an) *adj.-s.* plebeyo.
**plebiscite** (ple·bisait) *s.* plebiscito.
**plebs** (plebs) *s.* plebe.
**plectrum** (ple·ktrøm) *s.* plectro.
**pledge** (pledȳ) *s.* prenda [señal, garantía], rehén, fianza, caución, empeño: *as a ~ of*, en prenda. *3* brindis.
**pledge (to)** *tr.* dar en prenda, empeñar, comprometer: *to ~ one's word*, empeñar su palabra. *2* prometer, comprometerse. *3* hacer prometer. *4* brindar por.
**pledget** (ple·dȳit) *s.* CIR. compresa; tapón.
**pleiad** (pli·yæd) *s.* pléyade.
**Pleiades** (pli·yadiš) *n. pr.* MIT., ASTR. Pléyades.
**Pleistocene** (plai·stosin) *adj.-s.* GEOL. pleistoceno.
**plenary** (pli·neri) *adj.* pleno, lleno, completo, plenario.
**plenipotentiary** (plenipøte·nshieri) *adj.-s.* plenipotenciario.
**plenitude** (ple·nitiud) *s.* plenitud, abundancia.
**plenteous** (ple·ntiøs) *adj.* PLENTIFUL.
**plenteousness** (-nis) *s.* abundancia.
**plentiful** (ple·ntiful) *adj.* abundante, copioso, profuso, pingüe, opulento. *2* fértil, feraz.
**plentifulness** (-nis) *s.* abundancia, copia. *2* fertilidad.
**plenty** (ple·nti) *s.* copia, abundancia: *~ of*, mucho, de sobra.
**plenum** (pli·nøm) *s.* pleno. *2* espacio lleno.
**plenonasm** (pliønæšm) *s.* pleonasmo, redundancia.
**pleonastic (al** (pliønæ·stik(al) *adj.* pleonástico.
**plesiosaur** (plɪ·siøsoʳ) *s.* PALEONT. plesiosauro.
**plethora** (ple·zora) *s.* plétora.
**plethoric (al** (ple·zorik(al) *adj.* pletórico.
**pleura** (plu·ra) *pl.* **rae** (-ri) *s.*, ANAT. pleura.
**pleurisy** (-risi) *s.* MED. pleuresía; pleuritis.
**pleuronectid** (plurone·ktid) *adj.-s.* ICT. pleuronecto.
**plexiglass** (ple·ksiglæs) *s.* plexiglás.
**plexus** (ple·ksøs) *s.* ANAT. plexo.
**pliability** (plaiabi·liti) *s.* flexibilidad, docilidad.
**pliable** (plai·abøl) *adj.* flexible, dócil [fácil de trabajar]. *2* doblegable, dúctil, manejable.
**pliancy** (-ansi) *s.* flexibilidad, docilidad, ductilidad.
**pliant** (-ant) *adj.* flexible, cimbreño. *2* blando, dócil. *3* complaciente, obediente, adaptable.
**plicate (d** (plai·keit(id) *adj.* BOT., ZOOL. plegado.

**pliers** (plai·øʳš) *s. pl.* alicates, tenazas.
**plight** (plait) *s.* condición, estado; aprieto, apuro. *2* promesa, compromiso.
**plight (to)** *tr.* empeñar [la palabra, etc.]; prometer [fidelidad, etc.]. *2* prometer en matrimonio.
**plinth** (plinz) *s.* ARQ. plinto, orlo; zócalo.
**Pliny** (pli·ni) *n. pr.* Plinio.
**Pliocene** (plai·øsin) *adj.-s.* GEOL. plioceno.
**plod (to)** (plad) *intr.* afanarse, trabajar mucho o pesadamente. ¶ Pret. y p. p.: *plodded;* ger.: *-dding.*
**plodder** (-øʳ) *s.* el que se afana; el que trabaja con más aplicación que talento.
**plop** (pla·p) *s.* plaf [ruido sordo].
**plot** (plat) *s.* porción de terreno; cuadro, bancal; solar, parcela. *2* plano, mapa. *3* conspiración, complot, trama, maquinación. *4* trama, argumento [de una obra literaria].
**plot (to)** *tr.* (E.U.) dividir [en cuadros o parcelas]. *2* trazar el plano de. *3* tramar, urdir, fraguar. *4* *intr.* conspirar. ¶ Pret. y p. p.: *plotted;* ger.: *-tting.*
**plotter** (-øʳ) *s.* conspirador, tramador.
**plough** (plau) *s.* arado. *2* ENCUAD. ingenio. *3* ASTR. el Carro, la Osa Mayor.
**plough (to)** *tr.-intr.* arar. *2 tr.* surcar. *3* arrancar, quitar [con un arado, etc.]. *4 intr.* avanzar como el que ara.
**ploughland** (-lænd) *s.* tierra labrantía.
**ploughman** (-mæn) *s.* arador, labrador; rústico, gañán.
**ploughshare** (-sheʳ) *s.* reja del arado.
**ploughstaff** (-stæf) *s.* abéstola, aguijada.
**ploughtail** (-teil) *s.* esteva, mancera.
**ploughwright** (-rait) *s.* constructor de arados.
**plover** (pløˑvøʳ o plouˑvøʳ) *s.* ORN. nombre de varias aves, como el chorlito, el avefría, etc.
**plow, to plow,** etc. (E.U.) PLOUGH, TO PLOUGH, etc.
**pluck** (pløk) *s.* valor, resolución. *2* tirón, estirón. *3* asadura. *4* (Ingl.) suspenso, calabazas.
**pluck (to)** *tr.* coger, arrancar. *2* pelar, desplumar. *3* dar un tirón a. *4* MÚS. puntear, herir las cuerdas de. *5* pop. robar. *6* (Ingl.) catear, calabacear. *7 to ~ up courage*, cobrar ánimo. *8* intr. *to ~ at*, tirar de.
**plucky** (pløˑki) *adj.* valeroso, denodado.
**plug** (pløg) *s.* tapón, botana, espita, taco, pieza que entra en un agujero. *2* DENT. empaste. *4* ELECT. clavija; tapón fusible. *5* AUTO. bujía. *6* cala [de melón]. *7* tableta [de tabaco]. *8* fam. chistera. *9* fig. elogio o anuncio interpolado en un texto.
**plug (to)** *tr.* atarugar, tapar. *2* DENT. empastar. *3* ELECT. *to ~ in*, enchufar. *3* trabajar con ahínco. ¶ Pret. y p. p.: *plugged;* ger.: *-gging.*
**plum** (pløm) *s.* BOT. ciruela; ciruelo. *2* pasa [para repostería] *~ cake*, bizcocho con pasas; *~ pudding*, budín inglés con pasas. *4* fig. lo mejor; cargo provechoso, turrón.
**plumage** (plu·midȳ) *s.* plumaje.
**plumb** (pløm) *s.* plomo, plomada. *2* plomo, verticalidad: *in ~*, a plomo, *out of ~*, desaplomado. *3 adj.* vertical. *4* completo. *5 adv.* a plomo. *6* completamente; directamente.
**plumb (to)** *tr.* sondear. *2* ALBAÑ. aplomar. *3* plomar. *4* instalar cañerías en.
**plumbago** (plømbeiˑgou) *s.* plombagina, grafito. *2* BOT. belesa.
**plumbeous** (pløˑmbiøs) *adj.* plomizo. *2* plúmbeo.
**plumber** (pløˑmøʳ) *s.* plomero. *2* fontanero.
**plumbery** (pløˑmøri) *s.* plomería; fontanería.
**plumbic** (pløˑmbik) *adj.* plúmbico.

**plume** (plum) *s.* pluma [de ave]. *2* plumaje. *3* penacho, plumero. *4* fig. honor, galardón. *5* BOT. ~ *grass,* carricera.

**plume (to)** *tr.* desplumar, pelar. *2* emplumar, empenachar. *3* alisar el plumaje de. *4* ref. *to* ~ *oneself,* jactarse, vanagloriarse.

**plumeless** (-lis) *adj.* implume. *2* fig. sin dinero.

**plumiped** (plu·miped) *adj.* ORN. calzado.

**plummet** (plø·mit) *s.* plomo [de la plomada, la sonda, etc.].

**plumose** (plu·mous) *adj.* plumoso, plúmeo.

**plump** (plømp) *adj.* regordete, rollizo. *2* brusco, franco. *3* adv. a plomo. *4* de golpe. *5* bruscamente, sin ambages. *6 s.* caída brusca, pesada.

**plump (to)** *tr.* engordar, hinchar. *2* soltar, dejar caer, tirar. *3 intr.* engordar; hincharse, llenarse. *4* caer a plomo. *5* dejarse caer, desplomarse.

**plumule** (plu·miul) *s.* BOT. plúmula. *2* ORN. pluma de plumón.

**plumy** (plu·mi) *adj.* plumoso, plúmeo.

**plunder** (plø·ndø[r]) *s.* pillaje, saqueo, robo. *2* botín [de pillaje, robo, etc.].

**plunder (to)** *tr.* pillar, saquear, robar.

**plunderer** (-ø[r]) *s.* saqueador, ladrón.

**plunge** (plønd̄y) *s.* zambullida, chapuz, sumersión; salto, caída, acción de arrojarse o lanzarse. *2* MAR. hocicada. *3* MIN. buzamiento.

**plunge (to)** *tr.* zambullir, chapuzar, sumergir; hundir; arrojar, precipitar. *2 intr.* zambullirse, sumergirse; hundirse; abismarse; arrojarse, precipitarse. *3* hocicar [el buque].

**plunger** (-ø[r]) *s.* buzo. *2* MEC. émbolo; chupón. *3* jugador o especulador desenfrenado.

**pluperfect** (plupø·[r]fikt) *adj.-s.* GRAM. pluscuamperfecto.

**plural** (plu·ral) *adj.-s.* plural.

**pluralism** (-išm) *s.* pluralismo.

**plurality** (pluræ·liti) *s.* pluralidad. *2* mayor número. *3* mayoría de votos.

**pluralize (to)** (plu·ralaiš) *tr.* pluralizar.

**plurally** (plu·rali) *adv.* en plural.

**plus** (plus) *prep.* más. *2 adj.* MAT., ELECT. positivo. *3* adicional, de más. *4 s.* MAT. el signo más. *5* cosa añadida, de más. *6* ~ *fours,* pantalón de golf.

**plush** (pløsh) *s.* TEJ. felpa, peluche. *2 adj.* de felpa, afelpado. *3* fam. suntuoso.

**Plutarch** (plu·ta[r]k) *n. pr.* Plutarco.

**plutarchy** (plu·ta[r]ki), **plutocracy** (pluta·krasi) *s.* plutocracia.

**Pluto** (plu·tou) *n. pr.* MIT., ASTR. Plutón.

**plutocrat** (plu·tøkræt) *s.* plutócrata.

**Plutonic** (pluta·nik) *adj.* plutónico.

**Plutonism** (plu·tønišm) *s.* plutonismo.

**plutonium** (plutou·niøm) *s.* QUÍM. plutonio.

**pluvial** (plu·vial) *adj.* pluvial.

**pluviometer** (pluvia·mitø[r]) *s.* pluviómetro.

**pluvious** (plu·viøs) *adj.* lluvioso.

**ply** (plai) *s.* pliegue, doblez. *2* propensión, inclinación. *3* capa [de una tela, etc.]; cabo [de cuerda].

**ply (to)** *tr.* usar, manejar [con ardor]. *2* practicar, ejercer. *3* trabajar con ahínco en. *4 to* ~ *with,* acosar con [preguntas, etc.]; hacer beber o comer [algo]. *5 tr.-intr.* ir y venir regularmente, hacer el servicio entre. *7* afanarse; no parar.

**plywood** (-wud) *s.* CARP. contrachapado.

**pneumatic** (niumæ·tik) *adj.* neumático. ~ *tire,* neumático. *2* de aire comprimido.

**pneumatics** (-s) *s.* neumática.

**pneumonia** (niu·mounia) *s.* MED. neumonía, pulmonía.

**pneumothorax** (niumozo·ræks) *s.* MED. neumotórax.

**poach (to)** (pouch) *tr.* invadir [un vedado]; robar [caza o pesca] de un vedado. *2* escalfar [huevos]. *3 intr.* cazar o pescar furtivamente.

**poacher** (-ø[r]) *s.* cazador o pescador furtivo.

**poachy** (-i) *adj.* aguanoso, blando [terreno].

**pock** (pak) *s.* MED. viruela, pústula eruptiva.

**pocket** (pa·kit) *s.* bolsillo, faltriquera. *2* fig. bolsa, dinero. *3* bolsa [de papel, etc.]. *4* MIL. bolsa. *5* ANAT., MED. saco, bolsa. *6* BILLAR. tronera. *7* cavidad, hoyo. *8* MIN. depósito de pepitas de oro. *9* AVIA. bache, bolsa de aire. *10 adj.* ~ *battleship,* acorazado de bolsillo.

**pocket (to)** *tr.* embolsar. *2* embolsarse, apropiarse. *3* BILLAR. entronerar. *4* ocultar [el orgullo, el enojo]; tragarse [una injuria].

**pocketbook** (-buk) *s.* librito de memorias. *2* billetero, carta, portamonedas.

**pocketful** (-ful) *s.* lo que cabe en un bolsillo o en una bolsa.

**pocketknife** (-naif) *s.* cortaplumas.

**pockmark** (-pa·kma[r]k) *s.* hoyo de viruelas, cacaraña.

**pock-marked** (-t) *adj.* picado de viruelas.

**pod** (pad) *s.* BOT. vaina, cápsula, silicua.

**pod (to)** *tr.* desvainar. *2 intr.* BOT. criar vainas. *3* hincharse. ¶ Pret. y p. p.: *podded;* ger.: *-dding.*

**podagra** (pødæ·gra) *s.* MED. podagra, gota.

**podgy** (pa·dȳi) *adj.* gordinflón, regordete.

**podium** (pou·diøm) *s.* ARQ. podio.

**poem** (pou·em o pou·im) *s.* poema. *2* fig. poesía.

**poesy** (pou·isi) *s.* ant. poesía. *2* inspiración, genio poético.

**poet** (pou·et o pou·it) *s.* poeta, vate.

**poetaster** (pouetæ·stø[r]) *s.* poetastro.

**poetess** (poue·tis) *f.* poetisa.

**poetic (al** (poue·tik(al) *adj.* poético.

**poetics** (poue·tiks) *s.* poética.

**poetize (to)** (-taiš) *tr.* poetizar.

**poetry** (pou·etri) *s.* poesía. *2* No tiene el sentido de verso, poema. *3* poética.

**pogrom** (pou·gram) *s.* pogrom.

**poh** (pou) *interj.* ¡puf!, ¡bah!, ¡quía!

**poignancy** (poi·nansi) *s.* acerbidad. *2* calidad de agudo, penetrante, punzante, conmovedor.

**poignant** (-ant) *adj.* acerbo. *2* agudo, penetrante, punzante. *3* mordaz. *4* conmovedor.

**point** (poi·nt) *s.* punta [extremo, esp. agudo]. *2* buril, punzón, puñal; herramienta puntiaguda. *3* GEOGR. punta, promontorio; pico, picacho. *4* punto [en varios sentidos]: ~ *at issue,* punto que se discute; ~ *of honour,* punto o cuestión de honor; ~ *of view,* punto de vista; *at the* ~ *of death,* en el artículo de la muerte; *on,* o *upon, the* ~ *of,* a punto de; *to a certain* ~, hasta cierto punto. *5* tanto, punto [en el juego]. *6* signo [de puntuación], punto final. *7* punto [de cañamazo o encaje; encaje de aguja]. *8* peculiaridad. *9* lo esencial, el quid; la intención, el chiste. *10* fin, propósito: *to carry one's* ~, salirse con la suya. *11* agujeta. *12* BOLSA. entero. *13* MAR. cuarta. *14* grado [de escala]. *15* MÚS. punto. *16* FERROC. aguja. *17* otros sentidos: *beside the* ~, fuera de propósito, que no viene al caso; *in* ~, pertinente, a propósito; *in* ~ *of,* por lo que toca a; *in* ~ *of fact,* de hecho; *to make a* ~ *of,* insistir en; tener por principio o regla; *to come to the* ~, ir al grano; venir al caso; *to speak to the* ~, hablar atinadamente.

**point (to)** *tr.* aguzar, sacar punta a. *2* apuntar,

asestar, encarar: *to ~ one's finger at*, señalar con el dedo. *3* señalar, indicar, hacer notar. | Gralte. con *out*. *4* GRAM. puntuar. *5* ALBAÑ. rejuntar. *6* intr. *to ~ at, to* o *toward*, señalar, indicar, apuntar a o hacia. *7* MED. madurar [un absceso]. *8 tr.-intr.* parar, mostrar la caza [el perro].

**point-blank** (-blænk) *adj.* directo, hecho a quemarropa. *2* claro, categórico. *3 adv.* a quemarropa. *4* clara, categóricamente.

**pointed** (-tid) *adj.* puntiagudo. *2* intencionado, mordaz. *3* directo, acentuado. *4* punteado. *5* ARQ. apuntado, ojival.

**pointer** (-tø$^r$) *s.* ARTILL. apuntador. *2* indicador, índice; manecilla [de reloj]; fiel [de balanza]. *3* puntero, buril. *4* perro de muestra; pachón. *5* fam. indicación u observación útil.

**pointless** (-list) *adj.* obtuso, sin punta. *2* insubstancial, insulso.

**poise** (poiš) *s.* equilibrio, estabilidad, reposo. *2* serenidad. *3* contrapeso. *4* indecisión. *5* aire, continente.

**poise (to)** *tr.* equilibrar, balancear. *2* mantener en equilibrio. *3* contrapesar. *4* llevar [la cabeza de cierto modo]. *5 intr.* posarse, estar suspendido, cernerse.

**poison** (poi·šøn) *s.* veneno, ponzoña, tósigo: *~ gas*, gas tóxico.

**poison (to)** *tr.* envenenar, empozoñar.

**poisoner** (-ø$^r$) *s.* envenenador.

**poisonous** (-øs) *adj.* venenoso, ponzoñoso.

**poke** (pouk) *s.* empujón, codazo. *2* hurgonazo; metido. *3* bolsa, saquito. *4* BOT. hierba, carmín. *5* fam. posma. *6* adj. *~ bonnet*, capota [sombrero].

**poke (to)** *tr.* picar, aguijonear, atizar, hurgar: *to ~ the fire*, atizar el fuego. *2 to ~ one's nose into*, meter la nariz en. *3 to ~ fun at*, burlarse de. *4 intr.* hurgar [en]. *5* andar buscando, husmear, meterse [en]. *6* haronear. *7* sobresalir, proyectarse.

**poker** (-ø$^r$) *s.* hurgón, atizador; espetón. *2* aguja para el pirograbado. *3* poker [juego].

**pokeweed** (-wid) *s.* BOT. hierba carmín.

**polacre** (pola·kø$^r$) *s.* MAR. polacra.

**Poland** (pou·land) *n. pr.* GEOGR. Polonia.

**polar** (pou·la$^r$) *adj.* polar: *~ bear*, oso blanco.

**polarimeter** (poulari·mitø$^r$) *s.* polarímetro.

**Polaris** (pole·ris) *s.* ASTR. la estrella polar.

**polariscope** (polæ·riskoup) *s.* ÓPT. polariscopio.

**polarity** (polæ·riti) *s.* polaridad.

**polarize (to)** (pou·larais) *tr.* polarizar.

**pole** (poul) *s.* GEOM., GEOGR., ASTR., BIOL., ELECT. polo. *2* palo, pértiga, vara, asta, poste. *3* lanza [de carruaje]. *4* balancín [de volatinero]. *5* TOP. jalón. *6* percha [medida]. *7* (con may.) polaco; polaca.

**pole (to)** *tr.-intr.* impeler [un barco] con pértiga.

**poleax(e** (-æks) *s.* hacha de combate o de matadero.

**polecat** (-lkæt) *s.* ZOOL. turón.

**polemarch** (pa·lima$^r$k) *s.* polemarca.

**polemic** (pole·mik) *adj.* polémico [de la controversia]. *2 s.* polemista. *3* polémica [controversia].

**polemical** (-kal) *adj.* POLEMIC 1.

**polemics** (pole·miks) *s.* polémica, dialéctica.

**polemist** (pa·lemist) *s.* polemista.

**polemonium** (palimou·niøm) *s.* BOT. polemonio.

**polestar** (pou·lsta$^r$) *s.* estrella polar. *2* fig. norte, guía.

**police** (pøli·s) *s.* policía: *~ court*, tribunal correccional.

**police (to)** *tr.* mantener el orden en. *2* guarnecer de policía. *3* MIL. asear y ordenar.

**policeman** (-mæn) *s.* policía; guardia de seguridad o urbano.

**policewoman** (-wumæn) *s.* mujer policía.

**policy** (pa·lisi) *s.* política, línea de conducta; trastienda, maña. *2* póliza [de seguro].

**policyholder** (-jouldø$^r$) *s.* asegurado, titular de una póliza.

**poliomyelitis** (paliomaiølai·tis) *s.* MED. poliomielitis.

**Polish** (pou·lish) *adj.* polaco, polonés. *2 s.* polaco [lengua].

**polish** (pa·lish) *s.* pulimento. *2* lustre, brillo. *3* acabado. *4* urbanidad, cultura. *5* barniz, betún, lustre para los zapatos.

**polish (to)** *tr.* pulir, bruñir, lustrar, dar brillo a. *2* pulir, perfeccionar; educar, refinar. *3 intr.* pulirse.

**polisher** (-ø$^r$) *s.* pulidor, bruñidor.

**polishing** (-g) *s.* pulimento, bruñido: *~ wax*, cera de lustrar.

**polite** (pølai·t) *adj.* cortés, urbano, atento, bien educado. *2* culto, refinado.

**politeness** (-nis) *s.* cortesía, urbanidad, buena crianza. *2* cultura, refinamiento.

**politic** (pa·litik) *adj.* sagaz, astuto. *2* político, prudente. *3* POL. constitucional. *4 body ~*, cuerpo político.

**political** (pøli·tikal) *adj.* político: *~ economy*, economía política.

**politician** (pøliti·shan) *s.* político. *2* politicastro, politiquero.

**politics** (pa·litiks) *s. pl.* política.

**polity** (pa·liti) *s.* constitución política. *2* comunidad, estado.

**polka** (pou·lka) *s.* polca. *2* adj. *~ dot*, topo o lunar en el dibujo de una tela.

**poll** (poul) *s.* cabeza [pers.]: *~ tax*, capitación. *2* votación; su resultado. *3* lista electoral. *4 pl.* colegio electoral. *5* urnas electorales.

**poll (to)** *tr.* recibir y escrutar [los votos]. *2* dar [voto]. *3* obtener [votos]. *4* trasquilar. *5* desmochar. *6* descornar. *7 intr.* votar en las elecciones.

**pollack** (pa·lak) *s.* ICT. especie de bacalao.

**pollard** (pa·la$^r$d) *s.* árbol descopado. *2* res descornada.

**pollard (to)** *tr.* descopar. *2* descornar.

**pollen** (pa·løn) *s.* BOT. polen.

**pollination** (palinei·shøn) *s.* BOT. polinización.

**polling** (pou·ling) *s.* votación, escrutinio: *~ place*, sección o colegio electoral.

**pollinic** (pali·nik) *adj.* BOT. polínico.

**polliwog** (pa·liuag) *s.* ZOOL. renacuajo.

**pollute (to)** (pøliu·t) *tr.* impurificar, contaminar, manchar, mancillar.

**polluted** (-id) *adj.* poluto, contaminado.

**pollution** (poliu·shøn) *s.* ensuciamiento, contaminación, mancillamiento. *2* MED. polución.

**Pollux** (pa·løks) *s.* ASTR. pólux.

**Polly** (pa·li) *n. pr.* Mariquita.

**polo** (pou·lou) *s.* polo [juego].

**polonaise** (pa·lønei·š) *s.* polonesa [danza, vestido].

**polonium** (palou·niøm) *s.* QUÍM. polonio.

**poltroon** (paltru·n) *s.* cobarde.

**poltroonery** (-øri) *s.* cobardía.

**poly** (pa·li) *s.* BOT. zamarrilla, polio.

**polyandry** (pa·liændri) *s.* poliandria.

**polycarpic, -pous** (palika·$^r$pik, -pøs) *adj.* BOT. policárpico.

**polychrome** (pa·likroumi) *s.* policromía.
**polyclinic** (palikli·nik) *s.* policlínica.
**polygamist** (pali·gamist) *s.* polígamo.
**polygamous** (-gamøs) *adj.* polígamo.
**polygamy** (-gami) *s.* poligamia.
**polyglot** (pa·liglat) *adj.-s.* poligloto. 2 poliglota [biblia]. *3 s.* mezcla de lenguajes.
**polygon** (pa·ligan) *s.* GEOM. polígono.
**polygonal** (pøli·gønal) *adj.* poligonal.
**polygraph** (pa·ligræf) *s.* polígrafo [escritor]. 2 multicopista.
**polyhedral** (paliji·dral) *adj.* poliédrico, poliedro.
**polyhedron** (-drøn) *s.* GEOM. poliedro.
**polymer** (pa·limøʳ) *s.* QUÍM. polímero.
**polymorphic** (palimo·ʳfik) *adj.* polimorfo.
**polymorphism** (-fišm) *s.* polimorfismo.
**Polynesia** (palinı·shia) *n. pr.* GEOGR. Polinesia.
**Polynesian** (-an) *adj.-s.* polinesio.
**polynormial** (palinou·mial) *adj.* MAT. de varios términos. *2 m.* polinomio.
**polyp** (pa·lip) *s.* ZOOL., MED. pólipo.
**polypary** (pa·liperi) *s.* polipero.
**Polyphemus** (palifi·møs) *n. pr.* Polifemo.
**polyphonic** (palifa·nik) *adj.* polifónico.
**polyphony** (pøli·føni) *s.* MÚS. polifonía.
**polypody** (pa·lipoudi) *s.* BOT. polipodio.
**polypus** (pa·lipøs) *s.* ZOOL. pulpo. 2 MED. pólipo.
**polysepalous** (palise·paløs) *adj.* BOT. polisépalo.
**polyspermus** (palispø·ʳmøs) *adj.* BOT. polispermo.
**polysyllabic (al** (palisilæ·bik(al) *adj.* polisílabo.
**polysyllable** (pa·lisilabøl) *s.* polisílabo.
**polytechnic** (palite·knik) *adj.* politécnico. *2 s.* escuela politécnica.
**polytheism** (pa·liziˈišm) *s.* politeísmo.
**polyvalent** (-vei·lønt) *adj.* QUÍM. polivalente.
**pomace** (pø·mis) *s.* bagazo de manzanas.
**pomaceous** (pømei·shøs) *adj.* BOT. pomáceo.
**pomade** (pømei·d) *s.* pomada.
**pomander** (poumæ·ndøʳ) *s.* pomo [bola olorosa].
**pomatum** (poumei·tøm) *s.* pomada.
**pome** (poum) *s.* BOT. pomo.
**pomegranate** (pa·mgrænit) *s.* BOT. granada. 2 BOT. granado.
**pomelo** (pa·mølou) *s.* BOT. toronja, pomelo.
**Pomeranian** (pamørei·nian) *adj.-s.* pomerano, pomeranio. *2 s.* perro de Pomerania.
**pomfret** (pa·mfrit) *s.* ICT. castañola.
**pommel** (pø·møl) *s.* pomo [de la espada]. 2 perilla [del arzón]. *3* ARQ. bola, manzana.
**pommel (to)** *tr.* aporrear, dar golpes. ¶ Pret. y p. p.: *pommel(l)ed*; ger.: *-l(l)ing*.
**pomp** (pømp) *s.* pompa, fausto, aparato.
**pompadour** (pa·mpadoʳ) *s.* copete [peinado].
**Pompeian** (pampei·an) *adj.-s.* pompeyano.
**Pompeii** (pampe·i) *n. pr.* HIST. Pompeya.
**Pompey** (pa·mpi) *n. pr.* Pompeyo.
**pompon** (pa·mpan) *s.* pompón.
**pomposity** (pampa·siti) *s.* pomposidad.
**pompous** (pa·mpøs) *adj.* pomposo. 2 hueco, vanidoso. *3* magnífico, brillante.
**poncho** (pa·nchou) *s.* poncho.
**pond** (pand) *s.* estanque, alberca, embalse, charca. *2* fam. el océano.
**ponder (to)** (pa·ndøʳ) *tr.* ponderar, pesar, estudiar. *2 intr. to ~ on o over,* reflexionar, acerca de.
**ponderable** (-abøl) *adj.* ponderable.
**ponderal** (-al) *adj.* ponderal.
**ponderosity** (pandøra·siti) *s.* ponderosidad. 2 pesadez.
**ponderous** (pa·ndørøs) *adj.* ponderoso, pesado. 2 importante, grave. *3* tedioso, cansado.

**poney** (pou·ni) *s.* PONY.
**poniard** (pa·niaᵗd) *s.* puñal, almarada.
**poniard (to)** *tr.* apuñalar.
**Pontic** (pa·ntik) *adj.* póntico.
**pontifex** (pa·ntifeks) *s.* pontífice, sumo sacerdote.
**pontiff** (pa·ntif) *s.* HIST., ECLES. pontífice.
**pontifical** (panti·fikal) *adj.* pontifical, pontificio. *2 s. pl.* pontifical [ornamentos, libro].
**pontificate** (-fikit) *s.* pontificado.
**pontificate (to)** (-fikeit) *intr.* pontificar.
**pontil** (pa·ntil) *s.* puntel.
**pontlevis** (pantle·vis) *s.* puente levadizo.
**pontoneer, pontonier** (pantø·niʳ) *s.* MIL. pontonero.
**pontoon** (pantu·n) *s.* pontón [para hacer puentes; barcaza]. 2 flotador [de hidroavión].
**pony** (pou·ni) *s.* jaquita, caballito. 2 cosa pequeña en su línea; copita, vasito.
**poodle** (pu·døl) *s.* perro de lanas.
**pooh** (pu) *interj.* ¡bah!, ¡quiá!, ¡uf!
**pooh-pooh (to)** (pu-pu) *tr.* desdeñar, quitar importancia a. 2 hacer mofa de.
**pool** (pul) *s.* charco, charca, balsa. 2 alberca, estanque: *swimming ~,* piscina. 3 polla, puesta [en ciertos juegos]. *4* fondos en común; fusión de intereses o de empresas. 5 trucos [juego].
**pool (to)** *tr.-intr.* formar una polla. 2 mancomunar [intereses, etc.].
**poolroom** (pu·lrum) *s.* (E.U.) sala de billar. 2 sala de apuestas.
**poop** (pup) *s.* MAR. popa. 2 MAR. toldilla.
**poop (to)** *tr.* MAR. embarcar [agua] por la popa.
**poor** (pu·øʳ) *adj.* pobre: *~ in spirit,* pobre de espíritu; *~ thing,* pobrecito, pobrecita. 2 de mala calidad, malo: *~ health,* mala salud. 3 débil, abatido: *~ spirits,* abatimiento. 4 enfermo, indispuesto. 5 pl. *the ~,* los pobres.
**poorhouse** (-jaus) *s.* hospicio, casa de caridad, asilo de pobres.
**poorly** (-li) *adv.* pobremente. 2 mal. 3 *adj.* enfermo, indispuesto.
**poor-spirited** *adj.* abatido, cobarde.
**pop** (pap) *s.* estallido, detonación, taponazo, pistoletazo. 2 bebida gaseosa. 3 fam. (E.U.) papá.
**pop (to)** *tr.* hacer estallar o detonar. 2 hacer saltar [un tapón]. 3 sacar, asomar, poner [de sopetón]. 4 soltar, disparar: *to ~ the question,* declararse, pedir en matrimonio. 5 *intr.* estallar, detonar; saltar [un tapón]. 6 *to ~ in,* entrar, meterse [de sopetón]. 7 *to ~ off,* morir; quedarse dormido. 8 *to ~ out,* salir [de sopetón]. 9 *to ~ up,* aparecer [de sopetón]. ¶ Pret. y p. p.: *popped*; ger.: *-pping*.
**popcorn** (pa·pkoʳn) *s.* rosetas de maíz.
**Pope** (pou·p) *s.* papa, pontífice. 2 [con min.] pope.
**popedom** (pou·pdøm) *s.* papado.
**popery** (-pøri) *s.* desp. papismo, catolicismo.
**pop-eyed** *adj.* de ojos saltones.
**popgun** (pa·pgøn) *s.* tirabala.
**popinjay** (pa·pindÿei) *s.* ORN. loro, papagayo. 2 ORN. picamaderos. 3 pisaverde, petimetre.
**popish** (pou·pish) *adj.* desp. católico romano.
**poplar** (pa·plaʳ) *s.* BOT. álamo, chopo.
**poplin** (pa·plin) *s.* TEJ. popelina.
**popliteal** (popli·tial) *adj.* ANAT. poplíteo.
**poppy** (pa·pi) *s.* BOT. amapola. 2 BOT. adormidera.
**poppycork** (-kak) *s.* fam. majadería.
**populace** (pa·piulis) *s.* pueblo, plebe, populacho.
**popular** (-laʳ) *adj.* popular. 2 corriente, general. 3 generalmente estimado; que tiene muchas simpatías. 4 de moda.
**popularity** (papiulæ·riti) *s.* popularidad; estimación general.

**popularize (to)** (pa·piularaiš) *tr.* popularizar, vulgarizar. *2* democratizar.
**populate (to)** (-leit) *tr.* poblar. *2 intr.* propagarse, multiplicarse.
**population** (-ei·shøn) *s.* población, populación. *2* población [habitantes].
**populous** (-løs) *adj.* populoso.
**porbeagle** (po·ʳbɪgøl) *s.* ɪCT. especie de tiburón.
**porcelain** (po·ʳsølin) *s.* porcelana.
**porch** (poʳch) *s.* porche, atrio, pórtico. *2* vestíbulo, entrada.
**porcine** (po·ʳsain) *adj.* porcuno, porcino.
**porcupine** (po·ʳkiupain) *s.* zooL. puerco espín.
**pore** (poʳ) *s.* poro.
**pore (to)** *intr. to ~ on, upon* u *over,* mirar fijamente, escudriñar, inspeccionar de cerca; leer con atención; reflexionar, meditar sobre.
**porgy** (po·ʳdÿi) ɪCT. pagro, pargo.
**pork** (poʳk) *s.* cerdo, carne de cerdo.
**porker** (po·rkøʳ) *s.* cerdo [esp. el de engorde].
**pornographic** (pornagræ·fik) *adj.* pornográfico.
**pornography** (poʳna·grafi) *s.* pornografía.
**porosity** (pora·siti) *s.* porosidad.
**porous** (po·røs) *adj.* poroso, esponjoso.
**porphyry** (po·firi) *s.* PETROGR. pórfido.
**porpoise** (po·ʳpøs) *s.* zooL. marsopa, puerco de mar.
**porraceous** (pørei·shøs) *adj.* porráceo.
**porridge** (pa·ridÿ) *s.* gachas, puches, potaje.
**porringer** (pa·rindÿøʳ) *s.* escudilla.
**port** (poʳt) *s.* puerto [de mar o río]. *2* MAR. porta, cañonera. *3* MEC. abertura, lumbrera. *3* desveno. *5* MAR. babor. *6* porte, aire, continente. *7* vino de Oporto.
**port (to)** *tr.-intr.* MAR. poner o virar a babor. *2 tr.* MIL. llevar [el fusil] terciado.
**portable** (po·ʳtabøl) *adj.* portátil.
**portage** (po·ʳtidÿ) *s.* porte, transporte.
**portal** (po·ʳtal) *s.* portal, portada. *2* vestíbulo. *3 adj.* ANAT. porta [vena].
**portcullis** (poʳtkø·lis) *s.* FORT. rastrillo.
**porte-cochère** (po·ʳt-koshe·ʳ) *s.* puerta cochera.
**portend (to)** (poʳte·nd) *tr.* anunciar, presagiar.
**portent** (po·ʳtent) *s.* presagio. *2* portento, prodigio.
**portentous** (poʳte·ntøs) *adj.* ominoso, presagioso. *2* portentoso. *3* grave, solemne.
**porter** (po·ʳtøʳ) *s.* portero. *2* portador; faquín; mozo [de estación, hotel, etc.]. *3* (E.U.) camarero de coche cama. *4* cerveza negra y floja.
**porterage** (-øridÿ) *s.* porte, transporte.
**portfolio** (-fou·liou) *s.* carpeta, cartera. *2* cartera, ministerio. *3* cartera [de un banco, etc.].
**porthole** (-joul) *s.* MAR. porta, portilla. *2* FORT. tronera.
**portico** (po·ʳtikou) *s.* ARQ. pórtico, atrio.
**portière** (po·ʳtie·ʳ) *s.* portier, antepuerta.
**portion** (po·ʳshøn) *s.* porción, parte. *2* herencia, patrimonio, dote. *3* sino, suerte.
**portion (to)** *tr.* dividir, partir, distribuir. *2* dotar.
**portly** (po·ʳtli) *adj.* voluminoso, corpulento. *2* majestuoso, imponente.
**portmanteau** (poʳtmæ·ntou) *s.* maleta, maltín.
**Porto Rico** (po·ʳtori·kou) *n. pr.* GEOGR. Puerto Rico.
**Porto Rican** (ri·kan) *adj.-s.* portorriqueño.
**portrait** (po·ʳtrit) *s.* retrato.
**portraitist** (po·ʳtreitist) *s.* retratista.
**portraiture** (po·ʳtrei·chuʳ) *s.* retrato. *2* acción o arte de retratar.
**portray (to)** (poʳtrei·) *intr.* retratar.
**portrayal** (-al) *s.* retrato, descripción.
**portress** (po·ʳtris) *f.* portera [de convento].

**Portugal** (po·ʳchugal) *n. pr.* GEOGR. Portugal.
**Portuguese** (-ɪ·š) *adj.-s.* portugués.
**portulaca** (poʳchulæ·ka) *s.* BOT. verdolaga.
**pose** (pouš) *s.* actitud. *2* actitud afectada.
**pose (to)** *tr.* B. ART. colocar en cierta postura. *2* proponer, plantear [un problema, etc.]; hacer, formular [una pregunta]. *3* confundir con preguntas difíciles. *4 intr.* B. ART. posar. *5 to ~ as,* darse aires de, hacerse pasar por.
**poser** (-øʳ) *s.* pregunta difícil, pega. *2* comediante, fachendoso.
**posit (to)** (pa·šit) *tr.* LÓG. afirmar, proponer.
**position** (poši·shøn) *s.* posición. *2* postura, actitud. *3* situación, ubicación. *4* colocación, empleo. *5 to be in a ~ to,* estar en situación de.
**positive** (pa·šitiv) *adj.* positivo. *2* categórico, dogmático; preciso, definido. *3* indudable. *4* terco, porfiado. *5 s.* lo positivo. *6* GRAM., ELECT., FOT. positivo.
**positivism** (-išm) *s.* positivismo.
**positivist** (-ist) *s.* positivista.
**positron** (pa·šitran) *s.* FÍS. positrón.
**posology** (pøsa·lødÿi) *s.* posología.
**posse** (pa·si) *s.* destacamento, partida [de gente armada].
**possess (to)** (pøšue·s) *tr.* poseer. *2* tener, gozar de. *3* posesionar. *4* llenar [de un sentimiento, convicción, etc.]. *5 to ~ oneself,* dominarse.
**possessed** (-st) *adj.* dueño; dotado. *2* poseído, poseso. *3* frío, dueño de sí mismo.
**possession** (-shøn) *s.* posesión. *2* dominio de sí mismo. *3* posesiones; bienes.
**possessive** (-siv) *adj.* posesional, posesivo. *2 adj.-s.* GRAM. posesivo.
**possessor** (-søʳ) *s.* posesor, poseedor. *2* COM. portador.
**possessory** (-søri) *adj.* posesorio.
**possibility** (pasibi·liti) *s.* posibilidad. *2* contingencia; cosa posible.
**possible** (pa·sibøl) *adj.* posible: *as soon as ~,* cuanto antes.
**possibly** (pa·sibli) *adv.* posiblemente, quizá.
**post** (pou·st) *s.* poste, pilar, pie derecho. *2* MIL. puesto. *3* puesto, sitio, empleo, cargo. *4* factoría [comercial]. *5* posta [para viajar]: *~ chaise,* silla de posta. *6* correo, estafeta; correos: *~ card,* tarjeta postal; *~ office,* servicio o casa de correo: *by return of ~,* a vuelta de correo. *7 adv.* por la posta, con rapidez.
**post (to)** *tr.* anunciar [con carteles]; fijar [carteles]. *2* poner en lista expuesta al público. *3* apostar, situar. *4* enviar por correo, echar al correo. *5* COM. pasar los asientos de un libro al libro mayor. *6* enterar, poner al corriente. *7 intr.* viajar por la posta.
**postage** (-idÿ) *s.* porte de correos, franqueo: *~ stamp,* sello de correos.
**postal** (-al) *adj.* postal: *~ order,* giro postal.
**postbox** (-baks) *s.* buzón de correos.
**postboy** (-boi) *s.* postillón. *2* cartero.
**postdate** (-deit) *s.* posfecha.
**postdate (to)** (poustdei·t) *tr.* posfechar.
**poster** (pou·støʳ) *s.* cartel, anuncio. *2* fijador de carteles. *3* caballo de posta.
**poster (to)** *tr.* fijar carteles en.
**posterior** (pasti·rioʳ) *adj.* posterior. *2* trasero. *3 s. pl.* trasero, nalgas.
**posteriority** (pastiria·riti) *s.* posterioridad.
**posterity** (paste·riti) *s.* posteridad.
**postern** (pou·støʳn) *s.* FORT. poterna. *2* puerta falsa.

**postgraduate** (poustgræ·dẏuit) *s*. estudiante que ha recibido un grado y hace estudios superiores.
**posthaste** (pu·stjei·st) *adv*. a toda prisa, rápidamente.
**posthouse** (-jaus) *s*. posta, casa de postas.
**posthumous** (pa·stiumøs) *adj*. póstumo.
**postil** (po·stil) *s*. nota, apostilla.
**postil(l)ion** (pousti·lion) *s*. postillón.
**postman** (pou·stmæn) *s*. cartero.
**postmark** (-ma$^r$k) *s*. matasellos.
**postmaster** (-mæstø$^r$) *s*. administrador de correos.
**postmeridian** (-møri·dian) *adj*. postmeridiano, de la tarde.
**post mortem (examination)** (mo·$^r$tem) *s*. autopsia.
**post-office** *adj*. de correos: ~ *box*, apartado de correos, *casilla postal.
**postoperative** (-a·pøreitiv) *adj*. postoperatorio.
**postpaid** (-peid) *adj*. con franqueo pagado.
**postpone** (to) (poustpou·n) *tr*. aplazar, diferir, suspender. 2 posponer.
**postponement** (-mønt) *s*. aplazamiento. 2 posposición.
**postpose** (to) (-pou·s) *tr*. GRAM. posponer.
**postposition** (-pöi·shøn) *s*. posposición.
**postprandial** (-præ·ndial) *adj*. de sobremesa.
**postschool** (pou·stskul) *adj*. postescolar.
**postscript** (-skri·pt) *s*. posdata.
**postulant** (pa·schulant) *s*. postulante. 2 postulanta.
**postulate** (-leit) *s*. postulado.
**postulate** (to) *tr*. postular.
**postulation** (-ei·shøn) *s*. póstula, postulación.
**postulator** (pa·schuleitø$^r$) *s*. postulador.
**posture** (pa·schu$^r$) *s*. postura, actitud, posición. 2 estado, situación. 3 disposición [de ánimo].
**posture** (to) *tr*. poner en una actitud. 2 *intr*. adoptar una actitud.
**postwar** (pou·stuo$^r$) *s*. postguerra. 2 *adj*. de postguerra.
**posy** (pou·si) *s*. ramillete [de flores]. 2 ant. mote o cifra en verso.
**pot** (pat) *s*. marmita, olla, puchero, jarro: *to go to the* ~, fracasar, arruinarse; *to keep the* ~ *boiling*, ganarse la vida; mantener la actividad. 2 maceta, tiesto. 3 orinal. 4 polla [en el juego]. 5 gran cantidad [de dinero]
**pot** (to) *tr*. cocer en marmita. 2 conservar en potes. 3 poner en macetas. 4 fam. ganar, conseguir. 5 disparar contra. 6 *intr*. tirar, disparar. ¶ Pret. y p. p.: *potted*; ger.: *-tting*.
**potable** (pou·tabøl) *adj*. potable.
**potash** (pa·tæsh) *s*. QUÍM. potasa.
**potassic** (pøtæ·sik) *adj*. potásico.
**potassium** (-siøm) *s*. QUÍM. potasa.
**potation** (potei·shøn) *s*. potación, bebida. 2 trago.
**potato** (potei·tou) *s*. BOT. patata; *papa: ~ chips*, patatas fritas a la inglesa; *sweet* ~, batata, patata de Málaga, bonito. 2 fam. persona, tipo.
**potbellied** (pa·tbelid) *adj*. barrigón, panzudo.
**potbelly** (pa·tbeli) *s*. barriga, panza.
**potboy** (pa·tboi) *s*. (Ingl.) mozo de taberna.
**potence** (pou·tøns) *s*. potencia, fuerza.
**potency** (-i) *s*. potencia, poder. 2 autoridad. 3 fuerza, actividad. 4 potencia [procreadora]. 5 fig. potencia [pers. de poder o autoridad].
**potent** (-tønt) *adj*. potente, poderoso. 2 eficaz.
**potentate** (-tønteit) *s*. potentado.
**potential** (pøte·nshal) *adj*.-*s*. potencial.
**potentiality** (pøtønshiæ·liti) *s*. potencialidad. 2 potencia, posibilidad.
**potentilla** (poutønti·la) *s*. BOT. cincoenrama.

**potentiometer** (pøtenshia·mitø$^r$) *s*. ELECT. potenciómetro.
**pothanger** (pa·tjængø$^r$) *s*. llares.
**pother** (pa·ðø$^r$) *s*. nube de polvo o de humo asfixiante. 2 barahúnda, alboroto, agitación.
**pother** (to) *tr*. preocupar, atormentar. 2 alborotar. 3 *intr*. agitarse, alborotarse.
**potherb** (pa·tjø$^r$b) *s*. hortaliza.
**pothole** (pa·tjoul) *s*. GEOL. marmita.
**pothook** (-juk) *s*. llares. 2 garabato [en la escritura].
**pothouse** (-jaus) *s*. cervecería; taberna.
**potion** (pou·shøn) *s*. trago, toma [de medicina, etc.].
**potluck** (pa·tløk) *s*. comida sin cumplidos; lo que haya: *to take* ~, hacer penitencia, comer de lo que haya.
**potpourri** (poupuri·) *s*. baturrillo, mezcolanza. 2 MÚS. popurrí.
**potsherd** (pa·tshø$^r$d) *s*. tiesto, casco [pedazo de vasija].
**pottage** (pa·tidẏ) *s*. menestra, potaje.
**potter** (pa·tø$^r$) *s*. alfarero, ollero: *potter's wheel*, torno de alfarero.
**potter** (to) *intr*. ocuparse en fruslerías. 2 vagar, haraganear.
**pottery** (-i) *s*. alfarería. 2 vasijas de barro.
**pouch** (pauch) *s*. bolsa, saquito. 2 faltriquera. 3 cartuchera. 4 abazón. 5 ANAT., ZOOL. bolsa, saco.
**pouch** (to) *tr*. embolsar. 2 fruncir [los labios]; hinchar [los carrillos]. 3 dar forma de bolsa. 4 aguantar, sufrir. 5 *intr*. formar bolsa.
**poulard** (pula·$^r$d) *s*. polla cebada.
**poulp (e** (pulp) *s*. ZOOL. pulpo.
**poulterer** (pou·ltørø$^r$) *s*. pollero, gallinero, recovero.
**poultice** (pou·ltis) *s*. cataplasma, bizma.
**poultice** (to) *tr*. bizmar, poner una cataplasma a.
**poultry** (pou·ltri) *s*. pollería, aves de corral.
**pounce** (pauns) *s*. grasilla, arenilla. 2 polvo para estarcir: ~ *bag*, cisquero. 3 garra, zarpa. 4 zarpazo. 5 salto súbito.
**pounce** (to) *tr*. estarcir. 2 polvorear con grasilla, etc. 3 pulir, apomazar. 4 calar, adornar con agujeros. 5 repujar [oro o plata]. 6 *intr*. *to* ~ *in* o *into*, entrar de sopetón. 7 *to* ~ *at, on* o *upon*, saltar, abalanzarse sobre.
**pound** (paund) *s*. libra [peso de 16 onzas]. 2 libra esterlina. 3 corral de concejo, depósito público para el ganado. 4 prisión, encierro. 5 vivero de peces.
**pound** (to) *tr*. moler, majar, machacar. 2 golpear, aporrear. 3 encerrar, acorralar. 4 *intr*. golpear. 5 trabajar duro. 6 andar, etc., pesadamente.
**pounder** (-ø$^r$) *s*. golpeador, machacador. 2 mano de almirez, almirez. 3 cosa, pez, etc., que pesa una libra.
**pound-foolish** *adj*. gastador, derrochador.
**pour** (po$^r$) *s*. vestimiento; caída, lluvia.
**pour** (to) *tr*. verter, derramar, echar, arrojar, emitir. 2 *intr*. fluir, correr, caer. 3 salir a chorros. 4 ir, entrar, salir, etc., en gran número. 5 llover copiosamente, diluviar.
**pout** (paut) *s*. mohín [con los labios]; puchero. 2 ICT. nombre de varios peces. 3 *pl*. berrinche.
**pout** (to) *intr*. hacer mohines o pucheros; mostrar mal humor.
**pouter** (-ø$^r$) *s*. perrsona que pone mal gesto. 2 ORN. *pouter* o ~ *pigeon*, paloma buchona.
**poverty** (pa·vø$^r$ti) *s*. pobreza, indigencia.
**poverty-stricken** *adj*. muy pobre, indigente.

**powder** (pau·dǿ$^r$) *s.* polvo; polvillo. *2* polvos [de tocador]: ~ *box*, polvera; ~ *puff*, borla. *3* pólvora: ~ *magazine*, polvorín, santabárbara.

**powder (to)** *tr.* polvorear. *2* empolvar, poner polvos a. *3* pulverizar. *4 intr.* empolvarse, ponerse polvos. *5* pulverizarse.

**powdered** (-d) *adj.* pulverizado, en polvo.

**powdery** (-i) *adj.* pulverulento. *2* friable. *3* polvoriento. *4* empolvado.

**power** (pau·ø$^r$) *s.* poder, facultad, virtud. *2* poder, fuerza, pujanza, poderío. *3* poder, potestad, autoridad, dominio, influencia: *executive* ~, poder ejecutivo; *in one's* ~, en poder de uno; *the powers that be*, las autoridades constituidas. *4* DER. poder: ~ *of attorney*, poder, procuración. *5* facultad [física o moral]. *6* potencia [estado soberano]. *7* MAT., FÍS. potencia. *8* energía, fuerza mecánica o motriz: ~ *plant*, instalación generadora de fuerza motriz; central eléctrica; AUTO. grupo motor; ~ *reactor*, reactor, generador de energía; ~ *shovel*, excavadora mecánica. *9 pl.* potestades [angélicas].

**power (to)** *tr.* accionar, impulsar.

**powerful** (-ful) *adj.* poderoso. *2* fuerte. *3* intenso, potente. *4* fam. grande, considerable.

**powerhouse** (-jaus) *s.* central eléctrica.

**powerless** (-lis) *adj.* impotente, ineficaz. *2* sin autoridad o capacidad [para un acto].

**powwow** (pau·uau) *s.* hechicero indio. *2* (E.U.) ceremonia india, conferencia de los indios o con los indios. *3* fig. reunión, congreso.

**pox** (paks) *s.* MED. enfermedad que produce erupciones pustulosas. *2* MED. sífilis.

**pozz(u)olana** (patsøla·na) *s.* puzolana.

**practicability** (præktikabi·liti) *s.* practicabilidad.

**practicable** (præ·ktikabøl) *adj.* practicable. *2* factible, hacedero. *3* transitable.

**practical** (-al) *adj.* práctico. *2* virtual, de hecho. *3* ~ *joke*, broma, chasco.

**practically** (-i) *adv.* prácticamente. *2* de hecho, casi poco menos que.

**practice** (præ·ktis) *s.* práctica: *in* ~, en la práctica. *2* costumbre: *to make a* ~ *of*, tener por costumbre. *3* clientela. *4* arteria, estratagema.

**practice (to)** *tr.-intr.*, **practiced** *adj. s.* = TO PRACTISE, PRACTISED.

**practician** (prækti·shøn) *s.* persona práctica. *2* PRACTITIONER.

**practise (to)** (præ·ktis) *tr.-intr.* practicar. *2* ejercitarse en. *3* ejercer [una profesión]. *4 tr.* ejercitar, adiestrar.

**practised** (-t) *adj.* práctico, versado.

**practising** (-ing) *adj.* en ejercicio [médico, abogado, etc.].

**practitioner** (prækti·shønø$^r$) *s.* médico, etc., que ejerce: *general* ~, médico de medicina general.

**praetexta** (prite·ksta) *s.* pretexta.

**praetor** (pri·to$^r$) *s.* pretor.

**praetorial** (prito·rial) *adj.* pretorial.

**praetorian** (prito·rian) *adj.-s.* pretoriano.

**praetorium** (prito·riøm) *s.* pretorio.

**pragmatic (al** (prægmæ·tik(al) *adj.* pragmático. *2* oficioso, entrometido. *3* pedante, dogmático. *4* *pragmatic sanction*, pragmática sanción.

**pragmatism** (præ·gmætišm) *s.* pragmatismo.

**Prague** (preig) *n. pr.* GEOGR. Praga.

**prairie** (pre·ri) *s.* pradera, llanura, sabana: ~ *dog*, perro de las praderas; ~ *wolf*, coyote.

**praise** (preiš) *s.* alabanza, elogio, encomio, aplauso. *2* celeridad, fama.

**praise (to)** *tr.* alabar, encomiar, ensalzar: *to* ~ *to the skies*, poner en las nubes.

**praiseworthy** (-uø$^r$di) *adj.* laudable, loable, digno de encomio.

**praline** (pra·lin) *s.* almendra garapiñada.

**pram** (pram) *s.* (Ingl.) cochecito de niño.

**prance** (præns) *s.* cabriola, trenzado [del caballo].

**prance (to)** *intr.* cabriolar, trenzar [el caballo]. *2* cabalgar o andar pavoneándose.

**prancer** (-ø$^r$) *s.* caballo pisador o trenzador.

**prandial** (præ·ndial) *adj.* de la comida.

**prank** (prænk) *s.* travesura, retozo, broma.

**prank (to)** *tr.* adornar, emperifollar. *2 intr.* emperifollarse.

**prankish** (-ish) *adj.* travieso, retozón.

**prate** (preit) *s.* charla, cháchara.

**prate (to)** *tr.* charlar, parlotear.

**prater** (-ø$^r$) *s.* hablador, charlatán.

**pratique** (prati·k) *s.* MAR. libre plática.

**prattle** (præ·tøl) *s.* charla, cháchara, parloteo.

**prattle (to)** *intr.* charlar, chacharear, parlotear. *2* murmurar [un arroyo, etc.].

**prawn** (pron) *s.* ZOOL. camarón, quisquilla, langostino.

**pray (to)** (prei) *tr.-intr.* rogar, pedir, suplicar. *2* *pray tell me*, haga el favor de decirme. *3 intr.* orar, rezar.

**prayer** (pre·ø$^r$) *s.* ruego, súplica, petición. *2* rezo, oración, plegaria; ~ *book*, devocionario; *to say one's prayers*, rezar, decir sus oraciones. *3 pl.* preces.

**prayerful** (-ful) *adj.* piadoso, devoto.

**praying mantis** (prei·ing ma·ntis) *s.* ENT. mantis religiosa.

**preach (to)** (prɪ·ch) *tr.-intr.* predicar, semonear.

**preacher** (-ø$^r$) *s.* predicador.

**preachify (to)** (-ifai) *intr.* fam. predicar molestamente, sermonear.

**preaching** (-ching) *s.* predicación. *2* sermón.

**preachment** (-mønt) *s.* desp. prédica, arenga.

**preacquaint (to)** (prɪakuei·nt) *tr.* dar a conocer de antemano.

**preadamite** (prɪæ·damait) *adj.-s.* preadamita.

**preadmonition** (prɪædma·nishøn) *s.* advertencia previa.

**preamble** (prɪæ·mbøl) *s.* preámbulo.

**prearrange (to)** (prɪarei·ndў) *tr.* arreglar o disponer de antemano.

**prebend** (pre·bønd) *s.* prebenda. *2* prebendado.

**prebendary** (pre·bønderi) *s.* prebendado.

**precarious** (prike·riøs) *adj.* precario. *2* incierto, inseguro. *3* gratuito, infundado.

**precaution** (priko·shøn) *s.* precaución.

**precautionary** (-eri) *adj.* de aviso, de precaución.

**precede (to)** (prɪsɪ·d) *tr.-intr.* preceder. *2* tener derecho a preceder.

**precedence, -cy** (prɪsɪ·døns, -si) *s.* precedencia; derecho de precedencia. *2* prioridad, anterioridad.

**precedent** (prɪsɪ·dønt) *adj.* precedente, antecedente, anterior, prior. *2 s.* (pre·sødønt) precedente.

**preceding** (prɪsɪ·ding) *adj.* precedente, que precede.

**precentor** (prise·ntø$^r$) *s.* ECLES. chantre, capiscol.

**precept** (prɪ·sept) *s.* precepto. *2* DER. auto, mandato.

**preceptive** (prise·ptiv) *adj.* preceptivo. *2* didáctico.

**preceptor** (prise·ptø$^r$) *m.* preceptor.

**preceptorial** (-torial) *adj.* de preceptor.

**precession** (prise·shøn) *s.* ASTR. precesión.

**precinct** (prı·sinkt) *s.* recinto; interior de un edificio, etc. *2* distrito. *3 pl.* inmediaciones.
**preciosity** (preshia·siti) *s.* LIT. preciosismo.
**precious** (pre·shøs) *adj.* precioso, preciado. *2* caro, amado. *3* culterano. *4* fig. bueno, considerable. *5 adv.* mucho, muy: ~ *little*, muy poco.
**preciously** (-li) *adv.* preciosamente. *2* extremadamente, muy.
**precipice** (pre·sipis) *s.* precipicio, despeñadero.
**precipitance, -cy** (prisi·pitans, -si) *s.* precipitación.
**precipitant** (-pitant) *adj.* precipitado. *2* arrebatado, temerario. *3 s.* QUÍM. precipitante.
**precipitate** (-piteit) *adj.* precipitado. *2* súbito. *3 s.* QUÍM. precipitado.
**precipitate (to)** *tr.* precipitar, despeñar. *2* precipitar, apresurar. *3* QUÍM., METEOR. precipitar. *4 intr.* precipitarse.
**precipitation** (-ei·shøn) *s.* precipitación. *2* derrumbamiento.
**precipitous** (prisi·pitøs) *adj.* precipitoso, pendiente, escarpado.
**precise** (prisai·s) *adj.* preciso, claro, distinto; exacto, justo, mismo. *2* rígido, formal, meticuloso.
**preciseness** (-nis) *s.* precisión, distinción, claridad. *2* rigidez, meticulosidad.
**precisian** (prisi·ÿan) *s.* rigorista; formulista.
**precision** (prisi·ÿøn) *s.* precisión, exactitud.
**preclude (to)** (prikliu·d) *tr.* impedir, excluir, hacer imposible.
**precocius** (prikou·shøs) *adj.* precoz. *2* temprano.
**precocity** (prika·siti) *s.* precocidad.
**precognition** (prıkagni·shøn) *s.* precognición.
**pre-Columbian** (prıkølø·mbian) *adj.* precolombino.
**preconception** (prıkønse·pshøn) *s.* prejuicio, preocupación, idea preconcebida.
**preconization** (prıkønišei·shøn) *s.* preconización. *2* proclamación, publicación.
**preconize (to)** (prı·kønaiš) *tr.* preconizar. *2* proclamar, pregonar.
**precool** (prıku·l) *tr.* preenfriar. *2* enfriar [frutas, etc.] antes de embarcarlas.
**precordial** (prıko·ʳdial) *adj.* ANAT. precordial.
**precursor** (prikø·ʳsøʳ) *s.* precursor.
**precursory** (-sori) *adj.* precursor; premonitorio.
**predaceous, predacious** (pridei·shøs) *adj.* rapaz, de presa, de rapiña.
**predecease (to)** (prı·disıs) *tr.-intr.* premorir.
**predecessor** (pre·disesøʳ) *s.* predecesor, antecesor. *2* antepasado, abuelo.
**predella** (prede·la) *s.* predela.
**predestinate** (prıde·stinit) *adj.-s.* predestinado.
**predestinate (to)** (-tineit) *tr.* predestinar.
**predestination** (-ei·shøn) *s.* predestinación.
**predestine (to)** (prıde·stin) *tr.* predestinar.
**predeterminate** (prıditø·ʳmineit) *adj.* predeterminado.
**predetermination** (-ei·shøn) *s.* predeterminación.
**predetermine (to)** (prıditø·ʳmin) *tr.* predeterminar.
**predicable** (pre·dikabøl) *adj.* que puede afirmarse [de]. *2 adj.-s.* LÓG. predicable.
**predicament** (pridi·kamønt) *s.* LÓG. predicamento. *2* apuro, aprieto, situación desgraciada.
**predicant** (pre·dikant) *adj.* de predicadores [orden].
**predicate** (pre·dikit) *s.* LÓG., GRAM. predicado.
**predicate (to)** (pre·dikeit) *tr.* afirmar. *2* LÓG., GRAM. predicar.

**predication** (-ei·shøn) *s.* afirmación, aserción. *2* LÓG., GRAM. predicación.
**predict (to)** (pridi·kt) *tr.* predecir, vaticinar.
**prediction** (-kshøn) *s.* predicción, vaticinio.
**predictive** (-tiv) *adj.* que predice.
**predilection** (predile·kshøn) *s.* predilección.
**predispose (to)** (pridispou·š) *tr.* predisponer.
**predisposition** (prıdispøsi·shøn) *s.* predisposición.
**predominance, -cy** (prida·minans, -si) *s.* predominio, predominación.
**predominant** (-ønt) *adj.* predominante.
**predominate (to)** (-eit) *intr.* predominar, prevalecer.
**pre-eminence** (prı-e·minøns) *s.* superioridad, supremacía.
**pre-eminent** (-t) *adj.* preeminente.
**preen (to)** (prın) *tr.* limpiar y componer [sus plumas] el ave. *2* componerse, acicalarse.
**pre-engage (to)** (prı-engei·dÿ) *tr.* apalabrar; contratar de antemano.
**pre-exist (to)** (prı-egši·st) *intr.* preexistir.
**pre-existence** (-øns) *s.* preexistencia.
**pre-existent** (-ønt) *adj.* preexistente.
**prefabricate (to)** (prıfæ·brikeit) *tr.* prefabricar.
**preface** (pre·fis) *s.* prefacio, prólogo. *2* LITURG. prefacio.
**preface (to)** *tr.* prologar; introducir, comenzar.
**prefatory** (pre·fatori) *adj.* de introducción, preliminar.
**prefect** (prı·fekt) *s.* prefecto.
**prefector (i) al** (prıfekto·r(i)al) *adj.* prefectoral.
**prefecture** (prıfe·kchuʳ) *s.* prefectura.
**prefer (to)** (prifø·ʳ) *tr.* preferir, anteponer. *2* ascender, elevar, exaltar. *3* ofrecer, presentar. *4 intr.* escoger [entre]. ¶ Pret. y p. p.: *preferred;* ger.: *rring.*
**preferable** (pre·førabøl) *adj.* preferible.
**preference** (pre·førons) *s.* preferencia. *2* predilección. *3* DER. prioridad.
**preferential** (-shal) *adj.* preferente, de preferencia.
**preferment** (prifø·ʳmønt) *s.* ascenso, elevación, adelantamiento. *2* cargo, dignidad. *3* favorecimiento, apoyo. *4* DER. prioridad.
**prefiguration** (prıfigiurei·shøn) *s.* prefiguración.
**prefigure (to)** (prıfi·gioʳ) *tr.* prefigurar. *2* prever, imaginar de antemano.
**prefix** (prı·fiks) *s.* prefijo, afijo.
**prefix (to)** (prıfi·ks) *tr.* prefijar, anteponer.
**prefloration** (prıflorei·shøn) *s.* BOT. prefloración.
**prefoliation** (prıfouliei·shøn) *s.* BOT. prefoliación.
**pregnable** (pre·gnabøl) *adj.* expugnable.
**pregnancy** (-nsi) *s.* preñez, embarazo. *2* fertilidad, fecundidad.
**pregnant** (-ønt) *adj.* preñada, embarazada, encinta. *2* fértil, fecundo. *3* preñado, lleno. *4* importante, grave; significativo.
**preheat (to)** (prıjı·t) *tr.* calentar de antemano.
**prehensible** (prije·nsibøl) *adj.* prensil.
**prehension** (-shøn) *s.* prensión. *2* aprehensión [mental].
**prehistoric (al** (prıjista·rik(al) *adj.* prehistórico.
**prehistory** (prıji·stori) *s.* prehistoria.
**prejudge (to)** (prıdÿø·dÿ) *tr.* prejuzgar.
**prejudg(e)ment** (-mønt) *s.* acción de prejuzgar, prejuicio.
**prejudice** (pre·dÿudis) *s.* prejuicio, prevención, preocupación. *2* perjuicio, detrimento.
**prejudice (to)** *tr.* prevenir, predisponer. *2* perjudicar, dañar.
**prejudicial** (predÿudi·shal) *adj.* perjudicial.
**prelacy** (pre·lasi) *s.* prelacía, prelatura.

**prelate** (pre·lit) *s.* prelado.
**prelature** (pre·lachøʳ) *s.* prelatura. *2* episcopado.
**prelect (to)** (prile·kt) *intr.* disertar, hablar en público.
**preliminary** (prili·mineri) *adj.-s.* preliminar.
**prelude** (pre·liud) *s.* preludio.
**prelude (to)** *tr.-intr.* preludiar.
**preludial** (priliu·dial), **prelusive** (-siv) *adj.* preliminar, introductorio.
**premature** (prɪmachu·øʳ) *adj.* prematuro.
**prematurely** (-li) *adv.* prematuramente.
**premeditate (to)** (prime·diteit) *tr.* premeditar. *2 intr.* reflexionar de antemano.
**premeditation** (-ei·shøn) *s.* premeditación.
**premier** (prɪ·miøʳ) *adj.* primero, principal, el más antiguo. *2 s.* primer ministro.
**première** (premie·ʳ) *s.* TEAT. estreno. *2* primera actriz.
**premise** (pre·mis) *s.* LÓG. premisa. *2* cosa que se da por supuesta. *3 pl.* local, establecimiento, casa, finca.
**premise (to)** (pre·maiš) *tr.* sentar, establecer como premisas. *2* suponer preexistente.
**premium** (prɪ·miøm) *s.* premio, galardón. *2* COM. premio, prima, interés.
**premolar** (prɪmou·laʳ) *adj.-s.* premolar [diente].
**premonition** (prɪmoni·shøn) *s.* aviso, prenuncio, presentimiento.
**premonitory** (prɪma·nitori) *adj.* premonitorio.
**prenatal** (prɪnei·tal) *adj.* prenatal.
**prentice** (pre·ntis) *s.* fam. aprendiz.
**preoccupancy** (prɪa·kiupansi) *s.* ocupación previa. *2* preocupación.
**preoccupation** (-ei·shøn) *s.* preocupación. | No tiene el sentido de cuidado. *2* prejuicio. *3* PREOCCUPANCY.
**preoccupied** (prɪa·kiupaid) *adj.* preocupado.
**preoccupy (to)** (prɪa·kiupai) *tr.* preocupar [ocupar antes que otro]. *2* preocupar, absorber la atención; predisponer.
**preordain (to)** (prɪoʳdei·n) *tr.* preordinar.
**prepaid** (prɪpei·d) *adj.* pagado por adelantado; con porte pagado.
**preparation** (preparei·shøn) *s.* preparación. *2* apresto, preparativo. *3* preparado, confección.
**preparative** (pripæ·rativ) *adj.* preparatorio. *2 s.* preparativo, apresto.
**preparatory** (pripæ·ratori) *adj.* preparatorio.
**prepare (to)** (pripe·øʳ) *tr.* preparar. *2* prevenir, disponer, aprestar. *3* equipar, pertrechar. *4 intr.* prepararse. *5* hacer preparativos.
**preparedness** (pripe·ridnis) *s.* estado de preparación.
**preparer** (pripe·røʳ) *s.* preparador.
**prepay (to)** (prɪpei·) *tr.* pagar por adelantado. *2* franquear [una carta].
**prepayment** (-mønt) *s.* pago adelantado. *2* franqueo.
**prepense** (pripe·ns) *adj.* premeditado: *with malice ~*, DER. maliciosa y premeditadamente.
**preponderance, -cy** (pripa·ndørans, -si) *s.* preponderancia.
**preponderant** (-dørant) *adj.* preponderante.
**preponderate (to)** (-døreit) *tr.* preponderar.
**preposition** (prepøši·shøn) *s.* GRAM. preposición.
**prepositional** (-al) *adj.* GRAM. prepositivo.
**prepositive** (pripa·šitiv) *adj.* GRAM. antepuesto.
**prepossess (to)** (prɪpøše·s) *tr.* imbuir [de una idea, etc.]. *3* predisponer favorablemente, causar buena impresión.
**prepossessing** (-sing) *adj.* simpático, atractivo.

**prepossession** (-shøn) *s.* simpatía, preferencia, predisposición favorable.
**preposterous** (pripa·størøs) *adj.* absurdo, descabellado; ridículo.
**prepotence, -cy** (prɪpou·tøns, -si) *s.* prepotencia.
**prepotent** (-ønt) *adj.* prepotente.
**prepuce** (prɪ·pius) *s.* prepucio.
**prerequisite** (prɪre·kuišit) *adj.* previamente necesario. *2 s.* requisito previo.
**prerogative** (prira·gativ) *adj.* privilegiado. *2 s.* prerrogativa.
**presage** (pre·sidy̌) *s.* presagio. *2* pronóstico.
**presage (to)** (prisei·dy̌) *tr.* presagiar. *2* pronosticar.
**presbyope** (pre·šbioup) *s.* MED. présbite.
**presbyopia** (prešbiou·pia) *s.* MED. presbicia.
**presbyter** (pre·šbitøʳ) *s.* presbítero.
**Presbyterian** (presbiti·rian) *adj.-s.* presbiteriano.
**presbytery** (pre·šbiteri) *s.* presbiterio. *2* casa rectoral. *3* sínodo de una iglesia presbiteriana.
**prescience** (prɪ·shiøns) *s.* presciencia.
**prescient** (nt) *adj.* presciente.
**prescind** (prisi·nd) *tr.* abstraer. *2 intr.* to *~ from*, prescindir, hacer abstracción, de.
**prescribe (to)** (priskrai·b) *tr.* prescribir [ordenar; recetar]. *2 tr.-intr.* DER. prescribir.
**prescription** (priskri·pshøn) *s.* prescripción [orden, precepto, regla; receta]. *3* DER. prescripción.
**presence** (pre·šøns) *s.* presencia: *~ of mind*, presencia de ánimo; *in the ~ of*, en presencia de. *2* aire, porte. *3* persona de elevada dignidad; soberano. *4 adj. presence chamber*, salón de audiencias.
**present** (-nt) *adj.* presente: *to be ~*, estar presente, asistir. *2 adj.: ~ value*, valor actual. *3* GRAM. activo [participio]; presente [tiempo]. *4 s.* presente, la actualidad: *at ~*, actualmente; *for the ~*, por ahora. *5* presente, regalo.
**present (to)** (priše·nt) *tr.* presentar: *to ~ arms*, presentar armas; *to ~ oneself*, presentarse, personarse. *2* ofrecer [un aspecto, sus respetos, etc.]. *3* apuntar [un arma]. *4 to ~ with*, regalar, obsequiar con.
**presentable** (priše·ntabøl) *adj.* presentable.
**presentation** (prešøntei·shøn) *s.* presentación: *on ~*, COM. a presentación; *the Presentation*, fiesta de la Candelaria. *2* regalo, obsequio: *~ copy*, ejemplar de regalo con dedicatoria.
**present-day** *adj.* actual, de hoy, del día.
**presential** (priše·nshal) *adj.* relativo al presente.
**presentient** (priše·ntiønt) *adj.* que presiente.
**presentiment** (priše·ntimønt) *s.* presentimiento.
**presently** (pre·søntli) *adv.* presentemente. *2* dentro de poco, al poco rato.
**presentment** (priše·ntmønt) *s.* presentación; exhibición. *2* retrato, representación.
**preservation** (prešøʳvei·shøn) *s.* preservación. *2* conservación.
**preservative** (prišø·ʳvativ) *adj.* preservativo. *2* conservativo. *3 s.* preservativo.
**preserve** (prišø·ʳv) *s.* conserva, confitura. *2* vedado.
**preserve (to)** *tr.* perseverar, resguardar, proteger. *2* conservar, mantener. *3* conservar, curar, confitar.
**preserved** (prišø·ʳvd) *adj.* en conserva, confitado.
**preserver** (prišø·ʳvøʳ) *s.* preservador, conservador. *2* conservero; confitero.
**preside (to)** (prišai·d) *tr.-intr.* presidir; dirigir: *to ~ at* o *over*, presidir.
**presidency** (pre·šidønsi) *s.* presidencia.

**president** (pre·šidønt) *s.* presidente.
**presidential** (prešide·nshal) *adj.* presidencial.
**presidium** (priši·diøm) *s.* presidium [soviético].
**press** (pres) *s.* multitud, tropel, muchedumbre. *2* apretura. *3* empuje, presión, apretón. *4* pliegue [de una prenda planchada]. *5* prisa, apremio. *6* prensa [máquina; periódicos]: ~ *cutting*, ~ *clipping*, recorte de prensa: *in* ~, en prensa. *7* imprenta, estampa. *8* armario. *9* FOT. prensa. *10* MIT. leva, enganche.
**press (to)** *tr.* apretar. *2* apiñar. *3* impeler. *4* prensar, planchar, laminar. *5* estrujar, exprimir. *6* abrumar, oprimir; apurar: *to be pressed for money*, estar apurado de dinero. *7* apresurar, apremiar. *8* obligar. *9* instar. *10* insistir en: *to* ~ *one's point*, insistir uno en su punto de vista. *11* estrechar, acosar. *12* estrechar [en sus brazos]. *13* MIL. hacer leva de. *14 intr.* pesar, ejercer presión. *15* abrirse paso, avanzar; agolparse, apiñarse: *to* ~ *forward*, avanzar, arremeter. *16* urgir, apremiar.
**pressing** (-ing) *adj.* urgente, apremiante. *2* insistente, importuno.
**pressman** (-mæn) *s.* prensador. *2* prensista. *3* (Ingl.) periodista.
**pressmark** (-ma<sup>r</sup>k) *s.* signatura [de biblioteca].
**pressroom** (-rum) *s.* IMPR. sala de prensas.
**pressure** (pre·shø<sup>r</sup>) *s.* presión: ~ *gauge*, manómetro; ~ *group*, grupo de presión. *2* prensadura. *3* apretón. *4* impulso, empuje. *5* peso, opresión. *6* urgencia, premura, apremio. *7* ELECT. tensión.
**presswork** (pre·suø<sup>r</sup>k) *s.* IMPR. impresión, tirada.
**prestidigitation** (prestididỹitei·shøn) *s.* prestidigitación.
**prestige** (pre·stidỹ) *s.* prestigio.
**presumable** (prišiu·mabøl) *adj.* presumible. *2* de esperar, probable.
**presume (to)** (prišiu·m) *tr.* presumir, suponer, dar por sentado; contar con. *2 intr.* presumir. *3 to* ~ *to*, atreverse a, tomarse la libertad de.
**presumption** (-šø·mshøn) *s.* presunción, suposición. *2* presunción, orgullo.
**presumptive** (-tiv) *adj.* presunto, supuesto. *2* presuntivo. *3* probable.
**presumptuous** (-chuøs) *adj.* presuntuoso, presumido, atrevido.
**presuppose (to)** (prɪsøpou·š) *tr.* presuponer.
**pretence** (prite·ns) *s.* pretensión. *2* presunción, ostentación. *3* fingimiento, apariencia, pretexto: *under false pretences*, con engaño; *under* ~ *of*, so pretexto.
**pretend (to)** (prite·nd) *tr.* aparentar, fingir, simular: *to* ~ *to be*, fingirse, dárselas de. *2* intentar. *3 tr.-intr.* pretender, aspirar a.
**pretended** (-id) *adj.* falso, fingido, supuesto.
**pretender** (-ø<sup>r</sup>) *s.* pretendiente [a un trono, etc.]. *2* fingidor, hipócrita.
**pretense** (prite·ns) *s.* PRETENCE.
**pretension** (prite·nshøn) *s.* pretensión. *2* boato. *3* afirmación gratuita; pretexto.
**pretentious** (-shøs) *adj.* pretencioso, ostentoso, de pretensiones. *2* ambicioso, vasto.
**preterit(e** (pre·tørit) *adj.* pretérito, pasado. *2* GRAM. pretérito definido.
**preterition** (pretøri·shøn) *s.* preterición.
**preternatural** (pritø<sup>r</sup>næ·chural) *adj.* preternatural.
**pretext** (prite·kst) *s.* pretexto.
**pretext (to)** *tr.* pretextar.
**pretor** (prɪ·tø<sup>r</sup>) *s.* pretor.
**pretorial, pretorian** *adj.-s.* PRAETORIAL, PRAETORIAN.

**pretiffy (to)** (pri·tifai) *tr.* embellecer, adornar. ¶ Pret. y p. p.: *prettified*.
**prettily** (-li) *adv.* lindamente. *2* considerablemente. *3* bastante.
**prettiness** (-nis) *s.* lindeza, gentileza, bonitura.
**pretty** (pri·ti) *adj.* lindo, bonito; gracioso, elegante. *2* bueno, regular; considerable: *a* ~ *penny*, fam. un dineral, un buen pico. *3 adv.* bastante; ~ *well*, bastante bien.
**prevail (to)** (privei·l) *intr.* prevalecer, triunfar. *2* predominar; reinar, ser general o corriente. *3 to* ~ *upon* o *with*, convencer, persuadir, inducir.
**prevalence** (pre·valøns) *s.* predominio. *2* boga, uso o aceptación general.
**prevalent** (-ønt) *adj.* reinante, corriente, general, en boga.
**prevaricate (to)** (privæ·rikeit) *intr.* usar de equívocos o argucias; deformar la verdad, mentir. *2* DER. prevaricar.
**prevent (to)** (prive·nt) *tr.* prevenir, evitar, impedir, estorbar. *2* anticiparse a.
**preventative** (-tɑtiv) *adj.-s.* PREVENTIVE.
**prevention** (-shøn) *s.* evitación, estorbo, obstáculo, impedimento.
**preventive** (-tiv) *adj.* impeditivo. *2* preventivo; profiláctico.
**previous** (pri·viøs) *adj.* previo. *2* anterior, precedente. *3 adv.* ~ *to*, antes de.
**prevision** (prɪvi·ỹøn) *s.* previsión, presciencia; pronóstico.
**prewar** (prɪ·uo<sup>r</sup>) *adj.* antes de la guerra.
**prey** (prei) *s.* presa, rapiña, pillaje: *bird of* ~, ave de rapiña. *2* presa, botín, víctima: *to fall a* ~ *to*, ser presa de.
**prey (to)** *intr.* cazar y devorar. *2* rapiñar, pillar, hacer presa. *3 to* ~ *on, upon* o *at*, consumir, remorder, preocupar: *to* ~ *upon one's mind*, preocupar, enloquecer.
**Priam** (prai·æm) *n. pr.* Príamo.
**price** (prais) *s.* precio; coste, costa: *cost* ~, precio de coste; *set* ~, precio fijo; *at any* ~, a toda costa. *2* valor, importe. *3* curso [en Bolsa].
**price (to)** *tr.* apreciar, estimar, tasar, valuar, poner precio a.
**priceless** (-lis) *adj.* inapreciable, inestimable, que no tiene precio.
**prick** (prik) *s.* pinchazo, punzada, picadura, resquemor, escrúpulo: *pricks of conscience*, remordimientos. *2* aguijón, púa. *4* estímulo, acicate.
**prick (to)** *tr.* pinchar, punzar, picar, agujerear; marcar con agujeros. *2* aguijonear, espolear. Gralte. con *on* u *off*. *3* avivar, aguzar; enderezar. | Gralte. con *up*: *to* ~ *up one's ears*, aguzar los oídos o las orejas. *4 intr.* pinchar, punzar, escocer. *5* agriarse, torcerse. *6* aguzarse, enderezarse.
**pricker** (-ø<sup>r</sup>) *s.* punzón, aguijón. *2* espina, púa.
**prickle** (pri·køl) *s.* pincho, púa, espina. *2* ardor, comezón.
**prickle (to)** *tr.* punzar, producir picazón. *2 intr.* sentir una punzada o picazón.
**prickly** (pri·kli) *adj.* espinoso, lleno de púas: *prickly pear*, BOT. chumbera; higo chumbo. *2* que pica: ~ *heat*, erupción debida al calor.
**pride** (praid) *s.* orgullo: *to take* ~ *in*, enorgullecerse de. *2* soberbia, altivez, engreimiento. *3* dignidad, amor propio. *4* pompa, esplendor.
**pride (to)** *tr.* enorgullecer. *2 to* ~ *oneself on* o *upon*, enorgullecerse de.
**prideful** (-ful) *adj.* orgulloso. *2* altanero.
**prier** (prai·ø<sup>r</sup>) *s.* curioso, fisgón, husmeador.

**priest** (prɪst) *m.* sacerdote. 2 presbítero.
**priestcraft** (-kræft) *s.* intriga atribuida a los sacerdotes.
**priestess** (-is) *f.* sacerdotisa.
**priesthood** (-tjud) *s.* sacerdocio.
**prig** (prig) *s.* pedante, presuntuoso; gazmoño.
**priggish** (-ish) *adj.* pedantesco; presuntuoso; gazmoño.
**prim** (prim) *adj.* relamido, estirado. 2 riguroso, exacto.
**prim (to)** *intr.* poner gesto estirado. 2 *tr.-intr.* vestor con severidad afectada.
**primacy** (prai·masi) *s.* primacía, supremacía. 2 primacía [dignidad de primado].
**primal** (prai·mal) *adj.* prístino, original. 2 principal, fundamental.
**primarily** (prai·merili) *adv.* primariamente.
**primary** (-meri) *adj.* primario: ~ *coil*, ELECT. bobina primaria de inducción; ~ *school*, escuela primaria. 2 primero, prístino; de origen. 3 principal, fundamental. 4 elemental: ~ *colours*, colores elementales. 5 *s.* lo elemental. 6 POL. (E.U.) elección de compromisarios.
**primate** (-mit) *s.* el primero o superior. 2 primado. 3 ZOOL. primate.
**primatial** (praimei·shal) *adj.* primacial.
**prime** (praim) *adj.* primero, primario, principal: ~ *minister*, primer ministro; ~ *mover*, fuente de energía; alma [de una empresa]. 2 superior, excelente. 3 MAT. primo. 4 ~ *cost*, coste de fabricación. 5 *s.* prima [hora]. 6 principio, albor, amanecer. 7 flor, nata, lo mejor: *the* ~ *of life*, la flor de la edad; la edad viril. 8 ESGR. prima. 9 MAT. número primo. 10 minuto [de un grado].
**prime (to)** *tr.* cebar [una arma de fuego, una bomba, etc.]. 2 imprimar, dar la primera mano de color, etc., a. 3 preparar, aleccionar, instruir de antemano. 4 poner el signo (') a.
**primer** (pri·møʳ) *s.* abecedario, cartilla de lectura. 2 compendio [libro]. 3 (prai·møʳ) *s.* pistón fulminante.
**primeval** (praimɪ·val) *adj.* primitivo, prístino.
**primigenial** (-idȳi·nial) *adj.* primigenio.
**priming hole** (prai·ming) *s.* ART. oído.
**primipara** (-mi·para) *s.* primípara.
**primitive** (pri·mitiv) *adj.* primitivo. 2 primero, prístino.
**primitivism** (-išm) *s.* primitivismo.
**primness** (pri·mnis) *s.* remilgo, tiesura, afectación.
**primogenitor** (praimoudȳe·nitøʳ) *s.* antepasado.
**primogeniture** (-nichøʳ) *s.* primogenitura.
**primordial** (praimo·ʳdial) *adj.* primordial. 2 original, primitivo.
**primp** (primp) *tr.* vestir, arreglar. 2 *intr.* vestirse, acicalarse.
**primrose** (pri·mrouš) *s.* BOT. vellorita, primavera. 2 color amarillo verdoso claro. 3 *adj.* florido, gayo: ~ *path*, sendero florido, vida dada a los placeres.
**Primulaceae** (primiulei·shii) *s. pl.* primuláceas.
**prince** (prins) *s.* príncipe: ~ *consort*, marido de la reina; ~ *royal*, príncipe heredero.
**princedom** (-døm) *s.* principado.
**princeling** (pri·nsling) *s.* principillo.
**princely** (-li) *adj.* principesco, digno de un príncipe; munífico; noble, magnífico, regio.
**princeps** (-eps) *adj.* príncipe [edición].
**princess** (-is) *f.* princesa.
**principal** (prin·sipal) *adj.* principal. 2 *s.* principal,

jefe. 3 director [de un colegio]. 4 DER. principal, poderdante. 5 principal [de un rédito].
**principality** (prinsipæ·liti) *s.* principado. 2 *pl.* principados [espíritus angélicos].
**principate** (pri·nsipeit) *s.* principado.
**principle** (-pøl) *s.* principio [origen, fundamento; verdad fundamental, regla, ley]. 2 QUÍM. principio. 3 *in* ~, en principio; *on* ~, por principio.
**print** (print) *s.* impresión, huella. 2 impresión, estampa: *in* ~, impreso; en letra de molde; *out of* ~, agotado. 3 lámina, grabado, estampa. 4 TEJ. estampado. 5 FOT. impresión, prueba.
**print (to)** *tr.-intr.* imprimir, estampar: *printed matter*, impresos; *printed goods*, estampados. 2 *tr.* dar a la imprenta, publicar. 3 FOT. tirar [una prueba]. 4 imprimir o grabar [en la mente].
**printer** (-øʳ) *s.* impresor, tipógrafo: *printer's devil*, aprendiz de impresor. 2 estampador.
**printing** (-ing) *s.* impresión, estampación, estampado: ~ *office*, imprenta [establecimiento]. 2 imprenta, tipografía [arte]. 3 estampa, impreso. 4 FOT. impresión: ~ *frame*, prensa fotográfica.
**prior** (prai·øʳ) *adj.* anterior, previo. 2 que tiene prioridad. 3 *adv. prior to*, antes de. 4 *s.* prior.
**priorate** (-ørit) *s.* priorato.
**prioress** (-øris) *f.* priora.
**priority** (praia·riti) *s.* anterioridad. 2 prioridad.
**priory** (prai·øri) *s.* priorato [comunidad].
**prism** (prišm) *s.* GEOM., ÓPT. cristal, prisma. 2 ÓPT. *prism binocular*, prismáticos.
**prismatic** (prišmæ·tik) *adj.* prismático. 2 colorido, brillante.
**prison** (pri·šøn) *s.* prisión, cárcel; encierro: ~ *house*, cárcel; ~ *term*, condena [tiempo]; ~ *van*, coche celular.
**prison (to)** *tr.* encarcelar.
**prisoner** (pri·šnøʳ) *s.* preso; prisionero.
**pristine** (pri·stin) *adj.* prístino, primitivo.
**privacy** (prai·vasi) *s.* retiro, aislamiento, intimidad. 2 reserva, secreto.
**private** (-vit) *adj.* privado, personal, particular: ~ *affair*, asunto privado; ~ *hospital*, clínica. 2 reservado, confidencial. 3 secreto, excusado. 4 retirado, apartado, solo: *they wish to be* ~, quieren estar solos. 5 *in* ~, particularmente, en secreto. 6 *s.* soldado raso.
**privateer** (praivati·øʳ) *s.* MAR. corsario. 2 buque corsario.
**privateer (to)** *intr.* MAR. hacer el corso.
**privately** (prai·vitli) *adv.* privadamente. 2 reservadamente, secretamente.
**privation** (praivei·shøn) *s.* privación [carencia; necesidad].
**privative** (pri·vativ) *adj.* privativo [que causa o significa privación].
**privet** (pri·vit) *s.* BOT. alheña, ligustro.
**privilege** (pri·vilidȳ) *s.* privilegio. 2 prerrogativa; inmunidad, exención, derecho; honor.
**privilege (to)** *tr.* privilegiar. 2 eximir.
**privileged** (-d) *adj.* privilegiado.
**privily** (pri·vili) *adv.* privadamente; secretamente.
**privity** (pri·viti) *s.* conocimiento de algo reservado.
**privy** (pri·vi) *adj.* privado. | Ús. sólo en denominaciones como: ~ *council*, consejo privado; ~ *seal* (Ingl.) sello privado [del rey]. 2 oculto, secreto. 3 *privy to*, enterado; cómplice de.
**prize** (praiš) *s.* premio, recompensa: ~ *fighter*, boxeador profesional. 2 premio [de lotería]. 3 presa, captura. 4 presa, botín. 5 decomiso.

**prize (to)** *tr.* apreciar, estimar, valuar. *2* tener en estima. *3* apresar [un buque]. *4* alzaprimar.

**pro** (prou) *prep.* pro [por]; en pro de: ~ *forma*, COM. pro-forma: ~ *forma invoice*, factura pro-forma; ~ *rata*, a prorrata. *2 s.* pro, razón en favor: *the pros and the cons*, el pro y el contra. *3* fam. deportista profesional.

**probabilism** (pra·babilišm) *s.* probabilismo.

**probability** (prababi·liti) *s.* probabilidad. *2* verosimilitud.

**probable** (pra·babøl) *adj.* probable. *2* verosímil.

**probate** (prou·beit) *s.* DER. prueba legal de la validez de un testamento. *2* DER. copia auténtica de un testamento. *3 adj.* DER. testamentario.

**probation** (probei·shøn) *s.* probación; noviciado. *2* DER. libertad vigilada.

**probationer** (-ø') *s.* el que está a prueba. *2* novicio, delincuente en libertad vigilada.

**probative** (prou·bativ) *adj.* de prueba. *2* probatorio.

**probe** (proub) *s.* CIR. tienta, sonda, cala. *2* exploración, sondeo.

**probe (to)** *tr.* CIR. tentar, sondar. *2* examinar a fondo, sondear.

**probity** (prou·biti) *s.* probidad.

**problem** (pra·bløm) *s.* problema.

**problematic (al** (prablømæ·tik(al) *adj.* problemático. *2* enigmático.

**proboscidean, -dian** (proubøsi·dian) *adj.-s.* ZOOL. proboscídeo.

**proboscis** (proba·sis) *s.* ZOOL. probóscide, trompa.

**procedure** (prosi·dÿø') *s.* proceder. *2* procedimiento. *3* marcha [de una operación, etc.]. *4* DER. procedimiento, tramitación.

**proceed (to)** (prosɪ·d) *intr.* proseguir, seguir adelante. *2* proceder, provenir. *3* proceder, obrar; pasar a [hacer algo]. *4* DER. actuar, proceder: *to ~ against*, proceder contra.

**proceeding** (-ing) *s.* proceder, procedimiento. *2* marcha, proceso. *3* diligencia, trámite. *4 pl.* actas. *5* DER. actuaciones, autos.

**proceeds** (prou·sidš) *s. pl.* producto, beneficios.

**process** (pra·ses) *s.* proceso, progreso, marcha, transcurso: *in ~ of time*, con el tiempo. *2* proceso [serie de fenómenos, operaciones, etc.]: *in ~ of construction*, en construcción. *3* procedimiento, sistema. *4* ANAT., ZOOL., BOT. apófisis, protuberancia, apéndice. *5* IMPR. procedimiento fotomecánico. *6* DER. auto, citación; proceso.

**process (to)** *intr.* ir en procesión. *2 tr.* procesar, citar. *3* fotograbar. *4* IND. preparar por algún procedimiento especial.

**processal** (-sal) *adj.* DER. procesal.

**procession** (-shøn) *s.* procesión. *2* cortejo, desfile; cabalgata. *3* marcha, curso.

**processional** (-al) *adj.* procesional. *2 s.* procesionario.

**processionary** (-eri) *adj.* procesional. *2* ENT. ~ *moth*, procesionaria.

**proclaim (to)** (proklei·m) *tr.* proclamar. *2* promulgar. *3* pregonar. *4* proscribir, poner fuera de la ley.

**proclamation** (praklamei·shøn) *s.* proclamación; publicación. *2* proclama, bando, edicto.

**proclitic** (prokli·tik) *adj.* GRAM. proclítico.

**proclivity** (prokli·viti) *s.* proclividad.

**proconsul** (proka·nsøl) *s.* procónsul.

**proconsulate** (-nsiulit), **proconsulship** (-nsølship) *s.* proconsulado.

**procrastinate (to)** (prokræ·stineit) *tr.* diferir, apla-

zar. *2 intr.* pasar el tiempo sin obrar, sin decidirse.

**procrastination** (-ei·shøn) *s.* dilación, demora.

**procreate (to)** (prou·krieit) *tr.* procrear.

**procreation** (-ei·shøn) *s.* procreación.

**procreator** (prou·krieitø') *s.* procreador.

**proctor** (pra·ktø') *s.* DER. especie de procurador o abogado. *2* censor [de una universidad].

**procumbent** (prokø·mbent) *adj.* postrado, inclinado. *2* BOT. rastrero.

**procurable** (prokiu·rabøl) *adj.* asequible.

**procuration** (prakiurei·shøn) *s.* DER. procuración, poder. *2* negociación, gestión. *3* alcahuetería.

**procurator** (pra·kiureitø') *m.* procurador, apoderado.

**procure (to)** *tr.* lograr, obtener. *2* obtener o proporcionar para un trato ilícito. *3 intr.* alcahuetear.

**procurement** (-mønt) *s.* obtención, consecución. *2* gestión, manejo.

**procurer** (prokiu·rø') *s.* alcahuete, tercero.

**procuress** (-ris) *f.* alcahueta.

**prod** (prad) *s.* pincho, aguijada. *2* aguijonazo.

**prod (to)** *tr.* pinchar, picar, aguijonear. ¶ Pret. y p. p.: *prodded*; ger.: *-dding*.

**prodigal** (pra·digal) *adj.-s.* pródigo.

**prodigality** (pradigæ·liti) *s.* prodigalidad.

**prodigious** (prodi·dÿøs) *adj.* prodigioso, portentoso. *2* enorme, inmenso.

**prodigy** (pra·didÿi) *s.* prodigio, portento, maravilla.

**produce** (prodiu·s) *s.* producto, producción. *2* productos agrícolas.

**produce (to)** *tr.* presentar, exhibir. *2* producir. *3* criar, generar. *4* presentar al público; poner en escena. *5* GEOM. extender, prolongar.

**producer** (-ø') *s.* productor: *producer's goods*, ECON. bienes de producción. *2* TEAT. director. *3* CINE. productor.

**product** (pro·døkt) *s.* producto, producción. *2* resultado, efecto. *3* MAT., QUÍM. producto.

**productile** (-til) *adj.* extensible, dúctil.

**production** (-shøn) *s.* producción. *2* TEAT. dirección [escénica].

**productive** (-tiv) *adj.* productivo. *2* productor. *3* fértil, fecundo.

**productivity** (prodøkti·viti) *s.* productividad. *2* fertilidad.

**proem** (prou·em) *s.* proemio, prólogo.

**proemial** (prou·mial) *adj.* proemial.

**profanation** (profanei·shøn) *s.* profanación.

**profane** (profei·n) *adj.* profano. *2* irreverente, sacrílego, blasfemo. *3 s.* profano [no entendido].

**profane (to)** *tr.* profanar. *2* prostituir, envilecer.

**profaner** (profei·nø') *s.* profanador.

**profanity** (profæ·niti) *s.* profanidad. *2* irreverencia, blasfemia, reniego.

**profess (to)** (profe·s) *tr.* profesar. *2* declarar, confesar: *to ~ oneself a Catholic*, declararse católico. *3 intr.* profesar [en una orden]. *4* profesar [ser profesor].

**professed** (-t) *adj.* declarado. *2* ostensible. *3* alegado, supuesto. *4* profeso.

**profession** (-shøn) *s.* profesión. *2* declaración, manifestación. *3* fe, religión.

**professional** (-shønal) *adj.-s.* profesional.

**professionalism** (-išm) *s.* profesionalismo.

**professor** (profe·sø') *s.* el que profesa o declara. *2* profesor, catedrático de Universidad.

**professorate** (-eit) *s.* profesorado.

**professorship** (-ship) *s.* profesorado, cátedra.

**proffer** (pra·før) *s.* oferta, ofrecimiento, proposición.
**proffer (to)** *tr.* ofrecer, brindar, proponer.
**proficiency** (profi·shønsi) *s.* pericia, habilidad.
**proficient** (-shønt) *adj.* perito, diestro, versado.
**profile** (prou·fail) *s.* perfil, contorno. 2 perfil [postura]: *in* ~, de perfil.
**profile (to)** *tr.* dibujar de perfil; perfilar.
**profit** (pra·fit) *s.* provecho, ventaja, utilidad. 2 ganancia, beneficio; interés, renta: ~ *and loss*, COM. ganancias y pérdidas; ~ *sharing*, participación en los beneficios.
**profit (to)** *tr.* servir, aprovechar, ser útil a. 2 *intr.* aprovecharse, beneficiarse; adelantar, mejorar: *to* ~ *by*, aprovechar, sacar partido de.
**profitable** (-abøl) *adj.* provechoso, beneficioso, útil, lucrativo.
**profiteer** (prafiti·ø) *s.* explotador, logrero, acaparador.
**profiteer (to)** *intr.* logrear; aprovecharse de las circunstancias de un país para obtener beneficios excesivos.
**profitless** (pra·fitlis) *adj.* infructuoso.
**profligacy** (pra·fligasi) *s.* libertinaje, disolución.
**profligate** (pra·figleit) *adj.-s.* libertino, disoluto.
**profound** (profau·nd) *adj.* profundo. 2 hondo. 3 abstruso.
**profundity** (profø·nditi) *s.* profundidad, hondura.
**profuse** (profiu·s) *adj.* profuso. 2 pródigo, generoso.
**profusion** (profiu·ŷøn) *s.* profusión. 2 prodigalidad.
**progenitor** (prodŷe·nitø) *s.* progenitor.
**progeniture** (prodŷe·nichø), **progeny** (pra·dŷini) *s.* prole, descendencia, linaje.
**prognathism** (pra·gnazišm) *s.* prognatismo.
**prognosis** (pragnou·sis) *s.* prognosis. 2 MED. pronóstico.
**prognostic** (pragna·stik) *s.* pronóstico, presagio.
**prognosticate (to)** (-eit) *tr.* pronosticar.
**prognosticator** (-ø) *s.* pronosticador.
**program** (prou·græm) *s.* (E.U.) PROGRAMME.
**programme** *s.* (Ingl.) programa. 2 plan.
**programming** (-ing) *s.* programación.
**progress** (prou·gres) *s.* progreso. 2 progresos. 3 marcha, curso, carrera.
**progress (to)** *intr.* progresar. 2 marchar, avanzar. 3 *tr.* hacer progresar.
**progression** (progre·shøn) *s.* progresión, progreso; curso, marcha. 2 MAT., MÚS. progresión.
**progressist** (-sist) *s.* progresista.
**progressive** (-siv) *adj.* progresivo.
**prohibit (to)** (prouji·bit) *tr.* prohibir. 2 impedir.
**prohibition** (proujibi·shøn) *s.* prohibición. 2 (E.U.) prohibición de la fabricación y venta de bebidas alcohólicas: ~ *law*, ley seca.
**prohibitionism** (-išm) *s.* prohibicionismo.
**prohibitive** (prouji·bitiv) *adj.* prohibitivo.
**project** (prodŷe·kt) *s.* proyecto, plan, traza, idea.
**project (to)** *tr.* proyectar, idear. 2 proyectar [sombra, etc.], arrojar, despedir. 3 GEOM. proyectar. 4 *intr.* volar, salir fuera, sobresalir, resaltar.
**projectile** (-til) *adj.* proyectante. 2 arrojadizo. 3 *s.* proyectil.
**projection** (-shøn) *s.* proyección: ~ *machine*, CINE proyector. 2 proyecto, planeamiento. 3 saliente, resalte.
**projector** (-tø) *s.* proyectista, arbitrista. 2 proyector, aparato de proyecciones.
**projecture** (-chø) *s.* ARQ. proyectura, vuelo.

**prolegomenon** (prouliga·menan), *pl.* **-na** (-na) *s.* prolegómeno.
**proletarian** (proulite·rian) *adj.-s.* proletario.
**proletariate** (-riæt) *s.* proletariado.
**proliferate (to)** (proli·føreit) *tr.* BIOL. multiplicar [células, etc.]. 2 *intr.* proliferar.
**proliferation** (proliførei·shøn) *s.* proliferación.
**prolific (al** (proli·fik(al) *adj.* prolífico.
**prolix** (pro·liks) *adj.* prolijo, difuso. 2 pesado, latoso.
**prolixity** (proli·ksiti) *s.* prolijidad.
**prolocutor** (prola·kiutø) *s.* portavoz; representante. 2 presidente [de ciertas asambleas].
**prologize (to)** (prou·løgaiš) *tr.* prologar.
**prologue** (prou·lag) *s.* prólogo.
**prolong (to)** (prolo·ng) *tr.* prolongar, extender, continuar. 2 *intr.* dilatarse, entretenerse.
**prolongation** (prolongei·shøn) *s.* prolongación; continuación.
**promenade** (pramina·d) *s.* paseo [acción, lugar]: ~ *deck*, MAR. cubierta de paseo.
**promenade (to)** *intr.* pasear, pasearse. 2 *tr.* pasear. 3 pasearse por.
**Prometheus** (promı·ziøs) *n. pr.* MIT. Prometeo.
**prominence, -cy** (pra·minøns, -si) *s.* prominencia. 2 eminencia, altura. 3 relieve, distinción, eminencia.
**prominent** (-ønt) *adj.* prominente, saliente: ~ *eyes*, ojos saltones. 2 visible, notable. 3 distinguido, eminente.
**promiscuity** (pramiskiu·iti) *s.* promiscuidad.
**promiscuous** (prami·skiuøs) *adj.* promiscuo.
**promise** (pra·mis) *s.* promesa, promisión, ofrecimiento, palabra dada: *to break one's* ~, faltar a la palabra dada. 2 promesa, augurio.
**promise (to)** *tr.-intr.* prometer: *Promised Land*, Tierra prometida o de promisión.
**promising** (-ing) *adj.* prometiente. 2 prometedor, halagüeño.
**promissory** (-ori) *adj.* promisorio. 2 COM. ~ *note*, pagaré.
**promontory** (pra·møntori) *s.* promontorio.
**promote (to)** (prømou·t) *tr.* promover, adelantar, ascender. 2 promover, fomentar. 3 fundar, organizar [una empresa].
**promoter** (-tø) *s.* promotor, promovedor. 2 organizador de empresas industriales, etc.
**promotion** (-shøn) *s.* promoción.
**prompt** (prampt) *adj.* pronto, presto, listo, puntual: ~ *payment*, pronto pago; *for* ~ *cash*, al contado. 2 *s.* plazo para pagar una factura.
**prompt (to)** *tr.* mover, incitar, inducir, impulsar. 2 dictar, sugerir, soplar, apuntar. 3 TEAT. apuntar.
**prompter** (-ø) *s.* TEAT. apuntador, traspunte: *prompter's box*, concha.
**promptitude** (pra·mptitiud) *s.* prontitud, presteza. 2 puntualidad, diligencia.
**promulgate (to)** (promø·lgeit) *tr.* promulgar, publicar.
**pronation** (pronei·shøn) *s.* pronación.
**pronator** (-tø) *s.* ANAT. músculo pronador.
**prone** (proun) *adj.* prono, inclinado [a una cosa]. 2 prono, boca abajo. 3 inclinado, pendiente.
**prong** (prang) *s.* gajo, púa, diente, punta [de horca, tenedor, etc.]. 2 horca, horcón.
**pronged** (pra·ngd) *adj.* provisto de gajos o púas.
**pronominal** (prøna·minal) *adj.* GRAM. pronominal.
**pronoun** (prou·naun) *s.* GRAM. pronombre.
**pronounce (to)** (prønau·ns) *tr.* pronunciar [palabras, sentencias]. 2 declarar: *to* ~ *one a brave*

*man*, declarar que uno es un valiente. *3 intr.* pronunciarse [en pro o en contra].
**pronounced** (-t) *adj.* pronunciado, marcado, decidido.
**pronouncement** (-mønt) *s.* juicio, opinión. *2* declaración, proclama, manifiesto.
**pronunciamiento** (prønønšiamie·ntou) *s.* pronunciamiento militar.
**pronunciation** (-siei·shøn) *s.* pronunciación.
**proof** (pruf) *s.* prueba, demostración. *2* prueba, ensayo, experimento: *to put to the* ~, poner a prueba. *3* graduación normal de las bebidas alcohólicas. *4* DER., MAT., IMPR., FOT. prueba. *5 adj.* de prueba o pruebas. *6* a prueba [de], resistente [a]: *to be* ~ *against*, estar hecho a prueba de, ser resistente a. *7* de graduación alcohólica normal.
**proofreader** (-rɪdøʳ) *s.* IMPR. corrector de pruebas.
**proofreading** (-ing) *s.* IMPR. corrección de pruebas.
**prop** (prap) *s.* puntal, paral, tentemozo; apoyo, sostén. *2* MIN. entibo. *3* AGR. rodrigón.
**prop (to)** *tr.* apuntalar, sostener, apoyar. *2* MIN. entibar. *3* AGR. rodrigar. ¶ Pret. y p. p.: *propped;* ger.: *propping.*
**propaganda** (prapagæ·nda) *s.* propaganda.
**propagandist** (-dist) *s.* propagandista.
**propagandize** (-daiš) *tr.-intr.* hacer propaganda de o en.
**propagate (to)** (pra·pageit) *tr.* propagar. *2* espaciar,difundir. *3 intr.* propagarse.
**propagation** (-eishøn) *s.* propagación.
**propagator** (pra·pageitøʳ) *s.* propagador.
**proparoxytone** (proupæra·ksitoun) *adj.-s.* GRAM. proparoxítino.
**propel (to)** (prope·l) *tr.* propulsar, impeler, mover. ¶ Pret. y p. p.: *propelled;* ger.: *propelling.*
**propellent** (-ønt) *adj.-s.* propulsor, motor.
**propeller** (-øʳ) *s.* propulsor. *2* hélice [de buque o avión].
**propensity** (prope·nsiti) *s.* propensión, tendencia. *2* inclinación, afición.
**proper** (pra·pøʳ) *adj.* propio, característico, peculiar. *2* propio, a propósito, apropiado. *3* exacto, correcto [en su uso, aplicación, etc.]. *4* propiamente dicho. *5* GRAM. propio: ~ *noun*, nombre propio. *6* MAT. propia [fracción]. *7* correcto, decoroso, conveniente; exigente en cuestiones de decoro o etiqueta. *8 s.* propio [de la misa].
**properly** (-li) *adv.* propiamente: *more* ~, mejor dicho. *2* convenientemente. *4* decorosamente.
**property** (pra·pøʳti) *s.* propiedad [atributo, cualidad]. *2* propiedad [derecho]. *3* propiedad, finca. *4* fortuna, bienes, posesiones. *5 pl.* TEAT. guardarropía, accesorios.
**prophecy** (pra·føsi) *s.* profecía.
**prophesy (to)** (pra·føsai) *tr.-intr.* profetizar, predecir. ¶ Pret. y p. p.: *prophesied.*
**prophet** (pra·fit) *s.* profeta.
**prophetess** (-is) *s.* profetisa.
**prophetic (al** (profe·tik(al)) *adj.* profético.
**prophylactic** (proufilæ·ktik) *adj.* profiláctico.
**prophylaxis** (-sis) *s.* profilaxis.
**propinquity** (propi·nkuiti) *s.* propincuidad. *2* afinidad. *3* parentesco.
**propitiate (to)** (propi·shieit) *intr.* propiciar.
**propitiation** (-ei·shøn) *s.* propiciación.
**propitiatory** (propi·shiatori) *adj.* propiciatorio.
**propitious** (-shøs) *adj.* propicio. *2* favorable, feliz.
**proponent** (propou·nønt) *s.* proponedor, proponente.
**proportion** (prøpo·ʳshøn) *s.* proporción [relación, correspondencia debidas]; armonía, correla-

ción: *in* ~ *as*, a medida que; *in* ~ *to*, a medida de; *out of* ~, desproporcionado. *2* MAT. proporción. *3 pl.* proporciones, tamaño.
**proportion (to)** *tr.* proporcionar [una cosa a otra; disponer con proporción o armonía].
**proportionable** (-abøl) *adj.* proporcionado.
**proportional** (-al) *adj.* proporcional. *2 s.* MAT. término de una proporción.
**proportionate** (-it) *adj.* proporcionado.
**proportionate (to)** (-eit) *tr.* proporcionar, ajustar.
**proportioned** (-d) *adj.* proporcionado [bien o mal].
**proportionless** (-lis) *adj.* desproporcionado.
**proposal** (propou·šal) *s.* propuesta, proposición. *2* oferta. *3* declaración; proposición de matrimonio.
**propose (to)** (prøpou·š) *tr.* proponer. *2* proponerse, tener intención de. *3* brindar [por]. *4 intr.* declararse [a una mujer].
**proposer** (-øʳ) *s.* proponedor, proponente.
**proposition** (prapøši·shøn) *s.* proposición, propuesta. *2* LÓG., MAT., RET. proposición. *3* fam. (E.U.) asunto, negocio, cosa, ocupación, etc.
**propound (to)** (prøpau·nd) *tr.* proponer. *2* presentar, plantear.
**proprietary** (prøprai·øteri) *adj.* propietario. *2* de propiedad. *3* registrado [específico]. *4 s.* propiedad, pertenencia. *5* propietarios [en general].
**proprietor** (-øtøʳ) *s.* propietario, dueño, amo.
**proprietorship** (-øtøʳship) *s.* propiedad [dominio sobre una cosa].
**proprietress** (-øtris) *f.* propietaria.
**propriety** (-øti) *s.* propiedad, cualidad de apropiado. *2* corrección, decoro, decencia. *3 pl.* reglas de conducta, urbanidad.
**propulsion** (propø·lshøn) *s.* propulsión. *2* impulso.
**propulsive** (-siv) *adj.* propulsor, impelente.
**pro rata** (prou rei·ta) *adv.* a prorrata.
**prorate (to)** (prou·reit) *tr.* (E.U.) prorratear.
**prorogation** (prourougei·shøn) *s.* aplazamiento, suspensión.
**prorogue (to)** (prourou·g) *tr.* aplazar, suspender.
**prosaic** (prosei·ic) *adj.* prosaico.
**prosaist** (-ist) *s.* prosista. *2* persona prosaica.
**proscenium** (prosi·niøm) *s.* TEAT. proscenio.
**proscribe (to)** (proskrai·b) *tr.* proscribir.
**proscription** (proscri·pshøn) *s.* proscripción.
**proscriptive** (-tiv) *adj.* proscriptivo.
**prose** (prouš) *s.* prosa. *2* discurso pesado, lata.
**prose (to)** *tr.* poner en prosa. *2 intr.* escribir o hablar en estilo pesado.
**prosecute** (pra·sikiut) *tr.* proseguir, seguir, continuar. *2* ejercer [una profesión o actividad]. *3* DER. procesar, enjuiciar, demandar.
**prosecution** (-shøn) *s.* prosecución. *2* DER. proceso, demanda, acusación. *3* DER. parte actora. *4* DER. ministerio fiscal.
**prosecutor** (-tøʳ) *s.* DER. demandante; acusador privado. *2* DER. *public* ~, fiscal.
**proselyte** (pra·sølait) *s.* prosélito.
**proselytism** (-litišm) *s.* proselitismo.
**prosenchyma** (prase·nkima) *s.* BOT., ZOOL. prosénquima.
**prosily** (prou·šili) *adv.* prosaicamente. *2* pesadamente, fastidiosamente.
**prosodic** (prasa·dik) *adj.* métrico [relativo a la métrica].
**prosody** (pra·sødi) *s.* métrica.
**prosopopoeia** (prousoupøpi·a) RET. prosopopeya.
**prospect** (pra·spekt) *s.* perspectiva, paisaje, panorama. *2* mirada a lo lejos, en el futuro. *3* expectativa, esperanza, probabilidad, perspectiva: *in*

~, en perspectiva, probable; *man of good prospects*, hombre de porvenir. *4* situación, orientación. *5* MIN. indicio de veta.
**prospect (to)** *tr.* explorar [terrenos] en busca de oro, petróleo, etc. *2 intr. to ~ for*, buscar [oro, petróleo, etc.]
**prospecting** (-ing) *s.* MIN. prospección.
**prospective** (-tiv) *adj.* probable, posible, en perspectiva, futuro. *2 s.* vista, perspectiva.
**prospector** (-tøʳ) *s.* MIN. buscador.
**prospectus** (-tøs) *s.* prospecto, programa.
**prosper (to)** (pra·spøʳ) *tr.-intr.* prosperar.
**prosperity** (praspe·riti) *s.* prosperidad.
**prosperous** (pra·spørøs) *adj.* próspero. *2* favorable.
**prostate** (pra·steit) *s.* ANAT. próstata.
**prosthesis** (pra·szesis) *s.* CIR., GRAM. prótesis.
**prostitute** (pra·stitiut) *s.* prostituta.
**prostitute (to)** *tr.* prostituir. *2 intr.* prostituirse.
**prostitution** (prastitiu·shøn) *s.* prostitución.
**prostrate** (pra·streit) *adj.* postrado, prosternado. *2* postrado, abatido. *3* BOT. tendido.
**prostrate (to)** *tr.* postrar. *2* abatir. *3* arruinar. *4 intr.-ref.* postrarse, prosternarse.
**prostration** (prastrei·shøn) *s.* prostración.
**prosy** (prou·ši) *adj.* prosaico. *2* latoso, insulso.
**protagonist** (protæ·gønist) *s.* protagonista.
**protasis** (pra·tasis) *s.* GRAM. prótasis.
**protean** (prou·tian) *adj.* proteico.
**protect (to)** (prøte·kt) *tr.* proteger.
**protection** (-shøn) *s.* protección. *2* salvoconducto.
**protectionism** (-shønism) *s.* EC. POL. proteccionismo.
**protective** (-tiv) *adj.* protector. *2* proteccionista. *3 s.* protección, resguardo [cosa que protege].
**protector** (-tøʳ) *s.* protector.
**protectorate** (-tørit) *s.* protectorado.
**protectress** (-tris) *s.* protectora.
**proteic** (prou·tiik) *adj.* QUÍM. proteico.
**protein** (prou·tiin) *s.* QUÍM. proteína.
**pro-tempore** *adj.* interino.
**protest** (prou·test) *s.* protesta: *under ~*, protestando, con reservas. *2* protestación. *3* DER. protesto.
**protest (to)** (prote·st) *tr.* protestar [declarar, afirmar, confesar]. *2* protestar de o contra; recusar. *3* DER. protestar [una letra]. *4 intr.* protestar, hacer protestas.
**Protestant** (pra·tistant) *adj.-s.* protestante.
**Protestantism** (-išm) *s.* protestantismo.
**protestation** (pratestei·shøn) *s.* protesta; protestación.
**protester** (prote·støʳ) *s.* el que protesta.
**prothesis** (pra·zisis) *s.* CIR., GRAM. prótesis.
**prothonotary** (proza·nøteri) *s.* protonotario.
**prothorax** (prozou·ræks) *s.* ENT. protórax.
**protocol** (prou·tøkal) *s.* protocolo.
**protocol (to)** *tr.* protocolizar.
**protomartyr** (proutøma·ʳtøʳ) *s.* protomártir.
**proton** (prou·tan) *s.* Fís. y QUÍM. protón.
**protoplasm** (prou·tøplæsm) *s.* BIOL. protoplasma.
**prototype** (-taip) *s.* prototipo, arquetipo.
**protoxid** (prouta·ksaid) *s.* QUÍM. protóxido.
**protozoan** (proutøšo·uan) *adj.-s.* ZOOL. protozoo, protozoario.
**protract (to)** (protræ·kt) *tr.* alargar, prolongar, dilatar [esp. en el tiempo]. *2* levantar [un plano] por medio del transportador.
**protractile** (-til) *adj.* protráctil.
**protractor** (-tøʳ) *s.* prolongador. *2* transportador [instrumento]. *3* ANAT. músculo extensor.

**protrude (to)** (protru·d) *tr.* sacar, hacer salir o sobresalir. *2 intr.* salir fuera, sobresalir.
**protrusion** (protru·ẙøn) *s.* protrusión.
**protuberance** (protiu·børans) *s.* protuberancia.
**protuberant** (-ant) *adj.* prominente, saliente.
**protuberate (to)** (-reit) *intr.* sobresalir, abultar.
**proud** (praud) *adj.* orgulloso, soberbio, altanero, arrogante, engreído. *2* orgulloso, satisfecho, ufano: *to be ~ of*, enorgullecerse de. *3* magnífico, espléndido, noble, bello.
**prove (to)** (pruv) *tr.* probar, demostrar, evidenciar, justificar. *2* probar, experimentar, poner a prueba, comprobar. *3* establecer la validez de [un testamento]. *4* ARIT. hacer la prueba de. *5* IMPR. sacar una prueba de. *6 intr.* salir, resultar [bien, mal, etc.]; demostrar que se es [apto, etc.]. ¶ P. p.: *proved* o *proven*.
**provenance** (prou·vønans) *s.* PROVENIENCE.
**Provençal** (prouvansa·l) *adj.-s.* provenzal.
**Provence** (prouva·nš) *n. pr.* GEOGR. Provenza.
**provender** (pra·vøndøʳ) *s.* pienso, forraje.
**provenience** (provi·niøns) *s.* origen, procedencia.
**proverb** (pra·vøʳb) *s.* proverbio, refrán, sentencia. *2* nombre, pers. o cosa proverbial.
**proverbial** (prouvø·ʳbial) *adj.* proverbial. *2* sentencioso.
**provide (to)** (prøvai·d) *tr.* proveer, abastecer, equipar: *to ~ with*, proveer de. *2* suministrar, proporcionar. *3* estipular. *4 intr. to ~ for*, proveer a; sufragar los gastos de; dotar, colocar, proveer de medios de vida; estipular. *5 to ~ against*, prevenir, precaverse contra.
**provided** (-id) *conj.* ~ *that*, con tal que, siempre que, a condición de o que.
**providence** (pra·vidøns) *s.* providencia, previsión, economía. *2* providencia divina. *3* (con may.) la Providencia, Dios.
**provident** (-nt) *adj.* próvido, providente, previsor. *2* frugal, económico.
**providential** (pravide·nshal) *adj.* providencial.
**provider** (prøvai·døʳ) *s.* proveedor.
**province** (pra·vins) *s.* provincia. *2* región, distrito. *3* esfera, campo [de actividad, etc.]. *4* competencia, incumbencia.
**provincial** (prøvi·nshal) *adj.* provincial. *2* provinciano, rústico. *3 s.* provincial. *4* provinciano.
**provision** (prøvi·ẙøn) *s.* provisión, prevención. *2* aprovisionamiento. *3* medida, disposición, providencia: *to make ~ for*, proveer a; asegurar el porvenir de. *4* cláusula, estipulación. *5 pl.* provisiones.
**provision (to)** *tr.* aprovisionar, abastecer.
**provisional** (-al) *adj.* provisional.
**proviso** (prøvai·šou) *s.* estipulación, condición, requisito.
**provisory** (prøvai·šori) *adj.* provisorio. *2* condicional.
**provocation** (pravøkei·shøn) *s.* provocación. *2* cosa que irrita o exaspera.
**provocative** (prøva·kativ) *adj.* provocativo. *2* irritante, exasperador.
**provoke (to)** (prøvou·k) *tr.* provocar. *2* irritar, encolerizar. *3 intr.* ser irritante, causar enojo.
**provoking** (-ing) *adj.* provocativo. *2* irritante, exasperador.
**provost** (pra·vøst) *s.* preboste. *2* prepósito, deán. *3* (Ingl.) director de un colegio universitario.
**prow** (prau) *s.* proa. *2* MAR. tajamar.
**prowess** (prau·is) *s.* valor, bizarría. *2* proeza. *3* destreza.

**prowl (to)** (praul) *tr.-intr.* rondar [para robar, hacer presa, etc.], andar acechando, merodear.

**proximal** (pra·ksimal) *adj.* BIOL. proximal.

**proximate** (-it) *adj.* próximo, inmediato.

**proximity** (praksi·miti) *s.* proximidad.

**proximo** (pra·ksimou) *adv.* del próximo mes.

**proxy** (pra·ksi) *s.* procuración, poder, delegación: *by ~*, por poderes. 2 apoderado, delegado.

**prude** (prud) *s.* remilgada, mojigata, gazmoña.

**prudence** (pru·døns) *s.* prudencia.

**prudent** (-dønt) *adj.* prudente.

**prudential** (prude·nshal) *adj.* prudencial.

**prudery** (pru·døri) *s.* remilgo, mojigatería, gazmoñería, pudibundez.

**prudish** (-ish) *adj.* remilgado, mojigato, gazmoño.

**prune** (prun) *s.* ciruela pasa; ciruela.

**prune (to)** *tr.* podar, escamondar, mondar, recortar. 2 TO PREEN.

**pruning hook** o **knife** (-ing) *s.* podadera, podón.

**prurience, -cy** (pru·riøns, -si) *s.* comezón, prurito. 2 lascivia.

**prurient** (-ønt) *adj.* lascivo. 2 deseoso, curioso.

**prurigo** (prurai·gou) *s.* MED. prurigo.

**Prussian** (prø·shan) *adj.-s.* prusiano.

**prussic** (prø·sik) *adj.* prúsico.

**pry** (prai) *s.* atisbo, fisgoneo. 2 curioso, fisgón, entremetido. 3 palanca, alzaprima.

**pry (to)** *intr.* espiar, acechar, fisgar, escudriñar, entremeterse. | Gralte. con *into*. 2 *tr.* alzaprimar, apalancar; *to ~ open*, abrir, forzar [con palanca]. 3 *to ~ out*, arrancar, obtener.

**prying** (prai·ing) *adj.* curioso, fisgón, entrometido.

**psalm** (sam) *s.* salmo.

**psalmist** (sa·mist) *s.* salmista.

**psalmody** (sæ·lmødi) *s.* salmodia.

**psalter** (so·ltø[r]) *s.* salterio [libro].

**psaltery** (so·ltøri) *s.* MÚS. salterio.

**pseudo** (siu·dou) *adj.* pseudo, seudo.

**pseudonym** (siu·dønim) *s.* seudónimo.

**pshaw** (šho) *interj.* ¡bah!

**psi** (si) *s.* psi [letra griega].

**psoas** (sou·æs) *s.* ANAT. psoas [músculo].

**psychasthenia** (saikæszı·nia) *s.* MED. psicastenia.

**Psyche** (sai·ki) *n. pr.* MIT., Psique, Psiquis. 2 *s.* (con min.) psiquis, el alma.

**psychiater** (saikai·ætø[r]), **psychiatrist** (-trist) *s.* psiquiatra.

**psychiatry** (saikai·ætri) *s.* psiquiatría.

**psychic (al** (sai·kik(al) *adj.* psíquico, anímico.

**psychoanalysis** (saikoanæ·lisis) *s.* psicoanálisis.

**psychoanalyst** (saikoæ·nalist) *s.* psicoanalista.

**psychologic (al** (saikola·dyik(al) *adj.* psicológico.

**psychologist** (saika·lodyist) *s.* psicólogo.

**psychology** (saika·lodyi) *s.* psicología.

**psychometrics** (saikome·triks), **psychometry** (saika·metri), *s.* psicometría.

**psychopath** (si·kopæz) *s.* psicópata.

**psychopaty** (saika·pazi) *s.* psicopa.

**psychosis** (saikou·sis), *pl.* **-ses** (-siš) *s.* MED. psicosis.

**psychotherapy** (saikoze·rapi) *s.* MED. psicoterapia.

**ptarmigan** (ta·[r]migøn) *s.* ORN. perdiz blanca.

**pteridophyte** (te·ridofait) *s.* BOT. pteridofita.

**Ptolemaic** (talømei·k) *adj.* ptolemaico.

**Ptolemy** (ta·lømi) *n. pr.* Tolomeo.

**pub** (pøb) *s.* pop. (Ingl.) cervecería, taberna.

**puberty** (piu·bø[r]ti) *s.* pubertad.

**pubes** (piu·bis) *s.* ANAT. pubis [bajo vientre].

**pubescent** (piube·sønt) *adj.* pubescente. 2 púber.

**pubis** (piu·bis) *s.* ANAT. pubis [parte del hueso coxal].

**public** (pø·blic) *adj.* público: *~ health*, higiene pública, sanidad; *~ house*, posada; (Ingl.) cervecería, taberna; *~ prosecutor*, DER. fiscal; *~ school* (Ingl.), escuela secundaria con internado, principalmente para clases pudientes; (Esc., E.U.) escuela controlada por el estado; *~ servant*, funcionario público; *~ works*, obras públicas. 2 general, universal. 3 *s.* el público: *in ~*, en público.

**publican** (pø·blikan) *s.* publicano. 2 (Ingl.) taberno, hostelero.

**publication** (pøblikei·søn) *s.* publicación. 2 edición [acción de editar]. 3 promulgación.

**publicist** (pø·blisist) *s.* publicista. 2 agente de publicidad.

**publicity** (pø·blisist) *s.* publicidad: *~ agent*, agente de publicidad; *~ office*, agencia de publicidad. 2 notoriedad.

**public-spirited** *adj.* cívico, patriótico.

**publish (to)** (pø·blish) *tr.* publicar. 2 editar; *publishing house*, casa editorial. 3 promulgar; difundir, propalar. 4 *to ~ the banns*, correr las amonestaciones.

**publisher** (-ø[r]) *s.* publicador. 2 editor.

**puce** (pius) *adj.-s.* color de pulga.

**puck** (pøk) *s.* duende. 2 disco de caucho usado en el hockey sobre hielo.

**pucker** (pø·kø[r]) *s.* arruga, pliegue, frunce, fruncido.

**pucker (to)** *tr.* arrugar, plegar, coger, fruncir.

**puckish** (-ish) *adj.* travieso.

**pudding** (pu·din) *s.* budín, pudín. 2 embuchado: *black ~*, morcilla. 3 GEOL. *~ stone*, pudinga.

**puddle** (pø·døl) *s.* charco, poza. 2 mezcla de arcilla y arena. 3 fig. confusión, lío.

**puddle (to)** *tr.* METAL. pudelar. 2 enlodar, enfangar. 3 ensuciar, enturbiar. 4 cubrir con una mezcla de arcilla y arena. 5 *intr.* patullar [en el lodo, etc.].

**puddly** (pø·dli) *adj.* encharcado, cenagoso.

**pudency** (piu·dønsi) *s.* recato, pudor.

**pudge** (pø·dy) *s.* fam. persona o cosa rechoncha, regordeta.

**pudgy** (-i) *adj.* rechoncho.

**pudicity** (piudi·siti) *s.* pudicicia, ardor.

**puericulture** (piuørikø·lchø[r]) *s.* puericultura.

**pueriliti** (piuøri·liti) *s.* puerilidad.

**puerperal** (piuø·[r]pøral) *adj.-m.* puerperal.

**Puerto Rican** (pue·[r]touri·kan) *adj.-s.* portorriqueño.

**Puerto Rico** (-kou) *n. pr.* GEOGR. Puerto Rico.

**puff** (pøf) *s.* soplo, resoplido, bufido: *~ of wind*, ráfaga de aire. 2 bocanada, fumarada, ventada. 3 coc. bollo: *~ paste*, pasta de hojaldre. 4 COST. bollo, bullón. 5 masa esponjada. 6 chupada [de cigarro]. 7 reclamo, bombo, elogio exagerado. 8 *puff* o *powder ~*, borla [para empolvarse]. 9 *interj.* ¡bah!

**puff (to)** *intr.* soplar, resoplar, jadear; echar bocanadas o fumaradas. 2 *to ~ up*, hincharse; ahuecarse. 3 *tr.* echar [aliento, aire, humo]; empujar, desvanecer, apagar, etc., con el soplo. 4 hacer jadear. 5 hinchar; ahuecar; abollonar. 6 engreír. 7 bombear, hacer el reclamo de. 8 empolvar [con borla].

**puffball** (-bol) *s.* BOT. bejín.

**puffery** (-øri) *s.* bombo, propaganda.

**puffin** (-in) *s.* ORN. alca, frailecillo.

**puffy** (-i) *adj.* que sopla a intervalos. 2 jadeante. 3 hinchado. 4 campanudo.

**pug** (pøg) *s.* barro amasado. 2 ZOOL. *pug* o *dog*, perro pequeño y de nariz chata.

**pugilism** (piu·dýlišm) *s.* pugilismo.
**pugilist** (-list) *s.* pugilista, púgil.
**pugnacious** (pøgnei·shøs) *adj.* pugnaz, belicoso.
**pugnacity** (pøgnæ·siti) *s.* pugnacidad.
**pug-nosed** *adj.* de nariz respingona. *2* chato [perro].
**puke (to)** (piuk) *tr.-intr.* vomitar.
**pulchritude** (pø·lkritiud) *s.* pulcritud, belleza.
**pule (to)** (piul) *intr.* gemir, llorar [con voz débil].
**pull** (pul) *s.* tirón, sacudida, tracción. *2* tirador [botón, cordón, etc.]. *3* subida, cuesta, ascensión difícil; esfuerzo [prolongado o penoso]. *4* atracción [fuerza que tira o atrae]. *5* trago, tiento. *6* chupada [a un cigarro, etc.]. *7* ventaja, superioridad. *8* influencia, aldabas. *9* acto de refrenar un caballo para que no gane [en una carrera].
**pull (to)** *tr.* tirar de, halar, estirar, arrastrar. *2* arrancar, sacar, extraer. *3* romper, desgarrar. *4* torcer, distender [un ligamento, etc.]. *5* beber; chupar. *6* DEP. refrenar un caballo para que no gane. *7* (E.U.) sacar [un arma]. *8 to* ~ *apart*, separar con violencia, arrancar. *9 to* ~ *a long face*, poner cara larga. *10 to* ~ *back*, tirar hacia atrás, hacer recular. *11 to* ~ *down*, derribar, demoler, bajar, rebajar, abatir. *12 to* ~ *in*, halar, cobrar [una cuerda]. *13 to* ~ *off*, llevar a cabo. *14 to* ~ *on*, ponerse [las medias, etc.]. *15 to* ~ *oneself together*, recobrarse, serenarse. *16 to* ~ *one's leg*, tomar el pelo a uno. *17 to* ~ *out*, arrancar, sacar. *18 to* ~ *the trigger*, apretar el gatillo. *19 to* ~ *through*, sacar de un apuro; llevar a cabo. *20 to* ~ *up*, arrancar; refrenar [un caballo]; detener, parar; reprender.
     *21 intr.* tirar con esfuerzo, dar un tirón, ejercer tracción; trabajar, esforzarse. *22 to* ~ *apart*, romperse [por tracción]. *23 to* ~ *at*, tirar de, dar chupadas [una pipa, etc.]; beber de. *24 to* ~ *in*, detenerse; entrar; llegar [un tren] a la estación. *25 to* ~ *on*, tirar de. *26 to* ~ *out*, salir, partir. *27 to* ~ *round*, restablecerse. *28 to* ~ *through*, salir de un apuro. *29 to* ~ *up*, alcanzar a los demás; detenerse, pararse.
**pullet** (pu·lit) *s.* ZOOL. polla [gallina joven].
**pulley** (pu·li) *s.* polea, garrucha, motón; aparejo; polea de transmisión, tambor.
**Pullman car** (pu·lmæn) *s.* FERROC. vagón Pullman.
**pull-over** *s.* pulóver, elástica, jersey.
**pullulate (to)** (pø·liuleit) *intr.* pulular.
**pulmonate** (pø·lmønit) *adj.* pulmonado.
**pulmotor** (pø·lmoutø<sup>r</sup>) *s.* MED. pulmón de acero.
**pulp** (pølp) *s.* pulpa. *2* pasta [de papel]. *3* ANAT. bulbo [de diente].
**pulpit** (pu·lpit) *s.* púlpito. *2* tribuna, tarima.
**pulpous** (pø·lpøs), **pulpy** (-pi) *adj.* pulposo, carnoso, mollar.
**pulsate (to)** (pø·lseit) *intr.* pulsar, latir. *2* vibrar, estar lleno de actividad, etc.
**pulsatile** (pø·lsatil) *adj.* pulsátil. *2* MÚS. de percusión.
**pulsation** (pølsei·shøn) *s.* pulsación, latido. *2* vida, vibración.
**pulse** (pøls) *s.* pulso. *2* latido, vibración, esfuerzo. *3* legumbres [garbanzos, lentejas, etc.].
**pulse (to)** *intr.* pulsar, latir. *2* vibrar.
**pulsimeter** (pølsi·mitø<sup>r</sup>) *s.* pulsímetro.
**pultaceous** (pøltei·shøs) *adj.* pultáceo.
**pulverization** (pølvørisei·shøn) *s.* pulverización.
**pulverize (to)** (pø·lvøraiš) *tr.* pulverizar.
**pulverizer** (pølvørai·šø<sup>r</sup>) *s.* pulverizador.

**pulverulent** (pølve·rulønt) *adj.* pulverulento, polvoriento.
**puma** (piu·ma) *s.* ZOOL. puma.
**pumice** o **pumice stone** (pø·mis) *s.* piedra pómez.
**pumice (to)** *tr.* apomazar.
**pummel (to)** *tr.* TO POMMEL.
**pump** (pømp) *s.* MEC. bomba [para fluidos]: *force* ~, bomba impelente; *suction* ~, bomba aspirante. *2* fuente alimentada por una bomba. *3* *gasoline* ~, surtidor de gasolina. *4 pl.* zapatos bajos, zapatillas.
**pump (to)** *tr.* impeler, lanzar, sacar, etc., con bomba o como una bomba. *2* sacar agua, aire, etc. [con bomba]. *3* inyectar aire, hinchar [con bomba o fuelle]. *4* sacar, obtener [noticias, dinero, etc.]. *5* sondear, sonsacar. *6 intr.* dar a la bomba. *7 tr.-intr.* mover o moverse de arriba abajo.
**pumper** (-ø<sup>r</sup>) *s.* el que acciona una bomba. *2* ganzúa, sonsacador.
**pumpkin** (-kin) *s.* BOT. calabaza; calabacera. *2* fam. (E.U.) personaje; cosa importante.
**pump-priming** *s.* (E.U.) ayuda económica del Estado al comercio, la industria, etc.
**pun** (pøn) *s.* retruécano, juego de palabras.
**pun (to)** *intr.* hacer retruécanos, jugar del vocablo.
**punch** (pønch) *s.* ponche: ~ *bowl*, ponchera. *2* puñada, puñetazo. *3* empuje, energía, vigor. *4* punzón; contrapunzón. *5* sacabocados; máquina de taladrar. *6* embutidera.
**punch (to)** *tr.* picar, aguijar. *2* perforar, marcar, embutir, remachar, etc., con punzón, sacabocados, etc. *3* apuñear, dar puñetazos a.
**Punch** *n. pr.* Polichinela: *Punch-and-Judy show*, función de títeres.
**puncheon** (-øn) *s.* punzón [para estampar].
**punchinello** (pønchine·lou) *s.* pulchinela; títere.
**punchy** (pø·nchi) *adj.* rechoncho.
**punctilio** (pønkti·liou) *s.* puntillo; detalle nimio.
**punctilious** (-liøs) *adj.* puntilloso, mirado, meticuloso, etiquetero.
**punctual** (pø·nkchual) *adj.* puntual, exacto.
**punctuality** (pønkchuæ·liti) *s.* puntualidad, exactitud, formalidad.
**punctuate (to)** (pø·nkchueit) *tr.* puntuar. *2* interrumpir a intervalos. *3* acentuar, hacer resaltar.
**punctuation** (-ei·shøn) *s.* GRAM. puntuación.
**puncture** (pø·nkchø<sup>r</sup>) *s.* puntura, pinchazo, picadura. *2* CIR. punción.
**puncture (to)** *tr.* punzar, pinchar, agujerear, picar.
**pundit** (pø·ndit) *s.* sabio indio. *2* desp. sabihondo.
**pungency** (pø·ndyønsi) *s.* picante, punta, sabor. *2* acrimonia, mordacidad. *3* agudeza, viveza.
**pungent** (-ønt) *adj.* picante. *2* acre, mordaz. *3* agudo, vivo, penetrante, pungente.
**Punic** (piu·nik) *adj.* púnico.
**punish (to)** (pø·nish) *tr.* castigar, penar.
**punisher** (-ø<sup>r</sup>) *s.* castigador.
**punishment** (-mønt) *s.* castigo. *2* vapuleo.
**punitive, -tory** (piu·nitiv, -tori) *adj.* de castigo.
**punk** (pønk) *s.* yesca; hupe. *2 adj.* zocato [fruto]. *3* pop. (E.U.) inferior, malo.
**punster** (pø·nstø<sup>r</sup>) *s.* equivoquista.
**punt** (pønt) *s.* batea, barca plana. *2* MAR. plancha de agua. *3* DEP. puntapié dado al balón en el aire.
**punt (to)** *tr.* mover [una batea] con percha. *2* dar un puntapié [al balón] en el aire. *3 intr.* ir en batea o barca plana. *5* apuntar [en el juego].
**punter** (-ø<sup>r</sup>) *s.* punto [que apuesta en el juego]. *2* el que mueve una batea o barca plana.

**puny** (piu·ni) *adj.* endeble, canijo. 2 pequeño, diminuto.

**pup** (pøp) *s.* cachorro.

**pup (to)** *intr.* parir [la perra].

**pupa** (piu·pa) *s.* ENT. ninfa, crisálida.

**pupil** (piu·pil) *s.* discípulo, alumno. 2 DER. pupilo. 3 ANAT. pupila.

**pupilage** (-idẏ) *s.* DER. pupilaje. 2 alumnado.

**puppet** (pø·pit) *s.* títere, muñeco; maniquí. 2 juguete, instrumento [de otro].

**puppy** (pø·pi) *s.* cachorro, perrito. 2 joven fatuo o casquivano; petimetre.

**purblind** (pø·ʳblaind) *adj.* cegato. 2 ciego [mentalmente].

**purchase** (pø·ʳchas) *s.* compra, adquisición. 3 MEC., MAR. acción de mover, tirar de, subir, etc., con algún medio mecánico; este mismo medio: palanca, aparejo, maniobra, etc.

**purchase (to)** *tr.* comprar, adquirir. 2 mover, tirar de, subir, etc., por medio de palanca, aparejo, etc.

**purchaser** (pø·ʳchasøʳ) *s.* comprador.

**purchasing power** (-ing) *s.* poder adquisitivo [de la moneda].

**pure** (piu·øʳ) *adj.* puro.

**purebred** (piuʳbre·d) *adj.* de pura raza.

**purée** (piurei·) *s.* COC. puré.

**purgation** (pøʳguei·shøn) *s.* purgamiento. 2 DER. purgación.

**purgative** (pø·ʳgativ) *adj.* purgativo. 2 *adj.-s.* MED. purgante.

**purgatory** (-tori) *s.* purgatorio.

**purge** (pø·ʳdẏ) *s.* purga, purgante. 2 purgación.

**purge (to)** *tr.* purgar, limpiar, purificar. 2 DER., MED., MEC. purgar. 3 *intr.* purgarse.

**purification** (piurifikei·shøn) *s.* purificación. 2 depuración.

**purificator** (-tøʳ) *s.* purificador.

**purifier** (piu·rifaiøʳ) *s.* purificador.

**purify (to)** (piu·rifai) *tr.* purificar. 2 *intr.* purificarse. ¶ Pret. y p. p.: *purified.*

**purism** (piu·rišm) *s.* purismo.

**purist** (-rist) *s.* purista.

**Puritan** (-ritan) *adj.-s.* puritano.

**puritanic (al** (piuritæ·nik(al) *adj.* puritano.

**Puritanism** (piu·ritanišm) *s.* puritanismo.

**purity** (-riti) *s.* pureza.

**purl** (pø·ʳl) *s.* murmurio del agua. 2 onda, rizo. 3 borde u orla rizada.

**purl (to)** *tr.* orlar, adornar con fleco o guarnición rizada. 2 *intr.* murmurar [los arroyos, etc.]. 3 ondular, arremolinarse.

**purline** (pø·ʳlin) *s.* ARQ. correa [de la armadura].

**purloin** (pøʳloi·n) *tr.* hurtar, robar, substraer.

**purloiner** (pøʳloi·nøʳ) *s.* ladrón.

**purple** (pø·ʳpøl) *adj.* purpúreo, morado, rojo. 2 imperial, regio. 3 brillante, magnífico. 4 *s.* púrpura.

**purple (to)** *tr.* purpurar, teñir de púrpura.

**purplish** (pø·ʳplish) *adj.* algo purpúreo.

**purport** (pø·ʳpoʳt) *s.* significado, sentido, tenor.

**purport (to)** (pøʳpo·ʳt) *tr.* significar, querer decir, dar a entender. 2 *to ~ to be,* querer ser, aparentar ser.

**purpose** (pø·ʳpøs) *s.* propósito, fin, objeto, mira, intención, designio: *of set ~, on ~,* de propósito. 2 resolución, determinación. 3 efecto, resultado, uso, utilidad: *common purposes,* usos ordinarios; *to no ~,* inútilmente, en vano. 4 *to the ~,* a propósito, al caso.

**purpose (to)** *tr.-intr.* proponerse, intentar, proyectar, tener designio de.

**purposeful** (-ful) *adj.* resuelto, determinado. 2 que tiene un sentido, fin u objeto.

**purpurin (e** (pø·ʳpiurin) *s.* purpurina [colorante].

**purr** (þøʳ) *s.* ronroneo.

**purr (to)** *intr.* ronronear.

**purse** (pø·ʳs) *s.* bolsa, bolsillo, portamonedas. 2 bolsa, caudal, dinero. 3 bolsa [premio, subvención]. 4 dinero recogido, colecta. 5 bolsa [recipiente; cosa en forma de bolsa].

**purse (to)** *tr.* fruncir, arrugar [la frente, los labios]. 2 *intr.* fruncirse, arrugarse.

**purse-proud** *adj.* orgulloso de su dinero.

**purser** (-øʳ) *s.* MAR. contador, sobrecargo.

**purslane** (pø·ʳslein) *s.* BOT. verdolaga.

**pursuance** (pøʳsiu·ans) *s.* persecución, seguimiento. 2 prosecución. 3 cumplimiento, ejecución.

**pursuant** (-ant) *adj.* consiguiente. 2 conforme [a]. 3 *adv.* de conformidad [con], en cumplimiento [de].

**pursue (to)** (pøʳsiu·) *tr.* seguir, perseguir. 2 perseguir [un fin]. 3 seguir [una línea de conducta, estudios, etc.]. 4 seguir [con la vista o mentalmente]. 5 *intr.* proseguir, continuar.

**pursuit** (pøʳsiu·t) *s.* seguimiento, perseguimiento, caza, busca: *~ plane,* avión de caza. 2 pretensión, empeño. 3 prosecución, continuación. 4 ocupación, actividad.

**pursuivant** (pø·ʳsuivant) *s.* perseverante.

**pursy** (pø·ʳsi) *adj.* obeso. 2 asmático. 3 engreído por el dinero.

**purulent** (piu·rulønt) *adj.* purulento.

**purvey (to)** (pøʳvei·) *tr.* proveer, abastecer. 2 suministrar. 3 *intr.* ser proveedor.

**purveyance** (-ans) *s.* abastecimiento, suministro.

**purveyor** (-øʳ) *s.* proveedor, abastecedor.

**purview** (pø·ʳviu) *s.* esfera, extensión, alcance.

**pus** (pøs) *s.* MED. pus, materia.

**push** (push) *s.* empujón. 2 impulso, empuje. 3 embestida. 4 esfuerzo. 5 avance [venciendo obstáculos]. 6 cornada, hurgonazo. 7 fam. apuro, aprieto. 8 apreturas. 9 fam. energía, acometividad. 10 *push o ~ button,* pulsador, botón eléctrico.

**push (to)** *tr.* empujar, empellar, impeler: *to ~ aside,* hacer a un lado, rechazar, apartar; *to ~ back,* echar atrás, hacer retroceder; *to ~ on,* aguijonear, apresurar. 2 apretar [un botón]. 3 llevar, extender [sus conquistas, etc.]. 4 proseguir. 5 promover, impulsar. 6 apremiar, apretar, estrechar. 7 *intr.* empujar. 8 dar una cornada, un hurgonazo. 9 avanzar [contra obstáculos]: *to ~ forward,* abrirse paso, avanzar. 10 *to ~ off,* desatracar; irse, salir. 11 *interj. push on!,* ¡adelante!

**pushcart** (pu·shkaʳt) *s.* carretilla de mano.

**pusher** (pu·shøʳ) *s.* empujador. 2 fam. persona emprendedora. 3 AVIA. *pusher o ~ plane,* avión que lleva la hélice en la parte de atrás.

**pushpin** (pu·shpin) *s.* juego de los alfileres, crucillo. 2 chinche [clavito].

**push-pull** *adj.* RADIO. de contrafase, simétrico, push-pull.

**pusillanimity** (piusilani·miti) *s.* pusilanimidad.

**pusillanimous** (piusilæ·nimøs) *adj.* pusilánime.

**puss** (pus) *s.* minino, michito, gato: *Puss in Boots,* el gato con botas. 2 chiquilla, mozuela. 3 *~ in the corner,* juego de las cuatro esquinas.

**pussy** (-i) *s.* minino, michito. 2 chiquilla.

**pussyfoot** (pu·sifut) *adj.* fam. cauteloso, evasivo [proceder, política]. *2 s.* persona cautelosa, que no se compromete.

**pustule** (pø·chøl) *s.* MED. pústula.

**pustulous** (pø·schøløs) *adj.* pustuloso.

**put** (put) *s.* acción del verbo TO PUT. *2* golpe, tiro, lanzamiento. *3 to stay* ~, estar quieto, en su lugar.

**put (to)** *tr.* poner, colocar, situar. *2* obligar, incitar. *3* hacer, formular [una pregunta]. *4* presentar [para ser discutido]. *5* exponer, expresar. *6* atribuir [un significado, valor, etc.]. *7* achacar [a una causa o razón]. *8* DEP. arrojar, lanzar. *9 to* ~ *about,* enojar; desconcertar; MAR. hacer virar. *10 to* ~ *aside,* descartar, desechar; poner aparte; ahorrar. *11 to* ~ *away,* guardar [en un cajón, etc.].; ahorrar; rechazar, repudiar; apartar. *12 to* ~ *by,* guardar, ahorrar; desviar, apartar. *13 to* ~ *down,* poner [en el suelo, etc.]; sofocar, reprimir; deprimir, abatir; humillar; apuntar, anotar; rebajar; atribuir; hacer callar. *14 to* ~ *forth,* extender, alargar; mostrar, ejercer, poner en acción; presentar, proponer; echar [hojas, plumas, etc.]. *15 to* ~ *in,* introducir en; pasar, emplear [tiempo] en. *16 to* ~ *in an appearance,* aparecer, ir, dejarse ver. *17 to* ~ *in a word for,* interceder por. *18 to* ~ *in mind,* recordar. *19 to* ~ *into effect,* poner en vigor. *20 to* ~ *off,* diferir, aplazar; desechar; eludir; quitar, quitarse [una prenda]. *21 to* ~ *on,* poner sobre; ponerse, calzarse [ropa, zapatos,etc.]; engañar; fingir; dar [la luz, vapor, etc.]; TEAT. poner en escena. *22 to* ~ *on airs,* darse tono. *23 to* ~ *on weight,* engordar. *24 to* ~ *oneself out of the way,* molestarse, tomarse molestia o trabajo. *25 to* ~ *out,* sacar; echar fuera; alargar, extender; exhibir; invertir, colocar [dinero]; echar [brotes, etc.]; apagar [la luz, un fuego]; molestar, irritar; desconcertar; dislocar. *26 to* ~ *out of countenance,* avergonzar; desconcertar. *27 to* ~ *out of joint,* dislocar. *28 to* ~ *out of the way,* quitar de enmedio; matar; poner [algo] donde no estorbe. *29 to* ~ *over,* aplazar. *30 to* ~ *through,* llevar a cabo; poner en comunicación telefónica. *31 to* ~ *to bed,* acostar. *32 to* ~ *to death,* matar, ajusticiar. *33 to* ~ *together,* reunir, juntar; armar, montar [un artefacto]. *34 to* ~ *to rights,* poner en orden; arreglar; reconciliar. *35 to* ~ *to the sword,* pasar a cuchillo. *36 to* ~ *two and two together,* atar cabos. *37 to* ~ *up,* levantar, elevar, erigir; armar, montar; ahorrar, atesorar; presentar [como candidato]; empaquetar, envolver; ofrecer [dinero] como premio, etc.; urdir, inventar; alojar, dar posada; TEAT. poner en escena. *38 to* ~ *upon oath,* hacer prestar juramento.

*39 intr.* ir, dirigirse. *40* MAR. *to* ~ *about,* cambiar de rumbo; *to* ~ *in,* entrar en un puerto; *to* ~ *off,* desatracar; *to* ~ *to sea,* hacerse a la mar. *41 to* ~ *out,* irse, salir; MAR. zarpar. *42 to* ~ *up,* parar, hospedarse; presentarse [como candidato]. *43 to* ~ *up with,* aguantar, sufrir, tolerar; conformarse con. ¶ Pret. y p. p.: *put;* ger.: *putting.*

**putative** (piu·tativ) *adj.* putativo.

**putlog** (pu·tlag) *s.* ALBAÑ. almojaya.

**put-off** *adj.* desechado. *2* aplazado. *3 s.* retraso, aplazamiento, dilatorias. *4* excusa, evasiva.

**put-out** *adj.* enojado, contrariado.

**putrefaction** (piutrifæ·kshøn) *s.* putrefacción. *2* putridez.

**putrefy (to)** (piu·trifai) *tr.* pudrir, corromper. *2 intr.* pudrirse, corromperse. ¶ Pret. y p. p.: *putrefied.*

**putrescible** (piutre·sibøl) *adj.* putrescible.

**putrid** (piu·trid) *adj.* pútrido. *2* apestoso. *3* corrompido, ponzoñoso [moralmente].

**putt** (pøt) *s.* GOLF. golpe suave que hace rodar la pelota hasta que se mete en el hoyo.

**puttee** (pø·ti o pøti·) *s.* polaina.

**putter (to)** (pu·tø$^r$) *intr.* TO POTTER.

**putting green** (-ing) *s.* GOLF. terreno nivelado y cubierto de césped que rodea cada hoyo.

**putty** (pø·ti) *s.* masilla.

**putty (to)** *tr.* enmasillar.

**put-up** *adj.* tramado, urdido, preparado.

**puzzle** (pø·søl) *s.* embarazo, perplejidad. *2* enredo, embrollo. *3* acertijo, enigma, rompecabezas: *crossword* ~, crucigrama.

**puzzle (to)** *tr.* confundir, dejar perplejo. *2* enredar, embrollar. *3 to* ~ *out,* desenredar, descifrar. *4 intr.* estar perplejo o confuso. *5 to* ~ *over,* tratar de descifrar.

**puzzlement** (pø·sølmønt) *s.* perplejidad, confusión.

**puzzler** (pø·šlø$^r$) *s.* lo que confunde o tiene perplejo.

**puzzolan** (pu·tšolæn) *s.* puzolana.

**Pygmalion** (pigmei·liøn) *n. pr.* Pigmalión.

**pygmean** (pigmı·an), **pigmy** (pi·gmi) *adj.-s.* pigmeo, enano.

**pyjamas** (pidÿa·mæs) *s. pl.* pijama.

**pylon** (pai·lan) *s.* ARQ. pilón [de templo egipcio]. *2* AVIA., ELECT. torre [de señal, conducción, etc.].

**pylorus** (pailo·røs) *s.* ANAT. píloro.

**pyorrhea, pyorrhae** (paiørı·a) *s.* MED. piorrea.

**pyramid** (pi·ramid) *s.* pirámide.

**pyramid (to)** *tr.* acumular, amontonar. *2 intr.* aumentar, acumularse. *3* aumentar uno la extensión de sus operaciones, empleando el beneficio obtenido en cada una de ellas.

**pyramidal** (piræ·midal) *adj.* piramidal.

**Pyramus** (pi·ræmøs) *n. pr.* MIT. Píramo.

**pyre** (pai·ø$^r$) *s.* pira, hoguera.

**Pyrenean** (pirinı·an) *adj.* pirenaico.

**Pyrenees** (pi·rinı̌š) *n. pr.* GEOGR. Pirineos.

**pyrexla** (paire·ksia) *s.* MED. pirexia.

**pyriform** (pi·rifo'm) *adj.* piriforme.

**pyrites** (pirai·tiš) *s.* MIN. pirita.

**pyrogenous** (paira·dÿenøs) *adj.* pirógeno.

**pyrography** (paira·grafi) *s.* pirograbado.

**pyrolysis** (paira·lisis) *s.* QUÍM. pirólisis.

**pyrope** (pai·ropi) *s.* MIN. piropo.

**pyrotechnics** (pairotekniks) *s.* pirotecnia.

**pyrotechnist** (-nist) *s.* pirotécnico.

**pyroxylin** (paira·ksilin) *s.* piroxilina.

**Pyrrhic** (pi·rik) *adj.* pírrico. *2 s.* pirriquio.

**pyrrhonism** (pi·rønišm) *s.* pirronismo.

**Pyrrhus** (pi·røs) *n. pr.* Pirro.

**Pythagoras** (pizæ·gørøs) *n. pr.* Pitágoras.

**Pythagorean** (pizægorı·an) *adj.-s.* pitagórico.

**Pythian** (pi·zian) *adj.* pitio.

**python** (pai·zan) *s.* ZOOL., MIT. pitón.

**pythoness** (pai·zønis) *s.* pitonisa.

**pyx** (piks) *s.* píxide, copón. *2* caja de la brújula.

**pyxidium** (piksi·diøm) *s.* BOT. pixidio.

Q

**Q, q** (kiu) *s.* Q, q, decimoséptima letra del alfabeto inglés.
**quack** (kuæk) *s.* graznido [del pato]. *2* curandero, charlatán. *3 adj.* falso, de charlatán.
**quack (to)** *intr.* graznar, parpar. *2* echarlas de entendido, hacer el charlatán.
**quackery** (-øri) *s.* charlatanismo.
**quacksalver** (-sælvøʳ) *s.* curandero, charlatán.
**quad** (kuod) *s.* fam. (E.U.) patio cuadrangular [de una universidad]. *2* pop. cuadrillizo.
**quadragenarian** (kuadradŷine·rian) *adj.-s.* cuadragenario.
**Quadragesima** (-dŷe·sima) *s.* cuadragésima.
**quadrangle** (kua·dræŋgøl) *s.* cuadrángulo. *2* ARQ. patio cuadrado.
**quadrangular** (kuadræ·iŋgiulaʳ) *adj.* cuadrangular.
**quadrans** (kua·drans) *s.* cuadrante [moneda].
**quadrant** (-nt) *s.* GEOM., ASTR. cuadrante.
**quadrat** (kua·dræt) *s.* IMPR. cuadrado, cuadratín.
**quadrate** (-dreit) *adj.-s.* ANAT., ZOOL. cuadrado.
**quadrate (to)** *intr.* cuadrar, conformarse.
**quadratic** (kuadræ·tik) *adj.* MAT. cuadrático. *2 s.* MAT. ecuación cuadrática.
**quadrature** (kua·drachuʳ) *s.* MAT., ASTR. cuadratura.
**quadrennium** (kuadre·niøm) *s.* cuadrienio.
**quadriga** (kuadrai·ga) *s.* cuadriga.
**quadrille** (kuadri·l) *s.* contradanza. *2* cuatrillo [juego de naipes]. *3* cuadrilla [de toreros].
**quadrillion** (kuadri·liøn) *s.* cuatrillón.
**quadripartite** (kuadripa·ʳtait) *adj.* cuatripartito.
**quadrivium** (kuadri·viøm) *s.* cuadrivio.
**quadroon** (kuadru·n) *s.* cuarterón [pers.].
**quadrumane** (kuadru·mein) *s.* ZOOL. cuadrúmano.
**quadrumanous** (-manøs) *adj.* cuadrúmano.
**quadruped** (kua·druped) *adj.-s.* cuadrúpedo.
**quadrupedal** (kuadru·pedal) *adj.* cuadrúpedo.
**quadruple** (cua·drupøl) *adj.* cuádruple. *2 s.* cuádruplo.
**quadruple (to)** *tr.* cuadruplicar. *2 intr.* cuadruplicarse.
**quadruplet** (kua·druplit) *s.* serie de cuatro, cuatrillizo.
**quadruplicate** (kuadru·plikit) *adj.* cuadruplicado.
**quadruplicate (to)** (-plikeit) *tr.* cuadruplicar.
**quaestor** (kue·støʳ) *s.* cuestor [romano].
**quaetorship** (-ship) *s.* cuestura.

**quaff** (kuaf) *s.* trago, bebida.
**quaff (to)** *intr.-tr.* beber, beber a grandes tragos.
**quag** (kuæg) *s.* lugar pantanoso.
**quagga** (kuæ·ga) *s.* ZOOL. cuaga.
**quaggy** (-i) *adj.* pantanoso, cenagoso. *2* blando como lodo.
**quagmire** (-gmaiʳ) *s.* cenagal, tremedal, tembladal. *2* fig. atolladero.
**quahog** (kuo·jag) *s.* ZOOL. almeja redonda.
**quail** (kueil) *s.* ORN. codorniz.
**quail (to)** *intr.* abatirse, acobardarse. *2* cejar, ceder [por temor].
**quaint** (kueint) *adj.* raro, singular, curioso; de un primor o gracia anticuados. *2* elegante, afectado.
**quake** (kueik) *s.* temblor, estremecimiento. *2* terremoto.
**quake (to)** *intr.* temblar, estremecerse, trepidar.
**Quaker** (kuei·køʳ) *adj.-s.* cuáquero, cuákero. *2 s.* temblador.
**Quakeress** (-is) *f.* cuáquera, cuákero.
**Quakerism** (-išm) *s.* cuaquerismo.
**quaking** (kuei·kiŋ) *adj.* temblador, temblón: ~ *bog,* tremedal; ~ *grass,* BOT. tembladera.
**quaky** (-i) *adj.* temblón, tembloroso. *2* que tiembla como la gelatina, gelatinoso.
**qualifiable** (kua·lifaiabøl) *adj.* calificable.
**qualification** (kualifikei·shøn) *s.* calificación. | No tiene el sentido de nota. *2* condición, requisito, calidad, cualidad. *3* capacidad, idoneidad. *4* modificación, atenuación, restricción.
**qualified** (kua·lifaid) *adj.* calificado, apto, idóneo, competente. *2* modificado. *3* DER. limitado, restringido.
**qualify (to)** (-lifai) *tr.* calificar, habilitar, capacitar, hacer idóneo. *2* modificar, limitar, restringir. *3* atenuar, suavizar, templar. *4* GRAM. calificar. *5* *intr.* capacitarse, habilitarse. ¶ Pret. y p. p.: *qualified.*
**qualifying** (-lifaiiŋ) *adj.* calificativo. *2* que capacita, autoriza o prepara.
**qualitative** (-liteitiv) *adj.* cualitativo.
**quality** (-liti) *s.* calidad, cualidad: *in ~ of,* en calidad de. *2* clase. *3* excelencia. *4* propiedad, virtud. *5* ant. o vulg. *the ~,* la alta sociedad.
**qualm** (kuam) *s.* basca, desfallecimiento, angustia. *2* escrúpulo, remordimiento.
**qualmish** (-ish) *adj.* bascoso. *2* escrupuloso.

**quandary** (kua·nd*a*ri) *s.* incertidumbre, perplejidad. *2* aprieto, brete.

**quanta** (kua·nta) *s. pl.* de QUANTUM.

**quantitative** (kua·ntiteitiv) *adj.* cuantitativo.

**quantity** (-titi) *s.* cantidad, cuantidad; cuantía; tanto. *2* MÉTR., MÚS. cantidad. *3 sing.* y *pl.* gran cantidad, gran número.

**quantum** (-tøm), *pl.* **quanta** (kua·nta) *s.* tanto, cantidad. *2* FÍS. cuanto, quántum.

**quarantine** (kua·r*a*ntin) *s.* cuarentena [aislamiento]. *2* lazareto, estación de cuarentena.

**quarantine (to)** *tr.* poner en cuarentena, aislar.

**quarrel** (kua·røl) *s.* riña, reyerta, disputa, querella, desavenencia. *2* cuadrillo [saeta]. *3* vidrio o loseta cuadrados o en figura de rombo.

**quarrel (to)** *intr.* reñir, pelear, disputar, contender. *2* reñir, desavenirse. *3* estar disgustado [con], quejarse [de]. ¶ Pret. y p. p.: *quarrel(l)ed;* ger.: *-l(l)ing.*

**quarreller** (-ø*r*) *s.* quimerista, disputador.

**quarrelsome** (-søm) *adj.* pendenciero, rencilloso.

**quarrier** (kua·riø*r*) *s.* cantero, picapedrero.

**quarry** (kua·ri) *s.* cantera, pedrera. *2* presa, caza [que se persigue]. *3* MONT. carnada. *4* QUARREL 3.

**quarry (to)** *tr.* sacar [piedra] de una cantera. *2* sacar [datos, etc.] de libros, etc.

**1) quart** (kuo*r*t) *s.* cuarto de galón [medida].

**2) quart** (ka*r*t) *s.* ESGR. cuarta. *2* cuarta [en el juego de los cientos].

**quartan** (kuo·*r*tan) *adj.* cuartanal. *2* MED. cuartana.

**quarter** (-ø*r*) *s.* cuarto, cuarta [cuarta parte]. *2* cuarto [de hora; de la luna; de un animal]. *3* moneda de veinticinco centavos. *4* MAR. cuarta. *5* trimestre. *6* parte, punto, dirección: *from all quarters*, de todas partes. *7* barrio, vecindad. *8* BLAS. cantón, cuartel. *9* cuartel, clemencia: *to give no ~*, no dar cuartel. *10 pl.* cuartel, oficina; vivienda, alojamiento: *to take up quarters at*, establecerse o alojarse en. *11* m. adv. *at close quarters*, muy cerca uno de otro; a las manos.

**quarter (to)** *tr.* cuartear, dividir en cuatro partes. *2* descuartizar. *3* BLAS. cuartelar. *4* hospedar, alojar. *5* MIL. acuartelar, acantonar. *6 intr.* alojarse.

**quarter day** *s.* día en que principia o se paga un trimestre.

**quarter-deck** *s.* MAR. alcázar.

**quarter-final** *s.* DEP. cuarto de final.

**quarterly** (-li) *adj.* trimestral. *2 adv.* trimestralmente. *3 s.* publicación trimestral.

**quartermaster** (-mæ·stø*r*) *s.* MIL. administrador de... miento: ~ *general*, intendente del ejército... cabo de mar. *3* MIL. (E.U.) *Quarter*... Cuerpo de Intendencia.

**q...** (kø..*r*n) *s.* (Ingl.) cuarta [de varias me]... o ~ *loaf*, pan de cuatro libras... *s.* grupo de cuatro. *2* MÚS. cuar...

...*dj.* IMPR. en cuarto. *2 s.* libro en...

...S. MINER. cuarzo.

...*r.* aplastar, estrellar. *2* sofocar,... nular, invalidar; revocar.

...*adj.* cuasi: ~ *contract*, cuasicon...

...moudou) *s.* domingo de Cua...

...shia)*s.* BOT., FARM. cuasia.

**qu...** (kuatø·*r*neri) *adj.* cuaternario. *2* MAT... de base cuatro. *3 s.* grupo de cuatro. *4* (con may.) GEOL. cuaternario.

**quaternity** (-iti) *s.* cuaternidad.

**quatrain** (kua·trein) *s.* poét. cuarteta; redondilla.

**quatrefoil** (kæ·tø*r*foil) *s.* grupo, flor, ornamento, etc., de cuatro hojas.

**quaver** (kuei·vø*r*) *s.* temblor [esp. en la voz]; estremecimiento, vibración. *2* MÚS. trémolo; trino. *3* MÚS. corchea.

**quaver (to)** *intr.* temblar, estremecerse, vibrar. *2* MÚS. trinar, gorjear. *3 intr.-tr.* hablar, decir, etc., con voz trémula.

**quavery** (kuei·vøri) *adj.* tembloroso, trémulo.

**quay** (kı·) *s.* muelle, desembarcadero.

**quean** (kuın) *f.* mujerzuela. *2* moza, muchacha.

**queasy** (kuı·ši) *adj.* bascoso. *2* nauseabundo. *3* delicado, exigente, escrupuloso, melindroso.

**queen** (kuın) *s.* reina: ~ *dowager*, reina viuda; ~ *bee*, abeja reina. *2* naipe que equivale al caballo. *3* dama o reina de ajedrez. *4* BOT. ~ *of the meadow*, reina de los prados, ulmaria.

**queen (to)** *tr.* hacer reina. *2* gobernar como reina. *3 intr.* reinar [como reina].

**queenly** (-li) *adj.* regio, de reina.

**queer** (kuı*r*) *adj.* raro, extraño, curioso, estrafalario. *2* excéntrico: ~ *in the head*, fam. tocado, chiflado. *3* débil, indispuesto. *4* dudoso.

**queer (to)** *tr.* ridiculizar. *2* pop. comprometer; poner en mala situación. *3* pop. estropear; desbaratar: *to ~ the pitch for one*, estropearle a uno el negocio.

**quell (to)** (kuel) *tr.* reprimir, sofocar, sojuzgar, domar. *2* aquietar. *3* calmar, mitigar.

**queller** (-ø*r*) *s.* sojuzgador. *2* mitigador.

**quench (to)** (kuench) *tr.* apagar, extinguir, calmar [el fuego, la luz, la sed, una pasión]; templar el ardor de. *2* templar [el acero].

**quenchless** (-lis) *adj.* inextinguible; implacable.

**quenelle** (køne·l) *s.* albondiguilla.

**querist** (kuı·rist) *s.* inquisidor, preguntador.

**querulous** (kue·ruløs) *adj.* plañidero. *2* quejumbroso, quejicoso, quisquilloso.

**query** (kuı·ri) *s.* pregunta, cuestión. *2* duda. *3* interrogante.

**query (to)** *tr.* preguntar, inquirir. *2* interrogar. *3* poner en duda. *4 intr.* hacer preguntas. *5* dudar, expresar una duda.

**quest** (kuest) *s.* busca, demanda: *in ~ of*, en demanda de. *2* pesquisa, indagación.

**quest (to)** *intr.-tr.* buscar, perseguir. *2* indagar.

**question** (kue·schøn) *s.* pregunta, interrogación: ~ *mark*, signo de interrogación, interrogante. *2* DER. indagación, interrogatorio; cuestión de tormento. *3* objeción, duda, discusión: *to call in ~*, poner en duda, en tela de juicio; *beyond ~*, fuera de duda, indiscutible; *without ~*, sin duda. *4* cuestión, problema, asunto, caso [punto de que se trata]: *that is the ~*, he ahí el problema; *this is out of the ~*, esto es imposible, está descartado; *beside the ~*, impertinente, ajeno al asunto; *in ~*, de que se trata.

**question (to)** *tr.* preguntar, examinar, interrogar. *2* hacer objeciones a, recusar; discutir, poner en duda. *3 intr.* hacer preguntas, indagar.

**questionable** (-abøl) *adj.* cuestionable. *2* dudoso, sospechoso.

**questionary** (kue·schøneri) *s.* cuestionario.

**questioning** (-ing) *s.* interrogatorio. *2* dudas, preguntas. *3 adj.* interrogador. *4* de duda, que pone en duda o discute.

**questor** (kue·stø*r*) *s.* cuestor.

**quetzal** (ke·tsal) *s.* ORN. quetzal.

**queue** (kiu) *s.* coleta. *2* cola, hilera. *3* MÚS. cordal.

**queue (to)** *intr.* hacer cola. | A veces con *up*.
**quibble** (kui·bøl) *s.* sutileza; argucia, equívoco, subterfugio.
**quibble (to)** *intr.* sutilizar, valerse de equívocos o subterfugios; buscar escapatorias.
**quibbler** (kui·bløʳ) *s.* sofista, equivoquista.
**quick** (kuik) *adj.* vivo, animado, rápido, acelerado, pronto, impetuoso: ~ *time*, MIL. paso redoblado. *2* despierto, agudo, perspicaz. *3* vivo, irritable. ~ *temper*, genio vivo. *4* vivo, intenso, penetrante, ardiente. *5* movedizo [suelo, arena]. *6* vivo [agua, fuente]. *7* COM. ~ *assets*, activo fácilmente realizable. *8* BOT. ~ *grass*, grama. *9* *s.* carne viva, lo vivo, el alma: *to sting to the* ~, herir en lo vivo. *10* vivo, viviente: *the* ~ *and the dead*, los vivos y los muertos. *11* *adv.* QUICKLY.
**quick-acting** *adj.* de acción rápida.
**quilk-change artist** *s.* TEAT. transformista.
**quicken (to)** (-øn) *tr.* vivificar, dar vida, resucitar. *2* avivar, animar, excitar, aguzar. *3* apresurar, acelerar. *5* *intr.* revivir. *6* avivarse, animarse. *7* apresurarse, acelerarse.
**quick-fire** *adj.* ARTILL. de tiro rápido.
**quicklime** (-laim) *s.* cal viva.
**quickly** (-li) *adv.* vivamente, prontamente, con presteza, aprisa.
**quicksand** (-sænd) *s.* arena movediza.
**quickset** (-set) *s.* BOT. espino; planta para setos.
**quickset (to)** *tr.* cercar con seto vivo.
**quicksilver** (-silvøʳ) *s.* mercurio, azogue.
**quickstep** (kui·kstep) *s.* MÚS. paso doble, pasacalle. *2* MIL. paso redoblado.
**quick-tempered** *adj.* de genio vivo, irritable.
**quick-witted** *adj.* listo, despierto, perspicaz.
**quid** (kuid) *s.* mascada de tabaco. *2* pop. libra esterlina.
**quiddity** (-iti) *s.* quid, esencia. *2* argucia. *3* nadería.
**quidnunc** (-nønk) *s.* curioso, chismoso.
**quiescent** (kuaie·sønt) *adj.* quieto, en reposo; fijo, sin movimiento.
**quiet** (kuai·øt) *adj.* quieto, inmóvil. *2* callado, quedo, silencioso: *to be* ~, callar, callarse. *3* tranquilo, sosegado. *4* sencillo, modesto: serio [color, vestido]. *5* COM. encalmado, inactivo. *6* *s.* quietud, silencio, sosiego, calma, paz, tranquilidad. *7* pop. *on the* ~, a la chita callando.
**quiet (to)** *tr.* aquietar, sosegar, calmar, tranquilizar. *2* intr. *to* ~ *down*, aquitarse.
**quietness** (-nis) *s.* quietud. *2* sencillez, modestia.
**quietude** (-iud) *s.* quietud.
**quietus** (kuai·tøs) *s.* finiquito. *2* fig. despido; descanso; muerte.
**quill** (kuil) *s.* pluma [de ave]. *2* cañón [de pluma]. *3* la pluma, la profesión literaria. *4* púa [de puerco espín]. *5* canilla, broca, devanador, canutillo.
**quill (to)** *tr.* desplumar, pelar. *2* rizar, alechugar, encañonar. *3* encanillar.
**quillon** (kɪ·løn) *s.* gavilán [de la espada].
**quilt** (kuilt) *s.* colcha; cobertor acolchado.
**quilt (to)** *tr.* acolchar, acojinar. *2* meter [entre dos capas o partes].
**quilting** (-ing) *s.* colchadura. *2* piqué, tela acolchada.
**quina** (kɪ·na) *s.* BOT., FARM. quina.
**quince** (kuins) *s.* membrillo [árbol y fruto].
**quincunx** (kui·nkønks) *s.* disposición al tresbolillo.
**quindecennial** (kuindise·nial) *adj.* quindenial.
**quinin(e** (kui·nin) *s.* QUÍM. quinina.
**quinol** (-oul) *s.* QUÍM. hidroquinona.

**quinquagenarian** (kuinkuadÿine·rian) *adj.-s.* quincuagenario.
**Quinquagesima** (dÿe·sima) *s.* Quincuagésima.
**quinquennial** (kuinkue·nial) *adj.* quinquenal. *2* *s.* quinto aniversario.
**quinquennium** (-niøm) *s.* quinquenio.
**quinsy** (kui·nši) *s.* MED. angina [tonsilar].
**quint** (kuint) *s.* MÚS., NAIPES. quinta.
**quintain** (kui·ntin) *s.* estafermo [figura].
**quintal** (-al) *s.* quintal.
**quinte** (kæ·nt) *s.* ESGR. quinta.
**quintessence** (kuinte·søns) *s.* quinta esencia.
**quintet(te** (kuinte·t) *s.* grupo de cinco. *2* MÚS. quinteto.
**quintillion** (-ti·liøn) *s.* quintillón.
**quintuple** (kui·ntiupøl) *adj.-s.* quintuplo.
**quintuple (to)** *tr.* quintuplicar. *2* intr. quintuplicarse.
**quip** (kuip) *s.* pulla, sarcasmo. *2* ocurrencia.
**quip (to)** *intr.* mofarse, echar pullas. ¶ Pret. y p. p.: *quipped;* ger.: *-pping.*
**quire** (kuaiʳ) *s.* mano [de papel]. *2* pliego [de un libro].
**quirk** (kuøʳk) *s.* vuelta, recodo, torcimiento, desviación. *2* rasgo [de pluma]. *3* sutileza, argucia. *4* salida, ocurrencia. *5* arranque, capricho, rareza.
**quirt** (kuøʳt) *s.* látigo [de montar].
**quirt (to)** *tr.* azotar con el látigo de montar.
**quit** (kuit) *adj.* absuelto, descargado. *2* libre, exento: *to get* ~ *of*, librarse de.
**quit (to)** *tr.* dejar, abandonar, irse de, separarse de; dejarse de; desistir de; renunciar a: *to* ~ *an employment*, dejar un empleo; *to* ~ *jesting*, dejarse de bromas. *2* librar, descargar. *3* pagar, saldar. *4* intr. irse: *to give notice to* ~, despedir a un inquilino, arrendatario, etc. *5* parar, dejar de hacer algo. ¶ Pret. y p. p.: *quitted;* ger.: *-tting.*
**quite** (kuait) *adv.* completamente, enteramente, totalmente, absolutamente, del todo; realmente, verdaderamente. *2* fam. ~ *a man*, todo un hombre. *3* fam. ~ *so*, así es, en efecto. *4* ~ *a lot*, muchos.
**quits** (kuits) *adj.-interj.* desquitados, en paz: *to be* ~, estar en paz, haberse desquitado.
**quittance** (kui·tons) *s.* quitanza. *2* pago, recompensa.
**quiver** (-vøʳ) *s.* aljaba, carcaj. *2* vibración, temblor, estremecimiento.
**quiver (to)** *intr.* vibrar, temblar, estremecerse.
**quixotic** (kuiksa·tik) *adj.* quijotesco.
**quixotry** (kui·ksøtri) *s.* quijotería, quijotismo.
**quiz** (kuiš) *s.* burla, broma. *2* guasón. *3* (E.U.) interrogatorio, examen [esp. en la escuela].
**quiz (to)** *tr.* burlarse de. *2* mirar con curiosidad, con burla. *3* (E.U.) examinar, interrogar. ¶ Pret. y p. p.: *quizzed;* ger.: *-zzing.*
**quizzical** (-ikal) *adj.* raro, estrambótico, cómico, gracioso. *2* burlón, zumbón.
**quodlibet** (kua·dlibet) *s.* cuodlibeto. *2* MÚS. fantasía burlesca.
**quoin** (kuoin) *s.* ARQ. piedra angular. *2* ARQ. ángulo, esquina. *3* MEC., IMPR. cuña.
**quoin (to)** *tr.* acuñar, meter cuñas.
**quoit** (kuoit) *s.* tejo, herrón. *2* pl. juego del tejo.
**quondam** (kua·ndam) *adj.* antiguo, que fue.
**quorum** (kuo·røm) *s.* quórum.
**quota** (kuou·ta) *s.* cuota, cupo.
**quotable** (-tabøl) *adj.* citable. *2* COM. cotizable.
**quotation** (kuoutei·šøn) *s.* cita [texto citado]. *2* COM. cotización. *3* adj. ~ *marks*, comillas (").

**quote** (knont) *s.* cita [texto citado]. *2 pl.* comillas (").

**quote (to)** *tr.* citar [un texto, un autor]. *2* poner entre comillas. *3* COM. cotizar; dar el precio de.

**quoth** (kuouz) *pret.* del verbo desusado TO QUETH: *quoth I*, dije yo.

**quotidian** (kuoti·di*a*n) *adj.* cotidiano, diario.

**quotient** (kuou·sh*ø*nt) *s.* MAT. cociente.

# R

**R, r** (a<sup>r</sup>) *s.* R, r, decimoctava letra del alfabeto inglés.

**rabbet** (ræ·bit) *s.* CARP. rebajo, ranura, encaje: ~ plane, guillame.

**rabbet (to)** *tr.* CARP. ensamblar a rebajo, encajar. *2* CARP. hacer un rebajo en.

**rabbi** (ræ·bai), **rabbin** (ræ·bin) *s.* rabí, rabino.

**rabbit** (ræ·bit) *s.* ZOOL. conejo: ~ hole, conejera, gazapera: ~ *warren*, conejar.

**rabble** (ræ·bøl) *s.* populacho, chusma, gentuza, canalla. *2* multitud alborotada.

**rabic** (ræ·bik) *adj.* MED., VET. rábico.

**rabid** (ræ·bid) *adj.* MED., VET. rabioso, rábico. *2* furioso, violento; furibundo, exaltado.

**rabies** (rei·biš) *s.* MED., VET. rabia, hidrofobia.

**raccoon** (ræ·kun) *s.* ZOOL. mapache.

**race** (reis) *s.* raza; casta, estirpe, linaje: *human* ~, género humano; ~ *problem*, problema racial. *2* prole, descendencia. *3* carrera, regata: ~ *horse*, caballo de carreras. *4* competición. *5* curso, carrera [de un astro, de la vida, etc.]. *6* corriente de agua fuerte o rápida. *7* canal, caz, saetín. *8* MEC. canal, ranura, garganta. *9* sabor, fuerza, etc. peculiar de un vino.

**race (to)** *intr.* correr [en una carrera, regata, etc.]. *2* correr, moverse, afluir rápidamente. *3* dispararse [el motor]. *4* *tr.* hacer correr de prisa. *5* competir con [en una carrera].

**raceme** (ræsi·m) *s.* BOT. racimo [inflorescencia].

**racer** (rei·sø<sup>r</sup>) *s.* corredor, carrerista. *2* caballo o coche de carreras. *3* embarcación de regatas.

**raceway** (-uei) *s.* RACE 7 y 8. *2* conducto para hilos eléctricos.

**rachis** (ræ·kis), *pl.* **-chides** (-kidiš) *s.* ANAT., ZOOL., BOT. raquis. *2* ástil [de pluma].

**rachitic** (raki·tic) *adj.* raquítico.

**rachitism** (ræ·kitišm) *s.* MED. raquitismo.

**racial** (rei·shal) *adj.* racial.

**racily** (rei·sili) *adv.* de manera viva, picante.

**raciness** (-inis) *s.* viveza, picante. *2* nariz [del vino].

**racing** (-ing) *s.* carrera; regata.

**racism** (-išm) *s.* racismo.

**rack** (ræk) *s.* aparato de tortura. *2* fig. dolor, tormento. *3* estante, etc., para ciertas cosas: astillero [para lanzas], armero, taquera, espetera, perchero, red para el equipaje. *4* pesebre. *5* cremallera: ~ *railway*, ferrocarril de cremallera. *6* nube deshilachada. *7* trote cochinero. *8* destrucción: *to go to* ~ *and ruin*, perderse, arruinarse completamente.

**rack (to)** *tr.* torturar. *2* atormentar. *3* oprimir con exacciones. *4* mover sobre cremallera. *5* *to* ~ *one's brains*, devanarse los sesos. *6* *intr.* andar al trote cochinero.

**racket** (ræ·kit) *s.* raqueta [para el juego, para la nieve]. *2* alboroto: *to raise a* ~, armar alboroto. *3* diversión, holgorio. *4* prueba, dificultad. *5* pop. timo, engaño.

**racket (to)** *intr.* andar de fiestas. *2* hacer barullo. *3* *tr.* sacar dinero con engaños o amenazas.

**racketeer** (rækitı·<sup>r</sup>) *s.* (E.U.) el que saca dinero a personas o empresas comerciales con amenazas de violencia o de perjuicios causados a sus intereses.

**rackety** (ræ·kiti) *adj.* bullicioso. *2* jaranero.

**racking** (-ing) *adj.* torturador, desgarrador.

**rack-rent** (-rent) *s.* arriendo o alquiler exorbitante.

**rackwork** (-wø<sup>r</sup>k) *s.* mecanismo de cremallera.

**racoon** (ræ·kun) *s.* RACCOON.

**racquet** (ræ·kit) *s.* RACKET.

**racy** (rei·si) *adj.* que tiene el aroma o las cualidades de su clase o casta. *2* vivo, animado, chispeante.

**radar** (rei·da<sup>r</sup>) *s.* ELECT. radar: ~ *screen*, pantalla de radar.

**raddle** (ræ·døl) *s.* cañizo. *2* seto de ramas. *3* almagre.

**raddle (to)** *tr.* entretejer. *2* pintar con almagre.

**radial** (rei·dial) *adj.* radial, radiado.

**radian** (rei·dian) *s.* GEOM. radián, ángulo cuyo arco es igual al radio.

**radiance, radiancy** (rei·dians, -si) *s.* brillo, resplandor, fulgor, esplendor.

**radiant** (-iant) *adj.* FÍS. radiante. *2* radiante, radioso, resplandeciente.

**radiate** (-ieit) *adj.* radiado, radial. *2* *s.* ZOOL. radiado.

**radiate (to)** *tr.-intr.* radiar, irradiar. *2* *tr.* exponer a una radiación; iluminar. *3* difundir. *4* radiar [por radio].

**radiation** (-iei·shøn) *s.* radiación.

**radiator** (-ieitø<sup>r</sup>) *s.* radiador.

**radical** (ræ·dikal) *adj.* radical [en todas sus acepciones]. *2* esencial, fundamental. *3* *s.* raíz, fundamento. *4* GRAM., QUÍM., POL. radical.

**radicalism** (-išm) *s.* radicalismo.

**radicle** (ræ·dikøl) *s.* raicilla. *2* BOT. radícula.

**radio** (rei·diou) *s.* radio [radiodifusión, radiograma, radiorreceptor]: ~ *amateur,* ~ *fan,* radioaficiondo; ~ *beacon,* AVIA. radiofaro; ~ *listener,* radioescucha, radioyente; ~ *set,* aparato de radio; ~ *wave,* radioonda.

**radioactive** (-a·ktiv) *adj.* radiactivo.

**radiobroadcast (to)** (-bro·dkæst) *tr.* radiar, radiodifundir.

**radio-frequency** *adj.* de radiofrecuencia.

**radiogram** (rei·diougræm) *s.* radiograma. *2* radiografía [imagen].

**radiograph** (-græf) *s.* radiografía [imagen]. *2* actinógrafo.

**radiograph (to)** *tr.* radiografiar. *2* radiotelegrafiar a.

**radiography** (reidia·grafi) *s.* radiografía [acto, procedimiento].

**radiologist** (reidia·lodÿist) *s.* radiólogo.

**radiology** (-lodÿi) *s.* radiología.

**radiophony** (-foni) *s.* radiofonía.

**radioscopy** (-skøpi) *s.* radioscopia.

**radiosonde** (rei·diousand) *s.* radiosonda.

**radiotelegraph** (reidioute·løgræf) *s.* telégrafo sin hilos.

**radiotelegraph (to)** *tr.* radiotelegrafiar.

**radiotelegraphy** (-grafi) *s.* radiotelegrafia.

**radiotelephony** (-foni) *s.* radiotelefonía.

**radiotherapy** (-ze·rapi) *s.* radioterapia.

**radish** (ræ·dish) *s.* BOT. rábano.

**radium** (rei·diøm) *s.* QUÍM. radio.

**radiumtherapy** (reidiømze·rapi) *s.* radiumterapia.

**radius** (rei·diøs) *s.* GEOM., ANAT. radio. *2* radio, rayo. *3* radio [de acción, de influencia, etc.; espacio circular]. *4* ZOOL. plano radial.

**radix** (rei·diks) *s.* raíz, origen. *2* MAT. base [de un sistema].

**radula** (ræ·diul*a*), *pl.* **-la** (-li) *s.* ZOOL. rádula.

**raffia** (ræ·fi*a*) *s.* BOT. rafia.

**raffish** (ræ·fish) *adj.* canallesco. *2* disoluto.

**raffle** (ræ·føl) *s.* rifa. *2* fam. desecho, broza.

**raffle (to)** *intr.* tomar parte en una rifa. *2 tr. to* ~ *off,* rifar, sortear.

**raft** (raft) *s.* balsa [flotante]. *2* almadía, armadía, jangada. *3* masa flotante [de algas, etc.].

**raft (to)** *tr.* transportar en balsa. *2 intr.* servir de balsa.

**rafter** (-ø*r*) *s.* ARQ. viga; par.

**raftsman** (-smæn) *s.* almadiero.

**rag** (ræg) *s.* trapo, harapo, jirón, pingajo, guiñapo: ~ *doll,* muñeca de trapo; *in rags,* hecho jirones; andrajoso. *2* papelucho. *3* burla, broma, alboroto. *4 pl.* trapos o papeles rotos.

**rag (to)** *tr.* romper, hacer jirones. *2* reñir, regañar. *3* molestar con burlas o bromas.

**ragamuffin** (ræ·gamøfin) *s.* golfo, pelagatos.

**rage** (reidÿ) *s.* rabia, ira; arrebato de cólera. *2* furia, violencia, encarnizamiento. *3* vehemencia, ardor, entusiasmo. *4 to be all the* ~, estar en boga, estar de moda.

**rage (to)** *intr.* rabiar, encolerizarse. *2* hacer estragos. *3* arder furiosamente [el fuego].

**ragged** (ræ·gid) *adj.* andrajoso, harapiento. *2* roto, deshilachado; de borde mellado o dentado. *3* áspero, escabroso.

**raging** (rei·dÿing) *adj.* rabioso, furioso, bramador. *2* entusiasta, vehemente.

**raglan** (ræ·glæn) *s.* raglán.

**ragman** (ræ·gmæn) *s.* trapero.

**ragout** (rægu·) *s.* COC. guisado.

**ragpicker** (ræ·gpikø*r*) *s.*trapero.

**ragstone** (-stoun) *s.* (Ingl.) piedra de amolar.

**ragtag** (-tæg) *s.* canalla, chusma.

**ragtime** (-taim) *s.* música de ritmo sincopado.

**raid** (reid) *s.* correría, incursión, ataque, irrupción.

**raid (to)** *tr.* hacer una incursión en. *2* BOLSA to ~ *the market,* maniobrar para hacer bajar los precios.

**rail** (reil) *s.* barra [para apoyo, etc.]; pasamano, barandal; varal [de carro]. *2* antepecho, baranda, barandilla, barrera. *3* bance. *4* CARP. peinazo. *5* carril, rail, riel; ferrocarril: *by* ~, por ferrocarril. *6* ORN. rascón.

**rail (to)** *tr.* poner barandilla, cercar con valla, verja, etc. *2* transportar por ferrocarril. *3 intr. to* ~ *at,* injuriar, vituperar.

**railhead** (-jed) *s.* término de vía férrea en construcción. *2* parte superior del riel. *3* MIL. estación ferroviaria de víveres y municiones.

**railing** (-ing) *adj.* injurioso, vituperioso. *2 s.* barandilla, pasamano, balaustrada, barrera, valla, reja, verja.

**raillery** (-øri) *s.* burla, fisga. *2* bufonada.

**railroad** (-roud) *s.* ferrocarril, vía férrea. | Ús. esp. en los E.U.

**railroad (to)** *tr.* proveer de ferrocarriles. *2* (E.U.) transportar por ferrocarril. *3* (E.U.) apresurar, atropellar; hacer aprobar [una ley, etc.] con precipitación.

**railway** (-uei) *s.* ferrocarril, vía férrea. | Ús. esp. en Ingl.: ~ *man,* ferroviario. *2* línea de carriles para trasladar algo sobre ruedas.

**railway (to)** *tr.* (Ingl.) proveer de ferrocarriles.

**raiment** (rei·mønt) *s.* ropa, indumento, vestidos.

**rain** (rein) *s.* lluvia: ~ *gauge,* pluviómetro; ~ *water,* agua llovediza; ~ *or shine,* con buen tiempo o con mal tiempo; *the rains,* la época de las lluvias.

**rain (to)** *intr. impers.* y *tr.* llover: *it is raining,* llueve; *to* ~ *cats and dogs, to* ~ *pitchforks,* llover a cántaros.

**rainbow** (-bou) *s.* arco iris. *2* espectro solar.

**raincoat** (-kout) *s.* impermeable, chubasquero.

**raindrop** (-drap) *s.* gota de lluvia.

**rainfall** (-fol) *s.* aguacero. *2* lluvia, lluvias.

**rainpour** (-po*r*) *s.* aguacero.

**rainproof (to)** *tr.* impermeabilizar.

**rainstorm** (-sto*r*m) *s.* tempestad de lluvia.

**rainy** (rei·ni) *adj.* lluvioso: ~ *day,* día lluvioso; *to save up for a* ~ *day,* ahorrar para el día de mañana; ~ *season,* época de las lluvias.

**raise** (reiš) *s.* aumento, alza, subida [de precio, salario, etc.]; aumento de sueldo.

**raise (to)** *tr.* levantar, alzar, elevar; poner derecho, enhestar, erguir, erigir. *2* levantar [polvo, la voz, los ánimos, falsos testimonios, un sitio, etc.]. *3* elevar, subir [la temperatura, el tono, los precios, etc.]. *4* elevar, engrandecer; ascender. *5* despertar. *6* excitar, levantar, sublevar. *7* suscitar, promover, originar; dar lugar a. *8* prorrumpir en [gritos, etc.]. *9* presentar, hacer [una objeción]. *10* cultivar [plantas], criar [animales]. *11* (E.U.) criar, educar. *12* reunir, allegar, obtener. *13* levantar, reclutar. *14* evocar, llamar. *15* hacer surgir o aparecer. *16* leudar. *17* MAT. elevar [a una potencia]. *18 to* ~ *Cain, hell, the devil,* etc., armar un jaleo.

**raiser** (rei·sšø*r*) *s.* cultivador, productor; criador.

**raisin** (rei·šin) *s.* pasa [uva seca].

**raja(h** (ra·dÿa) *s.* rajá.

**rake** (reik) *s.* calavera, libertino. *2* AGR. rastro, rastrillo. *3* raqueta [de mesa de juego]. *4* rascador, raedera. *5* inclinación hacia popa [de un mástil, etc.]; inclinación hacia atrás. *6* MAR. lanzamiento.

**rake (to)** *tr.* AGR. rastrillar. *2* rascar, raer. *3* recoger, barrer. *4* atizar, hurgar [el fuego]. *5* registrar, buscar en. *6* MIL. barrer. *7* MÚS. rasguear. *8 to ~ over the coals,* criticar severamente. *9 to ~ together,* juntar, acumular. *10 intr.* buscar [en]. *11* estar inclinado hacia atrás.

**raker** (-ø$^r$) *s.* rastrillador. *2* AGR. rastrilladora mecánica. *3* raedera, rasqueta.

**raking** (-ing) *s.* AGR. rastrillaje. *2* reprimenda. *3 adj.* inclinado. *4* rápido, veloz.

**rakish** (-ish) *adj.* libertino. *2* airoso, gallardo, jacarandoso.

**râle** (ral) *s.* MED. estertor.

**rally** (ræ·li) *s.* unión, reunión [de tropas dispersas, de gente]. *2* recobro, restablecimiento.

**rally (to)** *tr.* reunir y reorganizar [tropas dispersas]. *2* reunir, concentrar [gente, energías, etc.]. *3* reanimar, fortalecer. *4* ridiculizar; embromar. *5 intr.* MIL. reunirse, rehacerse. *6* unirse [para una causa común]; dar su apoyo. *7* reponerse, rehacerse. *9* recobrar firmeza [los precios, el mercado]. ¶ Pret. y p. p.: *rallied.*

**Ralph** (rælf) *n. pr.* Rodolfo.

**ram** (ræm) *s.* ZOOL. morueco. *2* MIL. ariete. *3* ariete hidráulico. *4* MEC. martinete, pisón, émbolo percutor. *5* MAR. espolón; buque con espolón. *6* ASTR. (con may.) Aries.

**ram (to)** *tr.* apisonar. *2* golpear con martinete, pisón, espolón, ariete, etc. *3* hacer chocar [contra]. *4* clavar, meter [a golpes o por la fuerza]; atacar [un arma]; atestar, henchir. *5 intr.* chocar: *to ~ into,* dar contra, chocar con. ¶ Pret. y p. p.: *rammed;* ger.: *-mming.*

**ramble** (ræ·mbøl) *s.* paseo, excursión, correría, correteo. *2* divagación.

**ramble (to)** *intr.* pasear, vagar. *2* divagar. *3* extenderse libremente [una planta]. *4* serpentear [un río].

**rambling** (ræ·mbling) *adj.* paseador. *2* que divaga, incoherente. *3* BOT. trepador, rastrero. *4* grande y de planta irregular [casa].

**ramification** (ramifikei·shøn) *s.* ramificación.

**ramify (to)** (ræ·mifai) *tr.* dividir en ramas o ramales. *2 intr.* ramificarse.

**rammer** (ræ·mø$^r$) *s.* pisón. *2* atacador, baqueta. *3* MAR. espolón.

**rammish** (ræ·mish) *adj.* carneruno, maloliente. *2* libidinoso.

**ramose** (rei·mous), **ramous** (rei·møs) *adj.* ramoso.

**ramp** (ræmp) *s.* rampa, declive. *2* curva en la barandilla de una escalera. *3* salto o actitud agresiva.

**ramp (to)** *intr.* ARQ. elevarse o descender [un muro, etc.] a otro nivel. *2* saltar o avanzar amenazadoramente.

**rampage** (-idy̆) *s.* alboroto, furia, agitación, cólera: *to go on a ~,* alborotarse, enfurecerse.

**rampage (to)** *intr.* alborotarse, ponerse como un loco.

**rampancy** (-ansi) *s.* exuberancia, exceso.

**rampant** (-ant) *adj.* exuberante, excesivo. *2* fiero, violento. *3* general, extendido. *4* BLAS. rampante. *5* ARQ. por tranquil.

**rampart** (-a$^r$t) *s.* FORT. muralla, baluarte. *2* FORT. terraplén. *3* fig. defensa, amparo.

**ramrod** (ræ·mrad) *s.* baqueta [de fusil].

**ramshackle** (-shækøl) *adj.* desvencijado. *2* destartalado, ruinoso. *3* desarreglado, desordenado.

**ran** (ræn) *pret.* de TO RUN.

**ranch** (rænch) *s.* rancho, hacienda; *estancia.

**rancher** (-ø$^r$), **ranchman** (-mæn) *s.* ranchero, ganadero, vaquero.

**rancid** (ræ·nsid) *adj.* rancio, rancioso.

**ranco(u)r** (ræ·nkø$^r$) *s.* rencor, inquina, encono.

**rancorous** (-øs) *adj.* rencoroso, malévolo.

**random** (ræ·ndøm) *s.* azar, acaso: *at ~,* al azar, a la ventura. *2 adj.* ocasional, fortuito, impensado; hecho o dicho al azar.

**rang** (ræng) *pret.* de TO RING.

**range** (reindy̆) *s.* fila, línea, hilera: *range o mountain ~,* sierra, cordillera. *2* correría, viaje. *3* espacio [que recorre o cubre un cosa], recorrido. *4* esfera, campo [de una actividad, etc.]. *5* escala, gama, serie. *6* extensión de la voz. *7* alcance [de un arma, etc.]; distancia: *~ finder,* telémetro; *at close ~,* a quema ropa; *within the ~ of,* al alcance de. *8* autonomía [de un buque o avión]. *9* extensión de pastos. *10* clase, orden. *11* campo de tiro; línea de tiro. *12* línea [de dirección]: *in ~ with,* en línea con. *13* cocina económica. *14* pl. montañas.

**range (to)** *tr.* alinear. *2* arreglar, ordenar. *3* recorrer, ir y venir por o a lo largo de. *4* pasear [la mirada, etc.] por. *5* tener cierto alcance [un arma]. *6 intr.* alinearse; estar en línea. *7* correr, errar. *8* extenderse, variar, fluctuar [dentro de ciertos límites]. *9* contarse [entre]; ponerse de parte [de].

**ranger** (-ø$^r$) *s.* guardabosque. *2* perro ventor.

**rank** (rænk) *adj.* lozano, lujuriante, exuberante, vicioso. *2* fértil. *3* rancio; ofensivo [sabor, olor]. *4* grosero [lenguaje, etc.]. *5* malo, insalubre. *6* absoluto, extremado, insigne, acabado. *7 s.* línea, hilera, fila. *8* rango, categoría, grado. *9* MIL. graduación. *10* calidad, distinción. *11* la clase alta. *12* MIL. fila: *the ranks, the ~ and file,* la tropa; fig. la gente de abajo.

**rank (to)** *tr.* alinear, formar, poner en fila. *2* ordenar, arreglar, clasificar. *3* MIL. tener una categoría superior a. *4 intr.* formar o marchar en filas. *6* tener [una categoría]; figurar o contarse entre: *to ~ high,* tener un alto grado o categoría; ser tenido en gran estima, sobresalir; *to ~ with,* contarse entre, tener la misma categoría que.

**ranker** (-ø$^r$) *s.* MIL. oficial patatero.

**rankle (to)** (ræ·nkøl) *intr.* enconarse, ulcerarse, inflamarse, irritarse. *2* fig. roer, escocer.

**ransack (to)** (-sæk) *tr.* registrar, explorar. *2* saquear, pillar.

**ransom** (-søm) *s.* rescate, redención.

**ransom (to)** *tr.* rescatar, redimir. *2* hacer pagar rescate.

**rant** (rænt) *s.* lenguaje retumbante, declamación sin sentido, monserga; delirio.

**rant (to)** *intr.* declamar a gritos. *2* desbarrar, delirar; enfurecerse.

**ranula** (ræ·niula) MED., VET. ránula.

**ranunculus** (ranø·nkiuløs) *s.* ranúnculo.

**rap** (ræp) *s.* golpe seco: *~ on a door,* llamada a una puerta. *2* crítica, censura. *3* fam. *I don't care a ~,* no me importa un bledo.

**rap (to)** *tr.-intr.* golpear, dar un golpe seco: *to ~ at a door,* llamar a una puerta. *2 tr.* proferir vivamente. *3* (E.U.) criticar duramente. ¶ Pret. y p. p.: *rapped;* ger.: *-pping.*

**rapacious** (rapei·shøs) *adj.* rapaz. *2* codicioso. *3* voraz.

**rapacity** (-pæ·siti) *s.* rapacidad.
**rape** (reip) *s.* robo, rapiña; rapto. *2* violación, estupro. *3* BOT. colza. *4 pl.* orujo, brisa.
**rape (to)** *tr.* robar, raptar. *2* violar, estuprar.
**Raphael** (ræ·fiøl) *n. pr.* Rafael.
**raphe** (rei·fi) *s.* ANAT., BOT. rafe.
**raphia** (ra·fia) *s.* rafia [fibra].
**rapid** (ræ·pid) *adj.* rápido. *2 s.* rápido, rabión.
**rapidity** (rapi·diti) *s.* rapidez.
**rapier** (ræ·piøʳ) *s.* estoque, espadín.
**rapier-fish** *s.* ICT. pez espada.
**rapine** (ræ·pin) *s.* rapiña, pilaje.
**rapper** (ræ·pøʳ) *s.* golpeador. *2* llamador, aldabón.
**rapport** (ræ·po·ʳt) *s.* relación, armonía, conformidad.
**rapscallion** (ræpskæ·liøn) *s.* golfo, bribón, canalla.
**rapt** (ræpt) *adj.* arrebatado, transportado, enajenado, absorto.
**raptorial** (ræptou·rial) *adj.* rapaz, de rapiña.
**rapture** (ræ·pchøʳ) *s.* rapto, arrebato, arrobamiento, éxtasis.
**rapturous** (-øs) *adj.* arrobado, embelesado.
**rare** (re·øʳ) *adj.* raro [de poca densidad]; ralo. *2* raro [poco común, escaso]: ~ *bird,* rara avis, mirlo blanco. *3* raro, insigne, excelente, peregrino. *4* COC. poco cocido.
**raree-show** (re·rɪ-shou) *s.* tutilimundi, mundonuevo.
**rarefy (to)** (re·rifai) *tr.* rarefacer, rarificar, enrarecer. *2 intr.* rarificarse, encarecerse.
**rarity** (re·riti) *s.* rareza, raridad. *2* tenuidad. *3* preciosidad, primor. *4* curiosidad [cosa].
**rascal** (ræ·skal) *s.* bribón, pillo, granuja, canalla.
**rascally** (-i) *adj.* bribonesco. *2 adv.* ruinmente.
**rase (to)** (rei·š) *tr.* arrasar. *2* raer. *3* raspar, borrar.
**rash** (ræsh) *adj.* irreflexivo, precipitado; imprudente, temerario. *2 s.* salpullido.
**rasher** (ræ·shøʳ) *s.* lonja, magra.
**rashness** (ræ·shnis) *s.* irreflexión, temeridad.
**rasp** (ræsp) *s.* escofina. *2* rallador. *3* sonido estridente. *4* raspamiento. *5* ronquera, carraspera.
**rasp (to)** *tr.* raspar, escofinar, raer, rallar: fig. *to* ~ *the ear,* desgarrar los oídos.
**raspberry** (ræ·zberi) *s.* BOT. frambuesa; frambueso.
**rasper** (ræ·spøʳ) *s.* rallador, raspador.
**rasping** (-ping) *adj.* raspante. *2* áspero, bronco. *3* irritante, desagradable. *4 s.* raspamiento.
**rasure** (rei·šøʳ) *s.* raspadura, borradura.
**rat** (ræt) *s.* ZOOL. rata: ~ *trap,* ratonera; *to smell a* ~, sospechar algo malo; oler una intriga, etc. *2* pop. desertor. *3* pop. esquirol [obrero].
**rat (to)** *intr.* cazar ratas. *2* POL. volver casaca. *3* trabajar como esquirol. *4 tr.* emplear esquiroles u obreros no sindicados. ¶ Pret. y p. p.: *ratted;* ger.: *-tting.*
**ratable** (rei·tabøl) *adj.* sujeto a contribución, imponible. *2* valuable.
**ratafia** ( rætafi·a) *s.* ratafia.
**ratch** (ræch), **ratchet** (-it) *s.* MEC. trinquete; cremallera de trinquete: ~ *jack,* gato de cremallera; ~ *wheel,* rueda de trinquete.
**rate** (reit) *s.* razón, proporción, tanto [por ciento, etc.]; tipo [de interés o cambio]; velocidad. *2* tarifa, precio, tasa, valor, grado. *3* clase, orden: *first* ~, de primer orden, muy bien. *4* modo, manera. *5* arbitrio, impuesto. *6 at any* ~, al menos, de todos modos. *7 at the* ~ *of,* a razón de. *8 at this,* o *that* ~, a este paso, de este modo.
**rate (to)** *tr.* valuar, tasar, apreciar. *2* clasificar. *3* considerar como, contar entre. *4* reñir, repren-

der. *5 intr.* valer, ser estimado o considerado: *to* ~ *high,* ser tenido en gran estima.
**rather** (ra·ðøʳ) *adv.* bastante, algo, un tanto. *2* mejor, antes, más, más bien: *I had* ~, *I would* ~, me gustaría más, preferiría. *3* antes bien, al contrario. *4* mejor dicho. *5 the* ~, *the* ~ *as, the* ~ *that,* tanto más cuanto que. *6 interj.* ¡ya lo creo!
**ratification** (rætifikei·shøn) *s.* ratificación, confirmación.
**ratify (to)** (ræ·tifai) *tr.* ratificar, confirmar.
**rating** (rei·ting) *s.* valuación, justiprecio. *2* clasificación; grado, clase. *4* MEC. capacidad de trabajo. *5* reprimenda, peluca.
**ratio** (rei·shiou) *s.* relación, proporción. *2* MAT. razón.
**ratiocinate (to)** (ræshia·sineit) *intr.* raciocinar, razonar.
**ration** (ræ·shøn) *s.* MIL. ración. *2* ración, cupo.
**ration (to)** *tr.* racionar. *2* poner a ración.
**rational** (ræ·shønal) *adj.* racional. *2* cuerdo, razonable. *3 s.* racional [ser; ornamento].
**rationale** (ræshønæ·li) *s.* fundamento, razón. *2* exposición razonada.
**rationalism** (ræ·shønališm) *s.* racionalismo.
**rationality** (ræshønæ·liti) *s.* racionalidad. *2* lo razonable.
**rationalization** (ræshønališei·shøn) *s.* acción de hacer racional o explicable. *2* MAT., COM., IND. racionalización.
**rationalize (to)** (ræ·shønalaiš) *tr.* hacer racional o explicable. *2* MAT., COM., IND. racionalizar.
**rationing** (ræ·shøning) *s.* racionamiento.
**ratlin(e** (ræ·tlin), **ratling** (-ling) *s.* MAR. flechaste.
**ratsbane** (ræ·tsbein) *s.* arsénico.
**rattan** (ræt æ·n) *s.* rota, roten, junquillo, bejuco.
**rattle** (ræ·tøl) *s.* tableteo, matraqueo, ruido de algo que rueda, es sacudido, etc. *2* fig. charla, parloteo. *3* estertor. *4* cascabel [de serpiente]. *5* sonajero. *6* matraca, carraca. *7* fig. parlanchín.
**rattle (to)** *tr.* hacer sonar como una matraca, sacudir, mover, hacer de prisa y con ruido. *2* decir, proferir rápidamente. | Gralte. *con off. 3* desconcertar, agitar, aturrullar. *5 intr.* tabletear, matraquear, guachapear, repiquetear. *6* rodar con ruido [un carruaje, etc.]. *7* temblar [la voz, los cristales]. *8* parlotear. *9* tener estertor.
**rattlebox** (-baks) *s.* sonajero. *2* fig. charlatán.
**rattle-head** *s.* hablador, parlanchín. *2* casquivano.
**rattler** (ræ·tløʳ) *s.* parlanchín, tarabilla. *2* (E.U.) crótalo (serpiente).
**rattlesnake** (ræ·tølsneik) *s.* ZOOL. crótalo, serpiente de cascabel.
**rattletrap** (-træp) *adj.* desvencijado. *2 s.* objeto desvencijado, carraca. *3 pl.* retazos, chucherías.
**rattling** (ræ·tling) *adj.* ruidoso. *2* vivo, animado. *3* fam. estupendo.
**raucity** (ro·siti) *s.* ronquedad, bronquedad.
**raucous** (ro·køs) *adj.* rauco, ronco, bronco.
**ravage** (ræ·vidy) *s.* estrago, destrozo, destrucción, ruina, asolamiento. *2* saqueo, pillaje.
**ravage (to)** *tr.* asolar, talar, arruinar, destruir, hacer estragos en. *2* saquear, pillar.
**rave (to)** (reiv) *intr.* delirar, desvariarr, disparatar, despotricar. *2* bramar, enfurecerse. *3 to* ~ *about* u *over,* estar loco por.
**ravel** (ræ·vøl) *s.* RAVELLING. *2* RAVELMENT.
**ravel (to)** *tr.* deshilar, destejer, deshacer. *2* desenredar, desenmarañar. *3 intr.* deshilarse, destejercerse, deshacerse. *4* desenredarse. ¶ Pret. y p. p.: *ravel(l)ed;* ger.: *-l(l)ing.*
**ravelin** (ræ·vlin) *s.* FORT. revellín.

**ravel(l)ing** (ræ·vøling) *s.* hilacha, deshiladura.
**ravelment** (-mønt) *s.* enredo, maraña.
**raven** (rei·vn) *s.* ORN. cuervo. *2 adj.* negro y lustroso.
**raven (to)** *tr.* devorar. *2* apresar, rapiñar.
**ravenous** (ræ·vnøs) *adj.* voraz. *2* hambriento, famélico. *3* rapaz.
**ravin** (ræ·vin) *s.* rapacidad. *2* rapiña.
**ravine** (ravi·n) *s.* barranco, barranca, hondonada, quebrada; arroyada.
**raving** (rei·ving) *s.* delirio, desvarío. *2 adj.* delirante. *3* furioso: ~ *mad*, loco de atar.
**ravish (to)** (ræ·vish) *tr.* arrebatar, extasiar, embelesar,encantar. *2* arrebatar, robar. *3* raptar, forzar, violar.
**ravishment** (-mønt) *s.* éxtasis, embeleso, arrobamiento. *2* rapto; forzamiento, violación.
**raw** (rɔ) *adj.* crudo [sin cocer, sin preparar], en bruto, en rama: ~ *material*, materia prima. *2* puro, sin diluir [aguardiente, etc.]. *3* tosco, sin refinamiento. *4* llagado, desollado: ~ *flesh*, carne viva. *5* crudo, húmedo, frío [tiempo, viento]. *6* bisoño, novato, inexperto. *7* ~ *deal*, mala pasada. *8 s.* carne viva, llaga, matadura. *9 in the* ~, en estado crudo o natural; al desnudo.
**rawboned** (-bound) *adj.* esquelético, demacrado.
**rawhead** (-jed) *s.* coco, espantajo.
**rawhide** (-jaid) *s.* cuero crudo, sin curtir. *2* látigo de cuero crudo.
**ray** (rei) *s.* rayo [de luz, calor, etc.]: *X rays*, rayos X. *2* luz [de la luna, de la razón, etc.]. *3* GEOM. radio. *4* BOT. lígula. *5* ICT. raya. *6* BOT. ~ *grass*, ballico.
**ray (to)** irradiar. *2* exponer a una radiación. *3 intr.* radiar, resplandecer. *4* extenderse en forma radiada.
**rayon** (rei·øn) *s.* TEJ. rayón.
**raze (to)** (reiš) *tr.* arrasar, asolar. *2* rascar, rozar. *3* raspar, borrar. *4* afeitar.
**razor** (rei·šøʳ) *s.* navaja de afeitar: ~ *strop*, suavizador [para la navaja]. *2* ZOOL. ~ *clam*, ~ *shell*, navaja [molusco].
**razz** (ræš) *s.* (E.U.) burla, irrisión.
**razz (to)** *tr.-intr.* (E.U.) mofarse [de].
**razzia** (ræ·šia) *s.* razzia.
**razzle-dazzle** (ræ·šøl-dæ·šøl) *s.* bullicio, confusión, aturdimiento, borrachera. *2* especie de tíovivo.
**re** (rei) *s.* MÚS. re. *2 prep.* COM., DER. acerca de, referente a.
**reabsorb (to)** (riabso·ʳb) *tr.* reabsorber.
**reabsorption** (-pshøn) *s.* reabsorción.
**reaccess** (riæ·ksis) *s.* MED. recidiva.
**reach** (rɪch) *s.* acción de alcanzar [con la mano, etc.]. *2* alcance, poder, posibilidad: *within my* ~, a mi alcance. *3* distancia, extensión. *4* tramo, sección. *5* extensión de tierra o agua. *6* MAR. bordada.
**reach (to)** *tr.* alargar, extender, tender: *to* ~ *out one's hand*, alargar o tender la mano. *2* tocar, llegar a o hasta, alcanzar: *to* ~ *home*, llegar a casa. *3* llegar a las manos, a oídos, etc., de. *4* alargar, dar. *5* largar, atizar. *6* mover, influir sobre. *7* alcanzar, obtener. *8* comprender. *9 intr.* alargar el brazo, la mano, etc. [para tocar, alcanzar, etc.]. *10* extenderse, llegar, alcanzar [a o hasta]. *11* MAR. ceñir el viento. *12 to* ~ *after*, esforzarrse por obtener. *13 to* ~ *into*, meter la mano en, penetrar en.
**reach-me-down** *adj.* hecho [ropa]; de lance; de segunda mano.
**react (to)** (riæ·kt) *intr.* reaccionar.

**re-act (to)** *tr.* TEAT. volver a representar.
**reactance** (-tans) *s.* ELECT. reactancia.
**reaction** (-shøn) *s.* reacción.
**reactionary** (-shøneri) *adj.-s.* reaccionario.
**reactivate (to)** (-tiveit) *tr.* reactivar.
**reactive** (-tiv) *adj.* reactivo.
**reactor** (-øʳ) *s.* FÍS., ELECT. reactor. *2* QUÍM. reactivo.
**read** (red) *pret. y p. p.* de TO READ. *2 adj.* instruido, versado.
**read (to)** (rɪd) *tr.* leer. *2* interpretar. *3* descifrar [señales, indicios, etc.]. *4* aprender, estudiar. *5* indicar, registrar [díc. de un termómetro, etc.]. *6* IMPR. corregir [pruebas]. *7 to* ~ *one a lecture*, reprender vivamente. *8 to* ~ *out of*, expulsar de [una asociación, etc.]. *9 intr.* leer: *to* ~ *of* o *about*, leer acerca de, leer que; *to* ~ *through one*, leerle a uno el pensamiento; *to* ~ *for the bar*, prepararse para el foro. *10* decir, rezar [un escrito o impreso]: *the passage reads thus*, el pasage reza así. *11* dar conferencias. *12* leerse: *it reads easily*, se lee con facilidad. ¶ Pret. y p. p.: *read* (red).
**readable** (-abøl) *adj.* legible, leíble. *2* interesante, entretenido [libro, etc.].
**readapt (to)** (rɪadæ·pt) *tr.* readaptar.
**reader** (rɪ·døʳ) *s.* lector. *2* IMPR. corrector. *3* libro de lectura.
**readily** (re·dili) *adv.* prontamente. *2* fácilmente, sin esfuerzo. *3* de buena gana.
**readiness** (-nis) *s.* prontitud, expedición, facilidad. *2* disposición, buena voluntad. *3* disponibilidad.
**reading** (rɪ·ding) *s.* lectura, lección. *2* conferencia, disertación. *3* indicación [de un termómetro, etc.]. *4* leyenda [materia escrita]. *5 adj.* que lee; de lectura: ~ *book*, libro de lectura; ~ *desk*, atril, facistol; ~ *room*, gabinete de lectura.
**readjust (to)** (rɪadjø·st) *tr.* reajustar.
**readmit (to)** (rɪadmi·t) *tr.* readmitir.
**ready** (re·di) *adj.* preparado, pronto, listo, dispuesto, aparejado: *to make* ~, preparar, disponer; *prepararse*. *2* dispuesto, gustoso. *3* vivo, ágil, diestro. *4* fácil [método]. *5* pronto [pago, réplica, etc.]. *6* a la mano, disponible; contante, efectivo. *7* ~ *reckoner*, baremo.
**ready (to)** *tr.* preparar, apercibir, aprestar.
**ready-made** *adj.* ya hecho, confeccionado: ~ *clothes*, ropa hecha.
**ready-witted** *adj.* de ingenio vivo, pronto.
**reaffirm (to)** (rɪafø·ʳm) *tr.* reafirmar, reiterar.
**reafforest (to)** (rɪafo·røst) *tr.* repoblar de árboles.
**reagent** (rieidʸønt) *s.* QUÍM. reactivo.
**real** (ri·al) *adj.* real, verdadero. *2* sincero. *3* DER., FÍS. real. *4* DER. inmueble, raíz: ~ *estate*, bienes raíces; fincas.
**real-estate** *adj.* inmobiliario; de fincas.
**realgar** (riæ·lgaʳ) *s.* rejalgar.
**realism** (rɪ·alism) *s.* FIL., B. ART. realismo. *2* realismo, espíritu práctico.
**realistic** (rɪali·stik) *adj.* FIL., B. ART. realista. *2* práctico, realista.
**reality** (riæ·liti) *s.* realidad.
**realizable** (rɪ·alaišabøl) *adj.* realizable. *2* comprensible, perceptible.
**realization** (rɪališei·shøn) *s.* realización. *2* comprensión.
**realize (to)** (rɪ·alaiš) *tr.* comprender, ver, sentir, percatarse de. *2* realizar. *3* dar vida o realidad a. *4* obtener [un precio].
**really** (rɪ·ali) *adv.* realmente, de veras.
**realm** (relm) *s.* reino. *2* campo, dominio, región.

**realty** (rɪ·alti) *s.* DER. bienes raíces.
**ream** (rɪm) *s.* resma. 2 gran cantidad.
**ream (to)** *tr.* MEC. escariar.
**reamer** (rɪ·møʳ) *s.* escariador.
**reanimate (to)** (ɪræ·nimeit) *tr.* reanimar. 2 *intr.* reanimarse.
**reap (to)** (rɪp) *tr.* segar, guadañar. 2 recoger, cosechar.
**reaper** (rɪ·pøʳ) *s.* segador. 2 segadora mecánica.
**reaping machine** *s.* segadora mecánica.
**reappear (to)** (rɪapi·ʳ) *intr.* reaparecer.
**reappraise (to)** (rɪaprei·š) *tr.* retasar.
**rear** (rɪ·øʳ) *adj.* trasero, de atrás, de cola, último, posterior: ~ *admiral*, contralmirante; ~ *drive*, AUTO. tracción posterior; ~ *guard*, retaguardia. 2 *s.* trasera, zaga, parte de atrás; fondo [de una sala]; cola [de una fila]: *in the* ~, detrás, atrás, a la cola. 3 MIL. retaguardia.
**rear (to)** *tr.* levantar, alzar; erguir; erigir. 2 criar, cultivar; educar. 3 *intr.* empinarse, encabritarse.
**rearm (to)** (rɪ·aʳm) *tr.* MIL. rearmar. 2 *intr.* rearmarse.
**rearmost** (rɪ·øʳmoust) *adj.* último, de más atrás.
**rearrange (to)** (rɪarei·ndŷ) *tr.* volver a arreglar, disponer en un nuevo orden; refundir.
**rear-view mirror** *s.* AUTO. retrovisor.
**rearward** (rɪ·øʳuøʳd) *adj.* posterior, último. 2 *adv.* hacia atrás, hacia la cola. 3 *s.* retaguardia.
**reason** (rɪ·šøn) *s.* razón. | No tiene el sentido de razón en MAT. ni el de razón social. 2 ~ *of state*, razón de estado; *to bring to* ~, hacer entrar en razón; *to listen to* ~, atender a razones; *it stands to* ~, es razonable, es justo; *by* ~ *of*, por causa de.
**reason (to)** *tr.-intr.* razonar. 2 *intr.* raciocinar. 3 *tr.* discutir, debatir. 4 persuadir o disuadir con razones.
**reasonable** (-abøl) *adj.* racional [ser]. 2 razonable. 3 módico, de precio módico.
**reasoner** (-øʳ) *s.* razonador, discutidor.
**reasoning** (-ing) *s.* razonamiento.
**reasonless** (-lis) *adj.* irracional [privado de razón]. 2 sin razón o motivo. 3 desrazonable.
**reassume (to)** (-siu·m) *tr.* reasumir [volver a tomar]. 2 volver a adoptar [una actitud, etc.]; a ocupar [un sitio]. 3 reanudar.
**reassurance** (-shu·rans) *s.* confianza restablecida. 2 seguridad renovada, afirmación repetida. 3 COM. reaseguro.
**reassure (to)** (-shu·øʳ) *tr.* tranquilizar. 2 asegurar de nuevo. 3 COM. reasegurar.
**reassuring** (-ing) *adj.* tranquilizador.
**rebaptize (to)** (rɪbæ·ptaiš) *tr.* rebautizar.
**rebate** (rɪbei·t) *s.* disminución, rebaja, descuento. 2 ARQ., CARP. rebajo.
**rebate (to)** *tr.* disminuir, deducir, rebajar, descontar. 2 ARQ., CARP. hacer un rebajo en.
**rebatement** (-mønt) *s.* rebaja, descuento.
**Rebecca** (ribe·ka) *n. pr.* Rebeca.
**rebeck** (rɪ·bek) *s.* MÚS. rabel.
**rebel** (re·bøl) *adj.-s.* rebelde; insurgente.
**rebel (to)** (ribe·l) *intr.* rebelarse, sublevarse.
**rebellion** (-iøn) *s.* rebelión, sublevación.
**rebellious** (-øs) *adj.* rebelde. 2 insubordinado.
**rebind (to)** (rɪbai·nd) *tr.* reencuadernar. 2 volver a atar, a vendar. 3 COST. ribetear de nuevo.
**rebirth** (rɪbø·ʳz) *s.* renacimiento.
**reblossom (to)** (rɪbla·søm) *intr.* reflorecer.
**rebound** (rɪbau·nd) *s.* rebote, rechazo. 2 repercusión, eco. 3 salto, bote.

**rebound (to)** *intr.* rebotar, resurtir. 2 repercutir. 3 volver a adquirir actualidad o interés. 4 *tr.* devolver, rechazar, reflejar.
**rebounding** (-ing) *s.* rebote, rechazo.
**rebroadcast** (rɪbro·dkæst) *s.* RADIO. retransmisión.
**rebroadcast (to)** *tr.* RADIO. retransmitir.
**rebuff** (ribø·f) *s.* sofión, repulsa, desaire.
**rebuff (to)** *tr.* dar un sofión a, desairar, repulsar.
**rebuild (to)** (rɪbi·ld) *tr.* reconstruir.
**rebuke** (ribiu·k) *s.* reproche, censura, increpación, reprimenda.
**rebuke (to)** *tr.* increpar, reprender, reñir, censurar. 2 ser un reproche para.
**rebus** (ri·bøs) *s.* jeroglifico.
**rebut (to)** (ribø·t) *tr.* refutar, rebatir. ¶ Pret. y p. p.: *rebutted;* ger.: *-tting.*
**rebuttal** (ribø·tal) *s.* refutación.
**recalcitrant** (rikæ·lsitrant) *adj.* recalcitrante, obstinado, rebelde.
**recalcitrate (to)** (-sitreit) *intr.* recalcitrar.
**recall** (riko·l) *s.* llamada [para hacer volver]. 2 retirada [de un embajador]. 3 recordación. 4 anulación, revocación: *beyond* ~, irrevocable. 5 MIL. llamada [a la tropa].
**recall (to)** *tr.* llamar, hacer volver. 2 retirar [un embajador, unas palabras, etc.]. 3 recordar, acordarse de. 4 anular, revocar. 5 destituir.
**recant (to)** (rikæ·nt) *tr.* retractar, desdecirse de. 2 *intr.* retractarse, desdecirse.
**recantation** (-ei·shøn) *s.* retractación.
**recap (to)** (rɪkæ·p) *tr.* recauchutar [neumáticos].
**recapitulate (to)** (rɪkapi·chøleit) *tr.-intr.* recapitular, resumir.
**recapitulation** (-ei·shøn) *s.* recapitulación, resumen.
**recast (to)** (rɪkæ·st) *tr.* refundir. 2 reformar, rehacer. 3 calcular de nuevo. ¶ Pret. y p. p.: *recast.*
**recede (to)** (risɪ·d) *intr.* retroceder. 2 retirarse, alejarse; inclinarse hacia atrás. 3 desistir, volverse atrás.
**receipt** (risɪ·t) *s.* receta, fórmula. 2 recepción, recibo: *to aknowledge* ~, acusar recibo; *on* ~ *of*, al recibo de. 3 cobranza. 4 recibo, carta de pago, recibí. 5 *pl.* ingresos, entradas.
**receipt (to)** *tr.* poner el recibí en.
**receivable** (risɪ·vabøl) *adj.* recibidero. 2 cobradero: *bills* ~, cuentas por cobrar.
**receive (to)** (risɪ·v) *tr.* recibir: *received payment*, recibí. 2 tomar, aceptar. 3 acoger. 4 percibir, cobrar. 5 comprar, receptar [géneros robados].
**receiver** (-øʳ) *s.* receptor, recibidor. 2 DER. depositario. 3 cobrador, tesorero. 4 receptador [de géneros robados]. 5 ELECT., RADIO. receptor. 6 TELÉF. auricular. 7 receptáculo, recipiente [de ciertos aparatos]. 8 DER. síndico [de una quiebra].
**receiving** (-ing) *adj.* receptor: ~ *set*, RADIO. receptor; ~ *teller*, cobrador [de la caja de un banco].
**recense (to)** (rise·ns) *tr.* revisar [un texto].
**recension** (-shøn) *s.* revisión crítica. 2 texto revisado.
**recent** (rɪ·sent) *adj.* reciente. 2 moderno, nuevo.
**receptacle** (rise·ptakøl) *s.* receptáculo, recipiente. 2 BOT. receptáculo. 3 ELECT. parte fija de un enchufe.
**receptibility** (riseptibi·liti) *s.* receptividad.
**reception** (rise·pshøn) *s.* recepción. 2 admisión, aceptación; ingreso.
**receptionist** (-ist) *s.* recepcionista.
**receptive** (rise·ptiv) *adj.* receptivo.
**receptivity** (risepti·viti) *s.* receptividad.

receptor

**receptor** (rise·ptø<sup>r</sup>) *s.* DER. receptador. 2 TELÉF. auricular.

**recess** (rise·s) *s.* hueso, entrada, nicho, alcoba. 2 suspensión, descanso; recreo [escolar]. 3 retiro, lugar recóndito.

**recess (to)** *tr.* retirar, apartar. 2 hacer un hueco o entrada en. 3 *intr.* (E.U.) tomarse una vacación, un descanso.

**recession** (-shøn) *s.* retroceso, retirada. 2 parte que hace hueco o entrada. 3 DER. retrocesión.

**recharge** (ri·cha<sup>r</sup>dỹ) *s.* recarga. 2 carga de recambio.

**recharge (to)** *tr.* recargar [cargar de nuevo].

**recidivist** (risi·divist) *s.* criminal reincidente.

**recipe** (re·sipi) *s.* récipe, receta.

**recipient** (risi·piønt) *adj.-s.* receptor, recibidor.

**reciprocal** (risi·prøkal) *adj.* recíproco, mutuo. 2 GRAM. recíproco. 3 intercambiable, permutable; inverso. 4 alternativo, de vaivén. 5 MAT. lo recíproco o inverso.

**reciprocate (to)** (risi·prøkeit) *tr.* reciprocar. 2 cambiar, intercambiar. 3 corresponder a [un afecto, favor, etc.]. 4 MEC. dar movimiento alternativo o de vaivén a. 5 *intr.* ser recíproco o correspondiente. 6 corresponder a un cumplido, etc. 7 MEC. tener movimiento alternativo o de vaivén: *reciprocating engine*, máquina de émbolo o pistón.

**reciprocation** (-ei·shøn) *s.* reciprocación, reciprocidad. 2 intercambio; correspondencia. 3 MEC. movimiento alternativo.

**recision** (risi·ỹøn) *s.* rescisión.

**recital** (risai·tal) *s.* relación, narración; enumeración. 2 recitación. 3 MÚS. recital.

**recitation** (resitei·shøn) *s.* recitación.

**recitative** (risai·tativ) *adj.* recitativo. 2 *s.* (resitati·v) MÚS. recitado.

**recite (to)** (risai·t) *tr.-intr.* recitar. 2 *tr.* narrar. 3 dar o decir [la lección].

**reck (to)** (rek) *tr.* preocuparse por, hacer caso de, tener en cuenta. 2 *intr.* preocuparse.

**reckless** (-lis) *adj.* indiferente; que no hace caso. 2 temerario, atolondrado, inconsiderado.

**recklessness** (-nis) *s.* temeridad, atolondramiento.

**reckon (to)** (re·køn) *tr.-intr.* contar, calcular. 2 *tr.* considerar [como]; tener, reputar [por]; contar [entre]. 3 calcular, suponer, creer. 4 intr. *to* ~ *on* o *with*, contar con.

**reckoner** (-ø<sup>r</sup>) *s.* contador, calculador.

**reckoning** (-ing) *s.* cuenta, cómputo, cálculo. 2 cuenta [que se paga; que se da]; ajuste de cuentas. 3 MAR. estima.

**reclaim (to)** (riklei·m) *tr.* poner en cultivo, hacer utilizable [un terreno]; ganar [terreno] al mar. 3 salvar, poner a flote. 4 regenerar, redimir [a una pers.]. 5 regenerar [una materia]. 6 DER. reclamar.

**reclamation** (reclamei·shøn) *s.* regeneración, enmienda [de una pers.]. 2 regeneración [de una materia]. 3 puesta en cultivo, desecación, etc. [de terrenos]. 4 DER. reclamación.

**reclination** (reklinei·shøn) *s.* reclinación.

**recline (to)** (riklai·n) *tr.* reclinar, recostar. 2 *intr.* reclinarse, recostarse.

**recluse** (riklu·s) *adj.* retirado, solitario. 2 *s.* pers. retirada del mundo; monje, eremita.

**reclusion** (riklu·ỹøn) *s.* reclusión; retiro, aislamiento, recogimiento.

**recognition** (rekøgni·shøn) *s.* reconocimiento. 2 atención, caso [que se hace a uno], saludo amistoso.

**recognize (to)** (re·køgnaiš) *tr.* reconocer. | No tiene el sentido de examinar o registrar. 2 agradecer.

**recoil** (rikoi·l) *s.* retroceso, reculada, reacción. 2 rebote, rechazo. 3 coz, culatazo [de un arma]. 4 movimiento de repugnancia, temor, etc.

**recoil (to)** *intr.* retroceder, recular, retirarse. 2 dar coz o culatazo [un arma]. 3 sobrecogerse, arredrarse.

**Recollect** (re·kølekt) *adj.-s.* ECLES. recoleto.

**recollect (to)** (rekøle·kt) *tr.-intr.* recordar, acordarse.

**re-collect, recollect (to)** (rıkøle·kt) *tr.* recoger, reunir. 2 recobrar. 3 *to* ~ *oneself*, reponerse, serenarse; pensarlo mejor. 4 *intr.* reunirse, volver a juntarse.

**recollection** (rekøle·kshøn) *s.* recuerdo, memoria. 2 recolección, recogimiento [espiritual].

**recommence (to)** (rıkøme·ns) *tr.-intr.* comenzar de nuevo.

**recommend (to)** (rekøme·nd) *tr.* recomendar. 2 alabar. 3 encomendar [en las oraciones].

**recommendation** (rekømendei·shøn) *s.* recomendación. 2 consejo.

**recompense** (re·kømpens) *s.* recompensa. 2 compensación, indemnización.

**recompense (to)** *tr.* recompensar, pagar, retribuir. 2 compensar, indemnizar.

**recompose (to)** (rıkømpou·š) *tr.* tranquilizar, serenar de nuevo. 2 recomponer, rehacer.

**reconcilable** (re·kønsailabøl) *adj.* reconciliable. 2 conciliable, compatible.

**reconcile (to)** (re·kønsail) *tr.* reconciliar: *to become reconciled*, reconciliarse [dos o más pers.]. 2 conciliar, compaginar, hacer compatible. 3 *to* ~ *oneself to*, conformarse con, resignarse a.

**recondite** (re·køndait) *adj.* recóndito, secreto. 2 abstruso, profundo.

**recondition (to)** (rıkøndi·shøn) *tr.* reacondicionar.

**reconduct (to)** (rıkøndø·kt) *tr.* volver a conducir o acompañar.

**reconnaissance** (rika·nisans) *s.* MIL. reconocimiento.

**reconnoitre (to)** (rekønoi·tø<sup>r</sup>) *tr.* MIL. reconocer. 2 *intr.* MIL. hacer un reconocimiento.

**reconquer (to)** (rıka·nkø<sup>r</sup>) *tr.* reconquistar.

**reconquest** (-kuest) *s.* reconquista.

**reconsider (to)** (rıkønsi·dø<sup>r</sup>) *tr.* repensar. 2 volver a estudiar, a discutir.

**reconstitute (to)** (rıka·nstitiut) *tr.* reconstituir.

**reconstruct (to)** (rıkønstrø·kt) *tr.* reconstruir.

**reconvention** (rıkønve·nshøn) *s.* DER. reconvención.

**reconvey (to)** (rıkønvei) *tr.* devolver al punto de partida. 2 traspasar [a un propietario anterior].

**record** (re·ko<sup>r</sup>d) *s.* inscripción, registro. 2 partida, copia oficial. 3 acta, documento, relación, historia. 4 DER. expediente, autos. 5 hoja de servicios, historial. 6 rollo, disco [de fonógrafo, pianola, etc.]; cinta [magnetofónica]; grabación [en disco, etc.]. 7 DEP. récord, marca: *to beat* o *break the* ~, batir la marca. 8 *pl.* archivo, protocolo. 9 fastos, anales, memorias. 10 *adj.* nunca visto, de récord, de marca.

**record (to)** (riko·<sup>r</sup>d) *tr.* asentar, inscribir, registrar. 2 protocolizar [documentos]. 3 fijar en la memoria. 4 grabar en disco fonográfico, etc.

**recorder** (-ø<sup>r</sup>) *s.* archivero, registrador: ~ *of deeds*, registrador de la propiedad. 2 grabador de discos o cintas magnetofónicas. 3 MEC. indicador, contador.

**re-count** (rı·kaunt) *s.* recuento.

**re-count (to)** (rıkau·nt) *tr.* recontar.

**recount (to)** (rikau·nt) *tr.* referir, relatar, contar.

**recoup (to)** (riku·p) *tr.* resarcirse de. *2* resarcir, indemnizar. *3 intr.* resarcirse, indemnizarse.

**recourse** (riko·ʳs) *s.* recurso, refugio, auxilio: *to have ~ to*, recurrir a. *2* COM. *without ~*, sin responsabilidad por parte del endosante.

**re-cover (to)** (rıka·vøʳ) *tr.* volver a cubrir o tapar.

**recover (to)** (rika·vøʳ) *tr.* recobrar, recuperar. *2* curar; hacer volver en sí. *3* rescatar, librar. *4* DER. ganar, obtener, reivindicar. *5 to ~ oneself*, reponerse; recobrar el equilibrio. *6 intr.* restablecerse; volver en sí.

**recoverable** (-abøl) *adj.* recuperable, recobrable; cobrable.

**recovery** (-i) *s.* recobro, recuperación. *2* cobranza. *3* restablecimiento, convalecencia: *past ~*, sin remedio.

**recreant** (re·kriant) *adj.-s.* cobarde. *2* falso, desleal; apóstata.

**recreate (to)** (re·krieit) *tr.* recrear, divertir, deleitar. *2 intr.* recrearse.

**re-create (to)** (rı·criei·t) *tr.* recrear [crear de nuevo].

**recreation** (recriei·shøn) *s.* recreación, recreo.

**recreative** (re·krieitiv) *adj.* recreativo.

**recriminate (to)** (rikri·mineit) *tr.* recriminar.

**recrimination** (-ei·shøn) *s.* recriminación.

**recross (to)** (rıkro·s) *tr.* repasar, volver a cruzar.

**recrudesce (to)** (rıkriude·s) *intr.* recrudecer.

**recrudescence** (-øns) *s.* recrudecimiento.

**recruit** (rikriu·t) *s.* recluta, novato.

**recruit (to)** *tr.* reclutar, alistar. *2* reanimar, rehacer. *3 intr.* recobrarse, reponerse. *4* rehacerse [un ejército].

**recruitment** (-mønt) *s.* reclutamiento. *2* MIL. refuerzo.

**rectal** (re·ktal) *adj.* ANAT. rectal.

**rectangle** (re·ktøngøl) *s.* GEOM. rectángulo.

**rectangular** (rektæ·ngiulaʳ) *adj.* rectangular.

**rectification** (rektifikei·shøn) *s.* rectificación, corrección, enmienda. *2* GEOM., QUÍM., ELECT. rectificación.

**rectify (to)** (re·ktifai) *tr.* rectificar, corregir, enmendar. *2* COM., QUÍM., ELECT. rectificar. ¶ Pret. y p. p.: *rectified.*

**rectilineal** (rektili·nial), **rectilinear** (-aʳ) *adj.* rectilíneo.

**rectitude** (re·ktitiud) *s.* rectitud. *2* corrección, exactitud.

**recto** (re·ktou) *s.* folio recto.

**rector** (re·ktøʳ) *s.* rector, párroco. *2* rector [de una comunidad, de universidad].

**rectorate** (-it) *s.* curato. *2* rectorado.

**rectory** (-i) *s.* curato. *2* casa rectoral.

**rectrix** (re·ktriks) *s.* timonera [pluma].

**rectum** (-tøm) *s.* ANAT. recto.

**recumbent** (rikø·mbønt) *adj.* reclinado, recostado; yacente.

**recuperate (to)** (rikiu·pøreit) *tr.* recuperar, recobrar. *2 intr.* restablecerse, reponerse, rehacerse.

**recuperation** (-ei·shøn) *s.* recuperación, recobro. *2* restablecimiento [de la salud].

**recur (to)** (rikø·ʳ) *intr.* volver [a un tema]. *2* volver a ofrecerse [a la mente, etc.]. *3* volver a ocurrir, repetirse.

**recurrence** (rikø·røns), **recurrency** (-si) *s.* repetición, reaparición [esp. periódica].

**recurrent** (-ønt) *adj.* que se repite o reaparece; periódico. *2* ANAT., BOT. recurrente.

**recurve (to)** (rikø·ʳv) *tr.* recorvar. *2 intr.* recorvarse.

**recusation** (rekiušei·shøn) *s.* recusación.

**red** (red) *adj.* encarnado, colorado, rojo; enrojecido, encendido, sanguíneo, sangriento: *~ ball*, mingo [en el billar]; *~ blood*, sangre roja, vitalidad; *~ cabbage*, lombarda [col]; *~ cell*, *~ corpuscle*, hematíe, glóbulo rojo; *~ cross*, cruz de San Jorge; *Red Cross*, Cruz Roja; *~ currant*, grosella; *~ hat*, capelo [de cardenal]; (Ingl.) oficial de estado mayor; *~ heat*, calor al rojo; *~ herring*, arenque ahumado; *~ lead*, minio; *~ light*, luz roja; señal de peligro; *~ man*, indio norteamericano; *~ ocher*, almagre; *~ pepper*, pimentón, ají, chile; *~ rag*, trapo rojo; lo que excita o enfurece; *Red Ridinghood*, Caperucita Roja; *~ tape*, balduque; fig. formalismo burocrático, expendienteo; *~ wine*, vino tinto; *to see ~*, enfurecerse; *to turn ~*, ponerse colorado, sonrojarse. *2 adj.-s.* POL. rojo, revolucionario. *3 s.* rojo, encarnado [color, colorante].

**redact (to)** (ridæ·kt) *tr.* redactar, escribir. *2* rehacer, revisar [un artículo, etc.].

**redaction** (-shøn) *s.* redacción [acción de redactar o escribir]. *2* nueva redacción; revisión.

**red-bearded** *adj.* barbirrojo.

**redbird** (re·dbøʳd) *s.* ORN. nombre del pinzón real, del cardenal y de otros pájarros.

**red-blooded** *adj.* animoso. *2* fuerte, viril.

**redbreast** (-brest) *s.* ORN. petirrojo.

**redcap** (-kæp) *s.* (E.U.) mozo de estación. *2* (Ingl.) pop. miembro de la policía militar.

**redcoat** (-kout) *s.* fam. (Ingl.) soldado.

**redden (to)** (-øn) *tr.* enrojecer, embermejar. *2 intr.* enrojecerse. *3* enrojecer, ruborizarse.

**reddish** (-ish) *adj.* rojizo.

**reddle** (re·døl) *s.* almagre.

**redeem (to)** (ridı·m) *tr.* redimir. *2* cumplir [una promesa]. *3* compensar.

**redeemer** (-øʳ) *s.* redentor: *The Redeemer*, el Redentor, el Salvador.

**redeeming** (-ing) *adj.* redentor. *2* que salva o atenúa: *~ feature*, circunstancia atenuante.

**redemand (to)** (rıdimæ·nd) *tr.* volver a pedir o a preguntar.

**redemption** (ride·mpshøn) *s.* redención. *2* cumplimiento [de una promesa, etc.].

**redescend (to)** (rı·disend) *intr.* volver a bajar.

**red-haired** *adj.* pelirrojo.

**red-handed** *adj.* con las manos ensangrentadas. *2* con las manos en la masa, en flagrante.

**redheaded** (re·djedid) *adj.* pelirrojo. *2* de cabeza roja. *3* colérico.

**red-hot** *adj.* calentado al rojo, muy caliente. *2* acérrimo, muy entusiasta. *3* fresco, reciente [noticia, etc.].

**redintegrate (to)** (redi·ntigreit) *tr.* reintegrar, restablecer, renovar.

**redirect (to)** (rıdire·kt) *tr.* volver a dirigir.

**rediscount (to)** (rıdi·skaunt) *s.* COM. redescuento.

**rediscount (to)** COM. redescontar.

**redistribute (to)** (rıdistri·biut) *tr.* redistribuir.

**red-letter** *adj.* marcado con letra roja: *~ day*, día de fiesta; día señalado, feliz, memorable.

**redness** (-nis) *s.* rojez, rojura, bermejura.

**redolent** (re·dølønt) *adj.* fragante, oloroso. *2* impregnado. *3* que recuerda o tiene algo [de].

**redouble (to)** (rıdø·bøl) *tr.* reduplicar, redoblar, aumentar. *2 intr.* redoblarse. *3 tr.-intr.* BRIDGE. recontrar.

**redoubt** (ridau·t) *s.* FORT. reducto.

**redoubtable** (-abøl) *adj.* temible, formidable.

**redound (to)** (ridau·nd) *intr.* redundar, resultar. *2* refluir, recaer.

**redpoll** (re·dpoul) *s.* ORN. pajarel, pardillo.

**redraft** (rɪ·dræft) *s.* COM. resaca. *2* nuevo dibujo o borrador.

**redraw (to)** (rɪdrɔ·) *tr.* COM. recambiar. *2* hacer nuevo dibujo o borrador.

**redress** (ri·dres) *s.* reparación, desagravio. *2* remedio; compensación. *3* corrección, enmienda.

**redress (to)** (ridre·s) *tr.* deshacer, reparar [injusticias, etc.]. *2* resarcir, compensar, remediar. *3* corregir, enmendar. *4* AVIA. enderezar. *5* equilibrar [una balanza].

**re-dress (to)** (rɪ-dre·s) *tr.-intr.* vestir o vestirse de nuevo.

**redskin** (re·dskin) *s.* indio piel roja.

**red-tape** *adj.* burocrático, de expedienteo.

**reduce (to)** (ridiu·s) *tr.* reducir [disminuir; someter, obligar; convertir]. *2* rebajar, diluir. *3* MIL. degradar. *4* CIR., QUÍM., MAT. reducir. *5* FOT. rebajar. *6 intr.* reducirse.

**reducer** (-ɵʳ) *s.* reductor. *2* FOT. líquido para rebajar. *3* MEC. manguito o tubo de reducción.

**reduction** (ridø·kshøn) *s.* reducción. *2 ~ works*, instalación donde se queman las basuras de una población.

**redundance** (ridø·ndans), **-cy** (-si) *s.* redundancia.

**redundant** (-ant) *adj.* redundante.

**reduplicate** (ridiu·plikeit) *adj.* reduplicado, doblado.

**reduplicate (to)** *tr.* reduplicar, redoblar.

**redwing** (re·dwing) *s.* ORN. malvis.

**redwood** (-wud) *s.* BOT. secoya.

**re-echo (to)** (rɪe·kou) *intr.-tr.* resonar, repercutir, repetir [como un eco].

**reed** (rɪd) *s.* BOT. caña; carrizo; junco. *2* caña [material]. *3* MÚS. caramillo. *4* MÚS. instrumento de lengüeta. *~ organ*, armonio, concertina. *5* MÚS. boquilla. *6* ARQ. junquillo. *7* TEJ. peine. *8* poét. saeta. *9* BOT. *~ mace*, espadaña.

**re-educate (to)** (rɪe·dȳøkiet) *tr.* reeducar.

**re-education** (-eishøn) *s.* reeducación.

**reedy** (ri·di) *adj.* de caña o que lo parece. *2* abundante en cañas. *3* de tono delgado y agudo.

**reef** (rɪf) *s.* arrecife, bajío, escollo. *2* MIN. filón, vena. *3* MAR. rizo: *to take in a ~*, tomar un rizo.

**reef (to)** *tr.* MAR. arrizar: *to ~ one's sails*, fig. recoger velas.

**reefer** (-ɵʳ) *s.* chaquetón de paño grueso. *2* pop. (E.U.) cigarrillo de marihuana.

**reefy** (-i) *adj.* lleno de escollos.

**reek** (rɪk) *s.* vaho, vapor, humo, tufo, mal olor.

**reek (to)** *tr.* exhalar, echar [vaho, humo, tufo, etc.]. *2* ahumar. *3 intr.* humear, vahear; oler mal: *to ~ of*, oler a. *4* salir [un vaho, humo, etc.].

**reeky** (-i) *adj.* humeante; mal oliente.

**reel** (rɪl) *s.* devanadera, carrete, broca. *2* CINE. rollo [de película]. *3* danza escocesa muy animada. *4* tambaleo.

**reel (to)** *tr.* aspar, devanar. *2* hacer dar vueltas a. *3 to ~ off*, contar, recitar, fácil y prestamente. *4 intr.* dar vueltas [la cabeza]. *5* tambalearse, vacilar, retroceder.

**re-elect (to)** (rɪile·kt) *tr.* reelegir.

**re-embark (to)** (rɪemba·ʳk) *tr.* reembarcar.

**re-enact (to)** (rɪenæ·kt) *tr.* revalidar, promulgar de nuevo [una ley]. *2* volver a representar [un papel].

**re-engage (to)** (rɪengei·dȳ) *tr.* escriturar o contratar de nuevo.

**re-enlist (to)** (rɪenli·st) *tr.* reenganchar, volver a alistar. *2 intr.* reengancharse.

**re-enter (to)** (rɪe·ntøʳ) *tr.* volver a entrar en, reingresar en.

**re-entering** (-ing) *adj.* entrante [ángulo].

**re-establish (to)** (rɪestæ·blish) *tr.* restablecer, establecer de nuevo, instaurar.

**reeve (to)** (rɪv) MAR. hacer pasar [un cabo] por; asegurar [un cabo, etc.] en algo. *2* MAR. rozar [un bajío]. *3 intr.* MAR. laborear.

**re-examine** (riegšæ·min) *tr.* reexaminar, revisar.

**re-export (to)** (rɪe·kspoʳt) *tr.* reexportar.

**refection** (rife·kshøn) *s.* refacción, comida.

**refer (to)** (rifø·ʳ) *tr.* referir, remitir, enviar, dirigir; someter al juicio o decisión de. *3* referir, relacionar, atribuir. *4 intr.* referirse, aludir. *5* remitirse. *6* dirigirse, recurrir: *~ to drawer* (R/D), COM. dirigirse al librador [nota de un banquero, suspendiendo el pago de un cheque]. ¶ Pret. y p. p.: *referred*; ger.: *-rring*.

**referee** (reførɪ·) *s.* DEP. árbitro, juez. *2* DER. árbitro, componedor. *3* ponente.

**referee (to)** *tr.* arbitrar [juzgar como árbitro].

**reference** (re·førøns) *s.* referencia, relación. *2* alusión, mención. *3* referencia, remisión; consulta: *~ mark*, IMPR. llamada; *~ work*, obra de consulta. *4* pers. que da informes de otras; estos informes. *5* COM. referencias. *6* DER. arbitramento.

**referendum** (reføre·ndøm) *s.* referéndum.

**referent** (re·førønt) *adj.* referente.

**refill** (rɪ·fil) *s.* recambio de un producto para rellenar el envase especial con que se expende.

**refill (to)** (rɪfi·l) *tr.* rellenar [volver a llenar].

**refine (to)** (rifai·n) *tr.* refinar. *2* purificar, clarificar, afinar. *3* pulir, perfeccionar. *4 intr.* refinarse, pulirse. *5* sutilizar, discurrir sutilmente.

**refined** (-d) *adj.* refinado. *2* pulido. *3* fino, culto.

**refinement** (-mønt) *s.* refinamiento. *2* sutileza. *3* finura, urbanidad. *4* afectación. *5* refinación; afinación, afino. *6* perfeccionamiento.

**refinery** (-øri) *s.* refinería.

**refit (to)** (rɪfi·t) *tr.* volver a equipar; reparar, renovar.

**reflect (to)** (rifle·kt) *tr.* reflejar, reflectar. *2* hacer recaer en, traer consigo: *to ~ credit on one*, hacer honor a uno. *3 intr.* reflejarse. *5* reflexionar. *6 to ~ on o upon*, desprestigiar, desdorar.

**reflection** (-shøn) *s.* reflexión, reverberación. *2* reflejo, imagen. *3* tacha, descrédito. *4* ANAT. repliegue. *5* reflexión, consideración: *on ~*, después de reflexionarlo, bien pensado.

**reflective** (-tiv) *adj.* reflexivo, reflectante. *2* reflexivo, meditativo. *3* GRAM. reflejo [verbo].

**reflector** (-tøʳ) *s.* reflector, reverbero. *2* telescopio de reflexión.

**reflex** (rɪ·fleks) *adj.-s.* reflejo. *2 s.* acción refleja.

**reflex (to)** (rifle·ks) *tr.* doblar, encorvar o dirigir hacia atrás.

**reflexive** (-siv) *adj.* REFLECTIVE. *2* GRAM. reflexivo.

**refloat (to)** (rɪflou·t) *tr.* volver a poner a flote. *2 intr.* volver a flotar.

**reflourish (to)** (rɪflø·rish) *intr.* reflorecer.

**reflow (to)** (rɪflou·) *intr.* refluir.

**reflux** (rɪ·fløx) *s.* reflujo.

**reforest (to)** (rɪfa·rist) *tr.* repoblar de árboles.

**reform** (rifo·ʳm) *s.* reforma.

**reform (to)** *tr.* reformar, mejorar, enmendar; convertir [hacer volver a la vida honrada]. *2 intr.* reformarse, corregirse, enmendarse.

**re-form (to)** (rɪfo·ʳm) *tr.* reformar.

**reformation** (refoᵣmei·shøn) *s.* reforma [de costumbres, etc.]. *2* (con may.) Reforma [religiosa].
**reformatory** (rifo·ʳmatori) *adj.-s.* reformatorio.
**reformer** (-øʳ) *s.* reformador.
**refract (to)** (rifræ·kt) *tr.* ópt. refractar, refringir.
**refraction** (-shøn) *s.* ópt. refracción.
**refractive** (-tiv) *adj.* refractivo, de refracción.
**refractor** (-tøʳ) *s.* telescopio de refracción.
**refractory** (-tori) *adj.* terco, obstinado, rebelde. *2* repropio [caballo]. *3* refractario, resistente. *4* med. inmune.
**refrain** (rifrei·n) *s.* lit., mús. estribillo. *2* fig. cantilena.
**refrain (to)** *tr.* refrenar, contener, detener. *2 intr.* contenerse; abstenerse.
**reframe (to)** (rıfrei·m) *tr.* rehacer, reconstruir. *2* encuadrar de nuevo.
**refrangible** (rifræ·ndÿibøl) *adj.* refrangible.
**refresh (to)** (rifre·sh) *tr.* refrescar. *2* orear. *3* renovar, restaurar. *4* reparar las fuerzas de, descansar. *5* vivificar, reanimar. *6 intr.* refrescarse, descansar. *7* refrescar [beber].
**refresher** (-øʳ) *s.* refrescador. *2* fam. bebida. *3* recordativo. *4* cursillo de vacaciones.
**refreshment** (-mønt) *s.* refrescadura. *2* refresco, refrigerio. *3* renovación. *4* descanso, esparcimiento. *5 pl.* refrescos.
**refrigerate (to)** (rifri·dÿøreit) *tr.* refrigerar, helar.
**refrigerating** (rifri·dÿøreiting) *adj.* refrigerante, frigorífico; ~ *vault*, cámara frigorífica.
**refrigerator** (rifri·dÿøreitøʳ) *s.* refrigerador. *2* nevera, enfriadera. *3* quím. refrigerante.
**refringent** (rifri·ndÿøn·) *adj.* refringente.
**refuge** (re·fiudÿ) *s.* refugio, asilo, protección, guarida. *2* refugio, asilo [lugar, institución]. *3* recurso, pretexto, escapatoria.
**refugee** (refiudÿı·) *s.* refugiado. *2* asilado.
**refulgent** (rifø·ldÿønt) *adj.* refulgente.
**refund** (rı·fønd) *s.* reintegro, reembolso, amortización. *2* consolidación [de una deuda].
**refund (to)** (rifø·nd) *tr.* restituir, reintegrar, reembolsar, amortizar. *2* consolidar [una deuda].
**refurbish (to)** (rıfø·ʳbish) *tr.* volver a pulir. *2* renovar.
**refusal** (rifiu·šal) *s.* rechazamiento. *2* negativa, denegación, repulsa, desaire. *3* opción, preferencia.
**refuse** (re·fiuš) *s.* desecho, sobras, barreduras, basura. *2 adj.* de desecho.
**refuse (to)** (rifiu·š) *tr.* rehusar, rechazar, desechar, denegar, negar. *3* negarse a. *4* renunciar, abandonar.
**refutation** (refiutei·shøn) *s.* refutación, impugnación.
**refute (to)** (rifiu·t) *tr.* refutar, impugnar, rebatir.
**regain (to)** (rigei·n) *tr.* recobrar, recuperar, volver a ganar.
**regal** (rı·gal) *adj.* real, regio.
**regale (to)** (rigei·l) *tr.* regalar, agasajar. *2* recrear, deleitar. *3 ref.* regalarse.
**regalia** (rigei·lia) *s. pl.* regalías [del soberano]. *2* insignias, distintivos. *4* atavío.
**regality** (rıgæ·liti) *s.* realeza, soberanía.
**regard** (riga·ʳd) *s.* miramiento, consideración, cuidado, atención, caso: ~ *being had to*, en vista de; *without* ~ *to*, sin considerar, sin hacer caso de. *2* afecto, respeto. *3* relación, respecto: *with* ~ *to*, con respecto a, respecto de. *4* mirada. *5 pl.* memorias, recuerdos.
**regard (to)** *tr.* mirar, contemplar. *2* reparar, observar. *3* mirar, considerar, tener en cuenta. *4* mi-

rar o considerar [como]. *5* estimar, apreciar, respetar. *6* tocar a, concernir, referirse a: *as regards*, en cuanto a.
**regardful** (-ful) *adj.* atento, cuidadoso; que tiene en cuenta. *2* respetuoso, considerado. *3* observante.
**regarding** (-ing) *prep.* tocante a, respecto de.
**regardless** (-lis) *adj.* indiferente; que no hace caso, que no tiene en cuenta.
**regatta** (rigæ·ta) *s.* dep. regata.
**regency** (rı·dÿønsi) *s.* regencia [del reino].
**regenerate** (ridÿe·nørit) *adj.* regenerado.
**regenerate (to)** (-eit) *tr.* regenerar. *2 intr.* regenerarse.
**regenerative** (-ativ) *adj.* regenerador.
**regenerator** (-eitøʳ) *s.* regenerador.
**regent** (rı·dÿønt) *adj.* regente. *2 s.* pol. regente.
**regicide** (re·dÿisaid) *s.* regicidio. *2* regicida.
**regime** (redÿı·m) *s.* pol., med. régimen.
**regimen** (re·dÿimøn) *s.* régimen [político, de lluvias, etc.]. *2* med., gram. régimen.
**regiment** (re·dÿimønt) *s.* mil. regimiento.
**regiment (to)** (-ment) *tr.* regimentar.
**regimentals** (redÿime·ntals) *s. pl.* mil. uniforme.
**region** (rı·dÿøn) *s.* región.
**register** (re·dÿistøʳ) *s.* registro [libro; oficina, asiento]; archivo, protocolo. *2* mar. matrícula. *3* registro [cinta en un libro]. *4* índice [de un libro]. *5* regulador [de calefacción]. *6* mec. indicador, mecanismo registrador. *7* mús., impr. registro.
**register (to)** *tr.* registrar, inscribir, matricular. *2* registrar, señalar [dic. de un termómetro, etc.]. *3* mar. matricular; abanderar. *4* certificar [una carta, etc.]; facturar [el equipaje]. *5 intr.* registrarse, inscribirse, matricularse.
**registrar** (re·dÿistra·ʳ) *s.* registrador; archivero.
**registration** (-trei·shøn) *s.* registro, inscripción. *2* facturación [de equipajes], partida [de un registro].
**registry** (-tri) *s.* registro [inscripción; oficina]. *2* auto., mar. matrícula.
**regnant** (re·gnant) *adj.* reinante. *2* dominante.
**regorge (to)** (rıgo·ʳdÿ) *tr.* vomitar, devolver.
**regress** (rı·gres) *s.* retroceso. *2* astr. retrogradación.
**regress (to)** (rigre·s) *intr.* retroceder. *2* astr. retrodradar.
**regression** (-shøn) *s.* regresión.
**regressive** (-siv) *adj.* regresivo; retrógrado.
**regret** (rigre·t) *s.* pesar, sentimiento. *2* remordimiento. *3* añoranza. *4 pl. to send one's regrets,* enviar excusas al rehusar una invitación.
**regret (to)** *intr.* sentir, lamentar. *2* arrepentirse. *3* llorar, añorar. ¶ Pret. y p. p.: *regretted;* ger.: *-tting.*
**regretful** (-ful) *adj.* pesaroso.
**regrettable** (-abøl) *adj.* sensible, lamentable.
**regular** (re·giulaʳ) *adj.* regular. | No tiene el sentido de mediano. *2* ordenado, metódico. *3* normal, corriente. *4* fam. acabado, consumado. *5 s.* ecles. regular. *6* soldado regular. *7* obrero permanente.
**regularize (to)** (re·giularaiš) *tr.* regularizar.
**regulate (to)** (re·giuleit) *tr.* regular, arreglar, reglamentar. *2* regular, ajustar. *3* regularizar.
**regulation** (-ei·shøn) *s.* regulación. *2* reglamentación. *3* regla, orden. *4 pl.* reglas, reglamento, ordenanzas. *5 adj.* de reglamento, reglamentario, de rigor.
**regulative** (re·giulativ) *adj.* regulador, regulativo.

**regulator** (-leitø<sup>r</sup>) *s.* regulador [que regula]. *2* MEC., ELECT. regulador. *3* registro [de reloj].

**regulus** (re·giuløs) *s.* régulo.

**regurgitate (to)** (rɪgø·<sup>r</sup>dӯiteit) *tr.* regurgitar.

**rehabilitate (to)** (rɪjabi·liteit) *tr.* rehabilitar.

**rehash** (rɪ·jæsh) *s.* refundición. *2* fárrago.

**rehash (to)** (rɪjæ·sh) *tr.* desp. recomponer; refundir.

**rehearsal** (rijø·<sup>r</sup>sal) *s.* ensayo [de una comedia, etc.]. *2* relación, enumeración. *3* repetición, recitación.

**rehearse (to)** (rijø·<sup>r</sup>s) *tr.* ensayar [una comedia, etc.]. *2* repasar [lo estudiado]. *3* repetir, recitar.

**reheat (to)** (rɪjɪ·t) *tr.* recalentar. *2* recocer.

**reign** (rein) *s.* reino, soberanía. *2* reinado.

**reign (to)** *intr.* reinar. *2* imperar, estar en boga.

**reimburse (to)** (rɪimbø·<sup>r</sup>s) *tr.* reembolsar; indemnizar.

**reimbursement** (-mønt) *s.* reembolso; indemnización.

**reimpress (to)** (rɪimpre·s) *tr.* reimprimir.

**rein** (rein) *s.* rienda: *to give* ~, aflojar las riendas, dar rienda suelta; *to take the reins*, fig. tomar las riendas. *2* sujección, freno.

**rein (to)** *tr.* guiar, gobernar. *2* refrenar, contener. *3 intr.* obedecer a las riendas. *4* detener el caballo, pararse.

**reincarnate (to)** (rɪinka<sup>r</sup>nei·t) *tr.* reencarnar.

**reindeer** (rei·ndi<sup>r</sup>) *s.* ZOOL. reno.

**reinforce** (rɪinfo·<sup>r</sup>s) *s.* refuerzo.

**reinforce (to)** *tr.* reforzar. *2* armar [el hormigón]: *reinforced concrete*, hormigón armado.

**reinforcement** (-mønt) *s.* refuerzo. *2 pl.* MIL. refuerzos.

**reinstall (to)** (rɪinsto·l) *tr.* reinstalar, reponer, rehabilitar.

**reinstate (to)** (rɪinstei·t) *tr.* reponer [en un cargo]. *2* reparar, renovar.

**reinsurance** (rɪinshu·rans) *s.* COM. reaseguro.

**reinsure (to)** (rɪinshu·<sup>r</sup>) *tr.* COM. reasegurar.

**reinvest** (rɪinve·st) *tr.* reinvertir.

**reinvestment** (-mønt) *s.* reinversión.

**reiterate (to)** (rii·tøreit) *tr.* reiterar, repetir.

**reiteration** (-ei·shøn) *s.* reiteración, repetición.

**reject** (rɪ·dӯekt) *s.* desecho.

**reject (to)** (rɪdӯe·kt) *tr.* rechazar, rehusar, repeler. *2* denegar, desoír. *3* desechar, descartar, arrinconar. *4* arrojar, vomitar.

**rejection** (-shøn) *s.* rechazamiento. *2* denegación. *3* acción de desechar. *4* desecho. *5 pl.* excremento.

**rejoice (to)** (rɪdӯoi·s) *tr.* alegrar, regocijar. *2 intr.* alegrarse, regocijarse, gozarse.

**rejoicing** (rɪdӯoi·sing) *s.* alegría, gozo, regocijo, júbilo. *2* fiesta, festividad.

**rejoin (to)** (rɪdӯoi·n) *tr.* reunirse con, volver a juntarse con. *2 tr.-intr.* responder, replicar.

**rejoinder** (-dø<sup>r</sup>) *s.* respuesta, réplica. *2* DER. dúplica.

**rejoint (to)** (-t) *tr.* ALBAÑ. rejuntar.

**rejuvenate (to)** (rɪdӯu·vøneit) *tr.* rejuvenecer, remozar.

**rekindle (to)** (rɪki·ndøl) *tr.* volver a encender. *2* reavivar.

**relapse** (rɪlæ·ps) *s.* recaída. *2* reincidencia [en un vicio, etc.]. *3* MED. recidiva. *4* relapso.

**relapse (to)** *intr.* recaer, reincidir [en un vicio, etc.]; volver [a un estado]. *2* MED. recaer.

**relate (to)** (rɪlei·t) *tr.* relatar, referir, contar. *2* relacionar [una cosa con otra]. *3 intr.* relacionarse [guardar relación], referirse.

**related** (-id) *adj.* relacionado, conexo. *2* emparentado, afín.

**relating** (-ing) *adj.* referente, concerniente.

**relation** (-shøn) *s.* relación, relato. *2* relación [entre cosas o personas]; respecto: *in* ~ *to*, en relación con, respecto a. *3* parentesco, afinidad. *4* pariente, deudo.

**relationship** (-ship) *s.* relación [entre cosas o pers.]. *2* parentesco.

**relative** (re·lativ) *adj.* relativo. *2 s.* GRAM. pronombre relativo. *3* pariente, deudo, allegado.

**relatively** (-li) *adv.* relativamente.

**relativism** (-išm) *s.* FIL., FÍS. relativismo.

**relativity** (relati·viti) *s.* relatividad.

**relax (to)** (rɪlæ·ks) *tr.* relajar, aflojar, ablandar. *2* mitigar. *3* descansar, esparcir [el ánimo]. *4 intr.* relajarse, aflojarse, ablandarse. *5* remitir, amainar. *6* descansar, esparcirse.

**relaxation** (-ei·shøn) *s.* relajación, aflojamiento. *2* remisión, mitigación. *3* descanso, solaz, esparcimiento.

**relay** (rɪ·lei) *s.* parada, posta [caballerías, lugar]. *2* relevo, remuda. *3* ELECT. relevador, relé. *4* MEC. servomotor. *5* DEP. carrera de relevos.

**relay (to)** *tr.* relevar, mudar. *2* transmitir por relevos. *3* RADIO. retransmitir [una emisión].

**release** (rɪli·s) *s.* libertad, excarcelación. *2* descargo, exoneración. *3* quita, finiquito. *4* DER. cesión; escritura de cesión. *5* MEC. disparo; escape; descarga. *6* permiso de publicación, venta, etc., a partir de una fecha determinada.

**release (to)** *tr.* libertar, soltar. *2* librar, descargar, aliviar. *3* DER. ceder. *4* permitir [a partir de una fecha determinada] la publicación, venta, etc., de una obra.

**re-lease (to)** (rɪlɪ·s) *tr.* arrendar de nuevo.

**relegate (to)** (re·ligeit) *tr.* relegar. *2* confiar, delegar.

**relent (to)** (rɪle·nt) *intr.* ablandarse, aplacarse, ceder; enternecerse. *2* mitigarse.

**relentless** (-lis) *adj.* implacable, inexorable.

**relevant** (-ant) *adj.* pertinente, aplicable, que hace o viene al caso.

**reliable** (rɪlai·abøl) *adj.* confiable, digno de confianza, seguro, formal. *2* fidedigno.

**reliance** (-ans) *s.* confianza, seguridad.

**reliant** (-ant) *adj.* confiado [que confía].

**relic** (re·lik) *s.* reliquia. *2 pl.* restos, ruinas.

**relict** (re·likt) *s.* viuda [de]. *2* superviviente [de una raza o especie]. *3 pl.* restos [mortales].

**relief** (rɪli·f) *s.* ayuda, auxilio, socorro; limosna. *2* alivio. *3* aligeramiento. *4* descanso, solaz. *5* MIL. relevo. *6* relieve, realce. *7* DER. remedio, reparación.

**relieve (to)** (rɪli·v) *tr.* relevar, remediar, auxiliar, socorrer. *2* consolar. *3* aliviar, mitigar. *4* descargar. *5* desahogar. *6* animar, romper la monotonía de. *7* realzar, hacer resaltar. *8* MIL. relevar. *9* DER. reparar, hacer justicia.

**relieving arch** (-ing) *s.* ARQ. arco de descarga.

**relight (to)** (rɪlai·t) *tr.* volver a encender.

**religion** (rɪli·dӯøn) *s.* religión.

**religionist** (-ist) *s.* fanático religioso.

**religiosity** (rɪlidӯia·siti) *s.* religiosidad.

**religious** (rɪli·dӯøs) *adj.* religioso. *2* devoto, piadoso. *3 s.* religioso.

**relinquish (to)** (rɪli·nkuish) *tr.* abandonar, dejar; desistir de. *2* ceder, renunciar a.

**reliquary** (re·likuæri) *s.* relicario.

**relish** (re·lish) *s.* buen sabor, gusto, dejo. *2* gusto,

goce, fruición. *3* gusto [para apreciar]. *4* apetencia, inclinación. *5* condimento, entremés.
**relish (to)** *tr.* saborear, paladear. *2* gustarle a uno [una cosa]; hacer [algo] con fruición. *3* sazonar, condimentar. *4 intr.* gustar, agradar. *5* saber [a].
**reload (to)** (rɪlou·d) *tr.* recargar [volver a cargar].
**reluctance** (rilø·ktɑns) *s.* repugnancia, renuencia, aversión, mala gana. *2* ELECT. reluctancia.
**reluctant** (-ɑnt) *adj.* renuente, reacio.
**rely (to)** (rilai·) *intr.* [con *on* o *upon*], confiar o fiar en, contar con, fiarse de.
**remain (to)** (rimei·n) *intr.* quedar, sobrar, restar, faltar: *to ~ undone*, quedar por hacer. *2* quedarse. *3* permanecer, continuar.
**remainder** (-dø<sup>r</sup>) *s.* resto, remanente, sobrante. *2* MAT. resta, residuo.
**remains** (rimei·ns) *s. pl.* restos [mortales]. *2* sobras. *3* reliquias, ruinas. *4* obras póstumas.
**remake (to)** (rɪmei·k) *tr.* rehacer [volver a hacer].
**remand** (rima·nd) *s.* DER. reencarcelamiento.
**remand (to)** *tr.* DER. mandar de nuevo a la cárcel.
**remark** (rima·<sup>r</sup>k) *s.* observación [acción de observar o reparar]. *2* observación, nota, dicho, comentario.
**remark (to)** *tr.* observar, advertir, notar, reparar. *2* observar, hacer notar, decir.
**remarkable** (-ɑbøl) *adj.* observable. *2* notable, extraordinario.
**remarriage** (rɪmæ·ridŷ) *s.* segundas nupcias.
**remarrry (to)** (rɪmæ·ri) *tr.-intr.* volver a casar o casarse.
**remediable** (rimɪ·diɑbøl) *adj.* remediable.
**remedial** (-diɑl) *adj.* terapéutico, reparador.
**remedy** (re·mødi) *s.* remedio.
**remedy (to)** *tr.* remediar. *2* curar. *3* arreglar, reparar, corregir.
**remember (to)** (rime·mbø<sup>r</sup>) *tr.* recordar, acordarse de. *2* hacer presente; dar recuerdos: *~ me to him*, déle recuerdos de mi parte.
**remembrance** (rime·mbrɑns) *s.* recuerdo, memoria, recordación, rememoración. *2* memoria, retentiva. *3* recuerdo [objeto].
**remind (to)** (rimai·nd) *tr. to ~ of*, acordar, recordar [una cosa a uno], hacer presente.
**reminder** (-ø<sup>r</sup>) *s.* recordativo, recordatorio.
**reminiscence** (remini·søns) *s.* reminiscencia. *2 pl.* LIT. recuerdos.
**reminiscent** (remini·sønt) *adj.* recordativo, evocador. *2* lleno de recuerdos.
**remiss** (rimi·s) *adj.* remiso, negligente.
**remission** (rimi·shøn) *s.* remisión [perdón; disminución de intensidad]. *2* COM. remesa. *3* MED. remisión.
**remissive** (-siv) *adj.* remisivo.
**remissness** (-snis) *s.* flojedad, negligencia.
**remissory** (-sori) *adj.* remisorio.
**remit (to)** (rimi·t) *tr.* remitir [perdonar; someter a la decisión, etc.; diferir, aplazar]. *2* restituir [a un estado o condición]. *3* enviar, remitir, remesar. *4 tr.-intr.* remitir, disminuir, aflojar. ¶ Pret. y p. p.: *remitted;* ger.: *-tting.*
**remittal** (-ɑl) *s.* remisión [de una pena].
**remittance** (-ɑns) *s.* COM. remesa [de dinero], giro.
**remittent** (-ønt) *adj.* remitente [fiebre, etc.].
**remitter** (-ø<sup>r</sup>) *s.* remitente.
**remnant** (re·mnɑnt) *s.* remanente, resto, residuo. *2* vestigio. *3* retal, saldo.
**remodel (to)** (rima·del) *tr.* modelar de nuevo, rehacer, reconstruir.
**remonstrance** (rima·nstrɑns) *s.* protesta, queja,

amonestación, reconvención; razonamiento para disuadir. *2* memorial, representación.
**remonstrate (to)** (rima·nstreit) *intr.* protestar, objetar, reconvenir; tratar de persuadir.
**remora** (re·møra) *s.* ICT. rémora.
**remorse** (rimo·<sup>r</sup>s) *s.* remordimiento, compunción.
**remorseless** (-lis) *adj.* implacable, cruel.
**remote** (rimou·t) *adj.* remoto, lejano, apartado. *2* extraño, ajeno. *3* MEC. *~ control*, mando a distancia.
**remount** (rimau·nt) *s.* MIL. remonta.
**remount (to)** *intr.-tr.* volver a montar, volver a subir. *2* remontarse [a una fecha, etc.].
**removable** (rimu·vabøl) *adj.* trasladable; que se puede quitar. *2* amovible.
**removal** (rimu·val) *s.* acción de quitar o llevarse; remoción, levantamiento. *2* mudanza, traslado: *~ van*, camión de mudanzas. *3* destitución. *4* eliminación, supresión, alejamiento.
**remove** (rimu·v) *s.* traslado, mudanza. *2* distancia [que separa], grado, escalón, intervalo. *3* grado [de parentesco].
**remove (to)** *tr.* trasladar, mudar. *2* alejar. *3* remover, quitar, sacar, eliminar, extirpar. *4* quitar de enmedio; matar. *5* destituir. *6 intr.* trasladarse, mudarse; irse.
**remunerate (to)** (rimiu·nøreit) *tr.* remunerar.
**remuneration** (-shøn) *s.* remuneración.
**remunerative** (rimiu·nørativ) *adj.* remuneratorio. *2* remunerador.
**Remus** (rɪ·møs) *n. pr.* Remo.
**renaissance** (renøsa·ns) *s.* renacimiento. *2* HIST. *the Renaissance*, el Renacimiento.
**renal** (rɪ·nɑl) *adj.* ANAT. renal.
**renascence** (rinæ·søns) *s.* renacimiento.
**renascent** (-ønt) *adj.* renaciente.
**rencounter** (rinkau·ntø<sup>r</sup>) *s.* encuentro [casual]. *2* encuentro, combate; disputa.
**rencounter (to)** *tr.-intr.* encontrar; topar, encontrarse con.
**rend (to)** (rend) *tr.* rasgar, desgarrar, hender, rajar. *2* mesar [los cabellos]. *3* lacerar. *4* dividir, desunir. *5 intr.* rasgarse, rajarse. ¶ Pret. y p. p.: *rent.*
**render (to)** (re·ndø<sup>r</sup>) *tr.* dar, entregar. *2* devolver. *3* reflejar. *4* dictar [sentencia, etc.]. *5* hacer, administrar [justicia]. *6* rendir [tributo, etc.]. *7* prestar, hacer [ayuda, favor, etc.]. *8* volver, hacer, poner [en un estado]: *to ~ useless*, hacer inútil. *9* dar o rendir [cuenta]. *10* B. ART. representar, expresar, interpretar. *11* traducir [a una lengua]. *12* derretir, clarificar.
**rendezvous** (ra·ndøvu) *s.* cita [para encontrarse], reunión. *2* lugar de la cita.
**rendezvous (to)** *tr.-intr.* acudir, juntarse, reunirse.
**rendition** (rendi·shøn) *s.* rendición, entrega. *2* B. ART. interpretación, ejecución. *3* traducción.
**renegade** (re·nigeid) *s.* renegado, apóstata.
**renege (to)** (rini·g) *intr.* renunciar [en el juego de naipes]. *3* fam. volverse atrás, no cumplir lo prometido.
**renew (to)** (riniu·) *tr.* renovar. *2* reanudar. *3* COM. prorrogar. *4 intr.* renovarse, reanudarse.
**renewal** (-ɑl) *s.* renovación, renuevo. *2* reanudación. *3* COM. prórroga.
**reniform** (re·nifo<sup>r</sup>m) *adj.* reniforme, arriñonado.
**renitency** (reni·tønsi) *s.* renitencia.
**rennet** (re·nit) *s.* cuajo, cuajaleche: *~ bag*, cuajar.
**renounce (to)** (rinau·ns) *tr.* renunciar. *2* renegar; abjurar. *3* repudiar, rechazar, desconocer. *4 tr.-*

*intr.* no servir [al palo que se juega] por no tener naipe de él.
**renouncement** (-mønt) *s.* renuncia.
**renovate (to)** (re·noveit) *tr.* renovar, restaurar. *2* regenerar, revigorizar.
**renovation** (-ei·shøn) *s.* renovación.
**renown** (rinau·n) *s.* renombre, fama.
**renowned** (-d) *adj.* renombrado, famoso.
**rent** (rent) *s.* renta, arriendo, alquiler. *2* desgarrón; grieta, raja. *3* cisma, división. *4* p. p. de TO REND.
**rent (to)** *tr.* arrendar, alquilar. *2 intr.* alquilarse, arrendarse.
**rentable** (-abøl) *adj.* arrendable, alquilable.
**rental** (-al) *s.* renta, arriendo, alquiler.
**renter** (-ø<sup>r</sup>) *s.* arrendatario, inquilino.
**rentier** (rantiei·) *s.* rentista.
**renunciation** (rinønshiei·shøn) *s.* renuncia.
**reopen (to)** (ñou·pøn) *tr.* volver a abrir.
**reorganize (to)** (ño·<sup>r</sup>ganaiš) *tr.* reorganizar.
**rep** (rep) *s.* TEJ. reps.
**repaint (to)** (rɪ·peint) *tr.* repintar.
**repair** (ripe·<sup>r</sup>) *s.* reparación, restauración, remiendo, compostura. *2* estado, buen estado: *in ~, in good ~,* en buen estado; *out of ~,* descompuesto. *3* punto de reunión, lugar que se frecuenta.
**repair (to)** *tr.* reparar, remendar, componer, recorrer, renovar. *2* remediar, subsanar, restablecer. *3* reparar [daños, injusticias, etc.]. *4 intr. to ~ to,* ir o acudir a; refugiarse en.
**repairable** (-abøl) *adj.* reparable, remendable.
**reparable** (re·parabøl) *adj.* reparable [pérdida, etc.].
**reparation** (reparei·shøn) *s.* reparación.
**repartee** (repa<sup>r</sup>tɪ·) *s.* respuesta o réplica pronta y aguda; agudeza. *2* discreteo.
**repartee (to)** *intr.* dar respuestas prontas y agudas.
**repartition** (ñpa<sup>r</sup>ti·shøn) *s.* reparto, partición. *2* segunda partición.
**repass (to)** (ñpæ·s) *tr.* repasar [volver a pasar]. *2* volver a pasar delante de o a cruzarse con. *3 intr.* volver a pasar.
**repast** (ripæ·st) *s.* comida refacción.
**repatriate (to)** (ñpei·triet) *tr.* repatriar.
**repay (to)** (ripei·) *tr.* pagar, corresponder a. *2* pagar [lo que se debe]; reembolsar, compensar.
**repayment** (-mønt) *s.* pago, retorno, desquite.
**repeal** (ripɪ·l) *s.* abrogación, derogación, revocación, anulación.
**repeal (to)** *tr.* abrogar, derogar, revocar, anular.
**repeat** (ripɪ·t) *s.* repetición. *2* MÚS. signo de repetición. *3* TEAT. bisado.
**repeat (to)** *tr.* repetir, reiterar. *2* recitar. *3* repasar, ensayar. *4 intr.* repetir [lo que se ha comido]. *5* repetirse periódicamente.
**repeatedly** (-tidli) *adv.* repetidamente.
**repeating** (-ting) *adj.* repetidor; de repetición.
**repel (to)** (ripe·l) *tr.* repeler, rechazar. *2* repugnar. *3* MED. repercutir. ¶ Pret. y p. p.: *repelled;* ger.: *-lling.*
**repellent** (-ønt) *adj.* repelente. *2* repulsivo. *3* impermeable. *4 s.* tela impermeable.
**repent (to)** (ripe·nt) *intr.* arrepentirse. *2 tr.* arrepentirse de.
**repentance** (-ans) *s.* arrepentimiento.
**repentant** (-ant) *adj.-s.* arrepentido. *2 adj.* de arrepentimiento.
**repeople (to)** (ñpi·pøl) *tr.* repoblar.
**repercuss (to)** (ñpø·<sup>r</sup>kø·s) *tr.* rechazar, reflejar.

**repercussion** (ñpø·<sup>r</sup>kø·shøn) *s.* repercusión. *2* rechazo, reflexión, retumbo.
**repertoire** (repø·<sup>r</sup>tua·<sup>r</sup>) *s.* MÚS., TEAT. repertorio.
**repertory** (re·pø·<sup>r</sup>tori) *s.* repertorio, inventario.
**repetend** (re·pitend) *s.* MAT. período.
**repetition** (repiti·shøn) *s.* repetición. *2* repaso [de una lección, etc.]. *4* recitación. *5* copia, reproducción.
**repetitious** (repiti·shøs) *adj.* redundante; fastidioso.
**repine (to)** (ripai·n) *intr.* quejarse, lamentarse, afligirse. *2* consumirse, decaer.
**replace (to)** (riplei·s) *tr.* reponer, devolver, volver a poner. *2* reemplazar, substituir. *3* restituir. *4* cambiar [una pieza].
**replacement** (-mønt) *s.* substitución, cambio. *2* restitución. *3* pieza de recambio.
**replant (to)** (riplæ·nt) *tr.* replantar.
**replenish (to)** (riple·nish) *tr.* llenar, henchir. *2* rellenar, llenar de nuevo, reaprovisionar.
**replete** (riplɪ·t) *adj.* lleno, repleto. *2* gordo.
**repletion** (riplɪ·shøn) *s.* repleción. *2* ahíto.
**replica** (re·plika) *s.* B. ART. réplica. *2* MÚS. repetición.
**reply** (riplai·) *s.* respuesta, contestación.
**reply (to)** *tr.* responder, contestar. *2* DER. replicar.
**report** (ripo·<sup>r</sup>t) *s.* voz, rumor. *2* reputación. *3* noticia, información. *4* reseña [de un libro]. *5* relato. *6* parte, comunicado. *7* informe, dictamen. *8* denuncia. *9* DER. apuntamiento. *10* detonación, tiro.
**report (to)** *tr.* relatar, contar, dar cuenta o parte de. *2* repetir [lo que se ha oído]. *3* hacer reportaje de. *4* reseñar [un libro]. *5* informar sobre, dictaminar. *6* denunciar. *7* rumorear: *it is reported,* se dice. *8 intr.* dar noticias de sí mismo. *9* informar, dictaminar. *10* ser reportero. *11* presentarse.
**reporter** (-ø·<sup>r</sup>) *s.* reportero. *2* informador. *3* DER. relator.
**reportorial** (ripo·<sup>r</sup>to·rial) *adj.* reporteril.
**repose** (ripou·š) *s.* reposo. *2* descanso, sueño. *3* tranquilidad, calma, sosiego.
**repose (to)** *tr.* descansar, reclinar. *2* descansar [dar descanso a]. *3* poner, depositar [confianza, etc.]. *4 intr.* reclinarse, tenderse. *5* reposar, descansar.
**reposeful** (-ful) *adj.* sosegado, tranquilo.
**repository** (ripa·šitori) *s.* repositorio, depósito, almacén. *2* pers. a quien se confían penas, esperanzas, etc. *4* LITURG. monumento.
**repossess (to)** (ñpøše·s) *tr.* recobrar, recuperar. *2* volver a poner en posesión de.
**repoussé** (røpusei·) *adj.* repujado.
**reprehend (to)** (reprije·nd) *tr.* reprender, censurar.
**reprehension** (-nshøn) *s.* reprensión. *2* reprobación, censura.
**represent (to)** (repriše·nt) *tr.* representar. *2* exponer, hacer presente.
**re-present (to)** (ñpriše·nt) *tr.* volver a presentar.
**representation** (reprišentei·shøn) *s.* representación. | No tiene el sentido de dignidad o autoridad. *2* súplica, protesta, razonamiento.
**representative** (repriše·ntativ) *adj.* representativo. *2* típico. *3 s.* representante, apoderado, delegado; (E.U.) diputado. *4* tipo, símbolo.
**repress (to)** (ripre·s) *tr.* reprimir, contener, refrenar, dominar, sofocar. *2* cohibir.
**repression** (-shøn) *s.* represión.
**reprieve** (riprɪ·v) *s.* suspensión de la ejecución de una sentencia; indulto. *2* alivio, respiro, tregua.

**reprieve (to)** *tr.* suspender la ejecución [de un reo]; indultar. 2 aliviar, dar un respiro.

**reprimand** (re·primænd) *s.* reprimenda, reprensión.

**reprimand (to)** *tr.* reprender, reconvenir.

**reprint** (rɪpri·nt) *s.* reimpresión. 2 tirada aparte.

**reprint (to)** *tr.* reprochar. 2 reprender.

**reproachful** (-ful) *adj.* de reproche.

**reproachless** (-lis) *adj.* irreprochable.

**reprobate** (re·probeit) *adj.-s.* réprobo. 2 malvado, vicioso.

**reprobate (to)** *tr.* reprobar, condenar. 2 desaprobar.

**reprobation** (reprobei·ʃøn) *s.* reprobación, desaprobación.

**reproduce (to)** (rɪprødiu·s) *tr.* reproducir. 2 *intr.* reproducirse, propagarse.

**reproducer** (-ø*r*) *s.* reproductor. 2 aparato reproductor [de sonidos, etc.].

**reproduction** (rɪprødø·kʃøn) *s.* reproducción.

**reproof** (ripru·f), **reproval** (-val) *s.* reprobación, reprensión.

**reprove (to)** (ripru·v) *tr.* reprobar, reprender, censurar.

**reptant** (re·ptant) *adj.* BOT., ZOOL. rastrero, reptante.

**reptile** (re·ptil) *adj.-s.* ZOOL. reptil. 2 *adj.* rastrero, servil.

**reptilian** (repti·lian) *s.* ZOOL. reptil. 2 *adj.* de reptil.

**republic** (ripø·blik) *s.* república.

**republican** (-an) *adj.-s.* republicano.

**republication** (rɪpøblikei·ʃøn) *s.* nueva publicación o promulgación. 2 reedición.

**repudiate (to)** (ripiu·dieit) *tr.* repudiar. 2 desconocer, rechazar; recusar.

**repudiation** (-ei·ʃøn) *s.* repudiación, repudio. 2 rechazamiento, recusación.

**repugn (to)** (ripø·gn) *tr.-intr.* repugnar.

**repugnance, -cy** (-nans, -si) *s.* repugnancia.

**repugnant** (-ant) *adj.* repugnante. 2 hostil, reacio. 3 opuesto, contradictorio.

**repulse** (ri·pøls) *s.* repulsión, rechazamiento. 2 repulsa, negativa, desaire.

**repulse (to)** *tr.* rechazar, repeler. 2 repulsar.

**repulsion** (-ʃøn) *s.* repulsión.

**repulsive** (-siv) *adj.* de repulsión. 2 repulsivo.

**reputable** (re·piutabøl) *adj.* de buena reputación, estimable, honrado, honroso, lícito.

**reputation** (repiutei·ʃøn) *s.* reputación, fama. 2 buena reputación, nota, distinción.

**repute** (ripiu·t) *s.* reputación, estimación, fama, crédito: *of ill ~*, de mala fama.

**repute (to)** *tr.* reputar, estimar, juzgar, considerar, tener por.

**reputed** (-id) *adj.* reputado. 2 supuesto.

**reputedly** (-li) *adv.* según se cree.

**request** (rikue·st) *s.* ruego, petición, solicitud: *at the ~ of*, a petición, a instancias de. 2 demanda, salida: *in ~*, en boga, solicitado.

**request (to)** *tr.* rogar, pedir, solicitar, encargar.

**requiem** (rɪ·kuiem) *s.* LITURG. réquiem.

**require (to)** (rikuai·*r*) *tr.-intr.* requerir, pedir, demandar, exigir, necesitar.

**requirement** (-mønt) *s.* requisito, condición. 2 exigencia, necesidad. 3 demanda, requerimiento.

**requisite** (re·kuišit) *adj.* requerido, necesario, indispensable. 2 *s.* requisito, cosa esencial.

**requisition** (rekuiši·ʃøn) *s.* demanda, requerimiento. 2 requisición, requisa. 3 necesidad. 4 *to put in*, o *into ~*, poner a contribución.

**requisition (to)** *tr.* requisar. 2 requerir.

**requital** (rikuai·tal) *s.* paga, pago, correspondencia, compensación, recompensa. 2 desquite.

**requite (to)** (rikuai·t) *tr.* pagar, devolver, corresponder, compensar; pagar en la misma moneda.

**reredos** (ri·ø*r*das) *s.* retablo [de altar].

**resale** (rɪsei·l) *s.* reventa.

**rescind (to)** (risi·nd) *tr.* rescindir, anular.

**rescission** (risi·ɣøn) *s.* rescisión, anulación.

**rescript** (rɪskri·pt) *s.* rescripto. 2 edicto, decreto.

**rescue** (re·skiu) *s.* liberación, rescate, salvamento, socorro: *to go to the ~ of*, acudir en socorro de.

**rescue (to)** *tr.* librar, libertar, rescatar, salvar.

**rescuer** (-ø*r*) *s.* libertador, salvador.

**research** (risø·*r*ch) *s.* búsqueda, indagación, investigación.

**research (to)** *tr.* buscar, indagar, investigar.

**reseat (to)** (rɪsɪ·t) *tr.* sentar o asentar de nuevo. 2 poner asiento nuevo a.

**resect (to)** (risø·kt) *tr.* CIR. resecar.

**resection** (rise·kʃøn) *s.* CIR. resección.

**reseda** (risi·da) *s.* BOT. reseda.

**resell (to)** (rise·l) *tr.* revender.

**resemblance** (riše·mblans) *s.* parecido, semejanza.

**resemble (to)** (-bøl) *tr.* parecerse, asemejarse a.

**resent (to)** (riše·nt) *tr.* resentirse u ofenderse de o por; sentirse de, agraviarse por.

**resentful** (-ful) *adj.* resentido, ofendido. 2 rencoroso.

**resentment** (-mønt) *s.* resentimiento, enojo.

**reservation** (rešø*r*vei·ʃøn) *s.* reservación, reserva [acción]. 2 reserva, condición, salvedad. 3 terreno o sitio reservado.

**reserve** (rišø·*r*v) *s.* reserva, repuesto. 2 terreno reservado. 3 reserva [discreción; sigilo; frialdad]. 4 reservación, reserva, restricción: *without ~*, sin reserva. 5 COM., IND., MIL. reserva.

**reserve (to)** *tr.* reservar. 2 hacerse reservar [un asiento, etc.].

**reserved** (-d) *adj.* reservado.

**reservist** (-ist) *adj.-s.* MIL. reservista.

**reservoir** (-ua*r*) *s.* depósito [de agua, gas, etc.]. 2 cubeta [de barómetro]. 3 alberca, aljibe. 4 embalse. 5 fig. mina [de datos, saber, etc.].

**reset (to)** (rɪse·t) *tr.* volver a colocar, volver a engastar o montar; volver a componer [en imprenta].

**reshape (to)** (rɪshei·p) *tr.* reformar, volver a formar.

**reship (to)** (rɪshi·p) *tr.-intr.* reembarcar.

**reshipment** (rɪshi·pmønt) *s.* reembarco, reembarque.

**reside (to)** (risãi·d) *intr.* residir.

**residence** (re·sidøns) *s.* residencia; morada, mansión; obligación de residir; período en que se reside.

**residency** (-si) *s.* residencia del gobernador de un protectorado.

**resident** (re·šidønt) *adj.* residente. 2 ORN. no migratorio. 3 inherente. 4 *s.* residente, morador. 5 ministro residente. 6 gobernador de un protectorado.

**residential** (-shal) *adj.* residencial.

**residual** (riši·diual) *adj.* residual, restante.

**residuary** (riši·diueri) *adj.* residual, restante. 2 DER. *~ legatee*, heredero universal.

**residue** (re·šidiu) *s.* residuo, resto, remanente.

**residuum** (riši·diuøm) *s.* residuo, sobras. 2 hez [de la población].

**resign (to)** (risãi·n) *tr.* dimitir, renunciar a. 2 resignar, entregar: *to ~ oneself*, entregarse a; resignarse. *3 intr.* dimitir. *4* resignarse, conformarse. *5* AJED⌐ abandonar.

**resignation** (rešignei·shøn) *s.* dimisión, renuncia. *2* resignación, conformidad.

**resigned** (rišai·nd) *adj.* resignado.

**resignee** (rišaini·) *s.* resignatario.

**resigner** (rišai·nøʳ) *s.* dimitente. *2* resignante.

**resilience, -cy** (riši·liøns, -si) *s.* resalto, rebote. *2* resorte, elasticidad. *3* fig. capacidad para reaccionar; animación, viveza.

**resilient** (-ønt) *adj.* elástico. *2* que reacciona o se recobra fácilmente; alegre, animado, vivo.

**resin** (re·šin) *s.* resina: *gum* ~, gomorresina.

**resiniferous** (rešini·førøs) *adj.* resinífero.

**resinous** (re·šinøs) *adj.* resinoso.

**resipiscence** (resi·pisøns) *s.* reconocimiento del propio error, retorno al buen sentido.

**resist** (riši·st) *s.* IND. reserva.

**resist (to)** *tr.-intr.* resistir. | No tiene el sentido de tolerar, sufrir. *2 tr.* oponerse, resistirse a.

**resistance** (-ans) *s.* resistencia [acción de resistir o resistirse; capacidad para resistir]: *to offer* ~, oponer resistencia. *2* MEC., ELECT. resistencia. *3* BIOL. defensa.

**resistant** (-ant) *adj.* resistente.

**resistless** (riši·stlis) *adj.* irresistible. *2* indefenso.

**resole (to)** (rısou·l) *tr.* remontar [el calzado].

**resolute** (re·šoliut) *adj.* resuelto, determinado, decidido. *2* firme, inflexible.

**resoluteness** (-tnis) *s.* resolución, tesón.

**resolution** (re·søliushøn) resolución [acción de resolver o resolverse]. *2* resolución, denuedo. *3* propósito: *good resolutions*, buenos propósitos. *4* solución [de un problema, etc.]. *5* acuerdo [de una asamblea]; propuesta [de acuerdo]; conclusión.

**resolve** (riša·lv) *s.* resolución, acuerdo. *2* resolución, firmeza de propósito.

**resolve (to)** *tr.* resolver [en todas sus acepciones]. *2* decidir [a uno a que haga algo]. *3* acordar [en una asamblea]. *4 intr.* resolverse, decidirse. *5 to* ~ *into*, resolverse en.

**resolved** (-vd) *adj.* resuelto. *2* acordado, decidido. *3* persuadido, convencido.

**resonance** (re·šønans) *s.* resonancia. *2* resonación.

**resonate (to)** (re·šoneit) *intr.* resonar.

**resonator** (-øʳ) *s.* resonador.

**resorb (to)** (riso·ʳb) *tr.* resorber.

**resorption** (riso·ʳpshøn) *s.* resorción.

**resort** (rišo·ʳt) *s.* recurso, medio, refugio: *to have* ~ *to*, recurrir. *2* concurso, concurrencia. *3* lugar al que se acude: *health* ~, balneario, estación termal, etc.; *summer* ~, punto de veraneo.

**resort (to)** *intr.* acudir, concurrir, frecuentar. *2* recurrir, apelar, echar mano de.

**resound (to)** (rišau·nd) *intr.* resonar, retumbar, repercutir, formar eco. *2 tr.* devolver [el sonido]. *3* poét. cantar, celebrar.

**resource** (riso·ʳs) *s.* recurso, medio, expediente, remedio: *without* ~, sin remedio. *2* ingenio, maña˙. *3 pl.* recursos.

**resourceful** (-ful) *adj.* listo, ingenioso.

**respect** (rispe·kt) *s.* ˙respeto, atención, consideración. *2* acepción o aceptación de personas. *3* respeto, relación; concepto, punto de vista: *in* ~ *of*, *with* ~ *to*, respecto a o de; *in all respects*, por todos conceptos. *4 pl.* respetos, saludos [que se mandan].

**respect (to)** *tr.* respetar. *2* respectar: *as respects*, por lo que respecta a, tocante a.

**respectability** (rispektabi·liti) *s.* respetabilidad.

**respectable** (rispe·ktabøl) *adj.* respetable. *2* decente, presentable. *3* honroso. *4* correcto, que respeta las convenciones sociales.

**respectful** (-ful) *adj.* respetuoso.

**respecting** (-ing) *prep.* con respecto a, en cuanto a, relativamente a.

**respective** (-iv) *adj.* respectivo, de cada uno.

**respirable** (rispai·rabøl) *adj.* respirable.

**respiration** (rispirei·shøn) *s.* respiración, respiro.

**respiratory** (rispai·ratori) *adj.* respiratorio.

**respire (to)** (rispai·ʳ) *tr.-intr.* FISIOL., BOT. respirar. *2 intr.* resollar. *3* respirar [descansar, cobrar aliento].

**respite** (re·spit) *s.* respiro, tregua, descanso. *2* suspensión [esp. de la pena de muerte].

**respite (to)** *tr.* dar treguas o respiro a. *2* suspender, diferir, aplazar.

**resplendent** (risple·ndønt) *adj.* resplandeciente.

**respond (to)** (rispa·nd) *intr.* responder, contestar. *2* responder, corresponder [a una acción, un estímulo].

**respondent** (-ønt) *adj.-s.* díc. del que responde; correspondiente. *2* DER. demandado.

**response** (rispa·ns) *s.* respuesta, contestación, réplica. *2* respuesta [a una acción, un estímulo].

**responsibility** (rispansibi·liti) *s.* responsabilidad. *2* solvencia.

**responsible** (rispa·nsibøl) *adj.* responsable: *to be* ~ *for*, ser responsable de; ser la causa u origen de. *2* solvente. *3* autorizado, respetable.

**responsibleness** (-nis) *s.* responsabilidad.

**responsive** (rispa·nsiv) *adj.* que responde o corresponde [a una acción, un afecto], sensible; obediente; que se interesa.

**rest** (rest) *s.* descanso, reposo; sueño, sueño eterno: *to have a* ~, tomarse un descanso; *to lay to* ~, enterrar; *without* ~, sin descanso. *2* tregua, pausa. *3* inacción. *4* paz, tranquilidad. *5* parada, detención. *6* posada, descansadero. *7* apoyo, soporte. *8* diablo [de billar]. *9* cuja [para la lanza]. *10* ristre. *11* MÚS. pausa, silencio. *12* cesura. *13* resta, restante: *the* ~, lo demás; los demás. *14* saldo, superávit. *15* TENIS. rest. *16 at* ~, en reposo; tranquilo; dormido; en paz [muerto].

**rest (to)** *intr.* descansar, reposar, dormir; yacer; estar quieto, tranquilo. *2* cesar, parar. *3* posarse. *4* descansar, apoyarse, basarse [en], cargar [sobre]. *5* descansar, confiar [en]. *6* quedar, permanecer. *7 to* ~ *with*, depender de. *8 tr.* descansar, dar descanso a: *to* ~ *oneself*, descansar. *9* descansar, asentar, poner, apoyar, basar.

**restaurant** (re·storant) *s.* restaurante.

**restful** (re·stful) *adj.* quieto, sosegado. *2* que da descanso; reparador.

**restharrow** (-jærou) *s.* BOT. gatuña.

**resting place** (-ing) *s.* descansadero. *2* última morada. *3* meseta [de escalera].

**restitute (to)** (re·stitiut) *tr.* restituir.

**restitution** (restitiu·shøn) *s˙.* restitución, devolución. *2* indemnización, compensación.

**restitutive** (resti·tiutiv) *adj.* restitutorio.

**restive** (re·stiv) *adj.* ingobernable, reacio. *2* repropio [caballo]. *3* inquieto, impaciente, alborotado.

**restless** (-lis) *adj.* inquieto, intranquilo, agitado, impaciente. *2* bullicioso, revoltoso, levantisco. *3* desvelado, insomne.

**restock (to)** (rısta·k) *tr.* reaprovisionar. *2* repoblar [un acuario, etc.].

**restoration** (ristorei·shøn) *s.* restauración. *2* reno-

vación. *3* restablecimiento, recobro. *4* restitución, devolución.
**restorative** (risto·rativ) *adj.-s.* restaurativo. *2* reconstituyente.
**restore (to)** (risto·ʳ) *tr.* restaurar. *2* restablecer. *3* reponer [en el trono, etc.]. *4* restituir, devolver. *5 to* ~ *to life,* devolver la vida a.
**restrain (to)** (ristrei·n) *tr.* refrenar, contener, reprimir, coartar, impedir. *2* restringir, limitar. *3* encerrar, encarcelar.
**restraint** (ristrei·nt) *s.* refrenamiento, cohibición, restricción. *2* reserva, circunspección. *3* contención, moderación.
**restrict (to)** (ristri·kt) *tr.* restringir, limitar.
**restriction** (-shøn) *s.* restricción, limitación.
**restrictive** (-tiv) *adj.* restrictivo.
**result** (riso·lt) *s.* resultado. *2* consecuencia: *as a* ~ *of,* de resultas de, a consecuencia de.
**result (to)** *intr. to* ~ *from,* resultar, originarse, inferirse. *2 to* ~ *in,* dar por resultado, venir a parar en.
**resultant** (-ant) *adj.-s.* resultante.
**resume (to)** (rišiu·m) *tr.* reasumir, volver a tomar, a ocupar. *2* recobrar. *3* reanudar, continuar. *4* resumir, compendiar.
**résumé** (rešiumei·) *s.* resumen.
**resumption** (rišø·mpshøn) *s.* reasunción. *2* recobro. *3* reanudación.
**resurge (to)** (risø·ʳdỹ) *intr.* resurgir, renacer.
**resurgence** (-øns) *s.* resurgimiento.
**resurrect (to)** (rešøre·kt) *tr.-intr.* resucitar.
**resurrection** (-shøn) *s.* resurrección; renacimiento: *the Resurrection,* la Resurrección [del Señor].
**resuscitate (to)** (risø·siteit) *tr.-intr.* resucitar.
**resuscitation** (-ei·shøn) *s.* resurrección, restauración, renovación.
**ret (to)** (ret) enriar [cáñamo, lino, etc.]. ¶ Pret. y p. p.: *retted;* ger.: *-tting.*
**retable** (ritei·bøl) *s.* retablo.
**retail** (rɪtei·l) *s.* detall, menudeo, venta al por menor: ~ *trade,* comercio al por menor; *at* ~, al por menor.
**retail (to)** *tr.* detallar, vender al por menor.
**retailer** (-øʳ) *s.* detallista, vendedor al por menor.
**retain (to)** (ritei·n) *tr.* retener, guardar, quedarse con. *2* detener, contener. *3* tomar o tener a su servicio.
**retainer** (-øʳ) *s.* criado, dependiente, seguidor. *2* retenedor, mantenedor. *3* ajuste, empleo. *4* DER. retención.
**retaining** (-ing) *adj.* de retención, de contención, etc.: ~ *wall,* muro de contención.
**retake (to)** (rɪtei·k) *tr.* volver a tomar. *2* volver a fotografiar o a firmar.
**retaliate** (ritæ·lieit) *intr.* desquitarse, vengarse. *2 tr.* devolver [un daño, una injuria].
**·etaliation** (-ei·shøn) *s.* desquite, venganza, represalias.
**retaliative, tory** (ritæ·liativ, -tori) *adj.* de desquite, de venganza, vengador.
**retard** (rita·ʳd) *s.* retardo, retraso, demora.
**retard (to)** *tr.* retardar, retrasar, atrasar. *2* diferir, dilatar, demorar.
**retardation** (-ei·shøn) *s.* retardación, retardo, retraso, atraso.
**retch (to)** (rech) *intr.* arquear, tener náuseas. *2 tr.* vomitar.
**retention** (rite·nshøn) *s.* retención. *2* retentiva. .
**retiarius** (rɪsiei·riøs) *s.* reserva, taciturnidad, silencio. *2* RET. reticencia.

**reticent** (-ønt) *adj.* reservado, callado.
**reticle** (re·tikøl) *s.* ÓPT. retículo, retícula.
**reticular** (riti·kiulaʳ) *adj.* reticular.
**reticulate (to)** (riti·kiuleit) *tr.* dar forma de red. *2* proveer de retícula.
**reticule** (re·tikiul) *s.* ridículo [bolso]. *2* ÓPT. retículo, retícula.
**reticulum** (riti·kiuløm) *s.* ANAT., ZOOL. retículo.
**retina** (re·tina) *s.* ANAT. retina.
**retinue** (re·tiniu) *s.* séquito, acompañamiento; servidores [de un personaje].
**1) retire (to)** (ritai·ʳ) *intr.* retirarse, apartarse, retroceder. *2* retirarse, recogerse, irse a acostar. *3* retraerse. *4* retirarse; jubilarse. *5 tr.* retirar, apartar, sacar. *6* COM. retirar [de la circulación, etc.]. *7* retirar, jubilar.
**2) retire (to)** (ritai·ʳ) *tr.* poner neumáticos nuevos o llantas nuevas a.
**retired** (ritai·rd) *adj.* retirado, apartado, solitario. *2* íntimo, recóndito. *3* retraído. *4* retirado, jubilado.
**retirement** (-mønt) *s.* retiro [recogimiento; lugar retirado]. *2* retirada. *3* retraimiento. *4* retiro, jubilación.
**retiring** (-ing) *adj.* retraído, tímido, modesto. *2* que se retira. *3* del retiro o jubilación.
**retorsion** *s.* RETORTION.
**retort** (rito·ʳt) *s.* réplica mordaz. *2* QUÍM. retorta.
**retort (to)** *tr.-intr.* replicar. *2 tr.* retorcer, redargüir. *3* devolver [una ofensa, etc.].
**retortion** (rito·ʳshøn) *s.* retorsión. *2* represalia.
**retouch** (ritø·ch) *s.* retoque.
**retouch (to)** *tr.* retocar, pulir. *2* FOT. retocar.
**retrace (to)** (ritrei·s) *tr.* desandar: *to* ~ *one's steps,* volver sobre sus pasos. *2* seguir las huellas, buscar el origen de. *3* repasar [con los ojos, con la memoria], evocar. *4* relatar, contar.
**retract (to)** (ritræ·kt) *tr.* retractar, retractarse de. *2* retraer, encoger. *3 intr.* retractarse. *4* retraerse, encogerse.
**retractation** (-ei·shøn) *s.* retractación. *2* acción de desdecirse.
**retractile** (ritræ·ktil) *adj.* retráctil.
**retraction** (ritræ·kshøn) *s.* retractación. *2* retracción [de un órgano retráctil].
**retread** (rɪ·tred) *s.* neumático recauchutado.
**retread (to)** (rɪtre·d) *tr.* volver a pisar u hollar. *2* AUTO. recauchutar [neumáticos].
**retreat** (ritrɪ·t) *s.* retiro, retirada. *2* retiro, aislamiento. *3* refugio, asilo. *4* ECLES. retiro. *5* MIL. retirada. *6* MIL. retreta [toque]. *7* ARQ. parte entrante.
**retreat (to)** *intr.* retirarse, retroceder,·cejar. *2* refugiarse. *3* tener inclinación hacia atrás. *4 tr.* retirar, mover hacia atrás.
**retrench (to)** (ritre·nch) *tr.* cercenar, reducir. *2* quitar, suprimir. *3* atrincherar. *4 intr.* reducirse, economizar.
**retrenchment** (ritre·nchmønt) *s.* cercenamiento, reducción. *2* MIL. atrincheramiento, trinchera.
**retribute (to)** (retri·biut) *tr.* dar o hacer en pago o desquite.
**retribution** (retribiu·shøn) *s.* retribución, recompensa. *2* justo castigo, pago, pena merecida.
**retrieval** (ritrɪ·val) *s.* recobro, recuperación. *2* reparación. *3* cobra [en la caza].
**retrieve (to)** (ritrɪ·v) *tr.* recobrar, recuperar. *2* restablecer, rehacer, reparar, remediar. *3* desquitarse de. *4* cobrar [la caza]. *5 intr.* cobrar la caza.

**retriever** (ritrɪ·vø<sup>r</sup>) *s.* perro cobrador. *2* perdiguero.
**retroactive** (retroæ·ktiv) *adj.* retroactivo.
**retroactivity** (retroækti·viti) *s.* retroactividad.
**retrocede (to)** (re·trosid) *intr.* retroceder. *2 tr.* DER. hacer retrocesión de.
**retrocession** (retrose·shøn) *s.* retrocesión.
**retroflex** (re·trofleks) *adj.* vuelto hacia atrás.
**retrogradation** (retrogradei·shøn) *s.* retroceso. *2* ASTR. retrogradación.
**retrograde** (re·trogreid) *adj.* retrógrado.
**retrograde (to)** *intr.* retroceder. *2* ASTR. retrogradar.
**retrogress (to)** (re·trogres) *intr.* retroceder.
**retrogression** (retrogre·shøn) *s.* retroceso, empeoramiento.
**retrospect** (re·trospekt) *s.* mirada retrospectiva; *in* ~, retrospectivamente.
**retrospective** (retrospe·ktiv) *adj.* retrospectivo.
**retroussé** (røtrusei·) *adj.* respingona [nariz].
**retroversion** (retrovø·<sup>r</sup>shøn) *s.* retroversión.
**retting** (re·ting) *s.* enriado, enriamiento.
**return** (ritø·<sup>r</sup>n) *s.* vuelta, regreso, retorno: ~ *ticket*, billete de vuelta o de ida y vuelta; *many happy returns* [*of the day*], feliz cumpleaños; *by ~ mail*, *by ~ of post*, a vuelta de correo. *2* devolución, reexpedición: ~ *adress*, señas del remitente [en una carta]. *3* retorno, pago, correspondencia, cambio, desquite: *in* ~, en cambio, en recompensa. *4* respuesta, réplica. *5* vuelta, recodo. *6* beneficio, rédito, fruto; producción. *7* estado, declaración. *8* vuelta [billete]. *9 pl.* datos estadísticos, resultado: *election returns*, resultado del escrutinio.
**return (to)** *intr.* volver, retornar; regresar, reaparecer. *2* responder, replicar. *3 tr.* volver, devolver, restituir; reflejar; pagar, corresponder a, dar en cambio: *to ~ good for evil*, devolver bien por mal. *4* dar [un veredicto, una respuesta, las gracias]. *5* dar oficialmente [un informe, un estado]. *6* (Ingl.) elegir [como diputado]; anunciar como elegido.
**reunion** (rɪyu·niøn) *s.* reunión. *2* reconciliación.
**reunite (to)** (rɪyunai·t) *tr.* reunir, volver a unir, reconciliar. *2 intr.* reunirse, reconciliarse.
**revaccinate (to)** (rɪvæ·ksineit) *tr.* revacunar.
**revaluation** (rɪvaliuei·shøn) *s.* nueva valoración. *2* COM. revalorización.
**revalue (to)** (rɪvæ·liu) *tr.* revalorizar.
**revamp (to)** (rɪvæ·mp) *tr.* remendar, componer, renovar.
**reveal (to)** *tr.* revelar, descubrir, manifestar.
**reveille** (re·vøli) *s.* MIL. diana [toque].
**revel** (re·vøl) *s.* holgorio, jarana, francachela, fiesta; *farra.
**revel (to)** *intr.* jaranear, tomar parte en fiestas u orgías. *2* deleitarse, gozarse [en]. ¶ Pret. y p. p.: *revel(l)ed;* ger.: *-l(l)ing.*
**revelation** (-ei·shøn) *s.* revelación. *2* (con may.) Apocalipsis.
**revel(l)er** (re·vølø<sup>r</sup>) *s.* jaranero, juerguista, calavera.
**revelry** (re·vølri) *s.* jarana, juerga, orgía.
**revenant** (revna·nt) *s.* aparecido, espectro. *2* el que vuelve tras una larga ausencia.
**revenge** (rive·ndŷ) *s.* venganza, vindicta. *2* desquite.
**revenge (to)** *tr.* vengar, vindicar: *to be revenged, to ~ oneself*, vengarse. *2 intr.* vengarse.
**revengeful** (-ful) *adj.* vengativo.
**revenue** (re·vøniu) *s.* renta, rédito, ingresos. *2* rentas públicas; fisco: ~ *cutter*, escampavia; ~ *officer*, aduanero; agente del fisco; ~ *stamp*, póliza, timbre.
**reverberate (to)** (rivø·<sup>r</sup>børeit) *tr.* reflejar [la luz, etc.]. *2 intr.* reverberar, reflejarse, retumbar.
**reverberation** (-ei·shøn) *s.* reverberación, reflexión. *2* retumbo, eco, repercusión.
**reverberator** (rivø·<sup>r</sup>børeitø<sup>r</sup>) *s.* reverbero.
**reverberatory** (rivø·<sup>r</sup>børatori) *adj.* de reverbero.
**revere (to)** (rivi·<sup>r</sup>) *tr.* reverenciar, venerar.
**reverence** (re·vørøns) *s.* reverencia, respeto. *2* reverencia [saludo; tratamiento].
**reverence (to)** *tr.* reverenciar, acatar.
**reverend** (-ønd) *adj.* reverendo, venerable. *2* ECLES. reverendo [tratamiento]. *3 s.* clérigo.
**reverent** (-ønt) *adj.* reverente. *2* humilde, respetuoso.
**reverential** (revøre·nshal) *adj.* reverencial.
**reverie** (re·vøri) *s.* ensueño. *2* visión, fantasía.
**revers** (røvi·<sup>r</sup>), *pl.* **-vers** (-vi·<sup>r</sup>s) *s.* vuelta, vista, solapa [de un vestido].
**reversal** (rivø·<sup>r</sup>sal) *s.* inversión. *2* cambio completo [de la opinión, etc.]. *3* DER. revocación.
**reverse** (rivø·<sup>r</sup>s) *adj.* inverso, contrario. *2* de inversión, de marcha atrás. *3 s.* lo inverso o contrario: *quite the* ~, todo lo contrario. *4* inversión, cambio completo. *5* revés, contratiempo. *6* ESGR. revés. *7* reverso, revés, dorso. *8* MEC. contramarcha, marcha atrás.
**reverse (to)** *tr.* invertir, volver al revés, voltear, cambiar completamente. *2* MEC. poner en marcha atrás. *3* DER. revocar, anular. *4* invertirse; moverse en sentido contrario.
**reversely** (-li) *adv.* inversamente, al revés.
**reversible** (-ibøl) *adj.* reversible. *2* revocable. *3 s.* tejido de dos caras.
**reversion** (-shøn) *s.* reversión. *2* inversión, cambio en sentido opuesto. *3* BIOL. salto atrás.
**revert (to)** (rivø·<sup>r</sup>t) *intr.* DER. revertir. *2* volver [a un estado, lugar o tema]; retroceder. *3 tr.* volver a dirigir hacia atrás.
**revet (to)** (ri·vet) *tr.* revestir [un muro, etc.]. ¶ Pret. y p. p.: *revetted;* ger.: *-tting.*
**revetment** (-mønt) *s.* ALBAÑ., FORT., ING. revestimiento. *2* muro de contención.
**review** (riviu·) *s.* revista, inspección, repaso. *2* crítica, reseña [de una obra]. *3* revisión. *4* MIL. revista. *5* revista [periódico; espectáculo].
**review (to)** *tr.* rever. *2* revisar, repasar. *3* hacer el juicio crítico o la reseña de; analizar. *4* MIL. revistar.
**reviewer** (-ø<sup>r</sup>) *s.* crítico, revistero. *2* revisor [que revé].
**revile (to)** (rivai·l) *tr.* ultrajar, denigrar, injuriar, denostar, vilipendiar.
**revilement** (-mønt) *s.* ultraje, contumelia, denuesto, vilipendio.
**revindicate (to)** (rɪvi·ndikeit) *tr.* reivindicar.
**revisal** (rivai·šal) *s.* revisión; corrección.
**revise** (rivai·s) *s.* revisión. *2* IMPR. segunda prueba.
**revise (to)** *tr.* revisar, corregir.
**reviser** (-ø<sup>r</sup>) *s.* revisor [de un texto].
**revision** (revi·ŷøn) *s.* revisión, repaso.
**revisit (to)** (rɪvi·šit) *tr.* volver a visitar.
**revitalize (to)** (rɪvai·talaiš) *tr.* hacer revivir, galvanizar.
**revival** (rivai·val) *s.* reavivamiento, restauración, renacimiento, resurgimiento; despertar: *religious* ~, despertar religioso: *Revival of Learning*, Renacimiento humanístico. *2* TEAT. reposición [de obras antiguas].

**revive (to)** (rivai·v) *tr.* reanimar, reavivar, despertar. 2 restablecer, renovar, resucitar. *3* TEAT. reponer [obras antiguas]. *4 intr.* volver en sí. *5* revivir, renacer.
**revivify (to)** (rivi·vifai) *tr.* reivificar, reanimar, resucitar. *2* QUÍM. reactivar.
**revocable** (re·vøkabøl) *adj.* revocable.
**revocation** (-ei·shøn) *s.* revocación, derogación.
**revoke** (rivou·k) *s.* renuncio [en el juego de naipes].
**revoke (to)** *tr.* revocar, derogar. *2* renunciar [en el juego de naipes].
**revolt** (rivou·lt) *s.* revuelta, rebelión.
**revolt (to)** *intr.* sublevarse, amotinarse. *2* sublevarse, indignarse, sentir asco. *3 tr.* sublevar, levantar. *4* sublevar, indignar, dar asco.
**revolter** (-ø<sup>r</sup>) *s.* sublevado, amotinado.
**revolting** (-ing) *adj.* indignante, odioso. *2* repugnante, nauseoso.
**revolution** (revoliu·shøn) *s.* revolución.
**revolutionary** (-eri) *adj.-s.* revolucionario.
**revolutionist** (-ist) *s.* revolucionario.
**revolutionize (to)** (-naiš) *tr.* revolucionar.
**revolvable** (riva·lvabøl) *adj.* giratorio, rotatorio.
**revolve (to)** (riva·lv) *tr.* voltear; hacer girar. *2* revolver [en la mente]. *3 intr.* rodar, girar, dar vueltas.
**revolver** (-vø<sup>r</sup>) *s.* revólver.
**revolving** (-ving) *adj.* rotativo, giratorio: ~ *door*, puerta giratoria.
**revue** (riviu·) *s.* TEAT. revista.
**revulsion** (rivø·lshøn) *s.* MED. revulsión. *2* cambio repentino, reacción [esp. en los sentimientos o en las ideas].
**revulsive** (rivø·lsiv) *adj.-s.* revulsivo, revulsorio.
**reward** (riuø·<sup>r</sup>d) *s.* premio, recompensa, galardón. *2* pago, merecido.
**reward (to)** *tr.* premiar, recompensar, pagar.
**reweigh (to)** (riuei·) *tr.* repesar.
**reword (to)** (rɪ·uø<sup>r</sup>d) *tr.* redactar de nuevo.
**rewrite (to)** (rɪrai·t) *tr.* volver a escribir. *2* refundir [un escrito]. *3* (E.U.) arreglar [lo escrito por otro] para su publicación.
**rhabdomancy** (rab·dømɑnsi) *s.* rabdomancia.
**rhapsode** (ræ·psød), **rhapsodist** (ræ·psødist) *s.* rapsoda. *2* autor de rapsodias.
**rhapsodize (to)** (ræ·psodaiš) *tr.* recitar como una rapsodia. *2 intr.* hablar con entusiasmo exagerado.
**rhapsody** (ræ·psødi) *s.* rapsodia. *2* expresión o discurso entusiástico.
**rhea** (rɪ·ɑ) *s.* ORN. ñandú, avestruz americano.
**Rhenish** (re·nish) *adj.* renano.
**rheophore** (rɪ·ofo<sup>r</sup>) *s.* ELECT. reóforo.
**rheostat** (rɪ·ostæt) *s.* ELECT. reóstato.
**rhetoric** (re·tørik) *s.* retórica.
**rhetorical** (rita·rikal) *adj.* retórico.
**rhetorician** (ritari·shan) *s.* retórico.
**rheum** (rum) *s.* MED. resfriado, catarro. *2* poét. lágrimas.
**rheumatic** (rumæ·tik) *adj.-s.* reumático.
**rheumatism** (ru·matišm) *s.* reumatismo, reuma.
**rheumy** (ru·mi) *adj.* catarroso. *2* húmedo. *3* legañoso.
**Rhineland** (rai·nlænd) *n. pr.* GEOGR. Renania.
**rhinoceros** (raina·sørøs) *s.* ZOOL. rinoceronte. *2* ORN. ~ *hornbill*, cálao rinoceronte.
**rhinoplasty** (rai·noplæsti) *s.* rinoplastia.
**rhizoma** (raisou·ma), **rhizome** (rai·šoum) *s.* BOT. rizoma.
**rhizopod** (rai·šopad) *s.* ZOOL. rizópodo.

**Rhodes** (rou·dš) *n. pr.* GEOGR. Rodas.
**rhodium** (rou·dɪøm) *s.* QUÍM. rodio.
**rhododendron** (roudode·ndrøn) *s.* BOT. rododendro.
**rhomb** (ramb) *s.* GEOM. rombo. *2* BLAS. losange.
**rhombic** (-ik) *adj.* rombal. *2* CRISTAL. rómbico.
**rhombohedron** (rambouji·drøn) *s.* GEOM. romboedro.
**rhomboid** (ra·mboid) *s.* GEOM. romboide.
**Rhone** (roun) *n. pr.* GEOGR. Ródano.
**rhotacism** (rou·tasišm) *s.* rotacismo.
**rhubarb** (ru·ba<sup>r</sup>b) *s.* BOT. ruibarbo. *2* BOT. rapóntico.
**rhumb** (røm) *s.* MAR. rumbo, cuarta.
**rhyme** (raim) *s.* LIT. rima. *2* LIT. consonante. *3* *without* ~ *or reason*, sin ton ni son.
**rhyme (to)** *tr.* rimar. *2 intr.* rimar [hacer rima]. *3* consonar, armonizar. *4* versificar.
**rhymester** (-stø<sup>r</sup>) *s.* coplero, poetastro.
**rhythm** (rizm) *s.* ritmo. *2* MED. periodicidad.
**rhythmic(al** (-ik(al) *adj.* rítmico.
**rialto** (riæ·ltou) *s.* mercado, lonja.
**rib** (rib) *s.* ANAT., BOT., MAR. costilla. *2* ENT. nervio [de ala]. *3* cordoncillo [de tejido]. *4* varilla [de paraguas o abanico]. *5* ARQ. nervadura. *6* surco; caballón. *7* COST. vivo. *8* MEC. pestaña, reborde.
**rib (to)** *tr.* formar costillas, cordoncillos, etc., en. *2* COST. hacer un vivo en. *3* pop. tomar el pelo. ¶ Pret. y p. p.: *ribbed;* ger.: *-bbing.*
**ribald** (ri·bald) *adj.* grosero, obsceno. *2 s.* libertino, ribaldo.
**ribaldry** (-dri) *s.* lenguaje grosero, obsceno.
**riband** (ri·band) *s.* cinta [esp. de condecoración].
**ribbed** (ribd) *adj.* que tiene costillas, nervios, rebordes o pestañas.
**ribbing** (ri·bing) *s.* costillaje. *2* varillaje. *3* nerviación, nervadura.
**ribbon** (ri·bøn) *s.* cinta, galón, banda, tira. *2 pl.* cintas, perifollos.
**ribbon (to)** *tr.* encintar [adornar con cintas]. *2 intr.* extenderse como una cinta, serpentear.
**rice** (rais) *s.* BOT. arroz: ~ *field*, arrozal; ~ *paper*, papel de arroz.
**rich** (rich) *adj.* rico [en bienes, etc.; abundante; exquisito, costoso, suntuoso]. *2* suculento, muy condimentado. *3* muy dulce. *4* fértil, pingüe. *5* fragante. *6* vivo [color]. *7* lleno y pastoso, melodioso [voz, sonido]. *8* cómico, divertido.
**Richard** (ri·cha<sup>r</sup>d) *n. pr.* Ricardo.
**riches** (-iš) *s. pl.* riqueza, opulencia.
**richness** (-nis) *s.* riqueza, abundancia, suntuosidad, exquisitez. *2* fertilidad. *3* suculencia. *4* viveza [del color]. *5* plenitud [de la voz, del sonido].
**rick** (rik) *s.* niara, almiar.
**rick (to)** *tr.* amontonar [grano, paja, etc.].
**rickets** (ri·kits) *s.* raquitis, raquitismo.
**rickety** (ri·kiti) *adj.* raquítico. *2* desvencijado. *3* ruinoso, vacilante.
**ricksha** (ri·ksha), **rickshaw** (-sho) *s.* cochecito chino o japonés de dos ruedas y tirado por uno o más hombres.
**rictus** (ri·ktøs) *s.* rictus.
**rid (to)** (rid) *tr.* librar, desembarazar, zafar: *to get* ~ *of*, librarse, desembarazarse de; *to be well* ~ *of*, salir bien de. ¶ Pret. y p. p.: *rid* o *ridded;* ger.: *-dding.*
**riddance** (-ɑns) *s.* acción de librar o desembarazar.
**ridden** (-øn) *p. p.* de TO RIDE.

**riddle** (ri·døl) *s.* enigma, misterio, acertijo, adivinanza. *2* criba, harnero.

**riddle (to)** *tr.* resolver, descifrar. *2* cribar. *3* acribillar. *4 intr.* hablar enigmáticamente.

**ride** (raid) *s.* paseo o viaje a caballo, en bicicleta, en coche, etc. *2* camino de herradura.

**ride (to)** *intr.* cabalgar, montar; ir a hombros de una persona; ir, pasear o viajar a caballo, en bicicleta, en coche, etc.: *to ~ roughshod,* fig. no reparar en obstáculos; dominar, tiranizar, imponerse. *2* flotar. *3* ir por el espacio. *4* encabalgar, traslapar. *5* girar, funcionar. *6* andar, marchar [el caballo montado, el vehículo]. *7* MAR. *to ~ at anchor,* estar fondeado.
*8 tr.* montar, ir montado en [un caballo, una bicicleta, etc.]. *9* conducir, ir en [un vehículo]. *10* surcar [las olas]. *11* llevar montado, llevar a cuestas. *12* correr [una carrera]. *13* recorrer, atravesar, etc. [montado o en vehículo]. *14* llevar, impeler, empujar. *15* criticar, burlarse de. *16* oprimir. *17 to ~ down,* alcanzar [a uno] yendo montado; atropellar, pisotear, vencer. *18 to ~ out,* sortear, capear [un temporal, etc.]. *19 to ~ shank's mare,* fig. ir a pie. ¶ Pret.: *rode;* p. p. *ridden;* ger.: *riding.*

**rider** (-ø^r) *s.* jinete, amazona; picador; ciclista; el que va montado en algo. *2* hojuela pegada a un documento. *3* aditamento.

**ridge** (ridy̆) *s.* espinazo [de cuadrúpedo]. *2* arista, elevación larga y estrecha. *3* cerro, cresta, cordillera. *4* AGR. caballón, lomo. *5* caballete [de tejado]. *6* cordoncillo [de tejido].

**ridge (to)** *tr.* dar forma de lomo o cresta. *2 intr.* formar lomo o cresta. *3* tener lomos o arrugas; formar cordoncillo. *4* rizarse [el mar].

**ridgepiece** (-PIS), **ridgepole** (-poul) *s.* ARQ. parhilera.

**ridicule** (ri·dikiul) *s.* ridículo, irrisión: *to turn to ~,* ridiculizar, mofarse de.

**ridicule (to)** *tr.* ridiculizar, poner en ridículo.

**ridiculous** (ridi·kiuløs) *adj.* ridículo.

**riding** (rai·ding) *s.* cabalgata; paseo a caballo o en coche. *2* encaballamiento. *3* equitación, manejo; *~ coat,* redingote, capote; *~ habit,* traje de amazona; *~ school,* picadero. *4* MAR. fondeadero.

**rife** (raif) *adj.* corriente, común, general, frecuente, abundante. *2 ~ with,* lleno de.

**Riff** (rif) *n. pr.* GEOGR. Rif. *2 s.* rifeño.

**riffle** (rai·føl) *s.* (E.U.) rápido, rabión. *2* rizo [del agua].

**riffle (to)** *tr.* peinar [la baraja].

**riffraff** (ri·fræf) *s.* canalla, chusma. *2* bahorrina. *3 adj.* ruin, vil.

**rifle** (rai·føl) *s.* rifle, fusil. *2* raya [del fusil].

**rifle (to)** *tr.* pillar, saquear. *2* robar, llevarse. *3* rayar [un arma].

**rifleman** (rai·følmæn) *s.* fusilero.

**rifler** (rai·flø^r) *s.* saqueador, salteador.

**rift** (rift) *s.* hendedura, grieta, raja, rendija. *2* disensión, desavenencia.

**rift (to)** *tr.* hender, rajar. *2 intr.* henderse, rajarse, abrirse.

**rig** (rig) *s.* MAR. aparejo. *2* equipo, avíos, maquinaria. *3* carruaje con sus caballos. *4* traje, atavío, disfraz. *5* timo, engaño, mala partida.

**rig (to)** *tr.* MAR. aparejar, enjarciar. *2* equipar, preparar. *3* vestir, ataviar, disfrazar. *4* burlar, engañar. *5* arreglar o influir por medios fraudulentos.

**rigadoon** (rigadu·n) *s.* rigodón.

**rigging** (-ing) *s.* MAR. aparejo, jarcia. *2* equipo, instrumentos.

**right** (rait) *adj.* recto, derecho [no torcido]. *2* GEOM. recto. *3* ASTR. recta [ascensión]. *4* recto, justo, honrado. *5* bueno, correcto, verdadero, conveniente, apropiado, que se busca, que está bien, sano, cuerdo: *to be all ~,* estar bien; *in one's ~ mind,* en sus cabales. *6* que tiene razón: *you are ~,* usted tiene razón. *7* derecho, diestro; de la derecha. *8 the ~ side of,* el derecho, el haz de.
*9 adv.* derecho, en derechura. *10* inmediatamente: *~ afterwards,* acto seguido; *~ away, ~ off,* en seguida, en el acto. *11* exactamente, de lleno. *12* mismo; *~ now,* ahora mismo. *13* muy: *~ reverend,* reverendísimo. *14* correctamente, bien; justamente; con razón: *~ or wrong,* con razón o sin ella. *15* a la derecha: *~ and left,* a diestro y siniestro. *16* MIL. *~ about!,* ¡derecha!
*17 interj. all ~!,* ¡está bien!, ¡conformes!
*18 s.* derecho, justicia, razón: *to be in the ~,* tener razón; *by ~,* by rights, de derecho; propiamente. *19* derecho [que se tiene]: *rights of man,* derechos del hombre; *in one's own ~,* por derecho propio. *20* derecho [de una tela, etc.]. *21* derecha, diestra. *22* POL. derecha. *23 to put,* o *set, to rights,* poner en orden, arreglar.

**right (to)** *tr.* hacer justicia a. *2* enderezar, corregir: *to ~ a wrong,* deshacer un entuerto. *3* MAR. adrizar.

**rightabout-face** (rai·tabaut) *s.* vuelta a la derecha. *2* media vuelta.

**right-angled** *adj.* rectangular, rectángulo.

**righteous** (rai·chøs) *adj.* recto, justo. *2* honrado, virtuoso.

**rightful** (rai·tful) *adj.* justo, honrado, legítimo.

**right-hand** *adj.* derecho, de la derecha: *~ drive,* AUTO. conducción a la derecha; *~ man,* fig. hombre de confianza, brazo derecho.

**right-handed** *adj.* que no es zurdo. *2* para la mano derecha. *3* mañoso, hábil. *4* dado o hecho con la derecha. *5* que gira, etc., de izquierda a derecha.

**right-minded** *adj.* recto, honrado.

**rightness** (-nis) *s.* derechura. *2* rectitud, justicia. *3* corrección, exactitud; propiedad.

**right-wing** *adj.* POL. derechista, de la derecha.

**rigid** (ri·dy̆id) *adj.* rígido. *2* preciso, riguroso.

**rigidity** (ridy̆·diti) *s.* rigidez.

**rigmarole** (ri·gmaroul) *s.* galimatías.

**rigor** (ri·gø^r) *s.* rigidez. *2* rigor. *3* austeridad. *4 ~ mortis,* rigidez cadavérica.

**rigorism** (-išm) *s.* rigorismo.

**rigorist** (-ist) *s.* rigorista.

**rigorous** (-øs) *adj.* riguroso, rigoroso.

**rile** (rail) *tr.* fam. irritar, exasperar.

**rill** (ril) *s.* arroyuelo, riachuelo.

**rill (to)** *intr.* correr formando arroyuelo.

**rim** (rim) *s.* borde, margen, canto [esp. de algo curvo]. *2* reborde, pestaña. *3* aro, llanta [de rueda].

**rim (to)** *tr.* proveer de un borde. *2* enllantar [una rueda]. *3* correr alrededor del borde de; rodear. ¶ Pret. y p. p.: *rimmed;* ger.: *-mming.*

**rime** (raim) *s.* RHYME. *2* escarcha, helada.

**rime (to)** *tr.-intr.* TO RHYME. *2* cubrir o cubrirse de escarcha.

**rimester** (rai·mstø^r) *s.* RHYMESTER.

**rimple** (ri·mpøl) *s.* arruga. *2* rizo, onda [en el agua, etc.].

**rimple (to)** *tr.* arrugar, plegar. *2* rizar, hacer ondear [el agua, etc.].

**rimy** (rai·mi) *adj.* helado, cubierto de escarcha.

**rind** (raind) *s.* corteza. *2* cáscara, piel, hollejo.
**rind** (to) *tr.* descortezar. *2* pelar, mondar.
**ring** (ring) *s.* anillo, sortija. *2* ajorca. *3* anilla, anillo, aro, cerco. *4* argáneo. *5* ojera [en el ojo]. *6* grafila. *7* pista, arena, redondel. *8* BOX. ring, cuadrilátero. *9* corro, rueda, círculo. *10* pandilla. *11* sonido vibrante, resonante; clamor, estruendo; tañido [de campana]; sonido [de timbre]; llamada [de teléfono]. *12* juego de campanas. *13* tono especial: ~ *of defiance*, tono de desafío.
**1) ring** (to) *tr.* cercar, circundar. *2* poner anillo o anillas a. *3* quitar [a un árbol] una tira circular de corteza. *4* *intr.* moverse en círculo; formar círculo. ¶ Pret. y p. p.: *ringed.*
**2) ring** (to) *tr.* hacer sonar [un cuerpo metálico]; tocar, tañer, repicar [campanas]; tocar [un timbre o campanilla]. *2* anunciar, celebrar, convocar [con toque de campanas]. *3* repetir, reiterar. *4 to* ~ *up*, llamar; llamar por teléfono; TEAT. subir el telón. *5 intr.* hacer sonar el timbre o la campanilla, llamar. *6* sonar, tañer, retiñir. *7* resonar. *8* zumbar [los oídos]. *9 to* ~ *true*, sonar bien, sonar como verdadero. ¶ Pret.: *rang* o *rung;* p. p.: *rung.*
**ring-around-a-rosy** *s.* corro [juego].
**ringbolt** (-boult) *s.* perno con anillo.
**ringdove** (ri·ngdɒv) *s.* ORN. paloma.
**ringer** (ri·ngøʳ) *s.* campanero. *2* ELECT. llamador.
**ringing** (ri·nging) *adj.* resonante; retumbante. *2 s.* campaneo, repique; retintín. *3* zumbido [de oídos]. *4* anillamiento.
**ringleader** (ri·nglɪdøʳ) *s.* cabecilla, jefe de banda.
**ringlet** (ri·nglit) *s.* anillejo, pequeño círculo. *2* sortija, rizo.
**ringmaster** (ri·ngmæstøʳ) *s.* director de pista [en un circo].
**ring-shaped** *adj.* circular, en forma de anillo.
**ringworm** (-wøʳm) *s.*MED. culebrilla.
**rink** (rink) *s.* pista de patinar, patinadero.
**rinse** (to) (rins) *tr.* lavar con agua, aclarar, enjuagar.
**riot** (rai·øt) *s.* tumulto, alboroto, motín, bullanga. *2* desenfreno, exceso. *3* diversión bulliciosa. *4* orgía.
**riot** (to) *intr.* armar alboroto o motines. *2* entregarse al desenfreno. *3* ser exuberante. *4* moverse tumultuosamente.
**rioter** (-øʳ) *s.* alborotador, amotinado. *2* desenfrenado, libertino.
**riotous** (-øs) *adj.* amotinado. *2* desenfrenado, disoluto. *3* alborotado, bullicioso.
**rip** (rip) *s.* rasgadura, rasgón, hendedura. *2* descosido. *3* agua revuelta por la confluencia de dos corrientes. *4* fam. jamelgo. *5* fam. bribón.
**rip** (to) *tr.* rasgar, romper, abrir, destripar; descoser. | Con *up, open* u *off. 2* arrancar, cortar. | Gralte. con *out* o *away. 3* buscar a fondo, sondear, descubrir. | Con *up. 4 intr.* desgarrarse, abrirse, partirse. *5* fam. ir a toda marcha. ¶ Pret. y p. p.: *ripped;* ger.: *-pping.*
**riparian** (raipe·rian) *adj.* ribereño, riberiego.
**ripe** (raip) *adj.* maduro, sazonado. *2* en sazón, a punto, preparado. *3* hecho, acabado. *4* avanzada [edad]. *5* MED. maduro [tumor, etc.]. *6* rosado, colorado.
**ripen** (to) (-øn) *tr.* madurar, sazonar. *2 intr.* madurar, sazonarse. *3* MED. madurar.
**riposte** (to) (ripou·st) *intr.* ESGR. responder. *2* responder, replicar con viveza.
**ripper** (ri·pøʳ) *s.* rasgador, destripador. *2* arrancaclavos. *3* pop. pers. o cosa notable.

**ripping** (-ing) *s.* rasgadura. *2* descosedura. *3 adj.* magnífico, estupendo.
**ripple** (ri·pøl) *s.* onda, rizo, escarceo [del agua]. *2* pliegue, ondulación. *3* murmullo [de las aguas].
**ripple** (to) *intr.* rizarse, ondear [la superficie del agua, etc.]. *2* caer en ondas. *3* murmurar [el agua, etc.]. *4 tr.* rizar, formar ondas en.
**ripsaw** (to) (ri·pso) *tr.* aserrar [madera] al hilo.
**rise** (raiš) *s.* levantamiento, elevación, ascensión, subida. *2* resurrección. *3* salida [de un astro]. *4* pendiente, cuesta, altura, eminencia. *5* altura [de una cosa sobre otra]. *6* ING. peralte. *7* elevación [de la voz, del tono]. *8* crecida [de un río]. *9* encumbramiento; ascenso. *10* aumento, alza, subida [de precios, la temperatura, etc.]. *11* (Ingl.) aumento de sueldo. *12* fuente, causa, origen: *to give* ~ *to,* dar origen a.
**rise** (to) *intr.* subir, ascender, elevarse, alzarrse, remontarse. *2* resucitar. *3* salir [un astro]. *4* encumbrarse, ascender. *5* levantarse [de la cama, etc.; ponerse en pie]. *6* erizarse. *7* levantar la sesión. *8* alzarse, sublevarse. *9* subir, aumentar, crecer; encarecerse. *10* leudar. *11* nacer, salir, originarse. *12* surgir, aparecer, presentarse, ocurrir. *13* revolverse [el estómago]. *14 to* ~ *to,* estar o ponerse a la altura de. ¶ Pret.: *rose;* p. p.: *risen.*
**risen** (-øn) *p. p.* de TO RISE.
**riser** (rai·søʳ) *s.* el que se levanta. *2* sublevación. *3* conductor o tubo ascendente. *4* ARQ. contrahuella.
**risible** (ri·šibøl) *adj.* risible. *2* de la risa.
**rising** (rai·šing) *s.* subida, elevación, ascensión. *2* levantamiento. *3* alzamiento, insurrección. *4* resurrección. *5* ASTR. orto, salida. *6* protuberancia, grano. *7 adj.* ascendente. *8* pendiente, en cuesta. *9* creciente. *10* naciente. *11* próspero.
**risk** (risk) *s.* riesgo, exposición, peligro, albur.
**risk** (to) *tr.* arriesgar, aventurar, exponer. *2* correr el riesgo de, exponerse a.
**risky** (-i) *adj.* arriesgado, expuesto. *2* imprudente, temerario. *3* verde, escabroso.
**rite** (rait) *s.* rito.
**ritual** (ri·chual) *adj.-s.* ritual. *2* ceremonial.
**ritually** (-i) *adv.* según el ritual.
**rivage** (ri·vidy) *s.* ribera, costa, playa.
**rival** (rai·val) *adj.* competidor. *2 s.* rival.
**rival** (to) *tr.* competir, rivalizar con; emular a. ¶ Pret. y p. p.: *rival(l)ed;* ger.: *-l(l)ing.*
**rivalry** (-ri) *s.* rivalidad. *2* emulación.
**rive** (to) (raiv) *tr.* rajar, hender. *2 intr.* henderse. ¶ P. p.: *rived* o *riven.*
**river** (ri·vøʳ) *s.* río: ~ *basin,* cuenca de río; ~ *horse,* hipopótamo; *up the* ~, río arriba; *down the* ~, río abajo.
**riverain** (-ein) *adj.-s.* ribereño.
**riverhead** (-jed) *s.* nacimiento de un río.
**riverside** (-said) *s.* ribera, orilla de un río. *2 adj.* ribereño.
**rivet** (ri·vit) *s.* roblón, remache.
**rivet** (to) *tr.* roblar, remachar. *2* asegurar, afianzar. *3* fijar, absorber [la mirada, la atención, etc.].
**riveter** (-øʳ) *s.* remachador. *2* remachadora [máquina].
**rivulet** (ri·viulit) *s.* riachuelo, arroyo.
**roach** (rouch) *s.* ICT. pez de agua dulce. *2* cucaracha. *3* MAR. alunamiento.
**road** (roud) *s.* carretera, camino: *high* ~, camino real; ~ *mender,* peón caminero. *2* camino, vía, paso: *to be on the* ~, ir de pueblo en pueblo [un

viajante, una compañía teatral, etc.]; *in the* ~, estorbando el paso. *3 sing.* o *pl.* rada, ensenada.
**roadbed** (-bed) *s.* firme de carretera. *2* FERROC. explanación, balasto.
**roadhouse** (-jaus) *s.* parador.
**roadside** (-said) *s.* orilla del camino: ~ *inn*, parador, venta.
**roadstead** (-sted) *s.* MAR. rada, fondeadero.
**roadster** (-stǿʳ) *s.* automóvil abierto de turismo. *2* caballo de tiro y silla. *3* MAR. buque que puede fondear en las radas.
**roadway** (-wei) *s.* carretera, calzada.
**roam (to)** (roum) *intr.* rodar, vagar, errar. *2 tr.* rodar, vagar por.
**roan** (roun) *adj.* roano. *2 s.* caballo roano.
**roar** (roʳ) *s.* rugido, bramido. *2* estruendo: ~ *of laughter*, risotada. *3* grito; griterío.
**roar (to)** *intr.* rugir, bramar. *2* tronar, hacer estruendo. *3* roncar [un motor]. *4* gritar, alborotar. *5* reír a carcajadas.
**roaring** (-ing) *adj.* rugiente, bramador; ruidoso. *2* tremendo, enorme. *3* próspero, animado [negocio].
**roast** (roust) *s.* asado. *2* carne para asar. *3* tueste, tostadura. *4* crítica, burla. *5 adj.* asado, tostado: ~ *beef*, rosbif.
**roast (to)** *tr.* asar. *2* tostar. *3* METAL. calcinar. *4* criticar, ridiculizarr. *5 intr.* asarse. *6* tostarse.
**roaster** (-ǿʳ) *s.* el que asa, asador. *2* tostador. *3* pollo o lechón propio para asarse.
**rob (to)** (rab) *tr.* robar, hurtar, pillar, saquear: *to* ~ *Peter to pay Paul*, desnudar a un santo para vestir a otro. *2* robar [en el juego de naipes]. ¶ Pret.: *robbed*; ger.: *robbing*.
**robber** (-ǿʳ) *s.* ladrón: *highway* ~, salteador.
**robbery** (-ǿri) *s.* robo, latrocinio.
**robe** (roub) *s.* ropaje, traje talar, túnica; toga [de juez, letrado, etc.]. *3* bata. *4* vestido de mujer. *5* manta [de coche]. *6* fig. manto, capa.
**robe (to)** *tr.* vestir, ataviar. *2 intr.* vestirse, ataviarse, cubrir.
**robin** (ra·bin) *s.* ORN. pechicolorado, petirrojo.
**roborate (to)** (ra·børeit) *tr.* roborar.
**robot** (rou·bøt) *s.* robot; autómata.
**robust** (robø·st) *adj.* robusto. *2* fuerte, sólido.
**roc** (rak) *s.* rocho [ave fabulosa].
**rochet** (ra·chit) *s.* ECLES. roquete.
**rock** (rak) *s.* roca, peña, peñasco; escollo: ~ *bottom*, fondo, lo más profundo; ~ *crystal*, cristal de roca; ~ *dove*, paloma zurita; ~ *salt*, sal gema; *in the rocks*, perdido, arruinado. *2* peñón. *3* fig. defensa, sostén, refugio. *4* pop. diamante; piedra preciosa. *5* acción de mecer o de mecerse.
**rock (to)** *tr.* mecer, balancear, acunar. *2* sosegar, aquietar. *3* hacer tambalear, estremecer. *4 intr.* mecerse, balancearse, oscilar. *5* tambalearse.
**rocker** (-ǿʳ) *s.* el que mece o balancea. *2* mecedora. *3* columpio. *4* pie de cuna, mecedora, etc. *5* MEC. balancín; eje oscilante.
**rocket** (-it) *s.* cohete: ~ *bomb*, bomba volante; ~ *launcher*, MIL. lanzacohetes. *2* BOT. oruga, roqueta.
**rocket (to)** *intr.* subir o lanzarse como un cohete. *2 tr.* bombardear con cohetes.
**rocking** (-ing) *adj.* mecedor; vacilante, oscilante: ~ *chair*, mecedora; ~ *horse*, caballo mecedor.
**rock-ribbed** (-ribd) *adj.* que tiene costillas de roca. *2* fuerte, firme, inflexible.
**rockrose** (-rouš) *s.* roca o gruta artificial.
**rocky** (-i) *adj.* rocoso, roqueño, pedregoso: *Rocky*

*Mountains*, GEOGR. Montañas Rocosas. *2* fig. duro, endurecido.
**rococo** (røkou·kou) *adj.-s.* rococó.
**rod** (rad) *s.* vara, varilla, barra. *2* varilla de virtudes. *3* vara [de autoridad; para medir; para azotar]: *to give the* ~, dar azotes. *4* bastón de mando; cetro. *5* poder, opresión, castigo. *6* medida de 5'5 yardas. *7* caña [de pescar]. *8* MEC. barra, vástago; tirante. *9* ANAT. bastoncillo.
**rode** (roud) *pret.* de TO RIDE.
**rodent** (rou·dønt) *adj.-s.* ZOOL. roedor.
**rodeo** (rou·diou o roudei·ou) *s.* rodeo [del ganado].
**rodomontade** (radømantei·d) *s.* bravata, fanfarronada.
**rodomontade (to)** *intr.* bravear, fanfarronear.
**roe** (rou) *s.* hueva. *2* ZOOL. corzo. *3* ZOOL. cierva, gama. *4* ZOOL. ~ *deer*, corzo.
**rogations** (rougei·shøns) *s. pl.* LITURG. rogaciones.
**rogatory** (rou·gatori) *adj.* rogatorio.
**rogue** (roug) *s.* pícaro, bribón, tunante. *2* fam. picaruelo, pillín. *3* elefante fiero que vive separado del rebaño.
**roguery** (-øri) *s.* bellaquería, ruindad. *2* picardía, travesura.
**roguish** (-ish) *adj.* pícaro, ruin. *2* travieso, retozón, burlón.
**roll (to)** (roil) *tr.* enturbiar. *2* irritar, enojar.
**roister** (roi·støʳ) *s.* baladrón. *2* jaranero, calavera.
**roister (to)** *intr.* fanfarronear. *2* tomar parte en orgías o fiestas ruidosas.
**roisterer** (-ǿʳ) *s.* ROISTER.
**role, rôle** (roul) *s.* papel [que se hace o representa].
**roll** *s.* rollo [de papel, etc.]. *2* fajo [de billetes]; dinero: *bank* ~, dinero disponible. *3* pergamino, documento. *4* lista, rol, nómina, catálogo, registro: *to call the* ~, pasar lista. *5* bollo, panecillo. *6* rodillo, cilindro. *7* CIR. mecha. *8* ARQ. voluta. *9* tetumbo [del trueno]; tronar [del cañón]; redoble [del tambor]. *10* trino. *11* ondulación [del terreno]. *12* balanceo. *13* movimiento [de lo que rueda; de las olas], rodadura: ~ *of the waves*, oleaje.
**roll (to)** *tr.* hacer rodar o girar. *2* mover, llevar, recorrer sobre ruedas o como sobre ruedas, con movimiento fácil. *3* arrollar, enrollar. *4* liar [un cigarrillo]. *5* envolver, fajar. *6* laminar, cilindrar; alisar, allanar, pulverizar [con rodillo]. *7* tocar redobles [en el tambor]. *8* pronunciar [la *rr*] con sonido vibrante. *9* cantar con quiebro o trino. *10* mover [los ojos], ponerlos en blanco. *11 to* ~ *up*, arrollar, enrollar; amontonar [una fortuna]. *12 intr.* rodar, girar. *13* ir, etc. [en carruaje]; andar sobre ruedas. *14* revolverse, revolcarse. *15* ondular [un terreno]. *16* balancearse [un buque, el que anda]. *17* moverse [las olas; como las olas]. *18* arrollarse, hacerse una bola. *19* retumbar, tronar, resonar, retemblar. *20* redoblar [el tambor]. *21* trinar [hacer trinos]. *22* acumularse. *23 to* ~ *about*, rodar, andar de acá para allá; *to* ~ *down*, bajar rodando; *to* ~ *in money*, nadar en posibles.
**rolled oats** (-d) *s.* copos de avena.
**roller** (-ǿʳ) *s.* MEC. rodillo, cilindro, tambor: ~ *bearing*, cojinete de rodillos; ~ *towel*, toalla continua. *2* rollo [de cocina]. *3* rueda o ruedecita [de patín, etc.]. *4* CIR. venda, faja. *5* MAR. ola larga. *6* canario que trina. *7* ORN. variedad de paloma. *8* ~ *coaster*, montañas rusas.
**rollick (to)** (ra·lik) *intr.* juguetear, retozar, travesear.
**rollicking** (-ing) *adj.* jovial, juguetón, retozón.

**rolling** (rou·ling) *adj.* rodante, que rueda; de ruedas; laminador, allanador; ondulado, que retumba, etc. V. TO ROLL: ~ *stock*, FERROC. material rodante; ~ *chair*, sillón de ruedas; ~ *mill*, laminador; taller de laminarr; ~ *pin*, rollo de cocina; ~ *stone*, piedra movediza.

**Romaic** (roumei·ik) *adj.* romaico.

**Roman** (rou·man) *adj.* romano, romanesco: ~ *catholic*, católico romano; ~ *law*, derecho romano; ~ *nose*, nariz aguileña; ~ *numeral*, número romano. *2* latina [lengua]. *3 adj.-s.* IMPR. redonda [letra]. *4 s.* romano, neolatino.

**Romance** (romæ·ns) *adj.* romance, neolatino.

**romance** *s.* romance; novela; literatura novelesca: ~ *of chivalry*, libro de caballerías. *2* lo novelesco; interés, emoción, aventura; espíritu novelesco, idilio amoroso. *3* ficción, invención. *4* MÚS. romanza.

**romance (to)** *intr.* escribir novelas. *2* contar novelas, mentiras.

**romancer** (romæ·nsø<sup>r</sup>) *s.* novelista. *2* embustero; visionario.

**Romanesque** (roumane·sk) *adj.-s.* ARQ. románico.

**Romanic** (rouma·nik) *adj.* románico, neolatino.

**Romanism** (rou·manišm) *s.* romanismo. *2* desp. católico romano.

**Romanize (to)** (rou·manaiš) *tr.-intr.* romanizar. *2 tr.* catolizar. *3 intr.* hacerse católico.

**Romansh** (rou·mænsh) *s.* romanche.

**romantic(al** (romæ·ntik(al) *adj.* romántico.

**romanticism** (-tisišm) *s.* romanticismo.

**romanticize** (-tisaiš) *tr.* hacer romántico. *2 intr.* obrar, hablar de un modo romántico.

**Romany** (ra·mani) *adj.-s.* gitano.

**Rome** (roum) *n. pr.* GEOGR., HIST. Roma.

**Romish** (-ish) *adj.* desp. romano, católico.

**romp** (ramp) *s.* juego violento o bullicioso, retozo. *2* muchacha retozona; saltabardales.

**romp (to)** *intr.* jugar, correr, saltar, retozar, triscar.

**rompers** (-ø<sup>r</sup>s) *s. pl.* vestido holgado que se pone a los niños pequeños para que jueguen.

**rondeau** (ra·ndou) *s.* LIT. rondel. *2* MÚS. rondó.

**rondel** (ra·ndøl) *s.* LIT. rondel.

**rood** (rud) *s.* cruz, crucifijo. *2* medida de 1/4 de acre. *3* medida de longitud [7 u 8 yardas].

**roof** (ruf) *s.* techo, techado, tejado, cubierta: *flat* ~, azotea; ~ *garden*, azotea jardín; ~ *truss*, armadura de tejado. *2* techo [casa, habitación]. *3* imperial [de diligencia]. *4* cielo [de la boca].

**roof (to)** *tr.* cubrir, techar. *2* alojar, abrigar.

**roofless** (-lis) *adj.* destechado. *2* sin abrigo, sin hogar.

**rooftree** (-trı) *s.* cumbrera, parhilera. *2* techo, tejado. *3* fig. techo, hogar.

**rook** (ruk) *s.* ORN. grajo, chova. *2* trampista, estafador. *3* torre, roque [de ajedrez].

**rookery** (-øri) *s.* lugar donde anidan los grajos, los pingüinos, etc.; donde procrean las focas. *2* casa miserable de vecindad.

**room** (rum) *s.* cuarto, pieza, aposento, habitación, sala. *2* espacio, sitio; cabida: *to make* ~, hacer sitio, abrir paso, despejar. *3* causa, motivo: *there is no* ~ *for doubt*, no cabe duda. *4* ocasión, oportunidad.

**room (to)** *intr.* alojarse, ocupar una habitación.

**roomful** (-ful) *s.* los que llenan un aposento; cuanto cabe en él.

**roomy** (-i) *adj.* espacioso, holgado, amplio.

**roost** (rust) *s.* percha [de gallinero]; gallinero. *2*

lugar de descanso: *at* ~, en la percha [ave]; acostado, retirado a descansar.

**roost (to)** *intr.* dormir [las aves en la percha]. *2* fig. dormir, pasar la noche. *3 tr.* albergar, dar posada.

**rooster** (-ø<sup>r</sup>) *s.* gallo [ave].

**root** (rut) *s.* raíz [en todos sus sentidos]: *cube* ~, raíz cúbica; *to take* ~, arraigar. *2* tronco [de una raza o familia].

**root (to)** *intr.-tr.* hozar. *2 tr.* arraigar, implantar; clavar en el suelo. *3 to* ~ *up* o *out*, desarraigar, arrancar, estirpar. *4 intr.* arraigar, echar raíces.

**rooted** (-id) *adj.* arraigado.

**rootlet** (lit) *s.* raicilla.

**rootstock** (-stak) *s.* BOT. rizoma. *2* fig. origen.

**rooty** (-i) *adj.* lleno de raíces. *2* radicoso.

**rope** (roup) *s.* cuerda, soga, maroma, cabo, cable: ~ *railway*, ferrocarril aéreo; ~ *yard*, cordelería; *to be at the end of one's* ~, haber agotado todos los recursos; *to know the ropes*, conocer bien un asunto, etc. *2* cuerda, dogal. *3* (E.U.) lazo, cuerda. *4* sarta, ristra; guirnalda.

**rope (to)** *tr.* atar o cercar con cuerda. *2* ensogar. *3* (E.U.) coger con lazo. *4* fam. (E.U.) *to* ~ *in*, pescar, embaucar. *5 intr.* hacer madeja [un licor].

**ropedancer** (-dænsø<sup>r</sup>) *s.* funámbulo, volatín.

**ropemaker** (-meikø<sup>r</sup>) *s.* cordelero, soguero.

**ropewalk** (-wok) *s.* atarazana [de cordelería].

**ropewalker** (-wokø<sup>r</sup>) *s.* funámbulo, volatín.

**ropeway** (-wei) *s.* ferrocarril aéreo.

**ropy** (-i) *adj.* que hace hebra o madeja; viscoso. *2* que parece cuerda.

**rorqual** (ro·<sup>r</sup>kual) *s.* ZOOL. rorcual.

**rosace** (rou·šas) *s.* ARQ. rosetón [adorno].

**rosaceous** (roušei·shøs) *adj.* rosáceo.

**rosary** (rou·šari) *s.* rosario. *2* macizo de rosales; rosaleda.

**rose** (rouš) *s.* BOT. rosa: ~ *leaf*, pétalo de rosa; ~ *water*, agua de rosas; *under the* ~, secretamente. *3* rosa [color, adorno]. *4* rallo [de regadera]. *5* ARQ. rosetón [ventana]. *6* rosa náutica. *7* ~ *diamond*, diamante rosa. *8* BOT. ~ *apple*, pomarrosa; ~ *laurel*, laurel rosa; ~ *mallow*, malva real.

*9* pret. de TO RISE.

**Rose** *n. pr.* Rosa.

**roseate** (-lit) *adj.* rosado, róseo; de color de rosa.

**rosebay** (-bei) *s.* BOT. adelfa. *2* BOT. rododendro.

**rosebud** (-bød) *s.* capullo de rosa, pimpollo.

**rosebush** (-bøsh) *s.* BOT. rosal.

**rose-coloured** (-ard) *adj.* rosado, de color de rosa.

**rosemary** (-meri) *s.* BOT. romero, rosmarino.

**roseola** (rouši·øla) *s.* MED. roseola.

**roset** (rou·šet) *s.* rosicler.

**rosette** (rouše·t) *s.* rosa [lazo de cintas]; escarapela. *2* ARQ. rosetón, florón. *3* METAL. roseta.

**rosewood** (rou·šwud) *s.* palisandro; palo de rosa.

**rosily** (-ili) *adv.* con color de rosa. *2* con optimismo, lisonjeramente.

**rosin** (ra·šin) *s.* colofonia.

**rosolio** (rošo·lio) *s.* rosolí.

**roster** (ra·stø<sup>r</sup>) *s.* MIL. lista. *2* MIL. orden del día. *3* lista, nómina. *4* horario escolar.

**rostral** (ra·stral) *adj.* rostral.

**rostrate** (ra·streit) *adj.* rostrado.

**rostrum** (ra·strøm) *s.* ZOOL., BOT., MAR. rostro. *2* tribuna [de orador].

**rosy** (rou·ši) *adj.* rosado, sonrosado, color de rosa. *2* sonrojado. *3* risueño, lisonjero. *4* optimista.

**rosy-hued** *adj.* rosado. *2* de tez rosada.

**rot** (rat) *s.* putrefacción, podredumbre. *2* BOT. ulceración. *3* VET. modorra. *4* tontería, sandez. *5* *interj.* de disgusto, impaciencia, etc.

**rot (to)** *intr.* pudrirse, corromperse, echarse a perder. *2* ir a menos. *3 tr.* pudrir. *4* enriar. ¶ Pret. y p. p.: *rotted;* ger.: *-tting.*

**Rotarian** (rØtei·rian) *adj.-s.* rotario.

**rotary** (rou·tari) *adj.* rotatorio: ~ *press,* rotativa.

**rotate (to)** (rou·teit) *intr.* rotar, rodar, girar. *2* turnar, alternar. *3 tr.* hacer rodar o girar. *4* hacer turnar o alternar.

**rotation** (-ei·shØn) *s.* rotación. *2* turno, alternación: *in* ~, *by* ~, por turno.

**rotator** (-tØ^r) *s.* lo que hace rodar. *2* MAR. hélice [de la corredera].

**rotatory** (rou·tatori) *adj.* rotatorio. *2* turnante.

**rote** (rout) *s.* rutina; repetición rutinaria; estudio de memoria mecánica: *by* ~, de rutina.

**rotifer** (rou·tifØ^r) *s.* ZOOL. rotífero.

**rotogravure** (rotØgraviu·^r) *s.* rotograbado.

**rotor** (rou·tØ^r) *s.* MEC., ELECT. rotor.

**rotten** (ra·tØn) *adj.* podrido, corrompido. *2* cariado. *3* fétido. *4* malo, abominable, sucio, ofensivo. *5* poco firme, inseguro.

**rotter** (ra·tØ^r) *s.* pop. sinvergüenza.

**rotula** (ra·tiula) *s.* rótula.

**rotund** (rotØ·nd) *adj.* redondo; rechoncho. *2* rotundo [lenguaje].

**rotunda** (*-a*) *s.* ARQ. rotonda.

**rotundity** (-iti) *s.* redondez. *2* rotundidad.

**roué** (ruei·) *s.* libertino.

**rouge** (ru ̈y) *s.* colorete, arrebol. *2* JOY. colcótar.

**rouge (to)** *tr.* pintar, dar de colorete. *2* arrebolar. *3* *intr.* pintarse. *4* arrebolarse.

**rough** (rØf) *adj.* áspero, rugoso, tosco, basto. *2* peludo, hirsuto. *3* escabroso [terreno]. *4* agitado [mar]. *5* tempestuoso, borrascoso. *6* rudo, inculto. *7* brusco. *8* en bruto, mal acabado, de preparación: ~ *copy,* borrador; ~ *draft,* bosquejo; borrador. *9* aproximativo. *10* duro; penoso; rudo, violento: ~ *usage,* uso poco cuidadoso, maltrato. *11* bronco, discordante. *12* s. lo áspero, tosco, etc.: *in the* ~, en bruto, sin pulimento. *13* matón, persona brutal. *14* terreno escabroso.

**rough (to)** *tr.-intr.* poner o ponerse áspero. *2* *to* ~ *it,* vivir sin comodidades, hacer vida campestre. *3 tr.* hacer o labrar toscamente. *4* tratar con dureza.

**roughage** (-idȳ) *s.* material tosco o grosero.

**rough-and-ready** *adj.* tosco o rudo, pero eficaz.

**rough-and-tumble** *adj.* irregular, desordenado. *2 s.* lucha violenta y sin sujeción a reglas.

**roughcast** (-kæst) *s.* modelo tosco. *2* ALBAÑ. mezcla o mortero grueso.

**roughcast (to)** *tr.* bosquejar. *2* ALBAÑ. revocar con mortero grueso.

**roughdraw (to)** (-drø) *tr.* dibujar toscamente, bosquejar.

**roughdress (to)** (-dres) *tr.* desbastar, dar [a la piedra] una superficie tosca.

**roughdry** (-drai) *adj.* seco, sin planchar.

**roughdry (to)** *tr.* secar [ropa] sin plancharla.

**roughen (to)** (-Øn) *tr.-intr.* poner o ponerse áspero, rugoso o desapacible.

**roughew (to)** (-jiu) *tr.* esculpir toscamente.

**roughhouse** (-jauš) *s.* trapatiesta, alboroto.

**roughly** (-li) *adv.* ásperamente, bruscamente. *2* toscamente. *3* aproximadamente, en términos generales.

**roughride (to)** (-raid) *tr.-intr.* domar caballos. *2* dominar, tiranizar, imponerse.

**roughrider** (raidØ^r) *s.* desbravador o domador de caballos.

**roughshod** (-shad) *adj.* herrado con ramplones.

**roulade** (rula·d) *s.* MÚS. trino.

**rouleau** (rulou·) *s.* cartucho [de dinero]. *2* rollo, cucurucho. *3* MIL. fajina.

**roulette** (rule·t) *s.* ruleta.

**round** (raund) *adj.* ·redondo: ~ *table,* mesa redonda; ~ *number,* número redondo; ~ *trip,* viaje redondo, de ida y vuelta. *2* en corro: ~ *dance,* baile en corro. *3* rechoncho. *4* rotundo. *5* completo, cabal. *6* claro, fuerte [tono, voz]. *7* grande, cuantioso, liberal. *8* rápido, vivo. *9* claro, categórico; franco, sincero. *10* recto, honrado.

*11 s.* círculo, orbe, esfera; parte redonda; rodaja. *12* redondez. *13* corro. *14* circuito, recorrido, ronda: *to go one's rounds,* hacer uno su recorrido. *15* giro, rotación; ciclo, revolución periódica; serie [de sucesos, actos, etc.]; ronda; rutina. *16* salva [de aplausos]. *17* mano, tirada, asalto [en un juego o lucha]. *18* listón, travesaño [de silla], peldaño [de escala]. *19* descarga, salva, andanada; disparo. *20*·cartucho con bala. *21* MÚS. especie de canon.

*22 adv.* alrededor; por todos lados; siguiendo un circuito o ciclo: *to turn* ~, hacer girar o rodar; *to hand* ~ *the cigars,* pasar los cigarros; *muy head goes* ~, se me va la cabeza; *all the year* ~, todo el año. *23* ~ *about,* alrededor; del lado opuesto; de un modo indirecto; aproximadamente.

*24 prep.* alrededor de. *25* a la vuelta de: ~ *the corner,* a la vuelta de la esquina.

**round (to)** *tr.* redondear. *2* moverse alrededor de, rodear, cercar. *3* doblar [un cabo, una esquina]. *4* *to* ~ *off* u *out,* redondear, completar, acabar. *5* *to* ~ *up,* recoger [pers. o cosas dispersas]. *6* *intr.* redondearse. *7* volverse, revolverse. *8* *to* ~ *to,* reponerse; MAR. orzar.

**roundabout** (-abaut) *adj.* indirecto, hecho con rodeos. *2 s.* rodeo, circunloquio. *3* chaquetilla ajustada. *4* tiovivo.

**roundel** (-Øl) *s.* redondo, círculo. *2* corro. *3* rodela. *4* ARQ. ventana, nicho o panel circular. *5* LIT. rondel.

**roundelay** (-Ølei) *s.* canción con estribillo. *2* danza en corro.

**rounders** (-Ø^rs) *s.* juego inglés parecido al béisbol.

**round-faced** *adj.* carirredondo.

**roundhand** (-jænd) *s.* letra redonda.

**roundhead** (-jed) *s.* (Ingl.) cabeza redonda [apodo que se daba a los puritanos].

**roundhouse** (-jaus) *s.* MAR. camareta alta. *2* FERROC. casa de máquinas.

**roundish** (-ish) *adj.* redondeado.

**roundly** (-li) *adv.* redondamente. *2* rotundmente. *3* francamente. *4* vigorosamente. *5* en números redondos.

**roundsman** (-mæn) *s.* (E.U.) policía que hace rondas.

**roundup** (-øp) *s.* (E.U.) rodeo [del ganado]; recogida, redada.

**roup** (rup) *s.* pepita [de las aves].

**rouse** (rauš) *s.* despertar. *2* MIL. (Ingl.) diana [toque].

**rouse (to)** *tr.* despertar. *2* animar, mover, excitar, provocar. *3* levantar [la caza]. *4* *intr.* despertar.

**rousing** (-ing) *adj.* administrador, entusiasmador. *2* activo, animado. *3* vigoroso. *4* fam. estupendo.

**rout** (raut) *s.* rota, derrota, fuga desordenada. *2* turbamulta. *3* alboroto, tumulto. *4* séquito.

**rout (to)** *tr.* derrotar, poner en fuga. *2* arrancar hozando. *3 to ~ out*, sacar, echar; hacer salir a la fuerza. *4 intr.* huir a la desbandada. *5* hozar.

**route** (rut) *s.*,ruta, camino, vía. *2* itinerario.

**route (to)** *tr.* encaminar.

**routinary** (rutı·nari) *adj.* rutinario.

**routine** (rutı·n) *s.*rutina, hábito. *2* práctica diaria o regular.

**routinist** (-ist) *s.* rútinario.

**rove** (rouv) *s.* vagabundeo, correría, paseo. *2* TEJ. mecha; mecha estirada. *3* arandela de remache.

**rove (to)** *intr.* vagar, errar, corretear. *2* piratear. *3 tr.* pasar por un ojete. *4* TEJ. estirar [la mecha].

**rover** (-ø<sup>r</sup>) *s.* vagabundo, el que vaga o corre por·el mundo, el mar, etc. *2* ladrón, pirata. *3 boy scout* de cierta categoría.

**1) row** (rau) *s.* riña, pendencia, pelotera, alboroto.

**2) row** (rou) *s.* fila, hilera, línea, andana: *in a ~*, seguidos. *2* ALBAÑ. hilada. *3* remadura. *4* paseo en lancha o bote.

**1) row (to)** (rau·) *tr. fam.* pelearse con. *2* reñir, regañar. *3 intr.* pelearse, alborotar.

**2) row (to)** (rou·) *intr.* remar, bogar. *2 tr.* conducir o mover al remo.

**rowboat** (rou·bout) *s.* bote de remos.·

**rowdy** (rau·di) *adj.-s.* camorrista, bravucón, alborotador; bruto, bergante.

**rowel** (rau·øl) *s.* rodaja de espuela.

**rowel (to)** *tr.* espolear.

**rower** (rou·ø<sup>r</sup>) *s.* remero, bogador.

**rowlock** (-lak) *s.* MAR. chumacera. *2* ALBAÑ. sardinel.

**royal** (ro·ial) *adj.* real, regio. *2* magnífico, espléndido, estupendo. *3* tamaño de papel (19 × 24 pulgs. para escribir y 20 × 25 para imprenta). *4* MAR. sobrejuanete.

**royalism** (roi·ališm) *s.* realismo, monarquismo.

**royally** (-i) *adv.* regiamente.

**royalty** (-ti) *s.* realeza. *2* persona real. *3* las personas reales. *4* regalía. *5* derechos [que se pagan a un autor o inventor].

**rub** (røb) *s.* restregón, friega, frote, roce. *2* crítica, sarcasmo. *3* tropiezo, dificultad: *there's the ~*, ahí está la cosa.

**rub (to)** *tr.* estregar, restregar, fregar, frotar, friccionar. *2* bruñir, pulir. *3* irritar. *4 to ~ away* u *off*, quitar frotando. *5 to ~ in*, hacer penetrar frotando; encasquetar, machacar. *6 to ~ out*, borrar. *7 to ~ the wrong way*, frotar a contrapelo, irritar. *8 intr.* rozar. *9* pasar, penetrar, con fricción o dificultad. *10 fam. to ~ along*, *on* o *through*, ir tirando. ¶ Pret. y p. p.: *rubbed;* ger.: *-bbing.*

**rubber** (-rø·bø<sup>r</sup>) *s.* caucho, goma elástica: *~ band*, goma, banda de goma; *~ bulb*, pera de goma; *~ plantation*, cauchal. *2* goma de borrar. *3* frotador. *4* pulidor. *5* estropajo; aljofifa. *6* escofina. *7* [en ciertos juegos] partid entera o manga decisiva. *8 pl.* chanclos de goma.

**rubberize (to)** (-aiš) *tr.* engomar, cauchutar.

**rubberneck** (-nek) *s. fam.* (E.U.) turista que quiere verlo todo.

**rubberneck (to)** *intr.* (E.U.) *fam.* estirar el cuello o volver la cabeza para ver.

**rubber-stamp (to)** *tr.* sellar con sello de goma; estampillar. *2 fig.* aprobar ciegamente.

**rubbish** (rø·biš) *s.* basura, desecho, broza, escombros. *2 fam.* tonterías.

**rubble** (rø·bøl) *s.* ripio, cascote, cascajo; mampuestos.

**rubblework** (-wø<sup>r</sup>k) *s.* mampostería.

**rubdown** (rø·bdaun) *s.* fricción, masaje.

**rubefacient** (rubifei·shønt) *adj.-s.* rubefaciente.

**rubescent** (rube·sønt) *adj.* rubicundo, sonrojado.

**rubiaceous** (rubiei·shøs) *adj.* BOT. rubiáceo.

**rubican** (ru·bikan) *adj.* rubicán.

**rubicund** (ru·bikønd) *adj.* rubicundo.

**rubidium** (rubi·diøm) *s.* QUÍM. rubidio.

**rubiginous** (rubi·dÿinøs) *adj.* ruginoso.

**ruble** (ru·bøl) *s.* rublo.

**rubric** (ru·brik) *adj.* rubro, rojo. *2 s.* rúbrica.

**rubrical** (-al) *adj.* de rúbrica.

**rubricate (to)** (-ei) *tr.* marcar, iluminar o imprimir con color rojo. *2* poner rúbrica o epígrafe.

**ruby** (ru·bi) *s.* MINER. rubí: *~ spinel*, rubí espinela. *2 adj.* de color de rubí.

**ruby (to)** *tr.* rubificar.

**ruche** (rush) *s.* COST. lechuguilla.

**ruck** (røk) *s.* arruga, fruncido. *2* DEP. el pelotón [en una carrera]. *3 fig.* el vulgo; lo común.

**ruck (to)** *tr.* arrugar, ajar.

**rucksack** (-sæk) *s.* mochila, morral.

**ruction** (-shøn) *s. fam.* alboroto, tumulto.

**rudder** (rø·dø<sup>r</sup>) *s.* timón, gobernalle. *2 fig.* timón [dirección, gobierno].

**rudderpost** (-poust) *s.* MAR. codaste. *2* AVIA. eje del timón.

**ruddle** (rø·døl) *s.* almagre. *2* color rojo.

**ruddle (to)** *tr.* marcar con almagre.

**ruddy** (rø·di) *adj.* rojo, colorado, encendido, rubicundo. *2 fam.* maldito, condenado.

**rude** (rud) *adj.* rudo. *2* tosco. *3* escabroso [terreno]. *4* grande, fuerte. *5* duro, penoso. *6* chapucero, imperfecto. *7* inculto; inhábil. *8* brusco, descortés.

**rudeness** (-nis) *s.* rudeza. *2* tosquedad. *3* grosería. *4* descortesía. *5* rusticidad, incultura. *6* violencia.

**rudiment** (ru·dimønt) *s.* rudimento.

**rudimentary** (rudime·ntari) *adj.* rudimentario.

**rue** (ru) *s.* BOT. ruda.

**rue (to)** *tr.-intr.* llorar, lamentar, sentir, pesarle a uno, arrepentirse.

**rueful** (ru·ful) *adj.* lamentable, lastimoso. *2* triste, lloroso, afligido. *3* compasivo. *4* terrible.

**rufescent** (rufe·sønt) *adj.* rojizo.

**ruff** (røf) *s.* gorguera, cuello alechugado. *2* ZOOL., ORN. collar de pelo o pluma. *3* ORN. paloma de toca. *4* fallada [en los naipes]. *5 fam.* enojo.

**ruff (to)** *tr.-intr.* alechugar. *2* fallar [en los naipes].

**ruffian** (rø·fian) *adj.* brutal, cruel. *2 s.* hombre brutal, matón, forajido.

**ruffle** (rø·føl) *s.* lechuguilla, volante fruncido. *2* enojo, irritación. *3* rizo [en el agua]. *4* redoble apagado [de tambor].

**ruffle (to)** *tr.* rizar, alechugar, fruncir. *2* arrugar, ajar, descomponer. *3* irritar, incomodar, hacer perder la calma. *4* encrespar, erizar. *5 intr.* arrugarse, descomponerse; rizarse [el agua]. *6* irritarse, incomodarse.

**rufous** (ru·føs) *adj.* rufo, bermejo, leonado.

**rug** (røg) *s.* alfombra, alfombrilla, ruedo, felpudo. *2* (Ingl.) manta [de caballo, de viaje, etc.].

**Rugby (football)** (rø·gbi) *s.* DEP. rugby.

**rugged** (rø·gid) *adj.* rugoso, arrugado. *2* áspero, escabroso. *3* desapacible. *4* desgreñado. *5* rudo. *6* severo, regañón. *7* borrascoso. *8* recio.

**rugosity** (ruga·siti) *s.* rugosidad.

**ruin** (ruin) *s.* ruina. *2* destrucción. *3* perdición, deshonra. *4 pl.* ruinas.

**ruin (to)** *tr.* arruinar. *2* destruir. *3* seducir, perder. *4 intr.* arruinarse, perderse.

**ruination** (-ei·shøn) *s.* arruinamiento, ruina, perdición.

**ruinous** (rui·nøs) *adj.* ruinoso. *2* fatal, funesto.

**rulable** (ru·labøl) *adj.* gobernable, regulable. *2* conforme a regla.

**rule** (rul) *s.* regla, precepto, principio, máxima, pauta, norma: ~ *of three,* regla de tres; *to make it a* ~ *to,* tener por norma; *as a* ~, por regla general. *2* regla [de una orden]. *3* reglamento, régimen: *rules and regulations,* reglamento. *4* fallo [de un tribunal]. *5* gobierno, poder, mando, dominio, autoridad. *6* reinado. *7* regla [para trazar líneas; para medir]. *8* raya [en el papel]. *9* IMPR. filete.

**rule (to)** *tr.* gobernar, regir, dirigir: *to* ~ *the roast* o *the roost,* fig. ser el que manda. *2* decidir, fallar. *3* regular, reglar. *4* contener, reprimir. *5* reglar, rayar, pautar. *6* tirar [líneas]. *7* ordenar, arreglar. *8 to* ~ *out,* excluir; desechar. *9 intr.* mandar, regir, gobernar, reinar. *10* privar, estar en boga. *11* COM. mantenerse a un tipo.

**ruler** (-ǿ<sup>r</sup>) *s.* gobernante, soberano. *2* regla [para trazar líneas].

**ruling** (-ing) *adj.* gobernante. *2* predominante, imperante. *3* ~ *price,* precio medio. *4* ~ *pen,* tiralíneas.

**rum** (røm) *s.* ron, aguardiente. *2 adj.* extraño, singular. *3* ~ *customer,* persona o animal con quien no se puede jugar.

**Rumania** (rumei·nia) *n. pr.* GEOGR. Rumania.

**Rumanian** (-nian) *adj.-s.* rumano.

**rumble** (rø·mbøl) *s.* rumor, retumbo, ruido sordo y continuo. *2 rumble* o ~ *seat,* asiento descubierto en la trasera de un automóvil.

**rumble (to)** *intr.* retumbar, hacer un ruido sordo y continuo. *2* pasar con estruendo o ruido sordo. *3 intr.-tr.* hablar con voz grave y rumorosa.

**rumen** (ru·min) *s.* panza [del estómago de los rumiantes].

**ruminant** (ru·minant) *adj.-s.* ZOOL. rumiante. *2 adj.* meditativo, que rumia.

**ruminate (to)** (-eit) *tr.-intr.* rumiar [masticar por segunda vez]. *2* rumiar, reflexionar.

**rumination** (-ei·shøn) *s.* rumia, rumiadura. *2* reflexión, meditación.

**ruminative** (ru·minativ) *adj.* reflexivo, meditativo.

**rumly** (rø·mli) *adv.* extrañamente, singularmente.

**rummage** (rø·midy̆) *s.* búsqueda, registro que se hace revolviendo. *2* trastorno, desorden.

**rummage (to)** *tr.-intr.* registrar, revolver buscando. *2 to* ~ *out* o *up,* hallar [revolviendo], desenterrar.

**rummy** (rø·mi) *adj.* extraño, singular. *2 s.* pop. (E.U.) borracho. *3* juego de naipes.

**rumo (u) r** (ru·mø<sup>r</sup>) *s.* rumor, voz que corre.

**rumo (u) r (to)** *tr.* rumorear, propalar: *it is rumo(u)red,* se rumorea.

**rump** (rømp) *s.* ancas, cuarto trasero. *2* rabadilla [de ave]. *3* culata [de vaca]. *4* cola, resto, residuo.

**rumple** (rø·mpøl) *s.* doblez; arruga, arrugamiento, ajamiento.

**rumple (to)** *tr.* arrugar, chafar, ajar. *2* descomponer, desgreñar. *3 ref.* arrugarse, ajarse.

**rumpus** (rø·mpøs) *s.* bulla, alboroto, ruido.

**run** (røn) *s.* corrida, carrera. *2* curso, marcha, tendencia, dirección. *3* serie, continuación, racha. *4* TEAT. serie de representaciones de una obra. *5* asedio [de un banco] por los cuentacorrentistas. *6* funcionamiento. *7* operación, manejo: *to get the* ~ *of,* aprender el manejo de; hallar el modo de. *8* lo que sale, se produce, etc., en un tiempo u operación. *9* recorrido, distancia. *10* vida [de una cosa]. *11* hilo [del discurso]. *12* clase, tipo, etc., usual. *13* MAR. singladura. *14* carrera, competición. *15* viaje; paseo. *16* libertad de andar por un sitio, de hacer uso de algo. *17* terreno, extensión. *18* (E.U.) riachuelo. *19* MIN. buzamiento. *20* MÚS. carrerilla. *21* carrera [en las medias]. *22* TEAT. rampa. *23 in the long* ~, a la larga, tarde o temprano.

*24 p. p.* de TO RUN.

**run (to)** *intr.* correr. *2* girar, rodar. *3* extenderse [hacia, hasta, por]; llegar, alcanzar [hasta]. *4* pasar [a cierto estado]: *to* ~ *dry,* secarse [un pozo, etc.]. *5* fluir, manar, chorrear. *6* derretirse. *7* correrse [los colores]. *8* supurar. *9* ir, dirigirse. *10* decir, rezar: *the song runs as follows,* la canción dice así. *11* ser, durar, mantenerse. *12* TEAT. representarse seguidamente. *13* seguir, estar vigente; imperar, estar en boga. *14* funcionar, marchar. *15* POL. presentarse [para]; ser candidato [a]. *16 to* ~ *about,* correr, ir de un lado a otro. *17 to* ~ *across,* encontrar, dar con. *18 to* ~ *against,* chocar con; oponerse [a]. *19 to* ~ *along,* correr a lo largo de; correr, ir: ~ *along!,* ¡lárgate! *20 to* ~ *around with,* andar o juntarse con. *21 to* ~ *away,* huir desbocarse [un caballo], dispararse [un motor]; *to* ~ *away with,* fugarse con, arrebatar; llevarse. *22 to* ~ *down,* escurrir, gotear [un líquido]; pararse, habérsele acabado la cuerda, el vapor, etc. [a un reloj, un aparato]; agotarse, debilitarse. *23* MAR. *to* ~ *foul* o *foul of,* chocar con, abordar. *24 to* ~ *in,* entrar al pasar. *25 to* ~ *in the blood,* estar en la sangre. *26 to* ~ *off the track,* descarrilar. *27 to* ~ *on,* seguir, continuar. *28 to* ~ *out,* salir; salirse, derramarse; expirar; acabarse; extenderse; *to* ~ *out of,* acabársele a uno [una cosa]. *29 to* ~ *over,* rebosar, desbordarse; atropellar, pasar por encima. *30 to* ~ *through,* correr por, pasar por. *31 to* ~ *with,* estar chorreando o empapado de; abundar en.

*32 tr.* correr [un caballo]. *33* correr, cazar, perseguir. *34* pasar [una cosa por encima o a través de otra]. *35* recorrer, correr por. *36* hacer [un mandado]. *37* seguir [un camino, un curso]. *38* clavar, meter, introducir. *39* mover, empujar, llevar. *40* fundir, vaciar. *41* tirar [una línea]. *42* pasar de contrabando. *43* correr [un riesgo]. *44* derramar, verter, manar. *45* huir de. *46* regentar, dirigir, explotar [un negocio]. *47* conducir [un vehículo o máquina]. *48* MIL. burlar [un bloqueo]. *49* COST. bastear. *50 to* ~ *down,* dar caza a; derribar; atropellar [con un vehículo]; denigrar, difamar. *51 to* ~ *into,* clavar, hundir. *52 to* ~ *off,* escribir o pronunciar rápidamente; imprimir. *53 to* ~ *out,* sacar, extender; agotar. *54 to* ~ *through,* atravesar, pasar de parte a parte; examinar por encima; hojear; dilapidar. *55 to* ~ *to earth,* perseguir hasta su escondite; seguir hasta su origen. *56 to* ~ *up,* hacer subir [una cuenta]; sumar; edificar de prisa; COST. repasar, remendar; MAR. izar.

¶ Pret.: *ran;* p. p.: *run;* ger.: *running.*

**runabout** (-abaut) *s.* vagabundo. *2* birlocho. *3* automóvil pequeño. *4* canoa, automóvil ligero.

**runaway** (-auei) *adj.-s.* fugitivo. *2* desertor, tráns-

fuga. *3 adj.* desbocado [caballo]. *4* DEP. ganado fácilmente. *6 s.* fuga, escapatoria. *7* desbocamiento. *8* caballo desbocado.
**rundle** (rø·ndøl) *s.* RUNG 1. *2* rueda.
**rundlet** (rø·ndlet) *s.* barrilete, barrilejo.
**run-down** *adj.* agotado, debilitado; atropellado. *2* sin cuerda [reloj]. *3* ELECT. descargada [batería].
**rune** (ru·n) *s.* runa. *2* misterio; magia. *3 pl.* poemas rúnicos.
**rung** (rø·ng) *s.* escalón [de escala]. *2* travesaño [de silla]. *3* rayo [de rueda]. *4 pret.* y *p. p.* de TO RING.
**runic** (ru·nik) *adj.* rúnico, runo.
**runlet** (rø·nlit), **runnel** (-nøl) *s.* riachuelo.
**runner** (-ø^r) *s.* corredor [que corre]. *2* mensajero. *3* (E.U.) agente [de un hotel, vapor, etc.]. *4* contrabandista. *5* MEC. corredera. *6* anillo corredizo. *7* volandera [muela]. *8* cuchilla [de patín]; patín [de trineo]. *9* carrera [en las medias]. *10* pasillo [alfombra]. *11* camino de mesa. *12* BOT. estolón. *13* BOT. judía [planta].
**runner-up,** *pl.* **runners-up** *s.* DEP. jugador o equipo que queda en segundo lugar en un torneo.
**running** (-ing) *s.* carrera, corrida, curso. *2* marcha, funcionamiento. *3* dirección, manejo. *4* flujo. *5* supuración. *6 adj.* corredor. *7* corriente: ~ *water,* agua corriente. *8* corredizo: ~ *knot,* nudo corredizo. *9* corrida [letra]. *10* fluido, fácil [estilo]. *11* AUTO. ~ *board,* estribo. *12* MAR. ~ *lights,* luces de situación. *13* IMPR. ~ *title,* titulillo. *14 adv.* seguido: *three times* ~, tres veces seguidas.
**runt** (rø·nt) *s.* animal enano. *2* fam. enano, redrojo. *3* paloma de gran tamaño.
**runway** (rø·nwei) *s.* lecho, cauce. *2* vía; senda. *3* AVIA. pista de aterrizaje. *4* TEAT. pasarela.
**rupee** (rupi·) *s.* rupia.
**rupestrian** (rupe·strian) *adj.* rupestre.
**rupture** (rø·pchø^r) *s.* ruptura, rotura. *2* MED. hernia. *3* ruptura, desavenencia.
**rupture (to)** *tr.* romper. *2* producir hernia. *3 intr.* romperse. *4* quebrarse, sufrir hernia.
**rural** (ru·ral) *adj.* rural, rústico. *2 s.* rústico, campesino.
**ruse** (ruš) *s.* ardid, astucia, artimaña.
**rusé** (rušei·) *adj.* astuto.
**rush** (røsh) *s.* movimiento o avance impetuoso: *with a* ~, de golpe; impetuosamente. *2* torrente, tropel, afluencia: ~ *hour,* hora punta. *3* prisa, precipitación. *4* ímpetu, empuje. *5* ataque, embestida. *6* gran demanda [de una cosa]. *7* BOT. junco. *8* BOT. anea, espadaña. *9* fig. bledo, pito.
**rush (to)** *intr.* arrojarse, abalanzarse, precipitarse:

*to* ~ *forward,* avanzar, arrojarse con ímpetu: ~ *to* ~ *in upon,* sorprender; *to* ~ *through,* hacer precipitadamente; arrojarse [a los peligros]. *2 tr.* empujar o arrojar con violencia. *3* despachar con prontitud, apresurar. *4* embestir; tomar por asalto. *5* asediar con atenciones.
**rushlight** (-lait) *s.* vela de sebo y junco; su luz.
**rusk** (røsk) *s.* sequillo, galleta.
**russet** (rø·sit) *adj.* bermejo. *2 s.* color bermejo. *3* variedad de manzana. *4 adj.-s.* burdo [paño].
**russety** (rø·siti) *s.* bermejizo.
**Russia** (rø·sha) *n. pr.* GEOGR. Rusia. *2 Russia leather* o simplte. *russia,* piel de Rusia.
**Russian** (rø·shan) *adj.-s.* ruso.
**rust** (røst) *s.* moho, orín, herrumbre. *2* inacción, ociosidad. *3* BOT. roya, añublo. *4 adj.* rojizo [color].
**rust (to)** *tr.* enmohecer [oxidar; embotar]. *2* dar color de herrumbre. *3 intr.* enmohecerse [oxidarse; embotarse]. *4* aherrumbrarse. *5* BOT. arroyarse.
**rustic** (rø·stik) *adj.-s.* rústico. *2* campesino. *3 adj.* sencillo, campestre.
**rusticate (to)** (-ikeit) *intr.* rusticar. *2 tr.* enviar al campo. *3* expulsar temporalmente de una universidad.
**rusticity** (røsti·siti) *s.* rusticidad, rustiquez. *2* simplicidad. *3* grosería, rudeza.
**rustle** (rø·søl) *s.* susurro, crujido.
**rustle (to)** *intr.* susurrar, crujir. *2* (E.U.) menearse, obrar con energía. *3 tr.* hacer susurrar o crujir. *4* robar [ganado].
**rustler** (rø·slø^r) *s.* pop. (E.U.) persona activa. *2* (E.U.) ladrón de ganado.
**rusty** (rø·sti) *adj.* mohoso, herrumbroso. *2* enmohecido. *3* rojizo. *4* ronca [voz]. *5* rancio, anticuado.
**rut** (røt) *s.* brama, celo [de los animales]. *2* carril, rodada, surco. *3* rutina, costumbre, sendero trillado.
**rut (to)** *tr.* hacer rodadas o surcos en. *2* estar en celo. ¶ Pret. y p. p.: *rutted;* ger.: *-tting.*
**rutabaga** (rutabei·ga) *s.* BOT. naba.
**Ruth** (ruz) *n. pr.* Rut.
**Ruthenia** (ruzi·nia) *n. pr.* GEOGR. Rutenia.
**ruthenium** (ruzi·niøm) *s.* QUÍM. rutenio.
**ruthless** (ru·zlis) *adj.* cruel, despiadado, inhumano.
**rutile** (ru·til) *s.* MINER. rutilo.
**rutty** (rø·ti) *adj.* lleno de rodadas o surcos.
**rye** (rai) *s.* BOT. centeno. *2* (E.U.) whisky de centeno. *3* BOT. ~ *grass,* ballico, césped inglés.

# S

**S, s** (es) *s.* S, s, decimonona letra del alfabeto inglés.

**'s** de, el de (signo del llamado caso posesivo o posesivo sajón): *John's father*, el padre de Juan. *2 abrev.* de IS, HAS y US.

**Sabaean** (sabɪ·an) *adj.-s.* sabeo.

**Sabaism** (sa·baišm) *s.* sabeísmo.

**Sabbath** (sæ·baz) *s.* día de de descanso [sábado entre los judíos, domingo entre los cristianos].

**sabbatic (al** (sabæ·tik(al) *adj.* sabático.

**saber** (sei·bø<sup>r</sup>) *s.* sable.

**saber (to)** *tr.* acuchillar, herir a sablazos.

**Sabine** (sæ·bin) *adj.-s.* sabino.

**sable** (sei·bøl) *adj.-s.* BLAS. sable. *2* negro, obscuro. *3* ZOOL. marta cebellina. *4* su piel. *5 pl.* ropas de luto.

**sabot** (sæ·bou) *s.* zueco, almadreña.

**sabotage** (sæ·bøtidӯ) *s.* sabotaje.

**sabotage (to)** *tr.* sabotear.

**saboteur** (-tø<sup>r</sup>) *s.* saboteador.

**sabre** (sei·bø<sup>r</sup>) *s.* SABER.

**sabre (to)** *tr.* TO SABER.

**sabulous** (sæ·biuløs) *adj.* sabuloso, arenoso.

**saburra** (sabø·ra) *adj.* MED. saburra.

**sac** (sæ·k) *s.* ANAT., ZOOL., BOT. saco, cavidad.

**saccharimeter** (sækari·mitø<sup>r</sup>) *s.* sacarímetro.

**saccharin(e** (sæ·karin) *s.* QUÍM. sacarina.

**saccharine** *adj.* sacarino. *2* azucarado.

**saccharose** (-ous) *s.* QUÍM. sacarosa.

**saccule** (sa·kiul) *s.* ANAT. sáculo.

**sacerdocy** (sæ·sø<sup>r</sup>dosi) *s.* sacerdocio.

**sacerdotal** (sæsø<sup>r</sup>dou·tal) *adj.* sacerdotal. *2* clerical.

**sacerdotalism** (-išm) *s.* sacerdocio. *2* clericalismo.

**sack** (sæk) *s.* saco, costal. *2* saco, saqueo: *to put to* ~, meter a saco. *3* saco, chaqueta holgada. *4* vino blanco generoso. *5 fam. to give,* o *get, the* ~, despedir o ser despedido; dar o recibir calabazas.

**sack (to)** *tr.* ensacar, meter en saco. *2* saquear, pillar. *3* despedir; dar calabazas.

**sackbut** (-bøt) *s.* MÚS. sacabuche.

**sackcloth** (-kloz) *s.* harpillera. *2* cilicio.

**sacker** (-ø<sup>r</sup>) *s.* ensacador. *2* saqueador.

**sacking** (-ing) *s.* tela para sacos, harpillera.

**sacque** (sæk) *s.* saco, chaqueta holgada.

**sacral** (sa·kral) *adj.* ANAT. sacro. *2* sacral.

**sacrament** (sæ·cramønt) *s.* sacramento. *2* sacra-

mento del altar, eucaristía. *3* juramento solemne.

**sacramental** (sækrame·ntal) *adj.* sacramental. *2 s. pl.* sacramentales.

**sacrarium** (sækrei·riøm) *s.* sagrario.

**sacred** (sei·krid) *adj.* sagrado, sacro, santo: *Sacred College,* Sacro Colegio. *2* inviolable.

**sacrifice** (sæ·krifais) *s.* sacrificio; inmolación. *2* COM. *to sell at a* ~, vender sin beneficio.

**sacrifice (to)** *tr.* sacrificar; inmolar. *2* COM. vender sin beneficio. *3 intr.* sacrificar.

**sacrificial** (-shal) *adj.* de sacrificio, sacrificatorio.

**sacrilege** (sæ·krilidӯ) *s.* sacrilegio.

**sacrilegious** (sækrili·dӯøs) *adj.* sacrílego.

**sacring** (sa·kring) *s.* consagración [esp. en la misa]: ~ *tablet,* sacra.

**sacristan** (sæ·kristan) *s.* sacristán.

**sacristy** (-ti) *s.* sacristía.

**sacrosanct** (sæ·krosænct) *adj.* sacrosanto.

**sacrum** (sei·krøm) *s.* ANAT. sacro.

**sad** (sæd) *adj.* triste. *2* aciago. *3* malo, pobre, de inferior calidad.

**sadden (to)** (-øn) *tr.* entristecer. *2* ensombrecer. *3 intr.* entristecerse. *4* ensombrecerse.

**saddle** (sæ·døl) *s.* silla [de montar]: ~ *horse,* caballo de silla; *in the* ~, fig. en el poder; listo, dispuesto. *2* sillín. *3* COC. lomo, cuarto trasero. *4* paso [entre montañas]. *5* cosa o parte en figura de silla de montar.

**saddle (to)** *tr.* ensillar. *2* enalbardar. *3 to* ~ *with,* hacer cargar con.

**saddlebacked** (sæ·dølbækt) *adj.* ensillado, de lomo hundido.

**saddlebag** (sæ·dølbæg) *s.* alforja [para caballería]; maletín de grupa.

**saddlecloth** (-kloz) *s.* mantilla [del caballo].

**saddler** (sæ·dlø<sup>r</sup>) *s.* guarnicionero, talabartero.

**saddlery** (sæ·dløri) *s.* guarnicionería.

**saddletree** (sæ·døltrɪ) *s.* fuste [de la silla de montar].

**Sadducee** (sæ·diusɪ) *s.* saduceo.

**sad-iron** (sæd-aiø<sup>r</sup>n) *s.* plancha [para la ropa].

**sadism** (sei·dišm) *s.* sadismo.

**sadistic** (seidi·stik) *adj.* sádico.

**sadness** (sæ·dnis) *s.* tristeza. *2* melancolía.

**safe** (seif) *adj.* salvo, ileso, incólume: ~ *and sound,* sano y salvo. *2* seguro [exento de peligro]; pru-

dente. *3* seguro, confiable. *4* ~ *load*, carga máxima. *5 s.* arca, caja de caudales. *7* alacena.
**safe-conduct** *s.* convoy, salvoconducto.
**safeguard** (sei·fga<sup>r</sup>d) *s.* salvaguardia, resguardo. *2* escolta, salvoconducto.
**safeguard (to)** *tr.* salvaguardar, proteger.
**safe-keeping** *s.* guarda, custodia, depósito.
**safely** (-li) *adv.* seguramente, sin peligro, a salvo, sin novedad.
**safeness** (-nis) *s.* seguridad [estado o condición]. *2* prudencia [de una conducta].
**safety** (-ti) *s.* seguridad, protección, salvamento, incolumidad: ~ *belt*, salvavidas, cinturón de seguridad; ~ *island*, burladero [en una calle]; ~ *pin*, imperdible; ~ *razor*, maquinilla de afeitar; ~ *valve*, válvula de seguridad. *2* prudencia [de un proceder]. *3* seguro [de arma].
**safflower** (sæ·flauø<sup>r</sup>) *s.* BOT. alazor.
**saffron** (sæ·frøn) *s.* BOT. azafrán. *2 adj.* azafranado.
**sag** (sæg) *s.* combadura, comba, bolsa, hundimiento, depresión. *2* COM. baja [de precios].
**sag (to)** *tr.* combar, empandar. *2 intr.* combarse, pandear, hacer bolsa. *3* ceder, flojear. *4* bajar [los precios]. ¶ Pret. y p. p.: *sagged;* ger.: *-gging.*
**saga** (sa·ga) *s.* saga.
**sagacious** (sagei·shøs) *adj.* sagaz.
**sagacity** (sagæ·siti) *s.* sagacidad.
**sage** (seidỹ) *s.* BOT. salvia. *2* sabio, filósofo, hombre prudente. *3 adj.* cuerdo, prudente.
**sageness** (sei·dỹnis) *s.* sabiduría, cordura, prudencia.
**sagittal** (sæ·dỹital) *adj.* sagital.
**Sagittarius** (sædỹite·riøs) *s.* ASTR. Sagitario.
**sago** (sei·gou) *s.* sagú [fécula]. *2* BOT. *sago* o ~ *palm,* sagú [planta].
**Sahara** (saje·ra) *n. pr.* GEOGR. Sahara.
**sahib** (sa·ib) *s.* señor [usado por los persas e hindúes, esp. con el nombre de un europeo].
**said** (sed) *pret.* y *p. p.* de TO SAY.
**sail** (seil) *s.* MAR. vela: *to set* ~, hacerse a la vela. *2* buque de vela. *3* aspa [de molino].
**sail (to)** *intr.* navegar: *to* ~ *close to the wind,* ceñir el viento; fig. seguir la corriente; bordear lo ilícito. *2* hacerse a la vela. *3* ir o viajar [en un buque]. *4* deslizarse, flotar, volar. *5* moverse majestuosamente. *6 tr.* gobernar una embarcación. *7* navegar por, surcar.
**sailboat** (sei·lbout) *s.* buque o barca de vela, velero.
**sailcloth** (-kloz) *s.* lona, brin. *2* toldo.
**sailer** (sei·lø<sup>r</sup>) *s.* buque de vela, velero.
**sailing** (sei·ling) *s.* navegación, deporte de vela: ~ *master,* piloto; *plain* ~, fig. progreso fácil, coser y cantar. *2* salida [de un buque]. *3* viaje en barco.
**sailmaker** (sei·lmeikø<sup>r</sup>) *s.* velero [que hace velas de barco].
**sailor** (-ø<sup>r</sup>) *s.* marinero. *2* marino. *3* *sailor* o ~ *hat,* canotié, sombrero de paja.
**saint** (seint) *s.* santo, santa. *2* santo, san, santa [delante con un nombre]. | Suele escribirse con may. y se abrevia así: *St.*: *St. Elmo's fire,* fuego de Santelmo; *St. Martin's summer,* veranillo de San Martín; *St. Vitus's dance,* MED. corea, baile de San Vito.
**saint (to)** *tr.* canonizar. *2 intr.* obrar como un santo.
**sainted** (-id) *adj.* santo, canonizado. *2* santo, virtuoso, piadoso.
**saintliness** (-linis) *s.* santidad.
**saintly** (-li) *adj.* santo, pío, devoto.

**sake** (seik) *s.* causa, motivo, amor, consideración [que mueve a hacer algo]: *for my* ~, por mí, por mi causa; *for God's* ~, por Dios, por el amor de Dios; *art for art's* ~, el arte por el arte.
**saker** (-ø<sup>r</sup>) *s.* ORN., ARTILL. sacre.
**Sal** (sæl) *n. pr. dim.* de SARAH.
**sal** *s.* QUÍM., FARM. sal.
**salaam** (salæ·m) *s.* zalema.
**salaam (to)** *tr.-intr.* hacer zalemas.
**salability** (seilabi·liti) *s.* calidad de vendible, facilidad de venta, salida.
**salable** (sei·labøl) *adj.* vendible.
**salacious** (salei·shøs) *adj.* salaz.
**salacity** (salæ·siti) *s.* salacidad.
**salad** (sæ·lad) *s.* ensalada: ~ *bowl,* ensaladera; ~ *oil,* aceite de mesa; ~ *days,* fig. juventud inexperta.
**salamander** (sæ·lamændø<sup>r</sup>) *s.* ZOOL., MIT. salamandra. *2* COC. utensilio para calentar o tostar.
**salangane** (-længein) *s.* ORN. salangana.
**salaried** (sæ·larid) *adj.* asalariado. *2* retribuido [empleo].
**salary** (sæ·lari) *s.* salario, sueldo, paga.
**sale** (seil) *s.* venta; almoneda; liquidación: ~ *tax,* impuesto sobre las ventas; *for* ~, on ~, en venta. *3* salida, demanda [de un género].
**salesclerk** (-šklø<sup>r</sup>k) *s.* vendedor, dependiente.
**salesgirl** (-sgø<sup>r</sup>l·) *s.* vendedora, dependienta.
**Salesian** (sali·dỹan) *adj.-s.* salesiano.
**salesman** (-smæn) *s.* vendedor, dependiente. *2* viajante de comercio.
**saleswoman** (-swuman) *s.* vendedora, dependienta.
**salic** (sæ·lik) *adj.* sálico: ~ *law,* ley sálica.
**salicaceus** (sælikei·shøs) *adj.* BOT. salicáceo.
**salicylic** (sæ·lisilik) *adj.* QUÍM. salicílico.
**salient** (sei·liønt) *adj.* que brota o surte. *2* saliente, prominente. *3* saliente, notable.
**saliferous** (sali·førøs) *adj.* salífero.
**salification** (sælifikei·shøn) *s.* salificación.
**salify (to)** (sæ·lifai) *tr.* salificar.
**saline** (sei·lain) *adj.* salino. *2 s.* saladar. *3* salina. *4* substancia salina.
**salinity** (sali·niti) *s.* salinidad.
**salinous** (se·lainøs) *adj.* salino.
**saliva** (salai·va) *s.* saliva.
**salivary** (sæ·liveri) *adj.* salival.
**salivate (to)** (sæ·liveit) *tr.* producir salivación. *2 intr.* salivar.
**salivation** (-ei·shøn) *s.* salivación.
**sallet** (sæ·lit) *s.* celada [de la armadura].
**sallow** (sæ·lou) *adj.* pálido, amarillento, cetrino. *2 s.* BOT. sauce.
**sallowness** (-nis) *s.* palidez, color amarillento.
**Sally** (sæ·li) *n. pr. dim.* de SARAH.
**sally** *s.* MIL. salida. *2* excursión; paseo. *3* arranque, arrebato. *4* salida, ocurrencia. *5* ARQ. saliente, vuelo.
**sally (to)** *intr.* salir, hacer una salida. *2* salir o avanzar con ímpetu.
**salmagundi** (sælmagø·ndi) *s.* salpicón. *2* baturrillo, mezcolanza.
**salmi** (sæ·lmi) *s.* estofado de caza.
**salmon** (sæ·møn) *s.* ICT. salmón. *2* color de salmón.
**Salome** (sæ·lomi) *n. pr.* Salomé.
**Salomonic** (sæloma·nik) *adj.* salomónico [de Salomón].
**salon** (sæla·n) *s.* salón [pieza de recibir]. *2* salón [literario o artístico].
**saloon** (salu·n) *s.* salón [gran sala]. *2* cámara [de

un vapor]. *3* (E.U.) taberna, bar. *4* FERROC. (Ingl.) ~ *carriage*, coche salón.
**salpa** (sæ·lpa) *s.* ICT. salpa.
**salsify** (sæ·lsifi) *s.* BOT. salsifí.
**salt** (solt) *s.* QUÍM. sal. *2* sal común: *to be worth one's* ~, valer uno lo que come; *to take with a grain of* ~, considerar como exagerado. *3* sal, ingenio, agudeza. *4 old* ~, lobo de mar. *5 pl.* MED. sales. *6 adj.* de sal, para la sal; salado, salino; curado con sal: ~ *lick*, salegar; ~ *marsh*, marisma; ~ *meat*, cecina; ~ *shaker*, salero de mesa; ~ *water*, agua salada. *7* verde [cuento, etc.]. *8* exagerada [cuenta, factura].
**salt (to)** *tr.* salar. *2* sazonar con sal. *3* salpresar. *4* dar sal al ganado. *5* amañar [una cosa]; poner subrepticiamente mineral en [una mina] para darle apariencia de valor.
**saltatory** (sæ·ltatori) *adj.* perteneciente a la danza. *2* saltador. *3* que procede por saltos.
**saltcellar** (so·ltsela$^r$) *s.* salero [de mesa].
**salted** (-id) *adj.* salado. *2* experimentado; perito.
**salter** (-ø$^r$) *s.* salador. *2* salinero.
**saltern** (-ø$^r$n) *s.* salina.
**saltigrade** (sæ·ltigreid) *adj.* saltígrado.
**salting** (so·lting) *s.* saladura, salazón.
**saltish** (-ish) *adj.* salobre, un poco salado.
**saltmaker** (-meikø$^r$) *s.* salinero.
**saltness** (-nis) *s.* salsedumbre.
**salpeter, salpetre** (-pi·tø$^r$) *s.* nitro, salitre. *2* nitrato de Chile.
**saltus** (sæ·ltøs) *s.* salto, solución de continuidad.
**saltworks** (so·ltwø$^r$ks) *s.* salina.
**saltwort** (-wø$^r$t) *s.* BOT. barrilla, sosa.
**salty** (-i) *adj.* salado. *2* salobre.
**salubrious** (saliu·briøs) *adj.* salubre.
**salutary** (sæ·liuteri) *adj.* saludable; salutífero.
**salutation** (sæliutei·shøn) *s.* saludo. *2* salutación. *3* bienvenida.
**salutatory** (sæliu·tatori) *adj.* de salutación. *2 s.* (E.U.) saludo, discurso de salutación.
**salute** (saliu·t) *s.* saludo [ademán, actitud, beso]. *2* MIL. saludo; salva.
**salute (to)** *tr.-intr.* saludar. *2 intr.* MIL. cuadrarse.
**salvable** (sæ·lvabøl) *adj.* que puede salvarse.
**Salvador** (sæ·lvadø$^r$) *n. pr.* GEOGR. El Salvador.
**salvage** (sæ·lvidȳ) *s.* salvamento. *2* derecho de salvamento. *3* lo que se salva de un naufragio, fuego, etc.
**salvage (to)** *tr.* salvar [de un naufragio, ruina, etc.].
**salvation** (sælvei·shøn) *s.* salvación.
**salve** (sæv o sav) *s.* ungüento, pomada. *2* remedio, alivio. *3 fam.* adulación. *4* salve, Salve Regina.
**salve (to)** *tr.* untar. *2* aquietar, calmar, aliviar. *3* salvar [un buque, un cargamento, etc.].
**salver** (sæ·lvø$^r$) *s.* bandeja. *2* salvilla.
**salvia** (sæ·lvia) *s.* BOT. salvia.
**salvo** (sæ·lvou) *s.* salvedad, excepción. *2* excusa, subterfugio. *3* salva [de artillería, de aplausos].
**salvor** (sæ·lvø$^r$) *s.* pers. o buque que efectúa un salvamento.
**Sam** (sæm) *n. pr. fam.* Samuel.
**samara** (sæ·mara) *s.* BOT. sámara.
**Samaritan** (samæ·ritan) *adj.-s.* samaritano.
**samarium** (same·riøm) *s.* QUÍM. samario.
**sambo** (sæ·mbou) *s.* zambo [mestizo].
**sambuke** (sæ·mbiuk) MÚS. sambuca.
**same** (seim) *adj.-pron.* mismo, misma, etc.: *at the* ~ *time*, a la vez, al mismo tiempo; no obstante: *it is all the* ~ *to me*, me da lo mismo. *2 adv. the*

~, del mismo modo, igualmente. *3 all the* ~, a pesar de todo.
**sameness** (-nis) *s.* igualdad, identidad. *2* parecido exacto. *3* monotonía.
**samlet** (-lit) *s.* ICT. salmón joven.
**Samoan** (samou·an) *adj.-s.* samoano.
**Samotrace** (sæ·motreis) *n. pr.* GEOGR. Samotracia.
**samovar** (sæ·mova$^r$) *s.* samovar.
**sampan** (sæ·mpæn) *s.* MAR. sampán.
**samphire** (-fai$^r$) *s.* BOT. hinojo marino.
**sample** (-pøl) *s.* COM. muestra: ~ *case*, muestrario. *2* muestra [para analizar], cala, cata. *3* espécimen, ejemplo.
**sample (to)** *tr.* sacar una muestra, probar, calar, catar.
**sampler** (sæ·mplø$^r$) *s.* utensilio para sacar muestras. *2* dechado [labor].
**Sam(p)son** (sæ·mp(p)søn) *n. pr.* Sansón.
**sanative** (sæ·nativ) *adj.* sanativo, curativo.
**sanatorium** (sænato·riøm) *s.* sanatorio.
**sanctification** (sænktifikei·shøn) *s.* santificación.
**sanctifier** (sæ·nktifaiø$^r$) *s.* santificador.
**sanctify (to)** (-ifai) *tr.* santificar. *2* consagrar, hacer sagrado. ¶ Pret. y p. p.: *sanctified.*
**sanctimonious** (-imou·niøs) *adj.* santurrón.
**sanctimony** (-imouni) *s.* santurronería.
**sanction** (sæ·nkshøn) *s.* sanción.
**sanction (to)** *tr.* sancionar.
**sanctify** (sæ·nktiti) *s.* santidad. *2* carácter sagrado, inviolabilidad.
**sanctuary** (-chueri) *s.* santuario. *2* asilo, refugio, sagrado: *to take* ~, acogerse a sagrado.
**sanctum** (-tøm) *s.* lugar sagrado. *2* estudio, despacho, etc., privado.
**Sanctus** (-tøs) *s.* LITURG. Sanctus.
**sand** (sænd) *s.* arena: ~ *bar*, barra de arena; ~ *hill*, duna; ~ *grouse*, ORN. ganga. *2* playa, arenal. | A veces en plural. *3* pop. valor, aguante. *4* pop. dinero. *5* MED. arenas. *6* arenas [del reloj]; momentos de vida.
**sand (to)** *tr.* enarenar. *2* arenar. *3* pulir con arena o papel de lija.
**sandal** (sæ·ndal) *s.* sandalia. *2* BOT. sándalo.
**sandalwood** (-wud) *s.* sándalo [árbol; madera].
**sandbag** (sæ·ndbæg) *s.* saco o porra de arena.
**sandbank** (-bænk) *s.* banco de arena.
**sandblast** (-blæst) *s.* chorro de arena.
**sandblast (to)** *tr.* limpiar, grabar, etc., con chorro de arena.
**sandbox** (-baks) *s.* salvadera. *2* FERROC. arenero.
**sanders** (-ø$^r$s) *s.* BOT. sándalo rojo.
**sandglass** (-glæs) *s.* reloj de arena.
**sandpaper** (-peipø$^r$) *s.* papel de lija.
**sandpaper (to)** *tr.* lijar.
**sandpiper** (-paipø$^r$) *s.* ORN. lavandera.
**sandstone** (-stoun) *s.* piedra arenisca.
**sandstorm** (-sto$^r$m) *s.* tempestad de arena.
**sandwich** (-wich) *s.* emparedado, bocadillo: ~ *man*, hombre sandwich.
**sandwich (to)** *tr.* poner entre dos cosas iguales, intercalar.
**sandy** (-i) *adj.* arenoso, arenisco. *2* rufo, rojizo, de color de arena. *3* inestable.
**Sandy** *n. pr. dim.* de ALEXANDER.
**sane** (sein) *adj.* sano. *2* cuerdo. *3* razonable.
**sanforize (to)** (sæ·nførais) *tr.* sanforizar.
**sang** (sæng) *pret.* de TO SING.
**sangaree** (sængarı·) *t.* sangría [bebida].
**sang-froid** (san-frua) *s.* sangre fría.
**Sangrail** (sæ·ngreil) *s.* grial.
**sanguify (to)** (sæ·ngwifai) *tr.* sanguificar.

**sanguinary** (-neri) *adj.* sanguinario, cruel. *2* sangriento.
**sanguine** (-win) *adj.* colorado, rubicundo. *2* sanguíneo. *3* vehemente. *4* optimista. *5 s.* DIB. sanguina.
**sanguineous** (sangwi·niøs) *adj.* sanguíneo. *2* optimista.
**sanguinolent** (-nolønt) *adj.* sanguinolento.
**Sanhedrim, -drin** (sæ·njidrim, -drin) *s.* sanedrin.
**sanicle** (-nikøl) *s.* BOT. sanícula.
**sanify (to)** (sæ·nifai) *tr.* sanear [dar condiciones de salubridad]. ¶ Pret. y p. p.: *sanified.*
**sanitarian** (sænite·rian) *adj.-s.* sanitario.
**sanitarium** (-riøm) *s.* sanatorio.
**sanitary** (sæ·niteri) *adj.* sanitario, de sanidad: ~ *corps,* cuerpo de sanidad. *2* higiénico: ~ *napkin,* paño higiénico.
**sanitation** (sænitei·shøn) *s.* higienización, saneamiento.
**sanity** (sæ·niti) *s.* sanidad [estado sano]. *2* cordura, sano juicio, sensatez.
**Sanscrit, Sanskrit** (sæ·nskrit) *adj.-s.* sánscrito.
**Santa Claus** (sæ·ntikloš) *n. pr.* San Nicolás [que trae regalos a los niños en Nochebuena].
**santon** (sæ·ntøn) *s.* santón.
**sap** (sæp) *s.* savia. *2* vigor, vitalidad. *3* sámago. *4* fig. tonto, bobo. *5* FORT. zapa.
**sap (to)** *tr.* extraer la savia de; dejar sin savia. *2* zapar, minar. *3 intr.* MIL. hacer trabajos de zapa. *4* obrar bajo mano.
**sapful** (sæ·pful) *adj.* abundante en savia.
**saphead** (-jed) *s.* tonto, bobo.
**saphenous** (safi·nøs) *adj.* ANAT. safena.
**sapid** (sæ·pid) *adj.* sápido. *2* sabroso, agradable.
**sapience, -cy** (sei·piøns, -si) *s.* sapiencia.
**sapient** (-ønt) *s.* sabio.
**sapless** (sæ·plis) *adj.* sin savia, sin jugo; seco, estéril. *2* débil, sin vitalidad.
**sapling** (-ling) *s.* arbolillo, renuevo. *2* jovenzuelo.
**saponaceous** (sæponei·shøs) *adj.* saponáceo.
**saponification** (sapanifikei·shøn) *s.* saponificación.
**saponify (to)** (sapa·nifai) *tr.* saponificar. *2 intr.* saponificarse. ¶ Pret. y p. p.: *saponified.*
**sapor** (sei·pø[r]) *s.* sabor.
**sapper** (sæ·pø[r]) *s.* MIL. zapador, gastador.
**Sapphic** (sæ·fik) *adj.* sáfico. *2 s.* verso cálico.
**sapphire** (sæ·fai[r]) *s.* zafir, zafiro. *2* color de zafiro.
**Sappho** (sæ·fou) *n. pr.* Safo.
**sappy** (sæ·pi) *adj.* lleno de savia; jugoso. *2* vigoroso. *3* pueril. *4* ridículamente sentimental.
**saprophytic** (sæprofi·tik) *adj.* BOT. saprofita.
**sapwood** (sæ·pwud) *s.* BOT. albura; sámago.
**saraband** (sæ·rabænd) *s.* zarabanda.
**Saracen** (sæ·rasen) *s.* sarraceno.
**Saragossa** (særaga·sa) *n. pr.* GEOGR. Zaragoza.
**Sarah** (se·ra) *n. pr. f.* Sara.
**Saratoga trunk** (særatou·ga) *s.* baúl, mundo.
**sarbacane** (sæ·[r]bakein) *s.* cerbatana.
**sarcasm** (-kæšm) *s.* sarcasmo.
**sarcastic (al** (sa[r]kæ·stik(al) *adj.* sarcástico.
**sarcocarp** (-koka[r]p) *s.* BOT. sarcocarpio.
**sarcoma** (sa[r]kou·ma) *s.* MED. sarcoma.
**sarcophagus** (sa[r]ka·fagøs), *pl.* **-gi** (-dýai) o **-guses** *s.* sarcófago.
**Sardanapalus** (sa[r]danapei·løs) *n. pr.* Sardanápalo.
**sardine** (sa·[r]dın) *s.* ICT. sardina. *2* JOY. sardio.
**Sardinia** (sa[r]di·nia) *n. pr.* GEOGR. Cerdeña.
**Sardinian** (sa[r]di·nian) *adj.-s.* sardo.

**sardonic** (sa[r]da·nik) *adj.* sardónico.
**sardonyx** (sa·[r]døniks) *s.* MINER. sardónice.
**sargasso** (sa[r]gæ·sou) *s.* BOT. sargazo.
**Sarmatian** (sa[r]mei·shan) *adj.-s.* sármata.
**sarment** (sa·[r]mønt) *s.* BOT. sarmiento.
**sarsaparilla** (sa[r]sapari·la) *s.* BOT. zarzaparrilla.
**sartorial** (sa[r]to·rial) *adj.* sartorio. *2* de sastre; de sastrería.
**sash** (sæsh) *s.* faja, ceñidor, banda [de uniforme o de adorno]. *2* parte movible de la ventana de guillotina: ~ *window,* ventana de guillotina.
**sat** (-sæt) *pret.* y *p. p.* de TO SIT.
**Satan** (sei·tan) *n. pr.* Satán, Satanás.
**satanic (al** (seita·nik(al) *adj.* satánico.
**satchel** (sæ·chøl) *s.* maletín. *2* cartapacio [para llevar los libros, etc.].
**sate (to)** (seit) *tr.* saciar, hartar. *2* hastiar.
**sateen** (sætı·n) *s.* satén de algodón.
**sateless** (sei·tlis) *adj.* insaciable.
**satellite** (sæ·tølait) *s.* satélite.
**satiate** (sei·shieit) *adj.* saciado, satisfecho, harto.
**satiate (to)** *tr.* saciar. *2 intr.* saciarse.
**satlety** (satai·øti) *s.* saciedad, hartura. *2* hastío.
**satin** (sæ·tin) *s.* TEJ. raso.
**satinet** (-et) *s.* TEJ. rasete.
**satinwood** (-wud) *s.* árbol de madera lustrosa; esta madera; satín, doradillo.
**satiny** (sæ·tini) *adj.* arrasado, satinado.
**satire** (sæ·tai[r]) *s.* sátira.
**satiric (al** (sati·rik(al) *adj.* satírico.
**satirist** (sæ·tirist) *s.* escritor, satírico.
**satirize (to)** (sæ·tiraiš) *tr.* satirizar.
**satisfaction** (sætisfæ·kshøn) *s.* satisfacción.
**satisfactory** (-tori) *adj.* satisfactorio. *2* suficiente, adecuado, ventajoso. *3* expiatorio.
**satisfy (to)** (sæ·tisfai) *tr.* satisfacer. *2* contentar. *3* librar de duda, convencer: *I am satisfied that,* estoy seguro de que. *4* compensar, pagar. ¶ Pret. y p. p.: *satisfied.*
**satrap** (sei·træp) *s.* sátrapa. *2* tiranuelo.
**saturable** (sæ·churabøl) *adj.* saturable.
**saturate (to)** (sæ·chureit) *tr.* saturar. *2* empapar; llenar, colmar. *3* imbuir. *4* QUÍM. neutralizar.
**saturation** (-ei·shøn) *s.* saturación.
**Saturday** (sæ·tø·dei) *s.* sábado.
**saturn** (sæ·tø[r]n) *n. pr.* MIT., ASTR. Saturno.
**Saturnalia** (sætø[r]nei·lia) *s. pl.* saturnales.
**saturnine** (sæ·tø[r]nain) *adj.* saturnino, apático, taciturno, melancólico.
**satyr** (sæ·tø[r]) *s.* sátiro.
**sauce** (sos) *s.* salsa. *2* aderezo, condimento. *3* (E.U.) compota. *4* descaro, insolencia [de lenguaje].
**sauce (to)** *tr.* aderezar, sazonar. *2* templar, suavizar. *3* desvergonzarse, insolentarse con.
**sauceboat** (-bout) *s.* salsera.
**saucebox** (-baks) *s.* insolente, descarado.
**saucepan** (-pæn) *s.* cacerola, cazuela.
**saucer** (-ø[r]) *s.* platillo [plato pequeño].
**saucily** (-ili) *adv.* con descaro.
**saucy** (-i) *adj.* descarado, respondón. *2* elegante.
**sauerkraut** (sau·[r]kraut) *s.* chucruta.
**Saul** (sol) *n. pr.* Saúl.
**saunter** (so·ntø[r]) *s.* paseo; paso tranquilo [del que pasea].
**saunter (to)** *intr.* pasear; andar despacio y sin objeto; vagar.
**saurian** (so·rian) *adj.-s.* saurio.
**sausage** (so·sidý) *s.* salchicha, embutido.
**sauté** (sou·tei) *adj.* COC. salteado.
**sauté (to)** *tr.* COC. saltear.

**savage** (sæ·vidỹ) *adj.* salvaje. *2* fiero, bárbaro, brutal. *3 s.* salvaje.
**savageness** (-nis), **savagery** (-ri) *s.* salvajismo. *2* barbarie, ferocidad.
**savanna(h)** (savæ·na) *s.* GEOGR. sabana, pradera.
**savant** (sæ·vant) *s.* hombre de letras o de ciencia.
**save** (seiv) *prep.* salvo, excepto, menos. *2 conj.* si no fuera, a menos [que].
**save (to)** *tr.* salvar, librar. *2* guardar, preservar: *God ~ the Queen!*, ¡Dios guarde a la Reina! *3* ahorrar [dinero, trabajo, etc.]. *4* guardar; conservar. *5 to ~ appearances*, guardar las apariencias. *6 intr.* ahorrar.
**save-all** *s.* apuracabos. *2* delantal, mono.
**saveloy** (sa·vøloi) *s.* especie de salsicha seca.
**savin(e** (sæ·vin) *s.* BOT. sabina.
**saving** (sei·ving) *adj.* salvador. *2* ahorrador, económico. *3* que contiene salvedad. *4 s.* economía, ahorro. *5* salvedad. *6 pl.* ahorros: *savings bank*, caja de ahorros. *7 prep.* salvo, excepto.
**savio(u)r** (-viø<sup>r</sup>) *s.* salvador. *2 the Saviour*, el Salvador, el Redentor.
**savo(u)r** (-vø<sup>r</sup>) *s.* sabor; olor. *2* gusto, dejo.
**savo(u)r (to)** *tr.* saborear, dar sabor a. *2* dar un olor a. *3* saborear [apreciar con deleite]. *4 intr. to ~ of*, saber a, oler a; tener las cualidades de.
**savo (u) ry** (-vøri) *adj.* sabroso, apetitoso, agradable. *2* fragante. *3 s.* (Ingl.) especie de entremés. *4* BOT. ajedrea.
**Savoy** (savoi·) *n. pr.* GEOGR. Saboya.
**Savoyard** (savoi·a<sup>r</sup>d) *adj.-s.* saboyano.
**saw** (so) *s.* sierra [herramienta]. *2* dicho, refrán, proverbio. *3 pret.* de TO SEE.
**saw (to)** *tr.-intr.* serrar, aserrar. *2* mover o moverse como una sierra. *3 intr.* cortar [una sierra]. *4* aserrarse [bien, mal, etc., una materia]. P. p. *sawed* y *sawn*.
**sawbones** (-bouns) *s.* pop. cirujano.
**sawbuck** (-bøk) *s.* SAWHORSE.
**sawdust** (-døst) *s.* serrín, aserraduras.
**sawfish** (-fish) *s.* ICT. pez sierra, priste.
**sawhorse** (-jo<sup>r</sup>s) *s.* CARP. caballete, cabrilla, burro.
**sawings** (-ings) *s. pl.* aserraduras.
**sawmill** (so·mil) *s.* aserradero.
**sawn** (-to) *p. p. in* de TO SAW.
**sawney** (so·ni) *adj.* tonto, simple. *2 s.* simplón.
**saw-toothed** *adj.* BOT. serrado, aserrado.
**sawyer** (so·iø<sup>r</sup>) *s.* aserrador.
**saxatile** (sæ·ksatil) *adj.* saxátil.
**saxhorn** (-jø<sup>r</sup>n) *s.* MÚS. bombardón.
**saxifrage** (-ifridỹ) *s.* BOT. saxífraga.
**Saxon** (-øn) *adj.-s.* sajón. *2* anglosajón.
**Saxony** (-øni) *n. pr.* GEOGR. Sajonia.
**saxophone** (-foun) *s.* MÚS. saxofón.
**say** (sei) *s.* dicho, aserto; opinión. *2* turno para hablar; voz, derecho de hablar.
**say (to)** *tr.* decir: *to ~ good-bye*, decir adiós, despedir; *to ~ mass*, decir misa; *I should ~ so!*, ¡ya lo creo!; *it is said*, se dice; *no sooner said than done*, dicho y hecho; *say*, digamos, por ejemplo; *that is to ~*, es decir; *you don't ~ so!*, ¡no es posible!, ¿de veras? | No tiene el sentido de convenir o armonizar. *2* recitar, rezar. *3* contar, referir. *4 intr.* decir, hablar: *I say!*, ¡oiga!, ¡escuche! ¶ Pret. y p. p.: *said*.
**saying** (sei·ing) *s.* dicho, lo que se dice, relato. *2* dicho, sentencia, refrán.
**scab** (skæb) *s.* MED. costra, postilla. *2* VET. roña, escabro. *3* AGR. escabro. *4* fam. esquirol.
**scabbard** (skæ·ba<sup>r</sup>d) *s.* vaina, funda [de un arma].
**scabble (to)** (skæ·bøl) *tr.* desbastar.

**scabby** (skæ·bi) *adj.* costroso, postilloso. *2* VET. roñoso. *3* ruin, vil.
**scables** (skei·blš) *s.* MED. sarna.
**scabious** (-biøs) *adj.* SCABBY. *2 s.* BOT. escabiosa.
**scabrous** (-brøs) *adj.* áspero, rugoso. *2* escabroso [en sentido moral]. *3* difícil.
**scaffold** (skæ·fould) *s.* andamio. *2* tablado. *3* tribuna [al aire libre]. *4* cadalso, patíbulo.
**scaffold (to)** *tr.* proveer de andamios.
**scaffolding** (-ing) *s.* andamiaje. *2* armazón para varios usos.
**scagliola** (skøliou·la) *s.* escayola, estuco.
**scalar** (skei·la<sup>r</sup>) *adj.* MAT. escalar.
**scal(l)awag** (skæ·laueg) *s.* res raquítica. *2* fam. pícaro, bribón.
**scald** (skold) *s.* escaldadura. *2* SKALD.
**scald (to)** *tr.* escaldar. *2* calentar [un líquido] hasta casi hacerlo hervir.
**scald-head** *s.* MED. tiña, acores, usagre.
**scale** (skeil) *s.* platillo [de balanza]: *to turn the scales*, ser decisivo. *2* balanza, báscula, romana. *3* ZOOL., BOT., MED. escama. *4* escama, laminilla, costra, vaina, incrustación: *~ insect*, insecto cóccido. *5* escala [pitipié; serie graduada; proporción]: *on a large ~*, en gran escala; *on a small ~*, en pequeña escala. *6* MÚS. escala. *7 pl.* (con may.) ASTR. Libra.
**scale (to)** *tr.* pesar. *2* escamar [quitar las escamas]. *3* descostrar, descascarar, desvainar, pelar. *4* cubrir de escamas. *5* escalar, subir. *6* graduar, proporcionar, ajustar a escala. *7 intr.* descamarse; descascararse, pelarse. *8* cubrirse de incrustaciones. *9* subir en escala.
**scalene** (skeil·n) *adj.* GEOM., ANAT. escaleno.
**scaling** (skei·ling) *s.* escamadura. *2* escalamiento. *3* imbricación. *4* medición por escala.
**scall** (skol) *s.* MED. tiña.
**scallion** (skæ·liøn) *s.* BOT. chalote.
**scallop** (skæ·løp) *s.* ZOOL. venera, pechina. *2* concha de peregrino. *3* festón, onda, recorte.
**scallop (to)** *tr.* festonear, recortar en ondas. *2* COC. cocer al horno con pan rallado. *3* COC. cocer [ostras] en su concha.
**scalp** (skælp) *s.* cuero cabelludo.
**scalp (to)** *tr.* arrancar la cabellera, el cuero cabelludo a. *2* fig. criticar despiadadamente. *3* (E.U.) comprar y revender [localidades, etc.].
**scalpel** (-s) *s.* CIR. escalpelo.
**scalper** (-ø<sup>r</sup>) *s.* (E.U.) revendedor.
**scaly** (skei·li) *adj.* escamoso. *2* AGR. infestado por insectos cóccidos. *3* vil, ruin. *4* avaro.
**scammony** (skæ·møni) *s.* BOT. escamonea.
**scamp** (skæmp) *s.* pícaro, bribón, tuno.
**scamp (to)** *tr.* hacer [algo] mal o descuidadamente.
**scamper** (-ø<sup>r</sup>) *s.* huida precipitada, carrera rápida.
**scamper (to)** *intr.* correr o moverse precipitadamente. *2* huir, escaparse.
**scan (to)** *tr.* escandir. *2* examinar, escrutar; recorrer con la vista. *3* TELEV. explorar. ¶ Pret. y p. p.: *scanned*; ger.: *-nning*.
**scandal** (skæ·ndal) *s.* escándalo. | No tiene el sentido de alboroto. *2* ignominia. *3* cosa escandalosa. *4* difamación, maledicencia.
**scandalize (to)** (-aiš) *tr.* escandalizar. *2* difamar, murmurar de.
**scandalmonger** (-møngø<sup>r</sup>) *s.* difamador, murmurador.
**scandalous** (-øs) *adj.* escandaloso, vergonzoso. *3* difamatorio.

**Scandinavia** (skændinei·via) *n. pr.* GEOGR. Escandinavia.
**Scandinavian** (-vian) *adj.-s.* escandinavo.
**scansion** (skæ·nshøn) *s.* escansión.
**scant** (skænt) *adj.* escaso, corto, limitado, insuficiente, exiguo: ~ *of*, corto de.
**scant (to)** *tr.* escatimar. *2* reducir, limitar, estrechar. *3 intr.* MAR. caer [el viento].
**scantling** (-ling) *s.* poco, pequeña cantidad. *2* escantillón, escuadría. *3* cuartón. *4* caballete [para un barril].
**scanty** (skæ·nti) *adj.* escaso, insuficiente, exiguo. *2* mezquino, cicatero.
**scape** (skeip) *s.* BOT., ARQ. escapo.
**scapegoat** (skei·pgout) *s.* víctima propiciatoria, cabeza de turco.
**scapegrace** (skei·pgreis) *s.* pícaro, travieso.
**scapula** (skæ·piula) *s.* ANAT. escápula.
**scapular** (skæ·piula$^r$) *adj.* escapular. *2 s.* escapulario. *3* ANAT., ZOOL. escápula.
**scapular** (skæ·piula$^r$) *adj.* escapular. *2 s.* escapulario. *3* ANAT., ZOOL. escápula.
**scar** (ska$^r$) *s.* cicatriz. *2* chirlo, costurón. *3* raya, rasguño. *4* peñasco, farallón, roca pelada.
**scar (to)** *tr.* marcar con cicatriz, señalar. ¶ Pret. y p. p.: *scarred;* ger.: *-rring.*
**scarab** (skæ·rab) *s.* ENT. escarabajo, sagrado.
**scarce** (ske$^r$s) *adj.* escaso, raro, contado.
**scarcely** (-li) *adv.* escasamente, apenas, difícilmente. *2* apenas, no bien. *3* casi, casi no; ~ *ever*, casi nunca.
**scarceness** (-nis), **scarcity** (-iti) *s.* escasez, penuria, carestía. *2* rareza, raridad.
**scare** (ske$^r$) *s.* susto, alarma. *2* pánico [comercial].
**scare (to)** *tr.* asustar, amedrentar, alarmar. *2 to ~ away*, espantar, ahuyentar.
**scarecrow** (-krou) *s.* espantapájaros, espantajo.
**scaremonger** (-møngø$^r$) *s.* propagador de noticias alarmantes.
**scarf** (ska$^r$f), *pl.* **scarfs** o **scarves** *s.* echarpe. *2* pañuelo, bufanda, corbata, chalina. *3* banda, faja [de uniforme, etc.]. *4* tapete estrecho. *5* CARP. ensambladura a media madera.
**scarf (to)** *tr.* CARP. ensamblar a media madera.
**scarfpin** (-pin) *s.* alfiler de corbata.
**scarfskin** (-kin) *s.* ANAT. epidermis.
**scarification** (skærifikei·shøn) *s.* AGR., CIR. escarificación.
**scarify (to)** (skæ·rifai) *tr.* CIR., AGR. escarificar. *2* fig. flagelar, criticar duramente. ¶ Pret. y p. p.: *scarified.*
**scarlatina** (ska$^r$lati·na) *s.* MED. escarlatina.
**scarless** (ska·$^r$lis) *adj.* sin chirlos o cicatrices; ileso.
**scarlet** (ska·$^r$lit) *adj.* rojo, de color escarlata: ~ *fever*, MED. escarlatina; ~ *oak*, BOT. coscoja. *2 s.* escarlata, grana.
**scarp** (ska·$^r$p) *s.* escarpa, declive. *2* FORT. escarpa.
**scarp (to)** *tr.* escarpar [un terreno].
**scarred** (ska·$^r$d), **scarry** (ska·ri) *adj.* que tiene cicatrices. *2* pelado [roca, etc.].
**scary** (ske·ri) *adj.* fam. medrso, asustadizo.
**scat** (skæt) *interp.* ¡zape!
**scathe** (skeið) *s.* daño, perjuicio.
**scatheless** (-lis) *adj.* indemne, sano y salvo.
**scathing** (-ing) *adj.* acerbo, duro, mordaz.
**scatology** (skata·lødÿi) *s.* escatología [estudio de los excrementos].
**scatter (to)** (skæ·tø$^r$) *tr.* dispersar, poner en fuga. *2* disipar, desvanecer. *3* esparcir, difundir. *4 intr.* dispersarse. *5* disiparse.

**scatterbrain** (-brein), *s.*, **scatterbrained** (-breind) *adj.* ligero de cascos, atolondrado.
**scavenge (to)** (skæ·vindÿ) *tr.* recoger la basura.
**scavenger** (-ø$^r$) *s.* basurero, barrendero. *2* animal que se alimenta de basura.
**scenario** (sine·riou) *s.* TEAT., CINEM. guión.
**scenarist** (-rist) *s.* CINEM. guionista.
**scene** (sin) *s.* escena [en todas sus acepciones]: *to make a ~*, hacer una escena. *2* escenario. *3* TEAT. decorado: ~ *shifter*, tramoyista; *behind the scenes*, entre bastidores. *4* cuadro, vista, paisaje.
**scenery** (-øri) *s.* paisaje, panorama. *2* TEAT. decorado.
**scenic** (se·nik) *adj.* escénico. *2* pintoresco.
**scenographer** (sina·grafø$^r$) *s.* escenógrafo.
**scenography** (-græfi) *s.* escenografía.
**scent** (sent) *s.* olfato. *2* olor; fragancia. *3* rastro, pista, indicio. *4* perfume, esencia.
**scent** (sent) *s.* olfato. *2* olor; fragancia. *3* rastro, pista, indicio. *4* perfume, esencia.
**scent (to)** *tr.* oler, olfatear, husmear, ventear. *2* sospechar. *3* perfumar. *4 intr. to ~ of*, oler a.
**scepter** (se·ptø$^r$) *s.* centro [real].
**sceptic, scepticism** = SKEPTIC, SKEPTICISM.
**sceptre** *s.* SCEPTER.
**schedule** (ske·diul) *s.* lista, catálogo, inventario. *2* horario [de trenes, etc.]. *3* programa, plan.
**schedule (to)** *tr.* incluir en una lista, catálogo, etc. *2* incluir en un horario o programa; fijar el tiempo para.
**schema** (skı·ma) *s.* esquema, diagrama, cuadro.
**schematic** (skımæ·tik) *adj.* esquemático.
**scheme** (skı·m) *s.* esquema, diseño. *2* plan, proyecto, designio. *3* ardid, intriga, maquinación.
**scheme (to)** *tr.* proyectar, idear, trazar. *2 intr.* formar planes, intrigar.
**schemer** (-ø$^r$) *s.* proyectista. *2* maquinador, intrigante.
**schism** (si·šm) *s.* cisma; escisión.
**schismatic** (sišmæ·tik) *adj.-s.* cismático.
**schist** (shist) *s.* GEOL. esquisto.
**schizomycete** (skišomaisi·t) *s.* BOT. esquizomiceto.
**schizophrenia** (-frı·nia) *s.* MED. esquizofrenia.
**scholar** (ska·la$^r$) *s.* escolar, estudiante. *2* becario. *3* hombre docto, erudito: *classical ~*, humanista. *4 to be no ~*, tener poca instrucción.
**scholarly** (-li) *adj.* docto, erudito.
**scholarship** (-ship) *s.* saber, erudición. *2* beca [para estudiar].
**scholastic** (skølæ·stik) *adj.-s.* escolástico. *2 adj.* de erudito. *3* escolar, estudiantil.
**scholasticism** (-isišm) *s.* escolasticismo.
**scholium** (skou·liøm), *pl.* **-lia** (-liø) *s.* escolio.
**school** (skul) *s.* escuela. *2* colegio [de enseñanza]. *3* clase [sesión]. *4* facultad [de una universidad]. *5* banco de peces. *6 adj.* escolar; de enseñanza: ~ *year*, año escolar; ~ *board*, junta de enseñanza. *7* de clase, lectivo. *8* MAR. ~ *ship*, buque escuela.
**school (to)** *tr.* enseñar, instruir. *2* amaestrar, adiestrar, disciplinar. *3 intr.* ir en banco [los peces].
**schoolbook** (-buk) *s.* libro escolar.
**schoolboy** (-boi) *s.* muchacho de la escuela, colegial.
**schoolfellow** (-felou) *s.* condiscípulo.
**schoolgirl** (-gø$^r$) *s.* muchacha de la escuela, colegiala.
**schoolhouse** (-jaus) *s.* escuela [edificio].

**schooling** (-ling) *s.* instrucción, enseñanza. *2* experiencia. *3* precio de la escuela. *4* reprimenda.

**schoolman** (-mæn) *s.* escolástico. *2* humanista.

**schoolmaster** (-mæ·støʳ) *s.* profesora de instituto.

**schoolmate** (-meit) *s.* condiscípulo.

**schoolmistress** (-mistris) *s.* profesora de instituto.

**schoolroom** (-rum) *s.* aula, sala de clase.

**schoolyard** (-yaʳd) *s.* patio de escuela.

**schooner** (sku·nøʳ) *s.* MAR. goleta. *2* vaso grande para cerveza. *3* (E.U.) galera [carruaje] con toldo.

**schottische** (sha·tish) *s.* chotis.

**sciatica** (saiæ·tika) *s.* MED. ciática.

**science** (sai·øns) *s.* ciencia. *2* ciencias naturales.

**scientific** (al (saiønti·fik(al) *adj.* científico.

**scientist** (sai·øntist) *s.* hombre de ciencia.

**scimitar, -ter** (si·mitaʳ, -øʳ) *s.* cimitarra.

**scintilla** (sinti·la) *s.* chispa, leve asomo o indicio.

**scintillant** (si·ntilant) *adj.* centelleante, chispeante.

**scintillate (to)** (si·ntileit) *intr.* centellear, chispear.

**scion** (sai·øn) *s.* AGR. vástago, renuevo; esqueje, injerto, púa. *2* vástago, descendiente.

**scirrhus** (ski·røs) *s.* MED. cirro.

**scissel** (si·sel) *s.* cizallas, recortes de metal.

**scission** (si·shøn) *s.* corte, división; escisión.

**scissor (to)** (si·søʳ) *tr.* cortar [con tijeras].

**scissors** (-s) *s. pl.* tijeras.

**scissure** (si·shøʳ) *s.* cisura. *2* escisión.

**sclera** (skli·ra) *s.* ANAT. esclerótica.

**sclerenchyma** (sklire·nkima) *s.* BOT. esclerénquima.

**sclerosis** (sklirou·sis) *s.* MED. esclerosis.

**scoff** (skaf) *s.* mofa, burla, befa. *2* hazmerreír.

**scoff (to)** *intr.* mofarse, burlarse, hacer befa: *to ~ at,* mofarse de.

**scoffer** (-øʳ) *s.* mofador, despreciador.

**scold** (skould) *s.* mujer regañona, reñidora.

**scold (to)** *tr.* reñir, regañar.

**scolding** (-ing) *s.* regaño, reprensión.

**scoliosis** (skouliou·sis) *s.* MED. escoliosis.

**scolopendra** (skalope·ndra) *s.* ZOOL. escolopendra, ciempiés.

**scomber** (ska·mbøʳ) *s.* ICT. escombro, caballa.

**sconce** (skans) *s.* abrigo, defensa. *2* FORT. baluarte, reducto. *3* fam. cabeza, seso. *4* multa. *5* candelabro de pared.

**sconce (to)** *tr.* fortificar con baluarte, proteger. *2* multar.

**scone** (skan) *s.* COC. especie de bizcocho.

**scoop** (skup) *s.* cucharón grande, cazo. *2* pala de mano, cogedor, librador. *3* cuchara [de excavadora, draga, etc.]. *4* achicador. *5* instrumento en forma de cuchara. *6* cucharada, palada. *7* hoyo, cavidad. *8* buena ganancia. *9* noticia que da un periódico antes que los demás.

**scoop (to)** *tr.* sacar con pala o cuchara. *2* ganar, llevarse, obtener. *3* achicar, vaciar. *4* ahuecar, excavar.

**scoot** (skut) *s.* fam. carrera precipitada.

**scoot (to)** *intr.* salir, correr, deslizarse [de pronto o velozmente]. *2* fam. largarse.

**scooter** (-øʳ) *s.* patinete. *2* embarcación rápida y de poco calado. *3* motocicleta ligera.

**scope** (skoup) *s.* alcance, extensión. *2* campo, radio, esfera, oportunidad, libertad [de acción, etc.]. *3* mira, designio.

**scorbutic** (skoʳbiu·tik) *adj.-s.* MED. escorbútico.

**scorch** (skoʳch) *s.* chamusco, quemadura. *2* calor abrasador.

**scorch (to)** *tr.* chamuscar, socarrar. *2* abrasar, que-

mar, agostar. *3* intr. abrasarse, agostarse. *4* correr velozmente.

**scorching** (-ing) *adj.* ardiente, abrasador. *2* agostador. *3* fig. punzante.

**score** (skoʳ) *s.* muesca, entalladura. *2* raya, señal. *3* cuenta [de lo que se debe]; agravio: *to settle a ~,* saldar una cuenta. *4* tantos, tanteo [en el dep. o en el juego]: *~ board,* marcador. *5* razón, motivo, consideración: *on that ~,* a este respecto. *6* veintena. *7* MÚS. partitura. *8* pl. gran número.

**score (to)** *tr.* marcar con rayas o muescas; rayar. *2* poner en la cuenta. *3* azotar. *4* censurar severamente. *5* contar, marcar, valer [puntos o tantos]; ganar, lograr: *to ~ a point,* apuntarse un tanto. *6* MÚS. orquestar. *7* *to ~ out,* borrar, tachar. *8* intr. hacer rayas o señales. *9* ganar o marcar tantos; ganar, vencer.

**scoria** (sko·ria), pl. **scoriae** (sko·rii) *s.* escoria.

**scoring** (sco·ring) *s.* raya, rayado. *2* MÚS. orquestación. *3* CINEM. guión sonoro.

**scorn** (skoʳn) *s.* desdén, desprecio. *2* escarnio.

**scorn (to)** *tr.* desdeñar, despreciar. *2* escarnecer. *3* tener a menos.

**scornful** (-ful) *adj.* despreciativo, insolente.

**Scorpio** (sko·ʳpiou) *s.* ASTR. Escorpión.

**scorpion** (sko·ʳpiøn) *s.* ZOOL. escorpión, alacrán. *2* ICT. *~ fish,* escorpión, escorpina.

**scorpionwort** (-wo·ʳt) *s.* BOT. alacranera.

**Scot** (skat) *s.* escocés.

**scotch** (skach) *s.* corte, muesca. *2* calza, cuña. *3* obstáculo, impedimento.

**scotch (to)** *tr.* cortar, herir ligeramente. *2* calzar, poner cuñas. *3* estorbar, frustrar.

**Scotch** *adj.-s.* escocés: *~ pine,* pino albar. *2* *s.* whisky escocés, idioma escocés.

**Scotchman** (-mæn) *s.* escocés.

**scoter** (skou·tøʳ) *s.* ORN. pato negro.

**scot-free** (ska·tfri) *adj.* impune.

**scotia** (skou·shan) *s.* ARQ. escocia.

**Scotland** (ska·tland) *n. pr.* GEOGR. Escocia.

**Scotsman** (-smæn) *s.* escocés.

**Scottish** (-ish) *adj.* escocés [de Escocia o de los escoceses].

**scoundrel** (skau·ndrøl) *s.* granuja, bribón, canalla.

**scour** (skauʳ) *s.* acción limpiadora de una corriente rápida. *2* pl. diarrea del ganado.

**scour (to)** *tr.* fregar, estregar; limpiar, lavar [esp. con un chorro de agua]. *2* desgrasar [el paño]. *3* barrer, expulsar. *4* abrir [cauce] una corriente de agua. *5* purgar [dar una purga]. *6* recorrer, explorar, registrar. *7* batir [el monte].

**scourge** (skoʳdÿ) *s.* látigo, azote. *2* azote, calamidad.

**scourge (to)** *tr.* azotar, flagelar. *2* castigar, afligir.

**scout** (skaut) *s.* MIL. explorador, escucha. *2* buque de observación. *3* avión de reconocimiento. *4* muchacho explorador.

**scout (to)** *tr.-intr.* explorar, reconocer, espiar. *2* rechazar con desdén, burlarse de.

**scow** (skaw) *s.* MAR. chalana, barcaza.

**scowl** (skaul) *s.* ceño, sobrecejo. *2* ceño, aspecto amenazador.

**scowl (to)** *intr.* mirar con ceño; enfurruñarse. *2* tener aspecto amenazador. *3* tr. expresar, obligar, rechazar, etc., con el ceño.

**scrabble** (skræ·bøl) *s.* garabatos. *2* SCRAMBLE.

**scrabble (to)** *tr.-intr.* garabatear. *2* tr. arrebañar. *3* intr. arañar, escarbar, esforzarse [en busca de algo]. *4* trepar, gatear.

**scrag** (skræg) *s.* aleluya [pers. o animal flacos]. *2* pescuezo. *3* pedazo delgado y duro.

**scrag (to)** *tr.* pop. ahorcar, torcer el pescuezo a. ¶ Pret. y p. p.: *scragged;* ger.: *-gaing.*

**scragged** (skræ·gid) *adj.* flaco, descarnado.

**scraggy** (-i) *adj.* desigual, escabroso. *2* flaco, huesudo.

**scramble** (skræ·mbøl) *s.* lucha, arrebatiña. *2* gateamiento.

**scramble (to)** *intr.* trepar, gatear, arrastrarse. *2* andar a la arrebatiña; correr, luchar [por conseguir algo]. *3* extenderse irregularmente. *4 tr.* recoger precipitadamente. *5* barajar, revolver: *scrambled eggs,* huevos revueltos.

**scrap** (skræp) *s.* trozo, pedacito, mendrugo. *2* recorte. *3* pop. riña. *4 pl.* sobras, desperdicios; chatarra. *5 pork scraps,* chicharrones. *6* ~ *iron,* hierro viejo.

**scrap (to)** *tr.* desechar, echar a la basura. *2* desguazar [un buque]. *3* pop. reñir, pelear.

**scrapbook** (-buk) *s.* álbum de recortes.

**scrape** (skreip) *s.* raspadura, raedura, rasguño. *2* ruido de raspar. *3* restregadura de pies. *4* lío, aprieto. *5* riña.

**scrape (to)** *tr.* raspar, rascar, raer; arañar, rayar. *2* fig. rascar [el violín, etc.]. *3* restregar [los pies]. *4 to* ~ *acquaintance,* trabar conocimiento. *5 to* ~ *together* o *up,* rebañar; reunir poco a poco. *6* intr. *to* ~ *along,* ir tirando. *7 to* ~ *through,* salir bien [de algo] por milagro.

**scraper** (skrei·pø<sup>r</sup>) *s.* rascador, raspador; raedera. *2* fam. rascatripas. *3* CIR. legra.

**scrapings** (-ings) *s. pl.* raspaduras, raeduras. *2* ahorros.

**scratch** (skræch) *s.* arañazo; rasguño, raya; rascadura. *2* tachón, borradura. *3* fam. garabato [escrito]. *4* peluquín, bisoñé. *5* DEP. línea de salida: *to start from the* ~, fig. empezar sin nada, desde el principio. *5* BILL. chiripa. *7 pl.* VET. ajuagas. *8 adj.* casual, improvisado; allegadizo. *9* DEP. sin ventaja.

**scratch (to)** *tr.* arañar, rasguñar, rayar. *2* rascar, escarbar. *3* reunir [dinero, etc.]. *4* tachar, borrar. *5* garrapatear, borronear. *6 intr.* raspear [la pluma].

**scrawl** (skrol) *s.* escrito garrapateado. *2 pl.* garabatos, garrapatos.

**scrawl (to)** *tr.-intr.* garrapatear, borronear.

**scrawny** (skro·ni) *adj.* (E.U.) flaco, huesudo.

**screak** (skrik) *s.* chillido. *2* chirrido, rechinido.

**screak (to)** *intr.* chillar. *2* chirriar, rechinar.

**scream** (skrɪm) *s.* chillido, grito, alarido. *2* pitido [de locomotora]. *3* pop. cosa muy cómica.

**scream (to)** *intr.-tr.* chillar, gritar, vociferar. *2 intr.* pitar [la locomotora]. *3* ser chillón, llamativo.

**screamer** (-ø<sup>r</sup>) *s.* chillón, voceador. *2* titular sensacional [en un periódico].

**screaming** (-ing) *s.-adj.* chillón, gritador. *2* pop. muy divertido. *3* pop. estupendo.

**screech** (skrɪch) *s.* chillido, estridor. *2* alarido. *3* ululato.

**screech (to)** *intr.* chillar. *2* ulular.

**screechy** (-i) *adj.* chillón, agudo, estridente.

**screen** (skrɪn) *s.* pantalla: *the* ~, la pantalla, el cine. *2* biombo, mampara, cancel, persiana. *3* alambrera, enrejado [de ventana, etc.]. *4* reparo, abrigo, cosa que oculta. *5* criba, harnero. *6* trama [para el fotograbado]. *7* FOT. filtro. *8* tablón de anuncios.

**screen (to)** *tr.* ocultar, tapar. *2* abrigar, proteger. *3* reparar. *4* proyectar en una pantalla. *5* adaptar para el cine. *6* cribar.

**screenings** (-ings) *s. pl.* residuos de criba.

**screw** (skru) *s.* tornillo, rosca; tuerca: *female* ~, tuerca; ~ *eye,* armella; ~ *jack,* cric o gato de rosca; ~ *wrench,* desvolvedor, llave inglesa; *to have a* ~ *loose,* fam. faltarle a uno un tornillo. *2* tornillo [clavo]. *3* hélice [propulsor]. *4* vuelta de tornillo: *to put the screws on,* apretar los tornillos a. *5* pop. tacaño. *6* BILL. efecto.

**screw (to)** *tr.* atornillar. *2* apretar, oprimir, estrujar. *3* torcer, retorcer. *4* BILL. dar efecto a. *5* arrancar, sacar [dinero, etc.]. *6* dar cierta expresión [al semblante]. *7 to* ~ *down,* atornillar. *8 to* ~ *out,* desatornillar; sacar, sonsacar. *9 to* ~ *up one's courage,* darse ánimo. *10 intr.* atornillarse; retorcerse. *11 to* ~ *into,* insinuarse, introducirse.

**screwdriver** (-dri·vø<sup>r</sup>) *s.* destornillador.

**scribble** (skri·bøl) *s.* escrito desmañado. *2* garrapatos.

**scribble (to)** *tr.* escribir de prisa. *2* garrapatear.

**scribbler** (skri·blø<sup>r</sup>) *s.* escritorzuelo.

**scribe** (skraib) *s.* escriba. *2* escribiente. *3* amanuense, copista. *4* autor, escritor.

**scrimmage** (skri·midȳ) *s.* escaramuza, refriega, trapatiesta. *2* arrebatiña.

**scrimp** (skrimp) *adj.* corto, escaso, mezquino. *2 s.* avaro.

**scrimp (to)** *tr.* escatimar. *2* proveer con escasez.

**scrip** (skrip) *s.* cédula, documento. *2* título provisional de una acción u obligación. *3* vale, abonaré.

**script** (skript) *s.* DER. instrumento original. *2* letra, escritura. *3* letra cursiva. *4* TEAT. manuscrito.

**scriptural** (skri·pchø<sup>r</sup>) *adj.* escrito; relativo a la escritura. *2* bíblico.

**Scripture** (skri·pchø<sup>r</sup>) *s.* Sagrada Escritura.

**scrofula** (skra·fiula) *s.* MED. escrófula.

**scrofulous** (-løs) *adj.* escrofuloso.

**scroll** (skroul) *s.* rollo de papel o pergamino [esp. escrito]. *2* voluta. *3* rasgo, rúbrica.

**scrotum** (skrou·tøm) *s.* ANAT. escroto.

**scrub** (skrøb) *adj.* desmirriado, achaparrado: ~ *oak,* chaparro. *2* pobre, inferior. *3 s.* fregado, fregoteo. *4* enano. *5* monte bajo.

**scrub (to)** *tr.* fregar, estregar, aljofifar. ¶ Pret. y p. p.: *scrubbed;* ger.: *-bbing.*

**scrubbing** (-ing) *s.* fregado, etregón: ~ *brush,* cepillo para fregar.

**scrubby** (-i) *adj.* desmirriado, achaparrado, bajo. *2* despreciable. *3* hirsuto; mal afeitado. *4* lleno de maleza.

**scruff** (skrøf) *s.* pescuezo, nuca. *2* cuello [de la chaqueta]. *3* capa, superficie. *4* escoria.

**scrummage** (skrø·midȳ) *s.* RUGBY melée.

**scruple** (skru·pøl) *s.* escrúpulo [duda, recelo]. *2* escrúpulo [peso]. *3* cantidad ínfima.

**scruple (to)** *intr.* tener escrúpulo. *2* escrupulizar. *3 tr.* tener escrúpulo en.

**scrupulosity** (skrupiula·siti) *s.* escrupulosidad.

**scrupulous** (skru·piuløs) *adj.* escrupuloso.

**scrutineer** (skrutini·<sup>r</sup>) *s.* escrutador.

**scrutinize (to)** (skru·tinaiš) *tr.* escrutar, escudriñar, examinar atentamente.

**scrutiny** (skru·tini) *s.* escrutinio, examen.

**scud** (skød) *s.* carrera rápida. *2* nubes tenues que corren velozmente. *3* espuma, rocío [del mar].

**scud (to)** *intr.* correr, volar, deslizarse rápidamente.

**scuff** (skøf) *tr.* arrastrar [los pies]. *2* pisar, revolver [con los pies]. *3 intr.* arrastrar los pies. *4* ajarse, rayarse.

**scuffle** (skʌ·fəl) *s.* lucha, riña [en que hay carreras y empujones]; arrebatiña.
**scuffle (to)** *intr.* luchar, pelear [en confusión]; forcejear [unos con otros].
**scull** (skʌl) *s.* MAR. espadilla; remo.
**scull (to)** *intr.-tr.* cinglar. 2 remar o mover con remo.
**scullery** (skʌ·ləri) *s.* fregadero, trascocina.
**scullion** (skʌ·liən) *s.* galopín de cocina, sollastre.
**sculptor** (skʌ·lptər) *s.* escultor.
**sculptress** (-tris) *s.* escultora.
**sculptural** (-chərəl) *adj.* escultórico, escultural.
**sculpture** (skʌ·lpchər) *s.* escultura.
**sculpture (to)** *tr.* esculpir, cincelar.
**sculpturesque** (-esk) *adj.* escultural, estatuario.
**scum** (skʌm) *s.* espuma, nata. 2 escoria, hez. 3 canalla, chusma.
**scum (to)** *tr.* espumar, despumar. 2 *intr.* espumar, cubrirse de espuma.
**scummy** (skʌ·mi) *adj.* espumoso. 2 cubierto de escoria.
**scupper** (skʌ·pər) *s.* imbornal.
**scurf** (skʌrf) *s.* caspa; costra. 2 hez, chusma.
**scurfy** (skʌ·rfi) *adj.* casposo, costroso.
**scurrility** (skʌri·liti) *s.* chabacanería, procacidad, insolencia.
**scurrilous** (skʌ·riləs) *adj.* chabacano, grosero, procaz, insolente.
**scurry** (skʌ·ri) *s.* carrera [de pasos cortos], fuga precipitada. 2 ventolera, remolino.
**scurry (to)** *intr.* echar a correr [con pasos cortos y rápidos]; huir, escabullirse. 2 *tr.* poner en fuga.
**scurvy** (skʌ·rvi) *s.* MED. escorbuto. 2 *adj.* vil, ruin, indigno. 3 grosero.
**scut** (skʌt) *s.* cola corta, rabito.
**scutch** (skʌch) *s.* agramadera, espadilla. 2 agramiza.
**scutch (to)** *tr.* agramar, espadar.
**scutcheon** (skʌ·chən) *s.* ESCUTCHEON.
**scuttle** (skʌ·təl) *s.* escotillón, abertura. 2 MAR. escotilla pequeña; respiradero. 3 cubo del carbón. 4 cesta plana. 5 paso rápido; huida o partida precipitada.
**scuttle (to)** *tr.* MAR. barrenar, dar barreno a. 2 *intr.* correr, huir.
**scythe** (saið) *s.* guadaña, dalle.
**scythe (to)** *tr.* guadañar.
**sea** (si) *s.* mar; océano, golfo: *Sea of Marmara,* Mar de Mármara; *Sea of Tiberias,* lago de Tiberíades; *high ~,* mar gruesa; *high* o *open ~,* alta mar; *to go to ~,* embarcar, hacerse marino; *at ~,* en el mar; fig. perdido, perplejo, confuso; *by ~,* por mar. 2 oleaje, marejada. 3 oleada, ola grande. 4 *sing.* y *pl.* mar, mares [gran extensión o cantidad].
5 *adj.* del mar, marino; de las olas; de la marina; naval: *~ bank,* orilla del mar; rompeolas; *~ bread,* galleta de barco; *~ blue,* azul verdoso; *~ captain,* capitán de buque mercante; *~ chart,* carta de marear; *~ front,* paseo o línea de edificios frente al mar; *~ level,* nivel del mar; *~ power,* potencia naval; *~ room,* espacio para maniobrar sin peligro; *~ rover,* corsario, pirata; *~ wall,* rompeolas. 6 ORN. *~ eagle,* halieto; *~ goose,* barnacla. 7 ZOOL., ICT. *~ anemone,* anemone de mar; *~ bream,* besugo, pagro; *~ cow,* vaca marina; morsa; *~ dog,* DOGFISH, fig. lobo de mar; *~ hog,* marsopa; *~ horse,* caballo de mar; morsa; *~ lion,* león marino; *~ star,* estrellamar; *~ urchin,* erizo de mar.
**seabeach** (-bɪch) *s.* playa del mar.

**seaboard** (-bord) *s.* costa, litoral.
**sea-born** *adj.* nacido del mar.
**sea-borne** *adj.* transportado por mar.
**seacoast** (-koust) *s.* orilla del mar, costa, litoral.
**seadrome** (-droum) *s.* aeródromo flotante.
**seafarer** (-ferər) *s.* marinero, navegante.
**seafaring** (-fering) *s.* vida del marino o marinero. 2 *adj.* marinero, navegante.
**seafolk** (-fouk) *s.* gente de mar.
**seagirt** (-gərt) *adj.* rodeado de mar.
**seagoing** (-gouing) *adj.* de altura [buque]. 2 marinero, navegante.
**seal** (sil) *s.* ZOOL. foca; león marino. 2 sello, sigilo: *to set one's ~ to,* sellar, aprobar; *under the hand and ~ of,* firmado y sellado por. 3 timbre [para estampar]. 4 precinto. 5 sigilo, secreto. 6 lo que cierra u obtura: *water ~,* sifón.
**seal (to)** *tr.* sellar, precintar, marchamar, lacrar: 2 estampar [con sello]. 3 sellar [comunicar un carácter]. 4 confirmar, decidir irrevocablemente. 5 sellar, cerrar. 6 encerrar, aprisionar. 7 fijar, empotrar. 8 contrastar [pesos y medidas]. 9 *intr.* cazar focas.
**sealer** (-ər) *s.* sellador; cerrador. 2 cazador de focas.
**sealing wax** (-ing) *s.* lacre.
**sealskin** (-skin) *s.* piel de foca.
**seam** (sim) *s.* costura [serie de puntadas]. 2 grieta, juntura. 3 MAR. costura. 4 arruga. 5 costurón, cicatriz. 6 CIR. sutura. 7 MIN. veta delgada.
**seam (to)** *tr.* coser. 2 señalar con cicatrices o arrugas. 3 *intr.* arrugarse; henderse.
**seamaid** (-meid) *s.* MIT. sirena.
**seaman** (-mæn) *s.* marinero, marino.
**seamanship** (-ship) *s.* náutica. 2 pericia náutica.
**seamless** (si·mlis) *s.* inconsútil, sin costura.
**seamstress** (-stris) *s.* costurera.
**seamy** (-i) *adj.* con costura o cicatriz: *the ~ side,* fig. el lado peor.
**seapiece** (si·pis) *s.* PINT. marina.
**seaplane** (-plein) *s.* AVIA. hidroplano.
**seaport** (-port) *s.* puerto de mar.
**seaquake** (-kueik) *s.* maremoto.
**sear** (siər) *adj.* seco, marchito. 2 raído, gastado. 3 *s.* chamusco. 4 ARM. muelle real.
**sear (to)** *tr.* secar, agostar, marchitar. 2 tostar, chamuscar. 3 CIR. cauterizar. 4 fig. endurecer, empedernir.
**search** (sərch) 's. busca, búsqueda. 2 registro, reconocimiento: *~ warrant,* DER. orden de registro. 3 exploración, examen, indagación.
**search (to)** *tr.-intr.* buscar. 2 examinar, registrar, explorar. 3 escudriñar, penetrar. 4 indagar, inquirir, investigar. 5 CIR. tentar. 6 *to ~ after,* preguntar por, indagar, inquirir. 7 *to ~ into,* examinar, investigar. 8 *to ~ out,* descubrir buscando.
**searcher** (-ər) *s.* buscador, investigador. 2 vista, inspector. 3 veedor. 4 CIR. tienta, cala. 5 ÓPT. buscador.
**searching** (-ing) *adj.* escrutador, penetrante. 2 completo, minucioso.
**searchlight** (-lait) *s.* ELECT. proyector, reflector; foco eléctrico.
**seascape** (sɪ·skeip) *s.* vista del mar. 2 PINT. marina.
**seashore** (-shor) *s.* orilla del mar, costa, litoral; playa.
**seasick** (-sik) *adj.* mareado [en el mar].
**seasickness** (-nis) *s.* mareo [en el mar].
**seaside** (-said) *s.* SEASHORE. 2 *adj.* costanero; de la playa.

**season** (sɪ·sØn) *s.* estación [del año]. *3* estación, tiempo, temporada: ~ *ticket,* abono. *3* sazón, tiempo oportuno: *in due* ~, a su tiempo, en tiempo oportuno; *in* ~, a tiempo; a su tiempo; en sazón; *out of* ~, fuera de sazón, intempestivo.

**season (to)** *tr.* sazonar. *2* aliñar, aderezar. *3* moderar, templar. *4* habituar, aclimatar. *5* curar [la madera]. *6 intr.* sazonarse. *7* acostumbrarse. *8* curarse [la madera].

**seasonable** (-abØl) *adj.* oportuno, conveniente. *2* propio de la estación.

**seasonal** (-al) *adj.* estacional.

**seasoning** (-ing) *s.* sazonamiento. *2* condimento, sainete. *3* aclimatación. *4* cura [de la madera]. *5* sazón, punto.

**seat** (sɪt) *s.* asiento [para sentarse]: *to take a* ~, tomar asiento. *2* TEAT. localidad. *3* asiento [de silla, etc.]. *4* asiento, base, sitio, sede, residencia. *5* mansión, quinta. *6* situación. *7* fondillos.

**seat (to)** *tr.* sentar, asentar. *2* acomodar en asientos; tener asientos para. *3* poner asiento a [una silla]. *4* echar fondillos a [un pantalón]. *5* establecer, instalar. *6* fijar, afianzar.

**seating** (-ing) *s.* acción de sentar o de poner asiento. *2* MEC. asiento. *3* adj. ~ *capacity,* cabida, número de asientos.

**seaward** (sɪ·uaᵈd) *adv.* hacia el mar, mar adentro.

**seaway** (-uei) *s.* mar gruesa. *2* ruta marítima.

**seaweed** (-uid) *s.* alga marina.

**seaworthy** (-uØᶠði) *adj.* marinero [buque]; en buen estado para navegar.

**sebaceous** (sibei·shØs) *adj.* sebáceo.

**seborrhœa** (seborì·a) *s.* MED. seborrea.

**secant** (si·kænt) *adj.-s.* GEOM., TRIGON. secante.

**secede (to)** (sisi·d) *intr.* separarse [de una comunión].

**secession** (sise·shØn) *s.* secesión, separación.

**seclude (to)** (sikliu·d) *tr.* apartar, separar, aislar. *2* recluir, encerrar.

**seclusion** (-ȳØn) *s.* retraimiento, aislamiento, retiro, soledad. *2* reclusión, encierro.

**second** (se·kØnd) *adj.* segundo: ~ *best,* segundo [en calidad, mérito, etcétera]; mediocre: ~ *cabin,* MAR. segunda clase; ~ *sight,* doble vista, conocimiento de lo futuro. *2* secundario, subordinado. *3* inferior: *to be* ~ *to none,* no ser inferior a nadie. *4* de los segundos: ~ *hand,* segundero [de reloj]. *5* ~ segundo [pers.]. *6* padrino [en el duelo]. *7* segundo [división del minuto]. *8* dos [en las fechas]. *9* AUTO., MÚS. segunda. *10 pl.* COM. segundas.

**second (to)** *tr.* secundar, apoyar, apadrinar. *2* apoyar [una moción o proposición].

**secondary** (-eri) *adj.* secundario. *2* segunda [enseñanza]. *3* s. ELECT. secundario.

**second-class** *adj.* de segunda clase; inferior. *2 adv.* en segunda.

**seconder** (-Øᵣ) *s.* el que secunda o apoya.

**secondhand** (-jænd) *adj.* de segunda mano.

**second-rate** *adj.* de segunda clase; mediocre.

**secrecy** (sì·krØsi) *s.* secreto, sigilo, reserva. *2* clandestinidad. *3* SECRETIVENESS.

**secret** (sɪ·krit) *adj.* secreto: ~ *service;* espionaje; policía secreta. *2* recóndito, íntimo. *3* callado, reservado. *5 s.* secreto: *in* ~, en secreto. *6* LITURG. secreta.

**secretaire** (sekrØte·ᵣ) *s.* escritorio [mueble].

**secretariat(e** (sekrite·riit) *s.* secretaría. *2* secretariado.

**secretary** (se·kriteri) *s.* secretario, secretaría. *2* escritorio [mueble]. *3* ministro [del gobierno]. *4*

**Secretary of State,** (E.U.) ministro de asuntos exteriores; (Ingl.) título de varios ministros. *5* ORN. ~ *bird,* serpentario.

**secretaryship** (-ship) *s.* secretaría [cargo].

**secrete (to)** (sikrɪ·t) *tr.* esconder, ocultar, recatar, encubrir. *2* FISIOL. secretar.

**secretion** (sikrɪ·shØn) *s.* ocultación. *2* FISIOL. secreción.

**secretive** (sikrɪ·tiv) *adj.* callado, reservado. *2* FISIOL. secretorio.

**sect** (sekt) *s.* secta. *2* grupo, partido.

**sectarian** (sekte·rian) *adj.-s.* sectario. *2* secuaz.

**sectarianism** (sekte·rianišm) *s.* sectarismo.

**sectary** (sek·tari) *s.* sectario. *2* disidente.

**section** (se·kshØn) *s.* sección [acción de cortar; división, parte, grupo, etc.]. *2* corte microscópico. *4* región; barrio. *5* FERROC. tramo. *6* BIB., GEOM., MIL. sección. *7* H. NAT. grupo. *8* IMPR. párrafo [signo].

**sectional** (-al) *adj.* de la sección. *2* regional, local. *3* parcial, incompleto.

**sectionalism** (se·kshØnališm) *s.* localismo.

**sector** (se·ktØᵣ) *s.* sector. *2* compás de proporción.

**secular** (se·kiulaᵣ) *adj.* secular. *2 s.* eclesiástico secular. *3* seglar, lego.

**secularism** (se·kiularišm) *s.* POL. laicismo.

**secularization** (sekiularišei·shØn) *s.* secularización.

**secularize (to)** (se·kiularaiš) *tr.* secularizar.

**secundo** (si·kØndou) *adv.* en segundo lugar.

**secure** (sikiu·ᵣ) *adj.* seguro [libre de peligro o riesgo; que ofrece seguridad; bien guardado; cierto; confiado; confiable]. *2* tranquilo.

**secure (to)** *tr.* asegurar [resguardar; afianzar; prender]. *2* garantizar. *3* obtener; contratar; apoderarse de.

**security** (-iti) *s.* seguridad. *2* protección, salvaguardia. *3* garantía, prenda. *4* fiador, garante. *5* tranquilidad, confianza. *6 pl.* COM. pagarés, valores, efectos.

**sedan** (sidæ·n) *s.* silla de manos. *2* AUTO. sedán.

**sedate** (sidei·t) *adj.* sereno, tranquilo, ecuánime. *2* reposado, juicioso; grave, formal.

**sedative** (se·dativ) *adj.-s.* MED. sedativo. *2* calmante, sosegador.

**sedentary** (se·dØnteri) *adj.* sedentario.

**sedge** (sedȳ) *s.* BOL. juncia, ácoro; chufa.

**sediment** (se·dimØnt) *s.* sedimento. *2* heces, poso.

**sedimentation** (-ei·shØn) *s.* sedimentación.

**sedition** (sidi·shØn) *s.* sedición.

**seditionary** (-shØneri) *adj.-s.* sedicioso.

**seditious** (-shØs) *adj.* sedicioso, rebelde.

**seduce (to)** (sidiu·s) *tr.* seducir. *2* inducir, tentar.

**seducement** (-mØnt) *s.* seducción. *2* tentación, incentivo.

**seducer** (-Øᵣ) *s.* seductor.

**seduction** (sidØ·kshØn) *s.* seducción. *2* atractivo.

**seductive** (-tiv) *adj.* seductor, tentador.

**sedulity** (sidiu·liti) *s.* asiduidad, diligencia, aplicación.

**sedulous** (se·diulØs) *adj.* asiduo, aplicado, laborioso.

**see** (sɪ) *s.* ECLES. sede, silla: *Holy* ~, Santa Sede.

**see (to)** *tr.-intr.* ver: *to* ~ *a thing done,* ver hacer una cosa; *to* ~ *one another,* verse, visitarse; *to* ~ *the back of,* perder de vista, librarse de; *to* ~ *the light,* ver la luz, salir a luz; *let's* ~, veamos; *I* ~, ya veo; comprendo. *2* mirar, observar. *3* considerar, juzgar: *to* ~ *fit,* tener por conveniente. *4* acompañar: *to* ~ *one off,* ir a despedir a uno. *5 to* ~ *after,* cuidar, cuidar de; buscar. *6 to* ~ *into,* examinar; ver lo interior de. 7 *to ~ that, to ~ it that*, cuidar de que. *8 to ~ through*, penetrar; calar las intenciones de; llevar a cabo; ayudar a salir de un apuro. *9 to ~ to*, cuidar de, atender. *10 see!*, ¡mira!, ¡mirad! ¶ Pret.: *saw*; p. p.: *seen*.

**seed** (sɪd) *s*. BOT. semilla, simiente, grano, pepita: *~ bed*, semillero; *~ plant*, planta fanerógama; *to go, o to run, to ~*, dar en grana; fig. agotarse, decaer. *2* fig. semilla, origen.

**seed (to)** *tr.* sembrar. *2* despepitar, deshuesar. *3 intr.* sembrar, hacer la siembra. *4* granar.

**seedcake** (-keik) *s*. torta de semillas aromáticas.

**seeder** (-øʳ) *s*. sembradora [máquina]. *2* instrumento para despepitar. *3* pez que desova.

**seedling** (-ling) *s*. planta de semillero. *2* planta joven. *3* fig. semilla, germen.

**seedplot** (-plat) *s*. semillero.

**seedtime** (-taim) *s*. sementera [tiempo].

**seedy** (-i) *adj*. granado. *2* gastado, decaído. *3* andrajoso.

**seeing** (sɪ·ing) *s*. vista, acción de ver. *2* vidente, que ve.

**seek (to)** (sɪk) *tr.* buscar. *2* pedir. *3* perseguir, ambicionar; solicitar, cortejar. *4* intentar. *5* explorar, registrar. *6 to ~ one's life*, querer matar a uno. *7 intr. to ~ after, for o out*, buscar, perseguir, solicitar. ¶ Pret. y p. p.: *sought*.

**seem (to)** (sɪm) *intr.* parecer: *it seems to me*, me parece. *2* parecerle a uno: *I ~ to see him still*, me parece verlo todavía. *3* fingirse.

**seeming** (-ing) *adj*. aparente, especioso, fingido. *2* parecido. *3 s.* apariencia.

**seemingly** (-li) *adv.* aparentemente, al parecer.

**seemly** (sɪ·mli) *adj*. decente, decoroso, correcto. *2* agradable, bien parecido. *3 adv.* decentemente, correctamente.

**seen** (sɪn) *p. p.* de TO SEE.

**seep (to)** (sɪp) *intr.* filtrar, rezumarse, escurrirse.

**seepage** (-idɏ) *s*. filtración; lo que rezuma.

**seer** (sɪ·øʳ) *s*. profeta, vidente, adivino.

**seesaw** (sɪ·sɔ) *s*. columpio de tabla. *2* balanceo, vaivén. *3 adj.* de balanceo, de vaivén.

**seesaw (to)** *intr.* columpiarse, oscilar. *2* fig. vacilar, fluctuar.

**seethe (to)** (sɪð) *intr.* hervir [con el calor]. *2* fig. hervir, estar agitado. *3 tr.* hacer hervir. *4* empapar, macerar. ¶ P. p.: *seethed* o *sodden*.

**segment** (se·gmønt) *s*. segmento.

**segment (to)** *tr.* segmentar. *2 intr.* segmentarse.

**segmental** (segme·ntal) *adj*. segmentario. *2* ARQ. escarzano.

**segmentary** (-teri) *adj*. segmentario.

**segmentation** (-ei·shøn) *s*. segmentación.

**segregate** (se·grøgeit) *adj*. segregado, separado.

**segregate (to)** *tr.* segregar, separar. *2 intr.* segregarse, separarse.

**segregation** (-ei·shøn) *s*. segregación, separación.

**seigniory** (si·ñøri) *s*. señorío [dominio].

**Seine** (sen) *n. pr.* GEOGR. Sena.

**seine** *s*. red barredera.

**seism** (sai·søm) *s*. seísmo, terremoto.

**seismic** (-šmik) *adj*. sísmico.

**seismograph** (sai·šmogræf) *s*. sismógrafo.

**seizable** (sɪ·šabøl) *adj*. embargable.

**seize (to)** (sɪš) *tr.* asir, agarrar, tomar, coger. *2* apoderarse de; prender. *3* confiscar, embargar. *4* atar. *5* comprender. *6* aprovechar [la ocasión]. *7 to be seized of*, estar en posesión de. *8 to be seized with*, tener un ataque de; embargar, sobrecoger a uno [un afecto o pasión].

**seizin** (sɪ·šin) *s*. DER. posesión. *2* toma de posesión.

**seizure** (-ɏøʳ) *s*. asimiento, toma. *2* captura; prendimiento, prisión. *3* embargo, decomiso. *4* MED. ataque, acceso.

**selachian** (silei·kian) *adj.-s*. ICT. selacio.

**seldom** (se·ldøm) *adv.* raramente, rara vez.

**select** (sile·kt) *adj*. selecto, escogido. *2* delicado, exigente [al escoger].

**select (to)** *tr.* escoger, elegir, seleccionar.

**selection** (-shøn) *s*. selección. *2* trozo escogido. *3* COM. surtido.

**selective** (-tiv) *adj*. selectivo.

**selectivity** (-tiviti) *s*. RADIO. selectividad.

**selector** (-tøʳ) *s*. seleccionador. *2* ELECT. selector.

**selenium** (seli·niøm) *s*. QUÍM. selenio.

**selenography** (selina·grafi) *s*. selenografía.

**self** (self), *pl.* **selves** *adj*. mismo. | Se une a los pronombres personales, o algunos adjetivos posesivos y al pronombre *one* para formar pronombres reflexivos o para dar más fuerza a la expresión. V. *myself, yourself*, etc. *2 s.* yo, ser; personificación: *my other ~*, mi otro yo; *his former ~*, su ser anterior; *she is beauty's ~*, ella es la belleza misma. *2 one's ~*, ONESELF.

**self-** elemento de comp. Con el sentido de auto-, de sí mismo, por sí mismo, etc.,entra en gran número de voces.

**self-abashed** *adj*. avergonzado.

**self-acting** *adj*. automático.

**self-assured, self-reliant** *adj*. seguro de sí mismo.

**self-binder** *s*. AGR. segadora agavilladora.

**self-centered** o **-centred** *adj*. concentrado en sí mismo, egocéntrico.

**self-command** *s*. dominio de sí mismo.

**self-complacency** *s*. satisfacción de sí mismo.

**self-conceit** *s*. presunción, vanidad, engreimiento.

**self-confidence** *s*. confianza en sí mismo.

**self-concious** *adj*. tímido, cohibido, embarazado.

**self-consistent** *adj*. consecuente [pers.].

**self-contained** *adj*. completo, independiente, autónomo. *2* callado, reservado. *3* dueño de sí mismo.

**self-control** *s*. dominio de sí mismo. *2* autonomía.

**self-deception** *s*. propio engaño; vana ilusión.

**self-defeating** *adj*. contraproducente.

**self-defence** *s*. defensa propia.

**self-denial** *s*. abnegación.

**self-destruction** *s*. suicidio.

**self-determination** *s*. POL. libre determinación.

**self-effacement** *s*. modestia.

**self-esteem** *s*. propia estimación. *2* presunción.

**self-evident** *adj*. evidente, patente, palmario.

**self-excitation** *s*. ELECT. autoexcitación.

**self-existent** *adj*. existente por sí mismo.

**self-explanatory** *adj*. que se explica por sí mismo.

**self-expression** *s*. expresión de la propia personalidad.

**self-government** *s*. autonomía. *2* dominio de sí mismo.

**self-importance** *s*. orgullo, presunción.

**self-induction** *s*. ELECT. autoinducción.

**self-indulgence** *s*. satisfacción de los propios apetitos, falta de sobriedad, intemperancia.

**selfish** (se·lfish) *adj*. interesado, egoísta.

**selfishness** (-nis) *s*. egoísmo.

**selfless** (se·lflis) *adj*. desinteresado, generoso.

**self-love** *s*. amor propio, egoísmo.

**self-made** *adj*. que se ha hecho una posición por su propio esfuerzo.

**self-moving** *adj*. automotor.

**self-portrait** *s*. autorretrato.

**self-possessed** *adj*. sereno, dueño de sí mismo.

**self-propelled** *adj.* autopropulsado.
**self-reliant** *adj.* que confía en sí mismo.
**self-respect** *s.* dignidad, respeto de sí mismo.
**self-righteous** *adj.* pagado de su propia rectitud, farisaico.
**self-sacrifice** *s.* sacrificio personal, abnegación.
**self-same** (se·lfseim) *adj.* idéntico, mismísimo.
**self-satisfied** *adj.* satisfecho de sí mismo.
**self-seeker** *s.* egoísta.
**self-seeking** *s.* egoísmo. *2 adj.* egoísta.
**self-service** *adj.* de autoservicio.
**self-starter** *s.* MEC. arranque automático.
**self-styled** *adj.* que se titula o llama a sí mismo.
**self-sufficient** *adj.* que se basta a sí mismo. *2* presuntuoso, orgulloso.
**self-suggestion** *s.* autosugestión.
**self-will** *s.* voluntariedad, obstinación.
**self-willed** *adj.* voluntarioso, obstinado.
**self-winding** *adj.* de cuerda automática [reloj].
**sell** (sel) *s.* fam. engaño, estafa.
**sell (to)** *tr.* vender [enajenar; traicionar]: *to ~ oneself,* venderse [por dinero]. *2* pop. engañar. *3 to ~ out,* realizar, saldar; agotar [una edición]; vender, traicionar. *4 intr.* vender: *to ~ off,* liquidar. *5* venderse [un artículo]. ¶ Pret. y p. p.: *sold.*
**seller** (-øʳ) *s.* vendedor. *2* cosa que se vende bien: *best ~,* libro de mayor venta.
**Seltzer** o **Seltzer water** (-tsøʳ) *s.* agua de Seltz.
**selvage** (-vidÿ) *s.* orillo [del paño]. *2* orilla, orla.
**semantics** (simæ·ntiks) *s.* semántica.
**semaphore** (se·mafoʳ) *s.* semáforo. *2* FERROC. disco de señales.
**semasiology** (simeisia·lødÿi) *s.* semasiología.
**semblance** (se·mblans) *s.* semejanza. *2* aspecto, figura, semblante. *3* imagen, retrato. *4* apariencia, simulacro.
**semen** (sɪ·men) *s.* FISIOL. semen. *2* BOT. semilla.
**semester** (sime·støʳ) *s.* semestre. *2* semestre escolar.
**semi-** (se·mi) *pref.* semi-.
**semibreve** (se·mibrɪv) *s.* MÚS. semibreve.
**semicadence** (semikei·døns) *s.* mús. semicadencia.
**semicircle** (se·misøʳkøl) *s.* semicírculo.
**semicircular** (semisø·ʳkiulaʳ) *adj.* semicircular.
**semicolon** (semicou·løn) *s.* ORTOG. punto y coma.
**semiconsonant** (semika·nsønant) *s.* semiconsonante.
**semidiameter** (semidaiæ·metøʳ) *s.* semidiámetro.
**semifinal** (semifai·nal) *adj.-s.* dep. semifinal.
**semifluid** (semiflu·id) *adj.* semifluido.
**semilunar** (semiliu·naʳ) *adj.* semilunar.
**semimonthly** (semimø·nzli) *adj.* quincenal. *2 s.* publicación quincenal.
**seminal** (se·minal) *adj.* seminal. *2* germinal, originador. *3* embrionario.
**seminar** (se·mina·ʳ o semina·ʳ) *s.* seminario [en una Universidad].
**seminarist** (se·minerist) *s.* seminarista.
**seminary** (se·mineri) *s.* semillero, plantel. *2* SEMINAR. *3* colegio, academia. *4* ECLES. seminario.
**seminiferous** (semini·førøs) *adj.* seminífero.
**semiofficial** (semiofi·shal) *adj.* oficioso.
**semiquaver** (semikuei·vøʳ) *s.* MÚS. semicorchea.
**Semiramis** (sømi·ramis) *n. pr.* Semíramis.
**semispherical** (semisfe·rikal) *adj.* semiesférico.
**Semite** (se·mait) *adj.-s.* semita.
**Semitic** (simi·tik) *adj.* semítico. *2 s.* semita.
**semitone** (se·mitoun) *s.* MÚS. semitono.
**semivowel** (semivau·øl) *s.* letra semivocal.
**semolina** (semoli·na) *s.* sémola.
**sempitern(al** (sempitø·ʳnal) *adj.* sempiterno.

**sempstress** (se·mpstris) *s.* SEAMSTRESS.
**sen** (sen) *s.* sen [moneda japonesa].
**senate** (se·nit) *s.* senado.
**senator** (se·natøʳ) *s.* senador.
**senatorial** (senato·rial) *adj.* senatorial.
**senatorship** (se·natøʳship) *s.* senaduría.
**senatus consultum** (sinei·tøs consø·ltøm) *s.* senadoconsulto.
**send (to)** (send) *tr.* enviar, mandar, expedir, despachar. *2* lanzar; exhalar, despedir. *3* lanzar [un golpe]. *4* extender [las ramas, etc.]. *5 to ~ about one's business,* mandar a paseo. *6 to ~ forth,* exhalar, despedir; producir; exportar, publicar. *7 to ~ in one's papers,* dimitir. *8 to ~ word,* mandar recado. *9 tr.-intr.* RADIO [transmitir]. *10 intr. to ~ for,* enviar a buscar, mandar por. ¶ Pret. y p. p.: *sent.*
**sender** (-øʳ) *s.* remitente, expedidor. *3* TELEGR., RADIO. transmisor.
**send-off** (send-ɔf) *s.* envío. *2* despedida afectuosa.
**Senegalese** (senigali·š) *adj.-s.* senegalés.
**senescence** (sinø·søns) *s.* envejecimiento.
**seneschal** (se·nishal) *s.* senescal.
**senile** (sɪ·nail o sɪ·nil) *adj.* senil.
**senility** (sini·liti) *s.* chochez. *2* senectud.
**senior** (sɪ·niøʳ) *adj.* mayor, primero, padre [calificando a la de más edad de dos personas que llevan el mismo nombre]. *2* de mayor edad, categoría, etc.; más antiguo, decano. *3* (E.U.) del último curso de una facultad. *4 s.* anciano. *5* el que tiene más edad o es más antiguo que otro.
**seniority** (sinia·riti) *s.* mayor edad, categoría, etc.; antigüedad.
**senna** (se·na) *s.* BOT. sen, sena.
**sensation** (sensei·shøn) *s.* sensación. *2* sensacionalismo, efectismo.
**sensational** (-al) *adj.* sensacional. *2* melodramático. *3* efectista.
**sense** (sens) *s.* sentido [corporal]. *2* mente, inteligencia. *3* cordura, buen sentido: *common ~,* sentido común. *4* sentido [significado, acepción; razón de ser, finalidad]: *to make ~ out of,* entender, explicarse; *in a ~,* en cierto sentido. *5* sentido [de lo bello, del humor, humor, etc.]. *6* GEOM. sentido. *7* sensación, impresión, conciencia, sentimiento [de una cosa]. *8 to be out of one's senses,* estar loco. *9 to come to one's senses,* volver en sí; recobrar el buen sentido.
**sense (to)** *tr.* sentir, percibir; darse cuenta de.
**senseless** (-lis) *adj.* insensible, inerte, sin conocimiento. *2* sin sentido, absurdo. *3* insensato.
**sensibility** (sensibi·liti) *s.* sensibilidad.
**sensible** (se·nsibøl) *adj.* sensible. *2* perceptible. *3* cuerdo, razonable, juicioso, sensato. *4 to be ~ of,* sentir, tener conciencia de. *5 s.* MÚS. sensible.
**sensitive** (sen·nsitiv) *adj.* sensitivo. *2* sensible, impresionable. *3* sentido, susceptible. *4* sensorial. *5* sensible [instrumento, placa, etc.]. *6* MED., QUÍM., FOT. sensibilizado. *7* BOT. ~ *plant,* sensitiva.
**sensitivity** (sensiti·viti) *s.* sensibilidad. *2* susceptibilidad.
**sensitize (to)** (se·nsitaiš) *tr.* MED., QUÍM., FOT. sensibilizar. *2* hacer sensible.
**sensorial** (senso·rial) *adj.* sensorio.
**sensorium** (-riøm) *s.* sensorio.
**sensual** (se·nshual) *adj.* sensual. *2* materialista.
**sensualism** (-išm) *s.* sensualismo.
**sensuality** (senshuæ·liti) *s.* sensualidad.
**sensuous** (se·nshuøs) *adj.* sensual, sensitivo.
**sent** (sent) *pret. y p. p.* de TO SEND.

**sentence** (se·ntøns) *s.* sentencia, fallo; condena. *2* sentencia, máxima. *3* GRAM. oración, período.
**sentence (to)** *tr.* sentenciar, condenar.
**sententious** (sente·nshøs) *adj.* sentencioso. *2* conciso, enérgico, expresivo, lacónico.
**sentience** (se·nshiøns) *s.* sensibilidad [facultad de sentir]. *2* conciencia, percepción [de una cosa].
**sentient** (-ønt) *adj.* sensible [capaz de sentir físicamente]. *2* sensitivo. *3* ~ *of*, consciente de. *4 s.* ser sensible. *5* mente; conciencia.
**sentiment** (se·ntimønt) *s.* sentimiento. | No tiene el sentido de pena. *2* sensibilidad. *3* parecer, opinión. *4* concepto, frase; brindis.
**sentimental** (sentime·ntal) *adj.* sentimental.
**sentimentalism** (-išm) **sentimentality** (-iti) *s.* sentimentalismo.
**sentimentalize (to)** (-laiš) *tr.* hacer sentimental. *2* tratar sentimentalmente. *3 intr.* hacer el sentimental, afectar sentimiento.
**sentinel** (se·ntinøl) *s.* centinela: *to stand* ~, hacer centinela.
**sentry** (se·ntri) *s.* MIL. centinela.
**sepal** (se·pal) *s.* BOT. sépalo.
**separable** (se·parabøl) *adj.* separable.
**separate** (se·parit) *adj.* separado. *2* aparte; suelto. *3* distinto, diferente.
**separate (to)** (se·pareit) *tr.* separar. *2* despegar, desprender. *3 intr.* separarse. *4* despegarse, desprenderse.
**separately** (-li) *adv.* separadamente, por separado, aparte, de por sí.
**separation** (separei·shøn) *s.* separación. *2* porción.
**separatism** (se·paratišm) *s.* separatismo.
**separator** (se·pareitø^r) *s.* separador. *2* desnatadora.
**Sephardic** (sifa·^rdik) *adj.* sefardí, sefardita.
**Sephardim** (-im) *s. pl.* sefardíes, sefarditas.
**sepia** (sı·pia) *s.* ZOOL. sepia, jibia. *2* sepia [color].
**sepoy** (si·poi) *s.* cipayo. *2* policía indio.
**seps** (seps) *s.* ZOOL. eslizón.
**sepsis** (se·psis) *s.* sepsia.
**September** (septe·mbø^r) *s.* septiembre.
**septenary** (se·ptineri) *adj.-s.* septenario. *2 s.* septena. *3* septenio.
**Septentrion** (septe·ntriøn) *s.* ASTR. septentrión.
**septentrion(al** (septe·ntriøn(al) *adj.* septentrional.
**septet** (septe·t) *s.* septeto.
**septicaemia, -cemia** (septisı·mia) *s.* MED. septicemia.
**septicidal** (septisai·dal) *adj.* BOT. septicida.
**septillion** (septi·liøn) *s.* septillón.
**septime** (se·ptim) *s.* ESGR. séptima.
**septimole** (se·ptimoul) *s.* MÚS. septillo.
**septuagenarian** (sepchuadўine·rian) *adj.-s.* septuagenario.
**septuagenary** (sepchuæ·dўineri) *adj.* septuagenario.
**septuagesima** (sepchuadўe·sima) *s.* septuagésima.
**septum** (se·ptøm) *s.* BIOL. septo.
**septuor** (se·pchuø^r) *s.* MÚS. septeto.
**septuple** (se·ptiupøl) *adj.* séptuplo.
**septuple (to)** *tr.* septuplicar.
**sepulchral** (sepø·lkral) *adj.* sepulcral.
**sepulchre** (se·pølkø^r) *s.* sepulcro, tumba, sepultura.
**sepulchre (to)** *tr.* enterrar, sepultar.
**sepulture** (se·pølchø^r) *s.* sepultura. *2* entierro.
**sequel** (si·kuøl) *s.* secuela. *2* conclusión, inferencia. *3* continuación, lo que sigue.
**sequela** (sikui·la) *s.* secuaz, prosélito; grupo de secuaces. *2* secuela. *3* conclusión, inferencia.

**sequence** (si·kuøns) *s.* sucesión, continuación; serie. *2* consecuencia, secuela. *3* ilación. *5* LITURG., CINEM. secuencia. *5* escalera [en los naipes].
**sequent** (-ønt) *adj.* siguiente, subsiguiente.
**sequential** (sikue·nshal) *adj.* SEQUENT. *2* sucesivo, consecutivo. *3* consiguiente.
**sequester (to)** (sikue·stø^r) *tr.* separar, apartar, retirar. *2* DER. secuestrar.
**sequestered** (-d) *adj.* apartado, solitario.
**sequestrum** (sikue·strøm) *s.* CIR. secuestro.
**sequin** (sı·kuin) *s.* cequi. *2* lentejuela.
**sequoia** (sikuo·ia) *s.* BOT. secoya.
**seraglio** (siræ·liou) *s.* serrallo.
**seraph** (se·raf), *pl.* **-aphs** o **-afim** (-afim) *s.* serafín.
**seraphic(al** (seræ·fik(al) *adj.* seráfico.
**Serb** (sø^rb) *adj.-s.* servio.
**Serbia** (sø·^rbia) *n. pr.* GEOGR. Servia.
**Serbian** (sø·^rbian) *adj.-s.* servio.
**Serbo-Croatian** (sø·^rbo-krou·shan) *adj.-s.* servocroata.
**sere** (si^r) *adj.* seco, marchito; gastado.
**serenade** (serønei·d) *s.* serenata. *2* fam. cencerrada.
**serenade (to)** *tr.* obsequiar con una serenata. *2 intr.* dar una serenata.
**serene** (sirı·n) *adj.* sereno, claro, despejado; plácido, tranquilo.
**serene (to)** *tr.* serenar, tranquilizar.
**sereneness** (-nis) *s.* serenidad de ánimo, calma.
**serenity** (sire·niti) *s.* serenidad, bonanza. *2* sosiego, apacibilidad. *3* serenidad, sangre fría.
**serf** (sø^rf) *s.* siervo. *2* esclavo.
**serge** (sø·^rdў) *s.* TEJ. sarga.
**sergeancy** (sa·^rdўønsi) *s.* SERGEANTCY.
**sergeant** (sa·^rdўønt) *s.* MIL. sargento: ~ *major*, sargento auxiliar del ayudante. *2* ~ *at arms*, oficial que mantiene el orden en un cuerpo legislativo.
**sergeantcy** (-øntsi) *s.* sargentía.
**serial** (si·rial) *adj.* de serie, en serie. *2* de orden [número, etc.]. *3* consecutivo, sucesivo. *4* publicado por entregas; proyectado o radiado por episodios. *5 s.* obra que se publica por entregas. *6* CINEM., RADIO. serial.
**seriate (to)** (si·rieit) *tr.* disponer en serie.
**seriate (d** (si·rieit(id) *adj.* dispuesto en serie.
**seriatim** (siriei·tim) *adv.* punto por punto.
**seric** (se·rik) *adj.* de seda.
**seri(ci)culture** (seri(si)kø·lchø^r) *s.* seri(ci)cultura.
**seri(ci)culturist** (-ist) *s.* seri(ci)cultor.
**series** (si·riš) *s.* serie: *in* ~, ELECT. en serie.
**serin** (se·rin) *s.* ORN. especie de canario.
**seringa** (seri·nga) *s.* BOT. jeringuilla. *2* BOT. siringa.
**serio-comic(al** (siriou-ka·mik(al) *adj.* jocoserio.
**serious** (si·riøs) *adj.* serio. *2* verdadero, sincero.
**seriously** (si·riøsli) *adv.* seriamente, gravemente. *2* en serio.
**serjeant** (sa·^rdўønt) *s.* SERGEANT.
**sermon** (sø·^rmøn) *s.* sermón.
**sermonize (to)** (sø^rmønai·š) *intr.-tr.* predicar, sermonear.
**sermonizer** (sø·^rmønaišø^r) *s.* sermoneador.
**serosity** (sira·siti) *s.* serosidad.
**serous** (si·røs) *adj.* seroso.
**serpent** (sø·^rpønt) *s.* ZOOL. serpiente, sierpe. *2* pers. astuta y traidora. *3* PIROT. buscapiés. *4* MÚS. serpentón. *5* ARTILL. serpentín. *6* ASTR. Serpiente.
**serpent (to)** *intr.* serpentear.
**serpentine** (sø·^rpøntin) *adj.* serpentino. *2* sinuoso. *3 s.* MINER. serpentina.
**serpentine (to)** *intr.* serpentear.
**serpigo** (sø^rpai·gou) *s.* MED. serpigo.

**serrate (d** (se·reit(id) *adj.* dentado. *2* BOT. serrado.
**serried** (se·rid) *adj.* apretado, apiñado, espeso.
**serrulated** (se·riuleitid) *adj.* denticulado.
**serum** (si·røm) *s.* suero.
**servable** (sø·ʳvabøl) *adj.* servible.
**servant** (sø·ʳvant) *s.* sirviente, criado: ~ *girl*, criada. *2* servidor. *3* siervo.
**serve** (sø·ʳv) *s.* TENIS. servicio, saque.
**serve (to)** *tr.-intr.* servir: *to* ~ *as*, servir de; *to* ~ *for*, servir de o para. *2* servir, sacar [la pelota]. *3 tr.* llenar [un objeto]. *4* surtir, abastecer. *5* manejar [un cañón]. *6* dar cumplimiento a, ejecutar, notificar: *to* ~ *a summons*, entregar una citación. *7* cumplir [una condena]. *8* MAR. aforrar. *9* cubrir [el macho a la hembra]. *10 to* ~ *one's turn*, bastar, ser suficiente. *11 it serves me (you, him,* etc.) *right*, me (te, le, etc.) está bien empleado.
**server** (-vøʳ) *s.* servidor. *2* criado de mesa; mozo de comedor o de café. *3* saque [en el tenis, etc.]. *4* bandeja.
**Servia** (sø·ʳvia) *pr. n.* SERBIA.
**Servian** (-an) *adj.-s.* SERBIAN.
**service** (sø·ʳvis) *s.* servicio: ~ *entrance*, entrada de servicio; ~ *record*, hoja de servicios; *table* ~, servicio de mesa; *out of* ~, descompuesto; sin empleo. *2* utilidad, ventaja. *3* favor, ayuda. *4* función religiosa, oficio. *5* DER. entrega de una citación. *6* servicio, saque [de pelota]. *7* MAR. aforro. *8* cubrición. *9* reparación, montaje, etc. [de una máquina] ~ *station*, estación de servicio, taller de reparaciones. *10* BOT. *service* o ~ *tree*, serbal.
**service (to)** *tr.* instalar, conservar, reparar, suministrar lo necesario para; abastecer, surtir.
**serviceable** (sø·ʳvisabøl) *adj.* servible. *2* útil, provechoso. *3* duradero. *4* servicial.
**serviceberry** (-beri) *s.* BOT. serba.
**serviceman** (-mæn) *s.* reparador, mecánico. *2* militar; marino.
**servile** (sø·ʳvil) *adj.* servil.
**servility** (sø·ʳvi·liti) *s.* servilismo.
**servitor** (sø·ʳvitøʳ) *s.* servidor. *2* seguidor, secuaz.
**servitude** (-tiud) *s.* servidumbre, sujeción. *2* trabajos forzados. *3* DER. servidumbre.
**servomotor** (sø·ʳvomou·tøʳ) *s.* servomotor.
**sesame** (se·sami) *s.* BOT. sésamo, ajonjolí. *2 open* ~, ábrete sésamo.
**sesquioxide** (seskuia·csaid) *s.* QUÍM. sesquióxido.
**sessile** (se·sil) *adj.* BOT., ZOOL. sésil.
**session** (se·shøn) *s.* sesión. *2* período de sesiones; legislatura. *3* período escolar. *4* (Ingl.) sala de justicia.
**sessional** (-al) *adj.* perteneciente a la sesión o período de sesiones.
**sesterce** (se·støʳs) *s.* sestercio.
**set** (set) *s.* juego, servicio, surtido, colección; tren, grupo: ~ *of chairs*, sillería; ~ *of teeth*, dentadura. *2* aderezo [de diamantes]. *3* equipo, cuadrilla. *4* clase, gente, mundo, esfera. *5* aparato [de radio, etc.]. *6* dirección, curso, tendencia. *7* colocación, disposición; actitud, postura. *8* corte [de una prenda]. *9* traba [de una sierra]. *10* AGR. pie, estaca, bulbo [para plantar]. *11* TEAT., CINEM. decoración. *12* TENIS. set. *13* muestra [del perro de caza]. *14* endurecimiento [de la cola, etc.]; fraguado [de la cal, el yeso, etc.].
*15 pret.* y *p. p.* de TO SEAT.
*16 adj.* resuelto, determinado, empeñado; inflexible. *17* fijo, inmóvil, firme, persistente: ~ *price*, precio fijo. *18* regular, arreglado. *19* es-

tudiado, preparado. *20* intencionado, premeditado. *21* estrechado, en un aprieto.
**set (to)** *tr.* poner [en varios sentidos], asentar, colocar, situar, instalar, establecer. *2* poner a empollar. *3* destinar, fijar, señalar. *4* plantar, erigir. *5* preparar, ajustar, arreglar. *6* poner [un reloj] en hora. *7* azuzar, excitar [contra]. *8* dar [el tono]. *9* afilar [una navaja]. *10* triscar [una sierra]. *11* plantar [un terreno]. *12* adornar, sembrar. *13* engarzar, engastar, montar. *14* dar, atribuir [valor, precio]. *15* fijar, inmovilizar. *16* sujetar, apretar. *17* hacer obstinado, inflexible. *18* solidificar, cuajar, coagular. *19* mostrar [la caza] el perro. *20* IMPR. componer. *21* CIR. encajar [un hueso]. *22* armar, tender [un lazo, una trampa]. *23 to* ~ *about*, poner a; fam. atacar. *24 to* ~ *afloat*, poner a flote; hacer circular, esparcir. *25 to* ~ *ajar*, entornar, entreabrir. *26 to* ~ *an example*, dar ejemplo. *27 to* ~ *aside*, poner o dejar a un lado; descartar; reservar, ahorrar. *28 to* ~ *at naught*, despreciar. *29 to* ~ *back*, detener, estorbar; hacer retroceder; atrasar [el reloj]. *30 to* ~ *by the ears*, hacer reñir, enemistar. *31 to* ~ *down*, sentar; situar; bajar; humillar; anotar, poner por escrito; atribuir, achacar. *32 to* ~ *fire to, to* ~ *on fire*, pegar fuego a; encender, inflamar. *33 to* ~ *forth*, publicar; relatar; exponer, manifestar. *34 to* ~ *free*, libertar. *35 to* ~ *off*, adornar, embellecer; hacer resaltar; comparar, contraponer; compensar; destinar, reservar; disparar, hacer estallar. *36 to* ~ *one's cap at*, tratar de conquistar a [uno] para su novio. *37 to* ~ *one's heart on*, poner uno su esperanza en. *38 to* ~ *one's teeth*, apretar los dientes. *39 to* ~ *one's teeth on edge*, dar dentera. *40 to* ~ *out*, extender; exponer; señalar, asignar; trazar, proyectar. *41 to* ~ *right*, enderezar; enmendar. *42* MAR. to ~ *sail*, hacerse a la vela. *43 to* ~ *store by*, dar importancia a. *44 to* ~ *the table*, poner la mesa. *45 to* ~ *to rights*, poner en orden. *46 to* ~ *up*, alzar, llevar; ensalzar; erigir, levantar, fundar; montar, armar; exponer, presentar; poner en venta o subasta; IMPR. componer; *to* ~ *upon*, azuzar; atacar, acometer.
*47 intr.* empollar huevos. *48* sentar, caer bien [una prenda]. *49* ponerse [un astro]; declinar, acabar. *50* fluir, correr; tender. *51* dedicarse, ponerse a. *52* fraguar, cuajarse, solidificarse. *53* fijarse [un color]. *54* estar de muestra [un perro]. *55 to* ~ *about*, ponerse a. *56 to* ~ *forth*, salir, ponerse en camino. *57 to* ~ *in*, aparecer; cerrar [la noche]; correr o soplar hacia tierra. *58 to* ~ *off*, salir, partir. *59 to* ~ *out for*, salir para. *60 to* ~ *out to, to* ~ *to*, ponerse a. *61 to* ~ *up for*, hacerse pasar por.
¶ Pret. y p. p.: *set;* ger.: *setting.*
**setaceous** (siteis·shøs) *adj.* cerdoso.
**setback** (se·tbæk) *s.* revés, contrariedad, retroceso. *2* MEC. mecanismo de retroceso.
**setoff** (se·taf) *s.* adorno. *2* relieve, realce. *3* compensación, contrapeso. *4* ARQ. saliente, retallo. *5* salida, partida.
**seton** (sɪ·tøn) *s.* CIR. sedal.
**setscrew** (-skru) *s.* tornillo de presión.
**settee** (setɪ·) *s.* banco [para sentarse]; sofá.
**setter** (se·tøʳ) *s.* (en comp.) el que prepara, pone, ajusta, fija, coloca, monta, etc. *2* perro de muestra, perdiguero.
**setting** (-ing) *s.* puesta, ocaso. *2* fraguado, endurecimiento. *3* engaste, montura. *4* marco, escenario [de una narración, etc.]; medio circun-

dante, ambiente. *5* TEAT. decorado [de una obra]. *6* situación. *7* IMPR. composición. *8* compostura [de huesos]. *9* ~ *up*, establecimiento; montaje.

**settle** (se·tøl) *s.* escaño, banco. *2* escalón, grada.

**settle (to)** *tr.* colocar, asentar, establecer. *2* fijar, afirmar, asegurar. *3* colonizar, poblar. *4* dar estado, colocar, casar. *5* regular, ordenar; arreglar. *6* ajustar [cuentas]; zanjar [una disputa]; decidir, resolver. *7* pagar, liquidar, saldar. *8* sosegar, serenar, pacificar. *9* hacer posar las heces, etc., de. *10 to* ~ *on* o *upon*, dar en dote, asignar como herencia, pensión, etc., a. *11 intr.* posarse, asentarse, establecerse, instalarse. *12* hacer asiento [un edificio]. *13* posarse [las heces, el polvo]; reposarse [un líquido]. *14* fijarse, arraigar. *15* arreglar su vida; tomar estado, casarse. *16* sosegarse, serenarse. *17 to* ~ *down*, asentarse; fijarse; posarse; sentar la cabeza; ponerse [a]. *18 to* ~ *with*, liquidar o ajustar cuentas con.

**settle-bed** *s.* sofá cama.

**settlement** (se·tølmønt) *s.* establecimiento, instalación. *2* colonización. *3* colonia, poblado. *4* centro de acción benéfica y social. *5* sedimentación. *6* asignación de bienes, pensión, etc. *7* acomodo, empleo. *8* ajuste [de cuentas]. *9* arreglo, convenio. *10* pago, liquidación.

**settler** (se·tlø<sup>r</sup>) *s.* poblador, colono. *2* establecedor. *3* liquidador. *4* fam. lo que acaba o concluye; golpe de gracia.

**settlings** (-lings) *s. pl.* heces, poso, sedimento.

**set-to** *s.* fam. lucha, combate, disputa.

**setup** (se·tøp) *s.* cosa levantada o erigida. *2* posición, disposición, arreglo, organización. *3* tren, equipo, etc., de aparatos o instrumentos. *4* fam. (E.U.) invitación a beber.

**setwall** (se·twol) *s.* BOT. valeriana.

**seven** (se·vøn) *adj.-s.* siete: ~ *hundred*, setecientos; ~ *o'clock*, las siete.

**sevenfold** (-fould) *adj.* séptuplo. *2 adv.* siete veces.

**seventeen** (-tın) *adj.-s.* diecisiete.

**seventeenth** (-tınz) *adj.* decimoséptimo. *2* diecisiete [del mes]. *3* diecisieteavo.

**seventh** (-z) *adj.* séptimo. *2* siete [del mes]. *3 s.* séptimo [séptima parte]. *4* MÚS. séptima.

**seventhly** (-zli) *adv.* en séptimo lugar.

**seventieth** (-tiiz) *adj.-s.* septuagésimo, setentavo.

**seventy** (-ti) *adj.-s.* setenta.

**sever (to)** (se·vø<sup>r</sup>) *tr.* separar, dividir, desunir; cortar, romper. *2 intr.* separarse, desunirse, romperse.

**several** (-al) *adj.* varios, diversos, algunos. *2* diferentes, distintos. *3* individual, particular. *4* respectivo, respectivos. *5 pron.* algunos.

**severally** (-i) *adj.* separadamente. *2* respectivamente.

**severance** (se·vørans) *s.* separación, división, partición. *2* ruptura [de relaciones, etc.].

**severe** (sivi·<sup>r</sup>) *adj.* severo. *2* acerbo, agudo, grave, duro, fuerte, recio. *3* riguroso.

**severity** (sive·riti) *s.* severidad. *2* rigor, exactitud, rigorismo. *3* gravedad, agudeza, rigor, dureza, inclemencia.

**Sevillian** (sivi·lian) *adj.-s.* sevillano.

**Seville** (sivi·l) *n. pr.* GEOGR. Sevilla.

**sew (to)** (sou) *tr.-intr.* coser. ¶ P. p.: *sewed* o *sewn*.

**sewage** (siu·idÿ) *s.* aguas de albañal; aguas inmundas.

**1) sewer** (sou·ø<sup>r</sup>) *s.* cosedor.

**2) sewer** (siu·ø<sup>r</sup>) *s.* alcantarilla, cloaca, albañal. *2* HIST. maestresala.

**sewerage** (siu·øridÿ) *s.* desagüe de aguas inmundas. *2* alcantarillado. *3* SEWAGE.

**sewing** (sou·ing) *s.* costura [acción de coser]: ~ *machine*, máquina de coser.

**sex** (se·ks) *s.* sexo: *the fair* ~, el bello sexo. *2 adj.* sexual: ~ *appeal*, atracción sexual, encanto femenino.

**sexagenarian** (seksadÿine·rian) *adj.-s.* sexagenario.

**sexagenary** (seksæ·dÿineri) *adj.* sexagenario.

**Sexagesima** (seksadÿe·sima) *s.* sexagésima.

**sext** (se·kst) *s.* ECLES. sexta [hora].

**sextain** (-ein) *s.* LIT. sextilla.

**sextant** (-ant) *s.* sextante. *2* GEOM. sexta parte del círculo.

**sextet** (sekste·t) *s.* MÚS. sexteto. *2* LIT. sextilla. *3* grupo de seis.

**sexton** (se·kstøn) *s.* sacristán y enterrador.

**sextuple** (se·kstiupøl) *adj.* séxtuplo.

**sexual** (se·kshual) *adj.* sexual.

**sexuality** (sekshuæ·liti) *s.* sexualidad.

**sgraffito** (śgrafı·tou) *s.* B. ART. esgrafiado.

**shabbily** (shæ·bili) *adv.* andrajosamente. *2* mezquinamente.

**shabby** (shæ·bi) *adj.* raído, gastado, usado. *2* andrajoso, desaseado. *3* mezquino. *4* ruin, vil.

**shabby-genteel** *adj.* de señor tronado, cursi.

**shack** (shæ·k) *s.* (E.U. y Can.) cabaña, choza.

**shackle** (shæ·køl) *s.* grillete, grillo, esposa. *2* maniota, traba. *3* MEC. eslabón giratorio. *4* traba, estorbo. *5 pl.* hierros, prisiones.

**shackle (to)** *tr.* aherrojar. *2* manear, trabar. *3* estorbar, poner trabas.

**shad** (shæ·d) *s.* ICT. sábalo.

**shaddock** (shæ·døk) *s.* BOT. toronja, pamplemusa.

**shade** (shei·d) *s.* sombra [que dan los árboles, etc.; retiro; protección; aparición]. *2* PINT. sombra. *3* matiz, tinte; pequeña diferencia. *4* pantalla [de lámpara o para proteger los ojos]. *5* visillo, cortina, transparente. *6 pl.* sombras [de la noche]. *7* infierno, mundo de las sombras.

**shade (to)** *tr.* sombrear. *2* resguardar de la luz. *3* obscurecer. *4* matizar. *5* proteger, esconder, velar. *6 intr.* modificarse, convertirse gradualmente.

**shading** (-ing) *s.* PINT. sombreado, degradación. *2* matización.

**shadoof** (sha·duf) *s.* cigoñal [para sacar agua].

**shadow** (shæ·dou) *s.* sombra, obscuridad. *2* sombra [de un objeto]. *3* PINT. sombra. *4* sombra [defecto; lo que ensombrece; semejanza; pizca, señal; abrigo, amparo]. *5* sombra, espectro, imagen. *6* sombra [compañero inseparable; el que vigila a uno]. *7* retiro, vida, retirada. *8* ~ *play*, sombras chinescas.

**shadow (to)** *tr.* sombrear, dar sombra a. *2* anublar, ensombrecer. *3* espiar, seguir secretamente. *4* B. ART. sombrear. *5 to* ~ *forth* u *out*, indicar, representar vagamente, simbolizar.

**shadowy** (-i) *adj.* umbroso. *2* oscuro, tenebroso. *3* vago, indistinto. *4* espectral. *5* ilusorio. *6* simbólico.

**shady** (shei·di) *adj.* sombreado, umbrío. *2* sombrío. *3* sospechoso, equívoco, de dudosa moralidad. *4 on the* ~ *side of fifty*, pasados los cincuenta años.

**shaft** (shæft) *s.* astil [de saeta, herramienta o pluma]. *2* asta [de lanza o bandera]. *3* saeta, dardo. *4* fuste [de columna]. *5* MEC. árbol, eje. *6* lanza, vara [de carruaje]. 7 BOT. tronco, tallo, vástago. 8 ARQ. aguja, obelisco. 9 pozo, chimenea [de mina, etc.].

**shag** (shæg) s. lana o pelo áspero y enredado. 2 TEJ. pelo áspero y largo. 3 TEJ. felpa. 4 enredijo.

**shagbark** (-baʳk) s. BOT. nogal americano.

**shagged** (-id) adj. peludo, hirsuto. 2 SHAGGY. 3 JAGGED.

**shaggy** (-i) adj. lanudo, peludo, hirsuto. 2 afelpado. 3 áspero, rugoso. 4 desgreñado.

**shagreen** (shagrɪ·n) s. lija, piel de lija. 2 TEN. zapa, piel de zapa; chagrín.

**shake** (sheik) s. meneo, sacudida; sacudimiento. 2 temblor, estremecimiento. 3 apretón [de manos]. 4 fam. terremoto. 5 periquete, instante. 6 MÚS. trino. 7 grieta, hendedura. 8 acebolladura. 9 batido [de leche]. 10 to be no great shakes, no ser gran cosa.

**shake (to)** tr. sacudir, menear, agitar, blandir. 2 hacer temblar o retemblar. 3 sacudir, sacudirse, librarse de; dar esquinazo a. | Gralte. con off o out. 4 debilitar, hacer vacilar o flaquear. 5 desalentar; impresionar, afectar. 6 estrechar [la mano]. 7 MÚS. hacer trino en una [nota]. 8 to ~ down, vaciar, o hacer caer sacudiendo; fig. sacar dinero [a uno]. 9 intr. temblar, retemblar, estremecerse, tiritar. 10 vacilar, tambalearse. 11 MÚS. trinar. ¶ Pret.: shook; p. p.: shaken.

**shakedown** (-daun) s. cama improvisada. 2 acción de sacar dinero a uno.

**shaker** (shei·køʳ) s. temblador. 2 sacudidor, agitador. 3 coctelera. 4 espolvoreador.

**Shakespearian** (sheikspi·rian) adj. relativo a Shakespeare.

**shako** (shæ·kou) s. chacó.

**shaky** (shæ·ki) adj. trémulo. 2 inseguro, vacilante, ruinoso. 3 agrietado. 4 poco claro; que merece poco crédito.

**shale** (sheil) s. esquisto.

**shall** (shæl) aux. def. (con un inf. sin to). Con el pres. forma el futuro del segundo verbo. Al revés de lo que ocurre con to will, en las primeras personas, denota simple acción futura, posibilidad o contingencia, y en las segundas y terceras, voluntad, intención, permiso, mandato o amenaza: I shall go, yo iré; he shall go, tiene que ir. 2 El pret. should se usa a) como signo del subjuntivo: if you should come, si usted viniese; b) para formar el potencial; c) con la significación de deber o haber de: you should come, debería usted venir. V. SHOULD. ¶ Pres., 1.ª y 3.ª pers. sing.: shall; 2.ª pers.: shalt; pl. shall | Pret.: should.

**shallop** (shæ·løp) s. chalupa.

**shallot** (shala·t) s. BOT. chalote, ascalonia.

**shallow** (shæ·lou) adj. bajo, poco profundo, vadoso. 2 superficial, frívolo. 3 s. bajío; paraje vadoso.

**shallow (to)** tr. hacer menos profundo. 2 intr. hacerse menos profundo.

**shallowness** (shæ·lounis) s. poca profundidad. 2 superficialidad, ligereza de juicio, frivolidad.

**shaly** (chei·li) adj. esquistoso.

**sham** (shæm) s. fingimiento, simulación. 2 imitación, cosa falsa. 3 simulador, farsante. 4 adj. fingido, simulado, falso, postizo.

**sham (to)** tr.-intr. fingir, simular. ¶ Pret. y p. p.: shammed; ger.: shamming.

**shamble** (shæ·mbøl) s. paso torpe, vacilante.

**shamble (to)** intr. andar vacilando, arrastrar los pies.

**shambles** (shæ·mbøls) s. pl. (a veces construido como sing.) matadero, degolladero.

**shame** (sheim) s. vergüenza, bochorno; pudor: to put to ~, avergonzar. 2 vergüenza, deshonra: it is a ~, es una vergüenza; for ~!, ¡qué vergüenza!

**shame (to)** tr. avergonzar, abochornar. 2 afrentar, deshonrar.

**shamefaced** (-feist) adj. tímido, vergonzoso. 2 avergonzado.

**shameful** (-ful) adj. vergonzoso, ignominioso. 2 indecente, escandaloso.

**shameless** (-lis) adj. desvergonzado, descarado, sin vergüenza.

**shammer** (-øʳ) s. simulador, fingidor.

**shammy** (shæ·mi) s. CHAMOIS.

**shampoo** (shæmpu·) s. lavado [de la cabeza]. 2 champú.

**shampoo (to)** tr. dar champú a, lavar [la cabeza].

**shamrock** (shæ·mrak) s. BOT. trébol; aleluya; mielga azafranada. 2 emblema de Irlanda.

**shank** (shænk) s. zanca, pierna. 2 caña [del caballo]; zanca [del ave]; tibia [de insecto]. 3 canilla [de la pierna]. 4 MEC. astil, vástago, espiga. 5 caña [de ancla]. 6 tija [de llave]. 7 enfranque. 8 IMPR. árbol [del tipo]. 9 alacrán [de botón]. 10 cabo, extremo; fin.

**shan't** (shænt) abrev. fam. de SHALL NOT.

**shanty** (shæ·nti) s. cabaña, choza, casucha. 2 CHANTEY.

**shape** (sheip) s. forma, figura, hechura, cuerpo, estado: to put into ~, arreglar, poner en orden; to take ~, tomar forma o cuerpo; in bad ~, mal, en mal estado; out of ~, deformado; desarreglado, descompuesto. 2 giro, aspecto. 3 forma, molde.

**shape (to)** tr. formar, dar forma a; modelar. 2 expresar. 3 ahormar. 4 amoldar, ajustar. 5 dirigir [el curso, la conducta, etc.]. 6 disponer, idear. 7 concebir, figurarse. 8 intr. formarse, desarrollarse. 9 ocurrir [de cierto modo].

**shapeless** (-lis) adj. informe. 2 deforme.

**shapely** (-li) adj. bien formado o proporcionado. 2 de forma definida.

**shard** (sha·ʳd) s. tiesto, casco, fragmento. 2 ENT. élitro.

**share** (she·øʳ) s. parte, porción, cuota, cupo: to go shares, entrar o ir a la parte. 2 interés, participación. 3 COM. acción. 4 reja [de arado].

**share (to)** tr. dividir, distribuir, repartir. 2 repartirse, compartir, participar con otros en; usar en común. 3 intr. participar, tener o tomar parte.

**sharecropper** (-krapøʳ) s. AGR. aparcero.

**shareholder** (-jouldøʳ) s. COM. accionista.

**sharer** (-øʳ) s. partícipe, coparticipe.

**shark** (sha·ʳk) s. ICT. y fig. tiburón. 2 escualo. 3 estafador. 4 as [el que sobresale en algo].

**sharp** (sha·ʳp) adj. agudo, aguzado, afilado, cortante, punzante. 2 puntiagudo. 3 anguloso. 4 distinto, bien marcado. 5 repentino, brusco. 6 abrupto, escarpado. 7 áspero, acre, cáustico. 8 agudo, estridente. 9 vivo, penetrante, agudo, intenso, acerbo. 10 duro, severo, agrio, sarcástico. 11 fino, agudo [sentido]. 12 perspicaz, listo, astuto. 13 vivo, enérgico. 14 empeñado, reñido. 15 violento, impetuoso. 16 grande [apetito]. 17 codicioso. 18 atento, vigilante. 19 MÚS. agudo; sostenido; mayor, aumentado. 20 FONÉT. sordo. 21 ~ practice, estafa, dolo. 22 adv. SHARPLY. : look ~!, ¡ojo alerta! 23 en punto: at three o'clock ~, a las tres en punto. 24 s. pop. experto, perito. 25 estafador, fullero. 26 MÚS. sostenido.

**sharp (to)** *tr.* engañar, estafar, robar. *2* MÚS. subir el tono de; marcar con sostenido.
**sharp-edged** *adj.* afilado, aguzado.
**sharpen (to)** (-øn) *tr.* afilar, aguzar, amolar, adelgazar. *2* aguzar [los sentidos, etc.]. *3* hacer más áspero, severo, intenso, vehemente, etc. *4* hacer distinto o marcado. *5* MÚS. TO SHARP. *6* *intr.* aguzarrse. *7* afilarse.
**sharpener** (-ønøᵣ) *s.* afilador, amolador, aguzador. *2* cortalápices. *3* *knife* ~, chaira, afilón.
**sharper** (-øᵣ) *s.* estafador.
**sharp-featured** *adj.* de facciones enjutas.
**sharply** (-li) *adv.* grandemente; vivamente; ásperamente; mordazmente; bruscamente; nítidamente, etc.
**sharp-pointed** *adj.* puntiagudo.
**sharp-set** *adj.* ávido, ansioso.
**sharpshooter** (-shutøᵣ) *s.* buen tirador.
**sharp-sighted** *adj.* perspicaz; de vista penetrante.
**sharp-witted** *adj.* agudo, sutil, perspicaz.
**shatter** (shæ·tøᵣ) *s.* fragmento, astilla, añico.
**shatter (to)** *tr.* romper, hacer astillas o añicos. *2* destrozar, destruir. *3* quebrantar [la salud]; trastornar [el juicio]. *4* *intr.* romperse, hacerse añicos.
**shatterproof** (shæ·tøᵣpruf) *adj.* inastillable.
**shattery** (shæ·tøri) *adj.* quebradizo, friable.
**shave** (sheiv) *s.* afeitado, rasuración. *2* corte [de la hierba]. *3* rebanada fina; viruta. *4* *to have a close* ~, escaparse o salvarse de milagro.
**shave (to)** *tr.* afeitar, rasurar. *2* segar de raíz. *3* acepillar, alisar, rascar; cortar, rebanar finamente. *4* rozar [pasar rozando]. *5* *intr.* afeitarse. *6* ser duro en un trato; estafar.
**shaver** (shei·vøᵣ) *s.* barbero. *2* máquina de afeitar. *3* fam. jovencito, muchacho.
**shaving** (-ing) *s.* afeitado: ~ *brush*, brocha de afeitar. *2* viruta.
**shawl** (shol) *s.* chal, pañolón, mantón.
**shawm** (shom) *s.* chirimía, dulzaina.
**she** (shɪ) *pron. f.* ella [en nominativo]: ~ *who*, la que, aquella que. *2* (en composición) hembra: *she-ass*, borrica.
**sheaf** (shɪf), *pl.* **sheaves** (shɪvš) *s.* haz, gavilla. *2* manojo, atado, lío. *3* roldana.
**shear** (shɪᵣ) *s.* esquila, esquileo. *2* vellón, lana esquilada. *3* hoja de tijera.
**shear (to)** *tr.* cortar, esquilar, trasquilar. *2* tundir. *3* cizallar, cortar con cizallas. *4* recortar [una planta]. *5* fig. despojar, privar de. ¶ P. p.: *sheared* o *shorn*.
**shearer** (-øᵣ) *s.* esquilador. *2* tundidor.
**shears** (-s) *s. pl.* tijeras grandes. *2* cizallas.
**shearwater** (-wotøᵣ) *s.* ORN. meauca.
**sheatfish** (shɪ·tfish) *s.* ICT. siluro.
**sheath** (shɪz) *s.* vaina, funda, estuche, envoltura. *2* BOT. vaina [de hoja]. *3* cama [del arado].
**sheathe (to)** (shið) *tr.* envainar, enfundar; cubrir, forrar. *2* MAR. aforrar, embonar.
**sheathing** (shi·ding) *s.* forro exterior, cubierta, revestimiento. *2* MAR. aforro, embono.
**sheave** (shɪv) *s.* roldana, polea. *2* rueda excéntrica.
**sheave (to)** *tr.* agavillar, reunir en haz.
**shed** (shed) *s.* cobertizo, alpende. *2* hangar. *3* divisoria de aguas. *4* TEJ. calada.
**shed (to)** *tr.* verter, derramar. *2* lanzar, emitir, esparcir, despedir. *3* soltar, dejar caer; mudar [las plumas, la piel, etc.]. *4* *intr.* hacer la muda. ¶ Pret. y p. p.: *shed*; ger.: *-dding*.
**shedding** (-ing) *s.* derramamiento, efusión.
**sheen** (shɪn) *s.* lustre, brillo, resplandor.

**sheeny** (-i) *adj.* lustroso. *2* brillante, radiante.
**sheep** (shɪp) *s. sing.* y *pl.* ZOOL. carnero, oveja; carneros, ovejas: ~ *dog*, perro de pastor; ~ *tick*, garrapata; *to make sheep's eyes at*, fig. mirar lánguida y amorosamente. *2* papanatas, simplón. *3* badana.
**sheepcote** (-kout), **sheepfold** (-fould) *s.* aprisco, redil.
**sheepish** (-ish) *adj.* tímido, vergonzoso, encogido. *2* avergonzado.
**sheepshead** (-sjed) *s.* COC. cabeza de cordero. *2* estúpido, papanatas. *3* ICT. sargo.
**sheepshearer** (-shirøᵣ) *s.* esquilador. *2* esquiladora [máquina].
**sheepskin** (-skin) *s.* piel de cordero, zalea. *2* badana. *3* pergamino. *4* fam. (E.U.) diploma.
**sheepwalk** (shɪ·pwok) *s.* dehesa carneril.
**sheer** (shiᵣ) *adj.* puro, mero. *2* completo, absoluto. *3* empinado, escarpado. *4* TEJ. fino, ligero, transparente. *5* *adv.* completamente. *6* escarpadamente. *7* de golpe. *8* *s.* MAR. arrufadura. *9* desviación, cambio de rumbo.
**sheer (to)** *tr.* desviar. *2* *intr.* desviarse: *to* ~ *off*, apartarse, huir de.
**sheet** (shɪt) *s.* hoja, lámina, plancha. *2* hoja [de papel]; pliego [impreso]; carta; periódico. *3* sábana [de cama]. *4* mortaja. *5* extensión [de agua]; cortina [de fuego, de lluvia, etc.]. *6* poét. vela [de barco]; *to be*, o *tohave a* ~ *in the wind*, estar chispo, calamocano. *7* GEOL. capa. *8* MAR. escota. *9* MAR. ~ *anchor*, ancla de la esperanza.
**sheet (to)** *tr.* ensabanar. *2* disponer en capas. *3* *intr.* caer, extenderse, como una capa u hoja.
**sheeting** (shi·ting) *s.* lencería para sábanas. *2* acción de cubrir con planchas. *3* laminado. *4* HIDR., MIN. encofrado.
**sheik** (shɪk) *s.* jeque.
**shekel** (she·køl) *s.* siclo. *2* *pl.* fam. dinero.
**sheldrake** (she·ldreik) *s.* ORN. tadorna; mergánsar.
**shelf** (shelf) *s.* anaquel, entrepaño, tabla [de armario], repisa. *2* saliente de roca. *3* bajío.
**shell** (shel) *s.* ZOOL. concha, caparazón, carapacho: *to retire into one's* ~, meterse en su concha. *2* concha [materia]: ~ *comb*, peineta. *3* marisco. *4* cáscara, cascarón [de huevo]. *5* cáscara [de nuez, avellana, etc.]. *6* vaina [de legumbre]. *7* cáscara, concha, caja, cubierta; esqueleto o armazón exterior. *8* forro o casco [de buque]. *9* guarnición [de la espada]. *10* cuerpo [de caldera]. *11* caja [de motón]. *12* MÚS. caja [de tambor, de banjo, etc.]. *13* cubilete [pastel]. *14* MAR. yola. *15* cápsula [de cartucho]. *16* ARTILL. bomba, granada.
**shell (to)** *tr.* descascarar, desvainar, desgranar; romper [nueces, avellanas]. *2* ARTILL. bombardear. *3* intr. desgranarse. *4* descascararse. *5* fam. *to* ~ *out*, aflojar la mosca.
**shellac** (shølæ·k) *s.* goma laca.
**shellac (to)** *tr.* barnizar con laca. ¶ Pret. y p. p.: *shellacked*; ger.: *-cking*.
**shellbark** (she·lbaᵣk) *s.* BOT. nogal. americano.
**shellfire** (she·lfaiᵣ) *s.* cañoneo, bombardeo.
**shellfish** (-fish) *s.* marisco, mariscos.
**shellproof** (-pruf) *adj.* a prueba de bomba.
**shelly** (-i) *adj.* de conchas. *2* conchudo.
**shelter** (she·ltøᵣ) *s.* resguardo, abrigo, refugio, asilo, albergue, techo: *to take* ~, refugiarse.
**shelter (to)** *tr.* resguardar, proteger, amparar, guarecer, abrigar. *2* albergar, acoger. *3* intr. guarecerse, refugiarse, acogerse.

**shelterless** (-lis) *adj.* desamparado, sin hogar. *2* desabrigado, al descubierto.
**shelve (to)** (shelv) *tr.* proveer de anaqueles. *2* poner en un anaquel. *3* fig. arrinconar, archivar, dar carpetazo a. *4 intr.* estar en declive.
**shelves** (-š) *s. pl.* de SHELF.
**shelving** (-ing) *s.* anaquelería, estantería.
**shepherd** (she·pø<sup>r</sup>d) *s.* pastor: *the Good Shepherd*, el Buen Pastor. *2* BOT. *shepherd's purse*, bolsa de pastor.
**shepherd (to)** *tr.* pastorear.
**shepherdess** (she·pø<sup>r</sup>dis) *s.* pastora, zagala.
**sherbet** (shø·<sup>r</sup>bit) *s.* sorbete.
**sherd** (shø<sup>r</sup>d) *s.* tiesto, casco, tejoleta.
**sherif** (sherı·f) *s.* jerife.
**sheriff** (she·rif) *s.* funcionario superior de un distrito, encargado de hacer cumplir la ley, ejecutar los mandatos judiciales y mantener el orden.
**sherry** (she·ri) *s.* vino de Jerez.
**she's** (shıš) *contr.* de SHE IS y de SHE HAS.
**sheth** (shez) *s.* dental [del arado].
**shew (to)** (shou·) *tr.-intr.* (Ingl.) TO SHOW.
**shewbread** (-bred) *s.* panes de proposición.
**shibboleth** (shi·boliz) *s.* palabra que sirve de santo y seña.
**shield** (shıld) *s.* escudo, adarga. *2* escudo, defensa. *3* BLAS., ZOOL. escudo. *4* sobaquera [contra el sudor].
**shield (to)** *tr.* escudar, proteger, defender.
**shield-bearer** *s.* escudero.
**shift** (shift) *s.* recurso, expediente, esfuerzo, artificio, maña: *to make (a)* ~, componérselas [para]; arreglarse, pasar [con o sin]. *2* fraude; subterfugio. *3* muda [de ropa]. *4* tanda, turno [de obreros; de trabajo]. *5* cambio, desviación, sustitución, traslado: ~ *key*, tecla o palanca de mayúsculas.
**shift (to)** *tr.* cambiar, mudar; cambiar de posición o dirección, mover, trasladar: *to* ~ *gears*, AUTO. cambiar la marcha; *to* ~ *the blame*, echar [a otro] la propia culpa. *2* pop. comer, beber. *3 intr.* cambiar, mudar; moverse, trasladarse, correrse. *4* usar de subterfugios o evasivas; mañear. *5* ingeniarse: *to* ~ *for oneself*, arreglárselas.
**shiftiness** (-tinis) *s.* calidad de mudable o movedizo. *2* artificio, astucia; carácter evasivo.
**shiftless** (-tlis) *adj.* falto de recursos, de inventiva; inútil, perezoso.
**shifty** (-ti) *adj.* mudable, voluble. *2* movedizo, inquieto. *3* industrioso, mañoso, astuto, evasivo.
**shilling** (-shi·ling) *s.* chelín [vigésima parte de la libra esterlina].
**shilly-shally** (shi·li-shæ·li) *s.* irresolución, vacilación. *2* persona irresoluta.
**shilly-shally (to)** *intr.* vacilar, estar indeciso.
**shim** (shim) MEC. planchita con que se hacen ajustar entre sí dos partes de una máquina.
**shimmer** (shi·mø<sup>r</sup>) *s.* luz trémula, débil resplandor.
**shimmer (to)** *intr.* rielar, brillar débilmente.
**shimmery** (-i) *adj.* que luce con débil resplandor. *2* trémulo.
**shimmy** (shi·mi) *s.* shimmy [baile]. *2* fam. camisa de mujer. *3* AUTO. abaniqueo de las ruedas delanteras.
**shimmy (to)** *intr.* bailar el SHIMMY.
**shin** (shin) *s.* espinilla [de la pierna].
**shin (to)** *intr.-tr.* trepar, subir. *2 tr.* golpear en la espinilla. ¶ Pret. y p. p.: *shinned;* ger.: *-nning.*

**shindig** (shi·ndig) *s.* pop. (E.U.) juerga.
**shindy** (shi·ndi) *s.* fam. alboroto, trapatiesta.
**shine** (shai·n) *s.* brillo, resplandor, lustre, esplendor. *2* brillo, lustre [que se saca o se da]. *3* buen tiempo. *4* pop. (E.U.) afición, simpatía.
**shine (to)** *intr.* brillar, resplandecer, lucir. *2* brillar, distinguirse. *3* hacer sol o buen tiempo. *4 tr.* hacer brillar. *5* pulir, bruñir, lustrar; limpiar [el calzado]. ¶ Pret. y p. p.: *shone.*
**shiner** (-ø<sup>r</sup>) *s.* persona o cosa brillante. *2* pop. soberano [moneda]. *3* pop. ojo; ojo amoratado.
**shingle** (shi·ngøl) *s.* guijo, guijarros. *2* guijarro. *3* chilla, ripia [para techar]. *4* fam. (E.U.) letrero de despacho. *5* pelo de mujer corto y en disminución.
**shingle (to)** *tr.* cubrir con ripia. *2* cortar el cabello dejándolo corto y en disminución. *3* cinglar [el hierro].
**shingles** (shi·ngøls) *s.* MED. zoster, zona.
**shining** (shai·ning) *adj.* brillante, resplandeciente. *2* fig. brillante, distinguido.
**shinny** (shi·ni) *s.* cachava [juego y palo].
**shinny (to)** *intr.* jugar al *shinny*. *2* (E.U.) *to* ~ *up*, trepar, subir.
**Shinto** (shi·ntou), **Shintoism** (-išm) *s.* sintoísmo.
**shiny** (shai·ni) *adj.* brillante, luminoso. *2* claro, radiante. *3* lustroso. *4* raído.
**ship** (ship) *s.* MAR. buque, barco,nave, bajel, navío: ~ *biscuit*, galleta; ~ *carpenter*, carpintero de ribera; ~ *chandler*, proveedor de buques. *2* nave aérea, aeronave.
**ship (to)** *tr.* embarcar. *2* enviar, expedir, transportar. *3* armar [los remos, el timón, etc.]. *4* tomar como tripulante. *5 intr.* embarcarse. ¶ Pret. y p. p.: *shipped;* ger.: *-pping.*
**shipboard** (-bo<sup>r</sup>d) *s.* MAR. bordo: *on* ~, a bordo.
**shipbuilder** (-bildø<sup>r</sup>) *s.* constructor de buques.
**shipbuilding** (-bilding) *s.* arquitectura naval.
**shipload** (-loud) *s.* MAR. cargamento; todo lo que el buque puede llevar [de una cosa].
**shipmaster** (-mæstø<sup>r</sup>) *s.* MAR. patrón, capitán.
**shipmate** (-meit) *s.* compañero a bordo.
**shipment** (-mønt) *s.* embarque, cargamento. *2* envío, remesa, consignación, partida.
**shipowner** (-ounø<sup>r</sup>) *s.* naviero, armador.
**shipper** (-ø<sup>r</sup>) *s.* COM. cargador, embarcador; expedidor, remitente.
**shipping** (-ø<sup>r</sup>) *s.* embarque, envío, expedición: ~ *agent*, consignatario de buques. *2* buques, flota, tonelaje [de un puerto, país, etc.].
**shipplane** (-plein) *s.* avión de cubierta.
**shipshape** (-sheip) *adj.* en buen orden.
**shipworm** (-uø<sup>r</sup>m) *s.* ZOOL. broma, tiñuela.
**shipwreck** (-rek) *s.* naufragio. *2* buque náufrago.
**shipwreck (to)** *tr.* hacer naufragar. *2 intr.* naufragar.
**shipwright** (-rait) *s.* carpintero de ribera o de buque, calafate.
**shipyard** (-ya<sup>r</sup>d) *s.* MAR. astillero, arsenal.
**shire** (shai<sup>r</sup>) *s.* (Ingl.) distrito, condado.
**shirk** (shø<sup>r</sup>k) *s.* maula, el que huye del trabajo.
**shirk (to)** *tr.* eludir, evitar. *2 intr.* huir del trabajo, de hacer algo; faltar a una obligación.
**shirr** (shø<sup>r</sup>) *s.* COST. frunce, gandujado.
**shirr (to)** *tr.* COST. fruncir, gandujar. *2* COC. escalfar huevos en crema de leche.
**shirt** (shø<sup>r</sup>t) *s.* camisa [de hombre]: *in one's* ~ *sleeves*, en mangas de camisa.
**shirtband** (-bænd) *s.* tirilla [del cuello de la camisa].
**shirting** (-ing) *s.* tela para camisas.

**shirtwaist** (-weist) *s.* blusa camisera.
**shiver** (shi·vø$^r$) *s.* temblor, tiritón, escalofrío, estremecimiento. *2* pedazo, astilla, brizna.
**shiver (to)** *intr.* temblar, tiritar, estremecerse, vibrar. *2* romperse, hacerse añicos. *3 tr.* hacer temblar, estremecer. *4* romper, hacer añicos.
**shivery** (shi·vøri) *adj.* trémulo, tembloroso. *2* friolento, friolero. *3* friable, quebradizo.
**shoal** (shoul) *s.* bajo, bajío, banco de arena. *2* muchedumbre, multitud. *3* banco [de peces]. *4 adj.* poco profundo.
**shoal (to)** *intr.* MAR. disminuir gradualmente en profundidad. *2* reunirse en gran número.
**shoaly** (-i) *s.* vadoso, poco profundo. *2* lleno de bajíos.
**shoat** (shout) *s.* gorrino, cochinillo.
**shock** (shak) *s.* golpe, choque: ~ *absorber,* amortiguador. *2* conmoción, sacudida. *3* sobresalto, susto, impresión. *4* ofensa, escándalo, horror. *5* MED. choque. *6* hacina, tresnal. *7* greña, maraña.
**shock (to)** *tr.* chocar, ofender, escandalizar, horrorizar. *2* causar impresión, sobresaltar. *3* MED. someter al choque eléctrico. *4* sacudir, conmover. *5* hacinar. *6 intr.* chocar.
**shock-headed** *adj.* greñudo.
**shocking** (-ing) *adj.* chocante, ofensivo, repugnante, vergonzoso, escandaloso. *2* horrible.
**shod** (shad) *pret.* y *p. p.* de TO SHOE.
**shoddy** (sha·di) *s.* lana de desecho o regenerada. *2* bambolla, vulgaridad presuntuosa. *3 adj.* falso, de imitación.
**shoe** (shu) *s.* zapato, bota, botina; calzado: *in another's shoes,* en el pellejo de otro: ~ *polish,* crema o betún para los zapatos. *2* herradura. *3* suela [de trineo]. *4* zapato [de ancla; de freno]; galga [de carruaje]. *5* llanta [de rueda]; cubierta [de neumático]. *6* azuche, contera, regatón.
**shoe (to)** *tr.* calzar [a una pers.]. *2* herrar [a un animal]. *3* enllantar [una rueda]. *4* poner azuche o regatón a. ¶ Pret. y p. p.: *shod.*
**shoeblack** (-blæk) *s.* limpiabotas.
**shoehorn** (-jo$^r$n) *s.* calzador.
**shoemaker** (-meikø$^r$) *s.* zapatero.
**shoer** (shu·ø$^r$) *s.* herrador.
**shoeshine** (-shain) *s.* brillo, lustre que se da a los zapatos. *2* limpiabotas.
**shone** (shoun) *pret.* y *p. p.* de TO SHINE.
**shoo** (shu) *interj.* ¡so!, ¡oxe!; ¡fuera!
**shoo (to)** *tr.* oxear; ahuyentar.
**shook** (shuk) *pret.* de TO SHAKE.
**shoot** (shut) *s.* BOT. vástago, pimpollo, renuevo, retoño. *2* conducto inclinado [para granos, carbón, etc.]. *3* concurso de tiro; tiro al blanco, tirada. *4* cacería. *5* punzada [dolor].
**shoot (to)** *tr.* herir o matar [con un proyectil]; fusilar. *2* disparar, tirar, lanzar, arrojar, despedir. *3* vaciar, verter, precipitar. *4* sacar, proyectar, empujar hacia afuera. *5* recorrer, bajar rápidamente. *6* echar [brotes, renuevos]. *7* correr, descorrer [un cerrojo, un pestillo]. *8* disparar [una instantánea], fotografiar, filmar. *9* DEP. chutar, disparar. *10* esmaltar, salpicar. *11 to* ~ *down,* derribar a tiros. *12 to* ~ *off,* descargar [un arma]. *13 to* ~ *out,* extender [sus ramas un árbol]. *14 to* ~ *trouble,* localizar desperfectos o averías.
*16 intr.* tirar, hacer fuego. *17* cazar, ir de caza. *18* pasar, moverse rápidamente. *19* salir, proyectarse, extenderse, elevarse. *20* salir, en chorro. *21* brotar, retoñar, tallecer, crecer. *22* latir,

punzar [un dolor]. *23 to* ~ *at,* tirar a, disparar contra. *24 to* ~ *up,* crecer, brotar [las plantas]; alzarse, elevarse.
¶ Pret. y p. p.: *shot.*
**shooting** (-ing) *s.* caza con escopeta. *2* acción de tirar o de matar a tiros; tiro, tiros, tiroteo; fusilamiento. *3* CINEM. filmación, rodaje. *4 adj.* ~ *gallery,* tiro al blanco [lugar]; ~ *star,* estrella fugaz; ~ *pain,* punzada [dolor].
**shop** (shap) *s.* tienda, comercio, almacén, taller, negocio, ocupación: *to shut up* ~, cerrar la tienda; fig. dejar de hacer algo; *to talk* ~, hablar de negocios o de asuntos profesionales [fuera de sazón]. *2* fig. institución, establecimiento.
**shop (to)** *intr.* comprar en tiendas: *to go shopping,* ir de compras. *2 tr.* mandar [un auto, etc.] al taller de reparaciones. ¶ Pret. y p. p.: *shopped;* ger.: *-pping.*
**shopboard** (-bo$^r$d) *s.* mostrador de tienda.
**shopgirl** (-gø$^r$l) *s.* muchacha de tienda, dependienta.
**shopkeeper** (kɪpø$^r$) *s.* tendero.
**shoplifter** (liftø$^r$) *s.* rastro de tiendas; mechera.
**shoplifting** (-lifting) *s.* ratería en una tienda.
**shopman** (-mæn) *s.* tendero. *2* mancebo de tienda, dependiente.
**shopping district** *s.* barrio comercial.
**shopwalker** (-wokø$^r$) *s.* empleado de un comercio que vigila a los demás y atiende a los compradores.
**shopwindow** (-windou) *s.* escaparate de tienda.
**shore** (sho$^r$) *s.* orilla [del mar, de un río, de un lago], costa, playa, ribera: *in* ~, MAR. junto a tierra; *on* ~, en tierra. *2* ALBAÑ., MAR. puntal, escora. *3* MIN. entibo.
**shore (to)** *tr.* apuntalar, escorar, estibar.
**shoreless** (sho·$^r$lis) *adj.* sin riberas, ilimitado.
**shoring** (sho·ring) *s.* apuntalamiento, puntales.
**shorn** (sho·$^r$n) *p. p.* de TO SHEAR. *2 adj.* mocho.
**short** (sho·$^r$t) *adj.* corto [de poca extensión, longitud, duración o entidad; de poco valor o alcanza]; breve, escaso, poco: ~ *circuit,* ELECT. corto circuito; ~ *cut,* atajo; ~ *ton,* tonelada de 2.000 libras [907 kg.]; ~ *wave,* ELECT. onda corta; *to be* ~ *of,* estar falto o escaso de; estar lejos de, no alcanzar, no corresponder a; *to run* ~ *of,* acabársele a uno algo; *on* ~ *notice,* prontamente, con poco tiempo de aviso; *on* ~ *term,* a corto plazo. *2* bajo [de poca estatura]. *3* breve, sucinto: *to be* ~, para abreviar. *4 ANAT.* falsa [costilla]. *5* flaca [memoria]. *6* acelerado [pulso]. *7* anhelosa [respiración]. *8* seco, brusco. *9* pronto [genio]. *10* seco, sin diluir [licor]. *11* quebradizo, friable. *12* FONÉT. breve.
*13 adv.* brevemente, cortamente; bruscamente, en seco: *to cut* ~, interrumpir bruscamente; abreviar; *to stop* ~, parar en seco. *14* COM. al descubierto. *15 to fall* ~, escasear, faltar; no alcanzar el blanco, el objeto, etc.; fracasar. *16* ~ *of,* excepto, si no, a menos que.
*17 s.* lo corto, lo breve: *for* ~, para abreviar; *in* ~, en resumen. *18* COM. venta al descubierto. *19* CINEM. película corta. *20* forma abreviada: ~ *for,* forma abreviada de.
**shortage** (-idỹ) *s.* escasez, falta, carestía. *2* falta, merma, déficit.
**shortbread** (-bred) *s.* torta dulce y quebradiza.
**short-breathed** *adj.* corto de resuello, asmático.
**shortcoming** (-køming) *s.* defecto, falta, negligencia. *2* limitación, insuficiencia.
**short-dated** *adj.* a corta fecha.

**shorten (to)** (-øn) *tr.* acortar, reducir, abreviar. *2* cercenar. *3* hacer friable [la pastelería] con mantequilla, manteca, etc. *4 intr.* acortarse.
**shorthand** (-jænd) *s.* taquigrafía. *2 adj.* taquigráfico.
**short-handed** *adj.* que carece del número suficiente de criados, operarios, auxiliares, etc.
**shortish** (-ish) *adj.* algo corto, algo pequeño.
**short-legged** *adj.* de piernas cortas.
**short-lived** *adj.* efímero, de breve vida.
**shortly** (-li) *adv.* brevemente. *2* bruscamente. *3* luego, en breve: ~ *before*, poco antes; ~ *after*, poco después.
**short-range** *adj.* de poco alcance.
**shorts** (sho·ᵣts) *s. pl.* pantalones cortos para deporte. *2* calzoncillos cortos.
**short-sighted** *adj.* corto de vista, cegato. *2* poco perspicaz.
**short-tempered** *adj.* irascible, de mal genio.
**short-term** *adj.* COM. a corto plazo.
**short-winded** *adj.* corto de resuello.
**short-witted** *adj.* limitado, corto de alcances.
**shot** (sha·t) *pret. y p. p.* de TO SHOOT. *2 adj.* tornasolado, matizado. *3 s.* tiro, disparo, balazo, saetazo; fig. tentativa; conjetura: *to take a* ~ *at*, disparar un tiro a; probar a. *4* tiro, alcance; distancia: *not by a long* ~, ni por asomo; ni con mucho. *5* proyectil, bala; perdigones. *6* tirador: *good* ~, buen tirador. *7* pop. inyección; trago. *8* golpe, tirada, tacada, jugada [en ciertos juegos]. *9* fotografía, instantánea. *10* DEP. peso [que se lanza].
**shotgun** (-gøn) *s.* escopeta de caza.
**shot-put** *s.* DEP. lanzamiento.
**should** (shud) *pret.* de TO SHALL. ¶ V. SHALL. | V. el cuadro SUBJUNTIVO.
**shoulder** (shou·ldøᵣ) *s.* hombro: ~ *belt*, tahalí; ~ *blade*, paletilla, escápula; ~ *strap*, correa, etc., que pasa por el hombro; *to turn*, o *to give the cold* ~, tratar fríamente, volver la espalda; ~ *to* ~, hombro a hombro, codo a codo; *straight from the* ~, con toda franqueza. *2* codo [de cuadrúpedo]. *3* espaldilla [de cordero]. *4* CARP. espaldón. *5* parte saliente. *6 pl.* espaldas.
**shoulder (to)** *tr.* echarse sobre las espaldas o al hombro; llevar a hombros. *2* fig. cargar con, tomar sobre sí. *3* MIL. *shoulder arms*, armas al hombro. *4 intr.* empujar con el hombro.
**shout** (shaut) *s.* grito, exclamación, griterío, aclamación: ~ *of applause*, aclamación.
**shout (to)** *intr.-tr.* gritar, vocear, dar gritos. *2* vitorear, dar vivas.
**shouting** (-ing) *s.* gritería. *2* aclamación.
**shove** (shøv) *s.* empujón. *2* empuje, impulso.
**shove (to)** *tr.-intr.* empujar, empellar, impeler, dar empujones. *2 tr.* fam. meter. *3 intr.* avanzar dando empujones o a fuerza de remos: *to* ~ *off*, alejarse de la orilla; fig. salir, irse.
**shovel** (shø·vøl) *s.* pala [herramienta]. *2* palada [lo que coge una pala]. *3* sombrero de teja.
**shovel (to)** *tr.* traspalar, mover con palas. *2* cavar con pala. *3* meter a paladas. ¶ Pret. y p. p.: *shovel(l)ed;* ger.: *-l(l)ing.*
**shovelboard** (-boᵣd) *s.* especie de juego del tejo.
**shovel(l)er** (-øᵣ) *s.* palero.
**show** (shou) *s.* presentación, exhibición, muestra, demostración: ~ *bill*, cartel; ~ *case*, vitrina; ~ *window*, escaparate [de tienda]. *2* exposición [artística, comercial, etc.]. *3* espectáculo; función [de teatro, etc.]; sesión [de cine]: ~ *boat*, barco teatro. *4* ostentación, pompa; alarde,

gala: *to make a fine* ~, hacer gran papel; *to make a* ~ *of*, hacer gala de. *5* ficción, falsa apariencia. *6* señal, indicación, prueba. *7* pop. negocio, organización, conjunto, etc.
**show (to)** *tr.* mostrar, enseñar, exhibir, lucir: *to* ~ *the heels*, huir. *2* sacar, asomar. *3* hacer ver, demostrar, probar. *4* revelar, descubrir, manifestar. *5* indicar, señalar; dar [señales]. *6* guiar, introducir, acompañar: ~ *him in*, hágale pasar. *7* COM. arrojar [como resultado o saldo]. *8 to* ~ *how to*, enseñar a [hacer algo]. *9 to* ~ *up*, destacar; descubrir, desenmascarar. *10 intr.* mostrarse, aparecer, asomar. *11* TEAT. actuar. *12* TEAT. representarse. *13 to* ~ *off*, fachendear, pavonearse. *14 to* ~ *up*, destacarse; comparecer, dejarse ver. ¶ Pret.: *showed;* p. p.: *shown* o *showed.*
**showbread** (-bred) *s.* SHEWBREAD.
**shower** (shau·øᵣ) *s.* chubasco, chaparrón. *2* lluvia, copia, abundancia. *3* ~ *bath*, ducha.
**shower (to)** *tr.* regar, mojar. *2* derramar, hacer llover, dar en abundancia. *3 intr.* llover.
**showerless** (-lis) *adj.* sin lluvia.
**showery** (-i) *adj.* lluvioso.
**showman** (shou·mæn) *s.* director de espectáculos. *2* empresario de teatro, circo, etc.
**shown** (-n) *p. p.* de TO SHOW.
**showroom** (-rum) *s.* sala de exposición. *2* sala de muestras.
**showy** (-i) *adj.* vistoso, ostentoso, lujoso, suntuoso. *2* chillón, llamativo.
**shrank** (shrænk) *pret.* de TO SHRINK.
**shred** (shred) *s.* tira, jirón, andrajo, colgajo. *2* triza, fragmento.
**shred (to)** *tr.* hacer tiras, jirones o trizas. *2* cortar, desmenuzar. ¶ Pret. y p. p.: *shredded* o *shred;* ger.: *shredding.*
**shrew** (shru) *s.* arpía, mujer de mal genio. *2* ZOOL. musaraña, musgaño.
**shrewd** (shrud) *adj.* agudo, sagaz, perspicaz, listo, astuto. *2* vivo, penetrante.
**shrewdness** (-nis) *s.* agudeza, sagacidad, astucia.
**shrewish** (shru·ish) *adj.* regañón, mal humorado.
**shrewmouse** (-maus) *s.* ZOOL. musaraña, musgaño.
**shriek** (shrik) *s.* chillido, grito agudo, alarido.
**shriek (to)** *intr.* chillar, gritar.
**shrievalty** (shri·valti) *s.* cargo de SHERIFF.
**shrift** (shrift) *s.* confesión [de los pecados]. *2 to make short* ~ *of*, fam. despachar de prisa.
**shrike** (shraik) *s.* ORN. alcaudón.
**shrill** (shril) *adj.* agudo, penetrante, estridente, chillón.
**shrill (to)** *tr.-intr.* chillar.
**shrilly** (-i) *adj.* chillonamente.
**shrimp** (shrimp) *s.* ZOOL. camarón, quisquilla. *2* desp. enano, hombrecillo.
**shrine** (shrain) *s.* urna, relicario, sepulcro de santo; altar, capilla, santuario.
**shrine (to)** *tr.* TO ENSHRINE.
**shrink** (shrink) *s.* contracción, encogimiento.
**shrink (to)** *intr.* escoger, contraerse. *2* acortarse, estrecharse, disminuir, mermar. *3* encogerse, retroceder, estremecerse [por miedo, horror, etc.], huir [de]. *4 tr.* encoger, contraer, reducir, mermar. ¶ Pret.: *shrank* o *shrunk;* p. p.: *shrunk* o *shrunken.*
**shrinkage** (-idy̆) *s.* encogimiento, reducción. *2* COM. merma, pérdida.
**shrive (to)** (shraiv) *tr.* ant. confesar, oír en confesión. *3 intr.-ref.* confesarse. ¶ Pret.: *shrived* o *shrove;* p. p.: *shrived* o *shriven.*

**shrivel (to)** (shri·vøl) *tr.* arrugar, fruncir; encoger. *2* marchitar. *3 intr.* arrugarse, avellanarse, resecarse, encogerse, encarrujarse. *4* marchitarse. ¶ Pret. y p. p.: *shrivel(l)ed;* ger.: *-l(l)ing.*

**shriven** (shri·vøn) *p. p.* de TO SHRIVE.

**shroud** (shraud) *s.* mortaja, sudario. *2* manto, envoltura.

**shroud (to)** *tr.* amortajar. *2* envolver, cubrir.

**shrove** (shrouv) *pret.* de TO SHRIVE.

**Shrove** *s.* [sólo en composición] *Shrove Tuesday,* etc., martes, etc., de carnaval.

**Shrovetide** *s.* carnaval, carnestolendas.

**shrub** (shrøb) *s.* arbusto. *2* cierto licor.

**shrubbery** (-øri) *s.* arbustos. *2* plantación o grupo de arbustos.

**shrubby** (-i) *adj.* arbustivo. *2* cubierto de arbustos. *3* raquítico.

**shrug** (shrøg) *s.* encogimiento de hombros.

**shrug (to)** *tr.* encoger [los hombros]. *2 intr.* encogerse de hombros.

**shrunk** (shrønk) *pret.* y p. p. de TO SHRINK.

**shrunken** (-øn) *p. p.* de TO SHRINK.

**shuck** (shøk) *s.* cáscara, vaina, hollejo, zurrón. *2* (E.U.) concha [de ostra].

**shuck (to)** *tr.* descascarar, pelar, desvainar, deshollejar. *2* desbullar.

**shudder** (shø·dø<sup>r</sup>) *s.* temblor, estremecimiento.

**shudder (to)** *intr.* estremecerse. *2* tiritar.

**shuffle** (shø·føl) *s.* barajadura. *2* turno de barajar. *3* mezcla, confusión. *4* arrastramiento de pies. *5* evasiva, embuste.

**shuffle (to)** *tr.* barajar, revolver. *2* meter [entre otras cosas]. *3* arrastrar, restregar [los pies]. *4* mover de un lado a otro. *5 to ~ off,* quitarse, desprenderse de. *6 to ~ up,* hacer [algo] de cualquier modo. *7 intr.* barajar los naipes. *8* arrastrar o restregar los pies: *to ~ along,* ir arrastrando los pies; ir tirando. *9* andar con evasivas o embustes.

**shun (to)** (shøn) *tr.* rehuir, esquivar, eludir, evitar. *2* retraerse, apartarse de.

**shunt** (-t) *s.* desviación. *2* FERROC. desvío. *3* ELECT. derivación, shunt.

**shunt (to)** *tr.* desviar, poner a un lado. *2* FERROC. desviar, apartar. *3* ELECT. poner en derivación. *4 intr.* desviarse.

**shunter** (shø·ntø<sup>r</sup>) *s.* FERROC. (Ingl.) guardaagujas.

**shut** (shøt) *p. p.* de TO SHUT. *2 adj.* cerrado.

**shut (to)** *tr.* cerrar [una puerta, un abanico, los ojos, la boca, etc.]. *2* tapar, obstruir. *3* encerrar. *4* pillar, coger [un dedo, etc., en una puerta]. *5* excluir. *6 to ~ down,* cerrar [una fábrica]. *7 to ~ in,* encerrar. *8 to ~ off,* cortar [el gas, el agua, etc.]. *9 to ~ out,* impedir la entrada de; ocultar a la vista. *10 to ~ up,* cerrar bien; obstruir; encerrar, aprisionar; hacer callar. *11 intr.* cerrarse, cerrar. *12 to ~ down,* parar [una fábrica]. *13 to ~ up,* callarse. ¶ Pret. y p. p.: *shut;* ger.: *-tting.*

**shutdown** (-daun) *s.* cierre, paro.

**shutout** (-aut) *s.* DEP. triunfo en que el contrario no marca ningún tanto.

**shutter** (-ø<sup>r</sup>) *s.* cerrador. *2* postigo, persiana, contraventana; cierre metálico [de escaparate]. *3* cierre, obturador.

**shuttle** (shø·tøl) *s.* lanzadera.

**shuttlecock** (-kak) *s.* volante, rehilete.

**shy** (shai) *adj.* tímido, asustadizo. *2* recatado. *3* retraído, arisco. *4* cauteloso, prudente. *5* que escapa, rehuye o evita. *6* fam. (E.U.) falto, escaso.

*7 s.* huida, respingo [del caballo]. *8* sobresalto. *9* tiro, echada; ensayo, prueba.

**shy (to)** *intr.* hacerse a un lado, retroceder [ante algo]; respingar [el caballo]. *2 tr.* evitar, eludir. *3* lanzar, arrojar. ¶ Pret. y p. p.: *shied.*

**Shylock** (-lak) *s.* fig. usurero.

**shyness** (-nis) *s.* timidez. *2* vergüenza, recato. *3* esquivez, reserva.

**shyster** (-stø<sup>r</sup>) *s.* (E.U.) trapisondista.

**si** (si) *s.* MÚS. si.

**Siamese** (saiamı·s̆) *adj.-s.* siamés.

**Siberian** (saibi·rian) *adj.-s.* siberiano.

**sibilant** (si·bilant) *adj.* sibilante.

**sibilate (to)** (si·bileit) *tr.* pronunciar con *s* inicial.

**sibyl** (si·bil) *s.* sibila. *2* adivina.

**sibylline** (si·bilain) *adj.* sibilino, sibilítico.

**sic** (sik) *adv.* lat. sic.

**sicarian** (sikei·rian) *s.* sicario.

**siccative** (si·kativ) *adj.-s.* secante [que seca].

**Sicilian** (sisi·lian) *adj.-s.* siciliano, sículo.

**sick** (sik) *adj.-s.* enfermo: *the ~,* los enfermos. *2* de enfermo o de enfermedad. *3* mareado, con náuseas: *to be ~ at the stomach,* tener náuseas. *4* anheloso; nostálgico: *to be ~ for,* suspirar por. *5* asqueado, cansado, harto. *6* viciado, malsano. *7* pálido, débil. *8 ~ at heart,* acongojado, angustiado.

**sicken (to)** (-øn) *tr.* enfermar, poner enfermo. *2* dar asco o náuseas. *3* cansar, hartar; empalagar. *4* debilitar. *5 intr.* enfermar, ponerse enfermo. *6* nausear, tener asco. *7* cansarse, hartarse. *8* debilitarse.

**sickening** (-øning) *adj.* nauseabundo. *2* hastioso. *3* enfermo. *4* que pone enfermo.

**sickish** (-ish) *adj.* bascoso. *2* nauseabundo.

**sickle** (si·køl) *s.* hoz, segadera, segur.

**sickly** (si·kli) *adj.* enfermizo, achacoso. *2* insaluble. *3* empalagoso. *4* débil, lánguido, pálido.

**sickness** (-nis) *s.* enfermedad, mal, indisposición. *2* náusea, mareo. *3* hastío.

**side** (said) *s.* lado, costado, parte: *by the ~ of,* al lado de, junto a: *on all sides,* por todos lados, por todas partes; *on his mother ~,* por parte de madre; *right o wrong ~ of a cloth,* haz o envés [de una tela]. *2* orilla, margen. *3* falda, ladera. *4* GEOM. lado; cara. *5* MAR. costado, borda, banda. *6* lado, parte, partido, facción, bando: *to sake sides with,* tomar partido por. *7* ENCUAD. tapa.

*8 adj.* lateral; de lado, oblicuo; incidental, secundario: *~ door,* puerta lateral; puerta excusada; *~ glance,* mirada de soslayo; *~ issue,* cuestión secundaria; *~ light,* luz lateral; detalle o ilustración incidental; *~ table,* mesa auxiliar; trinchero; *~ wiskers,* patillas, chuletas.

**side (to)** *tr.* ponerse, ir o estar al lado de. *2* echar a un lado. *3 intr. to ~ with,* tomar partido por, ser de la opinión de.

**sideboard** (said·bo<sup>r</sup>d) *s.* aparador, copero, alacena.

**sideburns** (-bø·<sup>r</sup>ns) *s. pl.* patillas, chuletas.

**sidecar** (sai·dka<sup>r</sup>) *s.* sidecar.

**sideface** (sai·dfeis) *s.* perfil, rostro de perfil.

**sidelong** (-long) *adj.* lateral; oblicuo. *2* de soslayo. *3 adv.* lateralmente; oblicuamente.

**sidereal** (saidi·rial) *adj.* sideral, sidéreo.

**siderite** (si·dørait) *s.* MINER. siderita, siderosa.

**siderurgy** (si·dørø<sup>r</sup>ÿi) *s.* siderurgia.

**sidesaddle** (sai·dsædøl) *s.* silla para montar a mujeriegas. *2 adv.* a mujeriegas.

**sideslip** (-slip) *s.* AUTO., AVIA. patinazo o deslizamiento lateral.

**side-step (to)** *intr.* hacerse a un lado. *2 tr.* esquivar, evitar.

**sidetrack** (sai·dtræk) *s.* FERROC. vía muerta, apartadero.

**sidetrack (to)** *tr.* FERROC. desviar, apartar.

**sidewalk** (sai·dwok) *s.* acera, *vereda.

**sideward(s** (sai·dwø<sup>r</sup>dš) *adv.* de lado, hacia un lado.

**sideways** (sai·dueiš), **sidewise** (-uaiš) *adj.* dirigido hacia un lado. *2* indirecto. *3 adv.* de lado. *4* oblicuamente. *5* de soslayo, indirectamente.

**siding** (sai·aing) *s.* FERROC. apartadero, desvío. *2* adhesión a un partido, a un aopinión.

**sidle (to)** (sai·dǝl) *intr.* andar de lado, con timidez o furtivamente.

**siege** (sidẏ) *s.* sitio, asedio, cerco: ~ *artillery*, artillería de sitio.

**sienite** (sai·ønait) *s.* GEOL. sienita.

**sienna** (sie·na) *s.* tierra de Siena.

**sierra** (sie·ra) *s.* (E.U.) GEOGR. sierra.

**siesta** (sie·sta) *s.* siesta.

**sieve** (siv) *s.* cedazo, tamiz.

**sieve (to)** *tr.* TO SIFT.

**sift (to)** (sift) *tr.* cerner, tamizar. *2* espolvorear [con cedazo]. *3* separar, entresacar.

**sifter** (si·ftø<sup>r</sup>) *s.* cernedor, tamiz, harnero.

**siftings** (si·ftings) *s. pl.* cerniduras, granzas.

**sigh** (sai) *s.* suspiro.

**sigh (to)** *intr.* suspirar: *to ~ for*, suspirar por, anhelar. *2 tr.* decir suspirando. *3* lamentar.

**sight** (sait) *s.* vista, visión [sentido, órgano; acción de ver]: *to catch ~ of*, avistar, alcanzar a ver; *to come in ~*, aparecer; *at ~*, *on ~*, a primera vista; *by ~*, de vista; *eight days after ~*, COM. a ocho días vista. *2* vislumbre, atisbo. *3* vista, espectáculo. *4* aspecto. *5* visión, esperpento. *6* pínula. *7* mira, alza [de arma]. *8* opinión, parecer. *9* fam. la mar de. *10 pl.* sitios o cosas interesantes [de un lugar]. *11 adj.* visual. *12* COM. ~ *draft*, giro o letra a la vista. *13* ~ *reading*, lectura a primera vista.

**sight (to)** *tr.-intr.* ver, mirar, observar. *2 tr.* avistar, vislumbrar. *3* apuntar [un cañón, un fusil].

**sightless** (-lis) *adj.* ciego [que no ve]. *2* invisible.

**sightly** (-li) *adj.* hermoso, vistoso, agradable a la vista.

**sightseeing** (-sιing) *s.* turismo; visita de sitios o cosas interesantes.

**sigillography** (sidẏila·grafi) *s.* sigilografía.

**sigla** (sι·gla) *s.* sigla.

**sigma** (si·gma) *s.* sigma [letra griega].

**sigmoid** (sιgmoi·d) *adj.* sigmoideo.

**sign** (sain) *s.* signo, señal, seña; muestra, indicio: ~ *language*, dactilología; ~ *manual*, firma de propio puño; *to show sings of*, dar muestras de; *by signs*, por señas. *2* ASTR. signo [del Zodíaco]. *3* rastro, vestigio. *4* muestra, letrero.

**sign (to)** *tr.* signar. *2* hacer seña de. *3* firmar la cesión de. *4* contratar [a uno]. *5 intr.* hacer señas. *6* RADIO. *to ~ off*, terminar una emisión.

**signal** (si·gnal) *s.* señal [para indicar algo]; seña. *2* signo, indicio. *3 adj.* señalado, notable. *4* de señales: ~ *code*, código de señales.

**signal (to)** *tr.-intr.* señalar, indicar. ¶ Pret. y p. p.: *signal(l)ed;* ger.: *-nal(l)ing.*

**signalize (to)** (-aiš) *tr.* señalar, distinguir, particularizar.

**signalman** (-mæn) *s.* FERROC. guardavía.

**signalment** (-mønt) *s.* filiación, señas personales.

**signatory** (si·gnatori) *s.-adj.* signatario.

**signature** (-chø<sup>r</sup>) *s.* firma, rúbrica. *2* IMPR., MÚS. signatura. *3* RADIO. notas de sintonía.

**signboard** (sai·nbo<sup>r</sup>d) *s.* letrero, muestra.

**signer** (-ø<sup>r</sup>) *s.* firmante.

**signet** (si·gnit) *s.* sello, signáculo, estampilla.

**significance, -cy** (signi·fikans, -i) *s.* significación, significado. *2* importancia.

**significant** (-ant) *adj.* significante, significativo. *2* importante. *3* ARIT. significativa [cifra].

**signification** (-ei·shøn) *s.* significación, significado. *2* notificación.

**significative** (signi·fikeitiv) *adj.* significativo. *2* representativo, simbólico.

**signify (to)** (si·gnifai) *tr.* significar. *2* indicar, manifestar, notificar. *3 intr.* importar: *what does it ~?*, ¿qué importa? ¶ Pret. y p. p.: *signified.*

**signory** (si·ñøri) *s.* HIST. señoría [de Venecia, etc.].

**signpost** (sai·npoust) *s.* poste indicador.

**silage** (sai·lidẏ) *s.* forraje conservado en silo.

**silence** (sai·løns) *s.* silencio: ~ *gives consent*, quien calle otorga. *2* reserva, secreto. *3 interj.* ¡silencio!

**silence (to)** *tr.* imponer silencio, hacer callar.

**silencer** (-ø<sup>r</sup>) *s.* silenciador.

**silent** (sai·lønt) *adj.* silencioso; mudo: ~ *partner*, COM. socio comanditario; *to be ~*, callar, callarse. *2* callado, taciturno. *3* sigiloso.

**silex** (sai·leks) *s.* MINER. sílex.

**silhouette** (silu·t) *s.* silueta.

**silhouette (to)** *tr.* presentar en silueta.

**silica** (si·lika) *s.* MINER. sílice.

**silicate** (si·likeit) *s.* QUÍM. silicato.

**siliceous** (sili·shøs) *adj.* silíceo.

**silicon** (si·likan) *s.* QUÍM. silicio.

**silicosis** (silikou·sis) *s.* MED. silicosis.

**silique** (sili·k) *s.* BOT. silicua.

**silk** (silk) *s.* seda [materia, hilo, tejido]: ~ *cotton*, seda vegetal; ~ *growing*, sericultura; ~ *hat*, sombrero de copa; ~ *twist*, torzal. *2 pl.* sedería, géneros de seda.

**silken** (-øn) *adj.* de seda. *2* sedoso, sedeño. *3* suave, delicado. *4* meloso [lenguaje]. *5* lujoso, vestido de seda.

**silkman** (-mæn) *s.* sedero.

**silkworm** (-uø<sup>r</sup>m) *s.* gusano de seda.

**silky** (-i) *adj.* de seda, sedoso. *2* suave. *3* lustroso.

**sill** (sil) *s.* umbral. *2* antepecho [de ventana]. *3* ARQ. carrera, solera.

**silliness** (si·linis) *s.* tontería, simpleza.

**silly** (si·li) *adj.* tonto, necio. *2* absurdo, disparatado. *3* rústico, sencillo.

**silo** (sai·lou) *s.* silo, silero.

**silt** (silt) *s.* cieno, sedimento [de las aguas].

**silt (to)** *tr.-intr.* obstruir u obstruirse con el cieno.

**Silurian** (siliu·rian) *adj.-s.* silúrico.

**silvan** (si·lvan) *adj.-s.* SYLVAN.

**silver** (si·lvø<sup>r</sup>) *s.* plata [metal, moneda; objetos]. *2* color de plata. *3 adj.* de plata, argentado, argentino, plateado: ~ *fox*, zorro plateado; ~ *nitrate*, nitrato de plata; ~ *plating*, plateado, plateadura; ~ *wedding*, bodas de plata.

**silver (to)** *tr.* platear. *2* azogar [un espejo]. *3 intr.* volverse plateado.

**silverfish** (-fish) *s.* ENT. lepisma.

**silver-haired** *adj.* cano, de cabellos blancos.

**silvering** (-ing) *s.* baño de plata; plateado. *2* azogado [de un espejo].

**silver-plated** *adj.* plateado.

**silversmith** (-smiz) *s.* platero, orfebre.

**silverware** (-ue<sup>r</sup>) *s.* objetos de plata.

**silvery** (-i) *s.* plateado, argentino.

**silviculture** (silvikø·lchø<sup>r</sup>) *s.* silvicultura.
**simian** (si·mian) *adj.* simiesco. *2 s.* ZOOL. simio.
**similar** (si·mila<sup>r</sup>) *adj.* similar, semejante.
**simile** (si·mili) *s.* RET. símil.
**similitude** (simi·litiud) *s.* similitud. *2* símil, alegoría. *3* imagen, semejanza.
**similor** (si·milø<sup>r</sup>) *s.* similor.
**simitar** (si·mita<sup>r</sup>) *s.* cimitarra.
**simmer (to)** (si·mø<sup>r</sup>) *tr.* hacer cocer a fuego lento. *2 intr.* hervir con poco fuego; estar a punto de hervir. *3* fig. hervir [de ira, etc.].
**simoniac** (simou·niæk) *adj.-s.* simoníaco.
**simoom** (simu·m), **simoon** (-n) *s.* simún [viento].
**simper** (si·mpø<sup>r</sup>) *s.* sonrisa boba o afectada.
**simper (to)** *intr.* sonreír tontamente o con afectación.
**simple** (si·mpøl) *adj.* simple. *2* mero. *3* sencillo. *4* llano [accesible, sin presunción]. *5* humilde, plebeyo. *6* insignificante. *7* ingenuo. *8* mentecato. *9* MAT. de primer grado [ecuación]; incompleja [fracción]. *10 s.* simple, simplón. *11* cosa o idea simple. *12* pers. de humilde condición.
**simple-hearted** *adj.* sencillo, franco, sincero.
**simple-minded** *adj.* sencillo, cándido. *2* tonto.
**simpleton** (-tøn) *s.* simplón, bobo, papanatas.
**simplicity** (simpli·siti) *s.* simplicidad. *2* sencillez. *3* llaneza. *4* ingenuidad. *5* simpleza, bobería.
**simplification** (simplifikei·shøn) *s.* simplificación.
**simplify (to)** (si·mplifai) *tr.* simplificar. ¶ Pret. y p. p.: *simplified.*
**simulacrum** (simiulei·krøm), *pl.* -**cra** (-kra) *s.* simulacro.
**simulate (to)** (si·miuleit) *tr.* simular; imitar.
**simulation** (simiulei·shøn) *s.* simulación; imitación.
**simulator** (si·miuleitø<sup>r</sup>) *s.* simulador.
**simultaneity** (simøltanɪ·iti) *s.* simultaneidad.
**simultaneous** (simøltei·niøs) *adj.* simultáneo.
**sin** (sin) *s.* pecado: ~ *offering*, sacrificio expiatorio.
**sin (to)** *intr.* pecar. ¶ Pret. y p. p.: *sinned*; ger.: -*nning.*
**sinapism** (si·napišm) *s.* sinapismo.
**since** (sins) *adv.* desde, desde entonces; ha, hace tiempo: ~ *when?*, ¿desde cuándo?; *long* ~, hace mucho tiempo. *2 prep.* desde, después de. *3 conj.* desde que, después que. *4* ya que, puesto que, en vista de.
**sincere** (sinsɪ·<sup>r</sup>) *adj.* sincero. *2* verdadero, real.
**sincereness** (sinsɪ·<sup>r</sup>nis), **sincerity** (sinse·riti) *s.* sinceridad, franqueza.
**sinciput** (si·nsipøt) ANAT. coronilla.
**sine** (sain) *s.* MAT. seno.
**sinecure** (sai·nikiu<sup>r</sup>) *s.* sinecura, prebenda. *2* ECLES. beneficio simple.
**sinew** (si·niu) *s.* ANAT. tendón. *2* fuerza muscular. *3* energía, fibra, nervio, fortaleza.
**sinew (to)** *tr.* fortalecer.
**sinewy** (-i) *adj.* nervioso, nervudo. *2* fuerte, vigoroso.
**sinful** (si·nful) *adj.* pecador, pecaminoso.
**sing (to)** (sing) *tr.-intr.* cantar: *to* ~ *out*, vocear; *to* ~ *out of tune*, desafinar; *to* ~ *to sleep*, arrullar, adormecer. *2 intr.* murmurar [el agua]; silbar [un proyectil, el viento]; zumbar [los oídos]. ¶ Pret.: *sang* o *sung*; p. p.: *sung.*
**singe (to)** (sindÿ) *tr.* chamuscar, socarrar, sollamar. *2* fig. perjudicar. ¶ Ger.: *singeing.*
**singeing** (-ing) *s.* chamusco, socarra.
**singer** (-gø<sup>r</sup>) *s.* cantante, cantor, cantatriz. *2* pájaro cantor.

**Singhalese** (singali·š) *adj.-s.* cingalés.
**singing bird** (si·nging) *s.* pájaro cantor.
**singing master** *s.* maestro de canto.
**single** (si·ngøl) *adj.* único: *not a* ~, ni un solo. *2* célibe, de celibato: ~ *man*, soltero; ~ *life*, vida de celibato. *3* sencillo, simple: COM. ~ *entry*, partida simple. *4* de una sola pieza, movimiento, etc. *5* individual. *6* honrado, sincero. *7* ~ *combat*, singular combate. *8* ~ *file*, hilera, fila india. *9 s. pl.* TENIS. individuales.
**single (to)** *tr.* singularizar, distinguir; designar especialmente; escoger. | gralte. con *out* o *from.*
**single-acting** *adj.* MEC. de simple efecto.
**single-eyed** *adj.* tuerto. *2* perspicaz. *3* sincero.
**single-handed** *adj.* solo, sin ayuda. *2* con una sola mano.
**single-hearted** *adj.* sencillo de corazón.
**single-minded** *adj.* sencillo, sin doblez. *2* de un solo propósito o idea.
**single-phase** *adj.* ELECT. monofásico.
**single-pole** *adj.* ELECT. unipolar.
**singlet** (si·nglit) *s.* camiseta [prenda].
**singleton** (si·ngøltøn) *s.* BRIDGE única carta de un palo.
**singsong** (si·nsong) *s.* sonsonete, tonillo. *2* (Ingl.) fam. reunión para cantar. *3 adj.* monótono.
**singular** (si·ngiula<sup>r</sup>) *adj.* singular. *2* curioso, estrafalario. *3* individual. *4 s.* GRAM. número singular.
**singularity** (singiulæ·riti) *s.* singularidad. *2* individualidad. *3* peculiaridad.
**singularize (to)** (si·ngiularaiš) *tr.* singularizar, distinguir. *2* particularizar, individualizar.
**Sinic** (si·nik) *adj.-s.* sínico, chino, chinesco.
**sinister** (si·nistø<sup>r</sup>) *adj.* siniestro, izquierdo. *2* siniestro, avieso, funesto.
**sink** (sink) *s.* sumidero, sentina, albañal. *2* fregadero. *3* depresión, hoyo.
**sink (to)** *tr.* hundir, sumir, sumergir, echar a pique. *2* ahondar, excavar, grabar; abrir [un pozo]. *3* bajar [la voz, la mano, etc.]. *5* hundir, arruinar. *6* hundir, clavar. *7* deprimir, abatir. *8* ignorar, olvidar. *9 intr.* hundirse, sumergirse; irse a pique. *10* bajar [descender, disminuir]. *11* desaparecer. *12* decaer, declinar. *13* caer; dejarse caer. *14* abatirse. *15* engolfarse, embeberse. *16* penetrar. *17* grabarse [en la memoria]. *18* ARQ. asentarse. *19 to* ~ *down*, bajar; penetrar profundamente. ¶ Pret.: *sank* o *sunk*; p. p.: *sunk* o *sunken.*
**sinker** (si·nkø<sup>r</sup>) *s.* plomo [de caña de pescar]. *2* grabador en hueco.
**sinking fund** (-ing) *s.* COM. fondo de amortización.
**sinless** (si·nlis) *adj.* puro, libre de pecado.
**sinner** (si·nø<sup>r</sup>) *s.* pecador, pecadora.
**Sinology** (saina·løÿi) *s.* sinología.
**sinuate** (si·niueit) *adj.* sinuoso. *2* BOT. festoneado.
**sinuosity** (siniua·siti) *s.* sinuosidad, tortuosidad.
**sinuous** (si·niuøs) *adj.* sinuoso, tortuoso.
**sinus** (sai·nøs) *s.* seno [curva]. *2* ZOOL., ANAT., GEOGR. seno.
**sinusitis** (-aitis) *s.* MED. sinusitis.
**sinusoid** (-oid) *s.* GEOM. sinusoide.
**sip** (sip) *s.* sorbo.
**sip (to)** *tr.-intr.* beber a sorbos. ¶ Pret. y p. p.: *sipped*; ger.: -*pping.*
**siphon** (sai·føn) *s.* FÍS., ZOOL. sifón.
**siphon (to)** *tr.* vaciar con sifón. *2 intr.* pasar por un sifón.
**sippet** (si·pit) *s.* sopita, tostadita [que se moja].
**sir** (sø<sup>r</sup>) *s.* señor [término de cortesía]. *2* (Ingl.) tra-

tamiento que se antepone al nombre de pila de un caballero o baronet.

**sire** (sair) *s.* señor [tratamiento del soberano]. *2* progenitor. *3* animal padre, semental.

**siren** (sai·røn) *s.* MIT, sirena. *2* buena cantatriz. *3* mujer seductora. *4* sirena [pito].

**sirenian** (sairi·nian) *adj.-s.* ZOOL. sirenio.

**Sirian** (si·rian) *adj.-s.* siríaco, sirio.

**Sirius** (si·riøs) *s.* ASTR. Sirio.

**sirloin** (sø·rloin) *s.* solomillo, solomo.

**sirocco** (sira·kou) *s.* siroco.

**sirup** (si·røp) *s.* SYRUP.

**sisal** (si·sal) *s.* sisal, pita.

**sister** (si·stør) *s.* hermana. *2* sor, monja. *3* enfermera jefe; enfermera. *4* adj. ~ *language*, lengua hermana.

**sisterhood** (-jud) *s.* hermandad [parentesco entre hermanas]. *2* conjunto de hermanas. *3* cofradía de mujeres.

**sister-in-law** *s.* hermana política, cuñada.

**Sistine** (si·stin) *adj.* sixtino.

**sistrum** (si·strøm) *s.* MÚS. sistro.

**sit (to)** (sit) *tr.* sentar, asentar [colocar en asiento]. *2* montar [un caballo]. *3 to* ~ *out,* aguantar hasta el fin de; estar sin tomar parte en; quedarse más tiempo que [otro]. *4 intr.* sentarse, estar sentado. *5* posarse o empollar [las aves]. *6* estar, permanecer. *7* tener asiento [en un cuerpo o tribunal]; actuar [un juez]. *8* descansar, pesar [sobre]. *9* sentar, caer [bien o mal]. *10 to* ~ *down,* sentarse; establecerse; acampar. *11 to* ~ *for,* representar [un distrito] en el Parlamento; posar, servir de modelo para. *12 to* ~ *in judgement,* querer juzgar a los demás, criticar. *13 to* ~ *on* o *upon,* deliberar sobre; juzgar; fam. hacer callar; poner en su lugar; desairar. *14 to* ~ *still,* estarse quieto. *15 to* ~ *up,* estar bien sentado; incorporarse [el que estaba echado]; velar, estar levantado. ¶ Pret. y p. p.: *sat;* ger.: *sitting.*

**sit-down strike** *s.* huelga de brazos caídos.

**site** (sait) *s.* sitio, escenario [de algo]. *2* asiento, situación [de una población, edificio, etc.].

**sitter** (si·tør) *s.* el que está sentado. *2* el que posa o se hace retratar. *3* ave que empolla.

**sitting** (si·ting) *s.* acción de sentarse o estar sentado. *2* sentada, asentada: *at one* ~, de una sentada. *3* sesión. *4* empolladura; pollazón. *5 adj.* sentado. *6* para sentarse: ~ *room,* sala, estancia. *7* BOT. sésil.

**situate** (si·chueit) *adj.* situado.

**situation** (sichuei·shøn) *s.* situación. *2* posición, ubicación. *3* colocación, empleo.

**sitz bath** (sits) *s.* baño de asiento.

**six** (siks) *adj.-s.* seis: ~ *o'clock,* las seis.

**sixfold** (-fould) *adj.* séxtuplo. *2 adv.* seis veces.

**sixpence** (-pøns) *s.* seis peniques.

**sixpenny** (-peni) *adj.* de a seis peniques. *2* mezquino, de poco valor.

**sixteen** (-ti·n) *adj.-s.* dieciséis.

**sixteenth** (-tinz) *adj.-s.* decimosexto, dieciseisavo. *2* dieciséis [día].

**sixth** (-z) *adj.-s.* sexto. *2* seis [día]. *3 s.* MÚS. sexta.

**sixtieth** (-tiiz) *adj.-s.* sexagésimo.

**sixty** (-ti) *adj.-s.* sesenta.

**sizable** (sai·sabøl) *adj.* regular; de tamaño proporcionado.

**sizar** (sai·sar) *s.* (Ingl.) becario [estudiante].

**size** (saiš) *s.* medida, tamaño, dimensiones. *2* estatura, talla. *3* número [de calzado, etc.]; talla

[de vestido]; calibre [de un tubo, etc.]. *4* sisa, cola, goma, apresto.

**size (to)** *tr.* disponer, clasificar según tamaño. *2* medir el tamaño de. *3* apreciar, avaluar. *4* ajustar a un tamaño, medida, etc. *5* encolar, sisar, aprestar.

**sizzle** (si·šøl) *s.* sonido chirriante, chisporroteo.

**sizzle (to)** *intr.* chirriar [al freírse, etc.].

**skald** (skøld) *s.* escaldo.

**skate** (skeit) *s.* patín [para los pies]. *2* patinaje.

**skate (to)** *intr.* patinar [sobre patines]: *to* ~ *on thin ice,* fig. buscar el peligro.

**skater** (-ør) *s.* patinador.

**skating** (-ing) *s.* patinaje: ~ *ring,* pista de patinaje.

**skedaddle (to)** (sikidæ·døl) *intr.* fam. huir a la desbandada.

**skein** (skein) *s.* madeja, cadejo, capillejo.

**skeletal** (ske·løtal) *adj.* de esqueleto.

**skeleton** (ske·løtøn) *s.* esqueleto [osamenta; armazón]: ~ *in the cupboard, family* ~, fig. hecho deshonroso o humillante que se oculta a los extraños. *2* esbozo, esquema. *3 adj.* en esqueleto, en armazón. *4* ~ *key,* llave maestra.

**skeptic** (ske·ptik) *adj.-s.* escéptico.

**skepticism** (ske·ptisišm) *s.* escepticismo.

**sketch** (skech) *s.* boceto, esbozo, apunte, croquis. *2* TEAT., MÚS. pieza corta.

**sketch (to)** *tr.* esbozar, bosquejar, diseñar, hacer un croquis de. *2 intr.* hacer apuntes o bosquejos.

**sketchy** (-i) *adj.* abocetado. *2* ligero, incompleto, fragmentario.

**skew** (skiu·) *adj.* oblicuo, inclinado, sesgado. *2* oblicuidad, esviaje.

**skew (to)** *tr.* sesgar, poner de través. *2* torcer, tergiversar. *3 intr.* oblicuar; desviarse, girar.

**skewback** (-bæk) *s.* ARQ. salmer.

**skewer** (-ør) *s.* COC. brocheta. *2* HIL. huso.

**skewer (to)** *tr.* espetar, clavar.

**ski** (ski·) *s.* esquí.

**ski (to)** *intr.* esquiar.

**skid** (skid) *s.* madero, polín, rodillo. *2* calzo. *3* varadera. *4* AVIA. patín. *5* galga, freno. *6* deslizamiento, patinazo [de ruedas]: ~ *chain,* AUTO. cadena para impedir el deslizamiento.

**skid (to)** *tr.* hacer deslizar sobre maderos, polines, etc. *2* sostener con calzos. *3* proveer de varaderas. *4 intr.* patinar [una rueda]. ¶ Pret. y p. p.: *skidded;* ger.: *-dding.*

**skier** (ski·ør) *s.* esquiador.

**skiff** (skif) *s.* esquife, botecillo.

**skiff (to)** *intr.* navegar en esquife.

**skilful** (ski·lful) *adj.* diestro, hábil; experto, ducho.

**skill** (skil) *s.* habilidad, destreza, pericia, maña. *3* arte, ciencia.

**skilled** (-d) *adj.* práctico, experimentado; hábil, experto.

**skil(l)less** (-lis) *adj.* inexperto.

**skim** (skim) *s.* acción de espumar o desnatar. *2* espuma, nata. *3 adj.* desnatada [leche].

**skim (to)** *tr.* espumar, desnatar. *2* examinar rápida o superficialmente. *3* rasar, rozar [tocar ligeramente]. *4 intr.* cubrirse de espuma o nata. ¶ Pret. y p. p.: *skimmed;* ger.: *-mming.*

**skimmer** (-ør) *s.* espumadera.

**skimp (to)** (skimp) *tr.* escatimar. *2* chapucear. *3* intr. tacañear. *4* trabajar con poco cuidado.

**skin** (skin) *s.* piel, cutis, pellejo [de pers.]: *to be only* ~ *and bone,* estar en los huesos; *to save one's* ~, salvar el pellejo; *by the* ~ *of one's teeth,* por un pelo. *2* piel [de animal]. *3* odre. *4* BOT. piel, cáscara, hollejo. *5* telilla, cutícula, peli-

cula. 6 fam. avaro. 7 fam. tramposo. 8 ~ *game,* fullería.
**skin (to)** *tr.* desollar, despellejar. 2 fig. desplumar. 3 pelar, mondar. 4 abrir bien [los ojos]. 5 cubrir de piel. 6 *intr.* pelarse. 7 cubrirse de piel o tegumento: *to ~ over,* cicatrizarse.
**skin-deep** *adj.* superficial.
**skinflint** (-flint) *s.* avaro, vampiro.
**skink** (-k) *s.* ZOOL. escinco.
**skinner** (-øʳ) *s.* pellejero. 2 desollador. 3 petardista, estafador.
**skinniness** (-inis) *s.* flacura.
**skinny** (-i) *adj.* membranoso. 2 flaco, descarnado. 3 tacaño.
**skip** (skip) *s.* salto, brinco. 2 salto, omisión.
**skip (to)** *intr.* saltar, brincar. 2 botar, rebotar. 3 fam. largarse.ʾ4 *tr.* saltar [salvar de un salto]. 5 escaparse de. 6 *intr.-tr. to skip* o *to ~ over,* saltar, pasar por alto. ¶ Pret. y p. p.: *skipped;* ger.: *-pping.*
**skipper** (-øʳ) *s.* saltador. 2 gusanillo del queso. 3 patrón, capitán [de barco]. 4 DEP. capitán.
**skipping rope** (-ing) *s.* comba [para saltar].
**skirmish** (skøˑʳmish) *s.* escaramuza.
**skirmish (to)** *intr.* escaramuzar.
**skirmisher** (-øʳ) *s.* escaramuzador.
**skirt** (skøʳt) *s.* falda, saya; enaguas, refajo. 2 faldón [de una prenda; de la silla de montar]. 3 orilla, margen: *skirts of a town,* suburbios, alrededores, de una población.
**skirt (to)** *tr.-intr.* bordear, ladear, rodear, circundar. 2 *tr.* evitar, bordear [el peligro].
**skirting board** (-ing) *s.* zócalo, rodapié.
**skit** (skit) *s.* paso cómico; cuento satírico; parodia, burla, sátira.
**skitter (to)** (-øʳ) *intr.* ir rozando el agua [un ave marina]. 2 pescar haciendo deslizar el anzuelo sobre el agua.
**skittish** (-ish) *tr.* asustadizo [caballo]. 2 tímido. 3 retozón, frívolo, caprichoso.
**skittle** (ski·tøl) *s.* bolo [para jugar]. 2 *pl.* juego de bolos.
**skittle (to)** *intr.* jugar a los bolos.
**skua** (skiu·*a*) *s.* ORN. especie de gaviota.
**skulk (to)** (skølk) *intr.* esconderse, acechar sin ser visto, moverse furtivamente. 2 *tr.-intr.* huir del trabajo, etc.
**skull** (skøl) *s.* cráneo; calavera. 2 ANAT. coronilla. 3 cabeza, cerebro.
**skullcap** (-kæp) *s.* casquete, gorro.
**skunk** (skønk) *s.* ZOOL. mofeta; zorrillo, mapurite. 2 fig. canalla.
**sky** (skai) *s.* cielo [firmamento, atmósfera; mansión celestial]: *out of a clear ~,* inesperadamente, de repente. 2 ~ *blue,* color azul celeste.
**sky-blue** *adj.* azul celeste.
**skyey** (-i) *adj.* celeste, etéreo.
**skylark** (-laʳk) *s.* ORN. alondra.
**skylark (to)** *intr.* retozar, triscar, juguetear.
**skylight** (-lait) *s.* luz del cielo. 2 claraboya, lumbrera, tragaluz.
**skyline** (-lain) *s.* línea del horizonte; línea de los edificios, árboles, etc., contra el cielo.
**skyrocket** (-rakit) *s.* cohete volador.
**skyrocket (to)** *intr.* fam. subir como un cohete.
**skysail** (-seil) *s.* MAR. periquito.
**skyscraper** (skreipøʳ) *s.* rascacielos.
**skyward (s** (uaʳd(ś) *adv.* hacia el cielo. 2 *adj.* dirigido hacia el cielo.
**slab** (slæb) *s.* tabla, plancha, losa, laja. 2 loncha, tajada. 3 costero [de tronco].

**slabber (to)** (slæ·bøʳ) *intr.* babear, salivar.
**slack** (slæk) *adj.* flojo, laxo. 2 débil, poco firme. 3 lento, tardo. 4 negligente, remiso. 5 COM. encalmado. 6 ~ *water,* agua mansa; repunte de la marea. 7 *s.* seno [de un cabo]. 8 flojedad; inactividad, calma. 9 cisco [carbón]. 10 *pl.* pantalones anchos.
**slack (to)** *tr.* aflojar, relajar. 2 reducir, moderar. 3 apagar [la cal]. 4 *intr.* aflojar, amainar, ceder, cejar. 5 flojear. 6 huir del trabajo, remolonear. 7 *to ~ up,* reducir la marcha.
**slacken (to)** *tr.* moderar, retardar, hacer más lento. 2 aflojar. 3 *intr.* ser lento, remiso o negligente.
**slacker** (-køʳ) *s.* perezoso; remolón.
**slag** (-læg) *s.* escoria.
**slain** (slein) *p. p.* de TO SLAY.
**slake (to)** (sleik) *tr.* apagar [la sed, la cal, etc.]. 2 mojar, refrescar. 3 moderar, calmar. 4 *intr.* apagarse [la cal]. 5 desmenuzarse.
**slam** (slæm) *s.* golpe, portazo. 2 BRIDGE slam, bola.
**slam (to)** *tr.* cerrar de golpe; poner, dejar, etc., dando un golpe: *to ~ the door,* dar un portazo. 2 *tr.-intr.* BRIDGE hacer slam. 3 *intr.* cerrarse con estrépito. 4 trabajar con ruido. ¶ Pret. y p. p.: *slammed;* ger.: *-mming.*
**slander** (slæ·ndøʳ) *s.* calumnia, difamación.
**slander (to)** *tr.* calumniar, difamar, denigrar.
**slanderous** (-øs) *adj.* calumniador, difamador.
**slang** (slæng) *s.* lenguaje popular. 2 jerga, argot.
**slang (to)** *tr.* insultar, maltratar de palabra.
**slangy** (-i) *adj.* de argot.
**slant** (slænt) *s.* inclinación, oblicuidad; declive. 2 parecer, punto de vista. 3 *adj.* oblicuo, inclinado, en declive.
**slant (to)** *tr.* sesgar, inclinar. 2 *intr.* inclinarse, sesgarse.
**slanting** (-ing) *adj.-s.* SLANT.
**slap** (slæp) *s.* palmada, manotazo, bofetón. 2 insulto, desaire. 3 *adv.* de sopetón, directamente.
**slap (to)** *tr.* pegar, abofetear, dar una palmada, un manotazo. 2 poner, meter, etc., con prisa o violencia. ¶ Pret. y p. p.: *slapped;* ger.: *-pping.*
**slapdash** (-dæsh) *adj.* precipitado, atropellado. 2 *s.* cosa hecha atropelladamente. 3 *adv.* atropelladamente, impetuosamente.
**slash** (slash) *s.* cuchillada, tajo. 2 cuchillada [en un vestido]. 3 latigazo.
**slash (to)** *tr.* acuchillar, dar un tajo a; hacer un corte en. 2 fustigar. 3 hacer restallar [un látigo]. 4 rebajar considerablemente [sueldos, precios, etc.].
**slat** (slæt) *s.* tablilla, listón.
**slate** (sleit) *s.* pizarra, esquisto. 2 pizarra [para escribir]: ~ *pencil,* pizarrín. 4 (E.U.) lista de candidatos; programa de partido. 5 pizarra [para techar], teja plana. 6 color de pizarra.
**slate (to)** *tr.* empizarrar, cubrir. 2 POL. (E.U.) poner en lista o programa. 3 criticar, fustigar.
**slater** (-øʳ) *s.* pizarrero. 2 crítico severo.
**slattern** (slæ·tøʳn) *adj.* descuidado, desaliñado. 2 *s.* mujer desaseada, pazpuerca.
**slaty** (slei·ti) *adj.* pizarreño, esquistoso.
**slaughter** (slo·tøʳ) *s.* muerte, matanza, mortandad. 2 sacrificio [de reses].
**slaughter (to)** *tr.* matar. 2 sacrificar [reses].
**slaughterer** (-øʳ) *s.* asesino. 2 matarife.
**slaughterhouse** (slo·tøʳjaus) *s.* matadero.
**Slav** (slæ·v) *adj.-s.* eslavo.
**slave** (sleiv) *s.* esclavo, esclava: ~ *trade,* trata de esclavos.

**slave (to)** *intr.* trabajar como esclavo. *2 tr.* esclavizar.

**slaveholder** (sleiˑvjouldøʳ) *s.* dueño de esclavos.

**1) slaver** (slæˑvøʳ) *s.* mercader de esclavos; negrero. *2* buque negrero.

**2) slaver** (slæˑvøʳ) *s.* baba. *2* fig. adulación.

**slaver (to)** *intr.* babear. *2 tr.* babosear.

**slavery** (sleiˑvøri) *s.* esclavitud, servidumbre. *2* los esclavos.

**Slavic** (slæˑvik) *adj.* eslavo.

**slavish** (sleiˑvish) *adj.* servil. *2* bajo, abyecto. *3* esclavizado. *4* tiránico, opresivo.

**Slavism** (slaˑvišm) *s.* eslavismo.

**Slavonian** (slavouˑnian) *adj.-s.* esclavonio.

**slay** (slei) *s.* SLEY.

**slay (to)** *tr.* matar [quitar la vida]. ¶ Pret.: *slew;* p. p.: *slain.*

**slayer** (-øʳ) *s.* matador, asesino.

**sleazy** (slɪˑši) *adj.* ligero, tenue, delgado.

**sled** (sled) *s.* narria, rastra, trineo.

**sled (to)** *tr.* transportar en rastra o trineo.

**sledge** (sledȳ) *s.* trineo, rastra, narria. *2* *sledge* o ~ *hammer,* macho [martillo], acotillo.

**sledge (to)** *tr.-intr.* transportar o viajar en trineo. *2 tr.* golpear, martillar.

**sleek** (slɪk) *adj.* liso, bruñido. *2* zalamero, artero.

**sleek (to)** *tr.* pulir, alisar, asear.

**sleeky** (slɪˑki) *adj.* liso, lustroso. *2* suave, taimado.

**sleep** (slɪp) *s.* sueño [acto o gana de dormir]; descanso, muerte.

**sleep (to)** *intr.* dormir; *to* ~ *like a top,* dormir como un lirón; *to* ~ *on* o *upon,* consultar con la almohada; *to* ~ *away* o *on,* seguir durmiendo. *2 tr. to* ~ *away* o *out,* pasar [un tiempo durmiendo]. *3 to be slept in,* haber sido ocupada [una cama]. ¶ Pret. y p. p.: *slept.*

**sleeper** (-øʳ) *s.* durmiente [pers.]. *2* durmiente, vigueta; traviesa [de vía férrea]. *5* FERROC. coche cama. *6* ZOOL. lirón.

**sleepiness** (-inis) *s.* somnolencia, sueño.

**sleeping** (-ing) *adj.* durmiente, dormido: ~ *partner,* COM. socio comanditario. *2* de dormir, que hace dormir: ~ *bag,* saco de dormir; ~ *car,* coche cama; ~ *sickness,* MED. enfermedad del sueño.

**sleepless** (-lis) *adj.* insomne, desvelado. *2* sin dormir.

**sleeplessness** (-lisnis) *s.* insomnio.

**sleepwalker** (-wokøʳ) *s.* sonámbulo.

**sleepy** (-i) *adj.* soñoliento.

**sleet** (slɪt) *s.* cellisca.

**sleet (to)** *intr.* cellisquear.

**sleeve** (slɪv) *s.* manga [de vestido]: *to laugh in,* o *up, one's* ~, reírse con disimulo, para sus adentros; *up one's* ~, en reserva. *2* MEC. manguito. *3* camisa [incandescente].

**sleeveless** (slɪˑvlis) *adj.* sin mangas.

**sleigh** (sleiˑ) *s.* trineo: ~ *bell,* cascabel.

**sleigh (to)** *tr.-intr.* viajar o transportar en trineo.

**sleight** (slait) *s.* destreza, habilidad. *2* agilidad. *3* ardid, artificio. *4* ~ *of hand,* juego de manos, prestidigitación.

**slender** (sleˑndøʳ) *adj.* delgado, fino, esbelto. *2* leve, baladí. *3* corto, escaso. *4* frugal.

**slept** (slept) *pret.* y *p. p.* de TO SLEEP.

**sleuth** (sliuz) *s.* sabueso. *2* (E.U.) detective.

**sleuthhound** (-jaund) *s.* sabueso.

**slew** (sliu) *pret.* de TO SLAY.

**sley** (slei) *s.* TEJ. peine.

**slice** (slais) *s.* rebanada, lonja, rodaja. *2* COC. pala, estrelladera.

**slice (to)** *tr.* rebanar. *2* tajar, cortar, dividir.

**slick** (slik) *adj.* fam. diestro, mañoso. *2* astuto, meloso. *3* liso, lustroso. *4* s. parte lisa o lustrosa; lugar aceitoso en el agua. *5* adv. astutamente. *6* directamente, completamente.

**slick (to)** *tr.* alisar, pulir. *2* *intr.* componerse, acicalarse. | Gralte. con *up.*

**slicker** (-øʳ) *s.* timador, embaucador.

**slide** (slaid) *s.* resbalamiento, deslizamiento. *2* corrimiento de tierras. *3* MIN. falla. *4* resbaladero, declive. *5* MEC. corredera, ranura; ~ *rest,* soporte de corredera. *6* ÓPT. placa para proyectar; portaobjetos [de microscopio]. *7* MÚS. adorno en escala. *8* adj. que se desliza: ~ *bolt,* pestillo, pasador; ~ *caliper,* pie de rey; ~ *rule,* regla de cálculo; ~ *trombon,* trombón de varas; ~ *valve,* corredera [de máquinas de vapor].

**slide (to)** *intr.* resbalar, deslizarse. *2* escurrirse, escabullirse. *3* cometer un desliz. *4 to let* ~, dejar correr. *5 tr.* hacer deslizar. ¶ Pret.: *slid;* p. p.: *slid* o *slidden;* ger.: *slidding.*

**slider** (-øʳ) *s.* deslizador. *2* MEC. corredera.

**sliding** (-ing) *adj.* corredizo; variable, móvil: ~ *knot,* nudo, corredizo; ~ *scale,* escala móvil [de salarios, etc.]; regla de cálculo.

**slight** (slait) *adj.* ligero, leve. *2* pequeño, insignificante, escaso. *3* delgado, frágil, delicado. *4* s. desaire, desatención, feo, desprecio.

**slight (to)** *tr.* despreciar, no hacer caso de. *2* desairar, desdeñar. *3* desatender, descuidar.

**slighting** (-ing) *s.* desprecio. *2* adj. despreciativo.

**slim** (slim) *adj.* delgado, esbelto. *2* leve, pequeño. *3* fútil, baladí. *4* hábil, astuto.

**slime** (slaim) *s.* limo, légamo. *2* babaza, viscosidad.

**slime (to)** *tr.* enlegamar. *2* ensuciar.

**sling** (sling) *s.* honda. *2* hondazo, golpe. *3* braga, eslinga, balso. *4* CIR. cabestrillo. *5* portafusil; correa para llevar algo a la espalda. *6 pl.* MAR. grátil [de verga].

**sling (to)** *tr.* tirar con honda. *2* lanzar, arrojar. *3* embragar, eslingar, suspender. *4* poner en cabestrillo. ¶ Pret. y p. p.: *slung.*

**slinger** (-øʳ) *s.* hondero.

**slingshot** (-shat) *s.* tirador [de goma].

**slink (to)** (slink) *intr.* andar furtivamente: *to* ~ *away,* escurrirse. *2 tr.-intr.* VET. abortar. ¶ Pret. y p. p.: *slunk.*

**slip** (slip) *s.* resbalón, deslizamiento. *2* desliz, tropiezo, error: ~ *of pean,* lapsus cálami; ~ *of tongue,* lapsus linguae. *2* huida, esquinazo: *to give one the* ~, escaparse de uno, darle esquinazo. *4* AGR. esqueje, estaca. *5* tira [trozo estrecho]; trozo de papel. *6* fig. muchacho o muchacha pequeños de cuerpo. *7* funda [de mueble o almohada]. *8* combinación [de mujer]; delantal [de niño]; mono [de trabajo]. *9* slip [calzoncillos]. *10* grada [de astillero]. *11* GEOL. falla.

*12 adj.* que se desliza: ~ *knot,* nudo corredizo; ~ *cover,* sobrecubierta [de libro].

**slip (to)** *intr.* resbalar, deslizarse, escurrirse, salir de su sitio. *2* escapar; pasar sin ser notado. *3* borrarse de la memoria. *4* tener un desliz, equivocarse. *5 to* ~ *away* o *off,* escabullirse, huir, deslizarse. *6 to* ~ *by,* pasar inadvertido, pasar rápidamente. *7 to let* ~, dejar escapar.

*8 tr.* deslizar, meter, introducir. *9* escaparse de o a. *10* dejar escapar, soltar. *11* saltarse, pasar por alto. *12* soltar, desatar; desenganchar. *13* dislocarse [un hueso]. *14 to* ~ *off,* quitarse de encima; quitarse [una prenda] precipitadamente. *15 to ~ on*, poner o ponerse [una prenda] precipitadamente.

¶ Pret. y p. p.: *slipped;* ger.: *-pping.*

**slipcase** (-keis) *s.* estuche [para libros].

**slipknot** (sli·pno) *s.* lazo o nudo corredizo.

**slip-on** *s.* prenda de vestir que se pone por la cabeza o que se pone y quita con facilidad.

**slipper** (sli·pøʳ) *s.* zapatilla, babucha.

**slippered** (-øʳd) *adj.* con zapatillas.

**slippery** (-i) *adj.* resbaladizo. *2* escurridizo, huidizo. *3* astuto.

**slipshod** (sli·pshad) *adj.* en chancletas. *2* descuidado, desaliñado.

**slipslop** (-lap) *s.* aguachirle.

**slip-up** *s.* error, equivocación.

**slit** (slit) *s.* abertura, estrecha, corte, hendedura.

**slit (to)** *tr.* hender, cortar, dividir. ¶ Pret. y p. p.: *slit;* ger.: *-tting.*

**slither (to)** (sli·deʳ) *intr.* bajar, rodar, deslizarse, arrastrarse.

**sliver** (sli·vøʳ) *s.* raja, astilla, tira, brizna. *2* HIL. mecha, cinta.

**sliver (to)** *tr.* rajar, astillar, cortar en tiras o rodajas. *2* romperse, astillarse.

**slobber** (sla·bøʳ) *s.* baba. *2* fig. sensiblería.

**slobber (to)** *intr.* babear. *2 tr.* babosear. *3* estropear [un trabajo].

**sloe** (slou·) *s.* BOT. endrino. *2* endrina.

**slog** (slag) *s.* golpe, porrazo.

**slog (to)** *tr.* aporrear. *2 intr.* afanarse.

**slogan** (slou·gan) *s.* grito de combate. *2* eslogan, lema.

**sloop** (slup) *s.* MAR. balandra: *~ of war*, corbeta.

**slop** (slap) *s.* lodo blando; líquido derramado; suciedad líquida. *2* lavazas, agua sucia. *3* aguachirle. *4* vestido holgado. *5* ropa hecha de calidad inferior.

**slop (to)** *tr.* derramar [un líquido]; ensuciar, enlodar. *2 intr.* derramarse. *3 to ~ over*, estar demasiado efusivo. ¶ Pret. y p. p.: *slopped;* ger.: *-pping.*

**slope** (sloup) *s.* cuesta, pendiente, declive, inclinación. *2* falda, ladera. *3* GEOGR. vertiente.

**slope (to)** *intr.* inclinarse, estar en declive. *2 tr.* inclinar, sesgar.

**sloping** (-ing) *adj.* inclinado, pendiente. *2* deprimida [frente].

**sloppy** (sla·pi) *adj.* sucio, mojado, lodoso. *2* desaseado. *3* chapucero. *4* mal hecho [vestido].

**slosh** (slash) *s.* lodo, fango, aguachirle.

**slosh (to)** *intr.* andar chapoteando. *2* chapotear [el agua, etc.].

**slot** (slat) *s.* hendedura, abertura: *~ machine*, tragaperras. *2* pista, rastro.

**slot (to)** *tr.* hacer una hendedura en. *2* pasar por una hendedura.

**sloth** (sloz) *s.* pereza, galbana. *2* ZOOL. perezoso.

**slothful** (slo·zful) *adj.* perezoso.

**slouch** (slauch) *s.* pers. desmañada, perezosa. *2* actitud floja del cuerpo. *3* inclinación, caída. *4 adj.* caído, gacho.

**slouch (to)** *tr.* poner gacho. *2* bajar [el ala del sombrero]. *3 intr.* caer, estar gacho. *4* tomar una actitud floja; andar con la cabeza baja.

**slough** (slau·) *s.* cenagal. *2* (sliu·) (E.U.) pantano, marjal. *3* (sløf) piel que muda la serpiente. *4* MED. costra.

**slough (to)** *tr.* mudar, soltar [la piel, una costra, etc.]. *2 intr.* MED. formar costra. *3* desprenderse, caerse.

**sloughy** (slau·i) *adj.* fangoso, pantanoso. *2* (slø·fi) MED. que forma costra.

**Slovak** (slou·væk) *adj.-s.* eslovaco.

**sloven** (slø·vøn) *adj.* desaseado. *2* inculto. *3 s.* pers. desaseada.

**Slovene** (slou·vin) *adj.-s.* esloveno.

**slovenly** (slø·vønli) *adj.* desaliñado, desaseado. *2 adv.* desaliñadamente, descuidadamente.

**slow** (slou) *adj.* lento, tardo, pausado, detenido: *~ fire*, fuego lento. *2* paulatino. *3* calmoso. *4* lerdo, torpe. *5* que atrasa [reloj]: *to be ~*, atrasar. *6* atrasado [poco progresivo]. *7* aburrido. *8* encalmado. *9 adv.* despacio, lentamente.

**slow (to)** *tr.* retardar, hacer más lento. *2 intr. to ~ up o down*, hacerse más lento, ir más despacio.

**slow-motion** *adj.* lento, de movimiento lento.

**slowness** (-nis) *s.* lentitud. *2* cachaza. *3* torpeza, pesadez.

**slow-witted** *adj.* lerdo, tardo, torpe.

**slubber (to)** (slø·bøʳ) *tr.* manchar, obscurecer. *2* frangollar.

**sludge** (slødỹ) *s.* lodo, cieno, impurezas. *2* MAR. hielo nuevo que flota en el mar.

**sludgy** (slø·dỹi) *adj.* cenagoso.

**slue** (sliu·) *s.* giro, vuelta.

**slue (to)** *tr.* dar vuelta a, hacer girar. *2 intr.* girar, volverse. ¶ Gralte. con *round.*

**slug** (sløg) *s.* ZOOL. babosa. *2* animal o vehículo lento. *3* bala, posta. *4* IMPR. regleta; línea de linotipia.

**slug (to)** *tr.* pasar [un tiempo] ocioso. *2* aporrear, apuñear. *3 intr.* andar despacio; pasear.

**sluggard** (-aʳd) *adj.* lento, perezoso. *2 s.* haragán.

**sluggish** (-ish) *adj.* flojo, perezoso, indolente. *2* lento. *3* COM. encalmado.

**sluice** (slius) *s.* acequia, caz. *2* buzón, paradera. *3* compuerta; esclusa; agua detenida por una compuerta, etc., o que sale por ella. *4* lavadero de arenas auríferas.

**sluice (to)** *tr.* dar salida a, regar, limpiar [abriendo una compuerta]. *2* lavar [arenas auríferas].

**slum** (sløm) *s.* barrio miserable; barrio bajo.

**slum (to)** *intr.* visitar los barrios miserables. ¶ Pret. y p. p.: *slummed;* ger.: *-mming.*

**slumber** (slø·mbøʳ) *s.* sueño, sueño ligero. *2* adormecimiento, letargo.

**slumber (to)** *intr.* dormitar, dormir. *2* dormirse, descuidarse. *3* estar latente.

**slumberous** (-øs) *adj.* soñoliento. *2* dormido. *3* tranquilo, sosegado. *4* adormecedor.

**slump** (slømp) *s.* hundimiento, desplome. *2* COM. baja repentina, crisis.

**slump (to)** *intr.* caer, desplomarse. *2* fracasar. *3* dar un bajón [los precios, etc.]. *4 tr.* hacer bajar [los precios, etc.].

**slung** (sløng) *pret. y p. p.* de TO SLING. *2 ~ shot*, rompecabezas [arma].

**slunk** (slønk) *pret. y p. p.* de TO SLINK.

**slur** (sløʳ) *s.* mancha, borrón; tacha, desdoro. *2* cosa borrosa. *3* farfulla. *4* MÚS. ligadura.

**slur (to)** *tr.* manchar. *2* desdorar, rebajar. *3* pasar por alto, disimular, ocultar. *4* obscurecer, hacer borroso. *5* comerse [letras, sílabas]; farfullar. *6* MÚS. ligar. *7* IMPR. repintar. ¶ Pret. y p. p.: *slurred;* ger.: *-rring.*

**slush** (sløsh) *s.* nieve fangosa, lodo. *2* fig. sentimentalismo empalagoso; sensiblería. *3* grasa [para metales].

**slushy** (-i) *adj.* fangoso. *2* fig. empalagosamente sentimental.

**slut** (sløt) *s.* pazpuerca. *2* mujerzuela.

**sluttish** (-ish) *adj*. desaseado. *2* puerco, sucio.

**sly** (slai·) *adj*. astuto, socarrón, disimulado. *2* travieso. *3* secreto, furtivo: *on the* ~, a hurtadillas, callandito.

**slyly** (-li) *adv*. astutamente. *2* disimuladamente. *3* a hurtadillas.

**smack** (smæk) *s*. sabor, dejo, gustillo. *2* poquito, algo, punta. *3* tintura [noción superficial]. *4* restallido, chasquido, golpe, manotazo. *5* beso sonoro. *6* MAR. lancha de pesca. *7 adv*. de lleno; de golpe.

**smack (to)** *intr. to* ~ *of*, tener un gustillo de; fig. saber, oler a. *2 intr.-tr*. chasquear el látigo; chuparse los dedos; besar sonoramente. *3 tr*. dar un manotazo a.

**smacking** (-ing) *adj*. vivo, fuerte.

**small** (smol) *adj*. pequeño, chico, diminuto; insignificante: ~ *capital*, IMPR. versalita; ~ *change*, dinero suelto; ~ *fry*, freza; gente menuda; ~ *matters*, menudencias; ~ *wares*, mercería, artículos pequeños; *in a* ~ *way*, en pequeña escala. *2* menor; ~ *craft*, embarcaciones menores; ~ *game*, caza menor. *3* bajo [estatura]. *4* escaso; *to* ~ *purpose*, con poco resultado. *5* humilde, modesto. *6* mezquino. *7* flojo, diluido. *8* fino, delgado: ~ *intestine*, ANAT. intestino delgado. *9* ~ *hours*, primeras horas de la madrugada. *10* ~ *talk*, habladuría. *11 s*. parte pequeña de algo. *12* cosa o cantidad pequeña: *in* ~, en pequeño. *13 pl*. artículos menudos. *14* calzones cortos. *15 adv*. a trocitos: *to cut* ~, desmenuzar. *16* en tono bajo. *17* con desprecio: *to think* ~ *of*, tener en poco.

**smallclothes** (-klouðs) *s. pl*. calzones cortos. *2* ropa para niños. *3* ropa interior.

**smallish** (-ish) *adj*. algo pequeño o bajo.

**smallness** (-nis) *s*. pequeñez. *2* baja esatura. *3* bajeza, ruindad. *4* insignificancia.

**smallpox** (-paks) *s*. MED. viruelas.

**smalt** (smolt) *s*. esmalte, esmaltín.

**smart** (smaᵗt) *adj*. vivo, punzante, picante, acerbo. *2* fuerte, violento. *3* listo, ingenioso, astuto. *4* activo, diligente. *5* vivaracho. *6* agudo, gracioso, mordaz. *7* elegante, a la moda. *8* garrido. *9* distinguido: *the* ~ *set*, la gente distinguida, de buen tono. *10 s*. punzada, escozor. *11* dolor, aflicción.

**smart (to)** *intr*. escocer, doler. *2* sufrir, padecer. *3* sentir escozor [en el ánimo], sentir pesar o arrepentimiento.

**smarten (to)** (-tøn) *tr*. poner elegante, embellecer, animar.

**smarty** (-ti) *s*. (E.U.) el que las echa de agudo o gracioso.

**smash** (smæsh) *s*. rotura, destrozo. *2* choque [de vehículos]. *3* golpe violento. *4* fracaso, bancarrota. *5* ~ *hit*, éxito ruidoso.

**smash (to)** *tr*. romper, destrozar, estrellar, aplastar. *2* destruir, arruinar. *3* TENIS golpear la pelota por encima. *4 intr*. romperse, destrozarse. *5* quebrar, arruinarse.

**smatter** (smæ·tøᵗ), **smattering** (-ing) *s*. barniz, tintura, conocimiento superficial.

**smear** (smiᵗ) *s*. embadurnamiento, mancha. *2* BACT. frotis. *3* fig. mancha, desdoro.

**smear (to)** *tr*. embadurnar, untar, embarrar, tiznar. *2* fig. manchar, desdorar.

**smeary** (smi·ri) *adj*. graso, untuoso. *2* manchado.

**smell** (smel) *s*. olfato [sentido]. *2* olor [aroma, perfume, tufo, hedor]. *3* olor, traza.

**smell (to)** *tr*. oler [percibir con el olfato]. *2* olfa-

tear, husmear, ventear. *3* oler [adivinar]: *to* ~ *a rat*, sospechar algo malo. *4 intr*. oler [exhalar olor o hedor]: *to* ~ *of*, oler a. *5 to* ~ *at a rose*, oler una rosa. ¶ Pret. y p. p.: *smelled* o *smelt*.

**smeller** (sme·løᵗ) *s*. oledor, husmeador. *2* el que huele o echa un olor. *3* fam. nariz.

**smellfeast** (-fist) *s*. gorrista, gorrón.

**smelling** (-ing) *s*. olfato. *2* olfacción; husmeo. *3* olor. *4 adj*. que huele, oloroso; aromático.

**smelt** (smelt) *pret.* y *p. p.* de SMELL.

**smelt (to)** *tr*. fundir [minerales]. *2* extraer [metal] por fusión.

**smelter** (sme·ltøᵗ) *s*. fundidor de minerales.

**smelting** (-ing) *s*. fundición [de metales]: ~ *furnace*, horno de fundición.

**smile** (smail) *s*. sonrisa. *2* aspecto risueño.

**smile (to)** *intr*. sonreír: *to* ~ *at*, *on* o *upon*, sonreír a. *2* sonreírse. *3 tr*. expresar, decir, recibir, etc., con una sonrisa.

**smiling** (-ing) *adj*. risueño, sonriente.

**smirch** (smøᵗch) *s*. borrón, mancha.

**smirch (to)** *tr*. manchar, ensuciar. *2* mancillar.

**smirk** (smøᵗk) *s*. sonrisa boba o afectada.

**smirk (to)** *intr*. sonreírse tontamente o con afectación.

**smite (to)** (smait) *tr*. golpear, herir, pegar. *2* aplastar. *3* asolar, afligir, castigar. *4* aturdir, sobrecoger; conmover; remorder [la conciencia]. *5* prendar, enamorar. *6 intr*. dar golpes. ¶ Pret.: *smote*; p. p.: *smitten*.

**smith** (smiz) *s*. forjador. *2* el que trabaja en metales.

**smith (to)** *tr*. forjar [metales].

**smithereens** (smiðørɪ·nŝ) *s. pl*. fam. añicos.

**smithery** (smi·zøri) *s*. forja, herrería.

**smithy** (-zi) *s*. herrería, taller de herrero.

**smitten** (smi·tøn) *p. p.* de TO SMITE.

**smock** (smak) *s*. camisa, bata, delantal [de mujer]. *2* ~ *frock* o simplte. *smock*, blusa [de obrero, de pintor, etc.].

**smoke** (smouk) *s*. humo: ~ *screen*, cortina de humo. *2* sahumerio. *3* acción de fumar: *to have a* ~, fumar.

**smoke (to)** *tr*. ahumar. *2* fumigar. *3* sahumar, incensar. *4* fumar. *5* oler, descubrir. *6 to* ~ *out*, ahuyentar con humo. *7 intr*. humear, echar humo. *8* fumar.

**smoke-dry (to)** *tr*. secar o curar al humo.

**smokeless** (-lis) *adj*. sin humo.

**smoker** (-øᵗ) *s*. ahumador. *2* fumador. *3* compartimento para fumadores. *4* reunión en que se fuma.

**smokestack** (-stæk) *s*. chimenea.

**smoking** (-ing) *s*. acción de fumar: *no* ~, se prohibe fumar. *2 adj*. humeante. *3* de fumar: ~ *jacket*, batín; ~ *room*, fumadero.

**smoky** (-i) *adj*. humeante. *2* humoso. *3* ahumado.

**smolt** (smoult) *s*. ICT. murgón.

**smooth** (smuð) *adj*. liso, terso. *2* llano, igual, parejo. *3* uniforme, regular. *4* fácil, fluido. *5* blando, suave. *6* plácido. *7* afable. *8* meloso, lisonjero, hipócrita. *9* MÚS. ligado. *10 adv*. SMOOTHLY.

**smooth (to)** *tr*. alisar. *2* allanar, igualar. *3* cepillar, pulir. *4* facilitar [las cosas]. *5* suavizar. *6* calmar, apaciguar. *7 to* ~ *away*, hacer desaparecer [obstáculos, etc.] suavemente.

**smooth-faced** *adj*. barbilampiño. *2* liso. *3* meloso.

**smoothing** (-ing) *adj*. de alisar, cepillar, etc.: ~ *iron*, plancha; ~ *plane*, CARP. cepillo.

**smoothly** (-li) *adv.* lisamente. *2* fácilmente. *3* suavemente, melosamente.

**smooth-shaven** *adj.* bien afeitado.

**smooth-spoken, smooth-tongued** *adj.* meloso, lisonjero, adulador.

**smote** (smout) *pret.* de TO SMITE.

**smother** (smø·dø') *s.* humareda, polvareda, niebla, etc., sofocantes.

**smother (to)** *tr.* sofocar, ahogar [asfixiar; apagar; reprimir]. *2* COC. estofar. *3* cubrir. *4* ocultar. *5 intr.* ahogarse. *6* estar reprimido.

**smothery** (-i) *adj.* sofocante, asfixiante.

**smo (u) lder** (smou·ldø') *s.* fuego sin llama.

**smo (u) lder (to)** *intr.* arder sin llama, en rescoldo. *2* estar latente, reprimido.

**smudge** (smødý) *s.* mancha, tiznón. *2* humareda sofocante.

**smudge (to)** *tr.* manchar, tiznar. *2* embadurnar. *3* (E.U.) ahumar, proteger con humo.

**smug** (smøg) *adj.* compuesto, aseado. *2* satisfecho, pagado de sí mismo.

**smuggle (to)** (smø·gøl) *tr.* pasar de contrabando. *2 intr.* contrabandear.

**smuggler** (-glø') *s.* contrabandista.

**smuggling** (-gling) *s.* contrabando.

**smut** (smøt) *s.* suciedad, mancha, tiznón. *2* obscenidad. *3* AGR. añublo, tizón.

**smut (to)** *tr.* ensuciar, manchar, tiznar. *2* mancillar. *3* AGR. producir añublo. *4 intr.* AGR. atizonarse. ¶ Pret. y p. p.: *smutted;* ger.: *-tting.*

**smutch** (smøch) *s.* mancha, tiznajo.

**smutch (to)** *tr.* tiznar, manchar. *2* mancillar.

**smutty** (smø·ti) *adj.* tiznado, holliniento. *2* humoso, obscuro. *3* obsceno. *4* AGR. atizonado.

**snack** (snæk) *s.* porción, parte; sorbo, bocadito. *2* piscolabis, tentempié; ~ *bar,* bar donde se sirven bocadillos, etc.

**snaffle (-bit)** (snæ·føl) *s.* bridón [brida pequeña].

**snaffle (to)** *tr.* enfrenar. *2* refrenar, reprimir.

**snag** (snæg) *s.* tocón. *2* garrancho. *3* nudo [en la madera]. *4* raigón. *5* tronco o roca sumergidos. *6* obstáculo imprevisto.

**snagged** (-id), **snaggy** (-i) *adj.* nudoso. *2* lleno de tocones. *3* lleno de troncos o rocas sumergidos. *4* fig. lleno de obstáculos.

**snaggletooth** (snæ·gøltuz) *s.* sobrediente.

**snail** (sneil) *s.* ZOOL. caracol [esp. el terrestre]: babosa. *2* persona o cosa lenta.

**snake** (sneik) *s.* ZOOL. culebra, serpiente: ~ *in the grass,* fig. peligro oculto, enemigo secreto. *2* fig. serpiente [pers.].

**snake (to)** *tr.* arrastrar, mover sinuosamente. *2 intr.* serpentear.

**snakeroot** (-rut) *s.* BOT. serpentaria.

**snaky** (-i) *adj.* serpentino. *2* serpenteante. *3* traidor. *4* lleno de culebras.

**snap** (snæp) *s.* chasquido, estallido. *2* castañeta [con los dedos]. *3* acción rápida. *4* mordisco, dentellada. *5* disparo rápido, sin apuntar; FOT. instantánea. *6* broche de presión. *7* galletita. *8* energía, vigor, vida. *9* período breve [de frío, etc.]. *10* fam. canonjía; ganga. *11* observación o respuesta brusca. *12* fig. pito, bledo. *13 adj.* precipitado: ~ *judgement,* juicio precipitado. *14* de golpe, de resorte: ~ *bolt,* pestillo de golpe.

**snap (to)** *intr.* romperse con estallido; cerrarse dando chasquido o golpe. *2* dar chasquido, estallar. *3* echar chispas, llamear. *4 to* ~ *at,* tirar un bocado a; aceptar, asir prontamente; hablar o responder bruscamente a. *5 to* ~ *off,* soltarse; abrirse de golpe. *6 tr.* asir, agarrar, arrebatar. *7*

aceptar o tomar en el acto. *8* responder o expresar con acritud. *9* romper, cerrar, etc., con chasquido. *10* hacer chasquear: *to* ~ *one's fingers at,* burlarse de, despreciar. *11* FOT. hacer una instantánea. ¶ Pret. y p. p.: *snapped;* ger.: *-pping.*

**snapdragon** (-drægøn) *s.* BOT. dragón, becerra.

**snapper** (-ø') *s.* mordedor. *2* pers. gruñona. *3* tralla [del látigo].

**snappish** (-ish) *adj.* mordedor. *2* gruñón.

**snappy** (-i) *adj.* SNAPPISH. *2* chispeante, vivo. *3* elegante. *4* rápido.

**snapshot** (-shat) *s.* FOT. instantánea. *2* disparo rápido, sin apuntar.

**snapshot (to)** *tr.-intr.* hacer instantáneas. ¶ Pret. y p. p.: *snapshotted;* ger.: *snapshotting.*

**snare** (sne') *s.* lazo, armadijo. *2* celada, trampa, asechanza. *3* bordón [de tambor]. *4* CIR. lazo.

**snare (to)** *tr.* atrapar; hacer caer en una trampa, tender celadas o lazos a.

**snarl** (sna'l) *s.* gruñido. *2* regaño. *3* enredo, maraña; pelo enmarañado.

**snarl (to)** *tr.* regañar. *2* gruñir. *3* enredarse, enmarañarse. *4 tr.* enredar, enmarañar. *5* repujar [metales].

**snarly** (-i) *adj.* gruñón, regañón. *2* enredado, enmarañado.

**snary** (sne·ri) *adj.* enredoso, insidioso.

**snatch** (snæch) *s.* acción de coger o arrebatar. *2* trozo, pedacito. *3* rato: *by snatches,* a ratos.

**snatch (to)** *tr.* coger, agarrar precipitadamente; arrebatar, quitar. *2* intr. *to* ~ *at,* tratar de agarrar o arrebatar.

**snatchy** (-i) *adj.* irregular, intermitente.

**sneak** (snik) *s.* persona ruin, solapada. *2* fam. soplón. *3* movimiento furtivo. *4 sneak* o ~ *thief,* ratero, descuidero.

**sneak (to)** *intr.* moverse furtivamente, escabullirse. | Con *in, out, past, round, off, away,* etc. *2* obrar solapadamente o rastreramente; soplonear. *3 tr.* ṃover, sacar, meter, etc., furtivamente. *4* hurtar, ratear.

**sneaker** (-kø') *s.* SNEAK 1. *2 pl.* zapatos silenciosos; zapatos de playa o de gimnasia.

**sneaking** (-ing) *adj.* ruin, cobarde. *2* mezquino. *3* furtivo, husmeador. *4* secreto [no confesado]. *5* vago [idea, sospecha].

**sneaky** (-i) *adj.* ruin, cobarde. *2* solapado, furtivo.

**sneer** (sni') *s.* sonrisa, gesto o expresión despreciativa; burla, mofa.

**sneer (to)** *intr.* reírse o mirar con burla o desprecio; burlarse, mofarse. | Gralte. con *at.* *2 tr.* decir o expresar con burla o desprecio.

**sneering** (-ing) *adj.* burlón, despreciativo.

**sneeze** (sniš) *s.* estornudo.

**sneeze (to)** *intr.* estornudar.

**snell** (snel) *s.* hilo de tripa que une el sedal al anzuelo.

**snick** (snik) *s.* corte, tijeretazo. *2* ruido seco o metálico.

**snick (to)** *tr.* cortar. *2* pinchar, atravesar. *3* mover, sacar, etc., con ruido seco o metálico.

**snicker** (snikø') *s.* risita, risa ahogada.

**snicker (to)** *intr.* reír con risa ahogada, burlarse. *2* relinchar suavemente.

**sniff** (snif) *s.* olfato, husmeo. *2* sorbo [por las narices]; resoplido de desprecio.

**sniff (to)** *tr.* olfatear, husmear, oler. *2 intr.-tr.* absorber ruidosamente por la nariz; dar un resoplido: *to* ~ *at,* husmear; despreciar.

**sniffy** (sni·fi) *adj.* fam. desdeñoso, estirado.

**snifting-valve** (sni·fting) *s.* MEC. válvula de purga.

**snigger** (sni·gø<sup>r</sup>) s. SNICKER.

**snigger (to)** *intr.* TO SNICKER.

**snip** (snip) *s.* incisión, tijeretazo. *2* recorte, pedacito. *3* fam. persona pequeña o insignificante.

**snip (to)** *tr.* cortar, recortar [con tijeras o cosa parecida]. ¶ Pret. y p. p.: *snipped;* ger.: *-pping.*

**snipe** (snaip) *s.* ORN. agachadiza.

**snipe (to)** *intr.* cazar agachadizas. *2* tirar desde un sitio oculto: *to ~ at,* tirotear, paquear.

**sniper** (snai·pø<sup>r</sup>) *s.* tiroteador, paco.

**snippet** (sni·pit) *s.* recorte, pedacito.

**snivel** (sni·vøl) *s.* moco, moquita. *2* gimoteo.

**snivel (to)** *intr.* moquear. *2* sorberse la moquita; gimotear, hacer pucheros. ¶ Pret. y p. p.: *snivel(l)ed;* ger.: *-l(l)ing.*

**snivel(l)er** (sni·vlø<sup>r</sup>) *s.* lloraduelos, jeremías.

**snivelly** (sni·vli) *adj.* llorón, lloroso. *2* mocoso.

**snob** (snab) *s.* el que, por darse tono, imita a los que les parecen superiores o busca su trato; esnob. *2* el que rehuye el trato de los que tiene por inferiores; orgulloso.

**snobbery** (sna·børi) *s.* esnobismo. *2* orgullo, presunción.

**snooze** (snuš) *s.* fam. sueñecito, siestecita.

**snooze (to)** *intr.* fam. dormitar.

**snore** (sno<sup>r</sup>) *s.* ronquido [del que duerme, del mar, del viento].

**snore (to)** *intr.* roncar [el que duerme, el mar, el viento].

**snort** (sno<sup>r</sup>t) *s.* resoplido, bufido.

**snort (to)** *intr.* resoplar, bufar. *2* reírse ruidosamente con ira o desprecio.

**snout** (snaut) *s.* trompa [de elefante]. *2* hocico, jeta. *3* pitorro; nariz [de alambique]; lanza [de manguera]; cañón [de fuelle]. *4* MAR. proa. *5* promontorio. *6* ENT. ~ *beetle,* gorgojo.

**snouted** (-id) *adj.* hocicudo. *2* provisto de pitorro, etc. *3* en forma de hocico o pitorro.

**snow** (snou) *s.* nieve: ~ *flurry,* nevisca. *2* nevada. *3* pop. cocaína. *4* n. pr. *Snow White,* Blancanieves.

**snow (to)** *intr.* nevar. *2* *tr.* esparcir como nieve. *3* cubrir, obstruir, aprisionar, etc., con nieve. | Con *over, up, in, under.* *4* blanquear [el cabello].

**snowball** (-bol) *s.* bola de nieve. *2* BOT. mundillo.

**snowball (to)** *tr.-intr.* lanzar bolas de nieve. *2* *intr.* crecer como una bola de nieve.

**snowblind** (-blaind) *adj.* cegado por el reflejo de la nieve.

**snowbound** (-baund) *adj.* sitiado por la nieve.

**snowcapped** (-kæpt) *adj.* coronado de nieve.

**snowdrift** (-drift) *s.* nieve que lleva el viento, ventisca. *2* ventisquero.

**snowdrop** (-drap) *s.* BOT. campanilla blanca. *2* BOT. anémona.

**snowfall** (-fol) *s.* nevada, nevasca.

**snowflake** (-fleik) *s.* copo de nieve. *2* ORN. verderón de las nieves. *3* BOT. campanilla.

**snowplough, snowplow** (-plau) *s.* quitanieves.

**snowshoe** (-shu) *s.* raqueta para andar sobre la nieve.

**snowslide** (-laid), **snowslip** (-slip) *s.* alud.

**snow-white** *adj.* blanco como la nieve.

**snowy** (-i) *adj.* nevoso; nevado. *2* níveo.

**snub** (snøb) *s.* repulsa, desaire. *2* represión brusca. *3* fam. nariz chata. *4* *adj.* chata [nariz].

**snub (to)** *tr.* dar un sofión; reprender. *2* desairar, despreciar. *3* *to ~ up,* detener de repente.

**snub-nosed** *adj.* chato.

**snuff** (snøf) *s.* moco [de vela]. *2* rapé; polvo [que se toma].

**snuff (to)** *tr.* oler; absorber por la nariz. *2* olfatear,

husmear. *3* despabilar [una vela]. *4* *intr.* TO SNIFF *2.* *5* tomar rapé.

**snuffbox** (-baks) *s.* tabaquera, caja de rapé.

**snuffers** (-ø<sup>r</sup>s) *s. pl.* despabiladeras.

**snuffle** (-øl) *s.* respiración o inspiración ruidosa por la nariz. *2* gangueo. *3* *pl.* romadizo.

**snuffle (to)** *intr.* TO SNIFF *2.* *2* respirar con la nariz obstruida. *3* ganguear.

**snuffy** (-i) *adj.* sucio de rapé; tabacoso; desagradable.

**snug** (snøg) *adj.* cómodo, abrigado. *2* ajustado; apretado, compacto. *3* escondido. *4* tranquilo. *5* limpio, aseado.

**snug (to)** *tr.* poner cómodo; acomodar. *2* arreglar, asear. *3* hacer próspero.

**snuggery** (-øri) *s.* aposento cómodo.

**snuggle (to)** (-øl) *intr.-tr.* arrimar, arrimarse, poner o ponerse juntos, cómodos, abrigados.

**so** (sou) *adv.* así, de este modo; eso, lo mismo, lo: *if ~,* si es así; ~ *be it,* así sea; *I hope ~,* así lo espero; *quite ~, just ~,* eso mismo; *he is not too clever, but he is more ~ than many men,* no es muy listo, pero lo es más que muchos hombres. *2* de modo, de manera; ~ *that,* para que; de modo o de manera que. *3* también. *4* tan, tanto: ~ *good,* tan bueno; *it is not ~ good as,* no es tan bueno como. *5* y así, por tanto. *6* *pron.* cosa así, cosa de: *a year or ~,* cosa de un año. *7* *conj.* con tal que; para que. *8* *interj.* ¡bueno!; ¿eh? *9* Otras alocuciones: *and ~ forth* (o *on*), etcétera, y así sucesivamente; *how ~?,* ¿cómo es eso?; ~ *far as, in ~ far as,* hasta, hasta donde; ~ *long,* abur; ~ *long as,* mientras, con tal que; ~ *many,* tantos; ~ *much,* tanto; ~ *to say,* ~ *to speak,* por decirlo así.

**soak** (souk) *s.* remojo, remojón. *2* borrachín. *3* borrachera.

**soak (to)** *tr.* empapar, poner en remojo. *2* emborrachar. *3* pop. pegar, zurrar. *4* *to ~ up,* embeber, absorber. *5* *intr.* empaparse, estar en remojo. *6* emborracharse. *7* *to ~ into,* penetrar, filtrarse.

**soakage** (-idỹ) *s.* merma [por absorción].

**soaker** (-ø<sup>r</sup>) *s.* remojador. *2* borrachín. *3* chubasco.

**soaky** (-i) *adj.* empapado, mojado, calado.

**so-and-so** *s.* fulano, fulano de tal. *2* tal cosa.

**soap** (soup) *s.* jabón: ~ *dish,* jabonera; ~ *flakes,* escamas de jabón. *2* fam. lisonja. *3* fam. dinero. *4* BOT. ~ *plant,* jaboncillo.

**soap (to)** *tr.* jabonar. *2* dar jabón, adular.

**soapstone** (-stoun) *s.* esteatita, jabón de sastre.

**sopasuds** (-søds) *s. pl.* jabonaduras.

**soapy** (-i) *adj.* jabonoso.

**soar** (so<sup>r</sup>) *s.* vuelo, remonte.

**soar (to)** *intr.* elevarse, subir, remontarse, volar. *2* cernerse [en el aire]; AVIA. planear. *3* *tr.* elevarse, remontarse por.

**sob** (sab) *s.* sollozo. *2* suspiro [del viento, etc.].

**sob (to)** *intr.* sollozar.

**sober** (sou·bø<sup>r</sup>) *adj.* sobrio, moderado, templado. *2* sereno [que no está borracho]. *3* sereno, desapasionado, serio, sensato. *4* serio, discreto [color].

**sober (to)** *tr.* serenar, aquietar, ajuiciar; poner serio. *2* serenar [quitar la borrachera]. *3* *intr. to ~ down,* serenarse, ajuiciarse, sosegarse. *4* *to ~ up,* desemborracharse.

**soberness** (sou·bø<sup>r</sup>nes), **sobriety** (sobrai·øti) *s.* sobriedad. *2* moderación. *3* sensatez. *4* serenidad. *5* seriedad, gravedad.

**sobriquet** (soubrikei·) *s.* apodo, mote.

**so-called** *adj.* llamado, supuesto, pseudo.
**sociability** (soush*a*bi·liti) *s.* sociabilidad.
**sociable** (sou·sh*a*bøl) *adj.* sociable, tratable; comunicativo. *2* amistoso, familiar.
**social** (sou·sh*a*l) *adj.* social: ~ *security,* seguro social. *2* de trato o conversación, de sociedad: ~ *gathering,* reunión, fiesta de sociedad. *3* sociable. *4 s.* tertulia, reunión.
**socialism** (sou·sh*a*lišm) *s.* socialismo.
**socialist** (-ist) *adj.* socialista.
**socialize (to)** (sou·sh*a*laiš) *tr.* socializar.
**society** (sosai·øti) *s.* sociedad. *2* compañía, reunión, relación, trato social. *3* buena sociedad.
**Society Islands** *n. pr.* GEOGR. Islas de la Sociedad.
**sociology** (soshia·lodŷi) *s.* sociología.
**sock** (sak) *s.* calcetín. *2* sandalia. *3* fig. la comedia. *4* golpe, puñetazo.
**socket** (-it) *s.* hueco en que encaja algo; caja, cubo, mechero, portalámparas, etc.; cuenca [del ojo]; alvéolo [de diente].
**socle** (sa·køl) *s.* zócalo.
**sod** (sad) *s.* césped. *2* terrón; tepe; turba.
**sod (to)** *tr.* encespedar. ¶ Pret. y p. p.: *sodden;* ger.: *-dding.*
**soda** (sou·da) *s.* QUÍM. soda, sosa; carbonato de sodio: ~ *plant,* barrilla. *2* soda o ~ *water,* agua carbónica.
**sodality** (sodæ·liti) *s.* asociación, unión. *2* cofradía, hermandad.
**sodden** (sa·døn) p. p. de TO SEETHE. *2* mojado, empapado. *3* borracho; embrutecido. *4* mal cocido [pan].
**sodic** (sou·dik) *adj.* QUÍM. sódico.
**sodium** (sou·diøm) *s.* QUÍM. sodio.
**sodomite** (sa·dømait) *s.* sodomita.
**sodomy** (-i) *s.* sodomía.
**soever** (soe·vø<sup>r</sup>) *adv.* que sea; por más que sea: *in any way* ~, de cualquier modo que sea; *how great* ~, por grande que sea. *2* en modo alguno.
**sofa** (sou·fa) *s.* sofá.
**soffit** (sa·fit) *s.* ARQ. sofito; intradós.
**soft** (soft) *adj.* blando, maleable, flexible, mollar, fofo. *2* blando, muelle, suave, delicado. *3* melifluo. *4* dulce, grato. *5* blando, tierno, amoroso. *6* débil [de carácter]. *7* flojo, perezoso. *8* dulce [hierro]. *9* floja [bebida]. *10* FOT. débil. *11* COM. flojo, en baja. *12* FONÉT. suave. *13* MÚS. celeste. *14 adv.* blandamente, suavemente. *15 interj.* ¡quedo!; ¡despacio!
**soft-boiled** *adj.* pasado por agua [huevo].
**soften (to)** (so·føn) *tr.* ablandar, reblandecer. *2* dulcificar, mitigar, suavizar, amortiguar, ablandar. *3* bajar [la voz]. *4* debilitar. *5 intr.* ablandarse, resplandecerse. *6* dulcificarse, aplacarse. *7* debilitarse.
**softening of the brain** (-ning) *s.* MED. reblandecimiento cerebral.
**soft-hearted** *adj.* bondadoso, de buen corazón.
**softish** (-ish) *adj.* blanducho.
**softly** (-li) *adv.* blandamente, suavemente, dulcemente. *2* bajito: *speak* ~, hable usted bajito.
**soft-soap (to)** *tr.* fig. adular, dar jabón.
**soggy** (sa·gi) *adj.* empapado. *2* pesado y húmedo.
**soil** (soil) *s.* tierra, terreno, suelo. *2* suelo, país. *3* suciedad. *4* mancha, baldón. *5* abono, estiércol.
**soil (to)** *tr.* ensuciar, manchar. *2* mancillar. *3* abonar, estercolar. *4 intr.* ensuciarse.
**soirée** (suarei·) *s.* reunión nocturna, sarao.
**soja** (sou·ŷa) *s.* BOT. soja.
**sojourn** (sou·dŷø<sup>r</sup>n) *s.* estancia, estada.

**sojourn (to)** (soudŷø·<sup>r</sup>n) *intr.* estar, residir [por una temporada].
**sol** (soul) *s.* MÚS., QUÍM. sol. *2* sol [moneda del Perú].
**solace** (sa·lis) *s.*consuelo, alivio. *2* solaz.
**solace (to)** *tr.* consolar, confortar, aliviar. *2* solazar, divertir.
**solanaceous** (sa*l*anei·shøs) *adj.* BOT. solanáceo.
**solar** (sou·la<sup>r</sup>) *adj.* solar [del sol]: ~ *spot,* mancha solar; ~ *system,* sistema solar. *2* ANAT. ~ *plexus,* plexo solar.
**solarium** (søle·riøm) *s.* solarium.
**solatium** (sølei·shøm) *s.* compensación.
**sold** (sould) *pret.* y *p. p.* de TO SELL.
**solder** (sa·dø<sup>r</sup>) *s.* soldadura [material para soldar].
**solder (to)** *tr.* soldar. *2* unir. *3 intr.* soldarse.
**soldering** (-ing) *s.* soldadura.
**soldier** (sou·ldŷø<sup>r</sup>) *s.* soldado. *2* militar.
**soldier (to)** *intr.* servir como militar.
**soldierly** (-li) *adv.* soldadesco, militar, marcial.
**soldiery** (-ri) *s.* soldadesca, tropa.
**sole** (soul) *s.* planta [del pie]; palma [del casco del caballo]. *2* suela [del zapato]. *3* suelo, fondo, base. *4* ICT. lenguado. *5 adj.* solo, único. *6* exclusivo: ~ *right,* exclusiva.
**sole (to)** *tr.* solar, echar suelas a.
**solecism** (sa·løsišm) *s.* solecismo. *2* incongruencia. *3* incorrección.
**solemn** (sa·løm) *adj.* solemne. *2* grave, serio.
**solemnity** (søle·mniti) *s.* solemnidad. *5* formalidad, requisito.
**solemnize (to)** (sa·lømnaiš) *tr.* solemnizar. *2* celebrar solemnemente.
**solenoid** (sou·lønoid) *s.* ELECT. solenoide.
**sol-fa (to)** (sa·fa) *intr.-tr.* solfear.
**solfatara** (salfata·ra) *s.* solfatara.
**solfeggio** (salfe·dŷiou) *s.* solfeo.
**solicit (to)** (søli·sit) *tr.* solicitar. *2* rogar, importunar. *3* inducir, incitar, tentar, atraer.
**solicitation** (solisitei·shøn) *s.* solicitación. *2* ruego. *3* inclinación, requerimiento.
**solicitor** (søli·sitø<sup>r</sup>) *s.*especie de abogado o procurador.
**solicitous** (-tøs) *adj.* solícito. *2* inquieto, preocupado. *3* ávido, deseoso. *4* meticuloso.
**solicitude** (-tiud) *s.* solicitud, cuidado. *2* inquietud. *3* pl. cuidados, preocupaciones.
**solid** (sa·lid) *adj.* sólido. *2* macizo. *3* duro, firme. *4* serio, formal; solvente. *5* unánime. *6* continuo, seguido, entero. *7* MAT. cúbico; del espacio. *8 s.* FÍS., GEOM. sólido.
**solidarity** (salidæ·riti) *s.* solidaridad.
**solidary** (sa·lideri) *adj.* solidario.
**solidify (to)** (søli·difai) *tr.* solidificar. *2* consolidar. *3 intr.* solidificarse, consolidarse. ¶ Pret. y p. p.: *solidified.*
**solidity** (søli·diti) *s.* solidez. *2* macicez. *3* seriedad, solvencia. *4* sensatez.
**soliloquize (to)** (søli·løkuaiš) *intr.* soliloquiar.
**soliloquy** (-kui) *s.* soliloquio.
**soliped** (sa·liped) *s.* ZOOL. solípedo.
**solitaire** (sa·lite<sup>r</sup>) *s.* solitario [diamante; juego]. *2* solitario, ermitaño.
**solitariness** (-inis) *s.* soledad.
**solitary** (-ri) *s.* adj. solitario. *2* soledoso. *3* solo, único. *4* DER. ~ *confinement,* incomunicación. *5 s.* solitario, ermitaño.
**solitude** (-tiud) *s.* soledad, retiro. *2* soledad [lugar solitario].
**solmization** (salmišei·shøn) *s.* MÚS. solfa.

**solo** (sou·lou) *s.* MÚS. solo. 2 solo [juego]. *3 adj.* hecho por uno solo.
**soloist** (-ist) *s.* MÚS. solista.
**Solomon** (sa·lømøn) *n. pr.* Salomón.
**solstice** (sa·lstis) *s.* ASTR. solsticio.
**solstitial** (salsti·shal) *adj.* solsticial.
**solubility** (saliubi·liti) *s.* solubilidad.
**soluble** (sa·liubøl) *adj.* soluble.
**solution** (søliu·shøn) *s.* solución: ~ *of continuity,* solución de continuidad.
**solutive** (sa·liutiv) *adj.* solutivo.
**solvable** (sa·lvabøl) *adj.* soluble, resoluble.
**solve (to)** (salv) *tr.* resolver, aclarar, desentrañar. 2 solventar, solucionar; resolver [un problema].
**solvency** (sa·lvønsi) *s.* solvencia.
**solvent** (sa·lvønt) *adj.-s.* solvente, disolvente. 2 *adj.* COM. solvente.
**somatic(al** (somæ·tik(al) *adj.* somático.
**somber, sombre** (sa·mbø<sup>r</sup>) *adj.* obscuro, sombrío. 2 sombrío, tétrico, melancólico.
**sombrero** (sambre·rou) *s.* sombrero de fieltro de ala ancha.
**sombrous** (sa·mbrøs) *adj.* sombrío.
**some** (søm) *adj.* un, algún, cierto, unos, algunos, varios, ciertos: ~ *day,* un día, algún día, cierto día. 2 pop. us. para encarecer la importancia de algo: *this is* ~ *war!,* ¡esto es una guerra! *3* algo de, un poco de, una cantidad indeterminada de; unos, cosa de. | A veces no se traduce: *give me* ~ *bread,* déme pan. 4 *pron.* alguno, algunos. 5 *adv.* algo, un poco.
**somebody** (-badi) *pr.* alguien, alguno: ~ *else,* algún otro, otra persona.
**somehow** (-jau) *adv.* de algún modo. 2 ~ *or other,* de un modo u otro.
**someone** (so·muøn) *pr.* SOMEBODY.
**somersault** (sø·mø<sup>r</sup>solt), **somerset** (-set) *s.* salto mortal.
**somersault, somerset (to)** *intr.* dar un salto mortal, dar saltos mortales.
**something** (-zing) *s.* algo, alguna cosa. 2 persona o cosa de importancia. *3 to be* ~ *of a,* TO BE SOMEWHAT OF.
**sometime** (-taim) *adv.* algún día, alguna vez, en algún momento. 2 *adj.* antiguo, ex.
**sometimes** (-taims) *adv.* algunas veces, a veces.
**somewhat** (-juat) *s.* algo, un poco. *2 to be* ~ *of a,* tener algo de. *3 adv.* algo, algún tanto, un poco.
**somewhere** (-jue<sup>r</sup>) *adv.* en alguna parte.
**somnambulant** (samnæ·mbiulant) *adj.-s.* somnámbulo.
**somnambulism** (-lišm) *s.* somnambulismo.
**somniferous** (samni·førøs) *adj.* somnífero.
**somnific** (samni·fik) *adj.* soporífero.
**somnolence, -cy** (sa·mnøløns, -si) *s.* somnolencia, soñolencia.
**somnolent** (-ønt) *adj.* soñoliento. 2 soporífero.'
**son** (søn) *s.* hijo; descendiente [varón].
**sonant** (sou·nant) *adj.* FONÉT. sonoro.
**sonata** (søna·ta) *s.* MÚS. sonata.
**sonatina** (sønati·na) *s.* MÚS. sonatina.
**song** (søng o sang) *s.* canto [acción de cantar]. 2 MÚS., LIT. canción, canto, copla, cantar: *the Song of Songs,* el Cantar de los Cantares. *3 an old* ~, *a (mere)* ~, una bagatela. 4 *adj.* ~ *bird,* pájaro cantor; ~ *thrush,* ORN. malvis.
**songful** (-ful) *adj.* melodioso. 2 canoro.
**songster** (-tø<sup>r</sup>) *s.* cantor. 2 poeta. 3 pájaro cantor.
**songstress** (-stris) *s.* cantatriz, cantante.
**sonic** (sa·nik) *adj.* del sonido.
**son-in-law,** *pl.* **sons-in-law** *s.* yerno.

**sonnet** (sa·nit) *s.* LIT. soneto.
**sonneteer** (saneti·<sup>r</sup>) *s.* sonetista.
**sonny** (sa·ni) *s.* fam. hijito.
**sonority** (søno·riti) *s.* sonoridad.
**sonorous** (søno·røs) *adj.* sonoro; armonioso: resonante. ·
**soon** (sun) *adv.* pronto, luego; temprano: *as* ~ *as,* tan pronto como; ~ *after,* poco después; *too* ~, demasiado pronto o temprano. 2 prontamente.
**sooner** (-ø<sup>r</sup>) *adv. compar.* de SOON: más pronto, más temprano; antes: ~ *or later,* tarde o temprano;' *I would* ~ *die,* antes quisiera morir.
**soonest** (-ist) *adv. superl.* de SOON: lo más pronto posible: *at the* ~, cuanto antes.
**soot** (sut) *s.* hollín. 2 color negro de hollín.
**soot (to)** *tr.* cubrir o manchar de hollín.
**soothe (to)** (suđ) *tr.* aliviar, mitigar, calmar. 2 apaciguar. 3 agradar, halagar.
**soothing** (-ing) *adj.* consolador, confortante, calmante, tranquilizador.
**soothsayer** (su·zseiø<sup>r</sup>) *s.* adivino.
**sooty** (su·ti) *adj.* holliniento, fuliginoso. 2 tiznado.
**sop** (sap) *s.* sopa [pan empapado en caldo, etc.]. 2 dádiva para apaciguar, sobornar, etc.
**sop (to)** *tr.* ensopar, empapar: *to* ~ *up,* absorber.
**Sophia** (soufai·a) *n. pr.* Sofía.
**sophism** (sa·fišm) *s.* sofisma.
**sophist** (sa·fist) *s.* sofista.
**sophistic (al** (søfi·stik(al) *adj.* sofístico.
**sophisticate** (søfi·stikeit) *adj.* SOPHISTICATED.
**sophisticate (to)** *tr.* sofisticar. 2 hacer perder la ingenuidad; hacer complicado, refinado, mundano.
**sophisticated** (-tid) *adj.* sofisticado. 2 falto de ingenuidad, artificial, complicado, refinado, culto, mundano.
**sophistication** (-ei·shøn) *s.* sofisticación. 2 falta de espontaneidad o ingenuidad.
**sophisticator** (sofi·stikeitø<sup>r</sup>) *s.* sofisticador.
**sophistry** (sa·fistri) *s.* sofistería.
**sopor** (sou·pø<sup>r</sup>) *s.* sopor.
**soporiferous** (soupøri·førøs) *adj.* soporífero.
**soporific** (soupøri·fik) *adj.-s.* soporífero.
**soppy** (sa·pi) *adj.* mojado, empapado. 2 pop. tontamente sentimental; enamorado, chalado.
**soprano** (søpræ·nou) *s.* MÚS. soprano, tiple.
**sorb** (so<sup>r</sup>b) *s.* BOT. serbal, serbo: ~ *apple,* serba.
**sorbet** (sa·<sup>r</sup>bet) *s.* sorbete.
**sorcerer** (so·<sup>r</sup>sørø<sup>r</sup>) *s.* hechicero, brujo, encantador.
**sorceress** (so·<sup>r</sup>søris) *s.* hechicera.
**sorcery** (so·<sup>r</sup>søri) *s.* hechicería, brujería. 2 hechizo, sortilegio.
**sordid** (so·<sup>r</sup>did) *adj.* sórdido. 2 bajo, vil.
**sordine** (so·<sup>r</sup>din) *s.* MÚS. sordina.
**sore** (so<sup>r</sup>) *adj.* penoso, doloroso, enojoso. 2 violento. 3 extremo. 4 dolorido, inflamado, llagado: ~ *eyes,* mal de ojos; ~ *throat,* mal de garganta. 5 sensible, irritable. 6 dolorido, enojado, resentido. 7 *s.* herida [material o moral]; llaga, úlcera, matadura. 8 *adv.* SORELY.
**sorely** (-li) *adv.* penosamente. 2 sumamente.
**sorghum** (so·<sup>r</sup>gøm) *s.* BOT. sorgo, zahína.
**sorrel** (sa·røl) *adj.* alazán, rojo, canela. 2 *s.* color o caballo alazán. *3* BOT. acedera.
**sorrily** (sa·rili) *adv.* lastimosamente. 2 mal, malamente, pésimamente.
**sorrow** (sa·rou o sa·rou) *s.* dolor, pesar, pena, sentimiento. 2 arrepentimiento. 3 luto, duelo. 4 infortunio, sinsabor.
**sorrow (to)** *intr.* afligirse, sentir pena.

**sorrowful** (-ful) *adj.* afligido, pesaroso, desconsolado. *2* doloroso, lamentable. *3* triste, melancólico.
**sorrow-stricken** *adj.* agobiado de dolor.
**sorry** (sa·ri o so·ri) *adj.* afligido, pesaroso, triste, que siente o compadece: *I am* ~, lo siento; *I am* ~ *for him*, le compadezco. *2* arrepentido. *3* penoso, lastimoso. *4* malo, pobre, mezquino, ruin.
**sort** (so'rt) *s.* clase, especie, suerte: *a* ~ *of*, una especie de; *of sorts*, de varias clases, de clase mediocre. *2* modo, manera: *after a* ~, *in a* ~, en cierto modo. *3* *out of sorts*, indispuesto; de mal humor. *4* ~ *of*, algo, un tanto.
**sort (to)** *tr.* ordenar, clasificar. *2* escoger, entresacar. *3* *intr.* juntarse, andar con.
**sortie** (so·'tɪ) *s.* MIL. salida, surtida.
**sortilege** (so·'tilidӯ) *s.* sortilegio.
**sorus** (sou·røs), *pl.* **-ri** (-rai) *s.* BOT. soro.
**S.O.S.** (es ou es) *s.* S.O.S., llamada de auxilio.
**so-so** (sou-sou) *adj.* regular, mediano, pasadero.
**sot** (sat) *s.* borrachín.
**sottish** (sa·tish) *adj.* embrutecido por el vicio de la bebida. *2* borracho.
**soubrette** (subre·t) *s.* TEAT. graciosa, doncella.
**soubriquet** (sou·brikei) *s.* SOBRIQUET.
**Soudan** (sudæ·n) *n. pr.* GEOGR. Sudán.
**sough** (søf o sau) *s.* suspiro profundo. *2* murmullo, susurro [del viento].
**sough (to)** *intr.* suspirar, murmurar, susurrar.
**sought** (sot) *pret.* y *p. p.* de TO SEEK.
**soul** (soul) *s.* alma [en todos sus sentidos, menos en los de hueco, madero o pieza interior]: *every living* ~, todo bicho viviente; *poor* ~, pobre, pobrecito; *he is the* ~ *of honour*, es el honor mismo; *upon my* ~, en mi conciencia.
**soulful** (sou·lful) *adj.* conmovedor, lleno de sentimiento o que lo expresa; espiritual.
**soulless** (-lis) *adj.* desalmado, sin conciencia. *2* ruin, sin grandeza de alma.
**soul-pained** *adj.* afligido.
**sound** (saund) *adj.* sano: ~ *of mind*, en su cabal juicio. *2* ileso, incólume, entero, cabal. *3* cuerdo, sensato. *4* sólido, firme, seguro. *5* COM. solvente. *6* bueno, fuerte: *a* ~ *beating*, una buena paliza. *7* fiel, leal. *8* profundo [sueño]. *9* sonoro: ~ *film*, película sonora; ~ *wave*, FÍS. onda sonora. *10* *s.* son, sonido, tañido; ruido. *11* MAR., MED. sonda. *12* GEOGR. brazo de mar, estrecho.
**sound (to)** *intr.* sonar. *2* hacer ruido. *3* resonar; divulgarse. *4* echar la sonda. *5* sumergirse [la ballena]. *6* *tr.* tocar, tañer [un instrumento]; tocar [un toque, etc.]. *7* cantar, entonar [alabanzas]. *8* sondar; sondear; explorar. *9* auscultar.
**Sound** *n. pr.* GEOGR. Sund.
**soundboard** (-bo'd) *s.* SOUNDING BOARD.
**sounder** (-ø') *s.* tañedor. *2* sondeador. *3* CIR. sonda. *4* ELECT. resonador.
**sounding** (-ing) *adj.* sonoro, sonante, resonante: ~ *board*, tabla de armonía, secreto [del órgano]; tornavoz de púlpito. *2* de sondeo: ~ *lead*, MAR. escandallo; ~ *line*, sonda, sondaleza. *3* *s.* acción de sonar. *4* sondeo. *5* braceaje. *6* *pl.* MAR. aguas poco profundas.
**soundless** (-lis) *adj.* silencioso. *2* insondable.
**soundly** (-li) *adv.* sanamente. *2* cuerdamente. *3* firmemente. *4* vigorosamente. *5* profundamente, a pierna suelta.
**soundproof** (-pruf) *adj.* insonorizado.
**soup** (sup) *s.* COC. sopa: ~ *dish*, plato sopero; ~ *kitchen*, cocina de campaña; comedor de bene-

ficencia; ~ *tureen*, sopera. *2* fig. *in the* ~, en apuros.
**sour** (sau') *adj.* ácido, acedo, agrio. *2* rancio; fermentado. *3* verde [fruta]: ~ *grapes*, fig. están verdes. *4* agrio, áspero, desabrido, huraño, avinagrado. *5* desagradable. *6* BOT. ~ *cherry*, guindo; guinda.
**sour (to)** *intr.* agriarse. *2* enranciarse, fermentar. *3* malearse [la tierra]. *4* *tr.* agriar. *5* enranciar. *6* estropear, amargar.
**source** (so's) *s.* fuente, manantial: *to have from a good* ~, saber de buena tinta.
**sourdine** (su'di·n) *s.* MÚS. sordina.
**sourdough** (sau·'dou) *s.* levadura.
**sourish** (sau·rish) *adj.* agrillo, agrete.
**sourness** (sau·'nis) *s.* acidez, agrura. *2* aspereza.
**soursop** (-sap) *s.* BOT. guanábano; guanábana.
**souse** (saus) *s.* escabeche, encurtido; cabeza, mano u oreja de cerdo en vinagre. *2* zambullida, remojón.
**souse (to)** *tr.* escabechar, encurtir. *2* zambullir; remojar. *3* inundar. *4* (E.U.) emborrachar. *5* *intr.* mojarse, empaparse. *6* zambullirse. *7* (E.U.) emborracharse.
**soutane** (suta·n) *s.* sotana.
**south** (sauz) *s.* sur, mediodía. *2* *adj.* del sur, meridional: *South America*, América del Sur; *South American*, sudamericano; *South Pole*, Polo Sur. *3* *adv.* al sur; hacia el sur.
**southeast** (sauzɪ·st) *adj.-s.* sudeste. *2* *adv.* hacia el sudeste, del sudeste.
**southeastern** (sauzi·stø'n) *adj.* del sudeste.
**souther** (sau·zø') *s.* temporal o viento del sur.
**southerly** (sø·ðø'li) *adj.-adv.* del sur.
**southern** (sø·ðø'n) *adj.* del sur, meridional: *Southern Cross*, ASTR. Cruz del Sur.
**southernmost** (-moust) *adj.* más meridional.
**southernwood** (-wud) *s.* BOT. abrótano.
**southlander** (sau·zlændø') *s.* meridional.
**southpaw** (-po) *adj.-s.* DEP. zurdo.
**southward** (-uø'd) *adj.* situado hacia el sur. *2* *adv.* al sur, hacia el sur.
**southwest** (-ue·st) *adj.-s.* sudoeste.
**southwester** (-ø') *s.* temporal o viento del sudoeste. *2* MAR. sueste [sombrero].
**southwestern** (sauzue·stø'n) *adj.* del sudoeste.
**souvenir** (suveni·') *s.* recuerdo.
**sovereign** (sø·vrin) *adj.* soberano. *2* supremo, sumo. *3* *s.* soberano [monarca; moneda].
**sovereignty** (-ti) *s.* soberanía. *2* supremacía.
**soviet** (sou·viet) *s.* soviet. *2* *adj.* soviético: *Soviet Union*, Unión Soviética.
**sow** (sau) *s.* ZOOL. cerda, marrana. *2* ZOOL. ~ *bug*, cochinilla de la humedad.
**sow (to)** (sou) *tr.* sembrar: fig. *to* ~ *one's wild oats*, calaverear, pasar las mocedades. ¶ Pret.: *sowed*; p. p.: *sown* o *sowed*.
**sowbread** (sau·bred) *s.* BOT. pamporcino.
**sower** (sou·ø') *s.* sembrador. *2* sembradera.
**sown** (soun) *p. p.* de TO SOW.
**soy** (soi), **soya** (sou·ia), **soybean** (soi·bin) *s.* BOT. soja [planta y semilla].
**spa** (spa) *s.* balneario. *2* manantial de agua mineral.
**space** (speis) *s.* espacio. | No tiene el sentido de lentitud, tardanza: ~ *bar*, ~ *key*, espaciador [de máquina de escribir]. *2* trecho, distancia. *3* plaza, sitio. *4* tiempo, oportunidad.
**space (to)** *tr.* espaciar. *2* IMPR. regletear.
**spaceless** (-lis) *adj.* sin extensión.

**spacious** (spei·shøs) *adj.* espacioso; vasto, dilatado. *2* amplio, comprensivo.

**spadassin** (spadæ·sin) *s.* espadachín.

**spade** (speid) *s.* laya, pala [para remover la tierra]; zapa: *to call a ~ a ~*, llamar al pan, pan y al vino, vino. *2 pl.* picas [de la baraja inglesa].

**spade (to)** *tr.* layar, zapar, remover la tierra.

**spadix** (spei·diks) *s.* BOT. espádice.

**Spain** (spein) *n. pr.* GEOGR. España.

**spall** (spol) *s.* astilla.

**spall (to)** *tr.* romper, astillar [esp. piedra].

**span** (spæn) *s.* palmo, llave de la mano. *2* extensión; trecho, espacio, lapso; instante. *3* luz [de un arco]; ojo [de puente]. *4* tronco [de caballerías]. *5* envergadura [de aeroplano].

**span (to)** *tr.* medir por palmos; medir [en general]. *2* extenderse de un lado a otro de; tender un arco o puente sobre. *3* alcanzar, abarcar [en el espacio o en el tiempo]. ¶ Pret. y p. p.: *spanned;* ger.: *-nning.*

**spandrel** (spæ·ndrøl) *s.* ARQ. enjuta, embecadura.

**spangle** (spæ·ngøl) *s.* lentejuela; cosa brillante. *2* destello.

**spangle (to)** *tr.* adornar con lentejuelas o cosas brillantes. *2 intr.* destellar, centellear.

**Spaniard** (spæ·nia^rd) *s.* español.

**spaniel** (spæ·niøl) *s.* perro de aguas.

**Spanish** (spæ·nish) *adj.* español, hispano hispánico: *~ broom*, retama; *~ fly*, ENT. cantárida; *~ leather*, cordobán; *~ Main*, GEOGR. Tierra Firme; Mar del Caribe; *~ shawl*, mantón de Manila; *~ white*, yeso mate. *2 s.* lengua española o castellana. *3 pl.* the *Spanish*, los españoles.

**Spanish-American** *adj.-s.* hispanoamericano.

**Spanish-speaking** *adj.* de habla española.

**spank** (spænk) *s.* golpe, palmada, nalgada.

**spank (to)** *tr.* azotar, dar nalgadas. *2 intr.* correr, galopar.

**spanker** (-ø^r) *s.* azotador; azote. *2* pers. o cosa notable. *3* caballo veloz. *4* MAR. cangreja de mesana.

**spanking** (-ing) *s.* nalgada; azotaina. *2 adj.* rápido, veloz. *3* fuerte [viento]. *4* grande, notable.

**spanless** (spæ·nlis) *adj.* que no se puede abarcar o medir.

**spanner** (spæ·nø^r) *s.* MEC. llave de tuerca, llave inglesa.

**spanworm** (spæ·nwø^rm) *s.* ENT. oruga geómetra.

**spar** (spa^r) *s.* MINER. espato. *2* MAR. palo; verga; botalón. *3* pértiga. *4* hurgonazo. *5* boxeo, combate de boxeo. *6* riña de gallos. *7* riña, pelea. *8 adj.* MAR. *~ deck*, cubierta superior sin estructuras altas.

**spar (to)** *tr.* MAR. proveer de palos, vergas, etc. *2 intr.* boxear. *3* luchar a espolonazos [los gallos]. *4* reñir, disputar. ¶ Pret. y p. p.: *sparred;* ger.: *-rring.*

**spare** (spe·ø^r) *adj.* de repuesto, de recambio; sobrante; libre, disponible: *~ parts*, piezas de recambio; *~ time*, tiempo libre, ratos perdidos. *2* flaco, enjuto. *3* escaso, sobrio, frugal. *4* cicatero. *5 s.* pieza de recambio.

**spare (to)** *tr.* ahorrar, economizar, evitar, excusar: *to have (something) to ~*, tener [algo] de sobra; *to be spared the labour*, ahorrarse el trabajo. *2* prescindir de, pasar sin. *3* perdonar, hacer gracia de. *4* no maltratar. *5 to ~ oneself*, cuidarse; evitarse molestias. *6 intr.* economizar. *7* ser clemente.

**spare-built** *adj.* delgado, enjuto.

**sparerib** (-rib) *s.* chuleta de cerdo casi descarnada.

**sparing** (-ing) *adj.* económico, parco, sobrio, frugal. *2* escaso. *3* clemente.

**spark** (spa^rk) *s.* chispa; centella, chispazo: *~ arrester*, ELECT. parachispas; *~ coil*, bobina de inducción; *~ plug*, bujía [del motor]. *2* fig. chispa, átomo, pizca. *3* galán; lechuguino.

**spark (to)** *intr.* chispear, echar chispas, centellear.

**sparkle** (-øl) *s.* chispa, destello, brillo, centelleo. *2* viveza, animación. *3* chispa [diamante pequeño]. *4* chispa, átomo, pizca.

**sparkle (to)** *intr.* chispear, destellar, centellear, brillar. *2* espumar [un vino]. *3* tener viveza, animación.

**sparklet** (spa^r·kløt) *s.* centellita, chispita.

**sparkling** (-ing) *adj.* chispeante, centelleante. *2* vivo, animado. *3* espumoso [vino].

**sparrow** (spæ·rou) *s.* ORN. gorrión. *2* nombre de otros pájaros.

**sparrow-hawk** *s.* ORN. gavilán, esparver.

**sparse** (spa^rs) *adj.* esparcido, desparramado. *2* escaso, claro, ralo.

**sparsity** (-iti) *s.* raleza. *2* escasez, parquedad.

**Sparta** (spa·^rta) *n. pr.* GEOGR. Esparta.

**Spartan** (-tan) *adj.-s.* espartano.

**spasm** (spæʒm) *s.* MED. espasmo. *2* paroxismo.

**spasmodic** (spæsma·dik) *adj.* espasmódico. *2* intermitente.

**spat** (spæt) *pret.* y *p. p.* de TO SPIT. *2* cría [de los mariscos]. *3* golpecito. *4* gota, salpicadura. *5 pl.* botines [calzado].

**spat (to)** *intr.-tr.* desovar [los mariscos]. *2 intr.* sonar [la lluvia; un impacto]. *2 tr.* dar un golpecito. ¶ Pret. y p. p.: *spatted;* ger.: *-tting.*

**spate** (speit) *s.* (Ingl.) chaparrón. *2* (Ingl.) riada. *3* abundancia; torrente [de palabras]; fuerte emoción.

**spate (to)** *tr.* inundar.

**spathe** (spei·ð) *s.* BOT. espata.

**spathic** (spæ·zik) *adj.* MINER. espático.

**spatial** (spei·shal) *adj.* espacial.

**spatter** (spæ·tø^r) *s.* salpicadura, rociada. *2* chapoteo.

**spatter (to)** *tr.* salpicar, rociar. *2* difamar. *3 intr.* echar salpicaduras. *4* caer en gotas gruesas. *5* chapotear.

**spatterdashes** (-dæshiš) *s. pl.* polainas.

**spatula** (spæ·chøla) *s.* espátula [instrumento].

**spatulate** (spæ·chøleit) *adj.* espatulado.

**spavin** (spæ·vin) *s.* VET. esparaván.

**spawn** (spon) *s.* ICT. freza. *2* huevos de marisco. *3* desp. prole; producto, resultado.

**spawn (to)** *tr.-intr.* desovar [los peces, los mariscos]. *2* desp. producir, engendrar. *3 intr.* producirse en abundancia.

**spay (to)** (spei) *tr.* castrar [las hembras de los animales].

**speak (to)** (spik) *intr.* hablar: *to ~ for*, hablar por, ser prueba de; *to ~ out*, hablar claro, explicarse; hablar en voz alta; *to ~ through the nose*, ganguear; *to ~ well for*, decir mucho en favor de; *so to ~*, por decirlo así. *2 tr.* hablar, decir, expresar, proferir: *to ~ one's mind*, decir lo que uno piensa; *to ~ volumes*, decir mucho, ser muy significativo. *3* hablar [una lengua]. ¶ Pret.: *spoke;* p. p.: *spoken.*

**speakable** (-abøl) *adj.* decible.

**speakeasy** (-iši) *s.* fam. (E.U.) taberna clandestina.

**speaker** (-ø^r) *s.* el que habla. *2* orador. *3* presidente [de una asamblea]. *4* RADIO. locutor. *5* RADIO. altavoz.

**speaking** (-ing) *adj.* que habla, parlante para ha-

blar: ~ *tube*, tubo acústico; *to be on ~ terms*, hablarse, tratarse. *2 s.* habla, acto de hablar, discurso. *3* oratoria.
**spear** (spiᵣ) *s.* lanza, venablo. *2* fisga, arpón [para pescar]. *3* tallo, caña [de hierba].
**spear (to)** *tr.* alancear. *2* atravesar con arpón. *3 intr.* BOT. echar un tallo largo.
**spearhead** (-jed) *s.* moharra, punta de lanza.
**spearman** (-mæn) *s.* lancero.
**spearmint** (-mint) *s.* BOT. variedad de menta.
**spearwort** (-uøᵣt) *s.* BOT. ranúnculo.
**special** (spe·shal) *adj.* especial. *2* particular, peculiar. *3 ~ delivery*, correo urgente. *4 s.* tren, autobús, etc., especial. *5* carta urgente.
**specialism** (-išm) *s.* especialización.
**specialist** (-ist) *adj.-s.* especialista.
**speciality** (-iti) *s.* SPECIALTY.
**specialize (to)** (-aiš) *tr.* especializar. *2* detallar, particularizar. *3 intr.* especializarse. *4* entrar en detalles.
**specialty** (-i) *s.* especialidad. *2* peculiaridad, cualidad distintiva.
**specie** (spi·shi) *s.* efectivo, metálio.
**species** (spi·shiš) *s.* especie [imagen mental; apariencia]. *2* especie sacramental. *3* LÓG., H. NAT. especie. *4* especie, clase, suerte. *5* género humano.
**specific (al** (spisi·fik(al) *adj.* específico. *2* preciso, determinado. *3* peculiar, característico. *4 s.* FARM. específico.
**specification** (-eishøn) *s.* especificación. *2 pl.* presupuesto de una obra; pliego de condiciones. *3* instrucciones, detalles técnicos.
**specify (to)** (spi·sifai) *tr.* especificar, detallar. *2* estipular, prescribir. ¶ Pret. y p. p.: *specified*.
**specimen** (spe·simøn) *s.* espécimen, muestra, ejemplar. *2* fam. sujeto, individuo.
**specious** (spi·shøs) *adj.* especioso, engañoso.
**speck** (spek) *s.* manchita; motita, partícula. *2* pizca, átomo.
**speck (to)** *tr.* manchar, motear.
**speckle** (-øl) *s.* manchita, punto.
**speckle (to)** *tr.* manchar, motear, salpicar de manchitas, espolvorear, esmaltar.
**specs** (-s) *s. pl.* fam. gafas, anteojos.
**spectacle** (-tøkøl) *s.* espectáculo, exhibición. *2 pl.* gafas, anteojos.
**spectacular** (-tæ·kiulaᵣ) *adj.* espectacular. *2* sensacional, aparatoso.
**spectator** (spektei·tøᵣ) *m.* espectador.
**spectatress** (-tris) *s.* espectadora.
**specter** (spe·ktøᵣ) *s.* espectro, aparición.
**spectral** (-tral) *adj.* espectral.
**spectre** (-tøᵣ) *s.* SPECTER.
**spectroscope** (-trøskoup) *s.* espectroscopio.
**spectroscopy** (spektra·skøpi) *s.* espectroscopia.
**spectrum** (spe·ktrøm), *pl.* **spectra** (-tra) *s.* FÍS. espectro.
**speculate (to)** (spe·kiuleit) *intr.* especular, medi-
᾿  tar, teorizar [sobre]. *2* COM. especular.
**speculation** (-ei·shøn) *s.* especulación, conjetura, teoría. *2* COM. especulación.
**speculative** (spe·kiuleitiv) *adj.* especulativo, contemplativo. *2* teórico. *3* COM. especulador.
**speculator** (-tøᵣ) *s.* especulador, teórico. *2* COM. especulador. *3* TEAT. revendedor de billetes.
**speculum** (spe·kiuløm) *s.* CIR. espéculo.
**sped** (sped) *pret.* y *p. p.* de TO SPEED.
**speech** (spich) *s.* palabra, habla, lenguaje. *2* idioma, dialecto. *3* cosa hablada, oración, discurso. *4* TEAT. parlamento. *5* conversación.

**speechify (to)** (-ifai) *intr.* fam. discursear.
**speechless** (-lis) *adj.* mudo, callado, silencioso. *2* estupefacto, cortado, sobrecogido, sin hbla.
**speechmaker** (-meikøᵣ) *s.* orador.
**speed** (spid) *s.* rapidez, prisa, prontitud, presteza: *with all ~*, a toda prisa; *to make ~*, apresurarse, acelerarse. *2* marcha, andar, velocidad: *~ gear*, cambio de marchas; *~ limit*, máxima velocidad permitida; *full ~*, a toda velocidad. *3 adj.* rápido.
**speed (to)** *tr.* acelerar, avivar, apresurar, dar prisa a. *2* despachar, expedir. *3* prosperar, favorecer, ayudar. *4 intr.* apresurarse, correr. *5* llevar una velocidad excesiva. *6* prosperar, tener buen éxito. ¶ Pret. y p. p.: *sped* o *speeded*.
**speedboat** (-bout) *s.* canoa automóvil.
**speedometer** (spida·mitøᵣ) *s.* indicador de velocidad; taxímetro; odómetro.
**speed-up** (-nsøᵣ) *s.* aceleración, aumento de velocidad. *2* aumento de producción.
**speedway** (-wei) *s.* autopista.
**speedwell** (-wel) *s.* BOT. verónica.
**speedy** (-i) *adj.* rápido, veloz, ligero. *2* activo, pronto, diligente, expeditivo.
**spelean** (spili·æn) *adj.* troglodita.
**speleology** (spilia·lodŷi) *s.* espeleología.
**spell** (spel) *s.* hechizo, encanto, maleficio. *7* hechizo, fascinación. *3* relevo, turno, tanda. *4* rato, período, temporada: *by spells*, por turnos; *a ratos*.
**spell (to)** *tr.-intr.* deletrear. *2* escribir correctamente. *3* tr. indicar, significar. *4* descifrar. *5* hechizar, encantar. *6* relevar, reemplazar. ¶ Pret. y p. p.: *spelled* o *spelt*.
**spellbind (to)** (-baind) *tr.* hechizar, encantar, fascinar. ¶ CONJUG. pret. y p. p.: *spellbound*.
**spellbinder** (-baindøᵣ) *s.* orador persuasivo y arrebatador.
**spellbound** (-baund) *pret.* y *p. p.* de TO SPELLBIND.
**speller** (-øᵣ) *s.* deletreador. *2* silabario, cartilla.
**spelling** (-ing) *s.* deletreo; ortografía.
**spelt** (spelt) *p. p.* de TO SPELL. *2 s.* BOT. espelta.
**spelter** (spe·ltøᵣ) *s.* cinc, peltre.
**spelt-wheat** *s.* BOT. escanda, espelta.
**spencer** (spe·nsøᵣ) *s.* chaqueta corta de punto.
**spend (to)** (spend) *tr.* gastar, expender. *2* consumir, agotar. *3* pasar [un tiempo]. *4 intr.* gastar, hacer gastos. *5* consumirse, agotarse. ¶ Pret. y p. p.: *spent*.
**spendthrift** (-zrift) *s.* derrochador, malgastador, manirroto, pródigo.
**spent** (spent) *pret.* y *p. p.* de TO SPEND.
**sperm** (spøᵣm) *s.* esperma, semen. *2* espermatozoo. *3* esperma de ballena: *~ whale*, cachalote.
**spermaceti** (spøᵣmase·ti) *s.* esperma de ballena.
**spermatic (al** (spøᵣmæ·tik(al) *adj.* espermático.
**spermatozoön** (-tošou·øn) *s.* BIOL. espermatozoo.
**spew (to)** (spiu) *tr.-intr.* vomitar, arrojar.
**sphenoid** (sfi·noid) *adj.* esfenoidal. *2 s.* ANAT. esfenoides.
**sphere** (sfiᵣ) *s.* GEOM., GEOGR., ASTR. esfera. *2* globo, orbe. *3* astro. *4* poét. atmósfera, cielo. *5* esfera [de acción social, etc.].
**spheric** (sfe·rik) *adj.* esférico.
**spherical** (sfe·rikal) *adj.* esférico. *2* globular, orbicular. *3* de las esferas, celeste, astral.
**sphericity** (sfiri·siti) *s.* esfericidad.
**spheroid** (sfi·roid) *s.* esferoide.
**spheroidal** (sfiroi·dal) *adj.* esferoidal.
**spherometer** (sfira·metøᵣ) *s.* esferómetro.
**spherule** (sfe·riul) *s.* glóbulo.

**sphincter** (sfiˑnktøʳ) *s.* ANAT. esfínter.
**sphinx** (sfinks) *s.* MIT., ARQUEOL., ENT. esfinge. *2* fig. pers. enigmática.
**spice** (spais) *s.* especia. *2* sainete, picante, interés. *3* aroma, fragancia. *4* punta, algo, un poco.
**spice (to)** *tr.* condimentar con especias. *2* salpimentar, sazonar, dar picante o interés a.
**spicery** (-øri) *s.* especiería. *2* aroma, picante.
**spick-and-span** *adj.* nuevo, flamante, fresco. *2* pulcro, aseado, arreglado.
**spicula** (spiˑkiula) *s.* espícula.
**spicule** (spiˑkiul) *s.* espícula. *2* BOT. espiguilla. *3* aguja del hielo, de la nieve.
**spicy** (spaiˑsi) *adj.* sazonado con especias, picante, aromático. *2* fig. sabroso, picante. *3* vivo, pronto. *4* elegante, llamativo.
**spider** (spaiˑdøʳ) *s.* ZOOL. araña: *spider's web*, telaraña; ~ *lines*, ÓPT. retícula. *2* trébedes. *3* cazo o sartén con pies. *4* ZOOL. ~ *monkey*, mono araña.
**spidery** (-i) *adj.* parecido a una araña.
**spiffy** (spiˑfi) *adj.* fam. guapo, elegante.
**spigot** (spiˑgøt) *s.* espiche, botana, bitoque. *2* macho [de grifo o espita]. *3* (E.U.) grifo, espita.
**spike** (spaik) *s.* pincho, púa; punta de hierro. *2* clavo grande, alcayata. *3* BOT. espiga. *4* BOT. espliego. *5* (E.U.) gotas [de licor].
**spike (to)** *tr.* clavar [con clavos grandes]. *2* clavar [un cañón]. *3* atravesar, empalar. *4* acabar, poner fin a; inutilizar. *5* intr. formar espiga.
**spikelet** (-lit) *s.* BOT. espiguilla.
**spikenard** (-naʳd) *s.* BOT. espicanardo. *2* nardo [perfume].
**spiky** (-i) *adj.* puntiagudo. *2* erizado, armado de pinchos o púas.
**spile** (spail) *s.* botana, espiche. *2* estaca, pilote.
**spile (to)** *tr.* abrir [un barril]; ponerle botana o espita. *2* poner estacas o pilotes.
**spilikin** (spiˑlikin) *s.* SPILLIKIN.
**spill** (spil) *s.* astilla, alegrador [para encender]. *2* derramamiento. *3* fam. vuelco, caída.
**spill (to)** *tr.* verter, derramar. *2* contar, divulgar. *3* fam. despedir [de una montura, de un vehículo]. *4* MAR. quitar viento a [una vela]. *5* intr. verterse, derramarse. *6* pop. charlar [revelar lo secreto]. ¶ Pret. y p. p.: *spilled* o *spilt*.
**spillikin** (spiˑlikin) *s.* pajita [para jugar]. *2* pl. juego de las pajitas.
**spilt** (spilt) *pret.* y *p. p.* de TO SPILL.
**spin** (spin) *s.* giro, vuelta. *2* fam. paseo en coche o bicicleta. *3* AVIA. barrena.
**spin (to)** *tr.-intr.* hilar. *2* tejer [fantasías, etc.]; hacer, componer [una narración, etc.]: *to ~ a yarn*, contar un cuento increíble. *3* hacer girar. *4* hacer bailar [un trompo]. *5* *to ~ out*, alargar, prolongar, extender. *6* intr. dar vueltas, girar, pasar, rápidamente. *7* bailar [el trompo]. *8* AVIA. descender en barrena. ¶ Pret. y p. p.: *spun*; ger.: *spinning*.
**spinach** (spiˑnich) *s.* BOT. espinaca. *2* COC. espinacas.
**spinal** (spaiˑnal) *adj.* espinal: ~ *column*, espina dorsal; ~ *cord*, médula espinal.
**spindle** (spiˑndøl) *s.* HIL., BIOL. huso. *2* BOT. raquis, eje. *3* MEC. eje, mandril, varilla. *4* balustre. *5* BOT. ~ *tree*, bonetero.
**spindle (to)** *intr.* crecer muy alto y delgado.
**spindlelegs** (-legš) *s. pl.* piernas largas. *2* sing. persona flaquivana.
**spindle-shaped** *adj.* ahusado, fusiforme.
**spindrift** (spiˑndrift) *s.* rocío, roción [del mar].

**spine** (spain) *s.* espinazo. *2* fig. valor, energía. *3* fig. parte saliente y esquinada. *4* espina, púa.
**spinel** (spineˑl) *s.* MINER. espinela.
**spineless** (spaiˑnlis) *adj.* invertebrado. *2* fláccido, flojo; sin valor, sin energía. *3* sin espinas.
**spinet** (spiˑnit) *s.* MÚS. espineta.
**spinnaker** (spiˑnakøʳ) *s.* MAR. spinnaker.
**spinner** (spiˑnøʳ) *s.* hilador, hilandero. *2* máquina de hilar.
**spinneret** (-øret) *s.* ZOOL. hilera.
**spinney** (-i) *s.* bosquecillo, soto.
**spinning** (-spiˑning) *s.* hila, hilado, hilatura. *2* giro rápido. *3* que hila, de hilar: ~ *mill*, fábrica de hilados; ~ *wheel*, torno para hilar. *4* que gira: ~ *top*, trompo. *5* rápido, veloz.
**spinose** (spaiˑnous) *adj.* espinoso [que tiene espinas].
**spinous** (-nøs) *adj.* espinoso.
**Spinozism** (spinouˑšišm) *s.* espinosismo.
**spinster** (spiˑnstøʳ) *s.* soltera, solterona. *2* ant. hilandera.
**spinstress** (-tris) *s.* hilandera.
**spiny** (spaiˑni) *adj.* espinoso. *2* punzante.
**spiracle** (spiˑarakøl) *s.* ZOOL. espiráculo.
**spiral** (spaiˑral) *adj.* espiral. *2* helicoidal. *3* de caracol [escalera]. *4* *s.* GEOM. espiral; hélice; espira.
**spiral (to)** *intr.* moverse en espiral; tomar forma espiral. *2* AVIA. volar en espiral.
**spire** (spaiʳ) *s.* GEOM., ZOOL. espira. *2* GEOM. espiral. *3* cima, cúspide. *4* ARQ. aguja, chapitel. *5* BOT. brizna, caña o tallo largo y delgado.
**spire (to)** *tr.* elevarse [como un chapitel]; rematar en punta. *2* elevarse en espiral. *3* brotar, germinar.
**spirillum** (spairiˑløm) *s.* BACT. espirilo.
**spirit** (spiˑrit) *s.* espíritu [en todos sus sentidos]: *the Holy Spirit*, el Espíritu Santo; ~ *rapper*, espiritista: *in* ~, en espíritu. *2* aparecido, espectro. *3* estado de ánimo, humor, temple. | A veces en *pl.: in good spirits*, alegre, de buen humor. *4* ánimo, valor; vivacidad, animación; energía, ardor, fuego: *to break the* ~ *of*, desalentar; reprimir, domeñar. *5* pl. alcohol, bebida espirituosa. *6* *spirits* o *high spirits*, alegría, animación, viveza; *out of spirits*, triste, abatido. *7* *animal spirits*, vivacidad, fogosidad, energía.
**spirit (to)** *tr.* alentar, animar. | A veces con *up*. *2* infundir cierto espíritu. *3* *to ~ away* u *off*, llevarse, raptar, escamotear, hacer desaparecer.
**spirited** (-id) *adj.* vivo, brioso, espiritoso, fogoso.
**spiritedly** (-idli) *adv.* vivamente, briosamente, fogosamente, animosamente.
**spiritism** (-išm) *s.* espiritismo.
**spiritist** (-ist) *s.* espiritista.
**spiritless** (-lis) *adj.* exánime. *2* abatido, desanimado. *3* cobarde. *4* flojo, sin vigor.
**spiritual** (spiˑrichual) *adj.* espiritual. *2* mental, intelectual. *3* eclesiástico. *4* inteligente, agudo. *5* de los espíritus. *6* *s.* espiritual [canto religioso de los negros].
**spiritualism** (-išm) *s.* espiritualismo. *2* espiritualidad. *3* espiritismo.
**spiritualist** (-ist) *adj.-s.* espiritualista. *2* espiritista.
**spiritualistic** (spirichualiˑstik) *adj.* espiritista. *2* espiritualista.
**spirituality** (spirichuæˑliti) *s.* espiritualidad. *2* pl. bienes espirituales o eclesiásticos.
**spiritualize (to)** (spiˑrichualaiš) *tr.* espiritualizar.
**spirituous** (spiˑrichuøs) *adj.* espirituoso.

**spirituousness** (-nis) *s.* calidad de espirituoso.
**spirometer** (spaira·mitø$^r$) *s.* FISIOL. espirómetro.
**spirt** (spø$^r$t) *s.* SPURT.
**spirt (to)** *tr.* TO SPURT.
**spit** (spit) *s.* espetón, asador. *2* punta de tierra; banco de arena. *3* saliva, salivazo, escupitajo, esputo. *4* llovizna, nevisca.
**1) spit (to)** *tr.* espetar, ensartar, empalar. ¶ Pret. y p. p.: *spitted;* ger.: *-tting.*
**2) spit (to)** *tr.* escupir; esputar. *2* escupir, arrojar. *3 intr.* escupir. *4* lloviznar, neviscar. *5* chisporrotear. ¶ Pret. y p. p.: *spat;* ger.: *spitting.*
**spitball** (-bol) *s.* bolita de papel mascado.
**spitchcock** (spi·chkak) *s.* COC. anguila abierta o cortada y cocida.
**spitchcock (to)** *tr.* cortar y cocer. *2* tratar sumariamente.
**spite** (spait) *s.* despecho, rencor, inquina, resentimiento. *2 in ~ of*, a pesar de, a despecho de.
**spite (to)** *tr.* molestar, mortificar, irritar.
**spiteful** (spai·tful) *adj.* rencoroso, maligno, malévolo.
**spitfire** (spi·tfai$^r$) *s.* lo que escupe fuego; volcán, cañón, etc. *2* persona violenta, irascible.
**spittle** (spi·tøl) *s.* saliva, salivazo, escupidura.
**spittoon** (spitu·n) *s.* escupidera.
**spitz** (spits) *s.* perro de Pomerania.
**splash** (splæsh) *s.* salpicadura, rociada. *2* chapoteo. *3* mancha [de color]. *4* fig. *to make a ~*, llamar la atención, hacer sensación.
**splash (to)** *tr.* salpicar, rociar, manchar. *2* hacer saltar [el agua]. *3* chapotear, humedecer. *4 intr.* chapotear, chapalear.
**splashboard** (-bo$^r$d) guardabarros, alero.
**splashy** (-i) *adj.* cenagoso, lodoso. *2* llamativo; sensacional.
**splatter** (splæ·tø$^r$) *s.* SPATTER.
**splatter (to)** *tr.* rociar, salpicar; chapotear.
**splay** (splei) *adj.* ancho, extendido, desplegado. *2* abocinado, con derrame, capialzado. *3* tosco, pesado. *4 s.* extensión, expansión. *5* ARQ. alféizar, derrame, capialzo. *6* bisel, chaflán.
**splay (to)** *tr.* extender, desplegar. *2* VET. dislocar. *3* dar derrame, abocinar. *4* achaflanar.
**splayfoot(ed** (-fut(id) *adj.* de pies planos.
**spleen** (splin) *s.* ANAT. bazo. *2* bilis, rencor, mal humor. *3* esplín, melancolía.
**spleeny** (-i) *adj.* ·bilioso, irritable, enfadadizo. *2* melancólico.
**splendent** (sple·ndønt) *s.* brillante, esplendoroso.
**splendid** (-did) *adj.* espléndido [resplandeciente]. *2* ilustre, glorioso.
**splendo** (u) **r** (-ø$^r$) *s.* brillo, resplandor. *2* esplendor, magnificencia.
**splenetic** (spline·tik) *adj.* esplénico. *2* bilioso, rencoroso, malhumorado.
**splenic** (sple·nik) *adj.* ANAT. esplénico.
**splenius** (spli·niøs) *s.* ANAT. esplenio.
**splice** (splais) *s.* junta, empalme; ayuste.
**splice (to)** *tr.* empalmar, ayustar. *2* unir, juntar.
**splint** (splint) *s.* astilla. *2* tira estrecha. *3* CIR. tablilla, férula. *4* VET. sobrehueso.
**splint (to)** *tr.* CIR. entablillar.
**splinter** (-ø$^r$) *s.* astilla, esquirla. *2* rancajo. *3* cacho, añico. *4* CIR. tablilla.
**splinter (to)** *tr.* astillar. *2* CIR. entablillar. *3 intr.* astillarse, hacerse astillas.
**splintery** (-øri) *adj.* astilloso.
**split** (split) *s.* hendedura, grieta. *2* división, cisma, rompimiento. *3* astilla, raja. *4* media botella;

media copa. *5 pl.* despatarrada acrobática. *6 adj.* hendido, partido, rajado, dividido.
**split (to)** *tr.* hender, partir, rajar, dividir, separar: *to ~ one's sides*, desternillarse de risa. *2* reventar, romper. *3* revelar [un secreto]. *4 intr.* henderse, partirse, rajarse. *5* estallar, romperse. *6* separarse, dividirse. ¶ Pret. y p. p.: *split* o *splitted;* ger.: *-tting.*
**splitting** (-ing) *adj.* que raja o parte. *2* veloz. *3* muy cómico.
**splotch** (splach) *s.* mancha, borrón.
**splotch (to)** *tr.* manchar, salpicar.
**splurge** (splø$^r$dẏ) *s.* alarde, ostentación.
**splutter** (splø·tø$^r$) *s.* balbuceo, farfulla. *2* barullo, confusión. *3* rociada, salpicadura.
**splutter (to)** *tr.-intr.* balbucir, farfullar. *2* echar rociadas o salpicaduras.
**splutterer** (-ø$^r$) *s.* farfullador.
**spoil** (spoil) *s.* despojo, botín, presa. *2* saqueo, robo. *3 pl.* despojos, sobras.
**spoil (to)** *tr.* saquear, robar: *to ~ of*, privar de. *2* estropear, echar a perder. *3* viciar, corromper, pudrir. *4* mimar, malcriar. *5 intr.* estropearse, echarse a perder. ¶ Pret. y p. p.: *spoiled* o *spoilt.*
**spolit** (-t) *pret.* y *p. p.* de TO SPOIL.
**spoke** (spouk) *pret.* de TO SPEAK. *2 s.* rayo [de rueda]. *3* galga [freno]: *to put a ~ in one's wheel*, poner estorbos a uno. *4* travesaño [de escalera]. *5* cabilla [del timón].
**spoke (to)** *tr.* enrayar. *2* trabar, frenar.
**spoken** (-øn) *p. p.* de TO SPEAK.
**spokesman** (-smæn) *s.* portavoz, vocero. *2* orador.
**spoliation** (spouliei·shøn) *s.* expoliación, despojo, saqueo, rapiña.
**spoliator** (-tø$^r$) *s.* expoliador, saqueador.
**spondaic** (spandei·k) *adj.* espondaico.
**spondee** (spa·ndi) *s.* espondeo.
**sponge** (spøndẏ) *s.* esponja: *~ cake*, bizcocho muy ligero; *to thrown up the ~*, darse por vencido. *2* fig. gorrón, parásito. *3* ARTILL. lanada.
**sponge (to)** *tr.* lavar con esponja, borrar. *2* absorber, chupar. *3* sacar, exprimir. *4* esponjar [la masa]. *5 intr.* esponjarse. *6* pescar esponjas. *7 to ~ on*, vivir, etc., a costa de.
**sponger** (-ø$^r$) *s.* el que lava con esponja. *2* pescador de esponjas. *3* gorrón, sablista.
**spongy** (-i) *adj.* esponjoso. *2* fungoso. *3* flojo, sin consistencia. *4* mojado, lluvioso.
**sponsion** (spa·nshøn) *s.* acción de salir fiador o responder por otro.
**sponsor** (-sø$^r$) *s.* fiador, responsable. *2* padrino, madrina. *3* patrocinador.
**sponsor (to)** *tr.* salir fiador de, responder de [otro] o por [otro]. *2* apadrinar. *3* patrocinar.
**sponsorship** (-ship) *s.* fianza. *2* padrinazgo. *3* patrocinio.
**spontaneity** (spantanɪ·iti) *s.* espontaneidad.
**spontaneous** (spantei·niøs) *adj.* espontáneo.
**spook** (spuk) *s.* fam. fantasma, aparición.
**spool** (spul) *s.* carrete, canilla, carretel, bobina.
**spool (to)** *tr.* devanar en carrete, encanillar.
**spoon** (spun) *s.* cuchara: *~ cuchara: ~ hook*, anzuelo de cuchara. *2* cierto bastón de golf. *3 pop.* bobo; chalado.
**spoon (to)** *tr.* cucharear. *2* dar forma de cuchara. *4* ponerse tierno, acaramelado.
**spoonbill** (-bil) *s.* ORN. cuchareta; espátula.
**spoondrift** (-drift) *s.* rocío de las olas.
**spoonful** (-ful) *s.* cucharada.
**spoony** (-i) *adj.* amartelado, acaramelado. *2 s.* galán acaramelado.

**sporadic** (sporæ·dik) *adj.* esporádico.
**sporangium** (sporæ·ndÿiøm) *s.* BOT. esporangio.
**spore** (spo[r]) *s.* BIOL. espora.
**sporidium** (spori·diøm) *s.* BOT. esporidio.
**sporran** (spo·ran) *s.* escarcela de los montañeses de Escocia.
**sport** (spo[r]t) *s.* deporte. *2* juego, diversión, pasatiempo. *3* broma, burla: *in* ~, en broma; *to make* ~ *of*, burlarse de. *4* irrisión, hazmerreír. *5* juguete [de uno, de las pasiones, etc.]. *6* deportista, aficionado a los deportes. *7* fam. el que sabe perder; amigo, buen compañero. *8* BIOL. mutación.
**sport (to)** *tr.* ostentar, lucir. *2 intr.* jugar, divertirse, retozar, holgar. *3* bromear.
**sportful** (-ful) *adj.* juguetón. *2* chancero. *3* hecho ⸜ en broma, por juego.
**sporting** (spo·[r]ting) *adj.* deportivo. *2* que requiere cualidades deportivas; honrado, leal, arriesgado.
**sportive** (-iv) *adj.* juguetón. *2* alegre, festivo.
**sports** (-s) *adj.* deportivo, de deporte.
**sportsman** (-mæn) *m.* deportista. *2* hombre leal, que juega limpio, que sabe perder.
**sportsmanlike** (-mænslaik) *adj.* deportivo; leal, honrado.
**sportsmanship** (-mænship) *s.* destreza en los deportes; afición a ellos. *2* deportividad.
**sportswear** (-ue·[r]) *s.* ropa o trajes de deporte.
**sportswoman** (-wumæn) *s.* mujer deportista.
**sporty** (spo·[r]ti) *adj.* fam. deportivo. *2* alegre, disipado. *3* ostentoso, chillón.
**spot** (spat) *s.* mancha, borrón: ~ *remover*, quitamanchas. *2* lunar, pinta, punto; maca. *3* sitio, lugar, paraje, punto: *in spots*, aquí y allí; en algunos respectos; *on the* ~, en el sitio mismo; en el acto, al punto; alerta, despierto. *4 adj.* disponible, contante [dinero].
**spot (to)** *tr.* manchar. *2* motear, tachonar. *3* marcar, señalar. *4* reconocer, descubrir, divisar, observar; localizar. *5* colocar [una bola, etc.]. *6* diseminar. *7 intr.* mancharse. ¶ Pret. y p. p.: *spotted*; ger.: *-tting.*
**spotless** (-is) *adj.* limpio, inmaculado.
**spotlight** (-lait) *s.* reflector [de teatro], proyector orientable. *2* fig. vista o atención del público. *3* AUTO. faro piloto o giratorio.
**spotted** (-id) *adj.* manchado, moteado, pintado: ~ *fever*, tifus exantemático.
**spotter** (-ø[r]) *s.* pop. (E.U.) detective.
**spotty** (-i) *adj.* manchado.
**spousal** (spau·šal) *adj.* nupcial. *2 s. pl.* nupcias, bodas.
**spouse** (spauš) *s.* esposo; esposa; consorte.
**spout** (spaut) *s.* caño, espita, canilla [para líquidos]; pico, pitorro [de vasija]; gárgola, canalón. *2* chorro; surtidor. *3* aguacero. *4* pop. casa de empeños.
**spout (to)** *tr.* echar, arrojar [en chorro]. *2* pop. empeñar [un reloj, etc.]. *3 tr.-intr.* declamar. *4 intr.* chorrear, borbotar; brotar [un líquido].
**sprain** (sprein) *s.* MED. torcedura, esguince.
**sprain (to)** *tr.* MED. torcer: *to* ~ *one's ankle*, torcerse el tobillo.
**sprang** (spræng) *pret.* de TO SPRING.
**sprat** (spræt) *s.* ICT. arenque pequeño.
**sprawl** (sprol) *s.* postura del que yace, cae o se arrastra con las extremidades extendidas. *2* desparramamiento [de una planta].
**sprawl (to)** *intr.* yacer, caer, arrastrarse con las extremidades extendidas. *2* extenderse, despa-

rramarse [una planta]. *3 tr.* abrir, extender [los brazos, piernas, ramas, etc.].
**spray** (sprei) *s.* líquido pulverizado; rocío [del mar, de una cascada]. *2* ramita, ramaje.
**spray (to)** *tr.* esparcir [un líquido] en gotas finas. *2* rociar, pulverizar [con un líquido].
**sprayer** (-ø[r]) *s.* pulverizador; rociador.
**spread** (spred) *pret.* y *p. p.* de TO SPREAD. *2 adj.* extendido, etc. *3* BLAS. exployada [águila]. *4 s.* extensión, despliegue, desarrollo. *5* amplitud. *6* extensión [de terreno, etc.]. *7* difusión, propagación. *8* AVIA. envergadura. *9* cobertor; tapete; mantel. *10* mesa puesta, comida, festín.
**spread (to)** *tr.* extender, desplegar, desenvolver, alargar. *2* extender, esparcir, desparramar. *3* divulgar, publicar. *4* difundir, propagar. *5* emitir, exhalar. *6* ofrecer a la vista. *7* untar [con]; dar una mano [de]. *8* poner [la mesa], disponer, preparar. *9* fam. *to* ~ *oneself*, echar el resto; fachendear. *10 intr.* extenderse. *11* esparcirse, desparramarse. *12* difundirse, propagarse. *13* abrirse, separarse. ¶ Pret. y p. p.: *spread.*
**spread-eagle** *adj.*{(E.U.) patriotero [discurso, etc.].
**spree** (sprɪ) *s.* diversión, fiesta, juerga, parranda. *2* borrachera.
**spree (to)** *intr.* divertirse, ir de parranda. *2* emborracharse.
**sprig** (sprig) *s.* ramita, pimpollo. *2* hita, espiga [clavo].
**sprightly** (sprai·tli) *adj.* vivo, alegre, animado. *2* brioso, ágil, desenvuelto.
**spring** (spring) *s.* primavera [estación]. *2* fuente, manantial. *3* origen, principio; móvil. *4* salto, brinco. *5* muelle, resorte, ballesta. *6* resorte, elasticidad. *7* vigor, energía. *8* alabeo, combadura. *9* ARQ. arranque [de un arco]. *10 adj.* primaveral, de primavera. *11* de manántial. *12* de resorte, de muelle: ~ *latch*, cerradura de golpe; ~ *mattress*, colchón de muelles. *13* ~ *tide*, marea viva.
**spring (to)** *intr.* saltar, brincar; lanzarse, precipitarse, abalanzarse: *to* ~ *to one's feet*, *to* ~ *up*, levantarse de un salto. *2* salir, nacer, brotar; dimanar, provenir. *3* salir, aparecer, elevarse, crecer. | A veces con *forth, out* o *up*. *4* ARQ. arrancar [un arco]. *5* moverse, cerrarse, etc., por resorte, de golpe. *6* torcerse, alabearse, romperse. *7 tr.* hacer saltar. *8* levantar [la caza]. *9* sacar, presentar, dar, etc., de sopetón. *10* soltar [un resorte]; cerrar [con resorte]; meter o encajar haciendo muelle. *11* torcer, alabear, romper, rajar. *12* hacer estallar [una mina]; saltar [una valla, etc.]. *13 to* ~ *a leak*, hacer agua [un buque]. ¶ Pret.: *sprang* o *sprung*; p. p.: *sprung.*
**springboard** (-bo·[r]d) *s.* trampolín.
**springbook** (-bok) *s.* ZOOL. gacela del África del Sur.
**springer** (-ø[r]) *s.* saltador. *2* ojeador. *3* ARQ. imposta; sillar de arranque.
**springiness** (-inis) *s.* resorte, elasticidad.
**springtide** (-taid) *s.* primavera [estación].
**springy** (-i) *adj.* elástico. *2* abundante en fuentes o manantiales.
**sprinkle** (spri·nkøl) *s.* rocío, rociada. *2* llovizna. *3* pizca, poco.
**sprinkle (to)** *tr.* rociar, salpicar, regar, espolvorear, asperjar. *2* esparcir. *3 impers.* lloviznar.
**sprinkler** (spri·nklø[r]) *s.* regadera, aparato para regar.
**sprinkling** (-ing) *s.* rociadura, aspersión. *2* unas gotas, un poco, unos cuantos.

**sprint** (sprint) *s.* carrera corta y rápida. *2* corto período de esfuerzo.
**sprint (to)** *intr.* correr a toda velocidad, esp. por un corto espacio.
**sprit** (sprit) *s.* MAR. verga de vela de abanico.
**sprite** (sprait) *s.* duende, elfo, trasgo.
**spritsail** (spri·tseil) *s.* MAR. vela de abanico.
**sprocket** (spra·kit) *s.* MEC. diente que engrana con una cadena.
**sprout** (spraut) *s.* retoño, renuevo, brote. *2* pl. *sprouts* o *Brussels sprouts*, coles de Bruselas.
**sprout (to)** *intr.* germinar, brotar, retoñar, echar renuevos; crecer. *2 tr.* hacer germinar o brotar.
**spruce** (sprus) *adj.* pulcro, atildado, elegante, peripuesto. *2 s.* BOT. picea, abeto del Norte.
**spruce (to)** *tr.* asear, componer, vestir con elegancia. | Gralte. con *up.*
**sprung** (sprøng) *pret.* y *p. p.* de TO SPRING.
**spry** (sprai) *adj.* vivo, listo, ágil, activo.
**spud** (spød) *s.* laya larga y estrecha. *2* cosa corta y gruesa. *3* fam. patata.
**spue (to)** (spiu) *tr.-intr.* TO SPEW.
**spume** (spium) *s.* espuma. *2* espumarajo.
**spume (to)** *intr.* espumar, espumear.
**spumous** (-øs) *adj.* espumoso, espumajoso.
**spumy** (-i) *adj.* cubierto de espuma, espumoso.
**spun** (spøn) *pret.* y *p. p.* de TO SPIN.
**spun-out** *adj.* prolongado, prolijo.
**spunk** (spøŋk) *s.* fam. valor, denuedo; enojo. *2* yesca.
**spunky** (-i) *adj.* vivo, pronto. *2* valiente. *3* irritable, susceptible.
**spur** (spø<sup>r</sup>) *s.* espuela. *2* aguijón, estímulo, acicate: *on the ~ of the moment*, impulsivamente, sin reflexionar. *3* espolón. *4* uña puntiaguda. *5* pincho. *6* adj. *~ stone*, guardacantón; *~ timber*, MIN. ademe; *~ track*, FERROC. apartadero, vía muerta.
**spur (to)** *tr.* espolear, picar; aguijar, estimular: *to ~ on*, animar, incitar a seguir adelante. *2* poner o calzar espuelas. *3 intr.* picar espuelas, correr; seguir adelante. ¶ Pret. y *p. p.*: *spurred*; ger.: *-rring.*
**spurge** (spø<sup>r</sup>dȝ) *s.* BOT. euforbio; lechetrezna. *2 ~ laurel*, adelfilla.
**spurious** (spiu·riøs) *adj.* espurio. *2* BOT. falso, aparente.
**spurn** (spø<sup>r</sup>n) *s.* coz, puntapié. *2* desprecio.
**spurn (to)** *tr.* rechazar con desprecio, desdeñar, despreciar. *2* rechazar o echar a puntapiés.
**spurred** (spø<sup>.r</sup>d) *p. p.* de TO SPUR.
**spurrier** (spø·riø<sup>r</sup>) *s.* el que hace espuelas.
**spurry** (-i) *s.* BOT. espérgula.
**spurt** (spø<sup>r</sup>rt) *s.* chorretada, borbotón. *2* explosión [de ira, etc.]. *3* esfuerzo o aumento súbito. *4* rato, momento.
**spurt (to)** *intr.* brotar, salir en chorro. *2* estallar [una pasión], hacer un esfuerzo. *3 tr.* arrojar en chorro. *4* espurriar.
**sputter** (spø·tø<sup>r</sup>) *s.* rociada, esp. de saliva. *2* chisporroteo. *3* farfulla, barbulla.
**sputter (to)** *intr.* echar saliva al hablar. *2* chisporrotear. *3 intr.-tr.* farfullar, barbullar. *4 tr.* despedir [gotas o partículas].
**sputum** (spiu·tøm) *pl.* **sputa** *s.* MED. esputo.
**spy** (spai) *s.* espía, espión.
**spy (to)** *tr.* espiar; acechar, observar. *2* divisar, columbrar. *3 intr. to ~ on* o *upon*, espiar a. ¶ Pret. y *p. p.*: *spied.*
**spyglass** (spai·glæs) *s.* catalejo, anteojo.
**spyhole** (spai·joul) *s.* atisbadero.
**squab** (skuab) *adj.* regordete, rechoncho. *2* implume, recién salido de la cáscara. *3 s.* persona rechoncha. *4* pichoncillo. *5* cojín, almohadón. *6* sofá, otomana. *7 adv.* de golpe; a plomo.
**squabble** (skua·bøl) *s.* disputa, riña, pelotera.
**squabble (to)** *intr.* disputar, reñir.
**squabbler** (skua·blø<sup>r</sup>) *s.* reñidor, pendenciero.
**squabby** (skua·bi) *adj.* rechoncho.
**squad** (skuad) *s.* MIL. escuadra; pelotón, piquete.
**squadron** (skua·drøn) *s.* MAR. escuadra. *2* AVIA. escuadrilla. *3* MIL. escuadrón.
**squalid** (skua·lid) *adj.* escuálido, sucio, miserable.
**squall** (skuol) *s.* racha, chubasco, turbonada. *2* chillido.
**squall (to)** *impers.* hacer rachas, caer chubascos. *2 intr.-tr.* chillar.
**squally** (skuo·li) *adj.* borrascoso.
**squalor** (skua·lø<sup>r</sup>) *s.* escualidez, suciedad, miseria.
**squama** (skuei·ma), *pl.* **-mae** (-mi) *s.* BOT. y ZOOL. escama, escamilla.
**squamate** (-meit) *adj.* escamoso, con escamas.
**squamose, -mous** (-mous, -møs) *adj.* escamoso, lamelar.
**squander (to)** (skua·ndø<sup>r</sup>) *tr.* derrochar, despilfarrar, malgastar, disipar.
**squanderer** (-dørø<sup>r</sup>) *s.* derrochador, malgastador.
**square** (skue<sup>r</sup>) *adj.* cuadrado; *~ foot*, pie cuadrado; *~ measure*, medida cuadrada, de superficie; *~ root*, raíz cuadrada. *2* en cuadro: *two feet ~*, dos pies en cuadro. *3* cuadrangular. *4* en ángulo recto, escuadrado. *5* rehecho, fornido. *6* exacto, justo. *7* leal, recto, honrado. *8* saldado, en paz; empatado. *9* rotundo, categórico. *10* abundante [comida]. *11* MAR. de cruz, redonda [vela].
    *12 adv.* honradamente. *13* directamente. *14* firmemente. *15* en forma de cuadro.
    *16 s.* GEOM. cuadrado, cuadro. *17* MAT. cuadrado. *18* casilla, escaque. *19* cristal [de ventana]. *20* plaza [espacio abierto]. *21* manzana [de casas]. *22* escuadra, cartabón. *23* MIL. cuadro. *24 on the ~*, honradamente, de buena fe.
**square (to)** *tr.* cuadrar [dar figura de cuadro]. *2* GEOM., MAT. cuadrar. *3* escuadrar. *4* cuadricular. *5* medir en unidades cuadradas. *6* poner bien. *7* ajustar, saldar [cuentas]. *8* amoldar, ajustar, arreglar, regular. *9* pop. sobornar. *10 to ~ one's shoulders*, enderezar los hombros, cuadrarse. *11 to ~ oneself*, justificarse. *12 to ~ up*, enderezar. *13 intr.* concordar, conformarse [una cosa con otra]. *14* fam. pagar la cuenta. *15 to ~ up to*, tomar una actitud pugilística.
**square-toed** (-toud) *adj.* de punta ancha y corta [pie, zapato]. *2* fig. de ideas anticuadas.
**squash** (skuash) *s.* calabaza del gén. *Cucurbita*. *2* pulpa, cosa blanda o machacada. *3* golpe, caída [de algo blando]. *4* apretura [de gente]. *5* juego de pelota. *6* limonada.
**squash (to)** *tr.* aplastar, estrujar, machacar, despachurrar. *2* aplastar [dejar sin respuesta]. *3 intr.* aplastarse, despachurrarse. *4* apretarse, estrujarse.
**squashy** (-i) *adj.* blando y húmedo. *2* aplastado; fácil de aplastar.
**squat** (skuat) *adj.* en cuclillas, agachado. *2* rechoncho. *3 s.* postura que está en cuclillas.
**squat (to)** *intr.* sentarse en cuclillas. *2* agacharse, acurrucarse, alebrarse. *3* establecerse como colonizador en tierras baldías o del Estado, sin título o para adquirirlo.
**squatter** (-ø<sup>r</sup>) *s.* el que se establece como colonizador en tierras baldías o del Estado, sin título o para adquirirlo.

**squatty** (-i) *adj.* regordete, rechoncho.
**squaw** (skuo) *s.* (E.U.) mujer o esposa india: ∼ *man,* blanco casado con una india.
**squawk** (skuok) *s.* graznido, chillido. *2* queja.
**squawk (to)** *intr.* graznar, chillar. *2* quejarse.
**squeak** (skuık) *s.* chillido, chirrido, rechinido. *2 to have a narrow* ∼, escapar por milagro.
**squeak (to)** *intr.* chillar, chirriar, rechinar. *2* fam. hablar, cantar [confesar lo secreto, delatar].
**squeal** (skuıl) *s.* chillido, grito agudo.
**squeal (to)** *intr.* chillar, lanzar gritos agudos. *2* TO SQUEAK 2.
**squeamish** (skuı·mish) *adj.* delicado, escrupuloso, remilgado. *2* propenso a la náusea.
**squeegee** (skuı·dẏi) *s.* rodillo o escobilla de goma para restregar y secar superficies mojadas.
**squeegee (to)** *tr.* restregar con SQUEEGEE.
**squeeze** (skuiš) *s.* apretón, estrujón, abrazo estrecho. *2* comprensión. *3* apretura. *4* jugo exprimido. *5* facsímil obtenido por presión. *6* presión [para obligar]: *to put the* ∼ *on,* apretar los tornillos a. *7* fam. *tight* ∼, aprieto, apuro, brete.
**squeeze (to)** *tr.* apretar, comprimir. *2* estrujar, apretujar, prensar. *3* exprimir. *4* agobiar [con impuestos]. *5* obtener por presión. *6* apretar, obligar. *7 to* ∼ *in* o *through,* hacer entrar o hacer pasar apretando. *8 to* ∼ *out,* hacer salir apretando; exprimir. *9 intr.* apretujarse. *10* entrar, salir, pasar, apretando o entre apreturas. | Con *in, into, out* o *through.*
**squeezer** (skur·šø̈ʳ) *s.* exprimidera.
**squelch** (skuelch) *s.* aplastamiento, despachurro. *2* chapoteo.
**squelch (to)** *tr.* aplastar, despachurrar. *2* hacer callar, desconcertar. *3* sofocar, acabar con. *4 intr.* andar chapoteando.
**squib** (skuib) *s.* PIROT. carretilla, petardo. *2* escrito satírico.
**squib (to)** *intr.* tirar carretillas o petardos. *2 tr.* atacar con sátiras. ¶ Pret. y p. p.: *squibbed;* ger.: *-bbing.*
**squid** (skuid) *s.* ZOOL. calamar.
**squill** (skuıl) *s.* BOT. escila, esquila, cebolla albarrana. *2* ZOOL. esquila, quisquilla, camarón.
**squint** (skuınt) *s.* estrabismo; mirada bizca. *2* mirada de soslayo o furtiva. *3 adj.* estrábico [ojo]. *4* que mira de soslayo.
**squint (to)** *intr.* bizcar. *2* mirar de soslayo. *3* desviarse. *4 tr.* torcer [la mirada]. *5* entornar [los ojos].
**squint-eyed** (-aid) *adj.* bizco, bisojo, estrábico. *2* desconfiado, avieso, que mira atravesado.
**squire** (skuaiʳ) *s.* escudero. *2* (Ingl.) hacendado, esp. el más importante de una localidad. *3* fam. caballero [de una dama].
**squire (to)** *tr.* escoltar [a una dama].
**squirm (to)** *intr.* retorcerse, serpear: *to* ∼ *out of a difficulty,* salir con trabajo de un aprieto.
**squirrel** (skuø·rel) *s.* ZOOL. ardilla.
**squirt** (skuø̈ʳt) *s.* chorretada, chisguete. *2* jeringazo. *3* jeringa. *4* mequetrefe.
**squirt (to)** *tr.* lanzar en chorrito. *2* jeringar. *3* rociar. *4 intr.* salir en chorrito.
**squirting cucumber** *s.* BOT. cohombrillo amargo.
**stab** (stæb) *s.* puñalada, estocada, cuchillada.
**stab (to)** *tr.-intr.* herir con arma blanca, apuñalar, pinchar. ¶ Pret. y p. p.: *stabbed;* ger.: *-bbing.*
**stability** (stabi·liti) *s.* estabilidad. *2* firmeza, constancia. *3* cosa estable.
**stabilize (to)** (stei·bilaiš) *tr.* estabilizar.
**estabilizer** (-ø̈ʳ) *s.* estabilizador.

**stable** (stei·bøl) *adj.* estable. *2 s.* establo, cuadra, caballeriza.
**stable (to)** *tr.-intr.* poner, tener o estar en un establo o cuadra.
**stableboy** (-boi) *s.* mozo de cuadra.
**stack** (stæk) *s.* almiar. *2* pila, montón, rimero. *3* pabellón [de fusiles]. *4* cañón de chimenea. *5* cuba [de alto horno]. *6* montón, gran cantidad.
**stack (to)** *tr.* apilar, amontonar. *2* poner [los fusiles] en pabellón.
**stadholder** (sta·tjouldøʳ) *s.* STADTHOLDER.
**stadium** (stei·diøm) *s.* estadio.
**stadtholder** (stæ·tjouldøʳ) *s.* estatúder.
**staff** (stæf), *pl.* **staves** (esteivs) o **staffs** *s.* palo, vara, bastón, garrote. *2* báculo. *3* vara, bastón de mando. *4* asta [de bandera, lanza, etc.]. *5* TOP. mira, jalón. *6* MIL. estado mayor; plana mayor. *7* personal [esp. técnico o directivo], cuadro. *8* redacción [de un periódico]. *9* MÚS. pentagrama. *10* cartón piedra.
**staff (to)** *tr.* proveer de personal técnico, o directivo.
**stag** (stæg) *s.* ZOOL. ciervo, venado. *2* toro castrado. *3* hombre solo [en una fiesta]. *4* ENT. ∼ *beetle,* ciervo volante.
**stage** (steidẏ) *s.* TEAT. escenario, escena, tablas: ∼ *box,* palco de proscenio; ∼ *manager,* director de escena. *2* teatro [arte, profesión]. *3* escena, teatro, campo [de actividades]. *4* piso, alto [de un edificio]. *5* tablado, plataforma, andamio. *6* parada [de diligencia]; casa de postas. *7* diligencia [coche]. *8* etapa, jornada: *by easy stages,* por cortas etapas; fig. por grados, gradualmente. *9* estadio, fase, estado, grado, etapa, período. *10* platina [del microscopio]. *11* RADIO. paso.
**stage (to)** *tr.* poner en escena. *4* preparar [algo] para que ocurra de un modo teatral.
**stagecoach** (-kouch) *s.* diligencia [coche].
**stagecraft** (-kræft) *s.* arte escénico.
**stagehand** (-jænd) *s.* TEAT. tramoyista, metemuertos, metesillas.
**stager** (-øʳ) *s.* caballo de diligencia. *3* fig. *old* ∼, veterano, perro viejo.
**stagger** (stæ·gøʳ) *s.* tambaleo, vacilación.
**stagger (to)** *intr.* vacilar, tambalearse, temblar; hacer eses [al andar]. *2* vacilar, titubear, flaquear. *3 tr.* hacer vacilar. *4* causar vértigo. *5* asombrar, aturdir, asustar. *6* escalonar.
**staggerer** (-øʳ) *s.* cosa que aturde o desconcierta.
**staghound** (stæ·gjaund) *s.* sabueso.
**staging** (stei·dẏing) *s.* andamiaje. *2* tráfico en diligencias. *3* TEAT. puesta en escena.
**stagnancy** (stæ·gnɒnsi) *s.* estancamiento, paralización [estado].
**stagnant** (-nant) *adj.* estancado, estantío. *2* paralizado.
**stagnate (to)** (-neit) *intr.* estancarse, estar estancado; paralizarse.
**stagnation** (-ei·shøn) *s.* estancamiento, paralización.
**stagy** (stei·dẏi) *adj.* teatral.
**staid** (steid) *adj.* grave, serio, formal, sentado, juicioso. *2* fijo, decidido.
**stain** (stein) *s.* mancha, mácula. *2* tinte, tintura [materia colorante].
**stain (to)** *tr.* manchar. *2* teñir; colorar: *stained glass,* vidrio de color. *3* mancillar. *4 intr.* manchar; mancharse.
**stainless** (-lis) *adj.* limpio, inmaculado, sin mancha. *2* ∼ *steel,* acero inoxidable.
**stair** (steʳ) *s.* escalón, peldaño. *2 pl.* escalera,

tramo de escalera: *below stairs*, abajo, en el departamento de la servidumbre. *3 adj.* de escalera; ~ *well*, caja de escalera.

**staircase** (-keis) *s.* escalera; caja de escalera.

**stairway** (-wei) *s.* escalera.

**stake** (steik) *s.* estaca, piquete, jalón, estaquilla; poste, pilote. *2* AGR. rodrigón. *3* telero. *4* hoguera [suplicio]. *5* tas, bigorneta. *6* apuesta, puesta [en el juego]. *7* premio [de una contienda]. *8* lo que está en juego o se arriesga. *9 at* ~, en juego, comprometido, en peligro.

**stake (to)** *tr.* estacar [atar a una estaca; demarcar con estacas]. *2* rodrigar. *3* empalar. *4* apostar, arriesgar: *to* ~ *(one's) all*, jugar el todo por el todo.

**stalactite** (stǝlæ·ktait) *s.* estalactita.

**stalagmite** (stǝlæ·gmait) *s.* estalagmita.

**stale** (steil) *adj.* pasado, evaporado; rancio; viejo [pan]; picado [vino]. *2* gastado, viejo, trillado, sabido.

**stale (to)** *tr.* evaporar, enranciar, alterar. *2 intr.* pasarse, enranciarse. *3* perder la novedad, el interés.

**stalemate** (-meit) *s.* AJED. tablas por rey ahogado. *2* fig. estancamiento, punto muerto.

**stalemate (to)** *tr.* AJED. ahogar al rey. *2* estancar, paralizar.

**stalk** (stɔk) *s.* BOT., ZOOL. tallo, caña; caballo, pecíolo, pedúnculo. *2* pie [de copa]. *3* paso majestuoso. *5* caza al acecho.

**stalk (to)** *tr.* andar majestuosamente. *2* acercarse furtivamente a, espiar, acechar. *3* cazar al acecho, ocultándose.

**stalking-horse** (-ing) *s.* buey de cabestrillo. *2* máscara, capa, disfraz.

**stall** (stɔl) *s.* establo, cuadra; compartimiento de establo o cuadra. *2* puesto [de venta]. *3* silla de coro. *4* TEAT. luneta, butaca.

**stall (to)** *tr.* poner o tener en establo o cuadra. *2* atascar, atollar. *3* parar, ahogar [un motor]. *4 intr.* estar en un establo. *5* atascarse, atollarse. *6* pararse, ahogarse [un motor].

**stallion** (stæ·liǝn) *s.* caballo padre.

**stalwart** (stɔ·luaʳt) *adj.* fornido, forzudo. *2* valiente. *3* leal, acérrimo. *4 s.* persona forzuda o valiente. *5* POL. partidario acérrimo.

**stamen** (stei·men) *s.* BOT. estambre.

**stamina** (stæ·mina) *adj.* fornido, forzudo. *2* valiente. *3* leal, acérrimo. *4 s.* persona forzuda o valiente. *5* POL. partidario acérrimo.

**stamen** (stei·men) *s.* BOT. estambre.

**stamina** (stæ·mina) *s.* vitalidad, fibra, fuerza, vigor, resistencia.

**staminate** (stæ·mineit) *adj.* BOT. estamnífero.

**stammer** (stæ·mǝʳ) *s.* tartamudeo. *2* balbuceo, balbucencia.

**stammer (to)** *intr.* tartamudear. *2* balbucear, balbucir.

**stammerer** (-ǝʳ) *s.* tartamudo. *2* farfalloso.

**stamp** (stæmp) *s.* estampa, huella, señal, impresión. *2* sello, timbre [que se marca]; sello, póliza [que se pega]. *3* sello [utensilio]; carácter distintivo]. *4* estampilla. *5* cuño, troquel. *6* carácter, género, suerte.

**stamp (to)** *tr.* estampar, imprimir, marcar. *2* ditinguir, caracterizar. *3* sellar, timbrar, estampillar. *4* poner sello a. *5* estampar [en relieve]. *6* METAL. triturar. *7* patear; apisonar. *8 to* ~ *one's foot*, patalear. *9 intr.* patear, patalear.

**stampede** (stæmpɪ·d) *s.* huida en tropel, con pá-

nico; *estampida. *2* determinación repentina y unánime.

**stampede (to)** *intr.* huir o correr en tropel, con pánico. *2* obrar súbitamente y por común impulso. *3 tr.* hacer huir en desorden.

**stance** (stæns) *s.* posición, postura.

**stanch** (stanch) *adj.* estanco. *2* fuerte, sólido, seguro. *3* firme, leal, constante, fiel.

**stanch (to)** *tr.* estancar, restañar. *2* contener, detener. *3 intr.* restañarse.

**stanchion** (stæ·nshǝn) *s.* poste, puntal, montante, pie derecho. *2* MAR. candelero.

**stanchion (to)** *tr.* apuntalar, sostener.

**stand** (stænd) *s.* posición, puesto. *2* parada [de coches, etc.]. *3* alto, parada, detención. *4* resistencia: *to make a* ~, resistir, hacer frente; luchar. *5* tablado, tribuna. *6* puesto [en un mercado, etc.]; quiosco [de venta]. *7* velador, estante, pie, soporte.

**stand (to)** *intr.* estar o tenerse de pie o en pie. *2* ponerse en pie, levantarse, erguirse. *3* estar situado, hallarse. *4* estar, ponerse [de cierto modo]; tener [cierta altura]. *5* estar, permanecer, quedarse. *6* durar, subsistir; continuar en vigor. *7* pararse, detenerse; estancarse. *8* mantenerse firme, resistir. *9* ser [padrino]; salir [fiador]. *10* consistir. *11* ser compatible [con], conforme [a]. *12* presentarse [como candidato]. *13* descansar, estar sobre. *14* parar [el perro]. *15* MAR. dirigirse, hacer rumbo. *16 to* ~ *alone*, estar solo, ser el único. *17 to* ~ *at attention*, MIL. cuadrarse. *18 to* ~ *back*, retroceder; quedarse atrás. *19 to* ~ *by*, estar cerca, estar presente, quedarse allí; apoyar, defender; atenerse a; MAR., RADIO. estar listo. *20 to* ~ *for*, representar, significar; estar en lugar de; estar por, apoyar; presentarse para; MAR. hacer rumbo a. *21 to* ~ *in with*, estar en buenas relaciones con, gozar del favor de. *22 to* ~ *off*, apartarse, mantenerse apartado. *23 to* ~ *on*, descansar, estar colocado, sobre; depender de; insistir en. *24 to* ~ *on end*, ponerse de punta, erizarse. *25 to* ~ *out*, salir, sobresalir; resaltar, destacarse; mantenerse firme; MAR. alejarse de tierra. *26 to* ~ *to reason*, ser razonable, ser justo. *27 to* ~ *up*, estar derecho; levantarse, ponerse en pie. *28 to* ~ *up for*, defender, apoyar. *29 to* ~ *up to*, afrontar resueltamente.

*30 tr.* poner derecho, de pie. *31* sufrir, aguantar; soportar, someterse a. *33* atenerse a. *34* pagar, convidar a. *35 to* ~ *a chance*, tener probabilidad. *36 to* ~ *off*, tener a raya. *37 to* ~ *on end*, poner de punta; asentar sobre un extremo. *38 to* ~ *one's ground*, mantenerse firme.

¶ Pret. y p. p.: **stood**.

**standard** (stæ·ndaʳd) *s.* norma, regla establecida; tipo, nivel, medida; ~ *of living*, nivel de vida. *2* modelo, dechado. *3* marco [depesas y medidas]. *4* ley [de la moneda]. *5* patrón [monetario]. *6* base, pie, sostén; poste, pie derecho. *7* candelero alto. *8* estandarte, enseña. *9 adj.* establecido, de ley, oficial, normal, universal; standard: ~ *keyboard*, teclado universal; ~ *metre*, metro patrón; ~ *time*, hora oficial.

**standard-bearer** *s.* MIL. portaestandarte, abanderado. *2* jefe [de un movimiento].

**standardize (to)** (stæ·ndardaiš) *tr.* reducir a un tipo establecido, unificar, regularizar.

**stand-by** *s.* persona o cosa con quien se puede contar.

**stander** (stæ·ndǝʳ) *s.* persona que está de pie. *2* STANDARD 6.

**standing** (-ing) *adj.* derecho, en pie, de pie. *2* para estar de pie. *3* parado, estancado. *4* fijo, permanente, duradero: ~ *army*, ejército permanente; ~ *committee*, comisión permanente. *5* DER. vigente. *6* que tiene base o pie. *7* s. posición del que está en pie. *8* sitio, lugar. *9* reputación, crédito; posición social. *10* duración, antigüedad: *of old* ~, antiguo, de mucho tiempo.

**stand-off** *s.* reserva, frialdad. *2* empate, tablas. *3 adj.* STAND-OFFISH.

**stand-offish** *adj.* retraído, frío, reservado.

**standpat** (-pæt) *adj.-s.* fam. (E.U.) conservador [esp. en política aduanera].

**standpoint** (-point) *s.* punto de vista.

**standstill** (-stil) *s.* alto, parada, detención, estacionamiento. *2* pausa, descanso.

**stanhope** (-joup) *s.* especie de birlocho de un solo asiento.

**stank** (stænk) *pret.* de TO STINK.

**stanniferous** (stæni·førøs) *adj.* estannífero.

**stanza** (stæ·nša) *s.* estancia, estrofa.

**stapes** (stei·piš) *s.* ANAT. estribo.

**staphylococcus** (stæfiløkø·køs) *s.* BACT. estafilococo.

**staple** (stei·pøl) *s.* armella, grapa. *2* grapa para sujetar papeles. *3* artículo o producto principal [de un país, etc.]. *4* fig. base; tema principal. *5* materia prima, en bruto. *6* fibra, hebra [de materia textil]. *7 adj.* corriente, de uso general. *8* principal, importante.

**staple (to)** *tr.* sujetar con grapas. *2* clasificar hebras textiles según su longitud.

**stapler** (stei·pløʳ) *s.* clasificador de lanas. *2* máquina para coser papeles con grapa.

**star** (staʳ) *s.* ASTR. estrella, astro. *2* estrella [figura de estrella; asterisco]: *Stars and Stripes*, la bandera de los E.U. *3* placa, gran cruz. *4* estrella, hado, destino. *5* estrella [de cine, etc.]. *6 adj.* ~ *shower*, lluvia de estrellas; ~ *thistle*, BOT. cardo estrellado.

**star (to)** *tr.* estrellar, tachonar de estrellas. *2* marcar con asterisco. *3* TEAT., CINE. presentar como estrella. *4 intr.* ser estrella. ¶ Pret. y p. p.: *starred;* ger.: *-rring.*

**starblind** (-blaind) *adj.* medio ciego.

**starboard** (-boʳd) *s.* MAR. estribor. *2 adj.* de estribor. *3 adv.* a estribor.

**starch** (staʳch) *s.* almidón, fécula. *2* tiesura, empaque. *3* pop. (E.U.) energía, vigor, actividad.

**starch (to)** *tr.* almidonar. *2* dar tiesura.

**starchy** (-i) *adj.* amiláceo, de almidón. *2* almidonado. *3* tieso, entonado.

**stare** (steʳ) *s.* mirada fija, de hito en hito.

**stare (to)** *tr.-intr.* mirar fijamente, de hito en hito; clavar la vista. *2 to* ~ *one in the face* saltar a la vista, ser evidente; ser inminente. *3 intr.* ser llamativo o chillón. *4* erizarse [el cabello].

**starfish** (sta·ʳfish) *s.* ZOOL. estrellamar.

**stargaze (to)** (-geiš) *intr.* observar las estrellas. *2* estar distraído. *3* soñar despierto.

**staring** (ste·ring) *adj.* que mira fijamente. *2* chillón, llamativo. *3* que salta a la vista.

**stark** (staʳk) *adj.* tieso, rígido, yerto. *2* duro, severo. *3* desierto, desolado. *4* puro, completo, absoluto. *5 adv.* completamente, enteramente: ~ *mad*, loco de remate.

**starless** (staʳlis) *adj.* sin estrellas.

**starlet** (-lit) *s.* estrellita.

**starlight** (-lait) *s.* luz de las estrellas. *2 adj.* iluminado por las estrellas. *3* estrella [noche].

**starlike** (-laic) *adj.* estrellado [de figura de estrella]. *2* brillante, resplandeciente.

**starling** (-ing) *s.* ORN. estornino.

**starred** (staʳd) *adj.* estrellado, adornado con estrellas. *2* que tiene buena o mala estrella. *3* CINE., TEAT. presentado como estrella.

**starry** (sta·ri) *adj.* estrellado [lleno de estrellas; de forma de estrella]. *2* estelar, sidéreo. *3* brillante, resplandeciente.

**star-spangled** *adj.* estrellado, tachonado de estrellas.

**start** (staʳt) *s.* sobresalto, repullo, respingo, bote. *2* susto. *3* actividad intermitente: *by starts*, a ratos, a empujones. *4* salida, marcha, partida; principio, comienzo: *at the* ~, al principio. *5* impulso inicial: *to give a* ~ *to*, poner en marcha; ayudar [a uno] a establecerse. *6* ventaja, delantera: *to ge the* ~ *of*, coger la delantera.

**start (to)** *intr.* sobresaltarse, estremecerse, dar un salto, un respingo. *2* salir, partir, ponerse en marcha, arrancar: ~ *after*, salir en busca de; *to* ~ *for*, salir para. *3* comenzar, empezar: *to* ~ *with*, para empezar. *4* aflojarse, soltarse, salirse de sitio; moverse [un diente]. *5 to* ~ *off*, partir, ponerse en marcha. *6 to* ~ *up*, levantarse precipitadamente; aparecer de pronto; comenzar a funcionar. *7 tr.* levantar [la caza]; desemboscar. *8* poner en marcha, en movimiento; hacer funcionar; hacer o ayudar a empezar. *9* dar la salida a. *10* empezar, comenzar, originar, armar, iniciar, suscitar: ~ *a subject*, sacar un tema [de discusión]. *11* emprender [un negocio, etc.]. *12* aflojar, soltar, desencajar. *13 to* ~ *up*, poner en marcha.

**starter** (-øʳ) *s.* iniciador, el que comienza o sale. *2* MEC. mecanismo de arranque, motor de arranque. *3* DEP. juez de salida; el que da la salida.

**starting** (-ing) *s.* principio, comienzo; arranque, puesta en marcha, partida, salida. *2* sobresalto. *3 adj.* ~ *point*, punto de partida; ~ *post*, poste o línea de partida.

**startle (to)** (sta·ʳtøl) *tr.* asustar, sobresaltar, sorprender, alarmar. *2 intr.* saltar, sobresaltarse.

**startling** (sta·ʳtling) *adj.* notable, sorprendente.

**starvation** (staʳvei·shøn) *s.* hambre, inanición.

**starve (to)** (staʳv) *intr.* morir de hambre. *2* padecer hambre: *to* ~ *for*, sufrir por falta de. *3 tr.* matar de hambre, hambrear: *to* ~ *out*, MIL. rendir por hambre.

**starveling** (sta·ʳvling) *adj.-s.* extenuado por el hambre.

**starving** (-ing) *adj.* hambriento, famélico.

**starwort** (sta·ʳuøʳt) *s.* BOT. álsine, pamplina.

**stasis** (stei·sis) *s.* MED. éxtasis.

**state** (steit) *s.* estado, situación, condición: *married* ~, estado matrimonial; ~ *of siege*, estado de sitio. *2* FÍS. estado. *3* POL. estado: *State Department*, (E.U.) ministerio de relaciones exteriores; ~ *secret*, secreto de estado. *4* pompa, aparato, ceremonia: ~ *room*, salón de ceremonias; *to lie in* ~, estar en la capilla ardiente. *5* majestad, dignidad.

**state (to)** *tr.* exponer, enunciar, relatar, declarar, manifestar, decir, expresar, formular. *2* consignar [en un escrito]. *3* plantear [un problema]. *4* fijar, determinar.

**statecraft** (-kraft) *s.* gobierno, arte de gobernar.

**stateliness** (-linis) *s.* majestuosidad.

**stately** (-li) *adj.* majestuoso, imponente. *2* elevado, sublime. *3* digno, ceremonioso.

**statement** (-mønt) *s.* declaración, manifestación,

afirmación. *2* exposición, relación, resumen, relato, informe, estado. *3* estado de cuentas.

**stateroom** (-rum) *s.* MAR. camarote. *2* FERROC. departamento individual con cama.

**statesman** (-smæn) *s.* estadista, hombre de estado.

**statemanship** (-ship) *s.* calidad de estadista. *2* STATECRAFT.

**static** (stæ·tik) *s.* RADIO. parásito atmosférico.

**static(al** (-*a*l) *adj.* estático.

**statics** (-s) *s.* FÍS. estática.

**station** (stei·shøn) *s.* estación [de tren, meteorológica, etc.]. *2* parada, apeadero. *3* REL. estación. *4* puesto [militar; de un servicio]. *5* MAR. apostadero. *6* puesto, situación. *7* condición social.

**station (to)** *tr.* estacionar, situar, apostar.

**stationmaster** *s.* jefe de estación.

**stationary** (-eri) *adj.* estacionario; fijo.

**stationer** (-øʳ) *s.* librero; vendedor de objetos de escritorio.

**stationery** (-eri) *s.* objetos de escritorio.

**statism** (stei·tišm) *s.* estatismo.

**statist** (-ist) *s.* STATITIAN.

**statistic** (stæti·stik) *adj.* estadístico. *2 s.* estadística.

**statistical** (-*a*l) *adj.* estadístico.

**statistician** (stæti·stishan) *s.* estadista [perito en estadística].

**statistics** (-s) *s.* estadística.

**stator** (stæ·tøʳ) *s.* ELECT. estator.

**statuary** (stæ·chueri) *adj.* estatuario. *2 s.* estatuario. *3* estatuaria.

**statue** (stæ·chu) *s.* estatua, imagen.

**statuesque** (-esk) *adj.* estatuario. *2* escultural.

**statuette** (stæchue·t) *s.* estatuilla, figurilla.

**stature** (stæ·chøʳ) *s.* estatura, talla.

**status** (stei·tøs) *s.* estado legal. *2* estado, condición.

**statute** (stæ·chut) *s.* ley, decreto, ordenanza. *2* estatuto, reglamento. *3* ~ *mile*, milla ordinaria.

**statutory** (-ori) *adj.* estatuido, legal.

**staunch** (stonch) *adj.* STANCH.

**stave** (steiv) *s.* duela [de tonel]. *2* palo, garrote. *3* LIT. estrofa. *4* MÚS. pentagrama.

**stave (to)** *tr.* poner duelas a. *2* reventar, desfondar. *3* vencer, quebrantar. *4 to* ~ *off*, alejar, evitar. *5 intr.* romperse, desfondarse. ¶ Pret. y p. p.: *staved* o *stove*.

**staves** (-s) *s. pl.* de STAFF y de STAVE.

**stavesacre** (-šeikøʳ) *s.* BOT. estafisagria.

**stay** (stei) *s.* MAR. estay. *2* tirante, viento, riostra. *3* sostén. *4* ballena o varilla [de corsé]. *5* parada, detención. *6* suspensión, espera. *7* estancia, morada, permanencia. *8* estabilidad, duración. *9* resistencia, aguante. *10 pl.* corsé, cotilla.

**stay (to)** *tr.* sostener, apoyar, apuntalar. *2* fundar, basar. *3* resistir, soportar. *4* detener, contener, frenar, reprimir. *5* aplazar, suspender. *6* esperar, aguardar. *7* sosegar. *8 intr.* estar de pie. *9* estarse quieto, parar, pararse. *10* estar, permanecer, quedarse en casa; *to* ~ *up*, velar. *11* tardar, detenerse. *12* resistir [tener resistencia].

**stead** (sted) *s.* (precedido de *in*) lugar, vez; servicio, utilidad: *in* ~ *of*, en lugar de, en vez de; *to stand in (good)* ~, servir, ser útil.

**steadfast** (-fæst) *adj.* firme, fijo, inmóvil. *2* constante, invariable. *3* firme, resuelto.

**steadiness** (ste·dinis) *s.* firmeza, estabilidad. *2* constancia, regularidad. *3* morigeración.

**steady** (ste·di) *adj.* firme, seguro. *2* estable, continuo, regular. *3* tranquilo. *4* grave, juicioso, morigerado.

**steady (to)** *tr.* afianzar, sostener, dar firmeza. *2* tranquilizar. *3* ajuiciar. *4* hacer continuo, regular. *5 intr.* afianzarse. *6* sentar la cabeza. | Gralte. con *down*.

**steak** (stek) *s.* tajada [para asar o freír], biftec.

**steal** (stil) *s.* hurto, robo.

**steal (to)** *tr.-intr.* hurtar, robar. *2* plagiar. *3* mover, introducir, hacer, etc., furtivamente. *4 to* ~ *a march on*, sorprender, ganar por la mano. *5 intr.* moverse, pasar, deslizarse, etc., furtiva o insensiblemente: *to* ~ *away*, escabullirse; *to* ~ *upon*, aproximarse sin ruido a.

**stealing** (-ing) *s.* hurto, robo.

**stealth** (stelz) *s.* disimulo, cautela, secreto: *by* ~, a hurtadillas, a escondidas, con cautela.

**stealthy** (-zi) *adj.* furtivo, secreto; disimulado, cauteloso.

**steam** (stim) *s.* vapor [esp. de agua]: ~ *boiler*, caldera de vapor; ~ *engine*, máquina de vapor; ~ *gauge*, manómetro; ~ *roller*, apisonadora; *to blow of* ~, *to let off* ~, descargar vapor; fig. desahogarse; *to get up* ~, dar presión. *2* vaho. *3* fig. vigor, energía. *5* vapor [buque]. *6* guiso hecho al vapor.

**steam (to)** *tr.* cocer, preparar, etc., al vapor. *2* dar vapor a. *3* transportar por vapor. *4* empañar con vapor. *5 intr.* emitir vaho o vapor, vahear. *6* marchar a vapor. *7* evaporarse.

**steamboat** (-bout) *s.* vapor [buque].

**steamer** (-øʳ) *s.* vapor [buque]. *2* máquina o generador, etc., de vapor.

**steaming** (-ing) *adj.* humeante, vaheante.

**steamship** (-ship) *s.* vapor [buque].

**stearin** (stiari·n) *s.* QUÍM. estearina.

**steatite** (sti·atait) *s.* esteatita.

**steed** (sti·d) *s.* corcel.

**steel** (stil) *s.* acero [metal, arma]. *2* afilón, chaira. *3* eslabón [para sacar chispa]. *4* dureza, rigor; frialdad; resistencia. *5 adj.* de acero, acerado; fuerte, duro, insensible: ~ *wool*, estropajo metálico.

**steel (to)** *tr.* acerar. *2* endurecer, fortalecer, acorazar.

**steeliness** (-inis) *s.* dureza de acero.

**steelwork** (-uøʳk) *s.* obra de acero.

**steelworks** (-uøʳks) *s. pl.* acería, fábrica de acero.

**steely** (-i) *adj.* acerado. *2* duro, fuerte, inflexible.

**steelyard** (-yaʳd) *s.* romana.

**steep** (stip) *adj.* empinado, pendiente, escarpado. *2* excesivo, exorbitante. *3 s.* cuesta; precipicio. *4* empapamiento; maceración.

**steep (to)** *tr.* empapar, remojar; macerar. *2 intr.* estar en remojo.

**steeple** (sti·pøl) *s.* aguja, capitel, campanario.

**steeplechase** (-cheis) *s.* DEP. carrera [de caballos] de obstáculos.

**steer** (stiʳ) *s.* novillo castrado, buey.

**steer (to)** *tr.* gobernar [una embarcación]; conducir, pilotar [un vehículo, un avión]. *2* fig. guiar, dirigir, gobernar. *3 intr.* gobernar, obedecer al timón. *4* dirigirse, conducirse.

**steerage** (-idÿ) *s.* gobierno, dirección. *2* MAR. proa. *3* MAR. ~ *passenger*, pasajero de tercera.

**steering** (-ing) *s.* dirección, gobierno [esp. de un buque o automóvil]: ~ *gear*, AUTO. dirección; ~ *wheel*, MAR. rueda del timón; AUTO. volante.

**steersman** (-mæn) *s.* timonel, timonero.

**stele** (sti·li) *s.* ARQUEOL. estela.

**stellar** (ste·laʳ) *adj.* estelar, astral, sidéreo. *2* estrellado [de figura de estrella]. *3* fig. sobresaliente.

**stellate** (ste·leit) *adj.* estrellado, radiado.

**stem** (stem) *s.* BOT. tallo, tronco; vástago; pezón, pedúnculo, pecíolo. *2* tronco [de una familia]. *3* raíz [de una palabra]. *4* CARP. espiga. *5* MEC. vástago. *6* pie [de copa]. *7* cañón [de pipa, de pluma]. *8* árbol [de reloj]. *9* palo [de letra]. *10* rabillo [de una nota musical]. *11* MAR. roda; proa.

**stem (to)** *tr.* desgranar, despalillar. *2* estancar, represar. *3* contener, refrenar. *4* MAR. embestir por la proa; navegar contra [la corriente]. *5* resistir, oponerse a. *6 intr.* provenir, derivar. *7* detenerse, contenerse. ¶ Pret. y p. p.: *stemmed;* ger.: *-mming.*

**stemless** (-lis) *adj.* BOT. acaule.

**stemple** (ste·mpøl) *s.* MIN. estemple.

**stemson** (ste·msøn) *s.* MAR. contrarroda.

**stem-winder** *s.* remontuar [reloj].

**stench** (stench) *s.* hedor, tufo, peste.

**stencil** (-sil) *s.* estarcido. *2* patrón, color o tinta para estarcir.

**stencil (to)** *tr.* estarcir.

**stenograph** (ste·nøgræf) *s.* escrito taquigráfico. *2* máquina para escribir en taquigrafía.

**stenograph (to)** *tr.* taquigrafiar.

**stenographer** (stena·grafø$^r$) *s.* taquígrafo.

**stenography** (stena·grafi) *s.* taquigrafía.

**stentorian** (ste·ntørian) *adj.* estentóreo.

**step** (step) *s.* paso [del que anda o baila; manera de andar; acción]: *to keep ~ with,* llevar el mismo paso que; *to watch one's ~,* andarse con tiento; *in ~,* llevando el [mismo] paso; *de acuerdo;* ELECT. en fase; *~ by ~,* paso a paso. *2* paso [en el progreso]. *3* escalón, peldaño; umbral. *4* estribo [de coche]. *5* grado [de una escala]. *6* huella, pisada. *7* paso, diligencia, medida: *to take steps to,* dar pasos, tomar medidas, para. *8* RADIO. paso. *9* MAR. carlinga. *10* ARQ. resalto. *11* tejuelo. *12* diente de llave. *13 pl.* escalera [de mano]. *14* gradería; escalones de entrada.

**step (to)** *intr.* dar un paso o pasos; andar, caminar, ir: *to ~ aside,* apartarse; *to ~ back,* retroceder; *to ~ down,* bajar; *to ~ in,* entrar, intervenir; *to ~ out,* salir; *to ~ over,* atravesar; *to ~ up,* subir. *2* fam. andar de prisa. *3 to ~ on,* pisar, hollar. *4 tr.* poner, sentar [el pie]. *5* plantar [un mástil]. *6* escalonar. *7 to ~ down,* bajar, reducir. *8 to ~ off,* medir por pasos. *9 to ~ up,* elevar, aumentar. ¶ Pret. y p. p.: *stepped* o *stept;* ger.: *stepping.*

**stepbrother** (-brødø$^r$) *s.* hermanastro.

**stepdaughter** (-pdotø$^r$) *s.* hijastra, entenada.

**stepfather** (-fadø$^r$) *s.* padrastro.

**Stephen** (sti·vøn) *n. pr.* Esteban.

**step-ins** *s. pl.* pantalones de mujer.

**stepladder** (ste·plædø$^r$) *s.* escala, escalera de mano.

**stepmother** (-mødø$^r$) *s.* madrastra.

**steppe** (step) *s.* GEOGR. estepa.

**stepping-stone** *s.* estriberón, pasadera. *2* montadero. *3* fig. escabel.

**stepsister** (-sistø$^r$) *s.* hermanastra.

**stere** (sti$^r$) *s.* estéreo, metro cúbico.

**stereography** (steria·grafi) *s.* GEOM. estereografía.

**stereometry** (steria·metri) *s.* estereometría.

**stereophonic** (steriøfa·nik) *adj.* estereofónico.

**stereoscope** (ste·riøskoup) *s.* estereoscopio.

**stereotype** (ste·riøtaip) *s.* IMPR. estereotipo, clisé.

**stereotype (to)** *tr.* estereotipar, clisar.

**stereotyping** (-ing) *s.* estereotipia.

**stereotypist** (-ist) *s.* estereotipista.

**sterile** (ste·rail o -ril) *adj.* estéril. *2* improductivo.

**sterility** (steri·liti) *s.* esterilidad.

**sterilization** (steriliŝei·shøn) *s.* esterilización.

**sterilize (to)** (ste·rilaiŝ) *tr.* esterilizar.

**sterling** (stø·$^r$ling) *adj.* esterlina: *pound ~,* libra esterlina. *2* auténtico, puro, de ley.

**stern** (stø$^r$n) *adj.* duro, riguroso. *2* severo, austero. *3* torvo. *4* implacable. *5* firme, resuelto. *6 s.* MAR. popa: *~ chaser,* cañón de popa; *~ frame,* espejo de popa.

**sternal** (stø·$^r$nal) *adj.* esternal.

**sternmost** (stø·$^r$nmoust) *adj.* popel.

**sternpost** (-poust) *s.* MAR. codaste.

**sternum** (stø·$^r$nøm) *s.* ANAT. esternón.

**sternutative** (stø$^r$nui·tiv) *adj.* estornutativo, estornutatorio.

**sternway** (stø·$^r$nwei) *s.* MAR. marcha atrás.

**stertor** (stø·$^r$tø$^r$) *s.* estertor. *2* ronquido.

**stertorous** (-øs) *adj.* estertoroso.

**stethoscope** (ste·zoskoup) *s.* MED. estetoscopio.

**stevedore** (sti·vødo$^r$) *s.* estibador, cargador de muelle.

**stew** (stiu) *s.* COC. estofado, guisado. *2* fam. preocupación, apuro.

**stew (to)** *tr.* estofar, guisar. *2 intr.* cocerse [el estofado]. *3* ahogarse de calor. *4* preocuparse, apurarse.

**steward** (-a$^r$d) *s.* mayordomo, administrador. *2* senescal. *3* capataz. *4* despensero. *5* camarero [de buque o avión].

**stewardess** (-is) *s.* mayordoma, administradora. *2* camarera [de buque].

**stewed** (stiud) *adj.* estofado, cocido; *~ fruit,* compota de frutas.

**stewpan** (stiu·pæn) *s.* cazuela, cacerola.

**stewpot** (stiu·pat) *s.* olla.

**St. Gotthard** (sei·nt ga·ta$^r$d) *n. pr.* GEOGR. San Gotardo.

**stibium** (sti·biøm) *s.* estibio, antimonio.

**stick** (stik) *s.* palo, garrote, vara: *walking ~,* bastón de paseo. *2* leño. *3* varilla, palito, barrita. *4* batuta. *5* palillo [de escultor, de tambor]. *6* barra [de lacre]. *7* trozo, porción. *8* hurgonazo, estocada; pinchazo. *9* IMPR. componedor. *10* pegajosidad, adhesión. *11* obstáculo, estorbo. *12* demora, duda. *13 pl.* ramitas. *14* trastos. *15* fig. las piernas.

**stick (to)** *tr.* clavar, hincar. *2* poner, meter. *3* pegar, adherir. *4* pinchar, matar, punzar, picar. *5* atravesar, ensartar. *6* sacar, asomar. | Con *out* o *up.* *7* levantar, erguir. | Con *up.* *8* sufrir, tolerar. *9* untar. *10 intr.* estar clavado, pegado; clavarse, pegarse, adherirse. *11* aferrarse, mantenerse fiel o afecto; perseverar. *12* salir, sobresalir, resaltar. *13* atascarse. *14* detenerse, vacilar. *15 to ~ around,* estar o quedarse, por allí. *16 to ~ close,* mantenerse juntos. *17 to ~ to one's guns,* mantenerse firme. *18 to ~ up,* salir, proyectarse; estar de punta, erizado.

**sticker** (-ø$^r$) *s.* el que clava, fija, pega, etc. *2* espina, aguijón. *3* coma, cola. *4* etiqueta, papel engomado.

**stickiness** (-inis) *s.* tenacidad, glutinosidad.

**sticking** (-ing) *adj.* pegajoso, glutinoso, etc.: *~ plaster,* esparadrapo.

**stick-in-the-mud** *adj.-s.* retrógrado; rutinario [pers.].

**stickle (to)** (sti·køl) *intr.* disputar, porfiar por menudencias.

**stickler** (sti·klø$^r$) *s.* porfiador. *2* rigorista.

**sticky** (sti·ki) *adj.* pegajoso, viscoso, tenaz.

**stiff** (stif) *adj.* tieso [rígido; estirado]. *2* yerto, envarado. *3* duro, almidonado. *4* espeso. *5* tirante. *6* recio, fuerte, grande. *7* duro, difícil. *8* torpe, encogido. *9* terco, obstinado. *10* ~ *neck*, tortícolis; obstinación. *11 s.* fam. cadáver.

**stiffen (to)** (-øn) *tr.* atiesar. *2* envarar. *3* endurecer. *4* espesar. *5 intr.* atiesarse, ponerse tieso. *6* envararse. *7* endurecerse. *8* espesarse. *9* robustecerse. *10* obstinarse. *11* refrescar [el viento].

**stiff-necked** *adj.* obstinado, testarudo.

**stiffness** (-nis) *s.* tiesura, rigidez. *2* tirantez. *3* envaramiento.

**stifle** (stai·føl) *s.* VET. babilla.

**stifle (to)** *tr.* ahogar, sofocar. *2* apagar. *3* callar, ocultar.·*4 intr.* ahogarse.

**stifling** (stai·fling) *s.* ahogador, sofocante.

**stigma** (sti·gma), *pl.* **stigmas** o **-mata** (-ta) *s.* estigma [en todas sus acepciones].

**stigmatize (to)** (sti·gmataiš) *tr.* estigmatizar.

**stile** (stail) *t.* escalones de un portillo; portillo [en una valla]. *2* larguero, montante.

**stiletto** (stile·tou) *s.* estilete [puñal].

**still** (stil) *adj.* quieto, inmóvil: ~ *water runs deep*, fig. no te fíes del agua mansa. *2* tranquilo, sosegado. *3* silencioso, mudo. *4* suave [voz, ruido]. *5* muerto, inanimado: ~ *life*, naturaleza muerta. *6 adv.* aún, todavía. *7 conj.* no obstante, a pesar de eso. *9 s.* silencio, quietud. *10* alambique. *11* destilería.

**still (to)** *tr.* acallar. *2* aquietar, calmar. *3* detener, parar. *4 intr.* calmarse, aquietarse.

**stillborn** (sti·lboᶠn) *adj.* nacido muerto.

**stilly** (sti·li) *adj.* silencioso, tranquilo. *2 adv.* quietamente, silenciosamente.

**stilt** (sti·lt) *s.* zanco. *2* ORN. cigoñuela.

**stilted** (sti·ltid) *adj.* realzado, elevado. *2* altisonante, hinchado.

**stimulant** (sti·miulant) *adj.-s.* estimulante. *2 s. pl.* bebidas alcohólicas.

**stimulate (to)** (sti·miuleit) *tr.-intr.* estimular. *2* embriagar.

**stimulation** (stimiulei·shøn) *s.* excitación, estímulo.

**stimulus** (sti·miuløs) *s.* estímulo, incentivo.

**sting** (sting) *s.* picadura, punzada; mordedura [de serpiente]. *2* aguijón, estímulo. *3* escozor. *4* ZOOL., BOT. púa, aguijón.

**sting (to)** *tr.-intr.* picar, punzar, pinchar; morder [la serpiente]. *2* escocer, atormentar, remorder. *3* aguinojear, estimular. ¶ Pret. y p. p.: *stung*.

**stingaree** (-aɪ) *s.* ICT. pastinaca.

**stinginess** (sti·nÿinis) *s.* avaricia, tacañería.

**stingless** (stɪ·nglis) *adj.* sin púa o aguijón.

**stingy** (sti·nÿi) *adj.* avaro, tacaño. *2* mezquino, escaso.

**stink** (stink) *s.* hedor, peste.

**stink (to)** *intr.* heder, oler mal, apestar. ¶ Pret. *stank* o *stunk*; p. p.: *stunk*.

**stinkard** (sti·nkaᶠd) *s.* cosa o persona hedionda.

**stinker** (sti·nkøᶠ) *s.* cosa o persona hedionda. *2* fam. sujeto despreciable, canalla.

**stinking** (sti·nking) *adj.* hediondo, apestoso.

**stint** (stint) *s.* limitación, restricción: *without* ~, sin límite. *2* cuota o tarea asignada.

**stint (to)** *tr.* limitar, escatimar. *2 intr.* ser económico.

**stinted** (sti·ntid) *adj.* limitado, restringido. *2* corto, escaso.

**stipe** (staip) *s.* BOT. estipe; estípite.

**stipend** (stai·pend) *s.* estipendio, sueldo.

**stipendiary** (staipe·ndieri) *adj.-s.* estipendiario.

**stipple (to)** (sti·pøl) *tr.* B. ART., GRAB. puntear, granear.

**stipulate (to)** (sti·piuleit) *tr.* estipular.

**stipulation** (stipiulei·shøn) *s.* estipulación.

**stipule** (sti·piul) *s.* BOT. estípula.

**stir** (støᶠ) *s.* movimiento, actividad. *2* agitación, revuelo. *3* alboroto.

**stir (to)** *tr.* mover, menear, bullir. *2* agitar, revolver. *3* atizar, avivar. *4* conmover, inflamar, animar. *5* suscitar, promover; despertar, inspirar. *6* poner en movimiento. *7 intr.* moverse, menearse, agitarse; estar en movimiento. *8* fam. levantarse [por la mañana]. ¶ Pret. y p. p.: *stirred*; ger.: *-rring*.

**stirrup** (sti·røp) *s.* EQUIT., MEC. estribo: ~ *strap*, acción. *2* ZAP. tirapié. *3* ANAT. ~ *bone*, estribo [del oído].

**stitch** (stich) *s.* COST. puntada. *2* punto [de costura, bordado, etc.]. *3* CIR. punto. *4* punzada [dolor]. *5* trecho, distancia.

**stitch (to)** *tr.* coser, adornar con puntadas, pespuntar: *to* ~ *up*, remendar; CIR. dar puntos a. *2 intr.* coser, bordar.

**stithy** (sti·ði) *s.* yunque. *2* fragua.

**stoat** (stout) *s.* ZOOL. armiño [en verano].

**stock** (stak) *s.* BOT. tronco. *2* tronco [del cuerpo]. *3* tronco [origen]; estirpe. *4* zoquete. *5* pilar. *6* acopio, provisión, existencias; material: *in* ~, en existencia; *out of* ~, vendido, agotado. *7* TEAT. repertorio. *8* inventario. *9* ganado: ~ *raising*, ganadería. *10* capital de un negocio. *11* COM. título, acción, obligación; valores: ~ *company*, sociedad anónima; ~ *market*, mercado de valores. *12* muebles, enseres. *13* mango [de látigo, caña de pescar, etc.]; caja [de fusil; de cepillo o garlopa]. *14* patrón [de injerto]. *15* baceta [de la baraja]. *16* BOT. alhelí. *17* corbatín, alzacuello. *18 pl.* valores públicos. *19* cepo [castigo]. *20* VET. potro [máquina]. *21* MAR. basada. *22 adj.* común, usual, estereotipado.

**stock (to)** *tr.* tener en existencia, tener existencias de. *2* proveer, abastecer. *3* poblar [un estanque o río]. *4* sembrar hierba en. *5* almacenar, acoplar. *6* encepar.

**stockade** (stakei·d) *s.* empalizada, vallado.

**stockade (to)** *tr.* empalizar.

**stockbreeder** (stakbrɪ·døᶠ) *s.* ganadero.

**stockbroker** (-broukøᶠ) *s.* corredor de Bolsa.

**stockfish** (-fish) *s.* bacalao seco, pejepalo.

**stockholder** (-jouldøᶠ) *s.* accionista.

**Stockholm** (-joulm) *n. pr.* GEOGR. Estocolmo.

**stocking** (-ing) *s.* media, calceta. *2* fig. gato, dinero. *3* calzo [del caballo].

**stockish** (-ish) *adj.* estúpido.

**stockjobber** (-dÿabøᶠ) *s.* desp. (Ingl.) agente de corredores de Bolsa; (E.U.) bolsista, agiotista.

**stockman** (-mæn) *s.* ganadero. *2* encargado de las existencias.

**stockpile** (-pail) *s.* reserva de existencias.

**stockpile (to)** *tr.* acumular, reunir. *2 intr.* hacer acopio de existencias.

**stockroom** (-rum) *s.* GEOM. almacén.

**stock-still** *adj.* completamente inmóvil.

**stocky** (-i) *adj.* rechoncho. *2* achaparrado.

**stodgy** (sta·dÿi) *adj.* pesado, indigesto. *2* soso, aburrido. *3* rollizo.

**Stoic** (stou·ik) *s.* estoico.

**stoic (al** (stou·ik(al) *adj.* estoico.

**stoicism** (-isism) *s.* estoicismo.

**stoke (to)** (stouk) *tr.-intr.* atizar [el fuego]. *2* cargar, alimentar [un horno u hogar].

**stokehold** (-jould) *s.* MAR. cuarto de calderas. 2 puesto del fogonero.

**stokehole** (-joul) *s.* boca del horno; puesto del fogonero. 2 cuarto de calderas.

**stoker** (-ø$^r$) *s.* fogonero.

**stole** (stoul) *s.* estola.

**stole, stolen** (stoul, -øn) *pret.* y *p. p.* de TO STEAL.

**stolid** (sta·lid) *adj.* estólido. 2 impasible.

**stolon** (stou·lan) *s.* BOT. estolón.

**stoma** (-ma), *pl.* **-mata** (-mata) *s.* BOT. estoma.

**stomach** (stø·mak) *s.* ANAT. estómago: ~ *ache*, dolor de estómago. 2 fam. vientre, barriga. 3 apetito, deseo, afición. 4 ánimo, valor.

**stomach (to)** *tr.* tragar, digerir, sufrir, aguantar.

**stomacher** (-ø$^r$) *s.* peto, estomaguero.

**stomachic** (stømæ·kik) *adj.-s.* estomacal.

**stomachless** (stø·maklis) *adj.* desganado.

**stomatitis** (stomatai·tis) *s.* MED. estomatitis.

**stone** (stoun) *s.* piedra [materia o trozo de ella], canto, china: *Stone Age*, edad de piedra; ~ *cutter*, picapedrero, cantero: ~ *quarry*, cantera; *stone's throw*, tiro de piedra; *to leave no* ~ *unturned*, no dejar piedra sin mover. 2 ARQ. sillar. 3 muela [piedra]. 4 piedra preciosa. 5 MED. cálculo. 6 hueso, cuesco [de fruta]: ~ *fruit*, fruta de hueso; ~ *pine*, pino piñonero. 7 (Ingl.) peso de 14 libras. 8 IMPR. platina. 9 ficha [de dominó].

**stone (to)** *tr.* apedrear, lapidar. 2 despedregar. 3 deshuesar [un fruto]. 4 revestir de piedra.

**stone-blind** *adj.* completamente ciego.

**stone-broke** *adj.* arruinado, sin un éntimo.

**stonecrop** (-krap) *s.* BOT. uva de gato.

**stone-deaf** *adj.* completamente sordo.

**stonewall** (-uol) *adj.* fuerte [como una muralla]. 2 obstinado. 3 resuelto.

**stoneware** (-ue$^r$) *s.* especie de gres.

**stonework** (-uø$^r$k) *s.* obra de sillería.

**stony** (-i) *adj.* pedregoso. 2 de piedra, pétreo. 3 duro, insensible, empedernido.

**stony-hearted** *adj.* duro de corazón, cruel.

**stood** (stud) *pret.* y *p. p.* de TO STAND.

**stool** (stul) *s.* taburete, escabel, banquillo. 2 silico, retrete. 3 deposición, excremento. 4 antepecho [de ventana]. 5 cimillo. 6 cimbel, señuelo: ~ *pigeon*, cimbel [ave]; gancho [pers.]; confidente de la policía.

**stool (to)** *intr.* brotar, echar renuevos. 2 exonerar el vientre.

**stoop** (stup) *s.* inclinación del cuerpo, de la cabeza, encorvamiento. 2 dignación; rebajamiento. 4 (E.U.) escalinata de entrada.

**stoop (to)** *intr.* agacharse, doblar o encorvar el cuerpo. 2 andar encorvado. 3 inclinarse hacia abajo. 4 descender. 5 rebajarse; humillarse. 6 *tr.* inclinar, encorvar.

**stop** (stap) *s.* alto, parada, estancia; paro, detención; fin, pausa: ~ *light*, luz o señal de parada; *dead* ~, parada súbita; *to put a* ~ *to*, poner fin a; *without* ~, sin parar, sin detenerse. 2 parada, apeadero. 3 posada, parador. 4 obstrucción, estorbo. 5 tapón. 6 GRAM. punto: *full* ~, punto final. 7 MEC. tope, fiador. 8 MÚS. llave [de instrumento]; traste [de guitarra]; registro [de órgano]. 9 FOT. diafragma.

**stop (to)** *tr.* detener, parar, poner fin a. | *Stop thief!*, ¡al ladrón! 2 dejar de. 3 interrumpir, suspender. 4 refrenar, contener, atajar, poner coto a. 5 impedir, estorbar. 6 cerrar, tapar, cegar, atascar, obstruir; interceptar. 7 empastar [un diente]. 8 estancar, represar. 9 parar [un golpe]. 10 *intr.* pararse, detenerse, cesar; hacer alto, quedarse:

*not to* ~ *at*,·no pararse en; *to* ~ *short*, pararse en seco, quedarse cortado. *11* parar, hospedarse. ¶ Pret. y p. p.: *stopped*; ger.: -*pping*.

**stopcock** (-kak) *s.* llave o espita de paso.

**stopgap** (-gæp) *s.* lo que tapa una abertura. 2 recurso temporal, sustitutivo.

**stopover** (-ouvø$^r$) *s.* parada intermedia [en un viaje].

**stoppage** (-idy̆) *s.* detención, cesación, interrupción. 2 obstrucción, interceptación. 3 retención [sobre una paga]. 4 COM. suspensión [de un pago]. 5 MED. oclusión.

**stopper** (-ø$^r$) *s.* tapón, obturador.

**stopper (to)** *tr.* tapar, taponar.

**stopple** (-øl) *s.* tapón, bitoque.

**stopple (to)** *tr.* tapar, taponar.

**storage** (sto·ridy̆) *s.* almacenamiento: ~ *battery*. ELECT. batería de acumuladores, acumulador. 2 almacenaje. 3 espacio para almacenar.

**storax** (stou·ræks) *s.* estoraque.

**store** (sto$^r$) *s.* copia, abundancia; acopio, provisión. 2 tesoro. 3 almacén, depósito: *in* ~, almacenado en reserva. 4 (esp. E.U.) tienda, comercio. 5 *to set (great)* ~ *by*, tener en mucha estima. 6 *pl.* reservas, provisiones, pertrechos.

**store (to)** *tr.* proveer, abastecer. 2 guardar, acumular, atesorar, tener en reserva. 3 almacenar.

**storehouse** (-jaus) *s.* almacén.

**storekeeper** (sto·$^r$kıpø$^r$) *s.* guardalmacén. 2 (E.U.) tendero.

**storeroom** (-rum) *s.* almacén. 2 despensa.

**storey** (sto·ri) *s.* ARQ. piso, alto, planta.

**storied** (sto·rid) *adj.* B. ART. de temas históricos. 2 histórico, legendario. 3 de [tantos] pisos: *two-storied*, de dos pisos.

**storiette** (storie·t) *s.* cuento, historieta.

**stork** (sto$^r$k) *s.* ORN. cigüeña.

**storm** (sto$^r$m) *s.* tempestad, temporal, tormenta, borrasca: ~ *door*, guardapuerta, cancel. 2 fig. agitación, tumulto. 3 MIL. asalto: *to take by* ~, tomar por asalto; fig. arrebatar, entusiasmar.

**storm (to)** *tr.* tomar por asalto, atacar. 2 *intr.* haber tempestad. 3 rabiar, tempestear; alborotar.

**stormy** (-i) *adj.* tempestuoso, tormentoso, borrascoso. 2 violento, turbulento.

**story** (sto·ri) *s.* historia, leyenda, relato, cuento, anécdota, novela: *as the* ~ *goes*, según se cuenta. 2 fam. chisme, embuste. 3 trama, argumento. 4 ARQ. piso, alto.

**story (to)** *tr.* historiar. 2 adornar con escenas históricas. ¶ Pret. y p. p.: *storied*.

**stoup** (stup) *s.* frasco, jarro. 2 pila del agua bendita.

**stout** (staut) *adj.* fuerte, recio. 2 robusto, grueso, corpulento. 3 valiente, decidido. 4 firme, leal. 5 obstinado. 6 *s.* cerveza fuerte.

**stouthearted** (-ja$^r$tid) *adj.* valiente, intrépido.

**stove** (stouv) *s.* estufa; hornillo. 2 cocina económica de gas o de electricidad. 3 horno de cerámica. 4 JARD. estufa, invernáculo.

**stove** *pret.* y *p. p.* de TO STAVE.

**stow (to)** (stou) *tr.* apretar, hacinar. 2 guardar, esconder. 3 meter, alojar. 4 atestar, abarrotar. 5 MAR. arrimar, estibar. 6 *intr. to* ~ *away*, embarcarse clandestinamente.

**stowage** (-idy̆) *s.* almacenaje. 2 MAR. estiba.

**stowaway** (-auei) *s.* polizón, pasajero clandestino.

**stower** (-ø$^r$) *s.* estibador.

**strabismus** (strabi·smøs) *s.* MED. estrabismo.

**straddle** (stræ·døl) *s.* posición del que se esparranca o monta a horcajadas.

**straddle (to)** *intr.* esparrancarse. *2* montar o estar a horcajadas sobre. *3* extenderse. *4* *tr.-intr.* no comprometerse [entre dos partidos].

**stradiot** (stra·diat) *s.* estradiote.

**strafe (to)** (streif) *tr.* fam. bombardear violentamente. *2* ametrallar en vuelo bajo. *3* reprender, castigar.

**straggle (to)** (stræ·gøl) *intr.* rodar, andar perdido. *2* extraviarse; desbandarse, rezagarse. *3* desparramarse, estar esparcido.

**straggler** (stræ·gløʳ) *s.* paseante, vagabundo. *2* descarriado, rezagado. *3* el que se aparta o desvía. *4* rama extendida. *5* objeto aislado.

**straggly** (-i) *adj.* desparramado, esparcido, desordenado.

**straight** (streit) *adj.* recto, derecho; ~ *line*, línea recta. *2* directo, en línea recta. *3* erguido. *4* lacio [pelo]. *5* seguido. *6* correcto, exacto. *7* franco, sincero. *8* recto, justo, honrado. *9* serio, severo. *10* acérrimo. *11* en orden, arreglado. *12* puro, sin mezcla. *13* formando escalera [naipes]. *14* GEOM. ~ *angle*, ángulo de 180°. *15* *adv.* directamente, en línea recta. *16* continuamente. *17* erguidamente. *18* correctamente. *19* honradamente, francamente. *20* ~ *away*, ~ *off*, inmediatamente. *21* *s.* recta; plano. *22* escalera [en el poker].

**straighten** (-øn) *tr.* enderezar. *2* desalabear. *3* arreglar, poner en orden. *4* *intr.* *to* ~ *up*, enderezarse.

**straightforward** (-fo·ʳuaʳd) *adj.* recto, derecho. *2* honrado, íntegro. *3* franco, sincero.

**straightness** (strei·tnis) *s.* rectitud, honradez.

**straight-out** *adj.* fam. (E.U.) sincero, franco; completo, absoluto.

**straightway** (strei·tuei) *adv.* inmediatamente, al instante, en seguida.

**strain** (strein) *s.* tensión, tirantez; esfuerzo excesivo; exceso; fatiga. *2* torcedura, esguince. *3* MEC. deformación. *4* estirpe, linaje. *5* clase, suerte. *6* rasgo heredado. *7* vena [de loco, etc.]. *8* tono, acento, modo. *9* MÚS. aire, melodía. *10* estrofa, verso.

**strain (to)** *tr.* estirar, poner tirante. *2* aguzar [la vista, el oído]; someter a un esfuerzo; sobreexcitar, fatigar. *3* torcer, forzar, violentar, deformar. *4* extremar. *5* apretar, estrechar. *6* colar, tamizar. *7* *to* ~ *a point*, excederse, hacer una excepción. *8* *intr.* esforzarse. *9* soportar un esfuerzo. *10* pasar [por un filtro, etc.].

**strained** (-d) *adj.* forzado [risa, etc.]. *2* tirante [situación, relaciones].

**strainer** (-øʳ) *s.* tensor. *2* colador, cedazo.

**strait** (streit) *adj.* estrecho, apretado; ~ *jacket*, camisa de fuerza. *2* limitado. *3* difícil, apurado. *4* *s.* GEOGR. estrecho. *5* aprieto, apuro.

**straiten (to)** (-tøn) *tr.* estrechar, contraer. *2* reducir, limitar. *3* agobiar, apurar: *in straitened circumstances*, en situación apurada, sin dinero.

**strait-laced** *adj.* excesivamente rígido, mojigato.

**straitness** (-nis) *s.* estrechez. *2* apuro, escasez, penuria.

**strake** (streik) *s.* STREAK.

**stramineous** (strami·niøs) *adj.* pajizo. *2* sin valor.

**stramonium** (-mo·niøm) *s.* BOT. estramonio.

**strand** (-træn) *s.* playa, ribera. *2* hebra, cabo, ramal [de cuerda]; cuerda, trenza. *3* hilo [de perlas].

**strand (to)** *tr.-intr.* embarrancar. *2* *tr.* dejar perdido, desamparado. *3* romper un ramal de [una cuerda]. *4* torcer formando cuerda.

**strange** (streindỹ) *adj.* extraño, foráneo, desconocido. *2* ajeno. *3* extraño, raro, singular. *4* retraído, reservado.

**stranger** (-øʳ) *s.* extraño, forastero, desconocido. *2* *to be a* ~ *to*, ignorar, desconocer. *3* *you are a* ~, se vende usted muy caro.

**strangle (to)** (stræ·ngøl) *tr.* estrangular, asfixiar, ahogar. *2* fig. ahogar, sofocar, reprimir. *3* *intr.* ahogarse.

**strangulate (to)** (-giuleit) *tr.* apretar, ahogar. *2* MED. estrangular.

**strap** (stræp) *s.* correa, tira, faja, banda [esp. para atar o sujetar]. *2* SASTR. trabilla. *3* fleje. *4* ZAP. tirador. *5* suavizador [de navajas].

**strap (to)** *tr.* atar, sujetar con correas o tiras. *2* fajar, precintar. *3* azotar con correa. *4* asentar el filo de [una navaja]. *5* almohazar. ¶ Pret. y p. p.: *strapped;* ger.: *-pping*.

**strapper** (-øʳ) *s.* mozo de cuadra. *2* pers. o cosa corpulenta. *3* mentira colosal.

**strapping** (-ing) *adj.* robusto, fuerte; ~ *youth*, mocetón.

**Strasbourg** (stræ·sbøʳg) *n. pr.* GEOGR. Estrasburgo.

**stratagem** (stræ·tadỹem) *s.* estratagema, ardid.

**strategic(al** (stratɪ·dỹik(al) *adj.* estratégico.

**strategics** (stratɪ·dỹiks) *s.* estrategia.

**strategist** (stræ·tidỹist) *s.* estratega.

**strategy** (-tidỹi) *s.* estrategia.

**stratification** (strætifikei·shøn) *s.* estratificación.

**stratify (to)** (stræ·tifai) *tr.* estratificar. *2* *intr.* estratificarse. ¶ Pret. y p. p.: *stratified*.

**stratigraphy** (stratɪ·grafi) *s.* estratigrafía.

**stratosphere** (stræ·tøsfiʳ) *s.* estratosfera.

**stratum** (strei·tøm) *s.* estrato, capa.

**stratus** (strei·tus) *s.* METEOR. estrato.

**straw** (stro) *s.* paja: ~ *hat*, sombrero de paja; *the last* ~, fig. lo que faltaba; *to catch at* ~, fig. arrastrarse a un clavo ardiendo; *I don't care a* ~, me importa un bledo. *2* bálago. *3* fig. señal, indicio.

**strawberry** (-beri) *s.* BOT. fresa [planta y fruto]. *2* BOT. ~ *tree*, madroño.

**strawy** (-stro·i) *adj.* pajizo, de paja. *2* sin valor.

**stray** (strei) *adj.* descarriado, perdido, errante. *2* suelto, aislado, incidental. *3* *s.* o animal descarriado, perdido. *4* *pl.* RADIO. parásitos.

**stray (to)** *intr.* desviarse. *2* descarriarse, extraviarse, perderse, errar, vagar.

**streak** (strɪk) *s.* raya, línea, lista. *2* rayo o raya [de luz]: ~ *of lightning*, relámpago. *3* MIN. vena. *4* rastro, rasgo, un algo. *5* MAR. hilada. *6* (E.U.) racha [de suerte].

**streak (to)** *tr.* rayar, listar, gayar. *2* *intr.* ir como un rayo; viajar velozmente.

**streaky** (strɪ·ki) *adj.* rayado, listado, abigarrado. *2* desigual, variable [pers., carácter, humor].

**stream** (strɪm) *s.* corriente. *2* río, arroyo. *3* torrente, raudal; flujo, chorro: ~ *of words*, flujo de palabras. *4* rayo [de luz, de sol]. *5* curso [de la historia, de la vida].

**stream (to)** *intr.* correr, fluir, manar, chorrear. *2* salir a torrentes, derramarse. *3* pasar rápidamente. *4* ondear, tremolar. *5* extenderse en línea continua. *6* *tr.* verter, derramar. *7* hacer ondear.

**streamer** (-øʳ) *s.* flámula, gallardete. *2* cola [de un cometa]. *3* titulares de un periódico que ocupan todo el ancho de la página.

**streamlet** (-lit) *s.* arroyuelo, riachuelo.

**streamline** (-lain) *s.* línea que sigue una corriente. *2* línea aerodinámica. *3* *adj.* aerodinámico.

**streamline (to)** *tr.* hacer aerodinámico.

**streamlined** (-laind) *adj.* aerodinámico.

**streamy** (-i) *adj.* surcado por arroyos. *2* que sale como un chorro; radiante. *3* ondeante.

**street** (strıt) *s.* calle, vía pública: ~ *Arab,* golfillo, pilluelo; ~ *cleaner,* ~ *sweeper,* barrendero; barredera [máquina]; ~ *floor,* piso bajo, bajos; ~ *railway,* tranvía.

**streetcar** (-kaʳ) *s.* (E.U.) tranvía.

**streetwalker** (-wokøʳ) *s.* prostituta.

**strength** (strengz) *s.* fuerza, energía, vigor. *2* fortaleza, firmeza, solidez. *3* poder, pujanza. *4* intensidad. *5* concentración, cuerpo [de un líquido]. *6* fuerza legal. *7* MIL. fuerza [número].

**strengthen (to)** (-øn) *tr.* fortalecer, robustecer. *2* consolidar. *3* confirmar, corroborar. *4* animar, alentar. *5* reforzar. *6 intr.* fortalecerse. *7* hacerse más fuerte.

**strenuous** (stre·niuøs) *adj.* estrenuo, enérgico, activo, ardiente, celoso. *2* arduo.

**strepitous** (stre·pitøs) *adj.* estrepitoso, clamoroso.

**streptococcus** (streptøka·køs) *s.* BACT. estreptococo.

**streptomycin** (-mai·sin) *s.* estreptomicina.

**stress** (stres) *s.* fuerza [que obliga], presión, coacción, urgencia. *2* peso, importancia; fuerza, énfasis: *to lay ~ on,* dar importancia a, subrayar, insistir en. *3* esfuerzo, tensión. *4* MÚS., PROS. acento.

**stress (to)** *tr.* someter a un esfuerzo, una tensión, un peso. *2* acentuar. *3* recalcar, hacer hincapié en.

**stretch** (strech) *s.* extensión [acción de extender]. *2* estiramiento, dilatación. *3* tirantez, tensión. *4* estirón, esfuerzo. *5* interpretación forzada; exageración. *6* extensión, trecho, distancia: *at o on a ~,* de un tirón. *7* lapso, intervalo. *8* MAR. bordada.

**stretch (to)** *tr.* extender, alargar, tender. *2* estirar, atesar, distender. *3* ensanchar, dilatar. *4* violentar, forzar; extremar, exagerar. *5 to ~ forth,* alargar, extender. *6 to ~ oneself,* tenderse; desperezarse. *7 to ~ out,* estirar; alargar, tender. *8 to ~ a point,* hacer una concesión. *9 intr.* extenderse. *10* alargarse, dar de sí; estirarse; desplegarse. | Gralte. con *out. 11* esforzarse, menearse. *12* tenderse, tumbarse. *13* desperezarse.

**stretcher** (-øʳ) *s.* tendedor. *2* estirador, tensor. *3* ensanchador. *4* camilla, parihuelas. *5* CARP. viga, tirante. *6* fam. cuento, exageración.

**stretcher-bearer** *s.* camillero.

**strew** (stru) *s.* porción de cosas esparcidas.

**strew (to)** *tr.* esparcir, desparramar. *2* sembrar, salpicar, regar, espolvorear. ¶ Pret.: *strewed;* p. p.: *strewed* o *strewn.*

**stria** (strai·a) *s.* estría.

**striate (to)** (strai·eit) *tr.* estriar.

**stricken** (stri·køn) p. p. de TO STRIKE. *2 adj.* golpeado, herido. *3* gastado, cascado.

**strickle** (stri·køl) *s.* rasero. *2* escantillón.

**strict** (strikt) *adj.* estricto. *2* riguroso, escrupuloso. *3* rígido, severo.

**stricture** (stri·kchøʳ) *s.* crítica, censura. *2* MED. estrechez.

**stridden** (strai·døn) p. p. de TO STRIDE.

**stride** (straid) *s.* paso largo, tranco, zanzada.

**stride (to)** *intr.* andar a pasos largos. *2 tr.* pasar, salvar de un tranco. *3* recorrer a paso largo. *4* montar a horcajadas. ¶ Pret.: *strode;* p. p.: *stridden.*

**stridency** (strai·dønsi) *s.* estridencia.

**strident** (-ønt) *adj.* estridente.

**stridulate (to)** (stri·diuleit) *intr.* estridular.

**strife** (straif) *s.* disputa, contienda, lucha. *2* competición, emulación; porfía.

**strike** (straik) *s.* golpe. *2* huelga: ~ *breaker,* esquirol; *to go on ~,* declararse en huelga. *3* rasero. *4* descubrimiento de un filón. *5* golpe de suerte; ganga.

**strike (to)** *tr.* golpear. *2* herir. *3* batir, chocar con, dar contra. *4* hacer chocar. *5* dar [un golpe]. *6* quitar, cortar, etc., de un golpe. *7* embadurnar. *8* afligir, castigar. *9* encender [una cerilla]; sacar [fuego, chispa]. *10* producir un efecto súbito, una emoción: *to ~ dumb,* dejar mudo; asombrar; *to ~ with horror,* horrorizar. *11* sorprender, extrañar. *12* ocurrir [una idea]; parecer: *how does it ~ you?,* ¿qué le parece? *13* acuñar, troquelar. *14* echar [raíces]. *15* MÚS. tocar. *16* dar [la hora]. *17* hallar, dar con. *18* rasar, nivelar. *19* atraer; enamorar. *20* hacer [balance]; sacar [una cuenta]. *21* cerrar [un trato]. *22* bajar, arriar. *23* borrar, tachar. | Con *off* o *out. 24* tomar [una postura]. *25* levantar [las tiendas]. *26* trazar [una línea]. *27* IMPR. tirar. *28 to ~ down,* derribar, tumbar. *29 to ~ one's fancy,* antojársele a uno. *30 to ~ someone for a loan,* dar un sablazo a uno. *31 to ~ up,* ponerse a tocar o a cantar [algo]; trabar [amistad].

*32 intr.* golpear; luchar; atacar. *33* chocar, tropezar. *34* partir, avanzar, ir, entrar, pasar. *35* sonar, dar la hora. *36* declararse en huelga. *37* arriar el pabellón. *38* picar [el pez]. *39* AGR. arraigar. *40* MAR. embarrancar. *41 to ~ at,* amagar un golpe a, acometer. *42 to ~ into,* entrar en; echar por; ponerse a. *43 to ~ on,* ocurrirse [una idea]; hallar; impresionar.

¶ Pret.: *struck;* p. p.: *struck* o *stricken.*

**striker** (-øʳ) *s.* golpeador. *2* huelguista. *3* percutor.

**striking** (-ing) *adj.* notable, sorprendente. *2* manifiesto. *3* llamativo. *4* en huelga.

**string** (stri·ng) *s.* cordón, cinta, cordel. *2* hilo [con que se mueve una cosa]. *3* ristra, sarta. *4* cuerda [de un arco, de un instrumento]. *5* hebra, fibra, nervio, tendón. *6* BOT. ~ *bean,* judía verde. *7 pl.* MÚS. cuerda [instrumentos].

**string (to)** *tr.* atar [con cordón, etc.]. *2* encordar. *3* templar [un violín, etc.]. *4* poner tirante, en tensión. *5* sobreexcitar. *6* ensartar, enhebrar. *7* extender, alargar. *8* quitar las hebras a. *9 intr.* formar hilo. *10* marchar en hilera, extenderse en línea; prolongarse. ¶ Pret.: *strung;* p. p.: *strung* o *stringed.*

**stringboard** (-boʳd) *s.* zanca [de escalera].

**stringency** (stri·ndyønsi) *s.* fuerza convincente. *2* severidad, rigor. *3* estrechez, penuria.

**stringent** (-dyønt) *adj.* convincente. *2* rígido, severo. *3* COM. flojo [mercado].

**stringy** (stri·ngi) *adj.* fibroso, filamentoso. *2* viscoso, correoso.

**strip** (strip) *s.* tira, lista, cinta, faja, listón.

**strip (to)** *tr.* despojar, desnudar, desguarnecer. *2* quitar, arrancar [lo que cubre]. *3* privar [de], robar, arrebatar. *4* raer, limpiar. *5* MAR. desmantelar. *6* AGR. desgranar. *7* despalillar [tabaco]. *8 intr.* desnudarse, despojarse. *9* soltarse, caer [la piel, la corteza]. ¶ Pret. y p. p.: *stripped* y *stript;* ger.: *-pping.*

**stripe** (strai·p) *s.* raya, lista, franja, galón.

**stripe (to)** *tr.* rayar, listar, gayar. *2* azotar.

**striped** (-d) *adj.* rayado, listado.

**striping** (-ing) *s.* listas, franjas.

**stripling** (stri·pling) *s.* mozalbete, jovencito.

**strip-tease** *s.* espectáculo en que una artista se desnuda total o parcialmente.

**stripy** (strai·pi) *adj.* rayado, listado.

**strive (to)** (straiv) *intr.* esforzarse. *2* forcejear. *3* luchar, contender. ¶ Pret,: *strove;* p. p.: *striven.*

**strobile** (stra·bil) *s.* BOT. estróbilo.

**strode** (stroud) *pret.* de TO STRIDE.

**stroke** (strouk) *s.* golpe: ~ *of luck,* golpe de suerte; *at one* ~, de un golpe. *2* brazada [del que nada]; bogada; jugada; tacada. *3* MEC. carrera, embolada. *4* campanada [de reloj]. *5* MED. ataque [de apoplejía, parálisis, etc.]. *6* esfuerzo, acto, rasgo: ~ *of wit,* rasgo de ingenio. *7* trazo, toque, rasgo, pincelada: ~ *of pen,* plumada. *8* caricia [con la mano]. *9* DEP. *stroke* o ~ *oar,* primer remero.

**stroke (to)** *tr.* frotar suavemente; pasar la mano por; acariciar; alisar. *2* tildar, rayar.

**stroll** (stroul) *s.* paseo, paseíto, vuelta.

**stroll (to)** *intr.* pasear, pasearse [a pie]. *2* andar de un lugar a otro.

**stroller** (strou·lø^r) *s.* paseante. *2* vagabundo. *3* cómico ambulante. *4* cochecito de niño.

**stroma** (strou·ma) *s.* ANAT. estroma.

**strong** (strong) *adj.* fuerte: ~ *box,* caja fuerte; ~ *hand,* mano fuerte, dura. *2* robusto, fornido. *3* grande, poderoso. *4* marcado, pronunciado. *5* firme, arraigado. *6* ardiente, acérrimo. *7* espirituosa [bebida]; cargado [café, té]. *8* de olor fuerte u ofensivo. *9* firme [mercado]. *10 an army ten thousand* ~, un ejército de diez mil hombres. *11 adv.* fuertemente; sumamente.

**strong-handed** *adj.* de mano fuerte; duro.

**strong-headed** *adj.* obstinado, testarudo.

**stronghold** (stro·ngjould) *s.* fortaleza, plaza fuerte.

**strong-minded** *adj.* de espíritu independiente.

**strontium** (stra·nshiøm) *s.* QUÍM. estroncio.

**strop** (strap) *s.* suavizador [para navajas]. *2* MAR. estrobo.

**strop (to)** *tr.* suavizar [navajas].

**strophe** (strou·fi) *s.* estrofa.

**strove** (strouv) *pret.* de TO STRIVE.

**struck** (strøk) *pret.* y *p. p.* de TO STRIKE.

**structural** (strø·kchøral) *adj.* estructural. *2* ING. de construcción o construcciones.

**structure** (strø·kchø^r) *s.* estructura. *2* hechura, textura. *3* construcción, edificio, máquina.

**struggle** (strø·gøl) *s.* esfuerzo, lucha, brega, pugna, forcejeo. *2* contienda, disputa, pelea.

**struggle (to)** *intr.* esforzarse, luchar, bregar, pugnar, forcejear, batallar.

**strum (to)** (strøm) *tr.* arañar, aporrear [un piano, una guitarra, etc.]. *2* rasguear [la guitarra]. ¶ Pret. y p. p.: *strummed;* ger.: *-mming.*

**strumpet** (strø·mpit) *s.* ramera.

**strung** (strong) *pret.* y *p. p.* de TO STRING.

**strut** (strøt) *s.* andar arrogante; contoneo, pavoneo. *2* CARP. jabalcón, tornapunta, puntal, ademe.

**strut (to)** *intr.* andar con paso arrogante; contonearse, pavonearse. ¶ Pret. y p. p.: *strutted;* ger.: *strutting.*

**strychnin(e** (stri·knin) *s.* QUÍM. estricnina.

**Stuart** (stiu·a^rt) *n. pr.* Estuardo: *Mary* ~, María Estuardo.

**stub** (støb) *s.* tocón, cepa. *2* zoquete. *3* garrón, tetón. *4* resto, cabo. *5* colilla [de cigarro]. *6* matriz [de talonario]; ~ *book,* libro talonario.

**stub (to)** *tr.* arrancar, desarraigar. *2* limpiar de tocones. *3* aplastar. *4 to* ~ *one's toe,* tropezar [con un tocón, etc.].

**stubble** (stø·bøl) *s.* rastrojo. *2* barba sin afeitar.

**stubborn** (stø·bø^rn) *adj.* obstinado, terco; tenaz, inflexible, irreductible. *2* difícil de trabajar o manejar.

**stubby** (stø·bi) *adj.* lleno de tocones. *2* rechoncho. *3* grueso, corto y tieso; cerdoso.

**stucco** (stø·kou) *s.* estuco.

**stucco (to)** *tr.-intr.* estucar.

**stuccowork** (-wø^rk) *s.* obra de estuco.

**stuck** (støk) *pret.* y *p. p.* de TO STICK.

**stuck-up** *adj.* fam. tieso, estirado, orgulloso.

**stud** (stød) *s.* poste, montante [de tabique, de entramado]. *2* tachón, bollón, clavo de adorno. *3* refuerzo de eslabón. *4* gemelo [de camisa]. *5* yeguada, caballada; ~ *farm,* acaballadero, potrero.

**stud (to)** *tr.* tachonar, clavetear; adornar.

**studbook** (-buk) *s.* registro genealógico de caballos.

**student** (stiu·dønt) *s.* estudiante. *2* estudioso, investigador. *3* ~ *lamp,* quinqué.

**studhorse** (stø·djo^rs) *s.* semental, caballo padre.

**studied** (stø·did) *adj.* estudiado, premeditado.

**studio** (stiu·diou) *s.* estudio, taller. *2* CINEM., RADIO. estudio.

**studious** (stiu·diøs) *adj.* estudioso. *2* de estudio. *3* asiduo, solícito, deseoso. *4* estudiado.

**study** (stø·di) *s.* estudio [acción de estudiar]. *2* objeto, estudio. *3* B. ART., LIT. estudio. *4* despacho, estudio. *5* cuidado, esfuerzo, empeño. *6* meditación profunda.

**study (to)** *tr.-intr.* estudiar. *2* meditar. *3* discurrir, idear.

**stuff** (støf) *s.* material, materia prima. *2* carácter, aptitud, madera. *3* materia, substancia, artículo)s, producto)s : *food* ~, productos alimenticios. *4* tela, paño. *5* cosa, cosas, chismes, cachivaches. *6* pócima, mejunje. *7* deshecho, broza, tonterías, pataratas. *8 interj.* ¡tontería!

**stuff (to)** *tr.* llenar, atestar. *2* rellenar; emborrar; disecar [un animal]. *3* embutir, meter de cualquier modo. *4* tapar, atarugar. *5* atracar [de comida]. *6 intr.* atracarse, hartarse.

**stuffing** (stø·fing) *s.* relleno. *2* MEC. empaquetado: ~ *box,* prensaestopas.

**stuffy** (stø·fi) *adj.* mal ventilado, sofocante. *2* fam. soso, aburrido. *3* fam. (E.U.) malhumorado.

**stultify (to)** (stø·ltifai) *tr.* poner en ridículo; hacer parecer ridículo. *2* frustrar, anular.

**stumble** (stø·mbøl) *s.* tropiezo, tropezón, trompicón, traspié. *2* desliz.

**stumble (to)** *intr.* tropezar, dar un traspié: *to* ~ *on* o *upon,* tropezar con. *2* vacilar, embarullarse, tartamudear.

**stumbling-block, stumbling-stone** *s.* tropezadero, escollo; piedra de escándalo.

**stump** (stømp) *s.* tocón, tueco, cepa. *2* muñón [de miembro cortado]; raigón [de diente o muela]. *3* colilla [de cigarro]. *4* pequeña parte saliente. *5* DIB. esfumino. *6* fam. (E.U.) reto, desafío. *7* paso pesado. *8* (E.U.) tribuna al aire libre; discurso electoral. *9* pop. pierna. *10* poste [en el criquet]. *11* (E.U.) *up a* ~, en un brete.

**stump (to)** *tr.* cortar, mochar. *2* limpiar de tocones. *3* tropezar. *4* DIB. esfumar. *5* desafiar [a hacer algo]. *6* confundir, aplastar. *7* (E.U.) recorrer haciendo discursos electorales. *8 intr.* andar pesadamente; renquear, tropezar. *9* (E.U.) hacer discursos electorales.

**stumpy** (-i) *adj.* tozo, rechoncho, cachigordo. *2* lleno de tocones.

**stun (to)** (støn) *tr.* aturdir, atolondrar, dejar sin sentido. *2* atronar, asordar, ensordecer. *3* pasmar. ¶ Pret. y p. p.: *stunned;* ger.: *-nning.*
**stung** (støng) *pret.* y *p. p.* de TO STING.
**stunk** (stønk) *pret.* y *p. p.* de TO STINK.
**stunner** (stø·nø<sup>r</sup>) *s.* el o lo que aturde o atolondra. *2* fam. cosa pasmosa; mujer guapa.
**stunning** (-ing) *adj.* aturdidor. *2* fam. estupendo.
**stunt** (stønt) *s.* falta de crecimiento o desarrollo. *2* animal, planta, etc., raquíticos. *3* ejercicio de habilidad o destreza; acrobacia aérea. *4* truco propagandístico.
**stunt (to)** *tr.* impedir el crecimiento o desarrollo de. *2 intr.* hacer ejercicios de habilidad; hacer acrobacias aéreas.
**stunted** (-id) *adj.* desmedrado, raquítico, enano. *2* achaparrado.
**stupe** (stiup) *s.* MED. compresa, fomento.
**stupefacient** (stiupifei·shønt) *adj.-s.* estupefaciente.
**stupefaction** (stiupifæ·kshøn) *s.* estupefacción.
**stupefied** (stiu·pifaid) *pret.* y *p. p.* de TO STUPEFY.
**stupefy (to)** (stiu·pifai) *tr.* causar estupor, aturdir, atontar, entorpecer. *2* dejar estupefacto, pasmar. *3 intr.* atontarse, entorpecerse. ¶ Pret. y p. p.: *stupefied.*
**stupendous** (stiupe·ndøs) *adj.* estupendo, asombroso, enorme.
**stupid** (stiu·pid) *adj.-s.* estúpido, tonto. *2 adj.* atontado, aturdido.
**stupidity** (stiupi·diti) *s.* estupidez, tontería.
**stupor** (stiu·pø<sup>r</sup>) *s.* estupor, letargo, atontamiento.
**stuporous** (-øs) *adj.* letárgico.
**sturdiness** (stø·<sup>r</sup>dinis) *s.* robustez, fuerza, vigor. *2* firmeza. *3* tenacidad.
**sturdy** (stø·<sup>r</sup>di) *adj.* robusto, fornido, fuerte. *2* vigoroso. *3* resuelto, firme, tenaz, obstinado.
**sturgeon** (stø·<sup>r</sup>dȳøn) *s.* ICT. esturión, sollo.
**stutter** (stø·tø<sup>r</sup>) *s.* tartamudeo.
**stutter (to)** *intr.* tartamudear.
**stutterer** (-ø<sup>r</sup>) *s.* tartamudo.
**sty** (stai) *s.* pocilga, zahurda. *2* MED. orzuelo.
**Stygian** (sti·dȳian) *adj.* estigio.
**style** (stail) *s.* estilo [punzón, gnomon]. *2* BOT. estilo. *3* estilo [de un autor, escuela, etc.; modo, manera]. *4* distinción, elegancia; moda: *in ~,* de moda. *5* nombre, título, tratamiento.
**style (to)** *tr.* intitular, llamar, nombrar.
**stylet** (-it) *s.* estilete [puñal, punzón]. *2* CIR. estilete.
**stylish** (-ish) *adj.* elegante, a la moda.
**stylist** (-ist) *s.* estilista.
**stylistic** (-istik) *adj.* estilístico.
**stylite** (-ait) *s.* estilita.
**stylize** (-aiš) *tr.* estilizar.
**stylobate** (-øbeit) *s.* ARQ. estilóbato.
**stylograph** (-øgræf) *s.* estilográfica.
**styloid** (-oid) *adj.* ANAT. estiloides.
**stylus** (-øs) *s.* STYLE 1 y 2. *2* aguja [de fonógrafo]. *3* ZOOL. espícula.
**stymie** (stai·mi) *s.* GOLF. circunstancia de estar una pelota entre la del jugador y el hoyo.
**styptic** (sti·ptik) *adj.-s.* estíptico.
**styrax** (stai·ræks) *s.* BOT. estoraque.
**Styx** (stiks) *n. pr.* MIT. Estigia.
**suasion** (suei·ȳøn) *s.* persuasión.
**suasive** (-siv) *adj.* persuasivo, suasorio.
**suave** (sua·v) *adj.* suave, afable. *2* obsequioso, zalamero.
**suavity** (-iti) *s.* suavidad, afabilidad, dulcedumbre.

**sub** (søb) *s.* fam. subalterno; substituto. *2* submarino.
**sub-** *pref.* sub-, -a-, vice-.
**subacetate** (-æ·siteit) *s.* QUÍM. subacetato.
**subalpine** (-æ·lpain) *adj.* subalpino.
**subaltern** (-o·ltø<sup>r</sup>n) *adj.-s.* subalterno. *2 adj.* subordinado, dependiente.
**subaqueous** (-ei·kuiøs) *adj.* subacuático.
**subchanter** (-chæ·ntø<sup>r</sup>) *s.* sochantre.
**subchasser** (-chei·sø<sup>r</sup>) *s.* cazasubmarinos.
**subclass** (-klæs) *s.* subclase.
**subclavian** (-klei·vian) *adj.* ANAT. subclavio.
**subcommittee** (sø·bkømiti) *s.* subcomisión.
**subconscious** (søbka·nshøs) *adj.-s.* subconsciente.
**subcostal** (-ka·stal) *adj.* ANAT. subcostal.
**subcutaneous** (-kiutei·niøs) *adj.* subcutáneo, hipodérmico.
**subdeacon** (-dɪ·køn) *s.* subdiácono.
**subdean** (-dɪan) *s.* vice-decano.
**subdelegate** (-de·løgeit) *s.* subdelegado.
**subdivide (to)** (-divai·d) *tr.* subdividir.
**subdivision** (-divi·ȳøn) *s.* subdivisión.
**subdominant** (-da·minant) *adj.-s.* MÚS. subdominante.
**subdue (to)** (-diu·) *tr.* sojuzgar, someter, dominar, vencer. *2* domar, domeñar, amansar. *3* mitigar, amortiguar, suavizar. *4 subdued tone,* tono sumiso; voz baja; color apagado.
**suber** (siu·bø<sup>r</sup>) *s.* BOT. tejido suberoso.
**subereous** (siubi·riøs) *adj.* suberoso.
**subfamily** (søbfæ·mili) *s.* BIOL. subfamilia.
**subheading** (søbje·ding) *s.* subtítulo.
**subitaneous** (subitei·niøs) *adj.* súbito.
**subjacent** (søbdȳei·sønt) *adj.* subyacente.
**subject** (sø·bdȳekt) *adj.* sometido, supeditado. *2* sujeto, expuesto, propenso. *3 adj.-s.* súbdito, vasallo. *4 s.* sujeto, asunto, materia, tema; asignatura: *~ matter,* materia [de que se trata]. *5* ocasión, motivo. *6* GRAM., LÓG., FIL., PSIC. sujeto. *7* lo sometido a una operación o proceso.
**subject (to)** (søbdȳe·kt) *tr.* sujetar, someter, sojuzgar. *2* supeditar, subordinar. *3* someter, presentar, exponer.
**subjection** (-shøn) *s.* sometimiento. *2* sujeción.
**subjective** (-tiv) *adj.* subjetivo.
**subjectivity** (søbdȳekti·viti) *s.* subjetividad.
**subjoin (to)** (søbdȳoi·n) *tr.* añadir.
**subjugate (to)** (sø·bdȳugeit) *tr.* subyugar.
**subjugation** (-ei·shøn) *s.* subyugación.
**subjunctive** (-dȳø·nktiv) *adj.-s.* GRAM. subjuntivo.
**subkingdom** (sø·bkingdøm) *s.* BIOL. subreino.
**sublease** (sø·blɪs) *s.* subarriendo.
**sublease (to)** *tr.* subarrendar.
**sublet (to)** (søble·t) *tr.* subarrendar.
**sublimate** (sø·blimeit) *adj.-s.* QUÍM. sublimado. *2 adj.* refinado, elevado.
**sublimate (to)** *tr.* QUÍM. sublimar. *2* refinar, elevar.
**sublimation** (-ei·shøn) *s.* sublimación.
**sublime** (søblai·m) *adj.* sublime. *2 s. the ~,* lo sublime.
**sublime (to)** *tr.* sublimar [engrandecer, ensalzar]; refinar, purificar. *2* QUÍM. sublimar. *3 intr.* sublimarse.
**subliminal** (søbli·minal) *adj.* subliminar.
**sublimity** (søbli·miti) *s.* sublimidad.
**sublingual** (søbli·ngual) *adj.* ANAT. sublingual.
**sublunar** (-liu·na<sup>r</sup>) **sublunary** (-nari) *adj.* sublunar.
**submarine** (sø·bmarɪn) *adj.-s.* submarino.
**submaxillary** (søbmæ·ksilari) *adj.* ANAT. submaxilar.

**submerge (to)** (-mø·ʳdȳ) *tr.* sumergir. *2* inundar, anegar. *3 intr.* sumergirse.
**submergence** (-øns) *s.* sumersión.
**submergible** (-ibøl) *adj.* sumergible. *2 s.* MAR. sumergible, submarino.
**submerse (to)** (søbmø·ʳs) *tr.* TO SUMMERGE.
**submersion** (-shøn) *s.* sumersión.
**submersible** (-ibøl) *adj.-s.* SUBMERGIBLE.
**submission** (-mi·shøn) *s.* sumisión. *2* sometimiento. *3* DER. sometimiento a arbitraje. *4* conformidad, resignación.
**submissive** (-siv) *adj.* sumiso.
**submit (to)** (søbmi·t) *tr.* someter, remitir [a la decisión, etc., de uno]. *2* decir, afirmar. *3 intr.-ref.* someterse, ceder, conformarse, resignarse. ¶ Pret. y p. p.: *submitted;* ger.: *-tting.*
**submultiple** (-møl·tipøl) *s.* submúltiplo.
**subnormal** (-no·ʳmal) *adj.-s.* subnormal.
**suborder** (-o·ʳdøʳ) *s.* suborden.
**subordinacy** (-o·ʳdinasi) *s.* subordinación, sujeción.
**subordinate** (-o·ʳdinit) *adj.* subordinado, subalterno, secundario. *2 s.* subordinado.
**subordinate (to)** (-o·ʳdineit) *tr.* subordinar. *2* supeditar.
**subordination** (-ei·shøn) *s.* subordinación.
**suborn (to)** (søbo·ʳn) *tr.* sobornar.
**subornation** (-ei·shøn) *s.* soborno.
**subpoena** (søbpɪ·na) *s.* DER. citación, comparendo.
**subrogate (to)** (sø·brougeit) *tr.* subrogar.
**subscribe (to)** (-skraib) *tr.-intr.* subscribir, firmar. *2* intr. *to ~ for,* suscribirse a. *3 to ~ to,* subscribir, aprobar.
**subscription** (-skri·pshøn) *s.* firma. *2* subscripción. *3* cantidad subscrita.
**subsection** (-se·kshøn) *s.* subdivisión.
**subsequent** (-sikuønt) *adj.* subsecuente, subsiguiente; ulterior.
**subserve (to)** (søbsø·ʳv) *tr.* servir en condición subordinada. *2* servir, ayudar, favorecer.
**subservience, -cy** (søbsø·ʳviøns, -si) *s.* subordinación. *2* utilidad, ayuda. *3* servilismo.
**subservient** (-viønt) *adj.* subordinado. *2* útil. *3* servicial. *4* servil, rastrero.
**subside (to)** (-sai·d) *intr.* menguar, bajar [de nivel], posarse [un sedimento]. *2* hundirse. *3* calmarse. *4* dejarse caer.
**subsidence, -cy** (-sai·døns, -si) *s.* hundimiento, descenso. *2* desplome. *3* apaciguamiento.
**subsidiary** (-si·dieri) *adj.* subsidiario. *2* auxiliar, subordinado. *3 adj.-s.* COM. filial.
**subsidize (to)** (sø·bsidaiš) *tr.* subvencionar.
**subsidy** (sø·bsidi) *s.* subvención, subsidio.
**subsist (to)** (søbsi·st) *intr.* subsistir. *2 tr.* mantener, sustentar.
**subsistence** (-øns) *s.* subsistencia. *2* manutención, sustento.
**subsistent** (-ønt) *adj.* subsistente.
**subsoil** (sø·bsoil) *s.* subsuelo.
**substance** (-stans) *s.* substancia: *in ~,* en substancia, en lo esencial. *2* realidad, solidez. *3* caudal, bienes: *man of ~,* hombre rico.
**substantial** (søbstæ·nshal) *adj.* substancial. *2* substantivo. *3* real, positivo. *4* sólido, fuerte. *5* importante, cuantioso, copioso. *6* corpóreo, material. *7* acomodado, rico; solvente. *8 in ~ agreement,* de acuerdo en lo esencial.
**substantiality** (-shiæ·liti) *s.* substancialidad. *2* corporeidad. *3* solidez.
**substantiate (to)** (søbstæ·nshiet) *tr.* probar, establecer, demostrar, justificar, comprobar.

**substantiation** (søbstænshie·shøn) *s.* prueba, demostración, comprobación.
**substantival** (-tai·val) *adj.* GRAM. substantivo.
**substantive** (sø·bstantiv) *adj.* substantivo, real, positivo. *2* esencial; importante, considerable. *3 adj.-s.* GRAM. substantivo.
**substitute** (-titiut) *s.* sustitutivo, suplente. *2* substitutivo.
**substitute (to)** *tr.* sustituir.
**substitution** (søbstitiu·shøn) *s.* substitución, reemplazo.
**substratum** (-trei·tøm), *pl.* **substrata** (-ta) *s.* substrato.
**substructure** (-trø·kchøʳ) *s.* infraestructura.
**subtend (to)** (-te·nd) *tr.* GEOM. subtender.
**subtense** (-te·ns) *adj.* GEOM. subtensa.
**subterfuge** (sø·btøʳfiudȳ) *s.* subterfugio.
**subterranean** (søbtørei·nian), **subterraneous** (-niøs)*adj.* subterráneo.
**subtile** (sø·btil) *adj.* SUBTLE.
**subtileness** (-nis), **subtility** (søbti·liti) *s.* sutileza, sutilidad.
**subtilize** (-aiš) *tr.-intr.* sutilizar.
**subtitle** (sø·btaitøl) *s.* subtítulo.
**subtle** (sø·tøl) *adj.* sutil. *2* disimulado. *3* astuto.
**subtleness** (-nis), **subtlety** (-ti) *s.* sutileza. *2* agudeza, penetración. *3* astucia.
**subtract (to)** (søbtræ·kt) *tr.* substraer, deducir, quitar. *2* MAT. restar.
**subtraction** (-kshøn) *s.* substracción, deducción. *2* MAT. resta, descuento.
**subtrahend** (sø·btrajønd) *s.* MAT. substraendo.
**subtropic (al** (søbtra·pikɑl) *adj.* subtropical.
**suburb** (sø·bøʳb) *s.* suburbio. *2 pl.* inmediaciones.
**suburban** (søbø·ʳban) *adj.-s.* suburbano.
**suburbicarian** (-øʳbike·rian) *adj.* suburbicario.
**subvention** (-ve·nshøn) *s.* subvención, ayuda.
**subversion** (-ve·ʳshøn) *s.* subversión.
**subversive** (-vø·ʳsiv) *adj.* subversivo.
**subvert (to)** (-vø·ʳt) *tr.* subvertir.
**subway** (sø·bwei) *s.* paso subterráneo. *2* (E.U.) metropolitano, ferrocarril, subterráneo.
**succedaneous** (soksidei·niøs) *adj.* sucedáneo.
**succeed (to)** (søksɪ·d) *intr.* suceder [a una persona]. *2* suceder, seguir. *3* tener buen éxito; salir bien.
**succeeder** (-øʳ) *s.* sucesor.
**succeeding** (-ing) *adj.* subsiguiente, futuro.
**succentor** (-se·ntøʳ) *s.* sochantre.
**success** (søkse·s) *s.* éxito, buen éxito, logro, triunfo. *2* persona o cosa que tiene éxito.
**successful** (-ful) *adj.* que tiene éxito, airoso; afortunado, logrado. *2* próspero, venturoso.
**succession** (søkse·shøn) *s.* sucesión. *2* seguida, serie, continuación: *in ~,* uno tras otro.
**successive** (-siv) *adj.* sucesivo.
**successor** (-søʳ) *s.* sucesor.
**succin** (søksin) *s.* succino, ámbar.
**succinct** (søksi·nt) *adj.* sucinto. *2* conciso.
**succo(u)r** (sø·køʳ) *s.* socorro, auxilio, asistencia.
**succo(u)r (to)** *tr.* socorrer, auxiliar.
**succubus** (sø·kiubøs) *s.* súcubo.
**succulence, -cy** (sø·kiuløns, -si) *s.* suculencia, jugosidad.
**succulent** (-ønt) *adj.* suculento, jugoso.
**succumb (to)** (søkø·m) *tr.* sucumbir. *2* rendirse.
**such** (sø·ch) *adj.* tal, tales, semejante, semejantes, así: *~ love,* semejante, amor, un amor así; *no ~ a thing,* no hay tal; *~ and ~ thing,* tal y tal cosa. *2 pron.* tal, tales, éste, estos, estas: *~ is the result,* este es el resultado; *as ~,* como a tal. *3 ~ as,* el, la, los, las que; quien, quienes. *4 adv.* tan, así,

tal: ~ *a good man,* un hombre tan bueno; ~ *as it is,* tal cual, o como, es o está.

**suck** (søˑk) *s.* succión, chupada. *2* mamada, tetada: *to give* ~, amamantar.

**suck (to)** *tr.-intr.* chapuzar, absorber, sorber, libar. *2* mamar. *3* MEC. aspirar. *4 to* ~ *dry,* dejar seco o enjuto, agotar.

**sucker** (-øˑr) *s.* mamón, chupón. *2* lechón; cordero lechal. *3* ZOOL. ventosa. *4* ICT. rémora; lamprea. *5* émbolo o válvula [de bomba]. *6* AGR. retoño, chupón. *7* fig. primo, pagano. *8* fig. borrachín.

**suckle (to)** (søˑkøl) *tr.* amamantar, lactar, criar. *2 intr.* lactar, mamar, amamantarse.

**suckling** (søˑkling) *s.* lactación. *2 adj.-s.* niño de teta. *3* mamantón, recental.

**sucrose** (siuˑkrous) *s.* QUÍM. sacarosa.

**suction** (søˑkshøn) *s.* succión: ~ *cleaner,* aspirador de polvo; ~ *pump,* bomba aspirante.

**Sudan** (sudæˑn) *n. pr.* GEOGR. Sudán.

**Sudanese** (sudønrˑš) *adj.-s.* sudanés.

**sudatorium** (siudatoˑriøm) *s.* sudadero, baño turco.

**sudatory** (siuˑdatori) *adj.* sudatorio, sudorífico.

**sudden** (søˑdøn) *adj.* súbito, repentino, inesperado: *all of a* ~, *on a* ~, *of a* ~, de pronto, de repente. *2* súbito, pronto [de genio]; precipitado, violento. *3* improvisado.

**suddenness** (-nis) *s.* rapidez; precipitación. *2* brusquedad.

**sudoriferous** (siudoriˑførøs) *adj.* sudorífero.

**sudorific** (-fik) *adj.-s.* sudorífico.

**suds** (søds) *s. pl.* jabonaduras; espuma.

**sue (to)** (siu) *tr.-intr.* DER. demandar, poner pleito. *2* pedir, solicitar, instar. | Con *to o for. 3* hacer la corte, pretender.

**suède** (sueid) *s.* piel de Suecia.

**suet** (siuˑit) *s.* saín, sebo.

**suffer (to)** (søˑfør) *tr.-intr.* sufrir, padecer, experimentar: *to* ~ *from,* padecer de. *2* resistir, soportar, aguantar. *3* sufrir, tolerar.

**sufferable** (-abøl) *adj.* sufrible, soportable.

**sufferance** (-ans) *s.* tolerancia, consentimiento tácito. *2* sufrimiento, paciencia, aguante.

**suffering** (-ing) *s.* sufrimiento, padecimiento, pena. *2 adj.* doliente; enfermo. *3* sufrido.

**suffice (to)** (søfaiˑš) *intr.* bastar, ser suficiente o bastante, alcanzar. *2 tr.* bastar a.

**sufficiency** (søfiˑshønsi) *s.* lo suficiente o adecuado. *2* idoneidad, eficacia. *3* presunción. *4* medios suficientes, posición acomodada.

**sufficient** (-shønt) *adj.* suficiente, adecuado, amplio. *2* satisfactorio. *3* solvente; acomodado.

**suffix** (søˑfiks) *s.* sufijo.

**suffocate (to)** (søˑføkeit) *tr.* sofocar, asfixiar. *2 intr.* ahogarse, asfixiarse.

**suffocating** (-ing) *adj.* sofocante.

**suffocation** (-eiˑshøn) *s.* sofocación, asfixia.

**sufragan** (søˑfragan) *adj.-s.* ECLES. sufragáneo.

**suffrage** (søˑfridў) *s.* sufragio, voto.

**suffragette** (søfradўeˑt) *t.* sufragista [mujer].

**suffragist** (søˑfradўist) *s.* sufragista.

**suffuse (to)** (søfiuˑš) *tr.* bañar, cubrir, teñir [de un fluido]. *2* difundir.

**suffusion** (søfiuˑўøn) *s.* difusión, baño. *2* MED. sufusión.

**sugar** (shuˑgaʳ) *s.* azúcar: ~ *bowl,* azucarero [vasija]; ~ *beet,* remolacha; ~ *candy,* azúcar cande; ~ *cane,* caña de azúcar; ~ *mill,* trapiche, ingenio; ~ *pea,* tirabeque; ~ *tongs,* tenacillas [para el azúcar].

**sugar (to)** *tr.* azucarar, confitar; endulzar.

**sugar-coat (to)** *tr.* confitar, cubrir de azúcar. *2* fig. dorar, endulzar [lo desagradable].

**sugared** (-d) *adj.* endulzado, azucarado. *2* meloso, almibarado.

**sugarplum** (-pløm) *s.* confite, bombón.

**sugary** (-i) *adj.* dulce, azucarado. *2* melifluo. *3* goloso.

**suggest (to)** (søgdўeˑst) *tr.* sugerir. *2* hacer pensar en, recordar. *3* sugestionar.

**suggestible** (-tibøl) *adj.* sugestionable. *2* sugerible.

**suggestion** (-eiˑshøn) *s.* sugestión. *2* indicación, propuesta. *3* señal, indicio.

**suggestive** (-tiv) *adj.* sugestivo.

**suicidal** (siuisaiˑdal) *adj.* suicida.

**suicide** (siuˑsaid) *s.* suicidio: *to commit* ~, suicidarse. *2* suicida.

**suint** (siuˑint) *s.* churre, grasa de la lana.

**suit** (siuˑt) *s.* petición, súplica. *2* cortejo, galanteo. *3* DER. demanda; pleito. *4* terno, traje. *5* colección, serie, juego, surtido. *6* palo de la baraja.

**suit (to)** *tr.* vestir, trajear. *2 tr.-intr.* convenir, acomodar, ir o venir bien. *3* ajustarse, acomodarse. *4* agradar, satisfacer: ~ *yourself,* haga usted lo que guste.

**suitability** (siutabiˑliti) *s.* conformidad, conveniencia.

**suitable** (siuˑtabøl) *adj.* propio, conveniente, apropiado; conforme, satisfactorio.

**suitcase** (-keis) *s.* maleta.

**suite** (suiˑt) *s.* séquito, comitiva. *2* colección, serie: ~ *of rooms,* serie de habitaciones. *3* muebles [de una habitación]. *4* MÚS. suite.

**suitor** (siuˑtøʳ) *s.* DER. demandante. *2* solicitante, aspirante. *3* pretendiente, galán.

**sulcate(d** (søˑlkeit(ed) *adj.* surcado, acanalado.

**sulfate, sulfide,** etc. (E.U.) SULPHATE, SULPHIDE, etc.

**sulk** (søˑlk) *s.* enfurruñamiento, mal humor.

**sulk (to)** *intr.* estar enfurruñado, de mal humor; encerrarse en un silencio malhumorado.

**sulky** (-i) *adj.* enfurruñado, hosco, malhumorado. *2 s.* coche de dos ruedas y un solo asiento.

**sullage** (søˑlidў) *s.* basura; escoria.

**sullen** (søˑløn) *adj.* hosco, huraño, malhumorado. *2* triste, sombrío, lúgubre. *3* lento [río, etc.].

**sully** (søˑli) *s.* mancha, mancilla.

**sully (to)** *tr.* manchar, empañar. *2 intr.* mancharse, empañarse.

**sulphate** (søˑlfeit) *s.* QUÍM. sulfato.

**sulphate (to)** *tr.* sulfatar.

**sulphide** (-faid) *s.* QUÍM. sulfuro.

**sulphite** (-ait) *s.* QUÍM. sulfito.

**sulphur** (-øʳ) *s.* azufre.

**sulphur (to)** *tr.* azufrar.

**sulphurate (to)** (-iureit) *tr.* sulfurar, azufrar.

**sulphuret** (-rit) *s.* QUÍM. sulfuro.

**sulphuric** (søˑlfiuˑrik) *adj.* sulfúrico.

**sulphurous** (søˑlførøs) *adj.* sulfuroso.

**sulphydric** (søˑlfjaiˑdrik) *adj.* sulfhídrico.

**sultan** (søˑltan) *s.* sultán, soldán.

**sultana** (søˑltæˑna) *s.* sultana.

**sultanate** (søˑltaneit) *s.* sultanía, sultanato.

**sultriness** (søˑltrinis) *s.* bochorno, calor sofocante.

**sultry** (søˑltri) *adj.* bochornoso, sofocante.

**sum** (søm) *s.* MAT. suma. *2* cuenta, problema. *3* suma [cantidad, conjunto]; total, resumen. *4* suma, esencia; lo sumo.

**sum (to)** *tr.-intr.* sumar. *2 to* ~ *up,* sumar; resumir, recapitular. *3 to* ~ *to,* ascender a [un total]. ¶ Pret. y p. p.: *summed;* ger.: *-mming.*

**sumac (h** (sumæˑk) *s.* zumaque.

**Sumatra** (suma·tra) *n. pr.* GEOGR. Sumatra.
**sumless** (sø·mlis) *adj.* innumerable.
**summa** (sø·ma) *s.* suma [tratado].
**summarize (to)** (-raiš) *tr.* resumir, compendiar.
**summary** (-ri) *adj.* sumario, breve. *2 s.* sumario, resumen.
**summation** (sømei·shøn) *s.* suma [adición; total]. *2* resumen.
**summer** (sø·møʳ) *s.* estío, verano: ~ *resort*, lugar de veraneo. *2* ARQ. viga maestra; dintel; sotabanco. *3 pl.* años [de una pers.].
**summer (to)** *intr.* veranear, pasar el verano.
**summerhouse** (-jaus) *s.* glorieta, cenador.
**summering** (-ing) *s.* veraneo.
**summersault, -set** *s.* SOMERSAULT.
**summery** (-i) *adj.* veraniego, estival.
**summit** (sø·mit) *s.* ápice, cúspide, punta, cima, cumbre, pináculo.
**summon (to)** (sø·møn) *tr.* llamar, convocar; evocar. *2* DER. citar. *3* requerir, intimar. *4* hacer acopio de [valor, etc.].
**summons** (-š) *s.* llamada. *2* convocación. *3* DER. citación. *4* MIL. intimación [de rendición].
**sump** (sø·mp) *s.* sumidero. *2* MEC. colector de aceite.
**sumpter** (sø·mptøʳ) *s.* acémila.
**sumptuary** (-shueri) *adj.* suntuario.
**sumptuous** (-shuøs) *adj.* suntuoso. *2* espléndido, opíparo.
**sun** (søn) *s.* sol [astro; luz o calor del sol; día]: ~ *bath*, baño de sol; ~ *blind*, persiana, toldo; *in the* ~, al sol; *under the* ~, debajo del sol.
**sun (to)** *tr.* asolar, insolar. *2* secar, etc., al sol. *3 intr.* tomar el sol. ¶ Pret. y p. p.: *sunned;* ger.: *sunning.*
**sunbeam** (-bim) *s.* rayo de sol.
**sunbeat** (-bit) *adj.* asoleado.
**sunbright** (-brait) *adj.* resplandeciente.
**sunburn** (-bøʳn) *s.* quemadura del sol; bronceado, atezado.
**sunburn (to)** *tr.-intr.* quemar o quemarse, tostar o tostarse con el sol.
**sunburnt** (-bøʳnt) *adj.* tostado o bronceado por el sol, atezado.
**sunburst** (-bøʳst) *s.* salida del sol entre las nubes; rato de sol. *2* broche en figura de sol.
**Sunday** (-di) *s.* domingo: ~ *school*, escuela dominical; ~ *best*, fam. trapitos de cristianar.
**sunder** (-døʳ) *s.* separación, división: *in* ~, en dos, en trozos.
**sunder (to)** *tr.* separar, dividir, cortar. *2 intr.* separarse; romperse.
**sundial** (-daial) *s.* reloj de sol, cuadrante solar.
**sundown** (-daun) *s.* puesta del sol.
**sundries** (-driš) *s. pl.* COM. géneros diversos.
**sundry** (-dri) *adj.* varios, diversos. *2* sendos.
**sunfish** (-fish) *s.* ICT. rueda.
**sunflower** (-flauøʳ) *s.* BOT. girasol.
**sung** (søng) *pret.* y *p. p.* de TO SING.
**sunglasses** (sø·nglæsiš) *s.* gafas para el sol.
**sunk** (sønk) *pret.* y *p. p.* de TO SINK.
**sunken** (sø·nkøn) *adj.* sumido; hundido.
**sunless** (sø·nlis) *adj.* sombrío; sin luz; nublado.
**sunlight** (-lait) *s.* sol, luz del sol.
**sunlit** (-lit) *adj.* iluminado porˈel sol.
**sunny** (-i) *adj.* soleado, lleno de sol. *2* radiante, resplandeciente. *3 it is* ~, hace sol.
**sunrise** (-raiš) *s.* salida del sol, amanecer.
**sunset** (-set) *s.* ocaso, puesta del sol.
**sunshade** (-sheid) *s.* quitasol, sombrilla. *2* toldo. *3* visera contra el sol.

**sunshine** (-shain) *s.* sol [luz o calor del sol]; solana: *in the* ~, al sol.
**sunspot** (-spat) *s.* mancha solar.
**sunstroke** (-strouk) *s.* MED. insolación.
**sunstruck** (-strøk) *adj.* atacado de insolación.
**sunwise** (-uaiš) *adv.* como el sol, con el sol.
**sup** (søp) *s.* sorbo.
**sup (to)** *intr.-tr.* cenar. *2 tr.* dar de cenar. *3* beber, tomar a sorbos.
**super** (siu·pøʳ) *adj.* fam. superior, excelente. *2* fam. TEAT. comparsa.
**superable** (-abøl) *adj.* superable.
**superabound (to)** (siupørabau·nd) *intr.* superabundar, sobreabundar.
**superabundance** (-abø·ndans) *s.* superabundancia, sobreabundancia, plétora.
**superadd (to)** (-æ·d) *tr.* añadir, sobreañadir.
**superannuate** (-æ·nyueit) *adj.-s.* retirado, jubilado. *2 adj.* anticuado.
**superannuate (to)** *tr.* retirar, jubilar. *2* anticuar. *3 intr.* retirarse, jubilarse.
**superannuated** (-tid) *adj.-s.* SUPERANNUATE.
**superb** (siupø·ʳb) *adj.* soberbio, magnífico.
**supercargo** (siupøʳka·ʳgou) *s.* MAR. sobrecargo.
**supercilious** (-si·liøs) *adj.* arrogante, altanero, desdeñoso.
**superdominant** (-da·minant) *s.* MÚS. superdominante.
**superelevation** (-elivei·shøn) *s.* FERROC. peralte.
**supereminent** (-e·minønt) *s.* supereminente.
**supererogatory** (-ira·gatori) *adj.* supererogatorio.
**superexcellent** (-e·ksølønt) *adj.* óptimo.
**superficial** (-fi·shal) *adj.* superficial. *2* somero. *3* externo.
**superficiality** (-shiæ·liti) *s.* superficialidad. *2* exterioridad.
**superficies** (-fi·shiiš) *s.* superficie.
**superfine** (siu·pøʳfain) *adj.* superfino.
**superfluity** (siupøʳflu·iti) *s.* superfluidad.
**superfluous** (siupø·ʳfluøs) *adj.* superfluo.
**superfortress** (siu·pøʳfoʳtris) *s.* AVIA. superfortaleza.
**superhuman** (siupøʳjiu·man) *adj.* sobrehumano.
**superimpose (to)** (-impou·š) *tr.* sobreponer, superponer.
**superincumbent** (-inkø·mbønt) *adj.* que pesa o carga sobre; superyacente.
**superinduce (to)** (-indiu·s) *tr.* sobreañadir.
**superintendence, -cy** (-inte·ndøns, -si) *s.* superintendencia.
**superintendent** (-ønt) *s.* superintendente, inspector, director. *2* capataz.
**superior** (siupi·riøʳ) *adj.-s.* superior. *2* superiora. *3 adj.* de superioridad, orgulloso, desdeñoso.
**superioress** (-is) *s.* superiora.
**superiority** (siupiria·riti) *s.* superioridad.
**superlative** (siupø·ʳlativ) *adj.* superlativo. *2* exagerado. *3 s.* GRAM. superlativo.
**superman** (siu·pø·ʳmæn) *s.* superhombre.
**supermundane** (-møndein) *adj.* supramundano.
**supernal** (siupø·ʳnal) *adj.* superno, celestial.
**supernatural** (-næ·chural) *adj.-s.* sobrenatural.
**supernumerary** (-niu·møreri) *adj.* supernumerario. *2* superfluo. *3 s.* supernumerario.
**superphosphate** (-fa·sfeit) *s.* QUÍM. superfosfato.
**superpose (to)** (-pou·š) *tr.* sobreponer, superponer.
**supersaturate (to)** (-sa·chureit) *tr.* sobresaturar.
**superscribe (to)** (-skrai·b) *tr.* sobrescribir.
**superscription** (-skri·pshøn) *s.* sobrescrito.
**supersede (to)** (-si·d) *tr.* reemplazar, substituir, desalojar. *3* DER. sobreseer.

**supersensible** (-se·nsibøl) *adj.* suprasensible.
**supersensitive** (-se·nsitiv) *adj.* supersensible.
**supersonic** (-sa·nik) *adj.* supersónico.
**superstition** (-sti·shøn) *s.* superstición.
**superstitious** (-ti·shøs) *adj.* supersticioso.
**superstructure** (-strø·kchø ͬ) *s.* superestructura.
**supertax** (-æ·ks) *s.* impuesto suplementario.
**supervene (to)** (siupø ͬvi·n) *intr.* sobrevenir, supervenir, seguir.
**supervention** (-ve·nshøn) *s.* superveniencia.
**supervise (to)** (-vai·š) *tr.* inspeccionar, revisar, dirigir.
**supervisor** (-ø ͬ) *s.* inspector, director. *2* revisor [de una obra literaria].
**supination** (siupinei·shøn) *s.* supinación.
**supinator** (-tø ͬ) *adj.-s.* ANAT. supinador.
**supine** (siupai·n) *adj.* supino [tendido sobre el dorso, vuelto hacia arriba]. *2* indolente, negligente. *3 s.* GRAM. supino.
**supper** (sø·pø ͬ) *s.* cena: *to have ~,* cenar.
**supperless** (-lis) *adj.* sin cenar.
**supplant (to)** (søplæ·nt) *tr.* suplantar, desbancar. *2* reemplazar, substituir.
**supplanting** (-ing) *s.* suplantación.
**supple** (sø·pøl) *adj.* suave, flexible. *2* elástico, ágil. *3* dócil, complaciente, rastrero, servil.
**supple (to)** *tr.* suavizar, dar flexibilidad. *2* reducir, aliviar. *3 intr.* hacerse flexible, dócil.
**supplement** (sø·plimønt) *s.* suplemento.
**supplement (to)** *tr.* complementar, completar.
**supplemental▪-tary** (søplime·ntal, -teri) *adj.* suplementario.
**suppletory** (sø·plitori) *adj.* supletorio.
**suppliance** (sø·plians) *s.* ruego, súplica.
**suppliant** (-pliant), **supplicant** (-plikant) *adj.-s.* suplicante.
**supplicate (to)** (-plikeit) *tr.-intr.* suplicar, rogar.
**supplication** (-ei·shøn) *s.* súplica, ruego. *2* plegaria.
**supplier** (søplai·ø ͬ) *s.* suministrador, proveedor.
**supply** (søplai) *s.* suministro, provisión, abastecimiento. *2* respuesto, surtido. *3* COM. oferta, existencia: ~ *and demand,* la oferta y la demanda. *4 pl.* provisiones, pertrechos, víveres, materiales.
**supply (to)** *tr.* suministrar, proporcionar. *2* proveer, abastecer. *3* suplir. *4* satisfacer [las necesidades, la demanda].
**support** (søpo· ͬt) *s.* soporte, apoyo, sostén: *point of ~,* punto de apoyo. *2* ayuda, protección. *3* sostenimiento. *4* sustento, manutención.
**support (to)** *tr.* soportar [sostener, aguantar; sufrir, tolerar]. *2* sostener, defender, apoyar, proteger. *3* probar, justificar. *4* sustentar, mantener.
**supportable** (-abøl) *adj.* soportable, tolerable, llevadero. *2* sostenible, defendible.
**supporter** (-ø ͬ) *s.* mantenedor, sostenedor. *2* defensor, partidario. *3* apoyo, sostén. *4* tirante [para medias]. *5* sostén [prenda femenina]. *6* suspensorio.
**suppose (to)** (søpou·š) *tr.* suponer. *2* creer, pensar, figurarse.
**supposed** (-d) *adj.* supuesto, presunto.
**supposition** (søpøši·shøn) *s.* suposición, hipótesis.
**suppositional** (-al) *adj.* hipotético.
**supposititious** (søpøšiti·shøs) *adj.* suposticio.
**suppositive** (søpa·sitiv) *adj.* supositivo. *2* supuesto.
**suppository** (-sitori) *s.* MED. supositorio.
**suppress (to)** (søpre·š) *tr.* suprimir. *2* omitir. *3* re-

primir, contener. *4* ahogar, sofocar, acabar con. *5* callar, ocultar.
**suppression** (-shøn) *s.* supresión, omisión. *2* represión, contención. *3* MED. suspensión.
**supressive** (-siv) *adj.* supresivo. *2* represivo. *3* contentivo.
**suppurate (to)** (sø·piureit) *intr.* supurar.
**suppuration** (-ei·shøn) *s.* supuración.
**suprarenal** (siuprari·nal) *adj.* ANAT. suprarrenal.
**supremacy** (siupre·masi) *s.* supremacía.
**supreme** (siupri·m) *adj.* supremo, sumo, soberano. *2 s.* el más alto grado. *3 the Supreme,* el Altísimo.
**supremely** (-li) *adv.* supremamente, soberanamente. *2* sumamente.
**surah** (sura) *s.* surá.
**surbase** (sø· ͬbeis) *s.* cornisa de pedestal.
**surcharge** (sø ͬcha· ͬdÿ) *s.* sobrecarga. *2* recargo.
**surcharge (to)** *tr.* sobrecargar. *2* recargar.
**surcingle** (sø· ͬsingøl) *s.* sobrecincha.
**surcoat** (-kout) *s.* sobretodo, gabán. *2* sobrevesta.
**surd** (sø ͬd) *adj.* FONÉT. sordo. *2* MAT. irracional.
**sure** (shu· ͬ) *adj.* seguro [en sus varias acepciones]. *2* salvo. *3* cierto, convencido. *4* firme, estable. *5* seguro de sí mismo. *6 to be ~,* seguramente, sin duda; estar seguro; ser cierto. *7 to make ~,* asegurar (se; cerciorar se. *8 for ~,* de fijo, a punto fijo. *9 adv.* ciertamente, efectivamente.
**sure-footed** *adj.* de pie firme, seguro.
**surely** (-li) *adv.* ciertamente, sin duda.
**sureness** (-nis) *s.* seguridad [calidad de seguro]. *2* certeza, confianza.
**surety** (-ti) *s.* SURENES. *2* cosa segura o cierta. *3* seguridad, garantía, fianza. *4* fiador, garante: *to be ~ for,* salir fiador por.
**surexcitation** (søreksitei·shøn) *s.* MED. sobreexcitación.
**surf** (sø ͬf) *s.* oleaje que rompe en la playa, rompiente, resaca.
**surface** (sø· ͬfis) *s.* superficie; cara.
**surface (to)** *tr.* dar cierta clase de superficie a; alisar, igualar, pulir. *2 intr.* subir a la superficie [un submarino].
**surfacer** (-ø ͬ) *s.* máquina de alisar o cepillar.
**surfboard** (sø· ͬfbo ͬd) *s.* DEP. esquí acuático.
**surfeit** (sø· ͬfit) *s.* exceso, sobreabundancia. *2* ahíto, empacho. *3* empalago. *4* VET. encebadamiento.
**surfeit (to)** *tr.* ahitar, hartar, saciar. *2* encebadar. *3* empalagar. *4 intr.* hartarse.
**surge** (sø ͬdÿ) *s.* ola, oleada, oleaje. *2* ELECT. sobretensión.
**surge (to)** *intr.* hincharse, agitarse [el mar, las olas]. *2* surgir, levantarse, ondular. *3 tr.* hacer ondular. *4* MAR. largar, lascar.
**surgeon** (sø· ͬdÿøn) *s.* cirujano. *2* MIL. médico.
**surgery** (sø· ͬdÿøri) *s.* cirugía. *2* sala de operaciones.
**surgical** (sø· ͬdÿikal) *adj.* quirúrgico.
**surgy** (sø· ͬdÿi) *adj.* agitado; que se levanta en olas.
**surliness** (sø· ͬlinis) *s.* rudeza, brusquedad, hosquedad, desabrimiento, mal genio.
**surloin** (sø· ͬloin) *s.* solomillo.
**surly** (sø· ͬli) *adj.* rudo, brusco, desabrido, hosco, gruñón.
**surmise** (sø· ͬmai·š) *s.* conjetura, suposición.
**surmise (to)** *tr.* conjeturar, suponer.
**surmount (to)** (sø ͬmau·nt) *tr.* vencer, superar. *2* coronar [estar situado sobre]. *3* subir, escalar.
**surmullet** (sø ͬmø·lit) *s.* ICT. salmonete.
**surname** (sø· ͬneim) *s.* apellido. *2* sobrenombre.

**surname (to)** *tr.* apellidar, llamar.
**surpass (to)** (søᵣpæ·s) *tr.* sobrepujar, aventajar.
**surpassing** (søᵣpæ·sing) *adj.* superior, sobresaliente.
**surplice** (sø·ᵣplis) *s.* sobrepelliz.
**surplus** (sø·ᵣpløs) *s.* sobrante, excedente, exceso. 2 superávit.
**surprisal** (søᵣprai·šal) *s.* SURPRISE.
**surprise** (søᵣprai·š) *s.* sorpresa. 2 extrañeza, asombro, novedad.
**surprise (to)** *tr.* sorprender. 2 extrañar, maravillar a. 3 *to be surprised at*, sorprenderse de.
**surprising** (søᵣprai·šing) *adj.* sorprendente. 2 asombroso.
**surrealism** (sørɪ·ališm) *s.* surrealismo.
**surrender** (søre·ndøᵣ) *s.* rendición, sumisión. 2 entrega, renuncia, cesión.
**surrender (to)** *tr.* rendir, entregar. 2 abandonar, renunciar a. 3 *intr.* rendirse, entregarse.
**surreptitious** (sørepti·shøs) *adj.* subrepticio.
**surrey** (so·ri) *s.* especie de birlocho.
**surrogate** (sø·røgeit) *s.* sustituto, delegado.
**surround (to)** *tr.* rodear, cercar, circundar. 2 MIL. sitiar.
**surrounding** (-ing) *adj.* circundante. 2 *s.* acción de rodear, cerco. 3 *pl.* alrededores, contornos. 4 ambiente, medio.
**surtax** (sø·ᵣtaks) *s.* impuesto suplementario; recargo.
**surveillance** (søᵣvei·lans) *s.* vigilancia.
**surveillant** (søᵣvei·lant) *adj.* y *s.* vigilante.
**survey** (sø·ᵣvei·) *s.* medición, deslinde; plano [de un terreno]. 2 inspección, examen, estudio. 3 perspectiva, ojeada general.
**survey (to)** *tr.* medir, deslindar [tierras]. 2 levantar el plano de. 3 inspeccionar, examinar, reconocer. 4 dar una ojeada general. 5 *intr.* realizar operaciones de agrimensura o topografía.
**surveying** (-ing) *s.* agrimensura; topografía.
**surveyor** (-øᵣ) *s.* agrimensor; topógrafo. 2 inspector. 3 vista [de aduanas].
**survival** (søᵣvai·val) *s.* supervivencia. 2 resto, reliquia.
**survive (to)** (søᵣvai·v) *tr.* sobrevivir. 2 salir o quedar con vida.
**survivor** (-øᵣ) *s.* sobreviviente.
**Susan** (su·šan) *n. pr.* Susana.
**susceptibility** (søseptibi·liti) *s.* susceptibilidad, capacidad. 2 impresionabilidad. 3 *pl.* sentimientos.
**susceptible** (søse·ptibøl) *adj.* susceptible, capaz. 2 sensible, impresionable; enamoradizo.
**suspect** (søspe·kt) *adj.-s.* sospechoso.
**suspect (to)** *tr.* sospechar, recelar. 2 presumir, barruntar. 3 sospechar o desconfiar de.
**suspected** (-id) *adj.* sospechoso. 2 sospechado.
**suspend (to)** (søspe·nd) *tr.* suspender [colgar; interrumpir, diferir; absortar]. 2 tener en espera, indeciso. 3 suspender [de un cargo, etc.]. 4 COM. *to ~ payment*, hacer suspensión de pagos.
**suspenders** (-øᵣš) *s. pl.* ligas. 2 tirantes [de pantalón].
**suspense** (søspe·ns) *s.* suspensión, interrupción. 2 incertidumbre, ansiedad, espera. 3 estado indeciso.
**suspension** (-shøn) *s.* suspensión: *~ bridge*, puente colgante; *~ points*, puntos suspensivos.
**suspensive** (-siv) *adj.* suspensivo. 2 suspenso, indeciso.
**suspensory** (-sori) *adj.* suspensorio.

**suspicion** (søspi·shøn) *s.* sospecha. 2 recelo, desconfianza. 3 pizca. 4 indicio.
**suspicious** (-shøs) *adj.* sospechoso, receloso. 2 de sospecha. 3 suspicaz, desconfiado.
**suspiration** (søspairei·shøn) *s.* suspiro.
**suspire (to)** (søspai·ᵣ) *tr.* decir suspirando.
**sustain (to)** (søstei·n) *tr.* sostener. 2 mantener. 3 sustentar. 4 sufrir, experimentar [daño, pérdidas, etc.]. 5 defender, probar.
**sustenance** (sø·stinans) *s.* sostenimiento. 2 mantenimiento, sustento, alimentos.
**sustentation** (søstøntei·shøn) *s.* sustentación. 2 sostenimiento. 3 mantenimiento, conservación. 4 apoyo.
**susurrate (to)** (siusø·reit) *intr.* susurrar, murmurar.
**susurration** (siusørei·shøn) *s.* susurro.
**sutler** (sø·tløᵣ) *s.* vivandero.
**suture** (siu·chøᵣ) *s.* sutura. 2 BOT. rafe.
**suzerain** (siu·šørin) *adj.* soberano. 2 *s.* señor [de vasallos]. 3 estado soberano de otro.
**suzerainty** (-ti) *s.* soberanía, señoría.
**svelte** (svelt) *adj.* esbelto.
**swab** (suab) *s.* estropajo. 2 MAR. lampazo. 3 CIR. compresa, tapón.
**swab (to)** *tr.* limpiar con estropajo. 2 limpiar, enjugar.
**swaddle** (sua·døl) *s.* envoltura, faja, vendaje; *swaddling clothes*, pañales.
**swaddle (to)** *tr.* empañar, envolver [a un niño]. 2 fajar, vendar.
**swag** (suæg) *s. fam.* botín [de un robo]. 2 B. ART. guirnalda.
**swagger** (suæ·gøᵣ) *s.* andar arrogante, contoneo. 2 fanfarronería, jactancia.
**swagger (to)** *intr.* contonearse, fanfarrear. 2 *tr.-intr.* amenazar, intimidar.
**swaggerer** (-øᵣ) *s.* jactancioso, fanfarrón.
**swain** (suein) *s.* zagal. 2 enamorado.
**swale** (suei·l) *s.* terreno húmedo y bajo.
**swallow** (sua·lou) *s.* ORN. golondrina. 2 tragadero, gaznate. 3 engullida, trago.
**swallow (to)** *tr.-intr.* tragar, deglutir. 2 *tr.* tragar, tragarse [absorber, abismar; dar crédito a; aguantar, etc.]. 3 contener [la risa, etc.].
**swallowtail** (teil) *s. fam. frac.* 2 CARP. cola de milano.
**swallowwort** (-uøᵣt) *s.* BOT. celidonia. 2 BOT. vencetósigo.
**swam** (suæm) *pret. de* TO SWIM.
**swamp** (suamp) *s.* pantano, marisma, marjal.
**swamp (to)** *tr.* atollar. 2 sumergir, hundir. 3 inundar, encharcar. 4 abrumar [de trabajo]. 5 *intr.* empantanarse. 6 hundirse, irse a pique.
**swampy** (-i) *adj.* pantanoso, cenagoso.
**swan** (suan) *s.* ORN. cisne. 2 fig. poeta. 3 NAT. *~ dive*, salto del ángel.
**swap** (suap) *s.* cambio, cambalache.
**swap (to)** *tr.-intr. fam.* cambiar, cambalachear.
**sward** (suoᵣd) *s.* césped, tierra herbosa.
**sward (to)** *tr.* encespedar. 2 *intr.* cubrirse de hierbas.
**swarm** (suoᵣm) *s.* enjambre. 2 multitud, gentío, hormiguero.
**swarm (to)** *intr.* enjambrar. 2 pulular, hormiguear. 3 llegar en enjambre o multitud. 4 *to ~ with*, rebosar de. 5 *tr.* trepar.
**swart** (suoᵣt), **swarthy** (-ði) *adj.* moreno, atezado.
**swash** (suash) *s.* ruido o golpe del agua; chapoteo, chorro. 2 golpe de una sustancia blanda. 3 ruido, alboroto; fanfarria.

**swash (to)** *intr.* hacer ruido [el agua]. *2* golpear, etc., haciendo ruido. *3* meter bulla. *4* fanfarronear.

**swashbuckle** (-bøkøl) *intr.* fanfarronear.

**swashbuckler** (-bøklø$^r$), **swasher** (-ø$^r$) *s.* espadachín, fanfarrón, matasiete.

**swastika** (sua·stika) *s.* svástica.

**swat** (suat) *s.* golpazo, golpe abrumador.

**swat (to)** *tr.* golpear con fuerza; matar [moscas].

**swath** (suaz) *s.* camba [hierba segada].

**swathe** (suei·d) *s.* faja, venda. *2 pl.* pañales.

**swathe (to)** *tr.* fajar, vendar, envolver.

**sway** (suei) *s.* oscilación, vaivén. *2* inclinación, desviación. *3* poder, dominio, influjo.

**sway (to)** *intr.* oscilar, cimbrearse. *2* tambalear, flaquear. *3* inclinarse, ladearse, desviarse. *4 tr.-intr.* gobernar, dominar. *5* hacer oscilar. *6* inclinar, desviar. *7* influir en.

**swear (to)** (sue·ø$^r$) *intr.* jurar [prestar juramento; renegar, echar maldiciones]: *to ~ at*, maldecir; *to ~ by*, jurar por; poner toda su confianza en. *2 tr.* jurar. *3* pronunciar [un juramento]. *4* tomar juramento, juramentar. ¶ Pret.: *swore;* p. p.: *sworn.*

**sweat** (suet) *s.* sudor: *to be in a ~*, estar sudando. *2* trasudor. *3* exudación.

**sweat (to)** *intr.-tr.* sudar. *2* trasudar. *3* exudar. *4 tr.* hacer sudar. *5* explotar [al que trabaja]. *6* soldar, extraer, etc., por el calor.

**sweatband** (-bænd) *s.* badana [del sombrero].

**sweater** (-ø$^r$) *s.* el que suda. *2* explotador [de obreros]. *3* suéter.

**sweaty** (-i) *adj.* sudado, sudoroso, duro, laborioso.

**Swede** (suɪd) *s.* sueco.

**Sweden** (-øn) *n. pr.* GEOGR. Suecia.

**Swedish** (-ish) *adj.* sueco. *2 s.* idioma sueco.

**sweep** (suɪp) *s.* barrido, escobada. *2* barrendero. *3* deshollinador. *4* movimiento amplio o rápido en arco de círculo. *5* extensión, alcance, recorrido, golpe. *6* cigoñal [de pozo]. *7* remo largo. *8* cosa que se mueve rozando o barriendo.

**sweep (to)** *tr.* barrer, escobar. *2* limpiar, deshollinar. *3* pasar rápidamente por. *4* arrebatar, llevarse. *5* rastrear, dragar. *6* MÚS. rasguear, pulsar. *7* arrastrar [la cola]. *8* recorrer [con la vista, los dedos, etc.]; abarcar, dominar. *9* mover con amplio ademán. *10 to ~ one off his feet*, entusiasmar; convencer a uno. *11 tr.* pasar rápidamente. *12* andar majestuosamente. *13* extenderse. *14* describir una curva. ¶ Pret. y p. p.: *swept.*

**sweeper** (-ø$^r$) *s.* barrendero. *2* escoba mecánica.

**sweepstakes** (suɪ·psteiks) *s. sing.* y *pl.* DEP. combinación en que una sola persona puede ganar todas las apuestas.

**sweet** (suɪt) *adj.* dulce, azucarado. *2* dulce, grato, suave, amable, bondadoso. *3* benigno, apacible. *4* melodioso. *5* oloroso: *~ herbs*, hierbas aromáticas. *6* bello, lindo. *7* querido. *8* potable. *9 to be ~ on*, estar enamorado de. *10* BOT. *~ basil*, albahaca; *~ clover*, trébol oloroso; *~ flag*, ácoro; *~ potato*, batata, boniato; *~ william*, minutisa. *11 adv.* dulcemente, etc. *12 s.* dulzura. *13 pl.* dulces, golosinas.

**sweetbread** (-bred) *s.* lechecillas o mollejas de ternera.

**sweetbrier** (-braiø$^r$) *s.* BOT. agavanzo.

**sweeten (to)** (-øn) *tr.* endulzar, dulcificar. *2* suavizar. *3* purificar. *4* embalsamar, perfumar. *5 intr.* endulzarse. *6* dulcificarse.

**sweetheart** (-ja$^r$t) *s.* novio, amado; novia, amada; ser querido.

**sweetish** (-ish) *adj.* algo dulce.

**sweetly** (-li) *adv.* dulcemente.

**sweetmeat** (-mɪt) *s.* dulce, confitura, golosina.

**sweet-scented** *adj.* perfumado.

**sweet-spoken** *adj.* melifluo.

**sweet-tempered** *adj.* de carácter dulce.

**sweet-toothed** *adj.* goloso.

**swell** (suel) *s.* hinchazón. *2* bulto, prominencia. *3* ola, oleaje; crecida. *4* ondulación del terreno. *5* engrosamiento, aumento. *6* MÚS. crescendo y diminuendo. *7* MÚS. pedal de expresión. *8* fam. lechuguino. *9* fam. personaje. *10 adj.* fam. elegante. *11* fam. estupendo.

**swell (to)** *tr.* hinchar, inflar, dilatar. *2* abultar, engrosar, aumentar. *3* inflar, engreír. *4 intr.* hincharse, inflarse. *5* abultarse, engrosarse, aumentar, crecer. *6* entumecerse [un río]: embravecerse, agitarse [el mar]. *7* aumentar de intensidad [un sonido]. *8* inflarse, engreírse. ¶ Pret.: *swelled;* p. p.: *swelled* o *swollen.*

**swelling** (-ing) *s.* hinchazón. *2* aumento, crecida. *3* bulto, chichón.

**swelter** (sue·ltø$^r$) *s.* calor sofocante. *2* sudor copioso.

**swelter (to)** *tr.* sofocar [de calor]. *2 intr.* ahogarse de calor; sudar la gota gorda.

**swept** (suept) *pret.* y *p. p.* de TO SWEEP.

**swerve** (suø$^r$v) *s.* desviación, viraje. *2* vacilación.

**swerve (to)** *tr.* desviar, apartar. *2 intr.* desviarse, apartarse, torcer. *3* vacilar, flaquear.

**swift** (suift) *adj.* veloz, rápido. *2* pronto, presto. *3* repentino. *4* activo, diligente. *5* ORN. vencejo. *6* ZOOL. lagartija. *7* MEC. devandera, carrete.

**swift-footed** *adj.* ligero, veloz, de paso rápido.

**swiftly** (-li) *adv.* velozmente, rápidamente. *2* pronto.

**swig** (suig) *s.* fam. trago grande.

**swig (to)** *tr.-intr.* beber a grandes tragos.

**swill** (suil) *s.* bazofia. *2* tragantada.

**swill (to)** *tr.* enjuagar, lavar; inundar. *2* beber a grandes tragos. *3 intr.* emborracharse.

**swim** (suim) *s.* acción o rato de nadar. *2* espacio para nadar. *3* corriente [de los negocios, etc.].

**swim (to)** *intr.* nadar. *2* sobrenadar, flotar. *3* pasar, deslizarse. *4* anegarse, estar lleno o llenarse [de]. *5 my head swims*, se me va la cabeza. *6 tr.* hacer nadar o flotar. *7* pasar a nado. ¶ Pret.: *swam;* p. p.: *swum.*

**swimming** (-ing) *s.* natación. *2* vértigo, vahído. *3 adj.* que nada; para nadar: *~ bladder*, vejiga natatoria; *~ pool*, piscina. *4* arrasado [de lágrimas]. *5* desvanecido, con vértigo.

**swimmingly** (-li) *adv.* lisamente, sin tropiezo; prósperamente.

**swindle** (sui·ndøl) *s.* estafa, timo.

**swindle (to)** *tr.* estafar, timar.

**swindler** (-lø$^r$) *s.* estafador, timador.

**swine** (suain) *s. sing.* y *pl.* ZOOL. cerdo; cerdos; ganado de cerda. *2 fig.* cerdo, persona sensual.

**swineherd** (-jø$^r$d) *s.* porquero, porquerizo.

**swinery** (-ri) *s.* pocilga. *2* conjunto de cerdos.

**swing** (suing) *s.* oscilación, giro, balance, vaivén; ritmo. *2* impulso, ímpetu. *3* BOX. golpe de lado. *4* columpio, mecedor. *5* juego, operación, marcha, avance: *full ~*, plena operación; libre curso; apogeo. *6* MEC. carrera, recorrido. *7* período [de duración, acción, etc.]. *8* LIT., MÚS. ritmo sostenido.

**swing (to)** *tr.* balancear, hacer oscilar, hacer girar;

mecer, columpiar. *2* blandir [un bastón, etc.], lanzar con ímpetu. *3* suspender, colgar, engoznar. *4* (E.U.) manejar con éxito. *5 intr.* balancearse, oscilar, columpiarse. *6* colgar, ser ahorcado. *7* girar, dar vueltas: *to ~ about*, volverse. ¶ Pret. y p. p.: *swung*.

**swingeing** (sui·ndŷing) *adj.* fam. grande, enorme, estupendo.

**swinging** (-ging) *adj.* oscilante; colgante: *~ boom*, MAR. tangón; *~ door*, puerta giratoria.

**swingle** (sui·ngøl) *s.* espadilla [para espadar].

**swingle (to)** *tr.* espadar, espadillar.

**swinish** (suai·nish) *adj.* porcuno. *2* cochino, grosero, bestial.

**swipe** (suaip) *s.* golpe fuerte. *2* trago grande.

**swipe (to)** *tr.* dar o golpear fuerte. *2* hurtar, robar. *3 intr.* beber.

**swirl** (suø<sup>r</sup>l) *s.* remolino, torbellino.

**swirl (to)** *tr.* hacer girar. *2 intr.* arremolinarse. *3* girar, dar vueltas.

**swish** (suish) *s.* silbido del látigo o el bastón al cortar el aire. *2* frufrú; susurro.

**swish (to)** *tr.* golpear, dar latigazos. *2 intr.* silbar [el látigo, el bastón] al cortar el aire. *3* producir un frufrú, un susurro; crujir [las sedas, las hojas, etc.].

**Swiss** (suis) *adj.-s.* suizo, suiza. *2* BOT. *~ chard*, acelga.

**switch** (suich) *s.* vara flexible, verdasca; látigo, azote. *2* latigazo, verdascazo. *3* añadido [de pelo postizo]. *4* FERROC. aguja, desvío. *5* ELECT. conmutador, interruptor. *6* desviación, conmutación, cambio.

**switch (to)** *tr.* azotar, fustigar. *2* cambiar, desviar. *3* ELECT. *to ~ on*, conectar; dar [la luz]; *to ~ off*, desconectar; apagar [la luz]. *4 intr.* cambiar, pasar de una cosa a otra.

**switchback** (-bæk) *s.* camino o vía férrea en zigzag para subir una pendiente. *2* montaña rusa.

**switchboard** (-bo<sup>r</sup>d) *s.* ELECT., TELÉF. cuadro de distribución.

**switchman** (-mæn) *s.* guardagujas.

**Switzerland** (sui·tşø<sup>r</sup>lænd) *n. pr.* GEOGR. Suiza.

**swivel** (sui·vøl) *s.* pieza o eslabón giratorios: *~ chair*, silla o sillón giratorios; *~ door*, puerta giratoria.

**swivel (to)** *intr.-tr.* girar o hacer girar [esp. sobre la pieza que sujeta].

**swollen** (suo·løn) *p. p.* de TO SWELL.

**swoon** (swun) *s.* desmayo, síncope.

**swoon (to)** *intr.* desmayarse, desfallecer.

**swoop** (swup) *s.* descenso súbito; ataque.

**swoop (to)** *intr.* abatirse, precipitarse [sobre]. *2 tr.* barrer, arrebatar, llevarse.

**swoop** *s.*, **swoop (to)** *tr.-intr.* SWAP, TO SWAP.

**sword** (so<sup>r</sup>d) *s.* espada [arma]; *~ belt*, talabarte, cinturón; *~ lily*, BOT. estoque; *to be at sword's points*, estar a matar.

**swordfish** (-fish) *s.* ICT. pez espada.

**swordplay** (-plei) *s.* esgrima.

**swordsman** (-smæn) *s.* tirador de espada.

**swore** (suo<sup>r</sup>) *pret.* de TO SWEAR.

**sworn** (suo<sup>r</sup>n) *p. p.* de TO SWEAR.

**swum** (suøm) *p. p.* de TO SWIM.

**swung** (suøng) *pret.* y *p. p.* de TO SWING.

**Sybarite** (si·barait) *s.* sibarita.

**sybaritism** (-išm) *s.* sibaritismo.

**sycamore** (si·kamo<sup>r</sup>) *s.* BOT. sicómoro. *2* BOT. (E.U.) plátano falso.

**sycon** (sai·køn) *s.* ZOOL. sicón.

**syconium** (saikou·niøm) *s.* BOT. sicono.

**sycophant** (si·køfant) *s.* adulador; parásito. *2* sicofanta.

**syenite** (sai·enait) *s.* PETR. sienita.

**syllabary** (si·labari) *s.* silabario.

**syllabic(al** (silæ·bik(al) *adj.* silábico.

**syllabicate** (-bikeit), **syllabify** (-bifai), **syllabize** (-baiš) **(to)** *tr.* silabear.

**syllable** (si·labøl) *s.* sílaba. *2* palabra monosílaba.

**syllabus** (-bøs) *s.* sílabo. *2* sumario, resumen. *3* asignaturas de un curso; plan de estudios.

**syllepsis** (sile·psis) *s.* GRAM. silepsis.

**syllogism** (si·lødŷišm) *s.* LÓG. silogismo.

**syllogize (to)** (-aiš) *intr.* silogizar.

**sylph** (silf) *s.* silfo. *2* sílfide.

**sylva** (si·lva) *s.* selva. *2* descripción de los árboles de una región. *3* silva [colección].

**sylvan** (si·lvan) *adj.* selvático. *2* rústico.

**Sylvester** (silve·stø<sup>r</sup>) *n. pr.* Silvestre.

**symbiosis** (simbiou·sis) *s.* BIOL. simbiosis.

**symbol** (si·mbøl) *s.* símbolo.

**symbolic(al** (simba·lik(al) *adj.* simbólico.

**symbolism** (si·mbølišm) *s.* simbolismo.

**symbolize (to)** (-laiš) *tr.* simbolizar.

**symmetrical** (sime·trikal) *adj.* simétrico.

**symmetrize (to)** (si·mitraiš) *tr.* hacer simétrico.

**symmetry** (si·mitri) *s.* simetría. *2* proporción, armonía, conformidad.

**sympathetic** (simpaze·tik) *adj.* simpático. *2* simpatizante. *3* compasivo, que siente con los demás; comprensivo. *4* favorablemente dispuesto. *5* ANAT. *~ nervous system*, gran simpático.

**sympathize (to)** (si·mpazais) *intr.* simpatizar. *2* compadecerse, acompañar en un sentimiento. *3* comprender; sentir con los demás. *4* congeniar.

**sympathy** (-pazi) *s.* simpatía. *2* compasión, condolencia. *3* comprensión, benevolencia. *4* afinidad, armonía. *5* pésame.

**symphonic** (simfa·nik) *adj.* sinfónico. *2* armonioso. *3* homófono.

**symphony** (si·mfoni) *s.* sinfonía. *2* consonancia.

**symphysis** (si·mfisis) *s.* ANAT. sínfisis.

**symposium** (simpou·siøm) *s.* simpósium.

**symptom** (si·mptøm) *s.* síntoma.

**symptomatic (al** (simptømæ·tik(al) *adj.* sintomático.

**synaeresis** (sine·risis) *s.* sinéresis.

**synagogue** (si·nagag) *s.* sinagoga.

**synalepha** (sinali·fa) *s.* sinalefa.

**syncarpous** (sinka·<sup>r</sup>pøs) *s.* BOT. sincárpico.

**synchronism** (si·nkrønišm) *s.* sincronismo. *2* coetaneidad.

**synchronize (to)** (-naiš) *tr.-intr.* sincronizar.

**synchronous** (-nøs) *adj.* sincrónico. *2* coetáneo, simultáneo.

**synclinal** (sinklai·nal) *adj.* GEOL. sinclinal.

**syncopate (to)** (si·nkøpeit) *tr.* GRAM., MÚS. sincopar.

**syncopation** (-ei·shøn) *s.* GRAM., MÚS. síncopa.

**syncope** (sin·køpi) *s.* GRAM., MÚS. síncopa. *2* MED. síncope.

**syncretism** (si·nkritišm) *s.* sincretismo.

**syndic** (si·ndik) *s.* síndico.

**syndicalism** (-ališm) *s.* sindicalismo.

**syndicat** (sendika·) *t.* sindicato obrero.

**syndicate** (si·ndikit) *s.* sindicatura. *2* sindicato financiero, trust. *3* empresa distribuidora de artículos, fotografías, etc., para los periódicos.

**syndicate (to)** (-dikeit) *tr.* sindicar, asociar. *3 intr.* sindicarse.

**syndrome** (-drømi) *s.* MED. síndrome.

**synecdoche** (sine·kdoki) *s.* RET. sinécdoque.

**syneresis** (sine·risis) *s.* SYNAERESIS.

**synergy** (si·nø<sup>r</sup>dẙi) *s.* sinergia.
**synod** (si·nød) *s.* ECLES., ASTR. sínodo.
**synonym** (si·nønim) *s.* sinónimo.
**synonymous** (sina·nimøs) *adj.* sinónimo.
**synonymy** (sina·nimi) *s.* sinonimia.
**synopsis** (sina·psis) *s.* sinopsis.
**synovia** (sinou·via) *s.* ANAT. sinovia.
**syntactic (al** (sintæ·ktik(al) *adj.* sintáctico.
**syntax** (si·ntæks) *s.* GRAM. sintaxis.
**synthesis** (si·nzisis) *s.* síntesis.
**synthesize (to)** (si·nzišaiš) *tr.* SYNTHETIZE.
**synthetic (al** (sinze·tik(al) *adj.* sintético.
**synthetize (to)** (si·nzitaiš) *tr.* sintetizar.
**syntonic** (sinta·nik) *adj.* sintónico.
**syntonize (to)** (si·ntønaiš) *tr.* RADIO. sintonizar.
**syntony** (si·ntøni) *s.* RADIO. sintonía.
**syphilis** (si·filis) *s.* MED. sífilis.

**syphon** (sai·føn) *s.* SIPHON.
**Syracuse** (si·rakius) *n. pr.* GEOGR. Siracusa.
**Syria** (si·ria) *n. pr.* GEOGR. Siria.
**Syrian** (si·rian) *adj.-s.* sirio.
**syringa** (siri·nga) *s.* BOT. lila. *2* BOT. jeringuilla.
**syringe** (si·rindẙ) *s.* jeringa.
**syringe (to)** *tr.* jeringar. *2* inyectar [con jeringa].
**syrinx** (si·rinks) *s.* ORN. siringe. *2* ANAT. trompa de Eustaquio. *3* siringa, zampoña.
**syrup** (si·røp) *s.* jarabe. *2* almíbar.
**system** (si·støm) *s.* sistema. *2* método, orden.
**systematic (al** (sistømæ·tik(al) *adj.* sistemático. *2* taxonómico.
**systematize (to)** (si·stømataiš) *tr.* sistematizar. *2* organizar.
**systole** (si·støli) *s.* sístole.
**systyle** (-tail) *s.* ARQ. sistilo.
**syzygy** (si·šidẙi) *s.* ASTR. sicigia.

# T

**T, t** (ti) *s.* T, t, vigésima letra del alfabeto inglés.
**T** *s.* cosa en forma de T: *T square*, te (regla).
**'t** *contr.* de IT.
**tab** (tæb) *s.* parte saliente; pestaña. *2* oreja [de zapato]. *3* herrete [de cordón]. *4* cuenta [que se lleva].
**tabard** (tæ·ba<sup>r</sup>d) *s.* tabardo.
**tabby** (tæ·bi) *s.* TEJ. tabí. *2* gato de piel atigrada. *3* fig. mujer chismosa. *4 adj.* atigrado.
**tabernacle** (tæ·bø<sup>r</sup>nækøl) *s.* tabernáculo.
**tabes** (tei·biš) *s.* MED. tabes.
**table** (tei·bøl) *s.* mesa [mueble; comida; los que se sientan a una mesa]: ~ *linen*, mantelería; ~ *service*, vajilla; ~ *stone*, dolmen; ~ *tennis*, tenis de mesa. *2* tabla, plancha, losa. *3* tablero [de juego]. *5* ARQ. tablero. *6* PERSP. tabla. *7* mesa [de piedra preciosa]. *8* tabla [lista, índice, cuadro]: ~ *of contents*, índice; *the tables of the law*, las Tablas de la Ley.
**table (to)** *tr.* poner sobre la mesa. *2* poner en forma de tabla o índice. *3* dejar sobre la mesa, dar carpetazo a.
**tableau** (tæ·blou), *pl.* **-bleaux** *s.* cuadro vivo.
**tablecloth** (tei·bølkloz) *s.* mantel [de mesa].
**tableland** (-lænd) *s.* GEOGR. meseta.
**tablespoon** (-spun) *s.* cuchara de sopa.
**tablet** (tæ·blit) *s.* tabla, tablilla. *2* placa, lápida. *3* bloc [de papel]. *4* FARM. tableta, comprimido.
**tableware** (tei·bølue<sup>r</sup>) *s.* artículos para la mesa.
**tablier** (tablie·) *s.* delantal [de mujer].
**tabloid** (tæ·bloid) *adj.* breve, conciso, resumido. *2 s.* tableta, comprimido. *3* periódico ilustrado de noticias resumidas.
**taboo** (tabu·) *adj.-s.* tabú.
**taboo (to)** *tr.* declarar tabú, prohibir, proscribir.
**tabo(u)r** (tei·bø<sup>r</sup>) *s.* tamboril.
**tabo(u)ret** (tæbøre·t) *s.* taburete. *2* bastidor [de bordar].
**tabourine** (tæ·burin) *s.* MÚS. pandero, adufe.
**tabu** (tabu·) *s.* TABOO.
**tabular** (tæ·biula<sup>r</sup>) *adj.* tabular.
**tabulate (to)** (-leit) *tr.* disponer en forma de tabla o cuadro.
**tabulator** (-leitø<sup>r</sup>) *s.* tabulador.
**tachometer** (taka·metø<sup>r</sup>) *s.* tacómetro.
**tachycardia** (tækika·<sup>r</sup>dia) *s.* MED. taquicardia.
**tachygraphy** (tæki·grafi) *s.* taquigrafía.
**tachymeter** (tæki·mitø<sup>r</sup>) *s.* taquímetro.

**tacit** (tæ·sit) *adj.* tácito.
**taciturn** (tæ·sitø<sup>r</sup>n) *adj.* taciturno.
**tack** (tæ·k) *s.* tachuela. *2* hilván. *3* MAR. amura [cabo]. *4* MAR. bordada; virada. *5* política, línea de conducta.
**tack (to)** *tr.* clavar con tachuelas. *2* hilvanar, pegar, unir. *3 intr.-tr.* MAR. virar. *4 intr.* cambiar de política, de línea de conducta.
**tackle** (tæ·køl) *s.* equipo, aparejos, avíos. *2* MAR. jarcia; motonería. *3* aparejo [sistema de poleas]. *4* agarro, forcejeo.
**tackle (to)** *tr.* agarrar, forcejear con. *2* luchar, habérselas con. *3* abordar, [un problema, una dificultad]
**tackling** (-ling) *s.* MAR. jarcia, maniobra.
**tact** (tæ·kt) *s.* tacto, discreción, tiento, diplomacia.
**tactful** (-ful) *adj.* hábil, prudente, diplomático.
**tactic (al** (-ik(al) *adj.* táctico.
**tactician** (tækti·shan) *s.* táctico.
**tactics** (tæ·ktiks) *s. pl.* táctica.
**tactile** (-il) *adj.* táctil. *2* tangible, palpable.
**tactless** (-lis) *adj.* falto de tacto, impolítico.
**tactual** (tæ·kchual) *adj.* táctil.
**tadpole** (tæ·dpoul) *s.* ZOOL. renacuajo.
**tael** (teil) *s.* tael.
**tænia** (ti·nia) *s.* ARQ., ZOOL. tenia. *2* ANAT. tira, faja.
**taffeta** (tæ·fita), **taffety** (tæ·fiti) *s.* TEJ. tafetán.
**taffrail** (tæ·freil) *s.* MAR. coronamiento.
**taffy** (tæ·fi) *s.* especie de caramelo. *2* fam. (E.U.) coba.
**tag** (tæg) *s.* herrete. *2* marbete, etiqueta. *3* tirador [de zapato]. *4* punta [del rabo]. *5* cabo, resto. *6* trozo, cinta, etc., que cuelga; pingajo, colgajo. *7* mechón, vedija. *8* aditamento. *9* estribillo. *10* especie de marro [juego]. *11* TEAT. pie.
**tag (to)** *tr.* poner herretes a. *2* poner etiqueta a. *3* atar, unir. *4* seguir de cerca, perseguir. *5 intr. to* ~ *after*, andar detrás de [uno]. ¶ Pret. y p. p.: *tagged*; ger.: *tagging*.
**Tagal** (taga·l), **Tagalog** (-lag) *s.* tagalo.
**tagrag** (tæ·græg) *s.* RAGTAG.
**Tagus** (tei·gøs) *n. pr.* GEOGR. Tajo.
**Tahitian** (tajı·tian) *adj.-s.* tahitiano.
**tail** (teil) *s.* cola [de animal, de cometa, de vestido, etc.], rabo: ~ *end*, cola, parte de atrás; conclusión, final; ~ *light*, farol trasero, farol de cola. *2* cabo, apéndice. *3* cola, fila [de pers.]. *4* séquito. *5* SASTR. faldón: ~ *coat*, frac. *6* pie [de página]. *7*

LIT. estrambote. *8* DER. limitación de propiedad. *9 pl.* cruz [de moneda].

**tail (to)** *tr.* proveer de cola. *2* añadir, unir, empalmar, empotrar. *3* quitar los rabos a. *4* seguir, ir detrás de. *5 intr.* formar hilera; moverse en fila. *6 to ~ off* o *away*, dispersarse, desvanecerse.

**tailing** (-ing) *s.* cola [última parte]. *2* ARQ. cola, entrega [de sillar]. *3 pl.* residuos, restos.

**tailor** (-øᵣ) *s.* sastre.

**tailor (to)** *tr.* proveer de trajes, vestir. *2 intr.* ser sastre.

**tailoress** (-is) *s.* sastra, sastresa.

**tailoring** (-ing) *s.* sastrería [arte, oficio].

**tailpiece** (tei·lpis) *s.* cola, apéndice. *2* MÚS. cordal. *3* IMPR. florón, culo de lámpara.

**tain** (tein) *s.* hojalata delgada; hoja de estaño.

**taint** (teint) *s.* punta [de alguna mala cualidad]. *2* mancha, infección, corrupción.

**taint (to)** *tr.* manchar, inficionar, corromper, viciar. *2* inficionarse, corromperse.

**taintless** (-lis) *adj.* puro, sin mancha.

**take** (teik) *s.* toma, tomadura. *2* redada. *3* recaudación [dinero]. *4* atractivo.

**take (to)** *tr.* tomar. *2* coger. *3* asir, agarrar, apoderarse, posesionarse de. *5* apresar, capturar, prender; cazar, atrapar. *6* asumir. *7* escoger. *8* acometer [a uno una enfermedad, un deseo, etc.]. *9* deleitar, cautivar. *10* inferir, entender, suponer. *11* sacar, quitar; llevarse, robar. *12* restar, substraer. *13* cobrar, percibir. *14* aceptar, recibir, admitir. *15* ocupar, pedir, requerir [espacio, tiempo, etc.]. *16* llevar, conducir. *17* hallar [placer, etc.]. *18* saltar [una valla, etc.]. *19* dar [un golpe, un paseo, un salto, etc.]. *20* hacer [ejercicio, un viaje]. *21* someterse a, sufrir, aguantar. *22* sacar [una fotografía, una copia, etc.]; fotografiar. *23* prestar o tomar [juramento]. *24* forma locuciones equivalentes a un verbo reflexivo: *to ~ cold*, resfriarse; *to ~ offence*, ofenderse. *25 to ~ away*, quitar, sacar, llevarse. *26 to ~ back*, recobrar; devolver, retractar. *27 to ~ care*, cuidar, tener cuidado. *28 to ~ charge*, encargarse, tomar el mando. *29 to ~ down*, bajar, descolgar; desarmar, demoler; tragar; abatir, humillar; escribir, anotar. *30 to ~ fire*, encenderse; encolerizarse. *31 to ~ in*, entrar, llevar adentro; dejar entrar, admitir; recibir [como huésped], acomodar; observar, fijarse en; estrechar [una prenda]; recoger [una vela]; entender; abarcar, incluir; engañar; estar suscrito [a un periódico]. *32 to ~ off*, quitarse [una prenda]; quitar, llevarse; beber; sacar [copias]; saltar; remedar, parodiar. *33 to ~ on*, emprender; tomar [a bordo; a su servicio; como socio]; tomar, adoptar, asumir, arrogarse. *34 to ~ out*, quitar, sacar; sacar fuera; llevar [a comer, a paseo]; sacar, obtener. *35 to ~ up*, alzar, levantar; subir, llevar arriba; recoger; cobrar, recaudar; COST. fruncir; tomar; asumir; emprender; reanudar; absorber; ocupar, llenar; prender, arrestar; reprender; pagar [una letra, etc.]. *36 to ~ wind*, divulgarse. *37 intr.* arraigar [una planta]. *38* prender [el fuego; la vacuna]. *39* ser eficaz. *40* tener éxito. *41* pegar, adherirse. *42 to ~ after*, salir a, parecerse a; seguir el ejemplo de. *43 to ~ off*, partir de súbito; alzar el vuelo; despegar [el avión]. *44 to ~ on*, alborotarse; darse tono. *45 to ~ with*, juntarse con; prendarse de. *46 to ~ to*, dedicarse, entregarse a; retirarse a.

¶ Pret.: *took;* p. p.: *taken.*

**take-down** *adj.* desmontable. *2 s.* desarmadura, desmontadura. *3* fusil desmontable. *4* fam. humillación.

**take-in** *s.* fam. fraude, engaño.

**taken** (tei·køn) *p. p.* de TO TAKE.

**take-off** *s.* remedo, parodia, caricatura. *2* salto; raya desde donde se salta. *3* punto de partida. *4* AVIA. despegue.

**taking** (-ing) *adj.* atractivo, seductor. *2* contagioso. *3 s.* toma. *4* capura. *5* afecto, inclinación. *6 pl.* recaudación, ingresos.

**talaria** (tålei·ria) *s. pl.* talares.

**talc** (tælk), **talcum** (-øm) *s.* MINER. talco, *talcum powder*, polvos de talco.

**tale** (teil) *s.* cuento, fábula, conseja. *2* LIT. cuento. *3* relato, informe. *4* cuento, mentira, chisme. *5* cuenta, cómputo. *6* total.

**talebearer** (-berøᵣ) *s.* chismoso, soplón.

**talent** (tæ·lønt) *s.* talento [moneda]. *2* talento, aptitud, don. *3* persona de talento; artista.

**talented** (-id) *adj.* talentoso, hábil, dotado.

**taler** (ta·løᵣ) *s.* tálero.

**taleteller** (tei·lteløᵣ) *s.* cuentista, narrador de cuentos. *2* chismoso, soplón, enredador.

**talion** (tæ·liøn) *s.* talión.

**talisman** (tæ·lismøn) *s.* talismán.

**talk** (tok) *s.* conversación, plática, charla, conferencia. *2* rumor, hablilla. *3* comidilla, tema de conversación.

**talk (to)** *intr.* hablar; conversar: *to ~ about*, hablar de; *to ~ to*, hablar a; reprender; *to ~ up*, hablar claro. *2 tr.* hablar [una lengua]. *3* hablar de: *to ~ business*, hablar de negocios. *4 to ~ nonsense*, decir tonterías. *5 to ~ into*, persuadir, inducir a. *6 to ~ out of*, disuadir de. *7 to ~ over*, examinar, discutir. *8 to ~ up*, alabar.

**talkative** (-ativ) *adj.* hablador, comunicativo.

**talked-about** *adj.* de que se habla, sonado.

**talkie** (-i) *s.* película hablada. *2 pl.* cine hablado.

**talking** (-ing) *adj.* parlante. *2* hablador. *3* hablado [cine, película].

**tall** (tol) *adj.* alto [pers., árbol, mástil, etc.]; espigado, talludo. *2* fam. altisonante; exagerado, increíble.

**tallboy** (to·lboi) *s.* mueble con cajones, especie de cómoda.

**tallow** (tæ·lou) *s.* sebo.

**tallow (to)** *tr.* ensebar.

**tallowy** (-i) *adj.* seboso, sebáceo. *2* grasiento.

**tally** (tæ·li) *s.* tarja [para llevar una cuenta]. *2* cuenta [que se lleva]. *3* marbete, etiqueta. *4* copia, duplicado.

**tally (to)** *tr.* llevar la cuenta de. *2* marcar, señalar. *3* acomodar, ajustar. *4 intr.* cuadrar, concordar, corresponder.

**tallyho** (-jou) *interj.-s.* grito del cazador de zorras.

**Talmud** (tæ·lmød) *s.* Talmud.

**talon** (tæ·løn) *s.* garra. *2* monte [de la baraja]. *3* ARQ. talón [moldura].

**1) talus** (tei·løs), *pl.* **-li** (-lai) *s.* ANAT. astrágalo.

**2) talus**, *pl.* **-luses** (-løsiš) *s.* talud.

**tamable** (tei·måbøl) *adj.* domable, domesticable.

**tamale** (tama·li) *s.* tamal.

**tamandua** (tamandua·) *s.* ZOOL. tamanduá.

**tamarack** (tæ·maræk) *s.* BOT. alerce americano.

**tamarind** (tæ·marind) *s.* BOT. tamarindo.

**tamarisk** (tæ·marisk) *s.* BOT. tamarisco, taray.

**tambour** (tæ·mbuᵣ) *s.* MÚS., FORT., ARQ. tambor. *2 tambour* o *~ frame*, tambor de bordar.

**tambourine** (tæmbøri·n) *s.* pandero, pandereta.

**tame** (teim) *adj.* manso, dócil, sumiso. *2* amansado, domesticado. *3* insulso, aburrido.
**tame (to)** *tr.* domar, domeñar, domesticar, amansar. *2* suavizar [los colores]. *3 intr.* amansarse.
**tameless** (-lis) *adj.* indomado, indomable.
**taming** (-ing) *s.* doma, amansamiento.
**tamis** (tæ·mis) *s.* tamiz, cedazo.
**tam-o'-shanter** (tæmøshæ·ntøʳ) *s.* boina escocesa.
**tamp (to)** (tæmp) *tr.* atacar [un barreno; la pipa]. *2* apisonar; llenar apretando.
**tamper** (-øʳ) *s.* atacador; pisón.
**tamper (to)** *intr. to ~ with*, meterse en, enredar con; estropear, alterar, falsificar, sobornar.
**tampion** (-iøn) *s.* ARTILL. tapabocas.
**tampon** (-an) *s.* CIR. tapón.
**tampon (to)** *tr.* CIR. taponar.
**tamponage** (-ønidẏ), **tamponment** (-mønt) *s.* CIR. taponamiento.
**tan** (tæn) *s.* tanino. *2* casca [para curtir]. *3* tostadura, bronceado [del cutis]. *4* color tostado. *5 adj.* tostado, de color de canela.
**tan (to)** *tr.* curtir, adobar [las pieles]. *2* curtir, tostar, atezar [el cutis]. *3 fam.* zurrar, azotar. ¶ Pret. y p. p.: *tanned*; p. a.: *tanning.*
**tanager** (tæ·nødẏøʳ) *s.* ORN. tángara.
**tanbark** (tæ·nbaʳk) *s.* casca.
**tandem** (tæ·ndøm) *s.* tándem. *adj.-adv.* en tándem.
**tang** (tæng) *s.* dejo, sabor. *2* olor vivo. *3* sonido vibrante, tañido. *4* punzada. *5* espiga [de una herramienta].
**tang (to)** *intr.* sonar, retiñir. *2 tr.* hacer retiñir.
**tangency** (tæ·ndẏønsi) *s.* tangencia.
**tangent** (-ønt) *adj.-s.* tangente.
**Tangerine** (tæ·ndẏørin) *adj.-s.* tangerino. *2 s.* (con min.) mandarina [naranja].
**tangible** (tæ·ndẏibøl) *adj.* tangible, palpable.
**Tangier** (tænẏi·øʳ) *n. pr.* GEOGR. Tánger.
**tangle** (tæ·ngøl) *s.* enredo, maraña, confusión.
**tangle (to)** *tr.* enredar, enmarañar. *2* confundir. *3 intr.* enredarse, enmarañarse. *4* confundirse.
**tangly** (tæ·ngli) *adj.* enredado, enmarañado.
**tango** (tæ·ngou) *s.* tango [baile].
**tango (to)** *intr.* bailar el tango.
**tangram** (tæ·ngram) *s.* rompecabezas chino.
**tank** (tænk) *s.* tanque, aljibe, cisterna, alberca: *~ ship*, buque cisterna. *2* MIL. tanque.
**tankard** (-aʳd) *s.* jarro con tapa para beber.
**tanker** (-øʳ) *s.* MAR. buque cisterna. *2* camión cuba.
**tannage** (tæ·nidẏ) *s.* curtido, curtimiento.
**tannate** (tæ·neit) *s.* QUÍM. tanato.
**tanned** (tæ·nd) *pret.* y *p. p.* de TO TAN.
**tanner** (tæ·nøʳ) *s.* curtidor. *2 pop.* moneda de seis peniques.
**tannery** (-øri) *s.* tenería, curtiduría.
**tannic** (-ic) *adj.* QUÍM. tánico.
**tannin** (-in) *s.* QUÍM. tanino.
**tansy** (tæ·nsi) *s.* BOT. tanaceto.
**tantalize (to)** (tæ·ntalaiš) *tr.* atormentar, exasperar, mostrando lo inasequible.
**tantalum** (-løm) *s.* QUÍM. tantalio.
**Tantalus** (-løs) *n. pr.* Tántalo.
**tantamount** (tæ·ntamaunt) *adj.* equivalente.
**tantrum** (tæ·ntrøm) *s.* ataque de mal humor, berrinche, rabieta. *2* antojo, capricho.
**Taoism** (ta·uišm) *s.* taoísmo.
**tap** (tæp) *s.* grifo, espita, canilla: *on ~*, del barril. *2* tapón, bitoque. *3* calidad, clase [del vino, cerveza, etc.]. *4* mostrador [de taberna]. *5* ELECT. toma, derivación. *6* ZAP. media suela. *7* MEC. macho de aterrajar. *8* golpecito, palmada: *~ dance*, zapateado. *9 pl.* MIL. silencio [toque].

**tap (to)** *tr.* poner espita o canilla a; abrir [un barril]; sacar líquido de. *2* CIR. puncionar. *3* sangrar [un árbol]. *4* ELECT. derivar [una corriente]. *5* hacer una acometida en [una conducción]. *6* intervenir [un teléfono].·*7* MEC. aterrajar. *8* horadar; hacer [un agujero]. *9 tr.-intr.* dar golpecitos o palmadas [a o en]: *to ~ at a door*, llamar a una puerta. ¶ Pret. y p. p.: *tapped*; ger.: *-pping.*
**tape** (teip) *s.* cinta, galón: *~ line, ~ measure*, cinta de medir, cinta métrica; *~ recorder*, aparato magnetofónico de cinta.
**tape (to)** *tr.* atar o envolver con cinta. *2* medir con cinta. *3* grabar en cinta magnetofónica.
**taper** (tei·pøʳ) *s.* candela, velilla, cerilla; cirio. *2* afilamiento, disminución gradual. *3 adj.* afilado, cónico, piramidal.
**taper (to)** *intr.* afilarse, adelgazarse, ahusarse. *2* ir disminuyendo o cesando. *3 tr.* afilar, adelgazar, ahusar.
**tapestry** (tæ·pistri) *pl. s.* tapiz, colgadura, tapicería. *2* tela para tapizar. *3* papel que imita la tapicería.
**tapeworm** (tei·pwøʳm) *s.* ZOOL. tenia, solitaria.
**tapioca** (tæpiou·ka) *s.* tapioca.
**tapir** (tei·pøʳ) *s.* ZOOL. tapir, danta.
**tapis** (tæ·pis) *s. on the ~*, sobre el tapete.
**tappet** (tæ·pit) *s.* MEC. leva; alzaválvulas.
**taproom** (tæ·prum) *s.* taberna, bar.
**tapster** (-støʳ) *s.* mozo de taberna.
**tar** (taʳ) *s.* alquitrán, brea, pez líquida: *~ paper*, papel o cartón alquitranado.
**tar (to)** *tr.* alquitranar, embrear; untar o marcar con pez. ¶ Pret. y p. p.: *tarred*; ger.: *-rring.*
**tarantella** (tærante·la) *s.* tarantela.
**tarantula** (tæræ·nchula) *s.* ZOOL. tarántula.
**tardigrade** (ta·ʳdigreid) *adj.-s.* ZOOL. tradigrado.
**tardy** (ta·ʳdi) *adj.* lento, tardo. *2* retrasado, moroso. *3* tardío.
**tare** (teʳ) *s.* COM. tara. *2* BOT. arveja, algarroba. *3* BIB. cizaña.
**tare (to)** *tr.* COM. destarar.
**tarente** (tære·ntei) *s.* ZOOL. salamanquesa.
**targe** (tæ·ʳdẏ) *s.* tarja, escudo.
**target** (ta·ʳgit) *s.* blanco [al que se tira]; objetivo. *2* blanco, objeto [de críticas, burlas, etc.]. *3* escudo, rodela.
**tariff** (tæ·rif) *s.* tarifa. *2* arancel [de aduanas]: *~ protection*, protección arancelaria.
**tariff (to)** *tr.* tarifar.
**tarn** (ta·ʳn) *s.* lago pequeño entre montañas.
**tarnish** (ta·ʳnish) *s.* deslustre, empañadura.
**tarnish (to)** *tr.* empañar, deslucir; manchar, deshonrar. *2 intr.* empañarse, deslucirse.
**tarpaulin** (ta·ʳpo·lin) *s.* tela embreada, encerado. *2* sombrero embreado. *3 fam.* marinero.
**tarpot** (ta·ʳpat) *s.* caldero de alquitrán.
**tarragon** (tæ·ragøn) *s.* BOT. estragón.
**tarred** (ta·ʳd) *adj.* alquitranado, embreado.
**tarry** (ta·ri) *adj.* alquitranado, embreado. *2* píceo, negro, sucio.
**tarry (to)** (tæ·ri) *intr.* tardar, demorarse, entretenerse. *2* quedarse, esperar.
**tarsal** (ta·ʳsal) *adj.* ANAT., ZOOL. tarsal.
**tarsus** (ta·ʳsøs) *s.* ANAT., ZOOL. tarso.
**tart** (ta·ʳt) *adj.* acre, ácido, picante. *2* áspero, agrio; cáustico, mordaz. *3 s.* tarta.
**tartan** (ta·ʳtan) *s.* tartán. *2* MAR. tartana.
**tartar** (ta·ʳtaʳ) *s.* tártaro [del mosto]. *2* tártaro, sarro [de los dientes].
**Tartar** *adj.-s.* tártaro [de Tartaria]. *2* (con min.) persona violenta, intratable.

**tartare sauce** (ta·ʳtaʳ) s. coc. salsa tártara.
**tartaric** (taʳtæ·rik) adj. tartárico.
**Tartarous** (ta·ʳtarøs) s. mit. Tártaro, el infierno.
**Tartary** (ta·ʳtari) n. pr. geogr. Tartaria.
**tartlet** (ta·ʳtlit) s. tarta o pastel pequeño.
**tartrate** (ta·ʳtreit) s. quím. tartrato.
**task** (tæsk) s. tarea, labor, trabajo. 2 to take to ~, reprender, censurar.
**task (to)** tr. atarear, señalar tarea. 2 abrumar [de trabajo]. 3 poner a prueba. 4 acusar, tachar [de].
**tassel** (tæ·søl) s. borla, campanilla [adorno].
**tassel (to)** tr. adornar con borlas. ¶ Pret. y p. p.: tassel(l)ed; ger.: tassel(l)ing.
**tastable** (tei·stabøl) adj. gustable. 2 sabroso.
**taste** (teist) s. gusto [sentido]: ~ bud, anat. papila gustativa. 2 gusto, sabor. 3 gusto, afición: to have a ~ for, gustar de. 4 gusto [discernimiento de lo bello, armónico, etc.]: in good ~, de buen gusto; in bad ~, de mal gusto; man of ~, hombre de gusto. 5 bocadito, sorbo, un poco. 6 muestra, prueba.
**taste (to)** tr. gustar, saborear. 2 probar, catar. 3 gustar, experimentar. 4 intr. tener cierto sabor o gusto: to ~ of, saber a.
**tasteful** (-ful) adj. de buen gusto, elegante.
**tasteless** (-lis) adj. insípido, soso, insulso. 2 de mal gusto, falto de gusto.
**taster** (-tøʳ) s. probador, catador. 2 pipeta; catavino.
**tasty** (-ti) adj. de buen gusto. 2 fam. sabroso.
**tat** (to) (tæt) intr. hacer encaje de frivolité.
**tatou** (tatu·) s. zool. tato, tatú [armadillo].
**tatter** (tæ·tøʳ) s. harapo, andrajo, jirón, arambel.
**tatterdemalion** (tætøʳdimei·liøn) s. zarrapastrón.
**tattered** (tæ·tøʳd) adj. roto, desgarrado. 2 andrajoso.
**tatting** (tæ·ting) s. encaje de frivolité.
**tattle** (tæ·tøl) s. charla, parloteo. 2 chismorreo.
**tattle (to)** intr. charlar. 2 chismorrear. 3 soplonear. 4 tr. descubrir, revelar [charlando].
**tattler** (tæ·tløʳ) s. hablador. 2 chismoso. 3 soplón.
**tattoo** (tætu·) s. retreta [toque; fiesta]. 2 tabaleo, tamborileo. 3 tatuaje [dibujo].
**tattoo (to)** tr. tatuar. 2 intr. tocar retreta. 3 tabalear, tamborilear.
**tattooage** (-idȳ) s. tatuaje.
**tau** (tau) s. tau [letra griega]. 2 tao.
**taught** (tot) pret. y p. p. de to teach.
**taunt** (tont) s. reproche insultante, sarcasmo, insulto, provocación.
**taunt (to)** tr. reprochar con insulto, insultar, provocar.
**taurine** (to·rin) adj. taurino [de toro].
**tauromachy** (tora·maki) s. tauromaquia.
**Taurus** (to·røs) n. pr. astr. Tauro.
**taut** (tot) adj. tirante, tenso, tieso. 2 aseado, bien arreglado.
**tauten (to)** (to·tøn) tr. atirantar, tesar. 2 intr. ponerse tirante, tenso.
**tautology** (tota·lødȳi) s. ret. tautología.
**tavern** (tæ·vøʳn) s. taberna. 2 hotel, mesón.
**taw (to)** s. canica, bola.
**taw (to)** tr. curtir [pieles] en blanco.
**tawdry** (to·dri) adj. charro, chillón, llamativo.
**tawny** (to·ni) adj. moreno, tostado, atezado. 2 leonado. 3 orn. ~ owl, autillo.
**tax** (taks) s. impuesto, tributo, contribución. 2 carga, esfuerzo gravoso.
**tax (to)** tr. imponer tributo a, gravar. 2 fatigar; abusar de: to ~ one's patience, abusar de la pa-

ciencia de uno. 3 censurar, tachar, acusar. 4 der. tasar.
**taxable** (-abøl) adj. imponible; sujeto a tributación.
**taxation** (-ei·shøn) s. imposición de tributos. 2 tributo, impuesto; tributación.
**taxer** (tæ·ksøʳ) s. exactor. 2 acusador.
**taxi** (-i) s. taxi, taxímetro [coche].
**taxi (to)** tr.-intr. llevar o ir en taxi. 2 hacer correr [un avión] o correr [el avión] por tierra.
**taxicab** (-kæb) s. taxi.
**taxidermy** (tæksidø·ʳmi) s. taxidermia.
**taximeter** (tæksi·mitøʳ) s. taxímetro.
**taxonomy** (tæksa·nømi) s. taxonomía.
**taxpayer** (ta·kspeiøʳ) s. contribuyente.
**tea** (ti) s. té: ~ party, té [reunión]; ~ rose, rosa de té. 2 refacción de la tarde o prima noche. 3 tisana.
**teacart** (ti·kaʳt) s. carrito para el té.
**teach (to)** (ti·ch) tr.-intr. enseñar, instruir. 2 enseñar, profesar [una materia, etc.]. ¶ Pret. y p. p.: taught.
**teachable** (-abøl) adj. enseñable; dócil.
**teacher** (-øʳ) s. maestro, -tra, profesor, -ra.
**teaching** (-ing) s. enseñanza, instrucción. 2 adj. docente.
**teacup** (ti·køp) s. taza para té.
**teahouse** (-jaus) s. salón de té.
**teak** (ti·k) s. bot. teca [árbol].
**teakettle** (ti·ketøl) s. tetera.
**teal** (til) s. orn. trullo.
**team** (tim) s. tiro [de animales]; atelaje, tronco, junta. 2 grupo, equipo, cuadrilla. 3 dep. equipo.
**team (to)** tr. enganchar, uncir. 2 intr. guiar un tiro, una yunta, etc. 3 to ~ up, formar equipo.
**teammate** (-meit) s. compañero de equipo.
**teamwork** (-uøʳk) s. trabajo de equipo.
**teapot** (ti·pat) s. tetera.
**1) tear** (tiʳ) s. lágrima: ~ gas, gas lacrimógeno; ~ sac, anat. saco lacrimal. 2 pl. llanto, aflicción.
**2) tear** (teʳ) s. rotura, desgarro, desgarrón. 3 precipitación, furia.
**tear (to)** tr. romper, rasgar, desgarrar: to ~ open, abrir rompiendo o desgarrando. 2 mesar. 3 arrancar, separar con violencia: to ~ oneself away, arrancarse de un lugar. 4 to ~ down, desarmar; demoler. 5 to ~ up, arrancar; romper en pedazos. 6 intr. rasgarse. 7 moverse u obrar con furia, precipitadamente. ¶ Pret.: tore; p. p.: torn.
**teardrop** (ti·ʳdrap) s. lágrima.
**tearful** (ti·ʳful) adj. lloroso.
**tease** (ti·š) s. importunidad, broma, vaya. 2 embromador.
**tease (to)** tr. fastidiar, importunar, embromar, dar vaya. 2 cardar [el paño].
**teasel** (ti·šøl) s. bot. cardencha. 2 carda.
**teasel (to)** tr. cardar [el paño].
**teaser** (ti·šøʳ) s. cardador [de paño]. 2 embromador.
**teaspoon** (ti·spun) s. cucharilla, cucharita.
**teaspoonful** (ti·spunful) s. cucharadita.
**teat** (tit) s. teta, pezón [de teta]; teta.
**teazel** s., **teazel (to)** tr. teasel, to teasel.
**technic** (te·knik) adj. técnico. 2 s. tecnicismo.
**technical** (te·knikal) adj. técnico: ~ term, tecnicismo.
**technicality** (teknikæ·liti) s. carácter técnico. 2 tecnicismo. 3 detalle técnico.
**technician** (te·knishan) s. técnico.

**technics** (te·kniks) s. doctrina de las artes.
**technique** (tekni·k) s. técnica.
**technocracy** (tekna·krasi) s. tecnocracia.
**technology** (tekna·lodẏ) s. tecnología.
**techy** (te·chi) adj. TETCHY.
**tectonics** (tekta·niks) s. tectónica.
**Ted** (ted), **Teddy** (-i) n. pr. abrev. de Theodore y Edward.
**Teddy-bear** s. osito de trapo.
**Teddy-boy** s. gamberro.
**Te Deum** (tɪ-di·øm) s. tedéum.
**tedious** (tɪ·diøs) adj. tedioso, fastidioso, latoso.
**tedium** (-diøm) s. tedio, aburrimiento.
**tee** (tɪ) s. pieza en forma de T. 2 DEP. meta, hito. 3 GOLF. punto de saque.
**tee (to)** tr. GOLF poner [la pelota] sobre un TEE.
**teem (to)** (tɪm) tr. producir, engendrar. 2 intr. to ~ with, abundar en, hervir de.
**teen age** (tɪn) s. edad de los 13 a los 19 años.
**teen-ager** (-eidẏøʳ) s. joven de 13 a 19 años de edad.
**teens** (tɪ·nš) s. pl. números que terminan en TEEN. 2 edad de los 13 a los 19 años.
**teeny** (tɪ·ni) adj. fam. pequeñito, diminuto.
**teepee** (tɪ·pi) s. TEPEE.
**teeter** (tɪ·tøʳ) s. balance, vaivén.
**teeter (to)** intr. balancearse, columpiarse. 2 vacilar, andar vacilando.
**teeth** (tɪ·z) s. pl. de TOOTH: to cast, o throw, in one's ~, echar en cara; in the ~ of, contra, desafiando.
**teethe (to)** (tɪ·ð) intr. endentecer, echar los dientes.
**teething** (-ing) s. dentición.
**teetotal(l)er** (tɪtou·taløʳ) s. abstemio.
**teetotum** (-tøm) s. perinola.
**tegmen** (te·gmin) s. BOT., ZOOL. tegmen.
**tegument** (te·giumønt) s. tegumento.
**telamon** (te·lamøn) s. ARQ. atlante.
**telecast** (-likæst) s. transmisión por televisión.
**telecast (to)** tr. televisar.
**telecommunication** (telikømiunikei·shøn) s. telecomunicación.
**telegram** (te·ligræm) s. telegrama.
**telegraph** (-græf) s. telégrafo. 2 telegrama.
**telegrapher** (tile·graføʳ) s. telegrafista.
**telegraphy** (-fi) s. telegrafía.
**Telemachus** (tile·makøs) n. pr. MIT. Telémaco.
**telemeter** (tile·mitøʳ) s. telémetro.
**teleology** (tilia·lodẏ) s. teleología.
**teleost** (te·liast) adj. ICT. teleósteo.
**telepathy** (tile·pazi) s. telepatía.
**telephone** (te·lifoun) s. teléfono: ~ call, llamada telefónica; ~ directory, guía telefónica; ~ exchange, central telefónica.
**telephone (to)** tr.-intr. telefonear.
**telephonist** (-nist) s. telefonista.
**telephony** (tile·føni) s. telefonía.
**telephotography** (telifouta·grafi) s. telefotografía.
**telescope** (te·liscoup) s. telescopio.
**telescope (to)** tr.-intr. enchufar(se, empotrar(se [una cosa en otra]. 2 tr. acortar.
**teletype** (-taip) s. teletipo.
**teletype (to)** tr. transmitir por teletipo.
**teleview (to)** (-viu) tr.-intr. ver por televisión.
**televiewer** (-viuøʳ) s. telespectador.
**televise (to)** (-vaiš) tr. televisar.
**television** (-viẏøn) s. televisión.
**tell (to)** (te·l) tr. contar, numerar. 2 contar, relatar, narrar: ~ that to the marines, cuénteselo a su tía. 3 decir: to ~ volumes,decir mucho, ser significativo. 4 mandar, ordenar. 5 distinguir, conocer. 6 determinar. 7 MIL. to ~ off, destacar [para

un servicio]. 8 intr. to ~ on, notarse, dejarse ver; hacerse sentir en; delatar. ¶ Pret. y p. p.: told.
**teller** (-øʳ) s. narrador, relator. 2 escrutador de votos. 3 receiving ~, paying ~, cobrador, pagador [de la caja de un banco].
**telling** (-ling) adj. eficaz, notable. 2 s. acción de decir o contar: there is no ~, no es posible decir o prever.
**telltale** (-teil) adj.-s. chismoso, soplón. 2 s. indicador, contador. 3 adj. indicador, revelador.
**tellurian** (teliu·rian) adj. telúrico [de la Tierra].
**tellurium** (-riøm) s. QUÍM. telurio.
**telophase** (te·løfeiš) s. BIOL. telofase.
**temerarious** (temørei·riøs) adj. temerário.
**temerity** (time·riti) s. temeridad.
**temper** (te·mpøʳ) s. temple [del metal]. 2 punto [de una mezcla]. 3 genio; humor, temple. 4 cólera, mal genio. 5 to keep one's ~, contenerse, dominarse; to lose one's ~, perder la calma, encolerizarse.
**temper (to)** tr. templar, moderar, mitigar, atemperar. 2 mezclar, amasar. 3 templar [el metal].
**tempera** (te·mpøra) s. PINT. temple.
**temperament** (-mønt) s. temperamento [de una pers.]. 2 MÚS. temperamento.
**temperamental** (-al) adj. temperamental. 2 muy sensible o excitable.
**temperance** (te·mpørans) s. templanza, sobriedad.
**temperate** (-it) adj. templado [sobrio, moderado; tibio]. 2 templado [clima].
**temperature** (-achuʳ) s. temperatura.
**tempered** (te·mpøʳd) adj. templado, moderado, suavizado. 2 de genio o disposición: bad-tempered, de mal genio. 3 templado [metal, cristal].
**tempest** (te·mpist) s. tempestad.
**tempest (to)** tr. agitar. 2 intr. moverse con agitación, tempestear.
**tempestuous** (tempe·schuøs) adj. tempestuoso.
**Templar** (te·mplaʳ) s. templario.
**template** (te·mplit) s. TEMPLET 2.
**temple** (te·mpøl) s. templo. 2 ANAT. sien. 3 brazo [de anteojos]. 4 TEJ. templazo.
**templet** (te·mplit) s. templete. 2 plantilla, gálibo.
**tempo** (te·mpou) s. MÚS. tiempo. 2 ritmo.
**temporal** (te·mpøral) adj. temporal. 2 ANAT. hueso temporal.
**temporality** (-iti) s. temporalidad.
**temporalty** (-ti) s. propiedad secular. 2 los seglares.
**temporary** (te·mpøreri) adj. temporal, temporario, transitorio, provisional, interino.
**temporize (to)** (-aiš) intr. adaptarse a la ocasión, contemporizar; ganar tiempo; no comprometerse.
**tempt (to)** (tempt) tr. tentar, instigar, atraer.
**temptation** (-ei·shøn) s. tentación. 2 incentivo.
**tempter** (te·mptøʳ) s. tentador.
**tempting** (-ing) adj. tentador, atractivo.
**temptress** (-tris) s. tentadora.
**ten** (ten) adj.-s. diez: ~ o'clock, las diez. 2 s. decena.
**tenable** (te·nabøl) adj. defendible, sostenible.
**tenace** (te·neis) s. tenaza [en los naipes].
**tenacious** (tinei·shøs) adj. tenaz.
**tenacity** (tinæ·siti) s. tenacidad. 2 tesón.
**tenaille** (te·neil) s. FORT. tenaza.
**tenancy** (te·nansi) s. tenencia, arriendo, inquilinato.
**tenant** (-t) s. inquilino, arrendatario. 2 residente, morador.

**tenant (to)** *tr.* arrendar, alquilar. *2* tener en arriendo o alquiler.
**tenantry** (-tri) *s.* arriendo, inquilinato. *2* arrendatarios, inquilinos.
**tench** (tench) *s.* ICT. tenca.
**tend (to)** (tend) *tr.* cuidar, atender, guardar, vigilar. *2 intr.* tender [a un fin]; contribuir. *3* propender. *4* ir, dirigirse [a].
**tendance** (-ans) *s.* cuidado, atención, guarda.
**tendency** (te·ndønsi), *pl.* **-cies** (-siš) *s.* tendencia. *2* propensión.
**tendentious** (-shøs) *adj.* tendencioso.
**tender** (te·ndøʳ) *adj.* tierno. *2* delicado [escrupuloso; espinoso]. *3* dolorido. *4* susceptible, sentido. *5 s.* cuidador, guardador. *6* FERROC. ténder. *7* oferta. *8 legal* ~, moneda corriente, de curso legal.
**tenderfoot** (-fut), **-foots** o **-feet** *s.* novato, poco habituado a los rigores de un clima, una vida.
**tenderloin** (-løin) *s.* COC. filete. *2* (E.U.) barrio de la vida nocturna.
**tenderness** (-nis) *s.* terneza, ternura, suavidad. *2* debilidad, fragilidad. *3* sensibilidad.
**tendinous** (te·ndinøs) *adj.* tendinoso. *2* nervudo.
**tendon** (te·ndøn) *s.* tendón.
**tendril** (te·ndril) *s.* BOT. zarcillo, tijereta. *2* rizo [de pelo].
**tenebrous** (te·nibrøs) *adj.* poét. tenebroso.
**tenement** (te·nimønt) *s.* habitación, vivienda, piso: ~ *house*, casa de vecindad.
**tenet** (te·nit) *s.* principio, dogma, credo.
**tenfold** (te·nfould) *adj.* décuplo. *2 adv.* diez veces.
**tennis** (te·nis) *s.* tenis: ~ *court*, pista de tenis.
**tenon** (te·nøn) *s.* CARP. espiga, almilla.
**tenor** (te·nøʳ) *s.* tenor, contenido, significado, carácter, naturaleza. *2* curso, tendencia. *3* MÚS. tenor.
**tenpins** (te·npins) *s.* (E.U.) juego de bolos.
**tense** (tens) *adj.* tenso; tirante, tieso. *2* dramático, emocionante. *3 s.* GRAM. tiempo [de verbo].
**tensible** (-ibøl) *adj.* capaz de tensión.
**tensile** (-il) *adj.* TENSIBLE. *2* relativo a la tensión.
**tension** (te·nshøn) *s.* tensión. *2* atirantamiento. *3* tirantez. *4* esfuerzo mental; intensidad de sentimiento; ansiedad.
**tensive** (-iv) *adj.* tensor.
**tensor** (-øʳ) *s.* tensor. *2* ANAT. músculo tensor.
**tent** (tent) *s.* tienda [para alojamiento], tienda de campaña. *2* CIR. lechino, tapón.
**tent (to)** *intr.* acampar en tiendas. *2 tr.* alojar en tiendas. *3* CIR. poner un lechino a.
**tentacle** (te·økøl) *s.* ZOOL. tentáculo, tiento.
**tentacular** (tentæ·kiulaʳ) *adj.* tentacular.
**tentative** (te·ntativ) *adj.* tentativo. *2 s.* tentativa, ensayo, tanteo.
**tenter** (te·ntøʳ) *s.* rambla, máquina para estirar el paño. *2* TENTERHOOK.
**tenter (to)** *tr.* estirar, enramblar [el paño].
**tenterhook** (-juk) *s.* cada uno de los clavos con que se mantiene estirado el paño: *on tenterhooks*, fig. muy inquieto, en ascuas.
**tenth** (tenz) *adj.-s.* décimo, deceno. *2 s.* diez [día]. *3* MÚS. décima.
**tenuirostral** (tenuira·stral) *adj.* ORN. tenuirrostro.
**tenuity** (teniu·iti) *s.* tenuidad. *2* raridad [de un fluido]. *3* debilidad [de un sonido].
**tenuous** (te·niuøs) *adj.* tenue. *2* raro [poco denso].
**tenure** (te·niuʳ) *s.* tenencia, posesión. *2* ejercicio [de un cargo]; *right of* ~, inamovilidad.
**teocalli** (tiokæ·li) *s.* toecalí.

**tepee** (ti·pi) *s.* tienda de los indios norteamericanos.
**tepid** (te·pid) *adj.* tibio.
**tepidity** (tipi·diti) *s.* tibieza.
**teratology** (terata·lodẙi) *s.* teratología.
**terbium** (tø·ʳbiøm) *s.* QUÍM. terbio.
**terce** (tøʳs) *s.* TIERCE.
**tercel** (te·ʳsøl) *s.* ORN. terzuelo.
**tercet** (te·ʳsit) *s.* LIT. terceto. *2* MÚS. tresillo.
**terebinth** (te·ribinz) *s.* BOT. terebinto.
**teredo** (te·ridou) *s.* ZOOL. broma [molusco].
**Terence** (te·røns) *n. pr.* Terencio.
**tergal** (tø·ʳgal) *adj.* ZOOL. dorsal. *2 s.* tergal.
**tergiversate (to)** (te·ʳdẙivøʳseit) *intr.* usar de evasivas. *2* renegar, apostatar, abandonar una causa.
**term** (tøʳm) *s.* término, plazo, período, duración. *2* período de sesiones o de clases; período por el cual se hace un arrendamiento. *3* tiempo fijado para el pago de rentas, intereses, etc. *4* término, palabra. *5* LÓG., MAT., ARQ. término. *6 pl.* condiciones, estipulaciones. *7* COM. facilidades de pago. *8* términos o relación mutua: *to be in good terms*, estar en buenas relaciones. *9* acuerdo, arreglo: *to come to terms*, decidirse a un arreglo, ceder.
**term (to)** *tr.* nombrar, llamar.
**termagant** (tø·ʳmagant) *adj.* turbulento, pendenciero. *2 s.* fiera, furia, arpía.
**terminable** (tø·ʳminabøl) *adj.* limitable.
**terminal** (-al) *adj.* terminal. *2 s.* término, final. *3* ARQ. coronamiento. *4* ELECT. borne, terminal. *5* estación terminal.
**terminate (to)** (-eit) *tr.* limitar. *2 tr.-intr.* terminar, acabar.
**termination** (-ei·shøn) *s.* terminación, fin. *2* GRAM. terminación, desinencia.
**terminative** (tø·ʳminetiv) *adj.* terminativo. *2* terminante, definitivo.
**terminology** (tø·ʳmina·lodẙ) *s.* terminología.
**terminus** (tø·ʳminøs) *s.* término, final. *2* estación terminal. *3 n. pr.* MIT. Término.
**termite** (tø·ʳmait) *s.* ENT. termite.
**tern** (tøʳn) *s.* ORN. golondrina de mar. *2* terno [en la lotería].
**ternary** (tø·ʳnari) *adj.* ternario. *2* triple. *3 s.* terno [grupo de tres].
**terpene** (-pin) *s.* QUÍM. terpeno.
**Terpsichore** (tøʳsi·køri) *n. pr.* MIT. Terpsícore.
**terra** (te·ra) *s.* tierra [en ciertas denominaciones]: ~ *cotta*, terracota; ~ *firma*, tierra firme.
**terrace** (te·ris) *s.* terraza. *2* terrado, azotea. *3* hilera de casas sobre un terreno elevado.
**terrace (to)** *tr.* disponer en terrazas; terraplenar.
**terrain** (te·rein) *s.* terreno, campo [de batalla, de actividad, etc.]. *2 adj.* terreno, terrestre.
**terramycin** (teramai·sin) *s.* FARM. terramicina.
**terrapin** (te·rapin) *s.* ZOOL. tortuga acuática comestible de América.
**terraqueous** (terei·kuiøs) *adj.* terráqueo.
**terrene** (teri·n) *adj.* terreno, mundano.
**terreplein** (te·ʳplein) *s.* FORT. terraplén.
**terrestrial** (tere·strial) *adj.* terrestre, terreno.
**terrible** (te·ribøl) *adj.* terrible, tremendo.
**terribly** (te·ribli) *adv.* terriblemente.
**terrier** (te·riøʳ) *s.* terrier [perro].
**terrific** (teri·fik) *adj.* terrífico, terrorífico. *2* fig. tremendo, grande.
**terrify (to)** (te·rifai) *tr.* aterrar, aterrorizar. ¶ Pret. y p. p.: *terrified.*
**territorial** (terito·rial) *adj.* territorial.

**territory** (te·rit*o*ri) *s.* territorio. *2* región, distrito. *3* campo, dominio, esfera.

**terror** (te·r*ø*ʳ) *s.* terror.

**terrorism** (-iśm) *s.* terrorismo.

**terrorist** (-ist) *s.* terrorista. *2* alarmista.

**terrorize (to)** (-aiś) *tr.* aterrorizar.

**terse** (t*ø*·ʳs) *adj.* terso, conciso, limpio [estilo, lenguaje].

**tertian** (t*ø*·ʳsh*a*n) *adj.-s.* MED. terciana.

**tertiary** (t*ø*ʳshie·ri) *adj.-s.* terciario.

**tessellate (to)** (te·s*ø*leit) *tr.* cubrir con mosaico; taracear.

**tessera** (te·s*ø*ra), *pl.* **-ae** (-i) *s.* tesela. *2* tesera.

**tessitura** (tesitu·ra) *s.* MÚS. tesitura.

**test** (test) *s.* copela. *2* prueba, ensayo, examen: ~ *paper*, QUÍM. papel reactivo; ~ *pilot*, AVIA. piloto de pruebas; ~ *tube*, tubo de ensayo; probeta; *to put to the* ~, poner a prueba. *2* medio de prueba, piedra de toque. *3* PSIC., EDUC. test. *4* ZOOL. concha. *5* BOT. tegumento [de semilla].

**test (to)** *tr.* examinar, probar, ensayar, comprobar, hacer la prueba de, poner a prueba.

**testa** (te·sta), *pl.* **-tae** (-tı) *s.* TEST 4 y 5.

**testacean** (testei·sh*a*n) *adj.-s.* ZOOL. testáceo.

**testacy** (te·stasi) *s.* DER. circunstancia de haber testado.

**testament** (te·stam*ø*nt) *s.* testamento. *2 Old, New, Testament*, Antiguo, Nuevo, Testamento.

**testate** (te·steit) *adj.* testado.

**testator** (testei·t*ø*ʳ) *s.* DER. testador.

**testatrix** (-triks) *s.* DER. testadora.

**tested** (te·stid) *adj.* probado, ensayado.

**tester** (te·st*ø*ʳ) *s.* probador, ensayador. *2* QUÍM. reactivo. *3* pabellón de cama. *4* baldaquín, dosel.

**testicle** (te·stik*ø*l) *s.* testículo.

**testify (to)** (te·stifai) *tr.* testificar, atestiguar, testimoniar. *2 intr.* dar testimonio: *to* ~ *to*, dar testimonio de. ¶ Pret. y p. p.: *testified*.

**testimonial** (testimou·nial) *adj.* testimonial. *2* que sirve como testimonio de admiración, etc. *3 s.* certificado de buena conducta, aptitud, etc. *4* testimonio de admiración, respeto, etc.; homenaje.

**testimony** (te·stimouni) *s.* testimonio, atestación, fe. *2* la divina revelación, las Escrituras.

**testiness** (te·stinis) *s.* irritabilidad, susceptibilidad, mal humor, mal genio.

**testis** (te·stis) *s.* ZOOL. testículo.

**testudineous** (testiu·dini*ø*s) *adj.* testudíneo.

**testudo** (testiu·dou) *s.* testudo. *2* MED. talpa.

**testy** (te·sti) *adj.* irritable, susceptible, enojadizo.

**tetanus** (te·tan*ø*s) *s.* MED. tétano.

**tetchy** (te·chi) *adj.* quisquilloso, enojadizo.

**tête-à-tête** (teit-a-teit) *adv.* a solas [dos personas]. *2 adj.* privado, confidencial. *3 s.* entrevista a solas. *4* confidente [mueble].

**tether** (te·đ*ø*ʳ) *s.* cuerda, ramal [con que se tiene atado un animal]. *2* fig. *at the end of one's* ~, habiendo acabado las fuerzas, los recursos.

**tether (to)** *tr.* atar, estacar [a un animal].

**tetrachord** (te·trak*o*ʳd) *s.* MÚS. tetracordio.

**tetragon** (te·tr*a*gan) *s.* GEOM. tetrágono, cuadrilátero.

**tetragonal** (tetræ·g*ø*nal) *adj.* tetragonal.

**tetrahedron** (tetraji·dr*ø*n) *s.* GEOM. tetraedro.

**tetralogy** (tetræ·lodẏ) *s.* tetralogía.

**tetrameter** (tetræ·mit*ø*ʳ) *adj.-s.* tetrámetro.

**tetrarch** (te·tra·ʳk) *s.* tetrarca.

**tetrarchy** (te·trarki) *s.* tetrarquía.

**tetter** (te·t*ø*ʳ) *s.* herpe; empeine; serpigo.

**Teuton** (tiu·t*ø*n) *s.* teutón.

**Teutonic** (tiuta·nik) *adj.-s.* teutónico.

**Texan** (te·ksan) *adj.-s.* tejano.

**Texas** (-sas) *n. pr.* GEOGR. Tejas.

**text** (tekst) *s.* texto. *2* tema [de un discurso, etc.].

**textbook** (-buk) *s.* libro de texto. *2* libreto.

**textile** (te·kstil) *adj.-s.* textil.

**textual** (-chual) *adj.* textual.

**texture** (-chuʳ) *s.* textura. *2* tejido, obra tejida.

**Thailand** (tai·land) *n. pr.* GEOGR. Tailandia.

**thalamus** (zæ·lam*ø*s) *s.* tálamo.

**thaler** (ta·l*ø*ʳ) *s.* tálero.

**Thalia** (zalai·a) *n. pr.* MIT. Talía.

**thallium** (zæ·li*ø*m) *s.* QUÍM. talio.

**thallophyte** (zæ·lofait) *s.* BOT. talofita.

**thallus** (zæ·l*ø*s) *s.* BOT. talo.

**thalweg** (ta·lveik) *s.* vaguada.

**Thames** (temś) *n. pr.* GEOGR. Támesis.

**than** (đæn) *conj.* que [después de ciertos adverbios o adjetivos]: *softer* ~ *velvet*, más suave que el terciopelo; *nothing else* ~, nada más que. *2* en ciertas expresiones equivale a: de, de lo que, del que, etc.: *more* ~ *two*, más de dos; *more clever* ~ *you think*, más listo de lo que usted se figura. *3* con *whom* y *which*, forma expresiones que hay que traducir libremente: *my father* ~ *whom no one knew better this trade*, mi padre, que conocía este oficio mejor que nadie.

**thane** (zein) *s.* entre los antiguos anglosajones, gran señor.

**thank (to)** (zænk) *tr.* dar gracias, agradecer: ~ *you*, gracias; ~ *heaven!*, ¡gracias a Dios!

**thankful** (-ful) *adj.* agradecido.

**thankfulness** (-nis) *s.* agradecimiento, gratitud.

**thankless** (-lis) *adj.* desagradecido. *2* ingrato.

**thanks** (-s) *s. pl.* gracias, agradecimiento. *2* ~ *to*, gracias a; debido a.

**thanksgiving** (-sgi·ving) *s.* acción de gracias. *2* (E.U.) *Thanksgiving Day*, día de acción de gracias [cuarto jueves de noviembre].

**that** (đæt) *adj.* ese, esa, aquel, aquella. *2 pron. dem.* ése, ésa, eso, aquél, aquélla, aquello: ~ *is*, ~ *is to say*, eso es; es decir; *upon* ~, sobre eso o aquello; luego. *3* a veces se traduce por el, la, lo: ~ *which*, el que, la que, lo que. *4 at* ~, así, como está; aun así, de todos modos. *5 pron. rel.* que: *the money* ~ *you gave me*, el dinero que me diste. *6* en que, donde, cuando. *7 conj.* que, para que: *so* ~, para que. *8 adv.* así, tan: ~ *far*, tan lejos; ~ *much*, tanto.

**thatch** (zæch) *s.* techo de paja, cañas, etc.

**thatch (to)** *tr.* techar con paja, caña, etc.

**thaumaturge** (zo·mat*ø*rdẏ) *s.* taumaturgo.

**thaumaturgic (al** (-ik(al) *adj.* taumatúrgico.

**thaumaturgy** (-i) *s.* taumaturgia.

**thaw** (zo) *s.* deshielo, derretimiento.

**thaw (to)** *tr.* deshelar, derretir. *2 impers.* deshelar. *3 intr.* deshelarse, derretirse. *5* fig. ablandarse; perder la frialdad, la reserva.

**the** (di o đ*ø*) *art.* el, la, lo, los, las. *2 adv.* cuando, mientras, tanto [precediendo a un comparativo]: ~ *more ...*, ~ *more*, cuanto más o mientras más..., más o tanto más. | A veces no se traduce: *so much* ~ *better*, tanto mejor.

**theater, theatre** (zi·at*ø*ʳ) *s.* teatro.

**theatrical** (ziæ·trikal) *adj.* teatral. *2 s.* representación, comedia. *3 pl.* funciones teatrales. *4* fig. teatro, modo teatral de conducirse.

**Thebaid** (zibai·d) *n. pr.* GEOGR. Tebaida.

**Thebes** (zibs) *n. pr.* GEOGR. Tebas.

**theca** (zi·ka) *s.* BOT. teca [mitad de la antera].

**thee** (ði) *pron.* te, a ti [caso oblicuo de THOU].
**theft** (zeft) *s.* robo, hurto, latrocinio.
**their** (de$^r$) *adj.* su, sus [de ellos o ellas].
**theirs** (de$^r$s) *pron. pos.* (el) suyo, (la) suya, (los) suyos, (las) suyas [de ellos o de ellas].
**theism** (zɪ·ɪšm) *s.* teísmo.
**theist** (zɪ·ɪst) *s.* teísta.
**theistic** (al (zɪ·ɪstik(al) *adj.* teísta.
**them** (ðem) *pron.* [sin prep.] los, las, les [acusativo o dativo de THEY]. *2* [con prep.] ellos, ellas.
**thematic** (zɪmæ·tik) *adj.* temático.
**theme** (zɪm) *s.* tema [asunto; ejercicio]. *2* GRAM., MÚS. tema.
**themselves** (ðemse·lvš) *pron. pl.* se [reflexivo], si: *they wash* ~, ellos se lavan; *to* ~, a sí mismos o mismas. *2* ellos mismos, ellas mismas.
**then** (ðen) *adv.* entonces, en aquel tiempo: *by* ~, para entonces; ~ *and there*, en el acto, allí mismo. *2* luego, después. *3* además. *4 conj.* entonces, siendo así, luego pues, por consiguiente. *5 but* ~, pero entonces; pero, es que, pero por otra parte. *6 adj.* de entonces, de aquel tiempo.
**thence** (ðens) *adv.* de allí, desde allí. *2* desde entonces, de allí en adelante. *3* de ahí, por lo tanto, por eso.
**thenceforth** (ðensfo·$^r$z), **thenceforward** (-fo·$^r$ua$^r$d) *adv.* desde entonces, de allí en adelante, en adelante.
**theobromine** (zɪøbrou·min) *s.* QUÍM. teobromina.
**theocracy** (zɪa·krasi) *s.* teocracia.
**theodicy** (-disi) *s.* teodicea.
**theodolite** (-dølait) *s.* TOP. teodolito.
**Theodore** (zɪ·ødo$^r$) *n. pr.* Teodoro.
**Theodosius** (zɪødou·shøs) *n. pr.* Teodosio.
**theogony** (zɪa·gøni) *s.* teogonía.
**theologian** (zɪolou·dŷan) *s.* teólogo.
**theological** (zɪola·dŷikal) *adj.* teológico. *2* teologal: ~ *virtues*, virtudes teologales.
**theology** (zɪa·lodŷi) *s.* teología.
**theorem** (zɪ·orem) *s.* teorema.
**theoretic** (zɪore·tik) *s.* teoría, teórica. *2* teórico.
**theoretic(al** (zɪore·tik(al) *adj.* teórico.
**theorics** (zɪa·riks) *s.* teórica.
**theorize (to)** (zɪ·oraiš) *intr.* teorizar.
**theory** (zɪ·ori) *s.* teoría.
**theosophist** (zɪa·søfist) *s.* teósofo.
**theosophy** (-søfi) *s.* teosofía.
**therapeutics** (zɛrapiu·tikts) *s.* terapéutica.
**therapeutist** (-tist) *s.* terapeuta.
**therapy** (ze·rapi) *s.* terapia, terapéutica.
**there** (de$^r$) *adv.* allí, allá, ahí: ~ *he is*, helo ahí; *who goes there?*, ¿quién va?, ¿quién vive? *2 there* forma una con *to be* el verbo impersonal que corresponde al castellano *haber* en su uso impersonal: ~ *is*, ~ *are*, hay. *3* Ús. con otros verbos para dar fuerza a la frase: ~ *came a man*, vino un hombre. *4 interj.* ¡eh!, ¡toma!, ¡vaya!, ¡mira!
**thereabout(s** (-abauts) *adv.* por allí, cerca de allí. *2* cosa así, poco más o menos. *3* acerca de ello.
**thereafter** (-æ·ftø$^r$) *adv.* después de esto, de allí en adelante. *2* por lo tanto, en consecuencia.
**thereat** (æ·t) *adv.* allí, ahí. *2* en esto, entonces.
**thereby** (-bai) *adv.* en relación con esto. *2* así, de este modo; en consecuencia de esto.
**therefore** (-fo$^r$) *adv.* por esto, por ende, por lo tanto, por consiguiente.
**therefrom** (-fram) *adv.* de allí, de allá, de eso, de aquello.
**therein** (-i·n) *adv.* en esto, en eso, en aquello.
**thereinafter** (-inæ·ftø$^r$) *adv.* más adelante [en un escrito o discurso].

**thereof** (-a·v) *adv.* de eso, de aquello, de ello.
**thereon** (-a·n) *adv.* encima, encima de ello, sobre ello. *2* luego, en seguida.
**Theresa** (tøre·sa) *n. pr.* Teresa.
**thereto** (de$^r$tu·) *adv.* a aquello, a ello. *2* además.
**theretofore** (de$^r$tufo·$^r$) *adv.* hasta entonces.
**thereunder** (-o·ndø$^r$) *adv.* debajo de eso o ello. *2* menos de o que.
**thereunto** (-øntu·) *adv.* THERETO.
**thereupon** (-øpo·n) *adv.* por lo tanto, por consiguiente. *2* inmediatamente, al instante, en esto.
**therewithal** (-widol) *adv.* además. *2* al mismo tiempo.
**thermæ** (zø$^r$mi) *s. pl.* termas [de los romanos].
**thermal** (zø·$^r$mal) *adj.* termal. *2* térmico.
**thermic** (zø·$^r$mik) *adj.* térmico.
**thermionic** (zø$^r$mia·nik) *adj.* FÍS. termiónico.
**thermobarometer** (zø$^r$møbara·mitø$^r$) *s.* termobarómetro.
**thermocautery** (-ko·tøri) *s.* CIR. termocauterio.
**thermodynamics** (-dainæ·miks) *s.* termodinámica.
**thermoelectricity** (-ilektri·siti) *s.* termoelectricidad.
**thermology** (zø$^r$ma·lodŷi) *s.* termología.
**thermometer** (zø$^r$ma·mitø$^r$) *s.* termómetro.
**thermometry** (zø$^r$ma·metri) *s.* termometría.
**thermonuclear** (zermoniu·klia$^r$) *adj.* termonuclear.
**Thermopylæ** (zø$^r$ma·pilɪ) *s. pl.* GEOGR. Termópilas.
**thermos bottle** o **flask** (zø·$^r$mos) *s.* botella termos.
**thermosiphon** (zø$^r$møsai·føn) *s.* termosifón.
**thermostat** (zø·$^r$møstæt) *s.* termostato.
**thesaurus** (zeso·røs) *s.* tesauro, diccionario.
**these** (ðiš) *adj. y pron. pl.* de THIS.
**Theseus** (zɪ·siøs) *n. pr.* MIT. Teseo.
**thesis** (zɪ·sis), *pl.* **-ses** (-siš) *s.* tesis.
**Thespis** (ze·spis) *n. pr.* MIT. Tespis.
**Thessalonica** (zesalonai·ka) *n. pr.* GEOGR. Tesalónica, Salónica.
**Thessaly** (ze·sali) *n. pr.* GEOGR. Tesalia.
**theurgist** (zɪ·ø$^r$dŷist) *s.* teúrgo.
**theurgy** (-i) *s.* teúrgia.
**thews** (zɪuš) *s.* músculos, fuerza muscular. *2* energía, resolución.
**they** (ðei) *pron. pl.* de HE, SHE, IT: ellos, ellas [en nominativo].
**Thibetan** (zi·betan) *adj.-s.* tibetano.
**thick** (zik) *adj.* espeso, grueso: *two inches* ~, de dos pulgadas de grueso. *2* espeso, tupido, apretado, denso, consistente. *3* lleno: ~ *with*, lleno de. *4* seguido, continuado. *5* turbio; neblinoso, brumoso. *6* torpe, obtuso. *7* ronco, estropajoso, confuso [voz, pronunciación]. *8* duro [de oído]. *9* íntimo, muy amigo. *10 adv.* THICKLY. *11 s.* grueso, espesor. *12 the* ~ *of*, lo más espeso, denso, duro, reñido, etc. de. *13 through* ~ *and thin*, a pesar de todo, incondicionalmente.
**thick-bodied** *adj.* grueso, corpulento.
**thicken (to)** (zi·køn) *tr.* espesar, engrosar, reforzar. *2 intr.* espesarse, engrosarse, complicarse, enturbiarse.
**thickener** (zi·kønø$^r$) *s.* sustancia espesativa.
**thicket** (zi·kit) *s.* soto, espesura, maleza, matorral.
**thick-headed** *adj.* estúpido; testarudo.
**thick-knee** *s.* ORN. alcaraván.
**thick-lipped** *adj.* bezudo.
**thickly** (zi·kli) *adv.* espesamente, densamente: ~ *settled*, muy poblado. *2* seguido, seguidamente. *3* roncamente, estropajosamente.
**thick-necked** *adj.* cervigudo, de cuello grueso.

**thickness** (zi·knis) *s.* espesor, grueso. 2 densidad, consistencia. 3 parte más gruesa, espesa, etc. 4 capa [de una materia].

**thick-set** *adj.* denso, espeso. 2 grueso, rechoncho.

**thick-skinned** *adj.* paquidermo. 2 duro, insensible; de cara dura.

**thick-skulled** *adj.* lerdo, torpe, duro de mollera.

**thief** (zif) *s.* ladrón, ratero.

**thieve (to)** (zi·v) *intr.* robar, hurtar.

**thievery** (-øri) *s.* robo, latrocinio.

**thievish** (-ish) *adj.* ladrón, rapaz. 2 furtivo.

**thigh** (zai) *s.* ANAT. muslo.

**thighbone** (-boun) *s.* ANAT. fémur.

**thill** (zil) *s.* limonera [de carruaje].

**thimble** (zi·mbøl) *s.* dedal. 2 MEC. anillo de guía, refuerzo, etc. 3 BOT. digital.

**thin** (zin) *s.* delgado, fino, tenue. 2 flaco, enjuto. 3 claro, ralo. 4 claro, flojo, aguado. 5 raro, enrarecido. 6 ligero, transparente. 7 escaso, corto. 8 flaco, pobre [argumento, etc.]. 9 débil, agudo [voz, sonido].

**thin (to)** *tr.* adelgazar. 2 aclarar [hacer menos espeso]; enrarecer. 3 aguar. 4 disminuir. 5 *intr.* adelgazarse. 6 aclararse [hacerse menos espeso], ralear, hacerse escaso. ¶ Pret. y p. p.: *thinned;* ger.: *-nning.*

**thine** (ðain) *pron.* (el) tuyo, (la) tuya, (los) tuyos, (las) tuyas. 2 *adj.* tu, tus.

**thing** (zing) *s.* cosa; lo: *for one* ~, entre otras cosas; *the right* ~, lo justo, lo debido; *the* ~, la cuestión, lo importante, lo conveniente, lo elegante, etc. 2 fam. persona; *poor* ~*!*, ¡pobre!, ¡pobrecito! 3 *pl.* cosas, efectos, bártulos.

**think (to)** (zink) *tr.-intr.* pensar [en todos sus sentidos, menos en el de echar pienso a]: *to* ~ *fit, good* o *proper,* tener a bien, estimar conveniente: *to* ~ *nothing of,* tener en poco, no dar importancia a; creer fácil; *to* ~ *of,* pensar en; acordarse de; *to* ~ *over,* pensar bien [una cosa]; *to* ~ *well* o *ill of,* tener en buen o mal concepto; *I* ~ *so,* eso creo yo. 2 *tr.* juzgar, conceptuar, creer. 3 discurrir, idear. ¶ Pret. y p. p.: *thought.*

**thinkable** (-abøl) *adj.* pensable, concebible.

**thinker** (-ø<sup>r</sup>) *s.* pensador.

**thinking** (-ing) *s.* pensamiento, reflexión, pensar: *way of* ~, manera de pensar. 2 juicio, concepto.

**thinly** (zi·nli) *adv.* delgadamente. 2 flacamente. 3 esparcidamente, con poca densidad o espesor.

**third** (zø<sup>r</sup>d) *adj.-s.* tercero, tercera. 2 tres [día]. 3 *s.* tercio [tercera parte]. 4 MÚS., AUTO. tercera.

**third-class** *adj.* de tercera clase, de tercera.

**thirdly** (-li) *adv.* en tercer lugar.

**thirst** (zø<sup>r</sup>st) *s.* sed.

**thirst (to)** *intr.* tener o padecer sed. 2 *to* ~ *after* o *for,* tener sed o ansia de. 3 *tr.* hacer padecer sed.

**thirsty** (-i) *adj.* sediento: *to be* ~, tener sed.

**thirteen** (zø<sup>r</sup>ti·n) *adj.-s.* trece.

**thirteenth** (-nz) *adj.* decimotercio. 2 trezavo. 3 trece.

**thirtieth** (zø·<sup>r</sup>tiiz) *adj.* trigésimo. 2 treinta.

**thirty** (zø·<sup>r</sup>ti) *adj.-s.* treinta.

**this** (ðis) *adj.* este, está. 2 *pron.* éste, ésta, esto.

**thistle** (zi·søl) *s.* BOT. cardo. 2 ORN. ~ *finch,* jilguero. 3 (con may.) orden escocesa del Cardo.

**thistledown** (-daun) *s.* papo del cardo.

**thistly** (zi·sli) *adj.* lleno de cardos. 2 espinoso.

**thither** (di·ðø<sup>r</sup>) *adv.* allá, hacia allá: *hither and* ~, acá y allá. 2 *adj.* de allá, de la parte de allá.

**tho'** (ðou) *conj.* abr. de THOUGH.

**thole** (zoul), **tholepin** (-pin) *s.* MAR. escálamo, tolete.

**Thomas** (ta·mas) *n. pr.* Tomás.

**thomism** (tou·mišm) *s.* tomismo.

**thong** (zang) *s.* correa, tira de cuero, \*guasca.

**thoracic** (zoræ·sik) *adj.* torácico.

**thorax** (zo·ræks) *s.* ANAT., ZOOL. tórax.

**thorium** (zo·riøm) *s.* QUÍM. torio.

**thorn** (zo<sup>r</sup>n) *s.* espina, púa, pincho. 2 fig. espina, pesadumbre: *to be on thorns,* estar en ascuas. 3 BOT. espino. 4 BOT. abrojo. 5 ~ *apple,* estramonio.

**thornless** (zo·<sup>r</sup>nlis) *adj.* sin espinas.

**thorny** (-i) *adj.* espinoso, lleno de espinas. 2 espinoso, arduo.

**thorough** (zø·rou) *adj.* completo, total, acabado. 2 consumado, perfecto. 3 esmerado, cuidadoso. 4 MÚS. ~ *bass,* bajo continuo.

**thoroughbred** (-bred) *adj.* de pura raza. 2 bien nacido, distinguido. 3 *s.* animal de pura raza. 4 pers. bien nacida, distinguida.

**thoroughfare** (-fe<sup>r</sup>) *s.* vía pública, pasaje; camino. 2 paso, tránsito: *no* ~, prohibido el paso.

**thoroughgoing** (-gouing) *adj.* completo, esmerado, celoso, acérrimo.

**thoroughly** (-li) *adv.* completamente. 2 concienzudamente, a fondo.

**those** (ðous) *adj.-pron. pl.* de THAT: esos, esas, aquellos, aquellas; los, las: ~ *which,* ~ *who,* los o las que, quienes.

**thou** (ðau) *pron.* tú. | Úsase sólo en poesía o en lenguaje dialectal.

**thou (to)** *tr.* tutear.

**though** (dou) *conj.* aunque, aun cuando, si bien; sin embargo. 2 *as* ~, como si.

**thought** (zot) *pret.* y *p. p.* de TO THINK. 2 *s.* pensamiento [acción de pensar; cosa pensada; idea, intención]: ~ *reading,* adivinación del pensamiento; *on second* ~, pensándolo mejor. 3 consideración, atención, cuidado: *want of* ~, inadvertencia, descuido. 4 un poco, algo.

**thoughtful** (-ful) *adj.* reflexivo, meditativo. 2 pensativo, meditabundo. 3 atento, considerado. 4 solícito, cuidadoso. 5 previsor.

**thoughtless** (-lis) *adj.* irreflexivo, atolondrado, descuidado, incauto. 2 impróvido.

**thoughtlessness** (-nis) *s.* irreflexión, ligereza, indiscreción. 2 descuido, inadvertencia.

**thousand** (zau·sand) *adj.* mil. 2 *s.* mil, millar: *a* ~, *one* ~, mil.

**thousandth** (-z) *adj.-s.* milésimo. 2 *s.* milésima.

**Thrace** (zres) *n. pr.* GEOGR. Tracia.

**thrall** (zrol) *s.* siervo, esclavo. 2 esclavitud, servidumbre.

**thrall (to)** *tr.* esclavizar, avasallar.

**thral(l)dom** (-døm) *s.* esclavitud, servidumbre.

**thrash (to)** (zræsh) *tr.-intr.* AGR. trillar, desgranar: fig. *to* ~ *out a matter,* ventilar un asunto. 2 *tr.* golpear; apalizar; derrotar. 3 *intr.* revolcarse, agitarse.

**thrasher** (-ø<sup>r</sup>) *s.* trillador, desgranador. 2 trilladora; máquina de desgranar. 3 apalizador. 4 ORN. malvís americano.

**thrashing** (-ing) *s.* trilla, desgranar: ~ *floor,* era. 2 zurra, paliza.

**thread** (zred) *s.* hilo: *to hang on a* ~, pender de un hilo. 2 fibra, hebra, filamento. 3 MEC. filete [de rosca].

**thread (to)** *tr.* enhebrar, enhilar, ensartar. 2 pasar o hacer pasar por o entre. 3 MEC. aterrajar, labrar la rosca de [un tornillo]. 4 *intr.* pasar, correr, deslizarse.

**threadbare** (-be<sup>r</sup>) *adj.* raído, gastado. 2 fig. manido, trillado, gastado.

**threadworm** (-wøᵣm) *s.* lombriz intestinal.
**threat** (zret) *s.* amenaza. 2 amago.
**threaten (to)** (zre·tøn) *tr.-intr.* amenazar. 2 amagar.
**threatening** (-ing) *s.* amenaza. 2 *adj.* amenazador.
**three** (zrɪ) *adj.-s.* tres: ~ *o'clock*, las tres.
**three-colo(u)r** *adj.* tricolor; tricromo.
**three-cornered** *adj.* triangular. 2 de tres picos.
**three-decker** *s.* navío de tres puentes. 2 construcción de tres pisos. 3 novela muy larga.
**threefold** (-fould) *adj.* triplo, triple. 2 *adv.* tres veces más.
**three-legged** *adj.* de tres pies.
**threepenny** (zre·peni) *adj.* de a tres peniques, barato, despreciable.
**three-phase** *adj.* ELECT. trifásico.
**three-ply** *adj.* triple. 2 de tres capas.
**three R's** (aᵣš) *s. pl.* lectura, escritura y aritmética.
**threescore** (zrɪ·skoᵣ) *adj.-s.* sesenta.
**three-way** *adj.* de tres pasos, vías o direcciones.
**threnody** (zre·nodi) *s.* treno.
**thresh (to)** (zresh) *tr.-intr.* TO THRASH.
**thresher** (-øᵣ) *s.* TRASHER 1, 2 y 3.
**threshing** (-ing) *s.* THRASHING.
**threshold** (zre·should) *s.* umbral.
**threw** (zru) *pret.* de THROW.
**thrice** (zrais) *adv.* tres veces.
**thrift** (zrift) *s.* economía, frugalidad. 2 medro, crecimiento, desarrollo vigoroso.
**thriftiness** (-inis) *s.* economía, frugalidad.
**thriftless** (-lis) *adj.* manirroto, impróvido.
**thrifty** (-i) *adj.* económico, ahorrativo, frugal. 2 industrioso. 3 próspero, floreciente.
**thrill** (zril) *s.* temblor, estremecimiento, escalofrío, emoción.
**thrill (to)** *tr.* hacer temblar o estremecer, dar escalofríos, emocionar. 2 *intr.* temblar, estremecerse.
**thriller** (-øᵣ) *s.* cuento o drama espeluznante.
**thrilling** (-ing) *adj.* emocionante; espeluznante.
**thrive** (zraiv) *intr.* crecer, engordar. 2 medrar, prosperar. ¶ Pret.: *throve* o *thrived*; p. p.: *thrived* o *thriven*.
**thriving** (-ing) *adj.* próspero, floreciente.
**thro'** (zru·) *adv.* y *prep.* abrev. de THROUGH.
**throat** (zrout) *s.* garganta, cuello, gaznate: *to clear one's* ~, carraspear; *to cut the* ~ *of*, degollar. 2 fig. garganta, angostamiento. 3 fig. boca, entrada, paso. 5 ARQ. goterón.
**throatband** (-bænd) *s.* ahogadero [de brida].
**throatwort** (-uøᵣt) *s.* BOT. campanilla.
**throaty** (-i) *adj.* gutural, ronco.
**throb** (zrab) *s.* latido, palpitación, vibración.
**throb (to)** *intr.* latir, pulsar, palpitar, vibrar. ¶ Pret. y p. p.: *throbbed;* ger.: *-bbing.*
**throe** (zrou) *s.* angustia, agonía, dolor: *throes of childbirth*, dolores del parto.
**thrombosis** (zrambou·sis) *s.* MED. trombosis.
**throne** (zrou·n) *s.* trono.
**throne (to)** *tr.* entronizar, exaltar. 2 *intr.* reinar.
**throng** (zrong) *s.* muchedumbre, gentío, tropel.
**throng (to)** *intr.* apiñarse, agolparse. 2 *tr.* apiñar, apretar. 3 atestar, llenar.
**throstle** (zra·søl) *s.* ORN. zorzal.
**throttle** (zra·tøl) *s.* garganta, gaznate. 2 gollete [de botella]. 3 MEC. válvula reguladora; acelerador [de automóvil].
**throttle (to)** *tr.* ahogar, estrangular. 2 MEC. *to* ~ *down*, disminuir la marcha. 3 *intr.* ahogarse.
**through** (zru) *prep.* por, a lo largo de, a través de, por entre. 2 por medio o conducto de, gracias a,

a causa de. 3 *adv.* de un lado a otro, de parte a parte; de cabo a cabo, hasta el fin, completamente. 4 directamente [sin hacer paradas]. 5 *adj.* directo [tren, billete]. 6 de paso. 7 *to be* ~ *with*, haber acabado con, no querer ocuparse más de.
**throughout** (-aut) *prep.* por todo, en todo, durante todo, a lo largo de. 2 *adv.* de parte a parte; por todas partes; en todo; desde el principio hasta el fin.
**throve** (zrouv) *pret.* de TO TRIVE.
**throw** (zrou) *s.* lanzamiento, tiro, tirada, echada. 2 lance [de dados], jugada. 3 MEC. carrera, embolada.
**throw (to)** *tr.* lanzar, tirar, arrojar, echar, despedir. 2 derribar. 3 impeler, empujar. 4 despojarse de, soltar, perder. 5 poner [en un estado, condición, etc.]. 6 disponer, formar, expresar. 7 torcer [hilo]. 8 proyectar [luz, sombra]. 9 parir [la coneja, etc.]. 10 tender [un puente]. 11 *to* ~ *about*, esparcir. 12 *to* ~ *away*, tirar, desechar; desperdiciar. 13 *to* ~ *back*, devolver; replicar, rechazar. 14 *to* ~ *down*, derribar; echar por tierra. 15 *to* ~ *in*, intercalar, incluir; añadir, dar de más. 16 *to* ~ *off*, quitarse, despojarse de; improvisar [versos, discursos, etc.]. 17 *to* ~ *open*, abrir de par en par. 18 *to* ~ *out*, echar fuera; proferir, emitir; esparcir, exhalar. 19 *to* ~ *over*, echar por la borda, abandonar. 20 ~ *up*, echar al aire; elevar, levantar; abandonar, renunciar; construir precipitadamente; fam. vomitar.
    21 *intr.* jugar a los dados. 22 fam. *to* ~ *up*, vomitar.
    ¶ Pret.: *threw*; p. p.: *thrown*.
**throwback** (-bæk) *s.* retroceso. 2 BIOL. reversión, atavismo. 3 CINEM. escena retrospectiva.
**thrown** (-n) *p. p.* de TO THROW.
**thrum** (zrøm) *s.* TEJ. cadillos. 2 fleco, borla. 3 hilo basto. 4 tecleo, rasgueo, ruido monótono.
**thrum (to)** *tr.* teclear, rasguear, producir un ruido monótono en. 2 *intr.* sonar monótonamente. ¶ Pret. y p. p.: *thrummed*; ger.: *-mming*.
**thrush** (zrøsh) *s.* ORN. tordo; zorzal; malvís.
**thrust** (zrøst) *pret.* y *p. p.* de TO THRUST. 2 golpe de punta, estocada, lanzada, puñalada, cornada. 3 empujón. 4 arremetida. 5 MEC., ARQ. empuje.
**thrust (to)** *tr.* empujar, impeler: *to* ~ *aside*, rechazar, desechar. 2 extender [sus ramas, raíces, etc.]. 3 meter, introducir, hincar, clavar. 4 *to* ~ *out*, echar fuera, sacar. 5 *to* ~ *upon*, imponer, hacer aceptar. 6 *intr.* meterse, introducirse, abrirse paso. 7 empujar, apiñarse. 8 *to* ~ *at*, pinchar, tirar estocadas, dar cuchilladas, etc., a. ¶ Pret. y p. p.: *thrust*.
**thud** (zød) *s.* porrazo. 2 baque, golpe sordo.
**thud (to)** *intr.* moverse o golpear con golpe sordo. ¶ Pret. y p. p.: *thudded;* ger.: *-dding*.
**thuja** (zu·dỹa) *s.* BOT. tuya.
**thumb** (zøm) *s.* pulgar: ~ *nut*, tuerca de mariposa; *under the* ~ *of*, bajo la férula de.
**thumb (to)** *tr.* hojear [con el pulgar]. 2 manejar, tocar, ejecutar torpemente, sin arte.
**thumbnail** (-neil) *s.* uña del pulgar.
**thumbscrew** (-cru) *s.* tuerca o tornillo de cabeza prismática o moleteada. 2 empulgueras.
**thumbtack** (-tæk) *s.* chinche [clavito].
**thump** (zømp) *s.* golpe, porrazo, baque.
**thump (to)** *tr.-intr.* golpear, aporrear. 2 *tr.* meter, encasquetar [a golpes]. 3 *intr.* latir fuerte, dar porrazos. 5 andar con pasos resonantes.
**thumping** (-ing) *adj.* fam. pesado, enorme.

**thunder** (zø·ndø<sup>r</sup>) s. trueno. 2 estruendo. 3 fig. rayo, excomunión.

**thunder (to)** *impers.-intr.* tronar. 2 retumbar, moverse o avanzar con estrépito. 3 *tr.* lanzar, fulminar [censuras, excomuniones, etc.]. 4 expresar con aplausos, estrépito, etc.

**thunderbolt** (-boult) s. rayo, centella. 2 fulminación, censura. 3 piedra de rayo.

**thunderclap** (-klæp) s. trueno, estallido.

**thundering** (-ing) *adj.* atronador; estrepitoso. 2 fam. enorme, extraordinario.

**thundershower** (-shouø<sup>r</sup>) s. chubasco con truenos.

**thunderstorm** (-sto<sup>r</sup>m) s. tronada.

**thunderstruck** (-strøk) *adj.* aturdido, atónito, estupefacto.

**thurible** (ziu·ribøl) s. turíbulo.

**thurifer** (-fø<sup>r</sup>) s. turiferario.

**Thuringia** (ziuri·indẙia) *n. pr.* GEOGR. Turingia.

**Thursday** (zø·<sup>r</sup>šdi) s. jueves.

**thus** (ðøs) *adv.* así, tal, de este modo. 2 hasta este punto, tanto, tan: ~ *far*, hasta aquí, hasta ahora.

**thuya** (zu·ya) s. BOT. tuya.

**thwack** (zuæk) s. golpe, trastazo.

**thwack (to)** *tr.* golpear, pegar, zurrar.

**thwart** (zuø<sup>r</sup>t) s. MAR. banco de bogar. 2 *adj.* transversal, atravesado, oblicuo.

**thwart (to)** *tr.* desbaratar, frustrar, contrariar, contrarrestar.

**thy** (ðai) *adj. pos.* tu, tus. | Úsase con THOU.

**thyme** (taim) s. BOT. tomillo.

**thymelaeaceous** (taimiliei·shøs) *adj.* BOT. timeleáceo.

**thymol** (tai·moul) s. QUÍM. timol.

**thymus** (tai·møs) s. ANAT. timo [glándula].

**thyroid** (zai·roid) *adj.-s.* ANAT. tiroides. 2 *adj.* tiroideo.

**thyrse** (zø<sup>r</sup>s) s. BOT. tirso.

**thyrsus** (zø·<sup>r</sup>søs) s. MIT., BOT. tirso.

**thyself** (ðai·self) *pron.* tú mismo, ti mismo. | Úsase con THOU.

**tiara** (taie·ra o tia·ra) s. tiara. 2 diadema.

**Tibetan** (tibe·tan) *adj.-s.* tibetano.

**tibia** (ti·bia), *pl.* **-ae** (-i) o **-as** s. ANAT., MÚS. tibia.

**tic** (tik) s. MED. tic.

**tick** (tik) s. ZOOL. garrapata. 2 tela de colchón o almohada; cutí. 3 tictac; latido; clic. 4 fig. momento, segundo. 5 marca, señal. 6 fam. *to buy on* ~, comprar al fiado.

**tick (to)** *intr.* hacer tictac; hacer un clic; latir [el corazón]. 2 *tr.* marcar con señales. 3 señalar, marcar [el reloj, un taxímetro, etc.].

**ticker** (-ø<sup>r</sup>) s. teletipo.

**ticket** (ti·køt) s. billete, boleto, entrada, localidad, papeleta, ticket: ~ *office*, despacho de billetes o localidades; ~ *of leave*, (Ingl.) libertad condicional. 2 marbete, etiqueta. 3 POL. (E.U.) candidatura [lista]; programa.

**ticket (to)** *tr.* rotular, marcar.

**ticking** (ti·king) s. terliz, cutí.

**tickle** (ti·køl) s. cosquillas. 2 toque ligero.

**tickle (to)** *tr.* hacer cosquillas, cosquillear. 2 agradar, halagar; divertir. 3 coger truchas con la mano. 4 *intr.* tener cosquillas.

**tickler** (ti·klø<sup>r</sup>) s. el o lo que hace cosquillas. 2 fam. problema difícil.

**ticklish** (-ish) *adj.* cosquilloso. 2 picajoso, susceptible. 3 inestable, variable. 4 delicado, crítico.

**tick-tack** (tik-tak) s. tictac.

**tidal** (tai·dal) *adj.* de la marea o de la corriente: ~ *wave*, aguaje, ola de marea; fig. ola, marejada, conmoción popular. 2 periódico.

**tidbit** (ti·dbit) s. TITBIT.

**tide** (taid) s. marea; corriente: *high* o *full* ~, pleamar; *ebb* o *low* ~, bajamar; *to go with the* ~, seguir la corriente. 2 flujo [de la marea]. 3 curso, marcha [de las cosas]. 4 época, tiempo, ocasión. 5 *pl.* aguas [mareas].

**tide (to)** *tr.-intr.* llevar, ir, flotar, navegar [con la marea]. 2 *to* ~ *over*, ayudar; superar [una dificultad].

**tidemark** (-ma<sup>r</sup>k) s. señal que deja la marea.

**tidesman** (-smæn) s. aduanero de puerto.

**tidewater** (-wotø<sup>r</sup>) s. aguaje; agua que inunda la playa en la marea alta. 2 playa, litoral.

**tideway** (-wei) s. canal de marea.

**tidiness** (tai·dinis) s. aseo, pulcritud, orden.

**tidings** (tai·dings) s. pl. noticias, nuevas.

**tidy** (tai·di) *adj.* aseado, limpio, pulcro, ordenado. 2 fam. regular [bastante grande]. 3 s. cubierta de respaldo. 4 cajón para los retazos.

**tidy (to)** *tr.* asear, arreglar, poner en orden.

**tie** (tai) s. cinta, cordón, etc., para atar. 2 lazo, nudo, atadura. 3 fig. lazo, vínculo. 4 corbata. 5 MÚS. ligadura. 6 ARQ. tirante. 7 FERROC. traviesa. 8 empate. 9 pl. zapatos bajos.

**tie (to)** *tr.* atar. 2 liar, ligar, anudar. 3 unir, enlazar. 4 hacer [un nudo o lazo]. 5 *to* ~ *down*, sujetar. 6 *to* ~ *up*, atar; liar, envolver; vincular [la propiedad]; impedir, obstruir. 7 *tr.-intr.* empatar. ¶ Pret. y p. p.: *tied;* ger.: *tying.*

**1) tier** (-ø<sup>r</sup>) s. atador. 2 banda, ligadura.

**2) tier** (ti<sup>r</sup>) s. fila, hilera [esp. cuando están unas sobre otras]; capa, tonga. 2 TEAT. fila de palcos.

**tier (to)** *tr.* disponer en hileras o capas.

**tierce** (ti<sup>r</sup>s) s. tercerola [barril]. 2 tercera [en los naipes]. 3 MÚS. tercera. 4 ESGR., LITURG. tercia.

**tiercet** (ti·<sup>r</sup>set) s. TERCET.

**tie-up** s. enlace, conexión. 2 contubernio. 3 paro, paralización; embotellamiento.

**tiff** (tif) s. enfado, enojo. 2 pique, disgusto, desavenencia. 3 traguito, sorbo.

**tiff (to)** *intr.* estar enojado, de mal humor. 2 reñir, desavenirse. 3 *tr.* pop. beber.

**tiffin** (ti·fin) s. almuerzo; colación.

**tige** (tiẙ) s. ARQ. fuste [de columna]. 2 BOT. tallo.

**tiger** (tai·gø<sup>r</sup>) s. ZOOL. tigre. 2 ZOOL. ~ *cat*, gato cerval; ocelote. 3 BOT. ~ *flower*, flor de la maravilla; ~ *lily*, tigridia.

**tigerish** (-ish) *adj.* de tigre. 2 feroz, sanguinario.

**tight** (tait) s. bien cerrado, hermético, estanco. 2 tieso; firme; tirante. 3 apretado. 4 compacto. 5 ajustado, estrecho. 6 COM. retraído [dinero, mercado]. 7 listo, capaz. 8 duro, severo. 9 tacaño. 10 DEP. cerrado; igualado [juego]. 11 ~ *squeeze*, apuro, aprieto. 12 pop. borracho. 13 *adv.* apretadamente, firmemente, tiesamente.

**tighten** (to) (-øn) *tr.* apretar, estrechar. 2 estirar, atirantar, atiesar. 3 *intr.* apretarse; atirantarse.

**tight-fisted** *adj.* fam. agarrado, tacaño.

**tight-fitting** *adj.* muy ajustado.

**tightrope** (tai·troup) s. cuerda de volatinero.

**tights** (taits) s. pl. traje de malla [de los gimnastas, etc.].

**tigress** (tai·gris) s. f. tigresa.

**tigrish** (tai·grish) *adj.* TIGERISH.

**tike** (taik) s. TYKE.

**tilbury** (ti·lbøri) s. tilburí.

**tile** (tail) s. teja; losa, baldosa, azulejo: *to have a* ~ *loose*, fig. faltarle a uno un tornillo. 2 fam. sombrero de copa.

**tile (to)** *tr.* tejar. 2 embaldosar. 3 azulejar.

**tiler** (tai·lø<sup>r</sup>) s. tejero. 2 azulejero.

**tiliaceous** (tiliei·shøs) *adj.* BOT. tiliáceo.
**tiling** (tai·ling) *s.* tejado; embaldosado. *2* tejas, baldosas, azulejos.
**till** (til) *prep.* hasta. *2 conj.* hasta que. *3 s.* cajón o gaveta para el dinero.
**till (to)** *tr.-intr.* arar, labrar, cultivar.
**tillable** (ti·labøl) *adj.* arable, cultivable, labrantío.
**tillage** (ti·lidÿ) *s.* labranza, labor, cultivo.
**tiller** (ti·lø^r) *s.* labrador, agricultor. *2* MAR. caña [del timón]. *3* palanca, manija. *4* resalvo.
**tilt** (tilt) *s.* inclinación, ladeo; declive. *2* justa, torneo. *3* lanzada, golpe. *4* disputa. *5* toldo, entalamadura. *6 full ~*, a toda velocidad.
**tilt (to)** *tr.* inclinar, ladear. *2* verter, volcar. *3* dar lanzadas, acometer. *4* entoldar. *5 intr.* inclinarse, volcarse. *6* ajustar.
**tilter** (ti·ltø^r) *s.* justador. *2* vertedor de carbón.
**tilth** (tilz) *s.* labranza, cultivo. *2* tierra cultivada.
**tilting** (ti·lting) *s.* inclinación, ladeo. *2* justa, torneo.
**tiltyard** (ti·ltya^rd) *s.* liza, lugar de una justa.
**Tim** (tim) *n. pr. dim.* de TIMOTHY.
**timbal** (ti·mbal) *s.* MÚS. timbal.
**timbale** *s.* COC. timbal.
**timber** (-ø^r) *s.* madera [de construcción o carpintería], maderaje, maderamen. *2* madero, viga. *3* MAR. cuaderna. *4* bosque, árboles maderables.
**timber (to)** *tr.* enmaderar.
**timberland** (-lænd) *s.* tierra de bosques maderables.
**timbre** (ti·mbø^r) *s.* FONÉT., MÚS., BLAS. timbre.
**timbrel** (ti·mbrøl) *s.* MÚS. pandero, pandereta.
**time** (taim) *s.* tiempo. | No tiene el sentido de estado de la atmósfera: *~ clock*, reloj registrador; *to have a good ~*, pasarlo bien; divertirse; *at the same ~*, al mismo tiempo; sin embargo; *behind ~*, atrasado, retrasado, *behind the times*, anticuado; *for the ~ being*, por ahora, de momento; *in good ~*, a tiempo; pronto; *in no ~*, en un santiamén; *in ~*, a tiempo; con el tiempo; *in the course of ~*, andando el tiempo; *out of ~*, fuera de tiempo, de sazón. *2* hora, momento; *~ zone*, GEOGR. huso horario; *what ~ is it?*, ¿qué hora es? *3* duración del servicio militar; de una condena, etc.: *to do ~*, cumplir condena. *4* término del embarazo; de un período de trabajo, etc. *5* COM. prórroga, plazo. *6* vez: *at a ~*, de una vez; *at no ~*, nunca: *at times*, a veces; *from ~ to ~*, de vez en cuando; *~ about*, alternadamente. *7* MÚS. compás: *in ~*, a compás; *out of ~*, fuera de compás.
**time (to)** *tr.* escoger el momento: *well timed*, oportuno. *2* regular, poner a la hora. *3* cronometrar. *4* MÚS. llevar el tiempo a compás.
**timeful** (-ful) *adj.* oportuno.
**time-hono(u)red** *adj.* de reputación, consagrado, tradicional.
**timekeeper** (-kipø^r) *s.* reloj, cronómetro. *2* marcador de tiempo. *3* cronometrador.
**timeless** (-lis) *adj.* eterno, interminable. *2* independiente del tiempo.
**timely** (-li) *adv.* oportunamente. *2 adj.* oportuno, conveniente.
**timepiece** (-pis) *s.* reloj, cronómetro.
**timer** (-ø^r) *s.* contador de tiempo. *2* MEC. distribuidor del encendido.
**timeserver** (-sø^rvo^r) *s.* persona acomodaticia, oportunista.
**timetable** (-teibøl) *s.* guía, horario, itinerario.
**timeworn** (-uøn) *adj.* viejo, gastado. *2* anticuado.
**timid** (ti·mid) *adj.* tímido. *2* medroso.

**timidity** (timi·diti) *s.* timidez.
**timocracy** (taima·krasi) *s.* timocracia.
**timorous** (ti·mørøs) *adj.* temeroso, medroso.
**Timothy** (ti·mozi) *n. pr.* Timoteo.
**timpano** (ti·mpanou), *pl.* **-ni** (-ni) *s.* MÚS. tímpano.
**tin** (tin) *s.* estaño. *2* lata, hojalata: *~ plate*, hojalata. *3* lata, bote. *4* pop. dinero.
**tin (to)** *tr.* estañar, cubrir con estaño. *2* enlatar. | Pret. y p. p.: *tinned;* ger.: *-nning.*
**tinctorial** (tinkto·rial) *adj.* tintóreo.
**tincture** (ti·nkchø^r) *s.* tintura, color, tinte. *2* FARM. tintura. *3* fig. tinte, algo.
**tincture (to)** *tr.* teñir, colorar, tinturar.
**tinder** (ti·ndø^r) *s.* yesca, mecha [para encender].
**tinderbox** (-baks) *s.* yesquero.
**tine** (tain) *s.* púa, punta, diente, gajo.
**tinea** (ti·nia) *s.* MED. tiña.
**ting** (ting) *s.* tintín.
**ting (to)** *tr.* hacer tintinear. *2 intr.* tintinear.
**ting-a-ling** (tingøli·ng) *s.* tilín, tilín.
**tinge** (tindÿ) *s.* tinte, matiz. *2* punta, algo, dejo.
**tinge (to)** *tr.* matizar; dar un sabor, cualidad, etc., a. ¶ Ger.: *tingeing* *-ging.*
**tingle** (ti·ngøl) *s.* hormigueo, picazón. *2* estremecimiento, vibración.
**tingle (to)** *intr.* hormiguear, picar. *2* estremecerse, vibrar. *3* sonar en los oídos; zumbar [los oídos]. *4 tr.* producir hormigueo, picar. *5* estremecer, hacer vibrar.
**tinker** (ti·nkø^r) *s.* calderero remendón. *2* chapucero. *3* remiendo, chapucería.
**tinker (to)** *tr.-intr.* remendar vasijas de metal. *2* chafallar.
**tinkle** (ti·nkøl) *s.* tintineo.
**tinkle (to)** *intr.* retiñir, tintinear. *2 tr.* hacer sonar o retiñir.
**tinman** (ti·nmæn) *s.* TINSMITH.
**tinned** (tind) *adj.* estañado. *2* enlatado.
**tinny** (ti·ni) *adj.* de estaño. *2* de hojalata, de relumbrón. *3* que sabe a hojalata [conserva].
**tinsel** (ti·nsøl) *s.* TEJ. lama [de oro o plata]. *2* oropel, talco, bricho. *3* fig. oropel, relumbrón.
**tinsel (to)** *tr.* adornar con oropel. ¶ Pret. y p. p.: *tinsel(l)ed;* ger.: *-l(l)ing.*
**tinsmith** (ti·nsmiz) *s.* hojalatero, estañero.
**tint** (tint) *s.* tinte, matiz. *2* media tinta.
**tint (to)** *tr.* teñir, colorar, matizar.
**tintinnabulation** (tintinabiulei·shøn) *s.* tintineo, campanilleo.
**tinware** (ti·nue^r) *s.* objetos de hojalata.
**tiny** (tai·ni) *adj.* pequeñito, chiquito, diminuto.
**tip** (tip) *s.* extremo, punta, ápice: *from ~ to toe*, de pies a cabeza. *2* casquillo, contera, herrete. *3* BILLAR. suela. *4* ZAP. puntera. *5* propina, gratificación. *6* soplo, aviso confidencial. *7* golpecito. *8* inclinación, vuelco.
**tip** *s.* inclinar, ladear, volcar, verter. *2* poner casquillo, contera, etc., a; guarnecer el extremo de. *3* dar propina a. *4* dar un soplo o aviso confidencial a. *5* dar un golpecito. *6 to ~ one's hat*, tocarse el sombrero. *7 intr.* inclinarse, ladearse, volcarse. | A veces con *over*. ¶ Pret. y p. p.: *tipped;* ger.: *-pping.*
**tipcart** (-ka^rt) *s.* carro de vuelco, volquete.
**tipcat** (-kæt) *s.* tala [juego].
**tippet** (ti·pet) *s.* palatina, esclavina.
**tipple** (ti·pøl) *s.* bebida, licor.
**tipple (to)** *intr.* beber, beborrotear, libar.
**tippler** (ti·plø^r) *s.* bebedor.
**tipstaff** (ti·pstaf) *s.* vara [de alguacil, etc.]. *2* alguacil.

**tipsy** (ti·psi) *adj.* achispado. *2* vacilante.
**tiptoe** (ti·ptou) *s.* punta del pie. *2 adv. on* ~, de puntillas; alerta; con expectación.
**tiptoe (to)** *intr.* andar de puntillas.
**tiptop** (-tap) *s.* lo más alto, lo mejor.
**tipula** (ti·piula) *s.* ENT. típula.
**tirade** (ti·reid) *s.* andanada, distriba, invectiva.
**tire** (tai[r]) *s.* CARR. llanta, calce: *pneumatic* ~, neumático; ~ *chain*, AUTO. cadena antideslizante.
**tire (to)** *tr.* cansar, fatigar. *2* aburrir, fastidiar. *3* poner llanta o neumático a. *4 intr.* cansarse, fatigarse, aburrirse.
**tired** (tai[r]d) *adj.* cansado, fatigado; aburrido: ~ *out*, muerto de cansancio.
**tireless** (tai·[r]lis) *adj.* incansable, infatigable.
**tiresome** (-søm) *adj.* cansado, pesado, fastidioso.
**tiring** (-ing) *adj.* cansado, pesado.
**Tirol** (ti·roul) *n. pr.* TYROL.
**'tis** (tiš) *contr.* de IT IS.
**tisane** (tiša·n) *s.* tisana.
**tissue** (ti·shu) *s.* tisú, gasa: ~ *paper*, papel de seda. *2* tejido [de mentiras, etc.]. *3* BIOL. tejido.
**tissue (to)** *tr.* tejer, entretejer.
**tit** (tit) *s.* ORN. paro. *2* pezón [de teta]. *3* ~ *for tat*, golpe por golpe.
**Titan** (tai·tan) *n. pr.* MIT. Titán.
**titanic** (taitæ·nik) *adj.* titánico.
**titanium** (taitei·niøm) *s.* QUÍM. titanio.
**titbit** (ti·tbit) *s.* golosina; trozo escogido.
**titer** (tai·tø[r]) *s.* TITRE.
**tithe** (taið) *s.* diezmo. *2* décima parte. *3* pizca.
**tithe (to)** *tr.* diezmar [pagar el diezmo de].
**tither** (-ø[r]) *s.* diezmero.
**titi** (titi·) *s.* ZOOL. tití.
**titillate (to)** (ti·tileit) *intr.* titilar. *2 tr.* cosquillear, excitar agradablemente.
**titivate (to)** (ti·tiveit) *tr.* ataviar, componer. *2 intr.* ataviarse, componerse.
**titlark** (ti·tla[r]k) *s.* ORN. pitpit.
**title** (tai·tøl) *s.* título. | No tiene el sentido de título en química: ~ *page*, portada [de un libro]. *2* DER. ~ *deed*, título de propiedad.
**title (to)** *tr.* titular, intitular, llamar. *2* conferir un título a.
**titling** (ti·tling) *s.* ORN. gorrión silvestre.
**titmouse** (ti·tmaus) *s.* ORN. paro.
**titrate (to)** (tai·treit o ti·treit) *tr.* QUÍM. titular.
**titre** (tai·tø[r]) *s.* QUÍM. título.
**titter** (ti·tø[r]) *s.* TITTERING.
**titter (to)** *intr.* reír con risa ahogada o disimulada.
**tittering** (-ing) *s.* risita, risa ahogada o disimulada.
**tittle** (ti·tøl) *s.* tilde, punto. *2* partícula, ápice.
**tittle-tattle** (-tætøl) *s.* charla, chismorreo.
**tittle-tattle (to)** *intr.* charlar, chismorrear.
**titular** (ti·chula[r]) *adj.* del título. *2* honorario, nominal. *3 adj.-s.* titular.
**Titus** (tai·tøs) *n. pr.* Tito.
**to** (tu) *adv.* hacia una posición o estado normal, de contacto, de reposo, etc.: *to come* ~, volver en sí; *to pull a door* ~, entornar una puerta. *2* ~ *and fro*, de un lado a otro, de acá para allá. *3 prep.* a, hacia, para, para con, en comparación con, por, de, en, hasta, etc.: *face* ~ *face*, cara a cara; ~ *the right*, hacia la izquierda; *duty* ~ *humanity*, deber para con la humanidad; *work* ~ *do*, trabajo por hacer; *doctor* ~ *the king*, médico del rey; *from house* ~ *house*, de casa en casa; ~ *the end*, hasta el fin; *a quarter* ~ *five*, las cinco menos cuarto; *I will have* ~ *go*, tendré que irme. *4 to es*

el signo del infinitivo, que generalmente no se traduce: ~ *err is human*, de humanos es errar.
**toad** (toud) *s.* ZOOL. sapo. *2 fig.* persona odiosa.
**toadeater** (-itø[r]) *s.* parásito, adulador servil.
**toadflax** (-flæks) *s.* BOT. linaria.
**toadstool** (-stul) *s.* BOT. hongo; hongo venenoso.
**toady** (-i) *s.* adulador servil.
**toady (to)** *tr.-intr.* adular servilmente.
**to-and-fro** *adj.* alternativo, de vaivén.
**toast** (toust) *s.* tostada, pan tostado: ~ *water*, agua panada. *2* brindis.
**toast (to)** *tr.* tostar. *2* brindar por. *3 intr.* tostarse. *4* calentarse. *5* brindar.
**toaster** (-ø[r]) *s.* tostador. *2* el que brinda.
**tobacco** (tøbæ·kou) *s.* tabaco: ~ *pipe*, pipa para fumar; ~ *pouch*, petaca.
**tobaccoism** (-išm) *s.* MED. tabaquismo.
**tobacconist** (tobæ·kønist) *s.* tabaquero, estanquero.
**tobacconize (to)** (tobæ·kønaiš) *tr.* impregnar de tabaco, fumigar con tabaco.
**toboggan** (tøba·gan) *s.* tobogán [carrito o asiento]. *2* descenso rápido [de precios, etc.].
**toboggan (to)** *intr.* deslizarse por un tobogán, por una pendiente. *2* caer rápidamente [los precios, etc.].
**Toby** (tou·bi) *n. pr.* Tobías.
**toccata** (tøka·ta) *s.* MÚS. tocata.
**tocology** (tøka·lodŷi) *s.* tocología.
**tocsin** (ta·ksin) *s.* campana o toque de rebato.
**today, to-day** (tu·dei) *adv.* hoy. *2* hoy en día, actualmente. *3 s.* el día de hoy, la actualidad.
**toddle** (ta·døl) *s.* paso corto y vacilante; pinitos.
**toddle (to)** *intr.* andar con paso corto y vacilante, hacer pinitos.
**toddler** (ta·dlø[r]) *s.* niño pequeño.
**toddy** (ta·di) *s.* vino de palmera. *2* ponche.
**to-do** (tu·du) *s.* ruido, bullicio, alboroto.
**toe** (tou) *s.* dedo del pie: *great* ~, dedo gordo del pie; *on one's toes*, alerta, despabilado. *2* uña, pesuño. *3* punta del pie, del calzado, de la media.
**toe (to)** *tr.* tocar con la punta del pie: *to* ~ *the line*, fig. obrar como se debe, andar derecho. *2* dar un puntapié a. *3* poner punta o puntera a. *4 intr. to* ~ *in*, andar con las puntas de los pies hacia adentro.
**toenail** (-neil) *s.* uña de un dedo del pie.
**toffee, toffy** (to·fi o ta·fi) *s.* TAFFY.
**tog** (tag) *s.* fam. prenda de vestir, trapo.
**tog (to)** *tr.* acicalar, componer. ¶ Pret. y p. p.: *togged;* ger.: *-gging*.
**toga** (tou·ga) *s.* toga [romana].
**together** (tugeðø[r]) *adv.* junto; juntos, reunidos, juntamente; de consumo, de acuerdo; uno con otro, unos con otros; *to get* ~, reunir, juntar; reunirse, juntarse; ponerse de acuerdo; *to hang* ~, tener coherencia; *to sew* ~, coser [unir cosiendo]; ~ *with*, junto con, a una con. *2* al mismo tiempo, simultáneamente. *3* sin interrupción, de seguida.
**toggle** (ta·gøl) *s.* MAR. cazonete. *2* fiador atravesado. *3* palanca acodillada.
**toil** (toil) *s.* trabajo, labor, esfuerzo, fatiga, sudor, afán. *2 pl.* red, lazo.
**toil (to)** *intr.* afanarse, esforzarse. *2* avanzar o moverse con esfuerzo.
**toilet** (toi·lit) *s.* acto de vestirse; tocado, peinado; aseo de la persona. *2* tocador; cuarto de baño; retrete: ~ *articles*, artículos de tocador; ~ *paper*, papel higiénico. *3* traje, atavío [de la mujer].
**toilful** (toi·lful) *adj.* laborioso, trabajoso.

**toilsome** (-søm) *adj.* laborioso, trabajoso, cansado, fatigoso, penoso.

**token** (tou·køn) *s.* señal, signo, indicio, síntoma, prueba, prenda, recuerdo: *as a* ~ *of*, en señal o en prenda de. *2* distintivo, rasgo característico. *3* moneda, ficha.

**Tokio, Tokyo** (tou·kiou) *n. pr.* GEOGR. Tokio.

**told** (tou·ld) *pret.* y *p. p.* de TO TELL.

**tolerable** (ta·lørabøl) *adj.* tolerable, soportable. *2* pasadero, mediano.

**tolerance** (ta·lørans) *s.* tolerancia.

**tolerant** (-ant) *adj.* tolerante.

**tolerate (to)** (-eit) *tr.* tolerar.

**toleration** (talørei·shøn) *s.* tolerancia [esp. en materia religiosa].

**toil** (tou·l) *s.* tañido o doble de campana. *2* peaje, pontazgo, derecho, tributo: ~ *bar*, ~ *gate*, barrera de peaje o pontazgo; ~ *call*, TELÉF. conferencia interurbana. *3* maquilla [del molinero]. *4* fig. número de bajas o víctimas [en una batalla, un siniestro, etc.].

**toll (to)** *tr.* tañer [la campana] acompasadamente; doblar por. *2 intr.* doblar, sonar [la campana]. *3 tr.-intr.* cobrar o pagar peaje, pontazgo, tributo, etc.

**tollable** (-abøl) *adj.* sujeto al pago de derecho o tributo.

**tollgate** (-geit) *s.* barrera de peaje o pontazgo.

**tollkeeper** (-kıpøʳ) *s.* peajero, pontazguero.

**tolu** (tolu·) *s.* bálsamo de Tolú.

**toluene** (ta·liuin) *s.* QUÍM. tolueno.

**Tom** (ta·m) *n. pr. abrev.* de THOMAS.

**tom** *s.* macho de algunos animales: ~ *cat*, gato.

**tomahawk** (ta·majok) *s.* hacha de guerra de los indios norteamericanos.

**tomato** (toma·tou o tomei·tou) *s.* BOT. tomate.

**tomb** (tum) *s.* tumba, sepulcro, mausoleo.

**tombola** (tam·bøla) *s.* tómbola.

**tomboy** (ta·mboi) *s.* muchacha retozona, traviesa.

**tombstone** (tu·mstoun) *s.* lápida o piedra sepulcral.

**tomcat** (ta·mkæt) *s.* ZOOL. gato.

**tomcod** (ta·mkad) *s.* ICT. pez parecido al bacalao.

**tome** (tou·m) *s.* tomo, volumen.

**tomentose** (tome·ntous) *adj.* tomentoso.

**tomentum** (-tøm) *s.* BOT. tomento.

**tomfool** (tamfu·l) *s.* necio, mentecato.

**tomfoolery** (-øri) *s.* tontería, necedad. *2* payasada.

**Tommy** (ta·mi) *n. pr. dim.* de THOMAS. *2 s.* (con min.) soldado inglés.

**tomorrow** o **to-morrow** (tuma·rou) *adv.* mañana. *2 s.* día de mañana.

**tomtit** (ta·mtit) *s.* ORN. paro.

**tom-tom** (ta·m tam) *s.* gong. *2* tam-tam.

**ton** (tøn) *s.* tonelada: *long* ~, tonelada de 2.240 libras (1.016 kg); *short* ~, tonelada de 2.000 libras (907 kg); *metric* ~, tonelada métrica.

**tonal** (tou·nal) *adj.* MÚS. tonal.

**tonality** (tounæ·liti) *s.* tonalidad.

**tone** (toun) *s.* sonido [vocal o musical]; voz: ~ *control*, RADIO regulación del sonido. *2* MÚS. tono [intervalo]. *3* tono, acento, entonación, tonillo. *4* PINT., MED. tono. *5* tono [energía; nivel moral; carácter dominante].

**tone (to)** *tr.* dar tono o un tono a. *2* modificar el tono o el color de: *to* ~ *down*, bajar el tono de; suavizar; *to* ~ *up*, elevar el tono de; entonar, vigorizar. *3* FOT. virar. *4 intr.* tomar un tono o color; armonizar [con].

**tongs** (tangs) *s. pl.* tenazas, tenacillas, pinzas, alicates.

**tongue** (tøng) *s.* ANAT. lengua; ~ *twister*, trabalenguas; *to hold one's* ~, callar. *2* palabra, habla; lengua, lenguaje. *3* lengua [de tierra, de fuego, etc.]. *4* hebijón. *5* badajo. *6* MÚS., CARP. lengüeta. *7* fiel [de balanza]. *8* lancha [de coche].

**tongue (to)** *tr.* lamer. *2* CARP. engargolar. *3 intr.* salir como una lengua. *4 tr.-intr.* MÚS. producir con la lengua.

**tongue-lashing** *s.* fam. reprensión áspera.

**tongueless** (-lis) *s.* sin lengua. *2* mudo, sin habla.

**tongue-tied** *adj.* que tiene impedimento en el habla. *2* mudo, cortado, tímido.

**tonic** (ta·nik) *adj.* tónico, tonificante. *2* MÚS., FONÉT., PROS. tónico. *3 s.* MED. tónico. *4* MÚS. tónica.

**tonicity** (touni·siti) *s.* tonicidad.

**tonight** o **to-night** (tunai·t) *s.* esta noche.

**tonish** (tou·nish) *adj.* elegante, a la moda.

**tonka bean** (ta·nka) *s.* BOT. haba tonca; sarapia.

**tonnage** (tø·nidÿ) *s.* tonelaje, arqueo. *2* tonelaje [derecho]. *3* peso en toneladas.

**tonsil** (ta·nsil) *s.* ANAT. tonsila, amígdala.

**tonsil(l)itis** (tansilai·tis) *s.* MED. amigdalitis.

**tonsorial** (tanso·rial) *adj.* barberil.

**tonsure** (ta·nshøʳ) *s.* tonsura.

**Tony** (tou·ni) *n. pr. dim.* de ANTHONY.

**too** (tu) *adv.* demasiado. *2* fam. mucho. *3* también, además. *4* ~ *many*, demasiados. *5* ~ *much*, demasiado. *6* *it is* ~ *bad*, es una lástima; ~ *bad!*, ¡qué lástima!

**took** (tuk) *pret.* de TO TAKE.

**tool** (tul) *s.* instrumento, herramienta, utensilio. *2* fig. instrumento [pers.].

**toot** (tut) *s.* sonido de trompa; bocinazo; silbido, pitido.

**toot (to)** *tr.-intr.* tocar o sonar [la trompa, la bocina, el silbato], pitar.

**tooth** (tuz) *pl.* **teeth** (tız) *s.* ANAT. diente: ~ *decay*, caries dental; ~ *powder*, polvos dentífricos; *to cast in one's teeth*, echar a cara; *in the teeth of*, en la cara de; contra, a despecho de; ~ *and nail*, furiosamente, desesperadamente. *2* diente [de sierra, de rueda, etc.], púa, gajo, punta. *3* gusto, afición: *to have a sweet* ~, ser goloso.

**tooth (to)** *tr.* dentar. *2* endentar, engranar.

**toothache** (tou·zeik) *s.* dolor de muelas.

**toothbrush** (tu·zbrøsh) *s.* cepillo para los dientes.

**toothed** (tu·zt) *adj.* dentado, serrado.

**toothful** (tu·zful) *s.* bocado o trago.

**toothing** (tu·zing) *s.* ALBAÑ. adarajas.

**toothless** (tu·zlis) *adj.* desdentado.

**toothpick** (tu·zpik) *s.* mondadientes, palillo.

**toothsome** (tu·zsøm) *adj.* sabroso, apetitoso.

**toothy** (tu·zi) *s.* dentudo. *2* voraz.

**tootle (to)** (tu·tøl) *tr.* tocar la flauta o silbar suavemente.

**top** (tap) *s.* parte o superficie superior, lo alto, cima, cumbre, remate, pináculo, tejado, cabeza, cúspide, ápice: *from* ~ *to bottom*, de arriba abajo; *on (the)* ~ *of*, encima de, sobre; *on* ~, fig. con bien, con éxito. *2* auge, punto más alto; último grado: *at the* ~ *of one's voice*, a voz en cuello. *3* cabeza, primer puesto. *4* ANAT. cabeza, coronilla: *from* ~ *to toe*, de pies a cabeza. *5* copa [de árbol]. *6* tablero [de mesa]. *7* tejadillo o capota [de coche]. *8* MAR. cofa. *9* tapa, cubierta. *10* copete, tupé. *11* trompo, peón. *12* la flor, lo mejor. *13 adj.* superior, primero, principal; alto, de arriba; máximo: ~ *hat*, sombrero de copa; *at* ~ *speed*, a toda velocidad. *14* ZOOL. ~ *shell*, trompo [molusco].

**top (to)** *tr.* descabezar, desmochar. *2* cubrir, coronar. *3* acabar, rematar. *4* exceder, aventajar. *5* dominar. *6* llegar a la cima de. *7 to* ~ *off*, rematar, completar; MAR. embicar [una verga]. *8 intr.* sobresalir, ser excelente. *9* predominar. ¶ Pret. y p. p.: *topped;* ger.: *-pping.*

**topaz** (tou·pæš) *s.* MINER. topacio.

**topcoat** (ta·pkout) *s.* gabán; abrigo de entretiempo.

**tope (to)** (toup) *intr.* beber con exceso. *2* beber de un trago.

**topee** (tou·pɪ) *s.* salacot.

**toper** (tou·pø$^r$) *s.* borrachín.

**topful** (ta·pful) *adj.* lleno hasta el borde.

**topgallant** (tapgæ·lant) *s.* MAR. juanete.

**top-heavy** *adj.* demasiado pesado o grande por arriba. *2* COM. capitalizado por encima de su valor real.

**topi** (tou·pɪ) *s.* TOPEE.

**topic** (ta·pik) *s.* asunto, tema. *2 pl.* tópicos, lugares comunes.

**topic (al** (ta·pik(al) *adj.* tópico. *2* del tema o asunto. *3* referente a los asuntos del día. *4* MED. local.

**topknot** (ta·pnat) *s.* moño [de pelo, de plumas, de cintas].

**topman** (-mæn) *s.* MAR. gaviero.

**topmast** (-mæst) *s.* MAR. mastelero.

**topmost** (-moust) *adj.* más alto [de todos].

**topographer** (tøpa·grafø$^r$) *s.* topógrafo.

**topographic (al** (tapøgræ·fik(al) *adj.* topográfico.

**topography** (tøpa·grafi) *s.* topografía.

**toponymy** (-nimi) *s.* toponimia.

**topper** (ta·pø$^r$) *s.* fam. sombrero de copa. *2* persona o cosa excelente.

**topping** (-ing) *adj.* alto, elevado. *2* eminente, distinguido. *3* excelente, de primera. *4* (E.U.) tiránico, mandón.

**topple (to)** (ta·pøl) *tr.* hacer caer, derribar, volcar. *2 intr.* tambalearse, caer. | Gralte. con *down* u *over.*

**topsail** (ta·pseil) *s.* MAR. gavia.

**top-shell** *s.* ZOOL. trompo [molusco].

**topsoil** (-soil) *s.* capa superior del suelo.

**topsy-turvy** (ta·psi-tø·$^r$vi) *adv.* patas arriba, en confusión. *2 adj.* trastornado, revuelto, desordenado. *3 s.* desbarajuste, confusión.

**toque** (touk) *s.* toca [sombrero].

**tor** (to$^r$) *s.* tolmo, tormo.

**torch** (to$^r$ch) *s.* hacha, antorcha. *2* linterna eléctrica de bolsillo. *3* lámpara de soldar.

**torchbearer** (-berø$^r$) *s.* portador de antorcha.

**torchlight** (-lait) *s.* luz de antorchas.

**tore** (to$^r$) *pret.* de TO TEAR. *2 s.* ARQ. toro, torés.

**toric** (ta·rik) *adj.* tórico: ~ *lens*, lente tórica.

**torment** (to·$^r$mønt) *s.* tormento, tortura, pena.

**torment (to)** (to$^r$me·nt) *tr.* atormentar, torturar. *2* agitar. *3* molestar, inquietar. *4* violentar, tergiversar.

**tormenter, tormentor** (-ø$^r$) *s.* atormentador.

**torn** (to$^r$n) *p. p.* de TO TEAR. *2 adj.* roto, rasgado, desgarrado.

**tornado** (to$^r$nei·dou) *s.* tornado. *2* manga de viento.

**torpedo** (to$^r$pɪ·dou) *s.* MIL., ICT. torpedo: ~ *boat*, torpedero.

**torpedo (to)** *tr.* torpedear. *2* destruir, desbaratar.

**torpid** (to·$^r$pid) *adj.* tórpido. *2* torpe, aletargado, entorpecido, apático.

**torpidity** (to·$^r$pi·diti), **torpidness** (to·$^r$pidnis), **torpor** (to·$^r$po$^r$) *s.* torpeza, entorpecimiento, letargo, apatía.

**torque** (to$^r$k) *s.* torques. *2* MEC. impulso rotativo.

**torrefy (to)** (ta·rifai) *tr.* tostar, torrar. ¶ Pret. y p. p.: *torrefied.*

**torrent** (ta·rønt) *s.* torrente. *2* raudal.

**torrid** (ta·rid) *adj.* tórrido. *2* ardiente, inflamado.

**torridity** (tari·diti) *s.* calidad de tórrido.

**torsion** (to·$^r$shøn) *s.* torsión.

**tort** (to$^r$t) *s.* DER. agravio, perjuicio.

**torticollis** (to$^r$tika·lis) *s.* tortícolis.

**tortoise** (to·$^r$tøs) *s.* ZOOL. tortuga. *2 tortoise* o ~ *shell*, concha, carey.

**tortoise-shell** *adj.* de concha o carey.

**tortuous** (to·$^r$chuøs) *adj.* tortuoso, torcido, sinuoso. *2* tortuoso, solapado.

**torture** (to·$^r$chu$^r$) *s.* tortura, tormento, martirio.

**torture (to)** *tr.* torturar, martirizar. *2* violentar, tergiversar.

**torturer** (-ø$^r$) *s.* atormentador; verdugo.

**torus** (to·røs) *s.* ARQ. toro.

**Tory** (to·ri) *s.* POL. (Ingl.) tory, conservador.

**toss** (tos) *s.* sacudimiento, meneo; agitación. *2* lanzamiento [acción]. *3* tiro [distancia]. *4* cara o cruz; azar.

**toss (to)** *tr.* sacudir, zarandear, menear, agitar. *2* arrojar, lanzar; mover o levantar vivamente: *to* ~ *in a blanket*, mantear; *to* ~ *up*, echar al aire. *3* discutir, dar vueltas a un asunto. *4 intr.* moverse, agitarse; balancearse [un buque]; revolverse [en la cama]. *5 to* ~ *up for*, echar a cara o cruz.

**toss-up** *s.* cara y cruz. *2* probabilidad incierta.

**tot** (tat) *s.* chiquitín, na. *2* fam. suma. *3* fam. traguito.

**tot (to)** *tr.-intr.* sumar. ¶ Pret. y p. p.: *totted;* ger.: *-tting.*

**total** (tou·tal) *adj.* total. *2* global. *3* completo, absoluto. *4 s.* total, todo.

**total (to)** *tr.* sumar, ascender a.

**totalitarian** (toutælite·rian) *adj.-s.* POL. totalitario.

**totalitarianism** (-išm) *s.* totalitarismo.

**totality** (toutæ·lity) *s.* totalidad.

**totalize (to)** (tou·talaiš) *tr.-intr.* totalizar.

**totally** (tou·tali) *adv.* totalmente.

**totem** (tou·tøm) *s.* tótem.

**totemism** (-išm) *s.* totemismo.

**totter (to)** (to·tø$^r$) *intr.* vacilar, tambalearse; amenazar ruina. *2* vacilar [al andar].

**tottering** (-ing) *adj.* vacilante, tambaleante. *2* ruinoso.

**toucan** (tukæ·n) *s.* ORN. tucán.

**touch** (tøch) *s.* toque, tocamiento, tiento, palpamiento. *2* pulsación [en música y mecanografía]. *3* tacto [sentido; impresión táctil]. *4* contacto: *in* ~ *with*, en contacto, en comunicación con. *5* toque, prueba, piedra de toque. *6* toque, pincelada, detalle. *7* señal, huella. *8* sombra, ápice, algo. *9* mano, habilidad. *10* indicación, insinuación. *11* ~ *and go*, situación crítica, peligrosa.

**touch (to)** *tr.* tocar [con la mano, con un objeto] tentar, palpar. *2* tocar [tener contacto con; poner las manos en, ocuparse de, tratar un tema; comer, beber, etc.]. *3* rozar, tropezar. *4* MÚS. tocar, pulsar. *5* tocar, inspirar, aguijonear, conmover, afligir, irritar. *6* alcanzar, llegar a. *7* tocar a, concernir. *8* delinear, esbozar, retocar. *9* pop. robar; dar un sablazo a. *10 to* ~ *up*, corregir, retocar; espolear.

*11 intr.* tocar, tocarse, estar contiguo. *12 to* ~ *at, on, to* o *upon*, tocar; tocar a; frisar en, rayar en. *12* MAR. *to* ~ *at*, hacer escala en.

**touch-and-go** *adj.* hecho de prisa, incompleto. *2* crítico, peligroso.

**touchhole** (-joul) *s.* oído [de un cañón].

**touchiness** (-inis) *s.* susceptibilidad, irritabilidad.

**touching** (-ing) *prep.* tocante a, en cuanto a. *2 adj.* patético, conmovedor.

**touch-me-not** *s.* tema prohibido. *2* persona orgullosa. *3* BOT. balsamina.

**touchstone** (-stoun) *s.* piedra de toque.

**touchwood** (-wud) *s.* yesca, hupe.

**touchy** (-i) *adj.* susceptible, quisquilloso, irritable.

**tough** (tøf) *adj.* duro, correoso. *2* fuerte, vigoroso. *3* resistente. *4* terco, tenaz. *5* duro, arduo, penoso. *6* mala [suerte]. *7* (E.U.) malvado, pendenciero. *8 s.* (E.U.) matón.

**toughen (to)** (-øn) *tr.-intr.* endurecer o endurecerse. *2* hacer o hacerse correoso.

**toupee** (tupι·) *s.* peluquín, bisoñé.

**tour** (tuʳ) *s.* viaje, excursión, vuelta, gira. *2* circuito, recorrido. *3* turno.

**tour (to)** *intr.* viajar por. *2* hacer turismo.

**touring** (-ing) *s.* turismo: ~ *car*, turismo [coche].

**tourism** (-išm) *s.* turismo.

**tourist** (-ist) *s.* viajero, turista.

**tourmalin(e** (tu·ʳmalin) *s.* MINER. turmalina.

**tournament** (tu·ʳnamønt) *s.* torneo, justa. *2* certamen.

**tourney** (tu·ʳni) *s.* torneo, justa.

**tourney (to)** *intr.* justar, tomar parte en un torneo.

**tourniquet** (tu·ʳniket) *s.* CIR. torniquete.

**tousle** (tau·šøl) *s.* maraña [del cabello], greña.

**tousle (to)** *tr.* despeinar, desgreñar; desarreglar, maltratar.

**tout** (taut) *s.* corredor, gancho. *2* espía que vende informes relativos a las carreras de caballos.

**tout (to)** *tr.-intr.* buscar clientes, votos, etc. *2* espiar para obtener y vender informes relativos a las carreras de caballos.

**tow** (tou) *s.* estopa. *2* remolque [acción; lo que va remolcado; cabo, sirga]: *to take in* ~, remolcar, llevar a remolque. *3* remolcador.

**tow (to)** *tr.* remolcar, atoar.

**towage** (-idẏ) *s.* remolque [acción]. *2* derechos de remolque.

**toward** (toʳd o tuwo·ʳd), **towards** (-š) *prep.* hacia. *2* cerca de. *3* para. *4* con, para con.

**towboat** (tou·bout) *s.* remolcador.

**towel** (tau·øl) *s.* toalla: ~ *horse*, ~ *rack*, toallero.

**towel(l)ing** (-ing) *s.* género para toallas.

**tower** (tau·øʳ) *s.* torre, torreón. *2* campanario.

**tower (to)** *intr.* descollar, sobresalir. *2* elevarse, remontarse.

**towered** (-d) *adj.* guarnecido de torres.

**towering** (-ing) *adj.* alto, elevado. *2* que se remonta. *3* grande, exorbitante. *4* violento.

**towery** (-i) *adj.* guarnecido de torres. *2* alto, elevado.

**towheaded** (tou·jedid) *adj.* de cabello rubio pajizo.

**towhee** (tau·jι) *s.* ORN. especie de pinzón.

**towing** (tou·ing) *s.* remolque, atoaje: ~ *service*, AUTO. servicio de remolque.

**towline** (-lain) *s.* cuerda de remolque; sirga.

**town** (taun) *s.* población, ciudad, villa, pueblo; municipio: ~ *clerk*, secretario municipal; ~ *council*, ayuntamiento; ~ *hall*, casa del ayuntamiento; ~ *planning*, urbanismo. *2* (sin artículo) la metrópolis, la capital.

**township** (-ship) *s.* municipio, concejo, distrito municipal.

**townsman** (-mæn) *s.* ciudadano, vecino. *2* conciudadano.

**towpath** (tou·pæz) *s.* camino de sirga.

**towrope** (-roup) *s.* TOWLINE.

**tox(a)emia** (taksι·mia) *s.* MED. toxemia.

**toxic** (ta·ksik) *s.* tóxico.

**toxicity** (taksi·siti) *s.* toxicidad.

**toxicology** (taksika·lodẏ) *s.* toxicología.

**toxin(e** (ta·ksin) *s.* toxina. *2* ponzoña.

**toy** (toi·) *s.* juguete [para jugar]. *2* chuchería, fruslería. *3 adj.* de juguete; pequeñito.

**toy (to)** *intr.* jugar, juguetear, divertirse.

**toyshop** (toi·shap) *s.* juguetería [tienda].

**trace** (treis) *s.* huella, pisada, rastro. *2* vestigio, señal, indicio. *3* pizca. *4* trazo. *5* GEOM. traza. *6* tirante [de los arreos].

**trace (to)** *tr.* trazar, esbozar, escribir. *2* rastrear, seguir la pista de. *3* investigar, descubrir; buscar el origen de; atribuir una causa u origen a: *to* ~ *back to*, hacer remontar a.

**tracer** (-øʳ) *s.* trazador. *2* calcador. *3* punzón; tiralíneas. *4* rastreador, buscador. *5* MIL. ~ *bullet*, bala trazante.

**tracery** (-søri) *s.* ARQ. tracería.

**trachea** (trei·kia) *s.* ANAT., ZOOL., BOT. tráquea.

**tracheotomy** (trekia·tømi) *s.* CIR. traqueotomía.

**trachoma** (tracou·ma) *s.* MED. tracoma.

**tracing** (trei·sing) *s.* trazado, trazo. *2* calco: ~ *paper*, papel de calcar. *3* descubrimiento, rastreo.

**track** (træk) *s.* rastro, pista, huellas; señal, vestigio: *to keep* ~ *of*, fig. no perder de vista, estar al corriente de. *2* carril, rodada. *3* MAR. estela. *4* reguero. *5* camino, senda. *6* curso, rumbo, trayectoria. *7* DEP. pista. *8* banda [de tractor de oruga]. *9* vía [de tren, tranvía, etc.]. *10 off the* ~, descarrilado; fuera de camino, despistado.

**track (to)** *tr.* rastrear, seguir la pista de: *to* ~ *down*, llegar a descubrir o capturar. *2* trazar, trillar [un camino]. *3* sirgar.

**trackless** (-lis) *adj.* sin rastro. *2* sin caminos. *3* sin vías.

**tract** (trækt) *s.* área, región, espacio, trecho. *2* FISIOL. aparato, sistema. *4* LITURG. tracto. *5* folleto [esp. político o religioso].

**tractable** (-tabøl) *adj.* dócil, complaciente, tratable.

**tractate** (-teit) *s.* tratado, opúsculo, ensayo.

**tractile** (-til) *adj.* dúctil.

**traction** (-shøn) *s.* tracción. *2* servicio público de transportes. *3* FISIOL. contracción. *4* MEC. fricción adhesiva.

**tractive** (-tiv) *adj.* de tracción.

**tractor** (-tøʳ) *s.* tractor. *2* aeroplano de hélice delantera.

**Tracy** (tra·si) *n. pr. dim.* de THERESA.

**trade** (treid) *s.* profesión, ocupación; oficio, arte mecánica: ~ *union*, sindicato obrero. *2* gremio. *3* comercio, tráfico, trato, negocio: ~ *mark*, marca registrada. *4* parroquia, clientela. *5 the trades, the* ~ *winds*, los vientos alisios.

**trade (to)** *tr.* comerciar, traficar, negociar, tratar: *to* ~ *in*, tratar en; *to* ~ *on*, explotar, aprovecharse de. *2 tr.* comerciar o tratar en; vender; trocar, cambiar.

**trader** (-øʳ) *s.* comerciante, mercader, tratante, negociante. *2* buque mercante.

**tradesfolk** (-sfouk) *s.* tenderos. *2* artesanos; gentes del oficio.

**tradesman** (-mæn) *s.* comerciante, mercader, tendero. *2* artesano.

**tradespeople** (-spιpøl) *s. pl.* TRADESFOLK.

**trading** (-ing) *s.* comercio, tráfico. *2 adj.* comercial, mercantil: ~ *post*, factoría; ~ *stamp*, cupón prima.

**tradition** (tradi·shøn) *s.* tradición.

**traditional** (-*al*) *adj.* tradicional.

**traduce (to)** (tradiu·s) *tr.* difamar, calumniar.

**traffic** (træ·fik) *s.* tráfico, comercio. *2* tránsito, circulación, transporte, tráfico: ~ *jam*, embotellamiento del tráfico; ~ *light*, semáforo.

**traffic (to)** *intr.* comerciar, traficar. ¶ Pret. y p. p.: *trafficked;* ger.: *-cking.*

**trafficker** (-ø<sup>r</sup>) *s.* traficante.

**tragacanth** (træ·gakænz) *s.* BOT. tragacanto. *2* goma adragante.

**tragedian** (tradŷi·dian) *s.* trágico [autor; actor].

**tragedienne** (tradŷidie·n) *s.* actriz trágica.

**tragedy** (træ·dŷidi) *s.* tragedia.

**tragic (al** (-k(*al*) *adj.* trágico.

**tragicomedy** (trædŷika·mødi) *s.* tragicomedia.

**tragicomic (al** (-mik(*al*) *adj.* tragicómico.

**tragus** (trei·gøs) *s.* ANAT. trago.

**trail** (treil) *s.* cola [de vestido, cometa, etc.]. *2* rastro, huella, pista. *3* reguero. *4* estela [de luz]. *5* senda [esp. en una región deshabitada].

**trail (to)** *tr.* arrastrar, llevar arrastrando. *2* alargar, hacer durar. *3* rastrear, seguir la pista de. *4* ir detrás de. *5* dejar [un rastro]; trillar [un camino]. *6* *intr.* arrastrar, ir arrastrando. *7* arrastrarse. *8* rezagarse. *9* extenderse [un camino, etc.]. *10* dejar rastro. *11* *to* ~ *off*, perderse, ir desapareciendo.

**trailer** (-ø<sup>r</sup>) *s.* AUTO. remolque, coche habitación. *2* cosa que arrastra; planta rastrera. *3* rastreador, cazador. *4* rezagado. *5* CINEM. trailer.

**trailing** (-ing) *adj.* colgante, que arrastra. *2* BOT. rastrero. *3* MEC. trasero.

**train** (treín) *s.* FERROC. tren. *2* tren [de máquina, ondas, etc.]. *3* fila, recua; séquito, comitiva. *4* reguero [de pólvora]. *5* serie, encadenamiento. *6* cola [de cometa, vestido, etcétera].

**train (to)** *tr.* adiestrar, amaestrar, enseñar, educar. *2* DEP. entrenar. *3* AGR. poner en espaldera. *4* apuntar [un cañón, etc.]. *5* *intr.* adiestrarse, ejercitarse, entrenarse.

**trainbearer** (-berø<sup>r</sup>) *s.* caudatario.

**trainee** (treini·) *s.* el que se adiestra. *2* MIL. quinto.

**trainer** (trei·nø<sup>r</sup>) *s.* adiestrador, amaestrador. *2* DEP. preparador. *3* AVIA. avión de prácticas. *4* AGR. espaldera.

**training** (-ning) *s.* adiestramiento, instrucción, preparación, educación. *2* DEP. entrenamiento.

**trainman** (-mæn) *s.* FERROC. ferroviario.

**trait** (treit) *s.* toque, pincelada. *2* rasgo, peculiaridad. *3* rasgo, facción.

**traitor** (trei·tø<sup>r</sup>) *adj.-s.* traidor.

**traitorous** (-ørøs) *adj.* traidor, pérfido, alevoso.

**traitress** (trei·tris) *s.* traidora.

**trajectory** (tradŷe·ktori) *s.* trayectoria.

**tram** (træm) *s.* (Ingl.) tranvía. *2* vagoneta [de mina]. *3* carril, riel plano.

**tram (to)** *intr.* ir en tranvía.

**tramcar** (-ka<sup>r</sup>) *s.* tranvía.

**trammel** (træ·møl) *s.* trasmallo. *2* llares [de chimenea]. *3* compás de varas. *4* elipsógrafo. *5* traba, maniota. *6* traba, impedimento.

**trammel (to)** *tr.* trabar, sujetar, impedir, estorbar.

**tramp** (træmp) *s.* viajero a pie, viandante. *2* vagabundo. *3* caminata. *4* marcha pesada; ruido de pisadas. *5* MAR. vapor volandero.

**tramp (to)** *intr.* andar con paso fuerte. *2* viajar a pie, vagabundear. *3* *tr.* pisar, pisotear, apisonar. *4* recorrer a pie.

**tramper** (-ø<sup>r</sup>) *s.* vagabundo. *2* buen andador.

**trample** (træ·mpøl) *s.* pisoteo. *2* ruido de pisadas. *3* atropello.

**trample (to)** *tr.* hollar, pisar, pisotear. *2* *intr.* patullar, pisar fuerte. *3* *to* ~ *on*, pisotear, maltratar, atropellar.

**tramway** (træ·muei) *s.* (Ingl.) tranvía. *2* transbordador, funicular aéreo.

**trance** (træns) *s.* éxtasis, enajenamiento, ensimismamiento. *2* catalepsia; estado hipnótico.

**tranquil** (træ·nkuil) *adj.* tranquilo, apacible.

**tranquillize (to)** (-aiš) *tr.* tranquilizar.

**tranquillity** (trænkui·liti) *s.* tranquilidad, sosiego, paz, calma.

**transact (to)** (trænsæ·kt) *tr.* llevar a cabo, hacer, despachar [un negocio]. *2* *intr.* negociar, pactar.

**transaction** (-kshøn) *s.* despacho, negociación. *2* COM. transacción, operación. *3* DER. transacción, arreglo. *4* *pl.* actas, memorias [de una sociedad docta].

**transalpine** (trænsæ·lpin o -pain) *adj.* transalpino.

**transatlantic** (-ætlæ·ntik) *adj.* transatlántico.

**transcend (to)** (trænse·nd) *tr.* sobrepujar, sobrepasar; ir más allá de [los límites o facultades]. *2* *intr.* FIL., TEOL. trascender. *3* sobresalir.

**transcendence, transcendency** (-øns, -si) *s.* excelencia, superioridad. *2* FIL. transcendencia.

**transcendent** (-ønt) *adj.* sobresaliente, extraordinario. *2* FIL., TEOL. transcendente.

**transcendental** (trænsønde·ntal) *adj.* FIL. transcendental. *2* sobrenatural, sobrehumano.

**transcontinental** (trænskantine·ntal) *adj.* transcontinental.

**transcribe (to)** (-krai·b) *tr.* transcribir. *2* RADIO. grabar en disco.

**transcript** (træ·nskript) *s.* copia, traslado, trasunto. *2* transcripción [de taquigrafía].

**transcription** (trænskri·pshøn) *s.* transcripción. *2* copia.

**transept** (træ·nsept) *s.* ARQ. crucero, transepto.

**transfer** (træ·nsfø<sup>r</sup>) *s.* transferencia, traslado, transporte, transbordo. *2* DER. traspaso, cesión. *3* cosa o persona trasladada. *4* calco. *5* LITOG. reporte.

**transfer (to)** *tr.* transferir, trasladar, transportar, transbordar. *2* DER. traspasar, ceder. *3* LITOG. reportar. ¶ Pret. y p. p.: *transferred;* ger.: *-rring.*

**transferable** (trænsfø·rabøl) *adj.* transferible. *2* trasladable.

**transference** (-fø·røns) *s.* transferencia, traslado.

**transfigure (to)** (-figiurei·shøn) *s.* transfiguración.

**transfigure (to)** (-fi·giu<sup>r</sup>) *tr.* transfigurar.

**transfix (to)** (-fi·ks) *tr.* traspasar, atravesar.

**transfixion** (-fi·kshøn) *s.* transfixión.

**transform (to)** (-fo·<sup>r</sup>m) *tr.* transformar. *2* *intr.* transformarse.

**transformation** (-fo·<sup>r</sup>mei·shøn) *s.* transformación.

**transformer** (-fo·<sup>r</sup>mø<sup>r</sup>) *s.* transformador.

**transformism** (-fo·<sup>r</sup>mišm) *s.* BIOL. transformismo.

**transfuse (to)** (-fiu·š) *tr.* transfundir. *2* infundir, instilar.

**transfusion** (-fiu·ŷøn) *s.* transfusión.

**transgress (to)** (-gre·s) *tr.* transgredir, infringir, quebrantar. *2* traspasar los límites de. *3* *intr.* quebrantar la ley, pecar; propasarse.

**transgression** (-shøn) *s.* transgresión. *2* delito, pecado.

**transgressor** (-sø<sup>r</sup>) *s.* transgresor.

**tranship (to)** (træ·nship) *tr.* TRANSSHIP.

**transient** (træ·nshønt) *adj.* transitorio, pasajero;

rápido, momentáneo. *2* transeúnte, migratorio. *3 s.* huésped o viajero de paso.

**transiently** (-li) *adv.* transitoriamente, temporalmente, de paso.

**transistor** (trænsi·støʳ) *s.* ELECT. transistor.

**transit** (træ·nsit) *s.* tránsito, paso, pasaje. *2* tránsito, muerte. *3* ASTR., TOP. tránsito.

**transit (to)** *tr.-intr.* ASTR., TOP. pasar [por].

**transition** (trænsi·shøn) *s.* transición.

**transitional** (-shønal) *adj.* de transición.

**transitive** (træ·nsitiv) *adj.-s.* GRAM. transitivo.

**transitory** (træ·nsitori) *adj.* transitorio, pasajero.

**translatable** (trænslei·tabøl) *adj.* traducible.

**translate (to)** (trænslei·t) *tr.* traducir. *2* descifrar, interpretar. *3* trasladar [de un lugar a otro]. *4* TELEGR. retransmitir.

**translation** (-shøn) *s.* traducción, versión. *2* traslado. *3* B. ART. copia, interpretación.

**translator** (-tøʳ) *s.* traductor. *2* TELEGR. repetidor.

**translucence, translucency** (trænsliu·søns, -si) *s.* translucidez.

**translucent** (-sønt), **translucid** (-sid) *adj.* translúcido, trasluciente.

**transmigrate (to)** (-mai·greit) *intr.* transmigrar.

**transmigration** (-maigrei·shøn) *s.* transmigración.

**transmission** (-mi·shøn) *s.* transmisión. *2* AUTO. cambio de marchas.

**transmit (to)** (-mi·t) *tr.* transmitir. *2* enviar, remitir.

**transmitter** (-øʳ) *s.* transmisor.

**transmitting** (-ing) *adj.* transmisor: ~ *set*, RADIO. aparato transmisor; ~ *station*, emisora.

**transmutable** (miu·tabøl) *adj.* transmutable.

**transmutation** (-miutei·shøn) *s.* transmutación.

**transmute (to)** (miu·t) *tr.* transmutar.

**transoceanic** (-oushiæ·nik) *adj.* transoceánico.

**transom** (træ·nsøm) *s.* CARP. travesaño. *2* ARQ. dintel, puente. *3* montante [ventana]. *4* MAR. yugo.

**transpacific** (trænspasi·fik) *adj.* transpacífico.

**transpadane** (-pei·dein) *adj.* transpadano.

**transparence** (trænspe·røns) *s.* transparencia.

**transparency** (-rønsi) *s.* transparencia. *2* pintura, dibujo, etc., hechos para ser vistos por transparencia.

**transparent** (-rønt) *adj.* transparente, diáfano. *2* franco, ingenuo.

**transpierce (to)** (transpɪ·ʳš) *tr.* traspasar, atravesar.

**transpiration** (-pirei·shøn) *s.* transpiración.

**transpire (to)** (-pai·ʳ) *tr.-intr.* transpirar, sudar. *2 tr.* exhalar. *3 intr.* exhalarse, rezumarse. *4* transpirar, traslucirse. *5* fam. acaecer, suceder.

**transplant (to)** (-plæ·nt) *tr.* trasplantar.

**transplantation** (-plantei·shøn) *s.* trasplante.

**transport (to)** (træ·nspoʳt) *s.* transporte, acarreo. *2* transporte [buque]. *3* transporte, rapto, éxtasis. *4* deportado.

**transport (to)** (trænspo·ʳt) *tr.* transportar, acarrear. *2* transportar, enajenar. *3* deportar.

**transportation** (-ei·shøn) *s.* transporte, acarreo, sistemas de transporte. *2* (E.U.) coste del transporte; billete, pasaje. *3* deportación.

**transposal** (trænspou·šal) *s.* transposición.

**transpose (to)** (-pou·š) *tr.* transponer [mudar el orden o la posición relativa de]. *2* MÚS. transportar.

**transposition** (-pouši·shøn) *s.* transposición. *2* MÚS. transporte.

**transship (to)** (-shi·p) *tr.* MAR. transbordar.

**transshipment** (-mønt) *s.* MAR. transbordo.

**transubstantiation** (-søbstænshiei·shøn) *s.* transubstanciación.

**transude (to)** (-siud) *intr.* resudar, rezumar.

**transversal** (-vø·ʳsal) *adj.* transversal. *2 s.* GEOM. línea transversal.

**transverse** (-vø·ʳs) *adj.* transverso, travesero. *2 adv.* transversalmente.

**Transylvania** (trænsilvei·nia) *n. pr.* GEOGR. Transilvania.

**trap** (træp) *s.* trampa, armadijo, lazo. *2* bombillo, sifón [de desagüe]. *3* coche ligero. *4* DEP. lanzaplatos. *5* pop. (Ingl.) policía. *6* fam. la boca. *7 ~ door*, trampa [puerta]; escotillón. *8 pl.* MÚS. instrumentos de percusión. *9* equipaje, bártulos.

**trap (to)** *tr.* entrampar, hacer caer en la trampa, atrapar. *2* proveer de sifón. *3* engualdrapar. *4 intr.* cazar con trampa. ¶ Pret. y p. p.: *trapped*; ger.: *-pping*.

**trapan** (træpæ·n) *s.* TREPAN.

**trapeze** (trapɪ·š) *s.* GEOM., GIMN. trapecio.

**trapezing** (-šing) *s.* ejercicios en el trapecio.

**trapezist** (-šist) *s.* trapecista.

**trapezium** (-šiøm) *s.* GEOM. trapezoide; trapecio. *2* ANAT. trapecio [hueso].

**trapezius** (-šiøs) *s.* ANAT. trapecio [músculo].

**trapezoid** (træpišoi·d) *s.* GEOM. trapecio; trapezoide.

**trapper** (træ·pøʳ) *s.* trampero, cazador de pieles.

**trappings** (-ingš) *s. pl.* jaeces, caparazón, gualdrapa. *2* adornos, atavíos.

**traprock** (-rak) *s.* GEOL. roca volcánica, basalto.

**Trappist** (-ist) *s.* trapense.

**trash** (træsh) *s.* bagazo, hojarasca, broza, basura, desecho. *2* trastos, cosa inútil. *3* tontería, patarata. *4* gentuza.

**trashy** (-i) *adj.* inútil, malo, despreciable.

**trauma** (tro·ma) *s.* MED. trauma, herida.

**traumatism** (-tišm) *s.* MED. traumatismo.

**travail** (træ·veil) *s.* afán, trabajo, pena. *2* dolores del parto.

**travail (to)** *intr.* trabajar, afanarse. *2* estar de parto.

**travel** (træ·vøl) *s.* viaje, camino: ~ *bureau*, agencia de viajes. *2* MEC. curso, carrera. *3* tráfico, movimiento de viajeros.

**travel (to)** *intr.* viajar. *2* MEC. moverse, trasladarse. *3* propagarse [la luz, el sonido, etc.]. *4 tr.* viajar por, recorrer.

**travel(l)ed** (-d) *adj.* que ha viajado mucho. *2* frecuentado, recorrido por los viajeros.

**travel(l)er** (-øʳ) *s.* viajero, viajador: *travel(l)er's check*, cheque de viajero. *2* viajante. *3* MEC. carro.

**travel(l)ing** (-ing) *adj.* de viaje; que viaja. *2* MEC. móvil: ~ *crane*, grúa corredora.

**travelogue** (træ·vølog) *s.* conferencia sobre un viaje.

**traverse** (træ·vø·ʳs) *s.* travesaño. *2* cruce, paso, pasaje. *3* ARQ. galería transversal. *4* GEOM. línea transversal. *5* camino en zigzag [para una pendiente]. *6* MAR. bordada o ruta oblicua. *7* FORT. través. *8* DER. negación [de un hecho alegado]. *9* obstáculo, contrariedad, revés. *10 adj.* atravesado, transversal. *11 adv.* de través, transversalmente.

**traverse (to)** *tr.* cruzar, atravesar, recorrer. *2* estudiar detenidamente. *3* contrariar, oponerse a. *4* mover lateralmente. *5* DER. negar [un hecho alegado]. *6* ir y venir. *7* girar, dar vueltas.

**travesty** (træ·visti) *s.* disfraz, parodia.

**travesty (to)** *tr.* disfrazar, parodiar.

**trawl** (trɔl) *s.* especie de jábega. *2* ~ *line*, palangre.

**trawl (to)** *tr.* pescar a la rastra o con palangre.

**tray** (trei) *s.* bandeja. *2* cubeta [de baúl o maleta]. *3* FOT. cubeta.

**treacherous** (tre·chørøs) *adj.* traidor, traicionero, falso, engañoso.

**treachery** (tre·chøri) *s.* traición. *2* deslealtad, perfidia, alevosía.

**treacle** (trı·køl) *s.* melado. *2* fig. melosidad.

**tread** (tred) *s.* paso, pisada. *2* huella, rastro. *3* huella [del peldaño]. *4* suela [del zapato]. *5* superficie de rodadura [de la rueda, el neumático, etc.]. *6* galladura. *7* chalaza. *8* ORN. pisa.

**tread (to)** *tr.* pisar, hollar. *2* pisotear. *3* trillar, andar, seguir [un camino]. *4* ORN. pisar, gallear. *5* *intr.* pisar, andar, bailar. *6 to* ~ *on o upon*, pisar, pisotear. *7 to* ~ *on the heels of*, pisar los talones a: ¶ Pret.: *trod;* p. p.: *trodden* o *trod.*

**treadle** (-øl) *s.* cárcola, pedal. *2* chalaza.

**treadmill** (-mil) *s.* rueda de andar. *2* especie de noria. *3* rutina fatigosa, tráfago.

**treason** (trı·şøn) *s.* traición.

**treasonable** (-abøl) *adj.* traidor, traicionero.

**treasure** (tre·ÿør) *s.* tesoro. *2* preciosidad.

**treasure (to)** *tr.* atesorar. *2* guardar como un tesoro.

**treasurer** (tre·ÿurør) *s.* tesorero.

**treasurership** (-ship) *s.* tesorería [cargo].

**treasury** (tre·ÿuri) *s.* tesoro, erario, hacienda; ministerio de hacienda. *2* tesorería [oficina]. *3* tesoro [de noticias, etc.].

**treat** (trıt) *s.* agasajo, obsequio, convite, convidada. *2* regalo, placer, deleite.

**treat (to)** *tr.* tratar. *2* convidar, invitar, obsequiar, agasajar. *3 intr.* tratar, negociar: *to* ~ *for peace,* negociar la paz. *4 to* ~ *of,* tratar de.

**treatise** (-is) *s.* tratado [libro u opúsculo].

**treatment** (-mønt) *s.* trato, tratamiento [manera de tratar]. *2* MED., QUÍM., IND. tratamiento.

**treaty** (-i) *s.* tratado, convenio.

**treble** (tre·bøl) *adj.* triple, triplo, tríplice. *2* MÚS. de tiple, atiplado. *3* agudo, chillón [voz, sonido]. *4* *s.* MÚS. tiple.

**treble (to)** *tr.* triplicar. *2 intr.* triplicarse.

**trecento** (treishe·ntou) *s.* el siglo XIV.

**tree** (trı) *s.* BOT. y fig. árbol: ~ *of life,* árbol de la vida, tuya; ~ *of the knowledge of good and evil,* árbol de la ciencia del bien y del mal; *up a tree,* en un aprieto. *2* palo, pieza de madera [esp. en composición]: *shoe* ~, horma de zapato. *3 adj.* arborescente, arbóreo.

**tree (to)** *tr.* obligar [a una pers. o animal] a refugiarse en un árbol. *2* fam. acorralar. *3* poner [un zapato] en la horma.

**treeless** (-les) *adj.* pelado, sin árboles.

**treenail** (-neil) *s.* CARP. espiga, clavija.

**treetop** (-tap) *s.* cima, copa [de árbol].

**trefoil** (-foil) *s.* BOT. trébol, trifolio. *2* ARQ. trébol.

**trek** (trek) *s.* (Áf. del S.) viaje, migración [esp. en carromato].

**trek (to)** *tr.* tirar [de una carga]. *2 intr.* viajar, emigrar en carromatos. ¶ Pret. y p. p.: *trekked;* ger.: *-kking.*

**trellis** (tre·lis), **trelliswork** (-uoᵏk) *s.* enrejado, espaldera. *2* glorieta, emparrado.

**tremble** (tre·mbøl) *s.* temblor, estremecimiento.

**tremble (to)** *intr.* temblar. *2* tiritar. *3* estremecerse, trepidar.

**trembler** (tre·mbløᵣ) *s.* temblador. *2* cuáquero. *3* ELECT. vibrador automático.

**tremendous** (trime·ndøs) *adj.* tremendo.

**tremolo** (tre·mølou) *s.* MÚS. trémolo.

**tremor** (tre·møᵣ) *s.* tremor, temblor, estremecimiento.

**tremulous** (tre·miuløs) *adj.* trémulo, tembloroso. *2* palpitante. *3* tímido, medroso.

**trench** (trench) *s.* foso, zanja. *2* MIL. trinchera. *3* ~ *coat,* trinchera [abrigo].

**trench (to)** *tr.* abrir fosos o zanjas en. *2* avenar [un terreno]. *3* atrincherar. *4 intr.* hacer surco, abrir cauce. *5* atrincherarse. *6 to* ~ *on* o *upon,* usurpar, invadir, bordear, rayar en.

**trenchant** (-ant) *adj.* tajante, bien definido. *2* mordaz, incisivo, penetrante.

**trencher** (-øᵣ) *s.* trinchero, plato trinchero.

**trencherman** (-mæn) *s.* comilón. *2* compañero de mesa, parásito.

**trend** (trend) *s.* dirección, rumbo, curso, giro. *2* inclinación, tendencia.

**trend (to)** *intr.* dirigirse, tender.

**Trent** (trent) *n. pr.* GEOGR. Trento.

**trepan** (tripæ·n) *s.* CIR. trépano.

**trepan (to)** *tr.* CIR. trepanar.

**trepanation** (trepanei·shøn) *s.* CIR. trepanación.

**trepidation** (trepidei·shøn) *s.* trepidación, temblor. *2* sobresalto, alarma, agitación.

**trespass** (tre·spas) *s.* transgresión, infracción. *2* delito, pecado. *3* invasión, intrusión.

**trespass (to)** *intr. to* ~ *against,* infringir, violar; delinquir o pecar contra. *2 to* ~ *on* o *upon,* traspasar los límites de, entrar sin derecho en; invadir, usurpar; abusar de.

**tress** (tres) *s.* trenza [de pelo]; rizo, bucle.

**tressed** (-t) *adj.* trenzado.

**trestle** (tre·søl) *s.* caballete, asnilla. *2* bastidor de mesa. *3* TRESTLEWORK.

**trestlework** (-uøᵏk) *s.* obra de caballetes y riostras para sostener un puente, etc.

**trey** (trei) *s.* tres [en naipes, dados y dominó].

**triad** (trai·æd) *s.* tríada. *2* MÚS. acorde de tres notas.

**trial** (trai·al) *s.* prueba, ensayo, experimento: ~ *balloon,* globo sonda; ~ *trip,* viaje de prueba; *on* ~, a prueba. *2* probatura, tentativa. *3* prueba, aflicción, desgracia. *4* DER. juicio, vista de una causa.

**triangle** (-æŋgøl) *s.* GEOM., MÚS. triángulo. *2* escuadra [de dibujo]. *3* ASTR. Triángulo.

**triangled** (traiæ·ŋgøld), **triangular** (-giulaᵣ) *adj.* triangular; triangulado.

**triangulate (to)** (-giuleit) *tr.* triangular.

**triangulation** (-ei·shøn) *s.* triangulación.

**Triassic** (traiæ·sik) *adj.-s.* GEOL. triásico.

**tribal** (trai·bal) *adj.* tribal.

**tribasic** (traibei·sik) *adj.* QUÍM. tribásico.

**tribe** (traib) *s.* tribu.

**tribesman** (-smæn) *s.* miembro de una tribu.

**tribulation** (tribiulei·shøn) *s.* tribulación.

**tribunal** (traibiu·nal) *s.* tribunal. *2* juzgado.

**tribune** (tri·biun) *s.* tribuno. *2* tribuna.

**tribuneship** (-ship) *s.* tribunado.

**tributary** (tri·biuteri) *adj.-s.* tributario.

**tribute** (tri·biut) *s.* tributo. *2* homenaje, obsequio, elogio, encomio.

**trice** (trais) *s.* momento, instante: *in a* ~, en un santiamén.

**trice (to)** *tr.* MAR. izar y amarrar o trincar.

**tricennial** (traise·nial) *adj.* tricenal.

**triceps** (trai·seps) *adj.-s.* ANAT. triceps.

**trichina** (trikai·na) *s.* ZOOL. triquina.

**trichinosis** (trikinou·sis) *s.* MED. triquinosis.

**trichotomy** (traika·tømi) *s.* tricotomía.

**trick** (trik) *s.* treta, ardid, maña, trampa, engaño. *2* burla, travesura. *3* acción: *dirty* ~, mala pasada, jugarreta. *4* suerte [de destreza], truco, ilusión. *5* manera, arte, habilidad. *6* hábito, vicio. *7* baza [en los naipes]. *8* turno, guardia. *9 to do the* ~, servir, resolver el problema. *10 to play tricks,* hacer suertes; hacer travesuras, burlarse.

**trick (to)** *tr.-intr.* engañar, estafar, burlar. *2 tr.* inducir con engaño. *3 to* ~ *out* o *up,* vestir, ataviar.

**trickery** (-øri) *s.*engaño, superchería, malas artes.

**trickish** (-ish) *adj.* engañoso, trapacero. *2* habilidoso.

**trickle** (-øl) *s.* goteo, chorrillo, hilillo [de líquido].

**trickle (to)** *intr.* gotear, escurrir, destilar. *2* moverse, ir o salir de uno en uno.

**trickster** (-stø<sup>r</sup>) *s.* trampista, embaucador.

**tricksy** (-si) *adj.* travieso, juguetón. *2* marrullero.

**tricky** (-i) *adj.* trapacero, marrullero. *2* delicado, difícil, intrincado.

**triclinic** (traikli·nik) *adj.* CRISTAL. triclínico.

**triclinium** (-niøm) *pl.* **-a** (-a) *s.* triclinio.

**tricolo(u)r** (trai·kølø<sup>r</sup>) *adj.* tricolor. *2 s.* bandera tricolor.

**tricot** (tri·kou) *s.* tejido de punto.

**tricuspid** (traikø·spid) *adj.* tricúspide.

**tricycle** (trai·sikøl) *s.* triciclo.

**trident** (trai·dønt) *s.* tridente.

**tridentate** (-eit) *adj.* tridente.

**triduum** (tri·duøm) *s.* triduo.

**tried** (traid) *pret.* y *p. p.* de TO TRY. *2 adj.* probado, fiel, seguro.

**triennial** (traie·nial) *adj.* trienal.

**triennium** (-niøm) *s.* trienio.

**Triest** (trie·st) *n. pr.* Trieste.

**trifid** (trai·fid) *adj.* BOT. trífido.

**trifle** (-føl) *s.* fruslería, friolera, bagatela, baratija, nadería. *2* cierto plato de dulce.

**trifle (to)** *intr.* bromear, burlar, hablar u obrar con frivolidad. *2* holgar. *3 to* ~ *with,* jugar con; burlarse de [uno], engañarlo. *4 tr. to* ~ *away,* malgastar [el tiempo, etc.].

**trifler** (-flø<sup>r</sup>) *s.* persona frívola.

**trifling** (-ing) *adj.* fútil, ligero. *2* frívolo.

**trifoliate(d** (traifou·lieit(id) *adj.* BOT. trifoliado.

**trig** (trig) *adj.* arreglado, aseado. *2* peripuesto. *3* metódico; estirado. *4* sano, firme. *5 s.* calzo.

**trig (to)** *tr.* calzar o trabar [una rueda]. *2* acicalar, ataviar. ¶ Pret. y p. p.: *trigged;* ger.: *-gging.*

**trigeminal** (traidỹe·minal) *adj.-s.* ANAT. trigémino.

**trigger** (tri·gø<sup>r</sup>) *s.* gatillo, disparador.

**triglyph** (trai·glif) *s.* ARQ. triglifo.

**trigon** (-gan) *s.* GEOM., ASTROL. trígono. *2* MÚS. trigón.

**trigonometry** (trigøna·metri) *s.* trigonometría.

**trihedral** (traiji·dral) *adj.* GEOM. triedro.

**trihedron** (-ji·drøn) *s.* GEOM. ángulo triedro.

**trilingual** (-li·ngual) *adj.* trilingüe.

**triliteral** (-li·tøral) *adj.* trilítero.

**trilithon** (tri·lizøn) *s.* ARQUEOL. trilito.

**trill** (tril) *s.* FONÉT. vibración, sonido vibrante. *2* MÚS. trino. *3* quiebro, gorjeo.

**trill (to)** *tr.* pronunciar con vibración. *2* hacer trinos en. *3 intr.* trinar, gorjear. *4* gotear [caer gota a gota].

**trillion** (tri·liøn) *s.* (Ingl.) trillón. *2* (E.U.) billón.

**trilobate(d** (trailou·beit(id) *adj.* trilobulado.

**trilocular** (traila·kiula<sup>r</sup>) *adj.* trilocular.

**trilogy** (tri·lødỹ) *s.* trilogía.

**trim** (trim) *adj.* bien arreglado; en buen estado. *2* bonito, elegante. *3* pulcro, aseado, acicalado. *4 s.* disposición, condición, estado. *5* buen estado.

*6* adorno, aderezo. *7* traje, vestido. *8* MAR. asiento, disposición de un buque para navegar. *9* MAR. orientación [de las velas].

**trim (to)** *tr.* arreglar, disponer, adaptar. *2* cortar, recortar [arreglar cortando], atusar, podar. *3* CARP. alisar, desbastar. *4* despabilar, arreglar [una luz]. *5* pulir, componer; adornar, ribetear, guarnecer. *6* MAR. equilibrar [pesos]: *to* ~ *the hold,* estibar. *7* MAR. orientar las velas; disponer para la navegación. *8* reprender, castigar. *9 intr.* mantenerse neutral, nadar entre dos aguas. ¶ Pret. y p. p.: *trimmed;* ger.: *-mming.*

**trimester** (trai·mestø<sup>r</sup>) *s.* trimestre.

**trimestr(i)al** (-tr(i)al) *adj.* trimestral.

**trimmer** (tri·mø<sup>r</sup>) *s.* arreglador; guarnecedor. *2* máquina de recortar. *3* pastelero, oportunista. *4* RADIO. condensador de compensación.

**trimming** (-ing) *s.* acción de TO TRIM. *2* COST. guarnición, ribete, orla, franja. *3* represión, paliza. *4 pl.* adornos, accesorios. *5* recortes.

**trine** (train) *adj.* trino, triple. *2* (con may.) Trinidad.

**tringle** (tri·ngøl) *s.* vara de cortina. *2* ARQ. listel.

**Trinitarian** (trinite·rian) *adj.-s.* trinitario. *2* que cree en la Trinidad. *3 adj.* (con min.) trino.

**trinity** (tri·niti) *s.* trinca, trío. *2* (con may.) Trinidad.

**trinket** (tri·nkit) *s.* joya, dije. *2* baratija.

**trinomial** (trinou·mial) *adj.* de tres nombres o términos. *2 s.* MAT. trinomio.

**trio** (tri·ou) *s.* trío.

**triode** (trai·oud) *s.* RADIO. triodo.

**trip** (trip) *s.* viaje, excursión. *2* paso ágil o vivo. *3* tropezón, traspié. *4* tropiezo, desliz. *5* zancadilla. *6* MEC. trinquete, escape, disparo.

**trip (to)** *intr.* andar ligero, saltar, brincar. *2* tropezar, dar un traspié; equivocarse. *3 tr.* hacer tropezar o caer, echar la zancadilla a. *4* coger en falta, en error, etc. *5* MEC. soltar, disparar. *6* MAR. levar [el ancla]; inclinar [una verga]. ¶ Pret. y p. p.: *tripped;* ger.: *-pping.*

**tripartite** (trai·pa<sup>r</sup>tait) *s.* tripartito.

**tripe** (traip) *s.* COC. tripas, callos. *2* fig. cosa sin valor; tontería. *3* ʮEJ. tripe.

**trip-hammer** *s.* martillo pilón, martinete de fragua.

**triphthong** (tri·fzang) *s.* triptongo.

**tripinnate** (tri·pineit) *adj.* BOT. tripinado.

**triple** (tri·pøl) *adj.* triple, triplo, tresdoble.

**triple (to)** *tr.* triplicar, tresdoblar.

**triplet** (tri·plit) *s.* trinca, terno. *2* trillizo. *3* MÚS. tresillo. *4* LIT. terceto.

**triplex** (trai·pleks) *adj.* triple, tríplice. *2* MEC. de triple efecto.

**triplicate** (tri·plikit) *adj.-s.* triplicado.

**triplicate (to)** (-keit) *tr.* triplicar.

**tripod** (trai·pad) *s.* trípode.

**Tripolitan** (tripa·litan) *adj.-s.* tripolitano.

**tripper** (tri·pø<sup>r</sup>) *s.* (Ingl.) excursionista, turista. *2* saltarín. *3* tropezador. *4* MEC. disparador.

**tripping** (-ing) *adj.* ágil, ligero, vivo. *2* MEC. disparador.

**triptych** (tri·ptik) *s.* B. ART. tríptico.

**triptyque** (triptı·k) *s.* AUTO. tríptico.

**trireme** (trai·rim) *s.* trirreme.

**Trisagion** (trisei·giøn) *s.* ECLES. Trisagio.

**trisect (to)** (-saise·kt) *tr.* trisecar.

**trisection** (-kshøn) *s.* trisección.

**Tristram** (tri·stram) *n. pr.* Tristán.

**trisyllable** (traisi·labøl) *s.* palabra trisílaba.

**trite** (trait) *s.* gastado, trillado, trivial.

**triton** (trai·tøn) *s.* MIT., ZOOL. tritón.
**tritone** (trai·toun) *s.* MÚS. trítono.
**triturate (to)** (tri·chøreit) *tr.* triturar.
**triumph** (trai·ømf) *s.* triunfo, victoria. 2 júbilo, exultación.
**triumph (to)** *intr.* triunfar [recibir el triunfo]. 2 triunfar, vencer. 3 exultar, gozarse [en].
**triumphal** (traiø·mfal) *adj.* triunfal.
**triumphant** (-fant) *adj.* triunfante. 2 victorioso.
**triumvir** (-vøʳ) *s.* triunviro.
**triumvirate** (-virit) *s.* triunvirato.
**triune** (trai·un) *adj.* TEOL. trino y uno.
**trivet** (tri·vit) *s.* trébedes, trípode.
**trivial** (tri·vial) *adj.* trivial [del trivio]. 2 trivial, fútil, insignificante, frívolo, vulgar.
**triviality** (triviæ·liti) *s.* trivialidad, futilidad, frivolidad, insignificancia.
**trivium** (tri·viøm) *s.* trivio [las tres artes liberales].
**trocar** (trou·kaʳ) *s.* CIR. trocar.
**trochaic(al** (trokei·k(al) *adj.-s.* trocaico.
**trochanter** (trokæ·ntøʳ) *s.* ANAT., ENT. trocánter.
**trochee** (trou·kı) *s.* troqueo.
**trochoid** (trou·koid) *adj.* trocoideo. 2 *s.* GEOM. trocoide.
**trod** (tra·d) *pret.* y *p. p.* de TO TREAD.
**trodden** (tra·døn) *p. p.* de TO TREAD.
**troglodyte** (tra·glødait) *s.* troglodita. 2 ZOOL. mono antropoide.
**trogon** (trou·gan) *s.* ORN. ave de la familia del quetzal.
**troika** (troi·ka) *s.* troica.
**Trojan** (trou·dÿan) *adj.-s.* troyano. 2 *s.* persona valiente, esforzada.
**troll** (troul) *s.* MÚS. especie de canon. 2 repetición, rutina. 3 sedal y anzuelo rotatorios. 8 MIT. gnomo; gigante.
**troll (to)** *tr.* cantar por turno. 2 cantar, celebrar. 3 recitar sonora o rápidamente. 4 pescar con anzuelo desde un bote en movimiento. 5 *intr.* voltear, girar. 6 corretear. 7 cantar alegremente.
**trolley** (tra·li) *s.* polea del trole: ~ *bus*, trolebús; ~ *pole*, trole. 2 carrito, carretilla. 3 carrito aéreo.
**trollop** (tra·løp) *s.* pazpuerca. 2 ramera.
**trombone** (tra·mboun) *s.* MÚS. trombón [instrumento].
**trombonist** (-ist) *s.* trombón [músico].
**troop** (trup) *s.* tropa, cuadrilla, banda, tropel. 2 bandada, manada. 3 MIL. escuadrón [de caballería]. 4 *pl.* tropas, soldados.
**troop (to)** *intr.* atroparse, ir en grupo, en tropel: *to* ~ *away, to* ~ *off*, alejarse, retirarse en tropel.
**trooper** (-øʳ) *s.* soldado de caballería; su caballo. 2 MAR. transporte de tropas [buque].
**troopial** (tru·pial) *s.* TROUPIAL.
**trope** (troup) *s.* RET. tropo.
**trophy** (trou·fi) *s.* trofeo.
**tropic** (tra·pik) *adj.* tropical. 2 BIOL. del tropismo. 3 *adj.-s.* ASTR., GEOGR. trópico.
**tropical** (tra·pik(al) *adj.* tropical. 2 RET. trópico.
**tropism** (trou·pišm) *s.* BIOL. tropismo.
**troposphere** (tra·pøsfiʳ) *s.* troposfera.
**trot** (trat) *s.* trote: *at a* ~, al trote. 2 niñito.
**trot (to)** *intr.* trotar. 2 *tr.* hacer trotar.
**troth** (troz) *s.* fe, fidelidad; verdad, veracidad. 2 ant. esponsales.
**trotline** (-lain) *s.* especie de palangre.
**trotter** (tra·tøʳ) *s.* trotador, trotón. 2 COC. pie, mano [de carnero, cerdo, etc.].
**troubadour** (tru·badoʳ) *s.* trovador.
**trouble** (trø·bøl) *s.* perturbación, desorden, agita-

ción, inquietud. 2 pena, congoja; apuro, dificultad: *to be in* ~, estar en un apuro. 3 molestia, incomodidad, engorro. 4 inconveniente. 5 molestia, trabajo, pena [que se toma uno]: *to go to the* ~ *to, to take the* ~ *to*, molestarse en, tomarse la molestia de. 6 avería, accidente [en un mecanismo]: ~ *shooting*, localización de averías. 7 MED. afección, desarreglo, trastorno: *lung* ~, afección pulmonar.
**trouble (to)** *tr.* turbar, perturbar. 2 revolver, agitar, enturbiar. 3 inquietar, afligir, atribular. 4 incomodar, molestar. 5 *intr.-ref.* preocuparse, apurarse. 6 molestarse, tomarse trabajo o molestia.
**troublemaker** (-meikøʳ) *s.* agitador, alborotador.
**troublesome** (-søm) *adj.* molesto, gravoso, dificultoso, pesado, fatigoso. 2 enojoso, incómodo, fastidioso. 3 inquieto, enredador.
**troublous** (trø·bløs) *adj.* agitado, revuelto.
**trough** (trof) *s.* comedero; abrevadero. 2 artesa, batea, cubeta. 3 seno o depresión entre dos olas, montañas, etc. 4 canalón de tejado.
**trounce (to)** (trauns) *tr.* pegar, zurrar. 2 derrotar.
**troupe** (trup) *s.* TEAT. compañía.
**trouper** (-øʳ) *s.* miembro de una compañía teatral. 2 actor veterano.
**troupial** (tru·pial) *s.* ORN. trupial.
**trousers** (trau·søʳs) *s. pl.* pantalones, calzones.
**trousseau** (trousou·) *s.* ajuar de novia.
**trout** (traut) *s.* ICT. trucha.
**trouvère** (truve·ʳ) *s.* trovero.
**trowel** (trau·øl) *s.* ALBAÑ. trulla, llana; paleta, palustre. 2 JARD. desplantador.
**trowel (to)** *tr.* alisar o aplicar con llana.
**Troy** (troi) *n. pr.* GEOGR. Troya.
**troy, troy-weight** *s.* sistema de pesos para oro, plata y drogas medicinales cuya unidad es la libra de 12 onzas [373 gramos].
**truancy** (tru·ansi) *s.* acción o costumbre de hacer novillos; ociosidad.
**truant** (-ant) *s.* tunante, holgazán: *to play* ~, hacer novillos. 2 *adj.* ocioso; perezoso, errabundo.
**truant (to)** *intr.* hacer novillos; holgazanear.
**truce** (trus) *s.* tregua.
**truck** (trøk) *s.* carretilla [carro de mano]. 2 rueda pequeña y fuerte. 3 carro grande, camión: ~ *driver*, camionero. 4 FERROC. (Ingl.) furgón; batea. 5 cambio, trueque, trato. 6 efectos para trocar o vender. 7 artículos sin valor; desecho. 8 *pl.* trucos [juego].
**truck (to)** *tr.* trocar, traficar. 2 pagar los salarios en especie. 3 transportar en camión.
**truckage** (-idÿ) *s.* camionaje.
**trucker** (-øʳ) *s.* carretero, camionero.
**truckle** (trø·køl) *s.* ruedecita. 2 ~ *bed*, TRUNDLE BED.
**truckle (to)** *intr.* rodar sobre ruedecitas. 2 someterse servilmente.
**truckman** (trø·kmæn) *s.* carretero, camionero. 2 chamarilero.
**truculence** (trø·kiuløns) *s.* truculencia, crueldad.
**truculent** (-lønt) *adj.* truculento.
**trudge** (trødÿ) *s.* caminata; marcha penosa.
**trudge (to)** *intr.-tr.* andar, caminar, recorrer [esp. con fatiga o esfuerzo].
**true** (tru) *adj.* verdadero, cierto, real: ~ *ribs*, ANAT., costillas verdaderas; *it is true*, es cierto, es verdad. 2 verídico, veraz. 3 fiel, leal. 4 exacto, fiel, correcto: ~ *copy*, copia fiel. 5 puro, legítimo, genuino. 6 *adv.* TRULY.
**true (to)** *tr.* arreglar, corregir, rectificar.
**true-blue** *adj.* fiel, constante, leal.

**true-born** *adj.* legítimo, verdadero, de nacimiento.
**true-bred** *adj.* de casta legítima.
**true-hearted** *adj.* sincero, leal.
**truelove** (-lav) *s.* fiel amante. *2* amado, amada: ~ *knot*, lazada, lazo.
**truffle** (trø·føl) *s.* BOT. trufa.
**truffled** (-d) *adj.* trufado.
**truism** (tru·išm) *s.* verdad manifiesta; perogrullada.
**truly** (tru·li) *adv.* verdaderamente, realmente, en verdad. *2* sinceramente. *3* fielmente. *4* exactamente, correctamente, debidamente. *5 yours (very) truly*, su afectísimo o su seguro servidor.
**trump** (trømp) *s.* NAIPES triunfo; palo de triunfo: ~ *card*, triunfo [naipe]; fig. valioso recurso; *no* ~, sin triunfo. *2* poét. trompeta.
**trump (to)** *tr.* triunfar, fallar, jugar triunfo. *2 to* ~ *up*, inventar, forjar.
**trumpery** (trø·mpøri) *s.* oropel, relumbrón; vaciedades, tonterías. *2* ant. engaño, fraude.
**trumpet** (trø·mpit) *s.* trompeta, clarín: ~ *blast*, trompetazo. *2* sonido de la trompeta. *3* barrito, berrido [del elefante]. *4* zumbido [del mosquito].
**trumpet (to)** *tr.* pregonar a son de trompeta. *2* gritar, decir gritando. *3* abocardar. *4 intr.* trompetear. *5* berrear [el elefante].
**trumpeter** (-ø') *s.* trompetero, trompeta. *2* pregonero. *3* ORN. agamí.
**truncate (to)** *tr.* truncar, troncar. *2* mutilar. *3* abreviar.
**truncheon** (trø·nchøn) *s.* garrote, porra, cachiporra. *2* porra de policía.
**truncheon (to)** *tr.* golpear con cachiporra.
**trundle** (trø·ndøl) *s.* ruedecilla [esp. de mueble]. *2* carretilla de ruedas pequeñas. *3 trundle* o ~ *bed*, cama baja con ruedas.
**trundle (to)** *tr.* hacer rodar. *2 intr.* rodar.
**trunk** (trøŋk) *s.* tronco [de árbol; del cuerpo; de una familia, etc.]. *2* FERROC. línea principal. *3* cofre, baúl; portaequipaje [de automóvil]. *4* trompa de elefante. *5 pl.* pantalones cortos de deporte. *6 adj.* TELÉF. interurbano: ~ *call*, conferencia interurbana.
**trunkfish** (-fish) *s.* ICT. pez cofre.
**trunnion** (trø·ñøn) *s.* ARTILL. muñón.
**truss** (trøs) *s.* ING. armazón o armadura de sostén, viga de celosía. *2* mazorca. *3* CIR. braguero. *4* haz [de paja].
**truss (to)** *tr.* atar, liar. *2* recoger, empaquetar. *3* COC. atar [un ave] para asarla. *4* ARQ., ING. sostener; atirantar.
**trust** (trøst) *s.* confianza, fe [en una pers. o cosa]; esperanza. *2* depósito, cargo, cuidado, custodia; *Trust Company*, Banco de depósitos. *3* DER. fideicomiso. *4* COM. crédito: *to sell on* ~, vender a crédito. *5* trust, asociación de empresas.
**trust (to)** *tr.* confiar en, tener confianza o fe en. *2* confiar [algo] al cargo, custodia, etc., de alguno. *3* confiar, esperar [que]. *4* COM. hacer crédito a, fiar a. *5 intr.* confiar, esperar. *6* COM. fiar.
**trustee** (trøsti·) *s.* fideicomisario, fiduciario, depositario; administrador legal. *2 board of trustees*, patronato, consejo [de una universidad].
**trustful** (trø·stful) *adj.* confiado.
**trustworthy** (-uø'di) *adj.* fiable, confiable, fidedigno, seguro.
**trusty** (-i) *adj.* fiel, leal, honrado, fidedigno. *2* firme, fuerte, seguro. *3* confiado. *4 s.* persona honrada, digna de confianza.

**truth** (truz) *s.* verdad: *in* ~, en verdad. *2* exactitud, realidad. *3* veracidad. *4* fidelidad, constancia.
**truthful** (-ful) *adj.* veraz, verídico. *2* verdadero, exacto.
**truthless** (-lis) *adj.* falso; fementido.
**try** (trai) *s.* prueba, ensayo. *2* tentativa.
**try (to)** *tr.* probar a, intentar, tratar de. *2* probar, ensayar, hacer la prueba de: *to* ~ *on*, probarse [una prenda]. *3* poner a prueba, exasperar, cansar: *to* ~ *someone's patience*, poner a prueba la paciencia de uno. *4* DER. juzgar [a uno]; ver [una causa o litigio]. *5* CARP., MEC. ajustar, acabar. *6 to* ~ *out*, probar, someter a prueba. *7 intr.* probar, esforzarse. ¶ Pret. y p. p.: *tried*.
**trying** (-ing) *adj.* de prueba. *2* molesto, irritante, fatigoso.
**tryout** (-aut) *s.* prueba [que se hace de una persona o cosa].
**Tsar** (tsa') *s.* zar.
**tub** (tøb) *s.* tina, dornajo, batea. *2* bañera, baño. *4* cuñete, barrilito.
**tub (to)** *tr.* poner en tina. ¶ Pret. y p. p.: *tubbed;* ger.: *tubbing.*
**tuba** (tiu·ba) *s.* MÚS. tuba.
**tubage** (tiu·bidy) *s.* CIR. intubación.
**tubby** (tø·bi) *adj.* en forma de cubo, rechoncho.
**tube** (tiub) *s.* tubo: *inner* ~, cámara de neumático. *2* caño, cañuto. *3* ANAT. conducto, tubo. *4* RADIO. lámpara, válvula. *5 tube* o ~ *railway*, metro, ferrocarril subterráneo.
**tube (to)** *tr.* proveer de tubos. *2* entubar, conducir por tubos. *3* dar forma de tubo.
**tubercle** (tiu·bø'køl) *s.* ANAT., ZOOL., MED. tubérculo. *2* BOT. raíz tuberosa.
**tubercular** (tiubø·'kula') *adj.* tuberculoso, parecido a un tubérculo. *2 adj.-s.* tuberculoso.
**tuberculosis** (tiubø'kiuløu·sis) *s.* MED. tuberculosis.
**tuberculous** (tiubø·'kiuløs) *adj.* MED. tuberculoso.
**tuberose** (tiu·børoush) *s.* BOT. tuberosa, nardo.
**tuberosity** (tiubøra·siti) *s.* tuberosidad.
**tuberous** (tiu·børøs) *adj.* tuberoso.
**tubing** (tiu·bing) *s.* tubería, material para tubos.
**tubular** (tiu·biula') *adj.* tubular.
**tubulate (d** (tiu·biuleit(id) *adj.* tubular. *2* provisto de tubos.
**tuck** (tøk) *s.* alforza, pliegue, lorza. *2* ENCUAD. tapa con cartera. *3* pop. buena comida, golosinas.
**tuck (to)** *tr.* alforzar, recoger, arremangar. | Gralte. con *up*. *2* envolver, arropar. | Con *in, up*, etc. *3* meter: *to* ~ *in*, remeter bien [la ropa de la cama, etc.]; pop. engullir; *to* ~ *away*, esconder.
**Tuesday** (tiu·šdi) *s.* martes.
**tufa** (tiu·fa) *s.* toba, tufo.
**tufaceous** (tiufei·shøs) *adj.* tobáceo, toboso.
**tuft** (tøft) *s.* penacho, cresta, moño, copete, tupé. *2* mechón, borla. *3* manojo; grupo [de plantas]; mata espesa.
**tuft (to)** *tr.* empenachar. *2* adornar con borlas.
**tug** (tøg) *s.* tirón, estirón; lucha, forcejeo: ~ *of war*, DEP. juego de la cuerda. *2* tirante [guarnición]; cuerda [para arrastrar]. *3* remolcador.
**tug (to)** *tr.* tirar de, arrastrar. *2* halar, remolcar. *3 intr.* con fuerza, trabajar con esfuerzo.
**tuition** (tiui·shøn) *s.* enseñanza, instrucción. *2* lo que se paga por la enseñanza.
**tulip** (tiu·lip) *s.* BOT. tulipán. *2* BOT. ~ *tree*, tulipero.
**tulipwood** (-wud) *s.* palo de rosa [árbol y madera].
**tulle** (tul) *s.* tul.
**tumble** (tø·mbøl) *s.* caída, tumbo, vuelco, voltereta. *2* desorden, confusión.

**tumble (to)** *intr.* voltear, dar volteretas. *2* caerse, derrumbarse; dejarse caer. *3* hundirse, desplomarse. *4* correr, precipitarse. *5* agitarse, revolverse, revolcarse. *6 to* ~ *into, on* o *upon*, tropezar con, dar con, encontrar. *7 to* ~ *to*, comprender, entender, percatarse. *8 tr.* hacer caer, derribar, tumbar. *9* volcar. *10* desarreglar, trastornar. *11* zarandear, empujar de un lado a otro. *12* secar, pulir, etc., en un tambor giratorio.
**tumblebug** (-bøg) *s.* ENT. escarabajo pelotero.
**tumble-down** *adj.* destartalado, ruinoso.
**tumbler** (-ø$^r$) *s.* vaso [para beber], cubilete. *2* volteador, volatinero. *3* dominguillo. *4* tambor giratorio [para secar ropa, pulir metales, etc.]. *5* ORN. pichón volteador.
**tumbrel, tumbril** (tø·mbrøl) *s.* carro, carreta. *2* carro de artillería.
**tumefaction** (tiumifæ·kshøn) *s.* tumefacción.
**tumefy (to)** (tiu·mifai) *tr.* hinchar, producir tumefacción. *2 intr.* hincharse. ¶ CONJUG. pret. y p. p.: *tumefied.*
**tumid** (tiu·mid) *adj.* túmido, hinchado.
**tummy** (-mi) *s.* fam. estómago.
**tumo(u)r** (-mø$^r$) *s.* MED. tumor.
**tumular** (-miula$^r$) *adj.* tumulario.
**tumult** (-mølt) *s.* tumulto.
**tumultuary** (tiumø·lchueri) *adj.* tumultuario.
**tumultuous** (-chuøs) *adj.* tumultuoso.
**tumulus** (tiu·miuløs) *s.* túmulo [montecillo].
**tun** (tøn) *s.* tonel, cuba.
**tun (to)** *tr.* entonelar, encubar.
**tuna** (tu·na) *s.* BOT. tuna, higo chumbo. *2* ICT. atún.
**tunable** (tiu·nabøl) *adj.* afinable, templable. *2* armonioso, melodioso, agradable.
**tune** (tiun) *s.* aire, melodía, canción. *2* MÚS. afinación: *out of* ~, desafinado, destemplado. *3* concordancia, armonía: *in* ~ *with*, a tono con. *4* tono [con que se habla], actitud. *5* humor, disposición.
**tune (to)** *tr.* templar, afinar, acordar. *2* cantar, entonar. *3* ajustar, adaptar. *4* RADIO *to* ~ *in*, sintonizar. *5 to* ~ *up*, acordar [instrumentos]; poner a punto [un motor]. *6 intr.* armonizar.
**tuneful** (-ful) *adj.* armonioso, melodioso.
**tuneless** (-lis) *adj.* disonante, discordante.
**tuner** (-ø$^r$) *s.* afinador, templador. *2* ajustador. *3* RADIO. sintonizador.
**tungsten** (tøn·gstøn) *s.* QUÍM. tungsteno, volframio.
**tunic** (tiu·nik) *s.* túnica [vestidura]; blusa, guerrera. *2* ANAT., ZOOL., BOT. túnica.
**Tunicata** (tiunikei·ta) *s. pl.* ZOOL. tunicados.
**tunicle** (tiu·nikøl) *s.* ECLES. tunicela.
**tuning** (tiu·ning) *s.* MÚS. afinación, templadura. *2* RADIO. sintonización. *3 adj.* que sirve para afinar o sintonizar: ~ *fork*, diapasón; ~ *hammer*, ~ *key*, llave de afinador; ~ *coil*, bobina sintonizadora.
**Tunis** (tu·nis) *n. pr.* GEOGR. Túnez [ciudad].
**Tunisian** (tuni·shan) *adj.-s.* tunecí, tunecino.
**tunnel** (tø·nøl) *s.* túnel. *2* MIN. galería, socavón.
**tunnel (to)** *tr.* abrir un túnel a través de o debajo de; excavar. *2 intr.* abrir túnel o galería. ¶ Pret. y p. p.: *tunnel(l)ed; ger.: -l(l)ing.*
**tunny** (tø·ni) *s.* ICT. atún.
**turban** (tø·$^r$ban) *s.* turbante.
**turbary** (tiu·$^r$bæri) *s.* turbera.
**turbid** (tø·$^r$bid) *adj.* turbio, túrbido, turbulento.
**turbine** (tø·$^r$bin) *s.* MEC. turbina.
**turbojet** (tø·$^r$boudẏet) *s.* turborreactor.
**turbomotor** (-moutø$^r$) *s.* turbomotor.
**turbot** (tø·$^r$bot) *s.* ICT. rodaballo, rombo.

**turbulence, -cy** (tø·$^r$biuløns, -si) *s.* turbulencia, alboroto, tumulto.
**turbulent** (-ønt) *adj.* turbulento, agitado, tempestuoso. *2* levantisco, revoltoso.
**tureen** (tiurı·n) *s.* sopera. *2* salsera.
**turf** (tø·$^r$f) *s.* césped; tepe. *2* turba. *3 the* ~, el hipódromo; las carreras de caballos.
**turf (to)** *tr.* encespedar.
**turfy** (tø·$^r$fi) *adj.* abundante en césped o turba.
**turgescence** (tø·$^r$dẏe·søns) *s.* turgencia. *2* fig. hinchazón, pomposidad.
**turgescent** (-sønt), **turgid** (tø·$^r$dẏid) *adj.* turgente. *2* hinchado, ampuloso, pomposo.
**turion** (tiu·riøn) *s.* BOT. turión.
**Turk** (tø·$^r$k) *s.* turco, otomano.
**Turkestan** (tø·$^r$kø·stan) *n. pr.* GEOGR. el Turquestán.
**Turkey** (tø·$^r$k) *n. pr.* GEOGR. Turquía.
**turkey** *s.* ORN. pavo, gallipavo, *guajolote. *2* ORN. ~ *buzzard*, aura, gallinazo, *zopilote.
**Turkish** (-ish) *adj.* turco, turquí: ~ *blue*, azul turquí: ~ *towel*, toalla rusa. *2* ANAT. ~ *saddle*, silla turca. *3 s.* idioma turco.
**Turk's-head** *s.* escobón, deshollinador.
**turmalin(e** (tu·$^r$malin) *s.* TOURMALIN.
**turmeric** (tø·$^r$merik) *s.* BOT. cúrcuma.
**turmoil** (tø·$^r$moil) *s.* tumulto, agitación, alboroto, confusión, barahúnda.
**turmoil (to)** *tr.* agitar, inquietar, trastornar.
**turn** (tø·$^r$n) *s.* vuelta, giro, revolución. *2* vuelta, paseo. *3* recodo, vuelta; cambio, variación, desviación: ~ *of life*, FISIOL. menopausia. *4* viraje. *5* sobresalto, impresión. *6* aspecto, sesgo, giro, curso: *to take another* ~, tomar otro sesgo, cambiar de aspecto. *7* forma, hechura, estilo. *8* giro [de la frase]. *9* acción, comportamiento [respecto de otra pers.]: *friendly* ~, *good* ~, favor, servicio; *bad* ~, *ill* ~, mala pasada, jugarreta, trastada. *10* turno, tanda: *to take turns*, turnarse. *11* acto de destreza. *12* MÚS. grupeto. *13* COC. *to a turn*, en su punto.
**turn (to)** *tr.* volver, dar vuelta a; voltear, hacer rodar. *2* tornear [labrar al torno]. *3* formar, moldear, hacer, pergeñar. *4* volver, dirigir, encaminar. *5* remover [la tierra]. *6* trastornar, revolver: *to* ~ *the brain of*, trastornar el juicio a; *to* ~ *the stomach*, revolver el estómago. *7* volver del revés: *to* ~ *coat*, fig. volver casaca. *8* desviar, apartar, disuadir. *9* encauzar, dirigir. *10* aplicar, destinar. *11* rechazar, expulsar. *12* doblar [un cabo, una esquina], rebasar, dar la vuelta a: *to* ~ *the corner*, doblar la esquina. *13* cambiar, transformar, traducir. *14* poner [pálido, enfermo, etc.]. *15* encorvar, doblar, torcer. *16 to* ~ *a deaf ear*, hacerse sordo. *17 to* ~ *an honest penny*, ganar dinero honradamente. *18 to* ~ *around*, dar vuelta o la vuelta; hacer girar. *19 to* ~ *aside*, desviar. *20 to* ~ *away*, despedir, echar; desviar. *21 to* ~ *back*, volver atrás; devolver. *22 to* ~ *bridle*, volver grupas. *23 to* ~ *down*, poner boca abajo; bajar [el gas]. *24 to* ~ *on*, abrir [una llave o espita]; dar [la luz, el gas, etc.]; poner, abrir [la radio]. *25 to* ~ *out*, echar, expulsar, arrojar; producir, hacer; volver del revés; apagar [la luz]. *26 to* ~ *over*, volcar, invertir; revolver; revolver en la mente; traspasar, transferir; volver una hoja. *27 to* ~ *the scale* (*s*, fig. pesar, ser decisivo. *28 to* ~ *the tables*, volver las tornas. *29 to* ~ *to account*, *advantage* o *profit*, aprovechar, sacar partido de. *30 to* ~ *up*, volver, doblar o dirigir hacia arriba, subir [el cuello]; poner

más fuerte [la radio]; *to ~ up one's nose at,* desdeñar, hacer ascos a.
*31 intr.* girar, rodar, dar vueltas, voltear. *32* volverse [volver el cuerpo, el rostro]. *33* desviarse, torcer, virar. *34* dirigirse, tomar una dirección. *35* volverse, ponerse, hacerse: *to ~ pale,* ponerse pálido, palidecer. *36* volverse [contra]. *37* girar, versar [sobre]. *38* apartar la vista, la atención. *39* caer [la balanza]. *40* agriarse, torcerse, cortarse [un líquido]. *41* torcerse, doblarse. *42 to ~ about* o *around,* volver la cara, volverse, dar una vuelta. *43 to ~ aside,* desviarse. *44 to ~ away,* alejarse; volver la cara, la espalda. *45 to ~ from,* apartarse de, huir de. *46 to ~ in,* entrar; irse a la cama, acostarse. *47 to ~ into,* entrar en; volverse, convertirse en. *48 to ~ off,* desviarse, torcer. *49 to ~ out,* salir, resultar: *to ~ out badly,* salir mal; *to ~ out well,* salir bien. *50 to ~ over,* dar vueltas, revolverse; volcar [un vehículo]. *51 to ~ to,* tender, dirigirse a; ponerse, aplicarse a; acudir, recurrir a; volverse hacia; redundar en. *52 to ~ turtle,* MAR. zozobrar. *53 to ~ up,* estar vuelto hacia arriba; aparecer de pronto, reaparecer. *54 to ~ upside down,* volcarse, zozobrar.
**turnbuckle** (-bøkøl) *s.* tornillo tensor. *2* tarabilla [para tener abierta una ventana].
**turncoat** (-kout) *s.* POL. desertor, renegado.
**turndown** (-daun) *adj.* doblado hacia abajo, vuelto [cuello, etc.].
**turner** (-øʳ) *s.* tornero, torneador.
**turning** (-ing) *s.* giro, vuelta. *2* viraje. *3* revuelta, recodo, esquina. *4* tornería. *5 pl.* torneaduras. *6* piezas torneadas. *7 adj.* giratorio. *8 ~ point,* punto crucial o decisivo, crisis.
**turnip** (tøˑʳnip) *s.* BOT. nabo. *2* BOT. colinabo.
**turnkey** (tøˑʳnki) *s.* carcelero, llavero de cárcel.
**turnout** (tøˑʳnaut) *s.* salida [acción]. *2* reunión, concurrencia. *3* apartadero [en un camino o vía férrea]. *4* producción [de una fábrica, etc.]. *5* acabado, presentación. *6* vestido, atuendo.
**turnover** (-ouvøʳ) *adj.* doblado o vuelto hacia abajo. *2 s.* vuelco. *3* voltereta. *4* vuelta, parte doblada sobre otra. *5* empanadilla. *6* COC. estrelladera, pala. *7* cambio completo. *8* reorganización, cambio [de personal]. *9* COM. giro, movimiento. *10* COM. ciclo de compra y venta.
**turnpike** (-paik) *s.* barrera o camino de portazgo. *2* (E.U.) gran autopista de peaje.
**turnspit** (-spit) *s.* el que da vueltas al asador.
**turnstile** (-stail) *s.* torniquete [en un paso].
**turnstone** (-stoun) *s.* ORN. revuelvepiedras.
**turntable** (-teibøl) *s.* FERROC. placa giratoria. *2* disco giratorio del microscopio o del fonógrafo.
**turpentine** (tøˑʳpentain) *s.* trementina.
**turpitude** (tøˑʳpitiud) *s.* vileza, depravación.
**turquoise** (tøˑʳkois) *s.* MINER. turquesa.
**turret** (tøˑrit) *s.* torrecilla. *2* MAR. torre blindada.
**turtle** (tøˑʳtøl) *s.* ZOOL. tortuga [esp. de mar]. *2 adj.* de tortuga: *~ shell,* carey.
**turtledove** (-døv) *s.* ORN. tórtola.
**Tuscan** (tøˑskan) *adj.-s.* toscano.
**Tuscany** (tøˑskani) *n. pr.* GEOGR. Toscana.
**tusk** (tøsk) *s.* colmillo, defensa [de elefante, jabalí, morsa, narval, etc.].
**tussle** (tøˑsøl) *s.* pelea. *2* discusión, agarrada.
**tussle (to)** *intr.* luchar, pelear, forcejear.
**tussock** (tøˑsøk) *s.* mechón, penacho. *2* macizo de hierba espesa.
**tutelage** (tiuˑtølidy) *s.* tutela.
**tutelar** (-laʳ) *adj.* tutelar.

**tutelary** (-leri) *adj.* TUTELAR. *2 s.* divinidad o santo tutelar.
**tutor** (tiuˑtøʳ) *s.* preceptor, ayo. *2* tutor, curador.
**tutor (to)** *tr.* enseñar, instruir. *2* ser tutor de. *3* disciplinar, dominar. *4 intr.* ser preceptor, dar lecciones particulares.
**tutorial** (-ial) *adj.* preceptoral. *2* tutelar.
**tutorship** (-ship) *s.* preceptoria. *2* tutoría.
**tuxedo** (tuksiˑdou) *s.* (E.U.) traje de esmoquing.
**tuyere** (tuiyeˑʳ) *s.* tobera, alcribís.
**twaddle** (tuaˑdøl) *s.* charla, palabreo, palabrería.
**twaddle (to)** *intr.* charlar, decir tonterías.
**twain** (tuein) *adj.-s.* poét. dos.
**twang** (tuæng) *s.* sonido vibrante, como el de una cuerda punteada. *2* gangueo, tonillo nasal.
**twang (to)** *tr.* puntear [una cuerda, un instrumento]. *2* decir gangueando. *3 intr.* producir un sonido vibrante; sonar [una cuerda]. *4* ganguear.
**tweak** (tuɪk) *s.* pellizco retorcido.
**tweed** (tuɪd) *s.* TEJ. cierto paño de lana o mezcla y de dos o más colores. *2 pl.* ropa hecha de este paño. *3 adj.* hecho de este paño.
**tweedle (to)** (-øl) *intr.-tr.* cantar, silbar. *2* tocar un instrumento. *3 tr.* engaitar.
**tweet** (tuɪt) *s.* pío, gorjeo [de pájaro].
**tweezers** (tuɪˑsøʳš) *s. pl.* pinzas, tenacillas [para objetos menudos].
**twelfth** (tuelf) *adj.* duodécimo, doceno, doce. *2 adj.-s.* duodécimo. *3 s.* doce [del mes]. *4* MÚS. duodécima.
**Twelfth-day** *s.* día de Reyes, Epifanía.
**Twelfth-night** *s.* noche de Reyes.
**twelve** (tueˑlv) *adj.-s.* doce: *~ o'clock;* las doce.
**twelvemonth** (-manz) *s.* año, doce meses.
**twentieth** (tueˑntiiz) *adj.-s.* vigésimo, veintavo. *2 adj.* veinte [capítulo, etc.]. *3 s.* veinte [del mes].
**twenty** (tueˑnti) *adj.-s.* veinte.
**twice** (tuais) *adv.* dos veces. *2* el doble: *~ as much,* ~ *as many,* el doble.
**twiddle** (tuiˑdøl) *tr.* jugar, entretenerse con. *2* hacer dar vueltas [esp. a los pulgares para entretenerse]. *3 intr.* entretenerse, estar ocioso.
**twig** (tuig) *s.* BOT. ramita. *2* varita, vergueta. *3* ANAT. pequeña ramificación.
**twilight** (tuaiˑlait) *s.* crepúsculo, media luz: *at ~,* entre dos luces. *2 adj.* crepuscular; débilmente iluminado.
**twill** (tuil) *s.* tela cruzada o asargada.
**twill (to)** *tr.* TEJ. cruzar, asargar.
**twin** (tuin) *s.* gemelo, mellizo. *2 pl.* ASTR. Géminis. *3 adj.* gemelo. *4* doble, de dos.
**twin (to)** *tr.* juntar, emparejar, unir [dos cosas].
**twine** (tuain) *s.* cordel, bramante, guita. *2* abrazo, enroscadura, entrelazamiento.
**twine (to)** *tr.* torcer [hilos, hebras, etc., juntos]; tejer. *2* enroscar, enlazar, abrazar. *4 intr.* entrelazarse. *4* enroscarse. *5* serpentear.
**twin-engined** *adj.* AVIA. bimotor.
**twinge** (tuindy) *s.* punzada, dolor agudo. *2* remordimiento.
**twinge (to)** *tr.* punzar, causar dolor agudo. *2 intr.* sentir una punzada, un dolor agudo.
**twinkle** (tuiˑnkøl) *s.* titilación, centelleo, destello. *2* parpadeo. *3* instante.
**twinkle (to)** *intr.* titilar, centellear, destellar, chispear. *2* parpadear; guiñar. *3 tr.* hacer centellear. *4* abrir y cerrar [los ojos].
**twinkling** (-kling) *s.* TWINKLE: *in a ~, in the ~ of an eye,* en un abrir y cerrar de ojos.

**twirl** (tuǿl) s. giro o vuelta rápidos; molinete. 2 rasgo [hecho con la pluma].
**twirl (to)** tr. hacer girar o dar vueltas rápidamente. 2 retorcer, ensortijar. 3 intr. girar rápidamente. 4 retorcerse, enroscarse.
**twist** (tuist) s. torsión, torcedura. 2 enroscadura, vuelta. 3 sesgo, inclinación; propensión, tendencia. 4 rosca [de pan]. 5 rollo [de tabaco].
**twist (to)** tr. torcer, retorcer. 2 enroscar, enrollar. 3 entrelazar, trenzar. 4 estrujar, oprimir [torciendo]. 5 doblar, doblegar. 6 intr. torcerse, retorcerse. 7 enroscarse, arrollarse, ensortijarse. 8 serpentear. 9 dar vueltas.
**twisting** (tui·sting) s. TWIST. 2 adj. que tuerce, que se enrosca; serpenteante.
**twit** (to) (tuit) tr. reprochar, echar en cara. ¶ Pret. y p. p.: twitted; ger.: -tting.
**twitch** (tuich) s. crispamiento, temblor, contracción nerviosa. 2 tirón, sacudida. 3 VET. acial.
**twitch (to)** tr. tirar de, dar un tirón a. 2 intr. crisparse, moverse convulsivamente. 3 to ~ at, tirar de.
**twitter** (tui·tǿ) s. gorjeo, piar [de los pájaros]. 2 charla alegre. 3 risa ahogada. 4 agitación, inquietud.
**twitter (to)** intr. gorjear, piar. 2 reír con risa ahogada. 3 temblar, agitarse.
**two** (tu) adj.-s. dos: ~ o'clock, las dos; ~ of a kind, tal para cual.
**two-colo (u) r** adj. de dos colores, bicromático.
**two-cycle** adj. MEC. de dos tiempos.
**two-decker** s. MAR. navío de dos puentes.
**two-edged** adj. de dos filos.
**twofold** (-fould) adj. doble [duplo; de dos]. 2 adv. doble, doblemente.
**two-four** adj. MÚS. de dos por cuatro.
**two-legged** adj. de dos pies o patas. 2 bípedo.
**twopence** (tu·pøns) s. dos peniques.
**two-penny** adj. de dos peniques. 2 de tres al cuarto.
**two-phase** adj. ELECT. bifásico.
**two-ply** adj. de dos cabos o hilos. 2 de dos capas.
**two-seater** s. coche, aeroplano, etc., de dos asientos.
**two-step** s. paso doble [baile y música].
**two-stroke** adj. MEC. de dos tiempos.
**two-way** adj. de dos sentidos o direcciones.
**two-wheeler** s. vehículo de dos ruedas.
**tycoon** (taiku·n) s. magnate [de la industria, etcétera].

**tyke** (taik) s. fam. gozque. 2 fam. tipo, sujeto.
**tympan** (ti·mpan) s. MÚS. tambor. 2 ARQ., IMPR. tímpano.
**tympanic** (timpæ·nik) adj. ANAT., MED. timpánico.
**tympanist** (ti·mpanist) s. MÚS. timbalero.
**tympanites** (timpanai·tıš) s. MED. timpanitis.
**tympanitis** (-tis) s. MED. inflamación del tímpano.
**tympanum** (ti·mpanøm) s. ANAT., ZOOL., ARQ. tímpano. 2 TELEF. diafragma.
**type** (taip) s. tipo [símbolo, modelo, género, ejemplo característico]. 2 BIOL., H. NAT., IMPR. tipo. 3 NUMIS. figura.
**type (to)** tr. representar, ser el tipo de. 2 mecanografiar. 3 MED. determinar el grupo o tipo [de una sangre].
**typesetter** (-setǿ) s. IMPR. cajista, tipógrafo.
**typesetting** (-seting) s. IMPR. composición. 2 adj. IMPR. de componer.
**typewrite (to)** (-rait) tr. mecanografiar.
**typewriter** (-ǿ) s. máquina de escribir. 2 mecanógrafo, fa.
**typewriting** (-ting) s. mecanografía.
**typhoid** (tai·foid) adj. tifoideo. 2 s. fiebre tifoidea.
**typhoon** (taifu·n) s. METEOR. tifón.
**typhous** (tai·føs) adj. MED. tífico.
**typhus** (tai·føs) s. MED. tifo, tifus.
**typical** (ti·pikal) adj. típico; característico.
**typify (to)** (ti·pifai) tr. representar, simbolizar. 2 ser el tipo o ejemplo de. ¶ Pret. y p. p.: typified.
**typist** (tai·pist) s. mecanógrafo, fa; dactilógrafo, fa.
**typographer** (taipa·grafǿ) s. tipógrafo, impresor.
**typographic (al** (taipogræ·fik(al) adj. tipográfico.
**typography** (-grafi) s. tipografía, imprenta.
**tyrannic(al** (tiræ·nik(al) adj. tiránico, despótico.
**tyrannicide** (-nisaid) s. tiranicidio. 2 tiranicida.
**tyrannize (to)** (ti·ranaiš) tr. tiranizar. 2 intr. obrar con tiranía.
**tyrannous** (-nøs) adj. tiránico.
**tyranny** (ti·ranı) s. tiranía. 2 acto tiránico.
**tyrant** (tai·rant) s. tirano, déspota.
**Tyre** (tai·) n. pr. GEOGR. Tiro.
**tyre** s. TIRE.
**Tyrian** (ti·rian) adj.-s. tirio.
**tyro** (tai·rou) s. tirón, novicio.
**Tyrol (the)** (ti·roul) n. pr. GEOGR. el Tirol.
**Tyrolese** (tirøli·š) adj.-s. tirolés.
**Tyrrhenian** (tırı·nian) adj. tirreno: ~ Sea, Mar Tirreno.
**tzigane** (tši·gan) s. cíngaro, zíngaro.

# U

**U, u** (yu) *s*. U, u, vigésima primera letra del alfabeto inglés.
**ubiquitous** (yubi·kuitøs) *adj*. obicuo, omnipresente.
**ubiquity** (-ti) *s*. ubicuidad, omnipresencia.
**udder** (ø·dø<sup>r</sup>) *s*. ZOOL. ubre, teta.
**udometer** (yuda·mitø<sup>r</sup>) *s*. udómetro.
**ugh** (øg) *interj*. ¡uf!, ¡puf!, ¡fu!
**ugly** (ø·gli) *adj*. feo. 2 horroroso, horrible. 3 odioso, repugnante; malo, desagradable. 4 (E.U.) de mal genio.
**uhlan** (u·lan) *s*. MIL. ulano.
**ukase** (yu·keis) *s*. ucase.
**Ukraine** (yu·krein) *n. pr*. GEOGR. Ucrania.
**Ukrainian** (yukreini·an) *adj.-s*. ucranio, ucraniano.
**ulcer** (ø·lsø<sup>r</sup>) *s*. úlcera, llaga.
**ulcerate (to)** (-eit) *tr*. ulcerar. 2 *intr*. ulcerarse.
**ulceration** (ølsørei·shøn) *s*. ulceración.
**ulcerous** (ø·lsørøs) *adj*. ulceroso.
**ulema** (uløma·) *s*. ulema.
**uliginous** (yuli·dyinøs) *s*. uliginoso.
**ulmaceous** (ølmei·shøs) *adj*. BOT. ulmáceo.
**ulmic** (ø·lmik) *adj*. QUÍM. úlmico.
**ulna** (ø·lna) *s*. ANAT. cúbito. 2 ana [medida].
**ulster** (ø·lstø<sup>r</sup>) *s*. ruso [abrigo].
**ulterior** (ølti·riø<sup>r</sup>) *adj*. ulterior.
**ultima** (ø·ltima) *s*. última sílaba.
**ultimate** (ø·ltimit) *adj*. último, final. 2 fundamental, esencial, elemental. 3 MEC. máximo.
**ultimatum** (øltimei·tøm) *s*. ultimátum.
**ultimo** (ø·ltimou) *adj*. del mes próximo pasado.
**ultra-** (ø·ltra) *pref*. ultra-.
**ultra** *adj*. exagerado, extremo. 2 fanático, acérrimo. 3 *s*. extremista, exaltado.
**ultraism** (-iśm) *s*. extremismo, radicalismo.
**ultraist** (-ist) *s*. extremista, radical.
**ultramarine** (øltramarı·n) *adj*. ultramarino. 2 *s*. azul ultramaro o de ultramar.
**ultramicroscope** (-mai·kroskoup) *s*. ultramicroscopio.
**ultramontane** (-ma·ntein) *adj.-s*. ultramontano.
**ultramundane** (-ma·ndein) *adj*. ultramundano.
**ultravioleta** (-vai·ølit) *adj*. ultravioleta.
**ultravirus** (-vai·røs) *s*. ultravirus.
**ululate (to)** (ø·liuleit) *intr*. ulular, aullar.
**ululation** (øliulei·shøn) *s*. ululato. 2 aullido.
**Ulysses** (yuli·sis) *n. pr*. Ulises.

**umbel** (ø·mbøl) *s*. BOT. umbela.
**umbellate(d** (-eit(id) *adj*. umbelado.
**umbellifer** (ømbøli·fø<sup>r</sup>) *s*. BOT. umbelífera.
**umbelliferous** (-øs) *adj*. umbelífero.
**umber** (ø·mbø<sup>r</sup>) *s*. PINT. tierra de sombra. 2 ICT. tímalo. 3 *adj*. de color pardo oscuro.
**umbilical** (ømbi·likal) *adj*. umbilical.
**umbilicate** (ømbi·likit) *adj*. umbilicado.
**umbo** (ø·mbou) *s*. cazoleta de broquel.
**umbra** (ø·mbra), *pl*. **-brae** (-brı) *s*. sombra. 2 ASTR. cono de sombra. 3 ASTR. núcleo [de las manchas solares].
**umbrage** (ø·mbridý) *s*. sombra, umbría. 2 sombraje. 3 pique, resentimiento: *to take* ~ *at*, resentirse por.
**umbrage (to)** *tr*. sombrear, dar sombra a. 2 picar, ofender.
**umbrageous** (ømbrei·dýøs) *adj*. sombrío, umbroso. 2 receloso, resentido.
**umbrella** (ømbre·la) *s*. paraguas: ~ *stand*, paragüero [mueble]. 2 sombrilla. 3 ZOOL. umbrela.
**umbrous** (ø·mbrøs) *adj*. umbrátil, umbroso.
**umpire** (ø·mpai<sup>r</sup>) *s*. árbitro, juez árbitro. 2 DEP. árbitro.
**umpire (to)** *tr.-intr*. arbitrar [juzgar como árbitro].
**un-** (øn) *pref*. que denota contrariedad, oposición, negación, privación y equivale en muchos casos a des-, in-, no, sin, etc.
**unabashed** (ønabe·sht) *adj*. no avergonzado.
**unable** (-ei·bøl) *adj*. incapaz, imposibilitado. 2 *to be* ~ *to*, no poder [hacer una cosa].
**unabridged** (-abri·dýd) *adj*. sin abreviar, íntegro.
**unacceptable** (-akse·ptabøl) *adj*. inaceptable.
**unaccommodating** (-æka·mødeiting) *adj*. poco complaciente, poco servicial.
**unaccountable** (-ækau·ntabøl) *adj*. inexplicable, extraño, misterioso; irresponsable.
**unaccounted-for** (-tid) *adj*. no explicado.
**unadaptable** (-adæptabøl) *adj*. inadaptable.
**unaddressed** (-ædre·st) *adj*. sin dirección [carta, etc.].
**unadorned** (-ado·<sup>r</sup>nd) *adj*. sencillo, sin adornos.
**unadvisable** (-advai·śabøl) *adj*. que no es de aconsejar; poco cuerdo o prudente.
**unadvised** (-advai·śd) *adj*. sin consejo. 2 imprudente, precipitado, irreflexivo.
**unaffected** (-afe·ktid) *adj*. sencillo, natural, libre de afectación. 2 impasible, inalterado.

**unaided** (-ei·did) *adj.* sin ayuda.
**unalloyed** (-*aloi*·d) *adj.* puro, sin mezcla.
**unalterable** (-*o*·ltørabøl) *adj.* inalterable, inmutable.
**unaltered** (-*o*·ltørᵈd) *adj.* inalterado.
**unanimity** (yunani·miti) *s.* unanimidad.
**unanimous** (yunæ·nimøs) *adj.* unánime. 2 de acuerdo.
**unannounced** (ønanau·nst) *adj.* sin ser anunciado. 2 de improviso.
**unanswerable** (-æ·nsørabøl) *adj.* incontrovertible, incontestable, indisputable.
**unanswered** (-øᵈd) *adj.* por contestar, no contestado. 2 no correspondido.
**unappreciated** (-*apri*·shieitid) *adj.* no apreciado; mal comprendido.
**unapproachable** (-*aprou*·chabøl) *adj.* inaccesible, inabordable.
**unappropriate(d** (-*aprou*·pieit(id) *adj.* no concedido o aplicado [crédito, fondos]. 2 libre, baldío.
**unarmed** (-*a*·ʳmd) *adj.* desarmado, indefenso.
**unartistic** (-*a*ʳti·stik) *adj.* nada artístico, poco artístico.
**unasked** (-*a*·skt) *adj.* no pedido o solicitado. 2 sin ser llamado o invitado.
**unassailable** (-*asei*·labøl) *adj.* inexpugnable.
**unassisted** (-*asi*·stid) *adj.* sin ayuda.
**unassuming** (-*asiu*·ming) *adj.* modesto, sin presunción.
**unattached** (-*atæ*·cht) *adj.* suelto, despegado. 2 libre, sin compromiso. 3 DER. no embargado. 4 MIL. disponible.
**unattainable** (-*atei*·nabøl) *adj.* inasequible.
**unattended** (-*ate*·ndid) *adj.* no acompañado, solo.
**unattractive** (-*atræ*·ktiv) *adj.* poco atractivo.
**unau** (yu·nou) *s.* ZOOL. perezoso.
**unauthorized** (øno·zøraišd) *adj.* no autorizado.
**unavailable** (-*avei*·labøl) *adj.* no utilizable, no disponible. 2 agotado [libro].
**unavailing** (-*avei*·ling) *adj.* inútil, infructuoso, vano, ineficaz.
**unavoidable** (-*avoi*·dabøl) *adj.* inevitable, ineludible.
**unaware** (-*aue*·ʳ) *adj.* desprevenido, ignorante [de una cosa]; que no recela o hace caso [de ella].
**unaware (s** (-*aue*·ʳ(š) *adv.* sin premeditación, inadvertidamente. 2 inopinadamente, de improviso: *to catch unawares*, coger desprevenido.
**unbacked** (-bæ·kt) *adj.* sin ayuda, sin apoyo. 2 sin respaldo. 3 sin domar [potro].
**unbalanced** (-bæ·lanst) *adj.* desequilibrado.
**unbar (to)** (-ba·ʳ) *tr.* desatrancar, quitar la barra de.
**unbearable** (-be·rabøl) *adj.* insufrible, insoportable, inaguantable.
**unbeaten** (-bɪ·tøn) *adj.* no pisado o frecuentado. 2 invicto, imbatido.
**unbecoming** (-bika·ming) *adj.* que sienta o cae mal. 2 impropio, indecoroso.
**unbelief** (-bilɪ·f) *s.* descreimiento.
**unbeliever** (-vøʳ) *s.* descreído; infiel.
**unbend (to)** (-be·nd) *tr.* enderezar, desencorvar. 2 aflojar, relajar. 3 MAR. desenvergar. 4 *intr.* enderezarse. 5 ablandarse, humanizarse. 6 descansar, solazarse.
**unbending** (-ing) *adj.* inflexible.
**unbias(s)ed** (-bai·ast) *adj.* imparcial.
**unbind (to)** (-bai·nd) *tr.* desatar, desligar. 2 *intr.* desatarse, desligarse.
**unblemished** (-ble·misht) *adj.* puro, perfecto.

**unblushing** (-blø·shing) *adj.* que no se ruboriza. 2 sin rubor, desvergonzado.
**unbolt (to)** (-bou·lt) *tr.* desclavar [lo sujetado con pernos]. 2 abrir [corriendo el cerrojo]; desatrancar.
**unborn** (-boʳn) *adj.* no nacido, por nacer, futuro.
**unbosom (to)** (-bu·søm) *tr.* revelar, confesar: *to ~ oneself*, abrir su pecho, desahogarse.
**unbottomed** (-ba·tømd) *adj.* sin fondo. 2 insondable. 3 infundado.
**unbound** (-bau·nd) *pret.* y *p. p.* de TO UNBIND. 2 *adj.* desatado, suelto. 3 sin encuadernar.
**unbounded** (-id) *adj.* ilimitado, infinito. 2 libre, sin freno.
**unbraid (to)** (-brei·d) *tr.* destrenzar, destejer. 2 desembrollar.
**unbreakable** (-brei·kabøl) *adj.* irrompible.
**unbred** (-bre·d) *adj.* malcriado, grosero.
**unbridle (to)** (-brai·døl) *tr.* desembridar. 2 soltar, dar rienda suelta a.
**unbroken** (-brou·køn) *adj.* entero, intacto. 2 inviolado. 3 continuo, ininterrumpido. 4 indomado, indómito. 5 no labrado o cultivado [suelo].
**unbuckle (to)** (-bø·køl) *tr.* deshebillar, desatar, desabrochar.
**unburden (to)** (-bø·ʳdøn) *tr.* descargar [quitar un peso]; aliviar.
**unburied** (-be·rid) *adj.* insepulto.
**unbury (to)** (-be·ri) *tr.* desenterrar, exhumar.
**unbusinesslike** (-bi·šnislaik) *adj.* contrario a la práctica mercantil. 2 poco práctico.
**unbutton (to)** (-bø·tøn) *tr.* desabotonar, desabrochar.
**uncage (to)** (-kei·dŷ) *tr.* desenjaular.
**uncalled-for** (-ko·ld) *adj.* no requerido, innecesario, gratuito. 2 inmerecido.
**uncanny** (-kæ·ni) *adj.* misterioso, extraño, sobrenatural; del mundo de los fantasmas, duendes, etc.
**uncap (to)** (-kæ·p) *tr.* descubrir, destapar, quitar el casquillo.
**uncared-for** (ke·ʳd) *adj.* descuidado, abandonado, desatendido.
**unceasing** (-sɪ·sing) *adj.* incesante.
**unceremonious** (-serimou·niøs) *adj.* sin ceremonia; familiar, llano. 2 brusco, descortés.
**uncertain** (-sø·ʳtøn) *adj.* incierto, dudoso. 2 vago, indeterminado. 3 poco seguro o confiable. 4 precario. 5 variable, inconstante. 6 indeciso, irresoluto.
**uncertainty** (-ti) *s.* incertidumbre. 2 vaguedad. 3 precariedad. 4 inestabilidad. 5 indecisión.
**unchain (to)** (-chei·n) *tr.* desencadenar.
**unchangeable** (-chei·ndŷabøl) *adj.* inmutable, invariable, inalterable.
**unchanged** (-chei·ndŷd) *adj.* inalterado, igual.
**unchanging** (-chei·ndŷing) *adj.* inmutable, uniforme.
**uncharitable** (-chæritabøl) *adj.* poco caritativo, falto de caridad, duro.
**unchaste** (-chei·st) *adj.* incasto, deshonesto, impúdico, lascivo.
**unchastity** (-chei·stiti) *s.* deshonestidad, impureza, lascivia.
**unchecked** (-che·kt) *adj.* desenfrenado. 2 libre, sin que nada o nadie lo contenga. 3 COM. no comprobado.
**unchristened** (-kri·sønd) *adj.* no bautizado. 2 sin nombre.
**unchristian** (-stshan) *adj.* poco cristiano.
**uncinate** (ø·nsineit) *adj.* ganchudo.

**uncivil** (ønsi·vil) *adj.* incivil, descortés.
**uncivilized** (-sivilai·šd) *adj.* salvaje, tosco, inculto.
**unclad** (-klæ·d) *adj.* no vestido, desnudo.
**unclasp (to)** (-klæ·šp) *tr.* desabrochar.
**uncle** (ø·nkøl) *s.* tío. *2 Uncle Sam,* el tío Sam [los Estados Unidos].
**unclean** (ønkli·n) *adj.* sucio, desaseado. *2* inmundo. *3* impuro.
**uncleanly** (-kle·nli) *adj.* UNCLEAN. *2 adv.* suciamente.
**unclog (to)** (-cla·g) *tr.* desembarazar, desobstruir.
**unclose (to)** (-klou·š) *tr.* abrir. *2* descubrir, revelar.
**unclothe (to)** (-klou·ð) *tr.* quitar la ropa a, desnudar.
**unclouded** (-klau·did) *adj.* claro, despejado, sin nubes.
**uncock (to)** (-ka·k) *tr.* desmontar [un arma de fuego].
**uncoil (to)** (-koi·l) *tr.* desarrollar, desenrollar.
**uncollected** (-køle·ktid) *adj.* disperso. *2* por cobrar. *3* perturbado, desconcertado.
**uncombed** (-kou·md) *adj.* despeinado, sin peinar.
**uncomfortable** (-kø·mfø<sup>r</sup>tabøl) *adj.* penoso, incómodo, desagradable, molesto. *2* incómodo, molesto, embarazado; que no se siente bien.
**uncommon** (-ka·møn) *adj.* poco común o frecuente, insólito, raro, notable, extraordinario, excepcional.
**uncommunicative** (-kømiu·nikeitiv) *adj.* reservado, poco comunicativo.
**uncomplimentary** (-kamplime·ntari) *adj.* poco halagüeño o amable; ofensivo; desfavorable.
**uncompromising** (-kamprømai·šing) *adj.* inflexible, firme, intransigente.
**unconcerned** (-kønsø·<sup>r</sup>nd) *adj.* indiferente, frío, desinteresado. *2* no interesado.
**unconcluded** (-kliu·did) *adj.* inconcluso.
**unconditional** (-ndi·shønal) *adj.* incondicional.
**unconditioned** (-ndi·shønd) *adj.* no condicionado. *2* FIL. ilimitado, infinito, absoluto.
**unconformable** (-fo·<sup>r</sup>mabøl) *adj.* no conforme, proporcionado o correspondiente.
**unconformity** (-fø·<sup>r</sup>miti) *s.* disconformidad, contradicción, incompatibilidad.
**uncongenial** (-køndŷi·nial) *adj.* incompatible. *2* antipático, desagradable. *3* impropio, inadecuado.
**unconnected** (-køne·ktid) *adj.* inconexo. *2* incoherente. *3* desconectado.
**unconquerable** (-ka·nkørabøl) *adj.* inconquistable, invencible, indomable.
**unconscionable** (-shønabøl) *adj.* injusto, irrazonable. *2* desmedido. *3* sin conciencia.
**unconscious** (-shøs) *adj.* inconsciente. *2* desmayado, sin sentido. *3* ignorante, no sabedor o que no se percata [de]. *4* inanimado. *5 s. the ~,* lo inconsciente.
**unconstitutional** (-stitiu·shønal) *adj.* inconstitucional, anticonstitucional.
**uncontaminated** (-tæ·mineitid) *adj.* incontaminado.
**uncontrollable** (-trou·labøl) *adj.* ingobernable, indomable, irrefrenable.
**uncontrolled** (-trou·ld) *adj.* libre, sin freno.
**unconventional** (-ve·nshønal) *adj.* libre de trabas o reglas; que no sujeta a convenciones o costumbres, despreocupado; original.
**unconvincing** (-vi·nsing) *adj.* que no convence, poco convincente.
**uncork (to)** (ønko·<sup>r</sup>k) *tr.* descorchar, destapar.
**uncorrupted** (ønkørø·ptid) *adj.* incorrupto.

**uncouth** (-ku·z) *adj.* tosco, grosero. *2* rudo, rústico, inculto. *3* torpe, desmañado. *4* raro, extraño.
**uncover (to)** (-kø·vø<sup>r</sup>) *tr.* destapar, descubrir. *2* desabrigar, desarropar. *3* poner al descubierto, revelar. *4 intr.* descubrirse. *5* desabrigarse.
**uncreated** (-kriei·tid) *adj.* increado.
**uncrown (to)** (-krau·n) *tr.* destronar.
**unction** (ø·ncshøn) *s.* unción, ungimiento. *2* untamiento, untadura. *3* untura, ungüento. *4* lenitivo. *5* unción, fervor. *6* hipocresía.
**unctuous** (-chuøs) *adj.* untuoso. *2* meloso, zalamero, hipócrita.
**uncurl (to)** (ønkø·<sup>r</sup>l) *tr.* desrizar, desenroscar.
**uncut** (-køt) *adj.* sin cortar. *2* sin tallar, en bruto.
**undamaged** (-dæ·midŷd) *adj.* indemne, ileso.
**undaunted** (-do·ntid) *adj.* impávido, impertérrito, intrépido.
**undecagon** (-de·kagøn) *s.* GEOM. undecágono.
**undeceive (to)** (-disi·v) *tr.* desengañar, desimpresionar, sacar de un engaño o error.
**undecipherable** (-disai·førabol) *adj.* indescifrable.
**undeclinable** (-diklai·nabøl) *adj.* indeclinable. *2* inevitable.
**undefeated** (-difi·tid) *adj.* invicto.
**undefensible** (-dife·nsibøl) *adj.* indefendible.
**undefiled** (-difai·ld) *adj.* impoluto, limpio, libre de mancha.
**undefined** (-difai·nd) *adj.* indefinido.
**undeniable** (-dinai·abøl) *adj.* innegable, indiscutible, irrefragable.
**under** (ø·ndø<sup>r</sup>) *prep.* bajo, debajo de. *2* de menos de; en menos de, dentro; menos de, inferior o de grado inferior a: *all weights ~ two pounds,* todos los pesos de menos de dos libras; *~ an hour,* en menos de una hora, dentro de una hora. *3* en tiempo de, durante el reinado de. *4* conforme a, según: *~ the terms of,* según las condiciones de. *5* bajo la dirección o enseñanza de. *6* a o en, en frases como: *~ the care of,* al cuidado de; *~ discussion,* en discusión. *7* Otros usos: *~ arms,* MIL. sirviendo en el ejército; *~ cover,* al abrigo, a cubierto; *~ one's nose,* fam. en las barbas de uno; *~ sail,* navegando, con las velas desplegadas; *~ way,* en camino; en marcha; *to be ~ age,* ser menor de edad. *8 adv.* abajo, debajo, más abajo. *9 adj.* inferior. *10* subalterno, subordinado.
**under-** *pref.* que denota inferioridad, subordinación, etc., y que en muchos casos corresponde al español *sub-.*
**underbred** (øndø<sup>r</sup>bre·d) *adj.* que no es de pura raza. *2* tosco, vulgar.
**underbrush** (-brøsh) *s.* maleza [de un bosque].
**undercarriage** (ø·ndø<sup>r</sup>kæridŷ) *s.* soporte o armazón inferior. *2* AVIA. tren de aterrizaje.
**underclothes** (ø·ndø<sup>r</sup>kloudš), **underclothing** (-klou·ding) *s.* ropa interior.
**undercurrent** (-kørønt) *s.* corriente que pasa debajo de otra. *2* tendencia oculta. *3 adj.* que corre bajo la superficie; secreto, oculto.
**undercut** (-køt) *adj.* cortado por debajo. *2 s.* corte dado o hecho por la parte de abajo. *3* solomillo. *4* TENIS, BOX. golpe dado por debajo o de abajo arriba.
**undercut (to)** *tr.* cortar o vaciar por debajo, socavar. *2* TENIS, BOX. golpear por debajo o de abajo arriba.
**underdeveloped** (øndø<sup>r</sup>dive·løpt) *adj.* poco desarrollado. *2* subdesarrollado.
**underdog** (ø·ndø<sup>r</sup>dog) *s.* el que pierde [en una contienda]. *2* fig. oprimido, desvalido: *the underdogs,* los desvalidos, los de abajo.

**underdone** (-dǫn) *adj.* COC. poco asado, a medio asar.

**underdress (to)** (øndøˤdre·s) *intr.* vestirse menos de lo conveniente. 2 vestirse demasiado sencillamente para lo que requiere la ocasión.

**underestimate (to)** (-e·stimeit) *tr.* menospreciar, tener en poco. 2 valuar o calcular en menos del valor real.

**underexpose (to)** (-ekspou·š) *tr.* FOT. dar poca exposición a.

**underfeed (to)** (-fɪ·d) *tr.* alimentar insuficientemente, desnutrir.

**underfoot** (ø·ndˤfut) *adv.* bajo los pies. 2 en sujeción. 3 en secreto. 4 *adj.* pisoteado, oprimido.

**undergo (to)** (øndø·ˤgou) *tr.* sufrir, padecer, aguantar. 2 experimentar, ser sometido a.

**undergraduate** (-græ·diuit) *s.* estudiante que aún no tiene ningún grado académico.

**underground** (ø·ndøˤgraund) *adj.* subterráneo. 2 secreto, clandestino. 3 *s.* subterráneo. 4 subsuelo. 5 metro, ferrocarril subterráneo. 6 *adv.* bajo tierra. 7 en secreto, ocultamente.

**undergrown** (-groun) *s.* pequeño, raquítico. 2 cubierto de maleza.

**undergrowth** (-grouz) *s.* maleza, matas, hierbas [del bosque].

**underhand** (øndøˤjæ·nd) *adv.* bajo mano, por bajo cuerda, clandestinamente. 2 *adj.* secreto, clandestino.

**underhanded** (-id) *adj.* secreto, clandestino, disimulado, solapado.

**underlay** (-lei) *s.* IMPR. alza. 2 pieza que realza o sostiene. 3 UNDERCURRENT.

**underlay (to)** (-lei) *tr.* reforzar por debajo. 2 IMPR. calzar. 3 realzar [poniendo algo debajo].

**underlet (to)** (-lei·t) *tr.* subarrendar.

**underlie (to)** (-lai) *tr.* estar debajo de. 2 ser la base, fundamento o sostén de.

**underline** (ø·ndøˤlain) *s.* línea puesta debajo.

**underline (to)** (øndøˤlai·n) *tr.* subrayar.

**underling** (ø·ndøˤling) *s.* subordinado, inferior.

**underlying** (øndøˤlai·ing) *adj.* subyacente. 2 fundamental.

**undermine (to)** (-mai·n) *tr.* minar, socavar, zapar. 2 fig. minar [la salud, etc.].

**undermost** (ø·ndøˤmoust) *adj.* el más bajo. 2 ínfimo. 3 *adv.* debajo de todo.

**underneath** (øndøˤnɪ·z) *adv.* debajo. 2 *prep.* debajo de, bajo.

**undernourish (to)** (-nø·rish) *tr.* alimentar insuficientemente.

**underpass** (ø·ndøˤpæs) *s.* paso inferior.

**underpay (to)** (øndøˤpei·) *tr.* pagar poco, pagar mal.

**underpin (to)** (-pi·n) *tr.* socalzar, apuntalar.

**underprivileged** (-pri·vilidyͩd) *adj.* menesteroso, desheredado.

**underrate (to)** (ø·ndøˤreit) *tr.* desestimar, menospreciar, valorar demasiado bajo.

**underrun (to)** (øndøˤrøn) *tr.* correr por debajo de. 2 MAR. resacar.

**underscore (to)** (-sko·ˤ) *tr.* subrayar.

**undersecretary** (-se·krøteri) *s.* subsecretario.

**underset (to)** (-se·t) *tr.* apuntalar, sostener.

**undershirt** (ø·ndøˤshøˤt) *s.* camiseta.

**undershot** (-shot) *adj.* impulsada por debajo [rueda hidráulica]. 2 que tiene saliente la mandíbula inferior.

**undersign (to)** (øndøˤsai·n) *tr.* firmar, subscribir. 2 *the undersigned,* el infrascrito, el abajo-firmado.

**undersized** (ø·ndøˤsai·šd) *adj.* pequeño, de estatura o tamaño menor que los normales.

**underskirt** (-skøˤt) *s.* enaguas; refajo.

**understand (to)** (øndøˤstæ·nd) *tr.* entender, comprender: *to give to* ~, dar a entender; *to* ~ *each other,* entenderse, ir de acuerdo. 2 entender en. 3 ser sabedor de, tener entendido. 4 sobrentender.

**understanding** (-ing) *s.* inteligencia, comprensión, conocimiento [de una cosa]. 2 entendimiento, inteligencia [facultad]. 3 inteligencia, armonía, acuerdo: *to come to an* ~, llegar a un acuerdo. 4 *adj.* inteligente; comprensivo.

**understatement** (-stei·tmønt) *s.* declaración incompleta, en la que se dice menos de lo que hay.

**understood** (-stu·d) *pret. y p. p.* de TO UNDERSTAND.

**understudy** (ø·ndøˤstødi) *s.* TEAT. sobresaliente, suplente.

**understudy (to)** *tr.* aprender [un papel] para poder suplir a [otro actor].

**undertake (to)** (øndøˤtei·k) *tr.* emprender, acometer, intentar. 2 tomar por su cuenta, a su cargo; comprometerse a, encargarse de.

**undertaker** (-øˤ) *s.* empresario, contratista. 2 empresario de pompas fúnebres, dueño de una funeraria.

**undertaking** (-ing) *s.* empresa [acción de emprender, cosa que se emprende]. 2 contrata. 3 funeraria, empresa de pompas fúnebres. 4 DER. promesa, garantía.

**undertone** (ø·ndøˤtoun) *s.* voz baja. 2 color apagado.

**undertow** (-tou) *s.* MAR. resaca; contracorriente.

**undervalue (to)** (øndøˤvæ·liu) *tr.* desestimar, valuar por debajo del valor real.

**underwater** (-uø·tøˤ) *adj.* subacuático. 2 que se usa debajo del agua.

**underwear** (-uˤ) *s.* ropa interior.

**underwood** (ø·ndøˤwud) *s.* maleza, monte bajo.

**underworld** (-uøˤld) *s.* los profundos. 2 mundo subterráneo o submarino, de los insectos, de la vida inferior. 3 los antípodas. 4 el hampa, los bajos fondos de la sociedad.

**underwrite (to)** (øndøˤrai·t) *tr.* subscribir, firmar. 2 COM. subscribir [una emisión]. 3 COM. asegurar.

**underwriter** (-øˤ) *s.* firmante. 2 COM. suscriptor de una emisión. 3 COM. asegurador.

**undeserved** (-disø·ˤvd) *adj.* inmerecido.

**undeserving** (-disø·ˤving) *adj.* desmerecedor, indigno.

**undesigning** (dišai·ning) *adj.* sencillo, sin astucia, sincero, de buena fe.

**undesirable** (-dišai·rabøl) *adj.* indeseable, poco deseable.

**undetected** (-dite·ktid) *adj.* no descubierto.

**undetermined** (-ditøˤmind) *adj.* indeterminado. 2 indeciso, irresoluto.

**undeviating** (-dɪ·vieiting) *adj.* directo, sin rodeos; invariable, siempre igual.

**undies** (ø·ndiš) *s. pl.* fam. ropa interior femenina.

**undigested** (-didyͩe·stid) *adj.* no digerido.

**undignified** (-di·gnifaid) *adj.* poco digno o decoroso. 2 falto de seriedad, de gravedad.

**undine** (øndɪ·n) *s.* ondina.

**undisciplined** (-di·siplind) *adj.* no sujeto a disciplina. 2 rebelde, indócil, indisciplinado.

**undisguised** (-disgai·šd) *adj.* manifiesto, no disimulado.

**undismayed** (-dismei·d) *adj.* firme, impertérrito, no desanimado.

**undisturbed** (distø·ʳbd) *adj.* quieto, tranquilo. *2* impasible, sereno.

**undivided** (-divai·did) *adj.* entero, indiviso.

**undo (to)** (-du·) *tr.* abrir, desatar, desliar, soltar, desabrochar: *to ~ one's hair,* soltarse el cabello. *2* deshacer. *3* anular, desvirtuar. *4* destruir, arruinar, perder.

**undoing** (-du·ing) *s.* destrucción, pérdida, ruina.

**undone** (-døn) *p. p.* de TO UNDO: *to come ~,* desatarse, soltarse, desabrocharse; *to leave ~,* dejar por hacer.

**undoubted** (-dau·tid) *adj.* cierto, indudable, fuera de duda, indiscutido.

**undraw (to)** (-dro·) *tr.* abrir, descorrer [una cortina, etc.].

**undress** (-dre·s) *s.* traje de casa, deshabillé. *2* vestido de calle. *3* MIL. traje de diario.

**undress (to)** *tr.* desnudar, desvestir. *2* vestir a la ligera. *3* CIR. desvendar. *4 intr.* desnudarse.

**undressed** (-dre·st) *adj.* sin preparar, sin curtir; en rama, en bruto. *2* de trapillo. *3* vestido con traje de calle.

**undrinkable** (-dri·nkabøl) *adj.* impotable.

**undue** (-diu·) *adj.* indebido, excesivo, desmedido. *2* impropio. *3* ilegal, injusto. *4* COM. no vencido.

**undulant** (ø·ndiulant) *adj.* ondulante, undulante.

**undulate** (-diuleit) *adj.* ondulado, ondeado.

**undulate (to)** *intr.* ondular, ondear. *2* fluctuar. *3 tr.* hacer ondear o fluctuar. *4* ondular.

**undulation** (øndiulei·shøn) *s.* ondulación, ondeo.

**undulatory** (ø·ndiulatori) *adj.* ondulatorio, undoso.

**undutiful** (øndiu·tiful) *adj.* que falta a sus deberes; desobediente, irrespetuoso.

**undying** (-dai·ng) *adj.* imperecedero, eterno.

**unearned** (-ø·ʳnd) *s.* no ganado; inmerecido: *~ increment,* plusvalía.

**unearth (to)** (-ø·ʳz) *tr.* desenterrar.

**unearthly** (-ø·ʳzli) *adj.* no terrenal. *2* sobrenatural, supernatural. *3* terrible, fantástico.

**uneasiness** (-ɪ·šinis) *s.* intranquilidad, inquietud, desasosiego. *2* malestar, incomodidad.

**uneasy** (-ɪ·si) *adj.* intranquilo, inquieto, desasosegado. *2* molesto, incómodo. *3* torpe, cohibido.

**unedifying** (-e·difaiing) *adj.* poco edificante.

**uneducated** (-e·diukeitid) *adj.* inculto, indocto.

**unemployed** (-imploi·d) *adj.* desocupado, ocioso. *2* sin trabajo, parado. *3* no empleado.

**unemployment** (-mønt) *s.* desocupación, falta de trabajo, paro.

**unending** (-e·nding) *adj.* inacabable, interminable, perpetuo, eterno.

**unendurable** (-endiu·rabøl) *adj.* insoportable.

**unenlightened** (-enlai·tønd) *adj.* sin instrucción, ignorante.

**unequal** (-i·kual) *s.* desigual. *2* diferente. *3* desproporcionado. *4* insuficiente. *5* falto de fuerzas, capacidad, etc. [para algo].

**unequalled** (-d) *adj.* inigualado, sin par.

**unequivocal** (-ikui·vøkal) *adj.* inequívoco.

**unerring** (-ø·ring) *adj.* infalible. *2* certero.

**unessential** (-ese·nshal) *adj.* no esencial.

**unethical** (øne·zical) *adj.* contrario a la moral, o a las normas de la conducta profesional.

**uneven** (-ɪ·vn) *adj.* desigual, desnivelado, irregular, accidentado. *2* de longitud diferente. *3* impar, non.

**uneventful** (-ive·ntful) *adj.* exento de acontecimientos notables; tranquilo.

**unexampled** (-egšæ·mpøld) *adj.* sin ejemplo.

**unexceptionable** (ekse·pshønabøl) *adj.* intachable, irreprochable.

**unexpected** (-ekspe·ktid) *adj.* inesperado, imprevisto, inopinado. *2* repentino.

**unexperienced** (-pi·riønst) *adj.* inexperto. *2* no experimentado.

**unexplained** (-plei·nd) *adj.* inexplicado.

**unexplored** (-plo·ʳd) *adj.* inexplorado.

**unexpressive** (-pre·siv) *adj.* inexpresivo.

**unextinguishable** (-tingwi·shabøl) *adj.* inextinguible.

**unfading** (-fei·ding) *adj.* inmarcesible.

**unfailing** (-fei·ling) *adj.* inagotable. *2* cierto, seguro, indefectible. *3* infalible.

**unfair** (-fe·ʳ) *adj.* injusto, desleal, de mala fe.

**unfaithful** (-fei·zful) *adj.-s.* infiel.

**unfaltering** (-fo·ltøring) *adj.* resuelto, firme, inquebrantable.

**unfamiliar** (-fami·liaʳ) *adj.* poco familiar, desconocido. *2* que no conoce una cosa, que está poco familiarizado con ella.

**unfashionable** (-fæ·shønabøl) *adj.* no ajustado a la moda, que no la sigue.

**unfasten (to)** (-fæ·søn) *tr.* abrir, desatar, desabrochar, desprender, soltar, aflojar.

**unfathomable** (-fæ·dømabøl) *adj.* insondable. *2* impenetrable, inescrutable.

**unfavo(u)rable** (-fei·vørabøl) *adj.* desfavorable, contrario, adverso.

**unfeasible** (-fi·søbøl) *adj.* impracticable, no hacedero.

**unfed** (-fe·d) *adj.* falto de alimento; sin comer.

**unfeeling** (-fɪ·ling) *adj.* insensible, duro, cruel.

**unfeigned** (-fei·nd) *adj.* verdadero, no fingido.

**unfelt** (-fe·lt) *adj.* no percibido o sentido.

**unfetter (to)** (-fe·tøʳ) *tr.* quitar los hierros a; libertar.

**unfinished** (-fi·nisht) *adj.* inacabado, incompleto. *2* TEJ. sin acabar.

**unfit** (-fi·t) *adj.* incapaz, inepto. *2* inadecuado, impropio. *3* inservible, inútil. *4* en malas condiciones físicas.

**unfitting** (-fi·ting) *adj.* impropio. *2* indecoroso.

**unfix (to)** (-fi·ks) *tr.* desfijar, desprender.

**unflagging** (-flæ·ging) *adj.* persistente, incansable.

**unfledged** (-fle·dÿd) *adj.* ORN. implume. *2* fig. novel, inexperto.

**unflinching** (-flɪ·nching) *adj.* firme, resuelto.

**unfold (to)** (-fou·ld) *tr.* desplegar, desdoblar, extender, abrir. *2* descubrir, revelar, explicar. *3 intr.* abrirse, desplegarse, extenderse.

**unforeseen** (-fo·ʳsin) *adj.* imprevisto.

**unforgettable** (-fo·ʳge·tabøl) *adj.* inolvidable.

**unforgiving** (-fo·ʳgi·ving) *adj.* implacable, rencoroso, que no perdona.

**unfortunate** (-fo·ʳchønit) *adj.-s.* infortunado, desgraciado, desdichado. *2 adj.* infausto, aciago.

**unfortunately** (-li) *adv.* desgraciadamente, por desgracia.

**unfounded** (-fau·ndid) *adj.* infundado.

**unfrequently** (-frikue·ntli) *adv.* raramente, pocas veces.

**unfriendly** (-fre·ndli) *adj.* poco amistoso, hostil, enemigo. *2* desfavorable, perjudicial.

**unfruitful** (-fru·tful) *adj.* estéril, infecundo. *2* infructuoso.

**unfulfilled** (-fulfi·ld) *adj.* incumplido.

**unfurl (to)** (-fø·ʳl) *tr.* desplegar, extender.

**unfurnished** (-fø·ʳnisht) *adj.* desamueblado. *2* desprovisto.

**ungainly** (-gei·nli) *adj.* desgarbado, torpe, sin gracia.

**ungenerous** (-dẏe·nørøs) *adj.* poco generoso.

**ungentle** (-dẏe·ntøl) *adj.* rudo, brusco, duro.

**ungentlemanlike, ungentlemanly** (-ønẏe·ntølmanlaik, -li) *adj.* impropio de un caballero; incorrecto, descortés.

**ungird (to)** (-gø·ᵣd) *tr.* desceñir. 2 descinchar.

**unglazed** (-glei·šd) *adj.* sin vidrios. 2 sin vidriar. 3 deslustrado.

**unglue (to)** (-gliu·) *tr.* despegar [lo pegado]. 2 desencolar.

**ungodly** (-ga·dli) *adj.* impío. 2 malvado. 3 fam. atroz, enorme.

**ungraceful** (-grei·sful) *adj.* desgarbado, torpe, falto de gracia.

**ungracious** (grei·shøs) *adj.* brusco, desabrido.

**ungrammatical** (-gramæ·tikal) *adj.* antigramatical.

**ungrateful** (-grei·tful) *adj.* ingrato, desagradecido. 2 ingrato, desagradable.

**ungrounded** (-grau·ndid) *adj.* infundado, inmotivado. 2 ELECT. no conectado con la tierra.

**unguarded** (-ga·ᵣdid) *adj.* no guardado, indefenso. 2 desprevenido, descuidado. 3 imprudente.

**unguent** (ø·ngwønt) *s.* ungüento, unto.

**unguiculate** (øngwi·kiuleit) *adj.-s.* ZOOL. unguiculado.

**unguided** (-gai·did) *adj.* no dirigido, sin guía.

**unguis** (ø·ngwis) *s.* ANAT. unguis.

**ungulate** (-giuleit) *adj.-s.* ungulado.

**unhallowed** (ønjæ·loud) *adj.* no consagrado. 2 profano, impío.

**unhandy** (-jæ·ndi) *adj.* torpe, desmañado. 2 incómodo, de mal manejar.

**unhang (to)** (ø·njæng) *tr.* descolgar, desprender.

**unhappily** (ønjæ·pili) *adv.* infelizmente. 2 desgraciadamente, por desgracia.

**unhappiness** (-pinis) *s.* infelicidad, desdicha.

**unhappy** (-pi) *adj.* infeliz, desgraciado, desdichado. 2 poco oportuno o acertado. 3 triste.

**unharmed** (ønja·ᵣmd) *adj.* ileso, incólume.

**unharness (to)** (-ja·ᵣnis) *tr.* despojar de la armadura. 2 desenjaezar; desenganchar.

**unhealthy** (-je·lzi) *adj.* enfermo, enfermizo, achacoso. 2 malsano, insalubre.

**unheard** (-jø·ᵣd) *adj.* no oído; sin que se le haya oído. 2 ~ *of*, inaudito, nunca oído, extraño; obscuro, desconocido.

**unheeded** (-jɪ·did) *adj.* desatendido, sin que se le haga caso, inadvertido.

**unheeding** (-jɪ·ding) *adj.* desatento, descuidado, distraído.

**unhesitating** (-je·šiteiting) *adj.* resuelto, que no vacila. 2 hecho sin vacilar, rápido, pronto.

**unhinge (to)** (-ji·ndẏ) *intr.* desgoznar, desquiciar. 2 fig. trastornar, desequilibrar.

**unhitch (to)** (-ji·ch) *tr.* descolgar, desatar. 2 desenganchar [animales].

**unholy** (-jou·li) *adj.* profano [no sagrado].

**unhook (to)** (-ju·k) *tr.* desenganchar, desabrochar. 2 descolgar [de un gancho]. 3 *intr.* desengancharse, desabrocharse, descolgarse.

**unhoped-for** (-jou·pt) *adj.* inesperado.

**unhorse (to)** (-jo·ᵣs) *tr.* desmontar, desarzonar.

**unhurt** (-jø·ᵣt) *adj.* ileso, indemne.

**unicameral** (yunikæ·møral) *adj.* unicameral.

**unicellular** (-se·liula·ᵣ) *adj.* unicelular.

**unicity** (yuni·siti) *s.* unicidad.

**unicorn** (yu·niko·ᵣn) *s.* unicornio.

**unification** (yunifikei·shøn) *s.* unificación.

**uniform** (yu·nifo·ᵣm) *adj.* uniforme. 2 semejante, concorde, consonante. 4 *s.* uniforme.

**uniformity** (yunifo·ᵣmiti) *s.* uniformidad.

**unify (to)** (yu·nifai) *tr.* unificar, unir. 2 *intr.* unificarse, unirse.

**unilateral** (yunilæ·tøral) *adj.* unilateral.

**unimaginable** (ønimæ·dẏinabøl) *adj.* inimaginable.

**unimpaired** (-impe·ᵣd) *adj.* intacto, incólume, inalterado.

**unimpeachable** (-impɪ·chabøl) *adj.* intachable, irreprochable. 2 irrecusable.

**unimportant** (-impo·ᵣtant) *adj.* insignificante, sin importancia.

**uninflammable** (-inflæ·mabøl) *adj.* no inflamable.

**uninformed** (-infø·ᵣmd) *adj.* ignorante, indocto. 2 no informado.

**uninhabited** (-injæ·bitid) *adj.* inhabitado, desierto, despoblado.

**uninjured** (-indẏø·ᵣd) *adj.* indemne, incólume, sin daño.

**uninsured** (-inshu·ᵣd) *adj.* COM. no asegurado.

**unintelligible** (-inte·lidẏibøl) *adj.* ininteligible.

**unintentional** (-inte·nshønal) *adj.* involuntario.

**uninterested** (-i·ntørestid) *adj.* indiferente, distraído, apático.

**uninteresting** (-intøre·sting) *adj.* poco interesante, falto de interés, soso.

**uninterrupted** (-intøro·ptid) *adj.* ininterrumpido, continuo, incesante.

**union** (yu·niøn) *s.* unión: *the Union*, los Estados Unidos de América. 2 junta, juntura. 3 MEC. conexión, tubo de unión, etc. 4 (Ingl.) asociación o sindicato obrero. 5 emblema de la unión [en una bandera]: *Union Jack*, pabellón nacional de la Gran Bretaña.

**unionism** (-išm) *s.* unionismo. 2 (Ingl.) principios y sistema de los sindicatos obreros.

**unionist** (-ist) *s.* unionista. 2 (Ingl.) miembro de un sindicato obrero.

**unipersonal** (yunipø·ᵣsønal) *adj.* unipersonal.

**unique** (yuni·k) *adj.* único, solo. 2 sin igual, extraordinario. 3 extraño, raro.

**unisexual** (-se·kschual) *adj.* unisexual.

**unison** (yu·nisøn) *adj.* unísono. 2 *s.* MÚS. unisonancia: *in ~*, fig. al unísono.

**unisonous** (yuni·sønøs) *adj.* unísono.

**unit** (-nit) *s.* unidad: *~ figure*, cifra de las unidades. 2 MEC., ELECT. grupo.

**Unitarian** (yunite·rian) *s.* unitario [partidario del unitarismo].

**Unitarianism** (yunite·rianišm) *s.* unitarismo.

**unitary** (yu·niteri) *adj.* unitario.

**unite (to)** (yunai·t) *tr.* unir. 2 juntar, asociar. 3 *intr.* unirse. 4 juntarse,· asociarse. 5 obrar de acuerdo, concertarse.

**united** (-id) *adj.* unido: *United States*, Estados Unidos.

**unity** (yu·niti) *s.* unidad. 2 unión, concierto, armonía. 3 continuidad [de propósito o acción].

**univalence** (yuni·valøns) *s.* QUÍM. univalencia.

**univalve** (yu·nivælv) *adj.* univalvo.

**universal** (yunivø·ᵣsal) *adj.* universal. 2 general [de todos].

**universality** (-vø·ᵣsæ·liti) *s.* universalidad.

**universe** (yu·nivø·ᵣs) *s.* universo, mundo.

**university** (yunivø·ᵣsiti) *s.* universidad. 2 *adj.* universitario.

**univocal** (yuni·vøkal) *adj.* unívoco.

**unjudged** (øndẏø·dẏd) *adj.* no juzgado, pendiente de juicio, en litigio.

**unjust** (-dẏø·st) *adj.* injusto, inicuo. *2 s.* pecador.
**unjustifiable** (-dẏøstifai·abøl) *adj.* injustificable, inexcusable.
**unjustified** (-dẏø·stifaid) *adj.* injustificado.
**unkempt** (-ke·mpt) *adj.* desaliñado. *2* desgreñado, despeinado.
**unkind** (-kai·nd) *adj.* duro, cruel, falto de bondad. *2* adusto, seco, poco amable.
**unkindly** (-li) *adj.* UNKIND. *2 adv.* duramente, ásperamente.
**unknown** (-nau·n) *adj.* desconocido, ignorado, no sabido; ignoto: ~ *quantity,* incógnita; ~ *to me,* sin mi consentimiento, sin saberlo yo. *2* extraño. *3* incalculable, indecible.
**unladylike** (-lei·dilaik) *adj.* impropio de una dama. *2* poco femenino.
**unlawful** (-lo·ful) *adj.* ilegal, ilícito, ilegítimo.
**unlearned** (-lø·ʳnd) *adj.* indocto, ignorante. *2* no aprendido, ignorado. *3* natural, instintivo.
**unleavened** (-le·vønd) *adj.* ázimo.
**unless** (-le·s) *conj.* a menos que, a no ser que, como no sea, no siendo. *2* salvo, excepto, si no es.
**unlevel (to)** (-le·vøl) *tr.* desnivelar.
**unlevelled** (-d) *adj.* desnivelado.
**unlike** (-lai·k) *adj.* desemejante, diferente, distinto. *2 adv.* diferentemente, otramente, de diferente modo que. *3 prep.* a diferencia de.
**unlikelihood** (-lijud) *s.* improbabilidad. *2* inverosimilitud.
**unlikely** (-li) *adj.* improbable, remoto. *2* incierto, inseguro. *3* inverosímil. *4 adv.* improbablemente.
**unlimited** (ønli·mitid) *adj.* ilimitado. *2* vago, indefinido.
**unload (to)** (-lou·d) *tr.* descargar [un buque, una bestia, mercancías, etc.]. *2* descargar, exonerar, aligerar.
**unlock (to)** (-la·k) *tr.* abrir [una puerta, cajón, etc.], descubrir, revelar. *2* IMPR. desapretar [las formas].
**unlooked-for** (-lu·kt) *adj.* inopinado.
**unloose (n** (-lu·s(øn) *tr.* desatar, aflojar, soltar. *2 intr.* aflojarse, deshacerse.
**unlucky** (-lø·ki) *adj.* desafortunado, desgraciado, de mala suerte. *2* nefasto, aciago. *3* siniestro, de mal agüero.
**unmake (to)** (-mei·k) *tr.* deshacer, destruir, aniquilar.
**unman (to)** (-mæ·n) *tr.* dejar sin hombres, sin tripulación. *2* acobardar, desanimar, afeminar.
**unmanageable** (-mæ·nidẏabøl) *adj.* inmanejable, ingobernable, indomable.
**unmanly** (-mæ·nli) *adj.* impropio de un hombre. *2* falto de las cualidades de un hombre.
**unmannerly** (-mæ·nøʳli) *adj.* mal educado, grosero. *2 adv.* descortésmente.
**unmarried** (-mæ·rid) *adj.* soltero, soltera.
**unmask (to)** (-mæ·sk) *tr.* desenmascarar, quitar la careta. *2* descubrir, mostrar. *3 intr.* quitarse la careta.
**unmast (to)** (-mæ·st) *tr.* MAR. desarbolar.
**unmatched** (-mæ·cht) *adj.* único, sin par. *2* desapareado.
**unmeasurable** (-me·ẏørabøl) *adj.* inmensurable, incomensurable.
**unmentionable** (-me·nshønabøl) *adj.* que no se puede mencionar.
**unmerciful** (-mø·ʳsiful) *adj.* implacable, inclemente, despiadado, riguroso, cruel.
**unmerited** (-me·ritid) *adj.* inmerecido.

**unmindful** (-mai·ndful) *adj.* que olvida, que no atiende o considera.
**unmistakable** (-mistei·kabøl) *adj.* inequívoco, inconfundible, claro, evidente.
**unmitigated** (-mi·tigeitid) *adj.* no mitigado, duro. *2* acabado, de siete suelas.
**unmixed** (-mi·kst) *adj.* puro, sin mezcla.
**unmoor (to)** (-mu·ʳ) *tr.* MAR. desamarrar.
**unmoral** (-ma·ral) *adj.* amoral.
**unmounted** (-mau·ntid) *adj.* no montado, sin montar. *2* de a pie.
**unmoved** (-mu·vd) *adj.* firme, inmoble, en el mismo sitio. *2* impasible, frío, indiferente. *3* inflexible, inexorable.
**unmuzzle (to)** (-mø·šøl) *tr.* quitar el bozal a.
**unnatural** (-næ·chøral) *adj.* no natural, antinatural. *2* desnaturalizado, inhumano. *3* artificial, afectado, forzado.
**unnecessary** (-ne·søseri) *adj.* innecesario, inútil, superfluo.
**unnerve (to)** (-nø·ʳv) *tr.* enervar, acobardar, debilitar. *2* hacer perder la serenidad.
**unnoticed** (-nou·tist) *adj.* inadvertido, desadvertido, no observado.
**unnumbered** (-nø·mbøʳd) *adj.* innumerable; sin número.
**unobservant** (-øbsø·ʳvant) *adj.* distraído, poco observador.
**unobtainable** (-øbtei·nabøl) *adj.* inasequible.
**unobtrusive** (-øbtru·siv) *adj.* modesto, discreto.
**unoccupied** (øna·kiupaid) *adj.* desocupado, vacante, vacío. *2* desocupado [sin ocupación].
**unofficial** (-nøfi·shal) *adj.* no oficial; oficioso.
**unorthodox** (-o·ʳzødaks) *adj.* poco ortodoxo.
**unostentatious** (ønastentei·shøs) *adj.* sencillo, llano, modesto, no ostentoso.
**unpack (to)** (-pæ·k) *tr.* desempaquetar, desembalar, deshacer [baúles, maletas, etc.]. *2 intr.* deshacer los bultos o maletas.
**unpaid** (-pei·d) *adj.* sin pagar, por pagar, pendiente.
**unpalatable** (-pæ·latabøl) *adj.* ingustable, desagradable al gusto, fig. desagradable.
**unparalleled** (-pæ·raleld) *adj.* sin paralelo, único, sin par, sin igual.
**unpardonable** (-pa·ʳdønabøl) *adj.* imperdonable, inexcusable.
**unpaved** (-pei·vid) *adj.* sin empedrar.
**unpeople (to)** (-pɪ·pøl) *tr.* despoblar.
**unpleasant** (-ple·šant) *adj.* desagradable, ingrato, enfadoso, molesto.
**unploughed, unplowed** (-plau·d) *adj.* inculto, sin arar.
**unpolished** (-pa·lisht) *adj.* áspero, tosco. *2* sin pulir. *3* sin pulimentar.
**unpolluted** (-pøliu·tid) *adj.* impoluto, limpio.
**unpopular** (-pa·piulaʳ) *adj.* impopular. *2* que no goza de simpatías [en un mundo o esfera].
**unpractical** (-præ·ktikal) *adj.* poco práctico.
**unpractised** (-præ·ktist) *adj.* inexperto. *2* no practicado.
**unprecedented** (-pre·sidentid) *adj.* sin precedente, nunca visto, inaudito.
**unprejudiced** (-pre·dẏudist) *adj.* imparcial.
**unpremeditated** (-prime·diteitid) *adj.* impremeditado.
**unprepossessing** (-pripøše·sing) *adj.* poco atractivo.
**unpresentable** (-priše·ntabøl) *adj.* impresentable.
**unpretending, unpretentious** (-prite·nding, -shøs) *adj.* modesto, sencillo, sin pretensiones.

**unprincipled** (-pri·nsipøld) *adj.* inmoral, sin conciencia.

**unprofitable** (-pra·fitabøl) *adj.* improductivo, inútil, nada provechoso o lucrativo.

**unpronounceable** (-pronau·nsabøl) *adj.* impronunciable.

**unpropitious** (-prøpi·shøs) *adj.* desfavorable, adverso, poco propicio.

**unprotected** (-prøte·ktid) *adj.* sin protección, indefenso.

**unprovided** (-prøvai·did) *adj.* desproveído, desprovisto. *2* desprevenido.

**unpublished** (-pø·blisht) *adj.* inédito.

**unpunished** (-pø·nisht) *adj.* impune, sin castigo.

**unqualified** (-kua·lifaid) *adj.* inhábil, incapaz, incompetente. *2* absoluto, categórico; no modificado o condicionado; completo, entero.

**unquenchable** (-kue·nchabøl) *adj.* inextinguible.

**unquestionable** (-kue·schønabøl) *adj.* incuestionable, indiscutible, indudable.

**unquiet** (-kuai·øt) *adj.* inquieto, desasosegado, agitado, turbado. *2* nada silencioso.

**unravel** (to) (-ræ·vøl) *tr.* desenredar, desenmarañar. *2* aclarar, explicar, descifrar. *3* deshacer, deshilar. *4 intr.* desenredarse, desenmarañarse.

**unread** (-re·d) *adj.* no leído, por leer. *2* indocto.

**unready** (-re·di) *adj.* no listo o preparado.

**unreal** (-rɪ·al) *adj.* irreal, ilusorio, imaginario.

**unreasonable** (-rɪ·sønabøl) *adj.* irrazonable, desrazonable. *2* inmoderado, exorbitante.

**unrecognizable** (-re·køgnaišabøl) *adj.* desconocido, imposible de reconocer.

**unrecovered** (-ri·køvø<sup>r</sup>d) *adj.* no recuperado.

**unreeve** (to) (-rɪ·v) *tr.* MAR. despasar.

**unrefined** (-rifai·nd) *adj.* no refinado. *2* inculto, rudo.

**unregenerate** (-ridÿe·nørit) *adj.* no regenerado.

**unrelenting** (-rile·nting) *adj.* inexorable, implacable, inflexible. *2* que no cede o disminuye, tenaz.

**unreliable** (-rilai·abøl) *adj.* no confiable, de poca confianza. *2* informal.

**unreligious** (-rili·dÿøs) *adj.* irreligioso.

**unremitting** (-rimi·ting) *adj.* incesante, constante. *2* sostenido, incansable.

**unrepentant** (-ripe·ntant) *adj.* impenitente.

**unreserved** (-rišø·<sup>r</sup>vd) *adj.* no reservado, franco, abierto. *2* absoluto, ilimitado, incondicional.

**unresisting** (-riši·sting) *adj.* que no resiste, que no ofrece resistencia.

**unresolved** (-rišo·lvd) *adj.* no resuelto, sin solución. *2* irresoluto.

**unresponsive** (-rispa·nsiv) *adj.* que no responde [esp. a un sentimiento]; frío, insensible.

**unrest** (-re·st) *s.* inquietud, desasosiego.

**unrestrained** (-ristrei·nd) *adj.* libre, desenfrenado. *2* suelto, desembarazado.

**unriddle** (to) (-ri·døl) *tr.* resolver, descifrar, desembrollar.

**unrig** (to) (-ri·g) *tr.* MAR. desaparejar.

**unrighteous** (-rai·chøs) *adj.* malo, perverso. *2* injusto, inicuo.

**unripe** (-rai·p) *adj.* verde, en agraz; inmaduro.

**unrivalled** (-rai·vald) *adj.* sin rival, sin par.

**unrivet** (to) (-ri·vit) *tr.* desroblar.

**unrobe** (to) (-rou·b) *tr.* desnudar. *2 intr.* desnudarse.

**unroll** (to) (-rou·l) *tr.* desenrollar, desenvolver, desplegar. *2 intr.* abrirse, desenrollarse.

**unroot** (to) (-ru·t) *tr.* desarraigar, extirpar.

**unruffled** (-rø·føld) *adj.* tranquilo, sereno.

**unruly** (-ru·li) *adj.* indócil, díscolo, desobediente, indómito. *2* turbulento, levantisco.

**unsaddle** (to) (-sæ·døl) *tr.* desensillar. *2* desarzonar, derribar del caballo.

**unsafe** (-sei·f) *adj.* inseguro, peligroso.

**unsaid** (-se·d) *adj.* no dicho, por decir.

**unsal(e)able** (-sei·labøl) *adj.* invendible.

**unsalted** (-so·ltid) *adj.* no salado, sin salar.

**unsatisfactory** (-sætisfæ·ktori) *adj.* que no satisface, poco satisfactorio, inaceptable.

**unsatisfied** (-sæ·tisfaid) *adj.* no satisfecho. *2* descontento.

**unsavo(u)ry** (-sei·vøri) *adj.* insípido, soso, desabrido, de mal gusto. *2* mal oliente. *3* malo, desagradable.

**unscathed** (-skæ·did) *adj.* indemne, ileso.

**unscrew** (to) (-kru·) *tr.* destornillar.

**unscrupulous** (-skru·piuløs) *adj.* poco escrupuloso, inmoral.

**unseal** (to) (-sɪ·l) *tr.* abrir, desellar.

**unseasonable** (-sɪ·šønabøl) *adj.* intempestivo, inoportuno, prematuro o tardío.

**unseat** (to) (-sɪ·t) *tr.* quitar de un asiento. *2* desarzonar. *3* echar abajo [un ministerio].

**unseaworthy** (-sɪ·vø<sup>r</sup>dɪ) *adj.* MAR. sin condiciones marineras; innavegable [buque].

**unseemly** (-sɪ·mli) *adj.* impropio, indecoroso.

**unseen** (-sɪ·n) *adj.* no visto, inadvertido. *2* invisible.

**unselfish** (-se·lfish) *adj.* altruista, generoso, abnegado, desinteresado.

**unserviceable** (-sø·<sup>r</sup>visabøl) *adj.* inútil, inservible.

**unsettle** (to) (-se·tøl) *tr.* desquiciar, descomponer, desarreglar. *2* trastornar, agitar, turbar, alterar.

**unsettled** (-se·tøld) *adj.* desarreglado, descompuesto. *2* trastornado, inquieto, agitado. *3* turbio, revuelto. *4* inestable. *5* errante, sin residencia fija. *6* inhabitado. *7* irresuelto, indeterminado. *8* COM. pendiente, por pagar.

**unsew** (to) (-sou·) *tr.* descoser.

**unshackle** (to) (-shæ·køl) *tr.* libertar.

**unshaded** (-shei·did) *adj.* no sombreado, sin sombra.

**unshaken** (-shei·køn) *adj.* firme, inalterado, no conmovido.

**unshaven** (-shei·vøn) *adj.* sin afeitar.

**unsheathe** (to) (-shɪ·d) *tr.* desenvainar, sacar.

**unsheltered** (-sh·eltø<sup>r</sup>d) *adj.* desabrigado, sin abrigo, sin protección.

**unship** (to) (-shi·p) *tr.* MAR. desembarcar, descargar. *2* MAR. desmontar, desarmar [el timón, los remos, etc.].

**unshod** (-sha·d) *adj.* descalzo. *2* desherrado, sin herraduras.

**unshorn** (-sho·<sup>r</sup>n) *adj.* intonso; sin esquilar.

**unshrinkable** (shri·nkabøl) *adj.* inencogible.

**unsightly** (-sai·tli) *adj.* feo, deforme.

**unskilled** (-ski·ld) *adj.* UNSKILLFUL. *2* ~ *labo(u)rer*, obrero no especializado.

**unskillful** (-ful) *adj.* torpe, inhábil, inexperto, imperito.

**unsling** (to) (-sli·ng) *tr.* descolgar [lo que se lleva colgado].

**unsociable** (-sou·shabøl) *adj.* insociable, huraño, reservado.

**unsoiled** (ø·nsoild) *adj.* limpio, sin mancha.

**unsold** (ønsou·ld) *adj.* no vendido, por vender.

**unsoldierlike, unsoldierly** (-sou·lÿø<sup>r</sup>laik, -li) *adv.* poco militar o marcial. *2* impropio de un militar.

**unsolvable** (-sa·lvabøl) *adj.* insoluble, irresoluble.
**unsophisticated** (-søfi·stikeitid) *adj.* puro, no sofisticado. *2* ingenuo, natural, sencillo.
**unsought** (ø·nsɔt) *adj.* no buscado, no solicitado.
**unsound** (-sau·nd) *adj.* enfermo, achacoso. *2* defectuoso, erróneo, falso. *3* malsano, pernicioso. *4* insano, perturbado. *5* inseguro, poco sólido, rajado, podrido.
**unsparing** (-spe·ring) *adj.* liberal, generoso, profuso. *2* implacable, despiadado; cruel.
**unspeakable** (-spı·kabøl) *adj.* inefable, indecible. *2* atroz, execrable.
**unspecified** (-spe·sifaid) *adj.* no especificado o detallado.
**unspotted** (-spa·tid) *adj.* limpio, inmaculado.
**unstable** (-tei·bøl) *adj.* inestable. *2* inconstante, variable. *3* poco sólido.
**unstamped** (-stæ·mpt) *adj.* sin sellar. *2* sin franquear [carta].
**unsteadily** (-te·dili) *adv.* inseguramente. *2* con fluctuación, irregularmente. *3* inconstantemente.
**unsteady** (-šte·di) *adj.* inseguro, vacilante, inestable, movedizo. *2* fluctuante. *3* inconstante, irregular. *4* veleidoso.
**unstitch (to)** (-tı·ch) *tr.* descoser.
**unstop (to)** (-sta·p) *tr.* destapar, descorchar. *3* desobstruir.
**unstrained** (-strei·nd) *adj.* natural, no forzado.
**unstring (to)** (-stri·ng) *tr.* desensartar. *2* desencordar. *3* aflojar. *4* debilitar, aturdir.
**unstudied** (-stø·did) *adj.* no estudiado, no aprendido. *2* natural, no afectado.
**unsubstantial** (-søbstæ·nshal) *adj.* etéreo, incorpóreo; fantástico. *2* flojo, inconsistente.
**unsuccessful** (-søkse·sful) *adj.* infructuoso, desgraciado. *2* fracasado, sin éxito, sin suerte.
**unsufferable** (-sø·førabøl) *adj.* insoportable, insufrible.
**unsuitable** (ønsiu·tabøl), **unsuited** (-id) *adj.* impropio, inadecuado, poco apropiado o conveniente.
**unsupported** (-søpo·ʳtid) *adj.* sin apoyo, sin sostén.
**unsure** (-shu·ʳ) *adj.* inseguro. *2* incierto, precario.
**unsurmountable** (-søʳmau·ntabøl) *adj.* insuperable, invencible.
**unsurpassed** (-søʳpa·st) *adj.* excelente, insuperado.
**unsuspected** (-søspe·ktid) *adj.* insospechado. *2* que no es objeto de sospecha.
**unsuspecting** (-søspe·kting), **unsuspicious** (-søspi·shøs) *adj.* confiado, que no sospecha.
**unswerving** (-suø·ʳving) *adj.* firme, inmutable, resoluto.
**unsympathetic** (-simpaze·tik) *adj.* incompasivo, frío.
**untainted** (-tei·ntid) *adj.* impoluto, no inficionado.
**untamed** (-tei·md) *adj.* indomado, indómito, cerril, bravío.
**untasted** (-tei·stid) *adj.* sin probar, no gustado.
**untaught** (-tɔ·t) *adj.* no aprendido, natural, espontáneo. *2* sin instrucción.
**untenable** (-te·nabøl) *adj.* insostenible.
**untenanted** (-te·nantid) *adj.* desalquilado, desocupado.
**unthinkable** (-zi·nkabøl) *adj.* inconcebible.
**unthought-of** (-zo·t) *adj.* inimaginado. *2* impensado, inesperado.
**unthoughtful** (-zo·tful) *adj.* irreflexivo, inconsiderado.
**unthread (to)** (-zre·d) *tr.* desenhebrar, desensartar.
**untidy** (-tai·di) *adj.* desaliñado, desaseado, desordenado.

**untie (to)** (-tai·) *tr.* desatar, desligar, desanudar. *2* deshacer [un nudo]. *3* aflojar, soltar, zafar.
**until** (-ti·l) *prep.* hasta [con sentido temporal]. *2 conj.* hasta que.
**untilled** (-ti·ld) *adj.* inculto, baldío.
**untimely** (-tai·mli) *adj.* intempestivo, inoportuno. *2* prematuro. *3 adv.* intempestivamente. *4* prematuramente.
**untiring** (-tai·ring) *adj.* incansable, infatigable.
**unto** (ø·ntu) *prep.* poét. y ant. hacia, a, hasta, contra, en.
**untold** (øntou·ld) *adj.* no dicho, contado o narrado. *2* no revelado. *3* incontable, incalculable, vasto.
**untouchable** (-tø·chabøl) *adj.* intangible. *2 s.* intocable.
**untoward** (-to·aʳd) *adj.* indócil, terco, inmanejable. *2* inconveniente, indecoroso. *3* desgraciado, contrario, adverso.
**untractable** (-træ·ktabøl) *adj.* indócil, insumiso.
**untrained** (-trei·nd) *adj.* no ejercitado o entrenado, inexperto; indisciplinado. *2* MIL. bisoño.
**untranslatable** (-trænslei·tabøl) *adj.* intraducible.
**untravelled** (-træ·vøld) *adj.* no transitado, inexplorado, virgen. *2* que no ha visto mundo, provinciano.
**untried** (-trai·d) *adj.* no probado, no ensayado.
**untrimmed** (-tri·md) *adj.* desguarnecido, sin adornos. *2* sin cortar, sin arreglar.
**untrod(den** (-tra·d(øn) *adj.* no hollado.
**untroubled** (-trø·bøld) *adj.* quieto, sosegado, tranquilo.
**untrue** (-tu·) *adj.* falso, inexacto. *2* infiel, desleal.
**untrustworthy** (-trø·stuøʳdi) *adj.* poco fiable, poco seguro.
**untruth** (-tru·z) *s.* falsedad, error.
**untruthful** (-ful) *adj.* falso, mentiroso.
**untutored** (-tiu·tøʳd) *adj.* inculto, sin instrucción.
**untwine (to)** (-tuai·n) *tr.* desenlazar, desenroscar.
**untwist (to)** (-tui·st) *tr.* destorcer, desenroscar.
**unused** (-yu·šd) *adj.* no usado. *2* no habituado. *3* desusado.
**unusual** (-yu· yual) *adj.* extraordinario, excepcional, raro, insólito, no acostumbrado.
**unutterable** (-ø·tørabøl) *adj.* indecible.
**unvanquished** (-væ·nkuisht) *adj.* invicto.
**unvarying** (-ve·riing) *adj.* invariable, constante.
**unveil (to)** (-vei·l) *tr.* quitar el velo a, descubrir, revelar. *2 intr.* quitarse el velo, descubrirse.
**unvoiced** (-voi·sd) *adj.* mudo [no expresado en palabras].
**unwarned** (-wo·ʳnd) *adj.* no avisado. *2* desprevenido.
**unwarrantable** (-wa·rantabøl) *adj.* insostenible, injustificable, inexcusable.
**unwarranted** (-wa·rantid) *adj.* injustificado. *2* no autorizado. *3* sin garantía.
**unwary** (-we·ri) *adj.* descuidado, desprevenido, incauto. *2* imprudente, irreflexivo.
**unwatered** (-wo·tøʳd) *adj.* no regado, de secano.
**unwavering** (-wei·vøring) *adj.* que no tiembla o vacila; firme, determinado, resuelto.
**unwearied** (-wı·rid) *adj.* infatigable.
**unweave (to)** (-wı·v) *tr.* destejer, deshacer.
**unwelcome** (-we·lkøm) *adj.* mal acogido, mal recibido. *2* desagradable, inoportuno, indeseable.
**unwell** (-we·l) *adj.* enfermo, indispuesto, achacoso. *2* fam. que tiene la regla o menstruo.
**unwholesome** (-jou·lsøm) *adj.* insalubre, malsano. *2* dañino, pernicioso, nocivo.
**unwieldy** (-wı·ldi) *adj.* pesado, difícil de manejar,

embarazoso. 2 torpe, desmañado. 3 rebelde, ingobernable.

**unwilling** (-wi·ling) *adj.* reacio, renuente, mal dispuesto.

**unwind (to)** (-wai·nd) *tr.* devanar. 2 desenrollar. 3 desenredar, desenmarañar, desenvolver. ¶ Pret. y p. p.: *unwound.*

**unwise** (-wai·ŝ) *adj.* imprudente, poco cuerdo, necio. 2 ignorante.

**unwitting** (-wi·ting) *adj.* inconsciente, que no se percata, distraído.

**unwomanly** (-wu·manli) *adj.* impropio de una mujer.

**unwonted** (-wø·ntid) *adj.* desusado, desacostumbrado, inusitado, raro, poco común.

**unwooded** (-wu·did) *adj.* sin árboles.

**unworldly** (-wø·ʳldli) *adj.* no mundano, no terrenal, espiritual.

**unworn** (-wo·ʳn) *adj.* nuevo, no llevado, sin estrenar. 2 no usado o gastado.

**unworthy** (-wø·ʳdi) *adj.* indigno, desmerecedor.

**unwrap (to)** (-ræ·p) *tr.* desenvolver [quitar lo que envuelve], desabrigar.

**unwritten** (-ri·tøn) *adj.* no escrito. 2 en blanco. 3 oral, tradicional.

**unwrought** (-ro·t) *adj.* en bruto, no trabajado.

**unyielding** (-yi·lding) *adj.* inflexible, firme, inexorable. 2 terco, reacio.

**unyoke (to)** (-you·k) *tr.* desuncir; desunir. 2 *intr.* libertarse de un yugo.

**up** (øp) *adv.* hacia arriba, arriba, en lo alto, en o hacia una posición superior: ~ *above,* arriba, más arriba. 2 en o hacia una posición derecha, en pie. 3 en o hacia el centro más importante, la dirección, la oficina principal, etc. 4 en o hacia un estado de mayor actividad, fuerza, excitación, resolución, etc.: *to stir* ~, excitar, avivar. 5 en o hacia un estado de evidencia; manifestación o aparición. 6 a la altura, a la par de. 7 enteramente, completamente: *to burn* ~, quemar del todo. 8 de cara, en contacto, en proximidad: *to run* ~ *against,* topar con; *close* ~ *to,* tocando a. 9 a un lado, en reserva: *to lay* ~, guardar, acumular. 10 hasta: ~ *to now,* hasta ahora; ~ *to date,* hasta la fecha; al día, al corriente. 11 ~ *and down,* arriba y abajo, de un lado a otro. 12 up, con estos y otros sentidos modifica gran número de verbos formando locuciones que se encontrarán en los artículos respectivos. 13 *prep.* subido a, en o a lo alto de, hacia arriba de, a lo largo de [subiendo], hacia el interior de: ~ *a tree,* subido en un árbol; fig. en apuros; ~ *the river,* río arriba; ~ *the country,* hacia el interior del país. 14 *adj.* de arriba, dirigido hacia arriba, ascendente. 15 alto, levantado, derecho, en pie. 16 levantado [no acostado]. 17 vuelto hacia arriba. 18 en estado de actividad, excitado; levantado, sublevado. 19 que está en curso, en marcha: *what is* ~?, ¿qué ocurre?, ¿qué pasa? 20 igualado [con otro]. 21 entendido, enterado. 22 capaz, dispuesto. 23 acabado, terminado; *time is* ~, expiró el plazo; ha llegado la hora. 24 que está haciendo o se propone [algo]: *to be* ~ *to one's old tricks,* hacer uno de las suyas. 25 fam. ~ *against,* abocado a. 26 ~ *against it,* ante un obstáculo insuperable. 27 *hard* ~, apurado, a la cuarta pregunta. 28 *s.* movimiento o curva ascendente. 29 alza [de precios]. 30 *ups and downs,* altibajos, vaivenes.

*31 interj.* ¡arriba!, ¡aúpa!, ¡sus! *32* ~ *there!,* ¡alto ahí!

*33 up and,* seguido de infinitivo, indica que se inicia bruscamente la acción indicada por el verbo: ponerse de repente a + infinitivo.

**up-and-coming** *adj.* fam. (E.U.) listo, activo.

**upas** (yu·pas) *s.* bot. antiar. 2 upas [veneno]. 3 ponzoña.

**upbraid (to)** (øpbrei·d) *tr.* reconvenir, reprender.

**upbraiding** (-ing) *s.* reconvención, reproche.

**upbringing** (øpbri·nging) *s.* educación.

**upcast** (ø·pkæst) *adj.* lanzado o dirigido hacia arriba.

**upcountry** (ø·pkøntri) *s.* fam. interior [del país]. 2 *adj.* del interior [del país]. 3 *adv.* en el interior, hacia el interior, tierra adentro.

**upgrowth** (ø·pgrouz) *s.* crecimiento, desarrollo.

**upheaval** (øpjı·val) *s.* solevamiento, levantamiento [esp. de la corteza terrestre]. 2 trastorno, conmoción, cataclismo.

**upheave (to)** (-jı·v) *tr.* solevar, levantar. 2 *intr.* solevarse, levantarse.

**uphill** (ø·pjil) *adv.* cuesta arriba. 2 *adj.* que sube, ascendente. 3 penoso, trabajoso, dificultoso.

**uphold (to)** (øpjou·ld) *tr.* levantar; mantener derecho. 2 sostener, apoyar. 3 mantener, defender.

**upholster (to)** (øpjou·lstøʳ) *tr.* tapizar y emborrar [muebles]. 2 tapizar, colgar [habitaciones].

**upholsterer** (-øʳ) *s.* tapicero.

**upholstery** (-i) *s.* tapicería; colgaduras.

**upkeep** (ø·pkıp) *s.* conservación, manutención, entretenimiento.

**upland** (ø·plænd) *s.* altiplanicie, tierra alta. 2 tierra adentro, el interior.

**uplift** (øpli·ft) *s.* levantamiento, elevación.

**upon** (øpa·n) *prep.* sobre, encima. 2 corresponde a otras preposiciones, según los casos: *nothing to live* ~, nada con qué vivir; *to to turn* ~ *him,* volverse contra él; ~ *my honour,* por mi honor, a fe mía; ~ *pain of,* bajo pena de. 3 no se traduce cuando precede a una fecha o a algunos gerundios: ~ *the tenth of June,* el diez de junio; ~ *seeing this,* viendo esto.

**upper** (ø·pøʳ) *adj. compar.* de UP: superior, alto, más elevado, de encima, de arriba: ~ *case,* IMPR. caja alta; ~ *classes,* la clase alta; *Upper House,* cámara alta; ~ *works,* MAR. obra muerta. 2 dirigido hacia arriba. 3 ~ *s.* pala y caña del zapato: *on one's uppers,* con las suelas gastadas; fig. tronado; apurado.

**uppercut** (-køt) BOX. golpe dirigido hacia arriba.

**uppermost** (-moust) *adj.* el más alto o elevado; supremo, predominante. 2 el de encima de todo. 3 *adv.* en lo más alto; en primer lugar.

**uppish** (ø·pish) *adj.* fam. orgulloso, arrogante.

**upright** (ø·prait) *adj.* derecho, erguido, vertical, enhiesto: ~ *piano,* plano vertical. 2 recto, íntegro, honrado.

**uprise** (øprai·ŝ) *s.* levantamiento, ascensión. 2 pendiente enhiesta. 3 levantamiento, insurrección.

**uprise (to)** *intr.* levantarse [de la cama, etc.]. 2 levantarse, sublevarse. 3 elevarse, ascender. 4 crecer, aumentar [un sonido].

**uprising** (-ing) *s.* levantamiento; solevantamiento. 2 levantamiento, insurrección.

**uproar** (ø·proʳ) *s.* gritería, alboroto, tumulto.

**uproarious** (øpro·riøs) *adj.* estruendoso; ruidoso; bullicioso. 2 tumultuoso.

**uproot (to)** (øpru·t) *tr.* desarraigar, extirpar.

**upset** (-se·t) *adj.* volcado, tumbado. 2 trastornado, desarreglado, turbado. 3 indispuesto [malo]. 4

~ *price*, precio inicial en una subasta. *5 s.*
vuelco. *6* trastorno; desorden; indisposición. *7*
contratiempo.

**upset (to)** *tr.* volcar. *2* trastornar, descomponer,
desarreglar. *3* turbar, alterar, conmover. *4* contrariar, desbaratar. *5* indisponer, poner enfermo. *6 intr.* volcar.

**upshot** (ø·pshat) *s.* resultado final, conclusión.

**upside** (-said) *s.* lado o parte superior: ~ *down*, lo
de arriba abajo, al revés, patas arriba.

**upstairs** (øpste·ʳš) *adv.* arriba, a o en el piso de
arriba. *2 adj.* de arriba.

**upstanding** (-stæ·nding) *adj.* derecho, en pie. *2*
recto, honrado.

**upstart** (øpsta·ʳt) *adj.-s.* advenedizo; presuntuoso.

**upstream** (øpstrɪ·m) *adv.* aguas arriba, río arriba.

**upthrust** (ø·pzrøst) *s.* GEOL. solevantamiento.

**up-to-date** *adj.* que llega hasta la fecha, al corriente. *2* moderno, del día; de última moda.

**upturn** (-tøʳn) *s.* alza [de precios]. *2* mejoramiento.

**upturn (to)** (øptø·ʳn) *tr.* volver hacia arriba. *2* revolver, trastornar, volcar.

**upward** (ø·pwaʳd) *adj.* dirigido hacia arriba, ascendente.

**upward(s** *adv.* hacia arriba, para arriba, arriba.

**uraemia** (yurɪ·mia) *s.* (Ingl.) uremia.

**Ural Mountains** (yu·ral) *n. pr.* GEOGR. Montes Urales.

**Urania** (yurei·nia) *n. pr.* MIT. Urania.

**uranite** (yu·ranait) *s.* MINER. uranita.

**uranium** (yurei·niøm) *s.* QUÍM. uranio.

**uranography** (yurəna·grafi) *s.* uranografía.

**Uranus** (yu·ranøs) *s.* ASTR. Urano.

**urate** (yu·reit) *s.* QUÍM. urato.

**urban** (ø·ʳban) *adj.* urbano [de la ciudad].

**Urban** *n. pr.* Urbano.

**urbane** (øʳbei·n) *adj.* urbano, cortés.

**urbanity** (øʳbæ·niti) *s.* urbanidad. *2* fineza.

**urchin** (ø·ʳchin) *s.* pilluelo, granuja, bribonzuelo,
rapaz. *2* ZOOL. erizo: *sea* ~, erizo de mar.

**urea** (yurɪ·a) *s.* QUÍM. urea.

**uremia** (yurɪ·mia) *s.* (E.U.) uremia.

**ureter** (yurɪ·tøʳ) *s.* ANAT. y ZOOL. uréter.

**urethra** (yurɪ·zra) *s.* ANAT., ZOOL. uretra.

**urge** (ø·ʳdy̆) *s.* impulso. *2* ganas, deseo, estímulo.

**urge (to)** *tr.* encarecer, insistir en. *2* alegar. *3* proponer, recomendar. *4* instar, apremiar. *5* mover, incitar. *6* apresurar, acelerar.

**urgency** (-ønsi) *s.* urgencia. *2* insistencia; instancia. *3* URGE.

**urgent** (-ønt) *adj.* urgente. *2* insistente, apremiante.

**Uriah** (yurai·a) *n. pr.* Urías.

**uric** (yu·rik) *adj.* QUÍM. úrico.

**urinal** (yu·rinal) *s.* orinal. *2* urinario, mingitorio.

**urinary** (yu·rineri) *adj.* urinario: ~ *tract*, vías urinarias.

**urinate (to)** (yu·rineit) *intr.* orinar, mear.

**urine** (yu·rin) *s.* orina, orines.

**urn** (øʳ·n) *s.* urna. *2* jarrón.

**urodelan** (yurodi·lan) *adj.-s.* ZOOL. urodelo.

**urologist** (yura·lødy̆ist) *s.* urólogo.

**urology** (-i) *s.* urología.

**Ursa** (ø·ʳsa) *s.* ASTR. Osa: ~ *Major*, Osa mayor; ~
*Minor*, Osa menor.

**Ursidae** (ø·ʳsidɪ) *s. pl.* ZOOL. úrsidos.

**ursine** (-sin) *adj.* osuno. *2* peludo.

**Ursuline** (ø·ʳsiulin) *n. pr.* Ursulina.

**urticaceous** (øʳtikei·shøs) *adj.* urticáceo.

**urticant** (ø·ʳtikant) *adj.* urticante.

**urticaria** (øʳtike·ria) *s.* MED. urticaria.

**urubu** (ø·rubu) *s.* ORN. urubú.

**Uruguayan** (yurugwi·an) *adj.-s.* uruguayo.

**us** (øs) *pron.* [sin prep.] nos [acusativo o dativo de
WE]. *2* [con prep.] nosotros, nosotras.

**usable** (yu·šabøl) *adj.* que se puede usar.

**usage** (yu·sidy̆) *s.* trato, tratamiento. *2* uso, costumbre.

**use** (yus) *s.* uso, empleo, goce, aprovechamiento:
*out of* ~, desusado, pasado de moda. *2* utilidad,
servicio, provecho, objeto: *to put to* ~, aprovechar, sacar partido de; *of no* ~, inútil; *to have
no (further)* ~ *for*, no necesitar; no querer saber
nada o nada más de. *3* uso, usanza, práctica,
costumbre. *4* DER. uso.

**use (to)** *tr.* usar, emplear, gastar, servirse o valerse
de. *2* hacer, practicar. *3* tratar [bien, mal, etc.].
*4* acostumbrar, habituar. *5* soler ir o andar por.
*6 to* ~ *up*, gastar, consumir, agotar. *7 intr.* soler,
acostumbrar.

**used** (-d) *adj.* usado. *2* usual, acostumbrado. *3*
acostumbrado, habituado: ~ *to*, acostumbrado
a.

**useful** (-ful) *adj.* útil. *2* conveniente, provechoso,
beneficioso.

**useless** (-lis) *adj.* inútil. *2* inservible.

**usher** (yu·shøʳ) *s.* ujier, portero, introductor. *2*
TEAT. acomodador. *3* (Ingl.) ayudante de escuela.

**usher (to)** *tr.* introducir, anunciar, guiar.

**usherette** (-et) *s.* TEAT. acomodadora.

**ustion** (ø·schiøn) *s.* ustión.

**usual** (yu·y̆ual) *adj.·* usual, habitual, acostumbrado, ordinario, de costumbre: *as* ~, como de
costumbre, como de ordinario.

**usufruct** (yu·šiufrøkt) *s.* usufructo.

**usufructuary** (yusiufrø·kchueri) *adj.-s.* usufructuario.

**usurer** (yu·y̆ørøʳ) *s.* usurero.

**usurious** (yuy̆u·riøs) *adj.* usurario.

**usurp (to)** (yušø·ʳp) *tr.* usurpar.

**usurpation** (yušøʳpei·shøn) *s.* usurpación.

**usurper** (yušø·ʳpøʳ) *s.* usurpador.

**usury** (yu·y̆uri) *s.* usura.

**ut** (ut) *s.* MÚS. ut, do.

**utensil** (yute·nsil) *s.* utensilio. *2* útil, herramienta.

**uterine** (yu·tørin) *adj.* uterino.

**uterus** (-øs) *s.* ANAT., ZOOL. útero.

**utilitarian** (yutilite·rian) *adj.* utilitario.

**utilitarianism** (-išm) *s.* FIL. utilitarismo.

**utility** (yuti·liti) *s.* utilidad, ventaja, provecho. *2*
empresa de servicio público [agua, gas, electricidad, etc.]. *3* TEAT. ~ *man*, racionista.

**utilize (to)** (yu·tilaiš) *tr.* utilizar, emplear, aprovechar, explotar.

**utmost** (ø·tmoust) *adj.* sumo, extremo; más
grande, mayor, más alto, más distante, último.
*2 s.* lo más posible, lo sumo: *to do one's* ~, hacer
cuanto uno puede.

**utopia, Utopia** (yutou·pia) *s.* utopía.

**utopian, Utopian** (-n) *adj.* utópico. *2* utopista.

**utricle** (yu·trikøl) *s.* ANAT., BOT. utrículo.

**utter** (ø·tøʳ) *adj.* absoluto, completo, total. *2* categórico, terminante.

**utter (to)** *tr.* pronunciar, articular, proferir. *2* dar,
lanzar [un grito]. *3* decir, expresar, manifestar.

**utterance** (øtæ·rans) *s.* pronunciación, articulación, emisión [de sonidos, palabras, etc.]. *2* expresión, manera de hablar. *3* declaración, discurso.

**utterly** (-li) *adv.* absolutamente, completamente,
totalmente, del todo.

**uvate** (yu·veit) *s.* uvate.
**uvea** (yu·vi*a*) *s.* ANAT. úvea.
**uvula** (yu·viul*a*) *s.* ANAT. úvula.
**uvular** (-la<sup>r</sup>) *adj.* uvular.

**uxorial** (øxo·rial) *adj.* uxorial.
**uxoricide** (-isaid) *s.* uxoricidio. 2 uxoricida.
**uxorious** (-iøs) *adj.* gurrumino.

# V

**V, v** (vi) *s.* V, v, vigésima segunda letra del alfabeto inglés. *2* V, cifra romana.

**vacancy** (vei·kansi) *s.* ocio. *2* vacante, vacatura. *3* vacío, hueco, laguna. *4* vacuidad.

**vacant** (-kant) *adj.* vacante. *2* vacío, despreocupado. *3* ocioso, de ocio. *4* inexpresivo, vago. *5* distraído.

**vacate (to)** (vei·keit) *tr.* dejar vacante. *2* evacuar, desocupar. *3* anular, invalidar. *4 intr.* vacar, dedicarse.

**vacation** (veikei·shøn) *s.* vacación, descanso. *2* vacante. *3* DER. anulación.

**vaccinate (to)** (væ·ksineit) *tr.* vacunar.

**vaccination** (væksinei·shøn) *s.* vacunación.

**vaccine** (væ·ksin) *adj.* vacuno. *2* de vacuna: ~ *therapy*, vacunoterapia. *3 s.* vacuna.

**vacillate (to)** (væ·sileit) *tr.* vacilar. *2* fluctuar.

**vacillation** (væsilei·shøn) *s.* vacilación. *2* fluctuación.

**vacuity** (vakiu·iti) *s.* vacío. *2* hueco, blanco. *3* vaciedad. *4* ausencia [de ideas, emociones, etc.]; vaguedad.

**vacuole** (væ·kiuol) *s.* BIOL. vacuola.

**vacuous** (væ·kiuøs) *adj.* vacuo, vacío. *2* estúpido. *3* insulso. *4* ocioso, frívolo.

**vacuum** (va·kiuøm) *s.* vacío, vacuo: ~ *bottle* o *flask*, termos; ~ *cleaner*, aspirador eléctrico; ~ *tube*, ELECT. tubo o lámparra de vacío.

**vade mecum** (vei·di mi·køm) *s.* vademécum, manual.

**vagabond** (væ·gaband) *adj.* errabundo, nómada, vagabundo. *2 s.* vagabundo; vago.

**vagabondize (to)** (væ·gabandaiš) *intr.* vagabundear.

**vagary** (veige·ri) *s.* capricho, extravagancia, antojo, extravío, vagabundeo.

**vagina** (vadỹai·na) *s.* ANAT. vagina.

**vaginate** (væ·dỹineit) *s.* BOT. envainado.

**vagrancy** (vei·gransi) *s.* vagabundeo, vagancia. *2* extravío, capricho.

**vagrant** (-ant) *adj.* vagabundo, vagaroso, errante, errático. *2 s.* vago, vagabundo.

**vague** (veig) *adj.* vago, indefinido, indistinto. *2* incierto, dudoso.

**vain** (vein) *adj.* vano, fútil. *2* vano, infructuoso: *in* ~, en vano. *3* vano, vanidoso.

**vainglorious** (veinglo·riøs) *adj.* vanaglorioso.

**vainglory** (-ri) *s.* vanagloria.

**vair** (ve^r) *s.* vero [piel]. *2* BLAS. veros.

**valance** (væ·lans) *s.* cenefa colgante, doselera, sobrepuerta.

**vale** (veil) *s.* poét. valle: ~ *of tears*, valle de lágrimas.

**valediction** (vælidi·kshøn) *s.* adiós, despedida.

**valedictory** (-tori) *adj.* de despedida. *2 s.* discurso de despedida a fin de curso.

**valence, -cy** (vei·løns, -si) *s.* QUÍM. valencia.

**Valentine** (væ·løntain) *n. pr.* Valentín.

**valentine** *s.* tarjeta amorosa o jocosa enviada a una persona del sexo contrario el día de San Valentín. *2* novio o novia.

**valerian** (valr·rian) *s.* BOT., FARM. valeriana.

**valerianate** (-eit) *s.* QUÍM. valerianato.

**valet** (væ·lit o væ·lei) *s.* criado, ayuda de cámara. *2* planchador de trajes [en un hotel].

**valetudinarian** (vælitiudine·rian) *s.* valetudinario.

**valiant** (væ·liant) *adj.* valiente, valeroso.

**valid** (væ·lid) *adj.* válido. *2* valedero. *3* eficaz.

**validate (to)** (va·lideit) *tr.* validar.

**validity** (vali·diti) *s.* validez.

**valise** (valr·s) *s.* maleta, valija; *petaca.

**Valkyrie** (væ·lkiri) *s.* valquiria.

**valley** (væ·li) *s.* GEOGR. valle, cuenca, hoya. *2* ARQ. lima hoya.

**valor** (væ·lø^r) *s.* VALOUR.

**valorous** (-løøs) *adj.* valeroso, valiente.

**valour** (væ·lø^r) *s.* valor, valentía, fortaleza.

**valuable** (væ·liuabøl) *adj.* valioso, costoso, preciado. *2 s. pl.* joyas, objetos de valor.

**valuation** (væliuei·shøn) *s.* valoración, avalúo. *2* estimación, apreciación.

**value** (væ·liu) *s.* valor [de una cosa]; precio, mérito, valía, estimación, aprecio. *2* entidad, importancia. *3* MÚS., PINT. valor.

**value (to)** *tr.* valorar, valuar, tasar. *2* dar valor a, tener en mucho, estimar, considerar.

**valueless** (-lis) *adj.* sin valor, insignificante.

**valval, valvar** (væ·lval, -a^r) *adj.* BIOL. valvar.

**valve** (væ·lv) *s.* ANAT., MEC., RADIO. válvula. *2* BOT. ventalla. *3* ZOOL. valva. *4* compuerta [de canal, presa, etc.].

**valvular** (væ·lviula^r) *adj.* valvular.

**valvule** (-viul) *s.* valvulilla.

**vamp** (væmp) *s.* ZAP. pala, empella. *2* remiendo. *3* arreglo, improvisación. *4* fam. vampiresa, mujer fatal.

**vamp (to)** *tr.* remendar, componer. *2* arreglar, improvisar. *3 pop.* conquistar [una mujer a un hombre], coquetear con. *4 intr.* coquetear, hacer de mujer fatal.

**vamper** (-ø$^r$) *s.* remendón.

**vampire** (væ·mpai$^r$) *s.* vampiro. *2* vampiresa. *3* TEAT. escotillón.

**van** (væn) *s.* carromato. *2* carro de mudanzas; camión. *3* (Ingl.) furgón de equipajes. *4* vanguardia.

**vanadium** (vanei·diøm) *s.* QUÍM. vanadio.

**Vandal** (væ·ndal) *adj.-s.* vándalo.

**vandalism** (væ·ndališm) *s.* vandalismo.

**vane** (vein) *s.* veleta. *2* MAR. grímpola. *3* aspa [de molino]. *4* paleta, álabe. *5* barbas [de la pluma]. *6* pínula.

**vanguard** (væ·nga$^r$d) *s.* vanguardia.

**vanilla** (vani·la) *s.* BOT. vainilla.

**vanish (to)** (væ·nish) *intr.* desaparecer, desvanecerse, disiparse, esfumarse.

**vanity** (væ·niti) *s.* vanidad, envanecimiento: ~ *case,* polvera. *2* vanidad, inutilidad, futilidad.

**vanquish (to)** (væ·nkuish) *tr.* vencer, derrotar. *2* vencer, dominar.

**vantage** (væ·ntidȳ) *s.* ventaja, superioridad; situación favorable: ~ *ground,* posición ventajosa. *2* TENIS ventaja.

**vapid** (væ·pid) *adj.* soso, insípido, insulso.

**vapor** (vei·pø$^r$) *s.* VAPOUR.

**vapor (to)** *intr.-tr.* TO VAPOUR.

**vaporer** (vei·pørø$^r$) *s.* fanfarrón.

**vaporish** (-ish) *adj.* vaporoso. *2* histérico.

**vaporize (to)** (-aiš) *tr.* vaporizar. *2* volatilizar. *3* evaporar. *4 intr.* vaporizarse.

**vaporizer** (-aisø$^r$) *s.* vaporizador. *2* pulverizador.

**vaporose** (vei·pørous) *adj.* vaporoso, volátil.

**vaporous** (-øs) *adj.* calinoso, brumoso. *2* vaporoso, etéreo, fantástico. *3* vago, nebuloso.

**vapour** (-pø$^r$) *s.* vapor, gas, humo, vaho, exhalación. *2* niebla ligera. *3 fig.* humo, fantasía.

**vapour (to)** *intr.* evaporarse, vahear. *2* fanfarronear. *3 tr.* evaporar. *4* exhalar.

**vapo(u)ry** (-i) *adj.* vaporoso, calinoso.

**vapulate (to)** (vei·piulet) *tr.* vapulear.

**variability** (veriabi·liti) *s.* variabilidad.

**variable** (ve·riabøl) *adj.* variable. *2* inconstante, mudable. *3 s.* cosa variable. *4* MAT. variable. *5* GRAM. parte variable.

**variance** (ve·rians) *s.* variación, cambio. *2* discrepancia. *3* desavenencia, desacuerdo. *4 at* ~, en desacuerdo; desavenidos.

**variant** (ve·riant) *adj.* vario, distinto, diferente. *2 s.* variante.

**variation** (veriei·shøn) *s.* variación. *2* AJED. variante.

**varicolo (u) red** (ve·rikølø$^r$d) *adj.* multicolor.

**varicose** (væ·rikous) *adj.* varicoso.

**varied** (ve·rid) *adj.* vario, variado.

**variegate (to)** (ve·rigeit) *tr.* abigarrar, jaspear, vetear, matizar. *2* dar variedad a.

**variegated** (-id) *adj.* abigarrado, jaspeado, veteado, matizado, variado.

**variety** (varai·iti) *s.* variedad. *2* TEAT. variedades.

**variform** (varai·fo$^r$m) *adj.* diversiforme.

**variolous** (varai·oløs) *adj.* varioloso. *2* picado de viruelas.

**variometer** (veria·mitø$^r$) *s.* ELECT. variómetro.

**various** (ve·riøs) *adj.* vario [diverso; variable]. *2* variado. *3* varios, algunos.

**varix** (ve·riks), *pl.* **varices** (ve·risiš) *s.* MED. variz.

**varlet** (va·$^r$lit) *s. ant.* lacayo. *2 ant.* bribón.

**varnish** (va·$^r$nish) *s.* barniz. *2* charol. *3* CERÁM. vidriado.

**varnish (to)** *tr.* barnizar; charolar. *2* CERÁM. vidriar. *3 fig.* disimular, encubrir, paliar.

**varnishing** (-ing) *s.* barnizado [acción]: ~ *day,* B. ART. barnizado [de una exposición].

**varsity** (va·$^r$siti) *s.* fam. universidad.

**vary (to)** (ve·ri) *tr.-intr.* variar. *2 intr.* discrepar, diferenciarse. *3* desviarse, apartarse.

**varying** (ve·riing) *adj.* variante; variable.

**vascular** (væ·skiula$^r$) *adj.* vascular.

**vasculose** (-lous) *adj.* vasculoso.

**vase** (veis) *s.* jarrón; florero; jarro.

**vaseline** (væ·sølin) *s.* vaselina.

**vasomotor** (væsømou·tø$^r$) *s.* FISIOL., ANAT. vasomotor.

**vassal** (væ·sal) *adj.-s.* vasallo.

**vassalage** (væ·sølidȳ) *s.* vasallaje.

**vast** (væst) *adj.* vasto. *2* anchuroso. *3* inmenso; enorme, atroz. *4 s.* vastedad, inmensidad.

**vastly** (-li) *adv.* inmensamente, enormemente, muy, mucho, en sumo grado.

**vasty** (-i) *adj.* vasto, inmenso.

**Vatican** (væ·tikan) *n. pr.* Vaticano.

**vaticinal** (væti·sinal) *adj.* vatídico, profético.

**vaticinate (to)** (væti·sineit) *intr.* vaticinar.

**vaticination** (-ei·shøn) *s.* vaticinio.

**vaudeville** (vou·dvil) *s.* espectáculo de variedades. *2* especie de zarzuela. *3* canción popular satírica.

**vault** (volt) *s.* ARQ., ANAT. bóveda. *2 fig.* bóveda celeste. *3* sótano; cripta; tumba o panteón subterráneo. *4* salto [con pértiga, etc.].

**vault (to)** *tr.* abovedar, cubrir con bóveda. *2 tr.-intr.* saltar [por encima], voltear, saltar con pértiga.

**vaulted** (-id) *adj.* abovedado.

**vaunt** (vont) *s.* jactancia, vanagloria, alarde.

**vaunt (to)** *intr.* jactarse, vanagloriarse. *2 tr.* jactarse de, ostentar.

**vaunter** (-ø$^r$) *s.* jactancioso, fanfarrón.

**veal** (vil) *s.* ternera [carne].

**vector** (ve·ktø$^r$) *s.* MAT. radio vector.

**vectorial** (vekto·rial) *adj.* vector.

**Veda** (vei·da) *s.* Veda.

**vedette** (vide·t) *s.* MIL. centinela o escucha a caballo. *2* MAR. escampavía.

**veer (to)** (vi$^r$) *intr.* virar, girar, desviarse. *2* METEOR. cambiar [el viento]. *3 tr.* cambiar el rumbo o la dirección de.

**veering** (-ing) *s.* virada.

**veery** (vi·ri) *s.* ORN. tordo americano.

**vegetable** (ve·dȳitabøl) *adj.* vegetal: ~ *kingdom,* reino vegetal. *2* de hortalizas: ~ *garden,* huerto. *3 s.* vegetal, planta. *4* legumbre, hortaliza.

**vegetal** (ve·dȳital) *adj.* vegetal.

**vegetarian** (vedȳite·rian) *adj.-s.* vegetariano.

**vegetate (to)** (ve·dȳiteit) *intr.* vegetar.

**vegetation** (-shøn) *s.* vegetación. *2* vida monótona, vegetante.

**vegetative** (-tiv) *adj.* vegetativo.

**vehemence** (vɪ·jimøns) *s.* vehemencia. *2* violencia, intensidad.

**vehement** (-mønt) *adj.* vehemente. *2* violento, intenso.

**vehicle** (vɪ·jikøl) *s.* vehículo. *2* FARM. excipiente.

**veil** (veil) *s.* velo: *to take the* ~, tomar el velo, profesar. *2* disfraz, pretexto. *3* FOT. veladura.

**veil (to)** *tr.* velar [cubrir con velo]. *2* velar, ocultar, disimular, oscurecer.

**veilless** (-lis) *adj.* sin velo.
**vein** (vein) *s.* ANAT. vena. *2* BOT. vena, nervio. *2* ENT. nervio [de ala]. *4* vena, veta [de la piedra, la madera, etc.]. *5* MIN. vena, veta, filón. *2* humor, disposición.
**vein (to)** *tr.* cubrir de venas. *2* vetear, jaspear.
**veined** (-d) *adj.* venoso. *2* veteado.
**veinstone** (-stoun) *s.* MIN. ganga.
**velar** (vɪ·laʳ) *adj.* ANAT., FONÉT. velar.
**veld, veldt** (velt) *s.* en África del Sur, extensión de tierras cubiertas de hierba, arbustos o maleza.
**vellum** (vɪ·løm) *s.* pergamino, vitela.
**velocipede** (vila·sipid) *s.* velocípedo.
**velocity** (vila·siti) *s.* velocidad. *2* celeridad, rapidez.
**velodrome** (vɪ·lødroum) *s.* velódromo.
**velours** (velu·ʳ) *s.* felpa aterciopelada.
**velvet** (ve·lvit) *s.* terciopelo, velludo. *2* ZOOL. vellosidad. *3* pop. ganancia, ventaja.
**velveteen** (velvøtɪ·n) *s.* velludillo.
**velvety** (-i) *adj.* aterciopelado. *2* suave.
**venal** (vɪ·nal) *adj.* venal.
**venality** (vinæ·liti) *s.* venalidad.
**venatic** (vinæ·tik) *adj.* venatorio.
**vend (to)** (vend) *tr.* vender.
**vendee** (vendɪ·) *s.* DER. comprador.
**vender** (ve·ndøʳ) *s.* vendedor.
**vendible** (-ibøl) *adj.* vendible. *2* venal.
**vendor** (-øʳ) *s.* vendedor.
**vendue** (vendiu·) *s.* almoneda, subasta, *venduta.
**veneer** (vønɪ·ʳ) *s.* hoja para chapear, chapa. *2* revestimiento. *3* fig. apariencia.
**veneer (to)** *tr.* chapear, enchapar; revestir. *2* encubrir.
**venerable** (ve·nørabøl) *adj.* venerable. *2* venerado.
**venerate (to)** (-eit) *tr.* venerar, reverenciar.
**veneration** (venørei·shøn) *s.* veneración, reverencia.
**venereal** (vinɪ·rial) *adj.* venéreo.
**venery** (ve·nøri) *s.* venus, deleite sensual. *2* ant. montería.
**Venetia** (vinɪ·sha) *n. pr.* GEOGR. Venecia [comarca].
**Venetian** (vinɪ·shan) *adj.-s.* veneciano: ~ *blind*, persiana.
**Venezuelan** (venišui·lan) *adj.-s.* venezolano.
**vengeance** (ve·ndʒans) *s.* venganza. *2 with a* ~, con furia; extremadamente; con creces.
**vengeful** (-ful) *adj.* vengativo.
**venial** (vɪ·nial) *adj.* venial.
**Venice** (venis) *n. pr.* GEOGR. Venecia [ciudad].
**venison** (ve·nišøn) *s.* venado, carne de venado.
**venom** (ve·nøm) *s.* veneno. *2* ponzoña, rencor.
**venomous** (ve·nømøs) *adj.* venenoso. *2* rencoroso.
**venous** (vɪ·nøs) *adj.* venoso.
**vent** (vent) *s.* orificio, abertura, paso [para dar salida al aire, un fluido]; escape, respiradero. *3* oído, fogón [de un arma]. *4* ZOOL. ano. *5* salida, expansión, desahogo.
**vent (to)** *tr.* dar salida, expresión o libre curso a; desahogar, descargar.
**venter** (-øʳ) *s.* vientre.
**venthole** (-joul) *s.* orificio de escape; respiradero.
**ventilate (to)** (ve·ntileit) *tr.* ventilar, airear. *2* ventilar, discutir.
**ventilation** (-ei·shøn) *s.* ventilación.
**ventilator** (ve·ntileitøʳ) *s.* ventilador.
**ventose** (ve·ntous) *adj.* ventoso, flatulento.
**ventral** (ve·ntral) *adj.* ventral. *2* abdominal.
**ventricle** (ve·ntrikøl) *s.* ANAT., ZOOL. ventrículo.
**ventriloquism** (ventri·løkuišm) *s.* ventriloquía.
**ventriloquist** (-ist) *s.* ventrílocuo.

**venture** (ve·nchøʳ) *s.* ventura, azar, riesgo: *at a* ~, al azar. *2* especulación, empresa arriesgada.
**venture (to)** *tr.* aventurar, arriesgar. *2 intr.* aventurarse, arriesgarse, atreverse.
**venturesome** (-søm), **venturous** (-øs) *adj.* atrevido, temerario, emprendedor. *2* aventurado, arriesgado, azaroso.
**Venus** (vɪ·nøs) *n. pr.* ASTR., MIT. Venus. *2* fig. encanto, gracia.
**Venus'-comb** *s.* BOT. aguja de pastor o de Venus. *2* ZOOL. molusco del género *murex*.
**Venus's-flytrap** *s.* BOT. atrapamoscas, dionea.
**veracious** (virei·shøs) *adj.* veraz. *2* verídico.
**veracity** (viræ·siti) *s.* veracidad.
**veranda(h** (vøræ·nda) *s.* veranda.
**verb** (vøʳb) *s.* GRAM. verbo.
**verbal** (vøʳbal) *adj.* verbal: ~ *noun*, GRAM. sustantivo verbal. *2* literal.
**verbalism** (-išm) *s.* verbalismo. *2* palabrería.
**verbalize (to)** (-aiš) *tr.* convertir en verbo. *2* gastar muchas palabras, ser verboso.
**verbatim** (vøʳbei·tim) *adv.* literalmente, al pie de la letra.
**verbena** (vøʳbɪ·na) *s.* BOT. verbena.
**verbiage** (vøʳbiidẏ) *s.* verbosidad, palabrería.
**verbose** (vøʳbou·s) *adj.* verboso. *2* difuso, prolijo.
**verbosity** (vøʳba·siti) *s.* verbosidad.
**verdancy** (vøʳdansi) *s.* verdor. *2* fig. inocencia, sencillez, ingenuidad.
**verdant** (-dant) *adj.* verde [planta, campo, etc.]. *2* fam. ingenuo, sencillo.
**verdict** (vøʳdikt) *s.* veredicto. *2* dictamen.
**verdigris** (vøʳdigris) *s.* verdete. *2* cardenillo, verdín.
**verdure** (vøʳdẏuʳ) *s.* verde, verdura, verdor [de la vegetación]. *2* verdor, lozanía.
**verge** (vøʳdẏ) *s.* borde, orilla, límite: *on the* ~ *of*, al borde de, a punto de. *2* círculo, anillo. *3* ámbito, esfera. *4* vara [insignia], varilla. *5* fuste [de columna].
**verge (to)** *intr.* inclinarse, acercarse [a o hacia]. *2 to* ~ *on*, estar próximo a, estar al borde de, rayar en.
**verger** (-øʳ) *s.* macero. *2* pertiguero.
**veridical** (viri·dikal) *adj.* verídico.
**verification** (verifikei·shøn) *s.* verificación, comprobación, demostración.
**verify (to)** (ve·rifai) *tr.* verificar, comprobar, demostrar. *2* justificar, acreditar. *3* cumplir [una predicción, una promesa]. ¶ Pret. y p. p.: *verified*.
**verily** (ve·rili) *adv.* verdaderamente, en verdad.
**verisimilar** (verisi·milaʳ) *adj.* verosímil, verísimil.
**verisimilitude** (verisimi·litiud) *s.* verosimilitud.
**verism** (viri·šm) *s.* verismo.
**veritable** (ve·ritabøl) *adj.* verdadero.
**verity** (ve·riti) *s.* verdad, realidad.
**verjuice** (vøʳẏus) *s.* agraz. *2* agrazada. *3* acritud, aspereza [de carácter].
**vermicelli** (vøʳmise·li o -che·li) *s.* fideos.
**vermicide** (vøʳmisaid) *s.* vermicida.
**vermicular** (vøʳmi·kiulaʳ) *adj.* vermicular. *2* vermiforme.
**vermiculation** (vøʳmikiulei·shøn) *s.* movimiento vermicular. *2* dibujo u ornamentación vermiforme.
**vermiform** (vøʳmifoʳm) *adj.* vermiforme.
**vermifuge** (-fiuẏ) *s.* vermífugo.
**vermillion** (vøʳmi·liøn) *s.* bermellón. *2* rojo, carmín.

**vermin** (vø·ʳmin) *s.* bicho, sabandija. *2* bichos, sabandijas; alimañas.
**verminous** (-øs) *adj.* verminoso. *2* infestado de bichos o sabandijas.
**vermis** (vø·ʳmis) *s.* ANAT. vermis.
**verm(o)uth** (vø·ʳmuz) *s.* vermut.
**vernacular** (vøʳnæ·kiulaʳ) *adj.* vernáculo. *2 s.* lenguaje vernáculo o, por ext., profesional.
**vernal** (vø·ʳnal) *adj.* vernal. *2* BOT. ~ *grass*, grama de olor.
**vernier** (vø·ʳniøʳ) *s.* vernier, nonio.
**veronal** (ve·rønal) *s.* veronal.
**Veronica** (vira·nika) *n. pr.* Verónica. *2* la Santa Faz. *3* (con min.) BOT. verónica.
**Versailles** (veʳsai·o veʳse·lš) *n. pr.* GEOGR. Versalles.
**versatile** (vø·ʳsatil) *adj.* BOT., ZOOL. versátil. *2* versátil, voluble, inconstante. *3* vario, universal, de conocimientos variados.
**verse** (vøʳs) *s.* LIT. verso. *2* versículo.
**verse (to)** *intr.* versificar, hacer versos.
**versed** (vøʳst) *adj.* versado, instruido. *2* MAT. verso: ~ *sine*, seno verso.
**versemonger** (vø·ʳsmøngøʳ) *s.* coplero, poetastro.
**versicle** (vø·ʳsikøl) *s.* versículo. *2* verso corto.
**versification** (vøʳsifikei·shøn) *s.* versificación.
**versify (to)** (vø·ʳsifai) *tr.-intr.* versificar.
**version** (vø·ʳshøn) *s.* versión.
**verso** (vø·ʳsou) *s.* reverso. *2* folio verso.
**verst** (vøʳst) *s.* versta.
**versus** (vø·ʳsøs) *prep.* DER., DEP. contra.
**vertebra** (vø·ʳtibra), *pl.* **-bræ** (-brī) o **-bras** *s.* vértebra. *2 pl.* espinazo.
**vertebral** (vø·ʳtibral) *adj.* vertebral. *2* vertebrado.
**Vertebrata** (vøʳtibrei·ta) *s. pl.* ZOOL. vertebrados.
**vertebrate** (vø·ʳtibreit) *adj.-s.* ZOOL. vertebrado.
**vertebrated** (-id) *adj.* vertebrado.
**vertex** (vø·ʳteks) *s.* vértice. *2* cima, cumbre, cúspide, ápice. *3* ASTR. cenit.
**vertical** (vø·ʳtikal) *adj.* vertical.
**verticil** (vø·ʳtisil) *s.* BIOL. verticilo.
**vertiginous** (vøʳti·dȳinøs) *adj.* vertiginoso.
**vertigo** (vø·ʳtigou) *s.* vértigo.
**vervain** (vø·ʳvein) *s.* BOT. verbena.
**verve** (vøʳv) *s.* inspiración, brío.
**very** (ve·ri) *adj.* mismo, idéntico: *at the* ~ *moment*, en aquel mismo instante. *2* verdadero, exacto, puro, mero, solo: *the* ~ *truth*, la pura verdad. *3 adv.* muy, sumamente. *4* ~ *much*, mucho, muchísimo, muy.
**vesania** (visei·nia) *s.* MED. vesania.
**vesica** (visai·ka) *s.* ANAT. vejiga.
**vesicant** (ve·sikant) *adj.-s.* vesicante.
**vesicatory** (-tori) *adj.-s.* vejigatorio.
**vesicle** (ve·sikøl) *s.* vesícula, vejiguilla.
**vesicular** (visi·kiulaʳ) *adj.* vesicular.
**Vesper** (ve·spøʳ) *n. pr.* Véspero. *2 s.* (con min.) anochecer. *3 pl.* LITURG. vísperas. *4 adj.* vespertino.
**vespertine** (-tin) *adj.* vespertino.
**vespiary** (ve·spieri) *s.* avispero [de avispas].
**vessel** (ve·søl) *s.* vasija, vaso. *2* nave, embarcación. *3* AÑAT., ZOOL., BOT. vaso.
**vest** (vest) *s.* chaleco. *2* camiseta de punto; chaqueta [de mujer].
**vest (to)** *tr.* poét. vestir. *2 to* ~ *with*, investir con o de. *3 to* ~ *in*, dar, atribuir, conferir a. *4 intr.* poét. vestirse. *5* pasar, recaer [un derecho, propiedad, etc.].
**vestal** (ve·stal) *s.* vestal. *2* virgen, monja.
**vested interests** (ve·stid) *s. pl.* intereses creados.
**vestibule** (ve·stibiul) *s.* vestíbulo; zaguán, recibimiento. *3* ANAT. vestíbulo.

**vestige** (ve·stidȳ) *s.* vestigio.
**vestigial** (vesti·dȳial) *adj.* BIOL. rudimentario.
**vestment** (ve·stmønt) *s.* vestidura, vestido. *2* vestidura sagrada, ornamento.
**vestry** (ve·stri) *s.* sacristía. *2* junta parroquial.
**vestryman** (-mæn) *s.* miembro de la junta parroquial.
**Vesuvius** (visiu·viøs) *n. pr.* GEOGR. Vesubio.
**vetch** (vech) *s.* BOT. arveja, algarroba, veza.
**vetchling** (-ling) *s.* BOT. almorta.
**veteran** (ve·tøran) *s.-adj.* veterano.
**veterinarian** (vetørine·rian) *s.* veterinario, albéitar.
**veterinary** (ve·tørineri) *adj.* veterinario.
**veto** (vɪ·tou) *s.* veto.
**veto (to)** *tr.* poner el veto a. *2* vedar, prohibir.
**vex (to)** (veks) *tr.* vejar, molestar, incomodar, irritar, exasperar. *2* disgustar, desazonar. *3* discutir: *vexed point*, punto discutido.
**vexation** (veksei·shøn) *s.* molestia, mal trato. *2* chinchorrería. *3* disgusto, enojo, desazón.
**vexatious** (shøs) *adj.* molesto, enfadoso, enojoso, irritante.
**via** (vai·a) *prep.* via, por la via de, por.
**viability** (vaiabi·liti) *s.* viabilidad.
**viable** (-abøl) *adj.* viable [que puede vivir].
**viaduct** (-adøkt) *s.* viaducto.
**vial** (-al) *s.* redoma, frasco, ampolleta.
**viands** (-ands) *s. pl.* vituallas.
**viaticum** (vaiæ·tikøm) *s.* HIST., ECLES. viático.
**vibrant** (vai·brant) *adj.* vibrante.
**vibrate (to)** (-breit) *tr.* vibrar, hacer vibrar. *2 intr.* vibrar. *3* oscilar. *4* palpitar, trepidar.
**vibratile** (-bratil) *adj.* vibrátil.
**vibration** (vaibrei·shøn) *s.* vibración. *2* oscilación. *3* palpitación, trepidación.
**vibrator** (vai·breitøʳ) *s.* vibrador.
**vibratory** (-bratori) *adj.* vibratorio.
**vibrion** (vi·brian) *s.* BACT. vibrión.
**viburnum** (vaibø·ʳnøm) *s.* BOT. viburno; mundillo.
**vicar** (vi·kaʳ) *s.* vicario. *2* párroco anglicano que no cobra diezmos.
**vicarage** (vi·karidȳ) *s.* beneficio y casa del VICAR *2*.
**vicarial** (vike·rial) *adj.* delegado.
**vicarious** (vaike·riøs) *adj.* delegado. *2* hecho o sufrido por cuenta de otro o en su beneficio.
**vice** (vais) *s.* vicio. *2* VISE. *3* fam. sustituto, suplente.
**vice-** *pref.* vice-.
**vicegerent** (vaisdȳi·rent) *adj.-s.* lugarteniente, vicario: ~ *of God*, Vicario de Dios, el Papa.
**viceregal** (vaisri·gal) *adj.* virreinal.
**viceroy** (vai·sroi) *s.* virrey.
**vice versa** (vai·sivø·ʳsa) *adv.* viceversa.
**vicinage** (vi·sinidȳ) *s.* vecindad; vecindario.
**vicinal** (vi·sinal) *adj.* vecino, adyacente. *2* vecinal.
**vicinity** (visi·niti) *s.* vecindad, cercanía, proximidad. *2* alrededores, contornos.
**vicious** (vi·shøs) *adj.* vicioso [depravado; defectuoso]. *2* resabiado. *3* maligno, sañudo, rencoroso.
**vicissitude** (visi·sitiud) *s.* vicisitud.
**Vicky** (vi·ki) *n. pr. dim.* de VICTORIA.
**victim** (vi·ktim) *s.* víctima. *2* interfecto.
**victimize (to)** (-aiš) *tr.* hacer víctima, sacrificar. *2* estafar, embaucar.
**victor** (vi·ktøʳ) *m.* vencedor, triunfador. *2 n. pr.* Víctor.
**Victoria** (vikto·ria) *n. pr.* Victoria. *2 s.* (con min.) victoria [coche].
**Victorian** (-rian) *adj.-s.* victoriano.

**victorious** (-riøs) *adj.* victorioso. *2* triunfal.
**victory** (vi·ktori) *s.* victoria, triunfo.
**victress** (vi·ktris) *s.* vencedora, triunfadora.
**victual (to)** (vi·tøl) *tr.* avituallar. *2 intr.* avitua-
llarse. ¶ Pret. y p. p.: *victual(l)ed;* ger.: *-l(l)ing.*
**victual(l)er** (-ø$^r$) *s.* abastecedor. *2* tabernero.
**victuals** (-s) *s. pl.* vitualla, víveres.
**vicugna, vicuña** (viku·ña) *s.* ZOOL. vicuña.
**vide** (vai·di) *voz lat.* vide, véase.
**videlicet** (vide·liset) *adv.* a saber.
**video** (vi·diou) *s.* televisión (aparato); video. *2 adj.*
de televisión.
**vie (to)** (vai) *tr.* emular, competir, rivalizar. ¶ Pret.
y p. p.: *vied;* ger.: *vying.*
**Vienna** (vie·na) *n. pr.* GEOGR. Viena [de Austria].
**Viennese** (vieni·s̆) *adj.-s.* vienés.
**view** (viu) *s.* vista, visión, contemplación, inspección, consideración; mirada: *to take a ~ of,* ver,
examinar; *in ~ of,* en vista de; *on ~,* a la vista.
*2* vista, panorama, escena, perspectiva: *~
finder,* FOT. visor. *3* modo de ver, opinión, punto
de vista, aspecto. *4* mira, propósito: *with a ~ to,*
con el propósito de. *5* DIB. proyección.
**view (to)** *tr.* ver, mirar. *2* examinar, inspeccionar.
*3* considerar.
**viewer** (-ø$^r$) *s.* espectador. *2* inspector. *3* TELEV. telespectador.
**viewpoint** (-point) *s.* punto de vista.
**vigesimal** (vaidy̆e·simal) *adj.* vigésimo. *2* vigesimal.
**vigil** (vi·dy̆il) *s.* vigilia, desvelo, vela, velación. *2*
vigilancia. *3* ECLES. vigilia.
**vigilance, vigilancy** (-ans, -si) *s.* vigilancia.
**vigilant** (-ant) *adj.* vigilante, atento.
**vignette** (viñe·t) *s.* IMPR., FOT., GRAB. viñeta. *2* bosquejo literario.
**vigor** (vi·gø$^r$) *s.* VIGOUR.
**vigorous** (vi·gørøs) *adj.* vigoroso. *2* fuerte, enérgico.
**vigour** (vi·gø$^r$) *s.* vigor, fuerza, energía.
**viking** (vai·king) *s.* vikingo.
**vile** (vail) *adj.* vil, ruin. *2* malo, pésimo.
**vilification** (vilifikei·shøn) *s.* vilipendio, denigración.
**vilify (to)** (vi·lifai) *tr.* vilipendiar, denigrar.
**village** (vi·lidy̆) *s.* lugar, aldea, pueblo.
**villager** (-ø$^r$) *s.* lugareño, aldeano.
**villa** (vi·la) *s.* villa, quinta, hotel.
**villain** (vi·løn) *s.* bribón, canalla. *2* VILLEIN. *3* malo,
traidor [de un drama o novela].
**villainous** (-nøs) *adj.* villano, ruin, vil. *2* malo, detestable.
**villainy** (vi·løni) *s.* villanía, maldad, infamia.
**villein** (vi·lin) *s.* villano, pechero.
**villei(i)nage** (-idy̆) *s.* villanaje [condición].
**villosity** (vila·siti) *s.* vellosidad.
**villous** (vi·løs) *adj.* velloso. *2* BOT. pubescente.
**vim** (vim) *s. fam.* fuerza, vigor, energía.
**vinaceous** (vainei·shøs) *adj.* vinoso. *2* vinario.
**Vincent** (vi·nsønt) *n. pr.* Vicente.
**vincible** (vi·nsibøl) *adj.* vencible.
**vinculum** (vi·nkiuløm) *s.* vínculo.
**vindicate (to)** (vi·ndikeit) *tr.* vindicar, justificar. *2*
mantener, defender. *3* reivindicar.
**vindication** (-ei·shøn) *s.* vindicación, defensa.
**vindicative** (vindi·kativ) *adj.* vindicativo, justificativo.
**vindicatory** (-tori) *adj.* vindicatorio.
**vindictive** (vindi·ktiv) *adj.* vindicativo, vengativo.

**vine** (vain) *s.* BOT. planta rastrera o enredadera. *2*
vid, parra: *~ pest,* filoxera.
**vinedresser** (vai·ndresø$^r$) *s.* viñador.
**vinegar** (vi·niga$^r$) *s.* vinagre.
**vinegarish, vinegary** (vi·nigarish, -ri) *adj.* vinagroso. *2* avinagrado, agrio.
**vineyard** (vi·nya$^r$d) *s.* viña, viñedo.
**vinic** (vai·nik o vi·nik) *adj.* vínico.
**vinification** (vinifikei·shøn) *s.* vinificación.
**vinous** (vai·nøs) *adj.* vinoso. *2* vínico. *3* de color de
vino. *4* borracho.
**vintage** (vi·ntidy̆) *s.* vendimia. *2* cosecha [de vino].
*3* vino [esp. de calidad].
**vintager** (-ø$^r$) *s.* vendimiador, cosechero.
**vintner** (vi·ntnø$^r$) *s.* vinatero, tratante en vinos.
**viny** (vai·ni) *adj.* de vides o enredaderas. *2* sarmentoso.
**vinyl** (vi·nil) *s.* QUÍM. vinilo.
**viol** (vai·øl) *s.* MÚS. viola. *2* MAR. virador.
**viola** (viou·la) *s.* MÚS. viola, alto.
**violaceous** (vaiølei·shøs) *adj.* violáceo, violado.
**violate (to)** (vai·øleit) *tr.* violar.
**violation** (vaiølei·shøn) *s.* violación.
**violence** (vai·øløns) *s.* violencia. *2* ímpetu, ardor,
vehemencia.
**violent** (-lønt) *adj.* violento. *2* impetuoso, furioso.
*3* grande, extremo, intenso.
**violet** (vai·ølit) *s.* BOT. violeta. *2* color de violeta. *3*
*adj.* violado, de color de violeta.
**violin** (vaiøli·n) *s̆.* MÚS. violín.
**violinist** (-ist) *s.* violinista.
**violoncellist** (vaiølønche·list) *s.* violoncelista.
**violoncello** (-che·lou) MÚS. violoncelo.
**viper** (vai·pø$^r$) *s.* ZOOL. víbora. *2* persona mala o
traidora. *3* BOT. *~ grass,* escorzonera.
**viperine, viperish, viperous** (vai·pørin, -ish, -øs)
*adj.* viperino.
**virago** (virei·gou) *s.* virago. *2* arpía, mujer regañona.
**vire** (vī$^r$) *s.* vira [saeta].
**vireo** (vi·riou) *s.* ORN. víreo.
**virescent** (vaire·sønt) *adj.* verdoso.
**Virgil** (vø$^r$dy̆il) *n. pr.* Virgilio.
**virgin** (vø$^r$dy̆in) *s.* virgen, doncella: *the Virgin,* la
Santa Virgen. *2* ASTR. Virgo. *3 adj.* virgen. *4* virginal. *5* primero, inicial.
**virginal** (-al) *adj.* virgen, intacto. *2* virginal. *3* MÚS.
virginal.
**Virginia** (vø$^r$y̆i·nia) *n. pr.* Virginia.
**virginity** (-niti) *s.* virginidad.
**virgin's-bower** *s.* BOT. clemátide.
**Virgo** (vø$^r$gou) *s.* ASTR. Virgo.
**viridescent** (viride·sønt) *adj.* verdoso.
**virile** (vi·ril) *adj.* viril, masculino, varonil.
**virility** (viri·liti) *s.* virilidad.
**virose** (vai·rous) *adj.* ponzoñoso. *2* fétido.
**virtu** (vø$^r$tu·) *s.* afición a las curiosidades y objetos
de arte. *2* curiosidades, objetos de arte.
**virtual** (vø$^r$chual) *adj.* virtual.
**virtue** (vø$^r$chu) *s.* virtud: *by,* o *in, ~ of,* en virtud
de. *2 pl.* virtudes [espíritus angélicos].
**virtuosity** (vø$^r$chua·siti) *s.* virtuosismo, maestría.
**virtuoso** (vø$^r$chuou·sou) *s.* B. ART. virtuoso. *2* entendido en curiosidades u objetos de arte.
**virtuous** (vø$^r$chuøs) *adj.* virtuoso [que practica la
virtud o inspirado por ella]. *2* poderoso, eficaz.
**virulence** (vi·riuløns) *s.* virulencia.
**virulent** (-lønt) *adj.* virulento.
**virus** (vai·røs) *s.* virus.
**visa** (vi·s̆a) *s.* visado, visto bueno.

**visa (to)** *tr.* visar, refrendar. ¶ Pret. y p. p.: *visaed;* ger.: *visaing.*
**visage** (vi·sidȳ) *s.* rostro, semblante. *2* aspecto.
**viscacha** (viska·cha) *s.* VIZCACHA.
**viscera** (vi·søra) *s. pl.* vísceras.
**viscid** (vi·sid) *adj.* viscoso, pegajoso, glutinoso.
**viscose** (vi·skous) *s.* viscosa.
**viscosity** (viska·siti) *s.* viscosidad.
**viscount** (vai·kaunt) *s.* vizconde.
**viscountess** (-is) *s.* vizcondesa.
**viscous** (vi·skøs) *adj.* viscoso.
**vise** (vais) *s.* MEC. tornillo de banco.
**visé** (visei·) *s.* VISA.
**visibility** (višibi·liti) *s.* visibilidad.
**visible** (vi·šibøl) *adj.* visible.
**Visigoth** (vi·šigaz) *s.* visigodo.
**vision** (vi·ȳøn) *s.* vista [sentido]. *2* visión [acción o facultad de ver; cosa vista; aparición].
**visionary** (-eri) *adj.-s.* visionario. *2 adj.* imaginario, quimérico.
**visit** (vi·šit) *s.* visita [que se hace; registro, reconocimiento].
**visit (to)** *tr.* visitar. *2* afligir, castigar [con una desgracia, calamidad, etc.]. *2 intr.* hacer visitas. *3* visitarse.
**visitant** (-ant) *s.* visitante.
**visitation** (višitei·shøn) *s.* visita, visitación. *2* inspección. *3* TEOL. consuelo o trabajo que Dios envía. *4* aflicción, calamidad, castigo.
**visiting card** (vi·šiting) *s.* tarjeta de visita.
**visitor** (-ø^r) *s.* visita, visitante. *2* visitador.
**visor** (vai·šø^r) *s.* visera. *2* fig. máscara, disfraz.
**visor (to)** *tr.* cubrir con visera. *2* fig. cubrir, disimular.
**vista** (vi·sta) *s.* vista, panorama, perspectiva.
**visual** (vi·ȳual) *adj.* visual. *2* visible. *3 s.* visual.
**visuality** (viȳuæ·liti) *s.* visibilidad. *2* imagen, vislumbre.
**visualize (to)** (vi·ȳuælaiš) *tr.* hacer visible. *2* representarse en la mente.
**vital** (vai·tal) *adj.* vital. *2* fatal, mortal. *2* demográfico.
**vitalism** (-lišm) *s.* vitalismo.
**vitality** (vaitæ·liti) *s.* vitalidad. *2* animación, vigor.
**vitalize (to)** (vai·talaiš) *tr.* vivificar.
**vitals** (vai·tals) *s. pl.* órganos vitales, entrañas.
**vitamin(e** (vai·tamin) *s.* QUÍM. vitamina.
**vitaminize (to)** (-aiš) *tr.* vitaminar.
**vitelline** (vite·lin) *adj.* vitelino.
**vitellus** (-løs) *s.* BIOL. vitelo.
**vitiate (to)** (vi·shieit) *tr.* viciar [dañar, corromper; invalidar].
**vitiation** (-ei·shøn) *s.* corrupción. *2* invalidación.
**viticulture** (vitikø·lchø^r) *s.* viticultura.
**viticulturist** (-chørist) *s.* viticultor.
**vitreous** (vi·triøs) *adj.* vítreo, vidrioso.
**vitrification** (vitrifikei·shøn) *s.* vitrificación.
**vitrify (to)** (vi·trifai) *tr.* vitrificar. ¶ Pret. y p. p.: *vitrified.*
**vitriol** (vi·triøl) *s.* vitriolo. *2* virulencia, causticidad.
**vitriolic** (vitria·lik) *adj.* vitriólico. *2* fig. ferozmente cáustico o mordaz.
**vituperate (to)** (vaitiu·pøreit) *tr.* vituperar. *2* denostar.
**vituperation** (-ei·shøn) *s.* vituperación, vituperio.
**vivacious** (vaivei·shøs) *adj.* vivaz, vivaracho, vivo, alegre, animado. *2* vivaz [que vive mucho].
**vivacity** (vaivæ·siti) *s.* vivacidad. viveza, animación.

**vivandiere** (vivandie·^r) *s.* cantinera, vivandera.
**vivarium** (vaive·riøm) *s.* vivario.
**viva voce** (vai·va vou·si) *adj.* de viva voz.
**vivid** (vi·vid) *adj.* vívido. *2* vivo, intenso. *3* gráfico [que expresa vivamente].
**vividness** (-nis) *s.* viveza, intensidad.
**vivify (to)** (vi·vifai) *tr.* vivificar. *2* avivar, animar. ¶ Pret. y p. p.: *vivified.*
**viviparous** (vaivi·parøs) *adj.* vivíparo.
**vivisect (to)** (vi·visekt) *tr.* hacer la vivisección de.
**vivisection** (vivise·kshøn) *s.* vivisección.
**vixen** (vi·ksøn) *s.* ZOOL. zorra, raposa. *2* arpía, mujer colérica.
**viz** (viš) *abrev.* de VIDELICET, a saber. | Gralte. se lee *namely* o *to wit.*
**vizcacha** (viska·cha) *s.* ZOOL. viscacha, vizcacha.
**vizler, vizir** (višr·^r) *s.* visir, gran visir.
**vizor** (vi·šø^r) *s.* VISOR.
**vizor (to)** *tr.* TO VISOR.
**vocable** (vou·kabøl) *adj.* vocablo, voz, término.
**vocabulary** (vokæ·biuleri) *s.* vocabulario. *2* léxico.
**vocal** (vou·kal) *adj.* vocal: ~ *cords,* cuerdas vocales. *2* oral. *3* vocálico. *4* fig. hablador, elocuente. *5 s.* FONÉT. vocal.
**vocalic** (vokæ·lik) *adj.* vocálico.
**vocalist** (-ist) *s.* vocalista.
**vocalization** (voukališei·shøn) *s.* vocalización.
**vocalize (to)** (vou·kalais) *tr.* articular; cantar. *2* FONÉT. convertir en vocal. *3 intr.* MÚS. vocalizar.
**vocally** (-kali) *adv.* vocalmente. *2* oralmente.
**vocation** (vokei·shøn) *s.* vocación. *2* oficio, profesión.
**vocational** (-al) *adj.* de la vocación. *2* profesional. *3* de artes y oficios.
**vocative** (va·kativ) *s.* vocativo.
**vociferate (to)** (vosi·føreit) *intr.* vociferar.
**vociferation** (-ei·shøn) *s.* vociferación, griterío.
**vociferous** (vosi·førøs) *adj.* vociferante, vocinglero.
**vogue** (voug) *s.* boga, moda.
**voice** (vois) *s.* voz [del hombre, de los animales, etc.]. *2* habla, palabra. *3* voz, opinión, voto: *with one ~,* unánimemente. *4* GRAM. voz [del verbo].
**voice (to)** *tr.* expresar, decir, anunciar, rumorear; interpretar. *2* MÚS. regular el tono de. *3* FONÉT. hacer sonoro.
**voiceless** (-lis) *adj.* sin voz. *2* sin voto. *3* mudo, silencioso. *4* FONÉT. sordo.
**void** (voi·d) *adj.* vacío; desocupado, vacante. *2* desprovisto, falto [de]. *3* vano, inútil. *4* DER. nulo, inválido. *5 s.* vacío, hueco, claro. *6 the ~,* el vacío.
**void (to)** *tr.* vaciar, desocupar. *2* expeler, evacuar. *3* DER. anular.
**voidance** (-ans) *s.* vaciamiento, evacuación. *2* DER. anulación.
**volant** (vo·lant) *adj.* volador. *2* ágil, ligero.
**volatile** (va·latil) *adj.* volátil. *2* ágil, ligero, fugaz.
**volatility** (valati·liti) *s.* volatilidad. *2* fugacidad.
**volatilize (to)** (va·latilaiš) *tr.* volatilizar. *2 intr.* volatilizarse.
**volcanic** (valkæ·nik) *adj.* volcánico.
**volcano** (valkei·nou) *s.* volcán.
**vole** (voul) *s.* ZOOL. rata de agua; campañol. *2* bola [en el juego de naipes].
**volition** (voli·shøn) *s.* volición; voluntad.
**volitive** (va·litiv) *adj.* volitivo.
**volley** (va·li) *s.* descarga, andanada. *2* lluvia [de flechas, balas, etc.]. *3* DEP. voleo [de la pelota].
**volley (to)** *tr.* lanzar una descarga, una lluvia de. *2*

DEP. volear [la pelota]. *3 intr.* ser lanzado **en** descarga, volear.
**volplane** (va·lplein) *s.* vuelo planeado.
**volplane (to)** *intr.* planear, volar planeando.
**volt** (voult) *s.* ELECT. volt, voltio.
**voltage** (vou·ltidў) *s.* ELECT. voltaje, tensión.
**voltaic** (valtei·ik) *adj.* voltaico.
**Voltairian** (valte·rian) *adj.-s.* volteriano.
**voltameter** (valtæ·mitøʳ) ELECT. voltámetro.
**voltmeter** (vou·ltmitøʳ) *s.* ELECT. voltímetro.
**volubility** (valiubi·liti) *s.* ZOOL., BOT. volubilidad. *2* verbosidad, afluencia, facundia.
**voluble** (va·tiubøl) *2* verboso, afluente, fecundo.
**volume** (va·lium) *s.* volumen, tomo, libro. *2* GEOM., MÚS. volumen. *3* volumen, bulto, masa.
**volumetry** (voliu·metri) *s.* volumetría.
**voluminous** (voliu·minøs) *adj.* voluminoso. *2* copioso, prolijo.
**voluntary** (va·lønteri) *adj.* voluntario. *2* espontáneo, libre. *3 s.* ECLES. sólo de órgano.
**volunteer** (valønti·ʳ) *adj.* voluntario, espontáneo. *2* de voluntarios. *3 s.* voluntario.
**volunteer (to)** *tr.* ofrecer, dar voluntariamente. *2 intr.* ofrecerse o contribuir voluntariamente. *3* servir como voluntario.
**voluptuary** (volø·pchueri) *s.* voluptuoso, sibarita.
**voluptuous** (volø·pchuøs) *adj.* voluptuoso, sensual.
**volute** (voliu·t) *adj.* enroscado, en espiral. *2 s.* voluta, espiral. *3* ZOOL. espira.
**vomer** (vou·møʳ) *s.* ANAT. vómer.
**vomit** (va·mit) *s.* vómito. *2* vomitivo, emético.
**vomit (to)** *tr.-intr.* vomitar.
**vomitive** (va·mitiv) *adj.* vomitivo, emético.
**vomitory** (va·mitori) *adj.-s.* vomitorio, vomitivo. *2 s.* ARQ. vomitorio.
**voodoo** (vu·du) *s.* brujería, magia [esp. la de los negros de los E.U. y de las Antillas].
**voracious** (vorei·shøs) *adj.* voraz. *2* insaciable, ávido.
**voracity** (voræ·siti) *s.* voracidad.
**vortex** (vo·ʳteks), *pl.* **-texes** o **-tices** (-tisiš) *s.* vórtice. *2* vorágine, torbellino.
**vortical** (vo·ʳtikal) *adj.* vortiginoso.
**vorticella** (voʳtise·la) *s.* ZOOL. vorticela.
**votaress** (vou·taris) *s.* mujer dedicada o consagrada a; adepta, partidaria.
**votary** (-ari) *s.* persona dedicada o consagrada **a**

[Dios, etc.]. *2* adepto, devoto, partidario.
**vote** (vout) *s.* voto, votación, sufragio. *2* voto [derecho de votar].
**vote (to)** *tr.-intr.* votar [dar su voto]: *to ~ down*, rechazar por votación; *to ~ in*, elegir por votación.
**voter** (vou·tøʳ) *s.* votante. *2* elector.
**voting** (-ing) *s.* votación, acción de votar.
**votive** (-iv) *adj.* votivo.
**vouch (to)** (vauch) *tr.* testificar, certificar, dar fe de. *2* garantizar, responder de. *3 intr. to ~ for*, responder de o por.
**voucher** (-øʳ) *s.* garante, fiador. *2* documento justificativo, comprobante, resguardo, recibo.
**vouchsafe (to)** (vauchsei·f) *tr.* conceder, permitir, dignarse dar o hacer. *2* dignarse.
**voussoir** (vusua·ʳ) *s.* ARQ. dovela.
**vow** (vau) *s.* voto, promesa solemne. *2* voto, deseo; súplica.
**vow (to)** *tr.* hacer voto de; prometer solemnemente; consagrar.
**vowel** (va·uøl) *adj.-s.* GRAM. vocal.
**voyage** (voi·idў) *s.* viaje por mar, o por el aire, travesía.
**voyage (to)** *intr.* viajar, navegar. *2 tr.* recorrer o cruzar [un mar] viajando.
**voyager** (-øʳ) *s.* viajero, pasajero.
**Vulcan** (vø·lkan) *n. pr.* MIT. Vulcano.
**Vulcanism** (vø·lkanišm) *s.* vulcanismo.
**vulcanite** (-nait) *s.* vulcanita, ebonita.
**vulcanization** (vølkanišei·shøn) *s.* vulcanización.
**vulcanize (to)** (vø·lkanaiš) *tr.* vulcanizar.
**vulgar** (vø·lgaʳ) *adj.* vulgar. *2* común, ordinario, plebeyo, de mal gusto. *4 s. the ~*, el vulgo.
**vulgarism** (-išm) *s.* vulgarismo. *2* ordinariez.
**vulgarity** (vølgæ·riti) *s.* vulgaridad. *2* ordinariez.
**vulgarization** (vølgarišei·shøn) *s.* vulgarización.
**vulgarize (to)** (vø·lgaraiš) *tr.* vulgarizar. *2* adocenar.
**vulnerable** (vø·lnørabøl) *adj.* vulnerable.
**vulnerary** (vø·lnøræri) *adj.-s.* vulnerario.
**vulpine** (vø·lpain o -pin) *adj.* vulpino, zorruno. *2* astuto, taimado.
**vulture** (vø·lchuʳ) *s.* ORN. buitre, cóndor.
**Vulturidæ** (vølchu·ridi) *s. pl.* ORN. vultúridos.
**vulva** (vø·lva) *s.* ANAT. vulva.
**vying** (vai·ing) *ger.* DE TO VIE.

# W

**W, w** (dø·bøliu) *s.* W, w, vigésima tercera letra del alfabeto inglés.
**wabble** (ua·bøl) *s.* WOBBLE.
**wabble (to)** *intr.* TO WOBBLE.
**wabbly** (ua·bli) *adj.* WOBBLY.
**wad** (uad) *s.* porción de borra, algodón, etc., para rellenar, acolchar, etc. *2* guata. *3* ARTILL. taco. *4* fam. (E.U.) fajo [de billetes].
**wad (to)** *tr.* rellenar, acolchar, tapar, destruir. *2* atacar [un arma de fuego]. ¶ Pret. y p. p.: *wadded;* ger.: *wadding.*
**wadding** (-ing) *s.* relleno, borra, guata.
**waddle** (ua·døl) *s.* anadeo. *2* marcha torpe o vacilante.
**waddle (to)** *intr.* anadear, nanear. *2* andar o moverse con marcha torpe o vacilante.
**wade (to)** (ueid) *intr.* andar sobre terreno cubierto de agua, sobre lodo, nieve, arena, etc.; avanzar con dificultad. *2 to ~ in* o *into,* atacar, emprender resueltamente. *3 tr.* vadear.
**wadeable** (-abøl) *adj.* vadeable.
**wading bird** (ing) *s.* ORN. ave zancuda.
**wafer** (uei·føʳ) *s.* hostia, oblea. *2* barquillo.
**wafer (to)** *tr.* pegar o cerrar con oblea.
**wafery** (-i) *adj.* delgado y ligero.
**waffle** (ua·føl) *s.* COC. barquillo plano.
**waft** (uaft) *s.* mecedura, fluctuación, ondeo. *2* soplo, ráfaga [de aire o de olor].
**waft (to)** *tr.* mecer, hacer flotar, ondear. *2* llevar o enviar por el agua o el aire. *3 intr.* mecerse, flotar, ir flotando.
**wag** (uæg) *s.* meneo. *2* movimiento de cabeza. *3* bromista, guasón.
**wag (to)** *tr.* mover, menear [la cabeza, la cola, etc.]. *2 intr.* moverse, menearse; oscilar. *3* fam. irse. ¶ Pret. y p. p.: *wagged;* ger.: *gging.*
**wage** (ueidŷ) *s.* paga, jornal, sueldo, salario. | Ús. gralte. en plural.
**wage (to)** *tr.* emprender, sostener, empeñar, hacer: *to ~ war,* hacer guerra.
**wager** (uei·dŷøʳ) *s.* apuesta: *to lay a ~,* hacer una apuesta, apostar.
**wager (to)** *tr.-intr.* apostar [hacer una apuesta].
**waggery** (uæ·gøri) *s.* jocosidad, travesura. *2* broma, guasa, bufonada.
**waggish** (-gish) *adj.* juguetón.
**waggle** (-gøl) *s.* meneo, oscilación, balanceo.

**waggle (to)** *tr.* menear, mover de un lado a otro. *2* menearse, moverse de un lado a otro.
**Wagnerian** (vagni·rian) *adj.-s.* vagneriano.
**wag (g) on** (-gøn) *s.* carromato, furgón, camión. *2* FERROC. vagón de mercancías.
**wag (g) oner** (-øʳ) *s.* carretero, carromatero.
**wag (g) onette** (uægøne·t) *s.* carricoche.
**wagtail** (uæ·gteil) *s.* ORN. aguzanieves, motacilla, nevatilla, pizpita.
**waif** (ueif) *s.* cosa o animal sin dueño. *2* cosa o fragmento encontrado. *3* niño abandonado, golfillo, granuja.
**wail** (ueil) *s.* lamento, gemido, lloro.
**wail (to)** *tr.* lamentar, deplorar, llorar. *2 intr.* lamentarse, gemir, llorar.
**wailing** (-ing) *s.* WAIL.
**wainscot** (uei·nskat) *s.* revestimiento interior de una pared; zócalo, friso, arrimadillo.
**wainscot (to)** *tr.* enmaderar; poner friso o arrimadillo a.
**waist** (ueist) *s.* cintura, talle. *2* cinto, cinturón. *3* corpiño, jubón. *4* MAR. combés.
**waistband** (-bænd) *s.* pretina, cintura.
**waistcoat** (-kout o køt) *s.* chaleco. *2* justillo.
**wait** (ueit) *s.* espera, plantón. *2* pausa, detención, demora. *3 to lie in ~,* estar al acecho, en emboscada. *4 pl.* cantores de Nochebuena.
**wait (to)** *intr.-tr.* esperar, aguardar. | a veces con *for. 2 intr.* estar esperando órdenes, servir; ser mozo o camarero [de restaurante, etc.]: *to ~ at table,* servir a la mesa. *3 to ~ on* o *upon,* servir, atender, despachar; estar de servicio cerca de [alguien]; visitar; presentar sus respetos a; escoltar, acompañar.
**waiter** (-tøʳ) *s.* mozo, camarero [de café, restaurante, etc.]. *2* bandeja.
**waiting** (-ting) *s.* espera. *2* servicio. *3 adj.* de espera; de servicio: *~ room,* sala de espera; *~ maid* o *woman,* doncella [de una señora].
**waitress** (-tris) *s.* camarera [de restaurante, etcétera].
**waive (to)** (ueiv) *tr.* renunciar, abandonar; desechar. *2* desaprovechar. *3* abstenerse de. *4* diferir, aplazar.
**waiver** (-øʳ) *s.* DER. renuncia, abandono.
**wake** (ueik) *s.* MAR. estela, aguaje: *in the ~ of,* fig. detrás de. *2* vela, velatorio.
**wake (to)** [a veces con *up*] *intr.* despertar, desper-

tarse, despabilarse. *2* resucitar. *3* velar [no dormir]. *4 tr.* despertar. *5* excitar. *6* resucitar. *7* velar [un muerto]. ¶ Pret.: *waked* o *woke;* p. p.: *waked* o *woken.*

**wakeful** (-ful) *adj.* desvelado, insomne. *2* vigilante, alerta.

**waken (to)** (-øn) *tr.-intr.* despertar.

**wake-robin** *s.* BOT. aro, alcatraz.

**wale** (ueil) *s.* roncha, verdugo. *2* MAR. cinta. *3* TEJ. cordoncillo.

**wale (to)** *tr.* levantar roncha en; azotar.

**Wales** (ueilš) *n. pr.* GEOGR. Gales.

**walk** (uok) *s.* paso, andar [del que camina o pasea]. *2* paso [de un cuadrúpedo]. *3* paseo, caminata. *4* sitio para andar; paseo, alameda, acera, terraza, etc. *5* campo, esfera. *6* vida, conducta. *7* ~ *of life,* condición social; profesión, ocupación.

**walk (to)** *intr.* andar, caminar, marchar, ir a pie: *to* ~ *away,* irse, marcharse; *to* ~ *in,* entrar, pasar adelante; *to* ~ *on air,* fig. estar muy contento o ufano; *to* ~ *up to,* acercarse a. *2* pasear, pasearse: *to* ~ *with,* o *out with,* salir con, ser novio de. *3* ir al paso [la caballería]. *4* aparecer [fantasmas, espectros]. *5* obrar, conducirse.

*6 tr.* andar, pasear por, recorrer; hacer [un recorrido]: *to* ~ *the boards,* TEAT. pisar las tablas, ser actor; *to* ~ *the hospitals,* estudiar medicina. *7* hacer andar o pasear; sacar a paseo. *8* llevar [una caballería] al paso. *9* medir a pasos. *10 to* ~ *off a headache,* quitarse una jaqueca andando. *11 to* ~ *one off his legs,* rendir de fatiga a uno haciéndole andar.

**walkie-talkie** (uo·ki-to·ki) transmisor-receptor portátil.

**walking** (uo·king) *s.* marcha, paseo. *2* piso [de un camino, etc.]. *3 adj.* de paseo; para andar, que anda, ambulante: ~ *cane,* ~ *stick,* bastón; ~ *papers,* fam. despido [de un empleo].

**walkout** (-aut) *s.* fam. (E.U.) huelga [de obreros].

**walkover** (-ouvøʳ) *s.* fam. pan comido, victoria fácil.

**wall** (uol) *s.* pared, muro, tapia, seto: ~ *clock,* reloj de pared; ~ *fruit,* fruta de espaldera; ~ *louse,* ENT. chinche; ~ *paper,* papel pintado [de empapelar]; *to drive,* o *push, to the* ~, poner en un aprieto, poner entre la espada y la pared; *to take the* ~, tomarse la acera; *with one's back to the* ~, acorralado. *2* muralla. *3* pared [de un tubo, vasija o cavidad].

**wall (to)** *tr.* emparedar, tapiar. *2* cercar, murar. *3* amurallar. *4* separar con pared.

**wallaby** (ua·labi) *s.* ZOOL. especie de canguro.

**wallet** (ua·lit) *s.* zurrón, bolsa de cuero. *3* cartera [de bolsillo].

**wallflower** (uo·lflauøʳ) *s.* BOT. alhelí.

**Walloon** (ualu·n) *adj.-s.* valón.

**wallop** (ua·løp) *s.* golpe o puñada fuerte.

**wallop (to)** *tr.* pegar, zurrar. *2* dar un golpe fuerte.

**walloping** (-ing) *s.* zurra, tunda. *2 adj.* fam. grande, tremendo.

**wallow** (ua·lou) *s.* revuelco, revolcadero.

**wallow (to)** *intr.* revolcarse [en el agua, en el fango, etc.]. *2* nadar [en la abundancia]. *3* estar encenagado [en un vicio].

**wallwort** (uo·lwøʳt) *s.* BOT. parietaria, cañarroya.

**walnut** (uo·lnøt) *s.* BOT. nuez [del nogal]; nogal: ~ *tree,* nogal [árbol]; ~ *wood,* nogal [madera].

**walrus** (uo·lrøs) *s.* ZOOL. morsa.

**Walter** (uo·ltøʳ) *n. pr.* Gualterio.

**waltz** (uolts) *s.* vals.

**waltz (to)** *intr.* valsar. *2* dar vueltas rápidas. *3 tr.* hacer valsar.

**wan** (uan) *adj.* pálido, descolorido. *2* lánguido, triste, enfermizo.

**wand** (uand) *s.* vara, vergueta. *2* varita de virtudes. *3* vara [insignia]. *4* batuta.

**wander** (ua·ndøʳ) *s.* paseo, correría.

**wander (to)** *intr.* errar, vagar, rodar, corretear: *to* ~ *away,* extraviarse, perderse. *2* desviarse, apartarse. *3* delirar, divagar. *4 tr.* errar o vagar por.

**wanderer** (-øʳ) *s.* paseante, vagabundo, viajero.

**wandering** (-ing) *s.* correteo, viaje. *2* extravío, aberración. *3* delirio; divagación. *4 adj.* errante, errabundo: ~ *Jew,* judío errante. *5* extraviado, descaminado. *6* delirante; que divaga.

**wane** (uein) *s.* mengua, disminución. *2* declinación, decadencia. *3* marchitamiento. *4* menguante [de la luna]. *5 on the* ~, acabándose, declinando, en decadencia.

**wane (to)** *intr.* menguar, disminuir, decrecer. *2* declinar, decaer. *3* marchitarse.

**wangle (to)** (uæ·ngøl) *tr.* fam. sacar u obtener con maña, astucia o superchería. *2* fam. arreglar, amañar, falsear.

**wannish** (ua·nish) *adj.* algo pálido o macilento.

**want** (uant o uont) *s.* falta, necesidad, carencia, escasez: *for* ~ *of,* por falta de. *2* necesidad, indigencia, miseria.

**want (to)** *tr.* necesitar, tener falta o necesidad de. *2* carecer de. *3* querer, desear, anhelar. *4* buscar, reclamar [a uno]. *5* faltar [minutos, etc., para]. *6 intr.* pasar necesidad. *7 to* ~ *for,* necesitar.

**want ad** *s.* fam. anuncio clasificado.

**wantage** (-idỹ) *s.* falta, déficit, merma.

**wanting** (-ing) *adj.* falto, defectuoso, deficiente, escaso. *2* necesitado. *3* que falta: *to be* ~, faltar.

**wanton** (ua·ntøn) *adj.* alegre, juguetón, travieso. *2* irreflexivo, caprichoso. *3* lascivo. *4* licencioso, disoluto. *5* brutal, desconsiderado, injustificado, arbitrario. *6* pródigo, exuberante, lujuriante. *7 s.* mujer disoluta. *8* niño travieso.

**wanton (to)** *intr.* juguetear, jugar, retozar.

**wantonness** (-nis) *s.* retozo, picardía. *2* libertinaje. *3* brutalidad. *4* exuberancia.

**wapiti** (ua·piti) *s.* ZOOL. uapití.

**war** (uoʳ) *s.* guerra: ~ *dance,* danza guerrera; *War Department* (E.U.), *War Office* (Ingl.), Ministerio de la Guerra; ~ *horse,* corcel de batalla; fig. veterano; ~ *memorial,* monumento a los caídos. *2* arte de la guerra. *3* milicia, armas [profesión militar].

**war (to)** *intr.* guerrear, estar en guerra. ¶ Pret. y p. p.: *warred;* ger.: *warring.*

**warble** (uo·ʳbøl) *s.* trino, gorjeo, quiebro.

**warble (to)** *tr.-intr.* cantar con trinos y gorjeos; trinar, gorjear. *2* murmurar [un arroyo].

**warbler** (uo·ʳbløʳ) *s.* gorjeador. *2* pájaro cantor.

**ward** (uoʳd) *s.* guarda, custodia. *2* tutela. *3* pupilo, persona bajo tutela. *4* barrio, distrito [de una población]. *5* sala, cuadra [de hospital]. *6* ala, sección [de una cárcel]. *7* guarda [de llave o cerradura].

**ward (to)** *tr.* guardar, proteger. *2 to* ~ *off,* resguardarse de, parar, evitar, desviar.

**warden** (-øn) *s.* vigilante, guardián. *2* gobernador, jefe, director, alcaide. *3* fabriquero [de una parroquia].

**warder** (-øʳ) *s.* guarda, centinela. *2* carcelero.

**wardmaid** (-meid) *s.* camarera de hospital.

**wardrobe** (-roub) s. armario, guardarropa, ropero. 2 TEAT. guardarropía. 3 vestuario, ropa.

**wardroom** (-rum) s. MAR. cámara de oficiales [en un buque de guerra].

**wardship** (-ship) s. DER. tutela; pupilaje.

**ware** (ue·æ<sup>r</sup>) s. sing. o pl. géneros, artículos, mercancías; vajilla, cacharrería.

**warehouse** (ue·<sup>r</sup>jaus) s. almacén, depósito. 2 guardamuebles.

**warfare** (uo·<sup>r</sup>feø<sup>r</sup>) s. guerra, lucha. 2 arte militar.

**warfare (to)** intr. guerrear, combatir.

**warily** (ue·rili) adv. cautamente.

**wariness** (ue·rinis) s. cautela, precaución, prudencia.

**warlike** (uo·<sup>r</sup>laik) adj. bélico, belicoso, marcial.

**warm** (uo<sup>r</sup>m) adj. caliente, cálido, caluroso: I am ~, tengo calor; it is ~, hace calor; se está caliente. 2 de abrigo. 3 acalorado. 4 caluroso, ferviente, afectuoso, cordial. 5 ardiente, vivo, celoso, fogoso, apasionado, violento. 6 cómodo, confortable. 7 duro, difícil. 8 reciente, fresco. 9 PINT. cálido [color].

**warm (to)** tr. calentar. 2 caldear. 3 abrigar. 4 animar, enardecer, acalorar. 5 to ~ over, o up, recalentar [la comida]; AUTO. calentar [el motor]. 6 intr. calentarse. 7 animarse, acalorarse. 8 to ~ up, irse calentando, animando, etc. 9 to ~ to, to ~ up to, cobrar afecto a; sentir compasión de.

**warm-blooded** adj. ardiente, entusiasta. 2 ZOOL. de sangre caliente.

**warm-hearted** adj. de buen corazón, afectuoso.

**warming pad** (-ing) s. esterilla eléctrica.

**warming pan** s. calentador de cama.

**warmth** (-z) s. calor moderado. 2 calor, celo, ardor, afecto, cordialidad, entusiasmo, viveza.

**warn (to)** (uo<sup>r</sup>n) tr. avisar, advertir, prevenir. 2 amonestar, exhortar. 3 DER. desahuciar. 4 to ~ off, prohibir el paso, la entrada, etc.

**warning** (uo·<sup>r</sup>ning) s. aviso, advertencia. 2 amonestación. 3 lección, escarmiento. 4 despido [entre propietario e inquilino].

**warp** (uo<sup>r</sup>p) s. TEJ. urdimbre. 2 MAR. espía [cabo]. 3 alabeo. 4 torcimiento, deformación; prejuicio. 5 AGR. tarquín.

**warp (to)** tr. TEJ. urdir. 2 MAR. espiar. 3 alabear, abarquillar. 4 torcer, deformar, falsear, desviar. 5 AGR. entarquinar. 6 intr. alabearse, abarquillarse; torcerse, deformarse.

**warplane** (uo·<sup>r</sup>plein) s. avión militar.

**warrant** (ua·rant) s. autorización, poder. 2 orden, mandamiento, libramiento, despacho. 3 DER. orden de prisión, registro, etc. 4 justificante, comprobante. 5 COM. warrant. 6 garantía, seguridad. 7 derecho, razón, fundamento, autoridad.

**warrant (to)** tr. autorizar. 2 garantizar. 3 responder de, asegurar, certificar. 4 justificar.

**warrantee** (-i) s. persona en favor de la cual se establece una garantía.

**warranter, warrantor** (-ø<sup>r</sup>) s. garante.

**warranty** (-i) s. garantía. 2 autoridad, justificación.

**warren** (ua·røn) s. vedado. 2 conejar, vivar. 3 lugar donde habita mucha gente.

**warrior** (uo·riø<sup>r</sup>) s. guerrero, soldado.

**Warsaw** (uo·<sup>r</sup>so) n. pr. GEOGR. Varsovia.

**warship** (-ship) s. buque de guerra.

**wart** (uo<sup>r</sup>t) s. verruga, excrecencia. 2 ZOOL. ~ hog, facóquero.

**wartime** (uo·<sup>r</sup>taim) s. tiempo de guerra.

**warty** (uo·<sup>r</sup>ti) adj. verrugoso, averrugado.

**wary** (ue·ri) adj. cauto, cauteloso, prudente.

**was** (uaš o uøš) pret. de TO BE.

**wash** (uash) s. lavado, lavatorio, ablución. 2 WASHING 3. 3 lavazas; aguachirle. 4 loción. 5 chapaleo [del agua]: conmoción producida por la hélice en el agua o en el aire. 6 pincelada grande. 7 baño, capa. 8 PINT. lavado. 9 estuario; marjal. 10 aluvión.

**wash (to)** tr. lavar. 2 bañar, regar. 3 lamer [las aguas]. 4 barrer, arrastrar, llevarse [el agua]. 5 dar un baño o capa a. 6 to ~ away, off o out, quitar lavando; borrar; derrubiar; llevarse [el agua]. 7 intr. lavarse. 8 ser resistente al lavado. 9 correr, chapalear [el agua]. 10 ser arrastrado, llevado o desgastado por el agua. 11 to ~ up, lavar los platos.

**washable** (ua·shabøl) adj. lavable.

**washbasin** (-beisin) s. jofaina, palangana. 2 lavamanos.

**washboard** (-bo<sup>r</sup>d) s. tabla de lavar. 2 friso, rodapié. 3 MAR. falca.

**washbowl** (-boul) s. WASHBASIN.

**washcloth** (-kloz) s. paño [para lavarse].

**washed-out** adj. descolorido. 2 fig. extenuado.

**washed-up** adj. fam. extenuado. 2 fracasado [pers.].

**washer** (ua·shø<sup>r</sup>) s. lavador. 2 lavadora, máquina de lavar. 3 MEC. arandela.

**washerwoman** (-wumæn) s. lavandera.

**washhouse** (ua·shjaus) s. lavadero.

**washing** (ua·shing) s. acción de TO WASH. 2 MIN. lave. 3 colada, ropa lavada o para lavar. 4 adj. de lavar, que lava: ~ machine, lavadora.

**washy** (ua·shi) adj. aguado. 2 mojado. 3 flojo, débil. 4 insulso.

**wasn't** (ua·šønt) contr. de WAS NOT.

**wasp** (uasp) s. ENT. avispa: wasp's nest, avispero.

**waspish** (ua·spish) adj. de avispa. 2 irascible, gruñón.

**wast** (uast) 2.ª pers. sing. pret. de ind. de TO BE. | Ús. cuando se usa THOU.

**wastage** (ueis·tidž) s. merma, desgaste. 2 gasto inútil, desperdicio.

**waste** (ueist) adj. yermo, inculto. 2 desierto, desolado. 3 triste, sombrío. 4 devastado, arruinado. 5 inútil, desechado, sobrante, que se pierde: ~ paper, papeles rotos o usados. 6 s. extensión, inmensidad. 7 erial, desierto. 8 devastación, destrucción. 9 gasto inútil, pérdida, derroche. 10 desgaste, merma, consunción. 11 desechos, desperdicios; aguas sucias.

**waste (to)** tr. devastar, arruinar, destruir. 2 gastar, consumir, mermar, agotar. 3 debilitar, enflaquecer. 4 malgastar, desperdiciar, derrochar. 5 intr. gastarse, consumirse; debilitarse, demacrarse. | A veces con away.

**wasteful** (-ful) adj. asolador. 2 destructivo, ruinoso. 3 malgastador, pródigo, manirroto.

**waster** (-ø<sup>r</sup>) s. WASTREL 2 y 3. 2 cosa inútil, defectuosa.

**wastrel** (uei·strøl) s. desperdicio, desecho. 2 gastador, pródigo. 3 vago, golfo, perdido.

**watch** (uach) s. reloj de bolsillo: ~ strap, pulsera de reloj. 2 vela, vigilia: ~ night, noche vieja. 3 velatorio. 4 vigilancia, observación, cuidado: on the ~, alerta, sobre sí; de vigilancia. 5 centinela, vigilante; atalaya, vigía: ~ box, garita. 6 guardia [grupo que vigila o está de servicio]. 7 MAR., MIL. cuarto, guardia.

**watch (to)** intr. velar [estar despierto]. 2 velar, vigilar, estar alerta; tener cuidado: to ~ for, esperar, aguardar; *to* ~ *over,* velar por, cuidar de, vigilar, inspeccionar; *watch out!,* ¡cuidado! *3 tr.* vigilar, observar, contemplar, tener cuidado con: *to* ~ *one's step,* andarse con tiento. *4* esperar, aguardar. *5* seguir, espiar. *6* guardar, custodiar.

**watchdog** (-dog) *s.* perro guardián.

**watcher** (-ø͞ʳ) *s.* velador [que vela]. *2* observador. *3* vigilante.

**watchful** (-ful) *adj.* desvelado; en vela. *2* atento, vigilante, en guardia, cuidadoso.

**watching** (-ing) *s.* vigilia, desvelo. *2* vigilancia.

**watchmaker** (-meikø͞ʳ) *s.* relojero.

**watchman** (-mæn) *s.* vigilante, sereno, guardián.

**watchtower** (-tauø͞ʳ) *s.* atalaya, garita.

**watchword** (-wø͞ʳd) *s.* MIL. santo y seña, consigna.

**watchwork** (-wø͞ʳk) *s.* mecanismo de relojería.

**water** (uo·tø͞ʳ) *s.* agua: *to pour* o *throw cold* ~ *on,* fig. echar un jarro de agua fría; desanimar; *above* ~, a flote; *by* ~, por mar, por barco; *in deep* ~ o *waters,* en apuros; *in smooth* ~, sin dificultades. *2* marea. *3* FISIOL. linfa. *4* orina. *5* limpidez [de una piedra preciosa]; fig. calidad, clase: *of the first* ~, de lo mejor. *6* aguas, visos, reflejos. *7 pl.* aguas [territoriales; termales, etc.].
*8 adj.* de agua, acuático, hidráulico, para el agua: ~ *bath,* baño de María; ~ *carriage,* transporte por agua; conducción de agua; ~ *channel,* cuneta; ~ *clock,* reloj de agua; ~ *closet,* retrete con descarga de agua; ~ *colo(u)r,* acuarela; aguada; ~ *fowl,* ave o aves acuáticas; ~ *front,* orilla, ribera; barrio ribereño; ~ *gate,* compuerta, paradera; ~ *hammer,* martillo de agua; ~ *level,* nivel de agua; ~ *line,* MAR. línea de flotación, orilla del agua; ~ *parting,* divisoria de aguas; ~ *plane,* hidroavión; ~ *polo,* DEP. waterpolo; ~ *pot,* jarro, regadera; ~ *power,* energía hidráulica; ~ *spring,* manantial de agua; ~ *wave,* ondulación al agua [en el peinado]; ~ *wheel,* rueda hidráulica; turbina; ~ *wings,* nadaderas. *9* BOT. ~ *cress,* berro; ~ *fennel,* enante; ~ *germander,* escordio; ~ *lily,* nenúfar; ~ *parsnip,* berrera; ~ *plantain,* alisma. *10* ENT. ~ *skipper,* ~ *strider,* tejedor, zapatero. *11* ORN. ~ *hen,* polla de agua, gallineta. *12* ZOOL. ~ *flea,* pulga de agua; ~ *rat,* rata de agua; rata almizclada; ~ *snake,* culebra de agua.

**water (to)** *tr.* regar, rociar, mojar. *2* proveer de agua. *3* abrevar [el ganado]. *4* aguar, bautizar [el vino, etc.]. *5* dar visos a [una tela]. *6 intr.* chorrear agua o humedad. *7* llenar o llenarse de agua, lágrimas, etc.; llorar [los ojos], hacerse agua [la boca]. *8* abrevarse. *9* tomar agua. *10* MAR. hacer aguada.

**water-cooling** *s.* refrigeración por agua.

**watercourse** (-kø͞ʳs) *s.* corriente de agua, río, arroyo. *2* lecho de un río. *3* vaguada.

**waterfall** (-fol) *s.* cascada, catarata, salto de agua.

**wateriness** (-inis) *s.* acuosidad, humedad.

**watering** (-ing) *s.* riego, irrigación: ~ *can* o *pot,* regadera. *2* provisión o uso de agua; ~ *place,* abrevadero; aguada; balneario. *3* dilución. *4* acción de abrevar [a los animales]. *5* lagrimeo.

**waterish** (-ish) *adj.* acuoso, aguanoso. *2* húmedo, insípido.

**waterman** (-mæn) *s.* barquero. *2* el que cuida del agua o de dar agua.

**watermark** (-maʳk) *s.* señal indicadora del nivel del agua. *2* filigrana [en el papel].

**watermelon** (-meløn) *s.* BOT. sandía, melón de agua.

**waterproff** (-pruf) *adj.* impermeable. *2 s.* tela o abrigo impermeable.

**watershed** (-shed) *s.* GEOGR. divisoria de aguas. *2* GEOGR. cuenca; vertiente.

**waterside** (-said) *s.* orilla del agua, litoral.

**waterspout** (-spaut) *s.* manga, tromba marina. *2* turbión.

**watertight** (-tait) *adj.* estanco, hermético.

**waterworks** (-wø͞ʳks) *s. sing.* o *pl.* instalación o sistema de abastecimiento de agua. *2* fuente, juegos de agua.

**watery** (-i) *adj.* acuoso; aguanoso. *2* seroso. *3* lloroso. *4* húmedo. *5* claro [líquido]. *6* evaporado, insípido.

**watt** (uat) *s.* ELECT. vatio.

**wattle** (ua·tøl) *s.* zarzo. *2* sebe. *3* barbas [de ave]. *4* barba [de pez].

**wattle (to)** *tr.* cubrir o cercar con zarzos. *2* tejer, entretejer, entrelazar.

**wattmeter** (ua·tmitø͞ʳ) *s.* vatímetro.

**wave** (ueiv) *s.* ola. *2* onda: ~ *band,* RADIO. banda de ondas; ~ *length.* RADIO. longitud de onda; ~ *motion,* FÍS. movimiento ondulatorio. *3* ondulación. *4* temblor, oscilación. *5* aguas, visos. *6* ademán, señal [con la cabeza, la mano, una bandera].

**wave (to)** *intr.* flotar, ondear, ondular. *2* hacer señales. *3 tr.* blandir, agitar, tremolar. *4* mover [haciendo señales]; indicar, señalar [con la mano, un pañuelo, etc.]: *to* ~ *aside,* apartar; desechar. *5* ondular. *6* formar aguas [en una tela].

**wavelet** (-lit) *s.* ola u onda pequeña.

**waver** (-ø͞ʳ·) *s.* ondeo, oscilación, temblor. *2* ondulación [del cabello]. *3* tenacillas para ondular.

**waver (to)** *intr.* ondear, oscilar, temblar. *2* vacilar. *3* flaquear, ceder.

**wavy** (uei·vi) *adj.* ondoso, ondulante. *2* ondulado.

**wax** (uæks) *s.* cera: ~ *candle,* vela, cirio; ~ *end,* hilo encerado; ~ *paper,* papel parafinado; ~ *taper,* velita, candela. *2* objeto de cera. *3* cerumen. *4* fam. berrinche.

**wax (to)** *tr.* encerar. *2 intr.* crecer, aumentar. *3* hacerse, volverse, ponerse: *to* ~ *old,* envejecer.

**waxchandler** (uæ·kschændlø͞ʳ) *s.* cerero.

**waxen** (-øn) *adj.* de cera; encerado.

**waxwork** (-uø͞ʳk) *s.* obra o figura de cera.

**waxy** (-i) *adj.* céreo, ceroso. *2* blando, plástico.

**way** (uei) *s.* vía, camino, calle, canal, conducto. *2* camino, viaje, rumbo, curso, dirección, sentido: ~ *down,* bajada; ~ *up,* subida; *to go one's* ~, seguir uno su camino; irse, partir; *to look the other* ~, mirar a otro lado, desviar la mirada; *all the* ~, todo el camino; *on the* ~, de paso, al pasar; de camino; *the other* ~ *around,* al revés; *this* ~, por aquí. *3* paso [espacio o libertad para pasar]: ~ *in,* entrada; ~ *through,* paso, pasaje; ~ *out,* salida; *to be in the* ~, estorbar; *to get out of the* ~, quitarse de en medio, quitarse de encima [un trabajo, etc.]. *4* espacio, distancia, trecho: *a good* ~, *a long* ~, un buen trecho; *a long* ~ *off,* muy lejos. *5* marcha, progreso: *to make no* ~, no adelantar, no prosperar. *6* modo, manera: *any* ~, de cualquier modo o manera, de todos modos, como se quiera; *in a* ~, en cierto modo; *in a big* ~, en gran escala; *in a small* ~, en pequeña escala; *no* ~, nada, de ningún modo. *7* punto, lado, aspecto, respecto: *in a* ~, por un lado, en un aspecto; *in every* ~, en todos respectos. *8* medio, arbitrio. *9* sistema de vida, oficio, ocupa-

ción, hábito, costumbre: *it is not my* ~ *to*, ya no acostumbro a. *10* estado, condición: *in a bad* ~, mal, en mal estado. *11* impulso recibido. *12* MAR. marcha, andar, velocidad: *to gather* ~, ganar velocidad; *to get under* ~, levar, zarpar; *under* ~, en marcha, navegando; fig. empezando, haciéndose. *13 pl.* maneras, peculiaridades [de una pers.]. *14 to have a* ~ *with*, tener atractivo o poder de persuasión para; *to have one's* ~, salirse con la suya. *15 by* ~ *of*, pasando por; por vía de, a modo de, como. *16 by the* ~, a propósito, dicho sea de paso. *17 out of the* ~, fuera de camino; fuera del paso; impropio, inconveniente, extraordinario.
  *18 adj.* de camino, de tránsito: ~ *train*, tren tranvía.
**waybill** (uei·bil) *s.* hoja de ruta. *2* lista de pasajeros. *3* itinerario.
**wayfarer** (uei·ferø<sup>r</sup>) *s.* caminante. *2* viajero.
**waylay (to)** (uei·lei) *tr.* aguardar, acechar, asaltar [en el camino].
**waymark** (uei·ma<sup>r</sup>k), **waypost** (uei·poust) *s.* hito o poste indicador.
**wayside** (uei·said) *s.* orilla del camino.
**wayward** (uei·ua<sup>r</sup>d) *adj.* díscolo, voluntarioso. *2* adverso. *3* irregular, caprichoso.
**we** (uɪ) *pron. pers. pl.* de I; nosotros, nosotras.
**weak** (uɪk) *adj.* débil, flojo, flaco. *2* enclenque, delicado. *3* frágil, endeble, pobre, baladí. *4* ineficaz, impotente. *5* simple, recio. *6* GRAM., FONÉT. débil.
**weaken (to)** (-øn) *tr.* debilitar, enervar. *2* disminuir. *3 intr.* debilitarse. *4* flaquear, desfallecer.
**weak-headed** *adj.* de poca inteligencia.
**weak-hearted** *adj.* pusilánime.
**weak-kneed** *adj.* falto de energía, irresoluto.
**weakling** (ui·kling) *adj.-s.* persona débil, canija.
**weakly** (uɪ·kli) *adj.* débil, enclenque, enfermizo. *2 adv.* débilmente. *3* defectuosamente.
**weak-minded** *adj.* pobre de espíritu. *2* simple, mentecato.
**weaker sex** *s.* sexo débil.
**weakness** (uɪ·knis) *s.* debilidad, flaqueza. *2* flojedad. *3* fragilidad, endeblez. *4* decaimiento. *5* futilidad. *6* defecto. *7* lado débil.
**weal** (uɪl) *s.* cardenal, verdugón. *2* bien, salud, prosperidad: *public* ~, bien público.
**wealth** (uɪlz) *s.* riqueza. *2* fortuna, caudal. *3* opulencia. *4* copia, abundancia.
**wealthy** (uɪ·lzi) *adj.* rico, adinerado, opulento. *2* rico, abundante.
**wean (to)** (um) *tr.* destetar. *2 to* ~ *away from*, apartar gradualmente [de un afecto, hábito, etc.].
**weaning** (-ing) *s.* destete.
**weapon** (ue·pøn) *s.* arma [para atacar o defenderse].
**wear** (ue<sup>r</sup>) *s.* uso [de ropa, calzado, etc.]: *for everyday* ~, de uso diario; *in general* ~, de moda, que se lleva mucho: *the worse for the* ~, usado, deteriorado por el uso. *2* ropa, vestidos: *foot* ~, calzado. *3* gasto, desgaste: ~ *an tear*, uso, deterioro causado por el uso. *4* duración, resistencia.
**wear (to)** *tr.* traer puesto, usar, llevar: *to* ~ *the breeches*, llevar los calzones [la mujer]; *to* ~ *one's heart on one's sleeve*, llevar el corazón en la mano. *2* llevar, gastar [bigote, barba, etc.]. *3* llevar de cierto modo, color, etc. [el vestido, el pelo, etc.]. *4* tener [cierto aire o aspecto]. *5* gastar, desgastar, deteriorar. *6* agotar, fatigar, debilitar. *7 to* ~ *away*, gastar, consumir. *8 to* ~

*down*, desgastar con el roce; fig. gastar, acabar, convencer. *9 to* ~ *out*, desgastar; acabar con; cansar, fatigar; durar más que. *10 intr.* gastarse, consumirse, decaer. *11* pasar [un tiempo]. *12* resistir el uso. *13 to* ~ *away*, gastarse; pasar, decaer. *14 to* ~ *off*, borrarse; pasar; desaparecer. *15 to* ~ *out*, gastarse, inutilizarse. ¶ Pret.: *wore*; p. p.: *worn*.
**wearied** (uɪ·rid) *adj.* cansado, fatigado, agotado. *2* aburrido, fastidiado.
**weariness** (uɪ·rinis) *s.* cansancio, fatiga. *2* aburrimiento.
**wearing apparel** (we·ring) *s.* prendas de vestir.
**wearisome** (uɪ·risøm) *adj.* cansado, fatigoso. *2* pesado, aburrido, fastidioso.
**weary** (ui·ri) *adj.* cansado, fatigado. *2* abrumado, afligido. *3* cansado, aburrido, hastiado. *4* pesado, fatigoso, fastidioso.
**weary (to)** *tr.* cansar [fatigar, abrumar; aburrir, fastidiar]. *2 intr.* cansarse. *3* aburrirse. *4* hacerse pesado, aburrido.
**weasel** (uɪ·søl) *s.* ZOOL. comadreja.
**weather** (ue·ðø<sup>r</sup>) *s.* tiempo [estado de la atmósfera]: ~ *forecast(ing*, pronóstico del tiempo; ~ *report*, boletín meteorológico; ~ *strip*, burlete; ~ *vane*, veleta; *how is the* ~ *like?*, ¿qué tiempo hace? *2* mal tiempo, temporal, viento. *3* MAR. barlovento: ~ *side*, costado de barlovento. *4 pl.* vicisitudes de la suerte.
**weather (to)** *tr.* curar, secar, etc., a la intemperie. *2* capear, aguantar [el temporal; dificultades, etc.]. *3* MAR. doblar [un cabo]. *4 intr.* curarse, secarse, curtirse, etc., a la intemperie. *5* durar, resistir.
**weather-beaten** *adj.* curtido por la intemperie.
**weathercock** (kak) *s.* veleta.
**weathering** (-ing) *s.* acción de los agentes atmosféricos; desgaste, alteración que produce.
**weatherman** (-mæn) *s.* hombre del tiempo, meteorólogo.
**weatherproof** (-pruf) *adj.* a prueba de intemperie o de mal tiempo.
**weather-wise** *adj.* experto en prever los cambios de tiempo.
**weave** (uɪv) *s.* TEJ. tejido, textura, ligado.
**weave (to)** *tr.* tejer. *2* hilar [la araña, un insecto]. *3* entretejer. *4* urdir, trama. *5 to* ~ *one's way*, avanzar zigzagueando. *6 intr.* tejer. Pret.: *wove*; p. p.: *woven* o *wove*.
**weaver** (-ø<sup>r</sup>) *s.* ORN. tejedor, tejedora. *2* tramador.
**weaverbird** (-bø<sup>r</sup>d) *s.* ORN. tejedor [pájaro].
**web** (ueb) *s.* tejido, tela, obra tejida; telaraña. *2* enredo, red, trama. *3* ANAT. membrana. *4* ZOOL. membrana interdigital. *5* barbas [de una pluma]. *6* MEC. alma [de carril, etc.]; paletón [de llave]. *7* rollo [de papel continuo].
**webbed** (-d) *adj.* unido por una membrana; palmeado, palmípedo.
**webfoot** (-fut) *s.* ORN. pie palmeado. *2* palmípedo.
**web-footed** *adj.* ORN. palmípedo.
**we'd** (uid) *contr.* de WE HAD, WE SHOULD y WE WOULD.
**wed (to)** (ued) *tr.* casarse con. *2* casar [unir, dar en matrimonio]. *3* casarse. ¶ Pret. y p. p.: *wedded* o *wed*; ger.: *wedding*.
**wedded** (-id) *pret.* y *p. p.* de TO WED.
**wedding** (ue·ding) *s.* casamiento, boda, unión, enlace: ~ *cake*, pastel de boda. *2* aniversario de la boda: *silver* ~, bodas de plata; *golden* ~, bodas de oro.
**wedge** (uedȳ) *s.* cuña, calza, calce, alzaprima. *2*

GEOM. prisma triangular. *3* ZOOL. ~ *shell*, coquina.

**wedge (to)** *tr.* acuñar, apretar, partir o separar con cuña. *2* clavar, encajar o aprisionar [como una cuña]. *3 intr.* entrar o clavarse [como una cuña].

**wedlock** (ue·dlak) *s.* matrimonio, nupcias.

**Wednesday** (ue·nšdi) *s.* miércoles.

**wee** (uɪ) *adj.* fam. pequeño, chiquito.

**weed** (uɪd) *s.* yerbajo, mala hierba. *2* alga, planta acuática. *3* fam. tabaco; marihuana. *4 pl.* gasas, vestidos de luto.

**weed (to)** *tr.* escardar, desyerbar, limpiar; arrancar las malas hierbas. *2* quitar, extirpar.

**weedy** (uɪ·di) *adj.* lleno de yerbajos; parecido a un yerbajo. *2* algoso. *3* flaco, desgarbado.

**week** (uɪk) *s.* semana; ~ *end*, fin de semana; ~ *in*, ~ *out*, semana tras semana.

**weekday** (uɪ·kdei) *s.* día laborable.

**week-end (to)** *intr.* pasar el fin de semana.

**weekly** (uɪ·kli) *adj.* semanal, hebdomadario. *2 adv.* semanalmente, por semana. *3 s.* semanario [periódico].

**weep (to)** (uɪp) *intr.* llorar. *2 tr.* llorar, lamentar. *3* llorar, verter [lágrimas]. *4 to* ~ *one's eyes out*, hartarse de llorar. ¶ Pret. y p. p.: *wept*.

**weeper** (-øʳ) *s.* llorador, llorón. *2* plañidera. *3 pl.* velo de viuda.

**weeping** (uɪ·ping) *s.* llanto. *2 adj.* llorón: ~ *willow*, sauce llorón.

**weever** (uɪ·vøʳ) *s.* ICT. dragón marino.

**weevil** (uɪ·vøl) *s.* ENT. gorgojo.

**weft** (ueft) *s.* TEJ. trama. *2* tejido. *3* velo [de humo, niebla, etc.].

**weigh (to)** (uei) *tr.* pesar [determinar el peso de; ponderar, examinar]: *to* ~ *out*, pesar y distribuir. *2* sopesar. *3* contrapesar. *4* MAR. levar [un ancla]: *to* ~ *anchor*, levar anclas. *5 to* ~ *down*, abrumar, agobiar. *6 intr.* pesar [tener peso; hacer peso]. *7* pesarse. *8* MAR. levar anclas.

**weight** (ueit) *s.* peso, gravedad. *2* peso [de una cosa: *standard* ~, peso legal o normal; *to put on* ~, ganar peso, engordar; *by* ~, al peso. *3* unidad de peso. *4* sistema de pesos. *5* pesa. *6* peso, carga. *7* peso, importancia, fuerza, autoridad, influencia. *8* pisapapeles.

**weight (to)** *tr.* cargar con peso; aumentar el peso de; sobrecargar.

**weightless** (-lis) *adj.* ingrávido, ligero, leve.

**weighty** (-i) *adj.* pesado, ponderoso. *2* de peso, importante, serio, grave. *3* corpulento.

**weir** (uɪʳ) *s.* azud, presa [en un río]. *2* cañal, encañizada.

**weird** (uɪ·ʳd) *adj.* sobrenatural, fantástico, misterioso. *2* raro, extraño.

**welcome** (ue·lkøm) *adj.* bien venido, bien acogido, bien recibido. *2* grato, agradable, oportuno. *3 you are* ~, no hay de qué, de nada [en respuesta a *thank you*]. *4 you are* ~ *here*, está usted en su casa. *5 you are* ~ *to it*, está.a su disposición. *6 s.* bienvenida, buena acogida. *7 interj.* ¡bien venido!

**welcome (to)** *s.* dar la bienvenida. *2* acoger con agasajo. *3* recibir con gusto, aceptar.

**weld** (ueld) *s.* soldadura, unión. *2* BOT. gualda.

**weld (to)** *tr.* soldar [esp. a martillo]. *2* unir íntimamente, unificar. *3 intr.* soldarse.

**welder** (-øʳ) *s.* soldador.

**welding** (ue·lding) *s.* soldadura: ~ *torch*, lámpara de soldar.

**welfare** (-feʳ) *s.* bienestar, bien, felicidad, salud: ~ *work*, obra social o de beneficencia.

**we'll** (uɪl) *contr.* de WE SHALL y WE WILL.

**well** (uel) *s.* fuente, manantial, venero. *2* pozo [de agua, de petróleo, etc.]. *3* MAR. pozo; caja de bombas. *4* aljibe, cisterna. *5* ARQ. [caja de escalera o ascensor]. *6* vaso [de tintero]; depósito [de estilográfica].

**well** *adj.* bien hecho, satisfactorio, agradable, conveniente, bueno, sano, dichoso, apto, adecuado. | Us. gralte. como predicado y, en muchos casos, equivale al adverbio castellano «bien»: *all is* ~, todo va bien, no hay novedad:*is your father* ~?, ¿está bien su padre?; *very* ~, muy bien. *2 adv.* bien, felizmente, favorablemente, completamente, del todo: ~ *done*, bien hecho; COC. bien asado; ~ *off*, próspero, acomodado; *as* ~, además, también; ~ *then*, pues bien, conque. *3 interj.* ¡bien!, ¡bueno!, ¡vamos!

**well (to)** *intr.* manar, brotar. *2 tr.* manar.

**well-balanced** *adj.* bien equilibrado. *2* fig. equilibrado, cuerdo, sensato.

**well-behaved** *adj.* de buena conducta. *2* atento, cortés.

**well-being** *s.* bienestar.

**well-bred** *adj.* bien educado, bien criado.

**well-disposed** *adj.* bien dispuesto, favorable.

**well-favoured** *adj.* agraciado, bien parecido.

**well-founded** *adj.* bien fundado.

**wellhole** (ue·ljoul) *s.* caja u ojo de escalera. *2* boca de pozo.

**well-informed** *adj.* bien enterado. *2* culto, ilustrado.

**well-known** *adj.* conocido, bien conocido; familiar.

**well-meaning** *adj.* bienintencionado.

**well-nigh** *adv.* casi, cerca de.

**well-off** *adj.* próspero, acomodado.

**well-read** *adj.* leído, docto, erudito.

**wellspring** (ue·lspring) *s.* fuente, manantial.

**well-timed** *adj.* oportuno.

**well-to-do** *adj.* acomodado, próspero.

**well-worn** *adj.* gastado, raído. *2* fig. trillado.

**Welsh** (uelsh) *adj.* galés: ~ *rabbit* o *rarebit*, tostada cubierta de queso derretido en cerveza. *2 s.* idioma galés. *3 pl. the* ~, los galeses.

**Welshman** (ue·lshmæn) *s.* galés.

**welt** (uelt) *s.* COST. vivo, ribete. *2* ZAP. vira. *3* CARP. refuerzo. *4* roncha, verdugón.

**welt (to)** *tr.* ribetear. *2* ZAP. poner viras a. *3* CARP. reforzar. *4* levantar ronchas; zurriagar.

**welter** (ue·ltøʳ) *s.* agitación, tumulto. *2* confusión, revoltijo.

**welter (to)** *intr.* revolcarse. *2* encenagarse.

**welterweight** (ue·ltøʳueit) *s.* DEP. peso «welter».

**wen** (uen) *s.* lobanillo, lupia.

**wench** (uench) *s.* muchacha, jovencita. *2* moza, criada. *3* ant. ramera, coima.

**wend (to)** (uend) *tr.* dirigir, encaminar: *to* ~ *one's way*, dirigir sus pasos.

**went** (uent) *pret.* de TO GO.

**wept** (uept) *pret.* y *p. p.* de TO WEEP.

**we're** (uɪʳ) *contr.* de WE ARE.

**were** (uøʳ) *pret. pl.* de *ind.* y *sing.* y *pl.* de *subj.* de TO BE.

**Wesleyan** (ue·slian) *adj.-s.* wesleyano, metodista.

**west** (uest) *s.* oeste, occidente, poniente. *2* ~ *northwest*, oesnoroeste; ~ *southwest*, oessudoeste. *3 adj.* occidental, del oeste: *West Indies*, las Antillas. *4 adv.* al oeste, en el oeste o hacia el oeste.

**wester** (-øʳ) *s.* viento o temporal del oeste.

**westerly** (-øʳli) *adj.* occidental, del oeste. *2* que va hacia el oeste; que viene del oeste. *3 adv.* hacia el oeste. *4* viniendo del oeste.

**western** (-øʳn) *adj.* occidental, de occidente, del oeste: *Western Empire*, Imperio de Occidente. *3 s.* novela, cuento o película de la vida del Oeste [de los E.U.].

**westerner** (-øʳnøʳ) *s.* natural o habitante del oeste.

**Westphalia** (uestfei·lia) *n. pr.* GEOGR. Vestfalia.

**westward** (ue·stwaʳd) *adj.* que se dirige o está hacia el oeste; que mira al oeste. *2 s.* el Occidente [regiones, países].

**westwards** (-s) *adv.* hacia el oeste.

**wet** (uet) *adj.* mojado: ~ *blanket*, fig. aguafiestas, jarro de agua fría. *2* húmedo: ~ *cell*, ELECT. pila húmeda. *3* humedecido. *4* lluvioso. *5* que crece en terreno húmedo. *6* fam. achispado. *7* (E.U.) antiprohibicionista. *8* ~ *nurse*, ama de cría. *9 s.* humedad; tiempo lluvioso; agua, lluvia.

**wet (to)** *tr.* mojar: *to* ~ *one's whistle*, fam. mojar el gaznate, beber. *2* humedecer, humectar. ¶ Pret. y p. p.: *wet* o *wetted*; ger.: *-tting.*

**wether** (ue·ðøʳ) *s.* carnero castrado.

**whack** (juæk) *s.* fam. golpe, garrotazo. *2* pop. prueba, tentativa. *3* pop. porción, parte.

**whack (to)** *tr.* fam. golpear, pegar.

**whacking** (-ing) *adj.* fam. enorme, desmesurado.

**whale** (jueil) *s.* ZOOL. ballena, cachalote. *2* fig. (E.U.) cosa enorme, extraordinaria.

**whale (to)** *intr.* ir a la pesca de la ballena. *2* (E.U.) zurrar, apalizar.

**whaleboat** (-bout) *s.* MAR. ballenero [embarcación].

**whalebone** (-boun) *s.* ballena [lámina]. *2* ballena [de corsé].

**whaler** (-øʳ) *s.* ballenero. *2* buque ballenero. *3* WHALEBOAT.

**whaling** (-ing) *s.* pesca de la ballena.

**whang** (juæng) *s.* golpe fuerte, que resuena.

**whang (to)** *tr.* golpear con fuerza.

**wharf** (juoʳf) *s.* muelle, embarcadero.

**wharfage** (-idy̆) *s.* muellaje.

**wharfinger** (-ingøʳ) *s.* dueño o encargado de un muelle.

**what** (juat) *adj. y pron. interr.* qué; cuál: ~ *a man!*, ¡qué hombre!; ~ *is this?*, ¿qué es esto? ~ *for?*, ¿para qué?; ~ *is his name?*, ¿cuál es su nombre?, ¿cómo se llama? *2* a veces tiene el sentido de ¿y qué?», «¿qué importa?», «¿qué le parece?». *3 pron. rel.* lo que: ~ *followed*, lo que siguió; ~ *is* ~, lo que hay. *4 and* ~ *not*, y qué sé yo qué más. *5 adj. rel.* el, la, los, las... que; cuanto, cuantos, cuantas: *take* ~ *money you need*, tome el dinero que (o cuanto dinero) necesite. *6 adv.* parte, entre: ~ *with drink and* ~ *with fright*, entre la bebida y el miedo. *7 interj.* ¡eh!, ¡qué!

**whatever** (juate·vøʳ) *pron.* cualquier cosa que, sea, lo que sea que, cuanto, todo lo que. *2* fam. qué [interrogativo]: ~ *do you want?*, ¿qué quiere usted? *3 adj.* cualquiera que; de ninguna clase, en absoluto: ~ *be the issue*, cualquiera que sea el resultado; *no food* ~, ninguna clase de comida.

**whatnot** (jua·tnat) *s.* cosa, chisme. *2* estante, rinconera.

**whatsoever** (juatsoue·vøʳ) *pron. y adj.* WHATEVER.

**wheal** (juil) *s.* haba, roncha.

**wheat** (juit) *s.* BOT. trigo: ~ *field*, trigal.

**wheatear** (iøʳ) *s.* ORN. culiblanco.

**wheaten** (-øn) *adj.* de trigo.

**wheedle (to)** (ju·døl) *tr.* halagar, engatusar. *2* conseguir por medio de halagos.

**wheel** (juil) *s.* rueda [de carro, de reloj, etc.]: *on*

*wheels*, sobre ruedas. *2* rodaja, disco, polea. *3* rodezno. *4* torno [de alfarero o de hilar]. *5* PIROT. rueda. *6* rueda [suplicio]. *7* MAR. rueda del timón. *8* AUTO. volante. *9* fam. bicicleta. *10* giro, revolución. *11* MIL. conversión. *12 adj.* de ruedas, de figura de ruedas; del timón; que gira: ~ *base*, batalla [de un carruaje]; ~ *chair*, silla de ruedas; ~ *horse*, caballo de varas; ~ *window*, ARQ. rosa, rosetón.

**wheel (to)** *tr.* mover, llevar sobre ruedas; hacer rodar; hacer girar. *2* poner ruedas a. *3* labrar en el torno de alfarero. *4 intr.* girar, rodar, dar vueltas. *5* MIL. girar, efectuar una conversión. *6* ir en bicicleta. *7* rodar, marchar fácilmente.

**wheelbarrow** (-bærou) *s.* carretilla de mano.

**wheeler** (-øʳ) *s.* rodador, girador. *2* caballo de varas. *3* buque de ruedas. *4* fam. ciclista; motociclista.

**wheelhouse** (-jaus) *s.* MAR. timonera.

**wheelrace** (-reis) *s.* cárcavo.

**wheelwork** (-wøʳk) *s.* MEC. rodaje, ruedas.

**wheelwright** (-rait) *s.* CARTWRIGHT.

**wheeze** (juis) *s.* jadeo, silbido de la respiración fatigosa. *2* pop. chiste, broma, etc., gastados.

**wheeze (to)** *intr.* jadear, respirar produciendo un silbido.

**wheezy** (-i) *adj.* asmático, jadeante.

**whelk** (juelk) *s.* ZOOL. buccino, caracol de mar. *2* pápula, pústula, grano.

**whelp** (juelp) *s.* cachorro. *2* desp. mozalbete, granuja.

**whelp (to)** *intr.* parir [la perra, la loba, etc.].

**when** (juen) *adv. y conj.* cuando, al tiempo que, en cuanto, así que: *since* ~?, ¿desde cuándo? *2* en cuyo momento, y entonces. *3* en que: *the moment* ~, el momento en que. *4* estando, en caso de: ~ *in doubt*, en caso de duda. *5* aunque, a pesar de que.

**whence** (juens) *adv.* de donde, de qué lugar, origen, etc. *2* de donde, de ahí, por lo cual.

**whenever** (juene·vøʳ) *adv.* cuando quiera que, siempre que, en cualquier tiempo que o que sea, todas las veces que.

**where** (jueʳ) *adv. y conj.* donde, en donde, adonde, por donde. *2 pron.* adonde.

**whereabout** (jue·rabaut) *adv.* dónde, hacia dónde.

**whereabouts** (jue·rabauts) *s.* paradero.

**whereas** (jueræ·s) *conj.* considerando que. *2* mientras que, cuando por el contrario.

**whereby** (-bai) *adv.* con que, por medio de lo cual. *2* ¿cómo?

**wherefore** (-foʳ) *adv.* ¿por qué? *2* por lo cual, por consiguiente. *3 s.* porqué, razón, motivo.

**wherein** (jueri·n) *adv.* donde, en qué, con qué.

**whereto** (-tu·), **whereunto** (juerøntu·) *adv.* a lo cual, a que.

**whereupon** (-øpa·n) *adv.* entonces, después de lo cual. *2* sobre que, en que.

**wherever** (-e·vøʳ) *adv.* dondequiera que, adondequiera que, por dondequiera que.

**wherewith** (jue·ʳwiδ) *adv.* con que, con lo cual.

**wherry** (jue·ri) *s.* bote; chalana.

**whet** (juet) *s.* afiladura, amoladura, aguzadura. *2* filo [cortante].

**whet (to)** *tr.* afilar, amolar. *2* excitar, aguzar; abrir [el apetito].

**whether** (jue·δøʳ) *conj.* si: *I don't know* ~ *he will be there*, yo no sé si él estará allí. *2* sea, sea que, ora, ya, tanto si... (como): ~ *we go or not*, tanto si vamos como si no vamos.

**whetstone** (jue·tstoun) *s.* piedra de afilar.

**whetter** (-ø$^r$) *s.* amolador, afilador. *2* estimulante.
**whew** (jiu) *interj.* ¡eh!, ¡uf!, ¡cáspita!
**whey** (juei·) *s.* suero [de la leche].
**which** (juich) *adj.* y *pron. interrog.* ¿qué?, ¿cuál?, ¿cuáles?: ~ *way?*, ¿por qué camino?, ¿por dónde?; ~ *is* ~, quién, o cuál, es el uno y quién, o cuál, es el otro. *2 pron. rel.* lo que, lo cual: *all of* ~, *all* ~, todo lo cual. *3* que, el cual, los o las cuales [con referencia o cosas]: *both of* ~, los cuales, que [refiriéndose a dos]. *4* cualquiera que; el, los, etc., que: *take* ~ *you will*, tome el que quiera. *5 adj. rel.* Hay que traducirlo libremente: *three days, during* ~ *time*, tres días, durante los cuales.
**whichever** (-e·vø$^r$) *pron.* y *adj.* cualquiera, cualesquiera, quienquiera; el que.
**whidah-bird** (jui·da-bø$^r$d) *s.* ORN. viuda.
**whiff** (juif) *s.* soplo [de aire]. *2* vaharada, bocanada, fumarada, hálito, tufo; olor o hedor repentino.
**whiff (to)** *tr.* echar, exhalar [humo, olor, etc.]. *2* llevar o disipar con el soplo.
**whiffle (to)** (jui·føl) *tr.* soplar, exhalar, disipar, desvanecer. *2 intr.* soplar a rachas [el viento]. *3* vacilar, fluctuar.
**whiffletree** (-trɪ) *s.* CARR. volea, balancín.
**Whig** (juig) *adj.-s.* POL. (Ingl.) liberal, del partido liberal.
**while** (juail) *s.* rato, tiempo: *a little* ~, *a short* ~, un ratito; *for a* ~, por algún tiempo; *in a* ~, dentro de poco; *the* ~, entretanto; *to be worth* ~, o *one's* ~, valer la pena. *2 conj.* mientras, mientras que. *3* aun, aun cuando, si bien.
**while (to)** *tr.* pasar, entretener; distraer [el tiempo, el aburrimiento, etc.]. | Gralte. con *away*.
**whilst** (-st) *conj.* mientras, mientras que.
**whim** (juim) *s.* antojo, capricho, fantasía. *2* MIN. malacate.
**whimper** (-pø$^r$) *s.* gemido, gimoteo, lloriqueo.
**whimper (to)** *intr.* gemir, gimotear, lloriquear.
**whimsey** (-ši) *s.* WHIM.
**whimsical** (-šikɑl) *adj.* caprichoso, antojadizo. *2* caprichoso, fantástico, raro, extravagante.
**whimsy** (-ši) *s.* WHIM.
**whin** (juin) *s.* roca basáltica. *2* BOT. tojo.
**whine** (juain) *s.* gemido, plañido, gimoteo.
**whine (to)** *intr.* gemir, quejarse, gimotear.
**whinny** (jui·ni) *s.* relincho [esp. suave].
**whinny (to)** *intr.* relinchar [esp. suavemente].
**whip** (juip) *s.* látigo, fusta, zurriago, azote. *2* latigazo. *3* COC. batido de nata, huevos, etc. *4* movimiento de vaivén en arco de círculo. *5* MAR. tecle, andarivel. *6* POL. (Ingl.) miembro de una cámara encargado de velar por la disciplina de su grupo. *7* ~ *top*, peonza.
**whip (to)** *tr.* fustigar, zurriagar, azotar, dar latigazos a; zurrar, dar una paliza a. *2* COC. batir [huevos, nata, etc.]. *3* mover, sacar, meter, asir, etc., bruscamente, vivamente, con presteza. | Con *away, into, off, out*, etc. *4* sacudir [una alfombra, etc.]. *5* envolver [un cabo, palo, etc.] con cuerda o cordel. *6* COST. sobrecoser. *7 intr.* moverse, obrar, volverse, ir, pasar, etc., rápida o súbitamente. | Con *away, down, into, out, up*, etc. *8* ondear, restallar. ¶ Pret. y p. p.: *whipped;* ger.: *whipping.*
**whipcord** (-ko$^r$d) *s.* tralla [de látigo]. *2* catgut. *3* tela fuerte de estambre.
**whippersnapper** (jui·pø$^r$snæ·pø$^r$) *s.* quídam, mequetrefe.

**whippet** (-it) *s.* perro de una raza inglesa, muy corredora. *2* MIL. carro de asalto ligero.
**whipping** (-ing) *s.* azotamiento, flagelación, vapuleo, paliza. *2* ~ *top*, peonza.
**whippletree** (-øltrɪ) *s.* CARR. volea, balancín.
**whipstitch** (-stich) *s.* sobrecostura.
**whipstitch (to)** *tr.* sobrecoser.
**whir** (juø$^r$) *s.* zumbido; aleteo.
**whir (to)** *intr.* zumbar, rehilar. *2* moverse, volar, girar con zumbido. ¶ Pret. y p. p.: *whirred;* ger.: *rring.*
**whirl** (juø$^r$l) *s.* giro o vuelta rápidos; remolino, confusión. *2* espiral [de humo].
**whirl (to)** *intr.* girar, dar vueltas, volverse, pasar rápidamente; remolinar. *3 tr.* hacer girar, voltear. *4* arremolinar.
**whirligig** (-igig) *s.* perinola. *2* tiovivo. *3* fig. torbellino. *4* ENT. girino.
**whirlpool** (-pul) *s.* vórtice, vorágine, remolino de agua.
**wirlwind** (-uind) *s.* torbellino, remolino de viento.
**whirr** *s.* y **whirr (to)** *intr.* WHIR y TO WHIR.
**whish** (juish) *interj.* ¡zas! *2* ¡chitón!
**whish (to)** *intr.* TO SWISH. *2* TO WHIZ.
**whisk** (juisk) *s.* movimiento rápido, ligero [como el del que barre o roza algo]. *2* escobita, manojo [de paja, etc.]. *3* COC. batidor. *4* panoja [de mijo].
**whisk (to)** *tr.* barrer, arrastrar, cepillar. *2* mover, llevar, arrebatar: *to* ~ *out of sight*, escamotear. *3* COC. batir. *4 intr.* moverse rápidamente.
**whisker** (-ø$^r$) *s.* patilla; barba: *side whiskers*, patillas. *2 pl.* bigotes [del gato, el león, etc.].
**whiskey** *s.* WHISKY.
**whisky** (-i) *s.* whisky.
**whisper** (jui·spø$^r$) *s.* susurro, murmullo, cuchicheo.
**whisper (to)** *intr.-tr.* susurrar, murmurar, cuchichear; hablar o decir al oído.
**whispering** (-ing) *s.* susurro, rumor. *2 adj.* susurrador, murmurador. *3* cuchicheador.
**whist** (juist) *s.* whist [juego de naipes].
**whistle** (jui·søl) *s.* silbato, pito, chiflato. *2* fam. gaznate. *3* silbido, silbo, pitido.
**whistle (to)** *intr.-tr.* silbar, pitar: *to* ~ *for*, llamar con un silbido; fig. pedir en vano.
**whit** (juit) *s.* pizca: *not a* ~, nada.
**white** (juait) *adj.* blanco; albo: ~ *ant*, ENT. hormiga blanca; ~ *coal*, hulla blanca; ~ *corpuscle* FISIOL. glóbulo blanco; ~ *elephant*, elefante blanco; fig. carga, estorbo; cosa gravosa e improductiva; ~ *feather*, pluma blanca, símbolo de cobardía; ~ *friar*, carmelita; ~ *heat*, temperatura al rojo blanco; ~ *lead*, albayalde; ~ *lie*, mentirilla; ~ *matter*, ANAT. substancia blanca; ~ *monk*, monje cisterciense; ~ *oak*, roble albar; ~ *paper*, (Ingl.) informe oficial; *White Russia*, GEOGR. Rusia Blanca; *White Sea*, GEOGR. Mar Blanco; ~ *slavery*, trata de blancas. *2* cano. *3* pálido, descolorido. *4* rubio [trigo]. *5* puro, inmaculado. *6* feliz, propicio. *7* en blanco.
8 *s.* color blanco, blancura. *9* pureza, inocencia. *10* blanco [del ojo]. *11* clara [de huevo]. *12* vestido-blanco. *13* blanco, blanca [pers.]. *14* AJED. las blancas. *15 pl.* leucorrea. *16* flor de harina.
**whitebait** (-beit) *s.* boquerones.
**whitebeam** (-bɪm) *s.* BOT. mostellar.
**whitecaps** (-kæps) *s.* MAR. cabrillas.
**whitefish** (-fish) *s.* ICT. corégono.
**white-handed** *adj.* de manos blancas. *2* de manos limpias, inocente, puro.

**white-hot** *adj.* calentado al rojo blanco.
**white-livered** *adj.* cobarde. 2 envidioso.
**whiten (to)** (-øn) *tr.* blanquear, emblanquecer. 2 platear. 3 *intr.* emblanquecerse, volverse blanco, blanquear.
**whitening** (-ning) *s.* blanqueo; emblanquecimiento. 2 enjalbegadura; lechada.
**whitethorn** (-zoᵣn) *s.* BOT. espino blanco.
**whitewash** (-uash) *s.* preparación para blanquear, lechada. 2 blanquete, afeite.
**whitewash (to)** *tr.* blanquear, enjalbegar, encalar. 2 encubrir los vicios o faltas de uno o de algo.
**whitewood** (juai·twud) *s.* BOT. tulipero.
**whither** (jui·ðøʳ) *adv.* adonde, al lugar o punto donde. 2 ¿adónde?
**whiting** (juai·ting) *s.* blanco de España. 2 ICT. pescadilla. 3 ICT. ~ *pout,* faneca.
**whitish** (-ish) *adj.* blanquecino, blancuzco.
**whitlow** (jui·tlou) *s.* MED. panadizo.
**whitlowwort** (-louwøᵣt) *s.* BOT. nevadilla.
**Witsun** (-søn) *adj.* de Pentecostés.
**Whitsunday** (-dei) *s.* domingo de Pentecostés.
**Whitsuntide** (-taid) *s.* Pascua de Pentecostés.
**whittle** (jui·tøl) *s.* ant. cuchillo, cuchilla.
**whittle (to)** *tr.* dar forma, sacar pedazos, sacar punta [a un trozo de madera] con el cuchillo. 2 *to* ~ *away* o *down,* fig. reducir, cercenar poco a poco.
**whity** (juai·ti) *adj.* blanquizco.
**whiz** o **whizz** (juiš) *s.* zumbido; sonido entre zumbido y silbido.
**whiz** o **whizz (o)** *intr.* zumbar, silbar, rehilar, ir zumbando por el aire.
**who** (ju) *pron. rel.* quien, quienes, que, el que, los que, las que [refiriéndose a pers. y gralte. como sujeto]. 2 *he* ~, el que, quien. 3 *pron. interr.* ¿quién?, ¿quiénes?
**whoa** (juou) *interj.* ¡so!, ¡cho!
**whoever** (jue·vøʳ) *pron. rel.* quienquiera que, cualquiera que, quien.
**whole** (joul) *adj.* todo, entero, completo, total: *the* ~ *story,* toda la historia; ~ *note,* MÚS. semibreve, redonda; ~ *number,* número entero. 2 enterizo. 3 íntegro, intacto, sano, ileso. 4 *s.* todo, total, totalidad, conjunto: *as a* ~, en conjunto; *on the* ~, en suma, en general.
**whole-hearted** *adj.* sincero, cordial.
**wholesale** (-seil) *adj.-adv.* al por mayor, por mayor: ~ *dealer,* mayorista. 2 *adj.* extenso, general. 3 *s.* venta al por mayor.
**wholesome** (-søm) *adj.* sano, saludable; salutífero. 2 sano [en buena salud].
**whole-wheat** *adj.* integral, de todo el trigo.
**wholly** (-i) *adv.* totalmente, enteramente, del todo, completamente.
**whom** (jum) *pron.* (caso oblicuo de WHO) quien, quienes; que, el que, la que, etc.; el cual, la cual, etc. [precedidos de preposición].
**whoop** (jup) *s.* grito, alarido. 2 inspiración ruidosa propia de la tosferina.
**whoop (to)** *intr.* gritar, vocear. 2 silbar [el búho]. 3 inspirar ruidosamente después de un acceso de tos. 4 *tr.* decir, llamar, insultar, alabar, etc., a gritos.
**whooping cough** (-pin) *s.* MED. tos ferina.
**whop (to)** (juap) *tr.* zurrar, dar una paliza a.
**whopper** (-øʳ) *s.* fam. cosa enorme. 2 mentira colosal.
**whopping** (-ing) *adj.* fam. enorme, colosal.
**whore** (joᵣ) *s.* prostituta, ramera, puta.
**wore (to)** *intr.* fornicar.

**whorl** (juøᵣl) *s.* tortera [del huso]. 2 espiral, circunvolución. 3 BOT. verticilo. 4 ZOOL. espira [de caracol].
**whorled** (-d) *adj.* verticilado.
**whortleberry** (juøᵣtølberi) *s.* BOT. arándano.
**who's** (ju·š) *contr.* de WHO IS.
**whose** *pron.* (genitivo de WHO y WHICH) cuyo, cuya, cuyos, cuyas, del que, de la que, de los que, de las que, de quien, de quienes.
**why** (juai) *adv.* y *conj.* ¿por qué?, ¿cómo?; por qué, por el cual, por lo que, por... que. 2 *interj.* ¡cómo!, ¡toma!, ¡qué! 3 *s.* porqué, causa, razón.
**wick** (uik) *s.* pábilo, mecha torcida.
**wicked** (ui·kid) *adj.* malo, malvado, perverso. 2 maligno, mal intencionado. 3 travieso, revoltoso.
**wicker** (ui·køᵣ) *s.* mimbre. 2 tejido de mimbres. 3 *adj.* de mimbres, de cestería, recubierto de mimbres.
**wickerwork** (-uøᵣk) *s.* tejido de mimbres, obra de cestería.
**wicket** (ui·kit) *s.* postigo, portillo; ventanilla. 2 CRICQUET meta; turno de cada jugador con el palo.
**wide** (uaid) *adj.* ancho. 2 de ancho: *two feet* ~, de dos pies de ancho. 3 anchuroso, espacioso. 4 amplio, dilatado, extenso, variado. 5 alejado, desviado. 6 muy abierto. 7 *adv.* ampliamente. 8 lejos a distancia: ~ *of the mark,* sin dar en el blanco. 9 muy: ~ *apart,* muy separado; ~ *open,* muy abierto; de par en par.
**wide-awake** *adj.* muy despierto, despabilado.
**wide-eyed** *adj.* con los ojos abiertos. 2 asombrado.
**widely** (-li) *adv.* extensamente. 2 muy, mucho, ampliamente, holgadamente.
**widen (to)** (-øn) *tr.* ensanchar, dilatar, extender. 2 *intr.* ensancharse, extenderse.
**widespread** (-spred) *adj.* extendido [alas, brazos, etc.]. 2 muy difundido; general, extenso.
**widgeon** (ui·dÿøn) *s.* ORN. cierto pato silvestre.
**widow** (ui·dou) *s.* viuda.
**widow (to)***tr.* dejar viuda o viudo.
**widower** (-øʳ) *s.* viudo.
**widowhood** (-jud) *s.* viudez.
**width** (uidz) *s.* anchura, ancho.
**wield (to)** (uild) *tr.* manejar, esgrimir, empuñar. 2 ejercer [poder, autoridad].
**wieldy** (-i) *adj.* manejable.
**wife** (uaif), *pl.* **wives** (uai·vš) *s.* esposa, mujer.
**wifely** (-li) *adj.* de esposa.
**wig** (uig) *s.* peluca, peluquín. 2 fam. (Ingl.) juez.
**wigged** (-d) *adj.* con peluca.
**wigging** (-ing) *s.* fam. peluca, reprensión.
**wiggle** (-øl) *tr.* meneo. 2 culebreo.
**wiggle (to)** *tr.* menear [la cola, los dedos, etc.]. 2 *intr.* menearse, culebrear.
**wigwag** (-wæk) *s.* counicación con banderas.
**wigwam** (-wam) *s.* tienda o cabaña de ciertos indios norteamericanos.
**wild** (uaild) *adj.* salvaje, montaraz, silvestre [animal, planta]: ~ *ass,* onagro; ~ *boar,* jabalí; ~ *duck,* pato salvaje; ~ *fig,* cabrahigo; ~ *goat,* cabra montés; ~ *goose,* ánsar, ganso bravo; ~ *hazel,* nochizo; ~ *olive tree,* acebuche. 2 cimarrón. 3 inculto, sin cultivo, desierto. 4 salvaje [no civilizado]. 5 bravo, indómito, fiero. 6 turbulento, alborotado, borrascoso. 7 violento, impetuoso. 8 desenfrenado, desordenado. 9 alocado. 10 extraño, extravagante, disparato, loco. 11 *adv.* WILDLY. 12 sin gobierno, sin freno. 13 *s.* desierto, yermo, selva, tierra virgen.

**wildcat** (-kæt) *s.* ZOOL. gato montés. *2* (E.U.) locomotora suelta, sin tren. *3* pozo [de petróleo] de exploración. *4 adj.* poco seguro, arriesgado; fantástico, quimérico; ilícito.

**wilderness** (uiˈldøᵣnis) *s.* tierra inculta, desierto, soledad, extensión, inmensidad.

**wild-eyed** *adj.* con la mirada extraviada.

**wildfire** (uaiˈldfaiᵣ) *s.* fuego griego. *2* fuego fatuo. *3* fucilazo.

**wld-goose** *adj.* quimérico, inútil:~ *chase*, búsqueda o empresa inútil, quimérica.

**wildly** (-dli) *adv.* en estado salvaje, sin cultivo. *2* salvajemente, furiosamente, locamente,etc.

**wile** (uail) *s. pl.* ardid, maña, engaño, astucia.

**wile (to)** *tr.* inducir, atraer, engañar. *2 to ~ away*, pasar, entretener [el tiempo].

**wilful** (uiˈlful) *adj.* voluntarioso, testarudo. *2* voluntario, intencionado.

**wilfully** (-i) *adv.* voluntariosamente. *2* voluntariamente, intencionadamente.

**wilfulness** (-nis) *s.* obstinación, terquedad. *2* voluntariedad.

**Wilhelmina** (uiljelmiˈna) *n. pr.* Guillermina.

**will** (uiˈl) *s.* voluntad. No tiene el sentido de amor, cariño: ~ *power*, fuerza de voluntad; *at ~*, a voluntad, a discreción; *with a ~*, con toda el alma. *2* albedrío. *3* poder, arbitrio. *4* gana, inclinación, deseo. *5* DER. testamento.

**1) will (to)** *tr.* querer, determinar, ordenar, mandar. *2* legar, dejar en testamento. ¶ Pret. y p. p.: *willed;* ger.: *-lling.*

**2) will** *tr.-intr.* querer, desear, anhelar, gustar: *if you ~*, si usted quiere; *would (to) God*, plegue, o pluguiera, a Dios; ojalá. *2 aux.* (con un infinitivo sin *to*). Forma el futuro y el potencial del segundo verbo. En las primeras personas, denota especialmente voluntad, intención, promesa o amenaza; en las segundas y terceras, simple acción futura, posibilidad o contingencia: *I ~ not do it*, no lo haré, no quiero hacerlo; *it ~ be very pleasant*, será muy agradable. | A veces indica que la acción del segundo verbo es habitual, frecuente o persistente y se traduce por soler, acostumbrar, o se traduce libremente: *he would take nightly walks*, solía dar (o daba) paseos nocturnos. ¶ Pret. y SUBJ.: *would*. | Carece de INF. e IMPERS.

**willed** (-d) *pret.* y *p. p.* de TO WILL.

**willful** *adj.* **willfully** *adv.*, **willfulness** *s.* = WILFUL, WILFULLY, WILFULNESS.

**William** (uiˈliam) *n. pr.* Guillermo.

**willing** (uiˈling) *adj.* deseoso, dispuesto, inclinado, pronto. *2* gustoso, complaciente. *3* voluntario. *4* ger. de TO WILL: *God ~*, Dios mediante.

**willingly** (-li) *adv.* de buena gana, con gusto.

**willingness** (-nis) *s.* buena gana, gusto, complacencia.

**will-o'-the-wisp** *s.* fuego fatuo.

**willow** (uiˈlou) *s.* BOT. sauce. *2* BOT. mimbrera.

**willowy** (-i) *adj.* abundante en sauces o mimbres. *2* cimbreño, flexible, esbelto, juncal.

**willy-nilly** (uiˈli-niˈli) *adv.* velis nolis, de grado o por fuerza.

**wilt (to)** (uilt) *tr.* marchitar, secar. *2 intr.* marchitarse. *3* languidecer, descaecer. *4* acobardarse.

**wily** (uaiˈli) *adj.* astuto, artero, marrullero.

**wimble** (uiˈmbøl) *s.* berbiquí, barrena.

**wimple** (-pøl) *s.* toca, griñón.

**wimple (to)** *tr.* ondular, rizar [la superficie del agua]. *2 intr.* caer en pliegues. *3* rizarse [la superficie del agua].

**win (to)** (uin) *tr.* ganar, obtener, alcanzar, conquistar, lograr. *2* persuadir, atraer, convencer, ganar el afecto de. *3 intr.* vencer, triunfar, ganar. ¶ Pret. y p. p.: *won;* ger.: *winning.*

**wince** (uins) *s.* respingo.

**wince (to)** *intr.* cejar, retroceder, encogerse, acobardarse [ante una dificultad, un golpe, el dolor, etc.]; dar un respingo, respingar.

**winch** (uinch) *s.* manubrio, cigüeña. *2* torno, montacargas. *3* carrete [de caña de pescar].

**1) wind** (uind, *en poesía* uaind) *s.* viento, aire: ~ *sail*, MAR. manga [de ventilación]; ~ *sock*, AVIA. manga de viento; *to be in the ~*, tramarse; *to cast to the ~*, *to the winds*, esparcir, arrojar; abandonar; *to get* o *have the ~ up*, asustarse, ponerse nervioso; *against* o *up the ~*, contra el viento; *before the ~*, viento en popa; *between ~ and water*, en la línea de flotación; en sitio delicado o peligroso; *by the ~*, ciñendo el viento; *in* o *into, the wind's eye* o *the teeth of the ~*, de cara al viento; *under the ~*, a sotavento. *2* viento, rumbo, punto cardinal. *3* viento [olor que deja la caza]: *to get ~ of*, fig. oler, tener noticia de. *4* aliento, respiración, resuello. *5* flato, ventosidad: *to break ~*, ventosear. *6* BOX. boca del estómago. *7 sing.* y *pl.* MÚS. instrumento de viento.

**2) wind** (uaind) *s.* mecanismo para devanar. *2* devanado; espiral, vuelta, sinuosidad.

**1) wind (to)** (uind) *tr.-intr.* ventear, husmear, olfatear. *2 tr.* orear, airear. *3* quitar el resuello. *4* dejar recobrar el aliento. ¶ CONJUG. pret. y p. p.: *winded.*

**2) wind (to)** (uaind) *tr.* soplar. *2* tocar, hacer sonar [un instrumento de viento]. ¶ Pret. y p. p.: *wound.*

**3) wind (to)** *tr.* devanar, ovillar, encanillar. *2* arrollar, envolver, retorcer, ensortijar: *to ~ someone around one's fingers*, fig. manejar o gobernar a uno. *3* torcer; manejar. *4* dar cuerda a. *5* atirantar. *6* izar, elevar [con máquina]. *7 to ~ off*, desenrollar, desovillar. *8 to ~ one's way*, zigzaguear, serpentear. *9 to ~ up*, devanar, ovillar; dar cuerda a; atirantar; excitar; izar, elevar [con máquina]. *10 intr.* arrollarse, enrollarse, enroscarse. *11* serpentear, culebrear. *12* alabearse. *13 tr.-intr. to ~ up*, acabar, concluir, finalizar. ¶ Pret. y p. p.: *wound* (en términos náuticos, *winded*).

**windage** (uiˈndidȳ) *s.* ARTILL. viento. *2* ARTILL. desvío de un proyectil por efecto del viento.

**windbag** (-bæg) *s.* fam. palabrero, charlatán.

**wind-blown** *adj.* llevado o desarreglado por el viento.

**windbreak** (-brek) *s.* abrigo contra el viento.

**winded** (-id) *adj.* venteado. *2* sin aliento, sin resuello.

**winder** (uaiˈndøᵣ) *s.* devanador. *2* argadillo, devanadera; carrete. *3* llave para dar cuerda. *4* ARQ. escalón de abanico.

**windfall** (uiˈndfol) *s.* fruta caída del árbol por la fuerza del viento. *2* suerte inesperada.

**winding** (uaiˈnding) *s.* arrollamiento, enroscamiento, devanado, bobinado. *2* vuelta, revuelta, recodo, sinuosidad. *3* ELECT. arrollamiento. *4* alabeo. *5 ~ up*, acción de dar cuerda o de atirantar; final, conclusión. *6 adj.* sinuoso, tortuoso, etc. *7 ~ frame*, devanadera; ~ *sheet*, mortaja, sudario; ~ *stairs*, escalera de caracol.

**windlass** (uiˈndlas) *s.* torno [para elevar pesos]; malacate. *2* MAR. molinete.

**windmill** (-mil) *s.* molino de viento. *2* molinete [juguete]. *3* AVIA. turbina de aire.

**window** (ui·ndou) *s.* ventana: ~ *case*, ~ *frame*, marco de ventana; ~ *envelope*, sobre de ventanilla; ~ *screen*, sobrevidriera. *3* ventanilla. *4* escaparate [de tienda]: ~ *dresser*, decorador de escaparates; ~ *dressing*, arreglo de escaparates; fig. amaño para dar a ciertas cosas un aspecto favorable.

**windpipe** (ui·ndpaip) *s.* tráquea, gaznate.

**windscreen** (-skrɪn), **windshield** (-ʃɪld) *s.* AUTO. parabrisas: ~ *wiper*, limpiaparabrisas.

**wnd-up** *s.* conclusión, final, desenlace. *2* fam. estado de excitación, ansiedad, miedo, etc.

**windward** (-a<sup>r</sup>d) *s.* barlovento: *to sail to the* ~, barloventear. *2 adj.* de barlovento: *Windward Islands*, Islas de Barlovento. *3 adv.* hacia barlovento.

**windy** (-i) *adj.* ventoso. *2* ampuloso, hinchado. *3* palabrero. *4* vano, inconsistente.

**wine** (uain) *s.* vino: ~ *bag*, odre, pellejo; ~ *cellar*, bodega; ~ *press*, prensa para uva, lagar.

**wine-colo(u)red** *adj.* de color de vino, rojo oscuro.

**wineglass** (-glæs) *s.* copa para vino.

**winegrower** (-grouø<sup>r</sup>) *s.* viticultor, vinicultor.

**winesap** (-sæp) *s.* manzana roja de invierno.

**wineskin** (-skin) *s.* odre, pellejo.

**wing** (uing) *s.* ORN., ENT., ANAT., ARQ., FORT., MIL., POL. ala: *on*, o *upon*, *the* ~, volando; viajando con un pie en el estribo; *under the* ~ *of*, bajo la protección de. *2* vuelo [acción de volar]. *3* MEC. aleta, oreja: ~ *nut*, tuerca de orejas. *4* TEAT. bastidor.

**winged** (-d o -id) *adj.* alado, aligero. *2* herido del ala. *3* lleno de pájaros.

**winglet** (-lit) *s.* alita.

**wingspread** (-pred) *s.* ORN. envergadura.

**wink** (uink) *s.* parpadeo, pestañeo, abrir y cerrar de ojos. *2* guiño. *3* sueño corto: *not to steep a* ~, no pegar los ojos. *4* relámpago, destello.

**wink (to)** *intr.* pestañear, parpadear, abrir y cerrar los ojos. *2* hacer guiños, un guiño. *3* centellear, dar luz trémula. *4 to* ~ *at*, hacer la vista gorda, disimular.

**winker** (-ø<sup>r</sup>) *s.* guiñador. *2* BLINKER. *3* pop. pestaña.

**winkle** (ui·nkøl) *s.* PERIWINKLE.

**winner** (ui·nø<sup>r</sup>) *s.* ganador. *2* vencedor.

**winning** (-ing) *adj.* triunfante, ganador; ganancioso. *2* atractivo, encantador, persuasivo. *3* DEP. ~ *post*, poste de llegada.

**winnow (to)** (ui·nou) *tr.* aventar, ahechar. *2* fig. cerner, analizar, entresacar. *3* poét. batir [el aire] con las alas; recorrer volando.

**winsome** (ui·nsøm) *adj.* agradable, atractivo, simpático, seductor.

**winter** (ui·ntø<sup>r</sup>) *s.* invierno. *2 adj.* de invierno, invernal: ~ *cherry*, BOT. alquequenje; ~ *season*, invierno, invernada; ~ *solstice*, solsticio de invierno.

**winter (to)** *intr.* invernar, pasar el invierno.

**wintergreen** (-grɪn) *s.* BOT. gaulteria.

**wintering** (-ing) *s.* invernada.

**winterly** (-li), **wintry** (ui·ntri) *adj.* de invierno, invernizo; invernal, hiemal. *2* fig. frío, helado, triste.

**winy** (uai·ni) *adj.* vinoso. *2* embriagado.

**wipe** (uaip) *s.* limpión, limpiadura. *2* golpe, revés, manotazo.

**wipe (to)** *tr.* limpiar, secar, enjugar, restregar. *2* quitar, lavar, borrar, extirpar, destruir. ¶ Con

*away*, *off* o *out*. *3* pasar [la mano, un trapo, etc.] por.

**wiper** (-ø<sup>r</sup>) *s.* limpiador, enjugador. *2* fam. paño, trapo, toalla, pañuelo. *3* pop. WIPE 2. *4* ELECT. contacto deslizante.

**wire** (uai<sup>r</sup>) *s.* alambre; hilo o cuerda de alambre: ~ *cutter*, cortaalambres; ~ *edge*, filván; ~ *entanglement*, FORT. alambrada; ~ *fence*, alambrado; ~ *nail*, alfiler de París; ~ *rope*, cordón o cable metálico; ~ *screen*, alambrera, tela metálica. *2* alambrado. *3* telégrafo eléctrico. *4* telegrama. *5 pl.* hilos [con que se mueve una cosa]: *to pull the wires*, mover los hilos.

**wire (to)** *tr.* proveer de alambres; alambrar. *2* coger, atar, etc. con alambre. *3 tr.-intr.* telegrafiar.

**wiredraw (to)** (uai·<sup>r</sup>dro) *tr.* tirar [metales]. *2* alargar, hacer durar. *3* alambicar, sutilizar. ¶ Pret.: *-drew*; p. p.: *-drawn*.

**wiredrawing** (-droing) *s.* tirado [de metales].

**wire-haired** *adj.* de pelo áspero [perro].

**wireless** (-lis) *adj.* ELECT. inalámbrico, sin hilos; de telegrafía o telefonía sin hilos. *4* (Ingl.) radio, radiotelefonía; aparato de radio.

**wireless (to)** *tr.-intr.* comunicar o transmitir por radiotelegrafía o radiofonía.

**wiring** (-ing) *s.* ELECT. sistema e instalación de hilos y cables de distribución; conducción [eléctrica].

**wiry** (-i) *adj.* de alambre; como alambre. *2* delgado y fuerte; nervudo.

**wisdom** (ui·ṣdøm) *s.* sabiduría, sapiencia. *2* prudencia, cordura, juicio, discreción: ~ *tooth*, muela del juicio.

**wise** (uaiš) *adj.* cuerdo, prudente, juicioso, sensato. *2* fam. enterado, noticioso. *3* sabio, docto: *the Wise Men of the East*, los Magos de Oriente. *4 s.* modo, manera: *in no* ~, de ningún modo.

**wiseacre** (-eikø<sup>r</sup>) *s.* sabihondo.

**wisecrack** (-kræk) *s.* fam. chiste, bufonada.

**wish** (uiʃ) *s.* deseo, anhelo.

**wish (to)** *tr.* desear, anhelar, ansiar, querer: *to* ~ *one good morning*, dar los buenos días; *I* ~ *it were true!*, ¡ojalá fuera verdad! *2* intr. *to* ~ *for* o *after*, anhelar, desear.

**wishbone** (-boun) *s.* espoleta [de ave].

**wshful** (ui·ʃhful) *adj.* deseoso, anheloso, ansioso.

**wishy-washy** (ui·ʃhi-ua·ʃhi) *adj.* ñoño, insípido. *2* flojo, aguado [líquido].

**wisp** (uisp) *s.* mechón, manojito, trocito, jirón, pizca.

**wisteria** (uisti·ria) *s.* BOT. ṭ ɪcina.

**wistful** (uis·tful) *adj.* anhelante, ansioso. *2* pensativo, tristón.

**wit** (uit) *s.* agudeza, ingenio, sal, chispa. *2* ingenio [pers. ingeniosa], chistoso; conceptista. *3* talento, imaginación, inventiva: *to be at one's wits' end*, no saber qué hacer. *4* buen sentido. *5 pl.* juicio, razón, equilibrio mental: *to loose one's wits*, perder el juicio. *6* ingenio, habilidad, industria.

**wit (to)** *tr.* ant. saber. | Ús. sólo en *to* ~, a saber, es decir.

**witch** (uitch) *s.* bruja, hechicera. *2* bruja [mujer fea y vieja].

**witch (to)** hechizar.

**witchcraft** (-kræft); **witchery** (-øri) *s.* brujería, hechicería, encantamiento. *2* encanto, fascinación.

**witching** (-ing) *adj.* encantador. *2* brujesco.

**with** (uið) *prep.* con; contra; para con; a, de, en, entre, etc., expresando relaciones varias: ~ *me*,

conmigo; ~ *all speed,* a toda prisa; *charged* ~,
acusado de; *filled* ~, lleno de; *to abound* ~,
abundar en; *it was customary* ~ *the Greeks,* era
costumbre entre los griegos; *away* ~ *you!,* ¡fuera
de ahí!, ¡anda!

**whital** (uiđơ·l) *adv.* ant. además, también, al
mismo tiempo; con todo. *2 prep.* ant. con.

**withdraw (to)** (uiđdrơ·) *tr.* retirar. *2* apartar, separar, quitar, sacar. *3* descorrer [una cortina].
*4* distraer [de una ocupación]. *5 to* ~ *a statement,* retractarse. *6 intr.* retirarse.

**withdrawal** (-al) *s.* retiro, retirada. *2* recogida. *3*
retractación.

**withe** (uai·đ) *s.* mimbre, junco, vencejo.

**wither (to)** (ui·đơ ͬ) *tr.* marchitar, secar, poner
mustio, ajar. *2* debilitar, enflaquecer. *3* avergonzar. *4* marchitarse, secarse, ajarse. *5* debilitarse.

**withered** (-d) *adj.* marchito, mustio, seco.

**withers** (ui·đơ ͬš) *s. pl.* cruz [de un cuadrúpedo].

**withhold (to)** (ui·djould) *tr.* detener, contener; impedir. *2* suspender [un pago]. *3* negar, rehusar.
¶ Pret. y p. p.: *withheld.*

**within** (ui·đin) *prep.* dentro de, dentro de los límites de, en. *2* a, o a menos de [cierta distancia]. *3*
al alcance de: ~ *hearing,* al alcance del oído. *4
adv.* dentro, adentro, en o al interior. *5* por dentro. *6* en la casa, en la habitación.

**without** (-out) *prep.* sin. *2* falto de. *3* fuera de. *4
adv.* fuera, en el exterior, afuera. *5* por fuera,
exteriormente. *6 conj.* fam. si no, a menos que.

**withstand (to)** (ui·zstænd) *tr.* resistir, aguantar,
oponerse a, hacer resistencia a.

**withy** (ui·đ i) *s.* WHITE.

**witless** (ui·tlis) *adj.* necio, tonto, mentecato.

**witness** (-nis) *s.* testigo [pers.]. *2* testimonio, atestación, prueba: *to call to* ~, tomar por testigo;
*in* ~ *whereof,* en fe de lo cual.

**witness (to)** *tr.* dar testimonio de, atestiguar, dar
fe de. *2* presenciar, ver. *3* mostrar, demostrar. *4
intr.* dar testimonio, declarar.

**witted** (ui·tid) *adj.* ingenioso, inteligente.

**witticism** (ui·tisiŝm) *s.* agudeza, rasgo de ingenio,
chiste, ocurrencia.

**wittiness** (-inis) *s.* ingenio, agudeza, gracia.

**witty** (-i) *adj.* ingenioso, agudo, chistoso, ocurrente.

**wivern** (uai·vơ ͬn) *s.* BLAS. dragón alado.

**wives** (uai·vs) *s. pl.* de WIFE.

**wizard** (ui·šơ ͬd) *s.* brujo, hechicero.

**wizardry** (-ri) *s.* hechicería, magia.

**wizen (to)** (ui·šơn) *tr.* marchitar, secar, arrugar. *2
intr.* marchitarse, secarse, arrugarse, acarto-
narrse.

**wizened** (-d) *adj.* seco, marchito; arrugado, acartonado.

**woad** (uoud) *s.* BOT. y TINT. glasto, pastel.

**wobble** (ua·bơl) *s.* tambaleo, vacilación.

**wobble (to)** *intr.* balancearse, tambalear, vacilar.
*2* cambiar, ser inconstante.

**wobbly** (ua·bli) *adj.* tambaleante, vacilante.

**woe** (uou) *s.* pena, aflicción, calamidad, infortunio. *2 interj.* ¡ay!: ~ *is me!,* ¡ay de mí!

**wo(e)begone** (-bigon) *adj.* miserable, triste, abatido.

**wo(e)ful** (-ful) *adj.* triste, afligido. *2* desdichado. *3*
lastimero, doloroso. *4* ruin, pobre.

**wold** (uould) *s.* llanura; campiña ondulada.

**wolf** (wulf), *pl.* **wolves** (-š) *s.* ZOOL. lobo: ~ *cub,*
lobezno; *to keep the* ~ *from the door,* ponerse a
cubierto de la miseria.

**wolf (to)** *tr.* fam. engullir.

**wolfhound** (-jaund) *s.* mastín, perro lobero.

**wolfish** (-ish) *adj.* lobuno. *2* feroz, voraz.

**wolfram** (wu·lfram) *s.* QUÍM., MINER. volframio.

**wolfsbane** (wu·lfsbein) *s.* BOT. acónito.

**wolf's-milk** *s.* BOT. lechetrezna.

**wolverene, -rine** (wulvơri·n) *s.* ZOOL. carcayú.

**woman** (wu·mæn), *pl.* **women** (ui·min) *s.* mujer: ~
*writer,* escritora. *2* criada. *3 adj.* femenino, de
mujer.

**womanhood** (-jud) *s.* condición de mujer. *2* feminidad. *3* el sexo femenino.

**womanish** (-ish) *adj.* femenil, mujeril. *2* afeminado.

**womankind** (-kaind) *s.* las mujeres, el sexo femenino. *2* las mujeres de una familia o grupo.

**womanlike** (-laik) *adj.* WOMANLY.

**womanly** (-li) *adj.* femenino, femenil, mujeril. *2*
propio de la mujer adulta. *3 adv.* como mujer.

**womb** (wu·m) *s.* útero, matriz. *2* seno, entrañas.

**won** (uơn) *pret.* y *p. p.* de TO WIN.

**wonder** (uơ·ndơ ͬ) *s.* admiración, asombro, sorpresa: *no* ~, no es de extrañar. *2* incertidumbre,
perplejidad. *3* portento, prodigio, maravilla: *to
do wonders,* hacer maravillas.

**wonder (to)** *tr.* desear saber, preguntarse: *I* ~ *if it
will rain,* me pregunto si va a llover. | A veces no
se traduce y su sentido se expresa en forma de
pregunta: *I* ~ *what he wants,* ¿qué querrá? *2
intr.* sentir duda y curiosidad. *3* extrañarse, sorprenderse, maravillarse.

**wonderful** (-ful) *adj.* admirable, maravilloso,
asombroso, portentoso, prodigioso.

**wondering** (-ing) *adj.* asombrado, maravillado.

**wonderland** (uơ·ndơ ͬlænd) *s.* país de las maravillas; reino de las hadas.

**wonderment** (-mơnt) *s.* admiración, asombro. *2*
milagro, maravilla.

**wondrous** (uơ·ndrơs) *adj.* sorprendente, asombroso, maravilloso, portentoso.

**wont** (uơnt) *adj.* acostumbrado, sólito *to be* ~, soler, acostumbrar. *2 s.* costumbre, hábito.

**wont (to)** *intr.* acostumbrar, soler. ¶ Pret.: *wont;* p.
p.: *wont* o *wonted.*

**won't** *contr.* de WILL NOT.

**wonted** (-id) *adj.* acostumbrado, usual.

**woo (to)** (wu) *tr.* cortejar, pretender [a una mujer].
*2* buscar, perseguir [tratar de obtener]. *3 intr.*
cortejar.

**wood** (wud) *s.* bosque, selva, monte: *he cannot see
the* ~ *for the trees,* los árboles no le dejan ver el
bosque. *2* madera, palo, leña: *small* ~, chasca,
leña menuda. *3 adj.* de los bosques: ~ *louse,* cochinilla de humedad; ~ *pigeon,* paloma torcaz;
~ *sorrel,* acederilla. *4* de madera, en madera,
etc.: ~ *carver,* tallista; ~ *carving,* talla de la madera; ~ *engraving,* grabado en madera.

**wood (to)** *tr.* cubrir de bosque. *2* proveer de leña.

**woodbine** (-bain) *s.* BOT. madreselva.

**woodchuck** (-chơk) *s.* ZOOL. marmota de Norteamérica.

**woodcock** (-kak) *s.* ORN. chocha, becada.

**woodcraft** (-kræft) *s.* conocimiento y práctica de
todo lo referente a los bosques y a la vida en
ellos. *2* arte de trabajar la madera.

**woodcut** (-kơt) *s.* grabado en madera.

**woodcutter** (-kơtơ ͬ) *s.* leñador. *2* grabador en madera.

**wooded** (-id) *adj.* arbolado, cubierto de bosques.

**wooden** (-ơn) *adj.* de madera, de palo. *2* vago, sin

expresión [mirada, etc.]. *3* embotado, torpe; tosco, sin gracia.

**wooden-headed** *adj.* torpe, estúpido.

**woodland** (-lænd) *s.* monte, bosque, selva.

**wodlander** (-lændø<sup>r</sup>) *s.* habitante del bosque.

**woodless** (-lis) *adj.* sin árboles, sin bosques.

**woodman** (-mæn) *s.* leñador. *2* (Ingl.) guardabosque. *3* habitante del bosque.

**woodpecker** (-pekø<sup>r</sup>) *s.* ORN. pico, picamaderos, pájaro carpintero.

**woodpile** (-pail) *s.* pila de leña, leñera.

**woodruff** (-drøf) *s.* BOT. asperilla.

**woodshed** (-shed) *s.* leñera.

**woodsman** (-smæn) *s.* habitante del bosque; cazador, trampero, etc.

**wood-wind** *s.* MÚS. madera [instrumentos de viento].

**woodwork** (-uø<sup>r</sup>k) *s.* maderaje. *2* obra de carpintería.

**woody** (-i) *adj.* arbolado, selvoso. *2* leñoso.

**wooer** (wu·ø<sup>r</sup>) *s.* cortejador, pretendiente.

**woof** (wuf) *s.* TEJ. trama. *2* tejido, textura.

**wooing** (wu·ing) *s.* cortejo, galanteo.

**wool** (wul) *s.* lana: ~ *bearing,* lanar; *all* ~, pura lana; *to pull the* ~ *over one's eyes,* engañar. *2* cabello crespo.

**wooled** (-d) *adj.* lanudo.

**woolen** (-øn) *adj.* de lana; lanero. *2 s.* paño o tejido de lana. *3 pl.* géneros de lana.

**woolgatherer** (-gæðørø<sup>r</sup>) *s.* distraído; visionario.

**woolgathering** (-gæðoring) *s.* ensimismamiento.

**woollen** (-øn) *adj.-s.* WOOLEN.

**woolly** (-i) *adj.* de lana. *2* lanudo, lanoso. *3* coposo. *4* crespo, cabello. *5* confuso. *6 s.* prenda de lana.

**woolsack** (-sæk) *s.* saco de lana. *2* (Ingl.) asiento del Lord Canciller en la Cámara de los lores.

**word** (uø<sup>r</sup>d) *s.* palabra, vocablo, voz, término; cosa dicha: *the last* ~, la última palabra; *to have a* ~ *with,* hablar un poco con; *in a* ~, en una palabra; *in other words,* en otros términos; *in so many words,* literalmente; sin ambages. *2* palabra [expresión oral o escrita]: *in* ~, de palabra; *by* ~ *of mouth,* oralmente, verbalmente. *3* dicho, sentencia, adagio. *4* palabra [promesa, seguridad]: *to keep one's word,* cumplir su palabra; *to take one at his* ~, coger la palabra a uno; *on* o *upon my* ~, palabra de honor; a fe mía. *5* aviso, mensaje, noticia: *to leave* ~, dejar dicho, decar recado. *6* contraseña, santo y seña. *7* orden, voz de mando. *8 the Word,* el Verbo. *9 pl.* letra [de una canción]. *10* palabras, disputa: *to have words,* disputar.

**word (to)** *tr.* expresar [con palabras]; formular, redactar.

**wordiness** (-inis) *s.* verbosidad, palabrería.

**wording** (-ing) *s.* redacción, estilo, fraseología.

**wordy** (-i) *adj.* verbal. *2* verboso.

**wore** (uø<sup>r</sup>) *pret.* de TO WEAR.

**work** (uø<sup>r</sup>k) *s.* trabajo, labor, obra, tarea, faena; ocupación, empleo; operación, funcionamiento: *piece of* ~, trabajo, obra; *at* ~, trabajando; en operación; *out of* ~, sin trabajo. *2* obra [literaria, artística, etc.]. *3* COST. labor, bordado. *4* FORT. obra, trabajo. *5* obra, acto, acción. *6 pl.* fábrica, taller. *7* obras [públicas o de ingeniería]. *8* maquinaria [de un artefacto].

**work (to)** *intr.* trabajar; laborar: *to* ~ *at,* trabajar en. *2* obrar, surtir efecto, dar resultado. *3* funcionar, marchar. *4* moverse, avanzar, salir, entrar, etc. [gradualmente, con esfuerzo o por el uso, el movimiento, etc.]: *to* ~ *loose* o *free,* sol-

tarse, aflojarse. *5* moverse nerviosamente, agitarse. *6 to* ~ *out,* salir, resultar [bien o mal]; resolverse; DEP. entrenarse.

*7 tr.* trabajar, labrar, manufacturar. *8* formar, crear, fabricar, preparar, producir, causar, obrar, hacer. *9* explotar [una mina, etc.]. *10* hacer trabajar. *11* manejar, hacer funcionar. *12* obrar sobre, influir. *13* excitar, ir poniendo en cierto estado. *14* bordar. *15* resolver un problema. *16 to* ~ *in,* hacer entrar; intercalar. *17 to* ~ *off,* eliminar gradualmente; deshacerse de. *18 to* ~ *out,* hacer, realizar; borrar, expropiar; agotar [una mina]. *19 to* ~ *up,* excitar, inflamar; elaborar [un plan, etc.]; lograr, adquirir [con esfuerzo].

**workable** (-abøl) *adj.* explotable, laborable. *2* factible, viable.

**workaday** (-adei) *adj.* de diario. *2* prosaico.

**workbag** (-bæg) *s.* saco de labor.

**workbasket** (-bæskit) *s.* neceser, costurero.

**workday** (-dei) *s.* día laborable. *2* jornada [de trabajo]. *3 adj.* WORKADAY.

**worker** (-ø<sup>r</sup>) *s.* obrero, operario. *2* ENT. obrera.

**workhouse** (-jaus) *s.* (Ingl.) hospicio. *2* (E.U.) casa de corrección, taller penitenciario.

**working** (-ing) *adj.* de trabajo, trabajador, que trabaja: ~ *class,* clase obrera; ~ *day,* día laborable; jornada [de trabajo]. *2* activo, laborioso. *3* que se mueve o contrae nerviosamente [rostro, facciones]. *4* suficiente, eficaz. *5* MEC. motor. *6* MEC. de régimen. *7* que sirve de guía o modelo: ~ *drawing,* plano; ARQ. montea. *8* COM. ~ *capital,* capital circulante.

**workman** (-mæn) *s.* obrero, trabajador, oficial. *2* artesano. *3* artífice.

**workmanlike** (-laik), **workmanly** (-li) *adj.* primoroso, bien hecho, bien acabado.

**workmanship** (-ship) *s.* hechura, ejecución, obra. *2* arte o habilidad en el trabajo.

**workout** (uø·<sup>r</sup>kaut) *s.* prueba, ensayo. *2* DEP. ejercicio de entrenamiento.

**workroom** (-rum), **workshop** (-shap) *s.* taller, obrador.

**workwoman** (-wumæn) *s.* obrera, trabajadora.

**world** (uø<sup>r</sup>ld) *s.* mundo. | No tiene el sentido de baúl, mundo: *the* ~ *beyond,* el otro mundo; *for all the* ~, por nada del mundo; bajo todos los conceptos; ~ *without end,* por los siglos de los siglos. *2 adj.* mundano; mundial: ~ *map,* mapa mundi.

**worldling** (-ling) *s.* persona mundana.

**worldly** (-li) *adj.* mundano, mundanal. *2* terrenal. *3* seglar, secular.

**worldly-minded** *adj.* mundano, apegado a las cosas del mundo.

**worldly-wise** *adj.* que tiene mucho mundo.

**world-wide** *adj.* mundial, universal.

**worm** (uø<sup>r</sup>m) *s.* gusano, lombriz: fig. *the* ~ *of conscience,* el gusano de la conciencia. *2* oruga. *3* polilla, carcoma, coco. *4* rosca de barrena o de tornillo. *5* MEC. tornillo sin fin: ~ *gear,* engranaje de tornillo sin fin.

**worm (to)** *intr.-ref.* introducirse, insinuarse, deslizarse. *2 tr.* limpiar de cocos o lombrices. *3 to* ~ *one's way,* serpentear, arrastrarse. *4 to* ~ *out,* arrancar mañosamente, sonsacar.

**worm-eaten** *adj.* agusanado. *2* carcomido, apolillado.

**wormhole** (-joul) *s.* picadura de gusano, carcoma, etc.

**wormseed** (-sid) *s.* BOT. santónico.

**wormwood** (-wud) *s*. BOT. ajenjo.

**wormy** (-i) *adj*. agusanado, gusaniento. *2* bajo, rastrero.

**worn** (uɔ<sup>r</sup>n) *p. p.* de TO WEAR. *2 adj*. ~ out, usado, raído, gastado. *3* cansado, agotado.

**worried** (uɵ·rid) *adj*. angustiado, preocupado, inquieto.

**worrier** (uɵ·riɵ<sup>r</sup>) *s*. pesimista; aprensivo.

**worry** (uɵ·ri) *s*. cuidado, ansiedad, preocupación; molestia, tormento. *2* mordedura, desgarro.

**worry (to)** *tr*. inquietar, preocupar, apurar. *2* molestar, acosar. *3* morder, desgarrar, asir con los dientes y sacudir. *4* ajar, arrugar. *5 to* ~ *out*, hallar solución a. *6 intr*. inquietarse, preocuparse, apurarse.

**worse** (uɵ<sup>r</sup>s) *adj. y adv. compar*. peor: *to get* ~, empeorarse; ~ *and* ~, cada vez peor; *from bad to* ~, de mal en peor. *2 s*. lo peor; la peor parte: *to change for the* ~, empeorar; *to put to the* ~, derrotar.

**worsen** (-ɵn) *tr*. empeorar. *2 intr*. empeorarse.

**worship** (uɵ·<sup>r</sup>ship) *s*. culto, adoración. *2* veneración. *3 Your Worship*, su señoría, usía.

**worship (to)** *tr*. rendir culto a, adorar. *2* venerar. *3* idolatrar [querer mucho]. *4 intr*. hacer actos de culto. ¶ Pret. y p. p.: *worship(p)ed*; ger.: *-p(p)ing*.

**worshipful** (-ful) *adj*. adorable. *2* venerable, respetable, honorable. | Ús. como tratamiento. *3* adorador.

**worship (p) er** (-ɵ<sup>r</sup>) *s*. adorador. *2* fiel [que asiste a un acto religioso].

**worst** (uɵ<sup>r</sup>st) *adj. superl*. peor [en sentido absoluto]: *the* ~, el peor. *2 adv. superl*. peor, pésimamente, de la peor manera posible. *3 s*. lo peor: *the* ~ *(of it) is*, lo malo es, lo peor es; *at (the)* ~, en el peor estado; en el peor de los casos; *if the* ~ *comes to (the)* ~, si sucede lo peor.

**worst (to)** *tr*. vencer, derrotar, triunfar de.

**worsted** (wu·<sup>r</sup>stid) *s*. TEJ. estambre, lana peinada.

**worth** (uɵ·<sup>r</sup>z) *s*. valor, valía, precio: *twopence* ~ *of*, dos peniques de. *2* valor, valía, mérito. *3* utilidad, importancia. *4* riqueza, caudal. *5 adj*. que vale o posee: *to be* ~, valer; poseer [por valor de cierta cantidad]; *to be* ~ *while*, valer la pena. *6* digno, merecedor de; *to be* ~ *seeing*, ser digno de verse.

**worthily** (uɵ·<sup>r</sup>dili) *adv*. merecidamente.

**worthiness** (uɵ·<sup>r</sup>dinis) *s*. valía, mérito, dignidad.

**worthless** (uɵ<sup>r</sup>zlis) *adj*. sin valor, inútil, despreciable. *2* indigno.

**worthy** (uɵ·<sup>r</sup>di) *adj*. estimable, excelente, digno. *2* digno, merecedor, acreedor. *3 s*. persona ilustre, notable, personaje.

**would** (wud) *pret. y subj.* de TO WILL.

**would-be** *adj*. supuesto, seudo, presumido de. *2* aspirante, que quisiera ser.

**wouldn't** (wu·dɵnt) *contr*. de WOULD NOT.

**1) wound** (uaund) *pret. y p. p.* de TO WIND.

**2) wound** (wund) *s*. herida, llaga, lesión. *2* daño, ofensa.

**wound (to)** *tr*. herir, lastimar. *2* ofender, dañar.

**wounded** (-id) *adj*. herido, lastimado. *2 s*. herido; heridos.

**wove** (uouv) *pret. y p. p.* de TO WEAVE.

**woven** (uou·vɵn) *p. p.* de TO WEAVE.

**wrack** (ræk) *s*. naufragio, ruina: *to go to* ~, arruinarse. *2* WRECKAGE 2. *3* alga que se recoge en la playa.

**wrack (to)** *tr*. hacer naufragar. *2* arruinar, perder.

**wraith** (reiz) *s*. espectro, aparecido.

**wrangle** (ræ·ŋgɵl) *s*. disputa, altercado, discusión.

**wrangle (to)** *intr*. disputar, altercar. *2 tr.-intr*. debatir, discutir.

**wrangler** (ræ·ŋglɵ<sup>r</sup>) *s*. pendenciero, quimerista. *2* discutidor.

**wrangling** (-iŋ) *s*. disputa. *2* discusión.

**wrap** (ræp) *s*. envoltura. *2* abrigo, manta, capa, chal.

**wrap (to)** *tr.-intr*. cubrir (se, envolver (se, arropar (se; ocultar. | A veces con *up*. *2* enrollar (se, enroscar (se [alrededor de algo]. ¶ Pret. y p. p.: *wrapped*; ger.: *-pping*.

**wrapper** (-ɵ<sup>r</sup>) *s*. envolvedor. *2* cubierta, envoltura. *3* sobrecubierta [de libro]. *4* faja [de periódico]. *5* capa [de cigarro]. *6* bata, peinador.

**wrapping** (-iŋ) *s*. cubierta, envoltura.

**wrasse** (ræs) *s*. ICT. labro.

**wrath** (raez) *s*. cólera, ira, rabia, furor.

**wrathful** (-ful) *adj*. colérico, airado, furioso.

**wreak** (rik) *s*. venganza, cólera. *2* castigo.

**wreak (to)** *tr*. infligir. *2* descargar [un golpe, etc.]; desahogar [la cólera, etc.]; satisfacer. *3* tomar [venganza]. *4* aplicar, dedicar.

**wreath** (riz) *s*. corona, guirnalda. *2* anillo, espiral [de humo, etc.].

**wreathe (to)** (rið) *tr*. entrelazar. *2* tejer [coronas o guirnaldas]. *3* enguirnaldar. *4* ceñir, rodear. *5 wreathed in smiles*, sonriente [rostro]. *6 intr*. entrelazarse; enroscarse. *7* formar anillos o espirales [el humo].

**wreck** (rek) *s*. naufragio; choque, descarrilamiento; ruina, destrucción, destrozo: *to go to* ~, naufragar, arruinarse. *2* restos de un naufragio. *3* ruina, cosa arruinada.

**wreck (to)** *tr*. hacer naufragar. *2* destruir, arruinar; hacer fracasar. *3* hacer chocar o descarrilar [un tren]. *4 intr*. naufragar. *5* arruinarse; fracasar. *6* raquear.

**wreckage** (-idɏ) *s*. naufragio, ruina. *2* pecio. *3* ruinas, escombros.

**wrecker** (-ɵ<sup>r</sup>) *s*. el que hace naufragar; arruinador. *2* raquero. *3* salvador de buques. *4* WRECKING CAR.

**wrecking car** (-iŋ) *s*. AUTO. camión de auxilio.

**wren** (ren) *s*. ORN. reyezuelo. *2* mujer perteneciente al servicio auxiliar femenino de la Armada.

**wrench** (rench) *s*. tirón o torcedura violenta. *2* torcedura, esguince. *3* MEC. llave, desvolvedor.

**wrench (to)** *tr*. tirar de [torciendo]; arrancar, arrebatar. *2* torcer, dislocar. *3* torcer [el sentido de una frase].

**wrest** (rest) *s*. WRENCH 1. *2* MÚS. llave, templador.

**wrest (to)** *tr*. torcer violentamente. *2* arrancar; arrebatar. *3* torcer, pervertir, tergiversar.

**wrestle (to)** (re·sɵl) *intr*. luchar a brazo partido. *2* luchar, contender. *3* esforzarse. *4* disputar.

**wrestling** (re·sliŋ) *s*. lucha. *2* DEP. lucha grecorromana.

**wretch** (rech) *s*. miserable, desdichado. *2* miserable, canalla.

**wretched** (-id) *adj*. infeliz, desdichado. *2* miserable. *3* calamitoso. *4* vil. *5* malo, ruin.

**wriggle** (ri·gɵl) *tr*. retorcer, menear. *2 intr*. retorcerse. *3* serpentear, culebrear; *to* ~ *into*, insinuarse en; *to* ~ *out of*, escaparse, deslizarse, escurrirse.

**wriggling** (-iŋ) *s*. retorcimiento; culebreo, serpenteo.

**wright** (rait) *s*. artífice, artesano.

**wring (to)** (riŋ) *tr*. torcer, retorcer: *to* ~ *the neck of*, torcer el pescuezo a. *2* estrujar, exprimir, escurrir. *3* arrancar. *4* oprimir, punzar, atormentar. *5* torcer, tergiversar. ¶ Pret. y p. p.: *wrung*.

**wrinkle** (ri·nkøl) *s.* arruga, surco.

**wrinkly** (ri·nkli) *adj.* arrugado, lleno de arrugas.

**wrist** (rist) *s.* ANAT. muñeca: ~ *watch*, reloj de pulsera. *2* puño [de una prenda].

**wristlet** (-lit) *s.* mitón. *2* pulsera de reloj.

**writ** (rit) *s.* escrito, escritura: *The Holy Writ*, la Sagrada Escritura. *2* DER. auto, mandamiento.

**write (to)** (rait) *tr.-intr.* escribir: *to* ~ *down*, anotar, poner por escrito; *to* ~ *off*, escribir de corrido; cancelar [en una cuenta]; *to* ~ *out*, redactar; escribir sin abreviar; *to* ~ *up*, describir extensamente por escrito; poner al día; dar bombo a. *2* decretar, ordenar. ¶ Pret.: *wrote;* p. p.: *written*.

**writer** (-ø<sup>r</sup>) *s.* escritor, autor. *2* escribiente.

**write-up** *s.* relato; crónica. *2* bombo [elogio].

**writhe (to)** (raið) *tr.* torcer, retorcer [el cuerpo, etc.]. *2 intr.* serpentear. *3* contorcerse, retorcerse [esp. de dolor o angustia]; sufrir.

**writing** (rai·ting) *s.* escritura, letra: *in one's own* ~, de su puño y letra. *2* acción de escribir. *3* escrito. *4 adj.* de escribir: ~ *desk*, escritorio, pupitre; ~ *materials,* ~ *set,* recado de escribir.

**written** (ri·tøn) *p. p.* de TO WRITE.

**wrong** (rong) *adj.* malo, pecaminoso, injusto, que no está bien. *2* erróneo, equivocado, defectuoso; inconveniente, inoportuno; que no es el que corresponde, el que se busca, el que debería ser, etc.: *to take the* ~ *train,* equivocarse de tren; *in* *the* ~ *place,* mal colocado, fuera de lugar. *3 the* ~ *side,* el revés [de una tela]. *4 to be* ~, no tener razón, estar equivocado; ser un error. *5 to be* ~ *with,* pasarle algo a. *6 adv.* mal, al revés, equivocadamente: *to go* ~, descaminarse; resultar mal. *7 s.* agravio, injusticia, daño, perjuicio. *8* mal, pecado, mala acción. *9* culpa. *10* error, falta de razón: *to be in the* ~, no tener razón; tener culpa.

**wrong (to)** *tr.* agraviar, ofender, perjudicar, hacer mal a, ser injusto con. *2* calumniar.

**wrongdoer** (-duø<sup>r</sup>) *s.* el que obra mal.

**wrongful** (-ful) *adj.* injusto, inicuo. *2* perjudicial. *3* ilegítimo, ilegal.

**wrongheaded** (-jedid) *adj.* terco, obstinado.

**wrongly** (-li) *adv.* injustamente. *2* mal. *3* equivocadamente.

**wrote** (rout) *pret.* de TO WRITE.

**wroth** (roz) *adj.* enojado, furioso, exasperado.

**wrought** (rot) *pret.* y *p. p. irreg.* de TO WORK. *2 adj.* trabajado, labrado, forjado, manufacturado: ~ *iron,* hierro forjado.

**wrung** (røng) *pret.* y *p. p.* de TO WRING.

**wry** (rai) *adj.* torcido, ladeado: ~ *face,* gesto, mueca. *2* de desagrado, de disgusto. *3* deformado, tergiversado.

**wryly** (-li) *adv.* torcidamente.

**wryneck** (-nek) *s.* MED. tortícolis. *2* ORN. torcecuello.

**wye** (uai) *s.* i griega. *2* cosa en forma de Y

**X, x** (eks) *s.* X, x vigésimo cuarta letra del alfabeto inglés.
**xanthein(e** (šæ·nziin) *s.* QUÍM. xanteína, janteína.
**xanthic** (šæ·nzik) *adj.* QUÍM. xántico, jántico.
**Xanthipe** (šænzi·pi) *n. pr.* Jantipa. 2 *s.* fig. esposa regañona.
**Xanthophyl(l** (šæ·nzofil) *s.* QUÍM. xantofila, jantofila.
**Xavier** (šæ·viøʳ) *n. pr.* Javier.
**xebec** (ši·bek) *s.* MAR. jebeque.
**xenon** (ši·nan) *s.* QUÍM. xeno, xenón.
**xenophobia** (šenofou·biɑ) *s.* xenofobia.
**Xenophon** (še·nøføn) *n. pr.* Jenofonte.

**xerophil(e** (ši·rofil) *adj.* BOT. xerófilo.
**xerophthalmia** (širafzæ·lmia), **xerophthalmy** (širafzæ·lmi) *s.* MED. xeroftalmía.
**xerophyte** (ši·rofait) *s.* BOT. planta xerófila.
**xiphoid** (ši·foid) *adj.* ANAT. xifoideo. 2 *adj.-s.* ANAT. xifoides.
**Xmas** (kri·smas) *s.* abrev. de CHRISTMAS.
**X-ray** *adj.* radiográfico.
**X rays** (i·ks-reiš) *s. pl.* rayos X.
**xylem** (šai·lem) *s.* BOT. leño [parte del tallo].
**xylograph** (šai·løgræf) *s.* grabado en madera.
**xylography** (šaila·grafi) *s.* xilografía.
**xylophagous** (šaila·fagøs) *adj.* xilófago.
**Xylophone** (šai·lofoun) *s.* xilófono, xilórgano.

# Y

**Y, y** (uai) *s.* Y, y, vigésimo quinta letra del alfabeto inglés.

**yacht** (yat) *s.* MAR. yate.

**yacht (to)** *intr.* manejar un yate o navegar en él.

**yacht(s)man** (ya·t(s)mæn) *s.* dueño de un yate. *2* marinero especializado en tripular yates.

**yagua** (ya·gua) *s.* BOT. yagua.

**yak** (yak) *s.* ZOOL. yak [buey del Asia].

**yam** (yæm) *s.* BOT. ñame.

**yank** (yænk) *s.* fam. (E.U.) tirón, sacudida.

**yank (to)** *tr.* fam. (E.U.) dar un tirón; sacar de un tirón.

**Yankee** (yæ·nki) *adj.-s.* yanqui.

**Yankeedom** (-døm) *s.* Yanquilandia. *2* los yanquis.

**yap** (yæp) *s.* ladrido corto, gañido. *2* fig. parloteo.

**yap (to)** *intr.* ladrar con ladrido corto. *2* fig. parlotear.

**yard** (yaʳd) *s.* yarda [medida ingl. de longitud = 0'914 m.]. *2* MAR. verga. *3* patio, corral, cercado, terreno.

**yard (to)** *tr.* acorralar [encerrar en corral]. *2* almacenar, guardar, reunir [en patio o depósito].

**yardarm** (ya·ʳdaʳm) *s.* MAR. penol.

**yardstick** (ya·ʳdstik) *s.* vara de medir [de una yarda].

**yarn** (yaʳn) *s.* hebra, hilo, hilado, hilaza. *2* narración extraordinaria; cuento o historia increíble: *to spin a* ~, contar un cuento.

**yarrow** (yæ·rou) *s.* BOT. milenrama.

**yataghan** (yæ·tagæn) *s.* yatagán.

**yaw** (yo·) *s.* MAR. guiñada. *2* AVIA. desviación.

**yaw(to)** *intr.* MAR. guiñar. *2* AVIA. desviarse.

**yawl** (yol) *s.* MAR. yola; bote.

**yawn** (yon) *s.* bostezo. *2* abertura, boquete.

**yawn (to)** *intr.* bostezarr. *2* abrir la boca [con avidez]. *3* abrirse, formar una abertura.

**yawning** (-ing) *adj.* bostezante. *2* abierto.

**ye** (yɪ) *pron. pers.* plural de THOU.

**yea** (yei) *adv.* sí, ciertamente; y es más. *2 s.* sí [consentimiento].

**yean (to)** (yɪn) *intr.* parir [la cabra o la oveja].

**yeanling** (-ling) *s.* cabritillo, corderillo.

**year** (yi·øʳ) *s.* año: *once a* ~, una vez al año; ~ *in,* ~ *out,* año tras año. *2 pl.* años, edad: *to grow in years,* envejecer.

**yearbook** (-buk) *s.* anuario.

**yearling** (-ling) *adj.* primal, añal, añojo. *2 s.* niño, planta, etc., de un año.

**yearly** (-li) *adj.* anual. *2 adv.* anualmente.

**yearn** (yøʳn) *intr.* anhelar:*to* ~ *for* o *after,* anhelar, suspirar por. *2* sentir ternura o compasión.

**yearning** (-ing) *s.* anhelo, deseo ardiente. *2* ternura.

**yeast** (yɪst) *s.* levadura.

**yeasty** (-i) *adj.* de levadura. *2* espumoso. *3* ligero, frívolo.

**Yeddo** (ye·dou) *n. pr.* GEOGR. Yedo.

**yell** (yel) *s.* grito, alarido, aullido.

**yell (to)** *intr.* gritar, dar alaridos, aullar, vociferar. *2 tr.* decir a gritos.

**yellow** (ye·lou) *adj.* amarillo: ~ *bark,* ~ *chinchona,* calisaya; ~ *fever,* fiebre amarilla; ~ *spot,* ANAT. mácula lútea. *2* de raza amarilla. *3* bilioso, celoso, melancólico. *4* de cobarde o traidor; vil, ruin. *5* sensacionalista: ~ *press,* prensa sensacionalista. *6 s.* color amarillo. *7* yema [de huevo].

**yellow (to)** *tr.* poner amarillo. *2 intr.* amarillecer.

**yellowbird** (-bøʳd) *s.* ORN. jilguero americano. *2* ORN. oropéndola.

**yelloish** (-ish) *adj.* amarillento.

**yelp** (yelp) *s.* latido, gañido, ladrido.

**yelp (to)** *intr.* latir, gañir, ladrar. *2* gritar [el pavo salvaje].

**yen** (yen) *s.* yen [moneda japonesa].

**yeoman** (you·mæn) *s.* labrador acomodado. *2* hidalgo que servía en una casa real o noble. *3* ~ *of the guard,* alabardero de palacio. *4* miembro de una antigua milicia. *5* oficinista de un buque de guerra.

**yeomanry** (-ri) *s.* HIST. conjunto de los labradores acomodados. *2* ant. milicia. *3* guardia del rey.

**yes** (yes) *adv.* sí. *2 s.* sí [respuesta afirmativa].

**yesterday** (ye·støʳdei) *s.* y *adv.* ayer.

**yet** (yet) *adv.* todavía, aún: *as* ~, todavía, hasta ahora; *not* ~, todavía no, aún no. *2 conj.* aun así, no obstante, sin embargo.

**yew** (yu) *s.* BOT. tejo.

**Yiddish** (yi·dish) *s.* yiddish [dialecto judío].

**yield** (yɪld) *s.* producto, rendimiento, rédito, producción, cosecha. *2* rendición. *3* ING. acción de ceder o deformarse.

**yield (to)** *tr.* producir, rendir, dar. *2* exhalar, despedir. *3* dar de sí. *4* rendir, entregar, ceder. *5* otorgar, dar. *6 intr.* dar fruto, rendir. *7* rendirse, someterse. *8* sujetarse, conformarse. *9* ceder, deferir. *10* consentir, asentir. *11* ceder [a una fuerza o presión], doblegarse, flaquear.

**yielding** (-ing) *adj.* productivo, que rinde. *2* dúctil, complaciente, condescendiente.

**yodel** (you·døl) *s.* modo de cantar de los tiroleses.

**yodel (to)** *tr.* cantar, como los tiroleses, modulando la voz desde el tono natural al falsete y viceversa.

**yoga** (you·ga) *s.* yoga.

**yogi** (you·gi) *s.* yogi [asceta de la India].

**yoke** (youk) *s.* yugo [para uncir; para los vencidos; sujeción, esclavitud]. *2* yunta. *3* yugada. *4* yugo [de campana]. *5* MEC. horquilla. *6* culata [de imán]. *7* percha [para elevar pesos]. *8* hombrillo [de camisa].

**yoke (to)** *tr.* uncir, acoyundar. *2* acoplar, unir, casar.

**yoke-elm** *s.* BOT. carpe.

**yokel** (you·køl) *s.* rústico, patán.

**yolk** (youk) *s.* yema [de huevo]. *2* churre [de la lana].

**yon** (yan) *adj.* y *adv.* YONDER.

**yonder** (ya·ndø<sup>r</sup>) *adj.* aquel, aquella, aquellos, aquellas. *2* de más allá. *3 adv.* allí, allá; más allá.

**yore** (yo<sup>r</sup>) *s.* otro tiempo: *of* ~, en otro tiempo, antaño.

**you** (yu) *pron.* de *2.ª pers. sing.* y *pl.* tú, usted, vosotros, ustedes. *2* te, a ti; le, a usted; os, a vosotros; les, a ustedes. *3 for* ~, para ti, usted, vosotros o ustedes.

**young** (yøng) *adj.* joven: *a* ~ *lady*, una señorita; *a* ~ *man*, un joven. *2* mozo, juvenil. *3* nuevo, tierno, verde; reciente; que empieza. *4 s. the* ~,

los jóvenes. *5* hijuelos, cría [de los animales]. *6 with* ~, encinta; preñada.

**younger** (-ø<sup>r</sup>) *adj. comp.* de YOUNG: más joven, menor. *2 Pliny the* ~, Plinio el joven.

**youngest** (-ist) *adj. superl.* de YOUNG: el más joven, el menor.

**youngling** (-ling) *s.* pequeñuelo. *2* jovencito.

**youngster** (-stø<sup>r</sup>) *s.* muchacho joven, niño.

**your** (yu<sup>r</sup>) *adj. pos.* tu, tus, vuestro, vuestra, vuestros, vuestras; su, de usted, de ustedes.

**yours** (yu<sup>r</sup>š) *pron. pos.* (el) tuyo o vuestro, (la) tuya o vuestra, (los) tuyos o vuestros, (las) tuyas o vuestras; (el) suyo, (la) suya, (los) suyos, (las) suyas [de usted o ustedes]: *you and* ~, usted y los suyos; *a friend of* ~, un amigo suyo, o vuestro. *2* la suya [su carta de usted]; ~ *faithfully*, ~ *sincerely*, ~ *(very) truly*, su afectísimo, su atento, s. s., etc. [en las cartas].

**yourself** (yu<sup>r</sup>se·lf) *pron. pers.* tú, ti, usted, tú mismo, usted mismo; te, se [reflexivos].

**yourselves** (you<sup>r</sup>se·lvš) *pron.* pl. de YOURSELF.

**youth** (yuz) *s.* juventud, mocedad, adolescencia. *2* primer período de existencia. *3* joven, mozalbete. *4 sing.* y *pl.* la juventud, los jóvenes.

**youthful** (-ful) *adj.* joven. *2* mozo, juvenil. *3* fresco, vigoroso.

**you've** (yuv) *contr.* de YOU HAVE.

**yowl** (yaul) *s.* aullido, alarido.

**yowl (to)** *intr.* aullar, gritar.

**ytterbium** (itø·<sup>r</sup>biøm) *s.* QUÍM. iterbio.

**yttrium** (i·triøm) *s.* QUÍM. itrio.

**yucca** (yø·ka) *s.* BOT. yuca.

**Yugoslav** (yu·gouslav) *adj.-s.* yugoeslavo.

**Yugoslavia** (yu·gousla·via) *n. pr.* Yugoeslavia.

**yule** (yul) *s.* Navidad; Pascua de Navidad: ~ *log*, nochebueno [leño].

**yuletide** (-taid) *s.* Pascua de Navidad, Navidades.

# Z

**Z, z** (ši·) *s.* Z, z, vigésimo sexta y última letra del alfabeto inglés.
**Zaccheus** (šæki·øs) *n. pr.* Zaqueo.
**zany** (še·ni) *s.* bufón, truhán. 2 simplón.
**Zanzíbar** (šænši·ba$^r$) *n. pr.* GEOGR. Zanzíbar.
**zeal** (ši·l) *s.* celo, ardor, fervor, entusiasmo.
**Zealand** (ši·land) *n. pr.* GEOGR. Zelandia.
**zealot** (še·løt) *s.* partidario acérrimo; fanático.
**zealotry** (-ri) *s.* fanatismo.
**zealous** (še·løs) *adj.* celoso, entusiasta.
**Zebedee** (še·bidı) *n. pr.* Zebedeo.
**zebra** (ší·bra) *s.* ZOOL. cebra.
**Zebu** (ší·biu) *n. pr.* GEOGR. Cebú.
**zebu** *s.* ZOOL. cebú.
**Zechariah** (šekarai·a) *n. pr.* Zacarías.
**zed** (šed) *s.* (Ingl.) zeda, zeta, ceda [letra Z].
**Zend-Avesta** (šend-*avesta*) *s.* zendavesta.
**zenith** (ší·niz) *s.* cenit. 2 culminación, apogeo.
**zenithal** (ši·nizal) *adj.* cenital.
**zephyr** (še·fø$^r$) *s.* céfiro [viento; tela].
**Zeppelin** (še·pælin) *s.* zepelín.
**zero** (ší·rou) *s.* cero.
**zest** (šest) *s.* luquete [de limón o naranja]. 2 sabor, sainete. 3 deleite, gusto, entusiasmo.
**zeta** (ší·ta) *s.* zeta [letra griega].
**zeugma** (šiu·gma) *s.* RET. zeugma.
**Zeus** (šius) *n. pr.* Zeus, Júpiter.
**zigzag** (ši·gšæg) *s.* zigzag. 2 *adj.* en zigzag.
**zigzag (to)** *intr.* zigzaguear.
**zinc** (šink) *s.* QUÍM. cinc, zinc.
**zincite** (ši·nksait) *s.* MINER. cincita.
**zincograph** (-øgraf) *s.* cincograbado.
**zincography** (šinka·grafi) *s.* cincografía.
**zingaro** (ši·ngarou) *s.* cíngaro.
**Zion** (šai·øn) *n. pr.* Sion.
**Zionism** (šai·ønišm) *s.* sionismo.
**zip** (šip) *s.* silbido, zumbido [de una bala]. 2 fam. energía, vigor.
**zip (to)** *intr.* silbar o zumbar [como una bala].

**zipper** (ši·p$^r$) *s.* cierre relámpago, cremallera.
**zircon** (šø·$^r$kan) *s.* MINER. circón.
**zirconium** (šø$^r$kou·niøm) *s.* QUÍM. circonio.
**zither(n** (ši·zø$^r$(n) *s.* MÚS. cítara.
**zoanthropy** (šouæ·nzroupi) *s.* zoantropía.
**zodiac** (šou·diæk) *s.* ASTR. zodíaco. 2 circuito.
**zoetrope** (šoui·troup) *s.* zootropo.
**zonal** (šou·nal) *adj.* zonal.
**zone** (šoun) *s.* zona. | No tiene el sentido de erupción.
**zoned** (-d) *adj.* dividido en zonas. 2 marcado con fajas.
**zoo** (šu) *s.* parque zoológico; colección zoológica.
**zoogeography** (šouodÿia·grafi) *s.* zoogeografía.
**zoography** (šoua·grafi) *s.* zoografía.
**zooid** (šou·oid) *adj.-s.* zooide.
**zoolatry** (šoua·latri) *s.* zoolatría.
**zoolite** (šou·olait) *s.* GEOL. zoolito.
**zoological** (šouola·dÿkal) *adj.* zoológico.
**zoology** (šoua·lodÿi) *s.* zoología.
**zoom (to)** (šum) *intr.* AVIA. elevarse rápidamente.
**zoophagous** (šoua·fagøs) *adj.* zoófago.
**Zoophyta** (šou·ofita) *s. pl.* ZOOL. zoófitos.
**zoophyte** (-ofait) *s.* zoófito.
**zoospore** (-ospo$^r$) *s.* zoospora.
**zootechny** (-otecni) *s.* zootecnia.
**Zoroaster** (šouroæ·stø$^r$) *n. pr.* Zoroastro.
**Zoroastrian** (šouroæ·strian) *adj.* zoroástrico.
**zoster** (šo·stø$^r$) *s.* MED. zoster, zona.
**Zouave** (šua·v) *s.* zuavo.
**Zulu** (šu·lu) *adj.-s.* zulú.
**Zululand** (-lænd) *n. pr.* Zululandia.
**Zwinglian** (šui·nglian) *adj.-s.* zuingliano.
**zygomatic** (šaigømæ·tik) *adj.* ANAT. cigomático.
**zygomorphic** (šaigømo·$^r$fik), **zygomorphous** (-føs) *adj.* cigomorfo.
**zygospore** (šai·gøspø$^r$) *s.* zigospora.
**zygote** (šai·gout) *s.* BIOL. cigoto, zigoto.
**zymogen** (šai·modÿøn) *s.* BIOQUÍM. cimógeno.

# IDIOMS AND EXPRESSIONS / MODISMOS Y EXPRESIONES

## A

**A boca llena**
Openly, plainly

**A bordo**
On board

**A buena hora**
On time

**A buen santo te encomiendas**
To bark up the wrong tree

**A buen seguro**
Certainly, very probably

**A cada momento**
Continually, frequently

**A cada paso**
At every turn (or step)

**A cada rato**
Each time, all the time

**A cambio de**
In exchange for

**A campo raso**
In the open

**A campo traviesa**
Cross-country

**A casa**
Home

**A causa de**
On account of

**A ciegas**
Blindly

**A (or de) ciencia cierta**
With certainty

**A contrapelo**
Against the grain

**¿A cuánto(s) estamos?**
What is the date?

**A deshora(s)**
At all hours, unexpectedly; at an untimely moment

**A despecho de**
In spite of, despite

**A duras penas**
With great difficulty, hardly, scarcely

**A escape**
Rapidly, at full speed

**A escondidas**
On the sly, undercover

**A escondidas de**
Without the knowledge of

**A eso de**
At about

**A espaldas de**
Behind one's back

**A estas alturas**
At this point or juncture

**A falta de**
For want of, lacking

**A fin de cuentas**
After all, in the final analysis

**A fin de que**
In order that, so that

**A fines de**
Late, towards the end of a period (week, etc.)

**A flor de**
Flush with

**A fondo**
Fully, thoroughly

**A fuerza de**
By force of, by dint of

**A gatas**
On all fours, crawling

**A guisa de**
Like, in the manner of

**A hurto**
On the sly, stealthily

**A instancias de**
At the request of

**A la antigüita**
Old-fashioned

**A la buena (mala)**
Willingly (unwillingly)

**A la buena de Dios**
Without malice, without plan, at random

**A la carrera**
In haste, on the run

**A la fuerza**
By force

**A la larga**
In the long run

**A la moda**
Up to date, in the latest fashion

**A la noche**
Tonight, at night

**A la postre**
At last, when all is said and done

**A la redonda (or en redondo)**
All around, round about

**A la sazón**
Then, at that time

**A la ventura**
Aimlessly, haphazardly, at random

**A la verdad**
In truth, in earnest, truly

**A la vez**
Together, at the same time

**A la vista de**
In plain view of

**A la voluntad**
At will, as you like

**A la vuelta de**
Around the corner, on returning

**A la vuelta de la esquina**
Around the corner

**A la vuelta de los años**
Within a few years

**A lado de**
Beside

**A las claras**
Clearly, openly, frankly, publicly

**A las mil maravillas**
Beautifully, wonderfully well

**A lo largo (de)**
Along, alongside of, lengthwise, at full length

**A lo lejos**
In the distance

**A lo más**
At most, at worst

**A lo mejor**
Perhaps, maybe

**A lo sumo**
At most

**A los cuatro vientos**
In all directions

**A los pocos meses**
After a few months

**A (la) manera de**
Like, in the style of

**A mano**
By hand, at hand, handmade

**A mar de**
A lot of, lots of

**A más no poder**
To the utmost, full blast

**A más tardar**
At the very latest

**A más ver (or hasta más ver)**
Goodbye

**A mediados de**
About the middle of the (day, week, etc.), during the (week, etc.)

**A medida que**
As, in proportion to

**A medio camino**
Halfway (to a place)

**A medio hacer**
Incomplete, half-done

**A menos que**
Unless

**A menudo**
Often

**A merced de**
At the mercy (or expense) of

**A mi entender**
In my opinion, as I understand it

**A mi modo de ver**
In my opinion

**¡A mí qué!**
What's that to me? So what!

**A montones**
In abundance, heaps

**A ninguna parte**
Nowhere

**A no ser que**
Unless

**A ojo**
By sight, by guess

**A ojos cerrados**
Blindly

**A ojos vistas**
Visibly, clearly; before one's eyes

**A oscuras (or a obscuras)**
In the dark

**A partir de**
As of, beginning on

**A partir de hoy**
From today on

**A pedir de boca**
Exactly as desired, to one's heart's content

**A pesar de (todo)**
In spite of (everything)

**A pesar de que**
In spite of the fact that

**A pie**
On foot, by foot

**A piedra y lodo**
Shut tight

**A pie(s) juntillas**
With both feet together; believe strongly

**A poco**
Shortly after

**A pocos pasos**
At a short distance

**A porfía**
In competition

**A primera luz**
At dawn

**A principios de**
Towards, early in, about the first of (day, week, etc.)

**A propósito**
By the way, apropos; on purpose

**A prueba de**
—proof, safe against

**A puerta cerrada**
Secretly, behind closed doors

**A punto fijo**
With certainty

**A pura fuerza**
By sheer force

**A puros gritos**
By just shouting

**A que**
I bet…(not a real wager)

**¡A que no!**
I bet you don't!

**¿A qué viene eso?**
What is the point of that?

**A quema ropa (or a quemarropa)**
Very close, point blank, without warning

**A raíz de**
Soon after, close to

**A ras de (or al ras con)**
Flush (or even) with

**A ratos**
From time to time, at times

**A ratos perdidos**
In (at) odd or spare moments

**A rienda suelta**
Free rein, violently, swiftly

**A saber**
Namely, that is

**A sabiendas**
Knowingly, consciously

**A salvo**
Safe, unharmed

**A sangre fría**
In cold blood

**A secas**
Plain, alone, simply, to the point

**A semejanza de**
Like, as

**A su (debido) tiempo**
In due course or time

**A tiempo**
On time, in time

**A tientas**
Blindly

**A toda costa**
By all means, at whatever cost

**A toda hora**
At any time, at all times

**A toda prisa**
At greatest speed

**A toda vela**
Under full sail, at full speed

**A todas luces**
By all means, any way you look at it

**A todo correr**
At full speed

**A todo trance**
At all costs

**A todo trapo**
Under full sail, speedily

**A traición**
Deceitfully, treacherously

**A través de, al través de**
Across, through

**A última hora**
At the last moment

**A una brazada**
At arm's length

**A una voz**
Unanimously

**A un tiempo**
At one (the same) time

**A veces**
At times

**A ver (si)**
Let's see (if)

**A vista de**
Within view, in the presence of

**A vistas**
On approval

**A voluntad**
At will

**A vuelo de pájaro**
As the crow flies

**Abrir paso**
To make way, to clear the way

**Acabar de**
To have just (done something)

**Acabar por**
To end up by (doing something)

**Acerca de**
About, with regard to

**Acordar con**
To be on good terms with

**Acostarse con las gallinas**
To go to bed early

**¿Adónde va?**
Where are you going?

**Adondequiera que**
Wherever

**Agachar las orejas**
To hang one's head

**Aguantar el chubasco**
To weather the storm

**Águila o pico**
Heads or tails

**Águila o sello**
Heads or tails

**Aguzar las orejas (los oídos)**
To prick up one's ears

**¡Ahí está el detalle!**
That's the point!

**Ahogarse en poca agua**
To worry about nothing

**Ahora bien**
Now then, well now, however

**Ahora es cuando**
Now is the time; now is your chance

**Ahora mismo**
Right now, at once

**Al aire libre**
In the open air, outdoors

**Al azar**
By chance, at random

**Al cabo (de)**
Finally or after

**Al caer de la noche**
At nightfall

**Al centavo**
Just right, to the letter

**Al contado**
Cash

**Al contrario**
On the contrary

**Al cuidado de**
In care of

**Al derecho**
Right side out

**Al (or en) derredor**
Around

**Al descubierto**
Openly

**Al día**
Per day

**Al día siguiente**
On the following day

**Al filo de (las cinco)**
At about (5 o'clock)

**Al fin**
At the end, at last

**Al fin de cuentas**
In any case

**Al fin y al cabo**
In short, at last, anyway

**Al frente de**
In front of

**Al habla**
Within speaking distance;
speaking! (in answering a
telephone)

**Al igual**
Equally

**Al instante**
At once

**Al lado (de)**
At one's side, near at hand,
next to

**Al menos (or a lo menos)**
At least, at the least

**Al menudeo (or al por menor)**
At retail, in small quantities

**Al mismo tiempo**
At the same time

**Al oído**
Confidentially

**Al otro día**
On the following day

**Al otro lado de**
On the other side of

**Al pan, pan y al vino, vino**
Call a spade a spade

**Al parecer**
Apparently

**Al pelo**
Perfectly, agreed, just right

**Al pie de la letra**
Literally, to the letter

**Al (or a) poco rato**
In a short while, soon after

**Al presente**
Now, at present

**Al principio**
At first

**Al punto**
At once

**Al raso**
In the open air

**Al (or en) rededor**
Around, about

**Al remo**
At hard labor

**Al revés**
Backwards, wrong side out, in
the opposite way

**Al sereno**
In the night air

**Al sesgo**
On the bias, diagonally,
obliquely

**Al soslayo**
On the bias, slanting, obliquely

**Al tanteo**
Hit or miss, by guess

**Al través de**
Through, throughout

**Al trote**
Quickly

**Algo por el estilo**
Similar, something of the sort

**Algo sordo**
Hard of hearing

**Algo tarde**
Rather late

**Algún otro**
Somebody else, some other

**Alrededor de**
Around about, more or less

**Alzar el codo**
To drink too much

**Allá a las quinientas**
Once in a blue moon

**¡Allí está el toque!**
There is the heart of the matter!

**Amante de**
Fond of

**Amigo de**
Fond of (friend of)

**Amor propio**
Self-esteem, pride, vanity

**Andar a gatas**
To creep, crawl

**Andar agitado**
To be out of sorts

**Andar bien**
To keep good time (e.g., a
watch), to work well, to be right

**Andar (or ir) de parranda (or de
fiesta en fiesta)**
To go on a spree

**Andarse con rodeos**
To beat around the bush

**Andarse el tiempo**
Meantime, as time goes on

**Andarse por las ramas**
To beat around the bush

**Ante todo**
Especially, first of all, above all

**Antes de que**
Before

**Antes hoy que mañana**
The sooner the better

**Antes que**
Rather than

**Año antepasado**
Year before last

**Año entrante**
Next year

**Año bisiesto**
Leap year

**Aparte de eso**
Besides that, aside from that

**Aprender de memoria**
To learn by heart

**Aprendiz de todo y oficial
de nada**
Jack of all trades

**Aprovechar la ocasión**
To take advantage of the
situation

**Aquí cerca**
Around (near) here

**Aquí mismo**
Right here

**Arranque de cólera**
Fit of anger

**Así así**
So-so

**Así como**
Just as, the same as, as well as

**Así de largo**
That long

**Así es que**
So that, as soon as

**Así está bien**
This will do (be OK)

**Así nada más**
Just plain, just as is

**Así pues**
So then, therefore

**Así que**
So that, as soon as, so,
therefore

**¡Así se hace!**
Well done!, Bully for you!

**Así y todo**
In spite of that, even so,
anyhow

**Atrás de**
Behind, in back of

**Aun así**
Even so

**Aun cuando**
Even if, even though

**Aún no**
Not yet

**Ayer mismo**
Just yesterday

**Ayer por la tarde**
Yesterday afternoon

**Azotar el aire**
To work in vain

## B

**Bailar a secas**
To dance without music

**Baja el radio**
Turn down the radio

**Bajo techo**
Indoors

**Barrios bajos**
Slums

**Beber a pulso**
To gulp down

**Bien arreglado**
Neatly dressed

**Bien asado**
Well-done (well-cooked)

**Bien cocido**
Well-done (well-cooked)

**Bien me lo merezco**
It serves me right

**Bien parecido**
Good-looking

**Bien peinado**
Well-groomed, trim

**Bien que**
Although

**Boca abajo**
Face down, prone

**Boca arriba**
Face up, supine

**Bromas aparte**
All joking aside

**Buen mozo**
Handsome man

**¡Buen provecho!**
Good appetite! Enjoy your meal!

**Buen rato**
Pleasant (or long) time

**Buen tipo**
Good fellow

**Burlarse de**
To make fun of

**Buscarle tres (cuatro) pies al gato**
To look for trouble

**Buscar una aguja en un pajar**
To look for a needle in a haystack

## C

**Cada cual (or cada uno)**
Each one

**¿Cada cuánto tiempo?**
How often?

**Cada dos días**
Every other day

**Cada uno**
Apiece

**Cada vez menos**
Less and less

**Caer bien**
To fit well, to be becoming, to please

**Caer enfermo**
To fall ill

**Caer en gracia**
To please

**Caer en la cuenta**
To realize, to get the point

**Caer mal**
To fit badly, displease

**Caliente de cascos**
Hot-headed

**¡Cállate la trompa!**
Shut up!

**Calle abajo**
Down the street

**Calle arriba**
Up the street

**Callejón sin salida**
Blind alley, dead end

**Cambiar de tema**
To change the subject

**Caminar con pies de plomo**
To go cautiously

**Camino de**
On the way to, on the road to

**Camino trillado**
Beaten path

**Cara a cara**
Face to face

**Cara o cruz**
Heads or tails

**Cargar con**
To carry away, assume responsibility

**Cargar con el muerto**
To get the blame unjustly

**Carne de gallina**
Goosebumps

**Casarse con**
To marry (someone)

**Casi nunca**
Hardly ever

**Castañetear con los dedos**
To snap one's fingers

**Cerca de**
Near to, close to

**Cerrarse el cielo**
To become overcast, cloudy

**Cifrar la esperanza en**
To place one's hope in

**Claro que no**
Of course not, certainly not

**Claro que sí**
Of course, naturally

**Colmo de la locura**
Height of folly

**Como a costumbre**
At about

**Como de costumbre**
As usual

**Como dijo el otro**
As someone said, as the saying goes

**Como Dios manda**
According to Hoyle (the rules)

**Como en**
In about

**Como mínimo**
At least

**Como no**
Unless

**¡Cómo no!**
Of course, why not!

**Como por ensalmo**
As if by magic, in a jiffy

**Como que**
Since, inasmuch as

**Como quiera que**
Since, inasmuch as

**Como quiera que sea**
At any rate

**Como si**
As if

**Como si fuera**
As if it were

**Como siempre**
As usual, like always

**Como sigue**
As follows

**Como último recurso**
As a last resort

**Como una seda**
As smooth as silk, soft as silk

**Como visita de obispo**
Once in a blue moon

**Con anticipación**
In advance

**Con delirio**
Madly

**Con el propósito de**
With the aim of

**Con (or en or por) extremo**
Very much, extremely

**Con fuerzas para...(la tarea)**
Equal to...(the task)

**Con la lengua de corbata (or con la lengua de pechera)**
Out of breath, with tongue hanging out

**Con motivo de**
With the idea of, because of, on the occasion of, on account of

**¿Con qué cara?**
How can I (one) have the nerve?

**¡Con razón!**
No wonder!

**Con respecto a**
With regard to

**Con rumbo a**
In the direction of

**Con tal (de) que**
Provided that, so that

**Con tiempo**
In advance, in good time

**Con todo (or con todos) los obstáculos**
In spite of that

**Conciliar el sueño**
To get to sleep

**Confiar en**
To trust, rely on

**Conforme a**
In accordance with

**Conocer de vista**
To know by sight

**Consigo mismo**
To oneself

**Conspirar contra una persona**
To frame someone

**Consultar con la almohada**
To sleep on it

**Contar con**
To reckon with, rely on, count on

**Contra viento y marea**
Against all odds, come hell or high water, come what may

**Convenirle a uno**
To be to one's advantage

**Correr por cuenta de uno**
To be one's own affair, to be up to oneself

**Correr riesgo**
To take a chance, to risk

**Corrida del tiempo**
Swiftness of time

**Cortar el hilo**
To break the thread of a story, to interrupt

**Corto de oído**
Hard of hearing

**Corto de vista**
Nearsighted

**Cosa de**
Approximately, about

**Costar trabajo**
To be very difficult

**Costar un ojo de la cara**
To cost an arm and a leg, be very expensive

**Cruzarse con**
To meet

**Cualquier cosa**
Anything at all

**Cualquiera (or cualesquiera) de los dos**
Either of the two

**Cuando más tarde**
At the latest

**Cuando menos**
At least

**Cuando quiera**
Whenever

**Cuanto antes**
As soon as possible

**Cuatro letras**
A few lines

**Cuatro palabras**
A few words

**Cuento alegre**
Spicy story

**Cuento chino**
Cock and bull story

**Cueste lo que cueste**
At any cost

**Cumplir años**
To have a birthday

**Cumplir su palabra**
To keep one's word

## CH

**Chueco o derecho**
Hit or miss, happy-go-lucky

## D

**Dado caso**
Supposing

**Dado el caso que**
Provided that

**Dar a**
To face, look towards, give to

**Dar a conocer**
To make known

**Dar a entender**
To pretend

**Dar alas a**
To embolden, give courage

**Dar aliento**
To encourage

**Dar al traste con**
To ruin, destroy

**Dar al través con**
To ruin, destroy

**Dar ánimo**
To cheer up

**Dar atención**
To pay attention

**Dar batería**
To raise a rumpus, to work hard

**Dar calabazas**
To reject, to jilt

**Dar caza**
To pursue, track down

**Dar cima**
To complete, carry out

**Dar coba**
To flatter, play up to, softsoap

**Dar cuenta de**
To give a report on

**Dar de comer**
To feed, be fed

**Dar disgustos a**
To cause distress or grief to

**Dar el pésame por**
To extend condolences to or for

**Dar el visto bueno**
To approve, OK

**Dar en**
To hit or to hit upon

**Dar en cara**
To reproach, blame

**Dar en el clavo**
To hit the nail on the head

**Dar en (or dar con) el chiste**
To guess right, hit the nail on the head

**Dar en tierra con alguien**
To overthrow someone

**Dar esquinazo**
To "ditch," avoid meeting someone

**Dar fe de**
To vouch for

**Dar fin (a)**
To complete

**Dar gato por liebre**
To cheat or swindle

**Dar grasa**
To polish (shoes)

**Dar guerra**
To make trouble

**Dar la hora**
To strike the hour

**Dar la lata**
To annoy

**Dar la mano**
To help, shake hands

**Dar la noticia**
To break the news

**Dar la razón**
To agree, to be of same opinion

**Dar la razón a una persona**
To admit a person is right

**Dar (or darse) la vuelta**
To turn (to turn around)

**Dar largas**
To postpone or delay, or give someone the run around

**Dar las espaldas a**
To turn one's back on

**Dar las gracias**
To give thanks, to thank

**Dar lástima (de)**
To arouse pity or sorrow

**Dar lo mismo**
To make no difference

**Dar los recuerdos**
To give regards

**Dar lugar a**
To give cause for

**Dar lustre**
To polish

**Dar marcha atrás**
To back up

**Dar mucha pena**
To cause sorrow, to be disconcerting

**Dar parte**
To inform

**Dar pie**
To give opportunity (or occasion to)

**Dar por**
To consider as

**Dar por descontado**
To take for granted

**Dar por hecho**
To take for granted, to consider as done

**Dar por sabido**
To take for granted

**Dar por sentado**
To take for granted

**Dar por supuesto**
To take for granted

**Dar prestado**
To lend

**Dar propina**
To tip (give a gratuity)

**Dar que hacer**
To cause extra work

**Dar rabia**
To anger

**Dar razón**
To inform, give account

**Dar realce**
To enhance, emphasize

**Dar sepultura**
To bury

**Dar un paseo**
To take a walk or ride

**Dar un paseo en barco**
To go for a sail

**Dar un paso**
To take a step

**Dar un pisotón**
To step hard upon

**Dar un portazo**
To slam the door

**Dar un salto (or dar saltos)**
To leap, jump

**Dar un traspié**
To trip, stumble

**Dar un vistazo a**
To glance over, peruse

**Dar una cita**
To make an appointment

**Dar una fiesta**
To give (throw) a party

**Dar una pasada por**
To pass by, walk by

**Dar una pisada**
To step (stomp) on (upon)

**Dar una satisfacción**
To apologize

**Dar una vuelta**
To take a stroll

**Dar uno en la tecla**
To hit the nail on the head, find the right way to do something

**Darle a uno mala espina**
To arouse one's suspicion

**Darle lo mismo**
It makes no difference

**Darse aires a**
To put on airs

**Darse cuenta de (que)**
To realize (that), to notice

**Darse de baja**
To drop out

**Darse farol**
To show off, put on airs

**Darse la mano**
To shake hands

**Darse por vencido (or me doy)**
To give up (or I give up)

**Darse prisa**
To hurry

**Darse tono**
To put on airs

**Darse un tropezón**
To trip, stumble

**Darse un encontrón**
To collide with, bump into each other

**Darse un resbalón**
To slip

**Dárselas de**
To pose as

**De acuerdo con**
In accordance with

**De ahí en adelante**
From then on

**De ahí que**
Hence

**De ahora en adelante**
From now on, in the future

**De algún modo**
Somehow

**De algún tiempo para acá**
For some time now

**De alguna manera**
Somehow

**De arriba abajo**
From top to bottom

**De aquel tiempo en adelante**
From that time on

**De aquí en adelante**
From now on

**De aquí para allá**
To and fro, back and forth

**De broma**
Jokingly, in jest

**De buen tomo y lomo**
Bulky, important

**De buen tono**
In good taste, stylish

**De buen ver**
Good-looking

**De buena cepa**
Of good stock or quality

**De buena fe**
In good faith

**De buena gana (or de buen grado)**
Willingly, gladly

**De buena ley**
Of good quality

**De buenas a primeras**
All of a sudden, unexpectedly, on the spur of the moment

**De burla**
In jest

**De cabo a rabo**
From beginning to end

**De camino (or de camino real)**
On the way

**De canto**
On edge

**De copete**
High rank, important, proud

**De corrida**
Without stopping

**De cualquier modo**
At any rate

**De cuando en cuando**
Sometimes, occasionally

**De día**
By day, before dark

**De dientes afuera**
Insincerely

**¡De dónde!**
Nonsense!

**De dos caras**
Two-faced

**De dos en dos**
By twos, two by two

**De dos sentidos**
Two-way

**De ese modo (or de esa manera)**
In that way

**De espaldas**
On one's back, supine

**De este modo (or de esta manera)**
In this way

**De etiqueta**
Formal

**De golpe**
Suddenly

**De gorra**
At another's expense

**De grado en grado**
By degrees

**De hecho**
In fact

**De hilo**
Without stopping

**De hoy en adelante**
From now on

**De hoy en ocho días**
One week from today

**De hoy en quince días**
Two weeks from today

**De improviso**
Unexpectedly

**De lado**
Tilted, oblique, sideways

**De la noche a la mañana**
Overnight

**De lejos**
From a distance

**De lo contrario**
If not, otherwise

**De lo lindo**
Wonderfully, very much, to the
utmost

**De mal en peor**
From bad to worse

**De mal grado**
Reluctantly, unwillingly

**De mal gusto**
In poor taste

**De mal temple**
In a bad humor

**De mala fe**
In bad faith, deceitfully

**De mala gana**
Unwillingly

**De mala suerte**
Unlucky

**De manera que**
So that

**De marca**
Of excellent quality

**De memoria**
By heart

**De moda**
In vogue, stylish

**De modo que**
So what?, so that, and so

**De momento**
For the time being

**De nada**
Don't mention it; you're
welcome

**De ningún modo**
By no means

**¡De ninguna manera!**
By no means!, I should say not!

**De noche**
By (at) night

**De nuevo**
Again, once again

**De ocasión**
Reduced price, a bargain

**De (or al) oído**
By ear

**De oídos**
Rumor, hearsay

**De ordinario**
Ordinary, usual

**De otro modo**
Otherwise

**De palabra**
By word of mouth

**De par en par**
Wide open

**De parte a parte**
Through, from one side to
the other

**De parte de**
On behalf of, in favor of

**De paso**
In passing, at the same time, by
the way, in transit

**De pie**
Standing

**De pilón**
To boot, besides, in addition

**De poca monta**
Of little value or importance

**De poquito**
In small amounts

**De por sí**
Separately, by itself

**De prisa**
Quickly

**De pronto**
At once, suddenly

**De propósito**
On purpose

**De punta**
On end

**De puntillas (or de puntas)**
On tiptoes

**De punto**
By the minute

**De pura casualidad**
By pure chance

**De rebote**
On the rebound, indirectly

**De relieve**
In relief, outstanding,
prominent

**De remate**
Absolutely, without remedy

**De repente**
Suddenly, all of a sudden

**De repuesto**
Spare, extra

**De resultas**
As a result, consequently

**De rigor**
A "must," it must

**De rodillas**
On one's knees

**De seguida**
Continuously, without
interruption

**De segunda mano**
Secondhand

**De seguro**
For certain, for sure

**De sobra**
More than enough,
unnecessary

**De sol a sol**
Sunrise to sunset

**De soslayo**
Slanting, sideways

**De subida**
On the way up

**De súbito**
Suddenly

**De suerte que**
So that, and so, in such a way

**De su (propia) cosecha**
Of one's own making or
invention

**De suyo**
Naturally, by nature

**De tarde en tarde**
From time to time, now and
then, once in a blue moon

**De tejas abajo**
Here below, in this world

**De todas maneras**
Anyway, at any rate

**De todos modos**
At any rate, in any case,
anyhow, by all means

**De tránsito**
In transit, on the way, passing
through

**De través**
Across

**De un golpe**
All at once

**De un modo u otro**
Somehow, in some way or other

**De un momento a otro**
At any moment

**De un salto**
Quickly

**De un solo sentido**
One way (e.g., one-way street)

**De un tirón**
All at once

**De una pieza**
Solid, of one piece

**De una tirada**
All at once, in one fell swoop

**De una vez**
At once, at one time, at one
stroke, once and for all

**De una vez por todas**
Once and for all

**De uno en uno**
One at a time

**De unos**
Of about

**De uso**
Secondhand

**De veras (¿De veras?)**
Really, in truth, in earnest
(really?, is that so?)

**De verdad (¿De verdad?)**
Truly, truthfully (really?, is
that so?)

**De vez en cuando**
Now and then, occasionally

**De vicio**
As a (bad) habit

**De viva voz**
By word of mouth

**De (buena) voluntad**
Willingly, with pleasure

**De vuelta**
Again

**Debajo de**
Under, beneath

**Debe de ser**
It must be, it probably is

**Decir para sí**
To say to one's self

**Decir para su coleto (or capote)**
To say to one's self

**Dejar a uno plantado**
To "stand someone up," leave
someone in the lurch

**Dejar caer**
To drop

**Dejar de**
To stop

**Dejar de asistir**
To drop out

**Dejar de la mano**
To leave, abandon

**Dejar dicho**
To leave word

**Dejar en las astas del toro**
To leave in the lurch

**Dejar en paz**
To let be, to leave alone

**Dejar saber**
To let on, pretend

**Dejar tranquilo**
To leave alone

**Dejarse de cuentos**
Come to the point, stop beating
around the bush

**Dejarse de rodeos**
Stop the excuses, stop beating
around the bush

**Del mismo modo**
Of the same sort, in the
same way

**Del próximo pasado**
Of last month

**Del todo**
Wholly, at all

**Delante de**
In front of

**Dentro de**
Inside of, within

**Dentro de poco**
In a little while

**Dentro de un momento**
In a short time

**Dentro de una semana**
Within a week

**Desayunarse con la noticia**
To hear a piece of news early or
for the first time

**Descabezar el sueño**
To take a nap

**Desde ahora**
From now on

**Desde el principio**
All along, from the beginning

**Desde entonces**
Since then, ever since

**Desde hace**
Dating from, over a period of...

**Desde lejos**
From a distance, from afar

**Desde luego**
Actually, of course, at once

**Desde que**
Since

**Desde un principio**
From the beginning

**Desempeñar un papel**
To play a part

**Despedirse de**
To say goodbye to

**Después de eso**
Thereafter

**Después de todo**
After all

**Detrás de**
Behind, in back of

**Devanarse los sesos**
To rack one's brain

**Día de raya**
Payday

**Día de semana (or día de
trabajo)**
Weekday

**Día hábil**
Weekday, workday

**Día tras día**
Day after day

**Días de antaño**
Days of old

**Días de semana**
Weekdays

**Dicho y hecho**
Sure enough, no sooner said
than done

**Dificultar el paso**
To obstruct, impede

**Digno de**
Well worth it

**Digno de confianza**
Reliable, trustworthy

**Dinero contante y sonante**
Ready (or hard) cash

**Dinero menudo**
Change (re money)

**Doblar a la esquina**
To turn the corner

**Dolerle a uno la garganta**
To have a sore throat

**Dolor de cabeza**
Headache

**Donde no**
Otherwise, if not

**Dondequiera que (or por
dondequiera que)**
Wherever

**Dormir a pierna suelta**
To sleep soundly

**Dormir la mona**
To sleep it off

**Dormir la siesta**
To take an afternoon nap

**E**

**Echar a correr (or echarse a
correr)**
To begin running (to run away)

**Echar(se) a perder**
To spoil, to ruin

**Echar a pique**
To sink

**Echar al olvido**
To forget on purpose

**Echar de menos**
To miss

**Echar de ver**
To notice, to observe

**Echar en cara**
To reproach, blame

**Echar espumarajos**
To froth at the mouth, to be
very angry

**Echar flores**
To throw bouquets, to flatter,
to compliment

**Echar la casa por la ventana**
To spare no expense, squander
everything

**Echar la culpa a**
To blame

**Echar la garra**
To arrest, grab

**Echar la llave**
To lock the door

**Echar la uña**
To steal

**Echar la zarpa**
To grasp, to seize

**Echar leña al fuego**
To add fuel to the fire

**Echar mano**
To seize

**Echar pajas**
To draw lots

**Echar papas**
To fib

**Echar por tierra**
To knock down, demolish

**Echar raíces**
To take root, become firmly
fixed

**Echar suertes**
To draw lots

**Echar un piropo**
To compliment, flatter

**Echar un sueño**
To take a nap

**Echar (or soltar) un terno**
To say a bad word, to swear,
curse

**Echar un trago**
To take a drink

**Echar una cana al aire**
To go out for a good time or
fling

**Echar (una carta) al correo**
To mail (a letter)

**Echar una siesta**
To take a nap

**Echarle la bendición a una cosa**
To give something up for lost

**Echarse a**
To begin to (do something)

**Echarse al coleto**
To drink down, devour

**Echarse para atrás**
To back out, go back on one's
word

**El caso es**
The fact is

**El común de las gentes**
The majority of the people, the
average person

**El cuento del tío**
Deceitful story told to get
money

**El de**
The one with

**El día menos pensado**
When least expected,
unexpectedly

**El gusto es mío**
The pleasure is mine

**El más reciente**
The latter

**El mismísimo hombre**
The very man

**El mismo que (or lo mismo que)**
The same as

**El pro y el contra**
Pro and con

**El que**
The one who, the one which

**El sol poniente**
The setting sun

**El tren llegó con (x) minutos
de retraso**
The train was (x) minutes late

**El uno al otro**
Each other

**El uno o el otro (or uno u otro)**
Either, one or the other

**Empeñar la palabra**
To promise, pledge

**Empinar el codo**
To drink (too much)

**En abonos**
On installments

**En absoluto**
Absolutely *(not)*

**En adelante**
In the future, from now on

**En alguna otra parte**
Somewhere else

**En alguna parte**
Somewhere

**En ambos casos**
In either case

**En aquel tiempo (en aquel
entonces)**
At that time, in those days

**En balde**
In vain

**En breve**
Shortly

**En broma**
In jest, as a joke

**En buen romance**
In plain language

**En cambio**
On the other hand

**En casa**
At home, indoors

**En caso afirmativo**
If so

**En caso de**
In the event of

**En caso de que**
In case of (that)

**En concreto**
Concretely, to sum up

**En conformidad con**
In compliance with

**En conjunto**
As a whole

**En contra de**
Against, opposed to

**En cualquier caso**
Anyway

**En cuanto**
As soon as

**En cuanto a**
As for, with regard to

**En curso**
In progress

**En descubierto**
Uncovered, unpaid

**En días pasados**
In days gone by

**En efecto**
In fact, indeed, really

**En el acto**
Right away, at once

**En el extranjero**
Abroad, out of the country

**En el fondo**
At bottom, at heart, in
substance

**En el momento preciso**
In the nick of time

**En el quinto infierno (or los
quintos infiernos)**
Very far away

**En el sigilo (or silencio) de la
noche**
In the dead of the night

**En especial**
Especially, in particular

**En espera de**
Awaiting

**En fecha a próxima**
At an early date

**En fin**
In short, finally, in conclusion

**En fragante**
In the act

**En grande**
On a large scale

**En grueso**
In bulk, by wholesale

**En junto (or en conjunto)**
All together, in all

**En la actualidad**
At the present time

**En libertad**
Free

**En lo futuro**
In the future

**En lo más crudo del invierno**
In the dead of winter

**En lo sucesivo**
Hereafter, in future

**En lontananza**
In the distance, in the
background

**En lugar de**
Instead of, in place of

**En manga de camisa**
In shirtsleeves

**En marcha**
In progress

**En muchos puntos**
In many respects

**En (or a) ninguna parte**
Nowhere

**En obsequio de**
In honor of, for the sake of

**En otros términos**
In other words

**En parte**
Partly

**En particular**
Especially

**En pleno día**
In broad daylight

**En pleno rostro (or en plena cara)**
Right on the face

**En poder de**
In the hands of

**En prenda de**
As proof of, as a pledge

**En pro de**
On behalf of

**En pro y en contra**
For and against

**En punto**
On the dot, sharp

**En rama**
Crude, raw

**En realidad**
As a matter of fact

**En regla**
In order

**En resolución**
In brief

**En resumen**
Summing up, in brief

**En resumidas cuentas**
In short, after all

**En rigor**
In fact, in reality

**En rueda**
In turn, in a circle

**En salvo**
In safety, out of danger

**En sazón**
Ripe, in season

**En secreto**
Secretly

**En seguida**
At once, right now

**En señal de**
In proof of, in token of

**En serio**
Seriously

**En sueños**
In one's sleep

**En tal caso**
In such a case

**En tanto que**
While

**En todas partes**
Everywhere

**En todo caso**
In any event

**En un credo**
In a jiffy, in a minute

**En un chiflido**
In a jiffy, in a second

**En un improviso**
In a moment

**En un salto**
Quickly

**En un santiamén**
Instantly, in the twinkling of an eye

**En un soplo**
In a jiffy, in a second

**En vela**
On watch, without sleep

**En verdad**
Really, truly

**En vez de**
Instead of

**En vigor**
In force, in effect

**En vista de que**
Since, in view of

**En voz alta**
Aloud, loud voice

**En voz baja**
In a low voice, whispering

**Encargarse de**
To take charge of

**Encima de**
On, upon

**Encogerse de hombros**
To shrug one's shoulders

**Encontrarse con**
To come across, to meet

**Enfrentarse con**
To confront, meet face to face

**Enredarse con**
To have an affair with

**Entablar una conversación**
To start a conversation

**Entre azul y buenas noches**
Undecided, on the fence

**Entre bastidores**
Behind the scenes, offstage

**Entre la espada y la pared**
Between the devil and the deep blue sea

**Entre paréntesis**
By the way

**Entre semana**
During the week

**Entre tanto**
Meanwhile, all the while, at the same time

**Es cierto**
It's true

**Es decir**
That is to say, in other words

**Es (la) hora de (partir)**
It is time for, it is time to (go)

**Es lo de menos**
It makes no difference, that's the least of the trouble

**Eso corre prisa**
That is urgent

**Eso es**
That is it, that's right

**¡Eso es el colmo!**
That is the limit!

**Eso es harina de otro costal**
That's a horse of a different color

**Eso estriba en que**
The basis for it is that

**Eso no tiene quite**
That can't be helped

**Eso sí**
That was (or is) true

**Esperar en alguien**
To place hope (or confidence) in someone

**Esperar todo el santo día**
To wait the whole blessed day

**Está de más**
It is unnecessary, superfluous

**Está por hacer**
It is yet to be done

**Estamos a mano**
We are even, quits

**Estar a buen recaudo**
To be safe

**Estar a cargo de**
To be in charge of

**Estar a gusto**
To be contented or comfortable

**Estar a la altura de**
To be equal to (a task)

**Estar a la mira de**
To be alert for, on the lookout for

**Estar a punto de**
To be about to

**Estar al cabo de**
To be well-informed, up-to-date

**Estar al corriente de**
To be informed, to be up-to-date

**Estar afecto a**
To be fond of

**Estar afilando con (or afilar con)**
To flirt with

**Estar (or ponerse) ancho**
To swell with pride

**Estar arreglado**
To be in order

**Estar bien**
To be all right, OK. Ex.: Está bien. (It is) all right, (it's) OK

**Estar bien de salud**
To be in good health

**Estar bruja**
To be broke

**Estar con el agua al cuello**
To be in big trouble

**Estar de acuerdo**
To agree

**Estar de bote en bote**
To be crowded, be completely
filled up

**Estar de buen humor (or de
buen genio)**
To be in a good mood

**Estar de conformidad con**
To be in compliance with

**Estar de duelo**
To mourn, be in mourning

**Estar de luto**
To be in mourning

**Estar de malas**
To be out of luck

**Estar de mal humor (or de
mal genio)**
To be in a bad mood

**Estar (or quedar) de non**
To be left alone, without a
partner or companion

**Estar de paso**
To be passing through

**Estar de prisa**
To be in a hurry

**Estar de regreso**
To be back

**Estar de sobra**
To be in the way

**Estar de turno**
To be on duty

**Estar de vacaciones**
To be on vacation

**Estar de (or estar en) vena (para)**
To be in the mood (for)

**Estar de venta**
To be on sale

**Estar de viaje**
To be traveling, on the road

**Estar de vuelta**
To be back

**Estar desahogado**
To be well off

**Estar dispuesto**
To be willing

**Estar en buen uso**
To be in good condition (re a
thing)

**Estar en camino**
To be on the way

**Estar en curso**
To be going on, be under way

**Estar en las mismas**
To be in the same boat

**Estar en las nubes**
To daydream

**Estar en las últimas**
To be on one's last legs, to be at
the end of one's rope, out of
resources

**Estar en pañales**
To be in infancy, to possess
scant knowledge

**Estar en peligro**
To be in danger

**Estar en pugna con**
To be opposed to, to be in
conflict with, to be against

**Estar en todo**
To have a finger in everything

**Estar en un aprieto**
To be in a jam, to be in trouble

**Estar en un error**
To be wrong, to be mistaken

**Estar encargado de**
To have charge of, to be in
charge of

**Estar entre la espada y la pared**
To be between the devil and the
deep blue sea

**Estar (or andar) escaso de dinero**
To be just about out of money,
be short of money

**Estar fuera de la casa**
To be out of the house, away
from home

**Estar fuera de la ley**
To be against the law

**Estar harto de**
To be fed up with

**Estar hasta los topes**
To be filled up

**Estar hecho un costal de huesos**
To be very thin, nothing but skin
and bones

**Estar hecho una sopa**
To be sopping wet, soaked
through

**Estar mal templado**
To be in a bad humor

**Estar muy metido en**
To be deeply involved in

**Estar para**
To be about to

**Estar peor que antes**
To be worse off

**Estar por**
To be in favor of

**Estar ras con ras**
To be flush, perfectly even

**Estar regular**
To feel OK

**Estar salado**
To be unlucky; to be witty, salty

**Estar sobre sí (...sobre aviso)**
To be on the alert, cautious

**Estar torcido con**
To be on unfriendly terms with

**Estar uno en sus cabales**
To be in one's right mind

**Estar uno hasta el copete**
To be stuffed, fed up

**Estar uno hasta la coronilla**
To be fed up, satisfied

**Estarse parado**
To stand still

**Estirar la pata**
To die

**Estrechar la mano (a)**
To shake hands, grasp (or
squeeze) a hand

**Explicar una cátedra**
To teach a course

## F

**Falta de conocimientos**
Lack of instructions

**Falta de saber**
Lack of instructions

**Faltar a clase**
To cut class

**Faltar a su palabra**
To break one's word

**Faltar poco**
To be almost time

**Faltarle a uno un tornillo**
To have little sense, "to have a
screw loose"

**Fijarse en**
To notice, pay attention to

**Formar parte de**
To be a part (or member) of

**Forzar la entrada**
To break into

**Frente a**
In front of

**Fruncir el ceño**
To frown, scowl

**Fruncir el entrecejo**
To wrinkle one's brow

**Fruncir las cejas**
To frown, knit the eyebrows

**Fuera de broma**
All joking aside

**Fuera de lo corriente**
Unusual, out of the ordinary

**Fuera de propósito**
Irrelevant

**Fuera de sí**
Beside oneself

## G

**Ganar para comer**
To earn a living

**Ganar tiempo**
To save time

**Ganarse la vida**
To make one's living

**Gente de baja estofa**
Low-class people, rabble

**Guardar cama**
To stay in bed, to be confined in
bed

**Guardar rencor**
To bear or hold a grudge

**Guardar silencio**
To keep silent

**Gusano de la conciencia**
Remorse

# H

**Había una vez (or érase que se era; érase una vez; y va de cuento)**
Once upon a time

**Hablar al alma**
To speak frankly

**Hablar al caso**
To speak to the point, or in plain language

**Hablar alto (or en voz alta)**
To speak loudly

**Hablar en secreto**
To whisper

**Hablar para sus adentros**
To talk to oneself

**Hablar por los codos**
To talk too much, chatter constantly

**Hace (dos, tres, etc.) años**
(Two, three, etc.) years ago

**Hace buen (mal) tiempo**
It is good (bad) weather

**Hace caso omiso**
It (he, etc.) ignores

**Hace mucho que no (juego, etc.)**
It's been a long time since (I played, etc.)

**Hace mucho tiempo**
Long ago

**Hacer alto**
To stop

**Hacer arreglos**
To make arrangements

**Hacer buen papel**
To make a good showing

**Hacer burla de**
To make fun of

**Hacer caso a (or hacer caso de)**
To take into account, pay attention to

**Hacer caso omiso de**
To ignore

**Hacer cocos**
To make eyes at, flirt

**Hacer cola**
To form a line, wait in line

**Hacer como si**
To act as if

**Hacer cuco a**
To fool, make fun of

**Hacer de**
To act as

**Hacer de nuevo**
To do again, to do over

**Hacer deducciones precipitadas**
To jump to conclusions

**Hacer destacar**
To emphasize

**Hacer ejercicio**
To take exercise

**Hacer el favor de**
Please

**Hacer el (or hacer un) papel**
To play a role

**Hacer el ridículo**
To be ridiculous, act a fool

**Hacer escala (en)**
To stop over at

**Hacer falta**
To lack, be in need of

**Hacer favoritismos en prejuicio de**
To discriminate against

**Hacer frente (a)**
To face

**Hacer gala de**
To boast of

**Hacer garras**
To tear to pieces

**Hacer gestos**
To make faces at

**Hacer gracia**
To amuse, to make laugh

**Hacer juego**
To match

**Hacer la corte**
To court, woo

**Hacer la zanguanga**
To feign illness

**Hacer las maletas**
To pack, get ready to leave

**Hacer las paces**
To make up after a quarrel

**Hacer lo posible**
To do one's best

**Hacer mal papel**
To make a poor showing

**Hacer mala obra**
To hinder, interfere

**Hacer mella**
To make a dent or impression, to cause pain or worry

**Hacer memoria**
To remember, recollect

**Hacer muecas**
To make faces

**Hacer otra vez**
To do over

**Hacer pedazos**
To break into pieces

**Hacer pinta**
To play hooky, cut class

**Hacer por escrito**
To put in writing

**Hacer preguntas (or hacer una pregunta)**
To ask questions, to ask a question

**Hacer presa**
To seize

**Hacer puente**
To take a long weekend

**Hacer rajas**
To slice, to tear or cut into strips

**Hacer rostro**
To face

**Hacer rumbo a**
To head (or sail) towards

**Hacer sombra**
To shade, cast a shadow

**Hacer su agosto**
To make hay while the sun shines

**Hacer teatro**
To show off

**Hacer trizas**
To tear to pieces, to shred

**Hacer un pedido**
To place an order

**Hacer un trato**
To make a deal

**Hacer un viaje**
To go on a journey

**Hacer una mala jugada**
To play a mean trick

**Hacer una perrada**
To play a mean trick

**Hacer una plancha**
To make a ridiculous blunder

**Hacer una visita**
To pay a visit

**Hacer vida**
To live together

**Hacerle daño a uno**
To hurt or harm someone

**Hacerse a**
To get used to

**Hacerse a la derecha**
To pull over to the right

**Hacerse a un lado**
To step aside, move over

**Hacerse amigo**
To make friends with

**Hacerse cargo**
To take charge, to be responsible for

**Hacerse de rogar**
To be coaxed, to let oneself (or want to) be coaxed

**Hacerse duro**
To resist stubbornly

**Hacerse el desentendido**
To pretend not to notice

**Hacerse el sordo**
To pretend not to hear, turn a deaf ear

**Hacerse el tonto**
To play dumb, to act the fool

**Hacerse entender**
To make oneself understood

**Hacerse ilusiones**
To fool oneself

**Hacerse noche**
To grow late, get late in the evening

**Hacerse tarde**
To get late

**Hacerse un lío**
To get tangled up, become confused

**Hacerse uno rajas**
To wear oneself out

**Hacia adelante**
Forward

**Hacia atrás**
Backward

**Hasta aquí (or hasta ahí)**
Up to now, so far

**Hasta cierto punto**
In a way, up to a point

**¿Hasta dónde?**
How far?

**Hasta más no poder**
To the limit, utmost

**Hasta el tope**
Up to the top

**Hasta la fecha**
Up to date, up to now

**Hasta que**
Until

**Hasta que se llene**
Until full

**Hay gato encerrado**
There is more than meets the eye

**Hay moros en la costa**
Something is wrong; the coast is not clear; little pitchers have big ears

**Hay que**
One must, it is necessary to

**He aquí**
Behold, here is...

**Hecho y derecho**
Mature, full-fledged, grown up

**Hincarse de rodillas**
To kneel down

**Hoy (en) día**
Nowadays

**I**

**Ida y vuelta**
Round trip

**Idas y venidas**
Comings and goings

**Igual que**
The same as

**Impedir el paso**
To block the door, to obstruct the way

**Ímpetu de ira**
Fit of anger

**Inaplicable al caso**
Irrelevant

**Incurrir en el odio de**
To incur the hatred of

**Incurrir en un error**
To fall into (or commit) an error

**Ingresar en**
To join (a club, etc.)

**Ir a caballo**
To ride horseback

**Ir a medias (or ir a la mitad)**
To go halves (50-50)

**Ir a pie**
To walk, to go on foot

**Ir al centro**
To go downtown

**Ir al grano**
To get down to cases, come to the point

**Ir corriendo**
To be running

**Ir de compras**
To go shopping

**Ir de jarana**
To go on a spree

**Ir de pesca**
To go fishing

**Ir de vacaciones**
To go on vacation

**Ir del brazo**
To go arm in arm

**Ir entendiendo**
To begin to understand

**Ir para atrás**
To back up

**Irse (or andar) a la deriva**
To drift, be adrift

**Irse abajo**
To fall down

**J**

**Juego de palabras**
Pun, play on words

**Juego limpio**
Fair play

**Juego sucio**
Foul play

**Jugar limpio**
To play fair

**Jugarle una mala partida**
To play a bad trick on one

**Junto a**
Near to, or next to

**Junto con**
With, along with

**L**

**La comidilla de la vecindad**
The talk of the town

**La cosa no cuajó**
The thing did not jell (or work well)

**La cuestión palpitante**
The burning question

**La gota que derrama el vaso**
The last straw, the straw that broke the camel's back

**La mayoría (de)**
The majority (of), most of

**La mayor parte (de)**
The majority (of), most of

**La mera idea de**
The very thought of

**La mera verdad**
The real truth

**La rutina diaria**
The daily grind

**La verdad clara y desnuda**
The whole truth, the plain and simple truth

**Lado flaco**
Weak side

**Largas uñas**
A thief

**¡Largo de aquí!**
Get out of here!

**Largos años**
A long time, many years

**Lavarse las manos de**
To wash one's hands of

**Levantar a pulso**
To lift (something heavy) with the hand

**Levantar la mesa**
To clear the table

**Levantarse de malas (or levantarse con las malas, or levantarse con el santo de espaldas)**
To get up on (or out of) the wrong side of the bed

**Ligero de cascos (or alegre de cascos)**
Featherbrained

**Limpio de polvo y paja**
Net, entirely free, clear profit

**Lo antes posible**
The earliest possible

**Lo de menos**
Of little importance, the least of it

**Lo expuesto**
What has been said

**Lo más pronto posible**
As soon as possible

**Lo menos posible**
As little as possible

**Lo mismo da**
It makes no difference

**Lo que**
That which

**Lo que hizo**
Which caused

**Lo recién llegado**
A new arrival

**Lo siento mucho**
I'm very sorry

**Loco de remate**
Stark raving mad

**Los (las) demás**
The others, the rest of them

**Los que**
Those which, those who, the ones

**Luego que**
As soon as

## LL

**Llamar al pan pan, y al vino vino**
Call a spade a spade

**Llamar por teléfono**
To call on the telephone

**Llegar a saber**
To come to know

**Llegar a ser**
To become, to get to be

**Llenar un vacío**
To bridge a gap

**Lleno de bote en bote**
Full to the brim

**Llevar a cabo**
To carry through, to accomplish

**Llevar a efecto**
To carry out

**Llevar cuentas**
To keep accounts

**Llevar el compás**
To beat time

**Llevar la contra**
To oppose, to object to

**Llevar la cuenta (or llevar cuenta de)**
To keep track of

**Llevar puesto**
To wear

**Llevar ventaja**
To have the lead, to be ahead

**Llevarse adelante**
To carry out

**Llevarse bien (con)**
To get along well with

**Llevarse un chasco**
To be disappointed

**Llover a cántaros**
To rain cats and dogs (pitchforks)

**Llover sobre mojado**
To come one after another (bad luck, misfortune)

## M

**Mal genio**
Bad temper

**Mal mandado (or muy mandado)**
Ill-behaved

**Mal sufrido**
Impatient

**Malas tretas**
Bad tricks, bad habits

**Mandar una bofetada**
To slap

**Mandar una pedrada**
To throw a stone

**Mañana Dios dirá**
Tomorrow is another day

**Mañana por la mañana (temprano)**
Tomorrow morning (early)

**Mañana por la noche**
Tomorrow night

**Mañana por la tarde**
Tomorrow afternoon

**Más acá**
Closer

**Más acá de**
This side of, before you get to

**Más adelante**
Farther on, later on

**Más ahorita**
Right now

**Más allá (de)**
Beyond, farther away

**Más aún**
Furthermore, what is more

**Más bien**
Rather

**Más bien que**
Rather than

**Más de**
More than

**Más de una vez**
More than once

**Más pesado que una mosca**
Pesky as a fly

**Más que**
More than

**Más que nadie**
More than anyone

**Más que nunca**
More than ever

**Más vale...**
It is better...

**Más vale tarde que nunca**
Better late than never

**Matar dos pájaros de un tiro**
To kill two birds with one stone

**Matar el gusano**
To satisfy a need or desire (hunger, etc.)

**Me entró miedo**
I became afraid

**Me hace falta**
I need it

**Me lloran los ojos**
My eyes water

**Media cuchara**
A mediocre person

**Medio sordo**
Hard of hearing

**Medir las calles**
To walk the streets, be out of a job

**Mejor dicho**
Better yet, rather

**Memoria de gallo**
Poor memory

**Menor de edad**
A minor (person)

**Menos de (or menos que)**
Less than

**Menos mal**
At least

**Merecer la pena**
To be worthwhile

**Meter la pata**
To put one's foot in one's mouth

**Meterse con**
To pick a quarrel or fight with

**Meterse de por medio**
To intervene, meddle in a dispute

**Meterse en un lío**
To get oneself in a mess

**Mientras más...menos**
The more...the less...

**Mientras tanto**
Meanwhile

**Mil gracias**
A thousand thanks

**Mirada de soslayo**
Side glance

**Mirar con el rabo del ojo**
To look out of the corner of one's eye

**Mirar por alguien**
To take care of someone

**Mirar por encima**
To glance at

**Mirar por encima del hombro**
To look down on; despise

**Molestarse en (con)**
To bother about

**Muchas subidas y bajadas**
Many ups and downs, much going up and down

**Mudar de casa**
To move (change residence)

**Muy a menudo**
Very often

**Muy de mañana**
Very early in the morning

**Muy trabajador**
Hard-working

## N

**Nacer de pie (or pies)**
To be born lucky

**Nada de eso**
Nothing like that

**Nada de particular**
Nothing unusual

**Nada en absoluto**
Nothing at all

**Nada más**
Just, only

**Negarse a (contestar)**
To refuse to (answer)

**Ni con mucho**
Not by far, not by a long shot,
far from

**Ni esto ni aquello**
Neither this nor that

**Ni mucho menos**
Not by any means, not anything
like it

**Ni siquiera**
Not even, even though

**Ni yo tampoco**
Nor I either

**Ningún otro**
Nobody else

**No cabe duda (que)**
There is no doubt (that)

**No caer bien**
To displease, (with direct
object) not to fit well

**No da abasto a**
To be unable to cope with

**No dar pie con bola**
To make a mistake, not to get
things right

**No darse cuenta**
Not to realize

**No despegar los labios**
Not to say a word, not to open
one's mouth

**¡No diga!**
Is that so? You don't say!

**No es asunto mío (suyo, etc.)**
It's none of my (your, etc.)
business

**No es mucho que**
It is no wonder that

**No estar de humor**
To be out of sorts, not in a
laughing mood

**No estoy de acuerdo**
I disagree

**¡No faltaba más!**
That's the last straw! Why, the
very idea!

**No hallar vado**
To find no way out

**No hay de que**
You're welcome; don't mention
it

**No hay más remedio que**
There's no other way but to;
there's nothing to do except

**No hay para que**
There's no need to

**No hay prisa**
There's no hurry

**No hay que darle vueltas**
There's no way around it; there
are no two ways about it

**¡No importa!**
Never mind!

**No irle ni venirle a uno**
To make no difference to one

**No le hace**
It doesn't matter, it makes no
difference

**No más que**
Only

**No le haga caso**
Pay no attention to him

**No me da la gana**
I don't want to

**No nos debemos nada**
We are even (quits)

**No obstante**
Notwithstanding, nevertheless

**No pararse en pelillos**
Not to bother about trifles

**No poder con**
Not to be able to stand, endure,
control, carry

**No poder con la carga**
Not to be able to lift the load,
not equal to the burden

**No poder más**
To be exhausted, "all in"

**No poder menos de**
Not to be able to help... Ex.: No
puede menos de hacerlo;
he can't help doing it

**No quedar otro recurso**
No way out, no alternative

**No querer hacerlo**
To be unwilling to do it

**No saber ni papa (de eso)**
To know absolutely nothing
(about that)

**No saber una (or ni) jota**
Not to know anything

**No se dé usted prisa**
Don't hurry

**¡No se ocupe!**
Never mind! Don't worry!

**¡No se preocupe usted!**
Don't worry!

**No se trata de eso**
That's not the point; that's not
the question

**No sea que**
Or else, because

**No ser cosa de juego**
Not to be a laughing matter

**No ser ni chicha ni limonada**
To be worthless, neither fish nor
fowl

**No servir para nada**
To be good for nothing

**No sólo...sino también**
Not only...but also

**No tan a menudo**
Not so often

**No tener alternativa (or elección)**
To have no alternative, no way
out

**No tener entrañas**
To be cruel

**No tener nada que ver con**
To have nothing to do with

**No tener pelillos en la lengua**
To speak frankly

**No tener razón**
To be wrong

**No tener remedio**
To be beyond help or repair

**No tener sal en la mollera**
To be dull, stupid

**No tenga usted cuidado**
Don't worry about it; forget it

**No tiene remedio**
It can't be helped; it is hopeless

**No tiene vuelta de hoja**
There's no two ways about it

**No vale la pena**
It's not worthwhile

**No vale un pito**
Not worth a straw

**No vale una cuartilla**
Not worth a penny

**No ver la hora de**
To be anxious to

**No viene al cuento (or no viene al caso)**
It is not opportune, or to the
point

## O

**O sea que**
That is to say

**O si no...**
Or else...

**Oír decir que**
To hear that

**Oír hablar de**
To hear about

**Oler a**
To smell like

**Optar por**
To choose, decide upon

**¡Otra, otra!**
Encore!

**Otra vez**
Again

## P

**Pagado de sí mismo**
To be pleased with oneself

**Pagar el pato**
To be the scapegoat, get the
blame

**Pagarse de**
To be proud of, or boast of

**¡Palabrita de honor!**
Word of honor, honestly; no kidding?

**Para mis adentros**
To myself

**Para que**
In order that

**¿Para qué?**
What for? For what use?

**Para (or por) siempre (+ jamás)**
Forever (forever and ever)

**Para todos lados**
To right and left, on all sides

**Para unos fines u otros**
For one purpose or another

**Para variar**
For a change

**Parar en seco**
To stop short or suddenly

**Parar mientes en**
To consider, reflect on

**Pararse en pelillos**
To split hairs

**Parece mentira**
It seems to be impossible

**Parecido a**
Like, similar to

**Pasado de moda**
Out of style, out of date

**Pasado mañana**
Day after tomorrow

**Pasar a mejor vida**
To die

**Pasar como un relámpago**
To flash by

**Pasar de la raya**
To overstep bounds, take undue liberties

**Pasar de moda**
To go out of style

**Pasar el rato**
To while away time

**Pasar la noche en claro (or en blanco)**
Not to sleep a wink

**Pasar lista**
To call the roll

**Pasar por alto**
To omit, overlook

**Pasar revista a**
To review, to go over carefully

**Pasar un buen rato**
To have a good time

**Pasarse sin**
To do without

**Pasear a pie**
To take a walk

**Pasear en coche**
To go for a drive (by auto)

**Pata de gallo**
Crow's foot wrinkles

**Patas arriba**
Upside down

**Pecar de bueno**
To be too good

**Pecar de oscuro**
To be very unclear, too complicated

**Pedir prestado**
To borrow

**Pegar de soslayo**
To glance, to hit at a slant

**Pegar fuego**
To set afire

**Pegar un chasco**
To play a trick, surprise, disappoint

**Pegar un salto**
To take a jump

**Pegar un susto**
To give a scare

**Pensar en**
To intend, to think about

**Peor que**
Worse than

**Peor que peor**
That is even worse

**Perder cuidado**
Not to worry

**Perder de vista**
To lose sight of

**Perder el juicio**
To lose one's mind, go crazy

**Perder el tiempo**
To lose time

**Perder la razón**
To lose one's mind

**Perder la vista**
To go blind

**Perder prestigio**
To lose face

**Perderse de vista**
To vanish, to be lost from view, to drop out of sight

**Pesarle a uno**
To be sorry for someone, to regret

**Picar en**
To dabble in

**Picar muy alto**
To aim very high

**(X) Pies de altura (or de alto)**
(X) Feet tall

**(X) Pies de largo**
(X) Feet long

**Pillar una mona**
To get drunk

**Pintar venado**
To play hooky

**Pintarle un violín**
To break one's word

**Planchar el asiento**
To be a wallflower

**Poca cosa**
Not much

**Poco a poco**
Gradually, little by little

**Poco después (de)**
Shortly thereafter

**Poco para las (tres)**
To be nearly (3) o'clock

**Poco rato**
Very soon

**Poner a buen recaudo**
To place in safety

**Poner adelantado**
To set forward (e.g., a clock)

**Poner al corriente**
To inform, to bring up to date

**Poner casa**
To set up housekeeping

**Poner defectos**
To find fault with

**Poner el grito en el cielo**
To complain loudly, to "hit the ceiling"

**Poner en claro**
To clear up, to clarify

**Poner en conocimiento**
To inform

**Poner en duda**
To question, to doubt

**Poner en el cielo**
To praise, extol

**Poner en juego**
To set in motion, to coordinate

**Poner en limpio**
To make a clean copy, to recopy

**Poner en marcha**
To get going

**Poner en razón**
To pacify

**Poner en ridículo**
To humiliate, make a fool of

**Poner faltas**
To find fault with

**Poner la luz, (el radio, etc.)**
To turn on the light (radio, etc.)

**Poner la mesa**
To set the table

**Poner la mira**
To fix one's eyes on, aim at

**Poner por las nubes**
To praise to the skies

**Poner por obra**
To undertake, put into practice

**Poner todo de su parte**
To do one's best

**Poner una queja**
To file a complaint

**Ponerse a**
To begin, start

**Ponerse bien**
To get well

**Ponerse colorado**
To blush

**Ponerse de acuerdo**
To come to an agreement

**Ponerse de pie**
To get to one's feet

**Ponerse de rodillas**
To kneel

**Ponerse duro**
To resist stubbornly

**Ponerse en**
To reach

**Ponerse en camino**
To set out (on a trip, etc.)

**Ponerse en contra de**
To oppose, be against

**Ponerse en marcha**
To start, start out

**Ponerse en pie**
To get up, or rise

**Por acá (or por aquí)**
This way, over here

**Por accidente**
By accident

**Por adelantado**
In advance

**Por ahí (or por allá)**
Over there, about that

**Por ahora**
For the time being, for now

**Por algo**
For some reason; that's why

**Por allí**
That way

**Por amor de**
For the sake of

**Por aquí**
This way

**Por aquí cerca**
Around here, in this vicinity

**Por arriba**
Above

**Por casualidad**
By chance, by accident

**Por completo**
Completely

**Por (or en) consecuencia de**
Therefore, consequently

**Por consiguiente**
Consequently, therefore

**Por de (or por lo) pronto**
For the present

**Por delante**
Ahead

**Por dentro**
On the inside

**Por desgracia**
Unfortunately

**Por despecho**
Out of spite

**Por detrás**
From the rear

**Por día**
By the day

**¿Por dónde?**
Where, through, which? Which way?

**Por el estilo**
Such as that, of that kind

**Por el (or por la or por lo) presente**
For the present

**Por encima de**
On top of

**Por encima de todo**
Above all

**Por ende**
Hence, therefore

**Por entre**
Among, between

**Por esa razón**
For that reason, that is why

**Por escrito**
In writing

**Por eso**
For that reason, therefore

**Por extenso**
In detail, at length

**Por favor**
Please

**Por fin**
At last, finally

**Por fuera**
From the outside, on the outside

**Por hoy**
At present

**Por instantes**
Continually, moment to moment

**Por la mañana (or por la tarde, etc.)**
In the morning (afternoon, etc.)

**Por la mitad**
In half, in the middle

**Por la noche (or en la noche)**
At night, in the evening

**Por las buenas o por las malas**
Whether one likes it or not

**Por las nubes**
Sky-high

**Por lo común**
Generally

**Por lo cual**
Therefore

**Por lo demás**
Moreover, as for the rest (of us), aside from this

**Por lo general**
Usually, generally

**Por lo menos**
At least

**Por lo pronto**
For the time being

**Por lo regular**
Usually, as a rule

**Por lo que**
Because of which

**Por lo que pueda tronar**
Just in case

**Por lo tanto**
Therefore

**Por lo visto**
Apparently, by the looks of, evidently

**Por más que**
However much

**Por medio de**
By means of

**Por menudo**
In detail, retail

**Por mi parte**
As far as I'm concerned

**Por motivo**
On account of

**Por mucho que**
No matter how much

**Por ningún lado**
Nowhere

**Por ningún motivo**
Under no circumstances, no matter what

**Por otra parte**
On the other hand

**Por otro lado**
On the other hand (or side)

**Por poco**
Almost, nearly. Ex.: Por poco se muere; he almost died

**Por primera vez**
For the first time

**¿Por qué?**
Why?

**Por rareza**
Seldom

**Por regla general**
As a general rule, usually

**Por separado**
Separately

**Por si acaso**
In case, just in case

**Por sí solo**
By oneself

**Por su cuenta**
All by himself (oneself)

**Por su mano**
By oneself

**Por supuesto**
Of course

**Por término medio**
On an average

**Por (or a or en) todas partes**
All over, everywhere

**Por toda suerte de penalidades**
Through thick and thin

**Por todo el mundo**
All over the world

**Por todo lo alto**
Not sparing expense

**Por todos lados**
All over, everywhere, all sides

**Por última vez**
For the last time, finally

**Por último**
Finally, at last

**Porque si no**
Otherwise

**Preguntar por**
To ask about

**Prender el fuego**
To start the fire

**Prender fuego a**
To set fire to

**Preocuparse de**
To take care of

**Preocuparse por**
To worry about, to be
concerned about or for

**Presencia de ánimo**
Presence of mind, serenity

**Prestar atención**
To pay attention

**Profundamente dormido**
Fast asleep

**Prohibida la entrada**
No trespassing

**Prohibido el paso**
No trespassing, keep out

**Prohibido estacionarse**
No parking

**Puede ser que**
It may be that

**Pues bien**
Now then, well then, all right
then

**Pues mire**
Well, look

**Pues que(?)**
Since, so what?

**Puesta del sol**
Sunset

**Puesto que**
Although, since

## Q

**¡Qué barbaridad!**
What nonsense! What an
atrocity!

**¡Qué batingue!**
What a mess!

**¡Qué de!**
What a lot! How much!

**¡Qué desgracia!**
How unfortunate!

**¡Qué divino!**
What a beauty!

**¡Qué gusto!**
What a pleasure! I am
delighted!

**¿Qué haces?**
What's the matter? What is it?

**¿Qué hay?**
What's the matter?

**¿Qué hay de malo con eso?**
What's wrong with that? So,
what's so bad about that?

**¿Qué hay de nuevo?**
What's new(s)?

**¿Qué hora es? (or ¿qué horas
son?)**
What time is it?

**¡Qué horror!**
How awful!

**¿Qué hubo?**
How goes it? What's up?

**¡Qué lástima!**
Too bad! What a pity!

**¿Qué le pasa (a Ud.)?**
What's the matter with you?

**Que le vaya bien**
Good luck

**Que lo pase bien**
Have a good day, etc.

**¿Qué mosca te ha picado?**
What's eating you?

**¡Qué nombrecito!**
What a tonguetwister!

**¿Qué pasa?**
What's up? What's going on?

**¿Qué pasó?**
What happened?

**¿Qué quiere decir?**
What does it mean?

**¡Que se divierta!**
Have a good time

**¿Qué tal?**
Hello! How are you?

**¿Qué tiene de malo?**
What's wrong with...?

**Quebrarse uno la cabeza**
To rack one's brain

**Quedar bien (con)**
To come out well, to get along
well (with)

**Quedar contento con**
To be pleased with

**Quedar en**
To agree (to)

**Quedar entendido que**
To be understood, agreed to

**Quedarle bien**
To be becoming

**Quedarse con (re una cosa)**
To keep, to take (e.g., I'll take
it.)

**Quedarse en la casa**
To stay in

**Quejarse de**
To complain of

**Quemarse hasta el suelo**
To burn down

**Quemarse las pestañas (or las
cejas)**
To burn the midnight oil, study
hard

**Querer decir**
To mean, signify

**¿Quién sabe?**
Who knows? I don't know

**¿Quién te mete, Juan Copete?**
Mind your own business.
What's it to you?

**Quieras que no**
Whether you wish or not

**Quiere llover**
It is trying (is about) to rain

**Quince días**
Two weeks

**¡Quita allá!**
Don't tell me that!

**Quitar la mesa**
To clear the table

**Quitarse uno un peso de encima**
To be relieved of, to be a load
off one's mind

**Quitarse de una cosa**
To give up (or get rid of)
something

**¡Quítese de aquí!**
Get out of here!

## R

**Rabiar por**
To be very eager to (or for)

**Rara vez (or raras veces)**
Seldom

**Ratos perdidos**
Leisure hours

**Recibir noticias (de)**
To hear from

**Recuerdos a**
Regards to...

**Rechinar los dientes**
To gnash one's teeth

**Reírse para sus adentros**
To laugh up one's sleeve

**Remolino de gente**
Throng, crowd

**Repetidas veces**
Over and over again, various
times

**Repetir de carretilla**
To rattle off, repeat
mechanically

**Resarcirse de**
To make up for

**Respecto a**
With regard to, concerning,
about

**Reunión de confianza**
Informal gathering or party

**Reventar de risa**
To burst with laughter

**Romper a**
To start to

**Romper el alba**
To dawn

**Romperse los cascos**
To rack one's brain

**Rosario de desdichas**
Chain of misfortunes

**Rozarse con alguien**
To have connections (or dealings) with someone

### S

**Saber a**
To taste like

**Saber de memoria**
To know by heart

**Sacar a bailar**
To ask to dance

**Sacar a uno de quicio**
To exasperate someone

**Sacar el cuerpo**
To dodge

**Sacar en claro (or en limpio)**
To deduce, conclude

**Salida de pie de banco**
Silly remark, nonsense

**Salida del sol**
Sunrise

**Salir a**
To resemble, take after

**Salir a gatas**
To crawl out of a difficulty

**Salir al encuentro de**
To go out to meet, to oppose, take a stand against

**Salir bien**
To be successful, to come out well

**Salir de**
To leave, depart

**Salir del paso**
To get out of a difficulty

**Salir fiador de**
To vouch for

**Salir ganando**
To win, to come out ahead

**Salir mal**
To fail, to come out poorly

**Salirse con la suya**
To have one's own way

**Saltar a la vista**
To be obvious

**Saltar a tierra**
To disembark, to land

**Saltar las trancas**
To lose patience, lose one's head

**Salvar el pellejo**
To save one's skin

**Sano y salvo**
Safe and sound

**Santo y bueno**
Well and good

**Se aguó la fiesta**
The party was spoiled

**Se conoce (que)**
It is obvious

**Se dice**
It is said, they say

**Se ha acabado**
It is all over

**Se prohibe (fumar)**
It is forbidden (to smoke); no (smoking)

**Se solicita**
Wanted

**Se suena que**
It is rumored that

**Se ve que**
It is obvious that

**Se venció el plazo**
The time limit expired

**Seguir las pisadas**
To follow in the footsteps (of), emulate

**Según y conforme (or según y como)**
Exactly as, just as, that depends

**Seguro que están**
I bet they are

**Seguro que sí**
Of course

**Sentar bien a**
To fit well

**Sentarle bien**
To be becoming

**Sentarse en cuclillas**
To squat

**Sentir en el alma**
To be terribly sorry, to regret very much

**Sentirse destemplado**
Not to feel well, to feel feverish

**Ser aficionado a**
To be a fan, a buff

**Ser como un puño**
To be close-fisted

**Ser conocedor**
To be a judge of

**Ser de carne y hueso**
To be only human

**Ser de rigor**
To be indispensable, to be required by custom

**Ser de (or ser para) ver**
Worth seeing

**Ser duro de mollera**
To be stubborn

**Ser fuerza**
To be necessary

**Ser gente**
To be cultured, socially important

**Ser huésped en su casa**
To be seldom at home

**Ser oriundo de**
To hail from, come from

**Ser piedra de escándalo**
To be the object of scandal

**Ser plato de segunda mesa**
To play second fiddle

**Ser tan fuerte como un león**
To be as strong as a horse

**Ser tempranero**
To be an early riser

**Ser un cero a la izquierda**
To be of no account

**Ser un erizo**
To be irritable; a grouchy person

**Servir de**
To serve, act as, be used as

**Servir la mesa**
To wait table

**Servir para**
To be good for, used for

**Si acaso**
If at all

**Si alguna vez**
If even

**Si bien**
Although

**Si mal no recuerdo**
If I remember correctly

**Si me hace el favor**
If you would do me the favor

**Si no**
Or else

**Si no fuera por**
Except for

**Si no fuera porque**
Except for

**Siempre que**
Whenever, provided that, as long as

**Siempre y cuando**
Provided

**Sin ceremonia**
Informal

**Sin comentarios**
No comment

**Sin contar**
Exclusive of

**Sin disputa**
Without question

**Sin embargo**
However, nevertheless

**Sin falta**
By all means, without fail, without fault

**Sin fin**
An infinite quantity

**Sin hacer caso de**
Regardless of

**Sin igual**
Unequaled

**Sin novedad**
As usual (to be well, in good health)

**Sin par**
Peerless, without equal

**Sin que**
Without

**Sin qué ni para qué**
Without rhyme or reason

**Sin querer**
Unwillingly

**Sin rebozo**
Openly, frankly

**Sin recurso**
Without remedy, without appeal

**Sin remedio**
Unavoidable, without help

**Sin reserva**
Unreserved, frankly

**Sin sentir**
Without realizing, inadvertently, unnoticed

**Sin ton ni son**
Without rhyme or reason

**Sino que**
But

**Sobradas veces**
Repeatedly, many times

**Sobre manera**
Excessively

**Sobre mi palabra**
Upon my honor

**Sobre que**
Besides, in addition to

**Sobre seguro**
Without risk

**Sobre todo**
Especially, above all

**Soltar el hervor**
To come to a boil

**Soltar la rienda**
To let loose, act without restraint

**Sonar a**
To sound like, seem like

**Soñar con (or soñar en)**
To dream of

**Soñar despierto**
To daydream

**Su punto flaco**
His weakness, her weak side

**Subidas y bajadas**
Ups and downs

**Subir al tren**
To get on the train

**Subir de punto**
To increase, get worse

**Subirse de tono**
To put on airs

**Suceda lo que suceda**
Come what may, no matter what

**Sudar la gota gorda**
To sweat profusely, work hard, sweat blood, have a bad time

**Suerte negra**
Very bad luck

**Suma atención**
Close attention

**Supuesto que**
Supposing that, since

**Surtir efecto**
To come out as desired or expected, to give good results

## T

**Tal como (or tales como)**
Such as

**Tal cual**
Such as, so-so, fair

**Tal para cual**
Two of a kind

**Tal vez**
Maybe, perhaps

**Tal vez sea que**
It may be that

**Tan pronto como**
As soon as

**Tanto...como**
As much...as

**Tanto mejor**
So much the better

**Tanto peor**
So much the worse

**Tardar en**
To be long in, take a long time (in doing)

**Tarde o temprano**
Sooner or later

**Tener a la vista**
To have in sight

**Tener a raya**
To keep in bounds, hold in check

**Tener al corriente**
To keep up-to-date (informed, posted)

**Tener...años**
To be...years old

**Tener buena cara**
To look well

**Tener cabida con alguien**
To have influence with someone

**Tener calor**
To be hot

**Tener celos**
To be jealous

**Tener confianza con**
To be on intimate terms with

**Tener cosquillas**
To be ticklish

**Tener cuidado (con)**
To take care, watch out (for)

**Tener deseos de**
To want to, to be eager to

**Tener el pico de oro**
To be eloquent

**Tener en cuenta**
To consider, to take into account

**Tener en la mente**
To have in mind

**Tener en la punta de la lengua**
To have on the tip of one's tongue

**Tener en mucho**
To esteem highly

**Tener en poco a**
To hold in low esteem

**Tener entendido que**
To understand that...

**Tener éxito**
To be successful

**Tener frío**
To be cold

**Tener gana(s) de**
To feel like

**Tener gancho**
To be attractive, alluring

**Tener gracia**
To be funny

**Tener gusto en**
To be glad to

**Tener hambre**
To be hungry

**Tener la bondad de**
To be good enough to

**Tener la costumbre de**
To be used (accustomed) to...

**Tener la culpa**
To be to blame

**Tener la intención de**
To intend or mean to

**Tener la lengua larga**
To have a big mouth

**Tener la pena de**
To have the misfortune to

**Tener la vida en un hilo**
To be in great danger

**Tener lástima de**
To feel sorry for, take pity on

**Tener lugar**
To take place

**Tener miedo**
To be afraid

**Tener mucho copete**
To be arrogant, haughty

**Tener murria**
To be sulky, to have the blues

**Tener para sí**
To think, to be of the opinion

**Tener por**
To believe, judge, consider, to take for a...

**Tener presente (de or que)**
To bear in mind

**Tener prisa**
To be in a hurry

**Tener probabilidad**
To stand a chance

**Tener que**
To have to (do something)

**Tener que ver (con)**
To have to do with

**Tener razón**
To be right

**Tener roce con**
To have contact with a person

**Tener sed**
To be thirsty

**Tener sueño**
To be sleepy

**Tener suerte**
To be lucky

**Tener tiempo libre**
To have time off

**Tener vergüenza**
To be ashamed

**Tenerle tirria a una persona**
To have a dislike for (or grudge against) a person

**Tenerse en pie**
To keep one's feet

**Tirar de**
To pull

**Tirar las riendas**
To restrain, tighten the reins

**Tirarse una plancha**
To put oneself in a ridiculous situation

**Tocar de oído**
To play by ear

**Tocar en lo vivo**
To hurt to the quick, hit a nerve, touch a sore spot

**Tocar por fantasía**
To play by ear

**Tocarle a uno**
To be one's turn

**Tocarle a uno la suerte**
To be one's turn, to fall to one's lot, to be lucky

**Tocarse el sombrero**
To tip one's hat

**Toda clase de**
All kinds of

**Todas las veces (que)**
Every time, whenever

**Todavía no**
Not yet

**Todo el año**
All year round

**Todo el día**
All day

**Todo el mundo**
Everybody

**Todo el que**
Everybody who

**Todo el tiempo**
All the time

**Todo hombre**
Everyone

**Todo lo contrario**
Exactly the opposite

**Todo lo demás**
Everything else

**Todo lo posible**
All that is possible

**Todo sigue bien**
All goes well

**Todos los días**
Every day

**Tomar a broma**
To take as a joke

**Tomar a pecho(s)**
To take to heart, to take seriously

**Tomar a risa**
To laugh off, take lightly

**Tomarle el pelo**
To tease, pull one's leg

**Tomar el rábano por las hojas**
To put the cart before the horse, to misinterpret or misconstrue

**Tomar el sol**
To sunbathe

**Tomar en cuenta**
To consider, take into account

**Tomar en serio**
To take to heart

**Tomar la delantera**
To take the lead

**Tomar por cierto**
To take for granted

**Tomar por su cuenta**
To attend to personally

**Tomar tiempo libre**
To take time off

**Tomarlo con calma**
To take it easy

**Tonto de capirote**
Dunce, plain fool

**Traer puesto**
To wear, to have on

**Transporte de locura**
Fit of madness

**Tras de**
Behind, after, beside

**Tratar con**
To have dealings with

**Tratar de**
To try to; to treat, to deal with

**Tratar en**
To deal in

**Tratarse de**
To be a question of

**¡Trato hecho!**
It's a deal!

**Tronar los dedos**
To snap one's fingers

**Tropezar con**
To meet, come across, encounter

# U

**Un buen pasar**
Enough to live on

**Un día sí y otro no**
Every other day

**Un día sí y un día no**
Every other day

**Un hervidero de gente**
A swarm of people

**Un no sé qué**
Something indefinable

**Un nudo en la garganta**
A lump in the throat

**Un rato desagradable**
A hard time

**Un tanto**
Somewhat

**Una buena carcajada**
A hearty laugh

**Una infinidad de**
A large number of

**Una mala pasada**
A mean trick

**Una negativa rotunda**
A flat denial

**Una negativa terminante**
A flat denial

**Una que otra vez**
Once in a while

**Una y otra vez**
More than once, over and over again

**Unas cuantas (or unos cuantos)**
A few

**Uno a la vez**
One at a time

**Uno por uno**
One by one

**Unos a otros**
Each other

**Unos pocos**
A few

# V

**Valer la pena**
To be worthwhile. Ex.: No vale la pena, it's not worth the trouble

**Valer más**
To be better

**Valer por**
To be worth

**Valerse de**
To make use of

**Varias veces**
Several times

**Venir a las manos**
To come to blows

**Venir a menos**
To decline

**Venir a parar**
To turn out to be, to end up (as)

**Venir a (or al) pelo**
To come at the right moment, to suit perfectly, to be opportune

**Venir a ser**
To turn out to be

**Venir bien**
To suit

**Venir en**
To agree to

**Venir sobre**
To fall upon

**Venirse abajo**
To fall down, collapse, fail

**Ver de (or ver que)**
To try to, see to it that

**Verse obligado a**
To be obliged to or forced to

**Visto que**
Whereas, considering that

**Vivir de sus uñas**
To live by stealing

**Voltear la espalda**
To turn one's back

**Volver a**
To do...again

**Volver a las andadas**
To fall back into old habits

**Volver corriendo**
To hurry back

**Volver en sí**
To come to, regain consciousness

**Volver loco**
To drive crazy

**Volver por**
To return for, to defend

**Volverse atrás**
To go back, back out, go back on one's word

**Volverse loco**
To go crazy

# Y

**Y así sucesivamente**
And so on, et cetera

**Y pico**
(A) little more

**¿Y qué?**
So what?

**¿Y si?**
What if...?

**Ya es hora de**
It's time to

**Ya es tarde**
It's too late now

**Ya mero**
Very soon, just about to...

**¡Ya lo creo!**
I should say so! Yes, of course

**Ya no**
No longer

**Ya no sopla**
To be no good, of no use as...

**Ya que**
Since, although

**Ya se acabó**
It is all over

**Ya se ve**
Of course; it is clear

**Ya voy**
I am coming

# MODISMOS Y EXPRESIONES / IDIOMS AND EXPRESSIONS

## A

**About**
Acerca de, al (or en) rededor, alrededor de, cosa de, respecto a

**About that**
Por ahí, por allá

**About the first of...**
A principios de...

**About the middle of...**
A mediados de

**Above**
Por arriba

**Above all**
Ante todo, por encima de todo, sobre todo

**Abroad**
En el extranjero

**Absolutely**
De remate

**Absolutely (not)**
En absoluto

**Accomplish**
Llevar a cabo

**According to Hoyle; according to the rules**
Como Dios manda

**Across**
A través de, de través

**Act a fool**
Hacer el ridículo, hacerse el tonto

**Act as**
Hacer de, servir de

**Act as if**
Hacer como si

**Actually**
Desde luego

**Act without restraint**
Soltar la rienda

**Add fuel to the fire**
Echar leña al fuego

**Admit a person is right**
Dar la razón a una persona

**After (in position)**
Tras de

**After a few months (etc.)**
A los pocos meses

**After all**
A fin de cuentas, después de todo, en resumidas cuentas

**Again**
De nuevo, de vuelta, otra vez

**Against**
En contra de

**Against all odds**
Contra viento y marea

**Against the grain**
A contrapelo

**Agree**
Dar la razón, estar de acuerdo, quedar en

**Agree to**
Quedar en, venir en

**Ahead**
Por delante

**Aim at**
Poner la mira

**Aimlessly**
A la ventura

**Aim very high**
Picar muy alto

**A little more**
Y pico

**All along**
Desde el principio

**All around**
A la redonda, en redondo

**All at once**
De un golpe, de un tirón, de una tirada

**All by oneself (himself)**
Por su cuenta

**All day**
Todo el día

**All goes well**
Todo sigue bien

**All joking aside**
Bromas a un lado, fuera de broma

**All kinds of**
Toda clase de

**All of a sudden**
De buenas a primeras, de repente

**All over**
En todas partes, por todas partes, por todos lados

**All that is possible**
Todo lo posible

**All the time**
A cada rato, todo el tiempo

**All the while**
Entre tanto

**All together**
En conjunto, en junto

**All year round**
Todo el año

**Almost**
Por poco

**Alone**
A secas

**Along, alongside of**
A lo largo (de)

**Along with**
Junto con

**Aloud**
En voz alta, voz alta

**Although**
Bien que, puesto que, si bien, ya que

**Among**
Por entre

**Amuse**
Hacer gracia

**And so**
De modo que, de suerte que

**And so on**
Y así sucesivamente

**Anger, to make angry**
Dar rabia

**Annoy**
Dar la lata

**Anyhow**
Así y todo, de todos modos

**Anything at all**
Cualquier cosa

**Anyway**
Al fin y al cabo, de todas maneras, en cualquier caso

**Any way you look at it**
A todas luces

**Apiece**
Cada uno

**Apologize**
Dar una satisfacción

**Apparently**
Al parecer, por lo visto

**Approve**
Dar el visto bueno

**Approximately**
Cosa de

**Apropos**
A propósito

**Around (about)**
Al derredor, en derredor, al rededor, en rededor, alrededor de

**Around here**
Aquí cerca, por aquí cerca

**Around the corner**
A la vuelta de, a la vuelta de la esquina

**Arouse one's suspicions**
Darle a uno mala espina

**Arouse pity (or sorrow)**
Dar lástima (de)

**Arrest**
Echar la garra

**As**
A medida que, a semejanza de, según y conforme, según y como

**As a general rule**
Por regla general; por lo general

As a last resort
Como último recurso

As a matter of fact
En realidad

As a result (of)
A consecuencia de, de resultas

As a rule
Por lo regular

As a whole
En conjunto

As far as I'm concerned
Por mi parte

As follows
A continuación, como sigue

As for
En cuanto a

As for the rest (of us)
Por lo demás

Aside from that
Aparte de eso

Aside from this
Por lo demás

As if
Como si

As if by magic
Como por ensalmo

As if it were
Como si fuera

As I understand it
A mi entender

Ask about
Preguntar por

Ask a question (or questions)
Hacer una pregunta (preguntas)

Ask to dance
Sacar a bailar

As little as possible
Lo menos posible

As long as
Siempre que

As much as
Tanto como

As of
A partir de

As proof of
En prenda de

As smooth as silk
Como una seda

As soon as
Así es que, así que, en cuanto, luego que, tan pronto como

As soon as possible
Cuanto antes, lo más pronto posible

Assume responsibility
Cargar con

As the crow flies
A vuelo de pájaro

As the saying goes
Como dijo el otro

As time goes on
Andarse el tiempo

As usual
Como de costumbre, como siempre, sin novedad

As well as
Así como

As you like
A la voluntad

At about
A eso de, como a costumbre

At about...(time)
Al filo de...

At all
Del todo

At all costs
A toda costa, a todo trance

At all hours
A deshora(s)

At all times
A toda hora

At an early date
En fecha a próxima

At another's expense
De gorra

At an untimely moment
A deshora(s)

At any cost
Cueste lo que cueste

At any moment
De un momento a otro

At any rate
Como quiera que sea, de cualquier modo, de todas maneras, de todos modos

At any time
A toda hora

At arm's length
A una brazada

At a short distance
A pocos pasos

At bottom
En el fondo

At every turn
A cada paso

At first
Al principio

At full length
A lo largo (de)

At full speed (or greatest speed)
A escape, a toda prisa, a toda vela, a todo correr

At hand
A mano

At hard labor
Al remo

At heart
En el fondo

At home
En casa

At last
A la postre, al fin, al fin y al cabo, por fin, por último

At (the) least
Al menos, a lo menos, como mínimo, menos mal, por lo menos

At length
Por extenso

At most
A lo más, a lo sumo

At once
Ahora mismo, al instante, al punto, de pronto, de una vez, desde luego, en el acto, en seguida

At one stroke
De una vez

At one time
A un tiempo, de una vez

At present
Al presente, por hoy

At random
A la buena de Dios, a la ventura, al azar

Attend to personally
Tomar por su cuenta

At that time
A la sazón, en aquel tiempo

At the end
Al fin

At the last moment
A última hora

At the mercy of
A merced de

At the most
A lo sumo

At the present time
En la actualidad

At the request of
A instancias de

At the same time
A la vez, al mismo tiempo, de paso, entre tanto

At the very latest
A más tardar

At this point or juncture
A estas alturas

At times
A ratos, a veces

At whatever cost
A toda costa

At will
A la voluntad, a voluntad

At worst
A lo más

At your service
A sus órdenes, servidor de usted

Average person
El común de las gentes

Avoid someone
Dar esquinazo

Awaiting
En espera de

# B

**Back and forth**
De aquí para allá

**Back out**
Echarse para atrás, volverse atrás

**Back up**
Dar marcha atrás, ir para atrás

**Backward(s)**
Al revés, hacia atrás

**Bad habits**
Malas tretas

**Bad temper**
Mal genio

**Bark up the wrong tree**
A buen santo te encomiendas

**Be a buff**
Ser aficionado a

**Be about to**
Estar a punto de, estar para

**Be a fan of**
Ser aficionado a

**Be afraid**
Tener miedo

**Be against**
Estar en pugna con, ponerse en contra de

**Be agreed to**
Quedar entendido que

**Be ahead**
Llevar ventaja

**Be alert**
Estar a la mira de, ponerse chango

**Be all right, OK**
Estar bien

**Be alluring**
Tener gancho

**Be a load off one's mind**
Quitarse uno un peso de encima

**Be an early riser**
Ser tempranero

**Be anxious to**
No ver la hora de

**Be a part of**
Formar parte de

**Be a question of**
Tratarse de

**Bear or hold a grudge**
Guardar rencor

**Bear in mind**
Tener presente (de lo que)

**Be arrogant**
Tener mucho copete

**Be ashamed**
Tener vergüenza

**Be as strong as a horse**
Ser tan fuerte como un león

**Beat around the bush**
Andarse con rodeos, andarse por las ramas

**Beaten path**
Camino trillado

**Be at the end of one's rope or resources**
Estar en las últimas

**Beat (or mark) time**
Llevar el compás

**Be attractive**
Tener gancho

**Beautifully**
A las mil maravillas

**Be a wallflower**
Planchar el asiento

**Be away from home**
Estar fuera de casa

**Be back**
Estar de regreso, estar de vuelta

**Be becoming**
Caer bien, quedarle bien, sentarle bien

**Be beyond help or repair**
No tener remedio

**Be born lucky**
Nacer de pie (...de pies)

**Be broke**
Estar bruja

**Because**
No sea que

**Because of**
Con motivo de

**Because of which**
Por lo que

**Be cautious**
Estar sobre sí, estar sobre aviso

**Be close-fisted**
Ser como un puño

**Be coaxed**
Hacerse del rogar

**Become**
Llegar a ser

**Become confused**
Hacerse un lío

**Become effective**
Entrar en vigor (e.g., a law)

**Be contented**
Estar a gusto

**Be courageous**
Tener puños

**Be crowded**
Estar de bote en bote

**Be cruel**
No tener entrañas

**Be cultured**
Ser gente

**Be deeply involved in**
Estar muy metido en

**Be disappointed**
Llevarse un chasco

**Be disconcerting**
Dar mucha pena

**Be dull**
No tener sal en la mollera

**Be eager to**
Tener deseos de

**Be eloquent**
Tener el pico de oro

**Be equal to (a task)**
Estar a la altura de

**Be exhausted**
No poder más

**Be fed**
Dar de comer

**Be fed up**
Estar uno hasta el copete, estar uno hasta la coronilla

**Be fed up with**
Estar harto de

**Be filled up**
Estar hasta los topes

**Be flush (even with)**
Estar ras con ras

**Be fond of**
Estar afecto a

**Be forced to**
Verse obligado a

**Before**
Antes de que

**Before dark**
De día

**Beforehand**
Con tiempo

**Before one's (very) eyes**
A ojos vistas

**Be funny**
Tener gracia

**Begin**
Echarse a, ponerse a, romper a

**Beginning on**
A partir de

**Begin running**
Echar(se) a correr

**Begin to understand**
Ir entendiendo

**Be glad to**
Tener gusto en

**Be good for**
Servir para

**Be good for nothing**
No servir para nada

**Be haughty**
Tener mucho copete

**Behind**
Atrás de, detrás de, tras de

**Behind closed doors**
A puerta cerrada

**Behind one's back**
A espaldas de

**Behind the scenes**
Entre bastidores

**Behold**
He aquí

**Be in a bad mood**
Estar mal templado, estar de mal humor, mal genio

**Be in a good mood**
Estar de buen humor, buen genio

**Be in a hurry**
Estar (or andar) de prisa, tener prisa

**Be in a jam**
Estar en un aprieto

**Be in big trouble**
Estar con el agua al cuello

**Be in charge of**
Estar a cargo de, estar encargado de

**Be indebted to**
Estar en deuda con

**Be indispensable**
Ser de rigor

**Be in favor of**
Estar por

**Be in good condition (a thing)**
Estar en buen uso

**Be in good health**
Estar bien de salud, sin novedad

**Be in great danger**
Tener la vida en un hilo

**Be in infancy**
Estar en pañales

**Be in mourning**
Estar de duelo, estar de luto

**Be in need of**
Hacer falta

**Be in one's right mind**
Estar uno en sus cabales

**Be in order**
Estar arreglado

**Be in the mood (for)**
Estar de (or en) vena (para)

**Be in the same boat**
Estar en las mismas

**Be in the way**
Estar de sobra

**Be in trouble**
Estar en un aprieto

**Be irritable (or a grouchy person)**
Ser un erizo

**Be jealous**
Tener celos

**Be a judge of**
Ser conocedor

**Be just about out of money**
Estar (or andar) escaso de dinero

**Be left alone**
Estar de non, quedar de non

**Believe**
Tener por

**Believe strongly**
A pie(s) juntillas

**Be long (in doing)**
Tardar en

**Below**
A continuación

**Be lucky**
Tener suerte, tocarle a uno la suerte

**Be mistaken**
Estar en un error

**Be nearly...(o'clock)**
Faltar un poco para las...(horas)

**Beneath**
Debajo de

**Be necessary**
Ser fuerza

**Be obliged to**
Verse obligado a

**Be obvious**
Saltar a la vista

**Be of no account**
Ser un cero a la izquierda

**Be of no use**
Ya no sopla

**Be of the opinion**
Dar la razón, tener para sí

**Be on duty**
Estar de turno

**Be one's own affair**
Correr por cuenta de uno

**Be one's turn**
Tocarle a uno, tocarle a uno la suerte

**Be on good terms with**
Acordar con

**Be on intimate terms with**
Tener confianza con

**Be only human**
Ser de carne y hueso

**Be on one's last legs**
Estar en las últimas

**Be on the alert for**
Estar a la mira de, estar sobre sí, estar sobre aviso

**Be on the lookout for**
Estar a la mira de

**Be on unfriendly terms with**
Estar torcido con

**Be on vacation**
Estar de vacaciones

**Be opportune**
Venir a (or al) pelo

**Be opposed to**
Estar en pugna con

**Be out of a job**
Medir las calles

**Be out of luck**
Andar de malas, estar de malas, tener la de malas

**Be out of resources**
Estar en las últimas

**Be out of sorts**
Andar agitado, no estar de humor

**Be out of the house**
Estar fuera de la casa

**Be passing through**
Estar de paso

**Be perfectly even**
Estar ras con ras

**Be pleased with**
Quedar contento con

**Be pleased with oneself**
Pagado de sí mismo

**Be proud of (or vain about) something**
Pagarse de algo

**Be a question of**
Tratarse de

**Be relieved of**
Quitarse uno un peso de encima

**Be required by custom**
Ser de rigor

**Be responsible for**
Hacerse cargo de

**Be ridiculous**
Hacer el ridículo

**Be right**
Andar bien; tener razón

**Be safe**
Estar a buen recaudo

**Be satisfied**
Estar uno hasta la coronilla

**Be seldom at home**
Ser huésped en su casa

**Be short of money**
Estar (or andar) escaso de dinero

**Beside**
A lado de, tras de

**Beside oneself**
Fuera de sí

**Besides (to boot)**
Además de, de pilón, sobre que

**Beside that**
Aparte de eso

**Be sleepy**
Tener sueño

**Be soaked through**
Estar hecho una sopa

**Be sorry for someone**
Pesarle a uno

**Be stubborn**
Ser duro de mollera

**Be stuffed**
Estar uno hasta el copete

**Be stupid**
No tener sal en la mollera

**Be successful**
Salir bien, tener éxito

**Be sulky**
Tener murria

**Be terribly sorry**
Sentir en el alma

**Be the scapegoat**
Pagar el pato

**Be the object of scandal**
Ser piedra de escándalo

**Be thirsty**
Tener sed

**Be ticklish**
Tener cosquillas

**Be to blame**
Tener la culpa

**Be too complicated**
Pecar de oscuro

**Be too good**
Pecar de bueno

**Be to one's advantage**
Convenirle a uno

**Better late than never**
Más vale tarde que nunca

**Better yet**
Mejor dicho

**Between**
Por entre

**Between the devil and the deep blue sea**
Entre la espada y la pared

**Be unable to cope with**
No da abasto a

**Be understood**
Quedar entendido que

**Be unlucky**
Estar salado

**Be unwilling to do it**
No querer hacerlo

**Be up to date**
Estar al cabo de, estar al corriente de, estar en corriente

**Be up to oneself**
Correr por cuenta de uno

**Be used as**
Servir de

**Be used for**
Servir para

**Be used (or accustomed) to...**
Tener la costumbre de...

**Be very angry**
Echar espumarajos

**Be very eager to (or for)**
Rabiar por

**Be very difficult**
Costar trabajo

**Be very thin**
Estar hecho un costal de huesos

**Be very unclear**
Pecar de oscuro

**Be a wallflower**
Planchar el asiento

**Be well**
Sin novedad

**Be well-informed**
Estar al cabo de, estar al corriente de, estar en corriente

**Be well off**
Estar desahogado

**Be willing**
Estar dispuesto

**Be witty or salty**
Estar salado

**Be worse off**
Estar peor que antes

**Be worth**
Valer por

**Be worthless**
No ser ni chicha ni limonada

**Be worthwhile**
Merecer la pena, valer la pena

**Be wrong**
Estar en un error, no tener razón

**Be...years old**
Tener...años

**Beyond**
Más allá (de)

**Blame**
Dar en cara, echar en cara, echar la culpa a

**Blindly**
A ciegas, a ojos cerrados, a tientas

**Block the door**
Impedir el paso

**Blush**
Ponerse colorado

**Boast of**
Hacer gala de, pagarse de

**Borrow**
Pedir prestado

**Bother about**
Molestarse en

**Brand as (or accuse)**
Motejar de

**Break into**
Forzar la entrada

**Break into pieces**
Hacer pedazos

**Break one's word**
Faltar a su palabra, pintarle un violín

**Break the news**
Dar la noticia

**Break the thread of a story**
Cortar el hilo

**Bridge a gap**
Llenar un vacío

**Bring up to date**
Poner al corriente

**Bulky**
De buen tomo y lomo

**Bully for you!**
¡Así se hace!

**Bump into each other**
Darse un encontrón

**Burn down**
Quemarse hasta el suelo

**Burning question**
La cuestión palpitante

**Burn the midnight oil**
Quemarse las pestañas (or las cejas)

**Burst with laughter**
Reventar de risa

**Bury**
Dar sepultura

**But**
Sino que

**By all means**
A toda costa, a todas luces, de todos modos, sin falta

**By chance**
Al azar, por casualidad

**By dint of**
A fuerza de

**By ear**
Al oído, de oído

**By foot**
A pie

**By force (of)**
A fuerza (de), a la fuerza

**By guess**
A ojo, al tanteo

**By hand**
A mano

**By heart**
De memoria

**By itself**
De por sí

**By just shouting**
A puros gritos

**By means of**
Por medio de

**By mistake**
Por equivocación, por descuido

**By no means**
De ningún modo, de ninguna manera, ni modo

**By oneself**
Por sí solo, por su mano

**By pure chance**
De pura casualidad

**By sheer force**
A pura fuerza

**By sight**
A ojo

**By the looks of**
Por lo visto

**By the minute**
De punto

**By the roots**
De raíz

**By the way**
A propósito, de paso, entre paréntesis

**By twos**
De dos en dos

**By word of mouth**
De palabra, de viva voz

# C

**Call a spade a spade**
Al pan, pan y al vino, vino;
llamar al pan pan y al vino vino

**Call on the phone (telephone)**
Llamar por teléfono

**Call the roll**
Pasar lista

**Carry away**
Cargar con

**Carry out**
Dar cima, llevar a efecto,
llevarse adelante

**Carry through**
Llevar a cabo

**Cast a shadow**
Hacer sombra

**Catch cold**
Coger catarro, coger un
resfriado

**Catch fire**
Coger fuego

**Cause distress or grief to**
Dar disgustos a

**Cause extra work**
Dar que hacer

**Cause pain or worry**
Hacer mella

**Cause sorrow**
Dar mucha pena

**Cents off**
Rebaja de...centavos

**Certainly**
A buen seguro

**Certainly not**
Claro que no

**Chain of misfortunes**
Rosario de desdichas

**Change one's mind**
Cambiar de idea (...opinión,
...pensamiento)

**Change the subject**
Cambiar de tema

**Chatter constantly**
Hablar por los codos, hablar a
chorros

**Cheat (in a bargain or exchange)**
Dar gato por liebre

**Cheer up**
Dar ánimo

**Choose**
Optar por

**Clarify**
Poner en claro

**Clearly**
A las claras, a ojos vistas

**Clear the table**
Levantar la mesa, quitar la
mesa

**Clear the way**
Abrir paso

**Clear up**
Poner en claro

**Close attention**
Suma atención

**Closer**
Más acá

**Close to**
A raíz de, cerca de

**Coast is not clear, the**
Hay moros en la costa

**Cock and bull story**
Cuento chino

**Collide with**
Darse un encontrón

**Collapse**
Venirse abajo

**Come across (someone or
something)**
Encontrarse con, tropezar con

**Come at the right moment**
Venir a (or al) pelo

**Come from**
Ser oriundo de

**Come hell or high water**
Contra viento y marea

**Come one after another (bad
luck or misfortunes)**
Llover sobre mojado

**Come out ahead**
Salir ganando

**Come out as desired**
Surtir efecto

**Come out poorly**
Salir mal

**Come out well**
Quedar bien, salir bien, surtir
efecto

**Come to (regain consciousness)**
Volver en sí

**Come to a boil**
Soltar (or alzar) el hervor

**Come to an agreement**
Ponerse de acuerdo

**Come to blows**
Venir a las manos

**Come to know**
Llegar a saber

**Come to pass**
Llegar a suceder, ocurrir

**Come to the point**
Dejarse de cuentos, ir al grano

**Come what may**
Contra viento y marea, suceda
lo que suceda

**Comings and goings**
Idas y venidas

**Complain loudly**
Poner el grito en el cielo

**Complain of**
Quejarse de

**Complete**
Dar cima, dar fin (a)

**Completely**
De raíz, por completo

**Compliment**
Echar flores, echar un
piropo

**Concerning**
Respecto a

**Confidentially**
Al oído

**Confront**
Enfrentarse con

**Consciously**
A sabiendas

**Consequently**
De resultas, en consecuencia
de, por consecuencia de, por
consiguiente

**Consider**
Parar mientes en, tener en
cuenta, tener por, tomar en
cuenta

**Consider as**
Dar por

**Consider as done**
Dar por hecho

**Considering that**
Visto que

**Continually**
A cada momento, por instante

**Continuously**
De seguida

**Coordinate**
Poner en juego

**Cost an arm and a leg**
Costar un ojo de la cara

**Count on**
Contar con

**Crawl (or creep)**
Andar a gatas

**Crawling**
A gatas

**Crawl out of a difficulty**
Salir a gatas

**Cross-country**
A campo traviesa

**Crowd**
Hervidero de gente, remolino
de gente

**Crowded**
De bote en bote

**Crow's feet (wrinkles)**
Pata de gallo

**Crude**
En rama

**Curse**
Echar ternos, soltar un terno

**Cut class**
Faltar a (la) clase, hacer
pinta

**Cut into strips**
Hacer rajas

# D

**Dabble in**
Picar en

**Daily grind**
La rutina diaria

**Dance without music**
Bailar a secas

**Dating from**
Desde hace

**Day after day**
Día tras día

**Daydream**
Estar en las nubes, soñar
despierto

**Days of old**
Días de antaño

**Dead end**
Callejón sin salida

**Deal in**
Tratar en

**Deal with**
Tratar de

**Deceitfully**
A traición, de mala fe

**Deceitful story told to get money**
El cuento del tío

**Decide upon**
Optar por

**Decline**
Venir a menos

**Delay**
Dar largas

**Demolish**
Echar por tierra

**Depart**
Salir de

**Despite**
A despecho de

**Destroy**
Dar al traste con, dar al través
con

**Devour (eat up or drink down)**
Echarse al coleto

**Diagonally**
Al sesgo

**Die**
Estirar la pata, pasar a mejor
vida

**Disappoint**
Pegar un chasco

**Displease**
Caer mal, no caer bien

**Ditch (avoid)**
Dar esquinazo

**Do...again**
Hacer...de nuevo, volver a...

**Dodge the issue**
Evadir el tema

**Don't worry**
¡No se ocupe!, ¡No se preocupe
usted!

**Don't worry about it**
No tenga usted cuidado

**Do one's best**
Hacer lo posible, poner todo de
su parte

**Do over**
Hacer de nuevo, hacer otra vez,
volver a hacer

**Doubt**
Poner en duda

**Do without**
Pasarse sin, prescindir de

**Draw lots**
Echar pajas, echar suertes

**Dream of**
Soñar con (or en)

**Drift**
Andar a la deriva, irse a la
deriva

**Drink too much**
Alzar el codo, empinar el codo

**Drive someone crazy**
Volver loco a uno

**Drop**
Dejar caer

**Drop out (of)**
Darse de baja, dejar de asistir,
retirarse (de)

**Drop out of sight**
Perderse de vista

**Dunce**
Tonto de capirote, zopenco

**During the week**
A mediados de la semana, entre
semana

# E

**Each one**
Cada cual, cada uno

**Each other**
El uno al otro, unos a otros

**Each time**
A cada rato, cada vez

**Earliest possible, the**
Lo antes posible

**Early in (a period of time)**
A principios de

**Earn a living**
Ganar para comer, ganarse la
vida

**Either**
El uno o el otro, uno u otro

**Either of the two**
Cualesquiera (or cualquiera) de
los dos

**Emphasize**
Dar realce, hacer destacar

**Encore!**
¡Otra, otra!

**Encounter**
Tropezar con

**Encourage**
Dar aliento, dar alas a

**Endanger**
Poner al tablero, poner en
peligro

**End up as**
Venir a parar

**End up by (doing something)**
Acabar por

**Enhance**
Dar realce

**Enjoy your meal!**
¡Buen provecho!

**Equally**
Al igual

**Equal to or up to**
Con fuerzas para, estar a la
altura de

**Especially**
Ante todo, en especial, en
particular, sobre todo

**Esteem highly**
Tener en mucho, poner en (or
sobre) las nubes

**Et cetera**
Y así sucesivamente

**Even if**
Aun cuando

**Even so**
Así y todo

**Even though**
Aun cuando, ni siquiera

**Even with (flush)**
Al ras con, a ras de

**Ever since**
Desde entonces

**Everybody**
Todo el mundo

**Everybody who**
Todo el que

**Every day**
Todos los días

**Everyone**
Todo hombre

**Every other day**
Cada dos días, un día sí y otro
no, un día sí y un día no

**Everything else**
Todo lo demás

**Every time**
Todas las veces (que)

**Everywhere**
A todas partes, en todas partes,
por todas partes, por todos
lados

**Evidently**
Por lo visto

**Exactly as**
Según y como, según y
conforme

**Exactly as desired**
A pedir de boca

**Exactly the opposite**
Todo lo contrario

**Exasperate (someone)**
Sacar (a uno) de quicio

**Except for**
Si no fuera por, si no fuera
porque

**Excessively**
Sobre manera

**Exclusive of**
Sin contar

**Extend condolences to or for**
Dar el pésame por

**Extra**
De repuesto

**Extremely**
Con (or en or por) extremo

# F

**Face**
Dar a, hacer frente (a), hacer
rostro

**Face to face**
Cara a cara

**Fail**
Dejar de, salir mal, venirse
abajo

**Fair (or such as it is)**
Tal cual

**Fair play**
Juego limpio

**Fall back into old habits**
Volver a las andadas

**Fall down**
Irse abajo, venirse abajo

**Fall ill**
Caer enfermo, ponerse enfermo

**Fall to one's lot**
Tocarle a uno la suerte

**Fall upon**
Venir sobre

**Far from**
Ni con mucho

**Farther away**
Más allá de

**Farther on**
Más adelante

**Fast asleep**
Profundamente dormido

**Featherbrained**
Alegre de cascos, ligero de
cascos

**Feed**
Dar de comer

**Feel feverish**
Sentirse destemplado

**Feel like**
Tener gana(s) de

**Feel OK**
Estar regular

**Feel sorry for**
Tener lástima de

**Feign illness, to**
Hacer la zanguanga

**Few, a**
Unas cuantas, unos cuantos

**Few lines, a**
Cuatro letras

**Few words, a**
Cuatro palabras

**Fib**
Echar papas

**Finally**
Al cabo, en fin, por fin, por
última vez, por último

**Find fault with**
Poner defectos, poner faltas

**Find no way out**
No hallar vado

**First of all**
Ante todo

**Fit badly**
Caer mal

**Fit of anger**
Arranque de cólera, ímpetu
de ira

**Fit of madness**
Transporte de locura

**Fit well**
Caer bien, sentar bien a

**Fix one's eyes on**
Poner la mira

**Flash by**
Pasar como un relámpago

**Flat denial**
Una negativa rotunda, una
negativa terminante

**Flatter**
Dar coba, dar jabón (a), echar
flores, echar un piropo

**Flirt (with)**
Afilar con, coquetear, hacer
cocos

**Flush with**
A flor de, al ras con, a ras de

**Follow in the footsteps (of)**
Seguir las pisadas

**Fond of**
Amante de, amigo de

**Fool, to**
Hacer cuco a

**Fool oneself**
Hacerse ilusiones

**Foot the bill**
Pagar los gastos

**For a change**
Para variar

**For and against**
En pro y en contra

**For certain**
De seguro

**Forever**
Para siempre, por siempre

**For example**
Por ejemplo

**Form a line**
Hacer cola

**For now**
Por ahora

**For one purpose or another**
Para unos fines u otros

**For some reason**
Por algo

**For some time now**
De algún tiempo para acá

**For sure**
De seguro

**For that reason**
Por esa razón, por eso

**For the first time**
Por primera vez

**For the last time**
Por última vez

**For the present**
Por de pronto, por lo pronto,
por el (or la or lo) presente

**For the sake of**
En obsequio de, por amor de

**For the time being**
De momento, por ahora, por el
momento, por lo pronto

**For want of**
A falta de

**Forward**
Hacia adelante

**Foul play**
Juego sucio

**Frame someone**
Conspirar contra una persona

**Frankly**
A las claras, sin rebozo, sin
reserva

**Free**
En libertad

**Free rein**
A rienda suelta

**Frequently**
A cada momento, a menudo,
con mucha frecuencia

**Frighten**
Dar horror

**From a distance**
De lejos, desde lejos

**From afar**
Desde lejos

**From bad to worse**
De mal en peor

**From beginning to end**
De cabo a rabo

**From now on**
De ahora en adelante, de aquí
en adelante, de hoy en adelante,
desde ahora en adelante

**From one side to the other**
De parte a parte

**From that time on**
De aquel tiempo en adelante, de
aquel entonces

**From the beginning**
Desde el principio

**From then on**
De ahí en adelante

**From the outside**
Por fuera

**From the rear**
Por detrás

**From time to time**
A ratos, de tarde en tarde

**From today on**
A partir de hoy

**From top to bottom**
De arriba abajo

**Full-fledged**
Hecho y derecho

**Full to the brim**
Lleno de bote en bote

**Fully**
A fondo

**Furthermore**
Más aún

# G

**Generally**
Por lo común, por lo general

**Get along well with**
Llevarse bien con, quedar bien con

**Get down to cases**
Ir al grano

**Get drunk**
Pillar una mona

**Get going**
Poner en marcha

**Get late**
Hacerse tarde

**Get late in the evening**
Hacerse noche

**Get lost!**
¡Vete a bañar!

**Get married**
Contraer matrimonio

**Get oneself in a mess**
Meterse en un lío

**Get out of a difficulty**
Salir del paso

**Get out of here!**
¡Largo de aquí!, ¡Quítese de aquí!

**Get ready to leave**
Hacer las maletas

**Get tangled up**
Hacerse un lío

**Get the blame**
Pagar el pato

**Get the blame unjustly**
Cargar con el muerto

**Get the point**
Caer en la cuenta

**Get to one's feet**
Ponerse de pie

**Get to sleep**
Conciliar el sueño

**Get up**
Ponerse de pie, ponerse en pie

**Get up on the wrong side of the bed**
Levantarse de malas, levantarse con las malas, levantarse con el santo de espaldas

**Get well**
Ponerse bien

**Get worse**
Subir de punto

**Give account**
Dar razón

**Give a party**
Dar una fiesta

**Give a report on**
Dar cuenta de

**Give a scare**
Pegar un susto

**Give cause for**
Dar lugar a

**Give courage**
Dar alas a

**Give good results**
Surtir efecto

**Give it up**
Darlo por abandonado

**Given name**
Nombre de bautismo, nombre de pila

**Give opportunity (or occasion) to**
Dar pie

**Give regards**
Dar los recuerdos

**Give someone the run around**
Dar largas

**Give something up for lost**
Echarle la bendición a una cosa

**Give thanks**
Dar las gracias

**Give to**
Dar a

**Give up**
Darse por vencido

**Give up (or get rid of) something**
Quitarse de una cosa

**Gladly**
Con mucho gusto, de buena gana, de buen grado, de (buena) voluntad

**Glance at**
Mirar por encima

**Glance off**
Pegar de soslayo

**Glance over**
Dar un vistazo a

**Gnash one's teeth**
Rechinar los dientes

**Go arm in arm**
Ir del brazo

**Go back**
Volverse atrás

**Go back on one's word**
Echarse para atrás, volverse atrás

**Go blind**
Perder la vista

**Go cautiously**
Caminar con pies de plomo

**Go crazy**
Perder el juicio, volverse loco

**Go halves**
Ir a medias, ir a la mitad

**Go jump in the lake!**
¡Vete a bañar!

**Good-looking**
Bien parecido, de buen ver

**Good luck**
Que le vaya bien

**Go on a journey**
Hacer un viaje

**Go on a spree**
Andar (or ir) de parranda, andar (or ir) de fiesta en fiesta, ir de jarana

**Go on foot**
Ir a pie

**Go on vacation**
Ir de vacaciones

**Goosebumps**
Carne de gallina

**Go out for a good time or fling**
Echar una cana al aire

**Go out of style**
Pasar de moda

**Go out to meet**
Salir al encuentro de

**Go over carefully**
Pasar revista a

**Go over like a lead balloon**
Caer mal, caer gordo

**Go shopping**
Ir de compras

**Go to bed early**
Acostarse con las gallinas

**Grab**
Echar la garra

**Gradually**
Poco a poco

**Grasp**
Echar la zarpa

**Grow late**
Hacerse noche

**Grown up**
Hecho y derecho

**Guess right**
Dar en (or con) el chiste

# H

**Hail from**
Ser oriundo de

**Half done**
A medio hacer

**Halfway (to a place)**
A medio camino

**Hang one's head**
Agachar las orejas

**Haphazardly**
A la ventura

**Happy-go-lucky**
Chueco o derecho

**Hard cash**
Dinero contante y sonante

**Hardly**
A duras penas

**Hardly ever**
Casi nunca

**Hard of hearing**
Algo sordo, corto de oído,
medio sordo

**Hard time**
Un rato desagradable

**Hard-working**
Muy trabajador

**Have a bad time**
Sudar la gota gorda

**Have a big mouth**
Tener la lengua larga

**Have a birthday**
Cumplir años

**Have a finger in everything**
Estar en todo

**Have a good day**
Que lo pase bien

**Have a good time**
Pasar un buen rato

**Have (an illness)**
Estar con (una enfermedad)

**Have a screw loose**
Faltarle a uno un tornillo

**Have contact (or a lot to do)
with a person**
Tener roce con alguien

**Have dealings with**
Tratar con

**Have a dislike for someone**
Tenerle tirria a una persona

**Have influence with someone**
Tener cabida con alguien

**Have in mind**
Tener en la mente

**Have in sight**
Tener a la vista

**Have just (done something)**
Acabar de

**Have little sense**
Faltarle a uno un tornillo

**Have nothing to do with**
No tener nada que ver con

**Have no way out**
No tener alternativa (o
elección)

**Have on**
Traer puesto

**Have one's own way**
Salirse con la suya

**Have on the tip of one's tongue**
Tener en la punta de la lengua

**Have the blues**
Tener murria

**Have the lead**
Llevar ventaja

**Have the misfortune to**
Tener la pena de

**Have time off**
Tener tiempo libre

**Have to (do something)**
Tener que...

**Have to do with**
Tener que ver con

**Heads or tails**
Águila o pico, águila o sello,
cara o cruz

**Head toward**
Hacer rumbo a

**Heaps**
A montones

**Hear about**
Oír hablar de

**Hear news early or for the
first time**
Desayunarse con la noticia

**Hear from**
Recibir noticias de

**Hearsay**
De oídos

**Hear that**
Oír decir que

**Hearty laugh**
Una buena carcajada

**Height of folly**
El colmo de la locura

**Help**
Dar la mano

**Help yourself**
Sírvase usted

**Hence**
De ahí que, por ende

**Here!**
A sus órdenes

**Hereafter**
En lo sucesivo

**Here below**
De tejas abajo

**Hinder**
Hacer mala obra

**Hit (upon)**
Dar en

**Hit a nerve**
Tocar en lo vivo

**Hit at a slant**
Pegar de soslayo

**Hit or miss**
Al tanteo, chueco o derecho

**Hit the ceiling**
Poner el grito en el cielo

**Hit the nail on the head**
Dar en el clavo, dar en (o con)
el chiste, dar uno en la tecla

**Hold in check**
Tener a raya

**Hold in low esteem**
Tener en poco a

**Honestly!**
¡Palabrita de honor!

**Horrify**
Dar horror

**Hot-headed**
Caliente de cascos

**How awful!**
¡Qué horror!

**How can I (one) have the nerve?**
¿Con qué cara?

**How do you like...?**
¿Qué le parece...?

**How do you say...?**
¿Cómo se dice...?

**However**
Ahora bien, sin embargo

**However much**
Por más que

**How far?**
¿Hasta dónde?

**How goes it? (or how is it
going?)**
¿Qué hubo?

**How often?**
¿Cada cuánto tiempo?

**How should I know?**
¿Qué sé yo?

**How unfortunate!**
¡Qué desgracia!

**Humiliate**
Poner en ridículo

**Hurry**
Darse prisa

**Hurry back**
Volver corriendo

**Hurt or harm someone**
Hacerle daño a uno

**Hurt to the quick**
Tocar en lo vivo

# I

**I bet... (not a real wager)**
A que...

**I bet they are...**
Seguro que están

**I bet you don't!**
¡A que no!

**If at all**
Si acaso

**If even**
Si alguna vez

**If I remember correctly**
Si mal no recuerdo

**If not**
De lo contrario, donde no

**I forgot to tell you**
Se me pasó decirte

**If so**
En caso afirmativo

**Ignore**
Hacer caso omiso de

**Ill-behaved**
Mal mandado, muy mandado

**Impatient**
Mal sufrido

**Impede**
Dificultar el paso

**Important**
De buen tomo y lomo, de copete

**In a bad humor**
De mal temple

**In about**
Como en

**In abundance**
A montones

**In accordance with**
Conforme a, de acuerdo con

**In addition to**
Además de, a más de, sobre que

**In advance**
Con anticipación, con tiempo, de antemano, por adelantado

**Inadvertently**
Sin sentir

**In a jiffy**
Como por ensalmo, en un credo, en un chiflido, en un soplo

**In a little while**
Dentro de poco

**In all**
En junto, en conjunto

**In all directions**
A los cuatro vientos

**In a loud voice**
En voz alta

**In a low voice**
En voz baja

**In a minute**
En un credo

**In a moment**
En un improviso

**In a month of Sundays**
Como visita de obispo

**In any case**
Al fin de cuentas, de todos modos

**In any event**
En todo caso

**In a second**
En un chiflido, en un soplo

**In a short time**
Dentro de un momento

**In a short while**
A (or al) poco rato, dentro de poco

**Inasmuch as**
Como que, como quiera que

**In a way**
Hasta cierto punto

**In back of**
Atrás de, detrás de

**In bad faith**
De mala fe

**In brief**
En resolución, en resumen

**In broad daylight**
En pleno día

**In case**
Por si acaso

**In case of (that)**
En caso de (que)

**In cold blood**
En sangre fría

**In competition**
A porfía

**Incomplete**
A medio hacer

**In compliance with**
En conformidad con, estar de conformidad con

**In conclusion**
En fin

**In conflict with**
Estar en pugna con

**Increase**
Subir de punto

**In days gone by**
En días pasados

**Indeed**
En efecto

**In detail**
Por extenso, por menudo

**Indirectly**
De rebote

**Indoors**
Bajo techo, en casa

**In due course or time**
A su (debido) tiempo

**In earnest**
A la verdad, de veras

**In either case**
En ambos casos

**In exchange for**
A cambio de

**In fact**
De hecho, en efecto, en rigor

**In favor of**
De parte de

**Inform**
Dar parte, dar razón, poner al corriente, poner en conocimiento

**Informal**
Sin ceremonia

**Informal gathering or party**
Reunión de confianza

**In front of**
Al frente de, delante de, frente a

**In good faith**
De buena fe

**In good taste**
De buen tono, de buen gusto

**In good time**
Con tiempo

**In half**
Por la mitad

**In haste**
A la carrera

**In honor of**
En obsequio de

**In jest**
De broma, de burla, en broma

**In many respects**
En muchos puntos

**In my opinion**
A mi entender, a mi modo de ver

**In (at) odd moments**
A ratos perdidos

**In one fell swoop**
De una tirada

**In one's sleep**
En sueños

**In order**
En regla

**In order that**
A fin de que, para que

**In other words**
En otros términos, es decir

**In particular**
En especial

**In passing**
De paso

**In place of**
En lugar de

**In plain language**
En buen romance

**In plain view (of)**
A la vista (de)

**In poor taste**
De mal gusto

**In the presence of**
A vista de

**In progress**
En curso, en marcha

**In proof of**
En señal de

**In proportion to**
A medida que

**In safety**
En salvo

**In season**
En sazón

**In shirtsleeves**
En mangas de camisa

**In short**
Al fin y al cabo, en fin, en resumidas cuentas

**Inside of**
Dentro de

**Insincerely**
De dientes afuera

**In small quantities**
Al menudeo, al por menor, de poquito

**In some way or other**
De un modo u otro

**In (at) spare moments**
A ratos perdidos

**In spite of**
A despecho de, a pesar de

**In spite of everything**
A pesar de todo

**In spite of that**
Así y todo, con todo, con todos los obstáculos

**In spite of the fact that**
A pesar de que

**Instantly**
En un santiamén

**Instead of**
En lugar de, en vez de

**In such a case**
En tal caso

**In such a way**
De suerte que

**Intend or mean to**
Pensar en, tener la intención de

**Interfere**
Hacer mala obra

**Interrupt**
Cortar el hilo

**Intervene**
Meterse de por medio

**In that way**
De esa manera, de ese modo

**In the act**
En fragante

**In the background**
En lontananza

**In the dark**
A oscuras, a obscuras

**In the dead of the night**
En el sigilo (or silencio) de la noche, en las altas horas

**In the dead of winter**
En lo más crudo del invierno

**In the direction of**
Con rumbo a

**In the distance**
A lo lejos, en lontananza

**In the evening**
En la noche, por la noche

**In the event of**
En caso de

**In the final analysis**
A fin de cuentas

**In the future**
De ahora en adelante, en adelante, en lo futuro, en lo sucesivo

**In the hands of**
En poder de

**In the latest fashion**
A la moda

**In the long run**
A la larga

**In the manner of**
A guisa de

**In the middle**
Por la mitad

**In the morning (afternoon, etc.)**
Por la mañana (la tarde, etc.)

**In the nick of time**
En el momento preciso

**In the night air**
Al sereno

**In the open**
A campo raso

**In the open air**
Al aire libre, al raso

**In the opposite way**
Al revés

**In the same way**
Del mismo modo

**In the style of**
A (la) manera de

**In the twinkling of an eye**
En un abrir y cerrar de ojos, en un santiamén

**In this vicinity**
Por aquí cerca

**In this way**
De esta manera, de este modo

**In this world**
De tejas abajo

**In those days**
En aquel tiempo, en aquel entonces

**In time**
A tiempo

**In transit**
De paso, de tránsito

**In truth**
A la verdad, de veras

**In turn**
En rueda

**In vain**
En balde

**In view of**
En vista de que

**In vogue**
De moda

**In writing**
Por escrito

**Irrelevant**
Fuera de propósito, inaplicable al caso

**I should say not!**
¡De ninguna manera!

**I should say so!**
¡Ya lo creo!

**Is that so?**
¿De veras?, ¿de verdad?, ¡no diga!

**It can't be helped**
No hay remedio, no tiene remedio

**It doesn't matter**
No le hace, no tiene importancia

**It is all over**
Ha pasado, ha terminado, se ha acabado, ya se acabó

**It is all right**
Está bien

**It is better...**
Más vale...

**It is clear**
Ya se ve

**It is forbidden**
Se prohibe

**It is good (bad) weather**
Hace buen (mal) clima

**It is hopeless**
No tiene remedio

**It is necessary to**
Hay que

**It is not worth the trouble**
No vale la pena

**It is no wonder that**
No es mucho que

**It is obvious**
Se conoce (que)

**It is obvious that**
Se ve que

**It is rumored that**
Se suena que

**It is said**
Se dice

**It is time for**
Es (la) hora de

**It is time to go**
Es (la) hora de partir

**It is unnecessary (superfluous)**
Está de más

**It is yet to be done**
Está por hacer

**It makes no difference**
Darle lo mismo, es lo de menos, lo mismo da, no le hace

**It may be that**
Puede ser que, tal vez sea que

**It must**
De rigor

**It must be**
Debe de ser

**It must be true**
Ha de ser verdad

**It probably is**
Debe de ser

**It's a deal!**
¡Trato hecho!

**It's almost time**
Falta poco

**It's been a long time since (I played)**
Hace mucho que no (juego)

**It seems to be impossible**
Parece mentira

**It seems to me that**
Me parece que

**It serves me right**
Bien me lo merezco

**It's none of your (my) business**
No es asunto suyo (mío)

**It's not important**
No tiene importancia

**It's not opportune (not to the point)**
No viene al caso, no viene al cuento

**It's not worthwhile**
No vale la pena

**It's time to...**
Ya es hora de...

**It's too late now**
Ya es tarde

**It's true**
Es cierto

**It won't be long now**
Ya mero, ya merito

## J

**Jack of all trades**
Aprendiz de todo y oficial de nada

**Jilt**
Dar calabazas

**Join (a club, etc.)**
Ingresar en

**Jokingly**
De broma

**Judge**
Tener por

**Jump**
Dar un salto, dar saltos

**Jump to conclusions**
Hacer deducciones precipitadas

**Just**
Nada más

**Just about to**
Ya mero

**Just as**
Así como, según y como, según y conforme

**Just as is**
Así nada más

**Just in case**
Por lo que pueda tronar, por si acaso

**Just plain**
Así nada más

**Just right**
Al centavo, al pelo

**Just yesterday**
Ayer mismo

## K

**Keep (something)**
Quedarse con (una cosa)

**Keep accounts**
Llevar cuentas

**Keep good time (a watch)**
Andar bien

**Keep in bounds**
Tener a raya

**Keep one's feet**
Tenerse en pie

**Keep one's word**
Cumplir (con) su palabra

**Keep out!**
¡Prohibido el paso!

**Keep silent**
Guardar silencio

**Keep track of**
Llevar la cuenta, llevar cuenta de

**Keep up to date, informed, posted**
Tener al corriente

**Kick out**
Dar de baja

**Kill two birds with one stone**
Matar dos pájaros de un tiro

**Kneel**
Ponerse de rodillas

**Kneel down**
Hincarse de rodillas

**Knit the eyebrows**
Fruncir las cejas

**Knock down**
Echar por tierra

**Know absolutely nothing (about that)**
No saber ni papa (de eso)

**Know by heart**
Saber de memoria

**Know by sight**
Conocer de vista

**Know how to (sew, dance, etc.)**
Saber (coser, bailar, etc.)

**Knowingly**
A sabiendas

## L

**Lack**
Hacer falta

**Lacking**
A falta de

**Lame excuse**
Disculpa pobre

**Large number of**
Una infinidad de

**Last month**
El mes pasado

**Last straw**
La gota que derrama el vaso

**Last week**
La semana pasada

**Last year**
El año pasado

**Late**
A fines de

**Later on**
Más adelante

**Latter**
El más reciente

**Laugh at**
Reírse de

**Laugh off**
Tomar a risa

**Laugh up one's sleeve**
Reírse para sus adentros

**Leap year**
Año bisiesto

**Learn by heart**
Aprender de memoria

**Least of it**
Lo de menos

**Leave**
Dejar de la mano; salir de

**Leave alone**
Dejar en paz, dejar tranquilo

**Leave (someone) in the lurch**
Dejar (a uno) plantado, dejar en las astas del toro

**Leave word**
Dejar dicho

**Leisure hours**
Ratos perdidos

**Lend**
Dar prestado

**Lengthwise**
A lo largo (de)

**Less and less**
Cada vez menos

**Less than**
Menos de, menos que

**Let be**
Dejar en paz

**Let loose**
Soltar la rienda

**Let on**
Dejar saber

**Let oneself be coaxed**
Hacerse del rogar

**Let's see (if)**
A ver (si)

**Like**
A guisa de, a (la) manera de, a semejanza de, parecido a

**Like always**
Como siempre

**Literally**
Al pie de la letra

**Little by little**
Poco a poco

**Little more**
Y pico

**Little pitchers have big ears**
Hay moros en la costa

**Live by stealing**
Vivir de sus uñas

**Live together**
Hacer vida

**Long ago**
Hace mucho tiempo

**Long time**
Largos años

**Look**
Pues, mire

**Look down on**
Mirar por encima del hombro

**Look for a needle in a haystack**
Buscar una aguja en un pajar

**Look for trouble**
Buscarle tres (or cuatro) pies
al gato

**Look out of the corner of one's
eye**
Mirar con el rabo del ojo

**Look towards**
Dar a

**Look well**
Tener buena cara

**Lose face**
Perder prestigio

**Lose one's head**
Saltar las trancas

**Lose one's mind**
Perder el juicio, perder la razón

**Lose patience**
Saltar las trancas

**Lose sight of**
Perder de vista

**Lose time**
Perder el tiempo

**Lots of**
A mar de

**Loud voice**
En voz alta

**Lump in the throat**
Un nudo en la garganta

**M**

**Madly**
Con delirio

**Mail (a letter)**
Echar (una carta) al correo

**Majority of**
La mayoría (de), la mayor
parte (de)

**Majority of the people**
El común de las gentes

**Make a deal**
Hacer un trato

**Make a dent**
Hacer mella

**Make a fool of**
Poner en ridículo

**Make a good showing**
Hacer buen papel

**Make a mistake**
No dar pie con bola

**Make an appointment**
Dar una cita

**Make a poor showing**
Hacer mal papel

**Make a ridiculous blunder**
Hacer una plancha

**Make arrangements**
Hacer arreglos

**Make eyes at**
Hacer cocos

**Make faces**
Hacer gestos, hacer muecas

**Make friends with**
Hacerse amigo de

**Make fun of**
Burlarse de, hacer cuco a, hacer
burla de

**Make good**
Tener buen éxito

**Make hay while the sun shines**
Hacer su agosto

**Make known**
Dar a conocer

**Make laugh**
Hacer gracia

**Make no difference**
Dar lo mismo, no irle ni venirle
a uno

**Make oneself understood**
Hacerse entender

**Make one's living**
Ganarse la vida

**Make trouble**
Dar guerra

**Make up**
Inventar, imaginar

**Make up (after a quarrel)**
Hacer las paces

**Make up for**
Resarcirse de

**Make use of**
Valerse de

**Make way for**
Abrir paso para

**Many years**
Largos años

**Match, to**
Hacer juego

**Mature**
Hecho y derecho

**Maybe**
A lo mejor, tal vez

**Mean (intend)**
Querer decir

**Meantime**
Andarse el tiempo

**Mean trick**
Una mala pasada

**Meanwhile**
Entre tanto, mientras tanto

**Measure**
Tomar una providencia

**Meddle**
Meterse de por medio

**Mediocre person**
Media cuchara

**Meet**
Cruzarse con, encontrarse con,
tropezar con

**Meet face to face**
Enfrentarse con

**Mind your own business!**
¿Quién te mete, Juan Copete?

**Minor (in age)**
Menor de edad

**Misconstrue or misinterpret**
Tomar el rábano por las hojas

**Miss**
Echar de menos

**Moment to moment**
Por instante

**More or less**
Alrededor de

**Moreover**
Por lo demás

**More than**
Más de, más que

**More than anyone**
Más que nadie

**More than enough**
De sobra

**More than ever**
Más que nunca

**More than once**
Más de una vez, una y otra vez

**Most of**
La mayoría de, la mayor
parte de

**Mourn**
Estar de duelo

**Move over**
Hacerse a un lado

**N**

**Namely**
A saber

**Naturally**
Claro que sí

**Near at hand**
Al lado (de)

**Nearly**
Por poco

**Neatly dressed**
Bien arreglado(a)

**Neither fish nor fowl**
No ser ni chicha ni limonada

**Neither this nor that**
Ni esto ni aquello

**Never mind**
¡No importa!, ¡no se ocupe!

**Nevertheless**
No obstante, sin embargo

**Next to**
Al lado de, junto a

**No...(smoking, eating, etc.)**
Se prohibe...(fumar, comer, etc.)

**Nobody else**
Ningún otro

**No comment**
Sin comentarios

**No kidding!**
¡Palabrita de honor!

**No longer**
Ya no

**No matter how much**
Por mucho que

**No matter what**
Por ningún motivo, suceda lo que suceda

**Nonsense**
¡De dónde!; salida de pie de banco

**No parking**
Prohibido estacionarse

**Nor I either**
Ni yo tampoco

**No sooner said than done**
Dicho y hecho

**Not by a long shot**
Ni con mucho

**Not by any means**
Ni mucho menos

**Not by far**
Ni con mucho

**Not equal to the burden**
No poder con la carga

**Not even**
Ni siquiera

**Nothing at all**
Nada en absoluto

**Nothing like that**
Nada de eso

**Nothing unusual**
Nada de particular

**Notice**
Darse cuenta de, echar de ver, fijarse en

**Not in a laughing mood**
No estar de humor

**Not much**
Poca cosa

**Not only...but also**
No sólo...sino también

**No trespassing**
Prohibida la entrada, prohibido el paso, se prohibe entrar (pasar)

**Not so often**
No tan a menudo

**Not to be a laughing matter**
No ser cosa de juego

**Not to bother about trifles**
No pararse en pelillos

**Not to feel well**
Sentirse destemplado

**Not to fit well**
No caer bien

**Not to get things right**
No dar pie con bola

**Not to know anything**
No saber una (or ni) jota

**Not to my knowledge**
No que yo sepa

**Not to open one's mouth**
No despegar los labios

**Not to realize**
No darse cuenta

**Not to say a word**
No despegar los labios

**Not to sleep a wink**
Pasar la noche en claro (or en blanco)

**Not to worry**
Perder cuidado

**Notwithstanding**
No obstante

**Not worth a red cent**
No vale una cuartilla

**Not worth a straw**
No vale un pito

**Not yet**
Aún no, todavía no

**Now**
Al presente

**Nowadays**
Hoy (en) día

**Now and then**
De tarde en tarde, de vez en cuando

**No way out**
No quedar otro

**No way out of it**
No hay tu tía

**Nowhere**
A ninguna parte, en (or a) ninguna parte, por ningún lado

**No wonder!**
¡Con razón!

**Now then**
Ahora bien, pues bien

## O

**Object to**
Levantar la contra

**Obstruct (the way)**
Dificultar (el paso), impedir (el paso)

**Occasionally**
De cuando en cuando, de vez en cuando

**Of about**
De unos

**Of age**
Mayor de edad

**Of course**
Claro que sí, ¿cómo no?, desde luego, por supuesto, seguro que sí, ya se ve

**Of course not**
Claro que no

**Of last month**
Del próximo pasado

**Of little value or importance**
De poca monta, lo de menos

**Of one piece**
De una pieza

**Of one's own making or invention**
De su (propia) cosecha

**Often**
A menudo

**Of that kind**
Por el estilo

**Of the same sort**
Del mismo modo

**OK (to approve)**
Dar el visto bueno

**Omit**
Pasar por alto

**On (upon)**
Encima de

**On account of**
A causa de, con motivo de, por motivo

**On a large scale**
En grande

**On all fours**
A gatas

**On all sides**
Para todos lados

**On an average**
Por término medio

**On approval**
A vistas

**On behalf of**
De parte de, en pro de

**Once again**
De nuevo

**Once and for all**
De una vez, de una vez por todas

**Once in a blue moon**
Allá a las quinientas, como visita de obispo, de tarde en tarde

**Once in a while**
Una que otra vez

**Once upon a time**
Había una vez, érase que se era, érase una vez, y va de cuento

**One at a time**
De uno en uno, uno a la vez

**One by one**
Uno por uno

**On edge**
De canto

**One must**
Hay que

**On end**
De punta

**One of these (fine) days**
Un día de estos

**One or the other**
El uno o el otro, uno u otro

**One way**
De un solo sentido

**One week from today**
De hoy en ocho días

**On foot**
A pie

**Only**
Nada más, no más que

**Only yesterday**
Ayer mismo

**On one's back**
De espaldas

**On one's knees**
De rodillas

**On purpose**
A propósito, de propósito

**On returning**
A la vuelta de

**On the contrary**
Al contrario, por el contrario

**On the dot**
En punto

**On the fence**
Entre azul y buenas noches

**On the following day**
Al día siguiente, al otro día

**On the inside**
Por dentro

**On the lookout for**
Estar a la mira de

**On the occasion of**
Con motivo de

**On the other hand**
En cambio, por otra parte, por otro lado

**On the other side of**
Al otro lado de

**On the outside**
Por fuera

**On the rebound**
De rebote

**On the road to**
Camino de

**On the run**
A la carrera

**On the sly**
A escondidas, a hurto

**On the spur of the moment**
De buenas a primeras

**On the way**
De camino, de tránsito, (estar) en camino

**On time**
A buena hora, a tiempo

**On tiptoes**
De puntillas, de puntas

**On top of**
Por encima de

**On vacation**
De vacaciones

**On watch**
En vela

**Openly**
A boca llena, a las claras, al descubierto, sin rebozo

**Oppose**
Llevar la contra, ponerse en contra de, salir al encuentro de

**Opposed to**
En contra de

**Ordinary**
De ordinario

**Or else**
No sea que, o si no, si no

**Others**
Los (las) demás

**Otherwise**
De lo contrario, de otro modo, donde no, porque si no

**Out of breath**
Con la lengua de corbata, con la lengua de pechera

**Out of danger**
En salvo

**Out of date**
Pasado de moda

**Out of sorts**
No estar de humor

**Out of spite**
Por despecho

**Out of style**
Pasado de moda

**Out of the country**
En el extranjero

**Out of the ordinary**
Fuera de lo corriente

**Over and over again**
Repetidas veces, una y otra vez

**Over a period of (time)**
Desde hace

**Over here**
Por acá, por aquí

**Overlook**
Pasar por alto

**Overnight**
De la noche a la mañana

**Overstep the bounds**
Pasar de la raya

**Over there**
Por ahí, por allá

**Overthrow someone**
Dar en tierra con alguien

## P

**Pacify**
Poner en razón

**Pack**
Hacer las maletas

**Partly**
En parte

**Pass by**
Dar una pasada por

**Passing through**
De tránsito

**Pay attention (to)**
Dar atención, fijarse en, hacer caso (a or de), prestar atención

**Pay a visit**
Hacer una visita

**Pay by cash**
Pagar al contado

**Payday**
Día de raya

**Peerless**
Sin par

**Perchance**
Por ventura

**Per day**
Al día

**Perhaps**
A lo mejor, tal vez

**Pesky as a fly**
Más pesado que una mosca

**Pick a fight or quarrel with**
Meterse con

**Place hope in someone**
Esperar en alguien

**Place in safety**
Poner a buen recaudo

**Place one's hope in**
Cifrar la esperanza en

**Plain**
A secas

**Plain and simple truth**
La verdad clara y desnuda

**Plain fool**
Tonto de capirote

**Plainly**
A boca llena

**Play a bad (or mean) trick (on someone)**
Hacer una mala jugada, hacer una perrada, jugarle una mala partida

**Play a part**
Desempeñar un papel

**Play a role**
Hacer el (or un) papel

**Play a trick**
Pegar un chasco

**Play by ear**
Tocar de oído, tocar por fantasía

**Play dumb**
Hacerse el tonto

**Play fair**
Jugar limpio

**Play hooky**
Hacer pinta, pintar venado

**Play on words**
Juego de palabras

**Play second fiddle**
Ser plato de segunda mesa

**Play up to (someone)**
Dar coba a (alguien)

**Please (make contented)**
Caer bien, caer en gracia, dar gusto

**Pledge**
Empeñar la palabra

**Point blank**
A quema ropa, a quemarropa

**Poor memory**
Memoria de gallo

**Pose as**
Dárselas de

**Praise (to the skies)**
Poner en el cielo, poner por las nubes

**Presence of mind**
Presencia de ánimo

**Present!**
¡A sus órdenes!

**Pretend**
Dar a entender, dejar saber

**Pretend not to hear**
Hacerse el sordo

**Pretend not to notice**
Hacerse el desentendido

**Pretend to be dead**
Hacerse muerto

**Prick up one's ears**
Aguzar las orejas (or los oídos)

**Pride**
Amor propio

**Proud**
De copete

**Provided**
Siempre y cuando

**Provided that**
Con tal (de) que, dado el caso que, siempre que

**Publicly**
A las claras

**Pull**
Tirar de

**Pull one's leg**
Tomarle el pelo

**Pull over to the right**
Desviarse hacia la derecha, hacerse a la derecha

**Pun**
Juego de palabras

**Pursue**
Dar caza

**Put into practice**
Poner por obra

**Put in writing**
Hacer por escrito

**Put on airs**
Darse aires a, darse farol, darse tono, subirse de tono

**Put oneself in a ridiculous situation**
Tirarse una plancha

**Put one's foot in one's mouth**
Meter la pata

**Put the cart before the horse**
Tomar el rábano por las hojas

## Q

**Quarrel with**
Meterse con

**Question**
Poner en duda

**Quickly**
Al trote, de prisa, de un salto, en un salto

## R

**Rabble**
Gente de baja estofa

**Rack one's brain**
Devanarse los sesos, quebrarse uno la cabeza, romperse los cascos

**Rain cats and dogs**
Llover a cántaros

**Rain or shine**
Que llueva o no

**Raise a rumpus**
Dar batería

**Rapidly**
A escape

**Rather**
Más bien, mejor dicho

**Rather late**
Algo tarde

**Rather than**
Antes que, más bien que

**Rattle off**
Repetir de carretilla

**Reach**
Ponerse en

**Realize (that)**
Caer en la cuenta, darse cuenta de (que)

**Really**
De veras, en efecto, en verdad

**Real truth, the**
La mera verdad

**Reckon with**
Contar con

**Reflect on (think about)**
Parar mientes en

**Regardless of**
Sin hacer caso de

**Regards to**
Recuerdos a

**Regret**
Pesarle a uno

**Regret very much**
Sentir en el alma

**Reject**
Dar calabazas

**Reliable**
Digno de confianza

**Reluctantly**
De mal grado

**Rely on**
Confiar en, contar con

**Remember (or recollect)**
Hacer memoria

**Remorse**
Gusano de la conciencia

**Repeatedly**
Sobradas veces

**Repeat mechanically**
Repetir de carretilla

**Reproach**
Dar en cara, echar en cara

**Resemble**
Salir a

**Resist stubbornly**
Hacerse duro, ponerse duro

**Rest of them, the**
Los (las) demás

**Restrain**
Tirar las riendas

**Return for**
Volver por

**Right away**
En el acto

**Right here**
Aquí mismo

**Right now**
Ahora mismo, en seguida, más ahorita

**Right side out**
Al derecho

**Ripe**
En sazón

**Rise**
Ponerse en pie

**Risk**
Correr riesgo, poner al tablero

**Round about**
A la redonda, en redondo

**Ruin**
Dar al traste con, dar al través con, echar(se) a perder

**Rumor**
De oídos

**Run away**
Echar(se) a correr

## S

**Safe**
A salvo

**Safe against**
A prueba de

**Safe and sound**
Sano y salvo

**Same as, the**
El (or lo) mismo que, igual que

**Satisfy a need or desire**
Matar el gusano

**Save one's skin**
Salvar el pellejo

**Save time**
Ganar tiempo

**Say a bad word**
Echar (or saltar) un terno

**Say goodbye to**
Despedirse de

**Say to oneself**
Decir para sí

**Scarcely**
A duras penas

**Scowl**
Fruncir el ceño

**Secondhand**
De segunda mano, de uso

**Secretly**
A puerta cerrada, en secreto

**Seem like**
Sonar a

**See to it that**
Ver de, ver que

**Seize**
Echar la zarpa, echar mano, hacer presa

**Seldom**
Por rareza, rara vez, raras veces

**Self-esteem**
Amor propio

**Separately**
De por sí, por separado

**Serenity**
Presencia de ánimo

**Seriously**
En serio

**Serve**
Servir de

**Serve as**
Oficiar de

**Set forward (e.g., a clock)**
Poner adelantado

**Set in motion**
Poner en juego

**Set out (on a trip, etc.)**
Ponerse en camino

**Set the table**
Poner la mesa

**Set up housekeeping**
Poner casa

**Several times**
Varias veces

**Shake hands (with)**
Dar la mano, darse la mano, estrechar la mano (a)

**Sharp (on time)**
En punto

**Shortly**
En breve

**Shortly after**
A poco

**Shortly thereafter**
Poco después de

**Show off**
Darse farol, hacer teatro

**Shred**
Hacer trizas

**Shrug one's shoulders**
Encogerse de hombros

**Shut tight**
A piedra y lodo

**Sideways**
De lado, de soslayo

**Signify**
Querer decir

**Silly remark**
Salida de pie de banco

**Similar**
Algo por el estilo, parecido a

**Simply**
A secas

**Since**
Como que, como quiera que, desde que, en vista de que, pues que, puesto que, supuesto que, ya que

**Since then**
Desde entonces

**Sky high**
Por las nubes

**Slam the door**
Dar un portazo

**Slanting**
Al soslayo, de soslayo

**Slap**
Mandar una bofetada

**Sleep it off**
Dormir la mona

**Sleep on it**
Consultar con la almohada

**Sleep soundly**
Dormir a pierna suelta

**Slice**
Hacer rajas

**Slip**
Darse un resbalón

**Slowly**
A la larga

**Smell like**
Oler a

**Snap one's fingers**
Castañetear con los dedos, tronar los dedos

**So**
Así que

**So far**
Hasta aquí, hasta ahí

**Soft (or smooth) as silk**
Como una seda

**Softsoap or flatter (someone)**
Dar coba a, dar jabón a

**Somebody else**
Algún otro

**Someday**
Algún día

**Somehow**
De algún modo, de alguna manera, de un modo u otro

**Something indefinable**
Un no sé qué

**Something is wrong**
Hay moros en la costa

**Something of the sort**
Algo por el estilo

**Sometime**
Algún día, algún tiempo, alguna vez

**Sometimes**
Algunas veces, de cuando en cuando

**Somewhat**
Un tanto

**Somewhere**
En alguna parte

**Somewhere else**
En alguna otra parte

**So much the better**
Tanto mejor

**So much the worse**
Tanto peor

**Soon after**
A raíz de, al (or a) poco rato

**Sooner or later**
A la corta o a la larga, tarde o temprano

**Sooner the better, the**
Antes hoy que mañana

**So-so**
Así así, tal cual

**So that**
A fin de que, así es que, así que, con tal (de) que, de manera que, de modo que, de suerte que

**So then**
Así pues

**Sound like**
Sonar a

**So what?**
¡A mí qué!, ¿de modo que?, ¿pues que?, ¿y qué?

**Spare (extra)**
De repuesto

**Spare no expense**
Echar la casa por la ventana

**Speak frankly**
Hablar al alma, no tener pelillos en la lengua

**Speaking! (in answering a telephone)**
Al habla

**Speak loudly**
Hablar alto, hablar en voz alta

**Speak to the point**
Hablar al caso

**Speedily**
A todo trapo

**Spicy story**
Un cuento alegre

**Split hairs**
Pararse en pelillos

**Spoil**
Echar(se) a perder

**Stand a chance**
Tener probabilidad

**Standing**
De pie

**Stand someone up**
Dejar a uno plantado

**Stand still**
Estarse parado

**Stark raving mad**
Loco de remate

**Start to**
Ponerse a, ponerse en marcha, romper a

**Start a conversation**
Entablar una conversación

**Start a fire**
Prender el fuego

**Start out**
Ponerse en marcha

**Stay in**
Quedarse en la casa

**Stay in bed**
Guardar (la) cama

**Stealthily**
A hurto

**Step aside**
Hacerse a un lado

**Step hard upon**
Dar un pisotón

**Stomp or step on**
Dar una pisada

**Stop (smoking, etc.)**
Dejar de (fumar, etc.)

**Stop beating around the bush**
Dejarse de cuentos, dejarse de rodeos

**Stop over at**
Hacer escala en

**Stop short (or suddenly)**
Parar en seco

**Stop the excuses**
Dejarse de rodeos

**Straw that broke the camel's back**
La gota que derrama el vaso

**Strike the hour**
Dar la hora

**Study hard**
Quemarse las pestañas (or las cejas)

**Stumble**
Dar un traspié, darse un tropezón

**Stylish**
De buen tono, de moda

**Succeed**
Tener éxito

**Such as**
Tal como, tales como, tal cual

**Such as that**
Por el estilo

**Suddenly**
De golpe, de pronto, de repente, de súbito

**Suit**
Venir bien

**Suit perfectly**
Venir a (or al) pelo

**Summing up**
En resumen

**Superfluous**
Está de más

**Supposing**
Dado caso, supuesto que

**Sure enough**
Dicho y hecho

**Surprise**
Pegar un chasco

**Swarm of people**
Un hervidero de gente, un remolino de gente

**Swear (curse)**
Echar un terno, soltar un terno

**Sweat blood**
Sudar la gota gorda

**Sweat profusely**
Sudar la gota gorda

**Swell with pride**
Estar (or ponerse) ancho

**Swiftly**
A rienda suelta

**Swiftness of time**
Corrida del tiempo

**Swindle**
Dar gato por liebre

# T

**Take (something)**
Quedarse con (una cosa)

**Take a chance**
Correr riesgo

**Take a drink**
Echar un trago

**Take advantage of the situation**
Aprovechar la ocasión

**Take after (someone)**
Salir a

**Take a jump**
Pegar un salto

**Take a long time (in doing something)**
Tardar en (hacer algo)

**Take a long weekend**
Hacer puente

**Take an afternoon nap**
Dormir la siesta

**Take a nap**
Descabezar el sueño, echar un sueño, echar una siesta

**Take a stand against**
Salir al encuentro de

**Take a step**
Dar un paso, tomar una providencia

**Take a stroll**
Dar una vuelta

**Take a walk**
Pasear a pie

**Take a walk or ride**
Dar un paseo

**Take care**
Tener cuidado (con)

**Take care of**
Preocuparse de

**Take care of someone**
Mirar por alguien

**Take charge (of)**
Encargarse (de), hacerse cargo (de)

**Take exercise**
Hacer ejercicios

**Take for a...**
Tener por...

**Take for granted**
Dar por descontado, dar por hecho, dar por sabido (or sentado or supuesto), tomar por cierto

**Take into account**
Hacer caso a (or de), tener en cuenta, tomar en cuenta

**Take it easy**
Tomarlo con calma

**Take lightly**
Tomar a risa

**Take pity on**
Tener lástima de

**Take place**
Tener lugar

**Take root**
Echar raíces

**Take seriously**
Tomar a pecho(s)

**Take the lead**
Tomar la delantera

**Take time off**
Tomar tiempo libre

**Take to heart**
Tomar a (or en) pecho(s), tomar en serio

**Take undue liberties**
Pasar de la raya

**Talk of the town**
La comidilla de la vecindad

**Talk too much**
Hablar por los codos

**Talk to oneself**
Hablar para sus adentros

**Tear into strips**
Hacer rajas

**Tear to pieces**
Hacer garras, hacer trizas

**Tease**
Tomarle el pelo

**Thank (or give thanks)**
Dar las gracias

**That can't be helped**
Eso no tiene quite

**That depends**
Según y conforme, según y como

**That is**
A saber

**That is a horse of a different color**
Eso es harina de otro costal

**That is even worse**
Peor que peor

**That is it**
Eso es

**That is the limit!**
¡Eso es el colmo!

**That is to say**
Es decir, o sea que

**That is urgent**
Eso corre prisa

**That is why**
Por algo, por esa razón

**That long**
Así de largo

**That's not the point (or the question)**
No se trata de eso

**That's right**
Eso es

**That's the last straw!**
¡No faltaba más!

**That's the least of the trouble**
Es lo de menos

**That's the point**
¡Ahí está el detalle!

**That was (is) true**
Eso sí

**That way**
Por allí

**That which**
Lo que

**The coast is not clear**
Hay moros en la costa

**The fact is**
El caso es

**The more...the less**
Mientras más...mientras menos

**Then**
A la sazón

**The ones**
Los que

**Thereafter**
Después de eso

**There are no two ways about it**
No hay que darle vueltas, no tiene vuelta de hoja

**Therefore**
Así pues, así que, por (or en) consecuencia de, por consiguiente, por ende, por eso, por lo cual, por lo tanto

**There is more than meets the eye**
Hay gato encerrado

**There is no doubt (that)**
No cabe duda (que)

**There is no way around it**
No hay que darle vueltas

**There is the heart of the matter!**
¡Allí está el toque!

**There's no hurry**
No hay prisa

**There's no need to**
No hay para que

**There's no other way but to...**
No hay más remedio que...

**There's nothing to do except...**
No hay más remedio que...

**The same as**
Así como, el (or lo) mismo que

**They say**
Se dice

**Think (be of the opinion)**
Tener para sí

**Think about**
Pensar en

**Think not**
Creer que no

**Think so**
Creer que sí

**This side of**
Más acá de

**This way**
Por acá, por aquí

**This will do**
Así está bien

**Thoroughly**
Por completo

**Those which (or those who)**
Los (or las) que

**Thousand thanks, a**
Mil gracias

**Throng (of people)**
Remolino de gente

**Through or throughout**
A través de, al través de, de parte a parte, por conducto de, por donde

**Through thick and thin**
Por toda suerte de penalidades

**Throw a party**
Dar una fiesta

**Throw a stone**
Mandar una pedrada

**Tilted**
De lado

**Tip (give a gratuity)**
Dar propina

**Tip one's hat**
Tocarse el sombrero

**To and fro**
De aquí para allá

**To boot**
De pilón

**Together**
A la vez

**Tomorrow afternoon**
Mañana por la tarde

**Tomorrow is another day**
Mañana Dios dirá

**Tomorrow morning**
Mañana por la mañana, mañana temprano

**Tomorrow night**
Mañana por la noche

**To myself**
Para mis adentros

**Tonight**
A la noche, por la noche

**Too bad!**
¡Qué lástima!

**To oneself**
Consigo mismo

**To one's heart's content**
A pedir de boca

**To the letter (just right)**
Al centavo, al pie de la letra

**To the limit**
Hasta más no poder

**To the point**
A secas, de perlas

**To the utmost**
A más no poder, de lo lindo, hasta más no poder

**Touch a sore spot**
Tocar en lo vivo

**Towards (a period of time)**
A principios de

**Towards the end of (a period of time)**
A fines de

**Track down**
Dar caza

**Train was *x* minutes late**
El tren llegó con *x* minutos de retraso

**Treacherously**
A traición

**Treat (deal with)**
Tratar de

**Trip (or stumble)**
Dar un traspié, darse un tropezón

**Truly or truthfully**
A la verdad, de veras, de verdad, en verdad

**Trust**
Confiar en

**Trustworthy**
Digno de confianza

**Try to (attempt)**
Tratar de, ver de, ver que

**Turn (around)**
Dar(se) la vuelta

**Turn a deaf ear**
Hacerse el sordo

**Turn one's back (on)**
Dar las espaldas (a), voltear la espalda

**Turn out to be**
Venir a parar, venir a ser

**Turn the corner**
Doblar a la esquina

**Turn the page**
Darle vuelta a la hoja

**Two by two**
De dos en dos

**Two-faced**
De dos caras

**Two of a kind**
Tal para cual

**Two-way**
De dos sentidos

**Two weeks from today**
De hoy en quince días

## U

**Unanimously**
A una vez

**Unavoidable**
Sin remedio

**Uncovered**
En descubierto

**Undecided**
Entre azul y buenas noches

**Under**
Debajo de

**Undercover**
A escondidas

**Understand that...**
Tener entendido que...

**Undertake**
Poner por obra

**Under the table (underhanded)**
Bajo cuerda

**Unequaled**
Sin igual

**Unexpectedly**
A deshora(s), de buenas a primeras, de improviso, el día menos pensado

**Unfortunately**
Por desgracia

**Unharmed**
A salvo

**Unless**
A menos que, a no ser que, como no

**Unlucky**
De mala suerte

**Unnecessary**
De sobra

**Unnoticed**
Sin sentir

**Unpaid**
En descubierto

**Unreserved**
Sin reserva

**Until**
Hasta que

**Unusual**
Fuera de lo corriente

**Unwillingly**
A la mala, de mal grado, de mala gana, sin querer

**Upon**
Encima de

**Upon my honor**
Sobre mi palabra

**Ups and downs**
Subidas y bajadas

**Upside down**
Patas arriba

**Up to a point**
Hasta cierto punto

**Up to date**
A la moda, hasta la fecha

**Up to now**
Hasta aquí, hasta ahí, hasta la fecha

**Up to the top**
Hasta el tope

**Usual**
De ordinario

**Usually**
Por lo general, por lo regular, por regla general

## V

**Vanish**
Perderse de vista

**Vanity**
Amor propio

**Various times**
Repetidas veces

**Very bad luck**
Suerte negra

**Very close**
A quema ropa, a quemarropa

**Very early in the morning**
Muy de mañana

**Very far away**
En el quinto infierno

**Very much**
Con (or en or por) extremo, de lo lindo

**Very often**
Con mucha frecuencia, muy a menudo

**Very probably**
A buen seguro

**Very soon**
Poco rato, ya mero

**Very thought of, the**
La mera idea de

**Violently**
A rienda suelta

**Visibly**
A ojos vistas

**Vouch for**
Dar fe de, salir fiador de

## W

**Wait in line**
Hacer cola

**Wait table**
Servir la mesa

**Wait the whole blessed day**
Esperar todo el santo día

**Walk**
Ir a pie

**Walk by**
Dar una pasada por

**Walk the streets**
Medir las calles

**Wanted**
Se solicita

**Want to**
Tener deseos de

**Wash one's hands of**
Lavarse las manos de

**Watch out (for)**
Tener cuidado (con)

**Weakness (or weak side)**
Lado flaco, punto flaco

**Wear**
Llevar puesto, traer puesto

**Wear oneself out**
Hacerse uno rajas

**Weather the storm**
Aguantar el chubasco

**Week before last**
La semana antepasada

**Weekday(s)**
Día(s) de semana, día de trabajo, día hábil

**Weekend**
El fin de semana

**Welcome**
Dar la bienvenida

**Well and good**
Santo y bueno

**Well done!**
¡Así se hace!

**Well-done (well-cooked)**
Bien asado, bien cocido

**Well-groomed**
Bien peinado

**Well now**
Ahora bien

**Well then**
Pues bien

**Well worth it**
Digno de

**What a mess!**
¡Qué batingue!

**What an atrocity!**
¡Qué barbaridad!

**What a pleasure!**
¡Qué gusto!

**What does it mean?**
¿Qué quiere decir?, ¿qué
significa?

**What do you think of it?**
¿Qué le parece?

**What for?**
¿Para qué?

**What happened?**
¿Qué pasó?

**What has been said**
Lo expuesto

**What if...?**
¿Y si...?

**What is it?**
¿Qué haces?

**What is it about?**
¿De qué se trata?

**What is it good for?**
¿Para qué sirve?

**What is more**
Más aún

**What is the date?**
¿A cuánto(s) estamos?

**What is the point of that?**
¿A qué viene eso?

**What is the use of it?**
¿Qué ventaja tiene?

**What nonsense!**
¡Qué barbaridad!

**What's eating you?**
¿Qué mosca te ha picado?

**What's it to you?**
¿Quién te mete, Juan Copete?

**What's going on?**
¿Qué pasa?

**What's new?**
¿Qué hay de nuevo?

**What's so bad about that?**
¿Qué hay de malo con eso?

**What's that to me?**
¿A mí qué?

**What's the difference?**
¡Qué más da!

**What's the matter with you?**
¿Qué le (or te) pasa?

**What's up?**
¿Qué hubo?, ¿qué pasa?

**What's wrong with...?**
¿Qué tiene de malo...?

**What's wrong with that?**
¿Qué hay de malo con eso?

**What time is it?**
¿Qué hora es?, ¿qué horas son?

**When all is said and done**
A la postre

**Whenever**
Cuando quiera, siempre que,
todas las veces (que)

**When least expected**
El día menos pensado

**Whereas**
Visto que

**Wherever**
Adondequiera que,
dondequiera que, por
dondequiera que

**Whether one likes it or not**
Por las buenas o por las malas

**Whether you wish or not**
Quieras que no, quiera o no

**While**
En tanto que

**While away the time**
Pasar el rato

**Whisper**
Hablar en secreto

**Whispering**
En voz baja

**Whole truth, the**
La verdad clara y desnuda

**Wholly**
Del todo

**Wide open**
De par en par

**Willingly**
A la buena, con mucho gusto,
de buena gana, de buen grado,
de (buena) voluntad

**Win**
Salir ganando

**With**
Junto con

**With both feet together (or on
the ground)**
A pie(s) juntillas

**With certainty**
A (or de) ciencia cierta, a punto
fijo

**With great difficulty**
A duras penas

**Within**
Dentro de

**Within a few years**
A la vuelta de los años

**Within a week**
Dentro de una semana

**Within speaking distance**
Al habla

**Within view**
A vista de

**With no confidence**
De mala fe

**Without**
Sin que

**Without a plan**
A la buena de Dios

**Without equal**
Sin par

**Without fail**
Sin falta

**Without help**
Sin remedio

**Without interruption**
De seguida

**Without question**
Sin disputa

**Without realizing**
Sin sentir

**Without remedy**
De remate, sin recurso

**Without rhyme or reason**
Sin qué ni para qué, sin ton
ni son

**Without risk**
Sobre seguro

**Without sleep**
En vela

**Without stopping**
De corrida, de hilo

**Without the knowledge of**
A escondidas de

**Without warning**
A quema ropa, a quemarropa

**With pleasure**
De (buena) voluntad

**With regard to**
Acerca de, con respecto a, en
cuanto a, respecto a

**With the aim of**
Con el propósito de

**With the idea of**
Con motivo de

**With tongue hanging out**
Con la lengua de corbata, con
la lengua de pechera

**With your permission**
Con permiso

**Wonderfully**
De lo lindo

**Wonderfully well**
A las mil maravillas

**Word of honor!**
¡Palabrita de honor!

**Workday**
Día hábil

**Work hard**
Dar batería, sudar la gota
gorda

**Work in vain**
Azotar el aire

**Work well**
Andar bien

**Worry about**
Preocuparse por

**Worry about nothing**
Ahogarse en poca agua

**Worse than**
Peor que

**Worth seeing**
Ser de ver, ser para ver

**Wrinkle one's brow**
Fruncir el entrecejo

**Wrong side out**
Al revés

# Y

**Year before last**
Año antepasado

**Years ago**
Hace años

**Yes, of course**
Ya lo creo

**Yesterday afternoon**
Ayer por la tarde

**You don't say!**
¡No diga!

**You're welcome**
De nada, no hay de que

# SPANISH-ENGLISH
# ESPAÑOL-INGLÉS

# REMARKS

For ease of reference, the reader should note the following:

- Within each entry, the word or group of words corresponding to each of the meanings of the Spanish word constitutes a separate numbered subentry.

- Examples of usage, phrases, and idioms are included in each entry immediately following the meaning of the word to which they correspond.

- Examples of usage, phrases, and idioms are given in a fixed sequence within each item of the entry: word groups not containing a verb; expressions containing a verb; phrases or locutions (adverbial, prepositional, etc.).

- Expressions, phrases, etc. that do not directly correspond to a specific meaning of the word are numbered separately within the entry.

- Words given as equivalents of the main entry are clarified further, when necessary, by synonyms and definitions enclosed in brackets.

- Abbreviations indicate meaning and usage in specific subject areas and geographical regions, as well as in grammar. See "Abbreviations Used in This Dictionary."

- The letters *ch* and *ll*, which are distinct letters in the Spanish alphabet, are listed as such.

In addition to the explanations of grammar within individual entries, certain points of grammar have been explained in greater detail in an overview preceding the lexicon. These summaries treat specific instances of Spanish grammar that have proven most troublesome to English-speaking readers (e.g., direct and indirect object pronouns, the subjunctive). (An asterisk in one of the grammar notes signals a reference to another note on a related subject.)

- An asterisk in the body of an entry indicates that the word it precedes is used only in the Americas.

In order to assist the reader, reference sections on a variety of topics are included in this dictionary. Idioms and expressions—both Spanish-to-English and English-to-Spanish—can be found in the center of the dictionary.

The appendices include:

- False Cognates and "Part-Time" Cognates
- Monetary Units / Unidades monetarias
- Weights and Measures / Pesas y medidas
- Numbers / Numerales
- Temperature / La temperatura
- Abreviaturas más usadas en inglés
- Abbreviations Most Commonly Used in Spanish
- Business Correspondence in Spanish / La carta comercial en español
- Maps / Mapas

# ABBREVIATIONS USED IN THIS DICTIONARY

| | | | |
|---|---|---|---|
| abs. | absolute | GEOG. | geography |
| ACC. | accounting | GEOL. | geology |
| *adj.* | adjective | GEOM. | geometry |
| *adv.* | adverb | GER. | Gerund |
| AER. | aeronautics | GRAM. | grammar |
| AGR. | agriculture | GYM. | gymnastics |
| ALG. | algebra | | |
| Am. | Spanish America | HIST. | history |
| ANAT. | anatomy | | |
| ARCH. | architecture | | |
| ARCHEOL. | archeology | ICHTH. | ichthyology |
| Arg. | Argentina | *imper.* | imperative |
| ARITH. | arithmetic | imperf. | imperfect |
| *art.* | article | *impers.* | impersonal verb |
| ARTILL. | artillery | *indef.* | indefinite |
| ASTR. | astronomy | INDIC. | Indicative |
| *aug.* | augmentative | IND. | industry |
| AUTO. | automobile | INF. | Infinitive |
| *aux.* | auxiliary verb | INSUR. | insurance |
| | | *interj.* | interjection |
| BACT. | bacteriology | *interrog.* | interrogative |
| BIBL. | Bible; Biblical | *intr.* | intransitive verb |
| BILL. | billiards | iron. | ironic |
| BIOCHEM. | biochemistry | *irr., irreg.* | irregular |
| BIOL. | biology | | |
| BOOKBIND. | bookbinding | JEWEL. | jewelry |
| BOOKKEEP. | bookkeeping | | |
| BOT. | botany | Lat. | Latin |
| BULL. | bullfighting | LIT. | literature |
| | | LITURG. | liturgy |
| CARP. | carpentry | LOG. | logic |
| CHEM. | chemistry | | |
| coll. | colloquial | *m.* | masculine; masculine noun |
| collect. | collectively | MACH. | machinery |
| COM. | commerce | MATH. | mathematics |
| *comp.* | comparative | MECH. | mechanics |
| COND. | Conditional | MED. | medicine |
| *conj.* | conjunction | METAL. | metallurgy |
| CONJUG. | conjugation | Mex. | Mexico |
| COOK. | cooking | MIL. | military |
| *cop.* | copulative verb | MIN. | mining |
| | | MINER. | mineralogy |
| *def.* | defective; definite | MUS. | music |
| *dim.* | diminutive | MYTH. | mythology |
| ECCL. | ecclesiastic | *n.* | noun; masculine and feminine noun |
| ELEC. | electricity | | |
| ENG. | engineering | NAUT. | nautical |
| ENT. | entomology | NAV. | naval; navy |
| exclam. | exclamatory | *neut.* | neuter |
| | | not cap. | not capitalized |
| *f.* | feminine; feminine noun | | |
| F. ARTS. | fine arts | obs. | obsolete |
| FENC. | fencing | OPT. | optics |
| fig. | figuratively | ORN. | ornithology |
| FISH. | fishing | | |
| Fut. | Future | | |

| | |
|---|---|
| *pers.*, pers. | person; personal |
| PHIL. | philosophy |
| PHOT. | photography |
| PHYS. | physics |
| *pl.* | plural |
| POET. | poetry |
| POL. | politics |
| *poss.* | possessive |
| *p. p.* | past participle |
| *prep.* | preposition |
| Pres. | Present |
| *pres. p.* | present participle |
| Pret. | preterit |
| PRINT. | printing |
| *pr. n.* | proper noun |
| *pron.* | pronoun |
| | |
| RADIO. | radio; broadcasting |
| *ref.* | reflexive verb |
| *reg.* | regular |
| REL. | religion |
| RLY. | railway; railroad |

| | |
|---|---|
| scorn. | scornful |
| SUBJ. | Subjunctive |
| *superl.* | superlative |
| SURG. | surgery |
| SURV. | surveying |
| | |
| TELEV. | television |
| THEAT. | theater |
| THEOL. | theology |
| TOP. | topography |
| *tr.* | transitive verb |
| | |
| usu. | usually |
| | |
| V. | Vide; See |
| vul. | vulgar |
| | |
| WEAV. | weaving |
| | |
| ZOOL. | zoology |

# KEY TO PRONUNCIATION IN SPANISH

## VOWELS

| Letter | Approximate sound |
|---|---|
| a | Like *a* in English *far, father,* e.g., **casa, mano.** |
| e | When stressed, like *a* in English *pay,* e.g., **dedo, cerca.**<br>When unstressed, it has a shorter sound like in English *bet, net,* e.g., **estado, decidir.** |
| i | Like *i* in English *machine* or *ee* in *feet,* e.g., **fin, salí.** |
| o | Like *o* in English *obey,* e.g., **mona, poner.** |
| u | Like *u* in English *rule* or *oo* in *boot,* e.g., **atún, luna.**<br>It is silent in **gue** and **gui,** e.g., **guerra, guisado.** If it carries a diaeresis (ü), it is<br>   pronounced (see Diphthongs), e.g., **bilingüe, bilingüismo.**<br>It is also silent in **que** and **qui,** e.g., **querer, quinto.** |
| y | When used as a vowel, it sounds like the Spanish **i,** e.g., **y, rey.** |

## DIPHTHONGS

| Diphthong | Approximate sound |
|---|---|
| ai, ay | Like *i* in English *light,* e.g., **caigo, hay.** |
| au | Like *ou* in English *sound,* e.g., **cauto, paular.** |
| ei, ey | Like *ey* in English *they* or *a* in *ale,* e.g., **reina, ley.** |
| eu | Like the *a* in English *pay* combined with the sound of *ew* in English *knew,* e.g.,<br>**deuda, feudal.** |
| oi, oy | Like *oy* in English *toy,* e.g., **oiga, soy.** |
| ia, ya | Like *ya* in English *yarn,* e.g., **rabia, raya.** |
| ua | Like *wa* in English *wand,* e.g., **cuatro, cual.** |
| ie, ye | Like *ye* in English *yet,* e.g., **bien, yeso.** |
| ue | Like *wa* in English *wake,* e.g., **buena, fue, bilingüe.** |
| io, yo | Like *yo* in English *yoke,* without the following sound of *w* in this word, e.g., **región,**<br>**yodo.** |
| uo | Like *uo* in English *quote,* e.g., **cuota, oblicuo.** |
| iu, yu | Like *yu* in English *Yule,* e.g., **ciudad, triunfo, yunta.** |
| ui | Like *wee* in English *week,* e.g., **ruido, bilingüismo.** |

## TRIPHTHONGS

| Triphthong | Approximate sound |
|---|---|
| iai | Like *ya* in English *yard* combined with the *i* in *fight,* e.g., **estudiáis.** |
| iei | Like the English word *yea,* e.g., **estudiéis.** |
| uai, uay | Like *wi* in English *wide,* e.g., **averiguáis, guay.** |
| uei, uey | Like *wei* in English *weigh,* e.g., **amortigüéis, buey.** |

## CONSONANTS

| Letter | Approximate sound |
|---|---|
| b | Generally like the English *b* in *boat, bring, obsolete,* when it is at the beginning of a word or preceded by *m,* e.g., **baile, bomba.** <br> Between two vowels and when followed by *l* or *r,* it has a softer sound, almost like the English *v* but formed by pressing both lips together, e.g., **acaba, haber, cable.** |
| c | Before *a, o, u,* or a consonant, it sounds like the English *c* in *coal,* e.g., **casa, saco, cuba, acto.** <br> Before *e* or *i,* it is pronounced like the English *s* in *six* in American Spanish and like the English *th* in *thin* in Castillian Spanish, e.g., **cerdo, cine.** <br> If a word contains two *c*s, the first is pronounced like *c* in *coal,* and the second like *s* or *th* accordingly, e.g., **acción.** |
| ch | Like *ch* in English *cheese* or *such,* e.g., **chato, mucho.** |
| d | Generally like *d* in English *dog* or *th* in English *this,* e.g., **dedo, digo.** When ending a syllable, it is pronounced like the English *th,* e.g., **usted, libertad.** |
| f | Like *f* in English *fine, life,* e.g., **final.** |
| g | Before *a, o,* and *u;* the groups *ue* and *ui;* or a consonant, it sounds like *g* in English *gain,* e.g., **gato, gorra, aguja, guerra, guitar, digno.** <br> Before *e* or *i,* like a strongly aspirated English *h,* e.g., **general, región.** |
| h | Always silent, e.g., **hoyo, historia.** |
| j | Like *h* in English *hat,* e.g., **joven, reja.** |
| k | Like *c* in English *coal,* e.g., **kilo.** It is found only in words of foreign origin. |
| l | Like *l* in English *lion,* e.g., **libro, límite.** |
| ll | In some parts of Spain and Spanish America, like the English *y* in *yet;* generally in Castillian Spanish, like the *lli* in English *million;* e.g., **castillo, silla.** |
| m | Like *m* in English *map,* e.g., **moneda, tomo.** |
| n | Like *n* in English *nine,* e.g., **nuevo, canto, determinación.** |
| ñ | Like *ni* in English *onion* or *ny* in English *canyon,* e.g., **cañón, paño.** |
| p | Like *p* in English *parent,* e.g., **pipa, pollo.** |
| q | Like *c* in English *coal.* This letter is only used in the combinations *que* and *qui* in which the *u* is silent, e.g., **queso, aquí.** |
| r | At the beginning of a word and when preceded by *l, n,* or *s,* it is strongly trilled, e.g., **roca, alrota, Enrique, desrabar.** <br> In all other positions, it is pronounced with a single tap of the tongue, e.g., **era, padre.** |
| rr | Strongly trilled, e.g., **carro, arriba.** |
| s | Like *s* in English *so,* e.g., **cosa, das.** |
| t | Like *t* in English *tip* but generally softer, e.g., **toma, carta.** |
| v | Like *v* in English *mauve,* but in many parts of Spain and the Americas, like the Spanish **b,** e.g., **variar, mover.** |
| x | Generally like *x* in English *expand,* e.g., **examen.** <br> Before a consonant, it is sometimes pronounced like *s* in English *so,* e.g., **excepción, extensión.** <br> In the word **México,** and in other place names of that country, it is pronounced like the Spanish **j.** |
| y | When used as a consonant between vowels or at the beginning of a word, like the *y* in English *yet,* e.g., **yate, yeso, hoyo.** |
| z | Like Spanish **c** when it precedes *e* or *i,* e.g., **zapato, cazo, azul.** |

## ACCENTUATION / ACENTUACIÓN

### Rules of accentuation

All words in Spanish (except adverbs ending in -mente) only have one stressed syllable. The stressed syllable is sometimes indicated by a written accent.

In words with no written accent, the ending of the word determines the placement of stress.

- Words that end in a consonant (except *n* or *s*) stress the last syllable: pared, añil, capaz.
  —The final y as part of a diphthong is treated as a consonant: carey, Paraguay.

- Words that end in a vowel or in *n* or *s* stress the next to the last (penultimate) syllable: casa, pasan, libros.

*Note:* Adverbs ending in -mente retain the original stress (and written accent) of the root word as well as stress the first syllable of the adverbial ending: claramente, difícilmente, últimamente.

The written accent is used in the following cases:

- Words that end in a vowel or the consonants *n* or *s* and that stress the last syllable: café, talón, anís.

- Words that end in a consonant (except *n* or *s*) and that stress the next to the last syllable: árbol, quídam.

- All words that stress the third from the last (antepenultimate) syllable: párvulo, máximo, ánimo.

*Note:* Verbs having unstressed pronouns attached to them preserve the written accent when they ordinarily carry one: llevóme, apuréla.

### Other uses of the written accent

- The written accent is used to distinguish between two words with the same spelling but different meanings or functions:

| | |
|---|---|
| él (pronoun) | el (article) |
| tú (pronoun) | tu (possessive adjective) |
| mí (pronoun) | { mi (possessive adjective) <br> mi (musical note) |
| sí (adverb) <br> sí (pronoun) } | si (conjunction) |
| sé (of the verb *ser*) <br> sé (of the verb *saber*) } | se (reflexive pronoun) |
| más (adverb) | mas (conjunction) |
| dé (of the verb *dar*) | de (preposition) |
| té (noun) | te (pronoun) |
| éste <br> ése } (pronouns) <br> aquél | este <br> ese } (adjectives) <br> aquel |
| sólo (adverb) | solo (adjective) |

- The written accent is also used in the following cases:
  —Quién, cuál, cúyo, cuánto, cuán, cuándo, cómo, and dónde in interrogative and exclamatory sentences.
  —Qué, cúyo, cuándo, cómo, and porqué used as nouns: sin qué ni para qué, el cómo y el cuándo.
  —Quién, cuál, and cuándo having a distributive sense: quién más, quién menos.
  —Aún when it is interchangeable with todavía: no ha llegado aún.
  —The vowels *i* and *u* are accented when they are preceded or followed by another vowel and form a separate stressed syllable: llovía, baúl.
  —The conjunction o takes an accent when it comes between two arabic numerals to avoid mistaking it for zero (0): 3 ó 4.

# ARTICLES / ARTÍCULOS

The article in Spanish is a variable part of speech, agreeing with the noun in gender and number.

### Definite articles

|  | Masculine | Feminine |
|---|---|---|
| *Singular* | el libro (the book) | la cara (the face) |
| *Plural* | los libros (the books) | las caras (the faces) |

The neuter article **lo** is used to give a substantive value to some adjectives: **lo** bello (the beautiful, what is beautiful, beautiful things); **lo** profundo de sus pensamientos (the profoundness of his thoughts).

### Indefinite articles

|  | Masculine | Feminine |
|---|---|---|
| *Singular* | un hombre (a man) | una naranja (an orange) |
| *Plural* | unos hombres (some men) | unas naranjas (some oranges) |

**Special cases**
- The masculine article is used with feminine nouns that begin with a stressed **a**: el alma (the soul); un ave (a bird).

- With reflexive verbs, the definite article is equivalent to an English possessive adjective in sentences like: me lavo **las** manos, I wash my hands; ponte **el** sombrero, put on your hat.

- When followed by **de** or an adjective, the Spanish definite article may be used as a pronoun equivalent to *the one* or *the ones:* el **del** sombrero blanco, the one in the white hat.

# GENDER / GÉNERO

All nouns in Spanish have a gender: masculine, feminine, common, or epicene. Some adjectives having the value of a noun are in the neuter gender.

*Note:* For all practical purposes, common and epicene nouns are masculine or feminine and are treated as such in the entries of this dictionary.

**Some observations**
- Nouns denoting living beings usually have a different form for the masculine or feminine gender: **trabajador, trabajadora**, working man, working woman; **actor, actriz**, actor, actress; **oso, osa**, bear (male), bear (female); **buey, vaca**, ox, cow; **caballo, yegua**, horse, mare.

- Some nouns that denote persons have only one ending for both masculine and feminine genders. They are in the common gender, and the sex is indicated solely by the article: un pianista, una pianista, a pianist.

- Some masculine nouns and feminine nouns are used to denote animals of either sex. They are in the epicene gender, and the sex is indicated by the word **macho** or **hembra** following the noun: una serpiente **macho**, a male serpent; un rinoceronte **hembra**, a female rhinoceros.

- Nouns denoting material or spiritual things are never in the neuter gender but have either the masculine or feminine gender attributed to them. The reader is advised to look for the gender in the corresponding entries of this dictionary whenever a question arises.

# FORMATION OF THE PLURAL / PLURAL

The plural of Spanish nouns and adjectives is formed by adding s or es to the singular word.

The plural is formed by adding s to:

- Words ending in an unstressed vowel: casa, **casas**; blanco, **blancos**.
- Words ending in an accented é: café, **cafés**.

The plural is formed by adding es to:

- Words ending in an accented á, í, ó, or ú: bajá, **bajaes**; rubí, **rubíes**.
  Exception: **Papá, mamá, chacó,** and **chapó** add s; maravedí has three forms for the plural: **maravedis, maravedíes,** and **maravedises**.
- The names of the vowels: a, **aes**; e, **ees**; i, **íes**, etc.
- Nouns and adjectives ending in a consonant: árbol, **árboles**; anís, **anises**; cañón, **cañones**.
  Exception: Nouns of more than one syllable ending in an s preceded by an unstressed vowel do not change in the plural: lunes, **lunes**; crisis, **crisis**. Observe that nouns and adjectives ending in z change the z to c in their written plurals: vez, **veces**; feliz, **felices**.

## Proper names

When a proper name is used in the plural, all the preceding rules and exceptions are observed. Exception: Family names ending in z (Núñez, Pérez, etc.) do not change in the plural.

## Nouns of foreign origin

Usually nouns of foreign origin form the plural according to the preceding rules. However, the plural of lord is **lores**, and the plural of cinc or zinc is **cincs** or **zincs**.
Latin words, such as ultimátum, déficit, fiat, and exequátur, have no plural form.

## Compound nouns and adjectives

- When the elements of the compound noun or adjective are separate, only the first element takes the plural form: **ojos** de buey, **patas** de gallo.
- When the compound is imperfect, such as ricahembra, mediacaña, both the elements take the plural form: **ricashembras, mediascañas**.
- When the compound is perfect, the plural is formed at the end of the word: **ferrocarriles, patitiesos**.
- The plurals of cualquiera and quienquiera are **cualesquiera** and **quienesquiera**.

# DIRECT AND INDIRECT OBJECTS / COMPLEMENTOS DIRECTO E INDIRECTO

## Direct object

As a rule, the direct object is not preceded by a preposition. However, the positions of the subject and object in Spanish are often reversed, and the direct object is sometimes preceded by the preposition a to avoid confusion.

**Examples and exceptions:**

| Construction with **a** | Construction without **a** |
|---|---|
| César venció a Pompeyo. (Proper noun—name of a person) | Plutarco os dará mil Alejandros. (Proper noun used as a common noun) |
| Ensilló a Rocinante. (Proper noun—name of an animal) | Ensilló el caballo. (Common noun of an animal) |
| Conquistó a Sevilla. Conozco Madrid. Uncertain use. (Proper nouns—names of places without the article) | Visitó La Coruña. Veremos El Escorial. (Proper nouns—names of places preceded by the article) |

Busco al criado de mi casa.
(Common noun of a specified person)

Busco criados diligentes.
(Common noun of nonspecified persons)

Tienen por Dios al viento.
Temo al agua.
(Noun of a personified thing or of a thing to which an active quality is attributed)

Partiremos esta leña. Recojo el agua.
(Nouns of things in general)

No conozco a nadie.
Yo busco a otros, a alguien, a ti.
(Indefinite pronoun representing a person or personal pronoun)

No sabía nada. Di algo.
(Indefinite pronouns representing things)

Aquel a quien amo.

No sé quién vendrá.

## Indirect object

The indirect object is always preceded by the prepositions **a** or **para**: Escribo una carta a mi madre. Compro un libro **para** mi hijo. (I write a letter to my mother. I buy a book for my son.)

## ADJECTIVES / ADJETIVOS

The adjective in Spanish is a variable part of speech and must agree in gender and number with the noun it qualifies: libro **pequeño**, casa **pequeña**; libros **pequeños**, casas **pequeñas**.

Some adjectives, however, have the same ending for both masculine and feminine genders: hombre **fiel**, mujer **fiel**; hombres **fieles**, mujeres **fieles**.

### Placement of the adjective

Predicate adjectives usually follow the verb: la nieve es **blanca,** the snow is white.

Nevertheless, the order of the sentence can be reversed for emphasis or in some fixed expressions: ¡**buena** es ésta!, that is a good one!; ¡**bueno** está lo bueno!, leave well enough alone.

Adjectives that directly modify a noun may either precede or follow it.

### Special cases

- Adjectives that express a natural quality or a quality associated with a person or thing are placed before the noun: el **fiero** león, la **blanca** nieve.

- Indefinite, interrogative, and exclamative adjectives; the adjectives **medio, buen, mal, poco, mucho,** and **mero;** and adjectives expressing cardinal numbers are placed before the noun: **algún** día, some day; ¿**qué** libro prefiere usted?, which book do you prefer?; **dos** hombres, two men.

  **Alguno,** when placed after a noun, has a negative sense: no hay remedio **alguno,** there is no remedy.

- Some adjectives change meaning or connotation when they precede or follow a noun: un **simple** hombre, a mere man; un hombre **simple,** a simpleton.

- Some adjectives change in form when used before a noun. **Grande** may be shortened to **gran** when used in the sense of extraordinary or distinguished: un **gran** rey, a great king; una **gran** nación, a great nation.

- The masculine adjectives **alguno, ninguno, bueno, malo, primero,** and **tercero** drop the final o when placed before a noun: **algún** día, some day; **ningún** hombre, no man; **primer** lugar, first place; **tercer** piso, third floor.

- The masculine adjective **Santo** is shortened to **San** before all names of saints except Tomás, Toribio, and Domingo: **San** Juan, Saint John; **Santo** Tomás, Saint Thomas.

### Comparative degree

The English comparatives—*more...than, less...than,* and adjective + *er than*—are expressed in Spanish as **más...que, menos...que**: Pedro es **más** (or **menos**) atlético **que** Juan, Peter is more (or less) athletic than John.

In a comparative expression, when **que** is followed by a conjugated verb or a number, it is replaced by **de lo que** and **de,** respectively: esto es más difícil **de lo que** parece, this is more difficult than it seems; hay más **de** diez personas, there are more than ten people.

The English comparatives, *as...as* and *so...as,* are expressed in Spanish as **tan...como:** mi casa es **tan** hermosa **como** la de usted, my house is as beautiful as yours.

### Superlative degree

The English superlatives—*the most* (or *the least*)...*in* or *of* and adjective + *est...in* or *of*—are expressed in Spanish as **el más** (or **el menos**)...**de:** el barrio **más** populoso de la ciudad, the most populous quarter in the town.

- The absolute superlative is formed by placing **muy** before the adjective or by adding the ending **-ísimo** to the adjective: **muy** excelente, **excelentísimo,** most excellent.

- Adjectives ending in a vowel drop the vowel and add **-ísimo:** grande, **grandísimo;** alto, **altísimo.**

- Adjectives ending in **co** or **go,** change **c** to **qu** and **g** to **gu** and add **-ísimo:** poco, **poquísimo;** largo, **larguísimo.**

- Adjectives ending in **io** drop the ending and add **-ísimo:** limpio, **limpísimo.**

- Adjectives containing an accented diphthong—**ie** or **ue**—change **ie** to **e** and **ue** to **o** and add **-ísimo:** valiente, **valentísimo;** fuerte, **fortísimo.**

- Adjectives ending in **ble** change this ending to **bilísimo:** amable, **amabilísimo.**

- Some adjectives have special forms for the comparative and superlative degrees: bueno, mejor, óptimo; malo, peor, pésimo; grande, mayor, máximo; pequeño, menor, mínimo.

# NUMERALS / NUMERALES

### Observations

1) **Uno,** when it precedes a masculine noun, and **ciento,** when it precedes any noun and when used in a cardinal number, take the shortened forms **un** and **cien: un** libro; **cien** hombres; **cien** mil soldados.

2) The cardinal numbers between 20 and 30 are spelled **veintiuno, veintidós, veintitrés,** etc.

3) The cardinal numbers between 30 and 40, 40 and 50, etc. (under 100), use the conjunction **y:** treinta **y** uno, ochenta **y** tres.

4) The preceding rules apply to the spelling of any cardinal number over 100: **ciento** veintiuno, 121; **seiscientos** cuarenta y dos, 642; **cien** mil cuarenta, 100.040. Note that:
   —**Millón, billón,** and the like take the indefinite article **un;** however, **ciento, cien,** and **mil** do not: **un** millón, a million; **ciento,** a hundred; **mil,** a thousand; **cien mil,** one hundred thousand.

5) Ordinal numbers between 10th and 20th are: **undécimo, duodécimo, decimotercero** or **decimotercio, decimocuarto, decimoquinto, decimosexto, decimoséptimo, decimoctavo,** and **decimonoveno** or **decimonono.**

6) The ordinal numbers between 20th and 30th, 30th and 40th, etc. are formed by adding the first nine ordinal numbers to **vigésimo, trigésimo, cuadragésimo,** etc.: **vigésimo primero,** twenty-first; **trigésimo segundo,** thirty-second; **cuadragésimo tercero,** forty-third.

7) Most ordinal numbers may also be formed by adding the endings **-eno, -ena,** and **-avo, -ava** to the cardinal numbers. The ordinal numbers ending in **-avo** (except octavo) are used only to express fractions: una **dozava** parte, one twelfth part; el **dozavo** de, a twelfth of.

8) The cardinal numbers (except **uno**) may be used as ordinals. However, from 2 to 10, preference is given to the ordinal numbers for the names of kings, chapters of books, etc.
   —For the days of the month (except the first), only cardinal numbers are used: el **primero** de junio, el **dos** de octubre, el **catorce** de diciembre.

9) As a rule, cardinal numbers are placed before the noun; but when they are used as ordinal numbers, they are placed after the noun: dos libros, capítulo quince.

10) All the ordinal numbers and the cardinal numbers uno, doscientos, trescientos, through novecientos agree with the noun they qualify: la primera puerta, el tercer hombre, una casa, doscientos libros, trescientas cuatro personas.

## PERSONAL PRONOUNS / PRONOMBRES PERSONALES
### Subject pronouns

| Person | Singular | Plural |
|---|---|---|
| *1st* | yo | nosotros, nosotras, nos |
| *2nd* | usted, tú | ustedes, vosotros, vosotras, vos |
| *3rd* | él, ella | ellos, ellas |

- The subject pronoun in Spanish is used only for emphasis or to prevent ambiguity. When neither of these reasons for its use exists, its presence in the sentence makes the style heavy and should be avoided.

- Usted and ustedes are technically second person pronouns used out of courtesy. However, they take the verb in the third person.

- Nos is used by kings, bishops, etc. in their writings or proclamations in the same way as the English *royal we* and *us*. Nosotros is used by writers in the same way as the *editorial we* in English.

- Vos is used to address God, a saint, a king, etc. In some American countries tú is used.

### Object pronouns

**Direct Object Pronouns**

| Person | Singular | Plural |
|---|---|---|
| *1st* | me | nos |
| *2nd* | te, le, lo, la | os, los, las |
| *3rd* | le, lo, la | los, las |

**Indirect Object Pronouns (without a preposition)**

| Person | Singular | Plural |
|---|---|---|
| *1st* | me | nos |
| *2nd* | te, le | os, les |
| *3rd* | le | les |

**Object Pronouns (with a preposition)**

| Person | Singular | Plural |
|---|---|---|
| *1st* | mí | nosotros, nosotras |
| *2nd* | usted, ti | ustedes, vosotros, vosotras |
| *3rd* | él, ella, sí | ellos, ellas, sí |

- Sí is equivalent to *himself, herself, itself,* and *themselves* relating to the subject of the sentence: esto es malo de sí, this is bad in itself; habla de sí mismo, he speaks of himself.

- When the indirect object pronouns le and les must precede another third person pronoun, they are replaced by se. Incorrect: le lo mandaron, les las quitaron. Correct: se lo mandaron, se las quitaron.

Reflexive Pronouns

| Person | Singular | Plural |
|--------|----------|--------|
| *1st*  | me       | nos    |
| *2nd*  | te       | os     |
| *3rd*  | se       | se     |

- Se may also be:
  —An indication of the passive voice.
  —An impersonal subject equivalent to the English *one, you, they, people:* se habló de todo, they talked about everything. However, when the verb is reflexive, se cannot be used this way. Instead, **uno, alguno,** or **alguien** may be substituted as the impersonal subject.

Observations:
- When the verb is a gerund or a form of the imperative or infinitive mood, the object pronoun or pronouns are placed after the verb: diciéndolo, dámelo, observarnos. In compound tenses, they are placed after the auxiliary verb: habiéndome dado, haberos comprendido.
  When the gerund or infinitive is subordinate to another verb, the pronouns may pass to the main verb: quieren molestarte or te quieren molestar; iban diciéndolo or lo iban diciendo.

- Direct and indirect object pronouns may be placed before or after the verb when the verb is in the indicative, subjunctive, or conditional mood. In everyday language, it is usual to place them before the verb.

- When there are two object pronouns, the indirect precedes the direct, and a reflexive pronoun precedes another pronoun: me lo dio, se las prometí.

- Object pronouns that follow the verb are incorporated into the verb: **diciéndolo, molestarte.**
  Sometimes in this union, the final letter of the verb must be dropped to avoid a metaplasm: correct: **unámonos,** incorrect: **unamosnos;** correct: **sentaos,** incorrect: **sentados.**

Order of placement
When two or more pronouns accompany the verb, either preceding or following it, the second person pronoun is placed before the first person pronoun, and this before the third person pronoun. The pronoun se always precedes the others. (**Te me** quieren arrebatar. **Nos lo** ofrecen. **Se te** conoce en la cara.)


## POSSESSIVE PRONOUNS AND ADJECTIVES / POSESIVO (Adjetivo y pronombre)

- The Spanish possessive adjective and pronoun agree with the noun representing the possessed thing: **mi** sombrero, my hat; **mis** libros, my books; **tus** caballos, **vuestros** caballos, your horses.

- The third person possessive adjective or noun, especially in the form of **su,** is very ambiguous because it can mean *his, her, its,* and *their.* It is also equivalent to *your* when used in correlation with **usted** or **ustedes.** To prevent misunderstanding, the practice had been to add the possessor's name (or a pronoun representing it) preceded by **de:** su casa **de Luis;** su libro **de ellos;** su madre **de usted.** However, this use is now restricted to **su...de usted** or **su...de ustedes:** su libro **de usted,** su madre **de ustedes.** In most cases, it is preferable to reword the sentence to avoid ambiguity.

- **Nuestro** and **vuestro** denote only one possessor when the corresponding personal pronoun (**nosotros, nos,** or **vos**) denotes one person.

- In some sentences, the definite article replaces the possessive adjective: he dejado **los** guantes sobre la mesa, I have left my gloves on the table; te has olvidado **el** paraguas, you have forgotten your umbrella.

# CONJUGATION OF VERBS / CONJUGACIÓN

Regular verbs in Spanish fall into three groups: -ar verbs (first conjugation), -er verbs (second conjugation), and -ir verbs (third conjugation).

## Models of the three conjugations (simple tenses)

amar (to love)     temer (to fear)     recibir (to receive)

### Indicative Mood

Present

am-o, -as, -a; -amos, -áis, -an
tem-o, -es, -e; -emos, -éis, -en
recib-o, -es, -e; -imos, -ís, -en

Preterite

am-é, -aste, -ó; -amos, -asteis, -aron
tem ⎫
recib ⎭ -í, -iste, -ió; -imos, -isteis, -ieron

Imperfect

am-aba, -abas, -aba; -ábamos, -abais, -aban
tem ⎫
recib ⎭ -ía, -ías, -ía; -íamos, -íais, -ían

Future

amar ⎫
temer ⎬ -é, -ás, -á; -emos, -éis, -án
recibir ⎭

### Conditional

amar ⎫
temer ⎬ -ía, -ías, -ía; -íamos, -íais, -ían
recibir ⎭

### Subjunctive Mood

Present

am-e, -es, -e; -emos, -éis, -en
tem ⎫
recib ⎭ -a, -as, -a; -amos, -áis, -an

Imperfect
(s-form)

am-ase, -ases, -ase; -ásemos, -aseis, -asen
tem ⎫
recib ⎭ -iese, -ieses, -iese; -iésemos, -ieseis, -iesen

Imperfect
(r-form)

am-ara, -aras, -ara; -áramos, -arais, -aran
tem ⎫
recib ⎭ -iera, -ieras, -iera; -iéramos, -ierais, -ieran

Future

am-are, -ares, -are; -áremos, -areis, -aren
tem ⎫
recib ⎭ -iere, -ieres, -iere; -iéremos, -iereis, -ieren

### Past Participle

amado     temido     recibido

### Gerund

amando     temiendo     recibiendo

Compound tenses are formed by the auxiliary verb **haber** and the past participle of the conjugated verb: **he comido**, I have eaten; **habrá llegado**, he will have arrived; **habías temido**, you had feared.

## Irregular verbs

The conjugations of irregular verbs are given in the entries corresponding to their infinitives.

## Orthographic-changing verbs

Some verbs undergo spelling changes to preserve their regularity to the ear: tocar, **toque**; llegar, **llegue**; vencer, **venzo**; lanzar, **lance**, etc. These orthographic-changing verbs are neither considered nor treated as irregular verbs in this dictionary.

## PASSIVE VOICE / VOZ PASIVA

The Spanish language expresses the passive voice in two different ways:
1) By a form of the verb **ser** and a past participle: la serpiente **fue muerta** por Pedro, the snake was killed by Peter.
2) By the pronoun **se** preceding the verb: aquí **se habla** español, Spanish is spoken here.

The second form of the passive voice is often difficult to distinguish from the active voice in sentences where **se** is an impersonal subject.

## EXPRESSING NEGATION / NEGACIÓN

Negation is expressed by the adverb **no**, which is equivalent to the English *no* and *not*.

- No is always placed before the verb: la casa **no es** mía, the house is not mine; el niño **no come**, the child does not eat.
  —Other words, even whole sentences, may be placed between **no** and the verb: no **se lo** daré, I will not give it to him; no **todos los presentes** estaban conformes, not all those present agreed.
  —Whenever the meaning may not be clearly understood, **no** must accompany the words it modifies. For example: tu madre **no puede** venir, your mother cannot come; tu madre **puede no** venir, your mother may not come.

- Words expressing negation: **jamás, nunca, nada, nadie, ninguno,** and the phrases **en mi vida, en todo el día,** etc. are substituted for **no** when they precede the verb: **jamás** volveré, **nunca** lo sabrás, **nada** me falta, a **nadie** veo, **ninguno** sobra.
  —However, when these words follow the verb, **no** must be used in the sentence and precede the verb: **no** volveré **jamás**, **no** lo sabrás **nunca**, **no** me falta **nada**, **no** veo a **nadie**, **no** sobra **ninguno**.
  —When the sentence contains many words that express negation, only one of them can be placed before the verb: **nadie** me ayudó nunca en nada, **nunca** me ayudó nadie en nada.
  —If the verb is preceded by **no**, all other negative words must follow the verb: No me ayudó **nunca nadie** en **nada**.

- No may be used without expressing negation:
  —In sentences subordinate to a verb expressing fear or possibility, **no** is substituted for a **que**: temía **no** viniese, I feared that he should come.
  —As an expletive in sentences like: Nadie dudará que la falta de precisión... **no** dimane de..., No one will doubt that the lack of precision comes from (or is due to)....

## INTERROGATIVES / INTERROGACIÓN

### Construction of the interrogative sentence

**Sentences with no interrogative word:**

- The subject is placed after the verb. If a compound tense is used, the subject follows the participle. Remember that in Spanish the subject is expressed only for emphasis or when its presence is necessary for meaning.

  ¿Ha llegado tu padre?
  ¿Viene alguien?
  ¿Trae cada uno su libro?
  Llaman.— ¿Será él?
  ¿Vienes?
  ¿Viene usted?
  ¿Viene ella?

**Sentences with an interrogative word:**

- When the interrogative word is the subject, the sentence order is not reversed.
- When the interrogative word is an attribute, an object, or a complement, the sentence order is reversed.

  ¿Quién llama?
  ¿Qué dolor es comparable al mío?
  ¿Cuál es tu libro?
  ¿Qué quiere tu hermano?
  ¿Con quién habla usted?

Complement, object, or subject placed at the beginning of the sentence:

- For emphasis, a complement or object is placed at the beginning of a sentence. If a direct or indirect object is emphasized, it may be repeated by means of a pronoun: A este hombre, ¿lo conocían ustedes? A tu padre, ¿le has escrito? De este asunto, ¿han hablado ustedes?

- The subject can also be placed at the beginning of an interrogative sentence, but then the question is indicated only by the question marks and vocal intonation: ¿Los estudiantes estaban contentos? or Los estudiantes, ¿estaban contentos?

Interrogative sentences are punctuated with two question marks: the one (¿) at the beginning of the question and the other (?) at the end of the question.

## THE INFINITIVE / INFINITIVO

The infinitive in Spanish has practically the same uses as the infinitive in English.

*Exception:* In some subordinate sentences that express what is ordered, expected, desired, etc., the subjunctive or indicative mood is used; whereas in English, the infinitive would be used: El capitán ordenó a los soldados **que trajesen** al prisionero. (The captain ordered the soldiers *to bring* the prisoner.) Me pidió **que pagase** la cuenta. (He asked me *to pay* the bill.) Esperan **que se irá** pronto. (They expect him *to go* away soon.)

The Spanish infinitive is used as a noun in the same way as the English infinitive and sometimes gerund are used as nouns. **Errar** es humano. (To err is human.) El **comer** es necesario para la vida. (Eating is necessary for life.)

## PARTICIPLES / PARTICIPIOS

### Past participle

- The past participle is always invariable when it is used to form a compound tense: **he recibido** una carta, los libros que **he recibido.**
  —When the past participle is used as an adjective or an attribute, it agrees with its noun in number and gender: un problema **resuelto,** la obra está **terminada.**
  —When the past participle is used with the verbs **tener, llevar, dejar,** etc., it is made to agree in number and gender with a related noun: tengo **resueltos** los problemas, I have the problems solved; llevo **escritas** cuatro cartas, I have four letters written; la dejó **hecha** una furia, when he left her, she was in a rage.

- Many past participles in Spanish have both a regular and an irregular form. As a rule, the irregular forms of the past participles are only used as adjectives and sometimes as nouns: Dios le ha **bendecido,** God has blessed him; una medalla **bendita,** a blessed medal.

### Present participle

Very few Spanish verbs have a present participle (in the Latin sense). This participle has become an adjective. Only **concerniente, condescendiente, conducente, correspondiente,** and some others that can have the same complements and objects as the verb, retain something of their participial nature.

## THE GERUND / GERUNDIO

### Formation

The first conjugation adds -**ando** to the stem of the infinitive (amar, **amando**). The second and third conjugations add -**iendo** (temer, **temiendo**; recibir, **recibiendo**). The gerund does not change for number and gender.

**Observations**

- The gerund in Spanish never acts as a noun. It expresses an action occurring at the same time as or immediately preceding the action of the main verb: Lee **paseándose,** he reads while strolling; **viendo** a su padre, corrió hacia él, on seeing his father, he ran toward him; **habiendo estudiado** la proposición, me resuelvo a aceptarla, having studied the proposition, I resolve to accept it.

The gerund never expresses an action that occurs after the action of the main verb.

- When the gerund is related to the subject of the main sentence, it may be used only in an explanatory sense: el lobo, **huyendo de los perros**, se metió en el bosque. (The wolf, fleeing from the dogs, went into the woods.)

   The gerund is never used restrictively. *It is correct to say*: Los pasajeros, **llevando pasaporte**, pudieron desembarcar. (The passengers, having their passports, were able to disembark.) *It is incorrect to say*: Los pasajeros **llevando pasaporte** pudieron desembarcar. (Only the passengers having their passports could disembark.) This can be expressed as: Los pasajeros **que llevaban** pasaporte....

- When the gerund is related to the object of the main verb, the object then acts as the subject of the gerund. This use is only correct when the gerund expresses an action perceptible in its course, never a state, quality, or action not perceptible in its course. *It is correct to say*: Vi a un hombre **plantando** coles. (I saw a man planting cabbages.) *It is incorrect to say*: Envió una caja **conteniendo** libros. (He sent a box containing books.) In this case, it is necessary to say: Envió una caja **que contiene** libros.

- The gerund is often used in phrases that are independent of a main sentence, as in titles, captions, inscriptions on engravings, photographs, paintings, etc.: César **pasando** el Rubicón (Caesar passing the Rubicon); las ranas **pidiendo** rey (the frogs asking for a king).

- The gerund is frequently used as an adverb: Ella se fue **llorando** (she went away in tears); el tiempo pasa **volando** (time passes swiftly).

   As an adverb, the gerund may also express the way in which something is done or attained: hizo una cuerda **uniendo varias sábanas** (he made a rope by tying several sheets together).

## ADVERBS / ADVERBIOS

### Adverbs ending in -mente

Some adverbs are formed by adding -**mente** to the end of an adjective: fiel, **fielmente**. If the adjective can change gender, -**mente** is added to the feminine form: rico, rica, **ricamente**.

### Placement of the adverb

Generally, when the adverb is qualifying an adjective or another adverb, it immediately precedes the word it qualifies: un libro **bien** escrito, a well-written book; tan **lindamente** ilustrado, so beautifully illustrated.

When the adverb modifies a verb, it may precede or follow the verb: **mañana** llegará mi padre or mi padre llegará **mañana**; my father will arrive tomorrow.

The negative adverb is always placed before the verb: **no** conozco a este hombre, I don't know this man; **no** lo conozco, I don't know him.

When a direct or indirect object pronoun precedes the verb, the adverb cannot separate the pronoun from the verb: **ayer** la vi or la vi **ayer**, I saw her yesterday. The adverb usually never separates an auxiliary verb from the principal verb: ha vencido **fácilmente** a su adversario, he has easily defeated his opponent.

*Note:* When a word is qualified by two or more adverbs that end in -**mente**, only the last adverb has the ending -**mente**, the others retain the adjective form: ella habló **clara, concisa** y **elegantemente**; she spoke clearly, concisely, and elegantly.

### Comparative and superlative degrees

Adverbs can also be expressed in comparative and superlative degrees: **más claramente**, more clearly; **clarísimamente**, very clearly or most clearly.

## SYNTAX / SINTAXIS

Sentence construction in Spanish is very free. As a general rule its elements, with the exception of object pronouns may be placed in any order.

*Examples:*

| | |
|---|---|
| Pedro llegará a las tres. | Traigo un regalo para ti. |
| Pedro a las tres llegará. | Traigo para ti un regalo. |
| Llegará a las tres Pedro. | Un regalo traigo para ti. |
| A las tres llegará Pedro. | Un regalo para ti traigo. |
| A las tres Pedro llegará. | Para ti traigo un regalo. |
| | Para ti un regalo traigo. |

The use of any one of these constructions is a matter of style or of psychological or emotional intent. Nevertheless, the placement of the verb at the end of the sentence is considered affected, even though it is grammatically correct. It is rarely used in writing and not used at all in conversation.

### Special cases

There are some cases in which the subject must be placed after the verb. The more important ones are:

- In some interrogative sentences.

- In exclamatory sentences beginning with **qué, cuál, cuán, cuánto**: ¡Qué alegría tendrá **Juan**! ¡Cuál sería **su sorpresa**!

- After **cualquiera que** and **quienquiera que**, used with the verb **ser**, and after **por...que** and **por muy...que**, when the intervening word is an attribute: Cualquiera que fuese **su estado**. Por muy hábil que sea **tu hermano**.

- In parenthetic sentences using the verbs **decir, preguntar, responder, exclamar**, etc.: Nadie — dijo **Juan** — lo creería.

- In sentences expressing a wish or desire, a condition, or a supposition: ¡Viva **la Reina**! Si se presenta **la ocasión**. Si lo quiere **usted** así.

- In sentences beginning with the adverbs or phrases **cuando, apenas, en cuanto**, etc.: Cuando llegue **tu padre**. Apenas lo oyó **Juan**. En cuanto estemos **todos** reunidos.

- In imperative sentences having **usted** as a subject or having a subject that is to be emphasized: Oiga **usted**. Ven **tú** si no viene él.

**A, a** *f.* A, a, the first letter of the Spanish alphabet.
**a** *prep.* to [governing the indirect object]: *dáselo* ~ *Pedro*, give it to Peter. *2* at, by, in, on, to, after, like, etc.: ~ *la mesa*, at table; ~ *la una*, at one o'clock; ~ *dos pesetas la libra*, at two pesetas a pound; ~ *mano*, by hand; ~ *fuerza de*, by dint of; ~ *oscuras*, in the dark; ~ *tiempo*, in time; ~ *bordo*, on board; ~ *caballo*, on horseback; ~ *la mañana siguiente*, on the next morning; ~ *mi gusto*, to my taste; *de diez* ~ *doce*, from ten to twelve; *voy* ~ *jugar*, I am going to play; ~ *los ocho días de*, eight days after; ~ *la inglesa*, English style; after the English fashion; ~ *lo loco*, like a madman, recklessly, widly; ~ *no ser que*, unless. *3* if, had, but: ~ *no ser por José*, but for Joseph. *3* Generally it is not translated when used with the direct object of a verb: *César venció* ~ *Pompeyo*, Caesar defeated Pompey. See DIRECT OBJECT diagram. *5* It coalesces with the article *el*, forming *al*: *al niño*, to the child; *al contrario*, on the contrary; *al menos*, at least; *al principio*, at first; *al llegar yo*, on my arrival.
**Aaron** *pr. n.* Aaron.
**abacá** *m.* abaca, Manila hemp.
**abacería** *f.* grocer's shop, grocery store.
**abacero, -ra** *m.-f.* grocer, retail grocer.
**abacial** *adj.* abbatial.
**ábaco** *m.* ARCH. abacus. *2* abacus [calculating frame]. *3* MIN. washing trough.
**abad** *m.* abbot.
**abadejo** *m.* codfish.
**abadengo, -ga** *adj.* abbatial. *2 m.* abbatial states.
**abadesa** *f.* abbess.
**abadía** *f.* Abbey. *2* abbacy. *3* abbotship.
**abajeño, -ña** *adj.* (Am.) lowland. *2 n.* (Am.) lowlander.
**abajo** *adv.* down: *boca* ~, face down; *cuesta* ~, downhill; *hacia* ~, downwards; *muy* ~, low down. *2* below, under: *el hombre que está* ~, the man below. *3 interj.* down with!
**abalanzar** *tr.* to balance [a scale]. *2 ref.* to fall, pounce, throw oneself, rush impetuously.
**abalaustrado, -da** *adj.* BALAUSTRADO.
**abalizamiento** *m.* buoy-laying. *2* AER. airways marking.
**abalizar** *tr.* to buoy, buoy off. *2 ref.* NAUT. to take bearings.
**abalorio** *m.* glass bead. *2* glass beads, beadwork.

**abaluartar** *tr.* ABASTIONAR.
**abanderado** *m.* colour bearer, standard-bearer.
**abanderar** *tr.* to register [a ship].
**abanderizar** *tr.* to divide into parties or factions.
**abandonado, -da** *adj.* abandoned, forsaken. *2* forlorn. *3* negligent, slovenly.
**abandonar** *tr.* to abandon, leave, forsake. *2* to give up. *3 intr.* CHESS, DRAUGHTS to resign. *4 ref.* to give oneself up (to). *5* to despair, give in. *6* to neglect oneself, one's duties.
**abandono** *m.* abandon, abandonment. *2* forlornness. *3* CHESS, DRAUGHTS. resigning.
**abanicar** *tr.* to fan. *2 ref.* to fan oneself.
**abanico** *m.* fan [instrument]: *en* ~, fan-shaped; fan-like. *2* NAUT. derrick, crane.
**abaniqueo** *m.* fanning.
**abaniquero** *m.* fanmaker.
**abanto** *adj.* shy, timid [bull]. *2 m.* ORN. Egyptian vulture.
**abaratamiento** *m.* cheapening.
**abaratar** *tr.* to cheapen, lower the price of. *2 ref.* to cheapen, become cheap, fall in price.
**abarca** *f.* brogue, sandal.
**abarcar** *tr.* to clasp, grasp, take in, embrace, comprise, include. *2* to undertake [too many things at once]. *3* (Am.) to monopolize.
**abarloar** *tr.* to bring alongside.
**abarquillar** *tr.-ref.* to curl up, warp, curve, turn up at the edges.
**abarraganamiento** *m.* concubinage.
**abarrajarse** *ref.* (Am.) to stumble, fall. *2* (Am.) to become a ruffian.
**abarrancar** *tr.* to ravine. *2 ref.* to fall into a ravine. *3 intr.-ref.* to get into a jam.
**abarrotado, -da** *adj.* full, crammed; ~ *de gente*, crowded.
**abarrotar** *tr.* to bar, strengthen with bars. *2* to cram, pack; to overstock. *3* CARDS to finesse.
**abarrote** *m.* NAUT. stopgap, small package. *2 pl.* (Am.) groceries.
**Abasidas** *pr. n. pl.* HIST. Abbasids.
**abastardar** *intr.* fig. to degenerate, to degrade.
**abastecedor, -ra** *m.-f.* purveyor, supplier.
**abastecer** *tr.* to provision, purvey, supply. ¶ CONJUG. like *agradecer*.
**abastecimiento** *m.* supply, provision, purveyance.
**abastionar** *tr.* to fortify with bastions.

abasto *m.* purveyance, supply. *2* abundance. *3 dar* ~ *a*, to be sufficent for; to be able to attend to.
abatanar *tr.* WEAV. to full, beat [cloth].
abatatar *tr.* (Am.) coll. to frighten, to scare, to intimidate. *2 ref.* coll. to become listless or lethargic. *3 ref.* (Am.) coll. to become frightened, to lose one's nerve.
abate *m.* abbé.
abatible *adj.* folding, collapsible.
abatido, -da *adj.* dejected, despondent, dispirited, downcast. *2* low, weakened. *3* humbled. *4* abject, mean.
abatimiento *m.* dejection, low spirits. *2* abjectedness. *3* humiliation. *4* lowness, prostration. *5* NAUT., AER. drift, leeway.
abatir *tr.* to bring down, throw down, overthrow. *2* NAUT. to lower [a sail]. *3* to depress, dishearten. *4* to humble. *5 intr.* NAUT., AER. to drift. *6 ref.* to humble oneself. *7* to be disheartened. *8* [of a bird of prey] to swoop down.
abazón *m.* ZOOL. cheek pouch.
abdicación *f.* abdication.
abdicar *tr.* to abdicate, to renounce.
abdomen *m.* abdomen.
abdominal *adj.* abdominal.
abducción *f.* LOG., PHYSIOL. abduction.
abductor *adj.* ANAT. abducent. *2 m.* ANAT. abductor.
abecé *m.* ABC. *2* abecedary, primer.
abecedario *m.* alphabet. *2* abecedary, primer.
abedul *m.* BOT. birch, birch tree.
abeja *f.* ENT. bee, honeybee: ~ *reina*, queen bee; ~ *obrera*, worker [bee].
abejarrón *m.* ENT. bumblebee.
abejaruco *m.* ORN. bee eater.
abejero *m.* beekeeper. *2* ABEJARUCO.
abejón *m.* ENT. drone. *2* ENT. bumblebee.
abejorro *m.* ENT. bumblebee. *2* ENT. cockchafer.
Abel *pr. n. m.* Abel.
abellacado, -da *adj.* knavish.
abellotado *adj.* acorn-shaped.
abemolar *tr.* to soften [the voice]. *2* MUS. to flat.
aberenjenado, -da *adj.* eggplant-shaped. *2* eggplant-coloured.
aberración *f.* aberration [deviation].
aberrante *adj.* aberrant.
aberrar *intr.* to aberrate.
abertura *f.* opening, aperture, hole, slit, gap. *2* cove, inlet, small bay. *3* frankness.
abestiado, -da *adj.* beast-like.
abetal *m.* fir wood or grove.
abeto *m.* BOT. fir, silver fir: ~ *del Canadá*, hemlock.
abetunado, -da *adj.* bitumen-like, bituminous.
abiertamente *adv.* openly, declaredly, frankly.
abierto, -ta *p. p.* of ABRIR; opened. *2* open. *3* sincere, frank.
abigarrado, -da *adj.* variegated; motley, many-coloured.
abigeato *m.* gentle, light sound; rustling.
abigarrar *tr.* to variegate, motley.
ab intestato *adv.* intestate.
abintestato *m.* LAW settlement of an intestate state.
abisal *adj.* abyssal.
Abisinia *pr. n.* Abyssinia.
abisinio, -a *adj.-n.* Abyssinian.
abismal *adj.* abysmal, abyssal.
abismar *tr.* to plunge into an abyss. *2* to depress. *3 ref.* to plunge, be plunged [into]; to be buried or sunk [in thought, grief, etc.].
abismático, -ca *adj.* abysmal.
abismo *m.* abysm, abyss, gulf.

abitar *tr.* NAUT. to bitt.
abjuración *f.* abjuration; recantation.
abjurar *tr.* to abjure, forswear.
ablación *f.* SURG. ablation.
ablandabrevas *m.-f.* good-for-nothing.
ablandamiento *m.* softening. *2* mollification.
ablandar *tr.* to soften. *2* to mollify. *3* to loosen [the bowels]. *4* to appease [temper, anger]; to melt. *5 intr.-ref.* [of weather] to moderate. *6 ref.* to soften, become soft. *7* to relent, melt.
ablande *m.* (Am.) AUTO. running-in.
ablativo *m.* GRAM. ablative.
ablución *f.* ablution.
ablusado, -da *adj.* blouse-like.
abnegación *f.* abnegation, self-denial.
abnegado, -da *adj.* self-denying.
abobado, -da *adj.* silly, stupid. *2* stupefied.
abobar *tr.* to make silly. *2 ref.* to become silly. *3 tr.-ref.* EMBOBAR.
abobamiento *m.* amazement, stupefaction. *2* foolishness, stupidity.
abocado *adj.* dry-sweet [wine].
abocar *tr.* to mouth, seize with the mouth. *2* to bring near: *verse abocado a*, to be on the verge of. *3* to pour from one vessel to another. *4 intr.* NAUT. to enter the mouth of a channel, a strait, etc.
abocardado, -da *adj.* bell-mouthed.
abocardar *tr.* to widen the mouth of [a hole, tube, etc.]; to ream, trumpet.
abocelado, -da *adj.* torus-shaped.
abocetado, -da *adj.* sketchy, roughly outlined.
abocetar *tr.* to sketch; to make a rough model of.
abocinado, -da *adj.* trumpet-shaped. *2* ARCH. splayed [arch]. *3* droop-headed [horse].
abocinar *tr.* to shape like a trumpet, to flare. *2 intr.* coll. to fall on one's face.
abochornado, -da *adj.* blushing, ashamed.
abochornar *tr.* to overheat. *2* to shame, put to the blush. *3 ref.* to blush, be ashamed. *4* AGR. to wilt from excessive heat.
abofetear *tr.* to buffet, cuff, slap in the face.
abogacía *f.* law, legal profession.
abogada *f.* a female lawyer. *2* advocatress, mediatrix.
abogado *m.* advocate, lawyer, barrister: ~ *de secano*, quack lawyer. *2* advocate, intercessor.
abogar *intr.* to plead [in favour of]: to intercede.
abolengo *m.* ancestry, descent. *2* inheritance.
abolición *f.* abolition, abrogation.
abolicionismo *m.* abolitionism.
abolir *tr.* to abolish, abrogate. ¶ Only used in the forms having *i* in their terminations.
abolsado, -da *adj.* loose, baggy.
abolsarse *ref.* to become purse-shaped, to bag.
abolladura *f.* dent, bruise, bump.
abollar *tr.* to dent, batter, bruise, bump.
abollón *m.* ABOLLADURA.
abollonar *tr.* to emboss, to raise bosses on.
abombado, -da *adj.* convex. *2* (Am.) stunned, danzed. *3* merry, tipsy, fuddled.
abombar *tr.* to curve, make convex. *2* coll. to deafen, stun. *3 ref.* (Am.) to get drunk. *4* (Am.) to taint, become putrid.
abominable *adj.* abominable. *2* very bad.
abominación *f.* abomination.
abominar *tr.* to abominate. *2* to detest, abhor.
abonable *adj.* payable. *2* COM. creditable.
abonado, -da *m.-f.* subscriber; *commuter, season-ticket holder. *2 adj.* apt, capable.
abonanzar *intr.* [of the weather] to calm, clear up.

**abonar** *tr.* to approve, *approbate. 2 to guarantee, answer for. 3 to improve. 4 to fertilize, manure [soil]. 5 COM. to credit; to discount; to pay. 6 *tr.-ref.* to subscribe [for], to buy a season or commutation ticket [for].
**abonaré** *m.* COM. credit note.
**abono** *m.* approbation. 2 guarantee. 3 payment. 4 COM. discount, allowance. 5 COM. credit. 6 fertilizer. 7 subscription; season or commutation ticket.
**aboquillado, -da** *adj.* with a mouthpiece. 2 bell-shaped, wide-mouthed. 3 bevelled, chamfered.
**aboquillar** *tr.* to make bell-shaped.
**abordaje** *m.* NAUT. collision. 2 NAUT. the act of boarding a ship.
**abordable** *adj.* affordable, reasonable, within one's means. 2 within reach, attainable, accesible. 3 approachable.
**abordar** *tr.* NAUT. to board, come up against [a ship]. 2 to run foul of [a ship]. 3 to approach [a person, a matter, etc.]. 4 *intr.* NAUT. to land.
**aborigen** *adj.* aboriginal.
**aborígenes** *m. pl.* aboriginals, aborigines.
**aborrajarse** *ref.* to dry prematurely, to go bad or off.
**aborrascarse** *ref.* [of weather] to become stormy.
**aborrecer** *tr.* to abhor, hate. 2 to desert [brood or nest]. 3 to bore, annoy. ¶ CONJUG. like *agradecer*.
**aborrecible** *adj.* hateful, detestable.
**aborrecimiento** *m.* abhorrence, hate, dislike.
**aborregado** *adj.* fleecy, mackerel [sky].
**aborregarse** *ref.* to become covered with fleecy clouds (the sky). 2 (Am.) fig. to lose one's nerve, to get frightened.
**aborricarse** *ref.* to become coarse, to grow stupid.
**abortar** *intr.* to abort, miscarry. 2 BIOL. to abort.
**abortivo, -va** *adj.-m.* abortive.
**aborto** *m.* abortion, miscarriage. 2 monster.
**abotagado, -da** *adj.* bloated, swollen.
**abotagamiento** *m.* bloating, swelling.
**abotagarse** *ref.* to become bloted, swollen.
**abotonador** *m.* buttonhook.
**abotonadura** *f.* fastening [buttons].
**abotonar** *tr.* to button, button up. 2 *intr.* to bud. 3 *ref.* to button up [one's coat].
**abovedado, -da** *adj.* vaulted, fornicate(d.
**abovedar** *tr.* to vault, cove, make vault-shaped.
**aboyar** *tr.* to lay buoys in. 2 *intr.* to float.
**abozalar** *tr.* to muzzle.
**abra** *f.* GEOL. bay, cove, haven. 2 dale, valley. 3 fissure.
**abracadabra** *m.* abracadabra.
**Abrahán** *pr. n.* Abraham.
**abrasador, -ra** *adj.* burning, scorching, very hot.
**abrasar** *t.* to burn, sear, scorch, parch. 2 [of cold or frost] to nip [a plant]. 3 fig. to squander. 4 *ref.* to swelter, feel very hot. 5 AGR. to be nipped [by cold]. 6 *abrasarse de* o *en*, to burn with [thirst, love, etc.].
**abrasión** *f.* abrasion.
**abrasivo, -va** *adj.-m.* abrasive.
**abrazadera** *f.* clasp, clamp, cleat, brace. 2 band [of a gun]. 3 PRINT. brace, bracket.
**abrazamiento** *m.* embracing.
**abrazar** *tr.* to embrace, hug, clasp. 2 to include, comprise. 3 to embrace, espouse, adopt, follow [a cause, opinion, etc.]. 4 *ref.* to embrace, hug each other; to cling [to].
**abrazo** *m.* hug, embrace, clasp.
**ábrego** *m.* south wind.
**abrelatas** *m.* can or tin opener.

**abrevadero, abrevador** *m.* drinking trough. 2 watering, place for cattle.
**abrevar** *tr.* to water [cattle]. 2 *ref.* to drink.
**abreviación** *f.* abbreviation. 2 abridgement. 3 shortening. 4 hastening, acceleration.
**abreviadamente** *adv.* briefly, in short.
**abreviar** *tr.* to abridge, abbreviate, shorten. 2 to hasten, speed up.
**abreviatura** *f.* abbreviation.
**abridor** *m.* opener. 2 grafting knife.
**abrigadero** *m.* sheltered place for ships.
**abrigado, -da** *adj.* protected, covered, sheltered. 2 wrapped-up, warmly dressed. 3 cosy.
**abrigaño** *m.* place sheltered from the wind.
**abrigar** *tr.* to cover, wrap, keep warm. 2 to shelter, protect. 3 to entertain, harbour [fears, hopes, etc.]. 4 *ref.* to wrap oneself up. 5 to take shelter.
**abrigo** *m.* protection against the cold, keeping warm: *ropa de* ~, warm clothing. 2 shelter. 3 protection. 4 overcoat, wrap. 5 NAUT. haven.
**abril** *m.* April. 2 *pl.* years of early youth.
**abrileño, -ña** *adj.* [pertaining to] April, like April.
**abrillantador, -ra** *n.* polisher, lapidary, person who polishes. 2 *m.* polishing tool. 3 *m.* polishing substance or product.
**abrir** *tr.* to open. 2 to unfasten, uncover, unlock, unseal. 3 to cut or tear open; to split. 4 to bore [a hole, a well], to dig [a trench]. 5 to head, lead [a procession, etc.]. 6 to whet [the appetite]. 7 ~ *paso*, to make way; to clear the way. 8 *tr.-ref.* to spread out, to unfold. 9 *ref.* to open (be opened). 10 to split, to burst open. 11 [of flowers] to blossom. 12 to open up [to], confide [in]. ¶ Past. p.: *abierto*.
**abrochar** *tr.-ref.* to button, clasp, buckle; to fasten with hooks and eyes.
**abrogación** *f.* abrogation, repeal.
**abrogar** *tr.* to abrogate, repeal [an act, a bill, etc.].
**abrojal** *m.* ground abounding in caltrops.
**abrojo** *m.* BOT., MIL. caltrop. 2 *pl.* NAUT. hidden rocks. 3 fig. difficulties.
**abroncar** *tr.-ref.* to vex, annoy. 2 pop. to dress down.
**abroquelado, -da** *adj.* BOT. shield-shaped.
**abroquelar** *tr.* NAUT. to boxhaul. 2 to shield. 3 *ref.* to shield oneself.
**abrótano** *m.* BOT. abrotanum, southernwood.
**abrumado, -da** *adj.* overwhelmed, overcome.
**abrumador, -ra** *adj.* overwhelming, crushing. 2 oppressive, fatiguing.
**abrumar** *tr.* to overwhelm, crush. 2 to oppress, weary, fatigue. 3 *ref.* [of the weather] to become foggy.
**abrupto, -ta** *adj.* abrupt, steep, craggy.
**abrutado, -da** *adj.* brutish.
**absceso** *m.* MED. abscess.
**abscisa** *f.* GEOM. abscissa.
**abscisión** *f.* abscission.
**absentismo** *m.* absenteeism.
**ábside** *m.-f.* ARCH. apse, apsis.
**absidiola** *f.* ARCH. apse chapel.
**absidiolo** *m.* ARCH. apsidiole.
**absintio** *m.* absinthe, absinth.
**absolución** *f.* absolution. 2 LAW acquittal.
**absoluta** *f.* dogmatic statement. 2 MIL. discharge.
**absolutamente** *adv.* absolutely, completely, in every way. 2 not at all, in no way. 3 ~ *nada*, nothing at all, absolutely nothing.
**absolutismo** *m.* POL. absolutism.
**absoluto, -ta** *adj.* absolute. 2 *m. lo* ~, the absolute. 3 *en* ~, absolutely, by no means, at all.

**absolutorio, -ria** *adj.* absolutory, absolving.
**absolvederas** *f. pl.* coll. readiness to absolve.
**absolver** *tr.* to absolve. *2* to acquit. ¶ CONJUG. like *mover.*
**absorbente** *adj.-m.* absorbent. *2 adj.* absorbing, engrossing.
**absorber** *tr.* to absorb. *2* to engross.
**absorción** *f.* absorption.
**absorto, -ta** *adj.* amazed, ecstatic. *2* absorbed in thought.
**abstemio, -mia** *adj.* abstemious. *2 m.-f.* teetotal(l)er.
**abstención** *f.* abstention, refraining.
**abstencionismo** *m.* POL. abstentionism.
**abstencionista** *adj.* abstentionist. *2 n* abstentionist person.
**abstenerse** *ref.* to abstain, refrain, forbear.
**abstinencia** *f.* abstinence.
**abstinente** *adj.* abstinent.
**abstracción** *f.* abstraction. *2 hacer ~ de,* to leave aside.
**abstracto, -ta** *adj.* abstract: *en ~,* in the abstract.
**abstraer** *tr.* to abstract. *2 ref.* to be abstracted, lost in thought. *3 abstraerse de,* to become oblivious of, to leave aside.
**abstraído, -da** *adj.* abstracted, lost in thought.
**abstruso, -sa** *adj.* abstruse.
**absuelto, -ta** *irreg. p. p.* of ABSOLVER.
**absurdidad** *f.* absurdity.
**absurdo, -da** *adj.* absurd, nonsensical. *2 m.* absurdity, nonsense.
**abubilla** *f.* ORN. hoopoe.
**abuchear** *tr.* to boo, hoot.
**abucheo** *m.* booing, hooting.
**abuela** *f.* grandmother: *cuéntaselo a su ~,* fig. tell that to the marines. *2* old woman.
**abuelo** *m.* grandfather. *2* ancestor. *3* old man.
**abuhardillado, -da** *adj.* garret-like.
**abulense** *adj.-n.* AVILÉS.
**abulia** *f.* abulia.
**abúlico, -ca** *adj.* abulic.
**abultado, -da** *adj.* bulky, large, big.
**abultamiento** *m.* swelling, protuberance. *2* enlarging, exaggeration.
**abultar** *tr.* to enlarge, increase. *2* to exaggerate. *3 intr.* to bulge, be bulky.
**abundamiento** *m.* abundance. *2 a mayor ~,* moreover, furthermore, by the same token.
**abundancia** *f.* abundance, plenty.
**abundante** *adj.* abundant, copious, plentiful.
**abundar** *intr.* to abound [the plentiful]. *2* to abound, teem, be rich [in]. *3 ~ en una opinión,* to adhere to, or have, an opinion.
**¡abur!** *interj.* ¡AGUR!
**aburguesamiento** *m.* adoption of bourgeois customs and manners.
**aburguesarse** *ref.* to become or act as a bourgeois.
**aburrido, -da** *adj.* bored, weary. *2* boring, tedious, weary, irksome, tiresome.
**aburrimiento** *m.* boredom, weariness, ennui.
**aburrir** *tr.* to annoy, bore, tire, weary. *2* to hazard, to spend. *3 ref.* to get bored.
**abusar** *intr.* to go too far, to abuse. *2 ~ de,* to abuse [misuse, make bad use of]; to take advantage of; to impose upon.
**abusivo, -va** *adj.* abusive [implying misuse].
**abuso** *m.* abuse [misuse, bad use, immoderate use]. *2 ~ de confianza,* breach of faith or trust.
**abyección** *f.* abjection, abjectness.
**abyecto, -ta** *adj.* abject, base, servile.
**acá** *adv.* here, over here, hither, this way, this side;

*~ y acullá,* here and there; *de ~ para allá,* hither and thither. *2 desde entonces ~,* since that time; *¿de cuándo ~?,* since when?
**acabable** *adj.* which can be finished.
**acabado, -da** *adj.* finished. *2* complete, perfect, consummate; arrant. *3* spent, worn out, ruined. *4 ~ de hacer,* freshly done. *5 m.* last touch, touching up. *6* F. ARTS., WEAV. finish.
**acabador, -ra** *m.-f.* finisher.
**acaballadero** *m.* place and time for covering mares.
**acaballado, -da** *adj.* horselike.
**acaballar** *tr.* to cover [a mare].
**acaballonar** *tr.* AGR. to ridge.
**acabamiento** *m.* finish, finishing, completion. *2* end, death.
**acabar** *tr.* to finish, end, complete. *2* to make, achieve. *3* to consume, exhaust. *4* to finish, kill. *5 intr.* to end, finish. *6* to die. *7 ~ con,* to obtain; to use up; to destroy, put an end to. *8 ~ de,* to have just: *acaba de salir,* he has just come out. *9 ~ por,* to end by. *10 ¡acabáramos!,* at last! *11 ref.* to end, be over; to diminish, run out: *se acaba el pan,* the bread is running out; *¡se acabó!,* it is all up!
**acabestrar** *tr.* to accustom to a halter.
**acabóse** *m.* coll. limit, end: *ser el ~,* to be the limit, to be the end.
**acacalote** *m.* (Am.) ORN. cormorant.
**acacia** *f.* BOT. acacia.
**acachetear** *tr.* to slap.
**academia** *f.* academy. *2* special school. *3* F. ARTS academy figure.
**academicismo** *m.* academicism.
**académico, -ca** *adj.* academic, academical. *2* it is said of official studies, titles, degrees, etc. *3 m.* academic. *4* academician.
**acaecedero, -ra** *adj.* possible, that may happen.
**acaecer** *impers.* to happen, come to pass. ¶ CONJUG. like *agradecer.*
**acaecimiento** *m.* happening, event, occurrence.
**acalabrotar** *tr.* NAUT. to make a cable-laid rope.
**acalambrarse** *ref.* to get a cramp.
**acalefo** *adj.-n.* ZOOL. acalephan. *2 pl.* ZOOL. Acalephae.
**acalía** *f.* BOT. marshmallow.
**acaloradamente** *adv.* heatedly.
**acalorado, -da** *adj.* heated, excited, fiery.
**acaloramiento** *m.* heat, ardour, excitement.
**acalorar** *tr.* to warm, heat [with work or exercise]. *2* to excite, inflame. *3 ref.* to get overheated. *4* to become heated, excited.
**acallar** *tr.* to silence, hush, still, quiet.
**acamar** *tr.* [of rain or wind] to lay [plants] flat. *2 ref.* [of plants] to be laid flat [by rain or wind].
**acampanado, -da** *adj.* bell-shaped, flaring.
**acampanar** *tr.* to shape like a bell.
**acampar** *intr.-tr.* to camp, encamp.
**acanalado, -da** *adj.* blowing through a narrow place [wind]. *2* channeled, grooved, fluted.
**acanaladura** *f.* ARCH. flute, stria, striation.
**acanalar** *tr.* to shape like a gutter. *2* to groove, flute, striate, corrugate.
**acanallado, -da** *adj.* base, rabble-like.
**acanelado, -da** *adj.* cinnamon-coloured or flavoured.
**acantáceo, -a** *adj.* BOT. acanthaceous.
**acantilado, -da** *adj.* sheer, cliffy. *2* stepped [sea floor]. *3 m.* cliff, bluff.
**acanto** *m.* BOT., ARCH. acanthus.
**acantonamiento** *m.* cantonment.

**acantonar** *tr.* to canton, quarter [troops].
**acantopterigio, -a** *adj.-m.* ICHTH. acanthopterygian.
**acaparador, -ra** *adj.* monopolizer; one who corners.
**acaparamiento** *m.* monopolizing, cornering.
**acaparar** *tr.* to monopolize. *2* COM. to corner.
**acápite** *m* (Am.) paragraph. *2* (Am.) *punto* ~, full stop, new paragraph; period, new paragraph.
**acaracolado, -da** *adj.* spiral-shaped.
**acaramelado, -da** *p. p.* of ACARAMELAR. *2* overpolite, spoony, oversweet.
**acaramelar** *tr.* to cover with caramel. *2 ref.* to get over-polite, spoony, oversweet.
**acardenalar** *tr.* to bruise; to beat black and blue.
**acariciador, -ra** *adj.* caressing, fondling. *2 m.-f.* caresser, fondler.
**acariciar** *tr.* to caress, fondle. *2* to stroke, brush lightly. *3* to cherish [hopes, etc.].
**ácaro** *m.* ZOOL. mite, acarus.
**acarreador, -ra** *m.-f.* carrier, transporter.
**acarreamiento** *m.* ACARREO.
**acarrear** *tr.* to carry, cart, haul, transport. *2* to cause, occasion. *3 ref.* to bring upon oneself.
**acarreo** *m.* carriage, cartage, haulage. *2 de* ~, transported; alluvial: *tierras de* ~, alluvium.
**acarroñarse** *ref.* obs. to decay, to rot. *2* (Am.) coll. to get scared or intimidated, to lose one's nerve.
**acartonado, -da** *adj.* cardboard-like. *2* dried up, wizened [with age].
**cartonarse** *ref.* to become cardboard-like. *2* to dry up, become wizened [with age].
**caso** *m.* chance, accident. *2 adv.* by chance; maybe, perhaps: *por si* ~, just in case.
**acatable** *adj.* worthy of, or deserving respect.
**acatadamente** *adv.* obediently and respectfully.
**acatamiento** *m.* obedience and respect.
**acatar** *tr.* to obey and respect.
**acatarrado, -da** *adj.* MED. having a cold.
**acatarrar** *tr.* to give a cold. *2 ref.* to catch a cold.
**acaudalado, -da** *adj.* rich, opulent, wealthy.
**acaudalar** *tr.* to accumulate, acquire [money, knowledge, etc.].
**acaudillar** *tr.* to lead, command [troops, men].
**acaule** *m.-f.* BOT. acaulescent.
**Acaya** *pr. n.* Achaea.
**acceder** *intr.* to accede, agree, consent.
**accesible** *adj.* accessible.
**accesión** *f.* acceeding. *2* LAW. accession.
**accésit** *m.* accessit.
**acceso** *m.* access [approach; entry]. *2* access, attack, fit, outburst [of illness, anger, etc.]. *3* sexual intercourse.
**accesoria** *f.* outbuilding, outhouse.
**accesorio, -a** *adj.* accessory [said of things]; secondary. *2 m.* accessory, fixture.
**accidentado, -da** *adj.* stormy, agitated. *2* broken, uneven, rough. *3* GEOG. accidented.
**accidental** *adj.* accidental. *2* acting [doing duty temporarily]. *3 m.* MUS. accidental.
**accidentarse** *ref.* to have or to be involved in an accident.
**accidente** *m.* accident. *2* MED. sudden fit. *3* MUS. accidental.
**acción** *f.* action [acting, doing, operation], act: ~ *de gracias*, thanksgiving; *en* ~, in action, at work. *2* attitude. *3* action [of an actor or speaker]. *4* COM. share, *stock. *5* PHYS., CHEM., MIL. action. *6* LAW lawsuit. *7* THEAT. plot.
**accionamiento** *m.* working.

**accionar** *tr.* to gesticulate, gesture. *2* MECH. to move, drive, operate, work.
**accionista** *m.-f.* shareholder, stockholder.
**acebo** *m.* BOT. holly tree.
**acebolladura** *f.* shake [in wood].
**acebrado, -da** *adj.* striped.
**acebuche** *m.* BOT. oleaster, wild olive tree.
**acebuchina** *f.* wild olive [fruit].
**acecinar** *tr.* to salt and dry [meat].
**acechadero** *m.* lurking or spying place.
**acechanza** *f.* ACECHO.
**acechar** *tr.* to lurk, to watch stealthily. *2* to lie in wait, look out for.
**aceche** *m.* copperas.
**acecho** *m.* lurking, spying: *al* ~, in wait, on the watch.
**acedar** *tr.* to sour, acidify. *2* to sour, embitter. *3 ref.* to sour [become sour or acid].
**acedera** *f.* BOT. sorrel, sorrel dock.
**acederaque** *m.* BOT. azederach.
**acedía** *f.* acidity, sourness. *2* sournes of temper. *3* heartburn. *4* PLATIJA.
**acedo, -da** *adj.* acid, sour, tart. *2* sour, crabbed, harsh, disagreeable.
**acefalía** *f.* acephalia.
**acéfalo, -la** *adj.* acephalous.
**aceitar** *tr.* to oil.
**aceite** *m.* olive oil, salad oil: ~ *virgen*, crude olive oil. *2* oil: ~ *de hígado de bacalao*, codliver oil; ~ *de linaza*, linseed oil; *echar* ~ *al fuego*, fig. to add fuel to the flames.
**aceitera** *f.* oil can. *2* MEC. oil cup. *3* ENT. oil beetle. *4 pl.* cruet, cruetstand.
**aceitería** *f.* olive-oil shop.
**aceitero, -ra** *adj.* [pertaining to] oil. *2 m.-f.* olive-oil dealer.
**aceitoso, -sa** *adj.* oily, oleaginous; greasy.
**aceituna** *f.* olive [fruit]: ~ *zapatera*, stale olive.
**aceitunado, -da** *adj.* olive, olivaceous.
**aceitunero, -ra** *m.-f.* olive dealer. *2* olive picker.
**aceituní** *m.* an ancient oriental fabric. *2* ARCH. a kind of arabesque work.
**aceituno** *m.* BOT. olive tree.
**aceleración** *f.* acceleration. *2* haste.
**aceleradamente** *adv.* quickly, fast, rapidly.
**acelerado, -da** *adj.* quick, fast. *2* PHYS. accelerated, increasing speed gradually. *3* acceleration. *4* quick motion.
**acelerador, triz** *adj.* accelerating. *2* accelerative. *3 m.* ANAT., AUTO. accelerator.
**aceleramiento** *m.* ACELERACIÓN.
**acelerar** *tr.* to accelerate, hasten, quicken, hurry. *2 ref.* to accelerate [move or act faster].
**aceleratriz** *f. adj.* accelerative [power].
**acelerón** *m.* sudden acceleration.
**acelga** *f.* BOT. chard, swiss chard.
**acémila** *f.* mule, pack mule.
**acemilero, -ra** *adj.* of the muleteer's trade. *2 m.* muleteer.
**acendrado, -da** *adj.* pure, stainless.
**acendramiento** *m.* purifying. *2* purity, stainlessness.
**acendrar** *tr.* to purify. *2* to fine, refine [metals].
**acensar, acensuar** *tr.* to tax [a property].
**acento** *m.* accent [in every sense]; stress; ~ *ortográfico*, written accent; ~ *prosódico*, stress accent.
**acentuación** *f.* accentuation.
**acentuado, -da** *adj.* accented. *2* accentuated.
**acentuar** *tr.* to accent. *2* to accentuate, emphasize.
**aceña** *f.* water mill. *2* AZUD 1.

**acepción** f. acceptation, meaning. 2 respect [of persons].
**acepilladora** f. ENG. planer, planing machine.
**acepilladura** f. brushing [of clothes]. 2 planing, shaving. 2 pl. shavings.
**acepillar** tr. to brush [clothes, etc.]. 2 to plane, smooth [wood, metals].
**aceptabilidad** f. acceptability.
**aceptable** adj. acceptable, admissible.
**aceptación** f. acceptance. 2 approbation. 3 respect [of persons].
**aceptador, -ra** m.-f. accepter, acceptant. 2 acceptor.
**aceptante** adj. accepting. 2 m.-f. ACEPTADOR.
**aceptar** tr. to accept, receive. 2 to approve of. 3 COM. to accept [a bill].
**acequia** f. irrigation canal or ditch.
**acera** f. sidewalk, pavement. 2 side of a street: en la otra ~, across the street.
**aceráceas** f. pl. BOT. Aceraceae.
**acerado, -da** adj. steel, made of steel; steely. 2 sharp, incisive, mordant.
**acerar** tr. to acierate. 2 to steel.
**acerbidad** f. acerbity, harshness, bitterness, cruelty.
**acerbo, -ba** adj. harsh to the taste. 2 harsh, bitter, cruel.
**acerca de** adv. about, concerning, with regard to.
**acercamiento** m. approach, approximation. 2 rapprochement.
**acercar** tr. to bring or place near or nearer. 2 ref. to approach, come near or nearer; to come up [to]; gain [upon].
**acería** f. steel works.
**acerico, acerillo** m. pincushion.
**acero** m. steel. 2 sword; weapon. 3 pl. spirit, courage. 4 coll. appetite.
**acerola** f. azarole [fruit].
**acerolo** m. BOT. azarole tree.
**acérrimo, -ma** adj. very acrid. 2 very strong, utter [enemy], staunch [friend, supporter].
**acerrojar** tr. to bolt [fasten or lock with a bolt].
**acertado, -da** adj. right, fit, proper, opportune; successful, well-aimed, apposite.
**acertante** adj. winning, just right, to the point. 2 n. winner.
**acertar** tr. to hit [the mark]. 2 to hit upon, find. 3 to guess right; to divine. 4 to do well, right; to succeed in. 5 intr. to happen, chance: yo acertaba a estar allí, I chanced to be there. ¶ CONJUG. INDIC. Pres.: acierto, aciertas, acierta, aciertan. | SUBJ. Pres.: acierte, aciertes, acierte, acierten. | IMPER.: acierta, acierte, acierten.
**acertijo** m. riddle; conundrum.
**acervo** m. heap, pile. 2 common property.
**acetato** m. CHEM. acetate.
**acético, -ca** adj. CHEM. acetic.
**acetificar** tr. to acetify.
**acetileno** m. CHEM. acetylene.
**acetona** f. CHEM. acetone.
**acetre** m. small bucket. 2 holy-water vessel.
**aciago, -ga** adj. ill-fated, unlucky, sad, ominous.
**acial** m. VET. barnacles, twitch [for horses].
**aciano** m. BOT. bluet, bluebottle, cornflower.
**acíbar** m. BOT. aloe. 2 aloes. 3 bitterness, displeasure.
**acibarar** tr. to put aloes into. 2 to embitter.
**acicalado, -da** p. p. of ACICALAR. 2 adj. wellgroomed; trim, neat. 3 m. ACICALADURA.
**acicaladura** f., **acicalamiento** m. burnishing. 2 dressing, embellishing, adorning, trimming.

**acicalar** tr. to burnish, polish. 2 to dress, embellish, trim. 3 ref. to embellish oneself.
**acicate** m. one-pointed spur. 2 spur, incitement.
**acicatear** tr. to stimulate, to spur on, to motivate.
**acíclico, -ca** adj. acyclic.
**acidez** f. acidity, sourness.
**acidificar** tr. to acidify.
**acidímetro** m. acidimeter.
**ácido** adj. acid, sour, tart. 2 harsh, mordant. 3 adj.-m. CHEM. acid.
**acidosis** f. MED. acidosis.
**acidulado, -da** adj. acidulated.
**acidular** tr. to acidulate.
**acídulo, -la** adj. acidulous.
**acierto** m. good aim, hit. 2 good guess. 3 wisdom, prudence. 4 ability, address. 5 success.
**acierto, acierte,** etc. irr. V. ACERTAR.
**acije** m. ACECHE.
**ácimo, -ma** adj. ÁZIMO.
**acimut** m. ASTR. azimuth.
**ación** f. stirrup leather or strap.
**acirate** m. raised earthen boundary. 2 CABALLÓN. 3 walk between two rows of trees.
**aclamación** f. acclamation. 2 acclaim.
**aclamador, -ra** m.-f. acclaimer, applauder.
**aclamar** tr. to acclaim, cheer, hail, applaud. 2 to acclaim, proclaim.
**aclaración** f. explanation, elucidation. 2 rinsing.
**aclarar** tr. to clear, clarify. 2 to thin, thin out. 3 to rinse. 4 to clear, sharpen [faculties, etc.]. 5 to explain, elucidate. 6 intr. [of weather] to clear up. 7 to dawn. 8 ref. to become clear, to brighten up.
**aclaratorio, -ria** adj. explanatory.
**aclavelado, -da** adj. carnation-like.
**aclimatación** f. acclimatization, acclimation.
**aclimatable** adj. that can be acclimatized.
**aclimatar** tr.-ref. to acclimatize..
**aclínico, -ca** adj. aclinic.
**acmé** f. MED. acme.
**acné** f. MED. acne.
**acobardar** tr. to cow, daunt, dishearten. 2 ref. to be daunted, to lose courage.
**acobrado, -da** adj. copper-coloured.
**acochambrar** tr. (Am.) to dirty, to soil, to befoul, to defile.
**acochinar** tr. to murder, slaughter like a pig. 2 ACOQUINAR. 3 to corner [in draughts].
**acodado, -da** adj. elbow-shaped, elbowed, cranked.
**acodadura** f. HORT. layerage.
**acodalar** tr. ARCH. to prop, stay.
**acodamiento** m. leaning upon one's elbows.
**acodar** tr.-ref. to lean or rest the elbow. 2 tr. HORT. to layer. 3 ACODALAR.
**acodillar** tr. to bend into an elbow or angle.
**acodo** m. HORT. layer. 2 HORT. laying [of shoots].
**acogedor, -ra** adj. welcoming, inviting, cozy.
**acoger** tr. to receive, admit, take into one's house or company. 2 to shelter, protect. 3 to receive, accept [ideas, etc.]. 4 ref. to take refuge [in]; to resort [to]; to claim the benefit [of].
**acogida** f. reception; hospitality: dar buena ~, to receive favourably. 2 refuge, shelter. 3 acceptance, approval.
**acogido, -da** m.-f. inmate [in a home or asylum].
**acogimiento** m. ACOGIDA 1, 2 & 3.
**acogollar** tr. to cover up [plants]. 2 intr. [of plants] to sprout, bud.
**acogotar** tr. to kill by a blow on the back of the neck. 2 to overpower, to cow.

**acojinar** tr. to quilt. 2 MACH. to cushion.
**acojonamiento** m. vul. jitters.
**acojonar** tr. vul. to give someone the jitters, to put the wind up. 2 ref. to get the jitters, to get the wind up.
**acolada** f. accolade.
**acolchado, -da** adj. padded, quilted, upholstered. 2 stuffing, padding. 3 (Am.) mattress.
**acolchar** tr. to quilt. 2 CORCHAR.
**acolitado** m. acolythate.
**acólito** m. acolyte.
**acología** f. acology.
**acollador** m. NAUT. lanyard.
**acollarar** tr. to collar, put a collar on [an animal]. 2 to fasten dogs together by the collar.
**acollonar** tr.-ref. ACOBARDAR.
**acombar** tr. COMBAR.
**acometedor, -ra** adj. enterprising, go-ahead. 2 aggressive.
**acometer** tr. to attack, assail, charge, go at. 2 to undertake. 3 [of fear, sleep, an illness] to seize, overtake: le acometió el miedo, he was seized by fear.
**acometida** f. attack, assault. 2 intake [of a pipe or power line].
**acometividad** f. aggressiveness.
**acomodable** adj. adaptable. 2 suitable.
**acomodación** f. accommodation, adaptation.
**acomodadizo, -za** adj. adaptable, pliable.
**acomodado, -da** adj. convenient, fit, apt. 2 well off, well-to-do. 3 moderate [in price].
**acomodador, -ra** m.-f. THEAT. usher, usherette.
**acomodamiento** m. transaction, agreement. 2 convenience.
**acomodar** tr. to accommodate [adapt; supply; harmonize; reconcile]. 2 to take in, lodge. 3 to place, settle, usher. 4 to suit, fit. 5 ref. to come to an arrangement. 6 to install oneself. 7 to adapt oneself.
**acomodaticio, -cia** adj. adaptable, pliable.
**acomodo** m. employment, situation, place. 2 lodgings.
**acompañado, -da** adj. accompanied. 2 frequented.
**acompañamiento** m. accompaniment; attendance. 2 retinue, train, cortege. 3 MUS. accompaniment. 4 THEAT. supernumeraries.
**acompañanta** f. female companion; chaperon. 2 MUS. woman accompanist.
**acompañante** m. accompanier, attendant. 2 MUS. accompanist.
**acompañar** tr. to keep [someone] company. 2 to accompany, go with, attend, escort. 3 to enclose. 4 MUS. to accompany. 5 to share [feelings] with. 6 ref. to join, be accompanied. 7 MUS. to accompany oneself.
**acompasado, -da** adj. rhythmic, measured. 2 leisurely [in speech or action].
**acompasar** tr. to keep in time or in pace. 2 MUS. to mark the rhythm, to beat time. 3 fig. to adjust, to adapt.
**acomplejar** tr. to give a complex, to make someone feel inferior. 2 ref. to get a complex, to feel inferior.
**aconchabarse** ref. to gather together, to gang up.
**acondicionado, -da** adj. [well, ill] conditioned. 2 fitted, conditioned: con aire ~, air-conditioned.
**acondicionamiento** m. conditioning; ~ de aire, air conditioning.
**acondicionar** tr. to fit, condition, arrange.
**acongojar** tr. to distress, to anguish.
**acónito** m. BOT. aconite, wolf's-bane.

**aconsejable** adj. advisable.
**aconsejar** tr. to advise, counsel. 2 ref. to take advice.
**aconsonantar** tr.-intr. to rhyme.
**acontecer** impers. to happen, occur, befall. ¶ CONJUG. like agradecer.
**acontecimiento** m. event, happening, occurrence.
**acopado, -da** adj. shaped like the top of a tree. 2 VET. cup-shaped [hoof].
**acopar** tr. to trim [a tree] to a crown. 3 NAUT. to hollow.
**acopiar** tr. to gather, store up, stock.
**acopio** m. gathering, storing. 2 store, stock, supply.
**acopladura** f., **acoplamiento** m. coupling, joining.
**acoplar** tr. to couple; to join, connect, yoke. 2 to fit together. 3 tr.-ref. to pair, mate. 4 to become intimate.
**acoquinar** tr.-ref. ACOBARDAR.
**acorazado, -da** adj. ironclad, armoured. 2 m. battleship.
**acorazar** tr. to armour [ships, forts, etc.].
**acorazonado, -da** adj. heart-shaped, cordate.
**acorcharse** tr. to become spongy, corklike.
**acordadamente** adv. by common consent. 2 with mature deliberation.
**acordado, -da** p. p. of ACORDAR. 2 wise, judicious.
**acordar** tr. to decide, agree upon. 2 to reconcile. 3 MUS. to attune. 4 PAINT. to harmonize. 5 intr. to agree, correspond. 6 ref. to come to an agreement. 7 to remember, recall, recollect. ¶ CONJUG. like contar.
**acorde** adj. agreeing; coincident in opinion. 2 conformable, consonant. 3 MUS. in harmony. 4 m. MUS. chord.
**acordeón** m. accordion.
**acordeonista** m.-f. accordionist.
**acordonamiento** m. milling [of a coin]. 2 surrounding [by a cordon of men].
**acordonar** tr. to lace, to tie. 2 to mill, knurl [coins]. 3 to surround with a cordon of men, to draw a cordon round.
**acornar, acornear** tr. to horn [gore with the horns].
**ácoro** m. BOT. sweet flag.
**acorralar** tr. to corral, pen [cattle]. 2 to drive at bay, to corner. 3 to intimidate.
**acorrer** tr. to help, succour.
**acortamiento** m. shortening, reduction.
**acortar** tr. to shorten, diminish, abridge. 2 ref. to shorten [become short or shorter].
**acosamiento** m. close pursuit, persecution.
**acosar** tr. to pursue closely. 2 to persecute, harass, worry.
**acoso** m. ACOSAMIENTO.
**acostado, -da** adj. abed, in bed. 2 lying down. 3 HER. couchant.
**acostar** tr. to put to bed; to lay down. 2 NAUT. to bring alongside. 3 intr. to lean, have a list. 4 to reach the coast. 5 ref. to go to bed. ¶ CONJUG. like contar.
**acostumbrado, -da** adj. accustomed, used. 2 usual, habitual, customary.
**acostumbrar** tr. to accustom. 2 intr. to be wont, be used [to]. 3 ref. to accustom oneself, get used [to].
**acotación** f. annotation, marginal note. 2 THEAT. stage directions. 3 ACOTAMIENTO. 4 TOP. elevation marked on a map.
**acotamiento** m. boundary mark, landmark.
**acotar** tr. to preserve [ground]. 2 to delimitate,

restrict. *3* to accept, choose, take. *4* to mark elevations on [a map].
**acotiledóneo, -a** *adj.* acotyledonous. *2 f.* acotyledon.
**acotillo** *m.* sledge hammer.
**acoyuntar** *tr.* to yoke [oxen].
**acracia** *f.* acracy.
**ácrata** *adj.-n.* anarchist.
**acre** *adj.* acrid, tart, pungent. *2* acrimonious. *3 m.* acre.
**acrecencia** *f.* ACRECENTAMIENTO. *2* LAW accretion.
**acrecentamiento** *m.* increase, growth.
**acrecentar** *tr.* to increase, augment. *2* to advance, promote. *3 ref.* to increase [become greater].
**acrecer** *tr.* to increase. *2 intr.* to acquire by accretion. ¶ CONJUG. like *agradecer.*
**acrecimiento** *m.* increase.
**acreditado, -da** *adj.* of good repute, well-known.
**acreditar** *tr.* to accredit, authorize. *2* to prove to be. *3* to bring fame or credit. *4* ACC. to credit. *5 ref.* to win credit or fame; to gain reputation.
**acreditativo, -va** *adj.* crediting, proving.
**acreedor, -ra** *adj.* deserving, worthy. *2* ACC. favourable [balance]. *3 m.* COM. creditor.
**acribillar** *tr.* to riddle [pierce with many holes]. *2* to harass, plague, pester.
**acriminar** *tr.* to criminate, accuse.
**acrimonia** *f.* acridity. *2* acrimony.
**acrisolado, -da** *adj.* proven, unblemished.
**acrisolar** *tr.* to purify, refine. *2* to ascertain, prove [truth, virtue, etc.].
**acritud** *f.* ACRIMONIA.
**acrobacia** *f.* acrobatics; acrobatism.
**acróbata** *m.-f.* acrobat.
**acrobático, -ca** *adj.* acrobatic.
**acromático, -ca** *adj.* achromatic.
**acromatismo** *m.* achromatism.
**acromio, acromión** *m.* ANAT. acromion.
**acrópolis** *f.* acropolis.
**acróstico** *adj.-m.* acrostic.
**acrotera** *f.* ARCH. acroterium.
**acta** *f.* minutes [of a meeting, etc.]. *2* certificate of election. *3* statement of facts: ~ *notarial,* affidavit. *4* records, proceedings [of a learned society]. *5 actas de los mártires,* acta martyrum.
**actínico, -ca** *adj.* actinic.
**actinio** *m.* CHEM. actinium.
**actitud** *f.* attitude. *2* posture, position, pose.
**activar** *tr.* to activate. *2* to hasten, quicken.
**actividad** *f.* activity.
**activo, -va** *adj.* active. *2 m.* COM. assets. *3 en activo,* in active service.
**acto** *m.* act, action, deed: *en el* ~, at once; ~ *seguido,* inmediately afterwards. *2* ceremony, meeting, public function. *3* act [of a play]. *4* THEOL. act [of faith, etc.]. *5 Actos de los Apóstoles,* Acts of the Apostles.
**actor** *m.* THEAT. actor. *2* actor [in an affair].
**actor, -ra** *m.-f.* LAW actor, plaintiff, claimant.
**actriz** *f.* actress.
**actuación** *f.* action [of any agent], performance. *2 pl.* law proceedings.
**actual** *adj.* present, current, of the day. *2* THEOL. actual.
**actualidad** *f.* present time: *en la* ~, at present. *2* the state of being present, of the day: *ser de* ~, to be the topic of the day. *3* current events. *4 pl.* CINEM. newsreel.
**actualizar** *tr.* to bring up-to-date.
**actualmente** *adv.* at present, now, nowadays.
**actuar** *tr.* to put into action. *2 intr.* to act, to per-

form, to take action: ~ *de,* to act as. *3* LAW to perform judicial acts.
**actuario** *m.* clerk of a court of justice. *2* ~ *de seguros,* actuary.
**acuadrillar** *tr.* to band [unite in a band]. *2* to lead a band. *3 ref.* to band together.
**acuarela** *f.* PAINT. water colour, aquarelle.
**acuarelista** *m.-f.* aquarellist.
**acuario** *m.* aquarium. *2* ASTR. Aquarius.
**acuartelar** *tr.* to quarter [troops]. *2* to confine [troops] to barracks. *3* to quarter [to divide]. *4* NAUT. to flat in [sails]. *5 ref.* [of troops] to take quarters.
**acuático, -ca** or **acuátil** *adj.* aquatic, water.
**acucia** *f.* diligence, haste. *2* longing, eagerness.
**acuciamiento** *m.* stimulation, urge. *2* longing.
**acuciante** *adj.* pressing, urging.
**acuciar** *tr.* to stimulate, urge, incite, goad, hasten. *2* to long for.
**acucioso, -sa** *adj.* diligent, eager. *2* longing for.
**acuclillarse** *ref.* to squat, to crouch.
**acuchillado, -da** *adj.* slashed [garments].
**acuchillar** *tr.* to knife, stab, put to the sword. *2* to slash [a garment].
**acudir** *intr.* to go or come to: ~ *a una llamada,* to answer a call. *2* to frequent. *3* to come or go to the aid, or rescue [of]. *4* to have recourse [to], to resort [to].
**acueducto** *m.* aqueduct.
**ácueo, -a** *adj.* aqueous.
**acuerdo** *m.* accord, agreement, understanding, convention: *de* ~ *con,* in agreement with, in accordance with; *de común* ~, by mutual agreement: *estar de* ~, to agree; *poner de* ~, to make agree, to harmonize. *2* resolution: *tomar un* ~, to pass a resolution. *3* resolve. *4* advice, opinion. *5* reflection, prudence. *6* PAINT. accord. *7 estar uno en su* ~, to be in one's right senses.
**acuerdo, acuerde,** etc. *irr.* V. ACORDAR.
**acuesto, acueste,** etc. *irr.* V. ACOSTAR.
**acuífero, -ra** *adj.* aquiferous, that contains water.
**acuitar** *tr.* to distress, afflict, grieve.
**acular** *tr.* to back [a horse, a cart, etc.] against. *2* to corner [somebody].
**acullá** *adv.* yonder, over there, there.
**acuminado, -da** *adj.* BOT. acuminate.
**acumulación** *f.* accumulation, gathering.
**acumulador, -ra** *adj.* accumulating. *2 m.-f.* accumulator. *3 m.* MACH., ELECT. accumulator; storage battery.
**acumular** *tr.* to accumulate.
**acumulativo, -va** *adj.* accumulative, growing by additions. *2* LAW cumulative, non-concurring.
**acunar** *tr.* to rock, cradle [a child].
**acuñación** *f.* coinage, mintage.
**acuñador, -ra** *m.-f.* coiner, minter.
**acuñar** *tr.* to coin, mint. *2* to wedge, key.
**acuosidad** *f.* wateriness.
**acuoso, -sa** *adj.* watery, aqueous.
**acupuntura** *f.* MED. acupuncture.
**acurrucarse** *ref.* to huddle up, tu cuddle, nestle.
**acusación** *f.* accusation, charge, impeachment.
**acusado, -da** *adj.* accused. *2 m.-f.* accused, defendant.
**acusador, -ra** *adj.* accusing. *2 m.-f.* accuser: ~ *privado,* prosecutor.
**acusar** *tr.* to accuse, to charge [with], to prosecute, indict. *2* to denounce. *3* to acknowledge [receipt]. *4 ref.* to acknowledge one's sins.
**acusativo** *m.* GRAM. accusative.
**acusatorio, -ria** *adj.* accusatory.

**acuse** *m.* acknowledgement [of receipt].

**acusón, -na** *adj.* sneak, talebearer, telltale.

**acústica** *f.* PHYS. acoustics.

**acústico, -ca** *adj.* acoustic.

**acutángulo** *adj.* GEOM. acute-angled.

**achacar** *tr.* to impute, ascribe.

**achacoso, -sa** *adj.* sickly, ailing, unhealthy, infirm.

**achaflanar** *tr.* to chamfer, bevel.

**achampañado, -da** *adj.* champagne-like [wine].

**achantarse** *ref.* to submit, be daunted. *2* to hide during danger.

**achaparrado, -da** *adj.* low and spreading. *2* stumpy, stubby [person].

**achaque** *m.* ailment, indisposition. *2* weakness, habitual failing. *3* matter, subject. *4* excuse, pretext.

**achares** *m. pl.* coll. *dar ~*, to make jealous.

**achatamiento** *m.* flattening.

**achatar** *tr.* to flatten. *2 ref.* to become flat.

**achicado, -da** *adj.* diminished. *2* childish.

**achicador, -ra** *adj.* diminishing. *2 m.-f.* diminisher. *3 m.* NAUT. bailer, scooper.

**achicamiento** *m.* diminution, reduction. *2* humiliation.

**achicar** *tr.* to diminish, belittle. *2* to bail, bale, scoop [water]. *3* to humiliate, to cow. *4 ref.* to diminish. *6* to humble oneself; to be daunted.

**achicoria** *f.* BOT. chicory.

**achicharradero** *m.* inferno, hot place.

**achicharrar** *tr.* COOK. to burn. *2* to swelter, scorch with heat. *3* to bother. *4 ref.* to swelter, be scorched.

**achinelado, -da** *adj.* slipper-shaped.

**achique** *m.* NAUT., MIN. bailing, baling, scooping.

**achispado, -da** *adj.* tipsy.

**achispar** *tr.* to make tipsy. *2 ref.* to get tipsy.

**achocharse** *ref.* to begin to dote, to enter one's dotage.

**achubascarse** *ref.* to get showery.

**achuchar** *tr.* AZUZAR. *2* to crush [by a blow or weight]. *3* to push [a person] violently.

**achuchón** *m.* push, squeeze. *2* fit.

**achulado, -da** *adj.* jaunty, cocky.

**achularse, achularse** *ref.* to become or get jaunty or cocky.

**adagio** *m.* adage, proverb, saying. *2 adv.-m.* MUS. adagio.

**adalid** *m.* leader, chief.

**adamado, -da** *adj.* womanish, delicate [man].

**adamantino, -na** *adj.* adamantine.

**adamascado, -da** *adj.* WEAV. damasked.

**adamascar** *tr.* WEAV. to damask.

**Adán** *m. pr. n.* Adam.

**adán** *m.* coll. slovenly man.

**adaptable** *adj.* adaptable.

**adaptación** *f.* adaptation, fitting, accommodation.

**adaptador, -ra** *adj.* adapting. *2 m.-f.* adapter.

**adaptar** *tr.* to adapt, fit, suit, accommodate. *2 ref.* to adapt oneself, to fit, to suit.

**adaraja** *f.* ARCH. toothing.

**adarga** *f.* oval or heart-shaped leather shield.

**adarme** *m.* ancient weight [179 centigrams]. *2* whit, jot: *por adarmes*, very sparingly.

**adarve** *m.* FORT. walk behind the parapet on top of wall. *2* rampart.

**adaza** *f.* BOT. sorghum.

**adecentar** *tr.* to tidy. *2* to make decent. *3 ref.* to tidy oneself.

**adecuación** *f.* adequation. *2* adequacy, suitableness.

**adecuadamente** *adv.* appropriately, adequately, conveniently. *2* sufficiently.

**adecuado, -da** *adj.* adequate, fit, suitable.

**adecuar** *tr.* to fit, adapt, make suitable.

**adefesio** *m.* nonsense, absurdity. *2* ridiculous attire. *3* scarecrow, fright.

**adehala** *f.* bonus, extra, gratuity.

**adehesar** *tr.* to turn [land] into pasture.

**Adelaida** *pr. n.* Adelaide.

**adelantado, -da** *adj.* anticipated: *por ~*, in advance. *2* advanced. *3* proficient. *4* precocious. *5* fast [clock]. *6 m.* formerly, the governor of a province.

**adelantamiento** *m.* advance, advancing. *2* advancement, furtherance, promotion. *3* progress, improvement.

**adelantar** *tr.* to advance [move forward; hasten; further, promote]. *2* to advance [money, an event]. *3 tr.-ref.* to be in advance of; to outstrip, overtake; get ahead of. *4 intr.-ref.* [of a clock] to be fast. *5 intr.* to make progress, improve.

**adelante** *adv.* forward, ahead, onward, farther on: *ir ~, pasar ~*, to go on or further; *de tres libras en ~*, from three pounds up. *2 en ~, de aquí en ~*, henceforth; *más ~*, later on. *3 interj.* forward!, onward!, go on!, come in!

**adelanto** *m.* advance. *2* progress, improvement. *3* COM. advance, payment.

**adelfa** *f.* BOT. oleander, rosebay.

**adelfilla** *f.* BOT. spurge laurel.

**adelgazamiento** *m.* thinness, slenderness.

**adelgazar** *tr.* to attenuate, make thin or slender. *2* to subtilize. *3 intr.-ref.* to become thin or slender. *4* to taper off.

**Adelina** *pr. n.* Adeline.

**Adelita** *pr. n.* dim. of ADELA.

**ademán** *m.* gesture, attitude: *en ~ de*, in the attitude of. *2 pl.* manners.

**además** *adv.* moreover, besides, furthermore, yet, too, as well. *2 ~ de*, besides.

**adenoideo, -a** *adj.* ANAT. adenoid.

**adenoma** *m.* MED. adenoma.

**adentellar** *tr.* to bite, to set one's teeth in. *2* to leave a toothing in [a wall].

**adentrarse** *ref.* to penetrate, go into.

**adentro** *adv.* within, inside, in: *mar ~*, out at sea; *tierra ~*, inland. *2 m. pl.* inward mind or thoughts: *para sus adentros*, to oneself. *3 interj.* come in!; let's go in!

**adepto** *m.* adept, initiated. *2* adherent, follower.

**aderezamiento** *m.* dressing, seasoning. *2* adornment, embellishing.

**aderezar** *tr.* to adorn, embellish, dress. *2* to cook. *3* to season. *4* to arrange, prepare. *5* to repair. *6* to dress [salad]. *7* to direct.

**aderezo** *m.* adornment, dressing. *2* cooking, seasoning. *3* preparation. *4* set of jewelry. *5* trappings [of a horse].

**adeudado, -da** *adj.* owing, still to be paid. *2* indebted.

**adeudar** *tr.* to owe. *2* to be dutiable. *3* ACC. to debit, to charge. *4 intr.* EMPARENTAR.

**adeudo** *m.* debt. *2* customs duty. *3* ACC. charge debit.

**adherencia** *f.* adhesion [sticking together]. *2* BOT., PHYS., MED. adhesion. *3* adhesion.

**adherente** *adj.* adherent, adhesive. *2* adherent, attached. *3 m. pl.* equipment, accessories.

**adherido, -da** *p. p.* of ADHERIR. *2 m.-f.* adherent, follower.

**adherir** *intr.-ref.* to adhere, to stick (to). ¶ CONJUG. like *hervir.*
**adhesión** *f.* adherence, adhesion. *2* PHYS. adhesion.
**adhesivo, -va** *adj.-m.* adhesive.
**adiar** *tr.* to fix a date.
**adición** *f.* addition, adding, addendum. *2* MATH. addition.
**adicional** *adj.* additional.
**adicionar** *tr.* to add, join; to make additions to.
**adicto, -ta** *adj.* attached, devoted. *2 m.* supporter, follower.
**adiestrado, -da** *adj.* instructed, taught, trained. *2* HER. dexter.
**adiestrador, -ra** *adj.* who instructs or trains. *2 n.* instructor, trainer, teacher.
**adiestramiento** *m.* training, drilling, teaching.
**adiestrar** *tr.* to train, drill, school, teach, guide. *2 ref.* to train oneself, practise.
**adinerado, -da** *adj.* rich, moneyed.
**adintelado, -da** *adj.* ARCH. straight [arch].
**adiós** *interj.* good-by or -bye!, farewell!, adieu!
**adiposidad** *f.* adiposity.
**adiposo, -sa** *adj.* adipose.
**aditamento** *m.* addition, addendum.
**adivas** *f. pl.* VET. vives.
**adive** *m.* ZOOL. corsac.
**adivinación** *f.* divination.
**adivinanza** *f.* ADIVINACIÓN. *2* ACERTIJO.
**adivinar** *tr.* to divine, guess, foresee. *2* to solve [a riddle].
**adivino, -na** *m.-f.* diviner, soothsayer.
**adjetivación** *f.* use in adjectival form.
**adjetival** *adj.* GRAM. adjectival.
**adjetivar** *tr.* to make an adjective of. *2* to apply adjectives to.
**adjetivo, -va** *adj.-s.* adjective. *2 adj.* adjectival.
**adjudicación** *f.* awarding, adjudgement.
**adjudicador, -ra** *m.-f.* awarder.
**adjudicar** *tr.* to adjudge, award, assign. *2 ref.* to appropriate.
**adjudicatario, -ria** *m.-f.* awardee.
**adjuntar** *tr.* to attach, to join, to append. *2* to enclose, to include. *3* to give.
**adjunto, -ta** *adj.* adjunct, joined. *2* enclosed [in a letter]. *3 m.-f.* adjunct, associate. *4 m.* ADITAMENTO.
**adminículo** *m.* adminicle. *2 pl.* articles carried for emergency use.
**administración** *f.* administration, administering. *2* office of an administrator, manager, steward or trustee. *3 ~ de Correos,* Post Office; *~ militar,* Commissariat.
**administrador, -ra** *m.-f.* administrator, manager, steward, trustee. *2 ~ de Correos,* postmaster.
**administrar** *tr.* to administer, manage. *2* to administer.
**administrativo, -va** *adj.* administrative.
**admirable** *adj.* admirable. *2* wonderful.
**admiración** *f.* admiration. *2* wonder, astonishment. *3* exclamation mark (¡ !).
**admirado, -da** *adj.* wondering, astonished.
**admirador, -ra** *m.-f.* admirer.
**admirar** *tr.* to astonish, surprise. *2* to admire. *3 ref.* to wonder, be astonished, surprised: *admirarse de,* to wonder at.
**admirativo, -va** *adj.* admirative; of admiration; of wonder. *2* astonished.
**admisible** *adj.* admissible, allowable.
**admisión** *f.* admission.
**admitir** *tr.* to admit [in every sense except «to acknowledge»]. *2* to accept. *3* to allow, suffer.

**admonición** *f.* admonition, admonishment.
**admonitor** *m.* admonisher, admonitor.
**adnato, -ta** *adj.* BOT., ZOOL. adnate.
**adobado** *m.* pickled meat [esp. pork].
**adobar** *tr.* to dress, prepare. *2* to pickle, souse [meat]. *3* to cook. *4* to tan and dress [hides].
**adobe** *m.* adobe.
**adobo** *m.* dressing, preparing; tanning. *2* sauce for seasoning or pickling. *3* mixture for dressing skins or cloth.
**adocenado, -da** *adj.* common, ordinary, vulgar.
**adocenar** *tr.* to dozen. *2 ref.* to become common, ordinary, vulgar.
**adoctrinamiento** *m.* indoctrination, filling someone's mind with particular ideas or beliefs. *2* teaching.
**adoctrinar** *tr.* to indoctrinate, teach, instruct.
**adolecer** *intr.* to be ill. *2 ~ de,* to have [a specified defect, vice etc.]. ´*3 ref.* CONDOLERSE. ¶ CONJUG. like *agradecer.*
**adolescencia** *f.* adolescence.
**adolescente** *adj.-n.* adolescent.
**Adolfo** *pr. n.* Adolphus.
**adonde** *adv.* where. *2 interr.* where?, whither?
**adondequiera** *adv.* wherever, anywhere.
**Adonis** *m.* Adonis.
**adopción** *f.* adoption.
**adoptador, -ra; adoptante** *adj.* adopting. *2 m.-f.* adopter.
**adoptar** *tr.* to adopt. *2* to embrace [an opinion]. *3* to take [an attitude, a decision].
**adoptivo, -va** *adj.* adoptive.
**adoquín** *m.* paving stone. *2* fig. blockhead.
**adoquinado** *m.* cobblestone paving; stone-block pavement.
**adorable** *adj.* adorable.
**adoración** *f.* adoration, worship.
**adorador, -ra** *adj.* adoring. *2 m.-f.* adorer. *3* worshipper.
**adorar** *tr.* to adore; worship.
**adormecedor, -ra** *adj.* soporific, sleep-inducing. *2* fig. sedative.
**adormecer** *tr.* to make sleepy, to lull to sleep. *2* to lull, allay. *3 ref.* to drowse, fall asleep. *4* to grow benumbed. ¶ CONJUG. like *agradecer.*
**adormecimiento** *m.* drowsiness, slumber. *2* numbness.
**adormidera** *f.* BOT. opium poppy. *2* poppy-head.
**adormilarse** *ref.* to drowse.
**adormitarse** *ref.* ADORMILARSE.
**adornado, -da** *adj.* adorned, ornamented.
**adornar** *tr.* to adorn, beautify, grace, decorate, embellish, deck, garnish.
**adorno** *m.* adornment, ornament, decoration, embellishment, garnishment, trimming.
**adosar** *tr.* to back or lean [something] against. *2* HER. to place back to back.
**adquiero, adquiera,** etc. *irr.* V. ADQUIRIR.
**adquirente; adquiridor, -ra** *adj.* acquiring. *2 m.-f.* acquirer.
**adquirido, -da** *adj.* acquired, not inherent. *2* bought, purchased.
**adquirir** *tr.* to acquire. *2* to obtain, to buy. ¶ CONJUG. INDIC. Pres.: *adquiero, adquieres, adquiere, adquieren.* | SUBJ. Pres.: *adquiera, adquieras, adquiera, adquieran.* | IMPER.: *adquiere, adquiera, adquieran.*
**adquisición** *f.* acquisition; acquirement.
**adquisidor, -ra** *adj.* ADQUIRENTE.
**adquisitivo, -va** *adj.* LAW acquisitive.
**adragante** *adj. goma ~,* tragacanth [gum].

**adrales** *adv.* hurdles on the sides of cart.
**adrede** *adv.* purposely, on purpose.
**adrenalina** *f.* CHEM. adrenaline.
**Adrián** *m. pr. n.* Adrian.
**Adriático** *pr. n.* GEOGR. Adriatic Sea.
**adscribir** *tr.* to attribute, assign, ascribe. *2* to attach, or appoint [a person] to a service.
**adscrito, -ta** *p. p.* of ADSCRIBIR.
**adscripción** *f.* attachment, appointment.
**adsorbente** *m.-adj.* CHEM. adsorbent.
**adsorción** *f.* CHEM. adsorption.
**aduana** *f.* customhouse.
**aduanero, -ra** *adj.* [pertaining to] customs or the customhouse. *2 m.* customhouse officer.
**aduar** *m.* douar. *2* gipsy camp.
**aducción** *f.* PHYSIOL. adduction.
**aducir** *tr.* to adduce, cite, allegre. ¶ CONJUG. like *conducir.*
**aductor** *adj.-m.* ANAT. adductor.
**adueñarse** *ref.* ~ *de,* to seize, take possession of.
**aduja** NAUT. rope coil, fake.
**adujar** *tr.* NAUT. to coil, fake.
**adulación** *f.* adulation, flattery.
**adulador, -ra** *adj.* adulating, flattering. *2 m.-f.* adulator, flatterer.
**adular** *tr.* to adulate, flatter, fawn upon.
**adulón, -na** *m.-f.* adulator, gross flatterer.
**adúltera** *f.* adulteress.
**adulteración** *f.* adulteration.
**adulterado, -da** *adj.* adulterated, sophisticated.
**adulterar** *tr.* to adulterate, corrupt, sophisticate. *2 intr.* to commit adultery.
**adulterino, -na** *adj.* adulterine.
**adulterio** *m.* adultery.
**adúltero, -ra** *adj.* adulterous. *2 m.* adulterer. *3 f.* adulteress.
**adulto, -ta** *adj.-n.* adult, grown-up.
**adulzar** *tr.* to soften [metals]. *2* ENDULZAR.
**adustez** *f.* gloominess, sulleness, sternness.
**adusto, -ta** *adj.* burnt, hot. *2* gloomy, sullen, stern.
**advenedizo, -za** *adj.* foreign. *2 m.-f.* foreigner, stranger, newcomer. *3* upstart, parvenu.
**advenimiento** *m.* advent, arrival, coming. *2* accession [to the throne].
**advenir** *intr.* to come, to arrive.
**adventista** *adj.-n.* adventist.
**adventicio, -cia** *adj.* adventitious.
**adverbial** *adj.* adverbial.
**adverbio** *m.* GRAM. adverb.
**adversario, -ria** *m.-f.* adversary, opponent; foe.
**adversativo, -va** *adj.* GRAM. adversative.
**adversidad** *f.* adversity.
**adverso, -sa** *adj.* adverse.
**advertencia** *f.* admonition, warning, advice. *2* foreword. *3* notice. *4* awareness, knowledge.
**advertido, -da** *adj.* capable, knowing, clever.
**advertir** *tr.* to notice, observe, perceive, realize. *2* to advise, instruct, recommend, point out; to warn. *3* to admonish. ¶ CONJUG. like *discernir.*
**adviento** *m.* ECCL. advent.
**advierto, advierta** etc. *irr.* V. ADVERTIR.
**advocación** *f.* name under wich a church, altar, saint, etc., is known.
**adyacente** *adj.* adjacent, adjoining.
**adyuvante** *adj.* adjuvant.
**aeración** *f.* aeration.
**aéreo, -rea** *adj.* aerial. *2* air. *3* airy, ethereal, insubstantial.
**aeriforme** *adj.* aeriform.
**aerobio, -a** *adj.* aerobic, aerobious. *2 m.* aerobe.
**aerobús** *m.* airbus.

**aeroclub** *m.* flying club.
**aerodeslizador** *m.* hovercraft, anphibian craft supported on air cushions.
**aerodinámica** *f.* aerodynamics.
**aerodinámico, -ca** *adj.* aerodynamic. *2* streamline.
**aeródromo** *m.* aerodrome.
**aerograma** *m.* aerogram.
**aerolito** *m.* aerolite.
**aeromancia** *f.* aeromancy.
**aerómetro** *m.* aerometer.
**aeromodelismo** *m.* aeroplane modelling, aeromodelling.
**aeronauta** *m.* aeronaut.
**aeronáutica** *f.* aeronautics.
**aeronáutico, -ca** *adj.* aeronautic(al.
**aeronave** *f.* airship.
**aeroplano** *m.* aeroplane, airplane.
**aeropuerto** *m.* airport.
**aeroscopio** *m.* aeroscope.
**aerostación** *f.* aerostation.
**aerostática** *f.* aerostatics.
**aerostático, -ca** *adj.* aerostatic.
**aerostato** *m.* aerostat, air balloon.
**afabilidad** *f.* affability.
**afable** *adj.* affable.
**afamado, -da** *adj.* famous, renowned.
**afamar** *tr.* to make famous, give fame to.
**afán** *m.* toil, labour. *2* anxiety, eagerness, ardour, solicitude; desire.
**afanar** *tr.* to harass, worry. *2 intr.* to drudge. *3 ref.* to toil, labour, strive: *afanarse por,* to strive to.
**afanoso, -sa** *adj.* toilsome, laborious. *2* eager, anxious, desirous.
**afasia** *f.* MED. aphasia.
**afeamiento** *m.* disfiguring, making ugly. *2* blaming, reproaching.
**afear** *tr.* to disfigure, deface, make ugly. *2* to blame, reproach.
**afección** *f.* affection, inclination. *2* MED. affection.
**afectación** *f.* affectation, affectedness. *2* affecting. *3* impression, emotion.
**afectado, -da** *adj.* affected.
**afectar** *tr.* to make a show of; to feign. *3* to annex, áttach. *3* to affect [move; influence; concern]. *4* LAW to encumber. *5* MED. to affect. *6 ref.* to be affected, moved.
**afectivo, -va** *adj.* affective.
**afecto, -ta** *adj.* attached, fond. *2* LAW ~ *a,* subject to [some charge]. *3 m.* affection, love, attachment. *4* affect, feeling, passion.
**afectuosidad** *f.* affectionateness.
**afectuoso, -sa** *adj.* fond, affectionate, loving; kind.
**afeitar** *tr.* to shave [with razor]. *2* to beautify; to make up. *3* to trim [a plant; a horse's tail or mane]. *4 ref.* to shave. *5* to put on cosmetics, make up.
**afeite** *m.* cosmetics, paint, rouge, make-up.
**afelio** *m.* ASTR. aphelion.
**afelpado, -da** *adj.* plushy, velvety.
**afeminación** *f.* effeminacy.
**afeminado, -da** *adj.* effeminate, ladylike.
**afeminar** *tr.-ref.* to effeminate.
**aferente** *adj.* PHYSIOL. afferent.
**aféresis** *f.* GRAM. aphaeresis, apheresis.
**aferradamente** *adv.* obstinately.
**aferrado, -da** *adj.* clinging, holding fast [to an opinion or purpose].
**aferramiento** *m.* grasping, seizing, grappling. *2* NAUT. furling. *3* obstinacy, tenacity.
**aferrar** *tr.* to grasp, seize, grapple. *2* NAUT. to furl. *3* NAUT. to moor, anchor. *4 ref. aferrarse a,* to hold

fast to, cling to; to stick to [an opinion]. 5 [of boats] to grapple.
**afestonado, -da** *adj.* festooned.
**Afganistán** *pr. n.* GEOG. Afghanistan.
**afianzar** *tr.* to stand surety for. 2 to make firm or fast, to prop, to strengthen. 3 *ref.* to become firm or fast, to steady oneself, to hold fast [to].
**afición** *f.* fondness, liking, leaning. 2 ardour. 3 hobby. 4 coll. *la* ~, the fans, the public.
**aficionado, -da** *m.-f.* amateur. 2 fan, devotee.
**aficionar** *tr.* to give a liking for. 2 *ref.* to grow fond of, to take a liking to.
**afidávit** *m.* affidavit.
**áfido** *m.* ENT. aphid, aphis.
**afijo, -ja** GRAM. affixed. 2 *m.* GRAM. affix.
**afiladera** *f.* whetstone.
**afilado, -da** *adj.* sharp, keen, pointed. 2 taper.
**afiladura** *f.* sharpening, grinding, whetting.
**afilador, -ra** *adj.* sharpening, whetting. 2 *m.* tool or knife grinder.
**afilamiento** *m.* sharpness [of the face or nose], tapering [of fingers].
**afilar** *tr.* to sharpen, grind, whet, hedge, point; to taper. 2 *ref.* to grow thin; to taper.
**afiliación** *f.* affiliation [with a party, etc.].
**afiliado, -da** *adj.-s.* affiliate, member.
**afiliar** *tr.* to affiliate, associate. 2 *ref. afiliarse a,* to join, to affiliate with.
**afiligranado, -da** *adj.* filigree, filigreed. 2 delicate, slender, thin.
**afiligranar** *tr.* to filigree. 2 to give an exquisite finish to.
**afín** *adj.* contiguous, adjacent. 2 kindred, related, allied. 3 *m.-f.* relative by marriage.
**afinación** *f.* perfecting, finishing touch. 2 MUS. tune; tuning.
**afinado, -da** *adj.* well finished, perfected. 2 MUS. in tune, well tuned.
**afinamiento** *m.* AFINACIÓN. 2 FINURA.
**afinar** *tr.* to perfect, polish, refine. 2 to refine, try [metals]. 3 MUS. to tune. 4 MUS. to sing or play in tune. 5 *ref.* to become refined, polished.
**afincar** *intr.-ref.* FINCAR.
**afinidad** *f.* affinity.
**afino** *m.* refining, trying [of metals].
**afirmación** *f.* affirmation, assertion.
**afirmado** *m.* roadbed.
**afirmar** *tr.* to make firm, to firm, secure, steady. 2 to affirm, say. 3 *ref.* to steady oneself, to lean [upon]. 4 to maintain firmly.
**afirmativa** *f.* affirmative, affirmative proposition.
**afirmativo, -va** *adj.* affirmative, affirming.
**aflamencado, -da** *adj.* flamenco-like.
**aflautado, -da** *adj.* fluted, flutelike.
**aflechado, -da** *adj.* arrow-shaped.
**aflicción** *f.* affliction, grief, sorrow, distress.
**aflictivo, -va** *adj.* afflictive.
**afligido, -da** *adj.* afflicted, sorrowing, grieving.
**afligir** *tr.* to afflict. 2 to distress, grieve. 3 *ref.* to grieve, repine, sorrow.
**aflojadura** *f.,* **aflojamiento** *m.* slackening, relaxation, loosening.
**aflojamiento** *m.* loosening, slackening. 2 relaxation, laxity [of discipline, severity...]. 3 loosening [of ties, bonds...]. 4 abatement [of the wind, of a storm].
**aflojar** *tr.* to slacken, slack, loose, loosen, relax, ease, let out. 2 coll. to pay up. 3 *intr.* to slack, slacken, relent, let up, abate, weaken. 4 *ref.* to become slack, loose, relaxed.
**afloramiento** *m.* MIN. outcrop, outcropping.

**aflorar** *intr.* MIN. to outcrop, crop out.
**afluencia** *f.* affluence, inflow, flowing to. 2 affluence, abundance, plenty.
**afluente** *adj.* inflowing. 2 fluent, voluble. 3 *m.* affluent.
**afluir** *intr.* ~ *a,* to flow in, into, to or towards; to congregate in; [of a stream] to discharge into. ¶ CONJUG. like *huir.*
**aflujo** *m.* MED. afflux, affluxion.
**afluyo, afluyó, afluya,** etc. *irr.* V. AFLUIR.
**afofarse** *ref.* to soften, to become or to turn soft.
**afonía** *f.* MED. aphonia.
**afónico, -ca** *adj.* aphonic.
**áfono, -na** *adj.* PHONET. aphonic.
**aforar** *tr.* to appraise [goods]. 2 to gauge [a stream, a vessel, etc.].
**aforismo** *m.* aphorism.
**aforo** *m.* gauging; appraisement. 2 capacity [of a theatre, cinema, etc.].
**afortunado, -da** *adj.* lucky, fortunate, happy.
**afrancesado, -da** *adj.* Frenchified. 2 *adj.-n.* Francophile [during the Peninsular War].
**afrancesar** *tr.* to Frenchify. 2 *ref.* to become a Francophile [during Peninsular War].
**afrecho** *m.* SALVADO.
**afrenta** *f.* affront, outrage, dishonour.
**afrentar** *tr.* to affront, outrage, dishonour.
**África** *pr. n.* GEOG. Africa.
**africano, -na** *adj.* African.
**áfrico** *adj.* african. 2 *m.* ÁBREGO.
**afro, afra** *adj.* AFRICANO.
**afrodisíaco** *adj.-m.* aphrodisiac.
**afrontamiento** *m.* confrontation, facing.
**afrontar** *tr.* to put face [to]; to bring face to face. 2 to confront, face.
**afta** *f.* MED. aphta.
**afuera** *adv.* out, outside. 2 outward. 3 *interj.* out of the way! 4 *f. pl.* outskirts, environs.
**afusión** *f.* affusion.
**afuste** *m.* gun-carriage.
**agabachar** *tr.* to Frenchify.
**agachadiza** *f.* ORN. snipe.
**agachar** *tr.* to lower, bend down [a part of the body]: fig. ~ *las orejas,* to hang one's head. 2 *ref.* to stoop; to duck, cower; to crouch, squat [as a partridge].
**agáloco** *m.* BOT. agalloch, aloes wood.
**agalla** *f.* BOT. gall, gall-nut. 2 ~ *de ciprés,* cypress nut. 3 tonsil. 4 gill [of a fish]. 5 each side of a bird's head. 6 *pl.* coll. courage, guts.
**agallón** *m.* large gall-nut. 2 hollow silver bead. 3 large wooden bead of a rosary.
**agamí** *m.* ORN. agami, trumpeter.
**ágape** *m.* agape. 2 banquet, feast.
**agarbanzado, -da** *adj.* chick-pea coloured.
**agarbillar** *tr.* AGR. to sheaf, sheave.
**agareno, -na** *adj.-n.* Mohammedan.
**agárico** *m.* BOT. agaric.
**agarrada** *f.* altercation, wrangle, tussle.
**agarradero** *m.* hold, handle, grip. 2 fig. protection, pull. 3 NAUT. anchorage.
**agarrado, -da** *adj.* close-fisted, stingy, niggardly.
**agarrador** *m.* flatiron holder.
**agarrar** *tr.* to seize, take, catch; to clutch, grab, grasp. 2 to get, obtain. 3 *ref.* to grapple, take hold of each other. 4 *agarrarse a,* to take hold of, cling to, catch at.
**agarrotado, -da** *adj.* tied up tightly. 2 rigid, stiff. 3 stuck, jammed, seized-up [a motor]. 4 fig. restricted, tied down.
**agarrotamiento** *m.* tying up, bundling up, bin-

ding. *2* seizing up [of a motor]. *3* stiffness, rigidity. *4* garrotting, garotting.

**agarrotar** *tr.* to tighten; to hold tight, to press tightly. *2* to garrotte. *3* to oppress. *4 ref.* to stiffen.

**agasajar** *tr.* to fête, make much of. *2* to regale, entertain, feast.

**agasajo** *m.* attention shown, affectionate reception. *2* gift, treat, refreshment.

**ágata** *f.* agate.

**agaucharse** *ref.* (Am.) to adopt the gauchos' way of life.

**agavanza** *f.* BOT. hip [dog rose fruit].

**agavanzo** *m.* BOT. dog rose. *2* AGAVANZA.

**agave** *m.* BOT. agave, century plant.

**agavillar** *tr.* to sheave. *2* to band, collect in bands. *3 ref.* to band together.

**agazapar** *tr.* coll. to nab, seize. *2 ref.* to crouch, squat.

**agencia** *f.* agency, bureau. *2* (Am.) pawnshop.

**agenciar** *tr.* to carry out, negotiate. *2 tr.-ref.* to manage to get.

**agencioso, -sa** *adj.* diligent, active.

**agenda** *f.* note-book, memorandum book.

**agente** *m.* agent. *2* ~ *de cambio y bolsa*, stockbroker; ~ *de negocios*, business agent; ~ *de policía*, plain-clothes man or officer.

**agibílibus** *m.* industry, smartness.

**agigantado, -da** *adj.* gigantic. *2* uncommon, extraordinary.

**agigantar** *tr.* to enlarge, aggrandize. *2* to exaggerate.

**ágil** *adj.* agile, nimble, limber, quick.

**agilidad** *f.* agility, nimbleness, quickness.

**agilitar** *tr.* to make someone agile. *2* to make easy, to facilitate. *3* (Am.) to activate.

**agio, agiotaje** *m.* agio. *2* agiotage, stockjobbing.

**agiotador, agiotista** *m.* agioter, stockjobber.

**agitación** *f.* agitation, flurry, flutter, excitement.

**agitador, -ra** *adj.* agitating. *2 m.* agitator.

**agitanado, -da** *adj.* gypsylike.

**agitar** *tr.* to agitate; to flurry, excite. *2* to shake, to stir; to wave. *3 ref.* to be agitated, to flurry [of the sea] to be rough.

**aglomeración** *f.* agglomeration, crowding, crowd.

**aglomerado, -da** *adj.-m.* agglomerate. *2 m.* coal briquette.

**aglomerar** *tr.* to agglomerate. *2 ref.* to agglomerate [be agglomerated].

**aglutinación** *f.* agglutination.

**aglutinante** *adj.* agglutinating, agglutinative. *2 m.* agglutinating agent.

**aglutinar** *tr.* to agglutinate. *2 ref.* to be agglutinated.

**agnación** *f.* agnation.

**agnado, -da** *adj.-m.* agnate.

**agnosticismo** *m.* agnosticism.

**agnóstico, -ca** *adj.* agnostic(al. *2 m.-f.* agnostic.

**Agnusdéi** *m.* Agnus Dei.

**agobiado, -da** *adj.* bent over, weighed down, bowed. *2* overwhelmed, over burdened, loaded with worries. *3* too tired, exhausted. *4* round-shouldered, with the shoulders bent forward.

**agobiar** *tr.* to bow down, weigh down, overburden; to oppress.

**agobio** *m.* burden, oppression, fatigue.

**agolpamiento** *m.* crowding, thronging.

**agolpar** *tr.* to gather suddenly. *2 ref.* to crowd, throng; to rush [to].

**agonía** *f.* agony, death agony. *2* agony, anguish.

**agónico, -ca** *adj.* dying, in the death agony. *2* pertaining to the death agony.

**agonizante** *adj.* dying. *2 m.-f.* dying person. *3 m.* monk who assists the dying.

**agonizar** *intr.* to be dying. *2 tr.* to press, hurry. *3* to assist the dying.

**ágora** *f.* agora.

**agorafobia** *f.* MED. agoraphobia.

**agorar** *tr.* to predict superstitiously. ¶ CONJUG. like *contar*.

**agorero, -ra** *adj.* of ill omen [bird]. *2 m.-f.* diviner. *3* a prophet of evil. *4* a believer in omens.

**agorgojarse** *ref.* [of grains, seeds] to get weeviled.

**agostamiento** *m.* parching, drying up [plants].

**agostar** *tr.* to parch, dry up [plants]. *2 ref.* [of plants] to be parched, dried up.

**agostero** *m.* harvest-worker.

**agosto** *m.* August. *2* harvest time; harvest, reaping: *hacer uno su* ~, to feather one's nest.

**agotable** *adj.* exhaustible.

**agotador, -ra** *adj.* exhausting, tiresome.

**agotamiento** *m.* exhaustion.

**agotar** *tr.* to exhaust, to drain off, use up, work out, sell out, tire out. *2 ref.* to exhaust oneself; to be exhausted, to run out; to become sold out.

**agracejina** *f.* BOT. barberry [fruit].

**agracejo** *m.* stunted grape. *2* BOT. barberry [tree].

**agraciado, -da** *adj.* graceful, well-favoured, genteel. *2* having [a gift, etc.] bestowed on him; winner [of a lottery prize].

**agraciar** *tr.* to grace, adorn. *2* to bestow [on], to favour [with].

**agradable** *adj.* agreeable, pleasant, enjoyable.

**agradar** *tr.* to please, be agreeable to; to suit, gratify: *esto me agrada*, I like this. *2 ref.* to like, to be pleased with. *3* to like each other.

**agradecer** *tr.* to acknowledge [a favour]; to thank for, be grateful for. ¶ CONJUG. INDIC. Pres.: *agradezco.* | SUBJ. PRES.: *agradezco, agradezcas, agradezca; agradezcamos, agradezcáis, agradezcan.* IMPER.: *agradezca; agradezcamos, agradezcan.*

**agradecido, -da** *adj.* acknowledged [favour]. *2* grateful, thankful, obliged.

**agradecimiento** *m.* gratitude, thankfulness.

**agradezco, agradezca,** etc. *irr.* V. AGRADECER.

**agrado** *m.* affability, amiableness, graciousness. *2* pleasure, liking.

**agramadera** *f.* scutch, brake, breaker.

**agramado** *m.* scutching, braking.

**agramar** *tr.* to brake [flax or hemp].

**agramiza** *f.* scutch, flax or hemp tow.

**agrandamiento** *m.* enlargement, aggrandizement.

**agrandar** *tr.* to enlarge, aggrandize, magnify. *2 ref.* to enlarge [grow larger].

**agranujado, -da** *adj.* pimply. *2* rascally; urchin-like.

**agrario, -ria** *adj.* agrarian.

**agravación** *f.*, **agravamiento** *m.* aggravation. *2* getting worse.

**agravante** *adj.* aggravating, making worse. *2* aggravative.

**agravar** *tr.* to aggravate, make heavier or worse. *2* to burden with taxes. *3 ref.* to become more grave; to get worse.

**agraviador, -a** *m.-f.* offender, wronger.

**agraviar** *tr.* to offend, insult. *2* to injure, hurt, wrong. *3 ref.* to take offence.

**agravio** *m.* grievance, offence, insult. *2* injury, harm, wrong.

**agravioso, -sa** *adj.* offensive, insulting.

**agraz** *m.* unripe grape: *en* ~, fig. prematurely. *2*

grape verjuice. *3* AGRAZADA. *4* bitterness, sorrow.

**agrazada** *f.* drink made of grape verjuice.

**agrazón** *m.* wild grape. *2* gooseberry bush. *3* annoyance, vexation.

**agredir** *tr.* to assail, assault, attack. ¶ Def.: only used in forms having *i* in their terminations.

**agregable** *adj.* aggregable.

**agregación** *f.* aggregation, addition, joining.

**agregado** *m.* aggregate, collection. *2* annex. *3* attaché.

**agregar** *tr.* to aggregate, add, join, attach. *2 ref.* to join, to attach oneself.

**agremán** *m.* insertion, attachment.

**agremiación** *f.* forming into a guild or association.

**agremiar** *tr.-ref.* to form a guild or tradesmen's union.

**agresión** *f.* aggression, assault, attack.

**agresividad** *f.* aggressiveness.

**agresivo, -va** *adj.* aggresive.

**agresor, -ra** *adj.* aggressing. *2 m.-f.* aggressor, assaulter.

**agreste** *adj.* rustic, rural, wild. *2* rude, uncouth.

**agrete** *adj.* sourish.

**agriamente** *adv.* fig. sourly, sharply, harshly. *2* bitterly.

**agriar** *tr.* to sour [make sour]. *2* to exasperate, embitter. *3 ref.* to sour, turn sour.

**agrícola** *adj.* agricultural. *2 m.-f.* agriculturist.

**agricultor, -ra** *m.-f.* agriculturist, farmer.

**agricultura** *f.* agriculture.

**agridulce** *adj.* bittersweet.

**agrietar** *tr.* to crack, fissure, chap. *2 ref.* to crack, fissure, chap [be cracked].

**Agrigento** *pr. n.* GEOG. Agrigento.

**agrillo, -lla** *adj.* sourish, acidulous.

**agrimensor** *m.* land surveyor.

**agrimensura** *f.* survey, land surveying.

**agrimonia** *f.* BOT. agrimony.

**agrio, -gria** *adj.* sour, acid, crab. *2* bitter [orange]. *3* rough, uneven. *4* sour, tart, sharp, ungracious. *5* brittle [metal]. *6* PAINT. harsh. *7 m.* acid juice. *8 pl.* citrus fruits.

**agripalma** *f.* BOT. motherwort.

**agrisado, -da** *adj.* grayish.

**agro** *m.* land, countryside.

**agronomía** *f.* agronomics, agronomy.

**agrónomo** *m.* agronomist.

**agropecuario** *adj.* land and cattle.

**agrumar** *tr.* to clot, coagulate. *2 ref.* to clot [become clotted].

**agrupación** *f.* grouping. *2* groupment, group, union, association. *3* cluster.

**agrupar** *tr.* to group. *2* to cluster, bunch. *3 ref.* to group, cluster, crowd together.

**agrura** *f.* sourness, acidity. *2* acid juice. *3* citrus trees.

**agua** *f.* water [liquid, body of water, sea, stream, etc.]: ~ *bendita*, holy water; ~ *carbónica*, soda water; ~ *corriente*, running water; ~ *dulce*, fresh water; ~ *mansa*, still water; ~ *salada*, salt water; *aguas jurisdiccionales*, territorial waters; *¡hombre al agua!*, man overboard!; *estar con el ~ al cuello*, fig. to be in deep water, in great difficulties; *guárdate del ~ mansa*, fig. still waters run deep; *tan claro como el ~*, obvious, manifest; *aguas abajo*, downstream; *aguas arriba*, upstream. *2* water [solution, infusion, distillation, etc.]: ~ *de azahar*, orangeflower water; ~ *de borrajas* or *de cerrajas*, fig. unsubstantial thing; ~ *de Colonia*, eau-de-Cologne; ~

*de rosas*, rose water; ~ *fuerte*, agua fortis, nitric acid; AGUAFUERTE; ~ *oxigenada*, hydrogen peroxide; ~ *regia*, agua regia. *3* rain: ~ *nieve*, sleet; ~ *viento*, wind and rain. *4* slope of a roof. *5* NAUT. water leakage: *via de* ~, leak. *6* water, saliva: *se me hace la boca* ~, fig. my mouth waters. *7 pl.* tide, tides [in the sea]: *aguas de creciente*, rising tide; *aguas de menguante*, ebb tide. *8* water, urine. *9* water [of a precious stone, etc.].

**aguacatal** *m.* plantation of avocadoes.

**aguacate** *m.* BOT. avocado, alligator pear [tree and fruit]. *3* pear-shaped emerald.

**aguacero** *m.* rainstorm, heavy shower.

**aguacha** *f.* foul, stagnant water.

**aguachar** *m.* pool, puddle.

**aguachirle** *f.* inferior wine. *2* weak liquor; unsubstantial thing.

**aguada** *f.* watering place [place where water may be obtained]. *2* NAUT. supply of drinking water: *hacer* ~, take fresh water. *3* PAINT. water colour.

**aguaderas** *f. pl.* frame for carrying water-pitchers on horses.

**aguadero, -ra** *adj.* water, for water; waterproof [cloak]. *2 m.* watering place [for animals].

**aguado, -da** *adj.* watered, watery. *2* teetotaller.

**aguador, -ra** *m.-f.* water carrier.

**aguaducho** *m.* water-seller's stall. *2* freshet. *3* flood.

**aguafiestas** *m.-f.* kill-joy, marplot.

**aguafuerte** *m.* etching; etched plate.

**aguaje** *m.* AGUADERO 2. *2* NAUT. spring tide; tidal wave. *3* sea stream or current. *4* NAUT. wake.

**aguamala** *f.* MEDUSA 1.

**aguamanil** *m.* pitcher, ewer. *2* wash-basin. *3* washstand.

**aguamanos** *m.* water for washing the hands. *2* AGUAMANÍL 1.

**aguamar** *m.* MEDUSA 1.

**aguamarina** *f.* aquamarina, aquamarine.

**aguamiel** *f.* hydromel.

**aguanieve** *f.* sleet.

**aguanoso, -sa** *adj.* waterish, watery.

**aguantar** *tr.* to restrain, hold, hold back, control. *2* to bear, endure, suffer, sustain, support, stand, abide, resist. *3* to swallow [an affront, etc]. *4* NAUT. to haul tight. *ref.* to restrain oneself.

**aguante** *m.* patience, endurance. *2* strength, firmness.

**aguapié** *m.* small wine.

**aguar** *tr.* to water [dilute with water]. *2* to spoil, mar [fun, pleasure]. *3 ref.* to be spoiled, marred.

**aguará** *m.* ZOOL. a South-American fox.

**aguardada** *f.* awaiting, wait.

**aguardar** *tr.* to wait, to await or wait for. *2* to expect. *3 intr.* to stay, hold on, stop. *4* ~ *a*, to wait, to wait for.

**aguardentoso, -sa** *adj.* mixed with spirits. *2* harsh, hoarse [voice].

**aguardiente** *m.* spirit, firewater: ~ *de caña*, rum.

**aguarrás** *m.* turpentine, oil of turpentine.

**aguaturma** *f.* BOT. Jerusalem artichoke.

**aguaviento** *m.* rainy wind.

**aguazal** *m.* fen. swamp.

**aguazar** *tr.* ENCHARCAR.

**agudeza** *f.* acuteness, sharpness, acuity, keenness. *2* perspicacity. *3* wit, smartness. *4* witticism, sally.

**agudizar** *tr.* to render more acute.

**agudo, -da** *adj.* acute [sharp-pointed; sharp; keen; high-pitched; shrill; perspicacious]. *2* witty, smart, clever. *3* GEOM., GRAM., MED. acute. *4* oxytone [word].

**Agueda** *f. pr. n.* Agatha.

**agüero** *m.* augury, prediction. *2* sign, omen: *de mal ~*, of ill omen.

**aguerrido, -da** *adj.* inured to war; veteran.

**aguerrir** *tr.* to inure to war. ¶ Only used in forms having *i* in their terminations.

**aguijada** *f.* goad. *2* ploughstaff.

**aguijar** *tr.* to goad, spur, prick. *2* to incite, stimulate. *3 intr.* hurry along.

**aguijón** *m.* point of a goad: *dar coces contra el ~*, to kick against the pricks. *2* ZOOL., BOT. sting. *3* fig. spur, goad, stimulus.

**aguijonazo** *m.* thrust with a goad or prick; sting.

**aguijonear** *tr.* to goad, prick. *2* to sting. *3* to incite, stimulate.

**águila** *f.* eagle [bird; emblem; coin]: *~ barbuda*, lammergeyer; *~ caudal*, golden eagle; *ser un ~*, fig. to be very clever. *2* ICHTH. eagle ray.

**aguileña** *f.* BOT. columbine.

**aguileño, -ña** *adj.* aquiline. *2* hawk-nosed.

**aguilón** *m. aug.* of ÁGUILA. *2* jib of a crane. *3* ARCH. gable angle.

**aguilucho** *m.* eaglet.

**aguinaldo** *m.* Christmas box, Christmas gift.

**agüista** *m.* resorter, frequenter of a spa.

**aguja** *f.* needle: *~ de hacer calceta*, knitting needle; *~ mechera*, larding pin; *~ saquera*, pack needle; *~ de marear*, NAUT. compass; *buscar una ~ en un pajar*, to look for a needle in a haystack. *2* bodkin, hatpin. *3* hand [of clock]; pointer, index. *4* style [of dial, etc.]. *5* ARCH. spire, steeple. *6* ICHTH. needlefish. *7* BOT. Lady's-comb. *8* switch rail. *9 pl.* RLY. switch. *10* fore ribs [of an animal].

**agujereado, -da** *adj.* with a hole or full of holes.

**agujerear** *tr.* to pierce, bore, perforate.

**agujero** *m.* hole. *2* needle maker or seller.

**agujeta** *f.* costume point, tagged lace. *2 pl.* pains from overexercise.

**aguosidad** *f.* lymph, serosity.

**¡agur!** *interj.* coll. good-bye!, farewell!

**agusanamiento** *m.* maggotiness, grubbiness.

**agusanarse** *ref.* to get or become maggoty, grubby or wormy; to become worm-eaten.

**Agustín** *pr. n.* Augustin, Austin.

**agustino, -na** *adj.-n.* Augustinian, Austin [friar].

**agutí** *m.* ZOOL. (Arg., Par.) agouti.

**aguzadero, -ra** *adj.* whetting, sharpening.

**aguzado, -da** *adj.* sharp-edged or -pointed, keen.

**aguzamiento** *m.* sharpening, whetting.

**aguzanieves** *f.* ORN. wagtail.

**aguzar** *tr.* to sharpen, point, whet. *2* to spur, goad, estimulate. *3* to sharpen [the wits, the senses]. *4* to prick up [one's ears].

**¡ah!** *interj.* oh!, ha!

**ahebrado, -da** *adj.* fibrous, thready.

**ahechador, -ra** *adj.* sieving, sifting. *2 n.* sifter, small utensil used for sifting.

**ahechaduras** *f. pl.* siftings of grain.

**ahechar** *tr.* to sift [grain].

**aherrojamiento** *m.* chaining, putting in irons.

**aherrojar** *tr.* to iron, fetter, put in irons. *2* to oppress, hold in subjection.

**aherrumbrarse** *ref.* [of water] to become ferruginous. *2* [of iron] to rust.

**ahí** *adv.* there, in that place: *de ~ que*, hence, therefore; *por ~*, somewhere around; that way; *por ~ por ~*, more or less.

**ahijada** *f.* goddaughter.

**ahijado** *m.* godchild, godson. *2* protégé.

**ahijar** *tr.* to adopt [a person]. *2* to impute. *3 intr.* to procreate. *4* AGR. to bud.

**ahilar** *intr.* to go in single file. *2 ref.* to grow thin [from illness]. *3* [of wine] to turn ropy. *4* [of plants] to become etiolated; [of trees] to grow slender.

**ahincadamente** *adv.* hard, eagerly, earnestly.

**ahínco** *m.* eagerness, earnestness, ardour.

**ahitar** *tr.* to surfeit, cloy, satiate, pall. *2 ref.* to gorge oneself.

**ahíto, -ta** *adj.* cloyed, surfeited, gorged. *2* fed up, disgusted. *3 m.* surfeit, indigestion.

**ahogadero** *m.* crowded, stifling place. *2* throat-band.

**ahogadilla** *f.* ducking.

**ahogado, -da** *adj.* choked, suffocated, stifled, smothered. *2* drowned. *3* close, stuffy, illventilated. *4 m.-f.* drowned person.

**ahogamiento** *m.* suffocation, choking. *2* drowning.

**ahogar** *tr.* to chocke, stifle, smother, suffocate, strangle, quench. *2* to drown. *3* to oppress. *4 ref.* to chocke, stifle, etc. [be choked, etc.]. *5* to be drowned.

**ahogo** *m.* anguish, oppression, suffocation. *2* pinch, financial difficulties.

**ahoguijo, ahoguío** *m.* constriction of the chest.

**ahondamiento** *m.* deepening, excavation, digging, penetration. *2* fig. investigation.

**ahondar** *tr.* to deepen [a hole or cavity]; to excavate. *2 intr.-tr.* to go deep into, to penetrate.

**ahonde** *m.* deepening.

**ahora** *adv.-conj.* now; *~ mismo*, just now, right now; *por ~*, for the present; *~ bien*, now, now then. *2 conj.* whether... or.

**ahorcado, -da** *m.-f.* hanged man (woman).

**ahorcadura** *f.* hanging [of a person].

**ahorcajarse** *ref.* to sit astride.

**ahorcar** *tr.* to hang [kill by hanging]. *2* to give up [books, studies]: *~ los hábitos*, to give up clerical life. *3 ref.* to hang [oneself].

**ahorita** *adv.* (Am.) instantly, this very minute.

**ahormar** *tr.* to adjust, shape, mould; to block [a hat], to last [a shoe].

**ahornagarse** *ref.* [of soil & plants] to become parched or scorched.

**ahorquillado, -da** *adj.* forked, furcate.

**ahorquillar** *tr.* AGR. to stay, prop up [with a forked pole]. *2* to fork [give a forklike shape].

**ahorrado, -da** *adj.* saving, thrifty.

**ahorrador, -ra** *adj.* saving, thrifty. *2 m.-f.* economizer.

**ahorrar** *tr.* to save, economize, lay by, spare. *2 tr.-ref.* to spare, to spare oneself [trouble, labour, etc.].

**ahorrativo, -va** *adj.* saving, thrifty.

**ahorro** *m.* saving, economy. *2 pl.* savings.

**ahuecado, -da** *adj.* deep, low [voice]. *2* hollow, empty. *3* bouffant, full, flared [a dress].

**ahuecar** *tr.* to hollow; to inflate, puff out. *2* to loosen, soften, fluff. *3* to make [the voice] hollow or pompous. *4* fig. *~ el ala*, to beat it, go away. *5 ref.* to become puffed up.

**ahuesado, -da** *adj.* bone-coloured. *2* bone-hard.

**ahumado, -da** *adj.* smoked, smoky. *2 f.* smoke signal.

**ahumar** *tr.* to smoke [blacken, cure, etc., with smoke]; to fill with smoke. *2 intr.* to smoke [emit smoke]. *3 ref.* to be smoked. *4* fig. to get drunk.

**ahusado, -da** *adj.* spindle-shaped, fusiform.

**ahuyentar** *tr.* to drive away, to scare away, to put to flight. *2 ref.* to flee.

**ailanto** *m.* BOT. ailanthus.
**airadamente** *adv.* angrily.
**airado, -da** *adj.* angry, irate, wrathful. *2* loose, depraved [life].
**airar** *tr.* to anger, irritate. *2 ref.* to get angry.
**aire** *m.* air [fluid, atmosphere, wind]; ~ *colado,* cold draught; ~ *comprimido,* compressed air; *beber los aires por,* fig. to sight or long for or after; to be madly in love with; *hacer* ~ *a uno,* to fan someone; *mudar de aires,* to go for a change; *tomar el* ~, to take the air, take a walk; *al* ~ *libre,* in the open air, outdoors; *por el* ~, *por los aires,* swiftly, rapidly. *2* appearance, air, airs: *tener aires de salud,* to have a healthy appearance. *3* resemblance: *darse un* ~ *a,* to resemble. *4* pace, gait [of a horse]. *5* humour, temper. *6* ease, dexterity. *7* elegance, gracefulness. *8* vigor, violence. *9* MUS. movement. *10* MUS. air, melody.
**aireación** *f.* VENTILACIÓN.
**aireado, -da** *adj.* aired, ventilated. *2* sour, bitter, fermented.
**airear** *tr.* to air, ventilate. *2 ref.* to take the air.
**airón** *m.* ORN. European heron. *2* ORN. crest of feathers. *3* aigrette, panache, crest.
**airosamente** *adv.* gracefully, lively.
**airosidad** *f.* graceful deportment.
**airoso, -sa** *adj.* airy, windy [place]. *2* graceful, lively [in carriage or deportment]. *3 salir* ~, to acquit oneself well; to be successful.
**aislacionismo** *m.* isolationism.
**aislacionista** *adj.-n.* isolationist, supporter of isolationism.
**aisladamente** *adv.* isolatedly, singly, separately.
**aislado, -da** *adj.* isolate(d, separate. *2* insulate(d.
**aislador** *m.* PHYS., ELEC. isolator, insulator.
**aislamiento** *m.* isolation; insulation. *2* seclusion.
**aislante** *adj.* non-conducting, insulating. *2 m.* insulator.
**aislar** *tr.* to isolate, insulate. *2 ref.* to isolate or seclude oneself.
**¡ajá!** *interj.* aha!, that is right!
**ajada** *f.* a garlic sauce.
**ajamiento** *m.* withering, fading, crumpling.
**ajamonarse** *ref.* [of a woman] to grow plump and buxon.
**ajar** *tr.* to crumple, rumple, spoil, wither, fade. *2 ref.* to become spoiled, to wither.
**ajardinado, -da** *adj.* landscaped, arranged as a garden.
**aje** *m.* ACHAQUE 1. *2* BOT. a plant of the yam family.
**ajebe** *m.* alum.
**ajedrea** *f.* BOT. savory, savoury.
**ajedrecista** *m.-f.* chess player.
**ajedrez** *m.* chess [game].
**ajedrezado, -da** *adj.* checkered, chequered.
**ajenjo** *m.* BOT. wormwood. *2* absinth.
**ajeno, -na** *adj.* another's, alien, strange. *2* alien, foreign [to], inconsistent [with], improper [of]. *3* ignorant [of]. *4* ~ *de cuidados,* free from care.
**ajerezado, -da** *adj.* sherry-like.
**ajete** *m.* BOT. young garlic. *2* garlic sauce.
**ajetrearse** *ref.* to tire oneself out; to bustle about.
**ajetreo** *m.* fatigue; bustle.
**ají** *m.* (Am.) chili, chili pepper. *2* chili sauce.
**ajiaceite** *m.* a garlic and oil sauce.
**ajipuerro** *m.* BOT. wild leek.
**ajo** *m.* BOT. garlic. *2* garlic clove. *3* garlic sauce. *4* secret affair. *5* PALABROTA. *6* BOT. ~ *chalote,* shallot.
**ajobar** *tr.* to carry on the back.

**ajofaina** *f.* washbasin, washboul, washhand basin.
**ajolote** *m.* ZOOL. axolotl.
**ajomate** *m.* a green filamentous alga.
**ajonjera** *f.* BOT. carline thistle.
**ajonjolí** *m.* BOT. sesame [plant & seeds].
**ajorca** *f.* ring bracelet, anklet, bangle.
**ajornalar** *tr.* to hire [a person] by the day.
**ajuar** *m.* household furniture. *2* trousseau.
**ajuiciado, -da** *adj.* sensible, wise.
**ajuiciar** *tr.-intr.* to make or become sensible, wise.
**ajumarse** *ref.* to get canned or drunk.
**ajustado, -da** *adj.* adjusted. *2* just, right. *3* tight, close-fitting.
**ajustador** *m.* close-fitting waistcoat. *3* MEC. adjuster, fitter. *4* PRINT. pager.
**ajustar** *tr.* to adjust, adapt, fit, regulate. *2* to fit tight, to tighten. *3* to make [an agreement]: to agree upon, to arrange. *4* to reconcile. *5* to settle [accounts]. *6* to hire, engage. *7* PRINT. to page. *8 intr.* to fit tight. *9 ref.* to conform [to]. *10* to hire oneself. *11* to come to an agreement.
**ajuste** *m.* adjustement, fitting, fit. *2* agreement, contract. *3* settlement [of accounts]. *4* hire, engagement. *5* PRINT. paging.
**ajusticiado, -da** *adj.-n.* executed [person].
**ajusticiamiento** *m.* execution [of a culprit].
**ajusticiar** *tr.* to execute, put to death.
**al** *contr.* of A EL: to the; at or at the [foll. by a masc. noun]. *2* when used with an inf. it is equivalent to «on», «about», «on the point of»: ~ *verlo,* on seeing it; *está* ~ *llegar,* he is about to arrive.
**ala** *f.* ORN., ENT., ANAT., ARCH., FORT., MIL., POL. wing: *cortar las alas,* fig. to clip the wings. *2* ANAT. auricle [of the heart]: *caérselo a uno las alas del corazón,* fig. to be dismayed. *3* brim [of a hat]. *4* flap [of a table]. *5* blade [of a propeller]. *6* NAUT. studding sail. *7* row, line. *8* eaves. *9 pl.* courage, boldness: *dar alas,* to embolden.
**¡ala!** *interj.* come on!, hup hup la! *2* hey!
**Alá** *pr. n.* Allah.
**alabado** *m.* motet in praise of the Sacrament.
**alabador, -ra** *m.-f.* praiser.
**alabancioso, -sa** *adj.* boastful, vainglorious.
**alabanza** *f.* praise, commendation, eulogy.
**alabar** *tr.* to praise, commend, extol, applaud. *2 ref.* to praise oneself. *3* to boast.
**alabarda** *f.* halberd.
**alabardero** *m.* halberdier. *2* THEAT. clapper.
**alabastrado, -da** *adj.* alabastrine, alabaster-like.
**alabastrino, -na** *adj.* alabaster, alabastrine.
**alabastro** *m.* MINER. alabaster.
**álabe** *m.* drooping branch of a tree. *2* side mat [in carts]. *3* float, paddle [of a water wheel].
**alabear** *tr.* to warp, camber. *2 ref.* to have a camber.
**alabeo** *m.* warp, warping, camber.
**alacena** *f.* cupboard, closet.
**alacrán** *m.* ZOOL. scorpion. *2* shank [of button].
**alacranado, -da** *adj.* bitten by a scorpion. *2* tainted with some vice or disease.
**alacranera** *f.* BOT. scorpionwort.
**alacridad** *f.* alacrity, cheerful readiness.
**alacha** *f.* BOQUERÓN 2.
**alada** *f.* wing stroke or beat.
**aladares** *m. pl.* hair falling over the temples.
**Aladino** *m. pr. n.* Aladdin.
**aladierna** *f.,* **aladierno** *m.* BOT. alatern.
**alado, -da** *adj.* winged [having wings; swift]. *2* BOT. alate.
**alalimón** *m.* a children's game.

**alama** *f.* BOT. a fodder plant.
**alamar** *m.* frog [ornamental braiding]. 2 fringe, tassel.
**alambicado, -da** *adj.* distilled. 3 parsimoniously given. 4 subtle, finedrawn.
**alambicamiento** *m.* distillation. 2 subtility.
**alambicar** *tr.* to distill, rectify. 2 to investigate closely. 3 to subtilize, fine-draw.
**alambique** *m.* still, alembic: *por ~*, sparingly.
**alambrado, -da** *adj.* wired [fenced with wires]. 2 *f.* FORT. wire entanglement. 3 *m.* wire screen; wire cover; wire fence.
**alambrar** *tr.* to fence with wire.
**alambre** *m.* wire [metallic thread].
**alambrera** *f.* wire screen. 2 wire cover.
**alameda** *f.* poplar grove. 2 avenue, mall.
**álamo** *m.* BOT. poplar: *~ blanco*, white poplar; *~ negro*, black poplar; *~ temblón*, aspen.
**alamparse** *ref.* to crave after, long for, be very fond of.
**alancear** *tr.* to lance, to spear. 2 ZAHERIR.
**alano** *m.* a large dog. 2 *pl.* Alans.
**alantoides** *adj.-m.* ANAT. allantoid.
**alar** *m.* eaves. 2 horse-hair snare for partridges.
**alarde** *m.* display, show, ostentation.
**alardear** *intr.* to boast.
**alargadera** *f.* CHEM. adapter. 2 lengthening bar, tube, etc.
**alargado, -da** *adj.* long, elongated, oblong.
**alargador, -ra** *adj.* lengthening, extending, stretching.
**alargar** *tr.* to lengthen, elongate, extend, prolong, protract. 2 to increase. 3 to reach, stretch out. 4 to hand, pass [something to somebody]. 5 to pay out [a rope]. 6 *ref.* to lengthen, grow longer. 7 to expatiate.
**Alarico** *pr. n.* Alaric.
**alarido** *m.* yell, howl, scream.
**alarife** *m.* formerly, an architect or builder.
**alarije** *m.* variety of grape.
**alarma** *f.* MIL. alarm. 2 alarm [warning or apprehension of danger]: *timbre de ~*, alarm bell.
**alarmado, -da** *adj.* alarmed.
**alarmante** *adj.* alarming.
**alarmar** *tr.* to call to arms. 2 to alarm. 3 *ref.* to be alarmed.
**alarmista** *m.-f.* alarmist, scaremonger.
**Álava** *pr. n.* GEOG. Alava, a Basque province of Spain.
**alavés, -sa** *adj.-s.* of or from Álava.
**alazán, -na** *adj.-n.* sorrel [horse].
**alazor** *m.* BOT. safflower, bastard saffron.
**alba** *f.* dawn, daybreak. 2 beginning. 3 ECCL. alb.
**albacea** *m.* LAW testamentary executor. 2 *f.* LAW testamentary executrix.
**albaceazgo** *m.* LAW executorship.
**albaceteño, -ña, albacetense** *adj.* of or from Albacete, Spain. 2 *n.* inhabitant of Albacete.
**albacora** *f.* ICHTH. albacore. 2 BREVA 1.
**albahaca** *f.* BOT. sweet basil.
**albahaquero** *m.* flowerpot. 2 a stand for flowerpots.
**albaida** *f.* BOT. a leguminous plant.
**albalá** *m.-f.* royal letters patent. 2 voucher.
**albanés, -sa** *adj.-n.* Albanian.
**Albania** *pr. n.* GEOG. Albania.
**albañal, albañar** *m.* drain, sewer.
**albañil** *m.* mason, bricklayer.
**albañilería** *f.* masonry.
**albar** *adj.* white [plant or tree].

**albarán** *m.* white paper in window implying that the place is to let. 2 voucher. 3 delivery note.
**albarazado, -da** *adj.* variegated. 2 affected with white leprosy.
**albarda** *f.* pack saddle. 2 ALBARDILLA 6.
**albardado, -da** *adj.* characteristic of some animals which consists in having the back a different color from the rest of the body.
**albardilla** *f.* small saddle for breaking in colts. 2 coping. 3 flatiron handle-pad. 4 a pad on the eyes of shears. 5 water-carrier's cushion. 6 COOK. bard.
**albardín** *m.* BOT. hooded matweed.
**albardón** *m.* a large pack-saddle for riding.
**albaricoque** *m.* BOT. apricot.
**albaricoquero** *m.* BOT. apricot tree.
**albarillo** *m.* BOT. white apricot. 2 tune on the guitar.
**albarizo, -za** *adj.* whitish [soil].
**albarrada** *f.* dry wall. 2 earth fence.
**albarrana** *adj.* see CEBOLLA & TORRE.
**albarranilla** *f.* BOT. squill.
**albatros** *m.* ORN. albatross.
**albayalde** *m.* ceruse, white lead.
**albazano, -na** *adj.* dark chestnut [horse].
**albear** *intr.* to whiten, show white.
**albedrío** *m.* free will: *libre ~*, free will. 2 will, pleasure: *al ~ de uno*, at one's pleasure.
**albéitar** *m.* farrier, veterinarian.
**alberca** *f.* pond, pool, millpond, water reservoir.
**albérchigo** *m.* BOT. peach-tree. 2 peach [fruit].
**alberchiguero** *m.* BOT. peach tree.
**albergar** *tr.* to house, shelter, lodge, harbour. 2 *ref.* to take shelter; to lodge, harbour.
**albergue** *m.* housing, shelter, lodging, harbour, refuge. 2 lair, den. 3 orphanage, home.
**albero** *m.* a tract of whitish soil. 2 dishcloth.
**Alberto** *pr. n.* Albert.
**albigense** *adj.* albigensian. 2 *m. pl.* Albigenses.
**albinismo** *m.* albinism, albinoism.
**albino, -na** *adj.* albinic. 2 *m.* albino. 3 *f.* albiness.
**Albión** *pr. n.* GEOG. Albion.
**albitana** *f.* GARD. fence for plants. 2 NAUT. apron or inner post [in small boats].
**albo, -ba** *adj.* poet, white.
**albohol** *m.* BOT. the lesser bindweed.
**albóndiga, albondiguilla** *f.* COOK. meat ball.
**albor** *m.* whiteness. 2 *pl.* dawn, beginning.
**alborada** *f.* dawn, break of day. 2 MIL. action fought at dawn. 3 reveille. 4 aubade.
**alborear** *intr.* [of the day] to dawn.
**albornoz** *m.* burnoose, burnous. 2 bathing gown.
**alboronía** *f.* dish of tomatoes, pumpkins, sweet peppers, etc.
**alboroque** *m.* treat given at the close of a deal.
**alborotadamente** *adv.* disorderly, excitedly, noisily.
**alborotadizo, -za** *adj.* easily agitated, excitable.
**alborotado, -da** *adj.* hasty, thoughtless, rash.
**alborotador, -ra** *m.-f.* agitator, rioter. 2 noisy person.
**alborotar** *tr.* to disturb, agitate, excite. 2 to incite to riot. 3 ALBOROZAR. 4 *intr.* to make a racket, to shout. 5 *ref.* [of the sea] to get rough. 6 to get excited. 7 to riot.
**alboroto** *m.* uproar, noise. 2 excitement, agitation. 3 disturbance, disorder. 4 tumult, riot.
**alborozado, -da** *adj.* rejoicing, joyful, jubilant.
**alborozar** *tr.* to gladden, cheer, exhilarate.
**alborozo** *m.* joy, joyfulness, exhilaration.

**albricias** *f. pl.* reward for good news. *2 interj.* joy!, joy!
**albufera** *f.* lagoon, salt lake by the sea.
**álbum** *m.* album.
**albumen** *m.* BOT. albumen.
**albúmina** *f.* BIOCHEM. albumin.
**albuminoide** *m.* BIOCHEM. albuminoid.
**albuminoideo, -a** *adj.* albuminoid.
**albuminuria** *f.* MED. albuminuria.
**albur** *m.* chance, hazard. *2* ICHTH. dace.
**albura** *f.* whiteness. *2* ALBURNO.
**alburno** *m.* alburnum, sapwood.
**alca** *f.* ORN. auk, razorbill.
**alcabala** *f.* an ancient excise.
**alcacel, alcacer** *m.* green barley. *2* barley field.
**alcachofa** *f.* BOT. artichoke. *2* cardoon or thistle head.
**alcachofera** *f.* BOT. artichoke [plant].
**alcahueta** *f.* procuress, bawd, go-between.
**alcahuete** *m.* procurer, pander. *2* screener, concealer.
**alcahuetear** *tr.-intr.* to procure, pander, bawd. *2 intr.* to act as a screen or concealer [for something dishonourable].
**alcahuetería** *f.* bawdry, pandering. *2* screening, concealing.
**alcaico** *adj.* alcaic.
**alcaide** *m.* formerly, a warden [of a prison or castle].
**alcaidía** *f.* wardenship [of a prison or castle].
**alcaldada** *f.* abuse of authority.
**alcalde** *m.* Mayor, Lord Mayor; head of a town council.
**alcaldesa** *f.* Mayoress.
**alcaldía** *f.* Mayoralty. *2* the Mayor's office.
**alcalescencia** *f.* alkalescence or -cy.
**alcalescente** *adj.* alkalescent.
**álcali** *m.* CHEM. alkali.
**alcalinidad** *f.* alkalinity.
**alcalino, -na** *adj.* alkaline.
**alcalizar** *tr.* CHEM. to alkalize, alkalify or alkalinize.
**alcaloide** *m.* CHEM. alkaloid.
**alcaloideo, -a** *adj.* alkaloidal.
**alcance** *m.* pursuit, overtaking: *dar* ~, to overtake. *2* reach: *fuera del* ~ *de uno*, out of one's reach. *3* scope, range [of missile]; import, consequence; *de gran* ~, far-reaching. *4* stop-press [news]. *5* intellect, understanding: *cortos alcances*, meagre intellect. *6* COM. balance due. *7* POST. *buzón de* ~, late collection post-box.
**alcancía** *f.* child's bank, money box.
**alcándara** *f.* perch [for falcons].
**alcandía** *f.* ZAHÍNA.
**alcanfor** *m.* camphor. *2* BOT. camphor tree.
**alcanforar** *tr.* to camphorate.
**alcanforero** *m.* BOT. camphor tree.
**alcantarilla** *f.* sewer, drains. *2* culvert.
**alcantarillado** *m.* sewage [system of sewers].
**alcanzable** o **alcanzadizo, -za** *adj.* attainable, reachable, accessible.
**alcanzado, -da** *adj.* in debt. *2* short of, lacking in.
**alcanzadura** *f.* VET. attaint.
**alcanzar** *tr.* to overtake, catch up with. *2* to reach. *3* to get, obtain. *4* to understand. *5* COM. to find [one] debtor of. *6* to reach back to, to have known. *7 intr.* [of a weapon] to carry. *8* to reach, arrive [to]. *9* to suffice, be sufficient [to or for]. *10* ~ *a ver, a oír*, to se, to hear. *11 ref.* VET. [of horses] to overreach.
**alcaparra** *f.* BOT. caper [plant]. *2* caper [bud].

**alcaparro** *m.* BOT. caper [plant].
**alcaparrón** *m.* caper berry.
**alcaraván** *m.* ORN. thick-knee, stone curlew.
**alcaravea** *f.* BOT. caraway.
**alcarraza** *f.* porous earthenware water vessel.
**alcarria** *f.* high, barren land.
**alcatifa** *f.* carpet.
**alcatraz** *m.* CUCURUCHO. *2* BOT. cuckoopint. *3* ORN. white pelican.
**alcaucil** *m.* BOT. artichoke. *2* wild artichoke.
**alcaudón** *m.* ORN. shrike.
**alcayata** *f.* ESCARPIA.
**alcazaba** *f.* fortress [within a walied town].
**alcázar** *m.* fortress. *2* royal palace. *3* NAUT. quarterdeck.
**alce** *m.* ZOOL. elk; moose. *2* cut [at carts].
**Alcestes** *m. pr. n.* Alcestis.
**Alcibíades** m. pr. n. Alcibiades.
**alción** *m.* ORN. kingfisher, halcyon. *2* ASTR. Alcyone.
**alcionarios** *m. pl.* ZOOL. Alcyonaria.
**alcista** *f.* bull [stock speculator].
**alcoba** *f.* alcove [recess for bed], bedroom.
**alcohol** *m.* alcohol. *2* kohl. *3* GALENA.
**alcoholar** *tr.* CHEM. alcoholize. *2* to blacken with kohl.
**alcoholato** *m.* CHEM. alcoholate.
**alcohólico, -ca** *adj.-n.* alcoholic.
**alcoholímetro** *m.* alcoholometer.
**alcoholismo** *m.* alcoholism.
**alcoholizado, -da** *adj.* alcoholized. *2 adj.-m.* MED. alcoholic.
**alcoholizar** *tr.* to alcoholize.
**alcor** *m.* hill, hillock.
**Alcorán** *m.* Alcoran.
**alcornocal** *m.* plantation of cork oaks.
**alcornoque** *m.* cork oak. *2* fig. blockhead, dolt.
**alcorza** *f.* sugar and starch paste, sugar icing.
**alcorzar** *tr.* to ice [cakes] with ALCORZA.
**alcotán** *m.* ORN. lanner.
**alcotana** *f.* bricklayer's hammer.
**alcurnia** *f.* lineage, ancestry, parentage, blood.
**alcuza** *f.* can for oil used in kitchens.
**alcuzcuz** *m.* couscous.
**aldaba** *f.* door-knocker. *2* bolt, crossbar. *3* hitching ring. *4* fig. *tener buenas aldabas*, to have powerful protectors.
**aldabada** *f.* knock, knocking [at the street door].
**aldabilla** *f.* latching hook, fastening hook.
**aldabón** *m.* door knocker. *2* large handle [of a chest, coffer, etc.].
**aldabonazo** *m.* ALDABA.
**aldea** *f.* hamlet, village.
**aldeaniego, -ga** *adj.* ALDEANO 1 & 2.
**aldeano, -na** *adj.* of a hamlet. *2* village, rustic. *3 m.-f.* villager, countryman, countrywoman.
**aldehído, -da** *m.-f.* CHEM. aldehyde.
**aldehuela** *f.* hamlet, small village.
**aldeorrio, aldeorro** *m.* miserable hamlet.
**alderredor** *adv.* ALREDEDOR.
**¡ale!** *interj.* come on!
**álea** *m.* risk.
**aleación** *f.* alloyage. *2* alloy [of metals].
**alear** *tr.* to alloy [metals]. *2 intr.* to flutter, flap the wings [or the arms].
**aleatorio, -ria** *adj.* aleatory, contingent, uncertain.
**alebrarse** *ref.* [of a rabbit] to squat. *2* to cower.
**aleccionar** *tr.* to teach, instruct, drill, coach.
**aleche** *m.* fresh anchovy.
**alechugar** *tr.* to plait, flute, frill, curl in the shape of a lettuce leaf.

**aledaño, -ña** *adj.* bordering, adjacent. *2 m. pl.* borders, surroundings.
**alegación** *f.* allegation, plea, argument.
**alegar** *tr.* to allege, quote, adduce, plead, urge.
**alegato** *m.* plea, pleading. *2* reasoned allegation.
**alegoría** *f.* allegory, emblem.
**alegórico, -ca** *adj.* allegoric(al, allegoristic.
**alegorizar** *tr.* to allegorize.
**alegrar** *tr.* to cheer, gladden, make joyful. *2* to brighten, enliven. *3* to incite [the bull]. *4 ref.* to be glad. *5* to rejoice, cheer. *6* coll. to get tipsy.
**alegre** *adj.* glad, joyful. *2* cheerful, merry, jolly, light-hearted. *3* beaming, bright, gay. *4* tipsy. *5* reckless. *6* light, wanton. *7* ~ *de cascos,* scatter-brained.
**alegremente** *adv.* happily, merrily.
**alegreto** *adj., adv. & m.* MUS. allegretto.
**alegría** *f.* joy, pleasure. *2* glee, merriment, mirth, gaiety. *3* brightness. *4* BOT. sesame.
**alegro** *adj., adv. & m.* MUS. allegro.
**alegrón** *m.* a sudden intense joy. *2* flash, transitory blaze.
**alejado, -da** *adj.* far away, distant, remote, far-off. *2* far away from, a long way from. *3* aloof, apart, isolated.
**alejamiento** *m.* removal to a distance, distance, absence. *2* withdrawal, estrangement, aloofness.
**Alejandría** *pr. n.* GEOG. Alexandria.
**alejandrino, -na** *adj.* Alexandrine.
**Alejandro** *pr. n.* Alexander.
**alejar** *tr.* to remove to a distance, to move away. *2* to separate, estrange. *3 ref.* to go away, move away.
**Alejo** *pr. n.* Alexis.
**alelado, -da** *adj.* bewildered, dazed, stupefied. *2* stupid, slow-witted.
**alelar** *tr.* to bewilder. *2* to stupefy.
**alelí** *m.* ALHELÍ.
**aleluya** *f.* or *m.* hallelujah. *2 m.* Easter time. *3 f.* poor verses, doggerel. *4* BOT. wood sorrel.
**alemán, -na** *adj.-n.* German. *2 m.* German language.
**alemana, alemanda** *f.* allemande [a dance].
**Alemania** *pr. n.* GEOG. Germany.
**alemanisco, -ca** *adj.* germanic. *2* damask.
**alentada** *f.* long breath: *de uña* ~, without interruption, at one go.
**alentado, -da** *adj.* brave, courageous, spirited.
**alentador, -ra** *adj.* encouraging, cheering, heartening. *2 m.-f.* encourager.
**alentar** *intr.* to breathe. *2 tr.* to encourage, cheer, hearten. ¶ CONJUG. like *acertar.*
**alerce** *m.* BOT. larch tree.
**alergia** *f.* allergy.
**alérgico, -ca** *adj.* allergic.
**alero** *m.* eaves. *2* splashboard, mudguard [of a carriage].
**alerón** *m.* AER. aileron.
**alerta** *adv.* on the watch, on the alert. *2 interj.* look out! *3 m.* sentinel's call.
**alertar** *tr.* to alert, put on guard.
**alerto, -ta** *adj.* watchful, careful.
**aleta** *f.* small wing. *2* fin [of a fish]. *3* ARCH. alette. *4* MACH. wing. *5* ALA 5.
**aletada** *f.* a motion of the wings.
**aletargado, -da** *adj.* lethargic, drowsy.
**aletargamiento** *m.* lethargy.
**aletargar** *tr.* to lethargize. *2 ref.* to fall into a lethargy, to get drowsy.
**aletazo** *m.* stroke of wing or fin; flap.

**aletear** *intr.* to flutter, to flap the wings or the fins.
**aleteo** *m.* flapping of wings or fins. *2* palpitation [of the heart].
**aleudar** *tr.* to leaven. *2 ref.* to rise [the dough].
**aleve** *adj.* ALEVOSO.
**alevino** *m.* alevin, fry.
**alevosamente** *adv.* treacherously, wickedly, mischievously. *2* in cold blood.
**alevosía** *f.* treachery, perfidy.
**alevoso, -sa** *adj.* treacherous, perfidious.
**aleya** *f.* koran verse.
**alfa** *f.* alpha.
**alfabético, -ca** *adj.* alphabetical.
**alfabetización** *f.* teaching to read and write, teaching literacy. *2* literacy.
**alfabetizar** *tr.* to teach literacy, to alphabetize [someone]. *2* to put in alphabetical order.
**alfabeto** *m.* alphabet.
**alfajor** *m.* sort of gingerbread. *2* (Am.) macaroon.
**alfalfa** *f.* BOT. lucerne, lucern, alfalfa.
**alfalfal, alfalfar** *m.* lucerne field.
**alfaneque** *m.* ORN. buzzard.
**alfanje** *m.* kind of short scimitar.
**alfaque** *m.* bar of sand at a river's mouth.
**alfaquí** *m.* alfaqui.
**1) alfar** *m.* pottery [factory]. *3* clay, argil.
**2) alfar** *intr.* [of horses] to rear.
**alfarda** *f.* ARCH. rafter.
**alfarería** *f.* pottery [shop, factory, art].
**alfarero** *m.* potter [pottery maker].
**alfarje** *m.* grinding mill for olives. *2* carved and panelled ceiling.
**alfayate** *m.* obs. tailor.
**alféizar** *m.* ARCH. splay; embrasure.
**alfeñicado, -da** *adj.* weakly, delicate.
**alfeñique** *m.* sugar paste in thin bars. *2* frail, delicate person. *3* REMILGO.
**alferazgo** *m.* ensigncy; second lieutenancy.
**alferecía** *f.* MED. epilepsy [in children]. *2* ALFERAZGO.
**alférez** *m.* second lieutenant, ensign.
**alfil** *m.* CHESS. bishop.
**alfiler** *m.* pin [pointed metal piece]; ~ *de corbata,* tie-pin; *de veinticinco alfiles,* dressed up. *2* brooch. *3* ~ *de París,* wire nail. *4 pl.* pin money.
**alfilerazo** *m.* prick [with a pin].
**alfiletero** *m.* needlecase, pincase.
**alfombra** *f.* floor carpet, rug. *2* fig. carpet.
**alfombrar** *tr.* to carpet.
**alfombrilla** *f.* small carpet or rug.
**alfombrista** *m.* carpet seller. *2* carpet layer.
**alfoncigo, alfónsigo** *m.* BOT. pistachio [tree and nut].
**alfonsino, -na** *adj.* Alphonsine.
**Alfonso** *pr. n.* Alphonse.
**alforfón** *m.* BOT. buckwheat.
**alforja** *f.* wallet [long bag open at the middle and closed at the ends].
**alforjón** *m.* ALFORFÓN.
**alforza** *f.* tuck, pleat [in a garment].
**alga** *f.* BOT. alga; sea-weed. *2 pl.* BOT. Algae.
**algaida** *f.* thick forest. *2* MÉDANO.
**algalia** *f.* civet [a perfume]. *2* SURG. catheter. *3 m.* ZOOL. civet, cat.
**algara** *f.* old-time raiding cavalry party. *2* raid of an ALGARA.
**algarabía** *f.* arabic language. *2* jargon. *3* hubbub, uproar.
**algarada** *f.* ALGARA 2. *2* outcry. *3* ancient war engine for throwing stones.
**algarroba** *f.* carob bean. *2* BOT. vetch.

**algarrobilla** f. BOT. vetch, tare.
**algarrobo** m. BOT. carob tree, locuşt tree.
**algazara** f. din, clamour, joyful uproar.
**algazul** m. BOT. ice plant.
**álgebra** f. algebra. 2 bonesetting.
**algebrista** m. algebraist. 2 bonesetter.
**algidez** f. algidity.
**álgido, -da** adj. algid.
**algo** pron. something; aught, anything. 2 adv. somewhat, a little.
**algodón** m. cotton: ~ en rama, cotton wool, raw cotton; ~ hidrófilo, absorbent cotton; ~pólvora, guncotton. 2 cotton plant.
**algodonal** m. cotton plantation. 2 cotton plant.
**algodonar** tr. to fill with cotton.
**algodonero, -ra** adj. cotton. 2 m.-f. cotton dealer. 3 m. BOT. cotton plant.
**algodonoso, -sa** adj. cottony.
**algorín** m. place in oilmills for receiving olives.
**algoritmo** m. algorism, algorithm.
**alguacil** m. beadle, court apparitor. 2 obs. a kind of judge. 3 obs. a peace-officer. 4 ZOOL. jumping spider.
**alguacilillo** m. rider at the head of bullfighter's parade.
**alguien** pron. somebody, someone.
**algún** adj. some. | Used before sing. masc. noun. 2 adv. ~ tanto, a little, somewhat.
**alguno, -na** adj. some, any: ~ vez, sometimes; ~ que otro, some, a few. 2 pron. someone, anyone.
**alhaja** f. jewel. 2 a valuable thing, or ornament. 3 iron. buena ~, a bad one, a sly one.
**alhajar** tr. to jewel. 2 to furnish [a house or room].
**alharaca** f. fuss, ado, exaggerated show of feeling.
**alhárgama, alharma** f. BOT. African rue.
**alhelí** m. BOT. gillyflower.
**alheña** f. BOT. privet, henna. 2 privet powder.
**alheñar** tr. to dye with privet.
**alholva** f. BOT. fenugreek.
**alhóndiga** f. public granary or grain market.
**alhucema** f. ESPLIEGO.
**aliacán** m. ICTERICIA.
**aliado, -da** adj. allied, confederated. 2 m.-f. ally.
**aliadófilo, -la** adj. allied. 2 n. sympathiser of the allied in world wars I and II.
**aliaga** f. AULAGA.
**alianza** f. alliance, league. 2 alliance [by marriage].
**aliar** tr. to ally. 2 ref. to ally [become allied].
**aliaria** f. BOT. hedge garlic.
**alias** lat. adv. alias.
**alicaído, -da** adj. weak, drooping. 2 sad, crestfallen. 3 downfallen.
**alicántara** f., **alicante** m. ZOOL. a viper.
**alicantina** f. coll, artifice, stratagem.
**alicantino, -na** adj.-n. of Alicante.
**alicatado** m. a glazed-tile work in Moorish style.
**alicates** m. pl. pliers.
**Alicia** pr. n. Alice.
**aliciente** m. incentive, inducement, attraction.
**alicortar** tr. to cut the winds off. 2 to wound in the wing. 3 to clip someone's wings.
**alicuanta** adj. aliquant.
**alícuota** adj. aliquot; proportional.
**alidada** f. alidade.
**alienación** f. alienation. 2 MED. mental alienation.
**alienado, -da** adj. alienated. 2 m.-f. MED. alienated [person].
**alienar** tr. ENAJENAR.
**alienista** m. alienist.
**aliento** m. breath, breathing; respiration: tomar

~, to breathe, take breath: sin aliento, breathless, out of breath. 2 spirit, courage: dar ~, to encourage.
**aliento, aliente,** etc. irr. V. ALENTAR.
**alifafe** m. VET. tumour on a horse's hock. 2 chronic complaint.
**aliforme** adj. wing-shaped, aliform.
**aligación** f. alligation: regla de ~, MATH. alligation.
**aligeramiento** m. lightening, making lighter [of a burden, a load]. 2 reduction, cutting down [taxes, fees]. 3 lessening; reduction, diminution [of responsibilities]. 4 relief, ease, alleviation.
**aligerar** tr. to lighten [make less heavy]. 2 to alleviate. 3 to hasten. 4 ref. to lighten [become lighter].
**aligero, -ra** adj. poet. aligerous, winged. 2 fast, fleet.
**aligustre** m. ALHEÑA 1.
**alijador, -ra** m.-f. ginner. 2 NAUT. unloader. 3 m. NAUT. lighter.
1) **alijar** tr. NAUT. to lighten or unload [a ship]. 2 to gin [cotton].
2) **alijar** m. untilled land. 2 pl. common land.
**alijo** m. NAUT. unloading. 2 smuggled goods.
**alimaña** f. beast that destroys game, vermin.
**alimentación** f. alimentation, feeding, nourishment.
**alimentador, -ra** adj. nourishing. 2 m.-f. nourisher. 3 m. MECH. feeder.
**alimentar** tr. to feed, nourish, sustain, aliment. 2 MECH. to feed; to stoke. 3 to entertain, cherish, nurture, foster. 4 ref. to feed, nourish oneself: ~ de, to feed on.
**alimenticio, -cia** adj. alimentary, nourishing, nutritious.
**alimento** m. aliment, food, nourishment. 2 pabulum. 3 pl. LAW allowance for sustenance, alimony.
**alimentoso, -sa** adj. nourishing.
**alimoche** m. ABANTO 2.
**alimón (al)** adv. BULLF. with the cape held by two bullfighters. 2 together, conjointly.
**alindamiento** m. boundary marking or setting.
**alindar** tr. set landmarks to. 2 to embellish. 3 intr. LINDAR.
**alineación** f., **alineamiento** m. alignment, alinement.
**alineamiento** m. alignment, arrangement in a straight line, lining up; no ~, nonalignment.
**alinear** tr. to align, aline, put into line, range. 2 ref. to align, aline, fall in line, be in line.
**aliñar** tr. to adorn, dress, tidy. 2 to dress, season [food, drink]. 3 to prepare, arrange. 4 (Am.) to set [bones].
**aliño** m. adornment, tidiness. 2 dressing, seasoning. 3 arrangement.
**alioli** m. AJIACEITE.
**alípede** adj. poet. wing-footed, swift, fleet.
**alípedo, -da** adj. ALÍPEDE. 2 ZOOL. aliped.
**aliquebrado, -da** adj. broken-winged. 2 ALICAÍDO.
**alisador, -ra** adj. smoothing, polishing. 2 m.-f. smoother, polisher, planer.
**alisadura** f. smoothing, planing. 2 pl. shavings.
1) **alisar** tr. to smooth, slick, sleek. 2 to polish, plane; to surface. 3 ref. to become smooth.
2) **alisar** m. plantation of alder trees.
**alisios** adj. vientos ~, trade winds.
**alisma** f. BOT. water plantain.
**aliso** m. BOT. alder tree.
**alistado, -da** adj. enlisted, enrolled, recruited. 2 striped. 3 m. volunteer, recruit.

**alistamiento** *m.* enlistment, enrollment. *2* MIL. conscription. *3* conscripts of a year.
**alistar** *tr.-ref.* to enlist, enroll [a person]. *2* to prepare, make ready.
**aliteración** *f.* alliteration.
**aliterado, -da** *adj.* alliterate.
**aliviador, -ra** *adj.* alleviating, allaying, relieving. *2 m.-f.* alleviator, allayer, reliever. *3* helper.
**aliviar** *tr.* to lighten [make less heavy]. *2* to unburden. *3* to alleviate, allay, relieve, ease, assuage. *4* to hasten. *5 ref.* to ease up, subside. *6* to get better.
**alivio** *m.* alleviation, allay, relief, ease, assuagement, mitigation. *2* improvement [in an illness].
**aljaba** *f.* quiver [case for holding arrows].
**aljama** *f.* a Jewish or Moorish community in medieval Spain; a mosque, a synagogue.
**aljamía** *f.* Spanish written in Arabic characters.
**aljez** *m.* crude gypsum.
**aljibe** *m.* cistern; water tank. *2* NAUT. tank boat; tanker.
**aljofaina** *f.* washboul, washbasin, washhand basin.
**aljófar** *m.* seed pearl. *2* poet. drops of dew.
**aljofarar** *tr.* to adorn or cover with ALJÓFAR.
**aljofifa** *f.* mop [for floors].
**aljofifar** *tr.* to mop [floors].
**aljuba** *f.* a Moorish garment.
**alma** *f.* soul, spirit, ghost: ~ *de cántaro*, fig. senseless fool; ~ *de Dios*, fig. good soul; ~ *en pena*, soul in purgatory; fig. lonely, dejected person; ~ *mía, mi* ~, my dearest, my love; *entregar* or *rendir el* ~ *a Dios*, to die, give up the ghost; *estar con el* ~ *en un hilo*, fig. to have one's heart in one's mouth; to be on tenterhooks; *romper el* ~ *a uno*, fig. to break someone's head or neck; *como* ~ *que lleva el diablo*, as if the devil were after one; *con el* ~ *y la vida*, very willingly. *2* soul, person, inhabitant. *3* soul [leader, moving spirit]. *4* soul, strength, vigour. *5* bore [of a gun]. *6* core, heart [of a rope, a casting, etc.]. *7* web [of a rail, etc.]. *8* MUS. sound post.
**almacén** *m.* store, storehouse, warehouse, shop. *2* storeroom. *3* depot. *4* magazine, repository, reservoir. *5 pl.* department store.
**almacenaje** *m.* storage [charges].
**almacenamiento** *m.* storage, warehousing, keeping of goods. *2* supply, stock, goods available.
**almacenar** *tr.* to store, store up. *2* to hoard.
**almacenero** *m.* warehouse keeper.
**almacenista** *m.* storekeeper, wholesale merchant.
**almáciga** *f.* mastic. *2* seedbed [for later transplantation].
**almacigar** *tr.* to perfume with mastic.
**almácigo** *m.* ALMÁCIGA 2. *2* BOT. mastic tree.
**almádana, almádena** *f.* stone hammer.
**almadraba** *f.* tunny fishing or fishery. *2* net for catching tunnies.
**almadrabero** *m.* tunny fisher.
**almadreña** *f.* sabot, wooden shoe.
**almagesto** *m.* almagest.
**almagral** *m.* reddle deposit.
**almagrar** *tr.* reddle, ruddle. *2* to stigmatize.
**almagre** *m.* reddle, ruddle, red ocher.
**almajaneque** *m.* MAGANEL.
**almalafa** *f.* haik, haick.
**almanaque** *m.* almanac, calendar.
**almandina** *f.* MINER. almandine, almandite.
**almarada** *f.* triangular poniard.
**almarjal** *m.* marshy land.

**almarjo** *m.* any plant yielding barilla.
**almazara** *f.* oil mill.
**almea** *f.* alme, almeh. *2* storax; storax bark.
**almecina** *f.* hackberry, fruit of the nettle plant.
**almeja** *f.* ZOOL. quahog, round clam.
**almena** *f.* FORT. merlon.
**almenado, -da** *adj.* embattled, battlemented. *2 m.* FORT. battlement.
**almenaje** *m.* FORT. battlement.
**almenar** *tr.* FORT. to embattle, to crenel(l)ate.
**almenara** *f.* beacon, signal fire.
**almendra** *f.* BOT. almond: ~ *confitada*, sugar almond; ~ *garrapiñada*, praline. *2* BOT. kernel [of a drupe]. *3* cutglass drop. *4* coll, pebble.
**almendrado, -da** *adj.* almond-shaped. *2 m.* macaroon. *3 f.* almond milk.
**almendral** *m.* plantation of almond trees.
**almendro** *m.* BOT. almond tree.
**almendruco** *m.* green almond.
**almeriense** *adj.-n.* of Almería.
**almete** *m.* armet.
**almez** *m.* BOT. hackberry, nettle tree.
**almeza** *f.* hackberry [fruit].
**almezo** *m.* ALMEZ.
**almiar** *m.* haystack, straw stack.
**almíbar** *m.* syrup [as used in confectionery].
**almibarado, -da** *adj.* sugary, honeyed.
**almibarar** *tr.* to preserve in syrup. *2* to sweeten, honey [one's words].
**almidón** *m.* starch. *2* (Am.) paste [for gluing].
**almidonado, -da** *adj.* starched. *2* coll. spruce, dapper.
**almidonar** *tr.* to starch.
**almijar** *m.* place where olives and grapes are put to dry before pressing them.
**almilla** *f.* under waistcoat.
**alminar** *m.* minaret.
**almiranta** *f.* NAUT. obs. vice-admiral's ship. *2* admiral's wife.
**almirantazgo** *m.* NAV. court of Admiralty. *2* admiralship, admiralty.
**almirante** NAV. admiral.
**almirez** *m.* brass mortar.
**almizcate** *m.* space fo land between two houses.
**almizcle** *m.* musk [the substance].
**almizcleño, -ña** *adj.* musky. *2 f.* BOT. grapehyacinth.
**almizclera** *f.* ZOOL. musk rat.
**almizclero, -ra** *adj.* ALMIZCLEÑO. *2 m.* musk deer.
**almo, -ma** *adj.* nourishing, vivifying. *2* holy.
**almocafre** *m.* hoe, weeding hoe.
**almocárabe** *m.* ARCH. knotted ornament.
**almocela** *f.* hood.
**almocrí** *m.* reader of the Koran in a mosque.
**almófar** *m.* ARM. hood of mail, camail.
**almogávar** *m.* a medieval foot soldier or adventurer.
**almohada** *f.* pillow, bolster; cushion: *consultar con la* ~, to sleep on [something]. *2* pillowcase.
**almohadilla** *f.* small cushion, pad. *2* sewing cushion. *3* (Am.) pincushion. *4* ARCH. bulging front or cushion [in an ashlar].
**almohadillado, -da** *adj.* ARCH. cushioned. *2 m.* ARCH. bolsterwork.
**almohadón** *m.* cushion, large cushion. *2* ARCH. springer.
**almohaza** *f.* currycomb.
**almohazar** *tr.* to currycomb, curry [a horse].
**almojarifazgo** *m.* obs. former payment demanded by the government on certain goods imported or exported.

almóndiga, almondiguilla f. ALBÓNDIGA, ALBONDI-
GUILLA.
almoneda f. auction, auction sale. 2 bargain sale.
almonedar, almonedear tr. to sell by auction.
almoraduj, almoradux m. BOT. sweet marjoram.
almorávides m. Almoravides.
almorranas f. pl. MED. piles, haemorrhoids.
almorta f. BOT. bitter vetch.
almorzado, -da adj. having breakfasted.
almorzar intr. to breakfast, to lunch. 2 tr. to eat at
breakfast or lunch. ¶ CONJUNG. like contar.
almotacén m. inspector of weights and measures.
2 (Morocco) overseer of markets.
almud m. a dry measure.
almuecín, almuédano m. muezzin.
almuerzo m. breakfast, lunch.
almuerzo, almuerce, etc. irr. V. ALMORZAR.
alocación f. allocation, distribution, assignment.
alocadamente adv. wildly, recklessly.
alocado, -da adj. mad, foolish, wild, reckless.
alocución f. allocution, harangue, address.
alodio m. al(l)odium.
áloe m. BOT. aloe. 2 PHARM. aloes. 3 agalloch.
aloja f. drink made of water, honey and spices.
alojado m. MIL. billeted man. 2 (Am.) lodger, guest.
alojamiento m. lodging, quartering, billeting. 2
lodgings, lodgement, quarters, billet; housing.
alojar tr. to lodge, give lodgings, to house, to quarter, to billet. 2 ref. to lodge, lodge oneself or itself, to put up.
alomado, -da adj. ridged. 2 high-backed [horse].
alomar tr. to plough leaving wide ridges.
alón m. COOK. wing of fowl.
alondra f. ORN. lark, skylark.
Alonso pr. n. Alphonse.
alópata adj.-n. allopath, allopathist.
alopatía f. allopathy.
alopecia f. MED. alopecia.
aloque adj.-n. light red [wine].
alotropia f. CHEM. allotropy, allotropism.
alotrópico, -ca adj. allotropic.
alpaca f. ZOOL. alpaca. 2 alpaca [wool and cloth].
3 German silver.
alpargata f. rope-soled sandal.
alpargatería f. ALPARGATA shop or factory.
alpargatero, -ra m.-f. maker or seller of ALPARGA-
TAS.
alpargatilla f. crafty, artful, insinuating person.
alpechín m. dark, fetid liquid which runs from
piled-up olives before being pressed.
Alpes pr. n. GEOG. Alps.
alpestre adj. Alpestrine.
alpinismo m. alpinism.
alpinista m.-f. alpinist, alpestrian.
alpino, -na adj. alpine.
alpiste m. BOT. canary grass. 2 alpist, canary seed.
alquequenje m. BOT. winter cherry.
alquería f. grange, farmhouse.
alquilable adj. rentable, that may be rented or
hired.
alquiladizo, -za adj. for reñt, for hire. 2 adj.-n. hireling.
alquilador, -ra m.-f. hirer.
alquilar tr. to let, rent; to hire. 2 ref. to hire out,
serve for wages. 3 to be let or rented.
alquiler m. letting, renting. 2 rent, rental, hire
[price]. 3 de ~, for rent, for hire; hack, hackney.
alquimia f. alchemy.
alquimista m. alchemist.
alquitara f. ALAMBIQUE.

alquitarar tr. to distil. 2 fig. alquitarado, over refined, affected.
alquitrán m. tar; pitch: ~ mineral, coal tar.
alquitranado, -da adj. tarred, covered with tar. 2
m. NAUT. tarpaulin, tarred canvas. 3 m. tarring
[of the road, the roof, etc.]. 4 tarmac, tar and
gravel mixture used for paving roads, paths,
etc.
alquitranar tr. to tar.
alrededor adv. ~ de, around, about [on all sides of;
approximately]; a su ~, around or about him or
it. 2 m. pl. outskirts, surroundings.
Alsacia pr. n. GEOG. Alsace.
alsaciano, -na adj.-n. Alsatian.
alta f. an old court dance. 2 discharge [from hospital, etc]. 3 registration for fiscal purposes. 4
MIL. inscription in the muster book. 5 dar de ~,
to discharge [a patient from hospital, etc.]; MIL.
to enter or inscribe in the muster book. 6 darse
de ~, to register for fiscal purposes; to join [a
club, society, etc.].
altaico, -ca adj. altaic.
altamente adv. highly, strongly, extremely.
altanería f. haughtiness, arrogance. 2 falconry,
hawking.
altanero, -ra adj. haughty, arrogant. 2 flying high
[as a falcon].
altar m. altar; ~ mayor, high altar; el Sacramento
del ~, the Holy Eucharist. 2 altar stone.
altavoz m. RADIO. loudspeaker.
alterable adj. alterable, changeable.
alteración f. alteration, change. 2 unevenness [of
the pulse]. 3 strong emotion, agitation. 4 disturbance: ~ del orden público, breach of the peace.
alterado, -da adj. altered, changed. 2 disturbed,
agitated, upset.
alterar tr. to alter, change. 2 to excite, unsettle. 3
to disturb, upset. 4 ref. to become altered, changed, excited, disturbed, agitated.
altercación f., altercado m. altercation, dispute,
wrangle.
altercar tr. to altercate, dispute, wrangle.
alternación f. alternation.
alternadamente adv. ALTERNATIVAMENTE.
alternado, -da adj. alternate, altern.
alternador m. ELECT. alternator.
alternancia f. alternation, alternance.
alternante adj. alternating, alternate. 2 m. MATH.
alternant.
alternar tr.-intr. to alternate. 2 intr. to have social
intercourse, to mix.
alternativa f. alternative, option. 2 alternation. 3
admission of a bullfighter as a MATADOR.
alternativo, -va adj. alternate, alternating.
alterno, -na adj. alternate. 2 ELEC. alternating
[current]. 3 BOT., GEOM. alternate.
alteza f. height. 2 elevation, sublimity: ~ de miras,
high-mindedness. 3 Highness [a title].
altibajo m. FENC. downright blow. 2 pl. ups and
downs.
altilocuente; altilocuo, -cua adj. grandiloquent.
altillo m. hillock. 2 (Am.) garret.
altimetría f. altimetry.
altímetro m. altimeter.
altiplanicie f. plateau, tableland.
altiplano m. (Am.) high plateau, tableland.
altísimo, -ma adj. superl. of ALTO. 2 m. El Altísimo,
The Most High, God.
altisonancia f. pompousness, bombast.
altisonante, altísono, -na adj. altisonant, high
sounding, bombastic.

**altitud** *f.* height [above ground, from base to top, in the air]. *2* GEOG. altitude [above sea level].

**altivecer** *tr.* to make haughty. *2 ref.* to become haughty.

**altivez, altiveza** *f.* haughtiness, arrogance, pride.

**altivo, -va** *adj.* haughty, arrogant, proud, lofty.

**alto, -ta** *adj.* high: ~ *precio*, high price; ~ *relieve*, high relief, alto-relievo; *alta mar*, high seas; *alta traición*, high treason; *lo* ~, the top; *de lo* ~, from above. *2* tall. *3* upper: ~ *Egipto*, Upper Egypt. *4* [of things] elevated, noble, excellent. *5* [of time] high, late, advanced. *6* ACCUST. high, loud. *7* ~ *hornos*, blast furnace. *8 m.* high: *un metro de* ~, a metre high. *9* height, hillock, eminence. *10* storey, floor [of a house]. *11* MUS. viola. *12* halt, stop: *dar el* ~, to call to a halt, stop. *13 altos y bajos*, ups and downs. *14 adv.* high, on high, raised: *en* ~, on high, raised. *15* loudly. *16 interj.* halt!, stop!: ¡*alto ahí!*, stop there!

**altoparlante** *m.* (Am.) loudspeaker.

**altozano** *m.* height, hill. *2* highest part of a town.

**altramuz** *m.* BOT. lupine.

**altruismo** *m.* altruism.

**altruista** *adj.* altruistic.

**altura** *f.* height, hillock. *2* height, tallness. *3* summit, top. *4* elevation, excellence. *5* altitude [above sea level]. *6* ASTR., GEOM. altitude. *7* GEOM. height. *8* MUS. pitch. *9* NAUT. latitude. *10 a la* ~ *de*, opposite; on the same level as; *estar a la* ~ *de*, to be equal to [a task, etc.]. *11* NAUT. *de* ~, sea-going. *12 pl.* heights. *13* heavens. *14 a estas alturas*, at this point or juncture.

**alubia** *f.* BOT. bean, French bean.

**alucinación** *f.* hallucination.

**alucinador, -ra** *adj.* hallucinating, fascinating, deluding. *2 m.-f.* hallucinator, deluder.

**alucinante** *adj.* hallucinating, hallucinatory.

**alucinar** *tr.* to hallucinate. *2* to fascinate, delude. *3 ref.* to delude oneself.

**alucinógeno, -na** *adj.* hallucinogenic. *2 m.* hallucinogen.

**alud** *m.* avalanche, snowslip.

**aluda** *f.* ENT. winged ant.

**aludido, -da** *adj.* mentioned, talked about, above mentioned. *2 darse por* ~, to consider oneself object of allusion, to get the hint, to take it personal.

**aludir** *intr.* to allude, refer to, hint at.

**alumbrado, -da** *p. p.* of ALUMBRAR. *2 adj.* coll. tipsy. *3 m.* lighting, lights.

**alumbramiento** *m.* illumination, enlightening. *2* drawing out of subterranean waters. *3* childbirth.

**alumbrar** *tr.* to light, illuminate. *2* to light the way [for someone]. *4* to illuminate, enlighten. *5* to give or launch [a blow]. *7* to alum. *8 intr.* to shed light. *9* to be delivered of a child. *10 ref.* to get tipsy.

**alumbre** *m.* alum: ~ *de pluma*, feather alum.

**alúmina** *f.* CHEM. alumina, alumine.

**aluminio** *m.* CHEM. aluminium, aluminum.

**aluminita** *f.* MINER. aluminite.

**alumnado** *m.* pupils [in school] students, student body [in university].

**alumno, -na** *m.-f.* pupil, scholar, alumnus.

**alunado, -da** *adj.* whimsical, quaint, fanciful. *2* lunatic, mad, insane, extremely foolish.

**alunarse** *ref.* [of bacon] to become spoiled.

**alunizaje** *m.* landing on the moon.

**alunizar** *intr.* to land on the moon.

**alusión** *f.* allusion, reference, hint, mention.

**alusivo, -va** *adj.* allusive, hinting.

**aluvial** *adj.* alluvial.

**aluvión** *f.* alluvion. *2* alluvium, silt, wash.

**álveo** *m.* channel, bed, runway [of a stream].

**alveolado** *adj.* honeycombed, faveolate, alveolate.

**alveolar** *adj.* alveolar, alveolary.

**alvéolo** *m.* alveole, alveolus.

**alverja, alverjana** *f.* ARVEJA. *2* (Am.) GUISANTE.

**alza** *f.* advance, rise, lift [in prices]. *2* PRINT. overlay. *3* FIREARMS. leaf sight, rear sight. *4* flashboard.

**alzacuello** *m.* neck stock.

**alzada** *f.* height, stature [of horses]. *2* appeal to a higher administrative body or official.

**alzadamente** *adv.* for a lump sum.

**alzado, -da** *adj.* lump [sum]: *por un tanto* ~, for a lump sum. *2 m.* ARCH., DRAW. elevation. *3* BOOKBIND. gathering.

**alzamiento** *m.* raising, lifting. *2* uprising, insurrection. *3* ~ *de bienes*, fraudulent bankruptcy.

**alzapaño** *m.* curtain holder or loop.

**alzaprima** *f.* lever, pry, crowbar. *2* wedge [for raising something]. *3* MUS. bridge.

**alzaprimar** *tr.* to lever, pry [raise with a lever].

**alzar** *tr.* to raise, lift, hoist, uplift, heave. *2* to elevate [the Host]. *3* to erect, build. *4* to remove, carry off. *5* to clear [the table]. *6* to gather [a crop]. *7* to strike [tents]. *8* PRINT. to gather [signatures for binding]. *9* ~ *el vuelo*, to take wing. *10* ~ *velas*, to set sail; to flee, depart. *11 ref.* to rise; to get up, stand up. *12* to rise, rebel. *13* LAW to appeal. *14 alzarse con*, to appropriate, to run away with.

**allá** *adv.* there [in or at that place]: *más* ~, farther; *el más* ~, the Beyond, the future life; *por* ~, thereabouts. *2* ~ *en Francia*, over in France; ~ *por el año 1800*, about 1800; ~ *veremos*, we shall see; ~ *vosotros*, that's up to you; that's your lookout.

**allanamiento** *m.* levelling, smoothing, razing. *2* submission, consent. *3* LAW ~ *de morada*, forcing an entry into a house.

**allanar** *tr.* to level, smooth, flatten. *2* to raze, level to the ground. *3* to smooth out [difficulties, etc.]. *4* to pacify, subdue. *5* to force an entry into [a house]. *7 ref.* [of a building] to tumble down. *8* to yield, submit, consent.

**allegado, -da** *adj.* near, related, allied. *2 m.-f.* relative, friend; follower.

**allegar** *tr.* to gather, raise, collect. *2* to put [a thing] near another. *3* to add.

**allende** *adv.* on the other side. *2 prep.* beyond, over.

**allí** *adv.* there, in that place, yonder: ~ *mismo*, in that very place; *por* ~, that way; there, thereabouts. *2* then, at that moment.

**allozo** *m.* BOT. almond tree. *2* wild almond tree.

**ama** *f.* mistress, lady of the house: ~ *de casa*, housewife. *2* mistress, owner. *3* ~ *de gobierno*, or *de llaves*, housekeeper. *4* nurse [of a child]: ~ *de leche*, wet nurse; ~ *seca*, dry nurse.

**amabilidad** *f.* kindness, affability, amiability.

**amable** *adj.* kind, affable, nice, amiable, obliging. *2* lovable.

**amachetear** *tr.* to strike with a machete.

**Amadeo** *m. pr. n.* Amadeus.

**amado, -da** *m.-f.* love, loved one, beloved.

**amador, -ra** *m.-f.* lover.

**amadrinar** *tr.* to act as godmother to, to sponsor. *2* to couple [horses]. *3* NAUT. to join or couple [two things].

**amaestrado, -da** *adj.* taught, trained, drilled.

**amaestramiento** *m.* teaching, training, drill.
**amaestrar** *tr.* to teach, coach, train, drill.
**amagar** *tr.* to threaten, to show intention of [doing something]. *2 intr.* to threaten, impend, to show signs or symptoms.
**amago** *m.* threatening gesture, feint. *2* sign, hint, symptom.
**amainar** *tr.* NAUT. to lower or shorten [the sails]. *2 intr.* [of wind, anger, etc.] to abate, subside, die down. *3* to relax.
**amaine** *m.* NAUT. lowering [the sails]. *2* abating, subsiding, dying down.
**amajadar** *tr.* to fold [land] with sheep. *2* to fold [sheep] on a land. *3 intr.* [of sheep] to have fold in.
**amalecita** *adj.-n.* amalekite.
**amalgama** *f.* amalgam.
**amalgamación** *f.* amalgamation.
**amalgamiento** *m.* amalgamating.
**amalgamar** *tr.* CHEM. to amalgamate. *2* to amalgamate, mix.
**amamantamiento** *m.* nursing, suckling, lactation.
**amamantar** *tr.* to nurse, suckle, lactate.
**amán** *m.* in Morocco, pardon, amnesty.
**amancebamiento** *m.* concubinage.
**amancebarse** *ref.* to enter into concubinage.
1) **amanecer** *intr.* to dawn, to get light. *2* to be, or appear [at or in some place or state] at dawn. ¶ CONJUG. like *agradecer*.
2) **amanecer** *m.*, **amanecida** *f.* dawn, dawning, daybreak: *al ~*, at dawn.
**amaneradamente** *adv.* affectedly, in a manneristic way.
**amanerado, -da** *adj.* mannered, affected.
**amaneramiento** *m.* mannerism; affectation.
**amanerarse** *ref.* to fall into mannerism; to be or become affected.
**amanezco, amanezca**, etc. *irr.* V. AMANECER.
**amanita** *f.* BOT. amanita.
**amanojar** *tr.* to bunch, gather in a handful.
**amansador, -ra** *m.-f.* tamer. *3* (Am.) horsebreaker.
**amansamiento** *m.* taming subduing; appeasing.
**amansar** *tr.* to tame, domesticate. *2* to tame, subdue, soften. *3 ref.* to become tame; to soften [in character].
**amante** *adj.* loving, fond. *2 m.-f.* lover. *3* paramour; mistress. *4 m.* NAUT. pendant.
**amantillo** *m.* NAUT. lift.
**amanuense** *m.* amanuensis, clerk.
**amañado, -da** *adj.* skilful, clever, crafty. *2* fake. *3* fixed, rigged [a contest, a fight].
**amañar** *tr.* to arrange artfully, to cook, to fake. *2 ref.* to manage.
**amaño** *m.* cleverness, skill. *2* artifice, trick. *3 pl.* tools, implements. *4* machinations.
**amapola** *f.* BOT. red poppy, corn poppy.
**amar** *tr.* to love. *2* to like, be fond of.
**amaraje** *m.* AER. alighting on water.
**amarantina** BOT. globe amaranth.
**amaranto** *m.* BOT. amaranth.
**amarar** *tr.* AER. to alight on water.
**amargado, -da** *adj.-n.* embittered, soured [person].
**amargamente** *adv.* bitterly.
**amargar** *intr.* to taste bitter. *2 tr.* to embitter. *3* to spoil [an evening, a feast, etc.]. *4 ref.* to become embittered, to sour.
**amargo, -ga** *adj.* bitter [tasting bitter; painful; expressing pain or grief]. *2* sour [temper]. *3 s.* bitterness. *4* bitters [liquor].
**amargón** *m.* BOT. dandelion.

**amargor** *m.* AMARGURA. *2* bitterness. *3* sorrow, grief.
**amargura** *f.* bitterness. *2* sorrow, grief.
**amaricado, -da; amariconado, -da** *adj.* coll. effeminate, queer.
**amarilidáceas** *f. pl.* BOT. Amaryllidaceae.
**amarillear** *intr.* to show yellow, to be yellowish. *2* to pale.
**amarillecer** *intr.* to yellow, turn yellow.
**amarillento, -ta** *adj.* yellowish. *2* sallow, pale.
**amarilleo** *m.* showing yellow; yellowishness.
**amarillez** *f.* yellowness. *2* sallowness, paleness.
**amarillo, -lla** *adj.* yellow. *2* sallow, pale. *3 m.* yellow colour.
**amariposado, -da** *adj.* papilionaceous.
**amarro** *m.* BOT. clary.
**amarra** *f.* martingale [for horses]. *2* NAUT. mooring cable, fast. *3 pl.* friends at court, protection.
**amarradero** *m.* fastening or mooring post, ring, etc. *2* NAUT. moorings.
**amarrado, -da** *adj.* fig. tied down.
**amarradura** *f.* tying. *2* NAUT. circumvolution. *3* mooring.
**amarraje** *m.* NAUT. moorage [charge for mooring].
**amarrar** *tr.* to tie, fasten, rope. *2* NAUT. to moor [a ship].
**amarre** *m.* NAUT., AER. mooring, fastening.
**amartelado, -da** *adj.* infatuated, in love, starry-eyed.
**amartelamiento** *m.* making love. *2* absorption [of lovers in each other].
**amartelar** *tr.* to make jealous. *2* to make love to. *3* to charm, enamour. *4 ref.* to fall in love.
**amartillar** *tr.* MARTILLAR. *2* to cock [a gun, a pistol].
**amasadera** *f.* kneading trough.
**amasamiento** *m.* kneading; mixing. *2* MED. massage.
**amasar** *tr.* to knead, mould, mix. *2* to amass. *3* MED. to massage. *4* to arrange [matters] for some purpose.
**amasijo** *m.* batch of dough. *2* kneading, mixing. *3* mixed material; medley. *4* plot, machination.
**amatista** *f.* MINER. amethyst.
**amatorio, -ria** *adj.* amatorial, amatory.
**amaurosis** *f.* MED. amaurosis.
**amazacotado, -da** *adj.* heavy, thick, clumsy.
**amazona** *f.* MYTH. Amazon. *2* a courageous woman. *3* horsewoman, lady rider. *4* habit, riding habit.
**Amazonas** *pr. n.* GEOG. Amazon [river].
**amazónico, -ca** *adj.* Amazonian.
**ambages** *m. pl.* ambages: *hablar sin ~*, to speak plainly.
**ámbar** *m.* amber: *~ gris*, amber, ambergris. *2 ~ negro*, jet.
**ambarino, -na** *adj.* amber, amber-like.
**Amberes** *pr. n.* GEOG. Antwerp.
**ambición** *f.* ambition.
**ambicionar** *tr.* to desire ambitiously.
**ambicioso, -sa** *adj.* ambitious.
**ambidextro, -tra** *adj.* ambidexter, ambidextrous.
**ambientación** *f.* atmosphere, environment. *2* setting, scene. *3* RADIO. sound effects.
**ambiental** *adj.* environmental.
**ambientar** *tr.* to give an appropriate atmosphere or setting to.
**ambiente** *adj.-m.* ambient. *2 m.* atmosphere, environment, setting.
**ambigú** *m.* buffet [at a party, dance, etc.]. *2* bar [in a theater, etc.].
**ambiguamente** *adv.* ambiguously.
**ambigüedad** *f.* ambiguity, ambiguousness.

**ambiguo, -gua** *adj.* ambiguous.
**ámbito** *m.* circuit, compass, field, area, precinct.
**ambivalencia** *f.* ambivalence.
**ambivalente** *adj.* ambivalent.
**ambladura** *f.* ambling [of horses].
**amblar** *tr.* [of animals] to amble, to pace.
**ambo** *m.* two-number combination in lotto.
**ambón** *m.* ambo [a reading pulpit].
**ambos, bas** *adj.-pron.* both: ~ *a dos*, both, both together.
**ambrosía** *f.* ambrosia. *2* BOT. ragweed.
**ambrosíaco, -ca** *adj.* ambrosial.
**Ambrosio** *pr. n.* Ambrose.
**ambulancia** *f.* ambulance. *2* ~ *de correos*, RLY. mail car, *postal car.
**ambulante** *adj.* ambulatory, itinerant, walking, travelling. *2 m.* ~ *de correos*, railway mail clerk.
**ambulatorio, -ria** *adj.* MED. ambulatory.
**ameba** *f.* AMIBA.
**amedrentamiento** *m.* fright, fear, terror.
**amedrentar** *tr.* to frighten, scare, intimidate.
**amelocotonado, -da** *adj.* peachy.
**amén** *m.* amen, so be it. *2* ~ *de*, excepting, save; besides, not to mention.
**amenaza** *f.* threat, menace.
**amenazador, -a** *adj.* threatening, menacing, lowering.
**amenazar** *tr.* to threaten, menace. *2 intr.* to be impending.
**amenguar** *tr.* to diminish, lessen. *2* to dishonour, disgrace.
**amenidad** *f.* amenity, pleasantness.
**amenizar** *tr.* to render pleasant, to brighten. *2* to adorn [a speech, etc.].
**ameno, -na** *adj.* agreeable, pleasant, delightful.
**amenorrea** *f.* MED. amenorrhœa.
**amentáceo, -a; amentífero, -ra** *adj.* BOT. amentaceous or amentiferous.
**amento** *m.* BOT. ament, catkin.
**ameos** *m.* BOT. bishop's weed.
**amerengado, -da** *adj.* meringue-like. *2* fig. sugary, syrupy.
**América** *pr. n.* GEOG. America.
**americana** *f.* coat, sack coat [of a man's suit].
**americanismo** *m.* Americanism.
**americanista** *n.* americanist.
**americanización** *f.* americanization.
**americano, -na** *adj.-n.* American.
**amerindio, -a** *adj.* amerindian. *2 n.* american indian, amerind.
**amerizaje** *m.* landing on the sea. *2* splashdown, landing of a spacecraft in the sea.
**amerizar** *int.* to land on the sea. *2* to splashdown [a spacecraft].
**amestizado, -da** *adj.* like a half-breed or half-caste.
**ametralladora** *f.* machine gun.
**ametrallar** *tr.* to shrapnel. *2* to machine-gun.
**amianto** *m.* amianthus, earth flax, asbestos.
**amiba** *f.*, **amibo** *m.* ZOOL. amœba.
**amida** *f.* CHEM. amide.
**amiga** *f.* friend [female f.]. *2* mistress, concubine.
**amigable** *adj.* amicable, friendly. *2* LAW ~ *componedor*, arbitrator.
**amigacho** *m.* AMIGOTE.
**amigar** *tr.-ref.* AMISTAR. *2 ref.* AMANCEBARSE.
**amígdala** *f.* tonsil, amygdala.
**amigdaláceo, -a** *adj.* BOT. amygdalaceous.
**amigdalitis** *f.* MED. tonsilitis.
**amigo, -ga** *adj.* friendly. *2* fond of or advocating [something]. *3 m.-f.* friend: ~ *del alma*, bosom

friend; *hacerse* ~ *de*, to make friends with. *4* paramour [man].
**amigote** *m.* coll. friend, pal.
**amiláceo, -a** *adj.* amilaceous.
**amilanamiento** *m.* daunting. *2* spiritlessness.
**amilanar** *tr.* to daunt, cow. *2 ref.* to be daunted.
**amilasa** *f.* BIOL. amylase.
**Amílcar** *pr. n.* Hamilcar.
**amílico, -ca** *adj.* CHEM. amylic.
**amilo** *m.* CHEM. amyl.
**amillarar** *tr.* to assess [property] for taxes.
**aminorar** *tr.* MINORAR.
**amistad** *f.* friendship. *2* amity. *3* favour, good graces. *4* concubinage. *5 pl.* friends. *6 hacer las amistades*, to make up, to become reconciled.
**amistar** *tr.* to make [others] friends. *2* to reconcile. *3 ref.* to become friends. *4* to be reconciled.
**amistoso, -sa** *adj.* friendly, amicable.
**amito** *m.* amice.
**amnesia** *f.* MED. amnesia.
**amnios** *f.* ANAT., ZOOL. amnion.
**amnistía** *f.* amnesty.
**amnistiar** *tr.* to amnesty.
**amo** *m.* master [of a house], lord, owner. *2* master [of servants]; boss.
**amoblar** *tr.* to furnish, fit up with furniture. ¶ CONJUG. like *contar*.
**amodorrado, -da** *adj.* drowsy, sleepy.
**amodorramiento** *m.* drowsiness, sleepiness.
**amodorrarse** *ref.* to drowse, become drowsy.
**amojamar** *tr.* to salt and dry [tunny fish]. *2 ref.* ACECINARSE.
**amojonar** *tr.* to set landmarks marks to.
**amoladera** *f.* whetstone, grindstone.
**amolador** *m.* whetter, knife grinder or sharpener.
**amoladura** *f.* whetting, grinding, sharpening.
**amolar** *tr.* to whet, grind, sharpen. *2* to bother, annoy. ¶ CONJUG. like *contar*.
**amoldamiento** *m.* mo(u)lding, modelling, adjusting, adapting.
**amoldar** *tr.* to mo(u)ld, shape, model, adapt, adjust. *2 ref.* to adjust, adapt oneself.
**amomo** *m.* BOT. amomum. *2* grains of Paradise.
**amonedar** *tr.* to monetize, coin.
**amonestación** *f.* admonition, reproof, warning. *2 pl.* marriage banns.
**amonestar** *tr.* to admonish, reprove, warn. *2* to publish banns of, to ask.
**amoniacal** *adj.* ammoniacal.
**amoníaco** *m.* CHEM. ammonia. *2* ammoniac.
**amonio** *m.* CHEM. ammonium.
**amonita** *f.* ZOOL. ammonite. *2 m.-f.* BIBL. Ammonite.
**amontillado** *m.* pale dry sherry.
**amontonamiento** *m.* heaping, accumulation, pile, heap. *2* crowding [of people].
**amontonar** *tr.* to heap, pile, accumulate; to crowd. *2 ref.* to heap, be piled; to crowd, throng. *3* to fly into a passion.
**amor** *m.* love: ~ *mío*, my love; ~ *propio*, amour propre, pride; *hacer el* ~ *a*, to woo, court; *al* ~ *del agua*, with the current; *al* ~ *del fuego*, or *de la lumbre*, by the fire, at the fireside; *por* ~ *de*, for the sake of. *2* care, careful attention [in work]. *3 pl.* love, love affair: *mal de amores*, love sickness; *requerir de amores*, to woo. *4* willingness: *con*, or *de mil amores*, willingly. *5* BOT. hedgehog parsley.
**amoral** *adj.* amoral.
**amoratado, -da** *adj.* purplish. *2* livid, black-and-blue.

**amorcillo** *m.* dim. of AMOR. *2* F. ARTS cupid.
**amordazar** *tr.* to gag, muzzle.
**amorfo, -fa** *adj.* amorphous.
**amorío** *m.* love affair, amour.
**amormío** *m.* BOT. sea daffodil.
**amoroso, -sa** *adj.* loving, amorous, tender, affectionate; gentle. *2* love, of love.
**amortajar** *tr.* to shroud [a corpse], to dress for burial.
**amortecer** *tr.* to deaden. *2 ref.* to swoon, faint. ¶ CONJUG. like *agradecer.*
**amortiguador, -ra** *adj.* deadening, muffling, softening, damping. *2 m.* deadener, muffler. *3* MACH. shock absorber, buffer. *4* ELECT. damper.
**amortiguamiento** *m.* deadening, muffling, softening, damping.
**amortiguar** *tr.* to deaden [a blow, etc.], to muffle [a sound]; to lessen, soften, tone down. *2* to absorb [a shock]. *3* ELECT. to damp.
**amortización** *f.* amortization.
**amortizable** *adj.* amortizable.
**amortizar** *tr.* to amortize.
**amoscarse** *ref.* to get angry, take offence.
**amostazar** *tr.* to anger, irritate. *2 ref.* to get angry or irritated.
**amotinado, -da** *m.-f.* mutineer, rioter.
**amotinador, -ra** *m.-f.* mutineer, inciter to rebellion.
**amotinamiento** *m.* mutiny.
**amotinar** *tr.* to mutiny, incite to rebellion. *2 ref.* to mutiny, rebel.
**amovible** *adj.* removable.
**amparador, -ra** *adj.* protecting. *2 m.-f.* protector.
**amparar** *tr.* to protect, shelter, help, support. *2 ref.* to shelter, protect oneself; to avail oneself of the protection [of].
**amparo** *m.* protection, shelter, help, support: *al ~ de,* under cover of, protected by.
**amperímetro** *m.* ammeter, amperemeter.
**amperio** *m.* ELECT. ampere.
**ampliación** *f.* enlargement, ampliation, extension. *2* PHOT. enlargement.
**ampliador, -ra** *adj.* enlarging. *2 m.-f.* enlarger. *3 f.* PHOT. enlarger [camera].
**ampliamente** *adv.* largely, extensively.
**ampliar** *tr.* to enlarge, amplify, extend.
**amplificación** *f.* enlargement, amplification. *2* RHET. amplification.
**amplificador, -ra** *adj.* enlarging, amplifying. *2 m.-f.* enlarger, amplifier. *3* PHYS. amplifier.
**amplificar** *tr.* to enlarge, amplify, extend, magnify.
**amplio, -plia** *adj.* ample, extensive. *2* spacious, roomy, wide. *3* large, plentiful.
**amplísimo, -ma** *adj.* superl. of AMPLIO.
**amplitud** *f.* amplitude, extent. *2* ASTR., PHYS. amplitude.
**ampo** *s.* shining whiteness. *2* snowflake.
**ampolla** *f.* blister [on the skin]. *2* water bubble. *3* round-bellied bottle. *4* cruet. *5* MED. ampoule.
**ampollar** *tr.* to blister. *2* to make hollow. *3 ref.* to become blistered. *4* to bubble out.
**ampolleta** *f.* phial, smal cruet. *2* hourglass, sandglass.
**ampulosidad** *f.* turgidness, pompousness.
**ampuloso, -sa** *adj.* turgid, inflated, pompous.
**amputación** *adj.* amputation.
**amputar** *tr.* to amputate.
**Amsterdam** *pr. n.* GEOG. Amsterdam.
**amuchachado, -da** *adj.* boyish, childish.
**amueblar** *tr.* AMOBLAR.

**amueblo, amueble,** etc. *irr.* V. AMOBLAR.
**amuelar** *tr.* to gather grain into a pile.
**amulatado, -da** *adj.* mulatto-like.
**amuleto** *m.* amulet.
**amura** *f.* NAUT. bow [part of the side of a vessel]. *2* NAUT. tack [rope].
**amurada** *f.* NAUT. interior side of a ship.
**amurallar** *tr.* to wall [defend with walls].
**amusgar** *tr.* [of a horse, a bull, etc.] to throw back [the ears]. *2* to half-close [the eyes] to see better.
**Ana** *pr. n.* Ann, Anne, Hannah.
**ana** *f.* ell [a measure].
**anabaptismo** *m.* Anabaptism.
**anabaptista** *adj.-n.* Anabaptist.
**anacarado, -da** *adj.* pearly, pearl-coloured, like mother-of-pearl.
**anacardo** *m.* BOT. cashew. *2* cashew nut.
**anaconda** *f.* ZOOL. anaconda.
**anacoreta** *m.* anchoret, anchorite, hermit.
**Anacreonte** *m. pr. n.* Anacreon.
**anacreóntico, -ca** *adj.* Anacreontic.
**anacrónico, -ca** *adj.* anachronic, anachronistic.
**anacronismo** *m.* anachronism.
**ánade** *m.* ORN. duck, drake.
**anadear** *intr.* to waddle.
**anaerobio, -bia** *adj.* BIOL. anaerobic. *2 m.* anaerobe.
**anafe** *m.* portable cooker.
**anafilaxis** *f.* MED., BIOL. anaphylaxis.
**anafrodisíaco, -ca** *adj.-m.* anaphrodisiac.
**anáglifo** *m.* anaglyph.
**anagoge** *m.,* **anagogía** *f.* anagoge.
**anagrama** *f.* anagram.
**anal** *adj.* ZOOL. anal.
**analectas** *f. pl.* analects, analecta.
**anales** *m. pl.* annals.
**analfabetismo** *m.* illiteracy.
**analfabeto, -ta** *adj.-m.* illiterate.
**analgesia** *f.* MED. analgesia.
**analgésico, -ca** *adj.-m.* analgesic.
**análisis** *m.* analysis. *2* GRAM. parsing.
**analista** *m.* analyst. *2* annalist.
**analítico, -ca** *adj.* analytic(al).
**analizable** *adj.* analysable, analyzable.
**analizar** *tr.* to analyse, analyze. *2* GRAM. to parse.
**analogía** *f.* analogy. *2* GRAM. part of grammar studying parts of speech as such.
**analógico, -ca** *adj.* analogous. *2* GRAM. pertaining to ANALOGIA 2.
**análogo, -ga** *adj.* analogous, similar, parallel.
**Anam** *pr. n.* GEOG. Annam.
**anamita** *adj.-n.* Annamese.
**ananá, ananás** *f.* BOT. pineapple, ananas.
**anapesto** *m.* PROS. anapaest.
**anaquel** *m.* shelf [on a wall, in a cabinet, etc.].
**anaquelería** *f.* shelving, shelves.
**anaranjado, -da** *adj.* orange-coloured. *2* orange [colour].
**anarquía** *f.* anarchy.
**anárquico, -ca** *adj.* anarchic(al).
**anarquismo** *m.* anarchism.
**anarquista** *adj.-n.* anarchist. *2 adj.* anarchistic.
**anastasia** *f.* BOT. mugwort.
**anastomosis** *f.* ANAT., BOT. anastomosis.
**anatema** *m.-f.* anathema.
**anatematizar** *tr.* to anathematize.
**anatomía** *f.* anatomy.
**anatómico, -ca** *adj.* anatomical.
**anatomista** *m.* anatomist.
**anatomizar** *tr.* to anatomize.

**anca** *f.* haunch. *2* croup [in horses]: *a (las) ancas,* pillion riding [on horseback]. *3* hip [in men].

**ancianidad** *f.* old age.

**anciano, -na** *adj.* old, aged. *2 m.-f.* old man, woman or person; ancient; elder.

**ancla** *f.* NAUT. anchor: ~ *de leva,* bower anchor, bower; ~ *de la esperanza,* sheet or waist anchor; *sobre el* ~, at anchor.

**ancladero** *m.* NAUT. anchorage [anchoring place].

**anclaje** *m.* NAUT. anchorage.

**anclar** *intr.* to anchor, cast anchor.

**anclote** *m.* kedge anchor, kedge.

**ancón** *m.* little bay, cove. *2* (Am.) corner, nook.

**áncora** *f.* ANCLA. *2* HOROL. anchor.

**ancusa** *f.* BOT. bugloss, alkanet.

**ancho, -cha** *adj.* broad, wide. *2* too broad or wide. *3* loose fitting [garment, etc.]. *4* lax, elastic [conscience]. *5 m.* breadth, width: ~ *de vía,* gauge. *6 f. pl. a sus anchas,* free, comfortable, at one's ease.

**anchoa, anchova** *f.* ICHTH. anchovy.

**anchor** *m.* ANCHURA.

**anchura** *f.* breadth, width. *2* freedom, ease, comfort.

**anchuroso, -sa** *adj.* broad, wide, spacious.

**andadas** *f. pl.* traces [of game]. *2 volver a las andadas,* to go back to one's old tricks.

**andaderas** *f. pl.* gocart for learning to walk.

**andadero, -ra** *adj.* [of ground] easy. *2* gadding about.

**andador, -ra** *adj.* good at walking. *2* gadding about. *3 m.* good walker. *4* gadabout. *5* messenger. *6 pl.* leading strings.

**andadura** *f.* galt, pace. *2 paso de* ~, amble.

**Andalucía** *pr. n.* GEOG. Andalusia.

**andaluz, -za** *adj.-n.* Andalusian.

**andaluzada** *f.* exaggeration.

**andamiaje** *m.* scaffolding.

**andamio** *m.* scaffold [for workmen or spectators].

**andana** *f.* row, tier. *2 llamarse* ~, to go back on one's word.

**andanada** *f.* NAUT. broadside [discharge]. *2* reprimand. *3* covered, grandstand in bull-ring.

**andante** *adj.* walking. *2* errant [knight]. *3* MUS. andante.

**andanza** *f.* event. *2* [good or bad] fortune. *3 pl.* adventures.

1) **andar** *intr.* to walk, to go, to move; to ride: ~ *a gatas,* to go on all fours; ~ *a caballo, en coche,* to ride on horseback, in a carriage. *2* [of a clock] to go; [of a machine] to run, to work. *3* to be: ~ *enfermo,* to be ill; ~ *con cuidado,* to be careful. *4* to tamper, touch, handle. | With *con* or *en.* *5* NAUT. to sail. *6* Other senses: ~ *a derechas,* to act uprightly; ~ *en los treinta años,* to be about thirty; ~ *en los negocios,* to be engaged in business; *andando el tiempo,* in the course of time; *a todo* ~, at full speed; *¡anda!,* go on!, move ahead!; gracious! *7 tr.* to walk, cover [a distance]. *8 ref. andarse con,* to employ, indulge in. *9 andarse por las ramas,* to beat about the bush. ¶ CONJUG.: INDIC. Pret.: *anduve, anduviste, anduvo; anduvimos, anduvisteis, anduvieron.* | SUBJ. Imperf.: *anduviera, anduvieras, anduviera; anduviéramos, anduvierais, anduvieran,* or *anduviese, anduvieses,* etc. | Fut.: *anduviere, anduvieres,* etc.

2) **andar** *m.* gait, pace: *a largo* ~, in the long run.

**andariego, -ga** *adj.* good at walking. *2* gadding about.

**andarín** *m.* good walker.

**andarivel** *m.* ferry cable. *2* NAUT. safety rope.

**andas** *f. pl.* bier. *2* stretcher, portable plataform: *en* ~ in triumph.

**andén** *m.* platform [of a railway station]. *2* banquette [of bridge]. *3* footwalk. *4* quay.

**Andes** *pr. n.* GEOG. Andes.

**andino, -na** *adj.* Andean.

**andorga** *f.* coll, belly.

**Andorra** *pr. n.* GEOG. Andorra.

**andorra** *f.* gadder, gadabout [woman].

**andorrano, -na** *adj.-n.* Andorran.

**andorrear** *intr.* to gad about.

**andorrero, -ra** *adj.* gadabout. *2 m.-f.* gadder.

**andrajo** *m.* rag, tatter. *2* despicable person or thing.

**andrajoso, -sa** *adj.* ragged, in rags, in tatters.

**Andrés** *pr. n.* Andrew.

**androceo** *m.* BOT. andrœcium.

**andrógino, -na** *adj.* BIOL. androgynous, androgyne. *2 n.* BIOL. androgyne.

**androide** *m.* android.

**Andrómaca** *f. pr. n.* Andromache.

**Andrómeda** *f. pr. n.* ASTR. Andromeda.

**andrómina** *f.* humbug, artifice, lie.

**andullo** *m.* rolled tobacco leaf. *2* NAUT. canvas shield on harpings and blocks.

**andurriales** *m. pl.* out-of-the-way places.

**anduve, anduviera, anduviese,** etc., *irr.* V. ANDAR.

**anea** *f.* BOT. cattail, cattail flag, rush.

**aneblar** *tr.* to befog. *2* to cloud, darken. *3 ref.* to become foggy or cloudy. ¶ CONJUG. like *acertar.*

**anécdota** *f.* anecdote.

**anecdótico, -ca** *adj.* anecdotical.

**anegadizo, -za** *adj.* frequently inundated.

**anegar** *tr.* to flood, overflow, inundate. *2* to drown. *3 ref.* to be inundated. *4* to drown; to sink.

**anejar** *tr.* ANEXAR.

**anejo, -ja** *adj.* ANEXO. *2 m.* sucursal church. *3* hamlet annexed to a town.

**anélido** *m.* ZOOL. annelid.

**anemia** *f.* anaemia, anemia.

**anémico, -ca** *adj.* anaemic, anemic.

**anemófilo, -la** *adj.* BOT. anemophilous.

**anemómetro** *m.* anemometer.

**anémona, anémone** *f.* BOT. anemone. *2* ZOOL. ~ *de mar,* sea anemone.

**aneroide** *adj.-n.* aneroid [barometer].

**anestesia** *f.* anaesthesia.

**anestesiar** *tr.* anaesthetize.

**anestésico, -ca** *adj.-m.* anaesthetic.

**anestesista** *n.* anaesthetist, anesthetist.

**aneurisma** *m.* MED. aneurism.

**anexar** *tr.* to annex [a territory, etc.].

**anexión** *f.* annexion, annexation.

**anexionar** *tr.* to annex.

**anexionismo** *m.* annexationism.

**anexo, -xa** *adj.* annexed, joined. *2 m.* annex.

**anfibio, -bia** *adj.* amphibious. *2 adj.-n.* ZOOL. amphibian.

**anfibol** *m.* MINER. amphibole.

**anfibología** *f.* amphibology.

**anficción** *m.* amphyction.

**anfisbena** *f.* ZOOL. amphisbaena.

**anfiscios** *m. pl.* amphiscians, amphiscii.

**anfiteatro** *m.* amphitheatre.

**anfitrión** *m.* amphitryon, host, entertainer.

**ánfora** *f.* amphora.

**anfractuosidad** *f.* anfractuosity.

**anfractuoso, -sa** *adj.* anfractuous.

**angarillas** *f. pl.* handbarrow. *2* panniers [for pack animals]. *3* cruet stand, set of casters.

**ángel** *m.* angel; ~ *custodio* or *de la guarda*, guardian angel. *2* crossbar shot. *3* tèner ~, to be charming.
**angélica** *f.* BOT. angelica.
**angelical** *adj.* angelic(al, cherubic(al.
**angélico, -ca** *adj.* angelic.
**angelico, angelito** *m. dim.* little angel. *2* fig. baby.
**angelote** *m.* large figure of an angel. *2* ICHTH. angelfish. *3* a fat, sweet child.
**ángelus** *m.* Angelus.
**angina** *f.* MED. angina, sorethroat. *2* MED. ~ *de pecho*, angina pectoris.
**angiospermas** *f. pl.* BOT. angiospermae.
**anglesita** *f.* MINER. anglesite.
**anglicanismo** *m.* Anglicanism.
**anglicano, -na** *adj.-n.* Anglican.
**anglicismo** *m.* Anglicism.
**anglo, -gla** *adj.-n.* Anglian. *2* English. *3 m. pl.* Angles.
**anglófilo, -la** *adj.-n.* Anglophil(e.
**anglófobo, -ba** *adj.-n.* Anglophobe.
**anglosajón, -na** *adj.-n.* Anglo-saxon.
**Angora** *f. pr. n.* GEOG. Angora.
**angora** *f.* angora wool.
**angorina** *f.* a light fluffy wool for knitting.
**angostar** *tr.* to narrow [lessen the breadth]. *2 ref.* to narrow [become less broad].
**angosto, -ta** *adj.* narrow.
**angostura** *f.* narrowness. *2* narrows, narrow passage. *3* angostura [medicinal bark].
**angrelado** *adj.* HER. engrailed.
**anguila** *f.* ICHTH. eel. *2* NAUT. ~ *de cabo*, REBENQUE 1.
**angula** *f.* elver, young eel.
**angular** *adj.* angular. *2 piedra* ~, corner stone.
**ángulo** *m.* GEOM. angle: ~ *agudo, recto, obtuso*, acute, right, obtuse angle; ~ *de mira*, angle of sight; ~ *horario*, ASTR. hour angle. *2* angle, corner, quoin.
**anguloso, -sa** *adj.* angular, angulated, angulous.
**angustia** *f.* anguish, affliction, distress.
**angustiado, -da** *adj.* anguished, afflicted, distressed.
**angustiar** *tr.* to afflict, distress, worry.
**angustioso, -sa** *adj.* anguishing, distressing.
**anhelante** *adj.* panting. *2* desirous, longing.
**anhelar** *intr.* to pant, gasp. *2 tr.* to desire, to long or yearn for or to.
**anhelo** *m.* longing, yearning, desire.
**anheloso, -sa** *adj.* hard [breathing]. *2* painting. *3* anxious, desirous, wishful, eager.
**anhídrido** *m.* CHEM. anhydrid.
**anhidro, -dra** *adj.* CHEM. anhydrous.
**Aníbal** *pr. n.* Hannibal.
**anidar** *intr.* to nest, nidify. *2* to dwell, reside. *3 tr.* to harbour, cherish.
**anilina** *f.* CHEM. aniline.
**anilla** *f.* curtain ring; strap ring. *2 pl.* GYM. rings.
**anillado, -da** *adj.* curled. *2* ringed, annulated. *3 m.* ZOOL. annulate.
**anillar** *tr.* to form into rings. *2* to fasten with rings.
**anillo** *m.* ring, circlet, finger ring: ~ *de boda*, wedding ring; *venir como* ~ *al dedo*, to fit, to be opportune. *2* cigar band. *3* ARCH., ZOOL., BOT. annulet, annulus. *4* NAUT. grommet. *5* MACH. ring, collar.
**ánima** *f.* human soul. *2* soul in Purgatory. *3* bore [of a gun]. *4 pl.* ringing of bells at night for prayers for souls in Purgatory.
**animación** *f.* animation, liveliness, life. *3* bustle, movement.

**animado, -da** *adj.* animate. *2* animated, lively. *3* prompted. *4* heartened. *5* full of people.
**animador, -ra** *adj.* animating; comforting, inspiring; encouraging. *2 m.-f.* animator; comforter; inspirer; encourager.
**animadversión** *f.* hatred, ill will, antagonism. *2* animadversion.
**animal** *adj.* animal. *2* stupid. *3 m.* animal. *4* fig. stupid, rude person.
**animalada** *f.* stupidity.
**animálculo** *m.* animalcule.
**animalejo** *m.* small animal.
**animalidad** *f.* animality.
**animalizar** *tr.* to animalize.
**animalote** *m. aug.* big animal. *2* fig. very stupid person.
**animalucho** *m.* ugly, hideous animal.
**animar** *tr.* to animate. *2* to cheer up. *3* to encourage, impel, decide. *4* to enliven, brighten. *5 ref.* to become animated, enlivened. *6* to take heart. *7* to make up one's mind.
**anime** BOT. courbaril. *2* courbaril copal.
**anímico** *adj.* PSÍQUICO.
**animismo** *m.* animism.
**ánimo** *m.* mind, spirit. *2* courage, energy: *cobrar* ~, to take courage. *3* intention, purpose: *hacer* or *tener* ~ *de*, to mean, to purpose. *4* attention, thought. *5 interj.* ¡ánimo!, cheer up!
**animosidad** *f.* animosity, ill will. *2* courage.
**animoso, -sa** *adj.* brave, courageous.
**aniñado, -da** *adj.* childlish; girlish.
**anión** *m.* CHEM., PHYS. anion.
**aniquilación** *f.* annihilation, destruction.
**aniquilador, -ra** *adj.* annihilating, destroying; crushing. *2 m.-f.* annihilator.
**aniquilamiento** *m.* annihilation, complete destruction.
**aniquilar** *tr.* to annihilate, destroy, crush. *2 ref.* to be annihilated.
**anís** *m.* BOT. anise. *2* aniseed. *3* sugar-coated aniseed. *4* ANISADO 2.
**anisado, -da** *adj.* anise-flavoured. *2 m.* anise-flavoured brandy.
**anisar** *tr.* to flavour with anise.
**anisete** *m.* anisette.
**anisopétalo, -la** *adj.* BOT. anisopetalous.
**aniversario, -ria** *adj.* ANUAL. *2 m.* anniversary. *3* annual memorial service.
**Ankara** *f. pr. n.* GEOG. Ankara.
**ano** *m.* ANAT. anus.
**anoche** *adv.* last night, last evening, yesternight.
*1)* **anochecer** *intr.* to grow dark. *2* to be or reach somewhere at nightfall. ¶ CONJUG. like *agradecer*.
*2)* **anochecer** *m.*, **anochecida** *f.* nightfall, dusk, evening.
**anodino, -na** *adj.-n.* anodyne. *2* inane, ineffective.
**anódico, -ca** *adj.* PHYS. anodic.
**ánodo** *m.* ELECT. anode.
**anomalía** *f.* anomaly, irregularity. *2* ASTR. anomaly.
**anómalo, -la** *adj.* anomalous.
**anona** *f.* BOT. soursop.
**anonadado, -da** *adj.* crushed, thunderstruck.
**anonadamiento** *m.* annihilation. *2* humiliation. *3* prostration.
**anonadar** *tr.* to annihilite; to crush, overwhelm. *2* to humiliate. *3 ref.* to humble oneself; to be crushed.
**anonimato** *m.* anonimity.
**anónimo, -ma** *adj.* anonymous. *2* COM. joint-stock

[company]. *3 m.* annonym(e [person, author]. *4* anonymous letter. *5* anonymity.

**anorexia** *f.* MED. anorexia.

**anormal** *adj.* abnormal. *2 m.-f.* abnormal person.

**anormalidad** *f.* abnormality, abnormity.

**anosmia** *f.* anosmia.

**anotación** *f.* annotation. *2* note, entry.

**anotador, -ra** *m.-f.* annotator.

**anotar** *tr.* to annotate, note. *2* to write, put down; to enter, inscribe.

**anquilosamiento** *m.* MED. ankylosis, anchylosis. *2* fig. paralysis, inmobility; ~ *de las negociaciones*, paralysis of the negotiations.

**anquilosarse** *ref.* to ankylose.

**anquilosis** *f.* MED. ankylosis, stiff joint.

**ansa** *f.* Hanse.

**ánsar** *m.* ORN. graylag. *2* ORN. goose, gander.

**ansarino, -na** *adj.* anserine. *2 m.* ORN. gosling.

**ansarón** *m.* ORN. ÁNSAR. *2* ORN. gosling.

**anseático, -ca** *adj.* Hanseatic.

**ansia** *f.* throe, anguish, pang. *2* eagerness, avidity, longing, hankering. *3 pl.* NÁUSEAS.

**ansiar** *tr.* to wish, long for, covet.

**ansiedad** *f.* anxiety, uneasiness, worry. *2* MED. anxiety.

**ansioso, -sa** *adj.* anguished. *2* desirous, anxious, eager; greedy.

**anta** *f.* ZOOL. elk, moose. *2* ARCH. anta. *3* menhir.

**antagónico, -ca** *adj.* antagonistic(al.

**antagonismo** *m.* antagonism.

**antagonista** *m.* antagonist, adversary, opponent.

**antaño** *adv.* last year. *2* formerly, in olden times; of yore.

**antañón, -na** *adj.* very old.

**antártico, -ca** *adj.* antarctic.

**Antártida** *f. pr. n.* GEOG. Antarctica.

1) **ante** *m.* ZOOL. elk, moose. *2* ZOOL. bubal. *3* buff [leather], buckskin.

2) **ante** *prep.* before, in the presence of. *2* ~ *todo*, first of all; above all.

**antealtar** *m.* chancel.

**anteanoche** *adv.* night before last.

**anteayer** *adv.* day before yesterday.

**antebrazo** *m.* forearm.

**antecámara** *f.* antechamber, anteroom.

**antecedente** *adj.-m.* antecedent.

**antecedentemente** *adv.* antecedently, previously.

**anteceder** *tr.* to antecede, precede.

**antecesor, -ra** *m.-f.* antecessor. *2* ancestor, forefather.

**antecocina** *f.* pantry, scullery.

**antecolumna** *f.* ARCH. column of a porch.

**antecoro** *m.* antechoir.

**Antecristo** *m.* Antichrist.

**antedata** *f.* antedate.

**antedatar** *tr.* to antedate [a document].

**antedicho, -cha** *adj.* a)foresaid; a(forenamed.

**antediluviano, -na** *adj.* antediluvian.

**antefirma** *f.* description of the signatory before the signature.

**anteiglesia** *f.* church porch.

**antelación** *f.* anteriority, previousness.

**antemano (de)** *adv.* beforehand.

**antemeridiano, -na** *adj.* antemeridian.

**antena** *f.* NAUT. lateen yard. *2* ZOOL. antenna, horn. *3* RADIO. antenna, aerial.

**anteojera** *f.* spectacle case. *2* blinder, blinker [for horses].

**anteojo** *m.* spyglass. *2 pl.* binocular fieldglasses, opera glasses. *3* eyeglasses, spectacles.

**antepalco** *m.* THEAT. small anteroom to a box.

**antepasado, -da** *adj.* foregone. *2 m.* ancestor, forefather.

**antepecho** *m.* parapet, railing; window sill. *2* FORT., MAR. breastwork. *3* breastband [of harness]. *4* breast beam [of loom].

**antepenúltimo, -ma** *adj.* antepenultimate.

**anteponer** *tr.* to place before, to prefix. *2* to place before, give the preference to. ¶ CONJUG. like *poner*.

**anteportada** *f.* bastard title page.

**anteposición** *f.* putting before, anteposition.

**anteproyecto** *m.* first draft or a project.

**antepuerta** *f.* portière. *2* FORT. anteport.

**antepuerto** *m.* NAUT. outer port.

**antepuesto, -ta** *p. p.* of ANTEPONER.

**antera** *f.* BOT. anther.

**anteridio** *m.* BOT. antheridium.

**anterior** *adj.* anterior, foregoing, former, previous: *el día* ~, the day before. *2* anterior, fore, front, forward.

**anterioridad** *f.* anteriority, priority: *con* ~, previously; *con* ~ *a*, previously to; prior to.

**anteriormente** *adv.* previously, before.

**antes** *adv.* before, first, previously, formerly; soon, sooner; ~ *de*, ~ *de que*, ~ *que*, previous to, before; *cuanto* ~, as soon as possible; *de* ~, from before; of old. *2* sooner, rather: ~ *morir que mentir*, sooner die than lie. *3 conj. antes*, or ~ *bien*, rather, on the contrary. *4 adj.* before, previous: *el día* ~, the previous day.

**antesala** *f.* anteroom, antechamber: *hacer* ~, to wait in an antechamber.

**antevíspera** *f.* the day before the eve [of]; two days before.

**anti-** *pref.* anti-.

**antiaéreo, -a** *adj.* anti-aircraft.

**antiafrodisíaco, -a** *adj.* antiaphrodisiac.

**antialcohólico, -ca** *adj.* antialcoholic.

**antiar** *m.* BOT. antiar.

**antiartístico, -ca** *adj.* inartistic.

**antibiótico, -ca** *adj.-n.* antibiotic.

**anticatarral** *adj.* MED. anticatarrhal.

**anticiclón** *m.* METEOR. anticyclone.

**anticipación** *f.* anticipation, advance: *con* ~, in advance.

**anticipadamente** *adv.* in advance, beforehand, previously. *2* prematurely.

**anticipado, -da** *adj.* advanced, in advance; advance [payment]. *3* early, premature.

**anticipar** *tr.* to anticipate, advance, hasten. *2* to advance [money], to lend; to pay in advance. *3 ref.,* to occur before the regular time. *4 anticiparse a*, to anticipate, forestall, to get ahead of.

**anticipo** *m.* ANTICIPACIÓN. *2* advance, advance payment, money advanced.

**anticlerical** *adj.-n.* anticlerical.

**anticlinal** *adj.* GEOL. anticlinal.

**anticolonialismo** *m.* anticolonialism.

**anticonceptivo, -va** *adj.* birth-controlling, contraceptive. *2 m.* contraceptive.

**anticongelante** *adj.* antifreeze.

**anticonstitucional** *adj.* anticonstitutional.

**Anticristo** *m.* Antichrist.

**anticuado, -da** *adj.* antiquated, old-fashioned, obsolete.

**anticuar** *tr.* to antiquate. *2 ref.* to become antiquated.

**anticuario** *m.* antiquarian, antiquary. *2* antique dealer; old curiosity dealer.

**anticuerpo** *m.* BACT. antibody.

**antidemocrático, -ca** *adj.* antidemocratic.

**antideportivo, -va** *adj.* unsportmanlike; unsporting, unsporty.
**antideslizante** *adj.* AUTO. antiskid.
**antidetonante** *adj.* anti-knock [gasoline].
**antidiftérico, -ca** *adj.-m.* MED. antidiphteritic.
**antídoto** *m.* antidote.
**antiespasmódico, -ca** *adj.-n.* antispasmodic.
**antiestético, -c** *adj.* unaesthetic.
**antifaz** *m.* mask, veil, etc., covering the face.
**antífona** *f.* ECCL. antiphon, anthem.
**antífrasis** *f.* RHET. antiphrasis.
**antifricción** *adj.* MACH. anti-friction.
**antígeno** *m.* PHYSIOL. antigen.
**antigualla** *f.* antique; old-fashioned or out-of-date custom, object, etc.
**antiguamente** *adv.* anciently, in old times.
**antigüedad** *f.* antiquity. *2* seniority. *3 pl.* antiquities, antiques.
**antiguo, -gua** *adj.* ancient, old; antique: *Antiguo Testamento,* Old Testament; *a la antigua,* in the ancient manner. *2* of long standing, old. *3 más* ~, senior [in employments, etc.]. *4 m.* old [old time]: *de* ~, of old. *5* senior. *6 pl. los antiguos,* the ancients.
**antihigiénico, -ca** *adj.* unhygienic, unhealthy.
**antilogaritmo** *m.* MATH. antilogarithm.
**antilogía** *f.* antilogy.
**antílope** *m.* ZOOL. antelope.
**antillano, -na** *adj.-n.* Antillean, West-Indian.
**Antillas** *f. pl.* GEOG. Antilles, West Indies.
**antimilitarismo** *m.* antimilitarism.
**antimonio** *m.* CHEM. antimony.
**antinacional** *adj.* antinational.
**antinatural** *adj.* unnatural
**antinomia** *f.* antinomy.
**Antíoco** *n. pr.* Antiochus.
**Antioquía** *f. pr. n.* GEOG. Antioch.
**antipapa** *m.* antipope.
**antípara** *f.* screen, folding screen. *2* legging.
**antiparras** *f. pl.* coll, spectacles, barnacles.
**antipatía** *f.* antipathy, dislike, aversion.
**antipático, -ca** *adj.* antipathetic, disagreeable.
**antipatriótico, -ca** *adj.* unpatriotic.
**antipirético, -ca** *adj.-m.* MED. antipyretic.
**antipirina** *f.* CHEM. antipyrine.
**antípoda** *adj.* antipodal. *2 m. pl.* antipodes.
**antiquísimo, -ma** *adj. superl.* very ancient, very old.
**antirrábico, -ca** *adj.* antihydrophobic.
**antirreglamentario, -ria** *adj.* against the rules.
**antirreligioso, -sa** *adj.* antireligious; irreligious.
**antirrevolucionario, -ria** *adj.-n.* antirevolucionary.
**antiscios** *m. pl.* GEOG. antiscians, antiscii.
**antisemita** *m.-f.* anti-Semite.
**antisemítico, -ca** *adj.* anti-Semitic.
**antisemitismo** *m.* anti-Semitism.
**antisepsia** *f.* MED. antisepsis.
**antiséptico, -ca** *adj.-n.* antiseptic.
**antisocial** *adj.* antisocial.
**antistrofa** *f.* antistrophe.
**antitanque** *adj.* MIL. antitank.
**antítesis** *f.* antithesis.
**antitético, -ca** *adj.* antithetic.
**antitoxina** *f.* MED. antitoxin.
**antituberculoso, -sa** *adj.* antituberculous.
**antojadizo, -za** *adj.* capricious, whimsical, fickle.
**antojarse** *ref.* (used with a pers. pron.: *me, te, le, nos, os, les*) to arouse a whimsical desire, a fancy: *se le antoja este juguete,* he wants this toy.

*2* to seem probable, occur to the mind, be imagined: *se me antoja que,* I think or imagine that.
**antojo** *m.* caprice, whim, notion, fancy, freak, will: *a su* ~, as one pleases; arbitrarily. *2* birthmark.
**antología** *f.* anthology.
**antológico, -ca** *adj.* anthological.
**Antón** *pr. n.* ANTONIO.
**antónimo, -ma** *adj.* antonymous. *2 m.* antonym.
**Antonio** *m. pr. n.* Anthony.
**antonomasia** *f.* antonomasia.
**antorcha** *f.* torch, flambeau, cresset.
**antozoario, antozoo** *adj.-n.* ZOOL. anthozoan.
**antraceno** *m.* CHEM. anthracene.
**antracita** *n.* anthracite, hard coal.
**ántrax** *m.* MED. anthrax.
**antro** *m.* cavern, den.
**antropocéntrico, -ca** *adj.* anthropocentric.
**antropofagia** *f.* anthropophagy.
**antropófago, -ga** *adj.* anthropophagous. *2 m.-f.* anthropophagite. *3 pl.* anthropophagi.
**antropoide** *adj.* ZOOL. anthropoid.
**antropología** *f.* anthropology.
**antropológico, -ca** *adj.* anthropologic(al.
**antropólogo** *m.* anthropologist.
**antropometría** *f.* anthropometry.
**antropomorfismo** *m.* anthropomorphism.
**antropomorfo, -fa** *adj.* anthropomorphous.
**antruejo** *m.* carnival days.
**anual** *adj.* annual, yearly.
**anualidad** *f.* annual recurrence. *2* annuity, yearly rent; year's pay.
**anualmente** *adv.* every year, yearly, annually.
**anuario** *m.* annual, yearbook, trade directory.
**anubarrado, -da** *adj.* clouded, cloudy [sky].
**anublar** *tr.* to cloud, darken, obscure, dim. *2* AGR. to blast, blight. *3 ref.* to become clouded, dimmed. *4* AGR. to become blasted, blighted.
**anublo** *m.* AÑUBLO.
**anudar** *tr.* to knot [make nots in; join, unite]. *2* to take up, resume. *3 ref.* to be knotted, united. *4* to be stunted. *5 anudársele a uno la voz,* to become speechless with emotion.
**anuencia** *f.* consent, permission.
**anuente** *adj.* consenting.
**anulable** *adj.* revocable, that can be annulled, revoked, cancelled or invalidated.
**anulación** *f.* annulment, voiding, nullification.
1) **anular** *tr.* to annul, make void, nullify. *2* to deprive of authority or influence.
2) **anular** *adj.* annular. *2 dedo* ~, ring finger.
**anunciación** *f.* announcement, annunciation. *2* Annunciation [to the Virgin Mary].
**anunciador, -ra** *adj.* announcing. *2* advertising. *3 m.-f.* announcer. *4* advertiser. *5* ELEC. annunciator.
**anunciante** *adj.* advertising. *2 m.-f.* advertiser.
**anunciar** *tr.* to announce. *2* to indicate, foretell. *3* to advertise, to bill.
**anuncio** *m.* announcement, notice. *2* presage, sign. *3* advertisement. *4* COM. advice.
**anuo, -a** *adj.* annual.
**anuro, -ra** *adj.-m.* ZOOL. anuran.
**anverso** *m.* obverse [as opposed to reverse]. *2* PRINT. recto [of a page].
**anzuelo** *m.* fishhook. *2 fig.* lure, allurement, incitement: *picar en el* ~, *tragar el* ~, to swallow the bait.
**añada** *f.* AGR. good or bad year.
**añadido** *m.* hair switch. *2* PRINT. addition.

**añadidura** f. addition, additament: *por* ~, into the bargain; to boot.

**añadir** tr. to add, join. *2* to augment, increase.

**añagaza** f. lure, decoy [for birds]. *2* snare, trick.

**añalejo** m. ordinal, liturgical calendar.

**añejar** tr. to age [a thing]. *2 ref.* [of wine, etc.] to grow old, to age.

**añejo, -ja** adj. old, aged, of old vintage [wine]; old [bacon, vice, custom, etc.].

**añicos** m. pl. bits, shatters, smithereens: *hacerse* ~, to be smashed; fig. to take great pains.

**añil** m. anil, indigo [shrub, dye]. *2* indigo blue.

**año** m. year: ~ *bisiesto*, leap year; ~ *de luz*, light year; ~ *económico*, fiscal year; ~ *escolar*, school year; *día de* ~ *nuevo*, New Year's Day; *el* ~ *de la nanita*, donkey's years ago; *estar de buen* ~, to be healthy and fleshy; *al* ~ *de...*, a year after...; *por años*, by the year; *por muchos años*, many happy returns [of the day]. *2* AGRIC. crop, harvest. *3 pl.* years, age; *tener años*, to be old; *tener diez años [de edad]*, to be ten years old; *¿cuántos años tiene usted?*, how old are you?

**añojal** m. fallow land.

**añojo, -ja** m.-f. yearling calf or lamb.

**añoranza** f. regret, nostalgia, homesickness.

**añorar** tr. to pine for, miss [a lost or absent person, etc.].

**añoso, -sa** adj. old, stricken in years.

**añublo** m. BOT. smut; rust.

**aojar** tr. to cast the evil eye on, to bewitch.

**aojo** m. casting the evil eye, bewitching.

**aoristo** m. GRAM. aorist.

**aorta** f. ANAT. aorta.

**aovado, -da** adj. ovate, oviform, egg-shaped.

**aovar** tr. to lay eggs.

**apabullar** tr. to crush, flatten. *2* to squelch, disconcert, silence.

**apacentamiento** m. pasturage, grazing. *2* pasture, food.

**apacentar** tr. to pasture, graze [cattle]. *2* to feed [spiritually]. *3 ref.* [of cattle] to pasture, graze. *4* to feed one's spirit or mind. ¶ CONJUG. like *acertar*.

**apacibilidad** f. gentleness, mildness, placidity.

**apacible** adj. gentle, mild, sweet. *2* pleasant, placid, tranquil, untroubled.

**apaciguador, -ra** adj. pacifying, appeasing. *2 m.-f.* pacifier, appeaser.

**apaciguamiento** m. pacification, appeasement.

**apaciguar** tr. to pacify, appease, calm, placate. *2 ref.* to be appeased.

**apaciento, apaciente**, etc. *irr.* V. APACENTAR.

**apache** adj.-n. Apache [indian]. *2 m.* apache [ruffian].

**apadrinamiento** m. sponsoring, acting as a godfather or a second. *2* protection, support, patronage.

**apadrinar** tr. to sponsor, to act as godfather to; to act as second of [in a duel]. *2* to protect, favour, patronize, support.

**apagado, -da** adj. out, extinguished, quenched. *2* meek, dull [person]. *3* faint, pale, dead, dull, muffled. *4* dead [volcano]. *5* slaked [lime].

**apagador** m. extinguisher. *2* damper [in a piano].

**apagar** tr. to extinguish, to put out, blow out, turn out. *2* to quench. *3* to slake [lime]. *4* to dull, soften [colours]. *5* to deaden, muffle [sound]. *6 ref.* [of fire, light, etc.] to die out, go out. *7* to be quenched. *8* [of colours, sound] to deaden.

**apagavelas** m. candle extinguisher.

**apagón** m. sudden failure of lights. *2* blackout [as when electricity fails].

**apainelado** adj. ARCH. basket-handle [arch].

**apaisado, -da** adj. oblong [rectangular with the horizontal dimension the greater].

**apalabrar** tr. to agree [to something]. *2* to bespeak, reserve, engage, beforehand.

**apalancamiento** m. levering, leverage.

**apalancar** tr. to lever, pry.

**apaleado, -da** adj. beaten, hit repeatedly.

**apaleamiento** m. beating, cudgelling, thrashing.

**apalear** tr. to beat, cane, cudgel, thrash. *2* AGR. to winnow [grain] with a shovel.

**apaleo** m. winnowing grain with a shovel.

**apanalado, -da** adj. honeycombed.

**apancora** f. ZOOL. a Chilean crab.

**apandillar** tr.-ref. to form a gang or league.

**apanojado, -da** adj. BOT. paniculate(d.

**apañado, -da** adj. clothlike. *2* dexterous, skilful. *4* suitable.

**apañadura** f., **apañamiento** m. act of taking or grasping. *2* mending. *3* managing.

**apañar** tr. to take, seize; to steal. *2* to dress, adorn. *3* to wrap up [for warmth]. *4* to patch, mend. *5 ref.* to manage, contrive.

**apaño** m. patch, repair, mending. *2* knack, skill.

**apañuscar** tr. to crumple. *2* to seize, pilfer.

**aparador** m. sideboard, cupboard, buffet; dresser. *2* credence. *3* shop window, show window.

**aparasolado, -da** adj. umbrella-shaped.

**aparato** m. apparatus, appliance, device: ~ *de radio*, wireless set; ~ *de relojería*, clockwork; ~ *fotográfico*, camera. *2* coll. machine [airplane]. *3* coll. phone. *4* SURG. application, bandage. *5* PHYSIOL. apparatus, system: ~ *digestivo*, digestive system. *6* exaggeration. *7* pomp. ostentation, display, show. *8* signs, symptoms. *9* assemblage, paraphernalia.

**aparatosamente** adv. ostentaciously, showily, pretentiously. *2* spectacularly.

**aparatosidad** f. show, ostentation, pomposity.

**aparatoso, -sa** adj. pompous, showy. *2* exaggerating, fussy. *3* spectacular.

**aparcamiento** m. parking. *2* parking place, car park, parking lot. *3* lay-by [on the road].

**aparcar** tr. to park [cars, artillery, etc.].

**aparcería** f. share tenancy, partnership.

**aparcero, -ra** m.-f. share tenant, partner.

**apareamiento** m. pairing, matching, mating.

**aparear** tr. to pair, match [things]. *2* to pair, mate [animals]. *3 ref.* to form a pair. *4* [of animals] to pair, mate, couple.

**aparecer** intr.-ref. to appear, show up, turn up; to arise, heave in sight. *2* [of a ghost] to walk. ¶ CONJUG. like *agradecer*.

**aparecido** m. ghost, spectre, specter, wraith.

**aparejado, -da** adj. apt, fit, competent, ready.

**aparejador** m. architect's assistant. *2* NAUT. rigger.

**aparejar** tr. to prepare, get ready. *2* to saddle [horses, mules, etc.]. *3* NAUT. to rig, rig out. *4* to size, to prime [before gilding or painting]. *5 ref.* to get [oneself] ready.

**aparejo** m. preparation, arrangement. *2* gear, equipment. *3* riding gear; packsaddle. *4* NAUT. masts, rigging, sails, tackle [on a ship]. *5* tackle [pulleys]: ~ *de gata*, cat tackle. *6* MAS. bond. *7* PAINT., GILD. sizing, priming.

**aparentar** tr. to feign, pretend. *2* to look, seem.

**aparente** adj. apparent [not real], seeming. *2* apparent, visible. *3* fit, suitable.

**aparezco, aparezca** etc. *irr.* V. APARECER.

**aparición** f. apparition, appearance. 2 apparition, ghost, vision.
**apariencia** f. appearance, aspect, look, semblance. 2 likelihood. 3 pretence, show. 4 pl. appearances: *guardar las apariencias*, to keep up appearances.
**apartadero** m. RLY. sidetrack, siding. 2 turnout [beside a road, etc.]. 3 place where bulls are boxed.
**apartadizo** m. partitioned off space.
**apartado, -da** adj. retired, aloof; distant, remote, out-of-the-way. 2 different. 3 m. side room. 4 post-office box; mail for it. 5 penning of bulls. 6 section [of a law, bill, etc.].
**apartador, -ra** m.-f. sorter, separator.
**apartamiento** m. retirement, separation. 2 aloofness. 3 putting aside. 4 sorting. 5 secluded place. 6 apartment, flat.
**apartar** tr. to separate, divide part. 2 to push, draw or turn aside; to remove, move away. 3 to dissuade. 4 to sort. 5 RLY. to shunt. 6 ref. to part, become separated. 7 to move away, withadraw, hold off. 8 to stray [from path, etc.].
**aparte** adj. separate, other: *esto es cuestión ~*, this is another matter. 2 adv. apart, aside. 3 separately. 4 m. THEAT. aside. 5 paragraph: *punto y ~*, paragraph.
**apartidar** tr. to form a party or faction.
**aparvadera** f. wooden rake.
**aparvar** tr. to heap [grain].
**apasionadamente** adv. ardently, passionately. 2 in a biased way, with partiality.
**apasionado, -da** adj. ardent, fervid, impassioned. 2 loving. 3 devoted, passionately fond. 4 biased.
**apasionamiento** m. ardour, fervour, enthusiasm, vehemence. 2 bias, partiality.
**apasionante** adj. exciting, thrilling, stirring.
**apasionar** tr. to impassion, excite strongly, to appeal deeply to. 2 ref. to become impassioned, strongly excited; to become passionately fond [of]. 3 to be biased in one's judgement.
**apatía** f. apathy.
**apático, -ca** adj. apathetic.
**apátrida** adj. without a country, stateless [person].
**apeadero** m. horse block. 2 wayside rest. 3 RLY. stop, wayside station, flag stop. 4 temporary quarters.
**apeador** m. land surveyor.
**apear** tr. to dismount, bring down, help down or out [from horse or carriage]. 2 to hobble [a horse]. 3 to scotch [a wheel]. 4 to survey [land]. 5 to fell [a tree]. 6 to dissuade. 7 ARCH. to prop up. 8 ~ *el tratamiento*, to drop the title. 9 ref. to dismount, alight, get of, get out. 10 to be dissuaded.
**apechugar** intr. to push with the chest. 2 ~ *con*, to take or accept [something distasteful].
**apedreado, -da** adj. stoned. 2 variegated, mottled, spotted. 3 pockmarked.
**apedreamiento** m. stone-throwing. 2 stoning, lapidation. 3 damage from hail.
**apedrear** tr. to throw stones at. 2 to stone, lapidate. 3 impers. to hail. 4 ref. to be injured by hail.
**apedreo** m. stoning. 2 damage caused by hail [to the crop].
**apegadamente** adv. devotedly.
**apegado, -da** adj. attached, devoted.
**apegarse** ref. to become attached, to attach oneself [to].
**apego** m. attachment, affection, liking.

**apelable** adj. LAW appealable.
**apelación** f. LAW appeal: *interponer ~*, to appeal. 2 coll. remedy, help.
**apelado, -da** m.-f. LAW appellee.
**apelambrar** tr. to remove hair from [hides].
**apelante** adj. LAW appealing. 2 m.-f. LAW appellant.
**apelar** intr. LAW to appeal. 2 call upon, have recourse to.
**apelativo** adj.-m. GRAM. appellative.
**apelmazado, -da** adj. heavy, compact, compressed.
**apelmazamiento** m. sogginess, stodginess, clumpiness. 2 compressing, flattening [the soil].
**apelmazar** tr. to make heavy, compact, thick; to compress, to render less spongy or porous.
**apelotonar** tr. to form [hair, wool, etc.] into knots, tufts or balls. 2 ref. to form knots, tufts or balls. 3 [of people] to cluster.
**apellidar** tr. to call, name, surname. 2 to proclaim. 3 ref. to be called [have the name].
**apellido** m. family name. 2 surname, name.
**apenar** tr. to pain, cause sorrow to. 2 ref. to grieve.
**apenas** adv. scarcely, hardly. 2 as soon as, no sooner than.
**apencar** intr. ~ *con*, to take or accept [something distasteful].
**apendectomía** f. MED. appendicectomy, appendectomy.
**apéndice** m. appendage, appendix.
**apendicitis** f. MED. appendicitis.
**Apeninos** pr. n. GEOG. Apennines.
**apeñuscar** tr. to pack together, to cram together, to press something together.
**apeo** m. landmarking, surveying. 2 ARCH. proping; prop. 3 tree felling.
**apeonar** intr. [of partridges] to run.
**apercibimiento** m. preparedness. 2 admonishing, warning, admonition.
**apercibir** tr. to prepare. 2 to admonish, warn, advise. 3 to perceive, see. 4 ref. to prepare oneself, to get ready.
**apercollar** tr. to grab by the neck.
**apergaminado, -da** adj. parchment-like. 2 fig. wizened, dry and wrinkled: *piel apergaminada* wizened, old-looking skin.
**apergaminarse** ref. to dry up, become yellow and wrinkled.
**aperitivo, -va** m. apéritif, appetizer. 2 adj.-m. MED. aperitive.
**apero** m. farm implements. 2 equipment of a farm. 3 kit, tools. 4 (Am.) riding gear.
**aperreado, -da** adj. harassed, worried.
**aperreador, -ra** adj. harassing, fatiguing, worrisome.
**aperrear** tr. to set the dogs on. 2 to harass, worry, fatigue. 3 ref. EMPERRARSE.
**aperreo** m. harassment, worry, toil.
**apersogar** tr. to tether [an animal].
**apersonado, -da** adj. bien or mal ~, of good or bad appearance.
**apersonamiento** m. LAW. appearance.
**apertura** f. opening [of an assembly, a shop, etc.]. 2 reading [of a will]. 3 CHESS. opening.
**apesadumbrado, -da** adj. pained, distressed.
**apesadumbrar** tr. to pain, distress. 2 ref. to be pained, to grieve.
**apesaradamente** adv. grievingly, sorrowfully.
**apesarar** tr. APESADUMBRAR.
**apestado, -da** adj. infected with the plague. 2 *estar ~ de*, to be infested with; to be full of.

**apestar** *tr.* to infect with the plague. *2* to corrupt, vitiate. *3* to sicken, plague. *4 intr.* to stink.
**apestoso, -sa** *adj.* stinking. *2* sickening. *3* pestilent.
**apétalo, -la** *adj.* BOT. apetalous.
**apetecedor, -ra** *adj.* desirous.
**apetecer** *tr.* to desire, to feel an appetite for. *2 esto me apetece,* I wish to have or to do this. ¶ CONJUG. like *agradecer.*
**apetezco, apetezca,** etc. *irr.* V. APETECER.
**apetecible** *adj.* desirable.
**apetecido, -da** *adj.* desired, *resultado ~,* desired result.
**apetencia** *f.* appetence, appetency, desire. *2* appetite.
**apetitivo, -va** *adj.* appetitive.
**apetito** *m.* appetite: *abrir el ~,* to whet the appetite. *2* appetence.
**apetitoso, -sa** *adj.* appetizing, savoury, palatable, tasty.
**apezonado, -da** *adj.* nipple-shaped.
**apiadar** *tr.* to inspire pity. *2 ref. apiadarse de,* to pity, have pity on.
**apical** *adj.* apical.
**apicarado, -da** *adj.* roguish, knavish.
**ápice** *m.* apex, summit, top. *2* whit, iota. *3* crux.
**apícola** *adj.* apicultural, apiarian.
**apicultor, -ra** *m.-f.* apiculturist, bee-keeper.
**apicultura** *f.* apiculture, bee-keeping.
**apilada** *adj.* dried [chestnut].
**apilamiento** *m.* piling, heaping.
**apilar** *tr.* to pile, pile up, heap, heap up.
**apimplarse** *ref.* coll. to get merry or tipsy, to get tight.
**apiñado, -da** *adj.* shaped like a pine-cone. *2* packed, crowded, pressed together.
**apiñamiento** *m.* packing, crowding together. *2* crowd, press.
**apiñar** *tr.* to pack, press together, jam. *2 ref.* to press [become pressed together].
**apio** *m.* BOT. celery.
**apiolar** *tr.* to jess, gyve. *2* to tie [game] by the legs. *3* coll. to arrest [a person]. *4* coll. to kill.
**apiparse** *ref.* coll. to stuff oneself.
**apirexia** MED. apyrexia.
**apisonadora** *f.* road roller, steam roller.
**apisonar** *tr.* to tamp, pack down [earth, etc.]; to roll [roadways].
**apitonar** *intr.* [of a deer, etc.] to begin to grow horns. *2* [of trees] to bud, sprout. *3 tr.* to break with bill or point.
**apizarrado, -da** *adj.* slate-coloured.
**aplacamiento** *m.* appeasement, placation, calming.
**aplacar** *tr.* to appease, placate, calm. *2 ref.* to become appeased.
**aplacer** *tr.* to please, satisfy. ¶ CONJUG. like *agradecer.*
**aplanadera** *f.* levelling board, road drag.
**aplanador, -ra** *adj.* smoothing, levelling. *2* crushing. *3* disheartening.
**aplanamiento** *m.* smoothing, levelling, flattening. *2* depression, prostration.
**aplanar** *tr.* to smooth, level, make even; to planish. *2* to astound. *3 ref.* to tumble down, collapse. *4* to be discouraged or depressed.
**aplastado, -da** *adj.* flat, flattened. *2* dumbfounded.
**aplastamiento** *m.* flattening. *2* crushing, quashing. *3* dumbfounding.
**aplastante** *adj.* crushing. *2* dumbfounding.
**aplastar** *tr.* to flatten. *2* to crush, to quash. *3* to dumbfound. *4 ref.* to become flat.

**aplatanarse** *ref.* coll. to become lethargic, to get listless, to become apathetic.
**aplaudir** *tr.-intr.* to applaud.
**aplauso** *m.* applause. *2* handclapping.
**aplazamiento** *m.* postponement. *2* summons.
**aplazar** *tr.* to adjourn, put off, postpone. *2* to summon, convene.
**aplebeyar** *tr.-ref.* to render, or to become, coarse, base.
**aplicación** *f.* application [in every sense but the one of marking a request]. *2* assiduity, sedulousness, studiousness. *3* SEW. appliqué.
**aplicado, -da** *adj.* applied. *2* studious, industrious, sedulous.
**aplicar** *tr.* to apply. *2* to impute, attribute. *3* LAW to adjudge. *4 ref.* to apply [have a bearing]. *5* to apply or devote oneself. *6* to be diligent, studious.
**aplique** *m.* wall light, wall lamp.
**aplomado, -da** *adj.* self-possessed, calm, prudent. *2* plumb, perpendicular. *3* lead-coloured.
**aplomar** *tr.* MAS., ARCH. to plumb. *2 ref.* DESPLOMARSE. *3* to acquire aplomb.
**aplomo** *m.* aplomb, self-possession, gravity. *2* verticality, aplomb.
**apnea** *f.* MED. apnœa.
**apocado, -da** *adj.* diffident, timid. *2* humble, lowly.
**Apocalipsis** *m.* Apocalypse, Book of Revelation.
**apocalíptico, -ca** *adj.* apocalyptic(al.
**apocamiento** *m.* diffidence, timidity, pusillanimity. *2* dejection, depression.
**apocar** *tr.* to lessen. *2* to contract, restrict. *3* to humble, belittle. *4 ref.* to become diffident.
**apocináceo, -a** *adj.* BOT. apocynaceous.
**apocopar** *tr.* GRAM. to apocopate.
**apócope** *f.* GRAM. apocope; apocopation.
**apócrifo, -fa** *adj.* apocryphal. *2 m. pl.* Apocrypha.
**apodar** *tr.* to nickname, give a nickname to.
**apoderado, -da** *m.* proxy, [private] attorney, manager.
**apoderar** *tr.* to empower, grant power of attorney to. *2 ref. apoderarse de,* to seize, take hold or possesion of.
**apodo** *m.* nickname, sobriquet.
**ápodo, -da** *adj.* ZOOL. apodal.
**apódosis** *f.* GRAM. apodosis.
**apófisis** *f.* ANAT. apophysis, process.
**apogeo** *m.* ASTR. apogee. *2* fig. apogee, height.
**apolillado, -da** *adj.* moth-eaten, mothy.
**apolilladura** *f.* moth hole.
**apolillar** *tr.* [of moths] to eat or infest [clothes, wool, etc.]. *2 ref.* to become moth-eaten.
**apolíneo, -a** *adj.* Apolline, Apollonian.
**apolítico, -ca** *adj.* apolitical.
**Apolo** *pr. n.* Apollo.
**apologético, -ca** *adj.* apologetic [defending]. *2 f.* apologetics.
**apología** *f.* apology, defence, eulogy.
**apologista** *m.* apologist.
**apólogo** *m.* apologue.
**apoltronarse** *ref.* to grow lazy.
**apomazar** *tr.* to pumice.
**aponeurosis** *f.* ANAT. aponeurosis.
**apoplejía** *f.* MED. apoplexy.
**apoplético, -ca** *adj.-n.* apoplectic.
**aporcar** *tr.* AGR. to hill, bank up. ¶ CONJUG. like *contar.*
**aporreado, -da** *adj.* cudgelled. *2* wretched, miserable.
**aporreante** *adj.* bothering.

**aporrear** *tr.* to cudgel, club; to beat, pound. 2 to bother, annoy. 3 *ref.* to drudge, toil.

**aporreo** *m.* cudgelling, beating, pounding. 2 bother, bothering. 3 toiling, drudgery.

**aportación** *f.* contribution [to a fund, an enterprise, etc.].

**aportar** *tr.* to bring, furnish; to contribute [as one's share]. 2 *intr.* ~ *a*, NAUT. to arrive at [a port]; to reach [an unexpected place].

**aposentamiento** *m.* lodging.

**aposentar** *tr.* to put up, lodge. 2 *ref.* to take lodging.

**aposento** *m.* room or apartment. 2 lodging.

**aposición** *f.* GRAM. apposition.

**apósito** MED. bandaged application.

**aposta, apostadamente** *adv.* designedly, on purpose.

**apostadero** *m.* stand, station, post. 2 NAUT. naval station. 3 NAUT. naval district.

**apostador, -ra** *m.-f.* better, bettor.

1) **apostar** *tr.-ref.-intr.* to bet, wager: ~ *a or por*, to bet on, to back [a horse, etc.]; ~ *a que*, to bet that; *apostárseles a or con*, to compete with. ¶ CONJUG. like *contar*.

2) **apostar** *tr.-ref.* to place, post, station.

**apostasía** *f.* apostasy.

**apóstata** *m.-f.* apostate.

**apostatar** *intr.* apostatize.

**apostema** *f.* MED. aposteme, abscess.

**apostemarse** *ref.* to become abscessed.

**a posteriori** *Lat. adv.* a posteriori.

**apostilla** *f.* marginal note, annotation.

**apostillar** *tr.* to annotate [a text]. 2 *ref.* to break out in pimples.

**apóstol** *m.* apostle.

**apostolado** *m.* apostolate, apostleship.

**apostólico, -ca** *adj.* apostolic(al.

**apostrofar** *tr.* RHET. to apostrophize. 2 to scold.

**apóstrofe** *m.-f.* RHET. apostrophe. 2 taunt, insult.

**apóstrofo** *m.* GRAM. apostrophe.

**apostura** *f.* handsomeness, good looks [of a person].

**apotegma** *m.* apophthegm, apothegm.

**apotema** *m.* GEOM. apothem.

**apoteósico, -ca** *adj.* glorifying. 2 glorious, great.

**apoteosis**, *pl.* **-sis** *f.* apotheosis.

**apoyar** *tr.* to rest, lean [something on]. 2 to back, favour, support, countenance, abet. 3 to prove, confirm. 4 to prop. 5 *intr.-ref.* to rest lean [on]; to be supported [on or by]; to depend, be based [on]. 6 *ref.* to base one's arguments.

**apoyatura** *f.* MUS. appoggiatura.

**apoyo** *m.* prop, stay, support. 2 protection, help, support, countenance.

**apreciable** *adj.* appraisable, evaluable. 2 appreciable. 3 estimable, nice, fine.

**apreciación** *f.* appraisal; appreciation.

**apreciar** *tr.* to appraise, estimate, value. 2 to esteem, like. 3 to appreciate.

**apreciativo, -va** *adj.* appreciative. 2 appraising.

**aprecio** *m.* appraisement, valuation. 2 esteem, regard, liking.

**aprehender** *tr.* to apprehend, arrest. 2 to seize [contraband]. 3 PHIL. to apprehend.

**aprehensión** *f.* apprehension, arrest. 2 seizure [of contraband]. 3 PHIL. apprehension.

**aprehensor, -ra** *adj.* apprehending. 2 *m.-f.* apprehender, seizer.

**apremiante** *adj.* urgent, pressing.

**apremiar** *tr.* to urge, press. 2 to compel, constrain. 3 to dun.

**apremio** *m.* pressure, urgency. 2 constraint, judicial compulsion.

**aprendedor, -ra** *adj.* learning. 2 *m.-f.* learner.

**aprender** *tr.* to learn: ~ *a leer*, to learn to read.

**aprendiz, -za** *m.-f.* apprentice.

**aprendizaje** *m.* apprenticeship; act of learning.

**aprensar** *tr.* to press, to calender.

**aprensión** *f.* APREHENSIÓN. 2 scruple, squeamishness. 3 dread of contagion or illness. 4 unfounded opinion or idea.

**aprensivo, -va** *adj.* fearing contagion or illness.

**apresador, -ra** *adj.* capturing. 2 *m.-f.* captor.

**apresar** *tr.* NAUT. to seize, capture [a ship]. 2 to seize, cluth [with claws or teeth]. 3 APRISIONAR.

**aprestar** *tr.-ref.* to prepare, make ready. 2 *tr.* to dress [cloth].

**apresto** *m.* preparation, making ready. 2 outfit, equipment. 3 WEAV. dressing, sizing.

**apresuradamente** *adv.* hastily, hurriedly.

**apresurado, -da** *adj.* hasty, hurried, lively.

**apresuramiento** *m.* hastening. 2 haste.

**apresurar** *tr.* to hasten, quicken, hurry. 2 *ref.* to hasten, hurry, make haste.

**apretadamente** *adv.* tightly. 2 eagerly.

**apretado, -da** *adj.* tight [knot, screw, etc.]. 2 dense, compact. 3 difficult, dangerous. 4 coll. stingy. 5 coll. badly off.

**apretadura** *f.*, **apretamiento** *m.* compression, constriction. 2 tightening.

**apretar** *tr.* to squeeze, to hug. 2 to press, press down. 3 to tighten [bonds, screws]: *apretarse el cinturón*, to tighten or take in one's belt. 4 to clench [the fist], to set [the teeth]. 5 [of garments] to fit tight; [of shoes] to pinch. 6 to grip, clutch. 7 to compress, constrict; to press together, pack tight; to crowd. 8 to spur, urge, press. 9 to pursue, press closely. 10 to afflict, distress. 11 to treat with severity; to make more severe. 12 ~ *el paso*, to quicken the pace. 13 ~ *las clavijas*, fig. to put the screw on. 14 ~ *los talones*, to take to one's heels. 15 *intr.* to get more severe. 16 to insist. 17 ~ *a correr*, to start running. 18 *ref.* to crowd, throng, become pressed together. ¶ CONJUG. like *acertar*.

**apretón** *m.* squeeze, quick pressure: ~ *de manos*, handshake. 2 effort, dash, spurt. 3 press [of people]. 4 difficulty, fix.

**apretujar** *tr.* to press or squeeze hard.

**apretujón** *m.* hard pressure or squeeze.

**apretura** *f.* press [of people], jam, crush. 2 narrow place. 3 difficulty, fix.

**aprieto** *m.* straits, difficulty, scrape, fix. 2 press [of people], jam, crush.

**aprieto, apriete**, etc. *irr.* V. APRETAR.

**apriorismo** *m.* apriorism.

**aprisa** *adv.* fast, quickly, swiftly.

**apriscar** *tr.* to gather [sheep] in the fold.

**aprisco** *m.* sheepfold.

**aprisionar** *tr.* to imprison. 2 to shackle. 3 to hold fast.

**aproar** *intr.* NAUT. to turn the prow.

**aprobación** *f.* approbation, approval; applause.

**aprobado** *m.* EDUC. pass mark.

**aprobar** *tr.* to approve, approve of. 2 to pass [an examination; a student]. 3 to pass, adopt [a bill, a resolution, etc.]. ¶ CONJUG. like *contar*.

**aprobatorio, -ria** *adj.* approbative, approving.

**aproches** *m. pl.* FORT. approaches.

**aprontar** *tr.* to prepare, have ready. 2 to pay, deliver.

**apropiación** f. appropriation [taking to oneself]. 2 fitting, applying.

**apropiadamente** adv. fitly, appropriately.

**apropiado, -da** adj. fit, proper, appropriate.

**apropiar** tr. to make [something] the possession of one. 2 to fit, make suitable. 3 to apply fitly. 4 ref. to appropriate, take to oneself.

**aprovechable** adj. utilizable, available.

**aprovechado, -da** adj. made use of. 2 well spent [time]. 3 studious, advanced, proficient. 4 m.-f. ser un ~ or una aprovechada, to look after the main chance.

**aprovechamiento** m. utilization, use, exploitation, development. 2 progress, improvement, proficiency.

**aprovechar** tr. to utilize, make use or good use of, benefit from, profit by, improve, spend profitably. 2 to use up [remaining material, etc.]. 3 intr. to be useful, to avail. 4 ref. to avail oneself of, to take advantage of.

**aprovechón, -ona** adj. opportunist, selfish. 2 n. profiteer, advantage-taker, opportunist.

**aprovisionamiento** m. supplying. 2 supply, supplies.

**aprovisionar** tr. to supply, furnish, provision.

**aproximación** f. nearing, nearness. 2 aproximation.

**aproximadamente** adv. approximately.

**aproximado, -da** adj. approximate.

**aproximar** tr. to bring near. 2 to approximate. 3 ref. to approach, come near, approximate.

**aproximativo, -va** adj. approximate.

**ápside** m. ASTR. apsis.

**áptero, -ra** adj. ENT. apterous, wingless.

**aptitud** f. aptitude, fitness, ability, talent.

**apto, -ta** adj. able, competent. 2 apt, fit, suitable.

**apuesta** f. bet, wager.

**apuesto, -ta,** adj. handsome, good-looking. 2 elegant, spruce.

**apuesto, apueste,** etc. irr. V. APOSTAR.

**apuntación** f. note, memorandum. 2 MUS. notation. 3 share in a lottery ticket.

**apuntado, -da** adj. pointed: arco ~, pointed arch.

**apuntador** m. one who notes or marks. 2 THEAT. prompter. 3 ARTILL. pointer [gunner].

**apuntalamiento** m. propping.

**apuntalar** tr. to prop, prop up, shore, underpin.

**apuntamiento** m. pointing, aiming. 2 note, memorandum. 3 sketch. 4 judicial report.

**apuntar** tr. to aim, level, point [a gun, etc.]. 2 to point at, point out, indicate, mark. 3 to note, jot down, inscribe. 4 to point, sharpen. 5 to sketch. 6 to stitch, pin or tack lightly. 7 to prompt [at the theatre, etc.]. 8 to hint at, insinuate. 9 to stake [a sum] on a card. 10 intr. to break, dawn, begin to appear. 11 [of wine] to begin to turn.

**apunte** m. note, memorandum. 2 rough sketch. 3 THEAT. prompter; prompt-book. 4 punter [gambler]. 5 coll, rogue.

**apuntillar** tr. BULLF. to finish off or deal the coup de grâce to the bull with a dagger.

**apuñalar** tr. to poniard, stab with a dagger.

**apuñear** tr. to punch, strike with the fist.

**apuracabos** m. save-all [in a candlestick].

**apuradamente** adv. exactly. 2 with difficulty.

**apurado, -da** p. p. of APURAR. 2 adj. exhausted. 3 needy, hard up. 4 difficult, dangerous. 5 accurate, precise. 6 hard-pressed.

**apurador, -ra** adj. exhausting. 2 worrying.

**apurar** tr. to purify, refine. 2 to investigate or expound minutely. 3 to carry to extremes. 4 to drain, use up, exhaust. 5 to hurry, press. 6 to worry, annoy. 7 ref. to grieve, worry, fret. 8 to exert oneself.

**apuro** m. fix, predicament, difficulty. 2 need, want. 3 worry. 4 (Am.) haste, urgency.

**aquejado, -da** adj. having, suffering [an illness].

**aquejar** tr. to ail, afflict.

**aquel, aquella,** pl. **aquellos, aquellas** adj. that, that... there, those, those... there.

**aquél, aquélla,** pl. **aquéllos, aquéllas** pron. dem. that one, those ones: ~, or aquélla, que, he, or she, who. 2 the former, the first mentioned. 3 m. coll. charm, appeal, it.

**aquelarre** m. witche's Sabbath.

**aquello** pron. dem. neuter that, it; that thing, that matter.

**aquende** adv. on this side of.

**aquenio** m. BOT. achene.

**aqueo, -a** adj.-n. Achean.

**aquerenciarse** ref. [of animals] to become fond of [a place].

**aquí** adv. here: ~ dentro, in here; de ~, from here, hence; por ~, here, hereabouts; this way. 2 now: de ~ en adelante, from now on. 3 then, at that moment.

**aquiescencia** f. acquiescence, consent.

**aquietar** tr. to quiet, calm, lull, pacify. 2 ref. to quiet down, become calm.

**aquilatado, -da** adj. proven, tested, demonstrated.

**aquilatar** tr. to estimate the carats of. 2 to weigh the merit or character of. 3 to purify.

**aquilea** f. BOT. yarrow.

**Aquiles** pr. n. Achilles.

**aquilino, -na** adj. poet, aquiline.

**aquilón** m. north wind; north.

**aquillado, -da** adj. keel-shaped, keel-like.

**Aquisgrán** pr. n. Aix-la-Chapelle.

**Aquitania** f. pr. n. GEOG. Aquitaine. 2 HIST. Aquitania.

**ara** f. altar; altar slab. 2 (cap.) ASTR. Ara. 3 ORN. macaw. 4 en aras de, for the sake of.

**árabe** adj.-n. Arab, Arabic, Arabian. 2 m. Arabic [language]. 3 adj. ARCH. Moresque.

**arabesco, -ca** adj. Arabic. 2 m. F. ARTS arabesque.

**Arabia** pr. n. GEOG. Arabia.

**arábigo, -ga** adj. Arabic, Arabian. 2 m. Arabic [language].

**arabismo** m. Arabism, Arabicism.

**arabización** f. arabicization.

**arable** adj. arable, suitable for ploughing.

**arabista** m.-f. Arabist, Arabic scholar.

**aráceo, -a** adj. BOT. araceous. 2 f. pl. BOT. Araceae.

**arácnido, -da** adj.-n. ZOOL. arachnid, arachnidan.

**aracnoides** adj.-f. ANAT. arachnoid.

**arado** m. AGR. plough, *plow. 2 ploughing, *plowing.

**arador** m. ploughman, *plowman. 2 ZOOL. itch mite.

**Aragón** pr. n. GEOG. Aragon.

**aragonés, -sa** adj.-n. Aragonese.

**araguato** m. ursine howler, an american monkey.

**aralia** f. BOT. American spikenard.

**arambel** m. rag, tatter.

**arameo, -a** adj. Aramaean, Aramaic. 2 m.-f. Aramaean. 3 m. Aramaic [language].

**arana** f. trick, imposition, cheat.

**arancel** m. tariff [of fees, duties or customs].

**arancelario, -ria** adj. [pertaining to] tariff, customs.

**arándano** m. BOT. bilberry, whortleberry.

**arandela** *f.* socket pan [of candlestick]. *2* MECH. washer. *3* burr [on a lance].
**arandillo** *m.* ORN. marsh warbler.
**araña** *f.* ZOOL. spider. *2 fig.* go-getter, thrifty person. *3* chandelier. *4* ICHTH. weaver, stingbull. *5* ARAÑUELA 2. *6* ZOOL. ~ *de mar*, spider crab.
**arañar** *tr.* to scratch. *2* to scrape together, scrape up.
**arañazo** *m.* scratch [mark or injury].
**arañuela** *f.* little spider. *2* BOT. love-in-a-mist.
**arar** *tr.* to plough, plow; to furrow.
**araucano, -na** *adj.-n.* Araucanian.
**araucaria** *f.* BOT. araucaria.
**arbitraje** *m.* arbitration, arbitrage. *2* umpiring; refereeing. *3* COM. arbitrage.
**arbitral** *adj.* arbitral.
**arbitrar** *tr.* to arbitrate; to umpire; to referee. *2* to act freely. *3* to contrive, find [ways, means]; to raise [funds].
**arbitrariedad** *f.* arbitrary act. *2* arbitrariness.
**arbitrario, -ria** *adj.* arbitrary.
**arbitrio** *m.* free will. *2* power, choice, discretion: *al ~ de*, at the discretion of. *3* means, device. *4* arbitrament. *5 pl.* excise, taxes.
**arbitrista** *m.* utopic planner or schemer.
**árbitro, -tra** *adj.-n.* sole master, free to do. *2 m.* arbiter, arbitrator, umpire, referee.
**árbol** *m.* BOT. tree: ~ *de Judas*, Judas tree; ~ *de la ciencia del bien y del mal*, BIBL. tree of knowledge (of good and evil); ~ *de la cruz*, tree of the cross; ~ *de la vida*, BIBL., BOT. tree of life; ANAT. arbor-vitae; ~ *de Navidad*, Christmas tree; ~ *frutal*, fruit tree. *2* MECH. arbor, shaft, axle, spindle: ~ *de levas*, camshaft. *3* NAUT. mast. *4* PRINT. shank. *5* newel [of winding stairs]. *6* ~ *genealógico*, genealogical tree.
**arbolado, -da** *adj.* wooded. *2* NAUT. masted. *3 m.* trees [in a place].
**arboladura** *f.* NAUT. masting, mast and yards.
**arbolar** *tr.* to hoist, raise aloft. *2* to set upright against a wall, etc. *3* NAUT. to mast [a ship]. *4 ref.* [of a horse] to rear.
**arboleda** *f.* grove, wooded ground.
**arborecer** *intr.* to grow into a tree.
**arbóreo, -a** *adj.* arboreal.
**arborescencia** *f.* BOT. arborescence.
**arborescente** *adj.* arborescent.
**arborícola** *adj.* ZOOL. arboreal, living in the trees, tree-dwelling.
**arboricultor** *m.* arboriculturist.
**arboricultura** *f.* arboriculture.
**arbotante** *m.* ARCH. flying buttress.
**arbustivo, -va** *adj.* BOT. shrubby.
**arbusto** *m.* BOT. shrub.
**arca** *f.* coffer, chest, box. *2* strong-box, safe. *3* annealing oven [for glass]. *4* ark: ~ *de la Alianza*, Ark of the Covenant; ~ *de Noé*, Noah's ark. *5* ~ *de agua*, water tower, reservoir. *6 pl.* ANAT. costal cavities.
**arcabucear** *f.* to shoot with a harquebus.
**arcabucería** *f.* trop of harquebusiers. *2* harquebuses. *3* harquebus factory.
**arcabucero** *m.* harquebusier. *2* harquebus maker.
**arcabuz**, *pl.* **-buces** *m.* harquebus.
**arcada** *f.* ARCH. arcade. *2* arch [of a bridge]. *3 pl.* retching.
**Arcadia** *pr. n.* Arcadia.
**arcaduz** *m.* pipe, conduit. *2* bucket [of water-wheel].
**arcaico, -ca** *adj.* archaic. *2* GEOL. Archeozoic.
**arcaísmo** *m.* archaism.

**arcaizante** *adj.* archaistic.
**arcaizar** *tr.-intr.* to archaize.
**arcángel** *m.* archangel.
**arcano, -na** *adj.* arcane. *2 m.* arcanum.
**arce** *m.* BOT. maple tree: ~ *sacarino*, sugar maple.
**arcediano** *m.* archdeacon.
**arcén** *m.* border, brim, edge. *2* curbstone [of well].
**arcilla** *f.* clay: ~ *figulina*, potter's clay, argil.
**arcilloso, -sa** *adj.* clayey, argillaceous.
**arciprestazgo** *m.* archpriesthood.
**arcipreste** *m.* archpriest.
**arco** *m.* GEOM., ELEC. arc: ~ *voltaico*, voltaic arc. *2* ARCH., ANAT. arch.: ~ *de herradura*, horseshoe arch: ~ *de medio punto*, round arc. *3* bow [weapon]. *4* MUS. bow, fiddle-bow. *5* hoop [of a cask]. *6* METEOR. ~ *iris*, rainbow.
**arcón** *m.* large chest or bin.
**arconte** *m.* archon.
**archicofradía** *f.* arch-brotherhood.
**archiconocido, -da** *adj.* coll. well-known, known by everyone.
**archidiácono** *m.* archdeacon.
**archidiócesis** *f.* archdiocese.
**archiducado** *m.* archduchy, archdukedom.
**archiducal** *adj.* archducal.
**archiduque** *m.* archduke.
**archiduquesa** *f.* archduchess.
**archifamoso, -sa** *adj.* coll. world famous.
**archimandrita** *m.* archimandrite.
**archimillonario, -ria** *n.* multimillionaire, multimillionairess.
**archipiélago** *m.* archipelago.
**archisabido** *adj.* coll. very well-known.
**archivador** *m.* letter file, filing cabinet.
**archivar** *tr.* to deposit in the archives. *2* to file, file away [papers, etc.]. *3* coll. to pigeonhole.
**archivero, -ra** *m.-f.* archivist.
**archivo** *m.* archives; file, files.
**archivolta** *f.* ARCH. archivolt.
**Ardenas** *pr. n.* Ardennes.
**ardentía** *f.* ardour. *2* heartburn. *3* phosphorescence [of sea].
**arder** *tr.* to burn, to blaze. *2* POÉT. to shine. *3* ~ *de*, or *en*, to burn with [love, etc.]; ~ *en*, to be ablaze with [war, discord, etc.]. *4 ref.* to burn, be burning. *5* [of grain, tobacco, etc.] to be heated up.
**ardid** *m.* stratagem, trick, artifice.
**ardido, -da** *adj.* bold, intrepid.
**ardiente** *adj.* ardent, burning, fiery, hot. *2* red. *3* ardent, feverish, eager, vehement.
**ardientemente** *adv.* ardently, fervently, earnestly.
**ardilla** *f.* ZOOL. squirrel.
**ardimiento** *m.* burning. *2* intrepidity, courage.
**ardite** *m.* old spanish coin of little value: *no me importa un ~*, fig. I don't care a hang.
**ardor** *m.* ardour, heat. *2* ardour, vehemence, eagerness. *3* intrepidity, courage.
**ardorosamente** *adv.* ardently.
**ardoroso, -sa** *adj.* burning, ardent, vehement, eager.
**arduo, -dua** *adj.* arduous, hard, difficult.
**área** *f.* area [superficial extent]. *2* are [measure].
**areca** *f.* BOT. areca, betel palm.
**arena** *f.* sand, grit: ~ *movediza*, quicksand. *2* arena, circus. *3 pl.* MED. gravel, bladder stones.
**arenáceo, -a** *adj.* arenaceous, sandy.
**arenal** *m.* sandy ground, extent of quicksands. *2* sand pit.
**arenar** *tr.* ENARENAR. *2* to rub or polish with sand.
**arenero** *m.* RLY. sandbox.
**arenga** *f.* harangue, speech, address.

**arengar** *intr.-tr.* to harangue.
**arenilla** *f.* powder to dry writing. *2 pl.* MED. stones, gravel.
**arenisca** *f.* PETROG. sandstone.
**arenisco, -ca** *adj.* sandy, gritty.
**arenoso, -sa** *adj.* sandy.
**arenque** *m.* ICHTH. herring.
**aréola** *f.* ANAT., ZOOL., MED. areola, areole.
**areometría** *f.* areometry.
**areómetro** *m.* areometer, hydrometer.
**areopagita** *m.* areopagite.
**areópago** *m.* Aeropagus.
**arepa** *f.* (Am.) corn griddle cake.
**arestín** *m.* BOT. an umbelliferous plant. *2* VET. thrush.
**arete** *m.* small hoop or ring. *2* earring.
**arfada** *f.* NAUT. pitching [of a ship].
**arfar** *intr.* NAUT. [of a ship] to pitch.
**argadijo** *m.* ARGADILLO. *2* ARGAMANDIJO.
**argadillo** *m.* DEVANADERA. *2* bustling, restless person.
**argallera** *f.* croze, crozing saw.
**argamasa** *f.* MAS. mortar.
**argamasón** *m.* large dry piece of mortar.
**árgana** *f.* MECH. crane.
**árganas** *f. pl.* wicker baskets for packsaddle.
**arganeo** *m.* NAUT. anchor ring.
**Argel** *pr. n.* GEOG. Algiers.
**Argelia** *pr. n.* Algeria.
**argelino, -na** *adj.-n.* Algerian, Algerine.
**argemone** *f.* BOT. argemone, prickly poppy.
**argén** *m.* HER. argent.
**argentado, -da** *adj.* silver-plated. *2* silvery.
**argénteo, -a** *adj.* silvery, silver-white.
**argentería** *f.* embroidery in gold or silver.
**argentero** *m.* silversmith.
**argentífero, -ra** *adj.* argentiferous.
**Argentina (la)** *pr. n.* GEOG. the Argentine.
**argentinismo** *m.* argentine word, phrase or locution.
**argentino, -na** *adj.* argentine, silvery. *2* Argentine. *3 m.-f.* Argentine, Argentinean.
**argento** *m.* poet. silver. *2 ~ vivo,* quicksilver.
**argivo, -va** *adj.-n.* Argive.
**argo** *m.* CHEM. argon.
**Argólida (la)** *pr. n.* HIST. GEOG. Argolis.
**argolla** *f.* ring, metal ring. *2* bracelet. *3* old game similar to croquet.
**argón** *m.* CHEM. argon.
**argonauta** *m.* MYTH. Argonaut. *2* ZOOL. paper nautilus.
**Argos** *pr. n.* HIST. GEOG. Argos. *2* MITH. Argus. *3* MYTH., ASTR. Argo. *4 m.* Argus [watchful person].
**argucia** *f.* subtlety, sophistry.
**árguenas** *f. pl.* handbarrow. *2* ALFORJAS.
**argüir** *tr.* to infer. *2* to argue [imply, prove; accuse]. *3 intr.* to argue, reason. ¶ CONJUG. like *huir.*
**argumentación** *f.* argumentation.
**argumentador, -ra** *m.-f.* arguer, argumentator.
**argumentar** *tr.* to argue, dispute, reason.
**argumento** *m.* argument. *2* plot [of a story or play].
**aria** *f.* MUS. aria.
**Ariadna** *f. pr. n.* MYTH. Ariadne.
**aridecer** *tr.* to render aid. *2 ref.* to become arid. ¶ CONJUG. like *agradecer.*
**aridez** *f.* aridity, aridness.
**árido, -da** *adj.* arid. *2 m. pl.* dry commodities [esp. grains].
**Aries** *m.* ASTR. Aries.

**ariete** *m.* battering ram. *2* NAUT. ram. *3* PHYS. ~ *hidráulico,* hydraulic ram.
**arijo, -ja** *adj.* AGR. light, easily tilled.
**arilo** *m.* BOT. aril.
**arillo** *m.* earring.
**arimez** *m.* ARCH. projection [in a building].
**ario, -ria** *adj.-n.* Aryan.
**arísaro** *m.* BOT. wake-robin.
**arisco, -ca** *adj.* unsociable, surly, shy.
**arista** *f.* arris, edge. *2* BOT. awn, beard [of grain].
**aristado, -da** *adj.* BOT. bearded [wheat].
**aristarco** *m.* Aristarch, severe critic.
**Arístides** *m. pr n.* Aristides.
**aristocracia** *f.* aristocracy.
**aristócrata** *m.-f.* aristocrat.
**aristocrático, -ca** *adj.* aristocratic.
**aristocratizar** *tr.* to make aristocratic.
**Aristófanes** *pr. n.* Aristophanes.
**aristoloquia** *f.* BOT. birthwort.
**Aristóteles** *pr. n.* Aristotle.
**aristotélico, -ca** *adj.-n.* Aristotelian.
**aritmética** *f.* arithmetic.
**aritmético, -ca** *adj.* arithmetic(al. *2 m.-f.* arithmetician.
**arlequín** *m.* harlequin. *2* (cap.) Harlequin.
**arlequinado, -da** *adj.* parti-coloured [clothes].
**arlequinada** *f.* harlequinade, bufoonery.
**arlo** *m.* BOT. barberry.
**arma** *f.* weapon, arm: ~ *atómica,* atomic weapon; ~ *blanca,* steel, cold steel; ~ *de fuego,* firearm; *¡a las armas!,* to arms!; *alzarse en armas,* to rise up in arms; *medir las armas,* to fight; *presentar las armas,* to present arms; *tomar las armas,* to take up arms; *sobre las armas,* under arms. *2* MIL. arm [combatant branch of an army]. *3 pl.* arms [military profession]. *6* HER. arms, armorial bearings.
**armada** *f.* navy, naval forces. *2* fleet [of warships].
**armadía** *f.* raft, float.
**armadijo** *m.* trap, snare [for game]. *2* wooden frame.
**armadillo** *m.* ZOOL. armadillo.
**armado** *m.* man dressed as a Roman soldier [in Holy Week processions].
**armador** *m.* shipowner, ship-charterer. *2* assembler, adjuster. *3* jerkin.
**armadura** *f.* armo(u)r [defensive covering]. *2* frame, framework, truss. *3* ARCH. roof frame. *4* ELECT., MAGN. armature. *5* MUS. key signature.
**armajo** *m.* ALMARJO.
**armamentista** *adj.* arms, armaments: *política ~,* arms policy; *carrera ~,* arms race.
**armamento** *m.* armament. *2* arms [of a soldier]. *3* outfitting [a ship].
**Armando** *m. pr. n.* Herman.
**armar** *tr.* to array in armour. *2* to arm. *3* to fix [a bayonet]. *4* NAUT. to outfit, fit out [a ship]. *5* to supply [with]. *6* to assemble, set up, adjust. *7* to build, establish [on]. *8* to set [a trap]. *9* to start, make, rise, stir up: ~ *ruido,* to raise a disturbance; *armarla,* to kick up a shindy. *10* to form, prepare. *11* SEW. to stiffen. *12* ~ *caballero,* to knight. *13 ref.* to array oneself in armour. *14* to arm oneself. *15* to happen, arise, be raised or started. *16 armarse de valor,* to gather up one's courage; *armarse de paciencia,* to arm oneself with patience.
**armario** *m.* press, wardrobe, cabinet, closet.
**armatoste** *m.* hulk, cumbersome machine or object; big, clumsy person.

**armazón** f. assemblage, setting up. 2 frame, framework, structure. 3 ANAT. skeleton.
**armella** f. screw eye, eyebolt.
**Armenia** pr. n. GEOG. Armenia.
**armenio, -nia** adj.-n. Armenian.
**armería** f. arms museum. 2 armo(u)ry. 3 gunsmith craft or shop; arms shop.
**armero** m. armo(u)rer; gunsmith. 2 rack or stand for arms, armrack.
**armilar** adj. armillary.
**armilla** f. ARCH. astragal [of a column]. 2 ASTR. armilary sphere.
**armiñado, -da** adj. trimmed or lined with ermine fur. 2 ermine-white.
**armiño** m. ZOOL., HER. ermine. 2 ermine fur.
**armisticio** m. armistice.
**armón** m. ARTILL. limber.
**armonía** f. harmony. 2 MUS. harmonization.
**armónica** f. MUS. harmonica, mouth organ.
**armónicamente** adv. harmoniously, in a harmonic way, in harmony.
**armónico, -ca** adj. harmonic. 2 m. MUS., PHYS. harmonic.
**armonio** m. MUS. harmonium.
**armonioso, -sa** adj. harmonious.
**armonista** m.-f. harmonist.
**armonización** f. harmonization.
**armonizar** tr.-intr. to harmonize.
**armuelle** m. BOT. orach, orache.
**arnés** m. harness, armour. 2 pl. harness [of horses]. 3 gear, tackle, implements, tools.
**árnica** f. BOT., PHARM. arnica.
**aro** m. hoop, ring, rim. 2 hoop [plaything]: entrar por el ~, to be forced to yield. 3 BOT. cuckoopint.
**aroma** f. flower of the huisache. 2 aroma, fragrance. 3 m.-f. aromatic.
**aromático, -ca** adj. aromatic.
**aromatizador** m. (Am.) spray, atomizer.
**aromatizar** tr. to aromatize.
**aromo** BOT. huisache, sponge tree.
**aromoso, -sa** adj. aromatic.
**arpa** f. MUS. harp: ~ eolia, aeolian harp.
**arpado, -da** adj. serrated, toothed. 2 poet. singing [bird].
**arpar** tr. to scratch. 2 to tear, rend.
**arpegiar** intr. to arpeggio.
**arpegio** m. MUS. arpeggio.
**arpella** f. ORN. marsh harrier.
**arpeo** m. NAUT. grappling iron.
**arpía** f. MYTH. harpy. 2 harpy [rapacious person]. 3 shrew [woman]. 4 hag.
**arpillera** f. burlap, sackcloth.
**arpista** m.-f. harper, harpist.
**arpón** m. harpoon. 2 ARCH. clamp.
**arponear** tr. to harpoon.
**arponero** m. harpoon maker. 2 harpooner.
**arqueador** m. ship gauger. 2 wool beater.
**arqueamiento** m. NAUT. gauging, tonnage, standard measurement of a ship's capacity.
**arquear** tr. to arch, bend. 2 to beat [wool]. 3 to gauge [a ship]. 4 intr. to retch, be nauseated. 5 ref. to arch.
**arquegonio** m. BOT. archegonium.
**arqueo** m. arching, bending. 2 NAUT. gauging. 3 NAUT. tonnage. 4 COM. checking the contents of a cashbox.
**arqueología** f. archaeology.
**arqueológico, -ca** adj. archaeological.
**arqueólogo** m. archaeologist.
**arquería** f. ARCH. series of arches.
**arquero** m. archer, bowman. 2 bow maker.

**arqueta** f. small coffer.
**arquetipo** m. archetype.
**arquiepiscopal** adj. archiepiscopal.
**Arquímedes** pr. n. Archimedes.
**arquitecto** m. architect.
**arquitectónico, -ca** adj. architectonic, architectural.
**arquitectura** f. architecture; architectonics.
**arquitrabe** m. ARCH. architrave.
**arquivolta** f. ARCHIVOLTA.
**arrabal** m. suburb. 2 pl. environs, outskirts.
**arracada** f. earring with a pendant, eardrop.
**arracimarse** ref. to cluster, bunch.
**arraclán** m. BOT. alder buckthorn.
**arraigado, -da** adj. rooted, deep-rooted. 2 owning real estate, landed.
**arraigar** intr.-ref. to take root. 2 tr. to establish, to strengthen.
**arraigo** m. taking root. 2 root, settling [in a place]; landed property, connexions.
**arramblar** tr. [of streams] to cover [ground] with sand or gravel. 2 to sweep away. 3 ref. [of ground] to be covered with sand or gravel.
**arrancaclavos** m. nail puller.
**arrancada** f. sudden departure. 2 NAUT. starting speed. 3 sudden increase in speed. 4 sudden charge [of a bull].
**arrancadura** f., **arrancamiento** m. pulling out, extraction.
**arrancar** tr. to root up or out, to pull out, extract, extirpate: ~ de cuajo or de raíz, to uproot, eradicate. 2 to pluck [feathers, hairs, etc.]. 3 to tear out, snatch, snatch away. 4 to wrest, wrench, wring, extort, force [from]. 5 intr. to start: ~ a correr, to start running. 6 to set sail. 7 to come [from], originate [in]. 8 ARCH. [of an arch or vault] to spring.
**arrancarse** ref. ENRANCIARSE.
**arranque** m. pulling up. 2 start [of a motor, a car, etc.]. 3 MECH. starter, starting gear: ~ automático, self-starter. 4 impulse, outburst [of piety, anger, etc.]. 5 sally, lively remark. 6 ARCH. spring [of an arch]. 7 ANAT., BOT. base, root.
**arrapiezo** m. child, urchin. 2 rag, tatter.
**arras** f. security, earnest [of a contract], earnest money, handsel. 2 thirteen coins given by bridegroom to bride at weeding.
**arrasamiento** m. razing to the ground.
**arrasar** tr. to level, flatten. 2 to raze, demolish. 3 to level with a strickle. 4 to fill to the brim. 5 ref.-intr. [of the sky] to clear up. 6 ref. arrasarse los ojos de, or en, lágrimas, [of the eyes] to become filled with tears.
**arrastradamente** adv. coll. badly, poorly. 2 coll. miserably, wretchedly.
**arrastradero** m. log path. 2 BULLF. spot through which dead animals are dragged from the ring.
**arrastradizo, -za** adj. dangling, -trailing.
**arrastrado, -da** adj. wretched, miserable. 3 rascally. 4 suit-following [card game]. 5 m.-f. rascal, scamp.
**arrastrar** tr. to drag, drag along, on or down, to trail, to have: ~ los pies, to shuffle, drag one's feet. 2 to carry after oneself. 3 to drive, impel; to carry away, to wash down, urge along. 4 intr. to drag, trail [hang down to the ground]. 5 CARDS. to lead trumps. 6 intr. to crawl, creep, trail. 7 ref. fig. to crawl, cringe.
**arrastre** m. drag, dragging; haulage. 2 washing down [by waters]. 3 dragging dead bull from ring. 4 CARDS. leading a trump.

**arrayán** *m.* BOT. myrtle. *2* BOT. ~ *brabántico,* wax myrtle, bayberry.

**¡arre!** *interj.* gee!, gee up! *2* get away!

**arrear** *tr.* to urge on [horses, mules, etc.]. *2* to spur, to hurry. *3* to deliver [a blow]. *4* to dress, adorn. *5 intr.* to hurry: *¡arrea!,* get moving!; nonsense!

**arrebatadamente** *adv.* hurriedly, hastily. *2* impulsively, rashly.

**arrebatado, -da** *adj.* hasty, rash, impetuous, violent. *2* ruddy, flushed, inflamed [face].

**arrebatador, -ra** *adj.* captivating. *2* stirring, exciting, inflaming, enrapturing.

**arrebatamiento** *m.* carrying off. *2* fury, rage. *3* rapture, ecstasy.

**arrebatar** *tr.* to snatch, to carry or take away [by force]. *2* to carry away, move, captivate, enrapture. *3 ref.* to be led away [by emotionl, passion, etc.]. *4* COOK. to be burned.

**arrebatiña** *f.* scramble, scrimmage [to pick up something].

**arrebato** *m.* fit, rage, fury. *2* rapture.

**arrebol** *m.* red tinge in the clouds. *2* rouge, paint. *3 pl.* red clouds.

**arrebolar** *tr.* to give a red tinge to. *2 ref.* take a red tinge, to flush.

**arrebozar** *tr.* to coat, to cover [with flour, crumbs, etc.]. *2 ref.* to cover oneself, to muffle or wrap oneself. *3* to swarm, to hive [the bees, wasps, etc.].

**arrebujadamente** *adv.* confusedly.

**arrebujar** *tr.* to pick up [clothes, etc.] in a huddle or heap. *2* to tuck in; to wrap up. *3 ref.* to tuck oneself in; to wrap oneself up.

**arreciar** *intr.-ref.* to increase in strength or intensity, to wax stronger. *2 ref.* ARRECIRSE.

**arrecife** *m.* reef [in the sea]. *2* stone-paved road.

**arrecirse** *ref.* to grow stiff with cold. ¶ Only used in forms having *i* in their terminations.

**arrechucho** *m.* sudden impulse, fit, outburst. *2* sudden and passing indisposition.

**arredramiento** *m.* backing out, fright, intimidation.

**arredrar** *tr.* to frighten, intimidate; to make [one] draw back or back out through fear. *2 ref.* to be frightened; to flinch, draw back.

**arredro** *adv.* backwards.

**arregazado, -da** *adj.* tucked up. *2* turned up.

**arregazar** *tr.* to tuck up [the skirts].

**arreglado, -da** *p. p.* of ARREGLAR. *2 adj.* orderly, neat. *3* regular [without excesses]. *4* moderate, reasonable [price, etc.].

**arreglar** *tr.-ref.* to adjust, regulate. *2* to settle, arrange. *3* to put in order. *4* to dress, smarten up. *5* to mend, fix up. *6 ref. arreglarse con,* to come to an understanding with; to manage with. *7 arreglárselas,* to manage, to shift.

**arreglo** *m.* order, orderly state. *2* settlement arrangement; agreement, compromise. *3* arrangement, putting in order. *4* mending, fixing up. *5* MUS. arrangement. *6 con ~ a,* according to.

**arrellanarse** *ref.* to sit at ease, to make oneself comfortable [in a seat].

**arremangar** *tr.-ref.* to tuck up [one's] sleeves. *2* to take a firm decision.

**arremetedor, -ra** *adj.* attacking.

**arremeter** *intr.* to attack, rush [upon].

**arremetida** *f.* attack, rushing upon. *2* sudden start [of a horse].

**arremolinarse** *ref.* to crowd, press together.

**arrendable** *adj.* suitable for renting, rentable. *2* LAW. leasable.

**arrendado, -da** *adj.* rented, leased, farmed. *2* obedient to the reins.

**arrendador, -ra** *m.-f.* landlord, landlady, lessor. *2* lessee, tenant, farmer.

**arrendajo** *m.* ORN. jay. *2* fig. aper, mimic.

**arrendamiento** *m.* renting; leasing, letting, farming; lease. *2* rent.

**arrendar** *tr.* to rent, to lease, to farm [to someone or by someone]; to let. *2* to tie [a horse] by the reins. *3* to break [a horse] to the reins. ¶ CONJUG. like *acertar.*

**arrendatario, -ria** *m.-f.* lessee, tenant, farmer.

1) **arreo** *m.* dress, ornament. *2 pl.* harness, riding gear. *3* appurtenances.

2) **arreo** *adv.* successively, without interruption.

**arrepanchingarse** *ref.* to lounge, to sit back, to make oneself comfortable.

**arrepentido, -da** *adj.* repentant; regretful.

**arrepentimiento** *m.* repentance; regret.

**arrepentirse** *ref.* to repent: ~ *de,* to repent of, be sorry for, to regret. *2* to back down or out. ¶ CONJUG. like *hervir.*

**arrepiento, arrepintió, arrepienta,** etc. *irr.* V. ARREPENTIR.

**arrequesonarse** *ref.* [of milk] to curdle.

**arrequives** *m. pl.* finery, adornments. *2* circumstances or requisites.

**arrestado, -da** *adj.* bold, daring.

**arrestar** *tr.* to arrest, imprison. *2* MIL. to detain, confine. *3 ref. arrestarse a,* to dare, venture.

**arresto** *m.* arrest, detention. *2* MIL. confinement. *3 pl.* pluck, spirit.

**arrevesado, -da** *adj.* intricate, obscure.

**arrezagar** *tr.* to tuck up [sleeves, etc.].

**arriada** *f.* flood, overflowing, freshet. *2* NAUT. lowering of the sails.

**arrianismo** *m.* Arianism.

**arriano, -na** *adj.-n.* Arian.

**arriar** *tr.* NAUT. to lower, to strike. *2* NAUT. to pay out [a rope]. *3* to strike [a flag, etc.].

**arriate** *m.* narrow bed along the wall of a garden. *2* causeway. *3* trellis.

**arriba** *adv.* up, upwards: *cuesta ~,* uphill; *río ~,* upstream; *de cuatro pesetas ~,* from four pesetas up. *2* above, on high, at the top, aloft: *de ~ abajo,* from top to bottom; from beginning to end. *3* afore, before, above: ~ *dicho,* above mentioned. *4 interj.* up!

**arribada** *f.* NAUT. arrival, putting in: ~ *forzosa,* putting in by stress.

**arribaje** *m.* NAUT. arrival, putting into port.

**arribar** *intr.* to arrive. *2* NAUT. to put into port. *3* NAUT. to fall off to leeward.

**arribazón** *f.* seasonal influx of fish to coasts.

**arribismo** *m.* arrivism.

**arribista** *adj.* profit-seeking, self-seeking. *2 n.* arrivist, arriviste.

**arribo** *m.* NAUT. arrival [of a ship, of merchandise].

**arricés** *m.* buckle of a stirrup strap.

**arriendo** *m.* ARRENDAMIENTO.

**arriero** *m.* muleteer.

**arriesgado, -da** *adj.* risky, dangerous. *2* daring, bold, rash.

**arriesgar** *tr.* to risk, hazard, venture. *2 ref.* to expose oneself to danger. *3 arriesgarse a,* to dare, risk [to do something].

**arrimadero** *m.* support. *2* wainscot.

**arrimar** *tr.* to bring close [to], draw up [to], place [against]. *2* to put away, shelve. *3* to give [a blow, etc.]. *4* NAUT. to stow [the cargo]. *5 ref. arrimarse a,* to go near, to lean against, to press oneself close to; to seek the protection of; to associate with.

**arrimo** *m.* placing beside, near, against. *2* support, help, protection. *3* attachment, leaning.

**arrinconado, -da** *adj.* out-of-the-way. *2* shelved, ignored, forgotten.

**arrinconamiento** *m.* discarding, laying aside, ruling out.

**arrinconar** *tr.* to put in a corner. *2* to corner [a person]. *3* to shelve, ignore, neglect. *4* to lay aside, discard. *5 ref.* to retire, become a recluse.

**arriñonado, -da** *adj.* kidney-shaped.

**arriostrar** *tr.* ARCH. to shore up, to support, to prop up, to stay.

**Arrio** *pr. n.* Arius.

**arriscado, -da** *adj.* craggy. *2* bold, resolute. *3* easy, free, brisk.

**arriscamiento** *m.* boldness, resolution.

**arriscar** *tr.-ref.* ARRIESGAR. *2 ref.* [of sheep or cattle] to plunge over a crag.

**arritmia** *f.* MED. arrhythmy.

**arrítmico, -ca** *adj.* MED. arrhythmic.

**arrizar** *tr.* NAUT. to reef. *2* NAUT. to fasten, lash.

**arroaz** *m.* ZOOL. dolphin.

**arroba** *f.* weight of about 11¹/₂ kg. *2* liquid measure of varying value.

**arrobador, -ra** *adj.* enchanting, entrancing.

**arrobamiento** *m.* bliss, entrancement, ecstasy, rapture.

**arrobar** *tr.* to entrance, to enrapture. *2 ref.* to be entranced, enraptured.

**arrocero, -ra** *adj.* [pertaining to] rice. *2 m.-f.* rice grower; rice dealer.

**arrodilladura** *f.*, **arrodillamiento** *m.* kneeling.

**arrodillar** *tr.* to make kneel down. *2 ref.* to kneel, kneel down.

**arrodigrar, arrodrigonar** *tr.* to prop [vines].

**arrogación** *f.* arrogation.

**arrogancia** *f.* arrogance, haughtiness. *2* courage, spirit. *3* handsomeness, stately carriage.

**arrogante** *adj.* arrogant, haughty. *2* courageous, spirited. *3* handsome, stately.

**arrogantemente** *adv.* arrogantly. *2* bravely, courageously. *3* proudly, with dignity.

**arrogarse** *ref.* to arrogate to oneself.

**arrojadizo, -za** *adj.* easily thrown; for throwing, missile.

**arrojado, -da** *adj.* bold, intrepid, dashing, rash.

**arrojar** *tr.* to throw, fling, hurl, cast. *2* to shed, emit. *3* to put forth [leaves, shoots]. *4* to expel, throw out; to turn out, dismiss. *5* NAUT. to drive or cast [on rocks, etc.]. *6* to vomit. *7* to show [a total, a balance]. *8 ref.* to throw oneself. *9* to rush [at], fall [upon]. *10* to launch out upon [an enterprise].

**arrojo** *m.* boldness, dash, bravery.

**arrollador** *m.* rolling, winding. *2* violent, sweeping.

**arrollamiento** *m.* rolling, winding. *2* ELECT. winding.

**arrollar** *tr.* to roll, roll up. *2* to wind, coil. *3* to roll or sweep away. *4* to rout [the enemy]. *5* to trample down, to run over. *6* to confound [an opponent]. *7* to rock [a child].

**arromanzar** *tr.* to translate into Spanish.

**arropar** *tr.-ref.* to cover, wrap, wrap up [in clothes].

**arrope** *m.* must boiled to a syrup. *2* honey syrup.

**arropea** *f.* fetter. *2* hopple [for horses].

**arropía** *f.* kind of taffy made of honey.

**arrostrar** *tr.* to face, stand, brave. *2 ref.* to fight face to face.

**arroyar** *tr.* [of rain] to form gullies in. *2 ref.* AGR. [of grain] to become smutted.

**arroyo** *m.* brook, rivulet, stream. *2* gutter [in a street], street: *poner en el ~*, to put out in the street. *3* stream [of tears, etc.].

**arroyuelo** *m.* rill, small brook.

**arroz** *m.* BOT. rice.

**arrozal** *m.* rice field.

**arrufadura** *f.* NAUT. sheer [of a ship].

**arrufar** *tr.* NAUT. to form the sheer of. *2 intr.* [of a ship] to have a sheer.

**arrufianado, -da** *adj.* rascally, dishonest, mischeavous. *2* vulgar, coarse, uncouth.

**arruga** *f.* wrinkle; crease, crumple, rumple.

**arrugamiento** *m.* wrinkling, creasing, crumpling.

**arrugar** *tr.* to wrinkle; to crease, crumple, rumple. *2* SEW. to gather, fold. *3 ~ el entrecejo, la frente*, to frown, to knit the brow. *4 ref.* to wrinkle, crumple, shrivel [become wrinkled].

**arruinar** *tr.* to ruin, ruinate, demolish, destroy. *2* to become ruined; to fall into ruins.

**arrullador, -ra** *adj.* cooing. *2* lulling.

**arrullar** *tr.* to coo; to bill and coo. *2* to lull or sing to sleep, to croon.

**arrullo** *m.* coo. *2* billing and cooing. *3* lullaby.

**arrumaco** *m.* caress, show of affection.

**arrumaje** *m.* NAUT. stowage.

**arrumar** *tr.* NAUT. to stow. *2 ref.* NAUT. [of the horizon] to become overcast.

**arrumazón** *f.* NAUT. stowage. *2* overcast horizon.

**arrumbar** *tr.* to lay aside, put out of the way, reject, discard. *2* to confound [an opponent]. *3* to shelve, cast into oblivion. *4 intr.* NAUT. to fix the course. *6 ref.* NAUT. to take bearings.

**arrurruz** *m.* arrowroot [starch].

**arsenal** *m.* shipyard, dockyard, navy yard. *2* arsenal.

**arseniato** *m.* CHEM. arseniate.

**arsénico** *adj.-m.* CHEM. arsenic.

**Artajerjes** *m. pr. n.* Artaxerxes.

**arte** *m.-f.* art: *artes mecánicas*, manual arts; *bellas artes*, fine arts; *por ~ de birlibirloque* or *de encantamiento*, as if by magic; *no tener ~ ni parte en*, to have nothing to do with. *2* craft, skill, knack; cunning: *con malas artes*, by evil means. *3* fishing appliance.

**artefacto** *m.* manufacture, mechanical handiwork. *2* device, contrivance, appliance.

**artejo** *m.* knuckle [of finger]. *2* ZOOL. article.

**Artemisa** *pr. n.* MYTH. Artemis.

**artemisa, artemisia** *f.* BOT. mugwort; sagebrush.

**arteramente** *adv.* artfully, craftily, slyly.

**arteria** *f.* ANAT. artery. *2* fig. artery [main thoroughfare].

**artería** *f.* artfulness, craftiness; cunning, trick.

**arterial** *adj.* arterial.

**arteriola** *f.* ANAT. arteriole.

**arteriosclerosis** *f.* MED. arteriosclerosis.

**arteritis** *f.* MED. arteritis.

**artero, -ra** *adj.* artful, crafty, sly.

**artesa** *f.* trough [for kneading, washing ore, etc.].

**artesanado** *m.* craftmen, artisans.

**artesanía** *f.* craftsmanship. *2* craftsmen.

**artesano, -na** *m.-f.* artisan, craftsman, mechanic.

**artesiano, -na** *adj.-n.* Artesian.

**artesón** *m.* kitchen tub. *2* ARCH. caisson, coffer.

**artesonado, -da** *adj.* panelled [ceiling]. *2 m.* panelwork [in a ceiling].

**ártico, -ca** *adj.* arctic: *Océano ~*, Arctic Ocean.

**articulación** f. articulation. 2 MECH. joint.
**articulado, -da** adj. articulate, articulated. 2 m. the articles [of an act, law, etc.]. 3 adj.-m. articulate.
1) **articular** tr. to articulate. 2 ref. to articulate, be connected.
2) **articular & articulario, -ria** adj. articular.
**articulista** m.-f. writer of articles.
**artículo** m. article [in a writing, contract, law, act, etc.; literary composition]: ~ de fondo, leader, editorial. 2 entry [in a dictionary]. 3 article [of faith]. 4 article, commodity: artículos de consumo, consumer's goods. 5 GRAM. article. 6 ZOOL. articulation. 7 en el ~ de la muerte, in articulo mortis.
**artífice** m. artificier, craftsman, artist. 2 maker.
**artificial** adj. artificial.
**artificiero** m. MIL. artificer.
**artificio** m. artifice, skill. 2 artifice, cunning, trick. 3 device, contrivance.
**artificioso, -sa** adj. skilful, ingenious. 2 crafty, artful.
**artilugio** m. contraption, worthless mechanical contrivance.
**artillar** tr. to equip with artillery.
**artillería** f. artillery; ordnance.
**artillero** m. gunner, artilleryman.
**artimaña** f. trick, stratagem. 2 trap, snare.
**artiodáctilo, -la** adj.-m. ZOOL. artiodactyl.
**artista** m.-f. artist.
**artísticamente** adv. artistically.
**artístico, -ca** adj. artistic.
**artocarpáceo, -a** adj. BOT. artocarpous.
**artritis** f. MED. arthritis.
**artritismo** m. MED. arthritism.
**artrópodo, -da** adj.-m. ZOOL. arthropod. 2 m.-pl. ZOOL. Arthropoda.
**arturiano, -na; artúrico, -ca** adj. arthurian.
**Arturo** pr. n. Arthur.
**arúspice** m. haruspex.
**arveja** f. BOT. spring vetch, tare.
**arvejal, arvejar** m. vetch field.
**arzobispado** m. archbishopric.
**arzobispal** adj. archiepiscopal.
**arzobispo** m. archbishop.
**arzolla** f. BOT. kind of centaury. 2 BOT. milk thistle.
**arzón** m. ~ delantero, saddlebow; ~ trasero, cantle [in saddles].
**as** m. ace [in cards or dice]. 2 ace, king [good performer].
**asa** f. handle [of a basket, cup, valise, etc.]: en asas, fig. akimbo. 2 ASIDERO. 3 BOT. ~ fétida, asafœtida.
**asadero, -ra** adj. fit for roasting.
**asado, -da** adj. roasted: ~ al horno, baked [meat]; ~ a la parrilla, broiled. 2 m. roast.
**asador** m. spit [for roasting]. 2 roasting jack.
**asadura** f. entrails, haslet; liver. 2 coll. slowness, phlegm.
**asaetear** tr. to shoot, wound or kill with arrows. 2 to bother, harass.
**asalariado, -da** adj. salaried. 2 m. wage-earner.
**asalariar** tr. to employ, hire [a person].
**asalmonado, -da** adj. salmon-coloured.
**asaltante** adj. assailing. 2 m.-f. assailant.
**asaltar** tr. to assail, assault, storm. 2 to surprise, hold up. 3 [of a thought, fear, etc.] to strike, to assail; [of death] to overtake.
**asalto** m. assault, storm: tomar por ~, to take by storm. 2 FENC. assault. 3 BOX. round.
**asamblea** f. assembly [for deliberation or legislation]. 2 MIL. assembly.

**asambleísta** m.-f. member of an assembly. 2 m. assemblyman.
**asar** tr. to roast: ~ a la parrilla, to broil. 2 ref. fig. to roast [be roasted].
**asargado, -da** adj. twiled, sergelike.
**ásaro** m. BOT. asarabacca.
**asaz** adv. poet. enough; much, very.
**asbesto** m. MINER. asbestos.
**ascalonia** f. BOT. shallot.
**ascáride** f. ZOOL. ascarid.
**ascendencia** f. ancestry, line of ancestors.
**ascendente** adj. ascending, ascendant. 2 up [train].
**ascender** intr. to ascend. 2 to accede [to the throne]. 3 to amount or add up [to]. 4 to be promoted. 5 tr. to promote. ¶ CONJUG. like entender.
**ascendido, -da** adj. promoted.
**ascendiente** adj. ascending, ascendant. 2 m.-f. ancestor. 3 m. ascendancy, ascendency.
**ascensión** f. ascension, ascent. 2 ASTR. ascension. 3 la Ascensión, the Ascension, Ascension Day. 4 accession [to the throne].
**ascensional** adj. ascensional.
**ascenso** m. promotion.
**ascensor** m. lift, elevator.
**ascensorista** m. lift maker or operator.
**asceta** m. ascetic.
**ascético, -ca** adj. ascetic(al. 2 f. ascetics.
**ascetismo** m. ascetism.
**ascidia** f. ZOOL. ascidian.
**asciendo, ascienda,** etc. irr. V. ASCENDER.
**asco** m. nausea, loathing, disgust: dar ~, to turn the stomach, to disgust; hacer ascos a, to turn up one's nose at. 2 disgusting thing.
**ascomiceto** s. BOT. ascomycete.
**ascón** s. BOT. ascon.
**ascua** f. ember, live coal: ~ de oro, resplendent thing; estar en ascuas, to be on tenterhooks; arrimar uno el ascua a su sardina, to further one's own interests.
**Asdrúbal** pr. n. Hasdrubal.
**aseadamente** adv. neatly, tidily, in an orderly way. 2 cleanly.
**aseado, -da** adj. clean, neat, tidy.
**asear** tr. to clean, to tidy. 2 ref. to make [oneself] clean, to tidy [oneself] up.
**asechanza** f. snare, trap, pitfall.
**asechar** tr. to set traps [for somebody].
**asecho** m. ASECHANZA.
**asediador, -ra** adj. besieging. 2 m.-f. besieger.
**asediar** tr. to besiege, lay siege to. 2 fig. to besiege, beset, importunate.
**asedio** m. siege, blockade.
**aseguración** f. insurance.
**asegurado, -da** adj.-n. insured.
**asegurador, -ra** adj. assuring. 2 insuring. 3 m.-f. assurer. 4 insurer, underwriter.
**aseguramiento** m. securing; security. 2 insurance.
**asegurar** tr. to secure, fasten, fix. 2 to secure [make safe; guarantee; seize and confine]; to ensure. 3 to assure. 4 to assert, affirm. 5 COM. to insure. 6 ref. to make sure. 7 to hold fast. 8 to insure oneself.
**asemejar** tr. to liken, to compare. 2 intr.-ref. to resemble, be like or alike.
**asendereado, -da** adj. beaten, frequented. 2 overwhelmed with hardships.
**asenso** m. assent, credence.
**asentaderas** f. pl. coll, buttocks.
**asentado, -da** adj. situated, located. 2 fig. stable, settled, established.

**asentador** *m.* razor'strop. *2* wholesale provisioner.

**asentamiento** *m.* sitting down. *2* settling, establishment, situation. *3* location, emplacement. *4* COM. registration, entry, record of facts.

**asentar** *tr.* to seat. *2* to place, fix establish, found. *3* to give [a blow]. *4* to tamp down. *5* to iron [seams]. *6* to affirm, asume. *7* to enter [in a ledger, etc.]; to note down. *8* to make [a deal, a bargain]. *9* to strop, hone. *10 ref.* to sit down. *11* to settle, become established. *12* [of birds] to alight. *13* [of liquids, a building] to settle. *14* [of food] not to be digested. *15* [of a packsaddle] to hurt the horse, mule, etc. ¶ CONJUG. like *acertar.*

**asentimiento** *m.* assent.

**asentir** *intr.* to assent, to agree. ¶ CONJUG. like *hervir.*

**asentista** *m.* government, contractor.

**aseñorado, -da** *adj.* gentlemanly.

**aseo** *m.* cleanliness, tidiness. *2* cleaning, tidying: *cuarto de* ~, toilet room.

**asepsia** *f.* asepsis.

**aséptico, -ca** *adj.* aseptic.

**asequible** *adj.* accesible, obtainable, reachable.

**aserción** *f.* assertion, affirmation.

**aserradero** *m.* sawmill, sawing place.

**aserrador, -ra** *adj.* sawing. *2 m.* sawer, sawyer.

**aserradura** *f.* saw cut. *2 pl.* sawings, sawdust.

**aserrar** *tr.* to saw. ¶ CONJUG. like *acertar.*

**aserrín** *m.* sawdust.

**asertivo, -va** *adj.* assertive, affirmative, positive.

**aserto** *m.* assertion, affirmation, statement.

**asertorio** *m.* affirmatory.

**asesinar** *tr.* to assassinate, murder.

**asesinato** *m.* assassination, murder.

**asesino, -na** *adj.* murderous. *2 m.-f.* assassin, murderer.

**asesor, -ra** *m.-f.* adviser,' assessor.

**asesoramiento** *m.* advice [esp. professional advice].

**asesorar** *tr.* to advise, give professional advice to. *2 ref.* to take advice.

**asesoría** *f.* the post or office of an adviser, assessorship.

**asestar** *tr.* to aim, point, level, direct. *2* to strike, deal [a blow]; to fire [a shot].

**aseveración** *f.* asseveration.

**aseverar** *tr.* to asseverate.

**asexual** *adj.* asexual.

**asexuado, -da** *adj.* asexual.

**asfaltado, -da** *adj.* asphalt, asphalted. *2 m.* asphalting. *3* asphalt pavement.

**asfaltar** *tr.* to asphalt.

**asfalto** *m.* asphalt, asphaltum.

**asfixia** *f.* asphyxia; asphyxiation.

**asfixiado, -da** *adj.* suffocated, asphyxiated.

**asfixiante** *adj.* asphyxiating; suffocating.

**asfixiar** *tr.* to asphyxiate; to suffocate. *2 ref.* to be asphyxiated.

**asfódelo** *m.* BOT. asphodel.

**asgo, asga,** etc. *irr.* V. ASIR.

**así** *adv.* so, thus, in this way: *así, así,* so so, middling; ~ *como* ~, anyway; ~ *sea,* so be it; *así y todo,* yet, notwithstanding. *2* in the same manner, as well. *3* as soon: ~ *como,* ~ *que,* as soon as. *4 adj.* such: *un hombre* ~, such a man. *5 conj.* would that. *6 así,* ~ *pues,* ~ *que,* so then, therefore.

**Asia** *pr. n.* GEOG. Asia: ~ *Menor,* Asia Minor.

**asiático, -ca** *adj.-n.* Asiatic, Asian.

**asidero** *m.* handle, hold. *2* occasion, pretext.

**asiduamente** *adv.* assiduously. *2* frequently, regularly, often.

**asiduidad** *f.* assiduity, sedulity.

**asiduo, -dua** *adj.* assiduous, sedulous, frequent.

**asiento** *m.* seat [chair, etc.; place]: *tomar* ~, to take a seat. *2* site [of building, town, etc.]. *3* ARCH. settling [of materials or building]. *4* sediment. *5* settlement, establishment. *6* contract for supplies. *7* entry [in a ledger or register]. *8* indigestion. *9* stability, permanence. *10* judgment, wisdom.

**asiento, asiente,** etc. *irr.* V. ASENTAR.

**asiento, asienta,** etc. *irr.* V. ASENTIR.

**asierro, asierre,** etc. *irr.* V. ASERRAR.

**asignación** *f.* assignation, assignment, allotment. *2* assignation, amount assigned [as wages, etc.].

**asignado** *m.* assignat.

**asignar** *tr.* to assign, allot. *2* to assign, fix, appoint.

**asignatario, -ria** *n.* Am. legatee, heir, inheritor.

**asignatura** *f.* subject or course of study.

**asilar** *tr.* to place in a home or asylum.

**asilo** *m.* asylum, home [for the poor, etc.].

**asimetría** *f.* asymmetry.

**asimétrico, -ca** *adj.* asymmetric(al.

**asimiento** *m.* seizing, grasping. *2* affection, attachment.

**asimilación** *f.* assimilation.

**asimilar** *tr.* to assimilate. *2 intr.* to be similar. *3 ref.* to be assimilated. *4* to resemble.

**asimismo** *adv.* in like manner, likewise, also.

**asincrónico, -ca** *adj.* asynchronous.

**asíndeton** *m.* RHET. asyndeton.

**asintió, asintiera,** etc. *irr.* V. ASENTIR.

**asíntota** *f.* GEOM. asymptote.

**asir** *tr.* to seize, grasp, take: *asidos del brazo,* arm in arm. *2 intr.* to take root. *3 ref.* to take hold [of]; to hold [to]. *4* to avail oneself [of]. *5* to dispute, grapple. ¶ CONJUG.: INDIC. Pres.: *asgo, ases,* etc. | SUBJ. Pres.: *asga, asgas, asga; asgamos, asgáis, asgan.* | IMPER.: *ase, asga; asgamos,* asid, *asgan.*

**Asiria** *f. pr.* HIST. GEOG. Assyria.

**asirio, -ria** *adj.-n.* Assyrian.

**Asís** *m. pr. n.* Assisi.

**asistencia** *f.* attendance, presence. *2* assistance, aid: ~ *social,* social service. *3 pl.* allowance; alimony.

**asistenta** *f.* charwoman.

**asistente** *adj.-n.* attendant, present. *2 m.* assistant, helper. *3* MIL. a soldier assigned as a servant to an officer.

**asistido, -da** *adj.* assisted, helped, aided: *dirección* ~, power steering; *frenos* ~, power brakes.

**asistir** *intr.* to attend, be present, go: ~ *a la escuela,* to attend school. *2* CARDS to follow suit. *3 tr.* to assist, aid, help. *4* to attend, take care of [the sick]. *5 me asiste la razón,* I am right.

**asma** *f.* MED. asthma.

**asmático, -ca** *adj.-n.* asthmatic.

**asna** *f.* she-ass, jenny ass. *2 pl.* rafters.

**asnacho** *m.* BOT. restharrow.

**asnada** *f.* stupidity, foolish act.

**asnal** *adj.* donkey, asinine.

**asnería** *f.* asses. *2* stupidity, nonsense.

**asno** *m.* ZOOL. ass, donkey, jackass.

**asociación** *f.* association.

**asociacionismo** *m.* associationism.

**asociado, -da** *adj.* associated, associate. *2 m.-f.* associate, partner. *3* member [of an association].

**asociar** *tr.* to associate. *2 ref.* to associate, become associated; to join, enter into partnership.

**asolador, -ra** *adj.* razing, ravaging, devastating.
**asolamiento** *m.* ravage, desolation, devastation.
**asolar** *tr.* to raze, level with the ground, lay waste, desolate, devastate. *2 ref.* [of liquids] to settle. ¶ CONJUG. like *contar.*
**asolear** *tr.* to sun. *2 ref.* to become heated in the sun. *3* to become sun-tanned.
**asomada** *f.* peep, short appearance. *2* point from which something is first seen.
**asomar** *intr.* to begin to appear or to show. *2 tr.* to show, put out [through, behind or over an opening or a wall]. *3 ref.* to peep out, put one's head out, look out.
**asombradizo, -za** *adj.* ESPANTADIZO.
**asombrado, -da** *adj.* surprised. *2* amazed, astonished, astounded.
**asombrar** *tr.* to shade [throw a shadow on]. *2* to frighten. *3* to amaze, astonish. *4 ref.* to take fright. *5* to be astonished, amazed.
**asombro** *m.* fright. *2* amazement, astonishment.
**asombrosamente** *adv.* amazingly, surprisingly, wonderfully.
**asombroso, -sa** *adj.* amazing, astonishing, wonderful.
**asomo** *m.* peep, looking out. *2* sign, indication: *ni por ~,* by no means.
**asonada** *f.* riot, tumult, disturbance.
**asonancia** *f.* as ˊ ˋnance.
**asonantar** *tr.* to make assonant. *2 intr.* to assonate.
**asonante** *adj.-n.* assonant.
**asonar** *intr.* to assonate. ¶ CONJUG. like *contar.*
**aspa** *f.* X-shaped figure or cross: *~ de San Andrés,* St. Andrew's cross. *2* reel [for skeining]. *3* sail, vane [of windmill]. *5* HER. saltier.
**aspadera** *f.* reel [for skeining].
**aspado, -da** *adj.* X-shaped.
**aspar** *tr.* to skein [yarn]. *2* to crucify. *3* to vex, annoy. *4 ref.* to cry and writhe [with pain, anger, etc.].
**aspaviento** *m.* exaggerated demonstration of terror, admiration, or feeling.
**aspecto** *m.* aspect, look. *2* ARCH., ASTROL. aspect.
**aspereza** *f.* asperity, roughness. *2* tartness; harshness. *3* rudeness, gruffness. *4* rough place.
**asperges** *m.* coll. sprinkling, aspersion. *2* coll. aspergillum.
**asperilla** *f.* BOT. woodruff.
**asperillo** *m.* slight sour taste.
**asperjar** *tr.* to sprinkle; to sprinkle with holy water.
**áspero, -ra** *adj.* rough. *2* harsh. *3* sour, tart. *4* rude, gruff.
**asperón** *m.* sandstone; grindstone.
**aspersión** *f.* aspersion, sprinkling.
**aspersorio** *m.* sprinkler, aspergillum.
**áspid, áspide** *m.* ZOOL. asp, aspic.
**aspidistra** *f.* BOT. aspidistra.
**aspillera** *f.* MIL. loophole.
**aspiración** *f.* aspiration. *2* MUS. short pause.
**aspirado, -da** *adj.* PHON. aspirate.
**aspirador, -ra** *adj.* sucking. *2 m. ~ de polvo,* vacuum cleaner.
**aspirante** *adj.* suction, sucking. *2 m.* aspirant, candidate.
**aspirar** *tr.* to inhale. *2* to suck, draw in. *3* PHYS., PHON. to aspirate. *5 intr. ~ a,* to aspire after or to; to be a candidate for.
**aspiratorio, -ria** *adj.* aspiratory.
**aspirina** *f.* PHARM. aspirin.
**asquear** *tr.* to loathe, be nauseated at. *2* to disgust, nauseate.

**asquerosidad** *f.* dirtiness, filthiness.
**asqueroso, -sa** *adj.* loathsome, dirty, filthy.
**asta** *f.* shaft [of a lance or pike]. *2* lance, pike. *3* flagstaff: *a media ~,* at half mast. *4* horn, antler. *5* handle [of a brush].
**astado** *m.* bull. *2* Roman pikeman.
**astático, -ca** *adj.* PHYS. astatic.
**astenia** *f.* MED. asthenia.
**asténico, -ca** *adj.-n.* asthenic.
**asterisco** *m.* asterisc (*).
**asteroide** *adj.* asteroid, starlike. *2 m.* ASTR. asteroid.
**astigmático, -ca** *adj.* astigmatic.
**astigmatismo** *m.* astigmatism.
**astil** *m.* handle, helve [of hoe, ax, etc.]. *2* beam [of balance]. *3* shaft [of arrow, of feaher]. *4* neck [of guitar].
**astilla** *f.* chip, splinter.
**astillar** *tr.* to chip, to splinter. *2 ref.* to splinter [be splintered].
**astillero** *m.* shipyard, dockyard. *2* rack for lances or pikes.
**astracán** *m.* astrakhan, astrachan.
**astracanada** *f.* THEAT. cheap farce.
**astrágalo** *m.* ANAT., ARCH., ARTILL. astragal. *2* BOT. milk vetch.
**astral** *adj.* astral.
**astreñir** *tr.* ASTRINGIR.
**astricción** *f.* astriction.
**astringencia** *f.* astringency.
**astringente** *adj.* astringent.
**astringir** *tr.* to astringe. *2* to astrict, bind.
**astro** *m.* star, heavenly body. *2* fig. star, luminary.
**astrofísica** *f.* astrophysics.
**astrofísico, -ca** *n.* astrophysicist. *2 f.* astrophysics.
**astrolabio** *m.* astrolabe.
**astrología** *f.* astrology.
**astrológico, -ca** *adj.* astrological.
**astrólogo, -ga** *m.-f.* astrologer. *2 adj.* astrological.
**astronauta** *m.-f.* astronaut.
**astronáutica** *f.* astronautics.
**astronave** *f.* spacecraft, spaceship.
**astronomía** *f.* astronomy.
**astronómico, -ca** *adj.* astronomic(al.
**astrónomo** *m.* astronomer.
**astrosamente** *adv.* uncleanly, slovenly, shabbily.
**astroso, -sa** *adj.* unclean, shabby. *3* vile, contemptible.
**astucia** *f.* astuteness, cunning. *2* trick, artifice.
**astur, asturiano, -na** *adj.-n.* Asturian.
**Asturias** *f. pr. n.* GEOG. Asturias.
**astuto, -ta** *adj.* astute, cunning, sly, crafty.
**asueto** *m.* brief vacation, day off, school holiday.
**asumir** *tr.* to assume [responsibilities, command, great proportions, etc.].
**asunción** *f.* assumption [taking to oneself]. *2* elevation [to a great dignity]. *3* (cap.) ECCLES. Assumption [of the Virgin].
**asunto** *m.* matter, subject. *2* affair, business. *3* LIT. theme or plot.
**asustadizo, -za** *adj.* easily frightened, scary, skittish.
**asustar** *tr.* to frighten, scare. *2 ref.* to be frightened, to take fright.
**atabal** *m.* kettledrum. *2* kettledrummer. *3* timbrel.
**atacador** *m.* rammer, ramroad.
**atacante** *adj.* attacking, assaulting, assailing. *2 m.* attacker, assailant, aggressor.
**atacar** *tr.* to attack. *2* to assail. *3* to impugn. *4* to

fasten, button [a garment]. 5 to ram, tamp, pack, stuff.

**atadero** *m.* tying cord, rope, etc. 2 part of a thing by which it is tied: *no tiene ~*, there is nothing to do with him [or it].

**atadijo** *m.* small bundle.

**atado, -da** *adj.* spiritless, irresolute. 2 *m.* pack, bundle.

**atador, -ra** *adj.* binding. 2 string, rope, bond.

**atadura** *f.* tying, binding, fastening. 2 string, rope, bond. 3 union, connection.

**atafagar** *tr.* to stun [by strong odours]. 2 to pester, plague.

**ataguía** *f.* cofferdam.

**atajar** *intr.* to take a short cut. 2 *tr.* to head off. 3 to stop, interrupt. 4 to cut [someone] short. 5 to partition off. 6 *ref.* to stop short in confusion.

**atajo** *m.* short cut: *echar por el ~*, to take the easiest way out. 2 small herd or flock. 3 collection, lot.

**atalaya** *f.* watchtower; high lookout. 2 *m.* guard, lookout [man].

**atalayar** *tr.* to watch [from a watchtower]. 2 to spy on.

**ataludar** *tr.* to slope, batter.

**atanasia** *f.* BOT. costmary. 2 PRINT. English type.

**atanor** *m.* earthen water pipe.

**atañer** *impers.* to concern, respect, regard.

**ataque** *m.* attack. 2 impugnation. 3 fit, access, stroke.

**atar** *tr.* to tie, fasten, lace, knot, bind; *~ cabos*, to put two and two together. 2 to tie, stop: *~ la lengua*, to prevent from speaking. 3 *ref.* to bind oneself. 4 to become embarrassed or tied.

**atarantado, -da** *adj.* bitten by a tarantula. 2 restless, bustling. 3 bewildered, confused.

**atarantar** *tr.* to stun, to daze. 2 to bewilder.

**ataraxia** *f.* ataraxia, ataraxy, imperturbability.

**atarazana** *f.* shipyard, dockyard. 2 ropewalk.

1) **atardecer** *impers.* to draw towards the evening.

2) **atardecer** *m.* late afternoon, evenfall.

**atareado, -da** *adj.* busy.

**atarear** *tr.* to task, assign work to. 2 *ref.* to toil, busy oneself.

**atarjea** *f.* drain pipe, sewer.

**atarugamiento** *m.* confusion, dumbfoundedness.

**atarugar** *tr.* CARP. to fasten with pegs or wedges. 2 to plug [a cask]. 3 to stuff, fill. 4 to silence, confuse. 5 *ref.* to get confused.

**atasajar** *tr.* to jerk [meat].

**atascadero** *m.* mudhole. 2 difficulty, obstruction, blind alley, dead end.

**atascamiento** *m.* ATASCO.

**atascar** *tr.* to stop, clog, obstruct. 2 fig. to arrest [an affair]. 3 *ref.* to be bogged. 4 to get stuck.

**atasco** *m.* sticking in the mud. 2 obstruction.

**ataúd** *m.* coffin [for a corpse].

**ataujía** *f.* damascene work.

**ataviar** *tr.* to dress, dress up, deck out, adorn. 2 *ref.* to dress or adorn oneself.

**atávico, -ca** *adj.* atavistic.

**atavío** *m.* dress, adornment. 2 *pl.* adornments.

**atavismo** *m.* atavism.

**ataxia** *f.* MED. ataxia.

**ateísmo** *m.* atheism.

**atelaje** *m.* harness [for horses]; team [of horses].

**atemorizar** *tr.* to intimidate, to frighten. 2 *ref.* to become frightened.

**atemperar** *tr.* to temper, soften, moderate. 2 to adjust, accommodate.

**atenacear** *tr.* to tear off the flesh [of a person] with pincers. 2 to torture.

**Atenas** *f. pr. n.* GEOG. Athens.

**atenazar** *tr.* ATENACEAR. 2 to clench [one's teeth]. 3 to grip, tightly.

**atención** *f.* attention: *en ~ a*, considering, in view of. 2 civility, kindness. 3 *pl.* affairs, duties, obligations. 4 *interj. ¡atención!*, attention!

**atender** *intr.-tr.* to attend, pay attention. 2 to heed. 3 to take care [of]. 4 to attend, receive, serve, wait [upon]. 5 *tr.* to listen to [entreaties, advice, etc.]; to comply with [someone's wishes]. ¶ CONJUG. like *entender*.

**atendible** *adj.* worthy of consideration.

**atendré, atendría**, etc. *irr.* V. ATENERSE.

**ateneo** *m.* athenaeum [literary club].

**atenerse** *ref.* *~ a*, to abide by, stick to, keep to [an opinion, one's instructions, etc.]. ¶ CONJUG. like *tener*.

**ateniense** *adj.-n.* Athenian.

**atenta** *f. su ~*, yours, your favour [letter].

**atentado, -da** *adj.* prudent, moderate. 2 *m.* abuse of power. 3 outrage, crime. 4 murder or attempted murder [of a high-placed person].

**atentamente** *adv.* attentively. 2 politely.

**atentar** *intr. atentar contra*, to commit outrage against; to attempt the life of.

**atentatorio, -ria** *adj.* contrary to [morals, law, etc.].

**atento, -ta** *adj.* attentive; watchful. 2 polite, courteous: *su ~ seguro servidor*, yours truly, yours faithfully.

**atenuación** *f.* attenuation, extenuation. 2 RHET. litotes.

**atenuante** *adj.* attenuating, extenuating. 2 *m.* extenuating circumstance.

**atenuar** *tr.* to attenuate; to extenuate, diminish.

**ateo, -a** *adj.* atheist, atheistic. 2 *m.-f.* atheist.

**aterciopelado, -da** *adj.* velvety.

**aterido, -da** *adj.* stiff with cold.

**aterirse** *tr. def.* to become stiff with cold.

**aterrador, -ra** *adj.* terrifying, dreadful.

**aterrajar** *tr.* MACH. to thread [a screw], to tap [a nut].

1) **aterrar** *intr.* AER. to land. 2 NAUT. to stand inshore. 3 *tr.* to pull down, to demolish. ¶ CONJUG. like *acertar*.

2) **aterrar** *tr.-ref.* ATERRORIZAR.

**aterrizaje** *m.* AER. landing, alighting.

**aterrizar** *tr.* AER. to land, alight.

**aterrorizador, -ra** *adj.* terrifying, frightening, scary, terrific.

**aterrorizar** *tr.* to terrify. 2 to terrorize. 3 *ref.* to be terrified.

**atesorador** *m.* hoarder.

**atesoramiento** *m.* hoarding, amassing, treasuring-up.

**atesorar** *tr.* to treasure, hoard up. 2 to possess [virtues, perfections, etc.].

**atestación** *f.* attestation, testimony.

**atestado, -da** *adj.* crammed. 2 obstinate, stubborn. 3 *m.* LAW attestation, statement, certificate.

1) **atestar** *tr.* to pack, cram, stuff; to crowd. 2 *ref.* to stuff oneself. ¶ CONJUG. like *acertar*.

2) **atestar** *tr.* to attest, witness.

**atestiguar** *tr.* to attest, testify, bear witness to.

**atezado, -da** *adj.* tan, tanned [by sun], sunburnt. 2 black, blackened.

**atezar** *tr.* to tan, make sunburnt. 2 to blacken. 3 *ref.* to become sunburnt.

**atiborrar** *tr.* to pack, cram, stuff. *2* to stuff [with food]. *3 ref.* to stuff oneself.

**ático, -ca** *adj.-n.* Attic: *sal ática,* Attic salt. *3 m.* ARCH. attic.

**atiendo, atienda,** etc. *irr.* V. ATENDER.

**atiento, atiente,** etc. *irr.* V. ATENTARSE.

**atiesar** *tr.* to stiffen. *2* to tighten, tauten.

**atiesto, atieste,** etc. V. ATESTAR I).

**atigrado, -da** *adj.* marked like a tiger's skin.

**Atila** *m. pr. n.* Attila.

**atildado, -da** *adj.* neat, elegant.

**atildamiento** *m.* neatness, elegance. *2* rendering neat or elegant, tidying.

**atildar** *tr.* to render neat, to tidy, trim.

**atinado, -da** *adj.* right, judicious.

**atinar** *intr.-tr.* to hit [the mark]. *2* to hit upon, find, find out, guess, guess right.

**atinente** *adj.* concerning.

**atiplado, -da** *adj.* high-pitched, shrill, sharp; *voz* ~, high-pitched voice.

**atiplar** *tr.* MUS. to raise the pitch of [an instrument] to treble. *2 ref.* to rise to treble.

**atirantar** *tr.* to tighten, tauten. *2* ARCH. to stay, brace with ties.

**atisbar** *tr.* to peep, spy, observe.

**atisbo** *m.* ATISBADURA. *2* inkling.

**¡atiza!** *interj.* goodness me! oh my goodness! good Lord!

**atizador, -ra** *adj.* inciting, stirring. *2 m.* poker, fire poker.

**atizar** *tr.* to poke, stir [the fire]. *2* to trim [a lamp]. *3* to fan, stir up [passions, etc.]. *4* coll. to give [a blow]. *5 interj. ¡atiza!,* good gracious!

**atizonarse** *ref.* AGR. [of corn] to smut.

**atlantes** *m. pl.* ARCH. atlantes.

**atlántico, -ca** *adj. m. pr. n.* Atlantic.

**atlas** *m.* atlas [book of maps]. *2* ANAT. atlas.

**Atlas** *pr. n.* MYTH. Atlas. *2* GEOG. Atlas Mountains.

**atleta** *m.* athlete.

**atlético, -ca** *adj.* athletic. *2* robust [person].

**atletismo** *m.* athletics.

**atmósfera** *f.* atmosphere [in every sense].

**atmosférico, -ca** *adj.* atmospheric.

**atoar** *tr.* NAUT. to tow. *2* NAUT. to warp.

**atocinado, -da** *adj.* fig. coll. fat, fleshy, obese.

**atocinar** *tr.* to cut up [a pig]. *2* to make into bacon. *3* coll. to assassinate.

**atocha** *f.* ESPARTO.

**atole** *m.* (Am.) corn-flour gruel.

**atolón** *m.* GEOG. atoll.

**atolondrado, -da** *adj.* scatterbrained, giddy, thoughtless, inconsiderate. *3* bewildered, confused.

**atolondramiento** *m.* giddiness, thoughtlessness, inconsideration. *2* stunned state, bewilderment.

**atolondrar** *tr.* ATURDIR. *2 ref.* to become bewildered, confused.

**atolladero** *m.* ATASCADERO.

**atollar** *intr.-ref.* to get stuck in the mud. *2 ref.* to get stuck, obstructed.

**atómico, -ca** *adj.* atomic.

**atomismo** *m.* atomism.

**atomización** *f.* atomization, spraying.

**atomizador** *m.* atomizer, spray, pulverizer [for liquids].

**atomizar** *tr.* to atomize.

**átomo** *m.* atom.

**atonal** *adj.* MUS. atonal, toneless, atonic.

**atonalidad** *f.* MUS. atonality, tonelessness.

**atonía** *f.* MED. atony.

**atónito, -ta** *adj.* astonished, amazed, aghast.

**átono, -na** *adj.* GRAM., MED. atonic.

**atontado, -da** *adj.* stunned, confused. *2* stupid, silly.

**atontamiento** *m.* stunning, stunned state, stupefaction, bewilderment, confusion. *2* stupidity.

**atontar** *tr.* to stun, to stupefy. *2* to confuse, bewilder. *3 ref.* to become stunned, stupefied.

**atorar** *tr.* to obstruct, choke. *2 ref.* to become obstructed. *3* ATRAGANTARSE 2.

**atormentador, -ra** *adj.* tormenting. *2 m.-f.* tormentor, tormentress, torturer.

**atormentar** *tr.* to torment. *2* to torture. *3 ref.* to torment oneself, worry.

**atornillar** *tr.* to screw [turn a screw]. *2* to screw [on].

**atorrante** *m.* (Arg.) vagabond, loafer, beggar.

**atorrantismo** *m.* (Am.) vagrancy, vagabondage.

**atortolar** *tr.* to confound, rattle, intimidate.

**atosigamiento** *m.* poisoning. *2* pestering, annoyance, harassing.

**atosigar** *tr.* to poison. *2* to press, rush, harass. *3 ref.* to trouble, toil.

**atrabancar** *tr.-intr.* to hurry over, jump over.

**atrabiliario, -ria** *adj.* MED. atrabiliary, atrabilious. *2* bad-tempered. *3 m.-f.* bad-tempered person.

**atrabilis** *f.* black bile.

**atracadero** *m.* NAUT. landfall, landing place.

**atracador, -ra** *m.* bandit, robber, thief, raider.

**atracar** *tr.* to gorge [with food]. *2* to assault, *hold up. *3* NAUT. to bring alongside. *4 intr.* NAUT. to come alongside. *5 ref.* to gorge oneself.

**atracción** *f.* attraction.

**atraco** *m.* assault, robbery, *holdup.

**atracón** *m.* overeating, gorging.

**atractivo, -va** *adj.* attractive. *2* engaging, charming. *3 m.* charm, grace. *4* inducement, attraction.

**atraer** *tr.* to attract, draw. *2* to lure, allure. *3* to charm, captivate. ¶ CONJUG. like *traer.*

**atragantarse** *ref.* to chocke, stick in the throat. *2* to be choked [by something sticking in the throat]. *3* to get mixed up [in one's speech].

**atraigo, atraiga,** etc. *irreg.* V. ATRAER.

**atraillar** *tr.* to leash [dogs]. *2* to dominate, subjugate.

**atrampar** *tr.* to trap, entrap. *2 ref.* to fall in a trap. *3* [of a pipe] to become choked. *4* [of a lock] to become jammed. *5* to get stuck [in an affair].

**atrancar** *tr.* to bar [a door]. *2* to choke, obstruct. *3 intr.* coll. to take long strides. *4 ref.* to bar oneself in.

**atranco** *m.* ATOLLADERO. *2* snag, hole, difficulty.

**atrapamoscas** *m.* BOT. Venu's-fly-trap.

**atrapar** *tr.* to overtake, catch. *2* to catch, take; to get. *3* to trap, entrap, ensnare.

**atrás** *adv.* back, in the rear, behind: *dejar* ~, to leave behind; *volverse* ~, to turn back; *hacia* ~, backwards; *de* ~, back [adj.]; *la parte de* ~, the back. *2* ago: *días* ~, some days ago. *3 interj.* back!, go back!, back up!; go behind!

**atrasado, -da** *adj.* in debt, in arrears. *2* behindhand. *3* backward, dull. *4* behind the times. *5* slow [clock]. *6 número* ~, back number or copy. *7* ~ *de noticias,* ignorant of common things.

**atrasar** *tr.* to delay, postpone, retard. *2* to postdate [an event]. *3* to set back [a clock]. *4 intr.* [of a clock], to be slow. *5 ref.* to remain behind, lag, fall, back. *6* to be late. *7* to be in arrears, in debt.

**atraso** *m.* backwardness. *2* delay, lateness: *con*

*diez minutos de* ~, ten minutes late. *3* slowness [of a clock]. *4 pl.* arrearages, arrears.
**atravesado, -da** *adj.* pierced. *2* crossed, laid or stretched across. *4* cross-eyed, squint-eyed. *5* crossbred [animal]. *6* fig. wicked, treacherous.
**atravesar** *tr.* to cross [go across]. *2* to cross, span, bridge, lie across. *3* to put or lay across, athwart or crosswise. *4* to pierce; to transfix, run through; to pass through. *5* to interpose. *6* to bet, stake. *7 ref.* to come between; to be or come in the way of. *8* to butt in. *9* [of an obstacle, etc.] to interfere, arise, spring up. ¶ CONJUG. like *acertar.*
**atravieso, atraviese,** etc. *irr.* V. ATRAVESAR.
**atrayente** *adj.* attractive.
**atreverse** *ref.* to dare, venture, make bold. *2* ~ *con,* to be insolent to; to feel equal to.
**atrevidamente** *adv.* daringly, boldly, fearlessly. *2* insolently, rudely, shamelessly.
**atrevido, -da** *adj.* daring, bold. *2* forward, impudent.
**atrevimiento** *m.* daring, boldness. *2* forwardness, effrontery, impudence.
**atribución** *f.* attribution. *2* power, authority.
**atribuir** *tr.* to attribute. *2* to ascribe, impute. *3 ref.* to assume, take to oneself. ¶ CONJUG. like *huir.*
**atribulado, -da** *adj.* full of tribulation, distressed.
**atribular** *tr.* to grieve, afflict. *2 ref.* to be worried.
**atributivo, -va** *adj.* attributive.
**atributo** *m.* attribute.
**atrición** *f.* THEOL. attrition.
**atril** *m.* music stand; reading desk, lectern.
**atrincheramiento** *m.* MIL. entrenchment.
**atrincherar** *tr.* MIL. to entrench [surround with a trench]. *2 ref.* to entrench oneself, to dig in.
**atrio** *m.* ARCH., ZOOL. atrium.
**atrito, -ta** *adj.* THEOL. attrite.
**atrocidad** *f.* atrocity, atrociousness. *2* enormity, excess. *3* stupidity, foolish action.
**atrofia** *f.* atrophy.
**atrofiarse** *ref.* to atrophy [undergo atrophy].
**atronado, -da** *adj.* harebrained, reckless.
**atronador, -ra** *adj.* deafening, thundering.
**atronar** *tr.* to deafen. *2* to stun. *3* to kill [a bull] by a stab on the nape of the neck. ¶ CONJUG. like *contar.*
**atropar** *tr.-ref.* to troop, assemble in troops. *2 tr.* to pile [grain, hay, etc.].
**atropelladamente** *adv.* helter-skelter; hastily.
**atropellado, -da** *adj.* badly off. *2 adj.* headlong, hasty, impetuous, precipitate.
**atropellador, -ra** *adj.* brusque, precipitate, rash, hasty.
**atropellar** *tr.* to run down or over, trample, drive over. *2* to knock down, to push violently down or away. *3* to outrage, oppress, bully. *4* [of age, misfortune, etc.], to crush. *5* to do hastily. *6 tr.-intr.* to disregard [rights, difficulties, etc.]; to ride roughshod over. *7 ref.* to be hasty.
**atropello** *m.* running over [accident]. *2* high-handed proceeding, outrage, abuse.
**atropina** *f.* CHEM. atropine.
**atroz** *adj.* atrocious. *2* enormous, huge.
**atrozmente** *adj.* atrociously. *2* fig. awfully, terribly, horribly, dreadfully.
**atrueno, atruene,** etc. *irr.* V. ATRONAR.
**atuendo** *m.* dress. *2* pomp, ostentation.
**atufar** *tr.* to anger, irritate. *2 tr.-ref.* to overcome or be overcome [by fumes]. *3 ref.* to get angry. *4* [of food] to get smelly.
**atufo** *m.* anger, irritation.

**atún** *m.* ICHTH. tunny, tunny fish, tuna.
**atunero, -ra** *m.-f.* tunny dealer. *2 m.* tunny fisher.
**aturdido, -da** *p. p.* of ATURDIR. *2 adj.* ATOLONDRADO.
**aturdimiento** *m.* stunning. *2* bewilderment, giddiness. *3* amazement. *4* awkwardness.
**aturdir** *tr.* to stun, to deafen. *2* to make giddy. *3* to rattle, bewilder. *4* to amaze. *5 ref.* to be stunned, rattled, bewildered.
**aturrullamiento** *m.* ATOLONDRAMIENTO.
**aturrullar** *tr.* to rattle, confound.
**atusar** *tr.* to trim [the hair]; to comb or smooth [the hair]. *2* to trim [plants]. *3 ref.* to make oneself neat or trim, to dress elaborately.
**atuve, atuviste,** etc. *irr.* V. ATENERSE.
**audacia** *f.* audacity, boldness.
**audaz,** *pl.* **audaces** *adj.* audacious, bold.
**audible** *adj.* audible.
**audición** *f.* audition, hearing. *2* concert.
**audiencia** *f.* audience [formal interview]. *2* Spanish provincial or colonial high court.
**audífonos** *m. pl.* (Am.) earphones.
**audiofrecuencia** *f.* RADIO. audio-frequency.
**audiovisual** *adj.* audio-visual.
**auditivo, -va** *adj.* auditive.
**auditor** *m.* judge advocate. *2* ECCL. ~ *de la Rota,* auditor of the Rota.
**auditorio, -ria** *adj.* auditory. *2 m.* audience, auditory.
**auge** *m.* acme, culmination. *2* ASTR. apogee.
**augur** *m.* augur.
**augurar** *tr.* to augur, to augur of.
**augurio** *m.* augury; omen.
**Augusto** *m. pr. n.* Augustus.
**augusto, -ta** *adj.* august. *2 m.* august [clown].
**aula** *f.* class room, lecture room: ~ *magna,* assembly hall. *2* poet. palace.
**aulaga** *f.* BOT. furze, gorse.
**áulico, -ca** *adj.* aulic. *2 m.* courtier.
**aullador, -ra** *adj.* howling.
**aullar** *intr.* to howl.
**aullido** *m.* howl. *2* RADIO. howling, squealing.
**aúllo** *m.* AULLIDO.
**aumentar** *tr.-intr.-ref.* to augment, increase, magnify. *2 intr.-ref.* to grow, grow larger.
**aumentativo, -va** *adj.-n.* GRAM. augmentative.
**aumento** *m.* augmentation, increase, magnifying. *2* OPT. magnifying power.
**aun** *adv.* even, still: ~ *cuando,* although.
**aún** *adv.* yet, as yet, still.
**aunar** *tr.-ref.* to join, unite, combine. *2* to unify.
**aunque** *conj.* though, although, even though.
**¡aúpa!** *interj.* up, up! *2 de* ~, important.
**aupar** *tr.* to lift, to help up, give a leg up.
**aura** *f.* gentle breeze. *2* breath. *3* general favour, popularity. *4* MED., ORN. aura.
**áureo, -a** *adj.* golden, gold, aureous.
**aureola, auréola** *f.* THEOL., METEOR., ASTR. aureole. *2* fig. aureole, halo. *3* areola.
**aureolar** *tr.* to aureole.
**aureomicina** *f.* PHARM. aureomycin.
**aurícula** *f.* ANAT., BOT. auricle.
**auricular** *adj.* auricular. *2 m.* TELEPH. receiver, earpiece. *3* RADIO. earphone.
**aurífero, -ra** *adj.* auriferous, gold-bearing.
**auriga** *m.* poet, coachman, charioteer. *2* (cap.) ASTR. Auriga, Wagoner.
**aurora** *f.* aurora, dawn. *2* fig. dawn, beginning. *3* METEOR. ~ *austral,* aurora australis; ~ *boreal,* aurora borealis.
**auscultación** *f.* MED. auscultation.
**auscultar** *tr.* MED. to auscultate.

**ausencia** *f.* absence. *2* lack.
**ausentarse** *ref.* to absent oneself.
**ausente** *adj.* absent. *2 m.-f.* absentee. *3* LAW missing person.
**ausentismo** *m.* absenteeism.
**auspiciar** *tr.* to patronize, to favour.
**auspicio** *m.* omen, auspice, augury. *2* sponsorship: *bajo los ~ de...* sponsored by...
**austeridad** *f.* austerity.
**austero, -ra** *adj.* austere.
**austral** *adj.* austral.
**Australia** *f. pr. n.* GEOG. Australia.
**australiano, -na** *adj.-n.* Australian.
**Austria** *f. pr. n.* GEOG. Austria.
**austríaco, -ca** *adj.-n.* Austrian.
**austro** *m.* south. *2* south wind.
**autarquía** *f.* autarchy, self-sufficiency.
**auténtica** *f.* certification. *2* LAW authentic copy.
**autenticar** *tr.* to authenticate.
**autenticidad** *f.* authenticity, genuineness.
**auténtico, -ca** *adj.* authentic, genuine.
**autillo** *m.* ORN. tawny owl.
**auto** *m.* judicial decree, writ, warrant. *2* coll. auto, car. *3* religious or biblical play. *4 ~ de fe,* auto-da-fé. *5 pl.* LAW proceeding: fig. *poner en autos,* to inform.
**autobiografía** *f.* autobiography.
**autobombo** *m.* self-glorification.
**autobús** *m.* bus, autobus.
**autocamión** *m.* autotruck, motor truck.
**autocar** *m.* coach, bus.
**autoclave** *f.* autoclave.
**autocracia** *f.* autocracy.
**autócrata** *m.* autocrat.
**autocrítica** *f.* self-examination, self-criticism.
**autóctono, -na** *adj.* autochthonous. *7 m.-f.* autochthon.
**autodeterminación** *f.* POL. self-determination.
**autodidacto, -ta** *adj.* self-taught.
**autógeno, -na** *adj.* autogenous [welding].
**autogiro** *m.* autogiro.
**autografía** *f.* autography.
**autógrafo, -fa** *adj.-m.* autograph.
**autoinducción** *f.* ELEC. self-induction.
**automación** *f.* automation.
**autómata** *m.* automaton.
**automático, -ca** *adj.* automatic(al.
**automatismo** *m.* automatism.
**automatizar** *tr.* to automate: *~ la fábrica,* to automate the factory.
**automotor, triz** *adj.* automotive. *2 m.* railway motor coach.
**automóvil** *adj.-m.* automobile.
**automovilismo** *m.* automobilism, motoring.
**automovilista** *adj.* automobile, automobilist. *2 m.-f.* automobilist, motorist.
**autonomía** *f.* autonomy. *2* home rule. *3* cruising radius [of a boat, airplane, etc.].
**autonomista** *adj.* autonomous. *2 n.* autonomist.
**autonómico, -ca** *adj.* autonomic.
**autónomo, -ma** *adj.* autonomous, autonomic.
**autopista** *f.* expressway, motorway.
**autopropulsión** *f.* self-propulsion.
**autopsia** *f.* autopsy, post-mortem examination.
**autor, -ra** *m.-f.* author, maker. *2* author, authoress [writer]. *3* perpetrator [of a crime].
**autoría** *f.* THEAT. treasurership.
**autoridad** *f.* authority. *2* person exercising power or command. *3* ostentation, pomp.
**autoritario, -ria** *adj.* authoritative, overbearing. *2 adj.-n.* authoritarian.

**autoritarismo** *m.* authoritarianism.
**autorización** *f.* authorization. *2* permit, license.
**autorizadamente** *adv.* with authority.
**autorizado, -da** *adj.* authorized. *2* empowered. *3* legalized. *4* respectable, responsible.
**autorizar** *tr.* to authorize. *2* to empower. *3* to permit. *4* to legalize. *5* to approve.
**autorregulación** *f.* self-regulation.
**autorretrato** *m.* self-portrait.
**autostop** *m.* hitchhiking: *hacer ~,* to hitchhike.
**autosuficiencia** *f.* self-sufficiency.
**autosugestión** *f.* autosuggestion.
**autovía** *f.* railway motor coach. *2* AUTOPISTA.
**autumnal** *adj.* OTOÑAL.
**Auvernia** *f. pr. n.* Auvergne.
**auxiliador, -ra** *adj.* helping, aiding. *2 m.-f.* helper, aider.
1) **auxiliar** *tr.* to help, aid; to assist. *2* to succour. *3* to attend [a dying person].
2) **auxiliar** *adj.* auxiliary. *2 m.* GRAM. auxiliary verb. *3* second class clerk. *4* professor's assistant.
**auxilio** *m.* help, aid, relief, assistance.
**aval** *m.* COM. guarantor's signature [in a bill of exchange]. *2* POL. guarantee of conduct.
**avalancha** *f.* avalanche.
**avalar** *tr.* to put an AVAL on [a bill of exchange]. *2* to answer for [a person].
**avalentonado, -da** *adj.* swaggering, bullying.
**avalorar** *tr.* to render valuable.
**avaluar** *tr.* VALUAR.
**avalúo** *m.* VALUACIÓN.
**avance** *m.* advance [going forward; payment beforehand]. *2* COM. balance sheet. *3* COM. estimate.
**avantrén** *m.* ARTILL. limber.
**avanzada** *f.* MIL. outpost; advance guard.
**avanzado, -da** *adj.* advanced [in age, in ideas]. *2* far into [the night, etc.].
**avanzar** *intr.* to advance [move forward]. *2* to advance, progress. *3 intr.-ref.* [of night, winter, etc.] to be approaching its end.
**avaramente** *adv.* avariciously, niggardly.
**avaricia** *f.* avarice.
**avaricioso, -sa** *adj.* AVARIENTO.
**avariento, -ta** *adj.* avaricious, miserly. *2 m.-f.* miser.
**avaro, -ra** *adj.-n.* AVARIENTO. *2 m.-f.* stinter.
**avasallador, -ra** *adj.* overwhelming. *2* domineering. *3 m.-f.* subjugator.
**avasallar** *tr.* to subjugate. *2 ref.* to become a vassal; to submit.
**ave** *f.* ORN. bird: *~ de corral,* domestic fowl; *~ de paso,* bird of passage; *~ del Paraíso,* bird of Paradise; *~ de rapiña,* or *rapaz,* bird of prey; *~ lira,* lyrebird.
**avecilla** *f. dim.* little bird.
**avecinar** *tr.* AVECINDAR. *2 ref.* to approach, be coming.
**avecindar** *tr.* to domicile. *2 ref.* to take up residence [at or in].
**avechucho** *m.* ugly bird.
**avefría** *f.* ORN. lapwing.
**avejentar** *tr.-ref.* to age [before one's time].
**avejigar** *tr.* to blister. *2 ref.* to blister [become blistered].
**avellana** *f.* BOT. hazel nut; filbert [nut].
**avellanado, -da** *adj.* shriveled; wizened.
**avellanador** *m.* countersink [bit].
**avellanal, avellanar** *m.* hazel plantation.
**avellanar** *tr.* MACH. to countersink. *2 ref.* to shrivel.
**avellaneda** *f.,* **avellanedo** *m.* AVELLANAL.

**avellano** *m.* BOT. hazel, hazel tree, filbert.
**avemaría** *f.* Hail Mary: *en un ~*, in a twinkle. *2* Angelus bell; *al ~*, at dusk.
**¡Ave María!** *interj.* gracious goodnes!
**avena** *f.* BOT. oats. *2 ~ loca*, wild oats.
**avenar** *tr.* to drain [land].
**avenate** *m.* drink made with oatmeal.
**avendré, avendría**, etc. *irr.* V. AVENIR.
**avenencia** *f.* agreement, compact, coming to terms. *2* harmony, concord.
**avengo, avenga**, etc. *irr.* V. AVENIR.
**avenida** *f.* flood, freshet. *2* avenue. *3* wide street.
**avenido, -da** *adj. bien* o *mal ~, con*, on good or bad terms with; agreeing or disagreeing with.
**avenir** *tr.* to make agree, to reconcile. *2 ref.* to agree, to get along well together. *3* to agree, come to an agreement. *4* to consent, resign oneself to.
**aventador, -ra** *m.-f.* winnower. *2 f.* winnowing machine. *3 m.* winnowin fork. *4* esparto fan [for fanning fire].
**aventajado, -da** *adj.* notable, excellent. *2* advantageous.
**aventajar** *tr.* to surpass, excel. *2* to advance, better. *3 ref.* to better oneself.
**aventar** *tr.* to fan, to blow. *2* to winnow. *3* to strew to the wind. *4* fig. to expel, drive away. *5 ref.* to swell up [with air]. *6* coll. to flee. ¶ CONJUG. like *acertar.*
**aventura** *f.* adventure. *2* hazard, chance, risk.
**aventurado, -da** *adj.* venturesome, risky.
**aventurar** *tr.* to venture, hazard, risk. *2 ref.* to adventure, risk, take the risk.
**aventurero, -ra** *adj.* adventure-seeking. *2 m.* adventurer; gentleman of fortune. *3* mercenary. *4 f.* adventuress.
**avergonzar** *tr.* to shame, put to shame, confound; to abash. *2 ref.* to be ashamed or abashed, to blush. ¶ CONJ. like *contar.*
**avergüenzo, avergüence** etc. *irr.* V. AVERGONZAR.
**avería** *f.* COM. damage. *2* NAUT. average. *3* MACH. failure, breakdown. *4* AVERÍO.
**averiado, -da** *adj.* damaged [esp. said of goods].
**averiarse** *ref.* to be damaged [esp. said of goods].
**averiguación** *f.* inquiry, acertainment.
**averiguar** *tr.* to inquire, ascertain, find out.
**averno** *m.* Avernus. *2* poet, hell.
**averrugado, -da** *adj.* full of warts, warty.
**aversión** *f.* aversion, dislike, loathing.
**avestruz** *f.* ORN. ostrich.
**avetoro** *m.* ORN. bittern, European bittern.
**avezar** *tr.* to accustom, inure. *2 ref.* to become accustomed, inured.
**aviación** *f.* aviation. *2* aviation corps, air force.
**aviador, -ra** *adj.* preparing, equipping. *2* AER. air [pilot]. *3 m.-f.* preparer, equipper. *4* AER. aviator, aviatrix, airman, airwoman.
**aviar** *tr.* to prepare, arrange. *2* to equip, provide. *3* to hasten. *4 estar uno aviado*, to be in a mess.
**avícola** *adj.* bird-rearing.
**avicultor, -ra** *m.-f.* aviculturist.
**avicultura** *f.* aviculture.
**avidez** *f.* avidity, greed. *2* eagerness.
**ávido, -da** *adj.* avid, eager, greedy.
**aviene, avienes**, etc. *irr.* V. AVENIR.
**avieso, -sa** *adj.* crooked, irregular. *2* evil-minded, perverse, malicious, wicked.
**avilés, -a** *adj.-n.* of Ávila.
**avinagrado, -da** *adj.* vinegary, sour, crabbed.
**avinagrar** *tr.* to sour, make sour. *2 ref.* to sour, to turn sour or vinegary.

**avine, aviniera**, etc. *irr.* V. AVENIR.
**Aviñón** *m. pr. n.* GEOG. Avignon.
**avío** *m.* preparation, provision. *2 pl.* tools, tackel, equipment. *3 interj. ¡al avío!*, hurry up!
**avión** *m.* AER. airplane: *~ de caza*, pursuit plane; *~ de combate*, fighter; *~ de reacción*, jet plane; *~ de línea*, air liner. *2* ORN. martin.
**avioneta** *f.* AER. light airplane.
**avisado, -da** *adj.* prudent, wise, shrewd: *mal ~*, ill-advised.
**avisador** *m.* adviser. *2* warner. *3 ~ de incendios*, fire alarm.
**avisar** *tr.* to inform. *2* to send word. *3* to warn; to advise, admonish.
**aviso** *m.* notice, information; warning. *2* admonishment, advice. *3* prudence, attention, caution: *sobre ~*, on the alert. *4* NAUT. dispatch boat.
**avispa** *f.* ENT. wasp.
**avispado, -da** *adj.* keen-witted, clever, smart.
**avispar** *tr.* to whip, urge [horses]. *2* to make clever. *4 ref.* to become lively or clever.
**avispero** *m.* wasp's nest. *2* swarm of wasps. *3* MED. carbuncle.
**avispón** *m.* ENT. hornet.
**avistar** *tr.* to sight, descry, get sight of. *2 ref.* to have an interview.
**avitaminosis** *f.* MED. avitaminosis.
**avituallamiento** *m.* provisioning, food-supplying. *2* NAUT. victualling.
**avituallar** *tr.* to victual, to provision.
**avivado, -da** *adj.* quick, lively, bright, spirited. *2* made brighter or livelier [a color]. *3* made quicker, livelier [the pace]. *4* excited, provoked, roused [the anger].
**avivador, -ra** *adj.* enlivening, stirring up.
**avivar** *tr.* to enliven, to stir up. *2* to heat, inflame, intensify. *3* to quicken, hasten. *4* to revive [the fire]. *5* to heighten, brighten [light, colours]. *6 intr.-ref.* to acquire life, vigour; to revive.
**avizor** *adj.* watching: *ojo ~*, on the alert.
**avizorar** *tr.* to watch, spy.
**avocar** *tr.* LAW to remove [a lawsuit] to a superior court.
**avoceta** *f.* ORN. avocet.
**avutarda** *f.* ORN. great bustard.
**axial, axil** *adj.* axial, axile.
**axila** *f.* ANAT. axilla, armpit. *2* BOT. axil.
**axilar** *adj.* axillar, axillary.
**axioma** *m.* axiom.
**axiomático, -ca** *adj.* axiomatic.
**axis** *m.* ANAT. axis.
**ay, pl. ayes** *m.* sigh, moan.
**¡ay!** *interj.* alas!, ouch!: *¡~ de...!*, woe to ...!; *¡~ de mí!*, woe is me!, ah me!
**aya** *f.* governess. *2* dry nurse.
**ayeaye** *m.* ZOOL. aye-aye.
**ayer** *adv.-m.* yesterday.
**ayo** *m.* tutor [private teacher].
**ayuda** *f.* help, aid, assistance. *2* MED. enema. *3 ~ de cámara*, valet, valet de chambre.
**ayudante** *m.* aid, assistant. *2* substitute teacher. *3* MIL. aid, aide; adjutant.
**ayudantía** *f.* assistantship. *2* MIL. adjutancy.
**ayudar** *tr.* to help, aid, assist.
**ayuga** *f.* BOT. mock cypress.
**ayunar** *intr.* to fast.
**ayunas (en)** *adv.* fasting. *2* without [or before] eating breakfast: *estar en ~*, not to have eaten breakfast, to have no idea; *quedarse en ~*, not to understand a thing.
**ayuno, -na** *adj.* having taken no food. *2* deprived.

*3* uninformed. *4 adv.* **en ayunas** or **en ayuno**, before, breakfasting; having taken no food; uninformed; not understanding. *5 m.* fast, fasting.

**ayuntamiento** *m.* town or city council. *2* town or city hall. *3* sexual intercourse.

**ayustar** *tr.* NAUT. to splice.

**azabachado, -da** *adj.* jet, jet-black.

**azabache** *m.* MINER. jet. *2* ORN. coal titmouse.

**azacán, -na** *adj.* menial, drudging. *2 m.-f.* drudge.

**azada** *f.* AGR. hoe.

**azadilla** *f.* ALMOCAFRE.

**azadón** *m.* AGR. hoe. *2 ~ de pico*, mattock.

**azadonada** *f.* stroke with a hoe.

**azadonar** *tr.* to hoe, hoe up, dig with a hoe.

**azafata** *f.* lady of the queen's wardrobe. *2* AER. air hostess.

**azafate** *m.* flat basket, tray.

**azafrán** *m.* BOT. saffron [plant and dried stigmas].

**azafranado, -da** *adj.* saffron, saffroned.

**azafranal** *m.* saffron plantation.

**azafranar** *tr.* to saffron.

**azagaya** *f.* assagai, javelin.

**azahar** *m.* orange, lemon or citron blossom.

**azalea** *f.* BOT. azalea.

**azamboa** *f.* BOT. kind of citron [fruit].

**azamboero, azamboo** *m.* BOT. kind of citron [tree].

**azar** *m.* hazard, chance: *al ~*, at random, haphazard. *2* accident, mishap.

**azarado, -da** *adj.* troubled, rattled, flustered.

**azarosamente** *adv.* with difficulties.

**azaroso, -sa** *adj.* misfortunate, unlucky.

**ázimo, -ma** *adj.* azymous, unleavened.

**azimut** *m.* ACIMUT.

**aznacho** *m.* BOT. pinaster, cluster pine.

**azoar** *tr.* to azotize.

**ázoe** *m.* CHEM. azote.

**azófar** *m.* brass, latten.

**azogadamente** *adv.* agitatedly.

**azogado, -da** *adj.-n.* [person] affected with mercurialism: *temblar como un ~*, to shake like a leaf. *2 m.* quicksilvering [in a mirror].

**azogamiento** *m.* quicksilvering. *2* MED. mercurialism. *3* shaking, agitation.

**azogar** *tr.* to quicksilver, to silver [a mirror]. *2 ref.* to be affected with mercurialism. *3* to get troubled, agitated.

**azogue** *m.* mercury, quicksilver: *ser un ~*, to be restless. *2* market place.

**azoico, -ca** *adj.* CHEM., GEOL. azoic.

**azolar** *tr.* to adze. ¶ Conjug. like *contar*.

**azor** *m.* ORN. goshawk.

**azorado, -da** *adj.* embarrassed, flustered, confused and ashamed.

**azoramiento** *m.* trouble, fluster, embarrassment.

**azorar** *tr.* to trouble, rattle, startle. *2 ref.* to get troubled, rattled, startled.

**Azores** *f. pr. n.* GEOG. Azores.

**azorrarse** *ref.* to be drowsy from heaviness.

**azotacalles** *m.* gadabout, loafer, street lounger.

**azotado, -da** *adj.* variegated.

**azotaina** *f.* flogging; spanking.

**azotamiento** *m.* whipping, flogging.

**azotar** *tr.* to whip, flog. *2* to flagellate. *3* to spank. *4* [of sea, rain, etc.] to beat, lash.

**azotazo** *m.* troke, lash, lashing. *2* spank.

**azote** *m.* birch, thong, scourge, etc. [for flogging]. *2* AZOTAZO. *3 fig.* scourge. *4 pl.* public flogging.

**azotea** *f.* flat roof [of a house].

**azteca** *adj.-n.* Aztec.

**azúcar** *m.-f.* sugar: *~ blanco*, refined sugar; *~ cande*, rock candy; *~ de cortadillo*, lump sugar; *~ moreno*, brown sugar.

**azucarado, -da** *adj.* sugared, sweedtened, made sweet: *yogur ~*, sugared yogurt. *2* sweet. *3 fig.* sugary, syrupy, sweet.

**azucarar** *tr.* to sugar. *2* to coat or ice with sugar.

**azucarera** *f.* sugar bowl. *2* sugar factory.

**azucarero, -ra** *adj.* [pertaining to] sugar. *2 m.* sugar producer. *3* sugar bowl.

**azucarillo** *m.* spongy sugar bar.

**azucena** *f.* BOT. Madonna lily, white lily.

**azud, azuda** *f.* irrigation water wheel. *2* irrigation dam.

**azuela** *f.* adze.

**azufaifa** *f.* jujube [fruit].

**azufaifo** *m.* BOT. jujube [tree].

**azufrado, -da** *adj.* sulphured. *2* sulphur, sulphureous. *3 m.* sulphuring.

**azufrar** *tr.* to sulphur, sulphurate, sulphurize.

**azufre** *m.* CHEM. sulphur, brimstone.

**azufrera** *f.* sulphur mine.

**azul** *adj.-m.* blue: *~ celeste*, sky blue; *~ marino*, navy blue; *~ turquí*, indigo.

**azulado, -da** *adj.* blue, bluish.

**azular** *tr.* to colour blue, to dye blue.

**azulear** *tr.* to have a bluish cast. *2* to show blue.

**azulejo** *m.* Dutch tile, glazed tile.

**azulete** *m.* blue, bluing [powder].

**azulino, -na** *adj.* bluish.

**azumbre** *m.* a liquid measure [about 2 litres].

**azur** *adj.-m.* HER. azure.

**azurita** *f.* MINER. azurite.

**azuzar** *tr.* to set [the dogs] on. *2* to incite.

# B

**B, b** f. B, b, second letter of the Spanish alphabet.
**Baal** m. pr. n. Baal.
**baba** f. drivel, slaver, slobber: *caérsele a uno la ~*, to be silly; to be delighted. 2 BABAZA I.
**babada** f. BABILLA.
**babaza** f. mucus, slime. 2 ZOOL. slug.
**babear** intr. to drivel, slaver, slobber, drool.
**babel** f. babel, bedlam. 2 pr. n. (cap.) Babel.
**babeo** m. drivelling, slobbering [flow of saliva].
**babera** f. beaver [of helmet]. 2 BABERO.
**babero** m. bib, chin-cloth.
**Babia** f. *estar en ~*, to be absent in mind.
**babieca** adj. silly. 2 m.-f. simpleton.
**Babilonia** f. pr. n. HIST. GEOG. Babylon. 2 (not cap.) babel, bedlam, uproar.
**babilónico, -ca** adj. Babylonian.
**babilonio, -nia** adj.-n. Babylonian.
**babilla** f. VET. stifle.
**babirusa** m. ZOOL. babirusa.
**bable** m. Asturian [dialect].
**babor** m. port, larboard.
**babosa** f. ZOOL. slug.
**babosear** tr. to cover with saliva, to slaver. 2 intr. coll. BABEAR.
**baboseo** m. dribbling [a baby] slobbering, slavering. 2 foaming, frothing. 3 slime. 4 fig. drooling, drivelling.
**baboso, -sa** adj. slavering, drooling. 2 m.-f. slaverer, drooler. 3 adj.-m. spoony. 4 m. brat.
**babucha** f. babouche.
**babuino, -na** n. ZOOL. baboon.
**baca** f. top [of stagecoach]. 2 rainproof cover [for a stagecoach].
**bacalao** m. ICHTH. codfish.
**bacanal** adj. bacchanal, bacchanalian. 2 f. bacchanalia. 3 pl. *bacanales*, Bacchanalia.
**bacante** f. bacchante. 2 drunken, riotous woman.
**bacará** m. baccarat.
**bacelar** m. arbour with grapevines.
**bacía** f. basin; shaving basin.
**bacilar** adj. bacillary.
**baciliforme** adj. bacilliform, rod-shaped.
**bacilo** m. bacillus.
**bacín** m. chamber pot. 2 cur, despicable man.
**bacineta** f. small basin; alms plate.
**bacinete** m. basinet. 2 ANAT. pelvis.
**Baco** m. pr. n. Bacchus.

**baconiano, -na** adj.-n. baconian [of Francis Bacon].
**bacteria** f. bacterium. 2 pl. bacteria.
**bactericida** adj. bactericidal, germ-kill-ing. 2 m. bactericide, germicide.
**bacteriología** f. bacteriology.
**bacteriólogo** m. bacteriologist.
**báculo** m. stick, staff. 2 fig. support, relief, comfort, aid. 3 ~ *pastoral*, crozier, pastoral staff.
**bache** m. hole [in a road]. 2 AER. ~ *de aire*, air pocket.
**bachiller, -ra** adj. garrulous. 2 m.-f. babbler, gossip. 3 bachelor [holder of degree].
**bachillerato** m. baccalaureate.
**bachillerear** intr. to babble, to gossip.
**bachillería** f. babbling, gossiping.
**badajada** f. stroke [of bell]. 2 stupidity, nonsense.
**badajo** m. clapper [of bell]. 2 coll, stupid babbler.
**badajocense** adj.-n. of Badajoz.
**badana** f. basan, dressed sheepskin: fig. *zurrarle a uno la ~*, to tan someone's hide.
**badén** m. channel made by rain water. 2 paved trench for a stream across a road.
**badián** m. BOT. Chinese anise.
**badil** m., **badila** f. small fire shovel.
**badulaque** m. nincompoop, simpleton.
**baga** f. flax boll.
**bagaje** m. MIL. baggage. 2 MIL. beast of burden. 3 coll. a person's store of knowledge or information.
**bagatela** f. bagatelle, trifle.
**bagazo** m. flax chaff. 2 bagasse. 3 waste pulp [of olives, oranges, etc.].
**bagre** m. ICHTH. South American catfish.
**baguarí** m. ORN. (Am.) kind of stork.
**¡bah!** interj. bah!
**baharí** m. ORN. sparrow hawk.
**bahía** f. [sea] bay.
**bailable** adj. dance [music]. 2 m. THEAT. dance number.
**bailador, -ra** adj. dancing. 2 m.-f. dancer.
**bailar** intr. to dance. 2 [of a top] to spin. 3 tr. to dance [some dance]. 4 to dance; dandle.
**bailarín, -na** adj. dancing. 2 m.-f. dancer.
**baile** m. dance; ball: ~ *casero*, informal dance; ~ *de etiqueta*, dress ball, formal dance; ~ *de máscaras*, masked ball, masquerade; ~ *de San Vito*, MED. St. Vitu's dance. 2 obs. bailiff [in Aragon].

**bailiaje** *m.* bailiage. *2* commandery in the order of Malta.

**bailío** *m.* knight commander of Malta.

**bailotear** *intr.* to dance a lot and ungracefully.

**bailoteo** *m.* ungraceful dancing.

**baivel** *m.* bevel square with a curved leg.

**bajá**, *pl.* **bajaes** *m.* pasha.

**baja** *f.* fall, drop [in prices, in value, etc.]: *jugar a la ~*, COM. to bear [speculate for a fall]; *ir de ~*, to decline. *2* MIL. casualty. *3* cancelled subscription. *4 dar de ~*, to cross out from a list of members, subscribers, etc.; MIL. to muster out; *darse de ~*, to cease to be a subscriber; to resign membership [of] voluntarily.

**bajada** *f.* descent. *2 ~ de aguas*, rainwater pipe, leader. *3* sloping street.

**bajamar** *f.* low tide, low water.

**bajar** *intr.* to descend, come down, go down. *2* to fall, drop, lessen, diminish. *3* to descend, sink, slope downwards. *4* to alight, get down. *5 tr.* to bring down, get down, lower, drop. *6* to descend [stairs, a slope, etc.]. *7* to lower, bow [one's head, body, etc.]: *~ los ojos*, to cast one's eyes down. *8* to lower reduce [the price, etc.]. *9 ref.* to stoop, bend down. *10* to alight [from carriage, etc.].

**bajel** *m.* ship, boat, vessel.

**bajete** *m.* MUS. bariton. *2* MUS. counterpoint exercise.

**bajeza** *f.* baseness, meanness; lowliness. *2* low action.

**bajío** *m.* shoal, sand bank. *2* (Am.) lowland.

**bajista** *m.* bear [in stock market].

**bajo** *adv.* softly, in a low voice. *2 prep.* beneath, under; on: *~ mano*, underhandly, secretly; *~ pena de muerte*, on pain of death; *~ techado*, under a roof, sheltered.

**bajo, -ja** *adj.* low [in practically every sense]: *~ latín*, low latin; *~ relieve*, bass-relief; *por lo ~*, secretly. *2* short [not tall]. *3* downcast [head, eyes, etc.]. *4* base [gold, silver]. *5* dull [colour]. *6* base, vile. *7* lower: *la clase ~*, the lower classes. *8 piso ~*, *planta baja*, ground floor. *9 m.* hollow, deep. *10* shoal, sand-bank. *11 pl.* lower part of trousers or skirts. *12* ground floor; ground-floor rooms.

**bajón** *m.* MUS. bassoon. *2* bassoonist. *3* decline, drop [in health, wealth, etc.]. *4* great fall [in prices].

**bajonista** *m.* bassoonist.

**bajorrelieve** *m.* low relief, bas relief.

**bajuno, -na** *adj.* low, coarse [people].

**bajura** *f.* lowness.

**bakelita** *f.* bakelite.

**bala** *f.* bullet, ball, shot: *~ perdida*, stray bullet; fig. flighty person; *~ rasa*, solid cannon ball. *2* bale [of goods]. *3* ten reams [of paper].

**balada** *f.* ballad [poem].

**baladí** *adj.* trivial, trifling.

**baladrón** *m.* braggart, bully, rodomont.

**baladronada** *f.* boast, brag, bravado, rodomontade.

**baladronear** *intr.* to brag, to play the bully.

**bálago** *m.* straw, grain stalk.

**balaj, balaje** *m.* balas, balas ruby.

**balance** *m.* oscillation; [a single movement of] swinging, rocking, rolling. *2* vacillation. *3* COM. balancing, balance, balance sheet.

**balancear** *intr.-ref.* to rock, swing, roll. *2 intr.* to hesitate, waver. *3 tr.* to balance, counterpoise.

**balanceo** *m.* swinging, rocking, rolling.

**balancín** *pl.* **-nes** *m.* whippletree. *2* MACH. walking beam. *3* ropewalker's balancing pole. *4* small coining press. *5* balancer, halter [of insect].

**balandra** *f.* NAUT. sloop.

**balandro** *m.* NAUT. small sloop.

**bálano** *m.* ANAT. glans. *2* ZOOL. acorn barnacle.

**balanza** *f.* balance, scales. *2* comparative estimate, judgment. *3 ~ comercial*, balance of trade. *4 en ~*, undecided, in danger.

**balar** *intr.* to bleat, baa.

**balastar** *tr.* RLY. to ballast.

**balasto** *m.* RLY. ballast.

**balaustrada** *f.* balustrade, banisters.

**balaustrado, -da** *adj.* baluster-shaped.

**balaustre, balaústre** *m.* baluster.

**balazo** *m.* shot; bullet wound.

**balbucear** *intr.* to stammer, hesitate in speech. *2* [of a child] to babble.

**balbucencia** *f.*, **balbuceo** *m.* stammering. *2* babble [of a child].

**balbuciente** *adj.* stuttering, stammering. *2* babbling.

**balbucir** *intr.* BALBUCEAR. ¶ Only used in forms having *i* in their terminations.

**Balcanes (los)** *m. pr. n.* GEOG. the Balkans.

**balcánico, -ca** *adj.-n.* Balkan.

**balcón** *m.* balcony [of a house].

**balconaje** *m.* balconies [of a house].

**baldadura** *f.*, **baldamiento** *m.* physical disability.

**baldado, -da** *adj.* invalid, physically disabled.

**baldaquín, baldaquino** *m.* baldachin.

**baldar** *tr.* to cripple, disable physically. *2* to annoy.

**balde** *m.* bucket, pail. *2 adv. de ~*, free, for nothing. *3 en ~*, in vain.

**baldear** *tr.* to wash [decks or floors] with buckets of water. *2* NAUT. to bail.

**baldeo** *m.* washing the decks. *2* washing, cleaning.

**baldíamente** *adv.* in vain, vainly; idly.

**baldío, -día** *adj.* untilled, uncultivated. *2* vain, idle. *3* idle, lazy.

**baldón** *m.* insult, affront. *2* blot, disgrace.

**baldonar** *tr.* to insult, to affront.

**baldosa** *f.* floor tile.

**baldosado** *m.* tiling, flagging, paving with tiles or flagstones. *2* tiled flooring.

**baldosar** *tr.* to tile, to flag, to pave with tiles or flagstones.

**baldosín** *m.* small floor tile.

**baldragas** *m.* weak, soft fellow.

**balduque** *m.* red tape.

**balear** *tr.* (Am.) to shoot [wound or kill].

**balear, baleárico** *adj.* Balearic.

**balénidos** *m. pl.* ZOOL. whales.

**baleo** *m.* round mat.

**balido** *m.* bleat, bleating, baa.

**balín** *m.* small bullet, buckshot.

**balista** *f.* ballista.

**balístico, -ca** *adj.* ballistic. *2 f.* ballistics.

**baliza** *f.* buoy, beacon.

**balizar** *tr.* ABALIZAR.

**balneario, -ria** *adj.* [pertaining to] bath. *2 m.* [medicinal] baths; watering place, spa.

**balompié** *m.* football [game].

**balón** *m.* [a large inflated] ball; a football. *2* bag [for holding a gas]. *3* CHEM. balloon.

**baloncesto** *m.* basketball.

**balonmano** *m.* handball.

**balonvolea** *m.* volleyball.

**balota** *f.* ballot [small voting ball].

**balotaje** *m.* (Am.) voting. 2 tie, draw [in an election].

**balsa** *f.* pool, pond. 2 NAUT. raft, float. 3 ~ *de aceite*, fig. quiet place or assembly.

**balsadera** *f.*, **balsadero** *m.* ferry.

**balsámico, -ca** *adj.* balsamic, balmy.

**balsamina** *f.* BOT. balsam apple. 2 BOT. impatiens, garden balsam.

**bálsamo** *m.* BOT., PHARM. balsam, balm. 2 fig. balm [something soothing].

**balsear** *tr.* to ferry [a river] on rafts.

**balsero** *m.* ferryman.

**Baltasar** *m. pr. n.* Balthasar. 2 Belshazzar [from Babylonia].

**báltico, -ca** *adj.* Baltic. 2 *pr. n.* (cap.) Baltic Sea.

**baluarte** *m.* FORT. bastion. 2 fig. bulwark, defence.

**balumba** *f.* bulk, mass of many things thrown together.

**ballena** *f.* ZOOL. whale. 2 whalebone. 3 bone [of corset]. 4 *pr. n.* ASTR. Whale, Cetus.

**ballenato** *m.* young whale, whale calf.

**ballenera** *f.* NAUT. whaleboat.

**ballenero, -ra** *adj.* whale, whaling: *barco* ~, whaler. 2 *m.* whaler, whaleman.

**ballesta** *f.* crossbow, arbalest. 2 carriage spring.

**ballestería** *f.* hunting, chase. 2 crossbows. 3 crossbowmen's quarters. 4 crossbowmen's quarters.

**ballestero** *m.* crossbowman, arbalester. 2 maker of crossbows. 3 royal armourer.

**ballestilla** *f.* small singletree. 2 NAUT. cross-staff, forestaff. 3 VET. fleam.

**ballet** *m.* ballet [dance and music].

**ballico** *m.* BOT. Italian rye grass.

**ballueca** *f.* BOT. wild oats.

**bambalear** *intr.-ref.* BAMBOLEAR.

**bambalinas** *f. pl.* THEAT. flies, borders.

**bambarria** *m.-f.* dolt, fool. 2 *f.* fluke [at billiards].

**bamboche** *m.* short and chubby person.

**bambolear** *intr.-ref.* to sway, swing.

**bamboleo** *m.* swaying, swinging.

**bambolla** *f.* show, sham, pretence.

**bambollero, -ra** *adj.* bragging, boastful, swanky. 2 showy, flashy.

**bambú** *m.* BOT. bamboo.

**banal** *adj.* banal, commonplace, trivial, uninteresting.

**banalidad** *f.* banality, triviality, triteness.

**banana** *f.* BOT. banana.

**banano** *m.* BOT. banana [plant].

**banasta** *f.* large basket.

**banasto** *m.* large round basket.

**banca** *f.* COM. banking. 2 a card game. 3 bank [in gambling]. 4 bench. 5 washing box.

**bancada** *f.* MACH. bed, bedplate; sideframe. 2 NAUT. thwart, bank. 3 portion of masonry. 4 MIN. shelf.

**bancal** *m.* AGR. terrace. 2 AGR. oblong plot. 3 bench cover.

**bancario, -ria** *adj.* COM. bank, banking.

**bancarrota** *f.* bankruptcy: *hacer* ~, to go bankrupt.

**banco** *m.* bench, form; pew. 2 bench [working table]. 3 bank, shoal. 4 school [of fishes]. 5 MIN. bench. 6 GEOL. stratum. 7 COM. bank.

**banda** *f.* scarf, sash [worn baldric-wise]. 2 band, strip. 3 band, gang; flock, herd. 4 side, border: *cerrarse a la* ~, to stand firm. 5 side [of ship]: *dar a la* ~, to careen. 6 cushion [of billiard table]. 7 MUS., RADIO. band: ~ *de tambores*, drum corps. 8 CINEM. ~ *de sonido*, sound track.

**bandada** *f.* flock [of birds], covey.

**bandazo** *m.* NAUT. lurch [sudden roll to one side].

**bandear** *tr.* to cross, to go across. 2 to shoot through. 3 to pursue, to chase, to run after. 4 to wound, to harm. 5 to court, to woo [a woman]. 6 *ref.* to manage, to get by, to take care of oneself.

**bandeja** *f.* tray.

**bandera** *f.* flag, banner, ensign, colours: ~ *blanca*, white flag; ~ *negra*, black jack; *a banderas desplegadas*, openly; *con banderas desplegadas*, with flying colours; *de* ~, wonderful, extraordinary.

**bandería** *f.* faction, party.

**banderilla** *f.* BANDERITA. 2 barbed dart used in bullfighting: *clavar, poner una* ~ fig. to taunt, to be sarcastic to.

**banderillear** *tr.* to thrust banderillas into the neck of [a bull].

**banderillero** *m.* banderillero.

**banderín** *m.* small flag; camp colour. 2 recruiting post. 4 RLY. flag.

**banderita** *f.* small flag.

**banderizo, -za** *adj.* factional. 2 seditious. 3 *m.* factionist, partisan.

**banderola** *f.* banderole. 2 SURV. fanion.

**bandidaje** *m.* BANDOLERISMO.

**bandido** *m.* outlaw. 2 bandit. 3 rascal.

**bando** *m.* faction, party. 2 edict, proclamation.

**bandola** *f.* MUS. mandore. 2 NAUT. jury mast.

**bandolera** *f.* female brigand. 2 bandoleer, bandolier.

**bandolerismo** *m.* brigandage.

**bandolero** *m.* brigand, robber, highwayman.

**bandolina** *f.* bandoline.

**bandoneón** *m.* MUS. concertina.

**bandullo** *m.* coll. guts, bowels.

**bandurria** *f.* MUS. bandurria, bandore.

**baniano** *m.* banian.

**banjo** *m.* MUS. banjo.

**banquero** *m.* COM. banker. 2 banker [in gambling].

**banqueta** *f.* stool, footstool. 2 FORT. banquette. 3 little bench. 4 (Mex.) sidewalk.

**banquete** *m.* banquet, feast.

**banquetear** *intr.-tr.* to banquet.

**banquillo** *m.* stool, little bench. 2 prisoner's seat [in court], dock.

**banquisa** *f.* ice field, ice floe, sheet of floating ice.

**banzo** *m.* cheek [of a frame].

**bañadera** *f.* (Am.) bathtub.

**bañadero** *m.* place where wild animals bathe.

**bañado** *m.* (Am.) marsh, swamp, soft wet land.

**bañador** *m.* bathing suit.

**bañar** *tr.* to bathe. 2 to give a coating to. 3 *ref.* to bathe, take a bath.

**bañera** *f.* bath, bathtub.

**bañero, -ra** *m.* bathhouse owner or keeper. 2 *m.-f.* bath attendant.

**bañil** *m.* BAÑADERO.

**bañista** *m.* bather. 2 resorter, frequenter of a spa or a seaside resort.

**baño** *m.* bath: ~ *de asiento*, sitz bath; ~ *María*, double boiler. 2 bathtub. 3 coating. 4 bagnio [oriental prison]. 5 *pl.* bathing place. 6 spa.

**bao** *m.* NAUT. beam [cross timber].

**baobab** *m.* BOT. baobab.

**baptisterio** *m.* baptist(e)ry.

**baque** *m.* blow in falling, thud, thump, bump.

**baqueta** *f.* ramrod. 2 switch used as a whip. 3 ARCH. bead. 4 *pl.* drumsticks. 5 *carrera de baquetas*, running the gauntlet. 6 *a* ~, harshly, despotically.

**baqueteado, -da** *adj.* experienced [person].

**baquetear** *tr.* fig. to treat roughly, 2 to train, to harden, to season, to drill. 3 to bother, to put out, to upset, to disturb.

**baqueteo** *m.* bother, trouble, annoyance. 2 training, hardening, seasoning, drilling. 3 jolting, jerking, shaking.

**baquía** *f.* familiarity with roads, paths, rivers, etc., of a region. 2 (Am.) skill, manual dexterity.

**baquiano, -na** *adj.* skillful. 2 *m.* expert guide.

**báquico, -ca** *adj.* Bacchic. 2 bacchic.

**báquira** *f.*, **báquiro** *m.* ZOOL. peccary.

**bar** *m.* bar, barroom.

**barahúnda** *f.* uproar, tumult.

**baraja** *f.* pack, *deck [of cards].

**barajar** *tr.* to shuffle [cards]. 2 to mingle, jumble together. 3 *intr.* to quarrel. 4 *ref.* to get mingled.

**baranda** *f.* BARANDILLA. 2 border [of billiard table].

**barandado, barandaje** *m.* BARANDILLA.

**barandal** *m.* upper or lower support [of a balustrade]; handrail. 2 BARANDILLA.

**barandilla** *f.* balustrade, railing, banisters.

**baratería** *f.* MAR., LAW barratry.

**baratija** *f.* trinket, trifle, gewgaw.

**baratillero** *m.* seller of cheap articles.

**baratillo** *m.* cheap or second-hand goods or shop.

**barato, -ta** *adj.* cheap. 2 *adv.* cheaply. 3 *m.* bargain sale. 4 money exacted from winning gamblers. 5 *dar de* ~, to grant [for the sake of argument].

**báratro** *m.* poet, barathrum, hell.

**baratura** *f.* cheapness [of goods].

**baraúnda** *f.* BARAHÚNDA.

**barba** *f.* chin. 2 beard, whiskers: ~ *cerrada*, thick beard; *Barba Azul*, Bluebeard; *hacer la* ~, to shave; to annoy; to fawn on; *en las barbas de uno*, to one's face; *por* ~, apiece. 3 beard [of goat]. 4 wattle [of fowl]. 5 ~ *de ballena*, whalebone. 6 *m.* THEAT. old man. 7 *f. pl.* barbs [of feather]. 8 BOT. slender roots. 9 deckle edge [of paper].

**barbacana** *f.* FORT. barbican.

**barbacoa** *f.* barbecue.

**barbada** *f.* lower jaw [of horse]. 2 bridle curb. 3 ICHTH. a Mediterranean fish.

**barbado, -da** *adj.* bearded. 2 deckle-edged.

**Barbados** *pr. n.* GEOG. Barbados.

**Bárbara** *f. pr. n.* Barbara.

**bárbaramente** *adv.* barbarously. 2 enormously.

**barbaridad** *f.* barbarousness. 2 barbarity; atrocity; rash or preposterous act or saying. 3 awful amount.

**barbarie** *f.* barbarism, barbarousness. 2 barbarity, cruelty.

**barbarismo** *m.* barbarism [impurity of language]. 2 BARBARIE.

**barbarizar** *tr.* to fill with barbarisms.

**bárbaro, -ra** *adj.* barbarian, barbaric, barbarous. 2 rude, cruel, savage. 3 coll. rash. 4 coll. enormous. 5 *m.-f.* barbarian.

**barbechar** *tr.* to fallow.

**barbechera** *f.* series of fallows. 2 fallowing.

**barbecho** *m.* fallow. 2 ploughed land ready for sowing.

**barbería** *f.* barber's shop. 2 barbering.

**barberil** *adj.* tonsorial.

**barbero** *m.* barber.

**barbeta** *f.* barbette.

**barbián, -na** *adj.* coll, dashing, bold, handsome.

**barbicano, -na** *adj.* white-bearded.

**barbilampiño** *adj.* smooth-faced, beardless.

**barbilindo, barbilucio** *adj.* foppish [young man].

**barbilla** *f.* point of the chin. 2 barbel [of fish]. 3 CARP. bevel end for joining.

**barbinegro, -gra** *adj.* black-bearded.

**barbiquejo** *m.* chin strap. 2 NAUT. bobstay.

**barbirrojo** *adj.-m.* red-bearded, ginger-bearded.

**barbitúrico** *adj.-m.* CHEM. barbiturate.

**barbo** *m.* ICHTH. barbel: ~ *de mar*, red mullet.

**barbón** *m.* bearded man.

**barboquejo** *m.* chin strap.

**barbotar** *intr.-tr.* to mumble, to mutter.

**barboteo** *m.* mumbling, muttering, grumbling.

**barbudo, -da** *adj.* bearded, long-bearded.

**barbulla** *f.* hubbub.

**barbullar** *intr.* to jabber noisily and in spurts.

**barbullón** *m.* jabberer.

**barbuquejo** *m.* BARBOQUEJO.

**barca** *f.* boat, small boat: ~ *de pasaje*, ferry-boat.

**barcada** *f.* boatload. 2 boat trip.

**barcaje** *m.* transport by boat. 2 boat freight. 3 ferrying, ferriage.

**barcarola** *f.* MUS. barcarole.

**barcaza** *f.* lighter, barge.

**Barcelona** *pr. n.* GEOG. Barcelona.

**barcelonés, -sa** *adj.-n.* of Barcelona.

**barcia** *f.* chaff [from grain].

**barco** *m.* NAUT. boat, vessel, ship.

**barda** *f.* bard [horse armour]. 2 thatched top [of a wall or fence].

**bardaguera** *f.* BOT. kind of osier.

**bardal** *m.* BARDA 2.

**bardana** *f.* BOT. burdock.

**bardo** *m.* bard [poet.].

**baremo** *m.* ready reckoner.

**bargueño** *m.* a painted and inlaid cabinet.

**bario** *m.* CHEM. barium.

**barita** *f.* CHEM. baryta.

**barítono** *m.* MUS. baritone.

**barloventear** *intr.* NAUT. to beat to windward, to beat. 2 coll. to rove about.

**barlovento** *m.* NAUT. windward.

**barnacla** *m.* ORN. barnacle, barnacle goose.

**barniz** *m.* varnish. 2 glaze [on pottery]. 3 fig. smattering.

**barnizado** *m.* varnishing.

**barnizador, -ra** *m.-f.* varnisher.

**barnizar** *tr.* to varnish.

**barógrafo** *m.* barograph.

**barométrico, -ca** *adj.* barometrical, barometric.

**barómetro** *m.* barometer.

**barón** *m.* baron.

**baronesa** *f.* baroness.

**baronía** *f.* barony, baronage.

**baroscopio** *m.* baroscope.

**barquear** *tr.* to cross [a river, etc.] by boat. 2 *intr.* to go about in a boat.

**barquero** *m.* boatman; ferryman.

**barquichuelo** *m.* small boat or ship.

**barquilla** *f.* AER. basket; nacelle. 2 NAUT. ~ *de la corredera*, log, log chip.

**barquillero** *m.* maker or seller o BARQUILLOS.

**barquillo** *m.* thin rolled waffle; cone.

**barquín** *m.* large bellows.

**barquinazo** *m.* hard jolt or upset of a carriage.

**barra** *f.* bar. 2 MECH. lever, bar; beam, rod. 3 ingot, bar [of metal]. 4 bar, rail [in lawcourt]. 5 SPORT. bar. 6 sand-bar. 7 WEAV. gross-spun thread in cloth. 8 HER. stripe, bar. 9 NAUT. irons. 10 ~ *colectora*, ELECT. bus bar. 11 *sin pararse en barras*, regardless of obstacles.

**Barrabás** *m. pr. n.* BIBL. Barabas. 2 (non cap.) devil [evil or mischievous person].

**barrabasada** *f.* wrong, hasty, inconsiderate action.

**barraca** *f.* cabin, hut, booth, shanty. *2* farmhouse [in the Valencian countryside].

**barracón** *m.* large hut or booth.

**barracuda** *f.* barracuda.

**barrado, -da** *adj.* striped, lined, streaked. *2* HER. barred.

**barragana** *f.* concubine.

**barranca** *f.* BARRANCO 1 & 2.

**barranco** *m.* precipice. *2* ravine, gorge. *3* difficulty, setback.

**barrancoso, -sa** *adj.* full of ravines, broken.

**barredero, -ra** *adj.* sweeping: *red barredera*, dragnet, seine. *2 m.* baker's mop.

**barredor, -ra** *adj.* sweeping. *2 m.-f.* sweeper.

**barreminas** *m.* mine sweeper [ship].

**barrena** *f.* drill, auger, gimlet. *2* rock drill. *3* AER. spin: *entrar en* ~, to go into a spin.

**barrenado, -da [de cascos]** *adj.* scatter-brained.

**barrenar** *tr.* to drill, bore. *2* to scuttle [a ship]. *3* to foil, sap, thwart. *4* to violate, infringe.

**barrendero, -ra** *m.-f.* street sweeper.

**barrenillo** *m.* ENT. borer [insect].

**barreno** *m.* large drill. *2* bored hole: *dar* ~, to scuttle [a ship]. *3* blast hole.

**barreño** *m.* earthen tub, dishpan.

**barrer** *tr.* to sweep; to sweep away; to sweep clean. *2* NAUT. to rake.

**barrera** *f.* barrier: ~ *del sonido*, sound barrier. *2* RLY. crossing gate. *3* FORT. parapet. *4* MIL. barrage. *5* BULLF. fence around inside of bullring. *6* BULLF. first row of seats. *7* clay pit.

**barreta** *f.* small bar. *2* shoe lining.·

**barretear** *tr.* to fasten with bars.

**barretina** *f.* Catalan cap.

**barriada** *f.* city ward or district; suburb.

**barrial** *m.* claypit. *2* muddy place, mire, swampy ground.

**barrica** *f.* cask, barrel.

**barricada** *f.* barricade.

**barrido** *m.* sweeping.

**barriga** *f.* belly. *2* bulge [in a wall].

**barrigón, -na, barrigudo, -da** *adj.* big-bellied.

**barriguera** *f.* belly-band.

**barril** *m.* barrel, keg. *2* earthen water jug.

**barrilamen** *m.* stock of barrels or casks.

**barrilete** *m.* keg. *2* CARP. dog, clamp. *3* NAUT. mouse. *4* ZOOL. fiddler crab.

**barrilla** *f.* BOT., CHEM. barilla.

**barrio** *m.* town ward, quarter or district: ~ *extremo*, suburb; *barrios bajos*, slums; fig. *el otro* ~, the other world.

**barriobajero, -ra,** *adj.* vulgar, low-class, cheap, common.

**barrizal** *m.* muddy ground, muddy place.

**barro** *m.* mud. *2 pl.* pimples [on the face].

**barroco, -ca** *adj.* baroque.

**barroquismo** *m.* baroque style; baroque taste.

**barroso, -sa** *adj.* muddy. *2* pimpled, pimply.

**barrote** *m.* heavy bar. *2* bar [in a window, etc.]. *3* rung [of a chair]; crosspiece.

**barruntar** *tr.* to conjecture guess, suspect.

**barrunto** *m.* feeling, guess. *2* inkling, sign.

**bartola (a la)** *adv. tumbarse a la* ~, to lie back lazily; to do nothing.

**bartolillo** *m.* little custard pie.

**Bartolo, Bartolomé** *m. pr. n.* Bartholomew.

**bártulos** *m. pl.* tools, traps: *liar los* ~, coll. to pack up.

**barullo** *m.* noise, confusion, tumult, medley.

**barzón** *m.* saunter, stroll.

**barzonear** *intr.* to walk idly, to stroll about.

**basa** *f.* basis, foundation. *2* ARCH. base.

**basada** *f.* stocks [for shipbuilding].

**basal** *adj.* basal.

**basáltico, -ca** *adj.* basalt, basaltic.

**basalto** *m.* PETROG. basalt.

**basamento** *m.* ARCH. base and pedestal, basement.

**basar** *tr.* to base, found. *2 ref.* to be based. *4* to base oneself, one's statement, etc.

**basáride** *f.* ZOOL. cacomistle.

**basca** *f.* nausea, squeamishness.

**bascosidad** *f.* filth, dirt.

**báscula** *f.* platform scale or balance. *2* bascule.

**bascular** *intr.* to tilt, seesaw.

**basculante** *adj.* bascule: *puente* ~, bascule bridge.

**base** *f.* basis, base: *a* ~ *de*, on the basis of. *2* MATH., GEOM., CHEM., MIL., SURV. base.

**básico, -ca** *adj.* basic.

**basidio** *m.* BOT. basidium.

**basilar** *adj.* basilar.

**Basilea** *f. pr. n.* GEOG. Basle.

**basílica** *f.* basilica. *2 adj.* basilic [vein].

**Basilio** *m. pr. n.* Basil.

**basilisco** *m.* MYTH. basilisk, cockatrice: *estar hecho un* ~, to be furious. *2* ZOOL., MIL. basilisk.

**basquear** *intr.* to be nauseated. *2 tr.* to nauseate.

**basquiña** *f.* black outer skirt.

**basta** *f.* basting stitch.

**bastante** *adj.* enough, sufficient. *2 adv.* enough, fairly, pretty, rather, sufficiently.

**bastar** *intr.* to suffice, be enough. *2 ref. bastarse a sí mismo*, to be sufficient unto oneself. *3 ¡basta!*, that wil do; stop!

**bastardear** *tr.* to debase, to adulterate. *2 intr.* to bastardize, degenerate.

**bastardía** *f.* bastardy. *2* meanness, indignity.

**bastardilla** *adj.* italic [letter]. *2 f.* italics.

**bastardo, -da** *adj.* bastard. *2* mean, base. *3 m.-f.* bastard.

**baste** *m.* basting stitch. *2* saddle pad.

**bastear** *tr.* SEW. to baste.

**bastedad** *f.* coarseness, lack of polish.

**bastidor** *m.* sash, frame. *2* embroidery frame. *3* PHOT. plate holder. *4* chassis [of a car]. *5* wing [of stage scenery]: *entre bastidores*, behind the scenes.

**bastilla** *f.* SEW. hem.

**bastimento** *m.* supply of provisions. *2* NAUT. vessel.

**bastión** *m.* FORT. bastion.

**basto, -ta** *adj.* coarse, rough, inferior. *2* unpolished [person]. *3 m.* packsaddle. *4* ace of clubs. *5 pl.* clubs [in Spanish cards].

**bastón** *m.* cane, walking stick. *2* baton, staff, truncheon.

**bastonada** *f.,* **bastonazo** *m.* blow with a cane.

**bastoncillo** *m. dim.* stick, small cane. *2* ANAT. rod [in retina].

**bastonera** *f.* cane stand, umbrella stand.

**bastonero** *m.* cane maker or seller.

**basura** *f.* sweepings, rubbish, garbage.

**basurero** *m.* dustman, garbage man. *2* rubbish dump.

**bata** *f.* dressing gown, morning gown. *2* white coat [for doctors, etc.]. *3* obs. frock with train.

**batacazo** *m.* violent bump [in falling].

**batahola** *f.* din, hubbub, hurly-burly.

**batalla** *f.* battle: ~ *campal*, pitched battle. *2* joust, tournament. *3* PAINT. battle piece.

**batallador, -ra** *adj.* battling, fighting.

**batallar** *intr.* to battle, fight; to struggle. *2* to fence. *3* to waver, hesitate.

**batallón** *m.* battalion.

**batán** *m.* fulling mill. *2* WEAV. lathe, lay.

**batanar** *tr.* to full [cloth].

**batanear** *tr.* fig. coll. to beat, to give someone a thrashing or a hiding.

**batanero** *m.* cloth fuller.

**bataola** *f.* BATAHOLA.

**batata** *f.* BOT. sweet potato.

**bátavo, -va** *adj.-n.* Batavian.

**batayola** *f.* NAUT. fender rail.

**batea** *f.* painted wooden tray. *2* small tub. *3* NAUT. SCOW. *4* RLY. flatcar, platform car.

**bateador** *m.* batsman [in cricket], *2* batter [in baseball].

**bate** *m.* (Am.) baseball bat.

**batel** *m.* small boat.

**batelero** *m.* boatman.

**batería** *f.* MIL., NAV., ELECT., MUS. battery. *2* battery [set of instruments, etc.]: ~ *de cocina*, kitchen utensils. *3* THEAT. footlights. *4* MIL. breach.

**batiborrillo, batiburrillo** *m.* hodgepodge.

**baticola** *f.* crupper.

**batida** *f.* HUNT. battue, beat. *2* combing, search.

**batidero** *m.* constant beating or striking. *2* beating place. *3* rough ground. *4* NAUT. washboard.

**batido, -da** *adj.* beaten [path]. *2* shot [silk]. *3 m.* COOK. batter. *4* beaten eggs; milk shake.

**batidor** *m.* beater. *2* COOK. whisk. *3* MIL. scout. *4* one of the cavalry men heading a regiment on parade. *5* comb [for cleaning hair].

**batiente** *adj.* beating. *2 m.* jamb against which a door closes. *3* spot where the sea beats. *4* damper [of piano]. *5* leaf [of door].

**batihoja** *m.* goldbeater, silverbeater.

**batimetría** *f.* bathymetry.

**batín** *m.* smoking jacket.

**batintín** *m.* gong.

**batir** *tr.* to beat, to strike. *2* to batter, beat down. *3* [of water, waves, wind, etc.], to beat, dash against. *4* to flap [wings]. *5* to beat [a metal] into sheets. *7* to coin [money]. *8* to beat, defeat. *9* HUNT. to beat. *10* MIL. to range, reconnoitre. *11* MED. to couch [the cataract]. *12* ~ *la marca*, to beat the record. *13* ~ *palmas*, to clap hands. *14* *ref.* to fight.

**batista** *f.* cambric.

**batracio, -cia** *adj.-m.* ZOOL. batrachian.

**baturrillo** *m.* hodgepodge, medley.

**baturro, -rra** *m.-f.* a rustic or peasant of Aragon.

**batuta** *f.* MUS. baton: *llevar la* ~, to lead.

**baúl** *m.* luggage trunk: ~ *mundo*, Saratoga trunk.

**bauprés** *m.* NAUT. bowsprit.

**bautismal** *adj.* baptismal.

**bautismo** *m.* baptism. *2* christening.

**bautista** *m.* baptizer: *el Bautista*, John the Baptist.

**bautisterio** *m.* baptistery.

**bautizar** *tr.* to baptize, to christen. *2* to name, give a name to. *3* to water [wine].

**bautizo** *m.* christening; christening party.

**bávaro, -ra** *adj.-n.* Bavarian.

**Baviera** *pr. n.* GEOG. Bavaria.

**baya** *f.* BOT. berry.

**bayadera** *f.* bayadere [dancer].

**bayeta** *f.* baize.

**bayetón** *m.* kind of duffel [cloth].

**bayo, -ya** *adj.* bay. *2 m.* bay horse.

**Bayona** *f. pr. n.* GEOG. Bayonne.

**bayoneta** *f.* bayonet.

**bayonetazo** *m.* bayonet thrust. *2* bayonet wound.

**baza** *f.* trick [in cards]: *meter* ~ *en*, coll. to butt in.

**bazar** *m.* baza(a)r [in the East]. *2* baza(a)r, department store.

1) **bazo** *m.* ANAT. spleen.

2) **bazo, -za** *adj.* yellowish-brown.

**bazofia** *f.* refuse, scraps of food. *2* garbage.

**bazooka, bazuka** *m.* MIL. bazooka.

**bazucar, bazuquear** *tr.* to stir [a liquid] by shaking.

**be** *f.* name of the letter *b*: ~ *por* ~, in detail.

**beatería** *f.* sanctimoniusness.

**beaterio** *m.* kind of beguinage.

**beatificación** *f.* beatification.

**beatificar** *tr.* to beatify.

**beatífico, -ca** *adj.* beatific(al.

**beatísimo, -ma** *adj.* most holy. *2 beatísimo Padre*. Holy Father.

**beatitud** *f.* beatitude, blessedness. *2* (cap.) Beatitude [title given to the Pope].

**beato, -ta** *adj.* happy, blessed. *2* blessed [beatified]. *3* devout; sanctimonious. *4 m.* beatus. *5 m.-f.* devout or sanctimonious person. *6 f.* beata. *7* woman who lives in pious retirement.

**Beatriz** *pr. n.* Beatrice.

**bebé** *m.* baby. *2* doll.

**bebedero, -ra** *adj.* drinkable. *2 m.* drinking bowl, dish, etc. [for birds]. *3* spout [of a drinking vessel].

**bebedizo, -za** *adj.* drinkable. *2 m.* potion; philtre.

**bebedor, -ra** *adj.* drinking. *2 m.-f.* drinker; hard drinker, toper.

1) **beber** *m.* drink, drinking.

2) **beber** *tr.-ref.* to drink: ~ *a la salud de uno*, to drink someone's health; ~ *los vientos por*, to sigh or long for or after, to be madly in love with.

**bebible** *adj.* pleasant to drink, drinkable.

**bebida** *f.* drink; beverage, potion.

**bebido, -da** *adj.* drunk, intoxicated, tipsy.

**bebistrajo** *m.* unpalatable drink, nasty drink.

**beborrotear** *intr.* to sip often.

**beca** *f.* sash worn over the ancient academic gown. *2* scholarship, sizarship [allowance].

**becacina** *f.* AGACHADIZA.

**becada** *f.* ORN. woodcock.

**becafigo** *m.* ORN. figpecker.

**becario** *m.* holder of a scholarship; sizar.

**becerra** *f.* BOT. snapdragon. *2* calf, young cow.

**becerrada** *f.* BULLF. fight with young bulls.

**becerrillo, -lla** *m.-f.* young calf. *2* calfskin.

**becerro** *m.* calf, young bull: ~ *de oro*, golden calf, wealth. *2* calfskin. *3* ZOOL. ~ *marino*, seal.

**becuadro** *m.* MUS. natural sign.

**bechamela** *f.* béchamel sauce.

**bedel** *m.* beadle, apparitor [in a University].

**beduino** *m.* adj.-n. Bedouin. *2 m.* barbarian.

**befa** *f.* jeer, flout, scoff.

**befar** *tr.* to jeer, flout, scoff at.

**befo, -fa** *adj.* blobber-lipped. *2* knock-kneed. *3 m.* lip [of an animal]. *4* a kind of monkey.

**begonia** *f.* BOT. begonia.

**beguina** *f.* beguine.

**Beirut** *f. pr. n.* GEOG. Beyrouth.

**béisbol** *m.* baseball.

**bejín** *m.* BOT. puffball.

**bejuco** *m.* BOT. liana, liane; rattan.

**Belcebú** *m. pr. n.* Beelzebub.

**belcho** *m.* BOT. joint fir.

**beldad** *f.* beauty [of a woman]. *2* beauty, belle.

**Belén** *m. pr. n.* GEOG. Bethlehem. *2 m.* (not cap.)

Christmas crib. *3* confusion, bedlam. *4* bad business.
**beleño** *m.* BOT. henbane.
**belérico** *m.* BOT. myrobalan.
**belesa** *f.* BOT. leadwort.
**belfo, -fa** *adj.* blobber-lipped. *2 m.* lip (of an animal).
**belga** *adj.-n.* Belgian.
**Bélgica** *f. pr. n.* GEOG. Belgium.
**Belgrado** *f. pr. n.* GEOG. Belgrade.
**bélico, -ca** *adj.* warlike, martial.
**belicosidad** *f.* bellicosity.
**belicoso, -sa** *adj.* bellicose, pugnacious.
**beligerancia** *f.* belligerency.
**beligerante** *adj.-n.* belligerent.
**belígero, -ra** *adj.* poet. warlike.
**Beluchistán** *m. pr. n.* GEOG. Beluchistan.
**belvedere** *m.* ARCH. belvedere.
**bellaco, -ca** *adj.* wicked, knavish. *2* cunning, sly. *3 m.-f.* knave, scoundrel.
**belladona** BOT. belladonna, deadly nightshade.
**bellamente** *adv.* beautifully, prettily.
**bellaquería** *f.* knavery, knavish act. *2* slyness.
**belleza** *f.* beauty.
**bellido, -da** *adj.* beautiful, handsome.
**bello, -lla** *adj.* beautiful, fair, fine: ~ *sexo*, fair sex; *bellas artes*, fine arts.
**bellota** *f.* BOT. acorn. *2* acorn-shaped tassel. *3* ZOOL. ~ *de mar*, acorn barnacle.
**bellote** *m.* large round-headed nail.
**bemol** *adj.-m.* MUS. flat: *doble* ~, double flat.
**bemolado, -da** *adj.* MUS. flat [lowered a semitone].
**benceno** *m.* CHEM. benzene.
**bencina** *f.* benzine. *2* petrol [for motor-cars].
**bendecir** *tr.* to bless. *2* to consecrate; to invoke a blessing upon. ¶ CONJUG. like *decir*, except for the INDIC. fut.: *bendeciré*; the COND.: *bendeciría*, and the IMPER.: *bendice*.
**bendigo, bendije, bendiga,** etc. *irr. V.* BENDECIR.
**bendición** *f.* benediction, blessing: *que es una* ~, abundantly; with the greatest ease. *2 pl.* wedding ceremony.
**bendito, -ta** *adj.* sainted, holy, blessed: *agua bendita*, holy water. *2* happy. *3* annoying, bothersome. *4 m.* simple-minded soul.
**benedícite** *m.* benedicite.
**benedictino, -na** *adj.-n.* Benedictine. *2 m.* benedictine [liqueur].
**benefactor; -ra** *adj.* beneficent, beneficial. *2 n.* benefactor, benefactress.
**beneficencia** *f.* beneficence. *2* charity, poor relief, social service.
**beneficiado** *m.* ECCL. beneficiary. *2* THEAT. person, charity, etc., to whom the proceeds of a benefit go.
**beneficiar** *tr.* to benefit, to do good to. *2* to cultivate, improve [land]; to exploit, work [a mine]; to beneficiate, process [ores]. *3* COM. to sell [bills, etc.] at a discount. *4 ref.* to benefit, to profit.
**beneficiario** *m.* [feudatory or insurance] beneficiary.
**beneficio** *m.* benefaction. *2* benefit, advantage, profit. *3* COM. profit: ~ *neto*, clear profit. *4* THEAT. benefit. *5* [feudal] benefice. *6* ECCL. benefice. *7* cultivation [of land]; exploitation [of mines]; beneficiation, processing [of ores]. *8* LAW ~ *de inventario*, benefit of inventory.
**beneficioso, -sa** *adj.* beneficial, profitable.
**benéfico, -ca** beneficent, charitable. *2* beneficial.

**benemérito, -ta** *adj.* well deserving, worthy, meritorious.
**beneplácito** *m.* approval, consent.
**benevolencia** *f.* benevolence, kindness, goodwill.
**benévolo, -la** *adj.* benevolent, kind.
**Bengala** *pr. n.* GEOG. Bengal.
**bengala** *f.* rattan. *2* MIL. baton. *3* Bengal light.
**bengalí** *adj.-n.* Bengalese, Bengali. *2 m.* Bengali [language]. *3* ORN. Bengali.
**benignidad** *f.* benignity, benignancy.
**benigno, -na** *adj.* benign. *2* benignant.
**Benito** *pr. n.* Benedict.
**Benjamín** *pr. n.* Benjamín. *2 m.* (not cap.) baby [the youngest son].
**benjuí** *m.* benzoin.
**Beocia** *pr. n.* GEOG. Boeotia.
**beocio, -cia** *adj.-n.* Boeotian.
**beodo, -da** *adj.* drunk. *2 m.-f.* drunkard.
**beorí** *m.* ZOOL. American tapir.
**berberecho** *m.* ZOOL. cockle.
**Berbería** *pr. n.* GEOG. Barbary.
**berberí** *adj.-n.* BEREBER.
**berberís** *m.* BÉRBERO.
**berberisco, -ca** *adj.-n.* BEREBER.
**bérbero** *m.* BOT. barberry. *2* a barberry confection.
**berbiquí** *m.* brace, carpenter's brace, wimble.
**bereber** *adj.-n.* Berber.
**berenjena** *f.* BOT. eggplant.
**berenjenal** *m.* bed of eggplants: *meterse en un* ~, fig. to get into a mess.
**bergamota** *m.* bergamot [pear, lime, perfume].
**bergamote, bergamoto** *m.* BOT. bergamot [tree].
**bergante** *adj.* scoundrel, rascal.
**bergantín** *m.* NAUT. brig: ~ *goleta*, brigantine.
**beriberi** *m.* MED. beriberi.
**berilo** *m.* MINER. beryl.
**Berlín** *pr. n.* GEOG. Berlín.
**berlina** *f.* berlin [carriage]. *2* closed front compartment [of stagecoach]. *3 en* ~, in a ridiculous position.
**berlinés, -sa** *adj.-n.* of Berlin. *2 m.-f.* Berliner.
**berma** *f.* FORT. berm, berme.
**bermejear** *intr.* to be or show red.
**bermejizo, -za** *adj.* reddish.
**bermejo, -ja** *adj.* bright reddish.
**bermellón** *m.* vermilion.
**Bermudas (las)** *pr. n.* GEOG. Bermudas Islands.
**Berna** *pr. n.* GEOG. Bern.
**Bernabé** *pr. n.* Barnaby.
**Bernardo** *pr. n.* Bernard.
**bernardo, -da** *adj.* Bernardine. *2 m.* Bernardine monk. *3 f.* Bernardine nun.
**bernés, -sa** *adj.-n.* Bernese.
**berra** *f.* BOT. tall water cress.
**berrear** *intr.* to low [as a calf]. *2* to bawl.
**berreo** *m.* lowing, bawling.
**berrenchín** *m.* BERRINCHE.
**berrendo, -da** *adj.* two-coloured. *2* dappled [bull].
**berrera** *f.* BOT. water parsnip.
**berrido** *m.* cry of the calf; low. *2* bawl.
**berrinche** *m.* rage, tantrum. *2* child's rage.
**berrizal** *m.* water cress patch.
**berro** *m.* BOT. water cress.
**berroqueña** *adj.* ~ *piedra* ~, granite.
**berrueco** *m.* granite rock. *2* baroque pearl.
**Berta** *pr. n.* Bertha.
**berza** *f.* BOT. cabbage.
**besalamano** *m.* unsigned note, beginning with B.L.M. [kisses the hand].
**besamanos** *m.* reception at court.
**besante** *m.* bezant [coin]. *2* HER. bezant.

**besar** *tr.* to kiss. *2 ref.* to kiss [one another].
**besico, besito** *m. dim.* little kiss.
**beso** *m.* kiss. *2* bump [collision].
**bestezuela** *f.* little beast.
**bestia** *f.* beast: ~ *de carga*, beast of burden. *2* boor, dunce, idiot. *3 adj.* stupid, idiot.
**bestial** *adj.* beastly, bestial. *2 coll.* enormous, colossal.
**bestialidad** *f.* beastliness, bestiality. *2* stupidity.
**bestiario** *m.* bestiary.
**bestseller** *m.* best seller.
**besucar** *tr.* BESUQUEAR.
**besucón, -na** *adj.* fond of kissing.
**besugo** *m.* ICHTH. sea bream.
**besuguera** *f.* fish kettle.
**besuquear** *tr.* to kiss repeatedly.
**beta** *f.* beta [Greek letter]. *2* MAR. small rope.
**Betania** *pr. n.* GEOG. Bethany.
**betel** *m.* BOT. betel.
**Bética** *f. pr. n.* GEOG. Betica.
**bético, -ca** *adj.* Andalusian.
**betónica** *f.* BOT. betony.
**betún** *m.* bitumen. *2* shoe blaking. *3* ZULAQUE.
**bey** *m.* bey.
**bezo** *m.* blubber lip. *2* lip. *3* proud flesh.
**bezoar** *m.* bezoar.
**bezudo, -da** *adj.* thick-lipped, blobber-lipped.
**bibásico, -ca** *adj.* CHEM. dibasic.
**biberón** *m.* feeding bottle, nursing bottle.
**Biblia** *f.* Bible.
**bíblico, -ca** *adj.* Biblical.
**bibliofilia** *f.* bibliophilism.
**bibliófilo** *m.* bibliophile.
**bibliografía** *f.* bibliography.
**bibliomanía** *f.* bibliomania.
**biblioteca** *f.* library: ~ *circulante*, lending library.
**bibliotecario, -ria** *m.-f.* librarian.
**bical** *m.* ICHTH. male salmon.
**bicameral** *adj.* bicameral.
**bicarbonato** *m.* CHEM. bicarbonate.
**bicéfalo, -la** *adj.* bicephalous.
**bíceps** *m.* ANAT. biceps.
**bicerra** *f.* ZOOL. ibex, wild goat.
**bicicleta** *f.* bicycle.
**bicloruro** *m.* CHEM. dichloride, bichloride.
**bicoca** *f. obs.* small fort. *2* fig. trifle, bagatelle.
**bicolor** *adj.* bicolor, bicolour, two-tone, two-colour.
**bicóncavo, -va** *adj.* biconcave.
**biconvexo, -xa** *adj.* biconvex.
**bicorne** *adj.* poet, bicorn, two-horned.
**bicornio** *m.* two-cornered hat.
**bicúspide** *adj.* bicuspid.
**bicha** *f.* shake [in superstitious use]. *2* ARCH. grotesque animal figure.
**bicharraco** *m.* insect, ugly animal.
**bichero** *m.* boat hook.
**bicho** *m.* little animal, vermin. *2* domestic animal. *3* BULLF. bull. *4* ~ *raro*, odd fellow; *mal* ~, wicked person; *todo* ~ *viviente*, all living soul.
**bidé** *m.* bidet [a form of sitz bath].
**bidentado, -da** *adj.* bidentate, double-toothed. *2 m.* AGR. pitchfork.
**bidón** *m.* can, drum [for petrol, etc.].
**biela** *f.* MACH. connecting rod.
**bieldo, bielgo** *m.* winnowing fork.
1) **bien** *adv.* well, properly, right, perfectly, happily, successfully. *2* willingly, readily: *yo* ~ *lo haría, pero...*, I'd willingly do it, but... *3* very much, a good deal, fully, enough. *4* easily: ~ *se ve que...*, it is easy to see that... *5 tener a* ~, to see

fit, to deign. *6* ~... ~, either... or. *7 ahora* ~, now, now then. *8 bien a* ~, *de* ~ *a* ~, willingly. *9* ~ *que*, although. *10 más* ~, rather. *11 no* ~, as soon as, just as. *12 si* ~, although. *13 y* ~, well, now then.
2) **bien**, *pl.* **bienes** *m.* good [as opposed to evil]: *hombre de* ~, honest, straight man. *2* good, welfare, benefit: *hacer* ~, to do good; *en* ~ *de*, for the sake, good or benefit of. *3* fig. *mi* ~, my dearest, my love. *4 pl.* property, possessions, estate: *bienes de fortuna*, worldly possessions; *bienes inmuebles* or *raíces*, real estate; *bienes muebles*, movables, personal property.
**bienal** *adj.* biennial.
**bienamado, -da** *adj.-n.* well-loved.
**bienandante** *adj.* happy, fortunate.
**bienandanza** *f.* happiness, fortune.
**bienaventurado, -da** *adj.* happy, blessed. *2* simple, guileless.
**bienaventuranza** *f.* blessedness. *2* happiness. *3 pl.* *Las bienaventuranzas*, the Beatitudes.
**bienestar** *m.* well-being, comfort. *2* comfortable living. *3* happiness, peace of mind.
**bienhablado, -da** *adj.* well-spoken, civil.
**bienhadado, -da** *adj.* fortunate.
**bienhechor, -ra** *adj.* beneficent, beneficial. *2 m.* benefactor. *3 f.* benefactress.
**bienintencionado, -da** *adj.* well-meaning.
**bienio** *m.* biennium.
**bienmandado, -da** *adj.* obedient, submissive.
**bienoliente** *adj.* fragrant.
**bienquerencia** *f.*, **bienquerer** *m.* affection, good will.
**bienquerer** *tr.* to love, like, esteem.
**bienquistar** *tr.-ref.* to gain the esteem [of somebody].
**bienquisto, -ta** *adj.* well-liked; generally esteemed.
**bienvenida** *f.* happy arrival. *2* welcome: *dar la* ~, to welcome.
**bienvenido, -da** *adj.* welcome.
**bies** *m.* bias [obliquity].
**bifásico, -ca** *adj.* ELEC. diphase, twophase.
**bife** *m.* (Am.) beefsteak.
**bífido, -da** *adj.* BOT. bifid.
**bifocal** *adj.* bifocal.
**biftec** *m.* beefsteak.
**bifurcación** *f.* bifurcation, forking. *2* branch.
**bifurcado, -da** *adj.* bifurcated, forked.
**bifurcarse** *ref.* to fork, bifurcate.
**bigamia** *f.* bigamy.
**bígamo, -ma** *adj.* bigamous. *2 m.-f.* bigamist.
**bigardo** *m. obs.* licentious friar. *2* licentious vagabond.
**bigardón, -a** *m.-f.* licentious vagabond.
**bígaro, bigarro** *m.* a sea snail.
**bigornia** *f.* two-pointed anvil.
**bigote** *m.* m(o)ustache, mustachio. *2* whiskers [of cat]. *3* PRINT. dash rule.
**bigotera** *f.* mustache protector. *2* smear on upper lip. *3* folding carriage seat. *4* bow compass.
**bija** *f.* BOT. annatto tree. *2* annatto [dyestuff].
**bilabial** *adj.* PHON. bilabial.
**bilateral** *adj.* bilateral.
**bilbaíno, -na** *adj.-n.* of Bilbao.
**Bilbao** *m. pr. n.* GEOG. Bilbao.
**biliar; biliario, -ria** *adj.* biliary.
**bilingüe** *adj.* bilingual.
**bilioso, -sa** *adj.* bilious.

**bilis** *f.* bile, gall: fig. *descargar la* ~, to vent one's spleen.
**bilobulado, -da** *adj.* bilobate.
**billa** *f.* BILLIARDS hazard.
**billar** *m.* billiards. *2* billiard table. *3* billiard room. *4* billiard hall.
**billarista** *m.* billiardist, billiard player.
**billete** *m.* note, short letter. *2* love letter. *3* ticket [railway, theater, lottery, etc., ticket]: ~ *de ida*, one-way ticket; ~ *de ida y vuelta*, return ticket; ~ *kilométrico*, mileage book. *4* ~ *de banco*, bank note.
**billón** *m.* [British] billion; [U.S.A.] trillion.
**bimano, -na** *adj.* bimanous. *2 m.* ZOOL. bimane.
**bimba** *f.* coll. high hat, top hat.
**bimensual** *adj.* semimonthly.
**bimestral** *adj.* bimestral, bimonthly.
**bimestre** *adj.* BIMESTRAL. *2 m.* period of two months.
**bimetalismo** *m.* bimetallism.
**bimotor** *adj.* AER. two-motor.
**binar** *tr.* AGR. to plough a second time. *2 intr.* to celebrate two Masses on the same day.
**binario, -ria** *adj.* binary.
**binocular** *adj.* binocular.
**binóculo** *m.* binocle, binocular. *2* lorgnette.
**binomio** *m.* ALG. binomial.
**binza** *f.* pellicle [of eggshell or onion]. *2* any thin membrane.
**biofísica** *f.* biophysics.
**biogenia** *f.* biogeny.
**biografía** *f.* biography.
**biográfico, -ca** *adj.* biographic(al).
**biógrafo** *m.* biographer.
**biología** *f.* biology.
**biológico, -ca** *adj.* biologic(al).
**biólogo** *m.* biologist.
**biombo** *f.* folding screen.
**bioquímica** *f.* biochemistry.
**bióxido** *m.* CHEM. dioxide.
**bipartido, da; bipartito, -ta** *adj.* bipartite.
**bípede; bípedo, -da** *adj.* bipedal. *2 m.* biped.
**biplano** *m.* AER. biplane.
**bipolar** *adj.* bipolar.
**biricú** *m.* sword belt.
**birimbao** *m.* MUS. Jew's harp.
**birlar** *tr.* coll. ~ *la novia, un empleo*, etc., to pinch [somebody's] sweetheart, job, etc.
**birlibirloque** *m. por arte de* ~, by magic.
**birlocha** *f.* kite [toy].
**birlocho** *m.* barouche.
**Birmania** *f. pr. n.* GEOG. Burma.
**birmano, -na** *adj.-n.* Burmese.
**birrefringente** *adj.* OPT. birefringent.
**birreme** *adj.-f.* bireme.
**birreta** *f.* scarlet biretta. *2* cardinalate.
**birrete** *m.* scarlet biretta. *2* academic cap. *3* cap worn by judges, barristers, etc., with official dress.
**birretina** *f.* MIL. bearskin, hussar or grenadier's cap.
**birria** *f.* horror, horrible person or thing. *2* lousy, unworthy thing, piece of junk. *3* (Am.) mania.
**bis** *adv.-adj.* bis.
**bisabuelo, -la** *m.-f.* great-grandfather; great-grandmother. *2 m. pl.* great-grandparents.
**bisagra** *f.* hinge. *2* shoemaker's polisher.
**bisar** *tr.* to repeat [a song, performance, etc.].
**bisbisar** *tr.* to mutter, mumble.
**bisbiseo** *m.* muttering, mumbling.
**bisecar** *tr.* GEOM. to bisect.

**bisección** *f.* MATH. bisection.
**bisector, bisectriz** *adj.* GEOM. bisecting. *2 m.* bisector. *3 f.* bisectrix.
**bisel** *m.* bevel, bevel edge.
**biselado** *m.* bevelling. *2 adj.* bevel, bevelled.
**biselar** *tr.* to bevel.
**bisemanal** *adj.* semiweekly.
**bisexual** *adj.* bisexual.
**bisiesto** *adj.* bissextile, leap [year].
**bisílabo, -ba** *adj.* disyllabic. *2 m.* disyllable.
**bismuto** *m.* CHEM. bismuth.
**bisnieto, -ta** *m.-f.* great-grandchild. *2 m.* great-grandson. *3 f.* great-granddaughter.
**bisojo, -ja** *adj.-n.* BIZCO.
**bisonte** *m.* ZOOL. bison.
**bisoñé** *m.* toupee or small wig for front of head.
**bisoño, -ña** *adj.* green, inexperienced. *2* MIL. raw. *3 m.-f.* greenhorn, novice. *4* raw recruit.
**bistec** *m.* beefsteak.
**bistorta** *f.* BOT. bistort.
**bistre** *m.* bistre.
**bisturí** *m.* SURG. bistoury.
**bisulco, -ca** *adj.* bisulcate, cloven-footed.
**bisulfato** *m.* bisulphate.
**bisulfito** *m.* CHEM. bisulphite.
**bisutería** *f.* imitation jewelry.
**bita** *f.* NAUT. bitt.
**bitácora** *f.* NAUT. binnacle.
**bitongo** *adj. niño* ~, boy fond of acting like a child.
**bitoque** *m.* spigot [in a cask].
**bituminoso, -sa** *adj.* bituminous.
**bivalencia** *f.* CHEM. bivalence.
**bivalente** *adj.* CHEM. bivalent.
**bivalvo, -va** *adj.* bivalve.
**Bizancio** *f. pr. n.* GEOG., HIST. Byzantium.
**bizantinismo** *m.* Byzantinism. *2* idle discussion.
**bizantino, -na** *adj.-n.* Byzantine. *2 adj.* idle [discussion].
**bizarría** *f.* gallantry, courage. *2* generosity, grandness, splendour.
**bizarro, -rra** *adj.* gallant, courageous. *2* generous, grand, splendid.
**bizcar** *intr.* to squint. *2 tr.* to wink [the eye].
**bizco, -ca** *adj.* squint-eyed, cross-eyed. *2 m.-f.* cross-eyed person, squinter.
**bizcocho** *m.* biscuit, hardtack. *2* sponge cake. *3* biscuit, bisque [unglazed porcelain].
**bizcotela** *f.* frosted sponge cake.
**biznaga** *f.* BOT. bishop's-weed.
**biznieto, -ta** *m.-f.* BISNIETO, TA.
**bizquear** *intr.* to squint.
**blanca** *f.* old copper and silver coin: *estar sin* ~, to be broke. *2* MUS. minim.
**blanco, -ca** *adj.* white, hoar, hoary. *2* white, pale. *3* fair [complexion]. *4* white [person, race, metal]. *5* POL. white. *6 m.-f.* white person. *7 m.* white colour. *8* target, mark: *dar en el* ~, to hit the mark. *9* aim, goal. *10* gap, interval. *11* blank, blank space: *en* ~, blank [page, check, etc.]. *12* white [of the eye]. *13* ~ *de España*, whiting. *14 quedarse en* ~, to fail to grasp the point, to be disappointed.
**blancor** *m.* BLANCURA.
**blancura** *f.* whiteness. *2* fairness [of skin].
**blancuzco, -ca** *adj.* whitish.
**blandamente** *adv.* softly, gently.
**blandear** *intr.-ref.* to yield, give in. *2 tr.* to make [someone] change his mind.
**blandengue** *adj.* soft, weak, without energy.
**blandicia** *f.* flattery. *2* love of luxury, luxury.
**blandir** *tr.* to brandish, flourish, swing.

**blando, -da** *adj.* soft [yielding to pressure]. *2* soft, gentle, mild, bland. *3* soft, delicate. *4* cowardly. *5* watery [eyes]. *6* ~ *de boca,* tendermouthed [horse].

**blandón** *m.* thick wax candle. *2* large candlestick.

**blanducho, -cha; blandujo, -ja** *adj.* softish.

**blandura** *f.* softness. *2* gentleness, sweetness, blandness. *3* endearing word. *4* luxury, delicacy.

**blanqueador, -ra** *adj.* whitening; whitewashing; bleaching. *2 m.-f.* whitener; whitewasher; bleacher.

**blanquear** *tr.* to whiten, blanch. *2* to bleach. *3* to whitewash. *4 intr.* to whiten, turn white. *5* to show white.

**blanquecedor** *m.* blancher [of metals].

**blanquecer** *tr.* to whiten, to bleach. *2* to blanch [metals]. ¶ CONJUG. like *agradecer.*

**blanquecino, -na** *adj.* whitish.

**blanqueo** *m.* whitening, bleaching. *2* whitewashing.

**blanquete** *m.* white cosmetic.

**blanquillo, -lla** *adj.* whitish.

**blanquizco, -ca** *adj.* BLANQUECINO.

**Blas** *m. pr. n.* Blase.

**blasfemador, -ra** *m.-f.* blasphemer.

**blasfemar** *intr.* to blaspheme.

**blasfematorio, -ria** *f.* blasphemous.

**blasfemia** *f.* blasphemy.

**blasfemo, -ma** *adj.* blasphemous. *2 m.-f.* blasphemer.

**blasón** *m.* heraldry, blazon. *2* armorial bearings. *3* HER. charge. *4* honour, glory.

**blasonar** *tr.* HER. to emblazon. *2 intr.* to boast: *blasonar de,* to boast of being.

**blasonería** *f.* boasting, bragging.

**blástula** *f.* BIOL. blastula.

**bledo** *m.* BOT. blite: *no me importa un* ~, I don't care a straw.

**blenda** *f.* MINER. blende.

**blinda** *f.* FORT. blind.

**blindado, -da** *adj.* armoured [car, ship], steel-jacketed [bullet]. *2* ELECT. shielded.

**blindaje** *m.* FORT. blindage. *2* armour plate. *3* ELECT. shield.

**blindar** *tr.* to armour, armour-plate. *2* ELECT. to shield.

**blocao** *m.* FORT. blockhouse.

**blonda** *f.* blond lace.

**blondo, -da** *adj.* blond, blonde, fair.

**bloque** *m.* block [of stone, wood, paper, etc.].

**bloquear** *tr.* MIL., NAUT. to blockade. *2* MED., PRINT. to block. *3* COM. to block [an account].

**bloqueo** *m.* MIL., NAUT. blockade. *2* PRINT., COM. BLOCKING. *3* MED. block.

**blusa** *f.* smock. *2* blouse.

**boa** *f.* ZOOL. boa. *2* boa [neckpiece].

**boato** *m.* show, pomp.

**bobalicón, -na** *adj.* silly, simple. *2 m.-f.* nitwit.

**bobear** *intr.* to talk nonsense, play the fool; to fool around.

**bobería** *f.* silliness, foolishness. *2* silly action or remark; nonsense, trifle, foolery.

**bóbilis, bóbilis (de)** *adv.* for nothing.

**bobina** *f.* bobbin. *2* ELECT. coil: ~ *de encendido,* spark coil, ignition coil.

**bobinado** *m.* winding [yarn or wire].

**bobinadora** *f.* winder, winding machine.

**bobinar** *tr.* to wind [yarn or wire].

**bobo, -ba** *adj.* silly, foolish, gullible. *2 m.-f.* fool, simpleton. *3 m.* THEAT. fool.·

**bobote** *m.* coll. great fool.

**boca** *f.* mouth [of man or animal; speech]: ~ *de escorpión,* fig. evil tongue [person]; ~ *de oro,* fig. very eloquent person; *andar en* ~ *de todos, andar de* ~ *en* ~, to be the talk of the place, to be generally known; *hacer* ~, to work up an appetite [by eating or drinking something]; *írsele a uno la* ~, to talk imprudently; *meterse en la* ~ *del lobo,* to put one's head into the lion's mouth; *no decir esta* ~ *es mía,* not to say a word; *oscuro como* ~ *de lobo,* pitchdark; *quitárselo uno de la* ~, to deprive oneself for the sake of another; *torcer la* ~, to make a wry mouth; ~ *abajo,* face downwards, flat on one's face, prone; ~ *arriba,* face upwards, flat on one's back, supine; *a pedir de* ~, very well, according to one's desire. *2* mouth, entrance, opening; ~, or *bocas, de un río,* mouth of a river; ~ *del metro,* subway entrance; ~ *de agua,* hydrant; *a* ~ *de jarro,* [drinking] without measure; at close range; suddenly. *3* beginning: *a* ~ *de noche,* at nightfall. *4* approaches [of a tunnel]. *5* muzzle [of a gun]. *6* ZOOL. pincers [of a crustacean]. *7* cutting part of some tools. *8* peen [of hammer]. *8* ~ *del estómago,* pit of the stomach. *10* ~ *de fuego,* firearm [esp. artillery]; *11* BOT. ~ *de dragón,* snapdragon.

**bocacalle** *f.* street entrance.

**bocacaz** *f.* a dam's outlet for irrigation.

**bocacha** *f.* wide-mouthed blunderbuss.

**bocadillo** *m.* sandwich.

**bocadito** *m.* little bit.

**bocado** *m.* mouthful [of food], morsel, bit. *2* bit [of the bridle].

**bocajarro [a]** *adv.* point-blank.

**bocal** *m.* wide-mouthed pitcher.

**bocamanga** *f.* bottom part of a sleeve.

**bocamina** *f.* mine entrance.

**bocanada** *f.* mouthful [of liquid]. *2* puff [of tobacco smoke]. *3* ~ *de aire* or *de viento,* gust, blast of wind. *4* *echar bocanadas,* to boast, brag.

**bocaza** *f.* large mouth. *2 m.* indiscreet talker.

**bocazo** *m.* fizzle [in blasting].

**bocel** *m.* ARCH. torus [molding]: *medio* ~, half round; *cuarto* ~, quarter round.

**bocelar** *tr.* to cut a round molding on.

**bocera** *f.* smear on lips [after eating or drinking].

**boceto** *m.* PAINT. sketch. *2* SCULP. rough model.

**bocina** *f.* MUS. horn [instrument made of a horn]. *2* sea shell used as a horn. *3* foghorn, auto horn. *4* speaking trumpet, megaphone. *5* phonograph horn. *6* MECH. bushing.

**bocinar** *tr.* to blow the horn.

**bocinazo** *m.* honk, toot. *2* coll. scolding, telling off, rebuke.

**bocio** *m.* MED. goitre.

**bocón, -na** *adj.* bigmouthed, boastful. *2 m.-f.* braggard.

**bocoy** *m.* large barrel [for goods]; hogshead.

**bocudo, -da** *adj.* bigmouthed.

**bocha** *f.* bowl [ball]. *2 pl.* bowls, bowling.

**bochar** *tr.* BOWL. to hit and dislodge [a ball].

**boche** *m.* small hole in the ground [for boys games].

**bochinche** *m.* noise, row, riot, tumult.

**bochinchero, -ra** *adj.-n.* coll. rowdy, rough and noisy.

**bochorno** *m.* hot summer breeze. *2* sultry weather, suffocating heat. *3* blush, blushing. *4* embarrassment, shame.

**bochornoso, -sa** *adj.* hot, sultry. *2* disgraceful, shameful.

**boda** *f.* marriage, wedding: *bodas de plata, de oro,* silver, golden wedding; *bodas de Camacho,* banquet, lavish feast.
**bodega** *f.* cellar, wine cellar, wine vault. *2* wine shop. *3* pantry. *4* dock-warehouse. *5* NAUT. hold [of a ship].
**bodegón** *m.* cheap eating house. *2* still-life painting [esp. of edibles].
**bodeguero, -ra** *m.-f.* cellarer, keeper of a wine cellar. *2 m.* NAUT. one in charge of the hold.
**bodijo** *m.* coll. mesalliance. *2* coll. wedding with little ceremony.
**bodoque** *m.* clay ball or pellet shot from crossbow. *2* lump. *3* fig. dolt, dunce.
**bodoquera** *f.* mould for clay balls. *2* cradle [of a crossbow]. *3* blowgun, peashooter.
**bodorrio** *m.* BODIJO.
**bodrio** *m.* soup made of leavings; poorly cooked food.
**bóer** *adj.-n.* Boer.
**bofe** *m.* coll. lung; *echar el ~* or *los bofes,* to toil; to pant. *2 pl.* lights [of sheep, hogs, etc.].
**bofetada** *f.* slap in the face; buffet.
**bofetón** *m.* slap in the face.
**boga** *f.* vogue [acceptation, popularity]. *2* rowing. *3* ICHTH. boce.
**bogada** *f.* distance covered at one oar-stroke.
**bogador** *m.* rower.
**bogar** *intr.* to row. *2* to sail.
**bogavante** *m.* first rower [in a galley]. *2* ZOOL. homard, lobster.
**bogui** *m.* RLY. bogie.
**Bohemia** *pr. n.* Bohemia [country].
**bohemio, -mia** *adj.-n.* Bohemian [in every sense]. *2 f.* Bohemia; Bohemian life.
**bohío** *m.* (Am.) hut, *shack.
**bohordo** *m.* short spear or reed, formerly used in tournaments. *2* BOT. scape.
**boicot** *m.* boycott.
**boicotear** *tr.* to boycott.
**boicoteo** *m.* boycott, boycotting.
**boina** *f.* beret.
**boj, boje** *m.* BOT. box, boxwood. *2* boxwood [wood].
**bol** *m.* punch bowl. *2* bowl [cup without a handle]. *3 ~ arménico,* Armenian bole.
**bola** *f.* ball [spherical body]: *~ de nieve,* snowball; BOT. snowball; *~ negra,* blackball. *2* marble. *3* CARDS slam. *4* NAUT. ball [for signals]. *5* shoe blacking. *6* fib.
**bolada** *f.* throw [of a ball].
**bolardo** *m.* NAUT. bollard.
**bolchevique** *adj.-n.* Bolshevist.
**bolcheviquismo** *m.* Bolshevism.
**boleadoras** *f. pl.* bolas, lariat with balls at the ends used by South American cowboys.
**bolear** *intr.* BILL. to knock the balls about. *2 tr.* to throw, flunk. *3* (Am.) to lasso with bolas.
**bolero, -ra** *adj.* lying. *2 m.-f.* fibber, liar. *3 m.* bolero [dance; short jacket]. *4* bowling alley.
**boleta** *f.* MIL. billet. *2* (Am.) ballot.
**boletería** *f.* (Am.) box office, ticket office [theatre]. *2* ticket office, booking office [station].
**boletín** *m.* subscription form. *2* bulletin.
**boleto** *m.* (Am.) ticket.
**boliche** *m.* jack [small ball for bowling]. *2* bowls, skittles. *3* bowling alley. *4* cup and ball [toy]. *5* small dragnet. *6* NAUT. bowline of a small sail.
**bólido** *m.* bolide, meteor.
**bolígrafo** *m.* ball-point pen.
**bolilla** *f.* small ball. *2* marble.

**bolillo** *m.* bobbin [for making lace]. *2* VET. coffin bone.
**bolina** *f.* NAUT. bowline: *de ~,* close-hauled; *navegar de ~,* to sail close to the wind. *2* NAUT. sounding line. *3* noise, tumult.
**bolinear** *tr.* NAUT. to sail close-hauled, to sail close to the wind.
**bolívar** *m.* bolivar [Venezuelan coin].
**Bolivia** *f. pr. n.* GEOGR. Bolivia.
**boliviano, -na** *adj.-n.* of Bolivia.
**bolo** *m.* skittle, ninepin, tenpin. *2* dunce, idiot. *3* THEAT. snap; tour [in the country]. *4* newel [of winding stairs]. *5* large pill. *6* bolus. *7 ~ arménico,* Armenian bole. *8 pl.* skittles.
**Bolonia** *pr. n.* GEOG. Bologna.
**bolonio** *adj.* stupid, ignorant. *2 m.* dunce, donkey.
**boloñés, -sa** *adj.-n.* Bolognese.
**bolsa** *f.* bag, pouch [receptacle]. *2* purse [for carrying money; money, funds]: *la ~ o la vida,* your money or your life. *3* bag, pucker [in cloth, etc.]. *4* ZOOL. pouch. *5* MED. pouch, pocket. *6* MIN. pocket. *7* stock exchange, stock market: *jugar a la bolsa,* to speculate in stocks. *8 ~ del trabajo,* employment bureau. *9* BOT. *~ de pastor,* shepherd's-purse.
**bolsero, -ra** *m.-f.* maker or seller of bags or pouches.
**bolsillo** *m.* pocket [in a garment]: *de ~,* pocket, pocket-size. *2* purse [for money].
**bolsín** *m.* curb market.
**bolsista** *m.-f.* stockbroker; stock speculator.
**bolsita** *f. dim.* small purse.
**bolso** *m.* purse [for carrying money]: *~ de mano,* ladie's handbag. *2* NAUT. bulge [in a sail].
**bollar** *tr.* to bump. *2* to dent.
**bollería** *f.* bakery, pastry shop.
**bollo** *m.* bun, roll. *2* puff [in a dress]. *3* dent: *~ de relieve,* boss [round embossment]. *4* bump [swelling]. *5* row, shindy; confusion.
**bollón** *m.* stud [ornamental nail]. *2* button earring. *3* boss [round embossment].
**bollonado, -da** *adj.* studded [with nails or bosses].
**bomba** *f.* pump: *~ aspirante,* suction pump; *~ impelente,* force pump; *~ neumática,* air pump. *2* bomb: *~ atómica,* atomic bomb; *~ de mano,* handbomb; *~ volante,* flying bomb; *a prueba de ~,* bombproof; *caer como una ~,* to drop or to burst upon like a bombshell; *noticia ~,* surprising news. *3* globe [of lamp]. *4* MUS. slide [of an instrument].
**bombáceo, -a** *adj.* BOT. bombacaceous. *2 f. pl.* Bombacaceae.
**bombacho** *adj. calzón ~,* short, wide breeches; *pantalón ~,* loose-fitting trousers, fastened at the ankles.
**bombarda** *f.* bombard.
**bombardear** *tr.* MIL. to bombard; to bomb. *2* PHYS. to bombard.
**bombardeo** *m.* bombardment; bombing; *~ en picado,* AER. dive bombing.
**bombardero** *m.* bombardier. *2* bomber.
**bombardino** *m.* MUS. alto saxhorn.
**bombardón** *m.* MUS. bombardon.
**bombazo** *m.* explosion, detonation [of a bomb].
**bombear** *tr.* ARTILL. to bombard. *2* to puff, write up [praise exaggeratedly].
**bombeo** *m.* bulging, convexity.
**bombero** *m.* fireman [who puts out fires]. *2* pumpman.
**bombilla** *f.* ELECT. light bulb. *2* thief tube. *3* (Am.) small tube for drinking mate.

**bombillo** *m.* water-closet trap. *2* thief tube.
**bombín** *m.* coll. derby, bowler [hat]. *2* pump [of a bicycle].
**bombo, -ba** *adj.* dumfounded, stunned. *2 m.* MUS. bass drum. *3* bass-drum player. *4* puffing, writing up: *dar ~*, to puff, to write up [praise exaggerately]. *5* revolving lottery box.
**bombón** *m.* bonbon, sweetmeat, chocolate.
**bombona** *f.* carboy.
**bombonaje** *m.* BOT. jipijapa.
**bombonera** *f.* box for bonbons.
**bombonería** *f.* sweet shop, confectioner's shop.
**bonachón, -na** *adj.* kind, good-natured. *2 m.-f.* good soul.
**bonaerense** *adj.-n.* of Buenos Aires.
**bonancible** *adj.* fair [weather]; calm [sea]; moderate [wind].
**bonanza** *f.* NAUT. fair weather; calm sea. *2* MIN. bonanza. *3* prosperity.
**bonapartista** *adj.-n.* Bonapartist.
**bondad** *f.* goodness. *2* kindness, kindliness, good nature. *3* kindness, favour: *tenga la ~ de*, kindly, please to.
**bondadoso, -sa** *adj.* kind, good, good-natured.
**boneta** *f.* NAUT. bonnet.
**bonete** *m.* biretta. *2* college cap. *3* cap, skull cap. *4* FORT. bonnet. *5* ZOOL. bonnet, reticulum.
**bonetero** *m.* BOT. spindle tree.
**boniato** *m.* BUNIATO.
**Bonifacio** *pr. n.* Boniface.
**bonificación** *f.* allowance, discount.
**bonificar** *tr.* to improve. *2* COM. to credit.
**bonísimo, -ma** *adj.* *superl.* very good.
**bonitamente** *adv.* easily, artfully.
**bonito, -ta** *adj.* pretty, nice, dainty. *2* goodly, pretty good. *3 m.* ICHTH. bonito.
**bono** *m.* COM. bond, debenture. *2* charity foodticket.
**bonzo** *m.* bonze.
**boñiga** *f.* cow dung.
**boñigo** *m.* cake of cow dung.
**boqueada** *f.* gasp [of death].
**boquear** *intr.* to gape, to gasp. *2* to be dying; to be at the last gasp. *3 tr.* to utter.
**boquera** *f.* opening in an irrigation canal. *2* window in a hayloft. *3* MED. sore at angle of lips.
**boquerón** *m.* wide opening. *2* ICHTH. anchovy.
**boquete** *m.* gap, breach, opening, narrow entrance.
**boquiabierto, -ta** *adj.* open-mouthed, gaping.
**boquiduro, -ra** *adj.* hard-mouthed [horse].
**boquifresco, -ca** *adj.* tender-mouthed [horse]. *2* outspoken.
**boquilla** *f.* stem [of pipe]. *2* cigar holder; cigarette holder; tip [of cigarette]. *3* mouthpiece [of musical instrument]. *4* burner [of lamp]. *5* upper chape [of scabbard].
**boquirrubio, -bia** *adj.* loose-tongued, babbling. *2* simple, naive. *3 m.* pretty boy, conceited youth.
**borato** *m.* CHEM. borate.
**bórax** *m.* CHEM. borax.
**borbollar, borbollear** *intr.* to bubble up.
**borbollón** *m.* bubbling up [of water]: *a borbollones*, hastily, tumultuously.
**borbollonear** *intr.* BORBOLLAR.
**borbónico, -ca** *adj.* Bourbonian, Bourbonic.
**borbor** *m.* bubble, bubbling.
**borborigmo** *m.* rumbling of the bowels.
**boboritar** *intr.* BORBOTAR, BORBOLLAR.
**borbotar** *intr.* [of water] to bubble up, to burble.

**borbotón** *m.* BORBOLLÓN: *a borbotones*, bubbling, gushing.
**borceguí** *m.* half boot, buskin.
**borda** *f.* NAUT. gunwale: *arrojar por la ~*, to throw overboard. *2* CHOZA.
**bordada** *f.* NAUT. tack, board: *dar bordadas*, to beat to windward, to tack.
**bordado** *m.* embroidering; embroidery.
**bordador, -ra** *m.-f.* embroiderer.
**bordar** *tr.* to embroider. *2* to perform exquisitely.
**borde** *adj.* bastard [person]. *2* wild [plant]. *3 m.* border, edge, fringe, verge, brink; fig. *al ~ de*, on the verge of. *4* hem [of a garment]. *5* brim [of a vessel]. *6* NAUT. board.
**bordear** *intr.-tr.* to border, skirt. *2 tr.* to border, to verge. *4 intr.* NAUT. to beat to windward.
**bordelés, -sa** *adj.-n.* of Bordeaux.
**bordillo** *m.* ENCINTADO.
**bordo** *m.* NAUT. board [ship's side]: *a ~*, aboard; *de alto ~*, large [ship]; fig. of importance, high-up. *2* NAUT. tack.
**bordón** *m.* pilgrim's staff. *2* MUS. snare [of drum]; bass string; bourdon [in organ]. *4* refrain, burden [of poem]. *5* pet word, pet phrase.
**bordonear** *intr.* to pluck a guitar's bass string.
**bordoneo** *m.* sound of the guitar's bass string.
**boreal** *adj.* boreal, northern.
**bóreas** *m.* Boreas [north wind].
**Borgoña** *f. pr. n.* GEOG. Burgundy. *2 m.* Burgundy [wine].
**borgoñón, -na** *adj.-n.* Burgundian.
**bórico, -ca** *adj.* CHEM. boric.
**borinqueño, -ña** *adj.-n.* Puerto Rican.
**borla** *f.* tassel, tuft. *2* tassel in academic cap. *3* powder puff.
**borne** *m.* tip of a jousting lance. *2* ELECT. terminal, binding post. *3* BOT. cytisus. *4 adj.* hard and brittle [wood].
**bornear** *tr.* to turn, move, shift. *2* to model and carve [a column]. *3 intr.* NAUT. to swing at anchor. *4 ref.* to warp, to bulge.
**borní** *m.* ORN. marsh harrier.
**boro** *m.* CHEM. boron.
**borona** *f.* BOT. millet. *2* BOT. Indian corn.
**borra** *f.* yearling ewe. *2* coarse wool. *3* goat's hair [for stuffing]. *4* floss, fluff, fuzz, waste: *~ de algodón*, cotton waste. *5* lees. *6* fig. trash.
**borrachera** *f.* drunkenness, intoxication. *2* carousal. *3* high exaltation. *4* coll. great folly.
**borrachín** *m.* drunkard.
**borracho, -cha** *adj.* drunk, drunken, intoxicated. *2* violet-coloured. *3 m.-f.* drunk man or woman, drunkard.
**borrador** *m.* draft, rough copy. *2* blotter [book].
**borragináceo, -a** *adj.* BOT. boraginaceous.
**borraja** *f.* BOT. borage.
**borrajear** *tr.* to scribble, scrawl.
**borrar** *tr.* to cross, strike, rub or blot out; to obliterate, efface, erase. *2* to smudge, blur.
**borrasca** *f.* storm, tempest. *2* coll. orgy, revelry.
**borrascoso, -sa** *adj.* stormy, tempestuous.
**borregada** *f.* flock of sheep.
**borrego, -ga** *m.-f.* yearly lamb. *2* simpleton.
**borreguil** *adj.* [pertaining to] lamb; of lambs.
**borrica** *f.* she-ass. *2* stupid woman.
**borricada** *f.* drove of donkeys. *2* stupidity, asininity.
**borrico** *m.* ZOOL. ass, donkey. *2* fig. ass. *3* CARP. sawhorse.
**borrilla** *f.* fuzz, fur [of fruits].
**borriquillo, -lla** *m.* young ass. *2 f.* young she-ass.

**borrón** *m.* ink blot. *2* blot, blemish. *3* draft, rough copy. *4* first sketch.
**borronear** *tr.* BORRAJEAR. *2* to sketch.
**borroso, -sa** *adj.* smudgy, blurred, blurry, faded. *2* thick with sediment.
**borujo** *m.* BURUJO.
**borujón** *m.* BURUJÓN.
**boscaje** *m.* boscage. *2* PAINT. woodland scene.
**boscoso, -sa** *adj.* wooded.
**Bósforo** *m. pr. n.* GEOG. Bosphorus.
**bosnio, -nia** *adj.-n.* Bosnian.
**bosorola** *f.* dregs, sediment.
**bosque** *m.* forest, wood, grove, thicket; woodland.
**bosquecillo** *m.* small wood, grove, copse, copice.
**bosquejar** *tr.* to sketch, to outline.
**bosquejo** *m.* sketch, outline: *en ~,* sketchy.
**bosquimano, -na** *adj.-n.* Bushman.
**bosta** *f.* dung, manure.
**bostezar** *intr.* to yawn, gape [with drowsiness, etc.].
**bostezo** *m.* yawn.
**bota** *f.* small leather wine bag. *2* cask, butt [for liquids]. *3* boot: *~ de montar,* riding boot; *ponerse las botas,* fig. to make money.
**botador** *m.* pole [for pushing a boat]. *2* CARP. nail puller; nail set.
**botadura** *f.* NAUT. launching.
**botafuego** *m.* linstock, match staff. *2* quicktempered person.
**botafumeiro** *m.* incense burner, censer [in Santiago de Compostela].
**botalón** *m.* NAUT. boom.
**botana** *f.* plug, stopper. *2* patch, plaster. *3* scar.
**botánica** *f.* botany.
**botánico, -ca** *adj.* botanical. *2* *m.-f.* botanist.
**botar** *tr.* to throw, fling out. *2* to launch [a boat]. *3* *intr.* to bound, bounce. *4* to jump. *5* *ref.* [of horses] to buck.
**botaratada** *f.* folly, nonsense.
**botarate** *m.* fool, harebrain. *2* (Am.) spendthrift.
**botarel** *m.* ARCH. buttress, counterfort.
**botarga** *f.* old large breeches. *2* ridiculous costume.
**botasilla** *f.* MIL. boots and saddles.
**botavara** *f.* NAUT. spanker boom.
**bote** *m.* NAUT. small boat: *~ salvavidas,* lifeboat. *2* bound, bounce, jump. *3* jar, pot, canister; tin can. *4* MIL. *~ de metralla,* canister shot. *5 de ~ en ~,* crowded, crammed with people.
**botella** *f.* bottle. *2* ELECT. *~ de Leyden,* Leyden jar.
**botellazo** *m.* blow with a bottle.
**botellero** *m.* bottle maker or dealer. *2* bottle rack.
**botero** *m.* NAUT. boatman.
**botica** *f.* chemist's; apothecary's shop, *drug store. *2* medicines.
**boticaria** *f.* chemist wife. *2* female pharmacist.
**boticario** *m.* chemist, druggist, apothecary.
**botija** *f.* earthen jug with a narrow mouth.
**botijo** *m.* round earthen jug with spout and handle.
**botilla** *f.* booty, ankle boot. *2* half boot.
**botillería** *f.* obs. icecream and light drinks saloon.
**botín** *m.* spat [short gaiter]. *2* boot. *3* booty, spoils.
**botina** *f.* high shoe.
**botiquín** *m.* medicine case; first-aid kit. *2* (Am.) retail wine store.
**botivoleo** *m.* SPORT. hitting the ball on the bounce.
**boto, -ta** *adj.* blunt, dull.
**botón** *m.* button [of garment, foil, electric bell, etc.]. *2* knob: *~ de puerta,* doorknob. *3* BOT. but-

ton, bud. *4* SURG. *~ de fuego,* hot iron cautery. *5* BOT. *~ de oro,* buttercup.
**botonadura** *f.* set of buttons.
**botonazo** *m.* FENC. thrust with a foil.
**botonería** *f.* button maker's shop.
**botonero, -ra** *m.-f.* button maker or seller.
**botones** *m.* buttons, pageboy, bell boy.
**botulismo** *m.* MED. botulism.
**bou** *m.* fishing by casting a net between two boats.
**bóveda** *f.* ARCH., ANAT. vault: *~ esquifada,* cross vault; *~ en cañón,* barrel vault; *~ palatina,* ANAT. palatine vault. *2* crypt. *3 ~ celeste,* canopy of heaven.
**bovedilla** *f.* ARCH. cove, small vault. *2* NAUT. counter.
**bóvido, -da** *adj.-n.* ZOOL. bovid.
**bovino, -na** *adj.* bovine.
**boxeador** *m.* SPORT. boxer.
**boxear** *intr.* SPORT. to box.
**boxeo** *m.* SPORT. boxing.
**boya** *f.* NAUT. buoy. *2* float [of fishing net].
**boyada** *f.* drove of oxen.
**boyante** *adj.* NAUT. [of a ship] riding light. *2* prosperous, successful.
**boyar** *intr.* [of a ship] to float, be afloat again.
**boyardo** *m.* boyar.
**boyera, boyeriza** *f.* ox stable.
**boyero, boyerizo** *m.* ox driver; oxherd.
**boyuno, -na** *adj.* bovine.
**bozal** *m.* muzzle [mouth covering]. *2* muzzle bells.
**bozo** *m.* down [on upper lip]. *2* mouth, lips.
**braceada** *f.* impetuous movement of the arms.
**braceaje** *m.* coining, minting. *2* NAUT. depth of water.
**bracear** *intr.* to move or swing the arms. *2* to struggle. *3* to swim with overhead strokes. *4* [of horses] to step high. *5* NAUT. to brace.
**braceo** *m.* waving of the arms. *2* stroke [swimming].
**bracero** *m.* labourer [unskilled workman]. *2* *adv. de ~,* arm in arm.
**bracmán** *m.* BRAHMÁN.
**bráctea** *f.* BOT. bract.
**bractéola** *f.* BOT. bractlet, bracteole.
**braga** *f.* hoisting rope. *2* diaper [infant breechcloth]. *3 pl.* wide breeches. *4* panties, step-ins.
**bragado, -da** *adj.* having the BRAGADURA of a different colour from the rest of the body [animal]. *2* wicked, ill-disposed. *3* firm, resolute.
**bragadura** *f.* crotch [of the body, of the trousers]. *2* inner surface of the thighs [in animals].
**bragazas** *m.* man without energy; henpecked man.
**braguero** *m.* SURG. truss [for a rupture]. *2* breeching [rope] of a gun.
**bragueta** *f.* fly [of trousers].
**braguetazo** *m.* coll. marriage of convenience: *dar un ~,* to marry money.
**brahmán** *m.* Brahman.
**brahmánico, -ca** *adj.* Brahmanic(al.
**brahmanismo** *m.* Brahmanism.
**brahmin** *m.* BRAHMÁN.
**brama** *f.* rut [of deers].
**bramadera** *f.* bull-roarer [toy]. *2* shepherd's horn.
**bramador, -ra** *adj.* lowing [a cow]; bellowing, roaring [a bull].
**bramante** *m.* thin twine or hemp string. *2* *adj.* roaring.
**bramar** *intr.* to bellow, roar.
**bramido** *m.* bellow, roar.
**brancada** *f.* trammel net, trammel.

**branca ursina** f. BOT. acanthus.
**brancal** m. frame [of a gun carriage].
**brandal** m. NAUT. side-rope [of ladder]. 2 NAUT. backstay.
**branquia** f. ZOOL. branchia. 2 pl. branchiae.
**branquial** adj. branchial.
**braquial** adj. ANAT. brachial.
**braquicéfalo, -la** adj. ANTHROP. brachycephalic.
**braquiópodos** m. pl. brachiopodes.
**braquiuro** m. brachyuran.
**brasa** f. live coal: estar en brasas, to be on tenterhooks; estar hecho unas brasas, to be flushed; pasar como sobre brasas, to mention or touch upon superficially.
**brasca** f. lute.
**braserillo** m. small pan for burning coals.
**brasero** m. brazier [pan for burning coals].
**Brasil** m. pr. n. GEOG. Brazil.
**brasil** m. BOT. brazil tree. 2 brazil, brazilwood.
**brasileño, -ña** adj.-n. Brazilian.
**brasilete** m. BOT. brazilette tree. 2 braziletto.
**bravamente** adv. bravely, gallantly. 2 cruelly. 3 finely, extremely well. 4 abundantly.
**bravata** f. bluster, swagger, brag.
**bravear** intr. to talk big, bluster, swagger.
**braveza** f. bravery. 2 fierceness, ferocity [of animals]. 3 fury [of the sea, wind, etc.].
**bravío, -a** adj. ferocious, wild, untamed. 2 rustic [person]. 3 wild [plant].
**bravo, -va** adj. brave, courageous. 2 fine, excellent. 3 fierce, ferocious [animal]. 4 rough [sea, land]. 5 angry, violent. 6 sumptuous, magnificent. 7 interj. bravo!
**bravucón, -na** adj. swaggering. 2 f. swaggerer.
**bravuconada** f. bluster, swagger.
**bravura** f. bravery, courage. 2 fierceness, ferocity [of animals]. 3 BRAVATA.
**braza** f. NAUT. fathom. 2 NAUT. brace [rope].
**brazada** f. stroke [with arms]. 2 BRAZADO.
**brazado** m. armful, armload.
**brazal** m. ARM. brassart. 2 brassard, arm band. 3 irrigation ditch. 4 NAUT. headrail. 5 EMBRAZADURA.
**brazalete** m. bracelet, armlet.
**brazo** m. arm [of the body, a chair, lever, etc.]: cruzarse de brazos, to fold one's arms; fig. to remain idle; no dar su ~ a torcer, not to yield; ser el ~ derecho de uno, to be someone's right-hand man; a ~ partido, hand to hand; tooth and nail; asidos del ~, arm in arm; con los brazos abiertos, with open arms. 2 arm, power, might. 3 foreleg [of a quadruped]. 4 branch [of a river]. 5 pl. hands, workers.
**brazuelo** m. small arm. 2 forearm [of quadrupeds].
**brea** f. tar, wood tar: ~ seca, rosin. 2 NAUT. pitch.
**brear** tr. to ill-treat. 2 to make fun of, to tease.
**brebaje** m. beverage, unpalatable drink.
**breca** f. ICHTH. bleak.
**brécol** m., **brecolera** f. BOT. broccoli.
**brecha** f. breach, gap, opening [in wall or fortification]; fig. impression [on the mind].
**brega** f. fight, scrap. 2 struggle: andar a la ~, to work hard, to toil. 3 dar ~, to tease.
**bregar** intr. to fight. 2 to struggle. 3 to work hard, toil. 4 tr. to knead.
**Brema** pr. n. Bremen.
**breña** f., **breñal, breñar** m. bushy and craggy ground.
**breñoso, -sa** adj. bushy an craggy.

**breque** m. sea bream. 2 (Am.) handbrake, emergency brake.
**bresca** f. honeycomb.
**Bretaña** f. pr. n. Bretagne, Brittany. 2 Gran ~, Great Britain, Britain.
**brete** m. tight spot, difficult situation.
**bretón, -na** adj.-n. Breton. 2 m. pl. BOT. Brussels sprouts.
**breva** f. early fig. 2 flat cigar. 3 fig. plum, good thing.
**breve** adj. short, brief. 2 PHON. short. 3 m. apostolic brief. 4 f. MUS. breve. 5 adv. en ~, soon, shortly.
**brevedad** f. brevity, briefness. 2 a la mayor ~, as soon as possible.
**breviario** m. breviary. 2 PRINT. brevier.
**brezal** m. heath, moor.
**brezo** m. BOT. heath, heather.
**briba** f. vagrant life, loafing about.
**bribón, -na** adj. loafing. 2 rascally. 3 m.-f. loafer. 4 rascal, knave, scoundrel.
**bribonada** f. knavery, dirty trick.
**bribonería** f. life of loafing. 2 rascality.
**bribonzuelo, -la** m.-f. little rascal, rogue.
**bricbarca** f. NAUT. bark.
**brida** f. bridle [of riding gear]: a toda ~, at to speed. 2 MEC. splice bar, clamp; flange. 3 RLY. fishplate. 4 pl. SURG. filaments around the lips of a wound.
**bridón** m. small bridle. 2 snaffle bit. 3 steed, spirited horse.
**brigada** f. MIL. brigade. 2 MIL. train [of beasts]. 3 squad, gang. 4 MIL. sergeant-major.
**brigadier** m. brigadier, brigadier general.
**Brígida** f. pr. n. Bridget.
**brillante** adj. brilliant, shining, bright. 2 sparkling, glittering, glossy. 3 m. brilliant [diamond].
**brillantez** f. brillance. 2 success, splendour.
**brillantina** f. brilliantine. 2 metal polish.
**brillar** intr. to shine. 2 to sparkle, glitter, be glossy. 3 fig. ~ por su ausencia, to be lacking.
**brillo** m. brilliance, brightness, lustre; splendor.
**brin** m. fine canvas.
**brincar** intr. to spring, skip, leap, jump. 2 to take offence, to get excited.
**brinco** m. spring, skip, leap jump.
**brindar** intr. to toast: ~ por, to drink [a person's] health; to toast. 2 tr.-intr. to offer, present, afford; to invite: ~ a uno con una cosa, to offer something to someone. 3 ref. brindarse a, to offer to [do something].
**brindis** m. toast, drinking the health.
**brío** m. strength, spirit, determination. 2 grace, elegance, vivacity.
**briofita** adj. BOT. bryophyitic.
**briol** m. NAUT. buntline.
**brionia** f. BOT. bryony.
**bríos** interj. ¡voto a ~!, by the Almighty!
**briosamente** adv. bravely, courageously, valiantly. 2 resolutely, firmly. 3 vigorously, energetically, with spirit.
**brioso, -sa** adj. vigorous, spirited, lively.
**briqueta** f. briquet, briquette [of coal].
**brisa** f. northeast wind. 2 breeze. 3 bagasse of pressed grapes.
**brisca** f. a Spanish card game.
**briscar** tr. to brocade.
**brisote** m. stormy breeze.
**bristol** m. Bristol board, Bristol paper.
**británico, -ca** adj. British, Britannic.
**britano, -na** adj. British. 2 m.-f. Briton.
**briza** f. BOT. quaking grass.

**brizna** *f.* slender particle, filament; leaf [of grass]; string [in pods].

**broca** *f.* WEAV., SPIN. spindle, skewer: ~ *de lanzadera*, shuttle spindle. 2 conical drill bit. 3 shoemaker's tack.

**brocado, -da** *adj.* brocaded. 2 *m.* brocade.

**brocal** *m.* curbstone [of a well]. 2 steel rim [of a shield]; metal mouth [of a scabbard]. 3 mouthpiece [of a leather wine bag].

**brocamantón** *m.* diamond brooch.

**brocatel** *m.* brocatel, brocatelle [fabric; marble].

**bróculi** *m.* BRÉCOL.

**brocha** *f.* stubby brush [for painting]: *de ~ gorda*, house [painter]; crude, heavyhanded [literary work]. 2 ~ *de afeitar*, shaving brush.

**brochada** *f.* dab, stroke [with a stubby brush].

**brochazo** *m.* BROCHADA.

**broche** *m.* clasp, fastener, hook and eye; brooch. 2 hasp [for book covers].

**brocheta** *f.* COOK. skewer.

**brocho** *adj.-m.* BULLF. having horns close together.

**broma** *f.* fun, merriment; joke, jest, practical joke: *gastar una ~ a*, to play a joke on; *en ~*, in fun, jokingly. 2 ZOOL. shipworm.

**bromato** *m.* CHEM. bromate.

**bromatología** *f.* bromatology.

**bromazo** *m.* practical joke.

**bromear** *intr.* to joke, jest, make fun.

**bromeliáceo, -a** *adj.* BOT. bromeliaceous.

**brómico** *adj.* CHEM bromic.

**bromista** *adj.* full of fun. 2 *m.-f.* merry person, joker, practical joker.

**bromo** *m.* CHEM. bromin(e. 2 BOT. brome grass.

**bromuro** *m.* CHEM. bromide.

**bronca** *f.* row, shindy. 2 harsh reprehension.

**bronce** *m.* bronze: *la Edad de ~*, the Bronze Age. 2 poet. cannon, bell, trumpet.

**bronceado, -da** *adj.* bronze, bronze coloured. 2 tanned, sunburnt. 3 *m.* bronzing, bronze finish; bronze [colour].

**bronceador** *m.* suntan product.

**broncear** *tr.* to bronze. 2 to tan [the skin].

**broncíneo, -a** *adj.* brazen; bronzelike.

**broncista** *m.* bronzesmith.

**bronco, -ca** *adj.* coarse, rough. 2 brittle [metal]. 3 gruff, rude. 4 harsh, hoarse [sound, voice].

**bronconeumonía** *f.* MED. bronchopneumonia.

**broncoscopio** *m.* bronchoscope.

**bronquedad** *f.* coarseness, roughness. 2 brittleness [of metals]. 3 gruffness. 4 hoarseness.

**bronquial** *adj.* bronchial.

**bronquio** *m.* ANAT. bronchus. 2 *pl.* bronchi.

**bronquiolo** *m.* ANAT. bronchiole.

**bronquitis** *f.* MED. bronchitis.

**broquel** *m.* shield, buckler. 2 shield, protection.

**broqueta** *f.* COOK. skewer.

**brotadurà** *f.* budding, sprouting. 2 springing, gushing. 3 eruption, rash.

**brotar** *intr.* to germinate, to sprout; to bud, burgeon, shoot. 2 [of water, tears, etc.] to spring, gush. 3 [of pimples, etc.] to break out. 4 *tr.* to put forth [plants, gras, etc.]. 5 to shed.

**brote** *m.* bud, sprout. 2 outbreak, appearance.

**broza** *f.* underbrush. 2 brush, brushwood. 3 rubbish, trash.

**brozno, -na** *adj.* BRONCO. 2 slow-witted.

**bruces (a or de)** *adv.* face downward, on one's face.

**brucita** *f.* MINER. brucite.

**bruja** *f.* witch, sorceress. 2 coll. hag, shrew.

**Brujas** *pr. n.* GEOG. Bruges.

**brujería** *f.* witchcraft, sorcery, magic.

**brujir** *tr.* to trim the edge of a glass.

**brujo** *m.* wizard, sorcerer.

**brújula** *f.* magnetic needle, compass.

**brujulear** *tr.* to guess, smell out.

**brulote** *m.* fire ship.

**bruma** *f.* mist, fog [in the sea].

**brumazón** *m.* heavy fog, thick mist.

**brumoso, -sa** *adj.* foggy, hazy, misty.

**bruno, -na** *adj.* dark, brown.

**bruñido, -da** *adj.* burnished. 2 *m.* burnishing.

**bruñidura** *f.*, **bruñimiento** *m.* burnishing.

**bruñir** *tr.* to burnish.

**bruño** *m.* BOT. black plum.

**brusco, -ca** *adj.* brusque, rude, blunt, gruff. 2 sudden. 3 sharp [curve]. 4 *m.* BOT. butcher's-broom.

**Bruselas** *pr. n.* GEOG. Brussels.

**brusquedad** *f.* brusqueness, rudeness, bluntness, gruffness; rude action or treatment. 2 suddenness.

**brutal** *adj.* brutal, brutish. 2 coll. colossal. 3 *m.* brute, beast.

**brutalidad** *f.* brutality. 2 stupidity. 3 fig. *me gusta una ~*, I like it enormously.

**brutalizarse** *ref.* to brutalize [become like a brute].

**bruteza** *f.* brutality. 2 roughness, want of polish.

1) **bruto** *m.* brute, beast. 2 fig. brute; blockhead. 3 *pr. n.* (cap.) Brutus.

2) **bruto, -ta** *adj.* brute, brutish. 2 stupid, ignorant. 3 rough, unpolished. 4 *bruto* or *en ~*, in the rough, unwrought, crude; gross [without any deduction].

**bruza** *f.* horse brush. 2 printer's brush.

**bruzar** *tr.* to brush [horses or printing forms].

**bu** *m.* bogey man: *hacer el ~*, to scare, frighten.

**búa** *f.* pimple. 2 *m.* bubo.

**buba** *f.* MED. bubo.

**búbalo** *m.* ZOOL. bubal, bubale.

**bubón** *m.* MED. bubo.

**bubónico, -ca** *adj.* bubonic.

**bucal** *adj.* buccal.

**bucanero** *m.* buccaneer.

**Bucarest** *pr. n.* GEOG. Bucharest.

**búcaro** *m.* an odoriferous clay. 2 flower vase.

**buccino** *m.* ZOOL. whelk.

**buceador** *m.* diver. 2 pearl diver.

**bucear** *intr.* to dive; to swim under water. 2 fig. to dive [in], to explore.

**Bucéfalo** *m.* Bucephalus.

**buceo** *m.* diving.

**bucinador** *m.* ANAT. buccinator.

**bucle** *m.* long curl [of hair]. 2 AER. loop.

**buco** *m.* ZOOL. billy goat, buck. 2 opening, gap.

**bucólica** *f.* bucolic [poem]. 2 coll. food; meal.

**bucólico, -ca** *adj.* bucolic. 2 *m.* bucolic poet.

**buchada** *f.* mouthful.

**buche** *m.* craw [of animals]. 2 stomach [of man]. 3 bosom [thoughts, secrets]. 4 suckling ass.

**buchon, -na** *adj.* pouter [pigeon].

**Buda** *m. pr. n.* Buddha.

**budin** *m.* pudding.

**budión** *m.* ICHTH. peacock fish.

**budismo** *m.* Buddhism.

**budista** *adj.-m.* Buddhist.

**buen** *adj.* apocopated form of BUENO, used only before a masculine substantive.

**buenamente** *adv.* easily, without difficulty. 2 voluntarily, spontaneously.

**buenaventura** *f.* good luck, happiness. 2 fortune [as told by a fortuneteller]: *decirle a uno la ~*, to tell someone his fortune.

**Buenaventura** *m. pr. n.* Bonaventure.
**bueno, -na** *adj.* good. *2* kind. *3* fit, suitable. *4* well [in good health or condition]. *5* iron. extraordinary, fine: ~ *fuera que...,* it would be fine if... *6 a buenas, por la buena,* willingly, without reluctance; *¡buena es ésta!,* that is a good one! [surprise or disapproval]; *buenos días,* good day, good morning; *buenas noches,* good evening, good night; *buenas tardes,* good afternoon.; *de buenas a primeras,* from the very start. *7 adv. ¡bueno!,* well!, very well!; al right! that is enough!
**Buenos Aires** *m. pr. n.* GEOG. Buenos Aires.
**buey** *m.* ZOOL. ox, bullock, steer: *carne de ~,* beef. *2* ZOOL. ~ *del Tibet,* yak. *3* ~ *de cabestrillo,* stalking-horse.
**bufado, -da** *adj.* blown very thin [glass].
**búfalo** *m.* ZOOL. buffalo.
**bufanda** *f.* muffler [for the neck], scarf.
**bufar** *intr.* to puff and blow, to snort [with anger].
**bufete** *m.* writing desk. *2* lawyer's office or practice. *3* (Am.) snack, refreshment.
**bufido** *m.* angry snort or roar.
**bufo, -fa** *adj.* farcical buffoon: *ópera ~,* opera bouffe. *2 m.* buffoon. *3* buffo [actor].
**bufón, -na** *adj.* buffoon. *2 m.-f.* buffoon, jester.
**bufonada** *f.* buffoonery.
**bufonesco, -ca** *adj.* buffoon, farcical.
**buganvilla** *f.* BOT. bougainvillea.
**bugle** *m.* MUS. bugle [wind instrument with pistons].
**buglosa** *f.* BOT. bugloss.
**buharda, buhardilla** *f.* dormer, dormer window. *2* garret. *3* (Am.) skylight.
**buharro** *m.* ORN. scops owl.
**búho** *m.* ORN. eagle owl.
**buhonería** *f.* pedlary, peddlery [pedlar wares].
**buhonero** *m.* pedlar, peddler, hawker.
**buido, -da** *adj.* pointed, sharp. *2* grooved, striated.
**buitre** *m.* ORN. vulture.
**buitrón** *m.* fish trap [made of osier]. *2* partridge net. *3* snare for game.
**buje** *m.* axle box [bushing].
**bujería** *f.* gewgaw, knick-knack.
**bujía** *f.* wax or stearine candle. *2* candlestick. *3* PHYS. candlepower. *4* spark plug.
**bula** *f.* [papal] bull. *2* bulla.
**bulbillo** *m.* BOT. bulbil.
**bulbo** *m.* ANAT., BOT. bulb.
**bulboso, -sa** *adj.* bulbous.
**buldog** *m.* bulldog.
**buldozer** *m.* bulldozer.
**bulerías** *f. pl.* bulerias, dance and song from Andalusia.
**bulevar** *m.* boulevard.
**Bulgaria** *f. pr. n.* GEOG. Bulgaria.
**búlgaro, -ra** *adj.-n.* Bulgar, Bulgarian.
**bulo** *m.* canard, hoax, false report.
**bulto** *m.* volume, size, bulk: *de ~,* in sculpture; fig. obvious, striking. *2* shade, form, body: *buscar el* ~ *a uno,* to persecute, provoke [someone]; *escurrir el ~,* to evade a task, danger, etc. *3* swelling, lump. *4* statue. *5* bundle, pack, piece of luggage. *6 a ~,* broadly, roughly.
**bulla** *f.* noise, uproar, racket. *2* crowd.
**bullabesa** *f.* bouillabaisse.
**bullanga** *f.* tumult, racket, disturbance.
**bullanguero, -ra** *adj.* fond of noise. *2 m.-f.* noisy person, rioter.
**bullebulle** *m.-f.* coll. a lively, bustling person.
**bullicio** *m.* hubbub, noise, stir. *2* riot.

**bullicioso, -sa** *adj.* noisy, boisterous, restless, lively, merry. *2* riotous. *3 m.-f.* rioter.
**bullidor, -ra** *adj.* bustling, lively.
**bullir** *intr.* to boil. *2* to bubble up. *3* to seethe. *4* to bustle about. *5 intr.-ref.-tr.* to move, stir, budge.
**bullón** *m.* stud [for bookbindings]. *2* puff [in a dress].
**bumerang** *m.* boomerang.
**bungalow** *m.* bungalow.
**buniato** *m.* BOT. sweet potato.
**bunker** *m.* bunker.
**buñolería** *f.* fried cake shop.
**buñolero, -ra** *m.-f.* maker or seller of BUÑUELOS.
**buñuelo** *m.* doughnut, cruller; fritter. *2* botch, bungle.
**buque** *m.* NAUT. ship, vessel: ~ *de cabotaje,* coaster; ~ *de guerra,* warship; ~ *de vapor,* steamer, steamboat; ~ *de vela,* sailboat; ~ *cisterna,* tanker; ~ *escuela,* training ship; ~ *mercante,* merchant vessel; ~ *transbordador,* train ferry. *2* hull [of a ship]. *3* capacity.
**burbuja** *f.* bubble.
**burbujear** *intr.* to bubble.
**burbujeo** *m.* bubbling.
**burdégano** *m.* ZOOL. hinny.
**burdel** *m.* brothel, disorderly house.
**Burdeos** *pr. n. & m.* Bordeaux [town and wine].
**burdo, -da** *adj.* coarse. *2* clumsy [lie, work].
**bureo** *m.* amusement, diversion.
**bureta** *f.* CHEM. burette.
**burga** *f.* hot springs.
**burgado** *m.* ZOOL. a brown edible snail.
**burgalés, -sa** *adj.-n.* of Burgos.
**burgo** *m.* obs. hamlet.
**burgomaestre** *m.* burgomaster.
**burgrave** *m.* burgrave.
**burgués, -sa** *m.-f.* burgher. *2* bourgeois.
**burguesía** *f.* burgeoisie.
**buriel** *adj.* chestnut red. *2 m.* coarse woollen cloth.
**buril** *m.* burin.
**burilar** *tr.* to engrave with a burin.
**burjaca** *f.* pilgrim's scrip. *23* leather bag carried by pilgrims and beggars for carrying food and alms.
**burla** *f.* mockery, gibe, jeer, scoff: *hacer* ~ *de,* to mock, scoff, make fun of. *2* joke, jest: *de burlas,* in fun. *3* deception, trick.
**burladero** *m.* refuge in a bull ring. *2* safety island.
**burlador, -ra** *adj.* mocking, deceiving. *2 m.* mocker, deceiver. *3* seducer of women.
**burlar** *tr.* to mock. *2* to deceive. *3* to disappoint, to frustrate, to evade. *4 intr.-ref.* to make fun: *burlarse de,* to make fun of, to laugh at; *burla, burlando,* without noticing it; on the quiet.
**burlería** *f.* mockery. *2* illusion. *3* derision.
**burlesco, -ca** *adj.* burlesque, comical, jocular.
**burlete** *m.* weather strip or stripping.
**burlón, -na** *adj.* mocking. *2 m.-f.* mocker, joker.
**buró** *m.* writing desk, bureau.
**burocracia** *f.* bureaucracy.
**burócrata** *m.-f.* bureaucrat.
**burra** *f.* she-ass. *2* ignorant, stupid woman. *3* strong hardworking woman.
**burrada** *f.* drove of asses. *2* stupid act or expression.
**burrero** *m.* ass keeper who sells asses' milk.
**burro** *m.* ZOOL. donkey, ass: fig. ~ *de carga,* strong, hardworking man. *2* ignorant, stupid man. *3* sawbuck, sawhorse. *4* card game.
**bursátil** *adj.* stock, stock-market.

**burujo** *m.* knot [in wool], lump [in a matter]. *2* bagasse of pressed olives.

**burujón** *m.* aug. of BURUJO. *2* lump, swelling.

**busardo** *m.* ORN. buzzard.

**busca** *f.* search, hunt, quest: *en ~ de,* in quest of. *2* HUNT. party of beaters.

**buscador, -ra** *adj.* searching. *2 m.-f.* searcher, seeker; prospector. *3 m.* OPT. finder.

**buscapié** *m.* sounding remark [in conversation].

**buscapiés** *m.* serpent, snake [firework].

**buscapleitos** *m. pl.* troublemaker, litigious fellow.

**buscar** *tr.* to look for, search for, hunt for, seek. *2* to prospect. *3 ref.* to get; to bring upon oneself.

**buscarruidos** *m.-f.* troublemaker.

**buscavidas** *m.-f.* busybody. *2* hustler.

**busco** *m.* miter sill [of canal-lock gate].

**buscón, -na** *m.-f.* searcher, seeker. *2* petty thief. *3 f.* harlot.

**busilis** *m.* coll. rub, point: *ahí está el ~,* there's the rub; *dar en el ~,* to see the point.

**búsqueda** *f.* search, hunt, quest.

**busto** *m.* bust.

**butaca** *f.* easy chair. *2* THEAT. orchestra seat.

**butano** *m.* CHEM. butane.

**buten (de)** *adj.* coll, first-rate, ripping.

**butifarra** *f.* a kind of pork sausage.

**butilo** *m.* CHEM. butyl.

**butírico, -ca** *adj.* CHEM. butyric.

**buxáceo, -a** *adj.* BOT. buxaceous.

**buyo** *m.* buyo [chewing paste].

**buzamiento** *m.* GEOL. dip.

**buzar** *intr.* GEOL. to dip.

**buzo** *m.* diver: *campana de ~,* diving bell.

**buzón** *m.* outlet [of a pond]. *2* letter drop; letter box, mailbox, postbox; *~ de alcance,* late-collection postbox. *3* stopper, plug, bung.

# C

**C, c** *f.* C, c., third letter of the Spanish alphabet.

**¡ca!** *interj.* oh no! not at all!, no indeed!

**cabal** *adj.* exact, full, complete. *2* perfect, faultless. *3 adv.* exactly. *4 m. pl. no estar uno en sus cabales*, not to be in one's right mind.

**cábala** *f.* cabala. *2* cabal. *3* guess, divination.

**cabalgada** *f.* [in old times] raid by horsemen.

**cabalgador, -ra** *m.-f.* rider [on horseback].

**cabalgadura** *f.* mount, riding horse or animal. *2* beast of burden.

**cabalgar** *intr.* to horse, ride on horseback. *2 tr.* to ride, mount [a horse, mule o ass]. *3* to cover [a mare].

**cabalgata** *f.* cavalcade.

**cabalista** *adj.-n.* cabalist, cabbalist. *2* intriguer, schemer.

**cabalístico, -ca** *adj.* cabalistic.

**cabalmente** *adv.* exactly, completely, fully. *2* just.

**caballa** *m.* ICHTH. mackerel.

**caballada** *f.* drove of horses. *2* (Am.) stupidity.

**caballar** *adj.* equine.

**caballejo** *m.* little horse. *2* nag.

**caballeresco, -ca** *adj.* chivalric, chivalrous, chivalresque.

**caballerete** *m.* little gentleman, little dandy.

**caballería** *f.* riding animal; horse, mule, ass. *2* MIL. horse, cavalry. *3* knights, knighthood, chivalry, order of knights: ~ *andante*, errantry, knight errantry. *4* chivalric act.

**caballeriza** *f.* stable [for horses]. *2* royal mews. *3* stable, stud [horses kept]. *4* stable hands.

**caballerizo** *m.* head groom of a stable. *2* equerry: ~ *mayor del rey*, royal master of the horse.

**caballero, -ra** *adj.* riding, mounted. *2 m.* knight: ~ *andante*, knight errant; *armar* ~, to knight. *3* gentleman: fig. ~ *de industria*, gentleman crook, chevalier of industry; ~ *en plaza*, mounted toreador. *4* sir [in addressing a man].

**caballerosamente** *adv.* chivalrously.

**caballerosidad** *f.* chivalry, gentlemanly behaviour.

**caballeroso, -sa** *adj.* chivalrous, gentlemanly.

**caballete** *m.* small horse. *2* ridge [of a roof]. *3* horse [instrument of torture]. *4* trestle, carpenter's horse, gantry. *5* easel. *6* ridge [between furrows]. *7* chimney cap. *8* bridge [of nose]. *9* stand for saddles.

**caballista** *m.* horseman, good rider. *2* mounted highwayman.

**caballito** *m. dim.* little horse. *2* rocking-horse, hobby-horse. *3* ENT. ~ *del diablo*, dragonfly. *4 pl.* merry-go-round. *5* petits chevaux [game].

**caballo** *m.* ZOOL. horse: ~ *de batalla*, battle horse; fig. forte, specialty; fig. main point [in controversy]; ~ *de silla*, saddle horse; ~ *padre* or *semental*, stallion; *a* ~, on horse-back; *a* ~ *de*, astride. *2* knight [in chess]. *3* CARDS. queen. *4* ~ *de agua* or *marino*, ZOOL. river horse; ICHTH. sea horse. *5* MECH. ~ *de fuerza* or *de vapor*, horsepower. *6* MIL. ~ *de Frisa* or *de Frisia*, cheval-defrise. *7 pl.* MIL. horse, cavalry.

**caballón** *m.* ridge [between furrows]. *2* small ridge for dividing plots, directing water, etc.

**caballuno, -na** *adj.* equine; horselike.

**cabaña** *f.* cabin, hut, hovel. *2* large number of sheep or cattle. *7* balk [in billiards].

**cabañal** *adj.* sheep-and-cattle [path]. *2 m.* village of cabins.

**cabañuela** *f.* little cabin.

**cabaretera** *f.* cabaret entertainer.

**cabe** *m.* stroke on a ball: *dar un* ~ *a*, to hurt, harm. *2 prep.* near, at the side of.

**cabecear** *intr.* to nod [in drowsiness]. *2* [of horses] to raise and lower the head. *3* NAUT. to pitch. *4 tr.* to strengthen [new wine] with old wine. *5* to blend [wines]. *6* to bind the edge [of a carpet, etc.]. *7* to put the headband to [a book].

**cabeceo** *m.* nodding [of the head]. *2* NAUT. pitching.

**cabecera** *f.* beginning or principal part; upper end; head [of a table, bed, etc.]. *2* seat of honour. *3* headboard [of a bed]. *4* bedside. *5* headwaters. *6* main town. *7* PRINT. headpiece. *8* head or tail of the back [of a book].

**cabecero** *m.* headrest.

**cabecilla** *f.* little head. *2* wrong-headed person. *3 m.* ringleader, rebel leader.

**cabellera** *f.* hair, head of hair. *2* wig. *3* ASTR. tail [of comet].

**cabello** *m.* hair [of the human head, singly or collectively]: *asirse de un* ~, to seize upon any trivial pretext; *partir un* ~ *en el aire*, to be very shrewd; *traído por los cabellos*, farfetched. *2* corn silk. *3* ~ *de ángel*, sweetmeat made from a squash. *4 pl.* hair, head of hair.

**cabelludo, -da** *adj.* with an abundant head of hair. *2* BOT. hairy.

**caber** *intr.* to be containable [in], to go [in or into]; to have room or room enough: *en esta lata caben diez litros*, this can will hold ten litres; *usted no cabe entre nosotros*, there is no room for you among us; *no me cabe en la cabeza que*, fig. I never would have believed that. *2 me cabe el honor de*, I have the hono(u)r of. *3 todo cabe en*, all is possible in. *4 no cabe duda*, there is no doubt. *5 no caber en sí de*, to be bursting with [joy, etc.]. ¶ CONJUG.: IND. Pres.: *quepo, cabes, cabe*, etc. | Pret.: *cupe, cupiste, cupo; cupimos, cupisteis, cupieron*. | Fut.: *cabré, cabrás*, etc. | COND.: *cabría, cabrías*, etc. | SUBJ. Pres.: *quepa, quepas, quepa; quepamos, quepáis, quepan*. | Imperf.: *cupiera, cupieras*, etc., or *cupiese, cupieses*, etc. | Fut.: *cupiere, cupieres*, etc. | IMPER.: *cabe, quepa; quepamos, cabed, quepan*.

**cabestrante** *m.* capstan.

**cabestrar** *tr.* to put a halter on [a beast].

**cabestrillo** *m.* sing [for injured arm]. *2* little chain worn as a necklace.

**cabestro** *m.* halter [for horses]: *llevar* or *traer del cabestro*, to lead by the halter; fig. to lead by the nose. *3* leading ox.

**cabeza** *f.* head [of man or animal; mind, understanding; top part of end]: ~ *de chorlito*, scatterbrains; ~ *de puente*, bridgehead; ~ *de turco*, scapegoat; *mala* ~, ne'er-do-well; scapegrace; *de* ~, by heart; head first; *calentarse la* ~, to rack one's brains; *írsele a uno la* ~, to feel giddy; *levantar* ~, to get on one's feet [after misfortune]; to recover [from illness]; *pasarle a uno por la* ~ [*una cosa*], to cross one's mind; to come into one's head; *romperse la* ~, to cudgel or to rack one's brains; *sentar la* ~, to settle down; *subirse una cosa a la* ~, to go to one's head. *2* head [chief, leader; first place]: *a la* ~, at the head, in the lead. *3* headwaters, head [of a river]. *4* head, individual: *por* ~, per head. *5* main town: ~ *de partido*, country seat. *6* ~ *de ajo*, bulb of garlic.

**cabezada** *f.* blow with the head, butt. *2* nod [from drowsiness or in salutation]: *dar cabezadas*, to nod. *3* NAUT., AER. pitch, pitching, plunge. *4* headgear [of harness], headstall [of bridle]. *5* headband [of book].

**cabezal** *m.* small pillow. *2* long pillow, bolster. *3* SURG. bolster. *4* MIN., MACH. headstock.

**cabezazo** *m.* blow with the head, butt.

**cabezón, -na** *adj.-n.* CABEZUDO 1 & 2. *2 m.* opening for the head [in a garment]. *3* ~ *de serreta*, cavesson.

**cabezonada** *f.* obstinate act.

**cabezota** *f.* large head. *3 m.-f.* big-headed or obstinate person.

**cabezudo, -da** *adj.* big-headed. *2* obstinate. *3 m.-f.* big-headed or obstinate person. *4 m.* figure of a big-headed dwarf [in some processions]. *5* ICHTH. mullet.

**cabezuela** *f.* dim. small head. *2* coarse flour, middling. *3* BOT. capitulum, head [inflorescence].

**cabida** *f.* espace, room, capacity: *dar* ~ *a*, to make room for; *tener* ~, to apply, be applicable. *2* extent [of a field]. *3* favour, influence.

**cabildante** *m.* town councillor.

**cabildear** *intr.* to lobby.

**cabildeo** *m.* lobbying, intriguing.

**cabildo** *m.* chapter [of a cathedral or collegiate church]. *2* town council. *3* meeting of a CABILDO.

**cabilla** *f.* NAUT. driftbolt. *2* NAUT. belaying pin. *3* NAUT. wheel handle.

**cabillo** *m.* BOT. stem [of leaf, flower or fruit].

**cabina** *f.* AER., TELEPH. cabin.

**cabio** *m.* ARCH. joist. *2* ARCH. trimmer. *3* top piece or bottom piece [of a door frame].

**cabizbajo, -ja** *adj.* crestfallen; pensive.

**cable** *m.* cable, rope, hawser. *2* cable [cable's length; submarine cable; cablegram].

**cablegrafiar** *tr.* to cable.

**cablegráfico, -ca** *adj.* cable: *dirección cablegráfica*, cable address.

**cablegrama** *m.* cablegram.

**cabo** *m.* end, extremity: ~ *suelto*, fig. loose end; *atar cabos*, fig. to put two and two together; *estar al* ~ *de la calle*, to be informed [about something]; *de* ~ *a rabo*, from head to tail, from beginning to end. *2* end, termination, conclusion: *llevar a* ~, to carry out; *al* ~, finally; *al* ~ *de*, at the end of; *al* ~ *de un mes*, in a month. *3* bit, stump: ~ *de vela*, stump of candle. *4* strand [of rope or thread]. *5* haft. *6* NAUT. rope, cordage. *7* GEOG. cape: ~ *de Buena Esperanza*, Cape of Good Hope; ~ *de Hornos*, Cape Horn. *8* MIL. corporal. *9* mane, muzzle and feet [of horses].

**cabotaje** *m.* NAUT. cabotage, coasting trade.

**cabra** *f.* ZOOL. goat: ~ *de almizcle*, musk deer; ~ *montés*, wild goat. *2 pl.* marks on the legs from sitting near the fire.

**cabrahigar** *tr.* to caprificate.

**cabrahígo** *m.* BOT. caprifig, goat fig, wild fig.

**cabreado, -da** *adj.* coll. angry, furious, livid.

**cabrear** *tr.* coll. to get worked up, to get one's back up, to become annoyed. *2 intr.* (Am.) to prance about, to scamper about. *3 ref.* coll. to see red, to get furious, to get worked up.

**cabreo** *m.* coger un ~, to fly of the handle; *tener un* ~, to be annoyed, to be worked up; *dar un* ~ *a alguien*, to get someone worked up.

**cabrera** *f.* goatherdess. *2* goatherd's wife.

**cabrería** *f.* goat's milk dairy. *2* stable for goats.

**cabreriza** *f.* goatherd's cabin. *2* goatherd's wife.

**cabrerizo, cabrero** *m.* goatherd.

**cabrestante** *m.* capstan.

**cabria** *f.* crab, derrik [hoisting machine].

**cabrilla** *f.* ICHTH. cabrilla. *2* sawbuck. *3 pl.* CABRAS 2. *4* whitecaps [in the sea]. *5* ASTR. Pleiades.

**cabrillear** *intr.* [of the sea] to form whitecaps.

**cabrilleo** *m.* the forming of whitecaps.

**cabrio** *m.* common rafter.

**cabrío** *adj.* hircine, goat. *2 m.* herd of goats.

**cabriola** *f.* caper, sikp, gambol, tumble; capriole.

**cabriolar** *intr.* CABRIOLEAR.

**cabriolé** *m.* cabriolet.

**cabriolear** *intr.* to caper, gambol; to capriole.

**cabrita** *f.* she-kid.

**cabritilla** *f.* [dressed] kidskin.

**cabrito** *m.* kid [young of goat].

**cabrón** *m.* ZOOL. buck, billy-goat. *2* fig. acquiescing cuckold.

**cabronada** *f.* vulg. dirty trick, foul trick. *2* tough job.

**cabruno, -na** *adj.* hircine, goat, goatish.

**cabujón** *m.* JEWEL. cabochon.

**cabuya** *f.* BOT. century plant. *2* pita [fiber]. *3* pita rope. *4* NAUT. small ropes, cordages.

**caca** *f.* coll. human excrement. *2* dirt, filth.

**cacahual** *m.* cacao plantation.

**cacahuete** *m.* BOT. peanut.

**cacao** *m.* cacao [tree, seed]; cocoa [tree, powder, drink]. *2* (Am.) *pedir* ~, to beg mercy.

**cacaraña** *f.* pit [in the face], pockmark.
**cacarañado, -da** *adj.* pitted, pock-marked.
**cacarañar** *tr.* to pockmark, to scar. *2* (Am.) to pinch, to scratch.
**cacarear** *intr.* [of fowls] to cackle, crow. *2* coll. to boast, brag.
**cacareo** *m.* cackling, crowing [of fowls]. *2* coll. boasting, bragging.
**cacatúa** *f.* ORN. cockatoo.
**cacera** *f.* irrigation ditch.
**cacería** *f.* hunt, hunting party. *2* bag [game shot]. *3* PAINT. hunting scene.
**cacerina** *f.* cartridge pouch.
**cacerola** *f.* casserole, saucepan.
**cacicato, cacicazgo** *m.* dignity or territory of a cacique. *2* political fief.
**cacillo** *m. dim.* small dipper or ladle.
**cacique** *m.* cacique, Indian chief. *2* political boss.
**caciquismo** *m.* bossism.
**caco** *m.* thief, burglar. *2* coll, coward.
**cacodilato** *m.* CHEM. cacodylate.
**cacofonía** *f.* cacophony.
**cactáceo, -a, cácteo, -a** *adj.* BOT. cactaceous.
**cacto** *m.* BOT. cactus.
**cacumen** *m.* coll. acumen, brains, head.
**cacha** *f.* side of a razor or knife handle. *2* cheek. *3* buttock [of a rabbit].
**cachada** *f.* stroke of one top [toy] against another.
**cachafaz** *m.* (Am.) rogue, scoundrel, rascal.
**cachalote** *m.* ZOOL. cachalot, sperm whale.
**cachar** *tr.* to break in pieces, to split.
**cacharrería** *f.* crockery shop.
**cacharrero, -ra** *m.-f.* crockery seller.
**cacharro** *m.* crock, piece of crockery. *2* coll. rattletrap; rickety machine or car.
**cachava** *f.* shinny [game and stick]. *2* crook, hooked staff.
**cachaza** *f.* slowness, phlegm, coolness.
**cachazudo, -da** *adj.* slow, leisurely, phlegmatic, cool.
**cachear** *tr.* to search, frisk [a person].
**cachemir** *m.*, **cachemira** *f.* CASIMIR.
**Cachemira** *f. pr. n.* Kashmir.
**cacheo** *m.* searching, frisking [a person].
**cacheta** *f.* spring-catch [of a lock].
**cachetada,** *f.* **cachetazo** *m.* slap, whack, smack.
**cachete** *m.* punch [in the face or the head]. *2* plump cheek. *3* short dagger.
**cachetear** *tr.* to slap, to whack, to smack.
**cachetudo, -da** *adj.* plum-cheeked.
**cachifollar** *tr.* to squash, humiliate.
**cachimba** *f.* smoking pipe.
**cachipolla** *f.* ENT. dayfly, May fly.
**cachiporra** *f.* club, bludgeon.
**cachirulo** *m.* liquor container. *2* NAUT. small three-masted vessel.
**cachivache** *m.* vessel, pot, utensil.
**cacho, -cha** *adj.* GACHO. *2 m.* bit. piece, fragment. *3* a fresh-water fish. *4* card game.
**cachondearse** *ref.* to poke fun at somebody.
**cachondeo** *m.* coll. ragging, leg- pulling, jeering, joking, teasing: *armar ~,* to mess about, to lark about; *sin ~,* no messing about, no joking; *tomárselo a ~,* to take it as a joke.
**cachondez** *f.* heat, rut, readiness to mate. *2* lust, randiness, lechery.
**cachondo, -da** *adj.* on heat, in rut, rutting. *2* coll. randy, lusty. *3* hilarious, funny.
**cachorrillo** *m.* obs. small pistol.
**cachorro, -rra** *m.-f.* pup, puppy, whelp, cub. *2* CACHORRILLO.

**cachú** *m.* catechu.
**cachucha** *f.* small rowboat. *2* man's cap. *3* Andalusian dance.
**cachuchear** *tr.* to caress, to fondle.
**cachuela** *f.* stew.
**cachumbo** *m.* GACHUMBO.
**cachunde** *f.* cachou. *2* catechu.
**cachupín** *m.* (Am.) Spaniard who settles in Spanish America.
**cada** *adj.* each, every: *~ cual, ~ uno,* each one, every one, *~ y cuando que,* provided; as soon as; *~ dos días,* every other day. *2 m.* ENEBRO.
**cadalso** *m.* scaffold, platform, stage, stand. *2* scaffold for capital punishment.
**cadáver** *m.* corpse, cadaver.
**cadavérico, -ca** *adj.* cadaverous.
**cadejo** *m.* small skein. *2* tangled hair.
**cadena** *f.* chain [connected series of links; restraining force; sequence, series of events, mountains, etc.]: *~ de neumático,* tire chain; *~ de agrimensor,* surveyor's chain; *~ de montañas,* range, chain of mountains; *~ sin fin,* endless chain. *2* chain gang. *3* ARCH. pier [in a wall]. *4* LAW. imprisonment; *~ perpetua,* imprisonment for life. *5* CHEM. chain.
**cadencia** *f.* cadence, cadency, rhythm, rhythmical flow. *2* MUS. cadence.
**cadencioso, -sa** *adj.* cadenced, rhythmical.
**cadeneta** *f.* chain stitch.
**cadera** *f.* ANAT. hip. *2* coxa [of arthropod].
**cadete** *m.* MIL. cadet.
**cadí** *m.* cadi [Mohammedan judge].
**Cádiz** *pr. n.* GEOG. Cadiz.
**cadillo** *m.* BOT. hedgehog parsley. *2* BOT. burdock. *3* wart. *4 pl.* WEAV. [warp] thrums.
**cadmio** *m.* CHEM. cadmium.
**caducar** *intr.* to dote [from old age]. *2* to fall into disuse. *3* LAW., COM. TO LAPSE, TO EXPIRE.
**caduceo** *m.* caduceus, Mercury's staff.
**caducidad** *f.* caducity, lapse.
**caduco, -ca** *adj.* caducous.
**caedizo, -za** *adj.* easily falling. *2* BOT. deciduous.
**caer** *intr.-ref.* to fall, drop, fall down, come down; to tumble down; to fall off or out: *~ al suelo* or *en tierra,* to fall to the ground; *~ enfermo,* to fall ill; *~ en una trampa, en la miseria,* to fall into a trap, into poverty: *caerse de viejo,* to totter with age. *2* to realize; *~ en la cuenta de,* to realize; *ya caigo,* I see it, I understand now. *3* [of interests] to become due. *4* to fall, to come [by lot, inheritance, etc.]: *~ en suerte,* to fall to one's lot. *5* to lie, be located: *el camino cae a la derecha,* the way lies to the right. *6* [of the sun] to go down. *7* to fall, occur: *~ en viernes,* to fall on friday. *8* *caerse de su peso* or *de suyo,* to be self-evident. *9* [of the day] to decline; [of the night] to fall: *al ~ de la noche,* at nightfall. *10* *caérsele a uno la cara de vergüenza,* to be ashamed. *11* to fall [in battle]. *12* *~ bien* or *mal,* to suit, fit, become, or not to suit, fit, become. *13* *estar al ~* [of an event] to be imminent, about to happen. ¶ CONJUG.: IND. Pres.: *caigo, caes,* etc. | Pret.: *caí, caíste, cayó; caímos, caísteis, cayeron.* | SUBJ. Pres.: *caiga, caigas, caiga; caigamos, caigáis, caigan.* | Imperf.: *cayera, cayeras,* etc., or *cayese, cayeses,* etc. | Fut.: *cayere, cayeres,* etc. | IMPER.: *cae, caiga; caigamos, caed, caigan.* | GER.: *cayendo.*
**café** *m.* coffee [tree; seeds; beverage]. *2* café: *~ cantante,* café-chantant, cabaret.
**cafeína** *f.* CHEM. caffein.

**cafetal** *m.* coffee plantation.
**cafetera** *f.* coffee-pot: ~ *de filtro*, percolator.
**cafetería** *f.* coffee house, bar.
**cafetero, -ra** *adj.* [pertaining to] coffee. *2 m.-f.* coffee gatherer. *3* keeper of a café.
**cafetín** *m.* small café.
**cafeto** *m.* BOT. coffee tree or plant.
**cáfila** *m.* coll. multitude, large number.
**cafre** *adj.-n.* Kaffir. *2* savage, inhuman [person]. *3* rude, rustic [person].
**caftán** *m.* caftan.
**cagaaceite** *m.* ORN. missel thrush.
**cagachín** *m.* ENT. small reddish mosquito.
**cagada** *f.* flyspeck. *2* droppings. *3* coll. shit. *4* coll. crap.
**cagadero** *m.* coll. bog, loo, latrine, john.
**cagado, -da** *adj.* coll. cowardly, yellow, yellow-bellied. *2 estar* ~, to be shit-scared.
**cagafierro** *m.* iron slag or scoria.
**cagajón** *m.* horse, mule or ass dung.
**cagalera, cagaleta** *f.* coll. diarrhea, the runs. *2 tener* ~, to be shit-scared.
**cagar** *intr., tr.-ref.* vulg. to defecate, go to stool. *2 tr.* vulg. to soil, defile; to make a botch of. *3 ref.* vulg. to be cowed.
**cagarria** *f.* BOT. morel.
**cagarruta** *f.* goat or sheep dung.
**cagatinta** *m.* coll. penpusher.
**cagón, -na** *adj.* cowardly. *2 m.-f.* coward.
**cagueta** *adj.* yellow, yellow-bellied. *2* diarrheic. *3 n.* chicken. *4* diarrheic child.
**caid** *m.* kaid.
**caída** *f.* fall, drop; downfall; falling off or out. *2* fall, descent [on ground]. *3* lapse, spiritual ruin. *4* arrangement of folds [of drapery]. *5* NAUT. depth, hoist [of a sail]. *6 a la* ~ *del sol*, at sunset; *a la* ~ *de la tarde*, in the late afternoon. *7 pl.* witty remarks; native wit.
**caído, -da** *adj.* fallen. *2* weak, downhearted. *3* drooping [eyelids, shoulders, etc.]. *4 m. pl.* interest due. *5 los caídos*, the fallen [in battle].
**Caifás** *m. pr. n.* Caiaphas.
**caigo, caiga** etc. *irr.* V. CAER.
**caimán** *m.* ZOOL. alligator, cayman.
**caimiento** *m.* fall. *2* downheartedness, languidness.
**caimito** *m.* BOT. star apple.
**Caín** *m. pr. n.* Cain: *pasar las de Caín*, to have a terrible time.
**cairel** *m.* crown of false hair. *2* fringe trimming.
**Cairo (El)** *m. pr. n.* Cairo.
**caja** *f.* box, chest, case, casing: ~ *de cambios de marcha*, AUTO. gearshift box; ~ *de ingletes*, mitre box; ~ *del tambor* o *del tímpano*, ANAT. eardrum; ~ *de música*, musical box. *2* cash box, safe; cashier's office or desk: ~ *fuerte* or *de caudales*, safe, strong box; ~ *registradora*, cash register. *3* name of some institutions: ~ *de ahorros*, savings bank; ~ *de reclutamiento*, MIL. induction centre. *4* frame, shell [of pulley]. *5* coffin. *6* body [of carriage; of a violin, guitar, etc.]. *8* stock [of firearm]. *9* well [of staircase]. *10* MUS. drum. *11* socket, mortise; ~ *y espiga*, mortise and tenon. *12* BOT. capsule. *13* PRINT. case: ~ *alta*, upper case; ~ *baja*, lower case.
**cajel** *adj.* bittersweet [orange].
**cajero** *m.* box maker. *2* cashier.
**cajetilla** *f.* packet, pack [of cigarettes].
**cajetín** *m.* rubber stamp. *2* box [in a printing case].
**cajiga** *f.* QUEJIGO.

**cajigal** *m.* QUEJIGAL.
**cajista** *m.* PRINT. compositor.
**cajón** *m.* large box, bin. *2* drawer, till, locker: ~ *de sastre*, miscellany, odds and ends. *3* wooden stand or shed [for selling or working]. *4* (Am.) grocer's shop. *5* ENG. ~ *hidráulico*, caisson. *6 ser de* ~, to be customary, be a matter of course.
**cal** *f.* lime [burned limestone]: ~ *viva*, quicklime; ~ *muerta*, slaked lime; *de* ~ *y canto*, fig. firm, solid.
**cala** *f.* cove, small bay. *2* fishing ground. *3* plugging [a melon, etc.]. *4* plug [cut out of a melon, etc.]. *5* hole made in a wall to try its thickness. *6*). suppository. *7* SURG. probe. *8* NAUT. hold. *9* BOT. calla, calla lily.
**calabacear** *tr.* to fail, turn down [in examination]. *2* to refuse [a lover], to give the mitten to.
**calabacín** *m.* BOT. vegetable marrow. *2* fig. dolt.
**calabacino** *m.* gourd [used as a bottle].
**calabaza** *f.* calabash, gourd, pumpkin, squash [plant and fruit]: ~ *confitera*, pumpkin; ~ *vinatera*, bottle gourd; *dar calabazas*, fig. CALABACEAR. *2* fig. dolt.
**calabazada** *f.* knock with the head: *darse de calabazadas*, to rack one's brains.
**calabazar** *m.* AGR. pumpkin field, gourd field.
**calabazazo** *m.* knock on the head.
**calabazo** *m.* gourd, pumpkin. *2* calabash.
**calabobos** *m.* drizzle.
**calabocero** *m.* jailer.
**calabozo** *m.* dungeon. *2* cell [of jail]. *3* pruning sickle.
**calabrés, -sa** *adj.-n.* Calabrian.
**calabriada** *f.* mixture of wines. *2* medley.
**calabrote** *m.* NAUT. cable, laid rope.
**calada** *f.* soaking. *2* sinking [of a fishing net]. *3* swoop [of a bird of prey]. *4* WEAV. shed.
**caladio** *m.* BOT. caladium.
**calado** *m.* drawn work [in linen]; openwork [in metal, stone, etc.]; fretwork. *3* NAUT. draught. *4* NAUT. depth [of water].
**calafate** *m.* NAUT. caulker. *2* shipwright.
**calafateado** *m.* CALAFATEO.
**calafatear** *tr.* to caulk [a boat or crevice].
**calafateo** *m.* NAUT. caulking.
**calamar** *m.* ZOOL. squid, calamary.
**calambac** *m.* BOT. calambac.
**calambre** *m.* MED. cramp.
**calambuco** *m.* BOT. calaba tree.
**calamento** *m.* BOT. calamint.
**calamidad** *f.* calamity, grievous disaster. *2* fig. *ser una* ~, to be a nuisance.
**calamina** *f.* MINER. calamine.
**calaminta** *f.* BOT. calamint.
**calamita** *f.* MINER. lodestone.
**calamite** *m.* ZOOL. green toad.
**calamitoso, -sa** *adj.* calamitous.
**cálamo** *m.* ancient flute. *2* poet, reed. *3* poet. writing pen. *4* BOT. smooth stem [as in rushes]. *5* BOT. a graminaceous plant.
**calamocano** *adj.* coll. tipsy. *2* coll. doting.
**calamoco** *m.* icicle.
**calamón** *m.* ORN. purple gallinule. *2* roundheaded brass nail.
**calamorra** *f.* coll. head.
**calandrado** *m.* calendering.
**calandrajo** *m.* rag, talter. *2* despicable person.
**calandrar** *tr.* to calender.
**calandrero** *m.* calenderer.
**calandria** *f.* ORN. calander, lark. *2* calender, mangle [machine]. *3* hoisting treadmill.

**calaña** *f.* pattern, model. *2* kind, sort, nature.
**calañés** *adj.* designating a kind of Andalusian hat.
**cálao** *m.* ORN. hornbill.
**1) calar** *tr.* to soak, drench. *2* to go through, pierce, penetrate. *3* to make drawn work in [linen]; to cut open work in [paper, metal, etc.]. *4* to plug [a melon]. *5* to incline [pikes, etc.] ready to use them. *6* to fix [the bayonet]. *7* to size up, to see through [a person, his intentions, etc.]. *8* NAUT. to lower [a yard]. *9* to sink [a fishing net, etc.]. *10 intr.* NAUT. [of a ship] to draw. *11 ref.* to get soaked or drenched. *12* to enter, get in. *13* to pull on or down [one's hat or cap]. *14* [of birds] to swoop.
**2) calar** *adj.* calcareous. *2 m.* limestone quarry.
**calavera** *f.* [fleshless] skull; death's head. *2* madcap, gay blade, profligate.
**calaverada** *f.* reckless action, escapade.
**calaverear** *intr.* to act recklessly. *2* to have a ball, to whoop it up.
**calcado** *m.* calking, calquing, tracing.
**calcador, -ra** *n.* tracer.
**calcáneo** *m.* ANAT. calcaneum, calcaneus.
**calcañal, calcañar** *m.* heel [of the human foot].
**calcar** *tr.* to calk or calque; to trace, transfer [a drawing]. *2 fig.* to imitate.
**calcáreo, -a** *adj.* calcareous.
**calce** *m.* steel tire [of a wheel]. *2* shim, wedge; chock.
**calcedonia** *f.* MINER. chalcedony.
**calceolado, -da** *adj.* BOT. calceolate.
**calceolaria** *f.* BOT. calceolaria.
**calcés** *m.* NAUT. masthead.
**calceta** *f.* stocking, hose: *hacer ~,* to knit.
**calcetería** *f.* hosiery.
**calcetín** *m.* sock.
**cálcico, -ca** *adj.* CHEM. calcic.
**calcificación** *f.* calcification.
**calcificar** *tr.* to calcify.
**calcinación** *f.* calcination.
**calcina** *f.* concrete.
**calcinar** *tr.* to calcine. *2 ref.* to calcine [undergo calcination].
**calcio** *m.* CHEM. calcium.
**calcita** *f.* MINER. calcite, calcspar.
**calcitrapa** *f.* BOT. star thistle.
**calco** *m.* copy made by tracing. *2* copy, imitation.
**calcografía** *f.* chalcography.
**calcomanía** *f.* decalcomania.
**calculable** *adj.* calculable.
**calculadamente** *adv.* in a calculating way.
**calculador, -ra** *adj.* calculating. *2 m.-f.* calculator [person]. *3 f.* calculator [machine].
**calcular** *tr.-intr.* to calculate. *2 tr.* to conjecture, guess.
**calculista** *m.-f.* calculator, designer.
**cálculo** *m.* calculation, computation, estimate. *2* conjecture, guess. *3* MATH., MED. calculus.
**calculoso, -sa** *adj.* MED. calculous.
**calda** *f.* warming, heating. *2 pl.* hot springs, hot mineral-water baths.
**caldaico, -ca** *adj.* Chaldaic, Chaldean.
**Caldea** *f. pr. n.* Chaldea.
**caldeamiento** *m.* heating.
**caldear** *tr.* to warm, heat. *2 ref.* to heat [grow ot].
**1) caldeo** *m.* warming, heating.
**2) caldeo, -a** *adj.-n.* Chaldean.
**caldera** *f.* cauldron, cooper, kettle: *calderas de Pedro Botero,* coll. hell. *2* MACH. boiler: *~ de vapor,* steam boiler. *3* shell of a kettle-drum.
**calderada** *f.* cauldron [contents of cauldron].

**calderería** *f.* boilermaker trade or shop.
**calderero** *m.* boilermaker, coppersmith.
**caldereta** *f.* small cauldron. *2* holy-water pot. *3* fish-stew. *4* lamb-stew.
**calderilla** *f.* holy-water pot. *2* copper coins.
**caldero** *m.* semispherical kettle or small cauldron.
**calderón** *m.* large cauldron. *2* PRINT. paragraph mark [¶]. *3* MUS. hold, pause; its symbol.
**caldo** *m.* broth, bouillon: *~ de cultivo,* BACT. broth; *~ de la Reina,* eggnog; *hacer el ~ gordo a,* to play into the hands of. *2 pl.* COM. vegetable juices, as wine, oil, etc.
**caldoso, -sa** *adj.* having plenty of broth.
**calducho** *m.* hogwash.
**calé** *m.* Spanish gypsy.
**Caledonia** *f. pr. n.* GEOG. Caledonia. *Nueva ~,* New Caledonia.
**calefacción** *f.* heating; heating system.
**calefactor** *m.* heating engineer.
**caleidoscopio** *m.* kaleidoscope.
**calendario** *m.* calendar: *hacer calendarios,* fig. to muse; to make hasty forecasts.
**calendas** *f. pl.* calends: *~ griegas,* Greek calends.
**caléndula** *f.* BOT. pot marigold.
**calentador** *m.* heater; warming pan: *~ a gas,* gas heater *~ de cama,* warming pan.
**calentamiento** *m.* warming, heating.
**calentar** *tr.* to warm, heat, warm up, heat up: *~ las orejas a,* fig. to chide, dress down. *2* to beat, spank. *3 ref.* to warm oneself; to warm or heat up. *4* [of animals] to be in heat. ¶ CONJUG. like *acertar.*
**calentón** *m.* *darse un ~,* to take a bit of a warming.
**calentura** *f.* MED. fever, temperature.
**calenturiento, -ta** *adj.* feverish.
**calenturón** *m.* high fever.
**calesa** *f.* kind of calash.
**calesero** *m.* driver of a CALESA.
**caleta** *f.* small cove or creek.
**caletre** *m.* coll, judgement, acumen, brains.
**calibración** *f.* calibration.
**calibrado** *m.* boring [a cylinder]. *2* gauging.
**calibrador** *m.* cal(l)ipers, gauge.
**calibrar** *tr.* to calibrate; to gauge.
**calibre** *m.* calibre, bore, gauge. *2 fig.* size, importance.
**calicata** *f.* MIN. test pit.
**calicó** *m.* calico.
**calículo** *m.* BOT. calycle.
**calidad** *f.* quality. *2* capacity, position: *en ~ de,* in the capacity of. *3* character, nature. *4* rank, importance. *6 pl.* moral qualities, gifts.
**cálido, -da** *adj.* warm, hot [climate, country]. *2* hot, burning [as pepper]. *3* PAINT. warm [colour].
**calidoscopio** *m.* kaleidoscope.
**calientapiés** *m.* foot warmer.
**calientaplatos** *m.* hot plate, chaffing dish.
**caliente** *adj.* warm, hot. *2* in heat, in rut. *3* PAINT. warm [colour]. *4 adv. en ~,* while hot, at once.
**caliento, caliente,** etc. *irr.* V. CALENTAR.
**califa** *m.* caliph.
**califato** *m.* caliphate.
**calificable** *adj.* qualifiable.
**calificación** *f.* qualification, rating. *2* judgement, grading [of marks]. *3* mark [in examination].
**calificado, -da** *adj.* qualified, competent. *2* [of a thing] having all the necessary conditions.
**calificador, -ra** *m.-f.* qualifier, examiner, judge. *2 m.* ECCL. qualificator.
**calificar** *tr.* to determine, express or denote the

qualities or attributes of; to apply an epithet to: ~ *de*, to qualify, rate or class as, to call. *2* to ennoble, give credit to. *3* to award marks to [in examination].

**calificativo, -va** *adj.* GRAM. qualifying [adjective]. *2 m.* GRAM. qualifier [adjective]; epithet.

**California** *f. pr. n.* GEOG. California.

**californiano, -na** *adj.-n.* Californian.

**calígine** *f.* gloom, darkness.

**caliginoso, -sa** *adj.* misty, caliginous.

**caligrafía** *f.* calligraphy.

**calígrafo** *m.* calligrapher, calligraphist.

**calina** *f.* haze.

**calinoso, -sa** *adj.* hazy.

**Calíope** *f. pr. n.* MYTH. Calliope.

**calipso** *m.* calypso.

**calistenia** *f.* calisthenics.

**cáliz** *m.* chalice [cup]. *2* BOT. calyx, chalice. *3* ANAT. calyx. *4* fig. cup of sorrow.

**caliza** *f.* limestone.

**calizo, -za** *adj.* calcareous, limy.

**calma** *f.* METEOR. calm: ~ *chicha*, dead calm. *2* calm, inactivity, let-up. *3* allayment, cessation [of pain]. *4* peace, calmness. *5* calmness, composure. *6* slowness, phlegm. *7 en* ~, calm, quiet; motionless [sea].

**calmante** *adj.* assuaging, soothing. *2 m.* MED. calmative, sedative.

**calmar** *tr.* to calm, quiet, pacify. *2* to allay, soothe. *3 intr.* [of wind] to abate. *4 intr.-ref.* to abate, calm down. *5* to calm oneself; to be allayed.

**calmo, -ma** *adj.* barren, treeless. *2* at rest.

**calmoso, -sa** *adj.* calm, quiet. *2* slow, sluggard.

**calmuco, -ca** *adj.-n.* Kalmuck.

**caló** *m.* slang of gypsies and low-class people.

**calofrío** *m.* ESCALOFRÍO.

**calomelanos** *m. pl.* calomel.

**calor** *m.* heat, warmth, hotness: *hacer* ~, [of weather], to be hot: *tener* ~, [of a person] to feel warm, hot. *2* glow, heat, warmth [excitement, enthusiasm], ardour, heat, animation. *3* heat [of a battle, a debate, etc.].

**caloría** *f.* PHYS., PHYSIOL. calorie.

**calórico** *m.* caloric.

**calorífero, -ra** *adj.* heat-conducting. *2 m.* heater [for a room]. *3* foot warmer.

**calorífico, -ca** *adj.* calorific.

**calorífugo, -ga** *adj.* heat-resistant, uninflammable.

**calorimetría** *f.* calorimetry.

**calorimétrico, -ca** *adj.* calorimetric, calorimetrical.

**calostro** *m.* colostrum.

**calta** *f.* BOT. caltha, marsh marigold.

**calumet** *m.* calumet, peace pipe.

**calumnia** *f.* calumny, slander.

**calumniar** *tr.* to calumniate, to slander.

**calumnioso, -sa** *adj.* calumnious, slanderous.

**calurosamente** *adj.* warmly, heartily, enthusiastically. *2* hotly, passionately.

**caluroso, -sa** *adj.* hot [weather]. *2* [of a person] sensitive to heat. *3* warm, hearty, enthusiastic.

**calva** *f.* bald head, bald pate. *2* bald spot or patch [in head, fields, woods, fur, or velvet].

**Calvario** *m. pr. n.* Calvary. *2 m.* (not cap.) calvary. *3* series of debts.

**calvero** *m.* clearing, bare spot [in a wood].

**calvez, calvicie** *f.* baldness.

**calvinismo** *m.* Calvinism.

**calvinista** *adj.* Calvinistic. *2 adj.-n.* Calvinist.

**Calvino** *m. pr. n.* HIST. Calvin.

**calvo, -va** *adj.* bald, hairless, bald-headed, bald-pated. *2* bare, barren [land].

**calza** *f.* coll. stocking: ~ *de arena*, sandbag. *2* wedge. *3 pl.* hose; breeches: *calzas atacadas*, laced breeches.

**calzada** *f.* paved road, causey, causeway: ~ *romana*, Roman road.

**calzado, -da** *adj.* shod. *2* calced, calceate. *3* with feet of a different colour to the rest of the body [animal]. *4* braccate [bird]. *5 m.* footwear.

**calzador** *m.* shoehorn.

**calzadura** *f.* putting on shoes.

**calzapiés** *m.* toe clip.

**calzar** *tr.-ref.* to put on [any article of footwear; gloves; spurs]. *2 ref.* to put one's shoes on. *3 tr.* to shoe, put the shoes on [a person]. *4* to supply with shoes. *5* to wear [gloves or spurs]. *6* to take [a certain size of shoe or glove]: fig. ~ *poco* or *pocos puntos*, not to be very intelligent. *7* to shim, wedge up. *8* to scotch [a wheel]. *9* PRINT. to underclay.

**calzo** *m.* shim, wedge, chock, scotch. *2* NAUT. quoin, chuck. *3 pl.* stockings [of horses].

**calzón, calzones** *m. sing.* or *pl.* breeches, trousers: ~ *corto*, knee breeches; *llevar los calzones* [of a woman], to wear the trousers.

**calzonazos** *m.* weak, soft fellow.

**calzoncillos** *m. pl.* drawers, pants [for men].

**calzorras** *m.* coll. henpecked husband.

**callada** *m.* a meal of tripe. *2* silence, keeping silent: *dar la* ~ *por respuesta*, to give no answer; *a las calladas, de* ~, on the quiet, secretly.

**calladamente** *adj.* silently, quietly, secretly.

**callado, -da** *adj.* silent, quiet. *2* reserved, reticent.

**callandico, -dito** *adv.* silently, stealthily, softly.

**callar** *intr.-ref.* to be, keep or become silent; to shut up, be quiet: *callarse la boca*, to shut up; *quien calla otorga*, silence gives consent. *2 tr.-ref.* to keep to oneself, keep secret, not to mention. *3 interj.* ¡calla! or ¡calle!, why!, don't tell me!

**calle** *f.* street: ~ *mayor*, high street, main street; *dejar en la* ~, fig. to deprive of one's livelihood; *echar, poner* or *plantar a uno en la* ~, to dismiss someone; *echarse a la* ~, to go out into the street; to mutiny, rebel, riot; *llevarse a uno de* ~, to sweep away; to convince someone. *3* ~ *de árboles*, alley, glade. *4 abrir* ~, to make way, clear a passage.

**calleja** *f.* CALLEJUELA.

**callejear** *intr.* to lounge about the streets.

**callejeo** *m.* lounging about the streets.

**callejero, -ra** *adj.* [pertaining to the] street. *2* fond of lounging about the streets. *3 m.* street guide.

**callejón** *m.* lane, alley: ~ *sin salida*, blind alley, impasse.

**callejuela** *f.* little street, by-street, alley, lane.

**callicida** *m.* corn remover, corn eradicator.

**callista** *m.-f.* chiropodist, corn doctor.

**callo** *m.* callus, callosity; corn. *2 pl.* tripe.

**callosidad** *f.* callosity.

**calloso, -sa** *adj.* callous, horny.

**cama** *f.* bed, couch; bedstead; ~ *turca*, day bed; *estar en* ~, to be sick in bed; *guardar* ~, to keep one's bed. *2* lair [of wild animals]. *3* part of a melon resting on the ground. *4* brood, litter [young animals]. *5* sheath [of the plough]. *6* COOK. layer or thickness [of food]. *7* MACH. cam.

**camada** *f.* brood, litter [young animals]. *2* bed, layer. *3* gang, band [of thieves, etc.].

**camafeo** *m.* cameo.

**camal** *m.* halter. *2* (Am.) slaughterhouse.

**camaleón** m. ZOOL. & fig. chameleon.
**camalote** m. BOT. South-American river plant.
**camamila** f. CAMOMILA.
**camándula** f. trickery, hypocrisy: *tener muchas camándulas*, to be full of tricks.
**camandulería** f. prudery, hypocrisy.
**camandulero, -ra** adj. hypocritical, sly, tricky.
**cámara** f. chamber, room [in some cases]: ~ *nupcial*, nuptial chamber. 2 royal chamber. 3 grain loft; granary. 4 NAUT. stateroom ward-room; cabin. 5 chamber, house [legislative body]: ~ *alta*, senate; ~ *baja*, Chamber of Deputies; ~ *de compensación*, COM. clearing house. 6 chamber [cavity]; ~ *de aire*, air chamber. 7 OPT. camera: ~ *oscura*, camera obscura. 8 inner tube [of tire]. 9 PHYSIOL. stool.
**camarada** m. comrade, companion, pal, chum.
**camaradería** f. camaraderie, good-fellowship.
**camarera** f. head maid. 2 chambermaid. 3 waitress. 4 stewardess [on ship]. 5 lady in waiting.
**camarero** m. waiter. 2 steward [in a ship]. 3 papal chamberlain.
**camareta** f. NAUT. cabin [of a small ship]. 2 NAUT. mess-room. 3 NAUT. ~ *alta*, deckhouse.
**camarilla** f. coterie, clique, cabal.
**camarín** m. little chapel behind an altar. 2 THEAT. dressing room. 3 closet [private room]. 4 car [of a lift or elevator].
**camarista** f. lady in waiting.
**camarlengo** m. papal chamberlain.
**camarón** m. ZOOL. a marine shrimp or prawn.
**camaronero, -ra** m.-f. shrimp seller.
**camarote** m. NAUT. cabin, stateroom [for passengers].
**camarroya** f. BOT. wild chicory.
**camastro** m. wretched bed. 2 MIL. sleeping boards in a guardhouse.
**camastrón** m. cunning, sly person.
**cambalache** m. barter of cheap things. 2 (Am.) second-hand shop.
**cambalachear** tr. to barter, exchange.
**cámbaro** m. ZOOL. crab, green crab.
**cambiable** adj. changeable. 2 exchangeable.
**cambiadiscos** m. record changer.
**cambiadizo, -za** adj. inconsistent, changeable, variable.
**cambiador, -ra** adj. changing; exchanging. 2 s. changer.
**cambiante** adj. changing; fickle. 2 m.-f. money-changer. 3 m. pl. iridescence.
**cambiar** intr.-tr. to change, alter. 2 to change, shift: ~ *de ropa*, to change clothes. 3 tr. to change, convert: ~ *en*, to change into. 4 to change, exchange; ~ *por*, to exchange for. 5 to exchange [money]. 6 intr.-ref. [of the wind] to veer.
**cambiazo** m. *dar el* ~, to make a fraudulent substitution.
**cambio** m. change [alteration; substitution, etc.]; shift, shifting: ~ *de domicilio*, change of address. 2 change [of money]. 3 small change, exchange, barter: *libre* ~, free trade; *a* ~ *de*, in exchange for; *en* ~, in exchange. 4 market price [of bonds, shares, etc.]. 5 BOT. cambium. 6 AUTO., MECH. shift: ~ *de marchas*, gearshift. 7 RLY. switch.
**cambista** m.-f. money-changer. 2 m. banker.
**cambium** m. BOT. cambium.
**Camboya** f. pr. n. GEOG. Cambodia.
**camboyano, -na** adj.-n. Cambodian.
**cambray** m. cambric [linen].

**cambriano, -na; cámbrico, -ca** adj.-n. Cambrian.
**cambrón** m. BOT. boxthorn. 2 BOT. buckthorn. 3 BOT. bramble. 4 pl. BOT. Christ's-thorn.
**cambronal** m. thicket of boxthorn, buckthorn or brambles.
**cambronera** f. BOT. boxthorn.
**cambur** m. BOT. kind of banana.
**camedrio** m. BOT. germander, wall germander.
**camelar** tr. to court, flirt with. 2 to cajole.
**cameleo** m. coll. flattery.
**camelia** f. BOT. camellia.
**camelo** m. courting, flirtation. 2 deception.
**camelote** m. camlet. 2 BOT. a tropical weed.
**camella** f. ZOOL. she-camel. 2 GAMELLA.
**camellero** m. camel driver, camel keeper.
**camello** m. ZOOL., NAUT. camel.
**camellón** m. CABALLÓN.
**camerino** m. THEAT. dressing room.
**camero, -ra** adj. full-sized [bed]. 2 suitable for a full-sized bed.
**Camerún** m. pr. n. GEOG. Cameroons.
**Camilo** m. pr. n. Camillus.
**camilla** f. stretcher, litter. 2 small bed, couch. 3 table with a heater underneath.
**camillero** m. stretcher-bearer.
**caminador, -ra** adj. good-walking. 2 m.-f. good walker.
**caminante** m.-f. traveller, wayfarer.
**caminar** intr. to travel, journey. 2 to walk, march, go, move along. 3 fig. ~ *derecho*, to act uprightly. 4 tr. to cover [a distance] walking.
**caminata** f. long walk, hike, march, excursion.
**caminero, -ra** adj. [pertaining to] road: *peón* ~, road mender.
**camino** m. path, road, way, -track, course: ~ *cubierto*, FORT. cover or covered way; ~ *de herradura*, bridle path; ~ *de hierro*, railway; *abrirse* ~, to make a way for oneself; *allanar el* ~, to smooth the way; *ir por buen* ~, to be on the right track; *llevar* ~ *de*, to be on the way to. 2 way, journey, travel: *ponerse en* ~, to start, set off on a journey; *de* ~, in passing, by the way; *en* ~, on the way. 3 ~ *de mesa*, runner [on a table].
**camión** m. camion, lorry, truck, motor truck.
**camionaje** m. trucking, truck transport. 2 truckage.
**camionero** m. truck driver, lorry driver.
**camioneta** f. light motor van.
**camisa** f. shirt; chemise: ~ *de dormir*, nightgown, nightdress; ~ *de fuerza*, strait jacket; *dejar a uno sin* ~, to clean someone out; *meterse en* ~ *de once varas*, to meddle in something that is not one's concern; *no llegarle a uno la* ~ *al cuerpo*, to be frightened; to be anxious. 2 BOT. tegmen [of a seed]. 3 slough [of a serpent]. 4 FORT. chemise. 5 MECH. jacket, casing, lining. 6 folder [for papers]. 7 incandescent gas mantle. 8 PRINT. linen case [for roller].
**camisería** f. shirt factory. 2 shirt shop.
**camisero, -ra** n. shirt maker, outfitter. 2 adj. shirtlike: *blusa* ~, shirt blouse.
**camiseta** f. vest, undervest, undershirt.
**camisola** f. ruffled shirt. 2 shirt of fine linen.
**camisolín** m. dicky, dickey [false shirt front].
**camisón** m. nightshirt, nightgown, nightdress.
**camomila** f. BOT., PHARM. camomile, chamomile.
**camorra** f. row, quarrel: *armar* ~, to raise a row; *buscar* ~, to look for trouble. 2 Camorra.
**camorrista** adj. quarrelsome. 2 m.-f. quarrelsome person.
**campal** adj. pitched [battle].

**campamento** *m.* camp, camping; encampment.
**campana** *f.* bell [of church, tower, etc.]: *echar las campanas al vuelo*, to publish [something] jubilantly; 2 bell-shaped object: ~ *de buzo*, diving bell; ~ *de chimenea* or *de hogar*, mantel [of a chimney], hood [of a fireplace]; ~ *de vidrio*, bell glass, bell jar. 3 parish church, parish.
**campanada** *f.* stroke of a bell. 2 scandal; sensational happening.
**campanario** *m.* belfry, bell tower, campanile: *de* ~, fig. local, mean, narrow-minded.
**campanear** *intr.* to ring bells frequently.
**campaneo** *m.* bell ringing, chime.
**campanero** *m.* bell founder. 2 bell ringer. 3 ENT. praying cricket, mantis. 4 ORN. bellbird.
**campaniforme** *adj.* campanulate.
**campanil** *m.* CAMPANARIO. 2 *adj.* bell [metal].
**campanilo** *m.* bell tower, belfry, campanile.
**campanilla** *f.* small bell; hand bell, doorbell: *persona de campanillas*, person of great importance or distinction. 2 ANAT. uvula. 3 small tassel. 4 BOT. bellshaped flower.
**campanillazo** *m.* loud ring of a bell.
**campanillear** *intr.* [of a hand bell or a doorbell] to ring, keep on ringing.
**campanilleo** *m.* ringing of a hand bell or a doorbell.
**campanillero** *m.* bellman.
**campanología** *f.* campanology.
**campante** *adj.* satisfied, contented, cheerful.
**campanudo, -da** *adj.* pompous, high-sounding.
**campánula** *f.* BOT. campanula, bell flower.
**campaña** *f.* level country. 2 (Am.) fields, country. 3 [military, commercial, political, etc.] campaign.
**campañol** *m.* ZOOL. vole, meadow mouse.
**campar** *intr.* to excel, to stand out. 2 to camp, encamp. 3 ~ *por sus respetos*, to act according to one's will or fancy; [of things] to prevail.
**campeador** *m.* champion in battle.
**campear** *intr.* to go to pasture. 2 [of wild animals] to go about. 3 [of fields] to grow green. 4 to excel, stand out. 5 MIL. to be in the field.
**campechanía** *f.* frankness, heartiness, good humor.
**campechano, -na** *adj.* frank, open, hearty, good-humored. 2 generous.
**campeche** *m. palo* ~ or *de Campeche*, campeachywood, logwood.
**campeón** *m.* champion. 2 defender.
**campeona** *f.* championess.
**campeonato** *m.* SPORT. championship.
**campero, -ra** *adj.* unsheltered, in the open field. 2 sleeping in the open [cattle]. 4 (Arg.) good at farming.
**campesinado** *m.* peasantry, peasants [pl.].
**campesino, -na** *adj.* country, rural, peasant. 2 *m.-f.* peasant, countryman, countrywoman.
**campestre** *adj.* campestrian, field, rural, country.
**camping** *m.* camping: *ir de* ~, to go camping. 2 camping site or ground.
**campiña** *f.* stretch of arable land; fields, country.
**campista** *m.* camper. 2 (Am.) herdsman, livestock keeper.
**campo** *m.* fields, country, countryside: ~ *raso*, open fields; *a* ~ *raso*, in the open; *a* ~ *traviesa*, aocross the fields. 2 cultivated land, crops. 3 field, ground: ~ *de Agramante*, bedlam [place of confusion]; ~ *de instrucción*, MIL. drill ground; ~ *del honor*, field of honour; ~ *de minas*, MIL., NAV. mine field; ~ *santo*, cemetery. 4 GOLF. links.

5 ground [in painted stuffs, engravings, etc.]. 6 MIL. camp: *levantar el* ~, to raise camp. 7 MIL. army, side. 8 ~ *de concentración*, concentration camp.
**camposanto** *m.* cemetery, graveyard.
**camuflaje** *m.* MIL. camouflage.
**camuflar** *tr.* MIL. to camouflage. 2 to hide, to cover up, to conceal.
**can** *m.* ZOOL. dog. 2 trigger [of firearm]. 3 ARCH. bracket, corbel [projecting timber]; modillion. 4 Khan. 5 ASTR. *Can mayor*, Canis Major, Great Dog; *Can Menor*, Canis Minor, Little Dog.
**cana** *f.* white hair: *peinar canas*, to be old; *echar una* ~ *al aire*, fig. to have a gay time.
**canáceo, -a** *adj.* BOT. cannaceous.
**canaco, -ca** *m.-f.* Kanaka.
**Canadá (el)** *m. pr. n.* GEOG. Canada.
**canadiense** *adj.-s.* Canadian.
**canal** *m.* canal [artificial channel]: ~ *de Suez*, Suez Canal. 2 GEOG. channel, strait: ~ *de la Mancha*, English Channel. 3 channel [deeper part of a river, harbour, etc.]. 4 *m.-f.* natural underground watercourse or duct. 5 ANAT. canal, duct. 6 long, narrow dell. 7 valley, gutter [in a roof]; gutter tile. 8 ARCH. flute. 9 groove. 10 front edge [of a book]. 11 *abrir en* ~, to cut open from top to bottom.
**canalado** *adj.* grooved, fluted.
**canaladura** *f.* ARCH. vertical groove, flute.
**canalera** *f.* roof gutter.
**canalete** *m.* paddle [for canoeing].
**canalización** *f.* canalization, channeling. 2 mains, piping, wiring.
**canalizar** *tr.* to canalize. 2 to channel, pipe, wire.
**canalizo** *m.* NAUT. narrow channel.
**canalón** *m.* rain water pipe; roof gutter. 2 gargoyle.
**canalones** *m. pl.* canneloni, cannelons.
**canalla** *f.* rabble, riffraff. 2 *m.* cad, rascal, scoundrel.
**canallada** *f.* dirty trick, caddish trick.
**canallesco, -ca** *adj.* low, rabblelike. 2 low, caddish, rascally.
**canana** *f.* cartridge belt.
**cananeo, -a** *adj.-n.* Canaanite.
**canapé** *m.* couch, sofa. 2 canapé [appetizer].
**Canarias (islas)** *f. pr. n.* GEOG. Canary Islands.
**canario, -ria** *adj.-n.* Canarian. 2 *m.* ORN. canary, canary bird. 3 *interj.* by Jove!, Great Scott!, *gee!
**canasta** *f.* large round basket. 2 canasta [card game].
**canastilla** *f.* small basket: ~ *de la costura*, sewing basket. 2 layette. 3 trousseau.
**canastillo** *m.* wicker tray. 2 small basket.
**canasto** *m.* large basket. 2 *interj. ¡canastos!*, expression of surprise and annoyance.
**cáncamo** *m.* NAUT. eyebolt, ringbolt.
**cancamurria** *f.* coll gloominess, blues.
**cancamusa** *f.* ruse, trick.
**cancán** *m.* cancan.
**cáncana** *f.* ZOOL. kind of spider.
**cancanear** *intr.* to loiter about.
**cancaneo** *m.* (Am.) sttuttering, stammering. 2 faltering.
**cáncano** *m.* coll. louse.
**cancel** *m.* storm door, wooden screen in the entrance of a church, hall, etc. 2 (Mx.) folding screen.
**cancela** *f.* entrance grating.
**cancelación** *f.* cancellation.

**cancelar** *tr.* to cancel, annul.
**cancelaria** *f.* papal chancery.
**cáncer** *m.* MED. cancer. *2* (cap.) ASTR. Cancer.
**cancerado, -da** *adj.* MED. cancerous, affected with cancer. *2* evil, corrupt [heart, soul].
**Cancerbero** *m.* MYTH. & fig. Cerberus.
**cancerígeno** *adj.* MED. cancerigenic, cancerogenic.
**canceroso, -sa** *adj.* MED. cancerous.
**cancilla** *f.* gate, barrier [in a garden, barnyard, etc.].
**canciller** *m.* chancellor.
**cancillería** *f.* chancellery, chancery.
**canción** *f.* song: ~ *de cuna*, lullaby, cradlesong; ~ *popular*, folk-song. *2* lyric poem.
**cancionero** *m.* collection of lyrics. *2* song-book.
**cancionista** *m.-f.* song composer. *2* singer of songs.
**cancro** *m.* MED. cancer. *2* canker [of trees].
**cancroide** *m.* MED. cancroid tumor.
**cancha** *f.* court for playing pelota. *2* cockpit. *3* (Am.) game ground; tennis court; racecourse.
**canchal** *m.* rocky ground or region.
**cancho** *m.* rock, boulder. *2* rocky ground.
**candado** *m.* padlock.
**candaliza** *f.* NAUT. brail.
**cande** *adj. azúcar* ~, rock candy, sugar candy.
**candeal** *adj.* white [wheat]; *pan* ~, bread made of white wheat.
**candela** *f.* candle, taper. *2* candlestick. *3* chestnut flower. *4* fire [burning coals or wood]. *5 arrimar* ~ *a*, to beat, trash. *6* NAUT. *en* ~, in a vertical position.
**candelabro** *m.* candelabrum.
**candelada** *f.* bonfire.
**candelaria** *f.* BOT. great mullein. *2* (cap.) Candlemas.
**candelero** *m.* candlestick. *2* metal olive-oil lamp. *3* fishing torch. *4* NAUT. stanchion. *5 en* ~, in a position of authority.
**candelilla** *f. dim.* thin candle. *2* SURG. bougie. *3* BOT. catkin. *4* coll. *le hacen candelillas los ojos*, his eyes sparkle with the fumes of wine.
**candente** *adj.* candent, candescent. *2 cuestion* ~, burning question.
**candi** *adj.* candied, formed into sugar crystals, crystalized, rock candy.
**candidato, -ta** *m.-f.* candidate [to post or election].
**candidatura** *f.* list of candidates [to post, election, etc.]. *2* candidacy, *candidature. *3* ballot paper, voting paper.
**candidez** *f.* whiteness. *2* simplicity, naïvety.
**cándido, -da** *adj.* white, snowy. *2* guileless, naïve simple; easy to deceive.
**candil** *m.* open oil lamp. *2* Greek or Roman oil lamp. *3* tine [of antler]. *4* corner [of a cocked hat].
**candileja** *f.* inner receptacle of an oil lamp. *2 pl.* THEAT. footlights.
**candiota** *adj.-n.* Candiot, Candiote. *2 f.* wine barrel. *3* large earthen vessel for wine.
**candiotera** *f.* wine cellar.
**candonga** *f.* ruse, trick. *2* banter, mockery.
**candongo, -ga** *adj.* cunning, wheedling. *2* workshy.
**candonguear** *tr.* to tease, banter, mock. *2 intr.* to shirk work, swing the lead.
**candonguero, -ra** *adj.* jocose, reasing, mocking. *2 s.* teaser, mocker. *3* wheedler.
**candor** *m.* pure whiteness. *2* candour, ingenuousness.
**candoroso, -sa** *adj.* ingenuous, pure, naïve, innocent.
**caneca** *f.* glazed earthen bottle.

**canecillo** *m.* ARCH. bracket, corbel, modillion.
**canela** *f.* cinnamon [bark and spice]. *2* fig. anything exquisite, very fine.
**canelo, -la** *adj.* cinnamon-coloured [dog, horse]. *2 m.* BOT. cinnamon tree.
**canelón** *m.* CANALÓN. *2* icicle. *3* cinnamon candy. *4* tubular element of a fringe.
**canesú** *m.* a woman's corsage. *2* yoke of a shirt or blouse.
**cangilón** *m.* earthen or metal vessel for liquids. *2* bucket [of a wheel]. *3* dredge bucket, scoop. *4* fluting [of a ruff].
**cangreja** *f.* NAUT. *vela* ~, boom-sail, gaff-sail.
**cangrejero, -ra** *m.-f.* crab or crayfish catcher or seller. *2 f.* nest of crabs or crayfish.
**cangrejo** *m.* ZOOL. crab or crayfish: ~ *de río*, freshwater crayfish; ~ *de mar*, crab. *2* NAUT. gaff.
**canguelo** *m.* coll. fear.
**canguro** *m.* ZOOL. kangaroo.
**caníbal** *adj.-n.* Cannibal.
**canibalismo** *m.* Cannibalism.
**canica** *f.* marble [little ball]. *2 pl.* marbles [game].
**canicie** *f.* whiteness of the hair.
**canícula** *f.* dog days. *2* (cap.) ASTR. Canicula, Dog Star.
**canicular** *adj.* canicular.
**cánido, -da** *adj.* ZOOL. canine [animal]. *2 m.* ZOOL. canid. *3 pl.* ZOOL. Canidae.
**canijo, -ja** *adj.* weak, infirm, sickly.
**canilla** *f.* long bone of either extremity; arm bone, leg bone, shinbone. *2* tap, spigot [in a cask or barrel]. *3* WEAV. bobbin, spool, quill. *4* WEAV. unevenness of the woof in thickness or colour.
**canillera** *f.* ESPINILLERA.
**canino, -na** *adj.* canine. *2 m.* ANAT. canine tooth.
**canje** *m.* MIL., DIP., COM. exchange.
**canjeable** *adj.* exchangeable.
**canjear** *tr.* to exchange [prisoners, diplomatic notes, newspapers, etc.].
**cano, -na** *adj.* gray, gray-haired, hoary, white.
**canoa** *f.* canoe: ~ *automóvil*, motor boat.
**canódromo** *m.* dog track.
**canoero, canoísta** *m.* canoeist.
**canon**, *pl.* **cánones** *m.* canon [rule, law]. *2* ECCL., BIBL., MUS., PRINT. canon. *3* Canon [of the Mass]. *4* F. ARTS standard measurements of the human figure. *5* rent, rate, royalty. *6 pl.* canon law.
**canonesa** *f.* canoness.
**canonical** *adj.* canonical [pertaining to a canon or member of a chapter].
**canonicato** *m.* canonicate, canonry.
**canónico, -ca** *adj.* canonical, canonic. *2 derecho* ~, canon law.
**canónigo** *m.* canon, prebendary.
**canonista** *m.* canonist, canon lawyer.
**canonización** *f.* canonization.
**canonizar** *tr.* to canonize.
**canonjía** *f.* canonry. *2* coll. sinecure.
**canoro, -ra** *adj.* canorous. *2* sweet-singing, tuneful [bird].
**canoso, -sa** *adj.* gray-haired, hoary.
**canotié** *m.* straw hat with a low, flat crown.
**cansadamente** *adv.* wearily. *2* wearingly.
**cansado, -da** *adj.* tired, weary. *2* spent, worn-out, exhausted. *3* tiresome, wearisome.
**cansancio** *m.* fatigue, tiredness, weariness.
**cansar** *tr.* to fatigue, tire, weary. *2* to bore, harass. *3* to wear out, exhaust. *4 ref.* to fatigue, tire, grow weary; to become exhausted. *5 intr.* to be tiring or tiresome.

**cansera** f. coll. bother, nuisance. 2 tiredness, weariness.
**cansino, -na** adj. tired, exhausted [animal].
**cantable** adj. singable. 2 MUS. to be sung slowly. 3 m. musical passage [of a ZARZUELA]; words for it.
**cantábrico, ca; cántabro, bra** adj.-n. Cantabrian.
**cantador, -ra** m.-f. singer [of popular songs].
**cantalupo** m. BOT. cantaloupe, cantaloup.
**cantante** adj. singing. 2 m.-f. singer, professional singer.
**cantaor, -ra** n. flamenco singer.
1) **cantar** m. short poem apt for a folk song: fig. éste es otro ~, that's another story. 2 ~ de gesta, chanson de geste. 3 BIBL. Cantar de los Cantares, Song of Songs, Canticles.
2) **cantar** tr.-intr. to sing: cantarlas claras, fig. to call a spade a spade. 2 POET. to chant. 3 [at cards] to declare. 4 ~ misa, [of a priest] to say Mass for the first time. 5 intr. coll. to speak, squeak, confess: ~ de plano, to make a full confession. 6 [of cocks] to crow: en menos que canta un gallo, in a twinkling. 7 [of insects] to chirp, chirr. 8 NAUT. to chantey.
**cántara** f. CÁNTARO. 2 wine measure [32 pints].
**cantarela** f. MUS. treble string [of violin or guitar].
**cantarera** f. shelf for jars, or jugs
**cantarero, -ra** n. potter, dealer in earthenware.
**cantárida** f. ENT. cantharis, Spanish fly. 2 PHARM. cantharides. 3 blister raised by cantharides.
**cantarín, -na** adj. fond of singing; always singing. 2 m.-f. singer.
**cántaro** m. water jar. 2 variable liquid measure. 3 ballot box.
**cantata** f. MUS. cantata.
**cantatriz,** pl. **-trices** f. professional singer [woman].
**cantazo** m. blow given with a stone.
**cante** m. Andalousian singing or song.
**cantera** f. quarry, stone pit. 2 fig. talent, capacity.
**cantería** f. stone cutting [for building]. 2 cutstone work. 3 cut or dressed stone.
**cantero** m. stone cutter. 2 easy-to-break extremity of something hard: ~ de pan, crust of bread.
**cántico** m. canticle, song.
**cantidad** f. MATH., PHON., PROS. quantity. 2 quantity, amount. 3 sum [of money].
**cantiga** f. old poetical composition to be sung.
**cantil** m. shelf, ledge [on coast or under sea].
**cantilena** f. short lyric. 2 song, annoying repetition: la misma ~, the same old song.
**cantiléver** adj.-n. cantilever.
**cantillo** m. small pebble.
**cantimplora** f. siphon [to transfer liquids]. 2 water cooler. 3 canteen, water bottle.
**cantina** f. canteen [in barracks, etc.], railway buffet. 2 (Am.) barroom. 3 lunch box.
**cantinela** f. CANTILENA.
**cantinera** f. vivandière.
**cantinero** m. canteen-keeper.
**canto** m. singing, chant, song: ~ llano, plain chant, plain song. 2 poet. canto. 3 crow [of cock]; chirp, chirr [of insects]. 4 edge, arris. 5 corner, point. 6 edge, thickness: de ~, on edge. 7 back [of knife]. 8 stone: ~ rodado, boulder. 9 · ~ de pan, crust of bread.
**cantón** m. canton, district, region. 2 corner. 3 HER. canton. 4 cantonment.
**cantonal** adj. cantonal.
**cantonero, -ra** adj. loafing. 2 f. corner-plate, rein-

forcement or protection for a corner. 3 RINCONERA. 4 streetwalker.
**cantor, -ra** adj. singing: pájaro ~, song bird. 2 m.-f. singer, songster, songstress. 3 cantor.
**cantoral** m. choir book.
**Cantórbery** m. pr. n. GEOG. Canterbury.
**cantueso** m. BOT. French lavender.
**canturrear** intr. to hum, sing in a low voice.
**canturreo** m. humming, singing in a low voice.
**canturriar** intr. CANTURREAR.
**cánula** f. cannula.
**canutero** m. barrel of pen. 2 pin box, pin case. 3 fountain pen.
**canutillo** m. CAÑUTILLO.
**canzonetista** f. singer, vocalist.
**caña** f. cane [stem]; culm, stem of any graminaceous plant. 2 reed [plant and stem]: correr cañas. formerly, to joust with reed spears. 3 any reedlike plant: ~ de azúcar, cane, sugar cane; ~ de Bengala or de Indias, rotang, rattan palm. 4 long bone [of arm or leg]. 5 shank, cannon [of horse]. 6 leg [of boot]. 7 tall, narrow wine tumbler. 8 tipstock [of firearm]. 9 ~ de pescar, fishing rod. 10 NAUT. ~ del timón, tiller, helm.
**cañacoro** m. BOT. Indian shot, Indian reed.
**cañada** f. glen, dell, hollow. 2 cattle path.
**cañadilla** f. ZOOL. purple shell.
**cañaduz** f. sugar cane.
**cañafístola** or **cañafístula** f. BOT. drumstick tree. 2 PHARM. cassia fistula.
**cañaheja, cañaherla** f. BOT. giant fennel.
**cañamazo** m. hemp tow. 2 burlap. 3 canvas for embroidery. 4 embroidered canvas.
**cañamiel** f. BOT. sugar cane.
**cáñamo** m. hemp [plant and fiber]. 2 hempen cloth.
**cañamón** m. hempseed.
**cañaveral** m. reed plantation. 2 canebrake. 3 sugar plantation.
**cañería** f. conduit, water or gas pipe.
**cañí** m. coll. gypsy.
**cañizal, cañizar** m. CAÑAVERAL.
**cañizo** m. hurdle of reeds [for drying fruit, rearing silkworms, etc.].
**caño** m. short tube or pipe. 2 sewer. 3 spout. 4 wind trunk [of the organ]. 5 jet [of water]. 6 NAUT. narrow channel [of a harbour].
**cañón** m. tube, pipe. 2 barrel [of gun]. 3 organ pipe. 4 flue [of chimney]. 5 quill [of feather]. 6 pinfeather. 7 canyon. 8 ARTILL. cannon, gun: ~ antiaéreo, anti-aircraft gun.
**cañonazo** m. cannon shot; report of a gun.
**cañonear** tr. to shell, to bombard.
**cañoneo** m. cannonade, cannonading, cannonry.
**cañonera** f. FORT. NAUT. embrasure, porthole. 2 NAUT. armed launch. 3 (Am.) holster.
**cañonería** f. MUS. pipework [of organ]. 2 cannon; cannonry, ordnance.
**cañonero, -ra** adj. NAUT. armed [boat]. 2 m. gunboat.
**cañota** f. BOT. a reedlike grass.
**cañuto** m. internode [of cane or reed]. 2 small tube. 3 tale-bearer, squealer.
**caoba** f. BOT. mahogany [tree and wood].
**caobo** m. BOT. mahogany [tree].
**caolín** m. kaolin, kaoline.
**caos** m. chaos.
**caótico, -ca** adj. chaotic.
**capa** f. cloak, mantle, cape: ~ rota, fig. person sent under cover for an important affair; andar de ~ caída, to be on the decline; hacer uno de su ~ un

*sayo*, to do as one pleases in one's own affairs; *de* ~ *y espada*, cloak-and-sword. *2* ECCL. cope, cloak: ~ *magna*, pontifical cope. *3* cope, canopy [of heaven]. *4* cloak, pretence, disguise. *5* coat, coating, couch [of paint, etc.]. *6* stratum. *7* wrapper [of a cigar]. *8* colour [of an animal]. *9* hider, concealer. *10* NAUT. primage, hat money. *11* NAUT. *estar* or *ponerse a la capa*, to lie to.

**capacidad** *f.* capacity [power of holding, etc.], content, capaciousness. *2* capacity, capability, ableness, ability. *3* LAW., ELECT., PHYS. capacity.

**capacitado, -da** *adj.* qualified *2* LAW. competent, qualified, capable.

**capacitación** *f.* enabling, qualification, capacitation.

**capacitar** *tr.* to enable, qualify, capacitate.

**capacho** *m.* flexible two-eared basket of palmetto, esparto grass or rushes.

**capador** *m.* gelder, castrator. *2* gelder's whistle.

**capadura** *f.* gelding, castration.

**capar** *tr.* to geld, castrate, emasculate.

**caparazón** *m.* caparison. *2* covering [for a coach, etc.]. *3* nose bag. *6* carcass [of a fowl]. *5* carapace, shell [of tortoise and crustaceans].

**caparrosa** *f.* CHEM. vitriol: ~ *azul*, blue vitriol; ~ *blanca*, white vitriol; ~ *verde*, copperas.

**capataz** *m.* foreman, overseer, steward.

**capaz** *adj.* having room or capacity [for]. *2* capacious, roomy. *3* capable. *4* able, competent.

**capazo** *m.* large flexible basket. *2* blow given with a cloak.

**capciosidad** *f.* captiousness, insidiousness.

**capcioso, -sa** *adj.* captious, insidious, deceiving.

**capea** *f.* exciting the bull with a cloak. *2* amateur free-for-all bullfight.

**capeador** *m.* BULLF. novice bullfighter. *2* BULLF. cape man, bullfighter who uses the cape.

**capear** *tr.* BULLF. to play the bull with the cape. *2* to beguile. *3* to weather [a storm]. *4* *intr.* NAUT. to lie to.

**capelán** *m.* ICHTH. capelin.

**capelina** *f.* SURG. capeline.

**capelo** *m.* cardinal's hat. *2* cardinalate.

**capellada** *f.* toe piece [of a shoe].

**capellán** *m.* priest, clergyman. *2* chaplain: ~ *castrense*, army chaplain.

**capellanía** *f.* chaplaincy.

**capellina** *f.* ARMOUR., SURG. capeline. *2* formerly a peasant's hood.

**capeo** *m.* CAPEA.

**caperuceta, caperucita** *f. dim.* small pointed hood: *Caperucita Roja*, Little Red Ridinghood.

**caperuza** *f.* pointed hood. *2* chimney cap. *3* MACH. hood.

**Capeto** *m. pr. n.* Capetian.

**capialzado** *adj.* ARCH. splayed [arch].

**capialzar** *tr.* ARCH. to splay.

**capibara** *f.* ZOOL. capybara.

**capicúa** *m.* palindromic number.

**capilar** *adj.* [pertaining to] hair. *2* capillary.

**capilaridad** *f.* capillarity. *2* capillary atraction.

**capilla** *f.* hod, cowl [attached to a garment]. *2* chapel; oratory: ~ *ardiente*, chamber where a dead body lies in state; *estar en* ~, to be sentenced to death and awaiting execution; to be awaiting an important issue. *3* MUS. chapel. *4* coll. friar, monk. *7* PRINT. proof sheet.

**capillita** *f. dim.* little chapel.

**capillo** *m.* baby cap. *2* baptismal cap. *3* hood [of hawk]. *4* toe-piece lining [of shoe]. *5* bud, rosebud. *6* cocoon. *7* ANAT. prepuce.

**capirotazo** *m.* fillip [stroke with the finger].

**capirote** *m.* chaperon [medieval hood]. *2* conical hood or cap [worn in processions]. *3* doctoral hooded mozzetta. *4* hood [of hawk]. *5* hood [of carriage]. *6* CAPIROTAZO.

**capirucho** *m.* coll. CAPIROTE.

**capisayo** *m.* cloaklike garment. *2* bishop's vestment.

**capitación** *f.* capitation, poll tax.

**capital** *adj.* capital [pertaining to the head, chief, main, great]: *pena* ~, capital punishment. *2 m.* property, fortune. *3* ECON., SOCIOL. capital: ~ *social*, nominal capital, capital stock. *4* principal [sum invested or lent]. *5 f.* capital, chief town. *6* FORT. capital.

**capitalino, -na** *adj.* of the capital. *2 n.* native or inhabitant of the capital.

**capitalismo** *m.* capitalism.

**capitalista** *adj.* capitalist, capitalistic. *2 m.-f.* capitalist.

**capitalizable** *adj.* capitalizable.

**capitalización** *f.* capitalization.

**capitalizar** *tr.* to capitalize [compute the present value of an income]. *2* to compound [interest].

**capitán** *m.* captain, chief, leader, great soldier. *2* MIL. captain: ~ *general del ejército*, field marshal; ~ *general de una región*, commander of a large military district. *3* NAV. captain: ~ *de navío*, captain; ~ *de fragata*, junior captain, commander; ~ *de corbeta*, senior lieutenant, *lieutenant commander. *4* NAUT. captain, master [of a ship]. *5* SPORT. captain. *6* ~ *del puerto*, harbour master.

**capitana** *f.* admiral's ship. *2* captain's wife. *3* female leader.

**capitanear** *tr.* to captain, lead, command.

**capitanía** *f.* captaincy, captainship. *2* ~ *general*, post and office of the CAPITÁN GENERAL. *6* ~ *de puerto*, harbour-master's office.

**capitel** *m.* ARCH. capital. *2* ARCH. spire. *3* capital [of a still].

**Capitolio** *m. pr. n.* Capitol. *2 m.* capitol.

**capitoné** *m.* furniture van, removal van. *2* *adj.* (Am.) quilted, upholstered.

**capitoste** *m.* big chief, big boss, petty tyrant.

**capitulación** *f.* capitulation, agreement. *2* MIL. capitulation. *3 pl.* articles of marriage.

**capitular** *adj.-m.* capitular, capitulary. *2 pl.* HIST. capitularies.

**capitular** *intr.* to agree, conclude an agreement. *2* to capitulate [surrender on terms]. *3* to order, decree.

**capítulo** *m.* chapter [of a book]. *2* fig. chapter, subject, matter. *3* charge, impeachment: *llamar* or *traer a* ~, to call to account, bring to book. *4* chapter [meeting of members of a monastic or knightly order]. *5 pl. capítulos matrimoniales*, articles of marriage.

**capó** *m.* AUTO. hood, bonnet.

**capoc** *m.*, **capoca** *f.* Kapok.

**capón** *adj.* castrated, gelded. *2 m.* castrated man. *3* capon. *4* rap on the head.

**caponera** *f.* fattening coop for capons. *2* FORT. caponier. *3* coll. coop, jail.

**caporal** *m.* chief, leader. *2* (Am.) headman in a ranch.

**capot** *m.* AUT. hood, bonnet.

**capota** *f.* bonnet with strings, poke bonnet. *2* hood [of carriage]. *3* AER. cowling.

**capotar** *intr.* [of a car or airplane] to capsize, turn turtle, nose over.

**capotazo** *m.* a flick with the cloak to stop the bull.
**capote** *m.* kind of cloak with sleeves: *decir para su* ~, to say to oneself. *2* MIL. capote, greatcoat. *3* bullfighter's cape. *4 dar* ~, [in some card games] to win all the tricks.
**capotear** *tr.* CAPEAR 1 & 2. *2* to dodge, elude, evade difficulties, etc.
**capoteo** *m.* BULLF. passes with the cape. *2* coll. trickery, wiles. *3* shirking.
**capotillo** *m.* cape, mantlet.
**Capricornio** *pr. n.* ASTR. Capricorn.
**capricho** *m.* caprice, freak, whim, fancy. *2* longing, keen desire. *3* F. ARTS., MUS. caprice.
**caprichoso, -sa** *adj.* capricious, freakish, whimsical, fanciful.
**caprichudo, -da'***adj.* whimsical, willful.
**cápsico** *m.* BOT. capsicum.
**cápsula** *f.* capsule. *2* cartridge shell.
**capsulado** *m.* capping.
**capsulador** *f.* capping machine.
1) **capsular** *adj.* capsular.
2) **capsular** *tr.* to put a capsule on [a bottle].
**captación** *f.* winning, securing [good will, attention, etc.]. *2* collecting [spring waters]. *3* RADIO. picking up [signals].
**captar** *tr.-ref.* to win, secure [good will, esteem, attention, etc.]. *2 tr.* to collect [spring waters]. *3* RADIO. to get, pick up [signals].
**captura** *f.* capture, seizure.
**capturar** *tr.* to capture, seize.
**capucha** *f.* hood, cowl. *2* PRINT. circumflex accent.
**capuchina** *f.* BOT. capucine. *2* Capuchin nun.
**capuchino, -na** *adj.* pertaining to the Capuchin order. *2* ZOOL. *mono* ~, capuchin [monkey]. *3 m.* Capuchin [monk].
**capuchón** *m.* capuchin, cloak and hood [for women]. *2* short domino. *3* AUTO. valve cap. *4* cap [of fountain pen].
**capullo** *m.* cocoon: ~ *ocal*, double cocoon. *2* flower bud. *3* acorn cup. *4* foreskin.
**capuz** *m.* cowl. *2* hooded mantle. *3* dive, ducking.
**caquéctico, -ca** *adj.* MED. cachectic.
**caquexia** *f.* MED. cachexia.
**caqui** *m.* BOT. kaki, japanese persimmon. *2 adj.-m.* khaki [material and colour].
**cara** *f.* face, visage, countenance: ~ *de pascua*, cheerful face: ~ *de pocos amigos*, stern, forbidding countenance; *echar en* ~, to reproach, to throw in one's face; *dar la* ~, to face the consequences of one's actions; *dar la* ~ *por otro*, to answer for someone, to defend him; *hacer* ~, to face, resist; *verse las caras*, to meet in order to fight or dispute; to settle a difference; *a* ~ *descubierta*, openly; *de* ~ *a*, opposite, facing; ~ *a* ~, face to face. *2* look, mien, aspect: *tener* ~ *de*, to look as if; *tener buena* ~, to look well; to look good. *3* face, front, façade; outside, surface. *5* face, obverse, right side. *6* face, head [of a coin]: ~ *y cruz*, heads or tails. *7* side [of phonograph record]. *8 adv.* facing, towards.
**caraba** *f.* coll. *esto es la* ~, this is the limit, this is the last straw.
**carabao** *m.* ZOOL. carabao.
**cárabe** *m.* amber.
**carabela** *f.* NAUT. caravel.
**carabina** *f.* carbine: *ser la* ~ *de Ambrosio*, to be useless. *2* coll. chaperon.
**carabinero** *m.* carabineer. *2* revenue guard. *3* coll. kind of crayfish.
**cárabo** *m.* a small moorish vessel. *2* ENT. carabus. *3* ORN. tawny owl.

**caracal** *m.* ZOOL. caracal.
**caracará** *m.* ORN. caracara.
**Caracas** *f. pr. n.* GEOG. Caracas.
**caracol** *m.* ZOOL. snail. *2* snail shell. *3* spit curl. *4* HOROL. fusee. *5* caracole [of horse]. *6* ARCH. spiral: *escalera de* ~, winding staircase.
**caracola** *f.* conch or triton shell [used as a horn].
**caracolada** *f.* dish of snails.
**caracolear** *intr.* [of horses] to caracole.
**caracoleo** *m.* caracoling.
**¡caracoles!** *interj.* ¡CARAMBA!
**caracolillo** *m. dim.* of CARACOL. *2* BOT. garden flower. *3* a variety of coffee. *4* veined mahogany.
**carácter, *pl.* caracteres** *m.* character [sign, type, letter, hand]: ~ *de letra*, hand, handwriting. *2* character [distinctive qualities; moral strength]. *3* nature, disposition. *4* character, status. *5* F. ARTS, BIOL., THEOL. character.
**característica** *f.* characteristic [distinctive trait]. *2* LOG., MATH. characteristic. *3* THEAT. actress who enacts elderly characters.
**característico, -ca** *adj.* characteristic(al. *2 m.* THEAT. old man.
**caracterización** *f.* characterization. *2* THEAT. make-up.
**caracterizado, -da** *adj.* qualified, competent, distinguished.
**caracterizar** *tr.* to characterize [be characteristic of]. *2* to give distinction, honour, etc. *3* THEAT. to act a part properly. *4 ref.* THEAT. to dress and make up for a rôle.
**caracterología** *f.* characterology.
**caracul** *m.* karakul.
**caradura** *n.* coll. cad, rotter, shameless person, cheeky devil. *2* coll. cheek, nerve: *es muy* ~, he's got a lot of cheek!
**carajo** *m.* prick. *2* coll. ¡~! shit! hell! *¡vete al* ~, go to hell!
**caramanchel** *m.* NAUT. shed over the hatchways.
**¡caramba!** *interj.* confound it!, gracious me!
**carámbano** *m.* icicle.
**carambola** *f.* BILL. cannon, carom: fig. *por* ~, indirectly. *2* double effect of a single act. *3* BOT. carambola [fruit].
**carambolear** *intr.* BILL. to cannon, to carom.
**carambolista** *m.-f.* BILL. cannon or carom player.
**carambolo** *m.* BOT. carambola [tree].
**caramelizar** *tr.* to caramelize.
**caramelo** *m.* caramel [burnt sugar; sweetmeat].
**caramillo** *m.* flageolet; rustic flute. *2* BOT. kind of saltwort. *3* confused heap of things. *4* tale, lie, malicious gossip.
**carantoña** *f.* coll. ugly person. *2* coll. painted hag. *3 pl.* caresses, wheedling, cajolery.
**carantoñero, -ra** *m.-f.* wheedler, cajoler.
**carapacho** *m.* ZOOL. carapace.
**¡carape!** *interj.* ¡CARAMBA!
**caraqueño, -ña** *adj.-n.* of Caracas.
**carátula** *f.* mask [false face]. *2* wire mask [of beekeeper].
**caravana** *f.* caravan [of pilgrims, travellers, etc.].
**caravanero** *m.* caravaneer [leader of a caravan].
**caravaning** *m.* caravanning.
**caravasar** *m.* caravanserai.
**caray** *interj.* ¡CARAMBA!
**carbohidrato** *m.* carbohydrate.
**carbón** *m.* coal; charcoal: ~ *animal*, animal charcoal; bone black; ~ *mineral* or *de piedra*, coal, mineral coal; ~ *vegetal*, charcoal. *2* F. ARTS charcoal. *3* ELECT. carbon, crayon.

**carbonada** *f.* charge of coal [for a furnace]. *2* broiled mincemeat. *3* kind of pancake.

**carbonado** *m.* black diamond.

**carbonar** *tr.* to turn into charcoal, to make charcoal of.

**carbonario** *m.* Carbonaro, Carbonarist.

**carbonatación** *f.* carbonatation, carbonation.

**carbonatado, -da** *adj.* CHEM. carbonated.

**carbonatar** *tr.* to carbonate.

**carbonato** *m.* CHEM. carbonate.

**carboncillo** *m.* F. ARTS charcoal, charcoal pencil. *2* black sand. *3* wheat smut.

**carbonear** *tr.* to burn [wood] into charcoal. *2 intr.* NAUT. to coal [take in coal].

**carboneo** *m.* charcoal making. *2* NAUT. coaling.

**carbonera** *f.* wood prepared for burning into charcoal. *2* coal cellar, coal shed, coal bunker, coal bin.

**carbonería** *f.* coalyard; charcoal shop or store.

**carbonero, -ra** *adj.* [pertaining to] coal or charcoal; coaling. *2 m.* charcoal burner. *3* coal dealer, collier. *4 m.-f.* charcoal seller.

**carbónico, -ca** *adj.* carbonic.

**carbonífero, -ra** *adj.* carboniferous.

**carbonilla** *f.* fine coal; coal dust; cinders.

**carbonización** *f.* carbonization.

**carbonizar** *tr.* to carbonize, char. *2 ref.* to become carbonized.

**carbono** *m.* CHEM. carbon.

**carbonoso, -sa** *adj.* carbonaceous.

**carbunclo** *m.* CARBÚNCULO. *2* CARBUNCO.

**carbunco** *m.* MED., VET. carbuncle, anthrax.

**carbúnculo** *m.* carbuncle, ruby.

**carburación** *f.* carburation, carburetion.

**carburador** *m.* carburet(t)er, carburet(t)or.

**carburante** *adj.-m.* carburant.

**carburar** *tr.* to carburet.

**carburo** *m.* CHEM. carbide.

**carca** *adj.-n.* coll. square. *2* coll. carlist. *3* coll. reactionary.

**carcaj** *m.* quiver [for carrying arrows].

**carcajada** *f.* burst of laughter, cachinnation, guffaw.

**carcajearse** *ref.* to roar with laughter, to have a good laugh.

**carcamal** *m. adj.* coll. infirm, decrepit. *2 m.* infirm, decrepit person.

**cárcel** *f.* jail, gaol, prison. *2* coulisse [of a sluice gate]. *3* carpenter's clamp.

**carcelario, -ria** *adj.* [relating to] jail or prison.

**carcelero, -ra** *adj.* CARCELARIO. *2 m.* jailer, gaoler, warder. *3 f.* gaoleress, wardress.

**carcinógeno, -na** *adj.* MED. carcinogen.

**carcinoma** *m.* MED. carcinoma.

**carcinomatoso, -sa** *adj.* carcinomatous.

**cárcola** *f.* treadle [of a loom].

**carcoma** *f.* ENT. woodworm. *2* dust made by the woodworm. *3* fig. gnawing care. *4* fig. fritterer, corroder.

**carcomer** *tr.* [of the woodworm] to eat, gnaw. *2* fig. to gnaw away, consume, undermine.

**carcomido, -da** *adj.* worm-eaten. *2* consumed, decayed.

**carda** *f.* carding. *2* teaseling. *3* card [for carding wool, etc.]; carding machine. *4* card, teasel [for teaseling]. *5* coll. severe reproof.

**cardado** *m.* carding, combing. *2* back-combing [hair].

**cardador, -ra** *m.-f.* carder [of wool]. *2 m.* ZOOL. millepede.

**cardadura** *f.* carding [of wool].

**cardamina** *f.* BOT. MASTUERZO.

**cardamomo** *m.* BOT. cardamom.

**cardán** *adj.* MECH. Cardan.

**cardar** *tr.* to card. *2* to teasel, raise a nap.

**cardenal** *m.* ECCL., ORN. cardinal. *2* black-and-blue mark, ecchymosis.

**cardenalato** *m.* cardinalate.

**cardenalicio, -cia** *adj.* cardinalitian.

**cardencha** *f.* BOT. teasel, fuller's teasel.

**cardenillo** *m.* verdigris. *2* verditer, Paris green.

**cárdeno, -na** *adj.* purple, livid. *2* piebald [bull]. *3* opaline [water].

**cardíaco, -ca** *adj.* cardiac.

**cardialgia** *f.* MED. cardialgia.

**cardias** *m.* ANAT. cardiac orifice [of the stomach].

**cardillo** *m.* BOT. golden thistle.

**cardinal** *adj.* cardinal.

**cardiografía** *f.* cardiography.

**cardiográfico, -ca** *adj.* MED. cardiographic.

**cardiograma** *m.* cardiogram.

**cardiología** *f.* cardiology.

**cardiólogo, -ga** *m.* cardiologist.

**cardiotónico** *m.* MED. heart tonic.

**carditis** *f.* MED. carditis.

**cardizal** *m.* land covered with thistles and weeds.

**cardo** *m.* BOT. cardoon. *2* BOT. thistle: ~ *ajonjero*, carline thistle; ~ *borriqueño*, cotton thistle, scotch thistle; ~ *estrellado*, star thistle.

**cardón** *m.* card, teasel. *2* carding, teasing. *3* (Am.) giant cactus.

**cardoncillo** *m.* BOT. milk thistle.

**cardume, cardumen** *m.* school, shoal [of fishes].

**carear** *tr.* to confront, bring face to face. *2* to confront, compare. *3* to lead [cattle] toward some place. *4 ref.* to meet face to face.

**carecer de** *intr.* to lack, be without. ¶ CONJUG. like *agradecer*.

**carena** *f.* NAUT. careen, careening [caulking and repairing].

**carenadura** *f.* NAUT. careenage.

**carenar** *tr.* NAUT. to careen [caulk and repair].

**carencia** *f.* lack, want, deficiency, deprivation.

**carenero** *m.* NAUT. careenage [place for careening].

**carente** *adj.* ~ *de*, lacking, wanting.

**careo** *m.* confrontation [esp. of criminals or witness].

**carero, -ra** *adj.* selling dearly, charging high prices.

**carestía** *f.* scarcity, want; famine. *2* high cost.

**careta** *f.* mask [covering for the face]: *quitar la* ~, to unmask, expose. *2* fencing mask, face-guard.

**carey** *m.* ZOOL. tortoise-shell, turtle. *2* tortoise shell.

**carezco, carezca**, etc. *irr.* V. CARECER.

**carga** *f.* loading, lading; charging. *2* load, burden. *3* cargo, freight: *buque de* ~, freighter, cargo ship. *4* tax, impost. *5* duty, obligation, expenses. *6* charge [on real estate]. *7* charge [of gun, furnace, etc.]. *8* ELECT. charge, load. *9* ENG., ARCH. load. *10* HYDR. head. *11* MIL. charge: *volver a la* ~, fig. to insist. *12* measure for charcoal, fruit, grain, etc.

**cargadero** *m.* loading place, freight station. *2* ARCH. lintel.

**cargado, -da** *adj.* full, fraught. *3* sultry, cloudy [weather]. *4* strong, saturated: *café* ~, strong coffee. *5* ~ *de años*, up in years; ~ *de espaldas*, round-shouldered.

**cargador** *m.* shipper; freighter. *2* carrier, porter. *3* loader, charger. *4* clip [of cartridges]. *5* (Am.) street-porter.

**cargamento** *m.* NAUT. cargo, shipment.
**cargante** *adj.* coll. boring, annoying, tiresome.
**cargar** *tr.* to load. *2* to burden. *3* to charge [a furnace, battery, etc.]. *4* to impose or lay [taxes]. *5* to impute, ascribe. *6* to bore, annoy, tire. *7* ACCOUNT. to charge, to debit. *8* NAUT. to brail up [a sail]. *9* MIL. to charge. *10* ~ *la mano*, to pursue something eagerly; to overdo; to be too exacting. *11 intr.* to lean, incline towards. *12* to load up, take on a load: ~ *mucho* or *demasiado*, coll. to eat or drink too much. *13* PHON. [of an accent] to fall, have its place. *14* ~ *con*, to take, carry away; to assume [a responsibility]; to bear [the blame]. *15* ~ *en* or *sobre*, to bear, rest or lean on; to fall on. *16 ref.* to lean the body [towards]. *17* to burden oneself. *18* to get cloudy, overcast. *19* [of a patient] to run up a temperature. *20* ELEC. to become charged. *21* cargarse de, to fill oneself (or itself) up with: *cargarse de paciencia*, to arm oneself with patience.
**cargazón** *f.* NAUT. cargo, shipment. *2* heaviness [of head or stomach]. *3* mass of heavy clouds.
**cargo** *m.* loading. *2* burden, weight: ~ *de conciencia*, a load on one's conscience, responsibility. *3* ACCOUNT. charge, debit. *4* employment, post, office. *5* duty, charge, responsibility: *a* ~ *de*, under the charge of. *6* charge, accusation, reproach: *hacer cargos*, to lay charges, accuse. *7 hacerse* ~, to take charge; to be understanding; *hacerse* ~ *de*, to take charge of; to take into consideration, understand, realize.
**cargoso, -sa** *adj.* burdensome, onerous. *2* annoying, bothersome.
**carguero, -ra** *adj.* freight, freight carrying. *2 m.* (Arg.) beast of burden.
**cariacontecido, -da** *adj.* sad, troubled, crestfallen.
**cariado, -da** *adj.* carious [tooth, bone].
**cariancho, -cha** *adj.* broad-faced.
**cariar** *tr.* to cause caries. *2 ref.* to become carious, to decay.
**cariátide** *f. f.* ARCH. caryatid.
**Caribdis** *f. pr. n.* Charybdis.
**caribe** *adj.* Caribbean. *2 m.-f.* Carib. *3 m.* fig. brute, savage.
**caribú,** *pl.* **-búes** *m.* ZOOL. caribou.
**caricato** *m.* baso buffo [opera singer].
**caricatura** *f.* caricature; cartoon.
**caricaturesco, -ca** *adj.* caricatural.
**caricaturista** *m.-f.* caricaturist.
**caricaturizar** *tr.* to caricature.
**caricia** *f.* caress, petting, endearment.
**caridad** *f.* charity [virtue; gift, alms] charitableness.
**caridoliente** *adj.* sad-looking.
**caries** *f.* MED., DENT. caries, decay.
**carigordo, -da** *adj.* fat-faced.
**carilampiño, -ña** *adj.* beardless, smoothfaced, clean-shaven.
**carilargo, -ga** *adj.* long-faced.
**carilla** *f.* mask [of beekeeper]. *2* page, side [of writing paper].
**carilleno, -na** *adj.* plump-faced.
**carillo, -lla** *adj.* dim. rather dear or expensive.
**carillón** *m.* carillon.
**carimba** *f.,* **carimbo** *m.* branding iron. *2* brand.
**cariño** *m.* love, affection, fondness, tenderness; care, solicitude. *2 pl.* caresses, endearments.
**cariñoso, -sa** *adj.* loving, affectionate, kind; endearing.
**carioca** *adj.* of Rio de Janeiro. *2 n.* native or inhabitant of Rio de Janeiro.

**cariofiláceo, -a** *adj.* BOT. caryophylaceous.
**carioplasma** *m.* karyoplasm.
**cariópside** *f.* BOT. caryopsis.
**carirredondo, -da** *adj.* round-faced.
**carisma** *m.* THEOL. charism.
**carismático, -ca** *adj.* charismatic.
**caritativo, -va** *adj.* charitable.
**cariz** *m.* aspect, look [of weather, a business, etc.].
**carlanca** *f.* spiked collar [for dogs]. *2 pl.* fig. *tener muchas carlancas*, to be very crafty.
**carlina** *f.* BOT. carline thistle.
**carlinga** *f.* AER. cockpit. *2* NAUT. mast step.
**carlismo** *m.* Carlism.
**carlista** *m.* Carlist.
**Carlomagno** *m. pr. n.* Charlemagne.
**Carlos** *m. pr. n.* Charles.
**Carlota** *f. pr. n.* Charlotte.
**carmañola** *f.* carmagnole.
**carmelita** *adj.-m.* Carmelite. *2 f.* Carmelite nun.
**carmelitano, -na** *adj.* Carmelite.
**Carmen** *m.* carmen [song, poem]. *2* country house and garden [in Granada].
**Carmen** *f. pr. n.* Carmen. *2 m.* order of Our Lady of Mount Carmel.
**carmenador** *m.* large toothed comb. *2* carder, teasel.
**carmenadura** *f.* disentangling, combing [hair]. *2* carding, teasing [wool], unraveling [silk].
**carmenar** *tr.* to comb, disentangle [the hair: wool, silk, etc.]. *2* to rob, clean out.
**carmesí** *adj.-m.* crimson. *2 m.* crimson silk fabric.
**carmín** *m.* carmine.
**carminativo, -va** *adj.-m.* MED. carminative.
**carmíneo, -a** *adj.* carmine-coloured.
**carnación** *f.* flesh colour.
**carnada** *f.* bait [to entice prey].
**carnadura** *f.* flesh, robustness. *2* ENCARNADURA.
**carnal** *adj.* carnal. *2 hermano* ~, full brother; *primo* ~, cousin-german.
**carnaval** *m.* carnival [feast before Lent].
**carnavalada** *f.* carnival trick or frolic.
**carnavalesco, -ca** *adj.* carnivalesque.
**carnaza** *f.* bait. *3* abundance of flesh, fleshiness.
**carne** *f.* flesh [of man, animal or fruit]: fig. ~ *de gallina*, goose flesh, goose skin; *estar metido en carnes*, to be plump, stout; *criar carnes*, to put on flesh; *ser de* ~ *y hueso*, to be only human; *en* ~ *viva*, raw [skin or sore]. *2* flesh [human nature, carnality]. *3* meat, flesh [as food]: ~ *asada*, roasted meat; *carnes blancas*, meat of fowl and young animals; ~ *de pluma*, fowl flesh; ~ *de vaca*, beef; *ni* ~ *ni pescado*, neither fish, flesh nor good red herring. *4* fig. ~ *de cañón*, cannon fodder. *5* ~ *de membrillo*, quince jelly.
**carné, carnet** *m.* card: ~ *de conducir*, driving license; ~ *de socio*, membership card; ~ *de identidad*, identity card. *2* pocket notebook, bankbook.
**carneada** *f.* (Am.) slaughtering.
**carnear** *f.* (Am.) to slaughter [for food].
**carnecería** *f.* butcher's shop.
**carnerada** *f.* flock of sheep.
**carnerear** *tr.* to kill [trepassing sheep] for damage done.
**1) carnero** *m.* ZOOL. sheep; mutton: ~ *padre*, ram. *2* ~ *del Cabo*, albatross.
**2) carnero** *m.* charnel, charnel house, sepulchre.
**carneruno, -na** *adj.* [pertaining to] sheep. *2* sheeplike.
**carnestolendas** *f. pl.* carnival, Shrovetide.
**carnet** *m.* notebook. *2* dance or membership card.

3 ~ *de chófer,* driver's licence; ~ *de periodista,* reporter's card.

**carnicería** *f.* butcher's shop. 2 carnage, massacre.

**carnicero, -ra** *adj.* carnivorous [animal]. 2 bloodthirsty, sanguinary. 3 *m.-f.* butcher [meat seller]. 5 *m. pl.* ZOOL. Carnivora.

**cárnico, -ca** *adj.* meat; *productos ~,* meat products.

**carnicol** *m.* hoof [half of a cloven foot].

**carnívoro, -ra** *adj.* carnivorous. 2 *m.* ZOOL. carnivore. 3 *pl.* ZOOL. Carnivora.

**carnosidad** *f.* MED. proud flesh. 2 carnosity. 3 fleshiness.

**carnoso, -sa** *adj.* carnose.

**carnudo, -da** *adj.* fleshy.

1) **caro** *adv.* dear, dearly.

2) **caro, -ra** *adj.* dear, costly, high-priced; expensive. 2 dear, beloved: *cara mitad,* better half.

**carocha** *f.* some insects'eggs [pl.].

**Carolina** *f. pr. n.* Caroline. 2 GEOG. Carolina. 3 *Islas Carolinas,* Caroline Islands.

**carolingio, -gia** *adj.-n.* Carolingian.

**Caron** *m. pr. n.* MYTH. Charon.

**carota** *n.* coll. cheeky devil.

**caroteno** *m.* CHEM. carotin, carrotin, carotene, carrotene.

**carotenoide** *adj.-n.* CHEM. carotinoid, carotenoid.

**carótida** *f.* ANAT. carotid, carotid artery.

**carozo** *m.* cob of maize, corncob.

**carpa** *f.* ICHTH. carp: ~ *dorada,* goldfish. 2 (Am.) awning, tent.

**carpanel** *adj.* ARCH. basket-handle [arch].

**carpanta** *f.* coll, hunger, keen appetite.

**Cárpatos (Montes)** *m. pr. n.* Carpathian Mountains.

**carpe** *m.* BOT. hornbeam, witch-hazel.

**carpelo** *m.* BOT. carpel.

**carpeta** *f.* writing-table cover. 2 writing case. 3 portfolio. 4 folder, letter file.

**carpetazo** *m. dar ~,* to shelve, pigeonhole, lay aside.

**carpetovetónico, -ca** *adj.* Spanish to the core, terribly Spanish.

**carpiano, -na** *adj.* ANAT. carpal.

**carpincho** *m.* ZOOL. capybara.

**carpintería** *f.* carpentry, carpentering. 2 carpenter's shop.

**carpintero** *m.* carpenter: ~ *de carretas,* cartwright; ~ *de ribera,* ship carpenter, shipwright.

**carpo** *m.* ANAT. carpus.

**carpología** *f.* BOT. carpology.

**carpólogo** *m.* BOT. carpologist.

**carraca** *f.* NAUT. carrack [galleon]. 2 fig. clumsy old boat; rattletrap. 3 rattle [instrument]. 5 ratchet brace.

**carraco, -ca** *adj.* old, decrepit.

**carrada** *f.* cartload. 2 loads, heaps, a lot.

**carraleja** *f.* ENT. oil beetle, blister beetle.

**carranza** *f.* iron spike [in a dog collar].

**carrasca** *f.* BOT. small holm oak.

**carrascal** *m.* ground covered with CARRASCAS.

**carraspear** *intr.* to hawk, clear one's throat. 2 to suffer from hoarseness.

**carraspeo** *m.* clearing the throat. 2 hoarseness.

**carraspera** *f.* hoarseness, frog-in-the-throat.

**carrasposo, -sa** *adj.* very hoarse, having a sore throat. 2 (Am.) harsh, rough.

**carraspique** *m.* BOT. candytuft.

**carrasqueño, -ña** *adj.* rough, harsh.

**carrera** *f.* run, running: ~ *de baquetas,* MIL. gauntlet, running the gauntlet; *a ~ tendida, a la ~,* at full speed; *de ~,* speedily, without thinking. 2 road, highway. 3 course [of a star]. 4 route [followed by pageant or procession]. 5 race [contest of speed]: ~ *de armamento,* armament race. 6 row; line, range. 7 run, ladder [in a stocking]. 8 parting [in hair]. 9 career. 10 profession. 11 ARCH. girder. 12 MACH. stroke [of piston], travel [of valve]. 13 *pl.* horse racing, turf.

**carrerilla** *f.* short run. 2 MUS. run of an octave.

**carrerista** *m.-f.* racegoer, turfman; race fan. 2 bicycle racer.

**carrero** *m.* cart driver, carter, cartman.

**carreta** *f.* long, narrow cart.

**carretada** *f.* cartful, cartload. 2 great quantitv.

**carrete** *m.* spool, reel, bobbin. 2 ELECT. coil.

**carretear** *tr.* to cart, haul [goods]. 2 to drive [a cart].

**carretel** *m.* NAUT. log reel.

**carretera** *f.* road, high road, highway.

**carretería** *f.* carting business. 2 carts, wagons. 3 cartwright's yard.

**carretero** *m.* carter, cartman, teamster. 2 cartwright, wheelwright. 3 *adj. camino ~,* cartway.

**carretilla** *f.* wheelbarrow; truck, baggage truck, handcart. 2 gocart [for learning to walk]. 3 BUSCAPIÉS. 4 *de ~,* by heart, mechanically.

**carretillero** *m.* wheelbarrow man.

**carretón** *m.* small cart. 2 handcart. 3 wheeled frame for a portable grindstone.

**carricera** *f.* BOT. plume grass.

**carricoche** *m.* old coach.

**carricuba** *f.* street-watering cart.

**carril** *m.* rut, track, furrow. 2 cartway. 3 RLY. rail.

**carrillera** *f.* ZOOL. jaw. 2 chin strap.

**carrillada** *f.* fat of hog's jowls.

**carrillera** *f.* jaw [of some animals]. 2 chin strap.

**carrillo** *m.* cheek, jowl: *comer a dos carrillos,* to eat greedily; to have two sources of income.

**carrilludo, -da** *adj.* round-cheeked.

**carrizal** *m.* ground covered with ditch reeds.

**carrizo** *m.* BOT. ditch reed grass.

**carro** *m.* cart: ~ *de mudanzas,* moving van; *untar el ~,* to grease the palm, to bribe; *pare usted el ~,* hold your horses, restrain yourself. 2 (Am.) automobile; streetcar; railway car. 3 chariot. 4 MIL. car, tank. 5 cartload. 6 running gear [of carriage]. 7 ASTR. *Carro,* or *Carro Mayor,* Great Bear. 8 MACH. carriage [of typewriter, etc.]. 9 ~ *de tierra,* a land measure.

**carrocería** *f.* coachmaker's shop. 2 body [of motorcar].

**carrocero** *m.* coachmaker, coach builder.

**carrocín** *m.* chaise, gig [light carriage].

**carrocha** *f.* insect eggs.

**carrochar** *intr.* to lay eggs [an insect].

**carromato** *m.* long two-wheeled cart with a tilt.

**carroña** *f.* carrion [corrupted flesh].

**carroño, -ña** *adj.* carrion, corrupt, rotten.

**carroza** *f.* coach, stately carriage. 2 float [in processions]. 3 (Am.) hearse. 4 NAUT. companion [covering]; awning, tilt.

**carruaje** *m.* carriage, car, vehicle.

**carrusel** *m.* merry-go-round, carrousel, roundabout. 2 horse tattoo.

**carta** *f.* letter [written communication]: ~ *certificada,* registered letter; ~ *credencial* or *de creencia,* letters of credence, credentials; ~ *de presentación,* letter of introduction. 2 charter, chart, letters patent; deed: ~ *de fletamento,* ~ *partida,* charter party; ~ *de marca,* letters of marque; ~ *de venta,* deed of sale; *Carta Magna,* Magna

Charta. *3* chart, map: ~ *de marear*, marine chart. *4* playing card: ~ *falsa*, card of no value; *jugar a cartas vistas*, to act frankly, openly; to act on inside information; *poner las cartas boca arriba*, to put or lay one's cards on the table; *tomar cartas en un asunto*, to take a hand in an affair. *5* bill of fare: *a la* ~, à la carte. *6* ~ *blanca*, carte blanche, full powers. *7* ~ *de naturaleza*, privilege of naturalization; *adquirir* ~ *de naturaleza*, to become naturalized. *8* ~ *de pago*, acquittance, receipt, discharge in full. *9* ~ *partida por a, b, c*, indenture [indented document]. *10 a* ~ *cabal*, thoroughly.

**cartabón** *m.* drawing triangle. *2* carpenter's square. *3* size stick. *4* topographic octagonal prism.

**Cartagena** *f. pr. n.* GEOG. Cartagena.

**cartagenero, -ra** *adj.-n.* of Cartagena.

**cartaginense; cartaginés, -sa** *adj.-n.* Carthaginian.

**Cartago** *f. pr. n.* GEOG. Carthage.

**cártama** *f.*, **cártamo** *m.* BOT. safflower.

**cartapacio** *m.* notebook; schoolboy's copy book. *2* schoolboy's satchel. *3* papers in a folder.

**cartear** *intr.* to play low cards [to see how the game stands]. *2 ref.* to correspond by letter.

**cartel** *m.* poster, placard, bill: fig. *tener* ~, to have a reputation. *2* mural reading chart [for teaching children]. *3* cartel.

**cartelera** *f.* billboard, hoarding.

**cartelista** *n.* poster designer.

**cartelón** *m.* large poster.

**carteo** *m.* correspondence, intercourse by letters.

**cárter** *m.* MACH. housing, case.

**cartera** *f.* pocketbook, wallet. *2* portfolio [portable case for papers; office of cabinet minister; list of securities]. *3* brief case, letter-case. *4* satchel. *5* pocket flap.

**cartería** *f.* sorting room [in post office].

**carterista** *f.* pickpocket.

**cartero** *m.* postman, letter, carrier.

**cartesiano, -na** *adj.-n.* Cartesian.

**cartilaginoso, -sa** *adj.* cartilaginous.

**cartílago** *m.* ANAT. cartilage, gristle.

**cartilla** *f.* primer, *speller [spelling book]. *2* short treatise [about some trade or art]. *3* identity book. *4* ~ *de la caja de ahorros*, deposit book of savings bank; ~ *de racionamiento*, ration book.

**cartografía** *f.* cartography.

**cartógrafo** *m.* cartographer.

**cartomancia** *f.* cartomancy.

**cartón** *m.* cardboard, pasteboard; ~ *piedra;* staff, papier mâché. *2* cartoon [model for frescoes, tapestry, etc.].

**cartonaje** *m.* cardboard articles.

**cartoné** *m.* BOOKBIND. *en* ~, in boards.

**cartonería** *f.* cardboard factory or shop.

**cartuchera** *f.* cartridge box. *2* cartridge belt.

**cartucho** *m.* cartridge: *quemar el último* ~, fig. to use up one's last resource. *2* roll of coins. *3* paper cone or bag [for sweets].

**cartuja** *f.* Carthusian order or monastery.

**cartujo** *adj.* Carthusian. *2 m.* Carthusian monk. *3* fig. taciturn fellow, recluse.

**cartulario** *m.* cartulary.

**cartulina** *f.* light or fine cardboard, Bristol board.

**carúncula** *f.* ANAT., ZOOL. caruncle, wattle

**carvi** *m.* BOT. caraway. *2* caraway seeds.

**casa** *f.* house, building, establishment, institution, office: ~ *central*, head office; ~ *consistorial*, or *de la villa*, town hall; ~ *cuna* or *de expósitos*, founding hospital; ~ *de banca*, banking house;

~ *de caridad*, alms house, poorhouse; ~ *de empeños* or *de préstamos*, pawn shop; ~ *de huéspedes*, boarding house; ~ *de juego*, gambling house; ~ *de labor*, or *de labranza*, farming house; ~ *de locos* or *de orates*, madhouse, lunatic asylum; bedlam; ~ *de maternidad*, maternity hospital; ~ *de moneda*, mint; ~ *de salud*, private hospital; ~ *de socorro*, first-aid station; emergency hospital; ~ *de vecindad*, tenement house; ~ *editorial*, publishing house; ~ *matriz*, head office, mother house; ~ *mortuoria*, house of mourning, of deceased person; ~ *pública*, brothel; ~ *real*, royal palace; royal family; ~ *solariega*, manor. *2* home; house, household, family: *en* ~, at home; *en* ~ *de*, at the home, office, shop, etc., of; *la* ~ *de Borbón*, the house of Bourbon; *echar la* ~ *por la ventana*, to go to a lot of expense [to entertain, etc.]; *poner* ~, to set up housekeeping. *3* house, commercial house, firm. *4* square [of chessboard]. *5* ba(u)lk [in billards]. *6* ASTROL. house.

**casabe** *m.* cassava flour or bread.

**Casablanca** *pr. n.* GEOG. Casablanca.

**casaca** *f.* old long coat: *volver uno* ~, to become a turncoat. *2* diplomat's coat.

**casación** *f.* LAW cassation, -quashing.

**casacón** *m.* large CASACA; cassock.

**casadero, -ra** *adj.* marriageable.

**casado, -da** *adj.* married. *2 m.-f.* married person.

**casal** *m.* country house. *2* ancestral mansion.

**casamata** *f.* FORT. casemate.

**casamentero, -ra** *adj.* matchmaking. *2 m.-f.* matchmaker, marriage maker.

**casamiento** *m.* marriage, wedding.

**casaquilla** *f.* kind of coat with short tails.

1) **casar** *m.* hamlet.

2) **casar** *intr.-ref.* to marry, get married: ~ or *casarse con*, to marry, to be married to. *2* to marry [unite in wedlock; give in marriage]. *3* to marry, match, harmonize [things]. *4* to quash, annul. *5* *intr.* [of things] to match, suit, correspond.

**casca** *f.* tanning bark. *2* skin of pressed grapes. *3* CÁSCARA.

**cascabel** *m.* small spherical bell: *poner el* ~ *al gato*, to bell the cat; *ser un* ~, to be a rattlebrain; to be merry, gay. *2* cascabel [of cannon]. *3* ZOOL. *serpiente de* ~, rattlesnake.

**cascabelear** *tr.* to incite with vain hopes. *2 intr.* to behave in a featherbrained manner.

**cascabeleo** *m.* jingle, jingling of bells.

**cascabelero, -ra** *adj.* thoughtless, featherbrained.

**cascabelillo** *m.* BOT. a small sweet plum.

**cascada** *m.* cascade, waterfall.

**cascado, -da** *adj.* broken, cracked. *2* worn out, infirm, decayed. *3* weak, cracked [voice].

**cascadura** *f.* breaking, cracking.

**cascajal, cascajar** *m.* place full of gravel.

**cascajo** *m.* gravel, fragments of stone, rubbish. *2* a broken piece of crockery: *estar hecho un* ~, to be decrepit.

**cascanueces,** *pl.* **-ces** *m.* nutcracker [instrument]. *2* ORN. nutcracker.

**cascar** *tr.* to break, crack, chink. *2* to beat, thrash. *3* to break the health of. *4 intr.* to chatter. *5 ref.* to crack. *6* to become infirm, decrepit.

**cáscara** *f.* rind, peel [of orange, melon, etc.]; shell [of egg or seed]. *2* bark [of tree]. *3* hard covering, hull, shell crust: *ser de la* ~ *amarga*, to hold advanced views. *5 interj. ¡cáscaras!*, by Jove!

**cascarela** *f.* a card game.

**cascarilla** *f*. thin metal shell or covering. *2* BOT. cascarilla, bark. *3* PHARM. thin cinchona bark.
**cascarillo** *m*. BOT. a cinchona shrub.
**cascarón** *m*. aug. of CÁSCARA. *2* eggshell; broken eggshell [from which chick has emerged]. *3* ~ *de nuez*, cockleshell [flimsy boat].
**cascarrabias** *m.-f*. coll, crab, irritable person.
**casco** *m*. casque, helmet. *2* crown [of hat]. *3* skull, cranium. *4* coat [of onion]. *5* fragment of broken crockery. *6* cask, bottle [for liquids]. *7* hull [of ship]. *8* hoof [of horse, mule or donkey]. *9* ~ *de población*, a city excluding its suburbs. *10 pl*. brains [of a person]: *levantar de cascos*, to incite with false hopes: *ser alegre de cascos*, to be scatterbrained.
**cascote** *m*. piece of rubble. *2* rubble, debris.
**caseína** *f*. casein.
**cáseo** *adj*. caseous, cheesy. *2 m*. curd.
**caseoso, -sa** *adj*. caseous, cheesy.
**caserío** *m*. group of houses. *2* hamlet. *3* CASERÍA.
**caserna** *f*. FORT. casern.
**casero, -ra** *adj*. house, home, informal [dress, gathering, etc.]. *2* domestic; homemade; homespun. *3* home-loving. *4 m.-f*. landlord, landlady [who leases houses or flats]. *5* house-agent. *6* caretaker. *7* renter, tenant.
**caserón** *m*. large house. *2* large ramshackle house.
**caseta** *f*. small house, hut. *2* ~ *de baño*, bathhouse, bathing cabin.
**casi** *adv*. almost, nearly.
**casia** *f*. BOT. cassia.
**casicontrato** *m*. LAW quasi contract.
**casilla** *f*. booth, cabin, hut [of railway guard, etc.]; keeper's lodge. *2* square [of chess board]; point [of backgammon board]. *3* column or square [on sheet of paper]. *4* pigeonhole. *5* *sacar a uno de sus casillas*, to jolt someone out of his old habits; to vex someone beyond patience; *salir uno de sus casillas*, to lose one's temper.
**casillero** *m*. set of pigeonholes, rack.
**casimir** *m*., **casimira** *f*. cashmere; cassimere.
**Casimiro** *m. pr. n*. Casimir.
**casino** *m*. casino, club; clubhouse.
**Casio** *m. pr. n*. Cassius.
**casis** *f*. BOT. cassis, black currant.
**casita** *f. dim*. little house.
**caso** *m*. GRAM., MED. case. *2* case, event, happening, instance, circumstances: ~ *de conciencia*, case of conscience: ~ *fortuito*, chance, accident; LAW force majeure; *hacer* or *venir al* ~, to be to the purpose, to be relevant; *poner por* ~, to take as an example; *vamos al* ~, let's come to the point; *el* ~ *es que*, the fact or the thing is that; ~ *que*, *en* ~ *de que*, in case; *de* ~ *pensado*, on purpose; *en todo* ~, anyhow. *3* heed, notice, attention: *hacer* ~ *de*, to heed, mind, notice; to listen, pay attention to, take into account; to esteem; *hacer* ~ *omiso*, to take no notice, to leave aside.
**casón** *m*. large house.
**casorio** *m*. unwise marriage. *2* informal wedding.
**caspa** *f*. dandruff, scurf.
**caspio, -pia** *adj*. Caspian: *Mar Caspio*, Caspian.
**¡cáspita!** *interj*. gracious!, by Jove!
**casposo, -sa** *adj*. scurfy, full of dandruff.
**casquería** *f*. tripe shop.
**casquero** *m*. tripe seller.
**casquete** *m*. skullcap, calotte. *3* MACH. cap. *4* GEOM. ~ *esférico*, one-base spherical segment.
**casquillo** *m*. ferrule, socket, metal tip or cap. *2* cartridge case; cartridge cap. *3* iron arrowhead.
**casquivano, -na** *adj*. featherbrained, frivolous.

**cassette** *f*. cassette.
**casta** *f*. caste. *2* race, stock, breed. *3* lineage, kindred. *4* kind quality [of things].
**Castálidas** *f. pl*. MYTH. Castalides.
**castamente** *adv*. chastely.
**castaña** *f*. chestnut [fruit]: *sacar las castañas del fuego*, to pull the chestnuts out of the fire; *dar la* ~ *a uno*, fig. to play a trick on one. *2* demijohn. *3* knot of hair, chignon.
**castañal, castañar** *m*., **castañeda** *f*. chestnut grove or plantation.
**castañazo** *m*. coll. bash, punch, thump.
**castañero, -ra** *m.-f*. chestnut seller.
**castañeta** *f*. castanet. *2* snapping of the fingers.
**castañetazo** *m*. clap of castanets. *2* craking of a chestnut in the fire. *3* cracking of the joints.
**castañetear** *tr*. to play [a tune] with the castanets. *2 intr*. [of teeth] to chatter; [of kness] to crackle. *3* [of partridges] to cry.
**castañeteo** *m*. sound of the castanets. *2* chattering [teeth], cracking [bones], clicking, clattering.
**castaño, -ña** *adj*. chestnut, chestnut-coloured, brown, hazel. *2 m*. BOT. chestnut tree: ~ *de Indias*, horse-chestnut tree. *3* chestnut, brown, hazel [colour]: *pasar de* ~ *oscuro*, fig. to be the limit, be intolerable.
**castañola** *f*. ICHTH. pomfret.
**castañuela** *f*. castanet.
**castañuelo, -la** *adj*. chestnut, hazel [horse].
**castellana** *f*. mistress of a castle, chatelaine. *2* wife of a castellan.
**castellanismo** *m*. word or phrase characteristic of Castile.
**castellanizar** *tr*. to give Castilian form to.
**castellano, -na** *adj.-n*. Castilian. *2 m*. Castilian or Spanish language. *3* castellan; lord of a castle.
**casticidad** *f*. purity, correctness [in language].
**casticismo** *m*. love of purity [in language], of pure national nature [in customs, fashions, etc.].
**casticista** *adj.-n*. purist.
**castidad** *f*. chastity, continence.
**castigable** *adj*. punishable.
**castigador, -ra** *adj*. punishing. *2 m.-f*. punisher; castigator. *3 m*. coll. ladykiller.
**castigar** *tr*. to punish, chastise, penalize. *2* to chasten, castigate. *3* to mortify [the flesh]. *4* to cut down [expenses].
**castigo** *m*. punishment, chastisement; penance, penalty. *2* affliction, mortification. *3* castigation.
**Castilla** *f. pr. n*. GEOG. Castile.
**castillejo** *m*. small castle. *2* scaffolding [for hoisting heavy materials].
**castillo** *m*. castle: ~ *en el aire*, castle in the air, castle in Spain; ~ *de naipes*, house of cards. *3* ~ *de fuego*, fireworks. *4* NAUT. ~ *de proa*, forecastle.
**castina** *f*. limestone flux.
**castizo, -za** *adj*. of good breed; of good origin. *2* pure, correct [style, language, writer]. *3* prolific.
**casto, -ta** *adj*. chaste, pure.
**castor** *m*. ZOOL. beaver. *2* beaver [fur, hair, cloth].
**Cástor** *m. pr. n*. MYTH., ASTR. Castor.
**castoreño, -ña** *adj*. *sombrero* ~, beaver hat.
**castóreo** *m*. castor, castoreum.
**castración** *f*. castration, gelding; spaying. *2* extraction of honeycombs.
**castrado, -da** *adj*. castrated. *2* gelded [a horse]. *3 m*. eunuch.
**castrador** *m*. castrator, gelder.
**castrar** *tr*. to castrate, geld; to spay. *2* to prune. *3*

to extract combs from [hive]. *4* to weaken, emasculate.
**castrazón** *f.* extraction of honeycombs.
**castrense** *adj.* [pertaining to the] army; military.
**casual** *adj.* chance, accidental, fortuitous, casual.
**casualidad** *f.* chance, accident, coincidence: *por* ~, by chance. *2* chance event.
**casualmente** *adv.* by chance, by accident. *2* as it happens.
**casuario** *m.* ORN. cassowary.
**casucha** *f.*, **casucho** *m.* small, miserable house.
**casuista** *adj.* casuistic. *2 m.-f.* casuist.
**casuística** *f.* casuistry.
**casulla** *f.* chasuble.
**cata** *f.* tasting, sampling. *2* taste, small portion, sample. *3* (Am.) MIN. prospection.
**catacaldos** *m.-f.* one who starts many things and concentrates on none. *2* busybody.
**cataclismo** *m.* cataclysm.
**catacumbas** *f. pl.* catacombs.
**catador, -ra** *m.-f.* taster, sampler.
**catadura** *f.* tasting, sampling. *2* aspect, face, countenance.
**catafalco** *m.* catafalque.
**catalán, -na** *adj.* Cataian, Catalonian. *2 m.-f.* Catalan.
**catalanismo** *m.* Catalanism.
**catalejo** *m.* spyglass.
**catalepsia** *f.* MED. catalepsis, catalepsy.
**cataléptico, -ca** *adj.-n.* cataleptic.
**Catalina** *f. pr. n.* Catherine.
**catalisis** *f.* CHEM. catalysis.
**catalizador** *m.* CHEM. catalyzer, catalytic agent.
**catalogar** *tr.* to catalogue, cataloguize.
**catálogo** *m.* catalogue.
**catalpa** *f.* BOT. catalpa.
**Cataluña** *f. pr. n.* GEOG. Catalonia.
**cataplasma** *f.* poultice.
**cataplum** *interj.* bang!, boom!
**catapulta** *f.* catapult.
**catar** *tr.* to taste, try by the taste; to sample. *2* to look at, to examine. *3* to think, judge. *4* to cut combs out of [hive].
**cataraña** *f.* ORN. whithe heron. *2* ZOOL. a West Indian lizard.
**catarata** *f.* cataract, waterfall.
**catarral** *adj.* catarrhal.
**catarro** *m.* MED. catarrh; head cold.
**catarsis** *f.* catharsis.
**catártico, -ca** *adj.* MED. cathartic.
**catastral** *adj.* cadastral.
**catastro** *m.* cadastre, cadaster.
**catástrofe** *f.* catastrophe.
**catastrófico, -ca** *adj.* catastrophic, disastrous, calamitous.
**cataviento** *m.* NAUT. dogvane.
**catavino** *m.* cup for tasting wine.
**Catay** *m. pr. n.* GEOG. Cathay.
**cate** *m.* blow, slap. *2 dar* ~, to reject, *flunk [in an examination].
**catear** *tr.* to reject [in an examination]. *2* (Am.) to prospect [a district] for minerals.
**catecismo** *m.* catechism.
**catecú** *m.* catechu.
**catecúmeno, -na** *m.-f.* catechumen.
**cátedra** *f.* chair [seat of the professor; professorship]. *2* cathedra: ~ *del Espíritu Santo*, pulpit; ~ *de San Pedro*, Chair of Saint Peter [papal office].
**catedral** *adj.-f.* cathedral [church].
**catedralicio, -cia** *adj.* [pertaining to a] cathedral.

**catedrática** *f.* woman professor. *2* professor's wife.
**catedrático** *m.* university professor.
**categoría** *f.* category. *2* class, condition, kind; quality: *de* ~, of importance; prominent.
**categórico, -ca** *adj.* categoric(al.
**catenaria** *adj.-f.* MATH. catenary.
**cateo** *m.* (Am.) prospection.
**catequesis** *f.*, **catequismo** *m.* catechesis.
**catequista** *m.-f.* catechist.
**catequístico, -ca** *adj.* catechistic. *2* catechetical.
**catequizar** *tr.* to catechize, catechise. *3* to bring around, persuade.
**caterva** *f.* multitude, lot, great number.
**catéter** *m.* SURG. catheter.
**cateterismo** *m.* MED. catheterism.
**cateto** *m.* GEOM. leg [of a right-angled triangle]. *2* coll. yokel, rustic.
**catilinaria** *f.* oration of Cicero against Catiline. *2* vehement denunciation.
**catión** *f.* ELECT. cation.
**catirrino, -na** *adj.-m.* ZOOL. catarrhine.
**catite** *m.* light blow or slap.
**cato** *m.* catechu.
**catódico, -ca** *adj.* cathode, cathodic.
**cátodo** *m.* ELECT. cathode.
**catolicismo** *m.* catholicism. *2* Catholicism; Catholicity.
**católico, -ca** *adj.* catholic. *2 adj.-n.* Catholic, Roman Catholic. *3 no estar muy* ~, to feel out of sorts.
**catolizar** *tr.* to catholicize.
**Catón** *m. pr. n.* Cato.
**catón** *m.* severe censor. *2* primer, reading book.
**catóptrica** *f.* catoptrics.
**catorce** *adj.-n.* fourteen.
**catorceno, -na** *adj.* fourteenth.
**catorzavo, -va** *adj.-m.* fourteenth [part].
**catre** *m.* cot, light bed: ~ *de tijera*, folding cot.
**catrecillo** *m. dim.* camp canvas chair.
**Cátulo** *m. pr. n.* Catullus.
**caucásico, -ca** *adj.-n.* Caucasian [white].
**Cáucaso** *m. pr. n.* GEOG. Caucasus.
**cauce** *m.* bed [of watercourse]. *2* channel, ditch.
**caución** *f.* caution, precaution. *2* LAW surety.
**caucionar** *tr.* LAW to bail. *2* LAW to guard against loss or harm.
**cauchera** *f.* BOT. rubber plant.
**cauchero, -ra** *adj.* [pertaining to] rubber. *2 m.* rubber gatherer or worker.
**caucho** *m.* rubber, india-rubber, caoutchouc. *2* BOT. rubber plant.
**cauchutado** *m.* rubberizing, covering or furnishing with rubber.
**cauchutar** *tr.* to rubberize, to cover or furnish with rubber.
**caudal** *adj.* of great volume [river]. *2* ZOOL. caudal. *3 m.* fortune, wealth, means; plenty, abundance. *4* volume [of water].
**caudaloso, -sa** *adj.* of great volume of water, carrying much water. *2* rich, wealthy.
**caudatario** *m.* ECCL. train-bearer.
**caudillaje** *m.* leadership.
**caudillo** *m.* chief, leader. *2* military leader.
**caudinas** *adj. f. pl.* HIST. Caudine.
**caulescente** *adj.* BOT. caulescent.
**causa** *f.* cause, origin, reason, motive: *a* ~ *de, por* ~ *de*, because of, on account of. *2* cause [espoused or advocated]: *hacer* ~ *común con*, to make common cause with. *3* lawsuit. *4* case, trial at law.
**causahabiente** *m.* LAW asignee, trustee, executor.

**causal** *adj.* GRAM. causal, causative.
**causalidad** *f.* causality.
**causante** *adj.* causing, causative; occasioning. *2 m.-f.* causer, doer, occasioner, originator.
**causar** *tr.* to cause, do, create, occasion, originate.
**causativo, -va** *adj.* causative.
**causticidad** *f.* causticity.
**cáustico, -ca** *adj.* caustic(al. *2 m.* caustic. *3* vesicatory.
**cautamente** *adv.* cautiously.
**cautela** *f.* caution, wariness. *2* craft, cunning.
**cautelar** *tr.* to prevent. *2 ref. cautelarse de,* to guard against.
**cautelosamente** *adv.* cautiously, heedfully, warily, carefully.
**cauteloso, -sa** *adj.* cautious, wary, guarded.
**cauterio** *m.* cautery.
**cauterización** *f.* cauterization.
**cauterizar** *tr.* to cauterize.
**cautivador, -ra** *adj.* captivating, charming.
**cautivante** *adj.* captivating, fascinating.
**cautivar** *tr.* to take prisoner. *2* to win, hold [the attention, etc.]. *3* to captivate, charm.
**cautiverio** *m.,* **cautividad** *f.* captivity.
**cautivo, -va** *adj.-n.* captive.
**cauto, -ta** *adj.* cautious, wary, prudent.
**cava** *f.* digging, hoeing. *2* royal wine cellar.
**cavador** *m.* digger.
**cavar** *tr.* to dig, to hoe. *2 intr.* to dig [in]. *3* to go to the bottom [of a subject, etc.].
**cavatina** *f.* MUS. cavatina.
**cavazón** *m.* digging.
**caverna** *f.* cavern, cave. *2* MED. morbid cavity.
**cavernario, -ria** *adj.* cave, cavern.
**cavernícola** *adj.* cave-dwelling. *2 m.-f.* cave dweller. *3* coll. political reactionary.
**cavernoso, -sa** *adj.* cavernous. *2* hollow [voice, sound].
**caveto** *m.* ARCH. cavetto.
**cavia** *f.* ZOOL. guinea pig.
**cavial, caviar** *m.* caviar.
**cavicornio, -na** *adj.* ZOOL. cavicorn.
**cavidad** *f.* cavity.
**cavilación** *f.* rumination, brooding over. *2* unfounded apprehension; fancy.
**cavilar** *tr.* to ruminate, brood over, muse on.
**caviloso, -sa** *adj.* given to anxious ruminations.
**cayado** *m.* hooked staff, crook, shepherd's hook. *2* crozier [of bishop].
**Cayena** *f. pr. n.* GEOG. Cayenne.
**Cayetano** *m. pr. n.* Gaetan.
**cayo** *m.* cay, key.
**caz** *m.* millrace, flume, channel.
**caza** *f.* hunting, chase: *dar ~ a,* to hunt, give chase to; *a la ~ de,* hunting for. *2* game [animals]: *~ mayor* big game; *~ menor,* small game. *3 m.* AER. pursuit plane, fighter.
**cazabe** *m.* cassava bread.
**cazabombardero** *m.* fighter bomber.
**cazador, -ra** *adj.* hunting. *2 m.* hunter; huntsman, fowler: *~ furtivo,* poacher. *3* MIL. chasseur. *4 f.* huntress. *5* jacket, hunting jacket.
**cazar** *intr.* to hunt, to fowl. *2 ~ largo,* to be perspicacious. *3 tr.* to hunt, chase, to hunt for. *4* to catch, get: *cazarlas al vuelo,* fig. to be quick-witted. *5* NAUT. to haul tight [a sheet].
**cazasubmarinos,** *pl.* **-nos** *m.* NAV. submarine chaser.
**cazatorpedero** *m.* NAV. torpedo-boat destroyer.
**cazcarrias** *f. pl.* dried mud splashings on clothes.
**cazo** *m.* dipper; little saucepan. *2* back [of knife].

**cazolada** *f.* contents of a cooking pan.
**cazoleta** *f.* small cooking pan. *2* flashpan [of firearm]. *3* bowl [of tobacco pipe]. *4* hand guard [of sword]. *5* boss [of buckler].
**cazón** *m.* ICHTH. dogfish [a small shark].
**cazuela** *f.* earthen cooking pan; large casserole. *2* THEAT. gallery.
**cazumbre** *m.* cooper's oakum.
**cazurro, -rra** *adj.* taciturn, reticent.
**ce** *f.* name of the letter *c: ~ por be,* minutely, circumstancially.
**ceba** *f.* fattening [of animals]. *2* feeding [of a furnace].
**cebada** *f.* BOT. barley: *~ perlada,* pearl barley.
**cebadal** *m.* barley field.
**cebadera** *f.* barley bin. *2* nose bag. *3* METAL. furnace charger. *4* NAUT. spritsail.
**cebadero** *m.* barley dealer. *2* MIN. the mouth of a furnace. *3* lead mule. *4* feeding place.
**cebadilla** *f.* BOT. wall barley. *2* BOT. sabadilla.
**cebador** *adj.* fattening; feeding, priming. *2 m.* priming horn, powder flask.
**cebadura** *f.* fattening [animal]. *2* stoking [furnace]. *3* priming [gun]. *4* (Am.) load of mate leaves. *5* brewing, making [mate].
**cebar** *tr.* to fatten, to feed [animals]. *2* to feed [a furnace, fire, etc.]; to prime [a gun, pump, steam engine, etc.]; to bait [a fishook, a trap]; to lure with bait. *3* to nourish [sentiments, passions]. *4 intr.* [of a nut, a nail] to catch, take hold. *5 ref. cebarse en,* to be firmly bent upon [a thing]; to vent one's fury on.
**cebellina** *f.* ZOOL. sable. *2* sable fur.
**cebo** *m.* food given to animals; fattening food. *2* bait. *3* lure, incentive. *4* primer charge, priming. *5* ZOOL. an African monkey.
**cebolla** *f.* BOT. onion [plant and bulb]. *2* BOT. bulb. *3* BOT. *~ albarrana,* squill.
**cebollana** *f.* BOT. chive.
**cebollar** *m.* onion patch.
**cebolleta** *f.* tender onion. *2* BOT. Welsh onion.
**cebollino** *m.* onion seedling. *2* onion seeds. *3* CEBOLLANA.
**cebollona** *f.* (Am.) coll. spinster, old maid.
**cebolludo, -da** *adj.* bulbous, bulbaceous. *2* coarse, rude.
**cebón, -na** *adj.* fattened. *2 m.-f.* fattened animal.
**cebra** *f.* ZOOL. zebra.
**cebrado, -da** *adj.* striped [like the zebra].
**cebruno, -na** *adj.* deer-coloured.
**cebú,** *pl.* **cebúes** *m.* ZOOL. zebu.
**ceca** *f.* mint [where money is coined].
**Ceca** *f. andar de Ceca en Meca* or *de la Ceca a la Meca,* to go hither and thither.
**cecear** *intr.* to lisp.
**ceceo** *m.* lisping.
**ceceoso, -sa** *adj.* lisping. *2 m.-f.* lisper.
**Cecilia** *f. pr. n.* Cecilia.
**Cecilio** *m. pr. n.* Cecil.
**cecina** *f.* cornet and dried meat.
**cecinar** *tr.* to jerk, to cure, to cut into strips and dry in the sun.
**ceda** *f.* CERDA 1. *2* ZEDA.
**cedacero** *m.* sieve maker.
**cedacillo** *m.* BOT. quacking grass.
**cedazo** *m.* sieve, bolt, bolter.
**cedente** *adj.* grating, assigning, transferring. *2 n.* grantor, assignor.
**ceder** *tr.* to cede, transfer, yield, give up, resign. *2 intr.* to yield, submit, give in, give way. *3* [of wind, fever, etc.]. to abate, slacken. *4* [of a floor,

a rope, etc.] to fall, give way. *5* ~ *en,* to redound to. *6 no* ~ *en nada a,* to be by no means inferior to.
**cedilla** *f.* cedilla.
**cedrino, -na** *adj.* cedrine.
**cedro** *m.* BOT. cedar: ~ *deodara,* deodar. *2* cedar wood.
**cédula** *f.* piece or slip of paper or parchment written or to write upon; order, bill, certificate.
**cefalalgia** *f.* MED. cephalalgia.
**cefalea** *f.* headache.
**cefálico, -ca** *adj.* cephalic.
**cefalópodo** *adj.-m.* cephalopod.
**cefalotórax** *m.* ZOOL. cephalothorax.
**Cefeo** *n. pr.* ASTR., MYTH. Cepheus.
**céfiro** *m.* zephyr [wind; cloth].
**cefo** *m.* an African monkey.
**cegado, -da** *adj.* blinded. *2* blocked, walled up.
**cegador, -ra** *adj.* dazzling, blinding.
**cegar** *intr.* to go blind. *2 tr.* to blind [make blind]; to obfuscate. *3* to dazzle. *4* to wall up, close up, stop up [a door, well, channel, passage, etc.]. *5 ref.* to be blinded [by passion, love, etc.] ¶ CONJUG. like *acertar.*
**cegarra** *adj.-n.* cegato.
**cegarrita** *f.* weak-eyed.
**cegato, -ta** *adj.* short-sighted, weak-eyed.
**cegesimal** *adj.* PHYS. centimeter-gram-second, C.G.S.
**ceguedad** *f.* blindness.
**ceguera** *f.* blindness. *2* obfuscation [of mind].
**ceiba** *f.* BOT. silk-cotton tree. *2* BOT. sea moss.
**Ceilán** *m. pr. n.* Ceylon.
**ceilanés, -sa** *adj.-n.* Ceylonese.
**ceja** *f.* ANAT. brow, eyebrow: *quemarse las cejas,* to burn the midnight oil: *tener entre* ~ *y* ~, to dislike [someone]; to persist in [a purpose]. *2* projecting part, flange. *3* brow [of a hill]. *4* cloud cap. *5* MUS. nut [of guitar, etc.]. *6* MUS. capotasto.
**cejar** *intr.* to back up, go backward. *2* to relax, desist: *no* ~, to persist.
**cejijunto, -ta** *adj.* bushy-browed, with thick, heavy eyebrows. *2* frowning, grim, scowling.
**cejilla** *f.* MUS. nut [of a guitar]. *2* capotasto.
**cejo** *m.* morning mist over a river or stream.
**cejudo, -da** *adj.* beetle-browed.
**celacanto** *m.* ZOOL. coelacanth.
**celada** *f.* ambush, trap, snare. *2* ARM. sallet, helmet.
**celador, -ra** *adj.* watching. *2 m.-f.* watcher, inspector; warden, wardress.
**celaje** *m.* NAUT. mass of clouds. *2* cloud scenery, cloud effect. *3* skylight, window. *5 pl.* sky covered with many-coloured clouds.
**celandés, -sa** *adj.-n.* ZEELANDÉS.
**celar** *tr.* to see to [the observance of law, duties, etc.]. *2* to watch over [employees, etc.]. *3* to watch, spy on [through suspicion or jealousy]. *4* to hide, conceal. *5* to carve, engrave.
**celastro** *m.* BOT. staff tree.
**celda** *f.* cell [in convent, prison, honeycomb].
**celdilla** *f.* cell [in honeycomb]. *2* BIOL., BOT. cell. *3* niche, cavity.
**celebérrimo, -ma** *adj. superl.* most celebrated.
**celebración** *f.* celebration. *2* holding [of a meeting, etc.]. *3* praise, applause.
**celebrado, -da** *adj.* popular.
**calebrante** *m.* celebrant.
**celebrar** *tr.* to celebrate [a ceremony, a birthday, etc.]; to make [a festival]; to perform [a contract]; to hold [a meeting]. *2* to celebrate, ap-

plaud; to extol, to honour. *3* to be glad of. *4 intr.* to celebrate, say Mass.
**célebre** *adj.* celebrated, famous. *2* coll. funny, witty.
**celebridad** *f.* celebrity. *2* celebration, festival.
**celemín** *m.* a dry measure [about half a peck].
**celenterado, celenterio** *adj.-n.* ZOOL. cœlenterate.
**celeridad** *f.* celerity.
**celeste** *adj.* celestial. *2* sky-blue. *3* Celestial [Empire]. *4* MUS. celeste. *5* MUS. soft [pedal].
**celestial** *adj.* celestial. *2* heavenly; perfect, delightful.
**celestina** *f.* bawd, procuress.
**celíaco, -ca** *adj.* ANAT. cœliac.
**celibato** *m.* celibacy. *2* coll. bachelor, single man.
**célibe** *adj.* celibate, single, unmarried. *2 m.-f.* bachelor or spinster, unmarried person.
**celidonia** *f.* BOT. celandine.
**celinda** *f.* syringa.
**celo** *m.* zeal. *2* heat, rut. *3 pl.* jealousy.
**celofana** *f.* cellophane.
**celosía** *f.* lattice; lattice window. *2* jealousy.
**celoso, -sa** *adj.* zealous. *2* jealous. *3* suspicious.
**celsitud** *f.* elevation, grandeur.
**celta** *adj.* Celtic. *2 m.-f.* Celt.
**celtibérico, -ca; celtíbero, -ra** *adj.-n.* Celtiberian.
**céltico, -ca** *adj.* Celtic.
**célula** *f.* BIOL., ELECT. cell. *2* ~ *comunista,* communist cell.
**celulado, -da** *adj.* celled, cellated, cellular.
**celular** *adj.* cellular.
**celulitis** *f.* MED. cellulitis.
**celuloide** *m.* celluloid.
**celulosa** *f.* cellulose.
**celuloso, -sa** *adj.* cellulose, cellulous.
**cellisca** *f.* sleet, sleet storm.
**cellisquear** *intr.* to sleet.
**cello** *m.* hoop [of a barrel].
**cementación** *f.* METAL. cementation.
**cementar** *tr.* METAL. to cement.
**cementerio** *m.* cemetery, churchyard, graveyard.
**cemento** *m.* cement. *2* ~ *armado,* reinforced concrete.
**cementoso, -sa** *adj.* cement-like.
**cena** *f.* supper. *2 la Santa Cena,* the Last Supper.
**cenáculo** *m.* Cenacle. *2* cenacle [literary group].
**cenacho** *m.* esparto or palm bag.
**cenador, -ra** *adj.* supping. *2 m.-f.* supper [pers.]. *3 m.* arbo(u)r, bower, summerhouse.
**cenagal** *m.* slough, miry place. *2* fig. quagmire.
**cenagoso, -sa** *adj.* miry, muddy.
**cenar** *intr.* to sup [have supper]. *2 tr.* to have for supper.
**cenceño, -ña** *adj.* lean, slender, thin.
**cencerrada** *f.* charivari, tin-pan serenade.
**cencerrear** *intr.* to jingle cowbells continually. *2* to jangle, rattle. *3* to play out of tune.
**cencerreo** *m.* jingle of cowbells. *2* jangle, rattle.
**cencerro** *m.* cowbell: *a cencerros tapados,* stealthily, cautiously.
**cencuate** *m.* poisonous snake from Mexico.
**cendal** *m.* sendal, gauze, transparent fabric. *2* ECCL. humeral veil. *3* barbs of a feather.
**cendolilla** *f.* madcap [girl].
**cenefa** *f.* list or stripe on the border of a stuff, garment, etc.; border. *2* middle stripe in a chasuble. *3* ARCH. ornamental band or fret.
**cenicero** *m.* ash tray. *2* ash pan, ashpit; ash dump.
**ceniciento, -ta** *adj.* ashen, ash-gray. *2 f.* Cinderella.
**cenit** *m.* ASTR. zenith.
**cenital** *adj.* zenith, zenithal.

**ceniza** f. ash, ashes. 2 BOT. oidium. 3 pl. ashes, cinders. 4 ashes [mortal remains].

**cenizo, -za** adj. CENICIENTO. 2 m. BOT. goosefoot. 3 BOT. oidium. 4 hoodoo, jinx, Jonah [person who brings ill-luck].

**cenobial** adj. coenobitic, cenobitic, coenobitical, cenobitical.

**cenobio** m. cenoby, cenobium.

**cenobita** m. cenobite.

**cenotafio** m. cenotaph.

**censal** adj. CENSUAL. 2 m. rent charge.

**cenozoico, -ca** adj. GEOL. cenozoic, caenozoic.

**censar** tr. to take a census of.

**censatario** m. person paying a rent charge.

**censo** m. census [official enumeration of population, etc.]. 2 LAW census, rent charge.

**censor** m. censor. 2 censorious person.

**censorio, -ria** adj. censorial.

**censual** adj. [pertaining to the] rent-charge.

**censualista** m. rent charger.

**censura** f. censure. 2 censorship. 3 body of censors.

**censurable** adj. censurable, blamable, reprehensible.

**censurador, -ra** adj. censorious.

**censurar** tr. to censor. 2 to censure, blame, criticize.

**centaura, centaurea** f. BOT. centaury, knapweed.

**centauro** m. MYTH. centaur.

**centavo, -va** adj. hundredth. 2 m. hundredth; one-hundredth part. 3 cent [money].

**centella** f. lightning, thunderbolt. 2 spark, flash.

**centellante** adj. sparkling, glittering, flashing.

**centellar, centellear** intr. to sparkle, glitter, flash, scintillate; to twinkle.

**centelleante** adj. CENTELLANTE.

**centelleo** m. sparkling, glittering, scintillation.

**centén** m. old Spanish gold coin.

**centena** f. a hundred.

**centenada** f. hundred: a ~, by the hundred.

**centenal** m. hundred. 2 rye field.

**centenar** m. hundred: a centenares, by hundreds. 2 rye field.

**centenario, -ria** adj. centenary, centennial, centenarian. 2 m.-f. centenarian [person]. 3 m. centenary, centennial [centennial aniversary].

1) **centeno** m. BOT. rye.

2) **centeno, -na** adj. hundredth.

**centesimal** adj. centesimal.

**centésimo, -ma** adj. centesimal, hundredth. 2 m.-f. hundredth.

**centiárea** f. centiare, square metre.

**centígrado, -da** adj. centigrade.

**centigramo** m. centigram.

**centilitro** m. centilitre.

**centímetro** m. centimetre.

**céntimo** m. hundredth part. 2 centime, one-hundredth part of a peseta.

**centinela** m.-f. sentinel, sentry: ~ de vista, prisoner's guard; estar de ~, hacer ~, to be on sentry duty, to watch.

**centinodia** f. BOT. knotgrass.

**centolla** f. ZOOL. thornback [crab].

**centón** m. crazy quilt, patchwork. 2 LITER. cento.

**centrado, -da** adj. centred, centered. 2 balanced. 3 m. centring, centering.

**central** adj. central. 2 f. main office, headquarters. 3 TELEPH. exchange, central. 4 ELECT. power-house, generating station.

**centralilla, centralita** f. TELEPH. local exchange.

**centralismo** m. centralism.

**centralización** f. centralization.

**centralizador, -ra** adj. centralizing. 2 m. centralizer.

**centralizar** tr.-ref. to centralize.

**centrar** tr. to centre, to center. 2 to point, to aim, to focus [beam, ray]. 3 to base. 4 ref. to center, to centre, to be based. 5 ref. find one's feet, to concentrate.

**céntrico, -ca** adj. centric, central. 2 downtown.

**centrifugador, -ra** adj.-f. centrifugal [machine].

**centrifugar** tr. to centrifuge.

**centrífugo, -ga** adj. centrifugal.

**centrípeto, -ta** adj. centripetal.

**centrista** n. centrist, middle-of-the-roader. 2 adj. centre, center, belonging to the center.

**centro** m. center, centre: ~ de gravedad, center of gravity; estar en su ~, to be in one's element. 2 the central part of a town, city. 3 goal, aim. 4 club, association, social meeting place. 5 main office, headquarters. 6 ~ de mesa, centrepiece [of table].

**centroamericano, -na** adj.-n. Central American.

**centroeuropeo, -a** adj.-n. Central European.

**centrosfera** f. BIOL. centrosphere.

**centrosoma** m. BIOL. centrosome.

**centunviro** m. centumvir.

**centuplicar** tr. to centuple, centuplicate.

**céntuplo, -pla** adj.-m. centuple, hundredfold.

**centuria** f. century [a hundred years]. 2 HIST. [Roman] century.

**centurión** m. centurion.

**cénzalo** m. ENT. mosquito.

**ceñido, -da** adj. close-fitting. 2 thrifty, economical. 4 reduced, condensed.

**ceñidor** m. girdle, belt, sash [for the waist].

**ceñir** tr. to gird; to girdle, encircle. 2 to fasten around the waist. 3 to fit tight. 4 to shorten, to condense. 5 ~ espada, to wear a sword. 6 NAUT. to haul [the wind]. 7 ref. to reduce one's expenses. 8 to be concise. ¶ CONJUG. like reír.

**ceño** m. frown. 2 threatening aspect [of clouds, sea, etc.].

**ceñudo, -da** adj. frowning, stern, grim.

**ceo** m. ICHTH. dory.

**cepa** f. underground part of the stock [of tree or plant]. 2 grapevine; vine stem. 3 butt or root [of horn, tail, etc.]. 4 stock [of lineage]. 5 de buena ~, of good quality.

**cepillado,** m. cepilladura f. planing [carpintry]. 2 brushing [a suit]. 2 pl. shavings.

**cepillar** tr. ACEPILLAR.

**cepillo** m. brush [for cleaning]: ~ de dientes, toothbrush; ~ para el pelo, hairbrush. 2 CARP. plane; ~ bocel, fluting plane. 3 alms box, poor box.

**cepo** m. bough, branch [of tree]. 2 stock [of anvil]. 3 stocks, pillory. 4 iron trap. 5 alms box. 6 stock [of anchor]. 7 CEFO. 8 ¡cepos quedos!, hands off!

**cequí** m. sequin, zequin [old golden coin].

**cera** f. wax; beewax: ~ aleda, bee glue; ~ de los oídos, earwax; figuras de ~, waxworks. 2 ORN. cere. 3 pl. honeycomb.

**cerafolio** m. BOT. chervil.

**cerámica** f. ceramics. 2 ARCHEOL. study of ceramics.

**cerámico, -ca** adj. ceramic.

**ceramista** m.-f. ceramist.

**cerapez** f. cobbler's wax.

**cerasta** f., **ceraste, cerastes** m. ZOOL. cerastes.

**cerato** m. PHARM. ointment containing wax.

**cerbatana** f. blowgun. 2 peashooter, popgun. 3 ear trumpet. 4 small culverin.

**cerbero** m. CANCERBERO.

1) **cerca** f. enclosure, hedge, fence.
2) **cerca** adv. near, close, nigh: *aquí* ~, near here; *de* ~, from near; *seguir de* ~, to follow closely. |
Before a noun, pron. or adv., it requires *de*: ~ *de Madrid*, near Madrid. *2* ~ *de*, nearly, about: ~ *de un año*, nearly a year. *3* to, at the court of. *4 pl.* PAINT. objects in the foreground.
**cercado, -da** adj. fenced-in, walled-in. *2* MIL. surrounded. *3 m.* enclosure, fenced-in or walled-in garden or field. *4* fence, enclosure.
**cercanamente** adv. nearby, close by. *2* shortly, soon, in a short time.
**cercanía** f. nearness, proximity. *2 pl.* neighbourhood, vicinity; surroundings.
**cercano, -na** adj. near, close, nearing. *2* neighbouring, adjoining.
**cercar** tr. to fence, hedge, pale, wall in. *2* to encircle, surround, hem in; to crowd around. *3* MIL. to invest, lay siege to.
**cercén, a cercén** adv. to the root. *2* completely.
**cercenador** m. clipper. *2* curtailer, reducer.
**cercenamiento** m. clipping, retrenchment. *2* curtailment, reduction.
**cercenar** tr. to clip, to cut off the point or edges of. *2* to curtail, lessen, reduce.
**cerceta** f. ORN. garganey. *2 pl.* buds [of antlers].
**cerciorar** tr. to make [someone] sure of a fact. *2 ref.* ᵥcerciorarse de, to ascertain, make sure of.
**cerco** m. circle [about a thing]; hoop, ring, edge. *2* rim [of wheel]. *3* casing, frame [of door or window]. *4* halo. *5* circle, ring [of persons]. *6* MIL., siege, blockade.
**cerchar** tr. AGR. to layer [the vine].
**cerchearse** ref. to warp.
**cerchón** m. ARCH. truss.
**cerda** f. horsehair; bristle, hog bristle. *2* ZOOL. sow. *3 ganado de* ~, swine (collec.).
**cerdada** f. coll. foul trick, lousy trick, dirty trick. *2* mess.
**cerdamen** m. tuft of bristle or horsehair.
**Cerdaña** f. pr. n. GEOG. Cerdagne valley.
**cerdear** intr. [of horses or bulls] to falter in the forelegs. *2* [of stringed instruments] to sound harsh, to rasp. *3* to show reluctance.
**Cerdeña** f. pr. n. Sardinia.
**cerdito** m. dim. little pig.
**cerdo** m. ZOOL. swine [domestic] hog, pig. *2* pork [meat]. *3* fig. pig, swine [person].
**cerdoso, -sa** adj. bristly.
**cereal** adj.-m. cereal.
**cerealista** adj. pertaining to cereals. *2 m.-f.* grain producer; grain dealer.
**cerebelo** m. ANAT. cerebellum.
**cerebral** adj. cerebral.
**cerebro** m. ANAT. cerebrum. *2* fig. head, brains.
**cerebroespinal** adj. cerebrospinal.
**cereceda** f. cherry orchard.
**ceremonia** f. ceremony. *2* formality. *3* ceremoniousness. *4 de* ~, formal, with all due ceremony; *por* ~, as a matter of form.
**ceremonial** adj.-m. ceremonial.
**ceremonioso, -sa** adj. ceremonious.
**céreo, -a** adj. cereous, waxen.
**cerería** f. waxchandlery, waxchandler's shop.
**cerero** m. waxchandler; waxdealer.
**Ceres** f. pr. n. MYTH. Ceres.
**cereza** f. cherry [fruit]: ~ *gordal*, bigaroon.
**cerezal** m. cherry orchard.
**cerezo** m. BOT. cherry tree: ~ *silvestre*, dogwood.
**ceriflor** f. BOT. honeywort.
**cerilla** f. wax match, paper match. *2* wax taper.

**cerillera** f., **cerillero** m. matchbox.
**cerillo** m. wax taper.
**cerio** m. CHEM. cerium.
**cermeña** f. BOT. a variety of pear.
**cermeño** m. BOT. a variety of pear tree.
**cernada** f. leached ashes.
**cerne** m. heart [of tree].
**cernedero** m. place for sifting flour.
**cernedor** m. sifter, bolter [person]. *2* bolter [machine].
**cerneja** f. fetlock [tuft of hair in horses].
**cerner** tr. to sift, bolt [flour, etc.]. *2* to scan, observe. *3 intr.* [of some plants] to have flowers in a state of pollination. *4* to drizzle, mizzle. *5 ref.* to swing the body in walking. *6* [of birds] to soar, hover. *7* [of evil, storm, etc.] to impend, to hang [over], to gather, to threaten. ¶ CONJUG. like *entender*.
**cernícalo** m. ORN. kestrel, sparrow hawk. *2* fig. rude ignoramus.
**cernidillo** m. drizzle. *2* short minced pace.
**cernidura** f. sifting, bolting. *2 pl.* siftings.
**cernir** tr. CERNER.
**cero** m. zero, naught, nought, cipher: *ser un* ~ *a la izquierda*, to be a mere cipher.
**cerón** m. dross of honeycombs.
**ceroso, -sa** adj. waxen, waxy.
**cerote** m. shoemaker's wak. *2* coll. fright, fear.
**cerquillo** m. fringe of hair around tonsure. *2* welt [of shoe].
**cerquita** adv. dim. not far off, very near.
**cerrado, -da** adj. shut; close, closed; fastened; locked. *2* obscure, incomprehensible. *3* cloudy, overcast. *4* secretive, reserved. *5* sharp [curve]. *6* thick [beard]. *7* PHONET. close. *8* with a heavy local accent. *9* ~ *de mollera*, dense, stupid. *10 m.* CERCADO.
**cerrador** m.-f. shutter, closer, fastener. *2 m.* fastening, lock, etc.
**cerradura** f. CERRAMIENTO. *2* lock [fastening]: ~ *de golpe*, spring lock; ~ *de seguridad*, safety lock.
**cerraja** f. lock [fastening]. *2* BOT. sow thistle.
**cerrajería** f. locksmith trade. *2* locksmith's shop.
**cerrajero** m. locksmith.
**cerramiento** m. shutting, closing. *2* occlusion. *3* enclosure. *4* partition, partition wall.
**cerrar** tr. to close, shut: ~ *la boca*, to shut up; ~ *los oídos*, to turn a deaf ear. *2* to fasten, bolt, lock; ~ *de golpe*, to slam. *2* to clench [the fist]. *4* to block up, stop, obstruct, bar. *5* to wall, to fence. *6* to seal [a letter]. *7* to close [a shop, a business; a bargain, etc.]. *8* ELECT. to close [a circuit]. *9* to turn off [the water, the gas, etc.]. *10 intr.* [of a shop, theatre, etc.] to shut, to close its doors. *11* to shut [to admit of closing]. *12* ~ *con*, to attack. *13* ~ *la noche*, to get dark. *14 ref.* to close, to close itself. *15* to persist, to stand firm. ¶ CONJUG. like *acertar*.
**cerrazón** f. dark and cloudy weather. *2* ~ *de mollera*, density, stupidity.
**cerrejón** m. hillock.
**cerrero, -ra** adj. wild, roaming, untamed. *2* uncouth, coarse, rough. *3* (Am.) bitter.
**cerril** adj. broken, uneven [ground]. *2* unbroken, untamed [cattle]. *3* coll. unpolished, boorish.
**cerrillo** m. hillock. *2* BOT. couch grass.
**cerro** m. neck [of animal]. *2* back, backbone. *3* hill: *irse por los cerros de Úbeda*, to talk irrelevantly.
**cerrojazo** m. slamming the bolt.
**cerrojillo** m. ORN. coal titmouse.
**cerrojo** m. bolt [fastening]. *2* bolt [of a rifle].

**certamen** *m.* literary contest. *2* competition for a literary, artistic or scientific prize.
**certeramente** *adv.* surely, unerringly.
**certero, -ra** *adj.* good [shot]. *2* well-aimed well-directed, unerring. *3* certain, sure, well-informed.
**certeza, certidumbre** *f.* certainty, certitude.
**certificable** *adj.* certifiable, registrable.
**certificación** *f.* certification.
**certificado** *adj.* registered [letter, package]. *2 m.* registered letter or package. *2* certification, certificate.
**certificador** *m.* certifier.
**certificar** *tr.* to certify, to certificate [assure; attest formally]. *2* to register [a letter or package].
**certísimo, -ma** *adj. superl.* very or most certain.
**certitud** *f.* certainty, certitude.
**cerúleo, -lea** *adj.* cerulean, sky-blue.
**cerumen** *m.* cerumen, earwax.
**cerusa** *f.* CHEM. ceruse.
**cerval** *adj.* deer, deerlike: *miedo* ~, great fear.
**cervantino, -na** *adj.* pertaining or peculiar to Cervantes; in the style of Cervantes.
**cervantista** *adj.* Cervantist.
**cervatillo** *m.* new-born fawn. *2* ZOOL. musk deer.
**cervato** *m.* fawn.
**cervecería** *f.* brewery. *2* alehouse, beer saloon.
**cervecero, -ra** *adj.* [pertaining to] beer. *2 m.-f.* brewer. *3* alehouse keeper.
**cerveza** *f.* beer, ale.
**cervicabra** *f.* ZOOL. an Indian antelope.
**cervical, cervicular** *adj.* cervical.
**cérvidos** *m. pl.* ZOOL. Cervidae.
**cerviguillo** *m.* thick nape of the neck.
**Cervino** *pr. n. el monte* ~, the Matterhorn.
**cervino, -na** *adj.* cervine.
**cerviz,** *pl.* -vices *f.* cervix, neck, nape of the neck: *bajar* or *doblar la* ~, to humble oneself.
**cervuno, -na** *adj.* cervine. *2* deerlike.
**cesación** *f.*, **cesamiento** *m.* cessation, ceasing.
**cesante** *adj.* ceasing. *2* [of a civil servant] out of office; on part pay. *3 m.* civil servant out of office or put on part pay.
**cesantía** *f.* dismissal of public employment. *2* part pay, pension of a dismissed civil servant.
**cesar** *intr.* to cease, stop; to leave off [doing something]; *sin* ~, unceasingly, without cease. *2* [of a civil servant] to go out of office, leave a post.
**César** *m. pr. n.* Caesar.
**cesáreo, -rea** *adj.* Caesarean.
**cesarismo** *m.* Caesarism.
**cese** *m.* cessation of a civil servant in his functions.
**cesibilidad** *f.* LAW transferability.
**cesible** *adj.* LAW transferable.
**cesio** *m.* CHEM. cesium.
**cesión** *f.* cession; transfer, conveyance, assignment.
**cesionario, -ria** *m.-f.* cessionary.
**cesionista** *m.* transferrer, assigner.
**césped, céspede** *m.* thick short grass, sward. *2* turf, sod. *3* BOT. ~ *inglés,* Italian rye grass.
**cesta** *f.* basket, hamper: ~ *de costura,* sewing basket. *2* wicker scoop used in playing the game of pelota.
**cestada** *f.* basketfull.
**cestería** *f.* basketmaking; basketwork. *2* basket shop.
**cestero, -ra** *m.-f.* basketmaker. *2* basket dealer.
**cestilla, cestita** *f.*, **cestillo, cestito** *m.* small basket.
**cesto** *m.* basket, washbasket. *2* HIST. cestus.

**cestodo** *m.* ZOOL. cestode.
**cestón** *m.* large basket. *2* FORT. gabion.
**cesura** *f.* PROS. cæsure.
**ceta** *f.* ZETA.
**cetáceo, -cea** *adj.* ZOOL. cetacean, cetaceous. *2 m.* ZOOL. cetacean. *3 m. pl.* ZOOL. Cetacea.
**cetona** *f.* CHEM. ketone.
**cetrería** *f.* falconry, hawking.
**cetrero** *m.* falconer. *2* ECCL. verger.
**cetrino, -na** *adj.* sallow, greenish yellow. *2* melancholy. *3* citrine; made with citron.
**cetro** *m.* scepter: *empuñar el* ~, to ascend the throne. *2* ECCL. verge. *3* FALCON. perch.
**ceugma** *f.* zeugma.
**ceutí** *adj.-n.* of Ceuta.
**cía** *f.* hipbone.
**ciaboga** *f.* NAUT. *hacer* ~, to put [a boat] about.
**cianhídrico** *adj.* CHEM. hydrocyanic.
**cianosis** *f.* MED. cyanosis.
**cianotipo** *m.* cyanotype, blueprint.
**cianuro** *m.* CHEM. cyanide.
**ciar** *tr.* NAUT. to back water. *2* to go backwards. *3* to back out.
**ciático, -ca** *adj.* sciatic. *2 f.* MED. sciatica.
**Cibeles** *f. pr. n.* MYTH. Cybele.
**cibelina** *f.* zool. sable.
**cibernética** *f.* cybernetics.
**ciborio** *m.* ARCH. ciborium.
**cicatear** *intr.* coll. to act niggardly.
**cicatería** *f.* niggardliness, stinginess.
**cicatero, -ra** *adj.* niggardly, stingy. *2 m.-f.* niggard.
**cicatriz,** *pl.* -trices *f.* cicatrice, cicatrix, scar.
**cicatrizable** *adj.* likely to heal, that may heal.
**cicatrización** *f.* cicatrization.
**cicatrizante** *adj.* MED. cicatrizing, healing.
**cicatrizar** *tr.* to cicatrize, to heal [a wound or ulcer]. *2 ref.* [of a wound or ulcer] to cicatrize, heal, scar.
**cícero** *m.* PRINT. pica.
**Cicerón** *m. pr. n.* Cicero.
**cicerone** *m.* cicerone.
**cicindela** *f.* ENT. tiger beetle.
**Cícladas** *f. pr. n.* Cyclades.
**ciclamino** *m.* BOT. cyclamen.
**ciclamor** *m.* BOT. Judas tree.
**cíclico, -ca** *adj.* cyclic(al).
**ciclismo** *m.* cycling, cyclism.
**ciclista** *m.-f.* cyclist.
**ciclo** *m.* cycle. *2* series [of lectures].
**cicloidal, cicloideo** *adj.* MATH. cycloidal.
**cicloide** *f.* GEOM. cycloid.
**ciclomotor** *m.* autocycle, moped, small motorcycle.
**ciclón** *m.* cyclone.
**cíclope** *m.* MYTH. Cyclops.
**ciclópeo, -ea; ciclópico, -ca** *adj.* Cyclopean, Cyclopic.
**ciclorama** *m.* cyclorama.
**ciclotimia** *f.* MED. cyclothymia.
**ciclostilo** *m.* cyclostile, mimeograph.
**ciclotrón** *m.* PHYS. cyclotron.
**cicuta** *f.* BOT. hemlock, poison hemlock. *2* hemlock [poison]. *3* BOT. ~ *menor,* water hemlock.
**cid** *m.* strong, courageous man. *2 El Cid Campeador,* a medieval Spanish hero.
**cidra** *f.* BOT. citron [fruit]. *2* BOT. ~ *cayote,* a variety of squash.
**cidrada** *f.* preserved citron.
**cidro** *m.* BOT. citron tree.
**cidronela** *f.* BOT. balm *[Melissa officinalis].*

**ciegamente** *adv.* blindly. *2* fearlessly. *3 confiar ~*, to have blind faith.

**ciego, -ga** *adj.* blind [in practically every sense]; blinded: *~ de ira*, blind with anger. *2* [of a channel, pipe, etc.] stopped, blocked. *3 m.-f.* blind man, blind woman. *4 m.* ANAT. caecum, blind gut. *5 adv. a ciegas*, blindly; thoughtlessly.

**ciego, ciegue,** etc. *irr.* V. CEGAR.

**cielito** *m.* darling, dearest, dearie.

**cielo** *m.* sky, heaven: *llovido del ~*, heaven sent; *despejarse el ~*, [of the weather] to clear up; *estar hecho un ~*, to be splendid, brilliant; *poner por los cielos*, to praise to the sky; *ver uno el ~ abierto*, to see one's way out [of a difficulty]; *a ~ abierto*, open to the sky; *a ~ descubierto*, in the open air. *2* heaven, Heaven [celestial abode; God]; *bajado del ~*, excellent, perfect. *3* skies, climate, weather. *4* top, roof, covering: *~ de la cama*, canopy of bed; *~ de la boca*, roof of mouth; *~ raso*, flat celling [of room].

**ciempiés,** *pl.* **-piés** m. ZOOL. centipede, scolopendra. *2* coll. preposterous, disconnected work.

**cien** *adj.* hundred, a hundred, one hundred [used before nouns].

**ciénaga** *f.* marsh, miry or marshy place.

**ciencia** *f.* science; knowledge, learning; certainty; *a ~ y paciencia de*, with the knowledge or sufferance of.

**cienmilésimo, -ma** *adj.-n.* hundred-thousandth.

**cienmillonésimo, -ma** *adj.-n.* hundred-millionth.

**cieno** *m.* silt, slime, mire.

**científico, -ca** *adj.* scientific. *2 m.-f.* scientist.

**cientifismo** *m.* scientism.

**ciento** *adj.-m.* hundred, a hundred, one hundred [used when not before the noun]: *por ~*, per cent.

**cierne** *m.* fecundation of flowers [of some plants]: *en ~*, BOT. blossoming; fig. in the bud.

**cierno, cierna,** etc. *irr.* V. CERNER.

**cierre** *m.* closing, shutting [act of closing]. *2* fastening, snap, clasp; closing or shutting device: *~ de cremallera*, zipper; *~ metálico*, sliding metal shutter.

**cierro** *m.* closing, shutting. *2 ~ de cristales*, glass-enclosed balcony.

**cierro, cierre,** etc. *irr.* V. CERRAR.

**ciertamente** *adj.* certainly, surely.

**cierto, -ta** *adj.* certain, sure: *estar ~*, to be sure; *estar en lo ~*, to be right; *no, por ~*, certainly not; *sí, por ~*, certainly, surely; *por ~ que*, by the way. *2* certain, a certain, some: *~ día*, a certain day, one day.

**cierva** *f.* ZOOL. hind.

**ciervo** *m.* ZOOL. red deer; stag, hart. *2* ENT. *~ volante*, stag beetle.

**cierzo** *m.* cold north wind.

**cifosis** *f.* MED. kyphosis.

**cifra** *f.* cipher, figure, number. *2* amount. *3* cipher [secret writing], code. *4* cipher, monogram. *5* abbreviation. *6* sum, summary. *7 en ~*, in code; enigmatically; in brief.

**cifrado, -da** *adj.* ciphered, in code.

**cifrar** *tr.* to cipher [write in cipher]. *2* to summarize. *3* to base, to place: *~ la dicha en*, to base one's happiness on; *~ sus esperanzas en*, to place one's hope in.

**cigala** *f.* ZOOL. crustacean of the *Scyllarus* genus.

**cigarra** *f.* ENTOM. cicada, harvest fly, *locust.

**cigarral** *m.* country house with orchard [in Toledo].

**cigarrera** *f.* cigar maker or seller [woman]. *2* cigar cabinet. *3* pocket cigar case.

**cigarrillo** *m.* cigarette.

**cigarro** *m.* cigar: *~ puro*, cigar; *~ de papel*, cigarette.

**cigarrón** *m.* ENT. cicada. *2* ENT. grasshopper.

**cigomático, -ca** *adj.* ANAT. zygomatic.

**cigoñal** *m.* well sweep.

**cigoñino** *m.* ORN. young stork.

**cigoñuela** *f.* ORN. stilt.

**cigoto** *m.* BIOL. zygote.

**cigua** *f.* BOT. a tropical tree.

**cigüeña** *m.* ORN. stork. *2* MACH. crank, winch. *3* crank [of a bell].

**cigüeñal** *m.* CIGOÑAL. *2* MACH. crankshaft.

**cilantro** *m.* BOT. coriander.

**ciliado, -da** *adj.* ciliate, ciliated.

**ciliar** *adj.* ANAT. ciliary.

**cilicio** *m.* cilice.

**cilindrada** *f.* AUTO. cylinder capacity.

**cilíndrico, -ca** *adj.* cylindric(al.

**cilindro** *m.* GEOM., MACH., HOROL., PRINT. cylinder. *2* PRINT. roller, in roller.

**cilindroeje** *m.* ANAT. axon, axone.

**cilio** *m.* BIOL. cilium.

**cima** *f.* summit, top, head [of mountain]; top [of tree]. *2* top, height: *por ~*, POR ENCIMA. *3* BOT. cyme. *4 dar ~ a*, to carry out, to achieve.

**cimacio** *m.* ARCH. cymatium, cyma recta.

**cimarrón, -na** *adj.* (Am.) runaway [slave]; gone wild [animal]; wild [plant]. *2 m.* (Am.) maroon [slave].

**cimbalaria** *f.* BOT. Kenilwort ivy, ivywort.

**cimbalero, cimbalista** *m.* MUS. cymbalist.

**cimbalillo** *m.* small bell.

**címbalo** *m.* small bell. *2* MUS. cymbal.

**cimbel** *m.* decoy [bird]. *2* cord by which the decoy is tied.

**cimborio, cimborrio** *m.* ARCH. dome.

**cimbra** *f.* ARCH. centre, center, centring, centering. *2* ARCH. inside curvature of an arch or vault. *3* NAUT. bending of a board.

**cimbrado, -da** *adj.* centred. *2 m.* bend from the waist [dancing].

**cimbrar** *tr.* to vibrate [a flexible thing]. *2* to bend, sway [the body]. *3* ARCH. to build the centering for. *4 ref.* to vibrate, to sway. *5* to bend or sway one's body.

**cimbreante** *adj.* flexible, lithe, pliant; swaying.

**cimbrear** *tr.* CIMBRAR.

**cimbreño, -ña** *adj.* flexible, pliant.

**cimbreo** *m.* act of vibrating, bending, swaying.

**címbrico, -ca** *adj.* Cimbrian.

**cimentación** *f.* foundation; laying the foundation.

**cimentar** *tr.* to lay the foundation for; to found, ground, establish. ¶ CONJUG. like *acertar*.

**cimera** *f.* crest [of helmet]. *2* HER. crest.

**cimero, -ra** *adj.* top, uppermost, crowning.

**cimicaria** *f.* BOT. danewort.

**cimiento** *m.* foundation [of a building, etc.]; groundwork, basis.

**cimiento, cimiente** etc. *irr.* V. CIMENTAR.

**cimitarra** *f.* scimitar.

**cinabrio** *m.* MINER. cinnabar. *2* cinnabar, vermilion.

**cinamomo** *m.* BOT. bead tree, China tree. *2* an aromatic substance.

**cinc** *m.* CHEM. zinc.

**cincel** *m.* chisel.

**cincelado** *m.* chisel(l)ing.

**cinceladura** *f.* carving, chiselling.

**cincelador** *m.* chisel(l)er, sculptor, engraver.
**cincelar** *tr.* to chisel, carve, engrave.
**cinco** *adj.* five: *las* ~, five o'clock; *decir cuántas son* ~, to tell one what's what. *2 m.* five. *3* fifth [in dates].
**cincoenrama** *f.* BOT. cinquefoil.
**cincograbado** *m.* zincography. *2* zincograph.
**cincografía** *f.* zincography.
**cincuenta** *adj.-m.* fifty. *2* fiftieth.
**cincuentavo, -va** *adj.-n.* fiftieth.
**cincuentena** *f.* group of fifty.
**cincuentenario** *m.* semicentennial.
**cincuentón, -na** *adj.-n.* quinquagenarian.
**cincha** *f.* saddle girth, cinch.
**cinchar** *tr.* to girth, cinch up. *2* to band, hoop.
**cincho** *m.* belly band. *2* iron band or hoop. *3* ARCH. transverse rib.
**cine** *m.* cine, movies, pictures: ~ *sonoro*, talkies; ~ *mudo*, silent movies. *2* cinema, picture house.
**cineasta** *m.-f.* movie producer, actor or actress.
**cineclub** *m.* cine club, film club, film society.
**cinegético, -ca** *adj.* cynegetic. *2 f.* cynegetics.
**cinemateca** *f.* film library.
**cinemática** *f.* kinematics.
**cinematografía** *f.* cinematography.
**cinematográfico, -ca** *adj.* cinematographic.
**cinematógrafo** *m.* cinematograph. *2* cinema, movies [show]. *3* film projector.
**cineraria** *f.* BOT. cineraria.
**cinerario, -ria** *adj.* cinerary.
**cinéreo, -a** *adj.* cinereous, ash-gray.
**cinestesia** *f.* kinaesthesis, kinesthesis.
**cinético, -ca** *adj.* kinetic. *2 f.* kinetics.
**cingalés, -sa** *adj.-n.* Cingalese.
**cíngaro, -ra** *adj.* gypsy. *2 m.-f.* zíngaro.
**cingiberáceas** *f. pl.* BOT. zingiberaceae.
**cinglar** *tr.* to shingle [iron]. *2* NAUT. to propel [a boat] with only one oar aft.
**cíngulo** *m.* cingulum.
**cínico, -ca** *adj.* cynical. *2* barefaced, impudent. *3 m.-f.* cynic. *4 m.* Cynic.
**cínife** *m.* MOSQUITO.
**cinismo** *m.* cynicism. *2* barefacedness, impudence.
**cinocéfalo** *m.* ZOOL. baboon.
**cinoglosa** *f.* BOT. hound's tongue.
**cinta** *f.* ribbon, tape, band: ~ *magnetofónica*, recording tape; ~ *métrica*, decimal tape measure. *2* CINEM. film. *3* ARCH. fillet. *4* NAUT. wale.
**cintarazo** *m.* blow with the flat of the sword.
**cinteado, -da** *adj.* beribboned.
**cintería** *f.* ribbons. *2* ribbon trade. *3* ribbon shop.
**cintillo** *m.* ornamental hat cord. *2* small ring with precious stones.
**cinto, -ta** *adj.* girdled. *2 m.* belt, girdle. *3* waist [of a person].
**cintra** *f.* ARCH. curvature [of an arch or vault].
**cintrado, -da** *adj.* ARCH. arched.
**cintura** *f.* waist, waistline. *2* waistband [of dress]. *3* throat [of chimney]. *4* *meter en* ~, to discipline, bring into subjection.
**cinturón** *m.* belt [around the waist; around something]: ~ *de seguridad*, safety belt; ~ life belt.
**cipayo** *m.* sepoy.
**ciperáceo, -a** *adj.* BOT. cyperaceous.
**cipolino** *m.* cipolin, onion marble.
**ciprés** *m.* BOT. cypress.
**ciprino** *m.* cyprinid. *pl.* cyprinidae.
**Cipriano** *m. pr. n.* Cyprian.
**ciprio, -pria** *adj.-n.* Cyprian [of Cyprus].
**circense** *adj.* Circensian.

**circo** *m.* [Roman] circus. *2* GEOL. circus, cirque. *2* *circo* or ~ *equestre*, circus [show].
**circón** *m.* MINER. zircon.
**circonio** *m.* CHEM. zirconium.
**circuito** *m.* circuit: *corto* ~, ELECT. short circuit.
**circulación** *f.* circulation; currency. *2* traffic, movement [of vehicles, etc.].
**circulante** *adj.* circulating.
1) **circular** *adj.* circular. *2 f.* circular, circular letter.
2) **circular** *intr.* to circulate. *2* to walk, move, pass.
**circulatorio, -ria** *adj.* circulatory.
**círculo** *m.* circle: ~ *máximo*, ~ *polar*, ASTR. great circle; polar circle; ~ *vicioso*, vicious circle. *2* circumference. *3* club, casino.
**circumpolar** *adj.* circumpolar.
**circuncidar** *tr.* to circumcise.
**circuncisión** *f.* circumcision.
**circunciso, -sa** *adj.* circumcised.
**circundante** *adj.* surrounding.
**circundar** *tr.* to surround.
**circunferencia** *f.* circumference.
**circunferente** *adj.* circumscribing, surrounding, limiting.
**circunferir** *tr.* to circumscribe, to limit.
**circunflejo** *adj.* circumflex [accent].
**circunlocución** *f.*, **circunloquio** *m.* circumlocution.
**circunnavegación** *f.* circumnavigation.
**circunnavegar** *tr.* to circumnavigate.
**circunscribir** *tr.* to circumscribe. *3* *ref.* to confine oneself [to].
**circunscripción** *f.* circumscription. *2* district, territory.
**circunscripto, -ta; circunscrito, -ta** *adj.* circumscribed; circumscript.
**circunspección** *f.* circumspection. *2* decorousness, decorum, dignity.
**circunspecto, -ta** *adj.* circumspect.
**circunstancia** *f.* circumstance: *en las circunstancias presentes*, under the circumstances. *2* particular, detail.
**circunstanciado, -da** *adj.* circumstancial, minute, particular.
**circunstancial** *adj.* circumstantial [pertaining to, or depending on, circumstances].
**circunstancialmente** *adv.* temporarily, provisionally.
**circunstante** *adj.* present, surrounding. *2 m. pl.* persons that are present, bystanders, audience.
**circunvalación** *f.* circumvallation: *carretera de* ~, bypass, ring road.
**circunvalar** *tr.* to circumvallate.
**circunvecino, -na** *adj.* neighbouring, adjacent, surrounding.
**circunvolar** *tr.* to fly around.
**circunvolución** *f.* circumvolution.
**cirial** *m.* ECCL. processional candlestick.
**Cirilo** *pr. n.* Cyril.
**cirineo, -da** *adj.* CIRENEO. *2 m.* fig. helper, candle.
**cirio** *m.* ECCL. wax candle.
**Ciro** *m. pr. n.* Cyrus.
**cirrípedo, -da** *adj.* CIRRÓPODO.
**cirro** *m.* BOT., METEOR., ZOOL. cirrus. *2* MED. scirrhus.
**cirrópodo, -da** *adj.-m.* cirriped.
**cirrosis** *f.* MED. cirrhosis.
**cirrótico, -ca** *adj.* cirrhotic.
**ciruela** *f.* plum [fruit]: ~ *damascena*, damson; ~ *claudia*, greengage; ~ *pasa*, dry plum, prune.
**ciruelo** *m.* BOT. plum tree. *2* coll. dolt.

**cirugía** *f.* surgery [science or art].
**cirujano** *m.* surgeon.
**cisalpino, -na** *adj.* cisalpine.
**cisca** *f.* BOT. sedge.
**ciscar** *tr.* to dirty, soil. *2 ref.* to ease nature.
**cisco** *m.* broken up charcoal: *hacer* ~, to shatter, smash. *2* row, breeze, shindy.
**ciscón** *m.* clinker, ashes, a piece of slag. *2* (Am.) easily offended.
**cisión** *f.* cutting, cut, incision.
**cisma** *m.* schism. *2* discord.
**cismático, -ca** *adj.-n.* schismatic.
**cisne** *m.* ZOOL. swan. *2* fig. swan, poet.
**cisoide** *f.* GEOM. cissoid.
**cisoria** *adj. arte* ~, art of carving meat.
**cisquero** *m.* pounce bag.
**cista** *f.* cist, kist.
**cistel, císter** *m.* Cistercian order.
**cisterciense** *adj.-m.* Cistercian.
**cisterna** *f.* cistern, reservoir. *2* water tank.
**cístico** *adj.* ANAT. cystic [duct].
**cistitis** *f.* MED. cystitis.
**cisto** *m.* BOT. cistus.
**cistotomía** *f.* cystotomy.
**cisura** *f.* fissure. *2* ANAT. sulcus.
**cita** *f.* appointment, engagement, date [for a meeting]: *darse* ~, to make an appointment. *2* [in a bad sense] assignation. *3* citation, quotation.
**citación** *f.* citation, quotation. *2* LAW citation, summons.
**citador, -ra** *m.-f.* citator.
**citar** *tr.* to make an appointment with. *2* LAW to cite, summon. *3* to cite, quote. *4* BULLF. to incite [the bull].
**cítara** *f.* MUS. cithara. *2* MUS. cithern, cittern. *3* MUS. zithern.
**citarista** *m.-f.* citharist. *2* zithern player.
**Citerea** *pr. n.* MYTH. Cytherea.
**citerior** *adj.* hither, nearer: *España* ~, the northeastern part of Roman Spain.
**citiso** *m.* BOT. cytisus.
**citola** *f.* clapper [in a corn mill], millclapper.
**citoplasma** *m.* BIOL. cytoplasm.
**citrato** *m.* CHEM. citrate.
**cítrico, -ca** *adj.* CHEM. citric.
**ciudad** *f.* city, town: *Ciudad del Cabo*, Cape Town; ~ *jardín*, garden city. *2* city council.
**ciudadanía** *f.* citizenship.
**ciudadano, -na** *adj.* [pertaining to the] city or town. *2* civic. *3* citizenly. *4* *m.-f.* citizen, urbanite.
**ciudadela** *f.* FORT. citadel.
**civeta** *f.* ZOOL. civet cat.
**civeto** *m.* civet.
**cívico, -ca** *adj.* civic. *2* civil, polite.
**civilidad** *f.* civility, politeness, sociability.
**civil** *adj.* civil. *2 adj.-n.* civilian [non military person]. *3 m.* a member of the *Guardia civil*.
**civilización** *f.* civilization.
**civilizado, -da** *adj.* civilized.
**civilizar** *tr.* to civilize. *2 ref.* to become civilized.
**civismo** *m.* civism, good citizenship.
**cizalla** *f.* or **cizallas** *f. pl.* sheet-metal shears. *2* paper cutter. *3* metal clippings.
**cizallar** *tr.* to shear [metal sheets or paper].
**cizaña** *f.* BOT. darnel. *2* BIBL. tare. *3* corrupting vice, bad influence. *4* discord.
**cizañar** *tr.* to sow discord in.
**clac** *m.* opera hat, claque, collapsible hat.
**clamar** *tr.-intr.* to clamour, cry, cry out: ~ *contra*,

to clamour against; ~ *al cielo*, to cry to heaven. *2 intr.* [of things] to want, require, demand.
**clámide** *f.* chlamys.
**clamor** *m.* clamour, outcry. *2* plaint, cry of affliction. *3* knell, toll of bells.
**clamorear** *tr.* to clamour. *2 intr.* [of bells] to knell, toll.
**clamoreo** *m.* clamour, clamouring.
**clamoroso, -sa** *adj.* clamourous; crying.
**clan** *m.* clan.
**clandestinidad** *f.* clandestinity.
**clandestino, -na** *adj.* clandestine.
**claque** *f.* THEAT. claque.
**Clara** *f. pr. n.* Clara, Claire.
**clara** *f.* white of egg. *2* bald spot. *3* thinly woven spot [in cloth]. *4* break [in a rainy day]. *5 adv. a la* ~, *a las claras*, openly, manifestly.
**claraboya** *f.* skylight. *2* clerestory.
**clarear** *tr.* to make clear. *2 intr.* to dawn. *3* [of weather] to clear, clear up. *4 ref.* to be transparent. *5* to disclose one's intentions.
**clarecer** *intr.* to dawn. ¶ CONJUG. like *agradecer*.
**clareo** *m.* clearing [a thicket or woods].
**clarete** *m.* claret wine.
**claridad** *f.* light. *2* clarity. *3* clearness; distinctness; plainness. *4* brightness. *5 pl.* home truths, plain truths.
**clarificar** *tr.* to clarify.
**clarín** *m.* BUS. clarion; bugle. *2* clarion player.
**clarinete** *m.* MUS. clarinet. *2* clarinet(t)ist.
**clarión** *m.* white crayon, chalk.
**clarisa** *f.* Clare [nun].
**clarísimo, -ma** *m.* very clear. *2* most illustrious.
**clarividencia** *f.* clairvoyance, clear-sightedness.
**clarividente** *adj.* clairvoyant, clear-sighted.
**claro, -ra** *adj.* bright, full of light. *2* clear [pure, nitid, transparent]. *3* clear, plain, obvious, distinct, intelligible. *4* clear [vision, intellect, day, night, weather, etc.]. *5* thin [liquid]; thin, sparse [hair, vegetation, etc.]. *6* light [colour; in colour]. *7* unspoken. *8* clear, illustrious. *9 adv.* clearly, plainly, outspokenly. *10 interj.* ¡*claro!*, ¡*claro está!*, of course!, sure! *11 m.* gap, break, space, interval. *12* clearing [in woods]. *13* PAINT. light. *14* ARCH. light, opening. *15 poner en* ~, to make plain, to clear up, elucidate. *16 pasar la noche de* ~ *en* ~, not to sleep a wink.
**claroscuro** *m.* PAINT. clear obscure, chiaroscuro.
**clarucho, -cha** *adj.* coll. thin, watery.
**clase** *f.* class, classes, order: ~ *alta*, upper classes; *clases pasivas*, pensioners. *2* HIST. NAT., RLY., NAUT. class. *3* class, kind, sort: *toda* ~ *de*, all kind of. *4* EDUC. class; classroom. *5* MIL. *clases de tropa*, non commissioned officers.
**clasicismo** *m.* classicism.
**clasicista** *adj.* classicistic. *2 m.-f.* classicist.
**clásico, -ca** *adj.* classic(al. *2 m.* classic [author].
**clasificable** *adj.* classifiable.
**clasificación** *f.* classification. *2* sorting, filing.
**clasificado, -da** *adj.* classified.
**clasificador, -ra** *adj.* classifying. *2 m.-f.* classifier. *3 m.* filing cabinet, file.
**clasificar** *tr.* to class, classify. *2* to sort, file.
**claudia** *adj. f. ciruela* ~, *reina* ~, greengage.
**Claudia** *f. pr. n.* Claudia, Claudette.
**claudicación** *f.* limping. *2* being untrue to one's professed principles.
**claudicante** *adj.* halting, limping.
**claudicar** *intr.* to halt, limp. *2* to be untrue to one's professed principles.
**Claudio** *m. pr. n.* Claude, Claudius.

**claustral** *adj.* claustral; cloistral.
**claustro** *m.* ARCH., ECCL. cloister. *2* faculty, academic staff. *3* ~ *materno*, womb, matrix.
**claustrofobia** *f.* MED. claustrophobia.
**cláusula** *f.* clause [in a document], proviso. *2* GRAM. sentence, period.
**clausura** *f.* inner part of a monastery or convent. *2* cloister, monastic confinement. *3* official closing of a congress, court sessions, etc.
**clausurar** *tr.* to close [sessions, a congress, etc.].
**clava** *f.* club [stick].
**clavado, -da** *adj.* nailed. *2* nail-studded. *3* exact, precise. *4* fitting exactly, apposite.
**clavadura** *f.* prick in a horse's hoof.
**clavar** *tr.* to drive, stick, thrust [something pointed], to prick or stab with. *2* to nail, to pin. *3* to fix [eyes, etc.]. *4* to set [a precious stone]. *5* to spike [a cannon]. *6* *tr.-ref.* to deceive.
**clave** *f.* key [to a riddle, etc.]. *2* code, cryptography: ~ *telegráfica*, telegraphic code. *3* ARCH. keystone. *4* MUS. clef. *5* *m.* MUS. clavichord.
**clavecín** *m.* MUS. clavecin, harpsichord.
**clavel** *m.* BOT. pink, carnation: ~ *coronado*, grass pink; ~ *doble*, carnation; ~ *reventón*, large carnation.
**clavelito** *m.* BOT. sweet william.
**clavelón** *m.* BOT. marigold, African marigold.
**clavellina** *f.* BOT. pink: ~ *de pluma*, grass pink.
**clavero, -ra** *m.-f.* keeper of the keys. *2 m.* BOT. clove tree.
**claveteado** *m.* studding.
**clavetear** *tr.* to stud, nail [stud with nails]. *2* to tip, tag [a lace]. *3* to wind up, settle.
**clavicémbalo** *m.* MUS. clavicymbal, harpsichord.
**clavicordio** *m.* MUS. clavichord.
**clavícula** *f.* ANAT. clavicle, collar bone.
**clavija** *f.* pin, peg, dowel, treenail. *2* MEC. pintle. *3* MUS. peg, wrest pin [of a stringed instrument]. *4* ELECT. plug.
**clavijero** *m.* MUS. pegbox [of guitar, etc.]. *2* wrest block, wrest plank [of piano].
**clavillo** *m.* rivet, pin [of scissors or fan]. *2* clove [spice].
**clavo** *m.* nail [of metal]: ~ *de adorno*, stud; ~ *de rosca*, screw; *agarrarse a un* ~ *ardiendo*, to catch at a straw; *dar en el* ~, to hit the nail on the head; *de* ~ *pasado*, self-evident; easy. *2* corn [on the foot]. *3* headache. *4* grief, pain. *5* core [of boil]. *6* SURG. tent. *7* *clavo* or ~ *de especia*, clove [spice].
**clemátide** *f.* BOT. clematis, virgin's bower.
**clemencia** *f.* clemency, mercy, forbearance.
**clemente** *adj.* clement, merciful.
**clepsidra** *f.* clepsydra, water clock.
**cleptomanía** *f.* kleptomania.
**clerecía** *f.* clergy.
**clerical** *adj.* clerical [pertaining to the clergy]. *2 adj.-n.* POL. clerical.
**clericalismo** *m.* clericalism.
**clerigalla** *f.* [contempt.] priests, priesthood.
**clérigo** *m.* clergyman, priest. *2* HIST. clerk, scholar.
**clero** *m.* clergy.
**clerofobia** *f.* hatred of priests.
**cliché** *m.* cliché, stereotyped expression.
**cliente** *m.-f.* client. *2* customer.
**clientela** *f.* clientele, practice, customers.
**clima** *m.* climate. *2* clime.
**climatérico, -ca** *adj.* climacteric.
**climático, -ca** *f.* climatic(cal.
**climatología** *f.* climatology.
**climax** *m.* RHET. climax.

**clin** *f.* CRIN.
**clínica** *f.* clinic. *2* private hospital. *3* clinical medicine.
**clínico, -ca** *adj.* clinical. *2 m.-f.* clinician.
**Clío** *f.* *pr. n.* MYTH. Clio.
**clip** *m.* clip, paper clip. *2* clip, hairclip, hairpin. *3* earclip, earring.
**clíper** *m.* NAUT., AER. clipper.
**clisado** *m.* PRINT. plating, stereotyping.
**clisar** *tr.* PRINT. to plate, stereotype.
**clisé** *m.* PRINT. plate, stereotype plate.
**clistel, clister** *m.* MED. clyster, enema.
**clivoso, -sa** *adj.* poet. sloping.
**cloaca** *f.* sewer, cloaca. *2* ZOOL. cloaca.
**clocar** *intr.* CLOQUEAR.
**Clodoveo** *m.* *pr. n.* Clovis.
**cloquear** *intr.* [of a hen] to cluck.
**cloqueo** *m.* cluck, clucking.
**cloral** *m.* CHEM. chloral.
**clorato** *m.* CHEM. chlorate.
**clorhídrico, -ca** *adj.* CHEM. hydrochloric.
**cloro** *m.* CHEM. chlorine.
**clorofila** *f.* BOT., BIOCHEM. chlorophyll.
**cloroformizar** *tr.* to chloroform, chloroformize.
**cloroformo** *m.* CHEM. chloroform.
**cloroplasto** *m.* BOT. chloroplast.
**clorosis** *f.* MED. chlorosis.
**clorótico, -ca** *adj.* chlorotic.
**cloruro** *m.* CHEM. chloride.
**Clotilde** *f.* *pr. n.* Clotilda.
**clown** *m.* circus clown.
**club** *m.* club [association].
**clueco, -ca** *adj.* broody [hen]. *2* coll. decrepit, *f.* broody hen.
**cluniacense** *adj.-n.* Cluniac.
**coacción** *f.* coaction, coercion, compulsion.
**coaccionar** *tr.* to coerce, compel.
**coactivo, -va** *adj.* coactive, compelling.
**coacusado, -da** *m.-f.* LAW codefendant.
**coadjutor** *m.* coadjutor. *2* assistant to a parish priest.
**coadjutora** *f.* coadjutrix.
**coadministrador** *m.* coadministrator.
**coadquisición** *f.* joint purchase.
**coadyutorio, -ria** *adj.* helping, aiding.
**coadyuvante** *adj.* coadjuvant, co-operating.
**coadyuvar** *intr.* to aid, co-operate, contribute.
**coagente** *m.* helper, assistant, coadjutant.
**coagulable** *adj.* coagulable, likely to coagulate.
**coagulación** *f.* coagulation; curdling.
**coagulador, -ra** *adj.* coagulative, coagulant. *2* coagulator, coagulant.
**coagulante** *adj.* coagulative. *2 m.* coagulant.
**coagular** *tr.* to coagulate; to curdle, to clot. *2 ref.* to coagulate [undergo coagulation].
**coágulo** *m.* coagulum, curd, clot.
**coaita** *m.* MONO ARAÑA.
**coalición** *f.* coalition, league.
**coaligarse** *ref.* to associate, to ally, to unite. *2* to form a coalition, to coalesce.
**coana** *f.* ANAT. choana.
**coarrendador** *m.* joint lessor.
**coartación** *f.* limitation, restriction.
**coartada** *f.* alibi: *probar la* ~, to prove an alibi.
**coartar** *tr.* to limit, to restrict.
**coatí** *m.* ZOOL. coati.
**coautor, -ra** *m.-f.* co-author; joint doer.
**coaxial** *adj.* MATH. coaxial, coaxal.
**coba** *f.* humorous lie. *2* soft soap, flattery.
**cobalto** *m.* CHEM. cobalt.

**cobarde** *adj.* cowardly; timid. *2 m.-f.* coward, yellow.

**cobardear** *intr.* to be cowardly.

**cobardía** *f.* cowardice, faint-heartedness.

**cobayo** *m.* ZOOL. guinea pig.

**cobear** *tr.* COLL. to play up to, to butter up to, to suck up to, to soap up.

**cobertera** *f.* lid, cover [of pot, pan, etc.]. *2* fig. ALCAHUETA. *3* ORN. tail covert [feather].

**cobertizo** *m.* shed; lean-to. *2* penthouse.

**cobertor** *m.* bedcover, coverlet; counterpane.

**cobertura** *m.* cover, covering. *2* FINANCE coverage.

**cobija** *f.* ridge tile. *2* ORN. covert [feather]. *3* cover, covering. *4 pl.* (Am.) bedclothes.

**cobijar** *tr.* to cover, to shelter, give shelter. *2 ref.* to take shelter.

**cobijo** *m.* covering, sheltering, shelter: *hallar* ~, to find shelter. *2* lodgings.

**cobra** *f.* ZOOL. cobra. *2* HUNT. retrieving, retrieval. *3* yoke strap. *4* mares employed in threshing.

**cobrable; cobradero, -ra** *adj.* collectable, collectible.

**cobrador** *m.* collector [of money]; receiving teller. *2* tram or bus conductor. *3 adj.* retriever [dog].

**cobranza** *f.* recovery, collection, cashing.

**cobrar** *tr.* to collect, receive [money, taxes]; to cash [cheques]; to get paid. *2* COLL. to catch it. *3* to charge [a price]. *4* to recover. *5* to take, acquire, gather: ~ *ánimo*, to take courage; ~ *cariño*, to take a liking; ~ *fuerzas*, to gather strength . *6* to pull in [a rope]. *7* HUNT. to retrieve. *8* HUNT. to take [game]. *9 ref.* to recover, to come to.

**cobre** *m.* CHEM. copper. *2* brasses [kitchen utensils]. *3* MUS. brass, brasses.

**cobreño, -ña** *adj.* copper [of copper].

**cobrizo, -za** *adj.* coppery. *2* copper-coloured.

**cobro** *m.* cashing, collection. *2 poner en* ~, to put in a safe place; *poner* ~ *en*, to be careful, to be cautious about.

**coca** *f.* BOT. coca. *2* coca leaf. *3* little round berry. *4* a medieval boat. *5* kink [in a rope]. *6* coll. head, bean. *7* side hair of women. *8* BOT. ~ *de Levante*, India berry tree.

**cocaína** *f.* CHEM. cocaine.

**cocción** *f.* cooking, boiling. *2* baking [of bread, bricks, pottery, etc.].

**cóccix** *m.* ANAT. coccix.

**coceador, -ra** *adj.* kicking [animal].

**coceadura** *f.*, **coceamiento** *m.* kicking.

**cocear** *intr.* [of animals] to kick.

**cocedero, -ra** *adj.* easily cooked, boiled or baked.

**cocer** *tr.* to cook [food]. *2* to boil [a substance]. *3* to boil [bread, bricks, pottery, etc.]. *4* to digest [in the stomach]. *5 intr.* [of a liquid] to boil. *6* [of wine] to ferment. *7 ref.* to cook, to be cooked, boiled or baked. ¶ CONJUG. like *mover*.

**cocido, -da** *adj.* cooked, boiled, baked, done. *2 m.* Spanish dish of boiled meat and vegetables.

**cociente** *m.* MATH. quotient.

**cocimiento** *m.* COCCIÓN. *2* decoction.

**cocina** *f.* kitchen. *2* NAUT. galley. *3* kitchen stove: ~ *económica*, cooking range. *4* cookery, cooking, cuisine.

**cocinar** *tr.* to cook [food]. *2 intr.* to cook, do the cooking. *3* coll. to meddle.

**cocinero, -ra** *m.-f.* cook.

**cocinilla** *f. dim.* alcohol stove, camping stove.

**cóclea** *f.* Archimedean screw. *2* ANAT., BOT. cochlea.

**coclearia** *f.* BOT. scurvy grass.

**coco** *m.* BOT. coco, coconut palm or tree. *2* BOT. co-conut. *3* grub [larva]. *4* BACT. coccus. *5* bogey, bogy, bugbear. *6* face, grimace: *hacer cocos*, to cajole; to make eyes, to flirt.

**cocodrilo** *m.* ZOOL. crocodile.

**cócora** *adj.* bothersome, annoying. *2 m.-f.* bothersome person.

**cocotal** *m.* coconut grove.

**cocotero** *m.* BOT. coco palm, coconut palm or tree.

**coctel** *m.* cocktail; cocktail party.

**coctelera** *f.* cocktail shaker.

**cochambre** *m.* coll, greasy, stinking filth.

**cochambroso, -sa** *adj.* coll. filthy and stinking.

**coche** *m.* coach, carriage, car: ~ *de alquiler, de punto*, cab, hack; ~ *de camino*, stage-coach; ~ *fúnebre*, hearse. *2* AUT. car: ~ *de turismo*, touring car. *3* RLY. car, carriage: ~ *cama*, sleeping car; ~ *restaurante*, dining car. *4* tram car; omnibus.

**cochera** *f.* coach house, livery stable. *2* tramway depot. *3* coachman's wife.

**cochero** *m.* coachman, carriage driver: ~ *de punto*, cabby, hackman.

**cochevís** *m.* COGUJADA.

**cochifrito** *m.* fricassee of lamb or kid.

**cochina** *f.* ZOOL. sow.

**cochinada** *f.* dirty thing. *2* dirty trick.

**Cochinchina** *f. pr. n.* GEOG. Cochin China.

**cochinería** *f.* filth, dirt; dirty thing. *2* dirty, base, indecorous action.

**cochinero, -ra** *adj.* of hog; for hogs.

**cochinilla** *f.* ENT. cochineal insect. *2* cochineal [dyestuff]. *3* ZOOL. ~ *de la humedad*, sow bug.

**cochinillo** *m.* sucking pig.

**cochino, -na** *adj.* filthy, dirty; piggish. *2* paltry. *3 m.* ZOOL. pig, hog. *5 m.-f.* dirty person.

**cochitril** *m.* pigsty. *2* filthy room, hovel.

**cochura** *f.* COCCIÓN. *2* dough for a batch of bread.

**coda** *f.* MUS. coda. *2* CARP. corner block.

**codal** *m.* ARM. elbow-piece. *2* ARCH. horizontal strut. *3* frame side of bow saw.

**codaste** *m.* NAUT. sternpost.

**codazo** *m.* poke with the elbow; nudge.

**codear** *intr.* to elbow, move the elbows. *2 ref.* codearse con, to mix or hobnob with.

**codeína** *f.* CHEM. codein, codeine.

**codeo** *m.* elbowing, nudging. *2* hobnobbing.

**codera** *f.* elbow patch. *2* itch on the elbow. *3* NAUT. stern fast.

**codeso** *m.* BOT. a Spanish cytisus.

**codeudor, -ra** *m.-f.* joint debtor.

**códice** *m.* codex.

**codicia** *f.* covetousness, cupidity, greed.

**codiciable** *adj.* covetable.

**codiciado, -da** *adj.* much desired, coveted, yearned for.

**codiciar** *tr.* to covet.

**codicilo** *m.* LAW codicil.

**codiciosamente** *adv.* covetously, greedily.

**codicioso, -sa** *adj.* covetous, greedy, grasping. *2* desirous. *3* coll. industrious, hard-working.

**codificación** *f.* codification.

**codificar** *tr.* to codify.

**codificador** *n.* codifier.

**código** *m.* code [collection or body of laws; system of principles or rules]: ~ *civil*, civil code; ~ *militar*, military law; ~ *del honor*, code of honour. *2* NAUT. ~ *de señales*, signal code.

**codillera** *f.* tumour in a horse's elbow.

**codillo** *m.* elbow, shoulder [of quadruped]. *2* elbow, bend [in tube or pipe]. *4* stump [of branch]. *5* NAUT. end [of keel]. *6* a term at ombre, used when the game is lost by the challen-

ger; *tirar a uno al* ~, to do one's best to harm somebody.
**codirección** *f.* co-direction, joint management.
**codirector, -ra** *n.* co-director, co-directress, co-manager, co-manageress.
**codo** *m.* ANAT. elbow; *dar de* ~, or *del* ~, to nudge; to spurn. *2* CODILLO I. *3* elbow, bend [in tube or pipe]. *4* cubit [measure].
**codoñate** *m.* quince sweet.
**codorniz,** *pl.* **-nices** *f.* ORN. quail.
**coeducación** *f.* coeducation.
**coeficiente** *adj.-m.* coefficient.
**coercer** *tr.* to coerce.
**coerción** *f.* coertion.
**coercitivo, -va** *adj.* coercive.
**coetáneo, -a** *adj.-n.* contemporary.
**coexistencia** *f.* coexistence.
**coexistente** *adj.* coexisting, coexistent.
**coexistir** *intr.* to coexist.
**cofa** *f.* NAUT. top [platform].
**cofia** *f.* hair net. *2* women's cap. *3* ARM. coif.
**cofrade** *m.-f.* member of a confraternity.
**cofradía** *f.* confraternity, brotherhood, guild.
**cofre** *m.* coffer; trunk, chest. *2* ICHTH. trunkfish.
**cogedera** *f.* forked pole for gathering fruits.
**cogedor** *m.* dustpan. *2* coal or ash shovel.
**coger** *tr.* to take, seize, grasp; to take hold of; ~ *a uno de la mano*, to take someone by the hand. *2* to catch: ~ *un resfriado*, to catch a cold. *3* to get: ~ *la delantera*, to get the start. *4* to overtake. *5* to take, surprise: ~ *desprevenido*, to take unawares. *6* to find: ~ *a uno en casa*, to find someone at home. *7* to pick, gather, collect [flowers, fruits, etc.]. *8* to take up, absorb. *9* to hold [have capacity for]. *10* to cover, occupy. *11* BULLF. [of the bull] to gore [the bullfighter]. *12* ~ *la palabra a uno*, to hold someone to his promise.
**cogestión** *f.* co-partnership.
**cogida** *f.* picking, gathering, harvest. *2* act of the bull goring the bullfighter.
**cogido** *m.* gather [in cloth].
**cogitabundo, -da** *adj.* pensive, quietly thoughtful.
**cogitación** *f.* cogitation.
**cogitativo, -va** *adj.* cogitative.
**cognación** *f.* cognation [blood relationship].
**cognado, -da** *adj.* GRAM. cognate. *2* *m.-f.* cognate.
**cognición** *f.* cognition.
**cognomento** *m.* cognomen, appellation.
**cognoscible** *adj.* cognoscible.
**cognoscitivo, -va** *adj.* cognoscitive.
**cogollo** *m.* heart [of lettuce, cabbage, etc.]. *2* shoot [of plant]. *3* fig. cream, the best.
**cogorza** *f.* coll. drunkeness.
**cogotazo** *m.* slap on the back of the neck.
**cogote** *m.* back of the neck.
**cogotera** *f.* havelock. *2* sun-bonnet for carriage horses.
**cogotudo, -da** *adj.* thick-necked. *2* coll. proud, haughty. *3* *m.* (Am.) enriched commoner.
**cogujada** *f.* ORN. crested lark.
**cogulla** *f.* cowl, frock [of monk].
**cogullada** *f.* dewlap [of pig].
**cohabitar** *intr.* to cohabit.
**cohechar** *tr.* to bribe [a judge, etc.].
**cohecho** *m.* bribing, bribery.
**coheredar** *tr.* to inherit jointly.
**coheredero** *m.* coheir.
**coherencia** *f.* coherence. *2* PHYS. cohesion.
**coherente** *adj.* coherent.
**cohesión** *f.* cohesion.

**cohesivo, -va** *adj.* cohesive.
**cohesor** *m.* RADIO. coherer.
**cohete** *m.* rocket, skyrocket.
**cohibición** *f.* restraint; embarrassment.
**cohibido, -da** *adj.* restrained; embarrassed, ill at ease.
**cohibir** *tr.* to restrain. *2* to constrain, embarrass.
**cohombro** *m.* BOT. cucumber. *2* ZOOL. ~ *de mar*, sea cucumber.
**cohonestar** *tr.* to give an honest appearance to [an action].
**cohorte** *f.* cohort.
**coima** *f.* concubine.
**coincidencia** *f.* coincidence.
**coincidente** *adj.* coincident.
**coincidir** *intr.* to coincide.
**coito** *m.* coition, coitus.
**cojear** *intr.* to limp, halt, hobble. *2* [of a table, chair, etc.] to be unsteady. *3* to have a failing or a weakness: *saber de qué pie cojea uno*, to know someone's weakness.
**cojera** *f.* lameness, halt, limp, hobble.
**cojín** *m.* cushion.
**cojinete** *m.* small cushion; pad. *2* RLY. chair. *3* MAC. bearing, pillow block: ~ *de bolas*, ball bearing; ~ *de rodillos*, roller bearing.
**cojitranco, -ca** *adj.* bustling lame person.
**cojo, -ja** *adj.* lame [person, animal, leg]. *2* unsteady [table, chair, etc.]. *3* out of scan [line]. *4* *m.-f.* lame person, cripple.
**cojudo, -da** *adj.* not castrated.
**cojuelo, -la** *adj.* dim. of COJO.
**col** *f.* BOT. cabbage: *coles de Bruselas*, Brussels sprouts.
**cola** *f.* BOT. tail [of animal, bird or comet]: fig. *tener* or *traer* ~ *una cosa*, to have serious consequences. *2* train [of gown]. *3* tail, tail end. *4* queue, line: *hacer* ~, to queue up. *5* last place, end, rear [of queue, line, etc.]: *a la* ~, behind, in the rear. *6* ARQ. back [of ashlar]. *7* glue: ~ *de pescado*, fish glue, isinglass. *8* BOT. cola, kola [tree and nut]. *9* BOT. ~ *de caballo*, horsetail. *10* CARP. ~ *de milano* or *de pato*, dovetail.
**colaboración** *f.* collaboration.
**colaborador, -ra** *m.-f.* collaborator. *2* contributor [to a publication].
**colaborar** *intr.* to collaborate. *2* to contribute articles [to a publication].
**colación** *f.* conferring [of a degree, of an ecclesiastical benefice]. *2* collation [comparison]. *3* collation, light meal. *4* *sacar a* ~, to mention.
**colacionar** *tr.* to confer [an ecclesiastical benefice]. *2* to collate, compare. *3* LAW to collate.
**colada** *f.* bucking, bleaching [of washed clothes]. *2* buck, lye. *3* washing [washed clothes]. *4* cattle run. *5* narrow mountain pass. *6* tap [of blast furnace].
**coladera** *f.* strainer for liquors.
**coladero** *m.* strainer, colander. *2* narrow pass.
**colado, -da** *adj.* *hierro* ~, cast iron; *aire* ~, draught. *2* *estar colado por* ~, to be mad or crazy about, to have a crush on.
**colador** *m.* strainer, colander.
**coladura** *f.* straining [of liquids]. *2* slip, faux pas, blunder.
**colapez** *f.* fish glue, isinglass.
**colapso** *m.* MED. collapse. *2* fig. collapse, breakdown.
**colar** *tr.* ECCL. to confer [a benefice]. *2* to strain [pass through a strainer]. *3* to buck, bleach [washed clothes]. *4* *intr.* to pass through inters-

tices or a narrow space. 5 to pass [be accepted]: fig. *ésta no cuela*, I don't believe that. 6 *ref.* to slip or sneak in. 7 to make a slip, to blunder. ¶ CONJUG. like *contar*.
**colateral** *adj.* side, lateral. 2 collateral [relative].
**colcótar** *m.* CHEM. colcothar.
**colcrén** *f.* cold cream.
**colcha** *f.* counterpane, quilt.
**colchón** *m.* mattress: ~ *de muelles*, bedspring; ~ *de pluma*, feather mattress.
**colchonería** *f.* mattress shop. 2 wool shop.
**colchonero, -ra** *m.-f.* mattress maker.
**colchoneta** *f.* long cushion [for a bench, a lounge, etc.]. 2 NAUT. mattress [for a berth].
**cole** *m.* coll. school.
**coleada** *f.* shake of the tail.
**colear** *intr.* to shake or wag the tail. 2 fig. *todavía colea*, we haven't seen the end of it yet. 3 AER. to fishtail. 4 *tr.* (Am.) to throw [cattle] by pulling at their tails.
**colección** *f.* collection [of objects, etc.].
**coleccionar** *tr.* to collect [form a collection of].
**coleccionista** *m.* collector [of objects or specimens].
**colecta** *f.* collection [act of collecting money for charity, in church, etc.]. 2 LITURG. collect.
**colectar** *tr.* RECAUDAR.
**colectividad** *f.* collectivity; community, group.
**colectivismo** *m.* collectivism.
**colectivista** *adj.* collectivistic. 2 *m.-f.* collectivist.
**colectivización** *f.* collectivization.
**colectivizar** *tr.* to collectivize.
**colectivo, -va** *adj.* collective [pertaining to a group]. 2 GRAM. collective.
**colector** *adj.* collecting. 2 *m.* main sewer. 4 *canal* ~, collecting waters. 5 ELECT. collector; commutator.
**colédoco** *m.-adj. m.* choledoch.
**colega** *m.* colleague. 2 contemporary [newspaper].
**colegatario, -ria** *n.* col-legatee, joint legatee.
**colegiado** *adj.* collegiate. 2 *m.* member of a professional association.
**colegial** *adj.-f.* collegiate [church]. 2 [pertaining to a] school. 3 *m.* schoolboy. 4 collegian.
**colegiala** *f.* schoolgirl.
**colegiarse** *ref.* to form a professional association. 2 to join a professional association.
**colegiata** *f.* collegial church.
**colegio** *m.* school, academy. 2 college, body, association: ~ *cardenalicio*, College of Cardinals. 3 ~ *electoral*, polling station.
**colegir** *tr.* to collect, assemble. 2 to collect, infer, conclude. ¶ CONJUG. like *servir*.
**coleóptero, -ra** *adj.* ENT. coleopterous. 2 *m.* ENT. coleopteran. 3 *m. pl.* ENT. Coleoptera.
**cólera** *f.* PHYSIOL. bile. 2 anger, rage, wrath: *montar en* ~, to fly into a rage. 3 *m.* MED. cholera.
**colérico, -ca** *adj.* choleric, irascible; angry. 2 MED. choleric.
**colesterina** *f.* BIOCHEM. cholesterin.
**colesterol** *m.* BIOL. cholesterol.
**coleta** *f.* pigtail, queue: *cortarse la* ~, to give up bullfighting. 2 additional remark, rider.
**coletazo** *m.* blow, slash with the tail.
**coletilla** *f.* COLETA.
**coleto** *m.* buff coat. 2 fig. one's body, oneself: *echarse al* ~, to drink or eat [something]: to read through.
**colgadero** *m.* peg, hook, etc., to hang things on; clothes rack; hanger.

**colgadizo** *m.* penthouse [over a door, etc.].
**colgado, -da** *adj.* pending, uncertain. 2 *dejar* ~ *a uno*, to disappoint, to frustrate someone.
**colgador** *m.* PRINT. peel. 2 hanger, coat hanger.
**colgadura** *f.* hangings, drapery.
**colgajo** *m.* tatter, rag. 2 bunch of fruit hung up for keeping.
**colgamiento** *m.* hanging, suspending.
**colgante** *adj.* hanging, suspended; suspension. 2 *m.* pendant [jewel]. 3 ARCH. festoon.
**colgar** *tr.* to hang, suspend. 2 to hang [kill by hanging]. 3 to hang [adorn with hangings]. 4 to attribute, impute. 5 *intr.* to hang [be suspended], to dangle, to droop. ¶ CONJUG. like *contar*.
**colibrí** *m.* ORN. humming bird.
**cólico, -ca** *adj.* ANAT., MED. colic. 2 *m.* MED. colic.
**coliflor** *f.* BOT. cauliflower.
**coligación** *f.* union, alliance. 2 colligation.
**coligado, -da** *m.-f.* ally, confederate, leaguer.
**coligarse** *ref.* to confederate, ally: ~ *con*, to ally oneself with.
**colilla** *f.* butt, stub, stump of cigar or cigarette.
**colillero, -ra** *m.-f.* cigar-butt picker.
**colimador** *m.* OPT. collimator.
**colín** *adj.* bobtail (horse). 2 *m.* bread stick.
**colina** *f.* hill, small mountain. 2 cabbage seed. 3 cabbage nursery. 4 BIOCHEM. choline.
**colinabo** *m.* BOT. rutabaga.
**colindante** *adj.* adjacent, contiguous.
**colindar** *intr.* to be adjacent, to be contiguous, to adjoin.
**colipava** *adj.* fantail [pigeon].
**colirio** *m.* MED. collyrium, eyewash.
**coliseo** *m.* coliseum. 2 (cap.) Coliseum, Colosseum.
**colisión** *f.* collision. 2 clashing [of ideas, interests, etc.].
**colista** *m.-f.* queuer.
**colitigante** *m.-f.* co-litigant.
**colitis** *f.* MED. colitis.
**colmado, -da** *adj.* full, abundant. 2 *m.* wine shop, eating house. 3 grocer's,* foodstore.
**colmar** *m.* to fill to overflowing. 2 to fulfill [one's hopes, etc.]. 3 ~ *de*, to fill with, to shower, overwhelm with.
**colmena** *f.* beehive.
**colmenar** *f.* apiary.
**colmenero, -ra** *m.-f.* beekeeper.
**colmenilla** *f.* BOT. morel.
**colmillada** *f.* injury made with an eyetooth or tusk.
**colmillar** *adj.* [pertaining to] eyetooth.
**colmillo** *m.* canine tooth, eyetooth, fang; tusk: *escupir por el* ~, fig. to brag; *tener los colmillos retorcidos*, fig. to be an old dog, to be astute.
**colmilludo, -da** *adj.* having large eyeteeth; bigtusked. 2 fig. shrewd, astute.
**colmo, -ma** *adj.* brimful, full to the top. 2 *m.* fill, completion, crowning. 3 height, limit: *es el* ~, it's the limit. 4 thatched roof.
**colocación** *f.* placing, laying, putting [in place or in a place], location, emplacement. 2 placement. 3 investment [of capital]. 4 employment; place, situation, job.
**colocar** *tr.* to place, to put [in place, in a place]; to set, lay. 2 to place, to find or give [someone] a situation or job. 3 *ref.* to place oneself. 4 to get a situation, a job.
**colocasia** *f.* BOT. taro.
**colodión** *m.* CHEM. collodion.
**colofón** *m.* colophon.
**colofonia** *f.* colophony, rosin.

**coloidal** *adj.* colloidal.
**coloide** *adj.-m.* CHEM. colloid.
**Colombia** *f. pr. n.* GEOG. Colombia.
**colombiano, -na** *adj.* Colombian.
**colombino, -na** *adj.* of Christopher Columbus.
**colombofilia** *f.* pigeon breeding.
**colombófilo, -la** *m.-f.* pigeon fancier.
**colon** *m.* ANAT., GRAM. colon. *2* GRAM. principal part of a period.
**Colón** *m. pr. n.* Columbus.
**colón** *m.* silver coin of Costa Rica and El Salvador.
**colonato** *m.* cultivation of lands by tenant farmers.
**Colonia** *f. pr. n.* GEOG. Cologne: *agua de Colonia*, cologne, eau-de-Cologne.
**colonia** *f.* colony. *2* cologne, eau-de-Cologne.
**colonaje** *m.* (Am.) colonial period.
**colonial** *adj.* colonial. *2 m. pl.* colonial products.
**colonialismo** *m.* colonialism.
**colonialista** *adj.-n.* colonialist.
**colonización** *f.* colonization.
**colonizador, -ra** *adj.* colonizing. *2 m.-f.* colonizer, colonist.
**colonizar** *tr.* to colonize, to settle.
**colono** *m.* colonist, settler. *2* tenant farmer.
**coloquial** *adj.* of the colloquy. *2* colloquial.
**coloquíntida** *f.* BOT. colocynth, bitter apple.
**coloquio** *m.* colloquy. *2* talk, conversation.
**color** *m.* colo(u)r [of things]: *colores nacionales*, colo(u)rs of the flag; *de ~*, colo(u)red [dress, person]; *salirle a uno los colores a la cara*, to blush, be ashamed. *2* colo(u)r [colo(u)ring matter]: *~ al óleo*, oil colo(u)r; *~ sólido*, fast colo(u)r. *3* colo(u)r, pretext: *so ~*, under colo(u)r.
**coloración** *f.* colo(u)ration, colo(u)ring.
**colorado, -da** *adj.* colo(u)red. *2* red, ruddy: *ponerse ~*, to blush, redden. *3* risqué, off-colour.
**colorante** *adj.* colo(u)ring. *2 m.* colo(u)ring matter, colo(u)rant, dye, pigment.
**colorar** *tr.* to colo(u)r, tint.
**colorear** *tr.* COLORAR. *2* to colo(u)r, gloss, make plausible. *3 intr.* to show red. *4 intr.-ref.* [of fruit] to redden, begin to ripen.
**colorete** *m.* rouge.
**colorido** *m.* colo(u)r [of things]. *2* colo(u)r, false appearance.
**colorímetro** *m.* colorimeter.
**colorín** *m.* ORN. goldfinch, linnet. *2 pl.* gaudy colo(u)rs.
**colorista** *m.* colo(u)rist.
**colosal** *adj.* colossal, gigantic, enormous.
**colosalmente** *adv.* coll. marvellously, wonderfully, fabulously.
**coloso** *m.* colossus.
**cólquico** *m.* BOT. colchicum, autumn crocus. *2* PHARM. colchicum.
**Cólquida (la)** *f. pr. n.* Colchis.
**columbario** *m.* columbarium.
**columbino, -na** *adj.* columbine, dovelike; pure, innocent.
**columbrar** *tr.* to descry, glimpse. *2* to guess.
**columelar** *m.* ANAT. canine [tooth].
**columna** *f.* column [in practically every sense]: *~ salomónica*, ARCH. wreathed column; *~ cerrada*, MIL. close column; *~ vertebral*, vertebral column. *2* fig. *quinta ~*, fifth column.
**columnata** *f.* colonnade.
**columnista** *n.* columnist [journalist].
**columpiar** *tr.* to swing. *2 ref.* to swing, to seesaw. *3* to swing the body in walking.
**columpio** *m.* swing [apparatus], seesaw.

**colusión** *f.* LAW collusion.
**colza** *f.* BOT. colza, rape.
**colla** *f.* gorget, throatpiece [armor]. *2* fish trap, line of fishing nets. *3* leash. *4* storm, tempest. *5* team of dockers. *6 n.* inhabitant of Argentinian or Bolivian Andes mountains.
**collado** *m.* hill, hillock. *2* mountain pass, col.
**collar** *m.* necklace. *2* collar [of knighthood]; chain of office. *3* collar [of dog, serf, etc.]. *4* ORN., MACH. collar.
**collarín, collarino** *m.* ARCH. gorgerin.
**colleja** *f.* BOT. a salad herb.
**collera** *f.* horse collar. *2* chain gang.
**coma** *f.* GRAM. comma: *sin faltar una ~*, down to the last detail. *2* MUS. comma. *3 m.* MED. coma.
**comadre** *f.* midwife. *2* mother and godmother with respect to each other; godmother with respect to father. *3* gossip [woman]. *4* female gossip, crony.
**comadrear** *intr.* to gossip, go around gossiping.
**comadreja** *f.* ZOOL. weasel.
**comadreo** *m.* gossiping.
**comadrería** *f.* gossip, tittle tattle.
**comadrón** *m.* obstetrician, accoucheur.
**comadrona** *f.* midwife.
**comanche** *adj.-n.* comanche.
**comandancia** *f.* command [office, district of commander]. *2 ~ de marina*, naval district. *3* MIL. majority.
**comandanta** *f.* coll. major's wife.
**comandante** MIL. commander, commandant: *~ en jefe*, commander in chief. *2* MIL. major.
**comandita** *f.* COM. limited or silent partnership.
**comanditar** *tr.* to enter as a sleeping partner or a silent partner.
**comanditario, -ria** *adj.* pertaining to a COMANDITA. *2 m.* silent partner.
**comando** *m.* MIL. command. *2* MIL. commando.
**comarca** *f.* district, region, country.
**comarcal** *adj.* district, regional.
**comarcano, -na** *adj.* neighbouring.
**comatoso, -sa** *adj.* comatose.
**comátula** *f.* ZOOL. feather star.
**comba** *f.* curvature, bend, warp, bulge. *2* skipping rope. *3* game of skipping rope.
**combadura** *f.* curvature, bend, camber.
**combar** *tr.* to curve, bend, camber. *2 ref.* to become curved, bent, cambered.
**combate** *m.* combat, fight. *2* BOX. fight.
**combatible** *adj.* that may be attacked, open to attack.
**combatiente** *adj.-n.* combatant.
**combatir** *intr.* to combat, to fight. *2 tr.* to combat, fight, oppose. *3* to cotest, impugn. *4* [of wind, sea, etc.] to beat, buffet. *5* [of passions] to shake, agitate, buffet.
**combatividad** *f.* combativeness.
**combativo, -va** *adj.* aggressive, combative, full of fighting spirit.
**combinación** *f.* combining; combination. *2* CHEM., MATH. combination. *3* combination [undergarment]. *4* RLY. connection.
**combinado** *m.* cocktail.
**combinar** *tr.* to combine. *2 ref.* to combine [be combined]. *3 intr.* RLY. to connect.
**combinatorio, -ria** *adj.* MATH. combinatorial.
**combo, -ba** *adj.* curved, bent, cambered. *2 m.* stand for casks.
**combustible** *adj.* combustible. *2 m.* combustible; fuel.
**combustión** *f.* combustion.

**comedero, -ra** adj. eatable. 2 m. feeding vessel [for birds]; feeding trough.

**comedia** f. comedy, play: ~ de capa y espada, cloak-and-sword comedy. 2 farce, pretence: hacer la ~, to feign, pretend.

**comedianta** f. comedienne, actress.

**comediante, -ta** m.-f. hypocrite. 2 m. comedian, actor.

**comedido, -da** adj. courteous, polite. 2 moderate.

**comedimiento** m. courtesy, politeness. 2 moderation.

**comediógrafo** m. playwright, writer of comedies.

**comedirse** ref. to restrain oneself, be moderate. 2 to be courteous.

**comedón** m. MED. comedo, blackhead.

**comedor, -ra** adj. heavy-eating. 2 m. dining room. 3 eating place, restaurant.

**comején** m. ENT. kind of white ant.

**comejenera** f. nest of COMEJÉN.

**comendador** m. knight commander [of a military order]. 2 head of some religious houses.

**comendadora** f. mother superior of some convents.

**comendatario** adj. m. REL. commendatory.

**comensal** m.-f. commensal.

**comentador, -ra** m.-f. commenter, commentator.

**comentar** tr. to comment on.

**comentario** m. commentary. 2 comment. 3 talk, gossip.

**comentarista** m.-f. commentator.

**comento** m. commentation. 2 commentary, comment.

**comenzar** tr.-intr. to commence, to begin. ¶ CONJUG. like acertar.

1) **comer** tr.-ref. to eat [chew and swallow; take as food; consume, corrode], to eat up: ~ or comerse vivo a uno, [of passions, vermin, debts, etc.] to devour, to eat one up; no tener qué ~, to have nothing to live on; sin comerlo ni beberlo, having nothing to do with it. 2 to spend, waste, use up. 3 to omit [words]. 4 CHESS, DRAUGHTS to take. 5 intr. to eat, feed [take food]. 6 fig. to cause expenditure. 7 to dine; to take a meal.

2) **comer** m. eating; food.

**comerciable** adj. marketable. 2 affable, sociable.

**comercial** adj. commercial, mercantile.

**comercialización** f. commercialization, marketing.

**comercializar** tr. to commercialize.

**comerciante** adj. mercantile, trading. 2 m. merchant, trader, tradesman: ~ al por mayor, wholesaler; ~ al por menor, retailer.

**comerciar** intr. to trade, to deal.

**comercio** m. commerce, trade: ~ exterior, foreign trade; ~ interior, domestic trade. 2 merchants, tradesmen. 3 shop, store. 4 commerce, intercourse. 5 a card game.

**comestible** adj. eatable, comestible. 2 m. eatable, comestible, foodstuff.

**cometa** m. ASTR. comet. 2 f. kite [toy].

**cometer** tr. to entrust, to commit [an undertaking to someone]. 2 to commit, do, perpetrate.

**cometido** m. commission, charge, duty.

**comezón** f. itch. itching. 2 hankering, longing.

**comible** adj. coll. fit to eat.

**comicastro** m. THEAT. poor actor.

**comicial** adj. comitial.

**comicios** m. pl. comitia. 2 POL. elections, polls.

**cómico, -ca** adj. comic, dramatic [pertaining to the comedy]. 2 comic, comical, ludicrous, funny. 3 m. comedian, actor: ~ de la legua, strolling player. 5 f. comedienne, actress.

**comida** f. food, dressed food; fare. 2 eating, meal, repast. 3 diner.

**comidilla** f. gossip, talk. 2 hobby.

**comido, -da** adj. eaten. 2 having eaten.

**comienzo** m. commencement, beginning, opening, initiation, start.

**comienzo, comience** etc. irr. V. COMENZAR.

**comilón, -na** adj.-n. great eater, glutton.

**comilona** f. big meal, plentiful repast, spread.

**comillas** f. pl. quotation marks.

**comino** m. BOT. cumin. 2 cumin seed: no valer un ~, not to be worth a rush.

**comisar** tr. to seize, confiscate, forfeit.

**comisaría** f., **comisariato** m. commissariat [function, office of commissioner]: ~ de policía, police station.

**comisario** m. commissary, commissioner, delegate: alto ~, high commissioner. 2 commissar.

**comiscar** tr. to eat in small quantities.

**comisión** f. commission, trust, charge, order. 2 COM. commission. 3 commitee; deputation. 4 commission, perpetration.

**comisionado** m. commissioner, commissioned person.

**comisionar** tr. to commission.

**comisionista** m. COM. commission agent or merchant.

**comiso** m. seizure, confiscation. 2 confiscated goods.

**comisura** f. ANAT. commissure. 2 ANAT. suture.

**comité** m. committee.

**comitente** m.-f. committent.

**comitiva** f. suite, retinue, procession.

**cómitre** m. NAUT. galley slave driver.

**como** adv. how [the manner in which]. | Sometimes it is not translated: la manera ~ lo hizo, the way he did it. 2 as, like: se portó ~ un héroe, he behaved like a hero; ~ usted dice, as you say; tanto ~, as much as. 3 conj. the moment, as soon as: así ~, tan luego ~, as soon as. 4 if: ~ lo vuelvas a hacer..., if you do it again... 5 because, since, as [offen with que]: ~, or ~ que, estábamos a oscuras..., as we were in the dark... 6 ~ quiera que, since, as, inasmuch as. 7 ~ no sea, unless it be.

**cómo** adv. interr. how [in what manner]: ¿~ está usted?, how do you do?; ¡~ corre!, how he runs! 2 why, how is it that: ¿cómo no viniste?, why did you not come?; ¿cómo?, what?, what did you say? 4 interj. why!, how now!, you don't say! 5 m. the how.

**cómoda** f. chest of drawers.

**cómodamente** adv. comfortably.

**comodidad** f. comfortableness, comfort, convenience, ease, leisure. 2 commodiousness.

**comodín** m. CARDS joker, wild card. 2 something of general utility. 3 habitual pretext or excuse.

**cómodo, -da** adj. comfortable. 2 convenient, easy. 3 commodious.

**comodón, -na** adj. comfort-loving, ease-loving. 2 m.-f. comfort lover, ease lover.

**comodoro** m. NAV. commodore.

**compacidad, compactibilidad** f. compactness.

**compacto** adj. compact, solid, close, dense.

**compadecer** tr. to pity, to feel sorry for, to sympathize with. 2 ref. compadecerse de, to pity, to have pity on. 3 compadecerse con, to agree, be consistent with.

**compadraje** *m.* league for mutual protection or benefit [used in a bad sense].

**compadrazgo** *m.* spiritual relationship between godfather and parents of a child. *2* COMPADRAJE.

**compadre** *m.* father and godfather with respect to each other; godfather with respect to mother. *2* comrade, pal. *3* (Arg.) bully.

**compadrear** *intr.* coll. to be on familiar terms.

**compadrito** *m.* (Am.) bully.

**compaginación** *f.* making [things] compatible. *2* PRINT. paging.

**compaginador** *m.* PRINT. pager.

**compaginar** *tr.* to arrange, connect. *2* to make compatible. *3* PRINT. to page, page up. *4 ref.* to fit, agree, be consistent.

**compaña** *f.* coll. COMPAÑÍA 1 & 2.

**compañerismo** *m.* good fellowship; companionship.

**compañero, -ra** *m.-f.* companion, fellow, mate, comrade, partner, associate. *2* [of things] one of a pair or set, mate.

**compañía** *f.* company [act of accompanying]: *hacer ~ a uno*, to give or keep somebody company. *2* company [accompanying persons]. *3* company, society. *4* COM., MIL., THEAT. company: *~ anónima*, joint-stock company.

**comparable** *adj.* comparable.

**comparación** *f.* comparison.

**comparar** *tr.* to compare. *2* to confront, collate.

**comparativo, -va** *adj.* comparative.

**comparecencia** *f.* LAW appearance [in court].

**comparecer** *intr.* LAW to appear [before a judge, etc.]. ¶ CONJUG. like *agradecer.*

**compareciente** *adj.* LAW appearing. *2 n.* person appearing before a tribunal.

**comparendo** *m.* LAW summons.

**comparezco, comparezca,** etc. *irr.* V. COMPARECER.

**comparsa** *f.* THEAT. supernumeraries [as a body]. *2* masquerade. *3* THEAT. supernumerary.

**compartimentado, -da** *adj.* partitioned.

**compartimiento** *m.* division [of a whole in parts]. *2* compartment.

**compartir** *tr.* to divide [a whole in parts]. *2* to share [partake of, participate in].

**compás** *m.* compass, compasses, dividers: *~ de calibres*, or *de espesores*, caliper(s. *2* NAUT. compass. *3* MUS. bar, measure: *~ de espera*, whole rest; fig. brief interruption. *4* MUS. time, measure, rhythm: *llevar el ~*, to keep time, to beat time; *a ~*, in time. *5* rule, measure. *6* springs of a coach hood.

**compasado, -da** *adj.* moderate, prudent.

**compasar** *tr.* to measure with a compass. *2* to regulate. *3* MUS. to bar, divide into measures.

**compasible** *adj.* compassionate. *2* pitiable.

**compasillo** *m.* MUS. quadruple time measure.

**compasión** *f.* compassion, pity: *tener ~ de*, to have pity on; *¡por ~!*, for pity's sake.

**compasivo, -va** *adj.* compassionate, merciful.

**compatibilidad** *f.* compatibility.

**compatible** *adj.* compatible, consistent.

**compatricio, -cia, compatriota** *m.-f.* compatriot.

**compatriota** *n.* felow countryman or countrywoman, compatriot.

**compeler** *tr.* to compel, force, constrain.

**compendiar** *tr.* to epitomize, summarize, abridge.

**compendio** *m.* compendium, epitome, abstract.

**compendioso, -sa** *adj.* compendious, brief, succinct.

**compenetración** *f.* mutual understanding. *2* full accordance or agreement in thought, feeling, etc.

**compenetrarse** *ref.* to penetrate or pervade lach other. *2* to be in full agreement of thought, feeling, etc.

**compensación** *f.* compensation.

**compensador, -ra** *adj.* compensating. *2 m.* compensador.

**compensar** *tr.* to compensate. *2* to compensate for, make up for. *3 ref.* to be compensated.

**compensatorio, -ria** *adj.* compensatory, compensating.

**competencia** *f.* competence, fitness, ability. *2* competence [legal authority], qualification. *3* province, jurisdiction. *4* competition.

**competente** *adj.* competent, fit, able. *2* adequate. *3* competent, qualified [with due authority for].

**competer** *intr.* to behove, belong; be incumbent [on].

**competición** *f.* competition.

**competidor, -ra** *adj.* competing, rival. *2 m.-f.* competitor, rival.

**competir** *intr.* to compete. ¶ CONJUG. like *servir.*

**competitivo, -va** *adj.* competitive.

**compilación** *f.* compilation, compilement.

**compilador, -ra** *m.-f.* compiler, compilator.

**compilar** *tr.* to compile.

**compinche** *m.* coll. comrade, chum, pal, associate.

**complacencia** *f.* pleasure, satisfaction.

**complacer** *tr.* to please, to oblige, to humour. *2 ref.* to be pleased: *~ en*, to be pleased to, to delight in. ¶ CONJUG. like *agradecer.*

**complaciente** *adj.* complaisant, compliant, obliging. *2* indulgent.

**complazco, complazca,** etc. *irr.* V. COMPLACER.

**complejidad** *f.* complexity.

**complejo, -ja** *adj.* complex. *2* compound [number]. *3 m.* complex.

**complementar** *tr.* to complement.

**complementario, -ria** *adj.* complementary.

**complemento** *m.* complement. *2* GRAM. object: *~ directo*, direct object; *~ indirecto*, indirect object. *4* completion, perfection.

**completar** *tr.* to complete. *2* to finish, to perfect.

**completas** *f. pl.* LITURG. compline.

**completivo, -va** *adj.* completive.

**completo, -ta** *adj.* complete: *por ~*, completely. *2* full [bus, tram, etc.].

**complexión** *f.* PHYSIOL. constitution.

**complexo, -xa** *adj.* complex.

**complicación** *f.* complicating. *2* complication, complicacy.

**complicado, -da** *adj.* complicated, complicate.

**complicar** *tr.* to complicate. *2* to implicate, involve. *3 ref.* to become complicated. *4* to become involved.

**cómplice** *m.-f.* accomplice, accesory.

**complicidad** *f.* complicity.

**complot** *m.* complot, plot, conspiracy; intrigue.

**complotar** *intr.* to complot, to conspire.

**compondré, compondría,** etc. *irr.* V. COMPONER.

**componedor, -ra** *m.-f.* arranger, mender, repairer. *2* conciliator: *amigable ~*, LAW arbitrator. *3* composer. *4 m.* PRINT. stick, composing. stick.

**componenda** *f.* shady or dubious compromise.

**componente** *adj.-n.* component.

**componer** *tr.* to compose, compound, make up. *2* to compose, constitute. *3* LIT., MUS., F. ARTS. GRAM. to compose. *4* to prepare, mix [a drink]. *5* to repair, mend, put in order. *6* to adorn, trim, spruce. *7* to make up [the face]. *8* to reconcile. *9*

PRINT. to compose, set [type]. *10* coll. to restore, fortify. *11 ref.* to adorn oneself, to dress up, to make up. *12* to make up differences. *13 componerse de,* to be composed of, to consist in. *14 componérselas,* to manage, make shift, shift for oneself. ¶ CONJUG. line *poner.*

**compongo, componga** etc. *irr.* V. COMPONER.

**comportamiento** *m.* behavior, comportment.

**comportar** *tr.* to bear, to tolerate. *2 ref.* to behave, to comport oneself.

**composición** *f.* composition [in practically every sense]. *2* agreement, compromise. *3* PRINT. type that has been set. *4 hacer ~ de lugar,* to weigh the pros and cons.

**compositivo, -va** *adj.* GRAM. combining [particle].

**compositor, -ra** *m.-f.* MUS. composer.

**compostelano, -na** *adj.-n.* of Santiago de Compostela.

**compostura** *f.* making, mixing. *2* repair, reparation, mending. *3* making neat, adorning, making up. *4* modesty, circumspection.

**compota** *f.* compote [fruit cooked in syrup].

**compotera** *f.* compotier, compote.

**compra** *f.* buying, purchasing, purchase; day's marketing, shopping; *ir de compras,* to go shopping. *2* purchase [that which is bought].

**comprable** *adj.* purchasable, buyable.

**comprador- ra,** *n.* purchaser, buyer. *2* customer, shopper.

**comprar** *tr.* to purchase, to buy. *2* to buy [by bribing].

**compraventa** *f.* LAW *contrato de ~,* contract of sale.

**comprender** *tr.* to comprehend, comprise, embrace. *2* to comprehend, understand.

**comprensibilidad** *f.* comprehensibility, understandability.

**comprensible** *adj.* comprehensible, understandable.

**comprensión** *f.* comprehension, inclusion. *2* comprehension, understanding.

**comprensivo, -va** *adj.* comprehensive; comprising. *2* understanding, large-minded.

**compresa** *f.* MED. compress.

**compresibilidad** *f.* compressibility.

**compresible** *adj.* compressible.

**compresión** *f.* compression, compressure.

**compresivo, -va** *adj.* compressive.

**compresor, -ra** *adj.* compressing. *2 m.* compressor.

**comprimible** *adj.* compressible.

**comprimido, -da** *adj.* compressed. *2 m.* PHARM. tablet.

**comprimir** *tr.* to compress. *2* to control, restrain. *3 ref.* to become compressed. *4* to control, restrain oneself.

**comprobable** *adj.* verifiable, ascertainable.

**comprobación** *f.* verification, checking, substantiation. *2* proof.

**comprobante** *adj.* proving. *2 m.* proof, evidence. *3* voucher.

**comprobar** *tr.* to verify, check, control, ascertain, substantiate. *2* to prove, confirm.

**comprometedor, -ra** *adj.* compromising, committing.

**comprometer** *tr.* to arbitrate [submit to arbitration]. *2* to compromise, risk, jeopardize. *3* to bind, engage; to render accountable or answerable. *4 ref.* to commit oneself; to undertake, to engage or pledge oneself [to do something]; to become involved. *5* to become engaged, betrothed.

**comprometido, -da** *adj.* implicated, involved. *2*

embarassing, compromising: *situación ~,* embarassing situation. *3* committed, engaged.

**compromisario** *m.* delegate, representative. *2* electoral delegate.

**compromiso** *m.* power given to an electoral delegate. *2* commitment to arbitration. *3* commitment, pledge, engagement, obligation. *4* fix, predicament.

**compuerta** *f.* hatch, half door. *2* sluice, floodgate.

**compuestamente** *adv.* with modesty or circumspection. *2* orderly.

**compuesto, -ta** *adj.* composed. *2* composite, compound, compounded. *3* ARCH., BOT. composite. *4* GRAM., MATH. compound. *5* repaired, mended. *6* dressed up, bedecked. *7 m.* compound, composite. *8* preparation, mixture. *9* CHEM., GRAM. compound. *10 p. p.* of COMPONER.

**compulsa** *f.* collation [of documents].

**compulsar** *tr.* to collate [documents].

**compulsión** *f.* compulsion.

**compulsivo, -va** *adj.* compulsory.

**compunción** *f.* compunction. *2* sorrow, pity.

**compungido, -da** *adj.* remorseful. *2* sorrowful.

**compungir** *tr.* to make remorseful. *2 ref.* to feel compunction. *3* to be sorry, to feel pity.

**computable** *adj.* computable.

**compuse, compusiera,** etc. *irr.* V. COMPONER.

**computación** *f.* CÓMPUTO.

**computador** *m.* computer.

**computadora** *f.* computer.

**computar** *tr.* to compute.

**cómputo** *m.* computation, calculation.

**comulgante** *m.-f.* ECCL. communicant.

**comulgar** *tr.* to administer Holy Communion. *2 intr.* to communicate, to take Holy Communion.

**comulgatorio** *m.* communion rail, altar rail.

**común** *adj.* common: *por lo ~,* in general, generally. *2* public. *3* current, ordinary, usual. *4* mean, low, inferior. *5 m.* community, commonalty: *el ~ de las gentes,* most people; *en ~,* in common.

**comuna** *f.* (Am.) municipality.

**comunal** *adj.* common, communal.

**comunero, -ra** *adj.* popular, pleasing to the people. *2 m.* member of the party that rose in Castile against Charles I.

**comunicabilidad** *f.* communicability.

**comunicable** *adj.* communicable. *2* sociable.

**comunicación** *f.* communication. *2* official letter. *3 pl.* communications [means of communication].

**comunicado** *m.* communiqué.

**comunicante** *m.-f.* communicant [one who communicates something].

**comunicar** *tr.* to communicate. *2 ref.* to communicate [hold communication]. *3* [of rooms, etc.] to communicate. *4* [of the telephone] to be engaged.

**comunicativo, -va** *adj.* communicative. *2* open, unreserved.

**comunidad** *f.* community. *2* commonwealth. *3 pl. comunidades de Castilla,* uprisings in Castile under Charles I.

**comunión** *f.* communion. *2 la Comunión, la Sagrada Comunión,* the Holy Communion.

**comunismo** *m.* comunism.

**comunista** *adj.* communist, communistic. *2 m.-f.* communist.

**comunistoide** *adj.* coll. communistic. *2 n.* coll. communist sympathiser.

**comunitario, -ria** *adj.* of the community.

**comunizar** *tr.* to communize.
**comúnmente** *adv.* commonly, usually, generally. 2 frequently.
**con** *prep.* with [on nearly every sense]. 2 [before an infinitive]: a) in spite of: ~ *ser tan fuerte, no lo pudo resistir,* in spite of his being so strong, he could not resist it; b) by: ~ *enseñar la carta, disipó sus dudas,* by showing the letter, he dispelled his doubts. 3 ~ *que,* as long as, if. 4 ~ *tal que,* provided that. 5 ~ *todo,* nevertheless. 6 *para* ~, towards, to.
**conato** *m.* endeavour, effort, exertion. 2 act or crime attempted but not committed.
**concadenar** *tr.* to concatenate.
**concatenación** *f.,* **concatenamiento** *m.* concatenation.
**concatenado, -da** *adj.* linked up, concatenate.
**concausa** *f.* factor, cause, motive.
**concavidad** *f.* concavity.
**cóncavo, -va** *adj.* concave. 2 *m.* concavity, hollow.
**concebible** *adj.* mentally conceivable.
**concebir** *tr.-intr.* to conceive [become pregnant]. 2 *tr.* to conceive mentally. 3 to conceive, formulate, express. 4 to conceive, begin to have [a dislike, etc.]. ¶ CONJUG. like *servir.*
**conceder** *tr.* to grant, bestow, award. 2 to concede, admit.
**concedido, -da** *adj.* conceded, granted.
**concejal** *m.* alderman, town councillor.
**concejalía** *f.* aldermanship, town councillorship.
**concejil** *adj.* pertaining to a town council.
**concejo** *m.* municipal council of a small town or village; municipality. 2 council meeting.
**concentración** *f.* concentration.
**concentrado, -da** *adj.* concentrate(d.
**concentrar** *tr.* to concentrate, concenter. 2 *ref.* to concentrate, concenter [in intr. sense]. 3 to be absorbed [mentally].
**concéntrico, -ca** *adj.* concentric(al.
**concepción** *f.* conception. 2 *La Inmaculada Concepción,* the Immaculate Conception.
**conceptismo** *m.* conceptism.
**concepto** *m.* concept. 2 witty thought, concept. 3 opinion, judgement: *en mi* ~, in my opinion. 4 *en* ~ *de,* as: *en* ~ *de remuneración,* as a remuneration. 5 *bajo este* ~, from this point of view. 6 *por este* ~, on this head, on this score.
**conceptual** *adj.* conceptual.
**conceptualismo** *m.* conceptualism.
**conceptuar** *tr.* to deem, judge, think, to form an opinion of.
**conceptuoso, -sa** *adj.* sententious, full of conceits or witty turns of expression.
**concerniente** *adj.* concerning, relating: *en lo* ~ *a,* as for; with regard to.
**concernir** *intr.* (with *a*) to concern [belong to, relate to]: *por lo que concierne a,* as concerns. ¶ Def., only used in third persons and the forms *concerniendo* and *concerniente.*
**concertadamente** *adv.* orderly, regularly. 2 concertedly.
**concertado, -da** *adj.* concerted, planned, agreed upon.
**concertante** *adj.* MUS. concerted.
**concertar** *tr.* to assemble, fit together, to adjust; to put in order. 2 to harmonize. 3 to concert, to arrange [a marriage, a treaty]; to conclude [a bargain]; to agree upon [a price, etc.]. 4 to unite [efforts, means, etc.]. 5 MUS. to tune, attune, put in tune. 6 *intr.* to agree, be in concordance. 7 GRAM. to agree. 8 *ref.* to agree [come to an agreement]. ¶ CONJUG. like *acertar.*
**concertina** *f.* MUS. concertina.
**concertino** *m.* MUS. concertmaster.
**concertista** *m.-f.* MUS. concertist.
**concesión** *f.* concession. 2 grant.
**concesionario** *m.* concessionary, grantee.
**concesivo, -va** *adj.* concessive.
**concibo, conciba, concibiera,** etc. *irr.* V. CONCEBIR.
**conciencia** *f.* conscience: *en* ~, in conscience, in good faith. 2 consciousness; awareness: *tener* ~ *de,* to be conscious of. 3 conscientiousness: *a* ~, conscienciously.
**concienzudo, -da** *adj.* conscientious, thorough.
**concierne, concierna,** etc. *irr.* V. CONCERNIR.
**concierto** *m.* good order and arrangement. 2 agreement, covenant. 3 concert, agreement: *de* ~, in concert. 4 MUS. concert. 5 MUS. concerto.
**conciliable** *adj.* conciliable, reconciliable, capable of being conciliated.
**conciliábulo** *m.* secret meeting.
**conciliación** *f.* conciliation. 2 winning of good will, favor, estime, etc.
**conciliador, -ra** *adj.* conciliating, conciliatory. 2 *m.-f.* conciliator.
1) **conciliar** *adj.* conciliar. 2 *m.* ECCL. member of a council.
2) **conciliar** *tr.* to conciliate. 2 to reconcile. 3 ~ *el sueño,* to get some sleep. 4 *ref.* to win, conciliate.
**conciliatorio, -ria** *adj.* conciliatory.
**concilio** *m.* ECCL. council.
**concisión** *f.* conciseness, concision.
**conciso, -sa** *adj.* concise.
**concitar** *tr.* to excite [one against another], to instigate, stir up, raise [opposition, sedition, etc.].
**conciudadano, -na** *adj.* fellow citizen.
**cónclave** *m.* conclave.
**concluir** *tr.* to conclude, finish, end. 2 to conclude [a treaty, etc.]. 3 to conclude, to infer. 4 to silence [by reason or argument]. 5 *intr.-ref.* to conclude, finish, end [come to an end]. ¶ CONJUG. like *huir.*
**conclusión** *f.* conclusion: *en* ~, in conclusion.
**conclusivo, -va** *adj.* conclusive.
**concluso, -sa** *adj.* concluded, closed. 2 [of a trial] ready for sentence.
**concluyente** *adj.* conclusive, convincing.
**concluyo, concluyó, concluya,** etc. *irr.* V. CONCLUIR.
**concoide** *adj.* conchoidal. 2 *f.* GEOM. conchoid.
**concoideo, -a** *adj.* conchoidal.
**concomerse** *ref.* to shrug one's shoulders and wriggle. 2 fig. to be eaten up [with impatience, sorrow, etc.].
**concomitancia** *f.* concomitance.
**concomitante** *adj.* concomitant, accompanying.
**concordancia** *f.* concordance, conformity, agreement. 2 GRAM. concord. 3 MUS. accord, concord. 4 *pl.* concordance [verbal index].
**concordante** *adj.* concordant, agreeing.
**concordar** *tr.* to make agree, to harmonize. 2 GRAM. to make agree. 3 *intr.* to agree, accord, tally. 4 GRAM. to agree. ¶ CONJUG. like *contar.*
**concordatario, -ria** *adj.* [pertaining to a] concordat.
**concordato** *m.* concordat.
**concorde** *adj.* concordant, in agreement.
**concordia** *f.* concord, harmony, peace.
**concreción** *f.* concretion [concreted mass].
**concretamente** *adv.* concretely. 2 specifically, particulary. 3 exactly, accurately.
**concretar** *tr.* to combine, unite. 2 to summarize,

condense; to express concretely; to fix details. *4 ref.* to limit or confine oneself [to].

**concreto, -ta** *adj.* concrete [not abstract]; definite. *2* concrete [formed by concretion]. *3 m.* concretion, concrete. *4 adv. en* ~, to sum up; *nada en* ~, nothing definite.

**concubina** *f.* concubine.

**concubinato** *m.* concubinage.

**concuerdo, concuerde,** etc. *irr.* V. CONCORDAR.

**conculcación** *f.* violation [of rights, law, etc.].

**conculcar** *tr.* to tread upon. *2* to violate, infringe [rights, law, etc.].

**concupiscencia** *f.* concupiscence. *2* cupidity.

**concupiscente** *adj.* concupiscent.

**concurrencia** *f.* concurrence, coincidence. *2* concourse [of people]; attendance, audience. *3* aid, cooperation.

**concurrente** *adj.* concurrent. *2* attending, present. *3 m.-f.* attendant, present. *4* frequenter, habitué.

**concurrido, -da** *adj.* [of a place] frequented; [of a meeting, etc.] attended.

**concurrir** *intr.* to concur [happen together, coincide, act jointly; agree in opinion]. *2* to converge. *3* to be present [at], to attend, to frequent. *4* to contribute [money]. *5* to take part in a competition for a prize, a post, etc.

**concursante** *n.* participant, competitor, contestant. *2* candidate [for a job, a post].

**concursar** *tr.* LAW to declare insolvent.

**concurso** *f.* concourse [of people]. *2* concurrence, coincidence. *3* aid, co-operation, assistance. *4* call for tenders [for contracts]. *5* competition [for a prize, a post, etc.]. *7* LAW ~ *de acreedores,* meeting of creditors.

**concusión** *f.* MED. concussion. *2* LAW extortion.

**concusionario, -ria** *adj.* extortioner.

**Concha** *f. pr. n.* coll. Conception.

**concha** *f.* ZOOL. shell; concha: ~ *de peregrino,* scallop shell; *tener muchas conchas,* to be reserved, sly, cunning. *2* oyster. *3* tortoise-shell. *4* any shell-shaped object. *5* THEAT. prompter's box. *6* enclosed bay. *7* ARCH. concha.

**conchabanza** *f.* comfort. *2·*leaguing, banding together.

**conchabarse** *ref.* to plot, band together.

**conchífero, -ra** *adj.* conchiferous.

**condado** *m.* earldom; countship. *2* county.

**condal** *adj.* pertaining to an earl or count.

**conde** *m.* earl, count. *2* gypsy chief.

**condecoración** *f.* decoration [act of investing with an order, medal, etc.]. *2* decoration [order, medal, badge of honour].

**condecorar** *tr.* to decorate [award a decoration].

**condena** *f.* LAW sentence; term [of imprisonment]. *2* transcript of a sentence.

**condenable** *adj.* condemnable, blameworthy, reprehensible, worthy of disapproval. *2* damnable, deserving condemnation.

**condenación** *f.* condemnation. *2* damnation.

**condenado, -da** *adj.* sentenced, condemned. *2* doomed. *3* damned. *4* wicked, accursed. *5 m.-f.* sentenced person. *6* damned person.

**condenar** *tr.* to condemn [a pers.]. *2* to condemn, blame. *3* THEOL. to damn. *4* to wall up [a door or window]. *5 ref.* to condemn oneself. *6* THEOL. to be condemned.

**condenatorio, -ria** *adj.* condemnatory.

**condensación** *f.* condensation.

**condensador, -ra** *adj.* condensing. *2 m.* condenser.

**condensar** *tr.* to condense. *2 ref.* to condense [become condensed].

**condesa** *f.* countess.

**condescendencia** *f.* complaisance, obligingness.

**condescender** *intr.* to comply, to accede or yield [out of kindness]. ¶ CONJUG. like *descender.*

**condescendiente** *adj.* complaisant, obliging.

**condesciendo, condescienda,** etc. *irr.* V. CONDESCENDER.

**condestable** *m.* HIST. constable. *2* NAUT. master gunner.

**condición** *f.* condition, rank, class; abs. high bird. *2* nature, disposition. *3* condition [requisite, stipulation, etc.]: *a* ~ *de que, con la* ~ *de que,* on condition that, provided that. *4 pl.* condition [of a thing]: *en buenas condiciones,* in good condition. *5* position; trim: *estar en condiciones de,* to be in a position to; to be in trim for. *6* conditions, terms. *7* conditions, circumstances.

**condicionado, -da** *adj.* conditionated, conditional.

**condicional** *adj.* conditional.

**condicionamiento** *m.* conditioning.

**condicionar** *tr.* to condition. *2* to conditionate.

**cóndilo** *m.* ANAT. condyle.

**condimentación** *f.* seasoning.

**condimentar** *tr.* to dress, to season [foods].

**condimento** *m.* condiment, seasoning.

**condiscípulo, -la** *m.-f.* classmate, schoolfellow.

**condolencia** *f.* condolence.

**condolerse** *ref.* to condole, sympathize, feel sorry: ~ *de,* to sympathize with, feel sorry for. ¶ CONJUG. like *mover.*

**condominio** *m.* LAW condominium.

**condonación** *f.* remission, pardon.

**condonar** *t.* to remit, pardon.

**cóndor** *m.* ORN. condor. *2* condor [coin].

**conducción** *f.* conduction. *2* conveyance, transportation. *3* piping, wiring. *4* driving [of vehicles]. *5* AUTO. drive: ~ *interior,* enclosed drive.

**conducente** *adj.* conducing, leading, conducive.

**conducir** *tr.* to convey, transport. *2* to conduct, lead. *3* to conduct, direct, manage. *4* PHYS. to conduct. *5* to conduce. *6* to drive [a vehicle]. *7* to engage [services]. *8 ref.* to behave, conduct oneself. ¶ CONJUG. INDIC. Pres.: *conduzco,* conduces, etc. | Pret.: *conduje, condujiste, condujo; condujimos, condujisteis, condujeron.* | SUBJ. Pres.: *conduzca, conduzcas, conduzca; conduzcamos, conduzcáis, conduzcan.* | Imperf.: *condujera,* etc., or *condujese,* etc. | Fut.: *condujere,* etc. | IMPER.: conduce, *conduzca; conduzcamos,* conducid, *conduzcan.*

**conducta** *f.* conduct, behaviour. *2* conduct, direction, management. *3* medical services contracted for a fixed subscription.

**conductibilidad** *f.* PHYS. conductivity.

**conductivo, -va** *adj.* conductive, conducting.

**conducto** *m.* conduit, pipe, duct, -channel. *2* ZOOL., BOT. duct, canal: ~ *auditivo,* auditory canal. *3* channel, mediation, intermediary: *por* ~ *de,* through.

**conductor, -ra** *adj.* conducting, leading, guiding. *2* PHYS. conducting. *3 m.-f.* conductor, leader, guide. *4* driver [of a vehicle]; motorist. *5* PHYS., RLY. conductor.

**conduelo, conduela,** etc. *irr.* V. CONDOLERSE.

**condueño** *m.* joint owner.

**conduje, condujera,** etc. *irr.* V. CONDUCIR.

**condumio** *m.* food, food to be eaten with bread.

**conduzco, conduzca,** etc. *irr.* V. CONDUCIR.

**conectar** *tr.* to unite, connect, gear.

**coneja** *f.* ZOOL. female rabbit, doe rabbit.

**conejal, conejar** *m.* rabbit warren.

**conejera** *f.* burrow, rabbit hole. *2* rabbit warren. *3* fig. den, low haunt; warren.

**conejero, -ra** *adj.* rabbit-hunting [dog].

**conejillo** *m.* young rabbit. *2* ZOOL. ~ *de Indias*, guinea pig, cavy.

**conejo** *adj.* ZOOL. rabbit.

**conexión** *f.* connection, relation, coherence. *2* ELECT. connection. *3 pl.* [social] connections.

**conexo, -xa** *adj.* connected, related.

**confabulación** *f.* confabulation. *2* league, plot.

**confabular** *intr.* to confabulate. *2 ref.* to plot, enter into a secret understanding.

**confalón** *m.* gonfalon.

**confección** *m.* making, confection. *2* confection [ready-made article]. *3* PHARM. confection.

**confeccionar** *tr.* to make, to prepare, to form [esp. by hand]. *3* PHARM. confection.

**confeccionista** *m.-f.* manufacturer of articles of dress.

**confederación** *f.* confederation, federation; league.

**confederado, -da** *adj.-n.* confederate, federate.

**confederar** *tr.-ref.* to confederate, federate.

**conferencia** *f.* conference. *2* public lecture. *3* TELEPH. trunk-call.

**conferenciante** *m.-f.* lecturer.

**conferenciar** *intr.* to confer [converse, hold conference].

**conferir** *tr.* to confer [bestow; consult about; compare]. *2 intr.* to confer [hold conference]. ¶ CONJUG. like *hervir*.

**confesar** *tr.* to confess. *2* to confess [one's sins]. *3* to confess [hear in confession]. *4 intr.-ref.* to confess [make confession]. *5 ref.* to confess oneself [guilty, etc.]. ¶ CONJUG. like *acertar*.

**confesión** *f.* confession [act of confessing; avowal, admission].

**confesional** *adj.* confessional.

**confesionario** *m.* CONFESONARIO.

**confeso, -sa** *adj.* having confessed his or her guilt. *2* converted [Jew]. *3 m.* converted Jew. *4* lay brother.

**confesonario** *m.* confessional.

**confesor** *m.* confessor.

**confeti** *m.* confetti.

**confiable** *adj.* reliable, trustworthy.

**confiado, -da** *adj.* confiding, unsuspecting. *2* self-confident, presumptuous.

**confianza** *f.* confidence, reliance, trust: *de* ~, reliable; *en* ~, confidentially. *2* courage, enterprise. *3* self-confidence, assurance. *4* familiarity, informality: *de* ~, informal. *5 pl.* liberties, familiarities.

**confiar** *intr.* to confide, to trust, to rely. *2 tr.* to confide, entrust, commit [something to somebody]. *3 ref.* to be trustful. *4* to make confidences.

**confidencia** *f.* confidence, trust. *2* confidence, secret, confidential information.

**confidencial** *adj.* confidential.

**confidente, -ta** *adj.* trustworthy, reliable. *2 m.* confidant. *3* secret informer, police informer. *4* love seat, tête-à-tête. *5 f.* confidante.

**confiero, confiera,** etc. *irr.* V. CONFERIR.

**confieso, confiese,** *irr.* V. CONFESAR.

**configuración** *f.* configuration.

**configurar** *tr.* to configurate, form, shame.

**confin** *adj.* bordering. *2 m.* confine, border, boundary.

**confinamiento** *m.* LAW banishement to a definite place.

**confinar** *intr.* to border: ~ *con*, to border on. *2 tr.* LAW to banish [somebody] to a definite place.

**confinidad** *f.* proximity, contiguity.

**confirmación** *f.* confirmation.

**confirmadamente** *adv.* firmly, surely.

**confirmar** *tr.* to confirm [strengthen, sanction; ratify; corroborate]. *2* ECCL. to confirm.

**confirmatorio, -ria** *adj.* confirmatory.

**confiscable** *adj.* confiscable.

**confiscación** *f.* confiscation.

**confiscar** *tr.* to confiscate.

**confitado, -da** *adj.* candied, glacé, covered with sugar, iced.

**confitar** *tr.* to candy, to preserve [fruit]. *2* fig. to dulcify, sweeten.

**confite** *m.* small round sweet, sugarplum.

**confiteor** *m.* confiteor.

**confitera** *f.* sweet box or jar.

**confitería** *f.* confectionery. *2* confectioner's shop.

**confitero, -ra** *m.-f.* confectioner. ·

**confitura** *f.* candied or preserved fruit, jam, confection, comfit.

**conflagración** *f.* conflagration.

**conflictivo** *adj.* that has conflict. *2* conflicting.

**conflicto** *m.* conflict. *2* fix, dilemma.

**confluencia** *f.* confluence.

**confluente** *adj.* confluent. *2 m.* confluence.

**confluir** *intr.* [of streams or roads] to flow together, converge, meet. *2* [of people] to crowd, assemble [coming from different parts]. ¶ CONJUG. like *huir*.

**conformación** *f.* conformation, form, structure.

**conformar** *tr.* to conform, adapt. *2 intr.* to conform, agree. *3 ref.* to conform, to adapt oneself or itself. *4* to submit, yield, comply; to resign oneself. *5* to content oneself.

**conforme** *adj.* according, accordant, agreeable, conformable, consistent. *2* agreeing, of a mind. *3* correct, in order. *4* resigned, patient. *5 adv.* in accordance [with], according or agreeably [to]. *6 as* ~ *había estado*, as it had been.

**conformidad** *f.* conformity. *2* accordance: *en* ~ *con*, in accordance with, according to. *3* union, harmony: *de* ~, agreeing, at one. *4* symmetry. *5* patience, resignation.

**conformismo** *m.* conformism, conventionalism, orthodoxy. *2* REL. conformism.

**confort** *m.* comfort.

**confortable** *adj.* comforting; comfortable.

**confortación** *f.* comfort, consolation. *2* strengthening, invigoration.

**confortador, -ra** *adj.* comforting, comfortable. *2* invigorating. *3 m.-f.* comforter, consoler.

**confortante** *adj.* comforting, comfortable. *2* tonic, invigorating. *3 m.-f.* comforter. *4 m.* mitten.

**confortar** *tr.* to confort [console, cheer, encourage]. *2* to strengthen, invigorate.

**confortativo, -va** *adj.* comforting. *2 m.* comfort, consolation. *4* cordial, restorative.

**confraternidad** *f.* confraternity, brotherhood.

**confraternizar** *intr.* to fraternize.

**confrontación** *f.* confrontation.

**confrontar** *tr.* to confront [put face to face]. *2* to confront, collate, compare. *3 intr.* to border: ~ *con*, to border on. *4 intr.-ref.* to face [be facing; place oneself facing].

**confucianismo** *m.* Confucianism.

**Confucio** *m. pr. n.* Confucius.

**confundido, -da** *adj.* embarassed, confounded, bewildered. *2* mistaken, confused.

**confundir** *tr.* to mix, mingle. *2* to confuse. *3* to confound. *4* to defeat [in argument]. *5* to mistake: ~ *con*, to mistake for. *6 ref.* to get mixed. *7* to get lost or mingled [in a crowd, etc.]. *8* to be confused or confounded. *9* to make a mistake.

**confusamente** *adv.* confusedly.

**confusión** *f.* confusion. *2* humiliation, shame.

**confuso, -sa** *adj.* confused. *2* troubled, bewildered, awed. *3* obscure, unintelligible. *4* blurred, indistinct.

**congelación** *f.* congelation, congealment, freezing.

**congelador** *m.* freezer.

**congelar** *tr.* to congeal, freeze. *2* COM. to freeze [credits, etc.]. *3 ref.* to congeal, freeze [become congealed].

**congénere** *adj.* congeneric. *2 m.-f.* congener.

**congeniar** *intr.* to get along well together.

**congénito, -ta** *adj.* congenital.

**congestión** *f.* congestion.

**congestionar** *tr.* to congest. *2 ref.* to become congested.

**congestivo, -va** *adj.* congestive.

**conglobar** *tr.-ref.* to conglobate, conglobe.

**conglomerado, -da** *adj.* conglomerate(d. *2 m.* conglomerate.

**conglomerar** *tr.* to conglomerate. *2 ref.* to conglomerate [be conglomerated].

**conglutinación** *f.* conglutination.

**conglutinar** *tr.* to conglutinate. *2 ref.* to conglutinate [be conglutinate].

**Congo** *m. pr. n.* GEOG. Congo.

**congoja** *f.* anguish, agony.

**congojoso, -sa** *adj.* anguishing. *2* anguished.

**congoleño, -ña** *adj.-n.* Congoese, Congolese.

**congraciar** *tr.* to win the good will of. *2 ref.* to ingratiate oneself [with].

**congratulación** *f.* congratulation.

**congratular** *tr.* to congratulate. *2 ref. congratularse de*, to be glad of, be rejoiced at.

**congratulatorio, -ria** *adj.* congratulatory.

**congregación** *f.* congregation, assembly. *2* ECCL. congregation.

**congregante, -ta** *m.-f.* member of a congregation.

**congregar** *tr.* to congregate, to assemble. *2 ref.* to congregate, assemble, meet.

**congresista** *m.-f.* member of a congress or assembly; congressist.

**congreso** *m.* congress, assembly. *2 Congreso de los diputados*, Chamber of deputies.

**congrio** *m.* ICHTH. conger eel, congre.

**congrua** *f.* adequate income for one who is to be ordained a priest. *2* suplementary emolument.

**congruencia** *f.* congruence, congruity. *2* MATH. congruence.

**congruente** *adj.* congruent, congruous.

**congruo, -a** *adj.* congruous, fitting.

**conicidad** *f.* conicalness.

**cónico, -ca** *adj.* conic(al).

**conífero, -ra** *adj.* BOT. coniferous. *2 f.* BOT. conifer. *3 pl.* BOT. Coniferae.

**coniza** *f.* BOT. fleawort.

**conjetura** *f.* conjecture, surmise, guesswork.

**conjetural** *adj.* conjectural.

**conjeturar** *tr.* to conjecture, surmise, guess.

**conjugable** *adj.* conjugable, that can be conjugated.

**conjugación** *f.* conjugation.

**conjugado, -da** *adj.* conjugate(d. *2 f.* BOT. conjugate.

**conjugar** *tr.* to conjugate.

**conjunción** *f.* conjunction, union. *2* ASTR., ASTROL., GRAM. conjunction.

**conjuntamente** *adj.* conjointly, jointly.

**conjuntiva** *f.* ANAT. conjunctiva.

**conjuntivitis** *f.* MED. conjunctivitis.

**conjuntivo, -va** *adj.* conjunctive, uniting. *2* GRAM. conjunctive. *3* ANAT. conjunctive, connective.

**conjunto, -ta** *adj.* conjoint, conjunct, united. *2 m.* whole, ensemble: *de* ~, general; *en* ~, as a whole; *en su* ~, all together. *5 m.* MUS. ensemble. *6* THEAT. chorus.

**conjura, conjuración** *f.* plot, conspiracy.

**conjurado, -da** *m.-f.* conspirator.

**conjurador** *m.* conjurer [one who entreats].

**conjurar** *intr.* or *ref.* to swear together; to conspire, join in a conspiracy. *2 tr.* to swear in. *3* to conjure, entreat. *4* to exorcise. *5* to avert, ward off.

**conjuro** *m.* exorcism. *2* conjuration.

**conllevar** *tr.* to help somebody to bear [hardships, etc.]. *2* to bear with [somebody]. *3* to suffer with patience [hardships, etc.].

**conmemorable** *adj.* memorable, worthy of being remembered.

**conmemoración** *f.* commemoration.

**conmemorar** *tr.* to commemorate.

**conmemorativo, -va** *adj.* commemorative; memorial.

**conmensurable** *adj.* commensurable. *2* mensurable, measurable.

**conmigo** *pron.* with me, with myself.

**conminación** *f.* commination. *2* threatening order or summons.

**conminar** *tr.* to threaten. *2* to order or summon [under threat of punishment].

**conmiseración** *f.* commiseration, pity.

**conmoción** *f.* commotion, agitation, shock. *2* commotion, disturbance, riot. *3* MED. concussion.

**conmocionar** *tr.* MED. to concusse, to shock. *2* to upset, disturb, to cause turmoil.

**conmovedor, -ra** *adj.* moving, touching, pathetic.

**conmover** *tr.* to move, touch, affect, stir. *2* to shake, to upset. *3 ref.* to be moved, touched, affected. *4* to be shaken. ¶ CONJUG. like *mover*.

**conmuevo, conmueva**, etc. *irr.* V. CONMOVER.

**conmutabilidad** *f.* commutability.

**conmutable** *adj.* commutable.

**conmutación** *f.* commutation, exchange, substitution.

**conmutador** *m.* ELECT. commutator; switch, change-over switch.

**connatural** *adj.* connatural, inherent, natural.

**connaturalizarse** *ref.* to become adapted, accustumed [to], acclimated.

**connivencia** *f.* connivance. *2* secret understanding.

**connivente** *adj.* conniving. *2* ANAT., BOT. connivent.

**connotación** *f.* connotation.

**connotar** *tr.* to connote.

**connubial** *adj.* connubial.

**connubio** *m.* poet. marriage.

**cono** *m.* GEOM., BOT. cone.

**conocedor, -ra** *adj.* knowing, expert. *2 m.-f.* knower, connoiseur, judge.

**conocer** *tr.* to know [by the senses or by the mind]. *2* to be or get acquainted with, to meet [a person]. *3* LAW to have cognizance of. *4* to know [carnally]. *5* to own, avow. *6 intr.* ~ *de*, to be versed in. *7 ref.* to know oneself. *8* to be or get acquainted with each other. ¶ CONJUG. like *agradecer*.

**conocido, -da** *adj.* known, familiar. *2* wellknown, distinguished. *3 m.-f.* acquaintance [person].

**conocimiento** *m.* knowledge, cognition, cognizance; notice, information: *poner una cosa en ~ de uno*, to inform someone of something. *2* understanding, intelligence, sense. *3* skill, ability. *4* consciousness: *perder el ~*, to lose consciousness. *5* acquaintance [with a person or thing]. *6* COM. bill of lading [also called *~ de embarque*]. *7 pl.* knowledge, learning.

**conoidal** *adj.* conoidal.

**conoide** *adj.* conoid. *2 m.* GEOM. conoid.

**conozco, conozca**, etc. *irr.* V. CONOCER.

**conque** *conj.* so, so then, and so; well then. *2 m.* condition, terms.

**conquista** *f.* conquest.

**conquistable** *adj.* conquerable. *2* attainable.

**conquistador, -ra** *adj.* conquering. *2 m.-f.* conqueror. *3 m.* lady-killer. *4* conquistador.

**conquistar** *tr.* to conquer [by force of arms]; win, gain, attain. *2* to win the love of; to win over.

**Conrado** *m. pr. n.* Conrad.

**consabido, -da** *adj.* before-mentioned, in question.

**consagración** *f.* consecration.

**consagrado, -da** *adj.* consecrate, consecrated. *2* sanctioned, established. *3* stock [phrase]. *4 autor ~*, autor of established fame.

**consagrante** *adj.* consecrating. *2 m.* consecrator.

**consagrar** *tr.* to consecrate, hallow. *2* to consecrate, devote. *3* to authorize [a word or meaning]. *4* to erect [a monument] to. *5 tr.-intr.* to consecrate [in the Mass]. *6 ref.* to devote oneself.

**consanguíneo, -a** *adj.* consanguineous.

**consanguinidad** *f.* consanguinity.

**consciente** *adj.* conscious, aware. *2* responsible, knowing what he is about.

**conscripción** *f.* (Am.) conscription.

**conscripto** *adj. padre ~*, conscript father.

**consecución** *f.* obtainment, attainment.

**consecuencia** *f.* consequence, inference: *en ~, por ~*, consequently, therefore. *2* consequence, issue, result: *a ~ de*, because of, owing to. *3* consistency [of conduct]. *4 ser de ~*, to be important.

**consecuente** *adj.* following. *2* consistent [conduct, person]. *3 m.* LOG., MATH. consequent.

**consecutivo, -va** *adj.* consecutive.

**conseguir** *tr.* to obtain, attain, get. *2* [with an inf.] to succeed in, to manage to. ¶ CONJUG. like *servir*.

**conseja** *f.* fable, old wive's tale.

**consejero, -ra** *m.-f.* adviser. *2 m.* counselor, councilor. *3* COM. director. *4 f.* counselor's wife.

**consejo** *m.* advice, counsel; piece of advice. *2* council, board: *~ de administración*, COM. board of directors; *~ de guerra*, council of war; court-martial; *~ de ministros*, cabinet, council of ministers. *2* meeting of a council or board.

**consenso** *m.* consensus, assent, consent.

**consensual** *adj.* LAW consensual.

**consentido, -da** *adj.* spoiled, pampered [child]. *2* complaisant [husband]. *3* cracked, slightly disjointed, unsound.

**consentidor, -ra** *adj.* conniving. *2 m.-f.* conniver.

**consentimiento** *m.* consent, permission. *2* spoiling, pampering.

**consentir** *tr.* to allow, permit, tolerate. *2* to admit of. *3* to spoil, pamper. *4 intr. ~ en*, to consent to. *5 ref.* to begin to split, crack, or become unsound. ¶ CONJUG. like *hervir*.

**conserje** *m.* concierge, keeper, caretaker [of a palace or public building].

**conserjería** *f.* conciergerie.

**conserva** *f.* preserve, preserved food, conserve: *conservas alimenticias*, canned goods. *2* NAUT. convoy, consort.

**conservación** *f.* conservation, maintenance, upkeep. *2* preservation; self-preservation.

**conservador, -ra** *adj.* preserving, preservative. *2 adj.-n.* POL. conservative. *3 m.-f.* conserver. *4 m.* conservator, curator.

**conservaduría** *f.* conservatorship, curatorship [of a museum, etc.].

**conservadurismo** *m.* conservatism.

**conservar** *tr.* to conserve, keep, maintain, preserve: *bien conservado*, well-preserved [pers.]. *2* to preserve, can, pickle.

**conservatorio, -ria** *adj.* conservatory. *2 m.* conservatoire, conservatory.

**conservería** *f.* art of making preserves.

**conservero, -ra** *adj.* preserve-making, canning. *2 m.-f.* preserve maker, canner.

**considerable** *adj.* considerable, great, important.

**consideración** *f.* consideration [considering; reflection; esteem; respect; thoughtfulness]: *tomar en ~*, to take into consideration; *en ~ a*, considering; *tener consideraciones*, to show consideration; to be considerate. *2* meditation. *3 de ~*, severe, important.

**considerado, -da** *adj.* considerate. *2* considered, esteemed.

**considerando** *conj.* whereas. *2 m.* whereas [introductory clause or item in a law, etc.].

**considerar** *tr.* to consider [think over; bear in mind]. *2* to consider [treat with consideration]. *3* to consider [believe, judge].

**consigna** *f.* MIL. orders, instructions, watchword. *2* luggage room, *checkroom.

**consiento, consintió, consienta**, etc. *irr.* V. CONSENTIR.

**consignación** *f.* consignation. *2* COM. consignment. *3* assignment [on a budget], appropriation.

**consignador** *m.* COM. consignor.

**consignar** *tr.* to assign [a sum on a budget] to a specified use, to appropriate. *2* to consign, deposit. *3* to state in writing. *4* COM. to consign.

**consignatario** *m.* consignatary. *2* COM. consignee. *3* NAUT. shipping agent.

**consigo** *pron.* with him, with her, with one, with it; with them; with himself, with herself, with itself, with themselves, with oneself. *2* with you or yourselves [with people adressed as *usted*].

**consigo, consiguió, consiga**, etc. *irr.* V. CONSEGUIR.

**consiguiente** *adj.* consequent [following, resulting]. *2 m.* LOG. consequent. *3 por ~*, therefore.

**consistencia** *f.* consistence, consistency [firmness; solidity; density].

**consistente** *adj.* consistent, firm, solid. *2* consistent [as a syrup]. *3* consisting.

**consistir** *intr. ~ en*, to consist, lie, reside in.

**consistorial** *adj.* consistorial. *2 casas consistoriales*, town hall, city hall.

**consistorio** *m.* consistory. *2* town council.

**consocio** *m.* fellow member. *2* COM. partner.

**consola** *f.* console, console table, pier table.

**consolación** *f.* consolation.

**consolador, -ra** *adj.* consoling. *2 m.-f.* consoler.

**consolar** *tr.* to console, comfort, cheer, soothe. *2 ref.* to be consoled. ¶ CONJUG. like *contar*.

**consolidación** *f.* consolidation.

**consolidado, -da** *adj.* consolidated. *2* funded [debt]. *3 m. pl.* consols.

**consolidar** *tr.* to consolidate [make firm, solid]. *2* to fund [a floating debt]. *3 ref.* to consolidate [become firm, solid].

**consonancia** *f.* consonance, consonancy, accord, conformity. *2* MUS. consonance, consonancy. *3* PROS. rhyme.
**consonante** *adj.* consonant. *2* rhyming. *3 m.* PROS. rhyme word. *4 f.* GRAM. consonant.
**consonar** *intr.* to agree, harmonize. *2* PROS. to rhyme.
**consorcio** *m.* union, fellowship. *2* marital association. *3* consortium.
**consorte** *m.-f.* consort, partner. *2* consort [husband or wife]. *3 pl.* LAW join-parties. *4* LAW confederates.
**conspicuo, -cua** *adj.* conspicuous, eminent.
**conspiración** *f.* conspiracy, plot.
**conspirador, -ra** *m.-f.* conspirer, conspirator.
**conspirar** *intr.* to conspire, plot. *2* to conspire, concur [to an end].
**constancia** *f.* constancy, perseverance. *2* certainty, proof.
**Constancia** *f. pr. n.* Constance.
**Constancio** *m. pr. n.* Constance.
**constante** *adj.* constant. *2* known for certain. *3* consisting [of]. *4 f.* MATH. constant.
**constantemente** *adv.* constantly.
**Constantino** *m. pr. n.* Constantine.
**Constantinopla** *f. pr. n.* Constantinople.
**constar** *intr.* to be certain, proved; to be on record: *hacer ~,* to state, to put on record. *2* to consist of, be composed of. *3* [of verses] to scan.
**constatación** *f.* verification, proof. *2* recording.
**constatar** *tr.* GAL. to verify. *2* to state, to record.
**constelación** *f.* ASTR., ASTROL. constellation.
**constelado, -da** *adj.* starry, star-spangled, full of stars. *2* strewn, studded.
**constelar** *tr.* to spangle, to constellate.
**consternación** *f.* consternation, dismay.
**consternar** *tr.* to consternate, dismay.
**constipado, -da** *adj.* MED. suffering from a cold. *2 m.* MED. cold, chill.
**constipar** *tr.* MED. to constrict, to close the pores of. *2 ref.* to catch a cold.
**constitución** *f.* constitution [in every sense].
**constitucional** *adj.* constitutional. *2 m.* constitutionalist.
**constitucionalidad** *f.* constitutionality.
**constitucionalizar** *tr.* to constitutionalize.
**constituir** *tr.* to constitute. *2 ref.* to constitute oneself. *3 constituirse en sociedad, en república,* to form an association, a republic. ¶ CONJUG. like *huir.*
**constitutivo, -va** *adj.* constitutive, essential. *2 m.* constituent [essential part].
**constituyente** *adj.* constituent, component. *2* POL. constituent.
**constituyo, constituyó, constituya,** etc. *irr.* V. CONSTITUIR.
**constreñimiento** *m.* constraint, compulsion. *2* MED. constriction, stricture.
**constreñir** *tr.* to constrain, compel, force. *2* MED. to constrict. ¶ CONJUG. like *ceñir.*
**constricción** *f.* constriction.
**constrictor, -ra** *adj.* constricting. *2 m.* constrictor.
**constringente** *adj.* constringent.
**construcción** *f.* construction, building [act or art of constructing; thing constructed], erection, structure. *2* GRAM. construction.
**constructivo, -va** *adj.* constructive.
**constructor, -ra** *m.-f.* constructor, builder.
**construir** *tr.* to construct, build, make. *2* GRAM. to construct, construe. ¶ CONJUG. like *huir.*

**construyo, construyó, construya,** etc. *irr.* V. CONSTRUIR.
**consubstanciación** *f.* THEOL. consubstantiation.
**consubstancial** *adj.* consubstantial.
**consubstancialidad** *f.* consubstantiality.
**consuegra** *f.* mother-in-law of one's child.
**consuegro** *m.* father-in-law of one's child.
**consuelda** *f.* BOT. comfrey.
**consuelo** *m.* consolation, comfort, alleviation: *sin ~,* inconsolably: coll. without measure. *2* joy.
**consuelo, consuele,** etc. *irr.* V. CONSOLAR.
**consuetudinario, -ria** *adj.* consuetudinary, customary: *derecho ~,* common law.
**cónsul** *m.* consul: *~ general,* consul general.
**consulado** *m.* consulate.
**consular** *adj.* consular.
**consulta** *f.* consultation, consulting. *2* opinion, information given or asked. *3* MED. consultation.
**consultación** *f.* consultation [conference].
**consultante** *adj.* consulting [asking advice]. *2 m.-f.* consulter.
**consultar** *tr.-intr.* to consult.
**consultivo, -va** *adj.* consultative.
**consultor, -ra** *adj.* consulting. *2 m.-f.* consultant, adviser, counsellor. *3* consúlter.
**consultorio** *m.* technical advising bureau. *2* MED. clinic, institution where outpatients are treated; doctor's room or office.
**consumación** *f.* consummation. *2* end, extinction.
**consumado, -da** *adj.* consummated. *2* consummate, perfect, complete. *3 m.* consommé.
**consumar** *tr.* to consummate, accomplish, complete. *2* to commit [a crime].
**consumible** *adj.* consumable.
**consumición** *f.* consuming, consumption. *2* service [drink, etc., taken in a café, restaurant, etc.].
**consumido, -da** *adj.* consumed. *2* thin, emaciated.
**consumidor, -ra** *adj.* consuming. *2 m.-f.* consumer.
**consumir** *tr.* to consume. *2* to waste away, eat up, use up. *3* to worry, afflict, vex. *4* to take [the Eucharist] in the mass. *5 ref.* to be consumed. *6* to waste away, to be vexed, to fret.
**consumo** *m.* consumption [of food, full, goods, etc.]: *artículos de ~,* commodities, consumers' goods. *2 pl.* municipal customs.
**consunción** *f.* consumption, consuming. *2* MED. consumption.
**consuno (de)** *adv.* together, in accord.
**consuntivo, -va** *adj.* MED. consumptive.
**contabilidad** *f.* accounting, accountancy, bookkeeping.
**contabilizar** *tr.* ACCOUNT. to enter [as an item] into a book.
**contable** *adj.* countable. *2 m.* accountant.
**contacto** *m.* contact. *2* touch: *mantenerse en ~ con,* to keep in touch with.
**contado, -da** *adj.* counted, numbered. *2* scarce, rare, few: *contadas veces,* rarely. *3 m. al ~,* for cash, cash down. *4 de ~,* at once, right away. *5 por de ~,* of course, certainly.
**contador, -ra** *adj.* counting. *2 m.-f.* counter, computer. *3 m.* accountant, auditor. *4* counter, meter: *~ de gas,* gas meter; *~ de Geiger,* Geiger counter.
**contaduría** *f.* accountant's office. *2* THEAT. box office for advance booking.
**contagiar** *tr.* to communicate by contagion. *2* to infect with. *3* to corrupt, pervert. *4 ref.* to be contagious, infectious. *5 contagiarse de,* to be infected with.

**contagio** *m.* contagion. *2* contagious disease.
**contagioso, -sa** *adj.* contagious, infectious.
**contaminación** *f.* contamination, pollution.
**contaminador, -ra** *adj.* contaminating, polluting, infecting.
**contaminante** *adj.* polluting, defiling. *2 m.* polluting agent.
**contaminar** *tr.* to contaminate, pollute, infect. *2 ref.* to be contaminated.
**contante** *adj.* ready [money].
**contar** *tr.* to count, number, tell, reckon. *2* to number, rate, reckon [among]. *3* to charge [a price for]. *4* to tell, relate, narrate, spin: *cuénteselo a su abuela,* fig. tell that to the marines. *5 cuéntelo por hecho,* count it as done. *6 contar [tantos] años,* to be [so many] years old. *7 intr.* to count, to do sums. *8 ~ con,* to count, reckon, rely, depend on or upon; to have. ¶ CONJUG.: INDIC. Pres.: *cuento, cuentas, cuenta; contamos, contáis, cuentan.* | SUBJ. Pres.: *cuente, cuentes, cuente; contemos, contéis, cuenten.* | IMPER.: *cuenta, cuente; contemos, contad, cuenten.*
**contemplación** *f.* contemplation. *2 pl.* complaisance, leniency.
**contemplar** *tr.* to contemplate, view, look at. *2* THEOL. to contemplate. *3* to be complaisant or lenient towards [somebody], to pamper.
**contemplativo, -va** *adj.* contemplative.
**contemporaneidad** *f.* contemporariness.
**contemporáneo, -a** *adj.* contemporaneous, contemporary, coeval. *2 m.-f.* contemporary.
**contemporización** *f.* temporizing, compliance.
**contemporizador, -ra** *adj.* temporizing, yielding, complying.
**contemporizar** *intr.* to temporize, to yield, comply.
**contención** *f.* holding back, restraint, restraining, checking. *2* contention, contest. *5* LAW litigation.
**contencioso, -sa** *adj.* contentious.
**contender** *int.* to contend, contest. *2* to fight, combat, strive. ¶ CONJUG. like *entender.*
**contendiente** *adj.* contending. *2 m.-f.* contender, contestant.
**contendré, contendría,** etc. *irr.* V. CONTENER.
**contenedor, -ra** *adj.* containing. *2 m.* container.
**contener** *tr.* to contain, hold, comprise. *2* to contain, restrain, refrain, curb, check, stop. *3* to hold back. *4 ref.* to be contained. *5* to contain oneself. ¶ CONJUG. like *tener.*
**contengo, contenga,** etc. *irr.* V. CONTENER.
**contenido, -da** *adj.* moderate, prudent, temperate. *2 m.* contents. *3* tenor, context.
**contentadizo** *adj.* easily pleased, easily satisfied.
**contentamiento** *m.* contentment, joy, content.
**contentar** *tr.* to content, please, satisfy. *2 ref.* to be contented.
**contento, -ta** *adj.* contented, pleased, satisfied, glad. *2 m.* contentment, content, joy, gladness.
**contera** *f.* ferrule, tip [of cane, umbrella, etc.]; chape [at scabard's point]. *2 por ~,* coll. to clinch it.
**conterráneo, -a** *m.-f.* compatriot, fellow countryman or countrywoman.
**contertulio, -lia** *m.-f.* fellow member of a coterie.
**contestable** *adj.* contestable. *2* answerable.
**contestación** *f.* answer, reply. *2* debate.
**contestador** *m. ~ automático,* answering machine, answer phone.
**contestar** *tr.* to answer, to reply. *2* to answer [a summons, a letter]. *3* to confirm [another's statement].
**contexto** *m.* context. *2* intertexture.
**contextura** *f.* contexture.
**contienda** *f.* contest, fight, battle, dispute.
**contiendo, contienda,** etc. *irr.* V. CONTENDER.
**contigo** *pron.* with thee, with you, with thyself or yourself.
**contigüidad** *f.* contiguity.
**contiguo, -gua** *adj.* contiguous, adjoining.
**continencia** *f.* continence. *2* containing.
**continental** *adj.* continental.
**continente** *adj.* containing. *2* continent [temperate, chaste]. *3 m.* container. *4* countenance, bearing. *5* GEOG. continent.
**contingencia** *f.* contingency.
**contingente** *adj.* contingent [chance, that may happen]. *2 m.* contingent.
**continuación** *f.* continuation, continuance; prolongation; literary sequel: *a ~,* immediately, immediately afterwards.
**continuado, -da** *adj.* continued, constant.
**continuamente** *adv.* continuously, continually, incessantly.
**continuar** *tr.* to continue [pursue, carry on]. *2 intr.* to continue, go on, keep. *3 ref.* to be continued, to extend: *se continuará,* to be continued.
**continuativo, -va** *adj.* continuative. *2* GRAM. illative.
**continuidad** *f.* continuity.
**continuo, -a** *adj.* continuous. *2* continued, constant, continual. *3* MACH. endless. *4* ELECT. direct [current]. *5 de ~,* continually. *6 m.* continuum.
**contonearse** *ref.* to swing the hips and shoulders in walking.
**contoneo** *m.* swinging of the hips and shoulders in walking.
**contorcerse** *ref.* to twist oneself, to writhe.
**contornar, contornear** *tr.* to circle, go around [a place]. *2* to contour, outline.
**contorno** *m.* contour, outline: *en ~,* around. *2 sing.-pl.* environs, neighbourhood.
**contorsión** *f.* contortion.
**contorsionista** *m.-f.* contortionist.
**contra** *prep.* against; athwart, counter: *~ viento y marea,* stubbornly, in spite of all difficulties. *2* contrarily to. *3* facing: *~ oriente,* facing east. *4 m.* con, against. *5* MUS. organ pedal; lower bass [of organ]. *6 f.* opposition: *hacer, o llevar, la ~,* to oppose, contradict; *ir en ~ de,* to run counter to. *7* snag, drawback. *8* FENC. counter.
**contraalmirante** *m.* rear admiral.
**contraamura** *f.* NAUT. preventer-tack.
**contraatacar** *tr.-intr.* to counterattack.
**contrabajo** *m.* MUS. contrabass. *2* contrabassist. *3* MUS. double-bass [voice; singer].
**contrabalancear** *tr.* to counterbalance, counterpoise. *2* to compensate.
**contrabandear** *intr.* to smuggle.
**contrabandista** *m.-f.* smuggler, contrabandist.
**contrabando** *m.* smuggling, contraband: *pasar de ~,* to smuggle [goods].
**contrabarrera** *f.* BULLF. second barrier in the bullring.
**contracarril** *m.* RLY. guardrail.
**contracción** *f.* contraction, contracting, shrinking [drawing together, making smaller]. *2* GRAM. contraction.
**contracepción** *f.* MED. contraception.
**contraceptivo, -va** *adj.-n.* contraceptive.
**contracifra** *f.* key to a cipher.

**contraclave** *f.* ARCH. voussoir next to the keystone.
**contracorriente** *f.* countercurrent; back water.
**contráctil** *adj.* contractile.
**contracto, -ta** *irreg. p. p.* of CONTRAER.
**contractual** *adj.* contractual.
**contrachapado** *m.* plywood.
**contradanza** *f.* contradance, country-dance.
**contradecir** *tr.-ref.* to contradict, to gainsay.
**contradicción** *f.* contradiction, gainsaying. 2 opposition, inconsistency.
**contradictorio, -ria** *adj.* contradictory.
**contradique** *m.* counterdike.
**contraer** *tr.* to contract [draw together; cause to shrink; wrinkle, knit]. 2 GRAM. to contract. 3 to contract [marriage, debts, a disease, etc.]. 4 to limit, confine [to one idea, point, etc.]. 5 *ref.* to contract [be contracted], to shrink. 6 to limit, confine, oneself. ¶ CONJUG. like *traer.*
**contraescarpa** *f.* FORT. counterscarp.
**contraespionaje** *m.* counterespionage.
**contrafagot** *m.* US. double bassoon, contrabassoon.
**contrafilo** *m.* back edge near the point [of a weapon].
**contrafirma** *f.* countersignature.
**contrafirmar** *tr.* to countersign.
**contrafoque** *m.* NAUT. fore-topmast staysail.
**contrafoso** *m.* THEAT. subcellar. 2 FORT. outer ditch.
**contrafuego** *m.* backfire.
**contrafuero** *m.* infringement or violation of a charter, right or privilege.
**contrafuerte** *m.* counter [of shoe]. 2 spur [of mountain range]. 3 FORT. counterfort. 4 ARCH. counterfort, buttress.
**contrafuga** *f.* MUS. counterfuge.
**contragolpe** *m.* MED. counterstroke. 2 kick-back. 3 counterblow.
**contraguerrilla** *f.* anti-guerrilla warfare. 2 anti-guerrilla force or troops.
**contrahacer** *tr.* to counterfeit. 2 to imitate, to mimic. 3 *ref.* to feign oneself. ¶ CONJUG. like *hacer.*
**contrahecho, -cha** *p. p.* of CONTRAHACER. 2 *adj.* counterfeit. 3 deformed, hunchbacked.
**contrahilo** *m. a* ~, across the grain.
**contrahuella** *f.* riser [of a step].
**contraindicación** *m.* MED. contraindication.
**contraindicar** *tr.* MED. to contraindicate.
**contralmirante** *m.* CONTRAALMIRANTE.
**contralor** *m.* comptroller, auditor.
**contralto** *m.-f.* MUS. contralto.
**contraluz** *f.* view [of a thing] against the light: *a* ~, against the light.
**contramaestre** *m.* foreman. 2 NAUT. boatswain.
**contramano (a)** *adv.* in the wrong direction.
**contramarca** *f.* countermark.
**contramarcar** *tr.* to countermark.
**contramarcha** *f.* countermarch. 2 MACH. reverse.
**contramarchar** *tr.* to countermarch.
**contramarea** *f.* NAUT. opposing tide.
**contramina** *f.* MIL. countermine.
**contraminar** *tr.* to countermine.
**contramuralla** *f.*, **contramuro** *m.* FORT. countermure.
**contraofensiva** *f.* MIL. counteroffensive.
**contraoferta** *f.* counterferta.
**contraorden** *f.* countermand, counterorder.
**contrapartida** *f.* emendatory entry [in book-keeping]. 2 compensation.
**contrapaso** *m.* back step. 2 MUS. second part.
**contrapelo (a)** *adv.* against the hair, against the grain.

**contrapesar** *tr.* to counterbalance, counterpoise, compensate, offset, setoff.
**contrapeso** *m.* counterweight. 2 counterpoise, counterbalance. 3 makeweight. 4 ropedancer's pole.
**contraponer** *tr.* to set against, to compare. 2 *tr.-ref.* to oppose. ¶ CONJUG. like *poner.*
**contraposición** *f.* contraposition. 2 opposition.
**contraproducente** *adj.* self-defeating, producing the opposite of the desired effect.
**contraproposición** *f.* counterproposition.
**contraproyecto** *m.* alternative project or plan, counterplan.
**contrapuerta** *f.* storm door. 2 second door.
**contrapuesto, -ta** *adj.* set against, compared. 3 opposed.
**contrapuntear** *tr.* MUS. to sing in counterpoint. 2 *ref.* [of two persons] to be at odds.
**contrapunto** *m.* MUS. counterpoint.
**contrariamente** *adv.* contrarily.
**contrariar** *tr.* to oppose, run counter to, cross, thwart. 2 to mortify, chagrin, vex, disappoint.
**contrariedad** *f.* contrariety, opposition. 2 mortification, vexation. 3 set back, disappointment.
**contrario, -ria** *adj.* contrary, opposed, adverse, hostile. 2 harmful, unfavourable. 3 opposite, reverse. 4 *m.-f.* opponent, adversary. 5 *m.* the contrary, the opposite: *al* ~, *por el* ~, on the contrary; *de lo* ~, otherwise. 6 *f. llevar la contraria,* to contradict; to oppose.
**contrarreforma** *f.* Counter Reformation.
**contrarregistro** *m.* second examination.
**contrarréplica** *f.* rejoinder.
**contrarrestar** *tr.* to resist, oppose, counteract, neutralize.
**contrarresto** *m.* resistance, counteraction.
**contrarrevolución** *f.* counterrevolution.
**contrarrevolucionario, -ria** *adj.* counterrevolutionary. 2 *m.-f.* counterrevolutionist.
**contrarriel** *m.* check rail, guard rail.
**contrarroda** *f.* NAUT. apron.
**contrasellar** *tr.* to counterseal.
**contrasello** *m.* counterseal.
**contrasentido** *m.* contradiction in terms, inconsistency.
**contraseña** *f.* countersign, countermark. 2 MIL. countersign, watchword. 3 check [for a coat, hat, etc.].
**contrastable** *adj.* contrastable. 2 comparable.
**contrastar** *tr.* to resist, oppose. 2 to hall-mark. 3 to check [weights and measures]. 4 *intr.* to contrast.
**contraste** *m.* resistance, opposition. 2 contrast. 3 hall mark. 4 hallmarker. 5 assay office. 6 inspector of weights and measures; his office.
**contrata** *f.* contract [esp. for works, supplies, etc.]. 2 engagement [of an actor, artist, etc.].
**contratación** *f.* contracting [marking contracts]. 2 commerce, trade, business transaction.
**contratante** *adj.* contracting. 2 *m.-f.* contracting party, contractor.
**contratar** *tr.* to contract for. 2 to engage, hire.
**contratiempo** *m.* mishap, hitch, disappointment. 2 MUS. contretemps.
**contratista** *m.* contractor: ~ *de obras,* building contractor.
**contrato** *m.* contract [agreement]: ~ *leonino,* one-sided, unfair contract.
**contratorpedero** *m.* NAUT. torpedo-boat destroyer.
**contratuerca** *f.* check nut, lock nut.
**contravapor** *m.* MACH. back-pressure steam.

**contravención** f. contravention, infringement.
**contraveneno** m. counterpoison, antidote.
**contravenir** tr. to contravene, infringe.
**contraventana** f. window shutter.
**contraventor, -ra** adj. contravening. 2 m.-f. contravener, transgressor.
**contraviento** m. ARCH. windbrace.
**contrayente** adj. contracting marriage. 2 m.-f. contracting party [to a marriage].
**contribución** f. contribution [act of contributing]. 2 contribution, tax.
**contribuir** tr. to pay as a tax. 2 tr.-intr. to contribute [a sum]. 3 intr. ~ a, to contribute to. ¶ CONJUG. like huir.
**contributivo, -va** adj. [pertaining to] tax, imposition.
**contribuyente** adj. contributing, taxpaying. 2 m.-f. contributor, taxpayer.
**contrición** f. contrition.
**contrincante** m. competidor, opponent, rival.
**contristar** tr. to sadden, grieve.
**contrito, -ta** adj. contrite.
**control** m. GAL. control, check.
**controlable** adj. controlable, regulable. 2 verifiable, checkable.
**controlador** m. controller; ~ del tráfico aéreo, air traffic controller.
**controlar** tr. GAL. to control, check, verify.
**controversia** f. controversy, disputation.
**controversista** m. controversialist.
**controvertible** adj. controversial, polemical. 2 questionable, debatable, disputable.
**controvertir** tr.-intr. to controvert, to dispute. ¶ CONJUG. like hervir.
**contubernio** m. cohabitation, concubinage. 2 base or evil alliance.
**contumacia** f. contumacy, stubborn persistency in one's error. 2 LAW default.
**contumaz** adj. contumacious, stubborn in maintaining an error. 2 LAW guilty of default.
**contumelia** f. contumely, insult, abuse.
**contundencia** f. contusive properties of a weapon. 2 weight [of a reason].
**contundente** adj. contusive. 2 blunt [instrument]. 3 forceful, impressive [argument, proof, etc.].
**contundir** tr. to bruise, beat; to contuse.
**conturbación** f. disturbance, trouble, disquiet.
**conturbar** tr. to disturb, trouble, disquiet. 2 ref. to become disturbed, troubled.
**contusión** f. contusion.
**contusionar** tr. to contuse [cause contusion].
**contuso, -sa** adj. contused, bruised.
**contuve, contuviera,** etc. irr. V. CONTENER.
**convalecencia** f. convalescence.
**convalecer** intr. to convalesce, be convalescent, recover. ¶ CONJUG. like agradecer.
**convaleciente** adj. convalescent.
**convalezco, convalezca,** etc. irr. V. CONVALECER.
**convalidación** f. LAW confirmation.
**convalidar** tr. LAW to confirm.
**convecino, -na** adj. neighbouring. 2 m.-f. fellow neighbour.
**convencer** tr. to convince. 2 ref. to become convinced.
**convencido, -da** adj. convinced.
**convencimiento** m. conviction [convincing; being convinced]; belief.
**convención** f. convention, agreement. 2 convention, conventionality. 3 POL. convention.
**conventional** adj. conventional. 2 m. member of a convention.

**convencionalismo** m. conventionalism, conventionality.
**convencionalmente** adv. conventionally.
**convenido, -da** adj. agreed, settled by agreement.
**conveniencia** f. conformity, agreement. 2 fitness, suitability, desirability. 3 convenience, advantage, interest. 4 place, situation [as a servant]. 5 pl. income, property.
**conveniente** adj. convenient, fit, suitable, expedient, opportune. 2 good, useful, advantageous.
**convenio** m. covenant, agreement, pact.
**convenir** intr. to agree [be of the same mind]. 2 to meet, convene. 3 to befit, harmonize, agree. 4 to be convenient, advantageous, necessary; to suit one's interests: me conviene, it suits me. 5 conviene a saber, namely, to wit. 6 ref. to agree, come to an agreement. ¶ CONJUG. like venir.
**conventículo** m. conventicle.
**conventillo** m. (Am.) tenement house.
**convento** m. convent, monastery; nunnery.
**conventual** adj.-m. conventual.
**convergencia** f. convergence, concurrence.
**convergente** adj. convergent, converging.
**converger, convergir** intr. to converge, to concur.
**conversación** f. conversation, talk.
**conversador, -ra** m.-f. good conversationalist.
**conversar** intr. to converse, talk, chat. 2 to have intercourse. 3 MIL. to effect a conversion.
**conversión** f. conversion; transformation, change. 2 THEOL., MATH., FENC., FINANCE conversion.
**converso, -sa** adj. converted. 2 m. convert. 3 lay brother.
**conversor** m. PHYS. converter.
**convertible** adj. convertible, transformable.
**convertido, -da** adj. converted. 2 m.-f. convert.
**convertidor** m. ELECT., METAL. converter.
**convertir** tr. to convert. 2 ref. to be or become converted, to turn [into]. ¶ CONJUG. like discernir.
**convexidad** f. convexity.
**convexo, -xa** adj. convex.
**convicción** f. conviction, belief.
**convicto, -ta** adj. convicted [found guilty].
**convidada** f. coll. invitation to drink, treat.
**convidado, -da** m.-f. invited person, guest.
**convidar** tr. to invite [as a guest or participant]; to treat: ~ a uno con una cosa, to offer something to someone. 2 to move, incite, invite, tempt. 3 ref. to invite oneself.
**conviene, convienes,** etc. irr. V. CONVENIR.
**convierto, convierta,** etc. irr. V. CONVERTIR.
**convincente** adj. convincing.
**convite** m. invitation. 2 treat, entertainment, banquet.
**convivencia** f. living together with others.
**convivir** intr. to cohabit, to live together. 2 to co-exist.
**convocación** f. convocation, summoning, summons.
**convocar** tr. to convoke, convene, summon.
**convocatorio, -ria** adj. convoking, convocative. 2 f. letter of convocation, call, notice of meeting.
**convolvuláceo, -a** adj. BOT. convolvulaceous.
**convólvulo** m. BOT. bindweed. 2 ENT. vine inchworm.
**convoy** m. convoy. 2 railway train. 4 retinue. 5 cruet stand.
**convoyar** tr. to convoy, escort.
**convulsión** f. convulsion.
**convulsionar** tr. to convulse.
**convulsivo, -va** adj. convulsive.
**convulso, -sa** adj. convulsed.

**conyugal** *adj.* conjugal, matrimonial.
**cónyuge** *m.-f.* spouse, consort, husband or wife.
**coña** *f.* coll. joke; *tomárselo en* ~, to take it as a joke.
**coñac** *m.* cognac, brandy.
**coño** *m.* coll. cunt. *2 interj.* coll. shit! damn! Christ!
**coolí** *m.* coolie.
**cooperación** *f.* co-operation.
**cooperador, -ra** *adj.* co-operative. *2 m.-f.* cooperator.
**cooperar** *tr.* to co-operate.
**cooperativo, -va** *adj.* co-operative. *2 f.* co-operative [co-operative society, store or enterprise].
**cooptación** *f.* co-optation, co-option.
**coordenado, -da** *adj.* MATH. co-ordinate. *2 f.* MATH. co-ordinate.
**coordinación** *f.* co-ordination.
**coordinado, -da** *adj.* co-ordinate(d. *2* GRAM. co-ordinate.
**coordinamiento** *m.* co-ordinating, co-ordination.
**coordinar** *tr.* to co-ordinate.
**copa** *f.* cup, glass [with stem and foot], goblet, wineglass. *2* drink [of liquor]. *3* cup [trophy]. *4* brazier. *5* head, top [branches and foliage of a tree]. *6* crown [of a hat]. *7* CARDS suit corresponding to hearts.
**copado, -da** *adj.* having a head [tree].
**copaiba** *f.* BOT. copaiba [tree]. *2* PHARM. copaiba.
**copal** *m.* copal.
**copar** *tr.* to sweep [all posts in an election]. *2* MIL. to cut off the retreat of [a force] and capture it. *3* GAMBLING ~ *la banca*, to go banco.
**coparticipación** *f.* copartnership, joint partnership.
**copartícipe** *m.-f.* joint participator, copartaker.
**copayero** *m.* BOT. copaiba [tree].
**copear** *intr.* to sell wine or liquor by the glass. *2* to drink, have drinks.
**copeck** *m.* kopeck.
**copela** *f.* cupel.
**copelación** *f.* cupellation.
**copelar** *tr.* to cupel.
**Copenhague** *f. pr. n.* Copenhaguen.
**Copérnico** *m. pr. n.* Copernicus.
**copero** *m.* cupbearer. *2* cabinet for wineglasses.
**copete** *m.* topping, topknot; tuft, pompadour; crest [of a bird]; forelock [of a horse]. *2* ornamental top [on a piece of furniture]. *3* fig. arrogance, uppishness. *4 de alto* ~, of high rank, aristocratic.
**copetín** *m.* small drinking glass. *2* (Am.) cocktail, drink.
**copetudo, -da** *adj.* tufted, crested. *2* vain, uppish.
**copia** *f.* abundance, plenty. *2* copy [transcript, reproduction, imitation]. *3* duplicate.
**copiador, -ra** *adj.* copying. *2 m.-f.* copier. *3* letter book.
**copiar** *tr.* to copy [transcribe, make copy of, imitate]. *2* to mimic, ape.
**copiloto** *m.* copilot. *2* co-driver.
**copión** *m.* coll. poorly made copy.
**copiosidad** *f.* copiousness, abundance.
**copioso, -sa** *adj.* copious, plentiful, abundant.
**copista** *m.-f.* copyist.
**copla** *f.* stanza. *2* short poetical composition; song, folk song, ballad. *3 pl.* rhymes, poetry; *coplas de ciego*, doggerel.
**coplear** *intr.* to rhyme [make verses].
**coplero, -ra** *adj.* ballad seller. *2* poetaster.
**coplista** *m.* poetaster.
**copo** *m.* flake [of snow]. *2* clot. *3* bunch of wool,

flax, etc. [to be spun]. *4* bottom of purse net. *5* GAMBLING banco. *6* sweeping all posts [in an election]. *7* MIL. cutting off the retreat of a force and capturing it.
**copón** *m.* large goblet. *2* ECCL. ciborium, pyx.
**copra** *f.* copra.
**copropietario, -ria** *m.-f.* joint owner, coproprietor.
**copto, -ta** *adj.* Coptic. *2 m.-f.* Copt.
**copudo, -da** *adj.* thick-topped [tree].
**cópula** *f.* copula, link. *2* copulation. *3* GRAM., LOG. copula.
**copularse** *ref.* to copulate.
**copulativo, -va** *adj.* joining. *2* GRAM. copulative.
**coque** *m.* coke.
**coqueluche** *f.* MED. whooping cough.
**coqueta** *adj.* coquettish, flirtatious. *2 f.* coquette, flirt [woman].
**coquetear** *intr.* to coquet, flirt.
**coqueteo** *m.* coquetting, flirting, flirtation.
**coquetería** *f.* coquetry.
**coquetón, -na** *adj.* [of things], pretty, charming. *2* flirtatious [man]. *3 m.* flirt [man].
**coquina** *f.* ZOOL. wedge shell.
**coquito** *m.* gesture, face [to amuse a baby]. *2* BOT. a palm of Chile; its fruit.
**coracero** *m.* cuirassier. *2* coll. strong cigar.
**coracoides** *adj.-m.* ANAT. coracoid.
**coracha** *f.* leather sack.
**coraje** *m.* courage, mettle. *2* anger, irritation.
**corajina** *f.* fit of anger.
**corajudo, -da** *adj.* choleric, irritable.
**coral** *adj.* MUS. choral. *2 m.* MUS. choral, chorale. *3* coral, red coral [polyp and secretion]. *4 f.* ZOOL. coral snake. *5 m. pl.* coral beads.
**coralero, -ra** *m.-f.* worker or dealer in corals.
**coralífero, -ra** *adj.* coralliferous.
**coralillo** *m.* ZOOL. coral snake.
**coralina** *f.* ZOOL., BOT. coralline.
**coralino, -na** *adj.* coralline, coral-like, coral-red.
**corambre** *f.* hides, skins, pelts. *2* wineskin.
**Corán** *m.* Koran.
**coránico, -ca** *adj.* Koranic.
**coraza** *f.* cuirass. *2* armour [of a ship].
**corazón** *m.* ANAT., ZOOL. heart. *2* heart [soul, sensibility, love, cordiality, good will; courage, spirit]: *llevar el* ~ *en la mano*, to wear one's heart on one's sleeve; *me da* or *me dice el* ~, I have a feeling that; *no caberle a uno el* ~ *en el pecho*, to be bursting with anger, anxiety, etc.; to be big-hearted; *no tener* ~, to have no heart, be insensible; *se me parte el* ~, my heart bleeds; *tocarle a uno en el* ~, to move one for the best; *de* ~, heartily, sincerely. *3* heart, core, middle [of a thing]. *4* core [of apple, pear, etc.].
**corazonada** *f.* presentiment, foreboding, *hunch. *2* impulse [that moves to act]. *3* coll. ASADURA 1.
**corazoncillo** *m.* BOT. St.-John's-wort.
**corbata** *f.* tie, necktie, cravat, scarf: ~ *de lazo*, bow tie; ~ *de pala*, four-in-hand tie.
**corbatería** *f.* necktie shop.
**corbatero, -ra** *m.-f.* necktie maker or dealer.
**corbatín** *m.* bow tie. *2* stock [for the neck].
**corbeta** *f.* NAUT. corvette, sloop of war.
**Córcega** *f. pr. n.* Corsica.
**corcel** *m.* steed, charger.
**corcino** *m.* ZOOL. fawn [of roe deer].
**corcova** *f.* hump, hunch, crooked back or chest.
**corcovado, -da** *adj.* humpbacked, hunchbacked. *2 m.-f.* humpback, hunchback.
**corcovar** *tr.* to crook.
**corcovear** *intr.* [of a horse] to buck.

**corcoveta** f. small hump. 2 m.-f. CORCOVADO 2.
**corcovo** m. buck [of a horse]. 2 bend, crook.
**corchar** tr. NAUT. to lay [strands of rope].
**corchea** m. MUS. quaver, eighth note.
**corchero, -ra** adj. cork [industry, etc.]. 2 m. cork-tree peeler. 3 f. CORCHO 3.
**corcheta** f. eye [of a hook and eye].
**corchete** m. hook and eye. 2 hook [of a hook and eye]. 3 CARP. bench hook. 4 MUS., PRINT. brace, bracket. 5 bumbailiff, catchpole.
**corcho** m. cork. 2 cork mat. 3 cork bucket [for cooling drinks]. 4 cork-soled clog. 5 beehive.
**¡córcholis!** interj. gracious me!, by Jove!
**corchoso, -sa** adj. corky, corklike.
**corchotaponero, -ra** adj. corkmaking.
**cordaje** m. NAUT. rigging, cordage.
**cordal** m. MUS. tailpiece [of stringed instrument]. 2 adj. muela ~, wisdom tooth.
**cordel** m. string, twine, fine cord: ~ de la corredera, NAUT. log line; a ~, in a straight line.
**cordelería** f. ropemaking. 2 ropewalk. 3 rope shop.
**cordelero, -ra** adj. ropemaking. 2 m.-f. ropemaker, cordmaker. 2 rope seller.
**cordera** f. ewe lamb. 2 fig. lamb [meek woman].
**cordería** f. roping, cordage.
**corderillo** m. little lamb. 2 lambskin dressed with wool on it.
**cordero** m. ZOOL. lamb: ~ lechal, sucking lamb. 2 fig. lamb [meek man]. 3 lamb meat. 4 lambskin. 5 (cap.) Lamb [Christ]: Cordero de Dios, Divino Cordero, Lamb of God.
**cordezuela** f. dim. small rope.
**cordial** adj. cordial, invigorating. 2 cordial, hearty, warm, affectionate, sincere. 3 middle [finger]. 4 m. cordial [drink].
**cordialidad** f. cordiality, heartiness, warmth.
**cordillera** f. chain of mountains, mountain range.
**cordita** f. cordite [explosive].
**Córdoba** f. pr. n. Cordova.
**cordobán** m. cordovan, tanned goatskin.
**cordobés, -sa** adj.-n. Cordovan.
**cordón** m. cordon, cord, string [mostly ornamental]. 2 lace [of shoe, corset, etc.]. 3 string [of purse]. 4 cord girdle [of a monk]. 5 cordon [of an order]. 6 NAUT. sfrand [of rope]. 7 ELECT., ANAT. cord. 8 ARCH. torus. 9 cordon [line, circle of persons or posts]. 10 pl. MIL. aglets.
**cordonazo** m. blow with a cord.
**cordoncillo** m. dim. small cord. 2 rib, cord [on a textile fabric]. 3 milling [on edge of a coin].
**cordura** f. soundness of mind, sanity. 2 prudence, wisdom.
**Corea** f. pr. n. Corea, Korea.
**corea** f. MED. chorea, St. Vitus dance.
**corear** tr. to compose chorus music. 2 to chorus.
**coreo** m. PROS. choreus. 2 MUS. harmony of choruses.
**coreografía** f. choreography.
**coriáceo, -a** adj. coriaceous.
**coriambo** m. PROS. choriamb.
**corifeo** m. coryphaeus. 2 leader.
**corimbo** m. BOT. corymb.
**corindón** m. MINER. corundum.
**corintio, -tia** adj.-n. Corinthian.
**Corinto** f. pr. n. Corinth.
**corión** m. EMBR. chorion.
**corista** m.-f. chorist, chorister. 2 choir priest. 3 m. THEAT. chorus man. 4 f. THEAT. chorus girl.
**coriza** f. MED. coryza, cold in the head.
**cormofita** adj. BOT. cormophytic.
**cormorán** m. ORN. cormorant.

**cornac, cornaca** m. mahout.
**cornada** f. thrust with the horns.
**cornalina** f. MINER. carnelian, cornelian.
**cornalón** adj. big-horned [bull].
**cornamenta** f. horns, antlers [of an animal].
**cornamusa** f. MUS. cornemuse, bagpipe. 2 MUS. kind of brass horn. 3 NAUT. chock, cleat.
**córnea** f. ANAT. cornea: ~ opaca, sclera.
**cornear** tr. to horn [gore with the horns].
**corneja** f. ORN. jackdaw, daw. 2 ORN. scops owl.
**cornejo** m. BOT. cornel, dogwood, red dogwood.
**Cornelio** m. pr. n. Cornelius.
**córneo, -a** adj. horny, corneous.
**corneta** f. MUS. bugle: ~ de llaves, cornet. 2 swineherd's horn. 3 NAUT. broad pennant. 4 bugler. 5 cornetist.
**cornete** m. ANAT. turbinated bone.
**cornetilla** f. BOT. hot pepper.
**cornetín** m. MUS. cornet. 2 cornetist.
**cornezuelo** m. dim. small horn. 2 BOT., FARM. ergot.
**corniabierto, -ta** adj. with widespread horns.
**corniapretado, -da** adj. with close-set horns.
**cornicabra** f. BOT. terebinth tree. 2 BOT. wild fig tree.
**corniforme** adj. horn-shaped.
**cornijal** m. corner [of building, mattress, etc.]. 2 ECCL. altar napkin.
**cornisa** f. ARCH. cornice.
**cornisamento, cornisamiento** m. ARCH. entablature.
**corniveleto, -ta** adj. with high, straight horns.
**Cornualles** f. pr. n. GEOG. Cornwall.
**cornucopia** f. cornucopia. 2 sconce with mirror.
**cornudo, -da** adj. horned, antlered. 2 cuckolded. 3 m. cuckold [man].
**cornúpeta** m. coll. bull.
**coro** m. choir. 2 chorus: a ~, in chorus; hacer ~ a, to chorus, echo. 3 choir loft. 4 de ~, by heart.
**corografía** f. chorography.
**coroides** adj.-f. ANAT. choroid.
**corola** f. BOT. corolla.
**corolario** m. corollary.
**corona** f. crown; wreath. 2 crown [regal power; monarchy; reward, glory]. 3 coronet [of nobility; of horse's pastern]. 4 halo, nimbus. 5 clerical tonsure. 6 crown [of a tooth]. 7 crown [coin]. 8 ASTR., METEOR. corona. 9 FORT. crownwork. 10 crown, summit. 11 crowning, end.
**coronamento, coronamiento** m. coronation. 2 crowning, completion. 3 ARCH. crown, crest. 4 NAUT. taffrail.
**coronar** tr. to crown [in every sense].
**coronario, -ria** adj. coronary. 2 fine [gold].
**corondel** m. PRINT. column rule.
**coronel** m. MIL. colonel. 2 HER. coronet. 3 ARCH. top moulding.
**coronela** f. colonel's wife.
**coronilla** f. dim. little crown. 2 crown [of the head]: estar hasta la ~, coll. to be fed up.
**corosol** m. BOT. kind of soursop.
**coroza** f. conical pasteboard hat worn as a mark of infamy.
**corpachón, corpanchón** m. big body, big carcass.
**corpazo** m. big body.
**corpiño** m. sleeveless bodice, waist.
**corporación** f. corporation, official corporation or institution. 2 guild.
**corporal** adj. corporal, bodily. 2 m. ECCL. corporal.
**corporativamente** adv. as a body.
**corporativo, -va** adj. corporative.
**corporeidad** f. corporeity.

**corpóreo, -a** *adj.* corporeal.
**corpulencia** *f.* corpulence.
**corpulento, -ta** *adj.* corpulent, bulky.
**Corpus** *m.* Corpus Christi [festival].
**corpuscular** *adj.* corpuscular.
**corpúsculo** *m.* corpuscle.
**corral** *m.* yard, farm yard, poultry yard, barnyard. 2 corral, enclosure, fold. 3 weir [to take fish]. 4 formerly, a playhouse.
**corraliza** *f.* yard, farm yard, poultry yard.
**correa** *f.* leather strap, thong, leash. 2 MACH. belt, belting. 3 flexibility [of a pliant thing]. 4 CARP. purlin. 5 *tener ~*, to bear raillery; to have endurance for work.
**correaje** *m.* straps, leather straps, belting.
**correazo** *m.* blow, lash or stroke with a belt.
**correcalles** *m. pl.* coll. loafer, lazybones, loiterer.
**corrección** *f.* correction. 2 correctness. 3 correctitude, honesty. 4 adjustement [of an instrument].
**correccional** *adj.* correctional. 2 *m.* correctional, prison.
**correctivo, -va** *adj.* corrective, correcting. 2 *m.* corrective. 3 punishment.
**correcto, -ta** *adj.* correct. 2 properly behaved.
**corrector, -ra** *adj.* correcting, corrective. 2 *m.* corrector. 3 PRINT. proofreader. 4 *f.* correctress.
**corredera** *f.* runner, groove, rail, track [on which something slides]: 2 sliding panel. 3 NAUT. log [chip and line]; log line. 4 slide valve [of steam engine]. 5 ENT. cockroach.
**corredizo, -za** *adj.* running, sliding, slip [easy to be untied]: *nudo ~*, slipknot.
**corredor, -ra** *adj.* fast running. 2 *adj.-f.* ORN. ratite. 3 *m.* SPORT runner. 4 COM. broker, commercial agent, canvasser. 5 corridor, passage, gallery. 6 FORT. covert way.
**corredura** *f.* overflow [in measuring].
**correduría** *f.* profession of the broker or commercial agent. 2 brokerage.
**corregente** *m.* co-regent.
**corregible** *adj.* corrigible.
**corregidor, -ra** *adj.* correcting. 2 corregidor [Spanish magistrate]. 2 wife of a corregidor.
**corregir** *tr.* to correct. 2 to adjust [an instrument]. 3 to temper, mitigate. 4 PRINT. *~ pruebas*, to read proofs. 5 *ref.* to mend; to cure oneself. ¶ CONJUG. like *servir*.
**correinante** *adj.* jointly reigning.
**correlación** *f.* correlation.
**correlacionar** *tr.* to correlate.
**correlativo, -va** *adj.* correlative.
**correligionario, -ria** *m.-f.* one of the same religion or political opinions.
**correntío, -tía** *adj.* [of liquids] running. 2 easy, agile.
**correntón, -na** *adj.* gadabout. 2 jolly, full of fun.
**correntoso, -sa** *adj.* (Am.) rapid, having a strong current, swift [river].
**correo** *m.* courier. 2 post, post office, mail, mail service: *~ aéreo*, airmail; *~ urgente*, special delivery; *echar al ~*, to post, to mail [a letter]. 3 correspondence, mail [letters].
**correón** *m.* large leather strap.
**correoso, -sa** *adj.* leathery, tough [food]. 2 pliant, stringy.
**correr** *intr.* to run [move swiftly, go fast; contend in race; slide, roll; extend]: *a todo ~*, at full speed. 2 [of wind] to blow, move. 3 to ramble, roam, rove. 4 [of rumours, news, etc.] to spread, run. 5 to be accepted, circulate. 6 [of time] to

pass. 7 [of interest, rent, etc.] to run. 8 to hasten, hurry. 9 *corría el mes de mayo*, it was the month of May. 10 *~ una cosa por cuenta de*, to be the concern of; *~ uno con una cosa*, to take charge of something. 11 *tr.* to run [a distance]. 12 to go about, to travel, to wander or rove over: *~ los mares*, to rove over the seas. 13 to run [a horse]. 14 to chase, hunt, run. 15 to fight [a bull]. 16 to run [a chance, a risk]; to have, seek [adventures]. 17 to slide, to move to a side; to turn [a key]; to draw [a bolt, a curtain]. 18 to abash, confound. 19 to publish [the banns]. 20 *~ prisa*, to be pressing, urgent. 21 *~ un artículo*, COM. to take orders for a merchandise, acting as a commercial agent. 22 *correrla*, to go on a spree. 23 *ref.* to move to the right or left, to shift. 24 to slide, to slip. 25 [of candles] to gutter. 26 [of ink, colours] to run. 27 to go too far [in talking, offering, etc.].
**correría** *f.* wandering, excursion. 2 raid, foray.
**correspondencia** *f.* correspondence [of a thing to another]. 2 correspondence [intercourse by letters; letters]. 3 return, reciprocation. 4 connection [of subway, etc.].
**corresponder** *intr.* to correspond, to answer [to or with]. 2 to pertain, belong, fall [to], devolve [upon]. 3 to fall to one's lot. 4 to return, reciprocate, repay. 5 *ref.* [of things] to correspond with each other. 6 to correspond [by letters]. 7 to love each other.
**correspondiente** *adj.* corresponding. 2 respective. 3 *m.* correspondent [by letters]. 4 correspondent [corresponding member].
**corresponsal** *m.* newspaper's correspondent. 2 COM. correspondent.
**corresponsalía** *f.* correspondent's post [in a newspaper]. 2 correspondent's office.
**corretaje** *m.* brokerage.
**corretear** *tr.* to walk around, to ramble, wander, romp.
**correteo** *m.* walking around, ramble, wandering, romp.
**correvedile, correveidile** *m.-f.* gossip monger. 2 go-between.
**corrida** *f.* run [spell of running]. 2 coll. reprehension. 3 *~ de toros*, bullfight. 4 *de ~*, fast, easily, fluently.
**corrido, -da** *adj.* long, exceeding a specified weight or measure. 2 abashed, confused. 3 wordlywise. 4 dissipate [man]. 5 continuous, unbroken [balcony, eaves, etc.]. 6 flowing [handwriting]. 7 *de ~*, DE CORRIDA.
**corriente** *adj.* flowing, running: *agua ~*, running water. 2 current. 3 ordinary, average, common, usual: *~ y moliente*, plain, usual. 4 correct, afable. 5 *adv.* all right, O.K. 6 *f.* current, stream: *~ de aire*, air draft; *~ del Golfo*, Gulf stream; *seguir la ~*, to swim with the current. 7 ELECT. current. 8 *m.* current month. 9 *al ~*, up to date; informed.
**corrientemente** *adv.* currently, usually.
**corrijo, corrija**, etc. *irr.* V. CORREGIR.
**corrillo** *m.* group of talkers, clique.
**corrimiento** *m.* running [of colour or ink]. 2 guttering [of a candle]. 3 shame, confusion. 4 vine blight. 5 *~ de tierras*, landslide.
**corro** *m.* circle, ring of people [talkers, spectators, etc.]: *hacer ~*, to make place. 2 ring-around-a-rosy. 3 ring, circular space.
**corroboración** *f.* corroboration. 2 strengthening.

**corroborante** *adj.* corroborative. *2 adj.-m.* corroborant.

**corroborar** *tr.* to corroborate. *2* to strengthen.

**corroborativo, -va** *adj.* corroborative, corroborating.

**corroer** *tr.* to corrode. *2 ref.* to become corroded.

**corrompedor, -ra** *adj.* corrupting. *2 m.-f.* corrupter.

**corromper** *tr.* to corrupt. *2* to bribe. *3* to seduce, debauch. *4* to mar, spoil, vitiate. *5* to annoy. *6 intr.* to smell bad. *7 ref.* to corrupt [become corrupted]; to rot. ¶ P. P.: *corrompido* and *corrupto.*

**corrompido, -da** *adj.* corrupted. *2* depraved.

**corrosal** *m.* BOT. soursop.

**corrosión** *f.* corrosion.

**corrosivo, -va** *adj.-m.* corrosive.

**corrupción** *f.* corruption; corruptness. *2* vitiation, depravation. *3* pollution, filth. *4* stench.

**corruptela** *f.* corruption. *2* abuse, corrupt practice.

**corruptibilidad** *f.* corruptibility.

**corrupto, -ta** *adj.* corrupt, corrupted.

**corruptor, -ra** *adj.* corrupting. *2 m.-f.* corrupter.

**corrusco** *m.* coll. crust of bread.

**corsario** *m.* corsair, privateer; pirate.

**corsé** *m.* corset, stays.

**corsetería** *f.* corset shop.

**corsetero, -ra** *m.-f.* corset maker or seller.

1) **corso** *m.* privateering: *armar en* ~, NAUT. to arm as a privateer.

2) **corso, -sa** *adj.-n.* Corsican.

**corta** *f.* cutting, felling [of trees].

**cortaalambres** *m.* wire cutter.

**cortabolsas** *m.-f.* pickpocket, cutpurse.

**cortacallos** *m.* corn cutter, corn parer.

**cortacésped** *m.* lawnmower.

**cortacircuitos** *m.* ELECT. circuit breaker.

**cortada** *f.* (Am.) cut: ~ *de pelo*, haircut.

**cortadillo** *m.* small tumbler [drinking glass].

**cortado, -da** *adj.* cut. *2* chapped [skin]. *3* adapted, proportioned. *4* broken, in short sentences [style]. *5* abashed, confused. *6* HER. parted.

**cortador, -ra** *adj.* cutting. *2 m.* butcher. *3* cutter [esp. one who cuts out garments, etc.]. *4 f.* cutting or slicing machine.

**cortadura** *f.* cut, incision, slit, slash. *2* cut between two mountains. *3 pl.* cuttings, trimmings.

**cortafrío** *m.* cold chisel.

**cortafuego** *m.* FORESTRY fireguard. *2* ARCH. fire wall.

**cortalápices** *m.* pencil sharpener.

**cortamente** *adv.* scantily, sparingly.

**cortante** *adj.* cutting, sharp. *2* biting [air, cold]. *3 m.* butcher.

**cortapapeles** *m.* paper knife, paper cutter. *2* letter opener.

**cortapicos** *m.* ENT. earwig.

**cortapisa** *f.* condition, restriction, interference.

**cortaplumas** *m.* penknife, pocketknife.

**cortapuros** *m.* cigar cutter.

**cortar** *tr.* to cut, to slash; to cut away, off, out or up [make an incision in; divide, sever; remove or shape by cutting]. *2* to cut [carve, chop, cleave]. *3* to trim, pare, clip. *4* to hew, hack. *5* to cut, fell [trees]. *6* to cut, cross, intersect. *7* to cut [a deck of cards]. *8* to cut off, intercept: ~ *la retirada*, to cut the retreat. *9* to interrupt, cut short. *10* to stop, bar [the passage]; to stop the progress [of something]. *11* to cut off [the steam, the gas, etc.]. *12* to chap [the skin]. *13* to settle, decide. *14 tr.-intr.* [of air or cold] to cut,

pierce. *15 ref.* to stop short in confusion. *16* [of milk] to curdle. *17* [of the skin] to chap. *18* [of leather or cloth] to crack, to slit. *19* GEOM. to intersect each other.

**cortaúñas** *m.* nail clipper.

**cortavidrio** *m.* glass cutter.

**cortaviento** *m.* windshield, windbreak.

1) **corte** *m.* cutting edge. *2* cut, cutting. *3* art of cutting clothes. *4* length [of material for a garment]. *5* felling [of trees]. *6* compromise [to settle differences]. *7* ARCH. section, sectional view. *8* ELECT. break [of current]. *9* edge [of a book].

2) **corte** *f.* court [of sovereign]. *2 fig.* suite, retinue. *3* city where the sovereign resides. *4* barnyard; stable; sheepfold. *5* (Am.) court [of justice]. *6* court [paid to someone]; courtship, wooing: *hacer la* ~ *a*, to court, pay court to. *7 pl.* Parliament. *8 Cortes Constituyentes*, Constituent Assembly.

**cortedad** *f.* shortness, scantiness, insufficiency. *2* bashfulness, timidity, diffidence.

**cortejador, -ra; cortejante** *adj.* courting; wooing. *2 m.-f.* courter; wooer.

**cortejar** *tr.* to court, woo.

**cortejo** *m.* court, paying court, hommage. *2* courtship, wooing. *3* sweetheart. *4* paramour. *5* train, procession: ~ *fúnebre*, funeral procession.

**cortés** *adj.* courteous, civil, polite, gracious.

**cortesana** *f.* courtesan.

**cortesanía** *f.* courtesy, politeness, civility.

**cortesano, -na** *adj.* of the court, courtlike. *2* courteous, polite. *3 m.* courtier.

**cortesía** *f.* courtesy, courteousness, politeness. *2* compliment, attention, present, favor. *3* COM. days of grace. *4* curtsey, curtsy.

**corteza** *f.* bark, rind [of tree]; crust [of bread, a pie, etc.]; rind [of cheese, melon, etc.]; rind, peel [of orange, lemon, etc.]: ~ *terrestre*, crust of the earth. *2* crust, exterior surface. *3* rusticity [in a person].

**cortical** *adj.* cortical.

**cortijada** *f.* group of farm houses.

**cortijero, -ra** *m.-f.* caretaker of a CORTIJO.

**cortijo** *m.* farm, grange.

**cortina** *f.* curtain, shade, screen: ~ *de humo*, smoke screen. *3* FORT. curtain. *4* ~ *de muelle*, wharf, jetty.

**cortinaje** *m.* set or pair of curtains.

**cortinilla** *f.* little curtain; window shade or blind; carriage curtain.

**cortinón** *m.* large heavy curtain.

**cortisona** *f.* BIOL. cortisone.

**corto, -ta** *adj.* short [not long or not sufficiently long; brief]. *2* scant, scanty, wanting. *3* bashful, timid. *4* dull, short-witted. *5* ELECT. ~ *circuito*, short circuit. *6* ~ *de alcances*, short-witted; ~ *de genio*, timid, spiritless; ~ *de vista*, short-sighted. *7 de corta edad*, tender in years. *8 quedarse* ~, to underrate, to ask too little. *9 a la corta o a la larga*, sooner or later.

**cortón** *m.* ENT. mole cricket.

**Coruña (La)** *f. pr. n.* Corunna.

**coruñés, -sa** *adj.-n.* of Corunna.

**coruscante** *adj.* coruscant, shining.

**coruscar** *intr.* to coruscate, shine.

**corva** *f.* back of the knee.

**corvadura** *f.* bend, curvature.

**corvejón** *m.* VET. hock, gambrel. *2* ORN. cormorant.

**corveta** *f.* curvet.

**corvetear** *intr.* to curvet.

**córvido, -da** *adj.* ZOOL. corvine.
**corvina** *f.* ICHTH. a food fish in the Mediterranean.
**corvo, -va** *adj.* arched, curved. *2 m.* hook, gaff.
**corzo, -za** *m.-f.* ZOOL. roe deer.
**cosa** *f.* thing, matter: ~ *de*, about, a matter of; ~ *de ver*, something worth seeing; ~ *de risa*, laughing matter; ~ *rara*, strange thing; strange to say; *alguna* ~, something; *poquita* ~, weak, little person; *como el que no quiere la* ~, feigning unconcern, casually; *como si tal* ~, as if nothing had happened; *no hay tal* ~, this is not so; *no sea* ~ *que*, lest; *no ser* ~ *del otro jueves*, or *del otro mundo*, to be nothing out of the common, or out of the world; *ser* ~ *hecha*, to be as good as done. *2* affair: *esto es* ~ *tuya*, that is your affair. *3 pl.* peculiarities, oddities [of a person]. *4* coll. regards.
**cosaco, -ca** *adj.-n.* Cossack.
**cosario** *m.* carrier, messenger.
**coscoja** *f.* BOT. kermes, kermes oak. *2* dry leaves of the evergreen oak.
**coscojal, coscojar** *m.* plantation of kermes oaks.
**coscojo** *m.* kermes gall.
**coscorrón** *m.* bump, blow on the head.
**cosecante** *f.* TRIG. cosecant.
**cosecha** *f.* harvest, crop, yield. *2* harvest, harvesting, reaping: *de su propia* ~, fig. of one's own invention. *3* vintage. *4* harvest, harvest time.
**cosechadora** *f.* AGR. reaping machine, combine.
**cosechar** *tr.* to harvest, crop, reap, gather. *2 intr.* to harvest [gather the crop].
**cosechero, -ra** *m.* grower, crop grower.
**cosedora** *f.* sewing machine. *2* stitching machine.
**coselete** *m.* corselet [piece of armour]. *2* pikeman. *3* ENT. corselet, thorax [of insect].
**coseno** *m.* TRIG. cosine: ~ *verso*, coversed sine.
**coser** *tr.* to sew; to stitch: *esto es* ~ *y cantar*, this is very easy, it's a child's play. *2* to join, unite. *3* to stab repeatedly. *4 ref. coserse con* or *contra*, to stick close to.
**cosido, -da** *adj.* sewed, sewn. *2* sticking close [to]. *3 m.* sewing.
**cosilla, cosita** *f.* small thing, trifle.
**cosmético, -ca** *adj.-m.* cosmetic.
**cósmico, -ca** *adj.* cosmic(al.
**cosmogonía** *f.* cosmogony.
**cosmografía** *f.* cosmography.
**cosmógrafo** *m.* cosmographer.
**cosmología** *f.* cosmology.
**cosmonauta** *n.* cosmonaut, astronaut.
**cosmonave** *f.* spaceship.
**cosmopolita** *adj.-n.* cosmopolitan, cosmopolite.
**cosmopolitismo** *m.* cosmopolitanism, cosmopolitism.
**cosmorama** *m.* cosmorama.
**cosmos** *m.* cosmos [universe].
**coso** *m.* enclosure for bullfights or other public spectacles. *2* main street.
**cospel** *m.* blank [coin-disk before stamping].
**cosque** *m.* coll. COSCORRÓN.
**cosquillar** *tr.* COSQUILLEAR.
**cosquillas** *f.* tickling, ticklishness: *buscarle a uno las* ~, fig. to try to irritate someone; *hacer* ~, to tickle.
**cosquillear** *tr.* to tickle.
**cosquilleo** *m.* tickling, tickling sensation.
**cosquilloso, -sa** *adj.* ticklish [sensitive to tickling]. *2* touchy, easily offended.
1) **costa** *f.* cost, price, expense: *a* ~ *de*, at the expense of; by dint of; *a mi* ~, at my expense; *a toda* ~, at any cost, at any price. *2 pl.* LAW costs.

2) **costa** *f.* coast, shore. *2* GEOG. *Costa Azul*, Côte d'Azur; *Costa de Marfil*, Ivory Coast; *Costa de Oro*, Gold Coast.
**costado** *m.* side [of the human body, of a ship, of a thing]. *2* MIL. flank. *3 pl.* lines of descent, ascendance.
**costal** *adj.* ANAT. costal. *2 m.* large sack [for grain, flour, etc.].
**costalada** *f.*, **costalazo** *m.* blow one gets when falling on the back or the side.
**costanera** *f.* slope, steep ground. *2 pl.* CARP. rafters.
**costanero, -ra** *adj.* steep, sloping. *2* coastal, coasting; of the coast.
**costanilla** *f.* gentle slope. *2* short steep street.
**costar** *intr.* to cost [be had at a price; involve expenditure of, penalty, etc.]: *costarle a uno caro*, or *cara, una cosa*, to pay dearly for a thing; *cueste lo que cueste*, at any price; *cuesta trabajo creerlo*, it is hard to believe it. ¶ CONJUG. like *contar.*
**Costa Rica** *f. pr. n.* GEOG. Costa Rica.
**costarricense** *adj.-n.* Costa Rican.
**coste** *m.* cost, price.
**costear** *intr.* NAUT. to coast, to sail along the coast. *2 tr.* to defray the cost of. *3 ref.* to pay one's own [studies, travel, etc.]. *4* to pay for itself.
**costeño, -ña** *adj.* COSTANERO.
**costero, -ra** *adj.* coastal, coasting. *2 m.* slab [taken from a log]. *3* side wall [of blast furnace].
**costilla** *f.* ANAT., ZOOL., NAUT. rib. *2* rib [of a leaf, a fruit, etc.]; rib-like thing. *3* coll. wife, better half. *4 pl.* shoulders, back.
**costillaje, costillar** *m.* ANAT. ribs. *2* ribs, ribbing, framework.
**costilludo, -da** *adj.* coll. broad-shouldered.
**costo** *m.* cost, price, expense. *2* BOT. costusroot.
**costoso, -sa** *adj.* costly, expensive, dear. *2* hard, difficult to obtain.
**costra** *f.* crust [hard dry formation, incrustation]; scab, scale [on cut, wound, etc.].
**costroso, -sa** *adj.* crusty, scabby.
**costumbre** *f.* custom [usual practice]; habit: *de* ~, usual, customary; usually. *2 pl.* customs, ways, habits.
**costumbrista** *m.-f.* genre writer.
**costura** *f.* sewing, needlework: *hacer* ~, to do sewing. *2* seam [formed by sewing]: *sentar las costuras*, to press the seams; to take [someone] to task; *sin* ~, seamless. *3* NAUT. seam. *4* MACH. seam, joint.
**costurera** *f.* seamstress.
**costurero** *m.* sewing case or table. *2* sewing room.
**costurón** *m.* large or coarse seam. *2* large scar.
**cota** *f.* coat [of arms or mail]. *2* quota. *3* TOPOGR. figure indicating height above datum line.
**cotangente** *f.* TRIG. cotangent.
**cotarrera** *f.* gossipy woman.
**cotarro** *m.* formerly, night lodging for beggars: *alborotar el* ~, fig. to raise a rumpus.
**cotejable** *adj.* comparable.
**cotejar** *tr.* to collate, compare.
**cotejo** *m.* collation, comparison.
**coterráneo, -a** *adj.-n.* CONTERRÁNEO.
**cotí** *m.* CUTÍ.
**cotidiano, -na** *adj.* daily, everyday, quotidian.
**cotiledón** *m.* BOT. cotyledon.
**cotillear** *tr.* to gossip.
**cotilleo** *m.* gossiping.
**cotillero, -ra** *m.-f.* gossiper.
**cotillo** *m.* face [of hammer].
**cotillón** *m.* cotillion.

**cotizable** *adj.* COM. quotable.
**cotización** *f.* COM. quotation, current price, price list. *2* act of paying or collecting subscription fees to a trade union, etc.
**cotizar** *tr.* COM. to quote; to value at a price. *2* to pay or collect subscription fees to a trade union, etc.
**coto** *m.* reserved ground, preserve. *2* boundary mark. *3* limit, boundary. *4* stop, restriction: *poner ~ a*, to stop, check, put a limit to. *5* set of billiard games. *6* ICHTH. chub.
**cotorra** *f.* ORN. parrot, small parrot. *2 fig.* chatterbox, magpie.
**cotorrear** *intr.* to chatter, to gossip.
**cotorreo** *m.* gossiping, chattering [of women].
**cotorrón, -na** *adj.* affecting youth [old person].
**cotudo, -da** *adj.* cottony, hairy. *2* (Am.) goitrous.
**cotufa** *f.* Jerusalem artichoke [tuber]. *2* tidbit, delicacy.
**coturno** *m.* cothurnus, buskin: *de alto ~*, of high standing.
**cotutela** *f.* LAW joint guardianship.
**covacha** *f.* small cave.
**covachuela** *f. dim.* small cave. *2 coll.* public office.
**covachuelista** *m. coll.* public servant, clerk.
**coxal** *adj.* ANAT. coxal.
**coxcojilla, -jita** *f.* hopscotch [child's game]: *a coxcojita*, jumping on one foot.
**coxis** *m.* CÓCCIX.
**coy** *m.* NAUT. sailor's cot or hammock.
**coyote** *m.* ZOOL. coyote, prairie wolf.
**coyunda** *f.* strap for yoking oxen. *2* yoke, dominion, tyranny. *3* matrimonial union.
**coyuntura** *f.* ANAT. joint, articulation. *2* conjuncture, juncture, occasion, opportunity.
**coz** *f.* kick [from a beast], backward kick [of a person]: *dar coces contra el aguijón*, to kick against the pricks. *2* churlish act or word. *3* kick, kickback, recoil [of a firearm]. *4* butt [of a musket, pistol, etc.].
**crac** *m.* crash, failure, bankruptcy.
**cran** *m.* PRINT. nick [of a type].
**craneal; craneano, -na** *adj.* cranial.
**cráneo** *m.* ANAT. cranium, skull.
**craniano** *adj.* CRANEAL.
**crápula** *f.* crapulence, debauchery.
**crapuloso, -sa** *adj.* crapulous; debauched.
**crascitar** *intr.* [of a raven] to croak.
**crasitud** *f.* fat, greasiness.
**Craso** *m. pr. n.* Crassus.
**craso, -sa** *adj.* thick, fat, greasy. *2* crass, gross [ignorance, error, etc.].
**crasuláceo, -a** *adj.* BOT. crasulaceous.
**cráter** *m.* GEOL., MIL. crater. *2* ASTR. Crater, Cup.
**crátera** *f.* ARCHEOL. crater [vessel].
**creación** *f.* creation. *2 La Creación*, the Creation.
**creador, -ra** *adj.* creating. *2 m.-f.* creator. *3 El Creador*, the Creator.
**crear** *tr.* to create. *2* to make: *crearse una posición*, to make a position for oneself. *3* to institute, establish. *4* to invent, design.
**creativo, -va** *adj.* creative.
**crecedero, -ra** *adj.* able to grow. *2* [of a child's garment] large enough to allow for growth.
**crecer** *intr.* [of natural beings] to grow. *2* to grow, increase. *3* [of a stream] to rise, to swell. *4 ref.* to take courage; to grow daring. ¶ CONJUG. like *agradecer*.
**creces** *f. pl. con ~*, amply, with interest.
**crecida** *f.* freshet, flood, swelling [of a river].
**crecido, -da** *adj.* grown. *2* swollen [stream]. *3*

large, big, numerous. *4 m. pl.* widening stitches [in knitting].
**creciente** *adj.* growing, increasing. *2* ASTR. *cuarto ~*, first quarter [of moon]. *3 m.* HER. crescent. *4 f.* CRECIDA. *5 ~ de la Luna*, crescent. *6 ~ del mar*, flood.
**crecimiento** *m.* growth, growing.
**credencia** *f.* ECCL. credence.
**credencial** *adj.-f.* credential. *2 f. pl.* credential, credential letters.
**credibilidad** *f.* credibility.
**crediticio, -cia** *adj.* credit.
**crédito** *m.* credit, credence: *dar ~ a*, to believe. *2* credit, good reputation. *3* COM. credit: *a ~*, on credit. *4* bank-credit.
**credo** *m.* creed, credo: *en un ~*, fig. in a trice. *2* creed [set of opinions or beliefs].
**credulidad** *f.* credulity.
**crédulo, -la** *adj.* credulous.
**creedero, -ra** *adj.* believable, credible.
**creencia** *f.* belief, creed, tenet. *2* credence, credit.
**creer** *tr.-intr.-ref.* to believe: *~ en*, to believe in; *no me lo creo*, I don't believe it: *¡ya lo creo!*, coll. I should say so. *2 tr.* to think [think probable]. *3 ref.* to believe or think oneself.
**creíble** *adj.* credible, believable.
**creído, -da** *adj.* confident. *2* credulous. *3* vain, conceited.
**crema** *f.* cream [of milk]. *2 fig.* cream [of society]. *3* custard. *4* cream [cosmetic]. *5* GRAM. diaeresis.
**cremación** *f.* cremation, incineration.
**cremallera** *f.* MACH. ratch, ratchet. *2* rack, rack rail: *ferrocarril de ~*, rack railway. *3* zipper.
**crematístico, -ca** *adj.* chrematistic. *2 f.* chrematistics.
**crematorio, -ria** *adj.* crematory, incinerating.
**cremoso, -sa** *adj.* creamy.
**crémor** *m.* cream [of tartar].
**crencha** *f.* parting of the hair [line]. *2* hair at each side of the parting.
**creosota** *f.* CHEM. creosote.
**crepitación** *f.* crepitation, crackling. *2* MED. crepitation.
**crepitar** *intr.* to crepitate.
**crepuscular** *adj.* crepuscular.
**crepúsculo** *m.* crepuscle, twilight; dawn; dusk.
**cresa** *f.* eggs of the queen bee. *2* flyblow.
**crescendo** *adv.-m.* MUS. crescendo.
**Creso** *pr. n. & fig.* Croesus.
**crespo, -pa** *adj.* crispy, curly [hair]. *2* BOT. crisp, crisped [leaves]. *3* angry, irritated.
**crespón** *m.* crape. *2 ~ de China*, crêpe de Chine.
**cresta** *f.* crest, comb [of a bird], cock's comb. *2* ZOOL. crest. *3* crest [of helmet, of mountain, of wave]. *4* FORT. crest [of the glacis]. *5* BOT. *~ de gallo*, wild sage; cockscomb.
**crestería** *f.* ARCH. cresting. *2* FORT. battlement.
**crestón** *m.* large crest. *2* crest [of helmet]. *3* MIN. outcrop.
**Creta** *f. pr. n.* Crete.
**creta** *f.* chalk.
**cretáceo, -a** *adj.* cretaceous. *2 adj.-m.* GEOL. Cretaceous.
**cretense** *adj.-n*, Cretan.
**cretinismo** *m.* cretinism.
**cretino, -na** *adj.* cretinic. *2 m.-f.* cretin.
**cretona** *f.* cretonne.
**creyente** *adj.* believing. *2 m.-f.* believer.
**crezco, crezca**, etc. *irr.* V. CRECER.
**cría** *f.* nursing, suckling, fostering, bringing up. *2* rearing, breeding: *~ caballar*, horse breeding. *3*

suckling [child or animal]. *4* brood, litter, young [animals].

**criada** *f.* female servant, maid, housemaid.

**criadero, -ra** *adj.* prolific. *2 m.* tree nursery. *3* breeding place [for animals]; fish hatchery. *4* MIN. seam, vein.

**criadilla** *f.* testicle: ~ *de carnero*, lamb's fry. *2* potato. *3* ~ *de tierra*, truffle.

**criado, -da** *adj.* bred: *bien* ~, well-bred; *mal* ~, illbred. *2 m.* manservant.

**criador, -ra** *adj.* nursing, nurturing. *2 adj.-m.* [of God] creator: *el Criador*, the Creator. *3* rearer, raiser, breeder. *4* ~ *de vinos*, viniculturist.

**crianza** *f.* nursing, lactation. *2* rearing, bringing up, education. *3* breeding, manners: *buena* ~, good breeding.

**criar** *tr.* to create [said only of God]. *2* to nurse, suckle. *3* to raise, rear, breed, grow. *4* to produce, put forth: ~ *carnes*, to put on flesh. *5* to bring up, to educate.

**criatura** *f.* creature [anything created; one owing his position to another]. *2* baby, infant, child.

**criba** *f.* cribble, screen, sieve.

**cribado** *m.* screening, sifting.

**cribar** *tr.* to screen, to sift.

**cric** *m.* jack, jackscrew, lifting jack.

**cricoides** *adj.-m.* ANAT. cricoid.

**cricquet** *m.* SPORT. cricket.

**crimen** *m.* serious crime, felony.

**criminal** *adj.-n.* criminal.

**criminalista** *m.* criminalist.

**criminar** *tr.* to criminate; to censure.

**criminología** *f.* criminology.

**crin** *f.* mane [of horse, lion, etc.]. *2* horsehair: ~ *vegetal*, vegetable horsehair.

**crinado, -da** *adj.* poet. long-haired.

**crinolina** *f.* crinoline.

**crío** *m.* baby, infant.

**criolita** *f.* MINER. cryolite.

**criollo, -lla** *adj.-n.* Creole.

**cripta** *f.* crypt.

**criptógamo, -ma** *adj.* BOT. cryptogamous. *2 f. pl.* BOT. Cryptogamia.

**criptografía** *f.* cryptography.

**criptograma** *m.* cryptogram, cryptograph.

**cris** *m.* kris [Malayan dagger].

**crisálida** *f.* ENT. chrysalis, pupa.

**crisantema** *f.,* **crisantemo** *m.* BOT. chrysanthemum.

**crisis** *f.* crisis: ~ *de la vivienda*, housing shortage. *2* COM. depression.

**crisma** *m.-f.* ECCL. chrism. *2 f.* coll. head: *romper la* ~ *a uno*, to break someone's head.

**crismera** *f.* chrismatory.

**crismón** *m.* chrismon.

**crisoberilo** *m.* MINER. chrysoberyl.

**crisol** *m.* crucible.

**crispadura** *f.,* **crispamiento** *m.* muscular contraction, twitch.

**crispar** *tr.* to cause contraction or twitching: ~ *los nervios*, coll. to set the nerves on edge. *2 ref.* to be contracted, to twitch.

**cristal** *m.* CHEM., MINER., RADIO. crystal: ~ *de roca*, rock crystal. *2* crystal [glass], flint glass; ~ *de aumento*, magnifying glass; ~ *tallado*, cut glass. *3* window pane, pane of glass. *4* poet. crystal [clear water].

**cristalera** *f.* sideboard. *2* glass door.

**cristalería** *f.* glassworks. *2* glass shop. *3* glassware. *3* glass service.

**cristalino, -na** *adj.* crystalline. *2 m.* ANAT. crystalline lens.

**cristalización** *f.* crystallization.

**cristalizar** *tr.* to crystallize. *2 intr.-ref.* to crystallize [become crystallized].

**cristalografía** *f.* crystallography.

**Cristián** *m. pr. n.* Christian [man's name].

**cristianar** *tr.* coll. to christen, baptize.

**cristiandad** *f.* Christendom, Christianity. *2* observance of Christ's law.

**cristianismo** *m.* Christianism, Christianity. *2* Christendom. *3* baptism.

**cristianizar** *tr.* to Christianize.

**cristiano, -na** *adj.-n.* Christian. *2 m.* soul, person. *3 hablar en* ~, to speak clearly.

**Cristina** *f. pr. n.* Christine.

**cristino** *m.* supporter of Queen Regent Maria Cristina against the Carlists.

**Cristo** *m. pr. n.* Christ. *2 m.* crucifix.

**Cristóbal** *m. pr. n.* Christopher.

**criterio** *m.* criterion. *2* judgement, discernment.

**crítica** *f.* criticism, critique. *2* criticism, faultfinding, censure. *3* the critics [as a body].

**criticable** *adj.* blameworthy.

**criticador, -ra** *adj.* criticizing, faultfinding. *2 m.-f.* criticizer, faultfinder.

**criticar** *tr.* to criticize. *2* to blame.

**criticastro** *m.* criticaster.

**crítico, -ca** *adj.* critical. *2 m.* critic.

**criticón, -na** *adj.* censorious, faultfinding. *2 m.-f.* faultfinder.

**crizneja** *f.* braid of hair. *2* rope or plait of esparto, etc.

**Croacia** *f. pr. n.* Croatia.

**croar** *intr.* [of frogs] to croak.

**croata** *adj.-n.* Croatian.

**crocante** *m.* almond brittle.

**crol** *m.* crawl [swimming].

**cromar** *tr.* to cromium plate.

**cromático, -ca** *adj.* MUS., OPT. chromatic. *2 f.* PHYS. chromatics.

**cromo** *m.* CHEM. chromium, chrome. *2* chromo, chromolithograph.

**cromolitografía** *f.* chromolithography.

**cromosfera** *f.* ASTR. chromosphere.

**cromosoma** *m.* BIOL. chromosome.

**crónica** *f.* chronicle. *2* news chronicle.

**crónico, -ca** *adj.* chronic.

**cronicón** *m.* brief chronicle.

**cronista** *m.* chronicler; reporter.

**crónlech** *m.* ARCHEOL. cromlech.

**cronógrafo** *m.* chronographer. *2* chronograph.

**cronología** *f.* chronology.

**cronológico, -ca** *adj.* chronologic(al.

**cronólogo** *m.* chronologist.

**cronometrador, -ra** *m.-f.* SPORT. timekeeper.

**cronometraje** *m.* SPORT. clocking, timing.

**cronometrar** *tr.* SPORT. to clock, time.

**cronometría** *f.* chronometry.

**cronómetro** *m.* chronometer.

**Cronos** *m. pr. n.* MYTH. Cronus.

**croquet** *m.* croquet [game].

**croqueta** *f.* croquette.

**croquis** *m.* sketch, rough drawing.

**crótalo** *m.* ZOOL. rattlesnake. *2* MUS. crotalum, castanet.

**cruce** *m.* cross, crossing. *2* intersection. *3* crossing [of roads, etc.]. *4* ELECT. cross.

**crucería** *f.* ARCH. intersecting ribs [in Gothic vaulting]; Gothic architecture.

**crucero** *m.* crucifer, cross-bearer. *2* crossroads. *3*

ARCH. crossing. *4* NAUT., AER. cruise, cruising. *5*
NAV. cruiser. *6* PRINT. crossbar of a chase. *7* MIN.
cleavage plane.
**cruceta** *f.* MACH. crosshead [of connecting rod]. *2*
NAUT. crosstree.
**crucial** *adj.* crucial.
**cruciata** *f.* BOT. kind of crosswort.
**cruciferario** *m.* crucifer, cross-bearer.
**crucífero, -ra** *adj.* cruciferous [bearing a cross]. *2*
BOT. cruciferous. *3 m.* crucifer, cross-bearer. *4 f.*
BOT. crucifer.
**crucificado, -da** *adj.* crucified.
**crucificar** *tr.* to crucify. *2* fig. to vex, torment.
**crucifijo** *m.* crucifix.
**crucifixión** *f.* crucifixion.
**cruciforme** *adj.* cruciform, cross-shaped.
**crucigrama** *m.* crossword puzzle.
**crudeza** *f.* crudity, rawness. *2* bluntness, rudeness,
roughness. *3* bitterness [of weather].
**crudo, -da** *adj.* raw, uncooked, underdone [food].
*2* unripe [fruit]. *3* hard [water]. *4* ecru, unblea-
ched [silk, linen]. *5* raw [leather]. *6* raw, bitter
[weather]. *7* harsh, rough. *8* crude, blunt.
**cruel** *adj.* cruel.
**crueldad** *f.* cruelty.
**cruentamente** *adv.* with effusion of blood.
**cruento, -ta** *adj.* bloody, involving bloodshed.
**crujía** *f.* corridor, passage [in some buildings]. *2*
hospital ward. *3* NAUT. midship gangway.
**crujido** *m.* creak, creaking, crackle, crackling. *2*
rustle [of silk]. *3* gnash, gnashing [of teeth]. *4*
flaw [in a sword blade].
**crujiente** *adj.* creaking, crackling. *2* rustling.
**crujir** *intr.* to creak, to crackle. *2* [of silk] to rustle.
*3* [of teeth] to gnash.
**crúor** *m.* POET. blood. *2* MED. cruor, blood clot.
**crup** *m.* MED. croup.
**crural** *adj.* ANAT. crural.
**crustáceo, -a** *adj.* ZOOL. crustaceous. *2 adj.-m.* crustacean.
**cruz** *f.* cross: ~ *de Malta*, Maltese cross; ~ *gamada*,
swastica; *Cruz Roja*, Red Cross; *hacerse cruces
de*, to be astonished at; *de la* ~ *a la fecha*, from
beginning to end; *en* ~, with the arms extended;
crosswise; ~ *y raya*, no more of this. *2* tails [of
coin]. *3* withers [of quadruped]. *4* PRINT. dagger.
*5* crown [of anchor]. *6* NAUT. middle [of yard]. *7*
ASTR. *Cruz del Sur*, Southern Cross.
**cruzada** *f.* crusade. *2* crossroads.
**cruzado, -da** *adj.* crossed. *2* engaged in a crusade.
*3* WEAV. twilled. *4* cross, crossbred. *5* double-
breasted [garment]. *6 m.* crusader.
**cruzamiento** *m.* crossing. *2* cross-breeding.
**cruzar** *tr.* to cross [place crosswise; cause to intersect; lie across, intersect; go across]: ~ *la cara a
uno*, to slap or slash someone in the face. *2* to
cross [breeds]. *3* WEAV. to twill. *4* NAUT. to cruise.
*5 ref.* to take the cross. *6* to cross, pass each
other. *7* *cruzarse de brazos*, to cross one's arms,
do nothing.
**cu** *m.* name of the letter *q.*
**cuaderna** *f.* NAUT. frame. *2 cuaderna via*, a Spanish
medieval stance.
**cuadernal** *m.* NAUT. block.
**cuadernillo** *m.* quinternion.
**cuaderno** *m.* notebook, exercise book, writing
book: ~ *de bitácora*, NAUT. log book.
**cuadra** *f.* stable [for horses]. *2* hall, ward, dormitory [in works, hospital, etc.]. *3* NAUT. quarter
[of ship]. *4* croup [of horse]. *5* (Am.) block [of
houses].

**cuadrada** *f.* MUS. breve.
**cuadradillo** *m.* square ruler. *2* sugar in cubes.
**cuadrado, -da** *adj.* square, quadrate. *2* square
[measure; root]. *3* square-shouldered. *4* perfect,
complete. *5 m.* GEOM., MATH. square. *6* square ruler. *7* clock [of stocking]; gusset [of shirt]. *8*
PRINT. quadrat.
**cuadragenario, -ria** *adj.-n.* quadragenarian.
**cuadragésima** *f.* CUARESMA.
**cuadragesimal** *adj.* quadragesimal.
**cuadragésimo, -ma** *adj.-m.* fortieth.
**cuadrangular** *adj.* quadrangular.
**cuadrante** *m.* ASTR., GEOM. quadrant. *2* sundial. *3*
quarter [of the compass]. *4* quadrans [Roman
coin].
**cuadrar** *tr.* to square [give a square shape]. *2* to
square [the shoulders]. *3* MATH., GEOM. to square.
*4* PAINT. to graticulate. *5 intr.* to fit, suit. *6* to
please. *7 ref.* MIL. to stand at attention. *8* to assume a firm attitude.
**cuadratura** *f.* ASTR., MATH., ELECT. quadrature.
**cuadrícula** *f.* quadrille ruling, graticule.
**cuadriculado, -da** *adj.* cross-section squared [pa-
per].
**cuadricular** *tr.* to graticulate, to rule in squares.
**cuadrienal** *adj.* quadrennial.
**cuadrienio** *m.* quadrennium.
**cuadriga** *f.* quadriga.
**cuadril** *m.* haunch bone. *2* haunch; hip.
**cuadrilátero, -ra** *adj.-m.* quadrilateral.
**cuadrilongo, -ga** *adj.* oblong, rectangular. *2 m.*
oblong, rectangle.
**cuadrilla** *f.* party, crew, gang, band, squad, troop.
*2* BULLF. quadrille.
**cuadrimotor** *adj.-m.* AER. four-motor [plane].
**cuadrigentésimo, -ma** *adj.-m.* four-hundredth.
**cuadrinomio** *m.* ALG. quadrinomial.
**cuadripartito, -ta** *adj.* quadripartite.
**cuadriplicado, -da** *adj.* quadrupled.
**cruadriplicar** *tr-intr.* to quadruple, to quadruplicate.
**cuadrisílabo, -ba** *adj.* quadrisyllabic. *2 m.* quadrisyllable.
**cuadrivalente** *adj.* CHEM. quadrivalent, tetrava-
lent.
**cuadrivio** *m.* quadrivium.
**cuadro** *adj.* square, square-shaped. *2 m.* square or
rectangle: *a cuadros*, checkered, chequered. *3*
picture, painting. *4* frame [of picture, door,
bicycle, etc.]. *5* LIT. picture, description. *6* THEAT.
tableau. *7* picture, scene, view, spectacle. *8*
THEAT. a division of the act. *9* [flower] bed. *10*
PRINT. platen. *11* MIL. square. *12* MIL. cadre, staff
[of a regiment]. *13* table, synopsis. *14* ELECT., TE-
LEPH. ~ *de distribución*, switchboard; ~ *indicador*, anunciator. *15 en* ~, square: *dos metros en
~*, two meters square. *16 quedarse en* ~, to be
left friendless; to be broke, ruined; MIL. [of a
body of troops] to be left with officers only.
**cuadrumano, -na; cuadrúmano, -na** *adj.* ZOOL.
quadrumanous. *2 m.* ZOOL. quadrumane.
**cuadrúpedo** *adj.-m.* quadruped.
**cuádruple** *adj.* quadruple, fourfold.
**cuádruplex** *adj.* TELEG. quadruplex.
**cuadruplicar** *tr.* to quadruple, quadruplicate.
**cuádruplo, -pla** *adj.-m.* CUÁDRUPLE.
**cuaga** *f.* ZOOL. quagga.
**cuajada** *f.* curd [of milk]. *2* cottage cheese.
**cuajaleche** *f.* BOT. yellow bedstraw, cheese rennet.
**cuajamiento** *m.* curdling, coagulation.
1) **cuajar** *tr.* to curd, curdle, coagulate. *2* to fill

[with adornments]. *3 intr.* [of a thing] to be successful. *4* to please, suit. *5 ref.* to curd, curdle, coagulate [be coagulated]. *6* to become crowded.

2) **cuajar** *m.* ZOOL. rennet bag, abomasum.

**cuajarón** *m.* clot, grume.

**cuajo** *m.* rennet [for curling milk]. *2* ZOOL. rennet bag. *3* curdling, coagulation. *4* phlegm, sluggishness, patience. *5 de ~,* by the roots.

**cual, cuales** *rel. pron.* who, which. *2* as, such as. *3 el, la ~, los, las cuales,* who, which; *lo ~,* which. *4 por lo ~,* for which reason. *5 adv.* as, like: *~ lo exigen las circunstancias,* as circumstances demand.

**cuál, cuáles** *interr. pron.* which, what. *2* [in distributive sense] some: *~ más, ~ menos,* some more, some less. *3 adv.* how [exclamative].

**cualidad** *f.* quality [distinctive character, trait, etc.].

**cualificado, -da** *adj.* skilled [worker].

**cualitativo, -va** *adj.* qualitative.

**cualquier,** *pl.* **cualesquier** *indef. adj.* apocopated form of CUALQUIERA used only before nouns.

**cualquiera,** *pl.* **cualesquiera** *pron.* anyone, anybody. *2 ~ que,* whatever, whichever, whoever; *~ que sea el resultado,* whatever the result may be; *~ que lo diga,* whoever says so. *3 ¡~ se acuerda!,* who's going to remember that! *4 un, una ~,* despicable person. *5 adj.* any; any whatever.

**cuan** *adv.* as: *el castigo será tan grande ~ grande fue la culpa,* the punishment will be as great as great was the sin.

**cuán** *adv.* how: *¡~ grande es mi dolor!,* how great is my pain!

**cuando** *adv.* when. *2* even when, even though. *3* since: *~ tú lo dices,* since you say it. *4* at the time of: *~ la peste,* at the time of the plague. *5 ~ más, ~ mucho,* at most; *~ menos,* at least; *~ no,* if not; *~ quiera,* whenever; *de ~ en ~,* now and then.

**cuándo** *adv. interr.* when. *2* sometimes, now: *~ con motivo, ~ sin él,* sometimes (or now) with a reason, sometimes [or now] without it.

**cuantía** *f.* amount, quantity. *2* distinction, importance.

**cuántico, -ca** *adj.* quantum, quantic.

**cuantificación** *f.* PHIL. quantification. *2* PHYS. quantization.

**cuantimás** *adv.* all the more.

**cuantioso, -sa** *adj.* large, substantial, numerous.

**cuantitativo, -va** *adj.* quantitative.

1) **cuanto** *adv.* as far as concerns or regards: *~ a eso, en ~ a eso,* as far as regards that. *2* as long as: *durará la alegría ~ dure el dinero,* joy will last as long as the money lasts. *3 ~ antes,* as soon as possible. *4 ~ más ..., menos* [or *más*], the more... the less [or the more]. *5 ~ más que,* all the more because. *6 en ~,* no sooner. *7 por ~,* since, seeing that. *8 m.* quantum.

2) **cuanto, ta; cuantos, tas** *adj.* all the, every, as much, as many. *2 pron.* all [that], everything, as much as. *3* as many as; all who. *4 adj.-pron. unos cuantos, unas cuantas,* some, a few.

1) **cuánto** *adv.* how: *¡~ me duele!,* how it pains me! *2 pron.* how much; how long.

2) **cuánto, -ta; cuántos, -tas** [with interr. or exclam.] *adj.* how many, how much, what.

**cuáquero, -ra** *adj.-n.* Quaker. *2 f.* Quakeress.

**cuarenta** *adj.-n.* forty. *2* fortieth.

**cuarentavo, -va** *adj.-m.* fortieth.

**cuarentena** *f.* forty, two score. *2* forty days, months or years. *3* Lent. *4* quarantine. *5* fig. *poner en ~,* to entertain doubts about.

**cuarentón, -na** *m.-f.* person forty years old.

**cuaresma** *f.* Lent.

**cuaresmal** *adj.* Lenten.

**cuarta** *f.* fourth part, quarter. *2* span [measure]. *3* quart [in piquet]. *4* NAUT. point [of the compass]. *5* MUS. fourth. *6* FENC. carte. *7* (Am.) short whip.

**cuartana** *f.* MED. quartan.

**cuartear** *tr.* to quarter, to divide in four parts. *2* to zigzag up steep places. *3* (Mex.) to whip, lash. *4* NAUT. *~ la aguja,* to box the compass. *5 intr.-ref.* BULLF. to dodge. *6 ref.* [of a wall, roof, etc.] to crack.

**cuartel** *m.* quarter, fourth part. *2* ward [of a town]. *3* plot, section [of land]. *4* HER. quarter. *5* MIL. barracks. *6* MIL. quarters: *~ general,* headquarters. *7* MIL. quarter [granted to enemy]. *8* NAUT. hatch [trap-door].

**cuartelada** *f.* military insurrection or coup d'état.

**cuartelar** *tr.* HER. to quarter.

**cuartelazo** *m.* putsch.

**cuartelero, -ra** *adj.* [pertaining to] barracks.

**cuartelillo** *m.* MIL. station: *~ de bomberos,* fire station, *\*firehouse.

**cuarteo** *m.* quartering. *2* zigzagging up steep places. *3* BULLF. dogding. *4* crack [in wall or roof].

**cuarterón, -na** *m.-f.* quadroon. *2 m.* fourth part, quarter. *3* quarter pound. *4* panel [of door]. *5* shutter [of window]. *6* HER. quarter.

**cuarteta** *f.* REDONDILLA. *2* stanza of four octosyllabic lines the second and last of which are in assonance.

**cuarteto** *m.* quatrain [poem]. *2* MUS. quartet, quartette.

**cuartilla** *f.* sheet of writing paper. *2* pastern [of horse].

**cuartillo** *m.* dry measure (1.156 l.). *2* liquid measure (0.504 l.). *3* fourth part of a REAL.

**cuarto, -ta** *adj.* fourth. *2 m.* quarter [fourth part]. *3* flat, rooms. *4* room, chamber: *~ de baño,* bathroom; *~ de estar,* living room; *~ excusado,* water-closet. *4* ASTR. quarter [of the moon]: *~ creciente,* first quarter; *~ menguante,* last quarter. *5* quarter [of an hour, of a quadruped; of a quartered criminal]. *6* old copper coin of little value: *de tres al ~,* of little importance; *echar su ~ a espadas,* to butt into the conversation; *no tener un ~,* to be penniless. *7 ~ militar,* military attendants to a sovereign or chief of State. *8 en ~,* quarto [volume]. *9 pl.* cash, money. *10 tener buenos cuartos,* to be strong, sturdy.

**cuartucho** *m.* hovel, miserable dwelling or room.

**cuarzo** *m.* MINER. quartz. *2 ~ hialino,* rock crystal.

**cuasi** *adv.* CASI.

**cuasia** *f.* BOT., PHARM. quassia.

**cuasicontrato** *m.* LAW quasi contract.

**cuasidelito** *m.* LAW quasi delict, technical offence.

**cuasimodo** *m.* ECCL. Quasimodo.

**cuaternario, -ria** *adj.* quaternary. *2 adj.-m.* GEOL. quaternary.

**cuatrero** *m.* horse thief, cattlethief.

**cuatrifolio** *m.* ARCH. quatrefoil.

**cuatrillizos, -zas** *n. pl.* quadruplets.

**cuatrillo** *m.* a card game.

**cuatrillón** *m.* quadrillion.

**cuatrimestral** *adj.* four-monthly, every four months. *2* lasting four months.

**cuatrimestre** *adj.* four-month. *2 m.* period of four months.

**cuatrimotor** *m.-adj.* four engined, four engined airplane.

**cuatrirreactor** *adj.* four-engined. *2 m.* four-engined jet.

**cuatrisílabo** *adj.* quadrisyllabic, four-syllable. *2 m.* quadrisyllable.

**cuatro** *adj.* four. *2* fig. a few: ~ *letras*, a few lines. *3 las* ~, four o'clock. *4 más de* ~, many, many people. *5 m.* four. *6* fourth [in dates].

**cuatrocientos, -tas** *adj.-m.* four hundred.

**cuba** *f.* cask, barrel: *estar hecho una* ~, fig. to be drunk. *2* tub, vat. *3* fig. big-bellied person, tubby. *4* stack [of blast furnace].

**cubano, -na** *adj.-n.* Cuban.

**cubeba** *f.* BOT. cubeb.

**cubero** *m.* cooper.

**cubeta** *f.* small cask. *2* pail, bucket. *3* toilet bowl. *4* cup, cistern [of barometer]. *5* MUS. pedestal [of harp]. *6* PHOT., CHEM. tank, cuvette.

**cubicación** *f.* cubing. *2* calculation of volumes.

**cubicar** *tr.* to cube.

**cúbico, -ca** *adj.* cubic(al.

**cubículo** *m.* cubicle.

**cubierta** *f.* cover, covering. *2* envelope, cover [of letter]. *3* cover [of a paper-bound book]. *4* roof, roofing [of a building]. *5* MACH. case, casing. *6* shoe [of a pneumatic tire]. *7* pretext. *8* NAUT. deck.

**cubierto, -ta** *p. p.* of CUBRIR. *2 m.-f.* cover, roof, shelter, protection: *a* ~, *bajo* ~, sheltered, indoors; *a* ~ *de*, protected from; under cover of. *3* set of fork, spoon and knife. *4* cover, plate [service of food for one at a meal]. *5* meal for one at a fixed price.

**cubil** *m.* lair, den [of wild animals].

**cubilete** *m.* goblet. *2* dicebox. *3* COOK. a thimble-shaped mould. *4* small round mince pie.

**cubileteo** *m.* jugglery. *2* scheming, intrigue.

**cubilote** *m.* METAL. cupola [furnace].

**cubismo** *m.* F. ARTS cubism.

**cubista** *adj.-n.* F. ARTS cubist.

**cubital** *adj.* cubital.

**cúbito** *m.* ANAT. ulna, cubit.

**cubo** *m.* bucket, pail, tub. *2* hub, nave [of wheel]. *3* socket [of bayonet or candlestick]. *4* water reservoir [for a mill]. *5* barrel [of watch]. *6* FORT. round tower. *7* GEOM., MATH. cube.

**cuboides** *adj.-m.* ANAT. cuboid.

**cubrecadena** *m.* chain cover [on bicycle].

**cubrecama** *m.* counterpane, coverlet, bedspread.

**cubrecorsé** *m.* corset cover, underbodice.

**cubreobjeto** *m.* cover glass, cover slip [for microscopic preparations].

**cubrir** *tr.* to cover, cover up; to wrap, envelop, clak, clothe, drape, shroud, veil; to coat, face, overlay, spread, spread over. *2* to hide, mask, disguise. *3* MIL. to cover, protect. *4* to roof [a building]. *5* to cover [expenses, a shortage, etc.]. *6* to cover [a distance]. *7* to cover, serve [a female]. *8 ref.* to cover [oneself]; to be or become covered. *9* to cover one's expenses. *10* to protect or guard oneself [against losses, etc.]. ¶ Past. p.: *cubierto*.

**cucamonas** *f. pl.* CARANTOÑAS.

**cucaña** *f.* greased pole to be walked on or climbed for a prize; the sport itself.

**cucaracha** *f.* ENT. cockroach, black beetle. *2* ZOOL. pill bug, wood louse.

**cucarda** *f.* cockade.

**cuclillas (en)** *adv.* in a squatting or crouching position, sitting on one's heels.

**cuclillo** *m.* ORN. cuckoo. *2* fig. cuckold.

**cuco, -ca** *adj.* nice, pretty, dainty. *2* crafty, cunning. *3 m.* ORN. cuckoo. *4 m.-f.* crafty, cunning person.

**cucú** *m.* cuckoo [call of the cuckoo].

~ **cucurbita** *f.* cucurbit, retort.

**cucurbitáceo, -a** *adj.* BOT. cucurbitaceous.

**cucurucho** *m.* paper cone, cornet.

**cuchara** *f.* spoon: ~ *de sopa*, table spoon; *meter uno su* ~, to meddle, to put in one's oar. *2* ladle. *3* NAUT. scoop [for bailing water]. *4* scoop, bucket [of dredging machine]; dipper [of excavator].

**cucharada** *f.* spoonful: *meter uno su* ~, to meddle, to put in one's oar.

**cucharadita** *f.* teaspoonful.

**cuchareta** *f.* little spoon. *2* ORN. (Am.) shoveller.

**cucharetear** *intr.* coll. to meddle in other people's affairs.

**cucharilla** *f.* small spoon, teaspoon.

**cucharón** *m.* large spoon; soup ladle, kitchen ladle. *2* MACH. bucket, grab bucket.

**cuchichear** *intr.* to whisper, speak in whispers [to another].

**cuchicheo** *m.* whispering, talking in whispers.

**cuchichiar** *intr.* [of a partridge] to call or cry.

**cuchilla** *f.* large knife. *2* cutting tool. *3* blade [of cutting tool or weapon]. *4* POET. sword. *5* runner [of skate, sledge, etc.]. *6* ELECT. blade [of switch].

**cuchillada** *f.* stab, slash, gash [from a knife, sword, etc.]. *2 pl.* slashes [ornamental slits in a garment].

**cuchillería** *f.* cutlery. *2* cutler's shop.

**cuchillero** *m.* cutler.

**cuchillo** *m.* knife: ~ *de monte*, hunting knife; *pasar a* ~, to put to the sword. *2* gore [in a garment]. *3* ENG., ARCH. truss [of a bridge]; frame [of a roof]. *4* NAUT. *vela de* ~, fore-and-aft sail.

**cuchipanda** *f.* merry feast, banquet.

**cuchitril** *m.* COCHITRIL.

**cuchufleta** *f.* jest, quip.

**cuchufletero, -ra** *adj.* given to poking fun at others.

**cuelgacapas** *adj.* cloak hanger.

**cuelgo, cuelga,** etc. *irr.* V. COLGAR.

**cuelmo** *m.* pine torch.

**cuelo, cuele,** etc. *irr.* V. COLAR.

**cuellicorto, -ta** *adj.* short-necked.

**cuellilargo, -ga** *adj.* long-necked.

**cuello** *m.* ANAT., ZOOL. neck; throat. *2* neck [of a vessel, of an object]. *3* collar [of a garment; detachable collar]: ~ *blando*, soft collar; ~ *duro*, stiff collar; ~ *de pajarita*, wing collar; ~ *alechugado* or *escarolado*, ruff.

**cuenca** *f.* wooden bowl. *2* socket [of eye]. *3* walley. *4* GEOG. basin, river basin, watershed.

**cuenco** *m.* earthen bowl. *2* hollow, concavity.

**cuenta** *f.* bead [of rosary, etc.]. *2* account, count, counting, reckoning; bill, note; arithmetical operation: *cuentas del Gran Capitán*, fig. overcharged bill; *cuentas galanas*, castles in the air; *hacer cuentas*, to cast accounts; to do one's sums; *a fin de cuentas*, after all; *en resumidas cuentas*, in short, to sum up; *más de la* ~, too much. *3* account [in the commercial and kindred senses]: ~ *corriente*, current account, checking account; *abonar en* ~, *adeudar* or *cargar en* ~, to credit or to charge to [someone's account]; *a* ~, *a buena* ~, on account. *4* account [given or taken]; *dar* ~, *rendir cuentas, de*, to answer for; give account of. *5* account, behalf, care, duty, responsibility: *tomar uno por su cuenta [una cosa]*, to take upon oneself, to assume responsibility for; *esto es ~ mía*, that is my affair; *por ~ de*, for account of; on the behalf of. *6* report, information: *dar ~ de*, to inform of. *7 caer en la ~*, *darse ~*, to see, realize. *8 dar ~ de*, to use up, waste, destroy. *9 hacer* or *hacerse ~*, or *la ~*, to imagine; to take for granted. *10 tener en ~*, to take into account, to bear in mind. *11 tener ~*, to be profitable, advantageous. *12 a la ~*, *por la ~*, as it seems.

**cuentacorrentista** *m.-f.* depositor, person having a current account in a bank.

**cuentagotas** *m.* PHARM. dropper, medicine dropper.

**cuentahílos** *m.* cloth prover.

**cuentakilómetros** *m.* AUTO. speedometer.

**cuentarrevoluciones, cuentavueltas** *m.* revolution counter.

**cuentero, -ra** *adj.-n.* CUENTISTA 1 & 2.

**cuentista** *adj.* gossipy. *2 m.-f.* gossip, talebearer. *3* narrator or writer of tales; story writer.

**cuento** *m.* tale, narrative, story, short story: *~ de hadas*, fairy tale; *~ de nunca acabar*, endless affair; *~ de viejas*, old-wives' tale; *dejarse de cuentos*, to come to the point; *venir a ~*, to be pertinent; *traer a ~*, to drag in [a subject]. *2* tale, gossip; yarn, falsehood. *3* gist, difficulty. *4* quarrel, disagreement. *5* count, number: *sin ~*, numberless. *6* million. *7* ferrule, tip [of cane, pike, etc.]. *8* prop, support.

**cuento, cuente**, etc. *irr.* V. CONTAR.

**cuerda** *f.* rope, cord, string: *~ floja*, tight rope, acrobat's rope; *por debajo de ~*, secretly, underhandedly. *2* MUS. string, chord [of an instrument]. *3* MUS. voice [bass, tenor, contralto, soprano]; compass [of a voice]. *4* spring or chain [of clock or watch]: *dar ~ a un reloj*, to wind a clock or watch. *5* GEOM. chord. *6 ~ de presos*, chain gang. *9 pl.* ANAT. cords, tendons. *10* ANAT. *cuerdas vocales*, vocal cords.

**cuerdo, -da** *adj.* sane [mentally sound]. *2* sane, wise, prudent, discreet, sensible.

**cuerna** *f.* horn vessel or trumpet. *2* ZOOL. antler. *3* ZOOL. horns, antlers [óf an ox, deer, etc.].

**cuerno** *m.* horn [of an animal, of the moon]. *2* horn [material]: *saber a ~ quemado*, to be unpleasant, distasteful. *3* ENT. horn, feeler. *4* MUS. *cuerno* or *~ de caza*, horn [made of a horn]. *5* PALEONT. *~ de Amon*, ammonite. *6 ~ de la abundancia*, horn of plenty. *7* GEOG. *Cuerno de Oro*, Golden Horn. *8 pl.* hornlike ends of some object.

**cuero** *m.* hide, rawhide, pelt. *2* leather. *3* wine bag, wineskin. *4* (Am.) whip. *5* skin: *~ cabelludo*, scalp; *en cueros, en cueros vivos*, stark naked.

**cuerpo** *m.* body [distinct mass or portion of matter]: *~ celeste*, heavenly body. *2* GEOM. body, solid. *3* CHEM. body, substance. *4* body [of a person or animal; trunk]: *~ sin alma*, fig. dull, inactive person; *echar el ~ fuera*, fig. to side-step a difficulty, an obligation, etc.; *hacer del ~*, to go to stool; *huir* or *hurtar el ~*, to dodge, avoid a blow, a person, a difficulty, etc.; *pedirle a uno el ~ una cosa*, fig. to want, desire something; *a ~, en ~*, without overcoat or cloak; *a ~ de rey*, like a king, with all comfort; *a ~ descubierto*, unprotected; manifestly; *~ a ~*, at close quarters, hand to hand; *de ~ entero*, full-length [portrait]; *de medio ~*, half-length [portrait]. *5* figure, build [of a person]. *6* corpse: *estar de ~ presente*, [of a corpse] to lie in state. *7* body [of a garment],

bodice: *en ~ de camisa*, in shirt sleeves. *8* ANAT. corpus, body. *9* body [of a church, a structure, a document, etc.]. *10* corpus [of laws]. *11* body, thickness, bulk, importance: *tomar ~*, to grow, take shape, gather importance. *12* body politic. *13˙* body [of persons], corps, company, staff: *~ de ejército*, army corps; *~ de redacción*, editorial staff; *~ diplomático*, diplomatic corps. *14* MACH. *~ de bomba*, pump barrel. *15* MIL. *~ de guardia*, guard, post of guard, guardroom. *16* LAW *~ del delito*, corpus delicti.

**cuervo** *m.* ORN. raven, crow. *2* ORN. *~ marino*, cormorant. *3* ORN. *~ merendero*, rook.

**cuesco** *m.* stone [of fruit]. *2* coll. PEDO.

**cuesta** *f.* slope, rising ground, sloping ground: *~ abajo*, downhill; *~ arriba*, uphill; *hacérsele a uno ~ arriba una cosa* [of a thing], to be repugnant to one. *2* CUESTACIÓN. *3* adv. *a cuestas*, on one's back or shoulders; to one's charge or care.

**cuestación** *f.* collection for a charitable purpose.

**cuestión** *f.* question [problem, matter in discussion]; affair, business. *2* dispute, quarrel. *3* LAW *~ de tormento*, torture.

**cuestionable** *adj.* questionable, doubtful.

**cuestionar** *tr.* to controvert.

**cuestionario** *m.* questionnaire.

**cuesto, cueste**, etc. *irr.* V. COSTAR.

**cuestor** *m.* quaestor. *2* solicitor of contributions for a charitable purpose.

**cuestura** *f.* questorship.

**cueto** *m.* defended tor. *2* rocky hill.

**cueva** *f.* cave. *2* cellar. *3* den.

**cuévano** *m.* round basket or pannier.

**cuezo** *m.* mortar trough.

**cuezo, cueza**, etc. *irr.* V. COCER.

**cuidado** *m.* care, carefulness. *2* care, charge, keeping: *tener uno una cosa a su ~*, to have care or charge of a thing. *3* care, fear, anxiety, worry: *estar con ~*, to be worried, uneasy; *de ~*, dangerous; *estar uno de ~*, to be seriously ill. *5 no hay ~*, there is no danger. *6 interj.* take care!, beware!

**cuidador, -ra** *adj.* taking care. *2 m.-f.* caretaker; keeper, tender.

**cuidadoso, -sa** *adj.* careful, painstaking. *2* watchful.

**cuidar** *tr.* to execute with care. *2 tr.-intr. cuidar* or *~ de*, to take care of, to tend, keep, mind, look after, nurse; *~ de que*, to see that. *3 ref.* to take care of oneself. *4 cuidarse de*, to care, to mind, to take notice.

**cuita** *f.* trouble, sorrow, misfortune.

**cuitado, -da** *adj.* unfortunate. *2* spiritless.

**cuja** *f.* lance bucket. *2* bedstead.

**culantrillo** *m.* BOT. maidenhair fern.

**culantro** *m.* CILANTRO.

**culata** *f.* butt [of a firearm]. *2* breech [of a gun]. *3* MACH. head [of a cylinder]. *4* buttock, haunch. *5* rear part [of some things].

**culatazo** *m.* blow with the butt of a firearm. *2* kick, recoil [of a firearm].

**culebra** *f.* ZOOL. snake: *~ de cascabel*, rattlesnake.

**culebrear** *intr.* to twist, wriggle, wind along.

**culebreo** *m.* twisting, wriggling, winding along.

**culebrilla** *f.* MED. ringworm. *2* BOT. green dragon.

**culebrina** *f.* culverin [cannon].

**culebrona** *f.* intriguing woman.

**culera** *f.* dirty spot in a baby's swaddling clothes. *2* patch on the seat of trousers.

**culero, -ra** *adj.* lazy. *2 m.* baby's diaper.

**culinario, -ria** *adj.* culinary.

**culminación** f. culmination.
**culminante** adj. culminating. 2 predominant.
**culminar** intr. to culminate.
**culo** m. behind, bottom, seat, backside, buttocks, rump. 2 anus. 3 seat [of trousers]. 4 bottom [of anything]: ~ de vaso, fig. imitation stone.
**culombio** m. ELECT. coulomb.
**culón, -ona** adj. coll. big-bottomed, broad-bottomed. 2 m. disabled soldier.
**culote** m. base [of a projectile].
**culpa** f. guilt, fault, sin, blame: echar a uno la ~, to put the blame on; tener la ~ de, to be to blame for; esto es culpa mía, it's my fault.
**culpabilidad** f. culpability, guilt.
**culpable** adj. guilty. 2 culpable, blamable, blameworthy. 3 m.-f. culprit. 4 the one to blame.
**culpado, -da** adj. guilty. 2 m.-f. culprit.
**culpar** tr. to blame, to accuse. 2 ref. to blame oneself, to take the blame.
**cultalatiniparla** f. euphuistic language.
**cultedad** f. hum. affectation [in style].
**culteranismo** m. euphuism, cultism.
**culterano, -na** adj. euphuistic. 2 m.-f. euphuist, cultist.
**cultismo** m. euphuism, cultism.
**cultivado, -da** adj. cultured.
**cultivador, -ra** adj. cultivating. 2 m.-f. cultivator; tiller, farmer. 3 f. cultivator [implement].
**cultivar** tr. to cultivate, labour, till, farm [land, soil]. 2 to cultivate [plants, a branch of learning, etc.]. 3 BACT. to culture.
**cultivo** m. cultivation, culture. 2 BACT. culture.
1) **culto** m. cult, worship: ~ divino, public worship. 2 veneration, homage [to beauty, etc.]. 3 pl. acts or ceremonies of public worship.
2) **culto, -ta** adj. cultured, cultivated, educated. 2 enlightened, civilized. 3 learned [language].
**cultor, -ra** m.-f. worshiper.
**cultura** f. CULTIVO. 2 cultivation, refinement, learning; culture.
**cultural** adj. cultural.
**cumbre** f. summit, top [of mountain]. 2 fig. summit, top, acme, pinnacle.
**cumbrera** f. ARCH. ridge [of a ceiling], lintel. 2 (Am.) top, peak, summit, acme.
**cúmel** m. kümmel.
**cumpleaños** m. birthday.
**cumplidamente** adv. completely.
**cumplidero, -ra** adj. expiring [by a specified date]. 2 necessary [to some purpose].
**cumplido, -da** adj. full, complete, through, perfect. 3 large, ample, abundant. 4 courteous, polite. 5 m. act of courtesy, compliment, ceremony: visita de ~, formal call.
**cumplidor, -ra** adj. conscientious, dependable. 2 trustworthy, true to one's word. 3 m.-f. one who executes [an order], keeps [a promise], does [his duty], observes [a law, a precept].
**cumplimentar** tr. to compliment, to pay a complimentary visit to. 2 to carry out [an order].
**cumplimiento** m. accomplishment, carrying out, fulfilment. 2 observance [of law or precepts]. 3 lapse, expiration [of a term]. 4 perfection. 5 CUMPLIDO 5: por ~, as a matter of pure form.
**cumplir** tr. to accomplish, perform, fulfil. 2 to keep [a promise]. 3 to do [one's duty]. 4 to observe [a law, a precept]. 5 ~ una condena, to serve or finish a term in prison. 6 hoy cumplo treinta años, I am thirty today. 7 intr. to do one's duty: ~ con Dios, to do one's duty to God; por ~, as a matter of form. 8 to have served the time

required in the Army. 9 to behove: cúmpleme decir, it behoves me to say. 10 intr.-ref. [of a term or period of time] to expire. 11 ref. to be fulfilled, to come true.
**cumquibus** m. coll. money, wherewithal.
**cumulativo, -va** adj. cumulative.
**cúmulo** m. heap, pile. 2 METEOR. cumulus.
**cuna** f. cradle [for a baby; infancy]. 2 place of birth [of a person]. 3 birth, family, lineage. 4 foundling hospital. 5 pl. cat's cradle.
**cundir** intr. [of liquids; of news, etc.] to spread. 2 to increase in volume; to go a long way.
**cunear** tr. to rock [in the cradle]. 2 ref. coll. to rock, sway.
**cuneiforme** adj. cuneiform. 2 BOT. cuneate.
**cúneo** m. ARCHEOL. cuneus.
**cunero, -ra** adj.-m. foundling. 2 BULLF. unpedigreed [bull].
**cuneta** f. ditch [at the side of a road].
**cunicultura** f. rabbit raising, rabbit breeding.
**cuña** m. wedge, quoin. 2 ANAT. cuneiform [bone].
**cuñada** f. sister-in-law.
**cuñado** m. brother-in-law.
**cuñete** m. keg.
**cuño** m. die [for stamping coins, medals, etc.]. 2 stamp made by the die: de nuevo ~, fig. newly minted, newly made.
**cuota** f. quota, share. 2 membership fee.
**cuotidiano, -na** adj. COTIDIANO.
**cupe, cupiera**, etc. irr. V. CABER.
**cupé** m. coupé [automobile, carriage]. 2 coupé [of a Continental diligence].
**cupido** m. cupid. 2 (cap.) MYTH. Cupid.
**cuplé** m. variety song, music-hall song.
**cupletista** f. variety singer, music-hall singer.
**cupo** m. quota, contingent.
**cupón** m. coupon.
**cupresáceo, -a** adj. BOT. cupressineous.
**cúprico, -ca** adj. CHEM. cupric.
**cuprífero, -ra** adj. cupriferous.
**cuprita** f. MINER. cuprite.
**cuproníquel** m. cupronickel.
**cúpula** f. ARCH. cupola, dome. 2 NAUT. cupola, turret. 3 BOT. cupule.
**cupulífero, -ra** adj. BOT. cupuliferous.
**cura** m. Roman Catholic priest; parish priest: ~ párroco, parish priest; este ~, fig. I, myself. 2 cure, healing, treatment: no tener ~, to be incurable. 3 dressing [of a wound]. 4 ~ de almas, care of souls.
**curable** adj. MED. curable.
**curación** f. cure, curing, healing.
**curadillo** m. ICHTH. codfish.
**curador, -ra** adj. curing, healing. 2 caretaking. 3 m.-f. curer, healer. 4 curer, seasoner, tanner. 5 caretaker, overseer. 6 LAW curator, guardian.
**curaduría** f. LAW curatorship.
**curalotodo** m. cure-all.
**curanderismo** m. quackery, quack medicine.
**curandero** m. quack doctor.
**curar** intr.-ref. to cure, heal, recover, be cured. 2 to take care [of]; to mind. 3 tr. cure, heal. 4 MED. to treat; to dress [a wound]. 5 to cure [meat, fish]; to season [lumber]; to tan [hides]. 6 ref. to take treatment: curarse en salud, to guard against possible danger.
**curare** m. curare, curari.
**curasao** m. curaçao [liqueur].
**curatela** f. CURADURÍA.
**curativo, -va** adj. curative.
**curato** m. office of a parish priest. 2 parish.

**curda** f. drunkenness, drunken fit.
**curdo, -da** adj. Kurdish. 2 m.-f. Kurd.
**cureña** f. gun carriage. 2 gunstock in the rough. 3 stock [of crossbow].
**curia** f. HIST. curia. 2 barristers, solicitors and court clerks as a whole. 3 ecclesiastical court: *Curia romana*, Roman Curia.
**curialesco, -ca** adj. legal [language, style].
**curiana** f. CUCARACHA 1.
**curiosamente** adv. curiously. 2 neatly, tidily, cleanly. 3 carefully.
**curiosear** intr. to act with curiosity; to inquire, snoop.
**curiosidad** f. curiosity [inquisitiveness; strangeness]. 2 cleanliness, tidiness. 3 curiosity [curious thing]: curio.
**curioso, -sa** adj. curious. 2 clean, tidy. 3 m.-f. curious person.
**Curlandia** f. pr. n. Kurland.
**Curra, Currita** f. pr. n. Francis.
**currelar** intr. coll. to slog away, to toil, to drudge.
**Curro, Currito** m. pr. n. Frank.
**curruca** f. ORN. whitethroat.
**currutaco, -ca** adj. dandified. 2 m. fop, dandy, dude. 3 f. woman of fashion.
**cursado, -da** adj. versed, experienced.
**cursar** tr. to frequent. 2 EDUC. to attend lectures of, to study [a subject]. 3 to make [a petition, etc.] pass through the regular administrative channels.
**cursi** adj.-s. [person] poorly affecting distinction and elegance; shabby-genteel.
**cursilón, -ona** adj. pretentious, showy, flashy, affected, pseudo-refined, snobish. 2 n. flashy type, common but pretentious person, genteel person, snob.
**cursilería** f. poor afectation of distinction and elegance; shabby-gentility.
**cursillo** m. EDUC. short course of lectures on a subject.
**cursivo, -va** adj. cursive. 2 f. italics.
**curso** m. course [career, direction, progress]; lapse, succession. 2 route [of a procession]. 3 MACH. run, -travel [of part or device]. 4 passing of a petition or affair through the regular chan-

nels. 5 EDUC. course [of lectures]. 6 school year. 7 course, run, flow, circulation: *dar libre* ~, to give free course. 8 COM. current rate. 9 pl. diarrhœa.
**cursor** m. MECH. slide.
**curtido, -da** adj. tanned, curried [leather]. 2 tanned, sunburnt, weather-beaten. 3 hardened, experienced. 4 m. tanning. 5 tanning bark. 6 m. pl. tanned leather.
**curtidor** m. tanner, currier, leather dresser.
**curtiduría** f. tannery, tanyard.
**curtiembre** f. tannery.
**curtir** tr. to tan [hides]. 2 to tan, to sunburn. 3 to harden, to inure. 4 ref. to become tanned. 5 to be hardened or inured; to gain experience.
**curuguá** m. BOT. cassabanana.
**curul** adj. curule.
**curva** f. curve. 2 NAUT. knee.
**curvatura, curvidad** f. curvature, bend.
**curvilíneo, -a** adj. curvilinear.
**curvo, -va** adj. curve, curved, bent.
**cuscurro** m. crust of bread.
**cuscuta** f. BOT. common dodder.
**cuscús, cuzcuz** m. couscous.
**cúspide** f. GEOM. vertex [of cone or pyramid]. 2 peak [of mountain]. 3 cusp, apex, summit.
**custodia** f. custody, care, safe-keeping. 2 escort or guard [to a prisoner]. 3 ECCL. monstrance. 4 ECCL. tabernacle. 5 custody [of the Franciscan order].
**custodiar** tr. to guard, keep, take care of.
**custodio** m. custodian, guard.
**cutáneo, -a** adj. cutaneous.
**cúter** m. NAUT. cutter [vessel with one mast].
**cutí** m. ticking [fabric].
**cutícula** f. cuticle.
**cutis** m. skin [of the human body], complexion.
**cutre** adj. stingy, miserly. 2 m.-f. miser.
**cuyo, -ya,** pl. **cuyos, -yas** poss. pron. whose, of which; *mi hermana, cuyo marido es inglés*, my sister, whose husband is an Englishman. 2 m. coll. lover [of a woman].
**cuzco** m. small dog.
**czar** m. ZAR.
**czarevitz** m. ZAREVITZ.
**czarina** f. ZARINA.

# CH

**Ch, ch** *f.* fourth letter of the Spanish alphabet.
**chabacanada, chabacanería** *f.* coarseness, vulgarity, bad taste.
**chabacano, -na** *adj.* coarse, vulgar, in bad taste.
**chabola** *f.* hut, cabin, shanty.
**chabolismo** *m.* shanty or shacky towns, slums.
**chacal** *m.* ZOOL. jackal.
**chacarero, -ra** *adj.-n.* farmer, peasant, grower. 2 *f.* peasant dance in Argentina, Uruguay and Bolivia.
**chacina** *f.* CECINA. 2 pork seasoned for sausages.
**chacinería** *f.* porkbutcher's shop.
**chacó** *pl.* **-cós** *m.* shako.
**chacolí** *m.* light sour wine of Vizcaya.
**chacolotear** *intr.* [of a loose horseshoe] to clatter.
**chacoloteo** *m.* clatter [of a loose horseshoe].
**chacona** *f.* MUS. chaconne.
**chaconá, chaconada** *f.* jaconet [fabric].
**chacota** *f.* fun, noisy mirth: *hacer ~ de,* coll. to make fun of.
**chacoteo** *m.* fun, noisy mirth, mockery.
**chacra** *f.* (Am.) farm, country estate, cultivated land. 2 farmhouse. 3 farm products.
**chacha** *f.* coll. nurse, nursemaid.
**cháchara** *f.* prattle, idle talk. 2 chitchat.
**chacharear** *intr.* to chatter, prate, prattle.
**chacharero, -ra** *adj.* chattering. 2 *m.-f.* chatterer, prattler.
**chacho** *m.* coll. boy, lad.
**chafaldita** *f.* jest, banter.
**chafalmejas** *m.-f.* dauber [bad painter].
**chafalonía** *f.* (Am.) scrap gold or silver, worn out gold jewellery.
**chafallar** *tr.* to botch, to make or mend clumsily.
**chafallo** *m.* botch, clumsy mending.
**chafallón, -na** *adj.* botching. 2 *m.-f.* botcher.
**chafandín** *m.* conceited ass.
**chafar** *tr.* to flatten, crush, crumple, rumple. 2 fig. to squash, cut short, silence.
**chafarote** *f.* cutlass. 2 sword, sabre.
**chafarrinar** *tr.* to blot, to stain.
**chafarrinón** *m.* CHAFARRINADA.
**chaflán** *m.* chamfer, bevel.
**chaflanar** *tr.* to chamfer, to bevel.
**chah** *m.* shah.
**chaira** *f.* steel [for sharpening knives]. 2 shoemaker's blade.
**chal** *m.* shawl.

**chalado, -da** *adj.* fool, addlepated. 2 infatuated: *estar ~ por,* to be madly in love with.
**chaladura** *f.* coll. fancy or crazy idea, whim. 2 craze, old habit, mania. 3 stupid thing. 4 crush.
**chalán, -na** *m.-f.* horse dealer; wily, crafty dealer. 2 *m.* (Am.) horsebreaker.
**chalana** *f.* scow, flatboat.
**chalanear** *tr.* coll. to drive [deals] craftily.
**chalaneo** *m.* horse dealing; crafty dealing.
**chalanesco, -ca** *adj.* pertaining to craftiness in buying and selling.
**chalar** *tr.* to drive mad. 2 *ref.* to lose one's head. 3 to become madly in love.
**chalaza** *f.* EMBRYOL., BOT. chalaza.
**chaleco** *m.* waistcoat, vest.
**chalet** *m.* chalet.
**chalina** *f.* bowtie with long ends.
**chalote** BOT. shallot, scallion.
**chalupa** *f.* NAUT. a small two-mast boat. 2 NAUT. launch, lifeboat. 3 (Mex.) a small canoe.
**chámara, chamarasca** *f.* brushwood. 2 brush fire.
**chamarilero, -ra** *m.-f.* dealer in second-hand goods.
**chamariz** *m.* ORN. greenfinch.
**chamarra** *f.* jacket of coarse woollen cloth.
**chamba** *f.* coll. CHIRIPA.
**chambelán** *m.* chamberlain.
**chambergo** *m.* an old broad-brimmed hat with a cocked side. 2 (Arg.) soft hat.
**chambón, -na** *adj.* coll. clumsy, awkward [in games]; unskilled. 2 coll. lucky [attaining something by a fluke]. 3 *m.-f.* coll. blunderer. 4 lucky person.
**chambonada** *f.* blunder. 2 fluke, stroke of luck.
**chambra** *f.* femenine dressing jacket.
**chambrana** *f.* ARCH. trim [around a door, window, etc.].
**chamicera** *f.* strip of half-burnt woodland.
**chamiza** *f.* BOT. chamiso. 2 brushwood [for fuel].
**chamizo** *m.* half-burnt tree or log. 2 chamiso-thatched hut. 3 fig. den.
**chamorro, -rra** *adj.* with the head shorn. 2 beardless [wheat].
**champán** *m.* NAUT. sampan. 2 champagne [wine].
**champaña** *m.* champagne [wine].
**champiñón** *m.* mushroom.
**champú** *m.* shampoo.
**champurrar** *tr.* to mix [liquors].

**chamullar** *tr.* to speak, to talk: ~ *algo de inglés*, to speak some English.
**chamuscado, -da** *adj.* singed, scorched.
**chamuscar** *tr.* to singe, sear, scorch. 2 *ref.* to be singed, scorched.
**chamusquina** *f.* singe, singeing, scorching. 2 row, quarrel. 3 *oler a chamusquina*, coll. to look like a fight; coll. to smack of heresy.
**chancear** *intr.-ref.* to joke, jest, fool.
**chancero, -ra** *adj.* joking, jesting.
**chancla** *f.* old shoe worn down at the heel.
**chancleta** *f.* slipper: *en chancleta*, with shoes worn slipper-like.
**chancletear** *intr.* to go about wearing the shoes slipper-like.
**chancleteo** *m.* clatter of slipper.
**chanclo** *m.* clog, patten. 2 overshoe, galosh, *gum.
**chancro** *m.* MED. chancre.
**chanchada** *f.* (Am.) coll. dirty trick, vile ed.
**chanchería** *f.* (Am.) pork-butcher's shop.
**chancho, -cha** *adj.* (Am.) dirty, unclean. 2 (Am.) pig, hog.
**chanchullero, -ra** *m.-f.* underhand dealer.
**chanchullo** *m.* underhand deal.
**chandal** *m.* track suit.
**chanfaina** *f.* COOK. stew of chopped lights.
**changüí** *m.* coll. joke. 2 trick, hoax, swindle: *dar* ~, to trick, to swindle.
**chantaje** *m.* blackmail.
**chantajista** *m.-f.* blackmailer.
**chantar** *tr.* to put on [clothes]. 2 to tell [someone something] to his face.
**chantre** *m.* precentor [in a cathedral].
**chanza** *f.* joke, jest, fun.
**chanzoneta** *f.* old little song. 2 coll. CHANZA.
**chapa** *f.* sheet, plate, veneer. 2 small piece of metal plate, used as a badge, sign, token, etc. 3 rosy spot on the cheek. 4 *hombre de* ~, serious man. 5 *pl.* game of tossing up coins.
**chapado, -da** *adj.* plated, veneered. 2 ~ *a la antigua*, old-fashioned [person].
**chapalear** *intr.* [of water] to splash. 2 CHACOLOTEAR.
**chapaleo** *m.* splashing [of water]. 2 CHACOLOTEO.
**chapaleta** *f.* flap valve, clack valve.
**chapaleteo** *m.* dash, splashing [of water]. 3 patter [of rain].
**chapar** *tr.* CHAPEAR.
**chaparra** *f.* BOT. kermes oak. 2 CHAPARRO.
**chaparral** *m.* thicket of dwarf oaks.
**chaparreras** *f. pl.* (Am.) chaps [worn by cowboys].
**chaparro** *m.* BOT. dwarf oak, dwarf evergreen oak.
**chaparrón** *m.* downpour, violent shower.
**chapear** *tr.* to plate [cover with metal sheets]; to veneer. 2 *intr.* CHACOLOTEAR.
**chapeo** *m.* hat.
**chapería** *f.* sheet-metal ornament.
**chapeta** *f.* small metal plate. 2 rosy spot on the cheek.
**chapín** *m.* chopine [kind of patten].
**chápiro** *m.* coll. *¡voto al* ~*!*, by Jove!, by thunder!
**chapitel** *m.* ARCH. spire. 2 ARCH. capital. 3 NAUT. agate socket [of the needle].
**chapodar** *tr.* to trim, clear of branches [a tree].
**chapodo** *m.* branch lopped off a tree.
**chapotear** *tr.* to moisten [by dabbing at with a wet, sponge or cloth]. 2 *intr.* [of water] to make a splashing sound.
**chapoteo** *m.* moistening, dabbing. 2 splashing.
**chapucear** *tr.* to botch, bungle.
**chapucería** *f.* clumsiness [of a work]. 2 botch, bungle, clumsy work.

**chapucero, -ra** *adj.* botched, bungled. 2 botching, bungling. 3 *m.-f.* botcher, bungler.
**chapurrar, chapurrear** *tr.* to jabber [a language]; to speak [a language] brokenly.
**chapuz** *m.* duck, ducking [sudden dip of head under water]. 2 CHAPUZA.
**chapuza** *f.* slight work. 2 botch, bungle.
**chapuzar** *tr.-intr.-ref.* to duck [under water].
**chapuzón** *m.* coll. duck, ducking, diving.
**chaqué** *m.* cutaway coat, morning coat.
**chaqueta** *f.* jacket, sack coat.
**chaquete** *m.* backgammon.
**chaquetear** *intr.* coll. to take fright, to flee.
**chaquetilla** *f.* short jacket.
**chaquetón** *m.* pea-jacket. 2 short overcoat.
**charabán** *m.* charabanc.
**charada** *f.* charade.
**charanga** *f.* MUS. military brass band.
**charca** *f.* pool, pond [of stagnant water].
**charco** *m.* puddle, pool. 2 fig. *pasar el* ~, to cross the pond [the sea].
**charcutería** *f.* pork butcher's shop.
**charla** *f.* chatter, prattle. 2 chat, chatting. 3 talk, lecture. 4 ORN. missel thrush.
**charladuría** *f.* indiscreet talk, gossip, prattle.
**charlar** *intr.* to chatter, prattle. 2 to chat.
**charlatán, -na** *adj.* chattering, prattling, loquacious. 2 babbling. 3 *m.-f.* chatterer, chatterbox. 4 charlatan, quack, mountebank; humbug.
**charlatanería** *f.* garrulity. 2 charlatanry.
**charlatanismo** *m.* charlatanism.
**charnela** *f.* hinge [of door, box, etc.]. 2 MACH. knuckle. 3 ZOOL. hinge [of bivalve shell].
**charol** *m.* varnish, japan. 2 patent leather.
**charolado, -da** *adj.* shiny, lustrous. 2 varnished.
**charolar** *tr.* to varnish, to japan.
**charpa** *f.* formerly, a baldric for carrying pistols. 2 sling [for a broken arm].
**charquear** *tr.* (Am.) to jerk, dry [beef].
**charqui** *m.* (Am.) jerked beef, dry beef.
**charrada** *f.* tawdriness, gaudiness.
**charrán** *adj.* knave, rogue.
**charranada** *f.* dirty trick, knavery.
**charrasca** *f.* coll. trailing sword or sabre.
**charrería** *f.* tawdriness, gaudiness.
**charretera** *f.* epaulet. 2 garter.
**charro, -rra** *adj.* pertaining to the countryfolk of Salamanca. 2 rustic. 3 tawdry, gaudy, flashy. 4 *m.-f.* Salamanca countryman or countrywoman. 5 *m.* (Mex.) cowboy.
**chasca** *f.* small wood [for fuel].
**chascar** *intr.* to crack [emit a splitting sound]. 2 *tr.* to click [one's tongue]. 3 to crunch [food].
**chascarrillo** *m.* joke, funny story.
**chasco** *m.* trick, deceit. 2 disappointment. 3 *dar un* ~, to play a trick upon; to disappoint; *llevarse un* ~, to be disappointed.
**chasis** *m.* AUTO., RADIO. chassis. 2 PHOT. plateholder.
**chasponazo** *m.* scratch made by a bullet.
**chasquear** *tr.* to play a trick on, to fool, deceive. 2 to disappoint. 3 to crack, snap [a whip]. 4 *intr.* to crack, snap. 5 *ref.* to be frustrated.
**chasquido** *m.* crack, snap, click [sound].
**chata** *f.* CHALANA. 2 bedpan.
**chatarra** *f.* scrap iron. 2 iron slag.
**chatarrero, -ra** *m.-f.* scrap-iron dealer.
**chato, -ta** *adj.* flat-nosed. 2 flat [nose and other things]. 3 *m.-f.* flat-nosed person.
**chatón** *m.* JEWEL. the stone in a bezel or chaton.
**¡chau!** *interj.* (Am.) so long.

**chauvinismo** *m.* chauvinism.
**chauvinista** *adj.* chauvinistic. *2 m.-f.* chauvinist.
**chaval, -la** *adj.* coll. young. *2 m.* coll. lad. *3 f.* coll. lass.
**chavea** *f.* coll, boy, lad.
**chaveta** *f.* cotter pin; key, forelock, linchpin. *2* coll. *perder la ~*, to go off one's head.
**chayote** *m.* BOT. edible fruit of an American vine.
**che** *f.* name of the letter *ch*.
**checo, -ca** *adj.-n.* Czech.
**checoeslovaco, -ca** *adj.-n.* Czecho-Slovakian.
**Checoeslovaquia** *f. pr. n.* GEOG. Czecho-Slovakia.
**chelín** *m.* shilling.
**chepa** *f.* coll. hump, hunch.
**cheque** *m.* COM. cheque, check: *~ cruzado*, crossed check; *~ de viajero*, traveler's check.
**chequeo** *m.* MED. checkup. *2* AUTO. servicing, overhauling. *3* checking, verifying.
**cherna** *f.* ICHTH. a mediterranean grouper.
**cheviot** *m.* cheviot [fabric, wool].
**chibalete** *m.* PRINT. frame.
**chibuquí** *m.* chibouk [turkish pipe].
**chicada** *f.* childish action.
**chicle** *m.* chicle gum; chewing gum.
**chico, -ca** *adj.* small, little. *2* very young [person]. *3 m.* child, kid, youngster, boy, lad. *4* coll. fellow; old chap. *5 f.* child, kid, girl, lass. *6* coll. old girl.
**chicolear** *intr.* to address compliments to a woman.
**chicoleo** *m.* compliment [addressed to a woman].
**chicorro** *m.* sturdy youngster.
**chicote** *m.* sturdy boy. *2* coll, cigar. *3* (Am.) whip. *4* NAUT. end of rope; piece of rope.
**chicozapote** *m.* BOT. sapodilla, sapote.
**chicuelo, -la** *adj. dim.* little, small, very small. *2 m.* child, little boy. *3 f.* child; girl, little girl.
**chicha** *f.* alcoholic drink made from maize: *no ser ~ ni limonada*, to be neither fish nor fowl. *2 adj.* NAUT. *calma ~*, dead calm.
**chicharra** *f.* ENT. cicada. *2* a noisy toy.
**chicharrón** *m.* crackling, scratching [residue of hog fat]. *2* burned meat.
**chichón** *m.* bump [swelling on the head].
**chichonera** *f.* cap for protecting child's head.
**chifla** *f.* hissing, whistling [to express disapproval]. *2* whistle. *3* paring knife.
**chiflado, -da** *adj.* off one's head, crazy. *2 estar ~ por*, to be in love with, to dote on; to have a craze for. *3 m.-f.* crackbrain, crank.
**chifladura** *f.* craziness. *2* love, doting. *3* craze, mania.
**chiflar** *intr.* to whistle. *2 tr.-ref.* to hiss, to scoff. *3 tr.* to pare [leather]. *4* to gulp down [wine, liquors]. *5 ref.* to become crazy, unbalanced. *6 chiflarse por*, to go crazy on.
**chiflato** *m.* whistle [instrument].
**chiflido** *m.* whistle [instrument and sound].
**chilaba** *f.* Moorish hooded garment.
**Chile** *m. pr. n.* Chile.
**chile** *m.* chil(l)i; red pepper.
**chileno, -na; chileño, -ña** *adj.-n.* Chilean.
**chilindrina** *f.* trifle. *2* joke; jest, banter.
**chilindrinero, -ra** *adj.* waggish. *2 m.-f.* wag, joker.
**chilindrón** *m.* a card game.
**chillador, -ra** *adj.* shrieking, squeaking, screaming.
**chillar** *intr.* to shriek, screech, squeak, scream. *2* fig. to shout. *3* [of colours] to clash, to glare, be garish. *4* CHIRRIAR.
**chillería** *f.* screaming, shouting. *2* scolding.

**chillido** *m.* shriek, screech, squeak, scream.
**chillón, -na** *adj.* shrieking, screaming. *2* shrill, screechy. *3* loud, garish [colour].
**chimenea** *f.* chimney; smokestack. *2* NAUT. funnel. *3* hearth, fireplace, chimney: *~ francesa*, fireplace. *4* MIN. shaft.
**chimpancé** *m.* ZOOL. chimpanzee.
**China** *f. pr. n.* China.
**china** *f.* pebble, small stone. *2* BOT. chinaroot. *3* China silk or cotton stuff. *4* China, porcelain. *5* Chinese woman. *6* (Am.) Indian or half-breed maidservant.
**chinazo** *m.* blow with a pebble.
**chinchar** *tr.* coll. to bother, annoy. *2* coll. to kill.
**chincharrero** *m.* place swarming with bedbugs. *2* (Am.) fishing smack.
**chinche** *f.* ENT. bedbug. *2* drawing pin, thumb tack. *3* bore, nuisance [person].
**chincheta** *f.* drawing pin, thumbtack.
**chinchilla** *f.* ZOOL. chinchilla. *2* chinchilla [fur].
**chinchín** *m.* street music. *2* ballyhoo.
**chinchona** *f.* CHEM. cinchona, cinchona bark.
**chinchorrería** *f.* annoyance. *2* tale, gossip.
**chinchorrero, -ra** *adj.* annoying, pestering.
**chinchorro** *m.* kind of fishing net. *2* small rowing boat.
**chinchoso, -sa** *adj.* annoying, pestering [person].
**chinela** *f.* slipper, chopine.
**chinero** *m.* china cabinet.
**chinesco, -ca** *adj.* Chinese. *2 m.* MUS. bell tree.
**chingar** *tr.* coll. to drink, tipple. *2 ref.* to get drunk.
**chino, -na** *adj.* Chinese. *2 adj.-n.* (Am.) offspring of Indian and mestizo. *3 m.* Chinaman, Chinese. *4* Chinese language. *5* (Am.) manservant.
**chipé** *f.* coll. truth, goodness.
**chipén** *f.* coll. life, excitement. *2 de ~*, first-class, excellent.
**chipirón** *m.* ZOOL. squid, calamary.
**Chipre** *f. pr. n.* Cyprus.
**chipriota, chiprote** *adj.-n.* Cyprian.
**chiquero** *m.* pigsty. *2* in a bull ring, place where bulls are shut up.
**chiquilicuatro** *m.* CHISGARABÍS.
**chiquillada** *f.* childish action.
**chiquillería** *f.* children, crowd of children.
**chiquillo, -lla** *adj.* small. *2 m.-f.* little boy or girl, child, little one, youngster.
**chiquirritín, -na; chiquitín, -na** *adj.* tiny, small. *2 m.-f.* tiny child, tot, infant.
**chiquito, -ta** *adj.* tiny, very small: *hacerse ~*, to be modest. *2 m.-f.* CHIQUILLO *2. 3 f. no andarse con chiquitas*, not to shift, to be clear, direct.
**chiribita** *f.* BOT. daisy. *2 pl.* sparks. *3 hacer chiribitas los ojos*, to see spots before the eyes.
**chiribitil** *m.* crib, hovel, den, small narrow room.
**chirigota** *f.* joke, jest, banter.
**chirigotero, -ra** *adj.* fond of jesting or bantering.
**chirimbolo** *m.* utensil, implement, vessel.
**chirimía** *f.* MUS. kind of flageolet, hornpipe.
**chirimoya** *f.* cherimoya.
**chirinola** *f.* trifle. *2 estar de ~*, to be in good spirits.
**chiripa** *f.* fluke, piece of luck.
**chirivía** *f.* BOT. parsnip. *2* ORN. wagtail.
**chirla** *f.* ZOOL. a small clam.
**chirle** *adj.* coll. dull, insipid, tasteless, wishy-washy, flat. *2 m.* droppings.
**chirlata** *f.* gambling den.
**chirlo** *m.* long slash or scar in the face.
**chirona** *f.* coll. jug, jail, prison.
**chirriar** *intr.* to hiss, sizzle. *2* [of a wheel, etc.] to

squeak. *3* [of birds] to chirr, screech. *4* [of insects] to chirr, chirp.
**chirrido** *m.* hiss, sizzle. *2* squeak [of a wheel, etc.] *3* chirr, screech [of birds]. *4* chirr, chirping [of insects].
**chirrión** *m.* squeaky, two-wheeled dray.
**chirumen** *m.* coll. acumen, brains.
**¡chis!** *interj.* hush!, sh!, silence!
**chisgarabís** *m.* whippersnapper, insignificant meddlesome fellow.
**chisguete** *m.* drink, swallow, swig [of wine]. *2* squirt [of a liquid].
**chisme** *m.* mischievous tale, piece of gossip. *2* coll. implement, utensil.
**chismear** *tr.* to gossip, tattle, bear tales.
**chismografía** *f.* gossip, tattle.
**chismorrear** *intr.* CHISMEAR.
**chismorreo** *m.* gossip, gossiping, tale-bearing.
**chismoso, -sa** *adj.* gossipy. *2 m.-f.* gossip, tale bearer.
**chispa** *f.* spark, sparkle: *echar chispas*, fig. to be raging, hit the ceiling. *2* sparkle [little bit; small diamond]. *3* drop [of drizzling rain]. *4* sparkle, wit: *tener ~*, to be witty. *5* coll. *coger una ~*, to get drunk.
**chispazo** *m.* spark, flying off of a spark, flash.
**chispeante** *adj.* sparkling, scintillant.
**chispear** *intr.* to spark, to sparkle. *2* to scintillate. *3* to drizzle, sprinkle [rain lightly].
**chispero** *m.* blacksmith. *2* formerly, in Madrid, man of the lower classes.
**chispo, -pa** *adj.* tipsy, drunk.
**chisporrotear** *intr.* to spark, sputter.
**chisporroteo** *m.* sparking, sputtering.
**chistar** *intr.* to speak: *no ~*, not to say a word.
**chiste** *m.* joke, funny story: *contar chistes*, to crack jokes. *2* fun: *hacer ~ de*, to make fun of. *3 caer en el ~*, to see the point.
**chistera** *f.* top hat. *2* fish basket. *3* CESTA *2*.
**chistoso, -sa** *adj.* witty, funny. *2 m.* wit, funny fellow.
**chita** *f.* ANAT. ankle bone. *2* knucklebone [of sheep]. *3* a game like, quoits. *4 adv. a la ~ callando*, on the quiet, stealthily.
**chiticalla** *m.-f.* coll. reticent person, oyster, *clam. *2* coll. secret.
**chito** *m.* CHITA.
**¡chito!, ¡chitón!** *interj.* hush!, silence!
**chitón** *m.* ZOOL. chiton.
**chiva** *f.* ZOOL. female kid.
**chivar** *tr.* to annoy, to upset, to get on someone's nerves. *2 ref.* to tell, to split, to squeal, to inform [against].
**chivata** *f.* shepherd's club or stick. *2* coll. female informer or talebearer.
**chivatazo** *m.* coll. tip-off, telling, informing: *dar el ~*, to spill the beans, to split, to give a tip-off.
**chivato** *m.* ZOOL. kid. *2* coll. informer, talebearer.
**chivo** *m.* ZOOL. male kid.
**chocante** *adj.* provoking. *2* surprising. *3* funny.
**chocar** *intr.* to collide, come into collision; to clash, bump together. *2* to meet, fight. *3* to annoy, vex. *4* to surprise: *esto me choca*, I am surprised at this.
**chocarrear** *intr.* to crack vulgar jokes.
**chocarrería** *f.* vulgar joke, coarse humour.
**chocarrero, -ra** *adj.* coarse vulgar [joke humour]. *2 m.-f.* vulgar joker.
**choclo** *m.* clog, patten. *2* (Am.) green ear of maize.
**chocolate** *m.* chocolate.

**chocolatería** *f.* chocolate factory. *2* chocolate shop.
**chocolatero, -ra** *adj.* fond of drinking chocolate. *2 m.-f.* chocolate maker or seller. *3 f.* chocolate pot.
**chocolatín** *m.* chocolate tablet or drop.
**chocha, chochaperdiz** *f.* ORN. woodcock.
**chochear** *intr.* to dote, to be in one's dotage.
**chochera, chochez** *f.* dotage. *2* doting act or word.
**chocho, -cha** *adj.* dotard, doddering. *2* doting: *estar ~ por*, to dote on. *3 m.-f.* dotard.
**chófer** *m.* AUT. chauffeur, driver.
**chola** *f.* CHOLLA.
**cholla** *f.* coll. head, noodle, pate.
**chollo** *m.* soft job, plum, good number. *2* bargain, snip. *3* luck.
**chopo** *m.* BOT. black poplar. *2* coll. musket, gun.
**choque** *m.* collision, clash; shock, impact. *2* MIL. encounter, skirmish. *3* dispute, quarrel. *4* MED. shock [depression].
**choquezuela** *f.* ANAT. kneecap, kneepan.
**choricería** *f.* sausage shop.
**choricero, -ra** *m.-f.* sausage maker or seller.
**chorizo** *m.* smoked-pork sausage.
**chorlito** *m.* ORN. golden plover. *2* coll. scatter-brains.
**chorrada** *f.* extra dash of a liquid [for good measure].
**chorreado, -da** *adj.* [of cattle] with dark vertical stripes.
**chorrear** *intr.* to spout, to gush. *2* to drip. *3* to be dripping wet. *4* [of some things] to come trickling.
**chorreo** *m.* spouting, gushing. *2* dripping.
**chorrera** *f.* place whence a liquid drips. *2* mark left by dripping or running water. *3* rapid [in a stream]. *4* jabot, shirt frill. *5* coll. (Am.) string, stream [of things or people].
**chorretada** *f.* squirt, spurt. *2* CHORRADA.
**chorrillo** *m.* small jet or flow, trickle. *2* continual trickle [of some things]: *sembrar a ~*, to sow in a trickle.
**chorrito** *m.* small jet, trickle. *2* dash [of a liquid].
**chorro** *m.* jet, spout, gush, flow, stream [of liquid, etc.]: *~ de arena*, sandblast; *a chorros*, in abundance. *2 ~ de voz*, voice of large volume.
**chortal** *m.* pool fed by a spring at the bottom.
**chotacabras** *f.* ORN. goatsucker.
**chotearse** *ref.* to make fun [of someone].
**choteo** *m.* fun, mockery.
**chotis** *m.* schottische [dance].
**choto, -ta** *m.-f.* sucking kid. *2* calf.
**chova** *f.* ORN. chough. *2* ORN. jackdaw.
**choza** *f.* hut, cabin, hovel, shanty.
**chozo** *m.* small hut.
**chozpo** *m.* gambol.
**chubasco** *m.* shower, squall: fig. *aguantar el ~*, to stand a storm of words, difficulties, etc.
**chubasquero** *m.* raincoat.
**chucha** *f.* bitch [female dog]. *2* (Am.) opossum.
**chuchería** *f.* trinquet, knick-nack. *2* titbit, delicacy.
**chucho** *m.* coll. dog.
**chueca** *f.* stump [of tree]. *2* head [of a bone]. *3* game played with a ball and sticks.
**chueta** *m.-f.* in the Balearic Islands, a descendant of Christianized Jews.
**chufa** *f.* BOT. chufa, groundnut.
**chufero, -ra** *adj.* chufa or orgeat seller.
**chufleta** *f.* CUCHUFLETA.
**chufletear** *intr.* to poke fun [at others].

**chulada** *f.* low action. *2* pert, droll saying.
**chulapo, -pa** *m.-f.* CHULO 3.
**chulear** *tr.* to banter, rally wittily. *2 ref.* to make fun, be facetious.
**chulería** *f.* pertness. *2* assemblage of CHULOS.
**chulesco, -ca** *adj.* pertaining to CHULOS.
**chuleta** *f.* chop, cutlet. *2* coll. slap in the face.
**chulo, -la** *adj.* pert and droll. *2* CHULESCO. *3 m.-f.* man or woman of the lower class of Madrid who affects special airs and manners. *4 m.* bullfighter's assistant. *5* pimp, procurer. *6* man kept by a woman. *7* fig. knave.
**chumacera** *f.* MACH. journal bearing, pillow block. *2* NAUT. rowlock.
**chumbera** *f.* BOT. Indian fig, prickly pear [plant].
**chumbo, -ba** *adj. higo ~*, Indian fig, prickly pear [fruit]; *higuera ~*, CHUMBERA.
**chunga** *f.* fun, banter: *estar de ~*, to be joking; *tomar a ~*, to make fun of.
**chunguearse** *ref.* to joke, to make fun [of].
**chupa** *f.* an old undercoat or jacket: *poner como ~ de dómine*, to upbraid, to abuse.
**chupada** *f.* suck, sucking. *2* pull [at a pipe].
**chupadero, -ra** *adj.* sucking. *2 m.* CHUPADOR 2.
**chupado, -da** *adj.* lean, emaciated.
**chupador, -ra** *adj.* sucking; absorbent. *2 m.* pacifier, teething ring, baby's coral.
**chupadura** *f.* suck, sucking.
**chupaflor** *m.* ORN. a humming bird.
**chupar** *tr.* to suck, draw; fig. *chuparse los dedos*, to eat, do or say something with much pleasure. *2* to absorb, imbibe. *3* to drain [money, etc.]; to

sponge. *4* (Am.) to smoke. *5* (Am.) to drink. *6 ref.* to become lean, emaciated.
**chupatintas** *m.* coll. office clerk.
**chupete** *m.* pacifier [nipplelike device for babies to suck]. *2 de ~*, fine, splendid.
**chupetear** *tr.* to suck gently and by starts.
**chupeteo** *m.* frequent sucking.
**chupetón** *m.* hard suck.
**chupón, -na** *adj.* sucking. *2* blotting [paper]. *3 m.* sucker, sponger, parasite. *4* HORT. sucker. *5* MACH. sucker [piston].
**churrasco** *m.* (Am.) barbecued steak. *2* steak, choice piece of meat.
**churrasquear** *tr.* (Am.) to barbecue.
**churre** *m.* thick, dirty grease. *2* greasy dirt.
**churretada** *f.* large dirty spot [on hands or face].
**churrete** *m.* dirty spot [on hands or face].
**churrería** *f.* shop where CHURROS are made and sold.
**churrero, -ra** *m.-f.* maker or seller of CHURROS.
**churriento, -ta** *adj.* dirty, greasy.
**churrigueresco, -ca** *adj.* F. ARTS Churrigueresque.
**churro, -rra** *adj.* coarse-wooled [sheep]. *2* coarse [wool]. *3 m.* a long cylindrical fritter.
**churrusco** *m.* burnt piece of bread.
**churumbel** *m.* coll. child.
**churumbela** *f.* MUS. kind of flageolet.
**chuscada** *f.* joke, pleasantry.
**chusco, -ca** *adj.* droll, funny. *2 m.* funny [person].
**chusma** *f.* rabble, mob. *2* galley slaves.
**chutar** *intr.* FOOTBALL to shoot.
**chuzo** *m.* short pike: fig. *caer* or *llover chuzos*, to rain pitchforks.
**chuzón, -na** *adj.* crafty, sly. *2* BURLÓN.

# D

**D, d** f. D, d, the fifth letter of the Spanish alphabet.
**daca** (word formed by *da,* and *acá*) give me.
**Dacia** f. pr. n. GEOG. Dacia.
**dacio, -cia** adj.-m. Dacian.
**dactilar** adj. digital, finger: *huella* ~, fingerprint.
**dáctilo** m. dactyl.
**dactilografía** f. typewriting.
**dactilógrafo, -fa** m.-f. typist.
**dactilología** f. dactylology.
**dactiloscopia** f. dactyloscopy.
**dádiva** f. gift, present.
**dadivoso, -sa** adj. bounteous, liberal.
**dado, -da** adj. given. *2 conj. dado que,* assuming that, if. *3 m.* ARCH. dado, die. *4* MACH. block. *5* die [used in gaming].
**dador, -ra** m.-f. giver. *2* bearer [of a letter]. *3* drawer [of a bill of exchange].
**daga** f. dagger. *2* line of bricks in a kiln.
**daguerrotipo** m. daguerreotype.
**daifa** f. concubine.
**¡dale!** or **¡dale que dale!** interj. at it again! [expressing displeasure at another's obstinacy]. *2 estar* ~ *que* ~, to insist, to persist.
**dalia** f. BOT. dahlia.
**Dalila** f. pr. n. Delilah.
**Dalmacia** f. pr. n. GEOG. Dalmatia.
**dálmata** adj.-n. Dalmatian.
**dalmática** f. dalmatic [vestment].
**dalmático, -ca** adj. Dalmatian.
**daltonismo** m. MED. Daltonism.
**dallar** tr. to scythe [mow with a scythe].
**dalle** m. scythe.
**dama** f. lady, dame. *2* lady in waiting. *3* mistress, concubine. *4* king [in draughts]. *5* queen [in chess]. *6* THEAT. actress: *primera* ~, leading lady. *7* FOUN. dam. *8* GAMO. *9* BOT. ~ *de noche,* night jasmine. *10 pl.* draughts, *checkers.
**damaceno, -na** adj. DAMASCENO.
**damajuana** f. demijohn.
**damasceno, -na** adj.-n. Damascene. *2 adj.-f.* BOT. damson [plum].
**Damasco** f. pr. n. GEOG. Damascus.
**damasco** m. damask [fabric]. *2* BOT. a variety of apricot.
**damasquinado, -da** adj. damascened. *2 m.* damascene work.
**damasquinar** tr. to damascene.
**damasquino, -na** adj. Damascene.

**damería** f. affected nicety, mincing. *2* scruple.
**damisela** f. young lady, damsel. *2* courtesan.
**damnificado, -da** m.-f. injured party.
**damnificar** tr. to damage, hurt, injure.
**dandi** m. dandy.
**danés, -sa** adj. Danish. *2 m.-f.* Dane. *3 m.* Danish [language].
**dango** m. ORN. gannet.
**danta** f. ZOOL. elk. *2* ZOOL. tapir.
**dantesco, -ca** adj. Dantesque.
**Danubio** m. pr. n. Danube.
**danza** f. dance; dancing: ~ *de cintas,* maypole dance. *2* HABANERA. *3* dubious or entangled affair.
**danzador, -ra** adj. dancing. *2 m.-f.* dancer.
**danzante, -ta** m.-f. dancer. *2* coll. active person, hustler. *3* coll. whippersnapper.
**danzar** intr. to dance. *2* to be [in an affair].
**danzarín, -na** m.-f. good dancer. *2* professional dancer. *3* coll. whippersnapper.
**danzón** m. a Cuban dance.
**dañable** adj. harmful. *2* condemnable.
**dañado, -da** adj. evil, wicked. *2* [of food, fruits, etc.] damaged, spoiled, tainted.
**dañar** tr. to harm, damage, injure, hurt. *2* to spoil, taint. *3 ref.* to become damaged, to spoil; to get hurt.
**dañino, -na** adj. harmful, destructive. *2* evil, wicked.
**daño** m. harm, damage, detriment, injury: *daños y perjuicios,* damages; *en* ~ *de,* to the detriment of. *2* hurt.
**dañoso, -sa** adj. harmful, noxious, damaging.
**dar** tr. to give [in nearly every sense], hand, deliver, grant, confer. *2* to produce, bear, yield [fruits, profits, etc.]. *3* to deal [cards]. *4* to produce, cause, excite; ~ *lástima,* to excite pity. *5* to strike [the hours]: *el reloj da las cinco,* the clock strikes five. *6* to show [at theatre, etc.]. *7* with some nouns it expresses the action implied by the noun: ~ *cabezadas,* to nod; ~ *comienzo,* or *principio,* to begin; ~ *gritos* or *voces,* to shout; ~ *un abrazo,* to embrace; ~ *un paseo,* to take a walk. *8 dar como* or *por,* to suppose, assume, consider, hold: ~ *como cierto,* to hold as true; ~ *por bueno,* to approve. *9* ~ *de puñetazos, tiros,* etc., to punch, shoot, etc.; ~ *de barniz, de pin-*

*tura,* etc., to overlay with varnish, paint, etc. *10* other senses: ~ *a conocer,* to make known; ~ *a entender,* to hint; ~ *a luz,* to give birth to; to publish: ~ *crédito a,* to believe; ~ *de lado,* to shun; ~ *de mano,* to leave, abandon; ~ *la enhorabuena,* to congratulate; ~ *que decir,* to set tongues wagging; ~ *que hacer,* to give trouble; ~ *que pensar,* to arouse suspicions, to set one thinking; ~ *señales,* to show sign; *no da pie con bola,* he does nothing right.
*11 intr.* to feel, to be stricken with or by: *me dio un dolor,* I was stricken by or with a pain. *12* ~ *a:* a) to overlook, open on, face: *esta ventana da a la calle,* the window overlooks the street. b) to work: ~ *a la bomba,* to work the pump. *13* ~ *con,* to meet, to find. *14* ~ *consigo en,* to land in. *15* ~ *contra,* to knock against. *16* ~ *de:* a) to fall on [one's head, etc.]. b) to give [food or drink]: ~ *de comer,* to feed. *17* ~ *en:* a) to take to, to acquire the habit of: *dio en salir todos los días,* he took to going out every day. b) to strike, hit, fall against: ~ *en el clavo,* to hit the nail on the head. c) to hit upon, to guess. *18 darle a uno por,* to take it into one's head; to take to. *19* other senses: ~ *al traste con,* to spoil, destroy, shatter; ~ *con uno en tierra,* to throw or bring one to the ground; ~ *de sí,* to give, yield, stretch. *20 ref.* to give oneself. *21* to yield, surrender, give in. *22* to take to: *darse a la bebida,* to take to drink. *23* [of things, events, etc.] to happen, exist, to be, to be given: *se da el caso,* (as) it happens, the case is. *24* other senses: *darse [uno] a conocer,* to identify oneself, to make oneself known; to allow one's real character to be seen; *darse la mano,* to shake hands; *darse por muerto,* to give oneself up for dead; *darse por vencido,* to give up.
¶ CONJUG.: INDIC. Pres.: *doy, das, da; damos, dais, dan.* | Imperf.: *daba, dabas,* etc. | Pret.: *di, diste, dio; dimos, disteis, dieron.* | Fut.: *daré, darás,* etc. | COND.: *daría, darías,* etc. | SUBJ. Pres.: *dé, des, dé; demos, deis, den.* | Imperf.: *diera, dieras,* etc., or *diese, dieses,* etc. | Fut.: *diere, dieres,* etc. | IMPER.: *da, dé; demos, dad, den.* | PAST. P.: *dado.* | GER.: *dando.*

**dardabasí** *m.* ORN. kite.
**Dardanelos** *m. pr. n.* GEOG. Dardanelles.
**dardo** *m.* dart [missile]. *2* cutting remark. *3* ICHTH. bleak.
**dares y tomares** *m. pl.* coll. disputes, discussions.
**Darío** *m. pr. n.* Darius.
**dársena** *f.* inner harbour, dock, basin.
**darvinismo** *m.* Darwinism.
**dasocracia, dasonomía** *f.* science of forestry.
**data** *f.* date [in documents, etc.]. *2* ACC. credit. *3 de larga* ~, very ancient.
**datar** *tr.* to date [mark with date]. *2* ACC. to credit on an account. *3 intr.* ~ *de,* to date from.
**dátil** *m.* BOT. date [fruit]. *2* ZOOL. date shell.
**datilera** *f.* BOT. date palm.
**dativo** *m.* GRAM. dative.
**dato** *m.* datum, fact. *2* document, testimony. *3* MAT. datum.
**David** *m. pr. n.* David.
1) **de** *f.* name of the letter *d.*
2) **de** *prep.* of [in practically every sense]. *2* from, about, for, on, by, at, out of, with: *viene* ~ *Madrid,* he comes from Madrid; *goma* ~ *mascar,* gum for chewing; *llorar* ~ *alegría,* to weep for joy; *un libro* ~ *matemáticas,* a book on mathematics; *la casa* ~ *la derecha,* the house on the

right; *un cuadro* ~ *Velázquez,* a painting by Velázquez; ~ *día,* by day; ~ *noche,* at night; ~ *diez uno,* one out of ten; *loco* ~ *rabia,* mad with anger. *3* if, should [conditional]: ~ *ir a pie, llegaríamos tarde,* if we went on foot, we'd arrive late. *4* [preceded by *más* or *menos*] than. *5* Other uses: *María Suárez* ~ *López,* Mrs. López, née Suárez; *este diablillo* ~ *criatura,* this imp of a child; *el bueno* ~ *Juan,* that good fellow John; ~ *pie,* standing up; ~ *un,* ~ *una,* at a, in one; ~ *uno en uno,* one by one; *¡pobre* ~ *mí!,* woe is me!
**dé** *irr.* V. DAR.
**deambular** *tr.* to walk, stroll.
**deán** *m.* ECCL. dean.
**deanato, deanazgo** *m.* ECCL. deanship.
**debajo** *adv.* underneath: ~ *de,* under, beneath; *por* ~, underneath; *por* ~ *de,* under, below.
**debate** *m.* debate. *3* altercation.
**debatir** *tr.* to debate, discuss.
**debe** *m.* COM. debit, debtor side of an account.
**debelador, -ra** *m.-f.* conqueror.
**debelar** *tr.* to conquer, to vanquish [in war].
1) **deber** *m.* duty obligation. *2* school work, homework.
2) **deber** *tr.* to owe. *2 aux.* [with an inf.] must, have to; ought to, should: *debo salir,* I must go out. *3* ~ *de,* must [expressing conjecture]: *deben de ser las cinco,* it must be five o'clock.
**debidamente** *adv.* duly, properly.
**debido, -da** *adj.* owed. *2* due, just, proper, right: *como es* ~, rightly, well, as it should be.
**débil** *adj.* weak, feeble. *2* slight, faint. *3* faint, sickly.
**debilidad** *f.* weakness, debility, feebleness.
**debilitación** *f.* debilitation. *2* weakness.
**debilitar** *tr.* to weaken, enfeeble, debilitate. *2 ref.* to weaken, become feeble, lose strength.
**débito** *m.* debt. *2* ~ *conyugal,* conjugal duty.
**debut** *m.* GALL. debut [first performance].
**debutante** *n.* débutante. *2* beginner.
**debutar** *intr.* GALL. to make one's debut.
**década** *f.* decade.
**decadencia** *f.* decadence, decline, decay.
**decadente** *adj.* decadent, declining.
**decaedro** *m.* GEOM. decahedron.
**decaer** *intr.* to decline, decay, be in decadence, fall, fall off, lessen.
**decágono, -na** *adj.-m.* GEOM. decagon.
**decagramo** *m.* decagram.
**decaído, -da** *adj.* declining. *2* low [sick person]. *3* ~ *de ánimo,* disheartened.
**decaimiento** *m.* decline, decay. *2* weakness.
**decalitro** *m.* decaliter.
**decálogo** *m.* decalogue.
**decampar** *intr.* [of an army] to decamp.
**decanato** *m.* deanship, deanery [of a faculty]; doyenship [of a body].
**decano** *m.* dean [of a faculty]. *2* doyen, dean [of a body].
**decantación** *f.* decantation.
**decantar** *tr.* to decant. *2* to overpraise.
**decapante** *adj.* scaling. *2* scaling product, scaler [metals], remover [paint].
**decapitación** *f.* beheading, decapitation.
**decapitar** *tr.* to behead, decapitate.
**decápodo, -da** *adj.-n.* ZOOL. decapod.
**decárea** *f.* decare.
**decasílabo, -ba** *adj.* decasyllabic. *2 m.* decasyllable.
**decena** *f.* ten [ten unities]. *2 pl.* ARITH. tens.

**decenal** *adj.* decennial.
**decencia** *f.* decency, propriety. *2* decorum, modesty. *3* cleanliness, tidiness. *4* honesty.
**deceno, -na** *adj.* tenth.
**decentar** *tr.* to begin the use of, to cut the first slice of. *2* to begin to impair [the health, etc.]. *3 ref.* to get bedsores. ¶ CONJUG. like *acertar.*
**decente** *adj.* decent. *2* proper, decorous, modest. *3* clean, tidy. *4* correct, hono(u)rable.
**decenviro** *m.* decemvir.
**decepción** *f.* disappointment, disillusionment. *2* deceit.
**decepcionar** *tr.* to disappoint, disillusion.
**deciárea** *f.* deciare.
**decibel, decibelio** *m.* PHYS. decibel.
**decididamente** *adv.* decidedly. *2* resolutely.
**decidido, -da** *adj.* decided. *2* determined.
**decidir** *tr.* to decide, settle. *2* to decide, determine, resolve [bring or come to a resolution]. *3 ref.* to make up one's mind.
**decidor, -ra** *adj. m.-f.* good talker, witty talker.
**decigramo** *m.* decigram.
**decilitro** *m.* deciliter.
**décima** *f.* tenth [tenth part]. *2* a ten-line stanza.
**decimal** *adj.-m.* decimal. *2* pertaining to tithes.
**decímetro** *m.* decimetre, decimeter.
**décimo, -ma** *adj.* tenth. *2 m.-f.* tenth. *3 m.* tenth part of lottery ticket.
**decimoctavo, -va** *adj.* eighteenth.
**decimocuarto, -ta** *adj.* fourteenth.
**decimonono, -na** *adj.* nineteenth.
**decimoquinto, -ta** *adj.* fifteenth.
**decimoséptimo, -ma** *adj.* seventeenth.
**decimosexto, -ta** *adj.* sixteenth.
**decimotercero, -ra; decimotercio, -cia** *adj.* thirteenth.
1) **decir** *tr.* to say, to talk, tell, speak: ~ *bien de,* to say well of, to speak well of; ~ *entre sí* or *para sí,* to say to oneself; ~ *mentiras,* to tell lies; ~ *misa,* to say mass; ~ *por* ~, to talk for talking's sake; ~ *verdad,* to speak the truth; ¡*diga!,* hello! [answering the telephone]; *el qué dirán,* what people will say; *querer* ~, to mean; *como quien dice, como si dijéramos,* so to speak; *es* ~, that is to say; *mejor dicho,* more properly speaking, rather. *2* to denote, show. *3* [with *bien* or *mal*] to suit, become, or not to suit, not to become. *4 ref.* to say to oneself. *5* to pretend to be. *6 se dice,* they say, it is said. ¶ CONJUG.: INDIC. Pres.: *digo, dices, dice;* decimos, decís, *dicen.* | Imperf.: decía, decías, etc. | Pret.: *dije, dijiste, dijo; dijimos, dijisteis, dijeron.* | Fut.: *diré, dirás,* etc. | COND.: *diría, dirías,* etc. | SUBJ. Pres.: *diga, digas, diga; digamos, digáis, digan.* | Imperf.: *dijera, dijeras, dijera; dijéramos, dijerais, dijeran* or *dijese, dijeses, dijese; dijésemos, dijeseis, dijesen.* | Fut.: *dijere; dijeres,* etc. | IMPER.: *di, diga; digamos,* decid, *digan.* | PAST. PART.: *dicho.* | GER.: *diciendo.*
2) **decir** *m.* say, saying, language: *al* ~ *de,* according to [someone]; *es un* ~, it is a manner of speaking. *2 el* ~ *de las gentes,* the opinion of the people.
**decisión** *f.* decision [act], issue; judgement, verdict; order, command. *2* decision, resoluteness.
**decisivo, -va** *adj.* decisive, final, conclusive.
**declamación** *f.* declamation.
**declamar** *intr.-tr.* to declaim.
**declamatorio, -ria** *adj.* declamatory.
**declaración** *f.* declaration. *2* statement. *3* LAW deposition. *4* expounding, explanation. *5* proposal, declaration of love. *6* BRIDGE bid.

**declaradamente** *adv.* openly, declaredly.
**declarado, -da** *adj.* declared.
**declarante** *m.-f.* LAW deponent. *2* BRIDGE bidder.
**declarar** *tr.* to declare. *2* to state, make known, avow. *3* to expound, explain. *4* LAW to find [guilty or not guilty]; to decide. *5 intr.* to testify, make a statement. *6 ref.* to declare oneself. *7* to let one's feelings, purposes, etc., be known; to propose [to a woman]. *8* [of war] to be declared. *9* [of a fire, an epidemic, etc.] to start, break out.
**declaratorio, -ria** *adj.* explanatory. *2* LAW declaratory.
**declinable** *adj.* GRAM. declinable.
**declinación** *adj.* decline, fall, descent. *2* ASTR., MAGN. declination. *3* GRAM. declension.
**declinante** *adj.* declining.
**declinar** *intr.* to decline, lean, deviate. *4* to decline, decay, sink, fall off, decrease; draw to close. *4* ASTR., MAGN. to have declination. *5 tr.* to decline, renounce. *6* GRAM. to decline.
**declive** *m.* declivity, slope, descent.
**decocción** *f.* decoction.
**decolorar** *tr.* to decolo(u)rize.
**decolorante** *adj.-m.* decolorant.
**decomisar** *tr.* COMISAR.
**decomiso** *m.* COMISO.
**decoración** *f.,* **decorado** *m.* decoration, adorning. *2* decoration, adornment. *3* THEAT. scenery, setting.
**decorador, -ra** *m.-f.* decorator.
**decorar** *tr.* to decorate, adorn, embellish.
**decorativo, -va** *adj.* decorative.
**decoro** *m.* decorum, propriety, decency, dignity. *2* circumspection, gravity. *3* modesty, honour. *5* honour, respect, reverence [due to a person].
**decoroso, -sa** *adj.* decorous, decent.
**decrecer** *intr.* to decrease, diminish.
**decreciente** *adj.* decreasing, diminishing.
**decrecimiento** *m.* decrease, diminution.
**decremento** *m.* decrement, decrease.
**decrepitar** *intr.* to decrepitate [crackle under heat].
**decrépito, -ta** *adj.* decrepit.
**decrepitud** *f.* decrepitude.
**decretal** *adj.-f.* decretal.
**decretar** *tr.* to decree, ordain, resolve, determine.
**decreto** *m.* decree. *2* an order of a judge.
**decúbito** *m.* decubitus, lying down position.
**décuplo, -pla** *adj.-m.* decuple.
**decurión** *m.* decurion.
**decurso** *m.* course, lapse [of time].
**decusado, -da; decuso, -sa** *adj.* BOT. decussate(d.
**dechado** *m.* example, model, pattern. *2* sampler [to learn needlework].
**dedada** *f.* small portion [of honey, etc.].
**dedal** *m.* thimble. *2* thimbleful. *3* leather fingerstail.
**dedalera** *f.* BOT. foxglove.
**Dédalo** *m. pr. n.* MYTH. Daedalus.
**dédalo** *m.* labyrinth, maze.
**dedicación** *f.* dedication, consecration. *2* dedication [dedicatory inscription on a building].
**dedicar** *tr.* to dedicate [a church, a book, etc.]. *2* to autograph [a photograph]. *3* to dedicate, devote. *4 ref. dedicarse a,* to devote oneself to, to make a specialty of.
**dedicatoria** *f.* dedication [in a book, etc.]; autograph [on a photograph].
**dedil** *m.* fingerstall.
**dedillo** *m.* little finger. *2 saber una cosa al* ~, to have something at one's finger tips.

**dedo** *m.* finger; toe: ~ *de la mano,* finger; ~ *del pie,* toe; ~ *anular,* ring finger; ~ *meñique,* little finger; ~ *del medio* or *del corazón,* middle finger; ~ *gordo,* thumb; big toe; ~ *pulgar,* thumb; ~ *índice,* forefinger, index; *cogerse los dedos,* to burn one's fingers; *chuparse los dedos,* to enjoy, relish [something] greatly; *no mamarse el ~,* to be no fool; *poner el ~ en la llaga,* to put one's finger on the sore spot; *señalar a uno con el ~,* to point one's finger at someone. *2* finger's breath; fig. very small distance: *estar a dos dedos de,* to be within an ace of.

**deducción** *f.* deduction, inference, conclusion. *2* deduction, rebate, discount.

**deducible** *adj.* deducible, inferable. *2* COM. deductible, allowable.

**deducir** *tr.* to deduce, deduct, infer. *2* to deduct, rebate, discount. *3* LAW to put forward, allege. ¶ CONJUG. like *conducir.*

**deductivo, -va** *adj.* deductive.

**deduje, dedujera, deduzco, deduzca,** etc. *irr.* V. DEDUCIR.

**defalcar** *tr.* DESFALCAR.

**defecación** *f.* defecation.

**defecar** *tr.-intr.* to defecate.

**defasaje** *m.* ELECT. dephasing, phaseshift, phase difference. *2* gap, difference.

**defección** *f.* defection, desertion.

**defectillo** *m. dim.* slight fault or defect.

**defectivo, -va** *adj.* defective, faulty. *2* GRAM. defective.

**defecto** *m.* defect, fault, failing, blemish, imperfection. *2* default, lack: *en ~ de,* in default of.

**defectuoso, -sa** *adj.* defective, faulty.

**defendedor, -ra** *adj.* defending. *2 m.-f.* defender.

**defender** *tr.-ref.* to defend. ¶ CONJUG. like *entender.*

**defendible** *adj.* defensible.

**defensa** *f.* defence, *defense. *2* protection, guard. *3 m.* FOOTBALL back. *4 f. pl.* FORT. defences. *5* NAUT. fenders, skids. *6* horns [of bull], antlers [of deer], tusks [of elephant or boar].

**defensión** *f.* defence, protection.

**defensivo, -va** *adj.* defensive. *2 f.* defensive: *estar a la ~,* to be on the defensive.

**defensor, -ra** *adj.* defending, protecting. *2 m.-f.* defender. *3* advocate, supporter. *4* LAW counsel for the defence.

**deferencia** *f.* deference.

**deferente** *adj.* deferential. *2* deferring [to another's opinion]. *3* ANAT. deferent.

**deferir** *intr.* to defer [to another's wishes, opinions, etc.]. ¶ CONJUG. like *hervir.*

**deficiencia** *f.* defect, fault, deficiency.

**deficiente** *adj.* deficient, faulty.

**deficientemente** *adv.* insufficiently, poorly.

**déficit** *m.* deficit, shortage.

**deficitario, -ria** *adj.* showing a deficit.

**defiendo, defienda,** etc. *irr.* V. DEFENDER.

**defiero, defiera,** etc. *irr.* V. DEFERIR.

**definición** *f.* definition.

**definido, -da** *adj.* definite. *2* defined, sharp. *3 m.* defined thing.

**definidor, -ra** *adj.* defining. *2 m.-f.* definer. *3* ECCL. definitor.

**definir** *tr.* to define. *2* PAINT. to finish, complete.

**definitivamente** *adv.* finally. *2* for good, once and for all. *3* decisively.

**definitivo, -va** *adj.* definitive. *2 f. en definitiva,* after all, in conclusion, in short.

**deflación** *f.* ECON. deflation.

**deflagración** *f.* deflagration.

**deflagrar** *intr.* to deflagrate.

**deflector** *m.* deflector, baffle. *2* NAUT. deflector.

**deflegmar** *tr.* CHEM. to dephlegmate.

**defoliación** *f.* BOT. defoliation.

**deformación** *f.* deformation. *2* MECH. distorsion.

**deformar** *tr.* to deform, misshape, put out of shape. *2 ref.* to become deformed.

**deforme** *adj.* deformed, misshapen, ugly.

**deformidad** *f.* deformity, ugliness. *2* gross error.

**defraudación** *f.* defraudation.

**defraudador, -ra** *m.-f.* defrauder.

**defraudar** *tr.* to defraud, rob, cheat. *2* to frustrate, disappoint. *3* to deceive [hopes].

**defunción** *f.* death, decease, demise.

**degeneración** *f.* degeneration. *2* degeneracy.

**degenerado, -da** *adj.-n.* degenerate.

**degenerar** *intr.* to degenerate.

**deglución** *f.* deglutition, swallowing.

**deglutir** *tr.* to swallow.

**degollación** *f.* decollation, beheading.

**degolladero** *m.* neck [of animals]. *2* slaughterhouse. *3* scaffold where people were beheaded.

**degolladura** *f.* slash, gash in the throat. *2* joint [between bricks]. *3* slender part of balusters.

**degollante** *adj.* presumptuous, boring. *2 m.-f.* bore, nuisance.

**degollar** *tr.* to decollate, behead; to cut the throat. *2* to cut [a garment] low in the neck. *3* fig. to destroy, ruin. ¶ CONJUG. like *contar.*

**degollina** *f.* massacre, slaughter, butchery.

**degradación** *f.* degradation.

**degradante** *adj.* degrading.

**degradar** *tr.* to degrade. *2 ref.* to degrade oneself, to become degraded.

**degüello** *m.* decollation; throat-cutting: *entrar a ~,* to take a town without giving quarter. *2* slender part, neck [of dart, etc.].

**degüello, degüelle,** etc. *irr.* V. DEGOLLAR.

**degustación** *f.* tasting, degustation.

**dehesa** *f.* pasture ground.

**dehiscente** *adj.* BOT. dehiscent.

**deicida** *adj.* deicidal. *2 m.-f.* deicide [person].

**deicidio** *m.* deicide, slaying of Jesus.

**deidad** *f.* deity.

**deificar** *tr.* to deify. *2 ref.* THEOL. to become deified [by divine union].

**deífico, -ca** *adj.* deific.

**deísmo** *m.* deism.

**deísta** *adj.* deistic. *2m.-f.* deist.

**dejación** *f.* abandonment, relinquishment.

**dejadez** *f.* laziness, negligence. *2* slovenliness, neglect [of one's things or oneself].

**dejado, -da** *adj.* lazy, negligent, slovenly. *2* lowspirited. *3 p. p.* of DEJAR.

**dejamiento** *m.* DEJACIÓN. *2* laziness, slovenliness. *3* lassitude. *4* dejection. *5* indifference.

**dejar** *tr.* to leave: ~ *aparte,* to leave aside; ~ *atrás,* to leave behind; to excel, surpass; ~ *en paz,* to leave alone, let be; ~ *por hacer,* to leave undone, put off doing. *2* to abandon, relinquish, let go. *3* let: ~ *caer,* to let fall; ~ *que ruede la bola,* to let things alone. *5* to abandon, forsake. *6* to commit, entrust, leave in charge. *7* to give up. *8* to deposit. *9* to yield, bring [as a profit]. *10* to lend, *loan. *11* to bequeath. *12* ~ *de,* to omit, to stop, cease, desist; ~ *de escribir,* to stop writing; *no ~ de tener,* not to lack, not to be without. *13* COM. ~ *de cuenta,* to refuse delivery [of goods]. *14* ~ *frío* or *helado,* to surprise, astound. *15* ~ *plantado,* to abandon; to disappoint. *16* ~ *seco,* to kill dead. *17 ref.* to abandon oneself; to neglect oneself. *18* to allow or let oneself [die, be seen, etc.]. *19 dejarse caer* [of a person], to drop or fall down purposely; fig. to turn up unexpectedly; fig. to let drop, to hint something. *20 dejarse de rodeos*, to come to the point; *déjate de tonterías*, quit your nonsense. *21 dejarse olvidado*, to forget; to omit, leave out. *22 dejarse ver*, to show, be easy to see; to appear in public, at friend's homes, etc.

**deje** *m.* slight accent, lilt, special inflection.

**dejillo** *m.* DEJO 2. *2* DEJO 3.

**dejo** *m.* DEJACIÓN 1. *2* peculiar accent or inflexion in speaking. *3* aftertaste. *4* lassitude.

**de jure** *adv.* de jure.

**del** contraction of DE AND EL; OF THE.

**delación** *f.* accusation, denunciation, information.

**delantal** *m.* apron; pinafore.

**delante** *adv.* before, in front; ahead: ~ *de*, before, in front of, in the presence of: ahead of; in preference to; *por* ~, before; ahead.

**delantera** *f.* front, fore part. *2* front row [in theaters, etc.]. *3* lead, advance, advantage; *coger* or *tomar la ~ a*, to get ahead of, to outstrip, to get the start of: *tomar la ~*, to take the lead.

**delantero, -ra** *adj.* fore, front, foremost, first. *2 m.* SPORT. forward.

**delatar** *tr.* to accuse, denounce, inform against. *2* to betray, disclose. *3 ref.* to betray oneself.

**delator, -ra** *adj.* accusing, denouncing. *2* betraying, disclosing. *3 m.-f.* accuser, denouncer, informer.

**delco** *m.* AUTO. distributor.

**dele** *m.* PRINT. dele.

**delectación** *f.* delectation, pleasure.

**delegación** *f.* delegation. *2* office of a delegate. *3* COM. branch.

**delegado, -da** *adj.* delegated. *2 m.-f.* delegate, representative, commissioner, deputy.

**delegar** *tr.* to delegate.

**deleitable** *adj.* DELEITOSO.

**deleitar** *tr.* to delight, please. *2 ref.* to delight, take delight or pleasure.

**deleite** *m.* pleasure, delight, gratification.

**deleitoso, -sa** *adj.* delightful, pleasing, pleasurable.

**deletéreo, -a** *adj.* deleterious, poisonous.

**deletrear** *tr.* to spell, spell out [read by spelling].

**deletreo** *m.* spelling out [of words].

**deleznable** *adj.* frail, perishable, weak. *2* crumbly. *3* slippery.

**délfico, -ca** *adj.* Delphian, Delphic.

**delfín** *m.* dauphin. *2* ZOOL., ASTR. dolphin.

**delfina** *f.* dauphiness.

**delga** *f.* ELECT. commutator bar.

**delgadez** *f.* thinness, leanness, slenderness, tenuity. *3* acuteness, subtlety.

**delgado, -da** *adj.* thin, lean, slender, slim, lank. *2* tenuous, delicate. *3* acute, subtle. *4 m.* NAUT. dead rise. *5* flank [of an animal].

**delgaducho, -cha** *adj.* thinnish, rather emaciated.

**deliberación** *f.* deliberation [weighing in mind]. *2* deliberation, discussion, debate.

**deliberadamente** *adv.* deliberately, on purpose.

**deliberado, -da** *adj.* deliberate, intentional.

**deliberante** *adj.* deliberating, deliberative.

**deliberar** *intr.* to deliberate, consider, weigh in mind. *2* to deliberate, take counsel together, hold debate. *3 tr.* to determine, resolve.

**deliberativo, -va** *adj.* deliberative [pertaining to deliberation].

**delicadeza** *f.* delicateness, delicacy. *2* fineness. *3* softness, tenderness. *4* scrupulousness, honesty.

**delicado, -da** *adj.* delicate. *2* poor [health]. *3* subtle, ingenious. *4* touchy, fastidious. *5* scrupulous, honest.

**delicaducho, -cha** *adj.* sickly, of weak health.

**delicia** *f.* delight.

**delicioso, -sa** *adj.* delicious, delightful.

**delictivo, -va; delictuoso, -sa** *adj.* criminal, unlawful.

**delicuescente** *adj.* deliquescent.

**delimitación** *f.* delimitation.

**delimitar** *tr.* to delimit, delimitate.

**delincuencia** *f.* delinquency, criminality.

**delincuente** *adj.* delinquent, offending. *2 m.-f.* delinquent, criminal, offender.

**delineación** *f.* delineation, draft, drawing in outline.

**delineante** *adj.* delineating. *2* draughtsman, draftsman [who draws plans, etc.].

**delinear** *tr.* to delineate.

**delinquir** *intr.* to commit a transgression, offence or crime.

**deliquio** *m.* fainting, ecstasy, rapture.

**delirante** *adj.* delirious, raving.

**delirar** *intr.* to rave, wander, be delirious. *2* to rant, talk nonsense. *3* ~ *por*, to be mad for.

**delirio** *m.* delirium, raving.

**delirium tremens** *m.* MED. delirium tremens.

**delito** *m.* transgression, offence, crime.

**delta** *f.* delta [Greek letter]. *2* GEOG. delta.

**deltoides** *adj. m.* ANAT. deltoid [muscle].

**deludir** *tr.* to delude.

**delusorio, -ria** *adj.* delusive, delusory.

**demacración** *f.* emaciation.

**demacrar** *tr.* to emaciate. *2 ref.* to waste away become emaciated.

**demagogia** *f.* demagogism; demagogy.

**demagógico, -ca** *adj.* demagogic.

**demagogo, -ga** *m.-f.* demagogue.

**demanda** *f.* petition, request. *2* COM. demand. *3* question, inquiry. *4* enterprise, endeavour. *5* LAW claim, plaint, complaint: *entablar* ~, to begin an action at law. *6* search, quest: *ir en* ~ *de*, to go in search of, go looking for.

**demandadero, -ra** *m.-f.* messenger [in a convent, etc.].

**demandado, -da** *m.-f.* LAW. defendant.

**demandante** *m.-f.* LAW claimant, plaintiff.

**demandar** *tr.* to demand, ask for, beg, request. *2* to ask, inquire. *3* to wish for. *4* LAW to sue.

**demarcación** *f.* demarcation.

**demarcar** *tr.* to demarcate. *2* NAUT. to determine the bearings of [a ship].

**demás** *adj.* [with *lo, la, los, las*] the other, the rest of the. *2* in plural, may be used without article: *y* ~ *vehículos*, and other vehicles. *3 pron.* other, others, the rest: *los* ~, others, other people; *lo* ~, the rest; *por lo* ~, as to the rest, apart from this; *y* ~, and so on, etcetera. *4 adv.* besides. *5 por* ~, in vain; excessively.

**demasía** *f.* excess, superabundance: *en* ~, too much, excessively. *2* boldness, audacity. *3* insolence, disrespect. *4* outrage. *5* iniquity, misdeed.

1) **demasiado** *adv.* too, excessively; too much. *2 pron.* too much.

2) **demasiado, -da** *adj.* too much, too many.

**demencia** *f.* insanity, madness.

**demente** *adj.* demented, mad, insane. *2 m.-f.* lunatic, maniac, insane person.

**demérito** *m.* want of worth or merit. 2 demerit, that which divests of worth or merit.
**demiurgo** *m.* demiurge.
**democracia** *f.* democracy.
**demócrata** *adj.* democratic. 2 *m.-f.* democrat.
**democrático, -ca** *adj.* democratic.
**democratizar** *tr.* to democratize.
**Demócrito** *m. pr. n.* Democritus.
**demografía** *f.* demography.
**demoledor, -ra** *adj.* demolishing, destructive. 2 *m.-f.* demolisher.
**demoler** *tr.* to demolish, pull down, destroy.
**demolición** *f.* demolition, destruction.
**demoníaco, -ca** *adj.* demoniac(al.
**demonio** *m.* demon, devil, evil spirit: *ser un* ~, fig. to be very wicked, roguish or cleever. 2 *interj.* the deuce!
**demonolatría** *f.* demonolatry.
**demontre** *m.* coll. devil. 2 *interj.* the deuce!
**demora** *f.* delay: *sin* ~, without delay. 2 NAUT. bearing.
**demorar** *tr.* to delay, retard. 2 *intr.* to delay, tarry, linger. 3 NAUT. to bear.
**Demóstenes** *m. pr. n.* Demosthenes.
**demostrable** *adj.* demonstrable.
**demostración** *f.* demonstration, show. 2 demonstration, proof, evidence.
**demostrador, -ra** *m.-f.* demonstrator.
**demostrar** *tr.* to demonstrate, show, prove. 2 *ref.* to show oneself. ¶ CONJUG. like *contar*.
**demostrativo, -va** *adj.* demonstrative. 2 *adj.-m.* GRAM. demonstrative.
**demótico, -ca** *adj.* demotic.
**demudar** *tr.* to change, alter, vary. 2 *ref.* to become disturbed, change colour or countenance.
**demuelo, demuela,** etc. *irr.* V. DEMOLER.
**demuestro, demuestre,** etc. *irr.* V. DEMOSTRAR.
**denario, -ria** *adj.* denary. 2 *m.* denarius.
**dendrita** *f.* ANAT., GEOL. dendrite.
**denegación** *f.* denial, refusal.
**denegar** *tr.* to deny, refuse. ¶ CONJUG. like *acertar*.
**denegatorio, -ria** *adj.* denying.
**dengoso, -sa** *adj.* finicky, mincing, affected.
**dengue** *m.* mincing, affectation of delicacy. 2 MED. dengue, influenza.
**deniego, deniegue,** etc. *irr.* V. DENEGAR.
**denigrante** *adj.* denigrating; insulting.
**denigrar** *tr.* to denigrate, debase, vilify. 2 to insult.
**denodadamente** *adv.* bravely, boldly, intrepidly. 2 stoutly, determinedly.
**denodado, -da** *adj.* bold, brave, intrepid, resolute.
**denominación** *f.* denomination, name, designation.
**denominado** *adj.* MAT. compoud [number].
**denominador, -ra** *adj.* denominating. 2 *m.* MATH. denominator.
**denominar** *tr.* to denominate, call, give a name to.
**denostador** *m.-f.* reviler, railer, insulter.
**denostar** *tr.* to revile, rail, insult. ¶ CONJUG. like *contar*.
**denotación** *f.* denotation.
**denotar** *tr.* to denote.
**densidad** *f.* density [closeness, compactness]. 2 obscurity, confusion. 3 PHYS. density. 4 ~ *de población*, density of population.
**densificar** *tr.* to densify.
**denso, -sa** *adj.* dense, close, compact, thick. 2 dark, confused.
**dentado, -da** *adj.* dentate, toothed, cogged: *rueda dentada*, cogwheel. 2 *m.* MACH. teeth [of a wheel]. 3 PHILAT. perforation.

**dentadura** *f.* denture, set of teeth.
**dental** *adj.* dental. 2 *m.* ploughshare bed.
**dentar** *tr.* to tooth, furnish with teeth or cogs; to indent, cut into teeth. 2 *intr.* to teethe, cut one's teeth. ¶ CONJUG. like *acertar*.
**dentario, -ria** *adj.* dental.
**dentellada** *f.* bite, biting: *a dentelladas*, with the teeth. 2 mark made by the teeth.
**dentellado, -da** *adj.* dentated. 2 HER. dentelated.
**dentellar** *intr.* to have the teeth chattering.
**dentellear** *tr.* to bite, nibble at.
**dentellón** *m.* cam, tooth [of lock]. 2 ARCH. dentil. 3 ARCH. tooth [of toothing].
**dentera** *f.* tooth edge. 2 coll. envy. 3 coll. desire. 4 *dar* ~, to set the teeth on edge; to awaken desire
**dentición** *f.* dentition, teething.
**denticulado, -da** *adj.* denticulate.
**denticulo** *m.* ARCH. dentil. 2 denticle, dentation.
**dentífrico, -ca** *adj.* tooth [paste, powder, etc.]. 2 *m.* dentifrice.
**dentina** *f.* ANAT. dentine.
**dentirrostro, -tra** *adj.* ORN. dentirostral, dentirostrate. 2 *m.* ORN. dentiroster.
**dentista** *m.* dentist.
**dentón, -na** *adj.* DENTUDO. 2 *m.* ICHTH. dentex.
**dentro** *adv.* in, inside, within: ~ *de un sobre*, in an envelope; ~ *de una hora*, within an hour; ~ *de poco*, soon, shortly; *de* ~, from the inside; *por* ~, inside, inwardly, on the inside.
**dentudo, -da** *adj.* big-toothed.
**denudación** *f.* denudation.
**denudar** *tr.* ZOOL., BOOT., GEOL. to denude, lay bare. 2 *ref.* to be denuded.
**denuedo** *m.* bravery, intrepidity, vigor.
**denuesto** *m.* insult, abuse.
**denuncia** *f.* denouncement. 2 report [of a transgression]. 3 denunciation [of a treaty]. 4 MIN. registration [of a mine or claim].
**denunciación** *f.* denouncing, denouncement.
**denunciante** *adj.* denouncing. 2 *m.-f.* denouncer.
**denunciar** *tr.* to denounce. 2 to inform against, to accuse. 3 to report [the commission of a transgression or offence]. 4 to denounce [a treaty, etc.]. 5 MIN. to denounce.
**deontología** *f.* deontology.
**deontológico, -ca** *adj.* deontological.
**deparar** *tr.* to afford, furnish, offer, present.
**departamental** *adj.* departmental.
**departamento** *m.* department. 2 district. 3 compartment, section. 4 naval district. 5 (Am.) apartment.
**departir** *intr.* to chat, talk, converse.
**depauperar** *tr.* to depauperate, impoverish, weaken, exhaust. 2 *ref.* to become depauperate.
**dependencia** *f.* dependence, dependency [subordination, subjection]. 2 branch office, section. 3 affair, errand. 4 staff, personnel, employees. 6 *pl.* accessories. 7 outbuildings.
**depender** *intr.* ~ *de*, to depend on; be subordinate to.
**dependienta** *f.* female employee or shop assistant.
**dependiente** *adj.* depending, dependent, subordinate. 2 *m.* clerk, salesman, shop assistant, employee. 3 subordinate.
**depilación** *f.* depilation.
**depilar** *tr.* to depilate.
**depilatorio, -ria** *adj.-m.* depilatory.
**deplorable** *adj.* deplorable, sad, lamentable.
**deplorar** *tr.* to deplore, lament, regret.
**depondré, depondría,** etc. *irr.* V. DEPONER.

**deponente** *adj.* GRAM. deponent. *2 m.-f.* LAW deponent.

**deponer** *tr.* to lay aside, set aside [fears, etc.]. *2* to lay down [one's arms]. *3* to depose, remove from office. *4* to take down. *5 tr.-intr.* LAW to depose, depone. *6 intr.* to go to stool. ¶ CONJUG. like *poner.*

**depongo, deponga,** etc. *irr.* V. DEPONER.

**deportación** *f.* deportation, exile, transportation.

**deportar** *tr.* to deport, exile, transport.

**deporte** *m.* sport [outdoor pastime]. *2* amusement, recreation.

**deportismo** *m.* sports, sporting.

**deportista** *m.* sportsman. *2 f.* sportswoman. *3 m.-f.* sport fan.

**deportividad** *f.* sportsmanship.

**deportivo, -va** *adj.* sports, sporting, sportive. *2* sportsmanlike.

**deposición** *f.* exposition, declaration. *2* deposal, deposition [removal from office]. *3* LAW deposition; sworn evidence. *4* evacuation of bowels.

**depositante** *m. f.* depositor.

**depositar** *tr.* to deposit. *2* to place, put. *3* to check [luggage]. *4 intr.* [of dust, a sediment, etc.] to settle, deposit.

**depositaría** *f.* place where deposits are made. *2* public treasury.

**depositario, -ria** *m.-f.* depositary. *2* public treasurer.

**depósito** *m.* deposit; trust: *en* ~, on deposit; in trust. *2* precipitation, sediment. *3* depot, store, storehouse, warehouse, depository, repository. *4* tank, reservoir: ~ *de gasolina,* AUTO. gas tank. *5* well [of a fountain pen]. *6* ~ *de equipajes,* checkroom.

**depravación** *f.* depravation, depravity.

**depravado, -da** *adj.* bad, depraved.

**depravar** *tr.* to deprave, corrupt. *2 ref.* to become depraved, dissolute.

**deprecación** *f.* entreaty, prayer, imploration.

**deprecar** *tr.* to entreat, pray, implore.

**deprecativo, -va; deprecatorio, -ria** *adj.* entreating.

**depreciación** *f.* depreciation [in value].

**depreciar** *tr.* to depreciate [lessen in value]. *2 ref.* to depreciate [become depreciated].

**depredación** *f.* depredation. *2* malversation.

**depredar** *tr.* to depredate, plunder, pillage.

**depresión** *f.* depression [act of depressing]. *2* pression [sunken place], hollow, dip. *3* dejection, low spirits. *4* ASTR., MED., METEOR. depression.

**depresivo, -va** *adj.* depressive.

**depresor, -ra** *adj.* depressing. *2 m.* ANAT., SURG. depressor.

**deprimente** *adj.* depressing, depressive. *2* humiliating.

**deprimir** *tr.* to depress [press down, cause to sink]. *2* to humiliate, belittle. *3 ref.* to become depressed, sunken. *4* to feel humiliated. *5* [of a line or a surface] to dip.

**depuesto** *p. p.* of DEPONER.

**depuración** *f.* depuration, purification. *2* POL. purge.

**depurado, -da** *adj.* pure, purified.

**depurar** *tr.* to depurate, purify. *2* POL. to purge.

**depurativo, -va** *adj.-m.* MED. depurative.

**depuse, depusiera,** etc. *irr.* V. DEPONER.

**derecha** *f.* right; right-hand side, right side; *a la* ~, to the right, on the right-hand side. *2* right hand. *3* POL. right. *4 adv. a derechas,* well, right, rightly.

**derechazo** *m.* BULLF. pass with the right hand. *2* BOX. right.

**derechista** *m.-f.* POL. member of the right.

**derecho, -cha** *adj.* right, right-hand [opposite to left]. *2* straight. *3* standing, upright. *4* just, reasonable. *5* right-handed. *6 adv.* straight, straight on, directly. *7 m.* right [that to which one is entitled]: justice, equity: ~ *de propiedad literaria,* copyright; *derechos del hombre,* rights of man; *tener* ~ *a,* to be entitled to; *de* ~, de jure, by right. *8* law [body of rules or laws]: ~ *canónico,* canon law; ~ *civil,* civil law; ~ *mercantil,* commercial law; ~ *natural,* natural law. *9* law [legal science or learning]. *10* exemption, grant, privilege. *11* right side, outside [of cloth, etc.]. *12* straight way; *ir por derecho,* to go straight. *13 pl.* fees, dues, taxes, duties: *derechos de aduana,* customs duties; *derechos de autor,* royalties, copyright; *derechos reales,* inheritance tax; duty on transfer of property.

**derechura** *f.* straightness, right way: *en* ~, directly, straight.

**deriva** *f.* NAUT., AER. drift, drifting: *ir a la* ~, to drift, be adrift.

**derivable** *adj.* derivable.

**derivación** *f.* derivation, descent. *2* inference. *3* drawing off [water, etc.] from a stream or source. *4* GRAM., MATH., MED. derivation. *5* ELECT. branch. *6* ELECT. shunt, shunt connection: *en* ~, shunt, shunted.

**derivado, -da** *adj.* derived, derivative. *2 m.* GRAM., CHEM. derivative. *3 f.* MATH. derivate, derivative.

**derivar** *tr.* to lead, conduct. *2* to derive. *3* ELECT. to shunt. *4 intr.-ref.* to derive, be derived. *5* AER., NAUT. to drift.

**derivativo, -va** *adj.* GRAM. derivative. *2 adj.-m.* MED. derivative.

**derivo** *m.* derivation, origin.

**dermatoesqueleto** *m.* ZOOL. dermatoskeleton.

**dermatología** *f.* dermatology.

**dermatólogo** *m.* dermatologist.

**dérmico, -ca** *adj.* dermic, dermal.

**dermis** *f.* ANAT. derma, dermis.

**derogable** *adj.* repealable, that can be abolished or annulled.

**derogación** *f.* abolishment, repeal, revocation.

**derogar** *tr.* to abolish, repeal, revoke. *2* to destroy, reform.

**derrama** *f.* apportionment of a tax, assessment or contribution. *3* special tax.

**derramamiento** *m.* overflowing, spilling. *2* outpouring. *3* shedding [of tears, etc.]. *4* scatterring.

**derramar** *tr.* to pour out, to spill. *2* to shed [blood, tears, etc.]. *3* to scatter. *4* to spread [news]. *5 ref.* to overflow, run over; to spill [be spilled]. *6* to scatter, disperse [be dispersed].

**derrame** *m.* DERRAMAMIENTO. *2* leakage [of liquids]. *3* ARCH. splay. *4* declivity, slope. *5* NAUT. draft [of a sail]. *6* MED. effusion; discharge; ~ *cerebral,* cerebral haemorrhage.

**derramo** *m.* ARCH. splay.

**derrapar** *intr.* AUTO. to skid.

**derredor** *m. al* ~, *en* ~, around, round about.

**derrelicto** *m.* NAUT. derelict.

**derrengado, -da** *adj.* coll. done up, aching all over.

**derrengadura** *f.* hip dislocation or hurt. *2* hurt or wound in the spine.

**derrengar** *tr.* to hurt seriously the spine or the hip of; to dislocate the hip of. *2* to tilt, inclinate. *3 ref.* to hurt one's spine or hip.

**derretimiento** *m.* fusion, melting, thaw, thawing. 2 consuming love.

**derretir** *tr.* to fuse, melt, thaw. 2 to consume, expend, waste. 3 *ref.* to fuse, melt, thaw [become liquid]. 4 to burn, be consumed [with love, with impatience]. ¶ CONJUG. like *servir.*

**derribar** *tr.* to pull down, tear down, demolish. 2 to fell, knock down, throw, throw down. 3 to overthrow. 4 to bring down [game, etc.]. 5 *ref.* to tumble down, to throw oneself on the ground.

**derribo** *m.* pulling down, demolition. 2 *pl.* materials from demolished buildings.

**derrito, derrita,** etc. *irr.* V. DERRETIR.

**derrocamiento** *m.* throwing down. 2 pulling down, demolition. 3 overthrow.

**derrocar** *tr.* to precipitate from a rock. 2 to pull down, demolish. 3 to overthrow [from office, etc.].

**derrochador, -ra** *adj.* spending, extravagant. 2 *m.-f.* prodigal, spendthrift, squanderer, wastrel.

**derrochar** *tr.* to waste, squander, spend lavishly.

**derroche** *m.* waste, extravagance. 2 profusion.

**derrota** *f.* defeat, rout. 2 path, road. 3 NAUT. ship's curse.

**derrotar** *tr.* to defeat, rout. 2 to waste, dilapidate. 3 *ref.* NAUT. to drift from the course.

**derrote** *m.* upward thrust of a bull's horn.

**derrotero** *m.* NAUT. ship's course. 2 NAUT. navigation track. 3 route, course, way.

**derrotismo** *m.* defeatism.

**derrotista** *adj.-n.* defeatist.

**derrubiar** *tr.* to wash away [river banks].

**derrubio** *m.* washing away of banks by a stream.

**derruido, -da** *adj.* in ruins.

**derruir** *tr.* to pull down, demolish. ¶ CONJUG. like *huir.*

**derrumbadero** *m.* precipice.

**derrumbamiento** *m.* fall [over a precipice]. 2 collapse, abrupt falling. 3 MIN. caving in.

**derrumbar** *tr.* to precipitate, throw down. 2 *ref.* to fall over a precipice. 3 to collapse, tumble down. 4 MIN. to cave in.

**derrumbe** *m.* precipice. 2 MIN. landslide, cave in.

**derviche** *m.* dervish.

**desabastecer** *tr.* to leave unprovided, unsupplied. ¶ CONJUG. like *agradecer.*

**desabollar** *tr.* to knock the dents or bruises out of.

**desabonarse** *ref.* to drop one's subscription, to discontinue a subscription.

**desaborido, -da** *adj.* tasteless, insipid. 2 dull, insipid [person].

**desabotonar** *tr.* unbutton. 2 *ref.* to undo one's buttons. 4 to become unbuttoned.

**desabrido, -da** *adj.* tasteless, insipid. 2 gruff, surly, rude, disagreeable. 3 displeasing [weather].

**desabrigado, -da** *adj.* lightly, dressed, uncovered. 2 unsheltered, unprotected, exposed.

**desabrigar** *tr.* to uncover, undress, to take off someone's warm clothes. 2 to deprive of shelter or protection. 3 *ref.* to uncover oneself, to take off one's warm clothes.

**desabrigo** *m.* lack of covering, clothing, sheltering or protection. 2 desertion, destitution.

**desabrimiento** *m.* insipidity, flatness. 2 gruffness, surliness. 3 displeasure, bitterness.

**desabrir** *tr.* to give a bad taste to. 2 to displease, annoy. 3 *ref.* to be annoyed.

**desabrochar** *tr.* to unclasp, unfasten, unbutton. 2 *ref.* to undo one's buttons or fastenings. 3 to become unfastened or unbuttoned.

**desacalorarse** *ref.* to cool off.

**desacatar** *tr.-ref.* to be disrespectful or irreverent toward; to disobey.

**desacato** *m.* disrespect, irreverence, contempt. 2 disobedience.

**desacedar** *tr.* to remove the acidity from.

**desacertadamente** *adv.* unwisely, wrongly, erroneously.

**desacertado, -da** *adj.* unwise, wrong, mistaken.

**desacertar** *tr.* to be wrong, err, make a mistake. ¶ CONJUG. like *acertar.*

**desacierto** *m.* error, mistake, blunder.

**declimatado, -da** *adj.* unacclimatized.

**desacobardar** *tr.* to free from fear.

**desacomodamiento** *m.* uncomfortableness.

**desacomodar** *tr.* to deprive of ease or convenience. 2 to deprive [a servant] of his place. 3 *ref.* [of a servant] to lose his place.

**desacomodo** *m.* inconvenience. 2 unemployment.

**desacompañar** *tr.* to abandon, leave the company of.

**desaconsejado, -da** *adj.* ill-advised, imprudent.

**desaconsejar** *tr.* to dissuade.

**desacoplar** *tr.* to uncouple, disconnect.

**desacordar** *tr.* MUS. to put out of tune; to make discordant. 2 *ref.* MUS. to get out of tune. 3 to forget, be forgetful. ¶ CONJUG. like *contar.*

**desacorde** *adj.* MUS. discordant. 2 disagreeing, incongruous.

**desacostumbrado, -da** *adj.* disaccustomed. 2 unusual.

**desacostumbrar** *tr.* to disaccustom. 2 *ref.* to lose a habit.

**desacotar** *tr.* to open up a preserved or reserved ground; to remove boundary marks of.

**desacreditado, -da** *adj.* discredited.

**desacreditar** *tr.* to discredit, bring discredit on. 2 *ref.* to lose credit, good repute or estimation.

**desacuerdo** *m.* disagreement, disaccord. 2 error, mistake.

**desaderezar** *tr.* to disarrange, ruffle.

**desadormecer** *tr.* to awaken. 2 to free from numbness. ¶ CONJUG. like *agradecer.*

**desadornar** *tr.* to divest of adornments.

**desafecto, -ta** *adj.* disaffected; opposed. 2 *m.* disaffection, dislike.

**desaferrar** *tr.* to loosen, unfasten. 2 NAUT. to unfurl. 3 NAUT. to weigh anchor. 4 to bring [a person] to a change of mind or opinion.

**desafiador, -ra** *adj.* defiant, defying. 2 *m.-f.* challenger, defier.

**desafiante** *adj.* defiant. 2 challenging.

**desafiar** *tr.* to challenge, defy; to dare. 2 to rival, compete with.

**desafición** *f.* disaffection, indifference.

**desaficionar** *tr.* ~ *de,* to cause [one] to lose his liking, or inclination for.

**desafinación** *f.* being out of tune.

**desafinadamente** *adv.* out of tune.

**desafinado, -da** *adj.* out of tune.

**desafinar** *intr.* MUS. to be out of tune. 2 to speak indiscreetly or irrelevantly.

**desafío** *m.* challenge, defiance; daring. 2 rivalry, competition. 3 duel, combat.

**desaforado, -da** *adj.* reckless, lawless, outrageous. 2 huge, enormous.

**desaforar** *tr.* to encroach on the rights of someone, to deprive of one's privileges. 2 to act violently, to behave outrageously, to lose control, to get worked up.

**desafortunado, -da** *adj.* unlucky; unfortunate.

**desafuero** *m.* excess, outrage, violence.

**desagraciado, -da** *adj.* graceless, ungraceful.
**desagradable** *adj.* disagreeable, unpleasant.
**desagradar** *tr.* to be unpleasant to; to displease, offend. *2 ref.* to be displeased.
**desagradecer** *tr.* to be ungrateful for. ¶ CONJUG. like *agradecer.*
**desagradecido, -da** *adj.* ungrateful.
**desagradecimiento** *m.* ungratefulness, ingratitude.
**desagrado** *m.* displeasure.
**desagraviar** *tr.* to make amends to, to right a wrong made to.
**desagravio** *m.* satisfaction for an injury, righting of a wrong, amends.
**desagregación** *f.* separation, disgregation.
**desagregar** *tr.* to separate, disgregate.
**desaguadero, desaguador** *m.* water oulet, drain.
**desaguar** *tr.* to drain [free of water], to empty. *2* to waste, to squander. *3 intr.* [of streams] to empty, flow [into].
**desagüe** *m.* drainage, drain. *2* water outlet.
**desaguisado, -da** *adj.* unjust, unreasonable. *2 m.* wrong, offence, outrage.
**desaherrojar** *tr.* to unchain, to unshackle.
**desahogadamente** *adv.* easily, comfortably. *2* impudently.
**desahogado, -da** *adj.* forward, impudent, cheeky, fresh. *2* roomy, unencumbered. *3 posición desahogada,* comfortable circumstances.
**desahogar** *tr.* to relieve [one] from care, worry, etc.; to relieve, alleviate [care, worry, etc.]. *2* to give free rein to [passions]; to vent [anger, etc.]. *3 ref.* to find relief from heat, fatigue, etc. *4* to relieve oneself from worry, debt, etc. *5* to vent one's anger, etc.; to relieve one's feelings; to unbosom oneself.
**desahogo** *m.* relief, respite [from care, worry, etc.]. *2* comfort, ease. *3* comfortable circumstances. *4* ample room. *5* forwardness, impudence, cheek. *6* relieving one's feelings; unbosoming oneself.
**desahuciadamente** *adv.* without hope.
**desahuciar** *tr.* to take away all hope from. *2* to condemn [a patient]. *3* LAW to evict, disposses [a tenant].
**desahucio** *m.* LAW eviction [of a tenant].
**desairadamente** *adv.* gracelessly, clumsily.
**desairado, -da** *adj.* graceless, unattractive. *2* unsuccessful, slighted, cutting a poor figure.
**desairar** *tr.* to slight, disregard, snub. *2* to reject, ignore [a petition].
**desaire** *m.* gracelessness. *2* slight, disregard.
**desajustar** *tr.* to disarrange, to disadjust.
**desajuste** *m.* disarrangement, lack of adjustment.
**desalabear** *tr.* to straighten, unwarp.
**desalado,ˈ -da** *adj.* desalted. *2* hasty, swift. *3* anxious, eager.
**desalar** *tr.* to desalt. *2* to cut off the wings of. *3 ref.* to hurry, to go swiftly. *4 desalarse por,* to be eager to, to yearn for.
**desalentadamente** *adv.* with discouragement.
**desalentador, -ra** *adj.* discouraging.
**desalentar** *tr.* to put out of breath. *2* to discourage. *3 ref.* to be discouraged. ¶ CONJUG. like *acertar.*
**desalfombrar** *tr.* to take up the carpets from.
**desalhajar** *tr.* to dismantle [a room, a house].
**desaliento** *m.* discouragement. *2* faintness, weakness.
**desaliento, desaliente,** etc. *irr.* V. DESALENTAR.
**desalineación** *f.* desalignment.
**desalinear** *tr.* to desalign, to put out of alignment.

**desaliñado, -da** *adj.* untidy, unkempt, slovenly, slipshod. *2* untidy, careless, neglectful [person].
**desaliñar** *tr.* to disarrange, disorder, ruffle, make untidy. *2 ref.* to become disarranged, untidy.
**desaliño** *m.* untidiness, slovenliness; carelessness.
**desalmado, -da** *adj.* wicked, cruel, inhuman.
**desalmar** *tr.* to weaken [a thing]. *2* to disquiet, worry. *3 ref.* to be eager, to yearn [to or for].
**desalojamiento** *m.* dislodging, evacuation.
**desalojar** *tr.* to dislodge. *2* to evacuate. *3* NAUT., PHYS. to displace. *4* to empty. *5 intr.* to move out.
**desalojo** *m.* DESALOJAMIENTO.
**desalquilado, -da** *adj.* unrented, untenanted, vacant.
**desalquilar** *tr.* to leave, to vacate [a rented room or house].
**desalterar** *tr.* to calm, quiet.
**desamable** *adj.* unlovable.
**desamar** *tr.* to love no more. *2* to hate, dislike.
**desamarrar** *tr.* to untie, unfasten, loosen. *2* NAUT. to unmoor.
**desambientado, -da** *adj.* out of place. *2* that lacks athmosphere.
**desamistarse** *ref.* to quarrel, to become estranged.
**desamoblar** *m.* DESAMUEBLAR.
**desamor** *m.* disaffection, lack of love. *2* dislike, hate.
**desamorado, -da** *adj.* indifferent, cold.
**desamortización** *f.* freeing from mortmain.
**desamortizar** *tr.* to free from mortmain.
**desamotinarse** *ref.* to cease mutinying.
**desamparado, -da** *adj.* abandoned, deserted, helpless, unprotected. *2* needy, destitute.
**desamparar** *tr.* to abandon, forsake, desert, leave, helpless or unprotected. *2* to leave, quit [a place]. *3* NAUT. to dismantle.
**desamparo** *m.* abandonment, desertion; lack of protection; need, destitution.
**desamueblado, -da** *adj.* unfurnished.
**desamueblar** *tr.* to remove the furniture from.
**desandar** *tr.* to retrace, to go back over [the way travelled]: ~ *lo andado,* to retrace one's steps. ¶ CONJUG. like *andar.*
**desangelado, -da** *adj.* dull, insipid.
**desangrado, -da** *adj.* estar ~, to have lost blood; *morir ~,* to bleed to death.
**desangramiento** *m.* bleeding to excess.
**desangrar** *tr.* to bleed to excess. *2* to drain [a lake, etc.]. *3 fig.* to bleed, to impoverish. *4 ref.* to bleed copiously, to lose much blood.
**desanidar** *intr.* to leave the nest. *2 tr.* to dislodge from a haunt.
**desanimación** *f.* discouragement, downheartedness. *2* lack of animation, dullness, unliveliness.
**desanimado, -da** *adj.* discouraged, downhearted, dispirited. *2* lacking in animation, dull. *3* poorly attended [party, etc.].
**desanimar** *tr.* to discourage, dishearten. *3 ref.* to become discouraged, disheartened.
**desánimo** *m.* discouragement, downheartedness.
**desanudar** *tr.* to untie, unknot. *2* to clear up, disentangle.
**desaojar** *tr.* to dispel the evil eye for.
**desapacibilidad** *f.* disagreeableness.
**desapacible** *adj.* unpleasant, disagreeable, harsh.
**desaparear** *tr.* to separate [the two of a pair].
**desaparecer** *intr.-ref.* to disappear.
**desaparejar** *tr.* to unsaddle [a pack animal]. *2* NAUT. to unrig.
**desaparición** *f.* disappearance.
**desapasionado, -da** *adj.* dispassionate, unbiased.

**desapasionarse** *ref.* to free oneself of love or fondness, to become indifferent.

**desapegar** *tr.* to detach, loosen, unglue. *2 ref.* to detach or unglue itself. *3* to lose one's love or liking [for]; to become indifferent [to].

**desapego** *m.* lack of affection, indifference.

**desapercibido, -da** *adj.* unprovided, unprepared, unguarded, unaware. *2 m.-f.* unnoticed.

**desapercibimiento** *m.* unpreparedness.

**desaplicación** *f.* lack of studiousness, laziness.

**desaplicado, -da** *adj.* not studious, lazy. *2 m.-f.* bad student.

**desaplicarse** *ref.* to become a bad student.

**desaplomar** *tr.* to put out of plumb. *2 ref.* to get out of plumb.

**desaporderado, -da** *adj.* impetuous, precipitate. *2* unbridled, wild, violent.

**desapoderamiento** *m.* dispossession of powers. *2* boundless freedom or licence.

**desapoderar** *tr.-ref.* to dispossess.

**desapolillar** *tr.* to clear of moths.

**desapreciar** *tr.* not to appreciate.

**desaprender** *tr.* to unlearn.

**desaprensión** *f.* unscrupulousness.

**desaprensivo, -va** *adj.* unscrupulous.

**desapretar** *tr.* to loosen. ¶ CONJUG. like *acertar*.

**desaprobación** *f.* disapproval.

**desaprobar** *tr.* to disapprove, to disapprove of; to censure, blame. ¶ CONJUG. like *contar*.

**desapropiarse** *ref.* to divest oneself [of property].

**desaprovechado, -da** *adj.* wasted, unproductive. *2* unprofiting, unproficient, backward.

**desaprovechamiento** *m.* waste, ill use, poor use. *2* lack of progress in studies, etc.

**desaprovechar** *tr.* to waste, to make no use of; to use to no advantage. *2 intr.* to make little or no progress in studies, etc.

**desapuntalar** *tr.* to remove the props or supports of.

**desarbolar** *tr.* NAUT. to dismast.

**desarenar** *tr.* to clear of sand.

**desarmable** *adj.* dismountable, collapsible.

**desarmado, -da** *adj.* unarmed. *2* dismounted, disassembled, taken to pieces.

**desarmar** *tr.* to disarm. *2* to dismount, take apart, disassemble. *3* NAUT. to lay up [a ship]. *4 intr.* to disarm.

**desarme** *m.* disarmament, disarming. *2* dismounting, disassembling. *3* NAUT. laying up.

**desarmonizar** *tr.* to disharmonize.

**desarraigar** *tr.* to uproot, root out, eradicate. *2* to exile. *3 ref.* to be uprooted. *4* to leave one's country or place of abode.

**desarraigado, -da** *adj.* uprooted [tree], uprooted, rootless [person]. *2* wiped out, erradicated.

**desarraigo** *m.* uprooting, eradication.

**desarrapado, -da** *adj.* DESHARRAPADO.

**desarrebujar** *tr.* to uncover, unbundle [a person]. *2* to disentangle. *3* to explain, elucidate.

**desarregladamente** *adv.* disorderly.

**desarreglado, -da** *adj.* disarranged, disorderly. *2* dishevelled, slovenly. *3* intemperate, extravagant, immoderate.

**desarreglar** *tr.* to disarrange, put out of order, to derange. *2 ref.* to become disarranged. *3* to become disorderly.

**desarreglo** *m.* disarrangement, disorder.

**desarrimar** *tr.* to move [a thing] away [from something]. *2* to dissuade.

**desarrollado, -da** *adj.* developed: *poco* ~, underdeveloped [country].

**desarrollar** *tr.* to unroll, to unwind, to unfurl. *2* to develop [form or expand by a process of growth]. *3* to develop, expound, work out [a theory, etc.]. *4* MATH., MEC. to develop. *5 ref.* to unroll, unwind, unfurl. *6* to develop, to grow. *7* [of a scene, action, etc.] to take place.

**desarrollo** *m.* unrolling, unwinding, unfurling. *2* development, growth, increase. *3* development, unfolding, working out [of a theory, etc.]. *4* MATH., MEC. development.

**desarropar** *tr.-ref.* to uncover, to take off covering clothes.

**desarrugar** *tr.* to smooth out, unwrinkle: ~ *el entrecejo*, to unknit the brow.

**desarticular** *tr.* to disarticulate, to put out of joint. *2* to take apart, disconnect, disjoint. *3 ref.* to come out of joint.

**desartillar** *tr.* to take the guns out of [a fort or ship].

**desarzonar** *tr.* to unhorse, unsaddle.

**desaseado, -da** *adj.* untidy, dirty, slovenly.

**desasear** *tr.* to make untidy, dirty, slovenly.

**desasentar** *tr.* to displace, move, remove. ¶ CONJUG. like *acertar*.

**desaseo** *m.* untidiness, dirtiness, slovenliness.

**desasimiento** *m.* loosening, letting loose. *2* detachment, disinterest, disaffection.

**desasimilación** *f.* PHYSIOL. disassimilation.

**desasir** *tr.* to detach, to loosen. *2 ref. desasirse [de]*, to get loose, free oneself [of]; to let go; to give up. ¶ CONJUG. like *asir*.

**desasistir** *tr.* to abandon, forsake.

**desasnar** *tr.* to educate, polish, civilize.

**desasosegadamente** *adv.* uneasily, anxiously.

**desasosegar** *tr.* to disquiet, worry, disturb, make uneasy or anxious. ¶ CONJUG. like *acertar*.

**desasosiego** *m.* disquiet, uneasiness, anxiety.

**desastrado, -da** *adj.* wretched, unfortunate. *2* shabby, ragged, untidy.

**desastre** *m.* disaster, catastrophe.

**desastrosamente** *adv.* disastrously.

**desastroso, -sa** *adj.* disastrous, unfortunate. *2* very bad.

**desatadamente** *adv.* loosely, freely.

**desatado, -da** *adj.* loose, untied. *2* wild, fierce, violent.

**desatalentado, -da** *adj.* out of one's senses.

**desatancar** *tr.* to unclog [a pipe or channel].

**desatar** *tr.* to untie, undo, loose, loosen, unbind, unfasten. *2* to undo, solve, unravel. *3 ref.* to come untied. *4* to lose one's timidity or fear. *5* to burst forth, lose all restraint. *6* [of a storm, etc.] to break out, break loose.

**desatascar** *tr.* to pull out of the mud. *2* to unclog [a pipe, etc.]. *3* to extricate from difficulties. *4 ref.* to get out of the mud.

**desatención** *f.* inattention. *2* disregard, disrespect, discourtesy, slight.

**desatender** *tr.* to pay no attention to. *2* to be unheedful or unmindful of. *3* to neglect. *4* to disregard. ¶ CONJUG. like *entender*.

**desatentado, -da** *adj.* unjudicious, unwise. *2* excessive, wild, disorderly.

**desatentar** *tr.* to derange, perturb the mind. ¶ CONJUG. like *acertar*.

**desatentamente** *adv.* inattentively, carelessly. *2* rudely, impolitely, discourteously.

**desatento, -ta** *adj.* inattentive. *2* discourteous, impolite, unmannerly.

**desatinado, -da** *adj.* deranged, perturbed. *2* nonsensical, foolish, senseless.

**desatinar** tr. to perturb, rattle, derange. 2 intr. to talk nonsense, to act foolishly. 3 to lose one's sense of direction of bearings.

**desatino** m. absurdity, nonsense, folly, error.

**desatollar** tr. to pull out of the mud.

**desatornillar** tr. to unscrew.

**desatracar** tr. NAUT. to move [a boat] away [from]. 2 ref. [of a boat] to move away [from].

**desatraillar** tr. to unleash [dogs].

**desatrancar** tr. to unbar, unbolt [a door].

**desatufarse** ref. to get out of the close air; to clear one's head. 2 to calm down, to put off anger.

**desaturdir** tr.-ref. to rouse from a state of dizziness or stupor.

**desautorización** f. withdrawal of authority, disavowal.

**desautorizado, -da** adj. disauthorized, discredited.

**desautorizar** tr. to deprive of authority or credit, to disauthorize, to disavow.

**desavenencia** f. discord, disagreement, quarrel.

**desavenido, -da** adj. discordant, disagreeing, in bad terms.

**desavenir** tr. to make disagree. 2 ref. to disagree, be at variance, quarrel. ¶ CONJUG. like venir.

**desaventajado, -da** adj. disadvantageous, inferior.

**desavezar** tr.-ref. DESACOSTUMBRAR.

**desavisado, -da** adj. unadvised; uninformed.

**desavisar** tr. to cancel a notice or summons.

**desayunarse** ref. to breakfast; ~ con, to breakfast on. 2 fig. ~ de, to have first intelligence of.

**desayuno** m. breakfast.

**desazogar** tr. to remove the backing of [a mirror].

**desazón** f. insipidity. 2 displeasure, vexation, worry. 3 discomfort, uneasiness. 4 indisposition.

**desazonado, -da** adj. insipid. 2 annoyed, vexed. 3 uneasy. 4 indisposed.

**desazonar** tr. to render tasteless. 2 to displease, annoy; to cause discomfort or uneasiness. 3 ref. to be displeased, annoyed. 4 to feel ill.

**desbancar** tr. NAUT. to clear of benches. 2 [in gambling] to break the bank. 3 to supplant in the affection of another, to cut out.

**desbandada** f. disbandment: a la ~, helter-skelter, in disorder.

**desbandarse** ref. to disperse [be dispersed]. 2 to disband, to flee in disorder.

**desbarajuste** m. disorder, confusion, confused medley.

**desbaratado, -da** adj. disorderly; debauched.

**desbaratamiento** m. destruction, ruin. 2 frustration. 3 defeat.

**desbaratar** tr. to destroy, ruin, take to pieces. 2 to waste, squander. 3 to frustrate, foil, thwart. 4 MIL. to disperse, rout, break up. 5 intr.-ref. to talk nonsense, to act unreasonably.

**desbarbar** tr. to cut off filaments, slender roots, etc., of. 2 coll. to shave.

**desbarrar** intr. to glide, slide. 2 to talk nonsense, to act foolishly.

**desbarro** m. gliding. 2 nonsensical talk; foolish act.

**desbastar** tr. to take off the rough parts of a thing; to plane, roughdress, rough down. 2 to spend, consume. 3 to polish [a person].

**desbaste** m. roughdressing. 2 roughdressed state.

**desbecerrar** tr. to wean calves.

**desbloquear** tr. COM. to unfreeze.

**desbloqueo** m. COM. unfreezing.

**desbocado, -da** adj. wide-mouthed [gun]. 2 broken-faced [tool]. 3 broken-lipped, broken-mouthed [jar, vessel]. 4 runaway [horse]. 5 foul-mouthed.

**desbocamiento** m. running away [of a horse]. 2 foulmouthedness, abusiveness, obscenity.

**desbocar** tr. to break the lips or mouth of [a jar, etc.]; to break the face [of a tool]. 2 ref. [of a horse], to run away. 3 [of a person] to become insolent.

**desbordamiento** m. overflowing. 2 breaking all bounds.

**desbordante** adj. overflowing.

**desbordar** intr.-ref. to overflow. 2 ref. [of passions] to break all bounds.

**desborrar** tr. to burl [cloth].

**desbravador** m. horse breaker.

**desbravar** tr. to tame, break in [horses]. 2 intr.-ref. to become less wild or fierce. 3 [of a liquor] to go flat.

**desbridar** tr. SURG. to débride.

**desbriznar** tr. to shred, to divide in small shreds. 2 to remove the strings [of vegetables]. 3 to pluck the stamens [of saffron].

**desbrozar** tr. to clear [lands, etc.] of rubbish, underbrush, obstructions, etc.: ~ el camino, to clear the way.

**desbrozo** m. the act of clearing lands, etc., of rubbish, obstructions, etc. 2 rubbish from clearing lands, trenches, etc.

**desbulla** f. oyster shell.

**desbullador** m. oyster fork.

**desbullar** tr. to take [oysters] out of shell.

**descabal** adj. incomplete.

**descabalar** tr. to make incomplete, to take out a part of, to impair.

**descabalgar** intr. to dismount, to alight from a horse. 2 tr. to dismount [a gun].

**descabellado, -da** adj. dishevelled. 2 preposterous, wild, absurd.

**descabellar** tr. to dishevel, tousle the hair. 2 BULLF. to kill [the bull] by stabbing him in the back of the neck.

**descabello** m. BULLF. killing the bull by stabbing him in the back of the neck.

**descabestrar** tr. to unhalter.

**descabezado, -da** adj. decapitated, headless, beheaded. 2 light-headed, reckless, crazy, wild. 3 absurd, ridiculous. 4 absentminded, forgetful.

**descabezar** tr. to behead. 2 to top, lop, cut off the top of. 3 to begin to overcome [a difficulty]. 4 ~ el sueño, to take a nap. 5 ref. to cudgel one's brains.

**descabullirse** ref. ESCABULLIRSE. 2 to slip out of a difficulty; to elude the strenght of an argument.

**descacharrante** adj. coll. hilarious, killing, terribly funny.

**descaderar** tr. to injure the hips of. 2 ref. to injure one's hips.

**descaecer** intr. to decline, droop, languish. ¶ CONJUG. like agradecer.

**descaecimiento** m. weakness, debility. 2 dejection.

**descalabazarse** ref. coll. to cudgel one's brains.

**descalabrado, -da** adj. wounded in the head. 2 injured, worsted: salir ~, to come out worsted.

**descalabradura** f. wound in the head.

**descalabrar** tr. to wound in the head. 2 to hurt, injure. 3 to occasion losses to. 4 ref. to hurt one's head.

**descalabro** m. misfortune, damage, loss, defeat.

**descalcar** tr. NAUT. to remove oakum from [seams].

**descalce** m. undermining.

**descalcificación** f. MED. decalcification.
**descalificación** f. disqualification. 2 discrediting, discredit.
**descalificar** tr. to disqualify [render unfit]. 2 to discredit. 3 SPORT. to disqualify.
**descalzador** m. bootjack.
**descalzar** tr. to take off [somebody's] shoes or stockings. 2 to remove wedges or chocks from. 3 to dig under, undermine. 4 ref. to take off one's shoes or stockings. 5 to take off [one's shoes, stockings or gloves]. 6 [of a horse] to lose a shoe.
**descalzo, -za** adj. unshod, barefooted, in stockinged feet. 2 discalced, barefooted [friar, nun].
**descamar** tr. ESCAMAR 1. 2 ref. MED. to desquamate.
**descaminado, -da** adj. lost, on the wrong road. 2 mistaken, wrong. 3 misguided, ill-advised.
**descaminar** tr. to lead astray, mislead, misguide. 2 ref. to lose one's way, to go astray. 3 to go wrong.
**descamino** m. leading astray, going astray. 2 misguidance, error.
**descamisado, -da** adj. shirtless, ragged. 2 m.-f. poor person, ragamuffin.
**descampado, -da** adj.-m. open, clear [ground]: en ~, in the open country.
**descansadero** m. resting place.
**descansado, -da** adj. rested, refreshed. 2 free of toil, easy, tranquil, peaceful.
**descansar** intr. to rest [get repose; lie in sleep or death; stop work]. 2 to feel alleviation. 3 AGR. [of land] to rest. 4 to rest, rely, put trust [in a person]. 5 to rest [be supported]. 6 tr. to give rest to, to aid, help [someone] in labour. 7 to rest, lean [one's head, etc.].
**descansillo** m. landing [of stairs].
**descanso** m. rest, repose, refreshment. 2 sleep. 3 rest, alleviation. 4 aid, help. 5 peace, quiet. 6 landing [of stairs]. 7 MEC. rest, seat, support.
**descantear** tr. to smooth corners or edges in.
**descantillar** tr. to break the arris or edge of. 2 to substract [a part] of an amount.
**descañonar** tr. to take off the quills left on [a plucked fowl]. 2 to shave against the grain.
**descapotable** adj. convertible [car].
**descapotar** tr. to fold or take down the hood of [a carriage].
**descaradamente** adv. barefacedly. 2 openly.
**descarado, -da** adj. impudent, barefaced; saucy.
**descararse** ref. to behave in an impudent manner, to be saucy. 2 to lose all decency.
**descarbonatar** tr. CHEM. to decarbonate.
**descarburar** tr. to decarbonize.
**descarga** f. unloading, unburdening, discharge. 2 ARCH., ELECT. discharge. 3 discharge [of firearms], volley, round.
**descargadero** m. unloading place.
**descargador** m. unloader: ~ del muelle, dock labourer.
**descargar** tr. to unload, unburden, disburden, discharge. 2 to ease [one's conscience]. 3 to free, discharge [of a debt, etc.]. 4 to clear [of an accusation]. 5 to dump, empty. 6 to deal, strike [a blow]. 7 to vent [one's fury, etc.]. 8 to unload; to fire, discharge [a firearm]. 9 ELECT. to discharge. 10 intr. [of streams] to flow into, to empty. 11 [of a storm] to burst. 12 ref. to unburden oneself; to get rid of. 12 ref. to unburden oneself; to get rid of. 13 to clear oneself [of an accusation]. 14 to disburden one's cares, duties, etc. [upon another].
**descargo** m. unburdening. 2 COM. acquittance. 3

easement [of one's conscience]. 4 clearing, justification. 5 discharge [of an obligation].
**descargue** m. unloading [of goods, etc.].
**descariño** m. lack of affection, coolness.
**descarnadamente** adv. bluntly, without euphemisms.
**descarnado, -da** adj. thin, lean. 2 bare [bone]. 3 fig. bare, unadorned, crude, blunt.
**descarnador** m. DENT. scraper.
**descarnar** tr. to remove the flesh from. 2 to wear away, corrode, denudate. 3 to detach from earthly things. 4 ref. to lose flesh.
**descaro** m. impudence, effrontery, sauciness, nerve, cheek.
**descarriar** tr. to lead astray, mislead. 2 to separate [cattle] from the herd. 3 ref. to stray, go astray. 4 to go wrong.
**descarrilamiento** m. derailment.
**descarrilar** intr. to derail, to run off the track.
**descarrío** m. going astray or wrong; error, sin.
**descartar** tr. to leave aside, leave out. 2 ref. CARDS descartarse [de], to discard.
**descarte** m. leaving aside. 2 CARDS discard.
**descasamiento** m. annulment of marriage.
**descasar** tr. to annul the marriage of. 2 to disturb the arrangement of [well matched things].
**descascarar** tr. to peel, to shell. 2 ref. to peel off, to shell off.
**descascarillar** tr. to peel [rice]. 2 to remove the thin metal plate covering [an object]. 2 ref. [of an object] to lose its thin metal plate covering.
**descaspar** tr. to remove the dandruff of.
**descastado, -da** adj. showing little natural afection. 2 ungrateful.
**descendencia** f. descent, descendants, issue. 2 descent, lineage.
**descendente** adj. descendent, descending; down: tren ~, down train.
**descender** intr. to descend, to come or go down. 2 to stoop [to something mean, etc.]. 3 [of temperature] to drop. 4 to descend [from a stock, etc.]; to derive. 5 tr. to take down, bring, down. ¶ CONJUG. like entender.
**descendiente** adj. descendent. 2 m.-f. descendant, offspring.
**descendimiento** m. descent, taking down. 2 Descent from the Cross.
**descenso** m. descent, coming down. 2 drop, fall [of temperature, prices, etc.]. 3 decline, fall [in station, dignity, etc.].
**descentrado, -da** adj. out of centre, decentred.
**descentralización** f. decentralization.
**descentralizar** tr. to decentralize.
**descentrar** tr. to decentre, uncentre, place out of centre. 2 ref. to become uncentred.
**desceñir** tr. to ungird; to unbelt. 2 tr.-ref. to take off one's girdle, belt, etc. ¶ CONJUG. like reír.
**descepar** tr. to uproot [trees, shrubs]. 2 to exterminate.
**descercado, -da** adj. open, unfenced.
**descercar** tr. to destroy or tear down the wall or fence of. 2 MIL. to raise the siege of. 3 MIL. to force the enemy to raise the siege of.
**descerco** m. raising the siege.
**descerezar** tr. to pulp [coffee berries].
**descerrajadura** f. lock breaking, lock bursting.
**descerrajar** tr. to burst or force the lock. 2 ~ un tiro a, to shoot, let go a shot at.
**desciendo, descienda**, etc. irr. V. DESCENDER.
**descifrable** adj. decipherable.
**descifrador** m. decipherer; decoder.

**desciframiento** *m.* deciphering. *2* decoding.
**descifrar** *tr.* to decipher, make out; to decode.
**descinchar** *tr.* to ungirth [a horse or pack animal].
**desciño, desciña,** etc. *irr.* V. DESCEÑIR.
**desclavador** *m.* nail puller.
**desclavar** *tr.* to remove the nails from. *2* to unnail. *3* to take [a precious stone] out of setting.
**descoagulante** *adj.* decoagulating.
**descoagular** *tr.* to decoagulate.
**descobajar** *tr.* to separate [grapes] from the stem.
**descocado, -da** *adj.* bold, forward, brazen.
**descocar** *tr.* to clear [trees] of grubs. *2 ref.* to become bold, forward.
**descoco** *f. m.* boldness, forwardness, excessive freedom in manners.
**descoger** *tr.* to unfold, extend, spread.
**descogollar** *tr.* to strip [a tree or plant] of shoots. *2* to take the heart out of [vegetables].
**descolar** *tr.* to dock or crop the tail of [an animal].
**descolgar** *tr.* to unhang, take down. *2* to lower, let down [something suspended from a rope, etc.]. *3* to unhang, divest of hangings [a room, etc.]. *4 ref.* to show up unexpectedly. *5* to slip or let oneself down [from a window, etc.]; to come down [from a steep place]. *6 descolgarse con,* to say [something unexpected]. ¶ CONJUG. like *contar.*
**descolocado, -da** *adj.* out of place.
**descolonizar** *tr.* to decolonize.
**descoloramiento** *m.* decolourization.
**descolorante** *adj.* decolourizing. *2 m.* decolourizer.
**descolorar** *tr.* DESCOLORIR I.
**descolorido, -da** *adj.* decolourized. *2* pale, colourless, faded.
**descolorimiento** *m.* decoloration, fading, paleness.
**descolorir** *tr.* to decolourize, to discolour. *2* to fade, render pale.
**descolladamente** *adv.* haughtily, loftily.
**descollamiento** *m.* superiority.
**descollante** *adj.* outstanding.
**descollar** *intr.* to stand out, be prominent or conspicuous: ~ *entre* or *sobre,* to excel, surpass, tower above. ¶ CONJUG. like *contar.*
**descombrar** *tr.* to disencumber, to clear of obstacles.
**descombro** *m.* disencumbering, clearing of obstacles.
**descomedido, -da** *adj.* excessive, disproportionate, immoderate. *2* rude, disrespectful, impolite.
**descomedimiento** *m.* disrespect, impoliteness.
**descomedirse** *ref.* to be rude, disrespectful, impolite.
**descompaginar** *tr.* to disarrange, upset.
**descompás** *m.* excess, want of measure or proportion.
**descompasado, -da** *adj.* excessive, immoderate.
**descomponer** *tr.* to decompose. *2* MEC. to resolve [forces]. *3* to put out of order; to disarrange, disturb, unsettle, upset. *4* fig. to alienate, set at odds. *5 ref.* to decompose [be decomposed]; to become putrid or tainted. *6* to get out of order. *7* [of the body] to be indisposed. *8* [of the face] to be altered by emotions. *9* to lose one's temper. *10* [of the weather, etc.] to change for the worse. ¶ CONJUG. like *poner.*
**descomposición** *f.* decomposition. *2* MEC. resolution [of forces]. *3* ~ *de vientre,* looseness of bowels.
**descompostura** *f.* decomposition. *2* disarrange-

ment. *3* slovenliness, untidiness. *4* lack of restraint, of moderation. *5* disrespect, insolence.
**descompresión** *f.* decompression.
**descompuesto, -ta** *adj.* decomposed. *2* disarranged, out of order. *3* wild, insolent, impolite.
**descomulgado, -da** *adj.* coll. perverse, wicked.
**descomulgar** *tr.* to excommunicate.
**descomunal** *adj.* extraordinary, huge, enormous.
**desconceptuar** *tr.* to discredit. *2 ref.* to become discredited.
**desconcertadamente** *adv.* disorderly, in disorder. *2* disconcertedly.
**desconcertado, -da** *adj.* disorderly. *2* out of order. *3* dislocate [bones]. *4* disconcerted, baffled.
**desconcertante** *adj.* disconcerting, baffling.
**desconcertar** *tr.* to disconcert. *2* to disarrange, disturb, put out of order. *3* to dislocate [a bone]. *4 ref.* to become disarranged, to get out of order. *5* to disagree. *6* to be disconcerted. *7* [of a bone] to become dislocated. ¶ CONJUG. like *acertar.*
**desconcierto** *m.* disarrangement, disorder, confusion. *2* mismanagement. *3* disagreement. *4* disarrangement, disrepair. *5* disconcertment. *6* lack of restraint. *8* looseness of bowels.
**desconchado** *m.* scaled or peeled off part [of wall, etc.].
**desconchar** *tr.* to remove part of the coating, varnish, etc., of. *2 ref.* to lose part of its coating, varnish, etc.
**desconchón** *m.* DESCONCHADO.
**desconectar** *tr.* MACH., ELECT. to disconnect. *2 ref.* to become disconnected.
**desconfiadamente** *adv.* distrustfully, suspiciously.
**desconfiado, -da** *adj.* distrustful, suspicious.
**desconfianza** *f.* distrust, mistrust. *2* suspicious fear. *3* diffidence.
**desconfiar** *intr.* to have no confidence: ~ *de,* to distrust, to have little hope of.
**descongelar** *tr.* to defreeze.
**descongestión** *f.* removing or relieving of congestion.
**descongestionar** *tr.* to remove or relieve the congestion of. *2 ref.* to become less congested.
**desconocedor** *m.* not knowing, ignorant.
**desconocer** *tr.* not to know, to ignore, be unacquainted with. *2* to fail to recognize. *3* to disown, disavow, deny. *4* to disregard, ignore. *5 ref.* to be ignored. *6* to become unrecognizable. ¶ CONJUG. like *agradecer.*
**desconocido, -da** *adj.* unknown. *2* strange, unfamiliar. *3* ungrateful. *4* unrecognizable. *5 m.-f.* stranger, unknown person.
**desconocimiento** *m.* ignorance [of something]. *2* disregard. *3* ungratefulness, ingratitude.
**desconozco, desconozca,** etc. *irr.* V. DESCONOCER.
**desconsideración** *f.* inconsiderateness, disregard, inattention.
**desconsiderado, -da** *adj.* inconsiderate, rude, discourteous. *2* inconsiderate, rash, imprudent.
**desconsiderar** *tr.* to have no regard for.
**desconsolado, -da** *adj.* disconsolate, griefstricken.
**desconsolador, -ra** *adj.* distressing.
**desconsolar** *tr.* to distress, grieve. *2 ref.* to be distressed, to grieve. ¶ CONJUG. like *contar.*
**desconsuelo** *m.* disconsolation, disconsolateness, grief. *2* empty feeling [in the stomach].
**descontar** *tr.* to discount, deduct, abate. *2* to discount [a bill, etc.]. *3* to allow [for exaggeration, etc.]. *4* to take for granted. *5 ref.* to miscount. ¶ CONJUG. like *contar.*

**descontentadizo, -za** *adj.* hard to please, easily displeased, fastidious.

**descontentar** *tr.* to discontent, dissatisfy, displease. *2 ref.* to be displeased.

**descontento, -ta** *adj.* discontent, dissatisfied, displeased. *2 m.* discontent, displeasure.

**desconvenir** *tr.* to disagree, differ [in opinion]. *2* to disagree, be dissimilar, not to suit. ¶ CONJUG. like *venir.*

**descorazonadamente** *adv.* despondently.

**descorazonamiento** *adv.* discouragement, despondency.

**descorazonar** *tr.* to dishearten, discourage.

**descorchador** *m.* corkscrew. *2* bark stripper.

**descorchar** *tr.* to bark [a cork tree]. *2* to uncork.

**descorche** *m.* barking [of cork oaks]. *2* uncorking.

**descornar** *tr.* to dehorn. *2 ref.* to be dehorned. *3* coll. to rack one's brains. ¶ CONJUG. like *contar.*

**descoronar** *tr.* to uncrown.

**descorrer** *tr.* to draw back [a curtain, a bolt, etc.]. *2* to run back over [the same ground]. *3 intr.* [of a liquid] to drip, trickle.

**descortés** *adj.* discourteous, impolite, uncivil.

**descortesía** *f.* discourtesy, impoliteness.

**descortezador** *m.* decorticator.

**descortezamiento** *m.* removal of bark, rind or crust.

**descortezar** *tr.* to bark [a tree]; to peel, to unrind; to remove the crust of. *2* coll. to polish, civilize. *3 ref.* to peel [lose the bark or rind].

**descortezo** *m.* removing of bark.

**descosedura** *f.* unseaming, ripping.

**descoser** *tr.* to unstitch, to unseam, to rip. *2* fig. *no ~ los labios,* to be silent. *3 ref.* [of a garment, etc.] to rip. *4* fig. to babble.

**descosidamente** *adv.* excessively. *2* disorderly, desultorily.

**descosido, -da** *adj.* ripped, unstitched. *2* disorderly, disconnected. *3 m.* open seam, rip. *4 como un ~,* immoderately.

**descostillar** *tr.* to beat [someone] on the ribs. *2 ref.* to fall violently on one's back.

**descostrar** *tr.* to remove the crust, or the scab, from.

**descotar** *tr.* to cut low in the neck. *2 ref.* to wear a low-neck dress.

**descote** *m.* ESCOTE I.

**descoyuntado, -da** *adj.* disjointed, disconnected.

**descoyuntamiento** *m.* dislocation [of a joint]. *2* pain through overexertion.

**descoyuntar** *tr.* to dislocate, disjoint. *2* to annoy, bore. *3 ref.* to be dislocate: *descoyuntarse de risa,* to split one's sides with laughter.

**descrédito** *m.* discredit, loss of repute.

**descreer** *tr.* to disbelieve.

**descreído, -da** *adj.* unbelieving. *2 m.-f.* disbeliever, unbeliever.

**descreimiento** *m.* unbelief, lack of faith.

**descremar** *tr.* to skim.

**describir** *tr.* to describe.

**descripción** *f.* description [in every sense, except sort, kind, class]. *2* LAW inventory, schedule.

**descriptible** *adj.* describable.

**descriptivo, -va** *adj.* descriptive.

**descrismar** *tr.* to remove the chrism from. *2* coll. to hit violently on the head. *3 ref.* coll. to break one's skull. *4* to cudgel one's brains.

**descristianizar** *tr.* to dechristianize. *2 ref.* to become dechristianized.

**descrito, -ta** *irr. p. p.* of DESCRIBIR.

**descruzar** *tr.* to uncross.

**descuadernar** *tr.* to unbind [a book]. *2* to derange, upset, put out of order.

**descuajar** *tr.* to decoagulate, to liquefy. *2* AGR. to uproot. *3* to dishearten.

**descuajaringarse** *ref.* coll. to be broken down with fatigue, to fall to pieces.

**descuartizamiento** *m.* quartering, dividing into pieces. *2* quartering [punishment].

**descuartizar** *tr.* to quarter, to divide into pieces. *2* to quarter [as punishment].

**descubierta** *f.* MIL. reconnoitering. *2* NAUT. scanning of the horizon. *3 adv. a la ~,* openly.

**descubierto, -ta** *irr. p. p.* of descubrir. *2 adj.* patent, manifest. *3* bareheaded, uncovered. *4* open to attack, charges or accusations. *5 m.* deficit, overdraft: *en ~,* overdrawn; fig. unable to justify one's conduct. *6 adv. al ~,* in the open; openly. *7* COM. short.

**descubridor, -ra** *adj.* discovering. *2 m.-f.* discoverer. *3 m.* MIL. scout.

**descubrimiento** *m.* discovery. *2* uncovering. *3* revealing, disclosure.

**descubrir** *tr.* to discover, disclose, reveal, exhibit. *2* to make known, to betray [a secret, etc.]. *3* to uncover, lay bare, expose to view. *4* to discover [find out; suddenly realize]. *6* to catch sight of, descry, make out. *6 ref.* to uncover, to take off one's hat or cap. *7* to betray oneself.

**descuello** *m.* overtopping. *2* superiority, eminence. *3* haughtiness, loftiness.

**descuello, descuelle,** etc. *irr.* V. DESCOLLAR.

**descuento** *m.* discount, deduction, rebate. *2* BANK. discount.

**descuento, descuente,** etc. *irr.* V. DESCONTAR.

**descuernacabras** *m.* strong, cold north wind.

**descuidado, -da** *adj.* neglected. *2* careless, negligent. *3* slovenly, untidy. *4* unaware, off his guard.

**descuidar** *tr.* to relieve from care. *2* to divert the attention of. *3 tr.-intr. ref. descuidar, descuidar de, descuidarse o en,* to neglect, to fail to attend with due care. *4 intr. descuide usted,* depend on lit.

**descuidero** *m.* sneak thief.

**descuido** *m.* neglect. *2* negligence, carelessness. *3* slovenliness. *4* oversight, inadvertence. *5* slip, faux pas. *6* slight, lack of attention.

**descuitado, -da** *adj.* carefree.

**descular** *tr.* to break the bottom of.

**desde** *prep.* from, since: *~ ... hasta,* from... to; *~ ahora,* from now on; *~ entonces,* since then; ever since; *~ niño,* from a child: *~ que,* since; *está enfermo ~ hace un año,* he has been ill for a year. *2 adv. ~ luego,* immediately; of course.

**desdecir** *intr. ~ de,* to be unbecoming to; not to be in keeping with. *2 ref.* to retract, to unsay.

**desdén** *m.* disdain, scorn. *2* slight, disdainful behaviour.

**desdentado, -da** *adj.* toothless. *2 adj.-m.* ZOOL. edentate.

**desdeñable** *adj.* contemptible.

**desdeñar** *tr.* to disdain, scorn. *2 ref.* to disdain, scorn [doing something], not to deign to.

**desdeñoso, -sa** *adj.* disdainful, contemptuous.

**desdibujado, -da** *adj.* poorly drawn, badly outlined, blurred.

**desdibujarse** *ref.* to become blurred.

**desdicha** *f.* misfortune; unhappiness, misery.

**desdichado, -da** *adj.* unfortunate, unlucky. *2* miserable, unhappy, wretched. *3 m.-f.* wretch, unfortunate one. *4* spiritless person, poor devil.

**desdoblamiento** *m.* unfolding. *2* splitting, originating two things out of one: ~ *de la personalidad,* desintegration of the personality.

**desdoblar** *tr.* to unfold, to spread open. *2 tr.-ref.* to split, to originate two things out of one.

**desdorar** *tr.* to take off the gilding of. *2* to tarnish, to sully [reputation, etc.].

**desdoro** *m.* dishonor, blemish, blot.

**desdoroso, -sa** *adj.* disgraceful.

**deseable** *adj.* desirable.

**deseado, -da** *adj.* desired.

**desear** *tr.* to desire, to wish.

**desecación** *f.* DESECAMIENTO.

**desecamiento** *m.* desiccation, drying, draining.

**desecar** *tr.* to desiccate, exsiccate; to dry, dry up; to drain: ~ *un pantano,* to drain a swamp.

**desecativo, -va** *adj.-n.* dessicative.

**desechar** *tr.* to cast aside, banish, refuse, decline, reject. *2* to cast off. *3* to underrate. *4* to draw back [a bolt].

**desecho** *m.* refuse, rubbish, reject, remainder, scrap: *de* ~, cast off, discarded; scrap [iron, etc.]. *2* contempt. *3 pl.* MIN. tailings.

**deselectrizar** *tr.* to diselectrify.

**desellar** *tr.* to unseal.

**desembalaje** *m.* unpacking [of goods].

**desembalar** *tr.* to unpack [goods].

**desembaldosar** *tr.* to untile [a floor].

**desembarazado, -da** *adj.* clear, free, open, unobstructed. *2* easy, unrestrained [air, manners, etc.].

**desembarazar** *tr.* to clear, disembarrass, disencumber: ~ *de,* to clear, rid of. *2* to empty [a room]. *3 ref.* to get rid [of].

**desembarazo** *m.* disembarrassment. *2* freedom, lack of restraint, ease, naturalness.

**desembarcadero** *m.* landing place, wharf, pier.

**desembarcar** *tr.* to disembark, debark, land, put ashore. *2 intr.-ref.* to disembark, debark, land, go ashore. *3 intr.* [of a stairs] to end at a landing.

**desembarco** *m.* disembarkation, landing.

**desembargar** *tr.* to free, to remove impediments from. *2* LAW to raise the attachment or seizure of.

**desembargo** *m.* LAW raising of an attachment or seizure.

**desembarque** *m.* debarkation, landing, unloading.

**desembarrancar** *tr.* to refloat [a stranded ship]. *2 intr.* [of a stranded ship] to float again.

**desembarrar** *tr.* to clear of mud.

**desembaular** *tr.* to take out of a trunk, box, etc.

**desembebecerse** *ref.* to come out of one's absorption. ¶ CONJUG. like *agradecer.*

**desembelesarse** *ref.* to come out of one's rapture.

**desembocadura** *f.* mouth [of a river]. *2* outlet, exit [of a street, road, etc.].

**desembocar** *intr.* [of streams] to flow, disembogue. *2* [of streets, etc.] to end [at], lead [to].

**desembolsar** *tr.* to take out of a bag or purse. *2* to disburse, pay out.

**desembolso** *m.* disbursement, payment; expenditure.

**desemboscarse** *ref.* to come out of the thicket or woods. *2* to come out of ambush.

**desembotar** *tr.* to remove the dullness of wits, senses, etc.

**desembozar** *tr.* to unmuffle, to uncover. *2 intr.* to unmuffle, to uncover one's face.

**desembragar** *tr.* MACH. to unclutch, ungear, disconnect.

**desembrague** *m.* MACH. unclutching.

**desembriagar** *tr.* to sober, cure from intoxication. *2 ref.* to sober up, recover from intoxication.

**desembridar** *tr.* to unbridle.

**desembrollar** *tr.* to unravel, disentangle, disembroil.

**desembuchar** *tr.* [of birds] to disgorge. *2* coll. to speak out, to tell all one knows.

**desemejante** *adj.* dissimilar, unlike.

**desemejanza** *f.* dissimilarity, unlikeness, difference.

**desemejar** *intr.* to be dissimilar, be unlike. *2 tr.* to disfigure.

**desempacar** *tr.* to unpack, to unwrap [goods].

**desempachar** *tr.-ref.* to relieve or be relieved from indigestion. *2 ref.* to lose one's bashfulness or timidity.

**desempacho** *m.* ease, unconstraint.

**desempalagar** *tr.* to uncloy.

**desempalmar** *tr.* to disconnect, to unsplice.

**desempañar** *tr.* to clean [a glass, mirror, etc.] of steam or tarnish; to make recover its luster to. *2* to remove swaddling clothes from [children].

**desempapelar** *tr.* to unwrap [from paper]. *2* to strip [a wall, a room, etc.] of paper hangings.

**desempaque** *m.* unpacking.

**desempaquetar** *tr.* to unpack.

**desemparejar** *tr.* to make uneven or unequal.

**desempastar** *tr.* to remove the filling.

**desempatar** *tr.* SPORT. to break a tie between. *2* to break a tie-vote.

**desempate** *m.* breaking the tie between.

**desempedrar** *tr.* to unpave, to remove the paving stones of. ¶ CONJUG. like *acertar.*

**desempeñar** *tr.* to redeem [what was pledged], to take out of pawn. *2* to free from debt or obligation. *3* to discharge [a duty]; to acquit oneself of [a commission]. *4* to fill [an office]. *5* to act, play [a part]. *6 ref.* to get out of debts. *7* to get out of a difficulty.

**desempeño** *m.* redeeming a pledge; tacking out of pawn. *2* discharging [of debt]. *3* performance [of an obligation]; discharging [of duty]; fulfilment [of a function]; filling [an office]. *4* acting [a part].

**desempleado, -da** *adj.* unemployed, out of work. *2 n.* unemployed man or woman.

**desempleo** *m.* unemployment.

**desempolvadura** *f.* removal of dust or powder.

**desempolvar** *tr.* to dust, remove the dust from. *2* to remove the powder from [face, etc.].

**desemponzoñar** *tr.* to free from poison.

**desempotrar** *tr.* to remove, take out [something embedded in a wall, etc.].

**desenalbardar** *tr.* to unsaddle [a pack animal].

**desenamorar** *tr.* to destroy the love [for]. *2 ref.* to lose the love [for].

**desencabalgar** *tr.* MIL. to dismount [a gun].

**desencadenamiento** *m.* unchaining.

**desencadenar** *tr.* to unchain, to unfetter. *2* to free, unleash. *3 ref.* [of passions] to become unleashed, run wild; [of wind] to break loose; [of a storm] to break; [of a war] to break out.

**desencajado, -da** *adj.* disjointed, out of joint. *2* [of features] distorted.

**desencajamiento** *m.* disjointing, dislocation, unhingement. *2* distortion [of face or features].

**desencajar** *tr.* to disjoint, dislocate; to unhinge. *2 ref.* to be disjointed. *3* [of face or features] to become distorted.

**desencajonar** tr. to take out of a box. 2 BULLF. to remove [bulls] from the travelling boxes.

**desencalabrinar** tr.-ref. to clear [somebody's] head, or [one's] head, of fumes.

**desencallar** tr. to set [a stranded ship] afloat. 2 intr. [of a stranded ship] to float again.

**desencaminar** tr. to mislead, lead astray.

**desencantar** tr. to disenchant. 2 to disillusion. 3 ref. to be disenchanted. 4 to become disillusioned.

**desencanto** m. disenchantment, disillusionment.

**desencapotar** tr. to strip [one] of his great coat. 2 to reveal. 3 to make [a horse] keep its head up. 4 ref. [of the sky] to clear up. 5 to smooth one's brow.

**desencaprichar** tr. to dissuade from or cure of a whim or fancy. 2 ref. to give up or get over a whim or fancy.

**desencarcelar** tr. to set free, release from prison.

**desencargar** tr. to countermand.

**desenclavar** tr. DESCLAVAR. 2 to put [someone] violently out of his place.

**desenclavijar** tr. to take the pins or pegs out of. 2 to separate, disjoint.

**desencoger** tr. to unfold, to spread out, to extend. 2 ref. to lose one's timidity or constraint.

**desencogimiento** m. unfolding. 2 ease, naturalness.

**desencolar** tr. to unglue. 2 to unsize [fabrics].

**desencolerizarse** ref. to cool off, be appeased.

**desenconar** tr. to allay the inflammation of. 2 to appease. 3 ref. to abate, calm down, soften up.

**desencono** m. mitigation of anger, passion or bitterness.

**desencordar** tr. MUS. to unstring.

**desencorvar** tr. to straighten, unbend.

**desencrespar** tr. to uncurl, to unfrizzle.

**desencuadernar** tr. to unbind, take the binding off [a book].

**desenchufar** tr. to unplug, to disconnect.

**desendemoniar** tr. to drive evil spirits out of.

**desendiosar** tr. to humble the vanity of.

**desenfadaderas** f. pl. tener buenas ~, to be resourceful.

**desenfadadamente** adv. without inhibition, casually, confidently.

**desenfadado, -da** adj. easy, unconstrained, bold.

**desenfadar** tr. to appease, pacify [an angry person]. 2 ref. to calm down, cease to be angry.

**desenfado** m. ease, freedom, naturalness.

**desenfardar** tr. to unpack [bales of goods].

**desenfilar** tr. MIL., FORT. to defilade.

**desenfocado, -da** adj. out of focus.

**desenfocar** tr. to put out of focus, not to focus properly. 2 ref. to get out of focus.

**desenfoque** m. out of focus.

**desenfrenadamente** adv. wildly; unrestrainedly: correr ~, to run wildly. 2 licentiously, wantonly.

**desenfrenado, -da** adj. unbridled. 2 wild [course, run, etc.]. 3 licentious, wanton.

**desenfrenar** tr. to unbridle. 2 ref. [of passion, vices, etc.] to run wild. 3 to give oneself up to vice; to give rein to one's passions or desires.

**desenfreno** m. licentiousness, wantonness. 2 boundless freedom or licence. 3 unbridling [of passions].

**desenfundar** tr. to take out of a sheath, case, cover, etc.

**desenfurecer** tr. to quiet the fury or anger of. 2 ref. to calm down, quiet down.

**desenfurruñar** tr. to appease [someone], make [someone] cease being angry or sulking.

**desenganchar** tr. to unhook, unfasten, disengage. 2 to uncouple, to unhitch, to unharness.

**desengañadamente** adv. clearly, openly, frankly.

**desengañado, -da** adj. disabused, disillusioned.

**desengañar** tr. to undeceive, disabuse. 2 to disillusion. 3 ref. to be undeceived, to be desillusioned.

**desengaño** m. undeceiving, disabusal. 2 disillusion, disappointment; bitter lesson of experience.

**desengarzar** tr. to take [precious stones, etc.] out of a setting. 2 to unstring [pearls, etc.].

**desengastar** tr. DESENGARZAR 1.

**desengomar** tr. DESGOMAR.

**desengoznar** tr. DESGOZNAR.

**desengranar** tr. MACH. to unmesh, disengage.

**desengrasar** tr. to take the grease out of.

**desengrase** m. removal of grease.

**desenhebrar** tr. to unthread.

**desenhornar** tr. to take out of the oven.

**desenjaezar** tr. to take the trappings off [a horse].

**desenjalmar** tr. to unsaddle [a pack animal].

**desenjaular** tr. to uncage, let out of the cage.

**desenlace** m. outcome, issue, end. 2 denouement, unravelling [of drama, plot, etc.].

**desenladrillar** tr. to untile [a floor].

**desenlatar** tr. to open, to take out [of a can].

**desenlazar** tr. to untie. 2 to solve, to bring to an issue. 3 to unravel [a drama or plot]. 4 ref. to come untied. 5 to come to a denouement.

**desenlodar** tr. to clear of mud.

**desenlosar** tr. to take up the flagstones from.

**desenlutar** tr. to strip of mourning hangings. 2 ref. to leave off mourning garments.

**desenmallar** tr. to disentangle [fish] from the net.

**desenmarañar** tr. to disentangle, unravel. 2 to disembroil.

**desenmascaramiento** m. unmasking, exposure.

**desenmascarar** tr. to unmask, expose. 2 ref. to unmask, take off one's mask.

**desenmohecer** tr. to unrust, clear of rust.

**desenmudecer** tr. to make [someone] recover speech. 2 intr. to recover speech. 3 to break a long silence. ¶ CONJUG. like agradecer.

**desenojar** tr. to appease, dispel the displeasure of. 2 ref. to cease to be angry or displeased.

**desenojo** m. appeasement of anger.

**desenredar** tr. to disentangle. 2 to unravel, clear, free from confusion. 3 ref. to disentangle oneself or itself; to extricate oneself.

**desenredo** m. disentangling, unravelling.

**desenrollar** tr. to unroll, to unwind. 2 ref. to unroll, to unwind [itself].

**desenroscar** tr. to uncoil, to untwist. 2 to unscrew.

**desensamblar** tr. CARP. to disjoint.

**desensartar** tr. to unstring, unthread. 2 to unskewer.

**desensibilizar** tr. to desensitize. 2 ref. to become desensitized.

**desensillar** tr. to unsaddle [a horse].

**desensoberbecer** tr. to make humble. 3 ref. to become humble. ¶ CONJUG. like agradecer.

**desentablar** tr. to take up the boards from.

**desentarimar** tr. to take up the flooring boards from.

**desentenderse** ref. ~ de, to pretend not to understand, affect ignorance of; to take no part in, cease to be interested in. ¶ CONJUG. like entender.

**desentendido, -da** adj. disinterested [in]. 2 s. ha-

*cerse el* ~, to pretend not to understand or not to notice.

**desenterrador** *m.* exhumer, unearther.

**desenterramiento** *m.* unearthing. 2 disinterment, exhumation.

**desenterrar** *tr.* to unearth. 2 to disinter, exhume. 3 to recall [long-forgotten things]. ¶ CONJUG. like *acertar.*

**desentoldar** *tr.* to take off the awning from. 2 strip of ornaments.

**desentonado, -da** *adj.* out of tune. 2 disrespectful.

**desentonar** *tr.* to humble the pride of. 2 *intr.* MUS. to be out of tune. 3 to be out of harmony, to discord.

**desentono** *m.* MUS. being out of tune, discordance. 3 rude, disrespectful tone of voice.

**desentorpecer** *tr.* to free from numbness or torpor. 2 to make smart, to polish [a clumsy person]. 3 *ref.* to shake off numbness or torpor. 4 to become smart, lively. ¶ CONJUG. like *agradecer.*

**desentrampar** *tr.* to free of debts. 2 *ref.* to get out of debt.

**desentrañar** *tr.* to eviscerate, to disembowel. 2 to find out, solve, decipher. 3 *ref. desentrañarse por,* to give one's all to [someone], out of love.

**desentrenado, -da** *adj.* SPORT. out of training.

**desentrenamiento** *m.* SPORT. lack of training.

**desentrenarse** *ref.* SPORT. to go or get out of training.

**desentronizar** *tr.* to dethrone.

**desentumecer** *tr.* to free [a limb] from numbness. 2 *ref.* to shake off numbness.

**desentumecimiento** *m.* freeing from numbness.

**desentumir** *tr.-ref.* DESENTUMECER.

**desenvainar** *tr.* to unsheathe. 2 [of an animal] to stretch out or bare [the claws].

**desenvergar** *tr.* NAUT. to unbend [a sail].

**desenvoltura** *f.* easy and graceful delivery in talking; ease in acts or manners. 2 boldness, wantonness [chiefly in women].

**desenvolver** *tr.* to unfold. 2 to unwrap. 3 to develop [a theme, etc.], to evolve. 4 to unravel, decipher; to clear up. 5 *ref.* to develop [be developed]. 6 to come out [of a difficulty]. 7 to act or behave with ease or assurance. ¶ CONJUG. like *mover.*

**desenvolvimiento** *m.* unfolding, development.

**desenvueltamente** *adv.* with ease, naturally, confidently, gracefully. 2 boldly, rudely. 3 shamelessly, brazenly. 4 openly.

**desenvuelto, -ta** *p. p.* of DESENVOLVER. 2 easy, free [in talk or manners]. 3 brazen, excessively free.

**desenyesar** *tr.* to remove plaster from.

**desenzarzar** *tr.* to disentangle from brambles. 2 to separate or appease [quarrelers].

**deseo** *m.* desire; wish.

**deseoso, -sa** *adj.* desirous.

**desequilibrado, -da** *adj.* unbalanced, unpoinsed, disequilibrated. 2 unbalanced [mind; person]. 3 *m.-f.* unbalanced person.

**desequilibrar** *tr.* to unbalance. 2 *ref.* to become unbalanced.

**desequilibrio** *m.* lack of equilibrium; unbalanced condition. 2 ~ *mental,* unbalanced mental condition.

**deserción** *f.* MIL. desertion.

**desertar** *tr.-intr.* MIL. to desert. 2 *tr.* coll. to give up frequenting [friends, a place of meeting].

**desértico, -ca** *adj.* barren, desert, uncultivated. 2 deserted, uninhabited. 3 GEOG. desert.

**desertor** *m.* deserter.

**deseslabonar** *tr.* DESLABONAR.

**desespaldar** *tr.-ref.* to break or dislocate the shoulder of.

**desesperación** *f.* despair, desperation. 2 *ser una* ~, to be unbearable.

**desesperado, -da** *adj.* despairing. 2 hopeless. 3 desperate. 4 furious, mad. 5 *m.-f.* desperate person.

**desesperante** *adj.* exasperating, maddening.

**desesperanza** *f.* despair, want of hope.

**desesperanzar** *tr.* to deprive of hope, to discourage. 2 *ref.* to lose hope.

**desesperar** *tr.* to cause to despair. 2 to exasperate, drive mad or wild. 3 *intr.* to despair, to have no hope [of]. 4 *ref.* to be exasperate. 5 to be driven to despair.

**desespero** *m.* DESESPERACIÓN.

**desestañar** *tr.* to untin, to detin. 2 to unsolder.

**desesterar** *tr.* to remove the mates from [floor].

**desestima, desestimación** *f.* disesteem, misestimation, undervaluation. 2 refusal, denial.

**desestimar** *tr.* to disesteem, misestimate, undervalue. 2 to reject [a petition].

**desfacedor** *m.* ~ *de entuertos,* righter of wrongs.

**desfachatado, -da** *adj.* impudent, brazen, shameless.

**desfachatez** *f.* impudence, brazenness, effrontery.

**desfajar** *tr.* to ungird.

**desfalcador, -ra** *m.-f.* embezzler, defalcator.

**desfalcar** *tr.* to detract a part of. 2 to embezzle.

**desfalco** *m.* detracting, diminution. 2 embezzlement, defalcation.

**desfallecer** *tr.* to weaken, debilitate. 2 *intr.* to faint, faint away. 3 to lose courage or vigour.

**desfalleciente** *adj.* weak, fainting.

**desfallecimiento** *m.* faintness, languor. 2 fainting fit.

**desfasado, -da** *adj.* out of date, antiquated, old fashioned. 2 out of place. 3 out of phase.

**desfase** *m.* ELECT. phase difference, phase shift. 2 gap. 3 imbalance.

**desfavorecer** *tr.* to disregard, to cease favouring. 2 to disfavour, to discountenance; to oppose. 3 to injure, hurt.

**desfigurar** *tr.* to disfigure, change, alter. 2 to disguise. 3 to blur, to obscure. 4 to distort, to misrepresent. 5 *ref.* to become disfigured.

**desfiladero** *m.* defile, gorge, long narrow pass.

**desfilar** *tr.* to defile [march in file]. 2 to march past [in review, etc.] to parade. 3 to file out.

**desfile** *m.* defiling; marching past, parade.

**desflecar** *tr.* to form fringes by loosening threads.

**desflemar** *tr.* CHEM. to dephlegmate. 2 *intr.* to expel phlegm.

**desflocar** *tr.* DESFLECAR. ¶ CONJUG. like *contar.*

**desfloración** *f.* defloration.

**desfloramiento** *m.* defloration, violation.

**desflorar** *tr.* to deflower. 2 to treat [a matter] superficially.

**desfogar** *tr.* to vent, to make an opening in [a furnace, etc.] for fire. 2 to slack [lime]. 3 *tr.-ref.* to give vent [to one's anger or feelings].

**desfogue** *m.* opening a vent [in a furnace, etc.]. 2 venting [of anger or feelings].

**desfondar** *tr.* to break or remove the bottom of. 2 NAUT. to bilge [a ship]. 3 AGR. to dig [the soil] to a great depth. 4 *ref.* NAUT. [of a ship] to bilge.

**desfonde** *m.* breaking of the bottom. 2 AGR. digging of the soil to a great depth.

**desfrenar** *tr.-ref.* DESENFRENAR. 2 *tr.* to take the breaks off [a carriage].

**desfruncir** *tr.* to unpucker. 2 to unknit [the brow].

**desgaire** *m.* affected carelessness in dress and deportment: *al* ~, with affected carelessness. *2* scornful attitude.

**desgajar** *tr.* to tear off [a branch of a tree]. *2* to break, to rent, to separate. *3 ref.* [of a branch] to break off. *4* to come off, break off, break away.

**desgaje** *m.* act of tearing or breaking off.

**desgalichado, -da** *adj.* coll. untidy. *2* ungainly.

**desgana** *f.* lack of appetite. *2* indifference, reluctance: *a* ~, reluctantly.

**desganado, -da** *adj.* having no appetite.

**desganar** *tr.* to take away one's taste [for]. *2 ref.* to lose one's appetite. *3* to lose one's taste [for].

**desgano** *m.* DESGANA.

**desgañitarse** *ref.* to shout oneself hoarse.

**desgarbado, -da** *adj.* ungainly, ungraceful, gawky.

**desgarbo** *m.* clumsiness.

**desgaritar** *intr.-ref.* NAUT. to lose the course. *2* to lose the way, to go astray.

**desgarradamente** *adv.* with effrontery.

**desgarrado, -da** *adj.* torn, ripped. *2* brazen, shameless, licentious.

**desgarrador, -ra** *adj.* rending. *2* heart-rending.

**desgarrar** *tr.* to tear, rend. *2* to cough up [phlegm]. *3 ref.* to tear oneself away.

**desgarro** *m.* tear, rent. *2* effrontery, impudence. *3* swagger, swaggering.

**desgarrón** *m.* large rent or rip. *2* shred, tatter.

**desgastar** *tr.* to wear away, abrade, erode, consume. *2 ref.* to wear down or away.

**desgaste** *m.* wear, wearing down, abrasion, attrition.

**desglosar** *tr.* to separate [a question, matter, etc.] of others. *2* to detach [a part] of a book.

**desglose** *m.* separation, detachment [of questions, etc.].

**desgobernado, -da** *adj.* disorderly.

**desgobernar** *tr.* to upset the government of, to misgovern. *2* to dislocate [bones]. *4 ref.* to go through contortions. ¶ CONJUG. like *acertar*.

**desgobierno** *m.* disorder, mismanagement, misgovernment.

**desgomar** *tr.* to ungum, unsize [silk fabrics].

**desgonzar** *tr.* DESGOZNAR. *2* to disjoint, to upset.

**desgoznar** *tr.* to unhinge.

**desgracia** *f.* misfortune: *por* ~, unfortunately. *2* bad luck, mischance. *3* disfavour, loss of favour. *5* gracelessness, awkwardness. *6* accident, casualty.

**desgraciadamente** *adv.* unfortunately.

**desgraciado, -da** *adj.* unfortunate, unhappy, unlucky. *2* graceless. *3* disagreeable. *4 m.-f.* wretch, unfortunate.

**desgraciar** *tr.* to displease. *2* to spoil, mar; to cripple. *3 ref.* to spoil [be spoiled]; to fail, fall through. *4* to be crippled. *5* to fall out [with a pers.].

**desgranar** *tr.* to beat or shake out the grain [from cereals, etc.], to thresh, to flail; to shell [peas, beans, etc.]; to remove grapes [from bunch]. *2 ref.* [of cereals, etc.] to shed the grains. *3* [of a necklace, a string of beads, etc.] to come loose [scattering pearls, beads, etc.].

**desgrasar** *tr.* to remove the grease from [wool].

**desgrase** *s.* removal of grease.

**desgravación** *f.* lowering of duties or taxes.

**desgravar** *tr.* to lower the duties or taxes on.

**desgreñado, -da** *adj.* dishevelled, with disordered hair.

**desgreñar** *tr.* to dishevel [the hair]. *2 ref.* to get dishevelled. *3* to pull each other's hair, to quarrel.

**desguace** *m.* NAUT. breaking up [of a ship].

**desguarnecer** *tr.* to strip of trimming or ornaments. *2* to dismantle [a fort]; to leave without garrison. *3* to remove the accessories from. *4* to unharness [a horse].

**desguazar** *tr.* to roughdress [timber]. *2* NAUT. to break up [a ship].

**deshabitado, -da** *adj.* uninhabited, deserted. *2* untenanted.

**deshabituar** *tr.* to disaccustom, free from a habit. *2 ref.* to leave off a habit.

**deshacedor** *m.* undoer: ~ *de agravios*, righter of wrongs.

**deshacer** *tr.* to undo, unmake. *2* to undo, untie, open [a parcel]; to undo, loosen [a knot]. *3* to consume, destroy. *4* to divide, cut to pieces; to take apart. *5* to upset [plans]. *6* MIL. to rout. *7* to melt, liquefy; to dissolve. *8* to cancel [a deal]. *9* to right [wrongs]. *10 ref.* to come undone. *11* to be consumed, destroyed, to wear itself out. *12* to dissipate, evanesce. *13* to melt, dissolve: *deshacerse en la boca*, to melt in the mouth. *14* to work hard. *15* [of a deal] to fall through. *16* *deshacerse de*, to dispose of; to get rid of. *17* *deshacerse en cumplidos*, to be all civility. *18* *deshacerse en lágrimas*, to melt into tears. ¶ CONJUG. like *hacer*.

**desharrapado, -da** *adj.* ragged, in tatters. *2 m.-f.* tatterdemalion.

**desharrapamiento** *m.* misery, poverty.

**deshebillar** *tr.* to unbuckle.

**deshebrar** *tr.* to ravel into threads. *2* to separate into filaments.

**deshecha** *f.* dissimulation, dissembling.

**deshechizar** *tr.* to uncharm, disenchant.

**deshecho, -cha** *adj.* undone, destroyed, in pieces, melted, dissolved. *2* fig. broken, crushed, exhausted [person]. *3* violent [storm]. *4 p. p.* of DESHACER.

**deshelar** *tr.* to thaw, melt the ice of. *2 ref.* (of a thing) to thaw. ¶ CONJUG. like *acertar*.

**desherbar** *tr.* to weed [ground]. ¶ CONJUG. like *acertar*.

**desheredado, -da** *adj.* disinherited. *2* poor, destitute.

**desheredar** *tr.* to disinherit.

**desherrar** *tr.* to unshoe [a horse]. *2 ref.* [of a horse] to lose a shoe. ¶ CONJUG. like *acertar*.

**desherrumbrar** *tr.* to clean of rust.

**deshidratación** *f.* dehydration.

**deshidratado, -da** *adj.* dehydrated.

**deshidratar** *tr.* to dehydrate, deprive of water.

**deshielo** *m.* thaw, thawing.

**deshilachar** *tr.* to ravel out [a fabric]; to fray. *2 ref.* to fray, become ravelled out.

**deshilado, -da** *adj.* going in single file. *2 m.* drawn-work [in embroidery].

**deshiladura** *f.* ravelling out.

**deshilar** *tr.* to ravel out; to fray. *2* to shred [meat].

**deshilvanado, -da** *adj.* disjointed, disconnected, lose, desultory [speech, writing, thinking, etc.].

**deshilvanar** *tr.* SEW. to unbaste, remove basting threads from.

**deshinchar** *tr.* to deflate [a balloon, etc.]. *2* to reduce the swelling of. *3* to appease [anger]. *4 ref.* to become deflated. *5* to unpuff.

**deshipotecar** *tr.* to cancel the mortgage on.

**deshojar** *tr.* to strip [a tree] of its leaves, [a flower] of its petals. *2* to tear the leaves out of [a book]. *3 ref.* to defoliate.

**deshoje** *m.* defoliation, fall of leaves.

**deshollejar** *tr.* to skin [grapes]; to shell [beans].

**deshollinadera** *f.* DESHOLLINADOR 2.

**deshollinador** *m.* chimney sweeper. *2* longhanded broom or brush, Turk's-head.

**deshollinar** *tr.* to sweep [a chimney]. *2* to sweep or clean [ceilings] with a Turk's-head.

**deshonestidad** *f.* immodesty, indecency, lewdness.

**deshonesto, -ta** *adj.* immodest, indecent, lewd.

**deshonor** *m.* dishonour, disgrace.

**deshonorar** *tr.* to dishonour, disgrace. *2* to deprive of office or dignity.

**deshonra** *f.* dishonour, disgrace, shame. *2* seduction or violation [of a woman].

**deshonrabuenos** *m.* defamer. *2* degenerate.

**deshonrador, -ra** *m.-f.* dishonourer, disgracer, defamer. *2* violator, seducer.

**deshonrar** *tr.* to dishonour, disgrace. *2* to insult, defame. *3* to violate or seduce [a woman]. *4 ref.* to disgrace or dishonour oneself.

**deshonroso, -sa** *adj.* dishonourable, disgraceful.

**deshora** *f.* unseasonable or inconvenient time: *a ~, a deshoras,* untimely, inopportunely.

**deshornar** *tr.* DESENHORNAR.

**deshuesado, -da** *adj.* boned [meat], pitted, stoned [fruit].

**deshuesar** *tr.* to bone [meat, an animal]. *2* to stone [fruits].

**deshumanizar** *tr.* to dehumanize.

**deshumedecer** *tr.* to dehumidify, dry up. ¶ CONJUG. like *agradecer.*

**desiderativo, -va** *adj.* desiderative, expressing desire.

**desiderátum,** *pl.* **-data** *m.* desideratum.

**desidia** *f.* carelessness, negligence, indolence.

**desidioso, -sa** *adj.* careless, negligent, indolent.

**desierto, -ta** *adj.* deserted, uninhabited, lonely. *2 m.* desert, waste, wilderness.

**designación** *f.* designation, appointment.

**designar** *tr.* to design, purpose. *2* to design, designate, appoint. *3* to designate, denote.

**designio** *m.* design, purpose, intention.

**desigual** *adj.* unequal, unlike. *2* uneven; irregular, rough, broken. *3* arduous, difficult. *4* changeable, variable. *5* unsuitable [marriage]. *6 salir ~ una cosa,* to fail, fall through.

**desigualar** *tr.* to make unequal. *2* to make uneven.

**desigualdad** *f.* inequality, unequality, difference. *2* roughness, unevenness. *3* changeableness. *4* MATH. inequality.

**desilusión** *f.* disillusion, disillusionment, disenchantment, disappointment.

**desilusionar** *tr.* to disillusion, disenchant, disappoint. *2 ref.* to become disillusioned.

**desimanar, desimantar** *tr.* to demagnetize. *2 ref.* to become demagnetized.

**desimpresionar** *tr.* to undeceive.

**desinencia** *f.* GRAM. desinence, termination, inflection.

**desinencial** *adj.* desinential.

**desinfección** *f.* disinfection.

**desinfectante** *adj.-m.* disinfectant.

**desinfectar** *tr.* to disinfect.

**desinflamar** *tr.* to remove the inflammation from. *2 ref.* [of a wound, part of the body, etc.] to be cured of inflammation.

**desinflar** *tr.* to deflate.

**desinsectación** *f.* fumigation, freeing from insects.

**desinsectar** *tr.* to fumigate, free from insects.

**desintegración** *f.* disintegration.

**desintegrar** *tr.* to disintegrate. *2 intr.* to disintegrate [become disintegrated].

**desinterés** *m.* disinterest, disinterestedness.

**desinteresadamente** *adv.* disinterestedly, generously.

**desinteresado, -da** *adj.* disinterested. *2* uninterested.

**desinteresarse** *ref.* to lose interest [in something].

**desintoxicar** *tr.* MED. to cure of intoxication.

**desistimiento** *m.* desistance. *2* LAW waiving a right.

**desistir** *intr.* to desist: *~ de,* to desist from or to. *2* LAW to waive [a right].

**desjarretar** *tr.* to hamstring, hock [animals].

**desjuiciado, -da** *adj.* lacking judgment, senseless.

**desjuntar** *tr.* to disjoin, sever, separate.

**deslabonar** *tr.* to unlink; to disjoint, disconnect.

**deslavado, -da** *adj.* weak, faded, pale. *2* barefaced.

**deslavar** *tr.* to wash superficially. *2* to weaken, fade; to take away the colour or force of.

**deslavazar** *tr.* DESLAVAR.

**deslazar** *tr.* DESENLAZAR.

**desleal** *adj.* disloyal.

**deslealtad** *f.* disloyalty.

**desleimiento** *m.* dissolving [with a liquid].

**desleír** *tr.* to dissolve [with a liquid]. *2* to dilute [expressions, ideas, etc.]. ¶ CONJUG. like *reír.*

**deslenguado, -da** *adj.* impudent, insolent, foulmouthed.

**deslenguar** *tr.* to cut out the tongue of. *2 ref.* to speak impudently or insolently.

**desliar** *tr.* to untie [a package, etc.]. *2* to separate less from [wine]. *2 ref.* to come untied.

**desligadura** *f.* untying, unbinding.

**desligar** *tr.* to untie, unbind. *2* to unravel [immaterial things]. *3* to absolve, free [from obligation]. *4* MUS. to play or sing [a note] staccato. *5 ref.* to come untied. *6* to free oneself [from obligation, bonds, etc.].

**deslindamiento** *m.* DESLINDE.

**deslindar** *tr.* to demarcate, delimitate, fix the boundaries or limits of. *2* to explain, define.

**deslinde** *m.* demarcation, delimitation.

**deslío, deslía, desliera,** etc. *irr.* V. DESLEÍR.

**desliz** *m.* sliding, slipping. *2* fig. slip, blunder, false step, frailty.

**deslizadero** *m.* slippery place.

**deslizadizo, -za** *adj.* sliding. *2* slippery.

**deslizamiento** *m.* sliding, slipping, skidding.

**deslizante** *adj.* gliding.

**deslizar** *intr.-ref.* to slide, glide, skid; to slip. *2 tr.* to slip, to glide. *3 ref.* to make a slip or blunder. *4* to slip away.

**deslomadura** *f.* injuring or straining of the loins.

**deslomar** *tr.-ref.* to injure or strain the loins of. *2 tr.* to beat, thrash.

**deslucido, -da** *adj.* tarnished, spoilt, lacklustre. *2* dull, poor, flat, being a failure.

**deslucimiento** *m.* tarnishing, lack of brilliancy; dullness, flatness, failure.

**deslucir** *tr.* to tarnish, mar, spoil, to impair the lustre or splendour of. *2 ref.* to become tarnished, to get spoilt, to lose lustre. ¶ CONJUG. like *lucir.*

**deslumbrador, -ra** *adj.* dazzling, glaring.

**deslumbramiento** *m.* dazzle, dazzling.

**deslumbrante** *adj.* dazzling, glaring.

**deslumbrar** *tr.* to dazzle, daze.

**deslustrado, -da** *adj.* frosted, ground [glass]. *2 m.* frosting [of glass].

**deslustrar** *tr.* to tarnish, dull; to unglaze, remove

the luster from; to frost [glass]. 2 to impair the beauty, the fame, etc., of.

**deslustre** *m.* tarnishing, dulling. 2 unglazing, removal of the luster. 3 discredit, stain.

**desmadejamiento** *m.* lassitude.

**desmadejar** *tr.* to cause languor or lassitude. 2 *ref.* to feel languor or lassitude.

**desmadrar** *tr.* to separate [young animals] from their mothers.

**desmagnetización** *f.* demagnetization.

**desmagnetizar** *tr.* to demagnetize.

**desmajolar** *tr.* to pull up [new vines].

**desmallar** *tr.* to cut or undo the meshes of. 2 DESENMALLAR.

**desmán** *m.* excess, outrage. 2 mishap. 3 ZOOL. desman, muskrat.

**desmanarse** *ref.* to stray from a flock or herd.

**desmandado, -da** *adj.* disobedient, unruly. 2 insolent. 3 strayed, stray.

**desmandar** *tr.* to repeal an order. 2 to revoke a legacy. 3 *ref.* to be insolent. 4 to take undue liberties, to lose moderation. 5 to break away from [group, ranks, etc.].

**desmangado, -da** *adj.* handleless, without a handle.

**desmanotado, -da** *adj.* awkward, unhandy.

**desmantelado, -da** *adj.* dismantled, ill-furnished.

**desmantelar** *tr.* to dismantle. 2 NAUT. to unmast. 3 NAUT. to unrig.

**desmaña** *f.* clumsiness, awkwardness.

**desmañado, -da** *adj.* clumsy, awkward, unhandy.

**desmaño** *m.* untidiness, slovenliness.

**desmarcar** *tr.* to remove marks from. 2 *ref.* FOOTBALL to evade the marking of an opponent.

**desmarrido, -da** *adj.* sad, languid, weak.

**desmayado, -da** *adj.* faint, languid. 2 discouraged. 3 pale; wan [colour, light].

**desmayar** *tr.* to dismay, discourage. 2 *intr.* to lose courage. 3 *ref.* to faint, swoon.

**desmayo** *m.* languor, weakness. 2 discouragement. 3 fainting fit, swoon. 4 BOT. weeping willow.

**desmedido, -da** *adj.* excessive, disproportionate, out of measure.

**desmedirse** *ref.* to forget oneself, act insolently. ¶ CONJUG. like *servir*.

**desmedrado, -da** *adj.* small, stunted.

**desmedrar** *tr.* to deteriorate. 2 *intr.-ref.* to decay, lose strength.

**desmedro** *m.* deterioration, decline.

**desmejora** *f.*, **desmejoramiento** *m.* impairment, loss of health.

**desmejorar** *tr.* to impair the beauty or perfection of. 2 to impair the health of. 3 *intr.-ref.* to lose beauty or perfection. 4 to decline [in health].

**desmelenado, -da** *adj.* dishevelled, tousled.

**desmelenar** *tr.* to dishevel, disarrange the hair of.

**desmembración** *m.* dismemberment.

**desmembrar** *tr.* to dismember. 2 to divide, segregate. ¶ CONJUG. like *acertar*.

**desmemoriado, -da** *adj.* forgetful, having a poor memory.

**desmemoriarse** *ref.* to forget, lose the memory.

**desmenguar** *tr.* to lessen, to reduce, to decrease, to lower.

**desmentida** *f.* denial, act of giving the lie to.

**desmentir** *tr.* to give the lie to. 2 to contradict, deny. 3 to belie [give the lie to in conduct; be false to]. ¶ CONJUG. like *hervir*.

**desmenuzable** *adj.* crumbly, easily crumbled.

**desmenuzamiento** *m.* crumbling, breaking into small pieces or shreds. 2 minute scrutinizing.

**desmenuzar** *tr.* to crumble, to break into small pieces or shreds, to fritter. 2 to scrutinize.

**desmerecedor, -ra** *adj.* unworthy.

**desmerecer** *tr.* to be or become unworthy of. 2 *intr.* to lose worth. 3 ~ *de*, to be inferior to [another thing]. ¶ CONJUG. like *agradecer*.

**desmerecimiento** *m.* demerit.

**desmesura** *f.* excess, lack of moderation.

**desmesuradamente** *adv.* beyond measure.

**desmesurado, -da** *adj.* excessive, disproportionate. 2 impudent, discourteous, forward.

**desmesurar** *tr.* to disorder, disarrange. 2 *ref.* to be insolent, lose restraint, go too far.

**desmiento, desmienta**, etc. *irr.* V. DESMENTIR.

**desmigajar** *tr.* to crumb, break into small pieces. 2 *ref.* to crumble, fall into small pieces.

**desmigar** *tr.* to crumb [bread].

**desmilitarización** *f.* demilitarization.

**desmilitarizar** *tr.* to demilitarize.

**desmineralización** *f.* MED. demineralization.

**desmirriado, -da** *adj.* lean, emaciated, run-down.

**desmochar** *tr.* to lop or cut off the top of [a tree, etc.]; to dehorn [an animal]. 2 to cut [a literary work, a musical composition, etc.].

**desmoche** *m.* lopping or cutting off.

**desmonetizar** *tr.* to demonetize.

**desmontable** *adj.* that can be taken to pieces, dismountable, knockdown. 2 collapsible. 3 detachable. 4 ARCH. sectional, in sections, portable. 5 *n.* tyre lever.

**desmontadura** *f.* dismounting, demounting. 2 disassembling.

**desmontar** *tr.* to clear [a wood]. 2 to level [ground]. 3 to dismount, take, apart, disassemble. 4 to uncock [firearms]. 5 to dismount [deprive of horses]; to unhorse. 6 to dismount [cannon]. 7 *intr.* to dismount, alight.

**desmonte** *m.* clearing from trees or bushes. 2 levelling [of ground]; cut [for a railway, road, etc.]. 3 cleared or levelled ground.

**desmoralización** *f.* demoralization.

**desmoralizador, -ra** *adj.* demoralizing. 2 *m.-f.* demoralizer.

**desmoralizar** *tr.* to demoralize. 2 *ref.* to become demoralized. 3 MIL. to lose the morale.

**desmoronamiento** *tr.* crumbling, disintegration.

**desmoronar** *tr.* to crumble, disintegrate, erode; to destroy little by little. 2 *ref.* to crumble, fall to pieces.

**desmostarse** *ref.* [of grapes] to lose must.

**desmotar** *tr.* to burl [cloth].

**desmovilización** *f.* demobilization.

**desmovilizar** *tr.* to demobilize.

**desnacionalización** *f.* denationalization.

**desnacionalizar** *tr.* to denationalize.

**desnarigado, -da** *adj.* noseless; small-nosed.

**desnarigar** *tr.* to cut off the nose of. 2 *ref.* to bump one's nose.

**desnatadora** *f.* cream separator.

**desnatar** *tr.* to cream, draw off the cream from.

**desnaturalizado, -da** *adj.* denaturalized. 2 denatured. 3 unnatural [parent, child, etc.].

**desnaturalizar** *tr.* to denaturalize. 2 to denature.

**desnivel** *m.* unevenness, difference of level, drop.

**desnivelado, -da** *adj.* unlevelled, uneven.

**desnivelar** *tr.* to unlevel, make uneven. 2 *ref.* to become uneven.

**desnucamiento** *m.* breaking of the neck.

**desnucar** *tr.-ref.* to break or dislocate the neck of.

**desnudamente** *adv.* nakedly; clearly, plainly.
**desnudamiento** *m.* undressing. *2* denuding.
**desnudar** *tr.* to undress, unclothe. *2* to draw [the sword]. *4 ref.* to undress. *5* to become denuded; to divest oneself or itself.
**desnudez** *f.* nudity, nakedness.
**desnudo, -da** *adj.* naked, nude. *2* ill-clothed. *3* bare, uncovered, stripped. *4* destitute. *5 m.* F. ARTS nude; nude figure.
**desnutrición** *f.* MED. denutrition.
**desnutrirse** *ref.* to suffer from denutrition.
**desobedecer** *tr.* to disobey. ¶ CONJUG. like *agradecer.*
**desobediencia** *f.* disobedience.
**desobediente** *adj.* disobedient.
**desobstrucción** *f.* removal of obstructions.
**desobstruir** *tr.* to clear, remove obstructions from. *2* MED. to deobstruct. ¶ CONG. like *huir.*
**desocupación** *f.* leisure. *2* unemployment.
**desocupado, -da** *adj.* free, vacant, unoccupied. *2* at leisure, idle. *3* unemployed [person]. *4 m.-f.* idle or unemployed person.
**desocupar** *tr.* to vacate, leave, empty; to evacuate.
**desodorante** *adj.-m.* deodorant.
**desoír** *tr.* not to hear, not to heed, to be deaf to.
**desojarse** *ref.* to strain one's eyes, to look hard.
**desolación** *f.* desolation, destruction; solitariness. *2* desolation, grief.
**desolado, -da** *adj.* desolate. *2* disconsolate.
**desolador, -ra** *adj.* desolating. *2* grieving.
**desolar** *tr.* to desolate, lay waste. *2 ref.* to be desolate, disconsolate. ¶ CONJUG. like *contar.*
**desoldar** *tr.* to unsolder. *2 ref.* to come unsoldered. ¶ CONJUG. like *contar.*
**desolladero** *m.* slaughterhouse.
**desollado, -da** *adj.* skinned, flayed. *2* impudent, brazen, shameless.
**desollador, -ra** *m.-f.* skinner, flayer. *3* fleecer, extortioner.
**desolladura** *f.* skinning, flaying. *2* excoriation.
**desollar** *tr.* to skin, flay. *2* to excoriate. *3* to cause great harm or injure to [a person]. *4 ~ vivo,* fig. to skin alive; fig. to backbite. ¶ CONJUG. like *contar.*
**desollón** *m.* excoriation.
**desopilar** *tr.* MED. to deoppilate.
**desopinar** *tr.* to discredit.
**desorden** *m.* disorder [want of order], confusion, disarray. *2* disorder, disturbance, riot. *3* disorder, licence, excess.
**desordenado, -da** *adj.* disorderly. *2* disarranged. *3* careless, slovenly. *4* inordinate, immoderate. *5* licentious [life].
**desordenar** *tr.* to disorder, throw into disorder, disarrange, upset. *2 ref.* to become disarranged.
**desorejado, -da** *adj.* infamous, dissolute, degraded.
**desorejar** *tr.* to crop the ears of.
**desorganización** *f.* disorganization.
**desorganizar** *tr.* to disorganize. *2 ref.* to become disorganized.
**desorientación** *f.* disorientation, loss of one's bearings. *2* confusion, bafflement.
**desorientador, -ra** *adj.* confusing, baffling.
**desorientar** *tr.* to disorientate. *2* to confuse, bewilder. *3 ref.* to become disorientated.
**desosar** *tr.* DESHUESAR.
**desovar** *intr.* [of aquatic animals] to spawn.
**desove** *m.* spawning. *2* spawning season.
**desovillar** *tr.* to unwind [a ball of yarn]. *2* to clear up, unravel.

**desoxidación** *f.* deoxidization. *2* removal of the rust.
**desoxidar** *tr.* to deoxidize. *2* to remove the rust of.
**desoxigenar** *tr.* to deoxygenate, to deoxidize.
**despabiladeras** *f. pl.* snuffers.
**despabilado, -da** *adj.* wakeful, awake. *2* smart, quick-witted.
**despabilar** *tr.* to trim or snuff [a candle]. *2* to finish quickly. *3* to steal. *4* to smarten, enliven, sharpen the wits of. *5* coll. to kill. *6 ref.* to wake up, shake sleepiness. *7* to become alert.
**despacio** *adv.* slowly, deliberately. *2* (Am.) in a low voice. *3 interj.* easy there!, gently!
**despacioso, -sa** *adj.* slow, deliberate, phlegmatic.
**despacito** *adv.* slowly, gently. *2 interj.* DESPACIO *3.*
**despachaderas** *f. pl.* coll. surly manner of replying. *2* coll. resourcefulness.
**despachado, -da** *adj.* impudent, brazen. *2* resourceful.
**despachar** *tr.* to dispatch [get promptly done; send off; kill]. *2* to attend to [correspondence]. *3* to attend to, settle [business]. *4* to sell [goods]. *5* to wait upon [customers]. *6* to dismiss, discharge. *7* to clear [at the custom-house]. *8 intr.-ref.* to hasten, be quick. *9 ref.* to talk without restraint.
**despacho** *m.* dispatch, promptness. *2* attending [to correspondence]; settling [of business]. *3* sale [of goods]. *4* clearance [at the custom-house]. *5* dismissal. *6* shipment. *7* office, bureau, counting house: *~ de billetes,* ticket-office; *~ de localidades,* box-office. *8* library, study. *9* dispatch [message]. *10* title, commission, warrant.
**despachurrar** *tr.* to crush, squash. *2* fig. to make a mess of [a speech, etc.].
**despajar** *tr.* to separate straw from [grain].
**despaldillar** *tr.* to break or dislocate the shoulder of [an animal].
**despalmar** *tr.* NAUT. to careen, clean the bottom of [a ship]. *2* to pare [a horse's hoof].
**despampanante** *adj.* astounding; stunning, splendid, ripping.
**despampanar** *tr.* to prune [vines]. *2* coll. to astound. *3 ref.* to give oneself a hard bump.
**despancijar, despanzurrar** *tr.* to burst the belly of; to squash.
**desparejar** *tr.* to break the pair of.
**desparpajado, -da** *adj.* easy in speech and deportment.
**desparpajo** *m.* easiness in speech and deportment, unembarrassment.
**desparramado, -da** *adj.* spread, scattered.
**desparramamiento** *m.* spreading, scattering. *2* squandering, extravagance. *3* dissipation.
**desparramar** *tr.* to spread, scatter. *2* to squander, dissipate. *3 ref.* to spread, scatter. *4* to amuse , oneself, have a wild time.
**despasar** *tr.* NAUT. to unreeve. *2* SEW. to take [a string, etc.] out of a casing.
**despatarrada** *f.* split [in dancing].
**despatarrar** *tr.* to make [a person] open his legs wide. *2* coll. to astound, to dumbfound. *3 ref.* to fall flat with legs spread out.
**despatillar** *tr.* CARP. to tenon.
**despavesar** *tr.* to snuff [candles]. *2* to blow the ashes off [embers].
**despavorido, -da** *adj.* terrified.
**despavorir** *intr.-ref.* to feel dread, terror; to be or become terrified. ¶ Only used in the forms having *i* in their terminations.

**despearse** *ref.* to get one's feet or hoofs sore [by much walking].

**despectivamente** *adj.* contemptuously, scornfully. 2 pejoratively.

**despectivo, -va** *adj.* contemptuous. 2 GRAM. pejorative.

**despechadamente** *adv.* spitefully; despairingly.

**despechar** *tr.* to irritate, enrage; to cause despair.

**despecho** *m.* spite born from disappointment. 2 despair. 3 *a ~ de,* in spite of, despite.

**despechugar** *tr.* to carve off the breast of a [fowl]. 2 *ref.* coll. to bare one's breast.

**despedazamiento** *m.* tearing to pieces, cutting into pieces.

**despedazar** *tr.* to tear to pieces, cut into pieces. 2 to break [one's heart]; to tear to shreds [a reputation].

**despedida** *f.* farewell. 2 leave-taking.

**despedir** *tr.* to throw. 2 to emit, send forth, eject, discharge, dart. 3 to reject, expel, throw back. 4 to dismiss; discharge, give notice to. 5 to see off, escort to the door, say good-bye to. 6 *ref.* to part, say good-bye to: *despedirse de,* to take leave of; *despedirse a la francesa,* to take French leave. 7 to give up one's job, give notice. ¶ CONJUG. like *servir.*

**despedregar** *tr.* to clear of stones.

**despegado, -da** *adj.* detached, unglued. 2 cool, indifferent, detached, unaffectionate. 3 surly.

**despegar** *tr.* to detach, unglue, unstick; to separate. 2 *intr.* AER. to take off. 3 *ref.* to detach itself. 4 to move away from. 5 to lose affection for. 6 not to suit, not to go well with.

**despego** *m.* coolness, indifference.

**despegue** *m.* AER. take-off.

**despeinado, -da** *adj.* dishevelled, unkempt.

**despeinar** *tr.-ref.* to dishevel, disarrange, ruffle the hair of.

**despejado, -da** *adj.* assured, self-confident. 2 [of person, intelligence, etc.] bright. 3 [of space, forehead, etc.] clear, wide; [of the sky] cloudless.

**despejar** *tr.* to clear, free from encumbrance. 2 to clear up [a situation, etc.]. 3 ALG. to find value of [unknown quantify]. 4 *ref.* to acquire assurance, ease. 5 [of weather, the head, etc.] to clear up. 6 MED. to get rid of fever.

**despejo** *m.* clearing, freeing from encumbrance. 2 clearing up. 3 assurance, ease. 4 intelligence.

**despelotado, -da** *adj.* coll. stark-naked.

**despelotarse** *ref.* coll. to strip naked. 2 to take care of oneself.

**despeluzar** *tr.* to dishevel. 2 to make the hair [of a person] stand on end. 3 *ref.* to be horrified.

**despeluznante** *adj.* hair-raising, horrifying.

**despeluznar** *tr.* DESPELUZAR.

**despellejar** *tr.* to skin, flay. 2 fig. to flay, speak ill of.

**despenar** *tr.* to relieve from sorrow. 2 coll. to kill.

**despensa** *f.* pantry, larder, storeroom. 2 store of provisions.

**despensería** *f.* pantryman's post.

**despensero, -ra** *m.* pantryman, butler. 2 *f.* pantrywoman.

**despeñadero** *m.* precipice, craggy slope. 2 fig. danger [to which one exposes oneself].

**despeñar** *tr.* to precipitate, fling down a precipice.

**despepitar** *tr.* to remove the pips from [a fruit]; to gin [cotton]. 2 *ref. despepitarse por,* to be mad about.

**desperdiciar** *tr.* to waste, squander, misspend. 2 to

fail to take advantage of; to lose, miss [an opportunity, etc.].

**desperdicio** *m.* waste, squander, misspending. 2 (spec. *pl.*) waste, waste material, remains.

**desperdigar** *tr.* to scatter, disperse. 2 *ref.* to scatter, disperse [go in different directions].

**desperezarse** *ref.* to stretch, to stretch one's limbs.

**desperezo** *m.* stretching [one's limbs].

**desperfecto** *m.* slight damage, deterioration.

**desperfilar** *tr.* PAINT. to soften the contours of.

**despernar** *tr.* to cut or injure the legs of.

**despersonalizar** *tr.* to depersonalize.

**despertador, -ra** *adj.* awaking. 2 *m.-f.* awakener. 3 *m.* alarm clock, alarum-clock.

**despertar** *tr.* to wake, awaken, rouse [from sleep]. 2 awaken, rouse, stir up, excite. 3 *intr.-ref.* to wake up, awake; to revive. ¶ CONJUG. like *acertar.*

**despestañarse** *ref.* to look hard, strain one's eyes.

**despezonar** *tr.* to take off the stem [of a fruit].

**despiadado, -da** *adj.* pitiless, ruthless, unmerciful.

**despicar** *tr.* to satisfy, gratify. 2 *ref.* to have one's own back, to take revenge.

**despichar** *tr.* to expel [juice or moisture].

**despidiente** *m.* ARCH. *~ de aguas,* flashing.

**despido** *m.* farewell; leave taking. 2 dismissal, discharge, layoff.

**despido, despida,** etc. *irr.* V. DESPEDIR.

**despiertamente** *adv.* smartly, ingeniously.

**despierto, -ta** *adj.* awake. 2 lively, smart, quick-witted.

**despierto, despierte,** etc. *irr.* V. DESPERTAR.

**despilfarradamente** *adv.* lavishly, prodigally.

**despilfarrado, -da** *adj.* wasted, squandered. 2 ragged, in rags. 3 *adj.-n.* prodigal, spendthrift.

**despilfarrador, -ra** *adj.* squanderer, prodigal.

**despilfarrar** *tr.* to waste, squander, spend lavishly. 2 *ref.* to be prodigal of his money.

**despilfarro** *m.* waste, extravagance, lavishness.

**despimpollar** *tr.* to clear [a vine] of useless shoots.

**despintar** *tr.* to take the paint off. 2 to cause to turn out differently. 3 *ref.* [of a thing] to lose its paint, lose colour. 4 *no despintársele a uno una persona,* not to forget what a person is like.

**despinzar** *tr.* to burl [cloth].

**despiojar** *tr.* to delouse.

**despique** *m.* satisfaction, requital.

**despistar** *tr.* to throw off the scent. 2 *ref.* to loose the scent. 3 coll. to go off the track, get lost.

**despiste** *m.* swerve (car). 2 absentmindedness, confusion, bewilderment. 3 mistake; *tener un gran ~,* to be terribly absentminded.

1) **desplacer** *m.* pain, displeasure.

2) **desplacer** *tr.* to pain, to displease.

**desplanchar** *tr.* to rumple [something that was ironed].

**desplantador** *m.* garden trowel.

**desplantar** *tr.* to uproot. 2 to throw out of plumb.

**desplante** *m.* irregular posture [in dancing or fencing]. 2 arrogant or insolent act or words.

**desplayar** *intr.* [of the sea] to recede from the beach.

**desplazamiento** *m.* NAUT. displacement [of water].

**desplazar** *tr.* NAUT. to displace.

**desplegable** *m.* brochure, folder, pamphlet.

**desplegar** *tr.* to unfold, spread, lay out, open out. 2 to unfurl. 3 to unfold, explain. 4 to display [activity, etc.]. 5 MIL. to deploy. 6 *ref.* to unfold, open, expand, spread out. 7 MIL. [of troops] to deploy. ¶ CONJUG. like *acertar.*

**despliegue** m. unfolding; displaying. 2 MIL. deployment.

**desplomar** tr. to throw out of plumb. 2 ref. to get out of plumb. 3 [of a wall] to tumble down. 4 to crash down. 5 [of a pers.] to collapse.

**desplome** m. getting out of plumb. 2 tumbling down. 3 collapse, fall.

**desplomo** m. ARCH. deviation from the vertical.

**desplumar** tr. to pluck [a bird]. 2 fig. to pluck, fleece [someone]. 3 ref. [of a bird] to lose its feathers.

**desplume** m. plucking, deplumation.

**despoblación** f. depopulation. 2 stripping [a land] of trees; emptying [a river] of fishes.

**despoblado** m. uninhabited tract of land; open country.

**despoblar** tr. to depopulate. 2 to strip [a land] of trees, to deprive [the head, a spot] of hair; to empty [a river, etc.] of fishes. 3 ref. to become depopulated, desert. 4 to become bald, treeless or empty of fishes. ¶ CONJUG. like contar.

**despojar** tr. to despoil, deprive; to strip, divest. 2 LAW to dispossess. 3 ref. despojarse de, to take off [a garment]; to give up, to divest oneself of.

**despojo** m. depoilment, despoliation; stripping, divesting; dispossession. 2 spoils, booty. 3 pl. head, pluck and feet [of slaughtered animals]; gizzard, pinions, legs, head and neck [of fowl]. 4 leavings, scraps. 5 mortal remains.

**despolarizar** tr. PHYS., CHEM. depolarize.

**despolvorear** tr. to dust, dust off.

**desportillar** tr. to chip or break the edge of.

**desposado, -da** adj. newly married. 2 handcuffed. 3 m.-f. newlywed.

**desposar** tr. to marry [unite in wedlock]. 2 ref. to get married. 3 to be betrothed.

**desposeer** tr.-ref. to disposses, to divest.

**desposeimiento** m. dispossession.

**desposorios** m. pl. nuptials, marriage. 2 betrothal.

**déspota** m. despot, tyrant.

**despótico, -ca** adj. despotic.

**despotismo** m. despotism.

**despotricar** intr. to talk without restraint, to rant.

**despotrique** m. wild talk, ranting.

**despreciable** adj. despicable, contemptible. 2 negligible.

**despreciar** tr. to despise, contemn, scorn, slight. 2 to lay aside, to reject. 3 to set to nought, to undervalue.

**despreciativo, -va** adj. contemptuous, scornful.

**desprecio** m. contempt, scorn, disregard. 2 slight.

**desprender** tr. to detach, loose, separate. 2 to emit, send, give out [light, heat, etc.]. 3 ref. to come loose, detach itself; to detach or extricate oneself. 4 [of light, heat, etc.] to issue, come forth. 5 to dispossess oneself. 6 to follow, be inferred.

**desprendido, -da** adj. generous, disinterested.

**desprendimiento** m. detaching, coming loose. 2 emission [of light, heat, etc.]. 3 disinterestedness. 4 indifference. 5 PAINT. descent from the Cross. 6 landslide.

**despreocupación** f. freedom from bias. 2 unconventionality. 3 unconcernedness. 4 openmindedness.

**despreocupado, -da** adj. unprejudiced. 2 carefree, unconcerned. 3 unconventional. 4 broadminded.

**despreocuparse** ref. to abandon a prejudice. 2 ~ de, not to care or worry anymore about.

**desprestigiar** tr. to discredit, impair the prestige of. 3 ref. to fall into discredit, lose prestige.

**desprestigio** m. discredit, loss of prestige.

**desprevenido, -da** adj. unprovided, unprepared: coger a uno ~, to catch somebody unawares.

**desproporción** f. disproportion.

**desproporcionado, -da** adj. disproportionate.

**desproporcionar** tr. to disproportion.

**despropósito** m. absurdity, nonsense.

**desproveer** tr. to deprive of provisions, supplies or the necessaries of life.

**desprovisto, -ta** adj. unprovided. 2 deprived, void [of]; lacking [in].

**después** adv. after, afterwards, later; next. 2 ~ de, after, next to; ~ (de) que, after; ~ de todo, after all.

**despulpar** tr. to extract the pulp from [a fruit].

**despuntar** tr. to blunt, to break or wear out the point of. 2 intr. to show wit or intelligence; to excel. 4 ~ el alba, ~ el día, to dawn.

**desquejar** tr. HORT. to slip.

**desqueje** f. HORT. slipping.

**desquiciamiento** m. unhinging. 2 upsetting, unsetting, downfall.

**desquiciar** tr. to unhinge. 2 to disjoint, to upset, to unsettle. 3 ref. to become unhinged, disjointed, upset, unsettled.

**desquitar** tr. to compensate [someone] for loss, etc. 2 ref. to retrieve a loss, to win back one's money. 3 to take revenge, get even.

**desquite** m. retrieving [of one's loss], compensation. 2 revenge, requital, retaliation.

**desramar** tr. to strip of branches.

**desratizar** tr. to derat.

**desratización** f. deratting, deratization.

**desrizar** tr. to uncurl, unfrizzle.

**destacado, -da** adj. outstanding, distinguished.

**destacamento** m. MIL. detachment.

**destacar** tr. MIL. detach, detail. 2 PAINT. to make stand out, emphasize. 3 ref. MIL. [of a troop] to detach itself. 4 to stand out, be conspicuous.

**destaconar** tr. to wear down the heels of [shoes].

**destajador** m. forging hammer.

**destajar** tr. to settle the terms for [a job]. 2 to cut [cards].

**destajero, -ra & destajista** m.-f. pieceworker.

**destajo** m. piecework, taskwork: a ~, by the job; fig. eagerly, rapidly.

**destapar** tr. to uncover. 2 to take off the cover, lid or cap of; to uncork, unplug, open. 3 to reveal. 4 ref. to get uncovered.

**destapiar** tr. to pull down the walls enclosing [an open space].

**destaponar** tr. to remove the stopper from.

**destarar** tr. COM. to deduct the tare on.

**destartalado, -da** adj. ramshackle. 2 poorly furnished [house, room].

**destazar** tr. BUTCH. to cut up carcasses.

**destechar** tr. to unroof.

**destejar** tr. to untile the roof of.

**destejer** tr. to unweave or ravel, to unknit, to unbraid.

**destellar** tr. to sparkle, twinkle, flash, scintillate.

**destello** m. sparkling, twinkling. 2 sparkle, flash, scintillation; beam [of light].

**destemplado, -da** adj. MUS. out of tune. 2 PAINT. inharmonious. 3 intemperate, disagreeable.

**destemplanza** f. intemperance, unsteadiness [of the weather]. 2 MED. malaise. 3 want of moderation [in language or actions], rudeness.

**destemplar** tr. to disturb the harmony of. 2 MUS. to put out of tune. 3 ref. MUS. [of instruments] to get out of tune. 4 MED. to feel a malaise. 5 [of a metal] to lose its temper. 6 to lose moderation in language or actions.

**destemple** *m.* MUS. [of instruments] being out of tune. 2 MED. malaise. 3 unpleasantness [of weather]. 4 untempering. 5 want of moderation [in words, etc.]; rudeness.

**desteñir** *tr.* to undye; to discolour, fade. 2 *ref.* to lose the dye; to fade. ¶ CONJUG. like *teñir.*

**desternillarse** *ref.* to break one's gristles: ~ *de risa,* coll. to split one's sides with laughter.

**desterrado, -da** *adj.* exiled. 2 *m.-f.* exile, outcast.

**desterrar** *tr.* to exile, banish [a person]. 2 to banish [sadness, uses, etc.]. 3 *ref.* to go into exile. ¶ CONJUG. like *acertar.*

**desterronar** *tr.* to break or crumb the clods of.

**destetar** *tr.* to wean.

**destete** *m.* weaning.

**destiempo (a)** *adv.* inopportunely, untimely, out of season.

**destierro** *m.* banishment, exile. 2 place of exile. 3 remote and solitary place.

**destierro, destierre,** etc. *irr.* V. DESTERRAR.

**destilación** *f.* distillation. 2 catarrhal discharge.

**destilado, -da** *adj.* distilled.

**destilador, -ra** *adj.* distilling. 2 *m.-f.* distiller. 3 *m.* ALAMBIQUE.

**destilar** *tr.* to distil. 2 to filter. 3 *intr.* to distil, trickle down.

**destilería** *f.* distillery, distilling plant.

**destinación** *f.* destination, destining.

**destinar** *tr.* to destine. 2 to designate, appoint [to a post]. 3 to allot, assign.

**destinatario, -ria** *m.-f.* addressee. 2 consignee.

**destino** *m.* destiny, fate, fortune, doom. 2 destination: *con* ~ *a,* bound for, going to. 3 employment, post, job.

**destitución** *f.* dismissal, removal from office. 2 destitution, depriving.

**destituir** *tr.* to dismiss or remove from office. 2 to destitute, deprive. ¶ CONJUG. like *huir.*

**destocar** *tr.-ref.* to undo the coiffure of; to uncover the head of.

**destorcer** *tr.* to untwist. 2 to straighten. 3 *ref.* to untwist [become untwisted]. ¶ CONJUG. like *mover.*

**destornillado, -da** *adj.* unscrewed. 2 brainless, thoughtless, with a screw loose.

**destornillador** *m.* screwdriver.

**destornillamiento** *m.* unscrewing. 2 craziness.

**destornillar** *tr.* to unscrew. 2 *ref.* to go crazy.

**destrabar** *tr.* to unshackle, untie. 2 to loosen, separate.

**destraillar** *tr.* to uncouple, unleash [dogs].

**destral** *m.* hatchet, small axe.

**destramar** *tr.* to unweave.

**destrenzar** *tr.* to unbraid, to undo [a tress].

**destreza** *f.* skill, dexterity, address, mastery.

**destripacuentos** *m.-f.* untimely interrupter of an account or narrative.

**destripar** *tr.* to gut, disembowel. 2 to take the inside out of, to crush.

**destripaterrones** *m.* clodhopper, rustic.

**destriunfar** *tr.* CARDS to draw out the trumps from.

**destronamiento** *m.* dethronement.

**destronar** *tr.* to dethrone. 2 to overthrow [from power].

**destroncar** *tr.* to detruncate; to maim, to dislocate. 2 to cut [trees] at the trunk. 3 to deprive of means, bring to ruin. 4 to tire out, exhaust.

**destrozar** *tr.* to break in pieces, shatter, rend, des-

troy. 2 to spoil, ill-treat. 3 fig. to anihilate. 4 MIL. to destroy, inflict great losses.

**destrozo** *m.* breakage, destruction, havoc.

**destrozón, -na** *m.-f.* one who wears out clothes and shoes too quickly.

**destrucción** *f.* destruction.

**destructible** *adj.* destructible.

**destructivo, -va** *adj.* destructive.

**destructor, -ra** *adj.* destructive. 2 *m.-f.* destroyer. 3 *m.* NAV. destroyer.

**destruible** *adj.* destructible.

**destruir** *tr.* to destroy. 2 to deprive of means, bring to ruin. 3 to waste, dissipate. 4 *ref.* to destroy each other. 5 ALG. to cancel each other. ¶ CONJUG. like *huir.*

**destruyente** *adj.* destructive.

**destruyo, destruyó, destruya,** etc. *irr.* V. DESTRUIR.

**desubstanciar** *tr.* DESUSTANCIAR.

**desudación** *f.* topping the sweating.

**desudar** *tr.* to stop the sweating of.

**desuello** *m.* skinning, flaying. 2 effrontery.

**desuello, desuelle,** etc. *irr.* V. DESOLLAR.

**desuncir** *tr.* to unyoke.

**desunión** *f.* disunion.

**desunir** *tr.* to disunite. 2 *ref.* to disunite, fall apart.

**desuñar** *tr.* to tear off the nails or claws of. 2 to pull up the dead roots of [plants]. 3 *ref.* coll. to work hard with one's hands.

**desurdir** *tr.* to remove the warp from [a fabric]; to unweave. 2 to upset [a plot, etc.].

**desusado, -da** *adj.* out of use, obsolete. 2 unusual.

**desusar** *tr.* to discontinue the use of.

**desuso** *m.* disuse, obsoleteness, desuetude: *caer en* ~, to become obsolete.

**desustanciar** *tr.* to deprive of substance, to weaken. 2 *ref.* to lose substance, weaken.

**desvaído, -da** *adj.* pale, dull [colour]. 2 lank, ungainly [person].

**desvainar** *tr.* to shell [beans, peas, etc.].

**desvalido, -da** *adj.* helpless, unprotected, destitute.

**desvalijador, -ra** *n.* thief, robber. 2 burglar.

**desvalijar** *tr.* to take out or steal the contents of [a valise, suitcase, etc.]. 2 to rob, plunder, fleece.

**desvalimiento** *m.* helplessness, abandonment, destitution.

**desvalorización** *f.* devaluation.

**desvalorizar** *tr.* to devalue.

**desván** *m.* garret, loft.

**desvanecedor** *m.* PHOT. mask.

**desvanecer** *tr.* to melt, cause to vanish. 2 to dispel, dissipate [clouds, doubts, etc.]. 3 to efface [a recollection]. 4 to swell [with pride]. 5 *ref.* to melt, vanish, evanesce, evaporate. 6 to be dispelled, dissipated, effaced. 7 to swell [with pride]. 8 to faint, swoon. 9 RADIO. to fade. ¶ CONJUG. like *agradecer.*

**desvanecidamente** *adv.* proudly, with presumption.

**desvanecido, -da** *adj.* vain, proud, conceited, haughty. 2 smug, self-satisfied. 3 MED. fainted.

**desvanecimiento** *m.* melting, vanishing, dispelling. 2 pride, presumption. 3 giddiness, swoon, fainting fit. 4 RADIO. fading.

**desvarar** *intr.-ref.* to glide, slip. 2 *tr.* NAUT. to refloat, set afloat [a stranded ship].

**desvariado, -da** *adj.* delirious, raving. 2 wild, nonsensical.

**desvariar** *intr.* to be delirious, rave, rant.

**desvarío** *m.* delirium, raving. 2 wild act or speech,

nonsense. *3* monstrosity. *4* inconstancy, caprice, whim.

**desvelado, -da** *adj.* wakeful, sleepless. *2* careful, solicitous.

**desvelar** *tr.* to keep awake, make sleepless. *2 ref.* to be unable to sleep. *3* to spare no pains, watch carefully [over].

**desvelo** *m.* sleeplessness, wakefulness. *2* care, solicitude, concern.

**desvencijado, -da** *adj.* rickety, loose-jointed.

**desvencijar** *tr.* to disjoint, make rickety. *2 ref.* to become rickety.

**desvendar** *tr.* to take off a bandage from.

**desventaja** *f.* disadvantage; drawback.

**desventajoso, -sa** *adj.* disadvantageous, detrimental.

**desventura** *f.* unhappiness, misery. *2* misfortune.

**desventurado, -da** *adj.* unfortunate, wretched. *2* timid, spiritless. *3* miserly. *4 m.-f.* poor, spiritless person. *5* miser.

**desvergonzado, -da** *adj.* shameless; impudent. *2 m.-f.* shameless or impudent person.

**desvergonzarse** *ref.* to lose shame. *2 ~ con*, to be impudent or insolent to. ¶ Conjug. like *contar*.

**desvergüenza** *f.* shamelessness, effrontery. *2* impudence, insolence.

**desvestir** *tr.-ref.* to undress.

**desviación** *f.* deviation, deflection, diversion. *2* turning aside or away, wandering away, swerving, swerve. *3* MAGN. deviation.

**desviacionismo** *m.* deviationism.

**desviacionista** *adj.* deviationist.

**desviado, -da** *adj.* deviated; devious.

**desviar** *tr.* to deviate, deflect. *2* to turn aside, turn away, swerve. *3* to dissuade. *4* RLY. to switch. *5* to ward off [in fencing]. *6 ref.* to deviate, be deflected, turn aside, swerve, wander away.

**desvinculación** *f.* freeing, releasing. *2* breaking one's links with, severing one's connections with, discharging [from an obligation or commitment], separation, cutting-off.

**desvincular** *tr.* to free, to discharge, to release. *2* to break one's links with, to cut-off, to separate.

**desvío** *m.* deviation, deflection, turning aside or away. *2* coldness, indifference, dislike. *3* RLY. siding, sidetrack.

**desvirar** *tr.* to pare off the edges of [a sole]. *2* to trim [a book]. *3* NAUT. to reverse [a capstan].

**desvirgar** *tr.* to deflower [a woman].

**desvirtuar** *tr.* to deprive of import, meaning, force or efficacity.

**desvivirse** *ref. ~ por*, to do one's utmost for; to long for.

**desyemar** *tr.* AGR. to remove the buds from [plants].

**desyerbar** *tr.* DESHERBAR.

**deszumar** *tr.* to extract the juice from.

**detall** *m.* retail: *al ~*, at retail.

**detalladamente** *adv.* in detail.

**detallar** *tr.* to detail, particularize; to work in detail. *2* to retail, sell at retail.

**detalle** *m.* detail, particular. *2* detailed account.

**detallista** *m.-f.* painter or writer fond of, or skilled in, detail. *2* retailer.

**detección** *f.* RADIO. detection.

**detectar** *tr.* RADIO. to detect.

**detective** *m.* detective.

**detector** *m.* RADIO. detector.

**detención** *f.* detainment, detention, stopping. *2* halt, stop, delay. *3* detention [in jail]. *4* arrest, capture [of a person]. *5* care, thoroughness.

**detendré, detendría,** etc. *irr.* V. DETENER.

**detener** *tr.* to detain, stop; to check, hold, hold back, keep, refrain. *2* to arrest, capture, take into custody. *3* to keep, retain. *4 ref.* to stop, halt. *5* to delay, linger, tarry, pause. *6 detenerse a considerar*, to stop to consider. ¶ Conjug. like *tener*.

**detengo, detenga,** etc. *irr.* V. DETENER.

**detenido, -da** *adj.* careful, minute, thorough. *2* in custody, under arrest. *5 m.-f.* LAW prisoner.

**detenimiento** *m.* care, thoroughness.

**detentar** *tr.* to retain unlawfully, to deforce.

**detergente** *adj.-n.* detergent, detersive.

**deterger** *tr.* to deterge.

**deterioración** *f.* impairing, damaging, spoiling, deterioration.

**deteriorar** *tr.* to impair, damage, spoil, deteriorate. *2 ref.* to become damaged, spoiled.

**deterioro** *m.* DETERIORACIÓN. *2* injury, damage.

**determinación** *f.* determination, determining. *2* determination, decision, resolve. *2* resoluteness, firmness, daring.

**determinado, -da** *adj.* determinate. *3* fixed, appointed. *4* given, specified. *5* determined. *6* GRAM. definite [article].

**determinante** *adj.-m.* determinant.

**determinar** *tr.* to determine. *2* to fix, appoint [time or place]. *3* to determine on, resolve. *4 ref.* to determine, make up one's mind.

**determinativo, -va** *adj.* determinative.

**determinismo** *m.* PHILOS. determinism.

**determinista** *adj.-n.* PHIL. determinist.

**detersión** *f.* detersion.

**detersivo, -va; detersorio, -ria** *adj.* detersive.

**detestable** *adj.* detestable. *2* very bad.

**detestación** *f.* detestation.

**detestar** *tr.* to detest.

**detonación** *f.* detonation, report.

**detonador** *m.* detonator.

**detonante** *adj.* detonating, explosive. *2* stunning, shattering. *3 m.* explosive.

**detonar** *tr.* to detonate.

**detorsión** *f.* MED. sprain.

**detracción** *f.* detraction.

**detractar** *tr.* to detract, defame, denigrate.

**detractor, -ra** *m.-f.* detractor.

**detraer** *tr.* to detract. ¶ Conjug. like *traer*.

**detrás** *adv.* behind, back, in the rear. *2 ~ de*, behind, after, in pursuit of: *~ de la puerta*, behind the door; *ir ~ de*, to go after. *3 por ~*, from behind; behind one's back.

**detrimento** *m.* detriment, damage, harm.

**detrítico, -ca** *adj.* GEOL. detrital.

**detrito** *m.* detritus.

**detuve, detuviera,** etc. *irr.* V. DETENER.

**deuda** *f.* debt. *2* sin, fault, offence. *3* public debt; *~ consolidada*, funded debt.

**deudo, -da** *m.-f.* relative. *2* relationship.

**deudor, -ra** *adj.* indebted. *2 m.-f.* debtor.

**Deuteronomio** *m.* Deuteronomy.

**devalar** *intr.* NAUT. to drift from the course.

**devaluación** *f.* devaluation.

**devanadera** *f.* reel, winding frame.

**devanado** *m.* winding [of yarn, etc.].

**devanador, -ra** *adj.* winding. *2 m.-f.* winder.

**devanar** *tr.* to wind, reel, spool. *2 ref. devanarse los sesos*, to rack one's brains.

**devanear** *intr.* to rave, to act or talk nonsense.

**devaneo** *m.* raving, delirium, nonsense. *2* dissipation. *3* flirtation.

**devastación** *f.* devastation, destruction, waste, ruin.

**devastador, -ra** *adj.* devastating. *2 m.-f.* devastator.

**devastar** *tr.* to devastate, lay waste, ruin.

**devengar** *tr.* to earn [wages]; to draw [interest].

**devenir** *intr.* to happen. *2* PHIL. to become. ¶ CONJUG. like *venir.*

**devoción** *f.* devotion, devoutness. *2* strong attachment. *3 pl.* devotions, prayers.

**devocionario** *m.* prayer book.

**devolución** *f.* return, restitution.

**devolver** *tr.* to give back, pay back, put back, send back, return, restore. *2* to return [give in requital or recompense]. *3* coll. to vomit.

**devónico, -ca** *adj.-n.* GEOL. Devonian.

**devorador, -ra** *adj.* devouring. *2 m.-f.* devourer.

**devorar** *tr.* to devour.

**devotería** *f.* sanctimony.

**devoto, -ta** *adj.* devout, pious. *2* devotional. *3* devoted [to a person]. *4 m.-f.* devout person.

**dextrógiro, -ra** *adj.* PHYS. dextrorotary, dextrorotatory.

**dextrina** *f.* CHIM. dextrine.

**dextrorso, -sa** *adj.* BOT. dextrorse.

**dextrosa** *f.* CHEM. dextrose.

**dey** *m.* dey [ruler of Algiers].

**deyección** *f.* PHYSIOL. dejection. *2* GEOL. debris.

**dezmable** *adj.* tithable.

**di** *irr.* V. DAR & DECIR.

**día** *m.* day: ~ *de abstinencia* or *de vigilia,* day of abstinence; ~ *de año nuevo,* New Year's day; ~ *de asueto,* day off; ~ *de ayuno,* fast day; ~ *de fiesta,* feast day, holiday; ~ *del juicio,* Judgement day; ~ *de los difuntos,* All-Soul's Day; ~ *de los inocentes,* Innocents' Day; ~ *de Reyes;* Epiphany; ~ *de Todos los Santos,* All-Saint's Day, Hallowmass; ~ *feriado,* LAW court holyday; ~ *festivo,* holyday; ~ *laborable,* workday, weekday; *quince días,* a fortnight; *a días,* now and then; *al* ~, a day, per day; up to date; *antes del* ~, at dawn; *de* ~ *en* ~, from day to day; *el* ~ *de hoy, hoy* ~, today; now, the present time; *el* ~ *menos pensado,* when least expected; *el mejor* ~, some fine day; *en cuatro días,* in few days; *en su* ~, at the proper time; *¡buenos días!,* good morning!; *dar los buenos días,* to pass the time of day. *2* daytime, daylight. *3 pl.* birthday; saint's day [of a person]: *dar los días,* to wish [someone] many happy returns of the day.

**diabetes** *f.* MED. diabetes.

**diabético, -ca** *adj.-n.* diabetic.

**diablear** *intr.* to play pranks.

**diablejo** *m.* little devil; imp.

**diablesa** *f.* she-devil.

**diablillo** *m.* little devil, devilkin; imp. *2* mischievous, waggish person, rogue.

**diablo** *m.* devil [evil spirit]; wicked person: *como un* ~, like the deuce, like the devil; *darse al* ~, to get angry, to get wild; *del* ~, *de mil diablos, de todos los diablos,* the devil of a; *¡diablos!,* the devil! *2* bad-tempered, reckless, mischievous, shrewd or skilled person. *3 pobre* ~, poor devil. *4* BILL. rest, *bridge.

**diablura** *f.* devilry, mischievous or daring act.

**diabólico, -ca** *adj.* diabolic, diabolical, devilish.

**diábolo** *m.* diabolo [game].

**diaconado** *m.* DIACONATO.

**diaconato** *m.* deaconry, diaconate.

**diaconisa** *f.* deaconess.

**diácono** *m.* deacon.

**diacrítico, -ca** *adj.* diacritic(al.

**diacústica** *f.* diacoustics.

**diadelfo, -fa** *adj.* BOT. diadelphous.

**diadema** *f.* diadem. *2* tiara, coronet [worn by women]. *3* glory, halo.

**diafanidad** *f.* diaphaneity.

**diáfano, -na** *adj.* diaphane. *2* clear, transparent.

**diáfisis** *f.* ANAT. diaphysis.

**diafragma** *m.* diaphragm.

**diagnosis** *f.* MED. diagnosis.

**diagnosticar** *tr.* to diagnose.

**diagnóstico, -ca** *adj.* diagnostic. *2 m.* diagnostic.

**diagonal** *adj.* diagonal. *2 f.* GEOM. diagonal.

**diagrama** *m.* diagram.

**dial** *m.* dial [radio].

**dialectal** *adj.* dialectal.

**dialéctica** *f.* dialectics.

**dialéctico, -ca** *adj.* dialectic(al. *2 m.* dialectician.

**dialecto** *m.* dialect.

**diálisis** *f.* CHEM. dialysis.

**dializador** *m.* CHEM. dialyzer.

**dializar** *tr.* CHEM. to dialyze.

**dialogar** *intr.-tr.* to dialogue, dialogize.

**dialogismo** *m.* RHET. dialogism.

**diálogo** *m.* dialogue.

**dialoguista** *m.* dialogist [writer].

**diamante** *m.* MINER. diamond: ~ *rosa,* rose diamond.

**diamantífero, -ra** *adj.* diamantiferous.

**diamantino, -na** *adj.* diamantine. *2* adamantine.

**diamantista** *m.* diamond cutter or merchant.

**diametral** *adj.* diametral, diametrical.

**diametralmente** *adj.* diametrically.

**diámetro** *m.* diameter.

**Diana** *f. pr. n.* MYTH. Diana.

**diana** *f.* MIL. reveille. *2* bull's eye [of a target].

**dianche** *m.* coll. devil. *2 interj.* the deuce!

**diandro, -dra** *adj.* BOT. diandrous.

**diantre** *m.* DIANCHE.

**diapasón** *m.* MUS. diapason. *2* MUS. fingerboard [of violin, etc.]. *3* MUS. tuning fork; pitch pipe.

**diapente** *m.* MUS. diapente.

**diapositiva** *f.* PHOT. diapositive; lantern slide.

**diariamente** *adv.* daily, every day.

**diario, -ria** *adj.* daily; *a* ~, daily, every day. *2 m.* daily newspaper. *3* diary, journal: ~ *de navegación,* NAUT. log book. *4* BOOKKEEP. day book.

**diarismo** *m.* (Am.) journalism.

**diarista** *m.* diarist.

**diarrea** *f.* MED. diarrhœa, diarrhea.

**diartrosis** *f.* ANAT. diarthrosis.

**Diáspora** *f.* Diaspora.

**diastasa** *f.* BIOCHEM. diastase.

**diástilo** *m.* ARCH. diastyle.

**diástole** *f.* PHYSIOL., PROS. diastole.

**diatermia** *f.* MED. diathermia, diathermy.

**diatomea** *f.* BOT. diatom.

**diatónico, -ca** *adj.* MUS. diatonic.

**diatriba** *f.* diatribe.

**dibujante** *m.-f.* draftsman, draftswoman. *2* sketcher, designer, illustrator.

**dibujar** *tr.* to draw, make a drawing of; to sketch, to design. *2* to depict, describe vividly. *3 ref.* to be outlined. *4* to appear, be revealed.

**dibujo** *m.* drawing [act or art of drawing; product of this]: ~ *animado,* animated cartoon. *2* description. *3* pattern [of an embroidery, wall paper, etc.].

**dicción** *f.* word. *2* diction.

**diccionario** *m.* dictionary.

**diccionarista** *m.-f.* lexicographer.

**diciembre** m. December.
**dicotiledóneo, -a** adj. BOT. dicotyledonous. 2 f. dicotyledon. 3 pl. Dicotyledones.
**dicotomía** f. dichotomy.
**dicroísmo** m. PHYS. dichroism.
**dictado** m. dictation: escribir al ~, to take dictation. 2 title, epithet, appellation. 3 pl. dictates.
**dictador** m. dictator.
**dictadura** f. dictatorship.
**dictáfono** m. dictaphone.
**dictamen** m. opinion, judgment, advice. 2 expert's report; findings.
**dictaminar** intr. to give an opinion [on]. 2 [of an expert] ro report.
**dictamo** m. BOT. dittany.
**dictar** tr. to dictate [a letter, terms, etc.]. 2 to inspire, suggest. 3 to give [laws, precepts]; to pass [judgment].
**dictatorial** adj. dictatorial.
**dicterio** m. taunt, insult, insulting word.
**dicha** f. happiness. 2 fortune, good luck.
**dicharachero, -ra** adj. fond of using vulgar expressions.
**dicharacho** m. vulgar expression.
**dicho, -cha** p. p. of DECIR.: ~ y hecho, no sooner said than done. 2 adj. said, mentioned: arriba ~, above mentioned. 3 m. saying, proverb, sentence; remark, statement; del ~ al hecho, hay gran trecho, saying and doing are different things. 4 amusing sally.
**dichoso, -sa** adj. happy, fortunate, lucky. 2 coll. annoying, bothersome, wretched.
**didáctica** f. didactics.
**didáctico, -ca** adj. didactic(al.
**diecinueve** adj.-m. nineteen. 2 m. nineteenth.
**diecinueveavo, -va** adj.-m. nineteenth.
**dieciochavo, -va; dieciocheno, -na** adj.-m. eighteenth.
**dieciocho** adj.-m. eighteen. 2 m. eighteenth.
**dieciséis** adj.-m. sixteen. 2 m. sixteenth.
**dieciseisavo -va** adj.-m. sixteenth.
**diecisiete** adj.-m. seventeen. 2 m. seventeenth.
**diecisieteavo, -va** adj.-m. seventeenth.
**diedro, -dra** adj. GEOM. dihedral.
**Diego** m. pr. n. James.
**dieléctrico, -ca** adj.-m. dielectric.
**diente** m. ANAT., ZOOL. tooth: ~ canino, canine tooth, eyetooth; ~ incisivo, incisor, cutting tooth; ~ molar, molar, back tooth; aguzar los dientes, to whet one's appetite; apretar los dientes, to set one's teeth; dar ~ con ~, to be with teeth chattering; hablar, or decir, entre dientes, to mutter, mumble; hincar el ~ en, to misappropriate a part of [another's property]; to backbite, slander; to attack [a task, etc.]; tener buen ~, to be a hearty eater; a regañadientes, reluctantly, most unwillingly; de dientes afuera, insincerely. 2 fang [of serpent]. 3 tooth [of a comb, saw, etc.]; cog. 4 MAS. tooth. 5 clove [of garlic]. 6 BOT. ~ de león, dandelion.
**dientimellado, -da** adj. nick-toothed.
**diera, diese,** etc. irr. V. DAR.
**diéresis** f. diaeresis.
**diesi** f. MUS. diesis. 2 MUS. sharp.
**diestra** f. right side. 2 right hand.
**diestramente** adv. skilfully, cleverly.
**diestro, -tra** adj. right, right-hand. 2 dexterous, skilful, able, clever. 3 m. right hand; a ~ y siniestro, right and left, wildly. 4 skilful fencer. 5 bullfighter; matador. 6 halter or bridle.
**dieta** f. diet [prescribed or regulated food; assembly]. 2 allowance to public officials and members of Parliament.
**dietario** m. family acount book. 2 chronicler's record book.
**dietético, -ca** adj. dietetic(al. 2 f. dietetics.
**diez** adj.-m. ten; las ~, ten o'clock. 2 m. tenth [in dates].
**diezmar** tr. to decimate. 2 to tithe.
**diezmilésimo, -ma** adj.-m. then-thousandth.
**diezmo** m. tithe.
**difamación** f. defamation.
**difamador, -ra** adj. defaming. 2 m.-f. defamer.
**difamar** tr. to defame.
**difamatorio, -ria** adj. defamatory.
**diferencia** f. difference: hacer diferencias, to treat differently; a ~ de, unlike.
**diferenciación** f. differentiation.
**diferencial** adj.-f. differential.
**diferenciar** tr. to differentiate. 2 ref. to differ [be different]. 5 to make oneself noticeable. 3 BIOL. to differentiate.
**diferente** adj. different. 2 adv. differently.
**diferir** tr. to defer, delay, adjourn, postpone, put off. 2 intr. to differ [be different]. ¶ CONJUG. like hervir.
**difícil** adj. difficult, hard: ~ de creer, hard to believe. 2 improbable.
**difícilmente** adv. with difficulty, hardly.
**dificultad** f. difficulty. 2 objection.
**dificultar** tr. to make difficult; to hinder. 2 to consider difficult or improbable.
**dificultoso, -sa** adj. difficult. 2 m.-f. raiser of difficulties.
**difidente** adj. distrustful.
**difiero, difiera,** etc. irr. V. DIFERIR.
**difluir** intr. to be diffused. ¶ CONJUG. like fluir.
**difracción** f. PHYS. diffraction.
**difteria** f. MED. diphteria.
**difumar** tr. ESFUMAR.
**difuminar** tr. ESFUMINAR.
**difumino** f. ESFUMINO.
**difundir** tr. to diffuse. 2 to spread, divulge. 3 RADIO. to broadcast. 4 ref. to diffuse itself; to spread.
**difunto, -ta** adj. deceased, defunct, late. 2 m.-f. deceased.
**difusión** f. diffusion. 2 diffuseness. 3 spreading. 4 RADIO. broadcasting.
**difuso, -sa** adj. diffuse. 2 broad, widespread.
**difusor, -ra** adj. diffusing. 2 RADIO. broadcasting. 3 m. diffuser.
**digerible** adj. digestible.
**digerir** tr. PHYSIOL., CHEM. to digest. 2 to digest [assimilate mentally; bear, put up with]. ¶ CONJUG. like hervir.
**digestión** f. PHYSIOL., CHEM. digestion.
**digestivo, -va** adj. digestive.
**digesto** m. LAW digest.
**digestor** m. digester [apparatus].
**digiero, digiera,** etc. irr. V. DIGERIR.
**digitación** f. MUS. fingering.
**digitado, -da** adj. BOT., ZOOL. digitate.
**digital** adj. digital. 2 f. BOT. digitalis, foxglove.
**digitalina** f. CHEM., PHARM. digitalin.
**digitígrado, -da** adj.-m. ZOOL. digitigrade.
**dígito** adj. ARITH. número ~, digit.
**dignarse** ref. to deign, condescend.
**dignatario** m. dignitary, high official.
**dignidad** f. dignity. 2 dignified bearing. 3 ECCL. dignitary.
**dignificación** f. dignification.
**dignificar** tr. to dignify.

**digno, -na** *adj.* worthy, honorable. *2* worthy, deserving. *3* suitable, appropriate. *4* dignified.
**digo, diga,** etc. *irr.* V. DECIR.
**dígrafo** *m.* digraph.
**digresión** *f.* digression.
**dije** *m.* trinket, locket, small piece of jewelry.
**dije, dijera,** etc. *irr.* V. DECIR.
**dilaceración** *f.* rending, tearing; laceration.
**dilacerar** *tr.* to rend, tear, lacerate.
**dilación** *f.* delay, procrastination.
**dilapidación** *f.* dilapidation, squandering.
**dilapidador, -ra** *m.-f.* dilapidator, squanderer.
**dilapidar** *tr.* to dilapidate, squander.
**dilatabilidad** *f.* dilatability.
**dilatación** *f.* dilatation, dilation, expansion. *2* delay, prolongation. *3* diffuseness, prolixity.
**dilatado, -da** *adj.* vast, extensive, large; numerous.
**dilatar** *tr.* to dilate, expand, widen. *2* to spread [fame, etc.]. *3* to delay, retard. *4* ~ *el ánimo,* to comfort, cheer up. *5 ref.* to dilate, expand, spread, etc. [be dilated, expanded, etc.]. *6* to expatiate.
**dilatorio, -ria** *adj.* dilatory, delaying. *2 f.* delay, procrastination.
**dilección** *f.* love, affection.
**dilecto, -ta** *adj.* beloved, loved.
**dilema** *m.* dilemma.
**diletantismo** *m.* dilettantism.
**diligencia** *f.* diligence, activity, dispatch, speed. *2* errand; step, action. *3* judicial proceeding. *4* diligence, stagecoach.
**diligenciar** *tr.* to take the necessary steps to acomplish or obtain [something].
**diligente** *adj.* diligent; prompt, active.
**dilucidación** *f.* clearing up, elucidation.
**dilucidar** *tr.* to clear up, to elucidate.
**dilución** *f.* dilution.
**diluente** *adj.-m.* diluent.
**diluir** *tr.* to dilute. *2 ref.* to dilute [become diluted].
¶ CONJUG. like *huir.*
**diluvial** *adj.* diluvial, diluvian. *2* GEOL. diluvial.
**diluviar** *impers.* to pour, rain hard.
**diluvio** *m.* deluge. *2* hard raining, downpour. *3 el Diluvio,* the Deluge, the Flood.
**dimanante** *adj.* springing, originating, issuing.
**dimanar** *intr.* ~ *de,* to spring, issue, arise from; originate in.
**dimensión** *f.* dimension.
**dimensional** *adj.* dimensional.
**dimes** *m. pl. andar en dimes y diretes,* to bicker.
**diminutivo, -va** *adj.* diminishing. *2 adj.-m.* GRAM. diminutive.
**diminuto, -ta** *adj.* diminutive, minute, tiny.
**dimisión** *f.* resignation [of office].
**dimisionario, -ria; dimitente** *adj.* resigning [an office].
**dimitir** *tr.* to resign, to give up [office].
**dimorfismo** *m.* dimorphism.
**dimorfo, -fa** *adj.* dimorphous.
**dina** *f.* PHYS., dyne.
**Dinamarca** *f. pr. n.* GEOG. Denmark.
**dinamarqués, -sa** *adj.* Danish. *2 m.-f.* Dane.
**dinámica** *f.* dynamics.
**dinámico, -ca** *adj.* dynamic.
**dinamismo** *m.* dynamism.
**dinamita** *f.* dynamite.
**dinamitar** *tr.* to dynamite.
**dinamitero, -ra** *m.-f.* dynamiter.
**dinamo** *f.* ELECT. dynamo.
**dinamómetro** *m.* dynamometer.
**dinasta** *m.* dynast.

**dinastía** *f.* dynasty.
**dinástico, -ca** *adj.* dynastic(al.
**dineral** *m.* large sum of money.
**dinerillo** *m.* dim. coll. some money.
**dinero** *m.* money, currency, wealth: ~ *contante,* ~ *contante y sonante,* ready money; cash; *hombre de* ~, wealthy man. *2* ancient silver coin. *3* denier.
**dingo** *m.* ZOOL. dingo.
**dinosauro** *m.* PALEONT. dinosaur.
**dinoterio** *m.* PALEONT. dinothere.
**dintel** *m.* ARCH. lintel, doorhead.
**diñar** *tr.* vulg. to give: *diñarla,* to die.
**diocesano, -na** *adj.-m.* diocesan.
**diócesi, diócesis** *f.* diocese.
**Diocleciano** *m. pr. n.* Diocletian.
**diodo** *m.* diode.
**dioico, -ca** *adj.* BOT. diœcious.
**dionea** *f.* BOT. Venus's-flytrap.
**dionisíaco, -ca** *adj.* Dionysiac.
**Dionisio** *m. pr. n.* Dionysius, Denis.
**Dionisios, Dionisos** *m. pr. n.* MYTH. Dionysos, Dionysus.
**dioptría** *f.* OPT. diopter [unit].
**dióptrico, -ca** *adj.* dioptric(al. *2 f.* dioptrics.
**diorama** *m.* diorama.
**dios** *m.* MYTH. god. *2 pr. n.* (cap.) God: ~ *Hombre,* Jesus Christ; ~ *Padre,* God the Father; *¡adiós!,* adieu!, farewell, good-bye; *a la buena de* ~, artlessly; *¡anda con* ~*!, ¡vaya con* ~*!,* good-bye; *¡bendito sea* ~*!,* bless me!; ~ *dirá,* we shall see; ~ *los cría y ellos se juntan,* birds of a feather flock together; ~ *mediante,* God willing; *¡* ~ *mío!,* my God!, good Heavens!; ~ *me libre,* God forbid; *sabe* ~, goodness knows; *plegue a* ~, please God; *¡válgame* ~*!,* good God!
**diosa** *f.* goddess.
**diplodoco** *m.* PALEONT. diplodocus.
**diploma** *m.* diploma.
**diplomacia** *f.* diplomacy.
**diplomática** *f.* diplomatics.
**diplomático, -ca** *adj.* diplomatic. *2 m.-f.* diplomat. *3* diplomatist.
**dipsomanía** *f.* dipsomania.
**dipsómano, -na** *adj.-s.* dipsomaniac.
**díptero, -ra** *adj.* ENT. dipteran, dipterous. *2* ARCH. dipteros.
**díptica** *f.* diptych [tablets].
**díptico** *m.* diptych [tablets; picture].
**diptongar** *tr.* to diphthongize.
**diptongo** *m.* diphthong.
**diputación** *f.* deputation. *2* object of a deputation.
**diputado** *m.* deputy, delegate, representative. *2* POL. deputy, member of a Chamber of Deputies.
**diputar** *tr.* to delegate, to commission. *2* to consider, to judge to be.
**dique** *m.* dam, mole, dike. *2* fig. barrier, check. *3* NAUT. dry dock: ~ *flotante,* floating dock.
**diré, diría,** etc. *irr.* V. DECIR.
**dirección** *f.* direction [line of course, point to which one moves, looks, etc.]; ~ *única,* one way. *2* direction, management; leadership. *3* office of a director or a manager. *6* address [on a letter, etc.]. *7* AUTO. steering.
**directamente** *adv.* directly in a direct manner.
**directivo, -va** *adj.* directive, managing. *2 f.* board of directors. *3 m.* member of a board of directors, *executive.
**directo, -ta** *adj.* direct, straight. *2* GRAM. direct.
**director, -ra** *adj.* directing, leading, managing. *2 m.-f.* director, manager, *executive: ~ *de es-*

*cena*, stage manager. *3* editor [of a paper]. *4* principal, headmaster [of a school]. *5* MUS. conductor.
**directorio** *m.* directory [body of rules]. *2* POL. directory. *3* Directoire.
**directriz** *f.* GEOM. directrix.
**dirigente** *adj.* leading, governing. *2 m.-f.* leader, director, *executive.
**dirigible** *adj.* dirigible. *2 m.* AER. dirigible.
**dirigir** *tr.* to direct [in every sense, except to give an order or instruction to]. *2* to manage, govern; to lead, to head. *3* AUT. to steer. *4* MUS. to conduct. *5* to point [a gun, etc]. *6* to address [a letter, one's word, etc]. *7 ref. dirigirse a*, to be directed to; to go to; to address [a person], to apply, resort to.
**dirimente** *adj.* diriment.
**dirimir** *tr.* to annul, dissolve. *2* to settle [a quarrel, a controversy].
**discerniente** *adj.* discerning.
**discernimiento** *m.* discernment, judgment. *2* discrimination.
**discernir** *tr.* to discern, distinguish. *2* LAW to appoint [a guardian]. ¶ CONJUG.: INDIC. Pres.: *discierno, disciernes, discierne; disciernen.* | SUBJ. Pres.: *discierna, disciernas, discierna; disciernan.* | IMPER.: *discierne, discierna; disciernan.* | All other forms are regular.
**disciplina** *f.* discipline. *2* teaching, instruction. *3* art, science. *4 pl.* scourge [for flogging].
**disciplinadamente** *adv.* with discipline.
**disciplinado, -da** *adj.* disciplined.
**disciplinante** *m.* disciplinant.
**disciplinar** *tr.* to discipline. *2 ref.* to scourge oneself [as penance].
**disciplinario, -ria** *adj.* disciplinary.
**discípulo, -la** *m.-f.* disciple. *2* pupil [of a teacher].
**disco** *m.* disk. *2* SPORT. discus. *3* record [of phonograph].
**discóbolo** *m.* discobolous, discus thrower.
**díscolo, -la** *adj.* ungovernable, refractory, wayward.
**disconforme** *adj.* disagreeing.
**disconformidad** *f.* disagreement. *2* disconformity.
**discontinuación** *f.* discontinuance, discontinuation.
**discontinuar** *tr.* to discontinue.
**discontinuidad** *f.* discontinuity.
**discontinuo, -nua** *adj.* discontinuous.
**discordancia** *f.* discordance, disagreement.
**discordante** *adj.* discordant.
**discordar** *intr.* to discord [be discordant]. *2* to disagree [in opinion]. *3* MUS. to discord. ¶ CONJUG. like *contar*.
**discorde** *adj.* discordant, in disagreement. *2* MUS. discordant, dissonant.
**discordia** *f.* discord, disagreement, disunion.
**discoteca** *f.* collection of phonograph records.
**discreción** *f.* discretion: *a ~*, at discretion. *2* wit, gracefulness [in talk or expression].
**discrecional** *adj.* discretionary.
**discrepancia** *f.* discrepancy. *2* dissent, disagreement.
**discrepante** *adj.* discrepant; disagreeing.
**discrepar** *intr.* to differ, disagree. *2* to dissent.
**discretear** *intr.* to make a show of graceful talk.
**discreteo** *m.* show of graceful talk.
**discreto, -ta** *adj.* discret. *2* graceful in talk or expression. *3* MATH. discrete [quantity]. *4* coll. not bad; fairly good.
**discriminación** *f.* discrimination.

**discriminar** *tr.* to discriminate.
**disculpa** *f.* excuse, apology. *2* exculpation.
**disculpar** *tr.* to exculpate; to excuse. *2 ref.* to excuse oneself, apologize.
**discurrir** *intr.* to go about, roam. *2* [of a river, etc.] to flow. *3* [of time] to pass. *4* to reflect, reason, discourse [about a thing]. *5 tr.* to invent, think out, devise. *6* to infer.
**discursear** *intr.* coll. to perorate, make speeches.
**discursivo, -va** *adj.* meditative.
**discurso** *m.* discourse. *2* use of reason. *3* talk, speech. *4* course [of time].
**discusión** *f.* discussion, argument.
**discutible** *adj.* disputable, debatable; uncertain.
**discutidor, -ra** *adj.* argumentative [person].
**discutir** *tr.* to discuss, argue about, dispute. *2 intr.* to discuss, argue.
**disecador** *m.* dissecter; taxidermist.
**disecar** *tr.* to dissect. *2* to stuff [dead animals].
**disección** *f.* dissection, anatomy. *2* stuffing [of dead animals], taxidermy.
**disector** *m.* dissector.
**diseminación** *f.* dissemination, scattering.
**diseminar** *tr.* to disseminate, scatter. *2 ref.* to disseminate, scatter [be disseminated].
**disensión** *f.* dissension. *2* division, strife.
**disentería** *f.* MED. dysentery.
**disentimiento** *m.* dissent, disagreement.
**disentir** *intr.* to dissent, disagree. ¶ CONJUG. like *sentir*.
**diseñador** *m.* designer, delineator, sketcher.
**diseñar** *tr.* to design, draw, sketch, outline.
**diseño** *m.* design, drawing, sketch, outline.
**disertación** *f.* dissertation, disquisition.
**disertar** *tr.* to dissert, dissertate.
**diserto, -ta** *adj.* eloquent, fluent.
**disfasia** *f.* MED. dysphasia.
**disfavor** *m.* disfavour. *2* bad turn.
**disforme** *adj.* misshapen, hideous. *2* huge, monstruous.
**disfraz** *m.* disguise. *2* costume, fancy dress. *3* dissimulation, dissembling.
**disfrazar** *tr.* to disguise. *2* to dissemble. *3 ref.* to disguise oneself, to masquerade.
**disfrutar** *tr.* to enjoy, possess, have the use or benefit of. *2 intr.* to enjoy oneself, take enjoyment. *3 ~ de*, to enjoy, have the use of. *4 ~ con*, to take or find enjoyment in.
**disfumino** *m.* stump.
**disfrute** *m.* enjoyment, benefit, use.
**disgregación** *f.* scattering, disgregation.
**disgregar** *tr.* to scatter, disintegrate, disperse.
**disgustado, -da** *adj.* tasteless. *2* displeased. *3* sorry.
**disgustar** *tr.* to render tasteless, disagreeable. *2* to displease, annoy, anger; to pain, give sorrow. *3 ref.* to be displeased, or hurt. *4* to fall out, have a difference [with].
**disgustillo** *m. dim.* slight displeasure or difference.
**disgusto** *m.* unpleasantness [to the palate]. *2* displeasure, annoyance, vexation. *3* sorrow. *4* quarrel. *5 a ~*, against one's will; ill at ease.
**disidencia** *f.* dissidence. *2* dissent, nonconformity.
**disidente** *adj.* dissident. *2 m.-f.* dissenter.
**disidir** *intr.* to dissent, separate [from a creed, etc.].
**disiento, disienta**, etc. *irr.* V. DISENTIR.
**disimetría** *f.* dissymmetry.
**disímil** *adj.* dissimilar.
**disimilación** *f.* PHON. dissimilation.

**disimilitud** *f.* dissimilitude, dissimilarity.
**disimulable** *adj.* excusable.
**disimulación** *f.* dissimulation. *2* DISIMULO.
**disimuladamente** *adv.* stealthily, slyly.
**disimulado, -da** *adj.* dissembling, reserved, sly.
**disimulador, -ra** *m.-f.* dissembler. *2* tolerator.
**disimular** *tr.* to dissimulate, dissemble. *2* to disguise; conceal. *3* to overlook, excuse, pardon.
**disimulo** *m.* dissimulation. *2* sly proceeding: *con* ~, stealthily, slyly. *3* tolerance, indulgence.
**disipación** *f.* dissipation.
**disipado, -da** *adj.* dissipated. *2* *m.-f.* dissipated person.
**disipador, -ra** *adj.* squandering. *2* *m.-f.* squanderer, spendthrift.
**disipar** *tr.* to dissipate [dispel; squander]. *2 ref.* to dissipate, envanesce, disappear.
**dislate** *m.* nonsense, absurdity.
**dislocación, dislocadura** *f.* dislocation.
**dislocar** *tr.* to dislocate. *2 ref.* to come out of joint.
**disloque** *m.* coll. the (giddy) limit.
**disminución** *f.* diminution.
**disminuir** *tr.-intr.-ref.* to diminish, lessen, decrease. *2* to taper. ¶ CONJUG. like *huir.*
**disminuyo, disminuyó, disminuya,** etc. irr. V. DISMINUIR.
**disnea** *f.* MED. dyspnea.
**disociación** *f.* dissociation.
**disociar** *tr.* to dissociate. *2 ref.* to dissociate [undergo dissociation].
**disolubilidad** *f.* dissolubility.
**disoluble** *adj.* dissoluble.
**disolución** *f.* dissolution, dissolving. *2* dissolution, solution [in a solvent]. *3* dissoluteness.
**disoluto, -ta** *adj.* dissolute. *2* *m.-f.* debauchee.
**disolvente** *adj.* dissolving. *2* *m.* dissolvent, dissolver.
**disolver** *tr.* to dissolve.*2 ref.* to dissolve [be dissolved]. ¶ CONJUG. like *mover.*
**disón** *m.* MUS. dissonance, harsh sound.
**disonancia** *f.* harsh sound. *2* dissonance.
**disonante** *adj.* harsh, dissonant, discordant.
**disonar** *intr.* MUS. to sound harshly, be dissonant or discordant. *2* to disagree, be incongruous.
**dispar** *adj.* unlike, different, disparate.
**disparada** *f.* (Am.) flight, stampede, wild rush; *a la* ~, flat out, full plet; *de una* ~, at once, right away.
**disparadero** *m.* trigger: *poner en el* ~, PONER EN EL DISPARADOR.
**disparador** *m.* shooter. *2* trigger: *poner en el* ~, to drive one to do something rash. *3* escapement [of watch]. *4* release [of camera]. *5* NAUT. anchor tripper.
**disparar** *tr.* to discharge, fire, let off [a firearm; a bow]: ~ *un tiro*, to fire a shot. *2* to hurl, throw. *3 ref.* to dash off: to bolt. *4* [of a gun, alarm, clock, etc.] to go off. *5* to lose self-control.
**disparatado, -da** *adj.* absurd, nonsensical, foolish.
**disparatar** *tr.* to talk nonsense; to act foolishly.
**disparate** *m.* absurdity, nonsense; crazy idea. *2* foolish or preposterous act, blunder, mistake.
**disparejo, -ja** *adj.* DISPAR.
**disparidad** *f.* disparity, unlikeness, dissimilarity.
**disparo** *m.* shot, discharge. *2* MACH. release, trip, start.
**dispendio** *m.* excessive expenditure.
**dispendioso, -sa** *adj.* costly, expensive.
**dispensa** *f.* dispensation, exemption.
**dispensable** *adj.* dispensable. *2* excusable.

**dispensación** *f.* dispensation [granting; exemption].
**dispensador, -a** *m.-f.* dispenser.
**dispensar** *tr.* to dispense, give, grant. *2* to dispense, exempt. *3* to excuse, pardon: *¡dispense!, ¡dispénseme!,* excuse me!, beg pardon! *4 ref.* to excuse oneself [from doing something].
**dispensario** *m.* clinic [for the poor].
**dispepsia** *f.* MED. dyspepsia.
**dispéptico, -ca** *adj.-n.* dyspeptic.
**dispersar** *tr.* to disperse, scatter. *2* MIL. to put to flight. *3 ref.* to disperse [be dispersed].
**dispersión** *f.* dispersion, dispersal. *2* PHYS. dispersion.
**disperso, -sa** *adj.* dispersed, scattered.
**displicencia** *f.* coolness, indifference, disdain.
**displicente** *adj.* cool, disdainful. *2* peevish.
**dispondré, dispondría,** etc. *irr.* V. DISPONER.
**disponer** *tr.* to dispose, arrange. *2* to dispose [incline; bring into certain state; determine course of events]. *3* to prepare, get ready. *4* to order, decree. *5 intr.* ~ *de,* to have. *6 ref.* to get ready [for]; to be about [to]. ¶ CONJUG. like *poner.*
**dispongo, disponga,** etc. *irr.* V. DISPONER.
**disponibilidades** *f. pl.* resources, money on hand.
**disponible** *adj.* disposable. *2* available.
**disposición** *f.* disposition. *2* disposal. *3* state of health. *4* gift, natural aptitude. *5* figure [of a pers.]. *6* order, command, provision. *7 pl.* dispositions, steps, measures. *8 últimas disposiciones,* last will and testament.
**dispositivo, -va** *adj.* preceptive. *2* *m.* MACH. device, contrivance.
**dispuesto, -ta** *p. p.* of DISPONER. *2 adj.* disposed: *bien* ~, favourably disposed; *mal* ~, unfavourably disposed. *3* prepared, ready. *4* comely. *5* able, clever.
**dispuse, dispusiera,** etc. *irr.* V. DISPONER.
**disputa** *f.* dispute; disputation: *sin* ~, beyond dispute.
**disputable** *adj.* disputable, contestable.
**disputar** *tr.* to dispute, contest. *2 intr.* to argue, dispute; to altercate.
**disquisición** *f.* disquisition.
**distal** *adj.* ANAT., BOT. distal.
**distancia** *f.* distance: *a* ~, at a distance. *2* difference, disparity.
**distanciar** *tr.* to distance [place at a distance]. *2* to separate, estrange. *3 ref.* to become distant or estranged.
**distante** *adj.* distant, far, remote.
**distar** *intr.* ~ *de,* to be [so many miles, etc.] distant from; to be different from; ~ *mucho de,* to be far from.
**distender** *tr.* MED. to distend.
**distensión** *f.* MED. distension, distention.
**dístico, -ca** *adj.* BOT. distichous. *2* *m.* POET. distich.
**distinción** *f.* distinction. *2* distinctness. *3* *a* ~ *de,* in distinction from or to.
**distingo** *m.* LOG. distinction. *2* coll. subtle distinction.
**distinguido, -da** *adj.* distinguished, prominent.
**distinguir** *tr.* to distinguish. *2* to discriminate. *3* to show regard for. *4 ref.* to distinguish oneself. *5* to make oneself different. *6* to be distinguished or characterized.
**distintivo, -va** *adj.* distinctive. *2* *m.* distinctive peculiarity. *3* distinctive mark; badge, sign.
**distinto, -ta** *adj.* distinct. *2* different, separate.
**distorsión** *f.* distortion.
**distracción** *f.* distraction, diversion, amusement.

2 absent-mindedness. *3* oversight. *4* ~ *de fondos*, embezzlement. *5 por* ~, for amusement; through an oversight.

**distraer** *tr.* to divert, amuse, entertain. *2* to distract [the attention, the mind, etc.]. *2* to lead astray. *4* ~ *fondos*, to embezzle. *5 ref.* to amuse oneself. *6* to be inattentive, absent-minded.

**distraídamente** *adv.* without thinking.

**distraído, -da** *adj.* absent-minded, inattentive.

**distribución** *f.* distribution. *2* apportionment.

**distribuidor, -ra** *adj.* distributing. *2 m.-f.* distributer, distributor: ~ *automático*, slot machine.

**distribuir** *tr.* to distribute. *2* to sort [mail]. ¶ CONJUG. like *huir*.

**distributivo, -va** *adj.* distributive.

**distrito** *m.* district.

**disturbio** *m.* disturbance, outbreak, riot.

**disuadir** *tr.* to dissuade.

**disuasión** *f.* dissuasion.

**disuasivo, -va** *adj.* dissuasive.

**disuelto, -ta** *p. p.* of DISOLVER.

**disuelvo, disuelva,** etc. *irr.* V. DISOLVER.

**disuria** *f.* MED. dysuria.

**disyunción** *f.* disjunction.

**disyuntiva** *f.* disjunctive, dilemma.

**disyuntivo, -va** *adj.* disjunctive.

**disyuntor** *m.* ELECT. circuit-breaker.

**ditirambo** *m.* dithyramb.

**dítono** *m.* MUS. ditone.

**diurético, -ca** *adj.-m.* MED. diuretic.

**diurno, -na** *adj.* diurnal.

**diuturno, -na** *adj.* diuturnal.

**diva** *f.* poet. goddess. *2* diva [great woman singer].

**divagación** *f.* divagation, rambling, digression.

**divagar** *intr.* to divagate, ramble, digress.

**diván** *m.* divan.

**divergencia** *f.* divergence; divergency.

**divergente** *adj.* divergent.

**divergir** *intr.* to diverge. *2* to differ, disagree.

**diversidad** *f.* diversity. *2* variety, abundance.

**diversificar** *tr.* to diversify.

**diversión** *f.* diversion, amusement. *2* MIL. diversion.

**diverso, -sa** *adj.* diverse, different, various. *2 pl.* several, many.

**divertido, -da** *adj.* amusing, funny.

**divertimiento** *m.* diversion, amusement.

**divertir** *tr.* to divert, amuse, entertain. *2* to divert, turn away. *3 ref.* to amuse oneself, have a good time. ¶ CONJUG. like *hervir*.

**dividendo** *m.* MATH., COM. dividend.

**dividir** *tr.* to divide. *2 ref.* to divide [separate, be at odds].

**dividivi** *m.* BOT. dividivi.

**divierto, divierta,** etc. *irr.* V. DIVERTIR.

**divieso** *m.* MED. furuncle, boil.

**divinamente** *adv.* divinely. *2* admirably.

**divinatorio, -ria** *adj.* divinatory.

**divinidad** *f.* divinity, godhead. *2* MYTH. divinity. *3* beauty, very beautiful person or thing.

**divinizar** *tr.* to divinize, deify.

**divino, -na** *adj.* divine.

**divisa** *f.* badge, emblem. *2* BULLF. coloured bow serving as brand on bull. *3* HER. device. *4* principle. *5* foreign currency.

**divisar** *tr.* to descry, espy, perceive.

**divisibilidad** *f.* divisibility.

**divisible** *adj.* divisible.

**división** *f.* division [dividing; distribution; discord]. *2* LOG., MATH., MIL. division.

**divisional** *adj.* divisional.

**divisionario, -ria** *adj.* divisional, divisionary. *2* fractional [currency].

**divisor, -ra** *adj.* dividing. *2 m.* MATH. divisor: *máximo común* ~, greatest common divisor.

**divisorio, -ria** *adj.* dividing. *2 f.* GEOG. divide.

**divo, -va** *adj.* poet. divine. *2 m.* poet. god. *3* great singer [man]. *4 f.* diva.

**divorciado, -da** *adj.* divorced. *2 n.* divorcee.

**divorciar** *tr.* to divorce. *2 ref.* to divorce [get divorced]: ~ *de*, to divorce [one's husband or wife]; to become divorced from.

**divorcio** *m.* divorce. *2* disunion, breach.

**divulgación** *f.* divulgation. *2* popularization [of knowledge].

**divulgar** *tr.* to divulge, publish abroad. *2* to popularize [knowledge]. *3 ref.* to be spread about.

**do** *m.* MUS. C, do, ut. *2 adv.* poet. DONDE.

**dobladillar** *tr.* SEW. to hem.

**dobladillo** *m.* SEW. hem.

**doblado, -da** *p. p.* of DOBLAR. *2 adj.* thick-set. *3* uneven [land]. *4* deceitful, dissembling.

**doblaje** *m.* CINEM. dubbing.

**doblar** *tr.* to double [make double; amount to twice as much as]. *2* to double, fold. *3* to bend [curve; cause to yield]; to bow [one's head]; ~ *la rodilla*, to go down on one's knee; to humble oneself. *4* to turn [a page]. *5* to turn, double [a corner, a cape]. *6* CINEM. to dub; to double. *7 intr.* to toll, knell. *8 ref.* to double, double up. *9* to bend, yield, give in.

**doble** *adj.* double, twofold: *al* ~, doubly. *2* thick, heavy [cloth, etc.]. *3* thick-set, sturdy. *4* BOT. double [flower]. *5* two-faced, deceitful. *6 adv.* doubly. *7 m.* fold, crease. *8* toll, knell.

**doblegable** *adj.* easily bent; pliable, pliant.

**doblegar** *tr.* to bend, curve. *2* to bend, force to yield, subdue. *3 ref.* to yield, give in, submit.

**doblete** *m.* doublet [false stone]. *2* a stroke in billiards.

**doblez** *m.* fold, crease, ply. *2* cuff [of trousers]. *3 f.* duplicity, deceitfulness.

**doblón** *m.* doubloon [old Spanish gold coin].

**doce** *adj.-m.* twelve: *las* ~, twelve o'clock. *2 m.* twelfth [in dates].

**docena** *f.* dozen: ~ *de fraile*, baker's dozen.

**docente** *adj.* educational, teaching.

**dócil** *adj.* docile, obedient. *2* tame. *3* soft, easily worked.

**docilidad** *f.* docility, meekness.

**dócilmente** *adv.* docilely, meekly. *2* obediently.

**docto, -ta** *adj.* learned [person].

**doctor, -ra** *m.-f.* doctor, doctoress. *2 Doctor de la Iglesia*, Doctor of the Church.

**doctorado** *m.* doctorate, doctorship.

**doctoral** *adj.* doctoral.

**doctorar** *tr.* to doctor [confer a doctorate upon]. *2 ref.* to take the degree of doctor.

**doctrina** *f.* doctrine. *2* learning, knowledge. *3* catechism. *4* Sunday School.

**doctrinal** *m.* doctrinal.

**doctrinar** *tr.* to teach, instruct.

**doctrinario, -ria** *adj.-n.* doctrinaire, doctrinarian.

**doctrinarismo** *m.* doctrinairism, doctrinarianism.

**doctrino** *m.* charity boy.

**documentación** *f.* documentation. *2* papers [proving identity, authorization, etc.].

**documentado, -da** *adj.* documented. *2* well-documented, well-informed.

**documental** *adj.* documental, documentary. *2 m.* CINEM. documentary [film].

**documentar** *tr.-ref.* to document.

**documento** *m.* document.
**dodecaedro** *m.* GEOM. dodecahedron.
**dodecágono** *m.* GEOM. dodecagon.
**dodecafónico, -ca** *adj.* MUS. dodecaphonic.
**dodecasílabo, -ba** *adj.* dodecasyllabic. *2 m.* dodecasyllabic verse.
**dogal** *m.* halter, hangman's rope; *estar con el ~ al cuello,* to be in a tight spot.
**dogaresa** *f.* dogaressa.
**dogma** *m.* dogma.
**dogmático, -ca** *adj.* dogmatic(al.
**dogmatismo** *m.* dogmatism.
**dogmatizar** *tr.-intr.* to dogmatize.
**dogo, -ga** *adj.-n.* bulldog. *2 m.* doge.
**dogre** *m.* NAUT. dogger.
**doladera** *f.* cooper's adze.
**dolar** *tr.* to dress wood or stone.
**dólar** *m.* dollar [U.S. money].
**dolencia** *f.* ailment, complaint, disease, illness.
**doler** *intr.* to ache, hurt, pain: *me duele la cabeza,* my head aches. *2* to pain, be hateful to one: *me duele hacer esto,* I hate, to do this. *3 ref. dolerse de,* to repent; to be moved by [another's misfortune]; to complain of. ¶ CONJUG. like *mover.*
**dolicocéfalo, -la** *adj.* dolichocephalous.
**dolido, -da** *adj.* hurt, pained, grieved.
**doliente** *adj.* aching, suffering. *2* ill, sick. *3* sorrowful. *4 m.-f.* sufferer, sick person.
**dolmen** *m.* ARCHEOL. dolmen.
**dolo** *m.* guile, deceit, fraud.
**dolomía, dolomita** *f.* MINER. dolomite.
**dolor** *m.* pain, ache, aching: *~ de cabeza,* headache. *2* pain, sorrow, grief: *la Virgen de los Dolores,* Mary of the Sorrows. *3* repentance. *4 pl. dolores del parto,* labour pains, throes of childbirth.
**dolora** *f.* short sentimental and philosophic poem.
**dolorido, -da** *adj.* sore, aching, tender, painful. *2* sorrowful, grieving, pained.
**Dolorosa** *f.* Mater Dolorosa.
**doloroso, -sa** *adj.* painful. *2* dolorous, distressing; pitiful, regrettable.
**doloso, -sa** *adj.* guileful, deceitful, fraudulent.
**doma** *f.* taming, breaking in.
**domable** *adj.* tamable. *2* conquerable.
**domador, -ra** *m.-f.* tamer. *2* horsebreaker.
**domar** *tr.* to tame. *2* to break, break in [horses, etc.]. *3* to curb, subdue, conquer.
**domeñar** *tr.* to master, conquer, subdue.
**domesticación** *f.* domestication.
**domesticar** *tr.* to tame, domesticate. *2 ref.* to become tame.
**domesticidad** *f.* domesticity.
**doméstico, -ca** *adj.* domestic [of the home]. *2* domestic [animal]. *3 m.-f.* domestic, servant.
**Domiciano** *m. pr. n.* Domitian.
**domiciliado, -da** *adj.* resident. *2* domiciled: *letra domiciliada,* domiciled draft.
**domiciliar** *tr.* to domicile, domiciliate. *2 ref.* to domiciliate, take up residence.
**domiciliario, -ria** *adj.* domiciliary.
**domicilio** *m.* domicile, home, residence.
**dominación** *f.* domination. *2 pl.* dominations [order of angels].
**dominador, -ra** *adj.* dominating; domineering. *2 m.-f.* dominator.
**dominante** *adj.* domineering. *2* dominant. *3* commanding [height, position]. *4 adj.-f.* MUS. dominant.
**dominar** *tr.* to dominate *2* to domineer. *3* to rule

over. *4* to control, restrain. *5* to master [a subject]. *6 ref.* to control oneself.
**dómine** *m.* coll. latin teacher. *2* coll. pedant.
**Domingo** *m. pr. n.* Dominic.
**domingo** *m.* Sunday: *~ de Pasión,* Passion Sunday; *~ de Ramos,* Palm Sunday.
**dominguero, -ra** *adj.* Sunday [used on Sundays].
**domínica** *f.* ECCL. Lord's day, Sunday.
**dominical** *adj.* dominical. *2* feudal [fees].
**dominicano, -na** *adj.-n.* Dominican.
**dominico, -ca** *adj.* Dominican [pertaining to the Dominican order]. *2 m.* Dominican friar.
**dominio** *m.* dominium. *2* domination, control, rule. *3* mastery [of a subject]. *4* domain. *5 ~ público,* public property; public knowledge.
**dómino** *m.* dominoes [game]; domino [piece].
**dominó** *m.* DÓMINO. *2* domino [cloak].
**domo** *m.* ARCH. dome, cupola.
**dompedro** *m.* BOT. DONDIEGO. *2* coll. chamber pot.
**don** *m.* gift, present, donation. *2* natural gift or talent, knack: *~ de gentes,* charm, winning manners. *3* Don, Spanish title prefixed to Christian names of men.
**donación** *f.* donation, gift, bestowal. *2* LAW donation.
**donado, -da** *m.-f.* lay brother or sister.
**donador, -ra** *m.-f.* donor, giver.
**donaire** *m.* nimble-wit. *2* sally, lively remark. *3* graceful carriage.
**donante** *m.-f.* donor.
**donar** *tr.* to donate, bestow, make donation of.
**donatario** *m.* donee, grantee.
**donativo** *m.* gift, donative, donation, contribution.
**doncel** *m.* virgin man. *2* king's page.
**doncella** *f.* virgin, maiden, maid. *2* maidservant, lady's maid.
**doncellería, doncellez** *f.* virginity, maidenhood.
**donde** *adv.-pron.* where, wherein, whither, in which: *a ~, en ~,* where; *de ~,* from where, whence; *hasta ~,* up to where, how far; *¿por dónde?* whereabouts? [by] wich way?; why? | The *o* is accented in interrogative or exclamatory sentences.
**dondequiera** *adv.* anywhere, wherever.
**dondiego** *m.* BOT. *dondiego* or *~ de noche,* four-o'clock, marvel-of-Peru; *~ de día,* morning glory.
**donguindo** *m.* variety of pear tree.
**donjuanismo** *m.* Don Juanism.
**donosamente** *adv.* wittily, amusingly. *2* gracefully, elegantly.
**donoso, -sa** *adj.* nimble-witted; graceful.
**donostiarra** *adj.-n.* of San Sebastián.
**donosura** *f.* grace, gracefulness.
**doña** *f.* Spanish title used before the Christian name of a lady.
**dopar** *tr.* to dope, to drug.
**doquier, doquiera** *adv.* anywhere, wherever.
**dorada** *f.* ICHTH. gilthead.
**doradillo** *m.* fine brass wire. *2* satinwood.
**dorado, -da** *adj.* gilt, golden. *2 m.* gilt, gilding.
**dorador** *m.* gilder.
**doradura** *f.* gilding.
**dorar** *tr.* to gild. *2* COOK. to brown. *3 ref.* to take a golden tinge. *4* COOK. to turn brown.
**dórico, -ca** *adj.* Doric. *2 m.* Doric [dialect].
**dorio, -ria** *adj.-n.* Dorian.
**dormida** *f.* night's sleep. *2* sleeping period [of silkworms].
**dormidera** *f.* BOT. garden poppy, opium poppy.

**dormidero, -ra** *adj.* soporific. *2 m.* sleeping place for cattle.
**dormilón, -na** *adj.* sleepy. *2 m.-f.* sleepyhead. *3 f.* armchair for napping. *4* earring.
**dormir** *intr.* to sleep, to rest; ~ *a pierna suelta,* to sleep soundly and peacefully; ~ *la mona,* to sleep oneself sober. *2* to pass the night. *3 tr.* to put to sleep. *4 intr.-ref.* to be careless, to be unwary or inactive. *5 ref.* to go to sleep, fall asleep. *6* to get benumbed. ¶ CONJUG.: INDIC. Pres.: *duermo, duermes, duerme; dormimos, dormís, duermen.* | Pret.: *dormí, dormiste, durmió;* dormimos, dormisteis, *durmieron.* | SUBJ. Pres.: *duerma, duermas, duerma; durmamos, durmáis, duerman.* | Imperf.: *durmiera, durmieras,* etc.; or *durmiese, durmieses,* etc. | Fut.: *durmiere, durmieres,* etc. | IMPER.: *duerme, duerma; durmamos, dormid, duerman.* | GER.: *durmiendo.*
**dormitar** *intr.* to doze, to nap.
**dormitorio** *m.* bedroom. *2* dormitory.
**dornajo** *m.* small round trough.
**dornillo** *m.* DORNAJO. *2* wooden bowl.
**Dorotea** *f. pr. n.* Dorothy.
**dorsal** *adj.* dorsal.
**dorso** *m.* back [of a thing]. *2* dorsum.
**dos** *adj.* two: *las* ~, two o'clock; *los* ~, *las* ~, both; *de* ~ *en* ~, two abreast; by twos; *en un* ~ *por tres,* in a flash, in a twinkling. *2* second [of the month]. *3 m.* two [number]. *4* deuce.
**doscientos, -tas** *adj.-m.* two hundred.
**dosel** *m.* canopy, dais.
**doselete** *m.* ARCH. canopy.
**dosificación** *f.* dosage. *2* CHEM. titration.
**dosificar** *tr.* to dose [a medicine]; to proportion [ingredients].
**dosimétrico, -ca** *adj.* dosimetric.
**dosis** *f.* MED. dose. *2* quantity [of something].
**dotación** *f.* endowment [endowing; funds]. *2* dowering. *3* NAV. complement. *4* staff, personnel.
**dotado, -da** *adj.* endowed; gifted.
**dotal** *adj.* dotal.
**dotar** *tr.* to endow, dower, portion [with money, a dowry, gifts, talents, etc.]; to gift. *2* NAV. to man [a ship]. *3* to staff [an office, etc.].
**dote** *m.* or *f.* dowry, dower, marriage portion. *2 f. pl.* endowments, gifts, virtues, talents.
**dovela** *f.* ARCH. voussoir.
**doy** *irr.* V. DAR.
**dozavo, -va** *adj.-m.* twelfth.
**dracma** *f.* drachm, drachma [coin]. *2* drachma, dram [weight].
**draconiano, -na** *adj.* Draconian.
**draga** *f.* dredge [machine]. *2* dredger [boat].
**dragado** *m.* dredging.
**dragaminas** *m.* NAV. mine sweeper.
**dragar** *tr.* to dredge.
**drago** *m.* BOT. dragon tree.
**dragón** *m.* MYTH., ZOOL., BOT. dragon. *2* MIL. dragoon. *3* ASTR. Draco. *4* ICHTH. ~ *marino,* greater weever.
**dragona** *f.* female dragon. *2* MIL. shoulder knot.
**dragontea** *f.* BOT. green dragon.
**drama** *m.* drama.
**dramática** *f.* drama, dramatic art or literature.
**dramático, -ca** *adj.* dramatic. *2 m.-f.* dramatist. *3* dramatic actor or actress.
**dramatismo** *m.* dramatic effect.
**dramatizar** *tr.* to dramatize.
**dramaturgia** *f.* drama, dramatic art.
**dramaturgo, -ga** *m.-f.* dramatist, playwright.
**dramón** *m.* a badly written sensational drama.

**drapeado** *m.* drapery.
**drapear** *tr.* to drape.
**drástico, -ca** *adj.* drastic.
**drenaje** *m.* SURG. drainage.
**drenar** *tr.* SURG. to drain.
**Dresde** *f. pr. n.* GEOG. Dresden.
**dríada, dríade** *f.* MYTH. dryad.
**driblar** *tr.* SPORT. to dribble.
**dril** *m.* drill [fabric]. *2* ZOOL. drill [baboon].
**driza** *f.* NAUT. halyard.
**droga** *f.* drug. *2* chemical substance. *3* fib, lie.
**drogadicto, -ta** *adj.-n.* drug addict.
**drogado, -da** *adj.* doped, drugged. *2 n.* drug addict. *3 m.* doping.
**droguería** *f.* drugstore.
**droguero** *m.* druggist.
**dromedario** *m.* ZOOL. dromedary.
**druida** *m.* Druid.
**druidismo** *m.* Druidism.
**drupa** *f.* BOT. drupe, stone fruit.
**dual** *adj.-m.* GRAM. dual.
**dualidad** *f.* duality.
**dualismo** *m.* dualism.
**dubitativo, -va** *adj.* dubitative.
**ducado** *m.* duchy. *2* dukedom. *3* ducat.
**ducal** *adj.* ducal.
**dúctil** *adj.* ductile.
**ductilidad** *f.* ductility.
**ducha** *f.* douche, shower bath.
**duchar** *tr.* to douche, give a shower bath. *2 ref.* to douche, take a shower bath.
**ducho, -cha** *adj.* skilful, expert, experienced.
**duda** *f.* doubt; *sin* ~, doubtless, no doubt.
**dudable** *adj.* dubitable.
**dudar** *intr.-tr.* to doubt, question. *2 intr.* to doubt, waver, hesitate.
**dudoso, -sa** *adj.* doubtful, dubious.
**duela** *f.* stave [of barrel]. *2* ZOOL. fluke.
**duelista** *m.* duelist.
**duelo** *m.* duel: ~ *judiciario,* judicial combat. *2* grief, sorrow. *3* pity, compassion: fig. *sin* ~, abundantly. *4* mourning; bereavement. *5* mourners [at a funeral]. *6 pl.* hardships.
**duelo, duela,** etc. *irr.* V. DOLER.
**duende** *m.* goblin, hobgoblin.
**dueña** *f.* owner, proprietress, mistress. *2* duenna.
**dueño, -ña** *m.-f.* owner, proprietor, master, landlord: *hacerse* ~ or *dueña de,* to appropriate to oneself; to master; *ser* ~ *de,* to own; to be master of; to be at liberty to [do, etc.]; *ser* ~ *de sí mismo,* to be self-controlled. *2 mi* ~, my love.
**duermevela** *f.* doze, light sleep.
**duermo, duerma,** etc. *irr.* V. DORMIR.
**Duero** *m. pr. n.* GEOG. Douro.
**dueto** *m.* short duet.
**dulcamara** *f.* BOT. bittersweet.
**dulce** *adj.* sweet. *2* saltless, insipid. *3* fresh [water]. *4* soft [iron]. *5* PAINT. soft, agreeably coloured. *6 adv.* sweetly, softly. *7 m.* sweet [dessert]. *8* sweetmeat, confection.
**dulcémele** *m.* MUS. dulcimer.
**dulcera** *f.* preserve dish, compotier.
**dulcería** *f.* confectionery shop.
**dulcero, -ra** *m.-f.* confectioner.
**dulcificar** *tr.* to sweeten, dulcify.
**dulcinea** *f.* coll. sweetheart, beloved one [woman].
**dulcísono, -na** *adj.* poet, sweet-toned.
**dulía** *f.* dulia, worship of angels and saints.
**dulzaina** *f.* MUS. kind of flageolet.
**dulzarrón, -na; dulzón, -na** *adj.* sickeningly sweet.
**dulzor** *m.* sweetness.

**dulzura** *f.* sweetness. *2* mildness [of temper, of weather]. *3* gentleness, kindliness. *4* pleasantness. *5 pl.* endearments.

**dumdum** *adj.* dumdum: *bala* ~, dumdum bullet.

**duna** *f.* dune.

**Dunquerque** *f. pr. n.* GEOG. Dunkirk.

**dúo** *m.* MUS. duet.

**duodecimal** *adj.* duodecimal.

**duodécimo, -ma** *adj.-m.* twelfth.

**duodeno, -na** *adj.* twelfth. *2 m.* ANAT. duodenum.

**duplex** *adj.* TELEG. duplex.

**duplicado, -da** *adj.-m.* duplicate.

**duplicador, -ra** *adj.* duplicating. *2 m.* duplicator.

**duplicar** *tr.* to double, duplicate.

**duplicidad** *f.* duplicity.

**duplo** *adj.-m.* double [twice as much].

**duque** *m.* duke.

**duquesa** *f.* duchess.

**durabilidad** *f.* durability.

**durable** *adj.* durable, lasting.

**duración** *f.* duration, endurance, lasting.

**duradero, -ra** *adj.* durable, enduring, lasting.

**duramadre, duramater** *f.* ANAT. dura mater.

**duramen** *m.* BOT. duramen.

**durante** *prep.* during.

**durar** *intr.* to endure, last, continue. *2* [of clothes, etc.] to wear well.

**duraznero** *m.* BOT. peach tree.

**durazno** *m.* BOT. peach tree. *2* peach [fruit].

**dureza** *f.* hardness. *2* harshness, severity. *3* obstinacy. *4* MED. callosity.

**durillo, -lla** *adj.* rather hard. *2 m.* BOT. laurustine. *3* BOT. dogwood. *4* a small golden coin.

**durmiente** *adj.* sleeping, dormant. *2 m.-f.* sleeper [pers.]. *3 m.* ARCH. dormant.

**durmiera, durmiere,** etc. *irr.* V. DORMIR.

**duro, -ra** *adj.* hard: ~ *de corazón,* hard-hearted; ~ *de oído,* hard of hearing; *ser* ~ *para* or *para con,* to be hard on. *2* harsh, severe, rigorous, unbearable. *3* obdurate, unfeeling. *4* obstinate. *5* strong, hardy. *6* stingy. *7* stiff [collar]. *8 a duras penas,* hardly, scarcely. *9 adv.* hard. *10* Spanish dollar [coin worth 5 pesetas].

**duunvirato** *m.* duumvirate.

**duunviro** *m.* duumvir.

**dux** *m.* doge.

# E

**E, e** f. E, e, sixth letter of the Spanish alphabet.

**e** conj. and [used for y before words beginning with i or hi not followed by e].

**¡ea!** interj. used as an encouragement or to express determination.

**ebanista** m. cabinetmaker.

**ebanistería** f. cabinetwork. 2 cabinetmaker's shop.

**ébano** m. BOT. ebony. 2 ebony wood.

**ebonita** f. ebonite.

**ebriedad** f. drunkenness, intoxication.

**ebrio, ebria** adj. drunk, intoxicated. 2 fig. blind [with anger, etc.].

**ebullición** f. ebullition, boiling.

**eburnación** f. MED. eburnation.

**ebúrneo, -a** adj. eburnean, ivorylike.

**Eccehomo** m. Ecce Homo.

**Ezequiel** m. pr. n. Ezekiel.

**eclecticismo** m. eclecticism.

**ecléctico, -ca** adj.-n. eclectic.

**Eclesiastés** m. BIBL. Ecclesiastes.

**eclesiástico, -ca** adj. ecclesiastic(al. 2 m. ecclesiastic, clergyman.

**eclipsar** tr. ASTR. & fig. to eclipse. 2 ref. to disappear.

**eclipse** m. eclipse.

**eclíptica** f. ASTR. ecliptic.

**eclisa** f. RLY. fishplate.

**eco** m. echo: tener ~, fig. to spread, to be widely accepted. 2 distant sound. 3 (cap.) MYTH. Echo.

**economato** m. company store, commissary; cooperative shop.

**economía** f. economy: ~ dirigida, planned economy. 2 economics. 3 saving, thrift. 4 sparingness, scantiness. 5 pl. savings: hacer economías, to save up.

**económico, -ca** adj. economic. 2 economical. 3 thrifty, saving. 4 cheap, uncostly. 5 cheap [price].

**economista** m. economist.

**economizar** tr. to economize; to save, spare.

**ecónomo** m. acting parish priest.

**ectoblasto** m. BIOL. ectoblast.

**ectodermo** m. BIOL. ectoderm.

**ectropión** m. MED. ectropion.

**ecuación** f. MATH., ASTR. equation.

**Ecuador** m. pr. n. GEOG. Ecuador.

**ecuador** m. GEOM., GEOG., ASTR. equator.

**ecuánime** adj. equanimous. 2 just, impartial.

**ecuanimidad** f. equanimity. 2 impartiality.

**ecuatorial** adj.-m. equatorial.

**ecuatoriano, -na** adj.-n. Ecuadorian.

**ecuestre** adj. equestrian.

**ecuménico, -ca** adj. ecumenic(al.

**eczema** f. MED. eczema.

**echada** f. throw, cast. 2 SPORT. man's length.

**echar** tr. to throw, cast, fling, pitch, toss; to heave, drop: ~ anclas, to cast anchor; ~ la culpa a, to throw the blame on. 2 to put in or into, to add: ~ leña al fuego, to add fuel to the flame. 3 to emit, give off or out [sparks, smell, etc.]: ~ chispas, fig. to be wild with anger. 4 to dismiss, discharge, fire, expel, throw out: ~ con cajas destempladas, fig. to dismiss or turn away without ceremony. 5 to grow, begin to have [hair, teeth, feathers]. 6 to put forth, sprout, bear [leaves, fruit, etc.]. 7 to give, deliver [a speech, a sermon]. 8 to turn [a key]; to shoot home [a bolt]. 9 to pour [wine, etc.]. 10 to move, push: ~ a un lado, to push aside. 11 followed by some nouns, it expresses the idea implied by the noun: ~ cuentas, to reckon; ~ maldiciones, to utter curses; ~ suertes, to draw lots; ~ un trago, to take a drink. 12 Other senses: ~ abajo or por tierra, to throw down, overthrow, demolish; ~ a broma, to take as a joke; ~ a perder, to spoil, to ruin; ~ a pique, to sink [a vessel]; ~ de menos, to miss; ~ de ver, to notice, observe; ~ las cartas, to tell fortunes by cards; ~ mano a, to seize, take hold of; ~ mano de, to resort to; ~ raíces, to take root; ~ una mano, to lend a hand; ¿cuántos años le echa?, how old would you say he is?

13 intr. ~ calle arriba, to go or start up the street. 14 ~ por, to take [a road, etc.]; to turn to [the right, the left, etc.].

15 intr.-ref. ~ or echarse a correr, a reír, a saltar, etc., to begin to run, laugh, jump, etc., to start running, laughing, jumping, etc.

16 ref. to lie down, to throw oneself down, to stretch oneself at full length. 17 to throw oneself into. 18 echarse a perder, to spoil, get spoiled, to become stale, to go bad. 19 echarse atrás, to draw back, to back out. 20 echarse a un lado, to move aside. 21 echarse encima or sobre, to rush at, fall upon; to throw on or upon oneself. 22

*echárselas de*, to pretend or claim to be, to boast of being.

**echarpe** *f*. scarf, stole, shawl.

**echazón** *f*. throwing. 2 NAUT. jettison; jetsam.

**edad** *f*. age: ~ *madura* or *provecta*, mature age, maturity; *mayor* ~, majority, full age; *menor* ~, minority; ~ *de oro*, golden age; ~ *media*, Middle Ages; *¿qué* ~ *tiene usted?*, how old are you?

**edafología** *f*. edaphology.

**edecán** *m*. MIL. aide-de-camp.

**edema** *f*. MED. œdema, edema.

**Edén** *m*. Eden, paradise.

**edénico, -ca** *adj*. paradisiac.

**edición** *f*. edition. 2 issue [of a newspaper]. 3 publication [of a book].

**edicto** *m*. edict.

**edículo** *m*. ARCH. small building or niche.

**edificación** *f*. building, construction. 2 edification.

**edificante** *adj*. edifying.

**edificar** *tr*. to build, construct. 2 to edify.

**edificio** *m*. edifice, building, structure.

**edil** *m*. aedile, edile. 2 town councillor.

**Edimburgo** *m. pr. n*. GEOGR. Edinburgh.

**Edipo** *m. pr. n*. MYTH. Oedipus.

**editar** *tr*. to publish [a book, a newspaper, etc.].

**editor** *m*. publisher.

**editorial** *adj*. publishing. 2 leading [article]. 3 *f*. publishing house. 4 editorial, leader [article].

**editorialista** *m.-f*. writer of editorials.

**edredón** *m*. eider down. 2 down quilt.

**Eduardo** *m. pr. n*. Edward.

**educación** *f*. education. 2 breeding, manners; good breeding, good manners; politeness.

**educador, -ra** *adj*. educating. 2 *m.-f*. educator.

**educando, -da** *m.-f*. student, pupil.

**educar** *tr*. to educate; to train. 2 to give good breeding.

**educativo, -va** *adj*. educative.

**educción** *f*. eduction.

**educir** *tr*. to educe. ¶ CONJUG. like *conducir*.

**edulcorar** *tr*. PHARM. to edulcorate, sweeten.

**efe** *f*. Spanish name of the letter *f*.

**efebo** *m*. ephebus.

**efectismo** *m*. F. ARTS striving after effect.

**efectivamente** *adv*. really, actually. 2 as a matter of fact; indeed. 3 effectually.

**efectividad** *f*. reality, actuality. 2 effectuality.

**efectivo, -va** *adj*. effective, real, actual. 2 permanent [employment]. 3 *dinero* ~, cash. 4 *hacer* ~, to carry out; to cash. 5 *m*. cash, specie: *en* ~, in cash. 6 *pl*. MIL. effectives, troops.

**efecto** *m*. effect: *surtir* ~, to have the desired effect, to work; *poner en* ~, to put into effect, to carry out; *con* ~, *en* ~, in fact, indeed, really; *de simple* ~, *de doble* ~, MACH. single acting, double acting. 2 purpose, end: *al* ~, for the purpose. 3 impression; *hacer* ~, to be impressive. 5 BILL. side, *English. 6 COM. article of merchandise. 7 COM. draft, bill, security: *efectos a cobrar*, bills receivable; *efectos públicos*, public securities. 8 *pl*. effects, goods, movables.

**efectuar** *tr*. to effect, effectuate, do, carry out. 2 *ref*. to take place.

**efemérides** *pl*. diary, daily record. 2 events of the same day in former years.

**efendi** *m*. Effendi [Turkish title].

**eferente** *adj*. PHYSIOL. efferent.

**efervescencia** *f*. effervescence. 2 agitation.

**efervescente** *adj*. effervescent.

**Efeso** *f. pr. n*. HIST., GEOG. Ephesus.

**eficacia** *f*. efficacity, efficacy.

**eficaz** *adj*. efficacious, effective, effectual.

**eficiencia** *f*. efficiency.

**eficiente** *adj*. efficient.

**efigie** *f*. effigy, image.

**efímero, -ra** *adj*. ephemeral.

**eflorecerse** *ref*. CHEM. to effloresce.

**eflorescencia** *f*. CHEM., MED. efflorescence.

**efluvio** *m*. effluvium, emanation, exhalation.

**Efraín** *m. pr. n*. Ephraim.

**efugio** *m*. evasion, subterfuge, shift, way out.

**efundir** *tr*. to effuse, to pour.

**efusión** *f*. effusion, pouring out, shedding. 2 fig. warmth, effusion.

**efusivo, -va** *adj*. effusive, warm.

**Egeo (Mar)** *m. pr. n*. GEOG. Ægean Sea.

**égida, egida** *f*. aegis, egis.

**egipcio, -cia** *adj.-n*. Egyptian. 2 *m*. Egyptian [language].

**Egipto** *m. pr. n*. GEOG. Egypt.

**egiptología** *f*. Egyptology.

**égira** *f*. HÉGIRA.

**égloga** *f*. eclogue.

**egocéntrico, -ca** *adj.-n*. egocentric.

**egocentrismo** *m*. egocentrism, self-centredness, egocentrity.

**egoísmo** *m*. egoism, selfishness.

**egoísta** *adj*. egoistic, selfish. 2 *m.-f*. egoist.

**egolatría** *f*. self-worship.

**egotismo** *m*. egotism.

**egregio, -gia** *adj*. illustrious, eminent, egregious.

**egresado, da** *adj.-n*. graduate.

**egresar** *intr*. (Am.) to go away, to leave. 2 to graduate, to take one's degree. 3 to pass out [military academy].

**¡eh!** *interj*. he!, here!

**eider** *m*. ORN. eider, eider duck.

**eje** *m*. axis. 2 axle, axletree, shaft, spindle, arbor. 3 fig. main or central point, subject, idea, etc.

**ejecución** *f*. execution. 2 LAW distraint.

**ejecutante** *adj*. executing. 2 *m.-f*. performer, executant. 3 LAW distrainor.

**ejecutar** *tr*. to execute, carry out, perform. 2 to execute [put to death]. 3 LAW to distrain.

**ejecutivo, -va** *adj*. executive. 2 pressing. 3 prompt, active. 4 *m*. (Am.) executive.

**ejecutor, -ra** *m.-f*. executer, executor. 2 *m*. ~ *de la justicia*, executioner.

**ejecutoria** *f*. letters patent of nobility. 2 glorious deed.

**ejecutorio, -ria** *adj*. LAW firm.

**ejemplar** *adj*. exemplary. 2 *m*. exemplar, pattern, model. 3 exemplar, specimen. 4 copy [of a book, magazine, etc.]. 5 precedent: *sin* ~, exceptional. 6 example, warning.

**ejemplaridad** *f*. exemplary quality or character.

**ejemplarizar** *tr*. to exemplify, to set an example to, to demonstrate by example.

**ejemplificar** *tr*. to exemplify, illustrate.

**ejemplo** *m*. example: *dar* ~, to set an example; *sin* ~, unexampled. 2 instance: *por* ~, for instance, for example.

**ejercer** *tr*. to exercise [authority, a right, etc.]. 2 to exercise, discharge, perform [functions]. 3 to exercise, practice, follow [a profession]. 4 to exercise, exert [influence, etc.].

**ejercicio** *m*. exercise. 2 MIL. drill. 3 practice [of a virtue, ability, or profession]; holding, tenure [of an office]. 4 fiscal year.

**ejercitación** *f*. exercise, practice.

**ejercitante** *adj*. exercising. 2 *m.-f*. exercitant.

**ejercitar** *tr.* to practice [a trade, profession, etc.]. *2 tr.-ref.* to exercise, drill, train.
**ejército** *m.* army.
**ejido** *m.* commons, public land [nearing a village].
**el** *def. art. masc. sing.* the.
**él** *pers. pron. masc. sing.* he, him; it.
**elaboración** *f.* elaboration, manufacturing.
**elaborar** *tr.* to elaborate, manufacture, work. *2* to work [a material].
**elástica** *f.* knit vest, undervest.
**elasticidad** *f.* elasticity. *2* resilience.
**elástico, -ca** *adj.* elastic. *2 m.* elastic [fabric].
**Elba** *f. pr. n.* Elbe [river].
**ele** *f.* Spanish name of the letter *l*.
**eléboro** *m.* BOT. hellebore.
**elección** *f.* election. *2* choice. *3* free election. *4 pl.* POL. election.
**electivo, -va** *adj.* elective.
**electo, -ta** *adj.* elected, chosen. *2* elect [chosen for office].
**elector, -ra** *adj.* electing. *2 m.-f.* elector, electress. *3 m.* Elector [German prince].
**electorado** *m.* electorate.
**electoral** *adj.* electoral.
**electricidad** *f.* electricity.
**electricista** *m.-f.* electrician.
**eléctrico, -ca** *adj.* electric(al.
**electrificación** *f.* electrification [of a railroad, etc.].
**electrificar** *tr.* to electrify [a railroad, etc.].
**electrización** *f.* electrification, electrization.
**electrizante** *adj.* electrifying.
**electrizar** *tr.* to electrify, to electrize.
**electro** *m.* amber. *2* electrum, electron.
**electrocardiografía** *f.* electrocardiography.
**electrocardiograma** *m.* electrocardiogram.
**electrocinética** *f.* electrokinetics.
**electrocución** *f.* electrocution.
**electrocutar** *tr.* to electrocute.
**electrodinámica** *f.* electrodynamics.
**electrodo** *m.* electrode.
**electroencefalograma** *m.* electro-encephalogram.
**electróforo** *m.* electrophorus.
**electrógeno, -na** *adj.* generating electricity. *2 m.* electric generator.
**electroimán** *m.* electromagnet.
**electrólisis** *f.* electrolysis.
**electrólito** *m.* electrolyte.
**electrolizar** *tr.* to electrolyze.
**electromagnetismo** *m.* electromagnetism.
**electromecánico, -ca** *adj.* electromechanical.
**electrometría** *f.* electrometry.
**electrómetro** *m.* electrometer.
**electromotor, -ra** *adj.* electromotive. *2 m.* electromotor.
**electromotriz** *adj.-f.* electromotive [force].
**electrón** *m.* PHYS., CHEM. electron.
**electrónico, -ca** *adj.* electronic, electron: *microscopio* ~, electron microscope. *2 f.* electronics.
**electroquímica** *f.* electrochemistry.
**electroscopio** *m.* PHYS. electroscope.
**electrostático, -ca** *adj.* electrostatic. *2 f.* electrostatics.
**electroterapia** *f.* MED. electrotherapy.
**electrotérmico, -ca** *adj.* electrothermic.
**electrotipia** *f.* electrotypy.
**electrotipo** *m.* electrotype.
**elefancía** *f.* MED. elephantiasis.
**elefanta** *f.* ZOOL. female elephant.
**elefante** *m.* ZOOL. elephant.

**elegancia** *f.* elegance, gracefulness, neatness, style.
**elegante** *adj.* elegant, graceful, smart, stylish. *2 m.-f.* elegant, dandy.
**elegantizar** *tr.* to make elegant, give style to.
**elegía** *f.* elegy.
**elegíaco, -ca** *adj.* elegiac, mournful.
**elegible** *adj.* eligible.
**elegido, -da** *adj.* elected, chosen. *2 m.* THEOL., one of the elect.
**elegir** *tr.* to elect. *2* to choose, select. ¶ CONJUG. like *servir*.
**elemental** *adj.* elemental, elementary. *2* fundamental.
**elemento** *m.* element. *2 pl.* elements [atmospheric forces]. *3* elements, rudiments. *4* means, resources.
**Elena** *f. pr. n.* Helen, Elaine.
**elenco** *m.* catalogue, index. *2* THEAT. company.
**elevación** *f.* elevation, raising, rise, ascent. *2* elevation, height. *3* elevation [of mind, of the style]. *4* ecstasy, transport. *5* exaltation [to a dignity]. *6* elevation [in the Mass].
**elevado, -da** *adj.* elevated, raised, lifted; high. *2* exalted. *3* sublime.
**elevador, -ra** *adj.* elevating. *2 m.* elevator.
**elevamiento** *m.* elevation, ecstasy, rapture.
**elevar** *tr.* to elevate, raise, lift. *2* to hoist. *3* to exalt [to a dignity]. *4* MATH. to raise [to a power]. *5 ref.* to rise, ascend, soar.
**elfo** *m.* elf.
**elidir** *tr.* GRAM. to elide.
**elijo, elija,** etc. *irr.* V. ELEGIR.
**eliminación** *f.* elimination.
**eliminar** *tr.* to eliminate.
**eliminatorio, -ria** *adj.* eliminating.
**elipse** *f.* GEOM. ellipse.
**elipsis** *f.* GRAM. ellipsis.
**elipsoide** *m.* GEOM. ellipsoid.
**elíptico, -ca** *adj.* GEOM., GRAM. elliptic(al.
**Elisa** *f. pr. n.* Eliza.
**Eliseo** *m. pr. n.* BIBL. Elisha. *2* MYTH. Elysium.
**elíseo, -a** *adj.* Elysian.
**elisión** *f.* elision.
**élitro** *m.* ENT. elytron, shard.
**elixir, elíxir** *m.* elixir.
**elocución** *f.* elocution.
**elocuencia** *f.* eloquence.
**elocuente** *adj.* eloquent.
**elogiable** *adj.* praiseworthy.
**elogiar** *tr.* to praise, commend, eulogize.
**elogio** *m.* praise, eulogy.
**elogioso, -sa** *adj.* praising, eulogistic.
**elongación** *f.* ASTR., MED. elongation.
**elote** *m.* (Am.) ear of green Indian corn.
**elucidación** *f.* elucidation.
**elucidar** *tr.* to elucidate.
**elucubración** *f.* lucubration.
**eludir** *tr.* to elude, avoid, evade.
**ella** *pron. f. sing.* she, her, it.
**elle** *f.* Spanish name of the letter *ll*.
**ello** *pron. neuter sing.* it: ~ *es que*, the fact is that.
**ellos, ellas** *pron. m. & f. pl.* they, them.
**Ema** *f. pr. n.* Emma.
**emaciación** *f.* MED. emaciation.
**emanación** *f.* emanation.
**emanar** *intr.* to emanate, issue.
**emancipación** *f.* emancipation.
**emancipar** *tr.* to emancipate. *2 ref.* to free oneself.
**Emanuel** *m. pr. n.* BIBL. Immanuel.
**emasculación** *f.* emasculation.

**embabiamiento** *m.* absorption, fit of abstraction.
**embadurnador, -ra** *adj.* daubing. 2 *m.-f.* dauber.
**embadurnar** *tr.* to daub, bedaub, besmear.
**embaír** *tr.* to deceive, humbug. ¶ Only used in the forms having *i* in their terminations.
**embajada** *f.* embassy. 2 ambassadorship. 3 message, errand.
**embajador** *m.* ambassador.
**embajadora** *f.* ambassadress.
**embalaje** *m.* packing [of goods]. 2 packing case.
**embalar** *tr.* to pack, bale [goods]. 2 *intr.* SPORT. to sprint. 3 AUTO. to step on the gas.
**embaldosado** *m.* paving with tiles. 2 tile floor.
**embaldosar** *tr.* to tile, pave with tiles.
**embalsamador, -ra** *adj.* embalming. 2 *m.-f.* embalmer.
**embalsamamiento** *m.* embalming.
**embalsamar** *tr.* to embalm [a corpse]. 2 to embalm, to perfume.
**embalsar** *tr.* to gather in a pond or pool. 2 to dam up [water]. 3 *ref.* [of water] to gather in a pond or pool. '
**embalse** *m.* damming [of water]. 2 dam [for water].
**emballenar** *tr.* to bone [stiffen with whalebone].
**embanastar** *tr.* to put into a basket. 2 to huddle, crowd together, pack.
**embanderar** *tr.* to bedeck with flags or banners.
**embarazada** *adj.* pregnant, with child. 2 *f.* pregnant woman.
**embarazar** *tr.-ref.* to embarrass, encumber, hinder. 2 *tr.* to make pregnant.
**embarazo** *m.* obstruction, hindrance. 2 embarrassment, constraint. 3 pregnancy.
**embarazoso, -sa** *adj.* embarrassing, difficult. 2 cumbersome.
**embarbillar** *tr.* CARP. to join obliquely.
**embarcación** *f.* NAUT. boat, craft, ship, vessel.
**embarcadero** *m.* wharf, pier, jetty.
**embarcador** *m.* shipper.
**embarcar** *tr.* NAUT. to embark; to ship. 2 *tr.-ref.* to embark [engage or become engaged in an enterprise]. 3 *intr.-ref.* to embark [go on board].
**embarco** *m.* embarkation [of people].
**embardar** *tr.* BARDAR.
**embargable** *adj.* LAW attachable.
**embargar** *tr.* to impede, restrain. 2 [of emotions] to overcome, to paralyse. 3 LAW to attach, seize [property]. 4 to lay an embargo on.
**embargo** *m.* LAW attachment, seizure [of property]. 2 embargo. 3 *adv. sin* ~, notwithstanding, nevertheless, however.
**embarque** *m.* shipment [of goods].
**embarrancar** *tr.* NAUT. to run [a ship] aground. 2 *intr.* NAUT. [of a ship] to run aground. 3 *ref.* fig. to stick in the mud.
**embarrar** *tr.* to bemud; to splash with mud. 2 to bedaub, besmear.
**embarrilar** *tr.* to pack in barrels or kegs.
**embarullador, -ra** *adj.* muddling. 2 *m.-f.* muddler.
**embarullar** *tr.* to muddle, mix up, make a mess of. 2 *ref.* to muddle, act in a confused way.
**embasamiento** *m.* ARCH. foundation.
**embastar** *tr.* SEW. to baste.
**embaste** *m.* SEW. basting.
**embastecer** *intr.* to put on flesh. 2 *ref.* to become gross or coarse. ¶ CONJUG. like *agradecer.*
**embate** *m.* dash, buffet, dashing, buffeting [of waves, wind, etc.].
**embaucador, -ra** *adj.* deceiving. 2 *m.-f.* deceiver, humbug, bamboozler.

**embaucamiento** *m.* deceiving, humbugging.
**embaucar** *tr.* to deceive, humbug, bamboozle.
**embaular** *tr.* to pack in a trunk. 2 to gobble, eat greedily.
**embausamiento** *m.* absorption, abstraction.
**embebecer** *tr.* to enrapture, absorb, delight. 2 *ref.* to become enraptured, be absorbed. ¶ CONJUG. like *agradecer.*
**embebecimiento** *m.* rapture, absorption.
**embeber** *tr.* to absorb, imbibe, soak up. 2 to soak [in]. 3 to embed, insert, fit in. 4 SEW. to take in. 5 *intr.* [of cloth] to shrink. 6 *ref.* to become absorbed. 7 *fig. embeberse de,* to get well acquainted with [a subject].
**embebezco, embebezca,** irr. V. EMBEBECER.
**embelecar** *tr.* to delude, deceive, humbug.
**embeleco** *m.* deception, trick, humbug.
**embelesador, -ra** *adj.* charming, captivating.
**embelesamiento** *m.* EMBELESO.
**embelesar** *tr.* to charm, entrance, delight, captivate. 2 *ref.* to be charmed, become entranced.
**embeleso** *m.* delight, enchantment. 2 charm; charming thing.
**embellecer** *tr.* to embellish, beautify. ¶ CONJUG. like *agradecer.*
**embellecimiento** *m.* embellishment, beautifying.
**embermejar** *tr.* EMBERMEJECER.
**embermejecer** *tr.* to dye red; to redden. 2 *ref.* to redden, blush. ¶ CONJUG. like *agradecer.*
**emberrenchinarse, emberrincharse** *ref.* fam. to be enraged, fly into a rage.
**embestida** *f.* assault, attack, charge, onset.
**embestidor, -ra** *adj.* attacking. 2 charging [a bull].
**embestir** *tr.* to assail, attack, charge. 2 to accost [someone]. 3 *intr.* ~ *contra,* to rush against or upon. ¶ CONJUG. like *servir.*
**embetunar** *tr.* to bituminize. 2 to black [shoes].
**embicar** *tr.* NAUT. to top [a yard].
**embisto, embista,** etc. irr. V. EMBESTIR.
**emblandecer** *tr.* to soften. 2 *ref.* to soften, to turn soft. 3 to relent.
**emblanquecer** *tr.* to whiten. 2 *ref.* to turn white. ¶ CONJUG. like *agradecer.*
**emblanquecimiento** *m.* whitening.
**emblema** *m.* emblem.
**emblemático, -ca** *adj.* emblematic(al.
**embobado, -sa** *adj.* dumbfounded, flabbergasted, agape. 2 bewildered, dazed, stupefied.
**embobamiento** *m.* absorption, enchantment.
**embobar** *tr.* to enchant, hold in suspense. 2 *ref.* to be enchanted, absorbed; to stand gaping.
**embobecer** *tr.* to make foolish, make silly. 2 *ref.* to become foolish, get silly. ¶ CONJUG. like *agradecer.*
**embocado, -da** *adj.* dry-sweet [wine].
**embocadura** *f.* entrance by a narrow passage. MUS. embouchure, mouthpiece. 3 mouthpiece [of a bridle]. 4 flavour [of wine]. 5 rivermouth. 6 THEAT. proscenium arch.
**embocar** *tr.* to mouth, put into the mouth. 2 to enter or to put through [a narrow place]. 3 to gobble up. 4 MUS. to mouth [as instrument].
**embocinado, -da** *adj.* shaped like a trumpet.
**embodegar** *tr.* to store [wine, olive oil, etc.].
**embojar** *tr.* to put on branches, encouraging the formation of cocoons [silkworms].
**embolada** *f.* MACH. stroke [of piston].
**embolado** *m.* THEAT. minor role. 2 BULLF. bull with wooden balls on horns. 3 coll. trick, deception.
**embolar** *tr.* BULLF. to tip horns of [bull] with wooden balls.

**embolia** *f.* MED. embolism.

**embolismar** *tr.* to carry tales, to make mischief.

**embolismo** *m.* ASTR. embolism. 2 muddle, confusion, difficulty. 3 gossip, falsehood.

**émbolo** *m.* MECH. piston, plunger. 2 MED. embolus.

**embolsar** *tr.* to pocket [money].

**embonar** *tr.* to improve. 2 to sheathe [a ship].

**embono** *m.* sheathing [of a ship].

**emboquillar** *tr.* to tip, put a tip on [a cigarette].

**emborrachamiento** *m.* intoxication, drunkenness.

**emborrachar** *tr.* to intoxicate, make drunk. 2 *ref.* to become intoxicated, to get drunk. 3 [of colours] to run together.

**emborrascar** *tr.* to anger, irritate. 2 *ref.* to get angry. 3 [of weather] to get stormy.

**emborrazamiento** *m.* COOK. barding.

**emborrazar** *tr.* COOK. to bard [a fowl].

**emborronar** *tr.* to blot [paper]; to scribble.

**emborrullarse** *ref.* to wrangle.

**emboscada** *f.* ambuscade, ambush.

**emboscar** *tr.-ref.* to ambuscade, ambush [station or lie in ambush]. 2 *ref.* to enter or hide in the woods. 3 fig. to shirk work or danger by taking an easy job.

**embotado, -da** *adj.* blunt, dull.

**embotamiento** *m.* blunting, dulling. 2 bluntness, dullness.

**embotar** *tr.* to blunt, to dull. 2 to put [tobacco] in a jar. 3 *ref.* to become blunt or dull.

**embotellado, -da** *p. p.* of EMBOTELLAR. 2 *adj.* fig. prepared [speech, etc]. 3 *m.* bottling.

**embotelladora** *f.* bottling machine.

**embotellamiento** *m.* stoppage, jam, traffic jam.

**embotellar** *tr.* to bottle. 2 to bottle up. 3 fig. to stop, obstruct.

**embovedar** *tr.* to arch, vault. 2 to enclose in a vault.

**embozadamente** *adv.* covertly.

**embozado, -da** *adj.* muffled, wrapped up to the eyes. 2 covert, disguised. 3 *m.-f.* person wrapped up to the eyes.

**embozar** *tr.-ref.* to muffle or wrap up to the eyes. 2 *tr.* to mask, disguise [the meaning of]. 3 to muzzle [dogs, horses, etc.].

**embozo** *m.* part of cloak, etc., held over the face: *quitarse el* ~, fig. to remove one's mask. 2 strip of wool, silk, etc., lining the side of a cloak. 3 fold in top part of bedsheet. 4 disguise [of meaning, etc.]: *sin* ~, openly, frankly.

**embragar** *tr.* to sling [for hoisting]. 2 MECH. to engage the clutch, throw the clutch in.

**embrague** *m.* slinging [for hoisting]. 2 MECH. clutch. 3 MECH. throwing the clutch in.

**embravecer** *tr.* to irritate, enrage. 2 *ref.* to get angry. 3 [of the sea] to get rough; [of a storm] to gather violence. ¶ CONJUG. like *agradecer*.

**embravecido, -da** *adj.* furious, enraged [person.], wild, rough [sea], wild [wind].

**embravecimiento** *m.* anger, fury, rage.

**embrazadura** *f.* handle [of shield].

**embrazar** *tr.* to clasp [a shield].

**embreadura** *f.* tarring, pitching.

**embrear** *tr.* to tar, pitch.

**embriagado, -da** *adj.* intoxicated, inebriated; drunk.

**embriagador, -ra** *adj.* intoxicating, inebriating.

**embriagar** *tr.* to intoxicate, inebriate. 2 to make drunk. 3 *ref.* to get drunk, become inebriated.

**embriaguez** *f.* intoxication, inebriation, drunkenness.

**embridar** *tr.* to bridle [a horse].

**embriología** *f.* embryology.

**embrión** *m.* embryo: *en* ~, in embryo.

**embrionario, -ria** *adj.* embryonic.

**embrocación** *f.* MED. embrocation; embrocating.

**embrocar** *tr.* to empty [a vessel] into another. 2 BULLF. to catch between the horns.

**embrolladamente** *adv.* confusedly.

**embrollar** *tr.* to entangle, confuse, muddle; to embroil. 2 *ref.* to get muddled or confused.

**embrollo** *m.* tangle, muddle, mess. 2 lie, deception. 3 imbroglio.

**embrollón, -na** *m.-f.* embroiler, confuser. 2 liar, mischief-maker.

**embromado, -da** *adj. estar* ~, to be in a fix, having a tough time.

**embromar** *tr.* to play jokes on, to banter, chaff. 2 to fool, deceive. 3 (Am.) to annoy, vex; to do a bad turn.

**embrujamiento** *m.* bewitchment.

**embrujar** *tr.* to bewitch.

**embrujo** *m.* EMBRUJAMIENTO.

**embrutecedor, -ra** *adj.* besotting, brutifying.

**embrutecer** *tr.* to besot, brutify. 2 *ref.* to become besotted. ¶ CONJUG. like *agradecer*.

**embrutezco, embrutezca**, etc. *irr.* V. EMBRUTECER.

**embrutecimiento** *m.* sottishness, stupidity.

**embuchado** *m.* any kind of sausage. 2 stuffing [of a ballot-box]. 3 fraudulent affair.

**embuchar** *tr.* to stuff [guts] to make sausages. 2 to stuff [food] into a fowl's crop. 3 to gobble up [one's food].

**embudar** *tr.* to put a funnel into. 2 to trick, deceive.

**embudo** *m.* funnel. 2 trick, deception.

**emburujar** *tr.* to tangle [threads, etc.]. 2 to make lumpy. 3 to jumble.

**embuste** *m.* lie, falsehood, invention.

**embustería** *f.* lying, deceit.

**embustero, -ra** *adj.* lying. 2 *m.-f.* liar, deceiver.

**embutido** *m.* inlaid work, marquetry. 2 any kind of sausage.

**embutir** *tr.* to stuff [guts] to make sausages. 2 to inlay, set flush. 3 to stuff, cram. 4 to insert, put [into]. 5 *tr.-ref.* to gobble up [food].

**eme** *f.* Spanish name of the letter *m.*

**emergencia** *f.* emergence, emersion [act of emerging]. 2 happening, incident.

**emergente** *adj.* emergent.

**emerger** *intr.* to emerge.

**emérito** *adj.* emeritus.

**emersion** *f.* ASTR. emersion.

**emético, -ca** *adj.-m.* emetic.

**emetropía** *f.* MED. emmetropia.

**emigración** *f.* emigration.

**emigrado, -da** *m.-f.* emigree, émigré.

**emigrante** *adj.-n.* emigrant.

**emigrar** *intr.* to emigrate.

**emigratorio, -ria** *adj.* migratory, emigratory.

**Emilia** *f. pr. n.* Emily.

**Emilio** *m. pr. n.* Æmilius.

**eminencia** *f.* eminence. 2 (cap.) Eminence [cardinal's title].

**eminente** *adj.* eminent.

**eminentísimo, -ma** *adj. superl.* most eminent.

**emirato** *m.* emirate.

**emir** *m.* emir, ameer.

**emisario** *m.* emissary; envoy, messenger.

**emisión** *f.* emission. 2 COM. issuance, issue [of bonds, shares, etc.]. 3 RADIO. broadcasting, broadcast.

**emisor, -ra** *adj.* emitting. 2 broadcasting. 3 *m.* wireless transmitter. 4 *f.* broadcasting station.
**emitir** *tr.* to emit. 2 to issue [bonds, shares, etc.]. 3 RADIO. to broadcast.
**emoción** *f.* emotion [agitation of mind].
**emocionado, -da** *adj.* touched, moved, stirred. 2 upset.
**emocional** *adj.* emotional [of the emotions].
**emocionante** *adj.* moving, touching, thrilling.
**emocionar** *tr.* to move, touch, thrill, arouse emotion in. 2 *ref.* to be moved.
**emoliente** *adj.-m.* emollient.
**emolumento** *m.* emolument.
**emotividad** *f.* emotionality.
**emotivo, -va** *adj.* emotive, emotional.
**empacador, -ra** *m.-f.* packer, baler.
**empacar** *tr.* to pack, bale. 2 *ref.* to get obstinate, stubborn or sulky [about].
**empachado, -da** *adj.* surfeited. 2 troubled, ashamed. 3 awkward, timid.
**empachar** *tr.* to impede, embarrass. 2 to surfeit, give indigestion. 3 *ref.* to be embarrassed; to be ashamed. 4 to have an indigestion.
**empacho** *m.* awkwardness, embarrassment, shame. 2 hindrance, obstacle. 3 surfeit, overeating.
**empachoso, -sa** *adj.* embarrassing. 2 bashful.
**empadronamiento** *m.* census; taking of the census.
**empadronar** *tr.* to register in a census.
**empajar** *tr.* to cover or stuff with straw.
**empalagar** *tr.* to cloy, sicken, pall. 2 to weary, bore.
**empalago** *m.* cloying, sickening, palling. 2 boring.
**empalagoso, -sa** *adj.* cloying, sickening, palling.
**empalar** *tr.* to impale [on a stake].
**empaliar** *tr.* to adorn with hangings.
**empalizada** *f.* palisade, stockade.
**empalizar** *tr.* to palisade, strockade.
**empalmar** *tr.* to join end to end, to splice. 2 to join, connect. 3 *intr.* [of roads or railways] to connect.
**empalme** *m.* joint, connection, join, union. 2 junction [train, road], intersection. 3 connection [train, bus]. 4 kick on the volley [football].
**empalletado** *m.* NAUT. barricade.
**empanada** *f.* COOK. pie.
**empanadilla** *f. dim.* turnover, small pie.
**empanar** *tr.* COOK. to put into a pie. 2 COOK. to bread. 3 AGR. to sow with wheat.
**empantanar** *tr.* to make swampy. 2 to swamp [plunge into a swamp]. 3 to obstruct [a business]. 4 *ref.* to become swampy. 5 to stick in the mud.
**empañar** *tr.* to swaddle. 2 to dim, blur, dull, tarnish. 3 to sully [reputation, etc.]. 4 *ref.* to become dim, dull, tarnished.
**empapar** *tr.* to soak, drench, steep, saturate. 2 to soak up, absorb, imbibe. 3 *ref.* fig. to acquire a full knowledge [of]; to enter into the spirit [of]. 4 to get soaked, or soaked up.
**empapelado** *m.* papering, paper hanging. 2 wallpaper.
**empapelador, -ra** *m.* paper hanger.
**empapelar** *tr.* to wrap in paper. 2 to paper [a wall]; to wallpaper. 3 coll. to prosecute [a person].
**empaque** *m.* packing. 2 coll. mien, appearance. 3 stiffness, affected gravity.
**empaquetado** *m.* packing.
**empaquetadura** *f.* packing. 2 MACH. gasket.

**empaquetar** *tr.* to pack [goods]. 2 to pack, crowd.
**emparchar** *tr.* to cover with plasters.
**emparedado, -da** *adj.* immured. 2 *m.-f.* recluse. 3 *m.* sandwich.
**emparedar** *tr.* to immure, wall in.
**emparejar** *tr.* to pair, match. 2 to make [a thing] level with another. 3 to close [doors] flush. 4 *intr.* to come abreast, catch up [with another]. 5 to equal. 6 *ref.* to pair.
**emparentado, -da** *adj.* related [by marriage].
**emparentar** *intr.* to become related by marriage. ¶ CONJUG. like *acertar.*
**emparrado** *m.* vine arbour, bower.
**emparrar** *tr.* to form into a bower. 2 to embower.
**emparrillado** *m.* ARCH. & ENG. grillage.
**empastar** *tr.* to cover with paste. 2 to bind [books] in a stiff cover. 3 to fill [a tooth]. 4 PAINT. to impaste.
**empaste** *m.* covering with paste. 2 filling [of a tooth]. 3 PAINT. impasto.
**empastelar** *tr.* PRINT. to pi, pie.
**empatar** *tr.-intr.-ref.* to tie, be in a tie, equal, draw [in games or voting].
**empate** *m.* tie, draw [in games or voting].
**empavesada** *f.* NAUT. armings, waistcloths.
**empavesado** *m.* NAUT. dressing [of a ship], bunting.
**empavesar** *tr.* NAUT. to dress [a ship]. 2 to veil [a monument].
**empavonado, empavonamiento** *m.* blueing [of a metal].
**empecatado, -da** *adj.* confounded, incorrigible. 2 ill-starred, unlucky.
**empecer** *intr.* to be an obstacle. ¶ CONJUG. like *agradecer.*
**empecinado, -da** *adj.* (Am.) stubborn.
**empecinamiento** *m.* stubbornness, obstinacy, pigheadedness.
**empecinar** *tr.* to smear with pitch or slime. 2 *ref.* (Am.) to get obstinate [about].
**empedernido, -da** *adj.* hardened, hard-hearted. 2 inveterate.
**empedernir** *tr.* to harden. 2 *ref.* to harden; to become hard-hearted. ¶ Only used in the forms having *i* in their terminations.
**empedrado, -da** *adj.* stone-paved. 2 strewn. 3 cloud-flecked. 4 *m.* stone pavement.
**empedrador** *m.* stone paver.
**empedrar** *tr.* to pave with stones. 2 fig. ~ *de*, to strew, bespatter with.
**empegado** *m.* tarpaulin.
**empegar** *tr.* to coat with pitch. 2 to mark [sheep] with pitch.
**empeine** *m.* lower part of the abdomen. 2 instep. 3 vamp [of shoe]. 4 MED. tetter.
**empelotarse** *ref.* coll. to get muddled. 2 coll. to get into a row. 3 coll. to strip naked, to undress. 4 to be mad or crazy about, to fall in love with.
**empellar** *tr.* to push, shove, jostle.
**empellón** *m.* push, shove: *a empellones*, by pushing, roughly.
**empenachar** *tr.* to plume, adorn with plumes.
**empenaje** *m.* AER. empennage, tail unit.
**empeñadamente** *adv.* with a will, hard, insistently.
**empeñado, -da** *adj.* pledged. 2 pawned. 3 eager [to], bent [on]. 4 [of a dispute, etc.] hard, hot.
**empeñar** *tr.* to pledge; plight; to pawn. 2 to engage, compel. 3 to join [battle]; to start [a dispute]. 4 *ref.* to get into debt. 5 to bind oneself. 6 [of a battle, dispute, etc.] to begin. 7 *empeñarse*

*en*, to insist on, to set one's mind on. 8 *empeñarse por*, to intercede for.

**empeño** *m.* pledging [of one's word, etc.]. 2 pawning, pawn: *casa de empeños*, pawnshop. 3 pledge, obligation. 4 insistence, determination. 5 undertaking. 6 protector, recommender.

**empeoramiento** *m.* deterioration, worsening.

**empeorar** *tr.-intr.-ref.* to deteriorate, worsen [make or get worse].

**empequeñecer** *tr.* to make smaller, belittle, diminish. ¶ CONJUG. like *agradecer*.

**emperador** *m.* emperor.

**emperatriz** *f.* empress.

**emperejilar** *tr.* to dress up, adorn. 2 *ref.* to dress up, adorn oneself.

**emperezar** *intr.-ref.* to grow lazy.

**empergaminar** *tr.* to cover or bind with parchment.

**emperifollar** *tr.* EMPEREJILAR.

**empernar** *tr.* to bolt [secure with bolts].

**empero** *conj.* yet, however, notwithstanding.

**emperrarse** *ref.* to get obstinate; to stick doggedly [to an idea or purpose].

**empezar** *tr.-intr.* to begin: ~ *a*, to begin to, to start [doing something]; ~ *por*, to begin by. ¶ CONJUG. like *acertar*.

**empiezo, empiece,** etc. *irr.* V. EMPEZAR.

**empinada** *f.* AER. zooming. 2 *irse a la* ~, [of a horse] to rear.

**empinado, -da** *adj.* high; steep. 2 stiff, stuck-up.

**empinar** *tr.* to raise, lift. 2 ~ *el codo*, to crook the elbow, to tipple. 3 *intr.* to drink much. 4 *ref.* to stand on tiptoe. 5 [of a horse] to rear. 6 AER. to zoom. 7 to tower, rise high.

**empingorotado, -da** *adj.* of high social standing; stuck-up.

**empíreo, -a** *adj.-m.* empyrean.

**empírico, -ca** *adj.* empirical, empiric. 2 *m.-f.* empiric, empiricist.

**empirismo** *m.* empiricism.

**empitonar** *tr.* BULLF. to catch with the horns.

**empizarrado** *m.* slate roof.

**empizarrar** *tr.* to roof with slate.

**emplastar** *tr.* to apply plasters to. 2 to paint the face of. 3 *ref.* to paint one's face.

**emplástico, -ca** *adj.* sticky, glutinous.

**emplasto** *m.* PHARM. plaster; poultice. 2 coll. unsatisfactory compromise.

**emplazamiento** *m.* summoning, summons. 2 location, emplacement.

**emplazar** *tr.* to summon at a specified time. 2 to locate, place.

**empleado, -da** *m.-f.* employee; clerk; officeholder.

**emplear** *tr.* to employ [a person, time, etc.]. 2 to employ, use. 3 to spend, invest [money]. 4 *le está bien empleado*, it serves him right. 5 *ref.* to take employment. 6 to occupy oneself.

**empleo** *m.* employ, employment, post, job; occupation. 2 employment, use. 3 investment [of money].

**empleomanía** *f.* eagerness for civil employment.

**emplomado** *m.* leads [of roof or latticed windows].

**emplomar** *tr.* to lead [cover, fix, etc., with lead]. 2 to plumb [seal with lead].

**emplumar** *tr.* to feather [cover, adorn with feathers]. 2 to tar and feather.

**emplumecer** *intr.* to fledge, grow feathers. ¶ CONJUG. like *agradecer*.

**empobrecer** *tr.* to impoverish. 2 *intr.-ref.* to become poor. ¶ CONJUG. like *agradecer*.

**empobrecimiento** *m.* impoverishment.

**empobrezco, empobrezca,** etc. *irr.* V. EMPOBRECER.

**empolvar** *tr.* to cover with dust. 2 to powder [put powder on]. 3 *ref.* to get dusty. 4 to powder [one's face].

**empollado, -da** *adj.* hatched, incubated. 2 coll. primed for an examination.

**empollar** *tr.* to brood, hatch [eggs]. 2 coll. to grind, swot up [a subject]. 3 *intr.* [of bees] to brood.

**empollón, -na** *adj.* swotting. 2 *m.-f.* swot, grind [student].

**emponchado, -da** *adj.* (Am.) wearing a poncho. 2 suspicious.

**emponcharse** *ref.* (Am.) to put on a poncho.

**emponzoñamiento** *m.* poisoning.

**emponzoñar** *tr.* to poison. 2 *ref.* to become poisoned.

**emporcar** *tr.* to dirty, foul, soil. 2 to get dirty. ¶ CONJUG. like *contar*.

**emporio** *m.* emporium. 2 center of arts or culture.

**empotrar** *tr.* ARCH. to embed [in a wall or floor].

**emprendedor, -ra** *adj.* enterprising.

**emprender** *tr.* to undertake, engage in, enter upon; to begin: ~ *la marcha*, to start out. 2 ~ *a uno*, to accost, address someone; *emprenderla con*, to attack, set upon.

**empresa** *f.* enterprise, undertaking. 2 concern, firm, company. 3 management [of a theater]. 4 HER. device.

**empresarial** *adj.* management, managerial.

**empresario** *m.* contractor. 2 theatrical manager; impresario; showman. 3 ~ *de pompas fúnebres*, undertaker.

**empréstito** *m.* government or corporation loan.

**empujar** *tr.* to push, shove; to impel.

**empuje** *m.* push, pushing. 2 ARCH., ENG. pressure, thrust. 3 push, energy, enterprise.

**empujón** *m.* push, shove, violent push. 2 push [to a work, etc.]. 3 *a empujones*, pushing, roughly; by fits and starts.

**empuñadura** *f.* hilt [of sword].

**empuñar** *tr.* to take [a sword, cane, etc.] by the hilt or the handle: ~ *el cetro*, to begin to reign. 2 to clutch, grasp, grip.

**empuñidura** *f.* NAUT. earing.

**emú** *m.* ORN. emu.

**emulación** *f.* emulation.

**emular** *tr.* to emulate.

**émulo, -la** *adj.* emulous. 2 *m.-f.* emulator.

**emulsión** *f.* emulsion.

**emulsionar** *tr.* to emulsify.

**emulsor** *m.* emulsifier.

**en** *prep.* in, at, on, upon: ~ *la caja*, in the box; ~ *casa*, at home; ~ *aquella ocasión*, on that occasion. 2 into: *convertir* ~, to change or turn into. 3 for: ~ *adelante*, for the future. 4 [followed by infinitive] by: *le conocí* ~ *el andar*, I recognized him by his gait. 5 [followed by gerund] on, upon, once, no sooner, right after.

**enaceitar** *tr.* to oil.

**enaguachar** *tr.* to fill with water, make watery.

**enaguas** *f. pl.* petticoat, underskirt.

**enaguazar** *tr.* to flood, make swampy. 2 *ref.* to become swampy.

**enagüillas** *f. pl.* short skirt or petticoat; kilt.

**enajenable** *adj.* alienable.

**enajenación** *f.* alienation. 2 abstraction, rapture. 3 ~ *mental*, mental derangement, madness.

**enajenamiento** *m.* ENAJENACIÓN.

**enajenar** *tr.* to alienate. 2 [of emotions] to transport, carry away. *3 ref.* to dispossess oneself of. *4* to become estranged. *5* to become enraptured.

**enálage** *f.* GRAM. enallage.

**enalbardar** *tr.* to put a packsaddle on. *2* COOK. to bread, to cover with batter.

**enaltecedor, -ra** *adj.* ennobling. *2* exalting, extolling.

**enaltecer** *tr.* to ennoble. *2* to exalt, extoll. *3 ref.* to become exalted. ¶ CONJUG. like *agradecer.*

**enaltecimiento** *m.* ennobling. *2* exalting, extolling.

**enamoradizo, -za** *adj.* inclined to love, amorous.

**enamorado, -da** *adj.* in love, loving, enamoured. *2 m.-f.* lover; sweetheart.

**enamoramiento** *m.* love, infatuation. *2* enamouring, love-making.

**enamorar** *tr.* to make love to. *2* to infatuate, enamour; to charm. *3 ref.* to fall in love.

**enamoricarse** *ref.* coll. to be slightly in love.

**enanito, -ta** *m.-f.* little dwarf; gnome.

**enano, -na** *adj.* dwarf, dwarfish. *2 m.-f.* dwarf.

**enarbolar** *tr.* to raise on high, to hoist [a flag, etc.]. *2* to brandish [a cane, a pike, etc.]. *3 ref.* [of a horse] to rear. *4* to hoop [barrels].

**enarcar** *tr.* to raise [one's eyebrows], to arch. *2* to hoop, to put a hoop on.

**enardecer** *tr.* to inflame, fire, heat, kindle, excite. *2 ref.* to heat, to become inflamed, kindled. *3* [of a dispute] to become heated. *4* [of a part of the body] to burn. ¶ CONJUG. like *agradecer.*

**enardecimiento** *m.* inflaming, heating, excitement.

**enarenar** *tr.* to sand, cover with sand; to gravel. *2 ref.* NAUT. to run aground.

**enarmónico, -ca** *adj.* MUS. enharmonic.

**enastado, -da** *adj.* horned [having horns].

**enastar** *tr.* to put a handle or shaft on.

**encabalgar** *intr.* [of some things] to rest upon another thing. *2 tr.* to provide horses for.

**encaballar** *tr.* to lap over [as tiles]. *2 intr.* to rest upon another thing.

**encabestrar** *tr.* to halter [a horse, etc.]. *2* to make [wild bulls] be lead by tame ones.

**encabezamiento** *m.* heading, first words [of a letter, deed, etc.], caption. *2* tax roll. *3* registering on a tax roll.

**encabezar** *tr.* to head, put a heading to [a letter, deed, etc.]. *2* to head [a subscription list]. *3* to head, lead. *4* to register on a tax roll. *5* to fortify [wine] with another wine or alcohol.

**encabritarse** *ref.* [of horses] to rear. *2* AER., NAUT. to shoot up.

**encachado** *m.* stone or concrete lining in the bed of a canal, ditch, etc.

**encadenamiento** *m.* chaining. *2* enchainment, connection, linking, concatenation.

**encadenar** *tr.* to chain, enchain. *2* to enslave. *3* to connect, link together, concatenate.

**encajar** *tr.* to make [a thing] fit into another; to fit in, insert. *2* to put or force in. *3* to put in [a joke, a remark, etc.], to drop [a hint]. *4* to force or palm off [something] on someone. *5* to land [a blow, etc.]; to take [a blow, etc.]. *6 intr.* to fit: ~ *en* or *con*, to fit into. *7* to be relevant, to the purpose. *8 ref.* to squeeze [oneself into]. *9* to butt in. *10* to put on [a garment].

**encaje** *m.* fitting in, insertion. *2* socket, cavity, frame, etc., into which a thing is fitted or inserted. *3* lace [openwork tissue]. *4* inlaid work.

**encajero, -ra** *m.-f.* lacemaker. *2* lace dealer.

**encajonado** *m.* cofferdam. *2* MAS. wall made of packed earth.

**encajonamiento** *m.* boxing [putting in boxes]. *2* narrowing of rivers between steep banks.

**encajonar** *tr.* to box, put in boxes. *2* to put in a narrow place. *3 ref.* [of rivers] to narrow between steep banks.

**encalabrinado, -da** *adj.* obstinate about a thing.

**encalabrinar** *tr.* [of a vapour or odour] to affect the head, make dizzy. *2* to excite, irritate. *3 ref.* to get dizzy. *4* to get obstinate.

**encalador** *m.* whitewasher. *2* lime pit or vat [for liming hides].

**encaladura** *f.* whitewashing.

**encalar** *tr.* to whitewash. *2* to lime [treat with lime].

**encalmarse** *ref.* VET. to be overheated. *2* [of weather or wind] to become calm, still.

**encalladero** *m.* NAUT. shoal.

**encalladura** *f.* NAUT. grounding, stranding.

**encallar** *intr.* NAUT. to run aground. *2* fig. to get stuck.

**encallecer** *intr.-ref.* to get corns or callosities. *2 ref.* to become hardened or callous. ¶ CONJUG. like *agradecer.*

**encallecido, -da** *adj.* hardened, callous.

**encamarse** *ref.* coll. to take to bed, fall ill. *2* [of cattle and game] to lie down. *3* [of wheat, etc.] to be beaten down by rain, wind, etc.

**encaminar** *tr.* to direct, set on the way, put on the right road. *2* to bend [one's steps]. *3* to direct [to an end]. *4 ref.* to betake oneself, be on one's way [to]. *5* to be intended [to].

**encanallamiento** *m.* becoming base, vile.

**encanallar** *tr.* to make base, vile. *2 ref.* to contract base habits, to become base, vile.

**encanastar** *tr.* to put in baskets.

**encandelar** *intr.* to blossom with catkin.

**encandilado, -da** *adj.* hight, erect. *2* cocked [hat].

**encandilar** *tr.* to dazzle, daze. *2* coll. to stir [the fire]. *3 ref.* [of the eyes] to shine with lust or drink.

**encanecer** *intr.* to grow white, hoary, gray or gray-haired. *2* to become old. *3 tr.* to turn hoary. ¶ CONJUG. like *agradecer.*

**encanijamiento** *m.* weakness, sickliness.

**encanijar** *m.* to make [an infant] lean and sickly. *2 ref.* [of infants] to grow lean and sickly.

**encanillar** *tr.* WEAV. to wind on a quill.

**encantación** *f.* ENCANTAMIENTO.

**encantado, -da** *adj.* enchanted. *2* delighted, satisfied. *3* coll. abstracted. *4* hautned, rambling [house].

**encantador, -ra** *adj.* enchanting, charming, delightful. *2 m.-f.* charmer. *3 m.* enchanter. *4 f.* enchantress.

**encantamiento** *m.* enchantment.

**encantar** *tr.* to enchant, cast a spell on. *2* to enchant, charm, delight.

**encante** *m.* auction, public sale.

**encanto** *m.* enchantment. *2* charm, delight. *3* delightful thing. *4 pl.* charms [of a woman].

**encanutar** *tr.* to shape like a tube. *2* to put into a tube.

**encañado** *m.* conduit for water. *2* trellis of reeds.

**encañar** *tr.* to pipe [water]. *2* to drain [a land]. *3* to prop up [plants] with reeds.

**encañizada** *f.* weir [for fish]. *2* trellis of reeds.

**encañonar** *tr.* to convey through pipes. *2* to cover [with a firearm]. *3* to quill, ruff. *4 intr.* [of birds] to fledge out.

**encaperuzar** *tr.* to put a hood on.
**encapillar** *tr.* to hood [a falcon].
**encapirotar** *tr.* to put a hood on.
**encapotar** *tr.-ref.* to put a capote on. *2 ref.* to frown, look grim. *4* to become cloudy. *5* [of horses] to lower the head too much.
**encapricharse** *ref.* to take it into one's head. *2* ~ *por*, to take a fancy to.
**encapuchar** *tr.* to cover with a cowl or hood. *2 ref.* to put on one's cowl or hood.
**encarado, -da** *adj. bien* (or *mal*) ~, well- (or ill-) favoured [in looks].
**encaramar** *tr.* to raise, hoist. *2* to elevate [to a high post]. *3 ref.* to climb, mount. *4* to reach a high post.
**encarar** *tr.* to aim, point [a weapon]. *2 intr.-ref.* ~ or *encararse con*, to face, to place oneself face to face with.
**encarcelación** *f.* **encarcelamiento** *m.* imprisonment, incarceration.
**encarcelar** *tr.* to incarcerate, imprison.
**encarecedor, -ra** *adj.* extolling, praising. *2* extoller, praiser.
**encarecer** *tr.* to raise the price of. *2* to emphasize, enhance, exaggerate; to praise. *3* to recommend strongly. *4 intr.-ref.* to become dearer. ¶ CONJUG. like *agradecer*.
**encarecidamente** *adv.* earnestly, insistently.
**encarecimiento** *m.* increase in price. *2* emphasizing; praising. *3* earnestness: *con* ~, earnestly.
**encarezco, encarezca,** etc. *irr.* V. ENCARECER.
**encargado, -da** *m.-f.* person in charge, manager, foreman, forewoman. *2 m.* ~ *de negocios*, chargé d'affaires.
**encargar** *tr.* to entrust, put under the care of. *2* to recommend, charge, urge. *3* to order [goods, etc.]. *4 ref. encargarse de*, to take charge of; to attend, see to.
**encargo** *m.* charge, commission, job. *2* errand. *3* recommendation, warning. *4* order [for goods].
**encariñado, -da** *adj.* attached, fond of.
**encariñar** *tr.* to awaken affection or liking. *2 ref. encariñarse con*, to get fond of.
**encarnación** *f.* THEOL., incarnation. *2* incarnation, embodiment. *3* PAINT., SCULP. flesh colour.
**encarnado, -da** *adj.* incarnate. *2* flesh-coloured, incarnadine. *3* red. *4 m.* flesh colour, incarnadine, red.
**encarnadura** *f. buena* (or *mala*) ~, quick- (or slow) healing flesh.
**encarnar** *intr.* THEOL. to be incarnate. *2* SURG. to heal over, incarn. *3 tr.* to incarnate, embody, personify. *4* to bait [a fishhook]. *5* to give flesh colour to [a sculpture]. *6 ref.* to unite, incorporate with one another.
**encarnizadamente** *adv.* bloodily, fiercely, bitterly, brutally, cruelly.
**encarnizado, -da** *adj.* blood-shot. *2* bloody, fierce, furious, bitter, hard fought.
**encarnizamiento** *m.* cruelty, fierceness, fury, rage.
**encarnizar** *tr.* to make cruel, to infuriate. *2 ref.* to become infuriated; to fight bitterly. *3 encarnizarse con*, to persecute, treat mercilessly.
**encarpetar** *tr.* to put in a file or portfolio.
**encarrilar** *tr.* to put back on the rails. *2* to put [a matter] on the right track; to set right.
**encarrujarse** *ref.* to curl, kink. *2* to become corrugated, to shrivel.
**encartar** *tr.* to indict. *2* [in card games] to play a suit that opponent can follow.

**encarte** *m.* [in card games] having to follow suit. *2* order of cards at the close of a hand.
**encartonar** *tr.* to put cadboard on; to protect with cardboard. *3* to bind [books] in boards.
**encascabelar** *tr.* to bell, put sleigh bells on.
**encasillado** *m.* set of squares or pigeonholes. *2* list of government candidates.
**encasillar** *tr.* to classify, to distribute. *2* to assign [a government candidate] to a voting district.
**encasquetar** *tr.* to pull on or down [a hat, cap, etc.]. *2* to hammer [an idea, etc.] into one's head. *4 ref.* to pull on [a hat, etc.]. *5* to get it into one's head.
**encasquillar** *tr.* to put a cap or ferrule on. *2* (Am.) to shoe [horses]. *3 ref.* [of a bullet in a gun] to stick, get stuck.
**encastillado, -da** *adj.* castellated. *2* haughty, proud.
**encastillar** *tr.* to fortify with castles. *2* to pile up. *3 ref.* to make a stand in a castle or lofty place. *4* to take refuge in some high spot. *5* to stick to one's own opinion.
**encastrar** *tr.* MECH. to engage, mesh.
**encauchar** *tr.* to cover with rubber.
**encausar** *tr.* LAW to arraign, indict, prosecute.
**encauste, encausto** *m.* PAINT. *pintura al* ~, encaustic.
**encáustico, -ca** *adj.* encaustic. *2 m.* wax polish.
**encauzamiento** *m.* channeling [directing by a channel]. *2* directing, guiding, guidance.
**encauzar** *tr.* to channel [direct by, or confine in, a channel]. *2* to direct, guide.
**encebollado** *m.* beef stew with onions.
**encefálico, -ca** *adj.* encephalic.
**encefalitis** *f.* MED. encephalitis.
**encéfalo** *m.* ANAT. encephalon.
**encefalograma** *m.* MED. encephalogram, encephalograph.
**encelamiento** *m.* jealousy. *2* rut.
**encelar** *tr.* to make jealous. *2 ref.* to become jealous. *3* to be in rut.
**enceldar** *tr.* to put in a cell.
**encella** *f.* cheese mould.
**encenagamiento** *m.* bemudding. *2* wallowing in vice.
**encenagarse** *ref.* to get into the mud. *2* to get covered with mud. *3* to give oneself up to, or to wallow [in vice].
**encendaja** *f.* kindling [for starting a fire].
**encendedor, -ra** *adj.* lighting, kindling. *2 m.* lighter, lighting device: ~ *automático*, cigarette lighter.
**encender** *tr.* to light, set fire to, ignite, kindle. *2* to burn [the mouth, etc.]. *3* to inflame, excite. *5 ref.* to burn, be kindled, catch fire. *6* [of war] to break out. *7* to become inflamed. *8* to blush, to redden. ¶ CONJUG. like *entender*.
**encendidamente** *adv.* ardently.
**encendido, -da** *adj.* high [colour], high-coloured. *3* red, flushed. *4* ardent, inflamed. *5 m.* AUTO. ignition.
**encendimiento** *m.* ignition; kindling, lighting. *2* flush, ruddy colour. *3* ardour, inflammation.
**encentadura** *f.* bed sore.
**encentar** *tr.-ref.* DECENTAR.
**encerado, -da** *adj.* waxed. *2* wax-coloured. *3 m.* oilcloth, oilskin, tarpaulin. *4* blackboard. *5* waxing [of floors and furniture].
**encerador, -ra** *m.-f.* waxer [of floors].
**encerar** *tr.* to wax.

**encerradero** *m.* sheep pen. 2 pen holding bulls before fight.

**encerrar** *tr.* to shut in, confine, hem in, lock up or in. 2 to enclose, contain. 3 *ref.* to shut oneself in. 2 to retire, go into seclusion. 5 to be closeted. ¶ CONJUG. like *acertar*.

**encerrona** *f.* voluntary confinement. 2 plant, trap.

**encespedar** *tr.* to sward, turf.

**encestar** *tr.* to put in a basket.

**enceste** *m.* basket [in basketball].

**encía** *f.* gum [of the mouth].

**encíclica** *f.* encyclical.

**enciclopedia** *f.* encyclop(a)edia.

**enciclopedismo** *m.* Encyclop(a)edism.

**enciendo, encienda**, etc. *irr.* V. ENCENDER.

**encierro** *m.* shutting in or up, locking up, enclosing, penning, confinement. 2 seclusion, retirement. 3 place of confinement, prison.

**encierro, encierre**, etc. *irr.* V. ENCERRAR.

**encima** *adv.* on, upon, over, at the top: ~ *de*, on, upon; *por* ~, superficially, hastily; *por* ~ *de*, over, above; in spite of; *blanco por* ~, white at the top. 2 on, upon, with [a person, oneself]: *echarse* ~ [*ropas, una responsabilidad*], to throw [clothes] on, to take upon oneself [a responsability]; *quitarse [una cosa] de* ~, to be rid of [a thing]. 3 in addition, on top, to boot.

**encimar** *tr.* to raise hight, to put on top. 2 *ref.* to rise above.

**encina** *f.* BOT. evergreen oak, holm oak.

**encinal, encinar** *m.* evergreen-oak grove.

**encinta** *adj.* pregnant, with child.

**encintado** *m.* curb [of a sidewalk, etc.].

**encintar** *tr.* to adorn with ribbons. 2 ENG. to put the curb or curbs on.

**enclaustrar** *tr.* to cloister.

**enclavado, -da** *adj.* enclaved. 2 *m.* enclave.

**enclavar** *tr.* to nail. 2 to pierce, transfix. 3 coll. to deceive.

**enclave** *m.* enclave, small area, isolated area. 2 setting, situation, location.

**enclavijar** *tr.* to join, interlock. 2 to peg [a stringed instrument].

**enclenque** *adj.* weak, feeble, sickly.

**enclítico, -ca** *adj.-f.* GRAM. enclitic.

**encocorar** *tr.* to vex, annoy, nag.

**encofrado** *m.* MIN. plank lining. 2 form [for concrete].

**encofrar** *tr.* MIN. to plank, timber. 2 to build a form for [concrete].

**encoger** *tr.* to contract, draw back, draw in [a limb, etc.]. 2 to dispirit. 3 *intr.* [of cloth, wood, etc.] to shrink. 4 *ref.* to shrink. 5 to lose courage. 6 *encogerse de hombros*, to shrug one's shoulders.

**encogido, -da** *adj.* awkward, timid, bashful.

**encogimiento** *adj.* contraction, shrinking, shrinkage. 2 awkwardness, timidity. 3 ~ *de hombros*, shrug.

**encolado** *m.* clarification [of wine]. 2 WEAV. dressing.

**encoladura** *f.*, **encolamiento** *m.* gluing. 2 PAINT. sizing. 3 ENCOLADO.

**encolar** *tr.* to glue. 2 WEAV. to dress. 3 PAINT. to size. 4 to clarify [wine].

**encolerizar** *tr.* to anger, irritate. 2 *ref.* to become angry.

**encomendar** *tr.* to entrust, commit, commend, recommend. 2 to make [somebody] a knight commander. 3 *ref.* to commend oneself [to]. ¶ CONJUG. like *acertar*.

**encomendero** *m.* holder of an ENCOMIENDA.

**encomiar** *tr.* to praise, eulogize, extol.

**encomiasta** *m.-f.* panegyrist.

**encomiástico, -ca** *adj.* encomiastic.

**encomienda** *f.* charge, commission. 2 commandery [of a military order]. 3 knight's cross. 4 HIST. grant of land made by a Spanish king. 5 HIST. Indian territory committed to the care of a Spanish colonist. 6 praise, commendation. 7 care, protection. 8 (Am.) postal parcel. 9 *pl.* regards [sent].

**encomiendo, encomiende**, etc. *irr.* V. ENCOMENDAR.

**encomio** *m.* encomium.

**enconamiento** *m.* inflammation [of a wound or sore]. 2 bitterness, rancour.

**enconar** *tr.* to inflame, aggravate [a wound or sore]. 2 to embitter [the feelings]. 3 *ref.* to become inflamed, to rankle, fester. 4 to become embittered. 5 *enconarse con uno*, to treat someone bitterly.

**encono** *m.* bitterness, rancour.

**encontradamente** *adv.* oppositely.

**encontradizo, -za** *adj. hacerse el* ~, to try to meet someone seemingly by chance.

**encontrado, -da** *adj.* contrary, opposed.

**encontrar** *tr.* to find, meet, encounter. 2 to find [good, disagreable, etc.]. 3 *intr.* to meet, collide. 4 *ref.* to meet [come together]; to collide, be in opposition. 5 to be [in a place]. 6 to find oneself. 7 to feel [ill, well, at ease, etc.]. 8 *encontrarse con*, to meet with, run across; to find. ¶ CONJUG. like *contar*.

**encontrón, encontronazo** *m.* bump, collision.

**encopetado, -da** *adj.* presumptuous, stuck-up. 2 noble, aristocratic, of high social standing.

**encorajar** *tr.* to give courage to. 2 *ref.* to become enraged.

**encorajinarse** *ref.* to become enraged.

**encorar** *tr.* to cover with leather. 2 to grow a skin over [a sore]. 3 *intr.-ref.* [of a sore], to grow a new skin. ¶ CONJUG. like *contar*.

**encordadura** *f.* MUS. strings [on an instrument].

**encordar** *tr.* to string [a musical instrument or a tennis racket]. 2 to bind or wrap with a rope. ¶ CONJUG. like *contar*.

**encordonar** *tr.* to lace, tie with laces. 2 to adorn with cords.

**encornado, -da** *adj.* [of a bull or cow] horned.

**encornadura** *f.* horns; set of the horns.

**encorralar** *tr.* to corral, shut in [cattle].

**encorsetar** *tr.-ref.* to put a corset on.

**encortinar** *tr.* to put up curtains on or in.

**encorvadura** *f.*, **encorvamiento** *m.* bending, curving, curvature. 2 stoop [bend of back and shoulderss].

**encorvar** *tr.* to bend, curve. 2 *ref.* to bend over, to stoop. 3 [of horses] to buck.

**encostarse** *ref.* NAUT. to approach the coast.

**encostrar** *tr.* to encrust, cover with a crust. 2 *intr.-ref.* to crust; to develop a crust or a scab.

**encovar** *tr.* to put in a cave. 2 to keep, hide away. 3 to force to hide oneself. 4 *ref.* to hide oneself. ¶ CONJUG. like *contar*.

**encrespado, -da** *adj.* curly [hair]. 2 rough [sea].

**encrespador** *m.* curling iron.

**encrespadura** *f.* curling, crimping, crisping, frizzling.

**encrespamiento** *m.* curling, crisping, frizzling. 2 bristling, ruffling. 3 roughness [of the sea]. 4 anger, irritation.

**encrespar** *tr.* to curl, crisp, frizzle. 2 to bristle, ruffle. *3* to stir up [the waves]. *4* to anger, irritate. *5 ref.* to curl, crisp, frizzle [become curled, etc.]. *6* [of hair, feathers] to bristle, ruffle. *7* [of the sea] to become rough. *8* to bristle with anger, be infuriated.

**encrestarse** *ref.* [of birds] to stiffen the crest or comb.

**encrucijada** *f.* crossroads; street intersection. *2* ambush, snare.

**encrudecer** *tr.* to make raw; to make hard to cook. *2* to exasperate, irritate. *3 ref.* to become exasperated, irritated. ¶ Conjug. like *agradecer.*

**encruelecer** *tr.* to make cruel. *2 ref.* to become cruel. ¶ Conjug. like *agradecer.*

**encuadernación** *f.* bookbinding. *2* binding [of a book]: ~ *a la holandesa,* half binding; ~ *en pasta,* carboard binding. *3* bindery.

**encuadernador** *m.* bookbinder.

**encuadernar** *tr.* to bind [a book]: *sin* ~, unbound.

**encuadramiento** *m.* framing.

**encuadrar** *tr.* to frame [provide with a frame; enclose in a frame; serve as a frame to].

**encuadre** *m.* cinem. framing. *2* setting, background. *3* mill. officering [troop].

**encubar** *tr.* to cask [wine, etc.]. *2* min. to timber [a shaft].

**encubierta** *f.* fraudulent concealment.

**encubiertamente** *adv.* secretly, on the sly.

**encubierto, -ta** *p. p.* of encubrir: *palabras encubiertas,* veiled words.

**encubridor, -ra** *m.-f.* concealer, one who covers up. *3* law accessory after the fact.

**encubrimiento** *m.* concealment. *2* law being an accesory after the fact.

**encubrir** *tr.* to conceal, hide. *2* to cover up. *3* law to become an accesory after the fact.

**encuentro** *m.* meeting [act of meeting]; encounter: *mal* ~, unlucky encounter; *salir al* ~ *de,* to go to meet; to oppose; to meet half way. *2* clash, collision, opposition. *3* mil. encounter. *4* arch. angle, nook, corner. *5* zool. axilla. *6 pl.* [in quadrupeds] points of the shoulder blades.

**encuentro, encuentre,** etc. *irr.* V. encontrar.

**encuesta** *f.* inquiry.

**encuestador, -ra** *n.* pollster.

**encumbrado, -da** *adj.* high, lofty. *2* elevated, sublime. *3* mighty, high-placed.

**encumbramiento** *m.* elevation, height. *2* exaltation, climbing or rising to high station.

**encumbrar** *tr.* to raise high. *2* to exalt, elevate. *3* to climb on the top of. *4 ref.* to rise high. *5* to raise oneself [to high station]. *6* to become proud, haughty.

**encunar** *tr.* to put [a child] in the cradle. *2* bullf. to catch between the horns.

**encurtidos** *m. pl.* pickles.

**encurtir** *tr.* to pickle.

**enchalecar** *tr.* coll. to pocket, to pinch. *2* to put sómeone into a straightjacket. *3 ref.* to pocket.

**enchancletar** *tr.* to put slippers on. *2* to drag shoes. *3 ref.* to put slippers on.

**enchapado** *m.* veneer, veneering, covering of thin plates or sheets.

**encharcar** *tr.* to inundate, turn into a pool. *2 ref.* to be covered with puddles. *3* to upset the stomach by much drinking.

**enchiquerar** *tr.* bullf. to pen [the bull] before the fight. *2* coll. to jail.

**enchironar** *tr.* coll. to jail.

**enchufado, -da** *adj. p.p.* of enchufar. *2* coll. well in; *estar* ~, to have useful contacts, to have

friends in the right places, to have a cushy lob. *3* coll. *n.* wirepuller, one who has succeeded through contacts. *4* slacker [soldier].

**enchufar** *tr.* to fit [a tube or pipe] into another. *2* elect. to connect, to plug in. *3 ref.* to get a sinecure.

**enchufe** *m.* fitting [of a pipe into another]; joint [of two pipes]. *2* elect. plug; plug and receptacle. *3* sinecure, easy job.

**ende** *adv. por* ~, therefore.

**endeble** *adj.* weak, feeble, frail, flimsy.

**endeblez** *f.* feebleness, fragility, flimsiness.

**endecágono** *m.* geom. hendecagon, undecagon.

**endecasílabo, -ba** *adj.* hendecasyllabic. *2 m.* hendecasyllabe.

**endecha** *f.* dirge, doleful song. *2* assonanced sevensyllabled quatrain.

**endemia** *f.* med. endemic.

**endémico, -ca** *adj.* endemic.

**endemoniado, -da** *adj.* demoniac. *2* fig. devilish, very bad. *3* fig. tremendous, awful. *4 m.-f.* demoniac, possessed.

**endemoniar** *tr.* to possess with an evil spirit. *2* coll. to irritate, enrage.

**endentar** *tr.* mach. to furnish with teeth. *2 tr.-intr.* to engage, mesh. ¶ Conjug. like *acertar.*

**endentecer** *intr.* to teethe, cut one's teeth. ¶ Conjug. like *agradecer.*

**enderezamiento** *m.* straightening. *2* setting right.

**enderezar** *tr.* to straighten, unbend. *2* to right, set upright. *3* to address, dedicate. *4* to right, correct, put in order. *5* to fix, punish. *6* to bend [one's steps]. *7 ref.* to straighten up. *8* to be directed [to an end].

**endeudarse** *ref.* to fall into debt.

**endiablado, -da** *adj.* devilish. *2* ugly, deformed. *3* very bad. *4* furious, wild. *5* complicated, difficult.

**endibia** *f.* bot. endive.

**endiento, endiente,** etc. *irr.* V. endentar.

**endilgar** *tr.* coll. to direct, guide. *2* coll. to put, lodge. *3* coll. to land [a blow]; to spring [something unpleasant] on [a person].

**endino, -na** *adj.* coll. wicked, perverse.

**endiosamiento** *m.* haughtiness, pride, conceit.

**endiosarse** *ref.* to become haughty, proud.

**endocardio** *m.* anat. endocardium.

**endocarpio** *m.* bot. endocarp.

**endocrino, -na** *adj.* physiol. endocrine.

**endodermo** *m.* biol. endoderm. *2* bot. endodermis.

**endógeno, -na** *adj.* endogenous.

**endolinfa** *f.* physiol. endolymph.

**endomingado, -da** *adj.* in his Sunday best.

**endomingarse** *ref.* to put on one's Sunday best.

**endosante** *m.-f.* com. endorser.

**endosar** *tr.* com. to endorse, indorse. *2* to transfer [a burden, task, etc.] to another person, to saddle with.

**endosatario, -ria** *m.-f.* endorsee.

**endoselar** *tr.* to canopy.

**endósmosis** *f.* phys., chem. endosmosis.

**endoso** *m.* com. endorsement.

**endospermo** *m.* bot. endosperm.

**endrina** *f.* bot. sloe plum.

**endrino, -na** *adj.* sloe-coloured. *2 m.* bot. blackthorn, sloe tree.

**endulzar** *tr.* to sweeten. *2* to soften, make bearable.

**endurecer** *tr.* to harden. *2* to inure. *3 ref.* to harden [become hard]. 4 to become hardened, cruel. ¶ CONJUG. like *agradecer*.

**endurecido, -da** *adj.* hard, hardened. 2 obdurate.

**endurecimiento** *m.* hardening. 2 hardness. 3 obduracy. 4 hard-heartedness.

**endurezco, endurezca,** etc. *irr.* V. ENDURECER.

**ene** *f.* Spanish name of the letter *n.* 2 x [unknown quantity].

**enea** *f.* BOT. cattail, bulrush.

**eneágono, -na** *m.* GEOM. nonagon.

**Eneas** *m. pr. n.* MYTH. Æneas.

**enebrina** *f.* juniper berry.

**enebro** *m.* BOT. juniper.

**Eneida** *f.* Æneid.

**eneldo** *m.* BOT. dill.

**enema** *f.* enema, clyster.

**enemiga** *f.* enmity, hatred, ill-will.

**enemigo, -ga** *adj.* adverse, opposed [to]. 2 enemy, hostile. 3 *m.-f.* enemy, foe: *el ~ malo*, the Evil one.

**enemistad** *f.* enmity.

**enemistar** *tr.* to make enemices of. 2 *ref.* to become enemies: *enemistarse con*, to fall out with.

**energético, -ca** *adj.* energy. 2 *f.* energetics. 3 *m. pl.* fuels.

**energía** *f.* energy: *~ atómica*, PHYS. atomic energy. 2 MECH. power: *~ eléctrica*, electric power.

**enérgico, -ca** *adj.* energetic, vigorous, active, lively.

**energúmeno, -na** *m.-f.* energumen. 2 wild, frantic person.

**enero** *m.* January.

**enervación** *f.* enervation. 2 MED. nervous prostration.

**enervamiento** *m.* enervation.

**enervante** *adj.* enervating.

**enervar** *tr.* to enervate. 2 *ref.* to become enervate.

**enésimo, -ma** *adj.* MATH. nth.

**enfadadizo, -za** *adj.* easily displeased, peevish.

**enfadar** *tr.* to displease, annoy, anger. 2 to bore. 3 *ref.* to be displeased, get angry.

**enfado** *m.* displeasure, annoyance, irritation. 2 trouble, bother.

**enfadoso, -sa** *adj.* annoying, bothersome, boring.

**enfangar** *tr.* to bemud. 2 *ref.* to sink in the mud. 3 to mix [in dirty business]. 4 to sink [into vice].

**enfardar** *tr.* to pack, to bale.

**enfardelar** *tr.* to bundle, to pack.

**énfasis** *m.* emphasis [special impressiveness of expression]. 2 affectation in delivery.

**enfático, -ca** *adj.* emphatic, impressive.

**enfatizar** *tr.* to emphasize.

**enfatuarse** *ref.* to become vain or conceited.

**enfermar** *intr.* to fall ill, be taken ill. 2 *tr.* to make ill.

**enfermedad** *f.* illness, sickness, disease.

**enfermera** *f.* woman nurse [for the sick].

**enfermería** *f.* infirmary, sick-quarters.

**enfermero** *m.* male nurse [for the sick].

**enfermizo, -za** *adj.* sickly, unhealthy.

**enfermo, -ma** *adj.* sick, ill, diseased. 2 *m.-f.* sick person, patient.

**enfermucho, -cha** *adj.* sickish, sickly.

**enfervorizar** *tr.* to inspire fervour. 2 *ref.* to become inflamed with fervour.

**enfeudación** *tr.* infeudation, enfeoffment.

**enfeudar** *tr.* to enfeoff.

**enfilar** *tr.* to line up. 2 to aim, sight. 3 to go straight down or up [a street, etc.]. 4 to string [beads, etc.]. 5 ARTILL. to enfilade.

**enfisema** *m.* MED. emphysema.

**enfiteusis** *f.* LAW emphyteusis.

**enflaquecer** *tr.* to make thin or lean. 2 to weaken. 3 *intr.-ref.* to become thin or lean. ¶ CONJUG. like *agradecer*.

**enflaquecimiento** *m.* loss of flesh, emaciation.

**enflorar** *tr.* to flower [adorn with flowers].

**enfocar** *tr.* to focus. 2 to envisage, direct [an affair]; to approach [a problem, etc.].

**enfoque** *m.* focussing. 2 approach [to a problem, etc.].

**enfrascamiento** *m.* absorption.

**enfrascar** *tr.* to put in bottles. 2 *ref.* to become absorbed, become deeply engaged [in].

**enfrenamiento** *m.* bridling. 2 checking, restraining.

**enfrentar** *tr.* to confront, cause to face; to bring face to face. 2 *tr.-ref.* to face: *enfrentarse con*, to face, oppose, stand up to; to cope with.

**enfrente** *adv.* in front, opposite: *~ de*, in front of, opposite, facing, against.

**enfriadera** *f.* bottle cooler.

**enfriamiento** *m.* cooling, refrigeration. 2 MED. cold.

**enfriar** *tr.* to cool, make cool. 2 *ref.* to cool [become cool], cool off. 3 to get chilled.

**enfrontar** *tr.* to come face to. 2 *tr.-intr.* to face, oppose.

**enfundar** *tr.* to sheathe, case. 2 to muffle [a drum].

**enfurecer** *tr.* to infuriate, enrage. 2 *ref.* to rage, become infuriated. ¶ CONJUG. like *agradecer*.

**enfurecimiento** *m.* infuriation, fury.

**enfurezco, enfurezca,** etc. *irr.* V. ENFURECER.

**enfurruñamiento** *m.* anger, sulkiness.

**enfurruñarse** *ref.* to get angry, to sulk.

**enfurtir** *tr.* to full [cloth].

**engaitar** *tr.* to deceive, cozen, humbug, wheedle.

**engalanar** *tr.* to adorn, bedeck. 2 NAUT. to dress.

**engalgar** *tr.* to brake [a cart wheel].

**engallado, -da** *adj.* erect, upright. 2 haughty.

**engallador** *m.* checkrein.

**engallarse** *ref.* to draw oneself up arrogantly; to get cocky. 2 [of a horse] to have the head pulled up.

**enganchar** *tr.* to hook [grasp with a hook]; to hook on or up. 2 to hitch, harness. 3 RLY. to couple [carriages]. 4 to attract, hook [a person]. 5 MIL. to recruit, enlist. 6 BULLF. to hook with the horns. 7 *ref.* to get caught [on a hook, a nail, etc.]. 8 MIL. to enlist [enroll oneself].

**enganche** *m.* hooking. 2 hitching [of horses]. 3 RLY. coupling, coupler. 4 MIL. enlistment.

**engañabobos** *m.-f.* bamboozler. 2 *m.* catchpenny.

**engañador, -ra** *adj.* deceptive, deluding. 2 *m.-f.* deceiver.

**engañar** *tr.* to deceive, beguile, delude, dupe, fool, hoax, mislead, impose upon, take in. 2 to wheedle. 3 to beguile, while away [time, etc.]. 4 *ref.* to deceive oneself, be mistaken.

**engañifa** *f.* coll. deception, trick. 2 catchpenny.

**engaño** *m.* deception, deceit; falsehood; fraud imposition: *llamarse a ~*, to revoke an agreement, alleging fraud. 2 error, mistake. 3 lure, bait.

**engañoso, -sa** *adj.* deceptive, delusive. 2 deceitful.

**engarabatar** *tr.* to crook, gnarl, twist. 3 *ref.* to get crooked or gnarled.

**engarabitar** *intr.-ref.* to climb. 2 *ref.* [of fingers] to get crooked and stiff [from cold].

**engarce** *m.* JEWEL. linking, wiring; setting.

**engargantar** *tr.* to put into the throat. 2 *intr.* MACH. to mesh, engage.

**engargante** *m.* MACH. mesh, meshing.

**engargolado** *m.* groove for a sliding door.
**engargolar** *tr.* CARP. to groove [fix in a groove].
**engarzar** *tr.* JEWEL. to link, wire. *2* JEWEL. to enchase, set, mount. *3* to curl [hair].
**engastar** *tr.* JEWEL. to enchase, set, mount.
**engaste** *m.* JEWEL. enchasing, setting, mounting. *2* setting [of a gem]. *3* pearl flat on one side.
**engatillado, -da** *adj.* having a high, thick neck [horse or bull]. *2 m.* flat-lock seaming.
**engatillar** *tr.* to joint with flat-lock seams.
**engatusador, -ra** *m.-f.* cajoler, wheedler.
**engatusamiento** *m.* coaxing, wheedling, inveigleing.
**engatusar** *tr.* to cajole, coax, wheedle.
**engazar** *tr.* ENGARZAR. *2* NAUT. to strap [blocks].
**engendramiento** *m.* engendering, begetting, generation.
**engendrar** *tr.* engender, beget. *2* to generate, originate. *3* GEOM. to generate.
**engendro** *m.* foetus. *2* abortion, freak. *3* poor literary or artistic work. *4 mal ~,* perverse child.
**englobar** *tr.* to lump together, to include.
**engolado, -da** *adj.* HER. engouled. *2* presumptuous, pompous.
**engolamiento** *m.* arrogance, presumption, pretentiousness.
**engolfar** *intr.-ref.* NAUT. to go far out on the sea. *2 ref.* to be deeply engaged or absorbed.
**engolosinar** *tr.* to allure, tempt. *2 ref. engolosinarse con,* to get fond of.
**engomadura** *f.* gumming.
**engomar** *tr.* to gum [papers, fabrics, etc.].
**engordar** *tr.* to fatten. *2 intr.* to fatten [grow fat; become rich].
**engorde** *m.* fattening.
**engorro** *m.* encumbrance, nuisance, bother.
**engorroso, -sa** *adj.* cumbersome, annoying.
**engoznar** *tr.* to hinge.
**engranaje** *m.* MACH. mesh, meshing. *2* MACH. gear, gearing. *3* teeth of a gear.
**engranar** *intr.* MACH. to mesh, gear. *2* to interlock.
**engrandecer** *tr.* to enlarge, aggrandize. *2* to extol. *3* to enhance, exaggerate. *4* to elevate, exalt. *5 ref.* to be exalted. ¶ CONJUG. like *agradecer.*
**engrandecimiento** *m.* enlargement. *2* praise. *3* enhancement. *4* exaltation.
**engrane** *m.* MACH. mesh, meshing.
**engrapar** *tr.* MAS., CARP. to cramp.
**engrasador, -ra** *adj.* greasing. *2 m.-f.* greaser, oiler.
**engrasar** *tr.* to make greasy. *2* to grease, oil, lubricate. *3* to fertilize. *4* to dress [cloth].
**engrase** *m.* greasing, lubrication. *2* grease [for lubrication]. *3* fertilization [of land].
**engreído, -da** *adj.* vain, conceited.
**engreimiento** *m.* vanity, presumption, conceit.
**engreír** *tr.* to make vain or conceited. *2 ref.* to become vain or conceited. ¶ CONJUG. like *reír.*
**engrescar** *tr.* to incite to quarrel. *2* to incite to merriment. *3 ref.* to get into a row. *4* to get merry.
**engrifarse** *ref.* to take drugs, to drug oneself.
**engrosamiento** *m.* thickening. *2* enlargening [of a number].
**engrosar** *tr.* to thicken; to make fat or corpulent. *2* to enlarge [the number of]. *3 ref.* to thicken [grow thick]. *4* to grow fat or corpulent. ¶ CONJUG. like *contar.*
**engrudar** *tr.* to paste.
**engrudo** *m.* paste [of flour or starch and water].
**engruesar** *tr.-r.* ENGROSAR.
**engrueso, engruese,** etc. *irr.* V. ENGROSAR.

**engrumecerse** *ref.* to clot, to curdle.
**engualdrapar** *tr.* to caparison [a horse].
**enguantado, -da** *adj.* wearing gloves.
**enguijarrado** *m.* cobblestone paving.
**enguijarrar** *tr.* to cobble [pave with cobblestones].
**enguirnaldar** *tr.* to garland.
**engullir** *tr.* to swallow, gulp, gobble.
**enharinar** *tr.* to cover or smear with flour.
**enhebillar** *tr.* to bucle [a strap].
**enhebrar** *tr.* to thread [a needle]; to thread, string [beads].
**enhestadura** *f.* raising high; setting upright.
**enhestar** *tr.* to raise high. *2* to set upright. ¶ CONJUG. like *acertar.*
**enhiesto, -ta** *adj.* erect, upright, raised.
**enhilar** *tr.* ENHEBRAR. *2* ENFILAR. *3* to marshal, arrange [ideas] in order. *4* to direct to an end.
**enhorabuena** *f.* congratulations: *dar la ~ a,* to congratulate. *2 adv.* happily. *3* all right; well and good.
**enhoramala** *adv.* in an evil hour. *2 vete ~,* go to blazes!
**enhorcar** *tr.* to string [onions].
**enhornar** *tr.* to put into an oven.
**enigma** *m.* enigma, riddle.
**enigmático, -ca** *adj.* enigmatic(al.
**enjabonar** *tr.* to soap, to lather. *2* coll. to softsoap. *3* coll. to give a rubbing to.
**enjaezar** *tr.* to put trappings on [a horse].
**enjalbegadura** *f.* whitewashing.
**enjalbegar** *tr.* to whitewash. *2* to paint [the face]. *3 ref.* to paint one's face.
**enjalma** *f.* light packsaddle.
**enjambrar** *tr.* to hive, swarm [bees]. *2 intr.* [of bees] to swarm, to breed a new hive.
**enjambrazón** *f.* swarming [of bees].
**enjambre** *m.* swarm. *2* crowd, multitude.
**enjarciar** *tr.* NAUT. to equip with rigging.
**enjaretado** *m.* grating, lattice work.
**enjaretar** *tr.* to run [a string] through a casing. *2* to rattle off [a speech, etc.]; to do [something] in a rush. *3* to spring [something] on [a person].
**enjaular** *tr.* to cage. *2* coll. to imprison, confine.
**enjoyar** *tr.* to bejewel, adorn or cover with jewels. *2* to embellish. *3* to set with precious stones.
**enjuagadientes** *m.* mouthwash.
**enjuagadura** *f.* rinse, rinsing, wash.
**enjuagar** *tr.* to rinse [mouth, vessels, etc.].
**enjuague** *m.* rinse, rinsing. *2* rinsing water; mouthwash. *3* washbowl, rinsing cup. *4* fig. scheme, plot.
**enjugador, -ra** *m.-f.* drier. *2 m.* clotheshorse.
**enjugar** *tr.* to dry [free from moisture]; to wipe. *2* to dry [tears, sweat, etc.]. *3* to cancel, wipe out [a debt, etc.].
**enjuiciamiento** *m.* examining, judging. *2* LAW act of instituting and carrying out a judicial proceeding. *3* LAW prosecution.
**enjuiciar** *tr.* to submit [a matter] to study and judgment; to judge of. *2* LAW to institute a judicial proceeding against, to prosecute.
**enjundia** *f.* fat in the ovary of fowls. *2* fat of any animal. *3* substance, force.
**enjundioso, -sa** *adj.* having much fat. *2* substantial, important, solid.
**enjunque** *m.* NAUT. pig-iron, ballast, kentledge.
**enjuta** *f.* ARCH. spandrel.
**enjuto, -ta** *adj.* dry [free from moisture]. *2* lean, thin, skinny.
**enlace** *m.* lacing, interlacing, linking. *2* link,

union. *3* RLY. junction; connection. *4* wedding. *5* *oficial de ~*, MIL. liaison officer.

**enlaciar** *tr.-ref.* to render or to become lax or flabby.

**enladrillado, -da** *adj.* paved with bricks. *2 m.* brick pavement.

**enladrillar** *tr.* to pave with bricks.

**enlatar** *tr.* to can [food, etc.]. *2* to roof or cover with battens.

**enlazadura** *f.*, **enlazamiento** *m.* linking, connection.

**enlazar** *tr.* to lace, to interlace. *2* to link, join. *3* to lasso. *4 ref.* to marry. *5* to become laced or linked. *6* to be connected together.

**enligar** *tr.* to smear with birdlime. *2 ref.* to be caught with birdlime.

**enlistonado** *m.* CARP. lathing, lath work.

**enlistonar** *tr.* to lath, lay lathwork on.

**enlobreguecer** *tr.* to make dark or gloomy.

**enlodar** *tr.* to bemud, bemire. *2* to smirch. *3 ref.* to get muddy. *4* to soil oneself.

**enloquecedor, -ra** *adj.* maddening.

**enloquecer** *tr.* to madden, drive insane, distract. *2 intr.* to go mad, become insane. ¶ CONJUG. like *agradecer.*

**enloquecimiento** *m.* going mad. *2* madness, distraction.

**enlosado** *m.* flagstone paving.

**enlosar** *tr.* to pave with flagstones.

**enlozar** *tr.* (Am.) to enamel [iron, etc.].

**enlucido, -da** *adj.* MAS. plastered. *2 m.* MAS. plastering [of a wall]; coat of plaster.

**enlucimiento** *m.* MAS. plastering. *2* polishing.

**enlucir** *tr.* MAS. to plaster [walls]. *2* to polish [metals].

**enlutar** *tr.* to put in mourning, to crape. *2* to darken. *3* to sadden. *4 ref.* to put on mourning; to dress oneself in mourning.

**enllantar** *tr.* to rim, to shoe [a wheel].

**enmaderar** *tr.* to plank, board, wainscot. *2* to timber [a building].

**enmagrecer** *intr.* to grow lean, lose flesh. ¶ CONJUG. like *agradecer.*

**enmallarse** *ref.* [of a fish] to be caught in the meshes of a net.

**enmarañamiento** *m.* entanglement, tangle. *2* embroilment, confusion.

**enmarañar** *tr.* to entangle, tangle, ravel. *2* to embroil, confuse. *3 ref.* to get tangled, embroiled.

**enmararse** *ref.* NAUT. to take to the open sea.

**enmarcar** *tr.* to frame. *2* to surround, to provide the setting for.

**enmascaramiento** *m.* MIL. camouflage.

**enmascarar** *tr.* to mask. *2 ref.* to put on a mask.

**enmasillar** *tr.* to putty.

**enmendable** *adj.* emendable.

**enmendadura** *f.* emendation, correction.

**enmendar** *tr.* to emend, correct, amend. *2* to repair, make amends for. *3 ref.* to reform, mend. ¶ CONJUG. like *acertar.*

**enmienda** *f.* emendation, correction. *2* amends, reparation. *3* [in parliamentary procedure] amendment. *4 pl.* AGR. amendments.

**enmiendo, enmiende,** etc. *irr.* V. ENMENDAR.

**enmohecer** *tr.* to make mouldy, to mildew. *2* to rust. *3 ref.* to get mouldy. *4* to get rusty. ¶ CONJUG. like *agradecer.*

**enmohecido, -da** *adj.* mouldy, rusty.

**enmohecimiento** *m.* mouldiness, rustiness.

**enmohezco, enmohezca,** etc. *irr.* V. ENMOHECER.

**enmonarse** *ref.* (Am.) to get drunk.

**enmudecer** *tr.* to hush, silence. *2 intr.* to become dumb. *3* to be silent. ¶ CONJUG. like *agradecer.*

**enmudezco, enmudezca,** etc. *irr.* V. ENMUDECER.

**enmugrecer** *tr.* to soil, make greasy. ¶ CONJUG. like *agradecer.*

**ennegrecer** *tr.* to blacken, to darken. ¶ CONJUG. like *agradecer.*

**ennegrecimiento** *m.* blackening, darkening.

**ennegrezco, ennegrezca,** etc. *irr.* V. ENNEGRECER.

**ennoblecedor, -ra** *adj.* ennobling.

**ennoblecer** *tr.* to ennoble. ¶ CONJUG. like *agradecer.*

**ennoblezco, ennoblezca,** etc. *irr.* V. ENNOBLECER.

**ennoblecimiento** *m.* ennoblement.

**enojadizo, -za** *adj.* irritable, peevish, easily angered.

**enojar** *tr.* to anger, make angry. *2* to annoy, displease. *3 ref.* to become angry, get cross.

**enojo** *m.* anger, irritation, displeasure. *2* annoyance.

**enojosamente** *adv.* angrily.

**enojoso, -sa** *adj.* annoying, vexatious, bothersome.

**enología** *f.* œnology.

**enólogo, -ga** *n.* oenologist.

**enorgullecer** *tr.* to make proud. *2 ref.* to be or become proud; *enorgullecerse de,* to pride oneself on. ¶ CONJUG. like *agradecer.*

**enorgullecimiento** *m.* pride, haughtiness.

**enorgullezco, enorgullezca,** etc. *irr.* V. ENORGULLECER.

**enorme** *adj.* enormous. *2* wicked, heinous.

**enormemente** *adv.* enormously, extremely, tremendously, vastly.

**enormidad** *f.* enormousness. *2* enormity. *3* absurdity, nonsense.

**enquistarse** *ref.* MED. to encyst

**enrabiar** *tr.* to anger, enrage.

**enraizar** *intr.* to take root.

**enramada** *f.* bower; shelter of branches.

**enranciar** *tr.-ref.* to make or to become rancid or stale.

**enrarecer** *tr.* to rarefy [make less dense]. *2 ref.* to rarefy [become less dense]. *3 intr.-ref.* to become scarce. ¶ CONJUG. like *agradecer.*

**enrarecido, -da** *adj.* rarefied.

**enrarecimiento** *m.* rarefaction.

**enrasar** *tr.* MAS. to make level or flush. *2 intr.* to become level or flush.

**enrase** *m.* making or being level or flush.

**enrayar** *tr.* to spoke [a wheel].

**enredadera** *adj.* BOT. climbing. *2 f.* BOT. climbing vine, climber. *3* BOT. bindweed.

**enredador, -ra** *adj.* entangling, embroiling. *2* mischievous.

**enredar** *tr.* to tangle, entangle, mat, ravel. *2* to net [catch in a net]. *3* to set [nets] for birds, etc. *4* to embroil, sow discord between. *5* to involve, implicate. *6 intr.* [of children] to be mischievous, play pranks. *7* to fumble, meddle. *8 ref.* to be caught [in a net, etc.]. *9* to get entangled; to get involved. *10* to become complicated, embroiled. *11* [of an anchor] to foul.

**enredijo** *m.* tangle, entanglement.

**enredo** *m.* tangle, entanglement. *2* complication. *3* imbroglio. *4* falsehood, gossip, mischief.

**enredoso, -sa** *adj.* complicated, full of difficulties.

**enrejado** *m.* iron railing, grille. *2* grating, latticework, trellis.

**enrejar** *tr.* to close with a grille. *2* to fence with railing or trellis. *3* to fix the share to [a plough].

**enrevesado, -da** *adj.* REVESADO.

**enriar** *tr.* to ret [flox or hemp].

**Enrique** *m. pr. n.* Henry.
**enriquecedor, -ra** *adj.* enriching.
**enriquecer** *tr.* to enrich. *2 ref.* to become wealthy. *3* to be enriched. ¶ Conjug. like *agradecer.*
**enriquezco, enriquezca,** etc. *irr.* V. ENRIQUECER.
**enriquecimiento** *m.* enrichment.
**Enriqueta** *f. pr. n.* Henrietta, Harriet.
**enriscado, -da** *adj.* craggy [full of crags].
**enriscar** *tr.* to raise. *2 ref.* to go or take refuge among the rocks.
**enristrar** *tr.* to couch [the lance]. *2* to string [onions, etc.]. *3* to go straight to.
**enrocar** *tr.-intr.* CHESS to castle. *2 tr.* to put [flak or hemp] on the distaff.
**enrojar** *tr.* to redden. *2* to make red-hot.
**enrojecer** *tr.* to redden. *2* to make red-hot. *3 ref.* to redden, turn red. *4 intr.* to blush. ¶ Conjug. like *agradecer.*
**enrojecimiento** *m.* reddening, blushing, blush [face]. *2* reddening, glowing [metal].
**enrolamiento** *m.* enrolment, enrollment, signing-up. *2* MIL. enlistment.
**enrolar** *tr.* to enroll, to sign-up. *2* MIL. to enlist.
**enrollable** *adj.* roll-up.
**enrollar** *tr.* to roll, coil.
**enronquecer** *tr.* to make hoarse. *2 intr.-ref.* to get hoarse. ¶ Conjug. like *agradecer.*
**enroque** *m.* CHESS. castling.
**enroscar** *tr.* to coil, twist. *2* to screw on or in. *3 ref.* to coil, twist itself.
**ensacar** *tr.* to bag, sack [put in bags or sacks].
**ensaimada** *f.* cake made of a coiled lenght of puff paste.
**ensalada** *f.* salad. *2* hodge-podge, medley.
**ensaladera** *f.* salad bowl.
**ensaladilla** *f.* kind of salad with mayonnaise sauce. *2* hodge-podge.
**ensalivar** *tr.* to moisten with saliva.
**ensalmador, -ra** *m.-f.* bonesetter. *2* one who pretends to cure by spells.
**ensalmar** *tr.* to set [bones]. *2* to cure by spells.
**ensalmo** *m.* curing by spells: *como por ~,* as if it were by magic, in a jiffy.
**ensalzamiento** *m.* exalting, elevation. *2* extolling.
**ensalzar** *tr.* to exalt, elevate. *2* to praise, extoll.
**ensambladura** *f.,* **ensamblaje** *m.* CARP. joining, assembling; joint.
**ensamblar** *tr.* to join, fit together. *2* CARP. to joint.
**ensamble** *m.* joining. *2* joint.
**ensanchador** *m.* glove stretcher.
**ensanchamiento** *m.* widening, enlarging.
**ensanchar** *tr.* to widen, broaden, enlarge. *2* to let out [a garment]. *3 ~ el corazón,* to relieve, cheer up. *4 ref.* to widen, to expand. *5* to put on airs.
**ensanche** *m.* widening, enlargement, extension. *2* SEW. allowance [in seams] for future enlargement. *3* suburban development.
**ensangrentar** *tr.-ref.* to stain with blood. *2 ref.* to get violent or furious. ¶ Conjug. like *acertar.*
**ensañamiento** *m.* cruelty, ferocity.
**ensañar** *tr.* to irritate, enrage. *2 ref. ensañarse con,* to be cruel to, to wend one's fury on.
**ensartar** *tr.* to string [beads, etc]. *2* to spit, skew, pierce. *3* coll. to rattle off, say disconnectedly.
**ensayar** *tr.* to assay [metals]. *2* to try, try out, test. *3* to rehearse [a play, etc.]. *4* to train, practise. *5 ref.* to practise, train oneself.
**ensaye** *m.* assay [of metals].
**ensayista** *m.-f.* essayist, essay-writer.
**ensayo** *m.* assay [of metals]. *2* trying, testing, trial, test, experiment. *3* preparatory practice; re-hearsal: *~ general,* THEAT. dress rehearsal. *4* LIT. essay.
**ensebar** *tr.* to grease, tallow.
**enseguida** *adv.* at once, right away, inmediately.
**ensenada** *f.* cove, inlet, small bay.
**enseña** *f.* standard, ensign.
**enseñado, -da** *adj.* trained, accustomed, educated.
**enseñanza** *f.* teaching, instruction, education: *primera ~,* primary education; *~ superior,* higher education. *2* lesson, example.
**enseñar** *tr.* to teach. *2* to instruct, train, school. *3* to show [exhibit, let be seen]. *4* to show, point out.
**enseñoreamiento** *m.* mastery, domination.
**enseñorearse** *ref.* to make oneself the master [of], take possession [of].
**enseres** *m. pl.* chattels, household goods. *2* implements, utensils.
**ensilaje** *m.* ensilage, silage.
**ensilar** *tr.* to ensilage, to ensile.
**ensillado, -da** *adj.* saddle-backed.
**ensillar** *tr.* to saddle [a horse, etc.].
**ensimismado, -da** *adj.* pensive, lost in thought, thoughtful, absorbed.
**ensimismamiento** *m.* absorption in thought.
**ensimismarse** *ref.* to become absorbed in thought.
**ensoberbecer** *tr.* to make haughty, arrogant. *2 ref.* to become haughty, arrogant. ¶ Conjug. like *agradecer.*
**ensoberbecimiento** *m.* haughtiness, arrogance.
**ensombrecer** *tr.* to darken, cloud. *2 ref.* to darken [become dark or gloomy]. ¶ Conjug. like *agradecer.*
**ensombrezco, ensombrezca,** etc. *irr.* V. ENSOMBRECER.
**ensopar** *tr.* to dunk, to soak.
**ensordecedor, -ra** *adj.* deafening.
**ensordecer** *tr.* to deafen [make deaf]. *2 ref.* to become deaf. ¶ Conjug. like *agradecer.*
**ensordecimiento** *m.* deafening; deafness.
**ensordezco, ensordezca,** etc. *irr.* V. ENSORDECER.
**ensortijar** *tr.* to curl, crisp [hair, etc.]. *2 ref.* [of hair, etc.] to curl.
**ensuciamiento** *m.* soiling, staining.
**ensuciar** *tr.* to dirty, soil, stain, defile, pollute. *2 ref.* to get dirty. *3* to soil one's bed, clothes, etc. *4* to soil oneself.
**ensueño** *m.* dream, day-dream, fantasy.
**entablado** *m.* flooring [of boards]. *2* wooden framework.
**entablamento** *m.* ARCH. entablature.
**entablar** *tr.* to plank, board, cover with boards. *2* to start [a conversation, etc.]; to bring [a suit or action]. *3* SURG. to splint. *4 ref.* [of wind] to settle.
**entablillar** *tr.* SURG. to splint.
**entalamadura** *f.* awning [of cart or wagon].
**entalegar** *tr.* to put in a bag, to bag. *2* to save, to hoard, to stash away. *3* to pocket. *4 ref.* coll. to make, to earn.
**entalladura** *f.,* **entallamiento** *m.* carving, sculpture; engraving. *2* notch, mortise, incision.
**entallar** *tr.* to carve, sculpture, engrave. *2* to notch, make a cut in. *3* to make [a garment] fit to the waist. *4 intr.* [of a garment] to fit to the waist.
**entapizar** *tr.* to upholster. *2* to carpet [cover as with a carpet].
**entarimado** *m.* boarded or parqueted floor.
**entarimar** *tr.* to floor with boards.
**entarquinar** *tr.* to fertilize with slime. *2* to soil with slime. *3* to reclaim [a swamp] by siltation.

**entarugado** *m.* pavement of wooden blocks.
**ente** *m.* entity, being. *2* coll, fellow *guy.
**enteco, -ca** *adj.* weakly, sickly.
**entelequia** *f.* PHILOS. entelechy.
**entena** *f.* NAUT. lateen yard.
**entenada** *f.* stepdaughter.
**entenado** *m.* stepson.
**entendederas** *f. pl.* brains, understanding.
**entendedor, -ra** *m.-f.* one who understands: *al buen ~ pocas palabras,* a word to the wise is enough.
1) **entender** *m.* understanding; opinion: *a mi ~,* in my opinion.
2) **entender** *tr.* to understand, conceive, comprehend. *2* to intend, mean. *3* to think, believe; infer. *4 intr. ~ de* or *en,* to be an expert on; to be in charge [of an affair]; to have authority to pass on. *5 ref.* to be understandable. *6* to be understood. *7* to know what one's about. *8* to understand each other. *9* to have a secret understanding. ¶ CONJUG. IND. Pres.: *entiendo, entiendes, entiende;* entendemos, entendéis, *entienden.* | SUBJ. Pres.: *entienda, entiendas, entienda;* entendamos, entendáis, *entiendan.* | IMPER.: *entiende, entienda;* entendamos, entended, *entiendan.*
**entendido, -da** *p. p.* of ENTENDER: *tener ~,* to understand. *2 adj.* that understands; *no darse por ~,* to pretend not to understand. *3* able, expert, learned.
**entendimiento** *m.* understanding, comprehension. *2* understanding, intellect, mind, sense.
**entenebrecer** *tr.* to darken, obscure. *2 ref.* to get dark. ¶ CONJUG. like *agradecer.*
**enterado** *adj.* informed, well informed.
**enteramente** *adv.* completely, fully, entirely, quite.
**enterar** *tr.* to inform, acquaint, make cognizant. *2 ref. enterarse de,* to learn, be informed of; to inquire about.
**entercarse** *ref.* to get obstinate.
**entereza** *f.* entirety. *2* integrity. *3* fortitude, firmness, presence of mind. *4 ~ virginal,* virginity.
**enteritis** *f.* MED. enteritis.
**enterizo, -za** *adj.* in one piece.
**enternecedor, -ra** *adj.* affecting, moving, touching.
**enternecer** *tr.* to soften. *2* to touch, move to pity. *3 ref.* to be touched, be moved to pity. ¶ CONJUG. like *agradecer.*
**enternecimiento** *m.* tenderness, pity, compassion.
**entero, -ra** *adj.* entire, whole, complete. *2* sound, robust. *3* honest, upright. *4* firm, constant. *5* ARITH. whole [number]. *6* BOT. entire. *7* uncastrated. *8 m.* ARITH. integer. *9 por ~,* entirely, completely, fully.
**enterocolitis** *f.* MED. enterocolitis.
**enterrador** *m.* gravedigger, sexton.
**enterramiento** *m.* interment, burial. *2* sepulchre, tomb, grave.
**enterrar** *tr.* to bury; to inter. *2* to survive. *3 ref.* to retire, bury oneself. ¶ CONJUG. like *acertar.*
**entesar** *tr.* to stretch, tighten, tauten.
**entestado, -da** *adj.* stubborn, obstinate.
**entibación** *f.* MIN. timbering.
**entibar** *tr.* MIN. to shore up, timber. *2 intr.* to rest, lean.
**entibiar** *tr.* to cool, to make lukewarm. *2* to temper, moderate. *3 ref.* to become lukewarm, to cool down.
**entibo** *m.* MIN. timber, prop, strut.
**entidad** *f.* entity. *2* consequence, importance, moment. *3* association, corporation.

**entiendo, entienda,** etc. *irr.* V. ENTENDER.
**entierro** *m.* interment, burial, funeral. *2* grave, tomb. *3* buried treasure.
**entierro, entierre,** etc. *irr.* V. ENTERRAR.
**entimema** *m.* LOG. enthymeme.
**entintar** *tr.* to ink. *2* to stain with ink. *3* to dye.
**entoldado** *m.* covering with awnings. *2* awnings; overhead shelter made of awnings.
**entoldar** *tr.* to cover with awnings. *2* to adorn with hangings. *3 ref.* to get cloudy, become overcast.
**entomología** *f.* entomology.
**entomólogo** *m.* entomologist.
**entonación** *f.* ENTONO. *2* intonation, modulation, tone. *3* MED., PAINT. toning.
**entonado, -da** *adj.* haughty, stuck-up.
**entonamiento** *m.* ENTONACIÓN.
**entonar** *tr.* to sing in tune. *2* to sing [a song]. *3* to intone [for others to follow]. *4* MUS., PAINT., PHOT. to tone. *5* MED. to tone up. *6 ref.* to become stuck-up.
**entonces** *adv.* then, at that time: *por ~, por aquel ~,* at that time. *2* then, this being the case.
**entonelar** *tr.* to put in casks or barrels.
**entono** *m.* singing in tune. *2* haughtiness, arrogance, airs.
**entontecer** *tr.* to besot, hebetate, make silly. ¶ CONJUG. like *agradecer.*
**entorchada** *adj.* ARCH. wreathed [column].
**entorchado** *m.* bullion lace [in the cuffs of some uniforms]. *2* string covered with silk or wire.
**entornar** *tr.* to half-close [the eyes]; to set ajar [a door]. *2* to tilt, upset.
**entorpecedor** *adj.* dulling, blunting, benumbing. *2* delaying, obstructing.
**entorpecer** *tr.* to dull, blunt [the mind, the senses], to benumb. *2* to clog, delay, obstruct. *3 ref.* to become dull, blunt, awkward. *4* to get delayed, obstructed. ¶ CONJUG. like *agradecer.*
**entorpecimiento** *m.* dullness, bluntness, numbness; torpidity. *2* obstruction, delay.
**entorpezco, entorpezca,** etc. *irr.* V. ENTORPECER.
**entozoario** *m.* ZOOL. entozoan.
**entrada** *f.* entrance, gate, place of entrance, access; MIN. adit; MACH. intake, inlet. *2* entrance, entering, entry, ingress. *3* admission [to society, club, etc.]; admittance, opening. *4* entrance fee; admission ticket. *5* THEAT. house [audience]: *gran ~,* full house. *6* THEAT. receipt, takings. *7* first payment. *8* beginning [of a book, year, etc.]. *9* intimacy with. *10* COOK. entrée. *11* cash receipts. *12* invasion. *13* MUS. entrance. *14* THEAT. *~ general,* gallery. *15 pl.* income. *16* receding hair at the temples.
**entrado, -da** *adj. ~ en años,* advanced in years.
**entramado** *m.* MAR. timber framework, studwork.
**entrambos, -bas** *adj. pl.* both, both the.
**entrampar** *tr.* to trap, entrap, ensnare. *2* to trick. *3* to entangle [matters]. *4* to burden with debt. *5 ref.* to stick in the mud. *6* to run into debt.
**entrante** *adj.* entrant, entering, incoming. *2* coming, next: *el mes ~,* the next month. *3* re-entering [angle]. *4 m.-f. entrantes y salientes,* goers and comers.
**entraña** *f.* ANAT. vital or internal organ. *2* the innermost part, the bottom, the core. *3 pl.* vitals. *4* entrails. *5* heart, feeling: *no tener entrañas,* to be heartless. *6* temper, disposition: *de buenas entrañas,* kind, human.
**entrañable** *adj.* most affectionate. *2* deep [affection].
**entrañablemente** *adv.* dearly, deeply.

**entrañar** *tr.* to bury deep. *2* to contain, involve. *3 ref.* to penetrate to the core. *4* to become deeply attached.

**entrar** *intr.* to enter, go in, come in. *2* to charge, attack. *3* [of seasons, writings, etc.] to begin. *4* to play for the stakes [at cards]. *5* MUS. to strike in. *6* ~ *a*, to enter, begin, start: ~ *a reinar*, to begin to reign. *7* ~ *en*, to go into, enter, penetrate; to have access to; to join, become a member of; to enter into, to engage in; to be numbered among. *8* ~ *en deseo*, to be seized by a desire. *9* ~ *en juego*, to come into play. *10 entran cuatro peras en libra*, there's four pears to the pound. *11 no entrarle a uno una persona*, not to be able to bear somebody. *12 tr.* to introduce, bring, put in. *13* MIL. to invade. *14* to attack, to influence. *15 ref.* to enter, go in, penetrate.

**entre** *prep.* between, among, amongst. *2* ~ *mí*, ~ *sí*, in my, his, heart; to myself, to himself. *3* ~ *tanto*, meanwhile, in the interim.

**entreabierto, -ta** *adj.* half-open, ajar.

**entreabrir** *tr.* to half-open; to set ajar. ¶ Past. p.: *entreabierto*.

**entreacto** *m.* THEAT. entr'acte, interval.

**entreancho, -cha** *adj.* neither broad nor narrow.

**entrecano, -na** *adj.* grayish [hair or beard].

**entrecava** *f.* AGR. shallow digging.

**entrecejo** *m.* space between the eyebrows: *fruncir el* ~, to knit one's brow. *2* frown, frowning.

**entreclaro, -ra** *adj.* lightish.

**entrecoger** *tr.* to catch, corner.

**entrecoro** *m.* ECCL. chancel.

**entrecortado, -da** *adj.* broken, faltering [voice, sound].

**entrecortar** *tr.* to cut without severing.

**entrecruzar** *tr.* to intercross. *2 ref.* to intercross [be intercrossed].

**entrecubiertas** *f. pl.* NAUT. between decks.

**entrechocar** *intr.-ref.* to collide with one another, to clash.

**entredicho** *m.* interdiction, prohibition. *2* ECCL. interdict.

**entredós** *m.* SEW. insertion. *2* PRINT. long primer.

**entrefilete** *m.* short feature [in a newspaper].

**entrefino, -na** *adj.* of medium quality.

**entrega** *f.* delivery, handing over. *2* surrender. *3* fascicle, instalment [of a novel, etc.].

**entregar** *tr.* to deliver, hand over; to give up: ~ *el alma a Dios*, to give up the ghost. *2* to surrender. *3 ref.* to surrender, give oneself up. *4* to yield, submit. *5* to abandon oneself [to a feeling, etc.]. *6* to devote oneself [to something].

**entrelazamiento** *m.* interlacing, interweaving.

**entrelazar** *tr.* to interlace, braid, entwine, interweave.

**entrelínea** *f.* writing between the lines.

**entrelinear** *tr.* to interline, write between lines.

**entreliño** *m.* space between rows of trees or vines.

**entrelucir** *intr.* to show through. ¶ CONJUG. like *lucir*.

**entremediar** *tr.* to put between.

**entremedias** *adv.* in between; in the mean time: ~ *de*, between; among.

**entremés** *m.* hors d'oeuvre, side dish. *2* THEAT. short farce inserted between two acts of a play.

**entremeter** *tr.* to insert, place between. *2 ref.* to butt in, meddle, intermeddle, obtrude.

**entremetido, -da** *adj.* meddlesome, officious. *2 m.-f.* meddler, busybody.

**entremetimiento** *m.* meddling, meddlesomeness.

**entremezclar** *tr.* to intermingle, intermix.

**entrenador** *m.* SPORT. trainer, coach.

**entrenamiento** *m.* SPORT. training, coaching.

**entrenar** *tr.* SPORT. to train, coach. *2 ref.* SPORT. to train, be in training.

**entrenudo** *m.* BOT. internode.

**entreoír** *tr.* to hear vaguely; to half-ear. ¶ CONJUG. like *oír*.

**entrepaño** *m.* ARCH. pier [piece of wall]. *2* panel [of door]. *3* shelf.

**entrepernar** *intr.* to put one's legs between those of another. ¶ CONJUG. like *acertar*.

**entrepiernas** *f. pl.* inner surface of the thights.

**entrepiso** *m.* MIN. space between galleries. *2* Am. mezzanine, entresol.

**entrepuente** *m.* or *pl.* -tes NAUT. between-decks.

**entrerrenglonar** *tr.* to pick out, select. *2* to thin out [trees, hair, etc.].

**entresacar** *tr* to select, to pick out, to sift out, to prune [tree], to thin out [plants], to thin [hair, woods].

**entresijo** *m.* ANAT. mesentery. *2* anything secret or hidden: *tener muchos entresijos*, to be complicated; to be reserved, sly.

**entresuelo** *m.* entresol, mezzanine.

**entretalla, entretalladura** *f.* bas-relief.

**entretallar** *tr.* to carve in bas-relief. *2* to sculpture, engrave. *3* to make openwork on.

**entretanto** *adv.* meanwhile. *2 m.* meanwhile meantime: *en el* ~, in the meantime.

**entretejer** *tr.* to interweave, intertwine. *2* to insert, mix, intermix.

**entretejido** *m.* intertwining, interweaving, entwining.

**entretejimiento** *m.* interweaving.

**entretela** *f.* SEW. interlining. *2 pl.* heartstrings.

**entretelar** *tr.* SEW. to interline.

**entretener** *tr.* to delay, detain. *2* to make bearable [hunger, etc.]. *3* to entertain, amuse. *4* to maintain, keep up. *5* to delay, put off. *6 ref.* to delay, dally, linter. *7* to amuse oneself. ¶ CONJUG. like *tener*.

**entretenido, -da** *adj.* entertaining, amusing.

**entretenimiento** *m.* entertainment, amusement, pastime. *2* maintenance, upkeep.

**entretiempo** *m.* spring or autumn: *ropa de* ~, light clothing.

**entrever** *tr.* to glimpse, see imperfectly. *2* to guess, divine.

**entreverado, -da** *adj.* intermingled, intermixed; interlarded. *2 tocino* ~, streaky bacon.

**entreverar** *tr.* to intermingle, intermix. *2* to streak, to interlard.

**entrevero** *m.* (Am.) crowd, throng. *2* confusion, muddle, mix-up, jumble. *3* hand-to-hand fight [horse soldiers].

**entrevía** *f.* RLY. space between rails.

**entrevista** *f.* interview, meeting, conference.

**entrevistarse** *ref.* to meet, hold an interwiew.

**entripado** *m.* bellyache. *2* suppressed anger or displeasure.

**entristecedor, -ra** *adj.* sad, saddening.

**entristecer** *tr.* to sadden; to make gloomy. *2 ref.* to sadden, become sad. ¶ CONJUG. like *agradecer*.

**entristecimiento** *m.* saddening, sadness.

**entrojar** *tr.* to garner [grain].

**entrometer** *tr.-ref.* ENTREMETER.

**entrometido, -da** *adj.* meddlesome, interfering. *2 n.* meddler, interferer, busybody, intruder.

**entromparse** *ref.* coll. to get stewed, canned, tight. *2* (Am.) to get angry, to get cross.

**entroncar** *intr.* to be or become related [to a family] by marriage. *2 (Am.)* [of railways, roads, etc.] to connect.

**entronerar** *tr.* BILL. to pocket [a ball].

**entronización** *f.* enthronement, enthronization.

**entronizar** *tr.* to enthrone, enthronize. *2* to exalt.

**entronque** *m.* relationship between people of the same stock.

**entropión** *m.* MED. entropion.

**entruchada** *f.*, **entruchado** *m.* coll. plot, intrigue, dirty affair.

**entruchar** *tr.* to lure into a business.

**entubar** *tr.* to tube, to pipe. *2* to tube, to case. *3* MED. to tube.

**entuerto** *m.* wrong, injustice. *2 pl.* afterpains.

**entumecer** *tr.* to benumb, make torpid [a limb, etc.]. *2 ref.* [of limbs] to become numb. *3* [of sea, etc.] to swell. ¶ CONJUG. like *agradecer.*

**entumecimiento** *m.* numbness, torpor [of limbs]. *2* swelling [of sea, etc.].

**entumezco, entumezca,** etc. *irr.* V. ENTUMECER.

**entumirse** *ref.* [of a limb] to become numb.

**enturbiar** *tr.* to render turbid, to muddy. *2* to cloud, obscure, muddle, dim, confuse; to trouble [waters]. *3 ref.* to get or become turbid. *4* to get obscured.

**entusiasmar** *tr.* to awake the enthusiasm of; to enrapture. *2 ref.* to be filled with enthusiasm, be enraptured.

**entusiasmo** *m.* enthusiasm.

**entusiasta** *m.-f.* enthusiast.

**entusiástico, -ca** *adj.* enthusiastic.

**enumeración** *f.* enumeration.

**enumerar** *tr.* to enumerate.

**enunciación** *f.*, **enunciado** *m.* enouncement, enunciation, statement.

**enunciar** *tr.* to enounce, enunciate, state.

**envainador, -ra** *adj.* sheathing.

**envainar** *tr.* to sheathe.

**envalentonamiento** *m.* emboldening. *2* boldness.

**envalentonar** *tr.* to embolden, to make bold, daring. *2 ref.* to grow bold or daring.

**envanecer** *tr.* to make vain, conceited. *2 ref.* to become vain, conceited; to be proud [of], to boast [of]. ¶ CONJUG. like *agradecer.*

**envanecimiento** *m.* vanity, conceit, conceitedness.

**envanezco, envanezca,** etc. *irr.* V. ENVANECER.

**envaramiento** *m.* stiffness, numbness.

**envarar** *tr.* to stiffen, benumb.

**envasador, -ra** *m.-f.* filler, packer.

**envasar** *tr.* to pack, bottle, can, sack, put into a container. *2* to drink [wine, etc.].

**envase** *m.* packing, bottling, canning, etc. *2* container [package, bottle, can, sack, etc.].

**envejecer** *tr.* to age; to make look old. *2 intr.-ref.* to age, grow old. *3* to go out-of-date. ¶ CONJUG. like *agradecer.*

**envejecido, -da** *adj.* aged, looking old. *2* tried, experienced.

**envejecimiento** *m.* ageing, growing or looking old.

**envejezco, envejezca,** etc. *irr.* V. ENVEJECER.

**envenenador, -ra** *m.-f.* poisoner.

**envenenamiento** *m.* poisoning.

**envenenar** *tr.* to poison, to envenom.

**enverar** *intr.* to take on ripe colour.

**envergadura** *f.* breadth [of a sail]. *2* AER. span, spread. *3* wingspread [of birds].

**envergar** *tr.* NAUT. to bend [a sail].

**enverjado** *m.* iron railing [for closing or fencing].

**envés** *m.* back, wrong side, underside.

**enviado** *m.* messenger, envoy.

**enviajado, -da** *adj.* ARCH. oblique, sloping.

**enviar** *tr.* to send, dispatch; to ship.

**enviciamiento** *m.* corruption. *2* taking bad habits.

**enviciar** *tr.* to corrupt; to make [one] acquire bad habits. *2 intr.* [of plants] to have luxuriant foliage and little fruit. *3 ref.* to take [to], to become addicted [to].

**envidar** *intr.-tr.* to bid or bet against [at cards].

**envidia** *f.* envy, enviousness, jealousy.

**envidiar** *tr.* to envy.

**envidioso, -sa** *adj.* envious. *2 m.-f.* envious person.

**envigar** *tr.* to put the beams [in a building].

**envilecer** *tr.* to debase, degrade, vilify. *2 ref.* to degrade oneself. ¶ CONJUG. like *agradecer.*

**envilecimiento** *m.* debasement, degradation, vilification.

**envinagrar** *tr.* to put vinegar into.

**envío** *m.* sending, remittance; shipment.

**envión** *m.* push, shove.

**enviscar** *tr.* to smear with birdlime. *2* to irritate, anger. *3* AZUZAR.

**envite** *m.* bid, rise on the stake [at cards]. *2* offer, proffer. *3* push: *al primer ~,* right off.

**enviudar** *intr.* to become a widower or widow.

**envoltorio** *m.* bundle, parcel.

**envoltura** *f.* cover, envelope, wrapper. *2* AER., BOT. envelope. *3 pl.* swaddling clothes.

**envolvente** *adj.* enveloping.

**envolver** *tr.* to cover, envelop, wrap, wrap up; to make up in a packet. *2* to swaddle [an infant]. *3* to wind [thread, etc.]. *4* to floor [an opponent]. *5* to involve [in an affair]. *6* to contain, imply. *7* MIL. to envelop. *8 ref.* to wrap oneself up. *9* to become involved. ¶ CONJUG. like *mover.* | PAST. P.: *envuelto.*

**envolvimiento** *m.* wrapping, enveloping. *2* winding. *3* MIL. envelopment.

**envuelvo, envuelva,** etc. *irr.* V. ENVOLVER.

**envuelto, -ta** *p. p.* of ENVOLVER.

**enyesado** *m.* plastering [of wine]. *2* plasterwork.

**enyesar** *tr.* to plaster [walls, etc.]. *2* to treat with gypsum. *3* SURG. to put a plaster cast on.

**enzarzar** *tr.* to cover with brambles. *2* to set [people] disputing. *3 ref.* to get entangled in brambles. *4* to engage [in difficult business]. *5* to dispute, quarrel.

**enzima** *f.* BIOCHEM. enzyme.

**eñe** *f.* name of the letter ñ.

**eoceno, -na** *adj.-m.* GEOL. Eocene.

**eólico, -ca** *adj.* Æolian. *2 m.* Æolic [dialect].

**Eólida (la)** *f. pr. n.* GEOG. Æolis.

**eolio, lia** *adj.-n.* Æolian.

**eolítico, -ca** *adj.* eolithic.

**Eolo** *m. pr. n.* MYTH. Æolus.

**eón** *m.* æon.

**eoperlano** *m.* ICHTH. smelt.

**¡epa!** *interj.* (Am.) hello! *2* come on!

**épica** *f.* epic poetry.

**epicarpio** *m.* BOT. epicarp.

**epiceno, -na** *adj.* GRAM. epicene.

**epicentro** *m.* epicentre.

**epicicloide** *f.* GEOM. epicycloid.

**épico, -ca** *adj.* epic, epical.

**epicureísmo** *m.* Epicureanism.

**epicúreo, -a** *adj.-s.* epicurean. *2* Epicurean.

**epidemia** *f.* epidemic.

**epidémico, -ca** *adj.* epidemic(al.

**epidérmico, -ca** *adj.* epidermal, epidermic.

**epidermis** *f.* ANAT., BOT. epidermis.

**Epifanía** *f.* Epiphany.

**epifenómeno** *m.* epiphenomenon.

**epífisis** *f.* ANAT. epiphysis.
**epífito, -ta** *adj.* epiphytic. *2 f.* BOT. epiphyte.
**epifonema** *m.* RHET. epiphonema.
**epigastrio** *m.* ANAT. epigastrium.
**epiglotis** *f.* ANAT. epiglottis.
**epígrafe** *m.* epigraph. *2* title, headline.
**epigrafía** *f.* epigraphy.
**epigrama** *m.* epigram.
**epigramático, -ca** *adj.* epigrammatic(al.
**epilepsia** *f.* MED. epilepsy.
**epiléptico, -ca** *adj.-s.* epileptic.
**epilogar** *tr.* to epilogize. *2* to sum up.
**epílogo** *m.* epilogue. *2* summing up.
**Epiro (el)** *m. pr. n.* GEOG. Epirus.
**episcopado** *m.* episcopacy, episcopate, bishopric.
**episcopal** *adj.* episcopal. *2* Episcopal.
**episódico, -ca** *adj.* episodic(al.
**episodio** *m.* episode.
**epístola** *f.* epistle, letter. *2* ECCL. Epistle.
**epistolar** *adj.* epistolary.
**epistolario** *m.* collection of letters. *2* ECCL. epistolary.
**epitafio** *m.* epitaph.
**epitalamio** *m.* epithalamium.
**epitelio** *m.* ANAT. epithelium.
**epitelioma** *m.* MED. epithelioma.
**epíteto** *m.* GRAM. epithet.
**epítimo** *m.* BOT. clover dodder.
**epítome** *m.* epitome, abstract, summary.
**epizootia** *f.* epizootic.
**época** *f.* epoch, age, time.
**epodo** *m.* epode.
**epónimo, -ma** *adj.* eponymous.
**epopeya** *f.* epopee. *2* epic poem.
**épsilon** *f.* epsilon.
**eptágono, -na** *adj.* MATH. heptagonal. *2 m.* MATH. heptagon.
**equidad** *f.* equity; equitableness. *2* reasonableness [in prices, terms, etc.].
**equidistancia** *f.* equidistance, equal distance.
**equidistante** *adj.* equidistant.
**equidna** *m.* ZOOL. echidna.
**équido** *m.* ZOOL. equid.
**equilátero, -ra** *adj.* equilateral.
**equilibrado, -da** *adj.* sensible, well-balanced.
**equilibrar** *tr.* to equilibrate, balance, equipoise, equalize. *2 ref.* to balance [be equal].
**equilibrio** *m.* equilibrium, balance, equipoise: ~ *europeo*, European balance of power.
**equilibrista** *m.-f.* equilibrist.
**equimosis** *m.* ecchymosis.
**equino, -na** *adj.* equine. *2 m.* ZOOL., ARCH. echinus.
**equinoccial** *adj.* equinoctial.
**equinoccio** *m.* ASTR. equinox.
**equinodermo** *adj.-m.* ZOOL. echinoderm.
**equipaje** *m.* luggage, baggage. *2* equipment. *3* NAUT. crew.
**equipar** *tr.* to equip, fit out.
**equiparable** *adj.* comparable.
**equiparar** *tr.* to compare, to put on the same level.
**equipo** *m.* equipment, fitting out. *2* equipment, outfit: ~ *de novia*, trousseau. *3* crew, gang, squad [of workmen]. *4* SPORT. team.
**equiponderar** *intr.* to equiponderate.
**equis** *f.* Spanish name of the letter *x*.
**equisetáceo, -a** *adj.* BOT. equisetaceous.
**equitación** *f.* equitation, horsemanship, riding.
**equitativo, -va** *adj.* equitable. *2* reasonable [price].
**equivalencia** *f.* equivalence.
**equivalente** *adj.-m.* equivalent.

**equivaler** *intr.* to be equivalent; to be equal, tantamount. ¶ CONJUG. like *valer*.
**equivocación** *f.* mistake, error.
**equivocadamente** *adv.* by mistake. *2* erroneously.
**equivocado, -da** *adj.* mistaken. *2* erroneous.
**equívocamente** *adv.* ambiguously, equivocally.
**equivocar** *tr.-ref.* to mistake. *2* to make a mistake in, to take wrongly: ~ *la carrera*, to miss one's calling; *equivocarse de camino*, to take the wrong way. *3 ref.* to be mistaken.
**equívoco, -ca** *adj.* equivocal. *2 m.* equivocation quibble, ambiguity.
**era** *f.* era, age : ~ *cristiana*, Christian era. *2* GEOL. era. *3* threshing floor. *4* vegetable patch; garden bed.
**era, éramos,** etc. *irr.* V. SER.
**eral** *m.* two-year-old ox.
**erario** *m.* exchequer, public treasury; provincial or municipal treasury.
**ere** *f.* Spanish name of the letter *r*.
**eres** *2nd pers. sing. pres.* of SER.
**erebo** *m.* MYTH. Erebus.
**erección** *f.* erection [raising, building]. *2* PHYSIOL. erection. *3* foundation, establishment.
**eréctil** *adj.* erectile.
**eremita** *m.* eremite, hermit.
**eremítico, -ca** *adj.* eremite.
**erg** *m.* ERGIO.
**ergástula** *m.* slave prison.
**ergio** *m.* PHYS. erg.
**ergotismo** *m.* LOG., MED. ergotism.
**ergotizar** *intr.* to ergotize.
**erguimiento** *m.* raising, straightening up.
**erguir** *tr.* to raise, lift up, erect [the head, the body, etc.] *2 ref.* to stand erect. *3* to become arrogant. ¶ CONJUG.: INDIC. Pres.: *irgo* or *yergo, irgues* or *yergues, irgue* or *yergue; erguimos, erguís, irguen* or *yerguen.* | Pret.: *erguí, erguiste, irguió; erguimos, erguisteis, irguieron.* | SUBJ. Pres.: *irga* or *yerga, irgas* or *yergas, irga* or *yerga; irgamos* or *yergamos, irgáis* or *yergáis, irgan* or *yergan.* | Imperf.: *irguiera, irguieras,* etc., or *irguiese, irguieses,* etc. | Fut.: *irguiere, irguieres,* etc. | IMPER.: *irgue* or *yergue, irga* or *yerga; irgamos* or *yergamos, erguid, irgan* or *yergan.* | PAST. P.: erguido. | GER.: *irguiendo.*
**erial** *adj.* untilled, uncultivated. *2 m.* uncultivated land.
**ericáceo, -a** *adj.* BOT. ericaceous.
**erigir** *tr.* to erect, build. *2* to found, establish. *3 tr.-ref.* ~, or *erigirse en*, to set, or set oneself up as.
**erisipela** *f.* MED. erysipelas.
**Eritreo, -a** *adj.* Eritraean.
**erizado, -da** *adj.* bristled, bristling. *2* covered with bristles. *3* ~ *de*, bristling with [difficulties, etc.].
**erizar** *tr.* to set on end; to bristle. *2* to cause to be bristling [with difficulties, etc.]. *3 ref.* to stand on end, to bristle.
**erizo** *m.* ZOOL. hedgehog. *2* fig. hedgehog [person]. *3* BOT. a prickly pant. *4* BOT. bur [of chestnut, etc.]. *5* ZOOL. ~ *de mar*, sea urchin.
**ermita** *f.* hermitage. *2* isolated sanctuary or chapel.
**ermitaño** *m.* hermit. *2* keeper of an isolated sanctuary or chapel. *3* ZOOL. hermit crab.
**Ernesto** *m. pr. n.* Ernest.
**erogación** *f.* distribution. *2* (Am.) expenditure, payment. *3* (Am.) contribution.
**erogar** *tr.* to distribute. *2* (Am.) to pay, to spend. *3* (Am.) to contribute.
**Eros** *m. pr. n.* MYTH. Eros.

**erosión** f. erosion.
**erótico, -ca** adj. erotic. 2 f. erotic poetry.
**erotismo** m. erotism.
**errabundo, -da** adj. wandering.
**errada** f. BILL. miscue.
**erradicación** f. eradication.
**erradicar** tr. to eradicate.
**errado, -da** adj. mistaken, in error. 2 erroneous.
**erraj** m. fine coal made of crushed olive stones.
**errante** adj. errant, wandering. 2 errant, erring.
**errar** tr. to miss [the target, a blow, one's calling, etc.]. 2 to wander, roam. 3 intr.-ref. to err, to be mistaken. ¶ CONJUG. like acertar, changing the i for y in the irregular forms.
**errata** f. erratum.
**errático, -ca** adj. wandering. 2 GEOL., MED. erratic.
**errátil** adj. erratic, variable.
**erre** f. Spanish name of the letter rr.
**erróneo, -a** adj. erroneous.
**error** m. error. 2 mistake.
**eructar** intr. to belch, eructate.
**eructo** m. belching, eructation.
**erudición** f. erudition, learning.
**erudito, -ta** adj.-n. erudite.
**erupción** f. MED., GEOL. eruption.
**eruptivo, -va** adj. eruptive.
**esa** adj. f. of ESE.
**ésa** pron. f. of ÉSE.
**esbatimentar** tr. PAINT. to shade.
**esbatimento** m. PAINT. shade.
**esbeltez, esbelteza** f. graceful slenderness.
**esbelto, -ta** adj. slender and graceful, svelte.
**esbirro** m. catchpoll, myrmidon.
**esbozar** tr. to sketch, outline.
**esbozo** m. sketch, outline.
**escabechar** tr. to pickle [fish, meat]. 2 coll. to kill.
**escabeche** m. pickle [of fish, etc.]. 2 pickled fish.
**escabechina** f. coll. ravage.
**escabel** m. stool; footstool. 2 fig. stepping stone.
**escabiosa** f. BOT. scabious.
**escabrosidad** f. roughness, unevenness [of a ground]. 2 asperity [of temper]. 3 scabrousness.
**escabroso, -sa** adj. rough, rugged, uneven [ground]. 2 harsh, rude. 3 scabrous, risqué.
**escabullirse** ref. to slip.
**escacado, -da** adj. HER. checkered.
**escacharrar** tr. to break, smash.
**escafandra** f., **escafandro** m. diving suit.
**escala** f. ladder, stepladder: ~ de cuerda, rope ladder. 2 scale [series of degrees; size, proportion; ratio, etc.]: en grande ~, on a large scale. 3 MUS. scale. 4 NAUT. port of call: hacer ~ en, to call at. 5 MIL. army list.
**escalada** f. escalade. 2 scaling, climbing.
**escalador, -ra** m.-f. scaler, climber, mountain climber.
**escalafón** m. roll, list [showing rank, seniority, etc.]; army list.
**escalamiento** m. escalading. 2 scaling, climbing.
**escálamo** m. NAUT. thole, tholepin.
**escalar** tr. to escalade. 2 to scale, climb. 3 to break into or out of [a place] through a wall, roof, etc.
**Escalda** m. pr. n. Scheldt [river].
**escaldado, -da** adj. cautious, wary.
**escaldadura** f. scalding, scald. 2 chafing [of the skin].
**escaldar** tr. to scald. 2 to make red-hot. 3 to chafe [the skin].
**escaleno** adj. GEOM. scalene.
**escalera** f. stair, staircase: ~ mecánica, escalator; ~ de caracol, winding stairs; ~ de escape, fire

escape. 2 ladder; ~ de incendio, fire ladder; ~ de mano, ladder; ~ de tijera, stepladder. 3 irregular cut in hair. 4 sequence; straight [at cards].
**escalerilla** f. dim. short ladder, steps. 2 sequence of three or five [at cards].
**escalfado** adj. COOK. poached [egg].
**escalfador** m. barber's kettle. 2 chaffing dish.
**escalfeta** f. CHOFETA.
**escalinata** f. ARCH. perron, front steps.
**escalo** m. breaking a way into or out of a place. 2 breaking in: robo con ~, burglary.
**escalofriante** adj. chilling, blood-curdling.
**escalofrío** m. chill [feverish shivering], shudder.
**escalón** m. stair, step, rung. 2 fig. step, degree. 3 MIL. echelon.
**escalonado, -da** adj. spaced out, spread out. 2 staggered. 3 in stages, escheloned.
**escalonar** tr. to place at intervals. 2 MIL. to echelon. 3 to space, to string out.
**escalonia, escaloña** f. BOT. scallion.
**escalope** m. escalope, veal cutlet.
**escalpelo** m. SURG. scalpel.
**escama** f. ZOOL., BOT. scale. 2 scale [of armour, etc.]. 3 distrust, suspicion.
**escamado, -da** p. p. of ESCAMAR. 2 adj. distrustful, suspicious. 3 m. scalework.
**escamar** tr. to scale [fish]. 2 to cause distrust or suspicion. 3 to adorn with scalework. 4 ref. to become distrustful or suspicious.
**escamón, -na** adj. distrustful, suspicious.
**escamonda** f. ESCAMONDO.
**escamondar** tr. to trim, to prune [a tree, etc.].
**escamondo** m. trimming, pruning.
**escamonea** f. BOT. scammony.
**escamoso, -sa** adj. scaly, squamous.
**escamoteador, -ra** m.-f. conjurer, prestidigitator.
**escamotear** tr. to make disappear by sleight of hand. 2 to whisk out of sight; to spirit away.
**escamoteo** m. sleight of hand. 2 spiriting away.
**escampada** f. clear spell [on a rainy day].
**escampar** tr. to clear out [a place]. 2 intr. to stop raining. 3 [of weather] to clear up.
**escampavía** f. NAUT. scout. 2 NAUT. revenue cutter.
**escanciador, -ra** m.-f. cupbearer.
**escanciar** tr. to pour, serve [wine]. 2 intr. to drink wine.
**escandalera** f. racket, uproar.
**escandalizador, -ra** adj. scandalizing. 2 m.-f. scandalizer. 3 noisy, boisterous person.
**escandalizar** tr. to give scandal to. 2 to scandalize, shock. 3 to make a lot of noise. 4 ref. to be scandalized, be shocked.
**escándalo** m. scandal: dar ~, to give scandal; dar un ~, to make a scene. 2 tumult, noise, disturbance; shouting.
**escandaloso, -sa** adj. scandalous. 2 noisy. 3 shameful.
**escandallar** tr. NAUT. to sound.
**escandallo** m. NAUT. sounding lead.
**Escandinavia** f. pr. n. GEOG. Scandinavia.
**escandinavo, -va** adj.-n. Scandinavian.
**escandir** tr. to scan [verse].
**escantillar** tr. ARCH. to measure off.
**escantillón** m. pattern, scantling. 2 ESCUADRÍA.
**escaño** m. settle, bench with a back.
**escapada** f. escape, flight. 2 en una ~, in a jiffy.
**escapar** intr.-ref. to escape; to flee, run away, make one's escape; to slip away: ~ a, to escape [death, danger, etc.]: escapársele a uno [una cosa], not to notice; to let slip, say inadvertently. 2 ref. [of gas, water, etc.]. to escape, leak out.

**escaparate** *m.* show window. *2* glass cabinet.
**escapatoria** *f.* escape, getaway. *2* evasion, way out [of difficulty, etc.].
**escape** *m.* escape, flight: *a* ~, at full speed, in great haste. *2* escape, leak, leakage. *3* exhaust, valve. *4* HOROL. escapement.
**escapo** *m.* ARCH., BOT. scape.
**escápula** *f.* ANAT. scapula, shoulder blade.
**escapular** *adj.* scapular.
**escapulario** *m.* ECCL. scapular, scapulary.
**escaque** *m.* square [of chessboard]. *2* HER. square.
**escara** *f.* SURG. eschar, slough.
**escarabajear** *intr.* to crawl around. *2* to scribble, scrawl. *3* coll. [of worry, care, etc.] to gnaw.
**escarabajo** *m.* ENT. beetle, scarab: ~ *pelotero,* tumblebug. *2 pl.* fig. scrawl, scribbling.
**escaramujo** *m.* BOT. dog rose. *2* BOT. hip. *3* ZOOL. goose barnacle.
**escaramuza** *f.* skirmish. *2* dispute, quarrel.
**escaramuzar** *intr.* to skirmish.
**escarapela** *f.* cockade. *2* dispute, quarrel.
**escarbadientes** *m.* toothpick.
**escarbaorejas** *m.* earpick.
**escarbar** *tr.* to scratch [the ground]. *2* to clean out, pick [one's ears or teeth]. *3* to poke [the fire]. *4* to dig into, to investigate.
**escarcela** *f.* a pouch hanging from the waist. *2* game bag. *3* skirt [of plate armour].
**escarceo** *m.* small bubbling waves. *2 pl.* turns of spirited horses. *3* detour, circumlocution.
**escarcha** *f.* rime, hoarfrost, white frost.
**escarchada** *f.* BOT. ice plant.
**escarchar** *tr.* to frost [fruit; glass]. *2 impers.* to freeze, to rime: *anoche escarchó,* it froze last night.
**escarda** *f.* AGR. weeding. *2* weeding time. *3* weeding hoe.
**escardar, escardillar** *tr.* to weed. *2* to weed out.
**escardillo** *m.* weeding hoe.
**escariador** *m.* reamer [tool].
**escariar** *tr.* to ream [a hole].
**escarificador** *m.* SURG. scarifier, scarificator. *2* AGR. scarifier, cultivator.
**escarificar** *tr.* AGR., SURG. to scarify.
**escarlata** *adj.-f.* scarlet [colour; cloth].
**escarlatina** *f.* MED. scarlatina, scarlet fever.
**escarmenar** *tr.* CARMENAR. *2* to cheat.
**escarmentado, -da** *adj.* taught or warned by punishment or experience.
**escarmentar** *tr.* to inflict an exemplary punishment on. *2 intr.* to learn one's lesson, take warning. ¶ CONJUG. like *acertar.*
**escarmiento** *m.* lesson, warning; punishment.
**escarmiento, escarmiente,** etc. *irr.* V. ESCARMENTAR.
**escarnecedor, -ra** *adj.* mocking, jeering, scoffing. *2* shameful. *3 n.* mocker, jeerer, scoffer.
**escarnecer** *tr.* to mock, to jeer at, to scoff at, to ridicule.
**escarnio** *m.* scoffing, derision, mock.
**escaro** *m.* ICHTH. scarus, parrot fish.
**escarola** *f.* BOT. endive. *2* ruff [collar].
**escarpa** *f.* scarp, steep slope. *2* FORT. scarp.
**escarpado, -da** *adj.* abrupt, steep, cliffy.
**escarpadura** *f.* scarp, escarpment.
**escarpar** *tr.* to scarp, escarp. *2* SCULPT. to rasp.
**escarpelo** *m.* SURG. scalpel. *2* rasp.
**escarpia** *f.* hooked nail.
**escarpidor** *m.* wide toothed comb.
**escarpín** *m.* sock, thin-soled shoe. *2* woollen slipper.
**escarzano** *adj.* ARCH. segmental [arch].

**escasamente** *adv.* scarcely, hardly.
**escasear** *tr.* to give sparingly, to spare. *2 intr.* to be or become scarce.
**escasez** *f.* scarcity, dearth, shortness. *2* stinginess. *3* want, poverty.
**escaso, -sa** *adj.* scant, scanty, scarce. *2* stingy. *3* short: *andar* ~ *de,* to be short of. *4 dos millas escasas,* less than two miles.
**escatimar** *tr.* to stint, curtail, give sparingly.
**escatología** *f.* THEOL. eschatology. *2* scatology.
**escayola** *f.* scagliola. *2* stucco.
**escena** *f.* THEAT. stage: *poner en* ~, to stage [a play]. *2* scene. *3* THEAT. scenery.
**escenario** *m.* THEAT. stage, boards. *2* setting, environment.
**escénico, -ca** *adj.* scenic [pertaining to the stage].
**escenificación** *f.* adaptation for the scene.
**escenificar** *tr.* to adapt for the scene.
**escenografía** *f.* scenography. *2* scene painting.
**escenógrafo** *m.* scenographer. *2* scene painter.
**escepticismo** *m.* scepticism, skepticism.
**escéptico, -ca** *adj.* sceptical, skeptical. *2 m.-f.* sceptic, skeptic.
**escila** *f.* BOT. squill.
**escinco** *m.* ZOOL. skink.
**escindible** *adj.* divisible. *2* PHYS. fissionable.
**escindir** *tr.* to cut, divide, split.
**Escipión** *m. pr. n.* Scipio.
**escisión** *f.* scission, division, schism. *2* BIOL. fishion.
**esclarea** *f.* BOT. clary.
**esclarecer** *tr.* to light up, brighten. *2* to enlighten. *3* to ennoble, make illustrious. *4* to clear up, elucidate. ¶ CONJUG. like *agradecer.*
**esclarecido, -da** *adj.* noble, illustrious.
**esclarecimiento** *m.* enlightening. *2* clearing up, elucidation.
**esclarezco, esclarezca,** etc. *irr.* V. ESCLARECER.
**esclavina** *f.* cape, pelerine, tippet. *2* pilgrim's cloak.
**esclavitud** *f.* slavery.
**esclavizar** *tr.* to enslave.
**esclavo, -va** *adj.* enslaved. *2 m.-f.* slave. *3 f.* kind of bracelet.
**esclerénquima** *m.* BOT. sclerenchyma.
**esclerosis** *f.* MED. sclerosis.
**esclerótica** *f.* ANAT. sclera.
**esclusa** *f.* lock, canal lock, sluice.
**escoba** *f.* broom, besom. *2* BOT. broom.
**escobajo** *f.* old broom. *2* grape stem [with grapes removed].
**escobazo** *m.* blow with a broom.
**escobén** *m.* NAUT. hawsehole.
**escobilla** *f.* brush [for cleaning]. *2* ELECT. brush [of a dynamo]. *3* BOT. fuller's teasel. *4* BOT. broom heath.
**escobillar** *tr.* to brush.
**escobillón** *m.* brush or cleaner for firearms; swab.
**escobón** *m.* large broom.
**escocedura** *f.* chafe, soreness [skin irritation].
**escocer** *intr.* to smart, cause a burning sensation. *2* fig. to smart, to annoy. *3 ref.* to feel hurt. *4* [of skin] to chafe. ¶ CONJUG. like *mover.*
**escocés, -sa** *adj.* Scotch, Scottish. *2* plaid [fabric]. *3 m.-f.* Scot. *4 m.* Scotchman. *5* Scotch [language]. *6 f.* Scotchwoman.
**Escocia** *f. pr. n.* GEOG. Scotland.
**escocia** *f.* ARCH. scotia.
**escocimiento** *m.* ESCOZOR.
**escofieta** *f.* coif, woman's headdress of gauze.
**escofina** *f.* rough rasp.

**escoger** *tr.* to choose, select, pick, pick out, sort.
**escogido, -da** *adj.* chosen. *2* choice, select.
**escogimiento** *m.* choosing, choice, selection, picking out, sorting.
**escolanía** *f.* choir school. *2* choirboys.
**escolapio, -pia** *adj.* pertaining to the *Scuole Pie*. *2 m.* piarist.
**escolar** *adj.* [pertaining to] school, scholastic. *2 m.* pupil, student.
**escolaridad** *f.* schooling: ~ *obligatoria*, compulsory schooling.
**escolarización** *f.* schooling.
**escolasticismo** *m.* scholasticism.
**escolástico, -ca** *adj.* scholastic(al. *2 m.* PHIL. Scholastic. *3 f.* Scholasticism.
**escolio** *m.* scholium.
**escoliosis** *f.* MED. scoliosis.
**escolopendra** *f.* ZOOL. scolopendra, centipede. *2* BOT. hart's tongue.
**escolta** *f.* escort. *2* NAUT. convoy, convoying ship.
**escoltar** *tr.* to escort. *2* NAUT. to convoy.
**escollera** *f.* breakwater.
**escollo** *m.* NAUT. reef, rock. *2* fig. danger, difficulty.
**escombrar** *tr.* to clear of rubbish, obstacles, etc.
**escombro** *m.* debris, rubbish. *2* MIN. deads.
**esconce** *m.* angle, corner.
**esconder** *tr.* to hide, conceal. *2* to harbour, contain. *3 ref.* to hide, be hidden; to lurk, skulk.
**escondidas (a)** *adv.* secretly, on the sly. *2 a escondidas de*, without the knowledge of.
**escondite** *m.* hiding place, cache. *2* hide-and-seek.
**escondrijo** *m.* hiding place, cache.
**escopeta** *f.* shotgun, gun; fowling piece: ~ *de viento*, air gun.
**escopetazo** *m.* gunshot.
**escopetear** *tr.* to fire a gun [at someone] repeatedly. *2 ref.* to exchange compliments or insults.
**escopetería** *f.* musketry. *2* musketry fire.
**escopetero** *m.* musketeer. *2* gun-maker, gunsmith.
**escopetón** *m.* (scorn.) big musket or shotgun.
**escopleadura** *f.* chisel cut, mortise, notch.
**escoplear** *tr.* CARP. to chisel, mortise, notch.
**escoplo** *m.* CARP. chisel.
**escora** *f.* NAUT. shore [prop]. *2* NAUT. list, heel.
**escorar** *tr.* NAUT. to shore up. *2 intr.* NAUT. to list, heel.
**escorbuto** *m.* MED. scurvy, scorbutus.
**escordio** *m.* BOT. water germander.
**escoria** *f.* scoria, dross, slag. *2* fig. dregs [worthless part, refuse]. *3* scoria [cinderlike lava].
**escoriación** *f.* excoriation.
**escorial** *m.* slag dump; slag heap.
**Escorial (el)** *m. pr. n.* Escorial or Escurial.
**escoriar** *tr.* to excoriate.
**escorpena, escorpina** *f.* ICHTH. scorpion fish.
**escorpión** *m.* ZOOL. scorpion. *2* ICHTH. scorpion fish. *3* ASTR. Scorpio.
**escorzar** *tr.* PAINT. to foreshorten.
**escorzo** *m.* PAINT. foreshortening.
**escorzonera** *f.* BOT. viper's-grass.
**escota** *f.* NAUT. sheet.
**escotado, -da** *adj.* low-necked. *2* indented.
**escotadura** *f.* low cut in the neck [of a garment]. *2* THEAT. large stage trap. *3* indentation, cut.
**escotar** *tr.* to cut the neck of [a garment]; to cut an indentation in. *2* to club, pay one's share of a common expense.
**escote** *m.* low-neck. *2* tucker. *3* share, part paid [of a common expense].
**escotera** *f.* NAUT. sheet hole.

**escotero, -ra** *adj.* walking or travelling unburdened. *2* NAUT. sailing alone [ship].
**escotilla** *f.* NAUT. hatchway.
**escotillón** *m.* trap door. *2* THEAT. stage trap. *3* NAUT. scuttle.
**escozor** *m.* irritation, burning pain or sensation.
**escriba** *m.* scribe [teacher of Jewish law].
**escribanía** *f.* court clerkship. *2* court clerk's office. *3* inkstand. *4* writing desk.
**escribano** *m.* court clerk. *2* obs. notary.
**escribiente** *m.* amanuensis; clerk.
**escribir** *tr.-intr.* to write. *2 ref.* to hold correspondence. ¶ PAST. p. irreg.: *escrito*.
**escriño** *m.* casket, jewel case. *2* straw basket.
**escrito, -ta** *p. p. irreg.* of ESCRIBIR. *2 m.* writing [written paper, etc.]: *por ~*, in writing. *3* LAW brief, bill, written plea.
**escritor, -ra** *m.-f.* writer.
**escritorio** *m.* writing desk; cabinet. *2* office, study; countinghouse.
**escritorzuelo** *m. dim.* scribbler.
**escritura** *f.* writing: ~ *a máquina*, typewriting. *2* handwriting, hand, script. *3* LAW deed, instrument. *4 La Escritura*, the Scripture.
**escriturar** *tr.* LAW to establish by deed or legal instrument. *2* to engage [an artist].
**escrófula** *f.* MED. scrofula.
**escrofularia** *f.* BOT. figwort.
**escrofuloso, -sa** *adj.* scrofulous.
**escroto** *m.* ANAT. scrotum.
**escrúpulo** *m.* scruple. *2* ESCRUPULOSIDAD.
**escrupulosidad** *f.* scrupulosity, scrupulousness.
**escrupuloso, -sa** *adj.* scrupulous. *2* squeamish.
**escrutador, -ra** *adj.* searching. *2 m.-f.* searcher, examiner, scrutinizer. *3* teller of votes.
**escrutar** *tr.* to search, examine, scrutinize. *2* to tell the votes [at an election].
**escrutinio** *m.* scrutiny, examination. *2* telling or counting of votes [at an election].
**escuadra** *f.* NAV. fleet, squadron. *2* MIL. squad. *3* squad, gang. *4* angle iron. *5* carpenter's square, drawing triangle: *falsa ~*, bevel square; *a ~*, square, at right angles.
**escuadrar** *tr.* to square [form with right angles].
**escuadría** *f.* scantling [of timber].
**escuadrilla** *f.* NAV., AER. escadrille.
**escuadrón** *m.* MIL. squadron [of cavalry].
**escualidez** *f.* leanness, emaciation. *2* squalor.
**escuálido, -da** *adj.* lean, pale, emaciate. *2* squalid, filthy. *3 m. pl.* ICHTH. Squalidae.
**escualo** *m.* ICHTH. shark.
**escucha** *f.* act of listening: *estar a la ~*, to be listening. *2* MIL. night scout.
**escuchar** *tr.* to listen to. *2* to mind, heed [advice, etc.]. *3 intr.* to listen.
**escuchimizado, -da** *adj.* lean, weak.
**escudar** *tr.* to shield, protect. *2 ref.* to protect oneself. *3* to take refuge in [a law, authority, etc.].
**escudería** *f.* squiredom, squire post. *2* AUTO. stable.
**escudero** *m.* HIST. shield bearer, squire. *2* HIST. nobleman. *3* HIST. lady's page.
**escudete** *m.* escutcheon. *2* SEW. gusset.
**escudilla** *f.* bowl [hemispherical cup].
**escudo** *m.* shield, buckler. *2* shield, protection. *3* escutcheon. *4* ZOOL. scute. *5* escudo [money]. *6* ~ *de armas*, coat of arms.
**escudriñar** *tr.* to scrutinize, search; to investigate; to pry into.
**escuece, escueza,** etc. *irr.* V. ESCOCER.
**escuela** *f.* school [teaching establishment]: ~ *de artes y oficios*, trade school; ~ *dominical*, Sun-

day school; ~ *de la experiencia, de la vida,* fig. school of experience, of life. 2 school [philosophic, artistic, etc.]. 3 school-house.
**escuerzo** *m.* toad. 2 fig. little runt [person].
**escueto, -ta** *adj.* bare, plain, unadorned, strict, unqualified.
**Esculapio** *pr. n.* MYTH. Aesculapius.
**esculpir** *tr.* to sculpture, carve; to engrave.
**escultora** *f.* sculptress.
**escultor** *m.* sculptor.
**escultórico, -ca** *adj.* sculptural [of sculpture].
**escultura** *f.* sculpture [art and work].
**escultural** *adj.* sculptural, sculpturesque.
**escupidera** *f.* cuspidor, spittoon.
**escupir** *intr.* to spit [eject saliva, etc.]. 2 *tr.* to spit [saliva, etc.]. 3 to spit at. 4 to throw off, discharge.
**escupitajo** *m.,* **escupitina** *f.* spit [spitted saliva].
**escurreplatos** *m.* plate rack, dish-draining rack.
**escurridero** *m.* draining place.
**escurridizo, -za** *adj.* slippery.
**escurrido, -da** *adj.* narrow-hipped.
**escurridor** *m.* colander. 2 ESCURREPLATOS.
**escurriduras, escurrimbres** *f. pl.* heeltap, last dregs.
**escurrir** *tr.* to drain [a vessel, plates, a liquid, etc.]. 2 to wring [moisture out of]. 3 *intr.* to drip, ooze, trickle. 4 *intr.-ref.* to slip, glide. 5 *ref.* to slip away, slip out. 6 to say too much.
**esdrújulo, -la** *adj.-m.* GRAM. accented on the antepenult, proparoxytonic [word].
1) **ese** *f.* name of the letter *s.* 2 S-shaped link [of chain]. 3 MUS. sound hole [of violin]. 4 *hacer eses,* [of a drunken man] to zigzag.
2) **ese, esa,** *pl.* **esos, esas** *adj.* that, those [nearest to the one addressed].
**ése, ésa,** *pl.* **ésos, ésas** *pron.* that one, those [nearest to the one addressed]. 2 *ésa,* your town or city. 3 *ni por ésas,* nothing doing. 4 *¡a ése!,* at him!
**esencia** *f.* essence. 2 CHEM. essence, perfume. 3 *quinta ~,* quintessence.
**esencial** *adj.* essential.
**esenciero** *m.* scent bottle.
**esfenoides** *m.* ANAT. sphenoid, sphenoid bone.
**esfera** *f.* GEOM., ASTR., GEOG. sphere. 2 sphere [of action, influence, etc.]. 3 sphere, rank, social class. 4 dial [of clock].
**esfericidad** *f.* sphericity.
**esférico, -ca** *adj.* spherical.
**esferoidal** *adj.* spheroidal.
**esferoide** *f.* GEOM. spheroid.
**esfinge** *f.* sphinx. 2 ENT. hawk moth.
**esfinter** *m.* ANAT. sphincter.
**esforzadamente** *adv.* vigorously, bravely.
**esforzado, -da** *adj.* brave, courageous.
**esforzar** *tr.* to give strength. 2 to give courage. 3 *ref.* to exert oneself, try hard, strive.
**esfuerzo** *m.* effort, exertion. 2 ENG. stress. 3 courage, spirit, vigor.
**esfumar** *tr.* DRAW. to stump. 2 PAINT. to tone down, soften. 3 *ref.* to disappear, evanesce.
**esfuminar** *tr.* ESFUMAR.
**esfumino** *m.* DRAW. stump.
**esgrima** *f.* fencing [art].
**esgrimidor** *m.* fencer, swordsman.
**esgrimir** *tr.* to wield, brandish [a weapon]; to enforce, urge, make use of [arguments, reasons, etc.]. 2 *intr.* to fence, practice fencing.
**esguín** *m.* ICHTH. parr, young salmon.
**esguince** *m.* dodge [to avoid a blow]. 2 frown, wry face. 3 sprain [of a joint].

**eslabón** *m.* link [of a chain]. 2 steel [for sharpening knives; for striking sparks from flint].
**eslabonamiento** *m.* linking, sequence, concatenation.
**eslabonar** *tr.* to link, interlink, concatenate. 2 *ref.* to be linked or concatenated.
**eslavo, -va** *adj.* Slav, Slavic. 2 *m.-f.* Slavish. 3 *m.* Slavic [language].
**eslinga** *f.* NAUT. sling.
**eslingar** *tr.* NAUT. to sling up.
**eslizón** *m.* ZOOL. seps.
**eslogan** *m.* slogan.
**eslora** *f.* NAUT. length [of ship]. 2 NAUT. carling.
**eslovaco, -ca** *adj.-n.* Slovak, Slovakian.
**esloveno, -na** *adj.-n.* Slovene, Slovenian.
**esmaltado** *m.* enamelling.
**esmaltador** *m.* enameller.
**esmaltadura** *f.* enamelling.
**esmaltar** *tr.* to enamel. 2 to variegate with bright colors. 2 to adorn, embellish.
**esmalte** *m.* enamel. 2 enamel work. 3 smalt. 4 HER. tincture.
**esmaltín** *m.* smalt.
**esmeradamente** *adv.* carefully, with great care, neatly. 2 elegantly.
**esmerado, -da** *adj.* careful, conscientious, painstaking. 2 conscientiously done.
**esmeralda** *f.* emerald. 2 ~ *oriental,* corundum.
**esmeraldino, -na** *adj.* emeraldlike.
**esmerar** *tr.* to polish, brighten. 2 *ref. esmerarse en* or *por,* to do one's best to, to take pains to.
**esmerejón** *m.* ORN. goshawk. 2 ancient small cannon.
**esmeril** *m.* emery. 2 ancient small cannon.
**esmerilar** *tr.* to emery, to grind with emery.
**esmero** *m.* great care, conscientiousness, neatness.
**Esmirna** *pr. n.* GEOG. Smyrna.
**esmirriado, -da** *adj.* DESMIRRIADO.
**esmoquin** *m.* tuxedo, dinner jacket.
**esnob** *m.-f.* snob, foolish admirer of new things.
**esnobismo** *m.* snobism, fawning admiration of new things.
**esnórquel** *m.* snorkel.
**eso** *pron. neut.* that, that thing; that matter: ~ *es,* that is it; *por ~,* for that reason; *a ~ de la una,* about one o'clock.
**esófago** *m.* ANAT. esophagus.
**Esopo** *m. pr. n.* Aesop.
**esos, esas** *adj. pl.* of *ese, esa.*
**ésos, ésas** *pr. pl.* of *ése, ésa.*
**esotérico, -ca** *adj.* esoteric.
**esotro, -tra** *adj.-pron.* that other.
**espabiladeras** *f. pl.* snuffers.
**espabilado, -da** *adj.* wide-awake. 2 quick, smart, sharp.
**espaciador** *m.* spacer, space bar, spacing key.
**espacial** *adj.* spatial, space.
**espaciar** *tr.* to space, space out. 2 PRINT. to space, lead. 3 *tr.-ref.* to spread, diffuse. 4 *ref.* to expatiate. 5 to relax, amuse oneself.
**espacio** *m.* space. 2 room, capacity. 3 blank [empty space]. 4 delay, slowness.
**espacioso, -sa** *adj.* spacious, roomy. 2 slow, deliberate.
**espada** *f.* sword, rapier: *entre la ~ y la pared,* between the devil and the deep blue sea. 2 swordsman. 3 BULLF. matador. 4 ace of ESPADAS. 5 *pl.* CARDS suit equivalent to spades.
**espadachín** *m.* swordsman. 2 spadassin, bravo.
**espadaña** *f.* BOT. cattail, reed mace. 2 bell gable.

**espadar** *tr.* to scutch, swingle [flax or hemp].
**espádice** *m.* BOT. spadix.
**espadilla** *f.* scutch, swingle. 2 scull [oar]. 3 ace of ESPADAS. 4 hair bodkin.
**espadillar** *tr.* ESPADAR.
**espadín** *m.* narrow gala sword; rapier.
**espadón** *m.* aug. large sword. 2 high-up [person].
**espaguetis** *m. pl.* spaghetti.
**espalda** *f. sing. & pl.* back [of the human body, of a garment, etc.]; shoulders: *cargado de espaldas,* round-shouldered; *a espaldas de,* behind someone's back; *de espaldas,* backwards; *echarse una cosa a las espaldas,* not to bother oneself about a thing; *echarse una cosa sobre las espaldas,* to take on, assume something as a responsibility; *guardar las espaldas a uno,* to protect someone.
**espaldar** *m.* backpiece [of cuirass]. 2 carapace [of turtle]. 3 back [of a seat]. 4 HORT. spalier.
**espaldarazo** *m.* accolade; slap on the back.
**espaldera** *f.* HORT. spalier.
**espaldilla** *f.* shoulder blade. 2 shoulder [of mutton, pork, etc.].
**espaldón** *m.* CARP. shoulder. 2 FORT. entrenchment.
**espalmar** *tr.* DESPALMAR.
**espalto** *m.* PAINT. dark glaze.
**espantada** *f.* sudden flight [of an animal]. 2 sudden scare, sudden giving up from fear.
**espantadizo, -za** *adj.* scary, shy.
**espantajo** *m.* scarecrow; fright.
**espantamoscas** *m.* flyflap.
**espantapájaros** *m.* scarecrow.
**espantar** *tr.* to frighten, scare. 2 to chase, drive away, scare away. 3 *ref.* to take fright. 4 to marvel, be astonished.
**espanto** *m.* fright, terror. 2 astonishment.
**espantoso, -sa** *adj.* fearful, frightful, dreadful, awful. 2 astonishing, astounding.
**España** *f. pr. n.* GEOG. Spain.
**español, -la** *adj.* Spanish. 2 *m.-f.* Spaniard. 3 *m.* Spanish [language].
**españolismo** *m.* love of Spain, Spanish patriotism. 2 Spanishness. 3 Hispanicism.
**españolizar** *tr.* to make Spanish or Spanishlike.
**esparadrapo** *m.* court plaster, sticking plaster.
**esparaván** *m.* GAVILÁN 1. 2 VET. spavin.
**esparcido, -da** *adj.* scattered. 2 merry, gay, frank.
**esparcimiento** *m.* scattering, spreading, dissemination. 2 relaxation, recreation, amusement.
**esparcir** *tr.* to scatter, spread, disseminate. 2 to recreate, entertain. 3 *ref.* to scatter, spread [be spread]. 4 to amuse oneself.
**espárrago** *m.* BOT. asparagus. 2 awning pole. 3 peg ladder.
**esparraguera** *f.* BOT. asparagus [plant]. 2 asparagus bed. 3 asparagus dish.
**esparrancado, -da** *adj.* with one's legs wide apart. 2 spread apart.
**esparrancarse** *ref.* to spread the legs apart.
**Esparta** *f. pr. n.* HIST. Sparta.
**espartano, -na** *adj.-n.* Spartan.
**espartería** *f.* esparto goods. 2 esparto goods' shop.
**espartero, -ra** *m.-f.* maker or seller of esparto goods.
**esparto** *m.* esparto, esparto grass.
**espasmo** *m.* MED. spasm.
**espasmódico, -ca** *adj.* MED. spasmodic.
**espata** *f.* BOT. spathe.
**espatarrarse** *ref.* to open one's legs wide, to do the splits.
**espático, -ca** *adj.* spathic.
**espato** *m.* MINER. spar: ~ *flúor,* fluor spar.

**espátula** *f.* spatula; palette knife. 2 ORN. spoonbill.
**especería** *f.* ESPECIERÍA.
**especia** *f.* spice [condiment].
**especial** *adj.* especial. 2 special: *en* ~, specially.
**especialidad** *f.* speciality; specialty.
**especialista** *adj.-n.* specialist.
**especialización** *f.* specialization.
**especializar** *intr.-ref.-tr.* to specialize: *especializarse en,* to specialize in.
**especiar** *tr.* to spice.
**especie** *f.* NAT. HIST., PHIL. species. 2 species, kind, sort. 3 matter, notion, piece of news. 4 pretext, show. 5 THEOL. *especies sacramentales,* species. 6 *en* ~, in kind, not in money.
**especiería** *f.* epicery, spices. 2 spice shop.
**especiero** *m.* spice dealer. 2 spice box.
**especificación** *f.* specification [stating precisely, in detail].
**específicamente** *adv.* specifically.
**especificar** *tr.* to specify [state precisely, in detail]; to itemize.
**específico, -ca** *adj.* specific. 2 *m.* MED. specific. 3 patent medicine.
**espécimen** *m.* specimen.
**especioso, -sa** *adj.* specious. 2 neat, beautiful.
**espectacular** *adj.* spectacular.
**espectáculo** *m.* spectacle; show, pageant: *dar un* ~, to make a scene.
**espectador, -ra** *m.-f.* spectator. 2 *pl.* audience.
**espectral** *adj.* spectral, ghostly. 2 PHYS. spectral.
**espectro** *m.* spectre, ghost. 2 PHYS. spectrum.
**espectrograma** *m.* PHYS. spectrogram.
**espectroscopia** *f.* spectroscopy.
**especulación** *f.* speculation, consideration, reflection. 2 COM. speculation, venture.
**especulador, -ra** *adj.* speculating. 2 *m.-f.* speculator.
**especular** *tr.* to speculate about, consider attentively. 2 *intr.* COM. to speculate.
**especulativo, -va** *adj.* speculative.
**espéculo** *m.* SURG., MED. speculum.
**espejear** *intr.* to shine like a mirror.
**espejería** *f.* mirror factory or shop.
**espejismo** *m.* mirage. 2 fig. illusion.
**espejo** *m.* mirror, looking glass: ~ *de cuerpo entero,* pier glass. 2 mirror, model. 3 NAUT. ~ *de popa,* escutcheon.
**espejuelo** *m.* small looking glass. 2 MINER. selenite. 3 leaf of talc. 4 a lure for larks. 5 *pl.* spectacles.
**espeleología** *f.* speleology.
**espelta** *f.* BOT. spelt.
**espeluznante** *adj.* hair-raising, dreadful, horrifying.
**espeluznar** *tr.-ref.* DESPELUZAR.
**espeluzno** *m.* shuddering.
**espeque** *m.* handspike, lever. 2 prop.
**espera** *f.* wait, waiting; expectation: *sala de* ~, waiting room. 2 delay, respite: *esto no tiene* ~, this admits of no delay. 3 LAW stay. 4 patience, restraint.
**esperantismo** *m.* Esperantism.
**esperanto** *m.* Esperanto.
**esperanza** *f.* hope, hopes, hopefulness.
**esperanzado, -da** *adj.* hopeful [having hopes].
**esperanzar** *tr.* to give hopes.
**esperar** *tr.* to hope, hope for; to expect: ~ *que,* to hope that. 2 to look forward to. 3 *tr.-intr.* to await, wait [for]: ~ *a que,* to wait until. 4 *intr.* to hope, to trust: ~ *en Dios,* to trust in God. 5 to wait, stay.
**esperma** *f.* sperm. 2 ~ *de ballena,* spermaceti.

**espermatozoo** *m.* BIOL. spermatozoid.

**espernada** *f.* open end link [of chain].

**esperpento** *m.* fright, sight [ugly, slovenly person or thing]. 2 absurdity.

1) **espesar** *m.* thickness, deep [of a wooded land].

2) **espesar** *tr.* to thicken [inspissate; make closer]. 2 *ref.* to thicken [become thick or thicker].

**espeso, -sa** *adj.* thick, dense, close, heavy, thickset. 2 close-woven. 3 thick [wall, etc.]. 4 dirty, untidy.

**espesor** *m.* thickness.

**espesura** *f.* thickness. 2 thicket, dense wood. 3 dirtiness, untidiness.

**espetar** *tr.* to spit, skewer. 2 to run [a knife, etc.] through. 3 coll. to spring [something] on [one]. 4 *ref.* to stiffen, assume a solemn air. 5 to thrust oneself [into a place].

**espetón** *m.* spit; pocker; rapier. 2 large pin.

**espía** *m.-f.* spy [person]. 2 *f.* NAUT. warp.

**espiar** *tr.* to spy, spy on. 2 *intr.* NAUT. to warp.

**espicanardo** *m.* BOT. spikenard.

**espícula** *f.* ZOOL. spicule.

**espichar** *tr.* to prick. 2 *intr.* coll. to die.

**espiche** *m.* pointed instrument. 2 peg, spigot.

**espiga** *f.* BOT. spike, ear. 2 shank, tang [of knife, etc.]. 3 CARP. tenon. 4 brad, peg, treenail. 5 clapper [of bell]. 6 fuse [of bomb]. 7 NAUT. masthead.

**espigado, -da** *adj.* spikelike. 2 AGR. seeded. 3 tall, grown [young person or tree].

**espigador, -ra** *m.-f.* gleaner.

**espigar** *tr.-intr.* to glean. 2 *tr.* CARP. to tenon. 3 *intr.* [of grain] to ear. 4 *ref.* AGR. to run to seed. 5 [of a person] to grow tall.

**espigón** *m.* point of sharp tool or nail. 2 peaky hill. 3 breakwater, jetty.

**espigueo** *m.* gleaning. 2 gleaning season.

**espiguilla** *f.* spikelet. 2 BOT. meadow grass.

**espín** *m.* ZOOL. porcupine.

**espina** *f.* thorn: fig. *sacarse la ~,* to get even. 2 splinter. 3 fishbone. 4 spine, backbone: *~ dorsal,* spinal column. 5 scruple, suspicion: *dar mala ~,* to make one suspicious. 6 worry, pain.

**espinaca** *f.* BOT. spinach.

**espinal** *adj.* spinal.

**espinapez** *m.* herringbone [in parquetry floors].

1) **espinar** *m.* place full of thornbushes.

2) **espinar** *tr.* to prick with thorns. 2 fig. to prick, wound. 3 *ref.* to get pricked [with a thorn].

**espinazo** *m.* spine, backbone. 2 ARCH. keystone.

**espinel** *m.* FISH. trawl line.

**espinela** *f.* MINER. spinel ruby. 2 ten-line stanza.

**espineta** *f.* MUS. spinet.

**espingarda** *f.* long Moorish gun. 2 a small cannon.

**espinilla** *f.* shin bone. 2 MED. blackhead.

**espinillera** *f.* ARMOUR. greave, jambe. 2 shin guard.

**espino** *m.* BOT. thornbush, hawthorn: *~ albar* or *blanco,* hawthorn; *~ cerval,* buckthorn; *~ negro,* blackthorn. 2 *~ artificial,* barbed wire.

**espinosismo** *m.* Spinozism.

**espinoso, -sa** *adj.* spiny, thorny. 2 arduous, delicate.

**espionaje** *m.* spying, espionage.

**espira** *f.* GEOM. spiral; spire. 2 turn [of a winding]. 3 ZOOL. spire [of a shell].

**espiración** *f.* PHYSIOL. expiration. 2 THEOL. spiration.

**espiral** *adj.-f.* GEOM. spiral. 2 *f.* HOROL. hairspring.

**espirar** *tr.-intr.* PHYSIOL. to expire. 2 *tr.* to exhale [an odour]. 3 to infuse a divine spirit in.

**espirilo** *m.* BACT. spirillum.

**espiritado, -da** *adj.* coll. ghostlike [extremely thin].

**espiritismo** *m.* spiritualism, spiritism.

**espiritista** *adj.* spiritualistic, spiritistic. 2 *m.-f.* spiritualist, spiritist.

**espiritoso, -sa** *adj.* spirited, lively. 2 spirituous.

**espíritu** *m.* spirit [in practically every sense]: *~ de cuerpo,* esprit de corps; *el ~ y la letra,* the letter and the spirit; *pobre de ~,* poor in spirit, pusillanimous. 2 ghost: *Espíritu Santo,* Holy Ghost.

**espiritual** *adj.* spiritual, ghostly.

**espiritualidad** *f.* spirituality.

**espiritualismo** *m.* PHIL. spiritualism; idealism.

**espiritualista** *adj.* PHIL. spiritualistic. 2 *m.-f.* PHIL. spiritualist.

**espiritualizar** *tr.* to spiritualize.

**espiritualmente** *adv.* spiritually. 2 wittily.

**espirituoso, -sa** *adj.* ESPIRITOSO.

**espirómetro** *m.* spirometer.

**espiroqueta** *f.* ZOOL. spirochaete, spirochete.

**espita** *f.* cock, tap, faucet [for a cask, etc.].

**espitar** *tr.* to tap, to put a cock on [a cask, etc.].

**espito** *m.* PRINT. peel, hanger.

**esplendente** *adj.* resplendent, shining.

**esplender** *intr.* poet. to shine.

**esplendidez** *f.* splendour, magnificence. 2 abundance, liberality, generosity.

**espléndido, -da** *adj.* splendid, magnificent, grand. 2 liberal, generous. 3 resplendent.

**esplendor** *m.* splendour. 2 fulgency, radiance.

**esplendoroso, -sa** *adj.* splendid, resplendent, radiant.

**esplenio** *m.* ANAT. splenius.

**espliego** *m.* BOT. lavender.

**esplín** *m.* melancholy, spleen, the blues.

**espolada** *f.,* **espolazo** *m.* prick with a spur.

**espolear** *tr.* to spur; to incite, to stimulate.

**espoleta** *f.* fuse [of bomb]. 2 wishbone [of bird].

**espolín** *m.* spur fixed to the heel of boot.

**espolio** *m.* ECCL. spolium.

**espolique** *m.* groom who walks in front of his master's horse.

**espolón** *m.* spur [of bird; of flower; of a range of mountains]. 2 beak, ram [of warship]. 3 cutwater [of bridge]. 4 ARCH. buttress. 5 breakwater, jetty.

**espolvorear** *tr.* DESPOLVOREAR. 2 to sprinkle with a powdered substance.

**espondaico, -ca** *adj.* spondaic.

**espondeo** *m.* spondee.

**espongiarios** *m. pl.* ZOOL. spongiae.

**esponja** *f.* sponge.

**esponjado, -da** *adj.* spongy, fluffy [wool, hair]. 2 *m.* sugar bar.

**esponjar** *tr.* to make spongious or fluffy. 2 *ref.* to become elated, proud. 3 to glow with health.

**esponjera** *f.* sponge tray.

**esponjosidad** *f.* sponginess, spongiousness.

**esponjoso, -sa** *adj.* spongy, spongious, porous.

**esponsales** *m. pl.* betrothal, spousals.

**espontanearse** *ref.* to speak frankly.

**espontaneidad** *f.* spontaneity, spontaneousness.

**espontáneo, -a** *adj.* spontaneous.

**espora** *f.* BIOL. spore.

**esporádico, -ca** *adj.* sporadic.

**esporangio** *m.* BOT. sporangium.

**esporidio** *m.* BOT. sporidium.

**esportilla** *f.* ESPUERTA.

**esportillo** *m.* esparto basket.

**esposa** *f.* spouse, wife. 2 *pl.* handcuffs, manacles.

**esposar** *tr.* to handcuff.

**esposo** *m.* spouse, husband. *2 pl.* husband and wife.

**esprint** *m.* sprint.

**espuela** *f.* spur [pricking instrument; incitement]. *2* BOT. ~ *de caballero*, larkspur.

**espuerta** *f.* two-handed esparto basket.

**espulgar** *tr.* to delouse, to clean of lice or fleas. *2* to examine closely.

**espulgo** *m.* delousing. *2* close examination, scrutiny.

**espuma** *f.* foam, froth, lather, spume. *2* scum. *3* ~ *de mar*, meerschaum.

**espumadera** *f.* COOK. skimmer [utensil].

**espumajear** *intr.* to foam [at the mouth].

**espumajo** *m.* ESPUMARAJO.

**espumante** *adj.* ESPUMOSO.

**espumar** *tr.* to skim, scum. *2 intr.* to foam, froth. *3* [of wine] to sparkle.

**espumarajo** *m.* froth from the mouth: *echar espumarajos*, to be furious.

**espumoso, -sa** *adj.* foamy, frothy, lathery. *2* sparkling [wine].

**espurio, -ria** *adj.* spurious.

**espurrear, espurriar** *tr.* to sprinkle with water, etc. squirted from the mouth.

**esputar** *tr.* EXPECTORAR.

**esputo** *m.* spittle, sputum.

**esqueje** *m.* HORT. cutting, slip.

**esquela** *f.* note, short letter. *2* ~ *mortuoria*, death note, death notice.

**esquelético, -ca** *adj.* skeletal, thin, wasted.

**esqueleto** *m.* ANAT., ZOOL. skeleton. *2* skeleton [thin person]. *3* framework.

**esquema** *m.* schema, scheme.

**esquemático, -ca** *adj.* schematic.

**esquematizar** *tr.* to sketch, outline.

**esquenanto** *m.* BOT. camel grass.

**esquí** *m.* ski. *2* skiing.

**esquiador, -ra** *m.-f.* skier.

**esquiar** *intr.* to ski.

**esquiciar** *tr.* PAINT. to sketch.

**esquicio** *m.* PAINT. sketch, outline.

**esquife** *m.* skiff, small boat.

**esquila** *f.* sheepshearing. *2* cattle bell. *3* call bell. *4* ZOOL. marine prawn. *5* BOT. squill.

**esquilador, -ra** *m.-f.* shearer [of sheep, etc.]; clipper [of horses]; trimmer [of dogs].

**esquilar** *tr.* to shear, clip [animals].

**esquileo** *m.* shearing, clipping [of animals], sheepshearing. *2* shearing pen. *3* shearing time.

**esquilmar** *tr.* to harvest. *2* to impoverish [the soil]. *3* to squeeze dry [a source of wealth].

**esquilón** *m.* large call bell or cattle bell.

**esquimal** *adj.-n.* Eskimo.

**esquina** *f.* corner, outside angle: *las cuatro esquinas*, puss in the corner.

**esquinado, -da** *adj.* cornered, angular. *2* difficult [person].

**esquinar** *tr.-intr.* to form a corner with, to be on the corner of. *2 tr.* to square [timber]. *3* to set [one] against [another]. *4 ref.* to quarrel, fall out.

**esquinazo** *m.* corner: *dar* ~ *a*, to avoid [someone], to give the slip [to].

**esquirla** *f.* splinter [of bone, stone, glass, etc.].

**esquirol** *m.* coll. blackleg, scab, strike breaker.

**esquisto** *m.* GEOL. schist, slate.

**esquivar** *tr.* to avoid, elude, evade, shun, dodge. *2 ref.* to withdraw, shy off.

**esquivez** *f.* disdain, coldness; gruffness.

**esquivo, -va** *adj.* disdainful, cold, shy. *2* elusive.

**esquizofrenia** *f.* MED. schizophrenia.

**esquizofrénico, -ca** *adj.-n.* MED. schizophrenic.

**esquizoide** *adj.-n.* MED. schizoid.

**estabilidad** *f.* stability.

**estabilización** *f.* stabilization.

**estabilizador, -ra** *adj.* stabilizing. *2 m.* stabilizer.

**estabilizar** *tr.* to stabilize. *2 ref.* to become stabilized.

**estable** *adj.* stable, steady, firm, permanent.

**establecer** *tr.* to establish. *2* to decree, order. *3 ref.* to settle, establish oneself, to take up residence, to set up in business. ¶ CONJUG. like *agradecer*.

**establecimiento** *m.* establishment, establishing. *2* establishment [institution, house], shop, store. *3* statute, ordinance.

**establezco, establezca**, etc. *irr.* V. ESTABLECER.

**establo** *m.* stable; cattle barn.

**estabular** *tr.* to stable, to raise in a stable.

**estaca** *f.* stake, pale, picket. *2* HORT. cutting. *3* stick, cudgel. *4* clamp nail.

**estacada** *f.* stockade, palisade, paling. *2* lists; battlefield: *dejar en la* ~, to leave in the lurch.

**estacar** *tr.* to tie [an animal] to a stake. *2* to stake off.

**estacazo** *m.* blow with a stick or cudgel.

**estación** *f.* state, position. *2* season [of the year]; season, time. *3* halt, stop. *4* RLY., RADIO., TEL., SURG., BIOL., ASTR. station. *5* ~ *balnearia*, bathing resort.

**estacional** *adj.* seasonal. *2* ASTR. stationary.

**estacionamiento** *m.* stationing. *2* AUTO. parking. *3* remainting stationary.

**estacionar** *tr.* to station. *2* to park [a car, etc.]. *3 ref.* to station, be stationed, stop; [of a car, etc.] to park. *4* to remain stationary.

**estacionario, -ria** *adj.* stationary.

**estacha** *f.* harpoon rope. *2* NAUT. line, hawser.

**estada** *f.* stay, sojourn.

**estadal** *m.* linear measure of about 10 ft. 9 in.

**estadía** *f.* stop, stay. *2* COM. demurrage.

**estadio** *m.* stadium.

**estadista** *m.* statesman. *2* statistician.

**estadística** *f.* statistics.

**estado** *m.* state, condition: ~ *de guerra*, martial law; ~ *líquido*, liquid state; ~ *civil*, status [celibacy, married state, etc.]; *tomar* ~, to marry, take orders, become a nun; *en* ~, *en* ~ *interesante*, with child; *en mal* ~, in bad condition. *2* estate, order, class: ~ *llano*, the commons. *3* POL. state, government, State, Nation. *4* lineal measure. *5* statement [of accounts, etc.]. *6* MIL. ~ *mayor*, staff. *7 pl.* HIST. *Estados Generales*, States General.

**Estados Unidos de América** *m. pr. n.* GEOG. United States of America.

**estadounidense** *adj.-n.* [citizen] of the U.S.

**estafa** *f.* cheat, swindle.

**estafador, -ra** *m.-f.* cheat, swindler.

**estafar** *tr.* to cheat, swindle.

**estafermo** *m.* quintain. *2* fig. person who stands like a dummy.

**estafeta** *f.* courier, post. *2* post-office branch. *3* diplomatic mail.

**estafilococo** *m.* BACT. staphylococcus.

**estafisagria** *f.* BOT. stavesacre.

**estalactita** *f.* stalactite.

**estalagmita** *f.* stalagmite.

**estallar** *intr.* to burst, to explode. *2* [of a fire, a war, etc.] to break out. *3* to burst [with anger, joy, etc.]. *4* RESTALLAR.

**estallido** *m.* explosion, outburst; snap, crack, crash: *dar un ~*, to explode, to crash.

**estambre** *m.* worsted, woolen yarn. *2* WEAV. varp. *3* BOT. stamen.

**Estambul** *m. pr. n.* GEOG. Istanbul.

**estamento** *m.* state. *2* each of the four estates of Aragon. *3* each of the two legislative bodies in Spain in the nineteenth century. *4* stratum, class.

**estaminífero, -ra** *adj.* BOT. staminate.

**estampa** *f.* stamped picture, print, engraving. *2* fig. appearance, figure. *3* likeness, image; *la mismísima ~ de*, the very image of. *4* printing; *dar a la ~*, to publish. *5* footstep, imprint.

**estampación** *f.* print(ing), stamp(ing).

**estampado** *m.* impression, stamping. *2* cotton print. *3* stamped object.

**estampador** *m.* stamper. *2* printer [of fabrics].

**estampar** *tr.* to print. *2* to stamp [metals]. *3* to stamp, impress, imprint, mark. *4* coll. to dash against.

**estampero** *m.* picture or print maker or seller.

**estampía (de)** *adv.* suddenly.

**estampida** *f.* ESTAMPIDO. *2* (Am.) rush, stampede.

**estampido** *m.* explosion, report, crack, crash.

**estampilla** *f.* rubber stamp [for signature]. *2* (Am.) postage or revenue stamp.

**estampillar** *tr.* to stamp [with a rubber stamp].

**estancamiento** *m.* stagnation, stagnancy.

**estancado, -da** *adj.* stagnant [water]. *2* bogged down, at a standstill, deadlocked, blocked.

**estancar** *tr.* to make stagnant, to hold up or back, to stop. *2* [of the government] to monopolize the sale of certain goods. *3* ref. to stagnate.

**estancia** *f.* stay, sojourn. *2* room, living room. *3* day in hospital. *4* stanza. *5* (Am.) ranch.

**estanciero** *m.* (Am.) rancher.

**estanco, -ca** *adj.* stanch, watertight. *2 m.* shop for selling government monopolized goods, tobacconist's.

**estándar** *m.* standard.

**estandarte** *m.* standard, banner.

**estannífero, -ra** *adj.* stanniferous.

**estanque** *m.* reservoir, basin, pond.

**estanquero, -ra** *m.* pond-keeper. *2 m.-f.* tobacconist.

**estantal** *m.* MAS. abutment, buttress.

**estantalar** *tr.* MAS. to buttress.

**estante** *adj.* veing [in a place], fixed, permanent. *2 m.* shelving, bookcase.

**estantería** *f.* shelving.

**estantigua** *f.* phantom, vision; scarecrow.

**estañadura** *f.* tinning, tinwork.

**estañar** *tr.* to tin. *2* to solder with tin.

**estaño** *m.* CHEM. tin.

**estaquilla** *f.* brad [nail]. *2* CARP. clamp nail.

**estaquillar** *tr.* to fasten with pegs.

**estar** *tr.-ref.* to be, to keep, stay, remain [in or at some place; in some condition or state]: *~ en casa*, to be at home; *~ enfermo*, to be ill; *~ or estarse quieto*, to be or keep still; *están verdes*, fig. sour grapes. *2 intr.* followed by gerund it constitutes the progressive form; *~ comiendo*, to be dining. *3* [of garments] to be too [wide, large, long, etc.] for one. *4 ~ a*, to abide by; to be the; to be selling for: *~ a lo que resulte*, to abide by the result; *estamos a 4 de abril*, it is the fourth of April; *las peras están a diez pesetas*, pears are selling at ten pesetas. *5 ~ al caer*, to be about to happen. *6 ~ a matar*, to be at daggers drawn. *7 ~ bien*, to be good, all right, to

suit, fit, become [one]; [of a person] to be in a good way; to be well off; to be in good health; *¡está bien!*, all right! *8 ~ bien con*, to be on good terms with. *9 ~ de paseo*, to be taking a walk; *~ de vacaciones*, to be on holiday. *10 ~ de más*, to be unnecessary; to be in the way. *11 estar en*, to lie; to understand: *en eso está*, that is where it lies; *¿está usted?*, do you understand? *12 ~ en mí, en ti, en sí*, to know what one is saying or doing. *13 no está en mí hacerlo*, it is not in my power to do it. *14 ~ en que*, to believe, be of opinion that. *15 ~ mal*, to be wrong, improper, incorrect, unbecoming; not to suit, fit or become one; [of a person] to be in a bad way, badly off. *16 ~ mal con*, to be on bad terms with. *17 ~ sobre mí, sobre ti, sobre sí*, to be on one's guard, be wary. *18 ~ para*, to be about to, on the point of; to be in a humour for. *19 ~ por*, to be for, to advocate; to have half a mind to; to be still to be [seen, done, etc.]. *20 le está bien empleado*, serve him right. *21 ¿estamos?*, do you understand?

¶ CONJUG.: IND. Pres.: estoy, estás, está; estamos, estáis, están | Pret.: estuve, estuviste, estuvo; estuvimos, estuvisteis, estuvieron. | SUBJ. Pres.: esté, estés, esté; estemos, estéis, estén. | Imperf.: estuviera, estuvieras, estuviera; estuviéramos, estuvierais, estuvieran, or estuviese, estuvieses, estuviese; estuviésemos, estuvieseis, estuviesen. | Fut.: estuviere, estuvieres, estuviere; estuviéremos; estuviereis, estuvieren. | IMPER.: está, esté; estemos, estad, estén. | PAST. P.: estado. | GER.: estando.

**estarcido** *m.* pounce drawing, stencil.

**estarcir** *tr.* to stencil.

**estarna** *f.* ORN. gray partridge.

**estatal** *adj.* [pertaining to] the state.

**estático, -ca** *adj.* static(al. *2* dumfounded, speechless. *3 f.* statics.

**estatismo** *m.* statism. *2* static state.

**estator** *m.* MACH., ELECT. stator.

**estatorreactor** *m.* AER. ramjet.

**estatua** *f.* statue.

**estatuaria** *f.* statuary [art].

**estatuario, -ria** *adj. n.* statuary.

**estatúder** *m.* stadholder.

**estatuilla** *f. dim.* statuette.

**estatuir** *tr.* to establish, order, decree. ¶ CONJUG. like *huir*.

**estatura** *f.* stature.

**estatuto** *m.* statutes, regulations [of a corporation, society, etc.]. *2* statute [in international and Roman law].

**estay** *m.* NAUT. stay.

1) **este** *m.* east, orient. *2* east wind.

2) **este** *adj. m.*, **esta** *adj. f.* this.

**éste** *pron. m.*, **ésta** *pron. f.* this, this one, the latter. *2 ésta*, this town [from where I am writing].

**esté**, etc. *irr.* V. ESTAR.

**estearina** *f.* CHEM. stearin.

**esteatita** *f.* MINER. steatite.

**Esteban** *m. pr. n.* Stephen.

**estela** *f.* wake [of a ship]; trail [of a luminous body]. *2* ARCH. stele. *3* ESTELARIA.

**estelar** *adj.* stellar, sidereal.

**estelaria** *f.* BOT. lady's mantle.

**estemple** *m.* MIN. stemple.

**estenografía** *f.* stenography.

**estenografiar** *tr.* to stenograph.

**estenordeste** *m.* east-northeast.

**estenotipia** *f.* stenotypy, stenotype.

**estentóreo, -a** *adj.* stentorian.
**estepa** *f.* steppe. *2* BOT. rockrose.
**esteparío, -ria** *adj.* [pertaining to the] steppe.
**estepilla** *f.* BOT. white-leaved rockrose.
**Ester** *f. pr. n.* Esther.
**éster, ester** *m.* CHEM. ester.
**estera** *f.* mat, matting.
**esterar** *tr.* to cover [the floor] with a mat.
1) **estercolar** *m.* dunghill.
2) **estercolar** *tr.* to dung, manure. *2 intr.* [of animals] to void the excrements.
**estercolero** *m.* dunghill. *2* dung collector.
**estéreo** *m.* stere [one cubic metre].
**estereofonía** *f.* stereo, stereophony.
**estereofónico, -ca** *adj.* stereophonic.
**estereografía** *f.* stereography.
**estereometría** *f.* stereometry.
**estereoscopio** *m.* stereoscope.
**estereotipado, -da** *adj.* stereotyped.
**estereotipar** *tr.* to stereotype.
**estereotipia** *f.* stereotypography, stereotypy.
**estereotipista** *m.* stereotypist.
**esterería** *f.* mat factory or shop.
**esterero, -ra** *m.-f.* mat maker or seller.
**estéril** *adj.* sterile, barren, fruitless. *2* futile, vain.
**esterilidad** *f.* sterility, barrenness. *2* futility.
**esterilización** *f.* sterilization.
**esterilizador, -ra** *adj.* sterilizing. *2 m.* sterilizer.
**esterilizar** *tr.* to sterilize.
**esterilla** *f.* small mat, door mat: ~ *eléctrica*, electric mat. *2* straw plait. *3* gold or silver braid.
**esterlina** *adj. libra* ~, sterling pound.
**esternón** *m.* ANAT. sternum, breastbone.
**estero** *m.* matting, act of laying mats on [floors]; matting season. *2* estuary, tideland.
**estertor** *m.* MED. stertor. *2* death rattle.
**estertoroso, -sa** *adj.* stertorous.
**esteta** *n.* aesthete.
**estética** *f.* aesthetics.
**esteticismo** *m.* aestheticism.
**estético, -ca** *adj.* aesthetic. *2* beautiful, having an artistic effect. *3 m.-f.* aesthete.
**estetoscopio** *m.* stethoscope.
**esteva** *f.* plough handle, stilt.
**estevado, -da** *adj.* bowlegged.
**estiaje** *m.* low water [in a river, lake, etc.]; low-water season.
**estiba** *f.* NAUT. stowage. *2* ORD. rammer.
**estibador** *m.* stevedore.
**estibar** *tr.* NAUT. to stow. *2* to pack, to stuff.
**estiércol** *m.* dung, manure.
**Estige** *f. pr. n.* MYTH. Styx.
**estigio, -gia** *adj.* Stygian.
**estigma** *m.* stigma.
**estigmatizar** *tr.* to stigmatize.
**estilar** *tr.* to draw [a document, etc.], in due style. *2 intr.* to use, to be in the habit of. *3 ref.* to be the fashion, the style, to be usual.
**estilete** *m.* stylet. *2* stiletto. *3* style [tool].
**estilista** *m.* stylist, mater of style.
**estilita** *m.* ECCL., HIST. stylite.
**estilización** *f.* stylizing, stylization, styling.
**estilizar** *tr.* to stylize.
**estilo** *m.* style, stylus [instrument for writing]. *2* style, gnomon. *3* BOT., ARCH., LIT., ART. style. *4* style, manner; use, custom, fashion: *al* ~ *de*, after the custom or style of; *por el* ~, *por este* ~, like that, of that kind.
**estilóbato** *m.* ARCH. stylobate.
**estilográfica** *adj. pluma* ~ or *f. estilográfica*, fountain pen.

**estima** *f.* esteem. *2* NAUT. dead reckoning.
**estimable** *adj.* estimable.
**estimación** *f.* esteem, estimation, regard: *propia* ~, self-respect. *2* estimation, estimate, valuation.
**estimar** *tr.* to esteem, hold in regard, set a high value on: ~ *en poco*, to hold in low esteem. *2* to judge, think. *3* to estimate, value.
**estimativa** *f.* power of judging. *2* instinct.
**estimulación** *f.* stimulation.
**estimulante** *adj.* stimulating. *2 m.* stimulant.
**estimular** *tr.* to stimulate. *2* to incite, encourage.
**estímulo** *m.* stimulus. *2* inducement, incentive. *3* encouragement.
**estío** *m.* summer, summer time.
**estipe** *m.* BOT. stipe.
**estipendiario** *m.* stipendiary.
**estipendio** *m.* stipend, salary, pay, fee.
**estípite** *m.* ARCH. pilaster in the form of an inverted truncated pyramid. *2* BOT. columnar trunk.
**estíptico, -ca** *adj.* styptic. *2* costive. *3* miserly.
**estípula** *f.* BOT. stipule.
**estipulación** *f.* stipulation.
**estipular** *tr.* to stipulate.
**estirado, -da** *adj.* stretched, expanded, lengthened, drawn. *2* stiff, prim; stuck-up.
**estiramiento** *m.* stretching. *2* drawing [of wire].
**estirar** *tr.* to stretch [by pulling]. *2* to stretch, extend, lengthen, expand: ~ *la pierna*, coll. to die; ~ *las piernas*, coll. to stretch one's legs. *3* to draw [wire]. *4* to iron lightly. *5 ref.* to stretch, stretch one's limbs.
**estirón** *m.* pull, tug. *2* coll. *dar un* ~, to grow tall in a short time.
**estirpe** *f.* stock, lineage, family.
**estival; estivo, -va** *adj.* aestival, estival, summer.
**esto** *dem. pron. neut.* this; this subject, this matter, this point: *en* ~, at this point; *por* ~, for this reason.
**estocada** *f.* stab, thrust, lunge [with a sword].
**Estocolmo** *m. pr. n.* GEOG. Stockholm.
**estofa** *f.* quality, class.
**estofado, -da** *adj.* stewed. *2* quilted. *3* ornamented. *4 m.* COOK. stew, ragout.
**estofar** *tr.* COOK. to stew, ragout. *2* to paint on burnished gold. *3* to size [wood carvings] for gilding.
**estoicismo** *m.* stoicism. *2* Stoicism.
**estoico, -ca** *adj.* stoic(al.
**estola** *f.* stole [garment]. *2* ECCL. stole.
**estolidez** *f.* stupidity, imbecility.
**estólido, -da** *adj.* stupid, imbecile.
**estolón** *m.* BOT. stolon. *2* ECCL. deacon's stole.
**estoma** *m.* BOT. stoma.
**estomacal** *adj.-m.* stomachic.
**estomagar** *tr.* to give indigestion. *2* coll. to disgust.
**estómago** *m.* ANAT. stomach: *revolver el* ~, to turn the stomach.
**estomatitis** *f.* MED. stomatitis.
**estonio, -nia** *adj.-n.* Estonian.
**estopa** *f.* tow [of flax, hemp, etc.]. *2* burlap. *3* oakum.
**estopilla** *f.* finest part of tow. *2* lawn [fabric]. *3* coarse cotton cloth.
**estopor** *m.* NAUT. stopper.
**estoque** *m.* estoc, rapier, narrow sword. *4* BULLF. sword. *3* BOT. sword lily, gladiolus.
**estoquear** *tr.* to stab, with an estoc or sword.
**estoraque** *m.* BOT. storax tree. *2* storax [balsam].
**estorbar** *tr.* to hinder, obstruct, hamper, impede;

to be in the way of; to prevent [someone] from. 2 to annoy, inconvenience.

**estorbo** *m.* hindrance, obstruction, nuisance.

**estornija** *f.* washer [under linchpin].

**estornino** *m.* ORN. starling.

**estornudar** *intr.* to sneeze.

**estornudo** *m.* sneeze.

**estoy** *irr.* V. ESTAR.

**estrábico, -ca** *adj.* strabismic, strabismal.

**estrabismo** *m.* MED. strabismus, squint.

**estrada** *f.* road, way.

**estradiote** *m.* stradiot.

**estrado** *m.* formerly, a lady's drawing-room. 2 dais. 3 *pl.* courtrooms, halls of justice.

**estrafalario, -ria** *adj.* ridiculous, queer, eccentric, edd. 2 *m.-f.* queer fish, eccentric person.

**estragamiento** *m.* disorderr and corruption.

**estragar** *tr.* to corrupt, vitiate, deprave. 2 to ruin, spoil, ravage.

**estrago** *m.* havoc, ruin, ravage: *hacer estragos*, to play havoc.

**estragón** *m.* BOT. tarragon.

**estrambote** *m.* LIT. tail [of a sonnet, etc.].

**estrambótico, -ca** *adj.* odd, queer, strange.

**estramonio** *m.* BOT. stramonium, thorn apple.

**estrangulación** *f.* throttling, strangulation. 2 SURG. strangulation. 3 MACH. throttling, chocke.

**estrangular** *tr.* to strangle, throttle, chocke. 2 SURG., MED. to strangulate. 3 MACH. to throttle, choke.

**estraperlista** *m.-f.* black marketeer.

**estraperlo** *m.* black market.

**estrás** *m.* strass [glass].

**Estrasburgo** *f. pr. n.* GEOG. Strasbourg.

**estratagema** *f.* stratagem, ruse.

**estratega** *m.* strategist.

**estrategia** *f.* strategy, strategics.

**estratégico, -ca** *adj.* strategic(al. 2 *m.* strategist.

**estratificación** *f.* stratification.

**estratificar** *tr.-ref.* GEOL. to stratify.

**estratigrafía** *f.* stratigraphy.

**estrato** *m.* GEOL., ANAT. stratum, layer. 2 METEOR. stratus.

**estratosfera** *f.* METEOR. stratosphere.

**estraza** *f.* rag. 2 *papel de* ~, brown paper.

**estrechamiento** *m.* narrowing. 2 closing [making close]. 3 pressing [of siege, etc.].

**estrechar** *tr.* to narrow, contract, make less wide. 2 to take in [a garment]. 3 to constrain, compel. 4 to press, to follow or besiege closely. 5 to tighten [bonds, etc.]. 6 ~ *la mano de*, to shake hands with; ~ *entre los brazos*, to embrace, clasp in one's arms. 7 *ref.* to narrow [become narrower]. 8 to press together. 9 to cut down expenses. 10 to become more intimate.

**estrechez** *f.* narrowness. 2 tightness [of shoes, garments, etc.]. 3 strictness. 4 pressure [of time]. 5 closeness, intimacy. 6 jam, predicament. 7 penury, poverty.

**estrecho, -cha** *adj.* narrow. 2 tight [shoes, garments, etc.]. 3 close [relation, friendship, etc.]. 4 strict. 5 miserly. 6 *m.* jam, predicament. 7 GEOG. straits: ~ *de Gibraltar*, Straits of Gibraltar.

**estrechura** *f.* narrowness, narrow passage. 2 closeness, intimacy. 3 jam, predicament.

**estregadera** *f.* scrubbing brush.

**estregadura** *f.*, **estregamiento** *m.* rubbing, scrubbing.

**estregar** *tr.* to rub, scrub, scour. 2 to strike [matches]. ¶ CONJUG. like *acertar*.

**estregón** *m.* hard or rough rub.

**estrella** *f.* ASTR. star: ~ *fugaz*, shooting star; ~ *polar*, polestar; *poner sobre las estrellas*, to praise to the skies; *ver las estrellas*, fig. to see stars. 2 star [starlike figure or object]. 3 star [of the screen, etc.]. 4 stars, destiny, luck: *tener buena* ~, to be lucky. 5 ZOOL. ~ *de mar*, starfish.

**estrellado, -da** *adj.* starry, star-spangled. 2 star-shaped. 3 fried [egg].

**estrellamar** *f.* ZOOL. starfish.

**estrellar** *tr.* to strew with stars. 2 to smash [against], dash to pieces. 3 to fry [eggs]. 4 *ref.* to become strewn with stars. 5 to smash, dash, be smashed [against]; to fail.

**estremecedor, -ra** *adj.* frightful, fearful; thrilling.

**estremecer** *tr.* to shake, make tremble or shudder; to thrill. 2 *ref.* to shake, tremble, shudder; to thrill. ¶ CONJUG. like *agradecer*.

**estremecimiento** *m.* shaking, trembling, shuddering, shudder; thrill, thrilling.

**estrenar** *tr.* to use or wear for the first time; to handsel. 2 to perform [a play] or to show [a film] for the first time. 3 *ref.* to make one's debut. 4 to make the first sale of day. 5 [of a play] to open.

**estreno** *m.* first use. 2 THEAT. première. 3 début; first performance. 4 handsel.

**estreñido, -da** *adj.* constipated, costive. 2 stingy.

**estreñimiento** *m.* constipation, costiveness.

**estreñir** *tr.* to bind, constipate. 2 *ref.* to become constipated. ¶ CONJUG. like *ceñir*.

**estrépito** *m.* clatter, crash, din, loud noise. 2 display, show.

**estrepitosamente** *adv.* noisily, loudly, rowdily, deafeningly.

**estrepitoso, -sa** *adj.* deafening, crashing, loud, boisterous, noisy, obstreperous. 2 spectacular.

**estreptococo** *m.* BACT. streptococcus.

**estreptomicina** *f.* PHARM. streptomycin.

**estría** *f.* stria, flute, groove.

**estriar** *tr.* to striate, flute.

**estribación** *f.* GEOG. spur, counterfort.

**estribar** *intr.* ~ *en*, [of things] to rest on or upon; to be based on; to lie in.

**estribera** *f.* stirrup.

**estribillo** *m.* burden, refrain, chorus. 2 pet word, pet phrase.

**estribo** *m.* stirrup: *perder los estribos*, fig. to lose one's head. 2 footboard, step [of a carriage]. 3 AUTO. running board. 4 GEOG. spur. 5 ARCH. abuttment, buttress. 6 ANAT. stapes. 7 fig. base, support.

**estribor** *m.* NAUT. starboard.

**estricnina** *f.* CHEM. strychnine.

**estricto, -ta** *adj.* strict.

**estridencia** *f.* stridence; stridor.

**estridente** *adj.* strident; shrill.

**estridor** *m.* stridor, harsh screeching noise.

**estridular** *intr.* to stridulate, to chirp, to chirr.

**estro** *m.* inspiration, afflatus. 2 ENT. botfly.

**estróbilo** *m.* BOT. strobile.

**estrobo** *m.* NAUT. grommet, grummet, becket.

**estroboscopio** *m.* stroboscope.

**estrofa** *f.* stanza, strophe.

**estroncio** *m.* CHEM. strontium.

**estropajo** *m.* esparto scrub; dishcloth. 2 fig. worthless thing. 3 BOT. dishcloth gourd.

**estropajoso, -sa** *adj.* fig. thick, indistinct [utterance]. 2 fig. untidy, ragged. 3 coll. tough, stringy [meat, vegetables, etc.].

**estropear** *tr.* to spoil, ruin, damage, put out of order. 2 to maim, cripple. 3 *ref.* to get spoiled, ruined, out of order. 4 to get maimed or crippled.

**estropicio** *m.* coll, breakage, smash, crash [of fragile things]. 2 upset, mess.

**estructura** *f.* structure, make.

**estructuración** *f.* structuration.

**estructural** *adj.* structural.

**estructuralismo** *m.* structuralism.

**estructurar** *tr.* to structure, to build.

**estruendo** *m.* great noise, clangor, crash. 2 uproar, clamour, din, confusion. 3 ostentation, pomp.

**estruendoso, -sa** *adj.* noisy, loud, uproarius, clamorous. 2 showy.

**estrujamiento** *m.* squeezing, pressing, crushing.

**estrujar** *tr.* to squeeze, press, crush, jam. 2 to squeeze, drain, exhaust.

**estrujón** *m.* squeeze, crush.

**estuación** *f.* flow of the tide, flood tide.

**Estuardo** *pr. n.* Stuart: *María* ~, Mary Stuart.

**estuario** *m.* estuary.

**estucado** *m.* stuccoing, stuccowork.

**estucar** *tr.* to stucco.

**estuco** *m.* stucco.

**estuche** *m.* case [for jewels, instruments, etc.]. 2 case, cover, etui, etwee.

**estudiado, -da** *adj.* studied, affected, mannered.

**estudiante** *m.* student [of a university, etc.].

**estudiantil** *adj.* [pertaining to] students, college.

**estudiantina** *f.* musical band of students.

**estudiar** *tr.* to study; to read or study for. 2 to read lesson to. 3 ART. to draw from nature. 4 *intr.* to be a student.

**estudio** *m.* study [act or process of studying]. 2 study, paper [article, writing]. 3 F. ARTS, CINEM., RADIO. studio. 4 studio, library. 5 studied manner. 6 F. ARTS study, sketch. 7 *pl.* studies, learning, education.

**estudioso, -sa** *adj.* studious.

**estufa** *f.* stove, heater: ~ *de desinfección,* sterilizer. 2 heated room. 3 sweating room. 4 HORT. hothouse. 5 foot stove. 6 drying chamber.

**estufilla** *f.* foot stove. 2 small fire pan.

**estulticia** *f.* foolishness, stupidity.

**estulto, -ta** *adj.* foolish, stupid.

**estupefacción** *f.* stupefaction, amazement.

**estupefaciente** *adj.-m.* stupefacient, narcotic.

**estupefacto, -ta** *adj.* amazed, dumbfounded.

**estupendo, -da** *adj.* stupendous, wonderful, grand.

**estupidez** *f.* stupidity. 2 stupid act or remark, folly.

**estúpido, -da** *adj.* stupid, foolish, witless. 2 *m.-f.* stupid [person].

**estupor** *m.* MED. stupor. 2 amazement.

**estuprar** *tr.* to rape, violate.

**estupro** *m.* rape, violation.

**estuquista** *m.* stucco plasterer.

**esturión** *m.* ICHTH. sturgeon.

**estuve, estuviste,** etc. *irr.* V. ESTAR.

**esvarar** *intr.* to slide, glide.

**esvástica** *f.* swastika.

**esviaje** *m.* ARCH. obliquity, skew.

**eta** *f.* eta [greek letter].

**etalaje** *m.* bosh.

**etamín** *f.* etamine [fabric].

**etano** *m.* CHEM. ethane.

**etapa** *f.* MIL. stage [of journey]. 2 stage [of development, process, etc.].

**etcétera** *f.* et cetera.

**éter** *m.* PHYS., CHEM. ether. 2 poet. ether, heavens.

**etéreo, -a** *adj.* ethereal.

**eterificar** *tr.* CHEM. to etherify.

**eterizar** *tr.* to etherize.

**eternal** *adj.* eternal.

**eternidad** *f.* eternity. 2 fig. long time.

**eternizar** *tr.* to eternize, perpetuate; to prolong indefinitely. 2 *ref.* to become interminable.

**eterno, -na** *adj.* eternal, endless, everlasting. 2 *m.* *el Eterno,* the Eternal, God.

**etesio** *adj.-m.* etesian [wind].

**ética** *f.* ethics.

**ético, -ca** *adj.* ethical, moral. 2 *m.* ethicist, moralist. 3 *adj.-n.* HÉTICO.

**etileno** *m.* CHEAM. ethylene.

**etílico, -ca** *adj.* ethylic.

**etilo** *m.* CHEM. ethyl.

**etimología** *f.* etymology.

**etimólogo** *m.* etymologist.

**etiología** *f.* aetiology.

**etíope** *adj.-n.* Ethiopian. 2 *adj.* Ethiopic.

**Etiopía** *f. pr. n.* GEOG. Ethiopia.

**etiqueta** *f.* label, tag. 2 etiquette, ceremony, formality: *de* ~, full dress, formal.

**etiquetado** *m.* labelling.

**etiquetero, -ra** *adj.* ceremonious [person].

**etmoides** *adj.-m.* ANAT. ethmoid.

**Etna** *m. pr. n.* GEOG. Etna.

**etnia** *f.* ethnos.

**étnico, -ca** *adj.* ethnic(al). 2 GRAM. gentilic.

**etnografía** *f.* ethnography.

**etnología** *f.* ethnology.

**etnólogo** *m.* ethnologist.

**etrusco, -ca** *adj.-n.* Etruscan.

**eucalipto** *m.* BOT. eucalyptus.

**eucaristía** *f.* THEOL. Eucharist.

**eucarístico, -ca** *adj.* Eucharistic.

**Euclides** *m. pr. n.* Euclid.

**eucologio** *m.* euchology.

**eudiómetro** *m.* eudiometer.

**eufemismo** *m.* euphemism.

**eufonía** *f.* euphony.

**eufónico, -ca** *adj.* euphonic, euphonious.

**euforbiáceo, -a** *adj.* BOT. euphorbiaceous.

**euforia** *f.* euphoria, euphory.

**eufuismo** *m.* euphuism.

**eugenesia** *f.* eugenics.

**Eugenia** *f. pr. n.* Eugenia.

**Eugenio** *m. pr. n.* Eugene.

**eunuco** *m.* eunuch.

**eurasiático, -ca** *adj.-n.* Eurasian.

**euritmia** *f.* eurythmy.

**euro** *m.* east wind.

**Europa** *f. pr. n.* GEOG. Europe. 2 MYTH. Europa.

**europeizar** *tr.* to Europeanize.

**europeo, -a** *adj.-n.* European.

**euscalduna; euscaro, -ra** *adj.-m.* Basque [language].

**Eustaquio** *m. pr. n.* Eustace.

**eutanasia** *f.* euthanasia.

**eutrapelia** *f.* moderation in pleasures.

**Eva** *f. pr. n.* Eve.

**evacuación** *f.* evacuation. 2 discharge, carrying out [of commission, etc.].

**evacuar** *tr.* to evacuate, empty, vacate. 2 to discharge [bowels, etc.]. 3 to discharge, carry out, fulfil [comission, etc.]. 4 MED., MIL. to evacuate.

**evadido, -da** *adj.* escaped. 2 *m.-f.* escapee.

**evadir** *tr.* to evade, elude, avoid. 2 *ref.* to escape, sneak away.

**evaluación** *f.* evaluation.

**evaluar** *tr.* to evaluate.

**evangélico, -ca** *adj.* evangelical.

**evangelio** *m.* gospel, Gospel, Evangel. *2* fig. gospel truth.
**evangelista** *m.* Evangelist. *2* gospel chanter.
**evangelización** *f.* evangelization.
**evangelizar** *tr.* to evangelize.
**evaporación** *f.* evaporation.
**evaporar** *tr.* to evaporate. *2* to cause to vanish. *3 ref.* to evaporate; to vanish, disappear.
**evasión** *f.* escape. *2* evasion.
**evasiva** *f.* evasion, subterfuge.
**evasivo, -va** *adj.* evasive.
**evento** *m.* event, contingency: *a todo* ~, against every contingency.
**eventual** *adj.* eventual, contingent.
**eventualidad** *f.* eventuality, case, contingency.
**evicción** *f.* LAW eviction.
**evidencia** *f.* evidence, obviousness.
**evidenciar** *tr.* to evidence, show, render evident.
**evidente** *adj.* evident, obvious.
**evidentemente** *adv.* evidently, obviously, clearly.
**evisceración** *f.* SURG. evisceration.
**evitable** *adj.* avoidable.
**evitación** *f.* avoidance.
**evitar** *tr.* to avoid, elude, shun. *2* to prevent [keep from happening]. *3* to save [trouble, etc.].
**evo** *m.* poet, age, æon.
**evocación** *f.* evocation, evoking.
**evocar** *tr.* to evoke, call up; to conjure up.
**evocativo, -va** *adj.* evocative.
**evolución** *f.* evolution [development, change]. *2* BIOL., PHIL., MIL., NAV. evolution.
**evolucionar** *intr.* to evolve. *2* to change [in conduct, etc.]. *3* MIL., NAV. to perform evolutions.
**evolucionismo** *m.* evolutionism.
**evolutivo, -va** *adj.* evolutional, evolutive.
**ex** *prep.* ex-, former, late.
**ex abrupto** *adv.* abruptly, suddenly. *2 m.* impolite or misplaced outburst.
**exacción** *f.* exaction. *2* extortion.
**exacerbar** *tr.* to exacerbate. *2* to irritate, exasperate. *3 ref.* to become exacerbate.
**exacerbante** *adj.* exasperating, irritating, provoking.
**exactitud** *f.* exactness, accuracy. *2* punctuality.
**exacto, -ta** *adj.* exact, accurate, precise, punctual.
**exageración** *f.* exaggeration.
**exageradamente** *adv.* exaggeratedly. *2* exceedingly, exorbitantly.
**exagerado, -da** *adj.* exaggerated. *2* excessive. *3* exaggerative.
**exagerador, -ra** *adj.* exaggerating. *2 m.-f.* exaggerator.
**exagerar** *tr.* to exaggerate.
**exaltación** *f.* exaltation. *2* passion, excitement; hot-headedness.
**exaltado, -da** *adj.* exalted. *2* hot-headed, extreme.
**exaltar** *tr.* to exalt. *2* to extol. *3 ref.* to become excited, worked up.
**examen** *m.* examination. *2* inspection, survey.
**examinador, -ra** *adj.* examining. *2 m.-f.* examiner.
**examinando, -da** *m.-f.* examinee.
**examinar** *tr.* to examine. *2* to inspect, survey, look into, inquire into, search, scan. *3 ref.* to sit for examination.
**exangüe** *adj.* bloodless, pale. *2* exhausted, worn out. *3* lifeless, dead.
**exánime** *adj.* exanimate, lifeless. *2* weak, faint.
**exasperación** *f.* exasperation.
**exasperante** *adj.* exasperating.
**exasperar** *tr.* to exasperate. *2 ref.* to become exasperated.

**excarcelar** *tr.* LAW to relase, set [a prisoner] free.
**exavación** *f.* excavation.
**excavador, -ra** *adj.* excavating. *2 m.-f.* excavator [person]. *3 f.* excavator, power shovel.
**excavar** *tr.* to excavate [hollow out, make a hole]. *2* AGR. to loosen the soil around [a plant].
**excedencia** *f.* temporary retirement [from post].
**excedente** *adj.* excessive. *2* left over; surplus. *3* temporarily retiring [employee]. *4 m.* surplus.
**exceder** *tr.* to exceed, surpass, outdo. *2 intr.-ref.* to go too far: *excederse en sus atribuciones*, to exceed one's powers. *3 excederse a sí mismo*, to outdo oneself.
**excelencia** *f.* excellence, excellency: *por* ~, preeminently. *2* Excellency [title].
**excelente** *adj.* excellent, very good, very fine.
**excelentísimo, -ma** *adj. superl.* most excellent.
**excelsitud** *f.* loftiness, sublimity.
**excelso, -sa** *adj.* lofty, elevated, sublime.
**excentricidad** *f.* eccentricity.
**excéntrico, -ca** *adj.* eccentric(al. *2 m.-f.* eccentric, crank [person]. *3 f.* MACH. eccentric.
**excepción** *f.* exception.
**excepcional** *adj.* exceptional, uncommon, unusual.
**excepto** *adv.* except, excepting, save.
**exceptuar** *tr.* to except.
**excesivo, -va** *adj.* excessive.
**exceso** *m.* excess, surplus: *en* ~, excessively, to excess. *2* excess, intemperance, outrage.
**excipiente** *m.* PHARM. excipient.
**excisión** *f.* MED. excision.
**excitable** *adj.* excitable.
**excitación** *f.* exciting, excitation, excitement. *2* ELEC., PHYSIOL. excitation.
**excitador, -ra** *adj.* exciting, excitant. *2 m.* ELEC. exciter.
**excitante** *adj.* exciting. *2 adj.-m.* excitant.
**excitar** *tr.* to excite, stir up, move. *2* ELEC., PHYSIOL. to excite. *3 ref.* to get excited.
**exclamación** *f.* exclamation.
**exclamar** *intr.* to exclaim, cry out.
**exclamativo, -va** *adj.* exclamatory.
**exclaustrar** *tr.* to secularize [a monk or nun].
**excluir** *tr.* to exclude, bar, debar. ¶ CONJUG. like *huir*.
**exclusión** *f.* exclusion.
**exclusiva** *f.* sole or exclusive right, special privilege. *2* rejection, exclusion.
**exclusivamente** *adv.* exclusively, solely.
**exclusive** *adv.* exclusively, exclusive.
**exclusivismo** *m.* exclusive attachment to an idea, person, etc.
**exclusivo, -va** *adj.* exclusive, excluding. *2* sole: *agente* ~, sole agent.
**excogitar** *tr.* to excogitate, find, devise.
**excomulgado, -da** *adj.-n.* excomunicate. *2* fig. & coll. imp of mischief.
**excomulgar** *tr.* to excommunicate. *2* to anathematize.
**excomunión** *f.* excommunication.
**excoriación** *f.* excoriation.
**excoriar** *tr.* to excoriate. *2 ref.* to be excoriated.
**excrecencia** *f.* excrescence, excrescency.
**excreción** *f.* PHYSIOL. excretion.
**excremento** *m.* excrement.
**excretar** *intr.* to excrete. *2* to void excrements.
**excreto, -ta** *adj.* excreted.
**exculpación** *f.* exculpation, exoneration.
**exculpar** *tr.* to exculpate, exonerate.
**excursión** *f.* excursion, trip, outing, tour.

**excursionista** *adj.* [pertaining to] excursion. *2 m.-f.* excursionist, tripper.

**excusa** *f.* excuse, excusing. *2* excuse, apology.

**excusable** *adj.* excusable, pardonable. *2* that may be omitted.

**excusado, -da** *adj.* exempt. *2* superfluous, unnecessary. *3* private: *puerta excusada*, side door, private door. *4 m.* water-closet, toilet.

**excusar** *tr.* to excuse. *2* to avoid, prevent. *3* to exempt from. *4 excuso decir*, needless to say. *5 ref.* to excuse oneself, to apologize. *6 excusarse de*, to excuse oneself from.

**execrable** *adj.* execrable.

**execración** *f.* execration.

**execrando, -da** *adj.* execrable.

**execrar** *tr.* to execrate.

**exedra** *f.* ARCH. exedra.

**exégesis** *f.* exegesis.

**exégeta** *m.* exegete.

**exención** *f.* exemption.

**exentar** *tr.* to exempt.

**exento, -ta** *adj.* exempt. *2* free [from]; deprived, bare. *3* ARCH. isolated, disengaged.

**exequátur** *m.* esequatur.

**exequias** *f.* exequies, obsequies.

**exergo** *m.* NUMIS. exergue.

**exfoliación** *f.* exfoliation.

**exfoliar** *tr.* to exfoliate.

**exhalación** *f.* exhalation. *2* shooting star. *3* bolt of lightning. *4* fume, vapour.

**exhalar** *tr.* to exhale, breathe forth, emit. *2* to heave [a sigh]. *3 ref.* to exhale [be exhaled].

**exhaustivo, -va** *adj.* exhaustive.

**exhausto, -ta** *adj.* exhausted.

**exhibición** *f.* exhibition, exhibiting. *2* show off.

**exhibicionismo** *m.* showing off. *2* exhibitionism.

**exhibicionista** *n.* exhibitionist.

**exhibir** *tr.* to exhibit, show, display. *2* to produce [documents, etc.]. *3 ref.* to show oneself. *4* to show off.

**exhortación** *f.* exhortation.

**exhortar** *tr.* to exhort.

**exhorto** *m.* LAW letters rogatory.

**exhumación** *f.* exhumation.

**exhumar** *tr.* to exhume, disinter, dig up.

**exigencia** *f.* exactingness; fastidiousness. *2* exigency, demand, requirement.

**exigente** *adj.* exigent, exacting; fastidious.

**exigibilidad** *f.* liability to be demanded or required.

**exigible & exigidero, -ra** *adj.* exigible.

**exigir** *tr.* to exact. *2* to require, demand, need.

**exigüidad** *f.* exiguity.

**exiguo, gua** *adj.* exiguous.

**exiliado, -da** *adj.* exiled. *2 n.* exile.

**exilio** *m.* DESTIERRO.

**eximente** *adj.* exempting. *2* exonerating.

**eximio, -mia** *adj.* eminent, most excellent.

**eximir** *tr.* to exempt.

**existencia** *f.* existence. *2* life [of man]. *3 sing. & pl.* COM. stock [goods in hand]: *en ~*, in stock.

**existencialismo** *m.* PHIL. existentialism.

**existente** *adj.* existent, extant. *2* COM. in stock.

**existir** *tr.* to exist, to be.

**exitazo** *m.* great success.

**éxito** *m.* issue, end: *buen ~*, success; *mal ~*, failure. *2* success; hit: *tener ~*, to be successful; to be a hit.

**ex libris** *m.* ex libris, bookplate.

**éxodo** *m.* exodus. *2* (cap.) BIB. Exodus.

**exoneración** *f.* exoneration. *2* dismissal, deposal.

**exonerar** *tr.* to exonerate. *2* to unburden. *3* to dismiss, depose, deprive of office.

**exorar** *tr.* to beg, entreat.

**exorbitancia** *f.* exorbitance, exorbitancy.

**exorbitante** *adj.* exorbitant.

**exorcismo** *m.* exorcism.

**exorcizar** *tr.* to exorcise.

**exordio** *m.* exordium.

**exornar** *tr.* to adorn, embellish.

**exósmosis** *f.* PHYS. exosmosis.

**exotérico, -ca** *adj.* exoteric.

**exótico, -ca** *adj.* exotic, foreign. *3* odd, bizarre.

**exotismo** *m.* exoticism.

**expansibilidad** *f.* PHYS. expansibility.

**expansión** *f.* PHYS., ANAT., BOT. expansion. *2* emotional effusion. *3* relaxation, recreation.

**expansionarse** *ref.* to open one's heart.

**expansivo, -va** *adj.* PHYS. expansive. *2* expansive, effusive.

**expatriación** *f.* expatriation.

**expatriarse** *ref.* to expatriate [leave one's country].

**expectación** *f.* expectancy, suspense.

**expectante** *adj.* expectant.

**expectativa** *f.* expectancy, hope. *2 a la ~*, on the look out.

**expectoración** *f.* expectoration.

**expectorar** *tr.* to expectorate.

**expedición** *f.* dispatch, shipment. *2* issuance [of a certificate, etc.]. *3* expedition, dispatch, speed, ease, readiness. *4* [military, scientific, etc.] expedition.

**expedicionario, -ria** *adj.* expeditionary. *2 m.-f.* expeditionist.

**expedidor, -ra** *adj.* sender, dispatcher, shipper. *2* issuer [of a certificate, etc.].

**expediente** *m.* action, proceeding: *formar ~ a uno*, to investigate an official's conduct. *2* dossier, file of papers bearing on a case. *3* device, resource, expedient. *4* excuse, motive, reason. *5 cubrir el ~*, to keep up appearances.

**expedienteo** *m.* red tape [in public business].

**expedir** *tr.* to issue [a certificate, etc.]. *2* to send, ship. *3* to expedite, dispatch. ¶ CONJUG. like *servir*.

**expeditivo, -va** *adj.* expeditious, expeditive.

**expedito, -ta** *adj.* clear, free from encumbrance, open [way, etc.]. *2* expeditious. *3* ready to act.

**expeler** *tr.* to expel, eject, throw out.

**expendedor, -ra** *adj.* spending. *2 m.-f.* spender. *3* seller, retailer. *4 ~ de moneda falsa*, counterfeit distributor.

**expendeduría** *f.* [tobacco] shop.

**expender** *tr.* to spend. *2* to sell, retail. *3* to pass [counterfeit money].

**expendición** *f.* sale, retailing. *2* spending. *3* distribution [of counterfeit money].

**expensas** *f. pl.* expenses: *a ~ de*, at the expense of.

**experiencia** *f.* experience [knowledge, skill, etc., resulting from experience]. *2* experiment.

**experimentación** *f.* experimentation.

**experimentado, -da** *adj.* experienced [person].

**experimental** *adj.* experimental.

**experimentar** *tr.* to experiment, test, try. *2* to experience, feel, undergo.

**experto, -ta** *adj.* expert, skilful. *2 m.* expert.

**expiación** *f.* expiation, atonement.

**expiar** *tr.* to expiate.

**expiatorio, -ria** *adj.* expiatory.

**expido, expida**, etc. *irr.* V. EXPEDIR.

**expiración** *f.* expiration, end.

**expirar** *intr.* to expire [come to an end; die].
**explanación** *f.* levelling, grading [of ground]. *2* explanation, elucidation.
**explanada** *f.* esplanade.
**explanar** *tr.* to level, grade [ground]. *2* to explain, elucidate.
**explayar** *tr.* to extend, widen, dilate. *2 ref.* to extend, spread out; to dwell [upon a subject]. *3* to amuse oneself. *4* to open one's heart.
**expletivo, -va** *adj.-m.* expletive.
**explicable** *adj.* explicable, explainable, accountable.
**explicación** *f.* explanation. *2* accounting for.
**explicar** *tr.* to explain, expound. *2* to account for. *3 ref.* to express oneself. *4* to explain oneself. *5 explicarse una cosa,* to account for a thing.
**explicativo, -va** *adj.* explanatory.
**explícito, -ta** *adj.* explicit.
**exploración** *f.* exploration. *2* scanning [of the horizon, etc.]. *3* MIL. scouting.
**explorador** *m.-f.* explorer. *2 m.* MIL. scout. *4* boy scout. *5* TELEV. scanning disk.
**explorar** *tr.* to explore. *2* to scan [the horizon, etc.]. *3* MIL. to scout.
**exploratorio, -ria** *adj.* exploratory.
**explosión** *f.* explosion [exploding; outburst]: *hacer ~,* to explode; *motor de ~,* combustion engine. *2* PHON. explosion. *3* MIN. blast.
**explosivo, -va** *adj.* explosive.
**explotación** *f.* exploitation. *2* development [of natural resources], cultivation [of soil]; working [of a mine]. *3* works, plantation, etc.
**explotar** *tr.* to run, operate, work, exploit [a business, mine, etc.]; to develop [natural resources]; to cultivate [soil]. *2* to exploit [a person].
**expoliación** *f.* spoliation.
**expondré, expondría,** etc. *irr.* V. EXPONER.
**exponente** *m.-f.* exponent, expounder. *2 m.* MATH. exponent.
**exponer** *tr.* to expound, explain, set forth, state. *2* to expose, show, put on view. *3* to exhibit [goods, painting, etc.]. *4* PHOT. to expose. *5* to expose [put in danger], imperil, jeopardize; to stake. *6* to expose [an infant]. *7 ref.* to expone oneself. ¶ CONJUG. like *poner.*
**expongo, exponga,** etc. *irr.* V. EXPONER.
**exportable** *adj.* exportable.
**exportación** *f.* exportation, export: *derechos de ~,* export duties.
**exportador, -ra** *adj.* exporting. *2 m.-f.* exporter.
**exportar** *tr.* to export.
**exposición** *f.* exposition, expounding, explanation, statement. *2* address, petition. *3* exposition, exposure. *4* PHOT. exposure. *5* peril, risk, jeopardy. *6* exposition, public exhibition, show.
**expositivo, -va** *adj.* expositive.
**expósito** *m.-f.* foundling.
**expositor, -ra** *adj.* expounding. *2* exhibiting. *3 m.-f.* expositor, expunder. *4* exhibitor.
**exprés** *m.* express [train]. *2* espresso [coffee].
**expresado, -da** *adj.* aforesaid.
**expresamente** *adv.* expressly. *2* on purpose.
**expresar** *tr.* to express [in words, etc.]. *2 ref.* to express oneself.
**expresión** *f.* expression. *2* expressiveness. *3* squeezing [of fruits, etc.]. *4 pl.* regards.
**expresivo, -va** *adj.* expressive. *2* affectionate, kind.
**expreso, -sa** *adj.* expressed. *2* express. *3 m.* RLY. express. *4* express messenger.
**exprimidera** *f.* squeezer, lemon squeezer.
**exprimidor** *m.* squeezer.

**exprimir** *tr.* to express, squeeze, press out, wring, wring out. *2* to express, state, show.
**ex profeso** *adv.* expressly; on purpose.
**expropiación** *f.* expropriation.
**expropiar** *tr.* to expropriate.
**expuesto, -ta** *p. p.* of EXPONER. *2 adj.* exposed. *3* on view, exhibited. *4* liable, open [to]; in danger. *5* dangerous, hazardous.
**expugnable** *adj.* expugnable, pregnable.
**expugnar** *tr.* MIL. to take by storm.
**expulsar** *tr.* to expel, eject, drive out. *2* to remove from membership; to cashier.
**expulsión** *f.* expulsion.
**expulsor** *m.* ejector [of firearm].
**expurgación** *f.* expurgation.
**expuse, expusiera,** etc. *irr.* V. EXPONER.
**exquisitez** *f.* exquisiteness, excellence.
**exquisito, -ta** *adj.* exquisite [of consummate excellence or beauty]; delicious.
**extasiarse** *ref.* to go into ecstasies, be enraptured.
**éxtasis** *m.* ecstasy, rapture. *2* MED. ecstasy.
**extático, -ca** *adj.* ecstatic.
**extemporáneo, -a** *adj.* untimely, inopportune.
**extender** *tr.* to spread, extend. *2* to spread out, unfold. *3* to stretch out [a limb]. *4* to extend, make extensive, enlarge, widen, expand. *5* to draw up [a document]. *6 ref.* to extend spread; become extensive; become general or popular. *7* to stretch, extend [in time or space], to reach. *8* to expatiate, speak at lenght. ¶ CONJUG. like *entender.*
**extensamente** *adv.* extensively, at length.
**extensible** *adj.* extensible.
**extensión** *f.* extension, extending. *2* extent; range. *3* expanse, stretch. *4* length [of a discourse, etc.]. *5* GEOM., LOG., GRAM. extension.
**extensivo, -va** *adj.* ample, loose [sense]. *2* extensive.
**extenso, -sa** *adj.* extensive, vast. *2* long, lengthy: *por ~,* extensively, at length.
**extenuación** *f.* emaciation, wasting, exhaustion.
**extenuar** *tr.* to emaciate, exhaust, weaken, wear out. *2 ref.* to exhaust oneself.
**exterior** *adj.* exterior, external, outer, outside, outward. *2* foreing [commerce, debt, etc.]. *3 m.* exterior, outside. *4* [personal] appearance. *5* foreing countries.
**exterioridad** *f.* externals, outside things. *2* outward appearance, outward show. *3 pl.* pomp, show.
**exteriorizar** *tr.* to externalize, reveal, show, make manifest. *2 ref.* to apear outwardly.
**exterminador, -ra** *adj.* exterminating. *2 m.-f.* exterminator.
**exterminar** *tr.* to exterminate.
**exterminio** *m.* extermination.
**externado** *m.* day school.
**externo, -na** *adj.* external, outside. *2* day [scholar, pupil]. *3 m.-f.* day scholar, day pupil.
**extinción** *f.* extinction, extinguishment.
**extinguible** *adj.* extinguishable.
**extinguir** *tr.* to extinguish. *2* to quench, put out [fire, etc.]. *3 ref.* to become extinct; to die, go out.
**extinto, -ta** *adj.* extinct. *2* (Am.) late, deceased.
**extintor** *m.* extinctor, fire extinguisher.
**extirpación** *f.* extirpation.
**extirpador, -ra** *adj.* extirpating. *2 m.-f.* extirpator. *3 m.* AGR. cultivator [implement].
**extirpar** *tr.* to extirpate.
**extorsión** *f.* extortion. *2* damage, trouble.

**extra** *adj.* extra. *2 m.* extra [gratuity]. *3 m.-f.* CINEM. extra.

**extracción** *f.* extraction. *2* birth, origin. *3* drawing numbers [in lottery].

**extracorta** *adj.* RADIO. ultrashort.

**extractar** *tr.* to abstract, epitomize.

**extracto** *m.* abstract, summary. *2* PHARM. extract.

**extractor, -ra** *adj.* extracting. *2 m.-f.* extractor [person]. *3 m.* extractor [device, machine].

**extradición** *f.* extradition.

**extradós** *m.* ARCH. extrados.

**extraer** *tr.* to extract, draw out. *2* MATH. to extract [a root]. ¶ CONJUG. like *traer.*

**extraigo, extraiga, extraje,** etc. *irr.* V. EXTRAER.

**extrajudicial** *adj.* extrajudicial.

**extralimitarse** *ref.* to overstep one's power or authority, exceed the limit, go too far.

**extramuros** *adv.* outside the town or city.

**extranjerismo** *m.* foreignism.

**extranjerizar** *tr.* to introduce foreign customs in. *2 ref.* to adopt foreign ways.

**extranjero, -ra** *adj.* foreign [of another country], outlandish. *2 m.-f.* alien, foreigner. *3 m.* any foreign country: *al* or *en el* ~, abroad.

**extranjis (de)** *adv.* secretly.

**extrañamiento** *m.* banishment, exile.

**extrañar** *tr.* to banish, exile. *2* to surprise: *me extraña su actitud,* I am surprised at his attitude. *3* not to feel at home in [an unfamiliar place, etc.]. *4 ref.* to exile oneself. *5 extrañarse de,* to be surprised, or wonder, at.

**extrañeza** *f.* strangeness, oddity. *2* wonder, surprise, astonishment.

**extraño, -ña** *adj.* strange, foreign, alien, extraneous. *2* strange, odd, queer, peculiar.

**extraoficial** *adj.* extraofficial, unofficial.

**extraordinario** *adj.* extraordinary, uncommon. *2 m.* extra dish [at a meal]. *3* special messenger or courier.

**extrarradio** *m.* outskirts [of a town].

**extraterritorial** *adj.* extraterritorial.

**extraterritorialidad** *f.* extraterritoriality.

**extravagancia** *f.* oddness, wildness, folly, nonsense.

**extravagante** *adj.* odd, queer, wild, nonsensical.

**extravasarse** *ref.* to extravasate.

**extraversión** *f.* PSICH. extroversion.

**extraviado, -da** *adj.* out-of-the-way.

**extraviar** *tr.* to lead astray. *2* to mislay. *3* ~ *la vista, la mirada,* to have a set unseeing look. *4 ref.* to stray, to miss or lose one's way, to get lost. *5* to be mislaid. *6* [of a letter] to miscarry. *6* to go astray.

**extravío** *m.* straying, going astray. *2* mislaying, loss. *3* error, wrong, disorderly life.

**extremado, -da** *adj.* extreme, extremely good or bad.

**extremar** *tr.* to carry to extremes, carry to the limit. *2 ref.* to do one's best, strive hard.

**extremaunción** *f.* ECCL. extreme unction.

**extremeño, -ña** *adj.-n.* Extremenian.

**extremidad** *f.* extremity, end, tip. *2* extremity [the highest degree]. *3 pl.* extremities [limbs, hands, feet].

**extremismo** *m.* extremism.

**extremista** *adj.-n.* extremist.

**extremo, -ma** *adj.* extreme. *2* great, excessive. *3 m.* extreme, tip, end, extremity. *4* extreme, extremity [highest degree]; *en, con* or *por* ~, extremely, very much; *hasta tal* ~, to such a point. *5* utmost care. *6* point [of a conversation, letters, etc.]. *7* MATH., LOG. extreme. *8 pl. hacer extremos,* to make a great show [of pain, joy, love, etc.], to gush.

**extremoso, -sa** *adj.* demonstrative, effusive.

**extrínseco, -ca** *adj.* extrinsic.

**extroversión** *f.* MED. extroversion.

**exuberancia** *f.* exuberance.

**exuberante** *adj.* exuberant. *2* luxuriant.

**exudar** *intr.-tr.* to exude; ooze out.

**exultación** *f.* exultation.

**exultar** *intr.* to exult.

**exutorio** *m.* MED. issue [artificial ulcer].

**exvoto** *m.* ex-voto, votive offering.

**eyaculación** *m.* ejaculation.

**eyacular** *tr.* PHYSIOL. to ejaculate.

**Ezequías** *m. pr. n.* BIBL. Hezekiah.

**Ezequiel** *m. pr. n.* BIBL. Ezekiel.

# F

**F, f** *f.* F, f, seventh letter of the Spanish alphabet.
**fa** *m.* MUS. fa.
**fabada** *f.* in Asturias, stew made of pork and beans.
**fabiano, -na** *adj.-n.* Fabian.
**fabla** *f.* literary imitation of Old Spanish.
**fábrica** *f.* factory, works, mill, plant. *2* manufacture, fabrication, invention. *3* building, fabric. *4* masonry [brick of stone work]. *5* church funds.
**fabricación** *f.* manufacture, fabrication, make.
**fabricante** *m.* manufacturer, maker. *2* factory owner.
**fabricar** *tr.* to make, manufacture. *2* to build. *3* to fabricate, construct, invent, forge.
**fabril** *adj.* manufacturing; pertaining to factories or workmen.
**fabriquero** *m.* FABRICANTE. *2* church warden.
**fabuco** *m.* BOT. beechnut.
**fábula** *f.* fable. *2* rumor, gossip. *3* talk [of the town]. *4* mythology.
**fabulista** *m.-f.* fabulist, writer of fables.
**fabuloso, -sa** *adj.* fabulous. *2* enormous, extraordinary.
**faca** *f.* curved knife; large pointed knife.
**facción** *f.* faction. *2* insurgent party. *3* MIL. action, combat. *4* MIL. *estar de* ~, to be on duty. *5 pl.* features [of the face].
**faccioso, -sa** *adj.* factious, insurgent. *2 m.* rebel.
**faceta** *f.* facet.
**facial** *adj.* facial. *2* intuitive.
**fácil** *adj.* easy, facile. *2* easy, fluent [speech, style]. *3* probable, likely. *4* frail, wanton [woman].
**facilidad** *f.* ease, easiness, facility: ~ *de palabra*, fluency. *2 pl.* facilities: *facilidades de pago*, easy payments.
**facilitar** *tr.* to facilitate, make easy, expedite. *2* to furnish, provide with.
**facilón, -na** *adj.* coll. dead easy, very simple.
**facineroso, -sa** *m.-f.* habitual criminal. *2* villain, evil person.
**facistol** *m.* lectern, chorister's desk.
**facón** *m.* (Am.) gaucho's knife.
**facsímil, facsímile** *m.* facsimile.
**factible** *adj.* feasible, practicable.
**facticio, -cia** *adj.* factitious, artificial.
**factitivo, -va** *adj.* GRAM. factitive.

**factor** *m.* COM. factor, agent. *2* RLY. luggage clerk. *3* factor [for a result]. *4* MATH. factor.
**factoría** *f.* COM. factorage, agency. *2* commercial factory; commercial establishment in a colony.
**factótum** *m.* factotum. *2* busybody.
**factura** *f.* facture, execution. *2* COM. invoice, bill.
**facturación** *f.* invoicing, billing. *2* RLY. registration [of luggage].
**facturar** *tr.* COM. to invoice, to bill. *2* RLY. to register [luggage]; to remit [goods] by rail.
**fácula** *f.* ASTR. facula.
**facultad** *f.* faculty. *2* power, permission. *3* ability, skill. *4* science, art. *5* branch or college [of University]. *6 pl.* *facultades del alma*, mental powers.
**facultar** *tr.* to empower, authorize.
**facultativo** *adj.* facultative, optional. *2* [pertaining to a] faculty. *3* *adj.-n.* professional. *4 m.* doctor, physician, surgeon.
**facundia** *f.* fluency, eloquence.
**facundo, -da** *adj.* fluent, eloquent.
**facha** *f.* appearance, look. *2* ridiculous figure, fright. *3* NAUT. *ponerse en* ~, to lie to.
**fachada** *f.* ARCH. façade, front. *2* appearance [of a person].
**fachenda** *f.* vanity, ostentation. *2 m.* boaster.
**fachendear** *intr.* to boast, show off.
**fachendoso, -sa** *adj.* vain, boastful, ostentatious. *2* *m.-f.* boaster.
**fachoso, -sa** *adj.* odd-looking, weird-looking. *2* (Am.) swanky, snooty, conceited.
**fado** *m.* Portuguese popular song.
**faena** *f.* work, toil. *2* task, job, *chore.
**faenar** *intr.* to fish.
**faetón** *m.* phaeton.
**fagocito** *m.* PHYSIOL. phagocyte.
**fagot** *m.* MUS. bassoon.
**faisán** *m.* ORN. pheasant.
**faisana** *f.* hen pheasant.
**faja** *f.* sash, scarf [around the waist]; girder. *2* swaddling band. *3* newspaper, wrapper. *4* stripe, band, zone. *5* strip [of land]. *6* ARCH. fascia.
**fajamiento** *m.* banding, bandaging. *2* swaddling.
**fajar** *tr.* to band, bandage, girdle. *2* to swaddle.
**fajín** *m.* sash [worn by generals, etc., with their civilian clothes].

**fajina** *f.* brushwood, kindling. *2* FORT. fascine. *3* MIL. call to mess; call to quarters.

**fajo** *m.* bundle, sheaf, roll.

**falacia** *f.* fallacy, deception, deceit. *2* deceitfulness.

**falange** *f.* phalanx. *2* ANAT., ZOOL. phalange, phalanx. *3* (cap.) POL. Falange.

**falangero** *m.* ZOOL. phalanger.

**falangeta** *f.* ANAT. phalangette.

**falangina** *f.* ANAT. second phalanx.

**falangista** *adj.-n.* POL. Falangist.

**falansterio** *m.* phalanstery.

**falaz** *adj.* deceitful. *2* deceptive, fallacious.

**falcado, -da** *adj.* falcate. *2 carro* ~, scythed chariot.

**falciforme** *m.* falciform.

**falcón** *m.* ARTILL. falcon.

**falda** *f.* skirt [of dress; woman's garment]. *2* lap [of a person]. *3* ARM. skirt. *4* BUTCH. plate. *5* foot [of a mountain]. *6* brim [of hat]. *7 pl.* skirts; women.

**faldamenta** *f.*, **faldamento** *m.* skirt, long skirt.

**faldar** *m.* ARM. skirt of tasses.

**faldear** *tr.* to skirt [a hill or mountain].

**faldero, -ra** *adj.* [pertaining to] skirt. *2* fond of the company of women. *3* lap [dog].

**faldillas** *f. pl.* skirts of some dresses.

**faldistorio** *m.* faldstool.

**faldón** *m.* skirt, tall [of a garment], coat tail. *2* shirt tail. *3* flap [of a saddle]. *4* ARCH. triangular slope [of roof]. *5* mantel [of chimney].

**faldriquera** *f.* FALTRIQUERA.

**falibilidad** *f.* fallibility.

**falible** *adj.* fallible.

**fálico** *adj.* phallic.

**falo** *m.* phallus.

**falsario, -ria** *adj.* liar. *2* forger, counterfeiter.

**falsarregla** *f.* bevel square.

**falseamiento** *m.* counterfeiting. *2* adulteration, misrepresentation.

**falsear** *tr.* to counterfeit, falsify; to misrepresent. *2* CARDS to lead with a low card. *3* to pierce or split [armour]. *4* ARCH. to slant a surface. *5 intr.* [of things] to weaken, give way. *7* MUS. [of a string] to be out of tune.

**falsedad** *f.* falseness, falsity. *2* falsehood.

**falsete** *m.* MUS. falsetto, head voice. *2* plug, spigot [in barrels]. *3* smalll communication door.

**falsía** *f.* falseness, duplicity, perfidy.

**falsificación** *f.* falsification, forgery.

**falsificador, -ra** *m.-f.* falsifier, counterfeiter, forger, faker.

**falsificar** *tr.* to falsify, counterfeit, forge, fake.

**falsilla** *f.* guide-lines [for writing].

**falso, -sa** *adj.* false. *2* untrue. *3* sham, imitated. *4* treacherous, perfidious [person]. *5* vicious [horse]. *6* counterfeit [money]. *7* ~ *testimonio*, false witness, slander. *8 m.* SEW. reinforcement. *9 en* ~, falsely. *10 en* ~, *sobre* ~, without proper support. *11 envidiar en* ~, to bluff.

**falta** *f.* lack, want, absbence, deficiency, shortage: ~ *de pago*, nonpayment; ~ *de respeto*, disrespect; *a* ~ *de*, lacking, for want of. *2* fail: *sin* ~, without fail. *3* fault, infraction. *4* absence, non attendance. *5* SPORT. fault. *6* LAW fault, misdeed, slight offence. *7* mistake, error: ~ *de ortografía*, misspelling. *8* fault, defect, failing. *9 hacer* ~, to be necessary, to be needed; *me hizo usted mucha* ~, I missed you very much.

**faltante** *adj.* wanting, missing.

**faltar** *intr.* to be lacking, wanting or missing; to be short of: *faltan los víveres*, victuals are lacking; *faltaban dos tenedores*, two forks were missing. *2* to die. *3* not to go, not to attend, to be absent from. *4* [of a gun, a rope, etc.] to fail. *5* to be false to, untrue to; to sin or offend against; ~ *a la verdad*, to lie. *6* to fail somebody; to offend somebody. *7* to break [an appointment, one's word, etc.], fail to fulfil [one's engagement]. *8* impers. *faltan tres días para Navidad*, it is three days till Christmas; *faltó poco para que cayese*, he almost fell. *9 falta algo por hacer*, something remains to be done. *10 ¡no faltaba más!*, that goes without saying!; that would be the last straw!

**falto, -ta** *adj.* devoid, wanting, lacking, short: ~ *de*, devoid of, wanting in, short of, lacking.

**faltriquera** *f.* pocket [of a garment].

**falúa** *f.* NAUT. barge [of a flagship], harbour tender.

**falucho** *m.* NAT. felucca.

**falla** *f.* fault, flaw [in things]. *2* GEOL. fault, break. *3* one of the bonfires made in Valencia on St. Joseph's eve.

**fallar** *tr.* to judge, pass sentence. *2* to ruff, trump [at cards]. *3 intr.* to fail, miss, be deficient or wanting; to fail, break, give way.

**falleba** *f.* shutter bolt.

**fallecer** *intr.* to decease, die. ¶ CONJUG. like *agradecer*.

**fallecimiento** *m.* decease, death, demise.

**fallezco, fallezca,** etc. *irr.* V. FALLECER.

**fallido, -da** *adj.* unsuccessful, ineffectual. *2* irrecoverable, uncollectable. *3 adj.-n.* bankrupt.

**fallo, -lla** *adj.* out of a certain suit [at cards]. *2 m.* lack of a certain suit [at cards]. *3* decision, judgment, verdict.

**fama** *f.* fame, renown, reputation. *2* report, rumor: *es* ~, it is said.

**famélico, -ca** *adj.* hungry, famished.

**familia** *f.* family. *2* household. *3* relatives, kin.

**familiar** *adj.* [pertaining to the] family. *2* familiar [well-known]. *3* familiar, unceremonious, informal. *4* colloquial. *5* familiar [spirit]. *6 m.* friend; relative. *7* familiar spirit. *8* familiar [of a bishop; of the Inquisition].

**familiaridad** *f.* familiarity.

**familiarizar** *tr.* to familiarize. *2 ref. familiarizarse con*, to familiarize oneself with.

**familiarmente** *adv.* familiarly. *2* colloquially.

**familión** *m. aug.* large family.

**famoso, -sa** *adj.* famous. *2* iron, priceless.

**fámula** *f.* coll. maidservant.

**fámulo** *m.* famulus. *2* coll. manservant.

**fanal** *m.* harbour beacon. *2* light or lamp globe. *3* bell-shaped glass case.

**fanático, -ca** *adj.* fanatic(al. *2 m.-f.* fanatic.

**fanatismo** *m.* fanaticism.

**fanatizar** *tr.* to fanaticize.

**fandango** *m.* a lively Spanish dance. *2* coll. shindy.

**fanega** *f.* grain measure [about 1.60 bu.]. *2* ~ *de tierra*, land measure [about 1.59 acres].

**fanerógamo, -ma** *adj.* BOT. phanerogamous. *2 f.* BOT. phanerogam.

**fanfarrear** *intr.* FANFARRONEAR.

**fanfarria** *f.* coll. bravado, braggadocio, boast.

**fanfarrón, -na** *adj.* swaggering, bragging, boasting. *2 m.-f.* swaggerer, braggart, boaster.

**fanfarronada** *f.* fanfaronade, swagger, boast.

**fanfarronear** *intr.* to bluster, boast swagger.

**fanfarronería** *f.* blustering, boasting.

**fanfurriña** *f.* pet, huff.

**fangal, fangar** *m.* miry place, mudhole, slough.

**fango** *m.* mud, mire.
**fangoso, -sa** *adj.* muddy, miry.
**fantasear** *intr.* to let one's imagination run free. *2* to boast. *3 tr.* to fancy, imagine.
**fantasía** *f.* fancy, imagination. *2* fancy [mental image]. *3* fantastic fiction, tale, etc. *4* vanity, airs, conceit. *6* MUS. fantasía. *7 de ~*, fancy, not plain.
**fantasioso, -sa** *adj.* vain, conceited.
**fantasma** *m.* phantom. *2* ghost, apparition. *3* solemn, conceited person. *4* TELEV. ghost.
**fantasmagoría** *f.* phantasmagoria.
**fantasmagórico, -ca** *adj.* phantasmagoric.
**fantasmal** *adj.* phantasmal, ghostly, irreal. *2* phantasmal [of ghosts].
**fantasmón, -na** *m.* solemn, conceited person.
**fantástico, -ca** *adj.* fantastic, fanciful. *2* vain, conceited.
**fantoche** *m.* puppet, marionette. *2* coll. jackanapes; ridiculous and presumptuous fellow.
**faquín** *m.* porter, carrier, street porter.
**faquir** *m.* fakir.
**farad, faradio** *m.* ELEC. farad.
**faralá** *m.* SEW. flounce. *2* tawdry ornament.
**farallón** *m.* cliff, headland. *2* MIN. outcrop.
**faramalla** *f.* blarney, eyewash, claptrap. *2* empty show, hollow sham. *3* coll. blarneyer, boaster.
**faramallero, -ra** *adj.* coll. tattling, blarneying. *2 m.-f.* tattler, blarneyer.
**farandola** *f.* farandole [dance].
**farándula** *f.* obs. profession of farce players. *2* troupe of strolling players. *3* FARAMALLA.
**farandulear** *intr.* to boast, show off.
**farandulero, -ra** *m.-f.* comedian. *2* blarneyer.
**faraón** *m.* Pharaoh. *2* faro [card game].
**faraónico, -ca** *adj.* Pharaonic.
**faraute** *m.* herald, messenger.
**fardar** *tr.* to outfit, to dress. *2* to be classy: *farda mucho este coche*, this car looks classy. *3* to show off, to swank. to boast.
**fardel** *m.* bundle, package.
**fardo** *m.* bundle, bale, package.
**farfallón** *adj.* bungler, botcher.
**farfante, farfantón** *m.* braggadocio, boaster.
**fárfara** *f.* shell membrane [of egg].
**farfolla** *f.* husk [of Indian corn]. *2* empty show.
**farfulla** *f.* spluttering, shuttering. *2 m.-f.* splutterer, slutterer.
**farfullar** *tr.* fo splutter, stutter. *2* to stumble through [a task, etc.].
**farináceo, -a** *adj.* farinaceous.
**faringe** *f.* ANAT. pharynx.
**faríngeo, -a** *adj.* pharyngeal.
**faringitis** *f.* MED. pharyngitis.
**farisaico, -ca** *adj.* pharisaic(al. *2* Pharisaic.
**farisaísmo, fariseísmo** *m.* pharisaism. *2* Pharisaism.
**fariseo** *m.* pharise. *2* Pharisee.
**farmacéutico, -ca** *adj.* pharmaceutic(al. *2 m.-f.* chemist, *druggist, pharmacist, apothecary.
**farmacia** *f.* pharmacy. *2* chemist's, *drug-store.
**fármaco** *m.* medicine.
**farmacopea** *f.* pharmacopoeia.
**faro** *m.* lighthouse, beacon: *~ aéreo*, air beacon. *2* headlight [of car]: *~ piloto*, spotlight.
**farol** *m.* street lamp, lamppost. *2* lantern. *3* carriage lamp. *4* NAUT. light: *~ de situación*, position light. *5* boaster, show-off. *6* bluff: *echar un ~*, to bluff. *7* a feat in bullfighting.
**farola** *f.* many-branched lamppost. *2* harbour beacon.

**farolear** *intr.* to show off, to boast.
**farolería** *f.* lantern shop. *2* showing off, boast.
**farolero, -ra** *adj.* showing off, boasting. *2 m.* lamplighter. *3* show-off; boaster.
**farolillo** *m. dim.* small lantern. *2* BOT. Canterbury bell. *3* BOT. heartseed.
**farolón** *m.* FAROLERO 3. *2* large lamp of lantern.
**farpa** *f.* point of a scallop.
**farra** *f.* ICHTH. lavaret. *2* (Am.) spree, revelry.
**fárrago** *m.* farrago, medley.
**farragoso, -sa** *adj.* confused, disordered.
**farraguista** *m.-f.* muddlehead.
**farro** *m.* barley soaked, peeled and broken.
**farruco, -ca** *adj.* bold, fearless.
**farsa** *f.* THEAT. farce. *2* troupe of farce players. *3* farce, empty show, mockery, humbug.
**farsante** *adj.-n.* THEAT. farce player. *2* hypocrite.
**fas** *por ~* or *por nefas*, rightly or wrongly, for one thing or for another.
**fasces** *f. pl.* fasces.
**fascículo** *m.* fascicle, instalment [of a book]. *2* ANAT. fascicle.
**fascinación** *f.* fascination, bewitching, spell.
**fascinador, -ra** *adj.* fascinating. *2 m.-f.* fascinator.
**fascinante** *adj.* fascinating.
**fascinar** *tr.* to fascinate, bewitch.
**fascismo** *m.* Fascism.
**fascista** *adj.* fascist, fascistic. *2 m.-f.* fascist.
**fase** *f.* phase.
**fastidiar** *tr.* to cloy, sicken. *2* to do a bad turn to. *3* to bore. *4 ref.* to become annoyed or bored; to be disappointed.
**fastidio** *m.* distaste, nausea. *2* annoyance, botheration. *3* boredom, ennui.
**fastidioso, -sa** *adj.* cloying. *2* annoying, bothersome. *3* boring, tedious, tiresome.
**fastigio** *m.* apex, summit. *2* ARCH. fastigium.
**fasto, -ta** *adj.* lucky, happy [day, year]. *2 m.* pomp, magnificence. *3 pl.* fasti.
**fastuoso, -sa** *adj.* pompous, magnificent.
**fatal** *adj.* fatal, unavoidable. *2* fateful. *3* bad, evil, deadly, destructive. *4* LAW unpostponable.
**fatalidad** *f.* fatality. *2* mischance, misfortune.
**fatalismo** *m.* fatalism.
**fatídico, -ca** *adj.* fatidic, ominous.
**fatiga** *f.* fatigue [weariness, labour, toil]. *2* hard breathing. *3 pl.* hardships, pains, anguish.
**fatigante** *adj.* fatiguing, tiring, annoying.
**fatigar** *tr.* to fatigue, weary, tire. *2* to annoy, harass. *3 ref.* to tire, get tired, weary oneself.
**fatigoso, -sa** *adj.* fatiguing, wearisome. *2* hard [breathing].
**fatuidad** *f.* fatuity, stupidity. *2* foolishness, inanity. *3* ridiculous, presumption.
**fatuo, -tua** *adj.* fatuous, half-witted. *2* vain, conceited.
**fauces** *f. pl.* ANAT. fauces.
**fauna** *f.* fauna.
**fauno** *m.* MYTH. faun.
**fausto, -ta** *adj.* happy, fortunate [event, etc.]. *2 m.* pomp, magnificence.
**fautor, -ra** *adj.* helper, abettor.
**favor** *m.* help, succour. *2* favour, service, good turn: *hacer el ~ de*, to do [one] the favour of. *3* favour, good will, good graces. *4* favour [ribbon, etc.]. *5 a ~ de*, for, pro, in favour of; *a ~ del viento*, with the wind [taking advantage of the wind]; *a ~ de la oscuridad*, under cover of darkness.
**favorable** *adj.* favourable. *2* advantageous.

**favorecedor, -ra** *adj.* favouring. *2 m.-f.* favourer. *3* helper, supported. *4* client, customer.
**favorecer** *tr.* to help, aid, favour. *2* to favour, support. *3* to bestow a favour to. *4* to become, improve the appearance of. ¶ CONJUG. like *agradecer.*
**favorezco, favorezca,** etc. *irr.* V. FAVORECER.
**favoritismo** *m.* favoritism.
**favorito, -ta** *adj.* favorite, preferred, best liked, pet. *2 m.-f.* favorite.
**faz** *f.* face, visage. *2* face, aspect. *3* obverse.
**fe** *f.* faith: *dar* or *prestar* ~ *a,* to give credit to, to believe; *tener* ~ *en,* to have faith in; *de buena* ~, in good faith; *a* ~ *mía,* upon my faith. *2* assurance, certification: ~ *de bautismo,* certificate of baptism; *dar* ~, to attest, to certify; *hacer* ~, to be a valid assurance or certification. *3* PRINT. ~ *de erratas,* errata, list of errata.
**fealdad** *f.* ugliness, hideousness. *2* plainness, homeliness. *3* badness, foulness [of deeds, words, etc.].
**Febe** *f. pr. n.* MYTH. Phœbus.
**febrero** *m.* February.
**febricitante** *adj.* MED. feverish.
**febrífugo, -ga** *adj.-m.* febrifuge.
**febril** *adj.* febrile. *2* feverish.
**fecal** *adj.* faecal, fecal.
**fécula** *f.* fecula, starch.
**feculento, -ta** *adj.* starchy [food]. *2* feculent.
**fecundación** *f.* fecundation.
**fecundante** *adj.* fecundating.
**fecundar** *tr.* to fecundate, to fertilize.
**fecundidad** *f.* fecundity, fertility.
**fecundizar** *tr.* to fertilize.
**fecundo, -da** *adj.* fecund. *2* abundant.
**fecha** *f.* date [time]: *con* ~ *de,* under date of; *hasta la* ~, to date. *2* day [elapsed].
**fechar** *tr.* to date [a letter, etc.].
**fechoría** *f.* misdeed, villainy.
**federación** *f.* federation.
**federal** *adj.* federal. *2* federalistic.
**federalismo** *m.* federalism.
**federar** *tr.* to federate, federalize. *2 ref.* to federate [become federated].
**federativo, -va** *adj.* federative.
**Federica** *f. pr. n.* Frederica.
**Federico** *m. pr. n.* Frederick.
**Fedra** *f. pr. n.* MYTH. Phaedra.
**fehaciente** *adj.* LAW. authentic.
**feldespato** *m.* MINER. feldspar.
**felice** *adj.* poet. happy.
**felicidad** *f.* felicity, happiness. *2* good fortune.
**felicitación** *f.* felicitation, congratulation.
**felicitar** *tr.* to felicitate, wish joy to, congratulate.
**félidos** *m. pl.* ZOOL. Felidœ.
**feligrés, -sa** *m.-f.* ECCL. parishioner.
**feligresía** *f.* parish.
**felino, -na** *adj.* feline. *2 m.* ZOOL. feline.
**Felipe** *m. pr. n.* Philip.
**feliz** *adj.* happy, fortunate. *2* felicitous.
**felón, -na** *adj.* perfidious, treacherous, felonious. *2 m.-f.* traitor, felon, wicked person.
**felonía** *f.* perfidy, treachery, felony.
**felpa** *f.* plush. *2* coll. drubbing. *3* reprimand.
**felpilla** *f.* chenille.
**felpudo, -da** *adj.* plushy. *2 m.* plush mat, doormat.
**femenil** *adj.* feminine, womanish.
**femenino, -na** *adj.* female, feminine. *2* GRAM. feminine.
**fementido, -da** *adj.* false, unfaithful, treacherous.
**femineidad** *f.* feminity.

**feminismo** *m.* feminism.
**feminista** *adj.* feminist, feministic. *2 m.-f.* feminist.
**femoral** *adj.* femoral.
**fémur** *m.* ANAT. ENT. femur.
**fenecer** *tr.* to finish, conclude. *2 intr.* to die. *3* to come to an end. ¶ CONJUG. like *agradecer.*
**fenecimiento** *m.* death. *2* finish, termination.
**fenezco, fenezca,** etc. *irr.* V. FENECER.
**fenianismo** *m.* Fenianism.
**feniano** *m.* Fenian.
**fenicado, -da** *adj.* carbolized.
**Fenicia** *f. pr. n.* Phoenicia.
**fenicio, -cia** *adj.-n.* Phoenician.
**fénico** *adj.* CHEM. phenic, carbolic.
**fénix** *m.* MYTH. phœnix. *2* fig. phœnix, paragon.
**fenol** *m.* CHEM. phenol.
**fenomenal** *adj.* phenomenal. *2* great, enormous.
**fenómeno** *m.* phenomenon. *2* monster, freak.
**feo, -a** *adj.* ugly. *2* plain, homely. *3* unbecoming. *4* bad, dirty [word, deed]. *5* bad, serious, alarming. *6 m.* slight, affront.
**feracidad** *f.* feracity, fertility.
**feraz** *adj.* feracious, fertile.
**féretro** *m.* bier, coffin.
**feria** *f.* fair [gathering, exhibition]. *2* deal, agreement. *3* ECCL. feria. *4* rest, holiday.
**ferial** *adj.* ferial. *2 m.* fair; fairground.
**feriante** *adj.* fairgoing. *2 m.-f.* fairgoer. *3* trader at fairs.
**feriar** *tr.* to buy at a fair. *2* to buy, sell or barter.
**ferino, -na** *adj.* ferine. *2* MED. whooping [cough].
**fermentación** *f.* fermentation.
**fermentar** *intr.* to ferment. *2 tr.* to produce fermentation.
**fermento** *m.* CHEM. ferment.
**Fernando** *m. pr. n.* Ferdinand.
**ferocidad** *f.* ferocity.
**feroz** *adj.* ferocious. *2* fig. ravenous.
**ferrar** *tr.* to put an iron on; to garnish, cover or shoe with iron. ¶ CONJUG. like *acertar.*
**férreo, -a** *adj.* ferreous, iron: *vía férrea,* railroad. *2* strong, harsh, severe.
**ferrería** *f.* ironworks, foundry.
**ferretería** *f.* FERRERÍA. *2* ironmongery. *3* hardware.
**ferretero, -ra** *m.-f.* hardware dealer.
**férrico, -ca** *adj.* CHEM. ferric.
**ferrocarril** *m.* railway, railroad: ~ *aéreo,* aerial railway; ~ *de cremallera,* rack railway; ~ *funicular,* funicular railway.
**ferrocianuro** *m.* CHEM. ferrocyanide.
**ferroso, -sa** *adj.* CHEM. ferrous.
**ferroviario** *adj.* [pertaining to the] railway, railroad. *2 m.* railwayman, *railroader.
**ferruginoso, -sa** *adj.* ferruginous.
**fértil** *adj.* fertile.
**fertilidad** *f.* fertility.
**fertilizante** *adj.* fertilizing. *2 m.* fertilizer.
**fertilizar** *tr.* to fertilize [the soil].
**férula** *f.* ferule. *2* fig. authority, rule, yoke. *3* BOT. giant, fennel. *4* SURG. flexible splint.
**férvido, -da** *adj.* fervid, ardent.
**ferviente** *adj.* FERVOROSO.
**fervor** *m.* fervour.
**fervorín** *m.* short prayer.
**fervoroso, -sa** *adj.* fervent.
**festejar** *tr.* to feast, fête, celebrate, honour with a celebration. *2* to court, to woo.
**festejo** *m.* fête, fêting. *2* courting, courtship. *3 pl.* public rejoicings.
**festín** *m.* feast, banquet.

**festival** m. festival.
**festividad** f. feast, celebration. 2 feast day, holiday. 3 humour, esprit.
**festivo, -va** adj. humourous, witty. 2 merry, joyful. 3 día ~, feast day, holiday.
**festón** m. festoon. 2 scalloped border.
**festonar, festonear** tr. to festoon. 2 to scallop.
**fetal** adj. fœtal, fetal.
**fetén** adj. coll. fantastic, terrific, smashing, super. 2 hundred per cent, through and through, from head to toe.
**fetiche** m. fetish.
**fetichismo** m. fetishism.
**fetidez** f. fetidity: ~ de aliento, foul breath.
**fétido, -da** adj. fetid. 2 foul [breath].
**feto** m. fœtus, fetus.
**feúco, ca; feúcho, -cha** adj. rather ugly, plain.
**feudal** adj. feudal. 2 feudalistic.
**feudalismo** m. feudalism.
**feudatario, -ria** adj.-n. feudatory.
**feudo** m. LAW feud, fief. 2 vassalage.
**fez** m. fez.
**fi** f. phi [greek letter].
**fiable** adj. trustworthy, responsible.
**fiado** m. al ~, on credit.
**fiador, -ra** m.-f. guarantor, surety, bail: salir ~, to stand surety. 2 safety cord, strap; safety catch; catch, pawl, stop.
**fiambre** adj. cold [meat]. 2 fig. stale [news, etc.]. 3 m. cold meat, cold cut.
**fiambrera** f. lunch basket. 2 dinner pail.
**fiambrería** f. (Am.) sausage store, coldmeat store. 2 (Am.) delicatessen store.
**fianza** f. bail, guaranty, security, bond: bajo ~, on bail. 2 guarantor, guarantee, surety, bond.
**fiar** tr. to answer for, go surety for; to bail. 2 to entrust, confide. 3 tr.-intr. to sell on credit. 4 intr. to trust: ~ en, to trust in. 5 ref. fiarse de, to trust, to rely on.
**fiasco** m. failure, fiasco.
**fiat** m. fiat.
**fibra** f. fibre, fiber; staple. 2 grain [of wood]. 3 fig. energy, vigour, stamina.
**fibrilla** f. fibril.
**fibrina** f. CHEM. fibrin, fibrine.
**fibroma** m. MED. fibroma.
**fibroso, -sa** adj. fibrous.
**fíbula** f. ARCHEOL. fibula.
**ficción** f. fiction.
**ficticio, -cia** adj. fictitious.
**ficha** f. counter, chip. 2 domino [piece]. 3 filing card: ~ catalográfica, index card [of a library].
**fichar** tr. to play [a domino]. 2 to file particulars of [a person] in the police record.
**fichero** m. card index; filing cabinet.
**fideicomiso** m. LAW fideicommissum.
**fidelidad** f. fidelity, faithfulness, loyalty. 2 fealty. 3 fidelity, faithfulness, accuracy.
**fideos** m. pl. vermicelli.
**fiduciario, -ria** adj.-n. fiduciary.
**fiebre** f. MED. fever. 2 fever, excitement, agitation.
**fiel** adj. faithful, loyal, true, trustworthy. 2 faithful, true, accurate. 3 m. faithful [church member]. 4 pointer [of scales]. 5 public inspector: ~ contraste, inspector of weights and measures; hallmarker.
**fielato** m. office of the FIEL. 2 octroi [office].
**fieltro** m. felt. 2 felt hat. 3 felt rug.
**fiera** f. wild beast. 2 BULLF. bull. 3 cruel, fierce person. 4 ser una ~ para, to be the devil for [work, etc.].

**fierabrás** m. devil [wicked person or child].
**fiereza** f. fierceness, cruelty, ferocity. 2 ugliness.
**fiero, -ra** adj. fierce, cruel, ferocious. 2 wild [beast]. 3 ugly, hideous. 4 great, violent. 5 rough, rude. 6 m. bluster, threat: echar fieros, to bluster, to threaten.
**fiesta** f. feast, entertainment, party: fête, festival, public rejoicing; la ~ brava, la ~ nacional, bullfight; fin de ~, THEAT. grand finale; aguar la ~, to spoil the feast; tengamos la ~ en paz, let's have no disturbance. 2 feast, holiday, feast day: ~ de guardar or de precepto, holiday of obligation; ~ de la hispanidad, ~ de la raza, Columbus Day, Discovery Day; ~ del Trabajo, Labour Day; ~ nacional, national feast day, bank holiday; hacer ~, to take a day off. 3 merrymaking. 4 endearment, caress: hacer fiestas a, to caress, fondle; [of a dog, etc.] to fawn on. 5 pl. holidays. 6 public rejoicings.
**fiestero, -ra** adj. gay, jolly, fond of feasts.
**fígaro** m. fig. barber. 2 short jacket.
**figle** m. MUS. ophicleide. 2 ophicleidist.
**figón** m. cheap eating house.
**figulino, -na** adj. figuline.
**figura** f. figure [external form; person; representation]. 2 figure [of the human body]. 3 figure, drawing. 4 GEOM., F. ARTS, RHET., LOG., GRAM., DANC. figure: ~ retórica, figure of speech. 5 MUS. note. 6 THEAT. character; actor. 7 ridiculous person. 8 court card. 9 hacer ~, to cut a figure.
**figuración** f. figuration. 2 imagining, fancy: eso son figuraciones tuyas, that's wat you imagine.
**figuradamente** adv. figuratively.
**figurado, -da** adj. figured, represented, imagined. 2 figurative [language, sense, etc.].
**figurante, -ta** m.-f. THEAT. figurant.
**figurar** tr. to figure, depict, represent. 2 to feign. 3 intr. to be counted [among, in the number of]. 4 to cut a figure. 5 ref. to fancy, imagine.
**figurativo, -va** adj. figurative, representative.
**figurilla** f. figurine, statuette. 2 small person.
**figurín** m. fashion plate [design; person]. 2 small model [of dress].
**figurón** m. large figure: ~ de proa, NAUT. figurehead. 2 pretentious nobody.
**fijación** f. fixation, fixing. 2 appointment [of time or place]. 3 posting [of bills]. 4 immobilizing. 5 CHEM., PHOT. fixation.
**fijador, -ra** adj. fixing. 2 m. fixer, poster. 3 PHOT. fixing bath. 4 PAINT. fixing liquid.
**fijamente** adv. firmly, steadfastly, attentively.
**fijar** tr. to fix, nail, make fast. 2 to stick, paste up, placard, post [bills, etc.]. 3 PHOT., F. ARTS. to fix. 4 to fix, make firm, set, determine. 5 ref. to become fixed or set. 6 to pay attention, notice, observe.
**fijeza** f. firmness. 2 fixity, steadfastness.
**fijo, -ja** adj. fixed. 2 firm, immovable, set, intent: mirada fija, set look. 3 fast [colour]. 4 MACH. stationary. 5 de ~, surely. 6 ésa es la fija, that is a fact.
**fila** f. row, line, tier; file: ~ india, single file, Indian file; en ~, in a row; in single file. 2 MIL. rank [of soldiers]: estar en filas, to be in the Army. 3 coll. dislike, hatred.
**filacteria** f. phylactery.
**Filadelfia** f. pr. n. GEOG. Philadelphia.
**filamento** m. filament.
**filamentoso, -sa** adj. filamentous.
**filandria** f. ZOOL. filander.
**filantropía** f. philanthropy.

**filántropo** *m.* philanthropist.
**filaria** *f.* ZOOL. filaria.
**filarmonía** *f.* love of music.
**filarmónico, -ca** *adj.-n.* philharmonic.
**filástica** *f.* NAUT. rope yarn.
**filatelia** *f.* philately.
**filatélico, -ca** *adj.* philatelic. *2 m.-f.* philatelist.
**filete** *m.* ARCH. fillet, listel. *2* BOOKB., PRINT. fillet, ornamental line. *3* SEW. narrow hem. *4* small spit. *5* MACH. narrow edge; thread [of a screw]. *6* snaffle bit. *7* COOK. fillet. *8* COOK. sirloin.
**filetear** *tr.* to fillet. *2* BOOKB. to tool.
**filfa** *f.* lie, humbug, false news.
**filiación** *f.* filiation. *2* personal description.
**filial** *adj.* filial. *2* COM. branch, affiliated. *3 f.* branch of a commercial house.
**filiar** *tr.* to note down the personal description of. *2 ref.* to enlist.
**filibustero** *m.* filibuster, freebooter.
**filicales** *f. pl.* BOT. Filicales.
**filiforme** *adj.* filiform, threadlike.
**filigrana** *f.* filigree. *2* delicate, fanciful thing or work. *3* watermark [in paper].
**filipéndula** *f.* BOT. dropwort.
**filipense** *adj.-n.* Philippian. *2* Oratorian.
**filípica** *f.* Philippic. *2* philippic [invective].
**Filipinas** *f. pr. n.* GEOG. Philippine [islands].
**filipino, -na** *adj.-n.* Philippine.
**Filipo** *m. pr. n.* Philip [of Macedonia].
**filisteo, -a** *adj.-n.* BIBL. Philistine. *2 m.* tall, corpulent fellow.
**filmación** *f.* CINEM. filming.
**filmar** *tr.* CINEM. to film.
**filme** *m.* CINEM. film.
**filmoteca** *f.* film library.
**filo** *m.* [cutting] edge. *2* point or line dividing something in two equal-parts. *3* NAUT. ~ *del viento*, direction of the wind.
**filocomunista** *adj.-n.* procommunist.
**filodio** *m.* BOT. phyllode.
**filología, filológica** *f.* philology.
**filólogo** *m.* philologist.
**filomela, filomena** *f.* poet. philomel, nightingale.
**filón** *m.* MIN. vein, lode. *2* fig. mine.
**filosofal** *adj. piedra* ~, philosopher's stone.
**filosofar** *intr.* to philosophize.
**filosofía** *f.* philosophy.
**filosófico, -ca** *adj.* philosophic(al).
**filósofo, -fa** *adj.* philosophic. *2 m.* philosopher.
**filoxera** *f.* ENT. phylloxera.
**filtración** *f.* filtration. *2* fig. leakage.
**filtrador, -ra** *adj.* filtering. *2 m.* filter.
**filtrante** *adj.* filtering. *2* porous.
**filtrar** *tr.-intr.* to filtrate, filter, percolate. *2 intr.* to leak. *3 ref.* to ooze out or through; [of money] to leak away.
**filtro** *m.* filter, percolator. *2* ELEC., OPT. filter. *3* seaside fresh-water spring. *4* philtre, philter.
**filustre** *m.* coll. fineness, elegance.
**filló, filloa** *f.* kind of pancake.
**fimbria** *f.* border [of a skirt].
**fimosis** *f.* MED. phimosis.
**fin** *m.* end [conclusion, close, finish; extremity]: *dar* ~ *a*, to end, finish; *poner* ~ *a*, to put an end to; *a fines de*, towards the end of; *al* ~, at the end; finally, at last: *al* ~ *y al cabo*, in the end; after all; *en* ~, finally; in short; well [as an expletive]: *por* ~, at last, lastly. *2* end, purpose: *a* ~ *de*, in order to; *a* ~ *de que*, in order that, so that.
**finado, -da** *adj.* late, deceased. *2 m.-f.* deceased.

**final** *adj.* final, last, ultimate. *2* GRAM. final. *3 m.* end, termination. *4* MUS. finale. *5 f.* SPORT. finals.
**finalidad** *f.* PHILOS. finality. *2* end, purpose.
**finalista** *m.-f.* PHILOS., SPORT finalist.
**finalizar** *tr.-intr.* to end, finish, conclude.
**finamente** *adv.* finely, nicely, delicately. *2* politely.
**financiar** *tr.* to finance.
**financiero, -ra** *adj.* financial. *2 m.-f.* financier.
**finanzas** *f. pl.* finances.
**finar** *intr.* to die. *2 ref.* to long, yearn.
**finca** *f.* property [piece of real estate], land, house, farm, ranch.
**fincar** *intr.-ref.* to buy up real estate.
**finés, -sa** *adj.* Finnic, Finnish. *2 m.* Finnish [language]. *3 m.-f.* Finn [person].
**fineza** *f.* fineness [goodness, purity], delicacy, perfection. *2* civility, kindness, favour, little gift.
**fingido, -da** *adj.* feigned, sham, affected. *2* false, deceitful.
**fingidor, -ra** *adj.* feigning, dissembling. *2 m.-f.* feigner, dissembler.
**fingimiento** *m.* feigning, simulation, pretence.
**fingir** *tr.* to feign, simulate, sham, pretend. *2 ref.* to feign to be; to pretend to be.
**finiquitar** *tr.* to settle, to close [an account]. *2* to finish, conclude, close, end.
**finiquito** *m.* settlement [of an account].
**finito, -ta** *adj.* finite.
**finlandés, -sa** *adj.* Finnish. *2 m.* Finnish [language]. *3 m.-f.* Finn, Finlander.
**Finlandia** *f. pr. n.* GEOG. Finland.
**fino, -na** *adj.* fine [of high quality; pure, refined]. *2* thin; sheer; slender. *3* polite, wellbred. *4* affectionate, true. *5* shrewd. *6* subtle, nice. *7* sharp [point; sense].
**finta** *f.* feint [sham attack or blow].
**finura** *f.* fineness, perfection. *2* politeness, courtesy.
**fiord, fiordo** *m.* fiord.
**fioritura** *f.* MUS. fioritura. *2* embellishment.
**firma** *f.* signature, subscription, hand: ~ *en blanco*, blank signature. *2* [act of] signing. *3* letters, etc., brought to be signed. *4* COM. firm.
**firmamento** *m.* firmament.
**firmante** *adj.* signer, subscriber, signatory.
**firmar** *tr.* to sign, subscribe.
**firme** *adj.* firm [stable, strong, solid, steady]: *tierra* ~, mainland. *2* steadfast, unflinching. *3 m.* roadbed. *4 adv.* firmly. *5 de* ~, with a will, hard; violently. *6 en* ~, COM. firm: *oferta en* ~, firm offer. *7 ¡firmes!* MIL. attention!
**firmeza** *f.* firmness [stability; steadfastness].
**firuletes** *m. pl.* (Am.) ornaments, elaborate adornments, flourishes.
**fiscal** *adj.* fiscal. *2 m.* LAW public prosecutor; *district attorney. *3* busybody, prier. *4* ~ *de tasas*, official in charge of price control.
**fiscalía** *f.* office and post of a FISCAL.
**fiscalización** *f.* control, inspection. *2* prying.
**fiscalizar** *tr.* to control, to inspect. *2* to pry into [somebody's conduct], to censure.
**fisco** *m.* fisc, fisk, state treasury.
**fisga** *f.* fish-spear. *2* sly mockery, raillery.
**fisgar** *tr.* to fish, fish spear. *2* to smell out, pry, peep. *3 ref. fisgarse de*, to make fun of.
**fisgón, -na** *m.-f.* sly mocker. *2* prier, peeper.
**fisgonear** *tr.* to keep prying [into other people's business].
**fisgoneo** *m.* prying, constant prying.
**física** *f.* physics.

**físico, -ca** *adj.* physical. *2 m.* physicist. *3* physique, looks [of a person].
**fisicoquímica** *f.* physicochemistry.
**fisil** *adj.* fissile.
**fisiócrata** *m.-f.* physiocrat.
**fisiología** *f.* physiology.
**fisiológico, -ca** *adj.* physiological.
**fisiólogo** *m.* physiologist.
**fisión** *f.* PHYS., CHEM. fission.
**fisionomía** *f.* FISONOMÍA.
**fisioterapia** *f.* physiotherapy.
**fisípedo, -da** *adj.-n.* ZOOL. fissiped.
**fisirrostro, -tra** *adj.* ORN. fissirostral.
**fisonomía** *f.* physiognomy. *2* features, face.
**fisonómico, -ca** *adj.* physiognomic(al.
**fisonomista** *m.-f.*, **fisónomo** *m.* physiognomist. *2* one who has a good memory for faces.
**fístula** *f.* fistula, tube. *2* MED. fistula.
**fistular** *adj.* fistular.
**fisura** *f.* MED., MIN. fissure.
**fitófago, -ga** *adj.* ZOOL. phytophagous.
**fitografía** *adj.* phytography.
**fitopatología** *f.* plant pathology.
**flabelífero, -ra** *adj.* fan-carrying [in ceremonies].
**flabelo** *m.* flabellum.
**flaccidez** *f.* flaccidity, flabbiness.
**fláccido, -da** *adj.* flaccid, flabby.
**flaco, -ca** *adj.* lean, thin, lank, meagre. *2* weak, feeble. *3* frail, weak in resolution. *4 m.* weak point, foible.
**flacucho, -cha** *adj.* rather lean, thinnish.
**flacura** *f.* leanness, thinness [lack of flesh]. *2* weakness, feebleness.
**flagelación** *f.* flagellation, scourging.
**flagelado, -da** *adj.-n.* BIOL., BOT. flagellate.
**flagelante** *m.-f.* flagellant. *2* Flagellant.
**flagelar** *tr.* to flagellate, scourge. *2* to lash, flay [vice, etc.].
**flagelo** *m.* scourge. *2* BIOL. flagellum.
**flagrante** *adj.* blazing, flaming. *2 en ~* or *en delito*, in the very act.
**flama** *f.* flame. *2* reverberation.
**flamante** *adj.* blazing, flaming, brilliant. *2* splendid, magnificent, remarkable. *3* brand new.
**flamear** *intr.* to flame, blaze. *2* [of flags, etc.] to wave, flutter. *3 tr.* to flame [sterilize with flame].
**flamen** *m.* flamen.
**flamenco, -ca** *adj.-n.* Flemish. *2 adj.* Andalousian gypsy [dance, song, etc.]. *3* buxom. *4 m.* Flemish [language]. *5* ORN. flamingo. *6 ponerse ~*, to get cocky.
**flamenquería** *f.* swagger.
**flamígero, -ra** *poet.* flaming. *2* ARCH. flamboyant.
**flámula** *f.* streamer, pennon.
**flan** *m.* flan, solid custard.
**flanco** *m.* flank, side. *2* FORT., MIL., NAV. flank.
**Flandes** *f. pr. n.* GEOG. Flanders.
**flanquear** *tr.* to flank.
**flanqueo** *m.* flanking.
**flaquear** *intr.* to weaken, give way; to lose strength. *2* fig. to lose heart, weaken, flag.
**flaqueza** *f.* leanness, emaciation. *2* weakness [lack or strength]. *3* weakness, frailty, failing.
**flash** *m.* PHOT. flash, flashlight. *2* RADIO. newsflash.
**flato** *m.* flatus [gas].
**flatulencia** *f.* flatulence.
**flatulento, -ta** *adj.* flatulent.
**flauta** *f.* MUS. flute. *2* flautist, flutist.
**flautado, -da** *adj.* flutelike. *2 m.* flute [organ stop].
**flauteado, -da** *adj.* flutelike, sweet.

**flautín** *m.* MUS. piccolo, octave flute.
**flautista** *m.* flautist, flutist.
**flavo, -va** *adj.* flavid, golden yellow.
**flébil** *adj.* poet. sad, tearful, plaintive.
**flebitis** *f.* MED. phlebitis.
**fleco** *m.* fringe [ornamental border]. *2* ragged edge. *3* fringe [of hair].
**flecha** *f.* arrow. *2* FORT. flèche. *3* ASTR. Sagita. *4* AER. sweepback. *5* ENG., ARCH. deflection [of a beam, etc.].
**flechadura** *f.* NAUT. ratlines.
**flechar** *tr.* to fit an arrow to [the bow]. *2* to wound or kill with arrows. *3* coll. to inspire sudden love.
**flechaste** NAUT. ratline.
**flechazo** *m.* arrow shot. *2* arrow wound. *3* coll. sudden love, love at first sight.
**fleje** *m.* iron hoop or strap.
**flema** *f.* physiol., chem. phlegm. *2* phlegm, calmness: *gastar ~*, to be cold, phlegmatic.
**flemático, -ca** *adj.* phlegmatic(al.
**flemón** *m.* MED. phlegmon. *2* MED. gumboil.
**flequillo** *m.* small fringe. *2* FLECO 3.
**fletador** *m.* NAUT. freighter, charterer.
**fletamento** *m.* NAUT. freightment, charterage. *2* freight, charter party.
**fletante** *m.* shipowner [in the charter party].
**fletar** *tr.* NAUT. to freight, charter [a ship].
**flete** *m.* NAUT. freight, cargo. *2* NAUT. freightage.
**flexibilidad** *f.* flexibility.
**flexible** *adj.* flexible, pliant, lithe, supple. *2* soft [hat]. *3 m.* ELEC. cord, flex. *4* soft hat.
**flexión** *f.* flexion, bending. *2* GRAM. flexion.
**flexor, -ra** *adj.* bending. *2 m.* ANAT. flexor.
**flexuoso, -sa** *adj.* flexuous.
**flirtear** *intr.* to flirt.
**flirteo** *m.* flirtation.
**flocadura** *f.* SEW. fringe trimming.
**flojamente** *adv.* laxly, carelessly, negligently.
**flojear** *intr.* to slack. *2* to weaken [in one's efforts, etc.]. *3* FLAQUEAR.
**flojedad** *f.* laxity, weakness. *2* slackness, carelessness.
**flojera** *f.* FLOJEDAD.
**flojo, -ja** *adj.* loose [only lightly secured], slack [not tight]; flaccid. *2* weak [wine, tea, etc.]. *3* weak [spring]. *4* light [wind]. *5* lax, careless, negligent.
**floqueado, -da** *adj.* fringed, trimmed with fringe.
**flor** *f.* BOT. flower, bloom, blossom; *~ compuesta*, composite flower; *~ de amor*, amaranth; *~ de la maravilla*, tigerflower; *~ de la Trinidad*, pansy; *~ de lis*, fleur-de-lis; *en ~*, in flower, in bloom, in blossom. *2* bloom [dust covering certain fruits]. *3* flower, cream, elite: *la ~ y nata*, the pick and choice, the cream. *4* flowers [of wine]. *5* CHEM. flower: *flores de cinc*, zinc oxide. *6* flower [of life, youth, etc.]: *en la ~ de la edad*, in the prime. *7* METAL. floss. *8* iridiscence on quenched metal sheets. *9* compliment, flattering remark: *decir* or *echar flores*, to say flattering things to a lady. *10* a card game. *11* face [of leather]. *12* GAMBLING. trick. *12 a ~*, flush; *a ~ de agua*, close to, or on the surface of, the water; awash; *a ~ de tierra*, close to the ground. *13 dar uno en la ~ de*, to acquire the habit of.
**flora** *f.* flora. *2* (cap.) MYTH. Flora.
**floración** *f.* BOT. flowerring, florescence.
**floral** *adj.* floral. *2 Juegos florales*, Floral Games.
**flordelisado, -da** *adj.* HER. fleury.
**florear** *tr.* to flower [decorate with flowers]. *2* to

stack [cards]. *3* to bolt [flour]. *4 intr.* to strike a continuous flourish on the guitar. *5* to vibrate the sword. *6* to pay compliments. *7* (Am.) to choose the best.

**florecer** *intr.* to flower, bloom, blossom. *2* to flourish, prosper. *3 ref.* to become mouldy. ¶ CONJUG. like *agradecer.*

**floreciente** *adj.* flowering, florescent. *2* flourishing.

**florecimiento** *m.* flowering, blossoming. *2* flourishing, prosperity. *3* mouldiness.

**Florencia** *f. pr. n.* Florence. *2* GEOG. Florence.

**florentino, -na** *adj.-n.* Florentine.

**floreo** *m.* idle talk. *2* idle compliment. *3* act of vibrating the sword. *4* continuous flourish on the guitar.

**florería** *f.* florist's [shop].

**florero, -ra** *m.-f.* flower seller. *2 m.* flower vase. *3* flower pot, flower box. *4* PAINT. flower piece.

**florescencia** *f.* MED., CHEM. efflorescence. *2* BOT. florescence.

**floresta** *f.* pleasant woods or grove.

**florete** *m.* foil, fencing foil.

**florezco, florezca,** etc. *irr.* V. FLORECER.

**floricultor, -ra** *m.-f.* floriculturist.

**floricultura** *f.* floriculture.

**florido, -da** *adj.* flowery, blossomy. *2* flowery, florid. *3* choice, select. *4 Pascua florida,* Easter.

**florífero, -ra** *adj.* floriferous.

**florilegio** *m.* florilegium, anthology.

**florín** *m.* florin [coin].

**florista** *m.-f.* florist, flower seller, flower girl.

**florón** *m.* ARCH. rosette. *2* HER. fleuron [in a crown]. *3* glorious feat.

**flósculo** *m.* BOT. floscule.

**flota** *f.* NAUT. fleet. *2* ~ *aérea,* air fleet.

**flotación** *f.* flotation, floating: *línea de* ~, NAUT. waterline.

**flotador, -ra** *adj.* floating, swimming. *2 m.* floater, float.

**flotante** *adj.* floating.

**flotar** *intr.* to float [on a liquid, in the air]. *2* [of a flag, etc.] to wave.

**flote** *m.* flotation: *a* ~, afloat.

**flotilla** *f.* flotilla, small fleet.

**fluctuación** *f.* fluctuation, wavering.

**fluctuante** *adj.* fluctuating, fluctuant.

**fluctuar** *intr.* to fluctuate, to bob up and down. *2* to fluctuate, waver, hesitate. *3* to wave [to the wind]. *4* to totter, be in danger.

**fluencia** *f.* flowing, running. *2* source, spring.

**fluente** *adj.* flowing, running.

**fluidez** *f.* fluidity. *2* flowingness, fluidness.

**fluido, -da** *adj.* fluid [body]. *2* flowing, fluid [style]. *3 m.* fluid. *4* ~ *eléctrico,* electric current.

**fluir** *intr.* to flow. ¶ CONJUG. like *huir.*

**flujo** *m.* flowing, flux: ~ *magnético,* mágnetic flux. *2* flow, rising tide. *3* MED. flux, discharge. *4* CHEM., METAL. flux.

**flúor** *m.* CHEM. fluorin, fluorine. *2* MINER. fluor spar.

**fluorescencia** *f.* fluorescence.

**fluorescente** *adj.* fluorescent.

**fluoruro** *m.* CHEM. fluoride.

**fluvial** *adj.* fluvial, river.

**flux** *m.* flush [at cards].

**fluxión** *f.* MED. fluxion. *2* cold in the head.

**foca** *f.* ZOOL. seal.

**focal** *adj.* focal.

**focalizar** *tr.* PHYS. to focalize.

**focense** *adj.-n.* Phocian.

**Fócida (la)** *f. pr. n.* HIST., GEOG. Phocis.

**focino** *m.* goad for elephants.

**foco** *m.* GEOM., OPT., PHYS., MED., SEISM. focus. *2* fig. focus, source. *3* AUTO., THEAT. headlight, spotlight. *4* (Am.) electric light.

**fofo, -fa** *adj.* soft, spongy, flabby.

**fogata** *f.* blaze, bonfire. *2* MIL. fougasse.

**fogón** *m.* open fire for cooking. *2* touch-hole [of cannon]. *3* fire-box [of steam-engine boiler].

**fogonadura** *f.* NAUT. mast-hole.

**fogonazo** *m.* powder flash.

**fogonero** *m.* fireman, stoker.

**fogosidad** *f.* fire, spirit, vehemence.

**fogoso, -sa** *adj.* ardent, vehement. *2* fierce, spirited, mettlesome.

**foguear** *tr.* to scale [a gun]. *2* MIL. to accustom to the discharge of firearms. *3* to accustom to the hardships of a trade or state. *4* VET. to cauterize.

**fogueo** *m.* habituation to the discharge of firearms.

**foja** *f.* ORN. European coot.

**folía** *f.* light popular music. *2 pl.* Portuguese dance.

**foliáceo, -a** *adj.* foliaceous.

**foliación** *f.* foliation.

**foliar** *tr.* to foliate, folio [a book].

**folicular** *adj.* follicular.

**foliculario** *m.* scorn, pamphleteer, news writer.

**folículo** *m.* ANAT., BOT. follicle.

**folio** *m.* folio: ~ *recto,* recto; ~ *vuelto,* verso; *de a* ~, fig. great, enormous; *en* ~, in folio. *2* PRINT. running head.

**folíolo** *m.* BOT. foliole.

**folklore** *m.* folklore.

**folklórico, -ca** *adj.* folkloric, folkloristic.

**follaje** *m.* foliage, leafage. *2* ARCH. foliage. *3* gaudy ornament. *4* rhetoric trash.

**follar** *tr.* to blow (up) with bellows. *2 tr.-intr.* to fuck. *3 ref.* coll. to drop a silent one, to fart silently.

**folletín** *m.* feuilleton, newspaper serial.

**folletinesco, -ca** *adj.* serial, romantic, sensational.

**folletinista** *m.-f.* serial writer.

**folletista** *m.-f.* pamphleteer.

**folleto** *m.* pamphlet, brochure, tract.

**follón, -na** *adj.* lazy, indolent. *2* cowardly and knavish. *3 m.-f.* lazy person. *4* cowardly knave. *5 m.* noiseless rocket. *6* coll. shindy.

**fomentación** *f.* MED. fomentation.

**fomentar** *tr.* to foment, promote, encourage, foster. *2* MED. to foment.

**fomento** *m.* fomentation, promoting, encouraging, fostering; encouragement. *2* MED. fomentation.

**fonación** *f.* phonation, uttering of voice.

**fonda** *f.* inn, restaurant, eating house.

**fondeadero** *m.* NAUT. anchorage [place].

**fondear** *tr.* NAUT. to sound. *2* to search [a ship]. *3* to examine closely. *4 intr.* to cast anchor.

**fondeo** *m.* NAUT. searching. *2* NAUT. anchorage.

**fondillos** *m. pl.* seat [of trousers].

**fondista** *m.-f.* innkeeper, hotel keeper.

**fondo** *m.* bottom [of a cavity or hollow; of sea, river, etc.; farthest or inmost point]: *dar* ~, NAUT. to cast anchor. *2* bottom. *3* bottom, essence: *en el* ~, at bottom. *4* depth [down or inwards]. *5* farthest end [of a room]. *6* background. *7* ground [of a painting, etc.]. *8* disposition, nature: *tener buen* ~, to have a good disposition. *9* head [of a cask]. *10* FENC. *tirarse a* ~, to lunge. *11 s.-pl.* fund [of wisdom, knowledge, money, etc.]; common fund [in gambling];

funds [money, resources]: *fondos de amortización*, sinking funds: *estar en fondos*, to have available money. *12 adv.* thoroughly.
**fonducho** *m.* cheap eating house.
**fonema** *m.* phoneme.
**fonética** *f.* phonetics.
**fonético, -ca** *adj.* phonetic(al.
**foniatra** *m.* MED. phoniatrician.
**fónico, -ca** *adj.* phonic.
**fonocaptor** *m.* ELEC. pickup.
**fonográfico, -ca** *adj.* phonographic.
**fonógrafo** *m.* phonograph.
**fonograma** *m.* phonogram.
**fonolita** *f.* MINER. phonolite.
**fonología** *f.* phonology.
**fonoscopio** *m.* PHYS. phonoscope.
**fontana** *f.* poet. spring; fountain.
**fontanal** *adj.* fontal. *2 m.* spring, source [of water]. *3* place abounding in springs.
**fontanar** *m.* springs, source [of water].
**fontanela** *f.* ANAT. fontanel.
**fontanería** *f.* plumbing, pipelaying. *2* water supply system.
**fontanero** *m.* plumber, pipelayer.
**foque** *m.* NAUT. jib.
**forajido** *m.* outlaw, bandit, malefactor.
**foral** *adj.* pertaining to the rights and privileges of a region. *2* pertaining to a special jurisdiction.
**forámen** *m.* foramen.
**foráneo, -a** *adj.* foreign, strange.
**forastero, -ra** *adj.* foreign, outside. *2 m.-f.* stranger, outsider; guest, visitor [of a town].
**forcejar, forcejear** *intr.* to struggle, strive, make violent efforts. *2* to contend [with].
**forcejeo** *m.* struggle, strife, struggling, striving.
**fórceps** *m.* SURG. forceps.
**forense** *adj.* forensic, legal.
**forestal** *adj.* forest, forestal.
**forja** *f.* METAL. forge; forging: ~ *a la catalana,* Catalan forge or furnace. *2* ironworks, foundry. *3* silversmith's forge.
**forjado, -da** *adj.* wrought, forged [metal].
**forjador** *m.* forger [of metals]. *2* forger, inventer.
**forjar** *tr.* to forge, hammer into shape. *2* to forge, invent: *forjarse ilusiones,* to have false illusions.
**forma** *f.* form, shape: *en ~ de,* in the shape of. *2* form, style, mode of being. *3* form [of a sacrament]. *4* SPORT., PRINT. form. *5* small host [for giving Holy Communion]. *6* mould. *7* format. *8* manner, way, method, means: *de ~ que,* so that, in such a manner that; *en debida ~,* in due form; *en toda ~,* properly. *9 pl.* figure, configuration [of the human body].
**formación** *f.* formation, forming. *2* form, shape. *3* training, education. *4* GEOL., MIL. formation.
**formal** *adj.* formal [pertaining to the form]. *2* serious, steadygoing, reliable [person, firm, ▸etc.]; grave, sedate. *3* formal, explicit, definite.
**formalidad** *f.* seriousness, exactitude, reliability. *2* restraint, composure, gravity. *3* formality, established practice.
**formalismo** *m.* formalism.
**formalista** *adj.-n.* formalist.
**formalizar** *tr.* to put in final form. *2* to formalize, give definite shape or legal form to. *3* to formulate, state. *4 ref.* to become serious or earnest; to take offence.
**formalmente** *adv.* formally. *2* seriously.
**formar** *tr.* to form [in practically every sense]. *2* to shape, fashion, make, frame, model, mould. *3* to constitute, make out or up. *4* to train, educate,

develop. *5 tr.-intr.* MIL. to form, draw up. *6 ref.* to form, take form. *7* to grow, develop, become trained or educated.
**formativo, -va** *adj.* formative.
**formato** *m.* format.
**formero** *m.* ARCH. side arch of a vault.
**fórmico** *adj.* CHEM. formic.
**formidable** *adj.* formidable. *2* great, enormous, huge, immense. *3* coll. fantastic, magnificent.
**formol** *m.* CHEM. formol.
**formón** *m.* CARP. chisel.
**fórmula** *f.* formula. *2 por ~,* as a matter of form.
**formular** *tr.* to formulate, express, make: ~ *cargos,* to make charges. *2* MED. to prescribe.
**formulario, -ria** *adj.* formulary. *2* perfunctory. *3 m.* formulary, form.
**formulismo** *m.* formulism.
**fornicación** *f.* fornication.
**fornicar** *tr.* to fornicate.
**fornido, -da** *adj.* robust, sturdy.
**foro** *m.* forum. *2* bar [legal profession]. *3* THEAT. back [of the stage]. *4* LAW kind of leasehold.
**forofo, -fa** *n.* coll. supporter, fan.
**forraje** *m.* forage, green fodder [for animals]. *2* foraging. *3* unsubstantial hodgepodge.
**forrajeador** *m.* MIL. forager.
**forrajear** *tr.* to gather forage. *2 intr.* MIL. to forage.
**forrajera** *f.* shako guard.
**forrar** *tr.* to line [a garment, box, etc.]. *2* to cover [a book, etc.]; to plank [a ship].
**forro** *m.* lining [of a garment, etc.]. *2* protective cover [on a book]: *ni por el ~,* not in the least. *3* NAUT. sheathing, planking.
**fortachón, -na** *adj.* coll. strong, sturdy, burly.
**fortalecedor, -ra** *adj.* fortifying, strengthening.
**fortalecer** *tr.* to fortify, strenghten. *2* MIL. to fortify. *3 ref.* to grow strong. ¶ CONJUG. like *agradecer.*
**fortalecimiento** *m.* fortification, strengthening.
**fortaleza** *f.* fortitude. *2* strength, vigour. *3* fortress, stronghold. *4* AER. ~ *volante,* flying fortress.
**fortalezca, fortalezco,** etc. *irr.* V. FORTALECER.
**fortificable** *adj.* fortifiable.
**fortificante** *adj.* fortifying. *2 m.* fortifier, tonic.
**fortificar** *tr.* to fortify, strengthen. *2* MIL. to fortify.
**fortín** *m.* MIL. small fort.
**fortísimo, -ma** *adj.* super. very strong.
**fortuito, -ta** *adj.* fortuitous.
**fortuna** *f.* fortune, -chance, luck, good luck: *por ~,* fortunately, luckily. *2* fortune, fate. *3* fortune, wealth. *4 de ~,* makeshift.
**fortunón** *m.* aug. great fortune [wealth].
**forúnculo** *m.* FURÚNCULO.
**forzadamente** *adv.* by force, forcibly, forcedly. *2* with difficulty.
**forzado, -da** *adj.* forced, compelled, constrained. *2* forced, strained [not spontaneous, not natural]. *3 trabajos forzados,* hard labour. *4 m.* galley slave.
**forzamiento** *m.* forcing. *2* ravishing, violation.
**forzar** *tr.* to force, compel, constrain. *2* to force, break [a door, lock, etc.]. *3* MIL. to force, storm, take. *4* to strain [one's ears, eyes, etc.]. *5* to ravish, violate. ¶ CONJUG. like *contar.*
**forzosamente** *adv.* against one's will. *2* necessarily, per force.
**forzoso, -sa** *adj.* necessary, unavoidable. *2 heredero ~,* legal heir. *3 paro ~,* unemployment.
**forzudo, -da** *adj.* strong, vigorous.
**fosa** *f.* grave, sepulture. *2* ANAT. fossa.
**fosco, -ca** *adj.* sullen, frowning. *2* dark.
**fosfato** *m.* CHEM. phosphate.

**fosfaturia** *f.* MED. phosphaturia.
**fosfito** *m.* CHEM. phosphite.
**fosforado, -da** *adj.* phosphoretted or phosphoreted, phosphuretted or phosphureted.
**fosforecer** *intr.* to phosphoresce. ¶ CONJUG. like *agradecer.*
**fosforera** *f.* matchbox.
**fosforero, -ra** *m.-f.* match seller.
**fosforescencia** *f.* phosphorescence.
**fosforescente** *adj.* phosphorescent.
**fosfórico, -ca** *adj.* CHEM. phosphoric.
**fosforita** *f.* MINER. phosphorite.
**fósforo** *m.* CHEM. phosphorus. *2* match, friction match. *3* (cap.) Phosphor [morning star].
**fósil** *adj.-m.* fossil.
**fosilización** *f.* fossilization.
**fosilizarse** *ref.* to fossilize.
**foso** *m.* pit, hole [in the ground]. *2* FORT. ditch, moat, fosse, foss. *3* THEAT. cellar under the stage.
**fotingo** *m.* (Am.) jalopy.
**foto** *f.* col. photo.
**fotocalco** *m.* photoprint.
**fotocomposición** *f.* phototypesetting.
**fotocopia** *f.* photocopy.
**fotocopiadora** *f.* photocopier.
**fotoeléctrico, -ca** *adj.* photoelectric.
**fotofobia** *f.* MED. photophobia.
**fotogénico, -ca** *adj.* photogenic.
**fotógeno, -na** *adj.* photogenic.
**fotograbado** *m.* photoengraving, photogravure.
**fotograbador, -ra** *m.-f.* photoengraver.
**fotograbar** *tr.* to photoengrave.
**fotografía** *f.* photography. *2* photograph.
**fotografiar** *tr.* to photograph.
**fotógrafo** *m.* photographer.
**fotograma** *m.* photogram. *2* CINEM. still, shot.
**fotolito** *m.* photolitho, photolith.
**fotolitografía** *f.* photolithography. *2* photolithograph.
**fotometría** *f.* photometry.
**fotómetro** *m.* PHOT. exposuremeter, photometer.
**fotón** *m.* PHYS. photon.
**fotoquímica** *f.* photochemistry.
**fotosfera** *f.* ASTR. photosphere.
**fotosíntesis** *f.* BOT., CHEM. photosynthesis.
**fototerapia** *f.* phototherapeutics, phototherapy.
**fototipografía** *f.* phototypography.
**fototropismo** *m.* BIOL. phototropism.
**frac,** *pl.* **fraques** *m.* full-dress coat, swallow-tailed coat.
**fracasado, -da** *adj.* unsuccessful. *2 m.-f.* failure, person who has failed in life.
**fracasar** *intr.* to fail, be unsuccessful, to fall through.
**fracaso** *m.* failure, unsuccess. *2* disaster, calamity.
**fracción** *f.* fraction part. *2* breaking into parts. *3* LITURG. fraction. *4* MATH. fraction. *5* faction, party.
**fraccionamiento** *m.* breaking up, fractioning. *2* CHEM. fractionation.
**fraccionar** *tr.* to break up, fraction. *2* CHEM. to fractionate.
**fraccionario, -ria** *adj.* fractional, fractionary.
**fractura** *f.* breaking, fracture. *2* MINER., SURG. fracture: ~ *conminuta,* comminution.
**fracturar** *tr.* to break, fracture.
**fragancia** *f.* fragrance.
**fragante** *adj.* fragrant. *2* FLAGRANTE: *en ~,* in the very act.
**fragata** *f.* NAUT. frigate: ~ *ligera,* corvette.
**frágil** *adj.* fragile, brittle, breakable. *2* frail, weak.

**fragilidad** *f.* fragility, brittleness. *2* frailty.
**fragmentación** *f.* fragmentation.
**fragmentar** *tr.* to break into fragments. *2 ref.* to fragment.
**fragmento** *m.* fragment.
**fragor** *m.* noise, roar, crash, thunder.
**fragoroso, -sa** *adj.* noisy, thundering.
**fragosidad** *f.* roughness and thickness [of woods]. *2* rough and brambly spot.
**fragoso, -sa** *adj.* rough and brambly. *2* FRAGOROSO.
**fragua** *f.* forge [furnace].
**fraguar** *tr.* to forge [metals]. *2* to plan, plot, brew, concoct. *3 intr.* MAS. [of mortar, etc.] to set.
**fraile** *m.* friar, monk. *2* PRINT. friar.
**frailecillo** *m.* dim. little friar. *2* ORN. lapwing. *3* ORN. puffin.
**frailesco, -ca** *adj.* monkish.
**frailuno, -na** *adj.* monkish, friarlike.
**frambuesa** *f.* BOT. raspberry [fruit].
**frambueso** *m.* BOT. raspberry bush.
**francachela** *f.* merry meal, carousal, spread.
**francés, -sa** *adj.* French: *despedirse a la francesa,* to take French leave. *2 m.* Frenchman. *3* French [language]. *4 f.* Frenchwoman. *5 m. pl. los franceses,* the French [people].
**francesada** *f.* Frenchism. *2* French invasion of Spain in 1808.
**Francia** *f. pr. n.* GEOG. France.
**Francisca** *f. pr. n.* Frances.
**franciscano, -na** *adj.-n.* Franciscan.
**Francisco** *m. pr. n.* Francis.
**francmasón, -na** *m.-f.* Freemason.
**francmasonería** *f.* Freemasonry.
**franco, -ca** *adj.* frank, open, candid. *2* generous, liberal. *3* free, open, unobstruced. *4* free, exempt [of duty, tax, etc.]: ~ *de servicio,* off duty; ~ *a bordo,* free on board. *5* Frankish. *6 m.* franc [coin]. *7 pl.* HIST. *los francos,* the Franks.
**francófilo, -la** *adj.-n.* Francophile.
**francófobo** *adj.-n.* Francophobe.
**francolín** *m.* ORN. francolin, black partridge.
**francote, -ta** *adj.* frank, open-hearted.
**franela** *f.* flannel.
**frangollar** *tr.* coll. to bungle.
**frangollón, -na** *adj.* bungling, botching.
**franja** *f.* ornamental band or braid; stripe. *2* strip [of land].
**franjar, franjear** *tr.* to trim with bands, braids or stripes.
**franquear** *tr.* to free, exempt. *2* to grant liberally. *3* to clear, open [the way]. *4* to stamp, prepay [a letter or parcel]. *5* to free [a slave]. *6 ref.* to yield to another's wishes. *7 franquearse con,* to open one's heart to.
**franqueo** *m.* postage [of a letter or parcel].
**franqueza** *f.* frankness, candour: *con ~,* frankly, candidly. *2* freedom, liberty, exception.
**franquía** *f.* NAUT. sea-room: *en ~,* ready to sail.
**franquicia** *f.* exemption of taxes, duties, etc.: ~ *postal,* frank. *2* franchise, privilege.
**fraque** *m.* FRAC.
**frasco** *m.* vial, bottle, flask. *2* powder flask.
**frase** *f.* phrase, sentence: ~ *hecha,* set expression, cliché. *2* MUS. phrase.
**frasear** *tr.* to phrase.
**fraseología** *f.* phraseology. *2* verbosity.
**frasquera** *f.* bottle frame or case.
**fratás** *m.* MAS. plastering trowel.
**fraternal** *adj.* fraternal, brotherly.
**fraternidad** *f.* fraternity, brotherhood.

**fraternizar** *intr.* to fraternize.
**fraterno, -na** *adj.* fraternal, brotherly.
**fratricida** *adj.* fratricidal. *2 m.-f.* fratricide [person].
**fratricidio** *m.* fratricide [crime].
**fraude** *m.* fraud [criminal deception].
**fraudulencia** *f.* fraudulence.
**fraudulento, -ta** *adj.* fraudulent.
**fray** *m.* brother [prefixed to the names of friars].
**frazada** *f.* blanket [bed covering].
**frecuencia** *f.* frequency: *con* ~, frequently.
**frecuentación** *f.* frecuentation. *2* frequent practice.
**frecuentar** *tr.* to frequent. *2* to practice, or partake of, frequently.
**frecuente** *adj.* frequent.
**fregadero** *m.* scullery; kitchen sink.
**fregado** *m.* scrubbing. *2* doubtul affair.
**fregadura** *f.* scrubbing.
**fregamiento** *m.* friction.
**fregar** *tr.* to rub, scrub, scour. *2* to mop [the floor]; to wash [dishes]. *3* (Am.) to annoy, bother. ¶ CONJUG. like *acertar*.
**fregatriz, fregrona** *f.* coll. kitchenmaid.
**fregotear** *tr.* to scrub or wash up quickly and carelessly.
**fregoteo** *m.* quick, careless scrub or wash up.
**freidura** *f.* frying in a pan.
**freiduría** *f.* fried-fish shop.
**freír** *tr.* to fry in a pan: *al* ~ *será el reír*, he laughs best who laughs last. *2* to bother, pester. *3 ref.* [of food] to fry. *4 freírsela a uno*, to deceive someone premeditatedly. ¶ CONJUG. like *reír*.
**frenaje** *m.* braking.
**frenar** *tr.* to brake [apply the brake to]. *2* to bridle [a horse].
**frenesí** *m.* frenzy. *2* vehemence, distraction.
**frenético, -ca** *adj.* frantic, frenzied, mad.
**frenillo** *m.* ANAT. frenum. *2* muzzle [for an animal]. *3* NAUT. tarred rope, bobstay.
**freno** *m.* bridle, bit of the bridle: *tascar el* ~, to champ the bit; fig. to bear something with impatience. *2* MACH. brake. *3* fig. curb check, restraint: *sin* ~, without restraint.
**frenópata** *m.* alienist.
**frenopatía** *f.* phrenopathy.
**frente** *f.* forehead, brow, face, countenance: *hacer* ~ *a*, to face, to meet; *con la* ~ *levantada*, serenely, brazenly; ~ *a* ~, face to face. *2 m.* front, face, fore part: *al* ~ *de*, fig. at the head of, in charge of; ~ *por* ~, directly opposite. *3* obverse. *4* FORT. face [of a bastion]. *5* MIL., POL., METEOR. front. *6 de* ~, forward: facing, abreast. *7 adv.* before, opposite: ~ *a*, before, face to; *en* ~, opposite.
**freo** *m.* channel, strait.
**fresa** *f.* BOT. strawberry [plant and fruit]. *2* MACH. milling cutter.
**fresado** *m.* milling [of metals].
**fresadora** *f.* MACH. milling machine.
**fresal** *m.* strawberry patch.
**fresar** *tr.* to mill [metals].
**fresca** *f.* cool air; cool of the early morning or the evening. *2* blunt remark, piece of one's mind.
**frescachón, -na** *adj.* robust and fresh-looking. *2 viento* ~, fresh gale.
**frescal** *adj.* slightly salted [fish].
**frescales** *m.-f.* forward, careless person.
**fresco, -ca** *adj.* cool, fresh, moderately cold. *2* light [clothing]. *3* fresh [recent; not preserved or salted; not faded; not stale]. *4* fresh [wind]. *5* fresh

[complexion]; fresh,-buxom [person]. *6* cool, calm, unconcerned: *se quedó tan* ~, it left him unconcerned. *7* bold, cheeky, *fresh. *8 estar* ~, coll. to be in a pretty pickle. *9 m.* cool, coolness, cool air: *hacer* ~ [of weather], to be cool; *tomar el* ~, to get a bit of cool air. *10* fresh fish, fresh bacon. *11* PAINT. fresco: *al* ~, in fresco.
**frescor** *m.* cool, coolness, freshness. *2* PAINT. freshness of flesh-colour.
**frescote, -ta** *adj.* fresh, buxom, looking healthy.
**frescura** *f.* freshness, coolness [of things; of a verdant place]. *2* freshness [of complexion]. *4* cheek, forwardness, freshness. *5* coolness, unconcern.
**fresneda** *f.* plantation of ash trees.
**fresnillo** *m.* BOT. fraxinella.
**fresno** *m.* BOT. ash, ash tree. *2* ash [wood].
**fresón** *m.* BOT. Chilean strawberry.
**fresquera** *f.* meat-safe.
**fresquista** *m.-f.* fresco painter.
**fresquito, -ta** *adj.* rather cool, coolish. *2* recent, fresh, freshly made. *3 m.* cool, cool breeze.
**freza** *f.* dung, droppings. *2* spawning. *3* spawning season. *4* spawn [of fishes, etc.]; fry.
**frezar** *intr.* to eject the dung. *2* to spawn.
**friable** *adj.* friable.
**frialdad** *f.* coldness, frigidity. *2* coolness, calmness, indifference, unconcern. *3* dullness, gracelessness.
**fricandó** *m.* COOK. fricandeau.
**fricasé** *m.* COOK. fricassee.
**fricativo, -va** *adj.* PHON. fricative.
**fricción** *f.* friction, rubbing. *2* MEC. friction.
**friccionar** *tr.* MED. to rub.
**friega** *f.* medicinal rubbing or friction.
**friego, friegue**, etc. *irr.* V. FREGAR.
**Frigia** *f. pr. n.* GEOG. Phrygia.
**frigidez** *f.* frigidity.
**frígido, -da** *adj.* cold, frigid.
**frigio, -gia** *adj.-n.* Phrygian.
**frigorífico, -ca** *adj.* refrigerating: *cámara frigorífica*, cold-storage room. *2 m.* refrigerator.
**fríjol** *m.* BOT. kidney bean.
**fringílidos** *m. pl.* ORN. Fringillidae.
**frío, fría** *adj.* cold, frigid. *2* cool, calm. *3* cold, chill, indifferent, unconcerned, unmoved, unemotional. *4* dull, graceless, inexpressive. *5 m.* cold, coldness [of temperature]: *hacer* ~ [of the weather], to be cold; *tener* ~ [of a person], to be cold.
**frío, fría, friera**, etc. *irr.* V. FREÍR.
**friolento, -ta** *adj.* FRIOLERO.
**friolera** *f.* trifle.
**friolero, -ra** *adj.* chilly, very sensitive to cold.
**frisa** *f.* frieze [coarse cloth]. *2* FORT. fraise.
**frisado** *m.* frizzing [of cloth].
**frisar** *tr.* to frieze, frizz [cloth]. *2* to rub. *3 intr.* to be close to, to border, approach.
**Frisia** *f. pr. n.* GEOG. Friesland.
**friso** *m.* ARCH. frieze. *2* dado, mopboard, ornamental band [on a wall].
**frisón, -na** *adj.-n.* Frisian.
**fritada, fritanga** *f.* fry [dish of anything fried].
**frito, frita** *adj.* fried. *2* worried to death, exasperated. *3 m.* fry, fried food.
**fritura** *f.* FRITADA.
**frivolidad** *f.* frivolity, frivolousness.
**frívolo, -la** *adj.* frivolous. *2* trifling.
**fronda** *f.* BOT. frond; leaf. *2* SURG. sling-shaped bandage. *3 pl.* foliage, frondage.
**fronde** *m.* BOT. frond [of fern].
**frondosidad** *f.* abundance of foliage, leafiness.

**frondoso, -sa** *adj.* leafy, luxuriant.
**frontal** *adj.* frontal. 2 *m.* ANAT., ECCL. frontal.
**frontalera** *f.* front [of a bridle]. 2 yoke pad [for oxen].
**frontera** *f.* frontier, boundary, border. 2 ARCH. façade.
**fronterizo, -za** *adj.* frontier, border [situated on the frontier]. 2 facing, opposite.
**frontero, -ra** *adj.* facing, opposite, placed in front. 2 *adv.* in front.
**frontil** *m.* FRONTALERA 2.
**frontis** *m.* ARCH. frontispiece, façade.
**frontispicio** *m.* frontispiece. 2 coll. face [of person].
**frontón** *m.* ARCH. fronton, pediment. 2 main wall of pelota court. 3 pelota court.
**frotación** *f.* rubbing.
**frotar** *tr.* to rub.
**frote** *m.* rubbing, friction.
**fructífero, -ra** *adj.* fructiferous. 2 fruitful.
**fructificación** *f.* fructification.
**fructificar** *intr.* to fructify. 2 to yield profit.
**fructosa** *f.* CHEM. fructose.
**fructuoso, -sa** *adj.* fruitful, fructuous, profitable.
**frugal** *adj.* frugal.
**frugalidad** *f.* frugality.
**frugívoro, -ra** *adj.* frugivorous.
**fruición** *f.* fruition, pleasure, enjoyment.
**frunce** *m.* SEW. gather, gathering, *shirr, shirring.
**fruncido** *m.* SEW. gathering, *shirring.
**fruncimiento** *m.* knitting [of brow]; puckering [of mouth]. 2 FRUNCIDO.
**fruncir** *tr.* to knit [the brow]; to pucker [the mouth]. 2 SEW. to gather, *shirr.
**fruslería** *f.* trifle, triviality.
**frustración** *f.* frustration.
**frustrar** *tr.* to frustrate, baulk, foil, defeat, thwart. 2 *ref.* to miscarry, fail, fall through.
**frustratorio, -ria** *adj.* frustrative, defeating.
**fruta** *f.* fruit [edible fruit or piece of fruit]: ~ *prohibida*, forbidden fruit; ~ *seca*, dry fruits. 2 ~ *de sartén*, fritter.
**frutaje** *m.* PAINT. fruit piece.
**frutal** *adj.* fruit [tree]. 2 *m.* fruit tree.
**frutar** *intr.* to bear fruit.
**frutería** *f.* fruit shop; *fruit store.
**frutero, -ra** *adj.* fruit [boat, dish, etc.]. 2 *m.-f.* fruit seller. 3 *m.* fruit dish. 4 table centrepiece imitating fruit. 5 PAINT. fruit piece.
**frutescente** *adj.* FRUTICOSO.
**frútice** *m.* BOT. frutex.
**fruticoso, -sa** *adj.* BOT. frutescent, fruticose.
**frutilla** *f.* (Am.) strawberry.
**fruto** *m.* BOT. fruit. 2 any useful produce of the earth. 3 fruit, product, consequence: *sin* ~, fruitlessly, in vain.
**fu** *interj.* faugh!, fie! 2 *no hacer ni* ~ *ni fa*, to leave one indifferent.
**fucilar** *intr.* to flash with heat lightning. 2 to flash, to twinkle.
**fucilazo** *m.* heat lightning.
**fucsia** *f.* BOT. fuchsia.
**fuego** *m.* fire [in practically every sense]: ~ *de Santelmo*, St. Elmo's fire; ~ *fatuo*, ignis fatuus; ~ *graneado*, MIL. drumfire; *fuegos artificiales*, fireworks; *abrir* ~, to open fire; *atizar el* ~, to stir the fire; *echar* ~ *por los ojos*, to look daggers; *hacer* ~, to fire [discharge firearms]; *pegar* ~, to set fire to, to set on fire; *a* ~ *lento*, by slow fire. 2 light [to light a cigarette, etc.]. 3 beacon fire.

4 rash, skin eruption. 5 hearth, house. 6 *interj.* MIL. fire!
**fuelle** *m.* bellows [for blowing]. 2 PHOT. bellows [of a folding camera]. 3 folding carriage hood. 4 folding side of some things. 5 fold, pucker. 6 bag [of a bagpipe]. 7 coll. talebearer.
**fuente** *f.* water spring, spring, source; fountain: ~ *luminosa*, illuminated fountain. 2 fig. source, origin: *beber en buenas fuentes*, to be well informed. 3 font, baptismal font. 4 dish [for serving up food; dishful]. 5 SURG. issue. 6 *pl.* headwaters, source [of a stream].
**fuer** *m. a* ~ *de*, as, as behoves, in the manner of.
**fuera, fuere,** etc. *irr.* V. IR and SER.
**fuera** *adv.* out, outside, without; away, out of town: *de fuera*, exterior; *desde* ~, from the outside; *hacia* ~, outward(s); *por* ~, in the outside. 2 ~ *de*, out of, outside of; away from; apart from, short of, except, save. 3 ~ *de sí*, beside oneself. 4 *interj.* out! 5 off with...!
**fuero** *m.* exception, privilege. 2 jurisdiction. 3 name for some codes of laws. 4 ~ *interior, interno*, conscience, inmost heart. 5 *pl.* coll. arrogance.
**fuerte** *adj.* strong. [in practically every sense]. 2 intense, severe [pain]. 3 heavy [blow]. 4 healthy, serious, vigorous, extreme. 5 active, eficacious [remedy, etc.]. 6 loud [voice, sound]. 7 good, proficient. 8 *hacerse* ~, to entrench oneself, make a stand. 9 *m.* fort, fortress. 10 *adv.* strongly; heavily.
**fuerza** *f.* strength, force power [capacity to raise, move, resist, etc.]: ~ *bruta*, brute force; *hacer* ~, to struggle; to apply force; to carry weight; *hacer* ~ *de velas*, NAUT. to crowd sail: *sacar fuerzas de flaqueza*, to make an extraordinary effort. 2 MECH., PHYS. force, power: ~ *centrífuga*, centrifugal force; ~ *hidráulica*, water power; ~ *motriz*, motive power. 3 strength [innate quality of things]. 4 force, duress, compulsion: *ser* ~, to be necessary; *de por* ~, *por* ~, by force, forcibly; perforce, undoubtedly; *a viva* ~, by sheer or main force. 5 force, violence. 6 strength, vigour [of youth, etc.]. 7 force, efficacy [of an argument, etc.]. 8 ~ *mayor*, force majeure, act of God. 9 *a* ~ *de*, by dint of. 10 *sing.-pl.* MIL. force, forces: ~ *pública*, police force; *fuerzas armadas*, armed forces.
**fuerzo, fuerce,** etc. *irr.* V. FORZAR.
**fuetazo** *m.* (Am.) lash.
**fuete** *m.* (Am.) whip, horsewhip.
**fuga** *f.* flight, escape: *poner en* ~, to put to flight. 2 elopement. 3 leak, leakage. 4 ardour, impetuousity. 5 MUS. fugue.
**fugacidad** *f.* fugacity.
**fugarse** *ref.* to escape, run away. 2 to elope.
**fugaz** *adj.* fugacious, fugitive, fleeting, brief, transitory. 2 ASTR. *estrella* ~, shooting star.
**fugitivo, -va** *adj.* fugitive, fleeting. 2 *adj.-n.* fugitive, runaway.
**fuguillas** *m.* coll. hustler.
**fui, fuiste,** etc. *irr.* V. IR and SER.
**fuina** *f.* ZOOL. stone marten, beech marten.
**ful** *adj.* (slan.) bogus, sham.
**fulanito, -ta** *m.-f.* dim. of FULANO.
**fulano, -na** *m.-f.* so-and-so, what's-his-name. 2 fellow; woman. 3 *f.* mistress, paramour.
**fular** *m.* foulard [silk fabric].
**fulcro** *m.* MECH. fulcrum.
**fulero** *adj.* bungling. 2 *n.* bungler.
**fulgente** & **fúlgido, -da** *adj.* fulgent, resplendent.

**fulgor** *m.* light, brillancy.
**fulguración** *f.* flash, flashing.
**fulgurante** *adj.* flashing, shining.
**fulgurar** *intr.* to flash, shine, fulgurate.
**fulgurita** *f.* GEOL. fulgurite.
**fúlica** *f.* ORN. fulica, coot.
**fulminación** *f.* fulmination.
**fulminado, -da** *adj.* struck by lightning.
**fulminante** *adj.* fulminating, fulminant. *2* sudden. *3* MED. fulminant. *4 m.* explosive; fulminating powder [in a percussion cap].
**fulminar** *tr.* to fulminate, thunder, hurl [censures, excommunions, etc.]. *2* to strike with lightning.
**fulminato** *m.* CHEM. fulminate.
**fullería** *f.* cheating [esp. at games], trickery.
**fullero, -ra** *adj.* cheating, tricky. *2 m.-f.* cheat, sharper.
**fumada** *f.* puff [of tobacco smoke].
**fumadero** *m.* smoking room. *2 ~ de opio,* opium den.
**fumador, -ra** *m.-f.* smoker.
**fumar** *tr.-intr.* to smoke [a cigar, etc.]. *2 ref.* coll. to spend, blow. *3* coll. *fumarse la clase,* to play truant. *4 intr.* HUMEAR.
**fumarada** *f.* puff, whiff or blast of smoke.
**fumaria** *f.* BOT. fumitory.
**fumarola** *f.* GEOL. fumarole.
**fumigación** *f.* fumigation.
**fumigar** *tr.* to fumigate.
**fumista** *m.* stove maker, repairer or seller.
**fumistería** *f.* stove or heater shop.
**funámbulo, -la** *m.-f.* funambulist, ropewalker.
**función** *f.* function. *2* show, performance [in a theater, circus, etc.]. *3* MIL. action, battle.
**funcional** *adj.* functional.
**funcionamiento** *m.* functioning, operation, working, running.
**funcionar** *intr.* to function, work, run.
**funcionario** *m.* functionary, civil servant.
**funda** *f.* case, sheath, envelope, cover, slip: *~ de almohada,* pillowcase; *~ para la pistola,* holster.
**fundación** *f.* foundation, founding, establishing. *2* foundation [endowed institution].
**fundadamente** *adv.* with good reason or proof.
**fundador, -ra** *adj.* founding. *2 m.-f.* founder.
**fundamental** *adj.* fundamental. *2* foundation.
**fundamentar** *tr.* to lay the foundations of. *2* to establish on a basis, to base, ground, set firm.
**fundamento** *m.* foundation, groundwork. *2* foundation, basis, ground. *3* root, origine. *4* seriousness, sense.
**fundar** *tr.* to found [build, erect; set up, establish, base, ground]. *2 ref. fundarse en,* to be based on, to base oneself on.
**fundente** *adj.* CHEM. fusing, melting. *2 adj.-m.* MED. dissolvent. *3 m.* CHEM. flux.
**fundición** *f.* founding, melting, casting. *2* foundry [of metals]. *3* cast iron. *4* PRINT. font.
**fundidor** *m.* founder, foundryman, smelter.
**fundir** *tr.* to fuse, melt. *2* to found, smelt, cast. *3 ref.* [of interests, parties, etc.] to merge, fuse. *4* (Am.) to be or become ruined.
**fundo** *m.* LAW land, country property.
**fúnebre** *adj.* funeral: *honras fúnebres,* obsequies. *2* funereal, sad, lugubrious.
**funeral** *adj.* funeral. *2 m.* funeral pomp. *3 pl.* obsequies.

**funerala (a la)** *adv.* MIL. with arms inverted [as a token of mourning].
**funerario, -ria** *adj.* funerary, funeral. *2 f.* undertaker's shop.
**funéreo, -a** *adj.* poet, funereal, sad, mornful.
**funesto, -ta** *adj.* fatal, baneful, pernicious. *2* sad, unfortunate.
**fungicida** *adj.* fungicidal. *2 n.* fungicide.
**fungo** *m.* MED. fungus.
**fungoso, -sa** *adj.* fungous, spongy.
**funicular** *adj.* funicular. *2 m.* funicular railway.
**funículo** *m.* BOT., ZOOL. funicle, funiculus.
**furente** *adj.* poet, furious, raging.
**furgón** *m.* van, waggon. *2* RLY. waggon, boxcar.
**furgoneta** *f.* van, station wagon, shooting brake, estate car.
**furia** *f.* fury, rage. *2* fit of madness. *3* hurry, speed, violence [of action]. *4* (cap.) MYTH. Fury. *5 estar hecho una ~,* to be raging.
**furibundo, -da** *adj.* furious, angry, choleric.
**furioso, -sa** *adj.* furious, in a fury. *2* violently insane. *3* tremendous, excessive.
**furor** *m.* furor, fury, rage. *2* furor, enthusiasm [of poets]. *3* fury, violence, vehemence. *4* fig. *hacer ~,* to be the rage.
**furriel, furrier** *m.* MIL. fourrier quartermaster.
**furtivo, -va** *adj.* furtive, clandestine: *cazador ~,* poacher.
**furúnculo** *m.* MED. furuncle, boil.
**fusa** *f.* MUS. demisemiquaver.
**fusco, -ca** *adj.* fuscous, dark.
**fuselaje** *m.* AER. fuselage.
**fusibilidad** *f.* fusibility.
**fusible** *adj.* fusible. *2 m.* ELEC. fuse.
**fusiforme** *adj.* fusiform, spindle-shaped.
**fusil** *m.* rifle, gun, musket: *~ ametralladora,* submachine gun; *~ de chispa,* flintlock gun; *~ rayado,* rifle.
**fusilamiento** *m.* execution by shooting.
**fusilar** *tr.* to shoot [execute by shooting]. *2* coll. to plagiarize.
**fusilería** *f.* musketry. *2* body of fusiliers.
**fusilero** *m.* fusilier, musketeer.
**fusión** *f.* fusion. *2* COM. merger, amalgamation.
**fusionar** *tr.-ref.* to unite, merge, amalgamate.
**fusta** *f.* brushwood. *2* coachman's whip. *3* a woolen fabric. *4* NAUT. an ancient two-mast boat.
**fustal, fustán** *m.* fustian [cotton cloth].
**fuste** *m.* wood, timber. *2* saddle-tree. *3* shaft [of a lance]. *4* fust, shaft [of a column]. *5* importance, substance.
**fustete** *m.* BOT. fustic.
**fustigar** *tr.* to whip, lash.
**fútbol** *m.* football.
**futbolín** *m.* table football.
**futbolista** *m.* football player.
**futesa** *f.* trifle, bagatelle.
**fútil** *adj.* futile, trifling, unimportant.
**futileza** *f.* triviality, futility, trifling nature. *2* worthlessness. *3* trifle, unimportant thing.
**futilidad** *f.* futility, triviality.
**futura** *f.* coll. fiancée, bride-to-be.
**futurismo** *m.* futurism.
**futurista** *adj.* futuristic. *2 m.-f.* futurist.
**futuro, -ra** *adj.* future. *2 m.* future [time]. *3* GRAM. future. *4 m.-f.* future, fiancé, fiancée. *5 pl.* COM. futures.

# G

**G, g** *f.* G, g, eighth letter of the Spanish alphabet.
**gabacho, -cha** *adj.-n.* scorn. French; Frenchman, Frenchwoman.
**gabán** *m.* greatcoat, overcoat.
**gabardina** *f.* gabardine. *2* raincoat.
**gabarra** *f.* NAUT. barge, lighter.
**gabarrero** *m.* NAUT. lighterman.
**gabarro** *m.* GEOL. nodule. *2* fault [in a fabric].
**gabela** *f.* tax, duty, gabelle. *2* fig. burden.
**gabinete** *m.* lady's private sitting room. *2* library, study, room: ~ *de lectura*, reading room; *de* ~, parlour, theoretical. *3* collection [of art, science, etc]. *4* POL. cabinet [Ministry, Government].
**gablete** *m.* ARCH. gablet.
**gacel** *m.* ZOOL. male gazelle.
**gacela** *f.* ZOOL. gazelle.
**gaceta** *f.* gazette; politic or literary newspaper.
**gacetilla** *f.* column of short news, news in brief. *2* short news, news item. *3* coll. newsmonger.
**gacetillero** *m.* paragrapher, short new's writer.
**gacha** *f.* watery mass. *2 pl.* porridge, mush, pap. *3* coll. mud, mire.
**gacheta** *f.* spring catch [of lock].
**gachí** *f.* [in Andalousian slang] woman, girl.
**gacho, -cha** *adj.* turned or bent downwards. *2* down-curved [horn]. *3* slouch [hat]. *4* having down-curved horns. *5 a gachas*, on all fours.
**gachón, -na** *adj.* coll. sweet and graceful [person].
**gachupín** *m.* CACHUPÍN.
**gádido, -da** *adj.* ICHTH. gadid.
**gaditano, -na** *adj.-n.* Gaditan.
**gaélico, -ca** *adj.-m.* Gaelic. *2 m.-f.* Gael.
**gafa** *f.* hook [for bending a crossbow]. *2* cramp [for holding together]. *3* NAUT. grapple fork. *4 pl.* can hooks. *5* spectacles. *6* spectacle bows.
**gafe** *m.* coll. jinx.
**gafedad** *f.* MED. claw hand.
**gafete** *m.* hook and eye.
**gaita** *f.* MUS. large flageolet. *2* MUS. hurdy-gurdy. *3* coll. neck. *4* coll. bother. *5* MUS. ~ *gallega*, bagpipe. *6 templar gaitas*, to act in a smoothing way.
**gaitero** *m.* piper, bagpipe player.
**gaje** *m.* gage [symbol or challenge]. *2 pl.* emoluments, perquisites: *gajes del oficio*, unpleasant things that go with a job.
**gajo** *m.* branch, broken off branch [of tree]. *2* cluster [of cherries, plums, etc.]. *3* division of an

orange, a pomegranate, a bunch of grapes, etc. *4* prong, tine. *5* spur [of a mountain]. *6* BOT. lobe.
**gala** *f.* best dress: *de* ~, in gala dress, in full dress. *2* grace and elegance in speaking and doing. *3 ser la* ~ *de*, to be the flower or the pride of. *4 hacer* ~ *de*, to make a show of; *tener a* ~, to pride oneself on, to glory in. *5 pl.* regalia, dresses, jewels, ornaments.
**galabardera** *f.* BOT. dog rose [plant and fruit].
**galactogogo** *adj.-m.* MED. galactagogue.
**galáctico, -ca** *adj.* ASTR. galactic.
**galactita, galactites** *f.* MINER. galactite.
**galaico, -ca** *adj.* Galician.
**galán** *adj.* GALANO. *2 m.* handsome man. *3* gallant, lover, suitor. *4* THEAT. *primer* ~, leading man; ~ *joven*, juvenile. *5* BOT. ~ *de día*, day jasmine; ~ *de noche*, night jasmine.
**galancete** *m.* young man. *2* THEAT. juvenile.
**galano, -na** *adj.* spruce, smartly dressed. *2* beautiful, elegant, adorned. *3* beautifully turned [style].
**galante** *adj.* courteous, obliging; gallant [attentive to women]. *2 mujer* ~, courtesan.
**galanteador** *m.* courter, wooer. *2* flatterer.
**galantear** *tr.* to pay compliments [to a lady]. *2* to court, woo, pay attentions to.
**galanteo** *m.* paying compliments [to a lady]. *2* courtship, wooing.
**galantería** *f.* gallantry, polite attention, compliment. *2* generosity, liberality. *3* gracefulness.
**galantina** *f.* COOK. galantine.
**galanura** *f.* beauty, grace, elegance.
**galápago** *m.* ZOOL. tortoise, fresh-water tortoise. *2* NAUT. block flat on a side. *3* ingot [of copper, lead or tin]. *4* light saddle. *5* MIL. testudo.
**galardón** *m.* guerdon, reward, recompense.
**galardonar** *tr.* to reward, recompense.
**gálata** *adj.-n.* Galatian.
**galaxia** *f.* MINER. galactite. *2* ASTR. Galaxy.
**galbana** *f.* sloth, laziness.
**gálbano** *m.* galbanum.
**gálbula** *f.* BOT. cone of cypress.
**gálea** *f.* galea [Roman helmet].
**galeaza** *f.* NAUT. galleass.
**galena** *f.* MINER. galena.
**Galeno** *m. pr. n.* Galen.
**galeno, -na** *adj.* gentle, soft [breeze]. *2 m.* coll. Galen, physician.

**galeón** *m.* NAUT. galleon.
**galeota** *f.* NAUT. galliot.
**galeote** *m.* galley slave.
**galera** *f.* NAUT. galley [vessel]. *2* covered wagon. *3* ward [of hospital]. *4* women's prison. *5* PRINT. galley. *6* CARP. large plane. *7* ZOOL. mantis shrimp. *8 pl.* rowing on a galley [as punishment].
**galerada** *f.* wagonload. *2* PRINT. galley proof.
**galería** *f.* ARCH., FORT., MIN., NAUT., THEAT. gallery. *2* gallery, collection [of paintings]. *3* gallery, burrow.
**galerín** *m.* PRINT. small galley.
**galerita** *f.* ORN. crested lark.
**galerna** *f.* stormy northwest wind [on northern coast of Spain].
**Gales** *f. pr. n.* GEOG. Wales.
**galés, -sa** *adj.* Welsh. *2 m.* Welshman. *3* Welsh [language]. *4 f.* Welshwoman.
**galga** *f.* greyhound bitch. *2* large falling stone. *3* kind of brake for carts. *4* NAUT. back [of an anchor].
**galgo** *m.* greyhound.
**Galia (la)** *f. pr. n.* HIST., GEOG. Gaul.
**gálibo** *m.* NAUT. pattern, template. *2* RLY. gabarit. *3* fig. elegance.
**galicanismo** *m.* Gallicanism.
**galicano, -na** *adj.-n.* Gallican.
**Galicia** *f. pr. n.* GEOG. Galicia [in Spain].
**galicismo** *m.* Gallicism.
**gálico** *adj.* Gallic.
**Galilea** *f. pr. n.* HIST., GEOG. Galilee.
**galileo, -a** *adj.-n.* Galilean. *2 f.* galilee [porch].
**galillo** *m.* ANAT. uvula.
**galimatías** *m.* gibberish, rigmarole.
**galio** *m.* CHEM. gallium. *2* BOT. cheese rennet.
**galiparla** *f.* Frenchified Spanish.
**galo, -la** *adj.* Gallic. *2 m.-f.* Gaul. *3 m.* Gaulish [language].
**galocha** *f.* clog, wooden shoe.
**galón** *m.* galloon, braid. *2* MIL. stripe. *3* gallon [English measure].
**galoneadura** *f.* galloons, trimming.
**galonear** *tr.* to trim with galloons or braid.
**galop** *m.*, **galopa** *f.* galop [dance].
**galopada** *f.* a spell of galloping.
**galopante** *adj.* galloping.
**galopar** *intr.* to gallop.
**galope** *m.* gallop: *a* or *de ~*, at a gallop; in great haste; *a ~ tendido*, at full speed.
**galopeado, -da** *adj.* hastily done, botched. *2 m.* beating, punching.
**galopín** *m.* ragamuffin. *2* scoundrel. *3* shrewd fellow. *4* NAUT. cabin boy. *5 ~ de cocina*, scullion.
**galvánico, -ca** *adj.* galvanic.
**galvanismo** *m.* galvanism.
**galvanizar** *tr.* to galvanize. *2* to electroplate.
**galvano** *m.* PRINT. electroplate.
**galvanómetro** *m.* galvanometer.
**galvanoplastia, galvanoplástica** *f.* galvanoplasty, galvanoplastics. *2* electroplating.
**galladura** *f.* cicatricle, tread [of an egg].
**gallardamente** *adv.* gracefully, elegantly. *2* valiantly, bravely, dashingly. *3* nobly.
**gallardear** *intr.* to do things with grace and ease.
**gallardete** *m.* NAUT. pennant, streamer.
**gallardía** *f.* good carriage, graceful deportment. *2* gallantry, bravery.
**gallardo, -da** *adj.* handsome, graceful. *2* bold, brave, gallant. *3* great, excellent.

**gallareta** *f.* ORN. European coot.
**gallarón** *m.* ORN. little bustard.
**gallear** *tr.* [of a cock] to tread. *2 intr.* coll. to cock, crow. *3* coll. to stand out, excel.
**gallegada** *f.* number of Galicians. *2* action or saying peculiar to a Galician.
**gallego, -ga** *adj.-n.* Galician [of Spain]. *2 m.* northwest wind [in Castile].
**galleo** *m.* FOUND. flaw in casting.
**gallera** *f.* cockpit.
**gallero** *m.* breeder of gamecocks. *3* (Am.) cockfighting fan.
**galleta** *f.* hardtack, ship biscuit or bread. *2* briquet [of anthracite]. *3* biscuit [small cake], *cookie, *cracker. *4* coll. slap, buffet.
**galletería** *f.* biscuit shop.
**galletero** *m.* biscuit dish. *2* biscuit maker.
**gallina** *f.* hen: *~ de Guinea*, guinea hen; *acostarse con las gallinas*, to go to bed very early. *2* chicken-hearted person. *3 ~ ciega*, blindman's buff. *4 adj.* chicken-hearted.
**gallináceo, -a** *adj.* ORN. gallinaceous.
**gallinaza** *f.* GALLINAZO. *2* hen dung.
**gallinazo** *m.* ORN. turkey buzzard.
**gallinería** *f.* hens, poultry. *2* cowardice.
**gallinero, -ra** *m.-f.* poultry dealer. *2 m.* hencoop, henhouse, henroost. *3* THEAT. coll. paradise, top gallery. *6* fig. madhouse.
**gallineta** *f.* ORN. European coot. *2* ORN. woodcock. *3* (Am.) guinea hen.
**gallipato** *m.* ZOOL. an European salamandroid.
**gallipava** *f.* large variety of hen.
**gallipavo** *m.* ORN. turkey. *2* false note [in singing].
**gallito** *m.* cockerel. *2* fig. cock, cock of the walk.
**gallo** *m.* ORN. cock, rooster: *~ de pelea*, gamecock, fighting cock; *~ silvestre*, cock of the wood; *en menos que canta un ~*, in a short time; *otro ~ me, te, le, nos, os, les cantara*, how differently I, you, etc., should or would, have fared. *2* fig. cock, boss, cock of the walk. *3* false note [in singing]. *4* ICHTH. dory. *5 alzar el ~*, to show arrogance; *bajar el ~*, to lower one's tone.
**gallocresta** *f.* BOT. wild sage, vervain sage.
**gallofero, ra; gallofo, -fa** *m.-f.* tramp, vagabond.
**gallón** *m.* sod [piece of turf]. *2* ARCH. ecchinus.
**gama** *f.* ZOOL. doe, female of the fallow deer. *2* MUS. gamut. *3* fig. gamut.
**gamarra** *f.* martingale [of harness].
**gamba** *f.* ZOOL. a Mediterranean prawn.
**gamberrada** *f.* loutish act, piece of hooliganism, act of vandalism.
**gamberrear** *intr.* to behave loutishly, to act like a hooligan, to go around causing trouble.
**gámbaro** *m.* CAMARÓN.
**gamberro, -rra** *adj.-n.* libertine. *2* uncivil, illbred. *3 m.-f.* uncivil or ill-bred person.
**gambeta** *f.* DANCE crosscaper. *2* caper, prance.
**gambetear** *intr.* to caper, prance.
**gambito** *m.* CHESS GAMBIT.
**gamella** *f.* bow [of yoke]. *2* feed trough.
**gameto** *m.* BIOL. gamete.
**gamma** *f.* gamma [Greek letter].
**gamo** *m.* ZOOL. fallow deer.
**gamón** *m.* BOT. asphodel.
**gamopétalo, -la** *adj.* BOT. gamopetalous.
**gamosépalo, -la** *adj.* BOT. gamosepalous.
**gamuza** *f.* ZOOL. chamois. *2* chamois [leather].
**gamuzado, -da** *adj.* chamois-coloured.
**gana** *f.* apetite, desire, will: *~ de comer*, appetite; *darle a uno la ~* or *la real ~ de*, to choose to; *no me da la ~*, I won't; *tener ~* or *ganas de*, to wish,

to feel like; *de buena* ~, willingly; *de mala* ~, reluctantly.

**ganadería** *f.* cattle raising. *2* cattle, livestock. *3* breed, brand, stock [of cattle].

**ganadero, -ra** *adj.* cattle, cattle raising. *2 m.-f.* cattle raiser or dealer.

**ganado** *m.* cattle, livestock: ~ *caballar*, horses; ~ *cabrío*, goats; ~ *de cerda*, swine; ~ *lanar*, sheep; ~ *mayor*, cows and bulls, horses, asses mules; ~ *menor*, sheep, goats, etc. *2* stock of bees.

**ganador, -ra** *adj.* winning. *2 m.-f.* winner. *3* gainer; earner.

**ganancia** *f.* gaining. *2* gain, profit: *ganancias y pérdidas*, COM. profit and loss.

**ganancioso, -sa** *adj.* lucrative, profitable. *2* profiting, winning. *3 m.-f.* gainer, winner.

**ganapán** *m.* odd-job man. *2* rough coarse man.

**ganapierde** *m.* giveaway [game].

**ganar** *tr.-ref.* to gain, earn, win: *ganarse la vida*, to earn one's living; *ganársela*, coll. to get it. *2* to gain or win over. *3* to earn [wages, etc.]. *4 tr.* to gain, reach, arrive at. *5* to make, win [money]. *6* to win, take [a city, etc.]. *7* to gain [land from the sea]. *8* to defeat [in war or competition]; to surpass, to outstrip. *9* to draw [interest]. *10 intr.* to gain, improve.

**ganchero** *m.* raftsman, log driver.

**ganchillo** *m.* small hook. *2* crochet needle. *2* crochet work.

**gancho** *m.* hook, crook. *2* fig. attractiveness; *tener* ~ [of a woman], to have a way with the men. *3* fig. enticer, decoy. *4* fig. pimp. *5* shepherd's crook. *6* snag [branch stump]. *7* coll. pothook, scrawl. *8* (Am.) hairpin.

**ganchoso, -sa; ganchudo, -da** *adj.* hooked, curved.

**gándara** *f.* low wasteland.

**gandul, -la** *adj.* idling, loafing. *2 m.-f.* idler, loafer, vagabond.

**gandulear** *intr.* to idle, loaf.

**gandulería** *f.* idleness, loafing, laziness.

**ganga** *f.* MIN. gangue. *2* ORN. pin-tailed sand grouse. *3* bargain [advantageous purchase]; something obtained easily, *snap, *cinch.

**ganglio** *m.* ANAT., MED. ganglion.

**gangosidad** *f.* snuffle, snuffling, nasal twang.

**gangoso, -sa** *adj.* snuffling, nasal.

**gangrena** *f.* MED. gangrene.

**gangrenarse** *ref.* to gangrene [become gangrenous].

**gangrenoso, -sa** *adj.* gangrenous.

**gangsterismo** *m.* gangsterism.

**ganguear** *intr.* to snuffle, speak through the nose.

**gangueo** *m.* snuffle, speaking through the nose.

**Ganimedes** *m. pr. n.* MYTH. Ganymede.

**ganoso, -sa** *adj.* desirous, wishing.

**gansada** *f.* coll. stupidity, silly act, remark, etc.

**gansarón** *m.* ORN. male goose. *2* ORN. gosling. *3* coll. tall, lanky fellow.

**ganso, -sa** *m.* ORN. goose, gander. *2 m.-f.* slow, lazy person. *3* rustic person. *4 f.* ORN. female goose.

**Gante** *m. pr. n.* GEOG. Ghent.

**ganzúa** *f.* picklock [tool; thief]. *2* pumper of secrets.

**gañán** *m.* farm hand. *2* strong rough man.

**gañanía** *f.* farm hands. *2* lodge for farm hands.

**gañido** *m.* yelp.

**gañiles** *m. pl.* throat [of animals].

**gañir** *intr.* to yelp. *2* [of some birds] to croak.

**gañón, gañote** *m.* coll. throat, gullet.

**garabatear** *intr.* to throw a hook or graple [to

catch a thing]. *2 intr.-tr.* to scrawl, scribble. *3* coll. to beat about the bush.

**garabateo** *m.* hooking, grappling. *2* scrawling, scribbling.

**garabato** *m.* hook; meathook, pothook. *2* grappling iron. *3* weeding hoe. *4* charm, winsomeness, it [of a woman]. *5 pl.* pothooks, scrawls. *6* disorderly movements of hand or fingers.

**garaje** *m.* garage [for motor cars].

**garajista** *m.* garage owner, garage attendant, garage man.

**garambaina** *f.* frippery, tawdry ornament. *2 pl.* ridiculous grimacing or affectation.

**garante** *adj.* responsible. *2 m.-f.* guarantor.

**garantía** *f.* guarantee, guaranty. *2* COM. warranty, security, collateral. *3* LAW *garantías constitucionales*, constitutional rights.

**garantizar** *tr.* to guarantee, guaranty; to warrant. *2* to indorse, vouch for.

**garañón** *m.* stud jackass. *2* stud camel.

**garapiña** *f.* state of a liquid frozen or coagulated into grumes.

**garapiñado, -da** *adj.* frozen into grumes. *2* coated with grumous sugar: *almendra garapiñada*, praline [almond].

**garapiñera** *f.* ice-cream freezer.

**garapullo** *m.* small dart or arrow.

**garba** *f.* sheaf [of wheat, etc.].

**garbanzal** *m.* chickpea field.

**garbanzo** *m.* BOT. chickpea [plant and seed].

**garbar** *tr.* AGR. to sheaf, sheave.

**garbear** *intr.* to affect grace or elegance. *2 intr.-ref.* coll. to get or pull along.

**garbeo** *m.* coll. stroll. *2* trip, tour.

**garbera** *f.* AGR. shock [of sheaves].

**garbo** *m.* gracefulness, easy and graceful bearing; jauntiness. *2* grace and ease [in doing something]. *3* liberality, generosity.

**garbón** *m.* ORN. male partridge.

**garbosamente** *adv.* gracefully, elegantly, stylishly. *2* proudly and gracefully. *3* generously.

**garboso, -sa** *adj.* easy and graceful, airy, sprightly; jaunty. *2* liberal, openhanded, generous.

**garceta** *f.* ORN. lesser egret. *2* side lock [of hair]. *3* brow antler.

**gardenia** *f.* BOT. gardenia.

**garduña** *f.* ZOOL. beech marten, stone marten.

**garduño, -ña** *m.-f.* sneak thief.

**garete** *m.* NAUT. *al* ~, adrift.

**garfa** *f.* claw [sharp, curved nail].

**garfio** *m.* hook; drag hook; gaff.

**gargajear** *intr.* to expectorate, spit phlegm.

**gargajo** *m.* [expectorated] phlegm.

**garganta** *f.* ANAT. throat, gullet: *tener a uno atravesado en la* ~, not to be able to bear someone. *2* voice [of a singer]. *3* throat [front of neck]. *4* instep. *5* throat [of a river], gorge; narrow mountain pass; neck, throat [of some things]. *6* MECH. gorge, groove [of a sheave].

**gargantear** *intr.* to warble, quaver, trill [in singing]. *2 tr.* NAUT. to strap [a deadeye].

**gargantilla** *f.* necklace.

**gárgaras** *f. pl.* gargling: *hacer* ~, to gargle.

**gargarismo** *m.* gargle, gargling. *2* gargle [liquid].

**gárgol** *adj. m.* CARP. groove, gain, croze.

**gárgola** *f.* ARCH. gargoyle. *2* flax boll.

**garguero, gargüero** *m.* gullet; windpipe.

**garita** *f.* fortification turret. *2* sentry box. *3* box [for a guard]; railway-crossing box. *4* porter's lodge.

**garitero** *m.* keeper or frequenter of a gambling den.

**garito** *m.* gambling den.

**garla** *f.* coll. talk, -chat.

**garlar** *intr.* to chatter.

**garlito** *m.* fishtrap. *2* fig. trap, snare: *coger en el ~,* to catch in the act.

**garlopa** *f.* CARP. jack plane, trying plane.

**garnacha** *f.* gown, robe [worn by lawyers, judges, etc.]. *2* a sweet purple grape; wine made from it.

**Garona** *m. pr. n.* GEOG. Garonne.

**garra** *f.* paw, claw [of wild beast]; talon [of bird of prey]. *2* fig. claw, hand, clutch: *caer en las garras de,* to fall into the clutches of. *3* NAUT. hook [of the grappling iron].

**garrafa** *f.* carafe, decanter.

**garrafal** *adj.* great, big, whopping.

**garrafón** *m.* demijohn, carboy.

**garrancha** *f.* coll. sword. *2* BOT. spathe.

**garrancho** *m.* snag [branch stump].

**garrapata** *f.* ZOOL. tick. *2* MIL. disabled horse.

**garrapatear** *intr.* to scribble, scrawl.

**garrapato** *m.* pothook, scrawl.

**garrar, garrear** *intr.* NAUT. to drag the anchor.

**garrido, -da** *adj.* handsome, beautiful, elegant.

**garrocha** *f.* BULLF. picador's pike or lance. *2* staff with a barbed point.

**garrochazo** *m.* prick or blow with a GARROCHA.

**garrón** *m.* spur [of bird]. *2* heel of a dead animal by which it is hung. *2* snag [on a tree branch].

**garrotazo** *m.* blow with a stick or cudgel.

**garrote** *m.* thick stick, cudgel. *2* AGR. olive cutting. *3* garrote [for capital punishment].

**garrotillo** *m.* MED. croup.

**garrotín** *m.* a Spanish dance.

**garrucha** *f.* pulley.

**garrucho** *m.* NAUT. cringle.

**garrulería** *f.* prattle, chatter.

**garrulidad** *f.* garrulity.

**gárrulo, -la** *adj.* garrulous, loquacious. *2* [of bird, stream, etc.] garrulous, chirping, babbling.

**garúa** *f.* (Am.) NAUT. drizzle.

**garza** *f.* ORN. heron, purple heron: *~ real,* gray heron.

**garzo, -za** *adj.* blue [eye]; blue-eyed.

**garzón** *m.* boy, lad, youth. *2* male child.

**garzota** *f.* ORN. night heron. *2* aigrette, plume.

**gas** *m.* gas: *~ de los pantanos,* marsh gas; *gases asfixiantes,* MIL. poison gas; *gases lacrimógenos,* tear gas. *2* gaslight.

**gasa** *f.* gauze, chiffon. *2* antiseptic gauze. *3* crape [worn round a hat].

**gascón, -na; gasconés, -na** *adj.-n.* Gascon.

**Gascuña** *f. pr. n.* GEOG. Gascony.

**gasear** *tr.* to gas [treat or attack with gas].

**gaseiforme** *adj.* gasiform.

**gaseosa** *f.* soda water.

**gaseoso, -sa** *adj.* gaseous.

**gasificar** *tr.* to gasify.

**gasógeno** *m.* gasogene, gazogene. *2* gas generator.

**gasolina** *f.* gasoline, petrol.

**gasolinera** *f.* NAUT. boat with petrol engine. *2* gas station.

**gasómetro** *m.* gasometer. *2* gasholder.

**Gaspar** *m. pr. n.* Jasper.

**gastado, -da** *adj.* spent. *2* used-up, worn-out. *3* trite, hackneyed, stale.

**gastador, -ra** *adj.-n.* spendthrift. *2 m.* MIL. sapper. *3* MIL. pioneer.

**gastamiento** *m.* consumption, wearing out.

**gastar** *tr.* to expend, spend [money, time, etc.]. *2* to consume, use up, exhaust, wear out, fret. *3* to waste. *4* to lay waste. *5* to be, have, enjoy, use, etc., habitually: *~ mal humor,* to be bad tempered. *6* to wear: *~ bigote,* to wear a moustache. *7* to play [a joke or jokes]. *8 gastarlas,* coll. to act, behave, conduct oneself. *9 ref.* to be expended. *10* to become used up, to wear out, fray. *11* to become trite.

**gasterópodo, -da** *adj.* ZOOL. gast(e)ropodous. *2 m.* ZOOL. gast(e)ropod. *3 pl.* ZOOL. Gast(e)ropoda.

**gasto** *m.* expenditure, expense. *2* consumption, waste, use, wear. *3* PHYS. flow, rate of flow [of water, gas, electricity, etc.]. *4 pl.* expenses: *gastos de conservación* or *mantenimiento,* upkeep, maintenance [expenses]; *gastos de explotación,* operating expenses; *gastos generales,* overhead charges or expenses; *gastos menores,* petty expenses; *cubrir gastos,* to cover expenses.

**gastoso, -sa** *adj.* spendthrift.

**gastralgia** *f.* MED. gastralgia.

**gástrico, -ca** *adj.* gastric.

**gastritis** *f.* MED. gastritis.

**gastronomía** *f.* gastronomy.

**gastrónomo, -ma** *m.-f.* gastronomer, gourmet.

**gastrovascular** *adj.* ZOOL. gastrovascular.

**gástrula** *f.* BIOL. gastrula.

**gata** *f.* she-cat. *2* Madrilene [woman].

**gatada** *f.* catlike act. *2* mean trick.

**gatas (a)** *adv.* on all fours.

**gatatumba** *f.* dissembling, pretence.

**gatazo** *m.* aug. big cat.

**gatear** *intr.* to climb [a pole, tree, etc.]. *2* to go on all fours; [of children] to creep. *3 tr.* [of a cat] to scratch. *4* coll. to pilfer.

**gatera** *f.* cat's hole. *2* NAUT. cathole.

**gatería** *f.* cats, number of cats. *2* gang of ill-bred boys. *3* fake humility, cajolery.

**gatesco, -ca** *adj.* catlike, feline.

**gatillo** *m.* trigger, hammer, cock [of firearm]. *2* pelican, dentist's forceps. *3* nape [of bull, cow, etc.]. *4* clamping piece.

**gatita** *f.* dim. little she-cat, pussy, kitten.

**gatito** *m.* dim. little cat, pussy, kitten.

**gato** *m.* ZOOL. cat; tomcat: *~ cerval,* tiger cat, serval; *~ de algalia,* civet cat; *~ montés,* wild cat; *cuatro gatos,* fig. a few people; *~ encerrado,* fig. nigger in the woodpile; *dar ~ por liebre,* fig. to cheat [in a bargain]. *2* stocking, money [of a person]. *3* MECH. jack, lifting jack. *4* CARP. clamp. *5* Madrilene [man]. *6* fig. fox [shrewd fellow]. *7* sneak thief.

**gatuno, -na** *adj.* cat, catlike, feline.

**gatuña** *f.* BOT. restharrow.

**gatuperio** *m.* hodgepodge. *2* intrigue.

**gaucho, -cha** *adj.-s.* Gaucho.

**gaudeamus,** *pl.* **-mus** *m.* feast, merrymaking.

**gaultería** *f.* BOT. wintergreen.

**gavanza** *f.* dog rose [flower].

**gavanzo** *m.* BOT. dog rose [plant].

**gaveta** *f.* drawer [of writing desk].

**gavia** *f.* NAUT. topsail. *2* NAUT. maintopsail. *3* ditch. *4* ORN. gull. *5* MIN. gang of basket passers.

**gavial** *m.* ZOOL. gavial.

**gaviero** *m.* NAUT. topman.

**gavilán** *m.* ORN. sparrow hawk. *2* nib [of a quill pen]. *3* hair stroke [ending in a letter]. *4* quillon [of swords]. *5* pappus.

**gavilla** *f.* sheaf, bundle, gavel. *2* gang: *~ de pícaros,* gang of rogues.

**gavina** *f.* GAVIOTA.

**gavinote** *m.* ORN. young sea gull.
**gavión** *m.* FORT., HYD. gabion. 2 coll. large hat.
**gaviota** *f.* ORN. gull, sea gull.
**gavota** *f.* gavotte [dance and tune].
**gaya** *f.* stripe [on fabrics, etc.]. 2 ORN. magpie.
**gayar** *tr.* to trim or adorn with coloured stripes.
**gayo, -ya** *adj.* gay, bright, showy. 2 ~ *ciencia*, art of poetry.
**gayomba** *f.* BOT. kind of Spanish broom.
**gayuba** *f.* BOT. bearberry.
**gaza** *f.* NAT. strap, strop, eye.
**gazapa** *f.* coll. lie, fib.
**gazapatón** *m.* blunder, slip [in talking].
**gazapera** *f.* rabbit, hole, burrow or warren. 2 fig. den. 3 fig. brawl, row.
**gazapo** *m.* young rabbit. 2 sly fellow. 3 lie. 4 blunder, slip [in talking or writing].
**gazmoñería** *f.* prudery; demureness, affected modesty; sanctimony.
**gazmoño, -ña** *adj.* prude, prudish; demure, affectedly modest, sanctimonious.
**gaznápiro, -ra** *m.-f.* bumpkin, booby, simpleton.
**gaznate** *m.* gullet, throttle, windpipe.
**gazpacho** *m.* cold vegetable soup.
**gazuza** *f.* (coll.) keen appetite, hunger.
**ge** *f.* Spanish name of the letter *g*.
**gea** *f.* mineral kingdom of a region or country.
**Gedeón** *m. pr. n.* BIBL. Gideon.
**gedeonada** *f.* platitude, self-evident truth.
**gehena** *m.* Gehenna, hell.
**géiser** *m.* geyser [spring].
**gel** *m.* CHEM. gel.
**gelatina** *f.* gelatin(e, jelly.
**gelatinoso, -sa** *adj.* gelatinous.
**gélido, -da** *adj.* poet, gelid, chilly.
**gema** *f.* gem, precious stone. 2 BOT. bud, gemma.
**gemación** *f.* BOT., ZOOL. gemmation.
**gemebundo, -da** *adj.* groaning, moaning.
**gemelo, -la** *adj.-n.* twin. 2 *m.* ANAT. gemellus. 3 *pl.* cuff links. 4 binocular: *gemelos de campaña*, field glasses; *gemelos de teatro*, opera glasses. 5 ASTR. (cap.) Gemini.
**gemido** *m.* lamentation, moan, groan, wail.
**geminado, -da** *adj.* geminate(d.
**geminar** *tr.* to geminate.
**Géminis** *m.* ASTR. Gemini.
**gemir** *intr.* to moan, groan, wail, grieve. 2 [of wind, etc.] to wail. ¶ CONJUG. like *servir*.
**gen** *m.* BIOL. gene.
**genciana** *f.* BOT. gentian.
**gendarme** *m.* gendarme.
**gendarmería** *f.* gendarmerie.
**genealogía** *f.* genealogy.
**genealógico, -ca** *adj.* genealogical.
**genealogista** *m.* genealogist.
**generación** *f.* generation. 2 succession, lineage.
**generador, -ra** *adj.* generating. 2 *m.* ELEC., MACH generator.
**general** *adj.* general: *en* ~, *por lo* ~, in general, generally. 2 common, usual. 3 *m.* MIL., ECCL. general: ~ *de brigada*, brigadier general; ~ *de división*, major general; ~ *en jefe*, general in chief.
**generala** *f.* general's wife. 2 MIL. call to arms.
**generalato** *m.* generalship. 2 generals of an army.
**generalidad** *f.* generality.
**generalísimo** *m.* generalissimo.
**generalización** *f.* generalization.
**generalizar** *tr.-intr.* to generalize. 2 *ref.* to become general, usual or prevalent; to spread.
**generalmente** *adj.* generally.
**generar** *tr.* to generate.

**generativo, -va** *adj.* generative.
**generatriz,** *pl.* **-trices** *f.* GEOM. generatrix.
**genérico, -ca** *adj.* generic.
**género** *m.* kind, sort, description. 2 manner, way. 3 kind, race: ~ *humano*, mankind. 4 GRAM. gender. 5 BIOL., LOG. genus. 6 F. ARTS, LIT. genre. 7 COM. cloth, stuff, material, goods, merchandise: ~ *de punto*, knit goods, knitwear.
**generosidad** *f.* generosity.
**generoso, -sa** *adj.* generous, magnanimous, noble-minded. 2 generous, liberal, munificent. 3 excellent. 4 generous [wine].
**genésico, -ca** *adj.* genesic.
**génesis** *f.* genesis. 2 *m.* (cap.) BIBL. Genesis.
**genético, -ca** *adj.* genetic. 2 *f.* genetics.
**genial** *adj.* genial [denoting or marked with genius]. 2 endowed with genius, brillant, inspired. 3 temperamental. 4 cheerful, pleasant.
**genialidad** *f.* eccentricity, peculiarity.
**geniazo** *m.* strong or fiery temper.
**genio** *m.* temper, disposition, nature; *de buen* ~, good-tempered; *de mal* ~, evil-tempered. 2 coll. fire, spirit: *corto de* ~, timid. 3 hot temper. 4 genius. 5 peculiarities [of an language]. 6 MYTH. genie, jinnee, jinni. 7 ~ *del mal*, evil spirit.
**genital** *adj.* genital.
**genitivo, -va** *adj.* generative. 2 *adj.-m.* GRAM. genitive.
**genitor** *m.* begetter.
**genízaro, -ra** *adj.* JENÍZARO.
**genol** *m.* NAUT. futtok.
**genovés, -sa** *adj.* Genoese.
**gente** *f.* people, folk, folks: ~ *bien*, smart set; ~ *de bien*, honest people; ~ *de mar*, seamen; ~ *de pluma*, clerks; ~ *menuda*, children; ~ *principal*, important people. 2 troops. 3 retinue. 4 coll. family, folks. 5 clan, nation. 6 *pl.* Gentiles.
**gentecilla** *f. dim.* contemptible people.
**gentil** *adj.-n.* gentile, heathen, pagan. 2 *adj.* handsome, graceful, lively.
**gentileza** *f.* handsomeness, gracefulness, elegance. 2 show, splendour. 3 courtesy, graciousness.
**gentilhombre** *m.* obs. my good man. 2 gentleman [attendant to a person of high rank].
**gentilicio, -cia** *adj.* GRAM. gentile, gentilic.
**gentílico, -ca** *adj.* gentilic, heathen, pagan.
**gentilidad** *f.,* **gentilismo** *m.* gentilism, heathenism. 2 heathendom.
**gentilmente** *adv.* gracefully, elegantly. 2 courteously. 3 generously. 4 heathenishly.
**gentío** *m.* crowd, throng, multitude.
**gentuza** *f.* riff-raff, rabble.
**genuflexión** *f.* genuflexion.
**genuino, -na** *adj.* genuine, true, pure, real.
**geocéntrico, -ca** *adj.* geocentric(al.
**geoda** *f.* GEOL. geode.
**geodesia** *f.* geodesy.
**geofísica** *f.* geophysics.
**geogenia** *f.* geogeny.
**geognosia** *f.* geognosy.
**geografía** *f.* geography.
**geográfico, -ca** *adj.* geographic(al.
**geógrafo** *m.* geographer.
**geología** *f.* geology.
**geológico, -ca** *adj.* geologic(al.
**geólogo** *m.* geologist.
**geómetra** *m.* geometer, geometrician. 2 ZOOL. measuring worm.
**geometría** *f.* geometry.
**geométrico, -ca** *adj.* geometric(al.

**geopolítica** *f.* geopolitics.
**geórgica** *f.* georgic [poem].
**geotactismo** *m.*, **geotaxia** *f.* BIOL. geotaxis.
**geotropismo** *m.* BIOL. geotropism.
**geraniáceo, -a** *adj.* BOT. geraniaceous.
**geranio** *m.* BOT. geranium.
**Gerardo** *m. pr. n.* Gerald.
**gerbo** *m.* JERBO.
**gerencia** *f.* COM. management, managership. *2* manager's office.
**gerente** *m.* COM. manager.
**gerifalte** *m.* ORN. gerfalcon: *como un* ~, wonderfully.
**germanía** *f.* slang or jargon of the gypsies, thieves, etc.
**germánico, -ca** *adj.* Germanic. *2 m.* Germanic [language].
**germanio** *m.* CHEM. germanium.
**germanismo** *m.* Germanism.
**germanizar** *tr.* to Germanize.
**germano, -na** *adj.* Germanic, Teutonic. *2 m.-f.* German, Teuton [of ancient Germany].
**germen** *m.* germ. *2* fig. spring, origin.
**germinación** *f.* germination.
**germinal** *adj.* germinal.
**germinar** *intr.* to germinate.
**gerontología** *f.* gerontology.
**Gertrudis** *f. pr. n.* Gertrude.
**gerundense** *adj.-n.* of or from Gerona.
**gerundio** *m.* GRAM. gerund. *2* bombastic writer or speaker [esp. a preacher or theologist].
**Gervasio** *m. pr. n.* Gervas.
**gesta** *f.* gest, geste: *cantar de* ~, chanson de geste.
**gestación** *f.* gestation.
**gestatorio, -ria** *adj.* gestatorial.
**gestear** *intr.* to make faces or grimaces.
**gesticulación** *f.* expressive movement of the features.
**gesticular** *intr.* to make faces or expressive movements of the features.
**gestión** *f.* action, negotiation, steps, exertions. *2* administration, management.
**gestionar** *tr.* to take steps to; to negotiate.
**gesto** *m.* distortion of one's countenance; face, grimace: *hacer gestos a una cosa*, to make faces at a thing; *poner* ~, to look annoyed. *2* face, countenance.
**gestor** *m.* COM. manager, director. *2* COM. ~ *de negocios*, agent.
**Getsemaní** *pr. n.* BIBL. Gethsemane.
**giba** *f.* hump, hunch. *2* coll. annoyance, inconvenience.
**gibado, -da** *adj.* humped; hunchbacked.
**gibelino, -na** *adj.-n.* Ghibelline.
**gibosidad** *f.* gibbosity.
**giboso, -sa** *adj.* gibbous, crookbacked, hunchbacked.
**Gibraltar** *m. pr. n.* GEOG. Gibraltar.
**gibraltareño, -ña** *adj.-n.* of Gibraltar.
**giga** *f.* jig [dance].
**giganta** *f.* giantess. *2* BOT. sunflower.
**gigante** *adj.* giant, gigantic. *2 m.* giant. *3* giant pasteboard figure [borne in processions].
**gigantesco, -ca** *adj.* gigantic.
**gigantismo** *m.* MED. giantism, gigantism.
**gigantón, -na** *m.-f.* huge giant. *2* GIGANTE 3.
**gigote** *m.* chopped-meat stew.
**Gil** *m. pr. n.* Giles.
**Gilberto** *m. pr. n.* Gilbert.
**gilvo, -va** *adj.* honey-coloured.
**gimnasia** *f.* gymnastics.

**gimnasio** *m.* gymnasium.
**gimnasta** *m.* gymnast.
**gimnástico, -ca** *adj.* gymnastic. *2 f.* GIMNASIA.
**gimnoto** *m.* ICHTH. electric eel.
**gimotear** *intr.* to whine, to moan.
**gimoteo** *m.* whining.
**gindama** *f.* JINDAMA.
**Ginebra** *f. pr. n.* GEOG. Geneva. *2* MYTH. Guinevere.
**ginebra** *f.* gin [liquor].
**ginebrino, -na** *adj.-n.* Genevan, Genevese.
**gineceo** *m.* gynaeceum, gynaecium.
**ginecología** *f.* gynecology.
**ginecólogo** *m.* gynecologist.
**ginesta** *f.* RETAMA.
**gineta** *f.* ZOOL. genet.
**gira** *f.* trip, excursion, tour.
**girado, -da** *m.-f.* COM. drawee.
**girador, -ra** *m.-f.* COM. drawer.
**giralda** *f.* weathercock in the form of an animal or human figure. *2 la Giralda*, the Giralda.
**girándula** *f.* girandole [fireworks; fountain].
**girante** *m.* gyrating.
**girar** *intr.* to gyrate, revolve, rotate, turn, spin, swivel; to turn [to the right, the left, etc.]. *2* ~ *en torno de*, [of a discussion, etc.] to turn on, to center round. *3* COM. to trade. *4* *tr.-intr.* COM. to draw.
**girasol** *m.* BOT. sunflower.
**giratorio, -ria** *adj.* gyratory, revolving, swivel.
**girino** *m.* ENT. whirligig.
**giro** *m.* gyration, revolution, turn. *2* turn, course, bias: *tomar otro* ~, to take another course. *3* turn [of expression]. *4* COM. draft: ~ *postal*, money order. *5* COM. trade, circulation, bulk of business.
**girola** *f.* ARCH. apse aisle.
**girondino, -na** *adj.-n.* HIST. Girondist.
**giroscopio** *m.* gyroscope.
**giróstato** *m.* gyrostat.
**giste** *m.* froth of beer.
**gitana** *f.* gypsy woman or girl.
**gitanada** *f.* gypsylike trick, mean trick. *2* cajolerie.
**gitanería** *f.* gypsylike cajolery or wheedling. *2* gypsydom; assembly of gypsies.
**gitanesco, -ca** *adj.* gypsylike, gypsy.
**gitano, -na** *adj.* gypsy. *2* sly, honeymouthed. *3 m.-f.* gypsy, Spanish gypsy.
**glabro, -bra** *adj.* glabrous.
**glacial** *adj.* glacial. *2* fig. cold, chilly.
**glacis** *m.* FORT. glacis.
**gladiador** *m.* gladiator.
**gladio, gladiolo** *m.* BOT. gladiolus.
**glande** *m.* ANAT. glans penis.
**glándula** *f.* ANAT., BOT. gland: ~ *pineal*, pineal body, pineal gland.
**glandular** *adj.* glandular.
**glanduloso, -sa** *adj.* glandulous.
**glasé** *m.* glacé silk.
**glasear** *tr.* to calender, satin; to glaze.
**glasto** *m.* BOT. woad.
**glauco, -ca** *adj.* glaucous, light green.
**glaucoma** *m.* MED. glaucoma.
**gleba** *f.* clod or lump of earth.
**glena** *f.* ANAT. glenoid cavity.
**glicerina** *m.* glycerin.
**glicina** *f.* BOT., CHEM. glycine. *2* BOT. wisteria.
**glicógeno** *m.* GLUCÓGENO.
**glíptica** *f.* glyptics.
**gliptografía** *f.* glyptography.
**global** *adj.* taken in a lump, in all.
**globo** *m.* globe, ball, orb, sphere: ~ *terráqueo*,

globe, terrestrial globe. 2 globe [lampshade]. 3
balloon, air balloon: ~ *aerostático*, air balloon;
~ *sonda*, sounding balloon. 4 ANAT. ~ *del ojo*,
eyeball. 5 *en* ~, in bulk, as a whole, without details.

**globoso, -sa** *adj.* globose, globate.

**globular** *adj.* globular, globulous.

**globulina** *f.* BIOCHEM. globulina.

**glóbulo** *m.* globule. 2 PHYSIOL. corpuscle.

**glomérulo** *m.* BOT. glomerule.

**gloria** *f.* glory. 2 heaven, eternal bliss. 3 bliss, delight, keen pleasure: *estar en sus glorias*, to delight in what one is doing; *saber a* ~, to taste
heavenly. 4 boast, pride. 5 gloria [fabric]. 6 a
gauzy silk tissue. 7 *m.* ECCL. Glory.

**gloriarse** *ref.* ~ *de*, to pride oneself on, boast of; ~
*en*, to glory in.

**glorieta** *f.* arbour, bower, summerhouse. 2 circus
[circle or square with streets converging on it].

**glorificación** *f.* glorification. 2 praise, extolling.

**glorificar** *tr.* to glorify. 2 *ref.* GLORIARSE.

**glorioso, -sa** *adj.* glorious [possessing or conferring glory; illustrious, praseworthy]. 2 holy,
blessed. 3 proud, boastful.

**glosa** *f.* gloss, comment, explanation. 2 gloss
[poem]. 3 MUS. variation.

**glosar** *tr.* to gloss, annotate, comment. 2 to compose a gloss to [a stanza]. 3 MUS. to vary [a
theme].

**glosario** *m.* glossary.

**glosopeda** *f.* VET. foot-and-mouth disease.

**glotis** *f.* ANAT. glottis.

**glotón, -na** *adj.* gluttonous. 2 *m.-f.* glutton. 3 *m.*
ZOOL. glutton.

**glotonear** *intr.* to gluttonize, gormandize.

**glotonería** *f.* gluttony.

**glucemia** *f.* MED. glucemia, glucaemia.

**glucinio** *m.* CHEM. glucinium.

**glucógeno** *m.* CHEM. glycogen.

**glucosa** *f.* CHEM. glucose.

**glugú** *m.* gurgle, glug.

**gluma** *f.* BOT. glume.

**gluten** *m.* gluten. 2 glue.

**glúteo, -a** *adj.* ANAT. gluteal.

**glutinoso, -sa** *adj.* glutinous.

**gneis** *m.* GEOL. gneiss.

**gnomo** *m.* gnome.

**gnomon** *m.* gnomon.

**gnomónico, -ca** *adj.* gnomonic(al. 2 *f.* gnomonics.

**gnosticismo** *m.* Gnosticism.

**gnóstico** *adj.-n.* Gnostic.

**gobernación** *f.* governing. 2 *ministerio de la* ~,
Home Office; *Department of the Interior.

**gobernador, -ra** *adj.* governing. 2 *m.* governor [of-
ficial; ruler]. 3 *f.* woman governor. 4 governor's
wife.

**gobernalle** *m.* NAUT. rudder, helm.

**gobernante** *adj.* governing, ruling. 2 *m.-f.* ruler,
member of a government.

**gobernar** *tr.-intr.* to govern, rule. 2 *tr.* to direct,
manage, control. 3 NAUT. to steer [a ship]. 4 *intr.*
NAUT. to steer, obey the helm. 5 *ref.* to manage
one's affairs. ¶ CONJUG. like *acertar*.

**gobierno** *m.* governing, government, ruling. 2 direction, guidance, management, control: ~ *de
la casa*, nousekeeping; *para tu* ~, for your guidance. 3 NAUT. steering. 4 NAUT. rudder, helm. 5
control [of an automobile, an airplane, etc.]. 6
POL. government, cabinet, administration. 7 go-
vernorship; governor's office. 8 government
[district].

**gobierno, gobierne,** etc. *irr.* V. GOBERNAR.

**gobio** *m.* ICHTH. gudgeon.

**goce** *m.* enjoyment, fruition.

**godo, -da** *adj.-n.* Goth.

**Godofredo** *m. pr. n.* Godfrey.

**goflo** *m.* (Am.) roasted flour or maize meal.

**gofo, -fa** *adj.* ignorant and rude. 2 PAINT. dwarf
[figure].

**gol** *m.* SPORT. goal [making a goal].

**gola** *f.* ANAT. throat. 2 ARM., MIL. gorget. 3 ruff;
ruche [collar]. 4 FORT. gorge. 5 ARCH. cyma.

**goleta** *f.* NAUT. schooner.

**golf** *m.* SPORT. golf.

**golfear** *intr.* to loaf, idle.

**golfería** *f.* street Arabs, loafers, ` agabonds.

**golfillo** *m.* street Arab, guttersnipe.

**golfín** *m.* DELFÍN 2.

**golfista** *m.-f.* SPORT. golfer.

1) **golfo** *m.* GEOG. gulf, large bay. 2 sea, main. 3 a
card game.

2) **golfo, -fa** *m.-f.* loafer, vagabond, ragamuffin. 2
*m.* street Arab, guttersnipe.

**Gólgota** *m. pr. n.* BIBL. Golgotha.

**Goliat** *m. pr. n.* BIBL. Goliath.

**golilla** *f.* collar formerly worn by magistrates or
court clerks.

**golondrina** *f.* ORN. swallow. 2 ICHTH. swallow fish.
3 ORN. ~ *de mar*, tern.

**golondrino** *m.* young swallow. 2 wanderer, vagabond. 3 MIL. deserter. 4 MED. tumor in the armpit.

**golondro** *m. campar de* ~, to live at another's expense.

**golosamente** *adv.* eagerly, with relish.

**golosear** *tr.* GOLOSINAR.

**golosina** *f.* dainty, delicacy, sweet, titbit. 2 sweet
tooth, appetite for delicacies; appetite; yearning; greediness. 3 pleasing trifle.

**golosinar, golosinear** *intr.* to eat, or look for, delicacies and sweetmeats.

**golosmear** *intr.* GULUSMEAR.

**goloso, -sa** *adj.* sweet-toothed, fond of delicacies. 2
fond of [something].

**golpazo** *m.* heavy blow or knock.

**golpe** *m.* blow, bump, hit, knock, stroke; coup: ~
*de Estado*, coup d'état; ~ *de fortuna*, stroke of
luck; ~ *de gracia*, coup de grâce; finishing blow;
~ *de mar*, heavy sea [striking a ship, etc.]; ~ *de
remo*, oar stroke; ~ *de vista*, glance; view, sight;
*errar el* ~, to miss one's aim, to fail; *parar el* ~,
to stop or ward off the blow; *a golpes*, by knocking; brutally; at intervals; *de* ~, suddenly,
quickly; *de* ~ *y porrazo*, all of a sudden. 2 impact, impingement. 3 hurt, bruise. 4 abundance, great number or quantity [of some-
thing]. 5 hard blow, shock [sudden misfortune].
6 *dar* ~, to astonish. take, create a sensation. 7
witty sally or remark. 8 GAMBLING coup. 9 spring
bolt. 10 SEW. trimming of braid, beads, etc. [on
a dress]. 11 pocket flap. 12 MECH. stroke [of pis-
ton]; travel [of a valve].

**golpeadura** *f.* striking, beating, hitting, knocking.

**golpear** *tr.-intr.* to strike, beat, knock [repeatedly],
to pummel, pound.

**golpecito** *m. dim.* slight blow or stroke.

**golpeo** *m.* GOLPEADURA.

**golpete** *m.* door or window catch [to keep it open].

**golpetear** *tr.-intr.* to beat, knock, hammer or strike
repeatedly; to rattle.

**golpeteo** *m.* repeated beating; rattling.

**gollería** *f.* dainty, delicacy, superfluity.

**golletazo** *m.* blow on the neck of a bottle [to break it open]. *2* sudden termination of an affair. *3* BULLF. stab in the neck of bull.

**gollete** *m.* throat, neck. *2* neck [of bottle].

**goma** *f.* gum; rubber: ~ *adragante*, gum dragon, tragacanth; ~ *arábiga*, gum arabic; ~ *de mascar*, chewing gum; ~ *elástica*, gum elastic; ~ *laca*, lacker. *2* rubber band. *3* rubber eraser. *4* MED. gumma.

**gomero, -ra** *adj.* [pertaining to] gum, rubber. *2 m.* (Am.) rubber producer.

**gomía** *f.* bugbear. *2* glutton. *3* fig. waster.

**gomífero, -ra** *adj.* gummiferous.

**gomorresina** *f.* gum resin.

**gomosería** *f.* dandyism, foppishness.

**gomosidad** *f.* gumminess, stickiness.

**gomoso, -sa** *adj.* gummy, viscous. *2 m.* dandy, fop.

**gonce** *m.* GOZNE.

**góndola** *f.* gondola [boat]. *2* kind of omnibus.

**gondolero** *m.* gondolier.

**gonfalón** *m.* gonfalon.

**gonfalonier, -ro** *m.* gonfalonier.

**gong** *m.* gong.

**gongorismo** *m.* Gongorism.

**goniometría** *f.* goniometry.

**goniómetro** *m.* goniometer.

**gordal** *adj.* big, large-sized.

**gordiano** *adj.* Gordian.

**gordinflón, -na** *adj.* chubby, fat and flabby.

**gordito, -ta** *adj. dim.* somewhat fat, plump.

**gordo, -da** *adj.* fat, obese, stout. *2* bulky. *3* fat, greasy, oily. *4* thick [thread, paper, cloth, etc.]. *5* big, large, of importance: *premio* ~, first prize [in lotery]. *6* hard [water]. *7 dedo* ~, thumb; big toe. *8 hacer la vista gorda*, to pretend not to see, to wink at. *9 m.* fat, grease, suet. *10 f. se armó la gorda*, there was the devil of a row.

**gordolobo** *m.* BOT. mullein, great mullein.

**gordura** *f.* fatness. *2* fat, grease.

**gorgojo** *m.* ENT. weevil. *2* fig. tiny person.

**Gorgona** *f.* MYTH. Gorgon.

**gorgor** *m.* GORGOTEO.

**gorgoritear** *intr.* to trill, quaver [in singing].

**gorgorito** *m.* trill, quaver [in singing]: *hacer gorgoritos*, to trill.

**gorgoteo** *m.* gurgle, gurgling sound.

**gorguera** *f.* ruff [collar]. *2* ARM. gorget.

**gorigori** *m.* coll. chant at funerals.

**gorila** *m.* ZOOL. gorilla.

**gorja** *f.* gorje, throat.

**gorjal** *m.* ARM. gorget.

**gorjear** *intr.* to trill, warble. *2* [of a baby] to gurgle.

**gorjeo** *m.* trill, warble, warbling. *2* gurgle [of a baby].

**gormar** *tr.* to vomit.

**gorra** *f.* cap [headgear without a brim]: ~ *de visera*, cap [with a visor]. *2* bearskin, hussar's cap. *3* baby's bonnet. *4* coll. sponging: *de* ~, at other people's expense.

**gorrería** *f.* cap factory or shop.

**gorrero, -ra** *m.-f.* cap maker or seller. *2 m.* parasite, sponger.

**gorretada** *f.* doffing the cap [in greeting].

**gorrín** *m.* GORRINO.

**gorrinada** *f.* pigs, number of pigs. *2* dirty action.

**gorrinera** *f.* pigsty.

**gorrinería** *f.* dirt, dirtiness. *2* dirty action.

**gorrino, -na** *m.-f.* sucking pig. *2* hog; sow. *3* fig. slovenly person; pig.

**gorrión** *m.* ORN. sparrow.

**gorriona** *f.* female sparrow.

**gorrionera** *f.* den of vice.

**gorrista** *m.-f.* parasite, sponger.

**gorro** *m.* cap [without a visor]; coif: ~ *de dormir*, nightcap; ~ *frigio*, liberty cap. *2* baby's bonnet.

**gorrón, -na** *adj.* sponging. *2 m.-f.* sponger, parasite. *3 m.* large round pebble. *4* MACH. journal, gudgeon, pivot. *5 f.* harlot, strumpet.

**gorronería** *f.* sponging, parasitism.

**gorullo** *m.* BURUJO.

**gota** *f.* drop [of a liquid]; raindrop: ~ *a* ~, drop by drop; *no ver* ~, fig. to see nothing; *sudar la* ~ *gorda*, fig. to work one's head off. *2* ARCH. drop, gutta. *3* MED. gout. *4* MED. ~ *serena*, amaurosis.

**goteado, -da** *adj.* spotted, speckled.

**gotear** *intr.* to dribble, drip [fall in drops]. *2* to sprinkle [begin to rain].

**goteo** *m.* dribbling, dripping.

**gotera** *f.* leak, leakage [in a roof]. *2* dripping [from a roof]; mark left by dripping water. *3* valance [of canopy]. *4* chronical ailment.

**goterón** *m.* big raindrop. *2* ARCH. throat.

**gótico, -ca** *adj.* Gothic: *letra gótica*, black letter. *2* noble, illustrious. *3 m.* Gothic art.

**gotón, -na** *adj.-n.* Goth.

**gotoso, -sa** *adj.* gouty. *2 m.-f.* gout sufferer.

**goyesco, -ca** *adj.* [pertaining to] Goya; in the style of Goya.

**gozar** *tr.-intr.* to enjoy [have, posess, have the benefit of]: ~ *de buena salud*, to enjoy good health. *2 tr.* to have carnal knowledge of [a woman]. *3 intr.-ref.* to enjoy oneself; to enjoy, rejoice, take a pleasure in: *gozarse en*, to take pleasure in.

**gozne** *m.* hinge.

**gozo** *m.* joy, gladness, glee, pleasure: *no caber en sí de* ~, to be bursting with joy. *2 pl.* couplets in praise of the Virgin or a Saint.

**gozoso, -sa** *adj.* joyous, joyful, glad, gleeful.

**gozque** *m.* a little yapping dog.

**grabación** *f.* recording: ~ *en disco*, recording on phonograph record; ~ *en cinta magnetofónica*, wire or tape recording.

**grabado** *m.* engraving [art, process, plate, picture]; cut, print; gravure: ~ *al agua fuerte*, etching; ~ *al agua tinta*, aquatint. *2* picture [in a book, newspaper, etc.].

**grabador, -ra** *m.-f.* engraver; woodcutter; diesinker.

**grabadura** *f.* engraving [act].

**grabar** *tr.* to engrave; ~ *al agua fuerte*, to etch; ~ *en la mente*, to engrave in the mind. *2* to sink [a punch or die]. *3* to record [for reproduction]. *4 ref.* to become engraved.

**grabazón** *f.* engraved onlays.

**gracia** *f.* THEOL. grace: *estar en* ~, to be in state of grace. *2* grace, charm; gracefulness. *3* grace, favour, kindness: *de* ~, for nothing; *hacer* ~ *de*, to excuse from, to free from. *4* graciousness, affability. *5* grace, favour, good graces: *caer en* ~, to find favour with; to please, be liked; *más vale caer en* ~ *que ser gracioso*, better to be lucky than wise. *6* grace, pardon, mercy. *7* witticism; point [of a joke]. *8* comicalness, funniness, pleasantness: *hacer* ~, to raise a laugh, amuse, be funny; fig. to please, be liked: *¡qué* ~*!*, iron. how funny!, how fine! *9* name [of a person]. *10* facility, dexterity. *11 en* ~ *a*, in consideration of, for the sake of. *12 pl.* thanks: *¡gracias!*, thank you; *gracias a*, thanks to [owing to]; *gracias a Dios*, thank God. *13* grace [thanksgiving after a meal]: *dar gracias*, to say grace. *14* charms, accomplishments. *15* MYTH. *las Gracias*, the Graces.

**grácil** *adj.* gracile, slender, small.

**graciosidad** *f.* grace, gracefulness, beauty.

**gracioso, -sa** *adj.* graceful, charming. *2* gracious, gratuitous. *3* witty, facetious. *4* comical, funny. *5* *m.-f.* THEAT. actor, actress playing the funny rôles.

**Graco** *m. pr. n.* HIST. Graccus.

**grada** *f.* step [of stairs]. *2* gradin, tier of seats. *3* gradins of an amphitheatre, etc. *4* footpace [of altar]. *5* NAUT. slip [of shipyard]. *6* AGR. harrow. *7 pl.* stone steps [in front of a building].

**gradación** *f.* gradation. *2* RHET. climax.

**gradar** *tr.* AGR. to harrow.

**gradería** *f.* gradins, tier of seats [in an amphitheatre, etc.]; series of steps.

**gradiente** *m.* METEOR. gradient. *2* gradient, slope.

**gradilla** *f.* small stepladder. *2* brick mould. *3* CHEM. tube, rack. *4* gradin [of altar].

**gradina** *f.* gradine, sculptor's chisel.

**grado** *m.* step [of stairs]. *2* degree [in a scale or process]. *3* grade [degree in quality, value, etc.]. *4* [academic] degree. *5* EDUC. grade. *6* ALG., GEOM., MUS., GRAM. degree. *7* degree, measure: *en sumo ~*, in the highest degree. *8* degree [of relationship]. *9* MIL. brevet. *10* will, willingness: *de ~, de buen ~*, willingly; *de ~ o por fuerza*, willy-nilly; *mal de mi ~*, against my wishes, much to my regret. *11 pl.* ECCL. minor orders.

**graduable** *adj.* adjustable.

**graduación** *f.* graduation, grading. *2* strength [of spirituous liquors]. *3* MIL. rank, degree of rank. *4* EDUC. admission to a degree.

**graduado, -da** *adj.* graduated, graded. *2* MIL. brevetted. *3* *m.-f.* graduate.

**gradual** *adj.* gradual. *2* *m.* ECCL. gradual.

**graduando, -da** *m.-f.* candidate for a degree.

**graduar** *tr.* to regulate, adjust, set. *2* to graduate [in nearly every sense]. *3* to determine the degree or quality of. *4* MIL. to brevet. *5 ref.* EDUC. to *graduate, receive a degree.

**grafía** *f.* GRAM. graph.

**gráfico, -ca** *adj.* graphic, graphical. *2* ilustrated [newspaper, magazine, etc.]. *3* *m.* diagram. *4* *f.* graph.

**gráfila, grafila** *f.* circle of dots around field of coin.

**grafito** *m.* MINER. graphite.

**grafología** *f.* graphology.

**gragea** *f.* small coloured sugarplums. *2* PHARM. sugar-coated pill.

**graja** *f.* female rook.

**grajear** *intr.* to caw. *2* [of a baby] to gurgle.

**grajo** *m.* ORN. rook, crow, common rook.

**grama** *f.* BOT. Bermuda grass, scutch grass. *2* BOT. *~ del Norte*, couch grass, scutch grass. *3* BOT. *~ de color*, or *de los prados*, vernal grass.

**gramalla** *f.* an ancient robe. *2* coat of mail.

**gramática** *f.* grammar. *2* coll. *~ parda*, shrewdness.

**gramatical** *adj.* grammatical.

**gramático, -ca** *adj.* grammatical. *2* *m.-f.* grammarian.

**gramil** *m.* CARP. gauge, marking gauge.

**gramináceo, -a** *adj.* BOT. graminaceous.

**gramo** *m.* gram, gramme [weight].

**gramófono** *m.* gramophone.

**gramola** *f.* console phonograph. *2* portable gramophone.

**gran** *adj.* contr. of GRANDE, used before *m.* or *f.*

nouns in the singular: *~ bestia*, ZOOL. elk; *~ cruz*, grand cross; *~ visir*, grand vizier.

**grana** *f.* seeding. *2* seeding time. *3* small seed of some plants. *4* cochineal. *5* kermes [dyestuff]. *6* kermes berry. *7* scarlet colour. *8* a fine cloth. *9* BOT. *~ del Paraíso*, cardamom.

**Granada** *f. pr. n.* GEOG. Granada. *2 Nueva ~*, New Granada.

**granada** *f.* BOT. pomegranate [fruit]. *2* MIL. grenade, shell: *~ de mano*, hand grenade.

**granadera** *f.* grenadier's pouch.

**granadero** *m.* MIL. grenadier.

**granadilla** *f.* BOT. passionflower. *2* passion fruit.

**granadillo** *m.* BOT. granadilla tree, red ebony.

**granadina** *f.* grenadine [fabric; syrup].

**granadino, -na** *adj.* [pertaining to] pomegranate. *2 adj.-n.* of Granada [Spain]. *3* *m.* pomegranate flower.

**granado, -da** *adj.* choice, select. *2* distinguished, illustrious. *3* mature, expert. *4* tall, grown. *5* AGR. seedy. *6* *m.* BOT. pomegranate [tree].

**granalla** *f.* FOUND. granulated metal.

**granar** *intr.* [of plants] to seed.

**granate** *m.* garnet [stone and colour].

**granazón** *f.* seeding [forming seeds].

**Gran Bretaña** *f. pr. n.* GEOG. Great Britain.

**grande** *adj.* large, big; great, grand: *en ~*, as a whole; in a big way; grandly. *2* *m.* grandee; *~ de España*, Spanish grandee.

**grandeza** *f.* bigness, largeness. *2* size, magnitude. *3* greatness, grandeur. *4* magnificence. *5* grandeeship. *6* the grandees.

**grandilocuencia** *f.* grandiloquence.

**grandilocuente; grandílocuo, -cua** *adj.* grandiloquent, grandiloquous.

**grandiosidad** *f.* grandeur, magnificence.

**grandioso, -sa** *adj.* grandiose, grand, magnificent.

**grandor** *m.* size, magnitude.

**grandote** *adj.* biggish.

**grandullón, -na** *adj.* overgrown.

**graneado, -da** *adj.* grained. *2* spotted. *3* MIL. *fuego ~*, drumfire.

**granear** *tr.* to grain [powder; a lithographic stone]; to stipple [in engraving].

**granel (a)** *adv.* loose, in bulk. *2* in abundance.

**granelar** *tr.* to grain [leather].

**granero** *m.* granary, barn. *2* fig. granary [region].

**granillo** *m.* small grain. *2* small pimple.

**granítico, -ca** *adj.* granitic.

**granito** *m.* small grain or pimple. *2* MINER. granite.

**granívoro, -ra** *adj.* granivorous.

**granizada** *f.* hailstorm. *2* fig. hail, shower.

**granizado** *m.* iced drink: *~ de café*, iced coffee.

**granizar** *intr.* to hail. *2* *tr.* to hail, shower as hail.

**granizo** *m.* hail; hailstorm.

**granja** *f.* grange, farm. *2* dairy [farm or shop].

**granjear** *tr.* to gain, earn, acquire. *2* *tr.-ref.* to win [the affection, etc., of].

**granjería** *f.* gain, profit.

**granjero, -ra** *m.-f.* granger, farmer.

**grano** *m.* grain [of cereals]. *2* small seed. *3* berry, grape, bean: *~ de café*, coffee bean. *4* grain [small hard particle]. *5* grain [of the wood, the stone, the leather, etc.]. *6* grain [weight]. *7* pimple. *8* *ir al ~*, to come to the point. *9 pl.* COM. grain, corn, small seeds.

**granoso, -sa** *adj.* grained.

**granuja** *f.* loose grapes. *2* grapeseed. *3* *m.* gamin, waif, street Arab. *4* knave, rascal.

**granujada** *f.* scurvy trick, knavery.

**granujería** *f.* lot of gamins. *2* lot of rascals, rascaldom. *3* GRANUJADA.
**granulación** *f.* granulation.
**granulado, -da** *adj.* granulated.
*1)* **granular** *adj.* granular.
*2)* **granular** *tr.* to granulate. *2 ref.* MED. to granulate.
**gránulo** *m.* granule.
**granuloso, -sa** *adj.* granulose.
**granza** *f.* BOT. madder.
**granzas** *f. pl.* chaff, shiftings, screenings. *2* dross of metals.
**grao** *m.* beach used as a landing place.
**grapa** *f.* staple, cramp, cramp-iron.
**grapón** *m.* large staple or cramp.
**grasa** *f.* grease, fat. *2* lubricant grease. *3* greasy dirt.
**grasera** *f.* vessel for grease. *2* COOK. dripping pan.
**graseza** *f.* fattiness, greasiness.
**grasiento, -ta** *adj.* greasy, oily.
**grasilla** *f.* pounce [powder].
**graso, -sa** *adj.* greasy, fat. *2* CHEM. fat [acid]. *3 m.* GRASEZA.
**grasoso, -sa** *adj.* greasy [permeated with grease].
**grasura** *f.* GROSURA.
**grata** *f.* wire brush.
**gratificación** *f.* gratification, gratuity, tip; bonus.
**gratificar** *tr.* to gratify, reward, tip. *2* to gratify, please.
**grátil, gratil** *m.* NAUT. head [of sail]. *2* NAUT. slings [of a yard].
**gratitud** *f.* gratitude, gratefulness.
**gratis** *adv.* gratis.
**grato, -ta** *adj.* agreeable, pleasant, pleasing. *2* acceptable. *3 f. su grata*, your favour [letter].
**gratuito, -ta** *adj.* gratuitous.
**gratulación** *f.* congratulation. *2* rejoicing.
**grava** *f.* pebble gravel. *2* broken stone [for road-beds].
**gravamen** *m.* burden, obligation. *2* tax, impost, duty. *3* mortgage, lien, encumbrance.
**gravar** *tr.* to weigh on or upon. *2* to burden [with taxes, etc.], to tax. *3* to encumber [property].
**grave** *adj.* heavy [heaving weight]. *2* grave, weighty, important, serious. *3* difficult, troublesome. *4* grave, dignified, solemn. *5* elevated [style]. *6* grave [sound]; deep [voice]. *7* GRAM. grave [accent]. *8* GRAM. having the stress on the penultimate syllable [word]. *9* MED. serious, dangerous [illness, wound]; in a dangerous condition [patient].
**gravedad** *f.* PHYS. gravity. *2* MUS. gravity. *3* gravity, importance, seriousness: *herido de ~*, dangerously wounded. *4* gravity, graveness.
**gravidez** *f.* pregnancy, gravidity.
**grávido, -da** *adj.* gravid. *2* full [of], abundant [in].
**gravimetría** *f.* gravimetry.
**gravímetro** *m.* PHYS. gravimeter.
**gravitación** *f.* gravitation.
**gravitar** *intr.* to gravitate. *2* to weigh [upon].
**gravoso, -sa** *adj.* burdensome, onerous. *2* annoying, hard to bear.
**graznar** *intr.* [of a crow, rook or raven] to caw, croak. *2* [of a goose] to cackle, gaggle.
**graznido** *m.* caw, croak [of crow, rook or raven]. *2* cackle, gaggle [of goose].
**greba** *f.* ARM. greave.
**greca** *f.* fret, Greek fret.
**Grecia** *f. pr. n.* GEOG. Greece.
**grecizar** *tr.-intr.* to Grecize.
**greco, -ca** *adj.-n.* Greek.

**grecolatino, -na** *adj.* Greco-Latin.
**grecorromano, -na** *adj.* Greco-Roman.
**greda** *f.* clay, fuller's earth.
**gredoso, -sa** *adj.* clayey.
**gregal** *m.* northeast wind [in the Mediterranean].
**gregario, -ria** *adj.* gregarious [pertaining to a crowd]. *2* servilely following other people's initiatives.
**gregoriano, -na** *adj.* Gregorian.
**Gregorio** *m. pr. n.* Gregory.
**greguería** *f.* hubbub, uproar.
**gregüescos** *m. pl.* wide breeches.
**greguizar** *intr.* to Grecize.
**gremial** *adj.* (pertaining to a) guild. *2 m.* guildsman. *3* ECCL. gremial.
**gremio** *m.* guild, corporation. *2* body, pale [of the Church].
**greña** *f.* [usually *pl.*] shock, head of dishevelled hair: *andar a la ~* [of women], to pull each other's hair; to wrangle. *2* something tangled or matted.
**greñudo, -da** *adj.* shock-headed.
**gres** *m.* material for making pottery refractory to heat and acids.
**gresca** *f.* merry noise, hubbub. *2* shindy, brawl.
**grey** *f.* flock, herd. *2* fig. flock [Christian body; congregation; people, race, nation].
**grial** *m.* grail: *el Santo Grial*, the Holy Grail.
**griego, -ga** *adj.-n.* Greek, Grecian. *2 m.* Greek [Greek language; inintelligible language].
**grieta** *f.* crack, crevice, cleft, flaw. *2* chap [in skin].
**grifo, -fa** *adj.* kinky, tangled [hair]. *2 adj.-f.* PRINT. script [type]. *3 m.* faucet, tap, cock. *4* MYTH. griffin.
**grillarse** *ref.* [of a seed, potato, etc.] to sprout.
**grillete** *m.* fetter, shackle.
**grillo** *m.* ENT. cricket: *~ cebollero* or *real*, mole cricket. *2* sprout [of a seed, potato, etc.]. *3 pl.* fetters, irons.
**grillotalpa** *m.* ENT. mole cricket.
**grima** *f.* horror; vexation, irritation: *dar ~*, to cause horror; to vex, irritate.
**grímpola** *f.* NAUT. pennant, streamer.
**gringo, -ga** *m.-f.* scorn. (Am.) foreigner [esp. English or American]. *2 m.* coll. gibberish.
**griñón** *m.* wimple. *2* BOT. nectarine.
**gripal** *adj.* MED. grippal.
**gripe** *f.* MED. grippe, flu.
**gris** *adj.* grey, gray. *2* dull, cloudy [day]. *3* dull, monotonous. *4 m.* ZOOL. a Siberian squirrel and its fur. *5* cold, cold wind.
**grisáceo, -a** *adj.* greyish.
**grisalla** *f.* grisaille [decorative painting].
**gríseo, -a** *adj.* greyish.
**grisú** *m.* MIN. firedamp.
**grita** *f.* shouting. *2* hooting [in disapproval].
**gritador, -ra** *adj.* shouting. *2 m.-f.* shouter.
**gritar** *intr.-tr.* to shout, cry out; scream. *2* to hoot [in disapproval].
**gritería** *f.*, **griterío** *m.* shouting, outcry, uproar.
**grito** *m.* shout, cry, scream, hoot: *alzar el ~*, to talk loud and haughtily; *poner el ~ en el cielo*, to complain vehemently; *a ~ herido* or *pelado*, *a voz en ~*, at the top of one's voice. *2* cry [of an animal].
**gritón, -na** *adj.* bawling, vociferous. *2 m.-f.* shouter.
**groelandés, -sa; groenlandés, -sa** *adj.* Greenlandic. *2 m.-f.* Greenlander.
**Groenlandia** *f. pr. n.* GEOG. Greenland.
**groera** *f.* NAUT. rope hole.

**grog** *m.* grog [drink].
**grosella** *f.* currant, red currant [fruit]. *2 ~ silvestre,* gooseberry [fruit].
**grosellero** *m.* BOT. currant, red currant [plant]. *2 ~ silvestre,* gooseberry [plant].
**grosería** *f.* coarseness, roughness. *2* rusticity. *3* rudeness, ill-breeding; discourtesy, incivility.
**grosero, -ra** *adj.* coarse, rough. *2* gross [error, etc.]. *3* rustic, unpolished. *4* rude, uncivil, discourteous. *5 m.-f.* ill-bred person, boor, churl.
**grosor** *m.* thickness.
**grosura** *f.* fat, suet, grease.
**grotesco, -ca** *adj.* grotesque, ridiculous. *2 adj.-m.* F. ARTS. grotesque.
**grúa** *f.* MACH. crane, derrick crane.
**gruesa** *f.* gross [twelve dozen].
**grueso, -sa** *adj.* thick [not thin or slender]. *2* corpulent, bulky, stout. *3* big, heavy. *4* dull, slow [mind]. *5* ANAT. large [intestine]. *6 m.* bulk, mass, corpulence. *7* main body or part. *8* thickness [of a wall, etc.]. *9* GEOM. thickness. *10* heavy stroke [in writing]. *11* COM. *en ~,* in gross, in the gross.
**gruir** *intr.* [of a crane] to cry, crunk. ¶ CONJUG. like *huir.*
**grujidor** *m.* glazier's trimmer.
**grujir** *tr.* to trim [glass] with the GRUJIDOR.
**grulla** *f.* ORN. crane.
**grumete** *m.* NAUT. cabin boy, ship boy.
**brumo** *m.* clot, lump [coagulated mass]. *2* thick cluster.
**grumoso, -sa** *adj.* full of clots, clotted.
**gruñido** *m.* grunt, growl, grumble.
**gruñidor, -ra** *adj.* grunting, growling.
**gruñir** *intr.* to grunt. *2* to growl; to grumble. *3* to creak, squeak. ¶ CONJUG. like *mullir.*
**gruñón, -na** *adj.* grumbling, grumpy, cranky.
**grupa** *f.* croup, rump [of horse].
**grupada** *f.* squall, burst of wind or rain.
**grupera** *f.* crupper [of harness].
**grupo** *m.* group, set, knot, clump, cluster: *~ de presión,* pressure group. *2* MACH., ELEC. set, unit.
**gruta** *f.* grot, grotto.
**grutesco, -ca** *adj.-m.* F. ARTS. grotesque.
**guacamayo** *m.* ORN. red-and-blue macaw.
**guaco** *m.* BOT. guaco. *2* ORN. curassow.
**guachapear** *tr.* to dabble in [water] with the feet. *2* to botch, bungle. *3 intr.* to clap, clatter.
**guácharo, -ra** *adj.* sickly. *2* dropsical. *3 m.* birdling.
**guadalajareño, -ña** *adj.-n.* of Guadalajara.
**Gudalupe** *f. pr. n.* Guadeloupe.
**guadamací, guadamacil** *m.* GUADAMECÍ.
**guadamacilero** *m.* embossed-leather maker.
**guadamecí, guadamecil** *m.* embossed leather.
**guadaña** *f.* scythe.
**guadañar** *tr.* to scythe, mow.
**guadarnés** *m.* harness room. *2* harness keeper.
**guagua** *f.* trifle: *de ~,* free, for nothing.
**guaita** *f.* MIL. obs. night watch.
**guaja** *m.* coll, rogue, knave.
**guájar** *m.* or *f.,* **guájaras** *f. pl.* fastness, roughest part of a mountain.
**guajira** *f.* Cuban popular song.
**guajiro, -ra** *m.-f.* Cuban peasant.
**guajolote** *m.* (Am.) ORN. turkey.
**gualda** *f.* weld, woad, dyer's rocket.
**gualdera** *f.* sidepiece [of a ladder, of the stock of a gun-carriage, etc.].
**gualdo, -da** *adj.* yellow, weld.

**gualdrapa** *f.* housing, horse trappings. *2* coll. dirty rag hanging from clothes.
**gualdrapazo** *m.* NAUT. flap [of sail against rigging].
**gualdrapear** *intr.* NAUT. [of sails] to flap. *2 tr.* to place [things] head to tail.
**Gualterio, Gualtero** *m. pr. n.* Walter.
**guanábana** *f.* BOT. soursop, custard-apple [fruit].
**guanábano** *m.* BOT. soursop, custard-apple [tree].
**guanaco** *m.* ZOOL. guanaco.
**guanche** *m.-f.* ancient inhabitant of the Canary Islands.
**guanera** *f.* guano deposit.
**guanero, -ra** *adj.* [pertaining to] guano.
**guano** *m.* guano [fertilizer]. *2* (Am.) palm tree.
**guantada** *f.,* **guantazo** *m.* slap [blow with the open hand].
**guante** *m.* glove: *arrojar el ~,* to throw down the glove, or the gauntlet; *echar el ~ a,* to take, to seize; *poner a uno más suave que un ~,* to render tractable. *2 pl.* tip, bonus.
**guantelete** *m.* gauntlet [armoured glove].
**guantería** *f.* glove shop. *2* glovemaking.
**guantero, -ra** *m.-f.* glovemaker, glover.
**guañir** *intr.* [of little pigs] to grunt.
**guapamente** *adv.* coll. bravely. *2* coll. very well.
**guapear** *intr.* coll. to be courageous; to brag, swagger. *2* to dress in a showy manner.
**guapería** *f.* blustering, bullying.
**guapetón, -na** *adj.* coll. handsome, good-looking, buxom. *2 m.* blusterer, bully, rough.
**guapeza** *f.* coll. bravery, daring. *2* coll. showiness [in dress]. *3* blustering, swagger.
**guapo, -pa** *adj.* handsome, good-looking. *2* coll. well-dressed, smart. *3 m.* blusterer, bully, rough.
**guapote, -ta** *adj.* good-natured. *2* handsome, good-looking.
**guapura** *f.* coll. good looks.
**guaraní** *adj.-n.* Guaraní.
**guarapo** *m.* juice of the sugar cane.
**guarda** *m.-f.* guard, keeper, custodian: *~ de coto,* gamekeeper. *2 m.* (Am.) street-car conductor. *3 f.* ward, guard, care, trust, custody, safe-keeping. *4* observance [of law, etc.]. *5* guard [of sword]. *6* ward [of lock or key]. *7* BOOKBIND. flyleaf. *8* outside rib [of a fan]. *9* MEC. guard plate.
**¡guarda!** *interj.* look out!, beware!
**guardabarrera** *m.* RLY. gatekeeper.
**guardabarros,** *pl.* **-rros** *m.* mudguard, fender.
**guardabosque** *m.* forester, gamekeeper.
**guardabrazo** *m.* ARM. brassard.
**guardabrisa** *m.* AUTO. windshield. *2* glass shade [for candles].
**guardacabo** *m.* NAUT. thimble.
**guardacantón** *m.* spur stone; corner spur stone.
**guardacostas** *m.* NAUT. revenue cutter. *2* NAUT. coast-guard ship.
**guardado, -da** *adj.* reserved, reticent.
**guardador, -ra** *adj.* thrifty, careful. *2* observant [of law, etc.]. *3* stingy. *4 m.-f.* thrifty person. *5* observer [of law, etc.]. *6* niggard.
**guardafrenos** *m.* RLY. brakeman.
**guardagujas** *m.* RLY. switchman.
**guardainfante** *m.* farthingale. *2* NAUT. whelp [of capstan].
**guardalado** *m.* railling, parapet.
**guardalmacén** *m.* storekeeper, warehouseman.
**guardamalleta** *f.* lambrequin [over a curtain].
**guardamano** *m.* guard [of sword].
**guardameta** *m.* SPORT. goalkeeper.
**guardamonte** *m.* trigger guard. *2* kind of poncho.

**guardamuebles** *m.* warehouse for storing furniture.
**guardapelo** *m.* locket [little case].
**guardapesca** *m.* NAUT. boat used by officials controlling the observance of fishing laws.
**guardapiés** *m.* BRIAL.
**guardapolvo** *m.* dust cover. *2* dust coat, duster. *3* inner lid [of watch]. *4* flashing [over a door or window].
**guardapuerta** *f.* hangings before a door.
**guardar** *tr.* to keep, watch over, take care of. *2* to tend [a flock, etc.]. *3* to keep, guard, preserve, protect, shield, keep safe, save: *Dios os guarde,* God save you. *4* to keep, hold, retain. *5* to put away, lay up, store, save. *6* to keep [one's word, a secret, etc.]. *7* to keep, observe [commandments, etc.]. *8* to show [respect, regard, etc.]. *9* ~ *rencor,* to bear a grudge. *10* ~ *cama,* to keep one's bed; ~ *silencio,* to be silent. *11 guardársela a uno,* to bild one's time to take revenge on. *12 ref. guardarse de,* to guard, protect oneself against, avoid, beware; to take care not to [say, do, etc.].
**guardarropa** *m.* wardrobe, clothespress. *2* cloakroom, checkroom. *3 m.-f.* cloakroom attendant. *4* THEAT. property man or woman.
**guardarropía** *f.* THEAT. wardrobe.
**guardarruedas** *m.* GUARDACANTÓN.
**guardasilla** *f.* chair rail.
**guardavía** *m.* RLY. trackwalker, flagman, signalman.
**guardería** *f.* guardship, keepership. *2* ~ *infantil,* day nursery.
**guardesa** *f.* female guard. *2* guard's wife.
**guardia** *f.* guard [body of armed men]: ~ *civil,* gendarmery; ~ *de honor,* guard of honour; ~ *urbana,* city police; *montar la* ~, MIL. to mount guard. *2* guard, defence, protection. *3* guard duty; turn of persons on duty; *estar de* ~, to be on duty. *4* FENC. guard: *estar en* ~, to be on guard; fig. to be on one's guard. *5* NAUT. watch. *6 m.* guard; member of a GUARDIA: ~ *civil,* gendarme; ~ *urbano,* policeman. *7* NAV. ~ *marina,* midshipman.
**guardián, -na** *m.-f.* guardian, keep, watchman. *2* guardian [of a convent of Franciscans].
**guardilla** *f.* buhardilla.
**guarecer** *tr.* to shelter, protect. *2* to preserve [from harm]. *3 ref.* to take shelter or refuge. ¶ CONJUG. like *agradecer.*
**guarezco, guarezca,** etc. *irr.* V. GUARECER.
**guarida** *f.* haunt, den, lair [of wild animals]. *2* shelter, cover. *3* fig. haunt, lurking place.
**guarismo** *m.* ARITH. cipher, figure, number.
**guarnecer** *tr.* to adorn, decorate, garnish. *2* to equip, furnish, provide. *3* to trim, bind, edge, face [clothes]. *4* to enchase [a jewel]. *8* [of nails, a lining, ferrule, etc.] to adorn, protect, reinforce. *6* to harness [horses]. *7* MIL. to garrison. ¶ CONJUG. like *agradecer.*
**guarnés** *m.* GUADARNÉS.
**guarnezco, guarnezca,** etc. *irr.* V. GUARNECER.
**guarnición** *f.* SEW. trimming, binding, edge, facing, flounce, garniture. *2* JEWEL. setting. *3* guard [of a sword]. *4* MACH. packing [of a piston]. *5* MIL. garrison. *6 pl.* gear, harness [of mules and horses].
**guarnicionar** *tr.* to garrison [put a garrison in].
**guarnicionería** *f.* harness making. *2* harness maker's shop.
**guarnicionero** *m.* harness maker.

**guarnigón** *m.* young quail.
**guarnir** *tr.* GUARNECER. *2* NAUT. to rig [a tackle].
**guarro, -rra** *adj.* dirty, filthy. *2 m.* ZOOL. hog. *3 f.* ZOOL., sow. *4 m.-f.* fig. unclean person.
**¡guarte!** *interj.* look out!, beware!
**guasa** *f.* jest, fun; mocking, irony: *estar de* ~, to be in a jesting mood.
**guasca** *f.* (Am.) thong, piece of rope; whip.
**guasearse** *ref.* to make fun, to joke.
**guaso, -sa** *adj.* (Am.) coarse, unpolished; uncivil. *2 m.* (Am.) peasant.
**guasón, -na** *adj.* mocking. *2 m.-f.* jester, mocker.
**guata** *f.* wadding, cotton wool.
**Guatemala** *f. pr. n.* GEOG. Guatemala.
**guatemalteco, -ca** *adj.-n.* Guatemalan.
**guateque** *m.* noisy ball or dancing party. *2* fig. frolic, spree.
**guau** *m.* bowwow [of a dog].
**¡guay!** *interj.* poet. alack!, woe!
**guayaba** *f.* BOT. guava, guava apple. *2* guava jelly.
**guayabo** *m.* BOT. guava tree.
**guayacán, guayaco** *m.* BOT. guaiac, guaiacum.
**Guayana** *f. pr. n.* GEOG. Guiana.
**gubernamental** *adj.* governmental. *2* gubernatorial.
**gubernativo, -va** *adj.* government, governmental, administrative. *2* gubernatorial.
**gubia** *f.* gouge [chisel].
**guedeja** *f.* long hair. *2* lion's mane.
**güelfo, -fa** *m.-f.* Guelf, Guelph.
**guerra** *f.* war, warfare: ~ *a muerte,* war to death; ~ *bacteriológica,* germ war; ~ *civil,* civil war; ~ *fría,* cold war; *Guerra Mundial,* World War; *dar* ~, to annoy, cause trouble.
**guerreador, -ra** *adj.* warlike, warring. *2 m.-f.* warrior.
**guerrear** *intr.* to war, wage war; to struggle.
**guerrera** *f.* MIL. tunic.
**guerrero, -ra** *adj.* martial, warlike. *2* warring. *3 m.-f.* warrior, soldier.
**guerrilla** *f.* MIL. party of skirmishers. *2* band of guerrillas. *3* a card game.
**guerrillear** *intr.* to fight guerrilla warfare.
**guerrillero** *m.* guerrilla, partisan. *2* guerrilla leader.
**guía** *m.-f.* guide [leader; adviser, mentor]. *2* guide, cicerone. *3 m.* MIL. guide [in evolutions]. *4 f.* guide, guidance. *5* guide [manual]; guidebook; directory: ~ *de ferrocarriles,* RLY. timetable. *6* MACH. guide rope, etc. *7* NAUT. guy. *8* road marker [on mountain paths]. *9* HORT., MIN. leader. *10* leader [horse]. *11* MUS. lead [of a fugue]. *12* curled-up end [of moustache]. *13* handle bar [of bicycle]. *14* customhouse docket. *15 pl.* reins for driving the leading horses.
**guiadera** *f.* MACH. guide, guide bar.
**guiar** *tr.* to guide, lead. *2* to guide [advise; direct the course of]. *3* to train [plants]. *4* to drive, steer [a car, etc.]. *5* AER. to pilot. *6 ref. guiarse por,* to be guided by, to follow.
**Guido** *m. pr. n.* Guy.
**guija** *f.* pebble. *2* BOT. blue vetch.
**guijarral** *m.* place full of cobbles or large pebbles.
**guijarro** *m.* large pebble, cobble, cobblestone.
**guijarroso, -sa** *adj.* full of cobbles, cobbly.
**guijo** *m.* pebble gravel. *2* MACH. gudgeon.
**guijoso, -sa** *adj.* pebbly, gravelly.
**guilladura** *f.* CHIFLADURA.
**guillame** *m.* CARP. rabbet plane.
**guillarse** *ref.* to leave, to flee. *2* to become crazy.
**Guillermo** *m. pr. n.* William.

**guillotina** *f.* guillotine.
**guillotinar** *tr.* to guillotine.
**guimbalete** *m.* pump handle.
**guimbarda** *f.* CARP. grooving plane.
**guincho** *m.* prod, pointed stick.
**guinda** *f.* BOT. sour cherry [fruit]. *2* NAUT. height of masts.
**guindalera** *f.* sour-cherry plantation.
**guindaleza** *f.* NAUT. hawser.
**guindamaina** *f.* NAUT. dipping the flag [as a salute].
**guindar** *tr.* to hoist, hang up. *2 ref.* to hoist oneself up. *3* to let oneself down by a rope, etc.
**guindaste** *m.* NAUT. frame; sheet bitt.
**guindilla** *f.* BOT. Guinea pepper [fruit]. *2* BOT. a very pungent pepper. *3* coll. policeman.
**guindo** *m.* BOT. sour cherry [tree].
**guindola** *f.* NAUT. boatswain's chair. *2* NAUT. life buoy. *3* NAUT. log chip.
**guinea** *f.* guinea [coin; money]. *2 f. pr. n.* GEOG. Guinea.
**guineo, -a** *adj.* Guinea, Guinean. *2 m.-f.* Guinean.
**guinga** *f.* gingham.
**guinja** *f.* jujube.
**guinjo** *m.* BOT. jujube tree.
**guinjolero** *m.* GUINJO.
**guiñada** *f.* wink [with one eye]. *2* NAUT. yaw, lurch.
**guiñapo** *m.* rag, tatter. *2* ragged person, tatterdemalion. *3* degraded, despicable person.
**guiñar** *tr.* to wink [one eye]. *2* NAUT. to yaw, lurch. *3 ref.* to wink at each other.
**guiño** *m.* wink [with one eye].
**guión** *m.* hyphen; dash. *2* notes [for a speech]. *3* CINEM., RADIO. scenario, script. *4* cross [carried before a prelate]. *5* banner [carried before procession]. *6* leader, guide. *7* NAUT. loom [of an oar].
**guionista** *m.-f.* CINEM., RADIO. script writer.
**guipar** *tr.* vulg. to see.
**guipur** *m.* guipure.
**guipuzcoano, -na** *adj.-n.* of Guipuzcoa.
**güira** *f.* BOT. calabash [tree and fruit].
**guirigay** *m.* gibberish. *2* hubbub, confusion.
**guirindola** *f.* frill of a shirt.
**guirlache** *m.* roast almond brittle.
**guirlanda** *f.* garland, wreath [of flowers, leaves, etc.]. *2* BOT. globe amaranth.
**guisa** *f.* manner, fashion, way, wise: *a ~ de*, as, like, in the manner of.
**guisado, -da** *adj.* cooked. *2* fig. prepared. *3 m.* COOK. cooked dish; stew, ragout, fricassee.
**guisandero, -ra** *m.-f.* cook [one who cooks food].
**guisante** *m.* BOT. pea [plant and seed]: *~ de olor*, sweet pea.
**guisar** *tr.* to cook [food]. *2* to stew, to make into a ragout or fricassee. *3* fig. to arrange, cook.
**guiso** *m.* cooked dish.
**guisote** *m.* coarse, poorly cooked dish.
**guita** *f.* packthread, twine. *2* coll. money, tin.
**guitarra** *f.* MUS. guitar.
**guitarrazo** *m.* blow with a guitar.
**guitarreo** *m.* strumming on the guitar.
**guitarrería** *f.* lutherie.
**guitarrero, -ra** *m.-f.* luthier.

**guitarrillo** *m.* MUS. small four-stringed guitar. *2* MUS. small treble guitar.
**guitarrista** *m.-f.* guitarist.
**guitarro** *m.* GUITARRILLO.
**guitón, -na** *m.-f.* vagabond, vagrant.
**guitonear** *intr.* to loaf, lead a vagrant life.
**guizacillo** *m.* BOT. hedgehog grass.
**guizque** *m.* pole with a hook for reaching things.
**gula** *f.* gluttony, gormandize.
**gules** *m. pl.* HER. gules.
**gulusmear** *intr.* to eat titbits. *2* to sniff the cooking.
**gúmena** *f.* NAUT. cable, thick rope.
**gumia** *f.* Moorish dagger or poniard.
**gumífero, -ra** *adj.* gum-bearing, gummiferous.
**gurriato** *m.* ORN. young sparrow.
**gurrumina** *f.* uxoriousness.
**gurrumino, -na** *adj.* small, poor, stunty, puny. *2 m.* uxorious man, henpecked husband.
**gurullada** *f.* gang of good-for-nothings.
**gurullo** *m.* BURUJO.
**gusanear** *intr.* HORMIGUEAR.
**gusanera** *f.* nest of worms, wormy place. *2* coll. ruling passion.
**gusanería** *f.* multitude of worms.
**gusaniento, -ta** *adj.* wormy, grubby, maggoty.
**gusanillo** *m.* small worm: *matar el ~*, fig. to take a shot of liquor before breakfast. *2* SEW. gold, silver or silk twist. *3* screw point of gimlet or bit.
**gusano** *m.* ZOOL. worm. *2* worm, grub, maggot, caterpillar: *~ de luz*, glowworm; *~ de seda*, silkworm. *3* fig. worm, miserable, wretch. *4 ~ de la conciencia*, worm of conscience, remorse.
**gusarapiento, -ta** *adj.* wormy [liquid]. *2* rotten, filthy.
**gusarapo** *m.* any worm found in liquids.
**gustación, gustadura** *f.* gustation, tasting.
**gustar** *tr.* to taste [perceive by the sense of taste]. *2* to taste, experience. *3 intr.* to please, be pleasing [to]. | often to be rendered by a sentence with «to like»: *me gusta el café*, I like coffee; *a nadie gustó la obra*, nobody liked the play. *4* to like, please, will: have a liking for: *gusta de leer*, he likes to read.
**gustativo, -va** *adj.* gustative, gustatory.
**gustazo** *m.* coll. great pleasure.
**gustillo** *m.* a lingering taste or flavour.
**gusto** *m.* taste [sense]. *2* taste, relish, flavour. *3* taste [discernment or appreciation of beauty, fitness, etc.]: *de buen ~, de mal ~*, in good taste, in bad taste; *de gustos no hay nada escrito*, there is no accounting for tastes. *4* pleasure, gratification: *dar ~*, to please, gratify, oblige; *hallarse a ~ en*, to be pleased or comfortable in; *tengo mucho ~ en conocerlo*, I am very glad to meet you; *con mucho ~*, with pleasure; gladly. *5* will, choice, liking, fancy, whim: *hacer uno su ~*, to do one's own will; *ser del ~ de*, to be to the liking of; *tomar ~ a*, to take a liking for.
**gustoso, -sa** *adj.* tasty, savoury, palatable. *2* agreeable, pleasant, pleasing. *3* glad, willing, ready.
**gutapercha** *f.* gutta-percha.
**gutífero, -ra** *adj.* guttiferous.
**gutural** *adj.* guttural.
**guzla** *f.* MUS. gusla.

# H

**H, h** *f.* H, h, ninth letter of the Spanish alphabet.
**ha** *irr.* V. HABER & HACER.
**haba** *f.* BOT. bean, broad bean [plant, pod and seed]: ~ *panosa*, horse bean; *son habas contadas*, it is a sure thing; it is that and no more. *2* bean [of coffee, cocoa, etc.]. *3* GEOL., MIN. nodule. *4* welt, papule.
**habado, -da** *adj.* dappled [horse, etc.]. *2* mottled [fowl].
**Habana (La)** *f. pr. n.* GEOG. Havana.
**habanero, -ra** *adj.-n.* Havanese. *2 f.* habanera [dance and tune].
**habano, -na** *adj.* Havanese, Havana. *2 m.* Havana [cigar].
**habar** *m.* broad-bean patch.
1) **haber,** *pl.* **haberes** *m.* BOOKKEEP. credit side. *2* salary, pay, wages. *3 sing.-pl.* property, fortune [of a person].
2) **haber** *tr.* obs. to have, own, possess. *2* to catch, get, lay hands on: *los ladrones no pudieron ser habidos*, the thiefs could not be caught.
*3 aux.* to have. *4* (with *de*) to have to, to be obliged to, to be to: *he de trabajar*, I have to work, I must work.
*5 impers.* (3rd. pers. pres. ind. *hay*) to be [with *there* as a subject]; to take place: *hay un puente sobre el río*, there is a bridge on the river. | Sometimes it requires a different translation: *¿cuánto hay de aquí a...?* how far is it to...?; *lo que hay es*, the fact is; *no hay de qué*, you are welcome, don't mention it [when thanked]; *¿qué hay?*, how's things? *6* (with *que*) it is necessary to, it's got to: *hay que trabajar*, it is necessary to work; *hay que hacerlo*, it's got to be done. *7 ¡hay que ver!*, fancy!, look! *8* (3rd. pers. pres. ind. *ha*) It is used to express a lapse of time, often with the adverbial value of *ago: cinco días ha*, five days ago.
*9 ref. habérselas con*, to deal with, dispute or contend with, cope with. *10 ¡habráse visto!*, fancy!
¶ CONJUG: IND. Pres.: *he, has, ha* or *hay; hemos* or *habemos, habéis, han.* | Imperf.: *había, habías,* etc. | Pret.: *hube, hubiste, hubo; hubimos, hubisteis, hubieron.* | Fut.: *habré, habrás, habrá; habremos, habréis, habrán.* | COND: *habría, habrías, habría; habríamos, habríais, habrían.* | SUBJ. Pres.: *haya, hayas, haya; hayamos, hayáis,*

*hayan.* | Imperf.: *hubiera, hubieras, hubiera; hubiéramos, hubierais, hubieran* or *hubiese, hubieses, hubiese; hubiésemos, hubieseis, hubiesen.* | Fut.: *hubiere, hubieres, hubiere; hubiéremos, hubiereis, hubieren.* | IMPER : *he, haya; hayamos, habed, hayan.* | PAST. P.: habido. | GER.: habiendo.
**habichuela** *f.* BOT. kidney bean, French bean.
**habiente** *adj.* LAW having, possessing.
**hábil** *adj.* skilful, clever, dexterous. *2* LAW able, legally qualified. *3* LAW lawful [day].
**habilidad** *f.* ability, skill, cleverness. *2* talent [special aptitude].
**habilidoso, -sa** *adj.* skilful.
**habilitación** *f.* habilitation, act of qualifying or making apt. *2* making [a place, etc.] available for a specified use. *3* financing, outfitting. *4* employment or office of a paymaster.
**habilitado, -da** *adj.* habilitated, qualified. *2* made available for a specified use [place, etc.]. *3 m.* paymaster [appointed by a body, regiment, etc.].
**habilitar** *tr.* to habilitate, qualify; to make apt. *2* to make [a place, etc.] available for a specified use. *3* to finance; to outfit.
**habitabilidad** *f.* habitability, habitableness.
**habitable** *adj.* habitable.
**habitación** *f.* habitation, inhabiting. *2* habitation, dwelling, abode. *3* room, chamber, apartment. *4* BOT. habitat.
**habitáculo** *m.* habitation, dwelling [place].
**habitante** *adj.* inhabiting, residing. *2 m.-f.* inhabitant, dweller, citizen.
**habitar** *tr.-intr.* to inhabit; to dwell, live, reside in.
**hábito** *m.* habit, custom: *tener el ~ de*, to be in the habit of. *2 sing.* or *pl.* habit, dress, esp. dress of a religious or military order: *tomar el ~*, to profess, to take vows.
**habituación** *f.* habituation, inurement.
**habitual** *adj.* habitual.
**habituar** *tr.* to habituate, accustom, inure. *2 ref.* to become habituated, accustomed, inured; to get used.
**habla** *f.* speech [faculty of speaking]: *perder el ~*, to lose one's speech. *2* speaking, act of speaking: *al ~*, NAUT. within speaking distance; in comunication, in negotiations: *¡al ~!*, speaking! [ans-

wer to telephone]. *3* speech, talk. *4* speech, language, tongue, dialect.

**hablado, -da** *adj.* spoken: *bien* ~, well-spoken; polite; *mal* ~, ill-tongued, foul-mouthed.

**hablador, -ra** *adj.* talkative. *2* chattering, babbling. *3 m.-f.* chatterer. *4* gossip, babbler.

**habladuría** *f.* impertinent talk. *2* gossip, piece of gossip, idle rumour.

**hablanchín, -na** *adj.-n.* HABLADOR.

**hablar** *intr.* to speak, talk: ~ *a*, to speak, talk to; ~ *al alma*, to speak movingly, touchingly; ~ *bien*, to speak well; ~ *bien de*, to speak favourably of, to commend; ~ *claro*, to speak plainly; to call a spade a spade; ~ *con sentido*, to speak sense; ~ *de*, to speak or talk of, on or about; to mention; ~ *en plata*, to speak plainly; ~ *entre dientes*, to mutter, mumble; ~ *por*, to speak for; to speak in behalf of, intercede for; ~ *por boca de ganso*, to speak at second hand; ~ *por* ~, to talk to no purpose; ~ *por los codos*, to chatter, talk incessantly; ~ *por señas*, to talk by signs. *2* to converse, chat, speak, talk: ~ *con*, to talk with; to woo, court, go out with. *3 tr.* to speak, utter, talk: ~ *disparates*, to talk nonsense. *4* to speak, talk [a language]; *se habla inglés*, English spoken. *5 ref.* to speak to each other: *no hablarse con*, not to be on speaking terms with.

**hablilla** *f.* idle rumour, piece of gossip.

**hablista** *m.-f.* one who writes or talks with elegance and purity of language.

**habré, habrás,** etc. *irr.* V. HABER.

**hacanea** *f.* nag, sturdy small horse.

**hacecico, -llo, -to** *m.* dim. small sheaf; fascicle. *2* pencil [of luminous rays].

**hacedero, -ra** *adj.* feasible, practicable.

**hacedor** *m.* manager [of a farm]. *2* (cap.) Maker: *el Supremo Hacedor,* the Maker, the Creator.

**hacendado, -da** *adj.* landed, property-owning. *2 m.-f.* landholder; owner of real estate.

**hacendero, -ra** *adj.* industrious, thrifty.

**hacendista** *m.* financier, one skilled in the management of the public finances.

**hacendoso, -sa** *adj.* assiduous, industrious [in household works].

**hacer** *tr.* to make [create, construct, build, form, frame, compose, draw up, produce, inflict, cause to exist, bring about]: ~ *una casa*, to build a house; ~ *testamento*, to make a will; ~ *ruido*, to make a noise. *2* to make, do [perform, execute, carry out]: ~ *un mandado*, to make an errand; *no sabe qué* ~, he doesn't know what to do. *3* to do, bring: *esto le hace honor*, this does him credit. *4* to make, deliver [a speech, etc.]. *5* to make, prepare [a meal, a bed, etc.]. *6* to pack [luggage]. *7* to make [cause to be or become]: ~ *famoso a uno*, to make someone famous. *8* to make, amount to: *dos y dos hacen cuatro*, two and two make four. *9* to make [compose, constitute]. *10* to make [cause to act in a certain way, compel]: *no me hagas hablar*, don't make me talk. *11* to make [grimaces, signs]. *12* to make [money]. *13* to do, work [wonders, miracles, etc.]. *14* to project, shed, cast, raise [shadow, smoke, dust, etc.]. *15* to habituate, inure. *16* to lead [a life]. *17* to provide, supply [with]. *18 no lo hacía tan tonto*, I did not suppose him to be so silly. *19* ~ *agua*, NAUT. to leak. *20* ~ *aguas* or *aguas menores*, to make water [void urine]; ~ *aguas mayores*, to evacuate the bowels. *21* ~ *alarde*, to boast; ~ *burla de*, to mock. *22* ~ *pedazos*, to break to pieces. *23* ~

*juego*, [of things] to match. *24 hacerlo bien, mal*, to do it rightly, wrongly, to perform or acquit oneself well, badly. *25* ~ *de las suyas*, to be up to one's old tricks. *26 ¡buena la has hecho!*, now you have done it!

*27 tr.-intr.-ref.* to act, play, pretend to be, boast of being: ~ *el hombre*, to act the man; *hacerse el olvidadizo*, to pretend to forget.

*28 intr.* to be relevant, be to the purpose: *esto no hace al caso*, that is irrelevant. *29* [with *de*] to act or work as: ~ *de presidente*, to act as a chairman. *30* [with *por* o *para*] to do one's best, to try: *haré por venir*, I'll try to come.

*31 ref.* to grow, develop. *32* to turn to, to grow, become: *hacerse vinagre*, to turn to vinegar; *hacerse más fuerte*, to grow stronger; *hacerse fraile, médico*, etc., to become a monk, a doctor, etc. *33* to make oneself: *hacerse obedecer*, to make oneself obeyed. *34* to order or have [something] made for oneself. *35* to inflict upon oneself [a wound, etc.]. *36* to move, step, retire: *hacerse a un lado*, to move or step aside. *37 hacerse con*, to get, obtain, get hold of. *38 hacerse de rogar*, to like to be a coaxed.

*39 impers.* [referring to the weather] to be [with *it* as a subject]: *hace frío*, it is cold; *hace buen día*, it is a fine day.

*40* When used to express a lapse of time it is rendered by *ago*, *since*, *for* or *by to be* [sometimes with *it* as a subject]: *hace tres días*, three days ago; *hace un año que no lo veo*, it is a year since I saw him; *hace un mes que estoy aquí*, I have been here a month. *41 se hace tarde*, I is getting, growing or becoming late.

¶ IRREG. CONJUG.: INDIC. Pres.: *hago, haces, hace; hacemos, hacéis, hacen.* | Imperf.: *hacía, hacías,* etc. | Pret.: *hice, hiciste, hizo; hicimos, hicisteis, hicieron.* | Fut.: *haré, harás, hará; haremos, haréis, harán.* | CONDIC.: *haría, harías, haría; haríamos, haríais, harían.* | SUBJ. Pres.: *haga, hagas, haga; hagamos, hagáis, hagan.* | Imperf.: *hiciera, hicieras, hiciera; hiciéremos, hicierais, hicieran* or *hiciese, hicieses, hiciese; hiciésemos, hicieseis, hiciesen.* | Fut.: *hiciere, hicieres, hiciere; hiciéremos, hiciereis, hicieren.* | IMPER. *haz, haga; hagamos, haced hagan.* | PAST. P.: *hecho.* | GER.: *haciendo.*

**hacia** *prep.* towards, toward, to, for [in the direction of]: ~ *abajo*, downward; ~ *adelante*, forward; ~ *atrás*, backward; ~ *el mar*, seaward; *partir* ~, to leave for. *2* towards, toward, to, for [as regards, in relation to]: *su actitud* ~ *mí*, his attitude toward me. *3* toward, near, about: ~ *las tres*, toward three o'clock.

**hacienda** *f.* landed property, farm. *2* (Am.) ranch. *3* property, possessions: ~ *pública*, public finances, public treasury. *4* management or science of public finance. *5 pl.* household work.

**hacina** *f.* pile of sheaves, shock. *2* heap.

**hacinamiento** *m.* heaping, piling. *2* packing, crowding together. *3* heap, pile, accumulation.

**hacinar** *tr.* to pile sheaves. *2* to heap, pile, stack, accumulate. *3* to pack, crowd together. *4 ref.* to pile up. *5* to be packed, crowded together.

**hacha** *f.* ax, axe, hatchet: ~ *de armas*, battleax. *2* heavy wax candle with four wicks. *3* torch, flambeau.

**hachazo** *m.* blow or stroke with an axe.

**hache** *f.* name of the letter *h.*

**hachear** *tr.* to dress [wood] with an axe.

**hachero** *m.* torch stand. *2* axman, axeman.

**hacho** *m.* torch, link. *2* beacon hill.
**hachón** *m.* large torch. *2* cresset.
**hada** *f.* MYTH. fairy [supernatural female being].
**hado** *m.* fage, destiny.
**hagiografía** *f.* hagiography.
**hagiógrafo** *m.* hagiographer.
**hago, haga,** etc., *irr.* V. HACER.
**Haití** *m. pr. n.* GEOM. Haiti.
**haitiano, -na** *adj.-n.* Haitian.
**¡hala!** *interj.* get up!, go on!, move on!
**halagador, -ra** *adj.* flattering. *2* pleasing, gratifying. *4* promising, bright, rosy.
**halagar** *tr.* to flatter. *2* to adulate. *3* to please, gratify.
**halago** *m.* flattering. *2* flattery. *3* pleasure, gratification. *4 pl.* caresses, blandishments.
**halagüeño, -ña** *adj.* HALAGADOR.
**halar** *tr.* NAUT. to haul [on a rope, etc.]; to pull [an oar]. *2* to pull or draw to oneself.
**halcón** *m.* ORN. falcon, hawk: ~ *niego,* eyas.
**halconería** *f.* falconry.
**halconero** *m.* falconer.
**halda** *f.* skirt [garment]; skirt [of a garment].
**haldada** *f.* skirtful.
**haldeta** *f.* small skirt, flap [of a garment].
**haleche** *m.* BOQUERÓN 2.
**halieto** *m.* ORN. osprey, sea eagle.
**hálito** *m.* breath [from the mouth]. *2* vapour, effluvium. *3* poet. breath, gentle breeze.
**halo** *m.* METEOR., PHOT. halo. *2* F. ARTS halo, nimbus.
**hallado, -da** *adj.* found. *2 bien ~,* at ease, contented; *mal ~,* displeased [in or with a place, situation, etc.] *3 ¡bien ~!,* welcome!
**hallar** *tr.* to find, come across, light upon. *2* to find out, discover, detect, catch. *3* to find, ascertain. *4* to find [favour, means, leisure, expression, one's way, etc.]. *5* to find, think. *6* to see, observe. *7 ~ la solución de un problema,* to solve a problem. *8 ref.* to be, be present, be found [in some place]. *9* to be, feel [in some state, condition, etc.]: *hallarse enfermo,* to be ill; *hallarse incómodo,* to feel uncomfortable.
**hallazgo** *m.* find, finding, discovery [act of finding; something found]. *2* reward [for finding].
**hamaca** *f.* hammock [hanging bed].
**hamadríada** *f.* MYTH. hamadryad.
**hambre** *f.* hunger; starvation, famine: ~ *canina,* canine hunger; *matar de ~,* to starve [someone]; *morirse de ~,* [of someone] to starve; *tener ~,* to be hungry. *2* hunger [strong desire]: *tener ~ de,* to hunger for or after.
**hambrear** *tr.* to starve, famish. *2 intr.* to starve, go hungry.
**hambriento, -ta** *adj.* hungry: ~ *de,* hungry for. *2 m.-f.* hungerer, starveling.
**hambrón, -na** *adj.* hungry, greedy for food. *2 m.-f.* glutton.
**Hamburgo** *f. pr. n.* GEOG. Hamburg.
**hamburgués, -sa** *adj.-n.* of Hamburg.
**hampa** *f.* underworld [low or criminal people]. *2* underworld life.
**hampón** *m.* rowdy, bully, gangster, vagrant.
**hanega** *f.* FANEGA.
**hangar** *m.* AER. hangar.
**Hansa** *f.* Hanse.
**hanseático, -ca** *adj.* Hanseatic.
**haragán, -na** *adj.* idle, lazy, slothful. *2 m.-f.* idler, loafer, loiterer, idle or lazy person.
**haraganear** *intr.* to idle, loaf, hang around.
**haraganería** *f.* idleness, loafing, laziness.
**harapiento, -ta** *adj.* ragged, tattered.

**harapo** *m.* rag, tatter.
**haraposo, -sa** *adj.* ragged, tattered.
**haré, harás,** etc. *irr.* V. HACER.
**harem, harén** *m.* harem.
**harina** *f.* flour [wheat meal]: *ser ~ de otro costal,* to be a horse of another colour. *2* flour, meal, powder: ~ *de linaza,* linseed meal; ~ *de maíz,* corn meal.
**harinero, -ra** *adj.* [pertaining to] flour. *2 m.* flour dealer. *3* flour bin or chest.
**harinoso, -sa** *adj.* floury, mealy, farinaceous.
**harmonía, harmónico, harmonioso,** etc. ARMONÍA, ARMÓNICO, ARMONIOSO, etc.
**harmonio** *m.* ARMONIO.
**harnero** *m.* sieve, sifter.
**harón, -na** *adj.* lazy, slothful, sluggish. *2* balky.
**haronear** *intr.* to be slow or lazy; to dawdle.
**harpa** *f.* ARPA.
**harpado, -da** *adj.* ARPADO.
**harpía** *f.* ARPÍA.
**harpillera** *f.* burlap, sackcloth.
**hartar** *tr.* to sate, satiate, glut. *2* to fill, gorge [with]. *3* to give in abundance: ~ *de palos,* to beat soundly. *4* to tire, sicken. *5 ref.* to satiate; to stuff oneself. *6* to have or get one's fill [of]. *7* to tire, sicken, become fed up.
**hartazgo, hartazón** *m.* fill, glut, bellyful. *2 darse un hartazgo,* to eat one's fill: *darse un hartazgo de,* to have or get one's fill of.
**harto, -ta** *adj.* satiated, glutted. *2* tired, sick [of]; fed up [with]. *3* enough, more than enough. *4 adv.* enough, well, well enough.
**hartura** *f.* fill, satiety, repletion. *2* abundance. *3* full gratification.
**has** *irr.* V. HABER.
**hasta** *prep.* till, until; to, as far as; as much as, up to, down to: ~ *ahora,* till now, up to now; ~ *aquí,* so far; ~ *la vista,* so long, see you later; ~ *más no poder,* to the utmost; ~ *que,* till, until; *iremos ~ el punte,* we'll go so far as the bridge. *2 conj.* even: ~ *un niño lo haría,* even a child could do it.
**hastial** *m.* ARCH. gable wall. *2* MIN. side wall. *3* big coarse man.
**hastiar** *tr.* to cloy, sate, surfeit. *2* to weary, bore. *3 ref. hastiarse de,* to weary of.
**hastío** *m.* surfeit, disgust. *2* weariness, boredom, ennui.
**hatajo** *m.* small herd or flock. *2* coll. lot, bunch, set: *un ~ de mentiras,* a bunch of lies.
**hatillo** *m.* small bundle [made with one's belongings]: *tomar el ~,* to leave, depart.
**hato** *m.* outfit, belongings: *liar el ~,* to pack up; *menear el ~ a,* to beat up. *2* herd [of cattle], flock [of sheep]. *3* shepherd's place of sojourn. *4* provisions for shepherds. *5* lot, bunch, set [of knaves, lies, etc.].
**hawaiano, -na** *adj.-n.* Hawaiian.
**haxix** *m.* hasheesh, hashish.
**hay, haya,** etc. *irr.* V. HABER.
**Haya (La)** *f. pr. n.* GEOG. The Hague.
**haya** *f.* BOT. beech [tree]. *2* beech [wood].
**hayal, hayedo** *m.* beech forest or grove.
**hayuco** *m.* beechnut. *2 pl.* beech mast.
**1) haz** *m.* bunch, bundle [of sticks, etc., fastened together]; fagot, faggot; gavel, sheaf. *2* beam, pencil [of rays]. *3* BOT. fascicle. *4 f.* face, visage. *5* face [of the earth]; right side [of cloth, etc.]. *6 m. pl.* fasces.
**2) haz** *irr.* V. HACER.
**haza** *f.* AGR. piece of tillable land.

**hazaña** *f.* deed, feat, exploit, achievement.
**hazmerreír** *m.* laughing-stock.
1) **he** *adv.* used generally, as a demonstrative, with the adverbs *aquí, allí,* and the pronouns *me, te, la, le, lo, los, las:* ~ *aquí que,* behold; *heme aquí,* here I am.
2) **he** *irr.* V. HABER.
**hebdomadario, -ria** *adj.* hebdomadary.
**hebilla** *f.* buckle, clasp.
**hebillaje** *m.* buckles, set of buckles.
**hebra** *f.* needleful of thread. *2* TEXT. fibre, staple. *3* thread, filament. *4* fibre [of meat]. *5* grain [of wood]. *6* thread [of discourse]. *7 pl.* poet. threads, the hair. *8 pegar la* ~, to chat.
**hebraico, -ca** *adj.* Hebraic, Hebrew.
**hebraísmo** *m.* Hebraism.
**hebraísta** *m.* Hebraist [Hebrew scholar].
**hebraizante** *adj.* hebraizing. *2 m.* HEBRAÍSTA. *3* Hebraist, Judaizer.
**hebraizar** *intr.* to Hebraize [use Hebraisms].
**hebreo, -a** *adj.-n.* Hebrew. *2 m.* Hebrew [language]. *3* coll. usurer.
**Hébridas (las)** *f. pr. n.* GEOG. the Hebrides. *2 Las Nuevas Hébridas,* the New Hebrides.
**hebroso, -sa** *adj.* fibrous, stringy.
**hecatombe** *f.* hecatomb.
**hectárea** *f.* hectare.
**hectogramo** *m.* hectogram.
**hectolitro** *m.* hectolitre, hectoliter.
**hectómetro** *m.* hectometre, hectometer.
**hechicería** *f.* sorcery, witchcraft, witchery, wizardry, enchantment. *2* charm, fascination.
**hechicero, -ra** *adj.* bewitching, -charming, fascinating. *2 m.-f.* bewitcher. *3 m.* enchanter, sorcerer, wizard. *4 f.* enchantress, sorceress, witch. *5* enchantress, witch [charming woman].
**hechizar** *tr.* to bewitch, charm, enchant. *2* to entrance, fascinate.
**hechizo, -za** *adj.* false, artificial. *2 m.* charm, spell, magic ointment, etc. *3* charm, fascination, glamour. *4 pl.* charms [of a woman].
1) **hecho, -cha** *irr. p. p.* of HACER.
2) **hecho, -cha** *adj.* made, done, finished: ~ *de encargo,* made to order. *2* grown, full matured, ripe. *3* build, shaped, proportioned [animal, body, limbs]. *4* ready-made [clothing]. *5* turned into, quite, like: *el niño está* ~ *un hombrecito,* the boy is quite a little man; *se volvió hacia él* ~ *un león,* he turned on him like a lion. *6* accustomed, inured, used. *7* ~ *y derecho,* complete, finished, in every respect.
*8 m.* fact: *de* ~, in fact, as a matter of fact; actually; de facto; *de* ~ *y de derecho,* by deed and right. *9* happening. *10* deed act, action, feat. *11 Hechos de los Apóstoles,* Acts of the Apostles.
**hechura** *f.* make, making. *2* form, shape, cut, build. *3* creation, creature [of someone]. *4 sing. -pl.* workmanship, work, making [of a dress, etc.]; money paid for it.
**hedentina** *f.* stench, stink.
**heder** *intr.* to stink. *2 tr.* to be insufferable [to one]. ¶ CONJUG. like *entender.*
**hediondez** *f.* stench, evil smell, fetidness.
**hediondo, -da** *adj.* stinking, fetid. *2* annoying. *3* filthy, dirty, obscene.
**hedonismo** *m.* hedonism.
**hedonista** *adj.* hedonistic. *2 m.-f.* hedonist.
**hedor** *m.* stench, stink, foul smell.
**hegeliano, -na** *adj.-n.* Hegelian.
**hegemonía** *f.* hegemony.
**hégira, hejira** *f.* hegira, hejira.

**helada** *f.* freeze, freezing, frost: ~ *blanca,* hoarfrost, white frost.
**Hélade** *f. pr. n.* GEOG. Hellas [Greece].
**heladera** *f.* (Am.) freezer, refrigerator.
**helado, -da** *adj.* frozen. *2* frostbitten. *3* frigid, cold, chilly. *4* fig. *quedarse* ~, to be frozen [with amazement, fear, etc.]. *5 m.* frozen food, ice cream, sherbet, water ice.
**helamiento** *m.* congealment, congelation, freezing.
**helar** *tr.* to freeze, congeal, chill, ice. *2* to frostbite. *3* to astound, amaze. *4* to chill, discourage. *5 ref.* to freeze, congeal, be frozen. *6* to become frostbitten. *7 impers.* to freeze: *está helado,* it is freezing. ¶ CONJUG. like *acertar.*
**helechal** *m.* fern land, fernery.
**helecho** *m.* BOT. fern: ~ *arbóreo,* tree fern.
**helénico, -ca** *adj.* Hellenic.
**helenio** *m.* BOT. elecampane.
**helenismo** *m.* Hellenism.
**helenístico, -ca** *adj.* Hellenistic(al.
**heleno, -na** *adj.* Hellenic. *2 m.-f.* Hellene.
**helero** *m.* GEL. glacier.
**Helesponto** *m. pr. n.* GEOG. Hellespont.
**helgado, -da** *adj.* jagged-toothed.
**helíaco, -ca** *adj.* ASTR. heliacal.
**helianto** *m.* BOT. helianthus.
**hélice** *f.* ANAT., ARCH., GEOM. helix. *2* GEOM. spiral. *3* AER., NAUT. propeller, screw-propeller.
**helicoidal** *adj.* helicoidal.
**helicóptero** *m.* AER. helicopter.
**helio** *m.* CHEM. helium.
**heliocéntrico, -ca** *adj.* heliocentric.
**heliograbado** *m.* heliogravure.
**heliógrafo** *m.* heliograph.
**helióstato** *m.* heliostat.
**helioterapia** *f.* heliotherapy.
**heliotropo** *m.* BOT., MINER. heliotrope.
**helminto** *m.* ZOOL. helminth.
**Helvecia** *f. pr. n.* GEOGR. Helvetia.
**helvecio, -cia** or **helvético, -ca** *adj.* Helvetic. *2 adj. -n.* Helvetian.
**hematíe** *m.* PHYSIOL. red cell.
**hematina** *f.* CHEM. haematin, hematin.
**hematites** *f.* MINER. haematite, hematite.
**hematoma** *m.* MED. haematoma, hematoma.
**hematuria** *f.* MED. haematuria, hematuria.
**hembra** *adj.* female [animal or plant]. *2 f.* female [of an animal]. *3* BOT. female plant. *4* coll. female, woman. *5* eye [of hook an eye]. *6* MACH. nut [for a bolt or screw]; bolt staple; female part, tool, etc. *7* NAUT. *hembras del timón,* gudgeons of the rudder.
**hembrilla** *f.* MACH. small nut or staple; small female part or piece. *2* eyescrew.
**hemélitro** *m.* hemelytron.
**hemeroteca** *f.* newspaper and magazine library.
**hemiciclo** *m.* hemicycle. *2* in Spain, floor [of the House of Deputies].
**hemicránea** *f.* MED. hemicrania, megrim.
**hemihédrico, -ca** *adj.* CRYST. hemihedral.
**hemihedro** *m.* CRYST. hemihedron.
**hemiplejia** *f.* MED. hemiplegia.
**hemíptero, -ra** *adj.* ENT. hemipterous. *2 m.* ENT. hemipteran. *3 pl.* ENT. Hemiptera.
**hemisférico, -ca** *adj.* hemispherical.
**hemisferio** *m.* hemisphere.
**hemistiquio** *m.* PROS. hemistich.
**hemofilia** *f.* MED. haemophilia, hemophilia.
**hemoglobina** *f.* PHYSIOL. haemoglobin, hemoglobin.

**hemoptisis** *f.* MED. haemoptysis, hemoptysis.
**hemorragia** *f.* MED. haemorrhage, hemorrhage.
**hemostático, -ca** *adj.* haemostatic, hemostatic.
**henal** *m.* hayloft.
**henar** *m.* hayfield.
**henchidura** *f.*, **henchimiento** *m.* filling, stuffing.
**henchir** *tr.* to fill, stuff. *2 ref.* to be filled. *3* to stuff oneself. ¶ CONJUG. like *servir*.
**hendedura** *f.* HENDIDURA.
**hender** *tr.* to cleave, split, slit, crack, chink. *2* to cut through, to cleave [the air, the water]. *3 ref.* to cleave, split, crack [become cleaved, etc.]. ¶ CONJUG. like *entender*.
**hendidura** *f.* cleft, crevice, crack, fissure, slit, slot.
**hendiente** *m.* downstroke of a sword.
**hendimiento** *m.* cleaving, splitting, cracking.
**henequén** *m.* BOT. henequen, sisal.
**henificar** *tr.* to hay [cut and cure grass for hay].
**henil** *m.* hayloft, hay barn.
**henné** *m.* henna [dye].
**heno** *m.* hay. *2* BOT. an hay plant.
**heñir** *tr.* to knead [work up into dough]. ¶ CONJUG. like *reír*.
**hepático, -ca** *adj.* MED. hepatic(al. *2* BOT. hepatic. *3 f.* BOT. hepatica, liverwort.
**hepatitis** *f.* MED. hepatitis.
**heptacordio, heptacordo** *m.* MUS. heptachord.
**heptagonal** *adj.* heptagonal.
**heptágono, -na** *adj.* heptagonal. *2 m.* GEOM. heptagon.
**heptámetro** *m.* PROS. heptameter.
**heptarquía** *f.* heptarchy.
**heptasílabo, -ba** *adj.* heptasyllabic.
**Heptateuco** *m.* Heptateuc.
**heráldica** *f.* Heraldry.
**heráldico, -ca** *adj.* heraldic. *2 m.-f.* heraldist.
**heraldo** *m.* herald. *2* harbinger.
**herbáceo, -a** *adj.* herbaceous.
**herbaje** *m.* herbage, grass, pasture.
**herbario, -ria** *adj.* herbal. *2 m.* botanist; herbalist. *3* herbarium. *4* ZOOL. rumen [of ruminant].
**herbazal** *m.* grassland. *2* weedy place.
**herbecer** *intr.* [of grass] to begin to grow.
**herbero** *m.* gullet [of ruminants].
**herbívoro, -ra** *adj.* herbivorous.
**herbolario, -ria** *adj.* scatterbrained. *2 m.-f.* scatterbrain. *3 m.* herbalist. *4* herbman shop.
**herborización** *f.* herborization, botanizing.
**herborizar** *intr.* to herborize, botanize.
**herboso, -sa** *adj.* herby, grassy.
**hercúleo, -a** *adj.* Herculean. *2* herculean.
**heredable** *adj.* inheritable; hereditable.
**heredad** *f.* country property, country estate.
**heredado, -da** *adj.* inherited. *2* landed, owning real state. *3* having inherited.
**heredamiento** *m.* landed property.
**heredar** *tr.* to inherit. *2* to give possessions or real estate to. *3* to institute heir.
**heredero, -ra** *adj.* inheriting. *2 m.-f.* heir, heiress, inheritor.
**hereditario, -ria** *adj.* hereditary.
**hereje** *m.* heretic. *2* fig. shameless person.
**herejía** *f.* heresy. *2* insult, injurious expression.
**herencia** *f.* heritage, inheritance. *2* heredity.
**heresiarca** *m.* heresiarch.
**heretical; herético, -ca** *adj.* heretical.
**Heriberto** *m. pr.* Herbert.
**herida** *f.* wound, injury: *renovar la* ~, to open an old sore.
**herido, -da** *adj.* wounded, injured hurt: *mal* ~, se-

riously wounded, seriously injured. *2* struck. *3 m.-f.* wounded or injured person.
**herir** *tr.* to wound, injure, hurt [bodily or morally]. *2* to offend, pique. *3* to touch, move. *4* to strike, hit. *5* MUS. to finger, pluck. ¶ CONJUG. like *hervir*.
**hermafrodita** *adj.* hermaphrodite.
**hermana** *f.* sister; V. HERMANO.
**hermanable** *adj.* fraternal, brotherly. *2* compatible.
**hermanado, -da** *adj.* matched, mated, like, uniform.
**hermanamiento** *adj.* matching, mating, joining, making compatible.
**hermanar** *tr.* to join, match, mate; to harmonize, make compatible. *2* to make brothers or sisters [in a spiritual sense]. *3 ref.* to match, harmonize, be compatible. *4* to become brothers or sisters [in a spiritual sense].
**hermanastro, -tra** *m.* stepbrother. *2 f.* stepsister.
**hermandad** *f.* fraternity, brotherhood, sisterhood [fraternal tie; intimate friendship]. *2* correspondence, harmony. *3* confraternity, guild, religious association. *4 Santa Hermandad*, a Spanish rural police instituted in the fifteenth century.
**hermano, -na** *m.-f.* brother, sister: ~ or *hermana carnal*, full brother or sister; ~ or *hermana de leche*, foster brother, foster sister; ~, or *hermana, de madre* or *de padre*, half brother by the same mother or father; ~ *político, hermana política*, brother-in-law, sister-in-law; *her manos siameses*, Siamese twins; *Hermanos de la Doctrina Cristiana*, Brothers of the Christian Schools; *Hermanas de la Caridad*, Sisters of Charity. *2 adj. lenguas hermanas*, sister languages; *primo* ~, *prima hermana*, cousin german.
**hermenéutica** *f.* hermeneutics.
**hermenéutico, -ca** *adj.* hermeneutic(al.
**hermético, -ca** *adj.* hermetic(al, airtight. *2* impenetrable.
**hermetismo** *m.* secretiveness, secrecy.
**hermosamente** *adv.* beautifully. *2* perfectly.
**hermosear** *tr.* to beautify, embellish. *2 ref.* to beautify oneself.
**hermoso, -sa** *adj.* beautiful, beauteous, fair, lovely. *2* handsome, good-looking.
**hermosura** *f.* beauty, fairness, loveliness. *2* handsomeness, good looks. *3* belle, beauty.
**hernia** *f.* MED. hernia; rupture.
**herniado, -da** *adj.* MED. herniated, ruptured. *2 m.-f.* ruptured person.
**hernista** *m.* hernia surgeon.
**Herodes** *m. pr. n.* BIBL. Herod: *ir de* ~ *a Pilatos*, to go from pillar to post; from bad to worse.
**herodiano, -na** *adj.* Herodian.
**Herodías** *f. pr. n.* BIBL. Herodias.
**héroe** *m.* hero.
**heroicidad** *f.* heroicity, heroism. *2* heroic deed.
**heroico, -ca** *adj.* heroic: *verso heroico*, heroics.
**heroína** *f.* heroine. *2* CHEM. heroin.
**heroísmo** *m.* heroism.
**herpe, herpes** *m.-f.* MED. herpes.
**herpético, -ca** *adj.* MED. herpetic. *2 m.-f.* one who suffers from herpes.
**herpetología** *f.* herpetology.
**herrada** *f.* wooden bucket or pail.
**herradero** *m.* branding of cattle. *2* place where cattle are branded. *3* season for branding cattle.
**herrado** *m.* horseshoeing.

**herrador** *m.* horseshoer, farrier.

**herradura** *f.* horseshoe.

**herraje** *m.* ironwork, pieces of iron put on a door, coffer, etc. *2* horseshoes and their nails. *3* ERRAJ.

**herramental** *adj.-m.* tool bag, tool box.

**herramienta** *f.* tool, implement. *2* tools, set of tools. *3* coll, horns [of bull, cow, deer, etc.]. *4* coll. teeth, set of teeth, grinders.

**herrar** *tr.* to shoe [an animal]. *2* to brand [cattle, etc.]. *3* to cover or ornament with iron. ¶ CONJUG. like *acertar.*

**herrén** *m.* mixed grain for fodder.

**herrera** *f.* coll. blacksmith's wife.

**herrería** *f.* forge, ironworks. *2* smithy, blacksmith's shop; blacksmith's trade.

**herrerillo** *m.* ORN. blue titmouse. *2* ORN. great titmouse.

**herrero** *m.* blacksmith; iron forger, iron worker.

**herreruelo** *m.* ORN. coal titmouse.

**herrete** *m.* tag, aglet [of a lace, etc.].

**herretear** *tr.* to tag, to tip [a lace, etc.] with a tag.

**herrín** *m.* HERRUMBRE I.

**herrón** *m.* quoit.

**herrumbre** *f.* rust, iron rust. *2* iron taste. *3* rust [plant disease].

**herrumbroso, -sa** *adj.* rusty, rusted.

**hertziano, -na** *adj.* Hertzian.

**herventar** *tr.* COOK. to bring to a boil.

**hervidero** *m.* noise and agitation of a boiling liquid. *2* boiling spring. *3* MED. rumbling in the chest. *4* crowd, swarm, seething mass.

**hervir** *intr.* [of a liquid] to boil: *hacer ~,* to make boil: to boil [something]. *2* to bubble, effervesce. *3* [of sea, etc.] to boil, seethe, be agitated. *4* to seethe [with emotion, etc.]. *5 ~ en,* to swarm or teem with. ‖ IRREG. CONJUG.: INDIC. Pres.: *hiervo, hierves, hierve; hervimos, hervís, hierven.* | Pret.: *hervi, herviste, hirvió; hervimos, hervisteis, hirvieron.* | SUBJ. Pres.: *hierva, hiervas, hierva; hirvamos, hirváis, hiervan.* | Imper.: *hirviera, hirvieras,* etc., or *hirviese, hirvieses,* etc. Fut.: *hirviere, hirvieres,* etc. | IMPER. *hierve, hierva; hirvamos, hervid, hiervan.* | PAST. P.: *hervido.* | GER.: *hirviendo.*

**hervor** *m.* boiling, reaching the boiling point. *2* vehemence, ardour [of youth].

**hervoroso, -sa** *adj.* ardent, impetuous.

**Hesíodo** *m. pr. n.* Hesiod.

**Hesperia** *f. pr. n.* GEOG. Hesperia [Spain or Italy].

**Hespérides** *f. pl.* MYTH. Hesperides. *2* ASTR. Pleiades.

**hesperidio** *m.* BOT. hesperidium.

**Héspero** *m.* ASTR. Hesperus, the evening star.

**heteo, -a** *adj.-n.* Hittite.

**heterocerca** *adj.* ICHTH. heterocercal.

**heteróclito, -ta** *adj.* heteroclite.

**heterodino, -na** *adj.* RADIO. heterodyne.

**heterodoxia** *f.* heterodoxy.

**heterodoxo, -xa** *adj.* heterodox.

**heterogeneidad** *f.* heterogeneity.

**heterogéneo, -a** *adj.* heterogeneous.

**heterónomo, -ma** *adj.* heteronomous.

**heteroscios** *m. pl.* GEOG. heteroscians.

**hético, -ca** *adj.-n.* hectic, consumptive.

**hexacordo** *m.* MUS. hexacord.

**hexaedro** *m.* GEOM. hexahedron.

**hexagonal** *adj.* hexagonal.

**hexágono, -na** *adj.* hexagonal. *2 m.* GEOM. hexagon.

**hexámetro** *m.* PROS. hexameter.

**hexápodo, -da** *adj.-m.* hexapod.

**hexasílabo, -ba** *adj.* hexasyllabic.

**hexástilo** *m.* ARQ. hexastyle.

**hez** *f.* scum, dregs [vilest part]. *2 pl.* **heces** dregs, grounds, lees, sediment. *3* fœces, excrement.

**hialino, -na** *adj.* hyaline.

**hialografía** *f.* hyalography.

**hiato** *m.* GRAM., PROS. hiatus.

**hibernación** *f.* hibernation.

**hibernal** *adj.* hibernal.

**hibernés, -sa** *adj.-s.* Hibernian.

**hibridación** *f.* hybridization.

**híbrido, -da** *adj.-n.* hybrid.

**hice, hiciera, hiciese,** etc., *irr.* V. HACER.

**hidalgo, -ga** *adj.* noble, generous [person, act, etc.]. *2* of noble birth. *3 m.* hidalgo, nobleman. *4 f.* hidalga, noblewoman.

**hidalguía** *f.* quality, state or status of being an hidalgo. *2* nobility, nobleness, generosity.

**hidra** *f.* ZOOL. a poisonous sea snake. *2* ZOOL. hydra [polyp]. *3* (cap.) ASTR., MYTH. Hydra.

**hidrácido** *m.* CHEM. hydracid.

**hidrargirio** *m.* HIDRARGIRO.

**hidrargirismo** *m.* MED. mercurialism.

**hidrargiro** *m.* CHEM. hydrargyrum, mercury.

**hidratación** *f.* hydration, hydrating.

**hidratado, -da** *adj.* hydrated.

**hidratar** *tr.* CHEM. to hydrate.

**hidrato** *m.* CHEM. hydrate.

**hidráulica** *f.* hydraulics.

**hidráulico, -ca** *adj.* hydraulic. *2 m.* expert in hidraulics.

**hidria** *f.* hydria [ancient jar].

**hidroavión** *m.* AER. hydroplane, seaplane.

**hidrocarburo** *m.* CHEM. hydrocarbon.

**hidrodinámica** *f.* hydrodynamics.

**hidrodinámico, -ca** *adj.* hydrodynamic.

**hidroeléctrico, -ca** *adj.* hidroelectric.

**hidrófilo, -la** *adj.* absorbent: *algodón ~,* absorbent cotton.

**hidrofobia** *f.* MED. hydrophobia; rabies.

**hidrófobo, -ba** *adj.* MED. hydrophobe.

**hidrófugo, -ga** *adj.* nonabsorbent, moistureproof.

**hidrogenar** *tr.* to hydrogenate.

**hidrógeno** *m.* CHEM. hydrogen.

**hidrografía** *f.* hydrography.

**hidrográfico, -ca** *adj.* hydrographical.

**hidrólisis** *f.* CHEM. hydrolysis.

**hidrolizar** *tr.* CHEM. to hydrolyze.

**hidrología** *f.* hydrology.

**hidromel** *m.* hydromel.

**hidrómetro** *m.* hydrometer.

**hidromiel** *m.* HIDROMEL.

**hidropatía** *f.* MED. hydropathy, water cure.

**hidropesía** *f.* MED. dropsy.

**hidrópico, -ca** *adj.* dropsical, dropsied, hydropic(al. *2 m.-f.* dropsied person.

**hidroplano** *m.* AER. hydroplane, seaplane.

**hidroscopio** *m.* hydroscope.

**hidrosfera** *f.* hydrosphere.

**hidrostática** *f.* hydrostatics.

**hidrostático, -ca** *adj.* hydrostatic(al.

**hidrostato** *m.* hydrostat.

**hidrosulfuro** *m.* CHEM. hydrosulphide.

**hidroterapia** *f.* hydrotherapeutics.

**hidróxido** *m.* CHEM. hydroxide.

**hidroxilo** *m.* CHEM. hydroxil.

**hiedra** *f.* BOT. ivy.

**hiel** *f.* bile, gall: *echar la ~,* fig. to work hard. *2* fig. gall, bitterness, asperity, rancour.

**hielo** *m.* ice [frozen water]. *2* freezing, frost. *3*

ice, reserve, coldness: *romper el* ~, to break the ice.
**hielo, hiele,** etc., *irr.* V. HELAR.
**hiemación** *f.* wintering. 2 BOT. winter blooming.
**hiemal** *adj.* hibernal.
**hiena** *f.* ZOOL. hyena, hyaena.
**hiendo, hienda,** etc. *irr.* V. HENDER.
**hierático, -ca** *adj.* hieratic(al.
**hierba** *f.* herb, grass, weed: *mala* ~, weed; *sentir crecer,* or *nacer, la* ~, to be very sagacious; *en* ~, [of grain] green; *y otras hierbas,* fig. and many other things. 2 grass, herbage. 3 *pl.* years of age [of grazing cattle or horse]: *un potro de dos yerbas,* a colt two years old.
4 BOT. the word *hierba* forms the name of a great number of herbs and plants: ~ *buena,* mint; ~ *cana,* groundsel; ~ *de Santa María,* costmary, tansy; ~ *jabonera,* soapwort; ~ *luisa,* lemon verbena; ~ *pastel,* woad; ~ *sagrada,* vervain.
**hierbabuena** *f.* BOT. mind.
**hierbezuela** *f. dim.* small herb.
**hierofanta** or **hierofante** *m.* hierophant.
**hieroglífico, -ca** *adj.-m.* JEROGLÍFICO.
**hierosolimitano, -na** *adj.* JEROSOLIMITANO.
**hierro** *m.* iron [metal]: ~ *colado,* cast iron; ~ *dulce,* wrought iron; ~ *ondulado,* corrugated iron; *machacar en* ~ *frío,* to labour in vain. 2 iron, branding iron. 3 brand [mark]. 4 iron, head [of an arrow, lance, etc.]. 5 iron piece; steel, weapon: *quien a* ~ *mata, a* ~ *muere,* he who lives by the sword, will die by the sword. 6 *pl.* irons [fetters, chains, etc.].
**hierro, hierre,** etc. *irr.* V. HERRAR.
**hiervo, hierva, hirviera, hirviere,** etc. *irr.* V. HERVIR.
**higa** *f.* baby's fist-shaped amulet. 2 derisive gesture. 3 contempt, derision. 4 coll. *no dar dos higas por,* not to care a rap for. 5 *dar* ~ [of firearms] to miss fire.
**higadillo** *m.* liver [of birds and other small animals].
**hígado** *m.* liver. 2 *pl.* fig. courage. 3 *malos hígados,* evil disposition; *echar uno los hígados,* to work to excess; *hasta los hígados,* deeply, vehemently.
**higiene** *f.* hygiene, hygienics. 2 hygiene, cleanliness; sanitation.
**higiénico, -ca** *adj.* hygienic.
**higienista** *m.* hygienist.
**higienizar** *tr.* to sanitate, make sanitary.
**higo** *m.* fig: *no dársele a uno un* ~, not to care a fig; *de higos a brevas,* once in a while.
**higrometría** *f.* hygrometry.
**higrómetro** *m.* hygrometer.
**higroscopio** *m.* hygroscope.
**higuera** *f.* BOT. fig tree: ~ *chumba, de Indias* or *de tuna,* prickly pear; ~ *de Egipto,* caprifig, wild fig; *estar en la* ~, to be dreaming, to be in the clouds.
**higueral** *m.* plantation of fig trees.
**higuereta** *f.* BOT. castor-oil plant.
**hija** *f.* daughter. V. HIJO.
**hijastro, -tra** *m.-f.* stepson, stepdaughter.
**hijito, -ta** *m.-f. dim.* little son, sonny; little daughter; little child. 2 my son, my girl, my child, my dear. 3 young [of all animals].
**hijo, -ja** *m.-f.* son, daughter; child: ~ *adoptivo,* adopted child; citizen of honour; ~ *de confesión,* spiritual son; *Hijo de Dios,* Son of God, the Word; ~ *de leche,* foster child; ~ *legítimo,* legi-

timate child; ~ *natural,* illegitimate child; ~ *político,* son-in-law. 2 native [of a town or country]. 3 young [of an animal]. 4 fig. child, offspring, fruit, result. 5 junior: *Alejandro Dumas hijo,* Alexander Dumas Junior. 6 *m. pl.* sons, descendants.
**hijodalgo** *m.* HIDALGO.
**hijuela** *f. dim.* of HIJA. 2 accesory thing. 3 chalice pall. 4 irrigation channel. 5 BOT. palm seed; palmetto seed.
**hijuelo** *m. dim.* of HIJO. 2 BOT. offshoot, shoot.
**hila** *f.* file, row. 2 thin gut. 3 spinning [operation]. 4 *pl.* SURG. lint.
**hilacha** *f.,* **hilacho** *m.* thread, filament or shred ravelled out of cloth.
**hilada** *f.* file, row. 2 MAS. layer [of bricks], course. 3 NAUT. streak.
**hilado** *adj.* spun. 2 *m.* spinning [operation]. 3 yarn, spun yarn, thread.
**hilador, -ra** *m.-f.* spinner.
**hilandera** *f.* woman spinner.
**hilandería** *f.* spinning [art, business]. 2 spinning mill, spinnery.
**hilandero, -ra** *m.-f.* spinner. 2 *m.* spinning room.
**hilar** *tr.* to spin [wool, flax, silk, etc.]. 2 ~ *delgado,* to be exceedingly particular.
**hilarante** *adj.* laughable. 2 laughing [gas].
**hilaridad** *f.* hilarity.
**Hilario** *m. pr. n.* Hilary.
**hilaza** *f.* yarn, thread. 2 uneven thread. 3 *descubrir uno la* ~, to show one's true nature.
**hilera** *f.* file, line, row. 2 drawplate [for drawing wire]. 3 fine yarn. 4 ARCH. ridgepole. 5 MIL. file, single file. 6 *pl.* ZOOL. spinnerets.
**hilillo** *m. dim.* small thread. 2 trickle.
**hilo** *m.* thread [of flax, wool, hemp, etc.]: ~ *de empalomar,* packthread; ~ *de la vida,* thread of life; ~ *de perlas,* string of pearls; *pender de un* ~, to hang by a thread; *por el* ~ *se saca el ovillo,* a known detail leads to the knowledge of the whole. 2 thread [of conversation, narrative, etc.]. 3 fibre, grain. 4 direction, current: *irse tras el* ~ *de la gente,* to follow the current. 5 thin wire, wire thread. 6 trickle, thread [of water, etc.]. 7 linen [cloth]. 8 *al* ~, with the thread, with the grain. 9 *al* ~ *de medianoche,* on the stroke of midnight; *al* ~ *del mediodía,* at noon sharp.
**hilván** *m.* basting, tacking.
**hilvanar** *tr.* to baste, tack. 2 to string together, coordinate [phrases, ideas, etc.]. 3 to plan something hurriedly.
**himen** *m.* ANAT. hymen.
**himeneo** *m.* hymen, nuptials, marriage, wedding.
**himenóptero, -ra** *adj.* ENT. hymenopterous. 2 *m.* ENT. hymenopter.
**himnario** *m.* hymnal.
**himno** *m.* hymn, anthem: ~ *nacional,* national anthem.
**himplar** *intr.* [of a panther] to roar, bellow.
**hincadura** *f.* sticking, driving, thrusting in or into.
**hincapié** *m. hacer* ~ *en,* to insist upon, emphasize, lay special stress on.
**hincar** *tr.* to stick, introduce, drive, thrust in or into: ~ *el diente,* to bite, set one's teeth into. 2 to plant, set [a post, etc.]. 3 ~ *la rodilla,* to go down on one's knee. 4 *ref. hincarse de rodillas,* to kneel down.
**hincha** *f.* hatred, enmity. 2 *m.-f.* coll. football-club fan.

**hinchado, -da** *adj.* swollen, inflated, bloated, tumid. *2* vain, puffed up. *3* high-flown, tumid, turgid [style].

**hinchamiento** *m.* swelling.

**hinchar** *tr.* to inflate, puff up, blow up, bloat, swell. *2* to swell [a river, brook, etc.]. *3* to pad, puff up [news, etc.]. *4 ref.* to swell, blot [become swelled]. *5* to swell [with pride].

**hinchazón** *f.* swelling, tumefaction. *2* vanity, pride, haughtiness. *3* tumidness [of style].

**hincho, hinche,** etc. *irr.* V. HENCHIR.

**hindú** *adj.-n.* Hindu, Hindoo.

**hinduismo** *m.* Hinduism.

**hinojo** *m.* BOT. fennel: ~ *marino,* samphire.

**hinojos** *m. pl.* knees: *de hinojos,* on one's knees.

**hintero** *m.* baker's kneading table.

**hioideo, -a** *adj.* hyoid.

**hioides** *adj.* hyoid: *hueso* ~, hyoid bone.

**hipar** *intr.* to hiccup. *2* [of dogs on the scent] to pant, snuffle. *3* to whimper.

**hiper-** *pref.* hyper-.

**hipérbaton** *m.* RHET. hyperbaton.

**hipérbola** *f.* GEOM. hyperbola.

**hypérbole** *f.* RHET. hyperbole.

**hiperbólico, -ca** *adj.* hyperbolic.

**hiperbóreo, -a** *adj.* hyperborean.

**hiperclorhidria** *f.* hyperchlorhydria.

**hipercrítico, -ca** *adj.* hypercritical.

**hiperdulia** *f.* ECCL. hyperdulia.

**hiperestesia** *f.* hyperaesthesia.

**hipérico** *m.* BOT. hypericum, St. John's wort.

**hipermetropía** *f.* hypermetropia.

**hipersensible** *adj.* MED. hypersensitive.

**hipertensión** *f.* MED. hypertension.

**hipertrofia** *f.* hypertrophy.

**hipertrofiarse** *ref.* to hypertrophy.

**hipertrófico, -ca** *adj.* hypertrophic.

**hípico, -ca** *adj.* equine, pertaining to horses: *concurso* ~, riding competition.

**hipido** *m.* action of hiccuping. *2* whine, whimper.

**hipnosis** *f.* hypnosis.

**hipnótico, -ca** *adj.-n.* hypnotic.

**hipnotismo** *m.* hypnotism.

**hipnotizador, -ra** *adj.* hypnotizing. *2 m.-f.* hypnotizer, hypnotist.

**hipnotizar** *tr.* to hypnotize.

**hipo** *m.* hiccup. *2* fig. longing. *3* fig. dislike, hatred.

**hipocampo** *m.* ICHTH. sea-horse, hippocampus.

**hipocausto** *m.* hypocaust.

**hipoclorito** *m.* CHEM. hypochlorite.

**hipocondria** *f.* hypochondria.

**hipocondríaco, -ca** *adj.-n.* hypochondriac.

**hipocondrio** *m.* ANAT. hypochondrium.

**hipocrás** *m.* hippocras, spiced wine.

**Hipócrates** *m. pr. n.* Hippocrates.

**hipocresía** *f.* hypocrisy.

**hipócrita** *adj.* hypocritical. *2 m.-f.* hypocrite.

**hipocritón, -na** *m.-f.* coll. great hypocrite.

**hipodérmico, -ca** *adj.* hypodermic.

**hipódromo** *m.* hippodrome.

**hipófisis** *f.* ANAT. hypophysis.

**hipofosfito** *m.* CHEM. hypophosphite.

**hipogastrio** *m.* ANAT. hypogastrium.

**hipogeo** *m.* ARCH. hypogeum.

**hipogrifo** *m.* MYTH. hippogriff, hippogryph.

**Hipólito** *pr. n.* Hyppolytus.

**hipopótamo** *m.* ZOOL. hippopotamus.

**hiposo, -sa** *adj.* hiccuping, having hiccups.

**hipóstasis** *f.* hypostasis.

**hipostático, -ca** *adj.* hypostatic, hipostatical.

**hipoteca** *f.* mortgage, pledge. *2* LAW hypothec, hypothecation.

**hipotecar** *tr.* to mortgage, hypothecate, pledge.

**hipotecario, -ria** *adj.* hypothecary.

**hipotenusa** *f.* GEOM. hypotenuse.

**hipótesis** *f.* hypothesis.

**hipotético, -ca** *adj.* hypothetic(al.

**hipsometría** *f.* hypsometry.

**hipsómetro** *m.* hypsometer.

**hirco** *m.* ZOOL. wild goat.

**hircocervo** *m.* MYTH. hircocervus. *2* chimera, fantasy.

**hiriente** *adj.* cutting, smarting, offensive.

**hirsuto, -ta** *adj.* hirsute, hairy, bristly.

**hirviente** *adj.* boiling, seething.

**hisopada** *f.* a sprinkle with the aspergillum, aspersion.

**hisopar, hisopear** *tr.* to asperse, to sprinkle with the aspergillum.

**hisopo** *m.* BOT. hyssop. *2* aspergillum, sprinkler.

**hispalense** *adj.* Sevillan.

**hispánico, -ca** *adj.* Hispanic.

**Hispaniola** *f. pr. n.* GEOG. Haiti Island.

**hispanismo** *m.* hispanicism; interest in language, literature, and other Spanish things.

**hispanista** *m.-f.* Hispanist.

**hispano, -na** *adj.-n.* Hispanic, Spanish, Hispano.

**hispanoamericano, -na** *adj.* Spanish-American.

**hispanófilo, -la** *adj.* Hispanophile.

**híspido, -da** *adj.* BOT., ZOOL. hispid, shaggy, bristly.

**histéresis** *f.* PHYS. hysteresis.

**histérico, -ca** *adj.* hysteric, hysterical. *2 m.-f.* hysterical person. *3 m.* HISTERISMO.

**histerismo** *m.* hysteria.

**histología** *f.* histology.

**historia** *f.* history: ~ *natural,* Natural History; ~ *sacra* or *sagrada,* Sacred History; ~ *universal,* Universal History; *hacer* ~ *de,* to relate, to give an account of; *picar en* ~, to be more serious than it seems. *2* story, tale, fable; gossip: *dejarse de historias,* to come to the point.

**historiado, -da** *adj.* historiated [letter]. *2* F. ARTS storied. *3* excessively and badly adorned.

**historiador, -ra** *m.-f.* historian.

**historial** *adj.* historical. *2 m.* account of an affair, event, etc. *3* dossier, record [of a person].

**historiar** *tr.* to write or tell the history of; to chronicle, relate, give an account of.

**histórico, -ca** *adj.* historic, historical.

**historieta** *f.* short story or tale: ~ *cómica,* comic strip.

**historiografía** *f.* historiography.

**historiógrafo** *m.* historiographer.

**histrión** *m.* histrion.

**histriónico, -ca** *adj.* histrionic.

**histrionismo** *m.* histrionism.

**hita** *f.* headless nail. *2* landmark, mile-stone.

**hito, -ta** *adj.* fixed, firm. *2 m.* landmark. *3* game like quoits. *4* target, aim: *dar en el* ~, fig. to see the point, the difficulty. *5 mirar de* ~ *en* ~, to look fixedly, to stare at.

**hizo** *irr.* V. HACER.

**hobachón, -na** *adj.* fat, soft and lazy.

**hocicada** *f.* blow with the snout.

**hocicar** *tr.* [of hogs] to root. *2* coll. to kiss repeatedly. *3 intr.* to fall on one's face. *4* to knock one's face [against an object]. *5* NAUT. to pitch.

**hocico** *m.* snout, muzzle, nose [of animal]. *2* blubber-lipped mouth. *3* coll. pouting, sullen look: *estar de* ~, to be sulky. *4 sing. & pl.* coll. face [of a person]: *caer de hocicos*, to fall on one's face; *meter el ~ en*, to poke one's nose into.

**hocino** *m.* billhook. *2* glen, den; narrow gorge. *3 pl.* gardens in glens.

**hogaño** *adv.* this year. *2* nowadays, at present.

**hogar** *m.* hearth, fireplace. *2* furnace [of steam engine]. *3* home [house; family life].

**hogareño, -ña** *adj.* home [of the home]. *2* home-loving.

**hogaza** *f.* large loaf.

**hoguera** *f.* bonfire, fire, blaze.

**hoja** *f.* BOT. leaf [of tree or plant], blade [of grass]; petal: *~ de parra*, fig. leaf [on a statue]. *2* leaf [of a book, door, table, etc.]: *volver la ~*, to turn the page; to change the subject [of conversation]. *3* sheet [of paper], printed or written sheet; blank form: *~ de pedidos*, COM. order blank; *~ de ruta*, RLY. waybill; *~ de servicios*, service record; *~ suelta* or *volante*, leaflet, handbill, fly sheet. *4* leaf, sheet, foil, pane [of metal, wood, etc.]. *5* blade [of sword, knife, etc.]: *~ de afeitar*, razor blade. *6* blade, sword. *7* layer, flake [of pastry]. *8* flitch, side [of bacon]. *9* ground cultivated every other year. *10* flaw [in a coin].

**hojalata** *f.* tin, tinplate.

**hojalatería** *f.* tinware. *2* tin-shop.

**hojalatero** *m.* tinman, tinsmith.

**hojaldrado, -da** *adj.* flaky [paste, pastry].

**hojaldre** *m.* or *f.* flaky or puff paste or pastry.

**hojarasca** *f.* dead leaves. *2* excessive foliage. *3* empty or superfluous words, rubbish, trash.

**hojear** *tr.* to leaf through, to skim the pages of.

**hojita** *f. dim.* small leaf, leaflet. *2* small blade, sheet, foil, layer or flake.

**hojoso, -sa; hojudo, -da** *adj.* leafy.

**hojuela** *f. dim.* HOJITA.

**¡hola!** *interj.* hello! *2* NAUT. hoy!, ahoy!

**Holanda** *f. pr. n.* GEOG. Holland. *2 f.* (not cap.) holland [fabric].

**holandés, -sa** *adj.* Dutch. *2 m.-f.* Dutchman, Dutchwoman, hollander.

**holgachón, -na** *adj.* ease-loving.

**holgadamente** *adv.* amply, fully. *2* quite. *3* comfortably.

**holgado, -da** *adj.* idle. *2* large, ample, roomy. *3* loose [clothing]. *4* comfortable, well-to-do.

**holganza** *f.* leisure, rest. *2* idleness. *3* pleasure, amusement.

**holgar** *intr.* to rest [after exertion]. *2* to be idle. *3* to be needless: *huelga decir*, needless to say. *4 ref.* to enjoy oneself. *5 intr.-ref.* to be glad: *huélgome de ello*, I am glad of it. ¶ CONJUG. like *contar*.

**holgazán, -na** *adj.* idle, lazy, slothful. *2 m.-f.* idler, loafer, lazy person.

**holgazanear** *intr.* to idle, lounge.

**holgazanería** *f.* idleness, laziness, slothfulness.

**holgorio** *m.* merrymaking, frolic.

**holgura** *f.* roominess, ampleness. *2* ease, comfort. *3* merrymaking.

**holocausto** *m.* holocaust, burnt offering; sacrifice.

**hológrafo, -fa** *adj.-m.* OLÓGRAFO.

**holohedro** *m.* CRYST. holohedron.

**holoturia** *f.* ZOOL. holoturian.

**holladero** *m.* trampled part of a path or place.

**hollar** *tr.* to tread, tread on or upon, trample. *2* fig. to tread upon, to humiliate, scorn.

**hollejo** *m.* thin skin covering some fruits [as grapes, beans, etc.].

**hollín** *m.* soot.

**holliniento, -ta** *adj.* sooty, fuliginous.

**hombrachón** *m.* big sturdy man.

**hombrada** *f.* manly action.

**hombradía** *f.* manliness. *2* courage, firmness.

**hombre** *m.* man [male member of the human race; human being; mankind]: *~ bueno*, LAW conciliator; *~ de armas*, man-at-arms; *~ de bien*, honest man; *~ de corazón*, courageous, magnanimous man; *~ de dinero*, man of means; *~ de estado*, statesman; *~ de letras*, man of letters; *~ de mar*, seaman; *~ de mundo*, man of the world; *~ de negocios*, businessman; *~ de palabra*, man of his word; *~ de pelo en pecho*, strong, daring man; *~ de pro* or *de provecho*, honest, steady man; *~ público*, politician; *buen ~*, good man; *pobre ~*, poor fellow; *ser todo un ~*, to be every inch a man: *como un solo ~*, at one, unanimously; *~ prevenido vale por dos*, forewarned is forearmed. *2* coll. man, husband. *3* CARDS ombre. *4 interj.* why!, well!, well I never!

**hombrear** *intr.* [of a boy] to try to act fullgrown. *2 intr.-ref. hombrearse con*, to strive to equal.

**hombrecillo** *m. dim.* little man, manikin. *2* BOT. hop.

**hombrera** *f.* ARM. pauldron. *2* shoulder strap. *3* shoulder pad.

**hombretón** *m.* big man.

**hombría de bien** *f.* probity, honesty.

**hombrillo** *m.* yoke [of a shirt].

**hombro** *m.* ANAT., ZOOL., PRINT. shoulder: *arrimar el ~*, to put one's shoulder to the wheel; *cargado de hombros*, round-shouldered; *echar al ~*, to take upon oneself; to shoulder the responsibility for something; *encogerse de hombros*, to shrug one's shoulders; not to be able or willing to answer; *llevar a hombros*, to carry on the shoulders; *mirar a uno por encima del ~*, to look down upon one.

**hombrón** *m.* big, sturdy man.

**hombruno, -na** *adj.* mannish, masculine.

**homenaje** *m.* homage: *rendir ~*, to pay or do homage to. *2* tribute, attention.

**homenajear** *tr.* to pay homage to. *2* to show respect, admiration, etc., through a public ceremony.

**homeópata** *m.* homoeopath, homoeopathist.

**homeopatía** *f.* homoeopathy.

**homérico, -ca** *adj.* Homeric.

**Homero** *m. pr. n.* Homer.

**homicida** *adj.* homicide [killing].

**homilía** *f.* homily.

**hominicaco** *m.* ugly, worthless man.

**homocerca** *adj.* ICHTH. homocercal.

**homófono, -na** *adj.* homophonous.

**homogeneidad** *f.* homogeneity.

**homogéneo, -a** *adj.* homogeneous.

**homologación** *f.* homologation.

**homologar** *tr.* to homologate.

**homólogo, -ga** *adj.* homologous.

**homónimo, -ma** *adj.* homonymous. *2 m.* homonym. *3 m.-f.* namesake.

**homóptero, -ra** *adj.* ENT. homopterous.

**homosexual** *adj.-n.* homosexual.

**homúnculo** *m.* homunculus.

**honda** *f.* sling [for hurling stones; hoisting rope].

**hondamente** *adv.* deeply, profoundly. *2* with deep insight.

**hondazo** *m.* shot with a sling.

**hondero** *m.* HIST. slinger.

**hondo, -da** *adj.* deep, profound. *2* low [ground]. *3 m.* depth, bottom: *de* ~, in depth.

**hondón** *m.* bottom [of a hollow thing]. *2* hollow, dell. *3* footpiece [of a stirrup].

**hondonada** *f.* hollow, dell, ravine, bottom land.

**hondura** *f.* depth, profundity: *meterse en honduras*, fig. to go beyond one's depth.

**Honduras** *f. pr. n.* GEOG. Honduras.

**hondureño, -ña** *adj.-n.* Honduran.

**honestidad** *f.* purity, chastity; modesty, decency.

**honesto, -ta** *adj.* pure, chaste, modest, decent. *2* honest, upright. *3* reasonable, just.

**hongo** *m.* BOT. fungus, mushroom. *2* bowler, Derby [hat]. *3* MED. fungus.

**honor** *m.* honour: *hacer* ~ *a uno*, to do one credit; *hacer uno* ~ *a sus compromisos*, to fulfill one's engagements. *2* honesty. *3 pl.* honours [civilities]. *4* dignity, rank, office. *5 honores de guerra*, honours of war.

**honorabilidad** *f.* honourability.

**honorable** *adj.* honourable [worthy of honour].

**honorario, -ria** *adj.* honorary. *2 pl.* honorarium, professional fee.

**honorífico, -ca** *adj.* honorific. *2* honorary.

**honra** *f.* honour [reputation, good name], dignity. *2* honour, purity [of women]. *3* honour, respect. *4 tener a mucha* ~, to be proud of. *5 pl.* obsequies.

**honradez** *f.* honesty, probity, integrity, uprightness.

**honrado, -da** *adj.* honest, honourable, upright, fair.

**honramiento** *m.* honouring.

**honrar** *tr.* to honour. *2* to do honour to, be a credit to. *3 ref.* to deem it an honour [to oneself], be proud [of].

**honrilla** *f.* keen sense of honour: *por la negra* ~, out of concern for what people will say.

**honroso, -sa** *adj.* honourable [behaviour, etc.]. *2* creditable, honour-giving. *3* decent, decorous.

**hontanal, hontanar** *m.* place with water springs.

**hopa** *f.* long cassock.

**hopalanda** *f.* houppelande.

**hoplita** *m.* hoplite.

**hopo** *m.* bushy or woolly tail. *2* tuft [of hair].

**hora** *f.* hour; time of day; time, season [of doing something, for something to happen]: ~ *de comer*, mealtime, dinnertime; ~ *de verano*, daylight-saving time; ~ *oficial*, standard time; *horas de ocio*, leisure hours; *horas de trabajo*, working hours; *horas extraordinarias*, overtime; *horas punta*, rush hours; *noticias de última* ~, last-minute news: stop-press; *no ver la* ~ *de*, to be impatient for; *¿qué* ~ *es?*, what time is it?; *a estas horas*, coll. at this time, by now; *a última* ~, at the last moment, at the eleventh hour; *de* ~ *en* ~, unceasingly; *en buen* or *buena* ~, happily, luckily; all right; *en mal* or *mala* ~, in an evil hour, unluckily; *por horas*, by instants; by the hour. *2 pl.* ECCL. hours. *3* (cap.) MYTH. Hours. *4 adv.* now.

**horaciano, -na** *adj.* Horatian.

**Horacio** *m. pr. n.* Horace, Horatio.

**horadado, -da** *adj.* perforated, bored, pierced.

**horadar** *tr.* to perforate, bore, drill, pierce.

**horario, -ria** *adj.* horary, horal, hour. *2 m.* hour hand. *3* timepiece. *4* timetable, schedule of times: ~ *escolar*, school hours.

**horca** *f.* gallows, gibbet. *2* AGR. hayfork, pitchfork. *3* crotch, forked prop [for trees]. *4* sting [of

onions or garlic]. *5 Horcas Caudinas*, Caudine Forks.

**horcado, -da** *adj.* forked, forklike.

**horcadura** *f.* crotch, fork [of a tree].

**horcajadas (a)** *adv.* astride, astraddle.

**horcajadura** *f.* crotch [of human body].

**horcajo** *m.* yoke [for mules]. *2* fork [made by two streams].

**horcate** *m.* hames [of harness].

**horco** *m.* string [of onions or garlic].

**horcón** *m.* large pitchfork.

**horchata** *f.* orgeat.

**horchatería** *f.* orgeat shop.

**horda** *f.* orde.

**horizontal** *adj.-f.* horizontal.

**horizontalidad** *f.* horizontality.

**horizonte** *m.* horizon.

**horma** *f.* form, mould. *2* shoe tree, shoemaker's last: *hallar la* ~ *de su zapato*, to meet one's match. *3* hatter's block. *4* MAS. dry wall.

**hormaza** *f.* MAS. dry wall.

**hormiga** *f.* ENT. ant: ~ *blanca*, white ant; ~ *león*, lion ant; *ser una* ~, fig. to be very thrifty.

**hormigón** *m.* ENG. concrete: ~ *armado*, reinforced concrete.

**hormigonera** *f.* concrete mixer.

**hormiguear** *intr.* [of a part of the body] to creep. *2* [of people or animals] to swarm, to move in a swarm.

**hormigueo** *m.* crawling or creeping sensation. *2* swarming.

**hormiguero, -ra** *adj.* pertaining to the ants. *2 m.* anthill. *3* place swarming with people. *4* AGR. pile of dry leaves burned to serve as manure.

**hormiguillo** *m.* VET. disease of horses' hoofs. *2* line of people who pass materials or loads from hand to hand. *3* tickling or creeping sensation; itching.

**hormiguita** *f. dim.* small ant. *2* fig. very thrifty person.

**hormilla** *f.* buttonmould.

**hormón** *m.*, **hormona** *f.* PHYSIOL. hormone.

**hornablenda** *f.* MINER. hornblende.

**hornacina** *f.* ARCH. niche.

**hornachuela** *f.* cave or hut.

**hornada** *f.* batch, baking [quantity of bread, bricks, etc., baked at once]; melt [of a blast furnace].

**hornaguera** *f.* coal, hard coal, pit coal.

**hornaguero, -ra** *adj.* loose, too large. *2* spacious. *3* coal-bearing [ground].

**hornazo** *m.* Easter cake with hard-boiled eggs.

**hornear** *intr.* to bake bread, be a baker.

**hornera** *f.* baker's wife.

**hornero, -ra** *m.-f.* baker [one who makes bread].

**hornija** *f.* brushwood for an oven.

**hornilla** *f.* kitchen grate. *2* pigeonhole [for pigeons to nest in].

**hornillo** *m.* portable furnace or stove: ~ *de gas*, gas-ring.

**horno** *m.* oven; furnace; kiln: ~ *de cal*, limekiln; ~ *de cuba, alto* ~, blast furnace; *no está el* ~ *para bollos*, fig. this is not the moment for doing that.

**horópter(o** *m.* OPT. horopter.

**horóscopo** *m.* horoscope.

**horqueta** *f.* crotch, forked prop. *2* crotch [of a tree].

**horquilla** *f.* small forked piece. *2* hooked pole for propping or hanging things. *3* hairpin. *4* fork [of bicycle]. 5 cradle [of telephone]. 6 MACH. gab, jaw [of connecting rod].

**horrendo, -da** *adj.* horrendous, horrible, frightful.

**hórreo** *m.* granary, mow. 2 granary built on pillars.

**horrible** *adj.* horrible, fearful, hideous, heinous.

**hórrido, -da** *adj.* horrid, horrible.

**horrífico, -ca** *adj.* horrific, horrifying.

**horripilación** *f.* horror, fright. 2 MED. horripilation.

**horripilante** *adj.* hair-raising, horrifying.

**horripilar** *tr.* to horripilate. 2 to horrify. 3 *ref.* to feel horripilation. 4 to be horrified.

**horrisonante, horrísono, -na** *adj.* horrisonant.

**horro, -rra** *adj.* enfranchised. 2 free, untrammelled.

**horror** *m.* horror. 2 horrid thing.

**horrorizar** *tr.* to horrify. 2 *ref.* to be horrified.

**horroroso, -sa** *adj.* horrible, horrid. 2 hideous, frightful, ugly.

**horrura** *f.* filth, dirt, dross.

**hortaliza** *f.* vegetables, garden produce.

**hortelano, -na** *adj.* [pertaining to] garden or orchard. 2 *m.-f.* gardener, horticulturist. 3 *m.* ORN. ortolan.

**hortense** *adj.* garden, hortensial: *plantas hortenses*, vegetables.

**Hortensia** *f. pr. n.* Hortense.

**hortensia** *f.* BOT. hydrangea.

**hortera** *f.* wooden bowl. 2 *m.* in Madrid, shop clerk.

**hortícola** *adj.* horticultural.

**horticultor, -ra** *m.-f.* horticulturist.

**hosanna** *m.* ECCL. hosanna.

**hosco, -ca** *adj.* dark [colour of skin]. 2 sullen, surly; gloomy.

**hospedador, -ra** *m.-f.* host, one who gives lodging.

**hospedaje, hospedamiento** *m.* lodging, board. 2 cost of lodging or board.

**hospedar** *tr.* to lodge; to lodge an board. 2 *ref.* to lodge [in]; to stop, put up [at].

**hospedería** *f.* hostelry, inn. 2 hospice, place for guests [in a monastery].

**hospedero, -ra** *m.-f.* host, innkeeper.

**hospiciano, -na** *m.-f.* inmate of a poor-house.

**hospicio** *m.* hospice, poor-house; orphanage.

**hospital** *m.* hospital.

**hospitalariamente** *adv.* hospitably.

**hospitalario, -ria** *adj.* hospitable. 2 ECCL. charitable [order]. 3 [pertaining to] hospital.

**hospitalicio, -cia** *adj.* [pertaining to] hospitality.

**hospitalidad** *f.* hospitality. 2 hospitableness.

**hospitalizar** *tr.* to hospitalize.

**hosquedad** *f.* sullenness, surliness.

**hostal** *m.* HOSTERÍA.

**hostelero, -ra** *m.-f.* host, inkeeper.

**hostería** *f.* hostelry, inn, tavern.

**hostia** *f.* sacrificial victim or offering. 2 ECCL. Host; wafer. 2 sugar wafer.

**hostiario** *m.* ECCL. wafer box; wafer mould.

**hostigamiento** *m.* harassing, worrying, plaguing. 2 lashing, whipping, flogging.

**hostigar** *tr.* to harass, worry, plague. 2 to lash, whip, flog.

**hostil** *adj.* hostile.

**hostilidad** *f.* hostility. 2 *pl.* hostilities, warfare: *romper las hostilidades*, to start hostilities.

**hostilizar** *tr.* to harry, worry [the enemy]; to commit hostilities against.

**hotel** *m.* hotel. 2 villa, detached house.

**hotelería** *f.* keeping of hotels.

**hotelero, -ra** *adj.* [pertaining to] hotel. 2 *m.-f.* hotelkeeper.

**hotentote** *adj.-n.* Hottentot.

**hoy** *adv.* today; now; nowadays, at the present time: *de ~ en adelante*, from now on, henceforth; *~ día, ~ en día*, nowadays; *~ por ~*, at the present time.

**hoya** *f.* hole, hollow, pit [in the ground]. 2 grave. 3 valley, dale.

**hoyada** *f.* dip, hollow, depression [in the ground].

**hoyo** *m.* hole, pit, hollow. 2 dent. 3 pockmark. 4 grave.

**hoyuela** *f.* the depression at the front of the neck.

**hoyuelo** *m.* small hole or pit. 2 dimple. 3 a boys' game. 4 HOYUELA.

**hoz** *f.* AGR. sickle: *de ~ y de coz*, headlong. 2 gorge, ravine.

**hozadero** *m.* hogs' rooting place.

**hozadura** *f.* hole made by a rooting hog.

**hozar** *tr.* [of hogs] to root.

**Huberto** *m. pr. n.* Hobart, Hubert.

**hube, hubiera, hubiese,** etc. *irr.* V. HABER.

**hucha** *f.* large chest or coffer. 2 money-box, money bank. 3 savings, nest egg.

**huchear** *tr.-intr.* to hoot at, to hoot.

**hueco, -ca** *adj.* hollow [not solid]. 2 empty: *cabeza hueca*, empty brains. 3 vain, conceited, proud. 4 hollow, deep [voice]. 5 affected, pompous [style]. 6 puffed, inflated. 7 soft, spongy [soil, wool, etc.]. 8 *m.* hollow, cavity: *~ del ascensor*, elevator or lift shaft. 9 gap, void, interval. 10 socket [of bone]. 11 ARCH. opening [for a door, etc.]. 12 vacancy.

**huecograbado** *m.* photogravure for a rotary press.

**huélfago** *m.* VET. heaves.

**huelga** *f.* strike [of workmen]: *~ de brazos caídos*, sit-down strike; *~ de hambre*, hunger strike; *declararse en ~*, to go on strike. 2 leisure, recreation. 3 HUELGO 3.

**huelgo** *m.* breath, respiration. 2 room, space. 3 MACH. play, allowance [between two pieces].

**huelgo, huelga,** etc. *irr.* V. HOLGAR.

**huelguista** *m.-f.* striker [workman].

**huelguístico, -ca** *adj.* [pertaining to a] workers' strike.

**huella** *f.* tread, treading. 2 print, impression; trace, track, rut, footprint, footstep: *~ dactilar*, fingerprint; *seguir las huellas de*, to follow in the footsteps of. 3 ARCH. tread [of a stair].

**huemul** *m.* ZOOL. the Andes deer.

**huequecito** *m. dim.* small hollow, space or interval.

**huérfano, -na** *adj.-n.* orphan. 2 *adj.* orphaned.

**huero, -ra** *adj.* addle [egg]. 2 fig. addle, empty: *salir ~*, to flop, fall through.

**huerta** *f.* large vegetable garden or orchard. 2 irrigated region.

**huertano, -na** *m.-f.* inhabitant of some irrigated regions.

**huerto** *m.* orchard, fruit garden. 2 kitchen garden, vegetable garden.

**huesa** *f.* grave, tomb.

**huesarrón** *m. augm.* large bone.

**hueso** *m.* bone [piece of the skeleton]: *~ sacro*, sacrum; *la sin ~*, fig. the tongue; *calarse hasta los huesos*, to get soaked to the skin; *estar en los huesos*, to be nothing but skin and bones; *no dejar ~ sano a uno*, to pick somebody to pieces, to backbite; *tener los huesos molidos*, to be tired out. 2 bone [material]. 3 BOT. stone, pit [of fruit]. 4 fig. hard or unwelcome job: *~ duro* *de roer*, hard nut to crack. *5 pl.* bones, mortal remains.

**huesoso, -sa** *adj.* bony, osseous.

**huésped, -da** *m.-f.* guest; lodger, boarder: *casa de huéspedes*, boarding house. *2* host, hostess: *echar la cuenta sin la huéspeda*, to reckon without one's host. *3* BOT., ZOOL. host.

**hueste** or *pl.* **huestes** *f.* army, host. *2* followers.

**huesudo, -da** *adj.* bony, big-boned.

**hueva** *f.* roe [fish eggs].

**huevera** *f.* egg dealer [woman]. *2* oviduct [of birds]. *3* eggcup. *4* eggdish.

**huevería** *f.* egg shop.

**huevero, -ra** *m.-f.* egg dealer. *2 m.* eggcup.

**huevo** *m.* egg: ~ *de zurcir*, darning egg; ~ *duro*, hard-boiled egg; ~ *pasado por agua*, (Am.) ~ *tibio*, soft-boiled egg; ~ *escalfado*, poached egg; ~ *estrellado*, or *frito*, fried egg; *huevos revueltos*, (Am.) *huevos pericos*, scrambled eggs; *parecerse como un ~ a una castaña*, not to be alike at all. *2* ZOOL. ~ *de pulpo*, sea hare.

**Hugo** *m. pr. n.* Hugh.

**hugonote** *adj.-n.* Huguenot.

**huida** *f.* flight, escape. *2* shying [of a horse].

**huidero** *m.* cover, shelter [of animals].

**huidizo, -za** *adj.* fugitive, evasive.

**huir** *intr.* to flee, fly, escape, run away, slip away: ~ *de*, to run away from, to flee, fly, avoid, shun, evade. *2* [of the time, days, etc.] to fly, pass rapidly. *3 tr.* to flee, fly, avoid, shun. *3* ~ *la cara*, to avoid [someone]. ¶ CONJUG. INDIC. Pres.: *huyo, huyes, huye;* *huimos, huís, huyen.* | Pret.: hui, huiste, *huyó;* huimos, huisteis, *huyeron.* | SUBJ. Pres.: *huya, huyas*, etc. | Imperf.: *huyera, huyeras*, etc., or *huyese, huyeses*, etc. | Fut.: *huyere, huyeres*, etc. | IMPER.: *huye, huya; huyamos,* huid, *huyan.* | GER.: *huyendo.*

**hule** *m.* oilcloth, oilskin. *2* rubber, India rubber. *3* BOT. (Am.) rubber tree. *4* BULLF. blood, goring.

**hulla** *f.* coal, mineral [gen. bituminous] coal. *2* fig. ~ *blanca*, white coal, water power.

**hullero, -ra** *adj.* [containing or pertaining to] coal.

**humanamente** *adv.* humanely. *2* humanly.

**humanal** *adj.* human.

**humanar** *tr.-ref.* HUMANIZAR. *2 ref.* to become man [said of Jesus Christ].

**humanidad** *f.* humanity. *2* mankind. *3* humaneness. *4* human weakness. *5* coll. corpulence, fleshiness. *6 pl.* humanities [classic literature].

**humanista** *m.-f.* humanist, classical scholar.

**humanitario, -ria** *adj.* humanitarian. *2* humane, charitable, benevolent.

**humanitarismo** *m.* humanitarianism, humaneness.

**humanizar** *tr.* to humanize, soften [make humane]. *2 ref.* to humanize, soften [become humane].

**humano, -na** *adj.* human. *2* humane, compassionate. *3 m.* human, human being.

**humareda** *f.* cloud of smoke, a great deal of smoke.

**humazo** *m.* dense smoke. *2* smoke made to drive rats from ship or animals out of their lair.

**Humberto** *m. pr. n.* Humbert.

**humeante** *adj.* smoky, smoking [emiting smoke]. *2* steaming.

**humear** *intr.* to smoke [emit smoke]. *2* to steam [emit steam]; to emit fumes or vapours. *3* to get proud, take on airs. *4 tr.* (Am.) to fumigate.

**humectación** *f.* humidification.

**humectar** *tr.* to humidify, moisten.

**humedad** *f.* humidity, moisture, dampness.

**humedal** *m.* humid ground, marsh.

**humedecer** *tr.* to humidify, moisten, dampen, wet. *2 ref.* to become humid, moist. ¶ CONJUG. like *agradecer.*

**humedezco, humedezca,** etc. *irr.* V. HUMEDECER.

**húmedo, -da** *adj.* humid, moist, damp, wet.

**humeral** *adj.* ANAT. humeral. *2 m.* ECCL. humeral veil.

**húmero** *m.* ANAT. humerus.

**humildad** *f.* humility. *2* humbleness, lowliness.

**humilde** *adj.* humble; lowly. *2* meek, submissive.

**humillación** *f.* humiliation; humbling.

**humilladero** *m.* roadside crucifix or shrine.

**humillante** *adj.* humiliating.

**humillar** *tr.* to humiliate. *2* to humble, abase, crush, lower. *3* to bow [one's head], to bend [one's body or knees]. *4 ref.* to humble oneself.

**humillos** *m. pl.* vanity, pride.

**humo** *m.* smoke: *la del* ~, good riddance; *a* ~ *de pajas*, without a reason. *2* steam, vapour, fume. *3 pl.* conceit, pride, vanity: *bajarle a uno los humos*, to humble someone's pride.

**humor** *m.* PHYSIOL. humour. *2* humour, temper, mood: *buen* ~, good humour; *mal* ~, bad humour; *no estar de* ~ *para*, not to be in the mood to or for. *3* merry disposition. *4* humour, wit.

**humorada** *f.* whim. *2* whimsical or witty act or saying.

**humoral** *adj.* PHYSIOL. humoural.

**humorismo** *m.* humour [in speaking or writing]; humorous literature. *2* humorousness.

**humorista** *m.-f.* humorist [writer].

**humorístico, -ca** *adj.* humorous, jocular, funny.

**humosidad** *f.* smokiness.

**humoso, -sa** *adj.* smoky.

**hundimiento** *m.* sinking. *2* cave-in. *3* NAUT. foundering. *4* collapse, downfall, ruin.

**hundir** *tr.* to sink, submerge, plunge. *2* NAUT. to founder. *3* to cave in, stave in. *4* to drive in. *5* to confound, confute. *6* to crush, destroy, ruin. *7 ref.* to sink, go down, be submerged; to subside, cave in. *8* to collapse, be ruined.

**húngaro, -ra** *adj.-n.* Hungarian.

**Hungría** *f. pr. n.* GEOG. Hungary.

**huno, -na** *m.-f.* Hun.

**hupe** *f.* punk, touchwood.

**huracán** *m.* hurricane.

**huracanado, -da** *adj.* hurricane-like [wind].

**hurañía** *f.* sullenness, unsociableness.

**huraño, -ña** *adj.* sullen, unsociable.

**hurgar** *tr.* to poke, stir: *hurgarse la nariz*, to pick one's nose. *2* to stir up, incite.

**hurgón** *m.* poke [for poking the fire].

**hurgonazo** *m.* thrust with a poker. *2* coll. ESTOCADA.

**hurgonear** *tr.* to poke [the fire]. *2* coll. to make a thrust at.

**hurí** *f.* houri.

**hurón, -na** *adj.* sullen, unsociable. *2 m.* ZOOL. ferret. *3* fig. ferreter, prier. *4* fig. unsociable person. *5 f.* ZOOL. female ferret.

**huronear** *intr.* to ferret.

**huronera** *f.* ferret hole. *2* lair, hiding place.

**huronero** *m.* ferret keeper.

**¡hurra!** *interj.* hurrah!

**hurtadillas (a)** *adv.* stealthily, on the sly.

**hurtar** *tr.* to steal, thieve, pilfer. *2* to cheat [in weight or measure]. *3* to plagiarize. *4* to move away: ~ *el cuerpo,* to dodge, shy away. *5 ref.* to withdraw, hide.

**hurto** *m.* stealing, theft, pilferage. *2* stolen thing. *3 adv. a hurto,* by stealth, on the sly.

**husada** *f.* spindleful [of yarn].

**húsar** *m.* MIL. hussar.

**husero** *m.* brow antler [of a yearling fallow deer].

**husillo** *m. dim.* small spindle. *2* MACH. screw pin.

**husma** *f.* HUSMEO: *andar a la* ~, to nose around.

**husmeador, -ra** *adj.* scenting, nosing around. *2 m.- f.* scenter. *3* prier, inquisitive person.

**husmear** *tr.* to scent, wind, smell out. *2* to pry out, nose out. *3 intr.* [of meat] to become gamy or high, to smell bad.

**husmeo** *m.* scenting, smelling. *2* nosing around.

**husmo** *m.* high odour, gaminess. *2 andar al* ~, to go scenting or prying.

**huso** *m.* spindle [for hand spinning]. *2* TEXT. spindle. *3* HER. narrow lozenge. *4* MIN. drum of a windlass. *5* GEOM. ~ *esférico,* spherical lune. *6* GEOG. ~ *horario,* time zone.

**¡huy!** *interj.* of pain, grief, surprise, etc.

**huyo, huyó, huya, huyera,** etc. *irr.* V. HUIR.

**I**

**I, i** *f.* I, i, tenth letter of the Spanish alphabet.
**iba,** etc., *imperf.* of IR.
**Iberia** *f. pr. n.* GEOG. Iberia.
**ibérico, -ca; iberio, -ria** *adj.* Iberian.
**ibero, -ra** *adj.-n.* Iberian.
**iberoamericano, -na** *adj.-n.* Latin-American.
**íbice** *m.* ZOOL. ibex, wild goat.
**ibis,** *pl.* **ibis** *f.* ORN. ibis.
**Ibiza** *f. pr. n.* GEOG. Iviza [Balearic Island].
**icáreo, -a; icario, -ria** *adj.* Icarian.
**iceberg** *m.* iceberg.
**icneumón** *m.* ZOOL., ENT. ichneumon.
**icnografía** *f.* ARCH. ichnography.
**icono** *m.* icon.
**iconoclasta** *adj.* iconoclastic. *2 m.-f.* iconoclast.
**iconografía** *f.* iconography.
**iconología** *f.* iconology.
**iconostasio** *m.* ECCL. iconostasis.
**icor** *m.* MED. ichor.
**icosaedro** *m.* GEOM. icosahedron.
**ictericia** *f.* MED. jaundice.
**ictérico, -ca** *adj.* icteric(al. *2* jaundiced.
**ictíneo** *m.* submarine vessel.
**ictiófago, -ga** *adj.* ichthyophagous.
**ictiología** *f.* ichthyology.
**ictiosauro** *m.* PALEONT. ichthyosaurus.
**ida** *f.* going [to a place], departure: *viaje de ~ y vuelta,* round trip; *idas y venidas,* comings and goings. *2* FENC. attack. *3* HUNT. track, trail [of game].
**idea** *f.* idea; notion. *2* intent, purpose: *llevar ~ de,* to intend to; *mudar de ~,* to change one's mind. *3* opinion, estimate. *4* ingenuity, inventiveness.
**ideación** *f.* ideation.
**ideal** *adj.-m.* ideal. *2 adj.* perfectly suitable or proper.
**idealismo** *m.* idealism.
**idealista** *adj.* idealist, idealistic. *2 m.-f.* idealist.
**idealizar** *tr.* to idealize.
**idear** *tr.* to form an idea of. *2* to devise, contrive, plan, invent, *think up.
**ídem** *pron.* idem, ditto.
**idéntico, -ca** *adj.* identic(al.
**identidad** *f.* identity. *2* identicalness.
**identificación** *f.* identification.
**identificar** *tr.* to identify. *2 ref.* to be identified. *3 identificarse con,* to identify oneself with.
**ideografía** *f.* ideography.

**ideograma** *m.* ideogram.
**ideología** *f.* ideology.
**ideólogo** *m.* ideologist.
**idílico, -ca** *adj.* idyllic.
**idilio** *m.* idyll. *2* amorous talk. *3* love relations.
**idioma** *m.* idiom, language, tongue.
**idiomático, -ca** *adj.* idiomatic [pertaining to an idiom or language].
**idiosincrasia** *f.* idiosyncrasy.
**idiota** *adj.* idiotic. *2 m.-f.* idiot.
**idiotez** *f.* idiocy.
**idiotismo** *m.* ignorance. *2* idiom [peculiar expression].
**idólatra** *adj.* idolatrous. *2 m.* idolater. *3 f.* idolatress.
**idolatrar** *tr.-intr.* to idolize.
**idolatría** *f.* idolatry.
**idolátrico, -ca** *adj.* idolatrous.
**ídolo** *m.* idol.
**idoneidad** *f.* fitness, suitability; competence.
**idóneo, -a** *adj.* fit, suitable; able, competent.
**idus** *m.* ides.
**iglesia** *f.* church [in every sense]: *~ anglicana,* Anglican Church, Church of England; *~ católica,* Roman Catholic Church.
**Ignacio** *m. pr. n.* Ignatius.
**ignaro, -ra** *adj.* ignorant.
**ígneo, -a** *adj.* igneous.
**ignición** *f.* ignition [burning state].
**ignífugo, -ga** *adj.* ignifuge, protecting from fire.
**ignipotente** *adj.* poet. ignipotent.
**ignívomo, -ma** *adj.* poet. ignivomous.
**ignominia** *f.* ignominy.
**ignominioso, -sa** *adj.* ignominious.
**ignorado, -da** *adj.* unknown. *2* fameless, obscure.
**ignorancia** *f.* ignorance.
**ignorante** *adj.* ignorant. *2 m.-f.* ignoramus.
**ignorantón, -na** *adj.* ignorant. *2 m.-f.* ignoramus.
**ignorar** *tr.* not to know, be ignorant of.
**ignoto, -ta** *adj.* unknown; undiscovered.
**igual** *adj.* equal [the same in value, size, etc.]: *~ a,* equal to, the same as. *2* the same, indifferent: *es ~, me es ~,* it is all the same [to me]. *3* level, even, uniform. *4* equal, commensurate. *5* equable. *6* constant, unchanging. *7 m.* MATH. equality sign (=). *8* equal. *sin ~,* matchless, unrivalled. *9 adv. al ~,* equally; *~ que,* as well as; *por ~, por un ~,* equally, evenly.

**iguala** *f.* equalizing, equalization. *2* monthly or annual fee.
**igualación** *f.* equalization. *2* leveling, making even.
**igualado, -da** *adj.* equal, level, even.
**igualar** *tr.* to equalize; to equate. *2* to even, level, smooth, face. *3* to deem equal, match. *4 intr.-ref.* ~ *a, igualarse con,* to equal [be equal to]; to compare with. *5 ref.* to become equal. *6* SPORT. to tie [in scoring].
**igualdad** *f.* equality, sameness. *2* MATH. equality. *3* evenness, smoothness, uniformity. *4* ~ *de ánimo,* equability, equanimity.
**igualitario, -ria** *adj.* equalizing. *2* equalitarian.
**igualmente** *adv.* equally. *2* evenly, uniformly. *3* likewise, also. *4* coll. the same to you.
**iguana** *f.* ZOOL. iguana.
**iguanodonte** *m.* PALEONT. iguanodont.
**ijada** *f.* flank [of an animal]. *2* side [of a pers.]; pain in the side, stitch.
**ijar** *m.* IJADA I.
**ilación** *f.* illation. *2* connectedness.
**ilativo, -va** *adj.* illative.
**Ildefonso** *m. pr. n.* Alphonso.
**ilegal** *adj.* illegal, unlawful.
**ilegalidad** *s.* illegality, unlawfulness.
**ilegible** *adj.* illegible.
**ilegitimar** *tr.* to illegitimate.
**ilegitimidad** *f.* illegitimacy.
**ilegítimo, -ma** *adj.* illegitimate. *2* false, spurious.
**íleo** *m.* MED. ileus.
**ileon** *m.* ANAT. ileum. *2* ANAT. ilium.
**ileso, -sa** *adj.* unharmed, sound, unhurt, unscathed.
**iletrado, -da** *adj.* illiterate, uneducated.
**ilíaco, -ca** *adj.* ANAT. iliac. *2* Iliac, Trojan.
**Ilíada** *f.* Iliad.
**iliberal** *adj.* illiberal, stingy.
**ilícito, -ta** *adj.* illicit, unlawful.
**ilíquido, -da** *adj.* COM. unliquidated.
**iliterato** *adj.* illiterate, unlearned.
**ilógico, -ca** *adj.* illogical.
**ilota** *m.* helot.
**iluminación** *f.* illumination, lighting. *2* illumination, enlightenment. *3* F. ARTS illumination.
**iluminado, -da** *adj.* illuminated, lighted. *2* illuminated [mentally or spiritually]. *3* illuminated [manuscript, book, etc.]. *4 m.-f.* one of the illuminati. *5 pl.* illuminati.
**iluminador, -ra** *adj.* illuminating. *2 m.-f.* illuminator.
**iluminar** *tr.* to illuminate, illumine, light, light up. *2* to illuminate, illumine, enlighten. *3* F. ARTS to illuminate. *4 ref.* to illuminate; to light up, brighten.
**iluminarias** *f. pl.* LUMINARIAS.
**iluminismo** *m.* illuminism.
**ilusión** *f.* illusion. *2* false or groundless hope: *hacerse ilusiones,* to deceive oneself with false hopes. *3* hopeful anticipation.
**ilusionarse** *ref.* to indulge in groundless hopes or in hopeful anticipations.
**ilusionista** *m.-f.* illusionist, prestidigitator.
**ilusionismo** *m.* illusionism, prestidigitation.
**ilusivo, -va** *adj.* illusive, deceiving.
**iluso, -sa** *adj.* deluded, deceived, beguiled. *2* dreamer, visionary.
**ilusorio, -ria** *adj.* illusive, illusory. *2* vain, ineffectual.
**ilustración** *f.* illustration, illustrating. *2* enlightenment. *3* learning, erudition. *4* making illus-trious. *5* illustration picture. *6* illustrated or pictorial magazine.
**ilustrado, -da** *adj.* illustrated. *2* enlightened. *3* learned, informed, cultivated.
**ilustrar** *tr.* to illustrate. *2* to enlighten. *3* to educate, civilize. *4* THEOL. to illuminate. *5* to make illustrious. *6 ref.* to learn, become educated. *7* to distinguish oneself.
**ilustrativo, -va** *adj.* illustrative.
**ilustre** *adj.* illustrious, distinguished.
**ilustrísimo, -ma** *adj.* most illustrious: *su ilustrísima,* form of address when talking to a bishop.
**imagen** *f.* image: ~ *de bulto,* image in sculpture; ~ *real,* ~ *virtual,* PHYS. real image, virtual image; *a su* ~, in his own image.
**imaginación** *f.* imagination, imagining. *2* imagination, fancy [mental faculty]. *3* fancy, unfounded belief, arbitrary supposition.
**imaginar** *tr.* to imagine, conceive. *2 tr.-ref.* to imagine [represent to oneself], fancy, suppose, conjecture: *¡imagínese!,* just imagine!
**imaginaria** *f.* MIL. reserve guard.
**imaginario, -ria** *adj.* imaginary, fancied. *2* MATH. imaginary. *3* of account [money].
**imaginativa** *f.* imagination, fancy [faculty].
**imaginativo, -va** *adj.* imaginative.
**imaginería** *f.* religious imagery or statuary. *2* fancy embroidery in colours.
**imaginero** *m.* painter or sculptor of religious images.
**imago** *m.* ENT. imago.
**imán** *m.* magnet. *2* loadstone, lodestone. *3* fig. attraction, charm. *4* imam [Mohammedan priest].
**imanación** *f.* magnetization [of a needle, etc.].
**imanar** *tr.* to magnetize [a needle, etc.]. *2 ref.* to become magnetized.
**imantación** *f.* IMANACIÓN.
**imantar** *tr.-ref.* IMANAR.
**imbatido, -da** *adj.* SPORT. unbeaten.
**imbécil** *adj.-n.* imbecile.
**imbecilidad** *f.* imbecility; stupidity.
**imberbe** *m.* beardless.
**imbornal** *m.* scupper [of roof]. *2* NAUT. scupper.
**imborrable** *adj.* indelible, ineffaceable.
**imbricación** *f.* imbrication.
**imbricado, -da** *adj.* imbricate, imbricated.
**imbuir** *tr.* to imbue, infuse. ¶ CONJUG. like *huir.*
**imbuyo, imbuyó, imbuya,** etc. *irr.* V. IMBUIR.
**imitable** *adj.* imitable.
**imitación** *f.* imitation: *a* ~ *de,* in imitation of; *de* ~, imitation [as adj.].
**imitado, -da** *adj.* imitated; imitation, mock, sham
**imitador, -ra** *adj.* imitating. *2 m.-f.* imitator.
**imitar** *tr.* to imitate. *2* to ape, mimic. *3* to counterfeit.
**imitativo, -va** *adj.* imitative.
**impaciencia** *f.* impatience. *2* anxiousness, eagerness.
**impacientar** *tr.* to make [one] lose patience; to vex, irritate. *2 ref.* to lose patience, become impatient, -chafe.
**impaciente** *adj.* impatient; anxious, eager.
**impacto** *m.* impact.
**impalpable** *adj.* impalpable.
**impar** *adj.* unmatched. *2* MATH. odd, uneven [number].
**imparcial** *adj.* impartial, fair, unbiassed.
**imparcialidad** *f.* impartiality.
**imparisílabo, -ba** *adj.* GRAM. imparisyllabic.
**impartir** *tr.* to impart.
**impasable** *adj.* impassable.

**impasible** *adj.* impassible. 2 impassive, unmoved.
**impavidez** *f.* fearlessness, intrepidity.
**impávido, -da** *adj.* dauntless, fearless, undaunted.
**impecabilidad** *f.* impeccability. 2 faultlessness.
**impecable** *adj.* impeccable. 2 faultless.
**impedancia** *f.* ELECT. impedance.
**impedido, -da** *adj.* disabled, crippled, paralytic. 2 *m.-f.* cripple; paralytic person.
**impediente** *adj.* impeding.
**impedimenta** *f.* MIL. impedimenta.
**impedimento** *m.* impediment, hindrance, obstacle.
**impedir** *tr.* to impede, hinder, obstruct, prevent; ~ *el paso*, to block the way. ¶ CONJUG. like *servir.*
**impelente** *adj.* impellent. 2 force [pump].
**impeler** *tr.* to impel, drive forward, propel. 2 to impel, drive [to action, to do something].
**impenetrabilidad** *f.* impenetrability.
**impenetrable** *adj.* impenetrable.
**impenitente** *adj.* impenitent, obdurate.
**impensado, -da** *adj.* unexpected, unforeseen.
**imperante** *adj.* ruling, commanding. 2 prevailing.
**imperar** *intr.* to rule, command, hold sway. 2 to prevail, be prevailing, reign.
**imperativo, -va** *adj.* imperative, commanding. 2 *adj.-n.* GRAM. imperative. 3 *m.* PHIL. ~ *categórico,* categorical imperative.
**imperceptible** *adj.* imperceptible.
**imperdible** *adj.* unlosable. 2 *m.* safety pin.
**imperdonable** *adj.* unpardonable, unforgivable.
**imperecedero, -ra** *adj.* imperishable, undying.
**imperfección** *f.* imperfection; fault, blemish.
**imperfecto, -ta** *adj.* imperfect, defective, faulty. 2 *adj.-n.* GRAM. imperfect.
**imperial** *adj.* imperial. 2 *f.* imperial, upper-deck [of a coach, diligence, etc.].
**imperialismo** *m.* imperialism.
**impericia** *f.* inexpertness, unskilfulness.
**imperio** *m.* empire. 2 command, sway. 3 haughtiness, imperiousness.
**imperiosidad** *f.* imperiousness.
**imperioso, -sa** *adj.* imperious, imperative.
**imperito, -ta** *adj.* inexpert, unskilful.
**impermeabilidad** *f.* impermeability.
**impermeabilizar** *tr.* to waterproof; to make impermeable.
**impermeable** *adj.* impermeable; impervious. 2 waterproof. 3 *m.* raincoat, mackintosh, waterproof.
**impersonal** *adj.* impersonal.
**impertérrito, -ta** *adj.* dauntless, intrepid; unmoved.
**impertinencia** *f.* impertinence. 2 annoyance, importunity.
**impertinente** *adj.* impertinent. 2 annoying, peevish. 3 *m.-f.* impertinent [person]. 4 *m. pl.* lorgnette.
**imperturbable** *adj.* imperturbable, unperturbed.
**impétigo** *m.* MED. impetigo.
**impetración** *f.* impetration; beseeching.
**impetrante** *adj.* impetrating; beseeching.
**impetrar** *tr.* to impetrate. 2 to beseech.
**ímpetu** *m.* impetus, impulse, momentum. 2 impetuousness, violence.
**impetuosidad** *f.* impetuosity, impetuousness.
**impetuoso, -sa** *adj.* impetuous.
**impido, impida,** etc. *irr.* V. IMPEDIR.
**impiedad** *f.* impiety, ungodliness.
**impio, -pía** *adj.* impious, irreligious, godless. 2 cruel, pitiless. 3 *m.-f.* impious person.
**implacabilidad** *f.* implacability.
**implacable** *adj.* implacable, inexorable.
**implantación** *f.* implantation.

**implantar** *tr.* to implant, introduce [doctrines, customs, etc.]. 2 SURG. to implant.
**implicación** *f.* contradiction. 2 implication, involving.
**implicar** *tr.* to implicate, involve, entangle. 2 to imply. 3 *intr.* to contradict, be an obstacle.
**implícito, -ta** *adj.* implicit.
**imploración** *f.* imploration, supplication.
**implorar** *tr.* to implore.
**implume** *adj.* featherless, unfeathered; unfledged.
**impluvio** *m.* impluvium.
**impolítica** *f.* impoliteness, incivility, discourtesy.
**impolítico, -ca** *adj.* impolite. 2 impolitic.
**impoluto, -ta** *adj.* unpollute, untarnished.
**imponderable** *adj.* imponderable. 2 great, extraordinary, beyond all exaggeration or praise.
**impondré, impondría, impongo, imponga,** etc. *irr.* V. IMPONER.
**imponente** *adj.* imposing. 2 *m.-f.* depositor [one who deposits money in a bank].
**imponer** *tr.* to impose [taxes, penalties, silence, etc.]. 2 ECCL. to impose [the hands]. 3 to impute falsely. 4 to acquaint, instruct. 5 to command, inspire [respect, awe]. 6 to deposit [money in a bank]. 7 PRINT. to impose. 8 *ref.* to assert oneself. 9 to be imperative or necessary. *10 imponerse a,* to impose one's authority on. *11 imponerse de,* to learn, find out. ¶ CONJUG. like *poner.*
**imponible** *adj.* taxable, dutiable.
**impopular** *adj.* unpopular.
**impopularidad** *f.* unpopularity.
**importación** *f.* COM. importation, imports.
**importador, -ra** *adj.* COM. importing. 2 *m.-f.* importer.
**importancia** *f.* importance, consequence.
**importante** *adj.* important, material, momentous.
**importar** *intr.* to import, be important, be of consequence; to matter, concern: *no me importa,* I don't care; *¿qué importa?,* what does it matter? 2 *tr.* to amount to, to be worth. 3 to carry, involve, imply. 4 COM. to import.
**importe** *m.* COM. amount, value, cost.
**importunación** *f.* importuning, pestering.
**importunar** *tr.* to importune, pester.
**importunidad** *f.* importunity, importunateness.
**importuno, -na** *adj.* importunate. 2 inopportune.
**imposibilidad** *f.* impossibility.
**imposibilitado, -da** *adj.* unable. 2 disabled, crippled, paralytic.
**imposibilitar** *tr.* to make unable. 2 to make impossible; to prevent. 3 to disable, cripple.
**imposible** *adj.* impossible. 2 *m.* impossible thing, impossibility: *hacer los imposibles,* to do one's utmost.
**imposición** *f.* imposition. 2 false imputation. 3 sum which a person, deposits in a bank.
**imposta** *f.* ARCH. impost.
**impostor, -ra** *m.* impostor. 2 *f.* impostress. 3 *m.-f.* slanderer.
**impostura** *f.* imposture. 2 false imputation, slander.
**impotable** *adj.* undrinkable.
**impotencia** *f.* impotence, inability. 2 MED. impotence.
**impotente** *adj.* impotent, powerless, unable. 2 MED. impotent.
**impracticable** *adj.* impracticable, infeasible. 2 impracticable, impassable [road, etc.].
**imprecación** *f.* imprecation.
**imprecar** *tr.* to imprecate.
**imprecisión** *f.* imprecision, vagueness.
**impreciso** *adj.* imprecise, vague, indefinite.

**impregnar** *tr.* to impregnate, interpenetrate. *2 ref.* to become impregnate or interpenetrated.
**impremeditación** *f.* unpremeditation.
**impremeditado, -da** *adj.* unpremeditated.
**imprenta** *f.* printing [art of printing books, etc.]. *2* printing office or house, press. *3* press, printed matter: *libertad de* ~, freedom of the press.
**imprescindible** *adj.* essential, indispensable.
**imprescriptible** *adj.* imprescriptible.
**impresentable** *adj.* unpresentable.
**impresión** *f.* impression, impressing, stamping [of a mark]. *2* impression, impress, imprint, print [mark impressed]. *3* PRINT. print, printing, press-work. *4* PHOT. print. *5* impression [physical or moral effect]. *6* impression [vague notion, belief, etc.].
**impresionable** *adj.* emotional, impressionable.
**impresionante** *adj.* impressive.
**impresionar** *tr.* to impress [affect, influence]. *2* to touch, move deeply. *3* PHOT. to produce images on [a plate]. *4* to record sounds on [a gramophone disk, etc.]. *5* CINEMA. to film, to shoot [a film]. *6 ref.* to be impressed or moved.
**impresionismo** *m.* F. ARTS impressionism.
**impresionista** *adj.* impressionistic. *2 m.-f.* impressionist.
**impreso, -sa** *adj.* impressed, printed, stamped. *2 m.* print, printed paper or book. *3 pl.* printed matter, publications.
**impresor, -ra** *m.-f.* PRINT. printer [workman or owner]. *2 f.* printer's wife.
**imprevisible** *adj.* unforeseeable.
**imprevisión** *f.* lack of foresight, improvidence.
**imprevisor, -ra** *adj.* unforeseeing, improvident.
**imprevisto, -ta** *adj.* unforeseen, unexpected. *2 m. pl.* incidental or unforeseen expenses.
**imprimación** *f.* priming [of a surface].
**imprimar** *tr.* to prime [a surface].
**imprimir** *tr.* to impress, imprint, stamp. *2* PRINT. to print [a book, etc.]. *3* to impart, communicate [a motion, etc.].
**improbabilidad** *f.* improbability, unlikelihood.
**improbable** *adj.* improbable, unlikely.
**improbar** *tr.* to disapprove, reprobate.
**improbidad** *f.* improbity, dishonesty.
**improbo, -ba** *adj.* dishonest. *2* arduous, laborious.
**improcedencia** *f.* inappropriateness, unsuitability, inexpedience. *2* non-conformableness to law.
**improcedente** *adj.* inappropriate, unsuitable, inexpedient. *2* not conformable to law.
**improductivo, -va** *adj.* unproductive, unprofitable. *2* unemployed [money].
**impronta** *f.* cast, impression.
**impronunciable** *adj.* unpronounceable.
**improperio** *m.* insult, affront, taunt.
**impropiedad** *f.* impropriety [in the use of language].
**impropio, -pia** *adj.* improper, unsuited. *2* unfitting, unbecoming. *3* MATH. improper [fraction].
**improrrogable** *adj.* unextendible [term, time].
**impróvido, -da** *adj.* improvident, thoughtless.
**improvisación** *f.* improvisation, extemporization, impromptu.
**improvisado, -da** *adj.* improvised, extempore, off-hand. *2* extemporaneous.
**improvisador, -ra** *m.-f.* improviser, extemporizer.
**improvisar** *tr.* to improvise, to extemporize.
**improviso, -sa; improvisto, -ta** *adj.* unforeseen, unexpected: *al* ~, *de* ~, *a la improvista,* suddenly.
**imprudencia** *f.* imprudence, indiscretion.
**imprudente** *adj.* imprudent, indiscret, unwise.
**impúber; impúbero, -ra** *adj.* impuberate, immature.

**impublicable** *adj.* unpublishable.
**impudencia** *f.* impudence, shamelessness.
**impudente** *adj.* impudent, shameless.
**impudicia, impudicicia** *f.* impudicity, immodesty.
**impúdico, -ca** *adj.* immodest; shameless.
**impudor** *m.* immodesty. *2* barefacedness.
**impuesto, -ta** *p. p.* of IMPONER. *2 adj.* imposed. *3* informed, cognizant. *4 m.* tax, duty, impost.
**impugnación** *f.* impugnation, challenge, refutation.
**impugnar** *tr.* to impugn, challenge, refute.
**impulsar** *tr.* to impel. *2* to actuate, move, prompt. *3* MECH. to drive, force.
**impulsión** *adj.* impulsion, impulse, drive.
**impulsivo, -va** *adj.* impulsive.
**impulso** *m.* impulse [in every sense]. *2* prompting. *3* impetus, momentum.
**impulsor, -ra** *adj.* impelling. *2 m.-f.* impeller.
**impune** *adj.* unpunished.
**impunidad** *f.* impunity.
**impureza** *f.* impurity. *2* unchasteness.
**impurificar** *tr.* to make impure, defile; to adulterate.
**impuro, -ra** *adj.* impure. *2* defiled, adulterated. *3* unchaste, lewd.
**impuse, impusiera,** etc. *irr.* V. IMPONER.
**imputable** *adj.* imputable.
**imputación** *f.* imputation.
**imputar** *tr.* to impute, ascribe, lay at the door of.
**inabordable** *adj.* unapproachable.
**inacabable** *adj.* interminable, endless, ever-lasting.
**inaccesible** *adj.* inaccessible.
**inacción** *f.* inaction, inactivity, idleness.
**inaceptable** *adj.* unacceptable.
**inactividad** *f.* inactivity.
**inactivo, -va** *adj.* inactive. *2* idle, doing nothing.
**inadaptación** *f.* inadaptation.
**inadecuado, -da** *adj.* unsuited, unsuitable.
**inadmisible** *adj.* inadmissible.
**inadvertencia** *f.* inadvertence, oversight.
**inadvertido, -da** *adj.* unseen, unnoticed, unobserved.
**inagotable** *adj.* inexhaustible, exhaustless.
**inaguantable** *adj.* intolerable, unbearable.
**inalámbrico, -ca** *adj.* wireless.
**inalcanzable** *adj.* unattainable, unreachable.
**inalienable** *adj.* inalienable.
**inalterable** *adj.* unalterable, unchangeable.
**inalterado, -da** *adj.* unaltered, unchanged.
**inamovible** *adj.* irremovable, unremovable.
**inane** *adj.* inane, empty, void.
**inanición** *f.* MED. inanition.
**inanidad** *f.* inanity.
**inanimado, -da** *adj.* inanimate, lifeless.
**inapelable** *adj.* unappealable. *2* inevitable.
**inapetencia** *f.* inappetence, lack of appetite.
**inapetente** *adj.* inappetent, having no appetite.
**inaplazable** *adj.* undeferable.
**inaplicable** *adj.* inapplicable.
**inapreciable** *adj.* invaluable. *2* inappreciable.
**inarticulado, -da** *adj.* inarticulate.
**inartístico, -ca** *adj.* inartistic.
**inasequible** *adj.* unattainable, inaccessible.
**inastillable** *adj.* nonshatterable.
**inatacable** *adj.* unattackable.
**inaudible** *adj.* inaudible.
**inaudito, -ta** *adj.* unheard-of, extraordinary. *2* outrageous, monstrous.
**inauguración** *f.* inauguration, opening. *2* unveiling [of a statue].
**inaugural** *adj.* inaugural.

**inaugurar** *tr.* to inaugurate [enter upon; initiate public use of]; to open [an exhibition, etc.]; to unveil [a statue].

**inca** *m.* Inca. *2* a gold Peruvian coin.

**incaico, -ca** *adj.* Inca.

**incalculable** *adj.* incalculable.

**incalificable** *adj.* very bad, most reprehensible.

**incandescencia** *f.* incandescence.

**incandescente** *adj.* incandescent.

**incansable** *adj.* indefatigable, untiring.

**incapacidad** *f.* incapacity. *2* incompetence, disability. *3* incapability, stupidity.

**incapacitar** *tr.* to incapacitate. *2* to disqualify, disable. *3* LAW to declare incapable.

**incapaz,** *pl.* **-ces** *adj.* incapable. *2* unable.

**incasable** *adj.* unmarriageable.

**incasto, -ta** *adj.* unchaste.

**incautarse** *ref.* ~ *de* [of a court, the government, etc.], to seize [money or property].

**incauto, -ta** *adj.* incautious, unwary, innocent.

**incendiar** *tr.* to set on fire, set fire to. *2 ref.* to catch fire, be burnt.

**incendiario, -ria** *adj.-n.* incendiary.

**incendio** *m.* fire, conflagration [destructive burning]. *2* fig. fire, passion.

**incensada** *f.* swing of the thurible. *2* flattery.

**incensar** *tr.* to incense [burn incense to]. *2* fig. to flatter, overpraise. ¶ CONJUG. like *acertar.*

**incensario** *m.* censer, incensory, thurible.

**incentivo, -va** *adj.* incentive. *2 m.* incentive, inducement.

**incertidumbre** *f.* uncertainty, doubt.

**incesante** *adj.* incessant, unceasing, continual.

**incesto** *m.* incest.

**incestuoso, -sa** *adj.* incestuous.

**incidencia** *f.* incident. *2* GEOM., PHYS. incidence.

**incidental** *adj.* INCIDENTE 1.

**incidente** *adj.* incidental, happening as a subordinate event. *2* GEOM., PHYS. incident. *3 m.* incident.

**incidir** *intr.* PHYS. [of a ray] to fall [upon]. *2* to fall [into error, etc.].

**incienso** *m.* incense [gum, spice], frankincense. *2* fig. incense, flattery.

**incienso, inciense,** etc. *irr.* V. INCENSAR.

**incierto, -ta** *adj.* not certain, untrue. *2* uncertain, doubtful, problematical.

**incineración** *f.* incineration, cremation.

**incinerar** *tr.* to incinerate, cremate.

**incipiente** *adj.* incipient.

**incircunciso** *adj.* uncircumcised.

**incisión** *f.* incision, cut.

**incisivo, -va** *adj.* incisive, cutting: *diente* ~, incisor. *2* incisive, sarcastic. *3 m.* ANAT. incisor.

**inciso, -sa** *adj.* cut, incised. *2 m.* GRAM. parenthetic sentence.

**incitación** *f.* incitation, incitement.

**incitador, -ra** *adj.* inciting. *2 m.-f.* inciter.

**incitante** *adj.* inciting, exciting.

**incitar** *tr.* to incite.

**incivil** *adj.* uncivil.

**incivilidad** *f.* incivillity.

**inclasificable** *adj.* unclassifiable.

**inclemencia** *f.* inclemency, unmercifulness. *2* inclemency [of weather or climate].

**inclemente** *adj.* inclement.

**inclinación** *f.* inclination [inclining; slant, slope; leaning; propension, liking]. *2* bow, nod, obeisance.

**inclinado, -da** *adj.* inclined, slanting, sloping. *2* inclined, disposed.

**inclinar** *tr.* to incline, tilt, slant, bow. *2* to incline,

dispose, move. *3 ref.* to incline, tilt, lean, slope, bow [as intr.]. *4* to incline, lean, tend, be disposed. *5* to yield, defer.

**ínclito, -ta** *adj.* illustrious, renowned.

**incluir** *tr.* to include. *2* to enclose [in an envelope]. ¶ CONJUG. like *huir.*

**inclusa** *f.* foundling hospital.

**inclusero, -ra** *adj. m.-f.* foundling.

**inclusión** *f.* inclusion.

**inclusivamente, inclusive** *adv.* inclusively, inclusive.

**incluso, -sa** *adj.* included. *2* enclosed [in an envelope]. *3 adv.* including, even.

**incoar** *tr.* LAW to inchoate, initiate.

**incoativo, -va** *adj.* inchoative, inceptive.

**incobrable** *adj.* COM. irrecoverable, uncollectable.

**incoercible** *adj.* incoercible.

**incógnita** *f.* unknown quantity.

**incógnito** *adj.* unknown. *2 adj.-m.* incognito. *3 adv. de* ~, incognito.

**incognoscible** *adj.* unknowable.

**incoherencia** *f.* incoherence, disconnectedness.

**incoherente** *adj.* incoherent, disconnected.

**incoloro, -ra** *adj.* colourless.

**incólume** *adj.* unharmed, sound, safe, whole.

**incolumidad** *f.* soundness, safety, wholeness.

**incombustibilidad** *f.* incombustibility.

**incombustible** *adj.* incombustible, fireproof.

**incomible** *adj.* uneatable, inedible.

**incomodar** *tr.* to inconvenience, put to inconvenience, incommode, bother. *2* to annoy, anger. *3 ref.* to get annoyed or angered.

**incomodidad** *f.* inconvenience, uncomfortableness, discomfort. *2* annoyance.

**incómodo, -da** *adj.* [of things] incommodious, inconvenient, uncomfortable, unhandy, cumbersome. *2* [of persons] uncomfortable, ill at ease.

**incomparable** *adj.* incomparable, matchless.

**incompatibilidad** *f.* incompatibility, inconsistency; uncongeniality.

**incompatible** *adj.* incompatible, inconsistent; uncongenial.

**incompetencia** *f.* incompetence, incompetency.

**incompetente** *adj.* incompetent.

**incompleto, -ta** *adj.* incomplete.

**incomportable** *adj.* intolerable, unbearable.

**incomprensibilidad** *f.* incomprehensibility.

**incomprensible** *adj.* incomprehensible, inconceivable.

**incompresible** *adj.* incompressible.

**incomunicable** *adj.* incommunicable.

**incomunicación** *f.* isolation, lack of comunication. *2* solitary confinement.

**incomunicado, -da** *adj.* isolated, without communication. *2* in solitary confinement.

**incomunicar** *tr.* to isolate; to deprive of communication. *2* to put in solitary confinement.

**inconcebible** *adj.* inconceivable.

**inconciliable** *adj.* unconciliable. *2* irreconciliable.

**inconcluso, -sa** *adj.* unfinished.

**inconcuso, -sa** *adj.* incontrovertible, indisputable.

**incondicional** *adj.* unconditional.

**inconexión** *f.* lack of connection, disconnection.

**inconexo, -xa** *adj.* unconnected, disconnected.

**inconfesable** *adj.* unavowable, dishonourable.

**inconfeso, -sa** *adj.* unconfessing [that has not admitted his guilt].

**inconfidente** *adj.* unreliable.

**inconfundible** *adj.* unmistakable.

**incongruencia** *f.* incongruity, incongruousness.

**incongruente; incongruo, -grua** *adj.* incongruous, incongruent.
**inconmensurable** *adj.* incommensurable, incommensurate.
**inconmovible** *adj.* immovable, unmovable, firm. *2* unyielding, inexorable.
**inconquistable** *adj.* unconquerable.
**inconsciencia** *f.* unconciousness. *2* thoughtlessness.
**inconsciente** *adj.* unconcious. *2* unaware, unwitting. *3* thoughtless, unthinking.
**inconsecuencia** *f.* inconsistency [lack of harmony between conduct and principles].
**inconsecuente** *adj.* not consequent. *2* inconsistent [acting at variance with one's own principles]. *3 m.-f.* inconsistent person.
**inconsideración** *f.* inconsiderateness. *2* thoughtlessness, rashness.
**inconsiderado, -da** *adj.* inconsiderate, thougthless, rash.
**inconsistencia** *f.* inconsistency, flimsiness, unsubstantiality.
**inconsistente** *adj.* inconsistent; flimsy, unsubstantial.
**inconsolable** *adj.* inconsolable.
**inconstancia** *f.* inconstancy.
**inconstante** *adj.* inconstant.
**inconstitucional** *adj.* unconstitutional.
**inconsútil** *adj.* seamless.
**incontable** *adj.* uncountable, countless.
**incontaminado, -da** *adj.* uncontaminated, undefiled.
**incontestable** *adj.* incontestable, indisputable.
**incontinencia** *f.* incontinence.
**incontinente** *adj.* incontinent. *2 adv.* INCONTINENTI.
**incontinenti** *adv.* at once, immediately, instantly.
**incontrastable** *adj.* invincible, irresistible, unaswerable.
**incontrovertible** *adj.* incontrovertible.
**inconveniencia** *f.* inconvenience, uncomfortableness. *2* unsuitableness. *3* impoliteness. *4* impolite act or remark.
**inconveniente** *adj.* inconvenient. *2* impolite. *3 m.* drawback, obstacle, disadvantage, objection: *no tengo ~*, I have no objection.
**incordio** *m.* MED. bubo. *2* vulg. nuisance.
**incorporación** *f.* incorporation [union, combination]. *2* sitting up. *3* joining a body, regiment, etc.
**incorporar** *tr.* to incorporate [unite, combine]. *2* to raise to a sitting position. *3 ref.* to incorporate [become incorporated with]. *4* to join a body, regiment, etc. *5* to sit up [from a reclining position].
**incorpóreo, rea** *adj.* incorporeal.
**incorrección** *f.* incorrectness. *2* incorrect act.
**incorrecto, -ta** *adj.* incorrect.
**incorregible** *adj.* incorrigible.
**incorruptible** *adj.* incorruptible.
**incorrupto, -ta** *adj.* incorrupt.
**increado, -da** *adj.* uncreated.
**incredibilidad** *f.* incredibility.
**incredulidad** *f.* incredulity; unbelief.
**incrédulo, -la** *adj.* incredulous; unbelieving. *2 m. -f.* unbeliever, disbeliever.
**increíble** *adj.* incredible, unbelievable.
**incremento** *m.* increment, increase.
**increpación** *f.* upbraiding.
**increpar** *tr.* to upraid.
**incriminación** *f.* incrimination.
**incriminar** *tr.* to incriminate.
**incruento, -ta** *adj.* bloodless [offering].

**incrustación** *f.* incrustation, encrusting. *2* scale [in a boiler]. *3* F. ARTS inlaying, inlay.
**incrustar** *tr.* to incrust. *2* F. ARTS to inlay.
**incubación** *f.* incubation.
**incubadora** *f.* incubator [apparatus].
**incubar** *tr.* to incubate, hatch.
**íncubo** *m.* incubus.
**incuestionable** *adj.* unquestionable.
**inculcar** *tr.* to inculcate.
**inculpabilidad** *f.* inculpability, guiltlessness: *veredicto de ~*, verdict of not guilty.
**inculpación** *f.* inculpation.
**inculpar** *tr.* to inculpate. *2* to blame.
**inculto, -ta** *adj.* incult, uncultivated, untilled. *2* incult, uncultured, uneducated, uncivilized.
**incultura** *f.* lack of culture.
**incumbencia** *f.* incumbency, duty, concern.
**incumbir** *intr.* to be incumbent [on], be the duty [of].
**incumplido, -da** *adj.* unfulfilled, nonexecuted.
**incumplimiento** *m.* unfulfilment, nonexecution, breach.
**incumplir** *tr.* not to fulfil, fail to fulfil.
**incunable** *adj.* incunabular. *2 m.* incunabulum.
**incurable** *adj.* incurable, hopeless.
**incuria** *f.* negligence, carelessness.
**incurrimiento** *m.* incurring.
**incurrir** *en intr.* to incur, become liable to. *2* to commit [a fault, etc.], to fall into [error].
**incursión** *f.* MIL. incursion. *2* INCURRIMIENTO.
**incurso, -sa** *adj.* having incurred.
**incuso, -sa** *adj.* incuse.
**indagación** *f.* investigation, search, inquiry, inquest.
**indagar** *tr.* to investigate, search, inquire.
**indebido, -da** *adj.* undue, improper, illegal, illicit.
**indecencia** *f.* indecency.
**indecente** *adj.* indecent. *2* low, dirty [act, conduct].
**indecible** *adj.* unspeakable, unutterable.
**indecisión** *f.* indecision, irresolution.
**indeciso, -sa** *adj.* undecided [not yet determined]. *2* undecided, hesitant, irresolute.
**indeclinable** *adj.* undeclinable. *2* GRAM. indeclinable, undeclinable.
**indecoro** *m.* indecorum, indecorousness.
**indecoroso, -sa** *adj.* indecorous, improper. *2* indecent.
**indefectible** *adj.* indefectible, unfailing, certain.
**indefendible, indefensible** *adj.* indefensible.
**indefensión** *f.* defencelessness.
**indefenso, -sa** *adj.* defenceless.
**indeficiente** *adj.* unfailing, certain.
**indefinible** *adj.* undefinable.
**indefinido, -da** *adj.* indefinite, undefined, vague. *2* GRAM. indefinite.
**indehiscente** *adj.* BOT. indehiscent.
**indeleble** *adj.* indelible, ineffaceable.
**indeliberado, -da** *adj.* indeliberate, unpremeditated.
**indelicadeza** *f.* indelicacy; unscrupulousness.
**indelicado, -da** *adj.* indelicate; unscrupulous.
**indemne** *adj.* unharmed, unhurt, undamaged.
**indemnidad** *f.* indemnity, freedom from damage.
**indemnización** *f.* indemnification, indemnity.
**indemnizar** *tr.* to indemnify, compensate.
**indemostrable** *adj.* indemonstrable, undemonstrable.
**independencia** *f.* independence.
**independiente** *adj.* independent.
**independizar** *tr.-ref.* EMANCIPAR.

**indescifrable** *adj.* undecipherable.
**indescriptible** *adj.* indescribable.
**indeseable** *adj.* undesirable [pers.].
**indestructible** *adj.* indestructible.
**indeterminación** *f.* indetermination. *2* irresolution.
**indeterminado, -da** *adj.* indeterminate, undetermined. *2* undetermined, irresolute, hesitating. *3* GRAM. indefinite [article].
**indevoción** *f.* indevotion, lack of devotion.
**indevoto, -ta** *adj.* undevout. *2* undevoted.
**India** *f. pr. n.* GEOG. India. *2 pl.* Indies: *Indias Occidentales,* Spanish America; West Indies; *Indias Orientales,* India.
**indiada** *f.* (Am.) multitude of Indians.
**indiana** *f.* printed calico.
**indiano, -na** *adj.* of the Spanish America. *2* Indian [of India]. *3 adj.-n.* Spanish American. *4 m.-f.* one who returns rich from America.
**indicación** *f.* indication, sign. *2* hint, suggestion. *3* direction, instruction. *4* MED. indication.
**indicado, -da** *adj.* indicated. *2* proper, appropriate, suitable.
**indicador, -ra** *adj.* indicating, indicatory. *2 m.* indicator, pointer, index, gauge. *3* ELECT. annunciator disc.
**indicar** *tr.* to indicate, point out, show. *2* to indicate, betoken, be sign of. *3* to indicate [state briefly]. *4* to hint, suggest.
**indicativo, -va** *adj.* indicative. *2 adj.-m.* GRAM. indicative.
**índice** *m.* ANAT. index, forefinger. *2* sign, indication. *3* index [table of contents, list; pointer, hand; ratio]: ~ *cefálico,* cephalic index. *4* MATH. index. *5* ECCL. Index.
**indicio** *m.* sign, indication, clue, evidence. *2 pl.* CHEM. traces. *3* LAW *indicios vehementes,* circumstantial evidence.
**índico, -ca** *adj.* Indian, East-Indian: *Océano Índico,* Indian Ocean.
**indiferencia** *f.* indifference.
**indiferente** *adj.* indifferent: *me es* ~, it is all the same to me.
**indiferentismo** *m.* indifferentism.
**indígena** *adj.* indigenous, native. *2 m.-f.* native [person].
**indigencia** *f.* indigence, destitution, need.
**indigente** *adj.* indigent, destitute, needy.
**indigestarse** *ref.* to cause indigestion. *2* [of persons] to be disagreeable, cause aversion or dislike.
**indigestión** *f.* indigestion.
**indigesto, -ta** *adj.* indigestible. *2* indigested, undigested. *3* disagreeable [person].
**indignación** *f.* indignation.
**indignado, -da** *adj.* indignant, angry.
**indignamente** *adv.* unworthily. *2* with indignity.
**indignante** *adj.* irritating, causing indignation.
**indignar** *tr.* to irritate, make indignant, cause indignation. *2 ref.* to become indignant.
**indignidad** *f.* unworthiness. *2* indignity.
**indigno, -na** *adj.* unworthy. *2* low, contemptible.
**índigo** *m.* indigo.
**indino, -na** *adj.* mischievous, saucy.
**indio, dia** *adj.-n.* Indian [of Asia or America]. *2 m.* CHEM. indium. *3 adj.* blue, azure.
**indirecta** *f.* hint, insinuation, innuendo.
**indirectamente** *adv.* indirectly.
**indirecto, -ta** *adj.* indirect.
**indisciplina** *f.* indiscipline, lack of discipline.
**indisciplinado, -da** *adj.* undisciplined, unruly.

**indisciplinarse** *ref.* to become undisciplined.
**indiscreción** *f.* indiscretion [want of discretion].
**indiscreto, -ta** *adj.* indiscreet [wanting in discretion].
**indiscutible** *adj.* unquestionable, indisputable.
**indisolubilidad** *f.* indissolubility.
**indisoluble** *adj.* indissoluble.
**indispensable** *adj.* indispensable, necessary, essential.
**indisponer** *tr.* to indispose [make sick or ill]. *2* ~ *a una persona con otra,* to set a person against another. *3 ref.* to be indisposed, out of health. *4* [of two persons] to fall out. *5 indisponerse con,* to quarrel with.
**indisposición** *f.* lack of fitness, unpreparation. *2* indisposition, passing ailment.
**indispuesto, -ta** *adj.* indisposed, slightly ill. *3* on bad terms, at variance.
**indisputable** *adj.* indisputable.
**indistinguible** *adj.* undistinguishable.
**indistintamente** *adv.* indistinctly, indiscriminately.
**indistinto, -ta** *adj.* indistinct.
**individual** *adj.* individual.
**individualidad** *f.* individuality.
**individualismo** *m.* individualism.
**individualista** *adj.* individualistic. *2 m.-f.* individualist.
**individualizar** *tr.* to individualize.
**individuo, -dua** *adj.* individual. *2* indivisible. *3 m.* individual [single member of a class]. *4* member, fellow [of a board, society, etc.]. *5* individual, fellow, person. *6 f.* despicable woman.
**indivisibilidad** *f.* indivisibility.
**indivisible** *adj.* indivisible.
**indiviso, -sa** *adj.* LAW undivided.
**Indo** *m. pr. n.* GEOG. Indus.
**indo, -da** *adj.-n.* Indian, East-Indian.
**indócil** *adj.* indocile.
**indocilidad** *f.* indocility.
**indocto, -ta** *adj.* unlearned, uneducated.
**indocumentado, -da** *adj.* lacking the documents for identification. *2 m.-f.* nobody [person of no account].
**Indochina** *f. pr. n.* GEOG. Indo-China.
**indochino, -na** *adj.-n.* Indo-Chinese.
**indoeuropeo, -a** *adj.-n.* Indo-European.
**índole** *f.* disposition, nature. *2* class, kind.
**indolencia** *f.* indolence. *2* painlessness.
**indolente** *adj.* indolent.
**indoloro** *adj.* MED. indolent.
**indomable** *adj.* untamable, indomitable.
**indomado, -da** *adj.* untamed.
**indómito, -ta** *adj.* untamed. *2* indomitable. *3* unruly.
**Indostán** *m. pr. n.* GEOG. Hindustan.
**indostanés, -sa** *adj.-n.* Hindustani, Hidoostani.
**indostánico, -ca** *adj.* Hindustani [of Hindustan].
**indostano, -na** *adj.* INDOSTANÉS.
**indubitable** *adj.* indubitable, doubtless.
**inducción** *f.* inducing, instigation. *2* ELECT., LOG. induction.
**inducido** *m.* ELECT. armature [of motor or dynamo].
**inducir** *tr.* to induce, persuade, instigate. *2* ELECT., LOG. to induce. ¶ CONJUG. like *conducir.*
**inductancia** *f.* ELECT. inductance.
**inductivo, -va** *adj.* LOG., ELECT. inductive.
**inductor, -ra** *adj.* inducing. *2 m.-f.* inducer, instigator. *3 m.* ELECT. inductor, field.
**indudable** *adj.* indubitable, doubtless, certain.

**indujo, indujera,** etc. *irr.* V. INDUCIR.
**indulgencia** *f.* indulgence, leniency, forbearance. *2* ECCL. indulgence.
**indulgente** *adj.* indulgent, lenient, forbearing.
**indultar** *tr.* to pardon [free from penalty]. *2* to exempt [from an obligation].
**indulto** *m.* LAW pardon, commutation. *2* indult.
**indumentaria** *f.* clothing, dress, garb.
**indumento** *m.* VESTIDURA.
**induración** *f.* MED. induration.
**industria** *f.* industry. *2* ingenuity. *3 de* ~, designedly, on purpose.
**industrial** *adj.* industrial. *2 m.* industrialist, manufacturer.
**industrialismo** *m.* industrialism.
**industrializar** *tr.* to industrialize.
**industriar** *tr.* to train, teach. *2 ref.* to manage; to get along.
**industrioso, -sa** *adj.* industrious. *2* ingenious.
**induzco, induzca,** etc. *irr.* V. INDUCIR.
**inedia** *f.* inanition.
**inédito, -ta** *adj.* unpublished.
**inefabilidad** *f.* ineffability.
**inefable** *adj.* ineffable, unutterable.
**ineficacia** *f.* inefficacy, inefficiency, ineffectualness.
**ineficaz** *adj.* inefficacious, inefficient, ineffectual.
**inelegante** *adj.* inelegant.
**ineluctable** *adj.* ineluctable, inevitable.
**ineludible** *adj.* ineludible, unavoidable.
**inenarrable** *adj.* ineffable, inexpressible.
**inencogible** *adj.* unshrinkable.
**inepcia** *f.* silliness, ineptitude.
**ineptitud** *f.* incompetence. *2* ineptitude.
**inepto, -ta** *adj.* incompetent, incapable. *2* inept. *3 m.-f.* incapable [person].
**inequívoco, -ca** *adj.* unequivocal, unmistakable.
**inercia** *f.* inertia.
**inerme** *adj.* unarmed. *2* BOT., ZOOL. inerm, inermous.
**inerte** *adj.* inert.
**inervación** *f.* innervation.
**Inés** *f. pr. n.* Agnes.
**inescrutabilidad** *f.* inscrutability.
**inescrutable, inescudriñable** *adj.* inscrutable.
**inesperado, -da** *adj.* unexpected, unforeseen.
**inestabilidad** *f.* instability.
**inestable** *adj.* unstable, instable.
**inestimable** *adj.* inestimable, invaluable, priceless.
**inevitable** *adj.* inevitable, unavoidable.
**inexactitud** *f.* inexactness; inaccuracy.
**inexacto, -ta** *adj.* inexact; inaccurate. *2* untrue.
**inexcusable** *adj.* inexcusable. *2* unavoidable.
**inexhausto, -ta** *adj.* unexhausted; unexhaustible.
**inexistencia** *f.* inexistence.
**inexistente** *adj.* inexistent, nonexistent.
**inexorable** *adj.* inexorable, relentless.
**inexperiencia** *f.* inexperience.
**inexperto, -ta** *adj.* inexpert, inexperienced.
**inexplicable** *adj.* inexplicable, unaccountable.
**inexplorado, -da** *adj.* unexplored.
**inexpresable** *adj.* inexpressible.
**inexpresivo, -va** *adj.* inexpressive.
**inexpugnable** *adj.* inexpugnable, impregnable. *2* firm, stubborn.
**inextenso, -sa** *adj.* unextended [having no extension].
**inextinguible** *adj.* inextinguishable, unquenchable.
**inextricable** *adj.* inextricable.

**infalibilidad** *f.* infallibility.
**infalible** *adj.* infallible.
**infamación** *f.* defamation.
**infamador, -ra** *adj.* defaming. *2 m.-f.* defamer.
**infamante** *adj.* causing infamy, opprobious.
**infamar** *tr.* to defame, infamize, dishonour.
**infamatorio, -ria** *adj.* defamatory, libellous.
**infame** *adj.* infamous. *2* fig. very bad. *3 m.-f.* infamous, wicked person.
**infamia** *f.* infamy. *2* infamous act.
**infancia** *f.* infancy, babyhood.
**infando, -da** *adj.* frightful, unspeakable.
**infanta** *f.* female child. *2* infanta.
**infantado** *m.* territory assigned to an INFANTE or INFANTA.
**infante** *m.* male infant. *2* infante. *3* infantry soldier.
**infantería** *f.* MIL. infantry: ~ *de marina*, marines.
**infanticida** *m.* infanticide [murderer of an infant].
**infanticidio** *m.* infanticide [act].
**infantil** *adj.* infantile, infant. *2* infantile, childish, innocent. *3* children's.
**infantilismo** *m.* infantility. *2* MED. infantilism.
**infanzón** *m.* ancient nobleman.
**infanzona** *f.* ancient noblewoman.
**infarto** *m.* MED. infarct, infarction.
**infatigable** *adj.* indefatigable, untiring.
**infatuación** *f.* conceit, presumption.
**infatuar** *tr.* to make conceited or vain. *2 ref.* to become conceited or vain.
**infausto, -ta** *adj.* unlucky, unhappy, fatal.
**infección** *f.* infection.
**infeccioso, -sa** *adj.* MED. infectious.
**infectar** *tr.* to infect. *2 ref.* to become infected.
**infectivo, -va** *adj.* infective.
**infecto, -ta** *adj.* infected, foul, corrupt.
**infecundo, -da** *adj.* infecund, barren, sterile.
**infelice** *adj.* poet. unhappy, wretched.
**infelicidad** *f.* infelicity, unhappiness.
**infeliz** *adj.* unhappy, unfortunate, wretched. *2 m. -f.* unhappy person, wretch. *3 adj.-n.* coll. simple, good-natured [person].
**inferencia** *f.* inference.
**inferior** *adj.-n.* inferior. *2 adj.* lower, under [part].
**inferioridad** *f.* inferiority.
**inferir** *tr.* to infer, conclude. *2* to cause, inflict [a wound]; to offer [an insult]; to do [an injury]. ¶ CONJUG. like *hervir*.
**infernáculo** *m.* hopscotch [game].
**infernal** *adj.* infernal, hellish. *2* coll. infernal, confounded, detestable.
**infernalmente** *adv.* infernally, hellishly.
**infestación** *f.* infestation.
**infestar** *tr.* to infest, overrun. *2* to infect.
**infesto, -ta** *adj.* poet. harmful, prejudicial.
**infeudación** *f.* ENFEUDACIÓN.
**infeudar** *tr.* ENFEUDAR.
**inficionar** *tr.* to infect, corrupt, taint. *2 ref.* to be infected.
**infidelidad** *f.* infidelity, unfaithfulness. *2* the infidels as a whole.
**infidencia** *f.* breach of trust, unfaithfulness.
**infidente** *adj.* unfaithful, dishonest.
**infiel** *adj.* unfaithful, disloyal. *2* inaccurate, inexact. *3 adj.-n.* infidel, pagan.
**infiernillo** *m.* small alcohol stove.
**infierno** *m.* [often in the *pl.*] hell, inferno: *en los quintos infiernos,* fig. very far; far away.
**infiltración** *f.* infiltration.
**infiero, infiera,** etc. *irr.* V. INFERIR.
**infiltrar** *tr.* infiltrate. *2* to infuse, instill [ideas,

etc.]. *3 ref.* to infiltrate [be infiltrated]. *4* to insinuate itself.

**ínfimo, -ma** *adj.* lowest, least. *2* vilest, most abject. *3* most inferior [in quality].

**infinidad** *f.* infinity, infinitude; infinite number, no end.

**infinitesimal** *adj.* infinitesimal.

**infinitivo** *adj.-n.* GRAM. infinitive.

**infinito, -ta** *adj.* infinite. *2 m.* infinite, infinite space. *3* MATH. infinity. *4 adv.* infinitely.

**infinitud** *f.* infinitude, infiniteness.

**inflación** *f.* inflation. *2* conceit, vanity.

**inflacionista** *adj.* inflationary.

**inflamable** *adj.* inflammable.

**inflamación** *f.* inflammation.

**inflamar** *tr.* to inflame. *2 ref.* to inflame [become inflamed].

**inflamatorio, -ria** *adj.* inflammatory.

**inflar** *tr.* to inflate. *2* to exaggerate [news, etc.]. *3 ref.* to inflate. *4* to be puffed up with pride.

**inflexibilidad** *f.* inflexibility.

**inflexible** *adj.* inflexible.

**inflexión** *f.* inflection, bend. *2* GEOM., GRAM. inflection. *3* inflection, modulation [of the voice].

**infligir** *tr.* to inflict.

**inflorescencia** *f.* BOT. inflorescence.

**influencia** *f.* influence.

**influenciar** *tr.* (Am.) to influence.

**influenza** *f.* MED. influenza.

**influir** *tr.* to influence. *2 intr.* ~ *en* or *sobre,* to influence, have influence on; to affect. ¶ CONJUG. like *huir.*

**influjo** *m.* influence. *2* NAUT. rising tide.

**influyente** *adj.* influential.

**infolio** *m.* folio book, book in folio form.

**información** *f.* information [informing, telling, being told, intelligence, news]: *oficina de informaciones,* information bureau. *2* reportage. *3* inquiry, investigation. *4* PHILOS. information.

**informador, -ra** *m.-f.* newspaper reporter.

**informal** *adj.* informal [not according to due form]. *2* [of a pers.] not serious, unreliable.

**informalidad** *f.* informality [want of regular or prescribed form]. *2* lack of seriousness, unreliability. *3* nonfulfilment of a promise, engagement, etc.

**informante** *adj.* informing, reporting. *2 m.-f.* one who reports on something.

**informar** *tr.* to inform [tell, notify, make acquainted]. *2* PHIL. to inform. *3 intr.* to report [on something]. *4* LAW [of a lawyer] to plead before a court. *5 ref.* to inquire, find out: *informarse de,* to inquire into, find out about.

**informativo, -va** *adj.* informative, giving news. *2* PHIL. informative.

**informe** *adj.* shapeless, formless. *2 m.* information, report, account. *3* report [of an expert, a commitee]. *4* LAW plea. *5 pl.* references, character.

**infortunado, -da** *adj.* unfortunate, unlucky. *2 m.-f.* unfortunate [person].

**infortunio** *m.* misfortune, misery. *2* mishap, mischance.

**infracción** *f.* infraction, infringement, breach.

**infractor, -ra** *m.-f.* infractor, breaker, transgressor.

**infraestructura** *f.* AER. nonflying structures.

**in fraganti** *adv.* in the very act.

**infrangible** *adj.* infrangible, inviolable.

**infranqueable** *adj.* insurmountable.

**infrarrojo, -ja** *adj.* infrared.

**infrascripto, -ta; infrascrito, -ta** *adj.-n.* undersigned.

**infrecuente** *adj.* infrequent.

**infringir** *tr.* to infringe, break, transgress.

**infructífero, -ra** *adj.* unfruitful, unprofitable.

**infructuoso, -sa** *adj.* fruitless, unfruitful, unsuccessful.

**ínfula** *f.* infula. *2 pl.* conceit, airs: *darse ínfulas,* to put on airs.

**infumable** *adj.* unsmokable, bad [tobacco].

**infundado, -da** *adj.* groundless, baseless, unfounded.

**infundio** *m.* lie, canard, false report.

**infundir** *tr.* to infuse, instil [life, spirit, etc.], to imbue with. *2* to infuse [steep in liquid].

**infusible** *adj.* infusible.

**infusión** *f.* infusion.

**infuso, -sa** *adj.* infused [by God].

**infusorio, -ria** *adj.-n.* ZOOL. infusory.

**ingeniar** *tr.* to think up, contrive, devise. *2 ref.* to manage, to find a way.

**ingeniería** *f.* engineering [art, science, profession].

**ingeniero** *m.* engineer [one who follows as profession any branch of engineering]. *2* MIL. engineer [soldier].

**ingenio** *m.* inventive faculty, mind, talent. *2* talented person, talent [esp. author]. *3* ingenuity, cleverness, wit: *aguzar el* ~, to sharpen one's wits. *4* engine, machine, mechanical device. *5* BOOKBIND. plough. *6* ~ *de azúcar,* sugar mill; sugar plantation.

**ingeniosidad** *f.* ingeniousness, ingenuity.

**ingenioso, -sa** *adj.* ingenious.

**ingénito, -ta** *adj.* unbegotten. *2* innate, inborn.

**ingente** *adj.* huge, prodigious, very large.

**ingenuidad** *f.* ingenuousness, candour.

**ingenuo, -nua** *adj.* ingenuous, candid, guileless.

**ingerencia** *f.* INJERENCIA.

**ingerir** *tr.* to ingest. ¶ CONJUG. like *hervir.*

**ingiero, ingiera,** etc. *irr.* V. INGERIR.

**ingestión** *f.* ingestion, ingesting of food.

**Inglaterra** *f. pr. n.* GEOG. England. *2 la Nueva* ~, New England.

**ingle** *f.* ANAT. groin.

**inglés, -sa** *adj.* English. *2 m.* Englishman. *3* English [language]. *4 f.* Englishwoman. *5 m. pl. los ingleses,* the English [people].

**inglesismo** *m.* Anglicism.

**inglete** *m.* mitre, miter [angle of 45°].

**ingobernable** *adj.* ungovernable, uncontrollable, unruly.

**ingratitud** *f.* ingratitude, ungratefulness.

**ingrato, -ta** *adj.* ungrateful, thankless. *2* ungrateful, harsh, unpleasant. *3 m.-f.* ungrateful person.

**ingravidez** *f.* weightlessness. *2* lightness, tenuousness.

**ingrávido, -da** *adj.* weightless. *2* light, tenuous.

**ingresar** *intr.* to enter: ~ *en,* to enter [a school, etc.]; to become a member of; to join [a political party, etc.]. *2* [of money] to come in. *3 tr.* to deposit [money], to pay in.

**ingreso** *m.* entrance, ingress. *2* entrance [into a school, etc.]; joining, admision to [a political party, society, etc.]. *3* COM. coming in [of money]. *4 pl.* income, revenue. *5* COM. receipts, incomings.

**inguinal; inguinario, -ria** *adj.* ANAT. inguinal.

**ingurgitar** *tr.* MED. to ingurgitate.

**inhábil** *adj.* unable, unskilful. *2* tactless. *3* unfit, unqualified, incompetent: *día* ~, dies non.

**inhabilidad** f. unskilfulness. 2 inability, disability.
**inhabilitación** f. disqualification, incapacitation.
**inhabilitar** tr. to disable, disqualify, incapacitate. 2 to render unfit.
**inhabitable** adj. uninhabitable.
**inhabitado, -da** adj. uninhabited.
**inhalación** f. inhalation.
**inhalar** tr. to inhale.
**inherencia** f. inherence.
**inherente** adj. inherent.
**inhibición** f. LAW, PHYSIOL., PSYCHOL. inhibition. 2 act of keeping out of [an affair].
**inhibir** tr. LAW, PHYSIOL., PSYCHOL. to inhibit. 2 ref. to keep out of [an affair].
**inhospitalario, -ria** adj. inhospitable.
**inhospitalidad** f. inhospitableness.
**inhóspito, -ta** adj. inhospitable [affording no shelter].
**inhumación** f. inhumation, burial, interment.
**inhumanidad** f. inhumanity.
**inhumano, -na** adj. inhuman, barbarous, cruel.
**inhumar** tr. to inhume, bury, inter.
**iniciación** f. initiation.
**iniciado, -da** adj. initiate, initiated. 2 m.-f. initiate.
**iniciador, -ra** adj. initiating. 2 starting. 3 m.-f. initiator, initiatrix. 3 starter, originator.
**inicial** adj. initial. 2 f. initial, initial letter.
**iniciar** tr. to initiate, begin. 2 to initiate [a person]. 3 ref. [of a thing] to initiate, begin, commence. 4 [of a person] to be initiated.
**iniciativo, -va** adj. initiative. 2 f. initiative: tomar la ~, to take the initiative.
**inicuo, -cua** adj. iniquitous.
**inigualado, -da** adj. unequaled, unrivaled.
**inimaginable** adj. unimaginable, inconceivable.
**inimitable** adj. inimitable.
**inimitablemente** adv. inimitably.
**ininteligible** adj. unintelligible.
**iniquidad** f. iniquity.
**injerencia** f. interference, intermeddling.
**injerir** tr. to insert, introduce. 2 ref. to interfere, intermeddle. ¶ CONJUG. like hervir,
**injertador** m. HORT., SURG. grafter.
**injertar** tr. HORT., SURG. to graft, engraft.
**injerto** adj. HORT. grafted. 2 m. HORT., SURG. grafting. 3 HORT. graft, scion. 4 HORT. stock [grafted plant]. 5 SURG. graft.
**injiero, injiera,** etc. irr. V. INJERIR.
**injuria** f. offence, affront, insult, abuse. 2 wrong, injustice. 3 injury, damage.
**injuriante** adj. injuring, offending, insulting.
**injuriar** tr. to offend, insult, abuse. 2 to injure, damage.
**injurioso, -sa** adj. injurious, insulting, abusive.
**injusticia** f. injustice.
**injustificable** adj. unjustifiable, unwarrantable.
**injustificado, -da** adj. unjustified.
**injusto, -ta** adj. unjust.
**⁺inmaculado, -da** adj. immaculate: Inmaculada Concepción, Immaculate Conception.
**inmanejable** adj. unmanageable.
**inmanencia** f. immanence, immanency.
**inmanente** adj. immanent, inherent.
**inmarcesible** adj. unfading, unwithering.
**inmaterial** adj. immaterial, incorporeal.
**inmaturo, -ra** adj. immature.
**inmediación** f. immediacy. 2 contiguity. 3 pl. environs, neighbourhood.
**inmediato, -ta** adj. immediate. 2 contiguous, adjoining, close, next: ~ a, close to, next to.

**inmejorable** adj. that cannot be better, unsurpassable; most excellent.
**inmemorial** adj. immemorial.
**inmensidad** f. immensity, immenseness. 2 vastness. 3 great multitude or number.
**inmenso, -sa** adj. immense. 2 unbounded, infinite.
**inmensurable** adj. immensurable, unmeasurable.
**inmerecido, -da** adj. undeserved, unmerited.
**inmersión** f. immersion.
**inmerso** adj. immersed.
**inmigración** f. immigration.
**inmigrante** adj. immigrating, immigrant. 2 m.-f. immigrant.
**inmigrar** intr. to immigrate.
**inmigratorio, -ria** adj. [of] immigration.
**inminencia** f. imminence, nearness.
**inminente** adj. imminent, impending, near.
**inmiscuir** tr. to mix. 2 ref. to interfere, meddle, intermeddle. ¶ CONJUG. regular or like huir.
**inmobiliario, -ria** adj. real-estate.
**inmoble** adj. unmovable. 2 motionless. 3 firm, constant.
**inmoderado, -da** adj. immoderated.
**inmodestia** f. immodesty.
**inmodesto, -ta** adj. immodest.
**inmolación** f. immolation, sacrifice.
**inmolar** tr. to immolate. 2 to sacrifice. 3 ref. to sacrifice oneself.
**inmoral** adj. immoral.
**inmoralidad** f. immorality.
**inmortal** adj. immortal.
**inmortalidad** f. immortality.
**inmortalizar** tr. to immortalize. 2 ref. to become immortal.
**inmotivado, -da** adj. unmotivated.
**inmoto, -ta** adj. unmoved, motionless.
**inmóvil** adj. immobile, motionless, stationary, still, fixed, set. 2 constant, unchanging.
**inmovilidad** f. immobility.
**inmovilizar** tr. to immobilize.
**inmueble** adj. immovable, real [property] 2 m. building [as a property]. 3 pl. immovables, real property.
**inmundicia** f. dirt, filth, lewdness. 2 impurity.
**inmundo, -da** adj. dirty, filthy. 2 unclean, impure.
**inmune** adj. immune, exempt. 2 MED. immune.
**inmunidad** f. immunity, exemption. 2 MED. immunity.
**inmunización** f. immunization.
**inmunizar** tr. to immunize.
**inmunología** f. immunology.
**inmutabilidad** f. immutability.
**inmutable** adj. immutable.
**inmutar** tr. to change, alter. 2 ref. to change countenance, become disturbed.
**innato, -ta** adj. innate, inborn.
**innavegable** adj. unnavigable. 2 unseaworthy.
**innecesario, -ria** adj. unnecessary.
**innegable** adj. undeniable.
**innoble** adj. ignoble.
**innocuo, -cua** adj. INOCUO.
**innominado, -da** adj. nameless, innominate.
**innovación** f. innovation.
**innovador, -ra** adj. innovating. 2 m.-f. innovator.
**innovar** tr. to innovate.
**innumerable** adj. innumerable, numberless.
**innúmero, -ra** adj. INNUMERABLE.
**inobediente** adj. inobedient, disobedient.
**inobservancia** f. inobservance, nonobservance.
**inocencia** f. innocence, innocency.
**Inocencio** m. pr. n. Innocent.

**inocentada** *f.* simple, silly act or words. *2* practical, joke, esp. when played on Holy Innocents' Day.

**inocente** *adj.-n.* innocent: *día de los Inocentes,* Holy Innocents' Day.

**inocentón, -na,** *adj.-n.* innocent, simple, credulous. *2 m.-f.* simple and credulous person.

**inocuidad** *f.* innocuity.

**inoculación** *f.* inoculation.

**inocular** *tr.* to inoculate; to inoculate with. *2 ref.* to become inoculated with.

**inocuo, -cua** *adj.* innocuous, harmless.

**inodoro, -ra** *adj.* inodorous, odourless. *2 m.* water closet, toilet.

**inofensivo, -va** *adj.* inoffensive, harmless.

**inolvidable** *adj.* unforgettable.

**inoperable** *adj.* MED. inoperable.

**inoperante** *adj.* inoperative, producing no effect.

**inopia** *f.* poverty, indigence, penury.

**inopinado, -da** *adj.* unexpected, unforeseen.

**inoportunidad** *f.* inopportuneness, inopportunity.

**inoportuno, -na** *adj.* inopportune, unseasonable.

**inorgánico, -ca** *adj.* inorganic.

**inoxidable** *adj.* inoxidable; stainless [steel].

**in promptu** (Lat.) *adv.* impromptu, offhand.

**inquebrantable** *adj.* unbreakable. *2* unyielding. *3* firm, irrevocable.

**inquiero, inquiera,** etc. *irr.* V. INQUIRIR.

**inquietante** *adj.* disquieting, disturbing.

**inquietar** *tr.* to disquiet, disturb, worry, make uneasy. *2* to vex, harass, trouble. *3 ref.* to worry, be anxious, be uneasy.

**inquieto, -ta** *adj.* restless, never still. *2* restless, agitated. *3* worried, anxious, uneasy.

**inquietud** *f.* inquietude, disquietude, restlessness, anxiety, concern, worry. *2* disturbance, riot.

**inquilinato** *m.* tenancy [of house or apartment].

**inquilino, -na** *m.-f.* tenant [of house or apartment].

**inquina** *f.* aversion, dislike, ill will, grudge.

**inquinar** *tr.* to infect, contaminate.

**inquirir** *tr.* to inquire into, search, investigate. ¶ CONJUG. like *adquirir.*

**inquisición** *f.* inquisition, investigation. *2 pr. n.* Inquisition, Holy Office.

**inquisidor, -ra** *f.* inquiring, inquisitive. *2m.-f.* inquirer, examiner. *3 m.* Inquisitor.

**inquisitivo, -va** *adj.* inquisitive.

**inquisitorial** *adj.* inquisitional, inquisitorial.

**inri** *m.* I.N.R.I. [inscription on the cross]: *poner el ~ a,* to deride, to insult.

**insaciable** *adj.* insatiable.

**insalivación** *f.* insalivation.

**insalivar** *tr.* to insalivate.

**insalubre** *adj.* insalubrious, unhealthy.

**insalubridad** *f.* insalubrity, unhealthiness.

**insania** *f.* insanity, madness.

**insatisfecho, -cha** *adj.* unsatisfied.

**insano, -na** *adj.* insane, mad, crazy.

**inscribir** *tr.* to inscribe [words, etc., on metal, stone, etc.]. *2* GEOM. to inscribe. *3 ref.* to inscribe oneself; to register.

**inscripción** *f.* inscription. *2* registration.

**inscripto, -ta; inscrito, -ta** *irreg. p. p.* of INSCRIBIR.

**insecticida** *adj.* insecticidal. *2 m.* insecticide.

**insectívoro, -ra** *adj.* insectivorous.

**insecto** *m.* ZOOL. insect. *2 pl.* ZOOL. Insecta.

**inseguridad** *f.* insecurity, unsafety. *2* uncertainty.

**inseguro, -ra** *adj.* insecure, unsafe. *2* uncertain. *3* not firm.

**inseminación** *f.* insemination, impregnation.

**inseminar** *tr.* to inseminate, impregnate.

**insensatez** *f.* insensateness, stupidity, folly.

**insensato, -ta** *adj.* insensate, stupid, foolish.

**insensibilidad** *f.* insensibility, insensitiveness. *2* hard-heartedness, callousness.

**insensibilizar** *tr.* to insensibilize. *2 ref.* to become insensible.

**insensible** *adj.* insensible [incapable of sensation; unconscious; imperceptible]. *2* insentient. *3* insensible, unfeeling, callous.

**inseparable** *adj.-n.* inseparable. *2 adj.* undetachable.

**insepulto, -ta** *adj.* unburied, uninterred.

**inserción** *f.* insertion.

**inserir** *tr.* to insert, introduce. *2* HORT. to graft. ¶ CONJUG. like *hervir.*

**insertar** *tr.* to insert, introduce [esp. in written or printed matter]. *2 ref.* BOT., ZOOL. to be inserted.

**inservible** *adj.* unserviceable, useless.

**insidia** *f.* snare, insidious act.

**insidiar** *tr.* to insidiate, put snares for.

**insidioso, -sa** *adj.* insidious.

**insigne** *adj.* illustrious, eminent. *2* egregious.

**insignia** *f.* badge, emblem. *2* standard of a Roman legion. *3* NAUT. pennant. *4 pl.* insignia.

**insignificancia** *f.* insignificance, insignificancy.

**insignificante** *adj.* insignificant.

**insinceridad** *f.* insincerity.

**insinuación** *f.* insinuation, hint, innuendo, intimation. *2* insinuation [insinuating oneself].

**insinuante** *adj.* insinuating, ingratiating, engaging.

**insinuar** *tr.* to insinuate, hint, suggest. *2 ref.* to insinuate oneself. *3* [of feelings, virtues, etc.] to be instilled into [a person].

**insipidez** *f.* insipidity, insipidness.

**insípido, -da** *adj.* insipid, tasteless, flat, vapid.

**insistencia** *f.* insistence, insistency.

**insistente** *adj.* insistent.

**insistir** *intr.* to insist: *~ en,* to insist on; *~ en que,* to insist that.

**ínsito, -ta** *adj.* connatural, inborn, inherent.

**insociable, insocial** *adj.* unsociable.

**insolación** *f.* insolation. *2* MED. sunstroke.

**insolar** *tr.* to insolate. *2 ref.* to be sunstruck.

**insolencia** *f.* insolence.

**insolentar** *tr.* to make insolent. *2 ref.* to become insolent.

**insolente** *adj.* insolent. *2 m.-f.* insolent person.

**insólito, -ta** *adj.* unusual, unaccustomed.

**insoluble** *adj.* insoluble. *2* unsolvable.

**insolvente** *adj.* insolvent.

**insomne** *adj.* insomnious, sleepless.

**insomnio** *m.* insomnia, sleeplessness.

**insondable** *adj.* fathomless. *2* inscrutable.

**insonorizado, -da** *adj.* soundproof.

**insoportable** *adj.* insupportable, unbearable.

**insostenible** *adj.* untenable, indefensible.

**inspección** *f.* inspection, overseeing, survey. *2* inspectorship. *3* inspector's office.

**inspeccionar** *tr.* to inspect, oversee, survey.

**inspector, -ra** *adj.* inspecting. *2 m.-f.* inspector, overseer, surveyor, supervisor.

**inspiración** *f.* inspiration.

**inspirado, -da** *adj.* inspired: *~ poeta,* inspired poet.

**inspirador, -ra** *adj.* inspiring. *2 m.-f.* inspirer.

**inspirar** *tr.* PHYSIOL. to inspire. *2* to inspire [infuse thought, create feeling, animate, suggest, etc.], to awaken, excite. *3 ref.* to become inspired. *4*

*inspirarse en,* to take as a model or subject [in literary or artistic work].
**instable** *adj.* INESTABLE.
**instalación** *f.* installation, instalment. *2* installation, plant; fittings, appointments.
**instalar** *tr.* to install, induct. *2* to install, lay, set up, put in place. *3 ref.* to install or establish oneself.
**instancia** *f.* instance, request: *a ~ de,* at the request of. *2* earnestness, urgency [in asking]. *3* petition, memorial. *4* LAW instance.
**instantáneo, -a** *adj.* instantaneous. *2 f.* PHOT. snapshot.
**instante** *adj.* pressing, soliciting. *2 m.* instant, moment: *al ~,* immediately; *por instantes,* incessantly, every moment.
**instar** *tr.* to request, beg, press, urge. *2 intr.* to be pressing, urgent.
**instauración** *f.* restoration, renewal. *2* establishment, foundation [of a monarchy, etc.].
**instaurar** *tr.* to restore, re-establish, renew. *2* to establish, found [a monarchy, etc.].
**instigación** *f.* instigation.
**instigador, -ra** *adj.* instigating. *2 m.-f.* instigator.
**instigar** *tr.* to instigate, incite, urge.
**instilación** *f.* instillation.
**instilar** *tr.* to instil, instill.
**instintivo, -va** *adj.* instinctive.
**instinto** *m.* instinct: *por ~,* instinctively.
**institución** *f.* institution [instituting; established thing; establishment, foundation]. *2 pl.* institutes. *3* constitutional organs of the soverain power.
**institucional** *adj.* institutional.
**instituir** *tr.* to institute, establish, found. *2* LAW to institute, appoint [heir]. ¶ CONJUG. like *huir.*
**instituto** *m.* constitution, rule [esp. of a religious order]. *2* institute [society, organization]. *3 ~ de enseñanza media,* high school, secondary school.
**institutriz** *f.* governess [of a young person].
**instituyente** *adj.* instituting.
**instrucción** *f.* instruction, teaching, education. *2* instruction, knowledge, learning. *2* MIL. drill. *4* LAW institution or carrying out of proceedings. *5 pl.* instructions, directions, orders.
**instructivo, -va** *adj.* instructive.
**instructor** *m.* instructor. *2* LAW *juez ~,* examining magistrate.
**instruido, -da** *adj.* learned, informed, educated.
**instruir** *tr.* to instruct, teach, educate. *2* MIL. to drill. *3* to instruct, inform, advise. *4* LAW to institute or carry out proceedings. *5 ref.* to learn, to educate oneself. ¶ CONJUG. like *huir.*
**instrumentación** *f.* MUS. instrumentation, orchestration.
**instrumental** *adj.* MUS. instrumental. *2 m.* MUS. instruments of an orchestra, etc. *3* SURG. kit of instruments.
**instrumentar** *tr.* MUS. to instrument, instrumentate.
**instrumentista** *m.* instrument maker. *2* MUS. instrumentalist.
**instrumento** *m.* instrument, implement, tool, appliance, contrivance, apparatus. *2* instrument, medium, means. *3* MUS. instrument: *~ de cuerda,* stringed instrument. *4* LAW instrument.
**insuave** *adj.* rough, unpleasant.
**insubordinación** *f.* insubordination.
**insubordinar** *tr.* to incite to insubordination. *2 ref.* to become insubordinate, to rebel.

**insubstancial** *adj.* unsubstantial, insubstantial. *2* inane, vapid, pointless, trivial.
**insubstancialidad** *f.* insubstantiality. *2* inanity, vapidness, triviality.
**insubstituible** *adj.* irreplaceable.
**insuficiencia** *f.* insufficiency, inadequacy.
**insuficiente** *adj.* insufficient, inadequate.
**insuflar** *tr.* MED. to insufflate.
**insufrible** *adj.* unbearabie, intolerable, insufferable.
**ínsula** *f.* obs. isle, island. *2* fig. small village.
**insular** *adj.* insular. *2 m.-f.* islander.
**insulina** *f.* MED. insulin.
**insulsez** *f.* insipidity, vapidity, flatness, dullness.
**insulso, -sa** *adj.* insipid, vapid, flat, dull.
**insultante** *adj.* insulting.
**insultar** *tr.* to insult; to call names.
**insulto** *m.* insult, affront.
**insumergible** *adj.* insubmergible, unsinkable.
**insumiso, -sa** *adj.* disobedient, rebellious.
**insuperable** *adj.* insuperable, insurmontable, invincible. *2* unsurpassable.
**insurgente** *adj.-n.* insurgent.
**insurrección** *f.* insurrection, rebellion.
**insurreccionar** *tr.* to incite to insurrection. *2 ref.* to rise up, rebel.
**insurrecto, -ta** *adj.* insurgent, rebellious. *2 m.-f.* insurgent, insurrectionist, rebel.
**insustancial** *adj.* INSUBSTANCIAL.
**insustancialidad** *f.* INSUBSTANCIALIDAD.
**insustituible** *adj.* INSUBSTITUIBLE.
**intacto, -ta** *adj.* intact, unimpaired, whole, pure.
**intachable** *adj.* blameless, faultless, irreprochable.
**intangibilidad** *f.* intangibility.
**intangible** *adj.* intangible. *2* not to be touched.
**integérrimo, -ma** *adj.* superl. of ÍNTEGRO: most honest or upright, irreproachable.
**integración** *f.* integration.
**integrado, -da** *adj. ~ por,* consisting of.
**integral** *adj.* integral, constituent. *2 adj.-f.* MATH. integral.
**íntegramente** *adv.* entirely, wholly.
**integrante** *adj.* integral, integrant.
**integrar** *tr.* to integrate, compose, form, make up. *2* MATH. to integrate.
**integridad** *f.* integrity, wholeness. *2* integrity, honesty, uprightness.
**íntegro, gra** *adj.* integral, whole, complete. *2* honest, upright.
**integumento** *m.* integument.
**intelección** *f.* intellection.
**intelecto** *m.* intellect.
**intelectual** *adj.-n.* intellectual.
**intelectualidad** *f.* intellectuality. *2* the intellectuals.
**inteligencia** *f.* intelligence, intellect, mind, understanding. *2* intelligence, sagacity, ability. *3* understanding, comprehension, interpretation. *4* sense, meaning. *5* understanding [between persons]. *6 en la ~ de que,* on the understanding that.
**inteligente** *adj.* intelligent.
**inteligible** *adj.* intelligible.
**intemperancia** *f.* intemperance.
**intemperante** *adj.* intemperate [person].
**intemperie** *f.* inclemency [of weather]: *a la ~,* in the open air, outdoors, unsheltered.
**intempestivo, -va** *adj.* untimely, ill-timed, unseasonable.
**intención** *f.* intention, purpose, mind; meaning:

*segunda* ~, duplicity of meaning or purpose; *mudar de* ~, to change one's mind; *tener* ~ *de*, to intend, have in mind; *con* ~, *con toda* ~, deliberately, on purpose; *de primera* ~, on the first impulse. *2* pointed way of saying something. *3* THEOL., SURG. intention.

**intencionadamente** *adv.* deliberately, on purpose.

**intencionado, -da** *adj.* deliberate, made on purpose. *2* inclined, disposed: *mal* ~, evil-minded.

**intencional** *adj.* intentional.

**intendencia** *f.* intendance, intendancy. *2* MIL. administrative corps of the army.

**intendente** *m.* intendant. *2* administrator.

**intensidad** *f.* intensity, intenseness, vehemence. *2* PHYS., MUS. intensity.

**intensificar** *tr.* to intensify. *2 ref.* to intensify [become more intense].

**intensión** *f.* intension, intensity.

**intensivo, -va** *adj.* intensive.

**intenso, -sa** *adj.* intense, intensive, vehement.

**intentar** *tr.* to try, attempt, endeavour. *2* to intend, mean, purpose. *3* LAW to enter [an action].

**intento** *m.* intent, purpose: *de* ~, purposely, on purpose. *2* attempt, try, trial, effort.

**intentona** *f.* rash attempt.

**intercalación** *f.* intercalation, interpolation.

1) **intercalar** *tr.* to intercalate, interpolate.

2) **intercalar** *adj.* intercalary. *2* leap [day or year].

**intercambiable** *adj.* interchangeable.

**intercambio** *m.* interchange, reciprocation [of services, etc.].

**interceder** *intr.* to intercede.

**intercelular** *adj.* intercellular.

**interceptación** *f.* interception.

**interceptar** *tr.* to intercept.

**intercesión** *f.* intercession.

**intercesor, -ra** *m.-f.* intercessor.

**intercolumnio** *m.* ARCH. intercolumniation.

**intercontinental** *adj.* intercontinental.

**intercostal** *adj.* ANAT. intercostal.

**interdecir** *tr.* to interdict, forbid.

**interdicción** *f.* interdiction.

**interdicto** *m.* interdict.

**interdigital** *adj.* interdigital.

**interés** *m.* interest [advantage, profit, concern]. *2* interest [value of thing in itself]. *3* interest [on capital]: ~ *legal*, legal rate of interest. *4* interest [attention, curiosity, inclination towards pers. or thing; quality exciting them]. *5 pl.* worldly possessions. *6* interests; *intereses creados*, vested interests.

**interesado, -da** *p. p.* of INTERESAR. *2 adj.* interested, concerned. *3* mercenary, selfish. *4 m.-f.* person or party concerned.

**interesante** *adj.* interesting.

**interesar** *tr.* to interest. *2* to concern. *3* MED. to affect [an organ, etc.]. *4* ~ *en*, to interest [invest with a share; cause to share]. *5 intr.* to be interesting. *6* to be advantageous, or necessary. *7* to have a pecuniary share [in]. *8 ref. interesarse en* or *por*, to be interested.

**interfecto, -ta** *m.-f.* LAW murdered person, victim.

**interferencia** *f.* PHYS. interference.

**interferir** *intr.-ref.* PHYS. interfere.

**ínterin** *adv.-m.* interim, meanwhile.

**interinidad** *f.* provisionality, temporariness. *2* duration of temporary job or office.

**interino, -na** *adj.* provisional, temporary. *2* acting, holding a temporary job or office. *3 m.-f.* holder of a temporary job or office.

**interior** *adj.* interior, internal, inner, inside, inward; home, domestic [not foreign]: *comercio* ~, domestic trade. *2 m.* interior, inside, inner part; inland. *3* mind, soul.

**interioridad** *f.* interiority, inwardness.

**interioridades** *f. pl.* private matters.

**interjección** *f.* GRAM. interjection.

**interlínea** *f.* PRINT. lead, space line.

**interlineación** *f.* interlineation.

**interlinear** *tr.* to interline, interlineate.

**interlocución** *f.* interlocution, dialogue.

**interlocutor, -ra** *m.-f.* interlocutor.

**interludio** *m.* MUS. interlude.

**intermediar** *intr.* to be in the middle. *2* to intermediate, mediate.

**intermediario, -ria** *adj.* intermediary. *2 m.-f.* intermediary, mediator. *3* COM. middleman.

**intermedio, -dia** *adj.* intermediate, intervening. *2 m.* interval, interim. *3* THEAT. interlude.

**interminable** *adj.* interminable, endless.

**intermisión** *f.* intermission.

**intermitencia** *f.* intermittence.

**intermitente** *adj.* intermittent.

**intermitir** *tr.* to intermit, discontinue.

**internación** *f.* internment.

**internacional** *adj.* international.

**internacionalismo** *m.* internationalism.

**internacionalizar** *tr.* to internationalize.

**internado** *m.* boarding school; boarding school system. *2* state of being a boarding student.

**internar** *tr.* to lead or send inland. *2* to intern. *3 ref.* to go into the interior of. *4* to go deeply [into a subject].

**internista** *m.-f.* MED. internist.

**interno, -na** *adj.* internal, interior, inside. *2* boarding [student]. *3 m.-f.* boarding student. *4 m.* intern [in a hospital].

**internuncio** *m.* interlocutor. *2* internuncio.

**interparlamentario, -ria** *adj.* interparliamentary.

**interpelación** *f.* act of addressing oneself to another [asking for aid or explanations, etc.]. *2* interpellation [in parliamentary practice].

**interpelar** *tr.* to address oneself to [another] asking for aid or explanations. *2* to interpellate.

**interplanetario, -ria** *adj.* interplanetary.

**interpolación** *f.* interpolation.

**interpolar** *tr.* to interpolate.

**interponer** *tr.* to interpose, place between. *2* to set as a mediator. *3* LAW to present [an appeal]. *4 ref.* to interpose [be or come between]. *5* to interpose, intervene, mediate. ¶ CONJUG. like *poner*.

**interposición** *f.* interposition, interposal.

**interpretación** *f.* interpretation.

**interpretar** *tr.* to interpret.

**intérprete** *m.-f.* interpreter.

**interpuesto, -ta** *adj.* interposed, intervening.

**interregno** *m.* interregnum.

**interrogación** *f.* interrogation, question. *2* GRAM. interrogation mark, question mark.

**interrogante** *adj.* interrogating, questioning. *2 m.* GRAM. *interrogante* or *punto* ~, interrogation mark; question mark.

**interrogar** *tr.* to interrogate, question.

**interrogativo, -va** *adj.* interrogative.

**interrogatorio** *m.* interrogatory, questioning.

**interrumpido, -da** *adj.* interrupted, broken, discontinued.

**interrumpir** *tr.* to interrupt. *2* to obstruct, hinder. *3 ref.* to be interrupted, pause, break off.

**interrupción** *f.* interruption.

**interruptor, -ra** *adj.* interrupting. *2 m.-f.* interrupter. *3 m.* ELECT. switch, circuitbreaker.
**intersecarse** *ref.* GEOM. [of two lines, planes, etc.] to intersect.
**intersección** *f.* intersection.
**intersticio** *m.* interstice. *2* interval.
**intervalo** *m.* interval [intervening time or space]; break, gap. *2* MUS. interval.
**intervención** *f.* intervention, taking part; interference. *2* mediation. *3* supervision, control. *4* auditing [of accounts]. *5* SURG., INTERN., LAW intervention.
**intervencionismo** *m.* interventionism.
**intervenir** *intr.* to take part. *2* to intervene. *3* to intercede, plead [for another]. *4* to mediate [between parties]. *5 tr.* to audit [accounts]. *6* SURG. to operate upon [someone].
**interventor, -ra** *m.-f.* supervisor. *2* auditor [of accounts]. *3* election supervisor.
**interviev** *m.* Angl. journalistic interview.
**intervievar** *tr.* to interview [for journalistic purposes].
**intestado, -da** *adj.* intestate. *2 m.* intestate.
**intestinal** *adj.* intestinal.
**intestino, -na** *adj.* internal. *2* intestine, domestic, civil. *3 m.* ANAT. intestine. *4 pl.* ANAT. intestines.
**intimación** *f.* notification; order, calling upon.
**intimar** *tr.* to intimate, notify authoritatively. *2* to order, call upon. *3 intr.-ref.* to become intimate.
**intimidación** *f.* intimidation.
**intimidad** *f.* intimacy, closeness. *2* inwardness.
**intimidar** *tr.* to intimidate, daunt. *2 ref.* to become intimidated, daunted.
**íntimo, -ma** *adj.* intimate. *2* internal, innermost. *3* private, personal. *4* close [contact, relation].
**intitular** *tr.* to entitle [give the title of]. *2 ref.* to be called; to call oneself.
**intolerable** *adj.* intolerable, unbearable.
**intolerancia** *adj.* intolerance.
**intolerante** *adj.* intolerant.
**intonso, -sa** *adj.* poet. unshorn. *2* fig. ignorant. *3* [of a book] with untrimmed leaves.
**intoxicación** *f.* MED. intoxication, poisoning.
**intoxicar** *tr.* to poison. *2 ref.* MED. to suffer intoxication.
**intradós** *m.* ARCH. intrados.
**intraducible** *adj.* untranslatable.
**intramuros** *adv.* within the walls [of a town].
**intranquilidad** *f.* unrest, restlessness, uneasiness.
**intranquilizar** *tr.* to worry, disquiet, make uneasy. *2 ref.* to worry, to become uneasy.
**intranquilo, -la** *adj.* restless, worried, uneasy.
**intransferible** *adj.* untransferable.
**intransigencia** *f.* intransigence, intransigency, uncompromisingness.
**intransigente** *adj.* intransigent, uncompromising.
**intransitable** *adj.* impassable [road, etc.].
**intransitivo, -va** *adj.-n.* GRAM. intransitive.
**intratable** *adj.* intractable. *2* cantankerous, crossgrained, unsociable.
**intravenoso, -sa** *adj.* intravenous.
**intrepidez** *f.* intrepidity, courage, bravery.
**intrépido, -da** *adj.* intrepid.
**intriga** *f.* intrigue. *2* plot [of a play]; imbroglio.
**intrigante** *adj.* intriguing. *2 m.-f.* intriguer.
**intrigar** *intr.* to intrigue, plot, scheme. *2 tr.* to intrigue [arouse the interest or curiosity of].
**intrincación** *f.* intricacy, intricateness.
**intrincado, -da** *adj.* intricate.
**intrincar** *tr.* to complicate, entangle, confuse.

**intríngulis,** *pl.* **-lis** *m.* hidden reason or motive, enigma, mystery.
**intrínseco, -ca** *adj.* intrinsic, intrinsical.
**introducción** *f.* introduction [in every sense except introduction of a bill; of a person]. *2* preliminary step, preparation. *3* exordium.
**introducir** *tr.* to introduce [in every sense except introducing a person to another or a bill, etc., before Parliament]. *2* to insert. *3* to usher in. *4 ref.* to introduce oneself or itself; to enter, gain access [to]; worm oneself [into]. ¶ CONJUG. like *conducir.*
**introductor, -ra** *adj.* introducing. *2 m.-f.* introducer, introductor. *3* usherer.
**introito** *m.* introduction, beginning. *2* ECCL. introito.
**intromisión** *f.* interference, meddling.
**introspección** *f.* introspection.
**introspectivo, -va** *adj.* introspective.
**introversión** *f.* introversion.
**introverso, -sa** *adj.-n.* introverted.
**intrusarse** *ref.* to usurp [an office, authority, etc.].
**intrusión** *f.* intrusion [in office, profession, etc.].
**intrusismo** *m.* practice of a profession without authority.
**intruso, -sa** *adj.* intruding, usurping. *2 m.-f.* intruder, usurper. *3* unauthorized practitioner.
**intuición** *f.* intuition.
**intuir** *tr.* to intuit. ¶ CONJUG. like *huir.*
**intuitivo, -va** *adj.* intuitive.
**intumescencia** *f.* intumescence, swelling.
**inulto, -ta** *adj.* poet. unavenged.
**inundación** *f.* inundation, flood, deluge.
**inundar** *tr.* to inundate, flood, overflow, deluge. *2 ref.* to be flooded.
**inurbano, -na** *adj.* inurbane, uncivil, discourteous.
**inusitado, -da** *adj.* unusual.
**inútil** *adj.* useless. *2 adj.-n.* good for nothing.
**inutilidad** *f.* uselessness, inutility. *2* useless person.
**inutilizar** *tr.* to render useless; to disable; to spoil. *2 ref.* to become useless; to be disabled.
**inútilmente** *adv.* uselessly, to no purpose, in vain.
**invadeable** *adj.* unfordable.
**invadir** *tr.* to invade. *2* to encroach upon.
**invaginación** *f.* invagination.
**invaginar** *tr.* to invaginate.
**invalidación** *f.* invalidation.
**invalidar** *tr.* to invalidate, void, nullify.
**invalidez** *f.* invalidity.
**inválido, -da** *adj.* invalid, void, null. *2* invalid, disabled. *3 m.* invalid [pers. disabled for active service].
**invariable** *adj.* invariable, constant.
**invasión** *f.* invasion.
**invasor, -ra** *adj.* invading. *2 m.-f.* invader.
**invectiva** *f.* invective.
**invencible** *adj.* invincible, unconquerable.
**invención** *f.* invention. *2 Invención de la Santa Cruz,* Invention of the Cross.
**invendible** *adj.* unsalable.
**inventar** *tr.* to invent.
**inventariar** *tr.* to inventory.
**inventario** *m.* inventory: *hacer ~,* to take inventory.
**inventiva** *f.* faculty of invention, inventiveness.
**invento** *m.* invention.
**inventor, -ra** *adj.* inventing, inventive. *2 m.-f.* inventor.
**inverecundia** *f.* shamelessness, impudence.
**inverecundo, -da** *adj.* shameless, impudent.

**invernáculo** *m.* greenhouse, hothouse, conservatory.

**invernada** *f.* winter season.

**invernadero** *m.* winter quarters. *2* winter pastureland. *3* INVERNÁCULO.

**invernal** *adj.* hibernal, hiemal, wintry, winter.

**invernar** *intr.* to hibernate, winter. *2* to be winter. ¶ CONJUG. like *acertar*.

**invernizo, -za** *adj.* wintry, hiemal.

**inverosímil** *adj.* not verisimilar, unlikely.

**inverosimilitud** *f.* inverisimilitude, unlikeliness.

**inversión** *f.* inversion. *2* COM. investment.

**inverso, -sa** *adj.* inverse, inverted, opposite. *2 a*, or *por, la inversa*, on the contrary.

**inversor, -ra** *adj.* inversing; reversing. *2* COM. investing. *3 m.* reversing mecanism. *4* ELECT. reverser. *5* COM. investor.

**invertebrado, -da** *adj.-n.* invertebrate.

**invertido, -da** *adj.* inverted, reversed. *2* COM. invested [money or capital]. *3 adj.-m.* invert.

**invertir** *tr.* to invert. *2* to reverse. *3* to spend [time]. *4* COM. to invest [money or capital]. ¶ CONJUG. like *hervir*.

**investidura** *f.* investiture.

**investigación** *f.* investigation, research, enquiry.

**investigador, -ra** *adj.* investigating. *2 m.-f.* investigator, researcher.

**investigar** *tr.* to investigate, inquire into.

**investir** *tr.* to invest [endow, establish legally]: ~ *de*, or *con*, to invest with. ¶ CONJUG. like *servir*.

**inveterado, -da** *adj.* inveterate; confirmed.

**inveterarse** *ref.* to become inveterate.

**invicto, -ta** *adj.* unconquered, unvanquished.

**invierno** *m.* winter.

**inviolabilidad** *f.* inviolability.

**inviolable** *adj.* inviolable.

**invisibilidad** *f.* invisibility.

**invisible** *adj.* invisible.

**invitación** *f.* invitation.

**invitado, -da** *m.-f.* person invited, guest.

**invitar** *tr.* to invite.

**invocación** *f.* invocation, invoking.

**invocar** *tr.* to invoke.

**involución** *f.* BIOL. involution.

**involucrar** *tr.* to introduce irrelevantly.

**involucro** *m.* BOT. involucre.

**involuntario, -ria** *adj.* involuntary.

**involuto, -ta** *adj.* involute. *2 f.* GEOM. involute.

**invulnerable** *adj.* invulnerable.

**inyección** *f.* injection.

**inyectable** *adj.* injectable. *2 m.* MED. ampoule.

**inyectado, -da** *adj.* injected. *2 ojos inyectados en sangre*, bloodshot eyes.

**inyectar** *tr.* to inject.

**inyector** *m.* MECH. injector.

**ión** *m.* CHEM., PHYS. ion.

**ionización** *f.* ionization.

**iota** *f.* iota [Greek letter].

**ipsilon** *f.* upsilon [Greek letter].

**ipso facto** *adv.* at once, right away.

**ir** *intr.* to go, proceed, make one's way, move, walk, ride, travel: ~ *a casa*, to go home; ~ *de prisa*, to go, move or walk fast; ~ *a pie*, to go on foot; ~ *a caballo*, to ride, go on horseback; ~ *en tren*, to travel by train. *2* to go, go about, be: ~ *descalzo*, to be barefooted; ~ *sin afeitar*, to go unshaved. *3* to go, happen, be, be doing, fare: *las cosas van despacio*, things go slowly; ~ *bien*, to be all right, to be doing well; ~ *de mal en peor*, to grow worse and worse; *¿cómo le va?, ¿cómo vamos?*, how are you? *4* to fit, suit, become: *esto*

*no me va*, that doesn't suit me. *5* to go, lead: *esta carretera va a Madrid*, this road goes or leads to Madrid. *6* to go, extend [from point to point]. *7* to be at stake, to depend on; to affect, concern: *le va la vida en ello*, his life depends on that; *nada te va en ello*, it doesn't concern you in the least. *8* to be, elapse: *de mayo a julio van dos meses*, it is two months from May to July. *9* ARITH. to leave: *de 2 a 5 van 3*, 2 from 5 leaves 3. *10* to bet, lay, wager: *¿cuánto va...?*, what do you bet...? *11* to act: ~ *a una*, to act in unison; ~ *de buena fe*, to act sincerely. *12* to go, frequent, attend: ~ *a la escuela*, to go to school. *13* followed by a gerund, it constitutes the progressive form: *va oscureciendo*, it is getting dark. *14* ~ *a* [followed by an inf.], to go to; to be going to, to intend to; to go and: *ir a esperar a uno*, to go to meet someone; *iba a decir*, I was going to say; *vaya a verlo*, go and see it. *15* ~ *de*, to be clad in; to perform the action implied by the following noun: ~ *de uniforme*, to be in uniform; ~ *de caza*, to go hunting. *16* ~ *para largo*, to take time. *17* ~ *por*, to go for, to go to fetch. *18 ¿quién va?*, who is there?, who goes there? *19 ¡vamos!*, let's go, come on!; come!, why!, well! *20 vamos a ver*, let's see. *21 ¡vaya una idea!*, what an idea! *22 vaya usted con Dios*, farewell, God be with you. *23 vaya* or *vete a paseo*, go away, go and chop chips.

*24 ref.* to be going, go away, depart. *25* to wear out. *26* [followed by a gerund] to be, to be gradually: *se va acercando*, it is getting near. *27 irse abajo*, to fall down, topple down. *28* NAUT. *irse a pique*, to sink, founder. *29 írsele a uno la cabeza*, to become dizzy. *30 írsele a uno la mano*, to overdo oneself; to put too much [salt, etc.]: *írsele a uno los pies*, to slip. *31 irse todo en humo*, to go up in smoke.

¶ IRREG. CONJUG.: INDIC. Pres.: *voy, vas, va; vamos, vais, van*. | Imperf.: *iba, ibas, iba; íbamos, ibais, iban*. | Pret. *fui, fuiste, fue; fuimos, fuisteis, fueron*. | Fut.: *iré, irás*, etc. | COND.: *iría, irías*, etc. | SUBJ. Pres.: *vaya, vayas, vaya; vayamos, vayáis, vayan*. | Imperf.: *fuera, fueras*, etc., or *fuese, fueses*, etc. | Fut.: *fuere, fueres*, etc. | IMPER.: *ve, vaya; vayamos, id, vayan*. | PAST. P.: *ido*. | GER.: *yendo*.

**ira** *f.* ire, anger, wrath.

**iracundia** *f.* irascibility. *2* anger, wrath.

**iracundo, -da** *adj.* irascible. *2* angry, wrathful.

**Irak (el)** *m. pr. n.* GEOG. Irak, Iraq.

**Irán (el)** *m. pr. n.* GEOG. Iran.

**iranio, nia** *adj.-n.* Iranian.

**irascible** *adj.* irascible, irritable.

**Irene** *f. pr. n.* Irene.

**irgo, irga, irguió, irguiera**, etc. *irr.* V. ERGUIR.

**iridáceo, -a** *adj.* BOT. iridaceous.

**iridio** *m.* CHEM. iridium.

**iridiscencia** *f.* iridescence.

**iridiscente** *adj.* iridescent.

**iris** *m.* iris, rainbow: ~ *de paz*, fig. peacemaker. *2* ANAT., OPT. iris. *3* MINER. noble opal.

**irisación** *f.* iridiscence.

**irisado, -da** *adj.* irised, rainbow-hued.

**Irlanda** *f. pr. n.* GEOG. Ireland.

**irlandés, -sa** *adj.* Irish. *2 m.* Irishman. *3* Irish [language]. *4 f.* Irishwoman. *5 m. pl. los irlandeses*, the Irish.

**ironía** *f.* irony.

**irónico, -ca** *adj.* ironic, ironical.

**irracional** *adj.* irrational [not endowed with rea-

son]. *2* irrational, absurd. *3* MATH. irrational. *4 m.* irrational being.
**irracionalidad** *f.* irrationality.
**irradiación** *f.* irradiation, radiation.
**irradiar** *tr.* to irradiate, radiate [light, heat, etc.].
**irrazonable** *adj.* unreasonable.
**irreal** *adj.* unreal.
**irrealidad** *f.* unreality.
**irrealizable** *adj.* unrealizable, impracticable.
**irrebatible** *adj.* irrefutable.
**irreconciliable** *adj.* irreconcilable.
**irrecuperable** *adj.* irrecoverable, irretrievable.
**irrecusable** *adj.* irrecusable.
**irredentismo** *m.* irredentism.
**irredento, -ta** *adj.* unredeemed [region].
**irreductible** *adj.* irreducible. *2* stubborn, unyielding.
**irreemplazable** *adj.* irreplaceable.
**irreflexión** *f.* rashness, thoughtlessness.
**irreflexivo, -va** *adj.* unreflecting, inconsiderate, rash, thoughtless.
**irrefragable** *adj.* irrefragable.
**irrefrenable** *adj.* irrepressible, uncontrollable.
**irrefutable** *adj.* irrefutable.
**irregular** *adj.* irregular.
**irregularidad** *f.* irregularity.
**irreligión** *f.* irreligion.
**irreligioso, -sa** *adj.* irreligious.
**irremediable** *adj.* irremediable, hopeless.
**irremisible** *adj.* irremissible.
**irrenunciable** *adj.* unrenounceable.
**irreparable** *adj.* irreparable, irretrievable.
**irreprensible** *adj.* irreprehensible, blameless.
**irreprimible** *adj.* irrepressible.
**irreprochable** *adj.* irreproachable.
**irresistible** *adj.* irresistible.
**irresoluble** *adj.* unsolvable.
**irresolución** *f.* irresolution, indecision.
**irresoluto, -ta** *adj.* irresolute, wavering.
**irrespetuoso, -sa** *adj.* disrespectful.
**irrespirable** *adj.* unbreathable, suffocating.
**irresponsable** *adj.* irresponsible.
**irreverencia** *f.* irreverence.
**irreverente** *adj.* irreverent.
**irreversible** *adj.* LAW, MACH., BIOL. irreversible.
**irrevocable** *adj.* irrevocable.
**irrigación** *f.* MED. irrigation.
**irrigar** *tr.* MED. to irrigate.
**irrisible** *adj.* laughable, ridicule.
**irrisión** *f.* derision, ridicule. *2* laughing stock.
**irrisorio, -ria** *adj.* derisory, ridiculous. *2* insignificant, ridiculously small.
**irritabilidad** *f.* irritability.
**irritable** *adj.* irritable.
**irritación** *f.* irritation.
**irritante** *adj.* irritating, irritant. *2* LAW irritant. *3 m.* MED., PHYSIOL. irritant.
**irritar** *tr.* to irritate, anger, annoy. *2* MED., PHYSIOL., LAW to irritate. *4 ref.* to become irritated.
**irrogar** *tr.* to cause, occasion [harm, damage].
**irrompible** *adj.* unbreakable.
**irrumpir** *intr.* to make an irruption.
**irrupción** *f.* irruption, bursting in, invasion.
**irubú** *m.* ORN. (Am.) turkey buzzard.
**Isaac** *m. pr. n.* Isaac.
**Isabel** *f. pr. n.* Isabela, Elizabeth.
**isabelino, -na** *adj.* Isabelline; Elizabethan. *2 adj.*

*-n.* HIST. defender of Isabella II against the Carlists.
**Isaías** *m. pr. n.* BIBL. Isaiah.
**Isidoro** *m. pr. n.* Isidore.
**Isidro** *m. pr. n.* Isidore.
**isla** *f.* GEOG. isle, island: *islas Baleares*, Balearic Islands; *islas Británicas*, British Isles; *islas Canarias*, Canary Islands; *islas Filipinas*, Philipine Islands. *2* block [of houses]. *3* isolated grove or woodland.
**islam** *m.* Islam.
**islámico, -ca** *adj.* Islamic.
**islamismo** *m.* Islamism.
**islandés, -sa** *adj.* Icelandic. *2 m.-f.* Icelander. *3 m.* Icelandic [language].
**Islandia** *f. pr. n.* GEOG. Iceland.
**isleño, -ña** *adj.* insular. *2 m.-f.* islander.
**isleta** *f. dim.* small island, islet.
**islote** *m.* small barren island.
**Ismael** *m. pr. n.* Ishmael.
**ismaelita** *adj.* Ishmaelitic. *2 m.-f.* Ishmaelite.
**isobara** *f.* METEOR. isobar.
**isobárico, -ca** *adj.* METEOR. isobaric: *línea isobárica*, isobar.
**isoclino, -na** *adj.* isoclinal, isoclinic.
**isocromático, -ca** *adj.* OPT. isochromatic.
**isócrono** *adj.* isochronal, isochrone, isochronic.
**isodáctilo, -la** *adj.* ZOOL. isodactylous.
**isógono, -na** *adj.* CRIST. isogonic.
**isómero, -ra** *adj.* CHEM., BIOL. isomeric, isomerous.
**isométrico, -ca** *adj.* isometric.
**isomorfo, -fa** *adj.* MINER. isomorphic, isomorphous.
**isópodo, -da** *adj.-n.* ZOOL. isopod, isopodan.
**isósceles** *adj.* GEOM. isosceles.
**isotermo, -ma** *adj.* PHYS., METEOR. isothermic. *2 f.* METEOR. isotherm [line].
**isótopo** *m.* PHYS., CHEM. isotope.
**isótropo, -pa** *adj.* isotropic.
**isquiático, -ca** *adj.* ANAT. ischiatic.
**isquión** *m.* ANAT. ischium.
**Israel** *m. pr. n.* Israel.
**israelí** *adj.-n.* Israeli.
**israelita** *adj.* Israelitish. *2 m.-f.* Israelite.
**israelítico, -ca** *adj.* Israelitish.
**istmeño, -ña** *adj.* isthmian [of an isthmus].
**ístmico, -ca** *adj.* isthmian, isthmic.
**istmo** *m.* GEOG., ANAT. isthmus.
**Itaca** *f. pr. n.* HIST., GEOG. Ithaca.
**Italia** *f. pr. n.* GEOG. Italy.
**italianismo** *m.* Italianism.
**italiano, -na** *adj.-n.* Italian.
**itálico, -ca** *adj.* Italic. *2* PRINT. italic.
**italo, -la** *adj.-n.* poet. Italian.
**item** *m.* clause, article [of a deed, etc.]. *2 adv. item* or *item más*, also, likewise [in deeds, etc.].
**iteración** *f.* iteration.
**iterar** *tr.* to iterate.
**iterativo, -va** *adj.* iterative.
**iterbio** *m.* CHEM. ytterbium.
**itinerario, -ria** *adj.-m.* itinerary.
**itrio** *m.* chem. yttrium.
**izar** *tr.* NAUT. to hoist, haul up.
**izquierda** *f.* left hand. *2* left, left-hand side; *a la ~*, to the left, on the left. *3* POL. Left, Left wing.
**izquierdista** *adj.-n.* POL. leftist.
**izquierdo, -da** *adj.* left, left-hand. *2* left-handed [person]. *3* crooked.

# J

**J, j** *f*. J, j, eleventh letter of the Spanish alphabet.
**jabalcón** *m*. strut, brace.
**jabalí** *m*. ZOOL. wild boar.
**jabalina** *f*. javelin, boarspear. *2* SPORT. javelin. *3* ZOOL. wild sow.
**jabardillo** *m*. noisy swarm.
**jabato** *m*. young wild boar.
**jábega** *f*. sweep net [for fishing]. *2* fishing smack.
**jabeque** *m*. NAUT. xebec. *2* coll. knife wound in the face.
**jabillo** *m*. BOT. sandbox tree.
**jabladera** *f*. croze, crozer [cooper's tool].
**jable** *m*. croze [groove in staves].
**jabón** *m*. soap: ~ *de afeitar*, shaving soap; ~ *de olor* or *de tocador*, toilet soap; ~ *de sastre*, soapstone, French chalk. *2* fig. flattery: *dar* ~, to softsoap. *3* fig. severe reprimand: *dar un* ~ *a*, to haul over the coals.
**jabonado, -da** *adj*. soaped. *2 m*. soaping.
**jabonadura** *f*. soaping. *2* fig. severe reprimand. *3 pl*. soapsuds, lather.
**jabonar** *tr*. to soap; to lather. *2* fig. to reprimand severely.
**jaboncillo** *m*. cake of toilet soap. *2* BOT. soapberry tree. *3* ~ *de sastre*, JABÓN DE SASTRE.
**jabonera** *f*. soap dish. *2* BOT. soapwort.
**jabonería** *f*. soap factory. *2* soap shop.
**jabonero, -ra** *adj*. [pertaining to] soap. *2* yellowish, dirty white [bull]. *2 m*. soapmaker. *4* soap dealer.
**jaboneta** *f*., **jabonete** *m*. cake of toilet soap.
**jabonoso, -sa** *adj*. soapy.
**jaca** *f*. nag, cob, bidet, jennet.
**jácara** *f*. merry ballad. *2* a kind of dance. *3* group of merry singers walking the streets at night. *4* annoyance. *5* story, tale; fable, lie.
**jacarandá** *f*. BOT. jacaranda.
**jacarandoso, -sa** *adj*. jaunty, lively, gay.
**jacarero** *adj*. gay, merry, sportful [person].
**jácena** *f*. ARCH. girder.
**jacerina** *f*. coat of mail.
**jacinto** *m*., BOT., MINER. hyacinth: ~ *occidental*, topaz; ~ *oriental*, ruby.
**Jacinto, -ta** *m.-f. pr. n*. Hyacinth.
**jaco** *m*. jade, sorry nag. *2* short coat of mail.
**Jacob** *m. pr. n*. BIBL. Jacob.
**jacobino, -na** *adj*. Jacobin, Jacobinic. *2 m*. HIST., POL. Jacobin.

**jacobita** *adj*. Jacobite, Jacobitic. *2 m.-f*. Jacobite.
**Jacobo** *m. pr. n*. James.
**jactancia** *f*. boasting, bragging, vaunt.
**jactancioso, -sa** *adj*. boastful, bragging, vaunting. *2 m.-f*. boaster, braggard, vaunter.
**jactarse** *ref*. to boast, brag, vaunt: ~ *de*, to boast of.
**jaculatoria** *f*. ejaculation [short prayer].
**jade** *m*. MINER. jade.
**jadeante** *adj*. panting, out of breath.
**jadear** *intr*. to pant, heave.
**jadeo** *m*. panting.
**jaenés, -sa** *adj.-n*. of Jaén.
**jaez**, *pl*. **jaeces** *m*. ornament for horses. *2* kind, nature [of things]. *3 pl*. trappings [for horses].
**Jafet** *m. pr. n*. BIBL. Japheth.
**jaguar** *m*. ZOOL. jaguar.
**jaguarzo** *m*. BOT. rockrose.
**jaharrar** *tr*. MASON. to plaster.
**Jaime** *m. pr. n*. James, Jim.
**jaique** *m*. moorish hooded cloak.
**¡ja, ja, ja!** *interj*. ha, ha!; ho, ho!
**jalapa** *f*. BOT. jalap, jalapa.
**jalar** *tr*. to haul, to pull. *2* to attract.
**jalbegar** *tr*. ENJALBEGAR.
**jalbegue** *m*. whitewash. *2* whitewashing.
**jaldado, -da; jalde; jaldo, -da** *adj*. bright yellow.
**jalea** *f*. jelly [of fruit juices].
**jalear** *tr*. to encourrage [hounds] with shouts. *2* to animate [dancers, singers, etc.] by clapping hands or cheering.
**jaleo** *m*. clapping hands, cheering, etc., to encourage dancers, singers, etc. *2* Andalusian dance and its tune. *3* merry noise. *4* row, disturbance.
**jaletina** *f*. gelatine. *2* fine jelly.
**Jalifa** *m*. Moroccan prince governing Spanish Morocco.
**jalifato** *m*. dignity of the *Jalifa*. *2* territory under the *Jalifa*.
**jalón** *m*. flagpole, range pole, stake.
**jalonar** *tr*. to mark or stake out.
**jaloque** *m*. southeast wind.
**Jamaica** *f. pr. n*. GEOG. Jamaica.
**jamar** *tr*. coll. to eat.
**jamás** *adv*. never: *nunca* ~, never, nevermore. *2* ever: *el mejor libro que* ~ *se haya escrito*, the best book ever writen.
**jamba** *f*. ARCH. jamb.

jambaje *m.* ARCH. door frame, window frame.
jamelgo *m.* jade [horse].
jamón *m.* ham [thigh of hog salted and dried].
jamona *adj.-f.* coll. buxom middle-aged woman.
jándalo, -la *adj.-n.* coll. Andalusian.
jangada *f.* nonsense, silly sally. *2* dirty trick. *3* NAUT. raft, float.
Jano *m. pr. n.* MYTH. Janus.
jansenismo *m.* Jansenism.
Japón (el) *m. pr. n.* GEOG. Japan.
japón, -na; japonés, -sa *adj.-n.* Japanese. *2 m.* Japanese [language].
jaque *m.* CHESS check: ~ *mate,* checkmate; *dar ~ mate,* to checkmate; *tener en ~,* fig. to hold a threat over the head of. *2* coll. swaggerer, bully.
jaquear *tr.* CHESS to check. *2* MIL. to harass.
jaqueca *f.* migraine, megrim, headache.
jaqueado, -da *adj.* HER. checkered.
jaquetilla *f.* short jacket.
jaquetón *m.* VALENTÓN.
jáquima *f.* rope headstall and halter.
jara *f.* BOT. rockrose.
jarabe *m.* syrup. *2* sweet drink. *3 ~ de pico,* empty talk, idle promises, lip service.
jaral *m.* place full of rockrose; bramble, brake.
jaramago *m.* BOT. hedge mustard.
jarana *f.* noisy merrymaking of low people. *2* coll. row, rioting, uproar. *3* coll. trick, deception.
jaranear *intr.* to go merrymaking. *2* to engage in rows, to riot.
jaranero, -ra *adj.* merry, merrymaking, funloving.
jarcia *f.* NAUT. rigging, cordage [of a ship]. *2* fishing tackle. *4* jumble, mess.
jardín *m.* [flower] garden, gardens: ~ *botánico,* botanical gardens; ~ *zoológico,* zoological gardens. *2* NAUT. privy, latrine. *3* EDUC. ~ *de la infancia,* kindergarten.
jardinera *f.* woman gardener. *2* jardinière. *4* basket carriage. *5* open tramcar for summertime.
jardinería *f.* flower gardening, landscape gardening.
jardinero *m.* gardener [tender of a flower garden].
jareta *f.* SEW. casing. *2* NAUT. cat-harping.
jarra *f.* jar, pitcher. *2 de jarras, en jarras,* with arms akimbo.
jarrazo *m. augm.* large jar. *2* blow with a jar.
jarrete *m.* ANAT. ham, back of the knee. *2* upper part of the calf of the leg. *3* hock, gambrel.
jarretera *f.* garter. *2* Order of the Garter.
jarro *m.* ewer, jug, pitcher, pot: *echar un ~ de agua fría a,* to pour cold water on.
jarrón *m.* [ornamental or flower] vase. *2* ARCH. urn.
jaspe *m.* MINER. jasper. *2* veined marble.
jaspeado, -da *adj.* marbled, jaspery. *2 m.* marbling.
jaspear *tr.* to marble, mottle, vein.
jato, -ta *m.-f.* calf [young of cow].
Jauja *f. pr. n.* Cockaigne.
jaula *f.* cage [for birds, beasts, etc]. *2* crate. *3* MIN. cage.
jauría *f.* pack of hounds.
javanés, -sa *adj.-n.* Javanese.
Javier *m. pr. n.* Xavier.
jayán, -na *m.-f.* burly, strong person.
jazmín *m.* BOT. jasmine.
jebe *m.* alum, rock alum. *2* (Am.) India rubber.
jedive *m.* khedive.
jefa *f.* female chief or head.
jefatura *f.* headship, leadership. *2* headquarters: ~ *de policía,* police headquarters.
jefe *m.* chief, head, leader, boss, master: ~ *de estación,* RLY. stationmaster; ~ *del Estado,* head of the State, *chief executive; ~ *de un partido,* leader of a party; *en ~,* in chief. *2* MIL. field officer: ~ *de día,* day officer. *3* HER. chief, chef. *4 adj.* chief, in chief.
Jehová *m. pr. n.* Jehovah.
¡je, je, je! *interj.* ha, ha!
jeme *m.* distance from tip of the thumb to tip of the forefinger when extended. *2* coll. face [of woman].
jengibre *m.* ginger [plant & spice].
jenízaro, -ra *adj.* mixed, hybrid. *2 m.* Janizary.
Jenofonte *m. pr. n.* Xenophon.
jeque *m.* sheik [Arab chief].
jerarca *m.* hierarch.
jerarquía *f.* hierarchy.
jerárquico, -ca *adj.* hierarchic(al.
jerbo *m.* ZOOL. jerboa.
jeremiada *f.* jeremiad.
Jeremías *m. pr. n.* Jeremiah.
jeremías *m.-f.* coll. constant complainer.
jerez *m.* sherry wine.
jerezano, -na *adj.-n.* of Jerez.
jerga *f.* coarse woollen cloth. *2* straw mattress. *3* jargon [of a trade or group]. *4* jargon, gibberish.
jergón *m.* straw mattress.
jerguilla *f.* silk or worsted serge.
jerife *m.* sherif, shereef.
jerigonza *f.* JERGA 3 & 4.
jeringa *f.* syringe: ~ *hipodérmica,* hypodermic syringe. *2* enema [apparatus].
jeringar *tr.* to syringe. *2* to give an enema to. *3* coll. to annoy, bother. *4 ref.* coll. to support an annoyance.
jeringazo *m.* syringing. *2* injection, enema, clyster.
jeringuilla *f.* small syringe. *2* hypodermic syringe. *3* BOT. syringa, mock orange.
jeroglífico, -ca *adj.* hieroglyphic, hieroglyphical. *2 m.* hieroglyphic. *3* rebus.
Jerónimo *m. pr. n.* Jerome.
jerónimo, -ma *adj.-m.* Hieronymite.
jerosolimitano, -na *adj.-n.* Hierosolymitan.
jersey *m.* jersey, sweater [garment].
Jerusalén *f. pr. n.* GEOG. Jerusalem.
Jesucristo *m. pr. n.* Jesus Christ.
jesuita *adj.-m.* Jesuit.
jesuítico, -ca *adj.* Jesuitic, Jesuitical.
Jesús *m. pr. n.* Jesus: *el niño ~,* the infant Jesus; *en un decir ~,* in an instant; *¡Jesús!, ¡Jesús, María y José!,* good gracious!, my gracious. ¶ The name of Jesus is employed in Spain with no necessary implication of profanity.
Jesusa *f. pr. n.* Jesus.
jeta *f.* thick lips; protruding mouth. *2* hog's snout. *3* coll. phiz, mug, face.
jetón, -na, jetudo, -da *adj.* thick-lipped.
jíbaro, -ra *adj.-n.* (Am.) peasant.
jibia *f.* ZOOL. cuttlefish. *2* cuttlebone.
jibión *m.* cuttlebone.
Jibraltar *m. pr. n.* GEOG. Gibraltar.
jibraltareño, -ña *adj.* & of Gibraltar.
jícara *f.* chocolate cup. *2* (Am.) small calabash cup.
jifero, -ra *adj.* [pertaining to the] slaughterhouse. *2* coll. dirty, filthy, vile. *3 m.* slaughtering knife. *4* butcher [slaughterer of animals].
jiga *f.* GIGA.
jigote *m.* GIGOTE.
¡ji, ji, ji! *interj.* he, he, he!

**jilguero** *m.* ORN. goldfinch, linnet.
**jilote** *m.* (Am.) ear of green Indian corn.
**jindama** *f.* coll. fear.
**jineta** *f.* ZOOL. genet. *2 montar a la* ~, to ride with stirrups high and legs bent. *3 tener los cascos a la* ~, to be harebrained.
**jinete** *m.* horseman, rider. *2* obs. cavalryman. *3* spirited pure-bred horse.
**jingoísmo** *m.* jingoism.
**jínjol** *m.* AZUFAIFA.
**jinjolero** *m.* AZUFAIFO.
**jipio** *m.* HIPIDO.
**jipijapa** *f.* fine strip of jipijapa straw. *2 m.* jipijapa, Panama hat.
**jira** *f.* strip of cloth. *2* picnic, outing. *3* excursion, tour.
**jirafa** *f.* ZOOL. giraffe.
**jirón** *m.* shred, tatter. *2* bit, small part. *3* pennant, pointed banner. *4* HER. gyron.
**jironado, -da** *adj.* shredded, torn. *2* HER. gyronny.
**jiu-jitsu** *m.* jiujitsu, jujitsu.
**Joaquín** *m. pr. n.* Joachim.
**Job** *m. pr. n.* BIBL. Job.
**jocoserio, -ria** *adj.* jocoserious, seriocomic.
**jocosidad** *f.* jocosity, jocularity, humorousness.
**jocoso, -sa** *adj.* jocose, jocular, humorous.
**jocundidad** *f.* jocundity.
**jocundo, -da** *adj.* jocund, pleasant.
**jofaina** *f.* washbowl, washbain.
**jolgorio** *m.* HOLGORIO.
**jollín** *m.* coll. noisy merrymaking, uproar.
**Jonás** *m. pr. n.* BIBL. Jonah.
**Jonia** *f. pr. n.* HIST., GEOG. Ionia.
**jónico, -ca** *adj.* Ionian, Ionic. *2* ARCH. Ionic. *3 m.-f.* Ionian.
**jonio, -nia** *adj.* Ionian, Ionic. *2 m.-f.* Ionian.
**Jordán** *m. pr. n.* Jordan [river].
**Jordania** *f. pr. n.* Jordan [country].
**Jorge** *m. pr. n.* George.
**jorguín** *m.* wizard, sorcerer.
**jorguina** *f.* witch, sorceress.
**jornada** *f.* day's journey: *a grandes* or *largas jornadas*, by forced marches, fast, speedily; *al fin de la* ~, fig. in the end. *2* journey, travel. *3* military expedition. *4* workday, working day [number of hours of work]. *5* obs. act of a play. *6* fig. occasion, event.
**jornal** *m.* day wages: *a* ~, by the day. *2* day's work, daywork. *3* a land measure.
**joroba** *f.* hump, hunch. *2* coll. annoyance, bother.
**jorobado, -da** *adj.* humped, humpbacked, hunchbacked. *2 m.-f.* humpback, hunchback.
**jorobar** *tr.* coll. to annoy, bother.
**Josafat** *m. pr. n.* BIBL. Jehoshaphat.
**José** *m. pr. n.* Joseph.
**Josefa, Josefina** *f. pr. n.* Josepha, Josephine.
**Josefo** *m. pr. n.* Josephus.
**Josías** *m. pr. n.* BIBL. Josiah.
**Josue** *m. pr. n.* BIBL. Joshua.
**jota** *f.* name of the letter *j.* *2* jota [Spanish dance]. *3* jot, iota, whit: *no entender* ~, not to understand anything: *sin faltar* ~, in minute detail.
**joule** *m.* ELECT. joule.
**joven** *adj.* young. *2 m.-f.* youth, young man, young woman, young person: *de* ~, as a young man or woman; *los jóvenes*, the young people.
**jovencillo, -lla** & **jovencito, -ta** *m.-f.* youngster, lad, lass.
**jovial** *adj.* jovial, cheerful, pleasant, goodhumoured.
**jovialidad** *f.* joviality, cheerfulness, good humour.

**joya** *f.* jewel, piece of jewelry. *2* fig. jewel, gem [person or thing]. *3* ARCH., ARTIL. astragal. *4 pl.* jewels, trinkets. *5* a bride's outfit and jewels.
**joyante** *adj.* glossy [silk].
**joyel** *m.* small jewel.
**joyería** *f.* jewelry; jeweller's trade. *2* jeweller's shop.
**joyero** *m.* jeweller. *2* jewel case or box, casket.
**joyo** *m.* BOT. darnel, bearded darnel.
**Juan** *m. pr. n.* John: *buen* ~, candid soul; ~ *Lanas*, man who has no will of his own.
**juanas** *f. pl.* gove stretcher.
**Juana** *f. pr. n.* Joan, Jane, Jean.
**juanete** *m.* bunion. *2* prominent cheekbone. *3* NAUT. topgallant yard or sail.
**juanetudo, -da** *adj.* having bunions.
**Juanita** *f. pr. n.* Jenny, Jeannette.
**Juanito** *m. pr. n.* Jack, Johnny.
**jubilación** *f.* pensioning off, superannuation, retirement. *2* pension, superannuation, retiring allowance.
**jubilado, -da** *adj.* pensioned, superannuate, retired. *2 m.-f.* pensioner, superannuate.
1) **jubilar** *adj.* ECCL. [pertaining to the] jubilee.
2) **jubilar** *tr.* to pension off, superannuate, retire. *2* fig. to discard as useless. *3 intr.-ref.* to jubilate. *4 ref.* to be pensioned, to retire.
**jubileo** *m.* HIST., ECCL. jubilee. *2* fig. much going and coming of many people.
**júbilo** *m.* jubilation, joy, delight, rejoicing.
**jubiloso, -sa** *adj.* jubilant, joyful, rejoicing.
**jubón** *m.* doublet, jerkin.
**judaico, -ca** *adj.* Judaic, Jewish.
**judaísmo** *m.* Judaism.
**judaizante** *adj.* Judaizing. *2 m.-f.* Judaizer, Judaist.
**judaizar** *intr.* to Judaize.
**Judas** *m. pr. n.* BIBL. & fig. Judas.
**judería** *f.* Jewry, ghetto. *2* tax on Jews.
**judía** *f.* Jewess. *2* BOT. bean, kidney bean; string bean, French bean: ~ *colorada*, scarlet runner.
**judiada** *f.* dirty trick. *2* inhuman action. *3* usurious profit.
**judicatura** *f.* judgeship. *2* judicature.
**judicial** *adj.* judicial, judiciary: *poder* ~, judicial power.
**judiciario, -ria** *adj.* judicial [astrology]. *2* pertaining to the judicial astrology. *3 m.* astrologer. *4 f.* judicial astrology.
**judío, -a** *adj.* Jewish, Judean. *2* miserly; usurious. *3 m.* Jew, Hebrew, Judean. *4* miser; usurer.
**Judit** *f. pr. n.* Judith.
**judo** *m.* judo.
**juego** *m.* play, playing [for amusement]: ~ *limpio*, fig. fair play; ~ *sucio*, fig. foul play; *por* ~, in fun, for fun. *2* gambling, gaming; game: *casa de* ~, gambling house. *3* play, game: ~ *de ajedrez*, chess, game of chess; ~ *de azar*, game of chance; ~ *de bochas*, bowling; ~ *de bolos*, skittles, ninepins, tenpins; ~ *de cartas* or *naipes*, card game, cards; ~ *de damas*, draughts, *checkers; ~ *de manos*, legerdemain, sleight of hands, conjurer's trick; ~ *de pelota*, ball [game], pelota; ~ *de palabras*, play on words, pun; ~ *de prendas*, forfeits; *juegos malabares*, juggling, jugglery. *4* game, art, scheming: *verle el* ~ *a uno*, to read someone's intention; *hacerle el* ~ *a*, to play into the hands of. *5* hand [cards dealt to a player]: *descubrir uno su* ~, to show one's hand. *6* play [of water, light, colours, etc.]. *7* MACH. play. *8* play, action, working, operation: *poner en* ~, to

bring into play, to make use of. *9* set, service, suite: ~ *de botones*, set of buttons; ~ *de café*, coffee service; ~ *de dormitorio*, bedroom suite. *10 hacer* ~, to match [suit, correspond]. *11 pl.* games [public games]: *juegos olímpicos*, Olympian games, Olympic games.

**juego, juegue,** etc. *irr.* V. JUGAR.

**juerga** *f.* spree, revelry, carousal: *ir de* ~, to go on a spree.

**juerguista** *m.-f.* reveller, carouser.

**jueves** *m.* Thursday: ~ *gordo* or *lardero*, Thursday before Shrovetide; ~ *santo*, Maundy Thursday, Holy Thursday.

**juez** *m.* judge, justice: ~ *árbitro*, LAW arbitrator, umpire; ~ *de instrucción*, examining magistrate; ~ *de paz*, justice of the peace. *2* SPORT. ~ *de línea*, linesman; ~ *de llegada*, goal judge; ~ *de salida*, starter.

**jugada** *f.* play [particular act in a play or game], stroke, throw, move. *2* ill turn, mean trick. *3* ~ *de Bolsa*, speculation.

**jugador, -ra** *adj.* given to gambling. *2 m.-f.* player [of a game]: ~ *de manos*, conjurer, conjuror, legerdemainist. *3* gambler, gamester.

**jugar** *intr.* to play, sport, frolic, toy, dally. *2* to game, to gamble. *3* to play [take part in a game]: ~ *al fútbol*, to play football. *4* to play, throw, move, to be one's turn to play. *5* to speculate: ~ *a la Bolsa*, to speculate in stocks; ~ *al alza*, to bull; ~ *a la baja*, to bear. *6* to play, enter in action. *7* MACH. to play. *8* ~ *con*, to play with; to toy with, dally with. *9* ~ *en*, to have a part or hand in. *10 tr.* to play [a match, game, hand, etc., at a game]. *11* to play, move [a card, a domino, a pawn, etc.]. *12* to ply, wield [a weapon]. *13 tr.-ref.* to play, risk, stake: *jugarse el todo por el todo*, to stake all. *14* to play or gamble away.

¶ IRREG. CONJUG.: INDIC. Pres.: *juego, juegas, juega;* jugamos, *jugáis, juegan.* | SUBJ. Pres.: *juegue, juegues, juegue;* juguemos, juguéis, *jueguen.* | IMPER.: *juega, juegue;* juguemos, jugad, *jueguen.*

**jugarreta** *f.* mean trick, dirty trick.

**juglandáceo, -a** *adj.* BOT. juglandaceous.

**juglar** *m.* minstrel, jongleur.

**juglaría** *f.* minstrel's or jongleur's feats or manners.

**jugo** *m.* juice: ~ *gástrico*, PHYSIOL. gastric juice. *2* gravy. *3* fig. substance, profit: *sacar el* ~ *a*, to make the most of.

**jugosidad** *f.* juiciness, succulence.

**jugoso, -sa** *adj.* juicy, succulent.

**juguete** *m.* toy, plaything. *2* fig. sport [of wind, passions, etc.]. *3* short, slight musical piece. *4* THEAT. short play.

**juguetear** *intr.* to joy, play, sport, frolic, dally.

**jugueteo** *m.* playing, sporting, frolicking.

**juguetería** *f.* toy trade. *2* toy shop.

**juguetón, -na** *adj.* playful, frolicsome, wanton.

**juicio** *m.* judgement, discretion, discernment, prudence, sense, wisdom: *hombre de* ~, man of judgment; *muela del* ~, wisdom tooth; *tener* ~, to be sensible; to behave oneself. *2* sanity, saneness, soundness of mind: *estar en su* ~ or *en su cabal* ~, to be in one's right mind; *perder el* ~, to go crazy, go out of one's mind. *3* judgment [mental act of judging], opinion: *a mi* ~, in my opinion. *4* LAW trial: ~ *ejecutivo*, levy, execution; ~ *oral*, trial [in criminal law]. *5* THEOL. judgment: *el* ~ *final* or *universal*, the last Judgment. *6* HIST. ~ *de Dios*, ordeal.

**juicioso, -sa** *adj.* judicious, sensible, wise.

**julepe** *m.* PHARM. julep. *2* a card game. *3* scolding, reprimand.

**Julia** *f. pr. n.* Julia.

**Julián** *m. pr. n.* Julian.

**juliano, -na** *adj.* Julian. *2* COOK. julienne. *3 pr. n. Juliano el Apóstata*, Julian the Apostate.

**julio** *m.* July. *3* ELECT. joule.

**Julio** *m. pr. n.* Julius.

**julo** *m.* bell-cow. *2* lead mule.

**jumenta** *f.* jenny, jenny ass, she-ass.

**jumento** *m.* ass, donkey.

**jumera** *f.* HUMERA.

**juncáceo, -a** *adj.* juncaceous.

**juncal** *adj.* rushy. *2* willowy, flexible, graceful [human body]. *3 m.* JUNCAR.

**juncar** *m.* ground full of rushes.

**juncia** *f.* BOT. sedge.

**junco** *m.* junk [Chinese ship]. *2* BOT. rush, bulrush. *3* rush stem. *4* slender walking stick. *5* BOT. ~ *de Indias*, rattan.

**juncoso, -sa** *adj.* rushy.

**junio** *m.* June.

**junior** *m.* ECCL. junior.

**junípero** *m.* BOT. juniper.

**Juno** *f. pr. n.* MYTH. Juno.

**junquillo** *m.* BOT. jonquil. *2* BOT. rattan. *3* ARCH. reed, bead.

**junta** *f.* meeting, conference: ~ *de acreedores*, meeting of creditors; ~ *de médicos*, MED. consultation. *2* session, sitting. *3* board, council: ~ *de comercio*, board of trade; ~ *directiva*, board of directors, executive board. *4* collection, aggregate. *5* union, junction, joint, seam. *6* pipe joint, gasket.

**juntamente** *adj.* jointly, together.

**juntar** *tr.* to assemble, congregate. *2* to amass, collect, gather, lay up, store. *3* to join, unite; to connect. *4 ref.* to join, meet, assemble, gather, come into contact, come close to. *5* to associate [with]. *6* to copulate.

**junto** *adv.* near, close: ~ *a*, near to, close to, next to, by, beside. *2* ~ *con*, together with, along with. *3 en* ~, altogether, in all, all told. *4 por* ~, wholesale. *5 todo* ~, at the same time, all at once.

**junto, -ta** *adj.* united, assembled, together: *todos juntos*, all together. *2* being near or close: *muy juntos*, very close to each other.

**juntura** *f.* joint, juncture [place of union]. *2* ANAT., ZOOL. joint, articulation.

**Júpiter** *m. pr. n.* MYTH., ASTR. Jupiter.

**jura** *f.* oath. *2* solemn ceremony of taking an oath of allegiance.

*1)* **jurado** *m.* LAW jury, panel [for awarding prizes]. *3* juror, juryman.

*2)* **jurado, -da** *adj.* sworn. *2* coll. *tenérsela jurada a*, to have it in for.

**juramentar** *tr.* to swear, put to an oath. *2 ref.* to bind oneself by an oath.

**juramento** *m.* oath: ~ *falso*, perjury. *2 ref.* act of swearing. *3* swearword, curse.

**jurar** *intr.* to swear [take an oath]: ~ *en falso*, to commit perjury. *2* to swear [use profane language]. *3 tr.* to swear. *4* to swear allegiance or obedience to. *5* ~ *un cargo*, to take the oath before entering and office.

**jurásico, -ca** *adj.-m.* GEOL. Jurassic.

**juratorio, -ria** *adj.* LAW juratory.

**jurel** *m.* ICHTH. saurel.

**jurídico, -ca** *adj.* juridical; legal.

**jurisconsulto** *m.* jurisconsult, jurist, lawyer.
**jurisdicción** *f.* jurisdiction.
**jurisdiccional** *adj.* jurisdictional. *2 aguas jurisdic-cionales,* territorial waters.
**jurisperito** *m.* jurisprudent, jurist.
**jurisprudencia** *f.* jurisprudence.
**jurista** *m.* jurist.
**juro** *m.* right of perpetual ownership. *2 de* ~, certainly, necessarily.
**justa** *f.* joust, tilt. *2* contest.
**justador** *m.* jouster, tilter.
**justamente** *adv.* justly. *2* tightly, fitting tightly. *3* just, exactly. *4* at that time.
**justar** *intr.* to joust, to tilt.
**justicia** *f.* justice [in every sense except a judge]: *administrar* ~, to administer justice; *hacer* ~, to do justice; *de* ~, just, deserved. *2* officers of lawcourt, judge; judicial power: *ir por* ~, to go to court, to bring suit. *3* public punishment, execution.
**justiciero, -ra** *adj.* just, fair, righteous [person].
**justificable** *adj.* justifiable.
**justificación** *f.* justification.
**justificado, -da** *adj.* justified. *2* having adequate reason or motive, well-grounded.

**justificante** *adj.* justifying. *2 m.* proof, voucher.
**justificar** *tr.* to justify [an action, a person, etc.]. *2* to prove, vouch, establish. *3* THEOL., PRINT. to justify. *4 ref.* to clear oneself, to justify one's conduct.
**justificativo, -va** *adj.* justificative; justificatory.
**justillo** *m.* underwaist, corset cover.
**Justiniano** *m. pr. n.* Justinian.
**justipreciar** *tr.* to appraise, estimate.
**justiprecio** *m.* appraisal, estimation.
1) **justo** *adv.* justly, rightly. *2* exactly. *3* tightly, closely.
2) **justo, -ta** *adj.* just. *2* righteous. *3* exact, correct. *4* tight, close, close-fitting. *5 m.* just man [righteous before God]: *los justos,* the just.
**Jutlandia** *f. pr. n.* GEOG. Jutland.
**juvenil** *adj.* juvenile, youthful.
**juventud** *f.* youth [part or life; early period]. *2* youthfulness. *3* youth, young people.
**juzgado** *m.* LAW court or tribunal [of one judge]. *2* judicature, judgeship.
**juzgador, -ra** *adj.* judging. *2 m.-f.* judger.
**juzgar** *intr.* to judge: ~ *de,* to form a judgement or opinion about. *2 tr.* to judge, try. *3* to judge [form opinion about; consider, think, judge to be]: *a* ~ *por,* judging by or from.

# K

**K, k** *f*. K, k, twelfth letter of the Spanish alphabet.
**ka** *f*. name of the letter *k*.
**kaiser** *m*. kaiser.
**kan** *m*. khan [tartar chief].
**kantiano, -na** *adj.-n*. Kantian.
**kantismo** *m*. Kantism.
**kappa** *f*. kappa [Greek letter].
**kepis,** *pl.* **-pis** *m*. kepi.
**kerosén, keroseno** *m*. kerosene.
**kilo** *m*. kilo, kilogram, kilogramme.
**kilociclo** *m*. kilocycle.
**kilográmetro** *m*. kilogrammetre, kilogrammeter.
**kilogramo** *m*. kilogram, kilogramme.

**kilolitro** *m*. kilolitre, kiloliter.
**kilometraje** *m*. kilometrage.
**kilométrico, -ca** *adj.* kilometric, kilometrical. 2 fig. very long, interminable.
**kilómetro** *m*. kilometre, kilometer.
**kilovatio** *m*. kilowatt.
**kimono** *m*. kimono.
**kiosko** *m*. QUIOSCO.
**kirie** *m*. ECCL. kyrie eleison.
**kodak** *f*. kodak.
**krausismo** *m*. Krausism.
**Kremlin** *m*. Kremlin.
**kurdo, -da** *adj.-n*. CURDO.

**L, l** *f.* L, l, thirteenth letter of the Spanish alphabet.

1) **la** *def. art. fem. sing.* the.

2) **la** *pers. pron. fem. sing.* her, it [direct object]: ~ *veo*, I see her, I see it.

3) **la** *m.* MUS. la, A.

**lábaro** *m.* labarum.

**laberíntico, -ca** *adj.* labyrinthic(al), labyrinthine.

**laberinto** *m.* labyrinth; maze. *2* ANAT. labyrinth.

**labia** *f.* coll. fluency, winning eloquence.

**labiado, -da** *adj.* BOT. labiate.

**labial** *adj.-f.* labial.

**labiérnago** *m.* BOT. mock privet.

**labihendido, -da** *adj.* harelipped.

**lábil** *adj.* labile. *2* weak, feeble.

**labio** *m.* ANAT., ZOOL. lip: ~ *leporino*, harelip. *2* lip [of a wound, a vessel, etc.]. *3* ANAT., BOT., ZOOL. labium. *4 sing.-pl.* lips [organ of speech]: *morderse los labios*, coll. to bite one's tongue; *no morderse los labios*, coll. to be outspoken.

**labor** *s.* labour, toil, work, task. *2* ornamental work. *3* fancywork, embroidery, needlework, etc.: ~ *de encaje*, lacework; ~ *de ganchillo*, crocheting. *4* AGR. tillage. *5* ploughing or digging [instance of them]. *6 pl.* fancywork, embroidery, needlework, etc. *7* MIN. works, workings. *8 labores del campo*, farming, farm work.

**laborable** *adj.* workable. *2* arable, tillable [ground]. *3 día ~*, workday, working day, week day.

**laboral** *adj.* [pertaining to] labour.

**laborar** *tr.* to work. *2 intr.* ~ *por, en favor de*, to work or scheme to some end.

**laboratorio** *m.* laboratory.

**laborear** *tr.* to work, fashion. *2* to till [land]. *3* to work [a mine]. *4 intr.* NAUT. to reeve, run.

**laboreo** *m.* AGR. tillage. *2* MIN. working, development. *3* NAUT. reeving, running.

**laboriosidad** *f.* laboriousness, industriousness.

**laborioso, -sa** *adj.* laborious, industrious, fond of working. *2* laborious, arduous, painful.

**laborismo** *m.* British Labour party.

**laborista** *adj.* Labour [of the Labour party]. *2 m. f.* Labourist, Laborite.

**labra** *f.* working, carving, cutting [of stone, wood, metal, etc.].

**labrado, -da** *adj.* AGR. tilled. *2* wrought, fashioned. *3* cut, carved [stone, etc.]. *4* WEAV. figured. *5 m.* LABRA. *6 pl.* tilled fields.

**Labrador (Tierra del)** *f. pr. n.* GEOG. Labrador.

**labrador, -ra** *adj.* tilling. *2* peasant. *3 m.* tiller, ploughman. *4 m.-f.* peasant.

**labradorita** *f.* MIN. labradorite.

**labrantín** *m.* petty farmer, small farmer.

**labrantío, -a** *adj.* arable, tillable. *2 m.* tillable land.

**labranza** *f.* cultivation, farming, husbandry. *2* farm, farm land.

**labrar** *tr.* to work, fashion, carve, cut, dress. *2* to plough, till, cultivate. *3* to figure [a fabric]. *4* to build, erect. *5* to cause, build, bring about: ~ *una reputación*, to build a reputation.

**labriego, -ga** *m.-f.* rustic, peasant.

**labro** *s.* ZOOL. labrum. *2* ICHTH. wrasse.

**labrusca** *f.* BOT. wild grapevine.

**laburno** *m.* BOT. laburnum.

**laca** *f.* lac, gum lac, shellac. *2* lacquer [varnish; article]; japan. *3* lake [pigment].

**lacayo** *m.* lackey, lacquey, footman, groom.

**lacayuno, -na** *adj.* lackeylike, servile.

**lacear** *tr.* to trim or tie with bows. *2* to snare [small game].

**Lacedemonia** *f. pr. n.* HIST. GEOG. Lacedaemon.

**lacedemonio, -nia** *adj.-n.* Lacedaemonian.

**laceración** *f.* laceration.

**lacerado, -da** *adj.* lacerated. *2* wretched, unhappy.

**lacerar** *tr.* to lacerate. *2* to hurt, damage [the reputation, etc.].

**lacería** *f.* poverty, want. *2* trouble, hardship.

**lacería** *f.* ARCH. ornament, imitating bows.

**lacero** *m.* lassoer. *2* dogcatcher.

**lacertoso, -sa** *adj.* muscular, brawny, robust.

**lacinia** *f.* BOT. lacinia.

**lacio, -cia** *adj.* withered. *2* flaccid, flabby, languid. *3* straight, lank [hair].

**lacónico, -ca** *adj.* laconic.

**Laconia** *f. pr. n.* HIST., GEOG. Laconia.

**laconio, -nia** *adj.-n.* Laconian.

**laconismo** *m.* laconism.

**lacra** *f.* mark of trace left by illness. *2* fault, defect.

**lacrar** *tr.* to injure the health of; to infect with a disease. *2* to seal [with sealing wax].

**lacre** *m.* sealing wax.

**lacrimal** *adj.* lachrymal.

**lacrimatorio, -ria** *adj.-m.* lachrymatory.

**lacrimógeno, -na** *adj.* lachrymogenic.

**lacrimoso, -sa** *adj.* lachrymose, tearful.
**lactación** *f.* sucking [of mother's milk].
**lactancia** *f.* LACTACIÓN. *2* lactation.
**lactante** *adj.* sucking [child]. *2* suckling, nursing. *3 m.-f.* suckling, sucking child. *4 f.* mother or nurse giving suck.
**lactar** *tr.* to lactate, suckle. *2 intr.* to suck.
**lactario, -ria** *adj.* milky.
**lactasa** *f.* BIOCHEM. lactase.
**lácteo, -a** *adj.* lacteal, lacteous. *2* milky.
**lactescente** *adj.* lactescent.
**lacticinio** *m.* milk or milk food.
**láctico, -ca** *adj.* CHEM. lactic.
**lactosa** *f.* CHEM. lactose.
**lacustre** *adj.* lacustrine.
**lacha** *f.* ICHTH. anchovy. *2* coll. *tener poca* ~, to be shameless; to be silly, dull.
**ladear** *tr.* to tilt, tip, lean or incline [something] to one side. *2* to turn [something] sideways. *3 intr.* to go round the hillside. *4* to deviate. *5 ref.-intr.* [of something] to tilt, tip, lean or incline to one side; to turn sideways. *6 ref.* to incline [to an opinion, party, etc.].
**ladeo** *m.* tilting, tipping, inclination to one side.
**ladera** *f.* slope, hillside, mountainside.
**ladilla** *f.* ENT. crab louse.
**ladino, -na** *adj.* sagacious, cunning, sly. *2* speaking foreign languages.
**lado** *m.* side: *dejar a un* ~, to leave or set aside, *ponerse al* ~ *de*, to take sides with; *al* ~, close by, near by; next door; *al* ~ *de*, beside; ~ *a* ~, side by side; *por todos lados*, on all sides. *2* hand, way: *por otro* ~, on the other hand; *por un* ~ ... *por otro* ~, on the one hand... on the other hand. *2* room, space: *hacer* ~, to make room. *4* favour, protection. *5 pl.* patrons, protectors; advisers.
**ladra** *f.* barking.
**ladrador, -ra** *adj.* barking.
**ladrar** *intr.* [of a dog] to bark. *2* coll. to bark [threaten idly]: ~ *a la luna*, to bark at the moon.
**ladrido** *m.* bark, barking [of dogs]. *2* coll. backbiting, slander.
**ladrillar** *m.* brickyard.
**ladrillazo** *m.* blow with a brick.
**ladrillero** *m.* brick maker. *2* brick seller.
**ladrillo** *m.* brick, tile. *2* ~ *de chocolate*, cake of chocolate.
**ladrón, -na** *adj.* thieving, thievish. *2 m.-f.* thief, robber, burglar.
**ladronear** *intr.* to thieve, go about thieving.
**ladronera** *f.* den of thieves.
**ladronicio** *m.* LATROCINIO.
**ladronzuelo, -la** *m.-f.* young thief. *2* pickpocket, pilferer, petty thief.
**lagar** *m.* wine press; olive press; apple press.
**lagarta** *f.* ZOOL. female lizard. *2* ENT. gypsy moth. *3* coll. cunning, sly woman.
**lagartera** *s.* lizard hole.
**lagartija** *f.* ZOOL. green lizard; wall lizard.
**lagarto** *m.* ZOOL. lizard. *2* coll. cunning, sly fellow.
**lago** *m.* lake [body of water].
**lagotear** *intr.-tr.* to flatter, cajole.
**lagotería** *f.* flattery, cajolery.
**lagotero, -ra** *adj.* flattering. *2 m.-f.* flatterer, cajoler.
**lágrima** *f.* tear, teardrop: *lágrimas de cocodrilo*, crocodile tears; *llorar a* ~ *viva*, to shed bitter tears. *2* tear, drop [of sap; of a liquor]. *3* BOT. *lágrimas de David*, or *de Job*, Job's-tears.
**lagrimal** *adj.* lachrymal. *2 m.* ANAT., ZOOL. medial angle of the eye.

**lagrimear** *intr.* to shed tears frequently.
**lagrimeo** *m.* frequent shedding of tears.
**lagrimón** *m.* large tear.
**lagrimoso, -sa** *adj.* LACRIMOSO. *2* watery [eye].
**laguna** *f.* small lake, lakelet. *2* lagoon. | Esp. in ~ *de Venecia*, lagoon of Venice. *3* lacuna, blank, gap.
**lagunajo** *m.* pool, puddle.
**lagunar** *m.* ARCH. lacunar, caisson.
**laical** *adj.* laical.
**laicidad** *f.* laicity. *2* LAICISMO.
**laicismo** *m.* laicism, secularism.
**laicizar** *tr.* to laicize, secularize.
**laico, -ca** *adj.* laic, lay. *2* secularistic. *3 m.-f.* laic.
**laja** *f.* LANCHA. *2* NAUT. stone flat.
**lama** *f.* slime, silt, ooze. *2* gold or silver tissue. *3* *m.* lama [Tibetan monk].
**lamaísmo** *m.* Lamaism.
**lamasería** *f.* lamasery.
**lambda** *f.* lambda [Greek letter].
**lambrequín** *m.* HER. lambrequin, mantling.
**lamedal** *m.* miry place.
**lamedor, -ra** *adj.* licking. *2 m.-f.* licker.
**lamedura** *f.* [act of] licking.
**lamelibranquio, -quia** *adj.-n.* ZOOL. lamellibranch.
**lamelicornio, nia** *adj.-n.* ENT. lamellicorn.
**lamentable** *adj.* lamentable, deplorable, pitiable.
**lamentación** *f.* lamentation, lament, wail.
**lamentar** *tr.* to lament, deplore, regret, be sorry for. *2 ref.* to lament, wail. *3* to complain.
**lamento** *m.* lament, lamentation, wail.
**lamentoso, -sa** *adj.* lamentable, doleful.
**lamer** *tr.* to lick, lap.
**lamerón, -na** *adj.* coll. GOLOSO.
**lametón** *m.* greedy licking.
**lamia** *f.* MYTH. lamia. *2* ICHTH. shark.
**lamido, -da** *adj.* licked. *2* lean, pale [person]. *3* affected, prim, overnice.
**lámina** *f.* lamina, sheet, plate. *2* BOT., ZOOL. lamina. *3* copperplate, engraving plate. *4* engraving, cut, plate, print, picture [printed copy].
**laminado, -da** *adj.* laminate. *2* laminated, rolled [metal]. *3* lamination, rolling [of metals].
**laminador** *m.* rolling mill. *2* metal roller.
1) **laminar** *tr.* to laminate, roll [metals]. *2* to laminate [cover with laminae].
2) **laminar** *adj.* laminal, laminar.
**lamiscar** *tr.* coll. to lick greedily.
**lampacear** *tr.* NAUT. to swab.
**lámpara** *f.* lamp, light: ~ *de Aladino*, Aladin's lamp; ~ *de seguridad*, safety lamp; ~ *de pie*, floor lamp; ~ *de sobremesa*, table lamp; ~ *de soldar*, blowtorch; ~ *piloto*, pilot lamp. *2* RADIO. tube, valve. *3* grease stain [on clothing].
**lamparería** *f.* lamp factory or shop. *2* lamp store.
**lamparilla** *f. dim.* small lamp. *2* night lamp. *3* BOT. aspen. *4* (Am.) electric light bulb.
**lamparín** *m.* bracket or suspended circle for holding a small lamp [in churches].
**lamparón** *m.* grease stain [on clothing]. *2* MED. scrofula [in the neck]. *3* VET. a disease of horses.
**lampazo** *m.* BOT. burdock. *2* (Mex.) BOT. water lily. *3* NAUT. swab, mop.
**lampiño, -ña** *adj.* beardless. *2* BOT. hairless.
**lampo** *m.* poet. flash of light.
**lamprea** *f.* ICHTH. lamprey.
**lampuga** *f.* ICHTH. yellow mackerel.
**lana** *f.* wool [of sheep, alpaca, etc.], fleece. *2* wool [yarn, garment, cloth].
**lanar** *adj.* wool-bearing: *ganado* ~, sheep [collectively].

**lance** *m.* throw, cast. *2* catch [fish caught]. *3* critical situation; event, episode, incident, affair: ~ *de honor*, affair of honour, duel. *4* move, turn, situation [in a game]. *5* BULLF. a skilled play of the cape. *6 de* ~, secondhand.
**lancear** *tr.* ALANCEAR.
**lanceolado, -da** *adj.* BOT. lanceolate.
**lancera** *f.* rack for lances.
**lancero** *m.* lancer. *2* spearman. *3* rack for lances. *5 pl.* lancers [dance and music].
**lanceta** *f.* SURG. lancet.
**lancinante** *adj.* piercing [pain].
**lancinar** *tr.* to lancinate.
**lancurdia** *f.* ICHTH. small trout.
**lancha** *f.* NAUT. launch, boat. *2* flagstone, stone naturally flat and thin.
**lanchada** *f.* boatload.
**lanchero** *m.* launchman, boatman.
**lanchón** *m.* NAUT. large launch, barge, lighter.
**landa** *f.* moor, waste land.
**landgrave** *m.* landgrave.
**landó** *m.* landau [carriage].
**landre** *f.* small tumor [in glands of neck, armpit or groin]. *2* hidden pocket.
**lanería** *f.* wool shop. *2* woolen goods.
**lanero, -ra** *adj.* wool: *industria lanera*, wool industry. *2* ORN. *halcón* ~, lanner. *3 m.* dealer in wool.
**langosta** *f.* ENT. locust. *2* ZOOL. lobster, spiny lobster.
**langostín, langostino** *m.* ZOOL. a salt-water prawn.
**langostón** *m.* ENT. a large green grasshopper.
**languidecer** *intr.* to languish; to pine away. ¶ CONJUG. like *agradecer*.
**languidez** *f.* languidness, languor.
**languidezco, languidezca,** etc. *irr.* V. LANGUIDECER.
**lánguido, -da** *adj.* languid, faint, weak.
**lanífero, -ra** *adj.* poet. laniferous, woolly.
**lanificación** *f.* **lanicio** *m.* woolwork.
**lanilla** *f.* nap of cloth. *2* a light woollen fabric.
**lanosidad** *f.* BOT. down, pubescence.
**lanoso, -sa** *adj.* woolly.
**lansquenete** *m.* lansquenet [soldier].
**lanudo, -da** *adj.* wooly, fleecy.
**lanza** *f.* lance, spear: *correr lanzas*, to joust with lances; ~ *en ristre*, with the lance in rest; ready for action. *2* [in the Middle Ages] lance, lancer. *3* pole, tongue [of a carriage]. *4* nozzle [of a hose].
**lanzabombas,** *pl.* **-bas** *s.* AER. bomb release. *2* MIL. bomb thrower.
**lanzacabos** *adj.* NAUT. *cañón* ~, lifesaving gun.
**lanzacohetes,** *pl.* **-tes** *m.* MIL. rocket launcher.
**lanzada** *f.* thrust with a lance.
**lanzadera** *f.* WEAV., SEW. shuttle.
**lanzador, -ra** *m.-f.* thrower: ~ *de disco*, discus thrower. *2* BASEBALL pitcher.
**lanzallamas,** *pl.* **-mas** *m.* MIL. flame thrower.
**lanzamiento** *m.* cast, fling, hurl, throw. *2* NAUT. launching [of a boat]. *3* LAW eviction, dispossession. *4* NAUT. rake [of the stern].
**lanzaminas** *m.* mine layer, mine-laying boat.
**lanzar** *tr.* to throw, cast, dart, fling, hurl. *2* to launch [a boat, an attack, a new product, etc.]. *3* to cast [a glance]. *4* LAW to evict, dispossess. *6 ref.* to throw oneself, to rush, dart, launch [into, out, etc.], to jump. *7* SPORT. to sprint.
**lanzatorpedos** *adj.* torpedo tube.
**Lanzarote** *m. pr. n.* Lancelot [of Round Table].
**laña** *f.* clamp, clamper, staple. *2* green coconut.
**lañar** *tr.* to mend or strengthen with clampers.

**lapa** *f.* ZOOL. limpet. *2* BOT. burdock [genus *Lappa*].
**lapachar** *m.* swamp, marsh.
**lapicero** *m.* pencil holder. *2* LÁPIZ 1.
**lápida** *f.* tablet [for an inscription], mural tablet, memorial stone: ~ *sepulcral*, gravestone.
**lapidación** *f.* lapidation, stoning to death.
**lapidar** *tr.* to lapidate, stone to death.
**lapidario, -ria** *adj.* lapidary. *2 m.* lapidary. *3* dealer in gems.
**lapidificar** *tr.* to lapidify.
**lapislázuli** *m.* MINER. lapis lazuli.
**lápiz,** *pl.* **-ces** *m.* pencil [for drawing or writing]; crayon: ~ *tinta*, indelible pencil. *2* ~ *para los labios*, lipstick.
**lapo** *m.* coll. blow with a cane; blow with the flat of a sword. *2* coll. drink, swallow.
**lapón, -na** *adj.* Lappish. *2 m.-f.* Lapp, Laplander. *3 m.* Lappish [language].
**Laponia** *f. pr. n.* GEOG. Lapland.
**lapso** *m.* lapse [interval of time]. *2* fall, lapse, slip.
**lar,** *pl.* **lares** *m.* MYTH. lar. *2* fireplace. *3 pl.* home [house; family].
**lardar, lardear** *tr.* COOK. to baste.
**lardo** *m.* bacon fat. *2* fat [of an animal].
**lardoso, -sa** *adj.* greasy, oily.
**larga** *f.* longest biliard cue. *2* BULLF. play of cape, executed by holding it extended lenghtwise. *3 pl.* delay: *dar largas a*, to delay, put off.
**largamente** *adv.* at lenght, at large. *2* long, for a long time. *3* amply, largely. *4* liberally.
**largar** *tr.* to let go. *2* to utter, deliver [a speech]. *3* to deal, deliver [a blow]. *4* to heave [a sigh]. *5* NAUT. to let go, pay out. *6* NAUT. to unfurl. *7 ref.* to get out, leave: *¡lárgate!*, get out!
1) **largo** *adv.* largely, extendedly. *2 m.* long, length: *ocho metros de* ~, eight metres long. *3* MUS. largo. *4 pasar de* ~, to pass by, without stopping; to pass over, disregard. *5 ponerse de* ~, [of a young woman] to come out, debut. *6 interj. ¡largo!, ¡largo de ahí!*, get out!, get out of here!
2) **largo, -ga** *adj.* long: *traje* or *vestido* ~, evening dress, evening gown [for women]; ~ *de lengua*, fig. loose-tongued; ~ *de manos*, fig. ready-handed; ~ *de uñas*, fig. lightfingered, thievish; *a la larga*, lengthwise; in the long run; *a lenght; a lo* ~, lengthwise; far away; *a lo* ~ *de*, along, lengthwise of; throughout; *cuán* ~ *es* or *era*, at full length, stretched out. *3* liberal, generous. *4* copious, abundant. *5* shrewd, cunning. *6* NAUT. loose, free. *7 adj. pl.* many; odd: *largos años*, many years; *veinte millas largas*, twenty-odd miles.
**largor** *m.* length.
**larguero** *m.* CARP. jamp post; upright; sidepiece. *2* AER. longueron, spar. *3* bolster [long pillow].
**largueza** *f.* liberality, generosity. *2* length.
**larguirucho, -cha** *adj.* coll. tall and lean, lanky.
**largura** *f.* length.
**laringe** *f.* ANAT. larynx.
**laríngeo, -a** *adj.* laryngeal.
**laringitis** *f.* MED. laryngitis.
**laringoscopio** *m.* laryngoscope.
**larva** *f.* ZOOL. larva.
**larvado, -da** *adj.* MED. larvate(d.
**las** *def. art. f. pl.* the. *2* ~ *que*, those, or they, which. *3 pron. pers. f. pl.* [direct object] them: ~ *vi*, I saw them.
**lasca** *f.* chip [from a stone].
**lascar** *tr.* NAUT. to ease away, pay out.
**lascivia** *f.* lasciviousness, lewdness.

**lascivo, -va** *adj.* lascivious, lewd, lustful. *2* wanton, playful [wind, etc.].
**lasitud** *f.* lassitude, weariness, languor.
**laso, -sa** *adj.* wearied, weak, languid.
**lástima** *f.* pity, compassion: *dar*, or *hacer* ~, to be pitiful. *2* pitiful object: *estar hecho una* ~, to be in a pitiable state. *3* plaint, lamentation. *4 es* ~, it is a pity; too bad; *qué* ~, what a pity!
**lastimado, -da** *adj.* hurt, injured, sore.
**lastimadura** *f.* hurt, bruise, injure.
**lastimar** *tr.* to hurt, injure, damage; to bruise. *2* to pity. *3 ref.* to hurt oneself. *4* to feel sorry for. *5* to complain, lament.
**lastimero, -ra** *adj.* doleful, plaintive, sad, sorrowful, mournful. *2* hurtful.
**lastimoso, -sa** *adj.* pitiful, sad.
**lastra** *f.* LANCHA 2.
**lastrar** *tr.* NAUT., AER. to ballast.
**lastre** *m.* NAUT., AER. & fig. ballast.
**lata** *f.* tin plate [tinned iron plate]. *2* tin, can; can of tinned food: *en* ~, canned, tinned. *3* lath [strip of wood]. *4* bore [tedious speech, performance, etc.]: *dar la* ~, to bore.
**latamente** *adv.* at great lenght. *2* broadly.
**lataz,** *pl.* **-taces** *s.* ZOOL. sea otter.
**latente** *adj.* latent.
**lateral** *adj.* side, lateral.
**lateranense** *adj.* Lateran.
**latido** *m.* beat, throb, pulsation [of the heart, the arteries, etc.]. *2* yelp [of dog].
**latiente** *adj.* beating, throbbing.
**latifundio** *m.* large landed estate, latifundium.
**latifundista** *m.-f.* owner of a large landed estate.
**latigazo** *m.* lash [with a whip, etc.]. *2* crack of a whip. *3* unexpected hurt or damage.
**látigo** *m.* whip, horsewhip. *2* lash [part of a whip]. *3* cinch strap.
**latiguear** *intr.* to crack a whip.
**latiguera** *f.* cinch strap.
**latiguillo** *m.* small whip. *2* BOT. stolon. *3* claptrap, declamatory affectation [of an actor or speaker].
**latín** *m.* Latin [tongue]: ~ *de cocina*, dog Latin; *saber mucho* ~, fig. to be very shrewd. *2* Latin word or quotation.
**latinajo** *m.* dog Latin. *2* Latin word or quotation.
**latinidad** *f.* Latin [tongue]. *2* Latinity.
**latiniparla** *f.* language excessively interspersed with Latinisms or Latin words.
**latinismo** *m.* Latinism, latinism.
**latinista** *m.-f.* Latinist.
**latinizar** *tr.-intr.* to Latinize.
**latino, -na** *adj.* Latin. *2* NAUT. lateen [sail, rig]. *3 m.-f.* Latin [person].
**latir** *intr.* to beat, throb, pulsate. *2* [of a dog] to yelp, bark.
**latitud** *f.* breadth, width; extent. *2* GEOG., ASTR. latitude. *3* fig. latitude [climate, region].
**latitudinal** *adj.* latitudinal.
**lato, -ta** *adj.* broad, wide, large. *2* broad [meaning of word].
**latón** *m.* brass [alloy of copper and zinc].
**latonero** *m.* brassworker, brazier.
**latoso, -sa** *adj.* annoying boring.
**latria** *f.* THEOL. latria.
**laucha** *f.* (Am.) mouse.
**laúd** *m.* MUS. lute. *2* NAUT. catboat. *3* ZOOL. leatherback [turtle].
**laudable** *adj.* laudable, praiseworthy.
**láudano** *m.* PHARM. laudanum.
**laudatorio, -ria** *adj.* laudatory. *2 f.* eulogy.

**laude** *f.* inscribed tombstone. *2 pl.* ECCL. lauds.
**laudo** *m.* LAW award or finding of an arbitrator.
**lauráceo, -a** *adj.* laurellike. *2* BOT. lauraceous.
**laureado, -da** *adj.* laureate; laurelled.
**laurear** *tr.* to laureate; to honour, reward.
**lauredal** *m.* plantation of laurel trees.
**laurel** *m.* BOT. laurel. *2 pl.* fig. laurels.
**láureo, -a** *adj.* laurel [of laurel, made of laurel].
**lauréola** *f.* laurel wreath. *2* BOT. *lauréola* or ~ *macho*, daphne; ~ *hembra*, mezereon.
**lauro** *m.* BOT. laurel. *2* fig. laurel, glory.
**lauroceraso** *m.* BOT. cherry laurel.
**lava** *f.* lava. *2* MIN. washing.
**lavable** *adj.* washable.
**lavabo** *m.* washstand. *2* washroom; lavatory. *3* LITURG. Lavabo.
**lavacaras** *m.-f.* coll. flatterer.
**lavadero** *m.* washing place. *2* laundry.
**lavado** *adj.* washed. *2 m.* wash, washing, cleaning. *3* PAINT. water colour in a single tint.
**lavador, -ra** *adj.* washing. *2 m.-f.* washer, cleaner. *3 f.* washing machine.
**lavadura** *f.* LAVAMIENTO. *2* LAVAZAS.
**lavaje** *m.* washing [of woods]. *2* MED. lavage.
**lavajo** *m.* pool of rain water, water hole.
**lavamanos** *m.* washbasin.
**lavamiento** *m.* wash, washing, cleaning.
**lavandera** *f.* laundress, laundrywoman, washerwoman. *2* ORN. sandpiper.
**lavandería** *f.* (Am.) laundry.
**lavandero** *m.* launderer, laundryman.
**lavándula** *f.* BOT. lavender.
**lavaplato,** *pl.* **-tos** *m.-f.* dishwasher.
**lavar** *tr.* to wash, clean. *2* to cleanse, to purify. *3* to colour [a drawing] with water colour. *4 ref.* to wash oneself, to wash up.
**lavativa** *f.* clyster, enema, injection. *2* syringe, enema [apparatus]. *3* fig. bother, annoyance.
**lavatorio** *m.* lavation, wash, washing. *2* lavatory, washbasin. *3* PHARM. lotion. *4* ECCL. maundy. *5* LITURG. lavatory.
**lavazas** *f. pl.* wash water, slops.
**lave** *m.* MIN. washing.
**lavotear** *tr.* to wash hurriedly.
**lavoteo** *m.* hurried washing.
**laxación** *f.*, **laxamiento** *m.* laxation, loosening.
**laxante** *adj.* laxing, loosening. *2 m.* MED. laxative.
**laxar** *tr.* to laxate, loosen. *2* MED. to loosen the intestines. *3* MED. to give a laxative to.
**laxitud** *f.* laxity, laxness.
**laxo, -xa** *adj.* lax, slack. *2* lax [loose in morals].
**lay** *m.* lay [poem].
**laya** *f.* AGR. spade; spud. *2* kind, class, nature.
**layar** *tr.* AGR. to spade, spud.
**lazada** *f.* bowknot. *2* bow [ornamental knot].
**lazar** *tr.* to lasso.
**lazareto** *m.* lazaretto [for quarantine; for lepers].
**lazarillo** *m.* blind-person's guide.
**lazarista** *m.* Lazarist, Lazarite.
**Lázaro** *m. pr. n.* Lazarus.
**lazo** *m.* bow, knot [ornamental knot], truelove knot, hair knot. *2* ARCH. knot. *3* bowknot. *4* tie, bond. *5* snare [for small game]. *6* snare, trap [for persons]: *tender un* ~ *a*, to set a trap for. *7* lasso, lariat. *8* ~ *corredizo*, running knot.
**lazulita** *f.* MINER. lazulite. *2* MINER. lapis lazuli.
**le** *pers. pron. m. sing.* him [direct object]. *2 pers. pron. m. & f. sing.* him, her, it, to him, to her, to it [indirect object].
**leal** *adj.* loyal. *2* faithful [servant, dog, etc.]. *3* fair

[procceding]. 4 *según mi* ~ *saber y entender,* to the best of my knowledge.

**lealtad** *f.* loyalty. 2 fidelity. 3 fairness.

**Leandro** *m. pr. n.* Leander.

**lebrato, lebratón** *m.* young hare, leveret.

**lebrel** *m.* hare-huntig dog.

**lebrero, -ra** *adj.* hare-hunting. 2 *m.* harehound.

**lebrillo** *m.* metal or earthenware washtub.

**lebruno, -na** *adj.* leporine, harelike.

**lección** *f.* lesson: *dar la* ~, to recite one's lesson; *dar una* ~ *a,* to give or teach a lesson to. 2 ECCL. lection. 3 lecture, reading.

**leccionario** *m.* ECCL. lectionary.

**leccioncita** *f. dim.* short lecture or lesson.

**lecitina** *f.* BIOCHEM. lecithin.

**lectivo, -va** *adj.* school [day, year, etc.].

**lector, -ra** *m.-f.* reader. 2 ECCL. lector. 3 lecturer [in Colleges, etc.].

**lectorado** *m.* ECCL. lectorate.

**lectura** *f.* reading, lecture. 2 reading [interpretation of a passage]. 3 PRINT. pica.

**lecha** *f.* ICHTH. milt [secretion and gland].

**lechada** *f.* grout; whitewash. 2 pulp of rags. 3 liquid containing finely divided solids in suspension.

**lechal** *adj.* sucking [lamb, calf, etc.]. 2 milky [plant]. 3 *m.* milk [of a plant].

**leche** *f.* milk [secreted by female mammals]: ~ *condensada,* condensed milk; ~ *desnatada,* skim milk; ~ *en polvo,* milk powder. 3 milk [preparation]: ~ *de almendras,* milk of almonds.

**lechecillas** *f. pl.* sweetbread. 2 liver and lights.

**lechera** *adj.* milch: *vaca* ~, milch cow. 2 *f.* dairymaid, milk seller. 3 milk can, milk jug, milk pot.

**lechería** *f.* dairy [shop].

**lechero, -ra** *adj.* milk, milky. 2 *m.* milkman, dairyman.

**lechetrezna** *f.* BOT. sun spurge.

**lechigada** *f.* litter [young brought forth at a birth]. 2 coll. gang, lot.

**lechino** *m.* SURG. dossil.

**lecho** *m.* bed, couch. 2 bed [of a river, lake, etc.]. 3 bed, layer. 4 GEOL. stratum. 5 MAS. bed [of a stone in position].

**lechón, -na** *adj.* dirty, sluttish. 2 *m.* sucking pig. 3 pig, hog. 4 fig. pig [dirty man]. 5 *f.* sow [female hog; dirty woman].

**lechoso, -sa** *adj.* milky.

**lechuga** *f.* BOT. lettuce.

**lechuguilla** *f.* BOT. wild lettuce. 2 ruff; frill.

**lechuguina** *f.* stylish young lady.

**lechuguino, -na** *adj.* dandified, stylish. 2 *m.* young dandy or dude. 3 small lettuce.

**lechuza** *f.* ORN. barn owl, screeching owl.

**lechuzo, -za** *adj.* sucking [mule]. 2 *m.* coll. bill collector, summons server.

**ledo, -da** *adj.* joyful, cheerful, placid.

**leer** *tr.-intr.* to read. 2 *ref.* to read, to be read: *este libro se lee fácilmente,* this book reads easily.

**lega** *f.* ECCL. lay sister.

**legacía** *f.* legateship.

**legación** *f.* legation.

**legado** *m.* LAW legacy, bequest. 2 legate.

**legajo** *m.* bundle of papers; dossier, file.

**legal** *adj.* legal, lawful.

**legalidad** *f.* legality, lawfulness. 2 political regime as established by the constitution of the State.

**legalismo** *m.* legalism.

**legalización** *f.* legalization. 2 attestation of the authenticity of a signature.

**legalizar** *tr.* to legalize. 2 to attest the authenticity of [a signature].

**légamo** *m.* mud, silt, slime.

**legaña** *f.* rheum, gummy secretion of the eyelids.

**legañoso, -sa** *adj.* blear-eyed.

**legar** *tr.* to legate, bequeath. 2 to send as a legate.

**legatario, -ria** *m.-f.* LAW legatee.

**legenda** *f.* legend [saint's life].

**legendario, -ria** *adj.-m.* legendary.

**legible** *adj.* legible, readable.

**legión** *f.* legion.

**legionario, -ria** *adj.-n.* legionary.

**legislación** *f.* legislation [body of laws]. 2 science of laws.

**legislador, -ra** *adj.* legislating, legislative. 2 *m.* legislator. 3 *f.* legislatress.

**legislar** *tr.* to legislate.

**legislativo, -va** *adj.* legislative.

**legislatura** *f.* term or session of a legislature.

**legista** *m.* legist. 2 law student.

**legítima** *f.* LAW legitim.

**legitimación** *f.* legitimation.

**legitimar** *tr.* to legitimate.

**legitimidad** *f.* legitimacy. 2 genuineness.

**legitimista** *adj.-n.* legitimist.

**legítimo, -ma** *adj.* legitimate. 2 lawful. 3 genuine.

**lego, -ga** *adj.* lay [person]. 2 ignorant, uninformed. 3 *m.* laic, layman. 4 lay brother. 5 *f.* lay sister.

**legra** *f.* SURG. scraper.

**legua** *f.* league [measure of distance]: *a la* ~, *de cien leguas,* from far off, a great distance.

**leguleyo** *m.* pettifogger, petty lawyer.

**legumbre** *f.* legume, pod fruit. 2 *pl.* pulse, vegetables.

**leguminoso, -sa** *adj.* BOT. leguminous.

**leíble** *adj.* legible, readable.

**leído, -da** *p. p.* de LEER. 2 *adj.* well-read, well-informed.

**lejanía** *f.* distance, remoteness, distant place.

**lejano, -na** *adj.* distant, remote, far.

**lejas** *adj. pl. de* ~ *tierras,* from distant lands.

**lejía** *f.* lye. 2 coll. dressing down, reprimand.

**lejitos** *adv. dim.* pretty far, rather far.

**lejos** *adv.* far, far away, far off, a long way off, afar: *estar* ~ *de,* to be far from; ~ *de mí,* fig. far be it from me: *a lo* ~, in the distance, far away; *de* ~, *desde* ~, from afar. 2 appearance at a distance: *tener buen* ~, to look good at a distance. 3 PAINT. distant view, background.

**lelo, -la** *adj.* stupid, dull. 2 *m.-f.* simpleton, ninny. 3 *estar* ~ *por,* to dote upon.

**lema** *m.* lemma. 2 motto. 3 slogan.

**lemniscata** *f.* GEOM. lemniscate.

**lemnisco** *m.* lemniscus.

**lemosín, -na** *adj.* of the Limousin. 2 Limousin language.

**lémur** *m.* ZOOL. lemur.

**lémures** *m. pl.* MYTH. lemures.

**len** *adj.* soft, flossy [thread or silk].

**lencería** *f.* linen goods. 2 linen trade. 3 linendraper's shop. 4 linen room.

**lencero** *m.* linen draper, linen merchant.

**lendrera** *f.* comb for removing nits or lice.

**lene** *adj.* soft, light, sweet, pleasant.

**lengua** *f.* tongue [organ in the mouth: faculty of, or tendence in, speech]: *las malas lenguas,* the gossips; *andar en lenguas,* to be much talked of; *hacerse lenguas de,* to praise highly; *írsele a uno la* ~, to say more than one wishes, to blab; *no morderse la* ~, to speak out, not to mince words; *tirar de la* ~ *a uno,* to draw out a person; *trabár-*

*sele a uno la* ~, to become tongue-tied; *tener en la punta de la* ~, .to have on the tip of one's tongue. *2* tongue, language: ~ *madre*, mother language or tongue [tongue from wich others spring]; ~ *materna*, mother tongue [one's native tongue]; ~ *viva*, living language. *3* tongue, clapper [of a bell]. *4* tongue [of land, of fire]. *5* tongue, index [of a balance or scale]. *6* BOT. ~ *canina* or *de perro*, hound's tongue; ~ *de ciervo*, hart's-tongue; ~ *de buey*, bugloss.

**lenguado** *m.* ICHTH. sole.

**lenguaje** *m.* language. *2* tongue, parlance, speech.

**lenguaraz,** *pl.* **-races** *adj.* accomplished in languages. *2* foul-mouthed; impudent, insolent.

**lenguaz,** *pl.* **-guaces** *adj.* garrulous.

**lengüecica, -cilla, -cita** *f. dim.* small tongue.

**lengüeta** *f.* small tongue. *2* ANAT. epiglottis. *3* tongue, index [of balance or scale]. *4* MUS. tongue, reed. *5* barb [of an arrow, etc.]. *6* CARP. tongue. *7* MEC. tongue, feather.

**lengüetada** *f.* licking, lapping.

**lengüetería** *f.* MUS. reedwork, reed stops [of an organ].

**lengüilargo, -ga** *adj.* bold, impudent.

**lenidad** *f.* lenity.

**lenificar** *tr.* to soften, assuage.

**Leningrado** *m. pr. n.* GEOG. Leningrad.

**lenitivo, -va** *adj.-m.* lenitive.

**lenocinio** *m.* pandering: *casa de* ~, brothel.

**lente** *m.-f.* OPT. lens. *2* OPT. glass: ~ *de aumento*, magnifying glass. *3 m. pl.* eyeglasses, nose glasses.

**lentecer** *intr.-ref.* to soften, grow soft. ¶ CONJUG. like *agradecer*.

**lenteja** *f.* BOT. lentil. *2* bob or disk of a pendulum.

**lentejuela** *f.* spangle, sequin [stitched on a dress].

**lenticular** *adj.* lenticular. *2 m.* ANAT. lenticular ossicle.

**lentisco** *m.* BOT. mastic tree.

**lentitud** *f.* slowness, sluggishness.

**lento, -ta** *adj.* slow. *2* sluggish, tardy, heavy. *3 adj.-adv.* MUS. lento.

**leña** *f.* firewood, kindling wood: *echar* ~ *al fuego*, fig. to add fuel to the flame. *2* beating, drubbing.

**leñador, -ra** *m.-f.* firewood dealer. *2 m.* woodman. *3 f.* woodwoman.

**leñazo** *m.* blow with a cudgel.

**leñera** *f.* woodshed; woodbin; woodpile.

**leñero** *m.* firewood seller. *2* LEÑERA.

**leño** *m.* log [unhewn piece of felled tree]. *2* wood [substance]. *3* NAUT. a medieval vessel. *4* poet. boat, ship, vessel. *5* fig. dullard.

**leñoso, -sa** *adj.* ligneous, woody.

**Leo** *m. pr. n.* ASTR. Leo.

**León** *m. pr. n.* Leon [man's name]. *2* ASTR. Leo. *3* GEOG. León [a Spanish town and province].

**león** *m.* ZOOL. lion: ~ *de Nemea*, MYTH. Nemean lion. *2* fig. lion [bold, brave man]. *3* ENT. lion ant. *4* ZOOL. ~ *marino*, sea lion.

**leona** *f.* lioness. *2* fig. brave, haughty woman.

**leonado, -da** *adj.* lion-coloured, tawny, fulvous.

**Leonardo** *m. pr. n.* Leonard.

**leoncico, cillo, cito** *m. dim.* little lion, lion cub.

**leonera** *f.* cage or den of lions. *2* coll. gambling den. *3* coll. den, junk room.

**leonero** *m.* lion keeper.

**leonés, -sa** *adj.-n.* of León.

**leonino, -na** *adj.* leonine. *2* one-sided, unfair. *3 f.* MED. leontiasis.

**Leonor** *f. pr. n.* Eleanor, Leonora, Leonore.

**leontina** *f.* watch chain.

**leopardo** *m.* ZOOL. leopard.

**leopoldina** *f.* MIL. a Spanish shako.

**Leopoldo** *m. pr. n.* Leopold.

**lepidóptero, -ra** *adj.* ENT. lepidopterus.

**lepisma** *f.* ENT. silver fish.

**leporino, -na** *adj.* leporine, harelike.

**lepra** *f.* MED. leprosy.

**leproso, -sa** *adj.* MED. leprous. *2 m.-f.* leper.

**lercha** *f.* reed on which fish and birds are strung.

**lerdo, -da** *adj.* dull, slow-witted. *2* slow, heavy.

**leridano, -na** *adj.-n.* of Lérida.

**les** *pers. pron. m.-f. pl.* them, to them, you, to you [indirect object]. *2 pers. pron. m. pl.* them, you [direct object].

**lesbiano, -na; lesbio, -bia** *adj.-n.* Lesbian.

**lesión** *f.* hurt, wound, injury. *2* harm, damage. *3* MED., VET. lesion.

**lesionar** *tr.* to hurt, wound, injure, damage, harm.

**lesivo, -va** *adj.* prejudicial, injurious.

**lesna** *f.* LEZNA.

**leso, -sa** *adj.* hurt, injured, offended: *lesa majestad*, lese majesty.

**letal** *adj.* lethal, deadly, mortal.

**letanía** *f.* ECCL. and fig. litany.

**letárgico, -ca** *adj.* lethargic.

**letargo** *m.* lethargy.

**Leteo** *m. pr. n.* MYTH. Lethe [river].

**leteo, -a** *adj.* poet. Lethean.

**Leticia** *f. pr. n.* Letitia.

**letificar** *tr.* to exhilarate, gladden, cheer.

**letífico, -ca** *adj.* gladdening, bringing joy.

**letón, -na** *adj.* Lettish. *2 m.-f.* Lett.

**letra** *f.* letter [of the alphabet; printing type], character, characters, hand, handwriting: ~ *capital* or *mayúscula*, capital letter; ~ *de molde*, print, printed letter; ~ *menuda*, fine, small writing; fig. cunning, adroitness; ~ *muerta*, dead letter; *tener buena* ~, to write a good hand. *2* line: *cuatro letras*, a few lines. *3* letter [literal meaning]: *al pie de la* ~, to the letter. *4* inscription. *5* words [of a song]. *6* COM. *letra* or ~ *de cambio*, draft, bill of exchange; *a* ~ *vista*, at sight. *7 pl.* letters: *bellas* or *buenas letras*, belles-lettres, literature; *letras humanas*, humanities. *8 primeras letras*, elementary education.

**letrado, -da** *adj.* lettered, learned, erudite. *2* coll. posing as a learned person. *3 m.-f.* lawyer.

**Letrán (San Juan de)** *pr. n.* Saint John Lateran [church].

**letrero** *m.* label. *2* sign [lettered board, etc.]; notice, placard.

**letrilla** *f.* a kind of Spanish rondelet.

**letrina** *f.* latrine, privy. *2* fig. filthy place.

**leucemia** *f.* MED. leukemia.

**leucocito** *m.* PHYSIOL. leucocyte.

**leucoma** *f.* MED. leucoma.

**leudar** *tr.* to leaven, ferment [dough] with yeast. *2 ref.* [of dough] to yeast, rise, ferment.

**leudo, -da** *adj.* leavened, fermented [dough, bread].

**leva** *f.* NAUT. weighing anchor. *2* MIL. levy, press. *3* MACH. lever; cam. *4* vane [of water wheel].

**levadizo, -za** *adj.* that can be lifted or raised: *puente* ~, drawbridge, lift bridge.

**levador** *m.* MEC. cog, tooth, cam.

**levadura** *f.* leaven, yeast.

**levantada** *f.* getting up [from bed].

**levantado, -da** *adj.* elevated, raised. *2* elevated, lofty, sublime. *3* up [from bed].

**levantamiento** *m.* elevation, raising, erection. *2* lifting up. *3* getting up. *4* elevation, sublimity.

*5* insurrection, uprising. *6* ~ *de planos,* surveying.
**levantar** *tr.* to raise, lift, lift up, heave, hoist. *2* to raise, set up, build, erect. *3* to take up, pick up, gather. *4* to raise [a blister, the voice, a siege, an army]. *5* to strike, take down [a tent]. *6* HUNT. to rouse, start [game]. *7* to stir, stir up. *8* to incite to rebellion. *9* to cut [cards]. *10* to impute falsely: ~ *un falso testimonio,* to bear false witness. *11* ~ *acta,* to draw up a formal statement [of a fact]. *12* ~ *bandera,* to rebel. *13* ~ *cabeza,* to take courage. *14* TOP. ~ *el plano de,* to survey. *15* ~ *la casa,* to move. *16* ~ *la mesa,* to clear the table. *17* ~ *la sesión,* to adjourn, rise. *18 ref.* to rise [move upward, ascend; come to life again]. *19* to rise, get up [from bed, chair, etc.]; to stand up. *20* to rise, to rebel. *21* [of spirits] to rise. *22* [of game] to start. *23 levantarse la tapa de los sesos,* to blow out one's brains.
**levante** *m.* East, Orient. *2* east wind, levanter. *3* Mediterranean regions of Spain. *4* Levant.
**levantino, -na** *adj.-n.* Levantine. *2* of the Mediterranean regions of Spain.
**levantisco, -ca** *adj.* turbulent, restless.
**levar** *tr.* NAUT. to set sail.
**leve** *adj.* light [not heavy]. *2* slight, trivial, trifling, venial.
**levedad** *f.* lightness, levity. *2* slightness. *3* inconstancy.
**Leví** *m. pr. n.* BIBL. Levi.
**leviatán** *m.* BIBL. & fig. leviathan.
**levigar** *tr.* to levigate.
**levirato** *m.* BIBL., HIST. levirate.
**levita** *m.* BIBL., HIST. Levite. *2 f.* frock-coat.
**levitación** *f.* levitation.
**levítico, -ca** *adj.* levitical. *2 m.* (cap.) BIBL. Leviticus.
**levitón** *m.* heavy frock-coat.
**levulosa** *f.* CHEM. levulose.
**léxico, -ca** *adj.* lexical. *2 m.* lexicon. *3* language of a person.
**lexicografía** *f.* lexicography.
**lexicógrafo** *m.* lexicographer.
**ley** *f.* law [body of enacted or customary rules]; law, rule, precept, act, statute; ~ *antigua,* Old law, Mosaic law; ~ *nueva, de gracia,* Christ's law; ~ *del embudo,* coll. one-sided law; ~ *escrita,* revealed law, decalogue; ~ *marcial,* martial law; ~ *seca,* dry law; *con todas las de la* ~, perfect. *2* SCIENCE, ECON. law. *3* religion, dispensation. *4* loyalty, devotion, attachment: *tener* or *tomar* ~ *a,* to become attached to. *5* legal standard of quality, weight or measure: *de buena* ~, fig. sterling, good; *de mala* ~, fig. bad, low, base. *6* fineness [of coin, metal]: *oro, plata de* ~, fine, sterling gold or silver.
**leyenda** *f.* legend.
**lezna** *f.* awl.
**Lía** *f. pr. n.* BIBL. Leah.
**lía** *f.* plaited esparto rope. *2 sing.-pl.* lee, dregs.
**liar** *tr.* to tie, bind, tie up, wrap up. *2* to roll [a cigarette]. *3* coll. to involve, entangle [a person]. *4 liarlas,* coll. to flee, go away; to die. *5 ref.* to embroil oneself. *6* to enter into concubinage.
**liásico, -ca** *adj.-m.* GEOL. Liassic.
**libación** *f.* libation.
**Líbano** *m. pr. n.* GEOG. Lebanon.
**libar** *tr.* to suck the juice [of flowers, etc.]. *2* to taste, drink [a liquor]. *3 intr.* to make a libation.
**libelista** *m.* libeler, libelist [writer of libels].

**libelo** or **libelo infamatorio** *m.* libel [defamatory writing].
**libélula** *f.* ENT. libellula, dragonfly.
**líber** *m.* BOT. bast, liber.
**liberación** *f.* liberation, deliverance, release.
**liberal** *adj.* liberal, generous. *2 artes liberales,* liberal arts. *3 adj.-n.* POL. liberal.
**liberalidad** *f.* liberality, generosity.
**liberalismo** *m.* POL. liberalism. *2* liberal party.
**liberalizar** *tr.* to liberalize.
**libérrimo, -ma** *adj. superl.* most free.
**libertad** *f.* liberty, freedom: ~ *de acción,* liberty of action; ~ *de cultos,* freedom of worship; ~ *de imprenta,* freedom of the press; ~ *provisional,* liberation on bail; *poner en* ~, to set free; *en* ~, at liberty. *2* liberty [setting aside of rules; licence]. *3* liberty, freedom [undue familiarity]: *tomarse libertades,* to make free with. *4* freedom, ease [in action]. *5* free an easy manners. *6 pl.* liberties, privileges.
**libertado, -da** *adj.* freed. *2* free, unrestrained. *3* free, bold, forward.
**libertador, -ra** *adj.* liberating, delivering. *2 m.-f.* liberator, deliverer.
**libertar** *tr.* to set free, liberate, deliver. *2* to free, rid, clear. *3* to exempt [of obligation]. *4* to save, preserve [from death, danger, etc.].
**libertario, -ria** *adj.* anarchistic. *2 m.-f.* anarchist.
**liberticida** *adj.* liberticidal. *2 m.-f.* liberticide.
**libertinaje** *m.* libertinism, libertinage, profligacy.
**libertino, -na** *adj.-n.* libertine, profligate.
**liberto, -ta** *adj.-n.* freedman, freedwoman.
**Libia** *f. pr. n.* GEOG. Lybia.
**líbico, -ca** *adj.-n.* Lybian.
**libídine** *f.* lewdness, lust.
**libidinoso, -sa** *adj.* libidinous, lewd, lustful.
**libido** *f.* libido.
**libio, -bia** *adj.-n.* Lybian.
**libra** *f.* pound [weight; coin]: ~ *esterlina,* pound sterling. *2* (cap.) ASTR. Libra.
**libración** *f.* libration [vibration]. *2* ASTR. libration.
**librado, -da** *adj. salir bien* ~, to come off well, unscathed; *salir mal* ~, to come off in a bad state. *2 m.-f.* COM. drawee.
**librador, -ra** *m.-f.* deliverer, preserver. *2* COM. drawer [of a bill of exchange]. *3 m.* grocer's scoop.
**libramiento** *m.* delivering, preserving. *2* order for payment.
**libranza** *f.* draft [order for payment of money].
**librar** *tr.* to free, deliver, save, preserve [from ill, danger, etc.]. *2* place [one's hopes]. *3* to pass [sentence]. *4* to issue, draw [a bill, a draft, etc.]. *5* to join, give [battle]. *6 ¡Dios me libre!,* God forbid! *7 intr.* to be delivered of a child. *8 a bien* ~, *a buen* ~, at best. *9 ref. librarse de,* to free oneself of or from; to get rid of; to escape: *de buena nos hemos librado,* we have had a close shave.
**librazo** *m. aug.* big book.
**libre** *adj.* free [in practically every sense, except gratuitous and liberal, generous]: ~ *albedrío,* free will; ~ *cambio,* free change; ~ *curso,* free course; ~ *de impuestos,* tax free. *2* vacant [place, seat]. *3* disengaged, at leisure. *4* single, unmarried.
**librea** *f.* livery [worn by a servant].
**librecambio** *m.* free trade.
**librecambista** *adj.* free-trading. *2 m.-f.* freetradist, freetrader.
**librejo** *m.* worthless book.

**librepensador, -ra** *adj.* freethingking. *2 m.-f.* free thinker.
**librepensamiento** *m.* free thinking, free thought.
**librería** *f.* bookcase. *2* bookseller's shop, bookstore. *3* book trade, bookselling.
**librero** *m.* bookseller.
**libreta** *f.* notebook: ~ *de la Caja de ahorros*, bankbook [of savings bank]. *2* loaf of bread of 1 lb. weight.
**libretista** *m.-f.* librettist.
**libreto** *m.* libretto.
**librillo** *m.* small book, booklet. *2* small book of cigarette paper.
**libro** *m.* book: ~ *antifonal* or *antifonario*, antiphonal; ~ *borrador*, COM. blotter, record book; ~ *copiador*, COM. letter book; ~ *de actas*, minute book; ~ *de caballerías*, romance of chivalry; ~ *de caja*, COM. cashbook; ~ *de cocina*, cookbook; ~ *de texto*, textbook; ~ *diario*, COM. daybook; ~ *en rústica*, paperbound book; ~ *mayor*, COM. ledger; *hablar como un* ~, to speak very well. *2* MUS. libretto. *3* ZOOL. abomasum.
**librote** *m.* large book. *2* trashy book.
**licántropo** *adj.* lycanthrope.
**licencia** *f.* license, leave, permission. *2* license [abuse of freedom], licentiousness. *3* EDUC. degree of master or bachelor. *4* [poetic] license. *5* MIL. leave: ~ *absoluta*, discharge.
**licenciado, -da** *m.-f.* EDUC. licentiate, graduate, holder of the degree of master or bachelor. *2* lawyer. *3* ~ *del ejército*, discharged soldier.
**licenciamiento** *m.* LICENCIATURA. *2* MIL. discharge [of soldiers].
**licenciar** *tr.* to give leave or permission. *2* EDUC. to confer the degree of master or bachelor. *3* MIL. to discharge [soldiers]. *4* *ref.* to receive the degree of master or bachelor.
**licenciatura** *f.* degree of master or bachelor. *2* act of conferring the degree of master or bachelor. *3* studies leading to the graduation with a degree of master or bachelor.
**licencioso, -sa** *adj.* licentious, dissolute.
**liceo** *m.* lyceum. *2* name for some clubs.
**Licia** *f. pr. n.* HIST., GEOG. Lycia.
**licitación** *f.* bidding [at an auction].
**licitador** *m.* bidder [at an auction].
**licitar** *tr.* bid on or for [at an auction].
**lícito, -ta** *adj.* licit, permitted, lawful, right, just.
**licopodio** *m.* BOT. lycopodium.
**licor** *m.* liquor. *2* liqueur.
**licorera** *f.* cellaret.
**licorista** *m.-f.* liqueur distiller. *2* liqueur seller.
**licoroso, -sa** *adj.* generous, rich [wine].
**licuación** *f.* liquefaction. *2* METAL. liquation.
**licuar** *tr.* to liquefy. *2* METAL. to liquate. *3* *ref.* to liquefy [become liquid].
**licuefacción** *f.* liquefaction.
**Licurgo** *m. pr. n.* Lycurgus.
**lid** *f.* contest, fight. *2* dispute, argument.
**líder** *m.* Angl. political leader.
**Lidia** *f. pr. n.* HIST., GEOG. Lydia.
**lidia** *f.* fight, struggle. *2* bullfight.
**lidiador, -ra** *m.-f.* combatant, fighter. *2* bullfighter.
**lidiar** *intr.* to fight, contend. *2* to struggle. *3* ~ *con*, to face up; to try to cope with. *4* *tr.* to fight [bulls].
**liebre** *f.* ZOOL. hare. *2* fig. coward. *3* ZOOL. ~ *de mar*, sea hare.
**Lieja** *f. pr. n.* GEOG. Liège.
**liendre** *f.* nit [egg of louse].

**liento, -ta** *adj.* damp, moist.
**lienzo** *m.* [flax, hemp or cotton] cloth; linen. *2* handkerchief. *3* PAINT. canvas. *4* face [of a building]; stretch [of wall]. *5* FORT. curtain.
**liga** *f.* garter. *2* band, bandage. *3* BOT. mistletoe. *4* birdlime. *5* union, mixture. *6* alloy [of metals]. *7* league, alliance. *8* FOOTBALL. league.
**ligado** *m.* union of letters in writing. *2* MUS. ligature.
**ligadura** *f.* tie, bond, ligature. *2* subjection. *3* turn of rope, etc. tying something. *4* MUS. ligature.
**ligamaza** *f.* viscosity on some fruits or seeds.
**ligamento** *m.* tying, binding. *2* ANAT. ligament.
**ligar** *tr.* to tie, bind. *2* to alloy [metals]. *3* to join, unite. *4* to bind, obligate. *5* SURG. to ligate. *6* *ref.* to league together, to enter in a league [with]. *7* to join, combine [be combined]. *8* to bind oneself.
**ligazón** *f.* union, connection, linking.
**ligereza** *f.* lightness, swiftness, agility, nimbleness. *2* lightness [of weight]. *3* lightness, levity, frivolity. *4* thoughtless act, indiscretion.
1) **ligero, -ra** *adj.* light [not heavy; easy to endure or perform; not violent; not burdened]. *2* light, swift, agile, nimble. *3* light [clothes, food, wine, sleep, comedy, etc.]. *4* thin [cloth]. *5* light, flippant, jesting. *6* light, giddy, fickle. *7* light, wanton. *8* MIL. light: *caballería ligera*, light horse. *9* ~ *de cascos*, featherbrained; ~ *de ropa*, scantily clad. *10 a la ligera*, quickly, simply, unceremoniously. *11 de* ~, rashly.
2) **ligero** *adv.* fast, rapidly.
**ligio, -gia** *adj.* liege.
**lignificarse** *ref.* to lignify.
**lignina** *f.* BOT. lignin.
**lignito** *m.* MINER. lignite.
**ligula** *f.* BOT. ligule.
**ligur, ligurino, -na** *adj.-n.* Ligurian.
**ligustre** *m.* BOT. flower of the privet.
**ligustro** *m.* BOT. privet.
**lija** *f.* ICHTH. dogfish. *2* shagreen; sandpaper.
**lijar** *tr.* to sandpaper.
**Lila** *f. pr. n.* GEOG. Lille.
**lila** *f.* BOT. lilac [shrub and flower]. *2* lilac colour. *3* *adj.* silly, half-witted. *4* *m.-f.* fool, simpleton.
**liliáceo, -a** *adj.* BOT. liliaceous.
**liliputiense** *adj.-n.* Liliputian.
**Lima** *f. pr. n.* GEOG. Lima.
**lima** *f.* file [tool]. *2* finish, polishing. *3* BOT. sweet lime [fruit]. *4* BOT. sweet-lime tree. *5* ARCH. ~ *hoya*, valley. *6* ARCH. ~ *tesa*, hip.
**limadura** *f.* filing [smoothing]. *2 pl.* filings.
**limalla** *f.* filings [of metal].
**limar** *tr.* to file [smooth with a file]. *2* to polish, touch up. *3* to weaken, destroy.
**limaza** *f.* ZOOL. slug.
**limazo** *m.* viscosity, slime.
**limbo** *m.* THEOL. limbo: *estar en el* ~, fig. to be absent-minded. *2* edge, border. *3* limb.
**limen** *m.* poet. threshold.
**limeño, -ña** *adj.-n.* Limean.
**limero** *m.* BOT. sweet-lime tree.
**limeta** *f.* long-necked bottle.
**limitación** *f.* limitation. *2* boundary, district.
**limitado, -da** *adj.* limited. *2* short, scanty. *3* dull-witted.
**limitador, -ra** *adj.* limiting. *2 m.-f.* limiter.
**limitáneo, -a** *adj.* frontier, bordering.
**limitar** *tr.* to mark the boundaries of. *2* to limit. *3* to cut down, reduce. *4* *intr.* ~ *con*, to border on,

be contiguous to. *5 ref.* to reduce expense. *6 limitarse a,* to confine oneself to.

**límite** *m.* limit, bound: *sin límites,* illimited, unbounded. *2* boundary, border. *3* MATH. limit.

**limítrofe** *adj.* bordering, conterminous.

**limo** *m.* mud, slime.

**limón** *m.* BOT. lemon tree.

**limonada** *f.* lemonade.

**limonar** *m.* lemon plantation or grove.

**limonera** *f.* shaft [of a carriage].

**limonero, -ra** *adj.* shaft [horse]. *2 m.-f.* shaft horse. *3* lemon seller. *4 m.* BOT. lemon tree.

**limonita** *f.* MINER. limonite.

**limosidad** *f.* muddiness, sliminess.

**limosna** *f.* alms.

**limosnero, -ra** *adj.* almsgiving, charitable. *2 m.* almoner.

**limoso, -sa** *adj.* muddy, slimy.

**limpia** *f.* cleaning, cleansing.

**limpiabarros,** *pl.* **-rros** *m.* scraper, boot scraper.

**limpiabotas,** *pl.* **-tas** *m.* bootblack.

**limpiachimeneas,** *pl.* **-neas** *m.* chimneysweep(er.

**limpiador, -ra** *adj.* cleaning, cleansing. *2 m.-f.* cleaner, cleanser.

**limpiamente** *adv.* cleanly. *2* neatly. *3* skilfully, with ease. *4* purely, honestly. *5* sincerely, fairly.

**limpiaparabrisas,** *pl.* **-sas** *m.* windshield wiper.

**limpiar** *tr.* to clean, cleanse. *2* to wipe [a pen, the hands, etc.]. *3* to shine [shoes]. *4* to furbish [metals]. *5* to prune [a tree]. *6* to clear [from impurities, weeds, etc.]. *7* to purify. *8* coll. to steal, to pick. *9* coll. to clean up or out [in gambling]. *10 ref.* to clean oneself.

**limpiatubos,** *pl.* **-bos** *m.* tube cleaner.

**limpiauñas,** *pl.* **-ñas** *m.* nail cleaner.

**limpidez** *f.* poet. limpidity.

**límpido, -da** *adj.* limpid, clear, pure.

**limpieza** *f.* cleanness, cleanliness. *2* neatness. *3* purity, chastity. *4* integrity, honesty, fairness. *5* neatness, ease or skill of execution. *6* cleaning. *7* household cleaning.

1) **limpio, -pia** *adj.* clean, cleanly. *2* neat, tidy. *3* clear [free from impurities, guile, guilt, etc.]; pure, -chaste, honest. *4* clear, net [free from deductions]. *5* fair [play]. *6 poner en ~,* to make a clear copy of. *7 sacar en ~,* to conclude, infer, make out.

2) **limpio** *adv.* cleanly. *2* fair: *jugar ~,* to play fair.

**limpión** *m.* hasty cleaning.

**lináceo, -a** *adj.* BOT. linaceous.

**linaje** *m.* lineage, family, race: *~ humano,* mankind. *2* class, kind, description.

**linajista** *m.* genealogist.

**linajudo, -da** *adj.* of high lineage, of noble descent.

**lináleo** *m.* BOT. aloes.

**linaza** *f.* flaxseed, linseed.

**lince** *m.* ZOOL. lynx. *2* fig. keen, shrewd person. *3 adj.* keen [sight, eyes].

**linceo, -a** *adj.* lyncean. *2* keen [sight, eyes].

**linchamiento** *m.* lynching.

**linchar** *tr.* to lynch.

**lindamente** *adv.* prettily, neatly, finely.

**lindante** *adj.* bordering, adjoining, contiguous.

**lindar** *intr.* *~ con,* to border, verge, abut on.

**linde** *m.-f.* limit, boundary.

**lindero, -ra** *adj.* bordering, adjoining. *2 m.* limit, boundary.

**lindeza** *f.* prettiness, neatness, beauty, elegance. *2 pl.* pretty things. *3* iron. insults.

**lindo, -da** *adj.* beautiful, pretty, nice, fine, lovely. *2 de lo ~,* a great deal, greatly.

**lindura** *f.* LINDEZA.

**línea** *f.* GEOM. line. *2* line [twelfth part of an inch]. *3* line [threadlike mark, formation or appearance; direction, course]: *~ de agua, ~ de flotación,* NAUT. water line; *~ de fondo,* TENNIS base line, service line; FOOTBALL goal line; *~ de fuerza,* PHYS. line of force; *~ de puntos,* dotted line; *~ equinoccial,* GEOG. equinoctial line. *4* GEOG. the line, the equator. *5* course, line [of conduct]. *6* line [written or printed]: *unas líneas, cuatro líneas,* fig. a line [short, letter]. *7* line [of steamers, autobuses, etc.]: *~ aérea,* airline; *~ férrea,* railway line; *~ telegráfica,* telegraph line. *8* line [of family]: *~ directa,* direct line. *9* limit, boundary. *10* MIL., NAV. line: *~ de fuego,* firing line. *12* class, kind. *13 en toda la ~,* thoroughly.

**lineal** *adj.* lineal, linear.

**lineamento, lineamiento** *m.* lineament.

**linear** *adj.* BOT., ZOOL. linear.

**linfa** *f.* PHYSIOL. lymph. *2* poet, lymph, water.

**linfático, -ca** *adj.* lymphatic.

**linfatismo** *m.* MED. lymphatism.

**linfocito** *m.* ANAT. lymphocite.

**lingote** *m.* ingot, pig, bloom.

**lingual** *adj.* lingual.

**linguete** *m.* pawl, ratchet.

**lingüista** *m.* linguist.

**lingüística** *f.* linguistics.

**linimento, linimiento** *m.* liniment.

**lino** *m.* BOT. flax. *2* flax [fiber]. *3* linen [thread, cloth].

**linóleo** *m.* linoleum.

**linón** *m.* lawn [fabric].

**linotipia** *f.* linotype.

**linotipista** *m.* linotypist.

**lintel** *m.* DINTEL.

**linterna** *f.* lantern, lamp: *~ eléctrica,* electric torch, flashlight; *~ mágica,* magic lantern; *~ sorda,* dark lantern. *2* NAUT. lighthouse. *3* MACH., ARCH. lantern.

**linternazo** *m.* blow with a lantern. *2* fig. blow.

**liño** *m.* row of trees or plants.

**lío** *m.* bundle, parcel. *2* tangle, muddle, mess, imbroglio: *armar un ~,* to muddle things, to stir up trouble; *hacerse un ~,* to get muddled, confused. *3* liaison [illicit intimacy]. *4* lie, deception.

**Lión** *pr. n.* GEOG. Lyon, Lyons.

**lionés, -sa** *adj.-n.* Lyonese.

**lioso, -sa** *adj.* lying, mischief-making. *2* embroiled, difficult. *3 m.-f.* liar, mischief-maker.

**lipoma** *m.* MED. lipoma.

**liquen** *m.* BOT., MED. lichen.

**liquidación** *f.* liquefaction. *2* liquidation. *3* bargain sale.

**liquidador, -ra** *adj.* liquidating. *2 m.-f.* liquidator. *3 ~ de averías,* insurance adjuster.

**liquidámbar** *m.* liquidambar.

**liquidar** *tr.* to liquefy. *2* to liquidate. *3* fig. to squander; to destroy, murder. *4 intr.* to liquidate; to go into liquidation. *5 ref.* to liquefy [come into liquid condition].

**liquidez** *f.* liquidity, liquidness.

**líquido, -da** *adj.* liquid, aquiform. *2* COM. clear, net. *3 adj.-f.* PHONET. liquid. *4 m.* liquid, liquor. *5* COM. net.

**lira** *f.* lira [monetary unit]. *2* MUS. lyre. *3* a Spanish poem or fixed verse form. *4* inspiration, poetry [of a poet]. *5* ASTR. (cap.) Lyra, Lyre.

**lírico, -ca** *adj.* lyric, lyrical. *2 m.-f.* lyric poet. *3 f.* lyric poetry. .

**lirio** *m.* BOT. German iris. *2* BOT. iris, lily: ~ *blanco*, Madonna lily; ~ *de agua*, calla, calla lily; ~ *de los valles*, lily of the valley.
**lirismo** *m.* lyricism. *2* abuse of lyricism.
**lirón** *m.* ZOOL. dormouse: *dormir como un* ~, to sleep like a log. *2* coll. sleepyhead.
**lirondo** *adj.* V. MONDO Y LIRONDO.
**lis** *f.* BOT. iris, flower-de-luce. *2* HER. fleur-de-lis.
**lisa** *f.* ICHTH. a kind of loach. *2* ICHTH. striped mullet.
**Lisboa** *f. pr. n.* GEOG. Lisbon.
**lisboeta; lisbonense; lisbonés, -ra** *adj.-n.* of Lisbon.
**lisiado, -da** *adj.* crippled. *2 m.-f.* cripple.
**lisiar** *tr.* to injure, maim, cripple. *2 ref.* to become crippled.
**lisimaquia** *f.* BOT. loosestrife.
**liso, -sa** *adj.* smooth, even. *2* plain, unadorned. *3* ANAT. nonstriated [muscle]. *4* ~ *y llano*, simple, easy.
**lisonja** *f.* flattery; compliment. *2* HER. lozenge.
**lisonjeador, -ra** *adj.* flattering. *2 m.-f.* flatterer.
**lisonjear** *tr.* to flatter. *2 ref.* to flatter oneself.
**lisonjero, -ra** *adj.* flattering; complimentary. *2* pleasing; promising, rosy. *3 m.-f.* flatterer.
**lista** *f.* strip. *2* slip [of paper]. *3* list, stripe, band. *4* list, catalogue: ~ *de platos*, bill of fare, menu; ~ *negra*, black list. *5* muster, roll; *pasar* ~, to call the roll. *6* POST. ~ *de correos*, general delivery.
**listado, -da** *adj.* striped.
**listel** *m.* ARCH. listel, fillet.
**listeza** *f.* cleverness, sagacity, smartness.
**listo, -ta** *adj.* ready, prepared. *2* ready, quick, prompt. *3* finished, completed; having finished [with a task]. *4* clever, adroit, shrewd.
**listón** *m.* narrow ribbon. *2* ARCH. listel, fillet. *3* CARP. lath, batten, strip of wood.
**lisura** *f.* smoothness, evenness. *2* sincerity, candour.
**lite** *f.* LAW lawsuit.
**litera** *f.* litter [vehicle]. *2* berth [in boat or train].
**literal** *adj.* literal.
**literalmente** *adv.* literally.
**literario, -ria** *adj.* literary.
**literato, -ta** *adj.* literary [person]. *2 m.-f.* literary person, writer.
**literatura** *f.* literature.
**litiasis** *f.* MED. lithiasis.
**litigación** *f.* litigation.
**litigante** *adj.-n.* litigant.
**litigar** *tr.-intr.* to litigate.
**litigio** *m.* litigation, law suit. *2* dispute, contest.
**litigioso, -sa** *adj.* litigious.
**litio** *m.* CHEM. lithium.
**litis,** *pl.* **-tis** *f.* LAW lawsuit.
**litófago, -ga** *adj.* ZOOL. lithophagous, rock-boring.
**litografía** *f.* lithography.
**litografiar** *tr.* to lithograph.
**litógrafo** *m.* lithographer.
**litología** *f.* lithology.
**litoral** *adj.* littoral, coastal. *2 m.* littoral, coast, shore.
**litro** *m.* litre, liter.
**Lituania** *f. pr. n.* GEOG. Lithuania.
**lituano, -na** *adj.-n.* Lithuanian.
**liturgia** *f.* liturgy.
**litúrgico, -ca** *adj.* liturgic(al.
**liviandad** *f.* lewdness. *2* lightness [lack of weight]. *3* levity, frivolity.
**liviano, -na** *adj.* wanton, lewd. *2* light [not heavy].

*3* slight [unimportant]. *4* frivolous, fickle. *5 m. pl.* lights, lungs.
**lividez** *f.* lividness.
**lívido, -da** *adj.* livid.
**livor** *m.* livid colour. *2* fig. malignity, hatred, envy.
**liza** *f.* lists [place of combat]. *2* combat, contest.
**lizo** *m.* WEAV. warp thread. *2* WEAV. heddle, leash.
**lo** *art. neut.* [before a masc. form of adjective] the, that which is, the... thing or things: ~ *primero*, the first thing; ~ *bello*, the beautiful, beautiful things. | The adjective can often be translated by a corresponding noun: ~ *estúpido de su proceder*, the stupidity of his behaviour. *2* [before an adverb or an inflected adjective followed by *que*] how; so: *usted verá* ~ *bien que [ella] baila*, you will see how well she dances; *con* ~ *cansado que estaba*, being so tired. *3 a* ~ [followed by a noun], like, in the style of, *a* ~ *caballero*, like a gentleman. *4* ~ *más*, as... as: ~ *lo más pronto posible*, as soon as possible. *5 pers. pron. masc. & neut.* him, you [in correspondence with *usted*], it, that: ~ *vi*, I saw him, I saw it. *6* so: *ya te* ~ *dije*, I told you so. *7 a* ~ *que*, according to, from what; *a* ~ *que veo*, from what I see. *8* ~ *de ayer*, what happened yesterday; ~ *de siempre*, the same old story. *9* ~ *que*, what, that which; how much. *10* ~ *que es por*, as to, as for.
**loa** *f.* praise. *2* THEAT. prologue [of an ancient play]. *3* short dramatic panegyric.
**loable** *adj.* laudable, praiseworthy.
**loar** *tr.* to praise, eulogize.
**loba** *f.* ZOOL. she-wolf. *2* soutane, cassock.
**lobado, -da** *adj.* BOT., ZOOL. lobate.
**lobanillo** *m.* MED. wen.
**lobato** *m.* wolf cub.
**lobeliáceo, -a** *adj.* BOT. lobeliaceous.
**lobera** *f.* thicket where wolves make their lair.
**lobezno** *m.* wolf cub.
**lobina** *f.* RÓBALO.
**lobo** *m.* ZOOL. wolf. *2* ICHTH. louch. *3* BOT. lobe. *4* coll. drunkenness. *5* coll. ~ *de mar*, old salt, sea dog.
**loboso, -sa** *adj.* full of wolves.
**lóbrego, -ga** *adj.* dark, gloomy, murky.
**lobreguez** *f.* darkness, obscurity, gloominess.
**lobulado, -da** *adj.* BOT., ZOOL. lobate, lobed, lobulate.
**lóbulo** *m.* lobe, lobule.
**lobuno, -na** *adj.* wolfish.
**locación** *f.* LAW lease.
**local** *adj.* local. *2 m.* place, rooms, quarters, premises.
**localidad** *f.* locality. *2* place, village, town. *3* seat [in a theatre, show, etc.].
**localización** *f.* localization. *2* location, act of finding out where a person or thing is.
**localizar** *tr.* to localize. *2* to locate, to find out where [a person or thing] is.
**locatario, -ria** *m.-f.* ARRENDATARIO.
**loco, -ca** *adj.* mad, crazy, insane: ~ *de remate*, stark mad; ~ *de contento*, fig. mad with joy. *2* mad, wild, violent. *3* foolish, imprudent. *4* great, abundant, immoderate, excessive. *5* MACH. idle. *6 m.-f.* lunatic, insane person, madman, madwoman. *7* fool.
**locomoción** *f.* locomotion.
**locomotor, -ra** *adj.* locomotive, locomotor. *2 f.* RLY. locomotive.
**locomotriz** *f. adj.* locomotive.
**locomóvil** *adj.-f.* locomobile.
**locuacidad** *f.* loquacity, talkativeness.

**locuaz** adj. loquacious, talkative.

**locución** f. locution. 2 phrase, idiom.

**locuelo, -la** adj. frisky, madcap [youngster]. 2 m. -f. young madcap.

**lóculo** m. loculus.

**locura** f. madness, lunacy, insanity: con ~, madly. 2 folly, foolishness, imprudence.

**locutor, -ra** m.-f. radio announcer, radio speaker.

**locutorio** m. locutory, parlour [in a convent]. 2 call box, telephone booth.

**locha** f., **loche** m. ICHTH. loach.

**lodachar, lodazal, lodazar** m. muddy place, mudhole.

**lodo** m. mud, mire.

**lodoso, -sa** adj. muddy, miry.

**lofobranquio, -quia** adj.-m. ICHTH. lophobranch.

**logaritmo** m. MATH. logarithm.

**logia** f. lodge [of freemasons]. 2 ARCH. loggia.

**lógica** f. logic.

**lógico, -ca** adj. logical. 2 m.-f. logician.

**logística** f. MIL. logistics.

**logogrifo** m. logogryph, riddle.

**logomaquia** f. logomachy.

**lograr** tr. to get, acquire, attain, obtain, procure. 2 [with an inf.] to succeed in, manage to. 3 ref. [of a thing] to succeed; to attain perfection.

**logrería** f. usury, profiteering.

**logrero, -ra** m.-f. moneylender. 2 usurer, profiteer.

**logro** m. accomplishment, attainment. 2 gain, profit, interest. 3 usury.

**Loira** m. pr. n. GEOG. Loire.

**Lola, Lolita** f. pr. n. dim. of DOLORES.

**loma** f. eminence, down, slope, long little hill.

**lombarda** f. lombard [cannon]. 2 BOT. a red cabbage.

**Lombardía** f. pr. n. GEOG. Lombardy.

**lombardo, -da** adj.-n. Lombard. 2 Longobard.

**lombriz** f. ZOOL. earthworm. 2 ZOOL. ~ intestinal, intestinal worm. 3 ZOOL. ~ solitaria, tapeworm.

**lomear** intr. [of horses] to arch the back.

**lomera** f. backstrap [of harness]. 2 BOOKB. backing.

**lomo** m. the lower part of the back [of a person]. 2 back [of an animal, a book, a cutting tool]. 3 chine [of pork]. 4 ridge between furrows. 6 pl. ribs, loins [of a person].

**lona** f. canvas [for sails, tents, etc.], sailcloth.

**loncha** f. flagstone, slap. 2 LONJA 4.

**londinense** adj. [pertaining to] London. 2 m.-f. Londoner.

**Londres** m. pr. n. GEOG. London.

**longanimidad** f. long-suffering, forbearance, magnanimity.

**longaniza** f. long pork sausage.

**longevidad** f. longevity.

**longevo, -va** adj. longevous, long-lived.

**longirrostro, -tra** adj. ORN. longirostral.

**longitud** f. length, longitude. 2 ASTR., GEOG. longitude.

**longitudinal** adj. longitudinal.

**lonja** f. exchange, market. 2 grocer's shop. 3 ARCH. raised porch. 4 slice [of meat]; strip [of leather].

**lontananza** f. PAINT. background. 2 en ~, far away, far off, in the distance.

**loor** m. praise.

**loquear** intr. to act like a fool. 2 to frolic.

**loquero, -ra** m.-f. guard or attendant in an insane asylum. 2 f. (Am.) folly [foolish act].

**loquesco, -ca** adj. reckless, foolish. 2 merry, jesting.

**lord**, pl. **lores** m. lord [English title].

**lordosis** f. MED. lordosis.

**Lorena (la)** f. pr. n. GEOG. Lorraine.

**lorenés, -sa** adj. Lorrainese. 2 m.-f. Lorrainer.

**Lorenzo** m. pr. n. Laurence, Lawrence.

**loriga** f. lorica [cuirass]. 2 horse armour.

**loro** adj. tawny, dark brown. 2 m. ORN. parrot.

**lorza** f. SEW. tuck.

**los** art. def. m. pl. the. 2 ~ que, those, or they who or which. 3 pron. pers. m. pl. [direct object] them: ~ vi, I saw them.

**losa** f. flagstone, slab. 2 gravestone. 3 grave.

**losange** m. lozenge, diamond.

**lote** m. share, portion [of something to be distributed]. 2 lot [of land]. 3 prize [in a lottery]. 4 lot [set of articles].

**lotería** f. lottery. 2 lotto [game].

**lotero, -ra** m.-f. seller of lottery tickets.

**loto** m. BOT. lotus. 2 BOT. lotus tree. 3 fruit of the lotus tree.

**lotófago, -ga** adj. lotus-eating. 2 m.-f. lotus-eater.

**Lovaina** f. pr. n. GEOG. Lovain.

**loza** f. china, fine earthenware or crockery.

**lozanear** intr. [of plants] to be luxuriant. 2 [of persons] to be blooming, fresh, vigorous.

**lozanía** f. verdure, luxuriance. 2 bloom, freshness, vigour. 3 pride, haughtiness.

**lozano, -na** adj. verdant, luxuriant. 2 blooming, fresh, vigorous, full of life. 3 proud, haughty.

**lubina** f. RÓBALO.

**lubricación** f. lubrication.

**lubricán** m. twilight [in morning or evening].

**lubricante** m. lubricant.

**lubricar** tr. to lubricate.

**lubricidad** f. lubricity.

**lúbrico, -ca** adj. lubricous.

**lubrificación** f. LUBRICACIÓN.

**lubrificante** m. LUBRICANTE.

**lubrificar** tr. LUBRICAR.

**Lucas** m. pr. n. Luke.

**Lucerna** f. pr. n. GEOG. Lucerne.

**lucerna** f. large chandelier [hanging from the ceiling]. 2 skylight, light shaft. 3 ICHTH. lying gurnard.

**lucero** m. any bright star: ~ del alba or de la mañana, morning star; ~ de la tarde, evening star. 2 star [on the forehead of an animal]. 3 pl. poet, eyes.

**Lucía** f. pr. n. Lucy, Lucía.

**lucidez** f. lucidity.

**lucido, -da** adj. brilliant, successful. 2 splendid, magnificient. 3 generous.

**lúcido, -da** adj. poet. lucid, bright. 2 lucid [in thought or style]. 3 MED. lucid.

**luciente** adj. lucent, bright, shining, luminous.

**luciérnaga** f. ENT. glowworm, firefly.

**Lucifer** m. pr. n. Lucifer, Satan. 2 morning star.

**lucífero, -ra** adj. poet, shining, luminous. 2 m. morning star.

**lucífugo, -ga** adj. lucifugal, lucifugous.

**lucimiento** m. brilliancy, show, splendour. 2 skill, success [in performance].

**lucio, cia** adj. lucid, bright. 2 m. ICHTH. luce, pike.

**lucir** intr. to shine, glitter, glow. 2 to shine, excel, be eminent. 3 [of work, etc.] to prove profitable. 4 tr. to show, to display. 5 to plaster [walls]. 6 to illuminate, light up. 7 ref. to dress to advantage, to show off. 8 to acquit oneself well, to act splendidly. ¶ IRREG. CONJUG.: INDIC. Pres.: luzco, luces, luce; lucimos, lucís, lucen. | SUBJ. Pres.: luzca, luzcas, etc. | IMPER.: luce, luzcan; luzcamos, lucid, luzcan.

**lucrar** *tr.* to obtain. *2 ref.* to profit [get a pecuniary gain].
**lucrativo, -va** *adj.* lucrative, profitable.
**Lucrecia** *f. pr. n.* Lucrece, Lucretia.
**lucro** *m.* lucre, gain, profit.
**luctuoso, -sa** *adj.* mournful, sorrowful, sad.
**lucubración** *f.* lucubration.
**lucubrar** *tr.* to lucubrate.
**lucha** *f.* fight, battle, combat. *2* strife, struggle: ~ *de clases*, class struggle. *3* contention, dispute. *4* wrestling.
**luchador, -ra** *adj.* fighting. *2 m.-f.* fighter, struggler. *3* wrestler.
**luchar** *intr.* to fight. *2* to strive, to struggle. *3* to contend, dispute. *4* to wrestle.
**ludibrio** *m.* derision, mockery, scorn.
**ludir** *tr.-intr.* to rub.
**luego** *adv.* afterwards, next. *2* presently, immediately. *3* later. *4* ~ *de*, after, right after. *5 desde* ~, at once; of course. *6 hasta* ~, so long, see you later. *7 conj.* therefore, then.
**luengo, -ga** *adj.* long: *luengos años*, many years.
**lúes** *f.* MED. lues.
**lugar** *m.* place [part of space, space occupied; ordinal relation]: *en primer* ~, firstly, *fuera de* ~, out of place; irrelevant. *2* place, spot, town, city. *3* village. *4* place, stead: *en* ~ *de*, instead of, in lieu of. *5* space, room: *hacer* ~, to make room. *6* time, occasion. *7* employment, office. *8* cause, reason, rise: *dar* ~ *a*, to give rise to. *9* ~ *común*, privy, toilet. *10 lugares comunes*, commonplace topics. *11* LAW *no ha* ~, petition refused. *12* Gal. *tener* ~, to take place, happen.
**lugarejo** *m. dim.* small village, hamlet.
**lugareño, -ña** *adj.* [pertaining to a] village. *2 m.-f.* villager.
**lugarteniente** *m.* lieutenant, deputy, substitute.
**lugre** *m.* NAUT. lugger.
**lúgubre** *adj.* lugubrious, sad, gloomy, dismal.
**lugués, -sa** *adj.-n.* of Lugo.
**Luis** *m. pr. n.* Louis, Lewis.
**luis** *m.* louis [French coin].
**Luisiana (la)** *pr. n.* GEOG. Louisiana.
**lujación** *f.* LUXACIÓN.
**lujo** *m.* luxury: *de* ~, de luxe, luxurious, magnificent. *2* ~ *de*, excess or abundance of.
**lujoso, -sa** *adj.* luxurious, costly, magnificent.
**lujuria** *f.* lewdness, lust. *2* excess, profuseness.
**lujuriante** *adj.* luxuriant, rank. *2* lustful.
**lujurioso, -sa** *adj.* lustful, lecherous, lewd.
**luliano, -na** *adj.* Lullian.
**lulismo** *m.* system of Raymond Lully.
**lumbago** *m.* MED. lumbago.
**lumbar** *adj.* ANAT. lumbar.
**lumbre** *f.* fire [burning coals, wood, etc.]; light [to light a cigarette]: *dar* ~ *a*, to light someone's cigarette. *2* forepart [of horseshoes]. *3* light [natural agent; emanation of a lightgiving body]. *4* space through which light is admitted. *5* clearness, lustre, splendor. *6* ~ *del agua*, surface of the water. *7 pl.* tinder box.
**lumbrera** *f.* luminary, light-giving body. *2* luminary, light [person]. *3* skylight, louver, light shaft. *4* ventilating shaft, air duct. *5* MACH. port.
**lumen** *m.* lumen [unit of light].
**luminar** *m.* luminary [star; person].
**luminaria** *f.* ECCL. lamp kept burning before the Sacrament. *2 pl.* illuminations, festival lights.
**lumínico, -ca** *adj.* photic, pertaining to light.

**luminiscencia** *f.* luminiscence.
**luminosidad** *f.* luminosity.
**luminoso, -sa** *adj.* luminous.
**luminotecnia** *f.* lighting engineering.
**luna** *f.* ASTR. moon: ~ *de miel*, honeymoon; ~ *llena*, full moon; ~ *menguante*, waning moon; ~ *nueva*, new moon; *media* ~, half-moon; crescent; *estar en la* ~, fig. to be absent-minded; *quedarse a la* ~ *de Valencia*, to be disappointed. *2* moonlight. *3* ASTR. satélite. *4* whim; humour: *de buena* or *de mala* ~, (Am.) in good, or bad, humour. *5* mirror plate. *6* lens, glass [of spectacles]. *7* ICHTH. sunfish, moonfish.
**lunación** *f.* ASTR. lunation, lunar month.
**lunar** *adj.* lunar. *2 m.* mole, beauty spot: ~ *postizo*, patch, beauty spot. *3* flaw, blemish. *4 pl.* polka dots.
**lunático, -ca** *adj.* having fits of madness; moonstruck. *2 m.-f.* person who has fits of madness; moonstruck person.
**lunes,** *pl.* **-nes** *m.* Monday.
**luneta** *f.* lens, glass [of spectacles]. *2* lunette [ornament]. *3* ARCH., FORT. lunette. *4* THEAT. orchestra seat.
**luneto** *m.* ARCH. lunette.
**lunfardo** *m.* (Am.) underworld slang. *2* (Am.) thief.
**lúnula** *f.* GEOM. lune. *2* ANAT., ZOOL. lunule. *3* OPT. meniscus.
**lupa** *f.* magnifying glass.
**lupanar** *m.* bawdyhouse, brothel.
**lupino, -na** *adj.* lupine, wolfish. *2 m.* BOT. lupine.
**lúpulo** *m.* BOT. hop. *2* BOT. hops [hop cones].
**lupus** *m.* MED. lupus.
**lusitano, na** *adj.* *luso*, **-sa** *adj.-n.* Lusitanian; Portuguese.
**lustración** *f.* lustration.
**lustral** *adj.* lustral.
**lustrar** *tr.* to lustrate, purify. *2* to polish, shine.
**lustre** *m.* lustre, luster, gloss, polish, glaze. *2* lustre, luster, glory. *3* shoe-polish.
**lustrina** *f.* lustrine.
**lustro** *m.* lustrum.
**lustroso, -sa** *adj.* lustrous, glossy, shining.
**lúteo, -a** *adj.* muddy [of mud].
**luteranismo** *m.* Lutheranism.
**luterano, -na** *adj.-n.* Lutheran.
**Lutero** *m. pr. n.* Luther.
**luto** *m.* mourning: *estar de* ~, to mourn; *ir de* ~, to be in mourning. *2* grief, bereavement. *3 pl.* mourning draperies.
**lutria** *f.* NUTRIA.
**luxación** *f.* SURG. luxation, dislocation.
**Luxemburgo** *m. pr. n.* GEOG. Luxemburg.
**luz** *f.* light [natural agent; emanation of a lightgiving body; amount of illumination in a place; lamp, candle, firework, etc.]: ~ *de bengala*, Bengal light; ~ *de cruce*, AUT. dimmer; ~ *del día*, daylight; *media* ~, half-light; *dar a* ~, to give birth to; to publish; *salir a* ~, to come out, be published; to be divulged; *ver la* ~, to be born; to be published; *a la* ~ *de*, in the light of; *a todas luces*, every way, in every respect; *entre dos luces*, at twilight; coll. half-seas over, half drunk. *2* light [of the eyes]. *3* light [mental or spiritual enlightenment]. *4* ARCH. span. *5* PAINT. light. *6 pl.* lights, enlightenment, learning. *9* ARCH. lights, openings.
**Luzbel** *m. pr. n.* Lucifer, Satan.
**luzco, luzca,** etc. *irr.* V. LUCIR.

# LL

**Ll, ll** f. Ll, ll, fourteenth letter of the Spanish alphabet.

**llaga** f. ulcer, sore. 2 fig. sore, source of pain or sorrow. 3 MAS. joint, seam.

**llagar** tr. to ulcerate, make sore. 2 fig. to hurt, wound. 3 ref. to become ulcerated.

**llama** f. flame, blaze. 2 fig. flame [ardour, burning passion]. 3 ZOOL. llama.

**llamada** f. call, calling, summons. 2 knock, ring [at a door, etc.]; sign, signal [to call someone]. 3 TELEPH. call. 4 PRINT. reference mark. 6 MIL. call. 7 MIL. chamade.

**llamadera** f. goad [for urging cattle].

**llamado** m. call, calling, summons, appeal.

**llamador, -ra** m.-f. caller. 2 messenger. 3 knocker [of a door]; push button.

**llamamiento** m. call, calling, summons, appeal. 2 convocation.

**llamar** tr. to call [demand presence of], summon, convoke, cite: ~ por teléfono, to call up, to telephone. 2 to call [rouse from sleep]. 3 to attract. 4 to call, destine: estaba llamado a, he, or it, was destined to, was called to be; ~ la atención, to catch or arrest the attention, to be noticeable; ~ la atención a, to warn, to scold. 5 to call, name, call by the name; describe as: ~ al pan, pan y al vino, vino, to call a spade a spade. 6 intr. to knock [at a door]; to ring the bell. 7 ref. to be called or named. | Often constructed diferently: ¿cómo se llama usted?, what is your name?; me llamo Juan, my name is John.

**llamarada** f. flare-up, sudden blaze. 2 flare-up, burst [of anger, etc.]. 3 sudden flush [on the face].

**llamativo, -va** adj. showy, flashy, gaudy. 2 attracting attention, noticeable.

**llamazar** m. swamp, marsh.

**llambria** f. steep face of a rock.

**llameante** adj. blazing, flaming.

**llamear** intr. to blaze, flame.

**llana** f. MAS. trowel. 2 plain, flatland. 3 page [of a writing].

**llanada** f. plain, flatland, level ground.

**llanero, -ra** m. plainsman. 2 f. plainswoman.

**llaneza** f. plainness, simplicity. 2 familiarity, unceremoniousness.

**llano, -na** adj. flat, even, level, smooth. 2 easy [not difficult]; unobstructed. 3 plain, unadorned. 4 open, frank. 5 simple [style]. 6 clear, evident. 7 GRAM. accented on the penultimate [syllable]. 8 MUS. plain [chant]. 9 a la llana, simply, unceremoniously. 10 m. plain, flatland.

**llanta** f. long flat piece of iron. 2 steel tire [of a carriage wheel]. 3 metal rim [of the wheels of a car or bicycle]. 4 ~ de goma, rubber tire [in horse carriages].

**llantén** m. BOT. plantain.

**llanto** m. crying, weeping, flood of tears.

**llanura** f. evenness, flatness. 2 plain, flatland, large tract of level ground.

**llapa** f. YAPA.

**llares** pl. pothanger.

**llave** f. key [for a lock]: ~ maestra, master key, passkey; bajo ~, under lock and key. 2 key [in any figurative sense]. 3 MEC. key [wedge]. 4 cock, faucet: ~ de paso, stopcock. 5 wrench, spanner, key; ~ inglesa, monkey wrench; also, brass knuckles. 6 lock [of a gun], gunlock. 7 DENT. key. 8 clock winder. 9 MUS. key, piston. 10 MUS. clef. 11 PRINT., MUS. brace. 12 span [of the hand].

**llavero, -ra** m.-f. keeper of the keys. 2 m. key ring.

**llavín** m. latchkey.

**llegada** f. arrival, coming.

**llegar** intr. to arrive, come. 2 ~ a, to arrive at, to get at, reach [a place, point, etc.]: to come to [an agreement]; to come to, amount to; to go to [one's heart, etc.]; to get to [know, be, etc.]. 3 ~ a or hasta, to go as far as, or as high as. 4 ~ a or para, to suffice to, to be enough for. 5 ~ a las manos, to come to blows. 6 tr. to gather, collect. 7 to bring near. 8 ref. llegarse a, to come near to; to go to [some neighbouring place].

**llena** f. flood, overflow [of a stream].

**llenar** tr. to fill, fill up, fill out. 2 to stuff, pack. 3 to pervade. 4 to cover; to overwhelm, load. 5 to please, content, satisfy, convince. 6 to hold [an office or position] honourably. 7 intr. [of the moon] to be full. 8 ref. to fill, fill up [become full]. 9 to get crowded, packed. 10 to stuff oneself.

**lleno, -na** adj. full, filled, replete, crowded, packed: ~ hasta el borde, brimful. 2 m. coll. fill, plenty. 3 perfection, completeness. 4 THEAT. full house. 5 ASTR. full [of the moon]. 6 de ~, fully; squarely.

**llenura** f. fulness, plenty, abundance.

**lleva, llevada** *f.* carrying, conveying, -transport.

**llevadero, -ra** *adj.* bearable, tolerable.

**llevar** *tr.* to carry, convey, take, transport, conduct. *2* to bear, wear, be in, have on: ~ *espada,* to wear a sword; ~ *luto,* to wear, be in, mourning. *3* to carry, bear, hold [the body, the head, etc.]. *4* to lead, guide, conduct, take. *5* to carry, win [a prize, etc.]; to get [a thrashing, etc.]: ~ *lo mejor,* or *lo peor,* to get the best, or the worst. *6* to cut off, carry away. *7* to induce, bring [to an opinion]. *8* to lead [a certain kind of life]. *9* to bear, tolerate. *10* to lead [a horse]. *11* to keep [accounts, books]. *12* to manage, be in charge of. *13* to charge, ask [a price]. *14* to bear, yield [fruit]. *15* ARITH. to carry. *16* [with nouns implying time] to have been: *llevo muchos años aquí,* I have been here many years. *17* [with a past p.] to have: *llevo escritas diez páginas,* I have written ten pages. *18* to exceed, be ahead of, be taller, heavier, older, etc. [by a specified distance, height, weight, time, etc.]: *mi hijo lleva dos años al tuyo,* my son is two years older than yours. *19* ~ *adelante,* to carry on, continue. *20* ~ *las de perder,* to be at a disadvantage. *21 ref.* to take or carry away; to take off. *22* to win, carry off. *23 llevarse bien* or *mal,* to get, or not to get, along together; to be on good, or bad terms. *24 llevarse una sorpresa,* to be surprised.

**lloradera** *f.* coll. blubbering, weeping.

**lloraduelos** *m.* sniveller, querulous person.

**llorar** *intr.* to weep, cry. *2* to lament. *3* [of eyes] to water. *4* to drip. *5 tr.* to shed [tears]. *6* to weep, weep over, bewail, mourn, lament.

**llorera** *f.* coll. blubber, crying, continual crying.

**lloriquear** *intr.* GIMOTEAR.

**lloro** *m.* weeping, crying, tears.

**llorón, -na** *adj.* weeping, crying, who cries often or with little cause. *2* BOT. weeping. *3 m.-f.* weeper, whiner. *4 m.* BOT. weeping willow. *5* pendulous plume. *6 f.* weeper [hired mourner].

**lloroso, -sa** *adj.* tearful, weeping. *2* sad.

**llosa** *f.* AGR. large fenced-in field.

**llovedizo, -za** *adj.* leaky [roof]. *2* rain [water].

**llover** *impers.* METEOR. to rain: ~ *a cántaros,* to rain cats and dogs, to rain pitchforsk; *como llovido,* unexpectedly. *2* fig. to rain, shower, come down like rain. *3 ref.* [of roofs] to leak. ¶ CONJUG. like *mover.*

**llovido** *m.* stowaway [person].

**llovizna** *f.* drizzle, sprinkle.

**llovizar** *impers.* to drizzle, sprinkle.

**lluvia** *f.* METEOR. rain: ~ *menuda,* drizzle. *2* rain water. *3* rain, shower [of things].

**lluvioso, -sa** *adj.* rainy, wet [day, weather].

# M

**M, m** *f.* M, m, fifteenth letter of the Spanish alphabet.
**maca** *f.* bruise [on fruit]. *2* flaw, blemish. *3* trickery.
**Macabeos** *m. pl.* BIBL. Maccabees.
**macabro, -bra** *adj.* macabre.
**macaco** *m.* ZOOL. macaque.
**macadam** *m.* macadam.
**macadamizar** *tr.* to macadamize.
**macadán** *m.* MACADAM.
**macana** *f.* drug [unsalable commodity]. *2* (Am.) cudgel. *3* (Am.) lie, fib; nonsense.
**macanazo** *m.* blow with a MACANA or a cudgel.
**macanudo, -da** *adj.* coll. great, ripping, extraordinary.
**macareno, -na** *adj.* of the quarter of *la Macarena*, in Sevilla. *2* boasting, swaggering. *3 m.-f.* boaster, swaggerer.
**macareo** *m.* tide rip in a river.
**macarrón** *m.* macaroon. *2 pl.* macaroni.
**macarronea** *f.* macaronics [poem].
**macarrónico, -ca** *adj.* macaronic.
**macarse** *ref.* [of fruit] to rot from bruises.
**macear** *tr.* to maul, beat with a maul or a mallet.
**Macedonia** *f. pr. n.* HIST., GEOG. Macedonia.
**macedónico, -ca** *adj.* Macedonian.
**macedonio, -nia** *adj.-n.* Macedonian.
**maceración** *f.*, **maceramiento** *m.* maceration.
**macerar** *tr.* to macerate.
**macero** *m.* macer, mace-bearer.
**maceta** *f.* mallet [small maul]. *2* mason's hammer; stonecutter's hammer. *3* flowerpot. *4* vase for artificial flowers. *5* BOT. corymb.
**macetero** *m.* flowerpot stand.
**macferlán** *m.* inverness, inverness cape.
**macia** *f.* MACIS.
**macicez** *f.* massiveness, solidity.
**macilento, -ta** *adj.* emaciate, pale, wan.
**macillo** *m.* small mallet. *2* hammer [of a piano]. *3* ELECT. tapper [of a bell, etc.].
**macis** *f.* mace [spice].
**macizar** *tr.* to fill up, render solid.
**macizo, -za** *adj.* massive, solid. *2 m.* flower bed. *3* clump, mass [of buildings, etc.]. *4* massif, mountain mass. *5* ARCH. wall space.
**macla** *f.* MINER. macle.
**macolla** *f.* BOT. cluster of shoots, flowers or spikes.
**macrobiótica** *f.* macrobiotics.

**macrocéfalo, -la** *adj.* macrocephalous.
**macrocosmo** *m.* macrocosm.
**macrogameto** *m.* BIOL. macrogamete.
**macrosmático, -ca** *adj.* ZOOL. macrosmatic.
**macruro, -ra** *adj.* ZOOL. macrural. *2 m.* ZOOL. macruran. *3 m. pl.* ZOOL. Macrura.
**mácula** *f.* spot, stain, blemish. *2* ASTR., ANAT. macula.
**macular** *tr.* to maculate, stain, defile.
**maculatura** *f.* PRINT. spoiled sheet.
**macuto** *m.* (Am.) alms basket. *2* MIL. knapsack.
**machaca** *m.-f.* bore, tiresome person. *3 f.* tiresome insistence.
**machacador, -ra** *adj.* pounding, crushing. *2 m.-f.* pounder, crusher. *3 f.* crusher [machine].
**machacante** *m.* MIL. sergeant's attendant.
**machacar** *tr.* to pound, crush, mash. *2 intr.* to be tiresomely insistent, to harp on a subject.
**machacón, -na** *adj.* tiresomely insistent, monotonous, boring, importunate. *2 m.-f.* bore.
**machaconería** *f.* tiresome insistence, tiresomeness.
**machada** *f.* flock of billy goats. *2* coll. stupidity.
**machamartillo (a)** *adv.* firmly, solidly.
**machaqueo** *m.* crushing, pounding. *2* MACHAQUERÍA.
**machaquería** *f.* tiresome insistence, importunity.
**machar** *tr.* to pound, crush, mash.
**machetazo** *m.* blow or cut with a machete.
**machete** *m.* machete, matchet, cutlass.
**machetear** *tr.* to strike with a machete.
**machetero** *m.* one who clears ground with a machete. *2* sugar cane cutter.
**machiega** *adj.* queen [bee].
**machihembrar** *tr.* CARP. to feather or mortise.
**machina** *f.* crane, derrick. *2* pile driver, pile engine.
**macho** *adj.* male [animal or plant]. *2* strong, robust. *3* stupid. *4 m.* ZOOL. male, jack, buck, bull [male animal]: ~ *cabrío*, he goat, billy goat. *5* ZOOL. he-mule. *6* stupid fellow. *7* MACH. male piece or part. *8* hook [of hook and eye]. *9* sledge hammer. *10* square anvil. *11* small anvil block. *12* ARCH. pillar, buttress. *13* MACH. ~ *de aterrajar*, tap, screw tap.
**machón** *m.* ARCH. pillar, buttress.
**machorro, -rra** *adj.* barren, sterile. *2 f.* barren female animal.

**machote** *m.* maul, hammer.
**machucadura** *f.* **machucamiento** *m.* crushing, bruising.
**machucar** *tr.* to crush, bruise.
**machucho, -cha** *adj.* sedate, judicious. *2* elderly.
**madama** *f.* lady, madam.
**madamisela** *f.* DAMISELA.
**madapolán** *m.* madapollam.
**madeja** *f.* skein, hank: *enredar la* ~, fig. to embroil an affair; *hacer* ~, fig. to become ropy. *2* head of hair.
**Madera** *f. pr. n.* GEOG. Madeira. *2 m.* Madeira wine.
**madera** *f.* wood [substance]; lumber, timber: ~ *de construcción*, building timber; ~ *de sierra*, lumber [cut for use]; *descubrir uno la* ~, fig. to show one's true nature. *2* makings, essential qualities: *tiene* ~ *de estadista*, he has the makings of a statesman.
**maderable** *adj.* timber-yielding.
**maderada** *f.* lumber floated downstream.
**maderaje, maderamen** *m.* timber, timber work.
**maderería** *f.* lumber yard.
**maderero, -ra** *adj.* [pertaining to] lumber. *2 m.* lumber dealer. *3* raftsman. *4* carpenter.
**madero** *m.* log, piece of timber. *2* fig. ship, vessel. *3* coll. log [stupid or senseless person].
**madianita** *adj.-n.* BIBL. Midianite.
**mador** *m.* moisture, slight sweat.
**madrastra** *f.* stepmother. *2* callous mother.
**madraza** *f.* coll. doting mother.
**madre** *f.* mother: ~ *patria*, mother country: ~ *política*, mother-in-law. *2* bed [of a river]: *sacar de* ~, fig. to irritate; *salir de* ~, [of a river] to overflow. *3* main sewer. *4* main irrigation ditch. *5* sediment, dregs [of wine or vinegar].
**madrecilla** *f.* ovary [of a bird].
**madrecita** *f. dim.* little mother, dear mother.
**madreperla** *f.* ZOOL. pearl oyster; mother-of-pearl.
**madrépora** *f.* ZOOL. madrepore.
**madrero, -ra** *adj.* coll. attached to his or her mother.
**madreselva** *f.* BOT. honeysuckle.
**madrigado, -da** *adj.* coll. experienced [person].
**madrigal** *m.* madrigal.
**madrigalesco, -ca** *adj.* madrigalian, madrigallike.
**madriguera** *f.* hole, burrow [of rabbits, etc.]. *2* den [of wild animals, thieves, etc.].
**madrileño, -ña** *adj.-n.* Madrilenian.
**madrina** *f.* godmother. *2* woman attending a person who is being married, or who is to receive confirmation, holy orders, etc. *3* patroness, protectress. *4* wooden prop. *5* leading mare.
**madrinazgo** *m.* godmothership.
**madrona** *f.* main sewer. *2* over-indulgent mother.
**madroño** *m.* BOT. strawberry tree. *2* BOT. fruit of the strawberry tree. *3* berry-shaped tassel.
**madrugada** *f.* dawn, daybreak: *de* ~, at daybreak. *2* early rising.
**madrugador, -ra** *adj.* early-rising. *2 m.-f.* early riser.
**madrugar** *intr.* to rise or get up early. *2* to gain the start, to be beforehand.
**madrugón, -na** *adj.* early-rising. *2 m.* act of rising very early.
**maduración** *f.* maturation, ripening. *2* ripeness.
**maduramente** *adv.* maturely. *2* with reflection or attentive consideration.
**madurar** *tr.* to maturate, mature, ripen. *2* MED. to maturate. *3* to mature, complete, think out [plans, etc.]. *4 intr.* to mature, ripen [become ripe]. *5* to maturate. *6* to grow old, wise.

**madurativo, -va** *adj.-n.* maturative.
**madurez** *f.* maturity, ripeness. *2* wisdom, prudence.
**maduro, -ra** *adj.* mature, ripe. *2* wise, prudent. *3* [of a person] middle-aged, advanced in years. *4* *edad madura*, middle age.
**maese** *m.* obs. MAESTRO.
**maestra** *f.* mistress, woman teacher; schoolmistress. *2* mistress [woman well skilled in anything]. *3* female head of a workshop, etc. *4* master's or teacher's wife. *5* queen bee.
**maestral** *m.* northwest wind.
**maestrante** *m.* member of a MAESTRANZA.
**maestranza** *f.* a fraternity or order or knights skilled in riding. *2* arsenal, armoury [for the artillery or the navy].
**maestrazgo** *m.* dignity or jurisdiction of the grand master of a military order.
**maestre** *m.* grand master [of a military order]. *2* NAUT. obs. mate.
**maestresala** *m.* formerly, chief waiter [for a prince or nobleman].
**maestría** *f.* mastery, mastership, masterly skill.
**maestril** *m.* queen cell [in a beehive].
**maestrillo, -lla** *m.-f. dim.* insignificant teacher.
**maestro, -tra** *adj.* master, main, principal, great: *abeja maestra*, queen bee; *obra maestra*, masterpiece; *pared maestra*, ARCH. main wall; *viga maestra*, ARCH. girder. *2 m.* teacher, master; ~ *de armas*, fencing master; ~ *de escuela*, schoolteacher. *2* master [in religion, art, science, etc.; great artist]. *4* MUS. composer. *5* master [skilled workman]: ~ *de obras*, builder, master builder. *6* head, director: ~ *de cocina*, chef, head cook; ~ *de ceremonias*, master of ceremonies, marshal.
**Magallanes (estrecho de)** *m. pr. n.* GEOG. Strait of Magellan.
**magallánico, -ca** *adj.* Magellanic.
**magancería** *f.* trick, deceit.
**maganel** *m.* mangonel.
**Magdalena** *f. pr. n.* Magdalen, Magdalene: *Santa María Magdalena*, BIBL. Mary Magdalene. *2* fig. penitent woman: *estar hecha una* ~, to weep bitterly.
**magdalena** *f.* cake made of flour, sugar and eggs.
**magdaleniense** *adj.* GEOL. Magdalenian.
**magia** *f.* magic: ~ *blanca*, white magic; ~ *negra*, black magic, black art.
**magiar** *adj.-n.* Magyar.
**mágico, -ca** *adj.* magic, magical. *2* wonderful. *3 m.* magician, sorcerer. *4 f.* magic, sorceress.
**magín** *m.* coll. mind, fancy, imagination.
**magisterial** *adj.* teaching.
**magisterio** *m.* teaching, guidance, mastership. *2* teaching profession. *3* teachers as a class. *4* affected gravity. *5* OLD., CHEM. magistery.
**magistrado** *m.* magistrate. *2* justice, judge.
**magistral** *adj.* pertaining to the teaching or mastership. *2* magisterial, dogmatic. *3* masterly. *4* who has charge of preaching [canon]. *5 adj.-m.* PHARM., METAL. magistral.
**magistratura** *f.* magistracy.
**magma** *m.* magma [viscid mixture]. *2* GEOL. magma.
**magnanimidad** *f.* magnanimity.
**magnánimo, -ma** *adj.* magnanimous.
**magnate** *m.* magnate.
**magnesia** *f.* CHEM. magnesia.
**magnesiano, -na** *adj.* magnesian.
**magnesio** *m.* CHEM. magnesium. *2* PHOT. flashlight.

**magnesita** *f.* MINER. magnesite.
**magnético, -ca** *adj.* magnetic.
**magnetismo** *m.* magnetism.
**magnetita** *f.* MINER. magnetite.
**magnetización** *f.* magnetization.
**magnetizar** *tr.* to magnetize.
**magneto** *f.* ELECT. magneto.
**magnetófono** *m.* PHYS. magnetophon. *2* tape recorder, wire recorder.
**magnetofónica (cinta)** *f.* recording tape.
**magnificador, -ra** *adj.* extolling, exalting.
**magnificar** *tr.* to extoll, exalt.
**Magnificat** *m.* Magnificat.
**magnificencia** *f.* magnificence.
**magnífico, -ca** *adj.* magnificent. *2* fine, excellent.
**magnitud** *f.* magnitude.
**magno, -na** *adj.* great: *Alejandro Magno,* Alexander the Great.
**magnolia** *f.* BOT. magnolia.
**mago, -ga** *adj.* Magian. *2* skilled in magic. *3 m.* Magian, Magus. *4* magician, wizard. *5 f.* enchantress. *6 m. pl.* Magi: *los Reyes Magos,* the Magi, the Wise Men of the East.
**magra** *f.* rasher, slice of ham.
**magrez** *f.* meagreness, thinness, leanness.
**magro, -gra** *adj.* meagre, meager, thin, lean. *2* lean [meat]. *3 m.* coll. lean meat of pork.
**magrura** *f.* MAGREZ.
**maguer** *conj.* obs. although.
**magulladura** *f.,* **magullamiento** *m.* bruising. *2* bruise, contusion.
**magullar** *tr.* to bruise, mangle.
**Maguncia** *f. pr. n.* GEOG. Mainz.
**Mahoma** *m. pr. n.* Mohammed.
**mahometano, -na** *adj.-n.* Mohammedan.
**mahometismo** *m.* Mohammedanism.
**Mahón** *m. pr. n.* GEOG. Mahon, Port Mahon.
**mahón** *m.* nankeen [cotton cloth].
**mahonés, -sa** *adj.-n.* of Mahon. *2 salsa mahonesa,* mayonnaise sauce. *3 f.* COOK. mayonnaise [dish].
**maicena** *f.* fine maize flour.
**maído** *m.* MAULLIDO.
**mainel** *m.* ARCH. mullion.
**maitines** *m. pl.* ECCL. matins.
**maíz** *m.* BOT. maize, Indian corn.
**maizal** *m.* Indian-corn field.
**majada** *f.* sheepfold. *2* dung, manure.
**majadal** *m.* sheepfold. *2* pasture ground for sheep.
**majadear** *intr.* [of sheep] to take shelter for the night. *2* to manure.
**majadería** *f.* nonsense, foolish remark or act.
**majaderillo** *m.* bobbin [for making lace].
**majadero, -ra** *adj.* silly, stupid. *2 m.-f.* dolt, bore. *3 m.* pestle, pounder. *4* MAJADERILLO.
**majadura** *f.* crushing, pounding, mashing.
**majagranzas,** *pl.* **-zas** *m.* stupid bore.
**majar** *tr.* to crush, pound, pestle, mash. *2* coll. to pester, annoy.
**majencia** *f.* MAJEZA.
**majestad** *f.* majesty. *2* (cap.) Majesty [title]: *Su Divina Majestad,* the Lord, God.
**majestuosidad** *f.* majesty, stateliness.
**majestuoso, -sa** *adj.* majestic, grand, stately.
**majeza** *f.* freedom of manners and gaudiness of dress. *2* boastfulness. *3* prettiness, fineness.
**majo, -ja** *adj.* boastful: dressed up. *3* fine, pretty. *4 adj.-n.* applied to persons displaying a freedom of manners and a gaudiness of dress that are peculiar to some low classes.
**majolar** *m.* grove of white hawthorns.
**majoleta** *f.* MARJOLETA.

**majoleto** *m.* MARJOLETO.
**majuela** *f.* BOT. fruit of the white hawthorn.
**majuelo** *m.* BOT. white hawtorn. *2* vineyard.
1) **mal** *adj.* contr. of MALO, used only before masculine nouns: ~ *humor,* bad humour; ~ *gusto,* bad taste. *2 adv.* bad, badly, ill, wrongly, wickedly; poorly, deficiently; in a bad way or situation: ~ *adquirido,* ill-gotten: ~ *hecho,* badly done; misshapen; wrong; unjust: *estar ~ de salud,* to be in bad health; *de ~ en peor,* from bad to worse; ~ *de su grado,* unwillingly; ~ *que bien,* anyhow, anyway; ~ *que le pese,* in spite of him. *3 amiss: algo va ~,* something is amiss. *4* hardly, scarcely. *5 interj.* *¡mal haya...!,* confound...!, curses on...!
2) **mal,** *pl.* **males** *m.* evil, ill, harm, wrong, injury, misfortune: *el bien y el ~,* good and evil; *hacer ~,* to harm, injure; to be injurious; *llevar* or *tomar a ~,* to take ill, take offence at. *3* illness, disease, evil, ailment, complaint: ~ *de ojo,* evil eye; ~ *de piedra,* lithiasis.
**mala** *f.* English or French mail or post. *2* manilla.
**malabar** *adj.-n.* of Malabar. *2 juegos malabares,* juggling.
**malabarista** *m.* juggler.
**Malaca** *pr. n.* GEOG. Malay Peninsula.
**malacate** *m.* whim, whimsey [hoisting machine].
**malacia** *f.* MED. pica [depraved appetite].
**malacitano, -na** *adj.-n.* MALAGUEÑO.
**malacología** *f.* malacology.
**malaconsejado, -da** *adj.* ill-advised.
**malacopterigio, gia** *adj.* ICHTH. malacopterygian.
**malacostráceo, -a** *adj.-m.* ZOOL. malacostracan.
**Málaga** *f. pr. n.* GEOG. Malaga. *2 m.* (not cap.) Malaga wine.
**malagana** *f.* coll. faintness, swoon.
**malagueño, -ña** *adj.-n.* of Malaga. *2 f.* popular song of Malaga.
**malamente** *adv.* badly, poorly, wrongly.
**malandante** *adj.* unfortunate, unhappy.
**malandanza** *f.* misfortune, misery.
**malandrín** *adj.* wicked, rascally. *2 m.* rascal, scoundrel.
**Malaquías** *m. pr. n.* BIBL. Malachi.
**malaquita** *f.* MINER. malachite.
**malar** *adj.-m.* ZOOL. malar.
**malaria** *f.* MED. malaria.
**Malasia** *pr. n.* GEOG. Malaysia.
**malasio, sia** *adj.-n.* Malaysian.
**malavenido, -da** *adj.* displeased. *2* in disagreement.
**malaventura** *f.* misfortune, unhappiness.
**malaventurado, -da** *adj.* unfortunate, unhappy.
**Malaya** *f. pr. n.* GEOG. Malaya.
**malayo, -ya** *adj.-n.* Malay, Malayan.
**malbaratar** *tr.* to undersell. *2* to squander.
**malbaratillo** *m.* second-hand shop.
**malcarado, -da** *adj.* grim-faced.
**malcasado, -da** *adj.* undutiful [spouse].
**malcasar** *tr.* to mismate [in marriage]. *2 ref.* to be mismated [in marriage].
**malcaso** *m.* treachery, infamous act.
**malcomer** *tr.-intr.* to eat poorly.
**malcomido, -da** *adj.* underfed, that eats poorly.
**malcontento, -ta** *adj.* displeased, discontented. *2 adj.-n.* malcontent.
**malcriado, -da** *adj.* ill-bred, incivil. *2* spoiled [child].
**malcriar** *tr.* to spoil [a child].
**maldad** *f.* wickedness, badness. *2* wicked act.
**maldecir** *tr.* to curse, accurse. *2 intr.* to curse. *3* ~

*de,* to speak ill of, to backbite. ¶ Conjug. like *decir,* except the Indic. Fut.: *maldeciré,* etc.; the Cond.: *maldeciría,* etc., and the Past. p.: *maldecido* or *maldito.*

**maldiciente** *adj.* cursing. 2 slanderous, backbiting. 3 *m.-f.* slanderer, backbiter.

**maldición** *f.* malediction, curse.

**maldispuesto, -ta** *adj.* indisposed. 2 unwilling.

**maldije, maldiga,** etc. *irr.* V. maldecir.

**maldito, -ta** *adj.* accursed, damned. 2 wicked. 3 bad, mean. 4 nothing, no: ~ *lo que me importa,* I don't care a straw. 5 *m.* el Maldito, the Evil One, the Devil. 6 *f.* coll. la maldita, the tongue.

**maleabilidad** *f.* malleability.

**maleable** *adj.* malleable.

**maleador, -ra** *adj.* spoiling. 2 perverting, corrupting. 3 *m.-f.* spoiler. 4 perverter, corrupter.

**maleante** *adj.* maleador 1 & 2. 2 evildoing. 3 *m.-f.* evildoer, rogue.

**malear** *tr.* to spoil, damage. 2 to pervert, corrupt. 3 *ref.* to spoil, become corrupted. 4 to go bad, go wrong.

**malecón** *m.* dike, levee, mole, embankment.

**maledicencia** *f.* evil talk, slander, backbiting.

**maleficencia** *f.* maleficence.

**maleficiar** *tr.* to harm, injure. 2 to harm by a spell or incantation.

**maleficio** *m.* spell, incantation.

**maléfico, -ca** *adj.* maleficent, harmful. 2 malefic. 3 *m.* sorcerer.

**malejo, -ja** *adj.* baddish, rather bad.

**maléolo** *m.* anat. malleolus.

**malestar** *m.* malaise, discomfort, uneasiness.

**maleta** *f.* valise, suitcase: *hacer la* ~, to pack up, get ready for departure. 2 *m.* coll. bungler; unskilled bullfighter.

**maletero** *m.* valise maker or seller. 2 [station] porter.

**maletín** *m.* small valise, satchel, -traveller's handbag, *gripsac, *grip. 2 mil. ~ *de grupa,* saddlebag.

**malevolencia** *f.* malevolence, ill will.

**malévolo, -la** *adj.* malevolent, malignant.

**maleza** *f.* weeds. 2 underbrush, brake, thicket.

**malformación** *f.* med. malformation.

**malgache** *adj.-n.* Madagascan.

**malgastador, -ra** *adj.* extravagant, squandering. 2 *m.-f.* spendthrift, squanderer, wastrel.

**malgastar** *tr.* to misspend, waste, squander.

**malhablado, -da** *adj.* foul-mouthed.

**malhadado, -da** *adj.* ill-starred, unfortunate.

**malhechor, -ra** *m.-f.* evil-doer, malefactor, malefactress, criminal.

**malherir** *tr.* to wound badly.

**malhumorado, -da** *adj.* ill-humoured, peevish.

**malicia** *f.* malice. 2 malignity, evil intention. 3 cunning, slyness, sagacity. 4 suspiciousness, inclination to think ill. 5 suspicion.

**maliciar** *tr.-ref.* to suspect, fear. 2 *tr.* malear.

**malicioso, -sa** *adj.* suspicious, inclined to think ill. 2 malicious.

**málico, -ca** *adj.* chem. malic.

**malignante** *adj.* malignant, malicious.

**malignar** *tr.* to vitiate, corrupt, deprave.

**malignidad** *f.* malignance, malignity.

**maligno, -na** *adj.* malign, malignant, evil, wicked. 2 med. malign, malignant.

**malilla** *f.* manille. 2 a card game.

**Malinas** *f. pr. n.* geog. Malines, Mechlin.

**malintencionado, -da** *adj.* evil-disposed. 2 *m.-f.* evil-disposed person.

**malmandado, -da** *adj.* disobedient.

**malmaridada** *adj.* faithless [wife]. 2 *f.* faithless wife.

**malo, -la** (before a masculine noun, **mal**) *adj.* bad, evil, wicked, depraved, vicious. 2 bad, poor, inferior, deficient. 3 ill, bad [unfavourable; harmful; offensive; unsound]: *mala voluntad,* ill will; ~ *para,* bad for, injurious to. 4 naughty, mischievous. 5 foul, obscene. 6 ill, sick, unwell; diseased, sore: *dedo* ~, sore finger; *estar* ~, to be ill, be unwell. 7 unpleasant, disagreeable. 8 hard, difficult: ~ *de entender,* hard to understand. 9 *estar de malas,* to be out of luck. 10 *lo* ~ *es que,* the trouble is that. 11 *por las malas,* by force. 12 *por malas o por buenas,* willingly or unwillingly. 13 *interj.* ¡malo!, bad!, that is bad!

**malogrado, -da** *adj.* late [person]. 2 failed, frustrated.

**malograr** *tr.* to miss, waste, spoil [time, an opportunity, etc.]. 2 *ref.* to fail, fall through. 3 to have an untimely end.

**malogro** *m.* failure, frustration, spoiling. 2 loss [of an opportunity, etc.]. 3 untimely end.

**maloliente** *adj.* ill-smelling, malodorous.

**malón** *m.* (Am.) Indian raid. 2 (Am.) surprise attack. 3 (Am.) mean trick, ill turn.

**malparado, -da** *adj.* impaired, hurt, damaged.

**malparar** *tr.* to treat ill, hurt, damage, put in a bad way.

**malparir** *intr.* [of a woman] to miscarry.

**malparto** *m.* miscarriage, abortion.

**malquerencia** *f.* ill will, dislike.

**malquerer** *tr.* to dislike, hate.

**malquistar** *tr.* to estrange, set at odds or against. 2 *ref.* to incur dislike: *malquistarse con,* to incur the dislike of.

**malquisto, -ta** *adj.* disliked, unpopular.

**malrotar** *tr.* to misspend, squander.

**malsano, -na** *adj.* unhealthy, unhealthful, unwholesome. 2 unhealthy, sickly.

**malsín** *m.* mischief-maker, talebearer.

**malsonante** *adj.* ill-sounding.

**malsufrido, -da** *adj.* impatient, unresigned.

**Malta** *f. pr. n.* geog. Malta.

**malta** *m.* malt. 2 roast barley.

**maltés, -sa** *adj.-n.* Maltese.

**maltosa** *f.* chem. maltose.

**maltratamiento** *m.* abuse, ill treatment, ill usage, rough usage, maltreatment.

**maltratar** *tr.* to abuse, ill-use, ill-treat, maltreat, treat roughly. 2 to use roughly; to spoil.

**maltrato** *m.* maltratamiento.

**maltrecho, -cha** *adj.* badly off, battered, damaged.

**maltusiano, -na** *adj.-n.* Malthusian.

**maltusianismo** *m.* Malthusianism.

**malucho, -cha** *adj.* poorly (in health).

**malva** *f.* bot. mallow: *ser una* ~ *ser como una* ~, fig. to be meek and mild. 2 bot. ~ *arbórea, loca, real* or *rosácea,* rose mallow, hollyhock.

**malváceo, -a** *adj.* bot. malvaceous.

**malvado, -da** *adj.* wicked, evil, villainous. 2 *m.-f.* wicked person, villain.

**malvarrosa** *f.* bot. rose mallow, hollyhock.

**malvasía** *f.* malmsey, malvoisie.

**malvavisco** *m.* bot. marshmallow.

**malvender** *tr.* to undersell, sell at a loss.

**malversación** *f.* malversation. 2 embezzlement, peculation.

**malversador, -ra** *m.-f.* one who misapplies funds. 2 embezzler, peculator.

**malversar** *tr.* to misapply [funds]. 2 to embezzle.

**malvís, malviz** *m.* ORN. song thrush, redwing.
**malla** *f.* mesh [of net]; network. *2* meshed or netted fabric. *3* mail [of armour]. *4* WEAV. heddle. *5* THEAT. *traje de ~* or *mallas*, fleshings.
**mallete** *m.* mallet.
**mallo** *m.* maul, mall. *2* mall, pall-mall [game and alley].
**Mallorca** *f. pr. n.* GEOG. Majorca.
**mallorquín, -na** *adj.-n.* Majorcan.
**mama** *f.* ANAT., ZOOL. mamma, breast, udder. *2* mamma, mummy [mother].
**mamá** *f.* MAMA 2.
**mamacallos,** *pl.* **-llos** *s.* coll. simpleton.
**mamada** *f.* suck [act of sucking milk].
**mamadera** *f.* breast pump. *2* (Am.) nursing bottle.
**mamado, -da** *adj.* (Am.) drunk, intoxicated.
**mamador, -ra** *adj.* sucking.
**mamaíta** *f. dim.* mammy.
**mamantón, -na** *adj.* sucking [animal].
**mamar** *tr.* to suck [milk]. *2 tr.-ref.* coll. to swallow, devour. *3* coll. to get, obtain. *4 no mamarse el dedo*, not to be taken in easily. *5 ref.* (Am.) to get drunk. *6* (Am.) *mamarse a uno*, to kill, or to get the best of, someone.
**mamario, -ria** *adj.* mammary.
**mamarrachada** *f.* coll. grotesque or ridiculous act.
**mamarrachista** *m.* PAINT. coll. dauber.
**mamarracho** *m.* coll. grotesque or ridiculous figure. *2* PAINT. daub. *3* coll. despicable man.
**mamelón** *f.* mound, knoll, hillock; small peak. *2* SURG. nipplelike protuberance.
**mameluco** *m.* Mameluke. *2* coll. dolt, simpleton.
**mamella** *f.* one of the two appendages hanging on the neck of goats.
**mamey** *m.* BOT. mammee.
**mamífero, -ra** *adj.* ZOOL. mammalian. *2 m.* ZOOL. mammal. *3 m. pl.* ZOOL. Mammalia.
**mamila** *f.* ZOOL. breast or udder round the nipple. *2* ANAT. mamilla [in men].
**mamilar** *adj.* mamillary.
**mamola** *f.* chuck under the chin.
**mamón, -na** *adj.* sucking. *2* fond of sucking. *3 m.-f.* suckling. *4 m.* BOT. shoot, sucker. *5* BOT. genip tree.
**mamotreto** *m.* memorandum book. *2* coll. bulky book or bundle of papers.
**mampara** *f.* screen [before a door, etc.].
**mamparo** NAUT. bulkhead.
**mamporro** *m.* blow, bump.
**mampostería** *f.* rubble masonry, rubblework.
**mampuesta** *f.* MAS. course.
**mampuesto, -ta** *adj.* MAS. rubble, for rubblework. *2 m.* rough stone, rubble stone. *3* parapet, shelter. *4 de ~*, spare, extra; from a sheltered position.
**mamujar** *tr.-intr.* to suck intermittently.
**mamullar** *tr.* to chew as if sucking. *2* coll. to mumble, mutter.
**mamut** *m.* PALEONT. mammoth.
**maná** *m.* manna.
**manada** *f.* herd, flock, drove, pack. *2* handful.
**manadero, -ra** *adj.* flowing, running. *2 m.* source, sprint. *3* herdsman, shepherd.
**manantial** *adj.* spring [water]. *2 m.* source, spring. *3* source, origin.
**manantío, -a** *adj.* flowing, running. *2 m.* source.
**manar** *intr.* to flow, run, issue forth. *2* fig. to abound, be rich in. *3 tr.* to pour forth.
**Manasés** *m. pr. n.* BIBL. Manasseh.
**manatí** *m.* ZOOL. manatee, sea cow.
**manaza** *f. augm.* large hand.

**mancamiento** *m.* maiming. *2* lack, want, deficiency.
**mancar** *tr.* to maim [in the hand]. *2 ref.* to become maimed [in the hand].
**manceba** *f.* mistress, concubine.
**mancebía** *f.* bawdyhouse, brothel.
**mancebo** *m.* young man, youth. *2* bachelor [unmarried man]. *3* shopman, shopboy.
**mancera** *f.* plough handle, plow handle.
**mancilla** *f.* spot, blemish.
**manco, -ca** *adj.* handless, one-handed, armless, maimed. *2* fig. faulty, defective. *3 m.-f.* handless, one-handed or armless person.
**mancomún (de)** *adv.* jointly, in agreement.
**mancomunadamente** *adv.* DE MANCOMÚN.
**mancomunar** *tr.* to associate, join, combine, pool [persons, resources, exertions, etc.]. *2 ref.* to associate, unite, act in concert.
**mancomunidad** *f.* union, association. *2* LAW association of provinces or municipalities.
**mancuerda** *f.* rack [torture].
**mancha** *f.* stain, spot, blot, discolouration. *2* ASTR. spot, macula. *3* spot, speckle: *~ ocultar*, ZOOL. eyespot. *4* patch [of vegetation]. *5* fig. stain, spot, blot, blemish.
**manchado, -da** *adj.* stained, soiled. *2* spotted, speckled. *3* patched [with colour or vegetation].
**manchar** *tr.* to stain, soil, discolour. *2* to spot, speckle. *3* to patch [with colour or vegetation]. *4* fig. to stain, defile, blot, sully. *5 ref.* to soil, become soiled or stained. *6* to disgrace oneself.
**manchego, -ga** *adj.-n.* of La Mancha [region of Spain].
**manchón** *m.* large stain. *2* patch [in a field, heath, etc.] where vegetation is most thick.
**manchú,** *pl.* **-chúes,** *adj.-n.* Manchu.
**manda** *f.* bequest, legacy.
**mandadero, -ra** *m.-f.* messenger, errand boy or girl.
**mandado** *m.* order, command. *2* errand.
**mandamiento** *m.* mandate, order, command. *2* LAW writ. *3* commandment: *los mandamientos de la ley de Dios*, the ten commandments.
**mandante** *m.-f.* LAW constituent, mandator.
**mandar** *tr.* to command, order, direct, decree: *~ hacer, escribir*, etc., to order or have [something] done, written, etc.; *~ decir*, to send word; *~ venir*, to call, order to come. *2* to command, be in command of. *3* to will, leave, bequeath. *4* to send: *~ por*, to send for. *5* to control [one's horse]. *6 intr.* to command, govern [exercise direct authority]. *7 ref. mandarse* or *mandarse mudar*, to go away.
**mandarín** *m.* mandarin.
**mandarina** *adj.* mandarin [language; orange]. *2 f.* BOT. mandarin orange.
**mandarria** *f.* shipwright's iron maul or hammer.
**mandatario** *m.* mandatary, mandatory. *2* mandatee.
**mandato** *m.* mandate, command, order, injunction. *2* LAW, POLIT. mandate. *3* ECCL. maundy.
**mandíbula** ANAT., ZOOL. jaw, mandible.
**mandil** *m.* apron; leather or coarse apron. *2* apron [of Freemasons].
**mandilete** *m.* ARTIL. door of a porthole.
**mandilón** *m.* coll. mean-spirited fellow, coward.
**mandioca** *f.* manioc, cassava [plant and starch].
**mando** *m.* command [act of commanding; authority or power to command]: *alto ~*, high command; *tomar el ~*, to take command. *2* MACH. drive, control: *~ a distancia*, remote control; *~*

*doble*, AUTO. dual drive; ~ *único*, RADIO. single control.

**mandoble** *m.* two-handed blow [with a sword].

**mandolina** *f.* MUS. mandolin.

**mandón, -na** *adj.* imperious, domineering, *bossy. 2 *m.-f.* domineering person.

**mandrágora** *f.* BOT. mandrake.

**mandria** *adj.-m.* good-for-nothing [fellow].

**mandril** *m.* ZOOL. mandrill. 2 MACH. mandrel, mandril; chuck [of a lathe]. 3 MED. mandrin.

**manducación** *f.* coll. eating.

**manducar** *tr.-intr.* coll. to eat.

**manducatoria** *f.* coll. food, sustenance.

**manea** *f.* MANIOTA.

**manear** *tr.* to hobble or hopple [a horse]. 2 MANEJAR.

**manecilla** *f. dim.* small hand. 2 book clasp. 3 hand [of clock or watch]; index [on instruments]. 4 PRINT. index, fist. 5 BOT. tendril.

**manecita** *f. dim.* small hand, little hand.

**manejar** *tr.* to manage, handle, wield. 2 to manage control, conduct, govern. 3 EQUIT. to manage. 4 (Am.) to drive [a car]. 5 *ref.* to behave, manage. 6 to get around, move about.

**manejo** *m.* handling, wielding. 2 management, conduct. 3 manège, horsemanship. 4 (Am.) driving [a car]. 5 scheming, intrigue.

**maneota** *f.* MANIOTA.

**manera** *f.* manner, way, mode, fashion; manner, style [in literature or art]: *a la ~ de*, in the style of; *a ~ de*, kind of; like; by way of; *de ~ que*, so that; so then, and so; *de ninguna ~*, in no way, by no means; *de otra ~*, otherwise: *de todas maneras*, at any rate. anyhow; *en gran ~*, very much, to a great extent; *sobre ~*, exceedingly, beyond measure; *hacer por ~ que*, to contrive. 2 way, means: *no hay ~ de*, it is not possible to. 3 quality, class [of persons]. 4 *pl.* manners, behaviour.

**manero, -ra** *adj.* FALCON. trained, tame.

**manes** *m. pl.* manes.

**manga** *f.* sleeve: *en mangas de camisa*, in shirt sleeves; *hacer mangas y capirotes*, coll. to act arbitrarily; *tener ~ ancha*, fig. to be too indulgent; to be unscrupulous. 2 wheel seat [of axletree]. 3 kind of portmanteau. 4 hose [pipe]: ~ *de riego*, watering hose. 5 scoop net. 6 casting net. 7 NAUT. air duct, wind sail. 8 conical cloth strainer. 9 BRIDGE game. 10 NAUT. beam [ship's breadth]. 11 METEOR. waterspout [rotating column]. 12 ~ *de agua*, cloudburst, waterspout. 13 ~ *de viento*, METEOR. whirlwind; AER. wind sock. 14 *pl.* profits, extras.

**mangana** *f.* lasso, lariat.

**manganato** *m.* CHEM. manganate.

**manganear** *tr.* to lasso.

**manganeo** *m.* lassoing.

**manganeso** *m.* CHEM. manganese.

**manganilla** *f.* trick, stratagem.

**mangante** *m.* coll. beggar. 2 coll. loafer, vagabond.

**manglar** *m.* mangrove swamp.

**mangle** *m.* BOT. mangrove tree. 2 MACH. mangle.

**mango** *m.* handle, haft, helve: ~ *de escoba*, broomstick; ~ *de pluma*, penholder. 2 BOT. mango.

**mangonear** *intr.* to loiter, loaf around. 2 to meddle, intermeddle, play the boss.

**mangoneo** *m.* meddling, intermeddling.

**mangonero, -ra** *adj.* meddling, fond of meddling.

**mangosta** *f.* ZOOL. mongoose.

**mangostán** *m.* BOT. mangosteen [tree].

**mangosto** *m.* BOT. mangosteen [fruit].

**mangote** *m.* long, wide sleeve. 2 sleeve protector.

**mangual** *m.* flail [medieval weapon]. 2 MAYAL.

**manguardia** *f.* ARCH. wing wall [of a bridge].

**manguera** *f.* hose, watering hose. 2 NAUT. air duct, wind sail. 3 METEOR. waterspout.

**manguero** *m.* hoseman.

**manguitería** *f.* furriery. 2 fur shop.

**manguitero** *m.* furrier.

**manguito** *m.* muff [for hands]. 2 knitted half-sleeve. 3 sleeve protector. 4 MACH. muff, sleeve, shaft coupling, pipe coupling.

**maní**, *pl.* **manises** *m.* CACAHUETE.

**manía** *f.* MED. mania. 2 mania, craze, whim. 3 dislike.

**maníaco, -ca** *adj.-n.* MED. maniac.

**manialbo, -ba** *adj.* white-footed [horse].

**maniatar** *tr.* to tie the hands. 2 to hand-cuff.

**maniático, -ca** *adj.* queer, crazy. 2 *m.-f.* queer person; person who has a craze for it.

**manicomio** *m.* insane asylum, madhouse.

**manicordio** *m.* MUS. manichord.

**manicuro, -ra** *m.-f.* manicure, manicurist. 2 *f.* manicure [care of hands and nails].

**manida** *f.* abode, haunt, dep.

**manido, -da** *adj.* high, gamey [meat]. 2 trite, stale.

**manifacero, -ra** *adj.* coll. meddlesome.

**manifestación** *f.* manifestation, exhibition, display. 2 statement, declaration. 3 POL. public manifestation or demonstration.

**manifestador, -ra** *adj.* manifesting. 2 *m.-f.* manifester.

**manifestante** *m.-f.* manifestant, demonstrant.

**manifestar** *tr.* to manifest, show, reveal, display. 2 to state, declare. 3 ECCL. to expose [the Eucharist]. 4 *ref.* to manifest oneself or itself, to show, appear; to become manifest. 5 POL. to manifest. ¶ CONJUG. like *acertar*.

**manifiesto, -ta** *adj.* manifest, plain, obvious, evident: *poner de ~*, to make evident; to exhibit, expose. 2 *m.* manifest, manifiesto [public declaration]. 3 NAUT. manifest. 4 ECCL. exposing the Eucharist.

**manija** *f.* handle [of some implements]. 2 hobble, hopple [for horses]. 3 MACH. ring, clasp.

**manilargo, -ga** *adj.* long-handed. 2 ready-fisted. 3 open-handed.

**manilense; manileño, -ña** *adj.-n.* of Manila.

**maniluvio** *m.* MED. bath for the hands.

**manilla** *f.* bracelet. 2 hand-cuff, manacle.

**manillar** *m.* handle bar [of bicycle].

**maniobra** *f.* handling, operation. 2 NAUT. working [of a ship]. 3 NAUT. gear, rigging, tackle. 4 MIL., NAV. manœuvre. 5 fig. manœuvre, manœuvring, trick. 6 *pl.* MIL., NAV. manœuvres. 7 RLY. shift, shifting.

**maniobrar** *intr.* to manœuvre. 2 RLY. to shift.

**maniota** *f.* hobble, hopple [for horses].

**manipulación** *f.* manipulation.

**manipulador, -ra** *adj.* manipulating. 2 *m.-f.* manipulator. 3 *m.* TELEG. key, telegraph key.

**manipular** *tr.* to manipulate, handle, manage.

**manipuleo** *m.* manipulation, managing.

**manípulo** *m.* maniple.

**maniqueísmo** *m.* Manicheanism, Manicheism.

**maniqueo, -a** *adj.-n.* Manichean.

**maniquete** *m.* black lace mitten. 2 mitten.

**maniquí**, *pl.* **-quíes** *m.* manikin, mannequin, lay figure, dummy. 2 mannequin [woman].

**manir** *tr.-def.* COOK. to keep [meat or game] until it

becomes gamey. | Only used in the forms having *i* in their termination.

**manirroto, -ta** *adj.* prodigal. *2 m.-f.* spendthrift.

**manita** *f.* mannitol, manna sugar.

**manivacío, -cía** *adj.* coll. empty-handed.

**manivela** *f.* MACH. crank.

**manjar** *m.* food, dish.

**manjorrada** *f.* lot of ordinary victuals.

**mano** *f.* hand [of a person; person who does something; work, agency; ability; skill; power, control, direction; personal possession; aid]: ~ *de obra*, work, labour [as distinguished from materials]; labour, labourers; ~ *derecha* or *diestra*, right hand; ~ *izquierda, siniestra* or *zurda*, left hand; tact; cunning; *buena* ~, adroitness; *mala* ~, bad luck; awkwardness, lack of skill; *manos limpias*, clean hands, honesty; *manos muertas*, dead hand, mortmain; mortmain owners; *buenas manos*, skill; *abrir la* ~, to be generous; to become more lenient; *apretar la* ~, to squeeze someone's hand; to shake hands with; to increase the rigour; *caerse de las manos*, [of a book], to be boring; *cargar la* ~, to press, insist; to be very rigid; to charge an immoderate price; to spice too heavily; *dar de* ~, to reject; to leave, abandon; *dar en manos de*, to fall into the hands of; *dar la* ~ *a*, to shake hands with; to aid, protect, lend a hand to; *dar la última* ~ *a*, to finish, retouch; *darse las manos*, to shake hands; to be reconciled; *dejar de la* ~, to leave, abandon; *echar* ~, *la* ~, or *manos a*, to seize, take; *echar una* ~, to lend a hand; *echar* ~ *de*, to resort to, make use of; *poner manos a la obra*, to put one's hand to the plough, to get busy; *tener*, or *traer*, *entre manos*, to have in hand; *tener uno la* ~, to contain oneself; *tener* ~ *con uno*, to have a pull with someone; *tener* ~ *en*, to have a hand in; *tener* ~ *para*, to have a hand for; *untar la* ~ *de*, to bribe; *a la* ~, near, at hand, within reach; *a* ~ *airada*, violently; *a* ~ *derecha*, or *izquierda*, on the right hand, or left hand, side; *a manos llenas*, liberally, abundantly; *bajo* ~, underhandedly secretly; *con las manos en la masa*, redhanded; *cogidos de las manos*, hand in hand; *de* ~ *en* ~, from hand to hand; *de manos a boca*, suddenly, unexpectedly, with proximity; ~ *a* ~, in company, together, tête-à-tête; on equal footing, even; ~ *sobre* ~, idle; *si a* ~ *viene*, perhaps; it is possible that.

*2* hand [person, source]: *de buena* ~, on good authority; *de primera* ~, first-hand; *3* hand [pledge of marriage]. *4* and [of monkey]. *5* forefoot [of quadruped]. *6* BUTCH., COOK. foot, trotter. *7* hand, index [of a clock, etc.]. *8* pestle. *9* coat [of paint, varnish, etc.]. *10* quire [of paper]. *11* game, round. *12* first hand [at cards]: *ser* ~, to lead. *13* reprimand. *14 pl.* work, labour [as distinguished from materials].

**manojo** *m.* bundle, bunch [of flowers, herbs, etc.].

**Manolo** *m. pr. n.* MANUEL.

**manolo, -la** *m.-f.* formerly, a Madrilenian of low class affecting a peculiar mode of dress and manners.

**manómetro** *m.* manometer.

**manopla** *f.* gauntlet. *2* postilion's whip.

**manosear** *tr.* to handle, feel, paw [something] repeatedly.

**manoseo** *m.* repeated handling, feeling or pawing.

**manota** *f. augm.* large hand.

**manotada** *f.*, **manotazo** *m.* blow with the hand.

**manotear** *tr.* to beat with the hands. *2 intr.* to gesticulate with the hands.

**manoteo** *m.* gesticulation with the hands.

**manotón** *m.* MANOTADA.

**manquedad, manquera** *f.* lack of one or both hands or arms. *2* faultiness, imperfection.

**mansalva (a)** *adv.* without danger, without running any risk, in a cowardly manner.

**mansarda** *f.* ARCH. mansard roof.

**mansedumbre** *f.* meekness, mildness, gentleness. *2* tameness.

**mansejón, -na** *adj.* very tame.

**mansión** *f.* stay, sojourn. *2* abode, dwelling, mansion: ~ *celestial*, heavenly home.

1) **manso** *m.* MASADA.

2) **manso, -sa** *adj.* tame. *2* meek, mild, gentle. *3* soft, quiet, gentle, slow: *agua mansa*, slow water.

**mansurrón, -na** *adj.* excessively meek or tame.

**manta** *f.* blanket [bed covering]. *2* blanket [used by men as a shawl or muffler]. *3* horse blanket. *4* MIL. mantelet, mantlet. *5* beating, drubbing. *6* ~ *de coche*, ~ *de viaje*, lap robe, travelling rug. *7 a* ~, *a* ~ *de Dios*, coll. abundantly.

**manteamiento** *m.* tossing in a blanket.

**mantear** *tr.* to toss in a blanket.

**manteca** *f.* fat, lard; butter; fatty oil: ~ *de cerdo*, lard; ~ *de vaca*, butter; ~ *de cacao*, cocoa butter.

**mantecada** *f.* buttered toast and sugar. *2* cake made of flour, eggs, sugar and butter.

**mantecado** *m.* butter bun. *2* ice-cream.

**mantecón, -na** *m.-f.* milksop, mollycoddle.

**mantecoso, -sa** *adj.* greasy, buttery.

**mantel, pl. -teles** *m.* tablecloth. *2* altar cloth.

**mantelería** *f.* table linen.

**manteleta** *f.* manteleta [lady's shawl or short cape].

**mantelete** *m.* ECCL. mantelletta. *2* MIL. mantelet, mantlet [movable shelter]. *3* HER. mantling.

**mantellina** *f.* mantilla.

**mantenedor** *m.* president of a tournament, joust, etc.

**mantenencia** *f.* maintenance.

**mantener** *tr.* to maintain, support, keep. *2* to hold, sustain, hold up. *3 ref.* to maintain, support oneself. *4* to keep [continue, perservere]. *5 mantenerse en*, to remain firm in; to hold on to. ¶ CONJUG. like *tener.*

**mantenimiento** *m.* maintenance, support. *2* sustenance, food, living. *3* keeping, carrying on *4* maintenance, upkeep.

**manteo** *m.* long cloak worn by Roman Catholic ecclesiastics. *2* MANTEAMIENTO.

**mantequero, -ra** *adj.* [pertaining to] butter. *2 m.-f.* butter maker or seller. *3* butter dish, butter bowl. *4 f.* churn [for making butter].

**mantequilla** *f.* butter. *2* hard sauce.

**mantero, -ra** *m.-f.* blanket maker or seller.

**mantés, -sa** *adj.* scoundrely. *2 m.-f.* scoundrel.

**mantilla** *f.* mantilla. *2* saddlecloth. *3* PRINT. blanket. *4 pl.* swaddling clothes: *estar en mantillas* [of a work, undertaking, etc.], to be in its infancy.

**mantillo** *m.* humus, vegetable mould. *2* manure.

**mantis** *f.* ENT. mantis; ~ *religiosa*, mantis, praying cricket.

**mantisa** *f.* MATH. mantissa.

**manto** *m.* mantle [garment; something that covers or envelops]. *2* robe of state. *3* large mantilla. *4* mantel-front of chimney. *5* ZOOL. mantle.

**mantón, -na** *adj.* having drooping wings [bird]. *2*

*m.* large shawl: ~ *de Manila*, bright shawl, embroidered silk shawl.
**manuable** *adj.* handy, easy to handle.
**manual** *adj.* manual: *trabajo* ~, manual labour. *2 m.* manual, handbook.
**manubrio** *m.* handle, crank. *2* ANAT., ZOOL. manubrium.
**manucodiata** *f.* ORN. bird of paradise.
**Manuel** *m. pr. n.* Emmanuel.
**Manuela** *f. pr. n.* Emma.
**manuela** *f.* [in Madrid] open hackney carriage.
**manufactura** *f.* manufactured article. *2* manufactory, factory.
**manufacturar** *tr.* to manufacture.
**manufacturero, -ra** *adj.* manufacturing.
**manumisión** *f.* manumission.
**manumisor** *m.* manumitter.
**manumitir** *tr.* to manumit.
**manuscrito, -ta** *adj.-n.* manuscript.
**manutención** *f.* maintenance, sustenance, board. *2* upkeep, conservation.
**manzana** *f.* BOT. apple: ~ *de la discordia*, fig. apple of discord. *2* city block, block of houses. *3* pommel [of sword]. *4* round ornamental knob. *5* (Am.) Adam's apple.
**manzanal, manzanar** *m.* apple orchad.
**manzanilla** *f.* BOT., PHARM. camomile. *2* small round olive. *3* round, ornamental knob [on furniture, etc.]. *4* pad, cushion [of foot·of clawed animals]. *5* tip of the chin. *6* manzanilla [pale dry sherry]. *7* BOT. ~ *hedionda*, stinking camomile. *8 adj. aceituna* ~, MANZANILLA 2.
**manzanillo** *m.* BOT. manchineel. *2* BOT. *olivo* ~, olive tree yielding a small round olive.
**manzano** *m.* BOT. apple tree.
**maña** *f.* dexterity, skill, cunning, knack; address, cleverness, tact: *darse* ~, to manage, contrive. *2* trick, wile. *2* bad habit.
**mañana** *f.* morning, forenoon: *de* ~, early in the morning; *por la* ~, in the morning. *2 m.* morrow. *3 adv.* tomorrow; later, in time to come: *pasado* ~, the day after tomorrow.
**mañanear** *intr.* to get up early [by habit].
**mañanero, -ra** *adj.* early-rising.
**mañero, -ra** *adj.* shrewd, artful, cunning. *2* easy, handy.
**maño, -ña** *adj.-n.* coll. Aragonese. *2* (dial. & Am.) brother; sister. *3* (dial. & Am.) dear, darling.
**mañoco** *m.* tapioca.
**mañoso, -sa** *adj.* dexterous, skilful, clever, shrewd. *2* having bad habits.
**mañuela** *f.* wile, low trick. *2 pl.* crafty person.
**mapa** *m.* map, chart. *2 f.* coll. *llevarse la* ~, to be the best in its line.
**mapache** *m.* ZOOL. raccoon.
**mapamundi** *m.* world map, map of the world.
**mapurite** *m.* ZOOL. (Am.) skunk.
**maque** *m.* lacquer. *2* BOT. heaven tree.
**maquear** *tr.* to lacquer.
**maqueta** *f.* maquette. *2* PRINT. dummy.
**maqui** *m.* BOT. a Chilean shrub. *2* ZOOL. macaco.
**maquiavélico, -ca** *adj.* Machiavellic, Machiavellian.
**maquiavelismo** *m.* Machiavellism.
**maquila** *f.* toll corn, miller's toll. *2* a grain measure [½ CELEMÍN].
**maquilero** *adj.* applied to a mill where grain is taken as pay for grinding.
**maquillaje** *m.* THEAT. make-up.
**máquina** *f.* machine, engine: ~ *de afeitar*, safety razor; electric razor; ~ *de coser*, sewing ma-

chine; ~ *de escribir*, typewriter; ~ *de vapor*, steam engine; ~ *fotográfica*, camera; ~ *herramienta*, machine tool; *tragaperras*, slot machine; *a toda* ~, at full speed. *2* locomotive. *3* THEAT. machine. *4* LIT. machine, machinery. *5* imposing structure.
**maquinación** *f.* machination.
**maquinador, -ra** *m.-f.* machinator.
**maquinal** *adj.* mechanical, unconscious, automatic.
**maquinar** *tr.* to machinate, scheme, plot, concoct.
**maquinaria** *f.* machinery. *2* applied mechanics.
**maquinismo** *m.* ECON. mechanization.
**maquinista** *m.-f.* machinist [constructor of engines]. *2* machinist, engineer, engine runner or driver. *3* THEAT. machinist.
**mar** *m.* or *f.* sea, ocean: ~ *de las Indias*, Indian Ocean; ~ *Muerto*, Dead Sea; ~ *Negro*, Black Sea; *alta* ~, high sea, open sea; ~ *de costado* or *de través*, sea on the beam; ~ *de fondo* or *de leva*, ground swell; *hacerse a la* ~, to take to the sea. *2* fig. ocean, lot, lots, great deal: *la* ~ *de dificultades*, a lot of difficulties. *3 adv. la* ~, very much; *la* ~ *de difícil*, extremely difficult. *4 a mares*, abundantly, copiously.
**marabú** *m.* marabou [bird and trimming].
**marabuto** *m.* Mahomedan hermitage.
**maraca** *f.* MUS. maraca.
**maracayá** *m.* ZOOL. margay.
**maragato, -ta** *m.-f.* native of a region in León [Spain].
**maraña** *f.* thicket, bush. *2* tangle, entanglement [of thread, hair, etc.]. *3* complexity, puzzle. *4* tale, lie [for making mischief]; mischief, discord.
**marañero, -ra** *adj.* embroiling. *2 m.-f.* embroiler, mischief-maker.
**marañón** *m.* BOT. cashew. *2* cashew nut.
**marasmo** *m.* MED. marasmus. *2* inactivity, depression.
**Maratón** *m. pr. n.* HIST. and SPORT. Marathon.
**maravedí**, *pl.* **-dises** or **-díes** *m.* maravedi [old Spanish coin].
**maravilla** *f.* wonder, marvel: *a las mil maravillas*, *a* ~, wonderfully weil. *2* BOT. marigold. *3* BOT. four-o'clock, marvel of Peru. *4* BOT. ivy-leaved morning glory.
**maravillar** *tr.* to astonish, cause to marvel. *2 ref.* to wonder, marvel.
**maravilloso, -sa** *adj.* wonderful, marvellous, wondrous.
**marbete** *m.* label [slip of paper].
**marca** *f.* mark, brand [affixed, impressed, etc., distinguishing sign]: ~ *de fábrica*, trademark; ~ *registrada*, registered trademark. *2* marking, branding. *3* marking instrument. *4* make [origin of manufactured article]. *5* standard of measure. *6* NAUT. seamark, landmark. *7* SPORT. record. *8* HIST. march [frontier province]. *9 de* ~, *de* ~ *mayor*, great of its kind, exceeding the common measure.
**marcación** *f.* NAUT. bearing, relative bearing. *2* NAUT. taking a ship's bearings.
**marcado, -da** *adj.* marked, pronounced.
**marcador, -ra** *adj.* marking, branding. *2 m.-f.* marker [pers.]. *3 m.* SPORT. scoreboard. *4* PRINT. feeder [worker]. *5* hallmarker.
**marcar** *tr.* to mark, brand; to stencil. *2* to mark [linen]. *3* to mark [as noteworthy]. *4* to lay out, assign. *5* SPORT. to score. *6* SPORT. to mark. *7* TE-

LEPH. to dial [a number]. *8 ~ el paso*, to mark time. *9 ref.* NAUT. [of a ship] to take its bearings.

**marcasita** *f.* MINER. marcasite.

**Marcelo** *m. pr. n.* Marcellus.

**marcescente** *adj.* BOT. marcescent.

**marcial** *adj.* martial [pertaining to war], soldierly, warlike. *2* PHARM. martial.

**marcialidad** *f.* martialness.

**marciano, -na** *adj.-n.* Martian.

**marco** *m.* enclosing frame or case; picture frame, doorcase, windowcase. *2* mark [coin; weight]. *3* standard [of weights and measures]. *4* size stick.

**marconigrama** *m.* marconigram, wireless telegram.

**Marcos** *m. pr. n.* Mark.

**marcha** *f.* march [marching of troops; walk journey]: *marchas forzadas*, forced marches; *sobre la ~*, at once; right off. *2* MUS. march: *~ fúnebre*, funeral march; *~ nupcial*, wedding march. *3* march, progress, motion, course. *4* going, operation, running, working; *poner en ~*, to start, set going; *ponerse en ~*, to start, begin to move. *6* departure, setting out. *7* pace, speed, rate of speed: *a toda ~*, at full speed. *8* AUTO. *cambio de marchas*, gearshift. *9* MACH. *~ atrás*, reverse.

**marchamar** *tr.* to mark [goods] at the custom house.

**marchamo** *m.* custom house mark. *2* lead seal.

**marchapié** *m.* NAUT. footrope.

**marchar** *intr.* to march, walk. *2* [of things] to go, proceed, go ahead, make progress. *3* [of machines, vehicles, etc.] to work, run, go, move. *4* MIL. to march. *5* *intr.-ref.* to go away, leave, depart.

**marchitar** *tr.* to wither, wilt, fade. *2 ref.* to wither, wilt, fade [become withered or faded]. *3* to languish.

**marchitez** *f.* withered or faded condition.

**marchito, -ta** *adj.* withered, wilted, faded.

**marea** *f.* tide [of sea]: *~ alta*, high tide; *~ baja*, low tide; *~ creciente*, flood tide; *~ menguante*, ebb tide; *~ muerta*, neap tide; *~ viva*, spring tide. *2* gentle sea breeze. *3* dew, drizzle.

**mareado, -da** *adj.* nauseated, sick, seasick, carsick, airsick. *2* dizzy, giddy. *3* annoyed.

**mareaje** *m.* navigation, seamanship.

**mareante** *adj.* causing seasickness or carsickness. *2* making dizzy. *3* annoying. *4* navigating, seafaring. *5 m.* navigator, sailor, seafarer.

**marear** *tr.* to sail [a ship]. *2* to annoy, bother. *3 ref.* to become nauseated, sick, seasick, carsick, airsick. *4* to get dizzy.

**marejada** *f.* NAUT. surge, swell, ground sea. *2* commotion, stirring.

**maremagno, mare mágnum** *m.* coll. confusion, omnium-gatherum.

**maremoto** *m.* earthquake at sea.

**mareo** *m.* nausea, sickness, seasickness, carsickness, airsickness. *2* dizziness. *3* coll. annoyance.

**mareógrafo** *m.* mareograph.

**marero** *adj.* sea [wind].

**maretazo** *m.* surge, heavy sea.

**marfil** *m.* ivory. *2 ~ vegetal*, ivory nut.

**marfileño, -ña** *adj.* [pertaining to] ivory. *2* ivory-like.

**marga** *f.* marl, loam.

**margal** *m.* marlpit, marly ground.

**margallón** *m.* BOT. palmetto, dwarf fan palm.

**margarina** *f.* margarine.

**Margarita** *f. pr. n.* Margaret.

**margarita** *f.* BOT. daisy, marguerite. *2* ZOOL. periwinkle. *3* pearl.

**margen** *m.-f.* margin. *2* marginal note. *3* border, edge, verge, fringe. *4* bank [of river]. *5* occasion: *dar ~ a*, to give occasion for.

**marginal** *adj.* marginal.

**marginar** *tr.* to margin, to write marginal notes on. *2* to leave a margin on [a page].

**margoso, -sa** *adj.* marly, loamy.

**margrave** *m.* margrave.

**margraviato** *m.* margraviate.

**María** *f. pr. n.* Mary.

**Mariana** *f. pr. n.* Marianne, Marian.

**Mariano** *m. pr. n.* Marion.

**mariano, -na** *adj.* ECCL. Marian.

**marica** *f.* ORN. magpie. *2 m.* coll. milksop, effeminate man.

**Maricastaña** *f. en tiempos de ~*, in the days of yore; long, long ago.

**maricón** *m.* effeminate man. *2* sodomite. | Not in decent use.

**maridaje** *m.* conjugal affection and agreement. *2* union; agreement, harmony [of things].

**maridar** *intr.* to marry. *2* to live as man and wife. *3 fig.* to join, connect.

**maridillo** *m.* foot stove.

**marido** *m.* husband.

**mariguana, marihuana** *f.* marihuana.

**marimacho** *m.* virago, manish woman.

**marimanta** *f.* coll. bogle, hobgoblin.

**marimba** *f.* MUS. marimba.

**marimorena** *f.* row, shindy.

**marina** *f.* seashore, seaside. *2* PAINT. marine, seascape. *3* seamanship. *4* marine [vessels]: *~ de guerra*, navy; *~ mercante*, merchant marine.

**marinaje** *m.* MARINERÍA.

**marinar** *tr.* to salt, marinate [fish]. *2* NAUT. to man [a ship].

**marinear** *tr.* to be a sailor, work as a sailor.

**marinería** *f.* sailoring, nautical profession. *2* sailors [collect.]. *3* sailors of a ship, crew.

**marinero, -ra** *adj.* [pertaining to] marine, sea or sailor. *2* sailorlike: *a la marinera*, sailorfashion. *3* NAUT. seaworthy. *4 m.* mariner, sailor, seaman. *5 f.* sailor blouse; middy, middy blouse.

**marinesco, -ca** *adj.* sailorly.

**marinista** *m.* marine painter, seascapist.

**marino, -na** *adj.* marine, nautical, sea. *2 m.* mariner, sailor, seaman.

**Mario** *m. pr. n.* Marius.

**marioneta** *f.* puppet, marionette.

**mariposa** *f.* ENT. butterfly. *2* floating taper, night taper. *3* MACH. *de ~*, wing, butterfly.

**mariposear** *intr.* to change frequently one's occupations, fancies, etc. *2* to flutter around.

**Mariquita** *f. pr. n.* Molly, Polly.

**mariquita** *f.* ENT. ladybird. *2 m.* milkshop.

**marisabidilla** *f.* coll. blue-stocking.

**mariscal** *m.* MIL. marshal: *~ de campo*, field marshal. *2* farrier.

**marisco** *m.* shellfish.

**marisma** *f.* salt marsh.

**marista** *adj.-m.* Marist.

**marital** *adj.* marital.

**marítimo, -ma** *adj.* maritime, marine, sea.

**maritornes** *f.* mannish maidservant.

**marjal** *m.* marsh, moor, swamp.

**marjoleta** *f.* fruit of the hawthorn tree.

**marjoleto** *m.* BOT. hawthorn tree. *2* BOT. white hawthorn.

**marmita** *f.* kettle, pot, boiler.

**marmitón** *m.* scullion, kitchen boy.
**mármol** *m.* marble [stone; sculpture]. *2* marver [for rolling hot glass]. *3* PRINT. imposing stone.
**marmolejo** *m.* small marble column.
**marmolería** *f.* marblework. *2* marble shop or works.
**marmolillo** *m.* GUARDACANTÓN. *2* fig. dunce.
**marmolista** *m.* marble worker. *2* marble dealer.
**marmoración** *f.* stucco.
**marmóreo, -a** *adj.* marble, marbly, marmoreal.
**marmòsete** *m.* PRINT. vignette.
**marmota** *f.* ZOOL. marmot. *2* coll. sleepy-head.
**maro** *m.* BOT. germander. *2* BOT. clary.
**maroma** *f.* cable of hemp or esparto. *2* tightrope.
**maronita** *adj.-n.* Maronite.
**marqués** *m.* marquis, marquess.
**marquesa** *f.* marchioness. *2* awning over a field tent.
**marquesado** *m.* marquisate.
**marquesina** *f.* marquee [canopy over an entrance]. *2* MARQUESA *2*.
**marquetería** *f.* cabinet work. *2* marquetry.
**marrajo, -ja** *adj.* treacherous, vicious [bull]. *2* artful, wily, tricky. *3 m.* ICHTH. shark.
**marrana** *f.* sow, female pig. *2* dirty, slovenly woman. *3* unprincipled woman.
**marranada** *f.* filthiness. *2* dirty trick.
**marranería** *f.* MARRANADA.
**marrano, -na** *adj.* dirty. *2* base, vile. *3 m.* ZOOL. hog, pig. *4* coll. hog, pig, dirty man; cur.
**marrar** *intr.-tr.* to miss, fail. *2 intr.* to go astray.
**marras** *adv.* a long time ago. *2 de ~,* mentioned, aluded to.
**marrasquino** *m.* maraschino.
**marro** *m.* game resembling quoits. *2* a boys' game. *3* cat [used in tipcat]. *4* slip, miss. *5* dodge [to elude pursuer].
**Mar Rojo** *m. pr. n.* GEOG. Red Sea.
**marrón** *m.* kind of quoit used in playing MARRO *1*. *2 adj.* Gal maroon, brown.
**marroquí** *adj.-n.* Moroccan. *2 m.* morocco, morocco leather.
**marrubio** *m.* BOT. horehound.
**marrueco, -ca** *adj.-n.* Moroccan.
**Marruecos** *m. pr. n.* GEOG. Morocco.
**marrullería** *f.* cunning, wheedling.
**marrullero, -ra** *adj.* cunning, wheedling. *2 m.-f.* wheedler, cunning person.
**Marsella** *f. pr. n.* GEOG. Marseilles.
**marsellés, -sa** *adj.-n.* of Marseilles. *3 m.* a kind of short jacket. *4 f.* (cap.) Marseillaise [French national anthem].
**marsopa, marsopia** *f.* ZOOL. porpoise, harbour porpoise, sea hog.
**marsupial** *adj.-n.* marsupial.
**Marta** *f. pr. n.* Martha.
**marta** *f.* ZOOL. marten, pine marten. *2* marten [fur]. *3 ~ cebellina,* sable, Siberian sable; sable [fur].
**martagón, -na** *m.-f.* sly, shrewd person. *2 m.* BOT. Turk's-cap lily.
**Marte** *m. pr. n.* ASTR., MYTH. Mars.
**martellina** *f.* marteline.
**martes,** *pl.* **-tes** *m.* Tuesday: *~ de carnaval,* Shrove Tuesday.
**martillada** *f.* blow or stroke with a hammer.
**martillar** *tr.* to hammer. *2* to worry, torment.
**martillazo** *m.* blow with a hammer.
**martilleo** *m.* hammering. *2* clatter.
**martillo** *m.* hammer [instrument]; claw hammer: *a macha ~,* firmly; strongly but roughly cons-

tructed. *2* MUS. tuning hammer. *3* ANAT. hammer, malleus. *4* auction rooms. *5* MACH. *~ pilón,* drop hammer.
**Martín** *m. pr. n.* Martin.
**martín del río,** *pl.* **martines del río** *m.* ORN. night heron.
**martín pescador,** *pl.* **martín pescadores** *m.* ORN. kingfisher.
**martinete** *m.* ORN. night heron. *2* drive hammer, drop hammer. *3* hammer [of piano].
**martingala** *f.* trick, cunning.
**Martinica (la)** *f. pr. n.* GEOG. Martinique.
**mártir** *m.-f.* martyr.
**martirio** *m.* martyrdom.
**martirizador, -ra** *adj.* martyrizing, tormenting. *2 m.-f.* martyrizer, tormentor.
**martirizar** *tr.* to martyr, martyrize; to torment.
**martirologio** *m.* martyrology.
**marxismo** *m.* Marxism.
**marxista** *adj.-n.* Marxian, Marxist.
**marzo** *m.* March.
**marzoleto** *m.* MARJOLETO.
**mas** *conj.* but [in the adversative sense].
**más** *adv.* more: *~ de,* more than [with a numeral]; *~ o menos,* more or less; *ni ~ ni menos,* exactly, just so; *no hay ~,* that is all; *cuanto ~ que, tanto ~ que,* all the more because. *2* It can be expressed by the termination «-er»: *más grande,* bigger. *3* most, -est; *el ~ bello,* the most beautiful; *el ~ pequeño,* the smallest; *lo ~, todo lo ~, cuando ~,* at the most, at most. *4* other: *no tengo ~ amigo que tú,* I have no other friend but you. *5* faster, longer, oftener, etc. *6 a ~,* besides, what is more. *7 a ~ correr,* at full speed. *8 a ~ de,* besides, in addition to. *9 a ~ amor ~ dolor,* the greater the love, the greater the pain. *10 a ~ y mejor,* copiously, hard, to one's heart's content. *11 listo como el que ~,* clever as the cleverest. *12 de ~,* over, above, extra, in excess. *13 estar de ~,* to be superfluous; to be amiss; to be in the way. *14 en ~ de,* at more than. *15 en ~ que,* above, over and above, more than. *16 ~ bien,* rather. *17 ~ que,* more than; but, only; although, eventhough. *18 ~ vale,* better to. *19 poco ~ o menos,* little more or less, practically; *de poco ~ o menos,* insignificant. *20 por ~ que,* however much; no matter how much; although. *21 sin ~ ni ~,* suddenly, without warning, without any reason.
*22 prep.* plus.
*23 m.* MATH. plus. *24 los ~,* the majority.
**masa** *f.* pastry mixture; dough; mortar. *2* mass, aggregate, bulk. *3* lump, whole. *4* PHYS., PAINT. mass. *5* mass, crowd, body [of persons]: *las masas,* the masses; *en ~,* in a body [of persons]. *6* nature or disposition.
**masada** *f.* farm, farmhouse.
**masaje** *m.* massage.
**masajista** *m.* masseur. *2 f.* masseuse.
**mascada** *f.* (Am.) chew [of tobacco].
**mascador, -ra** *adj.* chewing. *2 m.-f.* chewer.
**mascadura** *f.* chewing.
**mascar** *tr.* to chew, masticate. *2* coll. to mumble.
**máscara** *f.* mask [cover for the face; false face: that which conceals]: *~ antigás,* gas mask; *quitar la ~ a,* to unmask. *2* mask, masker, masquerader. *3* masquerade; disguise. *4* PHOT. mask. *5 pl.* masquerade [assembly].
**mascarada** *f.* masquerade. *2* fig. mummery.
**mascarilla** *f.* half mask. *2* death mask.

**mascarón** *m. augm.* large mask. *2* ARCH. mask. *3* NAUT. ~ *de proa*, figurehead.

**mascota** *f.* mascot.

**mascujar** *tr.* to chew poorly or with difficulty. *2 fig.* to mumble.

**masculino, -na** *adj.* male, masculine. *2 adj.-m.* GRAM. masculine.

**mascullar** *tr.* to mumble, mutter.

**masera** *f.* kneading trough.

**masetero** *m.* ANAT. masseter.

**masicote** *m.* CHEM. massicot.

**masilla** *f.* putty, glazier's putty, mastic.

**maslo** *m.* root [of the tail of a quadruped].

**masón** *m.* Mason, Freemason.

**masonería** *f.* Masonry, Freemasonry.

**masónico, -ca** *adj.* masonic.

**masoquismo** *m.* masochism.

**mastelerillo** *m.* NAUT. topgallant or royal mast.

**mastelero** *m.* NAUT. topmast.

**masticación** *f.* mastication.

**masticar** *tr.* to masticate, chew.

**mástil** *m.* NAUT., RADIO. mast. *2* NAUT. topmast. *3* upright pole or post. *4* BOT. trunk, stem, stalk. *5* shaft [of feather]. *6* neck [of violin, guitar, etc.].

**mastín, -na** *m.-f.* ZOOL. mastiff.

**mástique** *m.* mastic [resin].

**mastodonte** *m.* PALEONT. mastodon.

**mastranto, mastranzo** *m.* BOT. apple mint.

**mastuerzo** *m.* BOT. pepper cress, pepergrass. *2* BOT. water cress. *3* coll. dolt, simpleton.

**masturbación** *f.* masturbation.

**mata** *f.* BOT. low shrub or frutescent plant; bush. *2* sprig [of mint, basil, etc.]. *3* patch [of trees]. *4* BOT. mastic tree. *5* ~ *de pelo*, head of hair [of a woman].

**matacán** *m.* BOT. nux vomica. *2* FORT. machicolation.

**matacandelas,** *pl.* **-las** *m.* candle extinguisher.

**matachín** *m.* coll. swashbuckler.

**matadero** *m.* slaughterhouse, abattoir. *2* coll. tiresome work.

**matador, -ra** *adj.* killing. *2 m.-f.* killer. *3 m.* BULLF., CARDS matador.

**matadura** *f.* sore, gall [on beasts].

**matafuego** *m.* fire extinguisher.

**matalahuga, matalahuva** *f.* BOT. anise. *2* anised.

**mátalas callando** *m.-f.* coll. hypocrite, sly dog.

**matalobos,** *pl.* **-bos** *m.* BOT. wolf's-bane, aconite.

**matalón, -na** *adj.* skinny and full of sores [horse].

**matalote** *adj.-n.* MATALÓN.

**matamoros,** *pl.* **-ros** *m.* coll. bully, braggard.

**matamoscas,** *pl.* **cas** *m.* fly swatter.

**matanza** *f.* killing. *2* slaughter, butchery, massacre. *3* swine slaughtering and the season for it. *4* pork products kept at home for food.

**mataperros,** *pl.* **-rros** *m.* coll. street urchin.

**matapolvo** *m.* light rain, sprinkling.

**matar** *tr.* to kill, slay, murder. *2* to butcher [animals for food]. *3* to put out [a fire, a light]. *4* to gall [the back of a horse]. *5* to slack [lime]. *6* to dull, mat [metals]. *7* PAINT. to tone down [a colour]. *8* to bevel or round off [edges]. *9* to lay [dust]. *10* CARDS to take [play a card higher than]. *11* to obliterate, cancel [a postage stamp]. *12 fig.* to kill [time, hunger, etc.]. *13* to ruin, destroy. *14* to harass, worry, vex. *15 estar a ~ con*, to be at daggers drawn with. *16 ref.* to kill oneself. *17* to get killed. *18* to drudge, overwork; to struggle. *19* to kill one another.

**matarife** *m.* butcher, slaughterman.

**matasanos** *m.* coll. unskilled doctor; quack, medical charlatan.

**matasellos,** *pl.* **-llos** *m.* post-office cancelling stamp.

**matasiete** *m.* coll. swaggerer, braggart.

**matatías,** *pl.* **-tías** *m.* coll. moneylender, usurer.

**mate** *adj.* dull, mat, lusterless. *2* dull [sound]. *3 m.* CHESS. checkmate: ~ *ahogado*, stalemate; *dar ~*, to checkmate. *4* maté [herb and beverage]. *5* maté gourd.

**matear** *tr.* (Am.) to checkmate. *2 intr.* (Am.) to drink maté.

**matemática** *f.*, **matemáticas** *f. pl.* mathematics.

**matemático, -ca** *adj.* mathematical. *2 m.-f.* mathematician.

**Mateo** *m. pr. n.* Matthew.

**materia** *f.* matter [physical substance]. *2* material, substance, stuff: *primera ~*, raw material. *3* MED. matter, pus. *4* matter, topic, subject, subject matter: *en ~ de*, in the matter of; *entrar en ~*, to go into the subject. *5* cause, occasion.

**material** *adj.* material [of matter, physical, not spiritual]. *2* crude, coarse. *3 m.* ingredient. *4* equipment, matériel: ~ *fijo*, RLY. permanent way; ~ *móvil* or *rodante*, RLY. rolling stock. *6 pl.* materials.

**materialidad** *f.* materiality. *2* outward appearance.

**materialismo** *m.* materialism.

**materializar** *tr.* to materialize. *2 ref.* to become materialistic.

**materialmente** *adv.* materially. *2* absolutely.

**maternal** *adj.* maternal, motherly.

**maternidad** *f.* maternity, motherhood; *casa de ~*, maternity hospital.

**materno, -na** *adj.* maternal, mother.

**Matías** *m. pr. n.* Matthias.

**matidez** *f.* dullness [lack of luster]. *2* dullness [of sound].

**Matilde** *f. pr. n.* Matilda.

**matinal** *adj.* matinal, morning, matutine.

**matiné** *m.* GAL. matinée.

**matiz,** *pl.* **-tices** *m.* tint, hue, shade, nuance.

**matizado, -da** *adj.* nuanced. *2* variegated.

**matizar** *tr.* to give a special hue or shade to. *2* to nuance, shade. *3* to variegate, to blend harmoniously the colours of.

**matojo** *m.* bush, small shrub.

**matón** *m.* bully, hector.

**matorral** *m.* bush, thicket, heath, brake.

**matraca** *f.* wooden rattle. *2* coll. pestering, importunity. *3* coll. *dar ~ a*, to chaff, bantem.

**matraquear** *intr.* to rattle [with a wooden rattle]. *2* to pester, importune. *3* to chaff, banter.

**matraqueo** *m.* rattling sound. *2* pestering, importunity. *3* chaff, banter.

**matraz** *m.* CHEM. matrass.

**matrero, -ra** *adj.* shrewd, cunning, sly.

**matriarcado** *m.* matriarchate.

**matriarcal** *adj.* matriarchal.

**matricaria** *f.* BOT. feverfew.

**matricida** *adj.* matricidal. *2 m.-f.* matricide [person].

**matricidio** *m.* matricide [act].

**matrícula** *f.* register, list, roll; matriculation; registration.

**matricular** *tr.* to register, enroll, matriculate. *2 ref.* to matriculate [be matriculated], to register.

**matrimonial** *adj.* matrimonial.

**matrimonio** *m.* matrimony, marriage: ~ *civil*, civil marriage. *2* matrimony [sacrament]. *3* married couple.

**matritense** *adj.-n.* MADRILEÑO.

**matriz** *adj.* first, main, chief, mother: *casa ~,* mother house [monastery]; headquarters [of a business]. *2 escritura ~,* original draft [of a deed]. *3 f.* ANAT. matrix, womb. *4* matrix, mould, die. *5* GEOL. matrix. *7* stub of a stub book.

**matrona** *f.* matron [mother of a family]. *2* midwife. *3* matron [in a custom house, etc.].

**maturranga** *f.* trick, cunning, craft.

**Matusalén** *m. pr. n.* BIBL. Methuselah.

**matute** *m.* smuggling. *2* smuggled goods.

**matutear** *intr.* to smuggle.

**matutinal; matutino, -na** *adj.* matutinal, matutine.

**maula** *f.* rubbish, -trash. *2* remnant, piece. *3* deceitful trick. *4 m.-f.* trickster; bad pay. *5* lazy person, shirk, shirker.

**maullar** *intr.* to meow, mew.

**maullido, maúllo** *m.* meow, mew.

**Mauricio** *m. pr. n.* Maurice, Morris.

**máuser** *m.* Mauser [firearm].

**mausoleo** *m.* mausoleum.

**maxilar** *adj.-m.* maxillary.

**máxima** *f.* maxim [rule, principle, saying]. *2* MUS. maxim, maxima.

**máxime** *adv.* principally, specially.

**máximo, -ma** *adj.* maximum, greatest, top: *~ común divisor,* MATH. greatest common divisor. *2 m.* maximum.

**maya** *f.* BOT. daysy. *2* May queen. *7 adj.-n.* Maya, Mayan.

**mayal** *m.* flail [threshing instrument].

**mayar** *intr.* to meow, mew.

**mayestático, -ca** *adj.* majestic.

**mayo** *m.* May [month]. *2* Maypole.

**mayólica** *f.* majolica ware.

**mayonesa** *adj.* mayonnaise [sauce].

**mayor** *adj.* bigger, greater, larger; older, elder. *2* biggest, greatest, largest; oldest, eldest, senior. *3* of age. *4* principal, chief, main, high, major: *misa ~,* high mass; *palo ~,* NAUT. mainmast; *premisa ~,* LOG. major premiss. *5* MUS., MIL. major: *tambor ~,* drum major. *6 ~ de edad,* majority, full age; *ser ~ de edad,* to be of age. *7* COM. *libro ~,* ledger. *8 al por ~,* wholesale. *9 f.* LOG. major. *10 m.* superior, head. *11 m. pl.* elders, superiors. *12* ancestors, forefathers.

**mayoral** *m.* head shepherd. *2* stagecoach driver. *3* foreman [of farm labourers].

**mayorana** *f.* MEJORANA.

**mayorazgo** *m.* entailed estate. *2* owner of an entailed estate. *3* first-born son. *4* primogeniture.

**mayordoma** *f.* steward's wife. *2* stewardess.

**mayordomía** *f.* administration, stewardship. *2* butlership. *3* steward's office.

**mayordomo** *m.* steward. *2* butler, majordomo.

**mayoría** *m.* majority [larger number or part]. *2* POL. majority, plurality. *3* majority, full age.

**mayoridad** *f.* majority, full age. *2* superiority.

**mayorista** *m.* wholesale merchant.

**mayormente** *adv.* chiefly, especially.

**mayúsculo, -la** *adj.* large. *2* coll. awful, tremendous. *3* capital [letter]. *4 f.* capital letter.

**maza** *f.* mace [weapon]; war club. *2* mace [staff]. *3* drumstick of a bass drum. *4* monkey, ram, tup [of a drop hammer or pile driver]. *5* thick end [of billiard cue]. *6* coll. bore [person].

**mazacote** *m.* CHEM. barilla. *2* concrete. *3* coll. tough, doughy food. *4* bore [person].

**mazamorra** *f.* NAUT. mess of broken hardtack. *2* fig. anything broken into small pieces.

**mazapán** *m.* marchpane, marzipan.

**mazar** *tr.* to churn [milk].

**mazazo** *m.* blow with a mace or maul.

**mazdeísmo** *m.* Mazdaism, Mazdeism.

**mazdeísta** *adj.* Mazdean. *2 m.-f.* Mazdaist.

**mazmorra** *f.* underground dungeon.

**mazo** *m.* maul, mallet, wooden hammer. *2* bundle [of some things]. *3* coll. bore [person].

**mazorca** *f.* BOT. thick ear or spike. *2* BOT. ear [of Indian corn]. *3* BOT. cacao pod. *4* spindleful [of yarn]. *5* spindle [in a baluster].

**mazorral** *adj.* crude, rough. *2* PRINT. solid.

**mazurca** *f.* mazurka [dance and tune].

**me** *pers. pron., 1st pers. sing.* [object of the verb and ref.] me; to me, for me; myself.

**meada** *f.* urination. *2* spot made by urine.

**meados** *m. pl.* urine.

**meaja** *f.* MIGAJA.

**meandro** *m.* meander.

**mear** *intr.-ref.* to urinate, make water.

**meauca** *f.* ORN. shearwater.

**Meca (la)** *f. pr. n.* GEOG. Meca.

**¡mecachis!** *interj.* ¡CARAMBA!

**mecánica** *f.* mechanics. *2* machinery, works [working parts of a machine, etc.]. *3* contemptible thing. *4* MIL. fatigue, fatigue duty: *traje de ~,* fatigue dress.

**mecanicismo** *m.* BIOL., PHIL. mechanism [doctrine].

**mecánico, -ca** *adj.* mechanical [in every sense, except unconcious, automatic]. *2* fig. low, mean. *3 m.* mechanic, repairman. *4* AUTO. driver, chauffeur. *5* mechanician.

**mecanismo** *m.* mechanism. *2* works [of a machine].

**mecanización** *adj.* mechanization.

**mecanizar** *tr.* to mechanize.

**mecanografía** *f.* typewriting.

**mecanografiar** *tr.* to typewrite, to type.

**mecanógrafo, -fa** *m.-f.* typist, typewriter.

**mecedor, -ra** *adj.* rocking, swinging. *2* stirring [a liquid]. *3 m.* stirrer [implement]. *4* COLUMPIO. *5 f.* rocker, rocking chair.

**mecenas** *m.* Maecenas, patron of art or literature.

**mecenazgo** *m.* support given by a Maecenas.

**mecer** *tr.* to stir [a liquid]. *2* to rock, swing. *3 ref.* to rock, swing [intr.]. *4* [of birds] to soar.

**meconio** *m.* meconium.

**mecha** *f.* wick. *2* fuse, match [for firing an explosive]. *3* COOK. strip of bacon for larding. *4* SURG. roll of lint. *5* TEXT. sliver, rove. *6* lock, tuft [of hair, wool, etc.]. *7* NAUT. heel [of a mast].

**mechar** *tr.* COOK. to lard [with bacon].

**mechazo** *m.* MIN. fizzle of a blast fuse.

**mechera** *f.* larding pin. *2* shoplifter [woman].

**mechero** *m.* lamp burner, gas burner. *2* socket [of candlestick]. *3* cigarette lighter.

**mechinal** *m.* MAS. putlog hole. *2* fig. hovel.

**mechón** *m.* lock, tuft [of hair, wool, etc.].

**medalla** *f.* medal. *2* ARCH. medallion.

**medallón** *m.* large medal. *2* ARCH. medallion. *3* JEW. locket.

**médano, medaño** *m.* dune. *2* sand bank.

**Media** *f. pr. n.* HIST., GEOG. Media.

**media** *f.* stocking [for foot and leg]. *2* MATH. mean: *~ proporcional,* geometrical mean, mean proportional.

**mediacaña** *f.* fluted moulding. *2* picture moulding. *3* straight gouge [chisel]. *4* half-round file. *5* curling tongs. *6* PRINT. double rule.

**mediación** *f.* mediation. *2* intercession.

**mediado, -da** *adj.* half-filled, half-full. *2 adv. a mediados de,* about the middle of [a period of time].

**mediador, -ra** *m.-f.* mediator. *4* intercessor.

**mediana** *f.* long billiard cue. *2* GEOM. median.

**medianejo, -ja** *adj.* coll. mediocre.

**medianería** *f.* party wall. *2* party-line fence or hedge.

**medianero, -ra** *adj.* middle, dividing. *2* mediating; interceding. *3* party [wall]. *4 m.-f.* mediator. *5* intercessor.

**medianía** *f.* moderate circumstances. *2* mediocrity [person].

**mediano, -na** *adj.* middling, medium, moderate. *2* coll. mediocre, bad, worthless.

**medianoche** *f.* midnight. *2* small meat pie.

**mediante** *adj.* intervening, interceding. *2 adv.* by means of, through. *3 Dios ~,* God willing.

**mediar** *intr.* to be at the middle, to be half over. *2* to mediate. *3* to intercede. *4* to intervene. *5* [of time] to elapse. *6 tr.* to make half-full.

**medias (a)** *adv.* halves: *ir a medias,* to go halves. *2* by halves: *hacer a medias,* to do or make by halves. *3* half: *dormido a medias,* half asleep. *4* half and half, between two.

**mediastino** *m.* ANAT. mediastinum.

**mediatizar** *tr.* to mediatize.

**mediato, -ta** *adj.* mediate.

**médica** *f.* woman physician. *2* doctor's wife.

**medicación** *f.* medication, medical treatment.

**medicamento** *m.* medicament.

**medicamentoso, -sa** *adj.* medicamental.

**medicar** *tr.* to treat, to cure by medicine.

**medicastro** *m.* medicaster.

**medicina** *f.* medicine [science & art]. *2* medicine, medicament.

**medicinal** *adj.* medicinal.

**medicinar** *tr.* to administer medicines to.

**medición** *f.* measuring, measurement, mensuration.

**médico, -ca** *adj.* medical. *2* Medic. *3 m.* doctor, physician: *~ de cabecera,* family physician.

**medicucho** *m.* unskilled doctor.

**medida** *f.* measure, measurement: *tomar las medidas a uno,* to take someone's measurements. *2* measurement, mensuration. *3* measure [instrument for measuring; unit of measurement]; *~ de longitud,* linear measure; *~ de superficie,* square measure; *~ de volumen,* cubic measure; *~ para áridos,* dry measure; *~ para líquidos,* liquid measure. *3* ARITH., PROS. measure. *4* proportion, correspondence: *a ~ de,* in proportion to, according to; *a ~ que,* as, in proportion as. *5* measure, step, suitable action. *6* moderation.

**medidor, -ra** *adj.* measuring. *2 m.-f.* measurer.

**mediero, -ra** *m.-f.* stocking maker o seller, hosier.

**medieval** *adj.* medieval, mediaeval.

**medievo** *m.* Middle Ages.

**medio, -dia** *adj.* half, half a: *~ libra,* half a pound); *medias tintas,* half measures; *las dos y media,* half past two [o'clock]. *2* middle, mean, average: *clase media,* middle class; *distancia ~,* mean distance; *término ~,* middle term; average. *3* medium. *4* medial, median. *5* mid: *a media tarde,* in mid afternoon.

**medio** *adv.* half, partially, halfway: *~ dormido,* half asleep; *a ~ hacer,* half done. *2 m.* ARITH. half. *3* middle, midst: *en ~ de,* in the middle of, in the midst of; notwithstanding. *4* means, agency,

medium: *por ~ de,* by means of. *5* medium, environment. *6* BIOL., PHYS. medium. *7* mean [between the extremes]. *8 de ~ a ~,* in the middle, smack; absolutely. *9 de por ~,* in between; *estar de por ~,* to be concerned, have to do with. *10 quitar de en ~,* to put out of the way; to do away with. *11 quitarse de en ~,* to get out of the way. *12 pl.* means [pecuniary resources].

**mediocre** *adj.* mediocre.

**mediocridad** *f.* mediocrity.

**mediodía** *m.* noon, midday. *2* GEOG. south.

**medioeval** *adj.* MEDIEVAL.

**medir** *tr.* to measure, gauge. *2* to measure [one's skill, etc., with]. *3* to scan [verse]. *4 ref.* to act with moderation. ¶ CONJUG. like *servir.*

**meditabundo, -da** *adj.* meditative, pensive, musing.

**meditación** *f.* meditation.

**meditar** *tr.-intr.* to meditate, think.

**mediterráneo, -a** *adj.-n.* mediterranean: *Mar Mediterráneo,* Mediterranean Sea.

**médium** *m.* [spiritualistic] medium.

**medo, -da** *adj.* Median. *2 m.-f.* Mede.

**medra** *f.* growth, thriving, prosperity.

**medrana** *f.* coll. fear.

**medrar** *intr.* to grow, thrive, prosper.

**medro** *m.* growth, thriving, prosperity. *2 pl.* progress, improvement.

**medroso, -sa** *adj.* fearful, timorous, fainthearted. *2* dreadful, frightful.

**medula, médula** *f.* ANAT. medulla, marrow: *~ espinal,* spinal marrow, spinal cord. *2* BOT. medulla, pith. *3* fig. marrow, pith, substance.

**medular** *adj.* medullar, medullary.

**medusa** *f.* ZOOL. medusa, jellyfish. *2* (cap.) MYTH. Medusa.

**Mefistófeles** *m. pr. n.* Mephistopheles.

**mefistofélico, -ca** *adj.* Mephistophelian.

**megáfono** *m.* megaphone.

**megalítico, -ca** *adj.* ARCHEOL. megalithic.

**megalito** *m.* ARCHEOL. megalith.

**megalomanía** *f.* megalomania.

**megaterio** *m.* PALEONT. megathere.

**megatón** *m.* megaton, one million tons.

**mego, -ga** *adj.* meek, mild, gentle.

**megohmio** *m.* ELECT. megohm.

**mejana** *f.* islet [in a river].

**mejicano, -na** *adj.-n.* Mexican.

**Méjico** *m. pr. n.* GEOG. Mexico. *2* Mexico City.

**mejido, -da** *adj.* beaten with sugar and milk [egg].

**mejilla** *f.* ANAT. cheek.

**mejillón** *m.* ZOOL. common mussel.

1) **mejor,** *pl.* **mejores** *adj. comp.-superl.* better, best; *lo ~,* the best; *el ~ día,* when least expected; *el ~ postor,* the highest bidder; *a lo ~,* perhaps, maybe, probably.

2) **mejor** *adv. comp.-superl.* better, best: *tanto ~,* so much the better. *2* rather: *~ dicho,* rather, more properly speaking.

**mejora** *f.* improvement, betterment. *2* higher bid [in auction].

**mejoramiento** *m.* amelioration, improvement.

**mejorana** *f.* BOT. sweet marjoram.

**mejorar** *tr.* to ameliorate, meliorate, better, improve, mend. *2* to better, surpass. *3* to raise [a bid]. *4 intr.-ref.* to ameliorate, improve, grow better. *5* to mend, recover, get better. *6* [of weather] to clear up. *7* to reform. *8* to progress.

**mejoría** *f.* amelioration, improvement. *2* improvement in health.

**mejunje** *m.* medicinal or cosmetic mixture.

**melado, -da** *adj.* honey-coloured. 2 *m.* cane-juice syrup.
**meláfido** *m.* GEOL. melaphyre.
**melancolía** *f.* melancholy. 2 melancholia.
**melancólico, -ca** *adj.-n.* MED. melancholic. 2 *adj.* melancholic, melancholy.
**Melanesia** *f. pr. n.* GEOG. Melanesia.
**melanita** *f.* MINER. melanite.
1) **melar** [of cane or fruit] sweet, honey-sweet.
2) **melar** *intr.* [of bees] to fill combs with honey.
**melaza** *f.* molasses. 2 dregs of honey.
**melcocha** *f.* paste of concentrated honey.
**Melchor** *pr.-n.* Melchior.
**melena** *f.* mane [of man or lion]. 2 loose hair [in women]. 3 forelock [in animals].
**meleno** *adj.* having a forelock [bull.]. 2 *m.* peasant, rustic.
**melenudo, -da** *adj.* long-haired.
**melero** *m.* honey dealer. 2 storage place for honey.
**meliáceo, -a** *adj.* BOT. meliaceous.
**melífero, -ra** *adj.* melliferous.
**melificación** *f.* honey making.
**melificado, -da** *adj.* mellifluous.
**melificar** *intr.* to make honey. 2 *tr.* to draw honey from [flowers].
**melifluo, flua** *adj.* mellifluent, mellifluous.
**meliloto, -ta** *m.* BOT. melilot, sweet clover.
**melindre** *m.* honey fritter. 2 a small cake. 3 narrow ribbon. 4 finicking, mincing, affectation of delicacy.
**melindrear** *intr.* to finick, mince, affect delicacy.
**melindrería** *f.* finickiness, daintiness.
**melindroso, -sa** *adj.* finicky, mincing, affecting delicacy.
**melinita** *f.* melinite.
**melis** *m.* BOT. a variety of pine; its wood.
**melisa** *f.* BOT. balm, garden balm, lemon balm.
**melocotón** *m.* BOT. peach [fruit]; peach tree.
**melocotonar** *m.* peach orchard.
**melocotonero** *m.* BOT. peach tree.
**melodía** *f.* MUS. melody. 2 melodiousness.
**melódico, -ca** *adj.* MUS. melodic.
**melodioso, -sa** *adj.* melodious.
**melodrama** *m.* melodrama.
**melodramático, -ca** *adj.* melodramatic(al).
**melojo** *m.* BOT. a variety of black oak.
**melolonta** *m.* ENT. cockchafer.
**melomanía** *f.* melomania.
**melómano, -na** *m.-f.* melomane, melomaniac.
**melón** *m.* BOT. melon, muskmelon. 2 ZOOL. MELONCILLO.
**melonar** *m.* muskmelon patch.
**meloncillo** *m. dim.* ZOOL. a variety of mongoose.
**melonero, -ra** *m.-f.* muskmelon raiser or dealer.
**melopea** *f.* MELOPEYA. 2 monotonous singing. 3 vulg. drunkenness.
**melopeya** *f.* melopoeia.
**melosidad** *f.* honeyedness.
**meloso, -sa** *adj.* honey-like. 2 honeyed, sweet, mealy; mealy-mouthed.
**melton** *m.* melton.
**mella** *f.* nick, notch, break, dent [in an edge]. 2 hollow, gap. 3 damage, hurt; impression: *hacer ~*, to make an impression; to harm, injure, affect.
**mellado, -da** *adj.* nicked, jagged [edge, tool]. 2 having lost a tooth or some teeth.
**mellar** *tr.* to nick, break, dent the edge of. 2 to injure [the honour, credit, etc.]. 3 *ref.* to get nicked, jagged.
**mellizo, -za** *adj.-n.* twin [brother, sister].

**memada** *f.* stupidity, piece of folly.
**membrana** *f.* membrane.
**membranoso, -sa** *adj.* membranous.
**membrete** *m.* letterhead, heading [printed on letter paper]. 2 note, memo.
**membrillate** *m.* quince paste.
**membrillero** *m.* BOT. quince tree.
**membrillo** *m.* BOT. quince tree. 2 BOT. quince [fruit]. 3 quince paste.
**membrudo, -da** *adj.* burly, sturdy, robust.
**memento** *m.* ECCL. Memento.
**memez** *f.* silliness, stupidity.
**memo, -ma** *adj.* silly, foolish. 2 *m.-f.* fool, simpleton.
**memorable** *adj.* memorable.
**memorando, -da** *adj.* MEMORABLE.
**memorándum** *m.* [diplomatic] memorandum. 2 notebook.
**memorar** *tr.-ref.* to remember.
**memoria** *f.* memory [faculty of remembering]: *ser flaco de ~*, to have a bad memory; *traer a la ~*, to recall, remember; to remind; *de ~*, by heart. 2 memory, recollection, remembrance, reminiscence: *hacer ~*, to try to remember; to remember; to remind; *en ~ de*, in memory of. 3 memoir, record, statement, report. 4 essay, paper. 5 *pl.* memoirs. 6 compliments, regards.
**memorial** *m.* memorial, petition. 2 notebook.
**memorialista** *m.* one who writes petitions, letters, etc., for other people.
**memorión, -na** *adj.-n.* having a retentive memory [person]. 2 *m.* great memory.
**memorioso, -sa** *adj.* having a retentive memory.
**mena** *f.* MIN. ore. 2 ICHTH. picarel.
**ménade** *f.* maenad.
**menaje** *m.* household furniture. 2 school equipment and supplies.
**mención** *f.* mention: *~ honorífica*, honourable mention.
**mencionar** *tr.* to mention.
**menchevique** *m.-f.* Menshevik.
**mendacidad** *f.* mendacity.
**mendaz** *adj.* mendacious.
**mendicación** *f.* begging.
**mendicante** *adj.-n.* mendicant.
**mendicidad** *f.* mendicity, mendicancy.
**mendigar** *tr.* to beg [ask for as a charity]. 2 to beg, supplicate for. 3 *intr.* to beg [go begging].
**mendigo, -ga** *m.-f.* beggar.
**mendoso, -sa** *adj.* mendacious. 2 wrong, mistaken.
**mendrugo** *m.* crumb, crust [dry scrap of bread].
**menear** *tr.* to shake, stir. 2 to wag, waggle, move. 3 to manage, direct. 4 *ref.* to wag, waggle, move [be in motion]. 5 to stir, bestir oneself, hustle, hurry up. 6 [of a tooth, etc.] to be loose.
**menegilda** *f.* coll. housemaid.
**meneo** *m.* shake, shaking, stir, stirring, wag, wagging. 2 hustling. 3 coll. drubbing, beating.
**menester** *m.* need, want: *haber ~*, to need; *ser ~*, to be necessary. 2 job, occupation, duty. 3 *pl.* bodily needs. 4 implements, tools [of a trade].
**menesteroso, -sa** *adj.* needy. 2 *m.-f.* needy person.
**menestra** *f.* vegetable soup or stew. 2 *pl.* dried vegetables.
**menestral** *m.* artisan, mechanic, handicraftsman.
**menestralia** *f.* artisans, mechanics [as a class].
**Menfis** *f. pr. n.* HIST., GEOG. Memphis.
**menfita** *adj.* Memphian. 2 *m.-f.* Memphite.
**mengano, -na** *m.-f.* So-and-So.
**mengua** *f.* diminution, decrease, waning. 2 deficiency, lack, want. 3 discredit, disgrace.

**menguado, -da** *adj.* diminished, short, poor; mean, paltry. *2* cowardly, pusillanimous. *3* mean, base, vile. *4* foolish, silly. *5* wretched. *6 m.-f.* coward. *8* wretch. *9 m. pl.* narrowing [in knitting].

**menguante** *adj.* diminishing, decreasing, waning. *2 f.* decay, decline. *3* low water [in rivers, etc.]. *4* NAUT. ebbtide. *5* waning [of the moon].

**menguar** *intr.* to diminish, decrease, lessen, wane. *2* to decay, decline. *3* to narrow [in knitting]. *4 tr.* AMENGUAR.

**mengue** *m.* coll. deuce, devil.

**menhir** *m.* ARCHEOL. menhir.

**menina** *f.* formerly, a young lady-in-waiting.

**meníngeo, -a** *adj.* ANAT. meningeal.

**meninges** *f. pl.* ANAT. meninges.

**meningitis** *f.* MED. meningitis.

**menino** *m.* formerly, a noble page of the queen or a young prince.

**menisco** *m.* PHYS., OPT., ANAT. meniscus.

**menopausia** *f.* PHYSIOL. menopause.

**menor** *adj.* smaller, less, lesser; younger. *2* smallest, least, youngest, junior. *3* minor [poet, prophet, etc.]. *4* LOG., MUS. minor. *5 ~ de edad,* ~, under age; minor. *6 ~ edad,* minority. *7 m.-f.* minor [person]. *8 m.* minorite. *9 f.* LOG. minor. *10 adv. al por* ~, retail. *11 por* ~, retail; minutely, in detail.

**Menorca** *f. pr. n.* GEOG. Minorca.

**menoría** *f.* minority [state or period of being under age].

**menorquín, -na** *adj.-n.* Minorcan.

**menos** *adv.* less, least: ~ *de,* ~ *que,* less than; *al* ~, *a lo* ~, at least; at the least; *a* ~ *de* [with an inf.], without; *a* ~ *que,* unless; *de* ~, less, missing, wanting; *echar de* ~, to miss, feel or notice the absence of; *en* ~ *de,* at less than; *en* ~ *que,* less, at less than; *en* ~ *que canta un gallo,* in an instant; *lo* ~, the least; at the least; *por lo* ~, at least; at the least; *venir a* ~, to decline, decay. *2* fewer; *no* ~ *de,* no fewer than. *3* still less. *4* minus, less: *cinco* ~ *dos,* five minus two. *5* to [in telling time]: *las tres* ~ *cuarto,* a quarter to three. *6* but, except. *7 m.* minus [sign].

**menoscabar** *tr.* to lessen, impair, detract from.

**menoscabo** *m.* lessening, impairing, injure, detriment, derogation: *con* ~ *de,* to the detriment of.

**menospreciable** *adj.* contemptible.

**menospreciar** *tr.* to underestimate, underrate, undervalue. *2* to contempt, despise, slight.

**menosprecio** *m.* underestimation, undervaluation. *2* scorn, contempt.

**mensaje** *m.* message.

**mensajería** *f.* stage coach, public conveyance. *2 pl.* transportation company, stage line. *3* shipping line.

**mensajero, -ra** *m.-f.* messenger [carrier of a message]. *2 adj.* carrier [pigeon].

**menstruación** *f.* menstruation. *2* menses.

**menstruar** *intr.* to menstruate.

**menstruo** *m.* menses, courses. *2* CHEM. menstruum.

**mensual** *adj.* monthly.

**mensualidad** *f.* monthly pay or allowance. *2* monthly instalment.

**ménsula** *f.* ARCH. bracket, corbel.

**mensura** *f.* MEDIDA.

**mensurable** *adj.* mensurable.

**mensuración** *f.* mensuration.

**mensurar** *tr.* to measure.

**menta** *f.* BOT. mint. *2* peppermint.

**mentado, -da** *adj.* mentioned. *2* famous, renowned.

**mental** *adj.* mental.

**mentalidad** *f.* mentality.

**mentar** *tr.* to name, mention. ¶ CONJUG. like *acertar.*

**mente** *f.* mind, intellect. *2* mind, intention.

**mentecato, -ta** *adj.* silly, foolish, stupid, crack-brained, half-witted. *2 m.-f.* fool, dolt.

**mentidero** *m.* gossiping place.

**mentido, -da** *adj.* false, delusive.

**mentir** *intr.* to lie [speak falsely, tell lies]. *2* [of things] to deceive, be false, delusive. *3 tr.* to feign. *4* to fail to keep [one's word, promise, etc.]. ¶ CONJUG. like *sentir.*

**mentira** *f.* lie, fib, falsehood: ~ *inocente,* ~ *oficiosa,* white lie; *parece* ~, it hardly seems possible. *2* error, mistake [in writing]. *3* coll. white spot [on fingernails].

**mentirijillas** or **mentirillas (de)** *adv.* in fun, in jest, for fun.

**mentiroso, -sa** *adj.* lying, mendacious. *2* deceptive, deceitful. *3 m.-f.* liar.

**mentís,** *pl.* **-tís** *m.* lie [charge of lying]: *dar un* ~ *a,* to give the lie to.

**mentol** *m.* PHARM. menthol.

**mentón** *m.* chin, point of the chin.

**mentor** *m.* mentor.

**menú** *m.* gal, menu, bill of fare.

**menudamente** *adv.* minutely. *2* in detail.

**menudear** *tr.* to do frequently, to repeat frequently. *2 intr.* to happen frequently; come down in abundance. *4* to go into details.

**menudencia** *f.* smallness. *2* trifle. *3* minuteness, minute accuracy. *4 pl.* pork products.

**menudeo** *m.* constant repetition, incessant happening or falling down. *2* retail: *al* ~, by retail.

**menudillo** *m.* fetlock joint. *2 pl.* giblets.

**menudo, -da** *adj.* small, little, minute, tiny. *2* trifling, unimportant. *3* common [people]. *4* small [money, -change]. *5* minute, exact. *6 pl.* small change. *7* blood and entrails [of butchered animals]. *8* giblets. *9 a* ~, often, frequently. *10 por* ~, minutely; by retail.

**meñique** *adj.* coll. tiny, very small. *2* little [finger].

**meollo** *m.* ANAT. marrow, pith. *2* BOT. pith. *3* fig. marrow, pith, substance. *4* fig. judgment, sense.

**meón, -na** *adj.* constantly urinating.

**meple** *m.* (Am.) BOT. maple.

**mequetrefe** *m.* coll. whippersnapper, jackanapes.

**mercachifle** *m.* merchant, petty merchant. *2* peddler, hawker.

**mercadear** *intr.* to deal, trade, traffic.

**mercader** *m.* merchant, dealer.

**mercadería** *f.* MERCANCÍA.

**mercado** *m.* market: ~ *de valores,* stock market; ~ *negro,* black market. *2* market place.

**mercancía** *f.* commerce, trade. *2* merchandise commodity. *3 pl.* goods, merchandise, wares.

**mercante** *adj.* merchant.

**mercantil** *adj.* mercantile, commercial.

**mercantilismo** *m.* mercantilism.

**mercar** *tr.* to buy, purchase.

**merced** *f.* gift, grant, favour, grace. *2* mercy, will, power, disposal: *a* ~ *de,* at the mercy of. *3 La Merced,* order of Our Lady of Mercy. *4 vuestra (vuesa, su) Merced,* you, sir; you, madam. *5 ~ a,* thanks to.

**mercedario, -ria** *adj.* pertaining to the order of Our Lady of Mercy. *2 m.-f.* Mercedarian.

**mercenario, -ria** *adj.* mercenary, hired. *2* MERCE-

**mercería**

DARIO. *3 m.* mercenary, stipendiary. *4 m.-f.* Mercedarian.
**mercería** *f.* small wares, haberdashery, *notions. *2* haberdarher's shop.
**mercerizar** *tr.* to mercerize.
**mercurial** *adj.* mercurial. *2* ASTR., MYTH. Mercurial. *3 f.* BOT. herb mercury.
**Mercurio** *m. pr. n.* ASTR., MYTH. Mercury.
**mercurio** *m.* CHEM. mercury.
**merdoso, -sa** *adj.* filthy.
**merecedor, -ra** *adj.* deserving, worthy.
**merecer** *tr.* to deserve, merit, be worthy of: *~ la pena*, to be worthwhile. *2* to attain, obtain. *3* to be worth. *4 intr.* to deserve, be deserving: *~ bien de*, to deserve the gratitude of. ¶ CONJUG. like *agradecer.*
**merecido, -da** *adj.* deserved. *2 m.* deserts, deserved punishment.
**merecimiento** *m.* merit, desert.
**merendar** *intr.* to take a light refreshment in the afternoon. *2* [in some places] to lunch. *3 ref.* to manage to get. ¶ CONJUG. like *acertar.*
**merendero** *m.* place [often out of town] where refreshments or light meals are served.
**merengue** *m.* meringue.
**meretricio, -cia** *adj.* meretricious [of a harlot].
**meretriz** *f.* harlot, strumpet.
**mergansar, mergo** *m.* ORN. cormorant.
**mericarpio** *m.* BOT. mericarp.
**meridiana** *f.* couch, lounge. *2* afternoon nap.
**meridiano, -na** *adj.* meridian [of midday]. *2* ASTR. meridian. *3* vright, dazzling. *4 m.* ASTR., GEOG., GEOM. meridian.
**meridional** *adj.* meridional, southern. *2 m.-f.* meridional, southerner.
**merienda** *f.* snack, light refreshment taken in the afternoon. *2* [in some places] lunch. *3 ~ de negros*, confusion, bedlam.
**merino, -na** *adj.* merino. *2* thick and curly [hair]. *3 m.* formerly, a royal judge. *4* head shepherd. *5* merino [sheep, wool and fabric].
**mérito** *m.* merit, dessert; worth, excellence, value: *de ~*, excellent, of value. *2* LAW *méritos del proceso*, merits of the case. *3 hacer ~ de*, to mention.
**meritorio, -ria** *adj.* meritorious. *2 m.* improver [employee].
**merla** *f.* ORN. blackbird.
**merlín** *m.* NAUT. marline.
**merlón** *m.* FORT. merlon.
**merluza** *f.* ICHTH. hake. *2* coll. drunk, drunken fit.
**merma** *f.* decrease, waste, loss, leakage, shrinkage. *2* curtailment, reduction.
**mermar** *intr.-ref.* to decrease, diminish, lessen, wear away, shrink. *2 tr.* to lessen, curtail.
**mermelada** *f.* marmalade.
**1) mero** *m.* ICHTH. a Mediterranean grouper.
**2) mero, -ra** *adj.* mere, pure, simple.
**merodeador, -ra** *adj.* marauding. *2 m.-f.* marauder.
**merodear** *intr.* to maraud.
**merodeo** *m.* marauding.
**merovingio, gia** *adj.-m.* Merovingian.
**mes** *m.* month. *2* monthly pay or allowance. *3* menses.
**mesa** *f.* table [article of furniture]: *~ de juego*, gaming table, gambling table; *~ de noche*, bedside table; *~ del altar*, ECCL. altar; *~ del billar*, billiard table; *~ redonda*, round table; table d'hôte; *poner la ~*, to set, or lay, the table; *quitar la ~*, to clear the table. *2* table, food, fare, cheer. *3* exe-

cutive board [of a meeting, etc.]. *4* desk [writing table]. *5* tableland, plateau. *6* landing [of a staircase]. *7* game [at billiards]. *8* table [of a gem]. *9* NAUT. *~ de guarnición*, channel.
**mesada** *f.* monthly pay or allowance.
**mesalina** *f.* fig. dissolute woman.
**mesana** *f.* NAUT. mizzen sail; mizzenmast.
**mesar** *tr.* to tear or pull the hair or beard.
**mescolanza** *f.* MEZCOLANZA.
**mesenterio** *m.* ANAT. mesentery.
**meseta** *f.* tableland, plateau. *2* landing [of a staircase].
**mesiánico, -ca** *adj.* Messianic.
**Mesías** *m. pr. n.* BIBL. Messiah.
**mesilla** *f. dim.* small table. *2* landing [of a staircase]. *3* window sill.
**mesita** *f. dim.* small table.
**mesmerismo** *m.* mesmerism.
**mesmo, -ma** *adj.* obs. or vulg. MISMO.
**mesnada** *f.* armed retinue, company of soldiers. *2* company, band; followers.
**mesocarpio** *m.* BOT. mesocarp.
**mesocracia** *f.* government by the middle class.
**mesón** *m.* inn, hostelry, tavern, roadhouse.
**mesonero, -ra** *adj.* [pertaining to an] inn or hostelry. *2 m.-f.* inkeeper, host, hostess.
**Mesopotamia** *f. pr. n.* GEOG. Mesopotamia.
**mesotórax, pl. -rax** *m.* ZOOL. mesothorax.
**mesozoico, -ca** *adj.-m.* GEOL. Mesozoic.
**mesta** *f.* a powerful union of cattle or sheep raisers.
**mester** *m.* obs. art, trade. *2 ~ de clerecía*, verse of clerics in the Middle Ages. *3 ~ de juglaría*, Spanish minstrelsy, verse of the minstrels in the Middle Ages.
**mestizaje** *m.* crossing of races.
**mestizo, -za** *adj.* mongrel, half-breed half-blooded. *2 m.-f.* half-breed [pers. of mixed blood].
**mesura** *f.* gravity, dignified deportment. *2* politeness, deference. *3* moderation, circumspection.
**mesurado, -da** *adj.* grave, dignified. *2* moderate, circumspect, temperate.
**mesurar** *tr.* to moderate, inspire moderation in. *2 ref.* to restrain oneself, to act with moderation.
**meta** *f.* SPORT. goal; finish line. *2* fig. goal, aim, purpose.
**metabólico, -ca** *adj.* PHYSIOL. metabolic.
**metabolismo** *m.* PHYSIOL. metabolism.
**metacarpo** *m.* ANAT. metacarpus.
**metafase** *f.* BIOL. metaphase.
**metafísica** *f.* metaphysics.
**metafísico, -ca** *adj.* metaphysical. *2 m.* metaphysician.
**metáfora** *f.* metaphor.
**metafórico, -ca** *adj.* metaphorical.
**metal** *m.* CHEM., HER. metal: *~ blanco*, nickel silver, white metal; *~ precioso*, rich metal; *el vil ~*, fig. money. *2* brass, latten. *3* MUS. brass. *4* timbre [of voice]. *5* quality, nature [of things].
**metalario** *m.* metallist, metal worker.
**metalepsis** *f.* RHET. metalepsis.
**metálico, -ca** *adj.* metallic. *2 m.* specie, hard cash, hard money, coin.
**metalífero, -ra** *adj.* metal-bearing, metalliferous.
**metalista** *m.* METALARIO.
**metalizar** *tr.* CHEM. to give metallic properties to. *2 ref.* to become metallized. *3* to become mercenary, money-mad.
**metalografía** *f.* metallography.
**metaloide** *m.* CHEM. metalloid, nonmetal.
**metalurgia** *f.* metallurgy.

**metalúrgico, -ca** *adj.* metallurgic, metallurgical. *2 m.* metallurgist.
**metámero** *m.* ZOOL. metamere.
**metamórfico, -ca** *adj.* metamorphic.
**metamorfismo** *m.* GEOL. metamorphism.
**metamorfosear** *tr.* to metamorphose, transform. *2 ref.* to metamorphose, be transformed.
**metamorfosis,** *pl.* **-sis** *f.* metamorphosis, transformation. *2* ZOOL. metamorphosis.
**metano** *m.* CHEM. methane.
**metaplasma** *m.* BIOL. metaplasm.
**metátesis,** *pl.* **-sis** *f.* GRAM. metathesis.
**metazoo** *adj.-m.* ZOOL. metazoan.
**metedor** *m.* baby's diaper.
**metempsicosis,** *pl.* **-sis** *f.* metempsychosis.
**meteórico, -ca** *adj.* meteoric.
**meteorito** *m.* meteorite.
**meteorizar** *tr.* MED. to meteorize. *2 ref.* AGR. [of soil] to be influenced by atmospheric phenomena. *3* MED. to become meteorized.
**meteoro, metéoro** *m.* meteor.
**meteorología** *f.* meteorology.
**meteorológico, -ca** *adj.* meteorologic(al.
**meteorólogo** *m.* meteorologist.
**meter** *tr.* to put, place, insert, thrust, introduce [in or between]; to enclose [in]; to get [in or into]. *2* to pocket [a billiard ball]. *3* to hole [a golf ball]. *4* to smuggle. *5* to make, cause, sow; ~ *miedo,* to frighten, cause fear; ~ *ruido,* to make a noise; to cause a sensation; ~ *cizaña,* to sow discord. *6* to tell [lies]. *7* to give [a beating]. *8* to take in [a seam]. *9* to pack, compress. *10 ref.* to go, get [in or into]. *11* to intrude, interfere, meddle [with], butt [in]: *no se meta en lo que no le importa,* mind your own business. *12* to plunge [into vice; business, etc.]. *13* to become [a friar, a nun, a soldier]. *14 meterse a,* to assume [a character, function, etc.], to set oneself up as; to take it upon oneself. *15 meterse con,* to pick a quarrel with. *16 meterse uno en sí mismo,* to keep one's own counsel.
**meticuloso, -sa** *adj.* meticulous.
**metido, -da** *p. p.* of METER: ~ *en carnes,* plump, fleshy: *letra metida,* close writing; *estar muy* ~ *en,* to be deeply involved in. *2 m.* punch given below the ribs. *3* SEW. material allowed in seams. *4* coll. lecture, dressing down.
**metílico, -ca** *adj.* CHEM. methylic.
**metilo** *m.* CHEM. methyl.
**metimiento** *m.* putting in. *2* favour, influence.
**metódico, -ca** *adj.* methodical.
**metodismo** *m.* Methodism.
**metodista** *adj.-n.* Methodist.
**metodizar** *tr.* to methodize.
**método** *m.* method. *2* technique.
**metodología** *f.* methodology.
**metonimia** *f.* RHET. metonymy.
**métopa** *f.* ARCH. metope.
**metraje** *m.* length in metres: *de corto* ~, *de largo* ~, short, full-length [cinema pictures].
**metralla** *f.* grapeshot, case shot; shrapnel.
**metrallazo** *m.* discharge of grapeshot or shrapnel.
**métrica** *f.* metrics, prosody.
**métrico, -ca** *adj.* metric, metrical.
**metrificar** *intr.-tr.* to versify.
**metro** *m.* metre, meter [unit]. *2* POET. metre, meter. *3* coll. underground, subway train.
**metrónomo** *m.* MUS. metronome.
**metrópoli** *f.* metropolis. *2* mother country.
**metropolitano, -na** *adj.-m.* metropolitan. *2* underground, subway train.

**mexicano, -na** *adj.-n.* Mexican.
**México** *m. pr. n.* GEOG. Mexico. *2 f.* Mexico City.
**mezcal** *m.* mescal.
**mezcla** *f.* mixing, mingling, blending. *2* mixture; blend. *3* MAS. mortar. *4* TEXT. mixed cloth.
**mezclar** *tr.* to mix, mingle, blend, intermix, intermingle. *2 ref.* to mix, mingle [be mixed, associate]. *3* to take part, meddle.
**mezclilla** *f.* light mixed cloth.
**mezcolanza** *f.* mixture, medley, jumble, hodgepodge.
**mezquindad** *f.* need, poverty. *2* meanness, stinginess. *3* smallness, paltriness. *4* wretchedness. *5* trifle, mean thing. *6* niggardly act.
**mezquino, -na** *adj.* needy, poor. *2* stingy, niggardly. *3* small, short, mean, paltry. *4* wretched.
**mezquita** *f.* mosque.
**mezquite** *m.* BOT. mesquite.
1) **mi** *m.* MUS. mi, E.
2) **mi** *poss. adj.* my.
**mí** *pers. pron.* (used as object of prepositions) me, myself. *2 ¡y a mí qué!,* I don't care!
**miaja** *f.* crumb [of bread]. *2* bit [small piece].
**miar** *intr.* MAULLAR.
**miasma** *m.* miasma. *2 pl.* miasmata.
**miau** *m.* mew, mewing.
**mica** *m.* MINER. mica.
**micado** *m.* Mikado.
**micción** *f.* micturition.
**micelio** *m.* BOT. mycelium.
**Micenas** *f. pr. n.* HIST., GEOG. Mycenae.
**mico** *m.* ZOOL. long-tailed monkey. *2* coll. lecherous man. *3 dar* ~, *hacer* ~, not to keep a date.
**micología** *f.* mycology.
**micra** *f.* MICRÓN.
**microbiano, -na** *adj.* microbial, microbian.
**microbicida** *adj.-m.* microbicide.
**microbio** *m.* microbe, germ.
**microbiología** *f.* microbiology.
**microcéfalo, -la** *adj.* microcephalic.
**micrococo** *m.* BACT. micrococcus.
**microcopia** *f.* microcopy.
**microcosmo** *m.* microcosm.
**microfilme** *m.* microfilm.
**micrófono** *m.* microphone.
**microfotografía** *f.* microphotography.
**microgameto** *m.* BIOL. microgamete.
**micrografía** *f.* micrography.
**microhmio** *m.* ELECT. microhm.
**micrométrico, -ca** *adj.* micrometric.
**micrón** *m.* micron.
**Micronesia** *n. pr. f.* GEOG. Micronesia.
**microorganismo** *m.* BIOL. micro-organism.
**micrópilo** *m.* ZOOL., BOT. micropyle.
**microscópico, -ca** *adj.* microscopic(al.
**microscopio** *m.* microscope.
**microsurco** *m.* microgroove.
**micrótomo** *m.* microtome.
**michino, -na** *m.-f.* coll. pussy, pussycat.
**micho** *m.* coll. puss [tomcat].
**mieditis** *f.* coll. fear, dread.
**miedo** *m.* fear, dread; apprehension; ~ *cerval,* freat fear; *dar* ~, to be dreadful; *dar* ~ *a,* to frighten; *tener* ~, to be afraid.
**miedoso, -sa** *adj.* fearful, timid, timorous.
**miel** *f.* honey: ~ *sobre hojuelas,* fig. added, pleasure, profit, etc. *2* molasses.
**mielga** *f.* BOT. lucerne. *2* ICHTH. kind of dogfish.
**miembro** *m.* ANAT. member, limb. *2* ANAT. penis. *3* member [of a body, class, etc.]. *4* ARCH., ENG., GRAM., LOG., MATH. member.

**mientes** *f. pl.* mind, thought: *parar*, or *poner*, ~ *en*, to consider, reflect on; *traer a las* ~, to remember; *venírsele a uno a las* ~, to come to one's mind.

**miento, mienta**, etc. *irr.* V. MENTIR.

**mientras** *adv.-conj.* while, whilst, when, meanwhile: ~ *tanto*, meanwhile. *2* whereas. *3* ~ *que*, while; whereas. *4* ~ *más (o menos)... más (o menos)*, the more (or the less)... the more (or the less).

**miera** *f.* juniper oil. *2* pine turpentine.

**miércoles**, *pl.* -**les** *m.* Wednesday: ~ *de ceniza*, Ash Wednesday.

**mierda** *f.* excrement; filth. | Not in decent use.

**mies** *f.* ripe grain in the field or before thrashing. *2* harvest time. *3 pl.* grain fields.

**miga** *f.* crumb, bit [small fragment or piece]. *2* crumb [soft part of bread]. *3* fig. marrow, pith, substance. *4 pl.* fried crumbs. *5 hacer migas*, or *buenas migas*, *con*, to get along with.

**migaja** *f.* crumb [small piece of bread]. *2* crumb, bit, grain, particle. *3 pl.* crumbs, leavings.

**migar** *tr.* to crumb [bread]. *2* to put crumbs of bread into [a liquid].

**migración** *f.* migration.

**migraña** *f.* MED. megrim, migraine, headache.

**migratorio, -ria** *adj.* migratory.

**Miguel** *m. pr. n.* Michael.

**mihrab** *m.* mihrab.

**mijo** *m.* BOT. millet, panic-grass.

**mil** *adj.-m.* thousand, one thousand: *a las* ~ *y quinientas*, coll. at an unearthly hour. *2* thousandth.

**miladi** *f.* milady.

**milagrería** *f.* tale of pretended miracles.

**milagrero, -ra** *adj.* miraclemongering.

**milagro** *m.* miracle, wonder: *de* ~, with difficulty; by a narrow escape: *por* ~, for a wonder.

**milagroso, -sa** *adj.* miraculous.

**milamores** *f.* BOT. red valerian.

**milanés, -sa** *adj.-n.* Milanese.

**milano** *m.* ORN. kite, European kite. *2* ORN. goshawk. *3* ICHTH. flying gurnard. *4* VILANO.

**mildieu, mildiu** *m.* AGR. mildew.

**milenario, -ria** *adj.-n.* millenary, millenarian. *2 m.* millennial.

**milenio** *m.* millenium.

**milenrama** *f.* BOT. milfoil, yarrow.

**milésima** *f.* thousandth [part].

**milésimo, -ma** *adj.-n.* thousandth.

**milesio, sia** *adj.-n.* Milesian.

**milhojas** *f.* MILENRAMA.

**miliar** *adj.* miliary. *2* milliary.

**miliárea** *f.* milliare.

**milicia** *f.* art of warfare. *2* military service. *3* militia, soldiery: ~ *nacional*, national guard.

**miliciano, -na** *adj.* military. *2 m.* militiaman.

**miligramo** *m.* milligram, milligramme.

**mililitro** *m.* millilitre, milliliter.

**milímetro** *m.* millimetre, millimeter.

**militante** *adj.* militant.

1) **militar** *adj.* military. *2* soldierly. *3 m.* military man, soldier. *4 pl. los militares*, the military.

2) **militar** *intr.* to serve in the army. *2* to militate. *3* ~ *en*, to belong to [a party, etc.].

**militara** *f.* wife, daughter or widow of a soldier.

**militarismo** *m.* militarism.

**militarizar** *tr.* to militarize.

**mílite** *m.* soldier.

**miloca** *f.* ORN. kind of owl.

**milonga** *f.* (Am.) a popular dance and song.

**milord**, *pl.* -**lores** *m.* milord. *2* barouche.

**milpiés**, *pl.* **piés** *m.* ZOOL. wood louse.

**milla** *f.* mile: ~ *marina*, nautical mile.

**millar** *m.* thousand: *a millares*, by the thousand.

**millarada** *f.* about a thousand.

**millón**, *pl.* **millones** *m.* million.

**millonario, -ria** *adj.-n.* millionaire.

**millonésimo, -ma** *adj.-n.* millionth. *2 f.* millionth [part].

**mimado, -da** *adj.* pampered, spoiled: *niño* ~, spoiled child.

**mimar** *tr.* to pet, fondle, cuddle. *2* to pamper, spoil.

**mimbre** *m.* osier, wicker, withe. *2* MIMBRERA.

**mimbrear** *intr.-ref.* to sway or move with flexibility.

**mimbreño, -ña** *adj.* osierlike, willowy.

**mimbrera** *f.* BOT. osier, velvet osier.

**mimesis** *f.* RHET. mimesis.

**mimético, -ca** *adj.* BOT., ZOOL. mimetic.

**mimetismo** *m.* BIOL. mimesis, mimetism, mimicry.

**mímica** *f.* pantomime, dumb show, sign language.

**mímico, -ca** *adj.* mimic.

**mimo** *m.* mime [actor and play]. *2* caress, petting. *3* pampering, overindulgence.

**mimógrafo** *m.* mimographer.

**mimosa** *f.* BOT. mimosa.

**mimoso, -sa** *adj.* caressing, petting. *2* soft, spoiled, fond of being petted.

**mina** *f.* mine [of coal, metal, etc.]. *2* fig. mine, storehouse, gold mine. *3* underground passage. *4* FORT., MIL., NAV. mine.

**minador, -ra** *adj.* mining. *2 m.* miner, sapper. *3* mining engineer.

**minar** *tr.* to mine, burrow. *2* to mine, sap, undermine; to consume. *3* MIL., NAV. to mine.

**minarete** *m.* minaret.

**mineraje** *m.* mining, work of a mine.

**mineral** *adj.* mineral. *2 m.* mineral. *3* ore. *4* water spring, fountain-head.

**mineralizar** *tr.* to mineralize. *2 ref.* to become mineralized.

**mineralogía** *f.* mineralogy.

**mineralogista** *m.* mineralogist.

**minería** *f.* mining [working of mines]. *2* mines [of a region or country]. *3* miners [as a class].

**minero, -ra** *adj.* mining. *2 m.* miner [worker]. *3* mine operator; mine owner. *4* mine [of coal, metal, etc.]. *5* fig. source, origin.

**Minerva** *f. pr. n.* MYTH. Minerva. *2 f.* (not cap.) PRINT. small press.

**mingitorio** *m.* urinal [enclosure].

**mingo** *m.* BILL. object ball, red ball.

**miniar** *tr.* to paint in miniature.

**miniatura** *f.* miniature: *en* ~, in miniature.

**miniaturista** *m.-f.* miniature painter.

**mínima** *f.* smallest thing. *2* MUS. minim.

**minimizar** *tr.* to diminish, lessen, undervalue.

**mínimo, -ma** *adj.* minimal, minimum, least, smallest. *2* minute. *3 m.* minimum. *4* ECCL. Minim.

**minimum** *m.* minimum.

**minino, -na** *m.-f.* coll. kitty, puss, cat.

**minio** *m.* minium, red lead.

**ministerial** *adj.* POL. ministerial. *2 m.* POL. ministerialist.

**ministerio** *m.* ministry, cabinet, government, administration. *2* ministry, office, administration [of a cabinet minister]. *3* ministry, department: ~ *de Asuntos Exteriores*, ~ *de Estado*, Foreign office; *Department of State*; ~ *de Hacienda*,

Exchequer; \*Department of the Treasury; ~ *de la Gobernación*, Home Office; \*Department of the Interior. *4* ministry, ministration, office, function, agency. *5* use, service.

**ministrador, -ra** *adj.* ministering, ministrant. *2 m.-f.* ministrant.

**ministrar** *tr.-intr.* to minister. *2 tr.* to supply, furnish.

**ministril** *m.* petty officer of justice. *2 obs.* musician [player].

**ministro** *m.* minister, agent. *2* ECCL. minister: ~ *de Dios*, priest. *3* server [at Mass]. *4* petty officer of justice. *5* envoy. *6* DIPL. minister: ~ *plenipotenciario*, minister plenopotentiary. *7* POL. minister, cabinet minister, Secretary of State, \*Secretary; *primer* ~, primer minister, premier.

**minorar** *tr.* to lessen, diminish. *2 ref.* to lessen, diminish [become diminished].

**minoría** *f.* minority [in number]. *2* POL. minority. *3* minority [being under age].

**minotauro** *m.* MYTH. Minotaur.

**minucia** *f.* trifle. *2 pl.* minutiae.

**minuciosidad** *f.* minuteness, attention paid to small details. *2* trifle, small detail.

**minucioso, -sa** *adj.* minute, detailed, scrupulous.

**minué** *m.* minuet [dance and music].

**minuendo** *m.* ARITH. minuend.

**minúsculo, -la** *adj.* small, tiny, trifling. *2* small, lower-case [letter]. *3 f.* small letter, lower-case letter.

**minuta** *f.* first draft, rough draft. *2* memorandum. *3* lawyer's bill. *4* roll, list. *5* bill of fare.

**minutar** *tr.* to make a draft of, to minute.

**minutario** *m.* notary's book of drafts.

**minutero** *m.* minute hand.

**minutisa** *f.* BOT. sweet william.

**minuto, -ta** *adj.* minute, small. *2 m.* minute [of an hour, of a degree]: *al* ~, at once, right away.

**miñona** *f.* PRINT. minion.

**mío, mía, míos, mías** *poss. adj.* (never used before the noun) my, my own, of mine, mine: *padre mío*, my father; *estos libros son míos*, these books are mine. *2 poss. pron.* mine; *el mío, la mía, los míos, las mías*, mine.

**miocardio** *m.* ANAT. myocardium.

**mioceno** *adj.-m.* GEOL. Miocene.

**miope** *adj.* MED. myopic, near-sighted. *2 m.-f.* myope.

**miopía** *f.* MED. myopia, near-sightedness.

**miosota, miosotis** *f.* BOT. myosotis, forget-menot.

**mira** *f.* sight [of firearms and some instruments]. *2* leveling rod. *3* aim, purpose, intention, view: *poner la* ~ *en*, to aim at, to have designs on. *4 estar a la* ~, to be on the lookout.

**¡mira!** *interj.* look!, lo!, behold!; take care!

**mirabel** *m.* BOT. mock cypress. *2* BOT. sunflower.

**mirada** *f.* look, glance, gaze, regard, eye: *echar una* ~ *a*, to cast a glance at, to take a look at.

**miradero** *m.* cynosure [of all eyes]; thing most watched. *2* lookout, observatory.

**mirado, -da** *adj.* [when preceded by *muy, tan, más, menos*] considerate, thoughtful, careful, nice, circumspect. *2* [when preceded by *bien, mal*], considered, reputed, thought-of. *3 adv. bien mirado*, after all, in fact.

**mirador, -ra** *adj.* looking, gazing. *2 m.* belvedere, open gallery. *3* oriel window, bay window.

**miraguano** *m.* BOT. fan palm yielding vegetable down.

**miramelindos,** *pl.* **-dos** BOT. garden balsam.

**miramiento** *m.* consideration, reflection. *2* attention, care, considerateness: *sin miramientos*, inconsiderately, roughly.

**miranda** *f.* elevated place with an extensive outlook.

**mirar** *tr.* to look, look at, on, upon, etc.; to eye, gaze, observe, regard, view, watch, contemplate, examine: ~ *de hito en hito*, to stare at; ~ *por encima del hombro*, to look down on or upon, to despise. *2* to aim at, to seek. *3* to look, consider, give heed to: *mira cómo te portas*, look how you behave. *4* to regard, consider, think. *5* to inquire, seek information about. *6* ~ *con buenos ojos*, to like, approve of; ~ *con malos ojos*, to dislike, disapprove. *7 intr.* to look: ~ *de través*, to squint. *8* to concern, respect, have regard [to]. *9* [of a building, etc.] to face. *10* ~ *por*, to look after, take care of. *11 intr.-ref. mirar*, or *mirarse, en ello*, to be wary [in taking a determination]. *12 ref.* to look oneself. *13 mirarse en una persona*, to love a person dearly; to take example after a person. *14 interj.* ¡*mira!*, ¡*mire!*, look!, behold!

**mirasol** *m.* BOT. sunflower.

**miríada** *f.* myriad.

**miriagramo** *m.* myriagram, myriagramme.

**miriámetro** *m.* myriametre, myriameter.

**miriápodo** *adj.-n.* MIRIÓPODO.

**mirífico, -ca** *adj.* marvellous, wonderful.

**mirilla** *f.* peephole [in doors]. *2* SURV. sight.

**miriñaque** *m.* crinoline [hooped petticoat]. *2* bauble, trinket.

**miriópodo** *adj.-m.* ZOOL. myriapod, myriapodan.

**mirística** *f.* BOT. nutmeg tree.

**mirlarse** *ref.* coll. to put on airs, to affect gravity.

**mirlo** *m.* ORN. blackbird: ~ *blanco*, coll. rare bird. *2* coll. affected gravity.

**mirón, -na** *adj.* onlooking. *2 m.-f.* looker-on, onlooker, spectator, bystander.

**mirra** *f.* myrrh.

**mirrino, -na** *adj.* myrrhic.

**mirtáceo, -a** *adj.* BOT. myrtaceous.

**mirto** *m.* BOT. myrtle.

**misa** *f.* ECCL., MUS. Mass: ~ *de campaña*, Mass in the field, outdoor Mass; ~ *de difuntos*, Mass for the dead; ~ *del gallo*, Christmas-eve Mass; ~ *mayor*, High Mass; ~ *rezada*, Low Mass; *no saber de la* ~ *la media*, coll. not to know what all is about.

**misacantano** *m.* celebrant at Mass. *2* priest who says his first Mass.

**misal** *m.* missal, Mass book. *2* PRINT. two-line pica.

**misantropía** *f.* misanthropy.

**misantrópico, -ca** *adj.* misanthropic(al.

**misántropo** *m.* misanthrope.

**miscelánea** *f.* miscellany, medley. *2* miscellanea.

**misceláneo, -a** *adj.* miscellaneous.

**miscible** *adj.* miscible.

**miserable** *adj.* miserable, wretched. *2* miserable, mean, poor. *3* miserly, mean, stingy. *4* wicked, rascally. *5 m.-f.* miser. *6* wretch, cur, knave.

**miseración** *f.* mercy, pity.

**miserere** *m.* ECCL. Miserere. *2* MED. ileus.

**miseria** *f.* misery, wretchedness. *2* misery, poverty, destitution, want. *3* miserliness. *4* coll. lice. *5* trifle, pittance, small quantity.

**misericordia** *f.* mercy, pity: *obras de* ~, works of mercy. *2* misericord [dagger; seat].

**misericordioso, -sa** *adj.* merciful.

**mísero, -ra** *adj.* miserable, wretched, unhappy. *2* miserly, mean, stingy.

**misérrimo, -ma** *adj. superl.* most miserable. 2 very miserly. 3 very short or scanty.
**misión** *f.* mission [in practically every sense].
**misionario** *m.* MISIONERO. 2 envoy, messenger.
**misionero, -ra** *adj.-n.* ECCL. missionary.
**Misisipi** *m. pr. n.* GEOG. Mississippi [river and state].
**misivo, -va** *adj.* missive. 2 *f.* missive, letter.
**mismamente** *adv.* coll. exactly.
**mismísimo, -ma** *adj. superl.* very, very same.
1) **mismo** *adv.* right [in the very instant, place, etc.]: *ahora* ~, right now; *aquí* ~, right here. 2 *así* ~, in like manner, likewise, also.
2) **mismo, -ma** *adj.* same, very, selfsame: *el* ~ *hombre*, the same man; *sus mismos criados se ríen de él*, his very servants laugh at him; *lo* ~, the same, the same thing; *lo* ~ *me da*, it's all the same to me; *por lo* ~, for the same reason, for that very reason. 2 [for emphasis] myself, yourself, herself, itself, etc.: *lo haré yo* ~, I'll do it myself.
**misógino** *adj.* misogynous. 2 *m.* misogynist.
**misoneísmo** *m.* misoneism.
**mistagogo** *m.* mystagogue.
**mistela** *f.* a refreshing beverage. 2 liquor made of must and alcohol.
**misterio** *m.* mystery. 2 sculpture or image representing one of the mysteries of the Rosary.
**misterioso, -sa** *adj.* mysterious.
**mística** *m.* mystical theology.
**misticismo** *m.* mysticism.
**místico, -ca** *adj.* mystic, mystical. 2 mystic, enigmatic. 3 *m.-f.* mystic [person].
**mistral** *m.* mistral [wind].
**Misuri** *m. pr. n.* GEOG. Missouri [river and state].
**mitad** *f.* half: *cara* ~, fig. better half: *a la* ~ or *a* ~ *de*, half-way through. 2 moiety. 3 middle: *en* ~ *de*, in the middle of.
**mítico, -ca** *adj.* mythical.
**mitigación** *f.* mitigation, alleviation, allaying.
**mitigador, -ra** *adj.* mitigating, alleviating, allaying. 2 *m.-f.* mitigator, alleviator, allayer.
**mitigar** *tr.* to mitigate, alleviate, allay, assuage. 2 *ref.* to be mitigated, alleviated.
**mitin** *m.* political meeting, rally.
**mito** *m.* myth.
**mitología** *f.* mythology.
**mitológico, -ca** *adj.* mythological. 2 *m.* mythologist.
**mitologista, mitólogo** *m.* mythologist.
**mitón** *m.* mitt [knitted glove without fingers].
**mitosis** *f.* BIOL. mitosis.
**mitra** *f.* mitre, miter [bishop's cap; bishopric].
**mitrado** *adj.* mitred, mitered. 2 *m.* bishop or archbishop.
**mitral** *adj.* ANAT. mitral: *válvula* ~, mitral valve.
**mixtifori** *m.* coll. medley, hodgepodge.
**mixtilíneo, -a** *adj.* GEOM. mixtilineal, mixtilinear.
**mixtión** *f.* mixture, commixture.
**mixto, -ta** *adj.* mixed, mingled. 2 mixed [school, mathematics, etc.]: *parejas mixtas*, SPORT. mixed doubles. 3 crossbred. 4 *m.* compound. 5 sulphur match.
**mixtura** *f.* mixture. 2 PHARM. compound.
**mixturar** *tr.* to mix, mingle.
**mízcalo** *m.* BOT. edible milk mushroom.
**mnemónica, mnemotecnia** *f.* mnemonics, mnemotechny.
**moaré** *m.* MUARÉ.
**mobiliario, -ria** *adj.* movable, personal [property]. 2 *m.* household furniture, suit of furniture.

**moblaje** *m.* household furniture.
**moca** *f.* Mocha coffee.
**mocasín** *m.* moccasin [shoe; snake].
**mocear** *intr.* to act like a youth. 2 to go around after women.
**mocedad** *f.* youth, age of youth. 2 wild oats.
**moceril** *adj.* youthful, juvenile.
**mocerío** *m.* young people.
**mocero** *adj.* lewd, woman-mad.
**mocetón** *m.* strapping youth, strapping lad.
**mocetona** *f.* strapping girl or lass.
**moción** *f.* motion, movement. 2 divine inspiration. 4 motion [in a deliberative assembly].
**mocito, -ta** *adj.* very young. 2 *m.-f.* youngster, lad, lass.
**moco** *m.* mucus, nasal mucus. 2 viscid matter. 3 snuff [of lamp or candle]. 4 slag [of iron]. 5 ~ *de pavo*, crest of a turkey; BOT. cockscomb; *no ser* ~ *de pavo*, coll. [of a thing]. not to be despicable.
**mocoso, -sa** *adj.* snivelly, full of mucus. 2 *m.-f.* ill-bred child, brat. 3 inexperienced youth.
**mocosuelo, -la** *m.-f. dim.* coll. child, brat.
**mochada** *f.* butt [with the head].
**mocheta** *f.* thick head of a hatchet, hoe, etc. 2 rebate in the edge of a door frame.
**mochila** *f.* MIL. knapsack. 2 haversack.
**mocho, -cha** *adj.* blunt, stub-pointed, stub-horned, truncated. 2 topped [tree]. 3 cropped, shorn. 4 *m.* butt, butt end.
**mochuelo** *m.* ORN. little owl. 2 PRINT. omission. 3 coll. *cargar con el* ~, to get a hard task.
**moda** *f.* fashion, mode, style, prevailing custom: *a la* ~, *a la última* ~, after the latest fashion; *a la* ~ *de*, after the fashion of; *de* ~, fashionable; *estar de* ~, to be in fashion; *pasado de* ~, out of fashion. 2 pl. *tienda de modas*, ladies' dress shop.
**modal** *adj.* modal.
**modales** *m. pl.* manners, breeding.
**modalidad** *f.* manner of being, mode, kind.
**modelado** *m.* F. ARTS. modelling, moulding, molding.
**modelar** *tr.* F. ART to model, mould, mold.
**modelista** *m.* mould maker. 2 model maker.
**modelo** *m.* model, pattern, example. 2 model [to be reproduced; representation of a thing]. 3 model [person]; fashion model, mannequin. 4 *adj.* model.
**moderación** *f.* moderation.
**moderado, -da** *adj.* moderate. 2 reasonable. 3 *m.* POL. moderate.
**moderador, -ra** *adj.* moderating. 2 *m.-f.* moderator.
**moderar** *tr.* to moderate, temper, restrain, curb. 2 *ref.* to moderate [become less violent, intense, etc.]. 3 to restrain or control oneself.
**modernamente** *adv.* recently, lately.
**modernidad** *f.* modernness, modernity.
**modernismo** *m.* modernism.
**modernista** *adj.* modernist, modernistic. 2 *m.-f.* modernist.
**modernizar** *tr.* to modernize. 2 *ref.* to modernize [adopt modern ways, etc.].
**moderno, -na** *adj.* modern. 2 *m. pl. los modernos*, the moderns.
**modestia** *f.* modesty.
**modesto, -ta** *adj.* modest.
**módicamente** *adv.* moderately, sparingly.
**modicidad** *f.* moderateness, cheapness.
**módico, -ca** *adj.* moderate, reasonable, low price.
**modificación** *f.* modification.
**modificador, -ra** *adj.* modifying. 2 *m.-f.* modifier.

**modificar** *tr.* to modify. *2 ref.* to modify [undergo modification].
**modificativo, -va** *adj.* modificative.
**modillón** *m.* ARCH. modillion, bracket.
**modismo** *m.* GRAM. idiom.
**modista** *f.* dressmaker, modiste. *2 ~ de sombreros*, milliner. *3 m.* modiste, ladies' tailor.
**modistilla** *f.* young dressmaker's helper.
**modo** *m.* moda, manner, way: *~ de ser*, nature, disposition; *a ~* or *al ~ de*, in the manner of, like, by way of; kind of; *a mi ~*, in my own way; *de cualquier ~*, anyway, anyhow, without care; *de ~ que*, so that; so, and so; *de ningún ~*, by no means; *de otro ~*, otherwise; *de todos modos*, anyhow, at any rate; *en cierto ~*, in or after a fashion; *por ~ de*, as, by way of. *2* moderation, temperance. *3* PHIL., LOG., MUS. mode. *4* GRAM. mood. *5* GRAM. [adverbial, conjunctive, etc.] phrase. *6 pl.* manners, civility: *con buenos modos*, politely; *con malos modos*, impolitely.
**modorra** *f.* drowsiness, heaviness. *2* VET. gid.
**modorro, rra** *m.-f.* dolt, ignoramus.
**modoso, -sa** *adj.* quiet, well-behaved.
**modulación** *f.* modulation.
**modulador, -ra** *adj.* modulating. *2 m.-f.* modulator.
**modular** *intr.* to modulate [in speaking or singing]. *2 tr.* RADIO. to modulate.
**módulo** *m.* HYDRAUL., ARCH., NUMIS. module. *2* PHYS., MATH. modulus.
**mofa** *f.* mockery, jeer, scoff, sneer: *hacer ~ de*, to mock, to jeer at.
**mofar** *intr.-ref.* to mock, jeer, scoff, sneer: *mofarse de*, to mock, jeer at, scoff at, make fun of.
**mofeta** *f.* mofette; chokedamp; noxious emanation [of mines, etc.]. *2* ZOOL. skunk.
**moflete** *m.* coll. chubby cheek, fat cheek.
**mofletudo, -da** *adj.* chubby-cheeked, fat-cheeked.
**mogol, -la** *adj.* Mongolian. *2 m.-f.* Mongol, Mongolian. *3 el Gran Mogol*, the Great Mogul.
**Mogolia** *pr. n.* GEOG. Mongolia.
**mogólico, -ca** *adj.* Mongolian.
**mogollón** *m. de ~*, sponging upon others, free, for nothing.
**mogón** *adj.* one-horned, broken-horned.
**mogote** *m.* hummock, knoll. *2* stack of sheaves. *3* budding antler.
**moharra** *f.* head [of a lance or spear].
**moharrache, moharracho** *m.* merry-andrew.
**mohatra** *f.* sham sale, fraud.
**mohín** *m.* face, grimace, pouting.
**mohína** *f.* annoyance, displeasure.
**mohíno, -na** *adj.* sad, melancholy, worried, displeased. *2* black [horse or cattle]. *3 m.* hinny. *4* ORN. blue magpie.
**moho** *m.* mo(u)ld, mildew [of organic matter]; must, mustiness. *2* rust [on iron]; verdigris. *3* rustiness, stiffness caused by disuse.
**mohoso, -sa** *adj.* mouldy, moldy, mildewed, musty. *2* rusty.
**Moisés** *m. pr. n.* Moses.
**mojadura** *f.* wetting, drenching, soaking, moistening.
**mojama** *f.* dry salted tunny-fish.
**mojar** *tr.* to wet, moisten, drench, soak. *2* coll. to stab. *3* to dip [bread, cake, etc., into milk, etc.]. *4 intr.* coll. to have a hand or part in [an affair]. *5 ref.* to get wet.
**mojarra** *f.* ICHTH. a basslike marine fish.
**moje** *m.* COOK. gravy, sauce.
**mojera** *f.* MOSTELLAR.

**mojicón** *m.* small cake, bun. *2* punch in the face.
**mojiganga** *f.* masquerade, morris dance. *2* mummery.
**mojigatería, mojigatez** *f.* prudishness, sanctimoniousness, false humility.
**mojigato, -ta** *adj.* prudish, sanctimonious, hypocritical. *2 m.-f.* prude, hypocrite.
**mojón** *m.* boundary stone; landmark. *2* pile, heap.
**mola** *f.* MED. mole.
**molar** *adj.* molar. *2 m.* ANAT. molar, molar tooth.
**moldavo, -va** *adj.-n.* Moldavian.
**molde** *m.* mould, mold, matrix; cast, pattern. *2* FOUND. frame. *3* model, ideal. *4* PRINT. form. *6 venir de ~*, to be to the purpose; to be just right.
**moldear** *tr.* to mould, mold [give shape]. *2* to cast [in a mould]. *3* MOLDURAR.
**moldura** *f.* ARCH., CARP. moulding, molding.
**moldurar** *tr.* to carve, cut or make mouldings on.
**mole** *adj.* soft. *2 f.* huge mass or bulk.
**molécula** *f.* molecule.
**molecular** *adj.* molecular.
**moledera** *f.* grinding stone. *2* coll. botheration.
**moledura** *f.* grinding, crushing, pounding.
**molendero, -ra** *m.-f.* grinder, miller. *2 m.* chocolate grinder.
**moleña** *f.* PEDERNAL 1.
**moler** *tr.* to grind, crush, pound, mill. *2* to fatigue, tire out, wear out. *3* to spoil, destroy. *4* to vex, bore, importunate. *5 ~ a palos*, to beat up, give a drubbing. ¶ CONJUG. like *mover*.
**molestar** *tr.* to vex, disturb, annoy, put to inconvenience. *2* to displease, offend. *3 ref.* to bother; *~ en*, to bother to, to take the trouble to. *4* to be annoyed, take offence.
**molestia** *f.* vexation, annoyance, disturbance, inconvenience, trouble, discomfort. *2* displeasure.
**molesto, -ta** *adj.* vexatious, annoying, troublesome, bothersome. *2* annoyed, displeased. *3* uncomfortable, ill at ease.
**moleta** *f.* muller. *2* glass polisher.
**moleteado** *m.* knurl.
**moletear** *tr.* to knurl.
**molibdeno** *m.* CHEM. molybdenum.
**molicie** *f.* softness. *2* love of luxury, effeminacy.
**molido, -da** *adj.* ground. *2* fig. tired out, worn out.
**molienda** *f.* grinding, crushing, milling. *2* grist [corn for grinding]; sugar cane, olives, etc., ground or crushed. *3* mill [for grinding]. *4* grinding or crushing time. *5* fatigue, weariness.
**molificación** *f.* mollification, softening.
**molificar** *tr.* to mollify, soften.
**molimiento** *m.* grinding, crushing, pounding. *2* fatigue, weariness.
**molinera** *f.* woman miller. *2* miller's wife.
**molinería** *f.* mill industry.
**molinero** *m.* miller [pers.].
**molinete** *m. dim.* little mill. *2* pin wheel, windmill [toy]. *3* ventilating wheel. *4* moulinet [with a sabre, etc.]. *5* NAUT. windlass. *6* PHYS. *~ hidráulico*, hydraulic tourniquet.
**molinillo** *m.* hand mill. *2* coffee grinder. *3* chocolate stirrer.
**molino** *m.* mill [for grinding, crushing, etc.]: *~ harinero*, flour mill; *~ de agua*, water mill; *~ de viento*, windmill. *2* fig. restless person.
**Moloc** *m. pr. n.* BIBL. Moloch.
**molondro, molondrón** *m.* lazy, stupid fellow.
**moltura** *f.* grinding [of corn, etc.].
**molturar** *tr.* to grind [corn, etc.].
**molusco** *m.* ZOOL. mollusc, mollusk.

**mollar** *adj.* soft, easily broken, easily shelled. *2* lean [meat]. *3* productive, profitable. *4* manageable; gullible.

**mollear** *intr.* [of a thing] to give, yield [to pressure]; to bend [from being soft].

**molledo** *m.* fleshy part [of leg, arm, etc.]. *2* crumb [soft part of bread].

**molleja** *f.* gizzard [of birds]. *2* sweetbread.

**mollera** *f.* crown of the head. *2* fontanel. *3* fig. brains, sense: *cerrado de ~*, dull-witted; *duro de ~*, obstinate; dull-witted.

**mollete** *m.* muffin. *2* chubby cheek. *3* fleshy part [of the arm].

**mollina, mollizna** *f.* LLOVIZNA.

**molliznar, molliznear** *intr.* LLOVIZNAR.

**momentáneo, -a** *adj.* momentary. *2* prompt.

**momento** *m.* moment, instant: *al ~*, at once, immediately; *de ~*, at the first; *de ~, por el ~*, for the present; *por momentos*, continually, progressively. *2* MECH. moment. *3* moment, weight, importance.

**momería** *f.* mummery, clowning.

**momia** *f.* mummy [embalmed or dried-up body].

**momificación** *f.* mummification.

**momificar** *tr.* to mummify. *2 ref.* to become a mummy.

**momio, mia** *adj.* lean, meogre. *2 m.* that which is got or given extra. *3* bargain, sinecure. *4 de ~*, free, gratis, for nothing.

**Momo** *m. pr. n.* MYTH. Momus.

**momo** *m.* funny grimace, burlesque action.

**momórdiga** *f.* BOT. balsam apple.

**mona** *f.* female monkey. *2* ZOOL. Barbary ape. *3* fig. ape, imitator. *4* coll. drunk, drunkenness: *dormir la ~*, to sleep off a drunk. *5* coll. drunk person. *6* old maid [game]. *7* Easter cake.

**monacal** *adj.* monachal, monastic.

**monacato** *m.* monachism; monasticism.

**monacillo** *m.* MONAGUILLO.

**monada** *f.* apery, apish action. *2* grimace. *3* tomfoolery. *4* pretty little thing. *6* pretty child, pretty girl. *7* cajolery.

**mónada** *f.* BIOL., CHEM., PHIL., ZOOL. monad.

**monadelfo, -fa** *adj.* BOT. monadelphous.

**monaguillo** *m.* acolyte, altar boy.

**monaquismo** *m.* MONACATO.

**monarca** *m.* monarch.

**monarquía** *f.* monarchy. *2* kingdom.

**monárquico, -ca** *adj.* monarchic(al. *2 adj.-n.* monarchist.

**monarquismo** *m.* monarchism.

**monasterio** *m.* monastery.

**monástico, -ca** *adj.* monastic(al.

**monda** *f.* cleaning, pruning; paring, peeling. *2* parings, prunings, peelings. *3* pruning season.

**mondadientes** *m.* toothpick.

**mondadura** *f.* cleaning, paring, peeling. *2 pl.* parings, peelings.

**mondaoídos, mondaorejas** *m.* earpick.

**mondar** *tr.* to clean [free from superfluous matter]. *2* to prune, trim. *3* to pare, peel; to hull. *4* to cut the hair of. *5* fig. to fleece. *6 mondarse los dientes*, to pick one's teeth.

**mondarajas** *f. pl.* peelings.

**mondo, -da** *adj.* clear of superfluities, admixtures or additions: *~ y lirondo*, only, without additions.

**mondongo** *m.* intestines, guts [of pork, etc.].

**monear** *intr.* coll. to monkey, to fool, to act ridiculously.

**moneda** *f.* coin, piece of money. *2* money: *~ co-*

*rriente*, currency; coll. common knowledge; everyday matter; *~ falsa*, counterfeit; *~ imaginaria*, money of account; *~ suelta*, change, small change.

**monedero** *m.* moneyer: *~ falso*, counterfeiter. *2* moneybag.

**monería** *f.* apery, apish action. *2* tomfoolery. *3* pretty, pleasant action of a child.

**monesco, -ca** *adj.* coll. apish.

**monetario, -ria** *adj.* monetary. *2 m.* collection of coins and medals.

**monetizar** *tr.* to monetize.

**mongol** *adj.-n.* MOGOL.

**Mongolia** *f. pr. n.* MOGOLIA.

**moniato** *m.* coll. BUNIATO.

**monicaco** *m.* coll. HOMINICACO.

**monigote** *m.* lay brother. *2* rag figure; grotesque figure; badly drawn, painted or carved figure. *3* whippersnapper.

**monín, -na** *adj. dim.* coll. pretty, dear. *2 m.-f. dim.* coll. pretty child, pretty one, darling.

**monipodio** *m.* coll. collusion, combine.

**monises** *m. pl.* coll. money, dough.

**monismo** *m.* PHIL. monism.

**mónita** *f.* tact, cunning, adroitness.

**monitor** *m.* monitor, adviser. *2* NAUT., RAD. monitor.

**monja** *f.* nun.

**monje** *m.* monk. *2* anchorite.

**monjía** *f.* monkhood.

**monjil** *adj.* nunnish. *2 m.* nun's dress.

**monjío** *m.* nunhood. *2* taking the veil.

**monjita** *f. dim.* little nun.

**mono, -na** *adj.* pretty, dainty, *cute. *2 m.* ZOOL. ape, monkey; *~ capuchino*, capuchin; *~ sabio*, trained monkey; fig. BULLF. assistant of a picador. *3* fig. monkey [pers.]. *4* badly drawn or painted figure. *5 ~ de mecánico, de aviador*, etc., overalls. *6 estar de monos*, to be at outs.

**monobásico, -ca** *adj.* CHEM. monobasic.

**monoclínico, -ca** *adj.* CRYST. monoclinic.

**monocordio** *m.* MUS. monochord.

**monocotiledóneo, -a** *adj.* BOT. monocotyledonous. *2 f.* BOT. monocotyledon.

**monocromo, -ma** *adj.* monochrome.

**monóculo** *m.* monocle.

**monodia** *f.* MUS. monody.

**monofásico, -ca** *adj.* ELECT. monophase, single-phase.

**monogamia** *f.* monogamy.

**monógamo, -ma** *adj.* monogamous.

**monografía** *f.* monograph.

**monográfico, -ca** *adj.* monographic(al. *2* special [course, lectures, etc.].

**monograma** *m.* monogram.

**monoico, -ca** *adj.* BOT. monoecious.

**monolítico, -ca** *adj.* monolithic.

**monolito** *m.* monolith.

**monologar** *intr.* to monologize, soliloquize.

**monólogo** *m.* monologue, soliloquy.

**monomanía** *f.* monomania.

**monometalismo** *m.* monometallism.

**monomio** *m.* ALG. monomial.

**monopétalo, -la** *adj.* BOT. monopetalous.

**monoplano** *m.* AER. monoplane.

**monopolio** *m.* monopoly.

**monopolista** *m.-f.* monopolist.

**monopolizador** *adj.* monopolizing. *2 m.-f.* monopolizer.

**monopolizar** *tr.* to monopolize.

**monóptero, -ra** *adj.* ARCH. monopteral.

**monosépalo, -la** *adj.* BOT. monosepalous.
**monosilábico, -ca** *adj.* monosyllabic(al.
**monosílabo, -ba** *adj.* monosyllabic. *2 m.* monosyllable.
**monospermo, -ma** *adj.* BOT. monospermous.
**monoteísmo** *m.* monotheism.
**monoteísta** *adj.* monotheistic. *2 m.-f.* monotheist.
**monotipia** *f.* PRINT. monotype [machine; method].
**monotonía** *f.* monotony.
**monótono, -na** *adj.* monotonous.
**monotrema** *m.* ZOOL. monotreme.
**monovalente** *adj.* CHEM. monovalent.
**monóxido** *m.* CHEM. monoxide.
**monseñor** *m.* monseigneur. *2* monsignor.
**monserga** *f.* coll. gibberish.
**monstruo** *m.* monster, monstrosity.
**monstruosidad** *f.* monstrosity, monstrousness.
**monstruoso, -sa** *adj.* monstrous. *2* hateful, execrable.
**monta** *f.* mounting [act]. *2* covering [of a mare]. *3* amount, sum total. *4* value, account, importance. *5* MIL. call to horse.
**montacargas,** *pl.* **-gas** *m.* lift, elevator [for goods].
**montadero** *m.* horse block, mounting block.
**montado, -da** *adj.* mounted: *policía montada,* mounted police.
**montador** *m.* mounter. *2* assembler, erector, fitter. *3* horse block, mounting block.
**montadura** *f.* mounting. *2* MONTURA 2 & 5.
**montaje** *m.* MACH. assembling, erection, setting up. *2 pl.* ARTILL. mount, gun carriage.
**montanera** *f.* acorn or mast pasture for hogs. *2* acorn-feeding or mast-feeding season.
**montanero** *m.* forester.
**montano, -na** *adj.* [pertaining to] wood or forest.
**montantada** *f.* braggadocio. *2* multitude, crow.
**montante** *m.* broadsword. *2* upright, post, standard, strut. *3* ARCH. mullion. *4* transom [window over a door]. *5* COM. amount. *6 f.* NAUT. flood tide.
**montaña** *f.* mountain. *2* highlands. *3* forested region. *4* ~ *rusa,* roller coaster; switchback [amusement railway].
**montañés, -sa** *adj.* [pertaining to a] mountain, mountaineer, highlander. *3* of the mountains in the province of Santander [in Spain].
**montañismo** *m.* mountaineering.
**montañoso, -sa** *adj.* mountainous.
**montar** *intr.-ref.* to mount, get on: ~ *a horcajadas en,* to straddle. *2 intr.* to ride [horseback; on a bicycle or motorcycle]. *3* to be of importance: *tanto monta,* it has the same importance. *4* ~ *en cólera,* to fly into a rage. *5 tr.* to mount, put [a person] on a horse, etc. *6* to ride [a horse, a bicycle, etc.]. *7* to cover [a mare]. *8* to amount to [reach a sum]. *9* to mount, assemble, set up. *10* JEWEL. to set [a gem]. *11* to cock [a gun]. *12* THEAT. to mount [a play, etc.]. *13* NAUT. to command [a ship]. *14* NAUT. to mount, carry [cannon]. *15* NAUT. to round [a cape].
**montaraz** *adj.* of the woods; wild, untamed. *2* uncouth, rude. *3 m.* forester.
**montazgo** *m.* toll for the passage of cattle through a forest.
**monte** *m.* mount, mountain, hill: *el* ~ *de los Olivos,* Mount Olivet; *los montes Urales,* the Ural Mountains. *2* woods, woodland: ~ *alto,* forest; trees of a forest; ~ *bajo,* thicket, brushwood. *3* talon, stock [in card playing]. *4* monte [card game]. *5* bank [in gambling]. *6* ~ *de piedad,* mount of piety.
**montea** *f.* hunting or beating the woods [for

game]. *2* ARCH. working drawing. *3* ARCH. rise [of an arch].
**montecillo** *m.* dim. mound, hillock.
**montepío** *m.* pension fund [for widows, etc.].
**montera** *f.* cloth cap. *2* skylight. *3* head [of the boiler of a still]. *4* NAUT. moonsail.
**montería** *f.* hunting, chase. *2* HUNT. big game.
**montero** *m.* beater [in hunting], huntsman.
**montés, -sa; montesino, -na** *adj.* wild [cat, goat, etc.].
**montículo** *m.* mound, hillock.
**monto** *m.* amount, sum total.
**montón** *m.* heap, pile: *a, de* or *en* ~, coll. together, taken together. *2* lot, crowd, great quantity: *a montones,* coll. in abundance. *3 ser del* ~, to be common, ordinary.
**montuno, -na** *adj.* pertaining to the woods, wild.
**montuosidad** *f.* mountainousness.
**montuoso, -sa** *adj.* mountainous, hilly.
**montura** *f.* mount [riding horse]. *2* gear [of a riding horse]. *3* mounting, assembling, setting up. *4* mounting [of a telescope, gem, etc.]. *5* JEW. setting.
**monumental** *adj.* monumental.
**monumento** *m.* monument.
**monzón** *m.-f.* monsoon [wind].
**moña** *f.* bow of ribbons worn on the head. *2* badge on the bull's neck. *3* doll.
**moño** *m.* chignon, bun [of hair]. *2* bow or knot of ribbons. *3* crest, tuft of feathers [on head of a bird]. *4 pl.* frippery: *ponerse moños,* fig. to put on airs.
**moquear** *intr.* to snivel, run at the nose.
**moquero** *m.* pocket handkerchief.
**moqueta** *f.* moquette.
**moquete** *m.* punch on the face, on the nose.
**moquillo** *m.* VET. distemper. *2* VET. pip.
**moquita** *f.* watery discharge [from the nose].
**mora** *f.* Moorish woman. *2* BOT. black mulberry [fruit]. *3* BOT. white mulberry [fruit]. *4* BOT. blackberry, brambleberry [fruit]. *5* LAW delay.
**morabito, morabuto** *m.* marabout, Mohammedan hermit. *2* Mohammedan hermitage.
**moráceo, -a** *adj.* BOT. moraceous.
**moracho, -cha** *adj.* light purple [in colour].
**morada** *f.* abode, dwelling, house. *2* stay, sojourn.
**morado, -da** *adj.-n.* purple, mulberry [colour].
**morador, -ra** *m.-f.* inhabitant, dweller, resident.
**moraga** *f.* handful of gleaned grain.
**moral** *adj.* moral. *2 f.* morals, ethics, morality. *3* morale. *4 m.* BOT. black mulberry [tree].
**moraleja** *f.* moral [of a table, etc.].
**moralidad** *f.* morality [of acts, conduct, etc.]. *2* moral [of a fable, etc.].
**moralista** *m.* moralist.
**moralizador, -ra** *adj.* moralizing. *2 m.-f.* moralizer.
**moralizar** *tr.* to moralize.
**morapio** *m.* coll. red wine.
**morar** *intr.* to inhabite, dwell, reside.
**moratoria** *f.* COM., LAW moratorium.
**morbidez** *f.* softness, delicacy.
**mórbido, -da** *adj.* soft, delicate. *2* morbid.
**morbo** *m.* MED. morbus, disease.
**morboso, -sa** *adj.* morbid, unwholesome, diseased.
**morcella** *f.* spark from a lamp.
**morcilla** *f.* blood pudding. *2* THEAT. gag [interpolation by an actor].
**morcillo, -lla** *adj.* reddish black [horse].
**mordacidad** *f.* mordacity, mordancy.

**mordaz** *adj.* mordant, mordacious, biting, caustic. 2 pungent, acrid. 3 corrosive.
**mordaza** *f.* gag [to prevent speech]. 2 pipe wrench. 3 MEC. clamp, jaw.
**mordedor, -ra** *adj.* biting. 2 backbiting. 3 *m.-f.* biter. 4 backbiter.
**mordedura** *f.* bite [act and result of biting].
**mordente** *m.* mordant. 2 MUS. mordent.
**morder** *tr.* to bite [with the teeth]: ~ *el polvo,* fig. to bite the dust or ground. 2 to nibble at. 3 [of things] to bite, take hold of. 4 to gnaw eat, wear away. 5 [of an acid] to eat, corrode. 6 to revile, backbite. ¶ CONJUG. like *mover.*
**mordicante** *adj.* biting, pungent. 2 acrid, corrosive. 3 fig. nibbling, carping.
**mordicar** *tr.* to bite, sting.
**mordiente** *adj.* biting. 2 *m.* mordant.
**mordiscar** *tr.* to nibble at, to bite.
**mordisco** *m.* bite [act of biting; piece detached by biting].
**mordisquear** *tr.* MORDISCAR.
**morena** *f.* ICHTH. moray. 2 GEOL. moraine.
**morenillo, -lla** *adj.-n.* brunet, brunette.
**moreno, -na** *adj.* brown, dark. 2 dark-complexioned, swarthy, tawny, brunette. 3 coll. coloured [pers.]. 4 *m.-f.* dark-complexioned person. 5 coll. coloured person. 6 *f.* brunette.
**morera** *f.* BOT. white mulberry tree.
**moreral** *m.* grove of white mulberry trees.
**morería** *f.* Moorish quarter. 2 Moorish land.
**moretón** *m.* coll. black-and-blue mark.
**Morfeo** *m. pr. n.* MYTH. Morpheus.
**morfina** *f.* CHEM. morphine.
**morfinismo** *m.* MED. morphinism.
**morfología** *f.* morphology.
**morga** *f.* juice that oozes from a heap of olives. 2 COCA DE LEVANTE.
**morganático, -ca** *adj.* morganatic.
**moribundo, -da** *adj.* moribund, dying. 2 *m.-f.* moribund, dying person.
**morigeración** *f.* moderation, temperance.
**morigerado, -da** *adj.* moderate, temperate.
**morigerar** *tr.* to moderate, restrain.
**morilla** *f.* BOT. morel.
**morillo** *m. dim.* little Moor. 2 firedog, and ron.
**morir** *intr.* to die, expire, decease, pass away, come to an end: ~ *vestido,* to die a violent death. 2 [of a river, road, etc.] to flow [into], to end [at]. 3 *ref.* to die, be dying. 4 [of a limb] be benumbed. 5 *intr.-ref.* [of fire, flame, light, etc.] to die, go out. 6 to die of or with; to suffer, feel, etc., excessively: ~ or *morirse de hambre,* to die of hunger; to starve; ~ or *morirse de risa,* to die of laughing. 7 ~ or *morirse por,* to love dearly; be crazy about; to be dying for or to. 8 *interj.* ¡*muera...!,* down with...! ¶ CONJUG. like *dormir.* | Past. p.: *muerto.*
**morisco, -ca** *adj.* Moorish, Moresque. 2 *adj.-n.* HIST. Morisco.
**morisma** *f.* the Moors. 2 crowd of Moors.
**morisqueta** *f.* Moorish trick. 2 mean trick. 3 (Am.) face, grimace.
**morlaco** *adj.-n.* BULLF. bull, big bull.
**mormón, -na** *m.-f.* Mormon.
**mormonismo** *m.* Mormonism.
**moro, -ra** *adj.* Moorish. 2 Moslem. 3 unbaptized. 4 coll. unwatered [wine]. 5 black with a white spot on the forehead [horse]. 6 *m.* Moor: *hay moros en la costa,* fig. let's be cautious.
**morocada** *f.* butt of a ram.

**morocho, -cha** *adj.-m.* hard [Indian corn]. 2 *adj.* (Am.) fresh, vigorous [person]. 3 (Am.) MORENO.
**morón** *m.* mound [of earth].
**morondanga** *f.* coll. medley, hodgepodge.
**morondo, -da** *adj.* bald, hairless; leafless.
**morosidad** *f.* slowness, tardiness, delay.
**moroso, -sa** *adj.* slow, tardy, full of delay, lingering. 2 delinquent [in payment].
**morra** *f.* top, crown [of head]. 2 mora [game].
**morrada** *f.* butting of two heads. 2 cuff, punch.
**morral** *m.* nose bag. 2 game bag. 3 knapsack. 4 wallet [bag for travelling]. 5 coll. boor, rustic.
**morralla** *f.* small fry [fish]. 2 rabble. 3 rubbish.
**morrillo** *m.* fleshy part of neck [of animals]. 2 fleshy nape of neck. 3 pebble, boulder.
**morriña** *f.* VET. sheep dropsy. 2 coll. blues, melancholy, sadness.
**morrión** *m.* morion. 2 MIL. bearskin.
**morro** *m.* knob, round end or projection. 2 knoll. 3 pebble. 4 muffle; thick lips. 5 *estar de* ~ or *de morros,* to have quarelled, to be at odds.
**morrocotudo, -da** *adj.* coll. very important or difficult.
**morrón** *adj.* NAUT. knotted [flag]. 2 BOT. bonnet [pepper].
**morrongo, -ga** *m.-f.* coll. kitty, puss, cat.
**morrudo, -da** *adj.* thick-lipped.
**morsa** *f.* ZOOL. walrus, morse.
**mortadela** *f.* Bologna sausage.
**mortaja** *f.* shroud, winding sheet. 2 CARP. mortise.
**mortal** *adj.* mortal [subject to death]. 2 mortal [deadly, deathly; long, tedious]. 3 deathly [pallor]. 4 sure, conclusive. 5 *m.* mortal.
**mortalidad** *f.* mortality [condition of being mortal]. 2 mortality, death rate.
**mortandad** *f.* mortality [death of large numbers]; massacre, butchery.
**mortecino, -na** *adj.* dying, dim, dull, pale, subdued [light, fire, colour, etc.].
**morterete** *m. dim.* small mortar [used for salvos and public festivities].
**mortero** *m.* mortar [for pounding]. 2 ARTILL. mortar. 3 MAS. mortar.
**mortífero, -ra** *adj.* death-dealing, deadly, fatal.
**mortificación** *f.* mortification. 2 annoyance.
**mortificador, -ra; mortificante** *adj.* mortifying. 2 annoying.
**mortificar** *tr.* to mortify [in every sense]. 2 to annoy, bother. 3 *ref.* to mortify [practice or undergo mortification].
**mortuorio, -ria** *adj.* mortuary, funeral. 2 *m.* funeral.
**morucho** *m.* BULLF. young bull with tipped horns.
**morueco** *m.* ram [male sheep].
**moruno, -na** *adj.* Moorish.
**mosaico, -ca** *adj.* Mosaic [of Moses]. 2 *adj.-m.* F. ARTS mosaic. 3 paving tile set like mosaic.
**mosaísmo** *m.* Mosaism.
**mosca** *f.* ENT. fly: ~ *de burro,* horse fly: ~ *de la carne,* blowfly; ~ *muerta,* person feigning meekness; *estar* ~, *tener la* ~ *en la oreja,* fig. to be distrustful; *papar moscas,* fig. to stand gaping; *por si las moscas,* fig. for what may happen. 2 tuft of hair under the lip. 3 coll. money: *aflojar la* ~, to pay. 4 coll. bore, nuisance. 5 *pl.* sparks [from a fire].
**moscada** *adj.* BOT. *nuez* ~, nutmeg.
**moscarda** *f.* ENT. blowfly, bluebottle, meat fly.
**moscardón** *m.* ENT. botfly. 2 ENT. bluebottle. 3 ENT. hornet. 4 fig. importuning fellow.
**moscareta** *f.* ORN. flycatcher.

**moscatel** *adj.-m.* muscat, muscatel [grape and wine].

**moscón** *m.* ENT. large fly. 2 ENT. bluebottle. 3 fig. bore, nuisance [person]. 4 BOT. maple.

**mosconear** *tr.-intr.* to bother, importune.

**mosconeo** *m.* bothering, importunation.

**Moscovia** *f. pr. n.* GEOG. Muscovia.

**moscovita** *adj.-n.* Muscovite.

**mosqueado, -da** *adj.* spotted, dotted.

**mosqueador** *m.* flyflap.

**mosquear** *tr.* to drive [flies] away. 2 to give a sharp retort to. 3 to beat, flog. 4 *ref.* to shake off [annoyances]. 5 to take offence.

**mosquero** *m.* flyflap.

**mosqueta** *f.* BOT. a variety of white rose.

**mosquete** *m.* musket.

**mosquetería** *f.* musketry [troops].

**mosquetero** *m.* musketeer.

**mosquetón** *m.* short carbine.

**mosquita** *f. dim.* small fly. 2 coll. ~ *muerta*, MOSCA MUERTA.

**mosquitera** *f.*, **mosquitero** *m.* mosquito net.

**mosquito** *m.* ENT. mosquito; gnat. 2 coll. tippler.

**mostacera** *f.*, **mostacero** *m.* mustard pot.

**mostacilla** *f.* mustard-seed shot. 2 tiny glass beads.

**mostacho** *m.* moustache. 2 coll. smudge on the face. 3 NAUT. shroud [of bowsprit].

**mostachón** *m.* macaroon.

**mostajo** *m.* MOSTELLAR.

**mostaza** *f.* mustard [plant, seed, seasoning]. 2 mustard-seed shot.

**mostear** *intr.* [of grapes] to yield must. 2 to put must into vats. 3 to mix must with old wine.

**mostela** *f.* AGR. gavel, sheaf.

**mostellar** *m.* BOT. whitebeam.

**mosto** *m.* must [grape juice].

**mostrador, -ra** *adj.* showing, pointing. 2 *m.-f.* shower, pointer. 3 *m.* counter [in a shop]. 4 bar [counter].

**mostrar** *tr.* to show, exhibit, display, reveal. 2 to show, point out. 3 to show, demonstrate, prove. 4 *ref.* to show oneself, prove to be. ¶ CONJUG. like contar.

**mostrenco, -ca** *adj.* unclaimed, ownerless. 2 coll. homeless, masterless. 3 coll. dull, stupid. 4 *m.-f.* dullard.

**mota** *f.* burl [in cloth]. 2 mote, speck. 3 slight defect or fault. 4 knoll, hummock.

**motacila** *f.* AGUZANIEVES.

**mote** *m.* motto, device. 2 nickname.

**motear** *intr.* to speck, speckle, mottle.

**motejar** *tr.* to call names to, to nickname.

**motejo** *m.* name-calling, nicknaming.

**motel** *m.* motel.

**motete** *m.* MUS. motet.

**motilidad** *f.* BIOL. motility.

**motilón, -na** *adj.* having short or cropped hair. 2 *m.* coll. lay brother.

**motín** *m.* mutiny, riot, uprising.

**motivar** *tr.* to motive, motivate. 2 to give a reason for.

**motivo** *m.* motive, reason: *con* ~ *de*, owin to; on the occasion of; *por ningún* ~, under no circumstances. 2 F. ARTS, MUS. motif.

**moto** *m.* MOJÓN. 2 coll. motorcycle.

**motocicleta** *f.* motorcycle.

**motociclista** *m.* motorcyclist.

**motón** *m.* NAUT. block, pulley.

**motonave** *f.* NAUT. motor ship.

**motonería** *f.* NAUT. blocks, pulleys, tackle.

**motor, -ra** *adj.* motor, motive. 2 ANAT., PHYSIOL. motor. 3 *m.* motor, mover. 4 MACH. motor, engine: ~ *a chorro*, jet engine; ~ *a gas*, gas engine; ~ *de explosión*, explosion engine; ~ *Diesel*, Diesel engine.

**motora** *f.* NAUT. small motorboat.

**motorismo** *m.* motoring, motorism.

**motorista** *m.-f.* motorcyclist. 2 motorist.

**motorizar** *tr.* to motorize.

**motriz** *f. adj.* motive: *fuerza* ~, motive power.

**movedizo, -za** *adj.* movable. 2 shaky, unsteady. 3 fickle, inconstant. 4 *arenas movedizas*, quicksand.

**mover** *tr.* to move [change position of]. 2 to move, stir, shake, wag [a limb, the head, the tail, etc.]. 3 to move, actuate, drive, propel. 4 to move, induce, impel, prompt, persuade. 5 to raise, start, excite, make. 6 ~ *a*, to move to, to inspire, excite: ~ *a compasión*, to excite piety; ~ *a risa*, to move to laughter. 7 *intr.* to abort, miscarry. 8 *ref.* to move, stir, budge; to get busy, bestir oneself. ¶ IRREG. CONJUG. IND. PRES.: *muevo, mueves, mueve*; movemos, movéis, *mueven*. | SUBJ. PRES.: *mueva, muevas, mueva*; movamos, mováis, *muevan*. | IMPER.: *mueve, mueva*; movamos, moved, *muevan*.

**movible** *adj.* movable: *fiesta* ~, movable feast.

**móvil** *adj.* moving, mobile. 2 *m.* moving body. 3 motive, incentive, inducement.

**movilidad** *f.* movableness, mobility.

**movilización** *f.* mobilization.

**movilizar** *tr.* to mobilize.

**movimiento** *m.* moving, movement, motion; gesture: *en* ~, in motion. 2 MEC., ASTR. motion: ~ *alternativo* or *de vaivén*, reciprocating motion; ~ *ondulatorio*, wave motion. 3 [political, literary, etc.]. movement. 4 mental motion, impulse. 5 stir, agitation, life. 6 traffic. 7 animation [of style]. 8 MUS. movement, tempo. 9 *pl.* movements, activities.

**moyuelo** *m.* fine bran.

**moza** *f.* girl, lass: *buena* ~, *real* ~, handsome girl or woman. 2 maid of all work. 3 mistress, concubine. 4 wash beetle. 5 last or winning game.

**mozalbete** *m. dim.* lad, youth, young fellow.

**mozallón, -na** *m.-f.* strapping young person.

**mozárabe** *adj.* Mozarabic. 2 *m.-f.* Mozarab.

**mozo, -za** *adj.* young, youthful: *la gente moza*, the youth. 2 single, unmarried. 3 *m.* young man, youth, lad: *buen* ~, *real* ~, handsome youth or man. 4 manservant, hand, waiter, porter: ~ *de café*, ~ *de restaurante*, waiter; ~ *de cordel* or *de cuerda*, street porter; ~ *de estación*, station porter; ~ *de estoques*, BULLF. manservant of a matador; ~ *de labranza*, farm hand. 5 cloak hanger.

**mozuelo, -la** *m.-f. dim.* young lad, young lass.

**muaré** *m.* moire, moiré [watered silk].

**mucama** *f.* (Am.) female servant.

**mucamo** *m.* (Am.) manservant, valet.

**muceta** *f.* ECCL. mozetta. 2 a kind of mozetta worn by holders of a doctor's or master's degree.

**mucilaginoso, -sa** *adj.* mucilaginous.

**mucílago, mucilago** *m.* mucilage.

**mucosa** *f.* ANAT. mucous membrane.

**mucosidad** *f.* mucosity.

**mucoso, -sa** *adj.* mucous.

**muchacha** *f.* girl. 2 maid, maidservant.

**muchachada** *f.* boyish or girlish act. 2 (Am.) assemblage of boys or girls, of youngsters.

**muchachil** *adj.* boylike, girl-like; of boys or girls.

muchacho, -cha *adj.* young [person]. *2 m.* boy lad. *3* manservant. *4 f.* girl, lass. *5* maidservant.
muchedumbre *f.* multitude, crowd.
muchísimo, -ma *adj.-adv.* superl. of MUCHO; very much, a very great deal.
1) mucho *adv.* much, very much, a good or great deal, a lot, dearly, hard, abundantly, excessively; *ni ~ menos*, not by a long shot, far from; *por ~ que*, however much. *2* often: *va ~ al teatro*, he often goes to the theatre. *3* long, longtime. *4 pron.* much, a great or indefinite quantity; something uncommon, considerable: *~ será que...*, it is unlikely that...; *con ~*, by far; *ni con ~*, not by a long shot, far from.
2) mucho, -cha *adj.* much, very much, a good or great deal of, a lot of. *2 pl.* many, a good or great deal of, a lot of, lots of.
muchos, -chas *pron.* many: *~ lo conocían*, many knew him.
muda *f.* change, alteration. *2* change of linen. *3* mo(u)lt, mo(u)lting. *4* mo(u)lting season. *5* change of voice, in boys.
mudable *adj.* changeable. *2* fickle, inconstant.
mudanza *f.* change, alteration, mutation. *2* removal, moving [chance of residence]. *3* DANCE. figure, motion. *4* inconstancy.
mudar *tr.* to change, alter, convert: *~ en*, to change to or into. *2* to change [take or adopt another instead of]. | Often with *de*: *~ de color*, to change colour. *3* to move, remove [to another place]. *4* to mo(u)lt, to shed. *5 ~ la voz*, [of a boy] to change voice. *6 ref.* to change [in conduct, affections, etc.]. *7* to change one's underclothing. *8* to move [change one's residence]. *9* coll. to leave, go away. *10 mudarse de ropa*, to change one's clothes.
mudéjar *adj.-n.* Mudejar.
mudez *f.* dumbness.
mudo, -da *adj.* dumb, mute, silent. *2* PHON. mute. *3 m.-f.* mute [dumb person].
mueble *adj.* movable. *2 m.* piece of furniture. *3* RADIO. cabinet. *4 pl.* furniture.
mueblista *m.* furniture maker or seller.
mueca *f.* face, wry face, grimace, grin.
muela *f.* upper millstone. *2* grindstone. *3* ANAT. molar, molar tooth, grinder. *4* knoll, flattopped hill. *5* BOT. flat pea.
muellaje *m.* wharfage.
muelle *adj.* soft, delicate. *2* voluptuous, easy, luxurious. *3 m.* NAUT. wharf, pier. *4* RLY. freight platform. *5* MACH., HOR. spring.
muérdago *m.* BOT. mistletoe.
muerdo, muerda, etc. *irr.* V. MORDER.
muermo *m.* VET. glanders.
muero, muera, etc. *irr.* V. MORIR.
muerte *f.* death: *dar ~*, or *dar la ~ a*, to kill, put to death; *a ~*, to the death; *de ~*, implacably; deadly [wounded]; hopelessly [ill]; *de mala ~*, mean, sorry. *2* Death [skeleton with a scythe]. *3* homicide, murder.
muerto, -ta *p. p.* of MORIR and MATAR. *2 adj.* dead. *3* faded, dull. *4* exhausted, tired out. *5* slacked [lime]. *6* bursting, perished, dying [with curiosity, cold, hunger, etc.]. *7 estar ~ por*, to be madly in love with. *8 m.-f.* dead person, corpse. *9* dummy [at bridge]. *10 echarle el ~ a*, to put the blame on. *11 tocar a ~*, to toll, knell.
muesca *f.* notch, nick, indentation. *2* CARP. mortise.
muestra *f.* signboard, sign [in front of shop, inn, etc.]. *2* sample, specimen. *3* copy, model, pattern. *4* face, dial [of clock]. *5* sign, show, token: *dar muestras de*, to show signs of. *6* set [of dog]: *perro de ~*, pointer, setter.
muestrario *m.* collection of samples, sample book.
muevo, mueva, etc. *irr.* V. MOVER.
mufla *f.* muffle [in a muffle furnace].
mufti *m.* mufti.
mugido *m.* low, lowing, moo [of cattle].
mugir *intr.* to low, moo. *2* to bellow, to roar.
mugre *f.* greasy dirt [of wool, clothes, etc.].
mugriento, -ta *adj.* greasy, dirty.
mugrón *m.* AGR. layer [of wine]. *2* shoot [of plant].
muguete *m.* BOT. lily of the valley.
mujer *f.* woman: *~ de gobierno*, housekeeper; *~ pública*, prostitute; *~ de su casa*, good housewife; *~ fatal*, vamp. *2* wife.
mujercilla *f.* little woman. *2* despicable woman.
mujercita *f. dim.* little woman. *2* little wife.
mujeriego, -ga *adj.* womanly. *2* womanish. *3* fond of women. *4 montar a mujeriegas*, to ride sidesaddle.
mujeril *adj.* feminine, womanly. *2* womanish.
mujerío *m.* women; gathering of women.
mujerona *f. augm.* big woman, strapping woman.
mujerzuela *f. dim.* little woman. *2* despicable woman.
mújil, mújol *m.* ICHTH. mullet, striped mullet.
mula *f.* ZOOL. she-mule: *en la ~ de San Francisco*, on shank's mare. *2* coll. stupid fellow.
muladar *m.* dungheap, dunghill. *2* filth, corruption.
muladí *m.-f.* HIST. Spaniard who embraced Mohammedanism.
mular *adj.* [pertaining to] mule.
mulatero *m.* mule hirer. *2* muleteer, muleman.
mulato, -ta *adj.* mulatto. *2 m.* mulatto [man]. *3 f.* mulatto woman.
mulero *m.* muleman.
muleta *f.* crutch [for lame person; prop. support]. *2* BULLF. matador's red flag.
muletilla *f.* MULETA 2. *2* crosshandle cane. *3* braid frog. *4* pet phrase or word.
muleto *m.* young mule. *2* mule not yet broken.
muletón *m.* Canton flannel.
mulo *m.* ZOOL. mule; hinny: *~ castellano*, mule.
mulso, -sa *adj.* honeyed [wine].
multa *f.* fine, amercement, mulct.
multar *tr.* to fine, amerce, mulct.
multicolor *adj.* many-colo(u)red, multicolo(u)r.
multicopista *m.* duplicator, copying machine.
multiforme *adj.* multiform.
multimillonario, -ria *adj.-n.* multimillionaire.
múltiple *adj.* multiple, manifold.
multiplicación *f.* multiplication.
multiplicador, -ra *adj.* multiplying. *2 m.-f.* multiplier. *3 m.* MATH. multiplier.
multiplicando *m.* MATH. multiplicand.
multiplicar *tr.* to multiply. *2 ref.* to multiply [increase in number].
multiplicidad *f.* multiplicity.
múltiplo *adj.-m.* MATH. multiple: *mínimo común ~*, least common multiple.
multitud *f.* multitude.
mullida *f.* litter, bedding [for animals].
mullido *m.* soft filling for cushions, etc.
mullir *tr.* to fluff, soften, loosen [make fluffy or less compact]. *2* to beat up, shake up [a bed]. *3* to arrange, engineer. *5 mullírselas a uno*, to punish, to mortify a person. ¶ IRREG. CONJUG: IND. Pret.: mullí, mulliste, *mulló;* mullimos, mullisteis, *mulleron.* | SUBJ. Imperf.: *mullera, mulleras,*

etc., or *mullese, mulleses*, etc. | Fut.: *mullere, mulleres*, etc. | GER.: *mullendo*.

**mundanal** *adj.* worldly, mundane.

**mundanalidad** *f.* worldliness, mundanity.

**mundanamente** *adv.* worldlily.

**mundano, -na** *adj.* mundane, worldly [things, pleasure, etc.]. *2* worldly [person].

**mundial** *adj.* world-wide, world.

**mundificar** *tr.* to mundify, cleanse.

**mundillo** *m.* arched clotheshorse. *2* cushion for making lace. *3* warming pan. *4* BOT. snowball. *5* little world [of artists, politicians, etc.].

**mundo** *m.* world [in practically every sense]: *el gran ~*, the fashionable society; *el ~ antiguo*, the Old World; *el Nuevo Mundo*, the New World; *el otro ~*, the next World; *medio ~*, a lot of people; *todo el ~*, everybody; *tener ~*, or *mucho ~*, to know life, know the world. *2* globe [terrestrial sphere]. *3* Saratoga trunk.

**mundología** *f.* knowledge of life, tact, savoir-faire.

**mundonuevo** *m.* peep show, portable cosmorama.

**munición** *f.* MIL. ammunition, munition, supplies. *2* charge of firearms; shot [collectively]. *3 de ~*, ammunition [supplied by the government].

**municionar** *tr.* to ammunition, provide with ammunition.

**municipal** *adj.* municipal. *2 m.* policeman.

**municipalidad** *f.* municipality; municipal body or corporation.

**municipalizar** *tr.* to municipalize.

**munícipe** *m.* citizen, denizen. *2* councilman.

**municipio** *m.* municipium. *2* municipality.

**munificencia** *f.* munificence.

**munífico, -ca** *adj.* munificent.

**muñeca** *f.* ANAT. wrist. *2* doll; *~ de trapo*, rag doll. *4* manikin, dress form. *5* sugar teat. *6* pounce bag. *7* polishing bag.

**muñeco** *m.* boy doll, puppet. *2* dummy, man's figure. *3* fig. effeminate coxcomb.

**muñeira** *f.* popular dance of Galicia [in Spain].

**muñequera** *f.* bracelet or strap for a wrist watch.

**muñidor** *m.* beadle. *2 ~ electoral*, electioneer.

**muñir** *tr.* to deliver summons [to meetings, etc.]. *2* to arrange, concert. ¶ CONJUG. like *mullir*.

**muñón** *m.* stump [of amputated limb]. *2* ARTIL. trunnion. *3* MACH. gudgeon pin, wrist pin.

**murajes** *m. pl.* BOT. pimpernel.

**mural** *adj.* mural.

**muralla** *f.* FORT. wall, rampart.

**murar** *tr.* to wall [surround with a wall].

**murciélago** *m.* ZOOL. bat.

**murena** *f.* ICHTH. moray.

**murga** *f.* band of street musicians.

**murgón** *m.* ICHTH. parr, samlet.

**múrice** *m.* ZOOL. murex. *2* poet, purple.

**múridos** *m. pl.* ZOOL. Muridae.

**murmujear** *intr.-tr.* to murmur.

**murmullo** *m.* murmur, ripple; whisper; rustle [of leaves, etc.]; purl [of a brook].

**murmuración** *f.* gossip, backbiting.

**murmurador, -ra** *adj.* murmuring. *2* gossiping, backbiting. *3 m.-f.* gossiper, backbiter.

**murmurar** *intr.* to murmur, whisper. *2* to mutter, grumble. *3* [of leaves, etc.] to rustle. *4* [or streams] to purl, ripple. *5* to gossip, backbite.

**murmurio** *m.* MURMULLO.

**muro** *m.* wall [in a building, garden, etc.]: *~ de*

*contención*, retaining wall. *2* FORT. wall, rampart.

**murria** *f.* coll. blues, dejection, sullenness.

**murrio, -rria** *adj.* sad, dejected, sullen.

**murta** *f.* BOT. myrtle. *2* BOT. myrtle berry.

**murtón** *m.* BOT. myrtle berry.

**mus** *m.* a card game.

**musa** *f.* MYTH. Muse. *2* fig. Muse, muse [inspiration, poetry]. *3 pl.* Muses, liberal arts.

**musáceo, -a** *adj.* BOT. musaceous.

**musaraña** *f.* ZOOL. shrew, shrewmouse. *2* insect, small animal. *3* coll. floating speck in the eye. *4* *pensar en las musarañas*, to be absentminded.

**musco, -ca** *adj.* dark brown. *2 m.* MUSGO 1.

**muscular** *adj.* muscular [of the muscles].

**musculatura** *f.* musculature.

**músculo** *m.* ANAT. muscle; brawn.

**musculoso, -sa** *adj.* muscular, brawny.

**muselina** *f.* muslin.

**museo** *m.* museum.

**muserola** *f.* noseband.

**musgaño** *m.* ZOOL. shrew, shrewmouse.

**musgo** *m.* BOT. moss. *2* BOT. *~ marino*, coralline.

**musgoso, -sa** *adj.* mossy. *2* moss-covered.

**música** *f.* music: *~ celestial*, coll. nonsense, empty talk, moonshine; *~ de fondo*, background music; *~ popular*, folk music; *con la ~ a otra parte*, get out; don't bother me. *2* band, music [body of musicians]. *3* sheet music.

**musical** *adj.* musical.

**musicalidad** *f.* musicality, musicalness.

**músico, -ca** *adj.* musical. *2 m.-f.* musician. *3* MIL. *~ mayor*, bandmaster.

**musicógrafo** *m.* musicographer.

**musicología** *f.* musicology.

**musiquero** *m.* music cabinet, music stand.

**musitar** *intr.* to mumble, mutter.

**musivo** *adj.* mosaic [gold].

**muslera** *f.* armour for the thigh, cuisse.

**muslime** *adj.-n.* Moslem, Muslim.

**muslímico, -ca** *adj.* Moslem, Muslim.

**muslo** *m.* ANAT., ZOOL. thigh. *2* drumstick [of cooked fowl].

**musmón** *m.* ZOOL. mouflon.

**mustango** *m.* (Am.) mustang.

**mustela** *f.* ICHTH. dog shark. *2* ZOOL. obs. weasel.

**mustio, tia** *adj.* withered, faded. *2* sad, dejected, melancholy.

**musulmán** *adj.-n.* Mussulman.

**muta** *f.* pack of hounds.

**mutabilidad** *f.* mutability.

**mutación** *f.* mutation. *2* THEAT. change of scene. *3* change of weather, unsettled weather.

**mutilación** *f.* mutilation.

**mutilado, -da** *adj.* mutilated, crippled. *2 m.-f.* cripple.

**mutis** *m.* THEAT. exit: *hacer ~*, THEAT. to exit: coll. to say nothing, to be silent.

**mutismo** *m.* mutism, silence.

**mutualidad** *f.* mutuality. *2* mutual aid. *3* mutual benefit society.

**mutualismo** *m.* system of organized mutual aid.

**mutuo, tua** *adj.* mutual, reciprocal. *2 m.* LAW mutuum.

**muy** *adv.* very, very much, greatly, most, too [always before adj. or adv.]. *2 ~ hombre*, very much of a man. *3 ~ señor mío*, Dear Sir [in a letter].

**muzárabe** *adj.-n.* MOZÁRABE.

# N

**N, n** *f.* N, n, sixteenth letter of the Spanish alphabet.

**naba** *f.* BOT. rutabaga.

**nabab, nababo** *m.* nabob, nawab.

**nabí** *m.* Moorish prophet.

**nabina** *f.* turnip seed.

**nabo** *m.* BOT. turnip. *2* turniplike root. *3* root, stock [of the tail of a horse, etc.]. *4* NAUT. mast. *5* newel [of winding stair].

**Nabot** *m. pr. n.* BIBL. Naboth.

**Nabucodonosor** *m. pr. n.* BIBL. Nebuchadnezzar.

**nácar** *m.* mother-of-pearl, nacre.

**nacarado, -da** *adj.* nacred.

**nacáreo, -a; nacarino, -na** *adj.* nacreous, nacrine.

**nacela** *f.* ARCH. scotia [moulding].

**macencia** *f.* growth, tumour.

**nacer** *intr.* to be born. *2* [of plants, hair, horns, etc.] to grow, bud, sprout. *3* [of streams, etc.] to spring, flow, have its source. *4* to originate, spring, start, emanate, derive. ¶ CONJUG.: INDIC. Pres.: *nazco, naces, nace,* etc. | SUBJ. Pres.: *nazca, nazcas,* etc. | IMPER.: nace, *nazca; nazcamos,* naced, *nazcan.*

**nacido, -da** *adj.* born: *bien ~,* of noble birth, honest; *mal ~,* lowborn, lowminded. *2 m.* living man. *3* growth, boil.

**naciente** *adj.* incipient, recent; growing, budding, sprouting. *2* rising [sun]. *3 m.* East.

**nacimiento** *m.* birth, coming to life: *de ~,* born, by birth. *2* growth, budding, sprouting. *3* rising [of sun]. *4* source [of river or spring]. *5* origin, issue. *6* birth, descent, lineage. *7* crèche, crib [Nativity scene].

**nación** *f.* nation: *Naciones Unidas,* United Nations; *de ~,* by nationality.

**nacional** *adj.* national. *2* home [of one's own country]; *productos nacionales,* home products. *3 m.* native.

**nacionalidad** *f.* nationality. *2* citizenship.

**nacionalismo** *m.* nationalism.

**nacionalización** *f.* nationalization. *2* naturalization.

**nacionalizar** *tr.* to nationalize. *2* to naturalize.

**nada** *f.* nothing, naught, nothingness. *2 indef. pron.* nothing, not anything, not a bit: little, very little; *~ de nuevo,* nothing new; *de ~,* little, of no account; don't mention it [after thanks]. *3*
*adv.* not, nothing, not at all, not a bit: *no me gusta ~,* I don't like it at all.

**nadaderas** *f.* water wings.

**nadadero** *m.* swimming place.

**nadador, -ra** *adj.* swimming. *2 m.-f.* swimmer.

**nadar** *tr.* to swim. *2* to float. *3* fig. to swim, be rolling in.

**nadería** *f.* triffle, insignificant thing.

**nadie** *indef. pron.* nobody, no one, none. *2* [after negative] anybody. *3 m.* nobody [person of no importance].

**nadir** *m.* ASTR. nadir.

**nado (a)** *adv.* swimming.

**nafta** *f.* naphtha.

**Naftalí** *m. pr. n.* Naphtali.

**naftalina** *f.* naphthalene.

**naipe** *m.* [playing] card. *2* cards, deck of cards: *tener buen ~,* to have good luck at cards. *3 pl.* cards: *jugar a los naipes,* to play cards.

**naire** *m.* mahout, elephant keeper.

**nalga** *f.* buttock, rump. *2 pl.* buttocks, nates.

**nalgada** *f.* slap on the buttocks, span. *2* blow with the buttocks. *3* ham [of hog].

**nalgatorio** *m.* coll. posteriors, seat, buttocks.

**nana** *f.* coll. grandma. *2* lullaby, cradlesong.

**nanquín** *m.* nankeen, nankin.

**nansa** *f.* fish trap. *2* fish pond.

**nansú, nanzú** *m.* nainsook.

**nao** *f.* ship, vessel.

**Napoleón** *m. pr. n.* Napoleon.

**napoleón** *m.* napoleon [coin].

**Nápoles** *m. pr. n.* GEOG. Naples.

**napolitano, -na** *adj.-n.* Neapolitan.

**naranja** *f.* BOT. orange: *~ agria,* sour orange; *~ de ombligo,* navel orange; *~ mandarina,* mandarin orange. *2 media ~,* coll. better half; ARCH. cupola, dome.

**naranjada** *f.* orangeade.

**naranjal** *m.* orange grove.

**naranjero, -ra** *adj.* [pertaining to] orange. *2* with a bell muzzle [blunderbuss]. *3 m.-f.* orange raiser or seller.

**naranjilla** *f.* small green orange for preserving.

**naranjo** *m.* BOT. orange tree. *2* coll. booby, lout.

**Narbona** *pr. n.* GEOG. Narbonne.

**narcisismo** *m.* narcissism.

**narciso** *m.* BOT. narcissus, daffodil. *2* fig. dandy, fop.

**narcosis** *f.* narcosis.
**narcótico, -ca** *adj.-m.* narcotic.
**narcotizar** *tr.* to narcotize.
**nardo** *m.* spikenard, nard [plant and ointment]. *2* BOT. tuberose.
**narguile** *m.* narghile.
**narigón, -na** *adj.* large-nosed. *2 m.-f.* largenosed person. *3* large nose.
**narigudo, -da** *adj.-n.* NARIGÓN 1 & 2.
**narigueta, nariguilla** *f. dim.* small nose.
**nariz** *f. sing.-pl.* [human] nose: ~ *aguileña*, Roman or aquiline nose; ~ *respingona*, turned-up nose; *hinchársele a uno las narices*, to get angry; *meter las narices en*, to poke one's nose into. *2 f. sing.* nose [of an animal; of a retort]. *3* nostril. *4* nose [sense of smell]. *5* bouquet [of wine]. *6* noseshaped catch [for a latch].
**narizota** *f. aug.* large nose.
**narración** *f.* narration, narrative.
**narrador, -ra** *adj.* narrating. *2 m.-f.* narrator.
**narrar** *tr.* to narrate, relate, tell.
**narrativa** *f.* narration, narrative.
**narrativo, -va; narratorio, -ria** *adj.* narrative.
**narria** *f.* drag [sledge for conveying heavy bodies].
**narval** *m.* ZOOL. narwhal.
**nasa** *f.* bow net. *2* fisherman's basket. *3* basket for flour, bread, etc.
**nasal** *adj.* nasal.
**nasalizar** *tr.* to nasalize.
**nasardo** *m.* MUS. nasard.
**nata** *f.* cream [of milk; of any liquor]. *2* fig. cream [the best]. *3 pl.* whipped cream with sugar. *4* NATILLAS.
**natación** *f.* natation, swimming.
**natal** *adj.* natal, native. *2 m.* birth. *3* birthday.
**natalicio** *m.* birthday. *2* nativity.
**natalidad** *f.* natality, birth rate.
**Natán** *m. pr. n.* BIBL. Nathan.
**Nataniel** *m. pr. n.* BIBL. Nathanael.
**natátil** *adj.* natant, floating.
**natatorio, -ria** *adj.* natatorial, natatory.
**natillas** *f.* custard.
**natividad** *f.* nativity. *2* (cap.) Christmas, Yuletide.
**nativo, -va** *adj.* MINER. native. *2* native, natal: vernacular. *3* ntive, born. *4* inborn, naturalborn.
**nato, -ta** *adj.* born: *criminal* ~, born criminal. *2* inherent in an office or position.
**natura** *f.* nature. *2* genital organs.
**natural** *adj.* natural. *2* artless, ingenuous. *3* MUS. natural. *4 adj.-n.* native [of a country or place]. *5 m.* disposition, nature. *6 al* ~, without dressing. *7* F. ARTS *del* ~, from life, from nature.
**naturaleza** *f.* Nature. *2* nature. *3* constitution [of a person]. *4* genitals. *5* sort, kind, description. *6* nationality [of a person]. *7 carta de* ~, privilege of naturalization. *8* F. ARTS ~ *muerta*, still life.
**naturalidad** *f.* naturalness. *2* nationality [of a person].
**naturalismo** *m.* PHIL., LIT. naturalism.
**naturalista** *adj.* naturalistic. *2 m.-f.* naturalist.
**naturalización** *f.* naturalization.
**naturalizar** *tr.* to naturalize. *2* to become naturalized.
**naturalmente** *adv.* naturally. *2* of course.
**naturismo** *m.* naturism.
**naufragar** *intr.* NAUT. to be wrecked, to sink; to be shipwrecked. *2* fig. to be wrecked, to fail, fall through.
**naufragio** *m.* shipwreck. *2* failure, run, disaster.
**náufrago, -ga** *adj.* NAUT. wrecked, castaway. *2 m.-f.* shipwrecked person, castaway.

**naumaquia** *f.* naumachia, naumachy.
**náusea** *f.* nausea, sickness, qualmishness; disgust: *tener náuseas*, to be nauseated, to be sick at the stomach; *dar náuseas*, to make sick, to disgust.
**nauseabundo** *adj.* nauseous, nauseating, sickening, loathsome.
**nausear** *intr.* to nauseate, be nauseated.
**nauta** *m.* mariner, sailor.
**náutica** *f.* nautics, navigation.
**náutico, -ca** *adj.* nautical. *2* water [sports].
**nautilo** *m.* ZOOL. nautilus.
**nava** *f.* hollow [plain surrounded by mountains].
**navaja** *f.* clasp knife, folding knife: ~ *de afeitar*, razor. *2* (Am.) penknife. *3* razor, tusk. *4* ZOOL. razor clam.
**navajazo** *m.* stab with a clasp knife.
**naval** *adj.* naval.
**Navarra** *pr. n.* GEOG. Navarre.
**navarro, -rra** *adj.-n.* Navarrese.
**navazo** *m.* kitchen garden in sandy marshland.
**nave** *f.* ship, vessel: ~ *aérea*, airship: *quemar las naves*, to burn one's boats. *2* ARCH. nave, aisle: ~ *lateral*, aisle. *3* large hall or division in a building.
**navecilla** *f. dim.* small ship. *2* ECCL. navicula, incense boat.
**navegable** *adj.* navigable [river, lake, etc.].
**navegación** *f.* navigation, sailing: ~ *aérea*, aeronautics, aviation. *2* sea voyage.
**navegador, -ra; navegante** *adj.* navigating. *2 m.-f.* navigator.
**navegar** *intr.* to navigate, to sail. *2* to go about.
**naveta** *f.* NAVECILLA. *2* small drawer.
**navícula** *f.* BOT. navicula.
**navicular** *adj.* ANAT., BOT. navicular.
**Navidad** *f.* Nativity, Christmas, Christmas Day. *2* Christmastide, Yuletide.
**navideño, -ña** *adj.* [pertaining to] Christmas.
**naviero, -ra** *adj.* ship, shipping. *2 m.* shipowner.
**navío** *m.* NAUT. ship, warship: ~ *de guerra*, warship; ~ *de línea*, ship of the line.
**náyade** *f.* MYTH. naiad.
**nazareno, -na** *adj.-n.* Nazarene. *2 m.* Nazarite. *3* penitent in Holy Week processions.
**nazi** *adj.-n.* Nazi.
**nébeda** *f.* BOT. catnip, catmint.
**nebli** *m.* ORN. kind of falcon.
**neblinoso, -sa** *adj.* foggy, misty.
**nebulón** *m.* sly fellow, hypocrite.
**nebulosa** *f.* ASTR. nebula.
**nebulosidad** *f.* nebulosity, nebulousness, cloudiness. *2* cloud, shadow.
**nebuloso, -sa** *adj.* nebulous, cloudy. *2* misty, hazy, vague. *3* gloomy.
**necear** *intr.* to talk nonsense. *2* to persist foolishly.
**necedad** *f.* foolishness, folly, stupidity, nonsense.
**necesaria** *f.* privy, water-closet.
**necesario, -ria** *adj.* necessary; needful.
**neceser** *m.* case, kit: ~ *de costura*, sewing case, workbasket; ~ *de tocador*, toilet case.
**necesidad** *f.* necessity; need, want: *de* ~, of necessity; *por* ~, from necessity; necessarily. *2* emergency. *3* want, destitution, poverty. *4* hunger. *5 pl. hacer sus necesidades*, to urinate, to go to stool.
**necesitado, -da** *adj.* necessitous, needy, poor. *2* ~ *de*, wanting. *3 m.* needy, poor person.
**necesitar** *tr.* to necessitate [force, compel]. *2* to need, want, lack. *3* to have to, need to. *4* intr. ~ *de*, to need, be in need of.

**necio, -cia** *adj.* ignorant, foolish, stupid; silly, unjudicious. *2 m.-f.* ignorant person, fool.
**necrología** *f.* necrology.
**necromancia** *f.* necromancy.
**necrópolis** *f.* necropolis.
**necrosis,** *pl.* **-sis** *f.* MED. necrosis.
**néctar** *m.* nectar.
**nectario** *m.* BOT. nectary.
**neerlandés, -sa** *adj.-n.* HOLANDÉS. *2* Netherlandish [language].
**nefando, -da** *adj.* nefandous, abominable.
**nefario, -ria** *adj.* nearious, wicked, iniquitous.
**nefasto, -ta** *adj.* sad, ominous. *2* funest, noxious.
**nefridio** *m.* ZOOL. nephridium.
**nefrítico, -ca** *adj.* MED. nephritic.
**nefritis** *f.* MED. nephritis.
**negable** *adj.* deniable.
**negación** *f.* negation. *2* GRAM. negative particle.
**negado, -da** *adj.* inapt, incompetent. *2* dull, stupid.
**negar** *tr.* to deny [declare untrue or non-existent]. *2* to deny, refuse. *3* to deny, disavow. *4* to forbid, prohibit. *5* to hide, conceal. *6* ~ *el saludo a*, to cut, not to speak to. *7 ref.* to decline, refuse [to do]. *8* to deny oneself [to callers]. *9 negarse a sí mismo,* to deny oneself, practice, self-denial. ¶ CONJUG. like *acertar.*
**negativa** *f.* negative [negative statement or reply], denial. *2* denial, refusal.
**negativo, -va** *adj.* negative. *2 m.* PHOT. negative.
**negligencia** *f.* negligence, neglect, carelessness.
**negligente** *adj.* negligent, careless, neglectful.
**negociable** *adj.* COM. negotiable.
**negociación** *f.* negotation. *2* business transaction.
**negociado** *m.* bureau, division. *2* business, affair.
**negociador, -ra** *adj.* negotiating. *2 m.-f.* negotiator.
**negociante** *m.* dealer, trader, businessman.
**negociar** *intr.* to deal, trade, do business. *2 intr.-tr.* to negotiate [arrange by negotiation]. *3 tr.* COM. to negotiate [a bill, cheque, etc.].
**negocio** *m.* business, affair, transaction, deal, bargain; matter, occupation, work. *2* commerce, trade. *3* concern, business: *un ~ de banca*, a banking concern. *4* profit, gain. *5 pl.* business, commercial affairs. *6* DIPLOM. affaires.
**negocioso, -sa** *adj.* active, diligent.
**negra** *f.* fencing sword. *2* MUS. crotchet, quarter note. *3* Negress, Negro woman.
**negrear** *intr.* to show black, appear black. *2* to be blackish.
**negrero, -ra** *adj.* slave-trading. *2 m.-f.* slave trader. *3* fig. slave-driver.
**negreta** *f.* ORN. black scoter.
**negrillo, -lla** *adj.* blackish. *2* PRINT. *letra negrilla,* boldfaced type, clarendon type. *3 m.* BOT. elm.
**negrito, -ta** *m.-f.* Negro boy, Negro girl. *2* Negrito.
**negro, -gra** *adj.* black [colour]. *2* black [in colour; dusky, gloomy; sinister; wicked, dismal]. *3* dark, brown. *4* unlucky, wretched: *pasarlas negras,* to have a terrible time. *5* Negro. *6 m.* black [colour, pigment]: ~ *animal,* boneblack; ~ *de humo,* lampblack; ~ *de marfil,* ivory black. *7* Negro, nigger. *8 f.* Negress.
**negror** *m.,* **negrura** *f.* blackness.
**negruzco, -ca** *adj.* blackish.
**neguijón** *m.* tooth decay.
**neguilla** *f.* BOT. corn cockle. *2* BOT. love-in-amist. *3* age mark [in horses's teeth].
**neguillón** *m.* BOT. corn cockle.
**Negus** *m.* Negus [title of the Ethiopian emperor].
**nema** *f.* seal or sealing of a letter.
**nematelminto** *m.* ZOOL. nemathelminth.

**nemátodo, -da** *adj.-m.* ZOOL. nematode.
**nemeo, -a** *adj.-n.* Nemean.
**Némesis** *f. pr. n.* MYTH. Nemesis.
**nemoroso, -sa** *adj.* poet, sylvan; wooded.
**nena** *f.* baby [girl]. *2* dear, darling.
**nene** *m.* baby [boy]. *2* dear, darling. *3* villain [used ironically].
**nenúfar** *m.* BOT. white water lily.
**neo** *m.* CHEM. neon.
**neoclásico, -ca** *adj.* neoclassic. *2 m.-f.* neoclassicist.
**neófito** *m.* neophyte.
**neolatino, -na** *adj.* Neo-Latin.
**neolítico, -ca** *adj.* neolithic. *2 m.* Neolithic era.
**neologismo** *m.* neologism.
**neón** *m.* CHEM. neon.
**neoplasia** *f.* MED. neoplasia.
**neoplatónico, -ca** *adj.* Neoplatonic. *2 m.-f.* Neoplatonist.
**neoyorquino, -na** *adj.* of New York. *2 m.-f.* New Yorker.
**neozoico, -ca** *adj.-m.* GEOL. Neozoic.
**neperiano, -na** *adj.* Napierian, Naperian.
**nepotismo** *m.* nepotism.
**Neptuno** *m. pr. n.* MYTH., ASTR. Neptune.
**nequáquam** *adv.* coll. by no means.
**nequicia** *f.* iniquity, perversity.
**nereida** *f.* MYTH. Nereid.
**Nerón** *m. pr. n.* Nero.
**nervadura** *f.* ARCH. rib. *2* BOT., ENT. nervation, nervures, ribbing.
**nérveo, -a** *adj.* nerval.
**nerviación** *f.* BOT., ENT. nerviation.
**nervio** *m.* ANAT. nerve [of the nervous system]: *ataque de nervios,* fit of nerves, hysterics. *2* nerve, vigour, enerrgy. *3* nerve, sinew, tendon. *4* BOT. nerve, rib, vein. *5* ENT. nervure, rib. *6* BOOKB. rib. *7* MUS. string. *8* ARCH. rib in the intrados of a vault. *9* NAUT. stay.
**nerviosidad** *f.* NERVOSIDAD. *2* NERVIOSISMO.
**nerviosismo** *m.* nervousness, nervous excitement.
**nervioso, -sa** *adj.* nerve: *centro ~,* nerve centre. *2* nervous: *poner ~,* to get on one's nerves. *3* vigorous, energetic. *4* BOT. nerved.
**nervosidad** *f.* nervosity. *2* flexibility [of some metals]. *3* strength, forcibleness [of arguments].
**nervoso, -sa** *adj.* NERVIOSO.
**nervudo, -da** *adj.* strong-nerved, sinewy.
**nervura** *f.* BOOKB. ribbing.
**nesciencia** *f.* nescience, ignorance.
**nesga** *f.* SEW. gore. *2* triangular piece.
**netamente** *adv.* clearly, distinctly.
**neto, -ta** *adj.* clear, pure. *2* net [weight, etc.]. *3 m.* ARCH. dado [of pedestal].
**neumática** *f.* PHYS. pneumatics.
**neumático, -ca** *adj.* pneumatic. *2 m.* tire, pneumatic tire.
**neumonía** *f.* MED. pneumonia.
**neumotórax** *m.* MED. pneumothorax.
**neuralgia** *f.* MED. neuralgia.
**neurastenia** *f.* MED. neurasthenia.
**neuritis** *f.* MED. neuritis.
**neurosqueleto** *m.* endoskeleton.
**neurología** *f.* neurology.
**neurólogo** *m.* neurologist.
**neurona** *f.* ANAT. neuron, neurona.
**neurópata** *m.-f.* neuropath.
**neuropatía** *f.* MED. neuropathy.
**neuróptero, -ra** *adj.-m.* ENT. neuropteran.
**neurosis** *f.* MED. neurosis.
**neurótico, -ca** *adj.-n.* MED. neurotic.

**neutral** *adj.-n.* neutral, neuter [taking no sides].
**neutralidad** *f.* neutrality.
**neutralización** *f.* neutralization.
**neutralizar** *tr.* to neutralize. *2* to counteract.
**neutro, -tra** *adj.* neutral [colour]. *2* CHEM., ELECT. neutral. *3* BOT., ENT. neutral, neuter. *4* GRAM. neuter.
**neutrón** *m.* PHYS., CHEM. neutron.
**nevada** *f.* snowfall.
**nevadilla** *f.* BOT. whitlowwort.
**nevado, -da** *adj.* snow-covered. *2* snow-white, snowy.
**nevar** *impers.* to snow. *2 tr.* to make snowwhite. ¶ CONJUG. like *acertar.*
**nevasca** *f.* NEVADA. *2* snowstorm.
**nevatilla** *f.* AGUZANIEVES.
**nevera** *f.* icebox, refrigerator. *2* fig. very cold place.
**nevero** *m.* place of perpetual snow. *2* perpetual snow.
**nevisca** *f.* light snowfall, sleet.
**neviscar** *impers.* to snow lightly, to sleet.
**nevoso, -sa** *adj.* snowy [place, weather].
**nexo** *m.* nexus, bond, link, connexion.
**ni** *conj.* neither, nor: ~ *aquí* ~ *allí,* neither here nor there. *2* not one, not a single: ~ *un amigo,* not a single friend. *3* ~ *siquiera,* not even.
**niara** *f.* straw rick.
**nicaragüeño, -ña** *adj.-n.* Nicaraguan.
**niceno, -na** *adj.-n.* Nicene.
**Nicolás** *m. pr. n.* Nicholas.
**nicotina** *f.* CHEM. nicotine.
**nictalopia** *f.* nyctalopia.
**nicho** *m.* niche [recess in a wall].
**nidada** *f.* nestful of eggs. *2* brood, hatch, covey.
**nidal** *m.* nest [where hen lay eggs]. *2* nest egg. *3* haunt. *4* cache, hiding place. *5* cause motive.
**nidificar** *intr.* to nest, build a nest or nests.
**nido** *m.* nest [of bird, insects, etc.]. *2* home, abode. *3* nest [of bird, insects, etc.]. *2* home, abode. *3* nest [of thieves, machine guns, etc.]. *4* NIDAL.
**niebla** *f.* fog, mist, haze. *2* fig. haze, confusion. *3* BOT. smut, rust.
**niego, niegue,** etc. *irr.* V. NEGAR.
**niel** *m.* niello, niello work.
**nielado** *m.* nielloing.
**nielar** *tr.* to niello.
**nieto, -ta** *m.-f.* grandchild. *2 m.* grandson. *3 f.* granddaughter.
**nieve** *f.* snow. *2* fig. pure whiteness.
**nigromancia** *f.* necromancy.
**nigromante** *m.* necromancer, magician.
**nigromántico, -ca** *adj.* necromantic. *2 m.* NIGRO-MANTE.
**nigua** *f.* ENT. chigoe.
**nihilismo** *m.* nihilism.
**nihilista** *adj.* nihilistic. *2 m.-f.* nihilist.
**Nilo** *m. pr. n.* GEOG. Nilè [river].
**nilón** *m.* nylon.
**nimbar** *tr.* to encircle with a halo.
**nimbo** *m.* nimbus, aureole, halo. *2* METEOR. nimbus.
**nimiedad** *f.* prolixity, minuteness. *2* smallness.
**ninfa** *f.* MYTH., ENT. & fig. nymph.
**ninfea** *f.* BOT. white water lily.
**ningún** *adj.* contr. of NINGUNO [used only before masculine nouns].
**ninguno, -na** *adj.* no, not one, not any. *2 indef. pron. m.-f.* none, not any, neither: ~ *de ellos,* none of them; *ninguna de estas dos casas,* neith-

er of these two houses. *3 indef. pron. m.* nobody, no one.
**Ninive** *f. pr. n.* HIST., GEOG. Nineveh.
**niña** *f.* female child or infant; little girl, young girl. *2* ANAT. ~ *del ojo,* pupil, apple of the eye. *3* fig. *niñas de los ojos,* apple of one's eyes.
**niñada** *f.* puerility, childishness, childish action.
**niñera** *f.* dry nurse, nursemaid.
**niñería** *f.* puerility, childish action. *2* trifle.
**niñero, -ra** *adj.* fond of children.
**niñez** *f.* childhood. *2* fig. infancy. *3* childish action.
**niño, -ña** *adj.* child [of the age of a child]. *2* childish, childlike. *3* young, inexperienced. *4 m.* male child or infant, boy, little boy: ~ *de teta,* child in arms, suckling babe; *el* ~ *Jesús,* the child Jesús; *de* ~, as a child; *desde* ~, from childhood. *5 pl.* children.
**niobio** *m.* CHEM. niobium.
**nipa** *f.* BOT. nipa palm.
**nipón, -na** *adj.-n.* Nipponese, Japanese.
**níquel** *m.* CHEM. nickel.
**niquelado** *m.* **niqueladura** *f.* nickel-plate; nickel-plating.
**niquelar** *tr.* to nickel-plate.
**nirvana** *m.* Nirvana.
**niscalo** *m.* MÍZCALO.
**níspero** *m.* BOT. medlar [tree and fruit]. *2* (Am.) BOT. sapodilla. *3* BOT. ~ *del Japón,* loquat.
**níspola** *f.* medlar [fruit].
**nitidez** *f.* neatness, clearness, sharpness.
**nítido, -da** *adj.* neat, clear. *2* sharp, well-defined.
**nitrato** *m.* nitrate. *2* ~ *de Chile,* Chile saltpetre.
**nítrico, -ca** *adj.* CHEM. nitric.
**nitro** *m.* nitre, niter, saltpetre, saltpeter.
**nitrocelulosa** *f.* CHEM. nitrocellulose.
**nitrogenar** *tr.* to nitrogenize.
**nitrógeno** *m.* CHEM. nitrogen.
**nitroglicerina** *f.* CHEM. nitroglycerin.
**nivel** *m.* level [instrument; uniform altitude]: ~ *del mar,* sea level; ~ *de vida,* standard of living. *2* levelness, equality.
**nivelación** *f.* levelling. *2* balancing [of the budget].
**nivelador, -ra** *adj.* levelling. *2 m.-f.* leveller.
**nivelar** *tr.* to level [make level; bring to a common level; make equal]. *2* ~ *el presupuesto,* to balance the budget. *3 ref.* to level off.
**níveo, -a** *adj.* poet, snowy, snowy white.
**Niza** *f. pr. n.* GEOG. Nice.
**nizardo, -da** *adj.-n.* of Nice.
**no** *adv.* no, nay [particle equivalent to a negative sentence]: *¿se va usted? —No,* are you going? —No. *2* not, no: ~ *lo sé,* I don't know; ~ *bien,* no sooner; ~ *obstante,* notwithstanding; ~ *sea que,* lest, or else; ~ *ya,* not only. *3 ¿no?* [question tag], isn't it?
**nobiliario, -ria** *adj.* nobiliary.
**nobilísimo, -ma** *adj. superl.* most noble.
**noble** *adj.* noble. *2 m.-f.* noble, nobleman, noble-woman.
**nobleza** *f.* nobility, nobleness. *2* nobility, noblesse [the class of nobles].
**noblote** *adj.* noble, open-hearted.
**noca** *f.* ZOOL. a variety of crab.
**noción** *f.* notion, idea. *2 pl.* rudiments, elements.
**nocivo, -va** *adj.* noxious, harmful, pernicious.
**noctámbulo, -la** *adj.* night-wandering. *2 m.-f.* night-wanderer.
**nocturnidad** *f.* LAW condition of nocturnal.
**nocturno, -na** *adj.* nocturnal, night. *2 m.* ECCL. nocturn. *3* MUS. nocturne.
**noche** *f.* night [in every sense]; evening [from sun-

set to bed]: ~ *buena*, Christmas Eve; ~ *toledana*, sleepless night; ~ *vieja*, New Year's Eve; *buenas noches*, good night; good evening; *media* ~, midnight; *prima* ~, evening; *hacer* ~ *en*, to spend the night in; *hacerse de* ~, to grow dark; *ayer* ~, last night; *de la* ~ *a la mañana*, unexpectedly suddenly; *de*, or *por*, *la* ~, at night, by night; *esta* ~, tonight; *muy de* ~, late at night.

**nochebuena** *f.* Christmas Eve.

**nochebueno** *m.* Christmas cake. 2 Yule log.

**nocherniego, -ga** *adj.* night-wandering.

**nochizo** *m.* BOT. wild hazel.

**nodal** *adj.* nodal. 2 nodical.

**nodátil** *adj.* ANAT. nodal.

**nodo** *m.* ASTR., GEOM., PHYS., MED. node.

**nodriza** *f.* wet nurse. 2 AUTO. vacuum tank.

**nódulo** *m.* nodule.

**Noé** *m. pr. n.* BIBL. Noah.

**nogal** *m.* BOT. walnut tree. 2 walnut wood.

**nogalina** *f.* walnut stain.

**noguera** *f.* NOGAL.

**nolición** *f.* nolition.

**nómada** *adj.* nomad, nomadic. 2 *m.-f.* nomad.

**nomadismo** *m.* nomadism, nomadic state.

**nombradía** *f.* renown, fame, reputation.

**nombramiento** *m.* naming, nomination, appointing, appointment. 2 MIL. commission.

**nombrar** *tr.* to name, mention. 2 to name, nominate, appoint, commission.

**nombre** *m.* name [of a person or thing]: ~ *de pila*, Christian name; ~ *y apellido*, full name; *no tener* ~, to be unspeakable; *en* ~ *de*, in the name of. 2 name, fame, reputation. 3 nickname. 4 GRAM. noun: ~ *apelativo*, or *común*, common noun; ~ *propio*, proper noun.

**nomenclador, nomenclátor** *m.* catalogue of names; gazeteer; technical glossary.

**nomenclatura** *f.* nomenclature.

**nomeolvides**, *pl.* **-des** *f.* BOT. forget-me-not.

**nómina** *f.* catalogue of names. 2 pay roll.

**nominal** *adj.* nominal. 2 COM. face [value].

**nominalismo** *m.* nominalism.

**nominar** *tr.* NOMBRAR.

**nominativo, -va** *adj.* COM. nominative, nominal [share]. 2 *adj.-m.* GRAM. nominative [case].

**nomparell** *f.* PRINT. nonpareil.

**non**, *pl.* **nones** *adj.* MATH. odd, uneven. 2 *m.* MATH. odd number: *pares y nones*, odd or even; *estar de* ~, fig. to be unmatched; *quedar de* ~, fig. to remain alone, without a partner. 3 *pl.* no, nay [denial, refusal]: *decir nones*, to say no.

**nona** *f.* HIST. none. 2 ECCL. none, nones. 3 *pl.* nones [in the Roman calendar].

**nonada** *f.* trifle, nothing.

**nonagenario, -ria** *adj.-n.* nonagenarian.

**nonagésimo, -ma** *adj.-m.* ninetieth.

**nonágono** *adj.-m.* ENEÁGONO.

**nonato, -ta** *adj.* not naturally born, extracted by Caesarean section. 2 unborn, still nonexistent.

**noningentésimo, -ma** *adj.-m.* nine hundredth.

**nonio** *m.* vernier, vernier scale.

**nono, -na** *adj.-n.* ninth.

**nopal** *m.* BOT. nopal, prickly pear.

**norabuena** *f.-adv.* ENHORABUENA.

**noramala** *adv.* ENHORAMALA.

**noray** *m.* NAUT. bollard, mooring.

**nordestal** *adj.* northeast.

**nordeste** *m.* northeast. 2 northeast wind.

**nórdico, -ca** *adj.-n.* Nordic. 2 Norse. 3 *m.* Norse [language].

**noria** *f.* noria, chain pump, draw wheel.

**norma** *f.* norm, model, pattern, regulation, standard.

**normal** *adj.* normal. 2 standard, model. 3 *f.* GEOM. normal. 4 normal school.

**normalidad** *f.* normality.

**normalista** *m.-f.* normal-school student.

**normalizar** *tr.* to normalize. 2 *ref.* to become normal.

**Normandía** *f. pr. n.* GEOG. Normandy.

**normando, -da** *adj.* Norman. 2 *m.* Norman. 3 Norseman, Northman.

**noroeste** *m.* northwest.

**nortada** *f.* norther, north wind.

**norte** *m.* north. 2 north wind. 3 North Pole. 4 North Star. 5 fig. lodestar, guide, direction.

**Norteamérica** *f. pr. n.* North America.

**norteamericano, -na** *adj.-n.* North American; American [of the U.S.A.].

**norteño, -ña** *adj.-n.* northern; norther [esp. of the North of Spain].

**nórtico, -ca** *adj.* north, northern.

**Noruega** *f. pr. n.* GEOG. Norway.

**noruego, -ga** *adj.-n.* Norwegian.

**norueste** *m.* NOROESTE.

**nos** *pers. pron. pl. m.-f.* [object of the verb], us, to us, for us; [recip.] each other; [ref.] ourselves. 2 we, us [used by the king, the bishops, etc.].

**nosología** *f.* nosology.

**nosotros, -tras** *pers. pron. pl. m.-f.* we [as subject of the verb]; us [as object of preposition]. 2 *nosotros mismos, nosotras mismas*, ourselves.

**nostalgia** *f.* nostalgia, homesickness. 2 regret [for something lost].

**nostálgico, -ca** *adj.* nostalgic. 2 regretful.

**nota** *f.* note [mark; annotation; brief record of facts, etc.]: *tomar* ~ *de*, to take note of. 2 [diplomatic] note. 3 MUS. note: ~ *de adorno*, grace note. 4 note, eminence, reputation. 5 COM. account, bill; statement, schedule: ~ *de precios*, price list. 6 EDUC. mark, *grade. 7 caer en* ~, to be talked about.

**notabilidad** *f.* notability [quality; person].

**notabilísimo, -ma** *adj.* most notable or remarkable.

**notable** *adj.* notable, remarkable, striking, noteworthy, prominent. 2 noticeable, perceptible. 3 *m.* EDUC. good mark. 4 *m. pl.* notables [persons].

**notación** *f.* notation.

**notar** *tr.* to note, mark. 2 to annotate. 3 to note, notice, observe. 4 to note, set down. 5 DICTAR. 6 to blame charge with [a fault].

**notaría** *f.* profession of notary. 2 notary's office.

**notariado, -da** *adj.* notarized. 2 *m.* profession of notary. 3 the notaries [as a body].

**notarial** *adj.* notarial.

**notario** *m.* notary, notary public.

**noticia** *f.* news, news item, notice, piece of news, report, tidings: *noticias de última hora*, late news. 2 knowledge, information, intelligence: *tener* ~ *de*, to be informed of.

**noticiar** *tr.* to give notice of.

**noticiario** *m.* CINEM. news reel. 2 RADIO. newscast.

**noticiero, -ra** *adj.* news-bearing, news-giving. 2 *m.-f.* newsman, reporter.

**notición** *f. augm.* coll. big news, great news.

**noticioso, -sa** *adj.* knowing, informed.

**notificación** *f.* notification; official notice.

**notificar** *tr.* to notify, announce, intimate, inform.

**notita** *f. dim.* of NOTA.

**noto** *m.* south wind.

**notoriedad** *f.* notoriety [being well-known]; self-evidence. *2* fame, renown.

**notorio, -ria** *adj.* notorious [well-known]; evident, manifest, glaring.

**novador, -ra** *m.-f.* innovator.

**novatada** *f.* hazing of a new comer [in a college, etc.]. *2* beginner's blunder.

**novato, -ta** *adj.* beginning. *2 m.-f.* novice, beginner, freshman.

**novecientos, tas** *adj.-n.* nine hundred.

**novedad** *f.* novelty. *2* newness. *3* change, alteration: *sin ~*, as usual well. *4* news. *5* recent fashion. *6* surprise, astonishment: *causar ~*, to surprise. *7 pl.* *novedades* or *géneros de ~*, fancy goods.

**novedoso, -sa** *adj.* novel, having novelty.

**novel** *adj.-m.* new, inexperienced.

**novela** *f.* LIT. novel, romance, fiction, story: *~ por entregas*, serial. *2* lie, yarn. *3* LAW novel.

**novelador, -ra** *m.-f.* novelist.

**novelar** *tr.* to novelize. *2 intr.* to write novels.

**novelería** *f.* fondness for novelty; curiosity. *2* fondness for fiction. *3* worthless fiction.

**novelero, -ra** *adj.* of novelty. *2* fond of fiction, romantical. *3* newsmongering. *4* fickle, inconstant.

**novelesco, -ca** *adj.* novelistic. *2* like a novel; romantic, fantastic.

**novelista** *m.-f.* novelist, novel-writer.

**novena** *f.* ECCL. novena.

**noveno, -na** *adj.-m.* ninth.

**noventa** *adj.-m.* ninety.

**noventavo, -va** *adj.-m.* ninetieth.

**noventón, -na** *adj.-n.* nonagenarian.

**novia** *f.* bride. *2* fiancée, girl-friend, sweetheart.

**noviazgo** *m.* engagement, betrothal; courtship.

**novicia** *f.* ECCL. novice [woman].

**noviciado** *m.* ECCL. noviciate. *2* apprenticeship.

**novicio, -cia** *adj.* new, inexperienced. *2 m.* ECCL. novice [man]. *3 m.-f.* novice, beginner, tyro.

**noviembre** *m.* November.

**novilunio** *m.* new moon.

**novilla** *f.* heifer, young cow.

**novillada** *f.* drove of young bulls. *2* BULLF. fight with young bulls.

**novillero** *m.* BULLF. fighter of young bulls. *2* truant.

**novillo** *m.* young bull. *2 pl.* BULLF. fight with young bulls. *3 hacer novillos*, to play truant.

**novio** *m.* bridegroom. *2* fiancé; boy-friend; suitor. *3 pl.* betrothed man and woman. *4* bride and bridegroom, new-married couple.

**novísimo, -ma** *adj. superl.* most new. *2 m.* each of the last stages of man: death, judgment, hell and heaven.

**nubada, nubarrada** *f.* shower of rain. *2* crowd [of certain things].

**nubarrado, -da** *adj.* clouded, variegated [fabric].

**nubarrón** *m.* large black cloud.

**nube** *f.* cloud: *~ de verano*, summer shower; fig. passing annoyance; *estar por las nubes*, to be sky-high [in price]; *poner en*, or *sobre, las nubes*, fig. to priase to the skies. *2* MED. film, spot [on the cornea].

**nubecita** *f. dim.* small cloud.

**núbil** *adj.* nubile.

**nubilidad** *f.* nubility.

**nublado, -da** *adj.* clouded, cloudy, overcast. *2 m.* storm cloud: *descargar el ~*, to rain, hail or snow hard; fig. to vent one's anger in explosive words. *3* impending danger. *4* shower, cloud [of certain things].

**nublar** *tr.-ref.* ANUBLAR.

**nubloso, -sa** *adj.* cloudy, overcast.

**nuca** *f.* nape or scruff of the neck.

**nuclear** *adj.* PHYS. nuclear.

**núcleo** *m.* nucleus. *2* ELECT. core [of an electromagnet]. *3* BOT. kernel [of nut]; stone [of fruit].

**nucléolo** *m.* BIOL. nucleolus.

**nudillo** *m.* knuckle [at finger-joint].

**nudismo** *m.* nudism.

**nudista** *adj.-n.* nudist.

1) **nudo** *m.* knot, noose, hitch: *~ corredizo*, slip knot; *~ en la garganta*, fig. lump in one's throat. *2* knot, bond, tie. *3* knot, tangle, difficulty. *4* knot [of a problem, a plot, etc.]. *5* NAUT. knot. *6* burl [in cloth]. *7* knot, gnarl [in wood]. *8* BOT. knot, node, joint. *9* knot [of mountains, etc.].

2) **nudo, -da** *adj.* nude, naked.

**nudoso, -sa** *adj.* knotty [having knots]. *2* gnarled.

**nuera** *f.* daughter-in-law.

**nuestro, -tra** *poss. adj.* our, of ours. *2 poss. pron.* ours. *3 los nuestros*, ours, our friends, our men, etc.

**nueva** *f.* news, tidings. *2 hacerse de nuevas*, to feign ignorance of a thing; *no me coge de nuevas*, I am not surprised at it.

**nuevamente** *adv.* again, anew. *2* newly, recently.

**Nueva Orleans** *f. pr. n.* GEOG. New Orleans.

**Nueva York** *f. pr. n.* GEOG. New York.

**Nueva Zelandia** *f. pr. n.* GEOG. New Zeland.

**nueve** *adj.-n.* nine: *las ~*, nine o'clock. *2 m.* ninth [of the month].

**nuevecito, -ta** *adj. dim.* of NUEVO, brand-new.

**nuevo, -va** *adj.* new, novel: *¿qué hay de ~?*, what's new? *2* new, fresh [another]. *3* newly arrived. *4* novice, beginner. *5 adv. de ~*, anew, again, once more.

**nuez** *f.* walnut. *2* nut [of some other plants]: *~ de cola*, kola nut; *~ moscada*, nutmeg; *~ vómica*, nux vomica. *3* Adam's apple. *4* nut [of a crossbow]. *5* MUS. nut, frog [of a violin bow].

**nueza** *f.* BOT. bryony.

**nugatorio, -ria** *adj.* nugatory, frustrating.

**nulidad** *f.* nullity. *2* inability, incompetence. *3* incapable or insignificant person.

**nulo, -la** *adj.* LAW null, void. *2* null, nonexistent. *3* incapable, incompetent.

**Numancia** *f. pr. n.* HIST., GEOG. Numantia.

**numen** *m.* MYTH. numen. *2* poetical or artistic inspiration.

**numeración** *f.* numeration, numbering. *2* ARITH. system or notation.

**numerador** *m.* numerator, numberer. *2* ARITH. numerator.

**numeral** *adj.* numeral.

**numerar** *tr.* to numerate, enumerate. *2* to number [assign a number to].

**numerario, -ria** *adj.* numerary. *2 m.* cash, coin, specie.

**numérico, -ca** *adj.* numerical.

**número** *m.* ARITH. number. *2* numeral, figure: *~ arábigo*, Arabic numeral; *~ romano*, Roman numeral. *3* number [of persons or things]: *gran ~*, great number; *sin ~*, numberless. *4* number [assigned to a person or thing]; ticket, etc. bearing a number]. *5* number, issue [of a newspaper]. *6* item [of a program]. *7* size [of shoes, gloves, etc.]. *8* GRAM., POET. number. *9 pl.* BIBL. numbers.

**numeroso, -sa** *adj.* numerous. *2* harmonious, rhythmical.

**númida** *adj.-n.* Numidian.

**numisma** *m.* coin, money.

**numismática** *m.* numismatics.
**numismático** *m.* numismatist.
**nunca** *adv.* never: ~ *jamás*, never more.
**nunciatura** *f.* nunciature.
**nuncio** *m.* messenger, harbinger, forerunner. *2* nuncio [Pope's ambassador].
**nupcial** *adj.* nuptial, hymeneal.
**nupcias** *f.* nuptials, marriage, wedding.

**nutación** *f.* ASTR., BOT. nutation.
**nutria** *f.* ZOOL. otter. *2* otter-fur.
**nutricio, -cia** *adj.* nutritious.
**nutrición** *f.* nutrition. *2* filling, increasing.
**nutrido, -da** *adj.* nourished. *2* full, abundant.
**nutrimento** *m.* nutrition. *2* nutriment.
**nutrir** *tr.* to nourish, to feed. *2* to fill, increase.
**nutritivo, -va** *adj.* nutritive, nourishing.

**Ñ, ñ** *f.* seventeenth letter of the Spanish alphabet.

**ñame** *m.* BOT. yam [vine and root].

**ñandú** *m.* ORN. nandu, American ostrich.

**ñapa** *f.* (Am.) additional amount; something over or extra: *de* ~, to boot, into the bargain.

**ñaque** *m.* junk, pile of junk.

**ñiquiñaque** *m.* trash, worthless person of thing.

**ñoclo** *m.* a kind of macaroon.

**ñoñería** *f.* silly remark, inanity.

**ñoñez** *f.* silliness, inanity.

**ñoño, -ña** *adj.* feeble-minded. *2* silly, inane.

**ñu** *m.* ZOOL. gnu.

**ñudo** *m.* NUDO.

**ñudoso, -sa** *adj.* NUDOSO.

# O

**O, o** *f.* O, o, eighteenth letter of the Spanish alphabet.

**o** *conj.* or; either: *el uno ~ el otro*, either the one or the other.

**oasis,** *pl.* **-sis** *m.* oasis.

**obcecación** *f.* mental obfuscation or blindness.

**obcecar** *tr.* to obfuscate, blind. *2 ref.* to become obfuscated.

**obduración** *f.* obduracy, obstinacy.

**obedecer** *tr.-intr.* to obey. *2* to respond, yield [to a force, stimulus, etc.]. *3* to be due [to], arise [from]. ¶ CONJUG. like *agradecer.*

**obediencia** *f.* obedience.

**obediente** *adj.* obedient.

**obelisco, obelo** *m.* obelisk. *2* PRINT. dagger (†).

**obencadura** *f.* NAUT. shrouds [collectively].

**obenque** *m.* NAUT. shroud.

**obertura** *f.* MUS. overture.

**obesidad** *f.* obesity, obeseness, fatness.

**obeso, -sa** *adj.* obese, fat, fleshy.

**óbice** *m.* obstacle, impediment, hindrance.

**obispado** *m.* bishopric, episcopate. *2* diocese.

**obispal** *adj.* episcopal.

**obispillo** *m.* boy bishop. *2* rump [of a fowl]. *3* large blood pudding.

**obispo** *m.* ECCL. bishop. *2* OBISPILLO 3.

**óbito** *m.* death, decease.

**obituario** *m.* ECCL. obituary.

**objeción** *f.* objection.

**objetante** *adj.* objecting. *2 m.-f.* objector.

**objetar** *tr.* to object [adduce, state as objection].

**objetivar** *tr.* to objectify, objectivate.

**objetividad** *f.* objectivity.

**objetivo, -va** *adj.* objective. *2 m.* objective [aim, end of action]. *4* MIL., OPT. objective.

**objeto** *m.* object [in practically every sense, except the grammatical one]. *2* thing. *3* subject matter. *4* objective, aim, end, purpose.

**oblación** *f.* oblation.

**oblata** *f.* ECCL. in the Mass, the bread and wine before Consecration.

**oblato, -ta** *m.-f.* ECCL. oblate.

**oblea** *f.* wafer [for sealing letters].

**oblicuar** *tr.* to cant, slant, give an oblique direction to. *2 intr.* MIL. to oblique.

**oblicuo, cua** *adj.* oblique, slanting. *2* GEOM. oblique.

**obligación** *f.* obligation. *2* duty, charge, engage-

ment, debt. *3* COM. debenture, bond. *5 pl.* family responsabilities. *6* COM. liabilities.

**obligacionista** *m.-f.* bondholder.

**obligado, -da** *adj.* obliged. *2 m.* MUS. obbligato.

**obligar** *tr.* to obligate, oblige, bind. *2* to compel, force. *3 ref.* to obligate or bind oneself.

**obligatorio, -ria** *adj.* obligatory, compulsory.

**obliteración** *f.* MED. obliteration, obstruction.

**obliterar** *tr.* MED. to obliterate, obstruct.

**oblongo, -ga** *adj.* oblong.

**óboe** *m.* oboe. *2* oboist.

**oboísta** *m.-f.* oboist.

**óbolo** *m.* obol. *2* mite [small contribution].

**obra** *f.* work, piece of work; task: *~ de manos*, handwork; *poner por ~*, to carry into effect or execution. *2* work, act, deed: *buena ~, ~ de caridad*, good work, charity. *3* THEOL. work. *4* work [piece of literary or musical composition, book, painting, etc.]: *~ de arte*, work of art; *~ de consulta*, reference work; *~ maestra*, masterpiece. *5* THEAT. piece, play, drama. *6* works [of an author]. *7* building under construction; repair work [in a building]. *8* FORT. work: *~ exterior*, outwork. *9* means, virtue, agence. *10* NAUT. *~ muerta*, upper works; *~ viva*, quickwork. *11 ~ pía*, charitable foundation. *12 pl. obras públicas*, public works.

*13 adv. ~ de*, a matter of, about.

**obrador, -ra** *adj.* working. *2 m.-f.* worker. *3 m.* workshop.

**obrar** *tr.* to work, fashion, make. *2* to work, do, effect. *3* to build, construct. *4 intr.* to act, behave, proceed. *5* to act [produce an effect]. *6* to evacuate bowels. *7 obra en mi poder*, I have in my possession.

**obrepticio, cia** *adj.* obreptitious.

**obrerista** *adj.* [pertaïning to] labour. *2 m.-f.* labo(u)rist, labo(u)rite.

**obrero, -ra** *adj.* working: *la clase obrera*, the working classes. *2 m.-f.* labourer, worker, workman, workwoman. *3 m.* churchwarden.

**obrita** *f.* dim. little work; booklet.

**obrizo** *adj.* pure, refined [gold].

**obscenidad** *f.* obscenity.

**obsceno, -na** *adj.* obscene, indecent, lewd.

**obscurantismo** *m.* obscurantism.

**obscuras (a)** *adv.* in the dark.

**obscurecer** *tr.* to obscure, darken. *2* to obscure [confuse, dim, outshine, tarnish]. *3* PAINT. to

shade. *4 impers.* to grow dark. *5 ref.* to darken [become dark]. *6* to become cloudy. ¶ CONJUG. like *agradecer.*
**obscurezco, obscurezca,** etc. *irr.* V. OBSCURECER.
**obscurecimiento** *m.* obscuration, darkening. *2* clouding. *3* PAINT. shading.
**obscuridad** *f.* obscurity. *2* darkness, gloom.
**obscuro, -ra** *adj.* obscure. *2* dark [gloomy; dusky; cloudy]. *3* dark [colour]. *4* uncertain, dubious. *5 m.* dark colo(u)r, dark clothes.
**obsecración** *f.* obsecration.
**obsecuencia** *f.* compliance, obedience.
**obsecuente** *adj.* compliant, obedient.
**obsequiador, -ra; obsequiante** *m.-f.* one who pays attentions, who gives presents, entertains, etc. *2* courter, wooer.
**obsequiar** *tr.* to pay attentions to; to make presents to; to treat, entertain: ~ *con,* to treat to; to present with. *2* to court, woo.
**obsequio** *m.* attention shown, courtesy; treat; present, gift: *en ~ de,* in honour of.
**obsequioso, -sa** *adj.* obsequious, obliging, attentive.
**observable** *adj.* observable, noticeable.
**observación** *f.* observation [noticing, being noticed; watching]: *en ~,* under observation. *2* MIL., ASTR. observation. *3* observation, remark, note.
**observador, -ra** *adj.* observing, observant. *2 m.-f.* observer.
**observancia** *f.* observance.
**observante** *adj.* observant, observing.
**observar** *tr.* to observe [take notice of; watch]. *2* to observe [law, command, etc.].
**observatorio** *m.* observatory.
**obsesión** *f.* obsession.
**obsesionante** *adj.* obsessing.
**obsesionar** *tr.* to obsess.
**obseso, -sa** *adj.* obsessed.
**obsidiana** *f.* MINER. obsidian.
**obsidional** *adj.* obsidional.
**obstaculizar** *tr.* to prevent, hinder, obstruct.
**obstáculo** *m.* obstacle.
**obstante (no)** *conj.* notwithstanding; nevertheless.
**obstar** *intr.* to stand in the way, be an obstacle.
**obstetricia** *f.* obstetrics, obstetricy.
**obstinación** *f.* obstinacy, stubbornness, obduracy.
**obstinado, -da** *adj.* obstinate, stubborn.
**obstinarse** *ref.* ~ *en,* to be obstinate in or about; to persist in, to insist on.
**obstrucción** *f.* obstruction.
**obstruccionismo** *m.* obstructionism.
**obstruir** *tr.* to obstruct, block, clog, stop up. *2* to obstruct, impede. *3 ref.* to become obstructed. ¶ CONJUG. like *huir.*
**obstruyo, obstruyó, obstruya,** etc. *irr.* V. OBSTRUIR.
**obtemperar** *tr.* to obey, to assent.
**obtención** *f.* attainment, obtaining, obtention.
**obtener** *tr.* to attain, obtain, get; to procure.
**obtentor** *m.* obtainer.
**obturación** *f.* obturation.
**obturador, -ra** *adj.* obturating, stopping. *2 m.* stopper, plug. *3* SURG. obturator. *4* PHOT. shutter, obturator. *5* AUTO. throttle.
**obturar** *tr.* to obturate, close, plug, stop up. *2* AUTO. to throttle.
**obtusángulo** *adj.* obtuse-angled.
**obtuso, -sa** *adj.* GEOM. obtuse. *2* obtuse [of blunt form]. *3* obtuse, dull, slow of perception.
**obús** *m.* ARTILL. howitzer.
**obvención** *f.* perquisite.

**obviar** *tr.* to obviate, remove, surmount.
**obvio, -via** *adj.* obvious, evident.
**oca** *f.* ORN. goose. *2* BOT. oca. *3* royal goose [game].
**ocarina** *f.* MUS. ocarina.
**ocasión** *f.* occasion, opportunity, chance. *2* occasion, cause. *3* occasion [time of an ocurrence]: *en ~ de,* on the occasion of. *4 de ~,* secondhand.
**ocasionado, -da** *adj.* liable, exposed [to a specified contingency, etc.].
**ocasional** *adj.* occasional, chance, accidental. *2* occasional [acting as the occasion].
**ocasionar** *tr.* to occasion, cause.
**ocaso** *m.* west. *2* setting [of any heavenly body]; sunset. *3* fig. decadence, decline.
**occidental** *adj.* occidental, western. *2* Occidental. *3 m.-f.* Occidental [person].
**occidente** *m.* occident, west. *2* Occident.
**occipital** *adj.* ANAT. occipital.
**occipucio** *m.* ANAT. occiput.
**occiso, -sa** *adj.* killed.
**Oceanía** *pr. n.* GEOG. Oceania.
**oceánico, -ca** *adj.* oceanic.
**océano** *m.* ocean.
**oceanografía** *f.* oceanography.
**ocelo** *m.* ZOOL. ocellus.
**ocelote** *m.* ZOOL. ocelot.
**ocena** *f.* MED. ozaena, ozena, foul breath.
**ocio** *m.* idleness, leisure. *2* pastime, diversion.
**ociosidad** *f.* idleness.
**ocioso, -sa** *adj.* idle [doing nothing]. *2* idle, useles; needless.
**ocluir** *tr.* MED. to occlude. ¶ CONJUG. like *huir.*
**oclusión** *f.* MED., PHON. occlusion.
**oclusivo, -va** *adj.* occlusive.
**ocozol** *m.* BOT. sweet gum, liquidambar tree.
**ocre** *m.* MINER. ocher: ~ *rojo,* red ocher.
**octaedro** *m.* GEOM. octahedron.
**octagonal** *adj.* octagonal.
**octágono, -na** *adj.* octagonal. *2 m.* octagon.
**octano** *m.* CHEM. octane.
**octava** *f.* ECCL., FENC., MUS., PROS. octave. *2* PROS. ~ *real,* hendecasyllabic octave, rhymed ababacc.
**octaviano, -na** *adj.* Octavian.
**octavilla** *f.* eighth part of a sheet of paper. *2* PROS. octosyllabic octave.
**octavín** *m.* MUS. piccolo [flute].
**Octavio** *m. pr. n.* Octavius.
**octavo, -va** *adj.-m.* eigth. *2* PRINT. *en ~,* octavo.
**octingentésimo, -ma** *adj.-m.* eight hundredth.
**octogenario, -ria** *adj.-n.* octogenarian.
**octogésimo, -ma** *adj.-m.* eightieth.
**octogonal** *adj.* OCTAGONAL.
**octógono, -na** *adj.-m.* OCTÁGONO.
**octosílabo, -ba** *adj.* octosyllabic. *2 m.* PROS. octosyllable.
**octubre** *m.* October.
**óctuplo** *adj.-m.* octuple.
**ocular** *adj.* ocular. *2 m.* OPT. ocular, eyepiece.
**oculista** *m.-f.* oculist, eye-specialist.
**ocultación** *f.* concealing. *2* ASTR. occultation.
**ocultar** *tr.* to conceal, hide, cover, secret: ~ *algo a uno,* to hide something from someone. *2* to occult. *3 ref.* to hide [intr.]. *4 no se me oculta que,* I see, I understand that.
**ocultismo** *m.* occultism.
**oculto, -ta** *adj.* hidden, concealed. *2* occult. *3 adv. de ~,* incognit; secretly.
**ocupación** *f.* occupation. *2* occupancy.
**ocupado, -da** *adj.* occupied, busy, engaged.
**ocupante** *adj.* occupying. *2 m.-f.* occupier, occupant.

**ocupar** *tr.* to occupy. *2* to employ, give work to. *3* to engage the attention of. *4 ref. ocuparse en* or *de,* to busy oneself with, be engaged in, to devote oneself to.
**ocurrencia** *f.* occurrence, event, occasion. *2* witticism, witty remark, sally. *3* bright idea.
**ocurrente** *adj.* occurring. *2* bright, witty [person].
**ocurrir** *intr.* to occur, befall, happen. *2 ref.* to occur, strike [come into one's mind].
**ochavado, -da** *adj.* eight-sided.
**ochavo** *m.* small copper coin.
**ochenta** *adj.-n.* eighty.
**ochentavo, -va** *adj.-m.* eightieth.
**ochentón, -na** *adj.-n.* octogenarian.
**ocho** *adj.-n.* eight: *las ~,* eight o'clock. *2 m.* eight [in dates].
**ochocientos, -tas** *adj.-m.* eight hundred.
**oda** *f.* ode.
**odalisca** *f.* odalisque.
**odeón** *m.* ARCHEOL. odeum.
**odiar** *tr.* to hate.
**odio** *m.* hatred, hate; odium.
**odioso, -sa** *adj.* odious, hateful.
**Odisea** *f. pr. n.* MYTH. Odyssey. *2 f.* fig. odyssey.
**odontoceto, -ta** *adj.-m.* ZOOL. odontocete.
**odontología** *f.* odontology.
**odontólogo** *m.* odontologist.
**odorante** *adj.* odorous, fragant.
**odorífero, -ra; odorífico, -ca** *adj.* odoriferous.
**odre** *m.* winebag, wineskin. *2* fig. drunkard.
**oeste** *m.* west. *2* west wind.
**ofendedor, -ra** *adj.-n.* OFENSOR.
**ofender** *tr.* to offend, attack, injure, hurt. *2* to offend, give offence. *3* to be offensive to [as a smell, etc.]. *4 ref.* to take offence.
**ofensa** *f.* offence, attack. *2* offence [wounding the feelings, umbrage]; insult.
**ofensión** *f.* offence, harm, wrong, injury.
**ofensiva** *f.* offensive.
**ofensivo, -va** *adj.* offensive.
**ofensor, -ra** *adj.* offending. *2 m.-f.* offender [one who attacks or gives offence].
**oferente** *adj.* offering. *2 m.-f.* offerer.
**oferta** *f.* offer. *2* offering, gift. *3* COM. *la ~ y la demanda,* supply and demand.
**ofertorio** *m.* ECCL. offertory.
**oficial** *adj.* official. *2 m.* journeyman [skilled worker]. *3* clerk [in an office]: *~ mayor,* chief clerk. *4* MIL., NAV. commissioned officer below major. *5* MAR. officer. *6* MIL. *~ general,* general.
**oficiala** *f.* skilled workwoman.
**oficialidad** *f.* official nature. *2* MIL., NAV. the officers [collectivelly].
**oficiante** *m.* ECCL. officiant.
**oficiar** *tr.* ECCL. to officiate. *2* to make known by official letter. *3 intr.* to officiate, act.
**oficina** *f.* office, bureau. *2* workshop. *3* pharmacist's laboratory.
**oficinal** *adj.* MED., PHARM. officinal.
**oficinesco, -ca** *adj.* office, clerical, bureaucratic.
**oficinista** *m.-f.* clerk, office worker.
**oficio** *m.* work, occupation, calling, -trade, craft, handicraft: *artes y oficios,* arts and crafts; *de ~,* by trade. *2* office [duty, function, role]. *3* office, service: *buenos oficios,* good offices. *4* official letter. *5* ECCL. office. *6 Santo Oficio,* Holy Office.
**oficiosidad** *f.* officiousness. *2* diligence. *3* obligingness.
**oficioso, -sa** *adj.* officious, meddlesome. *2* DIPL. officious. *3* unofficial. *4* diligent. *5* obliging.
**ofidio, día** *adj.-m.* ZOOL. ophidian.

**ofiuroideo, -a** *adj.-m.* ZOOL. ophiuroidean.
**ofrecedor, -ra** *m.-f.* offerer.
**ofrecer** *tr.* to offer, present, tender, hold out, proffer. *2* to offer, promise. *3* to offer [present to sight or notice]. *4* COM. to offer; to bid. *5 ref.* to offer, occur, present itself. *6* to volunteer, offer [to]. ¶ CONJUG. like *agradecer.*
**ofreciente** *m.-f.* offerer.
**ofrecimiento** *m.* offer, offering, promise.
**ofrenda** *f.* offering, religious offering.
**ofrendar** *tr.* to offer, make an offering of.
**ofrezco, ofrezca,** etc. *irr.* V. OFRECER.
**oftalmía** *f.* MED. ophthalmia.
**oftálmico, -ca** *adj.* ophthalmic.
**oftalmología** *f.* ophthalmology.
**ofuscación** *f.,* **ofuscamiento** *m.* obfuscation. *2* dazzling, dazzle [by excess of light].
**ofuscar** *tr.* to obfuscate. *2* to dazzle [by excess of light].
**ogro** *m.* ogre.
**¡oh!** *interj.* o!, oh!
**ohm, ohmio** *m.* ELECT. ohm.
**oíble** *adj.* audible.
**oída** *f.* hearing [act]. *2 de oídas,* by hearsay.
**oidio** *m.* BOT. oidium.
**oído** *m.* hearing [sense]; ear [organ of hearing]: *aguzar los oídos,* to prick up one's ears; *dar oídos a,* to listen favourably, to believe; *hacer oídos de mercader,* to turn a deaf ear; *tener ~, tener buen ~,* to have an ear for music; *al ~,* in the ear, confidentially; *de ~,* by ear. *2* ANAT. internal ear. *3* FIREARMS. vent, priming hole, touchhole.
**oidor, -ra** *m.-f.* hearer. *2 m.* formerly, a judge.
**oigo, oiga,** etc. *irr.* V. OÍR.
**oír** *tr.* to hear [perceive by the ear; listen; grant prayer, accept advice]: *~ hablar de,* to hear about, or of; *oí cantar a tu hermana,* I heard your sister singing; *¡oiga!, ¡oigan!,* I say, listen; the idea!, well!; *~ misa,* to hear Mass. ¶ CONJUG.: INDIC. Pres.: *oigo, oyes, oye;* oímos, oís, *oyen.* | Pret.: *oí,* oiste, *oyó;* oímos, oísteis, *oyeron.* | SUBJ. Pres.: *oiga, oigas, oiga; oigamos, oigáis, oigan.* | Imperf.: *oyera, oyeras,* etc., *o oyese, oyeses,* etc. | Fut.: *oyere, oyeres,* etc. | IMPER.: *oye, oiga;* oigamos, oíd, *oigan.* | Past. p.: *oído.* | GER.: *oyendo.*
**oíslo** *m.-f.* beloved one; wife.
**ojal** *m.* buttonhole. *2* eyelet, eyelet hole.
**¡ojalá!** *interj.* would to God!, God grant!, I wish!
**ojalar** *tr.* to make buttonholes in.
**ojaranzo** *m.* BOT. hornbeam. *2* ADELFA.
**ojazo** *m.* augm. large eye.
**ojeada** *f.* glance [brief look]: *echar una ~ a,* to cast a glance at.
**ojeador** *m.* HUNT. beater.
**ojear** *tr.* HUNT. to beat for [game]. *2* to chase away. *3* to eye.
**ojeo** *m.* HUNT. beating for game.
**ojera** *f.* eye cup, eyeglass. *2 pl.* rings under the eyes.
**ojeriza** *f.* animosity, grudge, spite, ill vill.
**ojeroso, -sa** *adj.* having rings under the eyes.
**ojete** *m.* eyelet, eye hole.
**ojimel, ojimiel** *m.* PHARM. oxymel.
**ojinegro, -gra** *adj.* coll. black-eyed.
**ojituerto, -ta** *adj.* coll. squint-eyed.
**ojiva** *f.* ARCH. ogive.
**ojival** *adj.* ARCH. ogival.
**ojizarco, -ca** *adj.* coll. blue-eyed.
**ojo** *m.* eye [organ of sight; attention, care, notice; way of thinking, estimation]: *ojos blandos* or *tiernos,* bleary eyes, watery eyes; *ojos saltones,*

bulging eyes, goggle eyes; *abrir los ojos a uno*, to open someone's eyes [disabuse him, make him realize]; *cerrar los ojos a uno*, to wait on a dying person; *costar un ~*, or *los ojos, de la cara*, to cost a mint of money; *echar el ~ a*, to have one's eyes on [regard with desire]; *írsele a uno los ojos por* or *tras*, to gaze longingly, to desire; *llenar el ~*, to please; *no pegar el ~* or *los ojos*, coll. not to sleep a wink; *poner los ojos en blanco*, to roll the eyes; *saltar a los ojos*, to be self-evident; *a ~* [of an estimation, etc.], by guess, without taking any measurement: *a ojos cerrados*, blindly, without examination; *a ojos vistas*, visibly, obviously; *en un abrir y cerrar de ojos*, in the twinkling of an eye; *¡ojo!, ¡mucho ~!*, look out!, beware!
2 eye, hole, perforation. 3 eye [of neddle, axe, spade, etc.]. 4 bow [of a key]. 5 eye [in cheese]; hole [in bread]. 6 speck of grease in soup. 7 well [of stairs]. 8 span, bay [of bridge]. 9 PRINT. face [of type]. 10 ~ *de buey*, BOT. oxeye; ARCH. bull's eye. 11 ~ *de gallo*, ~ *de pollo*, corn [on toe]. 12 ~ *de la cerradura*, keyhole. 13 RADIO. ~ *mágico*, magic eye.
**ojoso, -sa** *adj.* eyey.
**ojuelos** *m. pl.* small or sparkling eyes. 2 spectacles.
**ola** *f.* wave, billow, surge, swell [on a liquid]. 2 fig. wave [of heat, cold, etc.]. 3 surge [of heat, cold, etc.]. 3 surge [of a crowd].
**olé** *m.* an Andalusian dance. 2 *interj.* bravo!
**oleáceo, -a** *adj.* BOT. oleaceous.
**oleada** *f.* large wave, surge, swell. 2 surge [of a crowd]. 3 MIL. wave.
**oleaginoso, -sa** *adj.* oleaginous, oily.
**oleaje** *m.* surge, succession of waves, motion or rush of waves.
**oleastro** *m.* BOT., ACEBUCHE.
**oleato** *m.* CHEM. oleate.
**oledor, -ra** *adj.* smelling. 2 *m.-f.* smeller.
**oleico** *adj.* CHEM. oleic.
**óleo** *m.* oil, olive oil; chrism, holy oil: *los santos óleos*, the chrism, the holy oil. 2 PAINT. *al ~*, oil, in oil colours.
**oleoducto** *m.* pipe line.
**oleografía** *f.* oleograph.
**oleoso, -sa** *adj.* oleaginous, oily.
**oler** *tr.* to smell, scent, sniff, snuff [perceive odours, detect presence of by smell]. 2 to smell, scent [find out, suspect]. 3 fig. to pry into. 4 *intr.* to smell [emit an odour; suggest]: ~ *a*, to smell like, smell of, to smack of; *no ~ bien*, to look suspicious.
**olfacción** *f.* olfaction [act of smelling].
**olfatear** *tr.* to smell, scent, sniff [eagerly]. 2 fig. to pry into, to try to discover.
**olfativo, -va** *adj.* olfactory.
**olfato** *m.* smell, nose [sense of smell]. 2 fig. nose, sagacious sense.
**olíbano** *m.* frankincense.
**oliente** *adj.* smelling, odorous.
**oligarca** *m.* oligarch.
**oligarquía** *f.* oligarchy.
**oligoceno, -na** *adj.-n.* GEOL. Oligocene.
**Olimpia** *f. pr. n.* GEOG. Olympia.
**olimpíada** *f.* Olympiad. 2 Olympic games.
**olímpico, -ca** *adj.* Olympic, Olympian. 2 fig. haughty.
**Olimpo** *m. pr. n.* GEOG., MYTH. Olympus.
**oliscar** *tr.* to smell, sniff. 2 *intr.* [of meat] to be tainted, gamey.

**oliva** *f.* olive. 2 olive tree. 3 fig. olive branch, peace. 4 ORN. barn owl.
**oliváceo, -a** *adj.* olivaceous.
**olivar** *m.* olive plantation, oliveyard.
**olivarero, -ra** *adj.* olive [growing, industry, etc.].
**olivera** *f.* OLIVO 1.
**Oliverio** *m. pr. n.* Oliver.
**olivillo** *m.* BOT. a kind of mock privet.
**olivo** *m.* BOT. olive tree.
**olmeda** *f.*, **olmedo** *m.* elm grove.
**olmo** *m.* BOT. elm tree.
**ológrafo, -fa** *adj.-m.* LAW holograph.
**olor** *m.* odour, smell, fragance. 2 fig. promise, hope. 3 fig. ~ *de santidad*, odour of sanctity.
**olorizar** *tr.* to scent, perfume.
**oloroso, -sa** *adj.* odorous, fragrant.
**olvidadizo** *adj.* forgetful. 2 ungrateful.
**olvidado, -da** *adj.* forgotten. 2 forgetful; oblivious.
**olvidar** *tr.-ref.* to forget; to be forgotten: *lo he olvidado, se me ha olvidado*, I have forgotten it. 2 *ref.* *olvidarse de*, to forget.
**olvido** *m.* forgetfulness. 2 omission, oversight, neglect. 3 oblivion: *caer en el ~*, to fall into oblivion.
**olla** *f.* pot, boiler, kettle [bulging pot used in cooking]; ~ *de grillos*, fig. pandemonium; ~ *de presión*, pressure cooker. 2 COOK. dish of boiled meat and vegetables. 3 eddy, whirlpool [in a river].
**ollao** *m.* NAUT. eyelet hole.
**ollar** *m.* horse's nostril.
**ollería** *f.* pottery. 2 earthenware shop.
**ollero** *m.* potter. 2 dealer in earthenware.
**ombligo** *m.* ANAT., ZOOL. navel. 2 navel-string. 3 navel, centre, middle.
**omega** *f.* omega [Greek letter].
**omento** *m.* ANAT. omentum.
**ominoso, -sa** *adj.* ominous, of evil omen. 2 odious, execrable.
**omisión** *f.* omission.
**omiso, -sa** *adj.* neglectful, remiss, careless.
**omitir** *tr.* to omit, drop, leave out.
**ómnibus, pl. -bus** *m.* omnibus.
**omnímodo, -da** *adj.* all-embracing, full, absolute.
**omnipotencia** *f.* omnipotence.
**omnipotente** *adj.* omnipotent, almighty: *el Omnipotente*, the Almighty [God].
**omnipresencia** *f.* omnipresence.
**omnipresente** *adj.* omnipresent.
**omnisciencia** *f.* omniscience.
**omnisciente; omniscio, cia** *adj.* omniscient.
**omnívoro, -ra** *adj.* omnivorous.
**omóplato** *m.* ANAT. shoulder blade.
**onagro** *m.* ZOOL. onager.
**onanismo** *m.* onanism.
**once** *adj.-m.* eleven: *las ~*, eleven o'clock. 2 *m.* eleventh [in dates]. 4 FOOTBALL eleven [team].
**onceno, -na** *adj.-m.* eleventh.
**onda** *f.* wave, ripple [on surface of water]. 2 wave [in hair, cloth, etc.]. 3 SEW. scallop. 4 PHYS. wave: ~ *amortiguada*, ELECT. damped wave; ~ *luminosa*, light wave; ~ *portadora*, RADIO. carrier wave; ~ *sonora*, sound wave. 5 *pl.* fig. the water [of sea, river or lake].
**ondeante** *adj.* waving, undulating.
**ondear** *intr.* [of water] to rise in waves, to ripple. 2 to wave [as a flag, a field of corn, etc.], to flutter, undulate. 3 to be wavy. 4 *ref.* to wave, sway, swing.
**ondina** *f.* MYTH. undine.
**ondoso, -sa** *adj.* wavy.

**ondulación** *f.* undulation. *2* wave [of hair]: ~ *permanente*, permanent wave.
**ondulado, -da** *adj.* undulated; rippled. *2* wavy. *3* billowy [ground]. *4* corrugated. *5* scalloped.
**ondulante** *adj.* undulating, waving.
**ondular** *intr.* to undulate, wave, ripple, billow, roll. *2 tr.* to wave [the hair].
**ondulatorio, -ria** *adj.* undulatory.
**oneroso, -sa** *adj.* onerous, burdensome.
**ónice, ónique** *f.* MINER. onyx.
**onírico, -ca** *adj.* oneiric.
**ónix** *f.* ÓNICE.
**onomástico, -ca** *adj.* onomastic.
**onomatopeya** *f.* onomatopœia.
**onomatopéyico, -ca** *adj.* onomatopœic.
**onoquiles** *f.* BOT. alkanet.
**ontogenia** *f.* ontogeny.
**ontología** *f.* ontology.
**onza** *f.* ounce [weight]. *2* ZOOL. ounce. *3* ~ *de oro*, Spanish doubloon.
**onzavo, -va** *adj.-m.* eleventh.
**oosfera** *f.* BOT. oösphere.
**opacidad** *f.* opacity.
**opaco, -ca** *adj.* opaque [not transparent; dark; dull].
**opalescencia** *f.* opalescence.
**opalescente** *adj.* opalescent.
**opalino, -na** *adj.* opaline.
**ópalo** *m.* MINER. opal.
**opción** *f.* option, choice. *2* COM. option.
**ópera** *f.* opera: ~ *bufa*, opera bouffe.
**operación** *f.* operation [working, action, process, performance]. *2* COM., MATH., SURG. operation. *3 pl.* MIL. operations.
**operador, -ra** *m.-f.* operator.
**operante** *adj.* operating, operative, working.
**operar** *tr.* SURG. to operate upon. *2 intr.* to operate [produce an appropiate effect]. *3* COM., MIL., NAV., SURG. to operate.
**operatorio, -ria** *m.-f.* operative, worker, workman, working woman.
**operativo, -va** *adj.* operative, operating.
**operatorio, -ria** *adj.* operating, working. *2* SURG. operative.
**opérculo** *m.* BOT., ZOOL. operculum.
**opereta** *f.* operetta, light opera.
**opiato, -ta** *adj.-m.* opiate.
**opilación** *f.* MED. oppilation, obstruction.
**opimo, -ma** *adj.* rich, fruitful, abundant.
**opinable** *adj.* debatable, being a matter of opinion.
**opinante** *adj.* opiner.
**opinar** *intr.* to opine. *2 tr.* to judge, think, be of the opinion that.
**opinión** *f.* opinion: *mudar de* ~, to change one's mind; *tener en buena* ~, to have a good opinion of.
**opio** *m.* opium.
**opíparo, -ra** *adj.* sumptuous, plentiful [banquet, etc.].
**opondré, opondría**, etc. *irr.* V. OPONER.
**oponer** *tr.* to oppose [a thing to another]. *2* to offer [resistance]. *3 ref. oponerse a*, to oppose oneself to; to oppose [resist, antagonize, set oneself against; to stand opposite to]; go against, be contrary to. *4 ref.* to oppose each other. ¶ CONJUG. like *poner*.
**oponga**, etc. *irr.* V. OPONER.
**oponible** *adj.* opposable.
**Oporto** *m. pr. n.* GEOG. Oporto, Porto. *2 m.* port wine.

**oportunidad** *f.* opportunity; opportuneness.
**oportunismo** *m.* opportunism.
**oportunista** *adj.* opportunistic. *2 m.-f.* opportunist.
**oportuno, -na** *adj.* opportune, suitable, timely. *2* witty [in conversation].
**oposición** *f.* opposition [act of opposing; being opposed]. POL., ASTR.. opposition. *3* competitive examination.
**oposicionista** *m.* POL. memberr of the opposition.
**opositor, -ra** *m.-f.* opposer. *2* competitor [for a position or office].
**opoterapia** *f.* MED. organotherapy.
**opresión** *f.* oppression. *2* pressing.
**opresivo, -va** *adj.* oppressive.
**opreso, -sa** *adj.* oppressed.
**opresor, -ra** *adj.* oppressing. *2 m.-f.* oppressor.
**oprimir** *tr.* to press, press down, push, pinch, lay heavy on, weigh down. *2* to oppress.
**oprobiar** *tr.* to defame, revile, disgrace.
**oprobio** *m.* opprobium, ignominy, disgrace.
**oprobioso, -sa** *adj.* opprobrious, disgraceful.
**optar** *intr.* to opt, choose. *2* ~ *a*, to be a candidate for [a position or office].
**optativo, -va** *adj.* optional. *2* GRAM. optative.
**óptica** *f.* optics. *2* stereoscope.
**óptico, -ca** *adj.* optic, optical. *2 m.* optician.
**optimismo** *m.* optimism.
**optimista** *adj.* optimistic, sanguine. *2 m.-f.* optimist.
**óptimo, -ma** *adj.* optimal, optimum, best.
**optómetro** *m.* optometer.
**opuesto, -ta** *adj.* opposed. *2* opposite. *3* contrary, adverse. *4* BOT. opposite.
**opugnar** *tr.* oppugn. *2* to attack, assault, invest.
**opulencia** *f.* opulence.
**opulento, -ta** *adj.* opulent.
**opúsculo** *m.* opuscle, booklet, tract.
**opuse, opusiera**, etc. *irr.* V. OPONER.
**oquedad** *f.* hollow, cavity. *2* hollowness.
**oquedal** *m.* grove of lofty trees without underbrush.
**ora** *conj.* now, then, whether: ~ *ríe*, ~ *llora*, now he laughs, now [or then] he cries.
**oración** *f.* oration, discourse. *2* prayer, orison: ~ *dominical*, Lord's prayer; *hacer* ~, to pray. *3* dusk, sunset [the Angelus hour]. *4* GRAM. sentence, clause.
**oráculo** *m.* oracle.
**orador, -ra** *m.-f.* orator, speaker.
**oral** *adj.* oral [spoken, not written]. *2* ZOOL. oral.
**orangután** *m.* ZOOL. orang-outang.
**orante** *adj.* F. ARTS. praying.
**orar** *intr.* to pray: ~ *por*, to pray for. *2* to speak, make a speech.
**orate** *m.-f.* lunatic, madman, madwoman.
**oratoria** *f.* oratory, speaking.
**oratorio, -ria** *adj.* oratorical. *2 m.* oratory. *3* MUS. oratorio.
**orbe** *m.* orb, sphere. *2* the earth, the world.
**orbicular** *adj.* orbicular.
**órbita** *f.* ASTR. orbit. *2* sphere, field [of action, etc.]. *3* ANAT. orbit, eye-socket.
**orca** *f.* ZOOL. orca.
**Orcadas (Islas)** *f. pr. n.* GEOG. Orkney Islands.
**orcaneta** *f.* BOT. alkanet.
**órdago (de)** *adj.* coll. swell, grand, excellent.
**ordalías** *f. pl.* ordeals [trial by fire, water, etc.].
**orden** *m.* order [arrangement, succession; method; harmonious relation of things; condition in which every part is in its right place]: *por* ~,

in order; *por su* ~, in its turn. *2* order [public quiet; rule of law]: *llamar al* ~, to call to order. *3* order, class, degree. *4* MIL. order, array. *5* ARCH., BIOL., MATH. order. *6* respect, relation: *en* ~ *a*, in respect of. *7 m.-f.* ECCL. order [sacrament, degree]. *8 f.* order [fraternity or body]: ~ *religiosa*, religious order. *9* order, command: *a la* ~ *de*, COM. to the order of; *a sus órdenes*, at your service; *en espera de sus gratas órdenes*, awaiting your commands or your pleasure [in business letters]. *10* ~ *del día*, agenda [for a meeting]; MIL. order of the day.

**ordenación** *f.* order, arrangement. *2* ECCL. ordination. *3* order, command. *4* auditor's office. *5* ARCH., PAINT. ordonnance.

**ordenada** *f.* MATH. ordinate.

**ordenado, -da** *adj.* orderly, methodical, tidy.

**ordenador, -ra** *adj.* ordering, arranging. *2* ordaining. *3 m.-f.* orderer, arranger. *4* ordainer. *5 m.* auditor [in some offices].

**ordenamiento** *m.* ordering, arrangement, regulation. *2* edict, ordinance.

**ordenancista** *adj.* strict, rigid. *2 m.-f.* disciplinarian, martinet.

**ordenando** *m.* ECCL. ordinand.

**ordenanza** *f.* order, method. *2* order, command. *3* ordinance, regulation. *4 m.* MIL. orderly. *5* errand boy [in certain offices].

**ordenar** *tr.* to order, arrange, put in order. *2* to direct [things] to an end. *3* to order, command, decree, prescribe. *4* ECCL. to ordain, confer holy orders on. *5 ref.* ECCL. to take orders.

**ordeñar** *tr.* to milk [a cow, ewe, etc.]. *2* to pick [olives] by a milking motion.

**ordinal** *adj.-n.* ordinal.

**ordinariez** *f.* ordinariness, inferior quality. *2* coarseness, grossness, vulgarity.

**ordinario, -ria** *adj.* ordinary. *2* inferior, coarse, gross, vulgar. *3 m.* daily household expense. *4* ordinary [judge, bishop]. *5* carrier, messenger. *6 de* ~, ordinarily, usually.

**orea, oréada, oréade** *f.* MYTH. Oread.

**orear** *tr.* to air [expose to open air], ventilate. *2 ref.* to become aired. *3* to take an airing.

**orégano** *m.* BOT. wild marjoram.

**oreja** *f.* ANAT. ear [sense; organ; external ear]: *pabellón de la* ~, auricle, pinna; *aguzar las orejas*, to prick up one's ears; *calentar las orejas*, to chide, dress down; *enseñar la* ~, to show the cloven foot. *2* flap [of shoe]. *3* MEC. ear, lug. *4* claw [of hammer]. *5* BOT. ~ *de oso*, bear's-ear.

**orejeado, -da** *adj.* informed, warned.

**orejear** *intr.* [of an animal] to shake or prick the ears. *2* to act with reluctance.

**orejera** *f.* ear flap, ear lap; ear muff. *2* mouldboard [of a plough].

**orejón** *m.* strip of dried peach. *2* pull on the ear.

**orejudo, -da** *adj.* big-eared, long-eared.

**oreo** *m.* airing. *2* breeze, gentle wind.

**orfanato** *m.* orphanage [institution].

**orfandad** *f.* orphanage, orphanhood. *2* abandonment, neglect.

**orfebre** *m.* glodsmith, silversmith.

**orfebrería** *f.* gold or silver work.

**Orfeo** *m. pr. n.* MYTH. Orpheus.

**orfeón** *m.* choral society.

**orfeonista** *m.-f.* member of a choral society.

**órfico, -ca** *adj.* Orphic.

**organdí** *m.* organdy.

**organero** *m.* MUS. organ builder, organ maker.

**orgánico, -ca** *adj.* organic.

**organillero** *adj.* organ-grinder.

**organillo** *m.* barrel organ, hand organ.

**organismo** *m.* organism. *2* organization, body, institution.

**organista** *m.-f.* MUS. organist.

**organización** *f.* organization.

**organizador, -ra** *adj.* organizing. *2 m.-f.* organizer.

**organizar** *tr.* to organize. *2* to set up, start. *3 ref.* to organize [intr.].

**órgano** *m.* PHYSIOL. organ. *2* organ, instrument, medium. *3* organ [newspaper, magazine, etc.]. *4* MUS. organ, pipe organ.

**organografía** *f.* organography.

**orgasmo** *m.* PHYSIOL. orgasm.

**orgía** *f.* orgy, revel.

**orgiástico, -ca** *adj.* orgiastic.

**orgullo** *m.* pride. *2* haughtiness.

**orgulloso, -sa** *adj.* proud. *2* haughty, conceited.

**orientación** *f.* orienting. *2* orientation. *3* bearings.

**oriental** *adj.* oriental, eastern. *2 adj.-n.* Oriental.

**orientalista** *m.-f.* Orientalist.

**orientar** *tr.* to orient; to orientate. *2* NAUT. to trim [a sail]. *3 ref.* to orient oneself; to guide oneself; to find one's bearings.

**oriente** *m.* east, orient. *2* east wind. *3* orient [of a pearl]. *4* (cap.) GEOG. East, Orient.

**orificar** *tr.* DENT. to fill with gold.

**orífice** *m.* goldsmith.

**orificio** *m.* orifice, hole.

**oriflama** *f.* oriflamme. *2* flag, banner.

**origen** *m.* origin. *2* native country.

**original** *adj.* original. *2* queer, -quaint, odd. *3 m.* original [of a portrait, etc.]: ~ *de imprenta*, copy, manuscript. *4* original, eccentric [person].

**originalidad** *f.* originality.

**originalmente** *adv.* originally. *2* quaintly, eccentrically.

**originar** *tr.* to originate. *2* to create, start. *3 ref.* to originate, derive, arise, spring.

**originariamente** *adv.* originally, by its origin.

**originario, -ria** *adj.* originating, of origin. *2* original, come, derived, native [from or of].

**orilla** *f.* border, margin, edge, brink, hem. *2* bank, margin [of river]; shore. *3 a la* ~, near, on the brink.

**orillar** *tr.* to arrange, settle. *2* to surmount [a difficulty]. *3 intr.* SEW. to border, hem.

**orillo** *m.* selvage, list, listing [of cloth].

*1)* **orín** *m.* rust [on iron]: *tomarse de* ~, to get rusty.

*2)* **orín** *or pl.* **orines** *m.*, **orina** *f.* urine.

**orinal** *m.* chamber pot, urinal.

**orinar** *intr.-tr.* to urinate.

**oriniento, -ta** *adj.* rusty.

**oriol** *m.* OROPÉNDOLA.

**oriundo, -da** *adj.* coming [from], native [of].

**orla** *f.* border, edging [of a garment]. *2* ornamental border [around a drawing, etc.]. *3* HER. orle.

**orladura** *f.* border, ornamental border.

**orlar** *tr.* to border, edge [a garment]; to put an ornamental border to.

**orlo** *m.* Alpine horn.

**ornado, -da** *adj.* ornate, adorned.

**ornamentación** *f.* ornamentation.

**ornamental** *adj.* ornamental.

**ornamentar** *tr.* to ornament, adorn, decorate.

**ornamento** *m.* ornament, adornment, decoration. *2* gift, moral quality. *3* ARCH. ornament. *4 pl.* ECCL. ornaments.

**ornar** *tr.* to ornament, adorn, embellish.

**ornato** *m.* adornment, embellishment; show.

**ornitología** *f.* ornithology.
**ornitólogo** *m.* ornithologist.
**ornitorrinco** *m.* ZOOL. duckbill.
**oro** *m.* gold [metal; money, wealth; precious things]; ~ *batido*, gold leaf; ~ *de ley*, standard gold; *de* ~, of gold; gold golden; *como un* ~ [clean, beautiful, bright], like gold; *de* ~ *y azul*, all dressed up; *poner de* ~ *y azul*, to upbraid, to abuse. *2* HER. or. *3 pl.* card suit equivalent to diamonds.
**orobanca** *f.* BOT. broomrape.
**orogenia** *f.* GEOL. orogeny.
**orografía** *f.* orography.
**orográfico, -ca** *adj.* orographic(al).
**orondo, -da** *adj.* big-bellied [jar, etc.]. *2* hollow, puffed up. *3* self-satisfied, proud.
**oropel** *m.* tinsel, brass foil. *2* fig. tinsel [cheap glittering thing; false show].
**oropéndola** *f.* ORN. loriot, golden oriole.
**oropimente** *m.* MINER. orpiment.
**orozuz** *m.* BOT. licorice.
**orquesta** *f.* MUS., THEAT. orchestra.
**orquestación** *f.* orchestration.
**orquestar** *tr.* to orchestrate.
**orquídeo, -dea** *adj.* BOT. orchidaceous. *2 f.* BOT. orchid.
**ortega** *f.* ORN. sand grouse.
**ortiga** *f.* BOT. nettle. *2* ZOOL. ~ *de mar*, jellyfish.
**ortivo, -va** *adj.* ASTR. ortive.
**orto** *m.* rising [of sun or star].
**ortodoxia** *f.* orthodoxy.
**ortodoxo, -xa** *adj.* orthodox.
**ortogénesis** *f.* BIOL. orthogenesis.
**ortogonal** *adj.* orthogonal.
**ortografía** *f.* orthography.
**ortográfico, -ca** *adj.* orthographical.
**ortopedia** *f.* orthopa(e)dy, orthopa(e)dics.
**ortopedista** *m.-f.* orthopa(e)dist.
**ortóptero** *adj.* ENT. orthopterous.
**oruga** *f.* ENT., MACH. caterpillar. *2* BOT. rocket. *3* rocket sauce.
**orujo** *m.* marc of grapes or olives.
**orvalle** *m.* GALLOCRESTA.
**orza** *f.* NAUT. luff, luffing. *2* NAUT. centreboard. *3* crock, earthen jar.
**orzaga** *f.* BOT. orach.
**orzar** *intr.* NAUT. to luff.
**orzuelo** *m.* MED. sty [in one's eye].
**os** *pers. pron. pl. m.-f.* [object of the verb] you, to you, for you; [recip.] each other; [ref.] yourselves.
**osa** *f.* ZOOL. she-bear. *2* (cap.) ASTR. *Osa Mayor*, Great Bear; *Osa Menor*, Little Bear.
**osadía** *f.* audacity, boldness, daring, hardihood.
**osado, -da** *adj.* audacious, bold, daring, hardy.
**osambre** *m.* **osamenta** *f.* skeleton, bones.
1) **osar** *intr.* to dare, venture.
2) **osar, osario** *m.* charnel-house, ossuary.
**oscilación** *f.* oscillation.
**oscilador** *m.* ELECT., RADIO. oscillator.
**oscilar** *intr.* to oscillate.
**oscilatorio, -ria** *adj.* oscillatory.
**osculación** *f.* GEOM. oscullation.
**ósculo** *m.* kiss. *2* ZOOL. osculum.
**oscurantismo, oscurecer, oscuridad**, etc. = OBSCU-RANTISMO, OBSCURECER, OBSCURIDAD, etc.
**osecillo, osecito** *m.* dim. small bone, bonelet.
**óseo, -a** *adj.* osseous, bony.
**osera** *f.* den of bears.
**osezno** *m.* cub or whelp of a bear.
**osificarse** *ref.* to ossify [become ossified].

**osífraga** *f.*, **osífrago** *m.* QUEBRANTAHUESOS 2.
**osmanlí** *adj.-n.* Osmanli.
**osmio** *m.* CHEM. osmium.
**ósmosis** *f.* PHYS. osmosis.
**oso** *m.* ZOOL. bear: ~ *blanco*, polar bear; ~ *gris*, grizzly bear; ~ *pardo*, brown bear; *hacer el* ~, fig. to make a fool of oneself; to court a woman. *2* ZOOL. ~ *hormiguero*, anteater. *3* ZOOL. ~ *marsupial*, koala.
**ososo, -sa** *adj.* osseous, bony.
**¡oste!** *interj.* ¡OXTE!
**ostensible** *adj.* ostensible, visible, manifest.
**ostensión** *f.* show, manifestation.
**ostensivo, -va** *adj.* ostensive, showing.
**ostensorio** *m.* ECCL. ostensory, monstrance.
**ostentación** *f.* ostentation, parade, display, show, vain show. *2* exhibition, manifestation.
**ostentador, -ra** *adj.* ostentatious.
**ostentar** *tr.* to parade, display, show, to make ostentation of. *2* to exhibit, manifest.
**ostento** *m.* portent, prodigy.
**ostentoso, -sa** *adj.* ostentatious, sumptuous.
**osteología** *f.* osteology.
**osteópata** *m.* osteopath, osteopathist.
**osteopatía** *f.* osteopathy.
**ostiario** *m.* ECCL. ostiary.
**ostión** *m.* large oyster.
**ostra** *f.* ZOOL. oyster: ~ *perlera*, pearl oyster.
**ostracismo** *m.* ostracism.
**ostrería** *f.* oyster shop.
**ostrero, -ra** *adj.* [pertaining to the] oyster. *2 m.-f.* oyster seller. *3 m.* oyster bed, oyster farm.
**ostrícola** *adj.* oyster-rising.
**ostricultura** *f.* oyster culture, oyster farming.
**ostro** *m.* south. *2* south wind.
**ostrogodo, -da** *adj.-n.* Ostrogoth.
**ostrón** *m.* large, coarse oyster.
**ostugo** *m.* RINCÓN. . *2* bit, piece.
**osudo, -da** *adj.* HUESUDO.
**osuno, -na** *adj.* bearish, bearlike.
**otear** *tr.* to watch, observe, survey from a height. *2* to spy, search, examine.
**otero** *m.* hillock, knoll, buttle, height.
**otitis** *f.* MED. otitis.
**otocisto** *m.* ZOOL. otocyst.
**otolaringología** *f.* otolaryngology.
**otología** *f.* otology.
**otomano, -na** *adj.-n.* Ottoman.
**otoñada** *f.* autumn, autumn time.
**otoñal** *adj.* autumnal.
**otoño** *m.* autumn, fall. *2* autumn aftermath.
**otorgador, -ra** *adj.* granting. *2 m.-f.* grantor.
**otorgamiento** *m.* grant, granting. *2* awarding [of a prize]. *3* LAW execution [of deed, etc.].
**otorgante** *m.-f.* grantor. *2* LAW maker [of a deed, etc.].
**otorgar** *tr.* to grant, give. *2* to award [a prize]. *3* to grant, consent: *quien calla otorga*, silence gives consent. *4* LAW to execute [a deed, etc.].
**otorrinolaringología** *f.* otorhinolaryngology.
**otoscopio** *m.* otoscope.
**otramente** *adv.* otherwise, in a different way.
**otro, -tra** *adj.-pron.* another, other: *otra cosa*, something else; ~ *que tal*, another such; *otros tantos*, as many; *otra vez*, again; *algún* ~, someone or somebody else; *al* ~ *día*, on the next day; *por otra parte*, on the other hand; *uno a* ~, one another. *2 interj.* ¡*otra!*, again!
**otrora** *adv.* formerly, of yore.
**otrosí** *adv.* LAW furthermore.

**ova** *f.* BOT. a fresh-water alga. *2* ARCH. egg [in egg-and-dart ornaments]. *3 pl.* roe.
**ovación** *f.* ovation.
**ovacionar** *intr.* to give an ovation to.
**ovado, -da** *adj.* ovate, oval.
**oval; ovalado, -da** *adj.* oval.
**ovalar** *tr.* to make oval.
**óvalo** *m.* GEOM. oval. *2* OVA 2.
**ovar** *intr.* to lay eggs.
**ovárico, -ca** *adj.* ovarian.
**ovario** *m.* ANAT., ZOOL., BOT. ovary, ovarium.
**oveja** *f.* ewe, female sheep.
**ovejero, -ra** *m.-f.* shepherd, shepherdess.
**ovejuela** *f. dim.* young ewe.
**ovejuno, -na** *adj.* [pertaining to] sheep.
**overa** *f.* ovary of birds.
**overo, -ra** *adj.* blossom-coloured, peach-coloured [horse].
**ovetense** *adj.-n.* of Oviedo.
**Ovidio** *m. pr. n.* Ovid.
**óvidos** *m. pl.* ZOOL. Ovidae.
**oviducto** *m.* ZOOL. oviduct.
**ovillar** *intr.* to wind [thread, yarn] in a ball. *2 ref.* to huddle up; to coil oneself into a ball.
**ovillejo** *m. dim.* small ball [of thread or yarn]. *2* a kind of rondeau or rondel.
**ovillo** *m.* ball [of thread or yarn]: *hacerse un ~*, OVILLAR 2; to get all tangled up [in speech].

**ovíparo, -ra** *adj.* oviparous.
**oviscapto** *m.* ZOOL. ovispositor.
**ovoide; ovoideo, -a** *adj.* ovoid.
**óvolo** *m.* ARCH. ovolo.
**ovovivíparo, -ra** *adj.* ovoviviparous.
**óvulo** *m.* BIOL., BOT. ovule.
**oxálico, -ca** *adj.* CHEM. oxalic.
**oxear** *tr.* to shoo [fowls].
**oxhídrico, -ca** *adj.* CHEM. oxyhydrogen.
**oxidación** *f.* CHEM. oxidation.
**oxidante** *m.* CHEM. oxidizer.
**oxidar** *tr.* to oxidize, to rust. *2 ref.* to oxidize, to rust [become oxidized].
**óxido** *m.* CHEM. oxide.
**oxigenación** *f.* oxygenation.
**oxigenar** *tr.* to oxygenate, oxygenize. *2 ref.* to become oxygenated. *3* to take the air.
**oxígeno** *m.* CHEM. oxygen.
**oximel, oximiel** *m.* PHARM. oxymel.
**oxiuro** *m.* ZOOL. pinworm.
**¡oxte!** *interj.* shoo!, get out! *2 sin decir ~ ni moxte*, coll. without saying a word.
**oyente** *m.-f.* hearer. *2* listener [to the radio]. *3* auditor [in school]. *4 pl.* audience.
**ozonización** *f.* ozonization.
**ozonizar** *tr.* to ozonize.
**ozono** *m.* CHEM. ozone.

# P

**P, p** *f.* P, p, nineteenth letter of the Spanish alphabet.

**pabellón** *m.* pavilion. *2* canopy [over a bed, throne, etc.]. *3* stack [of rifles]. *4* bell [of a wind instrument]. *5* NAUT. flag, colours. *6* national colours. *7* ANAT. ~ *de la oreja*, auricle, external ear.

**pábilo, pabilo** *m.* wick or snuff [of candle].

**Pablo** *m. pr. n.* Paul: *¡guarda Pablo!*, beware!

**pábulo** *m.* pabulum, food, fuel, aliment, support: *dar ~ a*, to give food to, to encourage.

**paca** *f.* bale [of goods]. *2* ZOOL. paca, spotted cavy.

**Paca** *f. pr. n.* coll. Fanny.

**pacana** *f.* BOT. pecan tree. *2* BOT. pecan nut.

**pacato, -ta** *adj.* excessively timid and moderate.

**pacedero, -ra** *adj.* pasturable.

**paceño, -ña** *adj.-n.* of La Paz [Bolivia].

**pacer** *intr.-tr.* to pasture, to graze.

**paciencia** *f.* patience. *2* small almond cake.

**paciente** *adj.* patient [having patience]. *2 m.-f.* MED. patient. *3 adj.-m.* patient [as opposed to agent].

**pacienzudo, -da** *adj.* very patient.

**pacificación** *f.* pacification. *2* peace, quiet.

**pacificador, -ra** *adj.* pacifying. *2 m.-f.* pacifier; peacemaker.

**pacificar** *tr.* to pacify. *2 ref.* to calm down.

**pacífico, -ca** *adj.* pacific. *2* peaceable, peaceful. *3 adj.-n.* (cap.) GEOG. Pacific [Ocean].

**pacifismo** *m.* pacifism.

**Paco** *m. pr. n.* coll. Frank.

**paco** *m.* ZOOL. alpaca. *2* Moorish sniper.

**pacotilla** *f.* venture, goods carried by seamen of a ship free of freight. *2 de ~*, cheap, of inferior quality.

**pacotillero, -ra** *m.-f.* peddler.

**pactar** *tr.* to covenant, agree upon, stipulate. *2 intr.* to come to an agreement. *3* to temporize.

**pacto** *m.* pact, compact, agreement, covenant.

**pachá,** *pl.* **-caes** *m.* BAJÁ.

**pachón, -na** *adj.* pointer [dog]. *2* (Am.) wooly, shaggy. — *3 m.* phlegmatic fellow.

**pachorra** *f.* phlegm, sluggishness, indolence.

**pachorrudo, -da** *adj.* phlegmmatic, sluggish, indolent.

**pachucho, -cha** *adj.* overripe. *2 fig.* weak, drooping.

**pachulí** *m.* patchouli.

**padecer** *tr.* to suffer [undergo, be subjected to]. *2* to be a victim of [a mistake, illusion, etc.]. *3 intr.* to suffer. *4* MED. ~ *de*, to suffer from troubles in. ¶ CONJUG. like *agradecer*.

**padezco, padezca,** etc. *irr.* V. PADECER.

**padecimiento** *m.* suffering. *2* ailment.

**padrastro** *m.* stepfather. *2* bad father. *3* hangnail.

**padrazo** *m. augm.* indulgent father.

**padre** *m.* father: *Padre Eterno*, the Eternal; ~ *político*, father-in-law; *Padre Santo*, Holy Father; *de ~ y muy señor mío*, great, hard; terrific. *2* stallion, sire. *3 pl.* parents.

**padrenuestro** *m.* Lord's prayer.

**padrinazgo** *m.* act of standing godfather or sponsor at baptism, confirmation, etc. *2* title or charge of a godfather. *3* patronage, support, protection.

**padrino** *m.* godfather, sponsor. *2* second [at a duel]. *3* patron, protector. *4* ~ *de boda*, best man.

**padrón** *m.* census [of the population]. *2* pattern, model. *3* memorial column or post. *4* PADRAZO.

**paella** *f.* dish of rice with meat, chicken, fish, etc.

**¡paf!** *interj.* expressing the noise of a fall, blow, etc.

**paga** *f.* payment. *2* pay, salary. *3* satisfaction, amends. *4* requital, return.

**pagadero, -ra** *adj.* payable [at a specified time]. *2 m.* time and place of payment.

**pagado, -da** *p. p.* of PAGAR. *2* pleased, proud: ~ *de sí mismo*, self-satisfied, conceited.

**pagador, -ra** *m.-f.* payer, paymaster. *2 buen ~*, good pay [person]; *mal ~*, bad pay [person].

**pagaduría** *f.* disbursement office; paymaster's office.

**paganismo** *m.* heathenism, paganism.

**pagano, -na** *adj.-n.* heathen, pagan. *2 m.* coll. one who pays for others, one who pays the piper.

**pagar** *tr.* to pay [money, wages, a debt, etc.]; to fee: ~ *al contado*, to pay cash. *2* to pay for: ~ *el pato, los vidrios rotos*, coll. to be the scapegot; *me las pagarás*, you'll pay for it. *3* to expiate, atone, make amends for. *4* to repay, return [love, a kindness, etc.]. *5* to return [a call]. *6 ref.* *pagarse de*, to be fond of; be proud of.

**pagaré** *m.* COM. promissory note.

**pagel** *m.* ICHTH. red sea bream.

**página** *f.* page [of book, etc.].

**paginación** *f.* pagination.

**paginar** *tr.* to page, paginate.

**pago** *adj.* coll. paid, having been paid [pers.]. *2 m.* rural district. *3* payment. *4* repayment, return. *5 en ~*, in payment; in return.

**pagoda** *f.* pagoda.

**pagro** *m.* ICHTH. porgy, red porgy.

**paguro** *m.* ZOOL. hermit crab.

**paila** *f.* large pan, cauldron.

**pailebot, pailebote** *m.* NAUT. a small schooner.

**paipai** *m.* fan made of palm.

**pairar** *intr.* NAUT. [of a ship] to lie to.

**pairo** *m.* NAUT. lying to.

**país** *m.* country, nation. *2* country, land, region, territory. *3* F. ARTS landscape. *4* sheet [of a fan].

**paisaje** *m.* landscape.

**paisajista** *m.-f.* landscape painter.

**paisanaje** *m.* civilians. *2* peasantry, countryfolk. *3* fellow countrymanship.

**paisano, -na** *adj.* of the same country or place. *2 m.-f.* compatriot, countryman or woman. *3* peasant. *4 m.* civilian.

**paja** *f.* straw: *no dormirse en las pajas*, not to let the grass grow under one's feet; *por un quítame allá estas pajas* [to quarrel], over the smallest trifle. *2* fig. trash, rubbish.

**pajado, -da** *adj.* straw-coloured.

**pajar** *m.* haystack, rick of straw. *2* straw loft.

**pájara** *f.* bird. *2* kite [toy]. *3* crafty female. *4* PAJARITA 1.

**pajarear** *intr.* to go birdcatching. *2* to loaf, around.

**pajarera** *f.* aviary; large bird cage.

**pajarería** *f.* large number of birds. *2* bird shop.

**pajarero** *m.* birdcatcher. *2* bird fancier. *3* bird seller.

**pajarete** *m.* fine sherry wine.

**pajarilla** *f.* BOT. columbine. *2* ANAT. spleen, milt.

**pajarita** *f.* paper bird. *2* ORN. *~ de las nieves*, AGUZANIEVES.

**pájaro** *m.* bird; passerine bird: *~ bobo*, penguin; *~ carpintero*, woodpecker; *~ mosca*, hummingbird; *matar dos pájaros de un tiro*, to kill two birds with one stone. *2* fig. sly, crafty fellow. *3* fig. ~ *de cuenta*, man of importance; dangerous fellow; ~ *gordo*, big gun, swell.

**pajarota, pajarotada** *f.* hoax, canard.

**pajarraco** *m.* large ugly bird. *2* fig. sly fellow.

**paje** *m.* page [youth]: *~ de hacha*, link boy. *2* familiar [of a bishop]. *3* NAUT. cabin boy.

**pajecillo** *m. dim.* little page [boy]. *2* washstand.

**pajel** *m.* PAGEL.

**pajero** *m.* straw dealer.

**pajizo, -za** *adj.* made of straw. *2* thatched with straw. *3* straw-coloured.

**pajón** *m.* high coarse stumps of grain.

**pajoso, -sa** *adj.* strawy.

**pajote** *m.* straw mat for covering plants.

**pajuela** *f. dim.* short straw. *2* sulphur match.

**Pakistán (el)** *m. pr. n.* GEOG. Pakistan.

**pal** *m.* HER. pale.

**pala** *f.* shovel. *2* peel; baker's peel. *3* slice [for serving fish, etc.]. *4* wash, beetle. *5* racket [for ball games]. *6* blade [of a hoe, spade, etc.]. *7* bowl [of a spoon]. *8* vamp [of a shoe]. *9* leaf [of a hinge]. *10* BOT. joint [of a prickly pear].

**palabra** *f.* word [term; speech, thing said, remark, conversation]: *palabras cruzadas*, crossword puzzle; *palabras mayores*, insulting words; serious matter; *dos palabras*, a few words; *medias palabras*, covert suggestion; *juego de palabras*, pun; *comerse las palabras*, to omit words; *de ~*, by word of mouth; *en una ~*, in a word, to sum up; *~ por ~*, word by word. *2* act of speaking;

right, turn or permission to speak; *pedir la ~*, to ask for the floor; *tomar la ~*, to take the floor. *3* word [one's promise]: *¡palabra!*, honestly!; *dar*, or *empeñar, uno su ~*, to give, or pledge, one's word; *bajo su ~*, on one's word.

**palabreja** *f.* odd word.

**palabreo** *m.*, **palabrería** *f.* empty talk.

**palabrero, -ra** *adj.* talkative, wordy, windy. *2 m.-f.* chatterer, vain talker, windbag.

**palabrita** *f. dim.* small word. *2* pointed word.

**palabrota** *f.* coarse, obscene word or expression.

**palaciego, -ga** *adj.* [pertaining to the] palace; court. *2 m.* courtier.

**palacio** *m.* palace. *2* mansion house [oficial residence].

**palada** *f.* shovelful. *2* stroke [of an oar].

**paladar** *s.* ANAT. palate. *2* taste [of things]. *3* palate, taste [sense of taste; mental taste].

**paladear** *tr.-ref.* to taste with pleasure, to relish, to take small portions [of something] in order to relish it.

**paladeo** *m.* tasting, relishing.

**paladial** *adj.-f.* palatal.

**paladín** *m.* paladin. *2* champion, defender.

**paladino, -na** *adj.* open, public, manifest. *2 m.* PALADÍN.

**paladio** *m.* CHEM. palladium.

**paladión** *m.* palladium, safeguard.

**palafito** *m.* ARCHEOL. palafitte.

**palafrén** *m.* palfrey. *2* groom's horse.

**palafrenero** *m.* groom, stableman, hostler.

**palamenta** *f.* oarage, seat of oars, outfit of oars.

**palanca** *f.* MECH. lever. *2* MACH. lever, bar: *~ del timón*, AER. rudder bar. *3* fig. lever [agency, influence]. *4* pole for carrying a weight.

**palancada** *f.* move made with a lever.

**palancana, palangana** *f.* washbowl.

**palanganero** *m.* washstand [stand with washbowl and pitcher].

**palangre** *m.* boulter.

**palangrero** *m.* boulterer [fisherman].

**palanquera** *f.* wooden fence.

**palanqueta** *f.* jimmy [short crowbar]. *2* NAV. bar shot.

**palanquín** *m.* palankeen, palanquin. *2* street porter. *3* NAUT. clew-garnet. *4* NAUT. gun tackle.

**Palas** *f. pr. n.* MYTH. Pallas.

**palastro** *m.* sheet iron, sheet steel. *2* plate [of a lock].

**palatal** *adj.-f.* palatal.

**palatalizar** *tr.* PHONET. to palatalize.

**Palatinado (el)** *pr. n.* GEOG. Palatinate. *2 m.* palatinate.

**palatino, -na** *adj.* ANAT. palatine. *2 adj.-m.* palatine [count, earl, etc.].

**palazón** *m.* NAUT. masting. *2* woodwork, timber.

**palco** *m.* THEAT. box. *2* THEAT. *~ escénico*, stage.

**palear** *tr.* to winnow, fan [grain] with a shovel.

**palenque** *m.* palisade, wood fence, enclosure, lists.

**palentino** *adj.-n.* of Palencia.

**paleografía** *f.* pal(a)eography.

**paleolítico** *adj.* pal(a)eolithic(al.

**paleólogo** *m.* pal(a)eologist.

**paleontología** *f.* pal(a)eontology.

**paleozoico, -ca** *adj.-m.* Pal(a)eozoic.

**palería** *f.* art and practice of draining lands.

**Palestina** *pr. n.* GEOG. Palestine.

**palestra** *f.* pal(a)estra.

**paleta** *f.* PAINT. palette, .pallet. *2* small, flat, fire shovel. *3* MAS. trowel. *4* ANAT. shoulder blade. *5*

float, paddle [of a water wheel or paddle wheel]; vane [of a propeller, fan blower, etc.].
**paletada** *f.* trowelful.
**paletazo** *m.* VARETAZO.
**paletear** *intr.* to row ineffectively.
**paletero** *m.* two-year-old fallow deer.
**paletilla** *f.* ANAT. shoulder blade. *2* ANAT. sternum cartilage.
**paleto** *m.* ZOOL. fallow deer. *2* coll. rustic, yokel.
**paletó**, *pl.* -toes *m.* paletot [overcoat].
**paletón** *m.* bit, web [of a key].
**palia** *f.* ECCL. pall. *2* curtain before the tabernacle.
**paliar** *tr.* to palliate, extenuate. *2* to palliate, alleviate.
**paliativo, -va** *adj.-m.* palliative.
**palidecer** *intr.* to pale, turn pale; to wan, grow wan. ¶ CONJUG. like *agradecer*.
**palidez** *f.* paleness, pallor, wanness.
**palidezco, palidezca,** etc. *irr.* V. PALIDECER.
**pálido, -da** *adj.* pale, pallid, wan, ghastly.
**paliducho, -cha** *adj.* palish.
**palillero** *m.* toothpick holder.
**palillo** *m.* small stick. *2* knitting-needle holder. *3* wooden toothpick. *4* drumstick. *5* bobbin [for making lace]. *6* coll. chit-chat. *7 pl.* castanets. *8* small pins used in billiards. *9* chopsticks. *10* small sticks used by sculptors.
**palimpsesto** *m.* palimpsest.
**palingenesia** *f.* palingenesis.
**palinodia** *f.* palinode: *cantar la ~*, to recant, retract.
**palio** *m.* HIST., ECCL. pallium. *2* portable canopy. *3* fig. canopy [overhanging covering].
**palique** *m.* chit-chat, small talk.
**palisandro** *m.* palisander, palissander, rosewood.
**palitoque, palitroque** *m.* rough small stick.
**paliza** *f.* beating, drubbing, -trashing.
**palizada** *f.* palisaded enclosure. *2* palisaded embankment. *3* FORT. stockade.
**palma** *f.* BOT. palm, palm tree. *2* palm [leaf of palm; symbol of victory, etc.]: *llevarse la ~*, to excel, to surpass everybody. *3* palm [of the hand]. *4* VET. sole [of hoof]. *5 pl.* clapping of hands: *batir palmas*, to clap hands.
**palmáceo, -a** *adj.* BOT. palmaceous.
**palmada** *f.* slap, pat [with the hand]. *2* handclap: *dar palmadas*, to clap hands.
**palmado, -da** *adj.* PALMEADO.
1) **palmar** *adj.* ANAT. palmar. *2* VET. pertaining to the sole of the hoof. *3* measuring a span. *4* PALMARIO. *5 m.* palm grove.
2) **palmar** *intr.* coll. to die.
**palmario, -ria** *adj.* clear, obvious, evident.
**palmatoria** *f.* short candlestick with a handle.
**palmeado, -da** *adj.* BOT. palmate. *2* ZOOL. palmate; webbed.
**palmear** *intr.* to clap hands.
**palmera** *f.* BOT. date palm.
**palmeral** *m.* date palms grove or plantation.
**palmero** *m.* palm keeper. *2* palmer [pilgrim].
**palmesano, -na** *adj.-n.* of Palma de Mallorca.
**palmeta** *f.* ferule [for punishing boys].
**palmetazo** *m.* slap with a ferule.
**palmiche** *m.* BOT. royal palm. *2* fruit of the royal palm. *3* fruit of the palmetto or dwarf fanpalm.
**palmípedo, -da** *adj.* ORN. palmiped, web-footed.
**palmito** *m.* BOT. palmetto, dwarf fan-palm. *2* sprout of the dwarf fan-palm. *3* woman's face: *buen ~*, beautiful face.
**palmo** *m.* span [measure]: *dejar con un ~ de nari-*

*ces*, coll. to disappoint; *~ a ~*, inch by inch. *2* palm [hand breadth].
**palmotear** *tr.* to clap hands, applaud.
**palo** *m.* stick, staff, pole. *2* NAUT. mast: *~ mayor*, mainmast; *a ~ seco*, under bare poles; fig. without the customary complements. *3* blow with a stick: *dar de palos*, to beat, thrash; *llevar ~*, to get a drubbing. *4* stalk of fruit. *5* suit [at cards]. *6* long stroke [in handwriting]. *7* execution on the gallows or on the garrote. *8* wood [material]. *9* a name for some trees or kinds of wood: *~ aloe*, aloes wood; *~ brasil*, brazilwood; *~ campeche*, campeche wood; *~ de jabón*, soapbark; *~ santo*, lignum vitae. *10 pl.* billiard pins.
**paloma** *f.* ORN. dove, pigeon: *~ silvestre*, stock dove; *~ buchona*, pouter [pigeon]; *~ mensajera*, carrier pigeon, homer; *~ torcaz*, wood pigeon. *2* fig. dove [meek person]. *3 pl.* whitecaps.
**palomar** *m.* pigeon-house, dovecot. *2* adj. hard-twisted [twine].
**palomariego, -ga** *adj.* domestic [pigeon].
**palomero, -ra** *m.-f.* pigeon dealer. *2* pigeon breeder.
**palomilla** *f.* small butterfly. *2* fore part of the croup of a horse. *3* wall bracket. *4* MECH. journal bearing. *5 pl.* whitecaps.
**palomina** *f.* pigeon dung. *2* BOT. fumitory.
**palomino** *m.* young pigeon.
**palomita** *f. dim.* little pigeon. *2* (Am.) piece of popcorn. *3* (Am.) darling. *4 pl.* popcorn.
**palomo** *m.* cock pigeon. *2* ORN. wood pigeon.
**palor** *m.* pallor.
**palotada** *f.* stroke with a stick: *no dar ~*, to do or say nothing right; to do nothing.
**palote** *f.* stick, drumstick. *2* stroke [in learning to write].
**palpable** *adj.* palpable. *2* obvious, evident.
**palpablemente** *adv.* palpably.
**palpación** *f.* PALPADURA. *2* MED. palpation.
**palpadura,** *f.*, **palpamiento** *m.* touching, feeling.
**palpar** *tr.* to touch, feel. *2* to grope through. *3* to see as self-evident. *4* MED. to palpate. *5 intr.* to feel one's way, to grope in the dark.
**palpebral** *adj.* palpebral.
**palpitación** *f.* palpitation, pulsation, throbbing.
**palpitante** *adj.* palpitating. *2* burning [question].
**palpitar** *intr.* to palpitate, pulsate, throb, thrill. *2* to reveal itself [in an act, words, etc.].
**palpo** *m.* ZOOL. palpus [in arthropods].
**palúdico, -ca** *adj.* marshy. *2* malarial.
**paludismo** *m.* MED. paludism, malaria.
**palumbario** *adj.* dove-hunting [hawk].
**palurdo, -da** *adj.* rustic, rude. *2 m.-f.* rustic, yokel.
**palustre** *adj.* paludal, marshy. *2 m.* MAS. trowel.
**pallador** *m.* (S. Am.) wandering poet and singer.
**pallete** *m.* NAUT. fender mat.
**pallón** *m.* assay button [of gold or silver].
**pamela** *f.* woman's wide-brimmed straw hat.
**pamema** *f.* coll. trifle, nonsense. *2* coll. bunkum.
**pampa** *m.* pampa: *La Pampa*, the pampas.
**pámpana** *f.* grapevine leaf.
**pampanilla** *f.* loincloth.
**pámpano** *m.* grapevine tendril or shoot. *2* grapevine leaf. *3* ICHTH. gilthead.
**pampeano, -na** *adj.-n.* (S. Am.) pampean.
**pampear** *intr.* to go or travel over the pampas.
**pampero, -ra** *adj.-n.* pampean. *2 m.* pampero [wind].
**pampirolada** *f.* a garlic sauce. *2* coll. silly thing.
**pamplina** *f.* nonsense, trifle, silly thing. *2* BOT. chickweed. *3* BOT. a kind of yellow poppy.

**pamplinada** *f.* nonsense, trifle, silly thing.
**pamplinero, -ra; pamplinoso, -sa** *adj.* silly, nonsensical.
**pamplonés, -sa** *adj.-m.* of Pamplona.
**pamporcino** *m.* BOT. cyclamen, sowbread.
**pamposado, -da** *adj.* lazy, indolent.
**pan** *m.* bread; loaf: ~ *ázimo,* unleavened bread; ~ *candeal,* white-wheat bread; ~ *tierno,* fresh bread; ~ *duro,* stale bread; ~ *integral,* wholewheat bread; ~ *rallado,* bread crumbs; *panes de proposición,* BIBL. shewbread, showbread; *ganarse el* ~, to earn one's livelihood; *llamar al pan, pan, y al vino, vino,* to call a spade a spade; *contigo* ~ *y cebolla,* fig. love in a cottage. *2* pie or pastry dough. *3* anything in the shape of a loaf or a cake: ~ *de azúcar,* sugar loaf. *4* wafer. *5* leaf, foil [of gold, silver, etc.]. *6* wheat. *7 pl.* grain fields.
**pana** *f.* velveteen, corduroy. *2* NAUT. flooring board. *3* AUTO. break-down.
**panacea** *f.* panacea.
**panadear** *tr.* to make [flour] into bread. *2 intr.* to make bread [for sale].
**panadeo** *m.* making bread.
**panadería** *f.* bakery. *2* baking business.
**panadero, -ra** *m.-f.* baker. *2 f.* baker's wife.
**panadizo** *m.* MED. felon, whitlow.
**panal** *m.* honeycomb. *2* comb built by wasps. *3* AZUCARILLO.
**Panamá** *m. pr. n.* GEOG. Panama. *2 m.* (not cap.) panama, panama hat.
**panameño, -ña** *adj.-n.* Panamanian.
**panamericano, -na** *adj.* Pan-American.
**panarizo** *m.* PANADIZO.
**panarra** *m.* lazy simpleton.
**pancarta** *f.* parchment containing several documents. *2* placard, portable placard.
**pancellar** *m.,* **pancera** *f.* ARM. belly plate.
**pancista** *m.* POL. one who sits on the fence.
**pancracio** *m.* HIST. pancratium.
**páncreas, pl. -creas** *m.* ANAT. pancreas.
**pancreático, -ca** *adj.* pancreatic.
**Pancha, Panchita** *f. pr. n. coll.* Fanny.
**Pancho, Panchito** *m. pr. n. coll.* Frank.
**pancho** *m.* ICHTH. spawn of the sea bream.
**pandear** *intr.-ref.* [of a wall, beam, etc.] to sag, buckle, bulge, bend in the middle.
**Pandectas** *f. pl.* Pandects.
**pandemia** *f.* MED. pandemia, pandemic.
**pandemónium** *m.* Pandemonium; pandemonium.
**pandeo** *m.* sagging, bulging, bending of a wall, beam, etc.
**pandera** *f.* PANDERO.
**panderada** *f.* tambouriness. *2* coll. silly remark.
**pandereta** *f.* PANDERO I.
**panderete** *m. dim.* small tambourine.
**panderetear** *intr.* to sing, dance or make merry and play the tambourine.
**pandereteo** *m.* playing the tambourine.
**panderetear** *intr.* to sing, dance or make merry and play the tambourine.
**pandereteo** *m.* playing the tambourine.
**pandero** *m.* MUS. tambourine, timbrel. *2* kite [toy]. *3* coll. silly talker, jabberer.
**pandilla** *f.* gang, band, set, company, faction.
**pandillaje** *m.* action or influence of a sang.
**pando, -da** *adj.* sagging, bulging [wall, beam, etc.]. *2* slow-moving. *3 m.* plain between two mountains.
**pandorga** *f.* fat, bulky woman. *2* kite [toy].
**panecillo** *m.* roll [bread].

**panegírico, -ca** *adj.* panegyric(al. *2 m.* panegyric.
**panegirizar** *tr.* to panegyrize, eulogyze.
**panel** *m.* panel [in wainscot, door, etc.]. *2* ELECT. panel. *3* NAUT. removable floor board.
**panera** *f.* granary. *2* bread basket.
**paneslavismo** *m.* Pan-Slavism.
**panetela** *f.* broth with crumps, minced fowl, eggs, sugar, etc. *2* panetella [cigar].
**panfilismo** *m.* excessive gentleness or benignity.
**pánfilo, -la** *adj.* slow, sluggish [person]. *2 m.-f.* sluggard.
**panfleto** *m.* (Am.) pamphlet.
**pangermanismo** *m.* Pan-Germanism.
**pangolín** *m.* ZOOL. pangolin.
**paniaguado** *m.* servant, minion. *2* protégé.
**pánico, -ca** *adj.* panic, panicky. *2 m.* panic.
**panícula** *f.* BOT. panicle.
**panículo** *m.* ANAT. panniculus.
**panificable** *adj.* good for making bread [fluor].
**panificación** *f.* panification.
**panificar** *tr.* to make [flour] into bread.
**panislamismo** *m.* Pan-Islamism.
**panizo** *m.* BOT. panic grass, foxtail millet, Italian millet. *2* Indian corn.
**panocha** *f.* ear [of Indian corn]. *2* panicle [of millet or foxtail millet]. *3* bunch [of fruit hung up for keeping].
**panoja** *f.* PANOCHA. *2* BOT. panicle.
**panoplia** *f.* panoply [suit of armour]. *2* collection of arms. *3* wall trophy. *4* study of ancient weapons.
**panorama** *m.* panorama.
**panorámico, -ca** *adj.* panoramic.
**panormitano, -na** *adj.-n.* Palermitan.
**panoso, -sa** *adj.* mealy.
**pantagruélico, -ca** *adj.* Pantagruelian, Pantagruelic.
**pantalón** or *pl.* **pantalones** *m.* trousers, breeches, *pants: ~ bombacho,* loose-fitting trousers; *pantalones de golf,* knicker-bockers; *llevar· los pantalones,* fig. [of a wife] to wear the trousers. *2* woman's drawers; pantlets.
**pantalla** *f.* lamp shade. *2* fire screen [before a fireplace]. *3* PHYS., CINE., TELEV. screen. *4* RADIO. baffle. *5* fig. anything that obstructs the view. *6* *servir de* ~ *a uno,* to be a blind for someone.
**pantanal** *m.* swampland.
**pantano** *m.* swamp, marsh. *2* small lake or natural pond. *3* a large dam. *4* fig. obstacle, hindrance.
**pantanoso, -sa** *adj.* swampy, marshy.
**panteísmo** *m.* pantheism.
**panteísta** *adj.* pantheistic. *2 m.-f.* pantheist.
**panteón** *m.* Pantheon. *2* family tomb.
**pantera** *f.* ZOOL. panther. *2* MINER. yellow agate.
**pantógrafo** *m.* pantograph.
**pantomima** *f.* pantomime, dumb show.
**pantomimo** *m.* mimic, pantomimist.
**pantoque** *m.* NAUT. bilge.
**pantorrilla** *f.* calf [of the leg].
**pantorrillera** *f.* padded stocking.
**pantorrilludo, -da** *adj.* thick-calved.
**pantufla,** *f.,* **pantuflo** *m.* slipper, house slipper.
**panza** *f.* paunch, belly. *2* belly [of a vase]. *3* ZOOL. paunch, rumen [of ruminants].
**panzada** *f.* bellyfull. *2* push with the paunch.
**panzón, -na** *adj.* PANZUDO. *2 m.* big belly.
**panzudo, -da** *adj.* paunchy, big-bellied.
**pañal** *m.* swaddling cloth. *2* tail of shirt. *3 pl.* swaddling clothes; infancy.
**pañería** *f.* drapery [cloth, woollen stuffs in general]. *2* draper's shop.

**pañero, -ra** *adj.* [pertaining to] drapery. *2 m.* draper, clothier.
**pañete** *m.* light, thin cloth.
**paño** *m.* cloth [woollen stuff]: *conocer el* ~, to know the ropes. *2* by extension, cloth [any woven stuff]. *3* tapestry. *4* cloth [piece of fabric adapted for some specified use]: ~ *de cocina*, dish cloth; ~ *de lágrimas*, fig. one who simpathizes and consoles; ~ *calientes*, fig. inefficent efforts; half measures; *en paños menores*, undressed. *5* spot in the face. *6* blur [in a mirror, a precious stone, etc.]. *7* stretch [of a wall]. *8* NAUT. canvas, sails. *9* SEW. breadth. *10 pl.* PAINT., SCULPT. draperies.
**pañol** *m.* NAUT. storeroom.
**pañolería** *f.* handkerchief business.
**pañolero** *m.* NAUT. storeroom keeper, yeoman.
**pañoleta** *f.* woman's triangular shawl.
**pañolón** *m.* large square shawl.
**pañoso, -sa** *adj.* ragged, in rags. *2 f.* coll. woollen cloak.
**pañuelo** *m.* square shawl. *2* kerchief, handkerchief: ~ *de hierbas*, bandana; ~ *para el cuello*, neckerchief, neckcloth.
**papa** *m.* Pope [Roman Pontiff]. *2* coll. papa, dad. *3 f.* fib, canard. *4* potato. *5 no saber una* ~, not to know a thing. *6 pl.* pap, porridge.
**papá** *m.* coll. papa, dad.
**papacito** *m.* (Am.) daddy.
**papada** *f.* double chin. *2* dewlap.
**papadilla** *f.* flesh under the chin.
**papado** *m.* papacy.
**papafigo** *m.* ORN. figpecker. *2* ORN. golden oriole.
**papagayo** *m.* ORN. parrot. *2* fig. parrot [pers.]. *3* fig. chatterbox. *4* ICHTH. peacock fish.
**papahigo** *m.* winter cap [covering head, ears and neck]. *2* ORN. figpecker. *3* NAUT. lower sail.
**papal** *adj.* papal.
**papalina** *f.* a kind of woman's coif. *2* a cap covering the ears. *3* coll. drunk, drunken fit.
**papamoscas**, *pl.* **-cas** *m.* ORN. flycatcher. *2* PAPANATAS.
**papanatas**, *pl.* **-tas** *m.* simpleton, ninny.
**papandujo, -ja** *adj.* coll. too soft, overripe.
**papar** *tr.* to eat without chewing.
**páparo, -ra** *m.* rustic, simpleton.
**paparrucha** *f.* fib, hoax, humbug. *2* nonsense, silliness.
**papaveráceo, -a** *adj.* BOT. papaveraceous.
**papaya** *f.* BOT. papaya [fruit].
**papayo** *m.* BOT. papaya tree.
**papazgo** *m.* papacy, papalty.
**papel** *m.* paper [material, piece of paper]: ~ *blanco*, blank paper; ~ *cuadriculado*, cross-section paper; ~ *de barbas*, untrimmed handmade paper; ~ *de calcar*, tracing paper; ~ *de fumar*, cigarette paper; ~ *de estraza*, coarse brown paper; ~ *de lija*, sandpaper; ~ *de seda*, tissue paper; ~ *de tornasol*, litmus paper; ~ *pintado*, wallpaper; ~ *rayado*, ruled paper; ~ *secante*, blotting paper; ~ *sellado*, official stamped paper. *2* paper [document]: ~ *de Estado*, government securities; ~ *moneda*, paper money; *papeles mojados*, worthless documents. *3* COM. [collect.] the securities brought for sale to the stock market. *4* THEAT. part, rôle: *desempeñar el* ~ *de*, to act the part of. *5* rôle, function, duty, -character, figure: *hacer buen* ~, to acquit oneself well; *hacer* ~, to cut a figure. *6 pl.* papers [identity documents].

**papelear** *intr.* to rummage papers, to look through papers. *2* to cut a figure, to make a show.
**papeleo** *m.* looking through papers. *2* red tape.
**papelera** *f.* paper case. *2* waste basket.
**papelería** *f.* paper shop, stationery shop. *2* lot of papers.
**papelero, -ra** *adj.* [pertaining to] paper. *2* showing off. *3 m.-f.* paper manufacturer or dealer. *4* shower off.
**papeleta** *f.* slip of paper; card, file card, ticket; ~ *de votación*, ballot.
**papelista** *m.* paper manufacturer. *2* paper dealer. *3* paper hanger.
**papelito** *m. dim.* small piece of paper. *2* curl paper.
**papelón, -na** *adj.* showing off. *2 m.* despicable writing or paper. *3* thin cardboard. *4* (Am.) raw sugar. *5 m.-f.* shower off.
**papelonear** *intr.* to make a vain show of power, influence, etc.
**papelorio** *m.* jumble of papers.
**papelote, papelucho** *m.* despicable writing or paper.
**papera** *f.* goitre. *2* mumps. *3 pl.* scrofula.
**papila** *f.* ANAT., BOT. papilla: ~ *gustativa*, taste bud.
**papilionáceo, -a** *adj.* BOT. papilionaceous.
**papilla** *f.* pap [soft food].
**papillote** *f.* hair twisted in a curl paper.
**papión** *m.* ZOOL. papion.
**papiro** *m.* papyrus.
**papirotada** *f.*, **papirotazo** *m.* fillip.
**papirote** *m.* fillip. *2* fool, dolt.
**papisa** *f.* papess.
**papista** *adj.* Papistic. *2 adj.-n.* Papist.
**papo** *m.* ZOOL. dewlap. *2* crop, craw, maw [of birds]. *3* MED. goiter. *4* BOT. thistledown. *5* puff [in a slashed garment].
**papú, pl. -púes** *adj.-n.* Papuan.
**papudo, -da** *adj.* full-gorged [bird].
**pápula** *f.* MED. papule.
**paquear** *tr.* to snipe at.
**paquebot, paquebote** *m.* NAUT. packet boat.
**paqueo** *m.* sniping.
**paquete** *adj.* (Am.) dolled up. *2* (Am.) self-important. *3* (Am.) insincere. *4 m.* package, packet, pack, parcel: *por* ~ *postal*, by parcel post. *5* PAQUEBOTE.
**paquetería** *f.* COM. smallwares sold in packages.
**paquidermo** *m.* ZOOL. pachyderm.
**Paquita** *f. pr. n.* coll. Fanny.
**Paquito** *m. pr. n.* coll. Frank.
**par** *adj.* like, equal. *2* even [number]: *pares o nones*, odd or even [game]. *3 m.* pair, brace, couple, set of two. *4* PHYS., MECH. ELECT. couple. *5* peer, equal: *sin* ~, peerless, unequaled. *6* peer [nobleman]. *7* ARCH. principal rafter. *8* COM. par: *a la* ~, at par. *9 a la* ~, or *al* ~, equally, on a par, in the same manner; at the same time. *10* *abierto de* ~ *en* ~, wide open [door, etc.].
**para** *prep.* for, to, in order to: ~ *que*, in order that, so that; *¿* ~ *qué?*, what for? *2* for, to [introducing the indirect object]: *lo compró* ~ *ella*, he bought it for her; *ha sido bueno* ~ *ella*, he has been good to her. *3* toward [as a share for the support or payement of]. *4* by, to, on [indicating future time]: ~ *entonces*, by then; *lo aplazaron* ~ *el lunes*, they postponed it to Monday; *pagará* ~ *Navidad*, he'll pay on Christmas. *5* ~ *con*, toward, with, compared with. *6* ~ *eso*, for that. *7* ~ *mí*, ~ *sí*, to myself, to himself or herself; *pensé* ~ *mí*, I thought to myself; *estar* ~, to be on the point

of; to be about [to do something]. 8 *no estar* ~, to be in no mood for.

**parabién** *m.* congratulation, felicitation: *dar el* ~, to congratulate, felicitate.

**parábola** *f.* parable. 2 GEOM. parabola.

**parabólico, -ca** *adj.* parabolic.

**paraboloide** *m.* GEOM. paraboloid.

**parabrisas,** *pl.* **-sas** *m.* AUTO. windscreen, windshield.

**paracaídas,** *pl.* **-das** *m.* parachute.

**paracaidista** *m.* parachuter, parachutist. 2 MIL. paratrooper.

**Paracleto, Paráclito** *m. pr. n.* Paraclete, Holy Ghost.

**parachispas,** *pl.* **-pas** *m.* ELECT. spark arrester.

**parachoques,** *pl.* **-ques** *m.* AUTO. bumper.

**parada** *f.* stop, halt, standstill, stay: ~ *en seco,* dead stop. 2 stop [of a bus, tram, etc.]. 3 pause. 4 post [for keeping horses for relays]. 5 stud farm. 6 irrigation dam. 7 stake, bid [in gambling]. 8 SPORT. catch [of the ball]. 9 parry. 10 parade [muster of troops]. 11 ~ *de coches,* cabstand.

**paradera** *f.* sluice gate. 2 fishing seine.

**paradero** *s.* whereabouts. 2 stopping place. 3 end [last point, place, state, etc., to which a thing has come].

**paradigma** *m.* paradigm.

**paradisíaco, -ca** *adj.* paradisiacal.

**parado, -da** *adj.* stopped, arrested, motionless. 2 slow, awkward, timid. 3 unoccupied, unemployed [person]. 4 shut down [factory]. 5 *m. pl.* unemployed, unemployed people.

**paradoja** *f.* paradox.

**paradójico, -ca; paradojo, -ja** *adj.* paradoxical.

**parador** *m.* inn, hosterly, tavern, roadhouse.

**parafina** *f.* parafin.

**parafrasear** *tr.* to paraphrase.

**paráfrasis,** *pl.* **-sis** *f.* paraphrase.

**paragoge** *f.* GRAM. paragoge.

**paraguas,** *pl.* **-guas** *m.* umbrella.

**Paraguay** *m. pr. n.* GEOG. Paraguay.

**paraguayo, -ya** *adj.-n.* Paraguayan.

**paragüería** *f.* umbrella shop.

**paragüero, -ra** *m.-f.* umbrella maker or seller. 2 *m.* umbrella stand.

**parahuso** *m.* pump drill.

**paraíso** *m.* paradise: ~ *terrenal,* Paradise, Garden of Eden.

**paraje** *m.* spot, place.

**paral** *m.* putlog. 2 scaffold prop.

**paraláctico, -ca** *adj.* parallactic.

**paralaje, paralasis, paralaxi** *m.* ASTR. parallax.

**paralelepípedo** *m.* GEOM. parallelepiped.

**paralelismo** *m.* parallelism.

**paralelo, -la** *adj.* parallel. 2 *m.* parallel [comparison]. 3 ELECT., GEOG. parallel. 4 *f.* GEOM., FORT. parallel. 5 *f. pl.* GYMN. parallel bars.

**paralelogramo** *m.* GEOM. parallelogram.

**parálisis,** *pl.* **-sis** *f.* MED. paralysis.

**paraliticarse** *ref.* MED. to become paralyzed.

**paralítico, -ca** *adj.-n.* MED. paralytic.

**paralización** *f.* paralyzation. 2 COM. stagnation. 3 stoppage [of the traffic].

**paralizador, -ra** *adj.* paralyzing.

**paralizar** *tr.* to paralise. 2 to stop, immobilize. 3 COM. to make stagnant. 4 *ref.* to become paralyzed. 5 COM. to stagnate.

**paralogismo** *m.* LOG. paralogism.

**paramentar** *tr.* to adorn, bedeck.

**paramento** *m.* adornment, ornament; hangings. 2

ARCH. face [of a wall]. 4 ECCL. *paramentos sacerdotales,* vestments.

**paramera** *f.* bleak, barren country.

**parámetro** *m.* GEOM. parameter.

**páramo** *m.* paramo, moor, bleak windy spot.

**parangón** *m.* parallel, comparison.

**parangonar** *tr.* to parallel, compare.

**paraninfo** *m.* paranymph. 2 harbiguer of felicity. 3 hall, auditorium [of university].

**paranoia** *f.* MED. paranoia.

**paranoico, -ca** *adj.-n.* MED. paranoiac, paranoic.

**parapetarse** *ref.* to shelter behind a parapet. 2 to protect oneself.

**parapeto** *m.* parapet [low wall or railing]. 2 FORT. parapet, breastwork.

**parapoco,** *pl.* **-poco** *m.-f.* dull, timid person.

1) **parar** *m.* lansquenet [card game].

2) **parar** *tr.* to stop, arrest, detain, check. 2 to prepare, get ready. 3 to stake [at gambling]. 4 HUNT. to point [game]. 5 to put [in a state]. 6 FENC. to parry. 7 SPORT. to catch [a ball]. 8 (Am.) to stand, set upright. 9 ~ *atención a,* to notice; ~ *mientes en,* to consider, reflect on. 10 *intr.-ref.* to stop [cease to go on]. 11 *intr.* to stop, cease [in action or operation]. 12 [of a train, bus, etc.] to stop. 13 to stop, to put up, to stay, to lodge. 14 to come into the possession of, to end in; finally to get to. 16 to be ready to face a danger. 17 to stop, desist. 18 (Am.) to stand up. 19 *pararse a,* to stop to, to pause to.

**pararrayos,** *pl.* **-yos** *m.* lightning rod. 2 lightning arrester.

**paraselene** *f.* METEOR. paraselene, mock moon.

**parasitario, -ria** *adj.* parasitic(al.

**parasiticida** *adj.-m.* parasiticide.

**parasitismo** *m.* parasitiom.

**parásito, -ta** *adj.* parasitic. 2 *m.* BIOL. parasite. 3 parasite, hanger-on. 4 *pl.* RADIO strays: *parásitos atmosféricos,* atmospherics, static.

**parasitología** *f.* parasitology.

**parasol** *m.* parasol, sunshade. 2 BOT. umbel.

**parata** *f.* AGR. step terrace.

**paratífico, -ca** *adj.* paratyphoid.

**paratifoidea** *f.* MED. paratyphoid fever.

**parca** *f.* MYTH. Parca, fate. 2 poet. Death.

**parcamente** *adv.* sparingly, scantily.

**parcela** *f.* lot, parcel [piece of land]. 2 particle.

**parcelar** *tr.* to parcel, divide [land] in lots.

**parcelario, -ria** *adj.* pertaining to parcels of land.

**parcial** *adj.* partial [not complete]. 2 partial, biased. 3 *m.-f.* partisan, follower.

**parcialidad** *f.* partiality, bias. 2 faction, party; clique. 3 friendship, favour. 4 affableness.

**parco, -ca** *adj.* frugal, sparing, scanty. 2 moderate, parsimonious.

**parchazo** *m.* NAUT. bang of a sail against the mast. 2 coll. trick, deception.

**parche** *m.* PHARM. patch, plaster. 2 patch [stuck on something]. 3 MUS. drumhead. 4 MUS. drum. 5 daub, botch.

**parchís** *m.* parchesi.

**pardal** *adj.* country [people]. 2 *m.* ORN. sparrow. 3 ORN. linnet. 4 ZOOL. leopard. 5 coll. sly fellow.

**pardear** *intr.* to be or show brown or drab.

**pardela** *f.* ORN. a small sea gull.

**¡pardiez!** *interj.* coll. by Jove!

**pardillo** *adj.-m.* rustic. 2 *m.* ORN. linnet.

**pardo, -da** *adj.* brown, drab, reddish gray. 2 dark, cloudy. 3 flat [voice]. 4 *gramática parda,* shrewdness, know-how.

**pardusco, -ca** *adj.* brownish, drabbish, grayish.

**pareado** *m.* couplet [pair of verses].
**parear** *tr.* to pair, match, arrange in couples.
**parecencia** *f.* resemblance, likeness.
1) **parecer** *m.* opinion, mind, advice. *2* looks, personal aspect: *ser de buen ~*, to be good looking. *3* appearance: *por el bien ~*, to save appearances.
2) **parecer** *intr.* to appear, show [become or be visible]. *2* to turn up [after having been lost]. *3* to appear, seem, look like. *4 impers.* to seem, look like, strike; *~ mentira*, it seems incredible; *según parece, al parecer*, as it seems. *5 ref.* to resemble, resemble each other, be alike. *6 parecerse a*, to resemble, be like. ¶ Conjug. like *agradecer*.
**parecido, -da** *adj.* resembling, similar [to], like. *2 bien ~*, good-looking; *mal ~*, bad-looking. *3 m.* resemblance, likeness.
**pared** *f.* MAS., ANAT., BOT., MIN., PHYS. wall: *~ maestra*, main wall; *~ medianera*, party wall; *~ por medio* [of horses], adjoining, contiguous. *2* partition, brick partition. *3* wall [something resembling a wall].
**paredaño, -ña** *adj.* adjoining, separate by a wall.
**paredón** *m. augm.* large wall. *2* standing wall.
**pareja** *f.* pair, couple, yoke, team. *2* pair of soldiers or policemen. *3* dancing partner. *4* match [one of two equal or corresponding things]. *5 pl.* GAMES doubles. *6* pair [at cards]. *7 correr parejas*, to be on a par, to go together.
**parejo, -ja** *adj.* equal, like. *2* even, smooth. *3 por ~* or *por un ~*, alike, in like manner.
**parénquima** *m.* BOT., ZOOL. parenchyma.
**parentela** *f.* kindred, kinsfolk, relations.
**parentesco** *m.* kinship, relationship.
**paréntesis** *m.* parenthesis: *entre ~, por ~*, parenthetically; by the bye.
**pareo** *m.* pairing, coupling.
**paresa** *f.* peeress.
**paresia, paresis,** *f.* MED. paresis.
**parezco, parezca,** etc. *irr.* V. PARECER.
**pargo** *m.* PAGRO.
**parhelia** *f.*, **parhelio** *m.* METEOR. parhelion.
**parhilera** *f.* ARCH. ridgepole, ridgepiece.
**paria** *m.* pariah, outcast.
**parias** *f.* tribute, homage. *2* ANAT. placenta.
**parida** *f.* woman lately delivered of a baby.
**paridad** *f.* parity, equality; comparison.
**paridera** *adj.* prolific [female]. *2 f.* parturition [of cattle].
**pariente, -ta** *m.-f.* relation, relative, kinsman, kinswoman.
**parietal** *adj.* parietal. *2 m.* ANAT. parietal bone.
**parietaria** *f.* BOT. wall pellitory.
**parihuela** *f.*, or **parihuelas** *f. pl.* handbarrow. *2* litter, stretcher.
**paripinado, -da** *adj.* BOT. paripinnate.
**parir** *tr.* to give birth to, to bring forth. *2 intr.* to be delivered of a baby. *3* [of an animal] to bring forth young.
**París** *m. pr. n.* MYTH. Paris.
**París** *m. pr. n.* GEOG. Paris.
**parisién, parisiense** *adj.-n.* Parisian.
**parisino, -na** *adj.* Parisian.
**parla** *f.* facility in speaking, loquacity. *2* chatter.
**parlador, -ra** *m.-f.* chatterer.
**parlamentar** *intr.* to talk, converse. *2* to parley [discuss terms].
**parlamentario, -ria** *adj.-n.* parliamentary, parliamentarian.
**parlamentarismo** *m.* parliamentarism.

**parlamento** *m.* Parliament. *2* legislative body. *3* speech, address. *4* THEAT. speech. *5* parley.
**parlanchín, -na** *adj.* chattering, babbling. *2 m.-f.* chatterer, babbler.
**parlar** *intr.* to speak fluently. *2* to chatter, jabber, babble. *3* [of a bird] to talk.
**parlería** *f.* loquacity. *2* tale, gossip.
**parlero, -ra** *adj.* talkative. *2* babbling. *3* expressive [eyes]. *4* garrulous, warbling, bubbling.
**parlón, -na** *adj.* loquacious, garrulous.
**parlotear** *intr.* coll. to prattle, prate, chatter.
**parloteo** *m.* prattle, idle talk.
**Parnaso** *m.* GEOG., MYTH., LIT. Parnassus.
**parné** *m.* coll. money.
**paro** *m.* MACH. stop, stopping. *2* suspension of work or action; layoff, shutdown; *~ forzoso*, unemployment. *3* ORN. titmouse.
**parodia** *f.* parody.
**parodiar** *tr.* to parody.
**parodista** *m.-f.* parodist.
**parola** *f.* coll. fluency, volubility. *2* coll. idle talk.
**paronimia** *f.* paronymy.
**paronomasia** *f.* paronomasia.
**parótida** *f.* ANAT. parotid gland. *2* MED. mumps.
**paroxismo** *m.* MED. paroxysm. *2* extremity [of pain, feeling, passion, etc.].
**paroxítono** *adj.* PHONET. paroxytone.
**parpadear** *intr.* to blink, wink [move the eyelids].
**parpar** *intr.* [of a duck] to quack.
**parque** *m.* park, garden, gardens: *~ zoológico*, zoological garden. *2* MIL. park. *3* assemblage of engines, cars, etc., for a public service. *4* (Am.) AUTO. parking area.
**parquedad** *f.* sparingness, paucity.
**parquial** *adj.* parochial. *2 f.* parish church.
**parra** *f.* grapevine [esp. a large one with spreading arms]. *2* earthen jar, honey jar.
**parrado, -da** *adj.* spreading [tree].
**párrafo** *m.* paragraph. *2* paragraph mark. *3* chat.
**parral** *m.* bower of grapevines. *2* large earthen jar.
**parranda** *f.* spree, revel: *ir de ~*, to go out on a spree, to revel. *2* group of merry serenaders.
**parricida** *adj.* parricidal. *2 m.-f.* parricide [person].
**parricidio** *m.* parricide [act].
**parrilla** *f.* gridiron, grill, broiler. *2* grate [of a furnace]. *3* earthen jug.
**parrocha** *f.* small sardines.
**párroco** *m.* ECCL. parson, parish priest.
**parroquia** *f.* ECCL. parish. *2* parish church. *3* congregation of a parish. *4* COM. custom, customers, clientele.
**parroquial** *adj.* parochial. *2 f.* parish church.
**parroquiano, -na** *m.-f.* ECCL. parishioner. *3* COM. customer, client, patron.
**parsi** *adj.* Parsic. *2 m.-f.* Parsee, Parsi.
**parsimonia** *f.* parsimony, economy. *2* moderation.
**parsimonioso, -sa** *adj.* parsimonious, economical.
**parte** *f.* part [portion, piece, section, division]: *~ de la oración*, part of the speech; *en gran ~*, largely; *en ~*, in part, partly; *por partes*, by parts. *2* part [share, concern, interest]: *ir a la ~*, to go shares; *llevar uno la mejor*, or *la peor ~*, to have the best, or the worse, of it; *tomar ~ en*, to take part in, to share in; *por ~ de*, on the part of. *3* hand [share in action]: *tener ~ en*, to have a hand in. *4* construction, interpretation; *tomar a mala ~*, to take in evil part; to put a bad construction to. *5* party, part, side [in dispute]: *estar de ~ de*, to support; to side with. *6* LAW party. *7* THEAT. part, rôle. *8* MUS. part. *9* part [of the

body]. *10* part, place, region, side, direction: *de ~ a ~*, through; from side to side; *en ninguna ~*, nowhere; *por todas partes*, everywhere. *11 de algún tiempo a esta ~*, for some time past. *12 de ~ de*, from, by courtesy of; in the name of. *13 de ~ de padre*, on the father's side. *14 por una ~*, on one hand; *por otra ~*, on the other hand. *15 pl.* abilities, gifts. *16* parts, genitals [also called *partes pudendas* or *vergonzosas*]. *17* telegram, dispatch. *18* official communication, communiqué. *19* report [statement]: *dar ~*, to report, inform. *20 adv.* partly.

**partear** *tr.* to assist [women] in childbirth.
**parteluz** *m.* ARCH. mullion.
**partenogénesis** *f.* BIOL. parthenogenesis.
**Partenón** *m.* Parthenon.
**partera** *f.* midwife.
**parterre** *m.* flower bed.
**partesana** *f.* partisan [kind of halberd].
**partición** *f.* partition, distribution. *2* LAW partition. *3* MATH. division.
**participación** *f.* participation, share. *2* notification, announcement. *3* COM. copartnership.
**participante** *adj.* participating. *2* notifying. *3 m.-f.* participant, sharer. *4* notifier.
**partícipe** *adj.* participant, sharing. *2 m.-f.* participant, participator, sharer.
**participial** *adj.* GRAM. participial.
**participio** *m.* GRAM. participle.
**partícula** *f.* particle.
**particular** *adj.* particular, peculiar, personal, private. *2* particular, noteworthy. *3* extraordinary, odd. *4 m.* private individual. *5* particular, item, point. *6 en ~*, in particular.
**particularidad** *f.* particularity. *2* friendship, favour [shown to someone].
**particularizar** *tr.* to particularize. *2 ref.* to be distinguished or characterized [by].
**partida** *f.* departure, leave, starting. *2* fig. departure, death. *3* entry, record [in a register of births, marriages, etc.]. *4* certificate [of birth, marriage, death]. *5* BOOKKEEP. entry, item: *~ doble*, double entry; *~ simple*, simple entry. *6* item [in a bill, invoice, etc.]. *7* COM. lot, shipment, consignment. *8* game [at cards, chess, etc.]; match [at billiards], set [at tennis]. *9* squad, gang, band; band of armed persons. *10* excursion, party: *~ de campo*, outing, picnic; *~ de caza*, hunting. *11* part, place. *12* turn, deed [as it affects another]: *mala ~*, bad turn. *13 tragarse la ~*, to guess another's intentions.
**partidario, -ria** *adj.* partisan, supporting. *2* advocating, being for, [ideas, measures, etc.]. *3 m.-f.* partisan, follower, adherent, supporter. *4* advocate [of an idea, system, etc.].
**partidismo** *m.* partisanship, party spirit.
**partidista** *adj.* having a party spirit; partisan.
**partido, -da** *p. p.* of PARTIR. *2 m.* party [body of persons united in a cause, opinion, etc.]. *3* profit, advantage. *4* favour, support; popularity. *5* SPORT. team. *6* SPORT. game, match. *7* GAMES, SPORT. odds [equalizing allowance]. *8* deal, agreement. *9* decision, resolve, measure: *tomar un ~*, to make up one's mind. *10* side [in dispute, etc.]: *tomar ~*, to take sides. *11* territorial division or district. *12* match [person considered from the point of view of marriage]. *13 darse a ~*, to desist, yield.
**partidor** *m.* divider, separator. *2* cleaver, spliter. *3* ARITH. divisor.
**partimiento** *m.* partition, division.

**partir** *tr.* to divide [in parts], to split, cleave, cut: *~ por la mitad*, to divide in two. *2* to crack [a nut.]. *3* to divide, distribute, share. *4* MATH. to divide. *5 intr.-ref.* to depart, leave, set out, start: *~ para*, to leave for. *6 intr. ~ de*, to take [something] as the basis or starting point; to start from, to reckon from. *7 a ~ de*, from [some specified time, amount, etc.] onward. *8 ref.* to divide, part [be separated]. *9* to break, split. *10* to share [use jointly].
**partitivo, -va** *adj.* GRAM. partitive.
**partitura** *f.* MUS. score.
1) **parto, -ta** *adj.-n.* Parthian.
2) **parto** *m.* parturition, labour, childbirth, delivery: *estar de ~*, to be in labour. *2* production, product, offspring: *~ del ingenio*, brain child.
**parturienta** *adj.* parturient [woman]. *2 f.* woman in confinement.
**parva** *f.* light breakfast [on fast days]. *2* grain spread in the threshing floor. *3* heap, pile.
**parvedad, parvidad** *f.* smallness, shortness.
**parvo, -va** *adj.* small, little, short.
**parvulez** *f.* smallness. *2* simplicyty, innocence.
**párvulo, -la** *adj.* small. *2* simple, innocent. *3* humble. *4 m.-f.* little child.
**pasa** *f.* raisin: *~ de Corinto*, currant. *2* kink [of a Negro's hair]. *3* NAUT. channel.
**pasable** *adj.* PASADERO.
**pasacalle** *m.* MUS. a lively march.
**pasada** *f.* passage, passing: *de ~*, on the way; hastly. *2* SEW. long stitch. *3* WEAV. pick. *4* coll. *mala ~*, mean trick.
**pasadera** *f.* stepping stone. *2* footbridge.
**pasadero, -ra** *adj.* passable [capable of being passed]. *2* passable, tolerable. *3* sufferable. *4 m.* PASADERA.
**pasadizo** *m.* alley, passage, corridor, aisle, hall.
**pasado, -da** *adj.* past, gone by. *2* elapsed [time]. *3* last [week, month, year]. *4* overripe, spoiled [fruit]; tainted [meat]. *5 ~ de moda*, out-of-fashion, out-of-date. *6 ~ mañana*, day after tomorrow. *7 m.* past [past time; person's life].
**pasador** *m.-f.* one who passes something across; smuggler. *2 m.* bolt [door-fastening]. *3* pin [of hinge]. *4* hairpin, bodkin. *5* JEW. ring for a necktie or neckcloth. *6* MIL. a safety pin with a bar for wearing medals. *7* strainer; colander.
**pasagonzalo** *m.* coll. tap, flick, light blow.
**pasaje** *m.* passage; passing. *2* passage money. *3* passage way, way. *4* passage [on a ship]. *5* passengers in a ship. *6* NAUT. strait [between land and island]. *7* passage [in a speech or literary work]. *8* lane, alley, arcade. *9* MUS. transition.
**pasajero, -ra** *adj.* frequented [thoroughfare]. *2* passing, transient, transitory. *3 m.-f.* passenger.
**pasamanería** *f.* passementerie.
**pasamano** *m.* passement, passementerie. *2* handrail. *3* NAUT. gangway [in ancient ships].
**pasante** *adj.* HER. passant. *2 m.* assistant [of a teacher, lawyer or doctor].
**pasantía** *f.* profession or practice of a PASANTE.
**pasapán** *m.* coll. gullet, windpipe.
**pasapasa** *m.* legerdemain.
**pasaporte** *m.* passport. *2* fig. free license.
1) **pasar (un buen)** *m.* competency, sufficiency of means for living.
2) **pasar** *tr.* to pass, transfer [something to a place or person; someone to a place, post, etc.], to transmit; to promote. *2* to carry across. *3* to smuggle [goods]. *4* to pass, hand, hand over. *5* to pass [move over something]. *6* to pass [a

thread, a rope through or round something]. 7 to pass [through a filter, sieve, etc.]. 8 to pass, go over, cross. 9 to pass by, walk past. 10 to pass, surpass. 11 to pass, transgress [a limit]. 12 to penetrate, pierce. 13 to swallow [food or drink]. 14 to go through, experience, suffer. 15 to pass by, omit, overlook. 16 to pass, spend [time]. 17 to study, read [a lesson, a book]. 18 to dry [fruit]. 19 ~ a cuchillo, to put to the sword. 20 ~ el rato, to kill the time. 21 ~ lista, to call the roll. 22 pasarlo, to be; do [as regards health]; have a time; pasarlo bien, to have a good time; que lo pase usted bien, good-bye. 23 ~ por alto, to omit; to overlook. 24 ~ por las armas, to shoot [as penalty]. 25 intr. to pass, go, move, proceed [along, across, down, over, on, etc.]; to have or effect passage; to be transported. 26 to pass, go by. 27 to pass, circulate, be accepted [money, etc.]. 28 to pass, flow, run. 29 to pass [from one state to another]. 30 to live. 31 to pass away, die. 32 [of a garment, etc.] to last. 33 to pass [come to and end]. 34 [of time] to pass, elapse. 35 to pass [at cards or dominoes]. 36 to enter, go, come in or into. 37 ~ a [with an inf.], to proceed to [do, etc.]. 38 ~ de, to go beyond; to exceed. 39 ~ de largo, to pass without stopping. 40 ~ por, to pass or go along, by, through, etc.]; to be held, be regarded as; to call at [a place]. 41 ~ por encima de, to disregard [rules, difficulties, etc.]. 42 ~ por la imaginación, to cross the mind. 43 ~ sin, to do without. 44 ir pasando, to get along. 45 impers. to pass, happen; to be. the matter: ¿qué pasa?, what is the matter?; ¿qué le pasa?, what is the matter with him? 46 ref. to go over to another party. 47 to cease, finish. 48 to be forgotten. 49 to lose its force. 50 [of fruit] to become spoiled, overripe; [of meat] to become tainted; [of fire] to burn out. 51 [of a vessel] to leak. 52 [of a bolt, etc.] to be loose. 53 pasarse de, to be too; pasarse de cortés, to be too polite. 54 pasarse sin, to do without.

**pasarela** f. footbridge. 2 NAUT. gangplank. 3 NAUT. bridge [on a ship].

**pasatiempo** m. pastime.

**pasavante** m. NAUT. safe-conduct.

**pascua** f. Passover. 2 ECCL. Easter and each of the Church holidays: Twelfth-day, Pentecost and Christmas: ~ de Resurrección, or florida, Easter; ~ de Pentecostés, Pentecost. 3 pl. Pascuas de Navidad, Christmas holidays; estar como unas pascuas, to be as merry as a cricket; felices Pascuas, merry Christmas.

**pascual** adj. paschal.

**pascuilla** f. first Sunday after Easter.

**pase** m. pass [permit, ticket, etc.]. 2 exequatur. 3 pass [of hand]. 4 FENC. pass, feint. 5 CARDS, FOOTBALL pass. 6 BULLF. instance of inciting the bull and letting it pass by.

**paseante** m.-f. stroller, promenader.

**pasear** intr.-ref. to pace; to walk about, stroll, saunter, take a walk; to ride, drive or go on a boat for pleasure, to promenade. 2 tr. to walk [a horse]. 3 to take out to walk; to carry around with oneself; to promenade. 4 ref. to be idle.

**paseata** f. coll. walk, promenade; riding.

**paseo** m. walk, stroll; pleasure ride, drive or boating; promenade; dar un ~, to take a walk, ride, etc.; mandar a ~, to send about one's business. 2 public walk, parade, mall, promenade. 3 avenue, boulevard.

**pasera** f. place for drying fruit. 2 drying of fruit.

**pasibilidad** f. passibility.

**pasible** adj. passible.

**pasicorto, -ta** adj. walking with short steps.

**pasilargo, -ga** adj. walking with long steps.

**pasillo** m. corridor, narrow passage. 2 aisle [passage between rows of seats].

**pasión** f. passion [in every sense except rage, wrath]. 2 (cap.) Christ's Passion.

**pasionaria** f. BOT. passionflower.

**pasionero, pasionista** m. ECCL. Passion singer.

**pasito** m. dim. short step: ~ a ~, very leisurely or gently. 2 adv. gently, softly.

**pasitrote** m. short trot.

**pasividad** f. passiveness, passivity.

**pasivo, -va** adj. passive. 2 unresponsive. 3 GRAM. past, perfect [participle]; passive [voice]. 4 haber pasivo, retirement pension. 5 clases pasivas, pensionaries. 6 m. COM. liabilities.

**pasmar** tr. to chill. 2 to benumb, paralyse. 3 to astonish, amaze. 4 ref. to chill [be chilled]. 5 to be astonished or amazed.

**pasmarota, pasmarotada** f. coll. exaggerated show of astonishment, wonder or surprise.

**pasmo** m. MED. chill, cold. 2 MED. tetanus. 3 astonishment, wonder. 4 astonishing thing, prodigy.

**pasmoso, -sa** adj. astonishing, marvellous.

1) **paso, -sa** adj. dried [fruit].

2) **paso** m. step, pace, footstep: dar un ~, to take a step, seguir los pasos a, to trail, watch [someone]; seguir los pasos de, to follow in the footsteps of; volver uno sobre sus pasos, to retrace one's steps; a cada ~, fig. at every turn. 2 step [in dancing]. 3 step [short distance; degree in progress]; a pocos pasos, at a short distance; a este ~, at this rate; a grandes pasos, apace; por sus pasos contados, by its regular course. 4 step, pace, gait: apretar el ~, to hasten one's steps; aflojar el ~, to slow down; marcar el ~, MIL. to mark time. 5 step [of stairs]. 6 step, move, measure. 7 passage [passing; migration; transition; progress]; estar de ~, to be a transient; al ~ que, fig. while; de ~, in passing; by the way. 8 passage, way: abrir ~, to make way; dar ~, to afford a passage; to give place; salir al ~, to meet or stop on the way. 9 incident, event, situation: salir del ~, to get out of the difficulty. 10 each of the stages of the Christ's Passion; statue or group representing it. 11 THEAT. very short piece. 12 pass, strait. 13 exequatur. 14 basting stitch. 15 MECH. pitch [of nut; screw, etc.]. 16 RLY. ~ a nivel, grade crossing. 17 adv. gently, softly.

**pasquín** m. pasquinade or political writing posted in a public place.

**pasta** f. paste [soft, plastic mixture], mash. 2 paste, dough [for pastry]. 3 pulp [for making paper]. 4 coll. dough, money. 5 (Am.) cookie. 6 BOOKB. board binding. 7 ~ para sopa, alimentary paste. 8 buena ~, mild disposition.

**pastadero** m. pasture, grazing field.

**pastaflora** f. sweetmeat of flour, sugar and eggs.

**pastar** intr. [of sheep or cattle] to pasture, graze. 2 tr. to pasture, graze [lead or put to pasture].

**pastel** m. COOK. pie, pasty. 2 cake, piece of pastry. 3 fig. secret agrement or compromise. 4 BOT. woad. 5 PAINT. pastel.

**pastelear** intr. to trim, compromise [politically].

**pasteleo** m. secret dealing, trimming, temporization, compromising [in politics].

**pastelería** *f.* pastry. *2* pastry shop. *3* pastry cooking.

**pastelero, -ra** *m.-f.* pastry cook. *2* POL. trimmer, temporizer.

**pastelillo** *m. dim.* small pie, patty.

**pastelista** *m.* pastelist, pastellist.

**pasterización** *f.* pasteurization.

**pasterizar** *tr.* to pasteurize.

**pastilla** *f.* pastil, pastille, tablet, lozenge, drop. *2* cake [of soap, chocolate, etc.].

**pastinaca** *f.* BOT. parsnip. *2* ICHTH. sting ray.

**pastizal** *m.* pasture ground for horses.

**pasto** *m.* pasturing, gazing. *2* pasture [herbage for cattle or sheep]; pasture ground. *3* food [for cattle]. *4* fig. nourishment, pabulum. *5 a todo* ~, abundantly, unrestrictedly.

**pastor** *m.* shepher; herdsman. *2* ~ *protestante*, pastor, protestant minister.

**pastora** *f.* shepherdess.

**pastoral** *adj.* pastoral [of shepherds]. *2* LIT., ECCL. pastoral. *3 f.* pastoral [play]. *4* ECCL. pastoral [letter]. *5* MUS. pastorale.

**pastorear** *tr.* to shepherd [flocks or souls].

**pastorela** *f.* sepherd's song. *2* LIT. pastourelle.

**pastoreo** *m.* shepherding, pasturing.

**pastoril** *adj.* pastoral [of shepherds].

**pastosidad** *f.* pastiness, doughiness. *2* mellowness [of the voice]. *3* PAINT. pastosity.

**pastoso, -sa** *adj.* pasty, doughy. *2* mellow [voice]. *3* PAINT. pastose.

**pastura** *f.* pasture, fodder. *2* pasture ground.

**pata** *f.* paw, foot, hoof and leg [of animals]. *2* fig. leg [of human being]: *estirar la* ~, coll. to kick the bucket, to die: *meter la* ~, coll. to make a blunder; *a cuatro patas*, on all fours; *a la* ~ *coja*, hopping; *a* ~, on foot, walking. *3* leg [of a table, etc.]: ~ *de banco*, fig. absurdity, stupid remark; *patas arriba*, upside down, topsy-turvy. *4* ORN. duck [female of a drake]. *5* ~ *de gallo*, fig. crow's feet [wrinkles at outer corner of eye]; coll. absurdity, stupid remark. *6 tener mala* ~, to have bad luck.

**patacón** *m.* peso, silver dollar.

**patache** *m.* NAUT. tender.

**patada** *f.* kick [blow with the foot]: *dar la* ~ *a*, to kick out; *a patadas*, in abundance. *2* stamp [stamping the foot]. *3* footstep, footprint.

**patagón, -na** *adj.-n.* Patagonian.

**patalear** *intr.* to kick about violently. *2* to stamp one's feet [with rage, annoyance, etc.].

**pataleo** *m.* violent kicking. *2* stamping one's feet. *3* patter, tramp [sound].

**pataleta** *f.* fit or convulsion; feigned fit or convulsion.

**patán** *m.* rustic, churl, boor.

**patarata** *f.* rubbish, trash, paltry trifle, nonsense. *2* ridiculous affectation of feeling; overpoliteness.

**patas** *m.* coll. the Devil.

**patata** *f.* BOT. potato. *2* sweet potato [tuber].

**patatero, -ra** *adj.* potato-eating. *2* coll. up from the ranks [military officer]. *3 m.-f.* potato seller.

**patatín, patatán (que)** coll. subterfuges.

**patatús** *m.* coll. fit, fainting fit.

**patear** *tr.* coll. to kick, beat with the feet. *2* coll. to give a rough dressing down; to treat [someone] roughly. *3* coll. [of an audience] to express disapproval of by stamping the feet. *4* intr. coll. to stamp the feet [in anger, etc.]. *5* coll. to be very angry.

**patena** *f.* ECCL. paten.

**patentar** *tr.* to patent.

**patente** *adj.* patent, clear, evident. *2 f.* patent. *3* licence, certificate. *4* MIL. commission. *5* NAUT. ~ *de navegación*, certificate of registry; ~ *de sanidad*, bill of health.

**patentizar** *tr.* to show, reveal, make evident.

**pateo** *m.* stamping the feet.

**paternal** *adj.* paternal, fatherly.

**paternidad** *f.* paternity, fatherhood. *2* authorship. *3* ECCL. title given to a father [monk].

**paterno, -na** *adj.* paternal; from the male line.

**paternalmente** *adv.* paternally, fatherly.

**paternóster** *m.* Lord's Prayer, paternoster.

**pateta** *m.* coll. old Nick, the Devil.

**patético, -ca** *adj.* pathetic.

**patetismo** *m.* patheticalness.

**patiabierto, -ta** *adj.* bowlegged.

**patialbo, -ba; patiblanco, -ca** *adj.* white-footed.

**patibulario, -ria** *adj.* gallows, hideous, sinister [look, face, etc.]. *2* hair-raising.

**patíbulo** *m.* scaffold [for executions], gallows.

**paticojo, -ja** *adj.* lame, limping.

**patidifuso, -sa** *adj.* astonished, astounded, amazed.

**patiestevado, -da** *adj.* bandy-legged, bowlegged.

**patihendido, -da** *adj.* cloven-footed, cloven-hoofed.

**patilla** *f.* a posture of the left hand in playing the guitar. *2* chape [of buckle]. *3* SEW. pocket flap. *4* CARP. tenon. *5 pl.* whiskers, mutton chops, sideburns.

**patillas** *m.* coll. old Nick, the Devil.

**patín** *m.* ORN. a kind of petrel. *2* skate [implement]: ~ *de ruedas*, roller skate. *3* AER. skid. *4* ELECT. contact shoe.

**pátina** *f.* patina.

**patinadero** *m.* skating place, skating ring.

**patinador, -ra** *m.-f.* skater.

**patinaje** *m.* skating. *2* skidding [of a vehicle].

**patinar** *tr.* to patinate. *2 intr.* to skate. *3* [of vehicles] to skid, slip on the road. *4* coll. to make a blunder.

**patinazo** *m.* skid, sudden skid. *2* coll. blunder.

**patinillo** *m. dim.* small court or courtyard.

**patio** *m.* court, yard, courtyard, campus. *2* THEAT. pit.

**patita** *f. dim.* female duckling. *2* small paw, foot or leg: *poner de patitas en la calle*, coll. to throw out; to dismiss, to discharge.

**patitieso, -sa** *adj.* coll. stiff-legged. *2* coll. astonished, astounded, amazed. *3* stiff, haughty.

**patito** *m.* male duckling.

**patituerto, -ta** *adj.* crook-legged.

**patizambo, -ba** *adj.* knock-kneed.

**pato** *m.* ORN. duck: ~ *de flojel*, eider duck. *2* ORN. drake [male duck].

**patochada** *f.* blunder, stupidity, nonsense.

**patogenia** *f.* MED. pathogenesis, pathogeny.

**patógeno, -na** *adj.* MED. pathogenic, pathogenous.

**patojo, -ja** *adj.* lame, waddling like a duck.

**patología** *f.* pathology.

**patólogo** *m.* pathologist.

**patoso, -sa** *adj.* dull and cheaply witty [person].

**patraña** *f.* lie, falsehood, fabulous story, humbug.

**patria** *f.* one's country, native country, fatherland: ~ *celestial*, heavenly home. *2* fig. home [of the arts, etc.].

**patriarca** *m.* patriarch.

**patriarcado** *m.* patriarchate.

**patriarcal** *adj.* patriarchal.

**patriciado** *m.* patriciate.

**Patricio** *m. pr. n.* Patrick.
**patricio, -cia** *adj.-n.* patrician.
**patrimonio** *m.* patrimony.
**patrio, -tria** *adj.* of one's country, native, home. *2* paternal [of the father].
**patriota** *m.-f.* patriot.
**patriotería** *f.* exaggerated patriotism, jingoism.
**patriotero, -ra** *adj.* jingoistic. *2 m.-f.* jingoist.
**patriótico, -ca** *adj.* patriotic.
**patriotismo** *m.* patriotism.
**patrística** *f.* ECCL. patristics.
**patrocinador, -ra** *adj.* patronizing, protecting. *2* RADIO., TELEV. sponsoring. *3 m.-f.* patron, protector. *4* RADIO., TELEV. sponsor.
**patrocinar** *tr.* to patronize, protect favour. *2* RADIO., telev. to sponsor.
**patrocinio** *m.* patronage, protection, favour, auspices. *2* RADIO., TELEV. sponsorship.
**patrón, -na** *m.-f.* patron, patroness, protector, protectress. *2* ECCL. patron saint. *3* host, hostess, landlord, landlady. *4* master, mistress, boss. *5 m.* NAUT. skipper. *6* pattern [for making things]. *7* standard [of measure; of money]: ~ *oro* gold standard.
**patronal** *adj.* patronal. *2* pertaining to employers, employers'. *3 f.* employers' association.
**patronato** *m.* ECCL. patronage. *2* the employers [as a class]. *3* board of trustees. *4* patronage [institution]; foundation.
**patronazgo** *m.* patronage.
**patronear** *tr.* NAUT. to skipper, command.
**patronímico, -ca** *adj.-m.* patronymic.
**patrono, -na** *m.-f.* PATRÓN 1, 2 & 4.
**patrulla** *f.* patrol. *2* coll. gang, band.
**patrullar** *intr.* to patrol.
**patudo, -da** *adj.* coll. big-footed, big-pawed.
**patulea** *f.* coll. disorderly soldiers. *2* coll. mob. *3* coll. gang of noisy brats.
**patullar** *intr.* to tramp wildly. *2* coll. to bustle around. *3* coll. to chat.
**paúl** *m.* bog, marsh, morass.
**Paula** *f. pr. n.* Pauline.
**paular** *m.* marsh, muddy hole.
**paulatino, -na** *adj.* slow, gradual.
**Paulina** *f. pr. n.* Pauline.
**paupérrimo, -ma** *adj. superl.* very poor.
**pausa** *f.* pause [temporary stop]. *2* MUS. rest.
**pausado, -da** *adj.* slow, calm, deliberate. *2 adv.* slowly, deliberately.
**pausar** *intr.* to make a pause. *2* to slow down.
**pauta** *f.* instrument for ruling paper. *2* guide lines [for writing]. *3* rule, model, standard [for action, conduct, policy].
**pautado, -da** *adj.* ruled [paper]. *2 m.* MUS. staff.
**pautar** *tr.* to rule [paper for writing or with the musical staff]. *2* to give rules or directions for.
**pava** *f.* ORN. turkey hen: ~ *real*, peahen; *pelar la* ~, coll. [of lovers] to talk by night at the window. *2* fig. dull ungraceful woman. *3* (Arg.) kettle, teapot.
**pavada** *f.* flock of turkeys. *2* inanity, triviality.
**pavana** *f.* pavan [dance].
**pavero, -ra** *m.-f.* turkey raiser or dealer. *2 m.* Andalusian broadbrimmed hat.
**pavés** *m.* pavis [large shield].
**pavesa** *f.* spark [of ignited substance], flying cinder or ember.
**pavía** *f.* BOT. pavy [clingstone peach].
**pavimentación** *f.* paving, flooring.
**pavimentar** *tr.* to pave, to floor.
**pavimento** *m.* pavement, floor.

**pavipollo** *m.* young turkey.
**pavisoso, -sa** *adj.* dull, graceless.
**pavo** *m.* ORN. turkey; turkey cock. *2* fig. dull, gullible man. *3* ORN. ~ *real*, peacock.
**pavón** *m.* ORN. peacock. *2* ENT. peacock butterfly. *3* bluing, blacking or browning [of iron or steel].
**pavonar** *tr.* to blue, black or brown [iron or steel].
**pavonear** *intr.-ref.* to strut, to show off.
**pavor** *m.* dread, fright, terror.
**pavorde** *m.* ECCL. provost.
**pavorido, -da** *adj.* terrified.
**pavoroso, -sa** *adj.* dreadful, frightful, terrific.
**pavura** *f.* PAVOR.
**payador** *m.* (Am.) PALLADOR.
**payasada** *f.* buffoonery, clownish act.
**payaso** *m.* clown, circus clown, merry-andrew.
**payés, -sa** *m.-f.* Catalan or Balearic peasant.
**payo, -ya** *m.-f.* rustic, churl.
**paz** *f.* peace [quiet; cessation of war; mental calm; state of friendliness]: *dejar en* ~, to leave alone; *que en* ~ *descanse*, may he rest in peace; *hacer las paces con*, to make peace with. *2* peacefulness. *3* ECCL. pax. *4 estar en* ~, to be even; to be quits. *5 interj.* peace!
**pazguato, -ta** *adj.* dolt, simpleton.
**pazpuerca** *f.* slattern, slut.
**¡pche!, ¡pchs!** *interj.* pshaw!
**pe** *f.* name of the letter *p: de* ~ *a pa*, from A to Z.
**peaje** *m.* toll [for the use of a public road].
**peal** *m.* foot [of a stocking]. *2* knitted legging.
**peana, peaña** *f.* base, foot, pedestal [for a figure, statue, etc.]. *2* altar step.
**peatón** *m.* walker, pedestrian. *2* rural postman.
**pebete** *m.* aromatic burning stick. *2* coll. stinker [thing].
**pebetero** *m.* perfume censer, perfume burner.
**peca** *f.* freckle.
**pecadillo** *m. dim.* peccadillo.
**pecado** *m.* sin: ~ *capital*, deadly or capital sin. *2* fig. defect, fault, excess, imperfection.
**pecador, -ra** *adj.* sinning, sinful. *2 m.-f.* sinner.
**pecaminoso, -sa** *adj.* sinful, wicked.
**pecante** *adj.* sinning, peccant. *2* excessive.
**pecar** *intr.* to sin. *2* ~ *por* or *de*, to have [some defect], to be too: *esto peca por*, or *de, corto*, this is too short.
**pécari** *m.* ZOOL. peccary.
**pecatta minuta** (Lat.) coll. peccadillo, slight fault.
**pececillo** *m. dim.* small fish.
**peceño, -ña** *adj.* pitchy.
**pecera** *f.* fish globe, fish bowl, aquarium.
**pecezuelo** *m. dim.* small foot. *2* small fish.
**peciento, -ta** *adj.* pitchy, pitch-coloured.
**pecina** *f.* slime, viscous mud. *2* PISCINA 1.
**pecio** *m.* NAUT. flotsam, jetsam, wreckage.
**peciolo** *m.* BOT. petiole.
**pécora** *f.* head of sheep [individual]. *2* coll. *buena* ~, *mala* ~, shrewd, wicked woman.
**pecorear** *tr.* to steal [cattle]. *2 intr.* MIL. to maraud, to loot.
**pecoso, -sa** *adj.* freckled, freckly, freckle-faced.
**pectina** *f.* CHEM. pectin.
**pectoral** *adj.* pectoral. *2 m.* pectoral [breastplate of Jewish high priest]. *3* ECCL. pectoral cross. *4* PHARM. pectoral.
**pecuario, -ria** *adj.* [pertaining to] cattle.
**peculado** *m.* LAW peculation.
**peculiar** *adj.* peculiar.
**peculiaridad** *f.* peculiarity.
**peculio** *m.* peculium. *2* fig. one's money.
**pecunia** *f.* money, cash.

**pecuniario, -ria** *adj.* pecuniary, financial.
**pechar** *tr.* to pay [as a tax or tribute]. *2 intr.* ~ *con,* to accept, put up with [some disagreeable duty, work, etc.].
**pechera** *f.* chest protector. *2* front [of a shirt]; bosom [of dress]. *3* jabot, shirt, frill. *4* breast strap [of harness].
**pechero, -ra** *m.-f.* commoner, plebeian. *2 m.* bib.
**pechina** *f.* scallop, scallop shell. *2* ARCH. pendentive.
**pechirrojo** *m.* ORN. linnet.
**pechisacado, -da** *adj.* coll. vain, arrogant.
**pecho** *m.* ANAT., ZOOL. chest, breast, bosom: *a ~ descubierto,* unprotected; fig. openly, frankly. *2* breast, teat: *dar el ~ a,* to nurse, suckle. *3* breast, bosom, heart [seat of affections, emotions, etc.]: *abrir el ~,* to unbosom oneself. *4* courage, spirit, fortitude. *5* short steep incline. *6* obs. tax or tribute. *7 tomar a ~,* to take to heart; to take seriously.
**pechuga** *f.* breast [of fowl]. *2* coll. breast, bosom [upper front of the human body].
**pedagogía** *f.* pedagogy.
**pedagógico, -ca** *adj.* pedagogic, pedagogical.
**pedagogo** *m.* pedagogue.
**pedal** *m.* MACH. pedal, treadle. *2* MUS. pedal.
**pedalear** *intr.* to pedal.
**pedáneo** *adj.* LAW petty, inferior.
**pedante** *adj.* pedantic. *2 m.-f.* pedant.
**pedantería** *f.* pedantry.
**pedantón** *m.* augm. great pedant.
**pedazo** *m.* piece, fragment, bit: ~ *de animal,* or *de alcornoque,* dolt, imbecile, good-for-nothing; ~ *de pan,* crumb; song [small price]; insignificant salary; *hacer pedazos,* to break to pieces; *morirse por los pedazos de,* to be madly in love with; *ser un ~ de pan,* to be extremely good-natured.
**pederastia** *f.* pederasty.
**pedernal** *m.* flint. *2* flintiness, extreme hardness.
**pedernalino, -na** *adj.* flinty; very hard.
**pedestal** *m.* pedestal. *2* PEANA 1.
**pedestre** *adj.* pedestrian.
**pediatría** *f.* MED. pediatrics.
**pedicelo** *m.* BOT., ZOOL. pedicel.
**pedicoj** *m.* hop, jumb on one foot.
**pedicular** *adj.* pedicular.
**pedículo** *m.* BOT. pedicle.
**pedicuro, -ra** *m.-f.* chiropodist.
**pedido** *m.* COM. order. *2* request, petition.
**pedigón, -na; pedigüeño, -ña** *adj.* persistent in asking or begging. *2 m.-f.* importunate asker.
**pediluvio** *m.* MED. pediluvium, foot bath.
**pedimento** *m.* petition. *2* LAW claim, bill.
**pedir** *tr.* to ask, ask for, beg, request: ~ *algo a alguien,* to ask someone for something; ~ *limosna,* to beg; ~ *permiso para,* to beg leave for; *a ~ de boca,* according to desire. *2* to ask [a price]. *3* to ask in marriage. *4* COM. to order. *5* to wish, desire. *6* [of things] to ask, ask for, call for, demand, need, require. *7* ~ *cuenta,* to call to account. *8* ~ *prestado,* to borrow. *9 pedírselo a uno el cuerpo,* to long for it. *10 intr.* to beg. *11* to collect [for charitable purposes]. *12* ~ *por,* to inquire after [a person]. ‖ CONJUG. like *servir.*
**pedo** *m.* wind from the anus.
**pedorrera** *f.* flatulence, frequently breaking wind.
**pedorreta** *f.* sound made to imitate the breaking of wind.
**pedrada** *f.* throw of a stone. *2* hit or blow with a stone: *matar a pedradas,* to stone to death.

**pedrea** *s.* throwing of stones. *2* fight with stones. *3* fall of hail. *4* fig. small prizes in lottery.
**pedregal** *m.* stony ground.
**pedregoso, -sa** *adj.* stony, full of stones.
**pedrejón** *m.* boulder.
**pedreñal** *m.* blunderbuss fitted with a flintlock.
**pedrera** *f.* stone pit, -quarry.
**pedrería** *f.* jewelry, precious stones.
**pedrero** *m.* stonecutter. *2* slinger.
**pedrisco** *m.* METEOR. hail; hailstorm.
**pedrizo, -za** *adj.* stony, full of stones.
**Pedro** *m. pr. n.* Peter.
**pedrusco** *m.* stone, rough piece of stone.
**pedúnculo** *m.* ANAT., BOT., ZOOL. peduncle.
**peer** *intr.-ref.* to break wind.
**pega** *f.* sticking together. *2* pitch varnish. *3* coll. practical joke, trick. *4* coll. poser, catch question [in an examination]. *5* beating, drubbing. *6 de ~,* sham, worthless.
**pegadizo, -za** *adj.* sticky, adhesive. *2* catching, contagious, infectious. *3* catchy [music, tune]. *4* sponging [person]. *5* false [not natural].
**pegado** *m.* patch, sticking plaster.
**pegadura** *f.* gluing, sticking.
**pegajosidad** *f.* stickiness, glutinosity.
**pegajoso, -sa** *adj.* sticky, clammy, glutinous, viscous. *2* catching, contagious. *3* coll. mushy.
**pegamiento** *m.* gluing, sticking, joining.
**pegante** *adj.* sticking, adhesive, glutinous.
**pegar** *tr.* to glue, cement, stick, join. *2* to attach, fasten [by sewing, tying, etc.]. *3* to bring close [to], to place against. *4* to infect with, give [a disease, etc.]. *5* to set [fire]. *6* to give, deal, deliver [a blow, etc.]. *7* to beat [inflict blows on]. *8* to give, take, execute [shouts, jumps, etc.]. *9 pegársela a uno,* to make a fool of someone. *10 no ~ los ojos,* not to sleep a wink. *11 intr.* to be sticking. *12* to take root. *13* [of a fire] to catch. *14* to pass, go, be credible: *ésa no pega,* that is too thin, that won't go. *15* to be pertinent. *16* to suit, accord. *17* to join. *18* to hit, knock, strike. *19 ref.* to stick; adhere, cling. *20* to keep close. *21* COOK. to burn [adhere to the saucepan]. *22* to join [others] unasked. *23* to be infectious. *24* to come to blows.
**Pegaso** *m.* MYTH., ASTR. Pegasus.
**pego** *m.* cheating by sticking two cards together: *dar el ~,* coll. to cheat, deceive.
**pegote** *m.* pitch plaster, sticking plaster. *2* coarse patch. *3* crude or clumsy addition. *4* sticky mess. *5* sponger, parasite.
**pegotear** *intr.* coll. to sponge, live as a parasite.
**pegotería** *f.* coll. sponging.
**pegujal** *m.* small funds. *2* small farm or herd of cattle.
**pegujalero** *m.* small farmer or cattle owner.
**pegujón, pegullón** *m.* lump or ball of wool or hair.
**peguntar** *tr.* to mark [sheep] with pitch.
**peinada** *f.* combing [the hair].
**peinado** *m.* combing. *2* hairdressing, hairdo, coiffure.
**peinador, -ra** *adj.* combing. *2 m.-f.* comber. *3* hairdresser. *4 m.* wrapper, peignoir. *5 f.* combing machine.
**peinadura** *f.* combing. *2* combings.
**peinar** *tr.* to comb, dress or do [the hair]. *2* to comb [wool, cotton, etc.]. *3 ref.* to comb, dress or do one's hair.
**peinazo** *m.* CARP. crosspiece [of a door or window].
**peine** *m.* comb [for combing the hair]. *2* comb,

card [for wool, cotton, etc.]. *3* WEAV. reed [of the loom]. *4* cartridge clip. *5* coll. sly fellow.
**peinería** *f.* comb factory or shop.
**peineta** *f.* comb [for confining the hair or for adornment]; back comb.
**peje** *m.* ZOOL. fish: ~ *ángel*, angelfish; ~ *araña*, stingbull. *2* coll. cunning, crafty fellow.
**pejepalo** *m.* stockfish.
**pejesapo** *m.* ICHTH. angler.
**pejiguera** *f.* bother, botheration.
**pela** *m.* PELADURA.
**pelada** *f.* pelt, sheepskin stripped of wool.
**peladera** *f.* alopecia, loss of the hair.
**peladilla** *f.* sugar almond. *2* small pebble.
**pelado, -da** *adj.* bald, bare, hairless, featherless, treeless, leafless. *2* peeled. *3* naked [without addition]. *4* fig. penniless. *5* *canto* ~, pebble. *6* *m.* penniless person.
**peladura** *f.* peeling, plucking, stripping. *2* peelings.
**pelafustán, -na** *m.-f.* good-for-nothing.
**pelagatos,** *pl.* **-tos** *m.* penniless fellow, ragamuffin.
**pelágico, -ca** *adj.* pelagic, oceanic.
**pelagra** *f.* MED. pellagra.
**pelaje** *m.* pelage, coat, fur [of an animal]. *2* coll. clothes, apparel. *3* coll. sort, kind, description.
**pelambrera** *f.* shock of hair. *2* TAN. place in which hair is removed from hides. *3* alopecia.
**pelamesa** *f.* hair-pulling scuffle.
**pelandusca** *f.* coll. harlot, strumpet.
**pelantrín** *m.* small farmer, petty farmer.
**pelar** *tr.* to remove, cut, shave the hair of. *2* to pluck [a fowl]. *3* to peel, bark, hull. *4* fig. to fleece, clean out [strip of money or property]. *5* (Am.) to beat, thrash. *6* *duro de* ~, very difficult. *7* *ref.* to lose the hair. *8* to peel off. *9* coll. to get one's hair cut. *10* (Am.) to be confused. *11* (Am.) to slip away; to die.
**pelásgico, -ca** *adj.* Pelasgian, Pelasgic.
**pelazga** *f.* row, -quarrel, scuffle.
**peldaño** *m.* step [of stairs].
**pelea** *f.* fight; combat. *2* wrangle. *3* struggle.
**peleador, -ra** *adj.* fighting. *2* quarrelsome.
**pelear** *intr.* to fight. *2* to battle. *3* to quarrel. *4* to struggle. *5* *ref.* to fight [come to blows]. *6* to quarrel, fall out.
**pelechar** *intr.* [of animals] to begin to have hair of feathers; to fledge. *2* coll. to improve one's fortune or health.
**pelele** *m.* stuffed figure [of straw and rags]. baby's knitted sleeping suit. *3* coll. nincompoop.
**pelendengue** *m.* PERENDENGUE.
**peleón** *m.* cheap wine.
**peleona** *f.* quarrel, row.
**peletería** *f.* furriery. *2* fur shop.
**peletero** *m.* furrier.
**peliagudo, -da** *adj.* arduous, difficult. *2* sly, clever.
**peliblanco, -ca** *adj.* white-haired.
**pelícano** *m.* ORN. pelican. *2* DENT. pelican.
**pelicano, -na** *adj.* gray-haired.
**película** *f.* pellicle, film. *2* PHOT. film. *3* CINEM. film, moving picture. *4* moving-picture reel.
**peligrar** *intr.* to peril, be in danger.
**peligro** *m.* danger, peril, risk, hazard, distress: *barco en* ~, ship in distress.
**peligroso, -sa** *adj.* dangerous, perilous, risky.
**pelilargo, -ga** *adj.* long-haired.
**pelillo** *m.* tiny hair or fibre. *2* trifle, trifling difference: *pelillos a la mar*, coll. let bygones be bygones; *no reparar en pelillos*, coll. not to bother about trifles.

**pelilloso, -sa** *adj.* coll. touchy, peevish.
**pelinegro, -gra** *adj.* black-haired.
**pelirrojo, -ja** *adj.* red-haired.
**pelitre** *m.* BOT. pellitory of Spain.
**pelma, pelmazo** *m.* compressed mass. *2* coll. lump, sluggard [person]. *3* coll. bore [person].
**pelo** *m.* hair, fibre, filament: *agarrarse*, or *asirse de un* ~, fig. to seize upon any trivial pretext; *no tener pelos en la lengua*, coll. to be outspoken. *2* hair's breadth; *por un* ~, by a hair's breadth. *3* smallest thing or quantity: *no tener* ~ *de tonto*, coll. to be clever, shrewd. *4* hair [collect]; coat, fur [of animal]; pile, nap [of cloth]: *mata de* ~, head of hair; *tomar el* ~ *a*, to pull the leg of; *venir al* ~, to be to the point; to be opportune; to suit perfectly; *contra* ~, backwards; fig. against the grain; fig. untimely. *5* down [of birds or fruit]. *6* flaw [in gems or metals]. *7* difficulty: *tener pelos*, to be a hard nut or crack. *8* *pl.* hair [of head]; *estar hasta los pelos de*, coll. to be sick of.
**pelón, -na** *adj.* bald, hairless. *2* coll. poor, penniless. *3* *m.-f.* bald person. *4* coll. penniless person. *5* *m.* (Am.) dried peach.
**pelona** *f.* alopecia, loss of hair.
**Peloponeso** *m. pr. n.* GEOG. Peloponnesus.
**pelosilla** *f.* VELLOSILLA.
**peloso, -sa** *adj.* hairy.
**pelota** *f.* ball [used in games]; hand ball; ball game: ~ *vasca*, pelota; *la* ~ *está en el tejado*, fig. the matter is still undecided. *2* ball [of mud, snow, etc.]. *3* (Am.) boat made of leather. *4* coll. accumulation of debts. *5* COM. accomodation bill. *6* *en* ~, naked.
**pelotari** *m.* pelota player.
**pelotazo** *m.* blow or hit with a ball.
**pelote** *m.* goat's hair [for stuffing furniture].
**pelotear** *tr.* to check [an account]. *2* *intr.* to play or throw a ball [without playing a game]. *3* to argue, dispute, wrangle.
**pelotera** *f.* dispute, -quarrel, wrangle.
**pelotilla** *f. dim.* small ball. *2* coll. *hacer la* ~ *a*, to fawn on.
**pelotón** *m. augm.* large ball. *2* ball of tangled hair. *3* small party, squad, platoon: ~ *de ejecución*, MIL. firing party o squad; ~ *de los torpes*, MIL. awkward squad.
**peltre** *m.* pewter.
**peluca** *f.* wig. *2* coll. wig, wigging, reprimand.
**pelucón** *m. augm.* large wig.
**pelucona** *f.* coll. gold doubloon.
**peluche** *f.* plush.
**peludo, -da** *adj.* hairy, shaggy. *2* *m.* mat with shaggy pile.
**peluquera** *f.* hairdresser [woman].
**peluquería** *f.* hairdresser's [shop]; barber's shop.
**peluquero** *m.* hairdresser, barber. *2* wigmaker.
**peluquín** *m.* scratch wig. *2* bob wig, periwig.
**pelusa** *f.* down [of fruits or plants]. *2* flue, fluff, fuzz. *3* coll. childish jealousy or envy.
**pelvis,** *pl.* **-vis** *f.* ANAT. pelvis.
**pella** *f.* ball, lump [of soap, butter, etc.]. *2* tender head [of cauliflower, etc.]. *3* raw lard or fat of swine. *4* lump of money.
**pellada** *f.* MAS. lump or trowelful of mortar.
**pelleja** *f.* skin, hide, pelt. *2* dressed sheepskin [with the wool on]. *3* skin, hide [of a person]. *4* coll. strumpet.
**pellejería** *f.* skins, hides, pelts [collect.]. *2* skinnery. *3* skinner's trade.
**pellejero** *m.* skinner [dresser or seller of skins].
**pellejo** *m.* skin, hide, pelt; rawhide. *2* waterskin,

wineskin, wine bag. *3* coll. drunkard. *4* skin, hide [of a pers.]: *estar* or *hallarse en el ~ de otro*, coll. to be in somebody else's shoes or skin; *jugarse el ~*, to risk one's life; *salvar el ~*, to save one's hide or skin.

**pellejudo, -da** *adj.* having a flabby or baggy skin.

**pellica** *f.* coverlet of tine skins. *2* jacket of fine skins. *3* small dressed skin.

**pellico** *m.* sheepskin jacket.

**pelliza** *f.* pelisse [fur or fur-lined garment].

**pellizcar** *tr.* to pinch, nip [squeeze between tips of finger and thumb]. *2* to take a pinch of.

**pellizco** *m.* pinch [act of pinching], nip. *2* pinch, small quantity. *3 ~ de monja*, small cookie.

**pena** *f.* ORN. penna. *2* penalty, punishment, pain: *~ capital*, capital punishment. *3* pain, affliction, grief, sorrow. *4* pity: *dar ~*, to arouse pity. *5* hardship. *6* trouble, toil, difficulty. *7 valer la ~*, to be worth while, to be worth the trouble; *no vale la ~*, don't mention it. *8 a duras penas*, with a great difficulty, just, barely.

**penable** *adj.* punishable.

**penacho** *m.* ORN. crest, tuft of feathers. *2* crest plume, panache. *3* fig. arrogance, airs.

**penachudo, -da** *adj.* crested, tufted, plumed.

**penado, -da** *adj.* full of sorrows. *2* painful, arduous. *3 m.-f.* convict; prisoner serving a sentence.

**penal** *adj.* penal. *2 m.* penitentiary.

**penalidad** *f.* trouble, hardship. *2* LAW penalty.

**penalista** *m.* penologist.

**penar** *tr.* to punish, penalize [impose penalty on]. *2 intr.* to suffer, grieve, sorrow. *3* to suffer, be tormented [in purgatory]. *4 ~ por*, to long for, to pine for.

**penates** *m. pl.* penates.

**penca** *f.* pulpy leaf [of some plants]; pulpy part [of some leaves]. *2* cowhide [for flogging]. *3 hacerse de pencas*, coll. not to yield easily.

**penco** *m.* jade [horse].

**pendencia** *f.* dispute, quarrel, light.

**pendenciero, -ra** *adj.* quarrelsome.

**pender** *intr.* to hang, be suspended, dangle. *2* to depend, hang, rest: *~ de*, to depend or hang on. *3* to be pendent or pending [undecided].

**pendiente** *adj.* pendent, hanging, dangling. *2* pendent, pending [undecided]. *3* depending, hanging: *estar ~ de*, to depend on, to hang on. *4* sloping. *5 m.* earring. *6* pendant [hanging ornament]. *7* pitch [of a roof]. *8 f.* slope, declivity, grade, gradient, dip.

**péndola** *f.* pendulum [of clock]. *2* clock [with pendulum]. *3* PLUMA 1 & 3.

**pendolista** *m.* penman.

**pendolón** *m.* ARCH. king post.

**pendón** *m.* banner, standard, pennon. *2* coll. tall, ungainly, despicable woman.

**péndulo, -la** *adj.* pendulous, pendent, hanging. *2 m.* pendulum.

**pene** *m.* ANAT. penis.

**Penélope** *f. pr. n.* Penelope.

**peneque** *adj.* coll. drunk, intoxicated.

**penetrable** *adj.* penetrable. *2* comprehensible.

**penetración** *f.* penetration.

**penetrante** *adj.* penetrant, penetrating. *2* deep, keen, perspicacious. *3* acute, shrill, piercing.

**penetrar** *tr.-intr.* to penetrate. *2 intr.* to be acute, piercing. *3 ref. penetrarse de*, to become imbued with; to grasp, comprehend.

**pénfigo** *m.* MED. pemphigus.

**penicilina** *f.* PHARM. penicillin.

**península** *f.* GEOG. peninsula.

**peninsular** *adj.-n.* peninsular.

**penique** *m.* penny [English coin].

**penitencia** *f.* penance: *hacer ~*, to do penance; coll. to take potluck. *2* penitence, repentance.

**penitenciado, -da** *adj.* punished by the Inquisition.

**penitencial** *adj.* penitential.

**penitenciar** *tr.* to penance [impose penance on].

**penitenciaría** *f.* penitentiary [tribunal; prison].

**penitenciario, -ria** *adj.* penitentiary. *2 m.* ECCL. Cardinal chief of the penitentiary.

**penitenta** *f.* female confessant.

**penitente** *adj.* penitent, repentant. *2 m.-f.* penitent. *3* confessant.

**penol** *m.* NAUT. yardarm, peak.

**penoso, -sa** *adj.* painful. *2* laborious, arduous, fatiguing. *3* distressing. *4* embarrassing, unpleasant.

**pensado, -da** *adj.* thought-out. *2 bien ~*, proper, wise. *3 de ~*, on purpose, deliberately. *4 mal ~*, evilminded [tending to think ill].

**pensador, -ra** *adj.* thinking. *2 m.* thinker.

**pensamiento** *m.* thought, mind: *como el ~*, swiftly. *2* thought [thinking; idea, etc., produced by thinking; intention]. *3* thoughts. *4* pithy saying, maxim. *5* suspicion. *6* BOT. pansy, heartsease.

**pensar** *tr.* to think out, over, about: *pensarlo mejor*, to change one's mind. *2* to think [consider]: *~ que*, to think that. *3* to think of [a card, a number, etc.]. *4* to imagine. *5* to intend. *6* to feed [animals]. *7 intr.* to think. *8 ~ en*, to think of [direct one's thoughts to; remember; conceive]. *9 sin ~*, unexpectedly, thoughtlessly. ‖ CONJUG. as *acertar*.

**pensativo, -va** *adj.* pensive, thoughtful.

**pensil** *adj.* pensile. *2 m.* delightful garden.

**Pensilvania** *pr. n.* GEOG. Pennsylvania.

**pensión** *f.* pension, annuity, allowance. *2* board; price of board [in a boarding house or school]. *3* pension, boarding house.

**pensionado, -da** *adj.* pensioned. *2 m.-f.* pensioner [one in receipt of a pension].

**pensionar** *tr.* to grant a pension or allowance to.

**pensionista** *m.-f.* pensioner [one in receipt of a pension]. *2* boarder: *medio ~*, day boarder [in a school].

**pentadáctilo, -la** *adj.* pentadactyl.

**pentaedro** *m.* GEOM. pentahedron.

**pentagonal** *adj.* pentagonal.

**pentágono** *m.* GEOM. pentagon.

**pentagrama** *m.* MUS. staff, musical staff.

**pentámero, -ra** *adj.* BOT., ZOOL. pentamerous.

**pentámetro** *adj.-m.* PROS. pentameter.

**pentano** *m.* CHEM. pentane.

**pentápolis** *f.* pentapolis.

**Pentateuco** *m.* BIBL. Pentateuch.

**Pentecostés** *m.* Pentecost, Whitsuntide.

**penúltimo, -ma** *adj.* penult, penultimate.

**penumbra** *f.* penumbra.

**penuria** *f.* penury.

**peña** *f.* rock, boulder. *2* rock, crag. *3* group of friends, circle, club.

**peñascal** *m.* rocky or craggy place.

**peñasco** *m.* large rock, crag.

**peñascoso, -sa** *adj.* rocky, craggy.

**peñola** *f.* pen, quill [for writing].

**peñón** *m.* rock [hill of rock]: *~ de Jibraltar*, Rock of Gibraltar.

**peón** *m.* pedestrian. *2* foot soldier. *3* unskilled labourer: *~ de albañil*, hodman; *~ caminero*, road mender. *2* (Am.) farm hand. *5* top [toy]. *6* man [in draughts]. *7* pawn [in chess]. *8* beehive.

**peonaje** *m.* day labourers.

**peonia** *f.* BOT. peonia.

**peonza** *f.* whip top, whipping top [toy].

**peor** *adj.-adv. comp.* worse: ~ *que* ~, that is still worse; *tanto* ~, so much the worse. *2 adj.-adv. superl.* [with determinate article] worst; the worst.

**Pepa** *f. pr. n.* coll. Josephine.

**Pepe** *m. pr. n.* coll. Joseph, Joe.

**pepinillo** *m.* gherkin, small cucumber.

**pepino** *m.* BOT. cucumber: *no dársele a uno un* ~, not to care a pin.

**Pepita** *f. pr. n.* coll. Josephine.

**pepita** *f.* seed [of apple, melon, etc.], pip. *2* MIN. nugget. *3* VET. pip.

**Pepito** *m. pr. n.* coll. Joseph, Joe.

**pepitoria** *f.* giblet or fowl fricassee with egg sauce. *2* fig. medley, hodgepodge.

**peplo** *m.* peplum.

**pepónide** *f.* BOT. pepo.

**pepsina** *f.* BIOCHEM. pepsin.

**péptico, -ca** *adj.* peptic.

**peptona** *f.* BIOCHEM. peptone.

**pequeñez** *f.* littleness, smallness. *2* childhood. *3* pettiness. *4* meanness; mean act. *5* trifle.

**pequeño, -ña** *adj.* little, small. *2* petty. *3* young, of tender age. *4* low, humble. *5 m.-f.* child.

**pequeñuelo, -la** *m.-f.* young child, baby, tot.

**pera** *f.* BOT. pear: *pedir peras al olmo*, fig. to expect the impossible. *2* fig. sinecure. *3* imperial, goatee [beard]. *4* pear-shaped bulb [of camera shutter, etc.]: ~ *de goma*, bulb syringe. *5* ELECT. pear-shaped switch.

**perada** *f.* pear jam. *2* pear brandy.

**peral** *m.* BOT. pear tree.

**peraleda** *f.* orchard of pear trees.

**peralte** *m.* ARCH. stilting. *2* RLY. superelevation, rise.

**perborato** *m.* CHEM. perborate.

**perca** *f.* ICHTH. perch.

**percal** *m.* percale.

**percalina** *f.* percaline.

**percance** *m.* unfortunate accident, mishap.

**percatarse de** *ref.* to notice, become aware of. *2* to consider, heed.

**percebe** *m.* ZOOL. goose barnacle.

**percepción** *f.* perception. *2* percept. *3* collection, receiving [of money, rents, taxes, etc.].

**perceptible** *adj.* perceptible; perceivable. *2* collectable.

**perceptivo, -va** *adj.* perceptive.

**perceptor, -ra** *adj.* percipient. *2* collecting, receiving. *3 m.-f.* percipient. *4* collector, receiver.

**percibir** *tr.* to perceive. *2* to collect, receive.

**perclorato** *m.* CHEM. perchlorate.

**percuciente** *adj.* percussive, percutient.

**percusión** *f.* percussion, striking. *2* MED. percussion.

**percusor** *m.* percussor. *2* percussion hammer, firing pin.

**percutir** *tr.* to percuss, strike.

**percha** *f.* perch, roost [for birds]. *2* pole, bar, horizontal bar. *3* clothes rack, clothes tree. *4* snare [for birds]. *5* PERCA. *6* napping [of cloth].

**perchar** *tr.* to teasel, nap, raise the nap on [cloth].

**perchero** *m.* hat rack, clothes rack.

**percherón, -na** *adj.-n.* Percheron [horse].

**perdedor, -ra** *adj.* losing. *2 m.-f.* loser.

**perder** *tr.* to lose: ~ *de vista*, to lose sight of; *pierda*

*usted cuidado*, don't worry. *2* to mislay. *3* to forfeit. *4* to waste. *5* to miss [a train, an opportunity, etc.]. *6* to ruin [bring to ruin]; to spoil. *7* ~ *el miedo*, to cease to fear. *8* ~ *el respeto a*, to cease to respect; to be disrespectful to. *9 intr.* to lose. *10* to lose value or credit. *11* [of a fabric] to fade. *12 ref.* to lose oneself or itself. *13* to get lost. *14* to become ruined, destroyed [physically or morally]. *15* [of fruit or crops] to be spoiled, damaged. *16* fig. to love excessively. *17* to fall into disuse. *18* to be wasted. *19* to cease to be perceptible; to disappear. *20* ~ *de vista*, to disappear; fig. to be very clever or shrewd. ‖ CONJUG. like *entender*.

**perdición** *f.* perdition. *2* loss, ruin. *3* violent, unrestrained love.

**pérdida** *f.* loss: *pérdidas y ganancias*, COM. profit and loss; *vender con* ~, to sell at a loss. *2* waste [of time, etc.]; *sin* ~ *de tiempo*, without delay. *3* COM. shortage, leakage.

**perdidizo, -za** *adj.* supposed to be lost: *hacer* ~, to hide, conceal. *2* sneaking away.

**perdido, -da** *adj.* lost. *2* mislaid. *3* wasted, useless, vain. *4* stray: *bala perdida*, stray bullet; fig. harebrain. *5* vicious. *6* countersunk. *7 ratos perdidos*, idle hours. *8 estar* ~ *por*, to be madly in love with; to be mad about. *9 m.* vicious man. *10 f.* harlot.

**perdidoso, -sa** *adj.* losing, sustaining loss.

**perdigar** *tr.* COOK. to brown, to broil slightly.

**perdigón** *m.* young partridge. *2* shot [pellet], bird shot; *perdigones*, shot [collect.].

**perdigonada** *f.* shot with bird shot.

**perdiguero, -ra** *adj.* partridge hunting. *2 m.* setter [dog]. *3* partridge dealer, game dealer.

**perdimiento** *m.* PERDICIÓN, PÉRDIDA.

**perdis,** *pl.* **-dis** *m.* coll. gay blade, libertine.

**perdiz,** *pl.* **-dices** *f.* ORN. partridge. *2* ~ *blanca*, ptarmigan.

**perdón** *m.* pardon, forgiveness, grace: *con* ~, by your leave, begging pardon. *2* remission [of a debt].

**perdonable** *adj.* pardonable.

**perdonador, -ra; perdonante** *adj.* forgiving. *2 m.-f.* forgiver.

**perdonar** *tr.* to pardon, forgive. *2* to remit [a debt]. *3* to exempt, spare. *4* to excuse. *5 no* ~, not to pardon; not to omit; not to spare; not to miss.

**perdonavidas,** *pl.* **-das** *m.* bully, hector.

**perdulario, -ria** *m.-f.* careless, sloppy person. *2* vicious person.

**perdurable** *adj.* everlasting. *2* long-lasting.

**perdurar** *tr.* to last, to last long.

**perecedero, -ra** *adj.* perishable, not lasting, mortal.

**perecer** *intr.* to perish, come to an end, die. *2* to perish [suffer spiritual death]. *3* to be in great want. *4 ref. perecerse por*, to crave for, be dying for, be mad about. ‖ CONJUG. like *agradecer*.

**perecimiento** *m.* perishing, end, death.

**peregrinación,** *f.*, **peregrinaje** *m.* peregrination. *2* pilgrimage.

**peregrinamente** *adv.* rarely, strangely, curiously. *2* wonderfully.

**peregrinar** *intr.* to peregrinate, travel, roam. *2* to pilgrim.

**peregrino, -na** *adj.* wandering, traveling. *2* of passage [bird]. *3* going on a pilgrimage. *4* rare, strange, singular. *5* perfect, wonderful. *6 m.-f.* pilgrim; palmer.

**perejil** *m.* BOT. parsley. 2 *pl.* coll. frippery, showy ornaments. 3 coll. handles [titles, etc.].
**perencejo, -ja** *m.-f.* PERENGANO.
**perendengue** *m.* bauble, trinket.
**perene, perennal, perenne** *adj.* perennial, perpetual. 2 BOT. perennial.
**perengano, -na** *m.-f.* So-and-So.
**perennal** *adj.* PERENNE.
**perenne** *adj.* perennial, perpetual. 3 BOT. perennial.
**perennindad** *f.* perenniality.
**perentoriedad** *f.* peremtoriness. 2 urgency.
**perentorio, -ria** *adj.* peremptory, decisive. 2 urgent, pressing.
**pereza** *f.* laziness, sloth. 2 slowness [in actions].
**pereco, perezca,** etc. *irr.* V. PERECER.
**perezoso, -sa** *adj.* lazy, slothful, idle, indolent, slow, heavy. 2 *m.* ZOOL. sloth.
**perfección** *f.* perfection: *a la* ~, perfectly.
**perfeccionamiento** *m.* perfection [making perfect]; improvement; finish.
**perfeccionar** *tr.* to perfect; to improve.
**perfectible** *adj.* perfectible.
**perfectivo, -va** *adj.* perfective.
**perfecto, -ta** *adj.* perfect. 2 GRAM. perfect [tense].
**perfidia** *f.* perfidy.
**pérfido, -da** *adj.* perfidious, treacherous. 2 *m.-f.* perfidious person.
**perfil** *m.* profile: *de* ~, in profile. 2 outline. 3 thin stroke [of pen]. 4 *pl.* finishing touches. 5 niceties; fuss [in social behaviour].
**perfilado, -da** *p. p.* of PERFILAR. 2 *adj.* long and thin [face]. 3 well-formed [nose].
**perfilar** *tr.* to profile. 2 to outline. 3 to make fine strokes in. 4 to perfect. 5 *ref.* to show one's profile, to stand sideways.
**perfoliado, -da** *adj.* BOT. perfoliate.
**perfolla** *f.* husk of Indian corn, \*cornhusk.
**perforación** *f.* perforation, drilling, boring. 2 hole.
**perforador, -ra** *adj.* perforating, drilling. 2 *m.-f.* perforator. 3 *f.* perforator, drill.
**perforar** *tr.* to perforate, bore.
**perfumado, -da** *adj.* perfumed. 2 odoriferous.
**perfumador, -ra** *adj.* perfuming. 2 *m.-f.* perfumer. 3 *m.* perfuming pan. 4 perfume atomizer.
**perfumar** *tr.* to perfume.
**perfume** *m.* perfume. 2 odour, fragrance.
**perfumería** *f.* perfumery. 2 perfumer's shop.
**perfumero, -ra; perfumista** *m.-f.* perfumer.
**perfunctorio, -ria** *adj.* perfunctory.
**perfusión** *f.* perfusion.
**pergamino** *m.* parchment, vellum. 2 *pl.* nobiliary antecedents of a family or person.
**pergeñar** *tr.* to prepare, do, make, write.
**pergeño** *m.* coll. appearance, looks.
**pérgola** *f.* pergola. 2 roof garden.
**periantio** *m.* BOT. perianth.
**pericardio** *m.* ANAT. pericardium.
**pericarpio** *m.* BOT. pericarp.
**pericia** *f.* expertness, skill.
**pericial** *adj.* expert's: *dictamen* ~, expert's report.
**periclitar** *intr.* to be in danger. 2 to decline, decay.
**Perico** *m. pr. n.* coll. Peter. 2 ~ *de los palotes,* John Doe, So-and-So.
**perico** *m.* ORN. parakeet. 2 large fan. 3 large asparagus. 4 coll. chamber pot. 5 ZOOL. ~ *ligero,* sloth.
**pericón** *m.* large fan. 2 a popular Argentinean dance.
**periecos** *m. pl.* GEOG. periœci.
**periferia** *f.* periphery.

**periférico, -ca** *adj.* peripheric(al.
**perifollo** *m.* BOT. chervil. 2 *pl.* finery, frippery.
**perifrasear** *tr.* to periphrase.
**perifrasi, perifrasis,** *pl.* -sis *f.* RHET. periphrasis.
**perigallo** *m.* loose skin under the chin.
**perigeo** *m.* ASTR. perigee.
**perihelio** *m.* ASTR. perihelion.
**perilla** *f.* pear-shaped ornament. 2 goatee, imperial [beard]. 3 pommel [of saddlebow]. 4 lobe [of the ear]. 5 *de* ~, coll. apropos, to the point.
**perillán** *m.* rascal, sly fellow, sly dog.
**perímetro** *m.* perimeter.
**perinclito, -ta** *adj.* most ilustrious.
**perineo** *m.* ANAT. perineum.
**perinola** *f.* teetotum. 2 pear-shaped ornament.
**periódico, -ca** *adj.* periodic, periodical. 2 *m.* periodical, journal, newspaper.
**periodismo** *m.* journalism.
**periodista** *m.-f.* journalist, newspaperman.
**período** *m.* period [age, epoch; portion of time]. 2 MATH., PHYS., MED., RETH. period.
**periostio** *m.* ANAT. periosteum.
**peripatético, -ca** *adj.-n.* Peripatetic, Aristotelian. 2 *adj.* coll. ridiculous, wild [in his opinions].
**peripecia** *f.* peripeteia, vicissitude, incident.
**periplo** *m.* periplus.
**períptero** *adj.* ARCH. peripteral. 2 *m.* ARCH. peripteros.
**peripuesto, -ta** *adj.* coll. spruce, smart, dressed up.
**periquete** *m.* coll. jiffy, instant.
**Periquito** *m. pr. n.* coll. Peter.
**periquito** *m.* ORN. parakeet.
**periscios** *m. pl.* GEOG. periscii.
**periscopio** *m.* periscope.
**perisodáctilo, -la** *adj.-n.* ZOOL. perissodactyl.
**perista** *m.* coll. fence [receiver of stolen goods].
**peristáltico, -ca** *adj.* peristaltic.
**peristilo** *m.* ARCH. peristyle.
**peritación** *f.* examination or appraisal by experts.
**peritaje** *m.* PERITACIÓN. 2 one of the degrees to be obtained in some technical schools.
**perito, -ta** *adj.* skilful, skilled, expert. 2 *m.* expert. 3 one holding the degree called PERITAJE.
**peritoneo** *m.* ANAT. peritoneum.
**peritonitis** *f.* MED. peritonitis.
**perjudicar** *tr.* to hurt, damage, injure, prejudice.
**perjudicial** *adj.* harmful, injurious, prejudicial.
**perjuicio** *m.* harm, damage, injury, prejudice, detriment: *en* ~ *de,* to the detriment of.
**perjurar** *intr.-ref.* to commit perjury, to perjure oneself. 2 *intr.* to swear, be profane.
**perjurio** *m.* perjury.
**perjuro, -ra** *adj.* perjured. 2 *m.-f.* perjurer.
**perla** *f.* pearl. 2 *de perlas,* excellent, apropos.
**perlado, -da** *adj.* pearled. 2 *cebada perlada,* pearl barley.
**perlático, -ca** *m.-f.* affected with shaking palsy.
**perlería** *f.* collection of pearls.
**perlesía** *f.* MED. palsy, shaking palsy; paralysis.
**permanecer** *intr.* to remain, stay [in some place or condition], to last, endure. ‖ CONJUG. like *agradecer.*
**permanencia** *f.* stay, sojourn. 2 permanence, permanency, duration, fixedness, stability.
**permanente** *adj.* permanent. 2 *f.* permanent wave [in hair].
**permanezco, permanezca,** etc. *irr.* V. PERMANECER.
**permeable** *adj.* permeable.
**permisible** *adj.* permissible.
**permisión** *f.* permission, leave, licence, permit.

**permisivo, -va** *adj.* permissive.
**permiso** *m.* permission, leare, licence, permit: ~ *de conducir*, AUTO. drive's licence; *con su* ~, *by your leave*. 5 leave of absence.
**permitir** *tr.* to permit, allow. 2 to permit, consent; to admit of. 3 *ref.* to take the liberty [to]. 4 *poder permitirse*, to be able to afford.
**permuta** *f.* barter, exchange, permutation.
**permutación** *f.* interchange, exchange, barter, permutation. 2 MATH. permutation.
**permutar** *tr.* to interchange, exchange, barter. 2 MATH. to permute.
**pernaza** *f. augm.* big leg.
**perneador** *adj.* strong-legged.
**pernear** *intr.* to kick, shake the legs. 2 to hustle. 3 to fret, worry.
**pernera** *f.* leg [of trousers].
**pernetas (en)** *adv.* bare-legged.
**perniabierto, -ta** *adj.* bowlegged.
**pernicioso, -sa** *adj.* pernicious, harmful, injurious.
**pernigón** *m.* Genoese preserved plum.
**pernil** *m.* ham [thigh and buttock of an animal]. 2 leg [of trousers].
**pernio** *m.* door or window hinge.
**perniquebrar** *tr.* to break the leg or legs of. 2 *ref.* to break one's leg or legs. ‖ CONJUG. like *acertar*.
**perno** *m.* bolt [headed metal pin for holding things together]. 2 hook [of a door-hinge].
**pernoctar** *intr.* to pass the night.
**pero** *advers. conj.* but, yet, and yet. 2 *m.* objection, fault: *poner peros a*, to make objections to, to find fault with; *sin un* ~, faultless. 3 BOT. a variety of apple and apple tree.
**perogrullada** *f.* truism, platitude.
**perojo** *m.* BOT. a little round pear.
**perol** *m.* kettle in form of hemisphere.
**peroné** *m.* ANAT. fibula.
**peroración** *f.* peroration. 2 oration, harangue.
**perorar** *intr.* to perorate, declaim, deliver a speech.
**perorata** *f.* coll. tiresome speech.
**peróxido** *m.* CHEM. peroxide.
**perpendicular** *adj.-f.* GEOM. perpendicular.
**perpetración** *f.* perpetration.
**perpetrar** *tr.* to perpetrate.
**perpetua** *f.* BOT. globe amaranth. 2 BOT. ~ *amarilla*, everlasting flower.
**perpetuación** *f.* perpetuation.
**perpetuar** *tr.* to perpetuate. 2 *ref.* to be perpetuated; to continue unceasingly.
**perpetuidad** *f.* perpetuity.
**perpetuo, -tua** *adj.* perpetual, everlasting.
**perpiaño** *m.* ARCH. bondstone, perpend.
**Perpiñán** *pr. n.* GEOG. Perpignan.
**perplejidad** *f.* perplexity, hesitation, irresolution.
**perplejo, -ja** *adj.* perplexed, doubtful, hesitating.
**perquirir** *tr.* to seek out, investigate.
**perra** *f.* bitch [female dog]. 2 coll. drunk, drunkenness. 3 coll. child's rage or fit of temper. 4 coll. ~ *chica*, five-centime copper coin; ~ *gorda*, ten-centime copper coin.
**perrada** *f.* pack of dogs. 2 coll. dirty trick.
**perrera** *f.* doghouse, kennel. 2 RLY. dog-box. 3 coll. drudgery. 4 coll. child's rage.
**perrería** *f.* dogs [collect.]. 2 coll. dirty trick, mean action. 3 coll. insult, abuse.
**perrero** *m.* keeper of the dogs. 2 dog fancier. 3 dog-catcher.
**perrezno, -na** *m.-f.* whelp, puppy [young dog].
**perrillo, -lla** *m.-f.* puppy. 2 *m.* trigger [of firearm].
**perro, -rra** *adj.* hard wretched. 2 wicked. 3 (Am.) stubborn. 4 (Am.) selfish, mean. 5 *m.* ZOOL. dog; ~ *dálmata*, coach dog; ~ *de aguas*, ~ *de lanas*, poodle, water spaniel; ~ *del hortelano*, fig. dog in the manger; ~ *de muestra*, pointer; ~ *de presa*, ~ *dogo*, bulldog; ~ *faldero*, lap dog; ~ *galgo*, greyhound; ~ *lebrero*, hare dog; ~ *mastín*, mastiff; ~ *perdiguero*, setter; ~ *podenco*, hound; ~ *sabueso*, bloodhound; ~ *viejo*, fig. cautious, experienced person; *a otro* ~ *con este hueso*, tell that to the marines. 6 fig. dog [mean, worthless fellow].
**perroquete** *m.* NAUT. topgallant mast.
**perruno, -na** *adj.* [pertaining to] dog, canine.
**persa** *adj.-n.* Persian.
**persecución** *f.* pursuit, hunt, -chase. 2 pursuit [seeking after, aiming at]. 3 persecution.
**perseguidor, -ra** *m.-f.* pursuer. 2 persecutor.
**perseguimiento** *m.* pursuing, pursuit.
**perseguir** *tr.* to pursue, hunt, chase. 2 to pursue, seek after, aim at. 3 to persecute. ‖ CONJUG. like *servir*.
**Perseo** *m. pr. n.* ASTR., MYTH. Perseus.
**persevante** *m.* pursuivant at arms.
**perseverancia** *f.* perseverance.
**perseverante** *adj.* persevering.
**perseverar** *intr.* to persevere.
**persiano, -na** *adj.-n.* Persian. 2 *f.* flowered silk stuff. 3 Persian blind; Venetian blind. 4 slatted shutter.
**persicaria** *f.* BOT. persicary.
**pérsico, -ca** *adj.* Persian. 2 *m.* BOT. peach.
**persignarse** *ref.* to cross oneself.
**persistencia** *f.* persistence, persistency.
**persistente** *adj.* persistent, persisting.
**persistir** *intr.* to persist. 2 to endure, last long.
**persona** *f.* person: *primera* ~, first person; *en* ~, in person. 2 excellent man. 3 *pl.* people.
**personada** *adj.* BOT. personate [corolla].
**personaje** *m.* personage. 2 character [in play etc.].
**personal** *adj.* personal [one's own, private; done, made, etc., in person]. 2 *m.* personnel, staff.
**personalidad** *f.* personality. 2 person of note or distinction. 3 LAW legal capacity.
**personalizar** *intr.* to personalize, become personal. 2 *tr.* GRAM. to make personal.
**personarse** *ref.* to go, call, appear personally.
**personificación** *f.* personification.
**personificar** *tr.* to personify.
**personilla** *f. dim.* little person. 2 queer little person.
**perspectiva** *f.* perspective. 2 prospect, view, outlook. 3 deceptive appearance. 4 *pl.* prospect, prospects.
**perspicacia, perspicacidad** *f.* perspicaciousness, perspicacity. 2 keen sight.
**perspicaz** *adj.* keen-sighted. 2 perspicacious.
**perspicuidad** *f.* perspicuity.
**perspicuo, -cua** *adj.* perspicuous.
**persuadir** *tr.* to persuade. 2 *ref.* to persuade oneself, to become persuaded or convinced.
**persuasible** *adj.* credible, plausible.
**persuasión** *f.* persuasion, conviction.
**persuasivo, -va** *adj.* persuasive.
**persuasor, -ra** *m.-f.* persuader.
**pertenecer** *intr.* to belong; to pertain, concern. 2 to be incumbent [on]. ‖ CONJUG. as *agradecer*.
**perteneciente** *adj.* belonging, pertaining.
**pertenencia** *f.* belonging, ownership, property. 2 appurtenance, accesory. 3 MIN. claim.
**pertenezco, pertenezca,** etc. *irr.* V. PERTENECER.
**pértica** *f.* perch [measure of length].

**pértiga** *f.* long pole or rod; staff, verge. *2* SPORT. pole [used in pole vault].

**pértigo** *m.* pole, tongue [of cart or wagon].

**pertiguero** *m.* verger.

**pertinacia** *f.* pertinacity.

**pertinaz** *adj.* pertinacious.

**pertinencia** *f.* pertinence, fitness, relevancy.

**pertinente** *adj.* pertinent, apt, fitting, appropriate, relevant.

**pertrechar** *tr.* to supply, provide, equip. *2 ref.* to provide, equip oneself.

**pertrechos** *m. pl.* MIL. supplies, stores. *2* tools, implements [for a work or operation].

**perturbación** *f.* perturbation, disturbance. *2* unsettlement, disorder: ~ *mental*, mental disorder.

**perturbado, -da** *adj.* perturbed, disturbed. *2* insane. *3 m.-f.* insane person, lunatic.

**perturbar** *tr.* to perturb, disturb, unsettle. *2* to disconcert, confuse. *3 ref.* to be disturbed.

**peruano, -na** *adj.-n.* Peruvian.

**perulero, -ra** *adj.-n.* Peruvian. *2 m.-f.* person who has returned wealthy from Peru.

**perversidad** *f.* perversity, wickedness.

**perversión** *f.* perversion.

**perverso, -sa** *adj.* perverse, wicked, depraved.

**pervertir** *tr.* to pervert, garble. *2* to pervert, lead astray, deprave, corrupt. *3 ref.* to become perverted. ‖ CONJUG. as *hervir*.

**pervierto, pervierta,** etc. *irr.* PERVERTIR.

**pervigilio** *m.* sleeplessness, wakefulness.

**pesa** *f.* weight [for scales]; clock weight. *2* GYMN. dumbbell.

**pesacartas,** *pl.* **-tas** *m.* letter scales.

**pesada** *f.* weighing [quantity weighed].

**pesadamente** *adv.* heavily. *2* cumbrously. *3* tiresomely, annoyingly. *4* slowly, tardily. *5* clumsily.

**pesadez** *f.* heaviness. *2* burdensomeness. *3* tiresomeness, irksomeness. *4* drowsiness. *5* sultriness. *6* slowness. *7* clumsiness. *8* PHYS. gravity.

**pesadilla** *f.* nightmare.

**pesado, -da** *adj.* heavy, ponderous. *2* heavy, burdensome, hard to endure or accomplish. *3* annoying, tiresome, boring. *4* clumsy. *5* slow, sluggish. *6* deep [sleep]. *7* drowsy. *8* heavy, sultry, stuffy. *9* fat, corpulent. *10 m.-f.* bore, tiresome person.

**pesador, -ra** *m.-f.* weigher.

**pesadumbre** *f.* sorrow, grief, regret. *2* heaviness.

**pesalicores,** *pl.* **-res** *m.* hydrometer.

**pésame** *m.* condolences: *dar el* ~, to present one's condolences.

**pesantez** *f.* PHYS. gravity.

1) **pesar** *m.* sorrow, grief. *2* regret, repentance. *3 a* ~ *de*, in spite of, with all, notwithstanding; *a* ~ *mío*, against my will.

2) **pesar** *tr.* to weigh, scale. *2* to weigh [consider, ponder in the mind]. *3 intr.* to weigh. [have weight, be heavy; have influence]. *4* to cause sorrow, regret or repentance: *esto le pesará*, you'll be sorry for it. *5 pese a*, in spite of; *pese a quien pese*, whatever anybody says or does.

**pesario** *m.* SURG. pessary.

**pesaroso, -sa** *adj.* sorry, regretful, repentant. *2* sorrowful, sad.

**pesca** *f.* fishing. *2* angling. *3* catch [fish caught]. *4* salted codfish.

**pescada** *f.* MERLUZA 1.

**pescadería** *f.* fish market.

**pescadero, -ra** *m.-f.* fishmonger.

**pescadilla** *f.* ICHTH. a kind of hake.

**pescado** *m.* fish [caught]. *2* salted codfish.

**pescador, -ra** *adj.* fishing. *2 m.-f.* fisher; fisherman, fisherwoman: ~ *de caña*, angler. *3 m.* ICHTH. angler.

**pescante** *m.* coach box. *2* AUTO. front seat. *3* arm, bracket. *4* NAUT. davit.

**pescar** *tr.* to fish, catch [fish]. *2* to fish, draw [something out of water]. *3* to catch, take, get. *4* to catch [someone in a lie, etc.]. *5 intr.* to fish, angle: ~ *en río revuelto*, to fish in troubled waters.

**pescozada** *f.*, **pescozón** *m.* slap in the neck. *2* slap on the head.

**pescozudo, -da** *adj.* thick-necked.

**pescuezo** *m.* neck [part of body]. *2* fig. haughtiness.

**pesebre** *m.* crib, rack, manger.

**pesebrera** *f.* row of racks in a stable.

**pesebrón** *m.* boot [of a coach].

**peseta** *f.* peseta [monetary unit of Spain].

**pésete** *m.* curse, imprecation.

**¡pesia!** *interj.* confound it!

**pesillo** *m.* small scales for weighing coins.

**pesimismo** *m.* pessimism.

**pesimista** *adj.* pessimitic. *2 m.-f.* pessimist.

**pésimo, -ma** *adj.* very bad, very poor, wretched.

**peso** *m.* weight [of bodies]; heaviness, gravity: ~ *específico*, PHYS. specific gravity; *a* ~ *de oro*, at a very high price; *de su* ~, naturally. *2* weighing. *3* balance, scales. *4* due weight. *5* weight [importance, influence]. *6* judgement, good sense: *hombre de* ~, wise, sensible man. *7* weight, load, burden. *8* BOX. weight: ~ *gallo*, bantamweight; ~ *mosca*, flyweight. *9* peso [Spanish American monetary unit]. *10 en* ~, suspended in the air; in a body; undecided.

**pespuntar** *tr.* SEW to backstitch.

**pespunte** *m.* SEW. backstitch.

**pesquera** *f.* fishery, fishing grounds.

**pesquería** *f.* fishery [fishing; fishing grounds].

**pesquis** *m.* acumen, penetration.

**pesquisa** *f.* inquiry, investigation, search.

**pesquisar** *tr.* to inquire into, investigate.

**pestaña** *f.* ANAT. eyelash. *2* SEW. edging, fringe. *3* rim [narrow strip at the edge]. *4* MACH. flange. *5 pl.* BIOL. cilia.

**pestañear** *intr.* to wink, blink [move the eyelids]: *sin* ~, without batting an eye.

**pestañeo** *m.* winking, blinking.

**peste** *f.* pest, pestilence, plague. *2* epidemic. *3* stink, stench. *4* evil, corruption of manners. *5* coll. excess, superabundance. *6 pl. decir pestes de*, to speak ill of, to talk against.

**pestífero, -ra** *adj.* pestiferous. *2* stinking.

**pestilencia** *f.* pestilence. *2* stink, stench.

**pestilencial** *adj.* pestilential, pestiferous.

**pestilente** *adj.* pestilent. *2* stinking.

**pestillo** *m.* bolt [of a lock]: ~ *de golpe*, spring bolt. *2* door bolt, door latch.

**pestiño** *m.* honeyed fritter.

**pestorejo** *m.* CERVIGUILLO.

**pesuña** *f.* PEZUÑA.

**pesuño** *m.* ZOOL. each half of a cloven hoof.

**petaca** *f.* cigar case. *2* tobacco pouch. *3* (Am.) leather covered chest.

**pétalo** *m.* BOT. petal.

**petar** *tr.* coll. to please.

**petardear** *tr.* MIL. to blow open with petards. *2* fig. to cheat, swindle. *3 intr.* AUTO. to backfire.

**petardista** *m.-f.* cheat, swindler, sponger.

**petardo** *m.* MIL. petard. *2* petard, firecracker. *3* fig. cheat, swindle, deception.

**petate** *m.* (Am.) sleeping mat. *2* bedding and clothes of a sailor, a soldier or a prisoner; luggage: *liar el ~*, coll. to pack up and go; to die.

**petenera** *f.* Andalusian popular song: *salir por peteneras*, fig. to say something irrelevant.

**petición** *f.* petition, demand, prayer, request, asking. *2* LAW claim, bill. *3* LOG. *~ de principio*, begging of the question.

**peticionario, -ria** *m.-f.* petitioner.

**petifoque** *m.* NAUT. flying jib.

**petimetra** *f.* affected, stylish lady.

**petimetre** *m.* fop, coxcomb, dude.

**petirrojo** *m.* ORN. robin, redbreast.

**petitorio, -ria** *adj.* petitionary. *2 m.* PHARM. catalogue of drugs.

**peto** *m.* ARM. breastplate. *2* FENC. plastron. *3* BULLF. mattress covering to protect horses. *4* breast of a garment. *5* ZOOL. plastron [of a turtle].

**petral** *m.* breastplate [for a riding horse].

**petrel** *m.* ORN. petrel.

**pétreo, -a** *adj.* stony, of stone; rocky.

**petrificación** *f.* petrifaction, petrification.

**petrificar** *tr.* to petrify. *2 ref.* to petrify [become petrified].

**petrografía** *f.* petrography.

**petróleo** *m.* petroleum, mineral oil. *2* kerosene.

**petrolero, -ra** *adj.* [pertaining to] petroleum, oil. *2 m.* petroleur.

**petrolífero, -ra** *adj.* petroliferous, oil-bearing.

**petroso, -sa** *adj.* stony, petrous. *2* ANAT. petrous.

**petulancia** *f.* insolence, pertness, flippancy. *2* presumptuousness.

**petulante** *adj.* insolent, pert, flippant. *2* presumptuous.

**petunia** BOT. petunia.

**peyorativo, -va** *adj.* depreciatory. *2* GRAM. pejorative.

**1) pez** *m.* ZOOL. fish: *~ de colores*, goldfish; *~ espada*, swordfish; *~ luna*, sunfish, moonfish; *~ martillo*, hammerhead; *~ sierra*, sawfish; *~ volador*, flying fish; *estar como el ~ en el agua*, to be comfortably situated.

**2) pez** *f.* pitch, tar: *~ griega*, rosin, colophony.

**pezón** *m.* BOT. stem [of fruits]; stalk [of a leaf or flower]. *2* nipple [of a teat]. *3* BOT. umbo [of lemon, etc.]. *4* axletree's end.

**pezonera** *f.* linchpin. *2* nipple shield.

**pezpita** *f.*, **pezpítalo** *m.* AGUZANIEVES.

**pezuña** *f.* hoof, cloven-hoof.

**pi** *f.* MATH. pi.

**piada** *f.* peeping, chirping.

**piadoso, -sa** *adj.* pious, godly. *2* merciful, compassionate.

**piafar** *intr.* [of horses] to paw, stamp.

**pial** *m.* (Am.) lasso lariat. *2* (Am.) snare, trap.

**piamadre, piamáter** *f.* ANAT. pia mater.

**Piamonte (el)** *m. pr. n.* GEOG. Piedmont.

**pian, pian; pian, piano** *adv.* coll. slowly, softly.

**pianino** *m.* MUS. upright piano.

**pianista** *m.-f.* pianist. *2 m.* piano manufacturer.

**piano, pianoforte** *m.* MUS. piano: *~ de cola*, grand piano; *~ de manubrio*, piano organ; *~ de media cola*, baby grand; *~ vertical*, upright piano.

**pianola** *f.* pianola.

**piante** *adj.* peeping, chirping.

**piar** *intr.* to peep, chirp. *2* fig. to cry for.

**piara** *f.* herd [of swine, mares or mules].

**piastra** *f.* piaster.

**pica** *f.* pike [weapon]. *2* pikeman. *3* BULL. goad. *4* stonecutter's hammer. *5* pica.

**picacho** *m.* peak, sharp peak [of mountain].

**picada** *f.* peck [of bird]; bite [of insect or reptile]. *2* (Am.) path, trail [cut through a forest].

**picadero** *m.* riding school, manege.

**picadillo** *m.* hash, minced meat.

**picado, -da** *p. p.* of PICAR. *2 adj.* pinked, perforated. *3* cut [tobacco]. *4* choppy [sea]. *5* piqued, hurt. *6 ~ de viruelas*, pockmarked. *7 m.* AER. dive, diving. *8* MUS. staccato.

**picador** *m.* horsebreaker. *2* BULLF. mounted bullfigther who goads the bull. *3* COOK. chopping block.

**picadura** *f.* prick, sting. *2* bite [of insect or reptile]. *3* pinking [ornamental perforation]. *4* cut tobacco. *5* DENT. beginning of decay.

**picafigo** *m.* ORN. figpecker.

**picaflor** *m.* ORN. humming bird.

**picajón, -na; picajoso, -sa** *adj.* touchy, peevish.

**picamaderos** *m.* ORN. woodpecker.

**picante** *adj.* hot, pungent, piquant [to the taste]. *2* highly seasoned. *3* piquant, spicy, racy. *4* biting, cutting [word]. *5 m.* piquancy, pungency. *6* mordacity.

**picapedrero** *m.* stonecutter.

**picapica** *f.* itch-producing vegetable powder.

**picapleitos**, *pl.* **-tos** *m.* coll. litigious fellow. *2* coll. pettifogger.

**picaporte** *m.* thumb latch, spring latch; latchkey. *2* door knocker.

**picar** *tr.* to prick, pierce, puncture. *2* BULLF. to prick [the bull] with a goad. *3* [of insects or some reptils] to sting, bite. *4* [of birds] to peck at. *5* to take [the bait]. *6* to pink, perforate. *7* to spur [a horse]. *8* to spur, incite. *9* to mince, hash. *10* to pock. *11* to roughen with a pointed tool. *12* to train [a horse]. *13* to pique, annoy. *14* MUS. to staccato. *15* BILL. to strike [the ball]. *16 tr.-intr.* to itch, prickle. *17* to burn, be hot [as a spice]. *18 intr.* [of the sun] to burn. *19* to bite [take the bait]. *20* AER. to dive. *21 ~ alto*, to aim high. *22 ~ de*, to take or eat a small bit of. *23 ref.* to become moth-eaten. *24* [of fruit] to begin to rot. *25* [of wine] to begin to turn sour. *26* [of teeth] to begin to decay. *27* [of the sea] to get choppy. *28* to take offence. *29* (Am.) to get tipsy. *30 picarse de*, to boast of being.

**picardear** *intr.* to play the rogue. *2* to prank. *3 ref.* to acquire bad habits.

**Picardía (la)** *pr. n.* GEOG. Picardy.

**picardía** *f.* knavery, knavish action, mean trick. *2* slyness. *3* roguishness, archness. *4* prank, innocent practical joke. *5 pl.* insults, offensive words.

**picardihuela** *f. dim.* prank, roguish trick.

**picardo, -da** *adj.-n.* Picard.

**picaresca** *f.* rogues or picaros [collect.]. *2* the life of the rogues or picaros.

**picaresco, -ca** *adj.* roguish. *2* LIT. picaresque.

**pícaro, -ra** *adj.* knavish, roguish. *2* mischievous. *3* sly. *4 m.-f.* knave, rogue. *5* sly person. *6* rogue [used playfully]. *7 m.* LIT. picaro. *8 ~ de cocina*, scullion, kitchen boy.

**picarón, -na** *adj. augm.* roguish, mischievous. *2 m.-f.* great rogue.

**picatoste** *m.* buttered toast.

**picaza** *f.* ORN. magpie.

**picazón** *f.* itching, itch. *2* coll. annoyance, displeasure.

**picea** *f.* BOT. spruce.

**píceo, -a** *adj.* piceous, pitchy.

**pico** *m.* beak, bill [of bird]. *2 fig.* mouth [as a means of speech]; eloquence, fluency: *tener mucho ~,* to talk too much. *2* beak [of a vessel; pointed end or projection]. *3* corner [of a handkerchief; of a cocked hat]. *4* peak [of a mountain]. *5* pick [tool], pickaxe. *6* small surplus: *cuarenta pesetas y ~,* forty pesetas odd. *7* some money. *8* ORN. *pico,* or *~ carpintero,* woodpecker. *9* NAUT. *~ cangrejo,* gaff. *10 andar a picos pardos,* to loaf around; to go on a spree.

**picor** *m.* burning of the palate [from having eaten something pungent]. *2* itching, itch.

**picoso, -sa** *adj.* pock-marked.

**picota** *f.* pillory.

**picotada** *f.,* **picotazo** *m.* peck [blow with a beak]. *2* sting [inflicted by an insect].

**picotear** *tr.* to peck, peck at. *2 intr.* [of horses] to toss the head. *3* to chatter. *4 ref.* [of women] to bandy sharp words.

**picotería** *f.* loquacity, talkativeness.

**picotero, -ra** *adj.* chattering, prattling, talkative. *2 m.-f.* chatterer, prattler.

**pícrico** *adj.* CHEM. picric.

**picto, -ta** *adj.* Pictic. *2 m.-f.* Pict.

**pictografía** *f.* pictography, picture writing.

**pictórico, -ca** *adj.* pictorial.

**picudo, -da** *adj.* beaked, pointed. *2* long-snouted. *3* chattering, prattling.

**pichel** *m.* pewter tankard, mug.

**pichón, -na** *m.-f.* coll. darling, dearest. *2* ORN. young pigeon.

**pido, pida,** etc. *irr.* V. PEDIR.

**pidón, -na** *adj.-n.* PEDIGÜEÑO.

**pie** *m.* foot [of person, animal, stocking of piece of furniture]: *~ de banco,* fig. absurdity, nonsense; *andar con pies de plomo,* to proceed cautiously; *buscar cinco,* or *tres, pies al gato,* to be looking for trouble; *entrar con buen ~* or *~ derecho,* to make a good start; *faltarle a uno los pies,* to lose one's balance; *no dar ~ con bola,* fig. to do nothing right, *no tener pies ni cabeza,* fig. to be nonsensical; *poner pies en polvorosa,* coll. to flee; *ponerse de ~,* or *en ~,* to stand up; *saber de qué ~ cojea uno,* to know someone's weak point; *tenerse en ~,* to stay on one's feet; to stand; *a cuatro pies,* in all fours; *a los pies de usted,* at your service [said to a lady]; *a ~,* on foot; *a ~ firme,* steadfastly; *a ~ juntillas,* with feet together; fig. firmly; *en ~,* standing. *2* foot, bottom, lowest part: *al ~ de,* at the foot of. *3* stem [of goblet]. *4* foot, base, stand. *5* footing, ground. *6* footing [state, relative position]: *en ~ de igualdad,* on equal footing. *7* foot [metrical unit]. *8* PROS. metre, line. *9* foots, lees, sediments. *10* trunk, stalk [of tree or plant]. *11* individual tree, young tree. *12* motive, ground, occasion: *dar ~ a,* to give occasion for. *13* root; *tomar ~,* to take root. *14* THEAT. cue. *15 al ~ de la letra,* to the letter, literally. *16 ~ de imprenta,* imprint [printer's name, etc.]. *17 ~ de rey,* slide caliper.

**piececito, piecezuelo** *m. dim.* little foot.

**piedad** *f.* piety. *2* godliness. *3* pity, compassion, mercy; *¡por ~!,* for pity's sake!

**piedra** *f.* stone [rock, piece of stone; precious stone]: *~ de afilar,* or *de amolar,* grindstone, whetstone; *~ angular,* ARCH. cornerstone; fig. cornerstone, keystone; *~ de escándalo,* stumbling block, cause of moral ruin to others; *~ de toque,* touchstone; *~ filosofal,* philosopher's stone; *~ imán,* loadstone; *~ militar,* milestone;

*~ pómez,* pumice; *~ rodada,* boulder; *lanzar la primera ~,* to cast the first stone; *no dejar ~ por mover,* to leave no stone unturned; *no dejar ~ sobre ~,* to rage to the ground; *a ~ y lodo,* tightshut [door or window]. *2* METEOR. hail. *3* METEOR. hailstone. *4* MED. stone, calculus. *5* point [in some card games].

**piel** *f.* skin: *~ de gallina,* goose flesh; *ser de la ~ del diablo,* coll. to be limb of the devil. *2* hide, pelt. *3* leather. *4* fur. *5* peel, skin [of fruit]. *6 m. ~ roja,* redskin [American Indian].

**piélago** *m.* sea, high sea. *2 fig.* countless number.

**pienso** *m.* feed [of dry fodder]. *2* thought: *ni por ~,* by no means.

**pienso, piense,** etc. *irr.* V. PENSAR.

**pierdo, pierda,** etc. *irr.* V. PERDER.

**piérides (las)** *f. pl.* poet. the Muses.

**pierna** *f.* leg [of person or animal]: *a ~ suelta,* coll. at one's ease, without care. *2* branch, leg [of compass]. *3* long stroke [of some letters]. *4* MECH. shank, fork. *5 ~ de nuez,* lobe of a walnut.

**piernitendido, -da** *adj.* with legs extended.

**pietismo** *m.* pietism.

**pietista** *adj.* pietistic. *2 m.-f.* pietist, Pietist.

**pieza** *f.* piece, fragment. *2* piece, part [of a machine, structure, etc.]: *~ de recambio,* spare part; *quedarse en una ~,* or *hecho una ~,* coll. to be astonished. *3* a single article of a collection, set, etc. *4* piece, coin. *5* piece, cannon, gun. *6* game, quarry [hunted animal]. *7* MUS. piece. *8* THEAT. short piece. *9* piece, bolt, roll [of cloth, paper, etc.]. *10* CHESS., DRAUGHTS piece, man. *11* room [in a house]. *12 buena ~,* coll. fine fellow, rogue, sly fox.

**piezgo** *m.* foot of a hide or skin. *2* wineskin.

**piezómetro** *m.* piezometer.

**pífano** *m.* MUS. fife. *2* MUS. fifer.

**pifia** *f.* BILL. miscue. *2 fig.* blunder, mistake.

**pifiar** *intr.* BILL. to miscue. *2* MUS. to wheeze in playing the flute.

**pigargo** *m.* ORN. osprey, fish hawk.

**Pigmalión** *m. pr. n.* MYTH. Pigmalion.

**pigmentario, -ria** *adj.* BIOL. pigmentary.

**pigmento** *m.* BIOL., TEXT. pigment.

**pigmeo, -a** *adj.-n.* pygmy.

**pignoración** *f.* pledging, pawning.

**pignorar** *tr.* to pledge, pawn.

**pigre** *adj.* slothful, lazy.

**pigricia** *f.* sloth, laziness.

**pihuela** *f.* jess [on hawk's leg]. *2 pl.* shackles.

**pijama** *m.* pajamas, pyjamas.

**pijotería** *f.* coll. nuisance.

**pila** *f.* stone trough or basin. *2* ECCL. font, holywater font: *nombre de ~,* Christian name. *3* pile, heap. *4* pillar, pier [of bridge]. *5* PHYS., ELECT. pile, battery: *~ seca,* dry battery.

1) **pilar** *m.* basin, bowl [of a fountain]. *2* pillar, pier, post. *3 fig.* pillar, column [supporter, support]. *4* stone post.

2) **pilar** *tr.* to pound [grain].

**pilastra** *f.* ARCH. pilaster, square column.

**Pilatos** *m. pr. n.* Pilate.

**píldora** *f.* PHARM. pill, pellet. *2 fig.* pill, bad news: *dorar la ~,* to gild the pill.

**píleo** *m.* ARCHEOL. pileus.

**pileta** *f. dim.* small basin. *2* holy-water bowl.

**pilón** *m.* basin, bowl [of a fountain]. *2* watering trough. *3* mortar [for pounding grain, etc.]. *4* loaf [of sugar]. *5* drop, ball [of a steelyard]. *6* ARCH. pylon.

**pilongo, -ga** adj. thin, lean. 2 peeled and dried [chestnut].
**píloro** m. ANAT. pylorus.
**piloso, -sa** adj. pilose, pilous, hairy.
**pilotaje** m. NAUT., AER. pilotage. 2 piling, pilework.
**pilotar** tr. to pilot. 2 AUTO. to drive.
**pilote** m. ENG. pile.
**pilotear** tr. PILOTAR.
**piloto** m. NAUT., AER. pilot: ~ de pruebas, AER. test pilot. 2 fig. pilot, guide. 3 NAUT. mate, first mate. 4 AUTO. driver. 5 adj. pilot.
**piltraca, piltrafa** f. scrap of meat. 2 skinny flesh. 3 pl. scraps of food. 4 scraps, refuse.
**pilla** f. pillage, plunder.
**pillada** f. coll. knavery, knavish trick, dirty trick.
**pillaje** m. pillage, plunder, sack: theft, stealing.
**pillar** tr. to pillage, plunder, steal. 2 to catch, take. 3 to catch, surprise [in a lie, etc.].
**pillastre, pillastrón** m. rogue, rascal, big rascal.
**pillería** f. pack of rogues. 2 piece of rascality. 3 roguishness. 4 slyness, craftiness.
**pillete** m. dim. little rogue or scamp. 2 street Arab.
**pillín** m. dim. little rogue.
**pillo, -lla** adj. roguish, rascally. 2 shrewd, sly. 3 m. rogue, rascal. 4 shrewd, sly fellow.
**pilluelo, -la** m.-f. dim. little rogue, urchin.
**pimentero** m. pepper, black pepper [shrub]. 2 pepperbox. 3 BOT. ~ falso, pepper tree.
**pimentón** m. red pepper, Cayenne pepper, Spanish paprika [powder]. 2 pepper [vegetable].
**pimienta** f. pepper [spice]: ~ blanca, ~ negra, white, black, pepper; ~ inglesa, allspice; ser como una ~, to be alert, lively.
**pimiento** m. pepper, capsicum, Guinea pepper, red pepper, chili [plant and fruit]: ~ morrón, bonnet pepper; ~ picante, hot pepper. 2 PIMENTERO 1. 3 PIMENTÓN 1.
**pimpinela** f. BOT. burnet, salad burnet.
**pimplar** tr. coll. to drink [wine].
**pimpollear, pimpollecer** intr. to sprout, bud.
**pimpollo** m. young tree. 2 tender shoot or sprout, bud. 3 fig. handsome child; handsome young person, rosebud.
**pina** f. conical mound. 2 felloe [segment of a wheel's rim].
**pinabete** m. BOT. fir tree.
**pinacoteca** f. picture gallery.
**pináculo** m. pinnacle.
**pinado, -da** adj. BOT. pinnate.
**pinar** m. pine grove or forest, pinery.
**pinastro** m. BOT. pinaster, cluster pine.
**pinatífido, -da** adj. BOT. pinnatifid.
**pinaza** f. NAUT. pinnace.
**pincarrasca** f., **pincarrasco** m. BOT. Aleppo pine.
**pincel** m. brush, pencil [for painting]. 2 brush, pencil [painter style; painter; painting].
**pincelada** f. stroke [with a brush], touch.
**pincelar** tr. F. ARTS to paint. 2 to portray, picture.
**pinciano, -na** adj.-n. of Valladolid.
**pinchadura** f. pricking, prick, puncture.
**pinchar** tr. to prick, pierce, puncture: no ~ ni cortar, fig. to count for nothing. 2 fig. to spur, incite. 3 fig. to pique, provoke.
**pinchazo** m. prick, puncture, jab. 2 fig. anything said to spur or pique someone. 3 AUTO. puncture.
**pinche** m. scullion, kitchen boy.
**pincho** m. thorn, sharp point. 2 pointed instrument.
**pindárico, -ca** adj. Pindaric.
**pindonga** f. gadabout [woman].
**pindonguear** intr. [of a woman] to gad about.

**pineal** adj. ANAT. pineal.
**pineda** f. pine grove or forest.
**pinga** s. yoke [for carrying pails, etc.].
**pingajo** m. rag, tatter.
**pingo** m. coll. rag, tatter. 2 (Am.) nag. 3 pl. cheap woman's clothes.
**pingorotudo, -da** adj. coll. high, lofty.
**pingüe** adj. fat, greasy, oily. 2 fig. plentiful, substantial; fertile.
**pingüedinoso, -sa** adj. fatty, greasy.
**pingüino** m. ORN. penguin.
**pinillo** m. BOT. ground pine. 3 BOT. mock cypress.
**pinitos** m. pl. first steps [of a child or a convalescent]: hacer ~, to begin to walk.
**pinjante** m. ARCH., JEWEL. pendant.
**pinnípedo, -da** adj.-n. ZOOL. pinniped.
1) **pino** m. BOT. pine tree: ~ albar, Scotch pine; ~ carrasco, Aleppo pine; ~ piñonero, stone pine, nut pine; ~ marítimo or rodenó, pinaster, cluster pine; ~ negro, mountain pine. 2 pl. PINITOS.
2) **pino, -na** adj. steep [having a decided slope].
**pinocha** f. pine needle.
**pinocho** m. pine cone.
**pinoso, -sa** adj. piny.
**pinsapo** m. BOT. Spanish fir.
**pinta** f. spot, mark, speckle. 2 lines near the edge of Spanish playing cards showing the suit. 3 pint [measure]. 4 appearance, look.
**pintacilgo** m. JILGUERO.
**pintada** f. ORN. guinea fowl, guinea hen.
**pintado, -da** adj. spotted, mottled, speckled. 2 coll. el más ~, the best one, the cleverest one. 5 estar, or venir, ~ or como ~, to fit, to be just the thing.
**pintamonas,** pl. **-nas** m.-f. coll. dauber [poor painter].
**pintar** tr. to paint. 2 to draw [a letter, accent, etc.]. 3 to picture, depict; fancy, imagine. 4 fig. to exaggerate. 5 pintarla, to show off. 6 intr. [of fruits] to colour. 7 [of things] to seem to be going [badly, well, etc.]. 8 to have authority, influence, etc. 9 ref. to paint oneself. 10 pintarse solo para, to show great aptitude for.
**pintarrajar, pintarrajear** tr. coll. to daub [paint inartistically].
**pintarrajo** m. daub [inartistic or coarse painting].
**pintear** intr. to drizzle.
**pintiparado, -da** adj. exactly alike, closely resembling. 2 fit, fitting, just the thing.
**pinto, -ta** adj. (Am.) spotted, speckled.
**pintojo, -ja** adj. spotted, mottled, speckled.
**pintor** m. painter: ~ de brocha gorda, house painter, sign painter; dauber.
**pintora** f. female painter.
**pintoresco, -ca** adj. picturesque.
**pintorrear** tr. to daub, paint coarsely.
**pintura** f. painting [act or art]: ~ a la aguada, water colour; ~ al fresco, fresco; ~ al óleo, oil painting; ~ al temple, tempera. 2 picture, painting [work of art]. 3 paint, colour. 4 painting, portrayal, description.
**pinturero, -ra** adj. vain, conceitedly affected.
**pínula** f. pinnule, sight [of an instrument].
**pinzas** f. pl. tweezers, pincers, nippers, small tongs. 2 ZOOL. pincers [of crustaceans].
**pinzón** m. ORN. chaffinch. 2 ORN. ~ real, bullfinch.
**piña** f. BOT. pine cone. 2 BOT. cone. 3 BOT. pineapple: ~ de América, pineapple. 4 fig. cluster, knot.
**piñal** m. (Am.) pineapple plantation.
**piñata** f. pot. 2 hanging pot filled with sweetmeats wich is broken with a stick at a masked ball on the first Sunday of Lent.

**piñón** *m.* BOT. pine nut [seed]. *2* pine-nut kernel. *3* MECH., ORN. pinion. *4* nut [of a gunlock].
**piñonate** *m.* candied pine-nut kernel.
**piñoneo** *m.* click [of a gun being cocked]. *2* cry [of male partridges in rut].
**piñonero** *adj. pino* ~, stone pine, nut pine.
**Pío** *m. pr. n.* Pius.
*1)* **pío** *m.* peeping [of chickens or young birds]. *2* coll. yearning, vehement desire.
*2)* **pío, -a** *adj.* pious. *2* merciful, compassionate. *3* pied, piebald [horse, etc.].
**piocha** *f.* jeweled head adornment. *2* MAS. a trimming hammer.
**piojento, -ta** *adj.* lousy.
**piojería** *f.* lousiness. *2* coll. misery, poverty.
**piojillo** *m.* ENT. bird louse.
**piojo** *m.* ENT. louse: ~ *resucitado*, fig. upstart, parvenu.
**piojoso, -sa** *adj.* lousy. *2* mean, stingy.
**pión, -na** *adj.* peeping, chirping.
**piorrea** *f.* MED. pyorrhea, pyorrhœa.
**pipa** *f.* pipe, tobacco pipe. *2* pipe, cask, barrel. *3* pip, seed [of apple, melon, etc.].
**pipar** *intr.* to smoke a pipe.
**piperáceo, -a** *adj.* BOT. piperaceous.
**pipería** *f.* pipes or casks [collect]. *2* NAUT. water barrels of a ship.
**pipeta** *f.* pipette.
*1)* **pipí,** *pl.* **-píes** *m.* ORN. pitpit, honey creeper.
*2)* **pipí,** *pl.* **-pis** *m.* [child's word] urination.
**pipiar** *intr.* to peep, chirp.
**pipiolo** *m.* coll. novice, green horn.
**pipirigallo** *m.* BOT. sainfoin.
**pipiritaña, pipitaña** *f.* boy's flute made of a green barley stalk.
**piporro** *m.* MUS. coll. bassoon.
**pique** *m.* pique, resentment. *2* determined purpose to do something out of pride or emulation. *3* NAUT. crotch. *4 echar a* ~, to founder, sink [a ship]; fig. to ruin. *5* NAUT. *irse a* ~ [of a ship], to founder, sink; fig. to be ruined. *6 a* ~ *de*, in danger of; on the point of. *7 a* ~, sharp-cut [cliff].
**piqué** *m.* piqué [cotton fabric].
**piquera** *f.* entrance hole [in a hive]. *2* tap [in a barrel]. *3* taphole [of blast furnace]. *4* lamp burner.
**piquero** *m.* MIL. pikeman. *2* ORN. booby.
**piqueta** *f.* pick, pickaxe. *2* mason's hammer.
**piquete** *m.* prick, puncture. *2* small hole. *3* picket, short stake. *4* MIL. picket, squad.
**piquillo** *m.* dim. small beak or bill. *2* small amount.
**piquituerto** *m.* ORN. crossbill.
**pira** *f.* pyre. *2* funeral pile.
**piragua** *f.* NAUT. pirogue.
**piramidal** *adj.* pyramidal.
**pirámide** *f.* pyramid.
**Píramo** *m. pr. n.* Pyramus.
**pirata** *adj.* piratical. *2 m.* pirate.
**piratear** *intr.* to pirate, practice piracy.
**piratería** *f.* piracy. *2* fig. robbery.
**pirático, -ca** *adj.* piratical.
**pirenaico, -ca** *adj.* Pyrenean.
**pirexia** *f.* MED. pyrexia.
**piriforme** *adj.* pyriform, pear-shaped.
**Pirineos (los)** *m. pl.* GEOG. Pyrenees.
**pirita** *f.* MINER. pyrites.
**piróforo** *m.* CHEM. pyrophorus.
**pirogálico, -a** *adj.* CHEM. pyrogallic.
**pirógeno, -na** *adj.* pyrogenous.
**pirograbado** *m.* pyrography, pyrogravure.

**pirólisis** *m.* CHEM. pyrolisis.
**piropear** *tr.* to pay compliments to.
**piropo** *m.* MINER. pyrope. *2* MINER. carbuncle. *3* compliment, flattering remark.
**piróscafo** *m.* steamship.
**piroscopio** *m.* PHYS. pyroscope.
**pirosfera** *f.* GEOL. pyrosphere.
**pirosis** *f.* MED. pyrosis, heartburn.
**pirotecnia** *f.* pyrotechnics.
**pirotécnico, -ca** *adj.* pyrotechnical. *2 m.* pyrotechnist; fireworks manufacturer.
**pirrarse** *ref.* to long, to be very fond: ~ *por*, to long for, to be very fond of.
**pírrico, -ca** *adj.* Pyrrhic.
**pirriquio** *m.* PROS. pyrrhic, pyrrhichius.
**pirronismo** *m.* Pyrrhonism.
**pirueta** *f.* pirouette, caper.
**piruetear** *intr.* to pirouet.
**pisa** *f.* tread, treading. *2* pressing [of grapes, etc.]. *3* coll. volley of kicks.
**pisada** *f.* tread, footstep; footprint: *seguir las pisadas de*, to follow in the footsteps of. *2* stepping on someone's foot.
**pisador, -ra** *adj.* treading. *2* prancing, highstepping [horse]. *3 m.-f.* treader.
**pisapapeles** *m.* paper weight.
**pisar** *tr.* to tread on, step on. *2* to tread, press [grapes, etc.], to ram, tamp. *3* to trample under foot. *4* MUS. to press down [keys or strings]. *5* [of male birds] to tread. *6* to overlap.
**pisaverde** *m.* fop, coxcomb, dandy.
**piscicultor, -ra** *m.-f.* pisciculturist.
**piscicultura** *f.* pisciculture, fish culture.
**piscifactoría** *f.* fish hatchery.
**pisciforme** *adj.* pisciform, fish-shaped.
**piscina** *f.* fishpond; swimming pool. *2* piscina.
**piscívoro, -ra** *adj.* piscivorous, fish-eating.
**piscolabis** *m.* **-bis** *m.* snack, bite, luncheon.
**pisiforme** *adj.* pisiform.
**piso** *m.* tread, treading. *2* floor, pavement. *3* floor, storey: ~ *bajo*, ground floor. *4* flat, apartment. *5* MIN. level, level works. *6* GEOL. stage formation.
**pisón** *m.* rammer, tamper, paver's beetle.
**pisotear** *tr.* to trample, tread under foot. *2* to humble, despise, abuse.
**pisoteo** *m.* trampling, treading under foot.
**pisotón** *m.* heavy tread on someone's foot.
**pista** *f.* trail, trace, track, scent: *estar sobre la* ~, to be on the scent; *seguir la* ~ *a*, to be on the trail of. *2* clue. *3* SPORT. racetrack. *4* ring [of a circus]. *5* AER. runway. *6* ~ *de patinaje*, skating ring.
**pistachero, pistacho** *m.* BOT. pistachio [tree].
**pistar** *tr.* to pound, crush, squeeze.
**pistero** *m.* feeding cup [for invalids].
**pistilo** *m.* BOT. pistil.
**pisto** *m.* chicken broth [for the sick]. *2* dish of hashed peppers, tomatoes, onions, etc. *3* hodgepodge. *4* airs: *darse* ~, to put on airs.
**pistola** *f.* pistol: ~ *ametralladora*, submachine gun. *2* spray gun. *3* pistole [coin].
**pistolera** *f.* holster.
**pistolero** *m.* pistol-shooting gangster.
**pistoletazo** *m.* pistol shot.
**pistón** *m.* MACH., MUS. piston. *2* percussion cap.
**pistoneo** *m.* knock, knocking [of an internal combustion engine].
**pistonudo, -da** *adj.* coll. grand, stunning.
**pistoresa** *f.* a short dagger.
**pita** *f.* BOT. American Aloe, pita. *2* pita [fibre or tread]. *3* glass marble [toy]. *4* hissing, hooting, catcalling.

**pitaco** *m.* BOT. scape of the pita.
**pitada** *f.* blow of a whistle. 2 coll. nonsensical remark. 3 PITA 4. 4 (Am.) puff [on a cigar, etc.].
**Pitágoras** *m. pr. n.* Pythagoras.
**pitagórico, -ca** *adj.-n.* Pythagorean.
**pitanza** *f.* dole, ration. 2 daily food. 3 coll. price, stipend.
**pitaña** *f.* LEGAÑA.
**pitañoso, -sa** *adj.* LEGAÑOSO.
**pitar** *intr.* [of a whistle] to blow. 2 to blow a whistle.
**pitido** *m.* whistle. 2 whistling [of a bird].
**pitillera** *f.* cigarette case. 2 cigarette maker [woman].
**pitillo** *m.* cigarette.
**pítima** *f.* coll. drunk, drunkenness.
**pitio, -a** *adj.-n.* Pythian.
**pitío** *m.* coll. PITIDO.
**pito** *m.* whistle, catcall [instrument]. 2 a South American tick. 3 jackstone. 4 cigarette. 5 ORN. woodpecker. 6 coll. nothing, a straw: *no me importa un ~*, I don't care a straw. 5 *pl.* whistling [expressing disapproval].
**pitón** *m.* budding horn. 2 point, tip [of bull's horn]. 3 PITORRO. 4 small pointed protuberance. 5 ZOOL. python.
**pitonisa** *f.* pythoness. 2 BIBL. witch.
**pitorrearse** *ref.* to make fun [of].
**pitorreo** *m.* making fun.
**pitorro** *m.* conic spout of certain vessels.
**pitpit** *m.* ORN. pipit.
**pituita** *f.* pituite.
**pituitario, -ria** *adj.* pituitary.
**pituso, -sa** *adj.* tiny, graceful [child]. 2 *m.-f.* tot, little child.
**piular** *intr.* PIAR.
**píxide** *m.* ECCL. pyx.
**pixidio** *m.* BOT. pyxidium.
**piyama** *m.* PIJAMA.
**pizarra** *f.* MINER. shale; slate. 2 slate [piece of slate]. 3 slate [for writing]; blackboard.
**pizarral** *m.* slate quarry.
**pizarreño, -ña** *adj.* slaty; slate-coloured.
**pizarrín** *m.* slate pencil.
**pizarroso, -sa** *adj.* slaty. 2 abounding in slate.
**pizca** *f.* coll bit, jot, whit: *ni ~*, not a bit.
**pizco** *m.* PELLIZCO.
**pizmiento, -ta** *adj.* dark, pitch-coloured.
**pizpireta** *adj.* brisk, lively, smart [woman].
**pizpita** *f.*, **pizpitillo** *m.* AGUZANIEVES.
**pizzicato** *adj.-m.* MUS. pizzicato.
**placa** *f.* plaque [badge of honorary order]. 2 MED. plaque. 3 superposed plate or thin sheet. 4 doorplate. 5 ANAT., ELECT., RADIO., PHOT. plate. 6 RLY. ~ *giratoria*, turntable.
**placable** *adj.* placable.
**pláceme** *m.* congratulation.
**placenta** *f.* ANAT., BOT., ZOOL. placenta.
**placentero, -ra** *adj.* joyful, pleasant, agreeable.
1) **placer** *m.* pleasure, enjoyment, delight, content: *a ~*, pleased; at one's heart content. 2 pleasure, will, consent. 3 NAUT. large flat bank [in sea bed]. 4 MIN. placer. 5 (Am.) pearl-fishing.
2) **placer** *tr.* to please, gratify, content. ‖ CONJUG.: INDIC. Pres.: *plazco*, places, place, etc. | Pret.: plació or *plugo;* placieron or *plugieron.* | SUBJ. Pres.: *plazca, plazcas, plazca* or *plegue* or *plega, plazcamos, plazcáis, plazcan.* | Imperf.: placiera or *pluguiera;* placiese or *pluguiese.* | Fut.: placiere, or *pluguiere.* | IMPER.: place, *plazca; plazcamos,* placed, *plazcan.*

**placero, -ra** *adj.* [pertaining to the] market place. 2 *m.-f.* marketer, market vendor.
**placible** *adj.* agreeable, pleasurable.
**placidez** *f.* placidity.
**plácido, -da** *adj.* placid, peaceful, calm. 2 agreeable.
**plácito** *s.* opinion, judgement.
**plafón** *m.* ARCH. soffit.
**plaga** *f.* plague, affliction, calamity, scourge. 2 AGR. scourge, pest. 3 fig. plenty, superabundance [esp. of injurious things]. 4 ulcer, sore.
**plagar** *tr.* to plague, fill, infest. 2 *ref.* to become filled or infected [with].
**plagiar** *tr.* to plagiarize. 2 (Am.) to kidnap.
**plagiario, -ria** *a.-n.* plagiary, plagiarist.
**plagio** *m.* plagiarism, plagiary [literary theft].
**plagiotropismo** *m.* BOT. plagiotropism.
**plaid** *m.* plaid.
**plan** *m.* plan, project, design, scheme: ~ *de estudios*, EDUC. curriculum. 2 level, height. 3 plan [drawing, map]. 4 NAUT. floor [of ship's hold]. 5 MIN. mine floor.
**plana** *f.* page [of a sheet of paper]. 2 copy [of penmanship]: *enmendar la ~ a uno*, to find fault with a thing done by someone. 3 plain, flat country. 4 PRINT. page. 5 MAS. trowel. 6 MIL. ~ *mayor*, staff.
**plancton** *m.* plankton.
**plancha** *f.* plate, sheet [of metal]. 2 PRINT. plate. 3 iron, flatiron. 4 ironing [clothes]. 5 horizontal suspension [in gymnastics]. 6 coll. blunder, social blunder: *tirarse una ~*, to blunder, to put one's foot in it. 7 NAUT. gangplank, gangboard.
**planchado** *m.* ironing, pressing [of clothes].
**planchar** *tr.* to iron, press [clothes].
**planchear** *tr.* to plate, cover with metal plates.
**planeador** *m.* AER. glider.
**planear** *tr.* to plan, design, outline. 2 *intr.* AER. to volplane, glide.
**planeta** *m.* ASTR. planet.
**planetario, -ria** *adj.* planetary. 2 *m.* orrery, planetarium.
**planga** *f.* ORN. gannet.
**planicie** *f.* plain, flatland.
**planificar** *tr.* to plan [arrange beforehand].
**planilla** *f.* (Am.) list, roll, schedule.
**planimetría** *f.* plane survey; planimetry.
**planímetro** *m.* planimeter.
**planisferio** *m.* planisphere.
**plano, -na** *adj.* plane. 2 flat, even, smooth. 3 *m.* plane [plane surface]: ~ *inclinado*, inclined plane; *primer ~*, foreground. 4 AER. plane, wing. 5 plan [drawing, map]: *levantar un ~*, to make a survey. 6 *de ~*, openly, clearly; with the flat of the land, of a sword, etc.
**planta** *f.* BOT. plant. 2 planted ground. 3 sole [of foot]; fig. foot. 4 ENG. plan, design. 5 ARCH. plan [of a floor or building]. 6 plan, list of the sections and staff or personnel of [an office, institution, etc.]. 7 MIN. level. 8 ~ *baja*, ground floor. 9 *buena ~*, fine physique or appearance. 10 *de ~*, from the ground up.
**plantación** *f.* AGR. planting. 2 plantation.
**plantador, -ra** *adj.* planting. 2 *m.-f.* planter [person]. 3 *m.* dibble, planting stick.
**plantagináceo, -a** *adj.* BOT. plantaginaceous.
**plantaina** *f.* BOT. plantain [herb].
1) **plantar** *adj.* plantar.
2) **plantar** *tr.* AGR. to plant. 2 to plant, place, set up. 3 to plant, deliver [a blow, etc.]. 4 to put, throw: ~ *en la calle*, to throw into the street. 5

to plant, establish. *6 plantar* or *dejar plantado a uno*, to abandon, desert; to jilt; to fail to keep one's appointment with. *7 ref.* to plant oneself. *8 coll.* to go, get, arrive [in a short time]. *9 [of an animal]* to balk or baulk. *10* to refuse obstinately to do a thing.

**plante** *m.* revolt or protest [in prison, etc.].

**planteamiento** *m.* planning. *2* carrying out [of a plan, etc.]. *3* statement [of a problem]; posing, raising [a question].

**plantear** *tr.* to plan, outline. *2* to establish [a system, etc.]; to carry out [a reform]. *3* to state [a problem]; to pose, raise [a question].

**plantel** *m.* nursery, nursery garden. *2* nursery [of artists, scholars, etc.].

**plantificar** *tr.* to stablish [a system, institution, etc.]. *2* to carry out [a reform]. *3* PLANTAR 3 & 4. *5 ref.* PLANTAR 8.

**plantígrado, -da** *adj.-m.* ZOOL. plantigrade.

**plantilla** *f.* insole. *2* sole [of a stocking]. *3* plate [of gunlock]. *4* MACH. template, templet [pattern]. *5* ENG. plan, design. *6* PLANTA 6.

**plantío, -a** *adj.* tillable [land]. *2 m.* planted ground, patch of young plants. *3* AGR. planting.

**plantista** *m.* landscape gardener.

**plantón** *m.* AGR. young tree, cutting, slip [for planting]. *2* watchman [before the door of a building]. *3* long wait standing: *dar un ~*, to keep someone waiting; *estar de ~*, to stand around for a long time.

**planudo, -da** *adj.* NAUT. flat-bottomed.

**plañidero, -ra** *adj.* moaning, mournful, plaintive. *2 f.* weeper [professional mourner].

**plañido** *m.* moan, lamentation, crying.

**plañir** *intr.* to lament, grieve, bewail. *2 tr.* to lament, grive over. ‖ CONJUG. as *mullir.*

**plaqué** *m.* plate, plating [of gold or silver].

**plasma** *m.* PHYSIOL. plasma. *2 f.* MINER. plasma.

**plasmar** *tr.* to make, mould, shape.

**plasmático, -ca** *adj.* plasmatic.

**plasta** *f.* paste, soft mass, anything soft [as mud, etc.]. *2* flattened mass.

**plaste** *m.* filler, size [made of glue and plaster].

**plástica** *f.* plastic [art of modeling].

**plasticidad** *f.* plasticity.

**plástico, -ca** *adj.* plastic. *2 m.* plastic [substance].

**plastrón** *m.* FENC. plastron. *2* large cravat.

**plata** *f.* CHEM., MINER. silver: *~ labrada,* wrought silver, silverware; *como una ~,* coll. clean, shining; *en ~,* coll. plainly; briefly; in sum. *2* plate [utensils, etc., of silver]. *3* silver [silver coins]. *4* coll. money.

**plataforma** *f.* platform [flat surface; raised flooring]. *2* GEOGR., POL. platform. *3* MACH. index plate. *4* RLY. platform car.

**platal** *m.* large amount of money, lot of money.

**platanáceo, -a** *adj.* BOT. platanaceous.

**platanal, platanar** *m.* plantation of plane trees. *2* banana field or plantation.

**platanero** *m.* BOT. banana [plant].

**plátano** *m.* BOT. banana, plantain [plant and fruit]. *2* BOT. plane tree. *3* BOT. *~ falso,* sycamore maple.

**platea** *f.* THEAT. orchestra, parquet, pit.

**plateado, -da** *adj.* silvered, silver-plated. *2* silver, silvery [in colour]. *3 m.* silver plating.

**platear** *tr.* to silver [coat with silver; give silvery appearance to].

**platelminto** *m.* ZOOL. platyhelminth.

**plateresco, -ca** *adj.* ARCH. plateresque.

**platería** *f.* silversmith's shop or trade.

**platero** *m.* silversmith. *2* jeweller.

**plática** *f.* chat, talk. *2* ECCL. address, sermon.

**platicar** *intr.* to chat, talk, converse.

**platija** *f.* ICHTH. plaice.

**platillo** *m. dim.* small dish; saucer: *~ volante,* flying saucer. *2* pan [of scales]. *3* COOK. dish of meat and vegetables. *4* subject of gossip. *5* MUS. cymbal.

**platina** *f.* stage [of microscope]. *2* plate [of air pump]. *3* PRINT. imposing table. *4* platen.

**platinado, -da** *adj.* platinized. *2 rubia platinada,* platinum blonde.

**platinar** *tr.* to platinize [coat with platinum].

**platino** *m.* CHEM. platinum.

**platirrino, -na** *adj.-m.* ZOOL. platyrrhine.

**plato** *m.* plate, dish [vessel; content of this]: *comer en el mismo ~,* coll. to be close friends; *no haber quebrado un ~,* coll. to be innocent. *2* COOK. dish. *3* course [at meals]: *~ fuerte,* pièce de résistance; *ser ~ de segunda mesa,* to be disregarded, to be second fiddle. *4* pan [of scales]. *5* subject of gossip. *6* MACH. plate, disk.

**Platón** *m. pr. n.* Plato.

**platónico, -ca** *adj.* Platonic, Platonistic. *2* platonic. *3 m.-f.* Platonist.

**platonismo** *m.* Platonism.

**plausibilidad** *f.* reasonableness, acceptability. *2* laudableness.

**plausible** *adj.* reasonable, acceptable. *2* laudable.

**plausivo, -va** *adj.* applauding.

**plauso** *m.* applause.

**playa** *f.* beach, strand, sandy shore.

**playado, -da** *adj.* having a beach.

**playeras** *f. pl.* a popular Andalusian song.

**plaza** *f.* public square, circus: *sacar a la ~,* fig. to make public. *2* market place. *3* MIL. place [fortified town]. *4* place [space, seat]. *5* place, post, situation, employement. *6* room, space: *hacer ~,* to make room, clear the way. *7* COM. town, city. *8 ~ de toros,* bull ring, arena. *9* MIL. *sentar ~,* to enlist. *10 sentar ~ de,* to set up for.

**plazco, plazca,** etc. *irr.* V. PLACER.

**plazo** *m.* term [limited period]; time, date [for an action, payment, etc.]. *2* term [appointed day]. *3* instalment [of a sum payable]: *venta a plazos,* hire purchase, hire system.

**plazoleta, plazuela** *f. dim.* small public square.

**pleamar** *f.* NAUT. high tide, high water.

**plebe** *f.* plebs, common people. *2* populace.

**plebeyez** *f.* plebeianism; coarseness, vulgarity.

**plebeyo, -ya** *adj.-n.* plebeian.

**plebiscito** *f.* plebiscite; plebiscitum.

**plectro** *m.* MUS. plectrum. *2* poet. inspiration.

**plegable** *adj.* pliable. *2* folding, collapsible.

**plegadera** *f.* paper folder, paper knife.

**plegado** *m.* PLEGADURA.

**plegador, -ra** *adj.* folding. *2 m.* folding instrument. *3* WEAV. beam. *4 f.* folding machine.

**plegadura** *f.* folding, doubling, plaiting.

**plegamiento** *m.* PLEGADURA. *2* GEOL. fold.

**plegar** *tr.* to fold, double, plait, pleat. *2* SEW. to gather, pucker. *3 ref.* to fold, bend. *4* to yield, submit. ‖ CONJUG. as *acertar.*

**plegaria** *f.* prayer, supplication.

**plegue, plega,** etc. *irr.* V. PLACER.

**pleguería** *f.* folds [in robes and drapery].

**pleistoceno, -na** *adj. &* GEOL. Pleistocene.

**pleita** *f.* plaited strand of esparto grass.

**pleiteador, -ra** *m.-f.* litigant. *2* litigious person.

**pleiteante** *adj.* litigating. *2 m.-f.* litigant.

**pleitear** *tr.* to litigate.

**pleitesía** *f.* homage: *rendir ~,* to do homage.

**pleitista** *m.-f.* litigious person, pettifogger.
**pleito** *m.* litigation, lawsuit. *2* dispute, debate, contest, strife. *3* ~ *homenaje,* FEUD. homage.
**plenamente** *adv.* fully, completely.
**plenario, -ria** *adj.* complete, full. *2* plenary.
**plenilunio** *m.* full moon.
**plenipotenciario, -ria** *adj.-n.* plenipotentiary.
**plenitud** *f.* plenitude, fullness.
**pleno, -na** *adj.* full, complete. *2 en* ~ [with a noun], in broad, in the middle of, at the height of: *en* ~ *día,* in broad day. *3 m.* full assembly, plenum.
**pleonasmo** *m.* pleonasm.
**pleonástico, -ca** *adj.* pleonastic.
**plepa** *f.* coll. person or thing full of defects.
**plesiosauro** *m.* PALEONT. plesiosaur.
**pletina** *f.* narrow iron plate.
**plétora** *f.* plethora.
**pletórico, -ca** *adj.* plethoric.
**pleura** *f.* ANAT., ZOOL. pleura.
**pleuresía** *f.* MED. pleurisy.
**pleuritis** *f.* MED. pleuritis.
**pleuronecto, -ta** *adj.-m.* ICHTH. pleuronectid.
**plexiglás** *m.* perspex.
**plexo** *m.* ANAT. plexus.
**pléyade** *f.* pleiad.
**Pléyades** *f. pl.* ASTR., MYTH. Pleiades
**plica** *f.* sealed envelope.
**pliego** *m.* sheet of paper; folded paper. *2* PRINT. sheet [part of a book]. *3* sealed letter or document; *4* ~ *de condiciones,* specifications [for a contract].
**pliego, pliegue,** etc. *irr.* V. PLEGAR.
**pliegue** *m.* fold, plait, pleat, crease. *2* GEOL. fold.
**Plinio** *m. pr. n.* Pliny.
**plinto** *m.* ARCH. plinth [lower square member].
**plioceno** *adj.-m.* GEOL. Pliocene.
**plomada** *f.* plumb-line; souding line; plummet. *2* sinkers [of a fishing net].
**plomar** *tr.* to put a lead seal on.
**plombagina** *f.* MINER. plumbago, graphite.
**plomería** *f.* lead roofing; leadwork. *2* plumber's shop.
**plomero** *m.* lead worker, plumber.
**plomizo, -za** *adj.* leaden, plumbeous [made of lead; resembling lead]. *2* lead-coloured.
**plomo** *m.* CHEM. lead. *2* lead [piece of lead]; plumb bob, plummet, sinker. *3* fig. bullet. *4* coll. bore, dull person. *5 a* ~, perpendiculary. *6 caer a* ~, to fall plumb.
**plugo, pluguiera,** etc. *irr.* V. PLACER.
**pluma** *f.* feather, plume [of bird]. *2* feathers. *3* [writing] quill, pen: ~ *estilográfica,* fountain pen; *dejar correr la* ~, to write away. *4* fig. pen [hand, author, style of literary composition]. *5* ~ *de agua,* a variable measure for running water.
**plumada** *f.* stroke of pen. *2* brief writing.
**plumado, -da** *adj.* feathered [having feathers].
**plumaje** *m.* plumage. *2* crest, plume.
**plumazo** *m.* PLUMADA.
**plumazón** *f.* plumage. *2* plumes [ornamental bunches of feathers].
**plumbagina** *f.* PLOMBAGINA.
**plúmbeo, -a** *adj.* of lead. *2* plumbeous, heavy as lead.
**plúmbico, -ca** *adj.* CHEM. plumbic.
**plumeado** *m.* PAINT. hatching.
**plumear** *tr.* PAINT., DRAW. to hatch. *2* to write.
**plúmeo, -a** *adj.* plumose, feathered.
**plumero** *m.* feather duster. *2* crest, plume [bunch of feathers]. *3* box for pens and pencils.

**plumilla** *f. dim.* small feather. *2* small writing pen. *3* point [of fountain pen]. *4* BOT. plumule.
**plumista** *m.* scrivener, clerk. *2* plumist.
**plumón** *m.* down [of birds]. *2* feather bed.
**plumoso, -sa** *adj.* feathered, feathery, plumose.
**plúmula** *f.* BOT. plumule.
**plural** *adj.-m.* GRAM. plural.
**pluralidad** *f.* plurality.
**pluralizar** *tr.* to pluralize.
**plus** *m.* extra, bonus. *2* MIL. extra pay.
**pluscuamperfecto** *adj.-m.* GRAM. pluperfect.
**plusvalía** *f.* unearned increment.
**Plutarco** *m. pr. n.* Plutarch.
**plutocracia** *f.* plutocracy.
**Plutón** *m. pr. n.* MYTH., ASTR. Pluto.
**plutónico, -ca** *adj.* GEOL. plutonic. *2* MYTH. Plutonic.
**plutonio** *m.* CHEM. plutonium.
**plutonismo** *m.* GEOL. Plutonism.
**pluvial** *adj.* pluvial, rain. *2* ECCL. *capa* ~, pluvial.
**pluvímetro, pluviómetro** *m.* pluviometer, rain gauge.
**pluvioso, -sa** *adj.* rainy, pluvious.
**pobeda** *f.* white-poplar grove.
**población** *f.* population. *2* peopling, planting, settling, colonizing. *3* village, town, city.
**poblacho** *m.* sorry village.
**poblado** *m.* town, settlement, inhabited place.
**poblador, -ra** *adj.* peopling, populating. *2 m.-f.* inhabitant. *3* populator, colonizer, settler.
**poblar** *tr.* to inhabit, people. *2* to people, populate, settle, colonize; to plant [a river with fishes, a land with trees, etc.]. *3* [of hairs, leaves, plants, etc.] to cover, grow on. *4 ref.* to become peopled. *5* to become filled or covered [with hairs, leaves, plants, etc.]. ‖ CONJUG. as *contar.*
**pobo** *m.* ÁLAMO BLANCO.
**pobre** *adj.* poor: ~ *de espíritu,* poor in spirit: *¡~ de mí!,* poor me!; ~ *diablo,* poor devil; good-natured, insignificant fellow; ~ *hombre,* spiritless fellow. *2 m.-f.* poor person; pauper, beggar.
**pobrecico, -ca; -cillo, -cilla; -cito, -cita** *adj.* dim. of POBRE. *2 m.-f. dim.* little begar. *3* poor little thing.
**pobrete, -ta** *adj.* poor, wretched. *2 m.-f.* poor person. *3* good-natured, spiritless person.
**pobretería** *f.* poor people, beggars.
**pobretón, -na** *adj.* poor, needy. *2 m.-f.* poor person.
**pobreza** *f.* poverty, destitution, want. *2* poverty, poorness. *3* scanty possessions [of the poor]. *5* meanness of spirit.
**pocero** *m.* well digger. *2* cesspool cleaner.
**pocilga** *f.* pigsty, pigpen. *2* fig. dirty place.
**pocillo** *m.* chocolate cup.
**pócima** *f.* medicinal decoction; medicinal drink.
**poción** *f.* drink, beverage.
1) **poco** *adv.* little: *me gusta* ~, I like it little; ~ *hábil,* unskilled; ~ *más o menos,* more or less. *2* shortly, a short time: ~ *antes,* shortly before. *3 m.* little [small amount, time, etc.]: *un* ~ *de,* a little, some [foll. by noun]; *tener en* ~, to set little value on; *a* ~, shortly afterwards; *dentro de* ~, in a short time; *¡~ a* ~*!,* easy there!; *por* ~, almost, nearly.
2) **poco, -ca** *adj.* little [not much]. *2 pl.* few. *3 unos pocos,* a few, some.
**pocho, -cha** *adj.* coll. pale, pale-faced.
**poda** *f.* pruning. *2* pruning season.
**podadera** *f.* pruning knife, billhook.
**podador, -ra** *m.-f.* pruner [one who prunes].
**podagra** *f.* MED. gout, podagra.
**podar** *tr.* to prune, lop, trim.

**podenco** *m.* hound [dog].

1) **poder** *m.* power [authority, control]. *2* power [ability to act; capability of producing an effect; active property]; force, strength, might. *3* power, hands, possession: *en ~ de*, in the power, or in the hands, of. *4* POL. holding of office: *estar en el ~*, to be in office. *5 sing.-pl.* LAW. power, proxy, power of attorney. *6* power, authority [delegated power].

2) **poder** *tr.-intr.* to be able [to], can, may: *no ~ con*, not to be able to bear; to be no match for; *no ~ más*, to be unable to do more; to be exhausted; *no puedo menos de hacerlo*, I cannot help doing it; *a más no ~*, to the utmost; *como pueda, podamos*, etc., the best I, we, etc., can. | Notice the different senses of the verb in the negative sentences: *Juan no puede ir*, John cannot go; *Juan puede no ir*, John may not go. *2 intr.* to have power or influence. *3 impers.* to be possible, may: *puede que llueva*, it may rain. ‖ IRREG. CONJUG.: INDIC. Pres.: *puedo, puedes, puede;* podemos, podéis, *pueden.* | Pret.: *pude, pudiste, pudo; pudimos, pudisteis, pudieron.* | Fut.: *podré, podrás*, etc. | COND.: *podría, podrías*, etc. | SUBJ. Pres.: *pueda, puedas, pueda;* podamos, podáis, *puedan.* | Imperf.: *pudiera, pudieras*, or *pudiese, pudieses*, etc. | Fut.: *pudiere, pudieres*, etc. | IMPER.: *puede, pueda;* podamos, poded, *puedan.* | GER.: *pudiendo.*

**poderdante** *m.-f.* LAW constituent.

**poderhabiente** *m.-f.* LAW attorney, proxy.

**poderío** *m.* power, might. *2* sway, jurisdiction. *3* wealth, riches.

**poderosamente** *adv.* mightily. *2* forcibly.

**poderoso, -sa** *adj.* powerful, mighty. *2* forcible, efficacious. *3* rich, wealthy.

**podio** *m.* ARCH. podium.

**podón** *m.* large pruning knife, billhook.

**podre** *f.* pus.

**podré, podrás**, etc. *irr.* V. PODER.

**podrecer** *tr.-intr.-ref.* PUDRIR.

**podredumbre** *f.* rot, rottenness, decay. *2* pus.

**podredura, podrición** *f.* putrefaction, corruption.

**podredero** *m.* PUDRIDERO.

**podría, podrías**, etc. *irr.* V. PODER.

**podrigorio** *m.* person full of aches and ailments.

**podrir** *tr.-ref.* PUDRIR.

**poema** *m.* poem.

**poesía** *f.* poetry. *2* poem.

**poeta** *m.* poet.

**poetastro** *m.* poetaster.

**poética** *f.* poetics.

**poético, -ca** *adj.* poetic, poetical.

**poetisa** *f.* poetess.

**poetizar** *intr.-tr.* to poetize.

**poíno** *m.* gantry, barrelstand.

**póker** *m.* poker [card game].

**polaco, -ca** *adj.* Polish. *2 m.-f.* Pole [person]. *3 m.* Polish language.

**polacra** *f.* NAUT. polacre.

**polaina** *f.* legging.

**polar** *adj.* polar; pole: *estrella ~*, polestar.

**polaridad** *f.* polarity.

**polarímetro** *m.* polarimeter.

**polariscopio** *m.* polariscope.

**polarización** *f.* polarization.

**polarizar** *tr.* to polarize.

**polca** *f.* polka [dance].

**polea** *f.* pulley. *2* NAUT. tackle, tackle block.

**polemarca** *m.* polemarch.

**polémica** *f.* polemic, controversy. *2* polemics. *3* MIL. art of fortification and investment.

**polémico, -ca** *adj.* polemic, polemical.

**polemista** *m.-f.* polemic, polemist.

**polemonio** *m.* BOT. polemonium.

**polen** *m.* BOT. pollen.

**poleo** *m.* BOT. penny royal. *2* coll. stiff, cold wind.

**poliandria** *f.* polyandry.

**policárpico, -ca** *adj.* BOT. polycarpic, polycarpous.

**pólice** *m.* thumb.

**policía** *m.* policeman, police officer, detective. *2* police, police force: *~ secreta*, secret police. *3* politeness. *4* cleanliness, good order.

**policíaco, -ca** *adj.* [pertaining to the] police. *2 novela policíaca*, detective story.

**policial** *adj.* (S. Am.) POLICÍACO.

**policlínica** *f.* MED. polyclinic.

**policromar** *tr.* to polychrome.

**policromía** *f.* polychromy.

**policromo, -ma** *adj.* polychrome, many-coloured.

**polichinela** *m.* punchinello.

**poliédrico, -ca** *adj.* polyhedral, polyhedric.

**poliedro** *m.* GEOM. polyhedron.

**polifásico, -ca** *adj.* ELECT. polyphase, multiphase.

**Polifemo** *m. pr. n.* MYT. Polyphemus.

**polifonía** *f.* MUS. polyphony.

**polifónico, -ca; polífono, -na** *adj.* MUS. polyphonic.

**polígala** *f.* BOT. milkwort.

**poligamia** *f.* polygamy.

**polígamo, -ma** *adj.* polygamous. *2 m.* polygamist.

**poligloto, -ta** *adj.-n.* polyglot. *2 f.* polyglot [Bible].

**poligonal** *adj.* polygonal.

**polígono, -na** *adj.* polygonal. *2 m.* GEOM., FORT. polygon.

**polígrafo** *m.* expert in ciphers. *2* polygraph [writer].

**polilla** *f.* ENT. moth, clothes moth, carpet moth. *2* fig. waster, destroyer.

**polimería** *f.* CHEM. polymerism.

**polimerizar** *tr.* CHEM. to polymerize.

**polímero, -ra** *adj.* CHEM. polymeric. *2 m.* CHEM. polymer.

**polimorfismo** *m.* polymorphism.

**polín** *m.* roller, skid.

**Polinesia** *f. pr. n.* GEOG. Polynesia.

**polinesio, -sia** *adj.-n.* Polynesian.

**polínico, -ca** *adj.* BOT. pollinic, pollinical.

**polinización** *f.* BOT. pollination.

**polinomio** *m.* ALG. polynomial.

**polio** *m.* BOT. poly.

**poliomielitis** *f.* MED. poliomyelitis.

**polípero** *m.* ZOOL. polypary.

**pólipo** *m.* ZOOL. polyp. *2* MED. polyp, polypus. *3* PULPO.

**polipodio** *m.* BOT. polypody, sweet fern.

**polisépalo, -la** *adj.* BOT. polysepalous.

**polisílabo, -ba** *adj.* polysyllabic. *2 m.* polysyllable.

**polisón** *m.* bustle [of woman's dress].

**polispasto** *m.* tackle, hoisting tackle.

**polispermo, -ma** *adj.* BOT. polyspermous.

**polista** *m.-f.* polo player.

**politécnico, -ca** *adj.* polytechnic.

**politeísmo** *m.* polytheism.

**política** *f.* politics. *2* policy [course of action; sagacity, address]. *3* politeness.

**politicastro** *m.* politicaster.

**político, -ca** *adj.* politic, political. *2* politic, expedient; tactful. *3* polite, courteous. *4* -in-law: *padre ~*, father-in-law. *5 m.* politician.

**politiquear** *intr.* coll. to dabble in politics, to play politics.

**politiqueo** *m.* coll. dabbling in politics.
**politiquería** *f.* political chicanery.
**politiquillo** *m.* petty politician.
**polivalente** *f.* BACT., CHEM. polyvalent, multivalent.
**póliza** *f.* paybill. *2* COM. certificate, policy: ~ *de seguros,* insurance policy. *3* tax stamp.
**polizón** *m.* loafer. *2* stowaway [in a ship].
**polizonte** *m.* coll. cop, policeman.
**polo** *m.* GEOM., ASTR., GEOG., PHYS., BIOL.. pole. *2* SPORT. polo.
**polonés, -sa** *adj.* Polish. *2 m.-f.* Pole. *3 f.* polonaise [woman's dress]. *4* MUS. polonaise.
**Polonia** *f. pr. n.* GEOG. Poland.
**polonio** *m.* CHEM. polonioum.
**poltrón, -na** *adj.* lazy. *2 m.-f.* lazy person. *3 f.* easy chair.
**poltronería** *f.* laziness, sloth.
**polución** *f.* MED. pollution.
**poluto, -ta** *adj.* polluted, unclean, filthy.
**Pólux** *m. pr. n.* MYTH., ASTR. Pollux.
**polvareda** *f.* cloud of dust. *2* fig. dust, turmoil.
**polvera** *f.* compact, face-powder case.
**polvillo** *m. dim.* fine dust.
**polvo** *m.* dust: *limpio de ~ y paja,* fig. free of all charges, net. *2* powder [mass of dry particles]: *hacer ~,* to destroy; to beat completely; to tire out; *en ~,* powdered. *3* pinch [of snuff or powder]. *4 pl.* cosmetic or medicinal powder. *5 polvos de la madre Celestina,* fig. hocus-pocus, secret or miraculous means.
**pólvora** *f.* powder [explosive], gunpowder: *gastar la ~ en salvas,* fig. to waste time or energy: *ser una ~,* coll. to be a live wire. *2* fireworks. *3* fig. bad temper. *4* fig. liveliness, vivacity.
**polvorear** *tr.* to powder [sprinkle with powder].
**polvoriento, -ta** *adj.* dusty.
**polvorín** *m.* powder magazine. *2* powder flask. *3* (Am.) spitfire [person].
**polvorista** *m.* PIROTÉCNICO.
**polvorizar** *tr.* POLVOREAR. *2* PULVERIZAR.
**polvoroso, -sa** *adj.* dusty.
**polvorón** *m.* a kind of cake.
**polla** *f.* CARDS POOL. *2* ORN. pullet. *3* fig. girl, young woman. *4* ORN. coot. *5* ORN. water hen, gallinule.
**pollada** *f.* brood, hatch, covey.
**pollastre, pollastro** *m.* coll. sly fellow.
**poliazón** *f.* brood, hatch, hatching.
**pollera** *f.* female poulterer. *2* chicken roost. *3* chicken coop. *4* gocart. *5* hooped petticoat. *6* (Am.) skirt [woman's garment].
**pollería** *f.* poultry shop. *2* coll. young people.
**pollero, -ra** *m.-f.* poulterer. *2* chicken roost.
**pollina** *f.* young she-ass.
**pollino** *m.* donkey; young ass. *2* fig. jackass, dolt.
**pollito, -ta** *m.-f. dim.* little chicken, chick. *2 m.* coll. boy, youth. *3 f.* coll. girl.
**pollo** *m.* chicken. *2* nestling, young bird. *3* brood [of the bee]. *4* coll. young person.
**polluelo** *m. dim.* little chicken, chick.
**poma** *f.* BOT. apple.
**pomáceo, -a** *adj.* BOT. pomaceous.
**pomada** *f.* pomade, pomatum.
**pomar** *m.* orchard; apple orchard.
**pomarrosa** *f.* BOT. rose apple.
**pomelo** *m.* BOT. pomelo, grapefruit.
**pomerano, -na** *adj.-n.* Pomeranian.
**pómez (piedra)** *f.* pumice stone.
**pomo** *m.* BOT. pome. *2* pomander. *3* phial, vial, small bottle. *4* pomel [of sword-hilt].

**pompa** *f.* pomp: *pompas fúnebres,* funeral. *2* pageant. *3* bubble. *4* NAUT. pump.
**Pompeya** *f. pr. n.* HIST., GEOG. Pompeii.
**pompeyano, -na** *adj.-n.* Pompeian.
**Pompeyo** *m. pr. n.* Pompey.
**pomposidad** *f.* pomposity, pompousness.
**pomposo, -sa** *adj.* pompous [showy; self-important]. *2* pompous, inflated [style, etc.].
**pómulo** *m.* ANAT. cheekbone.
**ponche** *m.* punch [drink]: ~ *de huevo,* eggnog.
**ponchera** *f.* punch bowl.
**poncho, -cha** *adj.* soft, lazy; mild. *2 m.* poncho.
**ponderable** *adj.* ponderable.
**ponderación** *f.* ponderation. *2* balance, equilibrium. *3* judiciousness. *4* exaggeration; emphasizing: *sin ~,* without exaggeration.
**ponderado, -da** *adj.* prudent.
**ponderador, -ra** *adj.* pondering, weighing. *2* balancing. *3* exaggerating; emphasizing.
**ponderal** *adj.* ponderal.
**ponderar** *tr.* to weigh. *2* to ponder over. *3* to balance, poise. *4* to exaggerate. *5* to emphasize; to praise highly.
**ponderativo, -va** *adj.* exaggerating, hyperbolical.
**ponderoso, -sa** *adj.* ponderous, heavy. *2* grave, circumspect.
**pondré, pondría,** etc. *irr.* V. PONER.
**ponedero, -ra** *adj.* egg-laying. *2 m.* hen's nest. *3* nest egg.
**ponedor, -ra** *adj.* egg-laying. *2* trained to rear on the hind legs [horse]. *3* POSTOR.
**ponencia** *f.* the post or office of one who is designated to report on a matter; his report.
**ponente** *m.-f.* reporter, one who is designated to report on a matter.
**ponentino, -na** *adj.* western.
**poner** *tr.* to lay [eggs]. *2* to place, put, lay, set: ~ *a prueba,* to put to the test; ~ *a trabajar,* to set to work; ~ *fin a,* to put an end to; to bring to an end; ~ *en libertad,* to set free; ~ *en práctica,* to carry out; ~ *la mesa,* to set the table; ~ *uno sus esperanzas en,* to lay one's hopes in. *2* to suppose. *3* to wager, bet [money]. *4* to appoint; post, set to work as: ~ *de aprendiz,* to apprentice. *5* to apply, adapt. *6* to give [a name]. *7* to expose [to the sun, the air]. *8* to contribute [give as a contribution]. *9* to impose, lay on [a law, tax, etc.]. *10* to put on [a play, etc.]. *11* to cause [fear, etc.]. *12* to make, render, turn: ~ *furioso,* to render furious; ~ *enfermo,* to make ill. *13* ~ *al corriente,* to inform. *14* ~ *al día,* to bring up to date. *15* ~ *como nuevo, como un trapo,* ~ *de vuelta y media,* to abuse, revile, cover with insults; to dress down. *16* ~ *de manifiesto,* to make evident. *17* ~ *de relieve,* to emphasize, point out. *18* ~ *en duda,* to doubt. *19* ~ *en las nubes,* to praise to the skies. *20* ~ *mal a uno,* to discredit someone. *21* ~ *mala cara,* to frown, to show displeasure. *22* ~ *reparos,* to make objections. *23 ref.* to place, put or set oneself. *24* to put on [a garment, etc.]. *25* to become, get, turn. *26* [of the sun, stars, etc.] to set. *27 ponerse a,* to start to, begin to, set about. *28 ponerse a cubierto,* to shelter or protect oneself. *29 ponerse al corriente, al tanto,* to get informed. *30 ponerse bien con,* to get in with. *31 ponerse de acuerdo,* to agree. *32 ponerse de barro, tinta,* etc., to stain oneself with mud, ink, etc. *33 ponerse en marcha,* to begin to move; to set out. *34 ponerse en pie,* to stand up. *35 ponerse en la razón,* to be reasonable.

¶ CONJUG. INDIC. Pres.: *pongo, pones,* pone; po-
nemos, ponéis, ponen. | Pret.: *puse, pusiste,*
*puso; pusimos, pusisteis, pusieron.* | Fut.: *pondré,*
*pondrás,* etc. | COND.: *pondría, pondrías,* etc. |
SUBJ. Pres.: *ponga, pongas, ponga; pongamos,*
*pongáis, pongan.* | Imperf.: *pusiera, pusieras* or
*pusiese, pusieses,* etc. | Fut.: *pusiere, pusieres,*
etc. | IMPER.: *pon, ponga; pongamos,* poned, *pon-*
*gan.* | PAST. P.: *puesto.*
**pongo, ponga,** etc. *irr.* V. PONER.
**poniente** *m.* west. *2* west wind.
**ponimiento** *m.* placing, putting, laying, setting.
**pontaje, pontazgo** *m.* bridge toll, pontage.
**pontear** *tr.* to build a bridge over.
**póntico, -ca** *adj.* Pontic.
**pontificado** *m.* pontificate.
**pontifical** *adj.* pontifical. *2 m.* ECCL. pontifical
[book]. *3 pl.* ECCL. pontificals.
**pontificar** *intr.* to pontificate.
**pontífice** *m.* pontiff, pontifex.
**pontificio, -cia** *adj.* pontifical, papal.
**pontocón** *m.* PUNTAPIÉ.
**pontón** *m.* pontoon. *2* pontoon bridge, floating
bridge. *3* hulk [dismantled ship used as a store
vessel, hospital or prison].
**pontonero** *m.* MIL. pontoneer, pontonier.
**ponzoña** *f.* poison, venom.
**ponzoñoso, -sa** *adj.* poisonous, venomous.
**popa** *f.* NAUT. poop, stern: *a ~, en ~,* aft, abaft.
**popar** *tr.* to despise. *2* to fondle, caress. *3* to pamper.
**pope** *m.* pope [priest of the Orthodox Church].
**popel** *adj.* NAUT. sternmost.
**popelina** *f.* poplin.
**poplíteo, -a** *adj.* ANAT. popliteal.
**población** *f.* population [act of populating].
**populachería** *f.* cheap popularity, appeal to the
mob.
**populachero, -ra** *adj.* vulgar, common. *2* intended
to please the populace.
**populacho** *m.* populace, mob, rabble.
**popular** *adj.* popular.
**popularidad** *f.* popularity.
**popularizar** *tr.* to popularize. *2 ref.* to become popular, to become generally known or liked.
**populoso, -sa** *adj.* populous.
**popurrí,** *pl.* **-rríes** *m.* MUS. potpurri.
**poquedad** *f.* paucity, littleness, scantiness, scarcity. *2* trifle. *3* timidity.
**poquísimo, -ma** *adj. superl.* very little.
1) **poquito** *m.* very small quantity, very short time,
little bit. *2 adv.* very little: *~ a poco,* gently,
slowly.
2) **poquito, -ta** *adj.* very little. *2 pl.* very few.
**por** *prep.* by, for, as, along, around, across,
through, from, out of, at, in, on, to, etc.: *~ aquí,*
around here, here; *~ por casualidad,* by chance;
*~ compasión,* out of pity; *~ decirlo así,* so to say;
*~ Dios,* for heaven's sake; *~ docenas,* by the doz-
en; *~ escrito,* in writing; *~ ocho pesetas,* for
eight pesetas; *~ la noche,* in the night, at night;
*~ la ventana,* through the window; *~ lo que veo,*
from what I see; *~ mar,* by sea; *~ recomenda-*
*ción de,* on recommendation of; *dos ~ dos,* two
by two; *fui ~ agua,* I went for water; *hablé ~ él,*
I spoke for him; *lo cogió ~ el brazo,* he took him
by the arm; *lo tengo ~ justo,* I hold it just. *2*
however, no matter how: *~ bien que lo haga,* no
matter how well I do it. *3* other applications: *~*
*ciento,* per cent; *~ donde,* wherefore, whereby;
*~ entre,* through, in between, among: *~ tanto,*

*~ lo tanto,* therefore; *~ lo visto,* apparently; *~*
*más que, ~ mucho que,* however much, no matter how much; *~ mí,* as a far as I am concerned;
*¿~ qué?,* why?; *~ supuesto,* of course.
**porcachón, -na; porcallón, -na** *adj.* coll. dirty, hoggish. *2 m.-f.* coll. dirty person, hog.
**porcelana** *f.* porcelain, china.
**porcentaje** *m.* percentage.
**porcino, -na** *adj.* porcine. *2 m.* little pig.
**porción** *f.* portion, part, allotment. *2* quantity.
**porcipelo** *m.* coll. bristle [of hog].
**porciúncula** *f.* ECCL. Franciscan jubilee.
**porcuno, -na** *adj.* porcine, hoggish.
**porche** *m.* porch, portico, covered walk.
**pordiosear** *intr.* to beg, go begging.
**pordiosero, -ra** *adj.* begging, mendicant. *2 m.-f.*
beggar.
**porfía** *f.* insistence, importunity. *2* stubborness. *3*
dispute. *4 a ~,* in emulation, in competition.
**porfiado, -da** *adj.* insistent, persistent, importunate, stubborn.
**porfiar** *intr.* to insist, persist. *2* to ask with importunity. *3* to argue stubbornly.
**pórfido** *m.* porphyry.
**pormenor** *m.* detail, particular: *entrar en porme-*
*nores,* to go into detail.
**pormenorizar** *tr.* to detail, tell in detail, itemize.
**pornografía** *f.* pornography.
**pornográfico, -ca** *adj.* pornographic.
**poro** *m.* pore.
**porosidad** *f.* porosity.
**poroso, -sa** *adj.* porous.
**poroto** *m.* BOT. (Am.) bean.
**porque** *conj.* for, because. *2* in order that.
**¿por qué?** *conj. interr.* why?, wherefore?
**porqué** *m.* reason, motive. *2* coll. quantity,
amount.
**porquera** *f.* wild boar's lair or couch.
**porquería** *f.* coll. dirt, filth. *2* coll. poor food. *3* coll.
trifle, worthless thing. *4* coll. filthy act or word.
*5* coll. dirty trick.
**porqueriza** *f.* pigsty.
**porquerizo, porquero** *m.* swineherd.
**porqueta** *f.* ZOOL. wood louse.
**porra** *f.* bludgeon, club. *2* maul. *3* bore, nuisance
[pers.]. *4 mandar a la ~,* to send to the devil.
**porráceo, -a** *adj.* porraceous.
**porrada** *f.* blow. *2* stupidity, nonsense. *3* lot, heap,
great quantity or number.
**porrazo** *m.* blow, bump, knock.
**porrería** *f.* coll. stupidity, silliness. *2* sluggishness.
**porreta** *f.* green leaves of leeks, garlic or onions. *2*
coll. *en ~,* naked, stark naked.
**porrillo (a)** *adv.* abundantly, in abundance.
**porro** *m.* coll. stupid fellow, dolt. *2* PUERRO.
1) **porrón** *m.* kind of wine bottle with a long side
spout. *2* BOTIJO.
2) **porrón, -na** *adj.* slow, heavy, sluggish.
**porta** *f.* NAUT. port, porthole. *2 adj.* ANAT. portal
[vein].
**portaaviones** *m.* NAV. airplane carrier.
**portabandera** *f.* shoulder-belt for carrying a flag.
**portacaja** *m.* drum strap.
**portacartas,** *pl.* **-tas** *m.* pouch or bag for letters.
**portada** *f.* ARCH. portal, front, façade. *2* frontispiece. *3* PRINT. title page. *4* cover [of magazine].
**portado, -da** *adj.* dressed; behaved.
**portador, -ra** *adj.* carrying. *2* RADIO. carrier [wave].
*3 m.-f.* carrier, bearer. *4 m.* COM. bearer.
**portaequipaje** *m.* AUTO. trunk.
**portaequipajes,** *pl.* **-jes** *m.* baggage rack.

**portaestandarte** *m.* standart-bearer.
**portafusil** *m.* MIL. sling [of a musket].
**portaherramienta** *m.* MACH. chuck.
**portal** *m.* doorway, portal, vestibule. *2* porch, portico. *3* town's gate.
**portalada** *f.* portal, large gate.
**portalámparas**, *pl.* -**ras** *m.* ELECT. socket, lamp holder.
**portalápiz** *m.* pencil holder.
**portalibros**, *pl.* -**bros** *m.* book straps [for schoolboys].
**portalón** *m.* gateway, portal. *2* NAUT. gangway.
**portamantas**, *pl.* -**tas** *m.* blanket straps.
**portaminas**, *pl.* -**minas** *m.* mechanical pencil.
**portamonedas** *m.* pocketbook, purse.
**portante** *m.* pace, amble [of horse]. *2 tomar el* ~, coll. to leave, go away.
**portantillo** *m.* easy pace [of horse or ass].
**portaobjeto** *m.* slide [for microscope].
**portapaz** *m.-f.* ECCL. pax [tablet].
**portaplacas** *m.* PHOT. plate holder, chassis.
**portapliegos** *m.* bag for papers.
**portaplumas** *m.* penholder.
**portar** *tr.* to carry [arms]. *2* HUNT. to retrieve.
**portaviandas** *m.* dinner pail.
**portavoz** *m.* megaphone. *2* mouthpiece [person, newspaper]; spokesman.
**portazgo** *m.* toll, road toll. *2* tollhouse.
**portazguero** *m.* tollkeeper.
**portazo** *m.* bang or slam [of a door].
**porte** *m.* portage, porterage, carriage [act; cost]: ~ *pagado*, portage prepaid. *2* behaviour, bearing; dress, appearance [of a person]. *3* nobility, illustrious descent. *4* size, capacity; tonnage [of a ship].
**portear** *tr.* to carry, transport [for a price]. *2 intr.* [of doors or windows] to slam.
**portento** *m.* prodigy, wonder, portent.
**portentoso, -sa** *adj.* prodigious, portentous.
**porteño, -ña** *adj.-n.* of Buenos Aires.
**porteo** *m.* carrying, portage.
**portera** *f.* portress, concierge, woman doorkeeper.
**portería** *f.* porter's lodge. *2* employment of a porter or doorkeeper. *3* SPORT. goal.
**portero** *m.* doorkeeper, porter, janitor. *2* SPORT. goalkeeper.
**portezuela** *f. dim.* little door. *2* carriage door. *3* pocket flap.
**pórtico** *m.* porch. colonnade.
**portier** *m.* door-curtain, portière.
**portilla** *f.* gate, passage [in a fence]. *2* NAUT. porthole [for admission of air and light].
**portillo** *m.* opening [in a wall, fence, etc.]. *2* wicket [small door or gate]. *3* breach, gap. *4* nick [in an edge]. *5* pass between hills.
**portón** *m. augm.* large door. *2* inner front door.
**portorriqueño, -ña** *adj.-n.* Puerto Rican.
**portugués, -sa** *adj.-n.* Portuguese.
**porvenir** *m.* future, time to come. *2* fig. promise: *de mucho* ~, of great promise.
**pos (en)** *adv. en* ~ *de*, after, behind; in pursuit of.
**posada** *f.* lodging. *2* dwelling, home. *3* lodging house, inn. *4* boarding house. *5* camp.
**posadera** *f.* landlady, hostess, woman innkeeper.
**posaderas** *f. pl.* coll. buttocks.
**posadero** *m.* landlord, host, innkeeper.
**posar** *intr.* to lodge, board, put up. *2* to lay, rest. *3* F. ARTS to pose. *4 intr.-ref.* [of birds, etc.] to

alight, to perch, sit. *5 tr.* to lay down [a burden]. *6 ref.* [of sediment, dust, etc.] to settle.
**poscomunión** *f.* ECCL. Postcommunion.
**posdata** *f.* postscript.
**poseedor, -ra** *m.-f.* possessor, owner, holder.
**poseer** *tr.* to possess, own, hold. *2* to have a mastery of [art, language, etc.]. *3 ref.* to control oneself. ¶ CONJUG.: INDIC. Pret.: poseí, poseíste, *poseyó;* poseímos, poseísteis, *poseyeron.* | SUBJ. Imperf.: *poseyera, poseyeras,* etc., or *poseyese, poseyeses,* etc. | PAST. p.: *poseído & poseso.* | GER.: *poseyendo.*
**poseído, -da** *p. p.* of POSEER. *2* possessed. *3 m.-f.* POSESO 2.
**posesión** *f.* possession. *2 dar* ~, to give possession, induct, install [in an office, rank, etc.].
**posesional** *adj.* possessional.
**posesionar** *tr.* to put in possession; to give possession, induct, install. *2 ref.* to take possession, to be installed [in an office, rank, etc.].
**posesivo, -va** *adj.* possessive. *2* GRAM. *adj.-m.* possessive.
**poseso, -sa** *adj. irreg. p. p.* of POSEER. *2 m.-f.* person possessed by an evil spirit.
**posesor, -ra** *m.-f.* possessor, owner, holder.
**posesorio, -ria** *adj.* LAW. possessory.
**posfecha** *f.* postdate.
**posguerra** *f.* POSTGUERRA.
**posibilidad** *f.* possibility. *2* ability [to do something]. *3 pl.* means, property.
**posibilitar** *tr.* to render possible, facilitate.
**posible** *adj.* possible: *hacer todo lo* ~, to do one's best. *2 m. pl.* means, income, property.
**posición** *f.* position [posture; manner in which anything is placed; mental attitude]. *2* position, rank, status. *3* putting, placement. *4* MIL., ASTR., CHEM. position.
**positivismo** *m.* PHIL. Positivism. *2* [moral] materialism. *3* matter-of-factness.
**positivista** *adj.* positivistic. *2* practical, realistic, matter-of-fact. *3 m.-f.* positivist.
**positivo, -va** *adj.* positive [certain, real; affirmative; not speculative or theoretical]. *2* matter-of-fact. *3* BACT., ELECT., GRAM., LOG., MATH., LAW positive. *4 adj.-m.* PHOT. positive.
**pósito** *m.* public granary. *2* cooperative.
**positrón** *m.* PHYS. positron.
**positura** *f.* position, posture. *2* state, disposition.
**posma** *f.* dullness, slowness, sluggishness. *2 adj. n.* dull, slow, sluggish [pers.].
**poso** *m.* sediment, dregs, lees. *2* rest, repose.
**posología** *f.* MED. posology.
**pospondré, pospondría,** etc. *irr.* V. POSPONER.
**posponer** *tr.* to postpone [place after something in order of precedence, value, importance, etc.], to subordinate. *2* GRAM. to postpose. ¶ CONJUG. like *poner.*
**pospongo, posponga,** etc. *irr.* V. POSPONER.
**posposición** *f.* postponement, subordination. *2* GRAM. postposition.
**pospositivo, -va** GRAM. postpositive.
**pospuesto, -ta** *irreg. p. p.* of POSPONER.
**pospuse, pospusiera,** etc. *irr.* V. POSPONER.
**posta** *f.* relay [of post horses]. *2* post, posthouse. *3* post, stage. *4* slice, chop [of meat or fish]. *5* lead ball. *6* stake [at cards]. *7* memorial tablet. *8* ARCH. Vitruvian scroll. *9* person who travels post, postrider. *10 correr la* ~, to ride post; *por la* ~, riding post; fig. posthaste; *silla de* ~, post chaise. *11 a* ~, coll. on purpose.

**postal** *adj.* postal: *servicio* ~, post, mail service. *2 f.* postcard.

**postdata** *f.* POSDATA.

**postdiluviano, -na** *adj.* postdiluvian.

**poste** *m.* post [upright pole], pillar: ~ *indicador*, finger post, signpost; ~ *telegráfico*, telegraph post. *2 dar* ~, coll. to keep [someone] waiting.

**postema** *f.* MED. abscess. *2* coll. bore, nuisance.

**postergación** *f.* delay, postponement. *2* leaving [someone] behind in a promotion.

**postergar** *tr.* to delay, postpone. *2* to leave [someone] behind in a promotion.

**posteridad** *f.* posterity.

**posterior** *adj.* posterior, hinder, back, rear. *2* posterior [in time].

**posterioridad** *f.* posteriority.

**postescolar** *adj.* postschool.

**postguerra** *f.* postwar.

**postigo** *m.* back door; postern. *2* small door, wicket. *3* window shutter.

**postilla** *f.* scab [over a sore, pustule, etc.].

**postillón** *m.* postilion, postboy.

**postilloso, -sa** *adj.* scabby.

**postín** *m.* coll. airs, importance: *darse* ~, to put on airs, to give oneself airs.

**postizo, -za** *adj.* artificial, not natural, false. *2* detachable [collar]. *3 m.* false hair, switch. *4 f.* castanet.

**postmeridiano, -na** *adj.* postmeridian.

**postoperatorio, -ria** *adj.* postoperative.

**postor** *m.* bidder [at an auction]: *mayor*, or *mejor* ~, highest bidder.

**postración** *f.* prostration.

**postrado, -da** *adj.* prostrate(d.

**postrar** *tr.* to prostrate, to humble. *2* to overthrow. *3* to prostrate, exhaust. *4 ref.* to prostate oneself; to kneel down.

**postre** *adj.* POSTRERO. *2 m. sing. & pl.* dessert. *3* adv. *a la* ~, at last, finally.

**postremo, -ma** *adj.* last, final.

**postrer** *adj.* [before a noun] POSTRERO.

**postrero, -ra** *adj.* last. *2* hindermost. *3 n.* last, last one.

**postrimer** *adj.* [before a noun] POSTRIMERO.

**postrimerías** *f. pl.* last period; last years of life. *2* THEOL. last stages of man.

**postrimero, -ra** *adj.* last [in order].

**postulación** *f.* postulation. *2* request, petition.

**postulado** *m.* postulate.

**postulanta** *f.* ECCL. woman postulant.

**postulante** *adj.* postulating. *2 m.-f.* postulant.

**postular** *tr.* to postulate. *2* to beg, demand.

**póstumo, -ma** *adj.* posthumous.

**postura** *f.* posture, position. *2* bid [at an auction]. *3* stake, wager [at cards, etc.]. *4* egg laying. *5* egg [of bird].

**potabilidad** *f.* potability, potableness.

**potable** *adj.* potable, drinkable.

**potación** *f.* potation. *2* drink.

**potaje** *m.* pottage, soup. *2* stewed vegetables. *3* mixed drink. *4* meddley, hodge-podge.

**potar** *tr.* to drink.

**potasa** *f.* CHEM. potassium.

**potásico, -ca** *adj.* CHEM. potassic, potassium.

**potasio** *m.* CHEM. potassium.

**pote** *m.* pot, jar. *2* cooking pot.

**potencia** *f.* potency. *2* power [active property; faculty of mind]: *potencias del alma*, mental powers. *3* potentiality: *en* ~, in potentiality. *4* power [great state]: *las potencias europeas*, the European Powers. *5* MATH., MECH., PHYS. power.

**potencial** *adj.-m.* potential. *2* GRAM. conditional [mood].

**potencialidad** *f.* potentiality.

**potentado** *m.* potentate.

**potente** *adj.* potent, powerful, mighty. *2* strong, vigorous.

**poterna** *f.* FORT. postern.

**potestad** *f.* power, faculty. *2* power, dominion, jurisdiction. *3* podesta. *4* potentate. *5 pl.* powers [angels].

**potestativo, -va** *adj.* facultative, optional.

**potingue** *m.* hum, medicine, concoction.

**potísimo, -ma** *adj. superl.* very powerful.

**potosí** *m.* coll. great wealth; mint of money.

**potra** *f.* filly, young mare. *2* coll. rupture, scrotal hernia. *3* coll. luck: *tener* ~, to be lucky.

**potrada** *f.* herd of colts.

**potranca** *f.* filly, young mare.

**potrero** *m.* herdsman of colts. *2* pasture ground for horses. *3* (Am.) cattle ranch.

**potrillo, -lla** *m. dim.* young colt. *2 f. dim.* young filly.

**potro** *m.* colt, foal. *2* horse [for torture or gymnastics]: *estar en un* ~, fig. to be on pins and needles. *3* stocks, shoeing frame.

**potroso, -sa** *adj.* MED. ruptured. *2* coll. lucky.

**poyata** *f.* shelf for glasses and crockery.

**poyo** *m.* stone seat built against the wall.

**poza** *f.* puddle. *2* pool for retting hemp or flax.

**pozal** *m.* bucket, pail. *2* curbstone of a well.

**pozanco** *m.* puddle or pool in a river bank.

**pozo** *m.* well, pit: ~ *artesiano*, artesian well; ~ *negro*, cesspool; ~ *de ciencia*, fig. profoundly learned person. *2* MIN. shaft. *3* fish tank [in a boat].

**práctica** *f.* practice [performance, carrying out; habit; repeated exercise in art, etc.]: *poner en* ~, to put into practice; *en la* ~, in practice. *2* skill [by practice]. *3 pl.* training [for a profession].

**practicable** *adj.* practicable, feasible. *2* THEAT. practicable.

**practicaje** *m.* NAUT. pilotage.

**prácticamente** *adv.* in practice.

**practicante** *adj.* practising. *2 m.-f.* surgeon [for minor surgery]. *3* medical assistant. *4* PHARM. prescription clerk.

**practicar** *tr.* to practise, exercise, do habitually, put into practice. *2* to make, cut [a hole or opening]. *3* SURG. to perform [an operation]. *4 intr. -ref.* to practise [exercise oneself in].

**práctico, -ca** *adj.* practical. *2* skilful, practised. *3 m.* NAUT. pilot: ~ *de puerto*, harbour pilot.

**practicón, -na** *m.-f.* coll. practician.

**pradejón** *m.* small meadow.

**pradeño, -ña** *adj.* [pertaining to] meadow.

**pradera** *f.* prairie. *2* meadowland.

**pradería** *f.* meadowland.

**prado** *m.* meadow, grassland, lawn.

**Praga** *f. pr. n.* GEOG. Prague.

**pragmática** *f.* pragmatic, pragmatic sanction.

**pragmático, -ca** *adj.* pragmatic.

**pragmatismo** *m.* PHIL. pragmatism.

**pragmatista** *adj.-n.* pragmatist.

**pratense** *adj.* pratal.

**preadamita** *m.* preadamite.

**preámbulo** *m.* preamble.

**prebenda** *f.* ECCL. prebend, benefice. *2* fig. sinecure.

**prebendado** *m.* ECCL. prebendary.

**preboste** *m.* provost.

**precario, -ria** *adj.* precarious.

**precaución** *f.* precaution.

**precaver** *tr.* to prevent, provide against. *2 ref.* to be on one's guard. *3 precaverse contra* or *de,* to guard against.
**precavidamente** *adv.* cautiously.
**precavido, -da** *adj.* cautious, guarded, wary.
**precedencia** *f.* precedence.
**precedente** *adj.* preceding, foregoing. *2 m.* precedent.
**preceder** *tr.-intr.* to precede.
**preceptista** *m.* one who sets precepts.
**preceptivo, -va** *adj.* preceptive.
**precepto** *m.* precept, command: *los preceptos del Decálogo,* the Commandments; *día de ~,* holy day, holiday of obligation. *2* precept, rule.
**preceptor, -ra** *m.-f.* preceptor. *2 m.* tutor [private teacher].
**preceptuar** *tr.* to lay down as a precept; to prescribe.
**preces** *f. pl.* prayers, supplications.
**precesión** *m.* MEC., ASTR. precession.
**preciado, -da** *adj.* valuable, precious. *2* proud, boastful.
**preciar** *tr.* to value, prize. *2 ref. preciarse de,* to boast of being; to take pride or glory in.
**precinta** *f.* strap, band [for sealing].
**precintar** *tr.* to seal with a strap or band.
**precinto** *m.* sealing with a strap or band. *2* strap, band [for sealing packages or boxes].
**precio** *m.* price: *no tener ~,* to be priceless. *2* value, worth. *3* esteem.
**preciosidad** *f.* preciousness, worth. *2* precious or beautiful object; beauty.
**precioso, -sa** *adj.* precious [costly, valuable, dear]. *2* beautiful.
**precipicio** *m.* precipice. *2* violent fall. *3* ruin.
**precipitación** *f.* precipitation. *2* precipitance.
**precipitadamente** *adv.* precipitately, hastily.
**precipitadero** *m.* PRECIPICIO.
**precipitado, -da** *adj.* precipitate, hurried, hasty, rash, inconsiderate. *2 m.* CHEM. precipitate.
**precipitar** *tr.* to precipitate [throw headlong; hurl; to hasten, hurry]. *2* CHEM. to precipitate. *3 ref.* to throw oneself headlong, to rush. *4* to be hasty or rash. *5* CHEM. to precipitate.
**precipitoso, -sa** *adj.* precipitous. *2* hasty, rash.
**precipuo, -pua** *adj.* chief, principal.
**precisamente** *adv.* precisely, exactly. *2* just: *~ ahora,* just at this moment.
**precisar** *tr.* to state precisely, specify; to fix, determine with precision. *2* to compel, oblige.
**precisión** *f.* precision, preciseness. *2* necessity, obligation: *tener ~ de,* to need; to be obliged to.
**preciso, -sa** *adj.* precise. *2* necessary, indispensable: *es ~,* it is necessary.
**precitado, -da** *adj.* forecited, aforesaid.
**precito, -ta** *adj.-n.* damned, condemned to hell.
**preclaro, -ra** *adj.* illustrious, renowned.
**precocidad** *f.* precocity, precociousness.
**precognición** *f.* precognition.
**precolombino, -na** *adj.* pre-Columbian.
**preconcebir** *tr.* to preconceive.
**preconización** *f.* ECCL. preconization. *2* preconization [public commendation].
**preconizar** *tr.* ECCL. to preconize. *2* to preconize [commend publicly].
**preconocer** *tr.* to foreknow. ¶ CONJUG. as *conocer.*
**precordial** *adj.* ANAT. precordial.
**precoz** *adj.* precocious.
**precursor, -ra** *adj.* precursory. *2 m.-f.* precursor, forerunner.
**predecesor, -ra** *m.-f.* predecessor.

**predecir** *tr.* to predict, foretell, forecast. ¶ CONJUG. like *decir.*
**predela** *f.* predella.
**predestinación** *f.* predestination.
**predestinado, -da** *adj.* predestinated, predestined. *2 m.-f.* predestinate.
**predestinar** *tr.* to predestine, predestinate.
**predeterminación** *f.* predetermination.
**predeterminar** *tr.* to predetermine.
**predial** *adj.* praedial, predial.
**prédica** *f.* sermon, harangue.
**predicable** *adj.* preachable. *2 adj.-m.* LOG. predicable.
**predicación** *f.* preaching.
**predicado** *m.* LOG. predicate.
**predicador, -ra** *adj.* preaching. *2 m.-f.* preacher.
**predicamento** *m.* LOG. predicament. *2* esteem, reputation.
**predicar** *tr.-intr.* to preach. *2* coll. to lecture, sermonize. *3* LOG. to predicate.
**predicción** *f.* prediction, forecasting.
**predilección** *f.* predilection, special love.
**predilecto, -ta** *adj.* preferred, favourite.
**predio** *m.* property, piece of real estate: *~ rústico,* country property; *~ urbano,* town property.
**predisponer** *tr.* to predispose. *2* to prejudice. *3* to prearrange. ¶ CONJUG. like *poner.*
**predisposición** *f.* predisposition.
**predispuesto, -ta** *adj.* predisposed. *2* prejudiced.
**predominación, predominancia** *f.* predomination, predominance.
**predominante** *adj.* predominant, prevailing.
**predominar** *tr.* to predominate; to prevail. *2* to tower [over], be higher [than].
**predominio** *m.* predominance.
**preeminencia** *f.* pre-eminence. *2* privilege.
**preeminente** *adj.* pre-eminent.
**preexistencia** *f.* pre-existence.
**preexistente** *adj.* pre-existent.
**preexistir** *intr.* to pre-exist.
**prefacio** *m.* preface, introduction. *2* ECCL. preface.
**prefecto** *m.* prefect.
**prefectura** *f.* prefecture.
**preferencia** *f.* preference.
**preferente** *adj.* preferential. *2* preferred.
**preferible** *adj.* preferable.
**preferir** *tr.* to prefer. ¶ CONJUG. as *hervir.*
**prefiero, prefiera,** etc. *irr.* V. PREFERIR.
**prefiguración** *f.* prefiguration, foreshadowing.
**prefigurar** *tr.* to prefigure, foreshadow.
**prefijar** *tr.* to prefix, prearrange, predetermine. *2* GRAM. to prefix.
**prefijo, -ja** *adj.* prefixed. *2 m.* GRAM. prefix.
**prefloración** *f.* BOT. praefloration, estivation.
**prefoliación** *f.* BOT. praefoliation, vernation.
**pregón** *m.* proclamation or announcement by the crier. *2* cry [of merchandise].
**pregonar** *tr.* to proclaim, announce. *2* to cry, hawk [merchandise]. *3* to proscribe [a person].
**pregonero, -ra** *adj.* proclaiming, announcing. *2 m.* common crier, town crier.
**pregunta** *f.* question, inquiry: *estar a la cuarta ~,* coll. to be penniless; *hacer una ~,* to ask a question.
**preguntador, -ra** *adj.* questioning; inquisitive. *2 m.-f.* questioner; inquisitive person.
**preguntar** *tr.-intr.* to ask, inquire; to question; *~ por,* to ask, inquire, after or for. *2 ref.* to wonder [desire to know].
**preguntón, -na** *adj.* inquisitive. *2 m.-f.* inquisitive person.

**prehistoria** *f.* prehistory, prehistorics.
**prehistórico, -ca** *adj.* prehistoric.
**prejuicio** *m.* prejudice, bias. *2* prejudgement.
**prejuzgar** *tr.* to prejudge.
**prelacía** *f.* prelacy.
**prelación** *f.* preference, priority.
**prelado** *m.* prelate.
**prelatura** *f.* PRELACÍA.
**preliminar** *adj.-m.* preliminary.
**prelucir** *intr.* to shine in advance. ¶ CONJUG. like *lucir.*
**preludiar** *tr.-intr.* MUS. to prelude.
**preludio** *m.* prelude, introduction. *2* MUS. prelude.
**prelusión** *f.* preface, introduction.
**prematuramente** *adv.* prematurely.
**prematuro, -ra** *adj.* premature.
**premeditación** *f.* premeditation.
**premeditado, -da** *adj.* premeditated.
**premeditar** *tr.* to premeditate.
**premiador, -ra** *adj.* rewarding. *2 m.-f.* rewarder.
**premiar** *tr.* to reward. *2* to award a prize to.
**premio** *m.* reward, recompense. *2* prize, award. *3* prize [in lottery]. *4* ECON. premium.
**premiosidad** *f.* awkwardness, lack of facility [of action, speech, etc.]; stiffness [of style].
**premioso, -sa** *adj.* burdensome. *2* urging, pressing. *3* strict, rigid. *4* awkward, lacking facility [of action, speech, etc.]; stiff [style].
**premisa** *f.* LOG. premise. *2* basis [of inference].
**premolar** *adj.* ANAT. premolar.
**premonitorio, -ria** *adj.* MED. premonitory.
**premorir** *intr.* LAW. to predecease.
**premura** *f.* haste, hurry. *2* pressure, urgency.
**prenatal** *adj.* prenatal.
**prenda** *f.* pledge, security, pawn; token, proof: *en ~ de,* as a pledge of, as a proof of. *2* fig. beloved one. *3* garment, article or clothing, headgear or footwear. *4 pl.* natural gifts, moral qualities [of a person]. *6 juego de prendas,* game or forfeits.
**prendador** *m.-f.* pledger, pawner.
**prendar** *tr.* to pledge, pawn. *2* to charm, please, enamour. *3* ref. *prendarse de,* to fall in love with, to take a liking to.
**prendedero** *m.* hook, brooch. *2* fillet, bandeau.
**prendedor** *m.* apprehender. *2* brooch, breastpin. *3* fillet, bandeau.
**prender** *tr.* to seize, catch, catch hold of. *2* to attach, hook, pin. *3* to take, arrest [a person]. *4* to dress up [a woman]. *5* to set [fire]. *6 intr.* [of a plant] to take root. *7* [of fire, etc.] to catch, take hold. *8 ref.* [of a woman] to dress up.
**prendería** *f.* second-hand shop.
**prendero, -ra** *m.-f.* second-hand dealer.
**prendimiento** *m.* apprehension, arrest.
**prenombre** *m.* praenomen.
**prensa** *f.* press [machine for compressing, crushing, etc.]: *~ hidráulica,* hydraulic press. *2* press, printing press, printing; newspapers: *dar a la ~,* to publish [a book, etc.] *tener buena,* or *mala ~,* to have a good, or bad, press. *4* PHOT. printing frame.
**prensado** *m.* pressing [by press]. *2* luster, gloss [from pressing].
**prensador, -ra** *m.-f.* presser.
**prensadura** *f.* pressing [by press].
**prensar** *tr.* to press [compress, squeeze in a press].
**prensil** *adj.* prehensile.
**prensión** *f.* prehension.
**prensista** *m.* PRINT. pressman.
**prensor, -ra** *adj.* ORN. psittacine.
**preñado, -da** *adj.* pregnant, with child, with

young. *2* fig. pregnant [full, charged]. *3 m.* pregnancy.
**preñar** *tr.* EMPREÑAR. *2* fig. to fill.
**preñez** *f.* pregnancy. *2* fig. fullness.
**preocupación** *f.* preoccupation [prejudice; mental absortion]. *2* care, concern, worry.
**preocupado, -da** *adj.* preoccupied, prejudiced. *2* concerned, anxious, worried.
**preocupar** *tr.* to preoccupy. *2* to prejudice. *3* to concern, worry. *4 ref.* to concern oneself: *preocuparse de,* to concern oneself in; to take care of. *5* to worry.
**preopinante** *m.-f.* predecessor [in a debate].
**preordinar** *tr.* to preordain.
**preparación** *f.* preparation, preparing, getting ready. *2* preparation [medicine, etc.].
**preparado** *m.* PHARM. preparation.
**preparador, -ra** *adj.* preparing. *2 m.-f.* preparator.
**preparar** *tr.* to prepare, make ready. *2 ref.* to prepare, get ready, make preparations.
**preparativo, -va** *adj.* preparative, preparatory. *2 m. pl.* preparations.
**preparatorio, -ria** *adj.* preparatory.
**preponderancia** *f.* preponderance.
**preponderante** *adj.* preponderant.
**preponderar** *intr.* to preponderate.
**preposición** *f.* GRAM. preposition.
**preposicional** *adj.* prepositional.
**prepositivo, -va** *adj.* GRAM. prepositive.
**prepósito** *m.* ECCL. prelate, provost.
**preposterar** *tr.* to reverse, invert, upset.
**prepóstero, -ra** *adj.* reversed, out of place, upset.
**prepotencia** *f.* prepotence, prepotency.
**prepotente** *adj.* prepotent.
**prepucio** *m.* ANAT. prepuce, foreskin.
**prerrogativa** *f.* prerogative, privilege.
**presa** *f.* catch, clutch, grip, hold: *hacer ~ en,* to catch, lay hold of. *2* seizing, capture [act]. *3* capture, prize, booty. *4* prey: *ave de ~,* bird of prey; *~ de,* a prey to. *5* fang, claw. *6* dam, weir. *7* channel, ditch.
**presagiar** *tr.* to presage, betoken, forebode.
**presagio** *m.* presage, omen, token.
**presagioso, -sa; presago, -ga; présago, -ga** *adj.* presaging, foreboding.
**presbicia** *f.* presbyopia, farsightedness.
**présbita, présbite** *adj.* presbyopic. *2 m.-f.* presbyope.
**presbiterado, presbiterato** *m.* priesthood.
**presbiterianismo** *m.* Presbyterianism.
**presbiteriano, -na** *adj.-n.* Presbyterian.
**presbiterio** *m.* chancel, presbytery [of a church].
**presbítero** *m.* presbyter, priest.
**presciencia** *f.* prescience, foreknowledge.
**prescindible** *adj.* that can be dispensed with.
**prescindir** *intr. ~ de,* to dispense with, do without; to set aside, leave out, disregard, prescind of.
**prescribir** *tr.* to prescribe, decree, ordain. *2* MED. to prescribe. *3 intr.* LAW to prescribe. ¶ PAST. p.: *prescrito* or *prescripto.*
**prescripción** *f.* prescription, order, rule. *2* LAW, MED. prescription.
**prescriptible** *adj.* prescriptible.
**presea** *f.* gem, jewel, valuable thing.
**presencia** *f.* presence: *en ~ de,* in the presence of. *2* ostentation. *3 ~ de ánimo,* presence of mind.
**presencial** *adj.* [relating to] presence. *2 testigo ~,* eyewitness.
**presenciar** *tr.* to be present at, witness, see.
**presentable** *adj.* presentable.
**presentación** *f.* presentation [presenting, exhibi-

tion]. *2* introduction [of a person to another]. *3* MED., THEAT. presentation. *4* external appearance [of a book, etc.].

**presentador, -ra** *m.-f.* presenter.

**presentalla** *f.* ECCL. votive offering.

**presentáneo** *adj.* quick-acting.

**presentante** *m.-f.* presenter; introducer.

**presentar** *tr.* to present: ~ *armas*, MIL. to present arms. *2* to introduce [a person to another]. *3* to nominate, propose for office. *4 ref.* to present oneself or itself. *5* to appear, turn up. *6* to volunteer. *7* to introduce oneself.

**presente** *adj.* present: *la* ~, this letter; *hacer* ~, to remind of; *tener* ~, to bear in mind; *por lo* ~, for the present. *2* current [month, etc.]. *3 adj.-m.* GRAM. present [tense]. *4 m.* present, gift. *5* present [present time].

**presentimiento** *m.* presentiment, foreboding.

**presentir** *tr.* to have a presentiment of, to forebode. ¶ CONJUG. like *hervir*.

**preservación** *f.* preservation, conservation.

**preservar** *tr.* to preserve, guard, keep safe.

**preservativo, -va** *adj.* preservative, preserving. *2 m.* preservative, preventive.

**presidario** *m.* PRESIDIARIO.

**presidencia** *f.* presidency. *2* chair [at a meeting, etc.]; chairmanship. *3* speakership [of a parliamentary body]. *4* presidential term.

**presidencial** *adj.* presidential.

**presidenta** *f.* president's wife. *2* woman president. *3* chairwoman.

**presidente** *m.* president. *2* chairman. *3* speaker [of a parliamentary body].

**presidiario** *m.* convict.

**presidio** *m.* penitentiary. *2* hard labour. *3* fortress, citadel. *4* garrison [of soldiers].

**presidir** *tr.* to preside over or at. *2 intr.* to preside.

**presilla** *f.* small loop forming an eye or fastener [for a button, etc.]. *2* SEW. buttonhole stitching.

**presiento, presienta**, etc. *irr.* V. PRESENTIR.

**presión** *f.* pressure: ~ *arterial*, blood pressure.

**presionar** *tr.* (Am.) to press, urge.

**preso, -sa** *adj.* imprisoned; arrested. *2 m.-f.* prisoner. *3* convict.

**prestación** *f.* lending. *2* service, prestation.

**prestado, -da** *adj.* lent, borrowed: *dar* ~, to lend; *pedir* or *tomar* ~, to borrow.

**prestador, -ra** *m.-f.* lender.

**prestamente** *adv.* speedily, promptly, quickly.

**prestamista** *m.-f.* moneylender; pawnbroker.

**préstamo** *m.* loan; lending: *casa de préstamos*, pawnshop; *tomar a* ~, to borrow.

**prestancia** *f.* excellence.

**prestante** *adj.* excellent.

**prestar** *tr.* to lend, loan. *2* to lend, bestow, give, communicate. *3* to do, render [service, duty, etc.]. *4* to give [ear; help, aid]. *5* to pay [attention]. *6* to keep [silence]. *7* to show [patience]. *8* to take [oath]. *9 intr.* [of a piece of cloth, etc.] to give. *10 ref.* to lend oneself or itself. *11* to submit. *12* to give ground for.

**prestatario, -ria** *adj.* borrowing. *2 m.-f.* borrower.

**preste** *m.* ECCL. high mass celebrant.

**presteza** *f.* celerity, promptness, quickness, haste.

**prestidigitación** *f.* prestidigitation.

**prestidigitador** *m.* prestidigitator.

**prestigio** *m.* prestige. *2* spell, fascination.

**prestigioso, -sa** *adj.* prestigious, influential.

**prestimonio** *m.* loan.

1) **presto** *adv.* promptly, quickly. *2* soon.

2) **presto, -ta** *adj.* prompt, quick. *2* ready, prepared.

**presumible** *adj.* presumable.

**presumido, -da** *p. p.* of PRESUMIR. *2* vain, conceited.

**presumir** *tr.* to presume, conjecture. *2 intr.* to presume, be vain or conceited; to boast: ~ *de*, to boast of being.

**presunción** *f.* presumption. *2* presumptuousness, conceit.

**presunto, -ta** *adj.* presumed, supposed. *2* ~ *heredero*, heir presumptive.

**presuntuosidad** *f.* presumptuousness.

**presuntuoso, -sa** *adj.* presumptuous, conceited.

**presuponer** *tr.* to presuppose. *2* to budget. *3* to form an estimate of [a work, etc.]. ¶ CONJUG. like *poner*.

**presuposición** *f.* presupposition.

**presupuestar** *tr.* to budget.

**presupuestario, -ria** *adj.* [pertaining to a] budget.

**presupuesto, -ta** *adj.* presupposed. *2 m.* presupposition. *3* reason, pretext. *4* budget. *5* estimate [for a work].

**presura** *f.* anxiety. *2* haste. *3* eagerness.

**presuroso, -sa** *adj.* prompt, hasty, hurried, swift.

**pretender** *tr.* to pretend to; to seek, solicit. *2* to court, seek in marriage. *3* to try to, to intend.

**pretendienta** *f.* woman pretender or claimant.

**pretendiente** *m.* pretender, claimant. *2* office seeker. *3* suitor, wooer.

**pretensión** *f.* pretension, pretense, claim.

**pretenso, -sa** *irr. p. p.* of PRETENDER.

**preterición** *f.* preterition.

**preterir** *tr.* to pass over, omit, disregard.

**pretérito, -ta** *adj.* past, bygone. *2 adj.-m.* GRAM. past, preterit: ~ *imperfecto*, imperfect; ~ *indefinido*, preterit, past absolute; ~ *perfecto*, present perfect; ~ *pluscuamperfecto*, pluperfect; ~*anterior*, past anterior.

**preternatural** *adj.* preternatural.

**pretextar** *tr.* to pretext.

**pretexto** *m.* pretext, cover, excuse.

**pretil** *m.* parapet, railing.

**pretina** *f.* girdle, belt, waistband.

**pretinazo** *m.* blow with a belt.

**pretinilla** *f. dim.* ladies' belt or girdle.

**pretor** *m.* praetor, pretor.

**pretoriano, -na** *adj.* praetorial, pretorial. *2 adj.-m.* praetorian, pretorian.

**pretorio, -ria** *adj.* praetorial, pretorial. *2 m.* praetorium, pretorium.

**pretura** *f.* praetorship, pretorship.

**prevalecer** *intr.* to prevail. *2* to take root, to thrive. ¶ CONJUG. as *agradecer*.

**prevaleciente** *adj.* prevailing, prevalent.

**prevaler** *intr.* to prevail. *2 ref. prevalerse de*, to avail oneself of, to take advantage of. ¶ CONJUG. like *valer*.

**prevalezco, prevalezca**, etc. *irr.* V. PREVALECER.

**prevaricación** *f.* act of injustice or breach of faith committed by a public officer.

**prevaricador, -ra** *m.-f.* one who commits PREVARICACIÓN.

**prevaricar** *intr.* to act injustly or corruptly in the discharge of a public trust.

**prevaricato** *m.* corrupt practice. *2* LAW prevarication.

**prevención** *f.* preparation, anticipation of needs, danger, etc.: *a* ~, *de* ~, ready in case. *2* stock, supply. *3* foresight. *4* prevention. *5* prejudice, dislike. *6* warning. *7* police station. *8* MIL. guardroom.

**prevendré, prevendría, prevengo, prevenga,** etc. *irr.* V. PREVENIR.
**prevenidamente** *adv.* beforehand, with preparation.
**prevenido, -da** *adj.* ready, prepared. *2* stocked, supplied. *3* forewarned, cautious.
**prevenir** *tr.* to prepare, make ready. *2* to anticipate, foresee, forestall. *3* to prevent, avoid. *4* to warn, caution. *5* to prepossess, prejudice. *6 ref.* to prepare, get ready; to take precautions. *7* to provide oneself. ¶ CONJUG. like *venir.*
**preventivo, -va** *adj.* preventive. *2* warning.
**prever** *tr.* to foresee; to anticipate.
**previo, via** *adj.* previous.
**previne, previniera,** etc. *irr.* V. PREVENIR.
**previsión** *f.* prevision, foresight; forecast: ~ *del tiempo,* weather forecasting. *2* providence. *3* ~ *social,* social security.
**previsor, -ra** *adj.* far-seeing, foresighted. *2* provident.
**previsto, -ta** *adj.* foreseen.
**prez** *f.* honour, glory.
**Príamo** *m. pr. n.* MYTH. Priam.
**prieto, -ta** *adj.* tight, compact. *2* close-fisted. *3* dark, blackish.
**prima** *f.* female cousin. *2* premium, bonus. *3* COM. bounty. *4* INSUR. premium. *5* prime [hour]. *6* MUS. treble [string].
**primacía** *f.* primacy; primateship.
**primada** *f.* coll. deception, trick.
**primado, -da** *adj.* primatial. *2 m.* primacy. *3* ECCL. primate.
**primal, -la** *adj.-n.* yearling [sheep or goat].
**primario, -ria** *adj.* primary, chief, first. *2* primary, elementary. *3* ASTR., BIOL., ELECT., GEOL. primary.
**primate** *m.* personage, worthy. *2* ZOOL. primate.
**primavera** *f.* spring, springtime. *2* BOT. cowslip, primrose.
**primaveral** *adj.* [pertaining to the] spring, vernal.
**primazgo** *m.* cousinship. *2* primacy.
**primer** *adj.* apocopated form of PRIMERO used only before the noun: ~ *ministro,* prime minister.
**primera** *f.* FENC. prime. *2* RLY. first class: *viajar en* ~, to travel first-class. *3* AUTO. low speed. *4* COM. ~ *de cambio,* first of exchange. *5 de* ~, first-class, excellent; very well. *6* directly, without warning.
**primeramente** *adv.* PRIMERO 1 & 2.
**primerizo, -za** *adj.* novice, beginner.
1) **primero** *adv.* first, in the first place. *2* first, rather, sooner. *3 de* ~, first, before.
2) **primero, -ra** *adj.* first. *2* foremost. *3* chief, leading. *4* early, former. *5* ARITH. prime [number]. *6* primary [education]. *7* raw [material].
**primevo, -va** *adj.* primeval, primitive. *2* oldest.
**primicia(s** *f. sing.-pl.* first fruit.
**primigenio, -nia** *adj.* primigenial.
**primípara** *f. adj.* OBST. primipara.
**primitivo, -va** *adj.* primitive. *2 m.* F. ARTS primitive.
**primitivamente** *adv.* originally.
**primo, -ma** *adj.* first. *2* prime, excellent. *3* ÁRITH. prime [number]. *4* raw [material]. *5 m.-f.* cousin: ~ *carnal,* ~ *hermano,* first cousin, cousin-german. *6* coll. gullible person, dupe.
**primogénito, -ta** *adj.-n.* first-born.
**primogenitura** *f.* primogeniture.
**primor** *m.* care, skill, excellence of execution. *2* beauty, exquisiteness [of work]. *3* coll. beautiful or exquisite thing.

**primordial** *adj.* primordial, fundamental.
**primoroso, -sa** *adj.* beautiful, exquisite; beautifully or exquisitely wrought or executed.
**primuláceo, -a** *adj.* BOT. primulaceous.
**princesa** *f.* princess.
**principado** *m.* princedom. *2* principality, principate. *3* primacy. *4 pl.* principalities [angels].
**principal** *adj.* principal, main, chief, foremost, essential. *2* principal, illustrious. *3* GRAM. principal. *4* princeps [edition]. *5 m.* chief, boss, head [of a firm, etc.]. *6* principal, capital [as distinguished from interest]. *7* main, first floor or storey.
**príncipe** *m.* prince: ~ *de Asturias,* Crown Prince of Spain. *2* sovereign, ruler. *3 adj.* princeps [edition].
**principesco, -ca** *adj.* princely.
**principiante, -ta** *m.-f.* beginner, novice, tyro.
**principiar** *tr.* to commence, begin, start.
**principio** *m.* beginning, commencement, start: *al* ~, at first; *a principios de,* at the beginning of [a month, year, etc.]; *en un* ~, at the beginning. *2* source, origin. *3* principle. *4* rule of action. *5* entrée. *6 pl.* principles. *7* rudiments.
**pringar** *tr.* to dip or soak [bread, etc.] in gravy or grease. *2* to stain with grease. *3* coll. to stab, wound. *4 intr.* coll. to share, participate [in an affair]. *5 ref.* to stain oneself with grease.
**pringoso, -sa** *adj.* greasy.
**pringue** *m.-f.* grease, melted fat. *2* greasy dirt.
**prior** *adj.* PHIL. prior, preceding. *2* ECC. prior.
**priora** *f.* prioress.
**priorato** *m.* priorship, priorate. *2* priory.
**prioridad** *f.* priority.
**prisa** *f.* haste, dispatch, celerity; hurry, urgency: *correr* ~, to be pressing; *darse* ~, to hurry, make haste; *tener* ~, to be in a hurry; *a* ~, *de* ~, quickly, with haste. *2* rush [of buyers, etc.].
**prisión** *f.* seizure, capture, arrest. *2* prison. *3* imprisonment. *4* fig. bond, tie. *5 pl.* chains, fetters.
**prisionero, -ra** *m.-f.* MIL. prisoner. *2* fig. captive.
**prisma** *m.* GEOM., OPT., CRYST. prism.
**prismático, -ca** *adj.* prismatic. *2 m. pl.* field glasses.
**pristino, -na** *adj.* pristine, first, original.
**privación** *f.* privation, want, lack. *2* deprivation, deprival. *3* forbidding, being forbidden.
**privado, -da** *adj.* forbidden. *2* private, privy. *3* stunned, unconscious. *4 m.* favorite [of a king or magnate].
**privanza** *f.* favour, preference [of a king, etc.].
**privar** *tr.* to deprive. *2* to prohibit, forbid. *3* to impede. *4* to stun, render unconscious. *5 intr.* to be in favour; to prevail, be in vogue. *6 ref.* to deprive oneself. *7* to become unconscious.
**privativo, -va** *adj.* privative. *2* peculiar, particular.
**privilegiado, -da** *adj.* privileged. *2* uncommon, extraordinary [talent, gift, etc.].
**privilegiar** *tr.* to privilege.
**privilegio** *m.* privilege, grant, exemption, franchise, patent.
**pro** *m.-f.* profit, benefit, advantage: *el* ~ *y el contra,* the pros and cons; *en* ~ *de,* for, in support of; *for the benefit of. 2 hombre de* ~, man of worth.
**proa** *f.* NAUT. prow, bow, head. *2* AER. nose [of an airplane].
**probabilidad** *f.* probability, likelihood. *2* prospect, chance.
**probabilismo** *m.* THEOL. probabilism.
**probable** *adj.* probable, likely. *2* provable.
**probablemente** *adv.* probably, likely.

**probación** *f.* probation [in a religious body].
**probado, -da** *adj.* proved. *2* tried, tested. *3* approved, demonstrated.
**probador, -ra** *m.-f.* trier, tester. *3* fitter [of dress]. *4 m.* fitting-room.
**probadura** *f.* tasting.
**probar** *tr.* to prove [demonstrate]. *2* to prove, test, try out. *3* to sample. *4* to taste [ascertain the flavour of]. *5* to try on [clothes]. *6* ~ *fortuna*, to take one's chances. *7 intr.* to suit, to agree with. *8* ~ *a*, to attempt, endeavour to. *9* ~ *de*, to taste. ¶ CONJUG. like *contar*.
**probatorio, -ria** *adj.* probative, probatory.
**probeta** *f.* CHEM. test tube.
**probidad** *f.* probity, honesty, integrity.
**problema** *m.* problem.
**problemático, -ca** *adj.* problematic, problematical.
**probo, -ba** *adj.* honest, upright.
**proboscidio, -dia** *adj.* ZOOL. proboscidian.
**procacidad** *f.* impudence.
**procaz** *adj.* impudent.
**procedencia** *f.* origin, source; plane or point of origin or departure. *2* propriety, accordance with the law, rules or practice.
**procedente** *adj.* coming, originating, proceeding [from]. *2* proper, suitable.
1) **proceder** *m.* behaviour, conduct, proceeding.
2) **proceder** *intr.* to proceed [go in certain order]. *2* to proceed [to do something]. *3* to proceed, to behave. *4* to proceed, come, originate. *5* LAW to proceed. *6* to be proper or suitable.
**procedimiento** *m.* proceeding, procedure; process, method, way. *2* LAW procedure.
**proceloso, -sa** *adj.* stormy, tempestuous.
**prócer** *adj.* high, eminent, exalted. *2 m.* grandee, person of eminence.
**proceridad** *f.* eminence, elevation. *2* vigor, growth.
**procesado, -da** *adj.* indicted, accused. *2 m.-f.* LAW. accused, defendant.
**procesal** *adj.* processal.
**procesamiento** *m.* LAW indictment, indicting.
**procesar** *tr.* LAW to indict, accuse.
**procesión** *f.* procession [as a religious ceremony, etc.].
**procesional** *adj.* processional, processionary.
**procesionaria** *f.* ENT. processionary moth.
**proceso** *m.* process [progress; course; development]. *2* lapse of time. *3* LAW proceedings. *4* LAW criminal case or suit.
**proclama** *f.* proclamation, address. *2 pl.* banns.
**proclamación** *f.* proclamation. *2* acclamation.
**proclamar** *tr.* to proclaim [announce publicly]. *2* to proclaim [a sovereign]. *3* to aclaim.
**proclítico, -ca** *adj.* GRAM. proclitic.
**proclive** *adj.* inclined, disposed, prone.
**proclividad** *f.* proclivity.
**procomún, procomunal** *m.* public welfare.
**procónsul** *m.* proconsul.
**procreación** *f.* procreation.
**procreador, -ra** *adj.* procreating. *2 m.-f.* procreator.
**procrear** *tr.* to procreate.
**procura** *f.* PROCURACIÓN. *2* PROCURADURÍA 2. *3* careful management.
**procuración** *f.* care, management. *2* procuration, power of attorney, proxy. *3* employment of an attorney, agent or procurator.
**procurador** *m.* attorney, agent, procurator. *2* LAW

procurator, solicitor, attorney at law. *3* member of the modern Spanish legislative assembly.
**procuraduría** *f.* procuratorship. *2* procurator's, solicitor's or attorney's office.
**procurante** *adj.* solicitant.
**procurar** *tr.* to try to, endeavour, see that. *2* to get, obtain. *3* to manage [another's affairs], to act as an agent, attorney or solicitor.
**prodigalidad** *f.* prodigality. *2* lavishness.
**prodigar** *tr.* to lavish, squander; to give or bestow with profusion. *2 ref.* to show oneself in public too often.
**prodigio** *m.* prodigy, marvel.
**prodigiosidad** *f.* prodigiousness.
**prodigioso, -sa** *adj.* prodigious. *2* fine, exquisite.
**pródigo, -ga** *adj.-n.* prodigal. *2 adj.* extravagant; lavish.
**producción** *f.* production. *2* produce, yield, output.
**producente** *adj.* producing, causing.
**producir** *tr.* to produce [yield, bear, manufacture]. *2* to produce, cause, originate. *3* LAW to produce. *4 ref.* to happen, arise. *5* to express oneself. ¶ CONJUG. as *conducir*.
**productividad** *f.* productivity, productiveness.
**productivo, -va** *adj.* productive. *2* profitable.
**producto** *m.* product, produce. *2* proceeds, outcome, profit. *3* MATH., CHEM. product. *4 pl.* commodities, produce: *productos agrícolas*, farm produce.
**productor, -ra** *adj.* productive. *2 m.-f.* producer.
**produje, produjera**, etc. *irr.* V. PRODUCIR.
**produzco, produzca**, etc. *irr.* V. PRODUCIR.
**proel** *adj.* NAUT. fore. *2 m.* NAUT. bowman.
**proemio** *m.* proem, preface, introduction.
**proeza** *f.* prowess, feat. *2* coll. stunt.
**profanación** *f.* profanation, desecration.
**profanador, -ra** *adj.* profanatory. *2 m.-f.* profaner.
**profanar** *tr.* to profane.
**profanidad** *f.* profanity, profaneness. *2* immodesty.
**profano, -na** *adj.* profane, secular. *2* profane, irreverent. *3* worldly. *4* immodest [in dress, etc.]. *5 adj.-n.* profane, lay [not expert]. *6 m.-f.* worldly person.
**profecía** *f.* prophecy. *2 pl.* BIBL. the Prophets.
**proferir** *tr.* to utter, give, speak. ¶ CONJUG. like *adquirir*.
**profesante** *adj.* professing.
**profesar** *tr.-intr.* to profess. *2 tr.* to have, entertain [friendship, love, hate, etc.].
**profesión** *f.* profession, calling: *de* ~, by profession. *2* profession, professing [of principles, a religion, etc.]. *3* profession [taking vows].
**profesional** *adj.-n.* professional.
**profesionalismo** *m.* professionalism.
**profeso, -sa** *adj.* professed [monk or nun].
**profesor, -ra** *m.-f.* professor, teacher.
**profesorado** *m.* professorate, professorship.
**profeta** *m.* prophet.
**profético, -ca** *adj.* prophetic, prophetical.
**profetisa** *f.* prophetess.
**profetizador, -ra** *adj.* prophesying. *2 m.-f.* prophesier.
**profetizar** *tr.-intr.* to prophesy.
**proficuo, -cua** *adj.* profitable, advantageous.
**profiláctico, -ca** *adj.* prophylactic.
**profilaxis** *f.* prophylaxis.
**prófugo, -ga** *adj.-n.* fugitive [from justice]. *2* one who absents himself to evade military service.

**profundidad** *f.* profundity, profoundness, depth. *2* GEOM. depth. *3* deep [of space, etc.].

**profundizar** *tr.* to deepen [make deeper]. *2 tr.-intr.* to go deep into, get to the bottom of, fathom, penetrate.

**profundo, -da** *adj.* profound, deep. *2* profound, low [bow, obeisance]. *3 m.* profundity, the deep. *4* poet. deep, sea, hell.

**profusión** *f.* profusion, abundance.

**profuso, -sa** *adj.* profuse, abundant.

**progenie** *f.* descent, lineage, parentage.

**progenitor** *m.* progenitor, ancestor.

**progenitura** *f.* PROGENIE. *2* primogeniture.

**prognatismo** *m.* prognathism.

**prognosis** *f.* prognosis, forecasting.

**programa** *m.* program, programme. *2* THEAT. play-bill.

**programación** *f.* programming.

**progresar** *intr.* to progress, advance, develop.

**progresión** *f.* progression, advance. *2* MATH. progression.

**progresista** *adj.-n.* POL. progressist.

**progresivo, -va** *adj.* progressive.

**progreso** *m.* progress. *2 pl.* progress: *hacer progresos,* to make progress.

**prohibición** *f.* prohibition, forbidding, interdiction.

**prohibicionismo** *adj.* prohibitionism.

**prohibir** *tr.* to prohibit, forbid: *se prohibe fumar,* no smoking.

**prohibitivo, -va** *adj.* prohibitive, forbidding.

**prohibitorio, -ria** *adj.* prohibitory.

**prohijamiento** *m.* adoption [of a person, etc.].

**prohijar** *tr.* to adopt [a person, another's opinion, etc.].

**prohombre** *m.* master [of an ancient guild]. *2* notable.

**prójima** *f.* coll. despicable or disreputable woman.

**prójimo** *m.* fellow being, fellow creature, neighbour. *2* coll. fellow. *3 el ~,* the other people.

**prole** *f.* progeny, offspring, issue.

**prolegómenos** *m. pl.* prolegomena.

**proletariado** *m.* proletariat, proletariate.

**proletario, -ria** *adj.-n.* proletarian.

**proliferación** *f.* proliferation.

**proliferar** *intr.* to proliferate.

**prolífico, -ca** *adj.* prolific.

**prolijidad** *f.* prolixity. *2* trifling nicety, minuteness.

**prolijo, -ja** *adj.* prolix, tedious. *2* overcareful, triflingly nice, minute.

**prologar** *tr.* to prologize.

**prólogo** *m.* prologue. *2* preface, introduction.

**prolongación** *f.* prolongation, lengthening. *2* prolongation [part prolonged], extension.

**prolongado, -da** *adj.* prolongated, protracted, extended. *2* long, lingering. *3* oblong.

**prolongar** *tr.* to prolong, lengthen. *2* to extend, continue. *3* to protract. *4* GEOM. to produce. *5 ref.* to be prolonged, to extend, continue.

**promediar** *tr.* to divide into two equal parts. *2 intr.* [of a month, year, etc.] to be half over. *3* to mediate.

**promedio** *m.* middle [middle point]. *2* average [medial estimate].

**promesa** *f.* promise. *2* pious offering.

**prometedor, -ra** *adj.* promising. *2 m.-f.* promiser.

**Prometeo** *m. pr. n.* MYTH. Prometheus.

**prometer** *tr.* to promise. *2* to betroth. *3 intr.* to promise well, bid fair. *4 ref.* to promise oneself, to expect. *5* to become betrothed.

**prometido, -da** *adj.* promised. *2* betrothed. *3 m.-f.* fiancé, fiancée, betrothed.

**prometimiento** *m.* promise, promising.

**prominencia** *f.* prominence, elevation, protuberance.

**prominente** *adj.* prominent, projecting.

**promiscuidad** *f.* promiscuity.

**promiscuo, -cua** *adj.* promiscuous. *2* ambiguous.

**promisión** *f.* promise, promising.

**promisorio, -ria** *adj.* promissory.

**promoción** *f.* promotion, furtherance, advancement. *2* CHESS. promotion.

**promontorio** *m.* promontory, headland. *2* height.

**promotor, -ra; promovedor, -ra** *adj.* promotive. *2 m.-f.* promoter, furtherer, starter.

**promover** *tr.* to promote, further, start. *2* to promote, prefer, exalt, raise.

**promulgación** *f.* promulgation, publication.

**promulgar** *tr.* to promulgate, proclaim, publish.

**pronación** *f.* PHYSIOL. pronation.

**pronador** *m.* ANAT. pronator.

**prono, -na** *adj.* prone, inclined, disposed. *2* prone [lying face downwards].

**pronombre** *m.* GRAM. pronoun.

**pronominal** *adj.* GRAM. pronominal.

**pronosticador, -ra** *adj.* prognosticating, prognosticatory. *2 m.-f.* prognosticator.

**pronosticar** *tr.* to prognosticate, foretell.

**pronóstico** *m.* prognostic, prediction. *2* MED. prognosis.

**prontamente** *adv.* promptly, quickly, speedily.

**prontitud** *f.* promptitude, promptness, readiness. *2* dispatch, speed, celerity.

**pronto** *adv.* soon: *lo más ~ posible,* as soon as possible; *tan ~ como,* as soon as. *2* promptly, quickly. *3 m.* impulse, sudden impulse. *4 al ~,* at first. *5 de ~,* suddenly; without thinking. *6 por de ~,* for the present, provisionally.

**pronto, -ta** *adj.* prompt. *2* ready prepared; willing.

**prontuario** *m.* memorandum book. *2* handbook.

**pronunciación** *f.* pronunciation.

**pronunciamiento** *m.* pronunciamiento, military insurrection. *2* LAW item [in a judgment].

**pronunciar** *tr.* to pronounce, utter. *2* to deliver, make [a speech]. *3* LAW to pass [judgement]. *4 ref.* to decide [on]; to pronounce [on, for, against]. *5* to rebel.

**propagación** *f.* propagation.

**propagador, -ra** *m.-f.* propagator.

**propaganda** *f.* propaganda. *2* COM. advertising.

**propagandista** *adj.-n.* propagandist.

**propagar** *tr.* to propagate. *2 ref.* to propagate, be propagated. *3* to spread, be diffused.

**propalador, -ra** *m.-f.* publisher, divulger.

**propalar** *tr.* to publish, divulge, spread.

**proparoxítono, -na** *adj.* GRAM. proparoxytone.

**propasarse** *ref.* to go too far, to take undue liberties.

**propender** *intr.* to tend, incline, be inclined.

**propensión** *f.* propensity, tendency, predisposition.

**propenso, -sa** *adj.* inclined, prone; predisposed.

**propiamente** *adv.* properly. *2 ~ dicho,* proper [strictly so called or considered].

**propiciación** *f.* propitiation.

**propiciar** *tr.* to propitiate.

**propiciatorio, -ria** *adj.* propitiatory.

**propicio, cia** *adj.* propitious.

**propiedad** *f.* ownership, property. *2* property

[thing owned]; landed property, estate. *2* property [quality]. *4* LOG. property. *5* F. ARTS naturalness, likeness. *6* GRAM. propriety. *7* ~ *intelectual*, copyright.
**propietario, -ria** *adj.* owning, proprietary. *2 m.-f.* owner, proprietor, proprietress. *3* landlord, landlady.
**propileo** *m.* ARCH. propyleum.
**propina** *f.* tip, fee, gratuity. *2 de* ~, extra.
**propinar** *tr.* to give [a drink]. *2* to give, prescribe [a medicine]. *3* coll. to give a blow, etc.
**propincuidad** *f.* propinquity.
**propincuo, -cua** *adj.* near, close.
**propio, pia** *adj.* one's own. *2* proper, peculiar, typical. *3* proper, suitable. *4* natural, genuine. *5* same. *6* himself, herself, itself: *el* ~ *general*, the general himself. *7* F. ARTS very like. *8* GRAM., MATH. proper [noun; fraction].
**proponer** *tr.* to propose, propound, move. *2* to propose, nominate. *3 ref.* to purpose, plan, intend, mean.
**proporción** *f.* proportion [symmetry, ratio, commensurateness]: *a* ~, in proportion. *2* opportunity, occasion. *3* MATH. proportion. *4 pl.* proportions, dimensions.
**proporcionado, -da** *adj.* proportioned. *2* proportionate. *3* fit, suitable.
**proporcional** *adj.* proportional.
**proporcionar** *tr.* to proportionate [give due proportions to]. *2* to proportion, proportionate, commensurate, adapt, adjust. *3* to afford, furnish, give, provide, supply. *4 ref.* to get, obtain.
**proposición** *f.* proposition, proposal. *2* LOG., MATH., RHET. proposition. *3* motion, resolution [in a meeting, etc.].
**propósito** *m.* purpose, intention, aim: *a* ~, for the purpose, suitable; opportunely; apropos, by the way; *de* ~, on purpose. *2* subject, matter in hand: *a* ~ *de*, apropos of; *fuera de* ~, irrelevant; out of place.
**propuesta** *f.* proposition, proposal. *2* offer, tender. *3* proposal, nomination.
**propulsar** *tr.* to propel.
**propulsión** *f.* propulsion: ~ *a chorro*, jet propulsion.
**propulsor, -ra** *adj.* propellent, propulsive. *2 m.-f.* propeller, propellent.
**prorrata** *f.* prorate: *a* ~, pro rata, in proportion.
**prorratear** *tr.* to prorate, apportion.
**prorrateo** *m.* apportionment.
**prórroga** *f.* PRORROGACIÓN.
**prorrogable** *adj.* prolongable [for a specified time].
**prorrogación** *f.* prolongation, extension [for a specified time].
**prorrogar** *tr.* to prolong, extend [for a specified time]. *2* to prorogue, postpone.
**prorrumpir** *intr.* to break forth, burst out.
**prosa** *f.* prose. *2* verbiage.
**prosaico, -ca** *adj.* prosaic.
**prosapia** *f.* ancestry, lineage.
**proscenio** *m.* THEAT. proscenium.
**proscribir** *tr.* to proscribe. ¶ P. P.: *proscrito, proscripto.*
**proscripción** *f.* proscription.
**proscripto** or **proscrito, -ta** *adj.* proscribed. *2 m.-f.* exile, outlaw, proscribed person.
**prosecución** *f.*, **proseguimiento** *m.* prosecution, continuation. *2* pursuit, pursuing.
**proseguir** *tr.* to continue, carry on. *2 intr.* to continue, go on. ¶ CONJUG. like *servir.*

**proselitismo** *m.* proselytism.
**prosélito** *m.* proselyte.
**prosénquima** *f.* BIOL. prosenchyma.
**prosimio, -mia** *adj.* ZOOL. prosimian.
**prosista** *m.-f.* prosaist [prose author].
**prosodia** *f.* orthoëpy.
**prosopopeya** *f.* RHET. prosopopœia. *2* coll. pomposity, solemnity.
**prospecto** *m.* prospectus.
**prosperar** *tr.* to prosper. *2 intr.* to prosper, thrive.
**prosperidad** *f.* prosperity.
**próspero, -ra** *adj.* prosperous.
**próstata** *f.* ANAT. prostate.
**prosternarse** *ref.* to prostrate oneself.
**prostíbulo** *m.* brothel.
**prostitución** *f.* prostitution.
**prostituir** *tr.* to prostitute. *2 ref.* to prostitute oneself. *3* to become prostitued. ¶ CONJUG. like *huir.*
**prostituta** *f.* prostitute, harlot.
**protagonista** *m.* protagonist. *2* hero, heroine [in poem, novel, etc.].
**prótasis,** *pl.* **-sis** *f.* DRAMA, GRAM. protasis.
**protección** *f.* protection.
**proteccionismo** *m.* protectionism.
**protector, -ra** *adj.* protecting, protective. *2 m.* protector. *3 f.* protectress.
**protectorado** *m.* protectorate.
**protectorio, -ria** *adj.* protective.
**proteger** *tr.* to protect.
**protegido, -da** *adj.* protected. *2 m.* protégé.
**proteico, -ca** *adj.* protean. *2* BIOCHEM. proteic.
**proteína** *f.* BIOCHEM. proteid, protein.
**protervamente** *adv.* perversely, wickedly.
**protervia, protervidad** *f.* perversity, wickedness.
**protervo, -va** *adj.* perverse, stubbornly wicked.
**prótesis** *f.* GRAM., SURG. prosthesis, prothesis.
**protesta, protestación** *f.* protest, protestation, remonstrance. *2* protestation [of friendship, impartiality, etc.]. *3* LAW protest.
**protestación** *f.* PROTESTA. *2* ~ *de la fe*, profession of faith.
**protestante** *adj.* protesting, protestant. *2 adj.-n.* Protestant.
**protestantismo** *m.* Protestantism.
**protestar** *tr.* to protest, affirm solemnly. *2* COM. to protest [a bill of exchange]. *3* intr. ~ *contra*, to protest, protest against.
**protesto** *m.* COM. protest [of a bill of exchange].
**protético, -ca** *adj.* GRAM. prosthetic.
**protocolario, -ria** *adj.* protocolary, ceremonial.
**protocolizar** *tr.* to file with the original copies kept by a notary.
**protocolo** *m.* protocol. *2* diplomatic or Court ceremonial rules. *3* file of original copies kept by a notary.
**protomártir** *m.* protomartyr.
**protón** *m.* PHYS. & CHEM. proton.
**protonotario** *m.* prothonotary.
**protoplasma** *m.* BIOL. protoplasm.
**protórax,** *pl.* **-rax** *m.* ENT. prothorax.
**prototipo** *m.* prototype.
**protóxido** *m.* CHEM. protoxide.
**protozoario, -ria; protozoo, -a** *adj.-m.* ZOOL. protozoan.
**protráctil** *adj.* protractile.
**protuberancia** *f.* protuberance.
**provecto, -ta** *adj.* advanced in years, learning or experience; mature.
**provecho** *m.* advantage, benefit, good. *2* profit, gain. *3* utility: *de* ~, useful. *4* progress, advancement.

**provechoso, -sa** *adj.* profitable. *2* beneficial, good. *3* advantageous, useful.

**proveedor, -ra** *m.-f.* supplier, furnisher, purveyor.

**proveer** *tr.* to supply, furnish, provide, purvey; to stock with provisions. *2* to appoint a person to [a post or office]. *3* LAW to decide. *4 intr.* ~ *a*, to provide for, to take the necessary steps for. *5 ref.* to provide oneself. ¶ P. P.: *provisto.*

**proveimiento** *m.* providing, supplying.

**proveniente** *adj.* coming, originating, arising.

**provenir** *intr.* to come, originate, arise. ¶ CONJUG. like *venir.*

**provento** *m.* product, revenue.

**Provenza** *f. pr. n.* GEOG. Provence.

**provenzal** *adj.-n.* Provençal.

**proverbial** *adj.* proverbial.

**proverbio** *m.* proverb, adage, saying.

**próvidamente** *adj.* providently, carefully.

**providencia** *f.* providence, forethought. *2* provision, step, measure. *3* providence [care of God]; (cap.) Providence [God].

**providencial** *adj.* providential.

**providenciar** *tr.* LAW to decide, decree. *2* to take steps or measures.

**providente** *adj.* wise, prudent. *2* provident, careful.

**próvido, -da** *adj.* provident. *2* benevolent, propitious.

**provincia** *f.* province [administrative division].

**provincial** *adj.* provincial. *2 m.* ECCL. provincial.

**provinciano, -na** *adj.-n.* provincial [inhabitating a province].

**provisión** *f.* provision, providing. *2* supply, stock. *3* step, measure. *4* COM. ~ *de fondos*, funds, money [to pay a bill of exchange, check, etc.]. *5 pl.* provisions, supply.

**provisional** *adj.* provisional, interim.

**provisor** *m.* purveyor, provider. *2* ECCL. vicar general.

**provisorio, -ria** *adj.* provisional, temporary.

**provisto, -ta** *adj.* provided, stocked, supplied.

**provocación** *f.* provocation [instigation, challenging, stirring up].

**provocador, -ra** *adj.* provoking. *2 m.-f.* provoker.

**provocar** *tr.* to provoke, incite, dare, challenge. *2* to provoke, cause, bring about, stir up.

**provocativo, -va** *adj.* provocative, inciting.

**proxeneta** *m.-f.* go-between, procurer, procuress.

**proximal** *adj.* ANAT., ZOOL. proximal.

**próximamente** *adv.* soon, before long. *2* approximately.

**proximidad** *f.* proximity. *2* vicinity.

**próximo, -ma** *adj.* near, neighbouring, proximate, close. *2* next: *el mes* ~, next month. *3* ~ *pasado*, last [month, year, etc.].

**proyección** *f.* projection [projecting; projected image]. *2* GEOM. projection.

**proyectante** *adj.* projecting, designing.

**proyectar** *tr.* to project, throw, cast. *2* to project [light, shadow, an image, etc.]: to show [a moving picture]. *3* GEOM. to project. *4* to project, plan, intend. *5* to design [draw the plan of]. *6 ref.* [of a shadow, etc.] to fall.

**proyectil** *m.* projectile, missile.

**proyectista** *m.-f.* designer, maker of projects. *2* projector [person].

**proyecto** *m.* project, plan, design. *2* ~ *de ley*, bill [proposed law].

**proyector** *m.* projector [apparatus]; searchlight; spotlight.

**prudencia** *f.* prudence.

**prudencial** *adj.* prudential.

**prudente** *adj.* prudent. *2* cautious.

**prueba** *f.* proof, demonstration, evidence. *2* sign, mark, token. *3* proof, test, trial, probation: *poner a* ~, to put to the test, to try. *4* tasting, sampling; sample. *5* fitting, trying on [of an article of dress]. *6* ordeal, trial. *7* temptation. *8* SPORT. match, competition. *9* MATH., ENGRAV., PRINT., PHOT. proof. *10 a* ~ *de*, proof, proof against.

**pruebo, pruebe,** etc. *irr.* V. PROBAR.

**prurigo** *m.* MED. prurigo.

**prurito** *m.* MED. itching, pruritus. *2* fig. eagerness, desire.

**Prusia** *f. pr. n.* GEOG. Prussia.

**prusiano, -na** *adj.-n.* Prussian.

**prúsico, -ca** *adj.* CHEM. prusic.

**pseudo** *adj.* SEUDO.

**psi** *s.* psi [Greek letter].

**psicastenia** *f.* MED. psychasthenia.

**psicoanálisis** *m.* MED. psychoanalysis.

**psicoanalista** *m.-f.* psychoanalyst.

**psicología** *f.* psychology.

**psicológico, -ca** *adj.* psychological.

**psicólogo** *m.* psychologist.

**psicometría** *f.* psychometrics, psychometry.

**psicópata** *m.* psycopath.

**psicopatía** *f.* MED. psycopathy.

**psicosis** *f.* MED. psychosis.

**psicoterapia** *f.* MED. psychotherapy.

**psique, psiquis** *f.* psyche, the human soul. *2* (cap.) MYTH. Psyche.

**psiquiatra** *m.* psychiater.

**psiquiatría** *f.* psychiatry.

**psíquico, -ca** *adj.* psychic, psychical.

**pteridofita** *f.* BOT. pteridophyte.

**¡pu!** *interj.* ugh!

**púa** *f.* prick, sharp point, barb, thorn. *2* prong, tine. *3* spine, quill [of porcupine, etc.]. *4* tooth [of comb]. *5* HORT. graft, scion. *6* MUS. plectrum. *7* fig. crafty person.

**púber, -ra; púbero** *adj.* pubescent [having reached puberty]. *2 m.-f.* pubescent person.

**pubertad** *f.* puberty.

**pubescencia** *f.* pubescence.

**pubescente** *adj.* pubescent.

**pubis** *m.* ANAT. pubes. *2* ANAT., ZOOL. pubis.

**publicación** *f.* publication, publishing. *2* publication [paper, book, music, etc., published].

**publicano** *m.* Rom. HIST. publican.

**publicar** *tr.* to publish. *2* to issue [a decree, etc.]. *3* to cause to appear [in a newspaper, etc.].

**publicidad** *f.* publicity.

**publicista** *m.* publicist.

**público, -ca** *adj.* public. *2* generally known. *3 m.* public. *4* audience [assembly of spectators, etc.].

**puchera** *f.* dish of meat and vegetables.

**pucheritos** *m. pl.* PUCHERO 4.

**puchero** *m.* cooking pot. *2* PUCHERA. *3* fig. food, sustenance. *4 pl.* pouting [of a person about to cry]: *hacer pucheros*, to pout.

**puches** *m. pl.* gruel, pap, porridge.

**pude, pudiera,** etc. *irr.* V. PODER.

**pudelar** *tr.* METAL. to puddle.

**pudendo, -da** *adj.* shameful, obscene. *2 partes pudendas*, private parts, genitals.

**pudibundez** *f.* overmodesty; prudishness.

**pudibundo, -da** *adj.* PUDOROSO.

**pudicicia** *f.* modesty, chastity, pudicity.

**púdico, -ca** *adj.* modest, chaste.

**pudiente** *adj.* rich, well off.

**pudín** *m*. Ang. pudding.
**pudor** *m*. modesty, chastity, pudency.
**pudoroso, -sa** *adj*. modest, bashful, chaste.
**pudridero** *m*. rotting place. 2 temporary vault [for corpses].
**pudrigorio** *m*. PODRIGORIO.
**pudrimiento** *m*. putrefaction, rotting.
**pudrir** *tr*. to putrefy, rot, corrupt. 2 *ref*. to putrefy, rot [undergo putrefaction]. 3 to languish [in jail, etc.]. 4 fig. to fret, worry. 5 *intr*. to be dead and buried.
**pueblerino, -na** *adj*. belonging to a village; country, countrified.
**pueblo** *m*. town, village; settlement. 2 people [of a place or country]; common people. 3 people, nation.
**puedo, pueda,** etc. *irr*. V. PODER.
**puente** *m.-f*. bridge [across stream, ravine, etc.]: ~ *aéreo*, air bridge, airlift; ~ *levadizo*, drawbridge. 2 MUS., NAUT., DENT. bridge. 3 MUS. tailpiece. 4 NAUT. gun-carrying deck. 5 AUTO. ~ *de engrase*, grease lift.
**puerca** *f*. ZOOL. sow. 2 fig. sow, slut.
**puerco, -ca** *adj*. dirty, filthy. 2 slovenly, sluttish. 3 piggish, hoggish. 4 base, mean. 5 *m*. ZOOL. hog, pig. 6 fig. hog, pig [man]. 7 mean, base mean. 8 ZOOL. ~ *de mar*, sea hog. 9 ZOOL. ~ *espín*, porcupine.
**puericia** *f*. childhood.
**puericultura** *f*. puericulture.
**pueril** *adj*. puerile, childish.
**puerilidad** *f*. puerility.
**puerperal** *adj*. puerperal.
**puerro** *m*. BOT. leek.
**puerta** *f*. door, doorway; gate, gateway; entrance, access: ~ *de corredera*, silding door; ~ *excusada*, or *falsa*, back door, side door; ~ *giratoria*, revolving door; *coger* or *tomar la* ~, to leave, go away; *dar a uno con la* ~ *en las narices*, to slam the door on one's face; *estar a la* ~, or *a las puertas*, to be imminent; *a* ~ *cerrada*, in secret; with closed doors; *de* ~ *en* ~, from door to door.
**puertaventana** *f*. window shutter.
**puerto** *m*. NAUT. port, harbour, haven: ~ *franco*, free port. 2 fig. haven, refuge. 3 mountain pass. 4 AER. ~ *aéreo*, airport.
**Puerto Rico** *m. pr. n*. GEOG. Porto Rico, Puerto Rico.
**puertorriqueño, -ña** *adj.-n*. Porto Rican.
**pues** *conj*. because, for, since: ~ *que*, since, inasmuch as. 2 then [accordingly; in summary or recapitulation]: *así* ~, so then; ~ *bien*, now then, well then; all right then. 3 well [as an expletive or intensive]. 4 *adv*. yes, so, certainly, indeed. 5 (interrogatively) *¿*~*?, ¿y* ~*?*, why?, how is that?; so?; and what then?
**puesta** *f*. ASTR. set, setting: ~ *de sol*, sunset. 2 stake [at cards]. 3 ~ *a punto*, completion, perfection. 4 ~ *de largo*, coming out, social debut. 5 ~ *en marcha*, starting.
**puesto, -ta** *irreg. p. p.* of PONER. 2 *adj*. placed, put, set. 3 dressed, attired. 4 *conj. puesto que*, since, inasmuch as. 5 *m*. place [assigned or occupied]. 6 stall, stand, booth. 7 place, dignity, office, post, employment, job. 8 MIL. post, station: ~ *de socorro*, first-aid station. 9 blind [for hunters].
**¡puf!** *interj*. ugh!
**púgil** *m*. pugilist; prize, fighter, boxer.
**pugilato** *m*. pugilism, boxing.
**pugna** *f*. fight, struggle, strife, conflict; opposition, clashing.

**pugnacidad** *f*. pugnacity.
**pugnar** *intr*. to fight, struggle, strive. 2 ~ *con*, to conflict with, to be opposed to.
**pugnaz** *adj*. pugnacious.
**puja** *f*. push, effort. 2 outbidding, bid [at an auction].
**pujador, -ra** *m.-f*. bidder [at an auction].
**pujame, pujamen** *m*. NAUT. foot [of a sail].
**pujante** *adj*. puissant, powerful, strong, vigorous.
**pujanza** *f*. puissance, might, strength, vigour.
**pujar** *tr*. to push [a project, etc.]. 2 to raise [one's bid]. 3 *intr*. to falter; to grope for words. 4 coll. to pout, snivel.
**pujo** *m*. MED. tenesmus. 2 fig. irresistible impulse [to cry, laugh, etc.]; eagerness, strong desire.
**pulcritud** *f*. neatness, tidiness, cleanliness. 2 honesty [of conduct].
**pulcro, -cra** *adj*. neat, tidy, cleanly. 2 honest [conduct, person].
**Pulchinela** *m*. Punchinello.
**pulga** *f*. ENT. flea: *tener malas pulgas*, to be ill-tempered; *tener pulgas*, fig. to be restless, too lively. 2 ZOOL. ~ *de mar*, beach flea.
**pulgada** *f*. inch.
**pulgar** *m*. ANAT. thumb.
**pulgarada** *f*. pinch [of salt, etc.]. 2 blow given pressing the thumb. 3 PULGADA.
**pulgón** *m*. ENT. aphid, plant louse.
**pulguera** *f*. BOT. fleawort.
**pulguillas,** *pl*. -**llas** *m*. coll. restless, fretful fellow.
**pulicán** *m*. dentist's forceps.
**pulidez** *f*. beauty. 2 cleanliness, neatness.
**pulido, -da** *adj*. polished. 2 beautiful, pretty. 3 clean, neat; exquisitely made or wrought.
**pulidor, -ra** *m.-f*. polisher, furbisher, burnisher.
**pulimentar** *tr*. to polish, burnish.
**pulimento** *m*. polish, gloss.
**pulir** *tr*. to polish, burnish, furbish. 2 to polish [refine, finish]. 3 to adorn, beautify. 4 *ref*. to beautify oneself. 5 to become refined.
**pulmón** *m*. ANAT. lung. 2 ~ *de acero*, iron lung.
**pulmonado, -da** *adj*. ZOOL. pulmonate.
**pulmonar** *adj*. pulmonary, lung.
**pulmonía** *f*. MED. pneumonia.
**pulpa** *f*. pulp.
**pulpejo** *m*. soft fleshy part [of finger, ear, etc.].
**pulpería** *f*. (Am.) grocery, general store.
**púlpito** *m*. pulpit.
**pulpo** *m*. ZOOL. octopus, cuttlefish.
**pulposo, -sa** *adj*. pulpous, pulpy.
**pulque** *m*. a Mexican fermented drink.
**pulquérrimo, -ma** *adj*. superl. of PULCRO.
**pulsación** *f*. pulsation, beat. 2 MUS. touch, striking, fingering.
**pulsada** *f*. pulsation, pulse, beat [of the arteries].
**pulsador** *m*. push button. 2 WEAV. feeler.
**pulsar** *tr*. to push [a button]. 2 to feel the pulse of. 3 fig. to sound, examine [an affair]. 4 MUS. to strike, finger, play [a key, a string, an instrument]. 5 *intr*. [of the heart, an artery, etc.] to pulsate, beat, throb.
**pulsátil** *adj*. pulsatile.
**pulsatila** *f*. BOT. pasqueflower.
**pulsera** *f*. JEWEL. bracelet. 2 wristlet. 3 watch strap. 4 SURG. wrist bandage. 5 side lock of hair.
**pulso** *m*. PHYSIOL. pulse: *tomar el* ~ *a*, to feel the pulse of; to sound, examine [an affair]. 2 part of the wrist where pulse is felt. 3 steadiness of the hand: *a* ~, freehand [drawing]; with the strength of the hand; fig. by a persistent effort. 4 care, tact.

**pultáceo, -a** *adj.* pultaceous.
**pulular** *intr.* to pullulate. 2 to swarm, teem.
**pulverización** *f.* pulverization.
**pulverizador, -ra** *adj.* pulverizing. 2 *m.* atomizer, spray, sprayer.
**pulverizar** *tr.* to pulverize. 2 to atomize [a liquid]. 3 *ref.* to become pulverized; to spray.
**pulverulento, -ta** *adj.* pulverulent, powdery, dusty.
**pulla** *f.* quip, cutting remark, innuendo. 2 repartee, witty saying.
**¡pum!** *interj.* bang!
**puma** *m.* ZOOL. puma, cougar.
**pumita** *f.* pumice stone.
**puna** *f.* (Am.) arid table-land in the Andes.
**punción** *f.* MED. puncture.
**pundonor** *m.* dignity, honour, self-respect.
**pundonoroso, -sa** *adj.* dignified, self-respectful, nice about matters of honour.
**pungente** *adj.* pungent, prickling, stinging.
**pungir** *tr.* to prick, pierce. 2 fig. to sting.
**punible** *adj.* punishable.
**púnico, -ca** *adj.* Punic.
**punitivo, -va** *adj.* punitive.
**punta** *f.* point [sharp or tapering end]: *sacar ~ a,* to sharpen. 2 head [of an arrow or spear]. *3* tip, nib, end: *de ~,* on end. 4 apex, top. 5 butt, stub, stump [of cigar or cigarette]. 6 horn [of bull]. 7 tine [of antlers]. 8 GEOG. point, headland. 9 taint of sourness [in wine]. 10 trace, streak, tinge, somewhat. 11 point [of a joke]. *12 ~ de París,* wire nail. *13 estar de ~,* to be on bad terms. *14 de ~ en blanco,* all dressed up; directly. *16 pl.* scalloped lace.
**puntada** *f.* SEW. stitch. 2 hint. 3 (Am.) stitch [in the side].
**puntal** *m.* prop, stanchion. 2 fig. stay, support. *3* NAUT. depth of hold.
**puntapié** *m.* kick [with the tip of the shoe]: *echar a puntapiés,* coll. to kick out.
**punteado, -da** *adj.* dotted, stippled. 2 *m.* dotting, stippling. 3 dotted surface. 4 plucking the guitar.
**puntear** *tr.* to dot, tó stipple. 2 to sew, stitch. 3 to pluck [the guitar]. 4 *intr.* NAUT. to tack.
**puntel** *m.* pontil, punty.
**puntera** *f.* cap [of a shoe]. 2 new toe on stockings.
**puntería** *f.* pointing, aim, aiming [of a weapon, a missile]; marksmanship.
**puntero, -ra** *adj.* sharpshooting. 2 *m.* pointer [rod for pointing]. 4 stonecutter's pointed chisel.
**puntiagudo, -da** *adj.* sharp, sharp-pointed.
**puntilla** *f.* narrow lace edging. 2 BULLF. short dagger used in finishing a bull. *3 de puntillas,* softly, on one's tiptoes; on tiptoe.
**puntillazo** *m.* PUNTAPIÉ.
**puntillero** *m.* bullfighter wo finishes the bull with a short dagger.
**puntilio** *m.* punctillo. 2 MUS. dot.
**puntilloso, -sa** *adj.* punctilious.
**puntito** *m.* dim. small point, dot.
**punto** *m.* GEOM. point. 2 dot: *poner los puntos sobre las íes,* fig. to dot the i's and cross the t's. 3 GRAM. period; stop, mark: *~ final,* full stop; *~ y coma,* semicolon; *dos puntos,* colon; *puntos suspensivos,* suspension points. 4 nib [of a pen]. 5 front sight [of a firearm]. 6 SEW., SURG. stitch. 7 stitch, loop [in knitting or netting]; point [in embroidery or lacemaking]. 8 knitwork: *géneros de ~,* hosiery. 9 method of stitching, knitting, etc. 10 break [in stockings or a knited fabric]. *11* punch

hole [in a strap]. *12* PRINT. point [unit]. *13* point, place, spot: *~ de apoyo,* point of support; fulcrum; *~ de partida,* starting point; *~ de vista,* point of view. *14* cabstand. *15* point, mark [unit of award or estimation]. *16* SPORT. point. *17* punter [in gambling]. *18* minute part. *19* moment, instant: *al ~,* immediately. 20 nick of time, right moment. *21* subject, matter, point, detail: *~ por ~,* in detail. 22 state, condition attained. *23* perfect condition attained by a thing cooked, baked, etc. 24 PHYS. point, stage. 25 degree, extent: *hasta cierto ~,* to a certain extent, in a way. 26 point of honour, punctilio. 27 aim, purpose. 28 GEOG., ASTR. *~ cardinal,* cardinal point. *29 poner en su ~,* to perfect [a thing] at its true value. *30 a ~,* opportunely; ready. *31 a ~ de* [with an inf.], on the point of, about to. *32 a ~ fijo,* with certainty. *33 en buen ~,* luckily. *34 en mal ~,* unluckily. *35 en ~,* exactly, sharp.
**puntoso, -sa** *adj.* full of points. 2 punctilious; self-respectful.
**puntuación** *f.* GRAM. punctuation. 2 number of marks awarded or gained in an examination, etc.
**puntual** *adj.* punctual. 2 certain, sure. 3 suitable.
**puntualidad** *f.* punctuality; punctual habits.
**puntualizar** *tr.* to specify, detail, tell in detail. 2 to finish, perfect.
**puntuar** *tr.* GRAM. to punctuate, point. 2 to award a number of marks to [in examination].
**puntura** *f.* prick, puncture, sting. 2 PRINT. register point.
**punzada** *f.* prick, puncture, sting. 2 stitch, pang, shooting pain. 3 fig. sting, pang [of remorse, etc.].
**punzante** *adj.* prickling, piercing, sharp. 2 shooting [pain]. 3 fig. biting, caustic.
**punzar** *tr.* to prick, puncture, sting. 2 to give a shooting pain to. 3 [of remorse, etc.] to sting.
**punzó** *m.* flaming red [colour].
**punzón** *m.* punch, puncheon; awl, pick, bodkin; counterdie. 2 graver, burin.
**puñada** *f.* PUÑETAZO.
**puñado** *m.* handful.
**puñal** *m.* poniard, dagger.
**puñalada** *f.* stab [with a dagger]. 2 fig. blow [cause of sudden pain or grief].
**puñetazo** *m.* cuff, punch, blow with the fist.
**puño** *m.* fist [clenched hand]: *meter en un ~,* coll. to intimidate, subdue; *como un ~,* [of things normally small] big: [of things normally large] small, tiny. 2 hand, handwriting: *de su ~ y letra,* in his own hand. 3 handful. 4 fig. grasp. 5 cuff, wristband. 6 hilt [of a sword, dagger, etc.]. 7 grip [of a sabre]. 8 handle [of an umbrella]. 9 head [of a cane]. *10 pl.* strength, courage.
**pupa** *f.* MED. eruption in the lips. 2 scab over a pimple. 3 child's word to express pain.
**pupila** *f.* ANAT. pupil. 2 pupil, ward [girl under a guardian]. 3 woman boarder.
**pupilaje** *m.* pupilage, wardship [state of being under a guardian]. 2 boarding house.
**pupilo** *m.* pupil, ward [boy under a guardian]. 2 boarder.
**pupitre** *m.* writing desk; school desk.
**puramente** *adv.* purely.
**puré** *m.* COOK. purée. *2 ~ de patatas,* mashed potatoes.
**pureza** *f.* purity. 2 virginity.
**purga** *f.* MED. purge, purgative, physic. 2 MACH. drains [of a boiler, etc.].

**purgación** f. purgation. 2 expiation.
**purgador, -ra** adj. purgative. 2 expiation. 3 m.-f. purger. 4 expiator.
**purgamiento** m. purgation, purge, purging.
**purgante** adj. purging. 2 expiating. 3 adj.-m. MED. purgative.
**purgar** tr. MED. to purge, physic. 2 to purge, purify, cleanse. 3 to expiate. 4 LAW., MACH. to purge. 5 ref. to take a purge. 6 to purge or free oneself.
**purgativo, -va** adj. purgative, purging.
**purgatorio** m. purgatory.
**puridad** f. purity. 2 secret, secrecy.
**purificación** f. purification, purifying.
**purificador, -ra** adj. purifying. 2 m.-f. purifier. 3 m. ECCL. purificator.
**purificar** tr. to purify. 2 ref. to purify, to become purified.
**Purísima (la)** f. pr. n. the Virgin Mary.
**purísimo, -ma** adj. superl. of PURO.
**purismo** m. purism.
**purista** m. purist.
**puritanismo** m. Puritanism.
**puritano, -na** adj. puritan, puritanic, puritanical. 2 Puritan. 3 m.-f. puritan. 4 Puritan.
**puro, -ra** adj. pure: de pura raza, thoroughbred. 2

solid [gold]. 3 a ~, by dint of. 4 de ~ [followed by an adj.], through being so much. 5 m. cigar.
**púrpura** f. ZOOL. purple, purple shell, murex. 2 purple [die, colour, robe]. 3 purple [cardinalate]. 4 MED. purpura.
**purpurado** m. cardinal.
**purpurar** tr. to purple. 2 to dress in purple.
**purpurear** intr. to purple, have a purple tinge.
**purpúreo, -a** adj. purple.
**purpurina** f. purpurin. 2 bronze powder.
**purpurino, -na** adj. PURPÚREO.
**purulento, -ta** adj. purulent.
**pus** m. MED. pus.
**pusilánime** adj. pusillanimous.
**pústula** f. MED. pustule.
**pustuloso, -sa** adj. pustulous, pustular.
**puta** f. harlot, strumpet, whore.
**putativo, -va** adj. putative.
**putrefacción** f. putrefaction.
**putrefacto, -ta** adj. putrid, rotten.
**putrescible** adj. putrescible.
**putridez** f. putridity.
**pútrido, -da** adj. putrid, rotten.
**puya** f. goad iron or head.
**puyazo** m. jab or prick with a goad.
**puzol** m., **puzolana** f. PETROG. pozzolana.

# Q

**Q, q** *f.* Q, q, twentieth letter of the Spanish alphabet.

**que** *rel. pron.* that, which, who, whom: *a* ~, to which, to whom; *a lo* ~, to what; *de* ~, of which; about which, whereof; from which, wherefrom; *en* ~, in which, wherein; upon which, whereupon. *2* Preceded by the definite article: *el* ~, *la* ~, he who or that, she who or that, who, whom, the one who or that; *los* ~, *las* ~, those who or that; *lo* ~, what, which, that which. *3* when: *el día* ~ *llegaste*, the day when you arrived. *4 conj.* that [introducing clauses of statement, hypothesis, wish, result, reason or cause, and frequently omitted in the translation]. *5* to [in the construction called accusative-infinitive]: *dígale* ~ *venga*, tell him to come. *6* than [in comparative sentences]. *7* because, for, since. *8* so that. *9* and [used as an expletive]. *10* In elliptical sentences expressing command or desire, it is not translated or is rendered by let, *may*, *I wish*, etc.: ~ *entre*, let him come in. *11* When placed between the participle and the auxiliary in an inverted form of compound tense, it is rendered by *when, after, as soon as*: *escrito que hubo la carta*, when he had written the letter. *12 a menos* ~, unless. *13 con tal* ~, provided, that. *14* ~ *no*, without, but. *15 por ...* ~, however, no mater how. *16* ~ ... ~, whether... or.

**qué** *interrog. & exclamatory adj. & pron.* which, what, how, what a. *2* how much. *3 ¿a* ~*?*, *¿para* ~*?*, what for? *4 no hay de* ~, don't mention it, you are welcome [in answer to thanks]. *5 ¿por* ~*?*, why? *6 ¡*~*!*, what! *7 ¿*~*?*, how goes it? *8 ¡*~ *va!*, nonsense!, go on! [expressing disbelief]. *9 sin* ~ *ni para* ~, without cause or motive. *10 un no sé* ~, a certain something. *11 ¡y* ~*!*, what then!

**quebrada** *f.* gorge, ravine, *gulch.

**quebradero** *m.* ~ *de cabeza*, worry, concern.

**quebradizo, -za** *adj.* brittle, fragile. *2* fig. frail, delicate.

**quebrado, -da** *adj.* broken [thing]. *2* bankrupt. *3* MED. ruptured. *4* broken, rough [ground]. *5* ~ *de color*, sickly, pale. *6 m.* bankrupt. *7* MED. ruptured person. *8* MATH. fraction.

**quebradura** *f.* break, crack. *2* MED. hernia, rupture.

**quebraja** *f.* crack [in wood, iron, etc.].

**quebrantador, -ra** *adj.* breaking. *2* crushing. *3 m.-f.* breaker. *4* crusher.

**quebrantahuesos,** *pl.* **-sos** *m.* ORN. osprey. *2* ORN. lammergeier. *3* coll. bore [tiresome person].

**quebrantamiento** *m.* breaking. *2* crushing. *3* fatigue, exhaustion; breaking down [of health].

**quebrantante** *adj.* breaking, crushing.

**quebrantar** *tr.* to break [separate into parts]; to break, crush, bruise. *2* to break, weaken, diminish. *3* to break [resistance, one's will; prison, a promise, etc.]: to infringe, violate. *4* to exhaust, fatigue; to impair [the health]. *5* ~ *el corazón*, to move to pity. *6 ref.* to break [be broken, weakened, etc.].

**quebranto** *m.* breaking, crushing. *2* loss. *3* lassitude. *4* grief, pain. *5* pity, compassion.

**quebrar** *tr.* to break [separate into parts; to interrupt]. *2* to break, violate. *3* to bend [the body or something slender]. *4* to impair or dull [the colour or complexion] of a person. *5* to temper, moderate. *6 intr.* to weaken, give way. *7* COM. to fail; go bankrupt. *8 ref.* to break, be broken. *9* [of the body or a slender thing] to bend. *10* [of colour or complexion] to become dull or pale. *11* MED. to be ruptured. ¶ CONJUG. like *acertar*.

**queche** *f.* NAUT. ketch; smack.

**quechua** *adj.-n.* QUICHUA.

**queda** *f.* curfew. *2* curfew bell.

**quedada** *f.* stay, remaining [in a place].

**quedamente** *adv.* softly, gently, in a low voice.

**quedar** *intr.-ref.* to remain, stay behind, stay, stop, keep, be left [in or at a place]. *2* to remain, be left [in a condition or state]. *3* to be, become: ~ *atónito*, to be astonished. *4 intr.* to remain [continue to exist; to be left over]; to have left: *nos quedan diez pesetas*, we have ten pesetas left. *5* to agree: ~ *en*, to agree on or to. *6* ~ *a deber*, to remain owing. *7* ~ *bien* or *mal*, to acquit oneself well or badly; to keep or break an appointment, promise, etc.; to look well or poorly in a portrait. *8* ~ *por* or *sin* [hacer, etc.], to remain to be [done, etc.]. *9 por mi no quedará*, I'll do my best. *10 ref.* to take, choose [when buying]. *11 quedarse con*, to take, keep, retain.

**quedito** *adv.* very gently, very softly.

1) **quedo** *adv.* softly, gently. *2* in a low voice.

1) **quedo, -da** *adj.* quiet, still. *2* easy, gentle. *3* soft, low [voice]: *con voz queda*, in a low voice.

**quehacer** *m.* work, task, occupation, *chore.
**queja** *f.* lament, moan. *2* complaint, grievance.
**quejarse** *ref.* to lament, moan. *2* to complain.
**quejicoso, -sa** *adj.* querulous, complaining.
**quejido** *m.* lament, moan.
**quejigo** *m.* BOT. gall oak. *2* BOT. young oak.
**quejoso, -sa** *adj.* complaining, having a grievance.
**quejumbre** *f.* frequent complaining.
**quejumbroso, -sa** *adj.* querulous, habitually complaining. *2* querulous, whining.
**quelícero** *m.* ZOOL. chelicera.
**quelonio, -nia** *adj.-m.* ZOOL. chelonian.
**quema** *f.* burning. *2* fire, conflagration.
**quemada** *f.* burnt patch in a forest or thicket.
**quemadero, -ra** *adj.* for burning, to be burned. *2 m.* place where convicts were burned. *3* place for burning dead animals or damaged food.
**quemado** *m.* burning or burned thing: *oler a ~,* to smell of fire. *2* QUEMADA.
**quemador, -ra** *adj.* burning. *2 m.-f.* burner [person]. *3* incendiary. *4 m.* burner [in appatus].
**quemadura** *f.* burn, scald [sore or injury]. *2* scorch or nip [in plants]. *3* smut [plant disease].
**quemante** *adj.* burning [very hot].
**quemar** *tr.* to burn [by fire or acid]. *2* to burn, scald, scorch. *3* to scorch, nip [plants]. *4* to burn [the mouth with pepper, etc.]. *5* fig. to anger, irritate. *6 intr.* to burn, be burning [be too hot]. *7 ref.* to burn [be consumed by fire]; to get burned. *8* to be very hot [have the sensation of heat]. *9* [of plants] to be scorched, nipped. *10* fig. to become angry. *11* fig. to be warm [near the object sought for].
**quemazón** *f.* burning. *2* excessive heat. *3* itching.
**quepis, *pl.* -pis** *m.* MIL. kepi.
**quepo, quepa,** etc. *irr.* V. CABER.
**queratina** *f.* BIOCHEM. keratin.
**querella** *f.* complaint, lament. *2* quarrel, dispute. *3* LAW complaint.
**querellante** *m.-f.* LAW complainant.
**querellarse** *ref.* to lament, bewail. *2* LAW to complain, bring suit.
**querelloso, -sa** *adj.* complaining. *2* plaintive.
**querencia** *f.* affection, liking. *2* inclination of man or animals to return to a haunt or place of frequent resort; this place. *3* natural tendency.
*1)* **querer** *m.* love, affection.
*2)* **querer** *tr.* to love [hold dear; be in love with]. *2* to will, want, wish, desire, like. *3 ~ bien,* to love. *4 ~ decir,* to mean. *5 no ~ [hacer, dar,* etc.], to refuse to [do, give, etc.]. *6 no ~ nada con,* not to wish to have anything to do with. *7 como quiera que,* inasmuch, since, whereas. *8 como quiera que sea,* anyhow, anyway, in any case. *9 cuando quiera,* at any time, whenever. *10 donde quiera,* anywhere, wherever. *11 sin ~,* unintentionally, unwillingly. *12* impers. *parece que quiere llover,* it looks like rain.
¶ CONJUG. INDIC. Pres.: *quiero, quieres, quiere; queremos, queréis, quieren.* | Pret.: *quise, quisiste, quiso,* etc. | Fut.: *querré, querrás, querrá,* etc. | SUBJ. Pres.: *quiera, quieras, quiera, queramos, queráis, quieran.* | Imperf.: *quisiera, quisieras,* etc., or *quisiese, quisieses,* etc. | Fut.: *quisiere, quisieres,* etc. | IMPER.: *quiere, quiera;* queramos, quered, *quieran.*
**querido, -da** *adj.* dear, beloved. *2 m.-f.* paramour. *3 f.* mistress, paramour.
**quermes** *m.* kermes.
**querocha** *f.* CRESA.
**querub, querube, querubín** *m.* cherub.

**querré, querrás,** etc. *in.* V. QUERER.
**quesadilla** *f.* cheesecake. *2* a sweet pastry.
**quesear** *intr.* to make cheese.
**quesera** *f.* cheese maker or seller [woman]. *2* dairy [where cheese is made]. *3* cheese board. *4* cheese dish.
**quesería** *f.* dairy, cheese factory or shop.
**quesero, -ra** *adj.* caseous, cheesy. *2 m.-f.* cheese maker; cheesemonger.
**queso** *m.* cheese.
**quetzal** *m.* ORN. quetzal.
**quevedos** *m. pl.* pince-nez having circular glasses.
**¡quiá!** *interj.* come now!, oh, no!
**quicial** *m.* hinge-pole. *2* QUICIO.
**quicialera** *f.* hinge-pole.
**quicio** *m.* door jamb. *2* pivot hole [for a hinge pole]: *sacar de ~,* to strain [things]; to exasperate [a person]; *fuera de ~,* out of order.
**quid** *m.* gist, reason, essence [of a thing].
**quídam** *m.* coll. fellow, person. *2* coll. nobody.
**quiebra** *f.* break, crack, fissure. *2* ravine. *3* loss, damage. *4* COM. failure, bankruptcy.
**quiebro** *m.* bending of the body at the waist [as in dodging or dancing]. *2* MUS. trill.
**quiebro, quiebre,** etc. *irr.* V. QUEBRAR.
**quien** *(interrog. & exclam.* **quién**), *pl.* **quienes** *pron.* who, whom, he who, whoever, whomever.
**quienquiera** *pl.* **quienesquiera** *pron.* whoever, whomever, whosoever, whomsoever.
**quiero, quiera,** etc. *in.* V. QUERER.
**quietación** *f.* quieting, appeasing.
**quietamente** *adv.* quietly, calmly.
**quietismo** *m.* quietism.
**quieto, -ta** *adj.* quiet, still, motionless. *2* quiet, undisturbed, calm, peaceful. *3* orderly, virtuous.
**quietud** *f.* quietness, quietude, stillness; quiet, rest, repose, tranquillity.
**quijada** *f.* jaw, jawbone. *2* MACH. jaw.
**quijera** *f.* cheekpiece [of a bridle]. *2* cheek [of a crossbow].
**quijones,** *pl.* **-nes** *m.* BOT. an aromatic herb.
**quijotada** *f.* quixotism, quixotry [quixotic action].
**quijote** *m.* ARM. cuisse. *2* upper part of the haunch [of horses]. *3* Quixote, quixotic person.
**quijotería** *f.* quixotism, quixotry.
**quijotesco, -ca** *adj.* quixotic.
**quilatar** *tr.* AQUILATAR.
**quilate** *m.* carat, karat.
**quilífero, -ra** *adj.* ANAT. chyliferous.
**quilificación** *f.* PHYSIOL. chylification.
**quilo** *m.* KILO. *2* PHYSIOL. chyle: *sudar el ~,* coll. to work hard.
**quilogramo, quilolitro,** etc. = KILOGRAMO, KILOLITRO, etc.
**quilla** *f.* NAUT., BOT., ORN. keel: *dar de ~,* [of a ship] to keel.
**quimera** *f.* chimera, chimaera [monster: fanciful conception, impracticable idea]. *2* quarrel, row.
**quimérico, -ca** *adj.* chimerical.
**quimerista** *adj.-n.* visionary. *2 adj.* quarrelsome. *3 m.-f.* quarrelsome person.
**química** *f.* chemistry.
**químico, -ca** *adj.* chemical. *2 m.-f.* chemist [person skilled in chemistry].
**quimificación** *f.* PHYSIOL. chymification.
**quimo** *m.* PHYSIOL. chyme.
**quimono** *m.* kimono.
**quina** *f.* cinchona, Peruvian bark.
**quinado, -da** *adj.* prepared with QUINA [wine].
**quincalla** *f.* small metal wares.
**quincallería** *f.* small metal ware factory or shop.

**quincallero, -ra** *m.-f.* maker or seller of small metal wares.
**quince** *adj.-n.* fifteen. *2* fifteenth.
**quincena** *f.* fortnight. *2* semi-monthly pay.
**quinceno, -na** *adj.* fifteenth.
**quincuagenario, -ria** *adj.* having fifty units. *2 adj.-n.* quinquagenarian.
**quincuagésimo, -ma** *adj.-m.* fiftieth. *3 f.* ECCL. Quincuagesima.
**quindécimo, -ma** *adj.-m.* fifteenth.
**quingentésimo, -ma** *adj.-m.* five-hundredth.
**quingombó** *m.* BOT. okra.
**quinientos, -tas** *adj.-m.* five hundred.
**quinina** *f.* CHEM. quinine.
**quino** *m.* BOT. cinchona [tree].
**quínolas** *f.* four of a kind [at cards]. *2 pl.* a card game.
**quinona** *f.* CHEM. quinone.
**quinqué** *m.* student lamp, Argand lamp.
**quinquefolio** *m.* CINCOENRAMA.
**quinquenal** *adj.* quinquennial.
**quinquenio** *m.* quinquennium.
**quinta** *f.* country place, villa. *2* MIL. draft. *3* quint [at cards]. *4* MUS. fifth, quint. *5* FENC. quinte.
**quintaesencia** *f.* quintessence.
**quintal** *m.* quintal. *2 ~ métrico*, metric quintal.
**quintana** *f.* countryplace, villa.
**quintante** *m.* quintant [instrument similar to a sextant].
**quintañón, -na** *adj.-n.* centenarian.
**quintar** *tr.* to draw one out of five. *2* MIL. to draft [soldiers].
**quintería** *f.* farm, grange.
**quintero** *m.* farmer. *2* farm hand.
**quinteto** *m.* MUS. quintet.
**quintilla** *f.* stanza of five octosyllables with two rhymes. *2* any five-lina stanza with two rhymes.
**Quintín** *m. pr. n.* Quentin.
**quinto, -ta** *adj.* fifth: *quinta columna*, fifth column. *2 m.* one fifth. *3* constript, recruit.
**quíntuplo, -pla** *adj.* quintuple, fivefold.
**quinzavo, -va** *adj.-m.* fifteenth.
**quiñón** *m.* share of profit. *2* lot of land.

**quiosco** *m.* kiosk, pavilion. *2* newstand. *3* bandstand.
**quiquiriquí** *m.* cock-a-doodle-do.
**quiragra** *f.* MED. chiragra.
**quirie** *m.* KIRIE.
**quiromancia** *f.* chiromancy, palmistry.
**quiromántico, -ca** *adj.* chiromantic, chiromantical. *2 m.-f.* chiromancer, chiromancist, palmist.
**quiróptero, -ra** *adj.* ZOOL. cheiropterous.
**quirúrgico, -ca** *adj.* surgical.
**quise, quisiera,** etc. *irr.* V. QUERER.
**quisicosa** *f.* coll. enigma, riddle.
**quisque (cada)** coll. everyone.
**quisquilla** *f.* trifle. *2* ZOOL. marine shrimp.
**quisquilloso, -sa** *adj.* overnice, squeamish. *2* touchy.
**quiste** *m.* MED., ZOOL. cyst.
**quisto, -ta** *adj.* liked: *bien ~*, well-liked; *mal ~*, disliked.
**quita** *f.* LAW remission of debt.
**quitaipón** *m.* QUITAPÓN.
**quitamanchas** *m.* clothes cleaner, spot remover.
**quitamotas** *m.-f.* flatterer, obsequious person.
**quitanieves** *f.* snowplough, snowplow.
**quitanza** *f.* quittance, discharge [of debt].
**quitapón** *m.* headstall ornament for horses.
**quitar** *tr.* to remove, take off, take out, rub off, pick off: *de quita y pon*, detachable, removable. *2* to eliminate. *3* to take, take off, deduct, subtract. *4* to steal, to rob of, deprive of. *5* to clear [the table]. *6* to hinder, be an obstacle to. *7* to prevent, forbid; to make a person give up [a habit]. *8* to intercept [the light]. *9* to abolish, repeal. *10* to free from [pain, worry, an obligation, etc.]. *11 ref.* to move away; *¡quítate de aquí!*, get out of here! *12* to take off [one's hat, clothes, etc.]. *13 quitarse de encima*, to get rid of [something]. *14 quitarse de*, to give up [a habit].
**quitasol** *m.* parasol, sunshade.
**quite** *m.* FENC. parry, dodge. *2* BULLF. attracting the bull from a man in danger.
**quitina** *f.* BIOCHEM. chitin.
**quitinoso, -sa** *adj.* chitinous.
**quito, -ta** *adj.* free, exempt.
**quizá, quizás** *adv.* perhaps, maybe.
**quorum** *m.* quorum.

# R

**R, r** *f.* R, r, twenty-first letter of the Spanish alphabet.

**rabada** *f.* hinder quarter, rump.

**rabadán** *m.* head shepherd.

**rabadilla** *f.* coccygeal region. *2* ORN. rump, uropygium.

**rabanal** *m.* patch or field of radishes.

**rabanero, -ra** *adj.* coll. short [gown, skirt]. *2* forward, bold [manners, language]. *3 m.-f.* seller of radishes. *4 f.* fig. fishwife, coarse woman.

**rábano** *m.* BOT. radish: *tomar el ~ por las hojas*, coll. to be entirely mistaken.

**rabazuz** *m.* licorice extract.

**rabear** *intr.* to wag the tail.

**rabel** *m.* MUS. rebeck. *2* coll. breech, backside.

**rabeo** *m.* wagging the tail.

**rabera** *f.* tail end. *2* handle [of a crossbow].

**rabi,** *pl.* **-bíes** *m.* rabbi, rabbin.

**rabia** *f.* MED. hydrophobia. *2* rage, fury. *3 tener ~ a uno*, to hate; *tomar ~ a*, to take a dislike to.

**rabiar** *intr.* MED. to have rabies. *2* to rage, be furious. *3* to suffer racking pain. *4* fig. *~ por*, to wish eagerly. *5* coll. *estar a ~ con uno*, to be very angry with someone.

**rabiatar** *tr.* to tie by the tail.

**rabiazorras** *m.* coll. east wind.

**rabicorto, -ta** *adj.* short-tailed.

**rabieta** *f.* coll. fit of temper, tantrum.

**rabihorcado** *m.* ORN. frigate bird.

**rabilargo, -ga** *adj.* long-tailed.

**rabillo** *m.* little tail. *2* stalk, stem [of flower, leaf, etc.], peduncle. *3* corner [of the eye].

**rabínico, -ca** *adj.* rabbinic, rabbinical.

**rabino** *m.* rabbi, rabbin.

**rabión** *m.* rapids [in a river].

**rabioso, -sa** *adj.* rabid, mad, affected with rabies. *2* rabid, furious, violent. *3* enraged. *4* raging.

**rabisalsera** *adj.* forward, pert [woman].

**rabiza** *f.* tip of a fishing rod.

**rabo** *m.* tail [of an animal]: *con el ~ entre piernas*, fig. discomfited, humiliated. *2* fig. tail [hind part, taillike part]. *3* stalk, stem. *4* corner [of the eye]. *5* BOT. *~ de zorra*, foxtail.

**rabón, -na** *adj.* short-tailed, bobtailed.

**rabopelado** *m.* ZARIGÜEYA.

**rabosear** *tr.* to crumple; to fray.

**rabotada** *f.* insolent reply.

**rabudo, -da** *adj.* long-tailed, thick-tailed.

**rábula** *m.* charlatan lawyer, pettifogger.

**racel** *m.* NAUT. dead rise.

**racial** *adj.* racial, race.

**racima** *f.* grapes remaining on vines after vintage.

**racimo** *m.* BOT. raceme. *2* bunch, cluster.

**racimoso, -sa** *adj.* racemose. *2* having or giving forth many bunches or clusters [of fruit].

**raciocinar** *intr.* to ratiocinate, reason.

**raciocinio** *m.* reason [faculty of reasoning]. *2* ratiocination, reasoning.

**ración** *f.* ration. *2* portion [of food]. *3* allowance for food.

**racionabilidad** *f.* judgement, discernment.

**racional** *adj.* rational. *2* reasonable. *3 m.* rational being. *4* rational [breast plate].

**racionalidad** *f.* rationality, reasonableness.

**racionalismo** *m.* rationalism.

**racionalista** *adj.* rationalistic. *2 adj.-n.* rationalist.

**racionalización** *f.* COM., IND. rationalization.

**racionalizar** *tr.* COM., IND. to rationalize.

**racionamiento** *m.* rationing.

**racionar** *tr.* to ration.

**racha** *f.* gust [of wind]. *2* streak of [good or bad] luck. *3* RAJA.

**rada** *f.* NAUT. bay, roads, roadsted.

**radar** *m.* ELECT. radar.

**radiación** *f.* radiation. *2* broadcasting.

**radiactivo, -va** *adj.* PHYS. radioactive.

**radiado, -da** *adj.* irradiated. *2* radiated [arranged like rays]. *3* broadcast. *4* BOT., ZOOL. radiate. *5 m.* ZOOL. radiate.

**radiador** *m.* radiator.

**radial** *adj.* radial.

**radian** *m.* GEOM. radian.

**radiante** *adj.* PHYS. radiant. *2* radiant, beaming.

**radiar** *tr.-intr.* to radiate, to irradiate. *2* to radio, broadcast. *3 intr.* to beam, shine.

**radicación** *f.* radication.

**radical** *adj.* radical. *2 m.-f.* POL. radical. *3 m.* MATH., PHILOL., CHEM. radical.

**radicalismo** *m.* radicalism.

**radicar** *intr.-ref.* to take root. *2 intr.* to be, lie. *3 ref.* to settle, establish oneself.

**radícula** *f.* BOT. radicle.

**radio** *m.* GEOM., ANAT. radius. *2* radius, spoke [of wheel]. *3* radius, scope. *4* CHEM. radium. *5* coll. radio, radiogram. *6 f.* coll. radio, broadcasting. *7* coll. radio, wireless set.

**radiodifusión** f. RADIO. broadcast, broadcasting.
**radiodifusor, -ra** adj. RADIO. broadcasting.
**radioescucha** m.-f. radio listener.
**radiofaro** m. AER. radio beacon.
**radiofonía** f. radiophony.
**radiofónico, -ca** adj. radiophonic.
**radiofrecuencia** f. radio frequency.
**radiografía** f. radiography, X-ray photography. 2 radiograph, X-ray photograph.
**radiograma** m. radiogram, radio message.
**radiología** f. MED. radiology.
**radiólogo** m. radiologist.
**radiorreceptor** m. radio receiver, wireless set.
**radioscopia** f. radioscopy.
**radioso, -sa** adj. radiant, beaming.
**radiosonda** f. radiosonde.
**radiotelefonía** f. radiotelephony.
**radiotelegrafía** f. radiotelegraphy.
**radiotelegrafiar** tr. to radiotelegraph, to wireless.
**radiotelegrafista** m.-f. wireless operator.
**radioterapia** f. MED. radiotherapy. 2 MED. radium-therapy.
**radioyente** m.-f. RADIOESCUCHA.
**raedera** f. scraper [instrument].
**raedor, -ra** m.-f. scraper. 2 m. strickle.
**raedura** f. scraping. 2 pl. scrapings.
**raer** tr. to scrape [a surface]. 2 to scrape off. 3 to wear out [clothes]. 4 fig. to extirpate, wipe out. ¶ CONJUG. like caer.
**Rafael** m. pr. n. Raphael.
**ráfaga** f. gust [of wind]. 2 burst [of machinegun fire]. 3 small cloud. 4 flash [of light].
**rafe** m. ANAT., BOT. raphe. 2 ARCH. eaves.
**rafia** f. BOT. raffia.
**raglán** m. raglan.
**rahez** adj. vile, low, despicable.
**raicilla** f. dim. rootlet. 2 BOT. radicle.
**raído, -da** adj. threadbare [clothes]. 3 barefaced, shameless.
**raigambre** f. intertwined roots. 2 fig. deep rooted-ness.
**raigo, raiga,** etc. irr. V. RAER.
**raigón** m. augm. large root. 2 root of a tooth.
**rail** m. RLY. rail.
**raíz** f. root [of a plant, etc.]; stem [of a word]: echar raíces, to take root; a ~, close to the root of; on the occasion of; de ~, entirely, at the root. 2 MATH. root.
**raja** f. split, rent, crack. 2 part of a split piece of wood. 3 slice [of melon, etc.].
**rajá** m. raja, rajah.
**rajadura** f. splitting, cracking. 2 split, crack.
**rajar** tr. to split, rend. 2 to slice [a melon, etc.]. 3 intr. coll. to brag. 4 ref. to split, crack [be split or cracked]. 5 coll. to back down.
**rajatabla (a)** adv. at any cost, regardless of anything else.
**ralea** f. kind, nature, sort. 2 [scornful and applied to persons] race, breed.
**ralear** intr. [of cloth, hair, etc.] to become thin or sparse. 2 [of vines] to yield thin bunches.
**raleza** f. thinness, sparseness [of cloth, hair, etc.].
**ralo, -la** adj. thin, sparse [cloth, hair, teeth, etc.].
**rallador** m. kitchen grater.
**ralladura** f. mark left by a grater. 2 COOK. gratings.
**rallar** tr. to grate [with a kitchen grater].
**rallo** m. kitchen grater. 2 rose, rosehead [of water-ring pot].
**rama** f. branch, bough. 2 fig. branch [of family, learning, etc.]: andarse por las ramas, to beat

about the bush. 3 PRINT. chase. 4 en ~, raw, un-manufactured.
**Ramadán** m. Ramadan.
**ramaje** m. branchage, branches.
**ramal** m. branch [of railway, mountain range, etc.]. 2 strand [of rope]. 3 flight [of stairs]. 4 halter [for leading a horse].
**ramalazo** m. lash with a rope. 2 sudden pain. 3 fig. blow, sudden sorrow or grief.
**rambla** f. sandy or dry ravine. 2 tenter [for cloths].
**rameado, -da** adj. flowered [design].
**ramera** adj. harlot, strumpet.
**ramificación** f. ramification; branching off.
**ramificarse** ref. to ramify; to branch off.
**ramillete** m. bouquet, nosegay. 2 BOT. a clustery cyme. 3 centerpiece, epergne. 4 ornamental dish of sweets. 5 collection of choice things.
**ramilletero, -ra** m.-f. maker and seller of bou-quets. 2 f. flower girl. 3 m. flower vase.
**ramio** m. BOT. ramie.
**ramita** f. dim. sprig, twig.
**ramito** m. dim. small bunch. 2 sprig, small bough.
**ramo** m. bough, branch. 2 bunch, cluster. 3 string [of onions]. 4 branch [of science, etc.]; line [of business]. 5 touch, slight attack [of a disease].
**ramojo** m. brushwood [wood of small branches].
**Ramón** m. pr. n. Raymond.
**ramón** m. browse.
**ramonear** intr. to browse. 2 to trim trees.
**ramoneo** m. browsing; browsing season. 2 trim-ming of trees.
**ramoso, -sa** m. ramose, ramous.
**rampa** f. cramp [contraction of the muscles]. 2 ramp, inclined plane, sloping way.
**rampante** adj. HER. rampant.
**ramplón, -na** adj. heavy, coarse [shoe]. 2 vulgar, uncouth. 3 m. calk [of horseshoe].
**rana** f. ZOOL. frog. 2 coll. no ser ~, to be expert, clever. 3 pl. MED., VET. ranula.
**rancajo** m. splinter in the flesh.
**rancidez** f. rancidity, rankness, staleness.
**rancio, -cia** adj. rank, rancid, stale. 2 aged [wine]. 3 old [lineage, etc.]. 4 antiquated [ideas]. 5 old-fashioned [person]. 6 m. rancidness. 7 rancid bacon.
**rancioso, -sa** adj. rancid, stale.
**ranchear** intr. to form a settlement with huts.
**ranchería** f. settlement made of huts or shanties. 2 MIL. kitchen [in barracks].
**ranchero** m. kitchen attendant [of a regiment]. 2 (Am.) rancher, ranchman.
**rancho** m. cooked food for soldiers, prisoners, etc. 2 hut, rustic cottage. 3 settlement made of huts. 4 coterie. 5 (Am.) cattle ranch.
**randa** f. lace, needle-point lace.
**rangífero** m. RENO.
**rango** m. class, order, sort. 2 rank [social stan-ding]; high station.
**rangua** f. MACH. pivot bearing.
**ranilla** f. frog [of hoof].
**ránula** f. MED., VET. ranula.
**ranunculáceo, -a** adj. BOT. ranunculaceous.
**ranúnculo** m. BOT. buttercup, crowfoot.
**ranura** f. groove, rabbet: a ~ y lengüeta, CARP. ton-gue-and groove. 2 slot.
**raño** m. oyster rake. 2 ICHTH. scorpion fish.
**rapa** f. blossom of the olive tree.
**rapacería** f. childish action.
**rapacidad** f. rapacity.
**rapador** m. coll. barber.
**rapadura** f. shaving. 2 close haircut.

**rapapolvo** *m.* coll. scolding, dressing down.
**rapar** *tr.* to shave. *2* to crop [the hair].
1) **rapaz** *adj.* rapacious. *2* ORN. of prey, raptorial.
2) **rapaz, -za** *m.* boy, young boy. *2 f.* girl, young girl.
**rapazuelo, -la** *m. dim.* little boy. *2 f. dim.* little girl.
**rape** *m.* coll. hurried shave or hair-cut. *2 al* ~, cropped, cut close or short.
**rapé** *m.* snuff, rappee.
**rapidez** *f.* rapidity, quickness, swiftness.
**rápido, -da** *adj.* rapid, fast, quick, swift. *2 m.* rapids [in a river].
**rapiña** *f.* rapine, robbery. *2 ave de* ~, bird of prey.
**rapiñar** *tr.* coll. to steal, plunder.
**rapista** *m.* coll. barber.
**raposa** *f.* ZOOL. fox. *2* ZOOL. female fox, vixen. *3* fig. fox [crafty person].
**raposear** *intr.* to fox, act craftily.
**raposera** *f.* fox hole, fox den.
**raposería** *f.* foxiness, craftiness; crafty ways.
**raposo** *m.* ZOOL. [male] fox. *2* fig. fox, crafty person.
**rapsoda** *m.* rhapsode, rhapsodist.
**rapsodia** *f.* LIT., MUS. rhapsody.
**raptar** *tr.* to abduct, ravish [a woman], to kidnap.
**rapto** *m.* abduction, ravishment [of a woman], kidnapping. *2* rapture, ecstasy.
**raptor** *m.* abductor, ravisher, kidnapper.
**Raquel** *f. pr. n.* Rachel.
**raqueta** *f.* SPORT. racket. *2* SPORT. battledore. *3* badminton battledore and shuttlecock [game]. *4* racket [snowshoe]. *5* rake [used by croupiers].
**raquetero** *m.* racket maker or seller.
**raquis**, *pl.* **-quis** *s.* ANAT., BOT. rachis.
**raquítico, -ca** *adj.* MED. rachitic, rickety. *2* stunted. *3* feeble, poor, short, meagre, stinted.
**raquitismo** *m.* MED. rachitism.
**raramente** *adv.* rarely, seldom. *2* oddly, strangely.
**rarefacción** *f.* rarefaction.
**rarefacer** *tr.-ref.* ENRARECER 1. ¶ CONJUG. like *hacer*.
**rareza** *f.* rarity, rareness. *2* oddity, strangeness. *3* curiosity, freak. *4* eccentricity, peculiarity.
**raridad** *f.* rarity, rareness.
**rarificar** *tr.-intr.* ENRARECER.
**raro, -ra** *adj.* rare [gas]. *2* rare [uncommon, exceptional]. *3* scarce: *raras veces*, seldom. *4* odd, queer, strange.
**ras** *m.* evenness, flushness. *2 a* ~ *de*, close to, even with, flush with.
**rasa** *f.* thin spot [in a fabric]. *2* small tableland.
**rasante** *adj.* grazing [touching lightly in passing]. *2* ARTILL. horizontal [fire]. *3 f.* grade line.
**rasar** *tr.* to strike [level with a strickle]. *2* to graze, skim [touch lightly in passing].
**rasarse** *ref.* [of the sky] to clear up.
**rascacielos** *m.* skyscraper [very tall building].
**rascadera** *f.* scraper [implement]. *2* currycomb.
**rascador** *m.* scraper, scratcher [implement]. *2* ornamental hairpin.
**rascadura** *f.* scraping, scratching.
**rascar** *tr.* to scrape, to scratch.
**rascatripas**, *pl.* **-pas** *m.-f.* coll. scraper [fiddler].
**rascazón** *f.* itch, itching.
**rascón, -na** *adj.* tart, sharp [to the taste]. *2 m.* ORN. water hen, gallinule.
**rasero** *m.* strickle: *medir por el mismo* ~, *o por un* ~, fig. to make no difference.
**rasete** *m.* satinet.
**rasgado, -da** *adj.* wide [mouth]. *2* almond [eyes].
**rasgadura** *f.* tear, tearing, rent, rip.

**rasgar** *tr.* to tear, rend, rip [clothes, paper, etc.]. *2* RASGUEAR. *3 ref.* to tear, become torn.
**rasgo** *m.* flourish, stroke [of pen]. *2* flash [of wit], bright saying. *3* deed, feat, act, action: ~ *heroico*, heroic feat. *4* trait. *5 pl.* features [of the face]. *6* fig. *a grandes rasgos*, broadly, in outline.
**rasgón** *m.* tear, rent, rip.
**rasgueado** *m.* RASGUEO.
**rasguear** *tr.* to play flourishes on [the guitar]. *2 intr.* to flourish, make flourishes with the pen.
**rasgueo** *m.* playing flourishes on the guitar. *2* making flourishes with the pen.
**rasguñar** *tr.* to scratch [with the nails, etc.]. *2* DRAW. to sketch, outline.
**rasguño** *m.* scratch. *2* DRAW. sketch, outline.
1) **raso** *m.* satin.
2) **raso, -sa** *adj.* flat, level, open, clear, unobstructed: *campo* ~, open country; *al* ~, in the open air. *2* clear, cloudless [sky]. *3* skimming the ground. *4 soldado* ~, common soldier, private.
**raspa** *f.* stem of a bunch of grapes. *2* awn, beard [of wheat, barley, etc.]. *3* corncob. *4* spine, backbone [of a fish].
**raspado** *m.* SURG. scraping.
**raspador** *m.* eraser [instrument].
**raspadura** *f.* erasure, scraping out. *2 pl.* scrapings.
**raspajo** *m.* stem of a bunch of grapes.
**raspante** *adj.* rough, harsh to the taste [wine].
**raspar** *tr.* to rasp, scrape, scrape out, erase. *2* [of wine, etc.] to be harsh to [the palate].
**raspear** *intr.* [of a pen] to scratch.
**raspilla** *f.* BOT. myosotis, forget-me-not.
**rasqueta** *f.* NAUT. scraper. *2* (Am.) currycomb.
**rastillo** *m.* RASTRILLO.
**rastra** *f.* trace, track, trail. *2* AGR. rake. *3* AGR. harrow. *4* drag [rough sledge]. *5* anything trailing. *6* outcome, consequence. *7* NAUT. drag. *8 a la* ~, *a* ~, *a rastras*, dragging; unwillingly. *9* string [of onions, etc.].
**rastrear** *tr.* to trace, track, trail, scent out. *2* to drag, search [the sea-bottom, etc.]. *3 intr.* AGR. to drag. *4* to skim the ground, to fly very low.
**rastreo** *m.* dragging, searching.
**rastrero, -ra** *adj.* creeping, dragging, trailing. *2* that tracks [dog]. *3* flying low. *4* cringing, grovelling, abject, low, base.
**rastrillador, -ra** *m.-f.* hatcheler. *2* AGR. raker.
**rastrillaje** *m.* hatcheling. *2* AGR. raking.
**rastrillar** *tr.* to hackle, hatchel [flax or hemp]. *2* AGR. to rake.
**rastrillo** *m.* hackle, hatchel. *2* FORT. portcullis. *3* iron gate. *4* battery [of a flintlock]. *5* AGR. rake. *6* ward [of a key or lock].
**rastro** *m.* AGR. rake. *2* trace, track, trail, scent. *3* trace, vestige, sign. *4* slaughterhouse.
**rastrojera** *f.* stubble field.
**rastrojo** *s.* AGR. stubble, haulm.
**rasura** *f.* shaving. *2* scraping. *3 pl.* argol.
**rasurar** *tr.* to shave [the hair].
**rata** *f.* ZOOL. rat: ~ *de alcantarilla*, brown rat. *2* coll. sneak thief.
**ratafía** *f.* ratafia, ratafee [liquor].
**rataplán** *m.* rub-a-dub [sound of a drum].
**rata por cantidad** *adv.* pro rata.
**ratear** *tr.* to distribute proportionally. *2* to filch, pilfer. *3 intr.* to crawl, creep.
**rateramente** *adv.* meanly, vilely.
**ratería** *f.* petty theft.
**ratero, -ra** *m.-f.* pickpocket, pilferer, sneak thief.
**ratificación** *f.* ratification, confirmation.

**ratificar** tr. to ratify. 2 ref. *ratificarse en*, to confirm [one's previous statement].

**ratito** m. dim. short time, little while.

**rato** m. time, short time, while: *un buen* ~, a great while; a pleasant time; *un mal* ~, an unpleasant time; *un* ~, a while; *al poco* ~, presently, soon; *a ratos*, from time to time, occasionally; *a ratos perdidos*, in spare time; *largo* ~, a long time, a great while.

**ratón** m. ZOOL. mouse; ~ *almizclero*, muskrat; ~ *de campo*, field mouse.

**ratona** f. ZOOL. female mouse.

**ratonar** tr. [of mice] to eat or gnaw.

**ratoncito** m. dim. little mouse.

**ratonera** f. mousetrap. 2 mousehole. 3 nest of mice.

**ratonero, -ra; ratonesco, -ca; ratonil** adj. [pertaining to] mice, mousy.

**rauco, -ca** adj. raucous, hoarse, husky.

**raudal** m. stream, torrent, flow.

**raudo, -da** adj. rapid, swift, impetuous.

**raya** f. ICHTH. ray, skate. 2 line [long narrow mark]. 3 stroke [of pen or pencil], dash [in printing, writing and telegraphy]. 4 score, scratch [on a surface]. 5 stripe, streak: *a rayas*, striped. 6 crease [in trousers]. 7 parting [in the hair]. 8 rifle groove. 9 boundary, frontier. 10 *pasar de* ~, or *de la* ~, to go too far; *tener a* ~, to keep within bounds.

**rayadillo** m. striped cotton duck.

**rayado, -da** adj. stripped, streaky. 2 ruled [paper]. 3 rifled [gun barrel]. 4 m. ruling [of paper]. 5 stripes.

**rayano, -na** adj. bordering, verging.

**rayar** tr. to draw lines on, to rule. 2 to scratch [a surface]. 3 to stripe. 4 to cross out, cancel. 5 to underline. 6 intr. to excel. 7 ~ *con*, to border on; fig. to equal, match. 8 ~ *en*, to border upon, verge on. 9 ~ *el alba, el día*, to dawn.

**rayo** m. ray, beam [of light, etc.]: ~ *de sol*, sunbeam; *rayos catódicos*, cathode rays. 2 spoke [of a wheel]. 3 lighting, stroke of lightning, bolt, thunderbolt: *como el* ~, fig. like lightning. 4 sudden misfortune. 5 fig. lively person.

**rayón** m. rayon, artificial silk.

**rayuela** f. dim. of RAYA. 2 game of pitching pennies.

**raza** f. BIOL., ETHN. race: *razas humanas*, human races. 2 race, kindred, lineage, breed, strain: *de pura* ~, thoroughbred. 3 crack, fissure. 4 ray of light [coming through a crack, fissure, etc.]. 5 WEAV. light-woven stripe [in fabrics].

**rázago** m. burlap, sackcloth.

**razón** f. reason [in practically every sense]: ~ *de estado*, reason of State; *uso de* ~, discretion, discernment; *entrar en* ~, to become reasonable; *meter en* ~, to bring to reason; *perder la* ~, to go out of one's wits. 2 words, speech: *con razones corteses*, with courteous words. 3 right, justice, correctness; being right; *dar la* ~, to agree with, to approve; *tener* ~, to be right; *no tener* ~, to be wrong, to be mistaken; *con* ~ *o sin ella*, rightly or wrongly. 4 reasonableness [of prices, terms, etc.]; *ponerse en* ~, to be or become reasonable. 5 regard, respect: *en* ~ *a, en* ~ *de*, with regard to. 6 information, account, explanation: *dar* ~ *de*, to inform about, to give an account of. 7 rate [proportion]: *a* ~ *de*, at the rate of. 8 MATH. ratio: ~ *aritmética*, difference; ~ *geométrica*, geometrical ratio. 9 COM. ~ *social*, firm, firm name.

**razonable** adj. reasonable, sensible. 2 reasonable, moderate, fair.

**razonado, -da** adj. reasoned [exposition, petition].

**razonador, -ra** adj. reasoning. 2 m.-f. reasoner.

**razonamiento** m. reasoning, argumentation.

**razonar** intr. to reason, ratiocinate. 2 tr. to reason [explain, justify, etc., by adducing reasons].

**razzia** f. razzia, raid [plundering expedition].

**re** m. MUS. re, D.

**reabrir** tr. to reopen.

**reabsorber** tr. to reabsorb.

**reabsorción** f. reabsorption.

**reacción** f. reaction. 2 RADIO. regeneration.

**reaccionar** intr. to react.

**reaccionario, -ria** adj.-n. reactionary.

**reacio, -cia** adj. reluctant, unwilling, disobedient.

**reactancia** f. ELECT. reactance.

**reactivar** tr. MED. to reactivate.

**reactivo, -va** adj. reactive. 2 m. CHEM. reagent.

**reactor** m. ELECT., PHYS. reactor.

**readaptar** tr. to readapt.

**readmitir** tr. to readmit.

**reajustar** m. to readjust.

**real** adj. real, actual. 2 MATH., OPT., real. 3 royal, regal; kingly, queenly. 4 grand, magnificent, fine, handsome: ~ *moza*, handsome woman. 5 m. real [Spanish coin]. 6 MIL. army's camp: *levantar, el* ~ or *los reales*, to break camp; *asentar los reales*, to encamp. 7 ~ *de una feria*, place for a fair.

**realce** m. embossment, relief, raised work. 2 enhancement, emphasis. 3 lustre, splendor. 4 PAINT. high light.

**realengo, -ga** adj. royal [burgh, etc.]. 2 m. royal patrimony.

**realera** f. queen cell [of beehive].

**realeza** f. royalty, regal dignity or power.

**realidad** f. reality, fact. 2 truth, sincerity. 3 *en* ~, in reality, really.

**realismo** m. realism. 2 royalism.

**realista** adj. realistic. 2 royalistic. 3 m.-f. realist. 4 royalist.

**realizable** adj. realizable [hope, plan, etc.]; feasible, practicable. 2 COM. realizable.

**realización** f. realization, doing, accomplishing, achievement, fulfilment. 2 COM. realization.

**realizador, -ra** m.-f. accomplisher. 2 CINEM. producer.

**realizar** tr. to realize, accomplish, carry out, do, perform, fulfill. 2 COM. to realize. 3 ref. to be accomplished, fulfilled, carried out.

**realmente** adj. really, in reality, actually.

**realzar** tr. to raise, elevate. 2 to emboss. 3 to heighten, enhance, set off. 4 PAINT. to brighten up, light up.

**reanimar** tr. to reanimate, revive. 2 ref. to reanimate, revive [be reanimated].

**reanudar** tr. to renew, resume. 2 ref. to be renewed or resumed.

**reaparecer** intr. to reappear.

**reaparición** f. reappearance.

**rearmar** tr. to rearm.

**rearme** m. rearmament, rearming.

**reasegurador, -ra** adj. reinsuring. 2 m. reinsurer.

**reasegurar** tr. to reinsure.

**reaseguro** m. reinsurance.

**reasumir** tr. to reassume, resume, retake.

**reasunción** f. reassumption, resumption.

**reasunto** irreg. p. p. of REASUMIR.

**reata** f. rope to tie animals and keep them in a

single file; drove of animals going in a single file. *3* (Am.) rope, lasso.

**reatar** *tr.* to tie again. *2* to tie tight. *3* to tie in a single file.

**reavivar** *tr.* to revive, renew, reawake.

**rebaba** *f.* burr, fin, rough edge, rough flange.

**rebaja** *f.* diminution, deduction. *2* COM. rebate.

**rebajado, -da** *adj.* relieved of service [soldier]. *3* depressed, drop [arch].

**rebajamiento** *m.* lowering, reduction, diminution. *2* PAINT. toning down. *4* disparagement, humiliation; lowering oneself.

**rebajar** *tr.* to lower, cut down, reduce, rebate, discount. *2* to lower [reduce the height of]. *3* CARP. to rabbet, scarf; to shave down. *4* to reduce the strength of [a liquor]. *5* PAINT. to tone down. *6* to disparage, to humiliate. *7* to humble oneself: *rebajarse a,* to stoop to.

**rebajo** *m.* rabbet [cut along an edge or arris].

**rebalaje** *m.* current of waters.

**rebalsa** *f.* pool [in a stream].

**rebalsar** *tr.* to dam [flowing water]. *2 intr.-ref.* [of flowing water] to form a pool.

**rebanada** *f.* slice [esp. of bread].

**rebanar** *tr.* to slice.

**rebañadera** *f.* ARREBAÑADERA.

**rebañadura** *f. pl.* leavings gathered together, scrapings.

**rebañar** *tr.* to gather up [without leaving any remnants]. *2* to scrape [a plate].

**rebaño** *m.* herd, flock, fold, drove.

**rebasar** *tr.* to exceed, go beyond. *2* NAUT. to sail past.

**rebate** *m.* fight, encounter.

**rebatimiento** *m.* refutation.

**rebatiña** *f.* scramble [for something].

**rebatir** *tr.* to rebut, refute. *2* to repel, drive back, resist.

**rebato** *m.* alarm, alarm bell, tocsin: *tocar a ~,* to sound the tocsin. *2* MIL. sudden attack.

**rebautizar** *tr.* to rebaptize.

**Rebeca** *f. pr. n.* Rebecca.

**rebeca** *f.* a jacket of knit worsted for women.

**rebeco** *m.* ZOOL. chamois.

**rebelarse** *tr.* to rebel, to revolt.

**rebelde** *adj.* rebellious, insurgent, insubordinate, stubborn. *3* MED. rebellious. *4* LAW defaulting. *5 m.-f.* rebel, insurgent. *6* LAW defaulter.

**rebeldía** *f.* rebelliousness; stubbornness. *2* rebellious act. *3* LAW default: *en ~,* by default.

**rebelión** *f.* rebellion, revolt, rising, insurrection.

**rebelón, -na** *adj.* balky, restive [horse].

**rebenque** *m.* whip [for flogging galley slaves]. *2* (Am.) strong riding whip. *3* NAUT. short rope.

**rebién** *adv.* coll. very well.

**reblandecer** *tr.* to soften. *2 ref.* to soften, become soft. ¶ CONJUG. like *agradecer.*

**reblandecimiento** *m.* softening: *~ cerebral,* MED. softening of the brain.

**rebollar, rebolledo** *m.* grove of Turkey oaks.

**rebollo** *m.* BOT. Turkey oak.

**rebolludo, -da** *adj.* thick-set.

**rebombar** *intr.* to resound.

**reborde** *m.* flange, projecting rim.

**rebosadero** *m.* overflow [outlet], spillway.

**rebosar** *intr.-ref.* to overflow, overbrim, run over. *2 intr.* to be in abundance. *3 ~ de* or *en,* to overflow with, to burst with.

**rebotar** *intr.* [of a ball, etc.] to bound or bounce repeatedly; to rebound. *2 tr.* to clinch, bend the point of [a nail, etc.]. *2* to drive back [after impact]. *4* to vex, exasperate, upset.

**rebote** *m.* bound, bounce; rebound [of a ball, etc.]: *de ~,* indirectly.

**rebotica** *f.* back room in a shop.

**rebozar** *tr.* to muffle or cover [one's face] with one's cape or cloak. *2* COOK. to cover with batter, flour, honey, etc. *3 ref.* to muffle oneself up.

**rebozo** *m.* muffling oneself up. *2* a kind of mantilla. *3* fig. disguise, simulation. *4 sin ~,* frankly, openly.

**rebudiar** *intr.* HUNT. [of a wild boar] to grunt.

**rebufar** *intr.* to snort again. *2* to snort loudly.

**rebufe** *m.* snort, snorting [of the bull].

**rebufo** *m.* muzzle blast, air expansion when a gun is fired.

**rebujar** *tr.-ref.* ARREBUJAR.

**rebujo** *m.* woman's thick veil. *2* clumsy bundle.

**rebullicio** *m.* great bustle or hubbub.

**rebullir** *intr.-ref.* to stir, begin to move; give sings of life.

**rebumbar** *intr.* [of a cannon ball] to whiz.

**reburujar** *tr.* to make up in a clumsy bundle.

**reburujón** *m.* clumsy bundle.

**rebusca** *f.* careful research or seeking out.

**rebuscado, -da** *adj.* affected, unnatural, far-fetched.

**rebuscamiento** *m.* too careful research. *2* affectation, excessive elegance [in bearing, language, etc.].

**rebuscar** *tr.* to research, to seek out with care. *3* to gather fruit left by gatherers.

**rebuznador, -ra** *adj.* braying. *2 m.-f.* brayer.

**rebuznar** *intr.* to bray.

**rebuzno** *m.* braying [of a donkey].

**recabar** *tr.* to obtain by entreaty.

**recadero, -ra** *m.-f.* commissionaire, messenger.

**recado** *m.* message, errand: *hacer recados,* to do or run errands. *2* present, gift [sent with a letter]. *3* daily provision or marketing. *4* outfit, equipment: *~ de escribir,* writing materials. *5* (Am.) saddle and trappings. *7 pl.* compliments, regards.

**recaer** *intr.* to fall again, fall back. *2* to relapse. *3 ~ en* or *sobre* [of an heritance, election, responsibility, etc.] to fall to; to fall upon, devolve upon. ¶ CONJUG. like *caer.*

**recaigo, recaiga,** etc. *irr.* V. RECAER.

**recalada** *f.* NAUT. landfall.

**recalar** *tr.* to soak, saturate. *2 intr.* NAUT. *~ en,* to approach or reach [a place].

**recalcar** *tr.* to press [a thing with another]. *2* to cram, to pack, or stuff [things]. *3* to emphasize, lay stress upon [words]. *4 intr.* NAUT. to heel, list. *5* ARRELLANARSE.

**recalce** *m.* AGR. hilling. *2* ARCH. underpinning.

**recalcitrante** *adj.* recalcitrant. *2* stubborn.

**recalcitrar** *intr.* to recalcitrate.

**recalentamiento** *m.* reheating. *2* overheating.

**recalentar** *tr.* to reheat. *2* to overheat, superheat. *3* to excite sexually. *4 ref.* to become overheated. *5* to be spoiled by the excessive heat. ¶ CONJUG. like *acertar.*

**recaliento, recaliente,** etc. *irr.* V. RECALENTAR.

**recalmón** *m.* NAUT. lull [in wind or sea].

**recalvastro** *adj.* bald-pated.

**recalzar** *tr.* to hill [plants]. *2* ARCH. to underpin. *3* PAINT. to colour [a drawing].

**recalzo** *m.* ARCH. underpinning.

**recamado, -da** *adj.* adorned with raised embroidery.

**recamar** *tr.* to adorn with raised embroidery.

**recámara** *f.* chamber, breech [of a gun]. *2* MIL. blasthole [of a mine]. *3* fig. caution, reserve, cunning. *4* obs. wardrobe.

**recambiar** *tr.* to re-exchange, to rechange. *2* COM. to redraw.

**recambio** *m.* re-exchange. *2* rechange. *3* COM. redrawing. *4* MACH. *de* ~, spare [part, wheel, etc.].

**recamo** *m.* raised embroidery.

**recancamusa** *f.* CANCAMUSA.

**recancanilla** *f.* emphasis, stress laid on words to indicate special significance.

**recantación** *f.* recantation.

**recantón** *m.* spur stone.

**recapacitar** *tr.* to go over [in one's mind], to meditate upon.

**recapitulación** *f.* recapitulation, summing up.

**recapitular** *tr.* to recapitulate, summarize.

**recargar** *tr.* to reload, recharge. *2* to overload, overcharge. *4* to increase [a tax or duty]. *5* to adorn to excess. *6* ref. to have an increase of fever.

**recargo** *m.* recharge, new load. *2* surtax. *3* MED. increase of fever.

**recatado, -da** *adj.* cautious, circumspect. *3* modest, chaste.

**recatar** *tr.* to hide, conceal. *2* ref. to hide [oneself or one's actions].

**recato** *m.* caution, reserve. *2* modesty, decency.

**recauchutar** *tr.* to retread, recap [a tire].

**recaudación** *f.* collection [of rents, taxes, etc.]. *2* sum collected, receipt. *3* collector's office.

**recaudador** *m.* collector, taxgatherer.

**recaudar** *tr.* to collect [rents, taxes, etc.]. *2* to hold or put under care, in safe place.

**recaudo** *m.* RECAUDACIÓN 1. *2* precaution, care: *a buen* ~, under care, in safe place.

**recavar** *tr.* to dig a second time.

**recazo** *m.* guard [of a sword]. *2* back [of a knife].

**recebar** *tr.* to level [a roadbed] with gravel. *2* to refill [a cask].

**recelar** *tr.-ref.* to fear, distrust, suspect.

**recelo** *m.* fear, distrust, misgiving, suspicion.

**receloso, -sa** *adj.* fearful, distrustful, suspicious.

**recental** *adj.* sucking [calf or lamb].

**recentísimo, -ma** *adj. superl.* very recent.

**recepción** *f.* reception, receiving, receipt. *2* reception, admission [into Academy, etc.]. *3* reception [ceremony]. *4* RADIO. reception.

**receptáculo** *m.* receptacle.

**receptador** *m.-f.* LAW receptor [of fugitives of justice]; receiver [of stolen goods].

**receptar** *tr.* LAW to conceal, shelter [offenders], to receive [stolen goods, etc.].

**receptividad** *f.* receptiveness, receptivity.

**receptivo, -va** *adj.* receptive.

**receptor, -ra** *adj.* receiving. *2* *m.-f.* receiver, recipient [person]. *3* *m.* TELEF., TELEG., RADIO. receiver.

**recercar** *tr.* to fence in again. *2* to regird. *3* CERCAR.

**receso** *m.* deviation, separation. *2* (Am.) adjournment.

**receta** *f.* prescription, recipe, receipt.

**recetar** *tr.* MED. to order, prescribe [a medicine]. *2* coll. to ask for. *3* intr. MED. to prescribe.

**recetario** *m.* pharmacopœia. *2* receipt book. *3* apothecary's file.

**recetor** *m.* receiver, treasurer.

**recial** *m.* rapids, swift current [in rivers].

**reciamente** *adv.* strongly, solidly. *2* vigorously, impetuously.

**reciario** *m.* retiarius [gladiator].

**recibí** *m.* COM. receipt; received payment.

**recibidero, -ra** *adj.* receivable.

**recibidor, -ra** *m.-f.* receiver, recipient. *2* *m.* RECIBIMIENTO 3 & 4.

**recibimiento** *m.* reception, receiving. *2* reception [manner of receiving a person]; greeting, welcome. *3* drawing-room. *4* entrance room, hall [of a flat or appartment].

**recibir** *tr.* to receive [in practically every sense]. *2* to admit, let in. *3* to meet [go to a place to receive a person]. *4* to face [an attack or assailant]. *5* intr. to receive [receive company, be at home]. *6* ref. recibirse de, to graduate as, to be admitted to practice as.

**recibo** *m.* reception, receipt: *acusar* ~ *de*, to acknowledge receipt of. *2* COM. receipt, quittance. *3* reception [of callers]: *día de* ~, at-home day; *estar de* ~, to be dressed for receiving callers. *4* RECIBIMIENTO 4.

**recidiva** *f.* MED. relapse.

**reciedumbre** *f.* strength, solidity, vigour.

**recién** *adv.* recently, lately, newly, late, new. | Used only before a p. p.: ~ *casados*, newly married. *2* (Am.) just: ~ *ha llegado*, he has just arrived.

**reciente** *adj.* recent, fresh, late, new, modern.

**recinto** *m.* area, enclosure, precinct. *2* FORT. enceinte.

**1) recio** *adv.* RECIAMENTE. *2 de* ~, RECIAMENTE.

**2) recio, -cia** *adj.* strong, robust, vigorous. *2* thick, heavy. *3* stout, bulky. *4* hard, difficult to bear. *5* rigourous [weather]. *6* swift, impetuous.

**récipe** *m.* recipe, prescription.

**recipiendario** *m.* member received [into an Academy, etc.].

**recipiente** *adj.* recipient. *2* *m.* receptacle, vessel, container. *3* receiver [of an air pump].

**recíprocamente** *adv.* reciprocally, mutually. *2* conversely.

**reciprocar** *tr.* to reciprocate [to make mutual or correspondent].

**reciprocidad** *f.* reciprocity.

**recíproco, -ca** *adj.* reciprocal, mutual.

**recitación** *f.* recitation.

**recitado** *m.* MUS. recitative.

**recital** *m.* MUS. recital.

**recitar** *tr.* to recite.

**recitativo, -va** *adj.* MUS. recitative.

**reciura** *f.* strength, vigour. *2* thickness, stoutness.

**reclamación** *f.* claim, demand [of a thing as one's due]. *2* reclamation, complaint, protest.

**reclamante** *m.-f.* claimant, claimer [one who demands something as his due]. *2* reclaimant.

**reclamar** *tr.* to claim [demand as one's due; call for, require]. *2* INTERN. LAW to reclaim. *3* to decoy [a bird]. *4* intr. to reclaim, protest [against]; to put in a claim. *5* ref. [of birds] to call one another.

**reclame** *m.* NAUT. tie block.

**reclamo** *m.* decoy bird. *2* birdcall. *3* call [of a bird calling another bird]. *4* allurement, attraction. *5* advertising, publicity. *6* PRINT. catchword.

**reclinación** *f.* reclination, reclining.

**reclinar** *tr.* to recline, to lean. *2* ref. to recline, to lean [intr.].

**reclinatorio** *m.* kneeling desk, prie-dieu. *2* anything arranged for reclining on.

**recluir** *tr.* to confine, imprison, intern, shut up, seclude [a person]. *2 ref.* to confine or seclude oneself. ¶ CONJUG. like *huir*.

**reclusión** *f.* confinement, imprisonment, internment, seclusion. *2* place of confinement.

**recluso** *adj.* confined, imprisoned, interned, recluse. *3 m.-f.* prisoner [person kept in prison].

**recluta** *f.* RECLUTAMIENTO. *2 m.* MIL. recruit.

**reclutamiento** *m.* recruitment; conscription. *2* MIL. the conscripts of the same year.

**reclutar** *tr.* to recruit, ro conscript.

**recobrar** *tr.* to recover, regain, retrieve. *2 ref.* to recover [regain health, consciousness, etc.].

**recobro** *m.* recovery, recuperation.

**recocina** *f.* back kitchen.

**recodar** *intr.-ref.* to lean upon with the elbow. *2 intr.* [of a river, road, etc.] to turn, bend.

**recodo** *m.* turn, bend [of a river, road, etc.].

**recogedor, -ra** *m.-f.* gatherer. *2* shelterer. *3 m.* dustpan.

**recoger** *tr.* to retake, take back. *2* to gather, collect, pick up. *3* to gather [a piece of cloth]; to take in [a garment]; to tuck up or in. *4* to take away, put away. *5* to fetch, get. *6* to gather, accumulate. *7* to receive, give shelter to. *8* to intern [in a home or asylum]. *9* to retire, withdraw; to withdraw from circulation. *10 ref.* to retire [into a convent, etc.]. *11* to retire [go to bed]. *12* to abstract oneself from worldly thoughts.

**recogida** *adj.* withdrawal from circulation.

**recogido, -da** *adj.* recluse. *2* short-trunked [animal]. *3 m.-f.* inmate [of a home or asylum].

**recogimiento** *m.* abstraction of worldly thoughts, recollection.

**recolección** *f.* summary. *2* gathering [of fruits], harvesting. *3* collection [of money or taxes]. *4* recollection, spiritual meditation.

**recolectar** *tr.* to gather [as harvest].

**recolector** *m.* collector, taxgatherer.

**recoleto, -ta** *adj.-n.* ECCL. Recollect.

**recomendable** *adj.* commendable. *2* recommendable.

**recomendación** *f.* recommendation.

**recomendar** *tr.* to recommend. *2 ref.* to make oneself or itself recommendable. ¶ CONJUG. like *acertar*.

**recompensa** *f.* recompense, compensation, reward: *en ~*, in return.

**recompensar** *tr.* recompense, compensate, reward.

**recomponer** *tr.* to recompose, compose again. *2* to mend, repair. ¶ CONJUG. like *poner*.

**recompuesto, -ta** *p. p.* of RECOMPONER.

**reconcentración** *f.*, **reconcentramiento** *m.* concentration [bringing together to a point; intensity of hate, etc.]. *2* concentration, absorption.

**reconcentrar** *tr.* concentrate [bring together to a point]. *2* to keep secret and intense [one's hate, etc.]. *3 ref.* to become absorbed in thought.

**reconciliación** *f.* reconciliation.

**reconciliador, -ra** *adj.* reconciling. *2 m.-f.* reconciler.

**reconciliar** *tr.* to reconcile [restore to friendship]. *2* ECCL. to reconcile. *3 ref.* to become reconciled.

**reconcomerse** *ref.* CONCOMERSE.

**reconcomio** *m.* CONCOMIO. *2* itching, desire. *3 fam.* secret fear or suspicion.

**recóndito, -ta** *adj.* recondite, out of the way, hidden.

**reconocedor, -ra** *adj.* inspector, examiner.

**reconocer** *tr.* to inspect, examine. *2* MIL. to recon-

noitre, scout. *3* to recognize [identify as known before]. *4* to recognize, acknowledge, own [that]. *6* to be recognizant [to]. *7 ref.* to avow or own oneself. ¶ CONJUG. like *agradecer*.

**reconocidamente** *adv.* gratefully. *2* acknowledgedly.

**reconocido, -da** *adj.* recognized. *2* acknowledged. *3* recognizant, grateful.

**reconocimiento** *m.* inspection, examination. *2* MIL. reconnaissance, scouting. *3* survey. *4* recognition. *5* acknowledgment; admission. *6* gratitude.

**reconozco, reconozca,** etc. *irr.* V. RECONOCER.

**reconquista** *f.* reconquest.

**reconquistar** *tr.* to reconquer.

**reconstituir** *tr.* to reconstitute. *2* MED. to restore.

**reconstituyente** *adj.-m.* reconstituent.

**reconstruir** *tr.* to reconstruct, rebuild. ¶ CONJUG. like *huir*.

**recontar** *tr.* to re-count. *2* to recount, tell, narrate, relate. ¶ CONJUG. like *contar*.

**reconvención** *f.* charge, reproach, reprehension.

**reconvendré, reconvendría,** etc. *irr.* V. RECONVENIR.

**reconvengo, reconvenga,** etc. *irr.* V. RECONVENIR.

**reconvenir** *tr.* to reproach, to reprehend. *2* LAW to make a reconvention against. ¶ CONJUG. like *venir*.

**reconvine, reconviniera,** etc. *irr.* V. RECONVENIR.

**recopilación** *f.* summary, abridgment, compendium. *2* compilation, collection.

**recopilar** *tr.* to compile.

**récord** *m.* SPORT. record.

**recordación** *f.* remembrance, recollection.

**recordar** *tr.* to remember, recollect. *2* to remind: *~ algo a uno*, to remind one of something. ¶ CONJUG. like *contar*.

**recordativo, -va** *adj.* reminding. *2 m.* reminder.

**recordatorio** *m.* reminder, memento.

**recorrer** *tr.* to travel, traverse, walk, go over or through [a place; space, etc.]. *2* MACH. to travel in. *3* to make the round of. *4* to run one's eye over. *5* to overhaul, repair. *6* PRINT. to overrun.

**recorrido** *m.* course, run, circuit, beat, rounds. *2* MACH. travel, stroke. *3* overhaul, reparation. *4* coll. scolding, dressing-down.

**recortado, -da** *adj.* BOT. notched. *3 m.* cutout [figure].

**recortadura** *f.* cutting out, clipping. *2 pl.* clippings.

**recortar** *tr.* to cut away, cut off, clip, pare off, trim. *2* to cut out [figures]. *3* PINT. to outline.

**recorte** *m.* cutting, clipping. *2 pl.* cuttings, trimmings. *3 recortes de prensa*, newspaper clippings.

**recorvar** *tr.-ref.* ENCORVAR.

**recoser** *tr.* to sew again. *2* to mend [the linen].

**recostadero, -ra** *adj.* reclining place.

**recostar** *tr.* to lean, recline [the upper part of the body]. *2 ref.* to lean back, sit back, recline. ¶ CONJUG. like *contar*.

**recoveco** *m.* turning, winding, bend [of a passage, lane, stream, etc.]. *2 fig.* artifice, trick.

**recreación** *f.* recreation. *2* re-creation.

**recrear** *tr.* to recreate, amuse. *2* to please, delight. *3* to re-create. *4 ref.* to recreate, amuse oneself; to take delight.

**recreativo, -va** *adj.* recreation, recreative.

**recrecer** *tr.-intr.* to increase. *2* to occur or happen again. *2 ref.* to gather vigour, courage. ¶ CONJUG. like *agradecer*.

**recrecimiento** *m.* increase, growth.

**recreo** *m.* recreation. *2* place of amusement.
**recría** *f.* rearing of colts, etc., bred in another place.
**recriar** *tr.* to rear [colts, etc.] bred in another place. *2* to give new strength to.
**recriminación** *f.* recrimination.
**recriminar** *tr.-ref.* to recriminate.
**recrudecer** *intr.* to recrudesce, get worse. ¶ CONJUG. like *agradecer.*
**recrudecimiento** *m.*, **recrudescencia** *f.* recrudescence.
**recruzar** *tr.* to recross, cross again.
**recta** *f.* straight line. *2* straight [straight part].
**rectal** *adj.* ANAT. rectal.
**rectamente** *adv.* directly, straightly [in a straight line]. *2* honestly, righteously, rightly.
**rectangular** *adj.* rectangular.
**rectángulo** *adj.* rectangular. *2* right-angled. *3 m.* GEOM. rectangle.
**rectificación** *f.* rectification.
**rectificador, -ra** *adj.* rectifying. *2 m.-f.* rectifier.
**rectificar** *tr.* to rectify.
**rectilíneo, -a** *adj.* rectilinear, rectilineal.
**rectitud** *f.* rectitude, righteousness, uprightness. *2* straightness. *3* correctness.
**recto, -ta** *adj.* straight [without curve or bend; not leaning or inclining]. *2* righteous, just, fair, severe. *3* GEOM., ASTR. right. *4* literal [sense or meaning]. *5 m.* ANAT., ZOOL. rectum. *6 f.* straight line.
**rector, -ra** *adj.* governing, directing. *2 m.* director, head, rector. *3* ECCL. rector, parish priest.
**rectorado** *m.* rectorate, rectorship.
**rectoral** *adj.* [pertaining to the] rector or parish priest. *2 f.* rectory, house of the parish priest.
**rectoría** *f.* rectorate, rectorship. *2* rector's office.
**recua** *f.* drove of animals. *2* fig. multitude of things.
**recuadrar** *tr.* PAINT. to graticulate.
**recuadro** *m.* ARCH. square compartment.
**recubrimiento** *m.* covering, coating, lining, facing.
**recubrir** *tr.* to cover again. *2* to cover, coat, line, face, overlay. *3* RETEJAR 1.
**recudir** *tr.* to pay [one] his due. *2 intr.* [of a thing] to rebound, come or spring back.
**recuento** *m.* recount [counting again]. *2* count, telling, enumeration.
**recuento, recuente,** etc. *irr.* V. RECONTAR.
**recuerdo** *m.* remembrance, recollection, memory. *2* remembrance, keepsake, souvenir. *3 pl.* compliments, regards.
**recuerdo, recuerde,** etc. *irr.* V. RECORDAR.
**recuestar** *tr.* to request, ask, beg.
**recuesto** *m.* declivity, slope.
**recuesto, recueste,** etc. *irr.* V. RECOSTAR.
**reculada** *f.* recoil, falling back, backing up.
**recular** *intr.* to recoil, go back, fall back, back up.
**reculo, -la** *adj.* tailless [hen or chicken].
**reculones (a)** *adv.* going backwards, backing up.
**recuperable** *adj.* recoverable.
**recuperación** *f.* recovery, regain. *2* recuperation.
**recuperador, -ra** *adj.* recuperative. *2 m.-f.* recoverer. *3 m.* recuperator.
**recuperar** *tr.* to recover, regain. *2* to recuperate. *3 ref.* to recover oneself.
**recuperativo, -va** *adj.* recuperative.
**recurrente** *adj.* BOT. recurrent. *2* LAW appellant.
**recurrir** *intr.* to appeal, resort, have recourse [to]. *2* to revert, return. *3* LAW to appeal.
**recurso** *m.* recourse, resort. *2* resource. *3* written

petition. *4* reversion, return. *5* LAW appeal. *6 pl.* resources, means.
**recusación** *f.* refusal, rejection. *2* LAW challenge, recusation.
**recusar** *tr.* to refuse, reject. *2* LAW to challenge, recuse.
**rechazamiento** *m.* repulsion, driving back. *2* refusal, rejection. *3* impugnation.
**rechazar** *tr.* to repel, drive back. *2* to refuse, reject; to rebuff; to contradict, impugn.
**rechazo** *m.* rebound, recoil, repercussion: *de* ~, fig. indirectly, as a repercussion.
**rechifla** *f.* hissing [in derision]. *2* derision.
**rechiflar** *tr.* to hiss [in derision]. *2 ref.* to flout, jeer, mock, ridicule.
**rechinamiento** *m.* squeaking, creaking, grating. *2* gnashing, grinding [or teeth].
**rechinar** *intr.* [of a door, wheel, etc.] to squeak, creak, grate. *2* [of teeth] to gnash. *3* fig. to do a thing with reluctance.
**rechinido, rechino** *m.* RECHINAMIENTO.
**rechoncho, -cha** *adj.* chubby, thickset.
**rechupete (de)** *coll.* splendid, fine.
**red** *f.* net [meshed fabric], fishing net, tennis net, etc.: ~ *barredera,* dragnet, seine. *2* netting, network. *3* hair net. *4* fig. net, snare, trap. *5* network, system [of railways, telephones, etc.]. *6* grating, railing. *7* OPT. grating.
**redacción** *f.* redaction, drawing up, wording. *2* newspaper offices. *3* editorial staff.
**redactar** *tr.* to redact, draw up, word, edit.
**redactor, -ra** *m.-f.* redactor, writer. *2* editor, journalist, member of an editorial staff.
**redada** *f.* casting a net. *2* netful, catch [of fish]. *3* fig. catch, haul [of criminals, etc.].
**redaño** *m.* ANAT. caul, omentum. *2 pl.* fig. courage.
**redargüir** *tr.* to retort [say by way of counterargument]. *2* LAW to impugn. ¶ CONJUG. like *huir.*
**redecilla** *f.* small net. *2* netting. *3* hair net. *4* ZOOL. reticulum [of ruminant].
**redecir** *tr.* to say over and over again.
**rededor** *m.* surroundings. *2 al* ~, *en* ~, ALREDEDOR.
**redención** *f.* redemption. *2* deliverance from pain, poverty, etc.
**redentor, -ra** *adj.* redeeming. *2 m.-f.* redeemer. *3 m. pr. n. El Redentor,* the Redeemer.
**redescuento** *m.* COM. rediscount.
**redición** *f.* repetition, saying again.
**redicho, -cha** *adj.* affected [in speech].
**redil** *m.* fold, sheepfold.
**redimible** *adj.* redeemable.
**redimir** *tr.* to redeem. *2* to deliver from pain, poverty, etc.
**rédito** *m.* interest, income, revenue.
**redivivo, -va** *adj.* resucitated, revived.
**redoblado, -da** *adj.* redoubled. *2* thick, stout; thick-set, heavy-built. *3* MIL. quick [step].
**redoblante** *m.* MIL. long-frame drum.
**redoblar** *tr.* to double. *2* to redouble, reduplicate. *3* to clinch [a nail or rivet]. *4 intr.* to roll a drum. *5 ref.* to redouble [grow greater].
**redoble** *m.* roll [of a drum].
**redoblegar** *tr.* to bend, to clinch.
**redoblón** *m.* clinch-nail, rivet.
**redolente** *adj.* slightly aching [after pain or illness].
**redolor** *m.* dull, lingering aching or pain.
**redoma** *f.* phial, flask. *2* CHEM. balloon.
**redomado, -da** *adj.* artful, crafty, sly.
**redonda** *f.* neighbourhood. *2* MUS. whole note,

semibreve. *3 a la* ~, around, round, round about.

**redondamente** *adv.* in a circle. *2* roundly, plainly.

**redondeado, -da** *adj.* round, rounded.

**redondear** *tr.* to round [make round]. *2* to round off, round out [complete]. *3 ref.* to round [become round]. *4* to acquire a fortune.

**redondel** *m.* coll. round, circle. *2* round cape. *3* arena, bull ring.

**redondez** *f.* roundness. *2 la* ~ *de la Tierra*, the face of the Earth.

**redondilla** *f.* eight-syllable quatrain with rhyme abba. *2 adj. letra* ~, round hand [writing].

**redondo, -da** *adj.* round [in shape]. *2* round [number; hand; trip]. *3* square, plain, direct. *4* PRINT. roman [type]. *5 m.* round, circle, orb, round object. *6 en* ~, around, circularly; roundly, plainly, categorically.

**redondón** *m.* large circle or round.

**redopelo** *m.* rubbing the wrong way: *al* ~, *a* ~, against the hair; against the nature, forcedly. *2 traer al* ~, to treat rudely.

**redor** *f.* round mat. *2* poet. REDEDOR.

**redrojo** *m.* bunch of grapes remaining after vintage. *2* after bruit or blossom. *3* coll. runt, stunted boy.

**redropelo** *m.* REDOPELO.

**reducción** *f.* reduction.

**reducido, -da** *adj.* reduced, diminished, small, compact.

**reducir** *tr.* to reduce [bring down, lower, diminish; convert; subdue; compel]. *2* to persuade, convince. *3* CHEM., LOG., MAT., SURG. to reduce. *4 ref.* to reduce, be reduced. *5* to cut down one's expenses. *6 reducirse a*, to decide from necessity to; [of a thing] to be reduced to. ¶ CONJUG. like *conducir.*

**reducto** *m.* FORT. redoubt.

**reductor, -ra** *adj.* reducing. *2 m.* CHEM. reducer.

**reduje, redujera**, etc. *irr.* V. REDUCIR.

**redundancia** *f.* redundance, redundancy.

**redundante** *adj.* redundant.

**redundar** *intr.* to overflow, run over. *2* ~ *en*, to redound to, result in, lead to, bring.

**reduplicado, -da** *adj.* reduplicate, redoubled.

**reduplicar** *tr.* to reduplicate, redouble; to reiterate.

**reduzco, reduzca**, etc. *irr.* V. REDUCIR.

**reedificación** *f.* rebuilding.

**reedificar** *tr.* to re-edify, rebuild.

**reeditar** *tr.* to republish, reprint.

**reeducación** *f.* re-education.

**reeducar** *tr.* to re-educate.

**reelección** *f.* re-election.

**reelecto, -ta** *adj.* re-elected.

**reelegible** *adj.* re-elegible.

**reelegir** *tr.* to re-elect. ¶ CONJUG. like *servir.*

**reembarcar** *tr.* to re-embark, to reship. *2 ref.* to re-embark [go on board again].

**reembarque** *m.* re-embarkation; reshipment.

**reembolsar** *tr.* to reimburse, to refund. *2 ref.* to get back [disbursed or expended money].

**reembolso** *m.* reimbursement, refunding: *contra* ~, cash on delivery, collect on delivery.

**reemplazable** *adj.* replaceable, substitutable.

**reemplazar** *tr.* to replace. *2* to supersede.

**reemplazo** *m.* replacement, substitution. *2* MIL. annual enrollment.

**reencarnación** *f.* reincarnation.

**reencarnar** *tr.* to reincarnate. *2 ref.* to become reincarnated.

**reencuentro** *m.* collision. *2* MIL. engagement.

**reenganchar** *tr.* MIL. to re-enlist. *2 ref.* MIL. to re-enlist [enroll oneself again].

**reenganche** *m.* re-enlisting.

**reensayo** *m.* second test or trial. *2* second rehearsal [of a play, etc.].

**reenviar** *tr.* to send back. *2* to forward.

**reenvidar** *tr.* CARDS to raise [the bid].

**reenvite** *m.* CARDS raised bid.

**reestreno** *m.* revival [of a play].

**reexaminar** *tr.* to re-examine.

**reexpedir** *f.* to forward, reship. ¶ CONJUG. like *servir.*

**reexportar** *tr.* to re-export.

**refacción** *f.* refection, refreshment. *2* repair, mending. *3* extra, bonus.

**refajo** *m.* short flannel skirt. *2* flannel underskirt.

**refección** *f.* refection, refreshment. *2* repair.

**refectorio** *m.* refectory.

**referencia** *f.* account, narration. *2* reference. *3 pl.* references, information.

**referéndum** *m.* referendum.

**referente** *adj.* referring, relating.

**referible** *adj.* referable. *2* narrable.

**referir** *tr.* to relate, narrate, tell. *2* to refer, relate. *3 ref. referirse a*, to refer [make allusion; have reference] to; to refer oneself to. ¶ CONJUG. like *hervir.*

**refiero, refiera, refiriera**, etc. *irr.* V. REFERIR.

**refilón (de)** *adv.* obliquely, sideways. *2* in passing.

**refinación** *f.* refining, refinement [of metals, etc.].

**refinado, -da** *adj.* refined. *2* subtle, artful.

**refinamiento** *m.* refinement [state or quality of being refined]. *2* refined cruelty.

**refinar** *tr.* to refine. *2* to perfect; polish.

**refinería** *f.* refinery.

**refino, -na** *adj.* very fine, extra fine. *2 m.* REFINACIÓN.

**refitolero, -ra** *m.-f.* ECCL. refectorian. *2* busybody, meddler. *3 adj.* meddlesome.

**reflectante** *adj.* PHYS. reflecting.

**reflectar** *tr.* PHYS. to reflect.

**reflector, -ra** *adj.* reflecting. *2 m.* reflector. *3* searchlight.

**reflejar** *tr.* to reflect [heat, light, sound, etc.]. *2* [of countenance, actions, etc.] to show, reveal. *3 ref.* to be reflected.

**reflejo, -ja** *adj.* reflected. *2 adj.-m.* PHYSIOL. reflex. *3 m.* reflection [reflected light; image].

**reflexión** *f.* reflection [of heat, light, an image, etc.]. *2* reflection [mental consideration; remark, comment].

**reflexionar** *tr.-intr.* to reflect [consider, meditate].

**reflexivo, -va** *adj.* reflective, reflecting. *2* reflective, thoughtful. *3* GRAM. reflexive.

**reflorecer** *intr.* to blossom or flower again. *2* to reflourish. ¶ CONJUG. like *florecer.*

**refluir** *intr.* to flow back. *2* REDUNDAR 2. ¶ CONJUG. like *huir.*

**reflujo** *m.* reflux, ebb, ebb-tide.

**refocilación** *f.* cheering, amusement.

**refocilar** *tr.* to cheer, gladden, amuse. *2 ref.* to rejoice, to be cheered.

**reforma** *f.* reform, reformation. *2* alteration, improvement. *3* ECCL. Reformation.

**reformador, -ra** *adj.* reforming. *2 m.-f.* reformer.

**reformar** *tr.* to re-form, shape anew. *2* to reform. *3* to mend, improve. *4 ref.* [of a person] to reform.

**reformatorio, -ria** *adj.-m.* reformatory.

**reformista** *adj.-n.* POL. reformist.

**reforzador** *m.* PHOT. intensifier.

**reforzar** *tr.* to reinforce, strengthen. 2 PHOT. to intensify. ¶ CONJUG. like *contar.*
**refracción** *f.* OPT. refraction.
**refractar** *tr.* OPT. to refract. 2 *ref.* OPT. to be refracted.
**refractario, -ria** *adj.* refractory, rebellious. 2 ~ *a,* unwilling to accept [opinions, ideas, etc.]. 3 PHYS. refractory.
**refracto, -ta** *adj.* OPT. refracted.
**refrán** *m.* adage, proverb, saying, saw.
**refranero** *m.* collection of adages or proverbs.
**refregamiento** *m.* hard rubbing.
**refregar** *tr.* to rub hard, to scrub. 2 fig. to rub in, harp on [something unpleasant]. ¶ CONJUG. like *acertar.*
**refregón** *m.* hard rubbing.
**refreír** *tr.* to fry anew. 2 to fry well or too much. ¶ CONJUG. like *freír.*
**refrenada** *f.* SOFRENADA.
**refrenamiento** *m.* curbing, check, restraint.
**refrenar** *tr.* to rein, curb [a horse]. 2 fig. to curb, check, restrain.
**refrendar** *tr.* to countersign. 2 to visé [a passport].
**refrendario** *m.* countersigner.
**refrendo** *m.* countersigning. 2 countersignature.
**refrescante** *adj.* cooling. 2 refreshing.
**refrescar** *tr.* to cool, refrigerate. 2 to renew [a pain, etc.]; to refresh [the memory]. 3 *intr.* to refresh, get vigour again. 4 [of the weather] to get cool; [of the wind] to freshen. 5 *intr.-ref.* to cool, become cool. 6 to get a bit of cool air. 7 to refresh, take a drink.
**refresco** *m.* refreshment. 2 cooling drink. 3 refreshments. 4 *de* ~, new, fresh [troops, etc.].
**refriega** *f.* affray, encounter, fray, combat.
**refrigeración** *f.* refrigeration.
**refrigerador, -ra** *adj.* refrigerating. 2 *m.* refrigerator [apparatus].
**refrigerante** *adj.* refrigerating. 2 *m.* cooling bath [of a still].
**refrigerar** *tr.* to cool, refrigerate. 2 to refresh [restore strength].
**refrigerio** *m.* relief, comfort. 2 refreshment [light meal].
**refringente** *adj.* refracting, refringent.
**refrito, -ta** *adj.* fried again. 2 too fried. 3 *m.* fig. rehash [of a literary work].
**refuerzo** *m.* reinforcement. 2 *pl.* MIL. reinforcements.
**refugiado, -da** *m.-f.* refugee.
**refugiar** *tr.* to shelter, give refuge. 2 *ref.* to take refuge.
**refugio** *m.* shelter, refuge, asylum.
**refulgente** *adj.* refulgent.
**refulgir** *intr.* to shine.
**refundición** *f.* remelting. 2 recast, rehash [of a literary work].
**refundir** *tr.* to remelt, recast [metals]. 2 to recast, rehash [a literary work].
**refunfuñar** *intr.* to grumble, growl [mutter angrily].
**refutable** *adj.* refutable.
**refutación** *f.* refutal, refutation.
**refutar** *tr.* to refute.
**regadera** *f.* watering can, watering pot. 2 REGUERA.
**regadío, -día** *adj.* irrigated [land]. 2 *m.* irrigated land.
**regala** *f.* NAUT. gunwale, gunnel.
**regalado, -da** *adj.* sweet, delicate, dainty. 2 comfortable, luxurious.
**regalamiento** *m.* regalement.

**regalar** *tr.* to give, present, compliment with. 2 to caress, flatter: ~ *el oído a,* to say flattering things to. 3 to regale, delight. 4 *ref.* to regale, feast oneself.
**regalía** *f.* royal privilege. 2 privilege, exemption. 3 *pl.* perquisites.
**regalicia** *f.* REGALIZ.
**regalismo** *m.* regalism.
**regaliz** *m.,* **regaliza** *f.* BOT. licorice.
**regalo** *m.* gift, present: *de* ~, given as a present, complimentary. 2 pleasure, gratification. 3 comfort, luxury.
**regalón, -na** *adj.* comfort-loving. 2 soft, easy [life].
**regañadientes (a)** *adv.* reluctantly, grumblingly.
**regañado, -da** *adj.* split open [bread; plum].
**regañar** *intr.* [of a dog] to snarl. 2 [of a person] to snarl, grumble. 3 to quarrel, wrangle. 4 [of plums, chestnuts, etc.] to split or crack open. 5 *tr.* to scold, chide.
**regaño** *m.* snarl, angry words. 2 scolding. 3 burst crust [of a loaf of bread].
**regañón, -na** *adj.* grumbling. 2 scolding. 3 *m.-f.* grumbler, crabbed person. 4 scolder.
**regar** *tr.* to water, sprinkle; to irrigate. 2 [of a stream, etc.] to water [a region]. 3 fig. to sprinkle, to strew something on. ¶ CONJUG. like *acertar.*
**regata** *f.* rowing or sailing race, boat race; regatta. 2 furrow or small trench for irrigation.
**regate** *m.* dodge, quick side-movement.
**regatear** *tr.* to bargain, haggle over. 2 to spare, grudge. 3 to resell at retail. 4 *intr.* to bargain, haggle. 5 to dodge. 6 NAUT. to race.
**regateo** *m.* bargaining. 2 sparing, grudging.
**regato** *m.* rill, rivulet.
**regatón, -na** *adj.* retailing. 2 haggling. 3 *m.-f.* retailer. 4 haggler. 5 *m.* tip, ferrule.
**regatonear** *intr.* to resell at retail.
**regazo** *m.* lap [of one sitting]. 2 fig. lap.
**regencia** *f.* regency. 2 direction, management.
**regeneración** *f.* regeneration. 2 ELECT. feedback.
**regenerar** *tr.* to regenerate. 2 *ref.* to regenerate [become regenerate].
**regenerativo, -va** *adj.* regenerative.
**regentar** *tr.* to direct, manage. 2 to hold [an office].
**regente** *adj.* ruling, governing. 2 *m.-f.* regent. 3 *m.* pharmacist managing an apothecary shop. 4 PRINT. foreman.
**regicida** *adj.* regicidal. 2 *m.-f.* regicide [murderer].
**regicidio** *m.* regicide [murder].
**regidor, -ra** *adj.* ruling, governing. 2 *m.* alderman, councilman, town councillor.
**régimen,** *pl.* **regímenes** *m.* rule, system of government. 2 regime. 3 regimen. 4 GRAM. government. 6 MACH. rate.
**regimentar** *tr.* to regiment.
**regimiento** *m.* rule, government. 2 MIL. regiment.
**regio, -gia** *adj.* royal [of the king, of the queen]. 2 royal, regal, kingly, sumptuous, magnificent.
**región** *f.* region.
**regional** *adj.* regional.
**regionalismo** *m.* regionalism.
**regir** *tr.* to direct, govern, rule. 2 to conduct, guide. 3 GRAM. to govern. 4 *intr.* [of a law, rule, etc.] to be in force; [of a custom] to prevail. 5 [of an organ, a mechanism, etc.] to function or work well. 6 *ref.* to be governed, be guided. ¶ CONJUG. like *servir.*
**registrado, -da** *adj.* registered. 2 *marca registrada,* trademark.

**registrador, -ra** *adj.* registering. 2 registrar, recorder: ~ *de la propiedad*, recorder of deeds.

**registrar** *tr.* to search, examine, inspect. 2 to register, to record. 3 PRINT. to register. 4 to mark with a bookmark.

**registro** *m.* search, inspection. 2 registering, recording, registry. 3 register [in practically every sense]. 4 registry, register office: ~ *civil*, register of births, marriages and deaths; ~ *de la propiedad*, register of deeds. 5 manhole. 6 MUS. organ stop. 7 regulator [of a timepiece].

**regla** *f.* rule [percept, regulation, standard, normal state of things]: *en* ~, in due form, in order; *por* ~ *general*, as a rule. 2 rule [of a religious order]. 3 MATCH. rule. 4 limit, prudence, moderation. 5 menstruation. 6 rule, ruler, straight-edge: ~ *de cálculo*, side rule.

**reglado, -da** *adj.* subjected to rule or precept. 2 moderate, temperate.

**reglamentación** *f.* regulation, establishment of regulations. 2 rules, regulations.

**reglamentar** *tr.* to regulate, establish regulations.

**reglamentario, -ria** *adj.* pertaining to, or prescribed by, regulations, standing rules or bylaws.

**reglamento** *m.* regulations, standing rules, bylaw.

**reglar** *tr.* to rule [paper, etc.]. 2 to regulate [subject to rules]. 3 *ref.* to guide oneself.

**regocijado, -da** *adj.* merry, joyful, mirthful.

**regocijar** *tr.* to rejoice, gladden, exhilarate. 2 *ref.* to rejoice, be glad.

**regocijo** *m.* rejoicing, joy, gladness. 2 merriment, mirth. 3 *pl.* rejoicings.

**regodearse** *ref.* to take delight [in].

**regodeo** *m.* delight. 2 coll. diversion.

**regoldano, -na** *adj.* wild [chestnut].

**regoldo** *m.* BOT. wild chestnut tree.

**regolfar** *intr.-ref.* [of water] to flow back, eddy. 2 *intr.* [of the wind] to turn, be deflected.

**regolfo** *m.* flowing back [of water], eddy. 2 turning, deflection [of the wind]. 3 bay, inlet.

**regordete, -ta** *adj.* plump, chubby, pudgy.

**regraciar** *tr.* to thank, to show gratitude to.

**regresar** *intr.* to return, come back.

**regresión** *f.* regression, retrogression.

**regresivo, -va** *adj.* regressive.

**regreso** *m.* return, coming back.

**regruñir** *intr.* to growl; to grumble.

**reguera** *f.* irrigation ditch.

**reguero** *m.* trickle, narrow line formed by something dripping or dropped in small portions.

**regulación** *f.* regulation, adjustment, control.

**regulador, -ra** *adj.* regulating. 2 *m.* regulator. 3 MACH. governor. 4 RADIO. ~ *de volumen*, volume control.

1) **regular** *adj.* regular: *por lo* ~, as a rule. 2 middling, so-so; fair, fairly good.

2) **regular** *tr.* to regulate.

**regularidad** *f.* regularity.

**regularización** *f.* regularization.

**regularizar** *tr.* to regularize.

**regularmente** *adv.* regularly. 2 ordinarily, usually, as a rule. 3 middling, so so, fairly well.

**régulo** *m.* regulus. 2 ORN. kinglet.

**regurgitar** *intr.* MED. to regurgitate.

**rehabilitar** *tr.* to rehabilitate. 2 *ref.* to become rehabilitated.

**rehacer** *tr.* to do over, remake, rebuild. 2 to repair, renovate. 3 to give back or recover [strength]. 4 *ref.* to recover, rally. 5 to recover oneself. ¶ CONJUG. like *hacer*.

**rehago, rehaga,** etc. *irr.* V. REHACER.

**reharé, reharía,** etc. *irr.* V. REHACER.

**rehecho, -cha** *pp.* of REHACER. 2 *adj.* stocky, thickset, sturdy.

**rehén** or *pl.* **rehenes** *m.* hostage.

**rehenchir** *tr.* to refill, to stuff again. 3 to stuff [furniture]. ¶ CONJUG. like *ceñir*.

**reherir** *tr.* to repulse, drive back. ¶ CONJUG. like *hervir*.

**rehice, rehiciera,** etc. *irr.* V. REHACER.

**rehilandera** *f.* pin wheel [toy].

**rehilar** *tr.* to twist too hard [in spinning]. 2 *intr.* [of a thing] to tremble, quiver. 3 [of a flying arrow, etc.] to whiz, whir.

**rehilete** *m.* dart [used in game of darts]. 2 shuttlecock. 3 BULLF. banderilla, barbed dart. 4 dig, cutting hint or remark.

**rehílo** *m.* trembling, quivering [of a thing].

**rehogar** *tr.* COOK. to cook with a slow fire in lard or oil.

**rehoyo** *m.* deep hollow or ravine.

**rehuida** *f.* avoiding, shunning, shirking or shrinking from something.

**rehuir** *tr.* to avoid, evade, flee, shun, shirk, shrink from. 2 to refuse, decline. ¶ CONJUG. like *huir*.

**rehundido** *m.* ARCH. sunken face of the dado of a pedestal.

**rehundir** *tr.* to sink deeper. 2 to depen [a hole or excavation].

**rehusar** *tr.* to refuse, to decline.

**reidor, -ra** *adj.* jolly, full of laughter. 2 *m.-f.* laugher.

**reimpresión** *f.* reprint; reprinting.

**reimprimir** *tr.* to reprint. ¶ P. *p.: reimpreso.*

**reina** *f.* queen [sovereign]. 2 CHESS & fig. queen. 3 ENT. queen bee. 4 BOT. ~ *de los prados*, meadowsweet. 5 BOT. ~ *luisa*, lemon verbena. 6 ~ *mora*, hopscotch.

**reinado** *m.* reign.

**Reinaldo** *m. pr. n.* Reynold.

**reinante** *adj.* reigning. 2 prevailing, prevalent.

**reinar** *intr.* to reign [hold royal office]. 2 to reign, prevail.

**reincidencia** *f.* repetition [of a fault, offence, etc.].

**reincidir** *intr.* ~ *en*, to commit again [a fault, offence, etc.]; to relapse into.

**reincorporar** *tr.* to reincorporate. 2 *ref.* to rejoin [a body, regiment, etc.]; to be reunited.

**reingresar** *intr.* to re-enter, enter again.

**reingreso** *m.* re-entry.

**reino** *m.* kingdom, realm. 2 NAT. HIST. kingdom.

**reinstalar** *tr.* to reinstate, reinstall.

**reintegración** *f.* redintegration. 2 repayment.

**reintegrar** *tr.* to redintegrate. 2 to restore, refund, repay. 3 to affix a tax stamp to. 4 *ref. reintegrarse de*, to recover, get back.

**reintegro** *m.* REINTEGRACIÓN. 2 payment.

**reír** *intr.-ref.* to laugh; to giggle, titter: ~ *a carcajadas*, to guffaw; ~ or *reírse de*, to laugh at, make fun of; to make a fool of; ~ or *reírse para sus adentros*, to laugh in one's sleeve. 2 *tr.* to laugh one's applause of. ¶ CONJUG.: INDIC. Pres.: *río, ríes, ríe, reímos, reís, ríen.* | Pret.: *reí, reíste, rió; reímos, reísteis, rieron.* | SUBJ. Pres.: *ría, rías, ría; ríamos, riáis, rían.* | Imperf.: *riera, rieras, riera; riéramos, rierais, rieran,* or *riese, rieses,* etc. | Fut.: *riere, rieres, riere; riéremos, riereis, rieren.* | IMPER.: *ríe, ría; riamos, reid, rían.* | GER.: *riendo.*

**reiteración** *f.* reiteration.

**reiteradamente** *adv.* repeatedly.

**reiterar** *tr.* to reiterate, repeat.

**reiterativo, -va** *adj.* reiterative.

**reivindicación** *f.* claim, reivindication.
**reivindicar** *tr.* to regain possession. 2 to claim back.
**reja** *f.* grate, grating, grille. 2 CHEM., PHYS. lattice. 3 ploughshare, plowshare. 4 AGR. ploughing, plowing.
**rejalgar** *m.* MINER. realgar.
**rejilla** *f.* small lattice or grille; latticed wicket. 2 fire grate. 3 ELECT., RADIO. grid. 4 foot stove. 5 cane, split rattan [for seats of chairs, etc.].
**rejo** *m.* sharp point. 2 ZOOL. sting. 3 hob [for quoits]. 4 BOT. radicle.
**rejón** *m.* pointed iron bar. 2 BULLF. short spear that breaks off in bull's neck.
**rejoneador** *m.* bullfighter on horseback who uses the REJÓN.
**rejonear** *tr.* to thrust a REJÓN into [a bull].
**rejoneo** *m.* fighting bulls with a REJÓN.
**rejuela** *f.* small grate or grating. 2 foot stove.
**rejuvenecer** *tr.* to rejuvenate. 2 *intr.-ref.* to rejuvenate, become rejuvenated. ¶ CONJUG. like *agradecer.*
**rejuvenecimiento** *m.* rejuvenation.
**relación** *f.* relation, account, recital, narrative. 2 THEAT. speech. 3 relation, reference, respect, bearing. 4 statement or list of particulars. 5 *sing. & pl.* relation, rapport, connection, intercourse; dealings. 6 *pl.* relations, terms, footing. 7 betrothal, engagement: *tener relaciones,* to be betrothed. 8 connections, acquaintances, friends.
**relacionar** *tr.* to relate. 2 to state, enumerate. 3 *ref.* to relate [have reference, stand in some relation]. 4 to be acquainted or connected.
**relajación** *f.* relaxation [of an organ, the discipline, etc.]. 2 relaxation, recreation, rest. 3 dissoluteness.
**relajado, -da** *adj.* relaxed. 2 loose, dissolute.
**relajamiento** *m.* RELAJACIÓN.
**relajante** *adj.* relaxing.
**relajar** *tr.* to relax, loosen, slacken [an organ, the discipline, etc.]. 2 to give relaxation or rest. 3 to relax, remit partially [a penalty]. 4 *ref.* to relax, be relaxed, become lax or loose. 5 to grow loose or dissolute.
**relamer** *tr.* to lick again. 2 *ref.* to lick one's lips. 3 to gloat, ro relish.
**relamido, -da** *adj.* affected, prim, spruce.
**relámpago** *m.* lightning, flash of lightning. 2 flash of light. 3 flash of wit.
**relampaguear** *intr.* to flash, to sparkle. 2 *impers.* to lighten: *relampaguea,* it lightens.
**relampagueo** *m.* lightening, flashing, sparkling.
**relapso, -sa** *adj.* relapsed [into sin or heresy]. 2 *m.-f.* backslider.
**relativamente** *adv.* relatively.
**relatividad** *f.* relativity.
**relativismo** *m.* PHILOS. relativism.
**relativo, -va** *adj.* relative.
**relato** *m.* relation, account, report, narrative.
**relator, -ra** *m.-f.* relater, narrator. 2 LAW court reporter.
**relatoría** *f.* LAW office of a RELATOR.
**relavar** *tr.* to wash again.
**relazar** *tr.* to tie up.
**relé** *m.* (Angl.) ELECT. relay.
**releer** *tr.* to reread, read again. 2 to revise.
**relegar** *tr.* to relegate.
**releje** *m.* rut, track. 2 ARCH. batter. 3 tartar [on teeth].
**relente** *m.* night dew. 2 coll. cheek, assurance.

**relevador** *m.* ELECT. relay.
**relevante** *adj.* excellent, eminent, outstanding.
**relevar** *tr.* to emboss, work in relief. 2 PAINT. to make stand out. 3 to relieve [give relief to; help; free, release]. 4 to remove [from office]. 5 to relieve, relay [one in station, duty, etc.]. 6 to lift up, exalt.
**relevo** *m.* relief, relay. 2 removing [from office].
**relicario** *m.* reliquary, shrine. 2 locket [small case].
**relicto** *adj.* LAW [property] left at one's death.
**relieve** *m.* relief, relievo: *alto ~,* high relief, alto-relievo; *bajo ~,* low relief, basso-relievo. 2 raised work, embossment. 3 relief [of something]: *poner de ~,* to point out, emphasize. 4 *pl.* leavings.
**religar** *tr.* to tie again. 2 to bind more tightly.
**religión** *f.* religion. 2 religious or monastic order.
**religionario** *m.* Protestant.
**religiosidad** *f.* religiosity, religiousness.
**religioso, -sa** *adj.* religious. 2 *m.-f.* religious, monk, nun.
**relimpio, -pia** *adj.* coll. very clean.
**relinchar** *intr.* to neigh, whinny.
**relinchido, relincho** *m.* neigh, neighing, whinny.
**relinga** *f.* NAUT. boltrope. 2 cork or lead rope [of a fishing net].
**reliquia** *f.* relic. 2 habitual ailment remaining after an illness. 3 *pl.* relics.
**reliquiario** *m.* RELICARIO.
**reloj** *m.* timepiece, clock, watch: *~ de agua,* water clock, clepsydra; *~ de arena,* sandglass; *~ de bolsillo,* pocket watch; *~ de pulsera,* wrist watch; *~ de sol,* sundial; *~ despertador,* alarm clock; *~ registrador,* time clock.
**relojera** *f.* watchcase; watch stand.
**relojería** *f.* clock and watch making, horology. 2 watchmaker's shop. 3 *mecanismo de ~,* clockwork.
**relojero** *m.* watchmaker, clockmaker.
**reluciente** *adj.* relucent, bright, shining.
**relucir** *intr.* to be bright, to shine, glisten. 2 fig. to shine, be brilliant, excel.
**reluctante** *adj.* reluctant.
**relumbrante** *adj.* shining, resplendent.
**relumbrar** *intr.* to shine dazzlingly; to glare.
**relumbre** *m.* light, shine, dazzling brightness.
**relumbrón** *m.* flash of light. 2 tinsel; show, false show; *de ~,* tinsel, showy, cheaply splendid.
**rellano** *m.* landing [of stairs]. 2 terrace, level stretch [in a sloping ground].
**rellenar** *tr.* to refill; fill again. 2 to replenish, fill up, cram. 3 to stuff [a fowl, a mattres, etc.]. 4 SEW. to pad. 5 fig. to stuff [with food]. 6 *ref.* to stuff oneself.
**relleno, -na** *adj.* filled up, stuffed, padded. 2 *m.* stuffing [act or process]. 3 COOK. stuffing, forcemeat. 4 MEC. gasket. 5 SEW. padding. 6 fig. padding [in a literary work].
**remachado** *m.* riveting.
**remachar** *tr.* to clinch, rivet. 2 fig. to clinch [confirm conclusively].
**remache** *m.* clinching, riveting. 2 rivet.
**remador, -ra** *m.-f.* rower.
**remadura** *f.* rowing.
**remallar** *tr.* to mend [a net or netting].
**remanente** *m.* remnant, remaining part.
**remangar** *tr.-ref.* ARREMANGAR.
**remansarse** *ref.* [of flowing water] to become still.
**remanso** *m.* still water. 2 fig. sluggishness, tardiness.

**remar** *intr.* to row, paddle. *2* fig. to toil, struggle.

**remarcar** *tr.* to mark again.

**rematadamente** *adv.* entirely, absolutely, utterly.

**rematado, -da** *p. p.* of REMATAR. *2 adj.* absolute, hopeless: *loco* ~, raving mad.

**rematante** *m.* highest bidder [at an auction].

**rematar** *tr.* to end, finish, complete; to top off. *2* to finish off, kill [a dying person or animal]. *3* to knock down [at an auction]. *4* SEW. to fasten off the last stitch of. *5 intr.* to end, terminate.

**remate** *m.* end, conclusion. *2* end, top, upper end. *3* ARCH. top, finial. *4* knocking down [at an auction]; public sale. *5 de* ~, absolutely; *loco de* ~, raving mad.

**remedador, -ra** *m.-f.* imitator, mimicker.

**remedar** *tr.* to imitate. *2* to mimic, to mock.

**remediable** *adj.* remediable.

**remediar** *tr.* to remedy. *2* to help, relieve. *3* to help, prevent: *no lo puedo* ~, I can't help that.

**remedio** *m.* remedy, cure: *no tener* ~, to be hopeless; to be irremediable. *2* amendment. *3* help, relief. *4* help [prevention, avoidance]: *no hay* ~, *no hay más* ~, it can't be helped; *no hay más* ~ *que*, there is nothing else to do but. *5 sin* ~, hopeless; hopelessly; inevitably.

**remedir** *tr.* to remeasure.

**remedo** *m.* imitation, copy. *2* mimicking, mimicry, mockery.

**remellado, -da; remellón, -na** *adj.* dented, jagged.

**remembranza** *f.* remembrance, memory.

**rememoración** *f.* remembrance, recollection.

**rememorar** *tr.* to remember, recall, recollect.

**remendado, -da** *adj.* mended, patched, darned. *2* fig. spotted, patched, streaked.

**remendar** *tr.* to mend, repair. *2* SEW. to patch, piece, darn. ¶ CONJUG. like *acertar.*

**remendón, -na** *adj.* mending, repairing. *2* cobbler, mender of shoes. *3* tailor who does mending.

**remero, -ra** *m.-f.* rower, paddler.

**remesa** *f.* remittance, sending. *2* remittance [money sent]; goods, etc., sent at a time; shipment.

**remesar** *tr.* to remit, send, ship.

**remesón** *m.* tearing, plucking out of hair. *2* plucked hair. *3* stopping a horse in full gallop.

**remeter** *tr.* to put in again; to put in further.

**remiendo** *m.* patch, mending piece; mending, repair, reparation. *2* amendment, correction. *3* patch, spot, streak [on an animal]. *4* PRINT. job, job work.

**remiendo, remiende,** etc. *irr.* V. REMENDAR.

**remilgado, -da** *adj.* affectedly nice, delicate or graceful.

**remilgarse** *ref.* [of women] to act with an affectation of nicety, delicacy or grace.

**remilgo** *m.* affectation of nicety, delicacy or grace.

**reminiscencia** *f.* reminiscence. .

**remirado, -da** *adj.* prudent, careful, circumspect.

**remirar** *tr.* to look at or go over again, to examine again. *2 ref.* to take great pains [with]. *3* to contemplate or consider with pleasure.

**remisible** *adj.* remissible.

**remisión** *f.* sending, dispatching, remittance. *2* remission [of sins, of a debt, etc.]. *3* remission [diminution of intensity]. *4* postponement. *5* referring, reference.

**remisivo, -va** *adj.* remissive. *2* referring.

**remiso, -sa** *adj.* remiss. *2* slack, slow.

**remitente** *adj.* remitting, remittent. *2* sending, dispatching. *3 m.-f.* sender, dispatcher.

**remitir** *tr.* to remit, send, dispatch. *2* to remit [sins, debt, etc.]. *3* to remit, postpone. *4* to re-

mit, refer [a matter for decision, etc.]. *5* to refer [in a book]. *6 intr.-ref.* to remit, slacken. *7 ref.* to refer, refer oneself.

**remo** *m.* NAUT. oar, paddle: *a* ~, rowing. *2* fig. arm or leg [of a person or quadruped]; wing [of a bird]. *3* rowing. *4* fig. toil, hard labour.

**remoción** *f.* removal. *2* removal from office.

**remojar** *tr.* to steep, soak, drench. *2* coll. to celebrate with a drink.

**remojo** *m.* steep, soak [process of steeping or soaking].

**remolacha** *f.* BOT. beet; beetroot. *2* BOT. sugar beet.

**remolar** *m.* oar maker. *2* oar shop.

**remolcador, -ra** *adj.* NAUT. towing. *2 m.* NAUT. tug, tugboat, towboat.

**remolcar** *tr.* to tow, take in tow.

**remolinar** *intr.* to whirl, eddy. *2 ref.* ARREMOLINARSE.

**remolinear** *tr.* to whirl about. *2 intr.* REMOLINAR.

**remolino** *m.* whirl, eddy, whirlpool, whirlwind. *2* cowlick. *3* crowding in a disordered way. *4* commotion, disturbance.

**remolón, -na** *adj.* indolent, shirky. *2 m.-f.* shirker [one who shirks work, etc.]: *hacerse el* ~, to shirk, hang back.

**remolonear** *intr.* to hang back, demur, to shun work or effort.

**remolque** *m.* tow, towing, towage. *2* tow, towrope. *3* tow [what is towed]. *4* trailer [vehicle].

**remonta** *f.* shoe repair. *2* patch [on riding breeches]. *3* MIL. remount; remount cavalry.

**remontar** *f.* to frighten [game] away. *2* MIL. to remount [supply remounts to]. *3* to repair [shoes, saddles]. *4* to raise, elevate. *5* to go up [a river]. *6 ref.* [of birds] to rise, soar. *7* to remount, go back [to a time, source, etc.]; to date from.

**remonte** *m.* raising. *2* remounting. *3* rising, soaring.

**remoquete** *m.* punch, cuff, fisticuff. *2* cutting remark, witty saying, epigram. *3* APODO.

**rémora** *f.* ICHTH. remora. *2* fig. remora, hindrance.

**remordedor, -ra** *adj.* disturbing, causing remorse.

**remorder** *t.* to bite repeatedly. *2* to disturb, sting, to cause remorse. *3 ref.* to show one's worry, trouble or regret. ¶ CONJUG. like *mover.*

**remordimiento** *m.* remorse, compunction, qualm.

**remotamente** *adv.* remotely; vaguely.

**remoto, -ta** *adj.* remote. *2* slight, vague; unlikely.

**remover** *tr.* to remove [displace; eliminate]. *2* to disturb, upset. *3* to stir [with a spoon, etc.]. *4* to remove, discharge. *5 ref.* to move, stir [intr.]

**remozar** *tr.* to rejuvenate. *2 ref.* to rejuvenate, to acquire a youthful appearance.

**rempujar** *tr.* to push, jostle.

**rempujón** *m.* push, impulse.

**remudar** *tr.* to change, replace.

**remugar** *tr.* to ruminate.

**remuneración** *f.* remuneration, consideration.

**remunerador, -ra** *adj.* remunerative. *2 m.-f.* remunerator.

**remunerar** *tr.* to remunerate.

**remusgar** *intr.* to guess, suspect.

**remusgo** *m.* guess, suspicion. *2* sharp, cool breeze.

**renacentista** *adj.* [pertaining to the] Renaissance. *2 m.-f.* Renaissancist.

**renacer** *intr.* to be reborn, to spring up anew.

**renaciente** *adj.* renascent.

**renacimiento** *m.* renascence, rebirth, renewal. *2* (cap.) Renaissance.

**renacuajo** *m.* tadpole, polliwog. *2* fig. shrimp [person].

**renadío** *m.* aftermath, new crop.

**renal** *adj.* renal.

**Renania** *f. pr. n.* GEOG. Rhineland.

**renano, -na** *adj.* Rhenish. *2 m.-f.* Rhinelander.

**rencilla** *f.* quarrel, grudge.

**rencilloso, -sa** *adj.* quarrelsome, touchy.

**renco, -ca** *adj.* hipshot, lame.

**rencor** *m.* rancour, grudge, animosity.

**rencoroso, -sa** *adj.* rancorous, spiteful.

**rendición** *f.* rendition, surrender. *2* yield. *3* rendering, paying [of tribute, hommage, etc.]. *4* rendering [of an account].

**rendidamente** *adv.* humbly, with loving or deferential submission.

**rendido, -da** *adj.* fatigued, exhausted, worn-out. *3* submissive, attentive, devoted.

**rendija** *f.* chink, crack, rift, slit.

**rendimiento** *m.* humility; loving or deferential submission, devotion. *2* fatigue, exhaustion. *3* yield, profit, produce. *4* output [of a worker, machine, etc.]. *5* MECH. efficiency.

**rendir** *tr.* to conquer, subdue. *2* surrender, deliver, give up. *3* to render, give; to pay [tribute, etc.]: ~ *cuentas,* to render an account. *4* to exhaust, tire out. *5* to yield, bring, produce. *6* MIL. to lower [the arm or the flag] as a sign of submission or reverence. *7* MIL. ~ *las armas,* to surrender. *8* NAUT. ~ *viaje,* to arrive. *9 ref.* to surrender, yield. *10* to become exhausted, tired out. ¶ CONJUG. like *servir.*

**renegado, -da** *adj.-n.* renegade, apostate.

**renegar** *tr.* to deny vigorously. *2* to detest, abhor. *3 intr.* to renegade, apostatize. *4* to swear, blaspheme. ¶ CONJUG. like *acertar.*

**renegrido, -da** *adj.* blackish, black-and-blue.

**rengífero** *m.* RANGÍFERO.

**renglón** *m.* [written or printed] line: *a ~ seguido,* fig. right after, immediately after. *2* fig. line [of business]. *3* fig. item, article.

**renglonadura** *f.* ruled lines.

**reniego** *m.* blasphemy. *2* swearword, curse.

**reniego, reniegue,** etc. *irr.* V. RENEGAR.

**reniforme** *adj.* reniform, kidney-shaped.

**renitencia** *f.* renitency.

**renitente** *adj.* renitent.

**reno** *m.* ZOOL. reindeer.

**renombrado, -da** *adj.* renowned, famous.

**renombre** *m.* surname. *2* renown, fame.

**renovación** *f.* renewal, renewing; renovation.

**renovar** *tr.* to renew; to renovate. *2* to change, reform. *3 ref.* to renew, be renewed. ¶ CONJUG. like *contar.*

**renquear** *intr.* to limp, hobble.

**renta** *f.* rent. *2* interest, income, revenue. *3* annuity. *4* revenue [taxes, duties, etc.]. *5* public debt; Government bonds.

**rentado, -da** *adj.* living on his rents or income.

**rentar** *tr.* to yield, bring an income or profit.

**rentero, -ra** *adj.* tax-paying. *2 m.-f.* rural tenant.

**rentista** *m.-f.* financier. *2* one who lives on the interest of bonds, shares, etc.

**rentístico, -ca** *adj.* financial [pertaining to public finances].

**rentoso, -sa** *adj.* yielding profit or income.

**rentoy** *m.* a card game.

**renuencia** *f.* reluctance, repugnance, unwillingness.

**renuente** *adj.* reluctant, unwilling.

**renuevo** *m.* sprout, shoot.

**renuevo, renueve,** etc. *irr.* V. RENOVAR.

**renuncia, renunciación** *f.,* **renunciamiento** *m.* renouncement, renunciation, resignation, giving up, waiver.

**renunciante** *adj.* renouncing, resigning, waiving. *2 m.-f.* renouncer, renunciator, resigner.

**renunciar** *tr.* to renounce, give up, resign, forsake. *2* to waive [a right]. *3* to decline, refuse. *4* CARDS to renege, revoke. *5 ref. renunciarse a sí mismo,* to deny oneself.

**renuncio** *m.* CARDS renege, revoke. *2* fig. contradiction, lie, untruth.

**reñidamente** *adv.* strongly, bitterly.

**reñidero** *m.* fighting place: ~ *de gallos,* cockpit.

**reñido, -da** *adj.* on bad terms. *2* opposed [to], inconsistent [with]. *3* bitter, hardfought.

**reñidor, -ra** *adj.* quarrelsome. *2* scolding. *3 m.-f.* quarreller. *4* scolder.

**reñir** *intr.* to quarrel, dispute, fight. *2* to quarrel, be at a variance, fall out. *3 tr.* to fight [a battle]. *4* to scold. ¶ CONJUG. like *reír.*

**reo** *adj.* guilty. *2 m.-f.* offender, culprit; one deserving a penalty.

**reóforo** *m.* ELECT. reophore.

**reojo (mirar de)** *tr.* to look out of the corner of one's eye; to look askance at.

**reorganización** *f.* reorganization.

**reorganizar** *tr.* to reorganize.

**reóstato** *m.* ELECT. rheostat.

**repanchigarse, repantigarse** *ref.* to lounge or sprawl [in a seat].

**reparable** *adj.* reparable, remediable. *2* noticeable.

**reparación** *f.* reparation, repair. *2* reparation, atonement.

**reparada** *f.* sudden start, shy [of a horse].

**reparador, -ra** *adj.* repairing. *2* restorative, refreshing. *3* fault-finding. *4 m.-f.* repairer, mender. *5* fault-finder.

**reparar** *tr.* to repair, mend. *2* to repair, restore, reinvigorate. *3* to repair [make amends for] to atone for. *4* to observe, notice, remark. *5* to consider, heed; to regard, stop at. *6* to parry; defend oneself from. *7 intr.* to stop, make a halt.

**reparativo, -va** *adj.* reparative.

**reparo** *m.* repair, restoration, remedy. *2* reparation [in a building]. *3* observation, doubt, objection; fault: *poner reparos a,* to raise objections to, to find fault with. *4* defence, protection.

**reparón, -na** *adj.* carping, cavilling, fault-finding.

**repartible** *adj.* distribuable.

**repartición** *f.* distribution, division, dealing out.

**repartidor, -ra** *adj.* distributing. *2 m.-f.* distributor, dealer. *3 m.* delivery man.

**repartimiento** *m.* distribution, division, allotment. *2* assessment [of taxes, etc.].

**repartir** *tr.* to distribute, deal out, divide, allot. *2* to assess [taxes, etc.].

**reparto** *m.* REPARTIMIENTO. *2* delivery [of goods, mail, etc.]. *3* THEAT. cast of characters.

**repasar** *intr.-tr.* to repass [pass by, across, etc., again]. *2 tr.* to re-examine, retrace, review. *3* to check [accounts]; to go over [one's lesson, part, etc.]. *4* to scan, glance over. *5* to mend [clothes, linen]. *6* to finish, perfect.

**repasata** *f.* coll. chiding, dressing-down.

**repaso** *m.* review, revision. *2* checking [of accounts]; going over [one's lesson, part, etc.]. *3* overhaul. *4* mending [of clothes or linen]. *5* REPASATA.

**repatriación** *f.* repatriation.

**repatriado, -da** *adj.* repatriated. *2 m.-f.* repatriate.
**repatriar** *tr.* to repatriate. *2 ref.* to repatriate [return to one's native land].
**repechar** *intr.* to go up hill.
**repecho** *m.* slope, short steep incline: *a* ~, uphill.
**repelente** *adj.* repellent, repulsive.
**repeler** *tr.* to repel, repulse. *2* to refute, contradict.
**repelo** *m.* anything that rises or goes against the grain, nap, etc. *2* cross fiber; cross grain [in wood]. *3* coll. slight quarrel. *4* coll. reluctance.
**repelón** *m.* pull on the hair. *2* kink [in a stocking]. *3* small part torn from anything. *4* spurt [of a horse]. *5 de* ~, in passing; swiftly.
**repeloso, -sa** *adj.* cross-grained [wood]. *2* coll. touchy, peevish.
**repensar** *tr.* to reconsider; to think over. ¶ Conjug. like *acertar.*
**repente** *m.* sudden impulse. *2 de* ~, suddenly; offhand.
**repentinamente** *adv.* suddenly, on a sudden.
**repentino, -na** *adj.* sudden, unexpected.
**repentista** *m.-f.* MUS. improviser, sight reader.
**repentizar** *tr.* MUS. to improvise, perform at sight.
**repercusión** *f.* repercussion.
**repercutir** *intr.* to rebound. *2* [of sound] to echo, reverberate. *3* ~ *en*, to have a repercussion on. *4 ref.* [of light] to reverberate.
**repertorio** *m.* repertory. *2* repertoire.
**repesar** *tr.* to reweigh.
**repeso** *m.* reweight, reweighing. *2* weight office.
**repetición** *f.* repetition, reiteration; recurrence. *2* MUS., THEAT. repeat. *3* RHET. repetition. *6* repeating mechanism: *de* ~, repeating.
**repetidamente** *adv.* repeatedly.
**repetidor, -ra** *adj.* repeating. *2 m.-f.* repeater.
**repetir** *tr.* to repeat, reiterate [say, do, over again]. *2 intr.* [of food] to repeat. *3* ~ *de*, to have another helping of. *4 ref.* to repeat itself or oneself; to recur. ¶ Conjug. like *servir.*
**repicar** *tr.* to chop, hash, mince. *2* to ring [bells] or to play [castanets, etc.] merrily. *3* to reprick. *4* to repique [in piquet].
**repicotear** *tr.* to scallop.
**repintar** *tr.* to repaint. *2 ref.* to paint [one's face] elaborately.
**repique** *m.* peal, ringing [of bells]; lively playing [of castanets, etc.]. *2* tiff, slight quarrel. *3* repique [in piquet].
**repiquetear** *tr.* to ring [bells] or play [castanets, etc.] lively. *3 ref.* coll. to exchange biting words.
**repiqueteo** *m.* lively ringing of bells, playing of castanets, etc. *2* exchange of biting words.
**repisa** *f.* bracketlike ledge or shelf: ~ *de la chimenea*, mantelpiece.
**replantar** *tr.* to replant. *2* to transplant.
**replantear** *tr.* ARCH., ENG. to lay out on the ground the plan of. *2* to restate [a problem].
**repleción** *f.* repletion.
**replegar** *tr.* to fold over and over. *2* MIL. to make [the troops] fall back. *3 ref.* MIL. to fall back, retreat in order. ¶ Conjug. like *acertar.*
**repleto, -ta** *adj.* replete, full.
**réplica** *f.* answer, reply, rejoinder, retort, repartee. *2* F. ARTS replica. *3* LAW replication.
**replicar** *intr.* to answer, answer back, reply, rejoin, retort. *2* LAW to reply.
**replicón, -na** *adj.* coll. saucy.
**repliegue** *m.* fold, double fold, convolution. *2* MIL. falling back.
**repliego, repliegue**, etc. *irr.* V. REPLEGAR.

**repoblación** *f.* repopulation, restocking: ~ *forestal*, afforestation.
**repoblar** *tr.* to repeople, repopulate; to restock; to reafforest. ¶ Conjug. like *contar.*
**repollar** *intr.-ref.* [of a cabbage, etc.] to head.
**repollo** *m.* head, round head [of a cabbage, etc.]. *2* BOT. cabbage.
**repolludo, -da** *adj.* cabbage-headed, roundheaded [plant]. *2* chubby.
**repondré, repondría**, etc. *irr.* V. REPONER.
**reponer** *tr.* to put again. *2* to put back, to replace, restore. *3* to reinstate. *4* to replace [pay back]. *5* THEAT. to revive [a play]. *6* to answer, reply. *7 ref.* to recover. *8* to recover one's losses.
**repongo, reponga**, etc. *irr.* V. REPONER.
**reportación** *f.* calm, self-restraint, moderation.
**reportaje** *m.* JOURN. reporting; report, news report.
**reportamiento** *m.* check, restraint.
**reportar** *tr.* to check, repress, restrain. *2* to bring or get [profit, advantage, etc.]. *3* LITHOGR. to transfer. *4 ref.* to restrain, control oneself.
**reporte** *m.* news, report. *2* tale, piece of gossip. *3* LITHOGR. transfer.
**reporteril** *adj.* reportorial.
**reporterismo** *m.* newspaper reporting.
**reportero, -ra** *m.-f.* newspaper reporter.
**reposado, -da** *adj.* calm, quiet, peaceful.
**reposar** *intr.* to repose, rest; to lie [in the grave]. *2 intr.-ref.* to rest, take a nap. *3* [of a liquid] to settle.
**reposición** *f.* putting back, replacement, restoration, reinstatement. *2* replacement, repaying. *3* recovery. *4* THEAT. revival [of a play].
**repositorio** *m.* repository.
**reposo** *m.* repose, rest. *2* sleep. *3* calm, peace.
**repostería** *f.* confectionery, pastry. *2* confectionery shop, pastry shop. *3* pantry, larder.
**repostero** *m.* pastry cook. *2* square covering ornamented with a coat of arms.
**repregunta** *f.* LAW cross-question; cross examination.
**repreguntar** *tr.* LAW to cross-examine.
**reprender** *tr.* to reprehend, rebuke, chide, scold.
**reprensible** *adj.* reprehensible, blamable.
**reprensión** *f.* reprehension, chiding, scolding.
**reprensor, -ra** *m.-f.* reprehender.
**represa** *f.* dam, weir, millpond, sluice. *2* damming [of water]. *3* NAUT. recapture.
**represalia** *f.* reprisal; retaliation.
**represar** *tr.* to dam, bank, impound [water]. *2* NAUT. to recapture [a ship].
**representación** *f.* representation [in every sense, except remontrances]. *2* address, petition. *3* rank, distinction.
**representante** *adj.* representing. *2 m.-f.* representative. *3* THEAT. player. *4* COM. agent, representative.
**representar** *tr.* to represent. *2* THEAT. to act, play; impersonate. *3* to look [an age, one's age]. *4 ref.* to imagine, represent to oneself.
**representativo, -va** *adj.* representative.
**represión** *f.* repression, suppression, check, curbing.
**represivo, -va** *adj.* repressive.
**reprimenda** *f.* reprimand, dressing down.
**reprimir** *tr.* to repress, suppress, check, curb.
**reprobable** *adj.* reprehensible.
**reprobación** *f.* reprobation, reproof, reproval.
**reprobado, -da** *adj.* reproved. *2* failed [in an examination]. *3 adj.-n.* RÉPROBO.

**reprobador, -ra** *adj.* reprobatory, reproving.
**reprobar** *tr.* to reprobate, reprove. *2* to fail, flunk [in an examination]. ¶ CONJUG. like *contar.*
**réprobo, -ba** *adj.-m.* reprobate.
**reprochar** *tr.* to reproach: ~ *algo a uno,* to reproach one for.
**reproche** *m.* reproach, upbraiding.
**reproducción** *f.* reproduction.
**reproducir** *tr.* to reproduce. *2 ref.* to reproduce [produce its kind]. *3* to be reproduced. ¶ CONJUG. like *conducir.*
**reproductor, -ra** *adj.* reproducing, reproductive. *2* breeding [animal]. *3 m.-f.* reproducer. *4* breeder [animal].
**reproduje, reprodujera,** etc. *irr.* V. REPRODUCIR.
**reproduzco, reproduzca,** etc. *irr.* V. REPRODUCIR.
**repropiarse** *ref.* [of a horse, mule, etc.] to get balky.
**repropio, -pia** *adj.* balky, unruly [horse, mule, etc.].
**repruebo, repruebe,** etc. *irr.* V. REPROBAR.
**reps** *m.* rep [fabric].
**reptar** *intr.* to creep, crawl.
**reptil** *adj.-n.* ZOOL. reptile, reptilian.
**república** *f.* republic. *2* state, commonwealth.
**republicano, -na** *adj.-n.* republican.
**repúblico** *m.* prominent citizen, statesman. *2* patriot.
**repudiar** *tr.* to repudiate.
**repudio** *m.* repudiation [of one's wife].
**repudrir** *tr.* to rot completely. *2 ref.* to rot [become rotten] completely. *3* fig. to burn with [supressed feelings].
**repuesto, -ta** *irreg. p. p.* of REPONER. *2 adj.* replaced, restored, reinstated. *3* recovered [from illness, etc.]. *4 m.* store, stock, supply. *5* pantry. *6 de ~,* spare [held in reserve].
**repugnancia** *f.* repugnance, repugnancy.
**repugnante** *adj.* repugnant. *2* loathsome.
**repugnar** *tr.* to be repugnant to. *2* to be loath or reluctant to.
**repujado, -da** *adj.-m.* repoussé.
**repujar** *tr.* to do repoussé work on. *2* to emboss [leather].
**repulgado, -da** *adj.* affected [full of affectation].
**repulgar** *tr.* SEW. to hem. *2* to put an edging on [a pie].
**repulgo** *m.* SEW. hem. *2* edging [of a pie]: *repulgos de empanada,* fig. trifles, ridiculous scruples.
**repulido, -da** *adj.* spruce, smart.
**repulir** *tr.* to repolish. *2* to spruce, dress smartly or affectedly. *3 ref.* to spruce oneself up.
**repulsa** *f.* repulse, rebuke, refusal.
**repulsar** *tr.* to repulse, reject, refuse.
**repulsión** *f.* repulsion.
**repulsivo, -va** *adj.* repulsive. *2* repellent.
**repullo** *m.* small dart. *2* start, jump.
**repuntar** *intr.* [of the tide] to turn. *2 ref.* [of wine] to be on the turn. *3* to be displeased with one another.
**repunte** *m.* NAUT. turning of the tide.
**repuse, repusiera,** etc. *irr.* V. REPONER.
**reputación** *f.* reputation, repute.
**reputar** *tr.* to repute, judge, think. *2* to prize, value.
**requebrar** *tr.* to address flattering remarks to [a woman]. *2* to compliment, flatter. *3* to break again, to recrush. ¶ CONJUG. like *acertar.*
**requemado, -da** *adj.* burnt, brown, tanned.
**requemar** *tr.* to burn again. *2* to burn, overcook, overbake. *3* to sunburn. *4* to parch, dry [plants]. *5* to bite, sting [the mouth]. *6 ref.* to burn [be-

come charred]. *7* [of plants] to parch. *8* fig. to burn with suppressed feelings.
**requeriente** *m.-f.* requirer, requester.
**requerimiento** *m.* requisition, request; summons. *2* requirement.
**requerir** *tr.* to require, request, induce [to do something]. *2* to require, need, call for. *3* to examine [a thing]. *4* ~ *de amores,* to make love to. ¶ CONJUG. like *hervir.*
**requesón** *m.* cottage cheese, pot cheese. *2* curd.
**requetebién** *adv.* coll. very well.
**requiebro** *m.* compliment, flattering remark [addressed to a woman].
**requiebro, requiebre,** etc. *irr.* V. REQUEBRAR.
**réquiem** *m.* requiem [mass & music].
**requiero, requiera,** etc. *irr.* V. REQUERIR.
**requilorios** *m. pl.* coll. beating about the bush.
**requinto** *m.* MUS. small clarinet. *2* MUS. small guitar.
**requirente** *m.-f.* REQUERIENTE.
**requisa** *f.* inspection, round of inspection. *2* REQUISICIÓN.
**requisar** *tr.* MIL. to requisition.
**requisición** *f.* MIL. requisition.
**requisito, -ta** *adj.* requisite. *2 s.* requisite, requirement: ~ *previo,* prerequisite.
**res** *f.* head of cattle, beast. *2* HUNT. a game quadruped.
**resabiar** *tr.* to give a vice or bad habit to. *2 ref.* to contract a vice·or bad habit. *3* to become displeased. *4* to relish.
**resabido, -da** *adj.* well known. *2* affecting learning.
**resabio** *m.* unpleasant aftertaste. *2* vice, bad habit.
**resaca** *f.* undertow. *2* COM. redraft.
**resalado, -da** *adj.* coll. charming; nimblewitted.
**resalir** *intr.* ARCH. to jut out, project. ¶ CONJUG. like *salir.*
**resaltar** *intr.* to rebound. *2* to jut out, project. *3* to stand out.
**resalte** *m.* jut, projection, prominence, ledge, ridge.
**resalto** *m.* rebound. *2* RESALTE.
**resaludar** *tr.* to return a greeting or salute to.
**resalvo** *m.* stump sprout, sapling left in stubbing.
**resarcimiento** *m.* compensation, indemnification, making good.
**resarcir** *tr.* to compensate, indemnify, make good to. *2 ref. resarcirse de,* to recover, recoup [one's losses, etc.]; make good for.
**resbaladero, -ra** *adj.* slippery. *2 m.* slippery place; chute, slide.
**resbaladizo, -za** *adj.* slippery. *2* skiddy.
**resbalamiento** *m.* slipping, sliding, gliding.
**resbalar** *intr.-ref.* to slip, slide, glide. *2* to skid. *3* fig. to slip [fall into error or fault].
**resbalón** *m.* slip, slipping. *2* fig. slip, misstep.
**rescatar** *tr.* to ransom, redeem, rescue. *3* to recover [by money or force]. *3* to make up for [lost time].
**rescate** *m.* ransom, redemption, rescue. *2* ransom money.
**rescaza** *f.* ESCORPINA.
**rescindir** *tr.* to rescind [a contract].
**rescisión** *f.* rescission [of a contract].
**rescoldera** *f.* heartburn, pyrosis.
**rescoldo** *m.* embers, hot ashes. *2* scruple, doubt.
**rescontrar** *tr.* COM. to set off, balance.
**rescripto** *m.* rescript.
**rescuentro** *m.* COM. offset, balance.

**resecar** *tr.* to dry up, dry to excess. *2* SURG. to resect. *3 ref.* to become too dry.
**resección** *f.* SURG. resection.
**reseco, -ca** *adj.* very dry, too dry. *2* lean, thin, spare [person].
**reseda** *f.* BOT. reseda.
**resellar** *tr.* to reseal, to restamp. *2* to recoin. *3 ref.* fig. to go over to another party.
**resello** *m.* resealing, restamping. *2* recoining.
**resentido, -da** *adj.* offended, displeased. *2* resentful.
**resentimiento** *m.* resentment, umbrage.
**resentirse** *ref.* [of a thing] to begin to give way. *2* to be resentful, be offended or hurt. *3* ~ *de,* to suffer from; to have a pain in. *4* ~ *de,* or *por,* to resent. ¶ CONJUG. like *hervir.*
**reseña** *f.* brief account, report. *2* review [of a book]. *3* MIL. review. *4* description, signalment.
**reseñar** *tr.* to make a brief description or narration of, to report. *2* to review [a book].
**resequido, -da** *adj.* dried up, parched.
**reserva** *f.* reserve, reservation [for future use]: *de* ~, spare, in reserve. *2* reserve, reticence, circumspection. *3* secrecy: *con toda* ~, in strictest confidence. *4* reserve, reservation, restriction: *sin* ~, without reserve; openly, freely. *5* MIL. reserve. *7* ECCL. the act of putting the exposed Host back in the ciborium. *8* BIOCHEM., *finance* reserve. *9* IND. resist. *10* ~ *de indios,* Indian reservation [in U.S.A.].
**reservación** *f.* reserving, reservation.
**reservadamente** *adv.* secretly, confidentially.
**reservado, -da** *adj.* reserved [set apart]. *2* reserved, reticent. *3* discreet, circumspect. *4* private, confidential. *5 m.* place reserved for certain persons or uses.
**reservar** *tr.* to reserve. *2* to keep secret, conceal. *3* to exempt. *4* ECCL. to put [the exposed Host] back in the ciborium. *5 hacer* or *hacerse* ~, to reserve, book [a seat, a place, etc.]. *6 ref.* to bide one's time. *7* to be cautious or distrustful.
**reservista** *m.* MIL. reservist.
**resfriado** *m.* MED. cold, catarrh.
**resfriar** *tr.* to cool, chill. *2* to cool, moderate [ardour, fervour]. *3 intr.* [of weather] to begin to be cold. *4 ref.* to catch cold. *5* to cool, grow cold or indifferent.
**resfrío** *m.* MED. cold.
**resguardar** *tr.* to preserve, protect, shelter. *2 ref.* to protect oneself.
**resguardo** *m.* preservation, guard, protection. *2* COM. security, voucher. *3* watch to prevent smuggling. *4* NAUT. sea room.
**residencia** *f.* residence, stay. *2* residence, house, dwelling home. *3* ECCL. residence.
**residencial** *adj.* residentiary.
**residenciar** *tr.* to examine into the conduct of [a high official]; to impeach. *2* fig. to call to account.
**residente** *adj.* resident, residing. *2 m.-f.* resident. *3 m.* DIPLOM. minister resident.
**residir** *intr.* to reside.
**residual** *adj.* residual.
**residuo** *m.* remnant, remainder, residue, rest. *2* CHEM. residuum. *3* ARITH. difference.
**resigna** *f.* ECCL. resignation.
**resignación** *f.* resignation, handing over. *3* resignation [being resigned].
**resignadamente** *adj.* resignedly.
**resignar** *tr.* to resign, hand over [one's power or authority]. *3 ref.* to resign oneself, be resigned.

**resina** *f.* resin, rosin.
**resinación** *f.* extraction of resin.
**resinar** *tr.* to draw resin from [a tree].
**resinero, -ra** *adj.* [pertaining to] resin. *2 m.* resin extractor.
**resinífero, -ra** *adj.* resiniferous.
**resinoso, -sa** *adj.* resinous.
**resistencia** *f.* resistance [act of resisting; power to resist]: ~ *pasiva,* passive resistance. *2* reluctance. *3* endurance, strength. *4* PHYS., MEC., ELECT. resistance. *5* AER. ~ *al avance,* drag.
**resistente** *adj.* resistant, resisting. *2* strong, firm.
**resistible** *adj.* resistible, endurable.
**resistir** *intr.-ref.* to resist; to withstand. *2* to bear, endure, stand. *3 ref.* to refuse [to]. *4* to struggle, make resistance.
**resma** *f.* ream [of paper].
**resmilla** *f.* four quires of letter paper.
**resobado, -da** *adj.* trite, hackneyed.
**resobrina** *f.* grandniece, great-niece.
**resobrino** *m.* grandnephew, great-nephew.
**resol** *m.* sun's glare.
**resoluble** *adj.* resoluble. *2* resolvable, solvable.
**resolución** *f.* resolution [solving; resolving]. *2* MED., MUS., PHYS. resolution. *3* LAW nullification [of a contract]. *4* resolution, decision, decree. *5* resolution, resolve, resoluteness. *6 en* ~, in short, in sum.
**resolutivo, -va** *adj.* resolutive, analytical. *2 adj.-m.* MED. resolutive.
**resoluto, -ta** *adj.* resolute. *2* brief, compendious.
**resolutorio, -ria** *adj.* LAW resolutory.
**resolvente** *adj.* resolvent, resolving.
**resolver** *tr.* to resolve [decide upon]. *2* to sum up. *3* to resolve, solve [a problem, etc.]. *4* to resolve [disintegrate, analyze, convert]. *5* to undo, annul. *6* MED., MUS., PHYS. to resolve. *7 ref.* to resolve, dare, make up one's mind. *8* to resolve, resolve itself. ¶ CONJUG. like *mover.*
**resollar** *intr.* to breathe [use the lungs; take breath; speak]. *2* to breathe noisily. *3* CONJUG. like *contar.*
**resonador** *m.* resonator.
**resonancia** *f.* resonance. *2* fig. *tener* ~, to make a sensation.
**resonante** *adj.* resonant, resounding.
**resonar** *tr.* to resound, resonate. *2* to echo. ¶ CONJUG. like *contar.*
**resoplar** *intr.* to breathe hard, to puff; to snort.
**resoplido, resoplo** *m.* hard breathing, puffing; snort.
**resorber** *tr.* to resorb.
**resorción** *f.* resorption.
**resorte** *m.* spring [elastic device]. *2* spring, resilience, elasticity. *3* fig. lever, means [to attain an object]. *4* (Am.) rubber band.
1) **respaldar** *m.* back [of a seat].
2) **respaldar** *tr.* to endorse [write on the back of]. *2* to back, support, protect. *3 ref.* to lean back. *4* to get backing or support.
**respaldo** *m.* back [of a seat; of a sheet of paper]. *2* endorsement. *3* AGR. espalier.
**respectar** *intr.* to concern, regard, relate to.
**respectivamente** *adv.* concerning. *2* respectively.
**respective** *adv.* as regards, concerning.
**respectivo, -va** *adj.* respective.
**respecto** *m.* respect [reference, relation]: *al* ~, in the matter; *con* ~ *a,* or *de,* ~ *a* or *de,* with respect to, with regard to.
**respetabilidad** *f.* respectability.
**respetable** *adj.* respectable.

**respetador, -ra** *adj.* respecting, respectful.

**respetar** *tr.* to respect. *2 intr.* RESPECTAR.

**respeto** *m.* respect, reverence, dutifulness. *2* awe, fear. *3* attention, care, regard. *4* observance [of law, etc.]. *5 de ~*, extra, spare. *6 pl.* respects: *ofrecer sus respetos a*, to pay one's respects to.

**respetuosidad** *f.* respectfulness.

**respetuoso, -sa** *adj.* respectful. *2* dutiful, humble, obedient. *3* awesome, impressive.

**respigón** *m.* hangnail.

**respingar** *intr.* [of a horse] to jerk, start. *2* to obey unwillingly, to grumble. *3* [of the edge of a poorly made garment] to curl up.

**respingo** *m.* start [due to pain, surprise, etc.]. *3* gesture of unwillingness.

**respingona** *adj.* turned up, retroussé [nose].

**respirable** *adj.* respirable, breathable.

**respiración** *f.* respiration, breathing. *2* ventilation.

**respiradero** *m.* vent, air hole, air passage. *2* ARCH. loophole, louver. *2* fig. breather, respite.

**respirar** *intr.* to respire, breathe. *2* BOT. to respire. *3* to take breath, respire, breathe again, get rest or respite: *sin ~*, without stopping. *4* to speak, open one's lips. *5 ~ a*, to breathe of, smell of. *6 tr.* to breathe, take in [air etc.].

**respiratorio, -ria** *adj.* respiratory.

**respiro** *m.* respiration, breathing. *2* breath [moment of rest], respite. *3* COM. extension of time [for payment].

**resplandecer** *intr.* to shine, glitter, glow. *2* fig. to shine, stand out. ¶ CONJUG. like *agradecer*.

**resplandeciente** *adj.* resplendent, bright, shining, glittering; luminous, radiant.

**resplandor** *m.* resplendence, light, glitter, glow, radiance. *2* luster, splendour. *3* gleam, gleaming.

**responder** *tr.* to answer, reply, respond to. *2 intr.* to echo. *3* to requite, return. *4* to yield, be productive. *5* to answer, have the desired effect. *6* to reply, respond [perform answering action]. *7* to respond [to a stimulus, etc.]. *8* to answer, correspond. *9* to answer back, be saucy. *10* [of a building, ect.] to face. *11 ~ de* or *por*, to answer, be accountable for; to vouch for.

**respondón, -na** *adj.* coll. answering back, saucy.

**responsabilidad** *f.* responsibility. *2* liability.

**responsable** *adj.* responsible. *2* liable, answerable.

**responso** *m.* ECCL. responsory for the dead.

**responsorio** *m.* ECCL. responsory.

**respuesta** *f.* answer, reply, response.

**resquebradura** *f.* crack, crevice, chink, flaw, split.

**resquebrajadizo, -za** *adj.* easily cracked or split.

**resquebrajar** *tr.* to crack, split. *2 ref.* to crack [become cracked].

**resquebrarse** *ref.* [of a thing] to begin to break or crack. ¶ CONJUG. like *acertar*.

**resquemar** *tr.-intr.* to bite, sting [the mouth]. *2* to burn [food]. *3* fig. to smart, to annoy. *4 ref.* [of food] to burn.

**resquemazón** *f.*, **resquemo** *m.* bite, sting [of food]. *2* burnt taste [of food]. *3* fig. smarting, annoyance.

**resquemor** *m.* smarting, annoyance. *2* resentment.

**resquicio** *m.* chink, narrow opening.

**resta** *f.* ARITH. subtraction. *2* ARITH. difference.

**restablecer** *tr.* to re-establish, restore. *2 ref.* to recover [be restored from illness, loss, etc.].

**restablecimiento** *m.* re-establishment, restoration. *2* recovery [from illnes, loss, etc.].

**restallar** *intr.* to crack [like a whip]. *2* to crackle.

**restante** *adj.* remaining. *2 m.* remainder rest.

**restañar** *tr.* to stanch [blood or a wound]. *2* to retin. *3 intr.* RESTALLAR. *4 ref.* [of blood] to stanch.

**restaño** *m.* stanching [of blood]. *2* stagnation [of waters].

**restar** *tr.* to deduct. *2* to detract, take away. *3 intr.* to be left, remain. *4 tr.-intr.* MATH. to subtract.

**restauración** *f.* restoration, re-establishment. *4* restoration [of a painting, etc.]. *3* POL. restoration.

**restaurante** *adj.* restoring. *2 m.-f.* restorer. *3 m.* restaurant.

**restaurar** *tr.* to restore, re-establish. *2* to restore [a painting, etc.]. *3* POL. to restore.

**restaurativo, -va** *adj.-n.* restorative.

**restinga** *f.* NAUT. shoal, bar.

**restitución** *f.* restitution, restoration, return.

**restituible** *adj.* restorable, returnable.

**restituir** *tr.* to restore, give back, return. *2* to restore, bring back [to original state]. *3 ref.* to return to the place of departure. ¶ CONJUG. like *huir*.

**restitutorio, -ria** *adj.* restitutive. *2* restitutory.

**resto** *m.* rest, remainder, residue. *2* limit for stakes [at cards]: *echar el ~*, coll. to stake one's all; to do one's best. *3* MATH. remainder. *4 pl.* remains.

**restorán** *m.* (Am.) RESTAURANTE.

**restregar** *tr.* to rub [something] hard, to scrub. ¶ CONJUG. like *acertar*.

**restregón** *m.* hard rubbing.

**restricción** *f.* restriction, limitation, restraint: *~ mental*, mental reservation.

**restrictivo, -va** *adj.* restrictive.

**restringir** *tr.* to restrict, limit. *2* to constrict, contract.

**restriñir** *tr.* astrict, astringe, constrict, contract.

**resucitador, -ra** *adj.* resuscitative. *2 m.-f.* resuscitator, reviver.

**resucitar** *tr.* to resurrect, resuscitate, revive. *2 intr.* to be resurrected, to resuscitate, revive.

**resudar** *intr.* to sweat or perspire sightly. *2 ref.-intr.* [of a wall, vessel, etc.] to ooze.

**resudor** *m.* slight perspiration.

**resueltamente** *adv.* resolutely.

**resuelto, -ta** *p. p.* of RESOLVER. *2 adj.* resolute, determined, bold, daring. *3* prompt, quick.

**resuelvo, resuelva**, etc. *irr.* V. RESOLVER.

**resuello** *m.* breathing; hard breathing: *sin ~*, breathless; panting.

**resulta** *f.* result, effect, consequence: *de resultas de*, as a result of.

**resultado** *m.* result, effect, outcome, consequence.

**resultando** *m.* LAW whereas.

**resultante** *adj.* resulting, resultant. *2 f.* MECH. resultant.

**resultar** *intr.* to result. *2* to be, prove to be, turn out to be. *3* to be [wounded, awarded, etc.]; to come out [well, badly, etc.]. *4* coll. to be advantageous. *5* coll. to please.

**resumen** *m.* summary, abstract, résumé. *2* summing up: *en ~*, in short, to sum up.

**resumir** *tr.* to summarize, abstract, abridge, sum up. *2 ref. resumirse en*, to be reduced to; to be comprised in.

**resurgimiento** *m.* resurgence, revival, renewal.

**resurgir** *intr.* to resurge, revive, to spring up again.

**resurrección** *f.* resurrection, resuscitation, revival.

**retablo** *m.* retable, altarpiece.

**retacar** *tr.* BILL. to hit [the ball] twice.

**retaco** *m.* a kind of short musket. *2* BILL. short cue. *3* coll. chubby fellow.

**retador, -ra** *adj.* challenging. *2 m.-f.* challenger.

**retaguardia** *f.* MIL. rear, rear guard: *a* ~, in the rear.

**retahíla** *f.* series, string.

**retal** *m.* remnant, piece, clipping, scrap [of cloth, leather, metal plates, etc.].

**retallecer** *intr.* [of a plant] to sprout again. ¶ CONJUG. like *agradecer.*

**retallo** *m.* ARCH. offset, scarcement.

**retama** *f.* BOT. Spanish broom. *2* BOT. ~ *de escobas*, furze, broom. *3* BOT. ~ *de tintes*, dyer's-broom.

**retar** *tr.* to challenge [to combat or competition]; to dare.

**retardación** *f.* retardation.

**retardado, -da** *adj.* retarded. *2 m.-f.* EDUC. retardate.

**retardador, -ra** *adj.* retarding, delaying.

**retardar** *tr.* to retard, slow down, slacken. *2* to delay. *3 ref.* to retard [intr.].

**retardo** *m.* retard, retardation, delay.

**retasar** *tr.* to reappraise.

**retazar** *tr.* to cut to pieces.

**retazo** *m.* remnant, piece, scrap [of cloth]. *2* fragment, portion.

**retejar** *tr.* to retile, repair the tiles of [a roof].

**retejer** *tr.* to weave closely or tightly.

**retemblar** *intr.* to shake, tremble, quiver. ¶ CONJUG. like *acertar.*

**retén** *m.* store, stock, reserve. *2* MIL. troops held ready for emergency. *3* MEC. pawl, catch.

**retención** *f.* retention, retaining. *2* MED. retention.

**retendré, retendría,** etc. *irr.* V. RETENER.

**retener** *tr.* to retain; keep, hold, catch. *2* to detain in prison. ¶ CONJUG. like *tener.*

**retengo, retenga,** etc. *irr.* V. RETENER.

**retenida** *f.* guy [rope].

**retentar** *tr.* [of a disease, pain, etc.] to threaten with a relapse.

**retentiva** *f.* retentiveness, memory.

**reteñir** *tr.* to redye. *2 intr.* RETIÑIR. ¶ CONJUG. like *ceñir.*

**retesar** *tr.* to draw or stretch tighter; to stiffen.

**reticencia** *f.* a manner of saying a thing which is incomplete or suggests that more could be said about it.

**reticente** *adj.* using RETICENCIAS.

**retícula** *f.* RETÍCULO. *2* ASTR. Reticule.

**reticular** *adj.* reticular, reticulated, netlike, netted.

**retículo** *m.* reticulum [netlike structure]. *2* OPT. reticle. *3* ANAT., ZOOL., BOT. reticulum.

**retienes, retiene,** etc. *irr.* V. RETENER.

**retina** *f.* ANAT. retina.

**retinte** *m.* second dye. *2* RETINTÍN.

**retintín** *m.* tinkling, jingle, ringing [in the ears]. *2* sarcastic emphasis or tone of voice.

**retiñir** *intr.* to tinkle, jingle, ring. ¶ CONJUG. like *mullir.*

**retirada** *f.* withdrawal. *2* retirement [withdrawal from public life or circulation]. *3* MIL. retreat. *4* MIL. tatoo. *5* safety. *6* dry bed [left by changed course of a stream].

**retiradamente** *adv.* retiredly. *2* secretly.

**retirado, -da** *adj.* retired, secluded, remote. *2* retired, pensioned. *3 m.* retired officer.

**retiramiento** *m.* retirement, seclusion. *2* retired place.

**retirar** *tr.* to retire, withdraw. *2* to retire, call in. *3* to push back or aside; to put out of the way. *4*

to force to retire. *5* CHESS. to retreat [a man]. *6 intr.* to resemble, take after. *7 ref.* to retire, withdraw [go away]. *8* to retire, recede. *9* MIL. to retreat. *10* to retire, go into retirement.

**retiro** *m.* retirement, withdrawal. *2* retirement, seclusion, retreat, retired place. *3* ECCL. retreat. *4* MIL. retirement [of an officer].

**reto** *m.* challenge [to combat or competition]; dare, defiance.

**retocar** *tr.* to touch up, finish, retouch.

**retoñar** *intr.* [of a plant] to sprout, shoot. *2* [of a thing] to reappear, revive.

**retoñecer** *intr.* RETOÑAR. ¶ CONJUG. like *agradecer.*

**retoño** *m.* sprout, shoot, tiller. *2* fig. child.

**retoque** *m.* retouch, touching up.

**retor** *m.* twilled cotton fabric.

**retorcedura** *f.* RETORCIMIENTO.

**retorcer** *tr.* to twist, wring, wrench, screw, contort, convolve. *2* to retort [an argument]. *3* fig. to twist, distort, misconstrue. *4 ref.* to twist [become twisted]. *5* to writhe, squirm, wriggle. ¶ CONJUG. like *mover.*

**retorcimiento** *m.* twisting, wringing, writhing.

**retórica** *f.* rhetoric. *2 pl.* coll. sophistries, subtleties.

**retórico, -ca** *adj.* rethorical. *2 m.-f.* rethorician.

**retornar** *tr.* to return, give back. *2* to cause [a thing] to go back. *3 intr.* to return, come back.

**retorno** *m.* return, coming back. *2* return voyage. *3* return, repayment. *4* barrer, exchange.

**retorsión** *f.* twisting. *2* retortion, retaliation. *3* retorting [an argument].

**retorta** *f.* retort [vessel]. *2* twilled linen fabric.

**retortero** *m.* turn around: *andar al* ~, to bustle around; *traer al* ~, to harass, keep busy; to deceive with false promises.

**retortijar** *tr.* to twist, curl.

**retortijón** *m.* twist, twisting: ~ *de tripas*, bellyache.

**retozar** *intr.* to frisk, gambol. *2* to frolic, disport, play. *3* [of some emotions] to be aroused.

**retozo** *m.* frisk, gambol, frolic. *2* ~ *de la risa*, suppressed laughter.

**retozón, -na** *adj.* frisky, frolicsome, playful.

**retracción** *f.* retraction.

**retractación** *f.* retractation, recantation.

**retractar** *tr.* to retract, recant, take back. *2* LAW to purchase by prior right.

**retráctil** *adj.* retractile.

**retracto** *m.* LAW. prior right to purchase.

**retraer** *tr.* to bring back. *2* to dissuade. *3* LAW to purchase by prior right. *4 ref.* to take refuge. *5* to retire, go back. *6* to retract, draw back. *7* to withdraw from [political activities]. *8* to lead a retired life.

**retraigo, retraiga,** etc. *irr.* V. RETRAER.

**retraído, -da** *adj.* retiring, incommunicative, shy.

**retraimiento** *m.* retirement, retired life. *2* keeping aloof. *3* retiringness, shyness. *4* retreat, refuge.

**retraje, retrajera,** etc. *irr.* V. RETRAER.

**retranca** *f.* breeching [of a harness].

**retransmisión** *f.* RADIO. rebroadcasting.

**retransmitir** *f.* RADIO. to rebroadcast.

**retrasado, -da** *adj.* [mentally] retarded.

**retrasar** *tr.* to delay, defer, postpone, retard. *2* to set back [a timepiece]. *3 intr.* to fall behind [in studies, etc.]; to decline. *4 ref.* to be backward. *5* to delay, to be behind time, slow, too slow, late.

**retraso** *m.* delay, retard, lag.

**retratar** *tr.* to portray. *2 ref.* to portray oneself. *3* to sit for a photograph. 4 to show, be reflected. 5 *tr.-intr.* RETRACTAR.

**retratista** *m.-f.* portraitist; portrait painter; photographer.

**retrato** *m.* portrait, likeness, picture; photograph, portraiture. 2 fig. image, resemblance.

**retrechería** *f.* artifice, shift, evasion.

**retrechero, -ra** *adj.* artful, sly, deceitful. 2 attractive, charming.

**retrepado, -da** *adj.* leaning back.

**retreparse** *ref.* to lean back, to recline [in a chair].

**retreta** *f.* MIL. retreat, tatoo [signal, call]. 2 tatoo [evening military parade].

**retrete** *m.* toilet, water-closet. 2 boudoir.

**retribución** *f.* recompense, reward, fee, consideration.

**retribuir** *tr.* to recompense, reward, pay, fee, remunerate. ¶ CONJUG. like *huir.*

**retributivo, -va** *adj.* retributive.

**retroactividad** *f.* retroactivity.

**retroactivo, -va** *adj.* retroactive.

**retrocarga** *f. de ~,* breech-loading.

**retroceder** *intr.* to go back, move backwards, recede, retrocede; regress, retrograde.

**retrocesión** *f.* retrocession. 2 LAW. recession.

**retroceso** *m.* backward motion, receding, regression, retrocession, retrogradation; recoil. 2 MED. aggravation. 3 BILL. draw.

**retrogradar** *intr.* RETROCEDER. 2 ASTR. to retrograde.

**retrógrado, -da** *adj.* retrogade. 2 *adj.-n.* POL. reactionary.

**retronar** *intr.* to thunder, to rumble.

**retrospectivo, -va** *adj.* retrospective.

**retrotraer** *tr.* LAW to antedate.

**retrovender** *tr.* LAW to sell back to the vendor.

**retrucar** *intr.* BILL. to kiss.

**retruécano** *m.* pun, play on words.

**retumbante** *adj.* resounding, thundering, rumbling. 2 fig. pompous, bombastic, high-flown.

**retumbar** *intr.* to resound, thunder, rumble.

**retumbo** *m.* resounding, thunder, rumble, reverberation.

**retuve, retuviera,** etc. *irr.* V. RETENER.

**reucliniano, -na** *adj.* Reuchlinian.

**reuma** *m.* MED. rheumatism.

**reumático, -ca** *adj.* MED. rheumatic(al. 2 *m.-f.* rheumatic.

**reumatismo** *m.* MED. rheumatism.

**reunión** *f.* reunion [reuniting]: joining. 2 reunion, meeting, gathering, party.

**reunir** *tr.* to reunite; to rally. 2 to unite, join, collect. 3 to gather, assemble, call together. 4 *ref.* to reunite [be reunited]. 5 to join, gather, assemble, rally [come or meet together]. 6 *reunirse a* or *con,* to rejoin.

**revacunación** *f.* MED. revaccination.

**revacunar** *tr.* MED. to revaccinate.

**reválida** *f.* final examination [for a degree, etc.].

**revalidación** *f.* revalidation, confirmation.

**revalidar** *tr.* to revalidate, confirm, renew.

**revejecer** *intr.-ref.* to age [before one's time]. ¶ CONJUG. like *agradecer.*

**revejido, -da** *adj.* prematurely aged.

**revelación** *f.* revelation.

**revelado, -da** *adj.* revealed. 2 *m.* PHOT. development.

**revelador, -ra** *adj.* revealing. 2 *m.-f.* revealer. 3 *m.* PHOT. developer.

**revelamiento** *m.* revealing, revelation.

**revelar** *tr.* to reveal. 2 PHOT. to develop. 3 *ref.* to reveal itself [or oneself].

**revellín** *m.* FORT. ravelin.

**revendedor, -ra** *m.-f.* reseller, retailer. 2 scalper, ticket speculator.

**revender** *tr.* to resell, retail. 2 to scalp [tickets].

**reventa** *f.* reseale, retail. 2 scalping [of tickets, etc.].

**reventadero** *m.* rough ground. 2 drudgery, hard task.

**reventar** *intr.-ref.* to burst, explode, blow up. 2 *intr.* [of waves] to break. 3 [of a boil, bud, cloud, etc.] to burst. 4 to burst [with joy, envy, pride, etc.]. 5 coll. to die. 6 ~ *por,* to be dying to. 7 *tr.* to burst, break, crush. 8 to tire [a person] out. 9 to run [a horse] to death. 10 coll. to annoy, displease. 11 coll. to ruin. 12 *ref.* to toil, work, run, etc., to exhaustion. ¶ CONJUG. like *acertar.*

**reventazón** *f.* burst, bursting. 2 breaking [of the waves].

**reventón, -na** *adj.* bursting, seeming to burst. 2 *m.* burst, bursting. 3 AUTO. blowout. 4 tiring to death.

**rever** *tr.* to review, revise, to look over or examine again. 2 LAW to review. ¶ CONJUG. *ver.*

**reverberación** *f.* reverberation [of light].

**reverberar** *intr.* [of light] to reverberate.

**reverbero** *m.* reverberation [of light]. 2 reflecting surface. 3 reverberator. 4 (Am.) alcohol stove.

**reverdecer** *intr.* to grow green again. 2 to acquire new freshness and vigour. 3 *tr.* to give new freshness and vigour, to renew. ¶ CONJUG. like *agradecer.*

**reverdeciente** *adj.* growing green and fresh anew.

**reverencia** *f.* reverence, revering. 2 bow, curtsy. 3 ECCL. reverence [title].

**reverencial** *adj.* reverential.

**reverenciar** *tr.* to reverence, revere, venerate.

**reverendísimo, -ma** *adj. superl.* Most Reverend.

**reverendo, -da** *adj.* reverend.

**reverente** *adj.* reverent.

**reversible** *adj.* reversible.

**reversión** *f.* reversion [return to a previous state]. 2 BIOL., LAW reversion.

**reverso** *m.* back, wrong side. 2 reverse [in coins or medals]: *el ~ de la medalla,* the entire opposite.

**revertir** *intr.* LAW to revert. ¶ CONJUG. like *hervir.*

**revés** *m.* back, wrong side, reverse. 2 slap. 3 SPORT backhand [stroke]. 4 reverse, misfortune, setback. 5 *al ~,* on the contrary, the other way around; in the opposite or wrong way, backwards. 6 *al ~, del ~,* wrongly; inside out; wrong side out, before, etc. 7 *de ~,* diagonally, from left to right.

**revesado, -da** *adj.* intricate, obscure. 2 mischievous, unmanageable.

**revestimiento** *m.* covering, coat, coating, lining, facing, revetment [on a surface, wall, etc.].

**revestir** *tr.* to put [vestments] on; to clothe. 2 cover, coat, line, face, revet. 3 to clothe, invest [with dignity, etc.]. 4 to adorn, disguise. 5 to give an air or expression to. 6 *ref.* to put vestments on. 7 *revestirse de paciencia,* to prepare to be patient. 8 *revestirse de valor,* to summon one's courage. ¶ CONJUG. like VESTIR.

**revezar** *intr.* to alternate, work by shifts.

**revezo** *m.* working by shifts. 2 shift, relay.

**revirar** *tr.* to turn, twist. 2 to roll [one's eyes]. 3 *intr.* NAUT. to veer again.

**revisar** *tr.* to revise, review, re-examine. 2 LAW to review. 3 to check, verify. 4 to audit [accounts].

**revisión** *f.* revision, review, revisal. 2 check, verification. 3 audit [of accounts].

**revisor, -ra** *adj.* revising, revisory. *2 m.-f.* reviser, re-examiner. *3 m.* RLY. conductor, ticket collector. *4* auditor [of accounts].

**revista** *f.* review, examination, inspection. *2* MIL. review, muster; parade. *3* review [of a book, play, etc.]. *4* review, magazine [journal]. *5* THEAT. revue.

**revistar** *tr.* MIL. to review.

**revistero** *m.* a journalist who writes reports and reviews about shows, bullfightings, etc.

**revisto, revista, revistiera,** etc. *irr.* V. REVESTIR.

**revitalizar** *tr.* to revitalize.

**revivificar** *tr.* to revivify.

**revivir** *intr.* to revive. *2* to be renewed.

**revocable** *adj.* revocable, repealable, reversible.

**revocación** *f.* revocation, repeal, reversal.

**revocador, -ra** *adj.* revoking. *2 m.-f.* revoker. *3 m.* plasterer.

**revocar** *tr.* to revoke, repeal, reverse. *2* to dissuade. *3* to drive back [the smoke, etc.]. *4* MAS. to plaster.

**revocatorio, -ria** *adj.* revocatory, repealing.

**revolar** *intr.* [of birds] to fly again. *2* REVOLOTEAR. ¶ CONJUG. like *contar*.

**revolcadero** *m.* wallowing place [for animals].

**revolcar** *tr.* to knock down, roll over. *2* coll. to floor [an opponent]. *3 ref.* to wallow, roll over and over. ¶ CONJUG. like *contar*.

**revolcón** *m.* knocking down, rolling over. *2* defeat [in argument, etc.]. *3* wallowing.

**revolear** *intr.* to fly around and around.

**revolotear** *intr.* to flutter, flit, fly round about.

**revoloteo** *m.* fluttering, flitting, flying round about.

**revoltijo, revoltillo** *m.* mess, medley, jumble. *2* entanglement, confusion.

**revoltón** *m.* ENT. vine grub. *2* BOVEDILLA *1. 3* ARCH. turn in a moulding.

**revoltoso, -sa** *adj.* riotous, rebellious. *2* mischievous. *3 m.-f.* rioter, rebel.

**revolución** *f.* revolution.

**revolucionar** *tr.* to revolutionize.

**revolucionario, -ria** *adj.* revolutionary. *2 m.-f.* revolutionary, revolutionist.

**revólver** *m.* revolver [firearm].

**revolver** *tr.* to stir [with a spoon]; to shake. *2* to rummage, turn over. *3* to upset, disarrange. *4* to agitate, stir up agitation in. *5* to wrap up. *6* to revolve or turn over [in one's mind]. *7* to set [a person] against [another]. *8* to swing [a horse] around. *9 intr.-ref.* [of a thing] to revolve. *10 ref.* to turn upon, to turn and face. *11* to stir, move. *12* [of a horseman] to swing around. *13* ASTR. to revolve.

**revoque** *m.* MAS. plastering, rendering.

**revuelco** *m.* REVOLCÓN.

**revuelo** *m.* second flight [of a bird]. *2* flying around. *3* flutter, stir [of some things]. *4* commotion, sensation. *5 de* ~, as in passing.

**revuelta** *f.* revolt, riot, disturbance. *2* turning, winding [of a road, etc.]. *3* turn, change.

**revueltamente** *adv.* confusedly, disorderly.

**revuelto, -ta** *p. p.* of REVOLVER. *2 adj.* disordered, confused. *3* disturbed, agitated. *4* intricate. *5* changeable [weather]. *6* scrambled [egg].

**revuelvo, revuelva,** etc. *irr.* V. REVOLVER.

**revulsión** *f.* MED. revulsion.

**revulsivo, -va; revulsorio, -ria** *adj.-n.* MED. revulsive.

**rey** *m.* king [sovereign, ruler, etc.]: ~ *de armas,* HER. king-at-arms; *los Reyes Magos,* the Magi,

the Three Wise Men; *servir al* ~, to be in the army. *2* CHESS, CARDS king. *3* ORN. ~ *de codornices,* corn crake.

**reyerta** *f.* wrangle, quarrel, row, fight.

**reyezuelo** *m.* kinglet [petty king]. *2* ORN. kinglet.

**rezagado, -da** *adj.* straggling, lagging, left behind. *2 m.-f.* straggler; lagger; one who falls behind.

**rezagar** *tr.* to outstrip, leave behind. *2* to delay, defer, put off. *3 ref.* to fall behind, lag.

**rezar** *tr.* to say [prayers, mass]. *2 tr.-intr.* to say, state, read: *la carta reza así,* the letter reads thus. *3 intr.* to say prayers. *4* ~ *con,* to concern, have to do with.

**rezno** *m.* ENT. bot.

**rezo** *m.* saying [of prayers, of the divine office, of the mass]. *2* prayer, praying, devotions.

**rezongar** *intr.* to grumble, mutter.

**rezumadero** *m.* place where something is oozing.

**rezumar** *tr.* [of a vessel, wall, etc.] to exude, sweat. *2 intr.-ref.* [of a liquid] to exude, ooze out. *3 ref.* to transpire [become known].

**Rhin** *m. pr. n.* GEOG. Rhine.

**ría** *f.* estuary, firth.

**riachuelo** *m.* rivulet, streamlet, small river.

**riada** *f.* freshet, flood [of a stream].

**riba** *f.* RIBAZO.

**ribaldo, -da** *adj.* knavish. *2 m.* knave, rascal.

**ribazo** *m.* steep bank, slope.

**ribera** *f.* shore, strand. *2* bank [of a river], riverside.

**ribereño, -ña** *adj.-n.* riparian.

**ribete** *m.* SEW. binding, border, trimming. *2* addition, embellishment [to a tale]. *3 pl.* streak, touch.

**ribetear** *tr.* SEW. to bind.

**ricacho, cha** *m.-f.* coll. vulgar rich person.

**ricachón, -na** *m.-f.* coll. rich person.

**ricadueña, ricahembra** *f.* obs. noblewoman.

**ricahombría** *f.* the ancient high nobility of Castile.

**ricamente** *adv.* richly. *2* pleasantly, comfortably.

**Ricardo** *m. pr. n.* Richard.

**ricino** *m.* BOT. castor-oil plant, Palma Christi.

**rico, -ca** *adj.* rich [wealthy, abundant, abounding in; exquisite; splendid]. *2* delicious. *3* coll. dear. *4 m.-f.* rich person. *5* coll. darling.

**ricohombre** *m.* obs. grandee, nobleman.

**rictus,** *pl. -tus m.* convulsive grin.

**ricura** *f.* deliciousness. *2* coll. darling.

**ridiculez** *f.* ridiculousness. *2* ridiculous thing or action. *3* oddity, eccentricity. *4* coll. trifle.

**ridiculizar** *tr.* to ridicule; to laugh at.

**ridículo, -la** *adj.* ridiculous, ludicrous, risible. *2* odd, eccentric. *3* trifling, insignificant. *4 m.* ridicule: *poner en* ~, to expose to ridicule, to make a fool of; *ponerse en* ~, to make a fool of oneself. *5* reticule [lady's bag].

**riego** *m.* irrigation, watering.

**riel** *m.* RLY. rail. *2* small ingot.

**rielar** *intr.* poet. to glisten, glimmer.

**rienda** *f.* rein: *dar* ~ *suelta a,* to give free rein to; *tirar la* ~ or *las riendas a,* to check, restrain; *tomar las riendas,* to take the reins; *a* ~ *suelta,* loose-reined; swiftly; without restraint. *2* fig. restraint, moderation.

**riente** *adj.* laughing, smiling.

**riesgo** *m.* risk, hazard, danger, peril.

**Rif (el)** *m. pr. n.* GEOG. El Rif.

**rifa** *f.* raffle [kind of lottery]. *2* quarrel, row.

**rifar** *tr.* to raffle, raffle off. *2 intr.* to quarrel, dispute. *3 ref.* NAUT. [of a sail] to split.

**rifeño, -ña** *adj.-n.* Riffian.

**rifirrafe** *m.* coll. squabble, row.
**rifle** *m.* rifle [firearm].
**rigidez** *f.* rigidity. *2 ~ cadavérica,* rigor mortis.
**rígido, -da** *adj.* rigid, stiff. *2* rigid, strict, rigorous.
**rigodón** *m.* rigadoon [dance].
**rigor** *m.* rigour, rigor. *2* MED. rigidity. *3 de ~,* de rigueur, indispensable. *4 en ~,* strictly speaking.
**rigorismo** *m.* rigorism.
**rigorista** *adj.* rigorist, rigoristic. *2 m.-f.* rigorist.
**rigoroso, -sa** *adj.* RIGUROSO.
**riguroso, -sa** *adj.* rigorous. *2* absolute.
**rijoso, -sa** *adj.* lustful, sensual. *2* quarrelsome.
**rima** *f.* rhyme, rime: *2* RIMERO. *3 pl.* lyric poems.
**rimado, -da** *p. p.* of RIMAR. *2 adj.* versified.
**rimador, -ra** *m.-f.* rhymer.
**rimar** *tr.-intr.* to rhyme.
**rimbombante** *adj.* resonant, thundering. *2* fig. showy. *3* bombastic, pompous.
**rimbombar** *intr.* to thunder; to resound, echo.
**rimbombe, rimbombo** *m.* resonance, echo.
**rimero** *m.* pile, heap.
**Rin** *m. pr. n.* GEOG. Rhine.
**rincón** *m.* corner [hollow angle], nook. *2* corner [secret or remote place]. *3* patch, small piece [of land]. *4* fig. home, retreat.
**rinconada** *f.* corner [hollow angle].
**rinconera** *f.* corner cabinet, stand, bracket or table.
**rindo, rinda, rindiera,** etc. *irr.* V. RENDIR.
**ringla** *f.,* **ringle** *m.,* **ringlera** *f.* coll. line, file, row.
**ringorrango** *m.* flourish [in writing]. *2 pl.* superfluous ornaments; fripperies.
**rinitis** *f.* MED. rhinitis.
**rinoceronte** *m.* ZOOL. rhinoceros.
**rinoplastia** *f.* SURG. rhinoplasty.
**riña** *f.* fight, quarrel, row, wrangle, dispute.
**riño, riña, riñera,** etc. *irr.* V. REÑIR.
**riñón** *m.* ANAT., ZOOL. kidney: *costar un ~,* fig. to cost a mint of money. *2* fig. heart [central part]. *3 pl.* loins. *4 tener riñones,* to be brave.
**riñonada** *f.* layer of fat about the kidneys. *2* loins. *3* dish of kidneys.
**río** *m.* GEOG. river, stream. *2* fig. river, flood, stream [of blood, people, etc.].
**río, ría, riera,** etc. *irr.* V. REÍR.
**riostra** *f.* ARCH. brace, stay.
**ripia** *f.* shingle [slip of wood].
**ripio** *m.* refuse, debris. *2* MAS. rubble. *3* padding [in verse]. *4 no perder ~,* not to miss a word; not to miss the least occasion.
**riqueza** *f.* riches, wealth. *2* richness. *3 pl.* riches, wealth. *4* precious objects.
**risa** *f.* laugh, laughter: *estar muerto de ~,* to be extremely amused; *no ser cosa de ~,* to be no laughing matter.
**risada** *f.* RISOTADA.
**riscal** *m.* craggy place.
**risco** *m.* crag, cliff. *2* honey fritter.
**riscoso, -sa** *adj.* craggy, cliffy.
**risible** *adj.* risible. *2* laughable, ridiculous.
**risita** *f. dim.* feigned laugh. *2* giggle, titter.
**risotada** *f.* guffaw. *2* outburst of laughter.
**ríspido, -da; rispo, -pa** *adj.* harsh, gruff.
**ristra** *f.* string [of onions or garlic]. *2* coll. string, row, file.
**ristre** *m.* ARM. rest [for the lance].
**risueño, -ña** *adj.* smiling, riant, cheerful, gay, pleasant. *2* hopeful [prospect, etc.].
**rítmico, -ca** *adj.* rhythmic(al. *2 f.* rhythmics.
**ritmo** *m.* rhythm, cadence.

**rito** *m.* rite.
**ritual** *adj.-m.* ritual: *ser de ~,* to be ordained by custom.
**rival** *m.-f.* rival: *sin ~,* unrivalled.
**rivalidad** *f.* rivalry.
**rivalizar** *intr.* to vie, compete.
**rivera** *f.* brook, creek.
**riza** *f.* ravage, destruction.
**rizado, -da** *adj.* curly. *2* ripply. *3 m.* curling, frizzling, crimping. *4* curls, frizzle.
**rizar** *tr.* to curl, crisp, frizz, frizzle, crimp, flute, corrugate. *2* to ripple [water]. *3 ref.* to curl naturally. *4* [of water] to ripple.
**rizo, -za** *adj.* curly. *2 m.* curl, frizzle, ringlet. *3* ripple [small wave]. *4* AER. loop: *hacer,* or *rizar, el ~,* to loop the loop. *5* NAUT. reef, point; reef.
**rizoma** *m.* BOT. rhizome.
**rizópodo, -da** *adj.-m.* ZOOL. rhizopod.
**rizoso, -sa** *adj.* naturally curly.
**roano, -na** *adj.* roan [horse or mare].
**robador, -ra** *m.-f.* robber, stealer.
**róbalo, robalo** *m.* ICHTH. sea bass. *2* ICHTH. snook.
**robar** *tr.* to rob, pilfer, plunder, steal, thieve, rob of. *2* to abduct [a woman]. *3* [of a stream] to sweep away [banks, land]. *4* to draw [cards or dominoes]. *5 ~ el corazón,* to captivate, enamour. *6 intr.* to rob, thieve.
**robellón** *m.* BOT. edible milk mushroom.
**Roberto** *m. pr. n.* Robert.
**robín** *m.* rust [of metal].
**robladura** *f.* clinching, riveting.
**roblar** *tr.* to clinch, rivet [a nail, etc.].
**roble** *m.* BOT. oak, British oak: *~ albar,* durmast. *2* oak [wood]. *3* fig. strong, robust person or thing.
**robleda** *f.,* **robledal, robledo** *m.* woods of oak trees.
**roblón** *m.* rivet. *2* ridge of tiles.
**robo** *m.* theft, stealing, pilferage, larceny, robbery: *~ con escalo,* burglary. *2* plunder. *3* draw, drawing [at cards or domino].
**roborar** *tr.* to strengthen. *2* to corroborate.
**roborativo, -va** *adj.* roborant. *2* corroborative.
**robot** *m.* robot.
**robustecer** *tr.* to strengthen, make strong. *2 ref.* to become strong. ¶ CONJUG. like *agradecer.*
**robustez, robusteza** *f.* robustness.
**robusto, -ta** *adj.* robust, strong, hale, vigorous.
**roca** *f.* GEOL. rock. *2* rock [mass of rock standing up or cut; large detached stone]. *3* fig. rock.
**rocadero** *m.* knob or head of a distaff.
**rocalla** *f.* small fragments of rock. *2* stone chips. *3* large glass beads. *4* F. ARTS. rocaille.
**roce** *m.* rubbing, grazing, friction. *2* light touch [in passing]. *3* frequent intercourse.
**rociada** *f.* sprinkling, aspersion. *2* fig. shower, volley [of bullets, insults, etc.]. *3* fig. reprimand.
**rociadura** *f.,* **rociamiento** *m.* sprinkling, aspersion.
**rociar** *impers.* to dew. *2 tr.* to bedew, sprinkle, spray, asperse.
**rocín** *m.* hack, jade, sorry horse. *2* work horse. *3* fig. coarse, stupid fellow.
**rocinal** *adj.* pertaining to a jade or sorry horse.
**rocinante** *m.* jade, worn-out horse.
**rocino** *m.* ROCÍN.
**rocío** *m.* dew. *2* spray, sprinkle [of a liquid]. *3* NAUT. spindrift. *4* light shower.
**rococó** *adj.* rococo.
**rocoso, -sa** *adj.* rocky.
**rocho** *m.* ROC [a fabulous bird].
**roda** *f.* NAUT. stem.
**rodaballo** *m.* ICHTH. turbot; brill.

**rodada** *f.* rut, wheel track.
**rodadizo, -za** *adj.* easy-rolling.
**rodado, -da** *adj.* dapple, dappled [horse]. *2* rounded, fluent [sentence, period]. *3 canto* ~, boulder. *4 tráfico* ~, traffic of wheeled vehicles. *5 venir* ~, [of things] to happen in a favourable way.
**rodadura** *f.* rolling [act]: *superficie de* ~, tread [of a wheel].
**rodaja** *f.* disk, circular plate. *2* round slice. *3* rowel [of spur].
**rodaje** *m.* wheels, set of wheels. *2* shooting, filming [of a motion picture, of a scene, etc.].
**rodal** *m.* spot, patch [piece of ground].
**rodamiento** *m.* MACH. [ball or roller] bearing.
**Ródano** *m. pr. n.* GEOG. Rhone.
**rodante** *adj.* rolling, wheeled.
**rodapié** *m.* ARCH. baseboard [of a room wall]. *2* drapery around the bottom of a bed, table, etc.
**rodaplancha** *f.* main ward of a key.
**rodar** *intr.* to roll [as a ball, a wheel, etc.]. *2* to roll down [the stairs, etc.]; to fall rolling; to tumble. *3* to roll, turn, wheel [go on wheels or as on wheels]. *4* to turn, revolve, rotate. *5* to wander, go about or around, roam. *6* fig. to abound. *7* [of things] to happen one after another. *8 echarlo todo a* ~, to upset everything; to lose one's temper. *9 tr.* to shoot, film; to project, screen [a moving picture, a scene]. ¶ CONJUG. like *contar*.
**Rodas** *f. pr. n.* GEOG. Rhodes.
**rodeabrazo (a)** *adv.* swinging the arm [for a throw].
**rodear** *tr.* to encircle, surround. *2* MIL. to invest. *3* (Am.) to round up [cattle]. *4* to turn around. *5 intr.* to go around, make a detour. *6* fig. to beat about the bush. *7 ref.* to move, stir, turn about.
**rodela** *f.* buckler.
**rodeno** *adj.* BOT. *pino* ~, pinaster.
**rodeo** *m.* encircling, surrounding. *2* detour, roundabout way. *3* roundabout, evasion: *andar con* ~, to beat about the bush; *sin rodeos*, frankly, bluntly. *5* rodeo, roundup [of cattle].
**rodera** *f.* rut, wheel track, cart track.
**rodete** *m.* bun or knot of plaited hair. *2* padded ring [for carrying things on the head]. *3* belt pulley. *4* MECH. horizontal water wheel.
**rodezno** *m.* horizontal water wheel.
**rodilla** *f.* ANAT., ZOOL. knee: *de rodillas*, kneeling, on one's knees. *2* RODETE 2. *3* cleaning cloth.
**rodillazo** *m.* blow or push with the knee.
**rodillera** *f.* knee guard, knee cap. *2* ARM. genouillere. *3* baggy knee [of trousers]. *4* VET. knee injury [of a horse].
**rodillo** *m.* roller [cylinder of wood, metal, stone, etc.]. *2* road roller. *3* PRINT. inking roller; brayer. *4* COOK. rolling pin. *5* platen [of typewriter].
1) **rodio** *m.* CHEM. rhodium.
2) **rodio, -dia** *adj.-n.* Rhodian.
**rododendro** *m.* BOT. rhododendron.
**rodrigar** *tr.* to prop up [plants].
**Rodrigo** *m. pr. n.* Roderick.
**rodrigón** *m.* prop [for plants]. *2* coll. old retainer who escorted ladies.
**roedor, -ra** *adj.* gnawing. *2* biting, stinging, consuming. *3 adj.-n.* ZOOL. rodent.
**roedura** *f.* gnawing, nibbling. *2* place that has been nibbled.
**roer** *tr.* to gnaw, nibble. *2* to gnaw, eat away, wear away, fret, corrode. *3* to pick [a bone]. ¶ CONJUG. INDIC. Pres.: roo, *roigo*, o *royo* [for the 1rst. pers.], roes, roe, etc. | Pret.: roí, roíste, *royó*; roí-

mos, roísteis, *royeron*. | SUBJ. Pres.: roa, *roiga* or *roya*, roas, *roigas* or *royas*, etc. | Imperf.: *royera*, *royeras*, etc., or *royese*, *royeses*, etc. | Fut.: *royere*, *royeres*, etc. | IMPER.: roe; roa, *roiga* or *roya* [for the 3rd. pers.]; *roigamos*, roed, *roigan*. | PAST. P.: roído. | GER. *royendo*.
**rogaciones** *f. pl.* ECCL. rogations.
**rogador, -ra** *m.-f.* entreater, supplicant.
**rogar** *tr.* to ask, beg, entreat, pray [someone to do, give, etc., something]. ¶ CONJUG. like *contar*.
**rogativas** *f. pl.* public prayers to God.
**Rogerio** *m. pr. n.* Roger.
**rojear** *intr.* to redden, blush, be reddish, show red.
**rojez** *f.* redness, reddishness, ruddiness.
**rojizo, -za** *adj.* reddish, reddy, ruddy.
**Rojo (Mar)** *m. pr. n.* GEOG. Red Sea.
**rojo, -ja** *adj.* red [in colour]. *2* ruddy. *3* red [hair]; red-haired. *4 m.* red [colour]: *al* ~, to a red heat. *5 adj.-n.* POL. Red.
**rojura** *f.* redness.
**rol** *m.* roll, list. *2* NAUT. muster roll.
**roldana** *f.* sheave, pulley wheel.
**rolde** *m.* circle, ring [of persons or things].
**rollete** *m. dim.* small roll or roller.
**rollizo, -za** *adj.* round, cylindrical. *2* plump, stocky. *3 m.* round log.
**rollo** *m.* roll [cylindrical mass]. *2* roll [of paper, cloth, etc.]. *3* coil [of rope]. *4* round log. *5* roller: rolling pin. *6* cylindrical boulder.
**Roma** *f. pr. n.* GEOG. Rome.
**romadizo** *m.* cold in the head.
**romaico, -ca** *adj.-m.* Romaic.
**romana** *f.* steelyard.
**romanar** *tr.* to weigh with a steelyard.
**romance** *adj.* Romance, Romanic [language]. *2 m.* Spanish language. *3* narrative or lyric poem in octosyllable metre with alternate lines in assonance.
**romancero** *m.* collection of Spanish ROMANCES [poems].
**romanesco, -ca** *adj.* Roman [of the ancient Romans]. *2* NOVELESCO.
**románico, -ca** *adj.-n.* Romanesque [architecture, style]. *2 adj.* Romanic [language].
**romanillo, -lla** *adj.-f.* round-hand [style of penmanship]. *2* PRINT. roman.
**romanista** *m.-f.* Romanist [one versed in Roman law or in Romance languages].
**romanizar** *tr.* to Romanize, Latinize. *2 ref.* to become Romanized or Latinized.
**romano, -na** *adj.-n.* Roman. *2* BOT. romaine [lettuce].
**romanticismo** *m.* romanticism. *2* romance, romanticness.
**romántico, -ca** *adj.-n.* romantic. *2* romanticist.
**romanza** *f.* MUS. romance, romanza.
**romaza** *f.* BOT. sorrel.
**rómbico** *adj.* CRYST. rhombic, orthorhombic.
**rombo** *m.* GEOM. rhomb. *2* losenge, diamond.
**romboedro** *m.* GEOM. rhombohedron.
**romboidal** *adj.* rhomboidal.
**romboide** *m.* GEOM. rhomboid.
**romeral** *m.* place abounding with rosemary.
**romería** *f.* pilgrimage. *2* gathering at an out-of-town shrine on the saint's day.
**romero, -ra** *m.-f.* pilgrim, palmer. *2 m.* BOT. rosemary.
**romí** *adj.* bastard [saffron].
**romo, -ma** *adj.* blunt [without a point]. *2* blunt-nosed. *3* blunt, dull, stupid.

**rompecabezas,** *pl.* **-zas** *m.* puzzle [toy], jigsaw puzzle. *2* puzzle, riddle. *3* slung shot.
**rompedura** *f.* breakage.
**rompehielos,** *pl.* **-los** *m.* NAUT. iceboat, icebreaker.
**rompenueces,** *pl.* **-ces** *m.* nut cracker.
**rompeolas,** *pl.* **-las** *m.* breakwater, jetty, mole.
**romper** *tr.* to break, crack, fracture, shatter, smash. *2* to tear, rend; to wear out [clothes]. *3* to break up [new ground]. *4* to cleave [the air, water, etc.]. *5* to break [silence; bounds; a contract, etc.]. *6* MIL. to break [ranks]. *7* to rout, defeat. *8* ~ *el hielo,* fig. to break the ice. *9 de rompe y rasga,* free, determined. *10 intr.* [of waves] to break. *11* [of flowers] to burst open. *12* to break out. *13* to begin, start, burst into or out. *14* ~ *con,* to break, quarrel, with. *15 al* ~ *el alba* or *el día,* at daybreak. *16 ref.* to break, fracture, shatter, smash, tear [be broken, fractured, etc.]. *17* to acquire ease of manner. *18* coll. *romperse el alma,* to break one's neck. *19* fig. *romperse la cabeza,* to rack one's brains. ¶ P. P.: *roto.*
**rompiente** *adj.* breaking. *2 m.* reef, rock, shoal, shore where waves break.
**rompimiento** *m.* break, breakage. *2* breach [gap; infringment; quarrel]. *3* PAINT. opening in the background.
**ron** *m.* rum.
**roncas** *pl.* boastful threats, bluster: *echar* ~, to bluster.
**roncador, -ra** *adj.* snoring. *2 m.-f.* snorer.
**roncar** *intr.* to snore. *2* [of the wind, the sea] to roar. *3* to bluster, brag, play the bully.
**roncear** *intr.* to be slow, defer action [out of unwillingness]. *2* to wheedle, cajole.
**roncería** *f.* remissness, unwillingness. *2* coaxing, cajolery, cajoling expression.
**roncero, -ra** *adj.* slow, unwilling, grumbling. *2* wheedling, cajoling.
**ronco, -ca** *adj.* hoarse, husky, raucous.
**roncón** *m.* drone [of a bagpipe].
**roncha** *f.* wale, weal, welt. *2* black-and-blue mark. *3* round slice.
**ronchar** *intr.* to raise wales. *2 tr.* to crunch.
**ronda** *f.* night patrol. *2* rounds [by a night watch]; beat [of a constable, etc.]. *3* MIL. rounds. *4* party of night serenaders. *5* round [of drinks or cigars]. *6* round [in playing cards]. *7* way around a town or its walls.
**rondador** *m.* night stroller or serenader. *2* courter, wooer.
**rondalla** *f.* fable, story, tale. *2* RONDA 4.
**rondar** *intr.-tr.* to patrol, go the rounds [of a town, etc.] watching. *2* to walk [the street] by night. *3 tr.* to court, woo. *4* to hover about. *5* to prowl. *6* [of an illness, etc.] to be coming on [someone]. *8 intr.* MIL. to make rounds.
**rondel** *m.* POET. rondel.
**rondeño, -ña** *adj.-n.* of Ronda [andalusian town].
**rondó** *m.* MUS. rondo.
**rondón (de)** *adv. meterse de* ~, to enter suddenly, boldly, without calling at the door.
**ronquear** *intr.* to be hoarse with cold.
**ronquedad** *f.* hoarseness. *2* harshness [of a sound].
**ronquera** *f.* hoarseness [from cold].
**ronquido** *m.* snore. *2* harsh, raucous sound.
**ronzal** *m.* halter [for horses].
**ronzar** *tr.* to crunch. *2* NAUT. to move with a lever.
**roña** *f.* scab, mange [in sheep]. *2* crust of dirt. *3* rust [in metal]. *4* coll. meanness, stinginess. *5* moral infection.

**roñería, roñosería** *f.* meanness, stinginess.
**roñoso, -sa** *adj.* scabby, mangy [sheep]. *2* dirty, filthy. *3* rusty [metal]. *4* coll. mean, stingy.
**ropa** *f.* dry goods; stuff, fabric. *2* clothes, clothing, garments, dress: ~ *blanca,* linen; ~ *hecha,* ready-made clothes; ~ *interior,* underwear; ~ *sucia,* dirty linen; laundry [clothes to be washed]; *a quema* ~, pointblank; at close range. *3* robe, gown of office.
**ropaje** *m.* clothes, garb. *2* robe, gown. *3* F. ARTS drapery. *4* fig. wording, language.
**ropavejería** *f.* old-clothes shop.
**ropavejero, -ra** *m.-f.* old-clothes dealer.
**ropero, -ra** *m.-f.* ready-made clothier. *2* wardrobe, clothes closet. *3* charitable institution for the distribution of clothes.
**ropilla** *f.* a kind of doublet with sleeves.
**ropita** *f. dim.* child's clothing.
**ropón** *m.* wide, loose gown or robe.
**roque** *m.* CHESS rook, castle.
**roquedo** *m.* rock, crag.
**roqueño, -ña** *adj.* rocky. *2* hard, flinty.
**roquero, -ra** *adj.* rocky. *2* built on a rock.
**roquete** *m.* ECCL. rochet.
**rorcual** *m.* ZOOL. rorqual, finback.
**rorro** *m.* coll. baby, baby in arms.
**ros** *m.* MIL. Spanish shako.
**Rosa** *f. pr. n.* Rose.
**rosa** *f.* BOT. rose [flower]: ~ *de Jericó,* rose of Jericho; *color de* ~, rose, pink [colours]. *2* rose, rosette, anything shaped as a rose. *3* rose diamond. *4* ARCH. rose, rosace, rose window. *5* red spot [on skin]. *6* NAUT. ~ *náutica,* ~ *de los vientos,* compass card. *7 pl.* popcorn.
**rosáceo, -a** *adj.* rosaceous, rose-coloured. *2* BOT. rosaceous.
**rosado, -da** *adj.* rose, rosy, pinky. *2* rose [prepared or flavoured with roses].
**rosal** *m.* BOT. rose [bush or plant].
**rosaleda, rosalera** *f.* rosary, rose garden.
**Rosalía** *f. pr. n.* Rosalie.
**rosario** *m.* Rosary, rosary. *2* fig. string, series, succession. *3* coll. backbone. *4* chain pump.
**rosbif** *m.* COOK. roast beef.
**rosca** *f.* screw and nut. *2* screw thread: *pasarse de* ~, fig. to go too far. *3* turn [of a spiral]; coil, spiral. *4* roll twisted into a ring. *5* padded ring [for carrying things on the head]. *6* roll of fat [on neck, wrists, etc.]. *7* coll. *hacer la* ~ *a,* to flatter, cajole.
**roscar** *tr.* MACH. to thread.
**rosco** *m.* ring-shaped piece of bread or pastry.
**roscón** *m.* large ring-shaped piece of pastry.
**rosear** *intr.* to show rosy, to have a tinge of rose.
**Rosellón** *m. pr. n.* GEOG. Roussillon.
**róseo, -a** *adj.* roseate, rosy.
**roséola** *f.* MED. roseola.
**roseta** *f. dim.* small rose. *2* red spot on the cheek. *3* rose, rosehead [of watering pot]. *4 pl.* popcorn.
**rosetón** *m.* ARCH. rose, rosette. *2* ARCH. rose, rose window, wheel, window.
**rosicler** *m.* pink of dawn. *2* ruby silver.
**rosillo, -lla** *adj.* light red. *2* roan.
**rosita** *f. dim.* small rose. *2 pl.* popcorn. *3 de rositas,* free, for nothing.
**roso, -sa** *adj.* red. *2* threadbare. *3 a* ~ *y velloso,* totally, without exception or distinction.
**rosoli** *m.* rosolio [a sweet cordial].
**rosquilla** *f.* small ring-shaped cake.
**rostrado, -da** *adj.* rostrate.
**rostral** *m.* rostrate. *2* rostral.

**rostro** *m.* face, countenance: *hacer ~ a,* to face; to oppose; to accept. *2* NAUT., ORN. rostrum.
**rota** *f.* MIL. rout, defeat. *2* BOT. rattan. *3* Rota, Sacred Roman Rota.
**rotación** *f.* rotation.
**rotacismo** *m.* rhotacism, rotacism.
**rotar** *intr.* ro rotate.
**rotario, -ria** *adj.-n.* Rotarian.
**rotativo, -va** *adj.* PRINT. rotary [press.]. *2 f.* PRINT. rotary press. *3 m.* daily newspaper.
**rotatorio, -ria** *adj.* rotary, rotating.
**roten** *m.* rattan [palm & walking cane].
**rotífero, -ra** *adj.* ZOOL. rotiferous.
**roto, -ta** *irreg. p. p.* of ROMPER. *2 adj.* broken, cracked, shattered. *3* torn, worn out, ragged. *4* debaucher, licentious. *5 m.* ragged man.
**rotograbado** *m.* rotogravure.
**rotonda** *f.* rotunda. *2* rear section of a stagecoach. *3* RLY. roundhouse.
**rotor** *m.* ELECT. rotor.
**rótula** *f.* ANAT., ZOOL. rotula, kneecap.
**rotulación** *f.* labelling, lettering.
1) **rotular** *adj.* rotular, rotulian.
2) **rotular** *tr.* to label, letter, put a title to.
**rótulo** *m.* label, title. *2* sign [lettered board, etc.]. *3* poster, placard.
**rotundidad** *f.* roundness. *2* rotundity.
**rotundo, -da** *adj.* round, circular. *2* rotund [speech, style]. *3* flat, direct, round, categorical.
**rotura** *f.* breakage, breaking, fracture. *2* break, crack [broken place]. *3* tear, rent [in cloth, etc.].
**roturar** *tr.* AGR. to break up [new ground].
**roya** *f.* BOT. rust, mildew.
**roza** *f.* grubbing, weeding, clearing [of land].
**rozadura** *f.* rubbing. *2* chafing, abrasion. *3* chafe, gall [sore].
**rozamiento** *m.* rubbing, chaffing. *2* friction.
**rozar** *tr.* to grub, stub, weed, clear [land]. *2* to graze, browse, nibble [the grass]. *3* to scrape, rub, graze, fret, gall, chafe. *4 tr.-intr.* to graze [touch lightly in passing]. *5 ref.* [of a horse] to interfere. *6* to associate, to hobnob. *7* to have a resemblance or connection.
**roznar** *tr.* to crunch. *2* REBUZNAR.
**roznido** *m.* crunching noise. *2* REBUZNO.
**rozno** *m.* little donkey.
**rozón** *m.* short and broad scythe.
**rúa** *f.* street, village street. *2* cartway.
**ruana** *f.* a woollen fabric.
**ruano, -na** *adj.* ROANO.
**rubefaciente** *adj.-n.* MED. rubefacient.
**Rubén** *m. pr. n.* Reuben.
**rúbeo, -a** *adj.* reddish.
**rubéola** *f.* MED. German measles.
**rubescente** *adj.* rubescent.
**rubeta** *f.* ZOOL. a kind of frog.
**rubí** *m.* MINER. ruby. *2* HOROL. ruby, jewel.
**rubia** *f.* BOT. madder. *2* a fresh-water fish. *3* blonde [girl or woman]: *~ oxigenada,* peroxide blonde.
**rubiáceo, -a** *adj.* BOT. rubiaceous.
**rubial** *adj.* reddish [soil or plant].
**rubiales,** *pl.* **-les** *m.-f.* coll. blond, blonde [person].
**rubican** *adj.* rubican.
**rubicundo, -da** *adj.* rubicund, ruddy. *2* reddish [hair].
**rubidio** *m.* CHEM. rubidium.
**rubio, -bia** *adj.* golden, blond, fair. *2 m.-f.* blond, blonde [person]. *3 m.* ICHTH. red gurnard. *4 m. pl.* the middle of the withers [in bulls].
**rublo** *m.* ruble, rouble [Russian coin].
**rubor** *m.* red colour. *2* blush, flush; bashfulness.

**ruborizar** *tr.* to cause to blush. *2 ref.* to blush, flush [become red in the face].
**ruboroso, -sa** *adj.* blushing, bashful.
**rúbrica** *f.* paraph, flourish added to one's signature. *2* rubric, title, heading. *3* ECCL. rubric: *ser de ~,* coll. to be in accordance with ritual or custom.
**rubricar** *tr.* to sign [a letter, document, etc.] with one's peculiar mark or flourish. *2* to sign and seal. *3* to certify to, to attest.
**rubro, -bra** *adj.* red, red-coloured.
**rucio, -cia** *adj.* gray [animal]. *2* gray-haired [person]. *3 m.* gray horse, or donkey.
**ruda** *f.* BOT. rue.
**rudamente** *adv.* roughly, rudely, harshly.
**rudeza** *f.* rudeness, coarseness, roughness. *2* dullness, stupidity.
**rudimentario, -ria** *adj.* rudimentary; elementary.
**rudimento** *m.* rudiment. *2 pl.* rudiments, elements.
**rudo, -da** *adj.* rude [rough; impolite; hard, severe]. *2* crude, rugged. *3* dull, stupid.
**rueca** *f.* distaff [for spinning]. *2* twist, turn.
**rueda** *f.* wheel: *~ de andar,* treadmill; *~ del timón,* NAUT. steering wheel: *~ de molino,* millstone; *~ dentada,* gearwheel, cogwheel; *~ hidráulica,* water wheel; *~ loca,* idle wheel; *~ motriz,* driving wheel. *2* caster, roller. *3* circle, ring [of persons or things]. *4* round slice. *5* turn, successive order. *6* ICHTH. sunfish. *7* rack [torture]. *8 hacer la ~,* [of a peacock] to spread its tail. *9 hacer la ~ a,* fig. to flatter; to court.
**ruedecita** *f. dim.* small wheel. *2* caster, roller.
**ruedo** *m.* turn, rotation. *2* circuit, circumference. *3* edge, fringe [of something round]. *4* circle, round. *5* bull ring, arena. *6* round mat; mat, rug.
**ruego** *m.* entreaty, prayer, petition, request.
**ruezno** *m.* outer rind of a walnut.
**rufián** *m.* pimp, pander. *2* scoundrel, villain.
**rufianear** *adj.* ALCAHUETAR.
**rufianesco, -ca** *adj.* panderly. *2* scoundrelly, villainous. *3 f.* panders or scoundrels [collect.].
**rufo, -fa** *adj.* red, carroty, rufous-coloured. *2* curly-haired.
**rugido** *m.* roar. *2* rumbling in the bowels.
**rugiente** *adj.* roaring.
**ruginoso, -sa** *adj.* rusty [metal].
**rugir** *intr.* [of a lion] to roar. *2* [of persons, cannon, thunder, etc.] to roar, bellow.
**rugosidad** *f.* rugosity, ruggedness.
**rugoso, -sa** *adj.* rugous, rugose, rugged, wrinkled.
**ruibarbo** *m.* BOT. rhubarb.
**ruido** *m.* noise: *hacer ~,* to make a noise. *2* discussion, quarrel, row. *3* ado, fuss: *mucho ~ y pocas nueces,* much ado about nothing.
**ruidoso, -sa** *adj.* noisy, loud. *2* clamorous. *3* sensational.
**ruin** *adj.* mean, vile, base, despicable. *2* mean, poor, paltry, sorry. *3* little, stunted. *4* mean, niggardly, stingy. *5* low-minded, rascally, treacherous. *6* vicious [animal]. *7 m.* rascal, scoundrel.
**ruina** *f.* ruin: *amenazar ~,* to begin to fall to pieces. *2* wreck [person, building]. *4 pl.* ruins.
**ruindad** *f.* meanness, baseness, vileness. *2* meanness, stinginess. *3* mean or base action.
**ruinoso, -sa** *adj.* ruinous [in ruins, dilapidated, tottering]. *2* ruinous [bringing ruin].
**ruiseñor** *m.* ORN. nightingale.
**ruleta** *f.* roulette [gambling game].

**rulo** *m.* large ball. *2* conical stone [of olive-oil mills]. *3* roller, road roller.
**Rumanía** *f. pr. n.* GEOG. Rumania.
**rumano, -na** *adj.-n.* Rumanian.
**rumba** *f.* (Am.) rumba [dance and music].
**rumbo** *m.* NAUT. rhumb, bearing, course, direction: *con ~ a,* bound for, in the direction of. *2* fig. course, trend, way. *3* coll. pomp, ostentation. *4* coll. liberality, generosity.
**rumboso, -sa** *adj.* ostentatious, magnificent. *2* liberal, generous.
**rumi** *m.* [among the Moors] Christian.
**rumia** *f.* rumination.
**rumiadura** *f.* RUMIA.
**rumiante** *adj.* ZOOL. ruminant.
**rumiar** *tr.* to ruminate [chew the cud]. *2* to ruminate, meditate. *3* fig. to grumble.
**rumo** *m.* first hoop of a cask.
**rumor** *m.* rumbling sound, murmur. *2* buzz; noise of voices. *3* rumour, report.
**rumorearse** *impers.* to be rumoured.
**rumoroso, -sa** *adj.* noisy, rumbling, murmurous.
**runa** *f.* rune, runic character.
**runfla, runflada** *f.* string, series [of things].
**rúnico, -ca; runo, -na** *adj.* runic.
**runrún** *m.* rumour, report.
**runrunearse** *impers.* to be rumoured.
**ruñar** *tr.* to croze [a stave].
**rupestre** *adj.* rupestrian.

**rupia** *f.* rupee [indian coin]. *2* MED. rupia.
**ruptura** *f.* rupture [breach of harmonious relations]. *2* breaking, fracture.
**ruqueta** *f.* BOT. rocket. *2* BOT. hedge mustard.
**rural** *adj.* rural, country.
**Rusia** *f. pr. n.* GEOG. Russia.
**rusiente** *adj.* candent, red-hot.
**ruso, -sa** *adj.-n.* Russian. *2 m.* Russian [language]. *3* ulster [overcoat].
**rusticano, -na** *adj.* wild [plant].
**rusticar** *intr.* to rusticate.
**rusticidad** *adj.* rusticity.
**rústico, -ca** *adj.* rural. *2* rustic. *3* rough, clumsy. *4* unmannerly. *5* Vulgar [latin]. *6 m.* rustic, peasant. *7* BOOKB. *en rústica,* paperbound.
**ruta** *f.* route, way. *2* NAUT. navigation route, course.
**rutáceo, -a** *adj.* BOT. rutaceous.
**rutenio** *m.* CHEM. ruthenium.
**rutilante** *adj.* poet, shining, sparkling, scintillating.
**rutilar** *intr.* poet. to shine, sparkle, scintillate.
**rutilo** *m.* MINER. rutile.
**rútilo, -la** *adj.* golden, bright, shining.
**rutina** *f.* routine [course of action, etc., adhered to through force of habit]. *2* CHEM. rutin.
**rutinario, -ria** *adj.* routine, routinish. *2 m.-f.* routinist.
**ruzafa** *f.* garden, park.

# S

**S, s** *f.* S, s, twenty-second letter of the Spanish alphabet.

**Sabá** *f. pr. n.* HIST., GEOG. Sheba.

**sábado** *m.* Saturday: ~ *santo,* Holy Saturday. *2* Sabbath [among the Jews].

**sábalo** *m.* ICHTH. shad.

**sábana** *f.* sheet [for a bed]. *2* altarcloth.

**sabana** *f.* savanna, savannah [treeless plain].

**sabandija** *f.* nasty insect or small reptile. *2* fig. vile person, vermin.

**sabanero, -ra** *adj.* (Am.) [pertaining to the] savanna. *2 m.-f.* savanna, dweller.

**sabanilla** *f. dim.* small sheet or piece of linen [towel, napkin, etc.]. *2* outer altar cloth.

**sabañón** *m.* chilblain.

**sabático, -ca** *adj.* Sabbatical; sabbatical.

**sabatina** *f.* ECCL. Saturday office.

**sabatino, -na** *f.* [pertaining to] Saturday.

**sabedor, -ra** *adj.* knowing, informed.

**sabeísmo** *m.* Sabaism.

**sabelotodo** *m.-f.* SABIDILLO.

1) **saber** *m.* knowledge, learning, information.

2) **saber** *tr.* to know [have cognizance of, be apprised or informed of], to be wise to: *hacer* ~, to inform, to let know: *no sé cuantos,* so-and-so, what's his name; *no sé qué, cierto no sé qué, un no sé qué,* a certain something; *¡y qué sé yo!,* and what not, and so forth. *2* to know [posses in the memory]. *3* to know, be able, know how: *Pedro sabe escribir,* Peter can, or knows how to, write. *4 tr.-intr.* ~ *ir a,* ~ *a,* to know the way to. *5 intr.* to know: *a* ~, namely, viz.; *que yo sepa,* as far as I know. *6* to be learned, informed. *7* ~ *a,* to taste of, taste like; to smack of. ¶ CONJUG.: INDIC. Pres.: *sé,* sabes, sabe; sabemos, sabéis, saben. | Imperf.: sabía, sabías, etc. | Pret.: *supe, supiste, supo; supimos, supisteis, supieron.* | Fut.: *sabré, sabrás,* etc. | COND.: *sabría, sabrías,* etc. | SUBJ. Pres.: *sepa, sepas, sepa; sepamos, sepáis, sepan.* | Imperf.: *supiera, supieras, supiera; supiéramos, supierais, supieran,* or *supiese, supiese, supieses; supiese; supiésemos, supieseis, supiesen.* | Fut.: *supiere, supieres, supiere; supiéremos, supiereis, supieren.* | IMPER.: sabe, *sepa; sepamos,* sabed, *sepan.* | PAST. P.: sabido. | GER.: sabiendo.

**sabiamente** *adv.* wisely, prudently.

**sabidillo, -lla** *adj.-n.* coll. pedant, know-it-all.

**sabido, -da** *adj.* known. *2* learned, well-informed.

**sabiduría** *f.* knowledge, learning. *2* wisdom, sapience, sageness.

**sabiendas (a)** *adv.* knowingly, consciously.

**sabihondo, -da** *adj.* know-it-all. *2 m.-f.* know-it-all, wiseacre.

**sabina** *f.* BOT. savin.

**sabino, -na** *adj.* roan [horse]. *2 adj.-n.* HIST. Sabine.

**sabio, -bia** *adj.* knowing, learned; sage, sapient, wise. *2* skilled, skilful. *3* trained [animal]. *4 m.-f.* learned person, scholar, scientist; wise person.

**sablazo** *m.* stroke with a sabre; wound from a sabre. *2* coll. instance of borrowing or sponging.

**sable** *m.* sabre, saber. *2 adj.-n.* HER. sable.

**sablista** *m.* coll. sponger, one who asks for petty loans of money.

**sablón** *m.* coarse sand.

**saboga** *f.* SÁBALO.

**sabogal** *m.* net for catching shad.

**sabor** *m.* taste, flavour, relish, savour, sapor.

**saboreamiento** *m.* flavouring. *2* relishing.

**saborear** *tr.* to flavour, give a zest or relish to. *2* fig. to allure, entice. *3 tr.-ref.* to relish, enjoy.

**sabotaje** *m.* sabotage.

**saboteador, -ra** *m.-f.* saboteur.

**sabotear** *tr.* to sabotage.

**Saboya** *pr. n.* GEOG. Savoy.

**saboyano, -na** *adj.* Savoyard.

**sabroso, -sa** *adj.* savoury, tasty, palatable. *2* pleasant, delightful.

**sabucal** *m.* grove of elders.

**sabuco** *m.* SAÚCO.

**sabueso** *m.* hound, bloodhound [dog]. *2* fig. tracer, sleuth.

**sabugal** *m.* SABUCAL.

**sabuloso, -sa** *adj.* sabulous.

**saburra** *f.* MED. saburra. *2* MED. coat on the tongue.

**saburroso, -sa** *adj.* MED. saburral. *2* coated [tongue].

**saca** *f.* extraction. *2* exportation. *3* sack, large bag.

**sacabalas,** *pl.* **-las** *m.* ARTILL. bullet screw.

**sacabocado(s** *m.* hollow punch; ticket punch.

**sacabotas,** *pl.* **-tas** *m.* bootjack.

**sacacorchos,** *pl.* **-chos** *m.* corkscrew.

**sacadinero(s** *m.* coll. catchpenny. *2* coll. bamboozler.

**sacamiento** *m.* taking out, drawing out.

**sacamuelas,** *pl.* **-las** *m.* coll. tooth puller, dentist. *2* coll. charlatán, quack.
**sacanete** *m.* lansquenet [card game].
**sacaperras,** *pl.* **-rras** *adj.* slot, gambling [machine].
**sacar** *tr.* to draw, draw out, bring out, take out, pull out, extract. *2* to except, exclude. *3* to get out, free: ~ *de pobreza,* to free from poverty. *4* to withdraw, retire. *5* to draw, get, obtain, derive, elicit. *6* to extort. *7* to draw, infer, deduce, make out, solve: ~ *en claro,* or *en limpio,* to deduce, conclude clearly. *8* to publish, bring out, invent, produce. *9* to introduce [a fashion, etc.]. *10* to show, produce, exhibit. *11* to put forth [strength, etc.]. *12* to put out, thrust out, stick out, protrude. *13* to take [a photo], to make [a copy]. *14* to imitate, copy. *15* to take, buy [a ticket]. *16* to draw [a sword, a pistol]. *17* PELOTA. to serve [the ball]. *18* to cite, quote. *19* ~ *a bailar,* to lead out for a dance. *20* ~ *adelante,* to bring up, rear; to pull through. *12* ~ *a luz,* to print, publish; to reveal. *22* ~ *a relucir,* to mention, drag in. *23* ~ *de quicio,* to strain [things]; to exasperate. *24* ~ *la cara por uno,* to stand or to answer, for someone. *25* ~ *la cuenta,* to figure out.
**sacarímetro** *m.* saccaharimeter.
**sacarino, -na** *adj.* saccharine. *2 f.* CHEM. saccharine.
**sacarosa** *f.* CHEM. saccharose.
**sacasillas,** *pl.* **-sillas** *m.* THEAT. stage hand.
**sacatrapos,** *pl.* **-pos** *m.* ARTIL. wormer, wad hook.
**sacerdocio** *m.* priesthood.
**sacerdotal** *adj.* sacerdotal.
**sacerdote** *m.* priest. *2* Roman Catholic priest.
**sacerdotisa** *f.* priestess.
**sácere** *m.* BOT. maple.
**saciar** *tr.* to satiate, so sate. *2 ref.* to become satiated or sated.
**saciedad** *f.* satiety: *hasta la* ~, to satiety.
**saco** *m.* bag, sack: ~ *de noche,* handbag; *no echar en* ~ *roto,* coll. not to forget, not to overlook. *2* bagful, sackful. *3* ANAT., BOT., ZOOL. sac. *4* loose-fitting coat. *5* (Am.) coat [of a man's suit]. *6* sack, pillage, plunder; *entrar a* ~, to sack plunder, loot.
**sacra** *f.* ECCL. sacring tablet.
**sacramentado, -da** *adj.* transubstantiated: *Jesús Sacramentado,* the consecrated Host. *2* having received the last sacraments.
**sacramental** *adj.* sacramental.
**sacramentar** *tr.* THEOL. to transubstantiate. *2* to administer the last sacraments to.
**sacramento** *m.* ECCL. sacrament: *el Santísimo Sacramento,* the Blessed or Holy Sacrament.
**sacratísimo, -ma** *adj.* most sacred or holy.
**sacre** *m.* ORN., ARTIL. saker.
**sacrificador, -ra** *adj.* sacrificing. *2 m.-f.* sacrificer.
**sacrificar** *tr.* to sacrifice. *2* to slaughter [kill for the market]. *3 ref.* to sacrifice oneself. *4* to devote oneself to God.
**sacrificio** *m.* sacrifice: ~ *del altar, Santo Sacrificio,* Sacrifice of the Mass. *2* self-sacrifice.
**sacrilegio** *m.* sacrilege.
**sacrílego, -ga** *adj.* sacrilegious.
**sacristán** *m.* socristan, sexton, parish clerk.
**sacristana** *f.* sexton's wife. *2* nun in charge of the sacristy.
**sacristía** *f.* sacristy, vestry.
**sacro, -cra** *adj.* sacred, holy. *2* ANAT. sacral. *3 m.* ANAT., ZOOL. sacrum.
**sacrosanto, -ta** *adj.* sacred, sacrosanct.

**sacudida** *f.* shake, shaking, jerk, jolt. *2* shock, mental shock.
**sacudidor** *m.* duster [stick, etc., for dusting].
**sacudimiento** *m.* shake, shaking, jerk; shaking off.
**sacudir** *tr.* to shake, jerk, jolt. *2* to beat, dust; to beat out [the dust]. *3* to deal [a blow]. *4* to beat, drub [someone]. *5 ref.* to shake off.
**sáculo** *m.* ANAT. saccule.
**sachar** *tr.* AGR. to weed.
**sacho** *m.* weeder, weeding hoe.
**sádico, -ca** *adj.* sadist, sadistic. *2 m.-f.* sadist.
**sadismo** *m.* sadism.
**saduceo, -a** *adj.* Sadducean. *2 m.-f.* Sadducee.
**saeta** *f.* arrow [missile]. *2* hand, pointer [of watch, clock, etc.]. *3* magnetic needle. *4* a popular Andalousian spiritual song.
**saetada** *f.,* **saetazo** *m.* arrow shot. *2* arrow wound.
**saetero, -ra** *adj.* arrow, pertaining to arrows. *2 m.* archer, bowman. *3 f.* FORT. loophole.
**saetilla** *f. dim.* small arrow. *2* SAETA 2 & 3.
**saetín** *m.* millrace, flume. *2* brad.
**safena** *f. adj.* ANAT. saphenous.
**sáfico, -ca** *adj.-m.* PROS. Sapphic.
**saga** *f.* saga. *2* sorceress.
**sagacidad** *f.* sagacity, sagaciousness.
**sagaz** *adj.* sagacious, shrewd. *2* keen-scented [dog].
**sagita** *f.* GEOM. part of radius between the middle of an arc and its chord.
**sagitado, -da** *adj.* BOT., ZOOL. sagittate, sagittated.
**sagitaria** *f.* BOT. arrowhead.
**sagitario** *m.* archer. *2* (cap.) ASTR. Sagittarius.
**sagrado, -da** *adj.* sacred. *2* hallowed, holy. *3 m.* asylum, place of refuge, sanctuary.
**sagrario** *m.* sacrarium.
**sagú** *m.* BOT. sago, sago palm. *2* sago [starch].
**saguntino, -na** *adj.-n.* Saguntian.
**Sahara** *m. pr. n.* GEOG. Sahara.
**sahornarse** *ref.* [of the skin or a part of the body] to get sore or chafed.
**sahorno** *m.* chafe, chafing [of the skin].
**sahumador** *m.* perfuming pan. *2* clotheshorse.
**sahumar** *tr.* to perfume, fumigate [with odorous smoke].
**sahumerio, sahúmo** *m.* perfuming, fumigation. *2* odorous smoke. *3* aromatics burnt as perfumes.
**sain** *m.* grease, fat [of animals]. *2* greasiness [on clothes].
**sainete** *m.* THEAT. one-act comedy. *2* seasoning, sauce. *3* flavour, relish, spice, zest. *4* tidbit, delicacy.
**sainetero, sainetista** *m.* writer of one-act comedies.
**saíno** *m.* ZOOL. wild boar of South America.
**sajadura** *f.* cut, incision [on the flesh].
**sajar** *tr.* to cut, make incisions on [the flesh].
**sajón, -na** *adj.-n.* Saxon.
**Sajonia** *f. pr. n.* GEOG. Saxony, Saxe.
**sal** *f.* salt [sodium chloride]: ~ *gema,* rock salt. *2* fig. wit, wittiness: ~ *ática,* Attic salt or wit. *3* fig. charm, grace, winning manners. *4* CHEM. salt: ~ *de la Higuera,* Epsom salts. *5* CHEM. ~ *amoníaca* or *amoníaco,* sal ammoniac.
**sala** *f.* drawing-room, living room, parlour. *2* hall, large room, room: ~ *de clase,* classroom; ~ *de espectáculos,* auditorium [of a theatre, cinema, etc.]; ~ *de espera,* waiting-room. *3* ward [in a hospital]. *4* LAW division of an *Audiencia,* court, law court.
**salabardo** *m.* scoop net, dip net.
**salacidad** *f.* salacity, lechery.

**salacot** *m.* topee, topi, pith hat, pith helmet, sun helmet.
**saladar** *m.* salt marsh. *2* saline ground.
**saladero** *m.* salting place, salting house or room.
**salado, -da** *adj.* salty, briny; brine-soaked, salt, salted: *pesca salada*, salt fish, salted fish. *2* coll. witty, amusing. *3* coll. charming, graceful, winsome. *4* (Am.) expensive.
**salamandra** *f.* ZOOL., MYTH. salamander: ~ *acuática*, newt. *2* a kind of heating stove.
**salamandria** *f.* SALAMANQUESA.
**salamanquesa** *f.* ZOOL. tarente.
**salangana** *f.* ORN. salangane.
**salar** *tr.* to salt [season or preserve with salt], to corn [meat]. *2* COOK. to put too much salt on.
**salario** *m.* wages, salary.
**salaz** *adj.* salacious, lecherous.
**salazón** *f.* salting [of meat or fish]. *2* salt meat or fish. *3* salt-meat, salt-meat business.
**salceda** *f.*, **salcedo** *m.* willow grove, salicetum.
**salcochar** *tr.* COOK. to boil.
**salchicha** *f.* sausage.
**salchichón** *m.* aug. large sausage.
**saldado, -da** *adj.* paid [debt]; settled [account].
**saldar** *tr.* to settle, liquidate [an account]. *2* to sell [goods] at reduced prices.
**saldista** *m.-f.* liquidation broker; remnant dealer.
**saldo** *m.* COM. balance [of an account]. *2* settlement, liquidation. *3* remainder of goods sold at reduced prices.
**saldré, saldría**, etc. *irr.* V. SALIR.
**saledizo, -za** *adj.* projecting. *2 m.* SALIDIZO.
**salegar** *m.* place for giving salt to cattle.
**salero** *m.* salt cellar, saltshaker. *2* storage place for salt. *3* SALEGAR. *4* coll. nimble-wit, address, easy and graceful deportment.
**saleroso, -sa** *adj.* lively, charming, graceful, winsome.
**salesa** *adj.-f.* Salesian [of the Order of Visitation].
**salesiano, -na** *adj.* Salesian [of the order of men founded by Dom Bosco]. *2 m.* Salesian father.
**saleta** *f. dim.* little drawing room.
**salgar** *tr.* to feed salt to [cattle].
**salgo, salga**, etc. *irr.* V. SALIR.
**salicáceo, -a** *adj.* BOT. salicaceous.
**salicaria** *f.* BOT. loosestrife, purple loosestrife.
**salicilato** *m.* CHEM. salicylate.
**salicílico, -ca** *adj.* CHEM. salicylic.
**sálico, -ca** *adj.* Salic.
**salicor** *f.* BOT. saltwort, prickly saltwort.
**salida** *f.* going out, coming out, outgoing, outcoming, egress, exit, issue emergence. *2* start, departure, leaving. *3* excursion, outing. *4* MIL. sally, sortie. *5* discharge [of a liquid, etc.]. *6* springing, sprouting, growing [of buds, leaves, hair, etc.]. *7* rise [of the sun, the moon, etc.]. *8* coming out, publication. *9* outlay, expenditure. *10* COM. sale, salableness: *tener* ~, to sell well; fig. [of a young lady] to be popular with the young men. *11* exit, outlet, issue, vent, way out. *12* end [of a street; of the winter, summer, etc.]. *13* outlaying fields [near a town gate]. *14* issue termination. *15* sally, witty remark. *16* salient, jut, projection. *17* NAUT. headway. *18* lead [at games]. *19* SPORT. start. *20* ~ *de baño*, bathrobe. *21* ~ *de teatro*, opera cloak. *22* ~ *de tono*, rude or irrelevant remark.
**salidizo** *m.* ARCH. projection, ledge, corbel.
**salido, -da** *adj.* salient, projecting.
**saliente** *adj.* salient, projecting. *2* GEOM. salient

[angle]. *3* outgoing. *4 m.* salient, jut, prominence. *5* east, sunrise.
**salificar** *tr.* CHEM. to salify.
**salina** *f.* salt mine. *2* salt pit, salt pan, saltworks.
**salinero** *adj.* spotted red and white [bull]. *2 m.* salt maker, salt dealer, salter.
**salir** *intr.* to go out, come out, issue; to sally. *2* to depart, leave, start, set out. *3* to get out [of a vehicle]. *4* to project, protrude, start, stand out. *5* to appear. *6* THEAT. to enter. *7* [of a book, etc.] to come out. *8* to spring, come [of], issue [from], originate [in]. *9* to offer, present itself; to be offered to one. *10* [of a season] to end. *11* [of a stain] to come off. *12* [of the sun] to rise. *13* [of hair, plants, etc.] to spring, shoot, grow. *14* to come, result, turn out. *15* to come out [from a contest, etc.] to be: ~ *vencedor*, to win; to be the victor. *16* to be first to play [in certain games]. *17* to be drawn [in a lottery]. *18* to be elected [by ballot]. *19* to cost [a price]. *20* [of a stream] to debouch. *21* [of a street, road, etc.] to lead [to]. *22* to take after, resemble. *23* ~ *adelante*, to be successful. *24* ~ *al encuentro*, to come out to meet; to oppose. *25* ~ *bien*, to do well, come right. *26* ~ *con*, to come out with [an unexpected, or irrelevant remark, etc.]. *27* ~ *[uno] de sus casillas*, to lose one's temper. *28* ~ *mal*, to do badly; to fail. *29* salga lo que saliese, whatever may happen.
*30* ref. [of a vessel] to leak. *31* to run over, overflow. *32* to come out [of its socket, etc.]. *33* salirse con la suya, to have one's way.
¶ IRREG. CONJUG.: INDIC. Pres.: *salgo*, sales, sale: *salimos*, salís, salen. | Fut.: *saldré*, *saldrás*, *saldrá*; *saldremos*, *saldréis*, *saldrán*. | COND.: *saldría*, *saldrías*, *saldría*; *saldríamos*, *saldríais*, *saldrían*. | SUBJ. Pres.: *salga*, *salgas*, *salga*; *salgamos*, *salgáis*, *salgan*. | IMPER.: *sal*, *salga*; *salgamos*, salid, *salgan*.
**salitral** *adj.* SALITROSO. *2 m.* saltpetre bed.
**salitre** *m.* saltpetre, saltpeter, nitre, niter.
**salitroso, -sa** *adj.* saltpetrous, nitrous.
**saliva** *f.* saliva, spittle: *tragar* ~, coll. to suffer an offence, vexation, etc. in silence.
**salivación** *f.* salivation.
**salival** *adj.* salivary.
**salivazo** *m.* spit [spitted saliva].
**salmantino, -na** *adj.-n.* [of] Salamanca.
**salmear** *tr.* to sing psalms.
**salmista** *m.* psalmist. *2* ECCL. chanter of psalms.
**salmo** *m.* psalm.
**salmodia** *f.* psalmody. *2* fig. singsong.
**salmodiar** *intr.* to sing psalms, salmodize. *2 tr.* to singsong, sing monotonously.
**salmón** *m.* ICHTH. salmon.
**salmonado, -da** *adj.* salmon-like. *2* salmon [in colour].
**salmonete** *m.* ICHTH. red mullet, surmullet.
**salmuera** *f.* brine, pickle.
**salobral** *adj.* saline [ground]. *2 m.* saline ground.
**salobre** *adj.* brackish, briny, saltish.
**salobreño, -ña** *adj.* saline [ground].
**salobridad** *f.* saltiness, brackishness.
**saloma** *f.* NAUT. chantey.
**Salomé** *f. pr. n.* Salome.
**Salomón** *m. pr. n.* Solomon.
**salomónico, -ca** *adj.* Solomonic. *2* ARCH. twisted [column].
**salón** *m.* drawing room, reception room. *2* hall, large room, assembly hall: ~ *de baile*, ballroom. *3* saloon. *4* ~ *de belleza*, beauty parlour.

**salpicadero** *m.* dashboard [in cars].

**salpicadura** *f.* splash, splashing, spattering. *2 pl.* fig. indirect results.

**salpicar** *tr.* to splash, bespatter, sprinkle. *2* to intersperse. *3* fig. to read or touch on without order.

**salpicón** *m.* salmagundi. *2* SALPICADURA.

**salpimentar** *tr.* to season with pepper and salt. *2* fig. to spice, intersperse. ¶ CONJUG. like *acertar*.

**salpresar** *tr.* to preserve with salt.

**salpullido** *m.* rash, fine eruption. *2* flea bites.

**salpullir** *tr.* to cause a rash. *2 ref.* to break out [have a rash]. ¶ CONJUG. like *mullir*.

**salsa** *f.* COOK. gravy, dressing, sauce. *2* fig. sauce [something that adds piquancy].

**salsedumbre** *f.* saltiness.

**salsera** *f.* sauceboat; gravy boat, gravy dish.

**salserilla** *f. dim.* small saucer [to mix paints].

**salsifí** *m.* BOT. salsify.

**saltabanco(s** *m.* mountebank. *2* juggler, tumbler.

**saltación** *f.* saltation, leaping, dancing.

**saltadizo, -za** *adj.* jumping, leaping. *2* hopping [insect]. *3 m.-f.* jumper, leaper. *4 m.* skipping rope.

**saltamontes** *m.* ENT. grasshopper.

**saltante** *adj.* jumping, leaping. *2* salient.

**saltar** *intr.* to spring, jump, leap, bounce, hop, skip. *2* [of water, etc.] to spurt, jet, shoot up. *3* [of sparks, etc.] to fly. *4* to snap, burst, break off: ~ *en pedazos*, to fly into pieces. *5* [of a button, etc.] to come off. *6* to project, stand out. *7* to start, show emotion or resentment. *8* to come out with [an irrelevant or unexpected remark]. *9* NAUT. [of the wind] to shift. *10* ~ *a la vista*, to be self-evident. *11 tr.* to jump over, leap [a wall, ditch, etc.]. *12* to skip, to do [something] desultorily. *13 tr.-ref.* to skip, omit.

**saltarín, -na** *adj.* jumping, dancing. *2 m.-f.* jumper, dancer. *3 m.* feather-brained youth.

**salteador** *m.* footpad, highwayman.

**salteamiento** *m.* highway robbery, assault, holdup.

**saltear** *tr.* to hold up, rob on the high way. *2* to assault, attack. *3* to skip, to do [something] desultorily. *4* COOK. to sauté.

**salterio** *m.* Psalter. *2* Rosary. *3* MUS. psaltery.

**saltimbanco, saltimbanqui** *m.* SALTABANCO.

**salto** *m.* spring, jump, leap, bound, hop, skip: ~ *de altura*, SPORT. high jump; ~ *de agua*, waterfall, falls; ~ *de carnero*, bucking [of a horse]; ~ *en el vacío*, leap in the dark; ~ *mortal*, somersault; *dar un* ~, to jump, leap; *a* ~ *de mata*, flying and hiding; *en un* ~, in a flash, quickly. *2* SWIM. dive. *3* skip, omission. *4* palpitation [of heart]. *5* leapfrog.

**saltón, -na** *adj.* jumping. *2* prominent, protruding. *3 m.* ENT. small grasshopper.

**salubre** *adj.* salubrious, healthful.

**salubridad** *f.* salubrity, healthfulness.

**salud** *f.* health; ¡*a su* ~!, to your health!; *gastar* ~, to enjoy good health; *vender* or *verter* ~, to radiate health. *2* welfare. *3* salvation. *4 interj.* coll. greetings!, hello!

**saludable** *adj.* salutary, healthful, wholesome.

**saludador, -ra** *m.-f.* greeter, saluter. *3 m.* a kind of quack doctor.

**saludar** *tr.* to greet, salute, hail, to give greetings or regards to. *2* MIL. to salute. *3* MIL. to fire a salute to. *4* NAUT. to dip the flag to.

**saludo** *m.* greeting, salutation, salute, bow. *2* MIL. salute. *3 pl.* compliments, regards.

**salumbre** *f.* flower of salt.

**salutación** *f.* salutation, greeting.

**salutífero, -ra** *adj.* salutiferous, healthful, wholesome.

**salva** *f.* salvo: ~ *de aplausos*, salvo or round of applause. *2* salutation, welcome. *3* obs. tasting of viands before are served. *4* SALVILLA.

**salvabarros, ** *pl.* **-rros** *m.* mudguard.

**salvación** *f.* salvation, saving. *2* escape, deliverance.

**salvadera** *f.* sandbox [for sprinkling and on ink].

**salvado** *m.* bran.

**salvador, -ra** *adj.* saving, rescuing, delivering. *2 m.-f.* saviour, rescuer, deliverer: *el Salvador*, the Saviour; El Salvador [American country].

**salvaguarda** *f.* SALVAGUARDIA.

**salvaguardia** *f.* safeguard, protection, security. *2* safeguard, safe-conduct. *3 m.* guard watch.

**salvajada** *f.* savagery, brutal action. *2* stupid action.

**salvaje** *adj.* savage. *2* wild [country, land, beast, plant]. *3* brutish, rude, stupid. *4 m.-f.* savage.

**salvajería** *f.* SALVAJADA.

**salvajino, -na** *adj.* wild [beast, plant]; of wild beast. *3 f.* wild beasts. *4* game [flesh of wild beasts].

**salvajismo** *m.* savagery.

**salvamanteles** *m.* table mat.

**salvamento, salvamiento** *m.* saving, rescuing. *2* salvage. *3* lifesaving. *4* place of safety.

**salvante** *adj.* saving. *2 adv.* saving, excepting.

**salvar** *tr.* to save, rescue, deliver. *2* to save [in a spiritual sense]. *3* to salve, salvage. *4* to overcome [a difficulty]. *5* to go over, negotiate, bridge; to clear, surmount [an obstacle]; to cover [a distance]. *6* to make an exception of. *7 ref.* to be saved. *8* to escape danger: *sálvese el que pueda*, everyone for himself.

**salvavidas, ** *pl.* **-das** *m.* NAUT. life preserver, life belt: *bote* ~, lifeboat. *2* guard [in front of electric cars].

**¡salve!** *interj.* hail! *2 f.* salve, Salve regina.

**salvedad** *f.* reservation, exception, qualification.

**salvia** *f.* BOT. sage, salvia.

**salvilla** *f.* tray for glasses or cups.

1) **salvo** *adv.* save, saving, excepting, barring.

2) **salvo, -va** *adj.* saved, safe: *a* ~, safe, out of danger. *2* excepted, omitted: *dejar a* ~, to set aside, make an exception of.

**salvoconducto** *m.* safe-conduct.

**sallar** *tr.* AGR. to weed.

**sámago** *m.* sapwood.

**sámara** *f.* BOT. samara.

**samaritano, -na** *adj.-n.* Samaritan.

**samario** *m.* CHEM. samarium.

**sambenito** *m.* fig. dishonour, disgrace. *2* note of infamy; disgrace.

**samblaje** *m.* ENSAMBLADURA.

**sambuca** *f.* MUS. sambuke. *2* MIL. an ancient war engine.

**samio, mia** *adj.-n.* Samian.

**samnita, samnite** *adj.-n.* Samnite.

**samoano, -na** *adj.-n.* Samoan.

**Samotracia** *f. pr. n.* GEOG. Samothrace.

**samoyedo, -da** *adj.-n.* Samoyed, Samoyede.

**sampán** *m.* NAUT. sampan.

**san** *adj.* apocopated form of SANTO, used only before masculine names of saints, except Tomás, Tomé, Toribio and Domingo.

**sanable** *adj.* curable, healable.

**sanador, -ra** *adj.* healing. *2 m.-f.* curer, healer.

**sanar** *tr.* to heal, cure. *2 intr.* to heal; to recover sickness.
**sanativo, -va** *adj.* sanative, curative.
**sanatorio** *m.* sanatorium, sanitarium.
**sanción** *f.* sanction. *2* ratification of an act of Parliament by the king or the President.
**sancionable** *adj.* sanctionable.
**sancionar** *tr.* to sanction. *2* to ratify [an act of Parliament].
**sancochar** *tr.* COOK. to parboil [boil partially].
**sancocho** *m.* parboiled meat.
**sancta** *m.* fore part of tabernacle.
**sanctasanctórum,** *pl.* **-rum** *m.* sanctum sanctorum.
**sanctus** *m.* ECCL. Sanctus.
**sandalia** *f.* sandal.
**sándalo** *m.* BOT. sandalwood. *2* BOT. bergamot mint.
**sandáraca** *f.* sandarac.
**sandez** *f.* stupidity, silliness. *2* inanity, foolish or stupid act or remark, piece of nonsense.
**sandía** *f.* BOT. watermelon.
**sandio, -dia** *adj.* stupid, foolish, silly.
**sandunga** *f.* charm, easy and graceful deportment.
**sandunguero, -ra** *adj.* charming, graceful, winsome.
**sandwich** *m.* Angl. sandwich.
**saneado, -da** *adj.* free from charges or deductions [property, income, etc.].
**saneamiento** *m.* sanitation. *2* drainage [of land]. *3* reparation.
**sanear** *tr.* to improve the sanitary conditions of. *2* to drain [lands]. *3* to repair, improve.
**sanedrín** *m.* Sanhedrin.
**sangrador** *m.* bloodletter. *2* drain, outlet.
**sangradura** *f.* SANGRÍA 1 & 6. *2* drain, outlet.
**sangrar** *tr.* SURG. to bleed. *2* to drain, open an outlet in. *3* RESINAR. *4* PRINT. to indent. *5 intr.* to bleed [emit blood]. *6 ref.* to have oneself bled.
**sangre** *f.* blood [liquid; temperament; race, family]; gore; ~ *fría*, fig. cold blood; sangfroid; serenity; *mala* ~, wicked or revengeful disposition; *subírsele a uno la* ~ *a la cabeza*, to lose one's self-control; *tener* ~ *de horchata*, to be phlegmatic; *a* ~ *caliente*, impulsively; *a* ~ *fría*, in cold blood; *a* ~ *y fuego*, by fire and sword.
**sangría** *f.* SURG. bleeding, bloodletting. *2* fig. bleeding [draining of money, etc.]. *3* tap, tapping [in a pine, a furnace, etc.]. *4* PRINT. indentation. *5* inner pit of the arm opposite to the elbow. *6* sangaree.
**sangriento, -ta** *adj.* bleeding, bloody, gory. *2* sanguinary. *3* cruel, savage. *4* poet. blood-red.
**sangüesa** *f.* FRAMBUESA.
**sanguificación** *f.* PHYSIOL. sanguification.
**sanguijuela** *f.* ZOOL. leech. *2* fig. leech [person].
**sanguina** *f.* sanguine [crayon; drawing].
**sanguinaria** *f.* MINER. bloodstone. *2* BOT. ~ *mayor*, knotgrass; ~ *menor*, witlowwort.
**sanguinario, -ria** *adj.* sanguinary bloodthirsty.
**sanguíneo, -a** *adj.* sanguineous. *2* sanguine [temperament].
**sanguinolencia** *f.* sanguinolency.
**sanguinolento, -ta** *adj.* sanguinolent, bloody, bloodstained.
**sanguiñuelo** *m.* CORNEJO.
**sanguis** *m.* blood of Christ, consecrated wine.
**sanguisorba** *f.* BOT. burnet.
**sanícula** *f.* BOT. sanicle.
**sanidad** *f.* soundness, health, healthfulness; ~ *mi-*

*litar*, Army Medicine Corps; ~ *pública*, public health, health department.
**sanie, sanies** *f.* MED. sanies.
**sanitario, -ria** *adj.* sanitary. *2 m.* MIL. officer or soldier of the Medicine Corps.
**sanjuaneño, -ña, sanjuanero, -ra** *adj.* ripe by St. John's Day [fruit].
**sanjuanista** *m.* knight of St. John of Jerusalem.
**sanmiguelada** *f.* Michaelmastide.
**sano, -na** *adj.* healthy, in good health, hale, fit. *2* healthful; salutary, wholesome. *3* sound [body, mind, fruit, doctrine, policy, etc.]; harmless: ~ *y salvo*, safe and sound. *4* whole [not broken]. *5* wise, discreet. *6* fig. *cortar por lo* ~, to take drastic measures.
**sánscrito, -ta** *adj.-m.* Sanskrit.
**sanseacabó** *interj.* coll. finished!
**sansirolée** *m.-f.* simpleton.
**Sansón** *m. pr. n.* BIBL. & fig. Samson.
**santa** *f.* female saint. *2* Saint, St. [before feminine names]. *3* saintly, virtuous woman.
**santabárbara** *f.* NAUT. magazine, powder room.
**santaláceo, -a** *adj.* BOT. santalaceous.
**santamente** *adv.* in a saintly manner, like a saint, virtuously. *2* coll. well, discreetly, wisely.
**santanderino, -na** *adj.-n.* of Santander.
**Santelmo** *m. fuego de* ~, St. Elmo's fire.
**santero, -ra** *m.-f.* caretaker of a sanctuary. *3* collector of alms who carries a saint's image.
**Santiago** *m. pr. n.* James. *2* Saint James.
**santiagués, -sa** *adj.-n.* of Santiago de Compostela.
**santiaguino, -na** *adj.* pertaining to Santiago de Chile. *2 m.-f.* native or inhabitant of Santiago de Chile.
**santiaguista** *m.* knight of Santiago.
**santiamén (en un)** *adv.* in an instant, in a jiffy, in the twinkling of an eye.
**santidad** *f.* sanctity, saintliness, holiness, godliness. *3 Su Santidad*, His Holiness [the Pope].
**santificación** *f.* sanctification.
**santificador, -ra** *adj.* santifying. *2 m.-f.* sanctifier.
**santificar** *tr.* to sanctify. *2* to hallow. *3* ~ *las fiestas*, to keep holy days. *4 ref.* to become sanctified.
**santiguada** *f.* act of blessing or crossing oneself.
**santiguador, -ra** *m.-f.* person pretending to effect cures by crossing the patients.
**santiguar** *tr.* to bless, cross, make the sign of the cross upon. *2* to treat sickness superstitiously by signs of the cross. *3 ref.* to bless oneself, cross oneself.
**santimonia** *f.* sanctity, saintliness, holiness.
**santísimo, -ma** *adj. superl.* of SANTO. *2* most holy. *3 m. el Santísimo*, the blessed Sacrament.
**santito, -ta** *m.-f. dim.* little saint. *2* fig. good child.
**santo, -ta** *adj.* canonized by the Church. *2* saint, holy, sacred, blessed: *el Santo Patrón*, the Holy Father. *3* saintly, godly, virtuous. *4* ~ *varón*, simple, artless man. *5* coll. *en el* ~ *suelo*, on the naked ground; *su santa voluntad*, his own sweet will; *todo el* ~ *día*, the whole day long. *6 adv. santo y bueno*, good and well. *7 m.* saint: *Todos los Santos*, All Saints' Day. *8* fête, fête day. *9* image of a saint. *10* coll. picture [in a book]. *11 írsele a uno el* ~ *al cielo*, to forget what one was up to. *13 m.-f.* saintly, godly, virtuous person.
**Santo Domingo** *f. pr. n.* GEOG. Hispaniola [island].
**santón** *m.* Mohammedan ascetic. *2* coll. hypocrite. *3* coll. big man, boss.
**santónico** *m.* BOT. wormwood.

**santoral** *m.* calendar of saints' days. *2* the lives of the saints.

**santuario** *m.* sanctuary [church, shrine]. *2* sanctum sanctorum.

**santurrón, -na** *adj.* sanctimonious. *2 m.-f.* sanctimonious person.

**saña** *f.* rage, fury. *2* cruelty.

**sañoso, -sa; sañudo, -da** *adj.* furious, cruel.

**sapidez** *f.* sapidity.

**sápido, -da** *adj.* sapid [possessing flavour].

**sapiencia** *f.* sapience, wisdom. *2* BIBL. Wisdom of Solomon.

**sapiente** *adj.* sage, learned.

**sapillo** *m. dim.* little toad. *2* RÁNULA.

**sapindáceo, -a** *adj.* BOT. sapindaceous.

**sapo** *m.* ZOOL. toad: *echar sapos y culebras*, fig. to utter angry words.

**saponáceo, -a** *adj.* saponaceous, soapy.

**saponaria** *f.* BOT. soapwort.

**saponificar** *tr.* to saponify.

**sapotáceo, -a** *adj.* BOT. sapotaceous.

**sapote** *m.* ZAPOTE.

**saque** *m.* a drawing out: *tener buen* ~, coll. to be a heavy eater or drinker. *2* PELOTA serving of the ball.

**saqueador, -ra** *m.-f.* sacker, pillager, plunderer.

**saqueamiento** *m.* saqueo.

**saquear** *tr.* to sack, pillage, plunder, loot.

**saqueo** *m.* sack, sacking, pillage, plunder.

**saquera** *adj.* packing [needle].

**saquería** *f.* manufacture of sacks. *2* sacks [collect.].

**saquerío** *m.* sacks [collect.].

**saquito** *m. dim.* little sack or bag.

**Sara** *f. pr. n.* Sarah.

**sarampión** *m.* MED. measles.

**sarao** *m.* soirée, evening party.

**sarcasmo** *m.* sarcasm.

**sarcástico, -ca** *adj.* sarcastic.

**sarcocarpio** *m.* BOT. sarcocarp.

**sarcófago** *m.* sarcophagus.

**sarcoma** *f.* MED. sarcoma.

**sardana** *f.* a Catalonian dance and its music.

**Sardanápalo** *m. pr. n.* HIST. Sardanapalus.

**sardina** *f.* ICHTH. sardine: *como sardinas en banasta* or *en barril*, coll. packed like sardines.

**sardinal** *m.* sardine net.

**sardinel** *m.* MAS. rowlock.

**sardinero, -ra** *adj.* [pertaining to] sardine. *2 m.-f.* sardine dealer.

**sardineta** *f. dim.* small sardine. *2* MIL. a kind of chevron.

**sardo, -da** *adj.-n.* Sardinian.

**sardónice** *f.* MINER. sardonyx.

**sardónico, -ca** *adj.* sardonic.

**sarga** *f.* serge. *2* painted wall fabric. *3* BOT. a variety of willow.

**sargado, -da** *adj.* ASARGADO.

**sargatillo** *m.* BOT. a variety of willow.

**sargazo** *m.* BOT. sargasso, gulfweed.

**sargentía** *f.* sergeancy, sergeantship.

**sargento** *m.* MIL. sergeant.

**sargentona** *f.* coll. big rude virago.

**sargo** *m.* ICHTH. sargo.

**sarmentar** *intr.* to gather pruned vine shoots.

**sarmentoso, -sa** *adj.* sarmentous, vinelike. *2* thin and knotty.

**sarmiento** *m.* vine shoot.

**sarna** *f.* MED. itch, mange, scabies.

**sarnoso, -sa** *adj.* itchy, mangy, scabious.

**sarpullido** *m.* SALPULLIDO.

**sarraceno, -na** *adj.-n.* Saracen.

**sarracina** *f.* row, fight, scuffle.

**sarria** *f.* coarse net for carrying straw.

**sarrillo** *m.* death rattle. *2* BOT. arum.

**sarro** *m.* crust, incrustation [in vessels]. *2* tartar [on teeth]. *3* SABURRA. *4* BOT. rust, mildew.

**sarroso, -sa** *adj.* crusty, incrusted [vessel]. *2* full of tartar [teeth].

**sarta** *f.* string [of beads, pearls, etc.]. *2* fig. string, series: *una* ~ *de mentiras*, a string of lies.

**sartén** *f.* frying pan: *tener la* ~ *por el mango*, to have the upper hand.

**sartenada** *f.* contents of a frying pan.

**sartorio** *adj.* ANAT. sartorius [muscle].

**sasafrás** *m.* BOT. sassafras.

**sastra** *f.* tailor's wife. *2* tailoress.

**sastre** *m.* tailor.

**sastrería** *f.* tailor's trade. *2* tailor's shop.

**sastresa** *f.* SASTRA.

**Satán, Satanás** *m. pr.* Satan, Satanas, the Devil.

**satánico, -ca** *adj.* satanic, satanical.

**satélite** *m.* ASTR. satellite. *2* fig. satellite, follower.

**satén** *m.* sateen.

**satín** *m.* satinwood.

**satinar** *tr.* to satin, calender, glaze [paper or fabrics]. *2* PHOT. to burnish.

**sátira** *f.* satire.

**satírico, -ca** *adj.* satiric, satirical. *2* satyric. *3 m.* satirist.

**satirizar** *tr.* to satirize; to lampoon.

**sátiro** *m.* satyr [silvan god]. *2* fig. satyr [lustful man].

**satisfacción** *f.* satisfaction: *a* ~, fully, according to one wishes. *2* confidence, conceit: ~ *de sí mismo*, conceit.

**satisfacer** *tr.* to satisfy. *2* to comply with, to answer, meet. *3* to settle, pay. *4 ref.* to satisfy oneself; to be satisfied. ¶ CONJUG. like *hacer*.

**satisfactorio, -ria** *adj.* satisfactory.

**satisfago, satisfaga,** etc. *irr.* V. SATISFACER.

**satisfecho, -cha** *p. p.* of SATISFACER. *2* satisfied, content. *3* vain, conceited.

**satisfice, satisficiera,** etc. *irr.* V. SATISFACER.

**sativo, -va** *adj.* cultivated [plant].

**sátrapa** *m.* satrap.

**saturar** *tr.* to saturate. *2* to satiate.

**saturnal** *adj.* Saturnian. *2 f. pl.* Saturnalia.

**saturnino, -na** *adj.* saturnine, gloomy, morose. *2* CHEM., MED. saturnine.

**Saturno** *m.* ASTR. Saturn. *2* CHEM. lead.

**sauce** *m.* BOT. willow, white willow.

**sauceda** *f.*, **saucedal** *m.*, **saucera** *f.* willow plantation.

**saúco** *f.* BOT. elder [*Sambucus nigra*].

**sauquillo** *m.* BOT. snowball.

**saurio, -ria** *adj.-m.* ZOOL. saurian.

**sauzgatillo** *m.* BOT. agnus castus, chaste tree.

**savia** *f.* BOT. sap. *2* fig. sap.

**saxífraga** *f.* BOT. saxifrage. *2* BOT. sassafras.

**saxifragáceo, -a** *adj.* BOT. saxifragaceous.

**saxofón, saxófono** *m.* MUS. saxophone.

**saya** *f.* skirt [garment]; petticoat.

**sayal** *m.*, **sayales** *m.* a coarse woollen cloth.

**sayo** *m.* a kind of cassock or loose coat: *cortar un* ~ *a*, to talk behind the back of; *decir para su* ~, to say to oneself. *2* coll. any garment.

**sayón** *m.* medieval executioner.

**sazón** *f.* ripeness, maturity. *2* season, time, opportunity. *3* taste, flavour. *4 a la* ~, then, at that time; *en* ~, ripe; in season, opportunely.

**sazonado, -da** *adj.* seasoned, ripe. *2* seasoned, spiced.

**sazonador, -ra** *adj.* ripening. *2* seasoning.

**sazonar** *tr.* to ripen, mature. *2* to season [food]. *3* to season, flavour, give zest to. *4 ref.* to ripen, mature [grow ripe, become mature].

**se** *3rd person form of ref. pron. for every gender and number.* Its uses are: *1* As a ref. acc. or dat. case, equivalent to «himself», «oneself», «yourself», «themselves», «yourselves»; «to himself», «to herself», etc. *2* As a reciprocal pron., equivalent to: «each other», «one another», «to one another». *3* As a dat. case before the acc. *lo, la, los, las: yo ~ lo di,* I gave it to him [or her, it, you, them]. *4* to give a possessive value to the def. or indef. article: *él ~ lava las manos,* he washes his hands. *5* As an expletive forming verbs reflexive in form but transitive or intransitive in meaning: *el hombre ~ fue,* the man went away. *6* to form expressions of passive or impersonal character: *~ dice,* it is said, they say, people say; *no ~ puede negar,* it cannot be denied.

**sé** *irr.* V. SABER.

**sé, sea,** etc. *irr.* V. SER.

**sebáceo, -a** *adj.* sebaceous.

**sebo** *m.* tallow, suet; candle grease. *2* fat, grease.

**seborrea** *f.* MED. seborrhoea, seborrhea.

**seboso, -sa** *adj.* tallowy, fat, unctous; greasy.

**seca** *f.* drought, dry season. *2* NAUT. dry sand bank. *3 adv. a secas,* V. SECO.

**secadal** *m.* SEQUEDAL. *2* AGR. unwatered land.

**secadero, -ra** *adj.* fit for drying [fruit, tobacco]. *2 m.* drying place, drying shed or room.

**secador, -ra** *adj.* drying. *2 m.-f.* dryer. *3 m.* drying contrivance; drying room.

**secamente** *adj.* dryly, curtly, shortly, brusquely.

**secamiento** *m.* drying; desiccation.

**secano** *m.* AGR. unwatered land, dry land: *cultivo de ~,* dry farming. *2* NAUT. dry and bank.

**secante** *adj.* drying. *2* blotting [paper]. *3 adj.-f.* GEOM., TRIG. secant. *4 m.* drying oil. *5* blotting paper.

**secar** *tr.* to dry, dry up. *2* to dessicate. *3* to wipe dry. *4* to parch. *5* coll. to bore, annoy. *6 ref.* to dry oneself. *7* to dry, get dry. *8* [of plants] to wither. *9* [of moisture, a well, etc.] to dry up, run dry. *10* to become lean, meagre. *11* to be thirsty.

**secatón, -na** *adj.* coll. dull, vapid, insipid.

**sección** *f.* section [in practically every sense]. *2* division [of a bureau or department]. *3* department [of a store]. *4* column [in newspapers].

**seccionado, -da** *adj.* sectional, in sections.

**seccionar** *tr.* to section. *2* to cut, cut off.

**secesión** *f.* secession.

**seco, -ca** *adj.* dry [in practically every sense]. *2* dried up. *3* juiceless. *4* arid. *5* withered dead [plants, leaves, etc.]. *6* lean, thin, meagre [person or animal]. *7* unadorned, bare, undiluted, strict. *8* curt, short, brusque. *9* hard, unfeeling. *10 dejar ~,* coll. to kill. *11 a secas,* merely; and nothing more. *12 en ~,* high and dry; dry; by the dry process; without cause or reason: dead, short, suddenly.

**secoya** *f.* BOT. sequoia.

**secreción** *f.* PHYSIOL. secretion.

**secreta** *f.* ECCL. secret [in the Mass]. *2* coll. plainclothes men, detective service.

**secretar** *tr.* PHYSIOL. to secrete.

**secretaria** *f.* woman secretary. *2* wife of a secretary.

**secretaría** *f.* secretary's office. *2* secretaryship.

**secretariado** *m.* secretariat, secretariate.

**secretario** *m.* secretary.

**secretear** *intr.* coll. to whisper [converse privately].

**secreteo** *m.* coll. whispering [private talk].

**secreter** *m.* secretary [writing desk].

**secreto, -ta** *adj.* secret. *2 m.* secret; secrecy: *~ a voces,* open secret; *de ~,* secretly; *en ~,* secretly, in secret, confidentially. *3* secret drawer. *4* key, secret combination [for opening a lock]. *5* MUS. soundboard [of organ, etc.].

**secretor, -ra; secretorio, -ria** *adj.* PHYSIOL. secretory.

**secta** *f.* sect.

**sectador, -ra; sectario, -ria** *adj.* sectarian. *2 m.-f.* sectarian, sectary.

**sectarismo** *m.* sectarianism.

**sector** *m.* sector.

**secuaz** *m.* follower, henchman.

**secuela** *f.* sequel, result, consequence.

**secuencia** *f.* CINE., LITURG. sequence.

**secuestrar** *tr.* LAW to sequester, sequestrate. *2* to kidnap, abduct.

**secuestro** *m.* LAW sequestration. *2* kidnapping, abduction. *3* SURG. sequestrum.

**secular** *adj.* secular.

**secularizar** *tr.* to secularize. *2* to impropriate.

**secundar** *tr.* to second, aid, support.

**secundario, -ria** *adj.* secondary. *2* GEOL. Secondary.

**secura** *f.* dryness, condition of drought.

1) **sed** *f.* thirst: *tener ~,* to be thirsty. *2* need for water, dryness [of land or plants].

2) **sed** *imper.* of SER.

**seda** *f.* silk [fibre, yarn and fabric]: *como una ~,* smooth as silk; pliable; easily, without hitch or hindrance. *2* wild boar's bristle.

**sedal** *m.* fishline. *2* SURG. seton. *3* VET. rowel.

**sedalina** *f.* silkaline, schappe.

**sedán** *m.* AUTO. sedan.

**sedante** *adj.-m.* sedative.

**sedar** *tr.* to soothe, quit, allay.

**sedativo, -va** *adj.-m.* sedative.

**sede** *f.* ECCL. see: *Santa Sede,* Holy See. *2* seat, quarters, headquarters.

**sedentario, -ria** *adj.* sedentary.

**sedeño, -ña** *adj.* silky, silken. *2* silklike. *3* bristly.

**sedera** *f.* bristle brush.

**sedería** *f.* silks, silk stuff. *2* silk business or shop.

**sedero, -ra** *adj.* [pertaining to] silk. *2 m.-f.* silk weaver. *3* silk dealer.

**sedición** *f.* sedition.

**sedicioso, -sa** *adj.* seditious.

**sediento, -ta** *adj.* thirsty, thirsting.

**sedimentación** *f.* sedimentation.

**sedimentar** *tr.* to deposit [as a sediment]. *2 ref.* to settle, form a sediment.

**sedimento** *m.* sediment, settlings, lees, dregs.

**sedoso, -sa** *adj.* silky.

**seducción** *f.* seduction, seducement. *2* charm.

**seducir** *tr.* to seduce. *2* to allure, tempt. *3* to charm, captivate. ¶ CONJUG. like *conducir.*

**seductor, -ra** *adj.* seducing. *2* seductive, tempting. *3* charming, captivating. *4 m.-f.* seducer.

**seduje, sedujera,** etc. *irr.* V. SEDUCIR.

**seduzco, seduzca,** etc. *irr.* V. SEDUCIR.

**sefardí, sefardita** *adj.-n.* Sephardi. *2 m. pl.* Sephardim.

**segadera** *f.* sickle, reaping hook.

**segador, -ra** *m.-f.* harvester, harvestman, reaper, mower. *2 m.* ENT. harvestman, daddy-longlegs. *3 f.* harvester, mowing machine.
**segar** *tr.* AGR. to harvest, reap, mow. *2* fig. to mow, cut down, mow down. ¶ CONJUG. like *acertar.*
**seglar** *adj.* secular, lay. *2 m.-f.* layman, laywoman.
**segmento** *m.* segment.
**segoviano, -na** *adj.-n.* of Segovia.
**segregación** *f.* segregation. *2* PHYSIOL., BIOL. secretion [act or process].
**segregar** *tr.* to segregate. *2* PHYSIOL., BIOL. to secrete.
**segueta** *f.* buhl saw, fret saw.
**seguida** *f.* following. *2* succession, continuation: *de ~*, in succession, uninterruptedly; *de ~, en ~*, immediately.
**seguidamente** *adv.* consecutively, in succession. *2* forthwith, immediately after, right after that.
**seguidilla** *f.* a Spanish stanza of four or seven short verses partly assonant. *2 pl.* a popular Spanish dance and its music.
1) **seguido** *adv.* consecutively, continuously.
2) **seguido, -da** *adj.* consecutive, running, succesive, continued: *ocho días seguidos*, eight days running. *3* straight, direct.
**seguidor, -ra** *m.-f.* follower.
**seguimiento** *m.* following. *2* pursuit, chase. *3* continuation.
**seguir** *tr.* to follow [in practically every sense]: *como sigue*, as follows. *2* to pursue, chase, hunt. *3* to prosecute, continue [action], to go on, keep on [doing something]. *4 intr.* to continue, keep [in a place, state, direction, etc.]. *5* to be, do: *¿cómo sigue el enfermo?*, how is the patient? *6 ref.* to ensue, result, follow. ¶ CONJUG. like *servir.*
**según** *prep.* according to, according as, as. *2* depending on. *3* so. *4 ~ que*, according as. *5 adv* that depends. *6 ~ y como, ~ y conforme*, just as; that depends.
**segundar** *tr.* to do again. *2 intr.* to be second, follow next to the first.
**segundero** *m.* second hand [of timepiece].
**segundo, -da** *adj.* second: *segunda intención*, duplicity of meanings or purposes [in acts or words]; *de segunda mano*, second-hand. *2 segunda enseñanza*, secondary education. *3 m.* second [part of the minute]. *4* second in authority, assistant, mate. *5 sin ~*, unequalled. *6 f.* SEGUNDA INTENCIÓN. *7* MUS., AUTO. second.
**segundogénito, -ta** *adj.-n.* second born.
**segundón** *m.* any son born after the first.
**segur** *f.* ax, axe. *2* AGR. sickle.
**seguramente** *adv.* securely, safely. *2* surely. *3* probably, very probably.
**seguridad** *f.* security, safety: *de ~*, safety [as adj.]. *2* police service. *3* surety, bond. *4* custody, safe keeping. *5* certainty. *6* assurance: *tener la ~ de*, or *de que*, to be sure of or that.
**seguro, -ra** *adj.* secure, safe. *2* sure, firm, fast, steady. *3* sure, dependable, reliable; constant. *4* sure, certain. *5* sure [assured in mind], convinced. *6 m.* certainty: *a buen ~, al ~, de ~*, certainly, very probably. *7* place of safety. *8* COM. insurance. *9* safe conduct. *10* safety lock [of a firearm]. *11* MECH. click, pawl, stop.
**seis** *adj.* six. *2 m.* six. *3* sixth [of the month]. *4 f. pl. las ~*, six o'clock.
**seisavado, -da** *adj.* hexagonal.
**seisavar** *tr.* to make hexagonal.
**seisavo, -va** *adj.* sixth. *2 m.* sixth [sixth part].
**seiscientos, -tas** *adj.-m.* six hundred.

**seiseno, -na** *adj.* sixth.
**seisillo** *m.* MUS. sextolet.
**seísmo** *m.* seism.
**selacio, -cia** *adj.* ICHTH. selachian.
**selección** *f.* selection.
**seleccionador, -ra** *adj.* selecting. *2 m.-f.* selector.
**seleccionar** *tr.* to select, choose, pick out.
**selecto, -ta** *adj.* select, choice; distinguished.
**selenio** *m.* CHEM. selenium.
**selenografía** *f.* selenography.
**self** *f.* (Angl.) ELECT. self-induction coil.
**seltz (agua de)** *f.* Seltzer water; soda water.
**selva** *f.* forest, woods; jungle: *Selva Negra*, Black Forest [in Germany].
**selvático, -ca** *adj.* silvan, sylvan. *2* rustic, wild.
**selvoso, -sa** *adj.* silvan, sylvan. *2* wooded, woody.
**sellar** *tr.* to seal [with a seal]. *2* to seal, close.
**sello** *m.* seal [piece of wax, lead, etc.; impression, mark]. *2* signet. *3* seal, stamp [instrument; characteristic mark]. *4* PHARM. cachet. *5 ~ de correos*, postage, stamp.
**semáforo** *m.* semaphore. *2* traffic lights.
**semana** *f.* week: *~ Santa*, Holy Week; *entre ~*, during the week [but not on the first or last days]. *2* septenary [of years, etc.]. *3* week's pay.
**semanal** *adj.* weekly.
**semanalmente** *adv.* weekly.
**semanario, -ria** *adj.* weekly. *2 m.* weekly [publication].
**semántica** *f.* semantics, semasiology.
**semblante** *m.* face, countenance, mien, look, expression [of a person]; look, aspect [of things]: *componer el ~*, to put on a calm appearance: *mudar de ~*, to change colour.
**semblanza** *f.* biographical sketch.
**sembradío, -a** *adj.* AGR. fit for sowing [land].
**sembrado, -da** *adj.* sown. *2 m.* AGR. sown ground; field, grain field.
**sembrador, -ra** *adj.* seeding, sowing. *2 m.-f.* seeder, sower. *3 f.* seeder, seeding machine, sowing machine.
**sembradura** *f.* seeding, sowing: *tierra de ~*, grain field.
**sembrar** *tr.-intr.* to sow, seed. *2 tr.* to sow, scatter, disseminate, sprinkle, strew. ¶ CONJUG. like *acertar.*
**semejante** *adj.* resembling, similar, like, alike. *2* such, of that kind. *3* ALG. like. *4* GEOM. similar. *5 m.* resemblance, imitation. *6* fellow, fellow creature.
**semejanza** *f.* resemblance, similarity, similitude: *a ~ de*, like, as.
**semejar** *intr.-ref.* to resemble, to be alike.
**semen** *m.* semen, sperm. *2* BOT. seed.
**semental** *adj.* AGR. [pertaining to] seeding or sowing. *2* breeding [horse, bull, etc.]. *3 m.* breeding horse, bull, etc.
**sementera** *f.* AGR. seeding, sowing. *2* sown land. *3* seedtime, sowing season. *4* fig. hotbed.
**semestral** *adj.* six-month, six-monthly.
**semestre** *adj.* semestral. *2 m.* semester, six months.
**semi-** *pref.* semi-, half-, partly-.
**semibreve** *f.* MUS. semibreve, whole note.
**semicadencia** *f.* MUS. semicadence.
**semicircular** *adj.* semicircular.
**semicírculo** *m.* GEOM. semicircle.
**semicircunferencia** *f.* GEOM. semicircumference.
**semiconsonante** *adj.* PHONET. semiconsonant.
**semicorchea** *f.* MUS. semiquaver, sixteenth note.
**semidiámetro** *m.* semidiameter.

**semidiós** *m.* MYTH. demigod.
**semidiosa** *f.* MYTH. demigoddess.
**semieje** *m.* GEOM. semiaxis.
**semifluido, -da** *adj.* semifluid.
**semifusa** *f.* MUS. double demisemiquaver.
**semilunar** *adj.* semilunar.
**semilla** *f.* seed.
**semillero** *m.* AGR. seed bed, seed plot, nursery. 2 fig. hotbed, cause, seminary.
**seminal** *adj.* seminal.
**seminario** *m.* EDUC. seminary: ~ *conciliar*, ECCL. theological seminary. 2 SEMILLERO.
**seminarista** *m.* seminarist, theological student.
**seminífero** *adj.* seminiferous.
**semínima** *f.* MUS. crotchet.
**Semíramis** *f. pr. n.* HIST. Semiramis.
**semirrígido, -da** *adj.* AER. semirigid.
**semisalvaje** *adj.* half savage.
**semiseda** *f.* half silk.
**semisuma** *f.* ARITH. half the sum [of].
**semita** *m.-f.* Semite. 2 *adj.* Semitic.
**semítico, -ca** *adj.* Semitic.
**semitono** *m.* MUS. semitone.
**semivocal** *adj.* PHONET. semivowel.
**sémola** *f.* semolina, groats.
**semoviente** *adj. bienes semovientes*, livestock.
**sempiterno, -na** *adj.* sempiternal. 2 *f.* durance [fabric]. 3 BOT. globe amaranth.
**sen** *m.* BOT. senna.
**sena** *f.* six [on a die]. 2 BOT. senna.
**Sena** *m. pr. n.* GEOG. Seine [river].
**senado** *m.* Senate. 2 Senate house. 3 THEAT. audience.
**senadoconsulto** *m.* senatus consultum.
**senador** *m.* senator.
**senaduría** *f.* senatorship.
**senatorial; senatorio, -ria** *adj.* senatorial.
**sencillez** *f.* simplicity. 2 easiness. 3 plainness, unpretentiousness. 4 naturalness.
**sencillo, -lla** *adj.* simple [not complicated or elaborated]. 2 light, of light body [fabric, etc.]. 3 simple, single. 4 easy [to do]. 5 simple, plain, unadorned; natural, unaffected. 6 simple, artless. 7 *m.* coll. small change.
**senda** *f.*, **sendero** *m.* path, footpath, byway. 2 fig. path, way.
**sendos, -das** *adj.* one each, one to each or for each.
**Séneca** *m. pr. n.* Seneca. 2 fig. man of wisdom.
**senectud** *f.* old age, senility.
**senegalés, -sa** *adj.-n.* Senegalese.
**senescal** *m.* seneschal.
**senil** *adj.* senile.
**seno** *m.* breast [milk-secreting organ]. 2 bosom [space between breast and dress]. 3 womb [of woman]. 4 fig. bosom, lap, the midst: *el ~ de Abraham*, Abraham's bosom. 5 concave, cavity, hollow, sinus. 6 ANAT., ZOOL., SURG. sinus. 7 GEOG. gulf, bay. 8 belly [of sail]; bight [of rope]. 9 TRIG. sine: ~ *verso*, versed sine.
**sensación** *f.* sensation, feeling. 2 sensation [vivid emotion]: *hacer ~*, to cause a sensation.
**sensacional** *f.* sensational.
**sensatez** *f.* sense, good sense, wisdom.
**sensato, -ta** *adj.* sensible, judicious, wise.
**sensibilidad** *f.* sensibility. 2 sensitiveness.
**sensibilizar** *tr.* to sensitize.
**sensible** *adj.* sentient, sensible. 2 sensible, perceptible, appreciable. 3 sensitive [person, instrument, plate, etc.]. 4 GEOG. sensible [horizon]. 5 deplorable, regrettable. 6 *f.* MUS. sensible note.
**sensiblería** *f.* oversentimentality, mawkishness.

**sensiblero, -ra** *adj.* oversentimental, mawkish.
**sensitiva** *f.* BOT. sensitive plant.
**sensitivo, -va** *adj.* sense, sensitive [of the senses; that conveys sense impressions]. 2 sentient.
**sensorio, -ria** *adj.* sensorial. 2 *m.* sensorium.
**sensual** *adj.* sensual.
**sensualidad** *f.* sensuality.
**sensualismo** *m.* sensualism.
**sentada** *f.* sitting: *de una ~*, at one sitting.
**sentadillas (a)** *adv.* sidesaddle.
**sentado, -da** *adj.* seated, sitting down. 3 settled, established: *dar por ~*, to take for granted, to consider as settled. 4 sedate, judicious. 5 BOT. sessile.
**sentar** *tr.* to seat [cause to sit down]. 2 to set, establish. 3 *intr. sentar*, or ~ *bien, a*, to fit, become, suit; to please, be agreeable to; [of food, climate, etc.] to agree with. 4 *ref.* to sit down. 5 ASENTARSE. 6 [of a seam, etc.] to hurt. ¶ CONJUG. like *acertar*.
**sentencia** *f.* LAW judgement, sentence, decision. 2 award, decision [of an arbitrator]. 3 judgment, opinion. 4 pithy saying, maxim.
**sentenciar** *tr.* to sentence, pass judgement on. 2 to determine, decide.
**sentencioso, -sa** *adj.* sententious.
**sentidamente** *adv.* feelingly.
**sentido, -da** *adj.* felt, experienced. 2 heartfelt; feeling. 3 sensitive, touchy. 4 offended: *darse por ~*, to take offence. 5 *m.* sense [any one of the five senses]: *costar un ~*, coll. to cost a fortune; *con todos los cinco sentidos*, with the utmost care and attention. 6 sense [judgment, understanding, etc.]: ~ *común*, common sense; *buen ~*, good sense. 7 sense, meaning, import, effect: *doble ~*, double meanning; *en cierto ~*, in a sense; *en el ~ que*, to the effect that; *sin ~*, meaningless. 8 sense [of the humour, the ridicule, etc.]. 9 consciousness. 10 sense, direction. 11 GEOM. sense.
**sentimental** *adj.* sentimental.
**sentimentalismo** *m.* sentimentalism.
**sentimiento** *m.* sentiment, feeling. 2 sense [of duty, honour, etc.]. 3 grief, sorrow, regret.
**sentina** *f.* NAUT. bilge. 2 fig. foul, filthy place.
1) **sentir** *m.* sentiment, feeling. 2 view, opinion.
2) **sentir** *tr.* to feel [perceive by sensation]. 2 to hear. 3 to feel [pleasure, pity, etc.]. 4 to have, experience, suffer; ~ *frío*, to be cold; ~ *miedo*, to be afraid. 5 to feel [be aware of]; to have a presentiment of. 6 to regret; be or feel sorry [for]: *lo siento*, I am sorry. 7 to think, judge. 8 *sin ~*, without noticing, without being aware. 9 *ref.* to feel [well, bad, sad, sick, etc.]. 10 to begin to decay or rot. 11 *sentirse de*, to resent; to feel [an insult, etc.]; to have a pain in. ¶ CONJUG. like *hervir*.
**seña** *f.* sign, indication, token: *por más señas*, more by token. 2 sign [motion, action, gesture]. 3 mark, signal. 4 MIL. password. 5 *pl.* address [description of a place of residence or business]. 6 *señas personales*, personal description.
**señal** *f.* sign, mark, token, symptom: *dar señales*, to show signs of; *en ~ de*, as a sign of, in token of. 2 landmark. 4 reminder. 5 distinctive mark. 6 trace, vestige. 7 sign, signal: *hacer señales*, to signal, make signals. 8 image, representation. 9 sign, prodigy. 10 scar, cicatrice. 11 pledge [token]. 12 earnest, money. 13 ~ *de la cruz*, sign of the cross.

**señaladamente** *adv.* especially, remarkably signally.

**señalado, -da** *adj.* signal. *3* noted, distinguished.

**señalamiento** *m.* appointment, date. *2* LAW assignation [for a trial].

**señalar** *tr.* to mark [with a sign]. *2* to show, indicate, point at, point out. *3* to set, fix, determine, assign. *4* to appoint [place, time]. *5* to scar. *6* to signal. *7* *ref.* to distinguish oneself, to excel.

**señero, -ra** *adj.* solitary, alone. *2* unique, unequalled.

**señor, -ra** *adj.* noble, distinguished, not vulgar, gentlemanlike, ladylike. *2* coll. great, fine, strong, etc. *3 m.* mister, Mr., sir: *el ~ López*, Mr. López; *muy ~ mío*, Dear Sir [in letters]; *sí ~*, yes, sir. *4* man, gentleman. *5* master [of the house]. *6* feudal lord, lord, master. *7* (cap.) *el Señor*, the Lord, God; *Nuestro Señor*, Our Lord.

**señora** *f.* mistress, Mrs., madam; *la ~ López*, Mrs. López; *muy ~ mía*, Dear Madam [in letters]; *sí ~*, yes, madam. *2* woman, lady, gentlewoman: *~ de compañía*, companion, chaperon. *3* lady [wife]. *4* mistress, lady [owner, etc.]; lady [of the house]. *5* (cap.) *Nuestra Señora*, Our Lady.

**señorear** *tr.* to dominate, rule over. *2* to lord it over. *3* to dominate, tower over. *4* to control [one's passions]. *5* *tr.-ref.* to take, take hold of, bring under one's rule or control. *6* *ref.* to take on airs.

**señoría** *f.* dominion, lordship, control. *2* lordship, ladyship, title of distinction inferior to EXCELENCIA. *3* HIST. signory.

**señorial** *adj.* seignorial, manorial. *2* feudal [fees]. *3* lordly, noble, stately.

**señoril** *adj.* lordly, genteel, dignified, distinguished.

**señorío** *m.* dominion, lordship, control. *2* seigniory. *3* gravity or stateliness of deportment. *4* self-command. *5* nobility, gentry, gentlefolk.

**señorita** *f. dim.* young lady, miss, Miss. *2* title given by servants to a lady or to the mistress of the house.

**señoritingo** *m.* coll. young gentleman of no account.

**señorito** *m. dim.* young gentleman. *2* Master [youth or boy]. *3* title given by servants to a gentleman or to the master of the house. *4* coll. idle young gentleman.

**señorón, -na** *m.-f.* swell, bigwig.

**señuelo** *m.* decoy, lure. *2* fig. lure, bait, enticement.

**seo** *f.* cathedral church.

**sépalo** *m.* BOT. sepal.

**separable** *adj.* separable. *2* detachable, removable.

**separación** *f.* separation. *2* dissmissal, discharge. *3* POL. secession.

**separado, -da** *adj.* separate; apart: *por ~*, separately.

**separar** *tr.* to separate. *2* to dismiss, discharge. *3* *ref.* to separate [intr.]. *4* COM. to put an end to partnership.

**separata** *f.* reprint.

**separatismo** *m.* separatism, secessionism.

**sepedón** *m.* ESLIZÓN.

**sepelio** *m.* burial, interment.

**sepia** *f.* ZOOL. sepia, cuttlefish. *2* sepia [colour].

**septena** *f.* septenary, group of seven.

**septenario, -ria** *adj.* septenary. *2 m.* period of seven days.

**septenio** *m.* septenary, septenium.

**septeno, -na** *adj.* SÉPTIMO.

**septentrión** *m.* north. *2* north wind. *3* ASTR. septentrion.

**septentrional** *adj.* septentrional, northern.

**septeto** *m.* MUS. septet, septuor.

**septicemia** *f.* MED. septicaemia.

**septicida** *adj.* BOT. septicidal.

**séptico, -ca** *adj.* septic.

**septiembre** *m.* September.

**septillo** *m.* MUS. septimole, septuplet.

**séptimo, -ma** *adj.-m.* seventh. *2 f.* MUS. seventh. *3* FENC. septime.

**septingentésimo, -ma** *adj.-m.* seven hundredth.

**septo** *m.* ANAT., BOT. septum.

**septuagenario, -ria** *adj.-n.* septuagenarian.

**septuagésima** *f.* ECCL. Septuagesima.

**septuagésimo, -ma** *adj.* seventieth. *2* septuagesimal.

**septuplicar** *tr.* to septuple.

**séptuplo, -pla** *adj.* septuple, sevenfold. *2 m.* septuple.

**sepulcral** *adj.* sepulchral.

**sepulcro** *m.* sepulcher. *2* grave, tomb.

**sepultar** *tr.* to bury, entomb. *2* fig. to bury [hide, cover up, submerge, immerse].

**sepulto, -ta** *adj.* buried.

**sepultura** *f.* sepulture: *dar ~ a*, to bury.

**sepulturero** *m.* gravedigger, sexton.

**sequedad** *f.* dryness. *2* aridity. *3* gruffness, surliness.

**sequedal, sequeral** *m.* dry soil.

**sequía** *f.* drought, dry season.

**sequillo** *m.* sweet biscuit.

**sequío** *m.* SECANO.

**séquito** *m.* train, suite, cortege. *2* popularity.

**sequizo, -za** *adj.* easily dried.

**1) ser** *m.* being: *el Ser Supremo*, the Supreme Being, God. *2* life, existence.

**2) ser** *subst. v.* to be [exist, live]. *2 aux.* to be [forming passives]: *él es amado*, he is loved. *3 intr. & copulative* to be, be a: *el hombre es mortal*, man is mortal: *Juan es abogado*, John is a lawyer. *4* to cost: *¿a cómo son estas peras?*, what is the price of these pears? *5* to be, happen: *¿cómo fue ello?*, how did it happen? *6* to be [belong to]: *este libro es mío*, this book is mine. *7* It is used in impersonal sentences as: *es la una*, it is one o'clock; *es necesario que*, it is necessary that. *8 ~ de*, a) to belong to; b) to be from, come from, be native of [a place]; c) to be in [a specified material]; d) *es de creer, es de ver*, it is to be believed; it is worth seeing; e) *¿qué será de mí?*, what will become of me? *9 ~ para poco*, to be feeble, timid. *10 a no ~ que*, unless. *11 ¡cómo ha de ser!*, it cannot be helped! [to express resignation]. *12 érase que se era*, once upon a time. *13 esto es*, that is to say. *14 no sea que*, lest. *15 sea lo que sea*, or *fuere*, be that as it may; anyhow. *16 un es, no es*, or *un si es, no es*, a little bit. ¶ CONJUG.: INDIC. Pres.: *soy, eres, es; somos, sois, son.* | Imperf.: *era, eras, era; éramos, erais, eran.* | Pret.: *fui, fuiste, fue; fuimos, fuisteis, fueron.* | Fut.: *seré, serás*, etc. | COND.: *sería, serías*, etc. SUBJ. Pres.: *sea, seas, sea; seamos, seáis, sean.* | Imperf.: *fuera, fueras, fuera; fuéramos, fuerais fueran*, or *fuese, fueses, fuese*, etc. | Fut.: *fuere, fueres, fuere; fuéremos, fuereis, fueren.* | IMPER.: *sé, sea; seamos, sed, sean.* | PAST. P. *sido.* | GER.: *siendo.*

**sera** *f.* large esparto basket.

**seráfico, -ca** *adj.* seraphic(al).

**serafín** *m.* seraph.

**serafina** f. a flowered woollen fabric.
**serapino** m. SAGAPENO.
**serba** f. BOT. fruit of the service tree.
**serbal, serbo** m. BOT. service tree.
**serena** f. SERENO 5: *a la* ~, AL SERENO.
**serenar** tr. to serene, calm, pacify. 2 to clear up [make unclouded]. 3 to cool [water] in the night air. 4 intr.-ref. to become calm. 5 [of weather] to clear up. 6 to regain one's selfpossession.
**serenata** f. serenade. 2 MUS. serenata.
**serenidad** f. serenity, calm. 2 calmness, coolness, self-possession. 3 Serenity [title].
**serenísimo, -ma** adj. superl. extremely serene or calm. 2 Most Serene [title of princes].
**sereno, -na** adj. serene. 2 clear, cloudless. 3 calm, cool, self-possessed. 4 m. night watchman. 5 serein, night dew: *al* ~, in the night air.
**seriamente** adv. seriously. 2 gravely. 3 in earnest.
**seri(ci)cultor** m. seri(ci)culturist.
**seri(ci)cultura** f. seri(ci)culture, silk culture.
**sérico, -ca** adj. silken.
**serie** f. series. 2 *de* ~, stock. 3 *en* ~, standardized, mass [production]; ELECT. series, in series.
**seriedad** f. seriousness, gravity. 2 earnestness. 3 reliability. 4 sternness.
**serio, -ria** adj. serious. 2 grave, dignified. 3 stern. 4 solvent, reliable. 5 grave, sober [not light or gay, not showy].
**sermón** m. sermon.
**sermonar** intr. to preach, to preach sermons.
**sermonario** m. collection of sermons.
**sermonear** intr.-tr. to sermonize.
**sermoneo** m. coll. sermonizing.
**seroja** f., **serojo** m. dry leaves. 2 brushwood.
**serón** m. esparto basket or pannier.
**serosidad** f. MED. serosity.
**seroso, -sa** adj. serous.
**serpear** intr. SERPENTEAR.
**serpentario** m. ORN. secretary bird. 2 (cap.) ASTR. Serpent Bearer.
**serpentear** intr. to wind, meander, serpentine, wriggle.
**serpenteo** m. winding, meandering, wriggling.
**serpentín** m. worm [of a still], cooling coil. 2 cock [of firelock].
**serpentina** f. MIN. serpentine. 2 a rolled strip of coloured paper which is cast so as to unroll [in carnival, etc.].
**serpentino, -na** adj. serpentine. 2 slanderous, poisoned [tongue].
**serpentón** m. aug. large serpent. 2 MUS. serpent.
**serpezuela** f. dim. of SIERPE.
**serpiente** f. ZOOL. serpent, snake: ~ *de cascabel,* rattlesnake. 2 ASTR. Serpent.
**serpigo** m. MED. serpigo, ringworm.
**serpol** m. BOT. wild thyme.
**serpollar** intr. [of a tree] to shoot, sprout.
**serpollo** m. shoot, sprout [of a tree].
**serrado, -da** adj. serrate.
**serrador, -ra** m.-f. ASERRADOR.
**serrallo** m. seraglio, harem. 2 fig. brothel.
**serranía** f. mountainous country or region.
**serrano, -na** adj. mountain, highlander. 2 m.-f. mountaineer highlander.
**serrar** tr. to saw. ¶ CONJUG. like *acertar.*
**serrátil** adj. MED. irregular [pulse].
**serreta** f. dim. small saw. 2 cavesson [iron].
**serrijón** m. short mountain chain.
**serrín** m. sawdust.
**serrucho** m. handsaw.
**servato** BOT. hog's-fennel.

**serventesio** m. quatrain with rhyme abab. 2 sirviente [Provençal moral lay].
**servible** adj. serviceable, in good condition for use.
**servicial** adj. serviceable, helpful, obliging, kind.
**servicio** m. service, serving. 2 duty [assigned service]: *estar de* ~, to be on duty. 3 service [occupation of a servant; branch of public employ, etc.]: ~ *público,* public service. 4 servants, staff of servants. 5 service, good turn: *flaco* ~, ill turn. 6 use, benefit. 7 military or naval service. 8 service [set of dishes, cups, etc.]. 9 course [in a meal]. 10 chamber pot. 11 TENNIS service, serve.
**servido, -da** p. p. of SERVIR. 2 adj. *ser* ~, to please, deign, have the kindness [to].
**servidor, -ra** m.-f. servant, server, servitor: ~ *de usted,* your servant, at your service; *queda de usted atento* ~, yours respectfully.
**servidumbre** f. servitude, bondage, subjection. 2 inevitable obligation. 3 servants, staff of servants. 4 LAW servitude, easement.
**servil** adj. servile.
**servilismo** m. servility.
**servilleta** f. table napkin, serviette.
**servilletero** m. napkin-ring.
**servio, -via** adj.-n. Serbian.
**serviola** f. NAUT. cathead, anchor beam.
**servir** intr.-tr. to serve [be a servant to, do service to, be useful to], to wait [on or upon]. 2 to do [for], to serve, answer [a purpose or end]. 3 [in ball games] to serve. 4 intr. to serve, wait [at table]. 5 intr. to serve [in the army or navy], to be employed [in a public service, etc.]. 6 CARDS to follow suit. 7 ~ *de,* to act as, be used as, serve as or for. 8 ~ *para,* to be for, be good for, good for, be used for: *no* ~ *para nada,* to be of no use, to be good for nothing. 9 tr. to help, serve [food or drink]. 10 to serve [a gun; an office]. 11 to tend [a machine]. 12 to do a favour to. 13 to serve, attend, court [a lady]. 14 COM. to wait upon [a customer]. 15 ref. to serve oneself. 16 to help oneself [to food or drink]. 17 to please, be pleased to, deign to: *sírvase informarme,* please inform me. 18 *servirse de,* to employ, make use of. ¶ CONJUG. INDIC. Pres.: *sirvo, sirves, sirve;* servimos, servís, *sirven.* | Pret.: serví, serviste, *sirvió;* servimos, servisteis, *sirvieron.* | SUBJ. Pres.: *sirva, sirvas,* etc. | Imperf.: *sirviera, sirvieras,* etc., or *sirviese, sirvieses,* etc. | Fut.: *sirviere, sirvieres,* etc. | IMPER.: *sirve, sirva; sirvamos,* servid, *sirvan.* | GER.: *sirviendo.*
**servitud** f. servitude.
**servocroata** adj.-n. Serbo-Croatian.
**servomotor** m. MACH. servomotor.
**sésamo** m. BOT. sesame. 2 sesame [magic word].
**sesear** intr. to pronounce *z,* and *c* before *e* & *i* like *s* [as in Am. and some parts of Spain].
**sesenta** adj.-m. sixty. 2 sixtieth.
**sesentavo, -va** adj.-n. sixtieth.
**sesentón, -na** adj.-n. sexagenarian.
**seseo** m. pronouncing *z,* and *c* before *e* & *i,* like *s.*
**sesera** f. brainpan. 2 the entire brain.
**sesgado, -da** p. p. of SESGAR. 2 adj. SESGO 1 & 2.
**sesgar** tr. to slant, give an oblique direction to. 2 to cut on the bias.
**sesgo, -ga** adj. slanting, oblique, biased. 2 cut on the bias. 3 fig. stern-faced. 4 m. obliquity, slant, bias: *al* ~, obliquely, on the bias. 5 mean course. 6 turn [of an affair].
**sesgue** pret., subj. & imper. of SESGAR.
**sesil** adj. BOT. sessile.

**sesión** f. session, sitting, séance, meeting, conference. 2 show [in a picture theatre]: ~ *continua*, continuous showing.
**seso** m. ANAT. brain, brains. 2 fig. brains, intelligence; prudence, judgment: *no tener* ~, to have no sense; *perder el* ~, to go crazy.
**sesquióxido** m. CHEM. sesquioxide.
**sesteadero** m. shady place where cattle rest.
**sestear** intr. to take a siesta. 2 [of cattle] to rest in the shade.
**sestercio** m. sesterce.
**sesudez** f. wisdom, prudence, sageness.
**sesudo, -da** adj. wise, prudent, judicious, sage.
**seta** f. BOT. mushroom. 2 bristle [of hog].
**setecientos, -tas** adj.-m. seven hundred. 2 seven hundredth [in order].
**setena** f. group of seven.
**setenta** adj.-n. seventy. 2 seventieth [in order].
**setentavo, -va** adj.-n. seventieth.
**setentón, -na** adj.-n. septuagenarian.
**setiembre** m. SEPTIEMBRE.
**seto** m. hedge, inclosure: ~ *vivo*, hedge, quickset.
**seudo** adj. pseudo, false.
**seudónimo, -ma** adj. pseudonymous. 2 m. pseudonym, pen name.
**severidad** f. severity, rigour, strictness, sterness. 2 austerity, severity.
**severo, -ra** adj. severe, rigorous, rigid, strict, stern. 2 severe, grim, austere.
**sevicia** f. cruelty, cruel treatment.
**Sevilla** f. pr. n. Seville.
**sevillanas** f. pl. a Sevillian dance and tune.
**sexagenario, -ria** adj.-n. sexagenarian.
**sexagésima** f. ECCL. Sexagesima.
**sexagésimo, -ma** adj. sexagesimal, sixtieth.
**sexenio** m. period of six years.
**sexo** m. sex: *el bello* ~, the fair sex.
**sexta** f. ECCL. sext, sexte. 2 MUS. sixth. 3 FENC. sixte.
**sextante** m. sextant. 2 sextans [Roman coin].
**sexteto** m. MUS. sextet.
**sextil** adj. ASTROL. sextile.
**sextilla** f. sextain [stanza of six short lines].
**sexto, -ta** adj.-n. sixth.
**séxtuplo, -pla** adj. sextuple, sixfold. 2 m. sextuple.
**sexual** adj. sexual.
**sexualidad** f. sexuality.
1) **si** m. MUS. si, B [seventh note of the scale].
2) **si** conj. if, whether: *como* ~, as if, as though; *por* ~ *acaso*, just in case; ~ *acaso*, if by chance; ~ *bien*, although; ~ *no*, otherwise, else; unless. 2 how, to what extent. 3 when. 4 if only. 5 It may be used for emphasis or to denote doubt: *¡*~ *no lo quiero!*, indeed, I don't want it; *¿*~ *será él?* I wonder if it is he.
1) **sí** 3rd person form of ref. pron. for every gender and number (used as object of prepositions) himself, herself, itself, oneself, themselves: *de por* ~, apart, separately; by oneself, itself, etc.; *de* ~, of himself, herself, etc.; spontaneously; by nature; *entre* ~, each other, of each other, to each other; *por* ~ *y ante* ~, of his own accord, ignoring others; haughty.
2) **sí** adv. yes, yea; indeed, certainly: *por* ~ *o por no*, in any case; *un día* ~ *y otro no*, every other day; *¿sí?*, indeed? 2 m. yes, assent, permission: *dar el* ~, to say yes.
**siamés, -sa** adj.-n. Siamese.
**sibarita** adj.-n. Sybarite. 2 sybarite.
**sibaritismo** m. sybaritism.
**siberiano, -na** adj.-n. Siberian.
**sibila** f. sibyl.

**sibilante** adj. sibilant, hissing.
**sibilino, -na; sibilítico, -ca** adj. sibyline.
**sic** Lat. adv. sic.
**sicalipsis** f. pornography.
**sicario** m. sicarian, paid assassin.
**sicigia** f. ASTR. syzygy.
**Sicilia** f. pr. n. GEOG. Sicily.
**siciliano, -na** adj.-n. Sicilian.
**sicoanálisis** m. PSICOANÁLISIS.
**sicofanta, sicofante** m. sycophant.
**sicofísica, sicología, sicometría,** etc. = PSICOFÍSICA, PSICOLOGÍA, PSICOMETRÍA, etc.
**sicómoro** m. BOT. sycamore. 2 BOT. sycamore maple.
**sicón** m. ZOOL. sycon.
**sículo, -la** adj.-n. Sicilian. 2 HIST. Siculian.
**sideral; sidéreo, -a** adj. sidereal.
**siderosa** f. MINER. siderite.
**siderurgia** f. siderurgy.
**siderúrgico, -ca** adj. siderurgical.
**sidra** f. cider.
**siega** f. reaping, mowing, harvest.
**siembra** f. sowing, seeding. 2 sowing time. 3 sown ground.
**siempre** adv. always, ever: *de* ~, usual; *para* ~, forever, for good; *por* ~, forever, evermore; ~ *jamás*, forever and ever; ~ *que*, whenever; provided.
**sien** f. ANAT. temple.
**Siena** f. pr. n. GEOG. Sienna.
**siena** f. sienna.
**sienés, -sa** adj.-n. Sienese, Siennese.
**sierpe** f. serpent, snake. 2 fig. ugly-looking person; fierce or angry person. 3 fig. anything that winds or wrigles.
**sierpecilla** f. dim. small serpent.
**sierra** f. saw: ~ *de bastidor*, bucksaw; ~ *de mano*, handsaw; ~ *sin fin*, band-saw. 2 GEOG. jagged mountain-chain. 3 ICHTH. sawfish.
**Sierra Leona** f. pr. n. GEOG. Sierra Leone.
**sierrecilla** f. dim. small saw.
**siervo, -va** m.-f. serf, slave. 2 humble servant, servant: ~ *de Dios*, servant of God.
**sieso** m. ANAT. rectum.
**siesta** f. hottest part of the day. 2 siesta, afternoon nap.
**siete** adj.-m. seven. 2 seventh [of the month]. 3 V-shaped tear in garment. 4 CARP. dog, clamp. 5 f. pl. *las* ~, seven o'clock.
**sieteenrama** f. BOT. tormentil.
**sietemesino, -na** adj. born in seven months [baby]. 2 coll. puny coxcomb.
**sífilis** f. MED. syphilis.
**sifilítico, -ca** adj.-n. syphilitic.
**sifón** m. siphon. 2 siphon bottle. 3 siphon water. 4 trap [in a pipe].
**sifosis** f. kyphosis.
**sigilación** f. sealing, stamping. 2 concealment, keeping secret.
**sigilar** tr. to seal [stamp with a seal]. 2 to conceal, keep secret, not to disclose or reveal.
**sigilo** m. seal, stamp. 2 concealment, secrecy.
**sigilografía** f. sigilography.
**sigilosamente** adv. silently, secretly.
**sigiloso, -sa** adj. silent, reserved.
**sigla** f. sigla.
**siglo** m. century [hundred years]: *hasta la consumación de los siglos*, until the end of time; *por los siglos de los siglos*, world without end. 2 age,

epoch, period. *3* fig. ages [long time]. *4* world [worldly intercourse or matters].

**sigmoideo, -a** *adj.* sigmoid.

**signáculo** *m.* seal, signet.

**signar** *tr.* to sign [with a sign; with one's name]. *2* to cross [make the sign of the cross upon or over]. *3* ref. to cross oneself.

**signatario, -ria** *adj.-n.* signatory.

**signatura** *f.* sign, mark. *2* PRINT. signature. *3* press-mark, library number [on a book].

**significación** *f.* signification, signifying. *2* signification, meaning, import. *3* significance.

**significado, -da** *adj.* well-known, prominent. *2 m.* signification, meaning, sense.

**significante** *adj.* signifying, significant.

**significar** *tr.* to signify [be a sign of; make know]. *2* to signify, mean. *3 intr.* to signify, matter.

**significativo, -va** *adj.* significative, significant.

**signo** *m.* sign, indication [of something]. *2* sign, mark, symbol, character. *3* scroll or flourish [in a notary's signature]. *4* MATH. sign. *5* GRAM. mark: ~ *de admiración*, exclamation mark. *6* ASTR. ~ *del Zodíaco*, sign of the Zodiac.

**siguiente** *adj.* following, next.

**sílaba** *f.* syllable.

**silabario** *m.* reader [book to teach reading].

**silabear** *intr.* to syllabicate, syllabify, syllabize.

**silábico, -ca** *adj.* syllabic.

**sílabo** *m.* syllabus, list, index.

**silba** *f.* hiss, hissing [of disapproval].

**silbar** *intr.* to whistle. *2* [of a steam whistle] to hoot. *3* to hiss. *4* [of a bullet] to whiz. *5 tr.* to whistle [a tune]. *6* to hiss, catcall [an actor, play, etc.].

**silbato** *m.* whistle [instrument].

**silbido** *m.* SILBO. *2* ~ *de oídos*, ringing in the ears.

**silbo** *m.* whistle [sound]. *2* hissing [of a snake, etc.]. *3* hoot, hooting [of a steam whistle]. *4* whiz [of a bullet].

**silbón** *m.* ORN. a hissing widgeon.

**silenciador** *m.* silencer [device for firearms, etc.].

**silenciar** *tr.* to omit, keep silent about.

**silencio** *m.* silence: *guardar* ~, to keep silence; *pasar en* ~, to omit, not to mention. *2* stillness, quiet. *3* taciturnity. *4* MUS. rest.

**silencioso, -sa** *adj.* silent. *2* taciturn. *3* noiseless, still, quiet.

**silente** *adj.* silent, still, quiet.

**silepsis** *f.* RHET. syllepsis.

**silero** *m.* silo.

**silesiano, -na; silesio, -sia** *adj.-n.* Silesian.

**sílex** *m.* MINER. silex.

**silfide** *f.* MYTH. & fig. sylph.

**silice** *f.* CHEM. silica.

**silíceo, -a** *adj.* siliceous.

**silicio** *m.* CHEM. silicon.

**silicua** *f.* BOT. siliqua, silique.

**silícula** *f.* BOT. silicle, silicula.

**silo** *m.* AGR. silo. *2* fig. cavern, dark place.

**silogismo** *m.* LOG. syllogism.

**silogizar** *intr.* to syllogize, argue.

**silueta** *f.* silhouette.

**silúrico, -ca** *adj.* GEOL. Silurian.

**siluro** *m.* ICHTH. catfish, sheatfish.

**sila** *f.* miscellany. *2* a form of poem.

**Silvestre** *m. pr. n.* Silvester, Sylvester.

**silvestre** *adj.* wild [plant, animal]. *2* uncultivated, rustic.

**silvicultor, -ra** *m.-f.* forester, silviculturist.

**silvicultura** *f.* forestry, silviculture.

**silla** *f.* chair [seat for one]: ~ *de cubierta*, deck

chair; ~ *de manos*, sedan chair; ~ *giratoria*, swivel chair; ~ *poltrona*, easy chair. *2* ECCL. see. *3 silla* or ~ *de montar*, saddle. *4* ~ *de posta*, post chair.

**sillar** *m.* ashlar [stone]. *2* place for the saddle on the back of a horse.

**sillería** *f.* set of chairs. *2* stalls [in a choir]. *3* chair making, chair business or shop. *4* ARCH. ashlar, ashlar masonry.

**sillero, -ra** *m.-f.* maker or seller of chairs.

**silleta** *f. dim.* small chair. *2* bedpan.

**silletazo** *m.* blow with a chair.

**silletero** *m.* carrier of a sedan chair.

**sillico** *m.* chamber pot; basin of a close-stool.

**sillín** *m.* light riding saddle. *2* harness saddle. *3* saddle [of a bicycle, motorcycle, etc.].

**sillón** *m. aug.* armchair, easy chair: ~ *de ruedas*, wheel chair.

**sima** *f.* cave, abyss, chasm.

**simbiosis** *f.* BIOL. symbiosis.

**simbólico, -ca** *adj.* symbolical.

**simbolismo** *m.* symbolism.

**simbolizar** *tr.* to symbolize, symbol, tipify, stand for.

**símbolo** *m.* symbol. *2* ~ *de la fe* or *de los Apóstoles*, Apostles' Creed.

**simetría** *f.* symmetry.

**simétrico, -ca** *adj.* symmetric, symmetrical.

**simiente** *f.* seed. *2* semen, sperm.

**simiesco, -ca** *adj.* simian, apelike, apish.

**símil** *adj.* similar. *2 m.* simile, comparison.

**similar** *adj.* similar, like.

**similitud** *f.* similitude, similarity.

**similor** *m.* similor: *de* ~, fig. sham, tinsel.

**simio** *m.* ZOOL. simian, ape.

**simón** *m.* hack, cab; hackman [in Madrid].

**simonía** *f.* simony.

**simoníaco, -ca** *adj.* simoniac(al. *2 m.-f.* simoniac.

**simpatía** *f.* sympathy, congeniality, liking, favour. *2* winsomeness. *3* PHYSIOL. sympathy.

**simpático, -ca** *adj.* pleasant, nice, likable, winsome; agreeable, congenial. *2* ANAT., PHYSIOL., PHYS., MUS. sympathetic. *3 m.* ANAT. *gran* ~, sympathetic nervous system.

**simpatizante** *adj.* favouring, supporting. *2 m.-f.* sympathizer, supporter.

**simpatizar** *intr.* to be congenial, to feel a mutual liking. *2* ~ *con*, to like; to sympathize with, to favour [a party, idea, etc.].

**simple** *adj.* simple [not compund, not complicated]. *2* MAT., GRAM., BIOL. simple. *3* simple, mere. *4* single [not double or multiple]. *5* simple, ingenuous. *6* simple, foolish. *7 m.-f.* simpleton.

**simpleza** *f.* silliness, foolishness. *2* silly thing.

**simplicidad** *f.* simplicity.

**simplicísimo, -ma** *adj. superl.* extremely simple.

**simplificación** *f.* simplification.

**simplificar** *tr.* to simplify.

**simplón, -na** *m.-f.* simpleton.

**simulación** *f.* simulation, feigning.

**simulacro** *m.* simulacrum. *2* MIL. sham battle.

**simulado, -da** *adj.* simulated, imitated, feigned, pretended, sham.

**simulador, -ra** *m.-f.* simulator.

**simular** *tr.* to simulate, imitate, feign, sham.

**simultanear** *tr.* to accomplish or carry out simultaneously.

**simultaneidad** *f.* simultaneity.

**simultáneo, -a** *adj.* simultaneous.

**simún** *m.* simoom [wind].

**sin** *prep.* without: ~ *dificultad*, without difficulty;

~ *que yo le viese*, without my seeing him. *2* besides, without counting. *3* ~ *embargo*, nevertheless, however.
**sinagoga** *f.* synagogue.
**sinalefa** *f.* GRAM. synalepha.
**sinapismo** *m.* sinapism.
**sinceramente** *adv.* sincerely.
**sincerar** *tr.-ref.* to exculpate, excuse, justify.
**sinceridad** *f.* sincerity.
**sincero, -ra** *adj.* sincere.
**sinclinal** *adj.* GEOL. synclinal.
**síncopa** *f.* GRAM., MUS. syncope, syncopation.
**sincopado, -da** *adj.* syncopated.
**sincopar** *tr.* GRAM., MUS. to syncopate. *2* to abridge.
**síncope** *f.* MED. syncope. *2* SINCOPA.
**sincretismo** *m.* syncretism.
**sincrónico, -ca** *adj.* synchronous.
**sincronismo** *m.* synchronism.
**sincronizar** *tr.* to synchronize. *2 intr.* RADIO. ~ *con*, to tune in.
**sindéresis** *f.* discretion, good judgment.
**sindicado** *m.* syndicate [body of syndics].
**sindical** *adj.* syndical. *2* syndicalistic.
**sindicalismo** *m.* syndicalism; unionism.
**sindicar** *tr.* to accuse, denounce. *2* to syndicate. *3 ref.* to syndicate [unite to form a syndicate].
**sindicato** *m.* syndicate [association]. *2* trade union, labor union.
**síndico** *m.* syndic. *2* LAW. liquidator or receiver [in a bankruptcy].
**síndrome** *m.* MED. syndrome.
**sinécdoque** *f.* RHET. synecdoche.
**sinecura** *f.* sinecure.
**sineresis** *f.* GRAM. syneresis.
**sinergía** *f.* PHYSIOL. synergy.
**sinfín** *m.* no end, endless number, endless amount.
**sínfisis** *f.* ANAT., ZOOL. symphysis.
**sinfonía** *f.* symphony.
**sinfónico, -ca** *adj.* symphonic.
**singar** *intr.* NAUT. to scull over the stern.
**singladura** *f.* NAUT. a day's run. *2* NAUT. day [from noon to noon].
**singular** *adj.* singular [unique; extraordinary]. *3 en* ~, in particular.
**singularidad** *f.* singularity. *2* peculiarity. *3* oddity.
**singularizar** *tr.* to singularize, distinguish, single out. *2* GRAM. to use in the singular. *3 ref.* to distinguish oneself, to make oneself conspicuous.
**singulto** *m.* sob. *2* hiccough, singultus.
**sinhueso** *f.* coll. *la* ~, the tongue.
**sínico, -ca** *adj.* Sinic, Sinitic.
**siniestra** *f.* left hand.
**siniestrado, -da** *adj.* that has undergone damage or loss [from wreck, fire, etc.].
**siniestro, -tra** *adj.* left, left-hand. *2* sinister. *3 m.* disaster, casualty, wreck. *4* COM. damage or loss [from wreck, fire, etc.].
**sinnúmero** *m.* no end, great number.
**sino** *conj.* but, except. *2* solely, only. *3 no solo* ... ~ *(también)*, not only... but (also).
**sínodo** *m.* ECCL., ASTR. synod.
**sinología** *f.* sinology.
**sinonimia** *f.* synonymity, synonymy.
**sinónimo, -ma** *adj.* synonymous. *2 m.* synonym.
**sinopsis**, *pl.* **-sis** *f.* synopsis.
**sinovia** *f.* ANAT. synovia.
**sinrazón** *f.* wrong, injustice. *2* unreason, unreasonable act.
**sinsabor** *m.* displeasure, worry, trouble, sorrow.
**sinsonte** *m.* ORN. mockingbird.

**sinsubstancia** *f.* coll. frivolous person.
**sintáctico, -ca** *adj.* syntactic.
**sintaxis** *f.* GRAM. syntax.
**síntesis**, *pl.* **-sis** *f.* synthesis.
**sintético, -ca** *adj.* synthetic, synthetical.
**sintetizar** *tr.* to synthesize, synthetize.
**sintoísmo** *m.* Shinto, Shintoism.
**síntoma** *m.* symptom.
**sintomático, -ca** *adj.* symptomatic.
**sintonía** *f.* ELECT., RADIO. syntony, tune, tuning.
**sintónico, -ca** *adj.* ELECT. syntonic, syntonical.
**sintonización** *f.* ELECT., RADIO. syntonization, tuning.
**sintonizar** *tr.-intr.* ELECT., RADIO. to syntonize, tune: ~ *con*, to tune in.
**sinuoso, -sa** *adj.* sinuous.
**sinusoide** *adj.* sinusoidal. *2 f.* GEOM. sinusoid.
**sinusitis** *f.* MED. sinusitis.
**sinvergüencería** *f.* brazenness, shamelessness.
**sinvergüenza** *adj.* brazen, barefaced. *2 m.-f.* shameless person, rascal, scoundrel.
**sionismo** *m.* Zionism.
**siquiatría** *f.* PSIQUIATRÍA.
**síquico, -ca** *adj.* PSÍQUICO.
**siquier, siquiera** *conj.-adv.* although, though, even if. *2* even, so much as. *3 un poquito* ~, ever so little. *4* whether... or: ~ *venga*, ~ *no venga*, whether he comes or not.
**Siracusa** *f. pr. n.* GEOG. Syracuse.
**sirena** *f.* MYTH. siren. *2* MYTH. mermaid. *3* siren [instrument]; foghorn.
**sirenio, -nia** *adj.-n.* ZOOL. sirenian.
**sirga** *f.* towrope, towline [for tracking a boat from the bank]. *2* line for hauling nets.
**sirgar** *tr.* to track [a boat from the bank].
**Siria** *f. pr. n.* GEOG. Syria.
**siríaco, -ca** *adj.-n.* Syrian.
**siringa** *f.* MUS. syrinx. *2* BOT. seringa, rubber tree.
**siringe** *f.* syrinx [vocal organ of birds].
**Sirio** *m. pr. n.* ASTR. Sirius.
**sirio, -ria** *adj.-n.* SIRÍACO.
**sirle** *f.* sheep's dung.
**siroco** *m.* sirocco [wind].
**sirte** *f.* NAUT. shoal, submerged sand bank.
**sirvienta** *f.* female servant, servant girl, maid.
**sirviente** *adj.* serving. *2* LAW servient. *3 m.* domestic, manservant.
**sirvo, sirva, sirviera, sirviere**, etc. *irr.* V. SERVIR.
**sisa** *f.* SEW dart; armscye. *2* petty theft. *3* size [for gilding].
**sisar** *tr.* to pilfer, filch. *2* to curt darts or armscyes in a garment. *3* to size [for gilding].
**sisear** *intr.-tr.* to hiss [to express disapproval].
**sisimbrio** *m.* JARAMAGO.
**sísmico, -ca** *adj.* seismic.
**sismo** *m.* TERREMOTO.
**sismógrafo** *m.* seismograph.
**sisón, -na** *adj.* pilfering, filchering. *2 m.-f.* pilferer, filcher. *3 m.* ORN. little bustard.
**sistema** *m.* system. *2* coll. method, way.
**sistemático, -ca** *adj.* systematic; methodical.
**sistematizar** *tr.* to systematize.
**sistilo** *m.* ARCH. systyle.
**sístole** *f.* PROS., PHYSIOL. systole.
**sistro** *m.* MUS. sistrum.
**sitiador, -ra** *adj.* besieging. *2 m.-f.* besieger.
**sitial** *m.* chair [seat of honour, authority, etc.].
**sitiar** *tr.* to besiege, lay siege to. *2* to surround, hem in.
**sitio** *m.* place, spot: *dejar en el* ~, fig. to kill one

outright. *2* place, seat, room [space]: *hacer* ~, to make room. *3* location, site. *4* stand, station. *5* country seat, villa. *6* MIL. siege: *poner* ~ *a*, to lay siege to.

**sito, -ta** *adj.* situated, lying, located.

**situación** *f.* placing. *2* situation, location, position. *3* situation [set of circumstances, position in which one finds oneself]. *4* position [to do, state, etc.].

**situar** *tr.* to situate, locate, place, put. *2* COM. to place [funds]. *3 ref.* to take one's stand; to place or station oneself.

**sixtino, -na** *adj.* Sistine.

**smoking** *m.* dinner jacket, *tuxedo.

**so** *prep.* under: ~ *capa de*, under pretence of. *2 m.* emphatic word used with depreciatory adjectives: ~ *marrano*, you, dirty fellow.

**¡so!** *interj.* whoa! [to horses].

**soasar** *tr.* COOK. to half roast, roast lightly.

**soba** *f.* kneading. *2* pawing [a person]. *3* drubbing.

**sobaco** *m.* armpit, axilla. *2* BOT. axil.

**sobajar** *tr.* to paw, crumple, rumple.

**sobaquera** *f.* shield [for the armpit in a garment].

**sobaquina** *f.* sweat from the armpit.

**sobar** *tr.* to knead, rub, soften. *2* to paw [a person]. *3* to beat, drub. *4* to vex, annoy.

**sobarba** *f.* noseband. *2* double chin.

**sobarbada** *f.* SOFRENADA. *2* scolding.

**sobarcar** *tr.* to take or carry under the arm.

**soberanear** *intr.* to lord it, domineer.

**soberanía** *f.* sovereignty. *2* rule, sway. *3* haughtiness.

**soberano, -na** *adj.* sovereign. *2* coll. very good, great. *3 m.-f.* sovereign [ruler]. *4 m.* sovereign [coin].

**soberbia** *f.* arrogance, pride, haughtiness. *2* magnificence.

**soberbio, -bia** *adj.* arrogant, proud, haughty. *2* superb. *3* grand, magnificent. *4* fiery [horse].

**sobina** *f.* wooden pin, peg.

**sobón, -na** *adj.* given to excessive fondling and caressing.

**sobornar** *tr.* to suborn, bribe.

**soborno** *m.* subornation, bribery. *2* bribe. *3* (Arg., Bol., Chi.) SOBORNAL.

**sobra** *f.* excess surplus: *de* ~, more than enough, in excess; superfluous; too well: *estar de* ~, to be one too many; to be superfluous or unnecessary. *2 pl.* leavings, leftovers.

**sobradamente** *adv.* more than enough, in excess, too, too well.

**sobradillo** *m.* ARCH. penthouse [sloping roof over a door or window].

1) **sobrado** *m.* attic, garret. *2 adv.* SOBRADAMENTE.

2) **sobrado, -da** *adj.* excessive, more than enough. *2* rich, having in abundance.

**sobrancero, -ra** *adj.* disengaged, unemployed.

**sobrante** *adj.* remaining, leftover. *2 m.* leftover, surplus.

**sobrar** *intr.* to be in excess, be more than is necessary, be over and above: *sobrarle a uno* [*una cosa*], to have in excess, have to spare. *2* to be superfluous; to be in the way. *3* to remain, be left over.

**sobrasada** *f.* a Majorcan sausage.

**sobre** *prep.* on, upon. *2* over, above: ~ *todo*, above all. *3* about, concerning. *4* about [approximately]. *5* to, toward. *6* in addition to. *7* on, near [a river, etc.]. *8* COM. on: *girar* ~, to draw on. *9* COM. above: ~ *la par*, above par. *10* ~ *manera*, beyond measure. *11* ~ *sí*, attentive, on guard;

haughty. *12 m.* envelope [for letters]. *13* SOBRESCRITO.

**sobreabundancia** *f.* superabundance.

**sobreabundar** *intr.* to superabound.

**sobrealimentar** *tr.* to overfeed.

**sobrealzar** *tr.* to raise, to raise excessively.

**sobreañadir** *tr.* to superadd, superinduce.

**sobreasada** *f.* SOBRASADA.

**sobreasar** *tr.* COOK. to roast again.

**sobrebarrer** *tr.* to sweep lightly.

**sobrecalza** *f.* legging.

**sobrecama** *f.* coverlet, bedspread.

**sobrecarga** *f.* overload, extra load, overburden. *2* additional trouble. *3* PHILAT. surcharge.

**sobrecargar** *tr.* to overload, overburden, overcharge. *2* to surcharge [a postage stamp]. *3* SEW. to fell.

**sobrecargo** *m.* NAUT. purser, supercargo.

**sobrecarta** *f.* envelope [for a letter].

**sobreceja** *f.* part of the forehead over the eyebrows.

**sobrecejo, sobreceño** *m.* frown.

**sobrecerco** *m.* reinforcing hoop, ring or frame.

**sobrecielo** *m.* canopy.

**sobrecincha** *f.*, **sobrecincho** *m.* surcingle.

**sobrecoger** *tr.* to surprise, take unawares. *2 ref.* to be surprised, to be struck with awe, dread, etc.

**sobrecogimiento** *m.* surprise, awe, fear.

**sobrecoser** *tr.* SEW. to whip, to fell.

**sobrecrecer** *intr.* to grow too much.

**sobrecubierta** *f.* double cover or wrapping. *2* jacket [of a book].

**sobrecuello** *m.* top collar. *2* stock [kind of cravat].

**sobredicho, -cha** *adj.* above-mentioned, aforesaid.

**sobrediente** *m.* snaggletooth.

**sobredorar** *tr.* to gold-plate [a metal]. *2* fig. to gloss over.

**sobreentender** *tr.* SOBRENTENDER.

**sobreesdrújulo, -la** *adj.* SOBRESDRÚJULO.

**sobreexcitar** *tr.* SOBREXCITAR.

**sobrefalda** *f.* overskirt.

**sobrefaz**, *pl.* **-faces** *f.* surface, outside.

**sobrehaz** *f.* surface, outside. *2* cover. *3* superficial appearance.

**sobrehilado** *m.* SEW. overcast, overcasting.

**sobrehilar** *tr.* SEW. to overcast.

**sobrehumano, -na** *adj.* superhuman.

**sobrejuanete** *m.* NAUT. royal [sail].

**sobrelecho** *m.* MAS. under bed [of a stone].

**sobrellenar** *tr.* to fill up, fill full.

**sobrellevar** *tr.* to ease [another's burden], to aid another to bear [his burden]. *2* to bear, suffer with patience. *3* to overlook, be lenient about.

**sobremanera** *adv.* exceedingly, beyond measure.

**sobremesa** *f.* table cover. *2* sitting at table after eating: *de* ~, at table after eating. *3 de* ~, desk, table: *reloj de* ~, desk clock.

**sobremesana** *f.* NAUT. mizzen topsail.

**sobrenadar** *intr.* to float [on a liquid].

**sobrenatural** *adj.* supernatural.

**sobrenombre** *m.* surname. *2* nickname; agnomen.

**sobrentender** *tr.* to understand [something implied, not expressed]. *2 ref.* to be understood, go without saying. ¶ CONJUG. like *entender*.

**sobrepaga** *f.* extra pay.

**sobreparto** *m.* after chilbirth, confinement after childbirth.

**sobrepeine** *adv.* coll. slightly, superficially.

**sobrepelliz**, *pl.* **-llices** *f.* ECCL. surplice.

**sobreponer** *tr.* to put over or upon; to superpose. *2 ref. sobreponerse a*, to be superposed; to master,

overcome, be or make oneself superior to. ¶ CONJUG. like *poner*.
**sobreposición** *f.* superposition.
**sobreproducción** *f.* superproduction, overproduction.
**sobrepuerta** *f.* overdoor; lambrequin. *2* cornice over a door.
**sobrepuesto, -ta** *p. p.* of SOBREPONER. *2 adj.* superposed, superimposed. *3 m.* appliqué.
**sobrepujanza** *f.* great power, strength or vigor.
**sobrepujar** *tr.* to surpass, excel.
**sobrequilla** *f.* NAUT. keelson.
**sobrero** *adj.* BULLF. extra, spare [bull].
**sobresaliente** *adj.* projecting. *2* surpassing, excellent. *3* outstanding, remarkable. *4 m.* the highest examination mark. *5* THEAT. understudy. *6* BULLF. substitute.
**sobresalir** *intr.* to project, jut out. *2* to excel, distinguish oneself. *3* to stand out.
**sobresaltar** *tr.* to alarm, startle. *2* to assail suddenly. *3 intr.* [of figures in a painting] to be striking. *4 ref.* to be startled, to start.
**sobresalto** *m.* startle, shock, sudden alarm. *2 de ~*, suddenly, unexpectedly.
**sobresanar** *intr.* [of a wound] to heal superficially.
**sobresaturar** *tr.* CHEM. to supersaturate.
**sobrescribir** *tr.* to superscribe. ¶ PAST. P.: *sobrescrito, sobrescripto.*
**sobrescrito** *m.* superscription, address.
**sobresdrújulo, -la** *adj.* accented on any syllable preceding the antepenult.
**sobreseer** *intr.* LAW to stay a judgement. *2* to desist, yield.
**sobreseimiento** *m.* LAW stay of proceedings.
**sobrestadías** *f. pl.* NAUT. extra lay days.
**sobrestante** *m.* foreman, overseer.
**sobresueldo** *m.* extra pay, extra wages.
**sobretarde** *f.* late afternoon.
**sobretodo** *m.* overcoat.
**sobrevenir** *intr.* to come, happen. *2* to come unexpectedly. *3* to follow, supervene. ¶ CONJUG. like *venir*.
**sobrevesta, sobreveste** *f.* surcoat [over the armour].
**sobrevestir** *tr.* to put [a garment] over other clothes.
**sobrevidriera** *f.* window guard. *2* storm window.
**sobreviento** *m.* gust of wind.
**sobreviviente** *adj.* surviving. *2 m.-f.* survivor.
**sobrevivir** *intr.* to survive. *2 ~ a*, to outlive.
**sobrexcitación** *f.* overexcitement, overexcitation.
**sobrexcitar** *tr.* to overexcite. *2 ref.* to become overexcited.
**sobriedad** *f.* sobriety, frugality, moderation.
**sobrina** *f.* niece.
**sobrino** *m.* nephew.
**sobrio, -bria** *adj.* sober, temperate, moderate, frugal.
**socaire** *m.* NAUT. lee: *al ~ de*, under the lee of.
**socaliña** *f.* trick [to get something from someone].
**socaliñar** *tr.* to trick one out of [something].
**socalzar** *tr.* MASON. to underpin, underset.
**socapa** *f.* pretext, pretence: *a ~*, on the sly.
**socarra** *f.* singe, scorching. *2* slyness.
**socarrar** *tr.* to singe, scorch.
**socarrén** *m.* ARCH. eaves.
**socarrón, -na** *adj.* sly, cunning.
**socarronería** *f.* slyness, cunning, artfulness.
**socava** *f.* digging under, undermining. *2* hollow for water around a tree.
**socavar** *tr.* to undermine.

**socavón** *m.* cave, cavern. *2* MIN. adit.
**socaz** *m.* tailrace.
**sociabilidad** *f.* sociableness, sociability.
**sociable** *adj.* sociable, companionable.
**social** *adj.* social: *ciencias sociales*, social sciences; *trato ~*, social intercourse; *razón ~*, COM. firm, firm name.
**socialismo** *m.* socialism.
**socialista** *adj.* socialist, socialistic. *2 m.-f.* socialist.
**socializar** *tr.* to socialize.
**sociedad** *f.* society [social mode of life, community; companionship, company]. *2 sociedad* or *buena ~*, society [fashionable people]. *3* society, association, union, club. *4* COM. partnership: *hacer ~ con*, to be in partnership with. *5* COM. society, company, corporation: *~ limitada*, limited company.
**societario, -ria** *adj.* pertaining to the associations or to the trade unions.
**socio, -cia** *m.-f.* COM. partner: *~ capitalista*, financial partner; *~ comanditario*, silent partner, sleeping partner; *~ industrial*, working partner. *2* member, fellow [of a society, club, etc.]. *3* coll. fellow, guy.
**sociología** *f.* sociology.
**sociólogo, -ga** *m.-f.* sociologist.
**socolor** *m.* pretext, pretence. *2 adv.* under colour.
**socollada** *f.* NAUT. flapping [of a sail]. *2* NAUT. pitching.
**socorredor, -ra** *adj.* helper, aider, succourer.
**socorrer** *tr.* to assist, help, aid, succour.
**socorrido, -da** *adj.* ready to help. *2* handy, useful. *3* trite, hackneyed.
**socorro** *m.* assistance, help, aid, succour, relief.
**sochantre** *m.* ECCL. subchanter, succentor.
**soda** *f.* SOSA.
**sódico, -ca** *adj.* CHEM. sodic; sodium.
**sodio** *m.* CHEM. sodium.
**sodomía** *f.* sodomy.
**sodomita** *adj.-n.* Sodomite. *2* sodomite.
**soez** *adj.* coarse, base, vile.
**sofá** *m.* sofa.
**Sofía** *f. pr. n.* Sophia. *2* GEOG. Sofia.
**sofión** *m.* snort [of anger]; harsh refusal.
**sofisma** *m.* sophism, fallacy.
**sofista** *m.* Sophist. *2* sophist.
**sofistería** *m.* sophistry.
**sofisticación** *f.* sophistication, adulteration.
**sofisticar** *tr.* to sophisticate, adulterate.
**sofístico, -ca** *adj.* sophistic, sophistical.
**sofito** *m.* ARCH. soffit.
**soflama** *f.* faint glow or flame. *2* blush. *3* fig. flimflam, deceitful talk. *4* coll. harangue.
**soflamar** *tr.* to deceive, humbug. *2* to make [a person] blush. *3 ref.* COOK. to burn, scorch.
**sofocación** *f.* choking, suffocation, smothering, stifling.
**sofocar** *tr.* to choke, suffocate, smother, stifle [stop the breath of]. *2* to stifle, smother, quench. *3* to harass, importune. *4* to put to blush. *5 ref.* to blush.
**sofoco** *m.* suffocation. *2* blush, embarrassment. *3* annoyance, vexation, mortification.
**sofocón** *m.*, **sofoquina** *f.* coll. great vexation or mortification.
**sofreír** *tr.* COOK. to fry slightly. ¶ CONJUG. like *reír*. | PAST. P.: *sofreído & sofrito.*
**sofrenada** *f.* sudden checking of a horse. *2* harsh reprimand.

**sofrenar** *tr.* to check [a horse] suddenly. *2* to reprimand severely. *3* to check [a passion].

**sofrito, -ta** *irreg. p. p.* of SOFREÍR. *2 m.* anything sightly fried.

**soga** *f.* rope, esparto rope, halter. *2* MAS. face [of a brick or stone]. *3 hacer ~,* to lag behind.

**soguero** *m.* ropemaker; ropedealer. *2* street porter.

**sois** *irr.* V. SER.

**soja** *f.* BOT. soy, soy bean.

**sojuzgar** *tr.* to conquer, subject, subjugate, subdue.

**sol** *m.* sun [heavenly body; warmth from the sun, sunlight; day]: *rayo de ~,* sunbeam; *hace ~,* it is sunny; *no dejar a ~ ni a sombra,* to importune, not to leave in pace; *tomar el ~,* to bask or walk in the sun; *a ~ puesto,* at nightfall; *de ~ a ~,* from sunrise to sunset. *2* MUS. sol, G. *3* sol [Peruvian coin].

**solada** *f.* sediment, lees.

**solado** *m.* paving, flooring [act]. *3* pavement, tile floor.

**solador** *m.* paver, tiler.

**solamente** *adv.* only, solely. *2 ~ que,* provided that, if only.

**solana** *f.* sunny place. *2* sun gallery.

**solanáceo, -a** *adj.* BOT. solanaceous.

**solano** *m.* easterly wind. *2* hot wind.

**solapa** *f.* lapel. *2* pretence, dissembling: *de ~,* underhand, sneakingly.

**solapado, -da** *adj.* underhand, sneaky. *2* sly, hypocritical.

**solapar** *tr.* to put lapels on [o coat]. *2* to overlap. *3* to cloak, conceal. *4 intr.* [of a part of a garment] to overlap.

**solapo** *m.* SOLAPA. *2* overlapped part or piece. *3* coll. chuck under the chin.

1) **solar** *adj.* solar. *2 m.* site, groundplot [for a building]. *3* ancestral mansion. *4* noble house or lineage.

2) **solar** *tr.* to floor, pave. *2* to sole [shoes]. ¶ CONJUG. like *contar.*

**solariego, -ga** *adj.* pertaining to a noble house or lineage: *casa solariega,* ancestral mansion.

**solaz** *m.* solace, comfort, relief, recreation.

**solazar** *tr.* to solace, comfort. *2* to solace, amuse, divert. *3 ref.* to solace oneself, amuse oneself.

**solazoso, -sa** *adj.* recreating, amusing, delectable.

**soldada** *f.* wages, pay, salary.

**soldadesca** *f.* soldiery. *2* undisciplinated troops.

**soldadesco, -ca** *adj.* soldierly, soldierlike.

**soldado** *m.* soldier: *~ de caballería,* trooper, cavalryman; *~ de infantería,* infantryman; *~ raso,* private.

**soldador** *m.* solderer, welder. *2* soldering iron. *3* blowtorch.

**soldadura** *f.* soldering, welding: *~ autógena,* welding. *2* solder. *3* soldered joint, welded joint.

**soldar** *tr.* to solder, weld. *2* to solder, unite. *3* fig. to mend [a blunder]. ¶ CONJUG. like *contar.*

**solear** *tr.* to sun [expose to the sun]. *2 ref.* to sun oneself or itself.

**solecismo** *m.* GRAM. solecism.

**soledad** *f.* solitude, loneliness. *2* sorrow, bereavement. *3* solitude [lonely place]. *4 pl.* Andalusian tune, song and dance.

**soledoso, -sa** *adj.* solitary. *2* lonely, lonesome.

**solemne** *adj.* solemn. *2* coll. great, downright.

**solemnidad** *f.* solemnity. *2* festivity. *3 pl.* formalities.

**solemnizar** *tr.* to solemnize.

**solenoide** *m.* ELECT. solenoid.

**soler** *intr.* to be accustomed to, be wont to, use to; to generally: *yo solía tomar el autobús,* I used to take the bus; *suele nevar en este tiempo,* it generally snows at this time of the year. ¶ It is used only in the INDIC. Pres.: *suelo, sueles, suele; solemos, soléis, suelen;* in the imperf.: *solía, solías,* etc., and in the compound preterit: *he solido, has solido,* etc.

**solera** *f.* ARCH. girder. *2* stone base [for uprights]. *3* nether millstone. *4* bottom [of a furnace]. *5* mother [of vine].

**soleta** *f.* patch for the sole of a stocking. *2 picar de ~, tomar ~,* to hasten, run; to flee.

**solevación** *f.,* **solevamiento** *m.* raising up, pushing up, upheaval [lifting up from beneath]. *2* uprising, insurrection.

**solevantar** *tr.* to raise up, upheave. *2 ref.* to rise up, upheave. *3 tr.-ref.* SOLIVIANTAR.

**solevar** *tr.* to incite to revolt. *2 ref.* to rebel. *3 tr.-ref.* SOLEVANTAR 1 & 2.

**solfa** *f.* solmization. *2* musical annotation, notes. *3* fig. music. *4* coll. beating, drubbing. *5 poner en ~,* to put in a ridiculous light.

**solfatara** *f.* GEOL. solfatara.

**solfeador, -ra** *m.-f.* sol-faer.

**solfear** *intr.-tr.* MUS. to sol-fa, solmizate. *2 tr.* coll. to bear, drub.

**solfeo** *m.* MUS. sol-fa; sol-faing, solmization. coll. beating, drubbing.

**solfista** *m.-f.* sol-faer.

**solicitación** *f.* solicitation.

**solicitado, -da** *adj.* in good demand. *2* sought, popular.

**solícitamente** *adv.* solicitously. *2* diligently.

**solicitante** *m.-f.* petitioner, applicant.

**solicitar** *tr.* to solicit, ask for, beg, petition. *2* to solicit, invite, attract. *3* to woo.

**solícito, -ta** *adj.* solicitous, diligent, careful.

**solicitud** *f.* solicitude, diligence, care. *2* petition, demand, request, application.

**solidar** *tr.* to consolidate, harden, strengthen. *2* to render firm or stable.

**solidaridad** *f.* solidarity. *2* common cause.

**solidario, -ria** *adj.* solidary. *2* jointly liable; jointly binding. *3* making common cause.

**solidarizar** *tr.* to make solidary. *2 ref.* to become solidary, to make common cause.

**solideo** *m.* ECCL. calotte.

**solidez** *f.* solidity. *2* firmness, strength. *3* fastness [of colour].

**solidificar** *tr.* to solidify. *2 ref.* to solidify [become solid].

**sólido, -da** *adj.* solid. *2* COM. substantial [firm]. *3* fast [colour]. *4 m.* GEOM. solid.

**soliloquio** *m.* soliloquy.

**solimán** *m.* coll. corrosive sublimate.

**solio** *m.* throne [royal seat].

**solípedo, -da** *adj.-m.* ZOOL. soliped.

**solista** *m.-f.* MUS. soloist.

**solitaria** *f.* coll. tapeworm.

**solitario, -ria** *adj.* solitary, lone, lonely. *2* secluded [spot, life]. *3* BOT. solitary [flower]. *4 m.* solitary, hermit. *5* solitaire [diamond game].

**soliviantar** *tr.* to revolt, make hostile or rebellious. *2 ref.* to revolt, become hostile or rebellious.

**soliviar** *tr.* to lift up [from beneath]. *2 ref.* to rise partly, get up partly.

**solo, -la** *adj.* alone; by himself, itself, etc. *2* lone, lonely. *3* only, sole. *4 m.* MUS. solo. *5* a card game. *6 a solas,* alone [unaccompanied, unaided]; in private.

**sólo** *adv.* SOLAMENTE.
**solomillo, solomo** *m.* sirloin. *2* loin [of pork].
**solsticio** *m.* ASTR. solstice.
**soltar** *tr.* to untie, unfasten, loosen. *2* to turn loose. *3* to let out, set free, release, discharge. *4* to let go, drop. *5* to cast, shed [the skin, etc.]. *6* coll. to give, pay [money]. *7* coll. to give [a blow, etc.]; to fire [a shot]. *8* to utter, let out [a curse, a remark, etc.]. *9* to burst into [laughter, tears, etc.]. *10 ref.* to come off, come untied, get loose. *11* to get free. *12* to acquire ease. *13* to begin to [walk, talk, etc.]. ¶ CONJUG. like *contar.*
**soltería** *f.* celibacy, singleness; bachelorhood.
**soltero, -ra** *adj.* single, unmarried. *2 m.* bachelor, single man. *3 f.* single woman.
**solterón** *m.* old bachelor.
**solterona** *f.* old maid, spinster.
**soltura** *f.* release, setting at liberty. *2* ease, facility, agility. *3* fluency. *4* licentiousness.
**solubilidad** *f.* solubility.
**soluble** *adj.* soluble. *2* solvable.
**solución** *f.* solution: ~ *de continuidad,* solution of continuity, break.
**solucionar** *tr.* to solve. *2* to bring to a favorable issue.
**solutivo, -va** *adj.* MED. solutive.
**solvencia** *f.* COM. solvency. *2* ability, reliability.
**solventar** *tr.* SOLUCIONAR. *2* to settle, pay up.
**solvente** *adj.* COM. solvent. *2* able, reliable.
**sollado** *m.* NAUT. orlop.
**sollamar** *tr.* to scorch, singe.
**sollo** *m.* ESTURIÓN.
**sollozar** *intr.* to sob.
**sollozo** *m.* sob.
**somanta** *f.* coll. beating, drubbing.
**somatén** *m.* [in Catalonia] body of armed citizens gathering at the call of the alarm bell. *2* alarm bell.
**somático, -ca** *adj.* somatic.
**sombra** *f.* shade, shadow: *dar* ~, to cast a shadow; *hacer* ~ *a,* to stand in the light of; to protect; to outshine; *a la* ~, in the shade; coll. in jail; *ni por* ~, by no means. *2* shadow, phantom, ghost. *3* ASTR. umbra. *4* F. ARTS shade, shading. *5 tener buena* ~, to be pleasant; to be witty or funny; to bring good luck. *6 tener mala* ~, to be disagreeable; to bring bad luck. *7 pl.* shades, shadows, darkness. *8 sombras chinescas,* shadow play.
**sombraje** *m.* screen or roof made with branches, mats, etc., to afford shade.
**sombrajo** *m.* SOMBRAJE. *2* coll. shadow cast by getting in someone's light.
**sombreado** *m.* F. ARTS shading.
**sombrear** *tr.* to shade, shadow [throw a shadow upon]. *2* F. ARTS to shade.
**sombrerazo** *m.* aug. large hat. *2* blow with a hat. *3* coll. doffing of the hat [as a greeting].
**sombrerera** *f.* hatbox, bandbox. *2* hatter's wife.
**sombrerería** *f.* hattery, hat factory. *2* hat shop.
**sombrerero** *m.* hatter.
**sombrerete** *m.* dim. little hat. *2* BOT. cap [of mushroom]. *3* hood, bonnet [of chimney]. *4* spark catcher [of locomotive].
**sombrerillo** *m.* dim. little hat or bonnet.
**sombrero** *m.* hat [for men or women], bonnet [for women]: ~ *calañés,* Andalusian hat with turned-up brim and low cone-shaped crown; ~ *cordobés,* beaver hat with a flat brim and a cylindrical low crown; ~ *de teja,* shovel hat; ~ *de candil,* or *de tres picos,* cocked hat; three-cornered hat; ~ *de copa,* high hat, silk hat; ~ *de jipi-*

*japa,* Panama hat; ~ *flexible,* soft hat; ~ *hongo,* derby hat. *2* canopy [of pulpit]. *3* BOT. cap [of mushroom]. *4* drumhead [of capstan].
**sombría** *f.* UMBRÍA.
**sombrilla** *f.* parasol, sunshade.
**sombrío, -bría** *adj.* sombre, gloomy, dark, dismal, shady, overcast. *2* F. ARTS shaded, dark.
**sombroso, -sa** *adj.* shady [causing shade]. *2* shady, shadowy [abounding in shade].
**someramente** *adv.* slightly, superficially.
**somero, -ra** *adj.* slight, superficial. *2* shallow; in the surface, about the surface.
**someter** *tr.* to subject, subjugate, subdue. *2* to subject [to the action of something], to put [to a test, etc.]. *3* to submit [for consideration or decision]. *4 ref.* to submit, surrender, yield. *5* to go [through an operation, examination, etc.].
**sometimiento** *m.* subjection. *2* submission.
**somier** *m.* bedspring, spring mattres.
**somnambulismo** *m.* somnambulism, sleepwalking.
**somnámbulo, -la** *adj.* somnambulistic. *2 m.-f.* somnambulist, sleepwalker.
**somnífero, -ra** *adj.* somniferous, somnific.
**somnolencia** *f.* somnolence, drowsiness.
**somorgujar** *tr.* to plunge, submerge. *2 intr.* BUCEAR. *3 ref.* to dive, duck, plunge.
**somorgujo, somorgujón** *m.* ORN. dabchick, grebe.
**somos** *irr.* V. SER.
**sompesar** *tr.* SOPESAR.
**son** *m.* sound [of an instrument]: *a* ~, or *al* ~, *de,* at or to the sound of. *2* news, report, rumour. *3* pretext, motive: *¿a* ~ *de qué?,* why?, for what reason?; *sin ton ni* ~, without rhyme or reason. *4* manner, guise: *en* ~ *de guerra,* in a hostile manner.
**son** *irr.* V. SER.
**sonadero** *m.* handkerchief.
**sonado, -da** *adj.* noted, famous. *3* coll. much talked-about: *hacer una que sea sonada,* to do something that causes a lot of talk.
**sonaja** *f.* jingle [each pair of disks of the tambourine]. *2 pl.* jingle hoop.
**sonajero** *m.* baby's rattle.
**sonambulismo** *m.* SOMNAMBULISMO.
**sonámbulo, -la** *adj.-n.* SOMNÁMBULO.
**sonante** *adj.* sonant, sounding, sonorous, jingling.
**sonar** *tr.* to sound, play, ring [an instrument]. *2* to blow [someone's nose]. *3 intr.* to sound, ring. *4* [of a clock] to strike. *5* PHON. [of a letter] to be sounded. *6* to be mentioned. *7* to sound familiar, be vaguely remembered. *8* ~ *a,* to seem, have the appearance of being. *9* ~ *bien* or *mal* [of a word, expression, etc.], to be pleasing or offensive. *10 ref.* to blow one's nose. *11 impers. por ahí suena* or *se suena, que,* it is rumoured that. ¶ CONJUG. like *contar.*
**sonata** *f.* MUS. sonata.
**sonatina** *f.* MUS. sonatina.
**sonda** *f.* sounding. *2* NAUT. sound, lead. *3* drill [for boring soils]. *4* SURG. sound, probe; catheter.
**sondaleza** *f.* NAUT. lead line, sounding line.
**sondar, sondear** *tr.* NAUT. to sound, fathom. *2* to sound [the soil]. *3* to sound, probe [a wound, a person; a person's intentions].
**sondeo** *m.* sounding, fathoming, probing.
**sonecillo** *m.* dim. slight sound. *2* merry tune.
**sonetista** *m.-f.* sonneteer, sonnet writer.
**soneto** *m.* sonnet.
**sonido** *m.* sound [sensation produced through

the ear; vibrations causing this sensation]. *2* PHONET. sound.

**sonochada** *f.* evening [early part of the night].

**sonoridad** *f.* sonority.

**sonoro, -ra; sonoroso, -sa** *adj.* sonorous. *2* harmonious. *3* clear, loud.

**sonreír** *intr.* to smile. ¶ CONJUG. like *reír*.

**sonriente** *adj.* smiling.

**sonrisa** *f.* smile.

**sonrojar, sonrojear** *tr.* to make [one] blush. *2 ref.* to blush.

**sonrojo** *m.* blush, blushing. *2* word or remark that causes a blush.

**sonrosar, sonrosear** *tr.* to rose-colour, to flush. *2 ref.* to become rose-coloured.

**sonsaca** *f.,* **sonsacamiento** *m.* the act of SONSACAR.

**sonsacar** *tr.* to stealthily take [something] out of its place. *2* to draw out [a person or a secret]. *3* to coax [a servant or employee] away from another's service.

**sonsonete** *m.* rhythmical tapping. *2* fig. dull monotonous noise; singsong. *3* ironic or scornful tone.

**soñación** *f. ni por ~,* by no means.

**soñador, -ra** *adj.* dreaming. *2 m.-f.* dreamer.

**soñar** *tr.* to dream: *ni soñarlo,* not even in dreams. *2 intr.* to dream; to daydream: *~ con* or *en,* to dream of. ¶ CONJUG. like *contar*.

**soñarrera** *f.* sleepiness. *2* deep sleep.

**soñera** *f.* sleepiness.

**soñolencia** *f.* SOMNOLENCIA.

**soñoliento, -ta** *adj.* somnolent, sleepy, drowsy, heavy. *2* lazy. *3* soporiferous.

**sopa** *f.* sop [bread dipped in a liquid]: *hecho una ~,* coll. drenched, soaked to the skin. *2* COOK. soup: *comer la ~ boba,* coll. to live at other people's expense.

**sopalancar** *tr.* to lift with a lever.

**sopapear** *tr.* coll. to beat, slap.

**sopapina** *f.* beating, drubbing.

**sopapo** *m.* blow under the chin. *2* slap in the face.

**sopeña** *f.* space or cavity under a rock.

**sopera** *f.* tureen, soup tureen.

**sopero** *adj.* soup [plate].

**sopesar** *tr.* to heft, test the weight of by lifting.

**sopetear** *tr.* to sop [bread]. *2* to maltreat.

**sopetón** *m.* toast soaked in olive oil. *2* box, slap. *3 de ~,* suddenly.

**sopicaldo** *m.* very thin soup.

**sopita** *f. dim.* light soup.

**¡sopla!** *interj.* gracious!, what a thing!

**sopladero** *m.* vent, blowhole.

**soplado, -da** *adj.* coll. overnice, spruce. *3* coll. conceited, stuck up.

**soplador, -ra** *adj.* blowing. *2 m.-f.* blower. *3 m.* blowing fan. *4* SOPLADERO.

**sopladura** *f.* blowing. *2* FOUND. air hole.

**soplamocos** *m.* box or slap on the nose.

**soplar** *intr.* to blow [send forth air from mouth, from a pair of bellows, etc.]. *2* [of the wind] to blow. *3 tr.* to blow, blow upon, blow out. *4* to blow [glass]. *5* to fan [coals, a fire]. *6* to blow up; inflate. *7* to steal. *8* to huff [a man] in draughts. *9* to prompt, whisper [tell one what to say]. *10* to report, tattle. *11 ref.* to be puffed up. *12* to stuff oneself.

**soplete** *m.* blowpipe, blowtorch, torch.

**soplido** *m.* SOPLO I.

**soplillo** *m.* blowing fan. *2* a kind of silk gauze.

**soplo** *m.* blow, blowing [forcing the air from the mouth, etc.]. *2* breath, puff, gust [of wind]. *3*

instant, moment. *4* secret warning. *5* report, piece of talebearing.

**soplón, -na** *m.-f.* informer, talebearer.

**soplonear** *tr.-intr.* to inform, tell tales.

**soponcio** *m.* coll. fainting fit, swoon.

**sopor** *m.* MED. sopor, lethargy. *2* somnolence.

**soporífero, -ra** *adj.* soporiferous, soporific.

**soportable** *adj.* supportable, bearable, tolerable.

**soportal** *m.* ARCH. porch, portico, arcade.

**soportar** *tr.* to support [bear the weight or stress of]. *2* to support, endure, suffer, tolerate.

**soporte** *m.* support, bearing, rest, base.

**soprano** *m.-f.* MUS. soprano.

**sopuntar** *tr.* to underscore with dots.

**sor** *f.* sister [before the name of a nun].

**sorber** *tr.* to suck [drink by sucking]. *2* to sip. *3* to absorb, imbibe. *4* to swallow.

**sorbete** *m.* sherbet, water ice.

**sorbetera** *f.* ice-cream freezer.

**sorbito** *m. dim.* little sip.

**sorbo** *m.* absortion, imbibing. *2* sip, gulp, swallow [of a liquid]: *beber a sorbos,* to sip.

**sordedad, sordera, sordez** *f.* deafness.

**sordidez** *f.* dirtiness, squalidity. *2* sordidness.

**sórdido, -da** *adj.* dirty, squalid. *2* sordid.

**sordina** *f.* MUS. mute, sordine, damper.

**sordo, -da** *adj.* deaf: *~ como una tapia,* stonedeaf. *2* silent, still: *a la sorda,* noiselessly, imperceptibly. *3* muffled, dull, low [sound]. *4* dull [pain]. *5* MATH., PHONET. surd. *6 m.-f.* deaf person: *hacerse el ~,* to pretend to be deaf, to turn a deaf ear.

**sordomudo, -da** *adj.-n.* deaf and dumb, deafmute.

**sorgo** *m.* BOT. sorghum.

**soriano, -na** *adj.-n.* of Soria.

**sorna** *f.* sluggishness. *2* sly slowness in doing or saying something.

**soro** *m.* BOT. sorus.

**sorocharse** *ref.* (S. Am.) to become mountain sick.

**soroche** *m.* (Am.) mountain sickness. *2* (Am.) blush flush. *3* (Bol., Chi.) GALENA.

**sorprendente** *adj.* surprising.

**sorprender** *tr.* to surprise.

**sorpresa** *f.* surprise: *coger de ~,* to surprise [astonish; take unawares].

**sorra** *f.* side of tunny fish.

**sorrostrada** *f.* insolence, taunt, blunt remark.

**sorteamiento** *m.* SORTEO.

**sortear** *tr.* to draw lots for; to raffle. *2* to evade, get around [a difficulty, etc.]. *3* BULLF. to fight [the bull].

**sorteo** *m.* drawing [of numbers in a lottery]; drawing of lots; raffle. *2* evading or getting around [a difficulty, etc.]. *3* BULLF. fighting the bull.

**sortija** *f.* small ring; finger ring. *2* curl [of hair].

**sortilegio** *m.* sortilege.

**sortílego, -ga** *adj.* sortilegic, sortilegious. *2 m.-f.* sortileger.

**sosa** *f.* CHEM. soda. *2* BOT. glasswort. *3* soda ash.

**sosaina** *m.-f.* dull, colourless person.

**sosegadamente** *adv.* calmly, quietly, peacefully. *2* unhurriedly.

**sosegado, -da** *adj.* calm, quiet, peaceful; pacified.

**sosegador, -ra** *adj.* calming, quieting. *2 m.-f.* quieter, appeaser, soother, pacifier.

**sosegar** *tr.* to calm, quiet, appease, soothe, pacify. *2 intr.* to rest, repose. *3 intr.-ref.* to become calm, to quiet down. *4* to be pacified. ¶ CONJUG. like *acertar*.

**sosera, sosería** *f.* dullness, insipidity, vapidness.

**sosiego** *m.* calm, quiet, peace, tranquility.

**sosiego, sosiegue**, etc. *irr.* V. SOSEGAR.

**soslayar** *tr.* to place obliquely. *2* to elude, evade, pass over [a question, a difficulty].

**soslayo, -ya** *adj.* oblique. *2 al* ~, *de* ~, obliquely, askance; sideways; in passing.

**soso, -sa** *adj.* insipid, tasteless. *2* insipid, dull, uninteresting.

**sospecha** *f.* suspicion.

**sospechar** *tr.* to suspect [have an impression of the existence or presence of; to be inclined to think that]. *2 intr.* to suspect, be suspicious about: ~ *de una persona*, to suspect a person.

**sospechoso, -sa** *adj.* suspicious [arousing suspicion], suspect. *2* suspicious [feeling suspicion]. *3 m.-f.* suspect [person].

**sospesar** *tr.* SOPESAR.

**sostén** *m.* support. *2* sustenance. *3* brassière.

**sostenedor, -ra** *m.-f.* supporter. *2* defender, upholder.

**sostener** *tr.* to support, sustain, hold up, prop. *2* to support, aid, give strength to, encourage. *3* to support, endure, tolerate. *4* to support, maintain [a family]. *5* to hold [a conference]. *6* to maintain, affirm, contend. *7* to defend, maintain [by argument]. *8* to maintain, sustain, keep up. *9 ref.* to support oneself. ¶ CONJUG. like *tener*.

**sostenido, -da** *adj.* supported. *2* sustained. *3 adj.-m.* MUS. sharp.

**sostenimiento** *m.* support. *2* maintenance, sustenance. *3 muro de* ~, retaining wall.

**sota** *f.* CARDS jack, knave.

**sotabanco** *m.* attic, garret.

**sotabarba** *f.* beard under the chin.

**sotacola** *f.* ATAHARRE.

**sotana** *f.* cassock, soutane. *2* coll. beating, drubbing.

**sótano** *m.* cellar, basement.

**sotaventarse, sotaventearse** *ref.* NAUT. to fall to leeward.

**sotavento** *m.* NAUT. lee, leeward.

**sotechado** *m.* shed.

**soterrar** *tr.* to bury underground. *2* fig. to bury, hide away. ¶ CONJUG. like *acertar*.

**sotileza** *f.* leader [of a fishline].

**sotillo** *m. dim.* little grove.

**soto** *m.* grove. *2* thicket.

**soviet** *m.* soviet.

**soviético, -ca** *adj.* soviet, sovietic.

**sovoz (a)** *adv.* in a low tone, in an undertone.

**soy** *irr.* V. SER.

**spinnaker** *m.* NAUT. spinnaker.

**su,** *pl.* **sus** *poss. adj.* [for the 3rd person in every gender and number]: his, your, her, its, their.

**suabo, -ba** *adj.-n.* Swabian.

**suasorio, -ria** *adj.* suasive, persuasive.

**suave** *adj.* soft, smooth, delicate, mellow. *2* sweet [odour]. *3* soft, gentle, mild. *4* suave, tractable.

**suavidad** *f.* softness, smoothness. *2* delicateness, mellowness, sweetness. *3* gentleness, mildness, suavity.

**suavizador, -ra** *adj.* softening, smoothing, mollifylling. *2 m.* razor strop.

**suavizar** *tr.* to soften, smoothe. *2* to mollify, mitigate, ease, temper. *3* to strop [a razor].

**subacuático, -ca** *adj.* subaqueous.

**subalpino, -na** *adj.* subalpine.

**subalterno, -na** *adj.* subaltern, subordinate. *2 m.-f.* subaltern.

**subarrendador, -ra** *m.-f.* subletter, subleaser.

**subarrendar** *tr.* to sublet, sublease. ¶ CONJUG. like *acertar*.

**subarrendatario, -ria** *m.-f.* sublessee, subtenant.

**subarriendo** *m.* sublease.

**subasta** *f.* auction, auction sale.

**subastador** *m.* auctioneer.

**subastar** *tr.* to auction, auction off, sell at auction.

**subclase** *f.* BIOL. subclass.

**subclavio, -via** *adj.* ANAT. subclavian.

**subcomisión** *f.* subcommission, subcommitee.

**subconsciente** *adj.* subconscious.

**subcostal** *adj.* ANAT. subcostal.

**subcutáneo, -a** *adj.* subcutaneous.

**subdelegado, -da** *m.-f.* subdelegate.

**subdiácono** *m.* subdeacon.

**subdirección** *f.* office of an assistant director.

**subdirector, -ra** *m.-f.* assistant director.

**súbdito, -ta** *m.-f.* subject [of a state, etc.].

**subdividir** *tr.* to subdivide.

**subdivisión** *f.* subdivision.

**subdominante** *f.* MUS. subdominant.

**suberoso, -sa** *adj.* suberous, suberose.

**subestimar** *tr.* to underrate, undervalue.

**subfamilia** *f.* BIOL. subfamily.

**subgénero** *m.* BIOL. subgenus.

**subida** *f.* ascent, ascension, going up, climbing. *2* accession [to the throne, etc.]. *3* elevation, hoisting. *4* rise [of prices, tide, etc.]. *5* acclivity, rise.

**subido, -da** *adj.* raised, mounted [on]. *2* high, strong. *3* high [price]. *4* bright, deep [colour]. *5* ~ *de color*, fig. off-colour, risqué.

**subinspector** *m.* subinspector.

**subintendente** *m.* assistant intendant.

**subir** *intr.* to go up, come up, ascend, rise, climb, mount, soar. *2* accede [to the throne, etc.]. *3* [of a river, prices, temperature, etc.] to rise. *4* to rise [become higher; increase in amount; come to the surface, slope upward; be promoted, prosper]. *5* MUS. to rise. *6* ~ *de tono*, fig. to become more arrogant; to raise one's voice. *7 tr.* to raise, bring up, take up, hoist. *8* to ascend, climb, go up [the stairs, etc.]. *9* to raise [the voice, price, etc.]. *10 ref.* to climb, get [on]. *11 subirse a la cabeza*, to go to one's head.

**subitáneo, -a** *adj.* sudden, unexpected.

**súbito, -ta** *adj.* sudden. *2* hasty, precipitate, impulsive. *3 adv. súbito* or *de* ~, suddenly.

**subjefe** *m.* assistant chief; second in command.

**subjetividad** *f.* subjectivity.

**subjetivo, -va** *adj.* subjective.

**subjuntivo** *adj.-m.* GRAM. subjunctive.

**sublevación, sublevamiento** *f.* insurrection, revolt.

**sublevar** *tr.* to raise in rebellion. *2* to stir up the indignation of. *3 intr.* to revolt, rise in insurrection.

**sublimación** *f.* sublimation.

**sublimado, -da** *adj.* sublimated. *2 m.* CHEM. sublimate.

**sublimar** *tr.* to sublime, sublimate. *2* CHEM. to sublimate.

**sublime** *adj.* sublime: *lo* ~, the sublime.

**sublimidad** *f.* sublimity.

**subliminar** *adj.* PSYCHOL. subliminal.

**sublingual** *adj.* ANAT. sublingual.

**sublunar** *adj.* sublunar, sublunary.

**submarino, -na** *adj.* submarine, underwater. *2 m.* NAUT. submarine.

**submaxilar** *adj.* ANAT. submaxillary.

**submúltiplo, -pla** *adj.-n.* MATH. submultiple.

**subnormal** *adj.* subnormal.

**suboficial** *m.* MIL. noncommissioned officer next above a sergeant.
**suborden** *m.* BIOL. suborder.
**subordinación** *f.* subordination.
**subordinado, -da** *adj.* subordinate; subservient. *2* GRAM. subordinate. *3 m.-f.* subordinate.
**subordinar** *tr.* to subordinate.
**subproducto** *m.* by-product.
**subrayar** *tr.* to underline. *2* to emphasize.
**subrepticio, -cia** *adj.* surreptitious.
**subrogar** *tr.* LAW. to subrogate, surrogate, substitute.
**subsanar** *tr.* to mend, correct, remedy, repair, obviate. *2* to excuse, exculpate.
**subscribir** *tr.* to sign, subscribe. *2* to subscribe [to another's opinion]. *3* to enter someone for a subscription to or for. *4 ref.* to subscribe to or for. ¶ CONJUG. Past. p.: *subscripto & subscrito.*
**suscripción** *f.* subscription.
**subscriptor, -ra** *m.-f.* subscriber.
**subsecretaría** *f.* undersecretaryship.
**subsecretario, -ria** *m.-f.* undersecretary.
**subsecuente** *adj.* SUBSIGUIENTE.
**subseguir** *intr.,* **subseguirse** *ref.* to follow next. ¶ CONJUG. like *servir.*
**subsidiario, -ria** *adj.* subsidiary [furnishing aid]. *2* LAW subsidiary.
**subsidio** *m.* subsidy. *2 ~ familiar,* family allowance.
**subsiguiente** *adj.* subsequent.
**subsistencia** *f.* subsistence. *2 pl.* provisions.
**subsistente** *adj.* subsistent.
**subsistir** *intr.* to subsist. *2* to last. *3* to live, find sustenance.
**substancia** *f.* METAPH. substance. *2* substance, matter. *3* substance [essence, most important part]: *en ~,* in substance, in brief. *4* nutritious part of food. *5* extract, juice. *6* value, importance. *7* coll. sense: *hombre sin ~,* senseless man.
**substancial** *adj.* substantial [pertaining to the substance]. *2* substancial, essential. *3* nourishing.
**substantividad** *f.* substantivity.
**substanciar** *tr.* to abstract, abridge. *2* LAW to conduct the proceedings of [a case].
**substancioso, -sa** *adj.* juicy, nourishing. *2* substantial, pithy. *3* important.
**substantivar** *tr.* GRAM. to substantivize.
**substantivo, -va** *adj.* substantive. *2* substantival. *3 m.* GRAM. substantive noun.
**substitución** *f.* substitution.
**substituible** *adj.* replaceable.
**substituir** *tr.* to substitute, replace; to be a substitute for. ¶ CONJUG. like *huir.*
**substitutivo** *adj.* substitutive. *2 m.* substitute [thing].
**substituto** *m.-f.* substitute [person].
**substracción** *f.* subtraction, deduction. *2* MATH. subtraction. *3* abstraction, purloining, stealing.
**substraendo** *m.* MATH. subtrahend.
**substraer** *tr.* to subtract, deduct. *2* MATH. to subtract. *3* to purloin, steal. *4 ~ a,* to put away from. *5 ref.* to elude, evade [observation, duty, etc.]. ¶ CONJUG. like *traer.*
**substrato** *m.* PHILOS. substratum.
**subsuelo** *m.* subsoil.
**subtender** *tr.* GEOM. to subtend.
**subteniente** *m.* MIL. second lieutenant.
**subtensa** *f.* GEOM. subtense, chord.
**subterfugio** *m.* subterfuge.

**subterráneo, -a** *adj.* subterranean, underground. *2 m.* subterranean. *3* (Am.) subway.
**subtítulo** *m.* subtitle, subhead.
**suburbano, -na** *adj.* suburban. *2 m.-f.* suburbanite.
**suburbicario, -ria** *adj.* suburbicarian.
**suburbio** *m.* suburb.
**subvención** *f.* subvention, subsidy.
**subvencionar** *tr.* to subsidize.
**subvenir** *tr.* to provide for [the needs of a person, community, etc.]; to meet, defray [expenses]. ¶ CONJUG. like *venir.*
**subversivo, -va** *adj.* subversive.
**subvertir** *tr.* to subvert. ¶ CONJUG. like *hervir.*
**subvierto, subvierta, subvirtió,** etc. *irr.* V. SUBVERTIR.
**subyacente** *adj.* subjacent, underlying.
**subyugación** *f.* subjugation.
**subyugar** *tr.* to subjugate, subdue.
**succino** *m.* succin, amber.
**succión** *f.* suction.
**sucedáneo, -a** *adj.* succedaneous. *2 m.* succedaneum, substitute [thing].
**suceder** *intr.* ~ *a,* to succeed [follow in order, ensue, be the successor of]. *2 ref.* to follow one another, follow one after the other. *3 impers.* to happen, occur.
**sucedido** *m.* event, happening.
**sucesión** *f.* succession [following in order; succeeding to the throne, etc.]. *2* LAW succession. *3* issue, offspring.
**sucesivamente** *adv.* successively: *y así ~,* and so on.
**sucesivo, -va** *adj.* successive, consecutive. *2 en lo ~,* in the future, thereafter.
**suceso** *m.* event, happening. *2* issue, outcome. *3* course [of time].
**sucesor, -ra** *m.-f.* successor.
**suciedad** *f.* dirt, filth. *2* dirtiness, filthiness.
**sucinto, -ta** *adj.* succint, concise, brief.
**sucio, -cia** *adj.* dirty, filthy, foul, unclean. *2* soiled, stained. *3* untidy, slovenly. *4* tainted with guilt or sin. *5* obscene. *6* easily soiled. *7* blurred [colour]. *8* foul [play]. *9 adv.* foully.
**sucre** *m.* sucre [Ecuadorean silver coin].
**suculento, -ta** *adj.* succulent, juicy, nourishing.
**sucumbir** *intr.* to succumb. *2* LAW to lose a suit.
**sucursal** *adj.* COM. branch. *2 f.* branch [of a commercial house], branch office.
**sud** *m.* south. *2* south wind.
**sudadero** *m.* saddlecloth. *2* sweating place, sudatorium.
**sudado, -da** *adj.* sweating, sweaty, wet with sweat.
**sudafricano, -na** *adj.-n.* South African.
**sudamericano, -na** *adj.-n.* South American.
**Sudán** *m. pr. n.* GEOG. Sudan.
**sudanés, -sa** *adj.-n.* Sudanese.
**sudar** *intr.* to sweat, perspire. *2 fig.* to sweat, toil. *intr.-tr.* to sweat, exude. *4 tr.* to sweat [wet with perspiration].
**sudario** *m.* shroud, winding sheet.
**sudatorio, -ria** *adj.* sudorific.
**sudeste** *m.* southeast. *2* southeast wind.
**sudoeste** *m.* southwest. *2* southwest wind.
**sudor** *m.* sweat, perspiration, exudation. *2 fig.* sweat, toil.
**sudoriento, -ta** *adj.* wet with sweat.
**sudorífero, -ra; sudorífico, -ca** *adj.-n.* sudorific.
**sudoríparo, -ra** *adj.* ANAT. sudoriferous [gland].
**sudoroso, -sa** *adj.* sweating, perspiring freely.
**sudoso, -sa** *adj.* sweaty.
**sudueste** *m.* SUDOESTE.

**Suecia** *f. pr. n.* GEOG. Sweden.
**sueco, -ca** *adj.* Swedish. *2 m.-f.* Swede: *hacerse el* ~, coll. to pretend not to hear.
**suegra** *f.* mother-in-law.
**suegro** *m.* father-in-law.
**suela** *f.* sole [of a shoe]: *de siete suelas*, fig. arrant, confirmed. *2* sole leather. *3* leather tip [of billiard cue]. *4* ICHTH. sole.
**sueldo** *m.* salary, pay: *a* ~ *de*, in the pay of. *2* sol [ancient coin].
**sueldo, suelde**, etc. *irr.* V. SOLDAR.
**suelo** *m.* ground, earth [surface of the earth] floor, pavement: *arrastrarse por el* ~, to crawl, creep; to cringe, humble oneself; *venir* or *venirse al* ~, to fall to the ground; to fail; *por el* ~, *por los suelos*, in state of great depreciation. *2* soil, land: ~ *natal*, native soil. *3* earth, world. *4* bottom, underside. *5* dregs, lees, sediment.
**suelta** *f.* release, setting free or loose.
**suelto** *adj.* loose [free; slack; hanging partly free; composed of free particles]. *2* light, swift, easy, agile, nimble. *3* flowing, fluent. *4* odd, loose, separate, detached. *5* single [copy]. *6* blank [verse]. *7* ~ *de lengua*, outspoken. *8 m. suelto* or *dinero* ~, small change. *9 m.* newspaper paragraph.
**suelto, suelte**, etc. *irr* V. SOLTAR.
**sueno, suene**, etc. *irr.* V. SONAR.
**sueño** *m.* sleep: ~ *pesado*, deep sleep; *tener* ~, to be sleepy; *entre sueños*, while half asleep. *2* sleepiness, drowsiness. *3* dream: *en sueños*, dreaming; *ni por sueños*, by no means.
**sueño, sueñe**, etc. *irr.* V. SOÑAR.
**suero** *m.* BIOL., MED. serum. *2* whey.
**sueroterapia** *f.* serotherapy, serum therapy.
**suerte** *f.* chance, hazard; fortune, lot, fate, destiny. *2* luck: *buena* or *mala* ~, good or bad luck. *3* good luck: *tener* ~, to be lucky; *por* ~, luckily. *4* lot [in deciding or selecting by lot]: *le cayó* or *le tocó la* ~, the lot fell on him. *5* state, condition: *mejorar de* ~, to better oneself. *6* sort, kind, class. *7* manner, way: *de* ~ *que*, so that; and so. *8* BULLF. any of the parts in which a bullfight is divided.
**sueste** *m.* southeast. *2* NAUT. southwester [hat].
**suéter** *m.* (Angl.) sweater [thick woollen jersey].
**suevo, -va** *adj.-n.* Swabian.
**suficiencia** *f.* ability, efficiency: *aire de* ~, sufficiency, conceit.
**suficiente** *adj.* sufficient, sufficing, enough: *ser* ~, to suffice. *2* able, capable.
**sufijo, -ja** *adj.* suffixed. *2 m.* suffix.
**sufocar** *tr.-ref.* SOFOCAR.
**sufragáneo, -a** *adj.-m.* suffragan.
**sufragar** *tr.* to defray, pay [the expenses]. *2* to aid, assist. *3 intr.* (Am.) to vote.
**sufragio** *m.* suffrage. *2* help, assistance. *3* ECCL. prayer, etc., for the dead.
**sufragista** *adj.-n.* suffragist. *2 f.* suffragette.
**sufrible** *adj.* sufferable, bearable.
**sufrido, -da** *adj.* enduring, patient, long-suffering. *3* that does not show dirt [colour]. *4* complacent [husband].
**sufridor, -ra** *adj.* suffering. *2 m.-f.* sufferer.
**sufrimiento** *m.* suffering. *2* bearing, endurance, tolerance.
**sufrir** *tr.* to suffer [pain, loss, grief, punishment, etc.]. *2* to suffer, endure, bear up, permit, tolerate. *3* to undergo [a change, operation, etc.]. *4* to take [an examination]. *6 intr.* to suffer. *7* to worry.

**sufusión** *m.* MED. suffusion.
**sugerencia** *f.* (Am.) suggestion, hint.
**sugerir** *tr.* to suggest, hint. ¶ CONJUG. like *hervir*.
**sugestión** *f.* suggestion [suggesting; idea, etc., suggested]. *2* [hypnotic] suggestion.
**sugestionable** *adj.* suggestible, easily influenced.
**sugestionar** *tr.* to hypnotize. *2* to influence [a person].
**suicida** *adj.* suicidal. *2 m.-f.* suicide [person].
**suicidarse** *ref.* to commit suicide, destroy oneself.
**suicidio** *m.* suicide, self-murder.
**Suiza** *pr. n.* GEOG. Switzerland.
**suizo, -za** *adj.-n.* Swiss.
**sujeción** *f.* subjection. *2* subduing. *3* submission, obedience. *4* fastening. *5* accordance [with law, etc.].
**sujetador** *m.* holder, fastener, clamp, clip, etc.
**sujetapapeles**, *pl.* **-les** *m.* paper clip.
**sujetar** *tr.* to subject, subdue. *2* to check, hold, restrain. *3* to hold fast, catch, grasp; fasten, attach, tie. *4 ref.* to submit, be subjected. *5* to conform to.
**sujeto, -ta** *irr. p. p.* of SUJETAR. *2 adj.* held, grasped, attached. *3* subject [in subjection; liable, prone]. *4 m.* GRAM., LOG., PHILOS. subject. *5* subject, matter. *6* coll. individual, fellow.
**sulfatar** *tr.* to sulphate.
**sulfato** *m.* CHEM. sulphate.
**sulfhídrico, -ca** *adj.* CHEM. sulphydric.
**sulfito** *m.* CHEM. sulphite.
**sulfurar** *tr.* CHEM. to sulphurate. *2* fig. to anger, incense. *3 ref.* to get angry, get furious.
**sulfúreo, -a** *adj.* sulphureous, sulphury.
**sulfúrico, -ca** *adj.* CHEM. sulphuric.
**sulfuro** *m.* CHEM. sulphide.
**sulfuroso, -sa** *adj.* sulphurous.
**sultán** *m.* sultan.
**sultana** *f.* sultana, sultaness.
**sultanato** *m.*, **sultanía** *f.* sultanate.
**suma** *f.* sum [aggregate; addition; total]; ~ *y sigue*, carried forward. *2* sum [of money]. *3* summa. *4* sum, substance: *en* ~, in sum.
**sumador, -ra** *adj.* adding. *2 m.-f.* adder.
**sumamente** *adv.* exceedingly, extremely, highly.
**sumando** *m.* MATH. addend.
**sumar** *tr.* MATH. to add: *máquina de* ~, adding machine. *2* to amount to. *3* to add, join. *4* to sum up. *5 ref. sumarse a*, to be added to; to adhere to [an opinion]; to join [a group].
**sumaria** *f.* LAW written proceedings. *2* MIL. indictment.
**sumario, -ria** *adj.* summary. *2 m.* summary, abstract. *3* LAW indictment.
**sumarísimo, -ma** *adj.* LAW swift, expeditious.
**sumergible** *adj.* submersible. *2 m.* submersible boat.
**sumergir** *tr.* to submerge, sink. *2 ref.* to submerge, plunge, dive; be submerged.
**sumersión** *f.* submersion, immersion.
**sumidad** *f.* apex, top, tip.
**sumidero** *m.* sewer, drain, sink, sump.
**suministrador, -ra** *adj.* furnishing, providing, supplying. *2 m.-f.* furnisher, provider, supplier.
**suministrar** *tr.* to furnish, provide, supply.
**suministro** *m.* providing, supplying. *2* provision, supply.
**sumir** *tr.* to sink, plunge, engulf. *2* to take [the Eucharist] in the mass. *3 ref.* to sink, plunge, be engulfed. *4* [of cheeks, etc.] to be sunken.
**sumisión** *f.* submission; submissiveness.
**sumiso, -sa** *adj.* submissive, humble, obedient.

**summum** *m.* the limit, the highest degree.
**sumo, -ma** *adj.* very great or much, greatest, highest, extreme, utmost: *en ~ grado*, highly; *a lo ~*, at most. *2* high, supreme: *Sumo Pontífice*, Pontifex Maximus; Sovereign Pontiff.
**sunción** *f.* taking [of the Eucharist] in the mass.
**Sund** *m. pr. n.* GEOG. Sound.
**suntuario, -ria** *adj.* sumptuary.
**suntuosidad** *f.* sumptuousness.
**suntuoso, -sa** *adj.* sumptuous, gorgeous, magnificent.
**supeditación** *f.* subjection, subordination.
**supeditar** *tr.* to reduce to subjection. *2* to subordinate.
**superable** *adj.* superable, surmountable.
**superabundancia** *f.* superabundance.
**superabundar** *intr.* to superabound.
**superar** *tr.* surpass, exceed, excel. *2* to overcome, surmount.
**superávit** *m.* surplus [excess of revenue over expenditure].
**supercarburante** *m.* high-test fuel.
**superchería** *f.* fraud, deceit, humbug, trick.
**superdominante** *f.* MUS. superdominant.
**supereminente** *adj.* supereminent.
**superentender** *tr.* to superintend, inspect, supervise.
**supererogatorio, -ria** *adj.* supererogatory.
**superficial** *adj.* superficial; shallow.
**superficie** *f.* surface, superficies. *2* area [superficial extent].
**superfino, -na** *adj.* superfine, extra fine.
**superfluidad** *f.* superfluity, superfluousness.
**superfluo, -flua** *adj.* superfluous.
**superfosfato** *m.* CHEM. superphosphate.
**superhombre** *m.* superman.
**superintendencia** *f.* superintendence, superintendency, supervision.
**superintendente** *m.-f.* superintendent, supervisor.
**superior** *adj.* superior. *2* upper. *3* better, finer. *4* higher [algebra, mathematics, education, etc.]. *6 m.* superior.
**superiora** *f.* mother superior.
**superioridad** *f.* superiority, superiorness.
**superiormente** *adv.* superiorly, extremely well.
**superlativo, -va** *adj.* superlative, surpassing; highest. *2 adj.-m.* GRAM. superlative.
**superno, -na** *adj.* supreme, highest.
**supernumerario, -ria** *adj.* supernumerary.
**súpero** *adj.* BOT. superior [ovary].
**superponer** *tr.* to superpose, superimpose. ¶ CONJUG. like *poner*.
**superposición** *f.* superposition, superimposition.
**superpuesto, -ta** *p. p.* of SUPERPONER.
**supersensible** *adj.* supersensitive.
**supersónico, -ca** *adj.* supersonic. *2 f.* supersonics.
**superstición** *f.* superstition.
**supersticioso, -sa** *adj.* superstitious.
**supersubstancial (pan)** *m.* THEOL. the Host.
**supervenir** *intr.* SOBREVENIR. ¶ CONJUG. like *venir*.
**supervivencia** *f.* survival. *2* LAW survivorship.
**superviviente** *adj.* surviving. *2 m.-f.* survivor.
**supinación** *f.* supineness. *2* supination.
**supinador** *adj.-m.* ANAT. supinator.
**supino, -na** *adj.* supine [opposed to *prone*]. *2* stupid, crass. *3* GRAM. supine.
**súpito, -ta** *adj.* SÚBITO.
**suplantación** *f.* supplanting. *2* fraudulent alteration [in a writing].
**suplantar** *tr.* to supplant. *2* to alter [a writing] fraudulently.

**suplementario, -ria** *adj.* supplemental, supplementary.
**suplemento** *m.* supplement.
**suplente** *adj.* substituting. *2 m.-f.* substitute.
**supletorio, -ria** *adj.* suppletory, supplemental.
**súplica** *f.* supplication, entreaty, petition, request.
**suplicación** *f.* supplication. *2* rolled waffle.
**suplicante** *adj.* suppliant. *2 m.-f.* suppliant, supplicant.
**suplicar** *tr.* to supplicate, entreat, pray, beg.
**suplicatorio, -ria** *adj.* supplicatory.
**suplicio** *m.* torture. *2* LAW corporal punishment; execution; place of execution. *3* fig. anguish, suffering.
**suplir** *tr.* to supply [make up for deficiency, loss, need, etc.]. *2* to replace, serve as a substitute for.
**supondré, supondría**, etc. *irr.* V. SUPONER.
**suponedor, -ra** *m.-f.* supposer.
1) **suponer** *m.* supposition.
2) **suponer** *tr.* to suppose, assume. *2* to imply, presuppose. *3* to entail [expense, etc.]. *4 intr.* [of a person] to have weight or authority. ¶ CONJUG. like *poner*.
**supongo, suponga**, etc. *irr.* V. SUPONER.
**suportar** *tr.* SOPORTAR.
**suposición** *f.* supposition, assumption. *2* imposition, falsehood. *3* consequence, distinction.
**supositicio, -cia** *adj.* supposititious.
**supositivo, -va** *adj.* suppositive.
**supositorio** *m.* MED. suppository.
**supradicho, -cha** *adj.* aforesaid, above-mentioned.
**suprarrenal** *adj.* ANAT. suprarenal.
**suprasensible** *adj.* supersensible.
**supremacía** *f.* supremacy.
**supremo, -ma** *adj.* supreme.
**supresión** *f.* suppression, abolition, elimination, omission.
**supresivo, -va** *adj.* abolishing, eliminating, omitting.
**suprimir** *tr.* to suppress, abolish, eliminate, strike out, do away with. *2* to omit.
**supuestamente** *adv.* pretendedly, assumedly.
**supuesto, -ta** *irreg. p. p.* of SUPONER. *2 adj.* supposed, assumed, pretended: *nombre ~*, assumed name. *3 dar por ~*, to take for granted; *esto ~*, this being understood; *por ~*, of course, naturally; *~ que*, since, granting that. *4 m.* supposition, assumption, hypothesis.
**supuración** *f.* suppuration.
**supurar** *intr.* MED. to suppurate.
**supuse, supusiera**, etc. *irr.* V. SUPONER.
**suputar** *tr.* computate, calculate, reckon.
**sur** *m.* south. *2* south wind.
**surá** *f.* surah.
**surcado, -da** *adj.* furrowed, sulcate, sulcated.
**surcar** *tr.* AGR. to furrow, plough. *2* to furrow, groove. *3* to cut through [the water, the air].
**surco** *m.* furrow, groove, rut. *2* groove [of a phonographic record]. *3* wrinkle, line [in the face].
**sureste** *m.* SUDESTE.
**surgidero** *m.* NAUT. anchorage, anchoring place.
**surgir** *intr.* [of water] to spirt, spurt, spring. *2* to come forth, issue, appear, arise. *3* NAUT. to anchor. ¶ P. p.: *surgido & surto*.
**suripanta** *f.* formerly, a chorus girl.
**suroeste** *m.* SUDOESTE.
**surrealismo** *m.* surrealism.
**surtida** *f.* MIL. sally, sortie. *2* FORT. sally port. *3* NAUT. slipway.
**surtidero** *m.* outlet [of a pond]. *2* SURTIDOR 3.

**surtido** *adj.* COM. assorted. *2 m.* COM. assortment, stock. *3* COM. supply.
**surtidor, -ra** *adj.* supplying. *2 m.-f.* supplier. *3 m.* jet, spout, springing up fountain. *4 ~ de gasolina,* gasoline pump.
**surtimiento** *m.* supplying, furnishing.
**surtir** *tr.* to supply, furnish, provide, stock. *2 ~ efecto,* to work, to have the desired effect. *3 intr.* [of water] to spout, spirt, spurt, spring.
**surto, -ta** *adj.* NAUT. anchored.
**sus** *posses. adj. pl.* of SU.
**¡sus!** *interj.* up!, forward!, get going!
**Susana** *f. pr. n.* Susan.
**susceptibilidad** *f.* susceptibility. *2* touchiness.
**susceptible** *adj.* susceptible [admitting of]. *2* touchy, ready to take offence.
**suscitar** *tr.* to raise, stir up, provoke, originate. *2 ref.* to rise, start, originate.
**suscribir** *tr.-ref.* SUBSCRIBIR.
**suscripción** *f.* SUBSCRIPCIÓN.
**suscritor, -ra** *m.-f.* SUBSCRIPTOR.
**susodicho, -cha** *adj.* above-mentioned, above-named.
**suspender** *tr.* to suspend, hang up. *2* to suspend [stop, delay, interrupt]. *3* to adjourn [a meeting]. *4* to suspend [from office]. *5* to astonish, ravish. *6* to fail [in an examination]. *7 ref.* to be suspended, stopped or adjourned.
**suspensión** *f.* suspension: *en ~,* in suspension. *2* adjournment [of a meeting]. *3* astonishment, ravishment.
**suspensivo, -va** *adj.* suspending. *2* suspension [points].
**suspenso, -sa** *adj.* suspended: *en ~,* suspended, not decided; in suspense. *2* astonished, perplexed: *3 m.* EDUC. failing mark [in an examination].
**suspensorio, -ria** *adj.-m.* suspensory.
**suspicacia** *f.* suspicion, distrust. *2* suspiciousness.
**suspicaz** *adj.* suspicious, distrustful.
**suspirado, -da** *adj.* sighed for, longed for.
**suspirar** *intr.* to sigh. *2 fig. ~ por,* to sigh for; to love madly.
**suspiro** *m.* sigh: *exhalar el último ~,* to breathe one's last. *2* kind of cake. *3* glass whistle. *4* MUS. short rest.

**sustancia, sustancial, sustanciar, sustancioso,** etc. = SUBSTANCIA, SUBSTANCIAL, SUBSTANCIAR, SUBSTANCIOSO, etc.
**sustantivar** *tr.* SUBSTANTIVAR.
**sustantivo** *adj.-m.* SUBSTANTIVO.
**sustentable** *adj.* defensible [by argument].
**sustentación** *f.* support, sustentation. *2* AER. lift.
**sustentáculo** *m.* support, prop, rest, stay.
**sustentamiento** *m.* sustentation, sustenance.
**sustentar** *tr.* to sustain, maintain, support, feed. *2* to sustain, support, hold up. *3* to sustain, defend.
**sustento** *m.* sustenance, maintenance. *2* support.
**sustitución, sustituible, sustituir,** etc. = SUBSTITUCIÓN, SUBSTITUIBLE, SUBSTITUIR, etc.
**susto** *m.* fright, scare, shock: *dar un ~,* to frighten, scare, startle. *2* fear, aprehension.
**sustracción, sustraendo, sustraer** = SUBSTRACCIÓN, SUBSTRAENDO, SUBSTRAER.
**susurrante** *adj.* whispering; murmuring, murmurous, purling, rustling.
**susurrar** *intr.-tr.* to whisper: *se susurra que,* it is whispered or rumoured that. *2 intr.* [of wind, etc.] to murmur; [of a book] to purl; [of leaves, etc.] to rustle.
**susurro** *m.* whisper. *2* murmur, purling, rustle.
**sutás** *m.* soutache.
**sutil** *adj.* subtle, subtile. *2* thin, slender.
**sutileza** *f.* subtlety, subtility. *2* thinness, slenderness. *3* dexterity.
**sutilidad** *f.* subtlety.
**sutilizar** *tr.* to subtilize. *2* to render thin or slender. *3* to refine, polish. *4 intr.* to subtilize, split hairs.
**sutura** *f.* seam. *2* ANAT., BOT., ZOOL., SURG. suture.
**suyo, suya, suyos, suyas** *poss. adj.* (never used before the noun) his, her, its, their, of him, of her, of it, of them; of his, of hers, of its, of theirs. *2 de ~,* by nature; on his (her, their) own accord. *3 esto es muy ~,* this is like him. *4 poss. pron.* his, hers, its, theirs. *5 hacer de las suyas,* to be up to one's old tricks. *6 salirse con la suya,* to have one's way. *7 m. pl. los suyos,* his (her, their) family, people, etc.; yours [when using *usted*].
**suzón** *m.* BOT. groundsel.
**svástica** *f.* swastica.

# T

**T, t** *f.* T, t, twenty-third letter of the Spanish alphabet.

**¡ta!** *interj.* easy! *2* look! *3 ¡ta, ta!,* rat-a-tat! tut, tut!

**taba** *f.* anklebone. *2* knucklebone [of sheep]. *3* knucklebones [game].

**tabacal** *m.* tobacco field.

**tabacalero, -ra** *adj.* [pertaining to] tobacco. *2 m.-f.* tobacco grower or dealer.

**tabaco** *m.* tobacco: ~ *en polvo,* snuff. *2* snuff [powdered tobacco]: *tomar* ~, to snuff. *3* cigar. *4* black rot [in trees].

**tabalada** *f.* coll. slap, spank. *2* coll. fall on the behind.

**tabalario** *m.* coll. behind, posteriors.

**tabalear** *tr.* to rock, to shake. *2 intr.* to drum with the fingers.

**tabaleo** *m.* shaking. *2* drumming with the fingers.

**tabanazo** *m.* slap, spank.

**tabanco** *m.* stall for selling eatables.

**tábano** *m.* ENT. gadfly, horsefly.

**tabaque** *m.* small wicker basket.

**tabaquera** *f.* snuff box. *2* bowl [of a tobacco pipe].

**tabaquería** *f.* tobacco shop.

**tabaquero, -ra** *m.-f.* tobacconist. *2* cigar maker.

**tabaquismo** *m.* MED. tobaccoism.

**tabardillo** *m.* coll. sunstroke. *2* MED. typhus. *3* fig. wild, annoying person.

**tabardo** *m.* tabard.

**tabarra, tabarrera** *f.* bore [tedious, speech, performance, etc.].

**taberna** *f.* tavern, public house, wine shop, *saloon.

**tabernáculo** *m.* tabernacle.

**tabernario, -ria** *adj.* coarse, low, vulgar.

**tabernera** *f.* mistress of a wine shop. *2* wife of the keeper of a wine shop.

**tabernero** *m.* keeper of a public house or wine shop; *saloon keeper.

**tabes** *f.* MED. consumption, tabes.

**tabicar** *tr.* to wall up, close up.

**tabique** *m.* thin wall, partition. *2* BIOL. septum.

**tabla** *f.* board [thin piece of timber; wooden slab]: ~ *de armonía,* MUS. soundboard; ~ *de chilla,* clapboard; ~ *de salvación,* last recourse; *salvarse en una* ~, to have a narrow escape; *a raja* ~, at any cost, regardless of· anything else. *2* plank, slab, tablet. *3* board [for posting notices]. *4* PAINT. panel: ~ *rasa,* unpainted panel; untrained mind; *hacer* ~ *rasa de,* to disregard [all obstacles] in the way of something. *5* table diamond. *6* wide part [of a member of the body]. *7* AGR. strip of land, garden patch. *8* meat stall. *9* PERSP. table. *10 Tabla Redonda,* Round Table. *11* BILL. *por* ~, cushion [carom]; fig. indirectly. *12 sing.-pl.* table [of contents, of logarithms, etc.]: *tabla de la ley,* tables of the law. *13 pl.* draw [at chess & draughts]: *hacer tablas,* to draw, to come out even. *14* THEAT. boards, stage.

**tablacho** *m.* sluice gate.

**tablado** *m.* stage, scaffold, platform [of timber]. *2* flooring [made of boards]. *3* THEAT. stage boards.

**tablajería** *f.* meat stall, butcher's shop.

**tablajero** *m.* butcher [dealer in meat].

**tablar** *m.* set of garden plots. *2* calm stretch of a river. *3* side board [of a car].

**tablazón** *f.* boarding, planking. *2* NAUT. planking and deck flooring [of a ship].

**tablero** *m.* board [square or oblong piece of thin wood]: ~ *de anuncios,* board [for posting notices]; ~ *de instrumentos,* AUTO. dashboard. *2* slab. *3* ARCH., CARP. panel. *4* table top. *5* drawing board. *6* board [for certain games]: ~ *de ajedrez,* chessboard; ~ *de damas,* draughtboard, checkerboard. *7* shop counter. *8* TABLAR. *9* floor [of a bridge]. *10* wooden blackboard. *11* ~ *contador,* abacus.

**tableta** *f.* dim. small board, tablet. *2* floor board. *3* tablet, lozenge, pastil, pastille.

**tableteado, -da** *m.* rattling sound.

**tabletear** *intr.* to rattle clappers. *2* to sound like clappers.

**tableteo** *m.* rattling sound. *2* rattle [of machine-gun shots].

**tablilla** *f.* small board, tablet. *2* bulletin board. *3* SURG. splint.

**tablón** *m.* thick plank. *2* NAUT. plank, strake.

**tabú** *m.* taboo.

**tabuco** *m.* hovel, narrow room.

**tabulador** *m.* tabulator [of a typewriter].

**tabular** *adj.* tabular.

**taburete** *m.* tabouret, stool.

**tac** *m.* tick [of clock, heart, etc.].

**tacada** *f.* BILL. stroke.

**tacañear** *intr.* to be niggarly, stingy.

**tacañería** *f.* niggardliness, stinginess.

**tacaño, -ña** *adj.* niggardly, stingy, closefisted. *2 m.-f.* niggard, miser.

**tacazo** *m.* BILL. stroke.

**tácito, -ta** *adj.* tacit. *2* silent.

**taciturnidad** *f.* taciturnity.

**taciturno, -na** *adj.* taciturn.

**taco** *m.* plug. *2* short and thick piece of wood. *3* ARTILL. wad. *4* ramrod. *5* BILL. cue. *6* popgun. *7* almanac pad. *8* picker [in a loom]. *9* profane oath: *echar tacos,* to swear. *10 hacerse un ~,* to get muddled, confused. *11* (Am.) heel [of shoe].

**tacómetro** *m.* tachometer.

**tacón** *m.* heel [part of shoe or boot that supports the heel].

**taconazo** *m.* blow with the shoe heel.

**taconear** *tr.* to walk hard on one's heels, to strut on one's heels.

**taconeo** *m.* walking hard on one's heels. *2* noise made with the heels in walking.

**táctico, -ca** *adj.* tactical. *2 m.* tactician. *3 f.* tactics.

**táctil** *adj.* tactile.

**tacto** *m.* touch, sense of touch. *2* touching, feeling. *3* touch, feel [of a fabric, etc.]. *4* tact.

**tacha** *f.* fault, defect, blemish: *poner ~ a,* to find fault with.

**tachar** *tr.* to find a fault or defect in or with. *2* to accuse, censure. *3* to cancel, strike out.

**tachón** *m.* erasure. *2* short piece of ribbon or braid trimming. *3* stud, ornamental tack.

**tachonar** *tr.* to trim [clothes] with short pieces of ribbon or braid. *2* to adorn with ornamental tacks. *3* to stud, to spangle.

**tachuela** *f.* tack, hobnail.

**tael** *m.* tael [weight and coin].

**tafanario** *m.* coll. behind, posteriors.

**tafetán, pl. -nes** *m.* taffeta [silk fabric]. *2 ~ inglés,* court plaster. *3 pl.* fig. flags, colours. *4* coll. finery.

**tafia** *f.* tafia.

**tafilete** *m.* morocco leather.

**tafiletear** *tr.* to adorn with morocco leather.

**tagalo, -la** *m.-f.* Tagal, Tagalog.

**tagarnina** *f.* BOT. golden thistle. *2* coll. poor cigar.

**tagarote** *m.* ORN. sparrow hawk. *2* coll. escrivener. *3* coll. lanky fellow.

**tahalí** *m.* baldric.

**taheño** *adj.* red [hair]. *2* red-bearded.

**tahona** *f.* backery, baker's shop.

**tahonero** *m.* baker [breadmaker].

**tahur, -ra** *m.-f.* gambler, gamester. *3* cardsharp.

**taifa** *f.* faction, party. *2* coll. lot [of disreputable people].

**Tailandia** *f. pr. n.* GEOG. Thailand.

**taimado, -da** *adj.* sly, cunning, crafty. *2* (Chi.) sullen, stubborn.

**taimería** *f.* slyness, craftiness, rascality.

**taita** *f.* coll. dad, daddy.

**tajada** *f.* cut, slice. *2* hoarseness [from a cold]. *3* coll. drunk, drunken fit.

**tajadera** *f.* curved chopping knife. *2* cold chisel.

**tajadero** *m.* COOK. chopping block.

**tajado, -da** *adj.* steep, sheer.

**tajador, -ra** *adj.* cutting. *2 m.* chopping block.

**tajamar** *m.* cutwater [of bridge or ship]. *2* (Am.) dike; dam.

**tajante** *adj.* cutting, sharp. *2* peremptory [tone].

**tajar** *tr.* to cut, divide, slice.

**Tajo** *m. pr. n.* GEOG. Tagus.

**tajo** *m.* cut, incision. *2* steep cliff. *3* cutting edge. *4* chopping block; butcher's block; beheading block. *5* three-legged rustic stool. *6* cut [in a

mountain]. *7* FENC. cut. *8* line of progress of a gang of reapers, miners, etc.

**tal** *adj.* such, such a, the same as, like. *2 el ~, -la ~,* that, that man, that fellow, that woman; *el ~ drama,* that play; *el ~ Pedro,* that man Peter. *3 un ~, una tal,* one, a certain. *4 tal cual viajero,* a few travellers, an occasional traveller. *5 indef. pron.* someone. *6* such a thing. *7 ~ para cual,* two of a kind. *8 otro que ~,* another of the same kind. *9 adv.* so, thus, in such a way. *10 con ~ (de) que,* provided that. *11 no ~,* no, no; *sí ~,* yes, indeed. *12 ¿qué ~?,* how do you do?; how do you like it? *13 ~ cual,* such as; middling, so so.

**tala** *f.* felling of trees. *2* destruction, havoc. *3* tipcat [boy's game]. *4* cat [used in tipcat].

**talabarte** *m.* sword belt.

**talabartería** *f.* saddlery, harness shop.

**talabartero** *m.* saddler, harness maker.

**taladrador, -ra** *adj.* boring, drilling, piercing. *2 m.- f.* borer, driller. *3 f.* drilling machine.

**taladrante** *adj.* piercing, penetrating.

**taladrar** *tr.* to bore, drill, perforate. *2* to punch [a ticket]. *3* to pierce, penetrate.

**taladro** *m.* drill, auger, boring instrument. *2* bore, drill hole, auger hole.

**talamete** *m.* NAUT. forward deck [in small vessels].

**tálamo** *m.* bridal chamber; bridal bed. *2* BOT. thalamus, receptacle. *3* ANAT. thalamus.

**talán** *m.* ding-dong.

**talanquera** *f.* barrier, fence. *2* fig. defence, cover, place of refuge. *3* fig. safety.

**talante** *m.* mode or manner of doing anything. *2* mood, mien, countenance. *3* will, wish, pleasure. *4 de buen ~,* in a good mood; with good grace; *de mal ~,* in a bad mood; with bad grace.

1) **talar** *adj.* long, reaching to the ankles.

2) **talar** *tr.* to fell [trees]; to fell or cut the trees of. *2* to destroy, lay waste.

**talares** *m. pl.* MYTH. talaria [of Mercury].

**talayote** *m.* ARCHEOL. talayot.

**talco** *m.* MINER. talc, talcum. *2* tinsel [material].

**talcualillo, -lla** *adj.* coll. middling.

**talega** *f.* bag, sack; money bag. *2* bagful. *3* hair bag. *4* POL. coll. money, wealth.

**talegada** *f.* bagful.

**talego** *m.* bag, sack.

**taleguilla** *f. dim.* small bag. *2* bullfighter's breeches.

**talento** *m.* talent.

**talentoso, -sa; talentudo, -da** *adj.* talented, able, clever.

**tálero** *m.* thaler [old German coin].

**Talia** *f. pr. n.* MYTH. Thalia.

**talio** *m.* CHEM. thallium.

**talión** *m.* talion, retaliation.

**talismán** *m.* talisman.

**talmente** *adv.* the same as; in such a manner.

**Talmud** *m.* Talmud.

**talo** *m.* BOT. thallus.

**talofita** *adj.* BOT. thallophytic. *2 f.* BOT. thallophyte.

**talón** *m.* ANAT. heel: *apretar los talones,* to hurry; to fly; *pisar los talones a uno,* to be at one's heels. *2* heel [part of a shoe or stocking that covers heel of the foot]. *3* MUS. heel [of a bow]. *4* NAUT. heel [of the keel]. *5* ARCH. heel, talon [molding]. *6* a check, voucher, coupon, etc., detached from a stub book. *7* standard [in a monetary system].

**talonada** *f.* kick with the heels.

**talonario** *m.* stub book: *~ de cheques,* chequebook.

**talonazo** *m.* kick or blow with the heel.

**talonear** *intr.* coll. to walk fast, to dash along.
**talquita** *f.* MINER. talc schist.
**talud** *m.* talus, slope. *2* ARCH. batter.
**talla** *f.* F. ARTS carving, wood carving: *media* ~, half relief. *2* round [of certain card games]. *3* height, stature [of a person]. *4* size [of a person].
**tallado, -da** *p. p.* of TALLAR. *2 adj.* cut, carved. *3 bien* or *mal* ~, having a good or bad figure.
**tallador, -ra** *m.-f.* engraver, diesinker. *2* one who measures the height of persons.
1) **tallar** *adj.* ready for cutting [tree, forest]. *2 m.* forest ready for the first cut. *3* young growth of trees.
2) **tallar** *tr.* to carve, engrave. *2* to cut [a precious stone]. *3* to appraise. *4* to tax, impose tax on. *5 intr.* to be the banker [in certain card games].
**tallarín** *m.* noodle [alimentary paste].
**talle** *m.* form, figure, appearance [of a person]. *2* waist [of a person, of a garment]. *3* fit, adjustment [of a garment to the body].
**taller** *m.* shop, workshop, factory. *2* atelier, studio.
**tallista** *m.-f.* sculptor, wood carver.
**tallo** *m.* BOT. stem, stalk. *2* BOT. shoot, sprout.
**talludo, -da** *adj.* BOT. long-stemmed. *2* tall, overgrown [boy, girl]. *3* no longer young.
**tamal** *m.* tamale [a Mexican dish].
**tamanduá** *f.* ZOOL. tamandua, anteater.
**tamañamente** *adv.* as greatly.
**tamañito, -ta** *adj. dim.* so small. *2* very small. *3* humbled, confused.
**tamaño, -ña** *adj.* as big, or as small. *2* very large or very small: *abrir tamaños ojos*, to open one's eyes wide. *3* so great, such a great. *4 m.* size: ~ *natural*, full size.
**tamañuelo, -la** *adj. dim.* very small.
**támara** *f.* BOT. a date palm. *2* date palm field. *3 pl.* cluster of dates. *4* brushwood.
**tamarindo** *m.* BOT. tamarind [tree and fruit].
**tamarisco, tamariz** *m.* BOT. tamrisk.
**tambaleante** *adj.* staggering, tottering, reeling.
**tambalear** *intr.-ref.* to stagger, totter, reel.
**tambaleo** *m.* staggering, tottering, reeling.
**tambanillo** ARCH. tympanum.
**tambarillo** *m.* small chest with an arched lid.
**también** *adv.* also, too, as well, likewise.
**tambo** *m.* (Am.) inn. *2* (Am.) dairy.
**tambor** *m.* MUS., ARCH. drum, tambour. *2* MUS. drummer: ~ *mayor*, drum major. *3* coffee roaster. *4* MACH. drum, barrel. *5* MACH. band pulley. *6* tambour [for embroidering]. *7* FORT. drum. *8* ANAT. tympanum, eardrum.
**tambora** *f.* MUS. bass drum.
**tamborear** *intr.* to drum with the fingers.
**tamboril** *m.* tabor, tabour, timbrel [small drum].
**tamborilada** *f.*, **tamborilazo** *m.* coll. bump on one's behind. *2* coll. slap on the head or shoulders.
**tamborilear** *intr.* to drum.
**tamborilero** *m.* taborer, drummer.
**tamborilete** *m.* PRINT. planer.
**tamborín** *m.* TAMBORIL.
**tamborino** *m.* TAMBORIL. *2* TAMBORILERO.
**tamboritear** *intr.* TAMBORILEAR.
**tambucho** *m.* NAUT. hood.
**Támesis** *m. pr. n.* GEOG. Thames.
**tamiz** *m.* sieve, bolter.
**tamizar** *tr.* to sift, sieve.
**tamo** *m.* fuzz, fluff. *2* dust gathered under beds, etc.
**tampoco** *adv.* neither, not either: either: *si usted no va, yo* ~ *iré*, you don't go, neither shall I; *ni yo* ~, nor I either.
**tamtam** *m.* tom-tom.
**tamujo** *m.* BOT. a shrub of which brooms are made.
**tan** *adv. contr.* de TANTO so, as: ~ ... *como*, as ... as. *2* ~ *siquiera*, ever so, at least. *3* ~ *solo*, only. *4 qué* ... ~, what a: *¡qué casa* ~ *hermosa!*, what a beautiful house.
**tanaceto** *m.* BOT. tansy.
**tanato** *m.* CHEM. tannate.
**tanda** *f.* turn [to do something]. *2* shift, relay [of workmen]. *3* task. *4* layer, bed. *5* series, number.
**tándem** *m.* tandem bicycle.
**tanganillo** *m.* temporary prop or support.
**tángano** *m.* CHITO.
**tangencia** *adj.* tangency.
**tangencial** *adj.* tangential.
**tangente** *adj.-f.* GEOM. tangent: *escapar, irse* or *salir, por la* ~, fig. to resort to subterfuges.
**Tánger** *m. pr. n.* Tangier.
**tangerino, -na** *adj.-n.* Tangerine.
**tangible** *adj.* tangible.
**tango** *m.* tango [dance]. *2* CHITO.
**tangón** *m.* NAUT. swinging boom.
**tánico, -ca** *adj.* CHEM. tannic.
**tanino** *m.* CHEM. tannin.
**tanque** *m.* tank, water tank. *2* MIL. tank. *3* (Am.) reservoir.
**tantalio** *m.* CHEM. tantalum.
**Tántalo** *m. pr. n.* MYTH. Tantalus.
**tantán** *m.* gong. *2* tom-tom.
**tantarantán** *m.* rub-a-dub. *2* coll. hard smack.
**tanteador, -ra** *m.-f.* scorekeeper. *2 m.* score board.
**tantear** *tr.* to try, size up, test, feel, explore. *2* to consider carefully. *3* to sketch. *4 tr.-intr.* GAMES to keep the score [of].
**tanteo** *m.* trial, testing, trial and error. *2* rough calculation: *al* ~, by guess. *3* points, score [in a game].
1) **tanto** *adv.* so, so much, as much, thus so far, so hard, so long, so often, in such a manner, to such degree or extent: ~ *como*, as much, or so much, as; as well as; *algún* ~, *un* ~, a little, somewhat; ~ *más* (or *menos*) *que*, all the more [or the less] that, especially as; ~ *mejor*, so much the better; ~ *peor*, so much the worse. *2 pron.* so much, as much, that: *no ser para* ~, not to be so bad, so serious, etc., as that; *por lo* ~, *por* ~, therefore, then. *3 m.* amount, sum; rate: ~ *alzado*, lump sum; ~ *por ciento*, percentage, per cent; *otro* ~, as much, as much more; the same. *4* point [in games]: *apuntarse un* ~, to score a point. *5* counter, chip [to keep score]. *6* copy [of a writing]. *7 al* ~ *de*, informed about. *8 en* ~, *entre* ~, in the meantime.
2) **tanto, -ta** *adj.* as much, so much. *2* such a big: *tanta nariz*, such a big nose.
**tantos, -tas** *adj. pl.* as many, so many. *2 y tantos* (or *tantas*), odd, and more: *veinte y tantos*, twenty odd, twenty and more.
**tañedor, -ra** *m.-f.* MUS. player [of an instrument].
**tañer** *tr.* to play [a musical instrument], to ring, toll [bells]. *2 intr.* to drum with the fingers.
**tañido** *m.* sound, sounding [of a musical instrument]; tune. *2* ringing [of a bell].
**tañimiento** *m.* playing on an instrument.
**tao** *m.* tau cross [badge of some orders].
**taoísmo** *m.* Taoism.
**tapa** *f.* lid, cover, cap. *2* head [of a cylinder, a barrel, a cask]. *2* board cover [of a book]. *4* lift, layer [of a shoe heel]. *5* hoof crust [of horses].

**tapaboca** *m.* slap on the mouth. *2* muffler [worn for warmth]. *3* fig. squelch, squelcher. *4* ARTIL. ~ or *tapabocas*, tampion.

**tapacubo** *m.* AUTO. hub cap.

**tapaculo** *m.* BOT. hip.

**tapada** *f.* woman who hides her face with a mantle or veil.

**tapadera** *f.* loose lid, cover [of a pot, etc.]. *2* blind [person who shields another].

**tapadillo (de)** *adv.* secretly, covertly.

**tapadizo** *m.* COBERTIZO.

**tapado** *m.* (Am.) woman's or child's overcoat.

**tapafunda** *f.* flap of a holster.

**tapagujeros,** *pl.* **-ros** *m.* substitute, makeshift [person].

**tapar** *tr.* to cover [with a lid, cover, etc.]. *2* to stop, plug; to cap, cork [a bottle, etc.]; to bung [a cask]. *3* to close up, obstruct. *4* to hide, conceal, screen, veil. *5* to wrap up. *6* (Am.) to fill [a tooth]. *7* *ref.* to cover or veil oneself up.

**tápara** *f.* ALCAPARRA.

**taparrabo** *m.* loincloth. *2* trunks, bathing trunks.

**tapetado, -da** *adj.* dark, dark-brown.

**tapete** *m.* small carpet, rug. *2* cover [for a table, chest, etc.], table cover: ~ *verde*, gambling table: *estar sobre el* ~, to be on the carpet [under discussion].

**tapia** *f.* mud wall, adobe wall. *2* wall fence.

**tapial** *m.* form or mould for mud walls. *2* TAPIA.

**tapiar** *tr.* to wall, wall in [enclose with a wall]. *2* to wall [block up with a wall].

**tapicería** *f.* tapestries. *2* art of making tapestry. *3* tapestry shop. *4* upholstery. *5* upholstery shop.

**tapicero** *m.* tapestry maker. *2* upholsterer.

**tapido, -da** *adj.* closely woven.

**tapioca** *f.* tapioca.

**tapir** *m.* ZOOL. tapir.

**tapiz** *m.* tapestry.

**tapizar** *tr.* to tapestry [hang with tapestry]. *2* to upholster [chairs, etc.]. *3* fig. to carpet, cover.

**tapón** *m.* stopper, cork, bung, plug, cap. *2* ELECT. plug fuse. *3* SURG. tampon.

**taponamiento** *m.* SURG. tamponage, tamponment.

**tàponar** *tr.* to plug, stop up. *2* SURG. to tampon.

**taponazo** *m.* pop [of a cork].

**taponería** *f.* corks [collect.]. *2* cork factory or industry. *3* cork shop.

**taponero, -ra** *adj.* [pertaining to] cork. *2* *m.-f.* cork maker, cork cutter. *3* cork seller.

**tapujarse** *ref.* to cover or muffle one's face.

**tapujo** *m.* covering one's face; cover held over the face. *2* fig. concealment, subterfuge.

**taquera** *f.* rack or stand for billiard cues.

**taquicardia** *f.* MED. tachycardia.

**taquigrafía** *f.* shorthand, stenography.

**taquigrafiar** *tr.* to stenograph.

**taquigráfico, -ca** *adj.* shorthand, stenographic.

**taquígrafo, -fa** *m.-f.* stenographer.

**taquilla** *f.* ticket rack. *23* ticket window, ticket office. *3* take, gate [money received for tickets].

**taquillero, -ra** *m.-f.* ticket seller, ticket agent.

**taquimeca** *f.* COLL. TAQUIMECANÓGRAFA.

**taquimecanógrafo, -fa** *m.-f.* a stenographer and typewriter.

**taquimetría** *f.* tachymetry.

**taquímetro** *m.* SURV. tachymeter.

**tara** *f.* COM. tare [allowance made for weight of box, etc.]. *2* tally [stick for keeping accounts].

**tarabilla** *f.* clapper [of a mill], millclapper. *2* catch, turnbuckle [for fastening a window]. *3* coll. chatterbox. *4* coll. jabber, jabbering.

**taracea** *f.* marquetry, inlaid work, buhlwork.

**taracear** *tr.* to inlay, to adorn with marquetry.

**taraje** *m.* TARAY.

**tarambana** *adj.* scatterbrained. *2* *m.-f.* scatterbrains.

**tarantela** *f.* tarantella, tarantelle.

**tarántula** *f.* ZOOL. tarantula.

**tarara, tarará** *f.* sound of a trumpet.

**tararear** *tr.* to hum [a tune].

**tarareo** *m.* humming [a tune].

**tarasca** *f.* dragon [in Corpus Christi procession]. *2* coll. glutton. *3* coll. ugly, bad-tempered woman.

**tarascada** *f.* bite, wound with the teeth. *2* rude answer or rebuff.

**tarascar** *tr.* [of dogs] to bite.

**taray** *m.* BOT. tamarisk.

**tardador, -ra** *adj.* slow, tarrying.

**tardanza** *f.* delay, slowness, tardiness.

**tardar** *intr.-ref.* to take a long time or a specified time [in doing something], to be slow, long or late [in coming, etc.]: *no tardes*, don't be long, don't be late; *a más* ~, at the latest.

**tarde** *adv.* late; too late: *hacerse* ~, to grow late; *de* ~ *en* ~, once in a while; ~ *o temprano*, sooner or later. *2* *f.* afternoon; evening; *buenas tardes*, good afternoon. *3* fig. evening [of life].

**tardecer** *intr.* to draw towards the evening, to grow dark. ¶ CONJUG. like *agradecer*.

**tardecica** *f.* *dim.* late hours of the afternoon.

**tardigrado, -da** *adj.-m.* ZOOL. tardigrade.

**tardío, -día** *adj.* late, tardy [coming or done after the proper time]. *2* tardy, slow. *3* *m. pl.* late crops.

**tardo, -da** *adj.* tardy, slow, sluggish. *2* tardy, late. *3* dull, sense, slow: ~ *de comprensión*, dull-witted.

**tardón, -na** *adj.* sluggish. *2* slow, dull-witted.

**tarea** *f.* task, job. *2* work, toil.

**tarifa** *f.* tariff. *2* price list, rate, fare.

**tarifar** *tr.* to tariff.

**tarima** *f.* wooden platform, dais.

**tarja** *f.* tally [for keeping decounts]. *2* large shield. *3* tilting target. *4* (Am.) visiting card.

**tarjeta** *f.* card [bearing one's name, etc.]: ~ *de visita*, visiting card; ~ *postal*, post card. *2* ARCH. tablet. *3* title and imprint [on a map].

**tarjeteo** *m.* coll. social exchange of cards.

**tarjetero** *m.* card case.

**tarjetón** *m.* *augm.* large card; show card.

**tarlatana** *f.* tarlatan [fabric].

**tarquín** *m.* slime, ooze, mire.

**tarraconense** *adj.-n.* of Tarragona.

**tarreñas** *f.* a kind of earthen castanets.

**tarro** *m.* jar.

**tarsiano, -na** *adj.* tarsal.

**tarso** *m.* ANAT., ZOOL., ORNITH., ENT. tarsus.

**tarta** *f.* tart [piece of pastry].

**tártago** *m.* BOT. caper spurge. *2* coll. misfortune. *3* coll. poor joke, mean trick.

**tartajear** *intr.* to stutter.

**tartajeo** *m.* stutter, stuttering.

**tartajoso, -sa** *adj.* stuttering. *2* *m.-f.* stutterer.

**tartalear** *intr.* coll. to move in a trembling or irregular way. *2* coll. to stammer, be embarrased.

**tartamudear** *intr.* to stammer, stutter.

**tartamudeo** *m.* stammering, stuttering.

**tartamudez** *f.* defect of stammering or stuttering.

**tartamudo, -da** *adj.* stammering, stuttering. *2* *m.-f.* stammerer, stutterer.

**tartán** *m.* tartan [fabric].

**tartana** f. NAUT. tartan [vessel]. 2 two-wheeled round-top carriage.
**tartanero** m. driver of a TARTANA.
**tartáreo, -a** adj. poet. Tartary.
**tartárico, -ca** adj. CHEM. tartaric.
**Tártaro** m. pr. n. MYTH. Tartarus.
**tártaro, -ra** adj.-n. Tartar. 2 m. CHEM. tartar. 3 tartar [on teeth].
**tartera** f. baking pan for pastry. 2 dinner pail.
**tartrato** m. CHEM. tartrate.
**tártrico, -ca** adj. CHEM. tartaric.
**tartufo** m. hypocrite.
**tarugo** m. wooden pin or plug. 2 wooden paving blook.
**tarumba** m. coll. volver ~ a uno, to confuse, perplex, rattle.
**tasa** f. measure, due limitation: sin ~, without measure. 2 valuation, appraisement. 3 the price of a commodity as established by the Gov' rnment.
**tasación** f. valuation, appraisement.
**tasador** m. appraiser.
**tasajo** m. jerked beef.
**tasar** tr. to fix the price of. 2 to limit, moderate. 3 to appraise, estimate. 4 to stint.
**tasca** f. tavern, wine shop. 2 gambling den.
**tascador** m. scutch, scutcher, swingle.
**tascar** tr. to scutch [flax or hemp]. 2 to crunch [grass]. 3 ~ el freno, to champ the bit.
**tastana** f. AGR. hard crust of dry soil. 2 membrane inside a fruit [as in walnuts, oranges, etc.].
**tasto** m. spoiled taste [of food].
**tata** f. nursemaid [in child's language]. 2 (Am.) coll. dad, daddy.
**tatarabuela** f. great-great-grandmother.
**tatarabuelo** m. great-great-grandfather.
**tataranieta** f. great-great-granddaughter.
**tataranieto** m. great-great-grandson.
**¡tate!** interj. easy there!, beware! 2 behold!
**tato, -ta** adj. lisping and stammering.
**tatú** m. ZOOL. (Am.) giant armadillo.
**tatuaje** m. tatoo [on the skin]. 2 tatooing [the skin].
**tatuar** tr. to tattoo [mark the skin of].
**tau** m. tau [Greek letter]. 2 tau cross.
**taumaturgia** f. thaumaturgy.
**taumaturgo, -ga** m.-f. thaumaturge.
**taurino, -na** adj. taurine.
**Tauro** m. pr. n. ASTR. Taurus.
**taurómaco, -ca** adj. tauromachian, bullfighting. 2 m.-f. one versed in tauromachy.
**tauromaquia** f. bullfighting, tauromachy.
**tautología** f. RHET. tautology.
**taxativo, -va** adj. definite, precise.
**taxi** m. taxi, taxicab.
**taxidermia** f. taxidermy.
**taxímetro** m. taximeter. 2 taxi, taxicab.
**taxonomía** f. taxonomy.
**taza** f. cup [drinking vessel with a handle]. 2 cup, cupful. 3 basin, bowl [of a fountain]. 4 cup guard [of a sword].
**tazón** m. large cup, bowl.
1) **te** f. name the letter t. 2 T square.
2) **te** pers. pron. 2nd pers. sing. [object of the verb and ref.] thee, you; to thee, for you; thyself, yourself.
**té** m. tea [plant; leaves; drink; meal with tea]. 2 ~ del Paraguay, maté, paraguay tea.
**tea** f. candlewood, torch, firebrand.
**teatino, -na** m. Theatin, Theatine.
**teatral** adj. theatrical.

**teatralidad** f. theatricality.
**teatro** m. theatre, theater. 2 stage [sense, actor's profession].
**Tebaida** f. pr. n. HIST., GEOG. Thebaid.
**tebano, -na** adj.-n. Theban.
**Tebas** f. pr. n. HIST., GEOG. Thebes.
**teca** f. BOT. teak. 2 teakwood. 3 BOT. theca.
**tecla** f. key [of a piano, organ, typewriter, etc.]: ~ de escape, margin release; ~ de retroceso, backspacer; tocar una ~, to resort to some expedient. 2 fig. delicate point.
**teclado** m. keyboard [of a piano, organ, typewriter, etc.].
**tecle** NAUT. single purchase.
**teclear** intr. to finger a keyboard. 2 to drum with the fingers.
**tecleo** m. fingering a keyboard. 2 click [of typewriter]. 3 drumming with the fingers.
**técnica** f. technics. 2 technic, technique, methode. 3 technical ability.
**tecnicismo** m. technicality, technicism [technical term or expression].
**técnico, -ca** adj. technical. 2 m. technician, technical expert.
**tecnología** f. technology.
**techado, -da** p. p. of TECHAR. 2 adj. roofed, covered. 3 m. roof.
**techar** tr. to roof, to thatch.
**techo** m. roof, covering [of a building]. 2 ceiling [of a room]. 3 AER. ceiling. 4 fig. roof [house, home].
**techumbre** f. roof, roofing [of a building].
**tedero** m. torch holder, cresset.
**tedéum** m. ECCL. Te Deum.
**tedio** m. tedium, tediousness. 2 loathing.
**tedioso, -sa** adj. tedious, boring. 2 disgusting.
**tegumento** m. ANAT., ZOOL., BOT. tegument.
**teína** f. CHEM. thein, theine.
**teísmo** m. theism.
**teja** f. roof tile, pantile, gutter tile: a toca ~, coll. cash down; de tejas abajo, coll. in the order of nature; in this world; de tejas arriba, coll. in the supernatural order, in heaven. 2 shovel hat. 3 BOT. linden tree.
**tejadillo** m. dim. small roof. 2 roof [of carriage].
**tejado** m. roof, tiled roof.
1) **tejar** tr. brickyard, brick works.
2) **tejar** tr. to tile [a roof].
**tejaroz** m. eaves.
**tejavana** f. shed, tiled shed.
**tejedor, -ra** adj. weaving. 2 m.-f. weaver. 3 m. ENT. water skipper, water strider.
**tejedura** f. weaving. 2 texture [of a fabric].
**tejeduría** f. art of weaving. 2 weaving mill.
**tejemaneje** m. coll. address, skilful management. 2 (Am.) intriguing.
**tejer** tr. to weave. 2 to knit [stockings, etc.]. 3 to braid, plaid, interweave, wreathe.
**tejera, tejería** f. brickyard, tile works.
**tejero** m. brickmaker, tile maker.
**tejido, -da** adj. woven, knit, braided. 3 m. weave, texture [of a fabric]. 4 fabric, textile: ~ de punto, knitted fabric. 5 fig. tissue, web. 6 BIOL. tissue: ~ conjuntivo, connective tissue.
**tejo** m. disk, quoit. 2 MACH. pillow block, socketplate. 3 BOT. yew.
**tejoleta** f. broken tile, brickbat. 2 pl. TARREÑAS.
**tejón** m. ZOOL. badger. 2 gold ingot.
**tejonera** f. burrow of badgers.
**tejuelo** m. TEJO 1. 2 BOOKB. label; lettering. 3 MACH. pillow block.

**tela** *f.* cloth, fabric, stuff: ~ *metálica*, wire cloth, wire screen. *2* web: ~ *de araña*, cobweb. *3* skin, pellicle, membrane. *4* film [on a liquid; in the eye]. *5* subject, something to talk about. *6* BOOKB. cloth. *7* PAINT. canvas; painting. *8 poner en* ~ *de juicio*, to doubt, question.

**telamón** *m.* ARCH. telamon.

**telar** *m.* WEAV. loom: ~ *mecánico*, power loom. *2* THEAT. gridiron. *3* BOOKB. sewing press.

**telaraña** *f.* cobweb, spider web: *tener telarañas en los ojos*, coll. to be blind to what is going on. *2* fig. cobweb, flimsy thing.

**telecomunicación** *f.* telecommunication.

**telefonear** *intr.-tr.* to telephone.

**telefonema** *m.* telephone message.

**telefonía** *f.* telephony.

**telefonista** *m.-f.* telephonist, telephone operator.

**teléfono** *m.* telephone: ~ *automático*, dial telephone; ~ *inalámbrico* or *sin hilos*, wireless telephone.

**telefotografía** *f.* telephotography. *2* telephotograph.

**telegrafía** *f.* telegraphy: ~ *sin hilos*, wireless telegraphy.

**telegrafiar** *intr.-tr.* to telegraph.

**telegrafista** *m.-f.* telegrapher, telegraphist.

**telégrafo** *m.* telegraph: ~ *inalámbrico* or *sin hilos*, wireless telegraph.

**telegrama** *m.* telegram.

**teleguiado, -da** *adj.* guided by remote control.

**Telémaco** *m. pr. n.* MYTH. Telemachus.

**telémetro** *m.* telemeter. *2* MIL. range, finder.

**telendo, -da** *adj.* sprightly, lively, jaunty.

**teleología** *f.* teleology.

**teleósteo, -a** *adj.* ICHTH. teleost.

**telepatía** *f.* telepathy.

**telera** *f.* plow pin. *2* sheepfold. *3* cheek [of a vice]. *4* tiebeam [of a cart]. *5* transom [of a gun-carriage]. *6* NAUT. rack block.

**telero** *m.* stake [of a cart].

**telescopio** *m.* telescope.

**teletipo** *m.* teletype.

**televisar** *tr.* to televise.

**televisión** *f.* television.

**televisor, -ra** *adj.* televising, [pertaining to] television. *2 m.* television set.

**telilla** *f. dim.* light woollen stuff. *6* film, pellicle.

**telina** *f.* ZOOL. clam.

**telón** *m.* THEAT. curtain, drop curtain, drop: ~ *de boca*, drop curtain; ~ *de fondo*, backdrop. *2* fig. ~ *de acero*, iron curtain.

**telúrico, -ca** *adj.* tellurian.

**telurio** *m.* CHEM. tellurium.

**tema** *m.* theme, subject, text. *2* GRAM. theme, stem. *3* MUS. theme. *4 f.* persistence, obstinacy; fixed idea. *5* unreasonable animosity or grudge.

**temario** *m.* program of subjects, agenda.

**temático, -ca** *adj.* thematic, thematical. *2* TEMOSO.

**tembladal** *m.* TREMEDAL.

**tembladera** *f.* a bowl of very thin metal or glass. *2* jewel mounted on a spiral wire. *3* ICHTH. torpedo. *4* BOT. quaking grass.

**tembladero, -ra** *adj.* shaking, trembling. *2 m.* TREMEDAL.

**temblador, -ra** *adj.* shaking, trembling. *2 m.-f.* trembler. *3* Quaker.

**temblar** *intr.* to tremble, quake, shake, quaver, quiver, shiver. ¶ CONJUG. like *acertar*.

**tembleque** *adj.* shaking, trembling. *2 m.-f.* trembler [person]. *3 m.* TEMBLADERA 2.

**temblequear** *intr.* coll. to shake or tremble all the time. *2* coll. to fake a tremor.

**temblón, -na** *adj.* trembling, tremulous, shaking.

**temblor** *m.* tremble, tremor, shaking, quaver, quiver, shiver: ~ *de tierra*, earthquake.

**tembloroso, -sa; tembloso, -sa** *adj.* trembling, tremulous, quavering, shaking.

**temer** *tr.* to dread, fear, apprehend. *2* to be in awe of. *3* fig. be afraid that. *4 intr.* to fear: fear: ~ *por*, to fear for.

**temerario, -ria** *adv.* rash, reckless, hasty, foolhardy.

**temeridad** *f.* temerity, rashness, recklessness, imprudence, foolhardiness. *2* rash or hasty action.

**temerón, -na** *adj.* blustering. *2 m.-f.* blusterer.

**temeroso, -sa** *adj.* dread, fearful. *2* timorous, timid, cowardly. *3* afraid, fearing.

**temible** *adj.* to be dreaded, redoubtable.

**temor** *m.* dread, fear: ~ *de Dios*, dread of God.

**temoso, -sa** *adj.* persistent, obstinate.

**témpano** *m.* MUS. kettledrum. *2* drumhead, drumskin. *3* head [of a cask or barrel]. *4* ARCH. tympan. *5* flat piece of something hard. *6* flitch [of bacon]. *7* ~ *de hielo*, floe, iceberg.

**temperación** *f.* tempering.

**temperadamente** *adv.* temperately.

**temperamento** *m.* PHYSIOL., MUS. temperament. *2* TEMPERIE. *3* compromising measure.

**temperante** *adj.* tempering. *2* (Am.) abstemious. *3 m.-f.* (Am.) teetotaler.

**temperar** *tr.* to temper, moderate, soften. *2 intr.* (Am.) to go to a warmer climate. *3 ref.* to become temperate.

**temperatura** *f.* temperature. *2* TEMPERIE.

**temperie** *f.* atmospheric conditions.

**tempestad** *f.* tempest, storm.

**tempestear** *intr.* to storm, be stormy. *2* fig. to storm, rage.

**tempestivo, -va** *adj.* opportune, seasonable, timely.

**tempestuoso, -sa** *adj.* stormy, tempestuous.

**templa** *f.* PAINT. distemper. *2 pl.* ANAT. temples.

**templado, -da** *adj.* temperate. *2* tepid, lukewarm. *3* LIT. moderate [style]. *4* tempered [steel, glass, etc.]. *5* MUS. tuned. *6* brave, firm, calmy courageous.

**templador, -ra** *m.-f.* temperer. *2* MUS. tuner. *3 m.* MUS. tuning key.

**templadura** *f.* tempering. *2* MUS. tuning.

**templanza** *f.* temperance. *2* moderation, sobriety. *3* mildness [of climate].

**templar** *tr.* to temper, moderate, mitigate, soften, appease. *2* to warm [a liquid] slightly. *3* to temper, anneal [metals, glass]. *4* MUS. to tune [an instrument]. *5* NAUT. to trim [the sails] to the wind. *6* PAINT. to blend, harmonize [colours]. *7 intr.* [of the weather] to moderate. *8 ref.* to become temperate.

**templazo** *m.* WEAV. temple.

**templario** *m.* Templar, Knight Templar.

**temple** *m.* TEMPERIE. *2* TEMPERATURA. *3* temper [of metal, glass, etc.]. *4* fig. temper, humour, frame of mind. *5* fig. courage, energy, decision. *6* fig. compromise. *7* MUS. tune [of instruments]. *8* Order of the Templars. *9* PAINT. *al* ~, in distemper.

**templete** *m. dim.* small temple. *2* niche, tabernacle. *3* pavillon, kiosk.

**templo** *m.* temple [place of worship], church.

**temporada** *f.* spell, period of time, some time. *2* season: ~ *de ópera*, opera season.

**temporal** *adj.* temporary. *2* temporal, secular,

worldly. *3* GRAM., ANAT. temporal. *4 m.* tempest, storm. *5* ANAT. temporal bone.

**temporalidad** *f.* temporality. *2* temporariness.

**temporalizar** *tr.* to make temporal or temporary.

**temporalmente** *adv.* temporarily. *2* temporally.

**temporáneo, -a; temporario, -ria** *adj.* temporary.

**témporas** *f. pl.* ECCL. Ember days.

**temporero, -ra** *adj.* temporary [clerk, employee].

**temporizar** *intr.* CONTEMPORIZAR. *2* to pass the time.

**tempranal** *adj.* producing early fruits.

**tempranamente** *adv.* early. *2* too early, prematurely.

**tempranero, -ra** *adj.* TEMPRANO 1.

**tempranito** *adv.* coll. very early.

**temprano, -na** *adj.* early: *fruto* ~, early fruit. *2* young [age]. *3 m.* field yielding early crops. *4 adv.* early. *5* too early.

**ten con ten** *m.* tact, adroitness, moderation.

**tenacidad** *f.* tenacity, tenaciousness, pertinacity, firmness, persistence. *2* PHYS. tenacity.

**tenacillas** *f. pl.* small tongs. *2* sugar tongs. *3* curling irons. *4* tweezers. *5* snuffers.

**tenaz** *adj.* tenacious, pertinacious, stubborn, persistent. *2* tenacious, adhesive, tough.

**tenaza** *f.* BOT. tenaille. *2* CARDS tenace. *3 pl.* tongs, pair of tongs; pincers, pair of pincers.

**tenazón (a)** *adv.* without taking aim. *2* suddenly.

**tenca** *f.* ICHTH. tench.

**tención** *f.* holding, possessing.

**tendal** *m.* awning. *2* TENDEDERO. *3* things spread out, or clothes hung up, to dry.

**tendalera** *f.* coll. litter, things scattered in disorder.

**tendalero, tendedero** *m.* place where clothes, etc., are spread or hung up to dry. *2* (Am.) clothesline.

**tendel** *m.* MAS. levelling line. *2* MAS. layer of mortar.

**tendencia** *f.* tendency, drift, trend.

**tendencioso, -sa** *adj.* tendentious.

**ténder** *m.* RLY. tender.

**tender** *tr.* to spread, spread out. *2* to stretch out. *3* to hold out [one's hand, etc.]; to extend, stretch forth. *4* to hang up [washing, etc., to dry]. *5* to spread on the ground. *6* to lay [a cable, a track, etc.]. *7* to throw, build [a bridge]. *8 intr.* to tend, have a tendency. *9 ref.* to stretch, lie down. *10* CARDS to show down. *11* [of a horse] to run at full gallop. ¶ CONJUG. like *entender*.

**tenderete** *m.* stand, stall, booth. *2* a card game.

**tendero, -ra** *m.-f.* shopkeeper, *storekeeper. *2 m.* tent maker.

**tendidamente** *adv.* diffusely, diffusively.

**tendido** *adj.* full [gallop]. *2 m.* spreading or hanging up [of washing, etc., to dry]. *3* laying [of a cable, a track, etc.]. *4* throwing, building [of a bridge]. *5* uncovered tiers of seats [in a bull ring]. *6* (Am.) bedclothes.

**tendiente** *adj.* tending, having a tendency.

**tendinoso, -sa** *adj.* tendinous.

**tendón** *m.* ANAT. tendon.

**tendré, tendría,** etc. *irr.* V. TENER.

**tenducha** *f.,* **tenducho** *m.* small, mean shop.

**tenebrario** *m.* ECCL. Tenebrae hearse.

**tenebrosidad** *f.* gloominess, darkness.

**tenebroso, -sa** *adj.* gloomy, dark, tenebrous.

**tenedero** *m.* NAUT. anchoring ground.

**tenedor** *m.* holder, possessor. *2* fork, table fork. *3* COM. holder [of a bill, etc.]. *4* ~ *de libros,* bookkeeper.

**teneduría** *f.* position of bookkeeper. *2* ~ *de libros,* bookkeeping.

**tenencia** *f.* holding, possession. *2* MIL. lieutenancy. *3* ECCL. succursal church.

**tener** *tr.* to have [in many senses], to hold, keep; own, posses. *2* to keep [one's word or promise]. *3* to hold, keep [in a specified place, condition, etc.]. *5* to have, hold [conversation]; to hold [a meeting, etc.]. *6* to keep [a shop, inn, etc.]. *7* to have, bear [young, a baby]. *8* to be the matter with, to ail: *¿qué tiene usted?,* what is the matter with you?, what ails you? *9* [app. to dimensions, years, months, etc.] to be: *este árbol tiene seis metros de alto,* this tree is six metres high; *mi padre tiene sesenta años,* my father is sixty years old. *10* ~ *cuidado,* to take care. *11* ~ *calor,* ~ *frío,* [of a pers.] to be hot, to be cold; ~ *miedo,* to be afraid; ~ *prisa,* to be in a hurry. *12* ~ *a honra,* to regard it is an honour. *13* ~ *a menos,* to deem it beneath one [to do something]. *14* ~ *algo de,* to be somewhat of. *15* ~ *en mucho,* to value highly; ~ *en poco,* to think little of. *16* ~ *para sí,* to think, be of the opinion. *17* ~ *por,* to consider or regard as. *18 no tenerlas todas consigo,* to be uneasy, full of aprehension. *19 intr.* to have possesions. *20 aux.* to have: *tengo escritos dos libros,* I have written two books. *21* ~ *de* or ~ *que,* to have to, be obliged to, must. *22 tengo entendido que,* I understand that. *23 ref.* to hold fast or steady, to keep from falling. *24* to stand, rest [on something]. *25* to stop. *26 tenerse a,* to abide by, to stick to. *27 tenerse en pie,* to stand, keep on one's feet. *28 tenerse por,* to consider oneself as.

¶ CONJUG.: INDIC. Pres.: *tengo, tienes, tiene;* tenemos, tenéis, tienen. | Pret.: *tuve, tuviste, tuvo; tuvimos, tuvisteis, tuvieron.* | Fut.: *tendré, tendrás,* etc. | COND.: *tendría, tendrías,* etc. | SUBJ. Pres.: *tenga, tengas, tenga; tengamos, tengáis, tengan.* | Imperf.: *tuviera, tuvieras,* etc., or *tuviese, tuvieses,* etc. | Fut.: *tuviere, tuvieres,* etc. | IMPER.: *ten, tenga; tengamos, tened, tengan.*

**tenería** *f.* tannery.

**tengo, tenga,** etc. *irr.* V. TENER.

**tenia** *f.* ZOOL. taenia, tapeworm. *2* ARCH. taenia.

**tenida** *f.* (Am.) meeting, session.

**tenienta** *f.* lieutenant's wife.

**teniente** *adj.* coll. dull of hearing. *2* coll. niggardly. *3 m.* deputy, substitute. *4* MIL. lieutenant: ~ *coronel,* lieutenant colonel; ~ *general,* lieutenant general.

**tenis** *m.* lawn tennis.

**tenista** *m.-f.* tennis player.

**tenor** *m.* MUS. tenor. *2* tenor, nature, import: *a este* ~, like this; *a* ~ *de,* in accordance with.

**tenorio** *m.* Don Juan, lady-killer.

**tensión** *f.* tension: ~ *arterial,* arterial tension. *2* MECH. stress.

**tenso, -sa** *adj.* tense, tight, taut; strained.

**tensón** *f.* tenson, tenzon.

**tensor, -ra** *adj.* tensile. *2 m.* tension [device]. *3* tightener, turnbuckle. *4* ANAT. tensor.

**tentación** *f.* temptation.

**tentacular** *adj.* tentacular.

**tentáculo** *m.* ZOOL. tentacle, feeler.

**tentador, -ra** *adj.* tempting. *2* alluring. *3 m.-f.* tempter.

**tentar** *tr.* to feel, touch, examine by touch. *2* to feel [one's way]; to grope for. *3* to try, attempt. *4* SURG. to probe. *5* to tempt. ¶ CONJUG. like *acertar*.

**tentativa** f. attempt, trial, endeavour.
**tentativo, -va** adj. tentative.
**tentemozo** m. prop, support. 2 DOMINGUILLO.
**tentempié** m. coll. light meal, snack, bite.
**tenue** adj. tenuous, thin, slender, delicate, faint.
**tenuidad** f. tenuity, tenuousness. 2 trifle.
**tenuirrostro, -tra** adj. ORN. tenuirostral.
**teñido, -da** adj. dyed. 2 m. dyeing; staining.
**teñir** tr. to dye, colour, stain, tinge. 2 PAINT. to dark, sadden [a colour]. ¶ CONJUG. like reír.
**teocali** m. ARCHEOL. teocalli [Aztec temple].
**teocracia** f. theocracy.
**teodicea** f. theodicy.
**teodolito** m. theodolite.
**Teodoro** m. pr. n. Theodore.
**Teodosio** m. pr. n. Theodosius.
**teogonía** f. theogony.
**teologal** adj. theologic, theological.
**teología** f. theology, divinity.
**teológico, -ca** adj. theologic, theological.
**teólogo, -ga** m.-f. theologian.
**teorema** m. theorem.
**teoría** f. theory. 2 theoretics.
**teórica** f. theoretics.
**teórico, -ca** adj. theoretic, theoretical. 2 m.-f. theorist.
**teorizante** m.-f. theorizer.
**teorizar** intr. to theorize.
**teoso, -sa** adj. resinous [wood].
**teosofía** f. theosophy.
**teósofo** m. theosophist.
**tepe** m. sod, turf [used for making walls].
**tequila** f. (Mex.) tequila [distilled liquor].
**terapeuta** m.-f. therapeutist.
**terapéutica** f. therapeutics.
**teratología** f. teratology.
**terbio** m. CHEM. terbium.
**tercamente** adv. obstinately, stubbornly.
**tercer** adj. apocopated form of TERCERO used only before masculine singular nouns.
**tercera** adj.-f. third. 2 f. go-between. 3 third class. 4 CARDS, FENC. tierce. 5 MUS. third, tierce. 6 AUTO. third [third speed].
**terceramente** adv. thirdly.
**tercería** f. mediation, intermediation. 2 pondering. 3 LAW right of a third party.
**tercerilla** f. PROS. short-line triplet.
**tercero, -ra** adj.-n. third. 2 m. third party or person. 3 mediator, intermediator. 4 gobetween, procurer. 5 third storey [of a building].
**tercerola** f. short carbine. 2 tierce [cask].
**terceto** m. PROS. tercet, triplet. 2 MUS. trio.
**tercia** f. one third. 2 third of a VARA [measure]. 3 ECCL., CARDS tierce.
**terciana** f. MED. tertian, tertian fever.
**terciar** tr. to place sidewise or diagonally. 2 to divide into three parts. 3 to plough the third time. 4 MIL. to carry [arms]. 5 intr. to mediate, intervene. 6 to take part. 7 si se tercia, if an occasion comes to hand.
**terciario, -ria** adj. third [in order or degree]. 2 CHEM., MED. tertiary. 3 adj.-m. GEOL. Tertiary. 4 m.-f. ECCL. tertiary.
**tercio, -cia** adj. third [in order]. 2 m. third, third part. 3 Sp. HIST. regiment of infantry. 4 MIL. Foreign Legion. 5 MIL. division of the GUARDIA CIVIL. 6 hacer buen ~, to do a good turn; hacer mal ~, to do a bad turn. 7 hacer ~, to complete a number of people. 8 pl. strong limbs [of a man].
**terciopelado, -da** adj. ATERCIOPELADO.
**terciopelero** m. velvet weaver, velvet worker.

**terciopelo** m. velvet.
**terco, -ca** adj. obstinate, stubborn. 2 hard, intractable [metal, wood, etc.].
**terebinto** m. BOT. terebinth.
**terebrante** adj. boring, piercing [pain].
**Terencio** m. pr. n. Terence.
**Teresa** f. pr. n. Theresa.
**teresiana** f. a kind of kepi.
**tergiversación** f. twisting, distortion, perversion, misrepresentation [of facts, statements, etc.].
**tergiversar** tr. to twist, distort, pervert, misrepresent [facts, statements, etc.].
**terliz** m. ticking [fabric].
**termal** adj. thermal [pertaining to hot springs].
**termas** f. pl. thermae. 2 hot baths, hot springs, thermal springs.
**termes** m. TERMITE.
**térmico, -ca** adj. thermal, thermic, thermical.
**terminación** f. termination, conclusion, end, completion. 2 GRAM. termination, ending.
**terminacho** m. coll. vulgar term. 2 coll. barbarism.
**terminal** adj. terminal. 2 m. ELECT. terminal.
**terminante** adj. final, conclusive, positive, peremptory.
**terminar** tr. to terminate, close, end, finish, complete. 2 intr.-ref. to terminate, close, end, finish [come to an end]; to end [in].
**término** m. end [extreme or last point]. 2 end, conclusion, completion: llevar a ~, to carry out; poner ~ a, to put an end to. 3 boundary; boundary mark. 4 term [of a town]. 5 aim, end, goal. 6 term, word. 7 term [limited period]. 8 ARCH., LOG., MATH. term. 9 ~ medio, average. 10 F. ARTS primer ~, foreground; último ~, background. 11 pl. terms: estar en buenos términos, to be in good terms; en buenos términos, in a polite or euphemistic manner. 12 manner [of conducting oneself]. 13 state, condition. 14 términos hábiles, possibility.
**terminología** f. terminology.
**terminote** m. affected term or word, big word.
**termiónico, -ca** adj. thermionic. 2 f. thermionics.
**termite** m. ENT. termite, white ant.
**termitero** m. nest of white ants.
**termobarómetro** m. thermobarometer.
**termocauterio** m. thermocautery.
**termodinámico, -ca** adj. thermodynamic. 2 f. thermodynamics.
**termoelectricidad** f. thermoelectricity.
**termología** f. thermology.
**termometría** f. thermometry.
**termómetro** m. thermometer.
**termonuclear** adj. thermonuclear.
**Termópilas** f. pl. pr. n. HIST. Thermopylae.
**termo, pl. -mos** m. thermos bottle.
**termosifón** m. thermosiphon. 2 hot-water boiler [for heating running water in a building].
**termostato** m. thermostat.
**terna** f. list of three candidates presented for selection. 2 pair of threes [at dice]. 3 set of dice.
**ternario, -ria** adj. ternary. 2 MUS. triple, three-part.
**terne** adj. strong, husky. 2 persistent, stubborn. 3 affecting courage, bullying. 4 m. bully.
**ternera** f. female calf. 2 veal.
**ternero** m. male calf.
**terneza** f. TERNURA. 2 pl. endearing words, sweet words.
**ternilla** f. gristle.
**ternilloso, -sa** adj. gristly, cartilaginous.
**ternísimo, -ma** adj. superl. of TIERNO.

**terno** *m.* ternary, triad. *2* tern [in lottery]. *3* suit of clothes. *4* vestments for the high mass. *5* profane oath, curse: *echar ternos,* to swear, curse.

**ternura** *f.* tenderness, softness. *2* fondness, affectionateness.

**terpeno** *m.* CHEM. terpene.

**Terpsícore** *f. pr. n.* MYTH. Terpsichore.

**terquear** *intr.* to be stubborn.

**terquedad** *f.* obstinacy, stubbornness.

**terracota** *f.* terra cotta.

**terrado** *m.* terrace, flat roof [of a house].

**terraja** *f.* diestock. *2* modelling board.

**terral** *adj.* land [breeze]. *2 m.* land breeze.

**terramicina** *f.* PHARM. terramycin.

**Terranova** *f. pr. n.* GEOG. Newfoundland.

**terraplén** *m.* fill, embankment, terrace. *2* FORT. terreplein.

**terraplenar** *tr.* to fill [with earth], embank, terrace.

**terráqueo, -a** *adj.* terraqueous, terrestrial.

**terrateniente** *m.-f.* landowner, landholder.

**terraza** *f.* terrace. *2* border [in a garden]. *3* flat roof [of a house]. *4* sidewalk café. *5* glazed jar with two handles.

**terrazgo** *m.* piece of land for planting. *2* land rent.

**terrazo** *m.* PAINT. ground, earth [in a landscape].

**terrear** *intr.* [of thin crops] to show the ground.

**terremoto** *m.* earthquake.

**terrenal** *adj.* earthly, mundane, terrene, terrestrial.

**terrenidad** *f.* earthliness, terreneness.

**terreno, -na** *adj.* terrestrial. *2* earthly, mundane, terrain, terrene. *3 m.* ground [position, distance, etc.]: *ganar ~,* to gain ground, to gain upon; *minarle el ~ a uno,* to undermine one's work; *preparar el ~,* fig. to pave the way; *sobre el ~,* on the spot; with data in hand. *5* fig. field, sphere [of action, etc.]. *6* GEOL. terrane, terrain. *7* MIL. terrain. *8 sing.-pl.* grounds [gardens, lawns, etc.].

**térreo, -a** *adj.* earthen, earthy, terreous.

**terrero, -ra** *adj.* earthy, low, humble. *2* low [fly of a bird]. *3 m.* terrace, flat roof. *4* mound of earth. *5* alluvium. *6* MIN. dump. *7* ·mark, target [for shooting].

**terrestre** *adj.* terrestrial. *2* BOT. terraneous.

**terribilidad** *f.* terribleness.

**terrible** *adj.* terrible. *2* illtempered.

**terrícola** *m.-f.* terrestrial, inhabitant of the earth.

**terrífico, -ca** *adj.* terrific.

**territorial** *adj.* territorial [of a territory].

**territorio** *m.* territory.

**terrizo, -za** *adj.* earthen. *2 m.-f.* earthen tub.

**terromontero** *m.* mound, hillock.

**terrón** *m.* clod [of earth]. *2* lump [of sugar, salt, etc.]. *3 pl.* coll. clod, soil, land.

**terror** *m.* terror.

**terrorífico, -ca** *adj.* terrific, frightful.

**terrorismo** *m.* terrorism.

**terrorista** *adj.* terroristic. *2 m.-f.* terrorist.

**terroso, -sa** *adj.* earthy, earthlike.

**terruño** *m.* AGR. soil. *2* piece of ground. *3* country, native soil.

**tersar** *tr.* to make limpid; to polish, smooth.

**terso, -sa** *adj.* limpid, clear; smooth; shining. *2* terse [style].

**tersura** *f.* limpidness, smoothness. *2* terseness.

**tertulia** *f.* social gathering for conversation or entertainment: *hacer ~,* to gather for conversation, to talk. *2* billiard or card room [in a café].

**tertuliano, -na** *m.-f.* one who attends a TERTULIA.

**terzuelo** *m.* one third. *2* ORN. tercel, male falcon.

**Tesalia** *f. pr. n.* GEOG. Thessaly.

**Tesalónica** *f. pr. n.* GEOG. Thessalonica.

**tesar** *tr.* NAUT. to haul taut, to make taut. *2 intr.* [of yoked oxen] to back, pull back.

**tesauro** *m.* thesaurus.

**tesela** *f.* tessera [in mosaic work].

**Teseo** *m. pr. n.* MYTH. Theseus.

**tésera** *f.* HIST. tessera.

**tesis** *f.* thesis.

**tesitura** *f.* MUS. tessiture. *2* attitude [settled behaviour].

**teso, -sa** *adj.* taut, drawn tight. *2 m.* top, brow of a hill. *3* small bulge [on a smooth surface].

**tesón** *m.* constancy, firmness, pertinacity.

**tesonería** *f.* obstinacy, stubbornness.

**tesonero, -ra** *adj.* firm, persistent, stubborn.

**tesorería** *f.* treasury, treasurer's office. *2* treasurership.

**tesorero, -ra** *m.-f.* treasurer.

**tesoro** *m.* treasure. *2* treasury, exchequer. *3* thesauros.

**Tespis** *m. pr. n.* Thespis.

**tespíades** *f. pl.* poet. the Muses.

**testa** *f.* head [of man or animal]. *2* head, face or front part [of certain things].

**testáceo, -a** *adj.-m.* ZOOL. testacean.

**testado, -da** *p. p.* of TESTAR. *2 adj.* testate.

**testador** *m.* testator.

**testadora** *f.* testatrix.

**testaferro** *m.* figurehead, dummy, man of straw.

**testamentaría** *f.* testamentary execution.

**testamentario, -ria** *adj.* testamentary. *2 m.* executor [of a will]. *3 f.* executrix [of a will].

**testamento** *m.* testament, will. *2* BIBL. Testament: *Antiguo Testamento,* Old Testament; *Nuevo Testamento,* New Testament.

**testar** *intr.* to make a will or testament. *2 tr.* to cancel, obliterate.

**testarada** *f.* blow with the head. *2* piece of obstinacy.

**testarazo** *m.* blow with the head.

**testarrón, -na** *adj.* TESTARUDO.

**testarudez** *f.* obstinacy, stubborness.

**testarudo, -da** *adj.* obstinate, stubborn, pigheaded.

**testera** *f.* front, fore part. *2* forehead [of an animal]. *3* crownpiece [of harness]. *4* back seat [of a carriage]. *5* FOUND. wall [of a furnace].

**testero** *m.* TESTERA. *2* back plate [of a fireplace]; big log [in the fireplace].

**testículo** *m.* ANAT., ZOOL. testicle.

**testificación** *f.* attestation, testification.

**testifical** *adj.* LAW of witness.

**testificar** *tr.* to attest, testify, bear witness to.

**testigo** *m.-f.* witness [person]: *~ ocular,* eyewitness. *2* witness [anything that serves as testimony or proof].

**testimonial** *adj.* attesting, testificatory. *2 f. pl.* certificate, testificatory document.

**testimoniar** *tr.* to attest, testify to, bear witness to.

**testimonio** *m.* testimony, attestation, witness, proof. *2* affidavit. *3 testimonio* or *falso ~,* calumny, false charge; false witness.

**testón** *m.* ancient silver coin.

**testudíneo, -a** *adj.* testudineous.

**testudo** *m.* HIST. testudo.

**testuz, testuzo** *m.* nape or forehead [of certain animals].

**teta** *f.* breast [mammary gland], udder: *dar la ~,* to

nurse, suckle. *2* teat, nipple. *3* fig. hummock, knoll.

**tétano, tétanos** *m.* MED. tetanus.

**tetar** *tr.* ATETAR.

**tetera** *f.* teapot, teakettle.

**tetilla** *f.* dim. of TETA. *2* breast [gland in man or male animal]. *3* nipple [of nursing bottle].

**tetón** *m.* stub [of a pruned limb of tree].

**tetracordio** *m.* MUS. tetrachord.

**tetraedro** *m.* GEOM. tetrahedron.

**tetrágono** *m.* GEOM. tetragon.

**tetralogía** *f.* tetralogy.

**tetramotor** *m.* AER. four-motor plane.

**tetrarca** *m.* tetrarch.

**tetrarquía** *f.* tetrarchy.

**tetrasílabo, -ba** *adj.* four-syllable [word].

**tétrico, -ca** *adj.* dark, gloomy, sullen, dismal.

**tetuaní** *adj.-n.* of Tetuán.

**teucalí** *m.* TEOCALÍ.

**teucrio** *m.* BOT. germander.

**teucro, -cra** *adj.-n.* Trojan.

**teutón, -na** *adj.* teutonic. *2 m.-f.* teuton.

**teutónico, -ca** *adj.* teutonic. *2 m.* teutonic [language].

**textil** *adj.-m.* textile.

**texto** *m.* text: *fuera de* ~, full-page [illustration]. *2* textbook. *3* PRINT. great primer.

**textual** *adj.* textual, literal.

**textualmente** *adv.* textually, literally.

**textura** *f.* texture. *2* weaving.

**tez** *f.* complexion [of the face].

**ti** *pers. pron.* [used as object of prepositions] thee, thyself; you, yourself.

**tía** *f.* aunt: ~ *abuela*, grandaunt, great-aunt; *no hay tu* ~, coll. there's no use, nothing doing. *2* mother [term of address for an elderly woman]. *3* coll. coarse woman. *4* coll. prostitute.

**tiara** *f.* tiara.

**tibetano, -na** *adj.-n.* Tibetan.

**tibia** *f.* ANAT. tibia, shinbone. *2* MUS. flute.

**tibieza** *f.* tepidity, lukewarmness. *2* coolness, indifference.

**tibio, -bia** *adj.* tepid, lukewarm [moderately warm]. *2* fig. tepid, lukewarm, cool, indifferent.

**tibor** *m.* large Chinese or Japanese decorative jar.

**tiburón** *m.* ICHTH. shark.

**tic** *m.* tic.

**tiemblo** *m.* BOT. aspen, aspen tree.

**tiempo** *m.* time [duration; portion of time, epoch, moment; allotted or available portion of time]: ~ *medio*, ASTR. mean time; *los buenos tiempos*, the good, old days; *cuánto* ~, how long; *mucho* ~, long, for long, a long time; *poco* ~, a short time; *dar* ~ *al* ~, to wait patiently, to bide one's time; *ganar* ~, to save time; to temporize; *hacer* ~, to wait, to while the time away; *pasar el* ~, to be idle, to pass the time away; *perder el* ~, to waste time; *al poco* ~, within a short time; *a su* ~, in due time; *a* ~, in time, opportunely; *al mismo* ~, at the same time, also; *a un mismo* ~, *a un* ~, at the same time, simultaneously; *con el* ~, in time, in the course of time; *con* ~, beforehand, not late; opportunely; *de un* ~ *a esta parte*, for some time now; *en* ~ *de*, at the time of; *hace* ~, ~ *ha*, some time ago, a long time ago; *un* ~, formerly, in other times. *2* weather: *hacer buen* ~, to be clear, to be good weather; *hacer mal* ~, to be bad weather. *3* MUS. tiempo. *4* MUS. beat [in a measure]. *5* GRAM. tense: ~ *simple*, simple tense; ~ *compuesto*, compound

tense. *6* MACH. *de dos tiempos*, two-cycle; *de cuatro tiempos*, four-cycle.

**tienda** *f.* shop, *store: ir de tiendas*, to go shopping. *2* tent [portable shelter]: ~ *de campaña*, tent. *3* NAUT. awning. *4* tilt [for a cart].

**tiendo, tienda,** etc. *in.* V. TENDER.

**tienta** *f.* BULLF. testing the courage of young bulls. *2* sagacity. *3* sounding rod. *4 a tientas*, groping: *andar a tientas*, to grope, to grope in the dark; to feel one's way.

**tientaguja** *f.* sounding rod.

**tiento** *m.* touch, feeling: *a* ~, *por el* ~, gropingly. *2* blindman's stick. *3* BALANCÍN. *4* steady hand.' *5* care, caution: *andarse con* ~, to watch one's step. *6* blow: *dar un* ~ *a*, to give a blow; fig. to try, examine; fig. to take a draught from [a bottle, a jug]. *7* MUS. preliminary flourish. *8* maulstick. *9* ZOOL. tentacle. *10 tomar el* ~ *a*, to examine, sound.

**tiento, tiente,** etc. *irr.* V. TENTAR.

**tiernamente** *adv.* tenderly, lovingly.

**tierno, -na** *adj.* tender [soft; loving, affectionate]. *2* tender [age]. *3* fresh [bread]. *4* blear [eyes].

**tierra** *f.* earth [this planet]. *2* land [solid part of the earth's surface]: ~ *de nadie*, MIL. no man's land; ~ *firme*, mainland; solid ground; *tomar* ~, to land; *en* ~, NAUT. on land, ashore; ~ *adentro*, inland. *3* ground [surface of earth]: *irse*, or *venirse, a* ~, to fall down; collapse; be ruined; *perder* ~, to lose footing; to be swept off one's feet. *4* country [one's country], homeland. *5* country, land, soil, region, district: *Tierra Santa*, Holy Land; *por estas tierras*, in these parts. *6* land, landed property, tillable land; piece of land: ~ *de pan llevar*, wheat land, cereal-growing land. *7* AGR. soil, mould. *8* earth [matter], dust: ~ *de batán*, fuller's earth. *9* CHEM. earth. *10* RADIO. ground.

1) **tieso** *adv.* hard, firmly, strongly.

2) **tieso, -sa** *adj.* stiff, rigid [not flexible]. *2* strong, robust. *3* tight, taut. *4* fig. valiant. *5* fig. stiff, stuck-up. *6* fig. stiff, uncompromising, firm, obstinate. *7* coll. *tenérselas tiesas con*, to hold one's ground with.

**tiesta** *f.* edge of headings [of a cask or barrel].

**tiesto** *m.* potsherd. *2* flowerpot.

**tiesura** *f.* stiffness.

**tífico, -ca** *adj.* MED. typhous.

**tifo** *m.* MED. typhus.

**tifoideo, -a** *adj.* typhoid. *2 f.* MED. typhoid fever.

**tifón** *m.* typhoon. *2* METEOR. waterspout.

**tifus** *m.* MED. typhus.

**tigre** *m.* ZOOL. tiger. *2* fig. tiger [bloodthirsty person]. *3* ZOOL. (Am.) jaguar.

**tigresa** *f.* tigress.

**tigridia** *f.* BOT. tiger lily.

**tigrillo** *m.* ZOOL. (Am.) gray fox.

**tija** *f.* stem [of a key].

**tijera** *f. sing. y pl.* scissors, shears. *2 sing.* sawbuck, sawhorse. *3* backbiter, gossip. *4 catre de* ~, folding cot; *silla de* ~, folding chair. *5 hacer* ~, [of horses] to twist the mouth.

**tijerada** *f.* TIJERETADA.

**tijereta** *f.* dim. small scissors. *2* BOT. tendril [of vine]. *3* ENT. earwig.

**tijeretada** *f.,* **tijeretazo** *m.* cut with scissors, clip, snip.

**tijeretear** *tr.* to cut clumsily with scissors. *2* coll. to deal' arbitrarily with [another person's affairs].

**tila** f. BOT. linden tree. 2 flower of the linden tree. 3 linden-blossom tea.

**tilburí** m. tilbury.

**tildar** tr. to put a tilde or dash over. 2 to cancel, cross out. 3 ~ de, to accuse of, or charge with, being [negligent, niggardly, etc.].

**tilde** f. tilde, dash [on the letter ñ, etc.]. 2 fault, blemish, defect. 3 f. jot, tittle.

**tildío** m. ORN. killdee.

**tildón** m. cancelling line or mark.

**tilia** f. TILO.

**tiliáceo, -a** adj. BOT. tiliaceous.

**tilín** m. ting-a-ling. 2 coll. hacer ~, to please. 3 tener ~, to be attractive, winsome.

**tilo** m. BOT. linden tree.

**tilla** f. NAUT. part deck on a small boat.

**tillado** m. board floor.

**tillar** tr. to floor with boards.

**timador, -ra** m.-f. swindler.

**tímalo** m. ICHTH. grayling.

**timar** tr. to swindle. 2 ref. coll. to make eyes to each other.

**timba** f. gambling party. 2 gambling den.

**timbal** m. MUS. kettledrum. 2 MUS. tambourin, small drum. 3 COOK. timbale.

**timbalero** m. MUS. kettledrummer.

**timbrado, -da** adj. MUS. bien timbrada, having a good timbre [voice]. 3 papel ~, stamped paper.

**timbrar** tr. to stamp [put a stamp or seal on].

**timbrazo** m. loud ring [of a call or door bell].

**timbre** m. HER. timbre, crest. 2 stamp, seal [on a paper]. 3 revenue stamp. 4 call bell, electric bell. 5 MUS., HER. timbre. 6 deed of glory.

**timidez** f. timidness, timorousness, shyness.

**tímido, -da** adj. timid, timorous, shy. 2 fainthearted.

**timo** m. swindle, cheat: dar un ~ a, to swindle. 2 ANAT. thymus. 3 TÍMALO.

**timocracia** f. POL. timocracy.

**timol** m. CHEM. thymol.

**timón** m. NAUT. rudder; helm. 2 AER. rudder. 3 fig. helm [direction, guidance]. 4 beam [of plough]. 5 pole, tongue [of a cart].

**timonear** intr. NAUT. to helm, steer.

**timonel** m. NAUT. helmsman, steersman.

**timonera** f. ORN. rectrix. 2 NAUT. pilothouse.

**timonero** m. TIMONEL.

**timorato, -ta** adj. God-fearing. 2 pusilanimous.

**Timoteo** m. pr. n. Timothy.

**timpánico, -ca** adj. ANAT., MED. tympanic.

**timpanitis** f. MED. tympanites.

**timpanización** f. MED. meteorization.

**tímpano** m. MUS. tambourin. 2 MUS. glass harmonica. 3 ANAT. tympan, tympanum, eardrum. 7 ARCH. tympan, tympanum. 5 PRINT. tympan.

**tina** f. large earthen jar. 2 vat, tub.

**tinada** f. woodpile. 2 cattle shed.

**tinaja** f. large earthen jar.

**tinción** f. dyeing.

**tinelo** m. obs. servants' dinning room.

**tinerfeño, -ña** adj.-n. of Tenerife.

**tingladillo** m. NAUT. clinker work.

**tinglado** m. shed. 2 temporary board platform. 3 fig. intrigue, machination.

**tiniebla** f. sing. & pl. darkness [absence of light; state of ignorance or error]. 2 pl. ECCL. Tenebrae.

**tino** m. skill or facility for finding things in the dark. 2 good aim, skill for hitting the mark. 3 judgement, wisdom, tact. sacar de ~, to bewilder; to exasperate. 5 a buen ~, by guess. 6 a ~, gropingly. 7 sin ~, without moderation.

**tinta** f. ink: ~ china, India ink; saber una cosa de buena ~, to have a thing from a reliable source. 2 [applied] colour or pigment. 3 [process of] dyeing. 4 colour, tint, hue. 5 PAINT. tint.

**tintar** tr. to dye, colour, tint.

**tinte** m. [process of] dyeing. 2 dye [colour]. 3 dyeing establishment. 4 fig. colouring, false appearance.

**tintero** m. inkstand, inkwell: dejarse [una cosa] en el ~, coll. to forget, to omit. 2 PRINT. ink fountain.

**tintín** m. clink, chink. 2 jingle.

**tintinar, tintinear** intr. to clink; to jingle.

**tintineo** m. clink, clinking. 2 jingle, jingling.

**tinto, -ta** adj. dyed, coloured, stained. 2 darkred [grape or wine].

**tintóreo, -a** adj. tinctorial.

**tintorería** f. dyeing, dyer's trade. 2 dyeing establishment. 3 clothes cleaner's shop.

**tintorero, -ra** m.-f. dyer. 2 clothes cleaner. 3 f. (Am.) female shark.

**tintura** f. [process of] dyeing. 2 dye [colour]. 3 fig. paint [in the face]. 4 tincture [solution]. 5 fig. smattering.

**tinturar** tr. to dye, colour, tincture.

**tiña** f. MED. tinea, scald-head. 2 coll. stinginess; poverty.

**tiñería** f. coll. stinginess.

**tiño, tiña, tiñera**, etc. in. V. TEÑIR.

**tiñoso, -sa** adj. scabby. 2 coll. mean, stingy. 3 coll. poor, indigent.

**tío** m. uncle: ~ abuelo, granduncle, great-uncle. 2 term of adress for an eldery man. 3 coll. fellow, guy.

**tiovivo** m. carrousel, merry-go-round.

**tipejo** m. dim. ridiculous fellow.

**típico, -ca** adj. typical. 2 characteristic.

**tiple** m. MUS. treble or soprano voice. 2 MUS. treble guitar. 3 m.-f. MUS. soprano singer.

**tiplisonante** adj. coll. treble-toned.

**tipo** m. type [pattern, standard, symbol, class, etc.]. 2 BIOL., PRINT., NUMIS. type. 3 BOT., ZOOL. phylum. 4 COM. rate: ~ de descuento, discount rate. 5 build, figure [of a person]. 6 fellow, specimen, guy.

**tipografía** f. typography. 2 printing shop.

**tipográfico, -ca** adj. typographic(al.

**tipógrafo** m. typographer, typesetter.

**típula** f. ENT. crane fly, daddy-longlegs.

**tiquis miquis, tiquismiquis** m. pl. ridiculous or affected scruples, words, etc.

**tira** f. narrow strip [of paper, cloth, etc.]; strap, thong. 2 shred.

**tirabala** m. popgun.

**tirabeque** m. BOT. sugar pea.

**tirabotas** f. boot hook.

**tirabuzón** m. corkscrew. 2 corkscrew curl, hanging curl.

**tirada** f. throw, cast. 2 shooting [at a mark]. 3 distance, stretch. 4 series [of things said or written without stopping], tirade. 5 PRINT. printing [of a book, journal, etc.]: ~ aparte, reprint. 6 edition, impression [number of copies]. 7 de, or en una ~, at a stretch.

**tiradero** m. HUNT. shooting post.

**tirado, -da** adj. dirt-cheap, given away. 2 long and low [ship]. 3 running [handwriting]. 4 m. wire-drawing. 5 PRINT. printing, presswork.

**tirador, -ra** m.-f. thrower. 2 drawer [of metals, etc.]. 3 marksman, [good or bad] shot. 4 FENC. fencer. 5 m. bell pull, pull chain. 6 handle, knob [of a door, drawer, etc.], doorknob. 7 slingshot. 8 PRINT. pressman.

**tirafondo** m. wood screw, lag screw.

**tiralíneas,** pl. **-neas** m. ruling pen.

**tiramira** f. long, narrow range [of mountains]. 2 line, string, series. 3 distance, stretch.

**tiranía** f. tyranny.

**tyranicida** m.-f. tyrannicide [person].

**tiranicidio** m. tyrannicide [killing of a tyrant].

**tiránico, -ca** adj. tyrannic(al, tyrannous.

**tiranizar** tr. to tyrannize.

**tirano, -na** adj. tyrannical. 2 m.-f. tyrant.

**tirante** adj. tight, taut, tense, strained. 2 strained [relations]. 3 m. trace [of harness]. 4 ARCH., ENG. tie, tie beam, tie rod, truss rod. 5 pl. braces, suspenders [of trousers].

**tirantez** f. tenseness, tautness, tightness. 2 tension, strained condition [of relations].

**tiranuelo, -la** adj. dim. little tyrant.

**tirapié** m. shoemaker's stirrup.

**tirar** tr. to throw, cast, fling, pitch. 2 to throw away, cast off. 3 to fire [a shot]. 4 to give [a kick]. 5 to draw, stretch. 6 to withdraw. 7 to knock down, overthrow, pull down. 8 to waste, squander. 9 to draw [a line]. 10 PRINT. to print. 11 intr. to attract, excite love or interest. 12 [of a chimney, etc.] to draw. 13 to last, endure. 14 ~ a: a) to fence with; shoot with; b) to shoot at; c) to turn [in some direction]; d) to tend, incline; e) to seek to, aim at; f) [of colours] to have a tinge of: ~ a rojo, to be reddish. 15 ~ de: a) to draw, attract; b) to pull, pull at, pull on, to draw; c) to draw, take, take out [a weapon, instrument, etc.]. 16 coll. ~ de largo, or por largo, to spend lavishly; to make a liberal estimate. 17 coll. ir tirando, to get along. 18 coll. tira y afloja, blowing hot and cold. 19 a todo ~, at the most. 20 ref. to rush, to throw oneself. 21 [of a parachutist, etc.] to jump. 22 to lie down.

**tiratacos** m. popgun.

**tirilla** f. neckband [of a shirt].

**tirio, -ria** adj.-m. Tyrian.

**tiritar** intr. to shiver.

**tiritón** m. shiver: dar tiritones, to shiver.

**Tiro** f. pr. n. HIST., GEOG. Tyre.

**tiro** m. throw [act of throwing]. 2 shot [discharge of a firearm; charge for a firearm]; errar el ~, to miss the mark; salir el ~ por la culata, [of one's exertions, scheming, etc.] to work the wrong way: a tiros, with shots; ni a tiros, coll. by no means. 3 throw, shot, range [distance]; a ~, within range; fig. within reach. 4 report [of a gun]. 5 shooting practice or sport: ~ al blanco, target shooting; ~ al plato, trapshooting. 6 shooting grounds; shooting gallery. 7 fig. physical or moral injury. 8 fig. innuendo, allusive remark. 9 ARTIL. fire, direction of fire. 10 team [of draught animals]. 11 harness trace. 12 length [of a piece of cloth, etc.]. 13 flight [of stairs]. 14 draft, draught [of a chimney, etc.]. 15 MIN. shaft; depth of a shaft. 16 coll. de tiros largos, all dressed-up.

**tiroideo, -a** adj. ANAT. thyroid.

**tiroides** m. ANAT. thyroid [gland].

**Tirol (el)** m. pr. n. GEOG. the Tyrol.

**tirolés, -sa** adj.-n. Tyrolese.

**tirón** m. pull, jerk, haul, tug: de un ~, with a pull; fig. at one stroke; at a stretch. 2 ESTIRÓN. 3 tyro, novice.

**tirotear** tr. to snipe at, blaze away at. 2 ref. to exchange shots, fire at each other.

**tiroteo** m. firing, shooting, exchange of shoots.

**tirreno, -na** adj.-n. Tyrrhenian. 2 Etruscan.

**tirria** f. coll. aversion, dislike.

**tirso** m. BOT., MYTH. Thyrsus.

**tisana** f. medicinal tea.

**tísico, -ca** adj. MED. phthisical, consumptive. 2 m.-f. consumptive [person].

**tisis** f. MED. phthisis, consumption.

**tisú** m. gold or silver tissue.

**Titán** m. pr. n. MYTH. and fig. Titan.

**titanio** m. CHEM. titanium.

**títere** m. puppet, marionette: no dejar ~ con cabeza, to upset, destroy, entirely. 2 fig. whippersnapper. 3 pl. puppet show. 4 jugglers show, tumblers show, etc.

**titilación** f. slight tremor [of a part of the body]. 2 twinkling [of a luminous body].

**titilar** intr. [of a part of the body] to tremble slightly. 2 [of a luminous body] to twinkle.

**titirimundi** m. MUNDONUEVO.

**titiritaina** f. coll. merry noise.

**titiritar** intr. to shiver, shake [with cold or fear].

**titiritero** m. puppet showman. 2 juggler, tumbler.

**Tito** m. pr. n. Titus.

**titubear** intr. to waver, hesitate. 2 to stammer. 3 to stagger, totter.

**titubeo** m. wavering, hesitation. 2 stammering. 3 staggering, tottering.

**titulado, -da** adj. diplomaed. 2 titled. 3 so-called. 4 CHEM. titrated.

**titular** adj. titular [bishop, saint, etc.]. 2 m.-f. bearer, holder [of a passport, etc.]. 3 m. capital letter [used in newspaper headlines].

**titular** tr. to title, entitle, call, name. 2 CHEM. to titrate. 3 ref. to be called; to call oneself.

**titulillo** m. PRINT. running title.

**título** m. title. 2 heading, headline, caption. 3 diploma, professional degree. 4 qualification, desert. 5 COM. certificate, bond. 6 CHEM. titre, titer. 7 LAW ~ de propiedad, title dead. 8 a ~ de, as a, by way of: a ~ de información, unofficially.

**tiza** f. chalk. 2 whiting [for polishing metals]. 3 calcined stag's horn.

**tiznadura** f. smudging, smutting; smudge, stain.

**tiznajo** m. TIZNÓN.

**tiznar** tr. to soil with soot. 2 to smudge, smut, stain, soil, sully. 3 ref. to get soiled or smudged. 4 (Am.) to get drunk.

**tizne** m. soot, smut. 2 half-burned stick.

**tiznón** m. smut, smear, stain.

**tizo** m. half-burnt charcoal.

**tizón** m. partly burned stick, firebrand. 2 AGR. wheat-smut. 3 fig. stain. 4 MAS. header.

**tizona** f. coll. sword.

**tizonear** intr. to stir up a fire.

**toalla** f. towel: ~ rusa, Turkish towel.

**toallero** m. towel rack.

**toalleta** f. dim. small towel. 2 napkin.

**toar** tr. ATOAR.

**toha** f. tufa, calcareous tufa. 2 DENT. tartar. 3 fig. crust, cover.

**tobera** f. tuyère.

**Tobías** m. pr. n. Tobias.

**tobillera** f. flapper [young girl]. 3 SPORT. ankle support.

**tobillo** m. ankle.

**tobogán** m. toboggan.

**toboso, -sa** adj. tufaceous.

**toca** f. wimple. 2 cornet [headdress of the Sisters of Charity]. 3 coif, bonnet. 4 toque [hat].

**tocadiscos** pl. **-cos** m. record player.

**tocado, -da** adj. touched: estar ~ de la cabeza, to be

touched, crazed. 2 m. hairdress [esp. for women]. 3 hairdo, coiffure.

**tocador, -ra** m.-f. MUS. player. 2 m. dressing table; toilet case: *productos de tocador*, toilet articles. 3 dressing room, toilet room.

**tocamiento** m. touching, feeling. 2 playing [on an instrument]. 3 call, inspiration.

**tocante** adj. touching. 2 ~ a, concerning, as regards, touching, with reference to.

**tocar** tr. to touch [with a part of the body, with a stick, etc.], to feel, lay hands upon. 2 to hit, knock, strike (lightly): ~ *fondo*, NAUT. to strike ground. 3 to touch [with a touchstone]. 4 to find [by experience], to suffer [the consequences of]. 5 to touch, touch upon [a subject]. 6 PAINT. to touch. 7 MUS. to touch, strike [keys or strings]; to play, sound, blow, ring, beat [an instrument, a bell, a drum; a composition, an air, a call, etc.]: ~ a muerte, to toll, sound a knell. 8 to play [a phonograph record]. 9 to move, inspire. 10 to do, dress [the hair].
11 intr. ~ a or en, to touch, touch at [be in contact with, be contiguous to]. 12 ~ a, to appertain to, to behove, devolve on, be up to; to one's turn; to fall on one's lot; to be got by one, be the share of [in a distribution, etc.]; to be one's due; to be a relation of; to touch, relate, concern, regard: en or por, lo que toca a, as regads, with regard to. 13 NAUT. ~ en, to touch at [a port].
14 impers. *tocan a*, it is time for or to.
15 ref. to touch, be in contact, touch each other. 16 to do or dress one's hair. 17 to cover one's head [with a hat, bonnet, etc.].

**tocata** f. MUS. toccata. 2 coll. drubbing.

**tocayo, -ya** m.-f. namesake.

**tocinería** f. bacon and pork shop or stand.

**tocinero, -ra** m.-f. por seller.

**tocino** m. bacon; salt pork.

**tocología** f. tocology, obstetrics.

**tocólogo** f. tocologist, obstetrician.

**tocón** m. stump [of tree, arm or leg].

**tochedad** f. rusticity, crudeness, stupidity.

**tocho, -cha** adj. rustic, crude, stupid.

**tochura** f. TOCHEDAD.

**todavía** adv. still, even, yet: ~ *más*, even more, ~ *mejor*, still better; ~ *no*, not yet.

**todo, -da; todos, -das** adj. all, every, each, the whole of: ~ *aquel que*, whoever, everybody who; ~ *aquello que*, whatever. 2 a toda prisa, with all speed, hurriedly; *a toda velocidad*, at full speed. 3 m. all, whole, everything: *ante* ~, first of all; *con* ~, still, however; *del* ~, entirely, wholly; *en* ~ *y por* ~, wholly, absolutely; *en un* ~, as a whole; *sobre* ~, above all, specially. 4 m.-f. pl. everyone, everybody, all of them. 5 adv. entirely.

**todopoderoso, -sa** adj. all-powerful, almighty; *el Todopoderoso*, the Almighty [God].

**toga** f. toga [Roman garment]. 2 gown, robe [of professor, judge or lawyer].

**togado, -da** adj. togated. 2 wearing a gown or robe [judge, magistrate, etc.].

**toisón, toisón de oro** m. Golden Fleece.

**tojino** m. NAUT. cleat.

**tojo** m. BOT. gorse, furze, whin.

**toldar** tr. ENTOLDAR.

**toldilla** f. NAUT. poop, poop deck.

**toldo** m. awning. 2 tilt [cloth covering of a cart, etc.]. 3 coll. pride, pomp.

**tole tole** m. hubbub, uproar. 2 popular clamour

[against something]. 3 *tomar el tole*, to run away, leave in a hurry.

**toledano, -na** adj.-n. Toledan.

**tolerable** adj. tolerable, bearable, sufferable.

**tolerancia** f. tolerance, toleration. 2 MACH., MED. tolerance.

**tolerante** adj. tolerant.

**tolerar** tr. to tolerate. 2 to bear, suffer.

**tolete** m. NAUT. thole, tholepin.

**tolmo** m. pilarlike rock, tor.

**Tolomeo** m. pr. n. Ptolemy.

**tolondro, -dra** adj. scatterbrained. 2 m.-f. scatterbrain. 3 m. bump, swelling [from a blow].

**tolondrón, -na** adj. scatterbrainer. 2 m.-f. scatterbrain. 3 m. bump, swelling [from a blow].

**tolondrón, -na** adj.-n. TOLONDRO: a tolondrones, by fits and starts.

**Tolosa** f. pr. n. GEOG. Toulouse [French city]. 2 Tolosa [Spanish town].

**tolosano, -na** adj.-n. of Tolouse or Tolosa.

**Tolú (bálsamo de)** m. tolu, tolu balsam.

**tolueno** m. CHEM. toluene.

**tolva** f. hopper, chute [in mills, etc.].

**tolvanera** f. cloud of dust, dust whirl.

**tollo** m. ICHTH. spotted dogfish. 2 loin of a stag. 3 HUNT. blind. 4 quagmire.

**toma** f. take, taking, receiving, assuming: ~ *de posesión*, taking possession; induction into office. 2 take, taking, capture [of a fort, a city, etc.]. 3 MED. dose. 4 HYDR. intake, inlet, tap. 5 ELEC. ~ *de corriente*, current collecting; current collector, tap, plug. 6 RADIO. terminal.

**¡toma!** interj. well!, why!; of course!

**tomadero** m. handle. 2 water intake or inlet.

**tomador, -ra** adj. taking. 2 retrieving [dog]. 3 m.-f. taker. 4 COM. payee [of a bill]. 5 NAUT. gasket.

**tomadura** f. taking. 2 ~ *de pelo*, fun made of one, hoax, pulling one's leg.

**tomar** tr. to take [lay hold of, assume possession of; receive, accept; capture], seize, catch. 2 to take, have [eat, drink, etc.]. 3 to take [measurements, the temperature; advice, precautions, measures, a resolution, the train, etc.]. 4 to acquire [an habit]. 5 to take [as a servant or employee]. 6 to take [spouse, a partner]. 7 to take [hire, lease, rent, subscribe to, etc.]. 8 to take [interpret; regard in specified manner]. 9 to take, occupy. 10 to steal. 11 to take, choose, buy. 12 to take, assume. 13 to take, borrow [a verse, an idea, etc.]. 14 to take [the government; the lead, a liking, a dislike, etc.]. 15 to gather [strength]. 16 to take [someone] with oneself. 17 CARDS to take [a trick]. 18 ~ *a mal*, to take it ill, take offence at. 19 ~ *calor*, to get warm. 20 ~ *en cuenta*, to take account of, to take into account. 21 ~ *frío*, to catch a cold. 22 *tomarla con*, to oppose, attack, have a grudge against. 23 *tomarle a uno la risa, el sueño*, to be overcome with laughter, with sleep. 24 ~ *lenguas*, to take tidings. 25 ~ *para sí*, to take to oneself. 26 ~ *por*, to take for: *lo tomé a usted por otro*, I took you for someone else. 27 ~ *sobre sí*, to take upon oneself. 28 ~ *razón de*, to register, make a record of.
29 intr. to go or turn in a specified direction: ~ *por la derecha*, to take or turn to the right.
30 ref. to take, to have: *tomarse libertades*, to take liberties, make free; *tomarse un descanso*, to take a rest. 31 *tomarse de moho, de orín*, to get rusty. 32 *tomarse del vino*, to get drunk.

**Tomás** *m. pr. n.* Thomas: *Santo* ~, Saint Thomas; *Santo* ~ *de Aquino*, Saint Thomas Aquinas.
**tomatazo** *m.* blow with a tomato.
**tomate** *m.* BOT. tomato [plant or fruit].
**tomatera** *f.* BOT. tomato, tomato plant.
**tomavistas** *adj.* picture-taking. *2 m.* motion-picture camera.
**tómbola** *f.* tombolo. *2* charity raffle.
**tomento** *m.* BOT. tomentum. *2* coarse tow.
**tomentoso, -sa** *adj.* BOT. tomentose, tomentous.
**tomillo** *m.* BOT. thyme.
**tomismo** *m.* Thomism.
**tomiza** *f.* esparto rope.
**tomo** *m.* volume, tome. *2* coll. *de* ~ *y lomo*, great, important.
**ton** *m. sin* ~ *ni son*, without motive or cause, without rhyme or reason.
**tonada** *f.* tune, song.
**tonadilla** *f.* light song.
**tonadillera** *f.* woman singer of light songs.
**tonalidad** *f.* MUS., PAINT. tonality.
**tonante** *adj.* Tonans: *Júpiter* ~, Jupiter Tonans.
**tonca** *adj.* BOT. tonka: *haba* ~, tonka bean.
**tonel** *m.* barrel, cask, tun.
**tonelada** *f.* ton: ~ *de arqueo*, register ton; ~ *métrica*, metric ton.
**tonelaje** *m.* tonnage.
**tonelería** *f.* barrelmaking, cooperage. *2* coopery [cooper's workshop]. *3* barrels, casks [collec.].
**tonelero** *m.* barrelmaker, cooper, hooper.
**tonelete** *m. dim.* small cask, keg. *2* short skirt.
**tonga, tongada** *f.* coat, couch, bed, layer.
**tongo** *m.* SPORT. coll. trick of a player, boxer, etc., who engages to lose for a bribe.
**tonicidad** *f.* tonicity.
**tónico, -ca** *adj.* tonic, invigorating. *2* MUS. key [note]. *3* GRAM. tonic [accent]; accented [vowel or syllable]. *4 m.* MED. tonic. *5 f.* MUS. tonic, keynote.
**tonificante** *adj.* tonic, invigorating.
**tonificar** *tr.* MED. to invigorate, tone up.
**tonillo** *m.* singsong, monotonous tone. *2* accent [of a region].
**tonina** *f.* ATÚN. *2* DELFÍN *2.*
**tono** *m.* tone [in writing or speaking]. *2* MUS., ACOUST. pitch. *3* MUS. mode, key. *4* MUS. tone, step. *5* diapason normal. *6* tone, shade [of colour]. *7* vigour, energy. *8* MED., PHYSIOL. tone. *9* tune, sing. *10* tune, harmony: *a* ~ *con*, in tune with, in harmony with. *11* fig. *bajar el* ~, *mudar de* ~, to change one's tune; *subir de* ~, fig. to become arrogant. *12 dar el* ~, fig. to set the standard. *13 darse* ~, to put on airs. *14 de buen* ~, fashionable, smart; *de mal* ~, vulgar. *15 a este* ~, like this.
**tonsila** *f.* ANAT. tonsil.
**tonsura** *f.* hair cutting; shearing. *2* ECCL. tonsure.
**tonsurar** *tr.* to cut the hair of; to shear, fleece. *2* ECCL. to tonsure.
**tontada** *f.* silliness, nonsense.
**tontaina** *m.-f.* silly person, fool.
**tontear** *intr.* to talk nonsense. *2* coll. to flirt.
**tontedad, tontera** *f.* TONTERÍA.
**tontería** *f.* silliness, foolishness. *2* nonsense. *3* triviality, trifle.
**tontillo** *m.* hoop skirt, farthingale.
**tontina** *f.* tontine.
**tontivano, -na** *adj.* foolishly conceited.
**tonto, -ta** *adj.* silly, foolish, dull, stupid. *2* nonsensical. *3 m.-f.* fool, dolt: ~ *de capirote*, blockhead;

*hacerse el* ~, to play the fool. *4 a tontas y a locas*, recklessly, haphazard.
**tontuelo, -la** *m.-f. dim.* little fool.
**tontuna** *f.* TONTERÍA.
**topacio** *m.* MINER. topaz.
**topada** *f.* TOPETADA.
**topar** *tr.* to strike, knock against, run into. *2* tr., intr., ref. ~ *con* or *toparse con*, to run across, meet, meet with, fall in with. *3* intr. to butt [with the head or horns]. *4* coll. *tope donde tope*, strike where it may.
**tope** *m.* butt, end: *al* ~, *a* ~, end to end. *2* RLY. buffer, bumper. *3* MACH. stop. *4* fig. rub, trouble, difficulty. *5* NAUT. masthead, topmasthead: *hasta el* ~, fig. up to the top, to the limit; *estar hasta los topes*, NAUT. to be overloades; fig. to be sated [with]. *6* NAUT. edge or butt end of a plank. *7* TOPETÓN. *8* fig. row, quarrel.
**topera** *f.* molehole, molehill.
**topetada** *f.* butt [by a horned animal]. *2* fig. butt, bump [with the head].
**topetar** *tr.-intr.* to butt [with head or horns]. *2 tr.* to strike, collide with, knock against.
**topetazo** *m.* TOPETADA.
**topetón** *m.* knock, bump, collision. *2* TOPETADA.
**tópico, -ca** *adj.* topical, local. *2 m.* MED. external local application. *3 pl.* commonplaces, platitudes.
**topinera** *f.* TOPERA.
**topo** *m.* ZOOL. mole. *2* coll. awkward person; dolt. *3* polka dot.
**topografía** *f.* topography. *2* surveying.
**topográfico, -ca** *adj.* topographical.
**topógrafo** *m.* topographer; surveyor.
**toponimia** *f.* toponymy.
**toque** *m.* touch [act of touching]. *2* touchstone. *3* fig. trial, proof. *4* blow, tap. *5* sounding [of a bugle, etc.], ringing [of bells], beat [of a drum] for announcing or signalling; call: ~ *de diana*, reveille; ~ *de queda*, curfew. *6* warning, admonition, advice. *7* PAINT. touch.
**toquilla** *f. dim.* small toque. *2* triangular kerchief. *3* knitted shawl.
**torácico, -ca** *adj.* ANAT., ZOOL. thoracic.
**torada** *f.* drove of bulls.
**toral** *adj.* main, strongest: *arco* ~, ARCH. each one of the arches supporting a cupola.
**tórax, pl. -rax** *m.* ANAT., ZOOL. thorax.
**torbellino** *m.* whirlwind. *2* coll. lively, hustling person.
**torca** *f.* GEOL. circular depression.
**torcaz** *adj.* wild [pigeon].
**torcecuello** *m.* ORN. wryneck.
**torcedor, -ra** *adj.* twisting. *2 m.-f.* twister [person]. *3 m.* fig. anything causing constant grief or worry.
**torcedura** *f.* twisting. *2* SURG. sprain. *3* small vine.
**torcer** *tr.* to twist, wrench, bend, crook. *2* to twist, twine [a thread, rope, etc.]. *3* to turn, aside. *4* to twist, distort, pervert. *5* to make [one] change his mind. *6* ~ *el gesto*, to make a wry face. *7* intr. to turn [to the right, to the left, etc.]. *8* ref. to become twisted, bent or crooked. *9* to go crooked or astray. *10* to yield [to persuasion, etc.]. *11* to turn bad, to fail. *12* [of milk] to curdle; [of wine] to turn sour. *13 torcerse el tobillo*, to sprain one's ankle. ¶ CONJUG. like *mover*.
**torcida** *f.* wick [of a lamp or candle].
**torcido, -da** *adj.* twisted, twined. *2* twisted, bent, crooked. *4* oblique. *5* fig. twisted, perverted. *6* fig. crooked, dishonest. *7 m.* twisted silk.

**torcijón** *m.* twist, wrench. 2 bellyache, gripes.

**torcimiento** *m.* twist, twisting. 2 perversion, warping. 3 circumlocution.

**tordillo, -lla** *adj.* dapple-gray. 2 *m.-f.* dapple-gray horse.

**tordo, -da** *adj.* dapple-gray [horse]. 2 *m.* ORN. thrush. 3 ORN. (Am.) starling. 4 dapple-gray horse.

**toreador** *m.* bullfighter.

**torear** *intr.-tr.* to fight bulls in the ring. 2 *tr.* fig. to fool, deceive, make fun of.

**toreo** *m.* bullfighting. 2 banter, covert mockery.

**torera** *f.* a short, tight, unbuttoned jacket. 3 *saltarse [una cosa] a la ~*, to disregard [a rule, engagement, duty, etc.].

**torería** *f.* bullfighters [collect.].

**torero, -ra** *adj.* [pertaining to] bullfighting. 2 *m.-f.* bullfighter.

**torete** *m. dim.* little bull. 2 coll. difficult matter.

**toril** *m.* BULLF. pen for bulls before the fight.

**torio** *m.* CHEM. thorium.

**torito** *m. dim.* little bull.

**tormenta** *f.* storm, tempest. 2 turmoil.

**tormento** *m.* torment, pain, anguish. 2 torture [for extorting confession, etc.]: *dar ~*, to torture.

**tormentoso, -sa** *adj.* stormy, tempestuous.

**tormo** *m.* TOLMO.

**torna** *f.* giving back, return. 2 *volver las tornas*, to give tit for tat; to turn the tables.

**tornaboda** *f.* day after a weeding.

**tornada** *f.* coming back, return. 2 POET. envoy.

**tornadizo, -za** *adj.* changeable, fickle. 2 renegade. 3 *m.-f.* turncoat, deserter, renegade.

**tornado** *m.* tornado.

**tornamiento** *m.* change, turn.

**tornapunta** *f.* brace, prop.

**tornar** *tr.* to return, give back. 2 to turn, make. 3 *intr.* to return, come back. 4 *~ a*, to [do, etc.] again. 5 *~ en sí*, to recover, come to. 6 *ref.* to turn, become.

**tornasol** *m.* BOT. sunflower. 2 iridescence, shot colour. 3 CHEM. litmus.

**tornasolado, -da** *adj.* iridescent, changeable, shot.

**tornasolar** *tr.* to make iridescent. 2 *ref.* to become iridescent.

**tornátil** *adj.* changeable, fickle.

**tornaviaje** *m.* return trip.

**tornavoz** *m.* any device to direct sound to an audience; sounding board. 2 echo.

**torneado, -da** *adj.* turned [in a lathe].

**torneador** *m.* turner [lathe operator]. 2 tourneyer.

**torneaduras** *f. pl.* lathe shavings, turnings.

**tornear** *tr.* to turn [in a lathe]. 2 to tourney. 4 to muse.

**torneo** *m.* tournament. 2 VET. gid, staggers.

**tornera** *f.* doorkeeper of a nunnery.

**tornería** *f.* turnery. 2 turner's shop or workshop.

**tornero** *m.* turner [lathe operator].

**tornillo** *m.* screw, male screw: *~ de orejas*, thumbscrew; *~ sin fin*, worm gear; *apretar los tornillos a uno*, coll. to put the screw upon one: *faltarle a uno un ~*, coll. to have a screw loose. 2 *~ de banco*, screw vice.

**torniquete** *m.* bell crank. 2 turnstile. 3 SURG. tourniquet.

**torniscón** *m.* slap with the back of the hand.

**torno** *m.* windlass, winch. 2 lathe. 3 revolving server [for passing dishes, etc., through a wall]. 3 revolving machine: *~ de alfarero*, potter's wheel; *~ de hilar*, spinning wheel. 4 turn [of a river]. 6 turn around. 7 *en ~ [de]*, around; *en ~ a* or *de*, regarding about.

**toro** *m.* bull [uncastrated male of bovine animal]: *~ de lidia*, bull reared for bullfighting. 2 fig. bull [strong, husky man]. 3 ASTR. Taurus. 4 ARCH. torus. 5 *pl.* bullfighting, bullfight: *ciertos son los toros*, coll. indeed, it is true.

**toronja** *f.* grapefruit.

**toronjil** *m.* **toronjina** *f.* BOT. lemon balm, garden balm.

**toronjo** *m.* BOT. grapefruit tree.

**torozón** *m.* displeasure, annoyance. 2 VET. gripes.

**torpe** *adj.* awkward, clumsy. 2 slow, heavy, torpid. 3 dull, dull-witted. 4 lewd, lascivious. 5 infamous. 6 crude, ugly.

**torpedeamiento** *m.* TORPEDEO.

**torpedear** *tr.* to torpedo.

**torpedeo** *m.* torpedoing.

**torpedero, -ra** *m.* torpedo boat.

**torpedo** *m.* NAV., AUTO. torpedo. 2 ICHTH. torpedo, electric ray.

**torpeza** *f.* awkwardness, clumsiness. 2 slowness, heaviness, torpidness. 3 dullness, stupidity. 4 lewdness, lasciviousness. 5 infamy, turpitude.

**tórpido, -da** *adj.* MED. torpid.

**torpor** *m.* MED. torpor.

**torrado** *m.* roasted chick-pea.

**torrar** *tr.* to toast.

**torre** *f.* tower [building or structure]: *~ albarrana*, FORT. watch tower; *~ del homenaje*, FORT. donjon. 2 belfry, bell tower. 3 turret, belvedere. 4 ARTIL., NAV. turret. 5 CHESS. castle, rook. 6 country house.

**torrefacción** *f.* torrefaction, toasting.

**torrefacto, -ta** *adj.* torrefied, toasted.

**torreja** *f.* (Am.) TORRIJA.

**torrejón** *m.* small tower, ill-shaped tower.

**torrencial** *adj.* torrential.

**torrente** *m.* torrent [rushing stream]. 2 fig. torrent [rust, downpour]; rush of people.

**torrentera** *f.* ravine made by a torrent.

**torreón** *m.* large fortified tower.

**torrero** *m.* lighthouseman, lightouse keeper.

**torrezno** *m.* rasher of bacon, fried rasher of bacon.

**tórrido, -da** *adj.* torrid: *zona tórrida*, torrid zone.

**torrija** *f.* slice of bread soaked in milk, wine, etc., then fried and sweetened with honey.

**torsión** *f.* torsion, twisting.

**torso** *m.* F. ARTS torso. 2 trunk of the body.

**torta** *f.* cake: *costar la ~ un pan*, coll. to cost dearly; *tortas y pan pintado*, a mere trifle; a child's play. 2 coll. blow, slap, box.

**tortada** *f.* a cake containing eggs, fruit, etc.

**tortazo** *m.* coll. blow, slap, box.

**tortera** *f.* baking pan. 2 whorl [of spindle].

**torticero, -ra** *adj.* wrong, unjust.

**tortícolis, torticolis** *f.* MED. torticollis, stiff neck.

**tortilla** *f.* omelet: *hacer ~ a*, to crush, smash. 2 (Mex.) pancake.

**tórtola** *f.* ORN. turtledove.

**tortolito, -ta** *adj.* green, inexperienced.

**tórtolo** *m.* ORN. male turtledove. 2 *m.-f.* fig. turtledove [demonstrative lover].

**tortor** *m.* NAUT. heaver.

**tortuga** *f.* ZOOL. tortoise, turtle. 2 TESTUDO.

**tortuosidad** *f.* tortuosity, tortuousness.

**tortuoso, -sa** *adj.* tortuous, sinuous, winding. 2 fig. tortuous [devious, circuitous, crooked].

**tortura** *f.* torture.

**torturador, -ra** *adj.* torturing, torturous.

**torturar** *tr.* to torture, torment. *2 ref.* to torture oneself, to worry.

**torva** *f.* whirl of rain or snow.

**torvisco** *m.* BOT. spurge flax.

**torvo, -va** *adj.* fierce, stern, severe, grim, frowning.

**torzal** *m.* silk twist. *2* cord, twist.

**tos** *f.* couch; coughing: ~ *ferina* or *convulsiva*, MED. whooping cough.

**tosca** *f.* tufa, calcareous tufa. *2* DENT. tartar.

**Toscana (la)** *f. pr. n.* GEOG. Tuscany.

**toscano, -na** *adj.-n.* Tuscan.

**tosco, -ca** *adj.* coarse, rough, crude. *2* rude, uncouth.

**tosecilla** *f. dim.* slight cough.

**toser** *intr.* to cough. *2 coll. toserle a,* to defy, compete with.

**tosidura** *f.* coughing.

**tósigo** *m.* poison. *2 fig.* grief, anguish.

**tosigoso, -sa** *adj.* coughing. *2* poisonous, poisoned.

**tosquedad** *f.* coarseness, roughness, uncouthness.

**tostada** *f.* toast, piece of toast. *2 coll. dar,* or *pegar, la ~ a uno,* to cheat, dupe, take in.

**tostado, -da** *adj.* toasted, roasted. *2* tan, brown [colour]. *3* tanned, sunburnt. *4 m.* toasting, roasting.

**tostador, -ra** *adj.* toasting, roasting. *2 m.-f.* toaster, roaster [person]. *3 m.* toaster, roaster [utensil].

**tostadura** *f.* toasting, roasting.

**tostar** *tr.* to toast, torrefy. *2* to roast [coffee beans]. *3* to brown, sunburn, tan. ¶ CONJUG. like *contar.*

**tostón** *m.* roasted chick-pea. *2* toast dipped in new olive oil. *3* scorched piece of food. *4* roast pig. *5 coll.* wearisome speech, play, etc.

**total** *adj.* total. *2 m.* total, sum total. *3 adv.* brief, in short.

**totalidad** *f.* totality, aggregate, whole.

**totalitario, -ria** *adj.* POL. totalitarian.

**totalitarismo** *m.* POL. totalitarianism.

**totalizar** *tr.* to totalize.

**tótem** *m.* totem.

**totemismo** *m.* totemism.

**toxemia** *f.* MED. toxemia.

**toxicidad** *f.* toxicity.

**tóxico, -ca** *adj.-m.* toxic.

**toxicología** *f.* toxicology.

**toxina** *f.* MED. toxin.

**tozal** *m.* top of a hill.

**tozo, -za** *adj.* short, dwarfish, stumpy.

**tozudo, -da** *adj.* stubborn, obstinate, pigheaded.

**tozudez** *f.* stubbornness, obstinacy, pigheadedness.

**tozuelo** *m.* thick, fleshy neck [of an animal].

**traba** *f.* bond, clasp, locking device. *3* hobble, shackle, trammel. *4 fig.* clog, hindrance, restraint.

**trabacuenta** *f.* mistake in accounts. *2* dispute, argument.

**trabadura** *f.* binding, locking, uniting, union. *2* thickening, inspissation.

**trabajado, -da** *adj.* worked, wrought. *3* overworked, worn out. *4* full of hardships. *5* elaborate [literary work].

**trabajador, -ra** *adj.* industrious, laborious, hardworking. *2* working. *3 m.-f.* worker: workingman, workingwoman, labourer, hand.

**trabajante** *adj.* working.

**trabajar** *intr.* to work, labour. *2* to strive, endeavour. *3* [of soil, a machine, etc.] to work. *4* NAUT. [of a ship] to labour. *5 tr.* to work [fashion, shape]. *6* to till [the ground]. *7* to labour, ela-

borate. *8* to harass, worry, trouble. *9* to wear out [by toil or hardship].

**trabajo** *m.* work, labour, toil: ~ *a destajo,* piecework; ~ *a jornal,* timework; *trabajos forzados,* hard labour. *2* work [thing done]; piece of work. *3* labour [as distinguished from capital]. *4* task, job. *5* employment; *sin ~,* unemployed [worker]. *6* exertion, effort, trouble: *costar ~,* to be hard, difficult; *tomarse el ~ de,* to take the trouble to. *7* PHYS. work. *8 pl.* hardships, privations, difficulties.

**trabajosamente** *adv.* laboriously, painfully.

**trabajoso, -sa** *adj.* hard, arduous, laborious. *2* laboured [not easy]. *3* full of hardships.

**trabalenguas** *pl.* -**guas** *m.* tongue twister, jawbreaker.

**trabar** *tr.* to bind, clasp, join, lock. *2* to thicken, inspissate. *3* to catch, seize. *4* to hobble, trammel. *5* to set [a saw]. *6* to join [battle]; to strike up [a friendship]; to begin [a conversation, etc.]. *7 ref.* to become entangled. *8 trabarse de palabras,* to have words. *9 trabársele a uno la lengua,* to become tongue-tied.

**trabazón** *f.* union [of parts, etc.]. *2* connexion, relation [between things]. *3* thickness, consistence. *4* CARP. bond.

**trabe** *f.* ARCH. beam.

**trabilla** *f.* gaiter or trouser strap.

**trabucar** *tr.* to upset, overturn, invert the order of. *2* to confuse, disturb [the mind]. *3* to mix up, jumble. *4* to mix up [words, syllables or letters]. *5 ref.* to become confused or mixed up.

**trabucazo** *m.* shot with a blunderbuss. *2 coll.* anything causing a sudden fright or distress.

**trabuco** *m.* blunderbuss.

**trabuquete** *m.* catapult. *2* a small seine.

**traca** *f.* string of firecrackers.

**tracamundana** *f. coll.* noise, uproar, confusion.

**tracción** *f.* traction: ~ *de sangre,* horse traction.

**tracería** *f.* ARCH. tracery.

**Tracia (la)** *f. pr. n.* GEOG. Thrace.

**tracio, -cia** *adj.-n.* Thracian.

**tracista** *m.* designer. *2 fig.* schemer, trickster.

**tracoma** *m.* MED. trachoma.

**tracto** *m.* stretch, space, tract. *2* lapse, interval [of time]. *3* ECCL. tract, tractus [in the mass].

**tractor** *m.* tractor: ~ *de oruga,* caterpillar.

**tradición** *f.* tradition. *2* LAW tradition.

**tradicional** *adj.* traditional.

**tradicionalismo** *m.* traditionalism.

**traducción** *f.* translation.

**traducible** *f.* translatable.

**traducir** *tr.* to translate. *2* to express, interpret. *3 ref.* to be translated. *4* to result [in]. ¶ CONJUG. like *conducir.*

**traductor, -ra** *m.-f.* translator.

**traedizo, -za** *adj.* portable.

**traer** *tr.* to bring. *2* to draw, attract. *3* to bring over. *4* to bring about, cause, occasion, result in. *5* to make, keep: *esto le trae inquieto,* this makes him anxious. *6* to wear, have on [a garment]. *7* to adduce. *8 lo trae el periódico,* it is in the newspaper. *9* ~ *a cuento,* to mention. *10* ~ *a mal ~,* to treat roughly. *11* ~ *en bocas,* or *en lenguas,* to gossip about one. *12 intr. coll. traer y llevar,* to gossip. *13 tr.-ref.* to be engaged in, be up to: ~ or *traerse entre manos,* to have in hand. *14 ref. traérselas,* to be more important, difficult, cunning, etc., than it seems.

¶ CONJUG.: INDIC. Pres.: *traigo,* traes, trae; traemos, traéis, traen. | Pret.: *traje, trajiste, trajo; tra-*

*jimos, trajisteis, trajeron.* | Fut.: traeré, traerás, etc. | Cond.: traería, traerías, etc. | Subj. Pres.: *traiga, traigas, traigan.* | Imperf.: *trajera, trajeras, trajera; trajéramos, trajerais, trajeran,* or *trajese, trajeses, trajeseis, trajesen.* | Fut.: *trajere, trajeres, trajere; trajéremos, trajereis, trajeren.* | Imper.: trae, *traiga; traigamos, traed, traigan.* | Past. P.: traído. | Ger.: *trayendo.*

**trafagar** *intr.* to traffic, trade. *2* to travel, roam. *3* to bustle, hustle.

**tráfago** *m.* traffic, trade. *2* bustle, hustle.

**trafagón, -na** *adj.* bustling, hustling. *2 m.-f.* bustler, hustler.

**trafalmejas** *m.-f.* coll. rattlebrain.

**traficante** *adj.* trafficking, trading. *2 m.-f.* trafficker, trader.

**traficar** *intr.* to traffic, deal, trade. *2* to travel, roam.

**tráfico** *m.* traffic, trade. *2* traffic of vehicles.

**tragacanto** *m.* tragacanth [tree and gum].

**tragaderas** *f. pl.* gullet: *tener buenas tragaderas,* coll. to be gullible; to be excessively tolerant.

**tragadero** *m.* gullet. *2* fig. hole, gulf, etc., that swallows up anything.

**tragador, -ra** *m.-f.* swallower. *2* glutton, gobbler.

**trágala** *m.* an ancient song against absolutism. *2* forcing one to support something opposed to his opinions, feelings, etc.

**tragaldabas,** *pl.* **-bas** *m.-f.* glutton.

**tragaleguas,** *pl.* **-guas** *m.-f.* great walker.

**tragaluz** *m.* skylight [window in the roof, ceiling, etc.].

**tragantada** *f.* large draugth [of liquor]; big swig.

**tragantón, -na** *adj.* gluttonous. *2 m.-f.* glutton, gobbler. *3 f.* coll. big meal, big spread.

**tragaperras,** *pl.* **-rras** *f.* slot machine.

**tragar** *tr.-ref.* to swallow [food, drink; a lie; an affront; one's words]; to gulp down: ~ *el anzuelo,* fig. to swallow the bait. *3* fig. *no poder* ~ *a,* to dislike, not to be able to bear. *4* to gobble, devour. *5* to swallow, engulf.

**tragasantos** *m.-f.* coll. overdevout person.

**tragedia** *f.* tragedy.

**trágico, -ca** *adj.* tragic, tragical. *2 m.* tragedian. *3 f.* tragedienne.

**tragicomedia** *f.* tragi-comedy.

**trago** *m.* draught [of liquor], drink; swallow, gulp: *echar un* ~, coll. to take a drink. *2* coll. misfortune, mishap. *3* ANAT. tragus.

**tragón, -na** *adj.* gluttonous. *2 m.-f.* glutton.

**tragonería, -tragonía** *f.* gluttony.

**traición** *f.* treason; treachery: *a* ~, treacherously.

**traicionar** *tr.* to betray, to do treason to.

**traicionero, -ra** *adj.* treacherous, treasonable, traitorous. *2 m.-f.* traitor, traitress.

**traída** *f.* carrying, bringing, conduction: ~ *de aguas,* conduction of water to a town.

**traído, -da** *adj.* used, worn out [garment]. *2 traído y llevado,* beaten about, knocked about.

**traidor, -ra** *adj.* treacherous, treasonable, traitorous. *2 m.* traitor. *3* villain [of a play]. *4 f.* traitress.

**traigo, -traiga,** etc. *irr.* V. TRAER.

**trailla** *f.* leash [for dogs]. *2* hounds leashed together. *3* AGR. levelling harrow. *4* TRALLA.

**traína** *f.* deep-sea fishing net. *2* net for sardine fishing.

**trainera** *f.* sardine-fishing boat.

**traíña** *f.* TRAÍNA.

**traje** *m.* costume, dress, suit [of clothes], garb, gown: ~ *de baño,* bathing suit; ~ *de calle,* street clothes; ~ *de ceremonia* or *de etiqueta,* full dress, dress suit, evening dress; ~ *de luces,* bullfighter's costume; ~ *de malla,* tights; ~ *de paisano,* civilian clothes; ~ *largo,* lady's evening dress; ~ *sastre,* lady's tailor-made suit; ~ *talar,* robe, gown, soutane; *cortar un* ~ *a,* coll. to gossip about.

**traje, -trajera,** etc. *irr.* V. TRAER.

**trajear** *tr.* to clothe, costume, dress.

**trajín** *m.* carrying from place to place. *2* going and coming, bustle, hustle.

**trajinante** *m.* carrier, carter.

**trajinar** *tr.* to carry or cart from place to place. *2* to go back and forth, to bustle, hustle.

**trajiste,** etc., *irr.* V. TRAER.

**tralla** *f.* whipcord, whiplash; whip.

**trallazo** *m.* lash [with a whip]. *2* crack [of a whip].

**trama** *f.* WEAV. weft, woof. *2* texture, estructure. *3* plot [of novel or play]. *4* plot, scheme.

**tramar** *tr.* WEAV. to insert the weft in. *2* to contrive. *3* to plot, hatch, scheme. *4 intr.* [of trees, esp. olive trees] to blossom.

**tramilla** *f.* (Am.) twine.

**tramitación** *f.* transaction, negociation, carrying steps, procedure.

**tramitar** *tr.* to transact, negotiate, conduct [an affair].

**trámite** *m.* step [in the transaction of an affair].

**tramo** *m.* stretch, section [of a canal, road, etc.]. *2* flight [of stairs]. *3* span [of a bridge].

**tramontana** *f.* north wind. *2* fig. vanity.

**tramontano, -na** *adj.* tramontane.

**tramontar** *intr.* to pass over the mountain. *2* [of the sun] to sink behind the mountains.

**tramoya** *f.* THEAT. stage machinery. *2* fig. scheme, trick, fake.

**tramoyista** *m.* THEAT. stage machinist; scene shifter; stage hand. *2* fig. trickster, humbug.

**trampa** *f.* trap [for catching animals]. *2* fig. trap, snare, pitfall. *3* trapdoor. *4* hinged section of a counter. *5* bad debt. *6* fraud, trick, cheat [in games]: *hacer trampas,* to cheat. *7 llevárselo la* ~, [of an affair] to fall through.

**trampal** *m.* bog, quagmire.

**trampantojo** *m.* coll. trick, deception.

**trampear** *intr.* to shift, use expedients. *2* to manage, to get along. *3 tr.* to trick, deceive.

**trampilla** *f.* small trapdoor used as a peephole. *2* door of a coalbin. *3* fly [of trousers].

**trampista** *m.-f.* liar, cheat; bad pay.

**trampolín** *m.* springboard. *2* ski jump.

**tramposo, -sa** *adj.* lying, cheating, tricky. *2 m.-f.* liar, trickster, cheat. *3* bad pay.

**tranca** *f.* thick stick, club. *2* crossbar [for a door]. *3* coll. *a trancas y barrancas,* without regard to difficulties.

**trancada** *f.* long stride.

**trancahilo** *m.* stop knot [in threads or ropes].

**trancazo** *m.* blow with a stick or club. *2* MED. influenza, grippe.

**trance** *m.* critical moment: *a todo* ~, at any cost, at any risk; *en* ~ *de muerte,* at the point of death. *2* ~ *de armas,* combat, battle.

**tranco** *m.* long stride: *a trancos,* coll. hurriedly. *2* threshold.

**tranchete** *m.* cobbler's heel knife.

**tranquera** *f.* palisade [fence]. *2* (Am.) gate [in a fence].

**tranquil** *m.* ARCH. plumb line.

**tranquilidad** *f.* tranquillity, quiet, peace. *2* composure, ease of mind, reassurance.

**tranquilizador, -ra** *adj.* tranquillizing. 2 soothing, reassuring.
**tranquilizar** *tr.* to tranquillize, calm, quiet down. 2 to compose, soothe, reassure.
**tranquilo, -la** *adj.* tranquil, quiet, calm, peaceful. 2 easy in mind, unconcerned, reassured.
**tranquilo** *m.* knack.
**transacción** *f.* transaction [piece of commercial business]. 2 compromise, accommodation.
**transalpino, -na** *adj.* transalpine.
**transatlántico, -ca** *adj.* transatlantic. 2 *m.* transatlantic ship, transatlantic liner.
**transbordador, -ra** *adj.* transfer, transshipping. 2 *m.* ferry, transfer boat or car.
**transbordar** *tr.* to transfer, transship. 2 *intr.-ref.* to transfer, change trains.
**transbordo** *m.* transfer, transshipment.
**transcendencia** *f.* TRASCENDENCIA.
**transcendental** *adj.* TRASCENDENTAL. 2 PHILOS. transcendental.
**transcendente** *adj.* TRASCENDENTE.
**transcender** *intr.* TRASCENDER.
**transcontinental** *adj.* transcontinental.
**transcribir** *tr.* to transcribe. ¶ CONJUG. past. p.: *transcrito* or *transcripto*.
**transcripción** *f.* transcription.
**transcurrir** *intr.* to pass, elapse.
**transcurso** *m.* lapse, course [of time].
**transepto** *m.* ARCH. transept.
**transeúnte** *adj.-n.* transient. 3 *m.-f.* passer-by.
**transferencia** *f.* transference. 2 LAW transfer.
**transferible** *adj.* transferable.
**transferir** *tr.* to transfer. 2 to postpone. ¶ CONJUG. like *hervir*.
**transfiguración** *f.* transfiguration.
**transfigurar** *tr.* to transfigure. 2 *ref.* to be transfigured.
**transfijo, -ja** *adj.* transfixed [pierced].
**transfixión** *f.* transfixion.
**transflorar** *tr.* to copy or trace against the light. 2 TRANSFLOREAR. 3 *intr.* to show through.
**transflorear** *tr.* to adorn [metal] with painting.
**transformable** *adj.* transformable; convertible.
**transformación** *f.* transformation.
**transformador, -ra** *adj.* transforming. 2 *m.-f.* transformer [person]. 3 *m.* ELECT. transformer.
**transformar** *tr.* to transform. 2 *ref.* to transform, be transformed.
**transformismo** *m.* transformism.
**transformista** *adj.* transformistic. 2 *m.-f.* transformist. 3 THEAT. quick-change artist.
**tránsfuga** *m.-f.* fugitive. 2 deserter, turncoat.
**transfundir** *tr.* to transfuse. 2 *ref.* to be transfused.
**transfusión** *f.* transfusion.
**transgredir** *tr.* to transgrees, break, violate. ¶ Only used in forms having *i* in their terminations.
**transgresión** *f.* transgression, violation.
**transgresor, -ra** *m.-f.* transgressor.
**transición** *f.* transition.
**transido, -da** *adj.* overwhelmed, exhausted [with grief, hunger, etc.]. 2 mean, stingy.
**transigencia** *f.* compromising. 2 tolerance.
**transigente** *adj.* compromising, accommodating. 2 broad-minded, tolerant.
**transigir** *intr.* to compromise, make concessions. 2 ~ *con,* to accept, tolerate.
**Transilvania** *f. pr. n.* Transylvania.
**transistor** *m.* ELECT. transistor.
**transitable** *adj.* passable, practicable [road, etc.].
**transitar** *intr.* to pas, go, walk, along streets, roads, etc.

**transitivo, -va** *adj.-n.* GRAM. transitive.
**tránsito** *m.* transit, passage: *de ~,* in transit. 2 traffic [along streets, roads, etc.]. 3 death [of saint]. 4 stop [in journey]. 5 ASTR. transit.
**transitorio, -ria** *adj.* transitory.
**translación, -translaticio, cia,** etc. = TRASLACIÓN, TRASLATICIO, etc.
**translimitación** *f.* going beyond any limit [moral or material].
**translimitar** *tr.* to go beyond [any moral or material limit].
**translucidez** *f.* translucence, translucency.
**translúcido, -da** *adj.* translucent.
**transmigración** *f.* transmigration.
**transmigrar** *intr.* to transmigrate.
**transmisible** *adj.* transmissible.
**transmisión** *f.* transmission. 2 LAW transfer, conveyance. 3 ~ *del pensamiento,* thought transference.
**transmisor, -ra** *adj.* transmitting. 2 *m.-f.* transmitter. 3 *m.* TELEG., TELEPH., RADIO. transmitter.
**transmitir** *tr.* to transmit. 2 RADIO. to broadcast.
**transmudar** *tr.* TRANSMUTAR.
**transmutación** *f.* transmutation.
**transmutar** *tr.* to transmute, change.
**transoceánico, -ca** *adj.* transoceanic.
**transpacífico, -ca** *adj.* transpacific.
**transpadano, -na** *adj.* transpadane.
**transparencia** *f.* transparence.
**transparentarse** *ref.* to be transparent. 2 to show through.
**transparente** *adj.* transparent. 2 translucent. 3 *m.* window shade, roller blind. 4 stained glass window at the back of an altar.
**transpiración** *f.* transpiration. 2 perspiration.
**transpirar** *intr.* to transpire. 2 to perspire.
**transpirenaico, -ca** *adj.* trans-Pyrenean.
**transponer** *tr.* to transpose. 2 to disappear behind. 3 to turn [a corner]. 4 [of the sun, etc.], to set below [the horizon]. 5 *ref.* to doze off. ¶ CONJUG. like *poner.*
**transportable** *adj.* transportable.
**transportador, -ra** *adj.* transporting. 2 *m.-f.* carrier, transporter. 3 *m.* protractor [instrument].
**transportamiento** *m.* TRANSPORTE 1 & 5.
**transportar** *tr.* to transport, carry, convey. 2 to transpose. 3 to transfer [a drawing or pattern]. 4 *ref.* fig. to be enraptured.
**transporte** *m.* transportation, transport, carriage, conveyance. 2 NAUT. transport [ship]. 3 transfer [of a drawing or pattern]. 4 MUS. transposition. 5 transport, ecstasy, rapture.
**transposición** *f.* transposition.
**transpuesto, -ta** *p. p.* DE TRANSPONER.
**transubstanciación** *f.* transubstantiation.
**transvasar** *tr.* to decant, transvase.
**transverberación** *f.* transfixion.
**transversal** *adj.* transversal. 2 cross [street]. 3 collateral [kinsman, kinship].
**transverso, -sa** *adj.* transverse.
**tranvía** *m.* tram, tramway, tramcar, *streetcar.
**tranviario** *m.* tramwayman.
**trapa** *f.* tramp, tramping [of feet]. 2 noise, uproar. 3 NAUT. spilling line. 4 (cap.) ECCL. *la Trapa,* la Trappe.
**trapacear** *intr.* to cheat, practice trickery.
**trapacería** *f.* TRAPAZA.
**trapacero, -ra; trapacista** *adj.* tricky, crafty. 2 *m.-f.* trickster, cheat.
**trapajo** *m.* rag, scrap of cloth.
**trápala** *f.* coll. trick, deceit. 2 noise, uproar. 3 clat-

ter [of a running horse]. *4 m.* garrulity. *5 m.-f.* prattler, chatterbox. *6* liar, cheat.

**trapalear** *intr.* to chatter, jabber. *2* to lie, cheat, deceive. *3* to walk noisily.

**trapalón, -na** *m.-f.* liar, cheat, humbug.

**trapatiesta** *f.* coll. brawl, row, shindy.

**trapaza** *f.* trick, fraud, deceit.

**trapecio** *m.* GEOM. trapeze, trapezium, trapezoid. *2* GYMN. trapeze. *3* ANAT. trapezium. *4* ANAT. trapezius.

**trapense** *adj.-n.* Trappist.

**trapería** *f.* rags. *2* rag shop.

**trapero, -ra** *m.-f.* ragpicker. *2* rag dealer.

**trapezoidal** *adj.* trapezial.

**trapezoide** *m.* GEOM. trapezium, trapezoid.

**trapiche** *m.* sugar mill. *2* olive press. *3* ore crusher.

**trapichear** *intr.* coll. to scheme, contrive. *2* to deal at retail.

**trapicheo** *m.* coll. scheming, contriving.

**trapillo** *m.* coll. *de ~*, in house clothes.

**trapío** *m.* coll. easy and graceful carriage of certain women. *2* BULLF. mettle [of a bull].

**trapisonda** *f.* coll. row, shindy. *2* coll. trick, scheme, intrigue.

**trapisondear** *intr.* coll. to lie, scheme, intrigue.

**trapisondista** *m.-f.* coll. liar, schemer, trickster, schemer.

**trapo** *m.* rag [piece of cloth]; cleaning rag; *poner a uno como un ~*, coll. to rake over the coals. *2* NAUT. canvas, sails: *a todo ~*, full sail. *3* BULLF. cape, red flag. *4* coll. *soltar el ~*, to burst out crying or laughing. *5 pl.* coll. clothes: *trapos de cristianar*, Sunday best.

**traque** *m.* crack [report of a rocket].

**tráquea** *f.* ANAT., ZOOL., BOT. trachea.

**traqueal** *adj.* tracheal. *2* ZOOL. tracheate.

**traquear** *intr.* TRAQUETEAR.

**traquearteria** *f.* ANAT. trachea.

**traqueotomía** *f.* SURG. tracheotomy.

**traquetear** *intr.* to crack, make a loud noise. *2 tr.* to shake, jolt, jerk.

**traqueteo** *m.* crack, cracking [noise]. *2* shaking, jolting, jerking.

**traquido** *m.* crack, snap [noise].

**tras** *prep.* after, behind. *2* after [in pursuit of]. *3* besides, in addition to. *4 ~ de*, after, behind; in addition to.

**trasalpino, -na** *adj.* TRANSALPINO.

**trasaltar** *m.* space behind the altar.

**trasandino, -na** *adj.* TRANSANDINO.

**trasatlántico, -ca** *adj.-n.* TRANSATLÁNTICO.

**trasbordar** *tr.* TRANSBORDAR.

**trasbordo** *m.* TRANSBORDO.

**trasca** *f.* leather thong.

**trascantón** *m.* corner spur stone.

**trascendencia** *f.* penetration, perspicacity. *2* result, consequence. *3* importance. *4* PHILOS. transcendence.

**trascendental** *adj.* far-reaching. *2* highly important, momentous.

**trascendente** *adj.* trascendent.

**trascender** *intr.* to be fragant. *2* to leak out [come to be known]. *3* to have effects or consequences. *4* PHILOS. to trascend. *5 tr.* to penetrate, find out. ¶ CONJUG. like *entender*.

**trasciende, -trascienda**, etc. *irr.* V. TRASCENDER.

**trascocina** *f.* back kitchen.

**trascolar** *tr.* to strain, percolate. *2* fig. to pass over [a mountain, etc.]. *3 ref.* to ooze through.

**trascordarse** *ref.* to forget. ¶ CONJUG. like *contar*.

**trascoro** *m.* back choir.

**trascorral** *m.* fenced space back of a barnyard.

**trascribir, -trascripción**, etc. = TRANSCRIBIR, TRANSCRIPCIÓN.

**trascuarto** *m.* back room. *2* rear apartment.

**trascuenta** *f.* TRABACUENTA.

**trascurrir** *intr.* TRANSCURRIR.

**trascurso** *m.* TRANSCURSO.

**trasdós** *m.* ARCH. extrados.

**trasegar** *tr.* to upset, disarrange. *2* to move, transfer. *3* to transvase, decant. *4* coll. to drink [liquor]. ¶ CONJUG. like *acertar*.

**trasera** *f.* back, rear [of a house, carriage, etc.].

**trasero, -ra** *adj.* back, hind, rear: *puerta trasera*, back door. *2 m.* coll. behind, buttocks.

**trasferencia, trasfiguración, trasfixión, trasformación, trásfuga, trasfundir**, etc. = TRANSFERENCIA, TRANSFIGURACIÓN, TRANSFIXIÓN, TRANSFORMACIÓN, TRÁNSFUGA, TRANSFUNDIR, etc.

**trasgo** *m.* goblin, hobgoblin, sprite. *2* coll. imp [mischievous child].

**trasgredir** = TRANSGREDIR.

**trasgresión** = TRANSGRESIÓN.

**trasgresor, -ra** = TRANSGRESOR, RA.

**trashoguero, -ra** *adj.* lazy, stay-at-home. *2 m.* fireback. *3* big log [in a fireplace].

**trashojar** *tr.* to leaf through [a book, etc.].

**trashumante** *adj.* moving from winter to summer pasture or vice-versa.

**trashumar** *intr.* [of flocks or herds] to move from winter to summer pasture or vice-versa.

**trasiego** *m.* upset, disorder. *2* transvasing, decanting.

**trasiego, trasiegue**, etc. *in.* V. TRASEGAR.

**trasijado, -da** *adj.* thin-flanked. *2* lank, lean.

**traslación, trasladación** *f.* moving, transfer, translation. *2* translation [into another language]. *3* RHET. metaphor, tralatition.

**trasladable** *adj.* movable.

**trasladar** *tr.* to move, remove, transfer. *2* MECH. to translate. *3* to postpone, adjourn [to another day]. *4* to translate [into another language]. *5* to copy [a writing]. *6 ref.* to move [from place to place; change residence].

**traslado** *m.* moving, removal, transfer. *2* move [change of residence]. *3* copy, transcript. *4* resemblance, likeness. *5* LAW notification.

**traslapar** *tr.* to overlap.

**traslapo** *m.* overlapped part or piece.

**traslaticio, -cia** *adj.* tralatitious, figurative.

**traslúcido, -da; trasluciente** *adj.* TRANSLÚCIDO.

**traslucirse** *ref.* to be translucent. *2* fig. to be inferred. *3* fig. to transpire [come to be known]. ¶ CONJUG. like *lucir*.

**traslumbrar** *tr.* [of light] to dazzle. *2 ref.* to be dazzled [by light]. *3* to pass or vanish swiftly.

**trasluz** *m.* light seen through a translucent body: *al ~*, against the light. *2* glint, gleam.

**trasmallo** *m.* trammel net.

**trasmano** *m.* second player [at cards]. *2 a ~*, out of reach; out of the way, remote.

**trasmigración, trasmigrar, trasmisión, trasmitir, trasmudar, trasmutación, trasmutar**, etc. = TRANSMIGRACIÓN, etc.

**trasnochado, -da** *adj.* stale, spoiled [from standing overnight]. *2* fig. haggard, wan. *3* fig. stale, trite, hackneyed.

**trasnochador, -ra** *m.-f.* night hawk, one who keeps late hours.

**trasnochar** *intr.* to keep late hours. *2* to spend the night.

**trasoir** *tr.* to hear wrong, mis-hear.

**trasojado, -da** *adj.* haggard, wan, with sunken eyes.

**trasoñar** *tr.* to imagine wrongly, to dream.

**trasovado, -da** *adj.* BOT. obovate.

**traspadano, -na** *adj.-n.* TRANSPADANO.

**traspapelarse** *ref.* [of a paper] to be mislaid among other papers.

**trasparencia, trasparentarse, trasparente** = TRANSPARENCIA, TRANSPARENTARSE, TRANSPARENTE.

**traspasamiento** *m.* TRASPASO.

**traspasar** *tr.* to pass, transfer, move [from a place to another]. *2* to pass, cross, go over, go beyond, go through. *3* to exceed [bounds]. *4* to pierce, transfix. *5* to transgress. *6* LAW to transfer [esp. a lease or tenancy].

**traspaso** *m.* passing, transfer, moving [from a place to another]. *2* crossing, going over. *3* piercing, transfixion. *4* transgression. *5* LAW transfer. *6* money paid for the transfer of a lease. *7* grief, anguish.

**traspié** *m.* slip, stumble, trip: *dar traspiés*, to slip, stumble, trip; fig. to slip, err.

**traspintar** *tr.* to let see [one card] and play another. *2 ref.* [of writing, painting, etc.] to show through the paper, cloth, etc. *3* coll. so turn out differently.

**traspirable, traspiración, traspirar, traspirenaico** = TRANSPIRABLE, TRANSPIRACIÓN, TRANSPIRAR, TRANSPIRENAICO.

**trasplantar** *tr.* to transplant. *2 ref.* to migrate.

**trasplante** *m.* transplant, transplantation.

**trasponer, trasportador, trasportamiento, trasportar, trasporte, trasposición,** etc. = TRANSPONER, TRANSPORTADOR, TRANSPORTAMIENTO, TRANSPORTAR, TRANSPORTE, TRANSPOSICIÓN, etc.

**traspuesta** *f.* transposition. *2* rise, elevation [of ground]. *3* back [of a house]. *4* flight, hiding [of a person].

**traspunte** *m.* THEAT. prompter in the wings.

**traspuntín** *m.* under-mattress. *2* folding seat [in a car].

**trasquila** *f.* TRASQUILADURA.

**trasquilador** *m.* shearer [of animals].

**trasquiladura** *f.* shearing [of animals]. *2* clumsy cutting of the hair. *3* clipping, curtailing.

**trasquilar** *tr.* to shear [animals]. *2* to cut the hair of [a person] clumsily. *3* fig. to clip, curtail.

**trasquilimocho, -cha** *adj.* close shorn or cropped.

**trasquilón** *m.* coll. TRASQUILADURA: *a trasquilones*, irregularly; clumsily.

**trastabillar** *intr.* TRASTRABILLAR.

**trastada** *f.* bad turn, mean trick, dirty trick.

**trastazo** *m.* coll. blow, bump, knock, whack.

**traste** *m.* MUS. fret [of guitar, etc.]. *2 dar al ~ con,* to spoil, ruin, destroy.

**trastear** *tr.* to fret [a guitar]. *2* to play [a guitar]. *3* BULLF. to play [the bull] with the MULETA. *4* coll. to manage with tact. *5 intr.* to move things around.

**trastejar** *tr.* to retile. *2* to repair, overhaul.

**trasteo** *m.* BULLF. playing the bull with the MULETA. *2* tactful management.

**trastera** *f.* lumber room.

**trastero, -ra** *adj.* lumber [room].

**trastienda** *f.* back room [behind a shop]. *2* coll. tact, address, cunning.

**trasto** *m.* piece of furniture; utensil. *2* disused article of furniture, etc.: *trastos viejos*, lumber. *3* coll. worthless person, tricky person. *4 pl.* tools of trade, implements, utensils. *5 tirarse los trastos a la cabeza*, coll. to quarrel.

**trastocarse** *ref.* to become crazy, to go off one's head. ¶ CONJUG. like *contar*.

**trastornado, -da** *adj.* upset, disarranged. *3* disturbed [in mind].

**trastornadura** *f.*, **trastornamiento** *m.* TRASTORNO.

**trastornar** *tr.* to upset, turn upside down. *2* to upset, disarrange, disturb. *3* to disturb [in mind]; derange the mind of; to muddle [with drink]. *4* to win over, persuade.

**trastorno** *m.* upset, derangement, disturbance. *2* riot, disorder. *3* MED. disorder, trouble.

**trastrabarse** *ref. trastrabársele a uno la lengua,* coll. to stammer, to become tongue-tied.

**trastrabillar** *intr.* to trip, stumble. *2* to reel, sway, stagger. *3* to stammer, stutter.

**trastrocamiento** *m.* change, transmutation.

**trastrocar** *tr.* to change, transmute. ¶ CONJUG. like *contar.*

**trastrueco** *m.* TRASTROCAMIENTO.

**trasudar** *tr.* to sweat lightly.

**trasudor** *m.* slight perspiration.

**trasunto** *m.* copy, transcript. *2* likeness, faithful image.

**trasvasar** *tr.* TRANSVASAR.

**trasvenarse** *ref.* [of blood] to extravasate. *2* fig. to spill [be spilled].

**trasver** *tr.* to see through. *2* to see wrong. ¶ CONJUG. like *ver.*

**trasverberación, trasversal, trasverso** = TRANSVERBERACIÓN, etc.

**trasverter** *intr.* [of liquid in a vessel] to overflow, run over.

**trasvolar** *tr.* to fly over or across.

**trata** *f.* trade, slave trade: *~ de negros*, slave trade. *2 ~ de blancas*, white slavery.

**tratable** *adj.* courteous, sociable, reasonable, tractable.

**tratadista** *m.-f.* author, writer [on special subjects].

**tratado** *m.* treaty [between nations]. *2* treatise.

**tratamiento** *m.* treatment, usage. *2* MED., CHEM., IND. treatment. *4* title, form of address.

**tratante** *m.-f.* trader, dealer.

**tratar** *tr.* to treat, use [act towards, behave]. *2* to handle, manage. *3* to treat, deal with [a subject]. *4* MED., CHEM., IND. to treat. *5* to have acquaintance or friendship with. *6 ~ a uno de,* to address as, to give one the title of; to call, charge with being: *~ de tú*, to thou, address as *tú; ~ a uno de embustero*, to call someone a liar. *7 intr. ~ de, sobre* or *acerca de,* to treat of, deal with [a subject]. *8 ~ de* [foll. by an inf.], to try to, to endeavour to. *9 ~ con,* to have intercourse with; COM. to deal, to business with. *10* COM. *~ en,* to trade with, deal in. *11 ref.* to live [well or poorly]. *12* to be in speaking or friendly terms. *13 ¿de qué se trata?,* what is the matter?, what is it about?

**trato** *m.* treatment, usage, dealing: *~ doble*, double dealing; *mal ~,* ill usage. *2* agreement, deal, bargain: *~ hecho*, it is a deal. *3* negotiation. *4* title, form of address. *5* trade, commerce. *6* intercourse social intercourse, friendly relations; *~ de gentes,* savoir-vivre; *tener buen ~,* to be nice, affable.

**trauma** *m.* MED. trauma.

**traumatismo** *m.* traumatism.

**través** *m.* inclination, bias: *mirar de ~,* to squint. *2* fig. misfortune, reverse. *3* ARCH. cross-beam. *4* FORT. traverse. *5* NAUT. *por el ~,* on the beam; *dar al ~,* to be stranded; *dar al ~ con,* fig. to squander, misspend; to ruin, destroy. *6 al* ~, *de* ~, *across, athwart. 7 al* ~ *de, a* ~ *de,* through, across.

**travesaño** *m.* crosspiece, crossbar, traverse; transom [of a cross or window]; rung [of a chair, etc.]. *2* bolster [of a bed].

**travesar** *tr.-ref.* ATRAVESAR.

**travesear** *intr.* to prank, frolic. *2* fig. to talk sparklingly. *3* fig. to lead a debauched life.

**travesero, -ra** *adj.* cross, transverse. *2 m.* bolster [of a bed].

**travesía** *f.* crossroad, cross street. *2* distance [over land or sea]. *3* passage, sea voyage, crossing [the sea]. *4* crosswise or transverse position. *5* FORT. traverse works.

**travesura** *f.* prank, frolic, antic, escapade, mischief. *2* roguishness, archness. *3* sparkling wit.

**traviesa** *f.* distance [over land or sea]. *2* side bet. *3* RLY. tie, crosstie, sleeper. *4* ARCH. transverse wall. *5* MIN. cross gallery.

**travieso, -sa** *adj.* cross, transverse. *2* keen, sagacious. *3* naughty, mischievous [child]. *4* frolicsome, prankish, roguish.

**trayecto** *m.* distance, stretch, section [in a way]; course [distance travelled].

**trayectoria** *f.* trajectory.

**traza** *f.* plan, design, project. *2* scheme, contrivance; way, means: *darse trazas,* to manage. *3* appearance, look, looks: *tener trazas de,* [of a thing] to show signs of. *4* GEOM. trace.

**trazado** *m.* drawing, planning, tracing. *2* layout, location [of a railway line, a road, etc.].

**trazar** *tr.* to draw, trace [lines, etc.]. *2* to design, plan, devise, lay out. *3* to trace, sketch, describe. *4* RLY. to locate.

**trazo** *m.* delineation, outline. *2* line, stroke [of a pen or pencil]. *3* PAINT. fold in drapery.

**trébedes** *f.* trivet.

**trebejo** *m.* toy, plaything. *2* chess piece. *3 pl.* tools, implements, utensils.

**trébol,** *pl.* **-les** *m.* BOT. clover, trefoil: ~ *oloroso,* sweet clover. *2* club [playing card].

**trece** *adj.-m.* thirteen: *mantenerse uno en sus* ~, to persist in one's opinion. *2 adj.* thirteenth. *3 m.* thirteenth [of the month].

**trecientos, -tas** *adj.-s.* TRESCIENTOS.

**trecho** *m.* stretch, space, distance: *a trechos,* by intervals; *de* ~ *en* ~, from place to place, from time to time.

**tredécimo, -ma** *adj.* thirteenth.

**trefilería** *f.* wiredrawing.

**tregua** *f.* truce. *2* respite, rest, letup, intermission: *dar treguas,* to ease up; not to be urgent; *sin* ~, without letup, without intermission.

**treinta** *adj.-m.* thirty. *2 adj.-n.* thirtieth. *3 m.* thirtieth [of the month].

**treintaidosavo, -va** *adj.-m.* thirty-second [part].

**treintavo, -va** *adj.-n.* thirtieth.

**treintena** *f.* thirtieth [part]. *2* group of thirty units.

**treinteno, -na** *adj.* TRIGÉSIMO.

**tremebundo, -da** *adj.* dreadful, frightful, fearful.

**tremedal** *m.* quagmire, quacking bog.

**tremendo, -da** *adj.* tremendous, fearful, terrible. *2* awful, imposing. *3* coll. tremendous [very great].

**tremente** *adj.* trembling.

**trementina** *f.* turpentine.

**tremer** *intr.* to tremble.

**tremielga** *f.* ICHTH. torpedo, electric ray.

**tremó, tremol** *m.* pier glass.

**tremolar** *tr.* to wave [a flag]. *2* fig. to display.

**tremolina** *f.* noisy blowing of the air. *2* coll. row, shindy, uproar.

**trémolo** *m.* MUS. tremolo.

**tremor** *m.* tremor, trembling.

**trémulo, -la** *adj.* tremulous, quivering, flickering.

**tren** *m.* RLY. train: ~ *correo,* mail train; ~ *de mercancías,* goods train; ~ *expreso,* express train. *2* MIL., PHYS. train: ~ *de ondas,* wave train. *3* train, set, gear, outfit: ~ *de aterrizaje,* AER. landing gear. *4* show, ostentation. *5* SPORT. speed, fury.

**trenado, -da** *adj.* reticulated. *2* latticed. *3* braided.

**trenca** *f.* crosstree [in a beehive]. *2* main root.

**trencilla** *f.* braid [for trimming].

**treno** *m.* dirge, threnody.

**Trento** *f. pr. n.* GEOG. Trent.

**trenza** *f.* braid, plait. *2* tress [braided hair].

**trenzadera** *f.* knot of braided cord or ribbon.

**trenzado** *m.* braid, plait. *2* braiding, plaiting. *3* entrechat [in dancing]. *4* prancing [of a horse].

**trenzar** *tr.* to braid, plait, tress. *2 intr.* to perform entrechats [in dancing]. *3* [of a horse] to prance.

**trepa** *f.* climbing. *2* tumble. *3* perforation. *4* grain [of polished wood]. *5* coll. trick, deceit, fraud. *6* coll. beating, drubbing.

**trepado, -da** *adj.* RETREPADO. *2* strong, robust [animal]. *3 m.* SEW. wavy trimming. *4 f.* ORN. climber.

**trepajuncos,** *pl.* **-cos** *m.* ORN. marsh warbler.

**trepanación** *f.* SURG. trepanation.

**trepanar** *tr.* SURG. to trepan.

**trépano** *m.* trepan.

**trepar** *intr.-tr.* to climb, clamber. *2* BOT. to climb, creep. *3 tr.* to bore, perforate. *4* SEW. to put a waving trimming on. *5 ref.* RETREPARSE.

**trepatroncos** *m.* ORN. blue titmouse.

**trepe** *m.* coll. scolding, reprimand.

**trepidación** *f.* trembling, vibration. *2* ASTR. trepidation.

**trepidante** *adj.* trembling, vibrating. *2* mad [rhythm].

**trepidar** *intr.* to tremble, vibrate.

**tres** *adj.-m.* three: *las* ~, three o'clock. *2 adj.* third. *3 m.* third [of the month].

**tresbolillo (a or al)** *adv.* arranged in quincunxes.

**trescientos, -tas** *adj.-m.* three hundred. *2 adj.* three-hundredth.

**tresdoblar** *tr.* to treble. *2* to fold three times.

**tresdoble** *adj.-m.* triple.

**tresillista** *m.-f.* ombre player.

**tresillo** *m.* ombre [card game]. *2* MUS. triplet. *3* set of a sofa and two armchairs.

**tresnal** *m.* AGR. shock, stack [of sheaves].

**treta** *f.* trick, wile. *2* FENC. feint.

**trezavo, -va** *adj.-n.* thirteenth.

**tría** *f.* selecting, sorting.

**triaca** *f.* theriac.

**tríada, triade** *adj.* triad.

**triangulación** *f.* triangulation.

**1) triangular** *adj.* triangular.

**2) triangular** *tr.* to triangulate.

**triángulo, -la** *adj.* triangular. *2 m.* GEOM., TRIGON., MUS. triangle.

**triar** *tr.* to select, sort.

**triásico, -ca** *adj.* GEOL. Triassic. *2 m.* GEOL. Triassic, Trias.

**tribal** *adj.* tribal.

**tribásico, -ca** *adj.* CHEM. tribasic.

**tribu** *f.* tribe.

**tribulación** *f.* tribulation, affliction.

**tríbulo** *m.* BOT. caltrop.

**tribuna** *f.* tribune, rostrum, platform. *2* gallery [in a church or legislative chamber]: ~ *de la prensa*, press box. *3* grandstand.

**tribunado** *m.* tribunate. *2* tribuneship.

**tribunal** *m.* tribunal, court [of justice]: ~ *supremo*, Supreme Court. *2* EDUC. examining board.

**tribunicio, -cia** *adj.* tribunitial.

**tribuno** *m.* tribune [roman officer; political orator].

**tributación** *f.* paying taxes. *2* tax, duty. *3* system of taxes.

**tributar** *tr.* to pay taxes or tribute; to pay as tax or tribute. *2* to pay, render [homage, respect].

**tributario, -ria** *adj.-n.* tributary. *2* [pertaining to] tax or duty: *sistema* ~, system of taxes.

**tributo** *m.* tribute, tax, duty, imposition. *2* fig. pecuniary burden.

**tricentésimo, -ma** *adj.* three-hundredth.

**triceps** *m.* ANAT. triceps.

**triciclo** *m.* tricycle.

**tricípite** *adj.* tricipital, three-headed.

**triclinio** *m.* HIST. triclinium.

**tricolor** *adj.* tricolour.

**tricornio** *adj.* three-cornered. *2 m.* three-cornered hat.

**tricotomía** *f.* trichotomy.

**tricotosa** *f.* knitting machine.

**tricromía** *f.* three-coloured printing.

**tricúspide** *adj.* ANAT. tricuspid.

**tridente** *adj.* trident, tridentate. *2 m.* trident.

**triduo** *m.* ECCL. triduum.

**triedro** *adj.* GEOM. trihedral. *2 m.* GEOM. trihedron.

**trienal** *adj.* triennial.

**trienio** *m.* triennium.

**trifásico, -ca** *adj.* ELECT. three-phase.

**trifido, -da** *adj.* BOT. trifid.

**trifoliado, -da** *adj.* BOT. trifoliate.

**trifulca** *f.* coll. squabble, row.

**trigal** *adj.* wheat field.

**trigaza** *adj.* of wheat [straw].

**trigémino, -na** *adj.-m.* ANAT. trigeminal.

**trigésimo, -ma** *adj.* thirtieth.

**trigla** *f.* ICHTH. mullet.

**triglifo** *m.* ARCH. triglyph.

**trigo** *m.* BOT. wheat. *2* coll. dough, money. *3* BOT. ~ *sarraceno*, buckwheat. *4 pl.* wheat fields.

**trigón** *m.* MUS. trigon.

**trígono** *m.* ASTROL., GEOM. trigon.

**trigonometría** *f.* trigonometry.

**trigueño, -ña** *adj.* of a light brown complexion.

**triguero, -ra** *adj.* [pertaining to] wheat. *2 m.-f.* wheat dealer or grower.

**trilingüe** *adj.* trilingual.

**trilítero, -ra** *adj.* triliteral.

**trilito** *m.* ARCHEOL. trilithon.

**trilobulado, -da** *adj.* trilobate.

**trilocular** *adj.* trilocular.

**trilogía** *f.* trilogy.

**trilla** *f.* ICHTH. red mullet. *2* AGR. thrashing. *3* AGR. thrashing time. *4* TRILLO 1.

**trillado, -da** *adj.* beaten [path]. *2* trite, commonplace.

**trillador, -ra** *adj.* AGR. thrashing. *2 m.-f.* AGR. thrasher. *3 f.* AGR. thrashing machine.

**trillar** *tr.* AGR. to thrash, thresh. *2* to beat, frequent [a path, etc.]. *3* to beat, crush, maltreat.

**trillo** *m.* AGR. a kind of harrow for thrashing.

**trillón** *m.* trillion [British trillion].

**trimestral** *m.* trimestral, trimestrial, quarterly.

**trimestralmente** *adv.* quarterly.

**trimestre** *m.* trimester, quarter. *2* quarterly payment.

**trinado** *m.* MUS. trill, quaver, warble.

**trinar** *intr.* MUS. to trill, quaver, warble. *2* coll. to be very angry, or impatient.

**trinca** *f.* triad. *2* coll. gang. *3* NAUT. lashing.

**trincar** *tr.* to tie, fasten, lash. *2* to hold fast [someone] with one's arms or hands. *3* to drink [liquor].

**trincha** *f.* cloth strap for tightening garments.

**trinchante** *adj.* carving [food]. *2 m.* carver [at table]. *3* carving fork. *4* TRINCHERO.

**trinchar** *tr.* to carve [food].

**trinchera** *f.* trench, ditch. *2* MIL. trench, entrenchment. *3* trench coat.

**trinchero** *m.* side table, carving table.

**trineo** *m.* sledge, sleigh, sled.

**Trinidad** *f. pr. n.* THEOL. Trinity.

**trinitaria** *f.* BOT. pansy, heartsease.

**trinitario, -ria** *adj.-n.* ECCL. Trinitarian.

**trino, -na** *adj.* trine, trinitarian. *2* ternary. *3* ASTROL. trine. *4 m.* MUS. trill, shake.

**trinomio** *m.* ALG. trinomial.

**trinquete** *m.* NAUT. foremast; foresail; foreyard. *2* MACH. pawl, ratchet. *3* hall for playing *pelota*.

**trinquis,** *pl.* **-quis** *m.* coll. drink [of liquor].

**trío** *m.* MUS. trio. *2* trio [set of three persons]. *3* TRÍA.

**triodo** *m.* RADIO. triode.

**tripa** *f.* gut, bowel, intestine: *hacer de tripas corazón*, coll. to pluck up courage; *tener malas tripas*, coll. to be cruel. *2* coll. paunch, belly. *3* filling, filler [of a cigar]. *4 pl.* fig. insides.

**tripada** *f.* coll. bellyful.

**tripartito, -ta** *adj.* tripartite.

**tripería** *f.* tripery, tripe shop.

**tripero, -ra** *m.-f.* gut seller. *2 m.* bellyband.

**tripicallero, -ra** *m.-f.* seller of tripe.

**tripicallos** *m.* tripe [as food].

**tripinnado, -da** *adj.* BOT. tripinnate.

**triple** *adj.-m.* triple, treble.

**triplicado, -da** *adj.* threefold, triplicate. *2 m.* triplicate: *por* ~, in triplicate.

**triplicar** *tr.* to treble, triple, triplicate.

**tríplice** *adj.* triple.

**triplo, -pla** *adj.-m.* triple, treble.

**trípode** *m.* or *f.* tripod.

**tripolitano, -na** *adj.-n.* Tripolitan.

**tripón, -na** *adj.-n.* TRIPUDO.

**tríptico** *m.* triptych.

**triptongo** *m.* FONET. triphthong.

**tripudio** *m.* dance.

**tripudo, -da** *adj.* big-bellied, pot-bellied.

**tripulación** *f.* crew [of a ship, plane or airship].

**tripulante** *m.* crew member. *2 pl.* crew.

**tripular** *tr.* to man [a ship, plane, etc.]. *2* to be a member of the crew of [a ship, plane, etc.].

**trique** *m.* crack [noise]: *a cada* ~, coll. at every turn.

**triquina** *f.* ZOOL. trichine.

**triquinosis** *f.* MED. trichinosis.

**triquiñuela** *f.* coll. chicanery, wile, subterfuge.

**triquitraque** *m.* cracking, clacking, clatter. *2* firecracker.

**trirreme** *m.* NAUT. trireme.

**tris** *m.* clink [of breaking glass]. *2* coll. trice, ace: *en un* ~, almost, within an ace.

**trisa** *f.* SÁBALO.

**Trisagio** *m.* ECCL. Trisagion.

**trisca** *f.* crushing sound made with the feet. *2* noise, noisy fun, uproar.

**triscar** *intr.* to make a noise with the feet. *2* to frisk about, frolic, gambol. *3 tr.* to set [a saw].

**trisecar** *tr.* GEOM. to trisect.

**trisección** f. trisection.
**trisílabo, -ba** adj. trisyllabic. 2 m. trisyllable.
**triste** adj. sad. 2 gloomy, dismal. 3 deplorable. 4 painful. 5 paltry, sorry.
**tristeza** f. sadness. 2 gloom. 3 grief, sorrow.
**tristón, -na** adj. saddish, melancholy.
**tritón** m. MYTH. Triton. 2 ZOOL. triton, eft, newt.
**tritono** m. MUS. tritone.
**trituración** f. trituration, crushing.
**triturar** tr. to triturate. 2 fig. to tear to pieces [an argument, etc.].
**triunfador, -ra** m.-f. triumpher, victor.
**triunfal** adj. triumphal.
**triunfante** a. triumphant, victorious.
**triunfar** intr. to triumph, be successful, be the victor: ~ de, to triumph over, conquer. 2 coll. to make a great show. 3 to trump [at cards].
**triunfo** m. triumph. 2 victory, success. 3 trump [at cards].
**triunvirato** m. triumvirate.
**triunviro** m. triumvir.
**trivial** adj. trivial, commonplace, trite.
**trivialidad** f. triviality. 2 triteness.
**trivio** m. trivium. 2 junction of three roads.
**triza** f. bit, shred, fragment: hacer trizas, to smash to pieces, to tear to bits.
**trocamiento** m. TRUEQUE.
**trocánter** m. ANAT. trochanter.
**1) trocar** m. SURG. trocar.
**2) trocar** tr. to exchange, barter. 2 to change, convert: ~ en, to change into. 3 to take or say [a thing] for another. 4 ref. to change [undergo a change]. 6 to exchange seats. ¶ CONJUG. like contar.
**trocear** tr. to divide into pieces.
**trocoide** f. GEOM. trochoid.
**trocha** f. cross path, narrow path.
**trochemoche (a)** adv. in a disordered way, recklessly.
**trofeo** m. trophy. 2 fig. victory, triumph.
**troglodita** adj. troglodytic. 2 fig. gluttonous. 3 m.-f. troglodyte. 4 fig. glutton.
**troj, troje** m. granary, barn.
**trola** f. coll. lie, fib, deception.
**trole** m. ELECT. trolley pole.
**trolebús** m. trolley bus.
**trolero, -ra** adj. coll. lying. 2 m.-f. liar.
**tromba** f. METEOR. waterspout. 2 fig. avalanche, rush.
**trombón** m. MUS. trombone [instrument and player].
**trombosis** f. MED. thrombosis.
**trompa** f. MUS. horn [brass instrument]: ~ de caza, hunting horn. 2 poet. trump, trumpet. 3 humming top. 4 trunk [of an elephant]. 5 proboscis [of insect, of tapir]. 6 METEOR. waterspout. 7 ARCH. projecting vault. 8 ANAT. tube: ~ de Eustaquio, Eustachian tube. 9 m. horn player.
**trompada** f. blow with a top. 2 blow with the trunk [of an elephant]. 3 hard blow or knock.
**trompeta** f. MUS. trumpet. 2 MUS. bugle. 3 BOT. ~ de amor, sunflower. 4 m. trumpeter, bugler.
**trompetada** f. coll. silly remark.
**trompetazo** m. trumpet blast; bugle blast. 2 TROMPETADA.
**trompetear** intr. coll. to sound the trumpet.
**trompetería** f. trumpetry. 2 MUS. trumpets [of an organ].
**trompetero** m. trumpet maker. 2 trumpeter.
**trompetilla** f. dim. small trumpet. 2 trompetilla or

~ acústica, ear trumpet. 2 de ~, buzzing [mosquito].
**trompicar** tr. to make [one] stumble or knock repeatedly. 2 coll. to promote [a person] over another. 3 intr. to stumble or trip repeatedly.
**trompicón** m., **trompilladura** f. stumble.
**trompillar** tr.-intr. TROMPICAR.
**trompis** m. coll. punch, blow with the fist.
**trompo** m. top, whipping top, spinning top [toy]. 2 ZOOL. top shell. 3 coll. dolt.
**trompón** m. BOT. narcissus.
**tronada** f. thunderstorm.
**tronado, -da** adj. used, worn out. 2 decayed, ruined, impoverished.
**tronante** adj. thundering.
**tronar** impers.-intr. to thunder: ~ contra, to thunder at. 2 intr. coll. to become ruined [financially]. 3 coll. ~ con, to quarrel or break with. 4 coll. por lo que pueda ~, just in case. ¶ CONJUG. like contar.
**troncar** tr. TRUNCAR.
**tronco** m. trunk [of the body, of a tree, of an artery, etc.]. 2 stock, origin [of a family]. 3 truncated object. 4 GEOM. frustum. 5 log, billet: estar como un ~, be unconscious; to be fast asleep. 6 team [of two horses].
**troncón** m. trunk [of the body]. 2 stump.
**tronchar** tr. to break [a stem, a branch, a stick, etc.].
**troncho** m. stem of a cabbage, cauliflower, etc.
**tronera** f. FORT., NAUT. embrasure, port, porthole. 2 loophole, narrow window. 3 pocket [of a billiard table]. 4 m.-f. coll. harum-scarum.
**tronido** m. loud report. 2 show, ostentation.
**trono** m. throne. 2 pl. thrones [order of angels].
**tronquista** m. driver of a team of horses.
**tronzar** tr. to divide into pieces. 2 fig. to wear out, exhaust. 3 SEW. to pleat [a garment].
**tropa** f. troop, crowd. 2 coll. people of no account. 3 troops, soldiers. 6 MIL. assembly [call]. 7 pl. forces, army.
**tropel** m. throng, rush, hurry, bustle, confusion: en ~, in a throng, in confusion. 2 crowd [of things].
**tropelía** f. injustice, outrage. 2 hurry, confusion.
**tropezadero** m. stumbling place.
**tropezadura** f. stumbling.
**tropezar** intr. to trip, stumble; to knock, strike: ~ con, contra o en, to stumble over, to knock against. 2 fig. to trip, slip, err. 3 ~ con, to come upon, find, meet [with]; to quarrel with. 4 ref. [of horses] to interfere. ¶ CONJUG. like acertar.
**tropezón** m. TROPIEZO: dar un ~, to trip, stumble; a tropezones, coll. by fits and starts; falteringly.
**tropical** adj. tropical, tropic [of the tropics].
**trópico, -ca** adj. tropical, figurative. 2 tropical [year]. 3 m. ASTR., GEOG. tropic.
**tropiezo** m. trip, stumble. 2 fig. trip, slip, fault. 3 hitch, difficulty, mishap: sin ~, without difficulty, without a mishap. 4 stumbling block. 5 quarrel, dissension.
**tropiezo, tropiece**, etc. irr. V. TROPEZAR.
**tropismo** m. BIOL. tropism.
**tropo** m. RHET. trope.
**troposfera** f. METEOR. troposphere.
**troquel** m. die [for stamping coins and medals].
**troquelar** tr. to coin, to stamp in a die.
**troqueo** m. PROS. trochee.
**trotador, -ra** adj. trotting. 2 m. trotter [horse].
**trotamundos**, pl. **dos** m.-f. globe-trotter.

**trotar** *intr.* [of a horse or rider] to trot. *2* coll. to trot, hustle, hurry.

**trote** *m.* trot [of a horse]: ~ *cochinero*, jog trot; *tomar el* ~, coll. to dash off, to depart in haste; *a* ~, *al* ~, at a trot; coll. hurriedly. *2* fig. bustle, hurried and fatiguing work.

**trotón, -na** *adj.* trotting [horse]. *2 m.* horse.

**trotona** *f.* coll. chaperon, companion.

**trova** *f.* LIT. metrical composition, verse, song.

**trovador, -ra** *m.* troubadour. *2* poet. *3 f.* poetess.

**trovadoresco, -ca** *adj.* [pertaining to] troubadour.

**trovar** *tr.* to versify, write poetry.

**trovero** *m.* trouvère.

**Troya** *f. pr. n.* HIST., GEOG. Troy: *allí, ahí* or *aquí fue* ~, coll. and then the row started; *arda* ~, let happen what will.

**troyano, -na** *adj.-n.* Trojan.

**trozo** *m.* piece, chunk, part, fragment. *2* passage, selection.

**truco** *m.* trick, artifice, stratagem. *2 pl.* trucks [game].

**truculencia** *f.* truculence, truculency.

**truculento, -ta** *adj.* truculent.

**trucha** *f.* ICHTH. trout: ~ *salmonada*, salmon trout.

**truchimán, -na** *m.-f.* TRUJIMÁN. *2* coll. shrewd person.

**trueco** *m.* TRUEQUE: *a* ~ *de*, provided; *a* or *en* ~, in exchange.

**trueco, trueque,** etc. *irr.* V. TROCAR.

**trueno** *m.* thunder, thunderclap. *2* fig. loud report, detonation. *3* coll. harum-scarum, wild youth.

**trueno, truene,** etc. *in.* V. TRONAR.

**trueque** *m.* exchange, barter: *a* ~, *en* ~, in exchange.

**trufa** *f.* BOT. truffle. *2* lie, story, falsehood.

**trufar** *tr.* COOK. to stuff with truffles. *2 intr.* to lie, tell lies.

**truhán** *adj.* knavish, tricky. *2 m.-f.* knave, rascal, trickster. *3* buffoon, jester.

**truhanada** *f.* TRUHANERÍA.

**truhanería** *f.* rascality. *2* rascals [collect.]. *3* buffoonery.

**truhanesco, -ca** *adj.* knavish, rascally. *2* buffoon.

**trujal** *m.* wine press. *2* oil press. *3* oil mill.

**trujamán, -na** *m.-f.* dragoman [interpreter]. *2 m.* expert adviser [esp. in buying or selling].

**trujamanear** *intr.* to act as an interpreter. *2* to act as a broker or adviser; to barter.

**trujimán, -na** *m.-f.* TRUJAMÁN.

**trulla** *f.* noise, frolic. *2* troop, crowd. *3* trowel.

**trullo** *m.* ORN. teal.

**truncado, -da** *adj.* truncate, truncated.

**truncar** *tr.* to truncate. *2* fig. to cut, cut off, leave unfinished [a speech, writing, etc.].

**trunco, -ca** *adj.* truncated, mutilated, incomplete.

**trupial** *m.* ORN. troupial.

**truque** *m.* a card game.

**trusas** *f. pl.* trunk hose.

**trust** *m.* COM. trust.

**tsetsé, tsé-tsé** *adj.* ENT. tsetse [fly].

**tú** *pers. pron.* thou; you: *de* ~ *a* ~, intimately.

**tu,** *pl.* **tus** *poss. adj.* thy; your.

**tuba** *f.* MUS. tuba.

**tubérculo** *m.* BOT. tuber. *2* MED., ZOOL. tubercle.

**tuberculosis** *f.* MED. tuberculosis.

**tuberculoso, -sa** *adj.* tuberculous, tubercular. *2* MED. tuberculous. *3 m.-f.* MED. consumptive [person].

**tubería** *f.* tubing, piping; pipe line or system.

**tuberosa** *f.* tuberose.

**tuberosidad** *f.* tuberosity.

**tuberoso, -sa** *adj.* tuberose, tuberous.

**tubo** *m.* tube [long hollow cylinder], pipe: ~ *acústico*, speaking tube; ~ *de ensayo*, test tube. *2* ELECT. tube. *3* chimney [of a lamp]. *4* ANAT. canal: ~ *digestivo*, alimentary canal.

**tubular** *adj.* tubular: *caldera* ~, tubular boiler.

**tucan** *m.* ORN. toucan. *2* (cap.) ASTR. Toucan.

**tudel** *m.* MUS. crook [of a bassoon].

**tudesco, -ca** *adj.-n.* German.

**tueca** *f.*, **tueco** *m.* stump [of tree].

**tuerca** *f.* nut, female screw.

**tuerce** *m.* twist, twisting.

**tuero** *m.* big log [in a fireplace]. *2* firewood.

**tuerto, -ta** *adj.* one-eyed, blind in one eye. *2* twisted, bend. *3 m.* wrong, injury, injustice. *4 a* ~, injustly. *5 a tuertas o a derechas*, rightly or wrongly.

**tueste** *m.* TOSTADURA.

**tuesto, tueste,** etc. *irr.* V. TOSTAR.

**tuétano** *m.* marrow [of bone]; pith [of plants]: *hasta los tuétanos*, to the marrow; head over heels.

**tufarada** *f.* strong smell or odour.

**tufo** *m.* fume, reek, vapour; offensive smell. *2* coll. haughtiness, conceit. *3* GEOL. tufa. *4 pl.* locks of hair over the temples.

**tugurio** *m.* shepherds' hut. *2* fig. hole, small room.

**tul** *m.* tulle.

**tulipa** *f.* BOT. small tulip. *2* tulip-shaped lampshade.

**tulipán** *m.* BOT. tulip.

**tulipero, -ca** *adj.* BOT. tulip tree.

**tullido, -da** *adj.* disabled, crippled, paralytic.

**tullimiento** *m.* disableness, crippleness.

**tullir** *tr.* to disable, cripple, make [one] a paralytic. *2 ref.* to become disabled, crippled or paralytic.

**tumba** *f.* tomb, grave. *2* arched top of a coach. *3* TUMBO 1. *4* VOLTERETA.

**tumbacuartillos,** *pl.* **-llos** *m.-f.* coll. sot, toper.

**tumbado, -da** *adj.* vaulted, arched.

**tumbaga** *f.* tombac. *2* finger ring.

**tumbar** *tr.* to fell, throw down, knock down. *2* of wine, a powerful odour, etc.] to stun, overpower. *3 ref.* to lie down. *4* to ease up, give up working.

**tumbilla** *f.* frame for holding a bed warmer.

**tumbo** *m.* tumble, jolt, violent roll or sway. *2* rise and fall [of a wave]. *3* undulation [in the ground]. *4* thunder, loud noise.

**tumbón, -na** *adj.* coll. sly. *2* coll. lazy. *3 m.-f.* coll. sly person. *4* coll. lazy person.

**tumefacción** *f.* tumefaction.

**tumefacto, -ta** *adj.* tumefied.

**túmido, -da** *adj.* tumid, swollen.

**tumor** *m.* MED. tumour.

**tumoroso, -sa** *adj.* having tumours.

**tumulario, -ria** *adj.* tumular, tumulary.

**túmulo** *m.* tumulus. *2* raised sepulchre. *3* catafalque.

**tumulto** *m.* tumult. *2* riot.

**tumultuario, -ria** *adj.* tumultuary.

**tumultuoso, -sa** *adj.* tumultuous.

**tuna** *f.* BOT. prickly pear, Indian fig [plant and fruit]. *2* idle and vagrant life: *correr la* ~, to loaf, *to bum. *3* ESTUDIANTINA.

**tunanta** *adj.-f.* rascally, artful [woman].

**tunantada** *f.* mean trick.

**tunante** *adj.* loafing. *2* rascally, artful [man]. *3 m.* loafer, vagrant. *4* rascal, rogue, scamp.

**tunda** *f.* shearing of cloth. *2* coll. beating, drubbing.
**tundente** *adj.* beating, whipping. *2* CONTUNDENTE 1.
**tundición** *f.* shearing of cloth.
**tundidor, -ra** *m.-f.* cloth shearer. *2 f.* cloth shearing machine.
**tundir** *tr.* to shear [cloth]. *2* coll. to beat, drub.
**tundizno** *m.* shearings from cloth.
**tundra** *f.* tundra.
**tunear** *intr.* to loaf.
**tunecí; tunecino, -na** *adj.-n.* Tunisian.
**túnel** *m.* tunnel.
**Túnez** *pr. n.* GEOG. Tunis [city]; Tunisia [state].
**tungsteno** *m.* CHEM. tungsten.
**túnica** *f.* tunic [ancient garment], robe, gown, long loose garment. *2* ANAT., ZOOL., BOT. tunic.
**tunicado, -da** *adj.* ANAT., ZOOL., BOT. tunicate.
**tunicela** *f.* ECCL. tunicle.
**tuno, -na** *adj.-n.* TUNANTE.
**tuntún (al buen)** *adv.* thoughtlessly, carelessly; without knowing what it is about.
**tupé** *m.* toupet, tuft, pompadour. *2* coll. cheek, nerve, brass.
**tupido, -da** *adj.* close, compact [in texture], dense, thick. *3* coll. dense, dull obtuse.
**tupinambo** *m.* AGUATURMA.
**tupir** *tr.* to make dense or thick, to make close or compact [in texture]. *2 ref.* to become dense, thick, close. *3* coll. to stuff oneself.
**turba** *f.* crowd, mob. *2* peat, turf.
**turbación** *f* disturbance. *2* confusion, embarrassment.
**turbador, -ra** *adj.* disturbing. *2* troubling. *3* embarrassing. *4 m.-f.* disturber, perturber.
**turbamulta** *f.* rabble, mob, disorderly crowd.
**turbante** *m.* turban.
**turbar** *tr.* to disturb, upset. *2* to trouble, make turbid. *3* to confuse, embarrass. *4 ref.* to become disturbed. *5* to get confused or embarrassed.
**turbera** *f.* peat bog.
**túrbido, -da** *adj.* TURBIO.
**turbiedad, turbieza** *f.* turbidity.
**turbina** *f.* turbine.
**turbio, -bia** *adj.* turbid, muddy, cloudy. *2* troubled, turbulent. *3* indistinct, confused, obscure.
**turbión** *m.* squall, heavy shower. *2* fig. rush [of things].
**turbomotor** *m.* turbomotor.
**turbonada** *f.* storm, thunderstorm.
**turborreactor** *m.* turbojet.
**turbulencia** *f.* turbidness. *2* turbulence, turbulency.
**turbulento, -ta** *adj.* turbid. *2* turbulent.
**turca** *f.* coll. drunk, fit of drunkenness: *coger una ~,* to get drunk.
**turco, -ca** *adj.* Turkish. *2 m.-f.* Turk.

**turcople** *adj.-n.* Turko-Greek.
**túrdiga** *f.* strip of hide, leather thong.
**turgencia** *f.* turgidness, turgescence.
**turgente** *adj.* protuberant, prominent. *2* turgid, turgescent, swollen.
**túrgido, -da** *adj.* poet, protuberant, prominent.
**turibulario** *m.* ECCL. censer [one who censes].
**turíbulo** *m.* ECCL. thurible, censer.
**turiferario** *m.* ECCL. thurifer, censer bearer.
**turífero, -ra** *adj.* thuriferous, incense-bearing.
**turificar** *tr.* to thurify, cense.
**Turingia** *f. pr. n.* GEOG. Thuringia.
**turión** *m.* BOT. turion.
**turismo** *m.* tourism, touring. *2* touring car.
**turista** *m.-f.* tourist.
**turístico, -ca** *adj.* touristic, touristical.
**turma** *f.* lamb fry. *2* BOT. *~ de tierra,* truffle.
**turmalina** *f.* MINER. tourmaline.
**turnar** *intr.* to alternate, take turns, go or work by turns.
**turnio, -nia** *adj.* squinting [eye]. *2* squint-eyed.
**turno** *m.* turn [to do something]; turn, shift [alternation]: *por ~,* in turn, taking turns.
**turón** *m.* ZOOL. fitch, fitchew, polecat.
**turquesa** *f.* MINER. turquoise. *2* bullet mould.
**Turquestán (el)** *m. pr. n.* GEOG. Turkestan.
**turquí** *adj.* deep [blue].
**Turquía** *f. pr. n.* GEOG. Turkey: *~ Asiática,* Turkey in Asia; *~ Europea,* Turkey in Europe.
**turrar** *tr.* to roast, broil.
**turrón** *m.* a kind of sweetmeat made with almond paste, nougat. *2* coll. public office, sinecure.
**turronería** *f.* TURRÓN shop.
**turronero, -ra** *m.-f.* maker or seller of TURRÓN.
**turulato, -ta** *adj.* coll. dumbfounded, stupefied.
**turumbón** *m.* bump, swelling [from a blow].
**¡tus!, ¡tusa!** *interj.* used in calling dogs. *2* coll. *sin decir tus ni mus,* without saying a word.
**tusilago** *m.* BOT. coltsfoot.
**tute** *m.* a card game.
**tutear** *tr.* to thou. *2 rec.* to thou each other.
**tutela** *f.* LAW tutelage, guardianship. *2* tutelage, protection.
**tutelar** *adj.* tutelar, tutelary.
**tuteo** *m.* thouing.
**tutilimundi** *m.* MUNDONUEVO.
**tutiplén (a)** *adv.* abundantly.
**tutor** *m.* LAW tutor, guardian. *2* guardian, protector. *3* AGR. prop [for plants].
**tutora** *f.* LAW tutoress, guardian.
**tutoría** *f.* LAW tutelage, tutorage, guardianship.
**tuturutú** *m.* sound of a trumpet.
**tuve, tuviera, tuviese,** etc. *irr.* V. TENER.
**tuya** *f.* BOT. thuja.
**tuyo, -ya** *poss. adj.* your; thy [formal]. *2 poss. pron.* yours, of yours; thine [formal]. *3 los tuyos,* yours [your family or people].

# U

**U, u** *f.* U, u, twenty-fourth letter of the Spanish alphabet. *2 u valona*, w [the letter].
**u** *conj.* [used instead of *o* before a word beginning with the vowel sound *o*] or.
**uapití** *m.* ZOOL. wapiti.
**ubérrimo, -ma** *adj.* very or most abundant or fertile.
**ubicación** *f.* location, position, situation.
**ubicar** *intr.-ref.* to lie, be located, be situated. *2 tr.* (Am.) to place, locate.
**ubicuidad** *f.* ubiquity.
**ubicuo, -cua** *adj.* ubiquitous.
**ubiquidad** *f.* UBICUIDAD.
**ubre** *f.* dug, udder, teat [of female mammals].
**ucase** *m.* ukase.
**Ucrania** *f. pr. n.* GEOG. Ukraine.
**ucranio, -nia** *adj.-n.* Ukranian.
**udómetro** *m.* udometer.
**¡uf!** *interj.* humph!; pshaw!
**ufanarse** *ref.* to boast, to pride oneself.
**ufanía** *f.* pride, vainglory. *2* joy, pleasure.
**ufano, -na** *adj.* proud, conceited, vainglorious. *2* glad, pleased.
**ujier** *m.* usher [of a court, etc.].
**ulano** *m.* MIL. uhlan.
**úlcera** *f.* MED. sore, ulcer. *2* BOT. rot.
**ulceración** *f.* MED. ulceration.
**ulcerado, -da** *adj.* MED. ulcerated.
**ulcerar** *tr.* MED. to ulcerate. *2 ref.* MED. to ulcerate [undergo ulceration].
**ulceroso, -sa** *adj.* MED. ulcerous.
**ulema** *m.* Ulema.
**uliginoso, -sa** *adj.* uliginose, uliginous.
**Ulises** *m. pr. n.* MYTH. Ulysses.
**ulitis** *f.* MED. ulitis.
**ulmáceo, -a** *adj.* BOT. ulmaceous.
**ulmaria** *f.* BOT. meadowsweet.
**ulterior** *adj.* ulterior. *2* subsequent.
**ultimación** *f.* finish, completion.
**últimamente** *adv.* lastly, finally. *2* of late.
**ultimar** *tr.* to end, finish, complete.
**ultimátum** *m.* ultimatum.
**último, -ma** *adj.* last, latter. *2* latest: *la última moda*, the latest fashion. *3* ultimate, final. *4* farthest, remote. *5* best, utmost. *6 última pena*, capital punishment. *7 estar a las últimas* or *en las últimas*, to be near one's, or it's end. *8 a última hora*, at the last minute. *9 a últimos de*, in the latter part of [a month, etc.]. *10 por ~*, lastly; finally.
**ultra** *adv.* besides. *2 pref.* ultra.
**ultrajante** *adj.* injurious, insulting, outraging.
**ultrajar** *tr.* to injure, insult, offend, outrage.
**ultraje** *m.* injure, insult, offence, outrage.
**ultramar** *m.* place or country overseas: *de ~*, overseas; ultramarine.
**ultramarino, -na** *adj.* overseas. *2* ultramarine [blue]. *3 m. pl.* COM. overseas foodstuffs; groceries.
**ultramicroscopio** *m.* ultramicroscope.
**ultramontano, -na** *adj.-n.* ultramontane.
**ultramundano, -na** *adj.* ultramundane.
**ultranza (a)** *adv.* to death. *2* at all costs, resolutely.
**ultratumba** *adv.* beyond the grave.
**ultraviolado, ultravioleta** *adj.* PHYS. ultraviolet.
**ultravirus** *m.* BACT. ultravirus.
**ulular** *intr.* to ululate.
**ululato** *m.* ululation.
**umbela** *f.* BOT. umbel.
**umbelífero, -ra** *adj.* BOT. umbelliferous.
**umbilicado, -da** *adj.* navel-shaped, umbilicate.
**umbilical** *adj.* ANAT., ZOOL. umbilical.
**umbráculo** *m.* shaded place for plants.
**umbral** *m.* threshold. *2* ARCH. lintel [beam].
**umbralar** *tr.* ARCH. to lintel.
**umbrátil** *adj.* umbrageous, shading.
**Umbría (la)** *f. pr. n.* GEOG. Umbria.
**umbría** *f.* shady place, shady side.
**umbrío, -bría** *adj.* shady [place].
**umbroso, -sa** *adj.* umbrageous, shady.
**un, una** *indef. art.* a, an. *2 adj.* one [numeral]. ¶ The form *un* is used before masculine singular nouns and adjectives, and before feminine singular nouns and adjectives beginning with an accented *a*: *un alma*, a soul.
**unánime** *adj.* unanimous.
**unánimemente** *adv.* unanimously.
**unanimidad** *f.* unanimity: *por ~*, unanimously.
**uncinado, -da** *adj.* uncinate.
**unción** *f.* unction, anointing. *2* extreme unction. *3* unction [fervent quality; religious fervour].
**uncir** *tr.* to yoke [oxen, etc.].
**undecágono** *m.* undecagon.
**undécimo, -ma** *adj.-m.* eleventh.
**undoso, -sa** *adj.* waving, undulating.
**undulación** *f.* undulation. *2* PHYS. wave.

**undular** *intr.* to undulate, wave, wriggle.
**undulatorio, -ria** *adj.* undulatory.
**ungido** *adj.-m.* anointed.
**ungimiento** *m.* unction, anointment.
**ungir** *tr.* to anoint.
**ungüento** *m.* unguent, ointment, salve.
**unguiculado, -da** *adj.-m.* ZOOL. unguiculate.
**unguis,** *pl.* **-guis** *m.* ANAT. unguis.
**ungulado, -da** *adj.-m.* ZOOL. ungulate.
**únicamente** *adv.* only, solely.
**unicameral** *adj.* unicameral.
**unicelular** *adj.* unicellular.
**unicidad** *f.* unicity.
**único, -ca** *adj.* only, sole. *2* unique, unequalled.
**unicornio** *m.* MYTH. unicorn. *2* ZOOL. rhinoceros. *3* (cap.) ASTR. Unicorn.
**unidad** *f.* unity [oneness, due coherence of parts]. *2* union, concord. *3* unit. *4* RHET., MATH., F. ARTS unity.
**unido, -da** *adj.* united. *2* being in union or concord.
**unificación** *f.* unification.
**unificador, -ra** *adj.* unifying. *2 m.-f.* unifier.
**unificar** *tr.* to unify. *2 ref.* to be unified.
**uniformar** *tr.* to uniform [make uniform], to standardize. *2* to uniform [clothe in uniform].
**uniforme** *adj.* uniform. *2 m.* uniform; regimentals.
**uniformidad** *f.* uniformity.
**unigénito, -ta** *adj.* unigenital, only-begotten.
**unilateral** *adj.* unilateral.
**unión** *f.* union. *2* contiguity. *3* MACH. coupling, connecting, connection, joint. *4* COM. amalgamation.
**unionista** *adj.* unionistic. *2 m.-f.* unionist.
**unípara** *adj.* uniparous.
**unipersonal** *adj.* unipersonal.
**unir** *tr.* to unite, join. *2 ref.* to unite [become united, attached, etc.; get married]. *3* to coalesce. *4* to unite, join, adhere. *5* COM. to amalgamate.
**unisexual** *adj.* BOT. unisexual.
**unison** *adj.* UNÍSONO. *2* MUS. unison.
**unisonancia** *f.* MUS. unisonance. *2* monotony.
**unísono, -na** *adj.* unison, unisonant, unisonous. *2 al ~,* in unison, unanimously.
**unitario, -ria** *adj.* unitary. *2 m.-f.* POL. unitarian. *3* THEOL. Unitarian.
**unitivo, -va** *adj.* unitive.
**univalvo, -va** *adj.* ZOOL. univalve.
**universal** *adj.* universal. *2 m.* LOG. universal.
**universalidad** *f.* universality.
**universalizar** *tr.* to universalize.
**universidad** *f.* EDUC., HIST. university. *2* universality.
**universitario, -ria** *adj.* universitarian, university. *2 m.* university professor.
**universo, -sa** *adj.* universal. *2 m.* universe, world.
**unívoco, -ca** *adj.* univocal.
**uno, -na** *adj.* one: *todo es ~,* all is the same; *~ que otro, una que otra,* a few; occasionally. *2 pl.* a few; some: *unas [cuantas] pesetas,* a few pesetas; *unos veinte minutos,* some twenty minutes. *3 adj.-m.* one [numeral]: *el número ~,* the number one. *4 pron.* one [one person or thing]; one of them: *de ~,* one's; *~ a otro, los unos a los otros,* each other, one another; *~ a ~, de ~ en ~, ~ por ~,* one by one; *~ y otro,* both. *5 f. la una,* one o'clock. *6 a una,* of one accord; jointly.
**untadura** *f.* UNTURA.
**untar** *tr.* to anoint, grease, oil, smear. *2* fig. to grease, bribe. *3 ref.* to grease oneself, to get smeared. *4* fig. to practice embezzlement.

**unto** *m.* ointment, unguent. *2* grease, fat [of animal].
**untuosidad** *f.* unctuosity, greasiness.
**untuoso, -sa** *adj.* unctuous, greasy.
**untura** *f.* anointing, oiling, greasing. *2* MED. unction. *3* ointment.
**uña** *f.* ANAT., ZOOL. nail, fingernail, toenail; claw, talon: *enseñar las uñas,* fig. to show one's teeth; *estar de uñas,* fig. to be on bad terms; *ser largo de uñas,* fig. to be of a thievish disposition; *ser ~ y carne,* fig. to be hand and glove. *2* ZOOL. hoof: *a ~ de caballo,* at full gallop. *3* sting [of scorpion]. *4* BOT. thorn. *5* stub [of limb of tree]. *6* curved point. *7* nail hole [of a penknife, etc.]. *8* NAUT. fluke, bill [of anchor].
**uñada** *f.* nail scratch. *2* push with the nail.
**uñarada** *f.* nail scratch.
**uñero** *m.* ingrowing nail.
**¡upa!** *interj.* up, up!, hoop-la!
**upas** *m.* BOT. upas [tree and sap].
**Urales (los)** *m. pr. n.* GEOG. the Urals.
**Urania** *f. pr. n.* MYTH. Urania.
**uranio, -nia** *adj.* uranic. *2 m.* CHEM. uranium.
**uranita** *f.* MINER. uranite.
**Urano** *m. pr. n.* ASTR. Uranus.
**uranografía** *f.* uranography.
**urato** *m.* CHEM. urate.
**urbanamente** *adv.* courteously, politely.
**urbanidad** *f.* urbanity, civility, manners.
**urbanismo** *m.* city planning.
**urbanización** *f.* urbanization. *2* city planning.
**urbanizar** *tr.* to urbanize, render urbane. *2* to urbanize, develop [land].
**Urbano** *m. pr. n.* Urban.
**urbano, -na** *adj.* urban. *2* urbane, courteous, polite. *3 m.* town policeman.
**urbe** *f.* large city, metropolis.
**urceolado, -da** *adj.* urceolate.
**urchilla** *f.* archil, orchil [plant and dye].
**urdidor, -ra** *adj.* WEAV. warping. *2* fig. plotting. *3 m.-f.* WEAV. warper. *4* fig. plotter. *5 m.* WEAV. warping frame.
**urdidura** *f.* WEAV. warping.
**urdiembre, urdimbre** *f.* WEAV. warp. *2* WEAV. warping.
**urdir** *tr.* WEAV. to warp. *2* fig. to plot, contrive.
**urea** *f.* CHEM. urea.
**uremia** *f.* MED. uraemia.
**urente** *adj.* hot, burning, smarting.
**uréter** *m.* ANAT. ureter.
**uretra** *f.* ANAT. urethra.
**urgencia** *f.* urgency [being urgent]. *2* MED. emergency.
**urgente** *adj.* urgent, pressing.
**urgir** *intr.* to press, be urgent [demand immediate action].
**Urías** *m. pr. n.* BIBL. Uriah.
**úrico, -ca** *adj.* uric.
**urinario, -ria** *adj.* urinary. *2 m.* urinal [place].
**urna** *f.* urn, casket. *2* glass case. *3* ballot box.
**uro** *m.* ZOOL. aurochs.
**urodelo, -la** *adj.-n.* ZOOL. urodelan.
**urogallo** *m.* ORN. capercailye.
**urología** *f.* urology.
**urólogo** *m.* urologist.
**urraca** *f.* ORN. magpie. *2* coll. magpie [chatterer].
**úrsido, -da** *m. pl.* ZOOL. Ursidae.
**ursulina** *adj.-f.* Ursuline.
**urticáceo, -a** *adj.* BOT. urticaceous.
**urticante** *adj.* urticant.
**urticaria** *f.* MED. urticaria, nettle rash, hives.

**urubú** *m.* ORN. urubu, black vulture.
**uruguayo, -ya** *adj.-n.* Uruguayan.
**usado, -da** *adj.* used, employed. *3* worn-out, old [impaired by use]. *4* second-hand [clothes]. *5* inured, accustomed, skilled.
**usagre** *m.* MED. infantile eczema. *2* VET. mange.
**usanza** *f.* usage, custom, fashion.
**usar** *tr.* to use [make use of]. *2* to wear [an article of dress, etc.]. *3* *tr.-intr.* to use to, be wont or accustomed to. *4* *ref.* to be used, be in use or fashion.
**usarcé, usarced** *m.-f.* obs. your honour.
**useñoría** *m.-f.* obs. your grace, your lordship, your ladyship.
**usía** *m.-f.* USEÑORÍA.
**uso** *m.* use [using, employment, right of using]; wear, wearing, wear and tear: *en buen* ~, in good condition. *2* usage, custom, fashion: *al* ~, *a* ~, according to custom. *3* habit, practice. *4* LAW. usage. *5* ~ *de razón*, discretion, discernment.
**usted,** *pl.* **ustedes** *pron.* (used with the third of verb) you: *de* ~, *de ustedes*, your, yours.
**ustorio** *adj.* burning [glass].
**usual** *adj.* usual, customary. *2* affable, sociable.
**usuario, -ria** *adj.* usuary; user.
**usufructo** *m.* LAW usufruct. *2* fruits, profits.
**usufructuar** *tr.* to enjoy the usufruct of. *2* *intr.* to yield profit.
**usufructuario, -ria** *adj.-n.* usufructuary.
**usura** *f.* usury.
**usurario, -ria** *adj.* usurious.
**usurear** *intr.* to practice usury.

**usurero, -ra** *m.-f.* usurer.
**usurpación** *f.* usurpation.
**usurpador, -ra** *adj.* usurping. *2* *m.-f.* usurper.
**usurpar** *tr.* to usurp. *2* to encroach upon.
**utensilio** *m.* utensil. *2* *pl.* tools [of a trade].
**uterino, -na** *adj.* uterine.
**útero** *m.* ANAT. uterus, womb.
**útil** *adj.* useful, profitable. *2* LAW lawful, legal [time]. *3* MECH. effective, available. *4* *m. pl.* tools, implements.
**utilidad** *f.* utility, usefulness. *2* fruit, profit.
**utilitario, -ria** *adj.* utilitarian.
**utilitarismo** *m.* utilitarianism.
**utilizable** *adj.* utilizable, available.
**utilizar** *tr.* to utilize, use. *2* *ref.* *utilizarse de*, to profit by.
**utopía** *f.* Utopia.
**utópico, -ca** *adj.* Utopian.
**utopista** *adj.-n.* Utopian.
**utrículo** *m.* ANAT., BOT. utricle.
**uva** *f.* BOT. grape: ~ *pasa*, raisin; *estar hecho una* ~, coll. to be vey drunk. *2* BOT. berry of the barberry bush. *3* MED. uvular tumor. *4* wart on the eyelid. *5* BOT. ~ *crespa*, ~ *espina*, gooseberry; ~ *de gato*, stonecrop.
**uvada** *f.* abundance of grapes.
**uvaduz** *f.* GAYUBA.
**uvate** *m.* conserve of grapes.
**uve** *f.* name of the letter *v*.
**úvea** *f.* ANAT. uvea.
**úvula** *f.* ANAT. uvula.
**uvular** *adj.* uvular.
**uxoricida** *m.* uxoricide [man].
**uxoricidio** *m.* uxoricide [act.].

**V, v** *f.* V, v, twenty-fifth letter of the Spanish alphabet.

**va** *3rd. sing. pres. ind.* of IR.

**vaca** *f.* ZOOL. cow [female of bovine animal]: ~ *lechera*, milch cow. *2* beef [meat]. *3* cow leather, cowskin. *4* joint stock of two gamblers. *5* ENT. ~ *de San Antón*, ladybird, ladybug. *6* ZOOL. ~ *marina*, sea cow, manatee.

**vacación** *f.* vacancy [of a post]. *2 sing.-pl.* vacation, holidays.

**vacada** *f.* herd of bovine cattle.

**vacancia** *f.* vacancy [unoccupied post].

**vacante** *adj.* vacant, unoccupied. *2 f.* vacancy [unoccupied post]. *3* vacation [period].

**vacar** *intr.* to take a vacation. *2* [of a post, office, etc.], to be vacant. *3* ~ *a*, to attend to, devote oneself to. *4* ~ *de*, to lack, be devoid of.

**vacatura** *f.* vacancy [time].

**vaciadero** *m.* drain, drain pipe. *2* dumping place.

**vaciado** *m.* cast; casting [in a mould]. *3* ARCH. hollow, excavation. *4* honing [of razors].

**vaciamiento** *m.* emptying. *2* casting, moulding.

**vaciar** *tr.* to empty. *2* to cast [form in a mould]. *3* ARCH. to excavate, hollow out. *4* to hone [razors]. *5 intr.* [of a river] to empty, flow. *6* [of a river, etc.] to fall, decrease. *7 ref.* to empty [become empty].

**vaciedad** *f.* inanity, silliness, silly remark.

**vacilación** *f.* vacilation. *2* unsteadiness. *3* flickering. *4* hesitation.

**vacilante** *adj.* vacillating, wavering. *2* staggering, unsteady. *3* flickering. *4* hesitating, irresolute.

**vacilar** *intr.* to vacillate, waver. *2* to reel, stagger, totter. *3* to flicker. *4* to fluctuate, hesitate.

**vacío, -a** *adj.* empty void, vacuous. *2* vacant, unoccupied. *3* empty, vain, inane. *4* vain, useless. *5* idle. *6* concave, hollow. *7 m.* void [empty space]. *8* emptiness. *9* PHYS. vacuum. *10* gap, blank. *11* vacancy. *12* flank [of animals], side [of persons]. *13 hacer el ~ a*, to isolate, ignore [someone]. *14 de ~* unloaded [cart, etc.]; fig. idling; empty-handed, unsuccessfully.

**vacuidad** *f.* vacuity, emptiness. *2* inaneness.

**vacuna** *f.* cowpox. *2* vaccine.

**vacunación** *f.* vaccination.

**vacunar** *tr.* to vaccinate.

**vacuno, -na** *adj.* bovine. *2* of cowskin.

**vacuo, cua** *adj.* empty. *2* vacant, unoccupied. *3 m.* hollow, concavity.

**vacuola** *f.* BIOL. vacuole.

**vade** *m.* school portfolio, satchel.

**vadeable** *adj.* fordable. *2* fig. conquerable, superable.

**vadear** *tr.* to ford, wade [a stream]. *2* to overcome [a difficulty]. *3* to sound [a person]. *4* to penetrate, understand. *5 ref.* to conduct oneself.

**vademécum** *m.* vade mecum. *2* VADE.

**vadera** *f.* wide ford.

**vado** *m.* ford: *tentar el* ~, fig. to feel one's way. *2* fig. expedient, resource.

**vadoso, -sa** *adj.* fordy, shallow, shoaly.

**vagabundear** *intr.* to wander, roam, loiter about.

**vagabundeo** *m.* wandering, roaming, loitering about.

**vagabundo, -da** *adj.* vagabond. *2 m.-f.* vagabond, wanderer, vagrant, tramp.

**vagamundear** *tr.* VAGABUNDEAR.

**vagamundo, -da** *adj.-n.* VAGABUNDO.

**vagancia** *f.* idleness, loafing. *2* vacancy.

1) **vagar** *m.* leisure, time. *2* idleness.

2) **vagar** *intr.* to wander, roam. *2* to be idle. *3* to be at leisure. *4* [of a thing] to lie around.

**vagaroso, -sa** *adj.* poet. errant, wandering, fluttering.

**vagido** *m.* cry of the newborn child.

**vagina** *f.* ANAT. vagina.

**vago, -ga** *adj.* wandering, roaming. *2* idle, loafing. *3* vague, indistinct, loose, hazy. *4* blank [stare]. *5* unimproved [plot of ground]. *6 m.* idler, loafer. *7* vagrant. *8 en* ~, unsteadily; in vain; in the air, at nothing [blow].

**vagón** *m.* RLY. carriage, car, coach, wagon, van: ~ *cisterna*, tank car; ~ *restaurante*, dining-car; ~ *de carga*, goods wagon, freight car.

**vagoneta** *f.* small wagon, open railway truck.

**vaguada** *f.* thalweg.

**vaguear** *intr.* to wander, roam.

**vaguedad** *f.* vagueness. *2* vague remark.

**vaguido, -da** *adj.* dizzy, giddy. *2 m.* VAHÍDO.

**vaharada** *f.* breath, breathing, exhalation.

**vaharina** *f.* coll. vapour, mist.

**vahear** *intr.* to exhale or emit fumes or vapour.

**vahído** *m.* vertigo, dizziness, swoon.

**vaho** *m.* fume, vapour, exhalation, breath.

**vaída** *adj.* ARCH. Byzantine [vault].

**vaina** *f.* sheath, case, scabbard. *2* BOT. sheath. *3* BOT. pod, shell. *4* NAUT. tabling [of a flag or sail].
**vainica** *f.* SEW. hemstitch.
**vainilla** *f.* BOT. vanilla [plant and fruit]. *2* VAINICA.
**vais** *irr. 2nd. pers. pl. pres. ind.* of IR.
**vaivén** *m.* to-and-fro motion, seesaw, swing, fluctuation. *2* fig. inconstancy [of fortune or things]. *3* NAUT. ratline.
**vajilla** *f.* table service, dinner set, plate: ~ *de oro*, gold plate; ~ *de plata*, silver plate, silverware.
**valdré, valdría**, etc. *irr.* V. VALER.
**vale** *m.* promissory note. *2* receipt, voucher. *3* bonus given to schoolboys.
**valedero, -ra** *adj.* valid, efficacious.
**valedor, -ra** *m.-f.* protector, defender, helper.
**valencia** *f.* CHEM. valence, valency.
**valenciano, -na** *adj.-n.* Valencian.
**valentía** *f.* valour, bravery. *2* feat, heroic exploit. *3* LIT., F. ARTS dash, boldness. *4* brag, braggadocio.
**Valentín** *m. pr. n.* Valentine.
**valentino, -na** *adj.* Valencian.
**valentísimo, -ma** *adj. superl.* of VALIENTE.
**valentón, -na** *adj.* blustering, arrogant. *2 m.-f.* blusterer, braggard, hector, bully.
**valentonada** *f.* bluster, brag, braggadocio.
1) **valer** *m.* worth, merit, value.
2) **valer** *tr.* to protect, defend, help. *2* to produce, give, yield. *3* to bring, bring about, cause to get. *4* to be worth, be valued at, be equal or equivalent to: *no valer nada*, to be worth nothing. *5* ~ *la pena*, to be worth, be worth while; to be important. *6 valga lo que valiere*, come what may. *7 ¡válgame Dios!*, bless my soul! *8 intr.* to be of worth, be valuable; be useful, able, proficient; to have power, influence. *9* to avail. *10* to be valid, good; to hold, count. *11* to prevail [over or against]. *12 hacer ~*, to make feel; to turn to account; to assert [one's rights, etc.]. *13* ~ *más*, to be better; *más vale tarde que nunca*, better late than never. *14* ~ *para*, to be useful for. *15* ~ *por*, to be worth, to be as good as. *16* ~ *tanto como*, to be as much as. *17 ref.* to help or defend oneself; to take care of oneself: *no poder valerse*, to be helpless. *18 valerse de*, to make use of; to avail oneself of, to take advantage of.
¶ CONJUG. INDIC. Pres.: *valgo, vales, vale*, etc. | Fut.: *valdré, valdrás*, etc. | COND. *valdría, valdrías*, etc. | SUBJ. Pres.: *valga, valgas*, etc. | IMPER.: *val* or vale; *valgamos, valed, valgan*.
**valeriana** *f.* BOT. valerian, setwall.
**valerosidad** *f.* valour, bravery, courage.
**valeroso, -sa** *adj.* valorous, brave. *2* active, powerful.
**valetudinario, -ria** *adj.-n.* valetudinarian.
**valgo, valga**, etc. *irr.* V. VALER.
**valí** *m.* vali, wali.
**valía** *f.* value, worth. *2* VALIMIENTO 1. *3* ECON. *mayor* ~, *plus* ~, unearned increment.
**validar** *tr.* to validate.
**validez** *f.* validity.
**válido, -da** *adj.* valid. *2* strong, robust, powerful.
**valido, -da** *adj.* generally accepted or esteemed. *2 m.* court favorite, prime minister.
**valiente** *adj.* valiant, brave. *2* strong, vigorous. *3* fig. fine, excellent. *4* fig. great, excessive. *5 m.-f.* brave person. *6 m.* bully.
**valija** *f.* valise, suitcase. *2* mailbag. *3* mail, post: ~ *diplomática*, diplomatic mail.

**valimiento** *m.* favour, good graces; favour at court. *2* protection, defense, help.
**valioso, -sa** *adj.* valuable, important, powerful.
**valisoletano, -na** *adj.-n.* of Valladolid.
**valón, -na** *adj.-n.* Walloon. *2 f.* Vandyke collar.
**valor** *m.* value, worth: ~ *nominal*, par value, face value. *2* import. *3* amount. *4* importance. *5* validity, force. *6* valour, courage. *7* audacity, impudence. *8 pl.* COM. securities.
**valorar, valorear** *tr.* to value, appraise. *2* to increase the value of.
**valoría** *f.* value, worth.
**valquiria** *f.* MYTH. Valkyrie.
**vals** *m.* waltz.
**valsar** *intr.* to waltz.
**valuación** *f.* valuation, appraisal.
**valuar** *tr.* to value, appraise, rate.
**valva** *f.* BOT., ZOOL. valve.
**valvar** *adj.* BIOL. valval, valvar.
**válvula** *f.* MACH., RADIO., ANAT. valve: ~ *de seguridad*, safety valve.
**valvular** *adj.* valvular.
**valla** *f.* paling, fence, stockade, barrier. *2* fig. barrier, obstacle. *3* SPORT hurdle.
**valladar** *m.* VALLADO. *2* fig. barrier, defence.
**vallado** *m.* fence, stockade, inclosure.
**vallar** *tr.* to fence, palisade.
**valle** *m.* valley, vale: *este* ~ *de lágrimas*, fig. this vale of tears. *2* river basin.
**vallisoletano, -na** *adj.-n.* of Valladolid.
**vamos** *1st. pers. pl. pres. ind. &* imper. of IR. *2 interj.* well!, come now!; let's go!; stop!
**vampiresa** *f.* vampire, vamp [woman].
**vampiro** *m.* vampire, ghoul. *2* fig. vampire, usurer. *3* ZOOL. vampire.
**van** *3rd. pers. pl. pres. ind.* of IR.
**vanadio** *m.* CHEM. vanadium.
**vanagloria** *f.* vainglory, conceit.
**vanagloriarse** *ref.* to boast [of], to be vainglorious.
**vanaglorioso, -sa** *adj.* vainglorious, conceited.
**vanamente** *adv.* vainly. *2* in vain.
**vandalismo** *m.* vandalism.
**vándalo, -la** *adj.-n.* Vandal, vandal.
**vanguardia** *f.* MIL. van, vanguard: *a* ~, in the van.
**vanidad** *f.* vanity: *hacer* ~ *de*, to boast of. *2* empty word, inanity.
**vanidoso, -sa** *adj.* vain, conceited. *2 m.-f.* vain person.
**vanilocuencia** *f.* verbosity, empty talk.
**vano, -na** *adj.* vain: *en* ~, in vain. *2* hollow, empty. *3 m.* ARCH. opening [for a door or window].
**vapor** *m.* PHYS. vapo(u)r. *2* steam: *al* ~, fig. with all speed. *3* mist, exhalation. *4* NAUT. steamboat, steamship, steamer. *5 pl.* vapours, hysterics.
**vapora** *f.* coll. steam launch.
**vaporear** *tr.-ref.* EVAPORAR. *2 intr.* to exhale vapours.
**vaporizador** *m.* vaporizer.
**vaporizar** *tr.* to vaporize.
**vaporoso, -sa** *adj.* vaporous, vapoury, airy, ethereal.
**vapular** *tr.* VAPULEAR.
**vapuleador, -ra** *adj.* flogging, whipping. *2 m.-f.* flogger, whipper.
**vapulear** *tr.* to flog, whip, vapulate.
**vapuleo** *m.* flogging, vapulation.
**vaquería** *f.* VACADA. *2* cow-house, dairy.
**vaquerizo, -za** *adj.* [pertaining to] cattle. *2 m.* cowherd. *3 f.* cowherdess. *4* winter stable for cattle.
**vaquero, -ra** *adj.* pertaining to cowherds. *2 m.* cowherd, cowboy. *3 f.* cowherdess.

**vaqueta** *f.* calf leather.
**vara** *f.* stick, switch. *2* rod, wand, verge, staff, cane: *tener ~ alta*, fig. to have authority. *3* shaft, thill [of a carriage]. *4* BOT. flowered scape. *5* BULLF. thrust with the pike. *6* measure of length [2,8 ft]. *7* BOT. *~ de Jesé*, tuberose.
**varada** *f.* NAUT. beaching or running aground.
**varadera** *f.* NAUT. skid.
**varadero** *m.* NAUT. place where boats are taken ashore for safety. *2* repair dock.
**varal** *m.* long pole or perch. *2* upper rail of the side of a cart. *3* coll. tall, ungainly person.
**varapalo** *m.* long pole. *2* blow with a stick or pole. *3* fig. blow, loss, damage, reverse.
**varar** *tr.* NAUT. to beach [a boat]. *2 intr.* NAUT. to run aground. *3* fig. [of an affair] to come to a standstill.
**varaseto** *m.* lattice-work fence, trellis.
**varazo** *m.* blow with a rod or stick.
**vareaje** *m.* knocking of fruit off trees with poles.
**varear** *tr.* to knock off [fruit] with a pole. *2* to beat with a stick. *3* to prick [bulls, etc.] with a pike.
**varenga** *f.* NAUT. floor-timber. *2* NAUT. headrail.
**vareo** *m.* VAREAJE.
**varetazo** *m.* BULLF. side blow with the horn.
**varetón** *m.* young stag.
**varga** *f.* steepest part of a slope.
**vargueño** *m.* BARGUEÑO.
**variabilidad** *f.* variability.
**variable** *adj.* variable. *2 f.* MATH. variable.
**variación** *f.* variation, change. *2* MUS. variation.
**variado, -da** *adj.* varied, diverse. *3* variegated.
**variante** *adj.* variant, varying. *2 f.* variant.
**variar** *tr.* to vary, change, alter, diversify, variegate. *2 intr.* to vary, change. *3* to vary, differ. *4* NAUT. [of the compass] to vary, desviate.
**varice, várice** *f.* MED. varix.
**varicela** *f.* MED. varicella, chicken pox.
**varicoso, -sa** *adj.* varicose.
**variedad** *f.* variety; diversity. *2* variation, change. *3* changeableness. *4* BIOL. variety. *5 pl.* variety show.
**varilarguero** *m.* PICADOR [in bullfighting].
**varilla** *f. dim.* slender stick, twig; slender rod. *2* rib [of an umbrella]. *3* stick [of fan]. *4* wire spoke. *5 ~ de virtudes*, conjurer's wand.
**varillaje** *m.* ribs [of an umbrella]; sticks [of a fan].
**vario, -ria** *adj.* various, diverse, varied. *2* inconstant. *3* variegated. *4 pl.* various, several.
**varioloso, -sa** *adj.* MED. variolous.
**variómetro** *m.* ELECT. variometer.
**varita** *f. dim.* switch, twig, small stick or rod. *2 ~ de virtudes*, VARILLA DE VIRTUDES.
**variz** *m.* VARICE.
**varón** *m.* male [person]: *un niño ~*, a male child. *2* man; man of respectability.
**varoncito** *m. dim.* boy, male child.
**varonil** *adj.* manful, manly, virile, courageous.
**Varsovia** *f. pr. n.* GEOG. Warsaw.
**vasallaje** *m.* HIST. vassalage. *2* HIST. liege money. *3* vassalage, servitude, subjection, dependence.
**vasallo** *adj.* subject, dependent, feudatory. *2 m.-f.* vassal, subject.
**vasar** *m.* kitchen shelf, kitchen shelving.
**vasco, -ca** *adj.-n.* Basque.
**vascongado, -da** *adj.-n.* Basque.
**vascuence** *m.* Basque [language].
**vascular** *adj.* vascular.
**vaselina** *f.* vaseline.
**vasera** *f.* kitchen shelf. *2* rack for glasses.
**vasija** *f.* vessel [receptacle for liquids or eatables].

**vaso** *m.* glass, tumbler. *2* glassful, tumblerful. *3* vessel, receptacle, reservoir: *~ de elección*, chosen vessel. *4* hoof [of horse]. *5* ARCH. vase. *6* ANAT., BOT. vessel. *7 ~ de noche*, chamber pot.
**vasomotor** *adj.* PHYSIOL. vasomotor.
**vástago** *m.* shoot; scion, offspring. *2* MACH. piston rod, tiller.
**vastedad** *f.* vastness.
**vasto, -ta** *adj.* vast, immense, huge, of great extent.
**vate** *m.* bard, poet. *2* seer, diviner.
**Vaticano** *m. pr. n.* Vatican.
**vaticano, -na** *adj.* Vatican.
**vaticinar** *tr.* to vaticinate.
**vaticinio** *m.* vaticination, prediction, prophecy.
**vatídico, -ca** *adj.* prophetical.
**vatímetro** *m.* ELECT. wattmeter.
**vatio** *m.* ELECT. watt.
1) **vaya** *f.* banter, raillery.
2) **vaya**, etc. *irr.* V. IR. *2 interj.* go!, go to!; come!, indeed!, well!
1) **ve** *2d pers. sing. imper.* of IR.
2) **ve** *f.* name of letter v: *~ doble*, name of w.
**véase** *imper.* of VERSE. *2* see, vide [in references].
**veces** *f. pl.* of VEZ.
**vecinal** *adj.* local, vicinal.
**vecinamente** *adv.* near, contiguously.
**vecindad** *f.* status of being an inhabitant of a town. *2* vicinage, vicinity; neighbours, neighbourhood.
**vecindario** *m.* neighbourhood [people living near one another]; inhabitants of a town or quarter.
**vecino, -na** *adj.* near by, next, neighbouring. *2* fig. neighbouring, bordering upon, resembling. *3 m.-f.* neighbour. *4* tenant [in a tenement house]. *5* resident, citizen [of a town].
**vector** *adj.* MATH. vectorial. *2 m.* MATH. vector.
**veda** *f.* prohibition, interdiction. *2* close season. *3 m.* Veda.
**vedado, -da** *adj.* prohibited, interdicted. *2 m.* enclosure, game preserve, warren.
**vedar** *tr.* to prohibit, forbid. *2* to impede.
**vedegambre** *m.* BOT. white hellebore.
**vedija** *f.* tuft of wool. *2* entangled lock of wool or hair. *4* matted hair.
**veedor, -ra** *adj.* curious, prying. *2 m.-f.* prier, busybody. *3* [formerly] overseer, supervisor.
**vega** *f.* fertile lowland. *2* (Cu.) tobacco plantation.
**vegetación** *f.* vegetation.
**vegetal** *adj.* vegetable, vegetal. *2 m.* vegetable, plant.
**vegetar** *intr.* to vegetate.
**vegetariano, -na** *adj.-n.* vegetarian.
**vegetativo, -va** *adj.* vegetative.
**veguer** *m.* an ancient magistrate.
**veguero** *m.* tobacco planter. *2* cigar made of a single leaf.
**vehemencia** *f.* vehemence.
**vehemente** *adj.* vehement.
**vehículo** *m.* vehicle.
**veintavo, -va** *adj.-n.* twentieth.
**veinte** *adj.-m.* twenty. *2 adj.-n.* twentieth. *3 m.* twentieth [of the month].
**veintena** *f.*, **veintenar** *m.* score, set of twenty.
**veinteno, -na** *adj.-n.* twentieth.
**veinticinco** *adj.-m.* twenty-five. *2 adj.* twenty-fifth. *3 m.* twenty-fifth [of the month].
**veinticuatro** *adj.-m.* twenty four. *2 adj.* twenty fourth. *3 m.* twenty-fourth [of the month].
**veintidós** *adj.-m.* twenty-two. *2 adj.* twenty-second. *3 m.* twenty-second [of the month].

**veintinueve** adj.-m. twenty-nine. 2 adj. twenty-ninth. 3 m. twenty-ninth [of the month].

**veintiocho** adj.-m. twenty-eight. 2 adj. twenty-eighth. 3 m. twenty-eight [of the month].

**veintiséis** adj.-m. twenty-six. 2 adj. twenty-sixth. 3 m. twenty-sixth [of the month].

**veintisiete** adj.-m. twenty-seven. 2 adj. twenty-seventh. 3 m. twenty-seventh [of the month].

**veintitrés** adj.-m. twenty-three. 2 adj. twenty-third. 3 m. twenty-third [of the month].

**veintiún** adj. twenty-one [used only before the noun].

**veintiuno, -na** adj.-m. twenty-one. 2 adj. twenty-first. 3 m. twenty-first [of the month]. 4 f. twenty-one [card game].

**vejación** f. molestation, humiliation, ill-treatment, oppresion.

**vejamen** m. VEJACIÓN. 2 humorous reprehension.

**vejancón, -na** adj. coll. old. 2 m.-f. coll. old person.

**vejar** tr. to molest, humiliate, ill-treat, oppress.

**vejatorio, -ria** adj. molesting, humiliating, oppressive.

**vejestorio** m. coll. very old person.

**vejete** m. ridiculous old man.

**vejez** f. oldness. 2 old age. 3 peevishness of old age. 4 coll. platitude, old history.

**vejiga** f. bladder: ~ de la bilis, ANAT. gall bladder; ~ de la orina, ANAT. bladder, urinary bladder; ~ natatoria, air bladder, swimming bladder [of fish]. 2 pustule of smallpox.

**vejigatorio, -ria** adj.-m. vesicant, vesicatory.

**vejiguilla** f. dim. small blister or pustule. 2 vesicle.

1) **vela** f. vigil, watch [keeping awake]: en ~, awake, sleepless. 2 nightwork, night watch. 3 watching the sick or the dead. 4 ECCL. vigil before the Holy Sacrament.

2) **vela** f. candle [for giving light]: ¿quién le ha dado a usted vela en este entierro?, coll. you have no voice in this matter.

3) **vela** f. awning. 2 NAUT. sail: sailboat: ~ al tercio, lugsail; ~ cangreja, gaff-sail; de abanico, spritsail; ~ de cruz, square sail; ~ de cuchillo, fore-and-aft sail; ~ latina, lateen sail; ~ mayor, mainsail; hacerse a la ~, largar velas, to set sail; levantar velas, fig. to decamp; recoger velas, fig. to restrain oneself; a toda ~, a velas llenas, full sail.

**velación**, pl. -ciones f. vigil, watch [keeping awake]. 2 sing.-pl. ECCL. veiling at nuptial mass.

**velacho** m. NAUT. fore-topsail.

**velada** f. VELACIÓN 1. 2 social evening; soirée.

**velador, -ra** m.-f. watcher, guard, guardian. 2 wooden candlestick. 3 small table with one foot.

**veladura** f. PAINT. glaze, velatura.

**velaje, velamen** m. NAUT. canvas, sails [of a ship].

1) **velar** adj. PHONET. velar.

2) **velar** intr. to watch, keep vigil, stay up. 2 to work at night. 3 [with por] to watch over, protect, see to. 4 NAUT. [of rocks, etc.] to stick out of the water. 5 intr.-tr. ECCL. to assist by turns before the Holy Sacrament. 6 tr. to watch [the sick or the dead]. 7 to watch, observe. 8 to veil. 9 PAINT. to glaze. 10 PHOT. to fog. 11 ref. to veil oneself, become veiled. 12 PHOT. to fog [become fogged].

**velarte** m. broadcloth.

**velatorio** m. wake [beside a dead body].

**veleidad** f. caprice, whim. 2 inconstancy, fickleness.

**veleidoso, -sa** adj. capricious, inconstant, fickle.

**velería** f. candle shop.

**velero, -ra** adj. NAUT. swift-sailing. 2 m.-f. tallow chandler. 3 m. sailmaker. 4 NAUT. sailboat, sailer.

**veleta** f. weathercock, weather vane. 2 streamer [of a lance]. 3 m.-f. fig. weathercock, fickle person.

**velete** m. thin veil.

**velilla** f. small candle.

**velillo** m. dim. small veil.

**velis nolis** Lat. willy-nilly.

**velo** m. veil: correr, or echar, un ~ sobre, fig. to draw a veil over. 2 fig. cloud [in the mind]. 3 taking the veil. 4 ANAT. ~ del paladar, velum, soft palate.

**velocidad** f. velocity; speed; primera ~, AUTO. low gear; segunda ~, AUTO. second; tercera ~, AUTO. high gear; en gran ~, RLY. by express; en pequeña ~, RLY. by freight.

**velocípedo** m. velocipede.

**velódromo** m. velodrome.

**velomotor** m. light motorcycle.

**velón** m. metal olive-oil lamp.

**velorio** m. wake, watch [over a dead person].

**veloz**, pl. -loces adj. fast, fleet, quick, rapid, swift.

**veludillo** m. VELLUDILLO.

**vellido, -da** adj. VELLOSO.

**vello** m. down, soft hair [on the human body]. 2 down, fuzz, pubescence [on plants and fruits].

**vellocino** m. fleece: ~ de oro, MYTH. Golden Fleece.

**vellón** m. fleece. 2 unsheared sheepskin. 3 lock of wool. 4 copper and silver alloy. 5 [formerly] copper coin.

**vellorita** f. BOT. daisy. 2 BOT. primrose, cowslip.

**vellosidad** f. downiness, hairiness.

**vellosilla** f. BOT. mouse-ear.

**velloso, -sa** adj. downy, hairy. 2 BOT. villous, fuzzy.

**velludillo** m. velveteen.

**velludo, -da** adj. downy, hairy, shaggy. 2 m. velvet; plush.

**vena** f. ANAT., BOT. vein. 2 vein [in wood, marble, etc.]. 3 GEOL., MIN. vein, seam, lode. 4 vena or ~ de agua, flow of water underground. 5 poetical inspiration: estar en ~, to be inspired. 6 strain, streak: tener una ~ de loco, to have a strain of madness. 7 darle a uno la ~ de, to take it into one's head. 8 estar de ~, to be in the mood [for something].

**venablo** m. javelin, dart: echar venablos, fig. to be furious.

**venación** f. venerry, hunting.

**venado** m. deer, stag. 2 deer meat, venison.

**venal** adj. venous. 2 salable. 3 venal.

**venalidad** f. venality.

**venatorio, -ria** adj. venatic.

**vencedor, -ra** adj. vanquishing, conquering. 2 m.-f. vanquisher, conqueror; victor: salir ~, to win, gain the victory, be the victor.

**vencejo** m. ORN. black martin, European swift. 2 withe, band, etc., for tying sheaves.

**vencer** tr. to vanquish, conquer, beat, defeat. 2 to overcome, overpower. 3 to overcome, surmount. 4 to conquer, subdue [passions]. 5 to surpass, outdo, excel. 6 to prevail upon, persuade. 7 to turn, incline [a thing]. 8 intr. COM. to fall due, mature; to expire. 9 to win, be the victor. 10 ref. to control oneself. 11 to incline to a side.

**vencetósigo** m. BOT. swallowwort.

**vencida** f. VENCIMIENTO 1. 2 ir de ~, to be nearly beaten, conquered or finished.

**vencido, -da** *p. p.* of VENCER. *2 adj.* COM. mature, due.

**vencimiento** *m.* vanquishment, defeat. *2* COM. maturity, coming due; expiration.

**venda** *f.* bandage. *2* regal fillet.

**vendaje** *m.* SURG. bandage, dressing.

**vendar** *tr.* SURG. to bandage. *2 fig.* to blind, obfuscate. *3 ~ los ojos,* to blindfold.

**vendaval** *m.* strong south wind. *2* gale.

**vendedor, -ra** *adj.* selling. *2 m.-f.* seller. *3 m.* salesman. *4 f.* saleswoman, salesgirl.

**vender** *tr.* to sell [goods, etc.]. *2* to sell, sell out [betray]. *3 ref.* to sell, be sold, be for sale: *se vende,* for sale. *4* to sell oneself. *5* to give oneself away, betray one's feelings, etc. *6 fig.* venderse caro, to be seldom seen, be quite a stranger. *7 fig. venderse por,* to pretend to be.

**vendí,** *pl.* **-dies** *m.* COM. certificate of sale.

**vendible** *adj.* salable, vendible, marketable.

**vendimia** *f.* vintage, grape-gathering. *2 fig.* rich profit.

**vendimiador, -ra** *m.-f.* vintager, grape-gatherer.

**vendimiar** *tr.* to gather [grapes]. *2 fig.* to reap [an unjust profit]. *3 coll.* to kill, murder.

**vendré, vendría,** etc. *irr.* V. VENIR.

**venduta** *f.* (Am.) auction, public sale.

**Venecia** *f. pr. n.* GEOG. Venice [city].

**veneciano, -na** *adj.* Venetian.

**veneno** *m.* poison, venom. *2 fig.* venom [malignity].

**venenosidad** *f.* poisonousness, venomousness.

**venenoso, -sa** *adj.* poisonous, venomous, baneful.

**venera** *f.* pilgrim's scallop shell. *2* badge of a military order. *3* spring [of water].

**venerable** *adj.* venerable.

**veneración** *f.* veneration. *2* worship.

**venerando, -da** *adj.* venerable.

**venerar** *tr.* to venerate. *2* ECCL. to worship.

**venéreo, -a** *adj.* venereal. *2 m.* venereal disease.

**venero** *m.* spring [of water]. *2 fig.* source, origin. *3* MIN. bed, lode. *4* hour mark [on sundial].

**venezolano, -na** *adj.-s.* Venezuelan.

**vengador, -ra** *adj.* avenging, revenging. *2 m.-f.* avenger, revenger.

**venganza** *f.* vengeance, revenge.

**vengar** *tr.* to avenge. *2 ref.* to avenge oneself, to take revenge.

**vengativo, -va** *adj.* revengeful, vindicative.

**vengo, venga,** etc. V. VENIR.

**venia** *f.* permission, leave. *2* bow [with the head]. *3* pardon, forgiveness.

**venial** *adj.* venial.

**venida** *f.* coming, arrival. *2* return. *3* flood, freshet. *4* FENC. attack. *5 fig.* impetuosity, rashness.

**venidero, -ra** *adj.* coming, future: *en lo ~,* for the future, in future. *2 m. pl.* successors, posterity.

**venido, -da** *adj.* come: *bien ~,* welcome.

**venir** *intr.* to come [move hitherward; approach; be the next; appear; arise, result, follow; happen]: *el mes que viene,* next month. *2* to come [in order or succession]. *3* to come [to the mind], occur. *4* [of a desire, pain, etc.] to be felt: *me vino el deseo de,* I felt the desire of. *5 ~ bien,* to fit, suit, become; *~ mal,* not to fit, suit or become. *6 esto no me va ni me viene,* that does not concern or affect me. *7 vino a conseguir lo que se proponía,* he ended by attaining his ends; *esto viene a pesar dos libras,* this must weigh about two pounds. *8 ~ a las manos,* to come to blows. *9 ~ al caso,* to be relevant. *10 ~ a menos,* to decay, decline. *11 ~ al pelo, ~ de perilla,* to be

opportune. *12 ~ en,* to decide, resolve upon. *13 ~ en conocimiento,* to come to know. *14 ~ sobre,* to fall upon. *15 ¿a qué viene eso?,* what is the purpose of that? *16 en lo por ~,* hereafter, for the future. *17 venga lo que viniere,* come what will. *18 intr.-ref.* to yield, submit, agree. *19 ref.* to come, to return. *20* [of bread, wine] to ferment. *21 venirse abajo, a tierra,* to fall, collapse. *22 venirse al suelo,* to fall to the ground. ‖ CONJUG.: INDIC. Pres.: *vengo, vienes, viene, venimos, venís, vienen.* ‖ Pret.: *vine, viniste,* etc. ‖ Fut.: *vendré, vendrás,* etc. ‖ COND.: *vendría, vendrías,* etc. ‖ SUBJ. Pres.: *venga, vengas,* etc. ‖ Imperf.: *viniera, vinieras,* etc., or *viniese, vinieses,* etc. ‖ Fut.: *viniere, vinieres,* etc. ‖ IMPER.: *ven, venga; vengamos,* venid, *vengan.* ‖ PAST. P.: *venido.* ‖ GER.: *viniendo.*

**venoso, -sa** *adj.* venous. *2* veiny, veined.

**venta** *f.* sale, selling: *~ al por mayor,* wholesale; *~ al por menor,* retail sale, retailing; *~ pública,* public auction sale; *de ~, en ~,* for sale. *2* roadside inn.

**ventada** *f.* blast, gust of wind.

**ventaja** *f.* advantage. *2* odds [given at play]. *3* gain, profit. *4* extra pay.

**ventajoso, -sa** *adj.* advantageous. *2* profitable.

**ventalla** *f.* MACH. valve. *2* BOT. valve [of a pod].

**ventana** *f.* window; casement; sash: *~ de guillotina,* sash window. *2* ANAT. fenestra. *3 ~ de la nariz,* nostril.

**ventanaje** *m.* ARCH. fenestration.

**ventanal** *m.* large window, church window.

**ventanear** *intr.* coll. to be often at the window.

**ventanico** *m.* VENTANILLO.

**ventanilla** *f. dim.* small window. *2* window [of a carriage, ticket office, bank teller, etc.], wicket. *3 ~ de la nariz,* nostril.

**ventanillo** *m. dim.* small window. *2* peephole, wicket [in a door].

**ventano** *m.* small window.

**ventarrón** *m.* stiff wind, gale.

**ventear** *impers.* [of the wind] to blow. *2 tr.* [of animals] to sniff, scent, wind. *3 fig.* to investigate, inquire. *4* to air [expose to the wind]. *5 ref.* to become spoiled in the air. *6 coll.* to break wind.

**ventero, -ra** *adj.* scenting [dog]. *2 m.-f.* roadside innkeeper.

**ventilación** *f.* ventilation. *2* discussion, elucidation.

**ventilador** *m.* ventilator. *2* ventilating fan.

**ventilar** *tr.* to air, ventilate. *2* to discuss, clear up, elucidate.

**ventisca** *f.* snowstorm, blizzard, snowdrift.

**ventiscar** *impers.* to snow and blow.

**ventisquear** *impers.* VENTISCAR.

**ventisquero** *m.* VENTISCA. *2* height in a mountain most exposed to snowstorms. *3* snowdrift, glacier.

**ventolera** *f.* gust of wind. *2* pinwheel [toy]. *3 coll.* vanity, haughtiness. *4 coll.* whim, sudden fancy.

**ventolina** *f.* NAUT. light variable wind.

**ventor, -ra** *adj.-m.* scenting, pointer [dog].

**ventorrero** *m.* high, windy place.

**ventorrillo** *m.* small roadside inn. *2* lunchhouse in the country.

**ventorro** *m.* VENTORRILLO 1.

**ventosa** *f.* vent, air hole. *2* ZOOL. sucker, sucking disk. *3* SURG. cupping; cupping glass.

**ventosear** *intr.-ref.* to break wind.

**ventosidad** *f.* flatulence, windiness. *2* wind [in intestines or being expelled].

**ventoso, -sa** *adj.* windy, wind-swept. *2* windy [day, weather]. *3* flatulent.
**ventral** *adj.* ventral.
**ventrecha** *f.* belly [of fishes].
**ventregada** *f.* litter, brood. *2* rush [of things].
**ventrera** *f.* bellyband.
**ventricular** *adj.* ventricular.
**ventrículo** *m.* ANAT. ZOOL. ventricle.
**ventrílocuo, -cua** *m.-f.* ventriloquist.
**ventriloquia** *f.* ventriloquism.
**ventrudo, -da** *adj.* big-bellied.
**ventura** *f.* happiness. *2* luck, fortune. *3* chance, hazard; risk: *a la* ~, at a venture, at hazard; *por* ~, perhaps. *4 buena* ~, BUENAVENTURA.
**venturado, -da** *adj.* VENTUROSO.
**venturanza** *f.* happiness.
**venturero, -ra** *adj.* taking occasional jobs.
**venturoso -sa** *adj.* happy, lucky, fortunate.
**Venus** *m.* ASTR. Venus. *2 f.* MYTH. & fig. Venus. *3* (not cap.) venery.
**venustez, venustidad** *f.* beauty, gracefulness.
**venusto, -ta** *adj.* beautiful, graceful.
**veo, vea,** etc. *irr.* V. VER.
1) **ver** *m.* sight, sense of sight. *2* aspect, appearance, look, looks: *tener buen* ~, to be goodlooking, to have a good appearance. *3* opinion, way of thinking; *a mi* ~, in my opinion.
2) **ver** *tr.* to see [in practically every sense]: ~ *las estrellas*, fig. to see stars; ~ *visiones*, to see things, to dream; *hacer* ~, to show, demonstrate; *a más* ~, *hasta más* ~, coll. so long; *a* ~, *veamos*, let's see. *2* to look, look at: *vea usted esto*, look at this. *3* LAW to try [a case]. *4* ~ *venir*, fig. to wait and see. *5* ~ *venir a uno*, fig. to see what [someone] is up to. *6 no poder* ~, not to be able to bear; to detest. *7 intr.* ~ *de*, to try to. *8 ref.* to be seen. *9* to be obvious. *10* to see oneself. *11* to be: *verse obligado a*, to be obliged to. *12 verse con*, to see, meet, have a talk with. *13 véase*, see [in references]. *14 ya se ve*, of course, certainly. ‖ CONJUG.: INDIC. Pres.: *veo, ves, ve; vemos, veis, ven*. │ Imperf.: *veía, veías,* etc. │ Pret.: *vi, viste,* etc. │ Fut.: *veré, verás,* etc. │ COND.: *vería, verías,* etc. │ SUBJ. Pres.: *vea, veas, vea,* etc. │ Imperf.: *viera, vieras,* etc., or *viese, vieses,* etc. │ Fut.: *viere, vieres,* etc. │ IMPER.: *ve, vea; veamos, ved, vean.* │ PAST. P.: *visto.* │ GER.: *viendo.*
**vera** *f.* border, side: *a la* ~ *de*, near, beside.
**veracidad** *f.* veracity, truthfulness.
**veranada** *f.* summer season [for pasturing].
**veranadero** *m.* summer pasture.
**veranda** *f.* veranda(h.
**veraneante** *m.-f.* summer resident, summer vacationist.
**veranear** *intr.* to summer.
**veraneo** *m.* summering, summer vacation.
**veraniego, -ga** *adj.* [pertaining to] summer. *2* sickly in summer. *3* fig. light, unimportant.
**veranillo** *m.* ~ *de San Martín*, Indian summer.
**verano** *m.* summer [season].
**veras** *f.* truth, reality; earnestness: *de* ~, real, genuine; indeed, really; in earnest.
**veratro** *m.* BOT. white hellebore.
**veraz** *adj.* veracious, truthful.
**verba** *f.* loquacity, talkativeness.
**verbal** *adj.* verbal, oral. *2* GRAM. verbal.
**verbalismo** *m.* verbalism.
**verbasco** *m.* BOT. mullein, great mullein.
**verbena** *f.* BOT. verbena, vervain. *2* night festival on the eve of a saint's day.
**verbenáceo, -a** *adj.* BOT. verbenaceous.

**verbenear** *intr.* HORMIGUEAR.
**verbigracia** *adv.* for example, for instance.
**Verbo** *m. pr. n.* THEOL. Word [second person of the Trinity].
**verbo** *m.* word. *2* GRAM. verb.
**verborrea** *f.* excessive verbosity.
**verbosidad** *f.* verbosity, wordiness.
**verboso, -sa** *adj.* verbose, wordy.
**verdad** *f.* truth: *decir cuatro verdades*, to give a piece of one's mind; *faltar a la* ~, to lie; *ser* ~, to be true; *a la* ~, *en* ~, in truth, truly, really; *¿no es* ~?, *¿verdad?*, isn't that so?
**verdaderamente** *adv.* truly, really; indeed.
**verdadero, -ra** *adj.* true. *2* real, genuine; actual. *3* veracious, truthful.
**verdal** *adj.* green-coloured even when ripe [fruit].
**verdasca** *f.* switch, twig [cut from tree].
**vesdascazo** *m.* blow with a switch.
**verde** *adj.* green [green-coloured; verdant; unripe; sour]: *están verdes*, fig. sour grapes; *poner* ~, fig. to abuse, rake over the coals. *2* inmature. *3* young [years]. *4* gay, merry [old man; widow]. *5* risky, off-colour. *6 m.* green [colour]. *7* green barley or grass [given to horses]. *8* verdure, foliage.
**verdear** *intr.* to show green. *2* to be greenish. *3* [of fields, trees, etc.]. to green [become green].
**verdeceledón** *m.* celadon, celadon green.
**verdecer** *intr.* VERDEAR 3.
**verdegay** *adj.* light-green. *2 m.* light green.
**verdeguear** *intr.* VERDEAR.
**verdemar** *adj.* sea-green. *2 m.* sea green.
**verderol, verderón** *m.* ORN. green-finch. *2* ZOOL. cockle [mollusk].
**verdete** *m.* verdigris.
**verdín** *m.* verdure, fresh greenness [of plants]. *2* pond scum. *3* green mould. *4* verdigris.
**verdinegro, -gra** *adj.* dark green.
**verdiseco, -ca** *adj.* half dry [plant].
**verdolaga** *f.* BOT. purslane.
**verdor** *m.* greenness, green colour. *2* verdure, verdancy [of vegetation]. *3* freshness, vigour. *4 pl.* youth, young days.
**verdoso, -sa** *adj.* greenish.
**verdoyo** *m.* pond scum; green mould.
**verdugado** *m.* hoopskirt, farthingale.
**verdugo** *m.* executioner, hangman. *2* fig. cruel punisher or tormenter. *3* shoot, sucker [of a tree]. *4* slender estoc or rapier. *5* scourge, lash, switch. *6* wale, weal, welt. *7* VERDUGADO.
**verdugón** *m.* shoot, sucker [of a tree]. *2* wale, weal, welt.
**verduguillo** *m.* dim. of VERDUGO. *2* narrow razor.
**verdulera** *f.* greengrocer [woman]. *2* fig. coarse woman, fishwife.
**verdulería** *f.* greengrocery, greengrocer's shop.
**verdulero** *m.* greengrocer.
**verdura** *f.* greenness, green colour. *2* verdure, verdancy. *3* PAINT. foliage. *4 sing.-pl.* greens, vegetables [as food].
**verdusco, -ca** *adj.* dark greenish.
**verecundia** *f.* shame, modesty, bashfulness.
**verecundo, -da** *adj.* bashful, modest.
**vereda** *f.* path, footpath: *meter por* ~, fig. to set aright.
**veredicto** *m.* verdict.
**verga** *f.* NAUT. yard. *2* penis. *3* steel bow [of a crossbow].
**vergajazo** *m.* slash or blow with a pizzle.
**vergajo** *m.* pizzle [used as a flogging instrument].
**vergel** *f.* flower and fruit garden.

**vergonzante** *adj.* bashful, shamefaced.
**vergonzoso, -sa** *adj.* shameful, disgraceful, scandalous. *2* private [parts]. *3 m.-f.* bashful person.
**vergüenza** *f.* shame [feeling]; bashfulness, shyness, confusion; modesty: *darse* ~, *darle a uno* ~, to be ashamed; to be shy. *2* shame, disgrace; scandal: *ser una* ~, to be a shame, to be a scandal. *3* honour, self-respect, dignity. *4 no tener* ~, to be shameless, be a rascal. *5 sacar a la* ~, to put in the pillory. *6 pl.* privy parts.
**vericueto** *m.* rough, pathless place.
**verídico, -ca** *adj.* truthful, veridical.
**verificación** *f.* verification. *2* test [of gas meter, etc.]. *3* fulfilment, coming true.
**verificar** *tr.* to verify [establish the truth of]. *2* to check; to test [a gas meter, etc.]. *3* to accomplish, carry out. *4 ref.* to be accomplished; to take place. *5* to come true.
**verija** *f.* pubes, region of the genitals.
**veril** *m.* NAUT. edge of a sandbank or shoal.
**verisímil** *adj.* VEROSÍMIL.
**verismo** *m.* verism.
**verja** *f.* gate [made of a grating]; window grate or grating. *2* iron railing [enclosure].
**vermicida** *adj.* vermicidal. *2 m.* vermicide.
**vermicular** *adj.* vermicular.
**vermiforme** *adj.* vermiform.
**vermífugo, -ga** *adj.* vermifugal. *2 m.* vermifuge.
**vermut** *m.* vermouth.
**vernáculo, -la** *adj.* vernacular.
**vernal** *adj.* vernal: *equinoccio* ~, vernal equinox.
**vernier** *m.* vernier.
**vero** *m.* marten [fur]. *2 pl.* HER. vair.
**veronal** *m.* veronal.
**verónica** *f.* BOT. veronica. *2* BULLF. waiting for bull's attack with cape extended in both hands.
**verosímil** *adj.* likely, probable, credible, verisimilar.
**verosimilitud** *f.* verisimilitude, probability.
**verraco** *m.* boar [male uncastrated pig].
**verraquear** *intr.* to grunt, grumble. *2* [of a child] to cry long and loud.
**verraquera** *f.* violent crying [of a child]. *2* (Am.) drunkenness.
**verriondo, -da** *adj.* rutting, in heat [animal].
**verruga** *f.* wart. *2* coll. nuisance.
**verrugoso, -sa** *adj.* warty.
**versado, -da** *adj.* versed, conversant.
**versal** *adj.-f.* PRINT. capital [letter].
**versalita** *adj.-f.* PRINT. small capital [letter].
**Versalles** *m. pr. n.* GEOG. Versailles.
**versar** *intr.* to turn, go around. *2* ~ *acerca de* or *sobre*, to deal with, treat of or on. *3 ref.* to become versed.
**versátil** *adj.* versatile, fickle. *2* BOT., ZOOL. versatile.
**versatilidad** *f.* versatility, fickleness. *2* BOT., ZOOL. versatileness.
**versículo** *m.* ECCL. verse, versicle.
**versificación** *f.* versification.
**versificador, -ra** *m.-f.* versifier, verse maker.
**versificar** *tr.-intr.* to versify.
**versión** *f.* version.
**versista** *m.-f.* versifier; poetaster.
**verso** *adj.* TRIG. versed. *2 m.* verse, poem. *3* verse, line: ~ *blanco*, *libre* or *suelto*, blank verse. *4* ECCL. verse, versicle.
**versta** *f.* verst.
**vértebra** *f.* ANAT. vertebra.
**vertebrado, -da** *adj.* vertebrate, vertebrated. *2 m.* ZOOL. vertebrate.

**vertebral** *adj.* vertebral.
**vertedera** *f.* AGR. mouldboard [of a plough].
**vertedero** *m.* sink; dumping place. *2* spillway.
**vertedor** *m.* spillway, drain. *2* grocer's scoop. *3* NAUT. boat scoop.
**verter** *tr.* to pour. *2* to spill, shed. *3* to cast, shed [light, etc.]. *4* to empty, dump. *5* to translate. *6* to emit, utter [opinions, etc.]. *7 intr.* [of a stream] to run, flow. *8 ref.* to spill, flow, empty. ‖ CONJUG. like *entender*.
**vertible** *adj.* changeable.
**vertical** *adj.* vertical. *2 f.* vertical line. *3 m.* ASTR. vertical circle.
**verticalidad** *f.* verticality.
**vértice** *m.* vertex, apex. *2* GEOM., ANAT. vertex.
**verticilado, -da** *adj.* BOT. verticillate.
**verticilo** *m.* BOT. verticil, whorl.
**vertiente** *adj.* pouring, flowing. *2 f.* GEOG. slope [of a continent, etc.]. *3* ARCH. slope [of a roof].
**vertiginoso, -sa** *adj.* vertiginous, dizzy, giddy. *2* rapid.
**vértigo** *m.* vertigo, dizziness, giddiness. *2* fig. abnormally hurried activity. *3* fit of insanity.
**vesania** *f.* vesania, insanity.
**vesánico, -ca** *adj.* insane. *2 m.-f.* insane person.
**vesicante** *adj.-m.* vesicant, vesicatory.
**vesícula** *f.* vesicle, small blister. *2* ANAT., BOT., ZOOL. vesicle: ~ *biliar*, gall bladder.
**Véspero** *m.* Vesper, evening star.
**vespertino, -na** *adj.* vespertine, evening.
**Vesta** *f. pr. n.* MYTH. Vesta.
**vestal** *adj.-f.* vestal.
**veste** *f.* poet. dress, clothing.
**Vestfalia** *f. pr. n.* GEOG. Westphalia.
**vestibular** *adj.* ANAT. vestibular.
**vestíbulo** *m.* vestibule, hall, lobby. *2* ANAT. vestibule.
**vestido** *m.* dress, clothes, garb, costume, suit: ~ *de etiqueta*, evening dress; ~ *de noche*, evening gown. *2* fig. dress, vesture, covering.
**vestidura** *f.* clothing, vesture. *2 pl.* ECCL. vestiments.
**vestigio** *m.* vestige, trace, sign. *2 pl.* ruins, remains.
**vestiglo** *m.* horrible monster.
**vestimenta** *f.* VESTIDO. *2 pl.* VESTIDURAS.
**vestir** *tr.* to clothe, dress, garb, attire. *2* to make clothes for. *3* to clothe, cover, deck, adorn. *4* to cloak, disguise. *5* to put on; to wear [a dress or garment]. *6 intr.* to dress, be dressed [in a specified way]: ~ *de negro*, to dress in black. *7* [of a garment, material, colour] to be fit for dressing, give a well-dressed appearance. *8 ref.* to dress, dress oneself. *9* fig. to be clothed or covered. *10* to assume an air. ‖ CONJUG. like *servir*.
**vestuario** *m.* apparel, wardrobe, clothes, dress. *2* MIL. clothing, uniform. *3* THEAT. dressing rooms.
**Vesubio** *m. pr. n.* GEOG. Vesuvius.
**veta** *f.* GEOL. vein. *2* MIN. vein, lode. *3* vein [in wood or stone]. *4* streak, stripe.
**vetar** *tr.* to veto, put one's veto on.
**veteado, -da** *adj.* veined, streaked, streaky.
**vetear** *tr.* to vein, streak, variegate with stripes.
**veterano, -na** *adj.-n.* veteran.
**veterinaria** *f.* veterinary medicine.
**veterinario** *m.* veterinarian, veterinary.
**veto** *m.* veto.
**vetustez** *f.* antiquity, great age.
**vetusto, -ta** *adj.* very ancient or old.
**vez**, *pl.* **veces** *f.* turn [in order or alternation]: *le llegó la* ~, it was his turn; *a su* ~, in turn, in his,

her, etc., turn; on his, her, etc., part. *2* time [instance, occasion]: *a la ~*, at one time, at the same time; *a la ~ que*, while; *alguna ~*, sometimes; [in questions] ever; *alguna*, or *una, que otra ~*, *tal cual ~*, once in a while; *a veces*, sometimes; *cada ~*, every time; *cada ~ más*, more and more; *de una ~*, at once; *una ~ para siempre*, once for all; *de ~ en cuando*, from time to time; *dos veces mayor que*, twice as large as; *otra ~*, again; some other time; *pocas*, or *raras veces*, seldom, rarely; *tal ~*, perhaps, maybe; *una ~*, once; *una ~ hecho esto*, after doing this; *una ~ que*, since, inasmuch as. *3* stead, place: *en ~ de*, instead of; in place of. *4 pl. hacer las veces de*, to serve as, take the place of.

**vi** *pret*. of VER.

**vía** *f.* path, road, way, street: *~ aérea*, airway; *~ Apia*, Appian Way; *~ férrea*, railway, railroad; *~ pública*, public way, street, thoroughfare; *vías de comunicación*, communications; *por la ~ de*, vía. *2* RLY. track: *ancho de ~*, gauge; *~ muerta*, sidetrack. *3* ANAT. duct. *4* CHEM. process: *~ húmeda*, wet process. *5* way, manner: *por ~ de*, by way of, as. *6* NAUT. *~ de agua*, leak. *7* LAW *~ ejecutiva*, seizure, attachment. *8* ASTR. *Vía Láctea*, Milky Way. *9* MED. *por ~ bucal*, orally. *10 pl.* ANAT. tract: *vías urinarias*, urinary tract. *11 estar en vías de*, to be on the process of, to be on the way to.

**viabilidad** *f.* viability. *2* feasibility, practicability.

**viable** *adj.* viable. *2* feasible, practicable.

**Vía Crucis** *m.* Via Crucis, way of the Cross.

**viaducto** *m.* viaduct.

**viajante** *adj.* travelling. *2 m.* traveller, commercial traveller.

**viajar** *intr.* to travel, journey, voyage.

**viajata** *f.* coll. long walk, excursion.

**viaje** *m.* travel, journey, voyage, trip: *~ de ida y vuelta, ~ redondo*, round trip; *de ~*, travelling; *¡buen ~!*, bon voyage! *2* travel book. *4* ARCH. obliquity.

**viajero, -ra** *adj.* travelling [that travels]. *2 m.-f.* traveller; passenger.

**vial** *adj.* pertaining to roads or streets. *2 m.* avenue, lane [way among trees or shrubs].

**vialidad** *f.* road service, street service.

**vianda** *f. sing. & pl.* food, viands.

**viandante** *m.-f.* traveller, itinerant. *2* tramp.

**viaticar** *tr.* ECCL. to administer the viaticum to.

**viático** *m.* viaticum [travel allowance]. *2* ECCL. viaticum.

**víbora** *f.* ZOOL. viper. *2* fig. viper [person].

**viborezno, -na** *adj.* viperine. *2 m.* young viper.

**vibración** *f.* vibration, quivering. *2* PHYS. vibration.

**vibrante** *adj.* vibrant. *2* PHONET. thrilled [consonant].

**vibrar** *tr.* to vibrate. *2* to roll [utter with a thrill]. *3 intr.* to vibrate, quiver.

**vibrátil** *adj.* vibratile.

**vibratorio, -ria** *adj.* vibratory.

**vibrión** *m.* BACT. vibrion.

**viburno** *m.* BOT. viburnum.

**vicaría** *f.* vicarship. *2* vicarage.

**vicario, -ria** *m.-f.* vicar [deputy, substitute].

**vicealmirante** *m.* vice-admiral.

**vicecanciller** *m.* vice-chancellor.

**vicecónsul** *m.* vice-consul.

**vicenal** *adj.* vicennial.

**Vicente** *m. pr. n.* Vincent.

**vicepresidencia** *f.* vice-presidency.

**vicepresidente, -ta** *m.-f.* vice-president. *2 f.* wife of a vice-president.

**vicerrector** *m.* vice-rector.

**vicesecretario, -ria** *m.-f.* vice-secretary.

**vicésimo, -ma** *adj.-m.* twentieth.

**vicetesorero, -ra** *m.-f.* assistant treasurer.

**viceversa** *adv.* vice versa. *2 m.* illogical thing.

**viciado, -da** *p. p.* of VICIAR. *2* vitiated; foul.

**viciar** *tr.* to vitiate, corrupt, deprave. *2* to adulterate. *3* to vitiate, nullify. *4* to pervert, misconstrue. *5 ref.* to become vitiated. *6* to give oneself up to vice. *7* to contract a habit or a bad habit.

**vicio** *m.* vice [evil conduct, wickedness, corruption, etc.]. *2* vice, defect. *3* habit, bad habit. *4* overindulgence, pampering. *5* AGR. excessive luxuriance. *6* warping [in boards, etc.]. *7 quejarse de ~*, to complain without reason, out of habit.

**vicioso, -sa** *adj.* vicious [of the nature of vice; addicted to vice; faulty]. *2* spoiled [child]. *3* abundant, luxuriant. *4 m.-f.* vicious person.

**vicisitud** *f.* vicissitude.

**víctima** *f.* victim.

**victo** *m.* daily sustenance.

**¡víctor!** *interj.-m.* ¡VÍTOR!

**victorear** *tr.* VITOREAR.

**victoria** *f.* victory. *2* victoria [carriage]. *3* BOT. *~ regia*, victoria, victoria regia.

**victoriano, -na** *adj.* Victorian.

**victorioso, -sa** *adj.* victorious.

**vicuña** *f.* vicuña [animal; wool; fabric].

**vid** *f.* BOT. vine, grapevine.

**vida** *f.* life [in practically every sense]: *~ airada*, loose life, prostitution; *~ de perros*, fig. dog's life; *~ mía, mi ~*, my life, dearest; *dar mala ~ a*, to treat ill; *darse buena ~*, to live comfortably; *dar ~*, to give life, to enliven; *jugarse la ~*, to take one's life in one's hand; *tener siete vidas como los gatos*, to bear a charmed life; *con ~*, in life, alive, living; *de por ~*, for life; *en ~*, while living, during life; *en la ~, en mi [tu, su] ~*, never; *¡por ~!*, by Jove! *2* activity, animation, liveliness. *3* living, livelihood: *ganarse la ~*, to earn one's living.

**vide** *Lat.* vide, see [in references].

**vidente** *adj.* seeing, sighted [not blind]. *2 m.-f.* sighted person. *3* seer; prophet.

**vidita** *f.* coll. dearest, darling.

**vidriado, -da** *adj.* glazed [pottery]. *2 m.* glazing [of pottery]. *3* glazed pottery.

**vidriar** *tr.* to glaze [pottery]. *2 ref.* to become glassy or brittle.

**vidriera** *f.* glass window, glass door, French window, glass partition. *2* (Am.) shopwindow.

**vidriería** *f.* glassworks. *2* glass shop. *3* glassware.

**vidriero** *m.* glassworker. *2* glazier. *3* glass dealer.

**vidrio** *m.* glass [substance, article made of glass]: *~ de color*, stained glass; *~ deslustrado*, ground glass; *~ tallado*, cut glass. *2* pane, glass pane [of window or door].

**vidriosidad** *f.* vitreousness; brittleness. *2* touchiness.

**vidrioso, -sa** *adj.* brittle [as glass]. *2* slippery [from frost]. *3* glassy [eye]. *4* touchy.

**vidueño, viduño** *m.* variety or kind of grapevine.

**viejecito, -ta** *adj.* old, oldish. *2 m.-f.* old man, old woman.

**viejo, -ja** *adj.* old. *2* aged. *3* ancient, antique. *4* old-fashioned. *5 m.* old man: *~ verde*, gay old man, old rake. *6 f.* old woman.

**Viena** *f. pr. n.* GEOG. Vienna.

**viene, vienes, vienen** *irr.* V. VENIR.

**vienés, -sa** *adj.-n.* Viennese.
**vientecillo** *m. dim.* breeze, light wind.
**viento** *m.* wind: *corren malos vientos,* fig. things are not favourable; *ir ~ en popa,* to sail before the wind; fig. to be flourishing; *a los cuatro vientos,* to the four winds; *como el ~,* swiftly; *contra ~ y marea,* fig. against all odds. *2* smell, sense of smell [of some animals]. *3* ARTIL. windage. *4* guy [rope or chain].
**vientre** *m.* belly, paunch, venter. *2* bowels. *3* womb.
**viernes,** *pl.* **-nes** *m.* Friday: *Viernes Santo,* Good Friday; *comer de ~,* to fast, abstain from meat.
**vierteaguas,** *pl.* **-guas** *m.* ARCH. flashing.
**vierto, vierta,** etc., *irr.* V. VERTER.
**viga** *f.* beam, girder, joist, baulk, rafter: *~ maestra,* summer.
**vigencia** *f.* [of a law, a custom, etc.] state of being in force, in use.
**vigente** *adj.* in force, in use [law custom, etc.].
**vigésimo, -ma** *adj.-m.* twentieth.
**vigía** *m.-f.* watch, lookout [man]. *2 f.* watchtower, lookout. *3* NAUT. rock, shoal.
**vigilancia** *f.* vigilance, watchfulness. *2* watch watching, survellance.
**vigilante** *adj.* vigilant, watchful, careful. *2 m.* watch, watchman, guard.
**vigilar** *intr.* to watch, keep guard, take or have care. *2 tr.* to watch over, keep guard on; look out, for, take or have care of.
**vigilia** *f.* vigil, wakefulness. *2* night study. *3* eve. *4* ECCL. vigil. *5* ECCL. abstinence of meat.
**vigor** *m.* vigour, vigor. *2* force, effect [of a law]: *entrar en ~,* to go into effect.
**vigorizador, -ra** *adj.* invigorating. *2 m.* invigorant, tonic.
**vigorizar** *tr.* to invigorate; to strengthen. *2 ref.* to invigorate [gain vigour].
**vigoroso, -sa** *adj.* vigorous; lusty.
**viguería** *f.* beams or girders [of a building].
**vigués, -sa** *adj.-n.* of Vigo.
**vigueta** *f. dim.* small beam or joist.
**vihuela** *f.* MUS. a kind of guitar.
**vil** *adj.* vile, worthless, base, low, despicable. *2 m.-f.* treacherous person.
**vilano** *m.* BOT. pappus. *2* BOT. thistle flower.
**vileza** *f.* vileness, baseness; infamy.
**vilipendiar** *tr.* to vilipend, revile, denigrate.
**vilipendio** *m.* contempt, revilement. *2* opprobium.
**vilmente** *adj.* vilely, basely, infamously.
**vilo (en)** *adv.* suspended, in the air. *2* in suspense.
**vilordo, -da** *adj.* slow, lazy, slothful.
**vilorta** *f.* hoop made of a twisted twig. *2* MACH. washer. *3* game like lacrosse.
**vilorto** *m.* VILORTA 1. *2* BOT. a kind of clematis.
**villa** *f.* villa [country residence]. *2* town, market town. *3* town council.
**Villadiego** *pr. n.* of a Spanish town: *coger* or *tomar las de ~,* to decamp, bolt, go away.
**villaje** *m.* village.
**villanada** *f.* infamy, despicable act.
**villanaje** *m.* villeinage, villenage. *2* peasantry.
**villancico** *m.* Christmas carol.
**villanesco, -ca** *adj.* rustic.
**villanía** *f.* status of a villain; humble birth. *2* villainy, infamy, despicable act. *3* fig. vile remark.
**villano, -na** *adj.* of humble birth. *2* rustic, impolite. *3* villainous, base, despicable. *4 m.-f.* villain, villein; rustic, peasant. *5* knave, scoundrel.

**villar** *m.* village.
**villorrio** *m.* small village, mean village.
**vinagre** *m.* vinegar. *2* fig. grouch.
**vinagrera** *f.* vinegar cruet or caster. *2* BOT. sorrel. *3* (Am.) heartburn. *4 pl.* casters, cruet stand.
**vinagrero, -ra** *m.-f.* vinegarer.
**vinagreta** *f.* COOK. vinaigrette sauce.
**vinagrillo** *m.* toilet vinegar.
**vinagroso, -sa** *adj.* vinegarish, vinegary.
**vinajera** *f.* ECCL. cruet [for wine or water in the mass]. *2 pl.* ECCL. set of two cruets and a tray.
**vinatería** *f.* wine trade. *2* wine shop.
**vinatero, -ra** *adj.* [pertaining to] wine. *2 m.* vintner, wine merchant.
**vinaza** *f.* wine drawn from lees.
**vincapervinca** *f.* BOT. periwinkle.
**vinculación** *f.* tying, attaching [esp. with immaterial bonds]. *2* LAW entailment.
**vincular** *tr.* to tie, attach [esp. with immaterial bonds]. *2* to ground, found [hopes, etc.]. *3* LAW to entail.
**vínculo** *m.* vinculum, tie, bond. *2* LAW entail.
**vindicación** *f.* vindication. *2* revenge.
**vindicar** *tr.* to vindicate [defend, justify]. *2* to avenge. *3* LAW to vindicate.
**vindicativo, -va** *adj.* vindicative. *2* vindictive.
**vindicta** *f.* revenge. *2 ~ pública,* public punishment, censure of public opinion.
**vine,** etc. *irr.* V. VENIR.
**vínico, -ca** *adj.* vinic.
**vinícola** *adj.* wine; vinegrowing.
**vinicultor, -ra** *m.-f.* viniculturist.
**vinicultura** *f.* viniculture, wine-making.
**viniera, viniese,** etc. *irr.* V. VENIR.
**vinilo** *m.* CHEM. vinyl.
**vinillo** *m. dim.* weak wine, light wine.
**vino** *m.* wine: *~ de mesa, ~ de pasto,* table wine; *~ de postre,* or *generoso,* strong old wine; *~ rancio,* fine old wine; *~ tinto,* red wine; *tener mal ~,* to be a quarrelsome drunk.
**vinolencia** *f.* excessive use of wine.
**vinolento, -ta** *adj.* too fond of wine.
**vinoso, -sa** *adj.* vinous.
**viña** *f.* vineyard: *ser una ~,* fig. to be a mine.
**viñador** *m.* vinegrower.
**viñedo** *m.* vineyard.
**viñeta** *f.* PRINT. vignette.
**viola** *f.* MUS. viola. *2* BOT. violet. *3 m.-f.* MUS. viola player.
**violáceo, -a** *adj.* violaceous.
**violación** *f.* violation.
**violado, -da** *adj.* violaceous [of violet colour]. *2 m.* violet [colour].
1) **violar** *m.* patch or bed of violets.
2) **violar** *tr.* to violate. *2* to spoil, tarnish.
**violencia** *f.* violence. *2* compulsion. *3* constraint. *4* rape.
**violentar** *tr.* to do violence to. *2* to break, break into. *3* to strain, distort. *4 ref.* to force oneself.
**violento, -ta** *adj.* violent. *2* forced, unnatural, strained. *3* constrained, embarrassed, ill at ease.
**violeta** *f.* BOT. violet. *2* violet [colour]. *3 adj.* violet, violet coloured.
**violetera** *f.* violet seller [woman or girl].
**violetero** *m.* small vase for violets.
**violín** *m.* MUS. violin, fiddle. *2* violin, violin player. *3* BILL. bridge, cue rest.
**violinista** *m.-f.* violinist.
**violón** *m.* MUS. bass viol: *tocar el ~,* coll. to do something nonsensical. *2* bass viol player.

**violoncelo** *m.* VIOLONCHELO.
**violonchelista** *m.-f.* violoncellist.
**violonchelo** *m.* MUS. violoncello.
**viperino, -na** *adj.* viperine. 2 viperish, viperous.
**vira** *f.* vire [arrow]. 2 welt [of a shoe].
**virada** *f.* NAUT. tack, tacking. 2 VIRAJE.
**virador** *m.* PHOT. toning bath. 2 NAUT. viol.
**virago** *f.* mannish woman.
**viraje** *m.* PHOT. toning. 2 AUTO. turn, turning.
**virar** *tr.* PHOT. to tone. 2 NAUT. to turn [the capstan]. 3 *tr.-intr.* NAUT. to tack, veer. 4 *intr.* AUTO. to turn.
**virazón** *f.* sea breeze.
**virgen** *adj.-n.* virgin. 2 *f. pr. n.* Virgin [Mary]: *la Santísima Virgen*, the Blessed Virgin.
**virgiliano, -na** *adj.* Virgilian.
**Virgilio** *m. pr. n.* Virgil.
**virginal** *adj.* virginal, virgin. 2 *m.* MUS. virginal.
**virgíneo, -a** *adj.* virginal.
**virginiano, -na** *adj.-n.* Virginian.
**virginidad** *f.* virginity.
**virgo** *m.* virginity. 2 (cap.) ASTR. Virgo.
**vírgula** *f.* short dash or line.
**viril** *adj.* virile. 2 manly. 3 *m.* clear glass [for protecting something]. 4 ECCL. small monstrance with a larger one.
**virilidad** *f.* virility. 2 manhood.
**virola** *f.* ferrule [ring]. 2 check ring on a goad.
**virolento, -ta** *adj.* having smallpox. 2 pockmarked. 7 *m.-f.* person with smallpox.
**virote** *m.* bolt [arrow]. 2 coll. solemn, straightbacked fellow.
**virotillo** *m.* ARCH. short upright brace.
**virreina** *f.* vice-queen, vicereine.
**virreinal** *adj.* viceregal.
**virreinato, virreino** *m.* viceroyship; viceroyalty.
**virrey** *m.* viceroy.
**virtual** *adj.* virtual. 2 tacit, implicit.
**virtualidad** *f.* virtuality.
**virtud** *f.* virtue: *en ~ de*, by, or in virtue of. 2 virtuousness. 3 *pl.* virtues [order of angels].
**virtuoso, -sa** *adj.* virtuous. 2 *m.-f.* virtuous person. 3 virtuoso.
**viruela** *f. sing.* or *pl.* MED. small pox, variola: *viruelas locas*, chicken pox. 2 pock, pock mark.
**virulencia** *f.* virulence.
**virulento, -ta** *adj.* virulent.
**virus** *m.* MED. virus. 2 poison, contagion.
**viruta** *f.* shaving [of wood or metal].
**visado** *m.* visa, visé.
**visaje** *m.* face, grimace; wry face.
**visar** *tr.* to visa, to visé. 2 ARTIL., SURV. to sight.
**viscacha** *f.* VIZCACHA.
**víscera** *f.* ANAT. internal organ. 2 *pl.* viscera.
**visceral** *adj.* visceral.
**visco** *m.* lime, birdlime.
**vis cómica** *f.* vis comica, ability to evoke mirth.
**viscosa** *f.* viscose.
**viscosidad** *f.* viscosity. 2 viscous matter.
**viscoso, -sa** *adj.* viscous, sticky. 2 PHYS. viscous.
**visera** *f.* peak [of a cap]. 2 visor [of a helmet]. 3 eyeshade.
**visibilidad** *f.* visibility.
**visible** *adj.* visible. 2 evident. 3 conspicuous.
**visigodo, -da** *adj.* Visigothic. 2 *m.-f.* Visigoth.
**visigótico, -ca** *adj.* Visigothic.
**visillo** *m.* window curtain, window shade.
**visión** *f.* vision, sight: *ver visiones*, to dream, be seeing things. 2 coll. sight, scarecrow [person].
**visionario, -ria** *adj.-n.* visionary [person].
**visir** *m.* vizier, vizir.

**visita** *f.* visit, call; social call: *~ de cumplido*, formal call; *hacer una ~*, to make or pay a call. 2 MED. visit. 3 visitor, guest: *tener visitas*, to have visitors, guests, company. 4 visitation, inspection.
**visitación** *f.* visit. 2 ECCL. (cap.) Visitation: *Visitación de la Virgen*, Visitation of Our Lady.
**visitador, -ra** *adj.* calling frequently, given to frequent calling. 2 *m.-f.* frequent caller. 3 *m.* visitor, inspector. 4 ECCL. visitator.
**visitante** *adj.* visiting, calling. 2 *m.-f.* visitor, caller, visitant.
**visitar** *tr.* to visit. 2 to search [goods at the customhouse]. 3 *ref.* to visit, call on each other. 4 [of a patient] to go to the doctor.
**visiteo** *m.* frequent visiting.
**visitero, -ra** *adj.* coll. fond of making calls.
**visivo, -va** *adj.* visive [serving for vision].
**vislumbrar** *tr.* to glimpse, catch a glimpse of, perceive indistinctly. 2 to sumise, conjecture. 3 *ref.* to appear or be perceived indistinctly. 4 to be conjectured.
**vislumbre** *f.* glimmer [faint gleam]. 2 glimpse, inkling, conjecture. 3 vague resemblance.
**viso** *m.* changeable luster or colour: *hacer visos* [of a fabric, etc.], to be changeable. 2 slip [undergarment worn under a thin dress]; coloured lining for a transparent cloth. 3 fig. appearance [of things]; 4 height, outlook. 5 *de ~*, notable, prominent [person].
**visón** *m.* ZOOL. mink, American mink.
**visor** *m.* PHOT. finder. 2 AER. bomb sight.
**visorio, -ria** *adj.* of sight, visual. 2 *m.* inspection by an expert.
**víspera** *f.* eve [day before]. 2 *sing.-pl.* eve [time just before]: *en vísperas de*, on the eve of. 3 ECCL. vespers. 4 HIST. *Vísperas Sicilianas*, Sicilian vespers.
**vista** *f.* sight, vision, view; eye, eyes: *~ cansada*, farsightedness; *~ corta*, nearsightedness; *doble ~*, second sight; *bajar la ~*, to look down; *dar ~ a*, to sight; *echar la ~ a*, fig. to choose; *estar a la ~*, to be on the look out; [of a thing] to be evident; *hacer la ~ gorda*, to wink at, to overlook; *torcer la ~*, to squint: *a la ~*, in sight, at sight, on sight; COM. at sight; *a primera ~*, at first sight; *a simple ~*, at a glance; with the naked eye; *a ~ de pájaro*, from a bird's-eye view; *de ~*, by sight; *hasta la ~*, so long. 2 view [scene, prospect]. 3 glance, brief look: *echar una ~*, to keep an eye on. 4 view [intention, design]. 5 view [consideration]: *en ~ de*, in view of, considering. 6 looks, aspect. 7 LAW trial. 8 *m. ~ de aduana*, customs officer. 9 *f. pl.* facings [of a garment]. 10 windows, etc., affording an outlook: *tener vistas a*, to look out on.
**vistazo** *m.* look, glance.
1) **viste, vistió, vistiera**, etc., *irr.* V. VESTIR.
2) **viste, vistes**, etc. *irr.* V. VER.
1) **visto, -ta** *p. p.* of VER. 2 *adj.* seen, looked, etc.: *bien ~*, looked on with approval; *mal ~*, looked on with disapproval, improper; *no ~, nunca ~*, extraordinary, unheard of; *por lo ~*, as it seems; *~ está, está ~*, it is evident. 3 *conj.* *~ que*, seeing, since, considering that. 4 *adv.-m.* *~ bueno*, (V.° B.°), correct, approved [in official documents]. 5 *m.* LAW whereas.
2) **visto, vista**, etc. *irr.* V. VESTIR.
**vistosidad** *f.* brightness, showiness.
**vistoso, -sa** *adj.* gay, bright, showy.
**visual** *adj.* visual. 2 *f.* line of sight.
**visualidad** *f.* gay, pleasant appearance.

**vital** *adj.* vital [of life, essential to life; essential].
**vitalicio, -cia** *adj.* [of pensions, grants, etc.] life, for life; [of an office] held for life. *2 m.* life-insurance policy. *3* life annuity.
**vitalidad** *f.* vitality.
**vitalismo** *m.* vitalism.
**vitamina** *f.* vitamin, vitamine.
**vitaminar** *tr.* to vitaminize.
**vitando, -da** *adj.* odious, execrable.
**vitela** *f.* vellum.
**vitelino** *adj.* vitelline.
**vitelo** *m.* BIOL. vitellus.
**vitícola** *adj.* viticultural, grape-growing.
**viticultor, -ra** *m.-f.* viticulturist, grape grower.
**viticultura** *f.* viticulture, grape growing.
**vitola** *f.* size of cigars. *2* MIL. ball or bullet calibre. *3* fig. mien, appearance [of a person].
**vítor** *m.* vivat, acclamation. *2 interj.* long live!, hurrah!
**vitorear** *tr.* to cheer, acclaim.
**vitrificación** *f.* vitrification.
**vitrificar** *tr.* to vitrify.
**vitrina** *f.* showcase, glass case. *2* (Am.) shopwindow.
**vitriolo** *m.* CHEM. vitriol: *aceite de* ~, oil of vitriol.
**vituallas** *f. pl.* victuals, provisions.
**vituallar** *tr.* AVITUALLAR.
**vituperable** *adj.* vituperable, blameworthy.
**vituperación** *f.* vituperation.
**vituperar** *tr.* to vituperate.
**vituperio** *m.* vituperation. *2* affront.
**viuda** *f.* widow. *2* dowager. *3* BOT. mourning bride, mourning widow.
**viudedad** *f.* widow's pension.
**viudez** *f.* widowhood.
**viudo, -da** *adj.* widowed. *2 m.* widower.
**viva** *m.* viva, vivat. *2 interj.* long live!, hurrah!
**vivac** *m.* VIVAQUE.
**vivacidad** *f.* vivacity, liveliness. *2* animal spirits. *3* brightness, vividness [of colour].
**vivandero, -ra** *m.* sutler.
**vivaque** *m.* MIL. bivouac.
**vivaquear** *intr.* MIL. to bivouac.
**vivar** *m.* warren. *2* fishpond, hatchery.
**vivaracho, -cha** *adj.* vivacious, lively, dapper.
**vivaz** *adj.* vivacious, lively, active, vigorous. *2* keen, quick-witted. *3* long-lived. *4* BOT. vivacious.
**víveres** *m. pl.* food, provisions, victuals.
**vivero** *m.* tree nursery. *2* seedbed. *3* fishpond, hatchery; vivarium.
**viveza** *f.* liveliness, sprightliness, briskness, quickness. *2* warmth, vehemence [in words]. *3* keenness, quick-wittedness. *4* brightness, gaiety, vividness. *5* sparkle [in the eyes]. *6* liveliness [of a description, etc.]. *7* lively remark. *8* thoughtless word or act.
**vividero, -ra** *adj.* habitable, livable.
**vívido, -da** *adj.* LIT. based on life or experience.
**vívido, -da** *adj.* vivid.
**vividor, -ra** *adj.* living. *2* long-lived. *3* thrifty. *4 m.-f.* living person. *5* thrifty person. *6 m.* chevalier of industry.
**vivienda** *f.* dwelling, house; housing.
**viviente** *adj.* living, alive. *2 m.* liver, living person. *3 los vivientes,* the living.
**vivificación** *f.* vivification.
**vivificador, -ra** *adj.* vivifying. *2 m.-f.* vivifier.
**vivificante** *adj.* vivifying, life-giving.
**vivificar** *tr.* to vivify. *2* to comfort, refresh.
**vivífico, -ca** *adj.* of life, springing from life.

**vivíparo, -ra** *adj.* ZOOL. viviparous.
1) **vivir** *m.* life, living: *de mal* ~, loose, disreputable [person]. *2* livelihood.
2) **vivir** *intr.* to live: ~ *bien,* to live honestly; to live comfortably; ~ *mal,* to live viciously; to live uncomfortably; ~ *de,* to live on or upon, to live by; ~ *en,* to live or dwell in; ~ *para ver,* live and learn!; *¿quién vive?,* MIL. who goes there?; *dar el quién vive,* MIL. to challenge. *2 tr.* to live [an experience or adventure].
**vivisección** *f.* vivisection.
**vivo, -va** *adj.* alive, living, live. *2* live [blaze, fire, etc.]. *3* vivid. *4* lively, brisk, quick, smart. *5* keen, acute, sharp, intense. *6* vigorous. *7* deep [feeling, interest, etc.]. *8* hasty, quick-tempered. *9* expressive. *10* vehement, persuasive. *11* bright [colour]. *12* sharp [edge, angle]. *13* running [water]. *14* unslaked [lime]. *15* raw [flesh, sore]. *16* living [language]. *17* live [rock]. *18* MECH., MACH. live. *19 lo* ~, the quick: *herir en lo* ~, to cut or hurt to the quick. *20 m.* edge, edging, border. *21* SEW. piping, edge trimming. *22 pl. los vivos,* the living, the quick.
**vizcacha** *f.* ZOOL. viscacha, vizcacha.
**vizcaíno, -na** *adj.-n.* Biscayan.
**Vizcaya** *f. pr. n.* GEOG. Biscay.
**vizcondado** *m.* viscountcy, viscountship, viscounty.
**vizconde** *m.* viscount.
**vizcondesa** *f.* viscountess.
**vocablo** *m.* word, term: *jugar del* ~, to pun.
**vocabulario** *m.* vocabulary.
**vocación** *f.* THEOL. vocation. *2* vocation [calling to a particular state, business or profession]. *3* ADVOCACIÓN.
**vocal** *adj.* vocal. *2 adj.-f.* GRAM., PHONET. vowel. *3 m.-f.* membler [of a council, a board of directors, etc.].
**vocálico, -ca** *adj.* vocalic.
**vocalista** *m.-f.* vocalist.
**vocalización** *f.* MUS. vocalization.
**vocalizar** *intr.* MUS. to vocalize.
**vocativo** *adj.-m.* GRAM. vocative.
**voceador, -ra** *adj.* vociferating. *2 m.-f.* vociferator. *3 m.* town crier.
**vocear** *intr.* to vociferate, shout, cry out. *2 tr.* to cry, publish. *3* to cheer, acclaim.
**vocejón** *m.* loud, harsh voice.
**vocería** *f.,* **vocerío** *m.* shouting, outcry, uproar.
**vocero** *m.* spokesman.
**voces** *f. pl.* of VOZ.
**vociferación** *f.* vociferation.
**vociferante** *adj.* vociferating, vociferant.
**vociferar** *intr.-tr.* to vociferate.
**vocinglería** *f.* shouting, uproar. *2* prate, rant.
**vocinglero, -ra** *adj.* shouting, vociferous. *2* chattering. *3 m.-f.* shouter. *4* prater, chatterer.
**vodka** *f.* vodka.
**volada** *f.* short flight. *2* (Am.) trick, bad turn.
**voladero, -ra** *adj.* able to fly. *2* flying, fleeting. *3 m.* precipice.
**voladizo, -za** *adj.* ARCH. projecting, jutting out. *2* ARCH. projection, projecting member, corbel.
**volado, -da** *adj.* PRINT. superior [figure, letter]. *2 estar* ~, to be uneasy, on tenterhooks.
**volador, -ra** *adj.* flying. *2* fleeting, running fast. *3 m.* skyrocket. *4* ICHTH. flying gurnard.
**voladura** *f.* blasting, blowing up. *2* flying through the air.
**volandas (en)** *adv.* [carried] in the air, as if flying. *2* rapidly, quickly.

**volandera** *f.* MACH. washer. *2* millstone.
**volandero, -ra** *adj.* VOLANTÓN. *2* floating in the air. *3* accidental, casual. *4* wandering. *5* flying [report, etc.].
**volante** *adj.* flying, volant. *2* MIL. flying [column]. *3 m.* SEW. flounce. *4* MACH. flywheel. *5* HOROL. balance wheel. *6* coining press. *7* shuttlecock. *8* battledore and shuttlecock [game]. *9* AUTO. steering wheel. *10* note, order, etc., written on a narrow sheet of paper.
**volantín** *m.* line with several hooks for fishing. *2* (Am.) kite [toy].
**volantón** *adj.* newfledged. *2 m.* fledgling [bird].
**volapié** *m.* BULLF. stroke in which the matador runs toward the bull and stabs him.
**volar** *intr.* to fly [move in or through the air; float, soar in the air]. *2* AER. to fly. *3* to fly, fleet, pass swiftly, run fast, make great haste. *4* to fly, disappear. *5* [of news] to spread rapidly. *6* ARCH. to project, jut out. *7 tr.* to blast, blow up. *8* to fly [a hawk]. *9* to irritate, exasperate. *10* PRINT. to raise [a letter, etc.]. ‖ CONJUG. like *contar.*
**volatería** *f.* hawking, falconry. *2* poultry, fowls.
**volátil** *adj.* flying [that flies or can fly]. *2* volatile.
**volatilidad** *f.* CHEM. volatility.
**volatilizar** *tr.* volatilize. *2 ref.* to volatilize [be volatilized]. *2* coll. [of money, etc.] to disappear.
**volatín** *m.* acrobatic feat. *2* VOLATINERO.
**volatinero, -ra** *m.-f.* ropewalker, acrobat.
**volatizar** *tr.* VOLATILIZAR.
**volcán** *m.* GEOL. & fig. volcano: *estar sobre un* ~, fig. to be on the edge of a volcano.
**volcánico, -ca** *adj.* volcanic.
**volcar** *tr.* to upset, overturn, capsize; to tilt [a vessel]. *2* to dump. *3* to make dizzy [with a strong odour]. *4* to make [one] change his mind. *5 fig.* to irritate. *6 intr.* [of a vehicle] to upset, overturn. ‖ CONJUG. like *contar.*
**volea** *f.* whippletree. *2* volley [of a ball].
**volear** *tr.* to volley [a bail]. *2* AGR. to sow broadcast.
**voleo** *m.* volley [of a ball]. *2* slap or blow that makes one reel. *3* AGR. *sembrar al* ~, to sow boadcast.
**volframio** *m.* CHEM. wolfram.
**volición** *f.* volition.
**volitivo, -va** *adj.* volitive, volitional.
**volquearse** *ref.* to roll about, wallow.
**volquete** *m.* tilt cart, tip cart, dump truck.
**volt** *m.* ELECT. volt.
**voltaico, -ca** ELECT. voltaic: *arco* ~, voltaic arc.
**voltaje** *m.* ELECT. voltage.
**voltámetro** *m.* ELECT. voltameter.
**voltariedad** *f.* fickleness, inconstancy.
**voltario, -ria** *adj.* fickle, inconstant.
**volteador, -ra** *m.-f.* tumbler, acrobat.
**voltear** *tr.* to turn, revolve. *2* to turn around to. *3* ARCH. to build [an arch or vault]. *4 intr.* to turn in the air; to roll over; to tumble.
**voltejear** *tr.* to turn around. *2 intr.* NAUT. to tack.
**volteo** *m.* turning. *2* overturning. *3* turning in the air; tumbling.
**voltereta** *f.* tumble, handspring, somersault. *2* turning up a card to determine the trump.
**volteriano, -na** *adj.-n.* Voltairian.
**voltímetro** *m.* ELECT. voltmeter.
**voltio** *m.* ELECT. volt.
**volubilidad** *f.* volubility. *2* fickleness, inconstancy.
**voluble** *adj.* voluble [turning easily]. *2* versatile, fickle, inconstant. *3* BOT. voluble.

**volumen** *m.* volume [book]. *2* volume, bulk, mass. *3* GEOM., MUS. volume.
**volumetría** *f.* volumetry.
**voluminoso, -sa** *adj.* voluminous, bulky.
**voluntad** *f.* will [in every sense, except testament]; wish, pleasure: *mala* ~, ill will; *última* ~, last wish; last will and testament; *a* ~, at will; *de buena* ~, *de* ~, willingly. *2* affection, love, goodwill: *tener* ~ *a*, to love, feel affection for.
**voluntariado** *m.* MIL. volunteering.
**voluntariedad** *f.* voluntariness. *2* wilfulness.
**voluntario, -ria** *adj.* voluntary; wilful. *2* wilful, self-willed. *3 m.-f.* volunteer.
**voluntarioso, -sa** *adj.* wilfully, self-willed.
**voluptuosidad** *f.* voluptuousness.
**voluptuoso, -sa** *adj.* voluptuous. *2 m.-f.* voluptuary.
**voluta** *f.* ARCH. volute.
**volver** *tr.* to turn [cause to revolve]; to turn, turn up, turn over, turn upside down or inside out: ~ *la cara*, to turn one's head; ~ *la espalda a*, to turn one's back on; ~ *la hoja*, to turn the page; fig. to change the subject; to change one's mind. *2* to turn, direct, aim. *3* to return, restore. *4* to put back, bring back. *5* to give [change of coin or note]. *6* SPORT. to return [the ball]. *7* to vomit. *8* to translate [from a language]. *9* to make, drive, turn, convert: ~ *loco*, to drive crazy, distract. *10* to make [a person] change his mind. *11* to push or pull [a door] to. *12* to reflect [sound, etc.].
*13 intr.* to return, come back, go back. *14* to turn [to the right, to the left]. *15* ~ *a hacer, a leer*, etc., to do, read, etc., again, anew or over. *16* ~ *en sí*, to come to, recover consciousness. *17* ~ *por*, to defend, stand up for. *18* ~ *sobre sí*, to recover one's calm.
*19 ref.* to go back. *20* to turn, turn around, face about, look back. *21* [of wine, etc.] to turn sour. *22 volverse atrás*, to back out; withdraw from promise, etc. *23 volverse contra*, to turn on. ‖ CONJUG. like *mover.* ‖ PAST. P. *vuelto.*
**volvible** *adj.* turnable, reversible.
**vómer** *m.* ANAT. vomer.
**vómico, -ca** *adj.* vomitive.
**vomitar** *tr.* to vomit. *2* to eject, belch forth. *3* to break out into [insults, etc.]. *4* coll. to disgorge, give up. *5 intr.* to vomit.
**vomitivo, -va** *adj.-n.* vomitive, emetic.
**vómito** *m.* vomit, vomiting.
**vomitona** *f.* coll. violent vomiting.
**vomitorio, -ria** *adj.-n.* vomitory. *2 m.* vomitory [in Roman theatres].
**voracidad** *f.* voracity, voraciousness.
**vorágine** *f.* vortex, whirlpool.
**voraz** *adj.* voracious; greedy, ravenous. *2* destructive, fierce [fire, etc.].
**vórtice** *m.* vortex, whirlpool, whirlwind. *2* centre of a cyclone.
**vorticela** *f.* ZOOL. vorticella.
**vortiginoso, -sa** *adj.* vortical, vortiginous.
**vos** *pers. pron. sing. & pl.* you. ‖ It is used in adressing God, the saints and high-placed or venerable persons. Even if it is singular in meaning it takes plural form of verb. *2* In much of Spanish America, it is colloquially used instead of *tú.*
**vosotros, -tras** *pers. pron. pl.* (plural form of *tú*) you, ye.
**votación** *f.* votation, voting, casting of votes. *2* vote, ballot [votes collectively].
**votante** *m.-f.* voter.

**votar** *intr.-tr.* to vow [make promise to God or the saints]. *2 intr.* to vote [for, against, on]. *3* to swear, curse. *4 ¡voto a tal!,* confound it!, by Jove! *5 tr.* to vote, vote for, give one's vote for.

**votivo, -va** *adj.* votive.

**voto** *m.* vow. *2* wish, supplication to God: *hacer votos por,* to pray for, to wish. *3* curse, oath, execration; *echar votos,* to swear, curse. *4* vote: *~ de calidad,* casting vote; *~ particular,* minority report; *ser* or *tener ~,* to have a vote; fig. to have voice, be qualified for speaking [on a matter]. *5* advice, opinion.

**voy** *1st pers. sing. pres.* of IR.

**voz** *f.* voice [of man, the animals, etc.]: *alzar la ~,* to raise, or lift up, one's voice; *estar en ~,* MUS. to be in voice; *llevar la ~ cantante,* fig. to have the say, be the boss; *a media ~,* in an undertone; with a slight hint; *a una ~,* with one voice; *a ~ en cuello, a ~ en grito,* at the top of one's voice; *de viva ~,* viva voce; *en alta ~,* aloud; *en ~ baja,* in a low tone, in whispers. *2* call or sound [of a bell, trumpet, etc.]. *3* shout: *dar voces,* to shout, yell. *4* voice [right to speak]. *5* vote. *6* GRAM. voice [of verb]. *7* word, term. *8* rumour, public opinion: *corre la ~ que,* it is rumoured that.

**vozarrón** *m.* strong, heavy voice.

**vuecelencia, vuecencia** *m.-f.* (contr. of VUESTRA EXCELENCIA) your excellency.

**vuelco** *m.* overturn, turnover, upset.

**vuelco, vuelque,** etc. *irr.* V. VOLCAR.

**vuelillo** *m.* lace cuff trimming.

**vuelo** *m.* flight [going through the air; distance covered at a flight]; soaring, excursion of fancy, thought, etc.]: *~ planeado,* AER. volplane; *~ sin motor,* AER. glide, gliding; *alzar el ~,* to take flight; fig. to decamp; *levantar el ~,* to take flight; to raise one's mind; *al ~,* quickly; on the wing; on the fly; in passing; *echar las campanas al ~,* to ring a full peal; *de un ~, en un ~,* in a jiffy. *2* SEW. spread, wideness, flaring [of a skirt, etc.]. *3* VUELILLO. *4* ARCH. jut, projection. *5* importance: *tomar ~,* to grow, progress. *6* wings: *cortar los vuelos a,* to cut someone's wings.

**vuelta** *f.* turn [revolution, turning motion, reversal of position; motion around]: *media ~,* about-face; *dar media ~,* to face around; *dar la ~ a,* to make the round of, to go around [something]; *dar vueltas a un manubrio,* to turn a crank; *dar vueltas a una cosa,* fig. to keep going

over the same subject; *no hay que darle vueltas,* no use talking, no two ways about it; *dar vueltas* [abs.], to turn, revolve, spin, whirl; turn end over end; walk to and fro. *2* turn, stroll, tour, trip, excursion: *dar una ~ por,* to take a turn in. *3* turn, bend, curve. *4* turn, wind [of a rope, etc., about something]. *5* reverse, other side: *a la ~,* overleaf; round the corner; *no tener ~ de hoja,* fig. to be incontrovertible. *6* return, coming back, coming again: *estar de ~,* to be back, have returned; *a la ~,* on returning; *a ~ de correo,* return mail. *7* return, restitution. *8* change [of coin or note]. *9* repetition, iteration. *10* turn, shift, change. *11* CARDS turning up a card for trump. *12* ARCH. vault, ceiling. *13* facing [in garment]; cuff trimming. *14* burden [of song]. *15* beating, drubbing. *16 andar a vueltas con,* to struggle for, to endeavour to. *17 dar cien vueltas a,* to surpass, be far superior to. *18 poner de ~ y media,* to cover with insults. *19 a la ~ de,* within [a specified time].

**vuelto, -ta** *p. p. irreg.* of VOLVER. *2 adj.* PRINT. *folio ~,* verso. *3 m.* (Am.) change [money].

**vuelvo, vuelva,** etc. *irr.* V. VOLVER.

**vuesamerced, vuesarced** *m.-f.* (contr. of VUESTRA MERCED) you, sir; you, madam.

**vuestro, -tra; vuestros, -tras** *poss. adj.* your. *2 poss. pron.* yours. ‖ It is used in correspondence with *vos* and *vosotros.*

**vulcanismo** *m.* GEOL. vulcanism.

**vulcanita** *f.* vulcanite.

**vulcanización** *f.* vulcanization.

**vulcanizar** *tr.* to vulcanize.

**Vulcano** *m. pr. n.* MYTH., ASTR. Vulcan.

**vulgar** *adj.* vulgar.

**vulgaridad** *f.* vulgarity. *2* commonplace, platitude.

**vulgarismo** *m.* vulgarism [vulgar expression].

**vulgarización** *f.* vulgarization. *2* popularization.

**vulgarizar** *tr.* to vulgarize. *2* to translate into the vernacular. *3* to popularize [technical subjects].

**vulgata** *f.* Vulgate.

**vulgo** *m.* vulgar, common people.

**vulnerable** *adj.* vulnerable.

**vulnerar** *tr.* to wound. *2* to harm, injure, damage.

**vulnerario, -ria** *adj.-m.* vulnerary.

**vulpeja** *f.* ZORRA 1.

**vulpino, -na** *adj.* vulpine.

**vultúridos** *m. pl.* ORN. Vulturidae.

**vulva** *f.* ANAT. vulva.

# W

**W, w** *f.* W, w. This letter does not belong to the Spanish alphabet and it is mainly used in words taken from other languages.

**wat** *m.* ELECT. watt.

**water closet** *m.* water-closet.

**whisky, wiski** *m.* whisky.

**whist** *m.* whist [card game].

**X, x** *f.* X, x, twenty-sixth letter of the Spanish alphabet.
**xanteína** *f.* CHEM. xanthein.
**xántico** *adj.* CHEM. xanthic.
**xantofila** *f.* BIOCHEM. xanthophyll.
**xenofobia** *f.* xenophobia.
**xenófobo, -ba** *adj.* xenophobian. *2 m.-f.* xenophobe.

**xenon** *m.* CHEM. xenon.
**xerófilo, -la** *adj.* BOT. xerophilous.
**xi** *f.* xi [Greek letter].
**xifoideo, -a** *adj.* ANAT. xiphoid.
**xifoides** *adj.-m.* ANAT. xiphoid.
**xilófago, -ga** *adj.* ENT. xylophagous.
**xilófono** *m.* MUS. xylophone.
**xilografía** *f.* xylography. *2* xylograph.

# Y

**Y, y** *f.* Y, y, twenty-seventh letter of the Spanish alphabet.

**y** *conj.* and.

**ya** *adv.* already. *2* now. *3* at once, presently: ~ *voy*, I am coming. *4* later on, at another time: ~ *veremos*, we shall see. *5* Often used as an emphatic expletive: ~ *veo*, I see. *6* ~ *lo creo*, of course, certainly. *7* ~ *no*, no longer. *8* ~ *que*, since, inasmuch as. *9 si* ~, if. *10 conj. ya... ya*, now... now; whether... or. *11* I see; of course!

**yacaré** *m.* ZOOL. (Am.) cayman, alligator.

**yacente** *adj.* lying, jacent. *2* LAW abeyant. *3 m.* MIN. floor [of a vein].

**yacer** *intr.* to lie, be lying down. *2* to lie [in the grave], to rest. *3* to lie [have sexual intercourse]. *4* to lie, be [in a place]. ‖ CONJUG.: INDIC. Pres.: *yazco, yazgo* or *yago, yaces, yace*, etc. │ SUBJ. Pres.: *yazca, yazga* or *yaga; yazcas, yazgas* or *yagas*, etc. │ IMPER.: *yace* or *yaz; yazca, yazga* or *yaga; yazcamos, yazgamos* or *yagamos; yaced; yazcan, yazgan* or *yagan*.

**yacija** *f.* bed, couch. *2* tomb, grave.

**yacimiento** *m.* GEOL. bed, deposit, field.

**yagua** *f.* BOT. yagua.

**yaguar** *m.* JAGUAR.

**yak** *m.* ZOOL. yak.

**yámbico, -ca** *adj.-m.* PROS. iambic.

**yambo** *m.* PROS. iamb, iambus.

**yanqui** *adj.-n.* Yankee, American [of U.S.].

1) **yantar** *m.* obs. food, viands.

2) **yantar** *tr.* obs. to eat, to take a meal.

**yapa** *f.* (S. Am.) bonus, extra.

**yarda** *f.* yard [english measure].

**yaro** *m.* BOT. arum.

**yatagán** *m.* yataghan.

**yate** *m.* NAUT. yacht.

**yazco, yago,** etc. *irr.* V. YACER.

**ye** name of the letter *y.*

**yedra** *f.* HIEDRA.

**yegua** *f.* ZOOL. mare. *2* (Am.) cigar butt.

**yeguada** *f.* stud, herd of horses and mares.

**yeguar** *adj.* mare [pertaining to the mares].

**yegüería** *f.* YEGUADA.

**yegüerizo, -za** *adj.* YEGUAR. *2 m.* YEGÜERO.

**yegüero** *m.* keeper of a herd of horses and mares.

**yeísmo** *m.* pronunciation of Spanish *ll* like *y.*

**yelmo** *m.* ARM. armet, helmet.

**yema** *f.* BOT. bud. *2* BIOL., ZOOL. bud, gemma. *3* yolk [of an egg]: ~ *mejida*, eggnog. *4* candied egg yolk. *5* fig. cream [best part]. *6* ~ *del dedo*, fleshy part of the finger tip.

**yendo** *ger.* of IR.

**yente** *adj.* going.

**yerba** *f.* HIERBA.

**yerbajo** *m.* weed, wild herb.

**yergo, yerga,** etc. *irr.* V. ERGUIR.

**yermo, -ma** *adj.* waste, desert, uncultivated, barren. *2 m.* waste, desert, wilderness.

**yerno** *m.* son-in-law.

**yero** *m.* BOT. a kind of fare.

1) **yerro** *m.* error, fault, sin. *2* error, fault, mistake.

2) **yerro, yerra,** etc. *irr.* V. ERRAR.

**yerto, -ta** *adj.* stiff, rigid, motionless.

**yesal, yesar** *m.* gypsum pit or quarry.

**yesca** *f.* tinder, touchwood, *punk. *2* fig. fuel, incentive. *3 pl.* tinderbox.

**yesería** *f.* gypsum kiln. *2* plasterer's shop. *3* plaster objects; plasterwork.

**yesero, -ra** *adj.* [pertaining to] gypsum. *2 m.* maker of plaster. *3* seller of gypsum or plaster.

**yeso** *m.* gypsum. *2* plaster. *3* plaster cast. *4* chalk [for writing or drawing].

**yesón** *m.* rubbish of plaster.

**yesoso, -sa** *adj.* gypseous.

**yeyuno** *m.* ANAT. jejunum.

**yezgo** *m.* BOT. danewort, dwarf elder.

**yo** *pers. pron.* I. *2 m.* PHIL. I, ego.

**yodado, -da** *adj.* iodized.

**yodo** *m.* CHEM. iodine.

**yodoformo** *m.* CHEM. iodoform.

**yoduro** *m.* CHEM. iodide.

**yoga** *m.* yoga.

**yogurt** *m.* yogurt.

**yola** *f.* NAUT. yawl.

**yubarta** *f.* ZOOL. finback.

**yuca** *f.* BOT. yucca. *2* BOT. cassava.

**yugada** *f.* AGR. yoke of land. *2* yoke of oxen.

**yugo** *m.* yoke [for oxen, mules, etc.]. *2* ROMAN HIST. yoke. *3* fig. yoke [oppression, servitude]. *4* yoke [of a bell]. *6* NAUT. transom.

**Yugoeslavia** *f. pr. n.* GEOG. Yugoslavia.

**yugoeslavo, -va** *adj.-n.* Yugoslav.

**yugular** *adj.-f.* ANAT. jugular.

**yunque** *m.* anvil. *2* ANAT. anvil, incus.

**yunta** *f.* couple, yoke [of oxen, mules, etc.].

**yusera** *f.* horizontal stone in olive-oil mills.

**yuso** *adv.* ABAJO.
**yute** *m.* jute [plant, fibre, fabric].
**yuxtaponer** *tr.* to juxtapose. *2 ref.* to become jux-taposed. ‖ CONJUG. like *poner.*
**yuxtaposición** *f.* juxtaposition.
**yuyuba** *f.* BOT. jujube.

# Z

**Z, z** *f.* Z, z, twenty-eighth letter of the Spanish alphabet.
**zabida, zabila** *f.* BOT. aloe.
**zabordar** *intr.* NAUT. to run aground.
**zabullida** *f.* ZAMBULLIDA.
**zabullir** *tr.-ref.* ZAMBULLIR.
**zacapela, zacapella** *f.* shindy, row, noisy quarrel.
**Zacarías** *m. pr. n.* Zachary, Zechariah.
**zacatín** *m.* clothes market.
**zafada** *f.* NAUT. freeing, disentangling.
**zafado, -da** *adj.* forward, impudent.
**zafar** *tr.* NAUT. to free, clear, disengage. 2 to adorn, bedeck. 3 MACH. [of a belt] to slip off. 5 *zafarse de,* to avoid, elude, get out of.
**zafarrancho** *m.* NAUT. clearing of a part of a ship: ~ *de combate,* clearing for action; ~ *de limpieza,* general cleaning. 2 coll. breaking, destruction. 3 coll. shindy, row.
**zafiedad** *f.* clumsiness, rusticity, uncouthness.
**zafio, -fia** *adj.* clumsy, rustic, ignorant, uncouth.
**zafir** *m.,* **zafira** *f.* ZAFIRO.
**zafíreo, -a** *adj.* sapphire, sapphirine.
**zafiro** *m.* MINER. sapphire.
**zafo, -fa** *adj.* NAUT. free, clear. 2 safe, unharmed.
**zafra** *f.* olive-oil can. 2 drip pan [for olive-oil measures]. 5 sugar-making season. 6 MIN. rubbish.
**zaga** *f.* rear, back part: *a la* ~, *en* ~, behind; *no irle en* ~ *a uno,* not to be inferior to one. 2 load in the rear of a carriage.
**zagal** *m.* lad, youth. 2 strapping young felow, swain. 3 shepherd's helper. 4 asistant of the driver in a stagecoach. 5 underskirt.
**zagala** *f.* lass, girl, maiden. 2 young shepherdess.
**zagaleja** *f. dim.* young lass.
**zagalejo** *m. dim.* young lad, boy. 2 underskirt.
**zagalón, -na** *m.-f.* overgrown boy or girl.
**zagual** *m.* paddle [oar].
**zaguán** *m.* entry, entrance-hall, vestibule.
**zaguero, -ra** *adj.* rear, hind; lagging behind. 2 *m.* backstop [at the game of PELOTA].
**zahareño, -ña** *adj.* disdainful, unsociable. 2 wild, intractable, refractory. 3 haggard [falcon].
**zaheridor, -ra** *adj.* taunting, blaming, upbraiding. 2 *m.-f.* taunter, blamer, upbraider.
**zaherimiento** *m.* taunt, upbraiding.
**zaherir** *tr.* to taunt, blame, upbraid. ‖ CONJUG. like *hervir.*
**zahina** *f.* BOT. sorghum.

**zahones** *m. pl.* chaps, chaparajos.
**zahorí** *m.* person credited by the popular belief with the power to see hidden things. 2 rhabdomancer. 3 fig. perspicacious person.
**zahorra** *f.* NAUT. ballast.
**zahurda** *f.* POCILGA.
**zaino, -na** *adj.* false, treacherous. 2 dar-chestnut [horse]. 3 black [cattle]. 4 vicious [horse, mule].
**zalagarda** *f.* ambush. 2 trap, snare. 3 deceitful obsequiousness. 4 skirmish. 5 coll. row, shindy.
**zalama, zalamería** *f.* blandishment, cajolery, flattery.
**zalamero, -ra** *adj.* honeyed, caressing, flattering, cajoling. 2 *m.-f.* caresser, flatterer, cajoler.
**zalea** *f.* unsheared skeepskin.
**zalear** *tr.* to drag and shake around. 2 to chase away [dogs].
**zalema** *f.* salaam. 2 coll. bow, courtsy.
**zallar** *tr.* NAUT. to rig out, run out.
**zamacuco** *m.* dolt, blockhead. 2 sly fellow. 3 coll. drunk, drunken fit.
**zamarra** *f.* shepherd's jacket of unsheared sheepskin. 2 unsheared sheepskin.
**zamarrear** *tr.* [of dogs, etc.] to worry, shake and tear with the teeth. 2 coll. to treat roughly, to knock around.
**zamarro** *f.* worrying and tearing with the teeth. 2 rough treatment; knocking around.
**zamarrico** *m. dim.* wallet of unsheared sheepskin.
**zamarilla** *f.* BOT. poly.
**zamarro** *m.* ZAMARRA 1. 2 sheepskin. 3 coll. boor, rustic, dolt. 4 coll. sly fellow. 5 *pl.* (Am.) chaps, chaparajos.
**zambo, -ba** *adj.* knock-kneed. 2 (Am.) born of an Indian and a Negro.
**zambomba** *f.* a rustic instrument. 2 *interj.* whew!
**zambombazo** *m.* hard blow, bump or knock.
**zambombo** *m.* boor, dolt.
**zamborondón, -na; zamborotudo, -da** *adj.* thick, clumsy, ill-shaped. 2 clumsy [person].
**zambra** *f.* a Morisco festival or merrymaking. 2 fig. merrymaking; noise, hullabaloo.
**zambucar** *tr.* coll. to hide [a thing] by mixing it quickly among others.
**zambullida** *f.,* **zambullimiento** *m.* dive, plunge, ducking.
**zambullir** *tr.* to dive, plunge, duck [a person or thing] into water. 2 *ref.* [of a person or animal]

to dive, plunge, duck. *3* [of a submarine] to dive.
*4* to duck, hide.
**zamorano, -na** *adj.-n.* of Zamora.
**zampa** *m.* ENG. pile, bearing pile.
**zampar** *tr.* to thrust or put hurriedly [in order to
conceal]. *2* to eat hurriedly and gluttonously. *3*
*ref.* to enter, go in suddenly.
**zampatortas,** *pl.* **-tas** *m.-f.* glutton. *2* boor, rustic.
**zampeado** *m.* ENG., ARCH. grillage.
**zampear** *tr.* ENG., ARCH. to strengthen [ground]
with a grillage.
**zampoña** *f.* MUS. rustic flute, reed pipe; panpipe.
**zampuzar** *intr.*, ZAMBULLIR. *2* ZAMPAR.
**zanahoria** *f.* BOT. carrot.
**zanahoriate** *m.* preserved carrot.
**zanca** *f.* shank [of bird]. *2* coll. long leg or shank.
*3* ARCH. string, stringboard [of a stair].
**zancada** *f.* long stride.
**zancadilla** *f.* trip [tripping someone]: *echar la ~ a
uno,* to stick out one's foot and trip someone. *2*
trick, snare [to harm someone].
**zancajear** *intr.* to hurry about, rush around.
**zancajiento, -ta** *adj.* ZANCAJOSO.
**zancajo** *m.* heel bone; heel or torn heel [of a shoe
or stocking]. *2* coll. short, illshaped person.
**zancajoso, -sa** *adj.* duck-toed. *2* big-heeled [per-
son]. *3* wearing stockings with holes at the
heels.
**zancarrón** *m.* coll. leg bone without flesh. *2* coll.
skinny, dirty old fellow. *3* coll. ignoramus.
**zanco** *m.* stilt: *en zancos,* fig. in a high position.
**zancudo, -da** *adj.* long-legged, long-shanked. *2*
ORN. wading. *3* *f.* ORN. wader, wading bird. *4* *m.*
(Am.) mosquito.
**zanfonía** *f.* MUS. hurdy-gurdy.
**zangala** *f.* buckram.
**zangamanga** *f.* coll. trick, ruse, wile.
**zanganear** *intr.* to drone, idle, loaf.
**zanganería** *f.* idlenness, laziness.
**zángano** *m.* ENT. drone. *2* fig. drone, idler, loafer.
**zangarilleja** *f.* slatternly, gadabout girl.
**zangarrear** *intr.* coll. to scrape a guitar.
**zangolotear** *tr.* to jiggle. *2* *intr.* to fidget or fuss
about. *3* to shake, rattle, move loosely in its socket, on its hinges, etc.
**zangoloteo** *m.* jiggle, jiggling. *2* fussing about. *3*
loose motion, shaking, rattling.
**zangolotino, -na** *adj.* fond of acting like a child;
being made to pass as a child [grown boy or
girl].
**zangotear** *tr.-intr.* ZANGOLOTEAR.
**zangoteo** *m.* ZANGOLOTEO.
**zanguanga** *f.* malingering. *2* coll. LAGOTERÍA.
**zanguango, -ga** *adj.* slothful. *2* *m.-f.* slothful person.
**zanja** *f.* ditch, trench: *~ de desagüe,* drain.
**zanjar** *tr.* to dig ditches or trenches in. *2* to settle
[a matter or dispute]; to conclude, finish. *3* to
obviate, surmount.
**zanjón** *m.* augm. large deep ditch.
**zanquear** *intr.* to waddle in walking. *2* to run
about, to walk much and fast.
**zanquilargo, -ga** *adj.* long-shanked, long-legged.
**zanquituerto, -ta** *adj.* bandy-legged.
**zanquivano, -na** *adj.* coll. spindle-legged.
**Zanzíbar** *f.* pr. n. GEOG. Zanzibar.
**zapa** *f.* spade [used by sappers]. *2* FORT. sap, tren-
ching: *trabajo de ~,* fig. secret work, intrigue. *3*
shagreen, sharkskin. *4* shagreen [leather]. *5*
sharkskin finish [on metals].
**zapador** *m.* MIL. sapper.

**zapapico** *m.* mattock, pickax, pickaxe.
**zapar** *intr.* MIL. to sap, mine, excavate.
**zaparrastrar** *intr.* coll. to trail one's clothes.
**zaparrastroso, -sa** *adj.-n.* ZARRAPASTROSO.
**zapata** *f.* buskin, half-boot. *2* BUILD. bolster. *3*
NAUT. shoe [of an anchor]. *4* NAUT. false keel. *5*
MECH. shoe [of a brake, etc.].
**zapatazo** *m.* large shoe. *2* blow with a shoe. *3*
heavy fall or blow. *4* thud, thump, whack. *5*
NAUT. flap [of a sail].
**zapatear** *tr.* to strike with the shoe. *2* to tap with
the feet. *3* FENC. to touch repeatedly with the
button of the foil. *4* coll. to ill-treat. *5* *intr.* NAUT.
[of sails] to flap.
**zapatera** *f.* woman who makes or sells shoes. *2*
shoemaker's wife.
**zapatería** *f.* shoemaker's shop. *2* shoe shop. *3* shoemaker's trade.
**zapateril** *adj.* [pertaining to a] shoemaker.
**zapatero, -ra** *adj.* hard, poorly cooked [beans]. *2*
stale [olive]. *3* *m.* shoemaker: *~ de viejo, ~ remendón,* cobbler mender of shoes. *4* ENT. water
skipper, water strider. *5* CARDS. *quedarse ~,* to
take no tricks.
**zapateta** *f.* slap on the foot or shoe while jumping.
*2* caper, leap, jump.
**zapatilla** *f.* slipper, light shoe. *2* leather washer
[for keys of a wind instrument]. *3* FENC. leather
button [of a foil].
**zapato** *m.* shoe, low shoe: *saber uno donde le
aprieta el ~,* to know on which side one's bread
is buttered.
**zapatón,** *pl.* **-tones** *m.* augm. large, clumsy shoe.
**¡zape!** *interj.* used to frighten cats away.
**zapote** *m.* BOT. sapote [tree and fruit]. *2* *chico ~,*
CHICOZAPOTE.
**zapotero** *m.* BOT. sapote [tree].
**zapotillo** *m.* BOT. sapodilla.
**zaque** *m.* wineskin. *2* coll. drunk person.
**Zaqueo** *m.* pr. n. Zaccheus.
**zaquizamí** *m.* garret, cockloft. *2* fig. hovel, hole,
mean room.
**zar** *m.* czar, tzar.
**zarabanda** *f.* saraband. *2* fig. noise, bustle.
**zaragata** *f.* row, noise, tumult; noisy merrimak-
ing.
**zaragatero, -ra** *adj.* fond of engaging in rows and
tumults; noisy, merry, fond of tun.
**zaragatona** *f.* BOT. fleawort.
**Zaragoza** *f.* pr. n. GEOG. Saragossa.
**zaragozano, -na** *adj.-n.* of Saragossa.
**zaragüelles** *m. pl.* a kind of short, wide and plaited
breeches.
**zaragutear** *tr.* coll. to bungle.
**zaranda** *f.* sieve, screen. *2* colander.
**zarandajas** *f. pl.* coll. trifles, unimportant things.
**zarandar** *tr.* to sift, winnow [grain, etc.]. *2* to
strain [jelly]. *3* fig. to stir, move [things] about,
or to and fro, easily and swiftly. *5* *ref.* to move
briskly about or to and fro.
**zarandear** *tr.-ref.* ZARANDAR. *2* *tr.* to harass, overwork. *3* *ref.* to walk swinging affectedly hips and
shoulders.
**zarandeo** *m.* sifting, screening. *2* swift or brisk
moving about.
**zarandillo** *m. dim.* small sieve or screen. *2* fig. live
wire, active person. *3* fig. restless, mischievous
boy. *4* *traerle a uno como un ~,* coll. to keep
someone on the go.
**zarapito** *m.* ORN. curlew.
**zaraza** *f.* chintz.

**zarazo, -za** *adj.* half-ripe [fruit].
**zarceño, -ña** *adj.* [pertaining to] bramble.
**zarcero, -ra** *adj.* hunting in brambles [dog].
**zarceta** *f.* CERCETA 1.
**zarcillitos** *m. pl.* BOT. quaking grass.
**zarcillo** *m.* eardrop. *2* BOT. tendril. *3* weeding hoe.
**zarco, -ca** *adj.* light-blue [eyes or waters].
**zarevitz** *m.* czarevitch, tzarevitch.
**zarigüeya** *f.* ZOOL. opossum.
**zarina** *f.* czarina, tzarina.
**zarpa** *f.* paw [of a lion, tiger, etc.]. *2* CAZCARRIA. *3* NAUT. weighing anchor. *4* ARCH. footing.
**zarpada** *f.* blow with a paw.
**zarpar** *intr.* NAUT. to weigh anchor, set sail.
**zarpazo** *m.* ZARPADA. *2* BATACAZO.
**zarracatín** *m.* coll. greedy merchant.
**zarramplín** *m.* bungler. *2* good-for-nothing.
**zarramplinada** *f.* bungle, stupidity.
**zarrapastrón, -na** *adj.* tattered, shabby, slovenly, dirty. *2 m.* ragamuffin. *3 f.* slut.
**zarrapastroso, -sa** *adj.* ZARRAPASTRÓN.
**zarza** *f.* BOT. bramble, blackberry, blackberry bush.
**zarzal** *m.* blackberry patch, brambles.
**zarzamora** *f.* BOT. brambleberry. *2* bramble, blackberry [fruit]. *2* bramble, blackberry bush.
**zarzaparrilla** *f.* BOT. sarsaparrilla.
**zarzaperruna** *f.* ESCARAMUJO 1 & 2.
**zarzarrosa** *f.* BOT. dog rose [flower].
**zarzo** *m.* hurdle, wattle.
**zarzuela** *f.* zarzuela [Spanish musical comedy].
**zarzuelero, -ra** *adj.* [pertaining to the] zarzuela.
**¡zas!** *interj.* bang!
**zascandil** *m.* coll. busybody, good-for-nothing.
**zascandilear** *intr.* to meddle.
**zazo, -za; zazoso, -sa** *adj.* TARTAJOSO.
**Zebedeo** *m. pr. n.* BIBL. Zebedee.
**zebra** *f.* CEBRA.
**zeda** *f.* zed [letter Z].
**zedilla** *f.* CEDILLA.
**Zelanda, Zelandia** *f. pr. n.* GEOG. Zealand.
**Zendavesta** *m.* Zend-Avesta.
**zenit** *m.* CENIT.
**zepelín** *m.* Zeppelin [dirigible].
**zeta** *f.* zed [letra Z]. *2* zeta [Greek letter].
**zeugma, zeuma** *f.* GRAM. zeugma.
**zigomorfo, -fa** *adj.* BIOL. zygomorphic, zygomorphous.
**zigospora** *f.* BOT. zygospore.
**zigzag** *m.* zigzag.
**zigzaguear** *intr.* to zigzag.
**zinc** *m.* CINC.
**zipizape** *m.* coll. row, shindy, scuffle.
**¡zis, zas!** *interj.* bing, bang!
**zoantropía** *f.* MED. zoanthropy.
**zócalo** *m.* ARCH. socle. *2* ARCH. dadc [of a wall].
**zocato, -ta** *adj.* overripe [fruit]. *2* left-handed. *3 m.-f.* left-handed person.
**zoclo** *m.* ZOCO 2.
**zoco, -ca** *adj.-n.* ZOCATO 1 & 2. *2 m.* clog, wooden shoe. *4* Moroccan market or market place. *5* ARCH. socle.
**zodiacal** *adj.* zodiacal.
**zodíaco** *m.* ASTR. zodiac.
**zoilo** *m.* fig. malevolent critic, detractor.
**zollipar** *intr.* coll. to sob.
**zollipo** *m.* coll. sob.
**zona** *f.* zone. *2* belt, area, region. *3* MED. zoster, shingles.
**zonzo, -za** *adj.* dull, insipid, silly. *2 m.-f.* dull person. *4* simpleton.

**zonzorrión, -na** *adj.* very dull or silly.
**zoófago, -ga** *adj.* zoophagus.
**zoófito** *m.* ZOOL. zoophyte.
**zoografía** *f.* zoography.
**zooide** *adj.* zooidal. *2* BIOL., ZOOL. zooid.
**zoolatría** *f.* zoolatry.
**zoología** *f.* zoology.
**zoológico, -ca** *adj.* zoologic, zoological.
**zoólogo** *m.* zoologist.
**zoospora** *m.* BOT. zoospora.
**zootecnia** *f.* zootechny.
**zootropo** *m.* zoetrope.
**zopenco, -ca** *adj.* doltish, block-headed. *2 m.-f.* dolt, blockhead.
**zopilote** *m.* ORN. (Am.) turkey buzzard.
**zopo, -pa** *adj.* crooked, deformed [foot or hand]. *2 m.-f.* person having crooked or deformed feet or hands.
**zoquete** *m.* block, chunk [of wood]. *2* chunk [of bread]. *3* coll. short, fat, ugly fellow. *4* coll. blockhead.
**zoquetudo, -da** *adj.* clumsy, ill-shaped.
**zorcico** *m.* Basque song and dance.
**zoroástrico, -ca** *adj.* Zoroastrian.
**Zoroastro** *m. pr. n.* Zoroaster.
**zorongo** *m.* kerchief folded around the head, worn by Aragonese men. *2* flat chignon. *3* Andalusian dance and tune.
**zorra** *f.* ZOOL. fox. *2* ZOOL. female fox. *3* fig. fox [crafty person]. *4* coll. harlot. *5* coll. drunk, drunkeness. *6* truck, dray. *7* ICHTH. ~ *de mar*, fox shark.
**zorrastrón, -na** *m.-f.* crafty, sly person; fox.
**zorrera** *f.* fox hole.
**zorrería** *f.* foxiness; cunning, wile.
**zorrero, -ra** *adj.* fox-hunting [dog]. *2* crafty, cunning. *3* NAUT. heavy-sailing. *4* fig. lagging behind.
**zorrillo** *m.* ZOOL. (Am.) skunk.
**zorro, -rra** *adj.* crafty, cunning. *2 m.* ZOOL. fox, male fox. *3* fox [fur]. *4* fig. fox [crafty person]. *5* coll. *hacerse el* ~, to feign ignorance or absent-mindedness. *6 pl.* duster.
**zorzal** *m.* ORN. fieldfare. *2* fig. sly fellow. *3* (Am.) simpleton.
**zoster** *f.* MED. zoster, shingles.
**zote** *adj.* dull, ignorant. *2 m.* dolt, blockhead.
**zozobra** *f.* uneasiness, anxiety. *2* NAUT. [danger of] sinking or capsizing.
**zozobrar** *intr.* NAUT. to be in danger of sinking or capsizing. *2* NAUT. to founder, sink, capsize. *3* to be wrecked or ruined. *4* to be anxious, uneasy.
**zuavo** *m.* MIL. Zouave.
**zuda** *f.* AZUD.
**zueco** *m.* sabot, clog, wooden shoe.
**zuingliano, -na** *adj.-n.* Zwinglian.
**zulaque** *m.* a kind of mastic for packing pipe joints, etc.
**zulú, pl. -lús** or **-lúes** *adj.-n.* Zulu.
**Zululandia** *f. pr. n.* GEOG. Zululand.
**zulla** *f.* BOT. French honeysuckle. *2* coll. excrements.
**zullarse** *ref.* coll. to go to stool. *2* coll. to break wind.
**zullón, -na** *adj.* coll. breaking wind often. *2 m.* wind [from the bowels].
**zumaque** *m.* sumac(h [plant and material]. *2* coll. wine, grape, wine.
**zumba** *f.* bell worn by a leading mule or ox. *2* bull-roarer [toy]. *3* banter, chaff, mockery.

**zumbador, -ra** *adj.* humming, buzzing. *2 m.* ELECT. buzzer.

**zumbar** *intr.* to hum, buzz, drone, whizz. *2* [of the ears] to ring. *3 tr.* coll. to deal, deliver [a blow]. *4 ref. zumbarse de,* to make fun of.

**zumbel** *m.* string for spinning a top.

**zumbido** *m.* hum, buzz, drone, whizz. *2* ringing [in the ears]. *3* ping [of a bullet]. *4* coll. blow, box, smack.

**zumbón, -na** *adj.* bantering, rallying, mocking. *2* waggish. *3 m.-f.* mocker, jester, wag.

**zumiento, -ta** *adj.* exuding juice.

**zumillo** *m. dim.* little juice. *2* DRAGONTEA. *3* TAPSIA.

**zumo** *m.* juice [of plants, flowers, fruit, etc.], expressed juice. *2* fig. profit, advantage.

**zumoso, -sa** *adj.* juicy [full of juice].

**zuncho** *m.* strengthening hoop or band; ferrule.

**zupia** *f.* dregs [of wine]. *2* wine full of dregs. *2* coll. slops. *4* coll. scum, thrash.

**zurano, -na** *adj.* ZURITO.

**zurcido, -da** *m.* darn, darning, fine-drawing.

**zurcidor, -ra** *m.-f.* SEW. darner.

**zurcir** *tr.* SEW. to arn, mend; to fine-draw. *2* fig. to join, unite. *3* coll. to make a tissue of [lies].

**zurdo, -da** *adj.* left-handed [person]: *no ser ~,* fig. to be clever. *2* left [hand]. *3 m.-f.* lefthanded person. *4 f.* left hand.

**zurear** *intr.* [of doves] to coo.

**zurito, -ta** *adj.* wild, stock [pigeon, dove].

**zuro, -ra** *adj.* ZURITO. *2 m.* corncob.

**zurra** *f.* TAN. currying, dressing. *2* beating, drubbing.

**zurrador** *m.* leather currier or dresser.

**zurrapa** *f. sing. & pl.* lees, dregs, grounds, settlings. *2 f. sing.* coll. thrash, rubbish. *3* coll. ugly skinny boy.

**zurrapelo** *m.* coll. dressing down, sharp reprimand.

**zurrapiento** *adj.* dreggy, turbid, roily.

**zurrar** *tr.* TAN. to curry, dress [leather]. *2* to spank, flog, drub, thrash, wallop: *~ la badana a uno,* to tan someone.

**zurriagar** *tr.* to lash, whip. *2* to whip [a top].

**zurriagazo** *m.* lash, whip [stroke]. *2* fig. lash, blow, unexpected mishap or ill-treatment.

**zurriago** *m.* lash, whip. *2* whip [for spinning a top].

**zurribanda** *f.* sound drubbing. *2* noisy row or scuffle.

**zurriburri** *m.* coll. despicable fellow. *2* coll. rabble. *3* confusion, uproar.

**zurrido** *m.* buzz, whirr. *2* coll. blow with a stick.

**zurrir** *intr.* to buzz, whirr.

**zurrón** *m.* shepher's pouch. *2* game bag. *3* leather bag. *4* BOT. husk.

**zurullo** *m.* soft roll [of anything]. *2* coll. turd.

**zurumbático, -ca** *adj.* stunned, dumb-founded.

**zurupeto** *m.* unregistered stockbroker.

**zutano, -na** *m.-f.* So-and-so. | It is used after «fulano»: *fulano, ~ y mengano,* Tom, Dick and Harry.

**zuzón** *m.* BOT. groundsel.

# APPENDICES
# APÉNDICES

## FALSE COGNATES AND "PART-TIME" COGNATES

Some of the following Spanish words appear to be cognates of English words, but they are not: e.g., **"sopa"** in Spanish does *not* mean "soap" in English, and **"parientes"** does *not* mean "parents" in English. Other words sometimes suggest an English equivalent, but can also have a very different meaning: e.g., **"real"** in Spanish can be interpreted at times to mean "real" in English but more often should be translated as "royal," and **"equipo"** in Spanish can mean "equipment" in English but is more often translated as "team."

In the Spanish-to-English column, certain English words are in brackets to indicate that *only sometimes* the Spanish word has the meaning of the bracketed English word. In the English-to-Spanish column the abbreviations—(a.) = adjective, (n.) = noun, and (v.) = verb—are used in a few cases for clarity.

### Spanish-English

**acre:** sharp, sour, rude, harsh, [acre]

**actual:** current, present (re time)

**admirar:** to astonish, surprise, [admire]

**apuntar:** to point, aim; write down, make a note of

**asignación:** allowance, assignment, [assignation]

**asistir:** to attend, be present, to help, [to assist]

**atender:** to pay attention, take care of, [attend to]

**carpeta:** portfolio; file folder

**carta:** letter (re mail), charter, [playing card]

**cigarro:** cigarette

**colegio:** school (private or high school)

**conferencia:** lecture, interview, meeting, [conference]

**constipado:** suffering from a cold

**contar:** to tell, relate, [count]

**contento:** happy, glad, satisfied, [contented]

**costumbre:** custom

**decepción:** disillusionment, disappointment, [deception]

**desgracia:** misfortune, mishap, disfavor

**desgraciado:** unfortunate, wretched, unlucky

**deshonesto:** immodest, indecent

**dirección:** address (re mail), [direction]

**disgusto:** quarrel, annoyance, sorrow, [disgust]

**distinto:** different; clear; several; [distinct]

**embarazada:** pregnant

**equipo:** team; fittings; squad; [equipment]

**equivocación:** error, mistake

**éxito:** success

**expedir:** to issue (a decree); send, ship; dispatch, [expedite]

**explanar:** to level, grade (ground); [explain]

**fábrica:** factory, mill, structure, [fabric]

**falta:** shortage, lack; blemish; defect, [fault]

### English-Spanish

**acre:** acre, unidad de medida

**actual:** verdadero, real

**admire:** considerar con placer, admirar

**appoint:** nombrar, señalar

**assignation:** asignación, destinación

**assist:** ayudar, asistir

**attend:** asistir a, cuidar, atender

**carpet:** alfombra

**cart:** carro, carreta
**card:** tarjeta, naipe, carta

**cigar:** puro

**college:** universidad

**conference:** junta, sesión, entrevista, conferencia

**constipated:** estreñido

**count:** (v.) contar

**contented:** satisfecho, tranquilo, contento

**costume:** vestuario, traje

**deception:** engaño, fraude, decepción

**disgrace:** (n.) deshonra, vergüenza, ignominia

**disgraced:** deshonrado, avergonzado

**dishonest:** engañoso, falso, poco honrado

**direction:** dirección

**disgust:** hastío, asco, repugnancia, disgusto

**distinct:** claro, visible; inequívoco; diferente, distinto

**embarrassed:** turbado, desconcertado

**equipment:** aparatos, equipo

**equivocation:** equívoco; subterfugio, engaño

**exit:** salida

**expedite:** acelerar, facilitar; apresurar, despachar

**explain:** explicar, aclarar

**fabric:** tela, textura; fábrica; construcción

**fault:** (n.) culpa; defecto, falta

formal: reliable, trustworthy; grave; definite; [formal]

frase: sentence, [phrase]

fray: priest, friar

golpe: blow

gracioso: amusing, witty; graceful, charming

grande: large, big, great, [grand]

honesto: decent, pure, virtuous; reasonable; [honest]

idioma: language, [idiom]

ignorar: to be unaware or ignorant of

largo: long

lectura: reading

leer: to read

liar: to tie, bind, roll up

media: stocking

ordinario: coarse, vulgar; usual, [ordinary]

parientes: relatives

probar: to test, taste, try out

quitar: to take away, deprive of, subtract

real: royal, [real]

realizar: to fulfill, achieve, carry out; [realize]

recordar: to remember, recall, remind, awaken

regular: ordinary; so-so, fairly well; systematic, [regular]

renta: interest, revenue, [rent]

repente: start, sudden movement

replicar: to reply, answer, retort, [replicate]

ropa: clothes, clothing

ruin: vile, mean; petty, stingy; little

salvo: safe; easily; omitted

sano: healthy; sound; whole; [sane]

sauce: willow

sensible: sentient; sensitive; perceptible; [sensible]

simpático: agreeable, pleasant, cogenial

sopa: soup

suceder: to happen, come about, [succeed]

suceso: event, incident

taller: workshop; laboratory; studio

tuna: prickly pear; idle and vagrant life

tutor: guardian, [tutor]

vagón: railway car or coach

vale: note, sales slip, coupon

formal: convencional, ceremonioso, formal

phrase: expresión, frase

fray: (v.) raerse, deshilacharse; (n.) alboroto, riña

gulp: (n.) trago

gracious: afable, cortés; atractivo; bondadoso

grand: magnífico; grandioso, majestuoso; grande

honest: honrado, íntegro, recto; sincero

idiom: modismo; lenguaje

ignore: no hacer caso de; desconocer

large: grande

lecture: (n.) conferencia; lección; plática

leer: (v.) mirar de soslayo, mirar con injuria; (n.) mirada de soslayo

liar: (n.) mentiroso, embustero

media: (pl. of medium) medios; medios de comunicación (radio, televisión, etc.)

ordinary: corriente, común, ordinario; mediocre

parents: padres

probe: (v.) tentar; examinar a fondo; sondear; penetrar

quit: abandonar, cesar, parar, dejar (de hacer algo)

real: (a.) verdadero, real

realize: darse cuenta de; comprender; efectuar, llevar a cabo; realizar

record: (v.) registrar, apuntar, asentar, inscribir; grabar en disco

regular: metódico, ordenado, regular

rent: (v.) alquilar; (n.) arrendamiento, renta; rasgadura

repent: arrepentirse

replicate: (v.) duplicar, repetir, replicar

rope: (n.) soga, cuerda

ruin: (v.) arruinar, estropear; (n.) ruina, destrucción

salvo: salva; pretexto

sane: cuerdo; razonable; sano

sauce: salsa, condimento

sensible: sensato, razonable, juicioso

sympathetic: compasivo; simpatizante

soap: jabón

succeed: lograr(se); medrar, salir bien; suceder

success: éxito

taller: más alto

tuna: atún

tutor: (n.) maestro particular, tutor

wagon: carro, carreta, carretón

vale: valle, cañada

# MONETARY UNITS / UNIDADES MONETARIAS

| Country / País | Name / Nombre | Subdivision / Subdivisión | Symbol / Símbolo |
|---|---|---|---|
| THE AMERICAS / LAS AMÉRICAS | | | |
| Argentina | austral* | | A |
| Bahamas | dollar / dólar bahameño | 100 cents / centavos | B$ |
| Barbados | dollar / dólar de Barbados | 100 cents / centavos | $ |
| Belize / Belice | dollar / dólar | 100 cents / centavos | $ |
| Bolivia | peso | 100 centavos | $B |
| Brazil / Brasil | cruzeiro / nuevo cruzeiro | 100 centavos | $; Cr$ |
| Canada / Canadá | dollar / dólar canadiense | 100 cents / centavos | $ |
| Chile | peso** / peso chileno** | 1000 escudos | $ |
| Colombia | peso | 100 centavos | $; P |
| Costa Rica | colon / colón | 100 centimos / céntimos | ₵; ¢ |
| Cuba | peso | 100 centavos | $ |
| Dominican Republic / República Dominicana | peso | 100 centavos | RD$ |
| Ecuador | sucre | 100 centavos | S/ |
| El Salvador | colon / colón | 100 centavos | ₵; ¢ |
| Guatemala | quetzal | 100 centavos | Q; Q |
| Guyana | dollar / dólar guayanés | 100 cents / centavos | G$ |
| Haiti / Haití | gourde | 100 centimes / céntimos | Ø; G; Gde |
| Honduras | lempira | 100 centavos | L |
| Jamaica | dollar / dólar jamaicano | 100 cents / centavos | $ |
| Mexico / México | peso | | $ |
| Nicaragua | cordoba / córdoba | 100 centavos | C$ |
| Panama / Panamá | balboa | 100 centesimos / centésimos | B/ |
| Paraguay | guarani / guaraní | 100 centimos / céntimos | Ø; G |
| Peru / Perú | sol | 100 centavos | S/; $ |
| Puerto Rico | dollar / dólar | 100 cents / centavos | $ |
| Suriname / Surinam | guilder / gulder de Surinam | 100 cents / centavos | g |
| Trinidad and Tobago / Trinidad y Tabago | dollar / dólar trinitario | 100 cents / centavos | TT$ |
| United States / Estados Unidos | dollar / dólar | 100 cents / centavos | $ |
| Uruguay | peso | 100 centesimos / centésimos | $ |
| Venezuela | bolivar / bolívar | 100 centimos / céntimos | B |

*The Argentinian monetary unit, the peso, was replaced by the austral in 1985.
*El peso, la unidad monetaria argentina, fue reemplazado por el austral en 1985.
** The Chilean monetary unit, the escudo, was replaced by the peso in 1975.
** El escudo, la unidad monetaria chilena, fue reemplazado por el peso en 1975.

OTHER COUNTRIES / OTROS PAÍSES

| | | | |
|---|---|---|---|
| Australia | dollar / dólar australiano | 100 cents / centavos | $A |
| Austria | shilling / chelín | 100 groschen | S; Sch |
| Belgium / Bélgica | franc / franco belga | 100 centimes / céntimos | Fr; F |
| China | yuan / yüan | 100 fen | $ |
| East Germany / Alemania, R.D. | mark or ostmark / marco DDR | 100 pfennigs | M; OM |
| Egypt / Egipto | pound / libra egipcia | 100 piasters / piastras | £E |
| France / Francia | franc / franco | 100 centimes / céntimos | Fr; F |
| Greece / Grecia | drachma / dracma | 100 lepta | Dr |
| India | rupee / rupia | 100 paise / paisas | Re; Rs |
| Ireland / Irlanda | pound / libra irlandesa | 100 pence / peniques | £ |
| Israel | shekel / siclo | 100 argorot | |
| Italy / Italia | lira | 100 centesimi / centésimos | L; Lit |
| Japan / Japón | yen | 100 sen | ¥ ; Y |
| Portugal | escudo | 100 centavos | $; Esc |
| Soviet Union / Unión Soviética | ruble / rublo | 100 kopecks / kopeks | R; Rub |
| Spain / España | peseta | 100 centimos / céntimos | Pta; P |
| United Kingdom / Reino Unido | pound / libra esterlina | 100 pence / peniques | £ |
| West Germany / Alemania, R.F. | deutsche mark | 100 pfennigs | DM |

# WEIGHTS AND MEASURES

## Metric System

| Unit | Abbreviation | Approximate U.S. Equivalent | |
|------|--------------|-----------|---|
| **LENGTH** | | | |
| 1 millimeter | mm | 0.04 | inch |
| 1 centimeter | cm | 0.39 | inch |
| 1 meter | m | 39.37 | inches |
| | | 1.094 | yards |
| 1 kilometer | km | 3,281.5 | feet |
| | | 0.62 | mile |
| **AREA** | | | |
| 1 square centimeter | sq cm (cm²) | 0.155 | square inch |
| 1 square meter | m² | 10.764 | square feet |
| | | 1.196 | square yards |
| 1 hectare | ha | 2.471 | acres |
| 1 square kilometer | sq km (km²) | 247.105 | acres |
| | | 0.386 | square mile |
| **VOLUME** | | | |
| 1 cubic centimeter | cu cm (cm³) | 0.061 | cubic inch |
| 1 stere | s | 1.308 | cubic yards |
| 1 cubic meter | m³ | 1.308 | cubic yards |
| **CAPACITY (Liquid Measure)** | | | |
| 1 deciliter | dl | 0.21 | pint |
| 1 liter | l | 1.057 | quarts |
| 1 dekaliter | dal | 2.64 | gallons |
| **CAPACITY (Dry Measure)** | | | |
| 1 deciliter | dl | 0.18 | pint |
| 1 liter | l | 0.908 | quart |
| 1 dekaliter | dal | 1.14 | pecks |
| 1 hectoliter | hl | 2.84 | bushels |
| **CAPACITY (Cubic Measure)** | | | |
| 1 deciliter | dl | 6.1 | cubic inches |
| 1 liter | l | 61.02 | cubic inches |
| 1 dekaliter | dal | 0.35 | cubic foot |
| 1 hectoliter | hl | 3.53 | cubic feet |
| 1 kiloliter | kl | 1.31 | cubic yards |
| **MASS AND WEIGHT** | | | |
| 1 gram | g, gm | 0.035 | ounce |
| 1 dekagram | dag | 0.353 | ounce |
| 1 hectogram | hg | 3.527 | ounces |
| 1 kilogram | kg | 2.2046 | pounds |
| 1 quintal | q | 220.46 | pounds |
| 1 metric ton | MT, t | 1.1 | tons |

# PESAS Y MEDIDAS

## Sistema métrico

| Unidad | Abreviatura | Equivalente aproximado del sistema estadounidense | |
|---|---|---|---|
| LONGITUD | | | |
| 1 milímetro | mm | 0,04 | pulgada |
| 1 centímetro | cm | 0,39 | pulgada |
| 1 metro | m | 39,37 | pulgadas |
| | | 1,094 | yardas |
| 1 kilómetro | Km | 3.281,5 | pies |
| | | 0,62 | milla |
| ÁREA | | | |
| 1 centímetro cuadrado | cm² | 0,155 | pulgada cuadrada |
| 1 metro cuadrado | m² | 10,764 | pies cuadrados |
| | | 1,196 | yardas cuadradas |
| 1 hectárea | ha | 2,471 | acres |
| 1 kilómetro cuadrado | Km² | 247,105 | acres |
| | | 0,386 | milla cuadrada |
| VOLUMEN | | | |
| 1 centímetro cúbico | cm³ | 0,061 | pulgadas cúbicas |
| 1 metro cúbico | m³ | 1,308 | yardas cúbicas |
| CAPACIDAD (Medida líquida) | | | |
| 1 decilitro | dl | 0,21 | pinta |
| 1 litro | l | 1,057 | quarts |
| 1 decalitro | Dl | 2,64 | galones |
| CAPACIDAD (Medida árida) | | | |
| 1 decilitro | dl | 0,18 | pinta |
| 1 litro | l | 0,908 | quart |
| 1 decalitro | Dl | 1,14 | pecks |
| 1 hectolitro | Hl | 2,84 | bushels |
| CAPACIDAD (Medida cúbica) | | | |
| 1 decilitro | dl | 6,1 | pulgadas cúbicas |
| 1 litro | l | 61,02 | pulgadas cúbicas |
| 1 decalitro | Dl | 0,35 | pie cúbico |
| 1 hectolitro | Hl | 3,53 | pies cúbicos |
| 1 kilolitro | Kl | 1,31 | yardas cúbicas |
| MASA Y PESO | | | |
| 1 gramo | g | 0,035 | onza |
| 1 decagramo | Dg | 0,353 | onza |
| 1 hectogramo | Hg | 3,527 | onzas |
| 1 kilogramo | Kg | 2,2046 | libras |
| 1 quintal métrico | q | 220,46 | libras |
| 1 tonelada métrica | t | 1,1 | toneladas |

## U.S. Customary Weights and Measures /
## Unidades de pesas y medidas estadounidenses

**Linear measure / Medida de longitud**

| | | |
|---|---|---|
| 1 foot / pie | = | 12 inches / pulgadas |
| 1 yard / yarda | = | 36 inches / pulgadas |
| | = | 3 feet / pies |
| 1 rod | = | 5½ yards / yardas |
| 1 mile / milla | = | 5,280 feet / 5.280 pies |
| | = | 1,760 yards / 1.760 yardas |

**Liquid measure / Medida líquida**

| | | |
|---|---|---|
| 1 pint / pinta | = | 4 gills |
| 1 quart / quart líquido | = | 2 pints / pintas |
| 1 gallon / galón | = | 4 quarts / quarts líquidos |

**Area measure / Medida de superficie**

| | | |
|---|---|---|
| 1 square foot / pie cuadrado | = | 144 square inches / pulgadas cuadradas |
| 1 square yard / yarda cuadrada | = | 9 square feet / pies cuadrados |
| 1 square rod / rod cuadrado | = | 30¼ square yards / yardas cuadradas |
| 1 acre | = | 160 square rods / rods cuadrados |
| 1 square mile / milla cuadrada | = | 640 acres |

**Dry measure / Medida árida**

| | | |
|---|---|---|
| 1 quart | = | 2 pints / pintas áridas |
| 1 peck | = | 8 quarts |
| 1 bushel | = | 4 pecks |

## Some useful measures / Unas medidas útiles

**Quantity / Cantidad**

| | | |
|---|---|---|
| 1 dozen / docena | = | 12 units / unidades |
| 1 gross / gruesa | = | 12 dozen / docenas |

**Quantity of paper / Cantidad de papel**

| | | |
|---|---|---|
| 1 quire / mano | = | 24 or 25 sheets / hojas |
| 1 ream / resma | = | 500 sheets / hojas |
| | = | 20 quires / manos |

**Electricity / Electricidad**

| | |
|---|---|
| charge / carga | coulomb / culombio |
| power / potencia | watt / vatio |
| | kilowatt / kilovatio |
| resistance / resistencia | ohm / ohmio |
| strength / fuerza | ampere / amperio |
| voltage / voltaje | volt / voltio |

# NUMBERS / NUMERALES

| Cardinal Numbers | | Números cardinales | Cardinal Numbers | | Números cardinales |
|---|---|---|---|---|---|
| zero | 0 | cero | twenty | 20 | veinte |
| one | 1 | uno | twenty-one | 21 | veintiuno |
| two | 2 | dos | twenty-two | 22 | veintidós |
| three | 3 | tres | twenty-three | 23 | veintitrés |
| four | 4 | cuatro | twenty-four | 24 | veinticuatro |
| five | 5 | cinco | twenty-five | 25 | veinticinco |
| six | 6 | seis | twenty-six | 26 | veintiséis |
| seven | 7 | siete | twenty-seven | 27 | veintisiete |
| eight | 8 | ocho | twenty-eight | 28 | veintiocho |
| nine | 9 | nueve | twenty-nine | 29 | veintinueve |
| ten | 10 | diez | thirty | 30 | treinta |
| eleven | 11 | once | forty | 40 | cuarenta |
| twelve | 12 | doce | fifty | 50 | cincuenta |
| thirteen | 13 | trece | sixty | 60 | sesenta |
| fourteen | 14 | catorce | seventy | 70 | setenta |
| fifteen | 15 | quince | eighty | 80 | ochenta |
| sixteen | 16 | dieciséis | ninety | 90 | noventa |
| seventeen | 17 | diecisiete | one hundred | 100 | cien, ciento |
| eighteen | 18 | dieciocho | five hundred | 500 | quinientos |
| nineteen | 19 | diecinueve | one thousand | 1000 | mil |

| Ordinal Numbers | | Números ordinales | | |
|---|---|---|---|---|
| 1st | first | $1.^o$, $1.^a$ | primero, -a | |
| 2nd | second | $2.^o$, $2.^a$ | segundo, -a | |
| 3rd | third | $3.^o$, $3.^a$ | tercero, -a | |
| 4th | fourth | $4.^o$, $4.^a$ | cuarto, -a | |
| 5th | fifth | $5.^o$, $5.^a$ | quinto, -a | |
| 6th | sixth | $6.^o$, $6.^a$ | sexto, -a | |
| 7th | seventh | $7.^o$, $7.^a$ | séptimo, -a | |
| 8th | eighth | $8.^o$, $8.^a$ | octavo, -a | |
| 9th | ninth | $9.^o$, $9.^a$ | noveno, -a | |
| 10th | tenth | $10.^o$, $10.^a$ | décimo, -a | |
| 11th | eleventh | $11.^o$, $11.^a$ | undécimo, -a | |
| 12th | twelfth | $12.^o$, $12.^a$ | duodécimo, -a | |
| 13th | thirteenth | $13.^o$, $13.^a$ | decimotercero, -a decimotercio, -a | |
| 14th | fourteenth | $14.^o$, $14.^a$ | decimocuarto, -a | |
| 15th | fifteenth | $15.^o$, $15.^a$ | decimoquinto, -a | |
| 16th | sixteenth | $16.^o$, $16.^a$ | decimosexto, -a | |
| 17th | seventeenth | $17.^o$, $17.^a$ | decimoséptimo, -a | |
| 18th | eighteenth | $18.^o$, $18.^a$ | decimoctavo, -a | |
| 19th | nineteenth | $19.^o$, $19.^a$ | decimonoveno, -a decimonono, -a | |
| 20th | twentieth | $20.^o$, $20.^a$ | vigésimo, -a | |
| 21st | twenty-first | $21.^o$, $21.^a$ | vigésimo (-a) primero (-a) | |
| 22nd | twenty-second | $22.^o$, $22.^a$ | vigésimo (-a) segundo (-a) | |
| 30th | thirtieth | $30.^o$, $30.^a$ | trigésimo, -a | |
| 40th | fortieth | $40.^o$, $40.^a$ | cuadragésimo, -a | |
| 50th | fiftieth | $50.^o$, $50.^a$ | quincuagésimo, -a | |
| 60th | sixtieth | $60.^o$, $60.^a$ | sexagésimo, -a | |
| 70th | seventieth | $70.^o$, $70.^a$ | septuagésimo, -a | |
| 80th | eightieth | $80.^o$, $80.^a$ | octogésimo, -a | |
| 90th | ninetieth | $90.^o$, $90.^a$ | nonagésimo, -a | |
| 100th | hundredth | $100.^o$, $100.^a$ | centésimo, -a | |

# TEMPERATURE / LA TEMPERATURA

## Fahrenheit and Celsius / Grados Fahrenheit y grados Celsius

To convert Fahrenheit to Celsius, subtract 32 degrees, multiply by 5, and divide by 9.

Para convertir grados Fahrenheit a grados Celsius (centígrados), réstese 32 grados, multiplíquese por 5 y divídase por 9.

$$104°F - 32 = 72 \times 5 = 360 \div 9 = 40°C$$

To convert Celsius to Fahrenheit, multiply by 9, divide by 5, and add 32 degrees.

Para convertir grados Celsius (centígrados) a grados Fahrenheit, multiplíquese por 9, divídase por 5 y agréguese 32 grados.

$$40°C \times 9 = 360 \div 5 = 72 + 32 = 104°F$$

| | |
|---|---|
| At sea level, water boils at<br>Al nivel del mar, se hierve el agua a | 212°F / 100°C |
| Water freezes at<br>Se congela el agua en | 32°F / 0°C |
| Average human temperature<br>Temperatura promedia del ser humano | 98.6°F / 37°C |

## Some normal temperatures in the Americas / Algunas temperaturas normales en las Américas

| | Winter / Invierno | Summer / Verano |
|---|---|---|
| **North of the equator / Al norte del ecuador** | | |
| Churchill, Manitoba | -11°F / -23.9°C | 63°F / 17.2°C |
| Montreal, Quebec | 22°F / -5.6°C | 79°F / 26.1°C |
| Anchorage, Alaska | 12°F / -11.1°C | 58°F / 14.4°C |
| Chicago, Illinois | 24°F / -4.4°C | 75°F / 23.9°C |
| New York, New York | 32°F / 0°C | 77°F / 25°C |
| Dallas, Texas | 45°F / 7.2°C | 86°F / 30°C |
| Los Angeles, California | 57°F / 13.9°C | 73°F / 22.8°C |
| Phoenix, Arizona | 51°F / 10.6°C | 94°F / 34.4°C |
| Tegucigalpa, Honduras | 50°F / 10°C | 90°F / 32°C |
| **South of the equator / Al sur del ecuador** | | |
| Tierra del Fuego, Argentina | 32°F / 0°C | 50°F / 10°C |
| Sao Paulo, Brazil | 57.2°F / 14°C | 69.8°F / 21°C |
| Montevideo, Uruguay | 55.4°F / 13°C | 71.6°F / 22°C |
| Buenos Aires, Argentina | 52.3°F / 11.3°C | 73.8°F / 23.2°C |
| Lima, Peru | 59°F / 15°C | 77°F / 25°C |

# ABREVIATURAS MÁS USADAS EN INGLÉS*

| | | | |
|---|---|---|---|
| A., a. | absent; acceleration; acre; adult; alto; ampere; anode; answer; ante; anterior; area | bg. | background; bag |
| | | biog. | biographer; biography |
| | | bk. | bank; book; break; brook |
| AAR, a.a.r. | against all risks | bkg. | banking; bookkeeping |
| abbr. | abbreviated; abbreviation | bkt., bskt. | basket |
| abr. | abridged; abridgment | BL | bill of lading |
| AC, ac | alternating current; area code; before Christ; before meals | bl. | bale; barrel; black; blue |
| | | bldg. | building |
| ac. | account | blvd. | boulevard |
| acad. | academy | BO | box office; branch office |
| AD, A.D. | after date; anno Domini | bor. | borough |
| ad | advertisement | bot. | bottle; bottom |
| adm. | administration; administrative | BP | blood pressure; blueprint |
| adv. | advertisement; advisory | bp | baptized; birthplace |
| ad val. | ad valorem (to the value of) | b.p. | below par; boiling point |
| aff. | affirmative | BR | bills receivable |
| afft. | affidavit | br. | branch; brass; brown |
| aft. | afternoon | bro(s). | brother(s) |
| agcy. | agency | BS | balance sheet; bill of sale |
| agt. | agent | Btu. | British thermal unit |
| alt. | altitude | bu. | bureau; bushel |
| AM, A.M. | airmail; amplitude modulation; anno mundi; ante meridiem | bx. | box |
| amt. | amount | C | calorie; carat; circa |
| anal. | analogous; analogy | c | cent; center; copyright |
| anc. | ancient | CA | chronological age; current account |
| ann. | annals; annual | can., canc. | canceled; cancellation |
| anon. | anonymous | cap. | capacity; capital |
| ans. | answer | cath. | cathedral; cathode |
| app. | apparatus; appendix | CB | citizens' band (radio) |
| Apr. | April | CBD | cash before delivery |
| approx. | approximately | cc | cubic centimeter; carbon copy |
| apt. | apartment | CD | certificate of deposit; civil defense |
| ar., arr. | arrival; arrive | cen., cent. | central |
| arch. | archaic; archery | cent. | centigrade; centum; century |
| art. | artificial; artillery | cert. | certificate; certification; certified |
| assoc. | associate(s); association | CF | centrifugal force; cost and freight |
| asst. | assistant | cf. | compare |
| AT | air temperature | CFI | cost, freight, and insurance |
| at. | atomic | ch. | chain; chaplain; chapter; chief; child(ren); church |
| atm. | atmosphere; atmospheric | | |
| att. | attached; attention | CI | cast iron; certificate of insurance |
| att., atty. | attorney | cit. | citation; cited; citizen |
| at. wt. | atomic weight | civ. | civil; civilian |
| Aug. | August | ck. | check |
| aux., auxil. | auxiliary | CL | carload; civil law; common law |
| AV | ad valorem; audiovisual | cl. | class; clause; close |
| av., avdp. | avoirdupois | cml. | commercial |
| av., ave. | avenue | CN | credit note |
| av., avg. | average | CO | cash order; conscientious objector |
| | | co. | company; county |
| B | Bible | c/o | care of |
| b | bass; bat; before; born | COD | cash on delivery; collect on delivery |
| bal. | balance | COL | cost of living |
| bar. | barometer; barometric | coll. | collateral; collect; college |
| BC, B.C. | before Christ | com. | comedy; comic; comma |
| bd. | board; bound; boundary; bundle | com., comm. | command; commentary; commerce; commission; committee; common; communication |
| bdrm. | bedroom | | |
| BE | bill of exchange | | |
| bet. | between | | |
| BF | board foot; brought forward | | |
| bf. | boldface | | |

*V. Apéndice: Weights and Measures.

| | |
|---|---|
| comp. | compare; compensation; compiled; compiler; composed; composer; composition; compound; comprehensive |
| con. | conclusion; consolidated; consul; continued |
| conc. | concentrate; concentration; concrete |
| cong. | congregation; congress; congressional |
| cons. | conservative; constitution; construction; consulting |
| cont. | containing; contents; continent; continental; continued; control |
| cop. | copper; copy; copyright |
| cor. | corner; coroner |
| cor., corr. | correct; correction; correspondence; corrupt |
| corp. | corporation |
| cos. | cosine |
| cosec., csc. | cosecant |
| cp. | compare; coupon |
| cpd. | compound |
| CR | cathode ray; class rate; current rate |
| cr. | center; circular; cream; credit; crescendo |
| CS | capital stock; civil service; county seat |
| C/S | cycles per second |
| cs. | cases; census |
| ct. | carat; cent; count; court |
| ctn. | carton; cotangent |
| cur. | currency; current |
| cw. | clockwise |
| CWO | cash with order |
| cwt. | hundredweight |
| cyl. | cylinder |
| D., d. | date; daughter; day; dead; deceased; depart; diameter; dimensional; distance; drive |
| DA | days after acceptance; deposit account |
| DB | daybook |
| db. | debenture; decibel |
| dbl. | double |
| DC | da capo (from the beginning); direct current; double crochet |
| DD | days after date; due date |
| dd. | dated; delivered |
| Dec. | December |
| def. | defendant; defense; deferred; defined; definition |
| deg. | degree |
| del. | delegate; delegation; delete |
| dep. | depart; departure; deposed; deposit; depot; deputy |
| dept. | department |
| der., deriv. | derivation; derivative |
| DG | dei gratia (by the grace of God) |
| dia., diam. | diameter |
| diag. | diagonal; diagram |
| dict. | dictionary |
| dif., diff. | difference; different |
| dim. | dimension; diminished |
| dir. | director |
| dis., disc. | discount |

| | |
|---|---|
| dis., dist. | distance; district |
| div. | divided; dividend; division; divorced |
| do. | ditto |
| DOB | date of birth |
| doc. | document |
| dom. | domestic; dominant; dominion |
| doz., dz. | dozen(s) |
| DP, D.P. | data processing; dew point |
| DR, dr | dining room |
| Dr. | doctor |
| dr. | debtor; dram; drive; drum |
| DS | days after sight; document signed |
| DST | daylight saving time |
| DT | daylight time; delirium tremens; double time |
| DW | deadweight; delayed weather; dust wrapper |
| dy. | delivery; deputy; duty |
| E., e. | earth; east; eastern; error |
| ea. | each |
| E and OE | errors and omissions excepted |
| ed., edit. | edited; edition; editor |
| e.g. | for example |
| elem. | elementary |
| encyc. | encyclopedia |
| eng. | engine; engineer |
| eq. | equal; equation |
| eq., equiv. | equivalent |
| equip. | equipment |
| ESP | extrasensory perception |
| esp. | especially |
| EST | eastern standard time |
| est. | established; estimate(d) |
| ETA | estimated time of arrival |
| et al. | et alia (and others) |
| etc. | et cetera (and so forth) |
| ETD | estimated time of departure |
| et seq. | et sequens, et sequentia [and the following one(s)] |
| ex. | example; exchange; executive; express; extra |
| exc. | excellent; except |
| exec. | executive |
| exp. | expense; experiment; export; express |
| ext. | extension; exterior; external; extra; extract |
| F., f. | failure; false; family; finish; folio; force; forte; from; full |
| fac. | facsimile; faculty |
| fam. | familiar; family |
| FB | freight bill |
| F.D. | fire department; free dock |
| Feb. | February |
| fed. | federal; federation |
| fem. | female; feminine |
| ff. | folios; following; fortissimo |
| fig. | figure |
| fin. | finance; financial; finish |
| fl. | floor; fluid |
| FM | frequency modulation |
| fn. | footnote |
| fo., fol. | folio |
| FOB | free on board |
| FOR | free on rail |

| | | | |
|---|---|---|---|
| f.p. | freezing point | ICU | intensive care unit |
| fr. | father; from | id. | idem (something previously |
| freq. | frequency; frequent; frequently | | mentioned) |
| Fri. | Friday | i.e. | id est (that is) |
| frt. | freight | ill., illus. | illustrated; illustration; illustrator |
| frwy. | freeway | imp. | import(ed) |
| ft. | feet; foot; fort | inc. | including; incomplete; |
| fwd. | forward | | incorporated; increase |
| FYI, fyi | for your information | incl. | including; inclusive |
| | | incr. | increase; increased |
| g. | gauge; gender; genitive; gravity; | ind. | independent; index |
| | guide; gulf | inorg. | inorganic |
| GA | general agent; general average | inq. | inquire |
| GCD | greatest common divisor | insp. | inspector |
| GCF | greatest common factor | inst. | instant; institute; institution |
| GCT | Greenwich civil time | int. | intelligence; interest; interim; |
| gd. | good | | interior; internal; international |
| gen. | general; genitive; genus | intl., intnl. | international |
| GI | galvanized iron; gastrointestinal; | in trans. | in transit |
| | general issue; government issue | inv. | inventor; invoice |
| GMT | Greenwich mean time | I/O | input/output |
| GNI | gross national income | isl. | island |
| GNP | gross national product | isth. | isthmus |
| gov. | government; governor | ital. | italic; italicized |
| GP | general practice; general | itin. | itinerary |
| | practitioner; geometric | | |
| | progression | J., j. | jack; journal; judge; justice |
| gp. | group | JA | joint account |
| GPA | grade-point average | Jan. | January |
| GPO | general post office | jct., junc. | junction |
| gr. | grade; grain; gravity; gross | JHS | junior high school |
| gr. wt. | gross weight | jr., jun. | junior |
| gt. | great | jt., jnt. | joint |
| GTC | good till canceled | Jul. | July |
| gtd. | guaranteed | Jun. | June |
| | | juv. | juvenile |
| h. | half; harbor; hard(ness); height; | | |
| | high; humidity; hundred; husband | K., k. | karat; Kelvin; kindergarten; |
| hcap. | handicap | | kitchen; knit |
| HD | heavy duty | kn. | knot |
| hd. | head | | |
| hdbk. | handbook | L., l. | lady; lake; land; late; left; liquid; |
| hdqtrs., HQ | headquarters | | little; low |
| hex. | hexagon; hexagonal | lang. | language |
| HF | high frequency | lat. | latitude |
| hf. | half | LC | landing craft; left center; letter of |
| hgt., ht. | height | | credit |
| hgwy., hwy. | highway | lc. | lowercase |
| hld. | hold | LCD | least (or lowest) common |
| hon. | honor; honorable; honorary | | denominator |
| hosp. | hospital | LCM | least (or lowest) common multiple |
| hor. | horizontal | ld. | load; lord |
| hort. | horticultural; horticulture | ldg. | landing; loading |
| HP | half pay; high pressure; | ldr. | leader |
| | horsepower | leg. | legal |
| hr. | here; hour | leg., legis. | legislative; legislature |
| HS | high school | LF | ledger folio; low frequency |
| HT | half time; halftone; high-tension; | lf. | lightface |
| | high tide | lg. | large; long |
| ht. | heat; height | LH | left hand; lower half |
| HV | high velocity; high voltage | lib. | liberal; librarian; library |
| hvy. | heavy | lin. | lineal; linear |
| HW | high water; highway | liq. | liquid; liquor |
| Hz | hertz | lit. | literal; literary; literature |
| | | lith., litho. | lithographic; lithography |
| I., i. | initial; intelligence; island; isle | LL | lending library; lower left |
| ib., ibid. | ibidem (in the same place) | ll. | lines |
| ICE | internal combustion engine | LMT | local mean time |

| | |
|---|---|
| log. | logarithm; logic |
| LP, lp | low pressure; long-playing (record) |
| LR | living room; lower right |
| LS | left side |
| LT | long ton; low-tension |
| lt. | light |
| ltd. | limited |
| ltr. | letter; lighter |
| lub. | lubricant; lubricating |
| M., m. | mach; manual; medium; middle; mile; month; moon; morning |
| mag. | magazine; magnitude |
| maj. | major |
| man. | manual |
| manuf. | manufacture; manufacturing |
| Mar. | March |
| mar. | maritime |
| marg. | margin; marginal |
| masc. | masculine |
| max. | maximum |
| MD | medical doctor; months after date |
| mdnt. | midnight |
| mdse. | merchandise |
| meas. | measure |
| med. | median; medieval; medium |
| mem. | member; memoir; memorial |
| mer. | meridian |
| met. | metropolitan |
| MF | medium frequency; microfiche |
| mfd. | manufactured |
| mfg. | manufacturing |
| mfr. | manufacture; manufacturer |
| mgr. | manager |
| mgt. | management |
| mi. | mile; mileage; mill |
| MIA | missing in action |
| mid. | middle |
| min. | minimum; minor; minute |
| misc. | miscellaneous |
| mixt. | mixture |
| mktg. | marketing |
| MO | mail order; modus operandi; money order |
| mo(s). | month(s) |
| mod. | moderate; modern |
| mod., modif. | modification |
| mol. | molecular; molecule |
| MOM | middle of month |
| Mon. | Monday |
| mon. | monastery; monetary |
| morph. | morphology |
| MP, m.p. | melting point; metropolitan police; military police |
| MPG, mpg | miles per gallon |
| MPH, mph | miles per hour |
| MS(S)., ms(s). | manuscript(s) |
| msg. | message |
| MST | mountain standard time |
| mt. | mount; mountain |
| mtg. | meeting |
| mtg., mtge. | mortgage |
| mus. | museum; music |
| MV | motor vehicle (or vessel) |
| mxd. | mixed |
| m.y. | million years |

| | |
|---|---|
| N., n. | name; net; noon; north; note; number |
| NA | no account; not applicable; not available |
| nat. | native; natural |
| nat., natl. | national |
| nav. | navigable; navigation |
| NB | northbound; nota bene (mark well) |
| NC | no charge; no credit |
| NCV | no commercial value |
| ND; n.d. | no date |
| NE | no effects; northeast |
| neg. | negative |
| NF | no funds |
| NFS | not for sale |
| NNE | north-northeast |
| NNW | north-northwest |
| no. | north |
| no(s). | number(s) |
| norm. | normal |
| Nov. | November |
| NP | no protest; notary public |
| n.p. | no pagination; no place (of publication) |
| NS, n.s. | new series; new style; not specified; not sufficient |
| NTP | normal temperature and pressure |
| nt. wt., n. wt. | net weight |
| NU | name unknown |
| num. | numeral |
| NV | nonvoting |
| NW | northwest |
| O., o. | ocean; ohm; old; order; over |
| o/a | on or about |
| ob. | obiit (died); observation |
| obj. | object; objective |
| obl. | oblique; oblong |
| OC | off center; on center; on course |
| Oc., oc. | ocean |
| occas. | occasionally |
| Oct. | October |
| oct. | octavo |
| OD | on demand; overdraft; overdrawn |
| off. | office; officer |
| off., offic. | official |
| OJT | on-the-job training |
| OM | order of merit |
| OP | observation post; out of print |
| op. | opus |
| op. cit. | opere citato (in the work cited) |
| opp. | opposite |
| opt. | optional |
| OR | operating room; owner's risk |
| orch. | orchestra |
| org. | organic; organization; organized |
| orig. | origin; original; originator |
| OS | old series; old style; out of stock |
| OT | occupational therapy; overtime |
| P., p. | page; part; past; per; port; power; pressure; purl |
| PA | particular average; per annum; power of attorney; press agent; private account; public address; purchasing agent |
| pam. | pamphlet |
| P and L | profit and loss |

| | |
|---|---|
| par. | paragraph; parallel; parish |
| pass. | passenger |
| pat. | patent |
| path., pathol. | pathological; pathology |
| payt., pmt. | payment |
| PC | personal computer; post card |
| PC, pct. | percent; percentage |
| PD | per diem; police department |
| pd. | paid |
| PDD | past due date |
| PDT | Pacific daylight time |
| PE | physical education; printer's error; probable error |
| pen. | peninsula |
| peo. | people |
| per. | period; person |
| perf. | perfect; perforated; performance |
| perh. | perhaps |
| perm. | permanent |
| perp. | perpendicular |
| pers. | person; personal; personnel |
| pert. | pertaining |
| pf. | preferred |
| pg. | page |
| ph. | phase |
| phr. | phrase |
| phys. | physical; physician |
| pk. | park; peak; peck; pike |
| pkg(s). | package(s) |
| pkt. | packet; pocket |
| pkwy. | parkway |
| PL | partial loss; private line; public law |
| pl. | place; plate |
| plat. | plateau; platoon |
| plf. | plaintiff |
| PM, P.M. | postmeridiem; postmortem |
| pmk. | postmark |
| PN | promissory note |
| PNR | point of no return |
| PO | postal order; post office; purchase order |
| POD | pay on delivery |
| pop. | population |
| por. | portrait |
| pos. | position; positive |
| pot. | potential |
| POW, PW | prisoner of war |
| PP. | parcel post; postpaid; prepaid |
| pp. | pages; per procurationem (by proxy) |
| ppd. | postpaid; prepaid |
| ppt. | precipitate |
| PR | payroll; public relations |
| pr. | pair; price; printed |
| prec. | preceding |
| pref. | preface; preference; preferred; prefix |
| prem. | premium |
| prep. | preparation; preparatory |
| pres. | president |
| press. | pressure |
| prev. | previous; previously |
| prf. | proof |
| prim. | primary; primitive |
| prin. | principal; principle |
| priv., pvt. | private |
| prob. | probable; probably; problem |
| proc. | proceedings |

| | |
|---|---|
| prod. | production. |
| prof. | professional; professor |
| prom. | promontory |
| pron. | pronounced; pronunciation |
| prop. | property; proposition; proprietor |
| prov. | province; provisional |
| prox. | proximo (in the next month) |
| PS | postscript; public school |
| pseud. | pseudonym; pseudonymous |
| psi. | pounds per square inch |
| PST | Pacific standard time |
| psych. | psychology |
| pt. | part; payment; point; port |
| ptg. | printing |
| pty. | proprietary |
| PU | pickup |
| pub. | public |
| pub., publ. | publication; published; publisher |
| PUD | pickup and delivery |
| PVT | pressure, volume, and temperature |
| pwr. | power |
| PX | please exchange; post exchange |
| Q., q. | quarto; queen; query; question |
| qt., qty. | quantity |
| qu., ques. | question |
| quad. | quadrant |
| quot. | quotation |
| qy. | query |
| R., r. | radius; rain; range; rare; real; red; resistance; right; river; roentgen; rook; rough; run |
| rad. | radical; radius; radix |
| R & B | rhythm and blues |
| R and D | research and development |
| R and R | rest and recreation; rest and recuperation |
| rcpt., rec. | receipt |
| rct. | recruit |
| RD | refer to drawer; rural delivery |
| rd. | road; round |
| rec. | record; recording; recreation |
| rec'd., recd. | received |
| rect. | rectangle; rectangular; rectified |
| red. | reduce; reduction |
| ref. | reference; referred; refining; reformed; refunding |
| refr. | refraction |
| reg. | region; register; regular; regulation |
| reg., regd. | registered |
| rel. | relating; relative; released |
| rep. | repair; report; reporter; representative; republic |
| repl. | replace; replacement |
| rept. | report |
| res. | research; reserve; residence; resistance; resolution |
| resp. | respective; respectively |
| ret(d). | retain(ed); retired; return(ed) |
| rev. | revenue; reverse; review; reviewed; revised; revision |
| RFD | rural free delivery |
| RH | right hand |
| rh | relative humidity |
| RIP | requiescat in pace (rest in peace) |
| riv. | river |
| rm(s). | ream(s); room(s) |

| | | | |
|---|---|---|---|
| rnd. | round | soph. | sophomore |
| ROG | receipt of goods | SP | self-propelled; sine prole (without issue); specialist |
| ROM | read-only memory | | |
| rot. | rotating; rotation | sp. | species; specimen; spelling; spirit |
| RP | reply paid; reprint; reprinting | sp., spec. | special; specific; specifically |
| RPM, rpm | revolutions per minute | spp. | species |
| RPS, rps | revolutions per second | SPQR | small profits, quick returns |
| rpt. | repeat; report | sps | sine prole superstite (without surviving issue) |
| RR | railroad; rural route | | |
| RS | recording secretary; revised statutes; right side | SR | shipping receipt |
| | | sr. | senior; sister |
| RSVP | répondez s'il vous plaît (please reply) | SRO | single-room occupancy; standing room only |
| RT | radiotelephone; room temperature | SS | saints; same size; steamship; Sunday school; sworn statement |
| rt. | right | | |
| rte. | route | ss. | semis (one-half) |
| rwy., ry. | railway | SSE | south-southeast |
| | | ssp. | subspecies |
| S., s. | sabbath; saint; second; section; semi; series; sine; small; smooth; snow; society; son; south; southern; subject | SST | supersonic transport |
| | | SSW | south-southwest |
| | | St. | saint; stratus |
| | | st. | stanza; state; stitch; stone; street |
| Sat. | Saturday | sta. | station; stationary |
| SB | simultaneous broadcast; southbound | stat. | statim (immediately); statute |
| | | stbd. | starboard |
| sc. | scale; scene; science; small capital (letter) | std. | standard |
| | | Ste. | saint (female) |
| sch. | school | ster., stg. | sterling |
| sched. | schedule | stge. | storage |
| sci. | science; scientific; scientist | stk. | stock |
| script. | scripture | STP | standard temperature and pressure |
| SD | sight draft; sine die (without day); special delivery; stage direction; standard deviation | str. | steamer; strophe |
| | | stud. | student |
| | | sub. | subaltern; subtract; suburb |
| sd. | said; sewed | suff. | sufficient; suffix |
| SE | southeast; stock exchange; straight edge | Sun. | Sunday |
| | | sup. | superior; supply; supra |
| sec. | second; secondary; secundum (according to) | sup., supp., suppl. | supplement; supplementary |
| sec., sect. | section; sectional | supr. | supreme |
| sec., secy. | secretary | supt. | superintendent |
| sel. | select; selection | supvr. | supervisor |
| sem. | seminar; seminary | sur. | surface |
| sen. | senate; senator | surv. | survey; surveying; surveyor |
| sen., sr. | senior | svgs. | savings |
| sep. | separate; separated | SW | shipper's weight; shortwave; southwest |
| Sept., Sep. | September | | |
| seq., seqq. | the following | sym. | symbol; symmetrical |
| ser. | serial; series | sys., syst. | system |
| ser., serv. | service | | |
| SF | science fiction; sinking fund | T., t. | tablespoon; target; teaspoon; technical; temperature; time; ton; true |
| SG,s.g.,sp.gr. | specific gravity | | |
| sgd. | signed | | |
| sh. | share | taxon. | taxonomic; taxonomy |
| SIG | special interest group | TB | trial balance |
| Sig. | signa (label) | tb., tbs., tbsp. | tablespoon; tablespoonful |
| sig. | signal; signature | TBA, tba | to be announced |
| sing. | singular | tchr. | teacher |
| SL | salvage loss; sea level; south latitude | tec., tech. | technical; technician |
| sl. | slightly; slow | tech., technol. | technological; technology |
| sld. | sailed; sealed; sold | tel. | telegram; telegraph; telephone |
| sm. | small | temp. | temperance; temperature; template; temporal; temporary; tempore (in the time of) |
| SO | seller's option | | |
| so. | south; southern | | |
| soc. | social; society | ter., terr. | territory |
| sol. | solicitor; soluble; solution | tgt. | target |
| SOP | standard operating procedure | Th., Thurs. | Thursday |
| | | therm. | thermometer |

| | |
|---|---|
| tinc. | tincture |
| tk. | tank; truck |
| tkt. | ticket |
| TL | total loss; truckload |
| tlr. | tailor; trailer |
| TM | technical manual; trademark |
| TMO | telegraph money order |
| tn. | ton; town; train |
| tng. | training |
| tnpk. | turnpike |
| TOT | time on target |
| tot. | total |
| tp. | title page; township |
| TR | tons registered; transmit-receive |
| tr. | transpose; troop; trustee |
| tr., trans., transl. | translated; translation; translator |
| trag. | tragedy; tragic |
| trans. | transactions; transportation; transverse |
| transf., tfr. | transfer; transferred |
| trav. | travel; traveler |
| treas. | treasurer; treasury |
| trib. | tributary |
| trop. | tropic; tropical |
| tsp. | teaspoon; teaspoonful |
| TU | trade union; transmission unit |
| Tu., Tues. | Tuesday |
| TV | terminal velocity |
| twp. | township |
| typog. | typographer; typographical; typography |
| | |
| U. | university |
| u. | uncle; unit; upper |
| UC | undercharge; uppercase |
| UDC | universal decimal classification |
| ugt. | urgent |
| UH | upper half |
| UHF | ultrahigh frequency |
| ult. | ultimate; ultimo (in the last month) |
| univ. | universal; university |
| unp. | unpaged |
| uns. | unsymmetrical |
| UV | ultraviolet |
| UW | underwriter |
| ux. | uxor (wife) |
| | |
| V., v. | vector; velocity; verse; versus; very; vice; victory; voice; volt; volume |
| VA | visual aid; volt-ampere |
| vac. | vacuum |
| val. | value; valued |
| var. | variable; variant; variation; variety; various |
| VAT | value-added tax |
| VD | vapor density; various dates; venereal disease |
| vel. | vellum; velocity |
| Ven. | venerable |
| ver. | verse |
| vert. | vertebrate; vertical |
| VF | very fair (or fine); video frequency; visual field |
| VHF | very high frequency |

| | |
|---|---|
| VI | viscosity index; volume indicator |
| vi | vide infra (see below) |
| vic. | vicinity |
| vil. | village |
| vis. | visibility; visual |
| viz. | videlicet (namely) |
| VLF | very low frequency |
| vocab. | vocabulary |
| vol. | volcano; volume; volunteer |
| vou. | voucher |
| VP | variable pitch; vice president |
| VS | verse; versus; vide supra (see above) |
| vss. | verses; versions |
| VT | vacuum tube; variable time |
| VTR | video tape recorder |
| VU | volume unit |
| vv. | verses; vice versa |
| | |
| W., w. | warden; water; watt; week; weight; west; western; white; wide; width; wife; with; work |
| war., wrnt. | warrant |
| WB | water ballast; weather bureau; westbound |
| WC | without charge |
| wd. | wood; word; would |
| Wed. | Wednesday |
| WH, whr. | watt-hour |
| wh. | which; white |
| whf. | wharf |
| whs., whse. | warehouse |
| whsle. | wholesale |
| wid. | widow; widower |
| wk. | week; work |
| WL | waterline; wavelength |
| wmk. | watermark |
| WNW | west-northwest |
| w/o | without |
| WP | weather permitting; without prejudice |
| WPM, wpm | words per minute |
| wpn. | weapon |
| WR | warehouse receipt; without rights |
| WSW | west-southwest |
| wt. | weight |
| WW | warehouse warrant; with warrants; world war |
| | |
| X, x | ex; experimental; extra |
| XC, xcp. | ex coupon |
| XD, x. div. | ex dividend |
| XI, x. in., x. int. | ex interest |
| XL | extra large |
| XR | ex rights |
| XW | ex warrants |
| | |
| y., yd. | yard |
| y., yr. | year |
| YOB | year of birth |
| yr. | younger; your |
| | |
| z | zero; zone |
| ZPG | zero population growth |

# ABBREVIATIONS MOST COMMONLY USED IN SPANISH*

| | |
|---|---|
| A | Aprobado (*in examinations*) |
| a | área |
| (a) | alias |
| AA. | autores |
| ab. | abad |
| abr. | abril |
| A.C., A. de C. | Año de Cristo |
| admón. | administración |
| adm.<sup>or</sup> | administrador |
| afmo., affmo. | afectísimo |
| afto. | afecto |
| ago. | agosto |
| a la v/ | a la vista |
| a.m. | ante meridiem, antes del mediodía |
| anac. | anacoreta |
| ap. | aparte; apóstol |
| apdo. | apartado |
| art., art.º | artículo |
| att.º, atto. | atento |
| | |
| B | beato; Bueno (*in examinations*) |
| Barna. | Barcelona |
| B.L.M., b.l.m. | besa la mano; besa las manos |
| B.L.P., b.l.p. | besa los pies |
| bto. | bulto; bruto |
| | |
| c. | capítulo |
| c/ | caja; cargo; contra |
| C.A. | corriente alterna |
| c.ª | compañía |
| c/a. | cuenta abierta |
| cap. | capítulo |
| C.C. | corriente continua |
| cénts. | céntimos |
| cf. | compárese |
| C.G.S. | cegesimal |
| Cía., cía. | compañía |
| C.M.B., c.m.b. | cuya mano beso |
| comis.º | comisario |
| comp.ª | compañía |
| comps. | compañeros |
| Const. | Constitución |
| corrte. | corriente |
| C.P.B., c.p.b. | cuyos pies beso |
| cps. | compañeros |
| cs. | cuartos; céntimos |
| cta. | cuenta |
| cte. | corriente |
| c/u | cada uno |
| C.V. | caballo (*or* caballos) de vapor |
| | |
| D. | Don |
| D.ª | Doña |
| descto. | descuento |
| d/f., d/fha. | días fecha |
| dha., dho., dhas., dhos. | dicha, dicho, dichas, dichos |
| dic. | diciembre |
| dls. | dólares |
| dna., dnas. | docena, docenas |
| d/p. | días plazo |
| Dr., dr. | Doctor |

| | |
|---|---|
| dra., dro., dras., dros. | derecha, derecho, derechas, derechos |
| dupdo. | duplicado |
| d/v. | días vista |
| | |
| E | este (*east*) |
| E.M. | Estado Mayor |
| E.M.G. | Estado Mayor General |
| ENE | estenordeste |
| ene. | enero |
| E.P.D. | en paz descanse |
| E.P.M. | en propia mano |
| ESE | estesudeste |
| etc. | etcétera |
| | |
| f.ª, fact.ª | factura |
| f/ | fardo(s) |
| f.a.b. | franco a bordo |
| F.C., f.c. | ferrocarril |
| fcos. | francos |
| feb., febr. | febrero |
| F.E.M. | fuerza electromotriz |
| fha., fho. | fecha, fecho |
| f.º, fol. | folio |
| fra. | factura |
| fund. | fundador |
| | |
| g/ | giro |
| gde. | guarde |
| gobno. | gobierno |
| gob.ʳ | gobernador |
| gral. | general |
| gte. | gerente |
| | |
| Hno., Hnos. | Hermano, Hermanos |
| HP., H. P. | caballo (*or* caballos) de vapor |
| | |
| ib., ibíd. | ibídem (en el mismo lugar) |
| íd. | ídem |
| i. e. | id est (*that is*) |
| ít. | ítem |
| izq.ª, izq.º | izquierda, izquierdo |
| | |
| J.C. | Jesucristo |
| jul. | julio |
| jun. | junio |
| | |
| L/ | letra |
| L. | ley; libro |
| Ldo., ldo. | licenciado |
| lín. | línea |
| liq. | liquidación |
| liq.º | líquido |
| | |
| M. | Maestro; Majestad; Merced |
| m. | minuto, minutos; mañana |
| m/ | mes; mi, mis; mío, míos |
| mar. | marzo |
| m/cta. | mi cuenta |
| merc. | mercaderías |
| m/f. | mi favor |
| milés. | milésimas |

*See Appendix: Pesas y Medidas.

| | |
|---|---|
| m/L. | mi letra |
| m/o. | mi orden |
| m/p. | mi pagaré |
| m/r. | mi remesa |
| Mtro. | Maestro |
| m.a. | muchos años |
| M.S. | manuscrito |
| | |
| N | norte; Notable (*in examinations*) |
| n. | noche |
| n/ | nuestro, nuestra |
| N. B. | nota bene |
| n/cta. | nuestra cuenta |
| NE | nordeste |
| NNE | nornoreste |
| NNO | nornoroeste |
| NO | noroeste |
| nov., novbre. | noviembre |
| núm., núms. | número, números |
| nto. | neto |
| ntra., ntro., ntras., ntros. | nuestra, nuestro, nuestras, nuestros |
| | |
| O | oeste |
| o/ | orden |
| oct. | octubre |
| ONO | oesnoroeste |
| OSO | oessudoeste |
| | |
| P. | Papa; padre; pregunta |
| P.A., p.a. | por ausencia; por autorización |
| pág., págs. | página, páginas |
| paq. | paquete |
| Part. | Partida |
| Patr. | Patriarca |
| pbro. | presbítero |
| p/cta. | por cuenta |
| P.D. | posdata |
| p. ej. | por ejemplo |
| P.O., p.o. | por orden |
| PP. | Padres |
| P.P., p.p. | porte pagado; por poder |
| p. pd.º, ppdo. | próximo pasado |
| pral. | principal |
| pralte. | principalmente |
| prof. | profesor |
| pról. | prólogo |
| prov.ª | provincia |
| próx.º | próximo |
| P.S. | Post Scriptum |
| ps. | pesos |
| P.S.M. | por su mandato |
| pta., ptas. | peseta, pesetas |
| pte. | parte; presente |
| pza. | pieza |
| | |
| Q.B.S.M., q.b.s.m. | que besa su mano |
| Q.B.S.P., q.b.s.p. | que besa sus pies |
| Q.D.G., q.D.g. | que Dios guarde |
| q.e.g.e. | que en gloria esté |

| | |
|---|---|
| q.e.p.d. | que en paz descanse |
| q.e.s.m. | que estrecha su mano |
| qq. | quintales |
| q.s.g.h. | que santa gloria haya |
| | |
| R. | respuesta; Reprobado (*in examinations*) |
| Rbi. | Recibí |
| R.D. | Real Decreto |
| R.I.P. | Requiescat in pace (descanse en paz) |
| Rl., Rls. | real, reales (*royal*) |
| rl., rls. | real, reales (*coin*) |
| r.p.m. | revoluciones por minuto |
| | |
| S. | San, Santo; sur; Sobresaliente (*in examinations*) |
| s/ | su, sus; sobre |
| S.ª | Señora |
| s/c. | su cuenta |
| S.C., s.c. | su casa |
| s/cta. | su cuenta |
| S.D. | Se despide |
| SE | sudeste |
| sep., sept., sepbre. | septiembre |
| serv.º | servicio |
| serv.or | servidor |
| s. e. u o. | salvo error u omisión |
| sigte. | siguiente |
| Sn. | San |
| SO | sudoeste |
| S.r, Sr. | Señor |
| Sra., Sras. | Señora, Señoras |
| Sres. | Señores |
| Sría. | Secretaría |
| sria., srio. | secretaria, secretario |
| Srta. | Señorita |
| S. S.ª | Su Señoría |
| SSE | sudsudeste |
| SSO | sudsudoeste |
| S.S.S., s.s.s. | su seguro servidor |
| SS. SS. | seguros servidores |
| Sta. | Santa; Señorita |
| Sto. | Santo |
| suplte. | suplente |
| | |
| tít., tít.º | título |
| tpo. | tiempo |
| trib. | tribunal |
| | |
| U., Ud. | usted |
| Uds. | ustedes |
| | |
| V. | usted; Venerable; Véase |
| y | versículo |
| vencimto. | vencimiento |
| vers.º | versículo |
| vg., v.g., v. gr. | verbigracia |
| Vmd., V. | vuestra merced; usted |
| V.º B.º | Visto bueno |
| vol. | volumen; voluntad |
| vols. | volúmenes |
| VV. | ustedes |

## BUSINESS CORRESPONDENCE IN SPANISH/LA CARTA COMERCIAL EN ESPAÑOL

The following selected phrases are indicative of the style and tone of business letters in the Spanish-speaking world.

### Para acusar recibo

1. Tenemos el gusto de acusar recibo de su estimada carta del 17 del actual...

2. Tengo el gusto de acusar recibo de su atta. de fecha 5 del corriente...

3. Hemos recibido su estimada carta del...

4. Le(s) agradezco (agradecemos) su carta del 15 de agosto...

5. En respuesta a su amable carta de fecha 11 del actual...

6. En contestación a su estimada carta del...

7. Le(s) doy (damos) las gracias por su carta del...

8. Quedo (quedamos) muy agradecido(s) por su estimada carta del...

9. Con referencia a su estimada carta del...

10. Acusamos recibo de su carta del 8 de septiembre...

11. Le(s) rogamos tenga(n) la bondad de excusar el retraso en corresponder a su carta del 2 de enero...

### To acknowledge receipt

1. We have the pleasure of acknowledging receipt of your esteemed letter of the 17th of this month...

2. I have the pleasure of acknowledging receipt of your esteemed letter of the 5th of this month...

3. We have received your esteemed letter of the...

4. I am (we are) grateful for your letter of August 15... (or thank you for your letter of...)

5. In answer to your kind letter of the 11th of this month...

6. In answer to your esteemed letter of...

7. I (we) thank you for your letter of...

8. I (we) remain grateful for your esteemed letter of...

9. In reference to your esteemed letter of...

10. We acknowledge receipt of your letter of September 8...

11. Please forgive (or please have the kindness to excuse) the delay in responding to your letter of January 2...

### Para empezar el texto de una carta

1. Tenemos el gusto de participar (informar, avisar) a Vd. que...

2. Tengo el gusto de remitir a Vd....

3. Sírvase tomar buena nota de que a partir de...

4. Aprovechamos (aprovecho) la ocasión para...

5. Con gusto incluimos...

6. Adjunto le(s) remito...

7. Sentimos mucho tener que informar a Vd. que...

8. Sentimos que por circunstancias imprevistas...

### To begin the body of a letter

1. We have the pleasure of informing you that...

2. I have the pleasure of sending you...

3. Please note that beginning on...

4. We take (I take) this opportunity to...

5. With pleasure we enclose...

6. Enclosed, I am sending you...

7. We regret (are very sorry) to inform you that...

8. We regret that because of unforeseen circumstances...

### Para pedir respuesta

1. Sírvanse contestarnos tan pronto como sea posible...

2. Rogamos (ruego) a Vds. una contestación inmediata...

3. Espero su contestación...

4. En espera de su grata contestación me suscribo de Vds. muy cordialmente,

5. Confiamos en que su respuesta será afirmativa.

6. Le(s) quedaría muy agradecido si me pudiera(n) contestar lo antes posible...

### To request an answer

1. Please respond (answer us) at your earliest convenience (as soon as may be possible)

2. We (I) ask you for an immediate answer...

3. I await your answer...

4. Awaiting your favorable answer, I remain yours very cordially,

5. We trust that your answer will be favorable.

6. I would be very grateful (would appreciate it) if you would answer as soon as possible...

| Para terminar una carta comercial | To close a business letter |
|---|---|
| 1. En espera de sus gratas órdenes, quedamos muy atentamente,... | 1. Awaiting your (pleasing) orders, we remain yours truly, |
| 2. En espera de sus noticias al respecto, quedo muy atentamente,... | 2. Awaiting your news of the matter, I remain very truly,... |
| 3. Muy cordialmente a sus órdenes... | 3. Very cordially at your service... |
| 4. Con este motivo, reciba nuestros afectuosos saludos. | 4. With this in mind, please receive our kind regards. |
| 5. Agradeciéndoles de antemano sus atenciones... | 5. Thanking you in advance for your attention... |
| 6. Aprovechamos la oportunidad para saludarles muy cordialmente, | 6. We take this opportunity of greeting you very cordially, |
| 7. Esperando su respuesta, quedamos muy cordialmente, | 7. Awaiting your answer, we remain very cordially... |
| 8. Muy atentamente lo saludamos y quedamos suyos affmos. y Ss. Ss. | 8. With best regards, we remain yours faithfully (or truly) |
| 9. Sin otro particular, lo saluda respetuosamente su affmo. atto. y S.S. | 9. With no other particular, your faithful servant greets you respectfully... |
| 10. Reiterándole mis disculpas, reciba mis saludos muy cordiales. | 10. Repeating my apologies, please receive my very cordial greetings. |

## Useful Expressions / Expresiones útiles

### Spanish
### The greeting / El saludo
From one company to another company / De una compañía a otra compañía:

Muy señores nuestros:

Estimados señores:

From one person to a company / De una persona a una compañía:

Muy señores míos:

Estimados señores:

From a person or company to another person / De una persona o compañía a otra persona:

| | |
|---|---|
| Muy señor mío: | Sr. Secretario: |
| Distinguido señor: | Sr. Administrador: |
| Muy distinguido señor: | Sr. Ingeniero García: |
| Estimado señor: | Distinguida Srta. López: |
| Muy estimado señor: | Distinguida señorita: |
| Muy apreciable señor: | Muy estimada Srta. López: |
| Sr. Director: | Muy estimada señora: |

### English
### El saludo / The greeting

| | |
|---|---|
| Dear Sir: | Dear Ms. Johnson: |
| Dear Sirs: | Dear Mr. Kelly: |
| Dear Madam: | Dear Student (Customer, Client, etc.): |

### La despedida / The closing

| | |
|---|---|
| Yours truly, | Cordially yours, |
| Very truly yours, | Respectfully yours, |
| Sincerely, | |

# NORTH AMERICA / AMÉRICA DEL NORTE

# CENTRAL AMERICA / CENTRO AMÉRICA

COLOMBIA

PANAMA

Golfo de Panamá

Colón

Panamá

Canal de Panamá

Caribbean Sea / Mar Caribe

Limón

COSTA RICA

San José

Puntarenas

Laguna de Caratasca

NICARAGUA

Lago de Managua

Lago Nicaragua

León

Managua

ISLAS DE LA BAHÍA

HONDURAS

San Pedro Sula

Lago de Yojoa

Tegucigalpa

Belmopan

Golfo de
Honduras

BELICE

MÉXICO

Lago de Izabal

GUATEMALA

EL SALVADOR

Guatemala

Santa Ana

San Salvador

Quezaltenango

Lago de Atitlán

PACIFIC OCEAN /

OCÉANO PACÍFICO

# MEXICO / MÉXICO

UNITED STATES / ESTADOS UNIDOS

Gulf of Mexico / Golfo de México

Bahía de Campeche

PENINSULA DE YUCATÁN

Cozumel

Mérida

Campeche

BELICE

GUATEMALA

Matamoros

Reynosa

Monterrey

Nuevo Laredo

San Luis Potosí

Querétaro

Oaxaca

Veracruz

★ México, D.F.

Puebla

Cuernavaca

Acapulco

Río del Norte

Río Bravo

Río Grande / Río

Chihuahua

Ciudad Juárez

Durango

Mazatlán

Guadalajara

Morelia

Manzanillo

Puerto Vallarta

M É X I C O

Hermosillo

Nogales

Mexicali

Tijuana

BAJA CALIFORNIA

PACIFIC OCEAN / OCÉANO PACÍFICO

# WEST INDIES / INDIAS OCCIDENTALES

TRINIDAD AND TOBAGO

WINDWARD ISLANDS

BARBADOS

LEEWARD ISLANDS

DOMINICA

MARTINIQUE

SAINT LUCIA

ST. VINCENT

GRENADA

GUADELOUPE

Port of Spain

VIRGIN ISLANDS

San Juan

ST. CROIX

PUERTO RICO

Ponce

Mona Passage

VENEZUELA

L E S S E R   A N T I L L E S

ARUBA

CURAÇAO

ATLANTIC OCEAN / OCÉANO ATLÁNTICO

DOMINICANA REPÚBLICA

Santiago

ISLA ESPAÑOLA

Santo Domingo

HAITÍ

Cap de Haïtien

Port-au-Prince

Guantánamo

COLOMBIA

B A H A M A S

Nassau

ANDROS ISLAND

Camagüey

Santiago de Cuba

Kingston

JAMAICA

G R E A T E R   A N T I L L E S

C U B A

FLORIDA

Miami

Key West

Straits of Florida

La Habana

CAYMAN ISLANDS

ISLA DE LOS PINOS

Gulf of Mexico / Golfo de México

PANAMA

COSTA RICA

NICARAGUA

HONDURAS

C E N T R A L   A M E R I C A

# SOUTH AMERICA / AMÉRICA DEL SUR

# SPAIN AND PORTUGAL / ESPAÑA Y PORTUGAL

FRANCE

ANDORRA

MENORCA

MALLORCA

IBIZA

ISLAS BALEARES

Mediterranean Sea / Mar Mediterráneo

Barcelona

Valencia

Bilbao

Burgos

Valladolid

• Madrid

Toledo

León

ESPAÑA

Duero

Tajo

Granada

Córdoba

Málaga

Strait of Gibraltar / Estrecho de Gibraltar

AFRICA

Sevilla

Cádiz

Guadiana

La Coruña

Douro

Oporto

Duero

PORTUGAL

Lisboa

ATLANTIC OCEAN / OCÉANO ATLÁNTICO